U. S. Bureau of the Census.
Negroes in the United States, 1920-32. Prepared under the supervision of Z. R. Pettet, chief statistician for agriculture, by Charles E. Hall, specialist in Negro statistics. Washington, U. S. Govt. Print. Off., 1935.
xvi, 845 p. incl. maps, tables, diagrs.
Reprint ed., New York, Arno Press and The New York Times, 1969.
(continued next card)

THE AMERICAN NEGRO
HIS HISTORY AND LITERATURE

NEGROES IN THE UNITED STATES 1920-1932

Charles E. Hall

ARNO PRESS and THE NEW YORK TIMES
NEW YORK 1969

*

Library of Congress Catalog Card No. 69–18629

*

Manufactured in the United States of America

General Editor
WILLIAM LOREN KATZ

U. S. DEPARTMENT OF COMMERCE
DANIEL C. ROPER, *Secretary*

BUREAU OF THE CENSUS
WILLIAM LANE AUSTIN, *Director*

NEGROES IN THE UNITED STATES

1920-32

Prepared under the supervision of Z. R. PETTET, *Chief Statistician for Agriculture*
By CHARLES E. HALL, *Specialist in Negro Statistics*

UNITED STATES
GOVERNMENT PRINTING OFFICE
WASHINGTON : 1935

MAP OF UNITED STATES SHOWING GEOGRAPHIC DIVISIONS

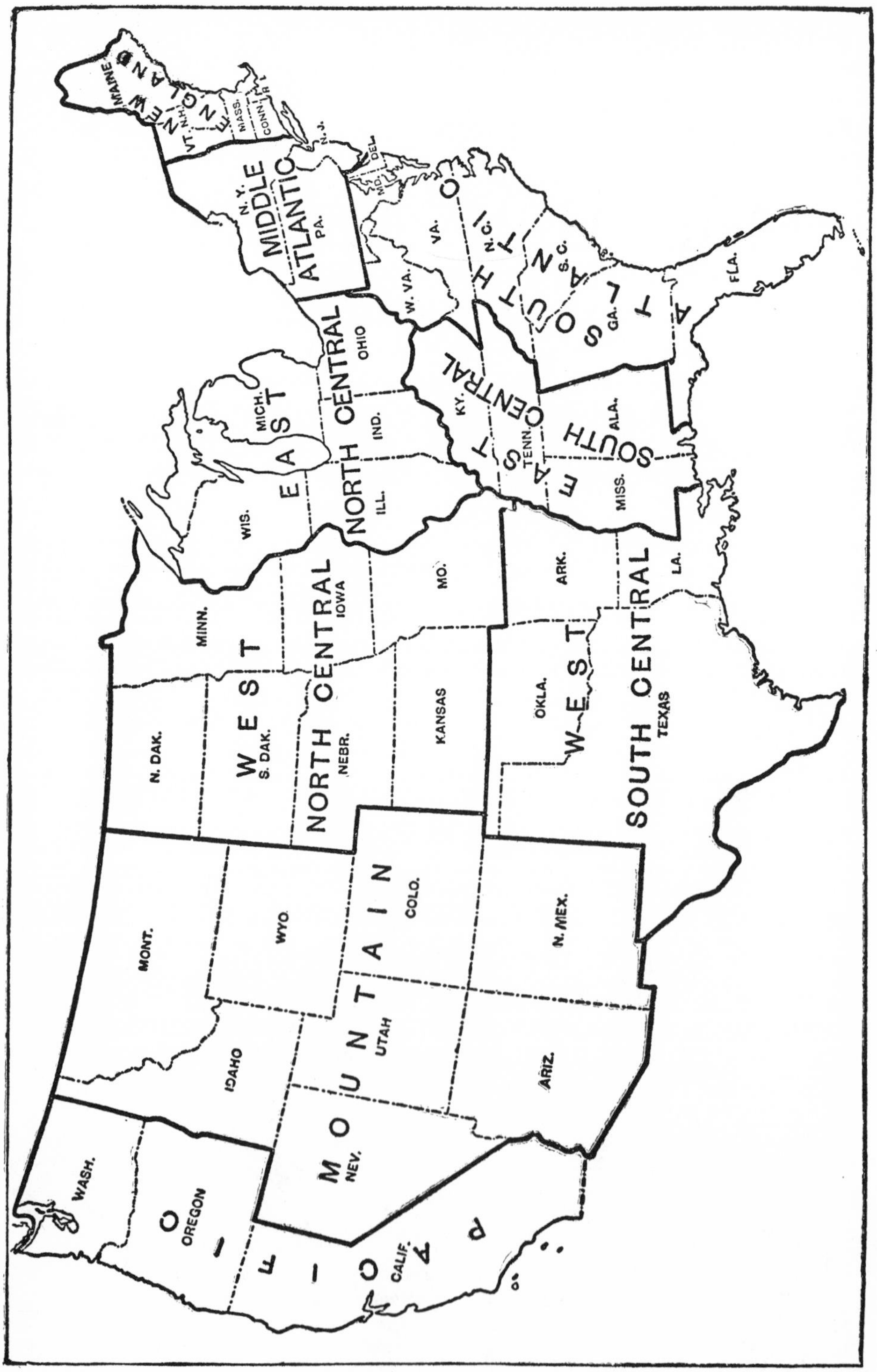

LETTER OF TRANSMITTAL

DEPARTMENT OF COMMERCE,
BUREAU OF THE CENSUS,
Washington, D. C., December 20, 1934.

SIR: I transmit herewith a report on the Negro population of the United States, entitled "Negroes in the United States: 1920-32", prepared under the supervision of Z. R. Pettet, chief statistician for the Division of Agriculture, by Charles E. Hall, specialist in Negro statistics, assisted by Charles W. White. This report supplements the volume, "Negro Population in the United States, 1790-1915", published by the Bureau of the Census in 1918. This, I believe, will prove to be a very valuable source of information regarding the progress and status of the Negro race in the United States.

The tabulations for this report were made by a corps of Negro clerks.

WILLIAM LANE AUSTIN,
Director of the Census.

Hon. DANIEL C. ROPER,
Secretary of Commerce.

CONTENTS

TABLES

Chapter IX.—MARITAL CONDITIONS

TABLES

Chapter X.—FERTILITY; PROPORTION OF CHILDREN TO WOMEN OF CHILDBEARING AGE

TABLES

CONTENTS

Chapter XIII.—FAMILIES

TABLES

Chapter XIV.—OCCUPATIONS

TABLES

Chapter XV.—VITAL STATISTICS, BIRTHS AN INFANT MORTALITY

MAP

TABLES

Chapter XVI.—VITAL STATISTICS—MORTALITY

Chapter XVII.—RETAIL BUSINESS

APPENDIX

NEGROES IN THE UNITED STATES 1920-32

INTRODUCTION

Source and scope of the data.—Statistics relating to The Negro race covering a period of 125 years from 1790—the date of the first United States census—to 1915, were published in volume form by the Bureau of the Census in 1918, and this supplementary report for the years 1920 to 1932 is designed to bring up to date the previous publication through the inclusion of additional data compiled by the Bureau of the Census since 1915, thus completing a statistical record of available data covering 142 years. The 1790 to 1915 volume was largely historical in character in that it embraced two important periods in the status of the American Negro—from 1790 to 1860, slavery— from 1870 to 1915, freedom. This report, however, differs from the previous one in that it is purely a factual presentation of available census data covering the years 1920 to 1932, and is simply another entry in the record of the activities and progress of the Negro population in continental United States. The statistics presented are for the United States as a whole, for the three main sections of the country (the South, the North, and the West), for the several States and the District of Columbia, for nine groups of States designated "geographic divisions", and for urban and rural areas. In some of the chapters, statistics are presented for counties and cities in which the Negro population constitute an important part of the total population.

Specifically, this volume presents statistics relative to the Negro race—growth by decades; geographical distribution in 1930 and changes in this distribution during the previous 10 years; movement to the North and to the cities; sex and age composition; marital condition; annual mortality and births in the registration area; school attendance and illiteracy; criminality insofar as this can be measured by the number of persons committed to State and Federal prisons and reformatories; number gainfully occupied; distribution according to occupation groups; ownership and value of homes; religious bodies and Sunday schools; retail business as conducted by Negro proprietors; farms, farm operators, and agricultural production.

The need for a special report arises from the fact that the census statistics relating to the subject must otherwise be sought for in many different volumes covering population, agriculture, occupation, mortality, retail business, and other general subjects. These statistics are not easily accessible to the public until they are brought together in a single publication. Much of the explanatory text of this volume is necessarily taken from the various general reports of the Bureau.

Part of the statistics presented in this chapter have been compiled from published tables of the Bureau of the Census, although in many tables the material has been reorganized from that previously published. This volume also presents much material which has never been published before by the Census Bureau.

Statistics on the Negro population have tended to become more comprehensive and detailed, not only as to the diversity of topics covered by schedule inquiries, but also in regard to tabulation made.

For the most part, the latest statistics presented here are for 1930. These data were secured in the censuses of agriculture, and population, taken as of April 1, 1930. For religious bodies, the latest available census data were for 1926. Many statistics on Negro births are presented here for the first time. Data on births, mortality, and persons in State and Federal prisons and reformatories are presented for 1931, since these data are compiled annually by the Bureau of the Census. Statistics on retail business as conducted by Negro proprietors were secured by a canvass in 1930 and reports were for the business of the year 1929.

Color and race.—In the main, tabulations of the population by color or race, three groups are distinguished, namely, Negroes, whites, and "other races." In some of the tables, the third group has been subdivided into its constituent parts such as Indian, Chinese, Japanese, Hindu, etc. In several of the tables, data are presented for the total population and for Negroes, and whites, omitting the relatively small numbers of "other races." The figures for "other races", however, are included in the totals and can be obtained, if needed, by adding the figures for Negro and white and subtracting the sum from the total. In other tables, only two classes of population are shown, namely, colored and white, because in carrying out the tabulation scheme, the figures were compiled in this manner. In such cases, "colored" includes Negro, Indian, Chinese, Japanese, etc.

Urban and rural areas.—Throughout many of the chapters in this volume, statistics are presented for the population classified as urban or rural. Urban population, as defined by the Bureau of the Census is, in general, that residing in cities or other incorporated places having 2,500 inhabitants or more, the remainder being classified as rural. In three States, New Hampshire, Massachusetts, and Rhode Island, conditions are exceptional in that the compactly built portions of the towns (townships) are not separately incorporated or politically distinct in any way from the rural territory within the same town; nor is it the usual practice to incorporate even the larger places as cities until they attain a population in excess of 10,000. Consequently, if only cities were counted as urban, the classification would be inadequate. In 1920 and 1910 all towns in these three States which had a population of 2,500 or more were classified as urban. This resulted in the inclusion of a considerable number of places that were mainly rural in their general characteristics. In 1930, the special rule for these three States was modified so as to place in the urban classification, in addition to the regularly incorporated cities, only those towns in which there was a village or thickly settled area having more than 2,500 inhabitants and comprising either by itself or when combined with other villages in the same town, more than 50 percent of the total population of the towns.

In 1930 another modification extended the classification or urban to include townships or other political subdivisions (not incorporated as municipalities, nor containing any area so incorporated) which had a total population of 10,000 or more and a population density of 1,000 or more per square mile. In the tables in this volume, the figures for 1910 and 1920 are presented as these statistics were then published, hence the data for these 2 years are not exactly comparable with those for 1930 for urban and rural areas.

Rural-farm and rural-nonfarm areas.—Rural population is subdivided into two classes, rural-farm and rural-nonfarm. The classification of the population as to rural-farm and rural-nonfarm is based on the reply to the question in the population schedule, reading: "Does this family live on a farm?" Those persons living on farms were classified as rural-farm and those living outside cities or other incorporated places having 2,500 inhabitants or more, who did not live on farms, as rural-nonfarm.

Fewer 75 percent Negro counties.—In 1930 there were 19 counties in which Negroes constituted 75 percent or more of the total population. Mississippi reported 8 of these counties; Alabama, 6, Georgia 2; and Arkansas, Louisiana, and Virginia, 1 each. At the Census of 1920 there were 36, and at the Census of 1910 there were 53 counties in which the Negro population formed 75 percent or more of the total county population. In 1930, Tunica County, Miss., reported 6,103 and Lowndes County, Ala., 6,048 Negroes per 1,000 whites. Negroes constituted 85.8 percent of the total population of each county.

School attendance.—For the United States as a whole, 60 percent of the Negro population 5 to 20 years of age attended school in 1930, as compared with 53.5 percent in 1920, 44.7 percent in 1910, and only 9.2 percent in 1870. Of the 15 cities having 50,000 or more Negro inhabitants, Cleveland, Ohio, reported the highest percentage of Negro children 7 to 15 years of age attending school. Chicago occupied second rank in this respect, and was followed in the order named by New York, Washington, Philadelphia, Pittsburgh, St. Louis, Houston, Baltimore, Memphis, Birmingham, Richmond, Detroit, New Orleans, and Atlanta. The percent attending school ranged from 97 in Cleveland to 86.6 in Atlanta.

Agriculture.—The farming activities of the Negro are generally listed as an asset to the agricultural resources and wealth of the Nation. Of the 13,853,599 bales of cotton produced in the Southern States in 1929, colored farmers produced 4,492,807, or 32.4 percent of the total. Colored farm owners produced 533,141 bales valued at $45,408,734. The value of farm products sold, traded, or used by the families of colored farm owners in the South amounted to $119,415,311.

Negroes engaged in principal professions.—In the total Negro population of 11,891,143 reported at the Census of 1930, there were 54,439 school teachers; 25,034 clergymen; 10,583 musicians and teachers of music; 5,728 trained nurses; 3,805 physicians and surgeons; 2,146 college presidents and professors; 1,746 dentists; and 1,230 lawyers, judges, and justices. Nearly 40 percent (39.3) of the physicians and surgeons were located in 7 northern States (New Jersey, New York, Pennsylvania, Ohio, Michigan, Illinois, and Missouri) and the District of Columbia, having a combined population of less than 19 percent of the total Negro population of the United States.

Negro home ownership.—During the 10 years, 1920 to 1930, there was an increase of 126,991 owned homes occupied by Negro families in the United States. The South reported an increase of 15.6 percent; the North, 67.4 percent; and the West an increase of 89.3 percent. Michigan led all other States with an increase of 183.1 percent, followed in the order named by Arizona, California, New York, District of Columbia, and New Jersey. Of the 15 cities having a Negro population of 50,000 or more, Philadelphia led with the greatest number of homes owned.

Decline of Negro illiteracy.—Of the 9,292,556 Negroes 10 years of age and over, 1,513,892 or 16.3 percent were reported illiterate, as compared with 2,789,689 or 81.4 percent in 1870, 60 years previous. South Carolina reported the highest percentage of Negro illiteracy for the United States in 1930, having displaced Louisiana where the highest percentage had been reported at each census since 1890. Alabama and Louisiana occupied second and third places, respectively, in 1930.

Marital condition in principal cities.—Of the 53 cities having 15,000 or more Negro inhabitants at the Census of 1930, Kansas City, Kans., reported the highest percentage of married males, Tulsa, Okla., widowed, and Beaumont, Tex., divorced males. For females, Gary, Ind., occupied first rank in the percentage married; Augusta, Ga., with widowed and Beaumont, Tex., with the highest percentage of divorced.

Infant mortality.—The highest colored infant mortality rate in 1931 for the seven cities with 100,000 or more Negro population was reported for Washington, D. C., with 115.2 deaths under 1 year per 1,000 live births. Baltimore, New York, New Orleans, Philadelphia, Detroit, and Chicago followed, in the order named.

Death rates from all causes.—For the seven cities having 100,000 or more Negro inhabitants as reported at the last census, the colored death rates from all causes per 1,000 estimated population (July 1, 1931), were as follows: New Orleans, 23.5; Washington, 22; Baltimore, 19.9; New York, 16.2; Philadelphia, 15.9; Chicago, 15.3; and Detroit, 13.2. Slightly higher rates were reported in 1931 than for 1930 for Baltimore and Washington while the New York rate remained unchanged. Decreased rates were reported for Chicago, Detroit, New Orleans, and Philadelphia.

Retail stores operated by Negro proprietors.—Of the 25,701 stores, 18,864 or 73.4 percent were in the South, 6,475, or 25.2 percent in the North, and 362, or 1.4 percent in the West, and of the $101,146,043 reported value of sales, the South with 78.7 percent of the total Negro population reported $57,036,307, or 56.4 percent of the total sales, the North with 20.3 percent of the Negro population reported $40,335,397, or 39.9 percent of the sales, and the West with 1 percent of the Negro population reported $3,774,339, or 3.7 percent of the total sales. Among the States, Texas reported the highest value of sales, $6,633,701, followed by Pennsylvania with sales amounting to $6,519,865; Illinois, $6,466,323; North Carolina, $5,770,830; New York, $5,625,743, and Georgia, $5,147,040. No other State reported sales valued at $5,000,000 or more. The Negro population of these six leading States, as reported at the Census of 1930, was 4,017,779, or 33.8 percent of the total Negro population of the United States.

CHAPTER I.—NEGRO POPULATION AND GROWTH IN THE UNITED STATES

Summarization of chapter.—In the 140 years from 1790 to 1930 the Negro population increased from three-quarters of a million to nearly 12 millions. Approximately one-third of this increase has taken place since 1900. The increase in Negro population from 1920 to 1930 was greater than the total Negro population shown in the census of 1800.

In nearly every decade (with two exceptions, 1800–10 and 1870–80), the percentage of increase for the Negro race has been below that for the white race. The large percentage of increase in the number of Negroes in the decade from 1800–10 was due to the importation of Africans prior to 1808, after which year the slave trade was prohibited by law. The rate of increase in the decades 1860–70 and 1870–80 were materially affected by the under count of Negroes in the census of 1870. If an adjusted figure for 1870 had been used for Negroes, the percentage of increase shown in table 1 would have been lower for the Negro than for the white race. The increase shown for the Negro population in the decade 1920–30 is equivalent to a constant annual increase of 1.28 percent, as compared with 0.63 percent for the decade 1910–20 and 1.07 percent for the decade 1900–10.

Usually the rate of increase for the Negro race has been very much lower than that of the white race. Immigration, which since the early part of the nineteenth century has been an important contributing factor in the growth of the white population, has contributed very little to the growth of the Negro population. Since 1810 the growth of the Negro population has been almost entirely due to natural increase by excess of births over deaths.

The rapid downward trend in the decennial rate of increase in Negro population from 1880 to 1920 is largely due to the decline in the birth rate. In the decade 1920–30 there appears a reversal of this downward trend. Death and birth registration figures, showing that the Negro death rate declined more rapidly than the Negro birth rate, substantiate the upward trend for the last decade.

Fluctuations in the decennial rates of increase in the Negro population are difficult to explain. For example: The rate of increase dropped from 11.2 percent in the decade 1900–10 to 6.5 percent in the decade 1910–20, followed by a rate of 13.6 percent between 1920 and 1930. Similar fluctuations occurred between the decades 1870–80 and 1880–90. These fluctuations have been so considerable as to be in themselves improbable and have been contrary in direction in successive decades. In the face of these fluctuations the Bureau of the Census has admitted an under count of Negroes in 1870 and the possibility of an under-count in 1890 and 1920. However, it is not correct to assume that the fluctuations between the decades 1900–10 and 1910–20 were due entirely to an incomplete enumeration. The influenza epidemic in 1918–19, together with shifts in Negro population caused by labor conditions, military service in the World War, and the advent of the bollweevil into areas of relatively high density of Negro population, contributed to the decrease in the birth rate, on the one hand, and the noticeable increase in the death rate, on the other.

In table 4 an attempt has been made to present data which eliminate the influence of the deficient enumeration in 1870 and 1890. In this table the increase during each decade has been determined by taking the increase in Negro population in the area included in the preceding census and not the increase in the United States as a whole. Fluctuations in the percentage increase are markedly reduced in table 4, even in the earlier decades, as compared with those shown in table 1.

Table 1.—NEGRO, WHITE, AND OTHER POPULATION OF THE UNITED STATES, WITH DECENNIAL INCREASE: 1790 TO 1930

[For a revision of figures in accordance with estimates of the Negro population for 1870 and 1890, and with reference to extensions of the area of census enumeration, see table 4]

CENSUS YEAR	All classes	NEGRO		White	Other races	INCREASE DURING PRECEDING 10 YEARS					
						Number			Percent		
		Number	Percent			All classes	Negro	White	All classes	Negro	White
1930	122, 775, 046	11, 891, 143	9. 7	108, 864, 207	2, 019, 696	17, 064, 426	1, 428, 012	14, 743, 833	16. 1	13. 6	15. 7
1920	105, 710, 620	10, 463, 131	9. 9	[1] 94, 120, 374	[1] 1, 127, 115	13, 738, 354	635, 368	12, 755, 927	14. 9	6. 5	15. 7
1910	91, 972, 266	9, 827, 763	10. 7	[1] 81, 364, 447	[1] 780, 056	15, 977, 691	993, 769	14, 555, 251	21. 0	11. 2	21. 8
1900	75, 994, 575	8, 833, 994	11. 6	66, 809, 196	351, 385	13, 046, 861	1, 345, 318	11, 707, 938	20. 7	18. 0	21. 2
1890	62, 947, 714	7, 488, 676	11. 9	55, 101, 258	357, 780	12, 791, 931	907, 883	11, 698, 288	25. 5	13. 8	27. 0
1880	50, 155, 783	6, 580, 793	13. 1	43, 402, 970	172, 020	11, 597, 412	1, 700, 784	9, 813, 593	30. 1	22. 0	29. 2
1870	38, 558, 371	4, 880, 009	12. 7	33, 589, 377	88, 985	7, 115, 050	438, 179	6, 666, 840	22. 6	21. 4	24. 8
1860	31, 443, 321	4, 441, 830	14. 1	26, 922, 537	78, 954	8, 251, 445	803, 022	7, 369, 469	35. 6	22. 1	37. 7
1850	23, 191, 876	3, 638, 808	15. 7	19, 553, 068	----------	6, 122, 423	765, 160	5, 357, 263	35. 9	26. 6	37. 7
1840	17, 069, 453	2, 873, 648	16. 8	14, 195, 805	----------	4, 203, 433	545, 006	3, 658, 427	32. 7	23. 4	34. 7
1830	12, 866, 020	2, 328, 642	18. 1	10, 537, 378	----------	3, 227, 567	556, 986	2, 670, 581	33. 5	31. 4	33. 9
1820	9, 638, 453	1, 771, 656	18. 4	7, 866, 797	----------	2, 398, 572	393, 848	2, 004, 724	33. 1	28. 6	34. 2
1810	7, 239, 881	1, 377, 808	19. 0	5, 862, 073	----------	1, 931, 398	375, 771	1, 555, 627	36. 4	37. 5	36. 1
1800	5, 308, 483	1, 002, 037	18. 9	4, 306, 446	----------	1, 379, 269	244, 829	1, 134, 440	35. 1	32. 3	35. 8
1790	3, 929, 214	757, 208	19. 3	3, 172, 006	----------	----------	----------	----------	----------	----------	----------

[1] A total of 700,541 and 367,510 Mexicans (estimated) have been excluded from the white population of 1920 and 1910, respectively, and added to "Other races." For census years prior to 1910 the white population includes Mexicans.

99576—35——1

TABLE 2.—POPULATION OF THE UNITED STATES AND INCREASE, BY CLASSES: 1930, 1920, AND 1910

RACIAL CLASS	1930	1920	1910	INCREASE OR DECREASE (—) 1920-30 Number	1920-30 Percent	1910-20 Number	1910-20 Percent
All classes	**122,775,046**	**105,710,620**	**91,972,266**	**17,064,426**	**16.1**	**13,738,354**	**14.9**
Negro	11,891,143	10,463,131	9,827,763	1,428,012	13.6	635,368	6.5
White	108,864,207	[1] 94,120,374	[1] 81,364,447	14,743,833	15.7	12,755,927	15.7
Mexican	1,422,533	700,541	367,510	721,992	103.1	333,031	90.6
Indian	332,397	244,437	265,683	87,960	36.0	−21,246	−8.0
Chinese	74,954	61,639	71,531	13,315	21.6	−9,892	−13.8
Japanese	138,834	111,010	72,157	27,824	25.1	38,853	53.8
Other races	50,978	9,488	3,175	41,490	437.3	6,313	198.8

[1] Figures for the white population in 1920 and 1910 are adjusted by deducting the estimated numbers of Mexicans which are shown separately.

TABLE 3.—INCREASE IN NEGRO AND WHITE POPULATION BY 20- AND 70-YEAR PERIODS: 1790 TO 1930

PERIOD	POPULATION AT BEGINNING OF PERIOD: Negro	POPULATION AT BEGINNING OF PERIOD: White	INCREASE DURING PERIOD: Number: Negro	Number: White	Percent: Negro	Percent: White	Negroes per 1,000 whites in the increase
1930	11,891,143	108,864,207					
20-year periods:							
1910–30	9,827,763	[1] 81,364,447	2,063,380	27,499,760	21.0	33.8	75
1890–1910	7,488,676	55,101,258	2,339,087	26,263,189	31.2	47.7	89
1870–90	4,880,009	33,589,377	2,608,667	21,511,881	53.5	64.0	121
1850–70	3,638,808	19,553,068	1,241,201	14,036,309	34.1	71.8	88
1830–50	2,328,642	10,537,378	1,310,166	9,015,690	56.3	85.6	145
1810–30	1,377,808	5,862,073	950,834	4,675,305	69.0	79.8	203
1790–1810	757,208	3,172,006	620,600	2,690,067	82.0	84.8	231
70-year periods:							
1860–1930	4,441,830	26,922,537	7,449,313	81,941,670	167.7	304.4	91
1790–1860	757,208	3,172,006	3.684,622	23,750,531	486.6	748.8	155

[1] A total of 367,510 Mexicans have been excluded from the white population for 1910. For census years prior to 1910 the white population includes Mexicans.

TABLE 4.—NEGRO POPULATION REVISED FIGURES OF INCREASE: 1790 TO 1930

[Figures in *italics* are estimated]

CENSUS YEAR	NEGRO POPULATION: Number	Increase during preceding 10 years: Total	Population of area enumerated first in the year specified	Increase within area enumerated at preceding census: Number	Increase within area enumerated at preceding census: Percent	Percent increase in white population within area enumerated at preceding census	Percent Negro in the total population	Negroes per 1,000 white population
1930	11,891,143	1,428,012		1,428,012	13.6	15.7	9.7	109
1920	10,463,131	635,368		635,368	6.5	15.7	9.9	111
1910	9,827,763	993,769		993,769	11.2	22.3	10.7	120
1900	8,833,994	*1,073,994*		*1,073,994*	*13.8*	21.2	11.6	132
1890	*7,760,000*	*1,179,207*	21,609	*1,160,571*	*17.6*	26.7	*12.3*	*142*
1880	6,580,793	*1,188,621*	452	*1,188,621*	*22.0*	*26.4*	13.1	152
1870	*5,392,172*	*950,342*		*950,342*	*21.4*	*27.5*	*13.5*	*157*
1860	4,441,830	803,022	830	802,222	22.0	36.8	14.1	165
1850	3,638,808	765,160	59,838	705,361	24.5	35.4	15.7	186
1840	2,873,648	545,006	284	544,818	23.4	34.3	16.8	202
1830	2,328,642	556,986	44,126	540,641	30.5	33.7	18.1	221
1820	1,771,656	393,848		393,848	28.6	34.2	18.4	225
1810	1,377,808	375,771	46,788	329,908	32.9	34.9	19.0	235
1800	1,002,037	244,829	[1] 4,480	240,349	31.7	34.0	18.9	233
1790	757,208						19.3	239

[1] Includes slaves only for western Georgia.

CHAPTER II.—GEOGRAPHIC DISTRIBUTION AND INCREASE

Negro distribution by sections and divisions.—The largest proportion of the Negro population resides in the South. Of the total Negro population in 1930, 78.7 percent was in the Southern States. Over 37 percent of the total was in the South Atlantic States alone. Approximately one-fifth of the total was in the North, and only 1 percent was in the West.

The greatest change in the distribution of the Negro race within the United States since 1790 occurred in the decade 1920–30. During the last decade there has been a marked shift northward. Previous to 1919 the proportion of the Negro population resident in the South did not vary greatly from census to census. In 1790, the proportion living in the South was 91.1 percent and this proportion increased in succeeding decades to a maximum proportion of 92.8 percent in 1830. It fell off in 1870, and declined slightly, from census to census, to 89 percent in 1910. It dropped from 89 percent to 85.2 percent from 1910 to 1920 and to 78.7 percent in 1930.

In the 140 years since 1790 the principal direction of migration has been westward and a large part of the growth of the Negro population within the South has taken place in the East South Central and West South Central divisions. In 1790, of the total Negro population, 88.9 percent was in the South Atlantic States. In 1930, only 37.2 percent of the total Negro population was resident in these States. The general westward migration brought an increase in the percentage living in the East South Central States from 2.2 percent in 1790 to 31.4 percent in 1860. This percentage has decreased at each census since 1860 to 22.4 percent in 1930.

Growth of Negro population and distribution of increase by divisions and sections.—Between 1920 and 1930 the Negro population increased over 1,400,000 as compared with about 600,000 for the period 1910–20. The growth of the Negro population during the 20 years, 1910–30, was less than during the period 1890–1910, or the period 1870–90.

More than two-thirds of the increase in the Negro population during the last two decades has taken place in the North. Between 1790 and 1830, and between 1870 and 1910, most of the growth of the Negro population occurred in the South Atlantic States. From 1830 to 1850 the largest part of the increase occurred in the East South Central States and from 1850 to 1870, in the West South Central States.

Negro distribution by States.—Over 40 percent of the Negro population in 1930 was in the 5 States having the largest number of Negroes: Georgia, Mississippi, Alabama, North Carolina, and Texas. These 5 States, together with 6 other Southern States, South Carolina, Louisiana, Virginia, Arkansas, Tennessee, and Florida, had 70.7 percent of the total Negro population in 1930. Two States, Georgia and Mississippi, each had more than a million Negroes in 1930, and 6 States, New Hampshire, Idaho, South Dakota, Vermont, Nevada, and North Dakota, had less than 1,000 each. Pennsylvania, New York, and Illinois had the largest number of Negroes of any of the Northern States. Between 1920 and 1930 the Negro population increased in 32 States and the District of Columbia and decreased in 16 States.

Negro population per square mile in 1930.—There were 4 Negroes per square mile in the United States in 1930 as compared with 41.3 persons for all the population and 36.6 for all whites. The Negroes numbered 10.7 per square mile in the South, 2.6 in the North, and only about 0.1 in the West. In the rural South there were 7.3 Negroes per square mile, whereas, in the rural areas of the North and West there was less than one Negro per square mile. In the North, the Negro population was almost completely urban, whereas most of the Negroes in the South lived in rural areas.

TABLE 1.—INCREASE BY 20-YEAR PERIODS FOR NEGRO AND WHITE POPULATION, BY SECTIONS, AND SOUTHERN DIVISIONS: 1790 TO 1930

PERIOD	INCREASE OF POPULATION													
	United States		The South								The North		The West	
			Total		South Atlantic division		East South Central division		West South Central division					
	Negro	White	Negro	White	Negro	White	Negro	White	Negro	White	Negro	White	Negro	White
	NUMBER													
1910–30	2,063,380	27,499,760	612,150	7,357,626	308,900	3,277,811	5,725	1,470,460	297,525	2,609,355	1,381,545	15,760,769	69,685	4,381,365
1890–1910	2,339,087	26,263,189	1,988,850	7,122,800	849,798	2,479,324	532,716	1,448,486	606,336	3,194,990	326,656	15,591,800	23,581	3,548,589
1870–90	2,608,667	21,511,881	2,339,766	5,330,244	1,045,985	1,596,911	655,545	1,366,577	638,236	2,006,756	248,200	14,220,026	20,701	1,961,611
1850–70	1,241,201	14,036,309	1,068,613	2,232,794	355,834	817,019	341,462	698,610	371,317	717,166	167,449	11,070,695	5,139	732,819
1830–50 [1]	1,310,166	9,015,690	1,190,313	2,084,451	331,588	701,750	621,203	926,099	237,522	456,602	118,612	6,758,980	1,241	177,577
1810–30	950,834	4,675,305	893,386	1,354,425	448,483	522,378	356,133	751,246	88,770	80,801	57,448	3,315,562	-------	-------
1790–1810	620,600	2,690,067	578,715	920,148	407,338	415,747	129,132	470,090	42,245	34,311	41,885	1,769,919	-------	-------
	PERCENT													
1910–30	21.0	33.8	7.0	36.2	7.5	40.6	0.2	25.6	15.0	40.2	134.4	28.9	137.5	68.2
1890–1910	31.2	47.7	29.4	54.0	26.0	44.2	25.1	33.6	44.0	96.9	46.6	39.9	87.1	123.6
1870–90	53.5	64.0	52.9	67.8	47.2	53.8	44.8	46.5	86.3	155.7	54.8	57.3	324.5	215.5
1850–70	34.1	71.8	31.9	39.7	19.1	29.0	30.4	31.2	100.8	125.4	58.7	80.5	414.1	412.7
1830–50	56.3	85.6	55.1	58.8	21.7	33.2	123.8	70.5	181.3	396.7	71.1	96.7	-------	-------
1810–30	69.0	79.8	70.4	61.8	41.5	32.8	244.8	133.4	210.1	235.5	52.6	90.3	-------	-------
1790–1810	82.0	84.8	83.9	72.4	60.5	35.3	791.2	505.2	-------	-------	62.1	93.1	-------	-------

[1] Total population for 1830 included 5,318 white persons on public ships in the service of the United States, not credited to any division or State.

TABLE 2.—GEOGRAPHIC DISTRIBUTION OF POPULATION BY RACE AND NATIVITY, BY SECTIONS, AND DIVISIONS: 1930

SECTION AND DIVISION	Total population	NEGRO			WHITE			MEXICAN			Indian	Chinese	Japanese	All other [1]
		Total	Native	Foreign born	Total	Native	Foreign born	Total	Native	Foreign born				
	NUMBER													
United States	122,775,046	11,891,143	11,792,523	98,620	108,864,207	95,497,800	13,366,407	1,422,533	805,535	616,998	332,397	74,954	138,834	50,978
THE SOUTH	37,857,633	9,361,577	9,347,049	14,528	27,673,879	27,141,704	532,175	698,090	429,494	268,596	116,836	4,194	1,126	1,931
South Atlantic	15,793,589	4,421,388	4,408,804	12,584	11,349,284	11,045,006	304,278	691	232	459	19,060	1,869	393	940
East South Central	9,887,214	2,658,238	2,657,706	532	7,224,614	7,166,949	57,665	1,403	724	679	2,106	743	46	64
West South Central	12,176,830	2,281,951	2,280,539	1,412	9,099,981	8,929,749	170,232	695,996	428,538	267,458	95,670	1,582	687	963
THE NORTH	73,021,191	2,409,219	2,327,183	82,036	70,388,367	59,001,814	11,386,553	104,986	36,076	68,910	78,237	25,877	6,039	8,466
New England	8,166,341	94,086	82,300	11,786	8,065,113	6,230,803	1,834,310	107	39	68	2,466	3,794	352	423
Middle Atlantic	26,260,750	1,052,899	988,334	64,565	25,172,104	19,903,062	5,269,042	6,757	1,528	5,229	7,709	14,005	3,662	3,614
East North Central	25,297,185	930,450	925,293	5,157	24,277,663	21,053,739	3,223,924	58,317	17,104	41,213	19,817	6,340	1,022	3,576
West North Central	13,296,915	331,784	331,256	528	12,873,487	11,814,210	1,059,277	39,805	17,405	22,400	48,245	1,738	1,003	853
THE WEST	11,896,222	120,347	118,291	2,056	10,801,961	9,354,282	1,447,679	619,457	339,965	279,492	137,324	44,883	31,669	40,581
Mountain	3,701,789	30,225	30,038	187	3,303,586	3,015,672	287,914	249,314	162,818	86,496	102,083	3,252	11,418	1,911
Pacific	8,194,433	90,122	88,253	1,869	7,498,375	6,338,610	1,159,765	370,143	177,147	192,996	35,241	41,631	120,251	38,670
	PERCENT DISTRIBUTION													
United States	100.0	100.0	100.0	100.0	100.0	100.0	100.0	100.0	100.0	100.0	100.0	100.0	100.0	100.0
THE SOUTH	30.8	78.7	79.3	14.7	25.4	28.4	4.0	49.1	53.3	43.5	35.1	5.6	0.8	3.8
South Atlantic	12.9	37.2	37.4	12.8	10.4	11.6	2.3	([2])	([2])	.1	5.7	2.5	.3	1.8
East South Central	8.1	22.4	22.5	.5	6.6	7.5	.4	.1	.1	.1	.6	1.0	([2])	.1
West South Central	9.9	19.2	19.3	1.4	8.4	9.4	1.3	48.9	53.2	43.3	28.8	2.1	0.5	1.9
THE NORTH	59.5	20.3	19.7	83.2	64.7	61.8	85.2	7.4	4.5	11.2	23.5	34.5	4.3	16.6
New England	6.7	.8	.7	12.0	7.4	6.5	13.7	([2])	([2])	([2])	.7	5.1	.3	.8
Middle Atlantic	21.4	8.9	8.4	65.5	23.1	20.8	39.4	.5	.2	.8	2.3	18.7	2.6	7.1
East North Central	20.6	7.8	7.8	5.2	22.3	22.0	24.1	4.1	2.1	6.7	6.0	8.5	.7	7.0
West North Central	10.8	2.8	2.8	.5	11.8	12.4	7.9	2.8	2.2	3.6	14.5	2.3	.7	1.7
THE WEST	9.7	1.0	1.0	2.1	9.9	9.8	10.8	43.5	42.2	45.3	41.3	59.9	94.8	79.6
Mountain	3.0	.3	.3	.2	3.0	3.2	2.2	17.5	20.2	14.0	30.7	4.3	8.2	3.7
Pacific	6.7	.8	.7	1.9	6.9	6.6	8.7	26.0	22.0	31.3	10.6	55.5	86.6	75.9

[1] Includes Filipino, Hindu, Korean, Hawaiian, Malay, Siamese, and Samoan.

[2] Less than 1/10 of 1 percent.

TABLE 3.—TOTAL AND NEGRO POPULATION BY SECTIONS, AND SOUTHERN DIVISIONS: 1830 TO 1930

SECTION AND DIVISION	POPULATION										
	1930	1920	1910	1900	1890	1880	1870	1860	1850	1840	1830
	TOTAL										
United States	**122,775,046**	**105,710,620**	**91,972,266**	**75,994,575**	**62,947,714**	**50,155,783**	**38,558,371**	**31,443,321**	**23,191,876**	**[1]17,069,453**	**[1] 12,866,020**
THE SOUTH	37,857,633	33,125,803	29,389,330	24,523,527	20,028,059	16,516,568	12,288,020	11,133,361	8,982,612	6,950,729	5,707,848
South Atlantic	15,793,589	13,990,272	12,194,895	10,443,480	8,857,922	7,597,197	5,853,610	5,364,703	4,679,090	3,925,299	3,645,75
East South Central	9,887,214	8,893,307	8,409,901	7,547,757	6,429,154	5,585,151	4,404,445	4,020,991	3,363,271	2,575,445	1,815,96
West South Central	12,176,830	10,242,224	8,784,534	6,532,290	4,740,983	3,334,220	2,029,965	1,747,667	940,251	449,985	246,12
THE NORTH	73,021,191	63,681,845	55,757,115	47,379,699	39,817,386	31,871,518	25,279,841	19,690,984	14,030,446	10,112,624	7,152,854
THE WEST	11,896,222	8,902,972	6,825,821	4,091,349	3,102,269	1,767,697	990,510	618,976	178,818	----------	----------
	NEGRO										
United States	**11,891,143**	**10,463,131**	**9,827,763**	**8,833,994**	**7,488,676**	**6,580,793**	**4,880,009**	**4,441,830**	**3,638,808**	**2,873,648**	**2,328,642**
THE SOUTH	9,361,577	8,912,231	8,749,427	7,922,969	6,760,577	5,953,903	4,420,811	4,097,111	3,352,198	2,641,977	2,161,885
South Atlantic	4,421,388	4,325,120	4,112,488	3,729,017	3,262,690	2,941,202	2,216,705	2,058,198	1,860,871	1,597,317	1,529,283
East South Central	2,658,238	2,523,532	2,652,513	2,499,886	2,119,797	1,924,996	1,464,252	1,394,360	1,122,790	830,306	501,587
West South Central	2,281,951	2,063,579	1,984,426	1,694,066	1,378,090	1,087,705	739,854	644,553	368,537	214,354	131,015
THE NORTH	2,409,219	1,472,309	1,027,674	880,771	701,018	615,038	452,818	340,240	285,369	231,671	166,757
THE WEST	120,347	78,591	50,662	30,254	27,081	11,852	6,380	4,479	1,241	----------	----------
	PERCENT DISTRIBUTION OF TOTAL POPULATION										
United States	**100.0**	**100.0**	**100.0**	**100.0**	**100.0**	**100.0**	**100.0**	**100.0**	**100.0**	**100.0**	**100.0**
THE SOUTH	30.8	31.3	32.0	32.3	31.8	32.9	31.9	35.4	38.7	40.7	44.4
South Atlantic	12.9	13.2	13.3	13.7	14.1	15.1	15.2	17.1	20.2	23.0	28.3
East South Central	8.1	8.4	9.1	9.9	10.2	11.1	11.4	12.8	14.5	15.1	14.1
West South Central	9.9	9.7	9.6	8.6	7.5	6.6	5.3	5.6	4.1	2.6	1.9
THE NORTH	59.5	60.2	60.6	62.3	63.3	63.5	65.6	62.6	60.5	59.2	55.6
THE WEST	9.7	8.4	7.4	5.4	4.9	3.5	2.6	2.0	.8	----------	----------
	PERCENT DISTRIBUTION OF NEGRO POPULATION										
United States	**100.0**	**100.0**	**100.0**	**100.0**	**100.0**	**100.0**	**100.0**	**100.0**	**100.0**	**100.0**	**100.0**
THE SOUTH	78.7	85.2	89.0	89.7	90.3	90.5	90.6	92.2	92.1	91.9	92.8
South Atlantic	37.2	41.3	41.8	42.2	43.6	44.7	45.4	46.3	51.1	55.6	65.7
East South Central	22.4	24.1	27.0	28.3	28.3	29.3	30.0	31.4	30.9	28.9	21.5
West South Central	19.2	19.7	20.2	19.2	18.4	16.5	15.2	14.5	10.1	7.5	5.6
THE NORTH	20.3	14.1	10.5	10.0	9.4	9.3	9.3	7.7	7.8	8.1	7.2
THE WEST	1.0	.8	.5	.3	.4	.2	.1	.1	(2)	----------	----------

[1] Includes white persons (6,100 in 1840 and 5,318 in 1830) on public ships in the service of the United States, not credited to any division or State.
[2] Less than 1/10 of 1 percent.

Table 4.—RANK OF STATES ACCORDING TO NEGRO POPULATION: 1790 TO 1930

STATE	1930	1920	1910	1900	1890	1880	1870	1860	1850	1840	1830	1820	1810	1800	1790
Alabama	3	3	3	3	4	5	3	3	4	5	9	9			
Arizona	33	35	38	37	39	46	47								
Arkansas	9	9	10	10	10	11	12	13	15	16	21	21			
California	25	27	27	30	29	30	30	26	28						
Colorado	32	32	31	32	33	32	37	39							
Connecticut	29	29	29	28	28	27	27	23	23	21	19	17	15	13	11
Delaware	28	28	26	26	24	23	22	19	19	17	15	14	13	10	8
District of Columbia	22	21	20	18	17	18	18	20	20	19	17	16	14	14	
Florida	11	11	11	13	13	14	14	14	16	14	16				
Georgia	1	1	1	1	1	1	1	2	3	3	4	4	5	5	5
Idaho	45	44	46	47	49	48	46								
Illinois	14	17	19	19	19	19	20	24	24	23	24	23	22		
Indiana	24	23	23	21	22	21	21	21	21	22	22	22	24	21	
Iowa	30	30	30	29	30	28	28	30	32	30					
Kansas	26	25	24	23	20	20	24	32							
Kentucky	17	14	12	11	11	10	10	9	9	8	5	5	6	6	9
Louisiana	7	7	5	6	7	7	7	7	7	7	8	8	8		
Maine	43	43	43	40	40	35	32	28	27	25	25	24	21	18	16
Maryland	16	13	13	12	12	12	11	11	10	10	6	5	4	4	2
Massachusetts	27	26	25	25	25	25	25	22	22	20	20	18	16	12	12
Michigan	21	24	28	27	27	26	26	25	26	27	28	27	25		
Minnesota	36	34	24	34	34	34	35	34	35						
Mississippi	2	2	2	2	2	2	4	4	6	6	10	11	12	16	
Missouri	18	18	15	14	14	13	13	12	11	11	13	15	18		
Montana	40	40	39	39	38	41	41								
Nebraska	31	31	33	33	31	33	34	37							
Nevada	48	49	49	49	48	39	38	40							
New Hampshire	44	46	48	45	44	38	36	33	31	28	27	26	20	17	15
New Jersey	19	20	21	20	21	22	19	18	18	15	14	13	11	8	7
New Mexico	38	37	40	38	36	37	43	36	36						
New York	13	15	17	16	18	17	17	16	14	12	11	10	9	7	6
North Carolina	4	5	6	7	6	6	6	6	5	4	3	3	3	3	4
North Dakota	49	48	47	48	47	[1] 47	[1] 45								
Ohio	15	16	18	17	16	16	16	17	17	18	18	19	19	20	
Oklahoma	20	19	16	22	26										
Oregon	39	39	42	41	41	40	39	35	33						
Pennsylvania	12	12	14	15	15	15	15	15	13	13	12	12	10	9	10
Rhode Island	35	33	32	31	32	29	29	27	25	24	23	20	17	15	13
South Carolina	6	4	4	4	3	4	5	5	2	2	2	2	2	2	3
South Dakota	46	45	45	46	46	[1] 44	[1] 45								
Tennessee	10	10	9	9	9	8	8	8	8	9	7	7	7	11	14
Texas	5	6	7	8	8	9	9	10	12						
Utah	42	41	44	44	45	45	44	38	34						
Vermont	47	47	41	43	42	36	33	31	29	26	26	25	23	19	17
Virginia	8	8	8	5	5	3	2	1	1	1	1	1	1	1	1
Washington	37	36	35	36	37	42	40	41							
West Virginia	23	22	22	24	23	24	23								
Wisconsin	34	38	36	35	35	31	31	29	30	29					
Wyoming	41	42	37	42	43	43	42								

[1] Dakota Territory.

Table 5.—RANK OF STATES IN NEGRO, WHITE, AND TOTAL POPULATION: 1930

STATE	Negro population, 1930	RANK OF STATE IN—			NEGRO POPULATION, 1930, CUMULATED BY STATES	
		Negro population	White population	Total population	Number	Percent
United States	**11,891,143**				**11,891,143**	**100.0**
Georgia	1,071,125	1	19	14	1,071,125	9.0
Mississippi	1,009,718	2	31	23	2,080,843	17.5
Alabama	944,834	3	22	15	3,025,677	25.4
North Carolina	918,647	4	16	12	3,944,324	33.2
Texas	854,964	5	7	5	4,799,288	40.4
South Carolina	793,681	6	33	26	5,592,969	47.0
Louisiana	776,326	7	29	22	6,369,295	53.6
Virginia	650,165	8	21	20	7,019,460	59.0
Arkansas	478,463	9	26	25	7,497,923	63.1
Tennessee	477,646	10	17	16	7,975,569	67.1
Florida	431,828	11	30	31	8,407,397	70.7
Pennsylvania	431,257	12	2	2	8,838,654	74.3
New York	412,814	13	1	1	9,251,468	77.8
Illinois	328,972	14	3	3	9,580,440	80.6
Ohio	309,304	15	4	4	9,889,744	83.2
Maryland	276,379	16	27	28	10,166,123	85.5
Kentucky	226,040	17	15	17	10,392,163	87.4
Missouri	223,840	18	10	10	10,616,003	89.3
New Jersey	208,828	19	9	9	10,824,831	91.0
Oklahoma	172,198	20	18	21	10,997,029	92.5
Michigan	169,453	21	6	7	11,166,482	93.9
District of Columbia	132,068	22	44	41	11,298,550	95.0
West Virginia	114,893	23	23	27	11,413,443	96.0
Indiana	111,982	24	11	11	11,525,425	96.9
California	81,048	25	5	6	11,606,473	97.6
Kansas	66,344	26	20	24	11,672,817	98.2
Massachusetts	52,365	27	8	8	11,725,182	98.6
Delaware	32,602	28	48	47	11,757,784	98.9
Connecticut	29,354	29	24	29	11,787,138	99.1
Iowa	17,380	30	14	19	11,804,518	99.3
Nebraska	13,752	31	28	32	11,818,270	99.4
Colorado	11,828	32	32	33	11,830,098	99.5
Arizona	10,749	33	46	44	11,840,847	99.6
Wisconsin	10,739	34	12	13	11,851,586	99.7
Rhode Island	9,913	35	36	37	11,861,499	99.8
Minnesota	9,445	36	13	18	11,870,944	99.8
Washington	6,840	37	25	30	11,877,784	99.9
New Mexico	2,850	38	45	45	11,880,634	99.9
Oregon	2,234	39	34	34	11,882,868	99.9
Montana	1,256	40	39	39	11,884,124	99.9
Wyoming	1,250	41	47	48	11,885,374	100.0
Utah	1,108	42	40	40	11,886,482	100.0
Maine	1,096	43	35	35	11,887,578	100.0
New Hampshire	790	44	41	42	11,888,368	100.0
Idaho	668	45	42	43	11,889,036	100.0
South Dakota	646	46	38	36	11,889,682	100.0
Vermont	568	47	43	46	11,890,250	100.0
Nevada	516	48	49	49	11,890,766	100.0
North Dakota	377	49	37	38	11,891,143	100.0

TABLE 6.—STATES ARRANGED BY PERCENT INCREASE IN NEGRO POPULATION: 1920 TO 1930

STATE	NEGRO POPULATION: Total number, 1930	NEGRO POPULATION: Increase or decrease (−), 1920-30: Number	NEGRO POPULATION: Increase or decrease (−), 1920-30: Percent	Percent increase or decrease (−) in white population, 1920-30
Total	**11,891,143**	**1,428,012**	**13.6**	**15.7**
Michigan	169,453	109,371	182.0	29.2
California	81,048	42,285	109.1	60.3
New York	412,814	214,331	108.0	19.5
Wisconsin	10,739	5,538	106.5	11.4
Illinois	328,972	146,698	80.5	15.4
New Jersey	208,828	91,696	78.3	26.1
Ohio	309,304	123,117	66.1	13.6
Pennsylvania	431,257	146,689	51.5	9.0
Nevada	516	170	49.1	17.3
Connecticut	29,354	8,308	39.5	16.0
Indiana	111,982	31,172	38.6	9.4
Arizona	10,749	2,744	34.3	30.2
West Virginia	114,893	28,548	33.1	17.2
Florida	431,828	102,341	31.1	62.2
New Hampshire	790	169	27.2	5.0
Missouri	223,840	45,599	25.6	5.5
North Carolina	918,647	155,240	20.3	25.3
District of Columbia	132,068	22,102	20.1	8.3
Oklahoma	172,198	22,790	15.3	17.1
Texas	854,964	113,270	15.3	21.4
Massachusetts	52,365	6,899	15.2	10.2
Kansas	66,344	8,419	14.5	5.9
Maryland	276,379	31,900	13.0	12.4
Louisiana	776,326	76,069	10.9	20.5
Mississippi	1,009,718	74,534	8.0	16.8
Delaware	32,602	2,267	7.5	6.8
Minnesota	9,445	636	7.2	7.2
Tennessee	477,646	25,888	5.7	13.4
Alabama	944,834	44,182	4.9	17.5
Colorado	11,828	510	4.5	5.6
Oregon	2,234	90	4.2	21.9
Nebraska	13,752	510	3.9	6.1
Arkansas	478,463	6,243	1.3	7.5
Washington	6,840	−43	−.6	15.3
Vermont	568	−4	−.7	2.0
Rhode Island	9,913	−123	−1.2	14.0
Kentucky	226,040	−9,898	−4.2	9.5
Virginia	650,165	−39,852	−5.8	9.4
South Carolina	793,681	−71,038	−8.2	15.3
Iowa	17,380	−1,625	−8.6	2.8
Wyoming	1,250	−125	−9.1	13.8
Georgia	1,071,125	−135,240	−11.2	8.8
Maine	1,096	−214	−16.3	3.9
North Dakota	377	−90	−19.3	4.9
South Dakota	646	−186	−22.4	8.1
Utah	1,108	−338	−23.4	12.5
Montana	1,256	−402	−24.2	−3.1
Idaho	668	−252	−27.4	3.1
New Mexico	2,850	−2,883	−50.3	9.9

TABLE 7.—INCREASE IN NEGRO AND WHITE POPULATION, BY SECTIONS, AND DIVISIONS: 1920 TO 1930

SECTION AND DIVISION	INCREASE OR DECREASE (−): Number: Negro	Number: White	Percent: Negro	Percent: White	Percent distribution: Negro	Percent distribution: White
United States	**1,428,012**	**14,743,833**	**13.6**	**15.7**	**100.0**	**100.0**
THE SOUTH	449,346	3,941,980	5.0	16.6	31.5	26.7
South Atlantic	96,268	1,700,728	2.2	17.6	6.7	11.5
East South Central	134,706	857,448	5.3	13.5	9.4	5.8
West South Central	218,372	1,383,804	10.6	17.9	15.3	9.4
THE NORTH	936,910	8,302,755	63.6	13.4	65.6	56.3
New England	15,035	749,118	19.0	10.2	1.1	5.1
Middle Atlantic	452,716	3,533,479	75.4	16.3	31.7	24.0
East North Central	415,896	3,346,384	80.8	16.0	29.1	22.7
West North Central	53,263	673,774	19.1	5.5	3.7	4.6
THE WEST	41,756	2,499,098	53.1	30.1	2.9	17.0
Mountain	−576	232,181	−1.9	7.6	(1)	1.6
Pacific	42,332	2,266,917	88.6	43.3	3.0	15.4

1 Less than 1/10 of 1 percent.

TABLE 8.—DENSITY OF NEGRO AND WHITE POPULATION, TOTAL AND RURAL, BY SECTIONS, AND SOUTHERN DIVISIONS: 1930

SECTION AND DIVISION	Land area in square miles	POPULATION PER SQUARE MILE: Total: All classes	Total: Negro	Total: White	Rural: Negro	Rural: White
United States	**2,973,776**	**41.3**	**4.0**	**36.6**	**2.3**	**15.5**
THE SOUTH	878,328	43.1	10.7	31.5	7.3	20.6
South Atlantic	269,073	58.7	16.4	42.2	11.0	26.5
East South Central	179,509	55.1	14.8	40.2	10.6	29.0
West South Central	429,746	28.3	5.3	21.2	3.6	13.4
THE NORTH	918,344	79.5	2.6	76.6	0.3	25.7
THE WEST	1,177,104	10.1	.1	9.2	(1)	3.7

1 Less than 1/10 of 1 percent.

TABLE 9.—PERCENT DISTRIBUTION OF NEGRO POPULATION BY SECTIONS, AND SOUTHERN DIVISIONS: 1790 TO 1930

CENSUS YEAR	United States	THE SOUTH: Total	South Atlantic division	East South Central division	West South Central division	The North	The West
1930	100.0	78.7	37.2	22.4	19.2	20.3	1.0
1920	100.0	85.2	41.3	24.1	19.7	14.1	.8
1910	100.0	89.0	41.8	27.0	20.2	10.5	.5
1900	100.0	89.7	42.2	28.3	19.2	10.0	.3
1890	100.0	90.3	43.6	28.3	18.4	9.4	.4
1880	100.0	90.5	44.7	29.3	16.5	9.3	.2
1870	100.0	90.6	45.4	30.0	15.2	9.3	.1
1860	100.0	92.2	46.3	31.4	14.5	7.7	.1
1850	100.0	92.1	51.1	30.9	10.1	7.8	(1)
1840	100.0	91.9	55.6	28.9	7.5	8.1	--------
1830	100.0	92.8	65.7	21.5	5.6	7.2	--------
1820	100.0	92.7	71.9	16.3	4.6	7.3	--------
1810	100.0	92.1	78.4	10.6	3.1	7.9	--------
1800	100.0	91.6	85.8	5.9	--------	8.4	--------
1790	100.0	91.1	88.9	2.2	--------	8.9	--------

1 Less than 1/10 of 1 percent.

TABLE 10.—NEGRO AND WHITE POPULATION PER SQUARE MILE, 1930, 1920, AND 1910, AND RURAL POPULATION, BY STATES, 1930

[States having Negro population less than 1 per square mile are omitted]

STATE	Land area in square miles, 1930	TOTAL POPULATION									RURAL POPULATION 1930	
		Negro			White			All classes			Negro	White
		1930	1920	1910	1930	1920	1910	1930	1920	1910		
United States	**2, 973, 776**	**4. 0**	**3. 5**	**3. 3**	**36. 6**	**31. 7**	**27. 4**	**41. 3**	**35. 5**	**30. 9**	**2. 3**	**15. 5**
District of Columbia	62	2, 130. 1	1, 773. 6	1, 574. 1	5, 708. 3	5, 271. 4	3, 935. 2	7, 852. 7	7, 292. 9	5, 517. 8	----	----
Maryland	9, 941	27. 8	24. 6	23. 4	136. 2	121. 2	106. 9	164. 1	145. 8	130. 3	11. 7	54. 3
New Jersey	7, 514	27. 8	15. 6	11. 9	509. 6	404..2	325. 5	537. 8	420. 0	337. 7	4. 5	88. 9
South Carolina	30, 495	26. 0	28. 4	27. 4	31. 0	26. 8	22. 3	57. 0	55. 2	49. 7	21. 5	23. 3
Mississippi	46, 362	21. 8	20. 2	21. 8	21. 5	18. 4	17. 0	43. 4	38. 6	38. 8	18. 9	17. 1
North Carolina	48, 740	18. 8	15. 7	14. 3	45. 9	36. 6	30. 8	65. 0	52. 5	45. 3	13. 8	34. 3
Alabama	51, 279	18. 4	17. 6	17. 7	33. 2	28. 2	24. 0	51. 6	45. 8	41. 7	13. 2	23. 9
Georgia	58, 725	18. 2	20. 5	20. 0	31. 3	28. 8	24. 4	49. 5	49. 3	44. 4	12. 8	21. 4
Louisiana	45, 409	17. 1	15. 4	15. 7	29. 0	24. 1	20. 7	46. 3	39. 6	36. 5	11. 4	16. 4
Delaware	1, 965	16. 6	15. 4	15. 9	104. 7	98. 0	87. 1	121. 3	113. 5	103. 0	8. 9	49. 7
Virginia	40, 262	16. 1	17. 1	16. 7	44. 0	40. 2	34. 5	60. 2	57. 4	51. 2	10. 8	29. 8
Tennessee	41, 687	11. 5	10. 8	11. 3	51. 3	45. 2	41. 1	62. 8	56. 1	52. 4	5. 7	35. 6
Pennsylvania	44, 832	9. 6	6. 3	4. 3	205. 0	188. 1	166. 6	214. 8	194. 5	171. 0	1. 3	67. 8
Rhode Island	1, 067	9. 3	9. 4	8. 9	634. 5	556. 7	499. 1	644. 3	566. 4	508. 5	. 8	47. 9
Arkansas	52, 525	9. 1	9. 0	8. 4	26. 2	24. 4	21. 5	35. 3	33. 4	30. 0	7. 4	20. 6
New York	47, 654	8. 7	4. 2	2. 8	255. 0	213. 4	188. 2	264. 2	217. 9	191. 2	. 5	42. 8
Florida	54, 861	7. 9	6. 0	5. 6	18. 9	11. 6	8. 1	26. 8	17. 7	13. 7	4. 0	8. 9
Ohio	40, 740	7. 6	4. 6	2. 7	155. 4	136. 7	114. 3	163. 1	141. 4	117. 0	. 9	51. 6
Massachusetts	8, 039	6. 5	5. 7	4. 7	521. 6	473. 1	413. 6	528. 6	479. 2	418. 8	. 8	51. 2
Connecticut	4, 820	6. 1	4. 4	3. 1	327. 1	281. 9	228. 0	333. 4	286. 4	231. 3	1. 0	97. 5
Illinois	56, 043	5. 9	3. 3	1. 9	129. 7	112. 3	98. 6	136. 2	115. 7	100. 6	. 4	35. 1
Kentucky	40, 181	5. 6	5. 9	6. 5	59. 4	54. 3	50. 5	65. 1	60. 1	57. 0	2. 7	42. 5
West Virginia	24, 022	4. 8	3. 6	2. 7	67. 2	57. 3	48. 2	72. 0	60. 9	50. 8	3. 5	48. 0
Missouri	68, 727	3. 3	2. 6	2. 3	49. 5	46. 9	45. 6	52. 8	49. 5	47. 9	. 8	25. 0
Texas	262, 398	3. 3	2. 8	2. 6	16. 3	13. 5	11. 4	22. 2	17. 8	14. 8	2. 0	9. 7
Indiana	36, 045	3. 1	2. 2	1. 7	86. 5	79. 0	73. 2	89. 8	81. 3	74. 9	. 2	39. 8
Michigan	57, 480	2. 9	1. 0	. 3	80. 9	62. 6	48. 5	84. 2	63. 8	48. 9	. 2	26. 5
Oklahoma	69, 414	2. 5	2. 2	2. 0	30. 6	26. 1	20. 8	34. 5	29. 2	23. 9	1. 5	20. 0

TABLE 11.—NEGRO AND FOREIGN-BORN WHITE POPULATION, BY SECTIONS, AND BY SOUTHERN DIVISIONS, AND STATES: 1930 AND 1920

SECTION, DIVISION, AND STATE	POPULATION										FOREIGN-BORN WHITES TO 1,000 NEGROES	
	1930		1920		Increase or decrease (−), 1920–30				Percent distribution, 1930			
					Number		Percent					
	Negro	Foreign-born white	Negro	Foreign-born white	Negro	Foreign-born white	Negro	Foreign-born white	Negro	Foreign-born white	1930	1920
United States	**11, 891, 143**	**13, 366, 407**	**10, 463, 131**	**13, 255, 394**	**1, 428, 012**	**111, 013**	**13. 6**	**0. 8**	**100. 0**	**100. 0**	**1, 124**	**1, 267**
THE SOUTH	9, 361, 577	532, 175	8, 912, 231	595, 570	449, 346	−63, 395	5. 0	−10. 6	78. 7	4. 0	57	67
South Atlantic	4, 421, 388	304, 278	4, 325, 120	315, 676	96, 268	−11, 398	2. 2	−3. 6	37. 2	2. 3	69	73
East South Central	2, 658, 238	57, 665	2, 523, 532	71, 698	134, 706	−14, 033	5. 3	−19. 6	22. 4	. 4	22	28
West South Central	2, 281, 951	170, 232	2, 063, 579	208, 196	218, 372	−37, 964	10. 6	−18. 2	19. 2	1. 3	75	101
THE NORTH	2, 409, 219	11, 386, 553	1, 472, 309	11, 348, 336	936, 910	38, 217	63. 6	. 3	20. 3	85. 2	4, 726	7, 708
THE WEST	120, 347	1, 447, 679	78, 591	1, 311, 488	41, 756	136, 191	53. 1	10. 4	1. 0	10. 8	12, 029	16, 688
The South												
SOUTH ATLANTIC:												
Delaware	32, 602	16, 885	30, 335	19, 785	2, 267	−2, 900	7. 5	−14. 7	. 3	. 1	518	652
Maryland	276, 379	95, 093	244, 479	102, 144	31, 900	−7, 051	13. 0	−6. 9	2. 3	. 7	344	418
District of Columbia	132, 068	29, 932	109, 966	28, 522	22, 102	1, 410	20. 1	4. 9	1. 1	. 2	227	259
Virginia	650, 165	23, 820	690, 017	30, 760	−39, 852	−6, 940	−5. 8	−22. 6	5. 5	. 2	37	45
West Virginia	114, 893	51, 520	86, 345	61, 864	28, 548	−10, 344	33. 1	−16. 7	1. 0	. 4	448	716
North Carolina	918, 647	8, 788	763, 407	7, 092	155, 240	1, 696	20. 3	23. 9	7. 7	. 1	10	9
South Carolina	793, 681	5, 266	864, 719	6, 397	−71, 038	−1, 131	−8. 2	−17. 7	6. 7	(1)	7	7
Georgia	1, 071, 125	13, 917	1, 206, 365	16, 163	−135, 240	−2, 246	−11. 2	−13. 9	9. 0	. 1	13	13
Florida	431, 828	59, 057	329, 487	42, 949	102, 341	16, 108	31. 1	37. 5	3. 6	. 4	137	130
EAST SOUTH CENTRAL:												
Kentucky	226, 040	21, 840	235, 938	30, 707	−9, 898	−8, 867	−4. 2	−28. 9	1. 9	. 2	97	130
Tennessee	477, 646	13, 066	451, 758	15, 443	25, 888	−2, 377	5. 7	−15. 4	4. 0	. 1	27	34
Alabama	944, 834	15, 710	900, 652	17, 617	44, 182	−1, 907	4. 9	−10. 8	7. 9	. 1	17	20
Mississippi	1, 009, 718	7, 049	935, 184	7, 931	74, 534	−882	8. 0	−11. 1	8. 5	. 1	7	8
WEST SOUTH CENTRAL:												
Arkansas	478, 463	10, 173	472, 220	13, 781	6, 243	−3, 608	1. 3	−26. 2	4. 0	. 1	21	29
Louisiana	776, 326	34, 910	700, 257	42, 976	76, 069	−8, 066	10. 9	−18. 8	6. 5	. 3	45	61
Oklahoma	172, 198	26, 753	149, 408	33, 655	22, 790	−6, 902	15. 3	−20. 5	1. 4	. 2	155	225
Texas	854, 964	98, 396	741, 694	117, 784	113, 270	−19, 388	15. 3	−16. 5	7. 2	. 7	115	159

[1] Less than 1/10 of 1 percent.

TABLE 12.—NEGRO AND WHITE POPULATION, BY SECTIONS, DIVISIONS, AND STATES: 1790 TO 1930

SECTION, DIVISION, AND STATE	1930				1920				1910		1900	
	Total	Negro	White	Other races	Total	Negro	White [1]	Other races [1]	Negro	White [1]	Negro	White
United States	**122,775,046**	**11,891,143**	**108,864,207**	**2,019,696**	**105,710,620**	**10,463,131**	**94,120,374**	**1,127,115**	**9,827,763**	**81,364,447**	**8,833,994**	**66,809,196**
The North	**73,021,191**	**2,409,219**	**70,388,367**	**223,605**	**63,681,845**	**1,472,309**	**62,085,612**	**123,924**	**1,027,674**	**54,627,598**	**880,771**	**46,413,758**
The South	**37,857,633**	**9,361,577**	**27,673,879**	**822,177**	**33,125,803**	**8,912,231**	**23,731,899**	**481,673**	**8,749,427**	**20,316,253**	**7,922,969**	**16,521,970**
The West	**11,896,222**	**120,347**	**10,801,961**	**973,914**	**8,902,972**	**78,591**	**8,302,863**	**521,518**	**50,662**	**6,420,596**	**30,254**	**3,873,468**
GEOGRAPHIC DIVISIONS:												
New England	8,166,341	94,086	8,065,113	7,142	7,400,909	79,051	7,315,995	5,863	66,306	6,480,468	59,099	5,527,026
Middle Atlantic	26,260,750	1,052,899	25,172,104	35,747	22,261,144	600,183	21,638.625	22,336	417,870	18,879.881	325,921	15,110,862
East North Central	25,297,185	930,450	24,277,663	89,072	21,475,543	514,554	20,931,279	29,710	300,836	17,926,513	257,842	15,710,053
West North Central	13,296,915	331,784	12,873,487	91,644	12,544,249	278,521	12,199,713	66,015	242,662	11,340,736	237,909	10,065,817
South Atlantic	15,793,589	4,421,388	11,349,284	22,917	13,990,272	4,325,120	9,648,556	16,596	4,112,488	8,071,473	3,729,017	6,706,058
East South Central	9,887,214	2,658,238	7,224,614	4,362	8,893,307	2,523,532	6,367,166	2,609	2,652,513	5,754,154	2,499,886	5,044,847
West South Central	12,176,830	2,281,951	9,099,981	794,898	10,242,224	2,063,579	7,716,177	462,468	1,984,426	6,490,626	1,694,066	4,771,065
Mountain	3,701,789	30,225	3,303,586	367,978	3,336,101	30,801	3,071,405	233,895	21,467	2,445,515	15,590	1,579,855
Pacific	8,194,433	90,122	7,498,375	605,936	5,566,871	47,790	5,231,458	287,623	29,195	3,975,081	14,664	2,293,613
NEW ENGLAND:												
Maine	797,423	1,096	795,183	1,144	768,014	1,310	765,693	1,011	1,363	739,991	1,319	692,226
New Hampshire	465,293	790	464,350	153	443,083	621	442,330	132	564	429,906	662	410,791
Vermont	359,611	568	358,965	78	352,428	572	351,816	40	1,621	354,298	826	342,771
Massachusetts	4,249,614	52,365	4,192,926	4,323	3,852,356	45,466	3,803,467	3,423	38,055	3,324,897	31,974	2,769,764
Rhode Island	687,497	9,913	677,016	568	604,397	10,036	593,976	385	9,529	532,488	9,092	419,050
Connecticut	1,606,903	29,354	1,576,673	876	1,380,631	21,046	1,358,713	872	15,174	1,098,888	15,226	892,424
MIDDLE ATLANTIC:												
New York	12,588,066	412,814	12,150,293	24,959	10,385,227	198,483	10,170,548	16,196	134,191	8,966,525	99,232	7,156,881
New Jersey	4,041,334	208,828	3,829,209	3,297	3,155,900	117,132	3,036,832	1,936	89,760	2,445,820	69,844	1,812,317
Pennsylvania	9,631,350	431,257	9,192,602	7,491	8,720,017	284,568	8,431,245	4,204	193,919	7,467,536	156,845	6,141,664
EAST NORTH CENTRAL:												
Ohio	6,646,697	309,304	6,331,136	6,257	5,759,394	186,187	5,570,951	2,256	111,452	4,654,758	96,901	4,060,204
Indiana	3,238,503	111,982	3,116,136	10,385	2,930,390	80,810	2,848,346	1,234	60,320	2,639,876	57,505	2,458,502
Illinois	7,630,654	328,972	7,266,361	35,321	6,485,280	182,274	6,294,999	8,007	109,049	5,526,241	85,078	4,734,873
Michigan	4,842,325	169,453	4,650,171	22,701	3,668,412	60,082	3,600,283	8,047	17,115	2,785,135	15,816	2,398,563
Wisconsin	2,939,006	10,739	2,913,859	14,408	2,632,067	5,201	2,616,700	10,166	2,900	2,320.503	2,542	2,057,911
WEST NORTH CENTRAL:												
Minnesota	2,563,953	9,445	2,538,973	15,535	2,387,125	8,809	2,368,586	9,730	7,084	2,059,143	4,959	1,737,036
Iowa	2,470,939	17,380	2,448,382	5.177	2,404,021	19,005	2,381,293	3,723	14,973	2,208,682	12,693	2,218,667
Missouri	3,629,367	223,840	3,398,887	6,640	3,404,055	178,241	3,221,661	4,153	157,452	3,133,570	161,234	2,944,843
North Dakota	680,845	377	671,243	9,225	646,872	467	639.912	6,493	617	569,845	286	311,712
South Dakota	692,849	646	669,453	22,750	636,547	832	619.052	16,663	817	563,747	465	380,714
Nebraska	1,377,963	13,752	1,353,702	10,509	1,296,372	13,242	1,276,473	6,657	7,689	1,179,994	6,269	1,056,526
Kansas	1,880,999	66,344	1,792,847	21,808	1,769,257	57,925	1,692,736	18,596	54,030	1,625,755	52,003	1,416,319
SOUTH ATLANTIC:												
Delaware	238,380	32,602	205,694	84	223,003	30,335	192,585	83	31,181	171,100	30,697	153,977
Maryland	1,631,526	276,379	1,354,170	977	1,449,661	244,479	1,204,690	492	232,250	1,062,627	235,064	952,424
District of Columbia	486,869	132,068	353,914	887	437,571	109.966	326,825	780	94,446	236,113	86,702	191,532
Virginia	2,421,851	650,165	1,770,405	1,281	2,309,187	690,017	1,617,871	1,299	671,096	1,389,802	660,722	1,192,855
West Virginia	1,729.205	114,893	1,613.934	378	1,463,701	86,345	1,377,180	176	64,173	1,156,811	43,499	915,233
North Carolina	3,170,276	918,647	2,234,948	16,681	2,559,123	763.407	1,783,769	11,947	697,843	1,500,508	624,469	1,263,603
South Carolina	1,738,765	793,681	944,040	1,044	1,683,724	864,719	818,532	473	835,843	679,159	782,321	557,807
Georgia	2,908,506	1,071,125	1,836,974	407	2,895,832	1,206,365	1,689,070	397	1,176,987	1,431,786	1,034,813	1,181,294
Florida	1,468,211	431,828	1,035,205	1,178	968,470	329,487	638,034	949	308,669	443,567	230,730	297,333
EAST SOUTH CENTRAL:												
Kentucky	2,614,589	226,040	2,388,364	185	2,416,630	235,938	2,180,462	230	261,656	2,027,926	284,706	1,862,309
Tennessee	2,616,556	477,646	2,138,619	291	2,337,885	451,758	1,885,939	188	473,088	1,711,417	480,243	1,540,186
Alabama	2,646,248	944,834	1,700,775	639	2,348,174	900,652	1,446,958	564	908,282	1,228,789	827,307	1,001,152
Mississippi	2,009,821	1,009,718	996,856	3,247	1,790,618	935,184	853,807	1,627	1,009,487	786,022	907,630	641,200
WEST SOUTH CENTRAL:												
Arkansas	1,854,482	478,463	1,374,906	1,113	1,752,204	472,220	1,279,479	505	442,891	1,130,878	366,856	944,580
Louisiana	2,101,593	776,326	1,318,160	7,107	1,798,509	700,257	1,093,991	4,261	713,874	939,789	650,804	729,612
Oklahoma [4]	2,396,040	172,198	2,123,424	100,418	2,028,283	149,408	1,813,217	65,658	137,612	1,441,577	55,684	670,204
Texas	5,824,715	854,964	4,283,491	686,260	4,663,228	741,694	3,529,490	392,044	690,049	2,978,382	620,722	2,426,669
MOUNTAIN:												
Montana	537,606	1,256	517,327	19,023	548,889	1,658	533,991	13,240	1,834	360,491	1,523	226,283
Idaho	445,032	668	437,562	6,802	431,866	920	424,540	6,406	651	319,074	293	154,495
Wyoming	225,565	1,250	214,067	10,248	194,402	1,375	188,146	4,881	2,235	139,990	940	89,051
Colorado	1,035,791	11,828	961,117	62,846	939,629	11,318	909,763	18.548	11,453	780,146	8,570	529,046
New Mexico	423,317	2,850	331,755	88,712	360,350	5,733	301,879	52,738	1,628	283,574	1,610	180,207
Arizona	435,573	10,749	264,378	160,446	334,162	8,005	202,985	123,172	2,009	122,360	1,848	92,903
Utah	507,847	1,108	495,955	10,784	449,396	1,446	440,699	7,251	1,144	366,425	672	272,465
Nevada	91,058	516	81,425	9,117	77,407	346	69,402	7,659	513	73,455	134	35,405
PACIFIC:												
Washington	1,563,396	6,840	1,521,099	35,457	1,356,621	6,883	1,319,393	30,345	6,058	1,108,967	2,514	496,304
Oregon	953,786	2,234	937,029	14,523	783,389	2,144	768,530	12,715	1,492	654,833	1,105	394,582
California	5,677,251	81,048	5,040,247	555,956	3,426,861	38,763	3,143,535	244,563	21,645	2,211,281	11,045	1,402,727

See footnotes at end of table.

TABLE 12.—NEGRO AND WHITE POPULATION, BY SECTIONS, DIVISIONS, AND STATES: 1790 TO 1930—Continued

SECTION, DIVISION, AND STATE	1890 [2]		1880		1870		1860		1850	
	Negro	White	Negro	White	Negro	White	Negro	White	Negro	White
United States	7, 488, 676	55, 101, 258	6, 580, 793	43, 402, 970	4, 880, 009	33, 589, 377	4, 441, 830	26, 922, 537	3, 638, 808	19, 553, 068
The North	701, 018	39, 035, 798	615, 038	31, 235, 267	452, 818	24, 815, 772	340, 240	19, 337, 997	285, 369	13, 745, 077
The South	6, 760, 577	13, 193, 453	5, 953, 903	10, 555, 427	4, 420, 811	7, 863, 209	4, 097, 111	7, 033, 973	3, 352, 198	5, 630, 414
The West	27, 081	2, 872, 007	11, 852	1, 612, 276	6, 380	910, 396	4, 479	550, 567	1, 241	177, 577
GEOGRAPHIC DIVISIONS:										
New England	44, 580	4, 653, 191	39, 925	3, 968, 789	31, 705	3, 455, 043	24, 711	3, 110, 480	23, 021	2, 705, 095
Middle Atlantic	225, 326	12, 468, 794	189, 492	10, 305, 055	148, 033	8, 662, 226	131, 290	7, 327, 548	126, 741	5, 771, 994
East North Central	207, 023	13, 253, 725	183, 298	11, 012, 047	130, 497	8, 987, 512	63, 699	6, 855, 644	45, 195	4, 478, 065
West North Central	224, 089	8, 660, 088	202, 323	5, 949, 376	142, 583	3, 710, 991	120, 540	2, 044, 325	90, 412	789, 923
South Atlantic	3, 262, 690	5, 592, 149	2, 941, 202	4, 654, 112	2, 216, 705	3, 635, 238	2, 058, 198	3, 305, 107	1, 860, 871	2, 818, 219
East South Central	2, 119, 797	4, 305, 668	1, 924, 996	3, 657, 593	1, 464, 252	2, 939, 091	1, 394, 360	2, 626, 376	1, 122, 790	2, 240, 481
West South Central	1, 378, 090	3, 295, 636	1, 087, 705	2, 243, 722	739, 854	1, 288, 880	644, 553	1, 102, 490	368, 537	571, 714
Mountain	12, 971	1, 117, 363	5, 022	614, 821	1, 555	301, 848	235	164, 092	72	72, 855
Pacific	14, 110	1, 754, 644	6, 830	997, 455	4, 825	608, 548	4, 244	386, 475	1, 169	104, 722
NEW ENGLAND:										
Maine	1, 190	659, 263	1, 451	646, 852	1, 606	624, 809	1, 327	626, 947	1, 356	581, 813
New Hampshire	614	375, 840	685	346, 229	580	317, 697	494	325, 579	520	317, 456
Vermont	937	331, 418	1, 057	331, 218	924	329, 613	709	314, 369	718	313, 402
Massachusetts	22, 144	2, 215, 373	18, 697	1, 763, 782	13, 947	1, 443, 156	9, 602	1, 221, 432	9, 064	985, 450
Rhode Island	7, 393	337, 859	6, 488	269, 939	4, 980	212, 219	3, 952	170, 649	3, 670	143, 875
Connecticut	12, 302	733, 438	11, 547	610, 769	9, 668	527, 549	8, 627	451, 504	7, 693	363, 099
MIDDLE ATLANTIC:										
New York	70, 092	5, 923, 955	65, 104	5, 016, 022	52, 081	4, 330, 210	49, 005	3, 831, 590	49, 069	3, 048, 325
New Jersey	47, 638	1, 396, 581	38, 853	1, 092, 017	30, 658	875, 407	25, 336	646, 699	24, 046	465, 509
Pennsylvania	107, 596	5, 148, 258	85, 535	4, 197, 016	65, 294	3, 456, 609	56, 949	2, 849, 259	53, 626	2, 258, 160
EAST NORTH CENTRAL:										
Ohio	87, 113	3, 584, 805	79, 900	3, 117, 920	63, 213	2, 601, 946	36, 673	2, 302, 808	25, 279	1, 955, 050
Indiana	45, 215	2, 146, 736	39, 228	1, 938, 798	24, 560	1, 655, 837	11, 428	1, 338, 710	11, 262	977, 154
Illinois	57, 028	3, 768, 472	46, 368	3, 031, 151	28, 762	2, 511, 096	7, 628	1, 704, 291	5, 436	846, 034
Michigan	15, 223	2, 072, 884	15, 100	1, 614, 560	11, 849	1, 167, 282	6, 799	736, 142	2, 583	395, 071
Wisconsin	2, 444	1, 680, 828	2, 702	1, 309, 618	2, 113	1, 051, 351	1, 171	773, 693	635	304, 756
WEST NORTH CENTRAL:										
Minnesota	3, 683	1, 296, 408	1, 564	776, 884	759	438, 257	259	169, 395	39	6, 038
Iowa	10, 685	1, 901, 090	9, 516	1, 614, 600	5, 762	1, 188, 207	1, 069	673, 779	333	191, 881
Missouri	150, 184	2, 528, 458	145, 350	2, 022, 826	118, 071	1, 603, 146	118, 503	1, 063, 489	90, 040	592, 004
North Dakota	373	182, 407	[3] 113	[3] 36, 192	[3] 94	[3] 12, 887	(3)	[3] 2, 576	—	—
South Dakota	541	328, 010	[3] 288	[3] 96, 955						
Nebraska	8, 913	1, 047, 096	2, 385	449, 764	789	122, 117	82	28, 696	—	—
Kansas	49, 710	1, 376, 619	43, 107	952, 155	17, 108	346, 377	627	106, 390	—	—
SOUTH ATLANTIC:										
Delaware	28, 386	140, 066	26, 442	120, 160	22, 794	102, 221	21, 627	90, 589	20, 363	71, 169
Maryland	215, 657	826, 493	210, 230	724, 693	175, 391	605, 497	171, 131	515, 918	165, 091	417, 943
District of Columbia	75, 572	154, 695	59, 596	118, 006	43, 404	88, 278	14, 316	60, 763	13, 746	37, 941
Virginia	635, 438	1, 020, 122	631, 616	880, 858	512, 841	712, 089	548, 907	1, 047, 299	526, 861	894, 800
West Virginia	32, 690	730, 077	25, 886	592, 537	17, 980	424, 033	—	—	—	—
North Carolina	561, 018	1, 055, 382	531, 277	867, 242	391, 650	678, 470	361, 522	629, 942	316, 011	553, 028
South Carolina	688, 934	462, 008	604, 332	391, 105	415, 814	289, 667	412, 320	291, 300	393, 944	274, 563
Georgia	858, 815	978, 357	725, 133	816, 906	545, 142	638, 926	465, 698	591, 550	384, 613	521, 572
Florida	166, 180	224, 949	126, 690	142, 605	91, 689	96, 057	62, 677	77, 746	40, 242	47, 203
EAST SOUTH CENTRAL:										
Kentucky	268, 071	1, 590, 462	271, 451	1, 377, 179	222, 210	1, 098, 692	236, 167	919, 484	220, 992	761, 413
Tennessee	430, 678	1, 336, 637	403, 151	1, 138, 831	322, 331	936, 119	283, 019	826, 722	245, 881	756, 836
Alabama	678, 489	833, 718	600, 103	662, 185	475, 510	521, 384	437, 770	526, 271	345, 109	426, 514
Mississippi	742, 559	544, 851	650, 291	479, 398	444, 201	382, 896	437, 404	353, 899	310, 808	295, 718
WEST SOUTH CENTRAL:										
Arkansas	309, 117	818, 752	210, 666	591, 531	122, 169	362, 115	111, 259	324, 143	47, 708	162, 189
Louisiana	559, 193	558, 395	483, 655	454, 954	364, 210	362, 065	350, 373	357, 456	262, 271	255, 491
Oklahoma [4]	21, 609	172, 554	—	—	—	—	—	—	—	—
Texas	488, 171	1, 745, 935	393, 384	1, 197, 237	253, 475	564, 700	182, 921	420, 891	58, 558	154, 034
MOUNTAIN:										
Montana	1, 490	127, 690	346	35, 385	183	18, 306	—	—	—	—
Idaho	201	82, 117	53	29, 013	60	10, 618	—	—	—	—
Wyoming	922	59, 324	298	19, 437	183	8, 726	—	—	—	—
Colorado	6, 215	404, 534	2, 435	191, 126	456	39, 221	46	34, 231	—	—
New Mexico	1, 956	142, 918	1, 015	108, 721	172	90, 393	85	82, 924	22	61, 525
Arizona	1, 357	55, 734	155	35, 160	26	9, 581	—	—	—	—
Utah	588	205, 925	232	142, 423	118	86, 044	59	40, 125	50	11, 330
Nevada	242	39, 121	488	53, 556	357	38, 959	45	6, 812	—	—
PACIFIC:										
Washington	1, 602	340, 829	325	67, 199	207	22, 195	30	11, 138	—	—
Oregon	1, 186	301, 982	487	163, 075	346	86, 929	128	52, 160	207	13, 087
California	11, 322	1, 111, 833	6, 018	767, 181	4, 272	499, 424	4, 086	323, 177	962	91, 635

See footnotes at end of table.

TABLE 12.—NEGRO AND WHITE POPULATION, BY SECTIONS, DIVISIONS, AND STATES: 1790 TO 1930—Continued

SECTION, DIVISION, AND STATE	1840		1830		1820		1810		1800		1790	
	Negro	White	Negro	White	Negro	White	Negro	White	Negro	White	Negro	White
United States	**2,873,648**	**14,189,705**	**2,328,642**	**10,532,060**	**1,771,656**	**7,866,797**	**1,377,808**	**5,862,073**	**1,002,037**	**4,306,446**	**757,208**	**3,172,006**
The North	**231,671**	**9,880,953**	**166,757**	**6,986,097**	**128,984**	**5,090,237**	**109,309**	**3,670,535**	**83,701**	**2,602,881**	**67,424**	**1,900,616**
The South	**2,641,977**	**4,308,752**	**2,161,885**	**3,545,963**	**1,642,672**	**2,776,560**	**1,268,499**	**2,191,538**	**918,336**	**1,703,565**	**689,784**	**1,271,390**
GEOGRAPHIC DIVISIONS:												
New England	22,657	2,212,165	21,379	1,933,338	20,927	1,639,144	19,906	1,452,067	18,652	1,214,359	16,987	992,421
Middle Atlantic	119,667	4,406,593	103,835	3,483,829	89,797	2,610,048	82,331	1,932,371	64,414	1,338,151	50,437	908,195
East North Central	29,345	2,895,383	15.883	1,454,135	7,691	785,028	3,454	268,870	635	50,371	---	---
West North Central	60,002	366,812	25,660	114,795	10,569	56,017	3,618	17,227	---	---	---	---
South Atlantic	1,597,317	2,327,982	1,529,283	2,116,469	1,273,399	1,787,664	1,080,800	1,594,091	859,690	1,426,804	673,462	1,178,344
East South Central	830,306	1,745,139	501,587	1,314,382	288,057	902,432	145,454	563,136	58,646	276,761	16,322	93,046
West South Central	214,354	235,631	131,015	115,112	81,216	86,464	42,245	34 311	---	---	---	---
NEW ENGLAND:												
Maine	1,355	500,438	1,192	398,263	929	297,406	969	227,736	818	150,901	538	96,002
New Hampshire	538	284,036	607	268,721	786	243,375	970	213,490	860	182,998	788	141,097
Vermont	730	291,218	881	279,771	903	235,078	750	217,145	557	153,908	271	85,154
Massachusetts	8,669	729,030	7,049	603,359	6,740	516,547	6,737	465,303	6,452	416,393	5,463	373,324
Rhode Island	3,243	105,587	3,578	93,621	3,602	79,457	3,717	73,214	3,684	65,438	4,355	64,470
Connecticut	8,122	301,856	8,072	289,603	7,967	267,281	6,763	255,179	6,281	244,721	5,572	232,374
MIDDLE ATLANTIC:												
New York	50,031	2,378,890	44,945	1,873,663	39,367	1,333,445	40,350	918,699	31,320	557,731	25,978	314,142
New Jersey	21,718	351,588	20,557	300,266	20,017	257,558	18,694	226,868	16,824	194,325	14,185	169,954
Pennsylvania	47,918	1,676,115	38,333	1,309,900	30,413	1,019,045	23,287	786,804	16,270	586,095	10,274	424,099
EAST NORTH CENTRAL:												
Ohio	17,345	1,502,122	9,574	928,329	4,723	576,711	1,899	228,861	337	45,028	---	---
Indiana	7,168	678,698	3,632	339,399	1,420	145,758	630	23,890	298	5,343	---	---
Illinois	3,929	472,254	2,384	155,061	1,374	53,837	781	11,501	---	---	---	---
Michigan	707	211,560	293	31,346	174	8,722	144	4,618	---	---	---	---
Wisconsin	196	30,749	---	---	---	---	---	---	---	---	---	---
WEST NORTH CENTRAL:												
Iowa	188	42,924	---	---	---	---	---	---	---	---	---	---
Missouri	59,814	323,888	25,660	114,795	10,569	56,017	3,618	17,227	---	---	---	---
SOUTH ATLANTIC:												
Delaware	19,524	58,561	19,147	57,601	17,467	55,282	17,313	55,361	14,421	49,852	12,786	46,310
Maryland	151,815	318,204	155,932	291,108	147,127	260,223	145,429	235,117	125,222	216,326	111,079	208,649
District of Columbia	13,055	30,657	12,271	27,563	10,425	22,614	7,944	16,079	4,027	10,066	---	---
Virginia	498,829	740,968	517,105	694,300	462,031	603,335	423,086	551,514	365,920	514,280	305,493	442,117
West Virginia	---	---	---	---	---	---	---	---	---	---	---	---
North Carolina	268,549	484,870	265,144	472,843	219,629	419,200	179,090	376,410	140,339	337,764	105,547	288,204
South Carolina	335,314	259,084	323,322	257,863	265,301	237,440	200,919	214,196	149,336	196,255	108,895	140,178
Georgia	283,697	407,695	220,017	296,806	151,419	189,570	107,019	145,414	60,425	102,261	29,662	52,886
Florida	26,534	27,943	16,345	18,385	---	---	---	---	---	---	---	---
EAST SOUTH CENTRAL:												
Kentucky	189,575	590,253	170,130	517,787	129,491	434,826	82,274	324,237	41,082	179,873	12,544	61,133
Tennessee	188,583	640,627	146,158	535,746	82,844	339,979	45,852	215,875	13,893	91,709	3,778	31,913
Alabama	255,571	335,185	119,121	190,406	42,450	85,451	---	---	---	---	---	---
Mississippi	196,577	179,074	66,178	70,443	33,272	42,176	17,328	23,024	3,671	5,179	---	---
WEST SOUTH CENTRAL:												
Arkansas	20,400	77,174	4,717	25,671	1,676	12,597	---	---	---	---	---	---
Louisiana	193,954	158,457	126,298	89,441	79,540	73,867	42,245	34,311	---	---	---	---

[1] Figures for white population in 1920 and 1910 are adjusted by deducting the estimated number of Mexicans and adding to "All Others."
[2] Includes persons specially enumerated in 1890 in Indian Territory and on Indian reservations—Negroes, 18,636; whites, 117,368.
[3] Dakota Territory.
[4] Includes population of Indian Territory for 1900 and 1890.

TABLE 13.—INCREASES IN THE NEGRO AND WHITE POPULATION, BY SECTIONS, DIVISIONS, AND STATES: BY PERIODS, 1790 TO 1930

[A minus sign (−) denotes decrease]

SECTION, DIVISION, AND STATE	1920-30				1910-20		1870-1910		1830-70		1790-1830	
	Negro		White		Negro	White	Negro	White	Negro	White	Negro	White
	Number	Percent	Number	Percent								
United States	**1,428,012**	**13.6**	**14,743,833**	**15.7**	**635,368**	**12,755,927**	**4,947,754**	**47,775,070**	**2,551,367**	**23,057,317**	**1,571,434**	**7,360,054**
The North	**936,910**	**63.6**	**8,302,755**	**13.4**	**444,635**	**7,548,014**	**574,856**	**29,811,826**	**286,061**	**17,829,675**	**99,333**	**5,085,481**
The South	**449,346**	**5.0**	**3,941,980**	**16.6**	**162,804**	**3,415,646**	**4,328,616**	**12,453,044**	**2,258,926**	**4,317,246**	**1,472,101**	**2,274,573**
The West	**41,756**	**53.1**	**2,499,098**	**30.1**	**27,929**	**1,882,267**	**44,282**	**5,510,200**	**6,380**	**910,396**	----------	----------
GEOGRAPHIC DIVISIONS:												
New England	15,035	19.0	749,118	10.2	12,745	835,527	34,601	3,025,425	10,326	1,521,705	4,392	940,917
Middle Atlantic	452,716	75.4	3,533,479	16.3	182,313	2,758,744	269,837	10,217,655	44,198	5,178,397	53,398	2,575,634
East North Central	415,896	80.8	3,346,384	16.0	213,718	3,004,766	170,339	8,939,001	114,614	7,533,377	15,883	1,454,135
West North Central	53,263	19.1	673,774	5.5	35,859	858,977	100,079	7,629,745	116,923	3,596,196	25,660	114,795
South Atlantic	96,268	2.2	1,700,728	17.6	212,632	1,577,083	1,895,783	4,436,235	687,422	1,518,769	855,821	938,125
East South Central	134,706	5.3	857,448	13.5	−128,981	613,012	1,188,261	2,815,063	962,665	1,624,709	485,265	1,221,336
West South Central	218,372	10.6	1,383,804	17.9	79,153	1,225,551	1,244,572	5,201,746	608,839	1,173,768	131,015	115,112
Mountain	−576	−1.9	232,181	7.6	9,334	625,890	19,912	2,143,667	1,555	301,848	----------	----------
Pacific	42,332	88.6	2,266,917	43.3	18,595	1,256,377	24,370	3,366,533	4,825	608,548	----------	----------
NEW ENGLAND:												
Maine	−214	−16.3	29,490	3.9	−53	25,702	−243	115,182	414	226,546	654	302,261
New Hampshire	169	27.2	22,020	5.0	57	12,424	−16	112,209	−27	48,976	−181	127,624
Vermont	−4	−0.7	7,149	2.0	−1,049	−2,482	697	24,685	43	49,842	610	194,617
Massachusetts	6,899	15.2	389,459	10.2	7,411	478,570	24,108	1,881,741	6,898	839,797	1,586	230,035
Rhode Island	−123	−1.2	83,040	14.0	507	61,488	4,549	320,269	1,402	118,598	−777	29,151
Connecticut	8,308	39.5	217,960	16.0	5,872	259,825	5,506	571,339	1,596	237,946	2,500	57,229
MIDDLE ATLANTIC:												
New York	214,331	108.0	1,979,745	19.5	64,292	1,204,023	82,110	4,636,315	7,136	2,456,547	18,967	1,559,521
New Jersey	91,696	78.3	792,377	26.1	27,372	591,012	59,102	1,570,413	10,101	575,141	6,372	130,312
Pennsylvania	146,689	51.5	761,357	9.0	90,649	963,709	128,625	4,010,927	26,961	2,146,709	28,059	885,801
EAST NORTH CENTRAL:												
Ohio	123,117	66.1	760,185	13.6	74,735	916,193	48,239	2,052,812	53,639	1,673,617	9,574	928,329
Indiana	31,172	38.6	267,790	9.4	20,490	208,470	35,760	984,039	20,928	1,316,438	3,632	339,399
Illinois	146,698	80.5	971,362	15.4	73,225	768,758	80,287	3,015,145	26,378	2,356,035	2,384	155,061
Michigan	109,371	182.0	1,049,888	29.2	42,967	815,148	5,266	1,617,853	11,556	1,135,936	293	31,346
Wisconsin	5,538	106.5	297,159	11.4	2,301	296,197	787	1,269,152	2,113	1,051,351	----------	----------
WEST NORTH CENTRAL:												
Minnesota	636	7.2	170,387	7.2	1,725	309,443	6,325	1,620,886	759	438,257	----------	----------
Iowa	−1,625	−8.6	67,089	2.8	4,032	172,611	9,211	1,020,475	5,762	1,188,207	----------	----------
Missouri	45,599	25.6	177,226	5.5	20,789	88,091	39,381	1,530,424	92,411	1,488,351	25,660	114,795
North Dakota	−90	−19.3	31,331	4.9	−150	70,067	[1] 1,340	[1] 1,120,705	[1] 94	[1] 12,887	----------	----------
South Dakota	−186	−22.4	50,401	8.1	15	55,305					----------	----------
Nebraska	510	3.9	77,229	6.1	5,553	96,479	6,900	1,057,877	789	122,117	----------	----------
Kansas	8,419	14.5	100,111	5.9	3,895	66,981	36,922	1,279,378	17,108	346,377	----------	----------
SOUTH ATLANTIC:												
Delaware	2,267	7.5	13,109	6.8	−846	21,485	8,387	68,879	3,647	44,620	6,361	11,291
Maryland	31,900	13.0	149,480	12.4	12,229	142,063	56,859	457,130	19,459	314,389	44,853	82,459
District of Columbia	22,102	20.1	27,089	8.3	15,520	90,712	51,042	147,835	31,133	60,715	12,271	27,563
Virginia	−39,852	−5.8	152,534	9.4	18,921	228,069	158,255	677,713	−4,264	17,789	211,612	252,183
West Virginia	28,548	33.1	236,754	17.2	22,172	220,369	46,193	732,778	17,980	424,033	----------	----------
North Carolina	155,240	20.3	451,179	25.3	65,564	283,261	306,193	822,038	126,506	205,627	159,597	184,639
South Carolina	−71,038	−8.2	125,508	15.3	28,876	139,373	420,029	389,492	92,492	31,804	214,427	117,685
Georgia	−135,240	−11.2	147,904	8.8	29,378	257,284	631,845	792,860	325,125	342,120	190,355	243,920
Florida	102,341	31.1	397,171	62.2	20,818	194,467	216,980	347,510	75,344	77,672	16,345	18,385
EAST SOUTH CENTRAL:												
Kentucky	−9,898	−4.2	207,902	9.5	−25,718	152,536	39,446	929,234	52,080	580,905	157,586	456,654
Tennessee	25,888	5.7	252,680	13.4	−21,330	174,522	150,757	775,298	176,173	400,373	142,380	503,833
Alabama	44,182	4.9	253,817	17.5	−7,630	218,169	432,772	707,405	356,389	330,978	119,121	190,406
Mississippi	74,534	8.0	143,049	16.8	−74,303	67,785	565,286	403,126	378,023	312,453	66,178	70,443
WEST SOUTH CENTRAL:												
Arkansas	6,243	1.3	95,427	7.5	29,329	148,601	320,722	768,763	117,452	336,444	4,717	25,671
Louisiana	76,069	10.9	224,169	20.5	−13,617	154,202	349,664	577,724	237,912	272,624	126,298	89,441
Oklahoma	22,790	15.3	310,207	17.1	11,796	371,640	137,612	1,441,577	----------	----------	----------	----------
Texas	113,270	15.3	754,001	21.4	51,645	551,108	436,574	2,413,682	253,475	564,700	----------	----------
MOUNTAIN:												
Montana	−402	−24.2	−16,664	−3.1	−176	173,500	1,651	342,185	183	18,306	----------	----------
Idaho	−252	−27.4	13,022	3.1	269	105,466	591	308,456	60	10,618	----------	----------
Wyoming	−125	−9.1	25,921	13.8	−860	48,156	2,052	131,264	183	8,726	----------	----------
Colorado	510	4.5	51,354	5.6	−135	129,617	10,997	740,925	456	39,221	----------	----------
New Mexico	−2,883	−50.3	29,876	9.9	4,105	18,305	1,456	193,181	172	90,393	----------	----------
Arizona	2,744	34.3	61,393	30.2	5,996	80,625	1,983	112,779	26	9,581	----------	----------
Utah	−338	−23.4	55,256	12.5	302	74,274	1,026	280,381	118	86,044	----------	----------
Nevada	170	49.1	12,023	17.3	−167	−4,053	156	34,496	357	38,959	----------	----------
PACIFIC:												
Washington	−43	−0.6	201,706	15.3	825	210,426	5,851	1,086,772	207	22,195	----------	----------
Oregon	90	4.2	168,499	21.9	652	113,697	1,146	567,904	346	86,929	----------	----------
California	42,285	109.1	1,896,712	60.3	17,118	932,254	17,373	1,711,857	4,272	499,424	----------	----------

[1] Dakota Territory.

CHAPTER III.—PROPORTION IN TOTAL POPULATION

Decrease in proportion of Negroes.—The proportion of Negroes in the total population has materially declined in the 140 years that have elapsed since the first census was taken in 1790, when almost one-fifth (19.3 percent) of the 3,929,214 persons were Negroes. In 1930, Negroes constituted only 9.7 percent of the total population. More than 60 percent of the Negro population lived in the States in which the proportion of the Negro population exceeded 25 percent of the total population. In fact, the 9 States, Mississippi, South Carolina, Louisiana, Georgia, Alabama, Florida, North Carolina, Virginia, and Arkansas, and the District of Columbia had 60.6 percent of the total Negro population in 1930 and only 12.5 percent of the total white population. In only the District of Columbia and 18 States, including 2 Northern States, Missouri and New Jersey, did the Negro population constitute 5 percent or more of the total population.

The steady decrease in the Negro proportion since 1810 has been due to the increase of the white population through the immigration of foreign-born white and several generations of their offspring, an accession that lowered the proportion of Negroes, whose growth of population is largely the result of natural increase. From 239 Negroes per 1,000 whites in 1790, the ratio has decreased to 109 Negroes per 1,000 whites in 1930.

Between 1920 and 1930 the proportion of Negroes to 100,000 whites increased in the District of Columbia and 19 States—3 Southern and 16 Northern and Western, decreased in 28 States—13 Southern and 15 Northern and Western, and did not change in Minnesota. Considered by States, the proportion of Negroes to whites in the South decreased generally in this decade, except in Maryland, Delaware, and West Virginia and the District of Columbia. Interstate migration has been an important factor in changing the proportion of Negroes to whites in several States.

Proportion of Negroes in the South.—The Negro population, though comprising less than 10 percent of the total population in the United States, comprises approximately one-fourth of the population of the South. More than one-half of the population of Mississippi was Negro in 1930. The percentage of Negroes was 45.6 for South Carolina, 36.9 for Louisiana, 36.8 for Georgia, and 35.7 for Alabama. All other States show less than one-third of the total population as being Negro. The percentage of Negroes in the population of the South has declined materially within the last 50 years. In 1880 it was 36 percent of the total population of the South. This was about the same as it had been since the first census in 1790. This percentage fell off to 33.8 in 1890, 32.3 in 1900, 29.8 in 1910, 26.9 in 1920, and 24.7 in 1930.

Proportion of Negroes in the North.—There has been a gradual increase in the percentage of Negro population in the North since 1860. A large part of this increase occurred in the decade 1920–30. However, even in 1930 the percentage of Negroes in the total population in the North was only 3.3. But this slight increase in the percentage reflects a very considerable increase in the number of Negroes in the North. It reflects also the striking change in the territorial distribution of the Negro population.

TABLE 1.—PERCENTAGE OF TOTAL NEGRO POPULATION AND NUMBER OF NEGROES PER 1,000 WHITES, BY SECTIONS AND SOUTHERN DIVISIONS: 1790 TO 1930

CENSUS YEAR	United States	THE SOUTH: Total	THE SOUTH: South Atlantic	THE SOUTH: East South Central	THE SOUTH: West South Central	The North	The West
	PERCENTAGE OF TOTAL NEGRO POPULATION						
1930	9.7	24.7	28.0	26.9	18.7	3.3	1.0
1920	9.9	26.9	30.9	28.4	20.1	2.3	.9
1910	10.7	29.8	33.7	31.5	22.6	1.8	.7
1900	11.6	32.3	35.7	33.1	25.9	1.9	.7
1890	11.9	33.8	36.8	33.0	29.1	1.8	.9
1880	13.1	36.0	38.7	34.5	32.6	1.9	.7
1870	12.7	36.0	37.9	33.2	36.4	1.8	.6
1860	14.1	36.8	38.4	34.7	36.9	1.7	.7
1850	15.7	37.3	39.8	33.4	39.2	2.0	.7
1840	16.8	38.0	40.7	32.2	47.6	2.3	-------
1830	18.1	37.9	41.9	27.6	53.2	2.3	-------
1820	18.4	37.2	41.6	24.2	48.4	2.5	-------
1810	19.0	36.7	40.4	20.5	54.4	2.9	-------
1800	18.9	35.0	37.6	17.5	-------	3.1	-------
1790	19.3	35.2	36.4	14.9	-------	3.4	-------

CENSUS YEAR	United States	THE SOUTH: Total	THE SOUTH: South Atlantic	THE SOUTH: East South Central	THE SOUTH: West South Central	The North	The West
	NUMBER OF NEGROES PER 1,000 WHITES						
1930	109	338	390	368	251	34	11
1920	111	376	448	396	267	24	9
1910	121	431	510	461	306	19	8
1900	132	480	556	496	355	19	8
1890	136	512	583	492	418	18	9
1880	152	564	632	526	485	20	7
1870	145	562	610	498	574	18	7
1860	165	582	623	531	585	18	8
1850	186	595	660	501	645	21	7
1840	203	613	686	476	910	23	-------
1830	221	610	723	382	1,138	24	-------
1820	225	592	712	319	939	25	-------
1810	235	579	678	258	1,231	30	-------
1800	233	539	603	212	-------	32	-------
1790	239	543	572	175	-------	35	-------

Table 2.—PERCENT DISTRIBUTION, BY RACIAL CLASSES, FOR SECTIONS, AND DIVISIONS: 1930 AND 1920

SECTION AND DIVISION	ALL CLASSES		NEGRO		WHITE [1]						MEXICAN		INDIAN		CHINESE, JAPANESE, AND ALL OTHERS	
					Total		Native		Foreign-born							
	1930	1920	1930	1920	1930	1920	1930	1920	1930	1920	1930	1920	1930	1920	1930	1920
United States	100.0	100.0	9.7	9.9	88.7	89.0	77.8	76.5	10.9	12.5	1.2	0.7	0.3	0.2	0.2	0.2
THE SOUTH	100.0	100.0	24.7	26.9	73.1	71.6	71.7	69.8	1.4	1.8	1.8	1.2	.3	.2	(2)	(2)
South Atlantic	100.0	100.0	28.0	30.9	71.9	69.0	69.9	66.7	1.9	2.3	(2)	(2)	.1	.1	(2)	(2)
East South Central	100.0	100.0	26.9	23.4	73.1	71.6	72.5	70.8	.6	.8	(2)	(2)	(2)	(2)	(2)	(2)
West South Central	100.0	100.0	18.7	20.1	74.7	75.3	73.3	73.3	1.4	2.0	5.7	3.9	.8	.6	(2)	(2)
THE NORTH	100.0	100.0	3.3	2.3	96.4	97.5	80.8	79.7	15.6	17.8	.1	.1	.1	.1	.1	(2)
New England	100.0	100.0	1.2	1.1	98.8	98.9	76.3	73.6	22.5	25.3	(2)	(2)	(2)	(2)	.1	.1
Middle Atlantic	100.0	100.0	4.0	2.7	95.9	97.2	75.8	75.1	20.1	22.1	(2)	(2)	(2)	(2)	.1	.1
East North Central	100.0	100.0	3.7	2.4	96.0	97.5	83.2	82.5	12.7	15.0	.2	(2)	.1	.1	(2)	(2)
West North Central	100.0	100.0	2.5	2.2	96.8	97.3	88.8	86.5	8.0	10.8	.3	.2	.4	.3	(2)	(2)
THE WEST	100.0	100.0	1.0	.9	90.8	93.3	78.6	78.5	12.2	14.7	5.2	3.0	1.2	1.2	1.8	1.7
Mountain	100.0	100.0	.8	.9	89.2	92.1	81.5	81.3	7.8	10.8	6.7	4.2	2.8	2.3	.4	.5
Pacific	100.0	100.0	1.1	.9	91.5	94.0	77.4	76.9	1.42	17.1	4.5	2.2	.4	.6	2.4	2.4

[1] Figures for white population in 1920 are adjusted by deducting the estimated number of Mexicans.
[2] Less than 1/10 of 1 percent.

Table 3.—NEGRO AND WHITE POPULATION, BY STATES, RANKED ACCORDING TO NEGRO PERCENTAGE OF TOTAL POPULATION: 1930

STATE	Negro percentage of total population	NEGRO POPULATION			WHITE POPULATION		
		Number	Cumulated by States		Number	Cumulated by States	
			Number	Percent		Number	Percent
Mississippi	50.2	1,009,718	1,009,718	8.5	996,856	996,856	0.9
South Carolina	45.6	793,681	1,803,399	15.2	944,040	1,940,896	1.8
Louisiana	36.9	776,326	2,579,725	21.7	1,318,160	3,259,056	3.0
Georgia	36.8	1,071,125	3,650,850	30.7	1,836,974	5,096,030	4.7
Alabama	35.7	944,834	4,595,684	38.6	1,700,775	6,796,805	6.2
Florida	29.4	431,828	5,027,512	42.3	1,035,205	7,832,010	7.2
North Carolina	29.0	918,647	5,946,159	50.0	2,234,948	10,066,958	9.2
District of Columbia	27.1	132,068	6,078,227	51.1	353,914	10,420,872	9.6
Virginia	26.8	650,165	6,728,392	56.6	1,770,405	12,191,277	11.2
Arkansas	25.8	478,463	7,206,855	60.6	1,374,906	13,566,183	12.5
Tennessee	18.3	477,646	7,684,501	64.6	2,138,619	15,704,802	14.4
Maryland	16.9	276,379	7,960,880	66.9	1,354,170	17,058,972	15.7
Texas	14.7	854,964	8,815,844	74.1	4,283,491	21,342,463	19.6
Delaware	13.7	32,602	8,848,446	74.4	205,694	21,548,157	19.8
Kentucky	8.6	226,040	9,074,486	76.3	2,388,364	23,936,521	22.0
Oklahoma	7.2	172,198	9,246,684	77.8	7,123,424	26,059,945	23.9
West Virginia	6.6	114,893	9,361,577	78.7	1,613,934	27,673,879	25.4
Missouri	6.2	223,840	9,585,417	80.6	3,398,887	31,072,766	28.5
New Jersey	5.2	208,828	9,794,245	82.4	3,829,209	34,901,975	32.1
Ohio	4.7	309,304	10,103,549	85.0	6,331,136	41,233,111	37.9
Pennsylvania	4.5	431,257	10,534,806	88.6	9,192,602	50,425,713	46.3
Illinois	4.3	328,972	10,863,778	91.4	7,266,361	57,692,074	53.0
Indiana	3.5	111,982	10,975,760	92.3	3,116,136	60,808,210	55.9
Kansas	3.5	66,344	11,042,104	92.9	1,792,847	62,601,057	57.5
Michigan	3.5	169,453	11,211,557	94.3	4,650,171	67,251,228	61.8
New York	3.3	412,814	11,624,371	97.8	12,150,293	79,401,521	72.9
Arizona	2.5	10,749	11,635,120	97.8	264,378	79,665,899	73.2
Connecticut	1.8	29,354	11,664,474	98.1	1,576,673	81,242,572	74.6
California	1.4	81,048	11,745,522	98.8	5,040,247	86,282,819	79.3
Rhode Island	1.4	9,913	11,755,435	98.9	677,016	86,959,835	79.9
Massachusetts	1.2	52,365	11,807,800	99.3	4,192,926	91,152,761	83.7
Colorado	1.1	11,828	11,819,628	99.4	961,117	92,113,878	84.6
Nebraska	1.0	13,752	11,833,380	99.5	1,353,702	93,467,580	85.9
Iowa	.7	17,380	11,850,760	99.7	2,448,382	95,915,962	88.1
New Mexico	.7	2,850	11,853,610	99.7	331,755	96,247,717	88.4
Nevada	.6	516	11,854,126	99.7	81,425	96,329,142	88.5
Wyoming	.6	1,250	11,855,376	99.7	214,067	96,543,209	88.7
Minnesota	.4	9,445	11,864,821	99.8	2,538,973	99,082,182	91.0
Washington	.4	6,840	11,871,661	99.8	1,521,099	100,603,281	92.4
Wisconsin	.4	10,739	11,882,400	99.9	2,913,859	103,517,140	95.1
Idaho	.2	668	11,883,068	99.9	437,562	103,954,702	95.5
Montana	.2	1,256	11,884,324	99.9	517,327	104,472,029	96.0
New Hampshire	.2	790	11,885,114	99.9	464,350	104,936,379	96.4
Oregon	.2	2,234	11,887,348	100.0	937,029	105,873,408	97.3
Utah	.2	1,108	11,888,456	100.0	495,955	106,369,363	97.7
Vermont	.2	568	11,889,024	100.0	358,965	106,728,328	98.0
Maine	.1	1,096	11,890,120	100.0	795,183	107,523,511	98.8
North Dakota	.1	377	11,890,497	100.0	671,243	108,194,754	99.4
South Dakota	.1	646	11,891,143	100.0	669,453	108,864,207	100.0

TABLE 4.—PERCENT NEGRO IN TOTAL POPULATION AT EACH CENSUS, BY DIVISIONS, AND STATES: 1790 TO 1930

DIVISION AND STATE	1930	1920	1910	1900	1890	1880	1870	1860	1850	1840	1830	1820	1810	1800	1790
United States	9.7	9.9	10.7	11.6	11.9	13.1	12.7	14.1	15.7	16.8	18.1	18.4	19.0	18.9	19.3
GEOGRAPHIC DIVISIONS:															
New England	1.2	1.1	1.0	1.1	0.9	1.0	0.9	0.8	0.8	1.0	1.1	1.3	1.4	1.5	1.7
Middle Atlantic	4.0	2.7	2.2	2.1	1.8	1.8	1.7	1.8	2.1	2.6	2.9	3.3	4.1	4.6	5.3
East North Central	3.7	2.4	1.6	1.6	1.5	1.6	1.4	.9	1.0	1.0	1.1	1.0	1.3	1.2	
West North Central	2.5	2.2	2.1	2.3	2.5	3.3	3.7	5.6	10.3	14.1	18.3	15.9	17.4		
South Atlantic	28.0	30.9	33.7	35.7	36.8	38.7	37.9	38.4	39.8	40.7	41.9	41.6	40.4	37.6	36.4
East South Central	26.9	28.4	31.5	33.7	33.0	34.5	33.2	34.7	33.4	32.2	27.6	24.2	20.5	17.5	14.9
West South Central	18.7	20.1	22.6	25.9	29.1	32.6	36.4	36.9	39.2	47.6	53.2	48.4	54.4		
Mountain	.8	.9	.8	.9	1.1	.8	.5	.1	.1						
Pacific	1.1	.9	.7	.6	.7	.6	.7	1.0	1.1						
NEW ENGLAND:															
Maine	.1	.2	.2	.2	.2	.2	.3	.2	.2	.3	.3	.3	.4	.5	.6
New Hampshire	.2	.1	.1	.2	.2	.2	.2	.2	.2	.2	.2	.3	.5	.5	.6
Vermont	.2	.2	.5	.2	.3	.3	.3	.2	.2	.3	.3	.4	.3	.4	.3
Massachusetts	1.2	1.2	1.1	1.1	1.0	1.0	1.0	.8	.9	1.2	1.2	1.3	1.4	1.5	1.4
Rhode Island	1.4	1.7	1.8	2.1	2.1	2.3	2.3	2.3	2.5	3.0	3.7	4.3	4.8	5.3	6.3
Connecticut	1.8	1.5	1.4	1.7	1.6	1.9	1.8	1.9	2.1	2.6	2.7	2.9	2.6	2.5	2.3
MIDDLE ATLANTIC:															
New York	3.3	1.9	1.5	1.4	1.2	1.3	1.2	1.3	1.6	2.1	2.3	2.9	4.2	5.3	7.6
New Jersey	5.2	3.7	3.5	3.7	3.3	3.4	3.4	3.8	4.9	5.8	6.4	7.2	7.6	8.0	7.7
Pennsylvania	4.5	3.3	2.5	2.5	2.0	2.0	1.9	2.0	2.3	2.8	2.8	2.9	2.9	2.7	2.4
EAST NORTH CENTRAL:															
Ohio	4.7	3.2	2.3	2.3	2.4	2.5	2.4	1.6	1.3	1.1	1.0	.8	.8	.7	
Indiana	3.5	2.8	2.2	2.3	2.1	2.0	1.5	.9	1.1	1.0	1.1	1.0	2.6	5.3	
Illinois	4.3	2.8	1.9	1.8	1.5	1.5	1.1	.5	.6	.8	1.5	2.5	6.4		
Michigan	3.5	1.6	.6	.7	.7	.9	1.0	.9	.7	.3	.9	2.0	3.0		
Wisconsin	.4	.2	.1	.1	.1	.2	.2	.2	.2	.6					
WEST NORTH CENTRAL:															
Minnesota	.4	.4	.3	.3	.3	.2	.2	.2	.6						
Iowa	.7	.8	.7	.6	.6	.6	.5	.2	.2	.4					
Missouri	6.2	5.2	4.8	5.2	5.6	6.7	6.9	10.0	13.2	15.6	18.3	15.9	17.4		
North Dakota	.1	.1	.1	.1	.2	[1] .3	[1] .7								
South Dakota	.1	.1	.1	.1	.2										
Nebraska	1.0	1.0	.6	.6	.8	.5	.6	.3							
Kansas	3.5	3.3	3.2	3.5	3.5	4.3	4.7	.6							
SOUTH ATLANTIC:															
Delaware	13.7	13.6	15.4	16.6	16.8	18.0	18.2	19.3	22.3	25.0	24.9	24.0	23.8	22.4	21.6
Maryland	16.9	16.9	17.9	19.8	20.7	22.5	22.5	24.9	28.3	32.3	34.9	36.1	38.2	36.7	34.7
District of Columbia	27.1	25.1	28.5	31.1	32.8	33.6	33.0	19.1	26.6	29.9	30.8	31.6	33.1	28.6	
Virginia	26.8	29.9	32.6	35.6	38.4	41.8	41.9	34.4	37.1	40.2	42.7	43.4	43.3	41.6	40.9
West Virginia	6.6	5.9	5.3	4.5	4.3	4.2	4.1								
North Carolina	29.0	29.8	31.6	33.0	34.7	38.0	36.6	36.4	36.4	35.6	35.9	34.4	32.2	29.4	26.8
South Carolina	45.6	51.4	55.2	58.4	59.8	60.7	58.9	58.6	58.9	56.4	55.6	52.8	48.4	43.2	43.7
Georgia	36.8	41.7	45.1	46.7	46.7	47.0	46.0	44.1	42.4	41.0	42.6	44.4	42.4	37.1	35.9
Florida	29.4	34.0	41.0	43.7	42.5	47.0	48.8	44.6	46.0	48.7	47.1				
EAST SOUTH CENTRAL:															
Kentucky	8.6	9.8	11.4	13.3	14.4	16.5	16.8	20.4	22.5	24.3	24.7	22.9	20.2	18.6	17.0
Tennessee	18.3	19.3	21.7	23.8	24.4	26.1	25.6	25.5	24.5	22.7	21.4	19.6	17.5	13.2	10.6
Alabama	25.7	38.4	42.5	45.2	44.8	47.5	47.7	45.4	44.7	43.3	38.5	33.2			
Mississippi	50.2	52.2	56.2	58.5	57.6	57.5	53.7	55.3	51.2	52.3	48.4	44.1	42.9	41.5	
WEST SOUTH CENTRAL:															
Arkansas	25.8	27.0	28.1	28.0	27.4	26.3	25.2	25.6	22.7	20.9	15.5	11.7			
Louisiana	36.9	38.9	43.1	47.1	50.0	51.5	50.1	49.5	50.7	55.0	58.5	51.8	55.2		
Oklahoma	7.2	7.4	8.3	[2] 7.0	[2] 8.4										
Texas	14.7	15.9	17.7	20.4	21.8	24.7	31.0	30.3	27.5						
MOUNTAIN:															
Montana	.2	.3	.5	.6	1.0	.9	.9								
Idaho	.2	.2	.2	.2	.2	.2	.4								
Wyoming	.6	.7	1.5	1.0	1.5	1.4	2.0								
Colorado	1.1	1.2	1.4	1.6	1.5	1.3	1.1	.1							
New Mexico	.7	1.6	.5	.8	1.2	.8	.2	.1	(3)						
Arizona	2.5	2.4	1.0	1.5	1.5	.4	.3								
Utah	.2	.3	.3	.2	.3	.2	.1	.2	.4						
Nevada	.6	.4	.6	.3	.5	.8	.8	.7							
PACIFIC:															
Washington	.4	.5	.5	.5	.4	.4	.9	.3							
Oregon	.2	.3	.2	.3	.4	.3	.4	.2	1.6						
California	1.4	1.1	.9	.7	.9	.7	.8	1.1	1.0						

[1] Dakota Territory.

[2] Includes population of Indian Territory.

[3] Less than 1/10 of 1 percent.

TABLE 5.—NUMBER OF NEGROES PER 100,000 WHITES AT EACH CENSUS, BY SECTIONS, DIVISIONS AND STATES: 1790 TO 1930

SECTION, DIVISION, AND STATE	1930	1920[1]	1910[1]	1900	1890	1880	1870	1860	1850	1840	1830	1820	1810	1800	1790
United States	10,923	11,117	12,079	13,223	13,591	15,162	14,528	16,499	18,610	20,252	22,110	22,521	23,504	23,268	23,872
The North	3,423	2,371	1,881	1,898	1,796	1,969	1,825	1,759	2,076	2,345	2,387	2,534	2,978	3,216	3,547
The South	33,828	37,554	43,066	47,954	51,242	56,406	56,221	58,247	59,537	61,317	60,968	59,162	57,882	53,907	54,254
The West	1,114	947	789	781	943	735	701	814	699	-----	-----	-----	-----	-----	-----
GEOGRAPHIC DIVISIONS:															
New England	1,167	1,081	1,023	1,069	958	1,006	918	794	851	1,024	1,106	1,277	1,371	1,536	1,712
Middle Atlantic	4,183	2,774	2,213	2,157	1,807	1,839	1,709	1,792	2,196	2,716	2,980	3,440	4,261	4,814	5,554
East North Central	3,833	2,458	1,678	1,641	1,562	1,665	1,452	929	1,009	1,014	1,092	980	1,285	1,261	-----
West North Central	2,577	2,283	2,140	2,364	2,588	3,401	3,842	5,896	11,446	16,358	22,353	18,867	21,002	-----	-----
South Atlantic	38,957	44,827	50,951	55,607	58,344	63,196	60,978	62,273	66,030	68,614	72,256	71,233	67,800	60,253	57,153
East South Central	36,794	39,634	46,097	49,553	49,233	52,630	49,820	53,091	50,114	47,578	38,161	31,920	25,829	21,190	17,542
West South Central	25,076	26,744	30,574	35,507	41,816	48,478	57,403	58,463	64,462	90,970	113,815	93,930	123,124	-----	-----
Mountain	915	1,003	878	987	1,161	817	515	143	99	-----	-----	-----	-----	-----	-----
Pacific	1,202	914	734	639	804	685	793	1,098	1,116	-----	-----	-----	-----	-----	-----
NEW ENGLAND:															
Maine	138	171	184	191	181	224	257	212	233	271	299	312	425	542	560
New Hampshire	170	140	131	161	163	198	183	152	164	189	226	323	454	470	558
Vermont	158	163	458	241	283	319	280	226	229	251	315	384	345	362	318
Massachusetts	1,249	1,195	1,145	1,154	1,000	1,060	966	786	920	1,189	1,168	1,305	1,448	1,549	1,463
Rhode Island	1,464	1,690	1,790	2,170	2,188	2,404	2,347	2,316	2,551	3,071	3,822	4,533	5,077	5,630	6,755
Connecticut	1,862	1,549	1,381	1,706	1,677	1,891	1,833	1,911	2,119	2,691	2,787	2,981	2,650	2,567	2,398
MIDDLE ATLANTIC:															
New York	3,398	1,952	1,497	1,387	1,183	1,298	1,203	1,279	1,610	2,103	2,399	2,952	4,392	5,616	8,270
New Jersey	5,454	3,857	3,670	3,854	3,411	3,558	3,502	3,918	5,166	6,177	6,846	7,772	8,240	8,658	8,346
Pennsylvania	4,691	3,375	2,597	2,554	2,090	2,038	1,889	1,999	2,375	2,859	2,926	2,984	2,960	2,776	2,423
EAST NORTH CENTRAL:															
Ohio	4,885	3,342	2,394	2,387	2,430	2,563	2,429	1,593	1,293	1,155	1,031	819	830	748	-----
Indiana	3,594	2,837	2,285	2,339	2,106	2,023	1,483	854	1,153	1,056	1,070	974	2,637	5,577	-----
Illinois	4,527	2,896	1,973	1,797	1,513	1,530	1,145	448	643	832	1,537	2,552	6,791	-----	-----
Michigan	3,644	1,669	615	659	734	935	1,015	924	654	334	935	1,995	3,118	-----	-----
Wisconsin	369	199	125	124	145	206	201	151	208	637	-----	-----	-----	-----	-----
WEST NORTH CENTRAL:															
Minnesota	372	372	344	285	284	201	173	153	646	-----	-----	-----	-----	-----	-----
Iowa	710	798	678	572	562	589	485	159	174	438	-----	-----	-----	-----	-----
Missouri	6,586	5,533	5,025	5,475	5,940	7,185	7,365	11,143	15,209	18,467	22,353	18,867	21,002	-----	-----
North Dakota	56	73	108	92	204	[2] 301	[2] 729	-----	-----	-----	-----	-----	-----	-----	-----
South Dakota	96	134	145	122	165			-----	-----	-----	-----	-----	-----	-----	-----
Nebraska	1,016	1,037	652	593	851	530	646	286	-----	-----	-----	-----	-----	-----	-----
Kansas	3,700	3,422	3,323	3,672	3,611	4,527	4,939	589	-----	-----	-----	-----	-----	-----	-----
SOUTH ATLANTIC:															
Delaware	15,850	15,751	18,224	19,936	20,266	22,006	22,299	23,874	28,612	33,340	33,241	31,596	31,273	28,928	27,610
Maryland	20,409	20,294	21,856	24,681	26,093	29,010	28,966	33,170	39,501	47,710	53,565	56,539	61,854	57,886	53,237
District of Columbia	37,316	33,647	40,000	45,268	48,852	50,503	49,167	23,560	36,230	42,584	44,520	46,100	49,406	40,006	-----
Virginia	36,724	42,650	48,287	55,390	62,290	71,705	72,019	52,412	58,880	67,321	74,479	76,580	76,714	71,152	69,098
West Virginia	7,119	6,270	5,547	4,753	4,478	4,369	4,240	-----	-----	-----	-----	-----	-----	-----	-----
North Carolina	41,104	42,797	46,507	49,420	53,158	61,261	57,725	57,390	57,142	55,386	56,074	52,392	47,578	41,549	36,622
South Carolina	84,073	105,643	123,070	140,249	149,117	154,519	143,549	141,545	143,480	129,423	125,385	111,734	93,801	76,093	77,683
Georgia	58,309	71,422	82,204	87,600	87,781	88,766	85,322	78,725	73,741	69,586	74,128	79,875	73,596	59,089	56,087
Florida	41,714	51,641	69,588	77,600	73,875	88,840	95,453	80,618	85,253	94,958	88,904	-----	-----	-----	-----
EAST SOUTH CENTRAL:															
Kentucky	9,464	10,821	12,903	15,288	16,855	19,711	20,225	25,685	29,024	32,118	32,857	29,780	25,375	22,839	20,519
Tennessee	22,334	23,954	27,643	31,181	32,221	35,400	34,433	34,234	32,488	20,437	27,281	24,367	21,240	15,149	11,838
Alabama	55,553	62,245	73,917	82,636	81,381	90,625	91,201	83,183	80,914	76,248	62,562	49,678	-----	-----	-----
Mississippi	101,290	109,531	128,430	141,552	136,287	135,647	116,011	123,596	105,103	109,774	93,945	78,888	75,261	70,882	-----
WEST SOUTH CENTRAL:															
Arkansas	34,800	36,907	39,163	38,838	37,755	35,614	33,738	34,324	29,415	26,434	18,375	13,305	-----	-----	-----
Louisiana	58,895	64,009	75,961	89,199	100,143	106,309	100,592	98,018	102,654	122,402	141,208	107,680	123,124	-----	-----
Oklahoma[3]	8,109	8,240	9,546	8,309	12,523	-----	-----	-----	-----	-----	-----	-----	-----	-----	-----
Texas	19,960	21,014	23,169	25,579	27,960	32,858	44,887	43,460	38,016	-----	-----	-----	-----	-----	-----
MOUNTAIN:															
Montana	243	310	509	673	1,167	978	1,000	-----	-----	-----	-----	-----	-----	-----	-----
Idaho	153	217	204	190	245	183	565	-----	-----	-----	-----	-----	-----	-----	-----
Wyoming	584	731	1,597	1,056	1,554	1,533	2,097	-----	-----	-----	-----	-----	-----	-----	-----
Colorado	1,231	1,244	1,468	1,620	1,536	1,274	1,163	134	-----	-----	-----	-----	-----	-----	-----
New Mexico	859	1,899	574	893	1,369	934	190	103	36	-----	-----	-----	-----	-----	-----
Arizona	4,066	3,944	1,642	1,989	2,435	441	271	-----	-----	-----	-----	-----	-----	-----	-----
Utah	223	328	312	247	286	163	137	147	441	-----	-----	-----	-----	-----	-----
Nevada	634	499	698	378	619	911	916	661	-----	-----	-----	-----	-----	-----	-----
PACIFIC:															
Washington	450	522	546	507	470	484	933	269	-----	-----	-----	-----	-----	-----	-----
Oregon	238	276	228	280	393	299	398	245	1,582	-----	-----	-----	-----	-----	-----
California	1,608	1,233	979	787	1,018	784	855	1,264	1,050	-----	-----	-----	-----	-----	-----

[1] Figures for white population in 1920 and 1910 are adjusted by deducting the estimated number of Mexicans.
[2] Dakota Territory.
[3] Includes Indian Territory in 1900 and 1890.

CHAPTER IV.—NATIVITY

Explanation of terms used.—"Native population", as the term is used here, comprises all persons born in continental United States and in any of the outlying possessions, and persons of native parentage born abroad or at sea and designated, respectively, "American citizens born abroad" and "American citizens born at sea." The term, "native population", when used in headings for tables which present statistics by States, does not indicate that these persons are native of specific States, but merely that they were born in the United States. Natives of individual States are designated in table headings as "population born in" specified States.

For a number of persons, the enumerators reported the place of birth as the United States without specifying the State. Persons for whom the place of birth was not specifically reported, and for whom the returns give no indication of foreign origin, have also been assumed to be natives of the United States, and included in the groups designated "United States, State not reported."

In measuring the movement of the population between sections, or States, the term "net gain or loss" is used. An example will indicate the method used in obtaining the net gain. For the North the net gain is obtained by subtracting the number of Negroes born in the North and living in the South from the number born in the South and living in the North.

It should be understood that the figures given in this chapter do not represent or measure the gross migration of the Negroes. The figures presented herein do not show the extent of interstate migration, but the net cumulative results of such migration in combination with mortality.

Native and foreign-born Negro population.—Less than 1 percent, or only 98,620, of the Negroes in the United States are of foreign birth, according to the census of 1930. However, the number of foreign-born Negroes in the United States in 1930 is almost five times as large as in 1900.

A very large percentage of the foreign-born Negro population in the United States in 1930 was born in the Western Hemisphere; mostly in the West Indies, in Canada, and the islands off the Atlantic Coast.

Year of immigration to the United States.—Over 40 percent of the total foreign-born Negro population immigrated to the United States between 1920 and 1930. The largest number of these immigrants arrived between 1920 and 1930. The number of male immigrants was approximately 20 percent greater than the number of female.

Place of residence of foreign-born Negro population.—Approximately six-tenths of the foreign-born Negro population resided in New York. Florida and Massachusetts each had about one-tenth of the total foreign-born Negro population.

Native Negro population by division of birth and division of residence.—More than 90 percent of the Negroes residing in the South (South Atlantic, East South Central, and West South Central divisions), in 1930, were born there, while the North had less than 36 percent of its Negro population born in the division of their residence.

Gain or loss of native Negro population by divisions.—The results of the migration of the native Negro population indicate the movement of the Negroes to the North. In the interval of 10 years, 1920–30, the number of Negroes living in the North, but born in the South, increased from 737,423 to 1,355,789. During the 20-year period, 1910–30, interdivisional migration resulted in a considerable loss in the South Atlantic and East South Central divisions but a large gain in the Middle Atlantic and East North Central divisions.

Place of birth and residence, 1930.—More than 58 percent of the Negroes living in the North and the West were born in the South, while less than 1 percent of the Negro population in the South in 1930 was born in the other sections.

The decreasing percentage of the native-born Negroes living in the State of birth indicates the increasing migration of the Negro population. This percentage was 73.8 percent in 1930, as compared with 79.2 percent in 1920 and 82.7 percent in 1910.

All of the Southern States, except Delaware, West Virginia, Florida, Arkansas, and Oklahoma, and the District of Columbia, showed a loss in Negro population in 1930 through interstate migration. There were gains as a result of interstate migration in all the Northern and Western States, except Maine, Vermont, and North Dakota.

The Negroes born in the northernmost of the Southern States have shown a tendency to move northward. For example, the largest number of the Negroes born in Maryland and living outside the State were living in Pennsylvania; the largest number born in North Carolina and living outside the State were living in Virginia; the largest number born in South Carolina and living outside the State were living in North Carolina.

The largest portion of the Negroes living in New England and the Middle Atlantic States, but born in other States, were born in Georgia, North Carolina, South Carolina, and Virginia. Most of the Negroes living in the East North Central States, but born in other States, were born in Alabama, Georgia, Kentucky, Mississippi, and Tennessee.

PERCENTAGE OF NEGROES IN THE TOTAL POPULATION, BY STATES: 1930

[District of Columbia, 27.1 per cent, not shown separately on the map]

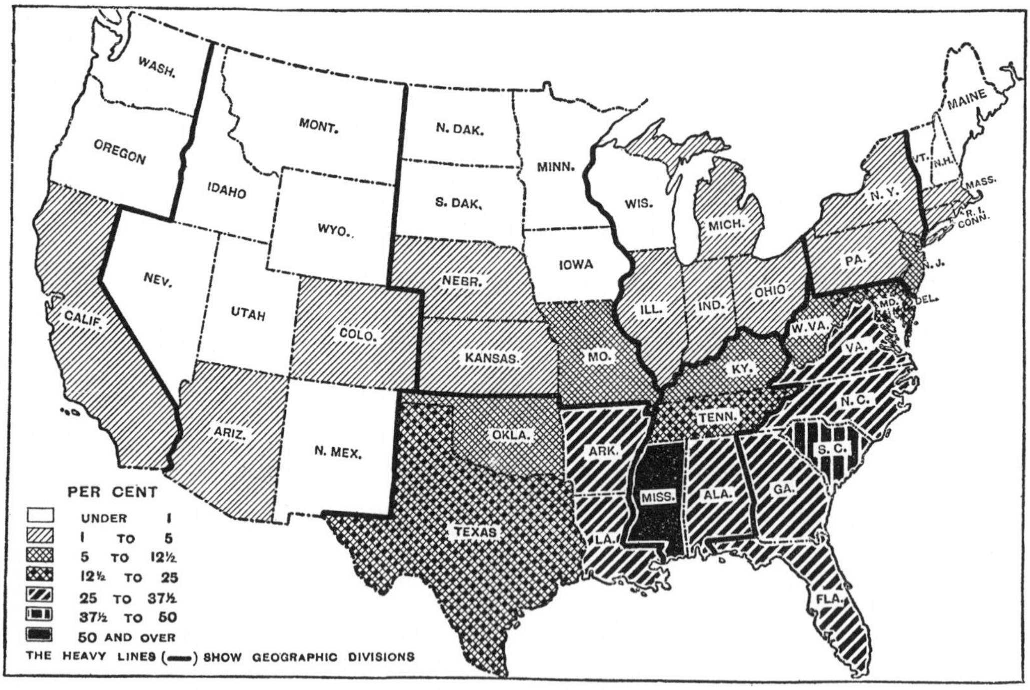

DISTRIBUTION OF THE TOTAL POPULATION, BY COLOR AND NATIVITY: 1850 TO 1930

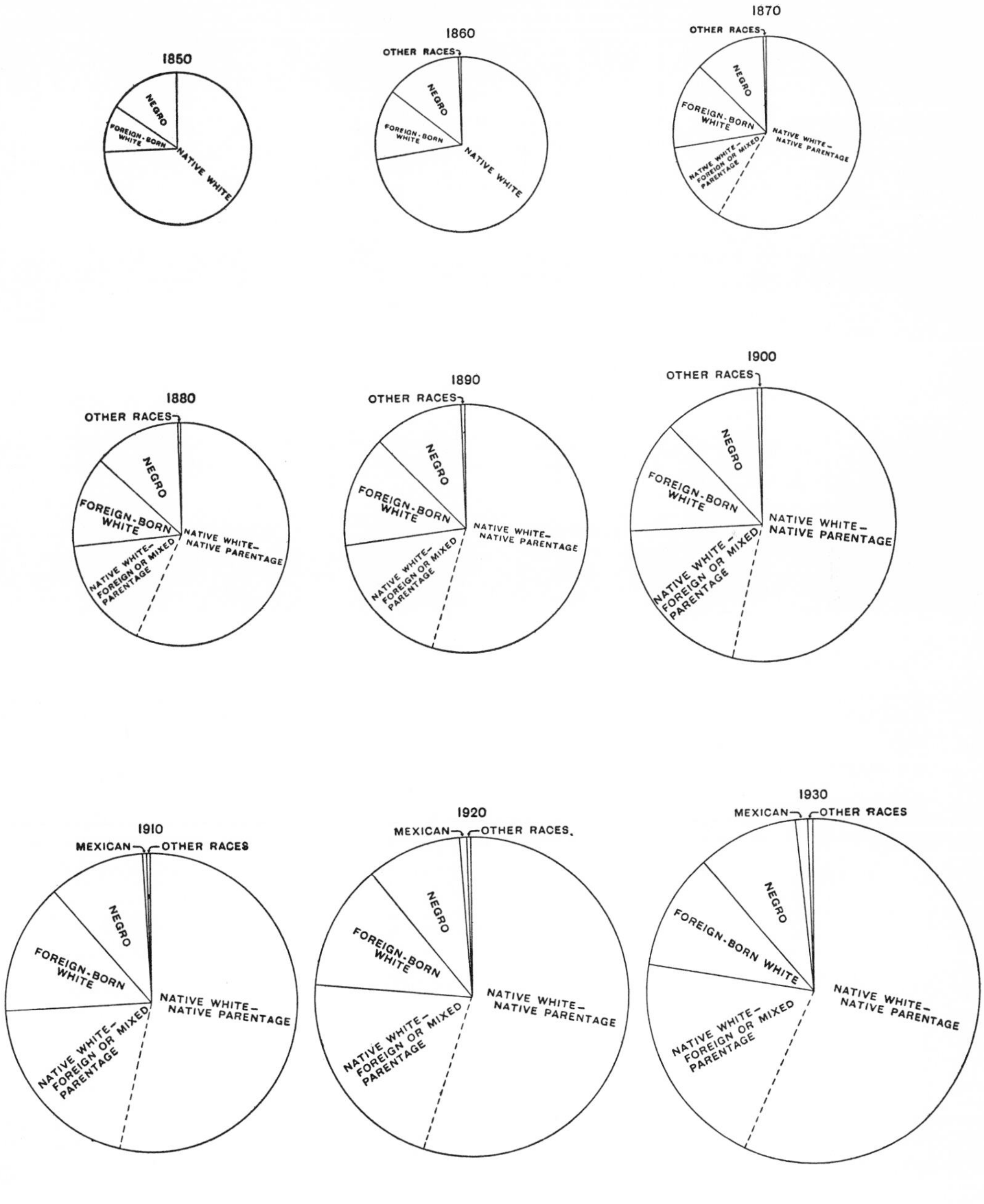

Negro Population, by States: 1930 and 1920

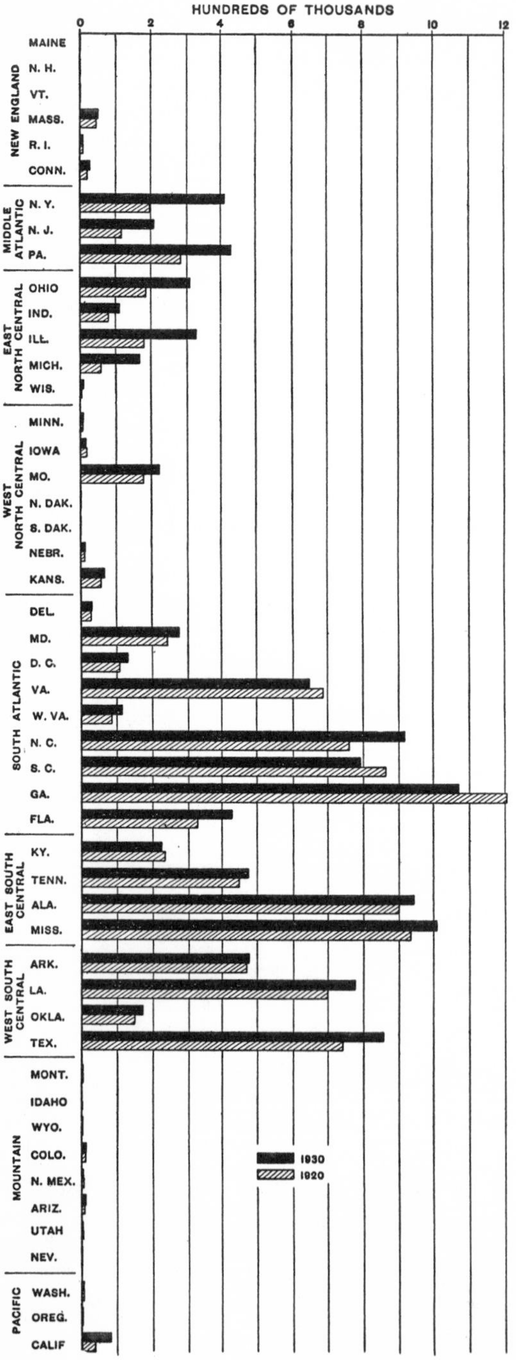

Color, Nativity, and Parentage, by States: 1930

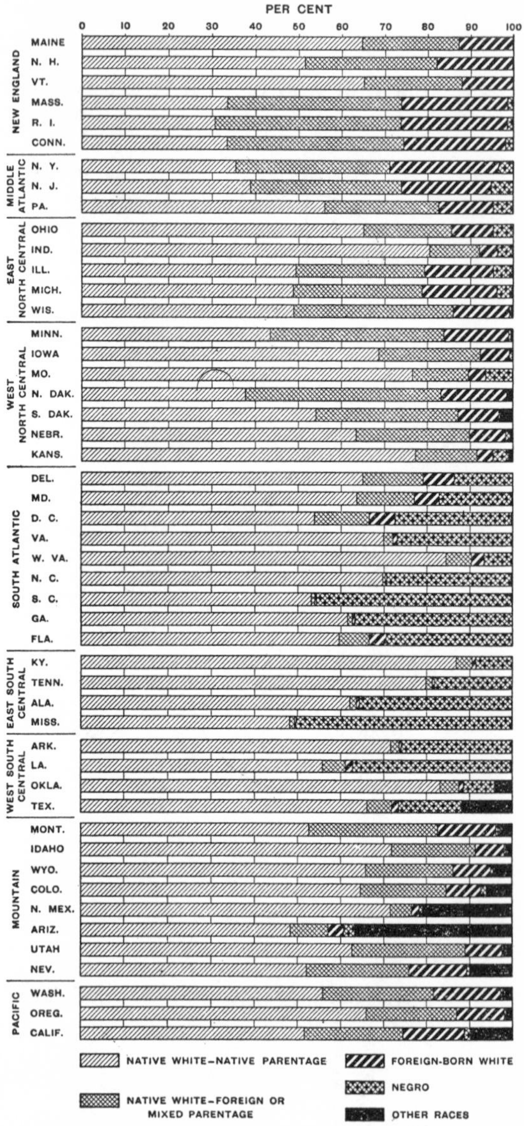

Table 1.—Native and Foreign-Born Negro Population and Foreign-Born White Population of the United States: 1900 to 1930

CENSUS YEAR	NEGRO POPULATION				FOREIGN-BORN WHITE POPULATION	
	Total	Native	Foreign born		Number	Percent of total white population
			Number	Percent of total		
1930	11,891,143	11,792,523	98,620	0.8	13,366,407	12.3
1920	10,463,131	10,389,328	73,803	.7	[1] 13,255,394	14.1
1910	9,827,763	9,787,424	40,339	.4	[1] 13,134,312	16.1
1900	8,833,994	8,813,658	20,336	.2	10,213,817	15.3

[1] Figures for white population in 1920 and 1910 are adjusted by deducting the estimated number of Mexicans.

Table 2.—Negro Population Distributed as Born in Division of Residence, in Other Divisions, or in Foreign Countries, by Divisions: 1930

GEOGRAPHIC DIVISION	Total Negro population [1]	Born in the United States, and with State of birth reported: Born in division of residence: Number	Percent	Born in other divisions: Number	Percent	Foreign born: Number	Percent
United States	**11,891,143**	**9,762,855**	**82.1**	**1,976,624**	**16.6**	**98,620**	**0.8**
New England	94,086	44,991	47.8	36,579	38.9	11,786	12.5
Middle Atlantic	1,052,899	354,910	33.7	611,497	58.1	64,565	6.1
East North Central	930,450	278,327	29.9	640,218	68.8	5,157	.6
West North Central	331,784	171,547	51.7	157,098	47.3	528	.2
South Atlantic	4,421,388	4,296,766	97.2	104,217	2.4	12,584	.3
East South Central	2,658,238	2,513,498	94.6	138,805	5.2	532	------
West South Central	2,281,951	2,077,617	91.0	197,058	8.6	1,412	.1
Mountain	30,225	6,122	20.3	23,591	78.1	187	.6
Pacific	90,122	19,077	21.2	67,561	75.0	1,869	2.1

[1] Includes Negroes born in the United States, State of birth not reported; Negroes born in outlying possessions, and born abroad or at sea. The combined numbers of these classes are 53,044, or 4/10 of 1 percent of the Negro population.

Table 3.—Country of Birth of the Foreign-Born Negro Population of the United States: 1930 and 1920

COUNTRY OF BIRTH	1930	1920	COUNTRY OF BIRTH	1930	1920
All foreign countries	98,620	73,803	Asia	44	27
America	87,094	63,684	China	1	6
Canada	5,817	5,651	India	29	------
Newfoundland	9	6	Other Asia	14	21
Cuba	2,362	1,934	Africa	986	556
Other West Indies	72,138	50,488	Australia	81	107
Mexico	915	3,123	Azores	177	206
Central America	2,662	816	Other Atlantic islands	5,411	5,143
South America	3,191	1,666	Pacific islands	96	40
Europe	4,632	3,996	Born at sea or not specified	99	44

Table 4.—Year of Immigration of the Foreign-Born Negro Population of the United States, by Sex

SEX	Total foreign-born negroes	1920 to 1930: Total	1925 to 1930	1920 to 1924	1911 to 1919: Total	1915 to 1919	1911 to 1914	1901 to 1910	1900 or earlier
Total	**98,620**	**39,515**	**8,576**	**30,939**	**33,012**	**20,597**	**12,415**	**17,453**	**8,640**
Male	54,081	19,944	4,414	15,530	18,215	11,248	6,967	10,644	5,278
Female	44,539	19,571	4,162	15,409	14,797	9,349	5,448	6,809	3,362

Table 5.—Summary of Data Indicating Results of the Migration of the Native Negro and White Population North and South, and East and West: 1920 to 1930

The small number of persons for whom State of birth was not reported is omitted from this table]

SECTION	Negro: 1930	Negro: 1920	White: 1930	White: 1920
Born in the South and living in the North	1,355,789	737,423	1,931,799	1,412,779
Born in the North and living in the South	52,338	44,536	1,821,678	1,675,085
Net gain of the North	1,303,451	692,887	110,121	----------
Net gain of the South	----------	----------	----------	262,306
Born east and living west of the Mississippi River [1]	320,589	342,931	4,820,182	4,882,520
Born west and living east of the Mississippi River [1]	177,158	96,110	1,458,154	939,017
Net gain of the West	143,431	246,821	3,362,028	3,943,503
Net gain of the East	----------	----------	----------	----------

[1] In the preparation of this table the entire States of Minnesota and Louisiana have been treated as living west of the Mississippi River.

Table 6.—NUMBER AND PERCENT NATIVE AND FOREIGN BORN IN THE TOTAL NEGRO POPULATION, WITH CLASSIFICATION OF NATIVE ACCORDING TO WHETHER BORN IN STATE OF RESIDENCE OR ELSEWHERE, FOR THE UNITED STATES: 1910 TO 1930

CENSUS YEAR	Total Negro population	Native Negro population: Total: Number	Total: Percent of total Negro population	With State of birth reported: Born in State of residence: Number	Born in State of residence: Percent of total Negro population	Born in other States: Number	Born in other States: Percent of total Negro population	Born in other States: Percent of native Negro population	State of birth not reported	Born in outlying possessions	American citizens born at sea	American citizens born abroad	Foreign-born Negro population: Number	Foreign-born: Percent of total Negro population
1930	11,891,143	11,792,523	99.2	8,774,754	73.8	2,964,725	24.9	25.1	32,384	17,625	39	2,996	98,620	0.8
1920	10,463,131	10,389,328	99.3	8,288,492	79.2	2,054,242	19.6	19.8	38,575	4,846	34	3,139	73,803	.7
1910	9,827,763	9,787,424	99.6	8,129,435	82.7	1,616,608	16.4	16.5	37,943	355	217	2,866	40,339	.4

TABLE 7.—PARENTAGE OF THE NEGRO AND THE WHITE POPULATION OF THE UNITED STATES: 1930 AND 1920

NATIVITY AND PARENTAGE	POPULATION											
	Number				Percent distribution				Increase			
	1930		1920		1930		1920		Number		Percent	
	Negro	White	Negro	White	Negro	White	Negro	White	Negro	White	Negro	White
Total	**11, 891, 143**	**108, 864, 207**	**10, 463, 131**	**94, 120, 374**	**100. 0**	**100. 0**	**100. 0**	**100. 0**	**1, 428, 012**	**14, 743, 833**	**13. 6**	**15. 7**
Native	11, 792, 523	95, 497, 800	10, 389, 328	80, 864, 980	99. 2	87. 7	99. 3	85. 9	1, 403, 195	14, 632, 820	13. 5	18. 1
Both parents native	11, 709, 162	70, 136, 614	10, 334, 151	58, 421, 957	98. 5	64. 4	98. 8	62. 1	1, 375, 011	11, 714, 657	13. 3	20. 1
1 or both parents foreign born	83, 361	25, 361, 186	55, 177	22, 443, 023	. 7	23. 3	. 5	23. 8	28, 184	2, 918, 163	51. 1	13. 0
1 parent foreign born, 1 native	39, 909	8, 361, 965	29, 334	6, 921, 188	. 3	7. 7	. 3	7. 4	10, 575	1, 440, 777	36. 1	20. 8
Father foreign born	26, 310	5, 459, 530	18, 193	(1)	. 2	5. 0	. 2	(1)	8, 117	(1)	44. 6	(1)
Mother foreign born	13, 599	2, 902, 435	11, 141	(1)	. 1	2. 7	. 1	(1)	2, 458	(1)	22. 1	(1)
Both parents foreign born	43, 452	16, 999, 221	25, 843	15, 521, 835	. 4	15. 6	. 2	16. 5	17, 609	1, 477, 386	68. 1	9. 5
Foreign born	98, 620	13, 366, 407	73, 803	[2] 13, 255, 394	. 8	12. 3	. 7	14. 1	24, 817	111, 013	33. 6	. 8

[1] Adjusted figures not available.

[2] Figures for white population in 1920 and 1910 are adjusted by deducting the estimated number of Mexicans.

TABLE 8.—NATIVE NEGRO AND WHITE POPULATION CLASSIFIED BY SECTION OF RESIDENCE, AND BY SECTION OF BIRTH: 1930

SECTION OF RESIDENCE	TOTAL		BORN IN—						STATE OF BIRTH NOT REPORTED, OR BORN IN OUTLYING POSSESSIONS [1]	
			The South		The North		The West			
	Negro	White	Negro	White	Negro	White	Negro	White	Negro	White
	NUMBER									
United States	**11, 792, 523**	**95, 497, 800**	**10, 699, 458**	**27, 891, 047**	**1, 004, 469**	**61, 783, 174**	**35, 552**	**5, 425, 014**	**53, 044**	**398, 565**
The South	9, 347, 049	27, 141, 704	9, 273, 245	25, 172, 567	52, 338	1, 821, 678	2, 378	96, 234	19, 088	51, 225
The North	2, 327, 183	59, 001, 814	1, 355, 789	1, 931, 799	933, 822	56, 551, 965	5, 556	269, 818	32, 016	248, 232
The West	118, 291	9, 354, 282	70, 424	786, 681	18, 309	3, 409, 531	27, 618	5, 058, 962	1, 940	99, 108
	PERCENT DISTRIBUTION BY SECTION OF BIRTH									
United States	**1. 000**	**100. 0**	**90. 7**	**29. 3**	**8. 5**	**64. 7**	**0. 3**	**5. 7**	**0. 4**	**0. 4**
The South	100. 0	100. 0	99. 2	92. 7	0. 6	6. 7	(2)	. 4	. 2	. 2
The North	100. 0	100. 0	58. 3	3. 3	40. 1	94. 8	. 2	. 5	1. 4	. 4
The West	100. 0	100. 0	59. 5	8. 4	15. 5	36. 4	23. 3	54. 1	1. 6	1. 1
	PERCENT DISTRIBUTION BY SECTION OF RESIDENCE									
United States	**100. 0**	**100. 0**	**100. 0**	**100. 0**	**100. 0**	**100. 0**	**100. 0**	**100. 0**	**100. 0**	**100. 0**
The South	79. 3	28. 4	86. 7	90. 3	5. 2	2. 9	6. 7	1. 8	36. 0	12. 9
The North	19. 7	61. 8	12. 7	6. 9	93. 0	91. 5	15. 6	5. 0	60. 4	62. 3
The West	1. 0	9. 8	0. 7	2. 8	1. 8	5. 5	77. 7	93. 3	3. 7	24. 9

[1] Includes American citizens born abroad or at sea.

[2] Less than 1/10 of 1 percent.

TABLE 9.—NATIVE NEGRO POPULATION, BY DIVISION OF BIRTH AND DIVISION OF RESIDENCE, 1930, WITH GAIN OR LOSS THROUGH INTERDIVISIONAL MIGRATION, 1930, 1920, AND 1910

[The small number of Negroes for whom State of birth was not reported is omitted from this table]

GEOGRAPHIC DIVISION	BORN IN THE SPECIFIED DIVISION			Born in and living in the specified division	LIVING IN THE SPECIFIED DIVISION			GAIN (+) OR LOSS (−) THROUGH INTERDIVISIONAL MIGRATION		
	Total	Living in other divisions			Total	Born in other divisions		1930	1920	1910
		Number	Percent			Number	Percent			
United States	**11,739,479**	**1,976,624**	**16.8**	**9,762,855**	**11,739,479**	**1,976,624**	**16.8**			
New England	57,530	12,539	21.8	44,991	81,570	36,579	44.8	+24,040	+21,325	+20,310
Middle Atlantic	394,022	39,112	9.9	354,910	966,407	611,497	63.3	+572,385	+296,664	+186,384
East North Central	323,198	44,871	13.9	278,327	918,545	640,218	69.7	+595,347	+296,111	+119,649
West North Central	229,719	58,172	25.3	171,547	328,645	157,098	47.8	+98,926	+68,222	+40,497
South Atlantic	5,195,040	898,274	17.3	4,296,766	4,400,983	104,217	2.4	−794,057	−455,410	−392,827
East South Central	3,193,449	679,951	21.3	2,513,498	2,652,303	138,805	5.2	−541,146	−405,511	−200,876
West South Central	2,310,969	233,352	10.1	2,077,617	2,274,675	197,058	8.7	−36,294	+127,350	+194,658
Mountain	12,327	6,205	50.3	6,122	29,713	23,591	79.4	+17,386	+20,085	+13,229
Pacific	23,225	4,148	17.9	19,077	86,638	67,561	78.0	+63,413	+31,164	+18,976

TABLE 10.—FOREIGN-BORN NEGRO POPULATION: 1930, 1920, AND 1910

DIVISION AND STATE	FOREIGN-BORN NEGROES			INCREASE OR DECREASE (−)	
	1930	1920	1910	1920 to 1930	1910 to 1920
United States	**98,620**	**73,803**	**40,339**	**24,817**	**33,464**
GEOGRAPHIC DIVISIONS:					
New England	11,786	12,256	7,710	−470	4,546
Middle Atlantic	64,565	37,625	16,322	26,940	21,303
East North Central	5,157	4,262	3,384	895	878
West North Central	528	1,049	807	−521	242
South Atlantic	12,584	12,962	8,075	−378	4,887
East South Central	532	636	625	−104	11
West South Central	1,412	2,991	1,869	−1,579	1,122
Mountain	187	581	373	−394	208
Pacific	1,869	1,441	1,174	428	267
NEW ENGLAND:					
Maine	203	274	237	−71	37
New Hampshire	195	70	40	125	30
Vermont	13	16	40	−3	−24
Massachusetts	8,934	9,037	6,152	−103	2,885
Rhode Island	1,063	1,496	872	−433	624
Connecticut	1,378	1,363	369	15	994
MIDDLE ATLANTIC:					
New York	57,895	31,971	12,851	25,924	19,120
New Jersey	3,719	2,634	1,487	1,085	1,147
Pennsylvania	2,951	3,020	1,984	−69	1,036
EAST NORTH CENTRAL:					
Ohio	1,077	951	655	126	296
Indiana	200	184	97	16	87
Illinois	1,566	1,245	928	321	317
Michigan	2,262	1,769	1,640	493	129
Wisconsin	52	113	64	−61	49
WEST NORTH CENTRAL:					
Minnesota	105	154	200	−49	−46
Iowa	50	107	55	−57	52
Missouri	209	376	326	−167	50
North Dakota	7	21	2	−14	19
South Dakota	7	14	9	−7	5
Nebraska	55	140	97	−85	43
Kansas	95	237	118	−142	119
SOUTH ATLANTIC:					
Delaware	87	51	35	36	16
Maryland	872	696	451	176	245
District of Columbia	457	364	238	93	126
Virginia	330	656	296	−326	360
West Virginia	119	127	82	−8	45
North Carolina	118	91	88	27	3
South Carolina	54	96	72	−42	24
Georgia	200	216	228	−16	−12
Florida	10,347	10,665	6,585	−318	4,080
EAST SOUTH CENTRAL:					
Kentucky	68	76	66	−8	10
Tennessee	100	111	99	−11	12
Alabama	268	313	282	−45	31
Mississippi	96	136	178	−40	−42
WEST SOUTH CENTRAL:					
Arkansas	70	86	80	−16	6
Louisiana	809	1,217	575	−408	642
Oklahoma	67	156	123	−89	33
Texas	466	1,532	1,091	−1,066	441
MOUNTAIN:					
Montana	14	48	61	−34	−13
Idaho	15	34	28	−19	6
Wyoming	8	30	38	−22	−8
Colorado	61	132	130	−71	2
New Mexico	14	96	34	−82	62
Arizona	53	178	31	−125	147
Utah	12	56	32	−44	24
Nevada	10	7	19	3	−12
PACIFIC:					
Washington	167	271	238	−104	33
Oregon	50	47	62	3	−15
California	1,652	1,123	874	529	249

TABLE 11.—NEGRO AND WHITE POPULATION DISTRIBUTED AS BORN IN STATE OF RESIDENCE, IN OTHER STATES, OR IN FOREIGN COUNTRIES, BY STATES: 1930

[Percent not shown where less than 1/10 of 1 percent]

STATE	NEGRO POPULATION							WHITE POPULATION						
	Total [1]	Born in the United States and with State of birth reported				Foreign born		Total [1]	Born in the United States and with State of birth reported				Foreign born	
		Born in State of residence		Born in other States					Born in State of residence		Born in other States			
		Number	Percent	Number	Percent	Number	Percent		Number	Percent	Number	Percent	Number	Percent
United States	11,891,143	8,774,754	73.8	2,964,725	24.9	98,620	0.8	108,864,207	72,821,481	66.9	22,277,754	20.5	13,366,407	12.3
NEW ENGLAND:														
Maine	1,096	659	60.1	212	19.3	203	18.5	795,183	628,614	79.1	62,285	7.8	100,368	12.6
New Hampshire	790	223	28.2	360	45.6	195	24.7	464,350	277,763	59.8	101,647	21.9	82,660	17.8
Vermont	568	347	61.1	197	34.7	13	2.3	358,965	254,898	71.0	59,031	16.4	43,061	12.0
Massachusetts	52,365	24,358	46.5	18,663	35.6	8,934	17.1	4,192,926	2,635,316	62.9	489,784	11.7	1,054,636	25.2
Rhode Island	9,913	5,242	52.9	3,556	35.9	1,063	10.7	677,016	390,680	57.7	113,780	16.8	170,714	25.2
Connecticut	29,354	10,503	35.8	17,250	58.8	1,378	4.7	1,576,673	901,184	57.2	289,029	18.3	382,871	24.3
MIDDLE ATLANTIC:														
New York	412,814	108,351	26.2	227,889	55.2	57,895	14.0	12,150,293	7,717,141	63.5	1,144,622	9.4	3,191,549	26.3
New Jersey	208,828	64,352	30.8	139,184	66.7	3,719	1.8	3,829,209	2,062,040	53.9	909,442	23.8	844,442	22.1
Pennsylvania	431,257	146,374	33.9	280,257	65.0	2,951	1.7	9,192,602	7,264,716	79.0	682,460	7.4	1,233,051	13.4
EAST NORTH CENTRAL:														
Ohio	309,304	99,479	32.2	206,717	66.8	1,077	.3	6,331,136	4,519,317	71.4	1,154,475	18.2	644,151	10.2
Indiana	111,982	35,727	31.9	75,110	67.1	200	.2	3,116,136	2,362,479	75.8	612,185	19.6	135,134	4.3
Illinois	328,972	76,069	23.1	249,401	75.8	1,566	.5	7,266,361	4,719,049	64.9	1,310,377	18.0	1,218,158	16.8
Michigan	169,453	29,121	17.2	136,315	80.4	2,262	1.3	4,650,171	2,793,520	60.1	997,352	21.4	840,268	18.1
Wisconsin	10,739	1,732	16.1	8,874	82.6	52	.5	2,913,859	2,153,245	73.9	368,463	12.6	386,213	13.3
WEST NORTH CENTRAL:														
Minnesota	9,445	2,384	25.2	6,834	72.4	105	1.1	2,538,973	1,646,808	64.9	497,312	19.6	388,294	15.3
Iowa	17,380	6,599	38.0	10,585	60.9	50	.3	2,448,382	1,791,435	73.2	485,032	19.8	165,735	6.8
Missouri	223,840	106,728	47.7	115,466	51.6	209	.1	3,398,887	2,461,546	72.4	778,050	22.9	149,390	4.4
North Dakota	377	94	24.9	267	70.8	7	1.9	671,243	384,016	57.2	179,870	26.8	105,148	15.7
South Dakota	646	175	27.1	458	70.9	7	1.1	669,453	371,588	55.5	230,453	34.4	65,648	9.8
Nebraska	13,752	3,123	22.7	10,351	75.3	55	.4	1,353,702	871,572	64.4	363,455	26.8	115,346	8.5
Kansas	66,344	27,665	41.7	37,916	57.2	95	.1	1,792,847	1,093,800	61.0	623,751	34.8	69,716	3.9
SOUTH ATLANTIC:														
Delaware	32,602	21,311	65.4	11,171	34.3	87	.3	205,694	134,264	65.3	54,289	26.4	16,885	8.2
Maryland	276,379	201,244	72.8	72,626	26.3	872	.3	1,354,170	1,005,259	74.2	249,507	18.4	95,093	7.0
District of Columbia	132,068	52,513	39.8	77,937	59.0	457	.3	353,914	128,226	36.2	192,714	54.5	29,932	8.5
Virginia	650,165	576,588	88.7	72,646	11.2	330	.1	1,770,405	1,486,280	84.0	258,137	14.6	23,820	1.3
West Virginia	114,893	46,834	40.8	67,724	58.9	119	.1	1,613,934	1,283,079	79.5	277,876	17.2	51,520	3.2
North Carolina	918,647	808,298	88.0	109,441	11.9	118	-------	2,234,948	2,019,223	90.3	205,201	9.2	8,788	.4
South Carolina	793,681	776,058	97.8	17,250	2.2	54	-------	944,040	819,156	86.8	118,822	12.6	5,266	.6
Georgia	1,071,125	996,411	93.0	73,373	6.9	200	-------	1,836,974	1,594,489	86.8	226,583	12.3	13,917	.8
Florida	431,828	259,635	60.1	159,923	37.0	10,347	2.4	1,035,205	480,405	46.4	492,011	47.5	59,057	5.7
EAST SOUTH CENTRAL:														
Kentucky	226,040	185,051	81.9	40,325	17.8	68	-------	2,388,364	2,110,461	88.4	253,990	10.6	21,840	.9
Tennessee	477,646	363,704	76.1	111,769	23.4	100	-------	2,138,619	1,812,763	84.8	309,108	14.5	13,066	.6
Alabama	944,834	883,289	93.5	60,117	6.4	268	-------	1,700,775	1,434,862	84.4	248,639	14.6	15,710	.9
Mississippi	1,009,718	938,911	93.0	69,137	6.8	96	-------	996,856	851,013	85.4	137,644	13.8	7,049	.7
WEST SOUTH CENTRAL:														
Arkansas	478,463	340,182	71.1	136,314	28.5	70	-------	1,374,906	1,006,271	73.2	355,651	25.9	10,173	.7
Louisiana	776,326	710,894	91.6	63,702	8.2	809	.1	1,318,160	1,076,094	81.6	205,186	15.6	34,910	2.6
Oklahoma	172,198	85,760	49.8	85,490	49.6	67	-------	2,123,424	1,005,882	47.4	1,083,967	51.0	26,753	1.3
Texas	854,964	755,017	88.3	97,316	11.4	466	.1	4,283,491	3,149,781	73.5	1,023,646	23.9	98,396	2.3
MOUNTAIN:														
Montana	1,256	299	23.8	919	73.2	14	1.1	517,327	204,507	39.5	236,679	45.8	72,961	14.1
Idaho	668	110	16.5	533	79.8	15	2.2	437,562	186,904	42.7	217,485	49.7	30,454	7.0
Wyoming	1,250	178	14.2	1,054	84.3	8	.6	214,067	68,422	32.0	125,246	58.5	19,658	9.2
Colorado	11,828	2,892	24.5	8,781	74.2	61	.5	961,117	386,451	40.2	486,106	50.6	85,406	8.9
New Mexico	2,850	515	18.1	2,277	79.9	14	.5	331,755	186,445	56.2	136,544	41.2	7,797	2.4
Arizona	10,749	1,113	10.4	9,469	88.1	53	.5	264,378	67,083	25.4	179,058	67.7	15,591	5.9
Utah	1,108	250	22.6	828	74.7	12	1.1	495,955	374,196	75.4	75,962	15.3	43,772	8.8
Nevada	516	47	9.1	448	86.8	10	1.9	81,425	24,262	29.8	44,381	54.5	12,275	15.1
PACIFIC:														
Washington	6,840	1,480	21.6	4,977	72.8	167	2.4	1,521,099	545,609	35.9	711,669	46.8	244,256	16.1
Oregon	2,234	351	15.7	1,779	79.6	50	2.2	937,029	372,797	39.8	450,667	48.1	105,475	11.3
California	81,048	16,514	20.4	61,537	75.9	1,652	2.0	5,040,247	1,706,570	33.9	2,468,131	49.0	810,034	16.1

[1] Includes persons born in the United States, State of birth not reported; persons born in outlying possessions; and American citizens born abroad or at sea. The combined number of these classes are 53,044 Negroes, or 4/10 of 1 percent of the Negro population, and 398,565 whites, or 4/10 of 1 percent of the white population.

Table 12.—MIGRATION OF NEGROES OUT OF AND INTO THE SOUTH, BY SECTIONS, DIVISIONS, AND STATES: 1910 TO 1930

SECTION, DIVISION, AND STATE OF RESIDENCE	1930	1920	1910	INCREASE OR DECREASE (—) Number 1920 to 1930	Number 1910 to 1920	Percent 1920 to 1930	Percent 1910 to 1920	PERCENT DISTRIBUTION 1930	1920	1910
	NEGRO POPULATION BORN IN THE SOUTH									
The North and West	1,426,213	780,794	440,534	645,419	349,260	82.7	77.2	100.0	100.0	100.0
THE NORTH	1,355,789	737,423	415,533	618,366	321,890	83.9	77.5	95.1	94.4	94.3
New England	31,323	26,010	22,600	5,313	3,410	20.4	15.1	2.2	3.3	5.1
Middle Atlantic	586,607	310,991	198,501	275,616	112,490	88.6	56.7	41.1	39.8	45.1
East North Central	593,273	299,298	128,547	293,975	170,751	98.2	132.8	41.6	38.3	29.2
West North Central	144,586	101,124	65,885	43,462	35,239	43.0	53.5	10.1	13.0	15.0
NEW ENGLAND:										
Maine	119	163	178	−44	−15	−27.0	−8.4	(1)	(1)	(1)
New Hampshire	197	139	169	58	−30	41.7	−17.8	(1)	(1)	(1)
Vermont	89	113	779	−24	−666	−21.2	−85.5	(1)	(1)	.2
Massachusetts	14,510	13,902	13,064	608	838	4.4	6.4	1.0	1.8	3.0
Rhode Island	2,331	2,723	3,191	−392	−468	−14.4	−14.7	.2	.3	.7
Connecticut	14,077	8,970	5,219	5,107	3,751	56.9	71.9	1.0	1.1	.12
MIDDLE ATLANTIC:										
New York	199,811	84,817	60,494	114,994	24,323	135.6	40.2	14.0	10.9	13.7
New Jersey	121,992	59,338	40,987	62,654	18,351	105.6	44.8	8.6	7.6	9.3
Pennsylvania	264,804	166,836	97,020	97,968	69,816	58.7	72.0	18.6	21.4	22.0
EAST NORTH CENTRAL:										
Ohio	190,048	105,084	44,439	84,964	60,645	80.9	136.5	13.3	13.5	10.1
Indiana	66,203	45,888	30,123	20,315	15,765	44.3	52.3	4.6	5.9	6.8
Illinois	213,862	108,670	50,314	105,192	58,356	96.8	116.0	15.0	13.9	11.4
Michigan	116,789	37,113	2,897	79,676	34,216	214.7	1,181.1	8.2	4.8	.7
Wisconsin	6,371	2,543	774	3,828	1,769	150.5	228.6	.4	.3	.2
WEST NORTH CENTRAL:										
Minnesota	3,386	3,268	2,502	118	766	3.6	30.6	.2	.4	.6
Iowa	5,016	6,137	4,452	−1,121	1,685	−18.3	37.8	.4	.8	1.0
Missouri	102,084	62,415	36,329	39,669	26,086	63.6	71.8	7.2	8.0	8.2
North Dakota	118	140	223	−22	−83	−15.7	−37.2	(1)	(1)	.1
South Dakota	160	176	249	−16	−73	−9.1	−29.3	(1)	(1)	.1
Nebraska	6,305	6,103	2,327	202	3,776	3.3	162.3	.4	.8	.5
Kansas	27,517	22,885	19,803	4,632	3,082	20.2	15.6	1.9	2.9	4.5
THE WEST	70,424	43,371	25,001	27,053	18,370	62.4	73.5	4.9	5.6	5.7
Mountain	17,691	17,702	10,140	−11	7,562	.1	74.6	1.2	2.3	2.3
Pacific	52,733	25,669	14,861	27,064	10,808	105.4	72.7	3.7	3.3	3.4
MOUNTAIN:										
Montana	448	584	682	−136	−98	−23.3	−14.4	(1)	.1	.2
Idaho	304	391	248	−87	143	−22.3	57.7	(1)	.1	.1
Wyoming	520	587	1,210	−67	−623	−11.4	−51.5	(1)	.1	.3
Colorado	5,752	5,383	5,212	369	171	6.9	3.3	.4	.7	1.2
New Mexico	1,912	4,203	889	−2,291	3,314	−54.5	372.8	.1	.5	.2
Arizona	7,996	5,783	1,251	2,213	4,532	38.3	362.3	.6	.7	.3
Utah	496	617	397	−121	220	−19.6	55.4	(1)	.1	.1
Nevada	263	154	251	109	−97	70.8	−38.6	(1)	(1)	.1
PACIFIC:										
Washington	2,668	2,840	2,992	−172	−152	−6.1	−5.1	.2	.4	.7
Oregon	1,060	942	620	118	322	12.5	51.9	.1	.1	.1
California	49,005	21,887	11,249	27,118	10,638	123.9	94.6	3.4	2.8	2.6
	NEGRO POPULATION BORN IN THE NORTH AND WEST									
The South	54,716	47,223	41,489	7,493	5,734	15.9	13.8	100.0	100.0	100.0
South Atlantic	28,869	22,771	15,651	6,098	7,120	26.8	45.5	52.8	48.2	37.7
East South Central	11,813	9,649	9,808	2,164	−159	22.4	−1.6	21.6	20.4	23.6
West South Central	14,034	14,803	16,030	−769	−1,227	−5.2	−7.7	25.6	31.3	38.6
SOUTH ATLANTIC:										
Delaware	1,614	1,477	1,397	137	80	9.3	5.7	2.9	3.1	3.4
Maryland	5,152	4,189	2,894	963	1,295	23.0	44.7	9.4	8.9	7.0
District of Columbia	4,772	3,751	2,542	1,021	1,209	27.2	47.6	8.7	7.9	6.1
Virginia	5,457	4,872	3,151	585	1,721	12.0	54.6	10.0	10.3	7.6
West Virginia	4,341	3,153	2,127	1,188	1,026	37.7	48.2	7.9	6.7	5.1
North Carolina	2,204	1,581	911	623	670	39.4	73.5	4.0	3.3	2.2
South Carolina	871	923	429	−52	494	−5.6	115.2	1.6	2.0	1.0
Georgia	2,145	1,307	1,146	838	161	64.1	14.0	3.9	2.8	2.8
Florida	2,313	1,518	1,054	795	464	52.4	44.0	4.2	3.2	2.5
EAST SOUTH CENTRAL:										
Kentucky	4,667	3,939	3,735	728	204	18.5	5.5	8.5	8.3	9.0
Tennessee	3,267	2,593	2,676	674	−83	26.0	−3.1	6.0	5.5	6.4
Alabama	1,965	1,460	1,412	505	48	34.6	3.4	3.6	3.1	3.4
Mississippi	1,914	1,657	1,985	257	−328	15.5	−16.5	3.5	3.5	4.8
WEST SOUTH CENTRAL:										
Arkansas	3,765	3,859	3,690	−94	169	−2.4	4.6	6.9	8.2	8.9
Louisiana	1,704	1,795	2,086	−91	−291	−5.1	−14.0	3.1	3.8	5.0
Oklahoma	5,185	5,406	6,096	−221	−690	−4.1	−11.3	9.5	11.4	14.7
Texas	3,380	3,743	4,158	−363	−415	−9.7	−10.0	6.2	7.9	10.0

1 Less than one-tenth of 1 percent.

TABLE 13.—NATIVE NEGRO POPULATION, BY STATE OF BIRTH AND STATE OF RESIDENCE, 1930, WITH GAIN OR LOSS THROUGH INTERSTATE MIGRATION, 1930, 1920, AND 1910

[The small number of Negroes for whom State of birth was not reported is omitted from this table]

STATE	NATIVE NEGRO POPULATION, 1930							GAIN (+) OR LOSS (−) THROUGH INTERSTATE MIGRATION		
	Born in the specified State			Born in and living in the specified State	Living in the specified State			1930	1920	1910
	Total	Living in other States			Total	Born in other States				
		Number	Percent			Number	Percent			
United States	**11,739,479**	**2,964,725**	**25.3**	**8,774,754**	**11,739,479**	**2,964,725**	**25.3**			
NEW ENGLAND:										
Maine	1,334	675	50.6	659	871	212	24.3	−463	−479	−473
New Hampshire	494	271	54.9	223	583	360	61.7	+89	−41	+9
Vermont	853	506	59.3	347	544	197	36.2	−309	−779	+501
Massachusetts	32,009	7,651	23.9	24,358	43,021	18,663	43.4	+11,012	+12,617	+12,563
Rhode Island	7,468	2,226	29.8	5,242	8,798	3,556	40.4	+1,330	+1,864	+3,196
Connecticut	15,372	4,869	31.7	10,503	27,753	17,250	62.2	+12,381	+8,143	+4,514
MIDDLE ATLANTIC:										
New York	125,964	17,613	14.0	108,351	336,240	227,889	67.8	+210,276	+83,334	+58,449
New Jersey	80,937	16,585	20.5	64,352	203,536	139,184	68.4	+122,599	+59,923	+42,450
Pennsylvania	187,121	40,747	21.8	146,374	426,631	280,257	65.7	+239,510	+153,407	+85,485
EAST NORTH CENTRAL:										
Ohio	129,116	29,637	23.0	99,479	306,196	206,717	67.5	+177,080	+95,465	+33,599
Indiana	53,032	17,305	32.6	35,727	110,837	75,110	67.8	+57,805	+39,270	+25,018
Illinois	101,878	25,809	25.3	76,069	325,470	249,401	76.6	+223,592	+116,476	+57,577
Michigan	35,906	6,785	18.9	29,121	165,436	136,315	82.4	+129,530	+42,374	+2,940
Wisconsin	3,266	1,534	47.0	1,732	10,606	8,874	83.7	+7,340	+2,526	+515
WEST NORTH CENTRAL:										
Minnesota	3,990	1,606	40.3	2,384	9,218	6,834	74.1	+5,228	+5,189	+3,950
Iowa	12,410	5,811	46.8	6,599	17,184	10,585	61.6	+4,774	+7,038	+5,966
Missouri	159,113	52,385	32.9	106,728	222,194	115,466	52.0	+63,081	+29,463	+6,030
North Dakota	377	283	75.1	94	361	267	74.0	−16	−103	+295
South Dakota	504	329	65.3	175	633	458	72.4	+129	−30	+287
Nebraska	5,882	2,759	46.9	3,123	13,474	10,351	76.8	+7,592	+8,569	+4,551
Kansas	47,443	19,778	41.7	27,665	65,581	37,916	57.8	+18,138	+18,096	+19,418
SOUTH ATLANTIC:										
Delaware	32,184	10.873	33.8	21,311	32,482	11,171	34.4	+298	−892	−1,597
Maryland	275,093	73,849	26.8	201,244	273,870	72,626	26.5	−1,223	−20,915	−31,177
District of Columbia	72,018	19,505	27.1	52,513	130,450	77,937	59.7	+58,432	+46,518	+41,235
Virginia	908,551	331,963	36.5	576,588	649,234	72,646	11.2	−259,317	−195,515	−206,764
West Virginia	64,898	18,064	27.8	46,834	114,558	67,724	59.1	+49,660	+40,456	+27,316
North Carolina	1,028,538	220,240	21.4	808,298	917,739	109,441	11.9	−110,799	−113,716	−109,751
South Carolina	1,095,214	319,156	29.1	776,058	793,308	17,250	2.2	−301,906	−152,423	−121,479
Georgia	1,403,856	407,445	29.0	996,411	1,069,784	73,373	6.9	−334,072	−121,576	−75,274
Florida	314,688	55,053	17.5	259,635	419,558	159,923	38.1	+104,870	+62,653	+84,664
EAST SOUTH CENTRAL:										
Kentucky	292,365	107,314	36.7	185,051	225,376	40,325	17.9	−66,989	−68,432	−62,878
Tennessee	539,556	175,852	32.6	363,704	475,473	111,769	23.5	−64,083	−63,557	−46,194
Alabama	1,133,771	250,482	22.1	883,289	943,406	60,117	6.4	−190,365	−134,344	−65,365
Mississippi	1,227,757	288,846	23.5	938,911	1,008,048	69,137	6.9	−219,709	−139,178	−26,439
WEST SOUTH CENTRAL:										
Arkansas	449,451	109,269	24.3	340,182	476,496	136,314	28.6	+27,045	+106,639	+105,516
Louisiana	882,024	171,130	19.4	710,894	774,596	63,702	8.2	−107,428	−52,784	−15,741
Oklahoma	115,284	29,524	25.6	85,760	171,250	85,490	49.9	+55,966	+69,994	+85,062
Texas	864,210	109,193	12.6	755,017	852,333	97,316	11.4	−11,877	+3,501	+19,821
MOUNTAIN:										
Montana	937	638	68.1	299	1,218	919	75.5	+281	+712	+1,041
Idaho	372	262	70.4	110	643	533	82.9	+271	+540	+140
Wyoming	596	418	70.1	178	1,232	1,054	85.6	+636	+902	+1,832
Colorado	6,062	3,170	52.3	2,892	11,673	8,781	75.2	+5,611	+6,332	+7,583
New Mexico	1,293	778	60.2	515	2,792	2,277	81.6	+1,499	+4,318	+636
Arizona	2,265	1,152	50.9	1,113	10,582	9,469	89.5	+8,317	+6,454	+1,407
Utah	627	337	60.1	250	1,078	828	76.8	+451	+675	+482
Nevada	175	128	73.1	47	495	448	90.5	+320	+152	+108
PACIFIC:										
Washington	2,998	1,518	50.6	1,480	6,457	4,977	77.1	+3,459	+3,582	+4,045
Oregon	746	395	52.9	351	2,130	1,779	83.5	+1,384	+1,449	+989
California	19,481	2,967	15.2	16,514	78,051	61,537	78.8	+58,570	+26,133	+13,942

TABLE 14.—NATIVE NEGRO POPULATION OF EACH DIVISION AND STATE, BY DIVISION AND STATE OF BIRTH: 1930

DIVISION AND STATE	Total native Negro population	NEGRO POPULATION BORN IN— United States	Geographic divisions: New England	Middle Atlantic	East North Central	West North Central	South Atlantic	East South Central	West South Central	Mountain	Pacific	United States, State not reported	Other native Negro population [1]
United States	**11,792,523**	**11,771,863**	**57,530**	**394,022**	**323,198**	**229,719**	**5,195,040**	**3,193,449**	**2,310,969**	**12,327**	**23,225**	**32,384**	**20,660**
GEOGRAPHIC DIVISIONS:													
New England	82,300	81,889	**44,991**	4,273	606	234	28,985	1,779	559	53	90	319	411
Middle Atlantic	988,334	971,731	8,366	**354,910**	11,629	3,141	530,748	45,196	10,663	637	1,117	5,324	16,603
East North Central	925,293	923,862	1,260	12,503	**278,327**	30,927	197,435	321,256	74,582	1,249	1,006	5,317	1,431
West North Central	331,256	331,040	182	991	9,935	**171,547**	11,267	74,868	58,451	1,012	392	2,395	216
South Atlantic	4,408,804	4,408,136	1,950	17,707	6,919	1,507	**4,296,766**	68,944	6,404	331	438	7,153	668
East South Central	2,657,706	2,657,548	150	1,101	7,493	2,654	85,861	**2,513,498**	41,131	208	207	5,245	158
West South Central	2,280,539	2,280,163	148	770	3,433	8,509	31,026	151,998	**2,077,617**	668	506	5,488	376
Mountain	30,038	29,939	74	353	1,125	3,976	2,387	4,418	10,886	**6,122**	372	226	99
Pacific	88,253	87,555	409	1,414	3,734	7,224	10,565	11,492	30,676	2,047	**19,077**	917	698
NEW ENGLAND:													
Maine	893	884	723	20	5	3	103	7	9		1	13	9
New Hampshire	595	592	326	31	24	3	156	31	10	1	1	9	3
Vermont	555	545	401	41	5	4	62	24	3	1		1	10
Massachusetts	43,431	43,176	26,081	1,859	351	130	13,332	869	309	34	56	155	255
Rhode Island	8,850	8,828	6,020	400	31	24	2,243	65	23	3	11	30	22
Connecticut	27,976	27,864	11,437	1,922	190	92	13,089	783	205	14	21	111	112
MIDDLE ATLANTIC:													
New York	354,919	339,125	5,823	123,015	5,074	1,641	182,077	11,904	5,830	314	562	2,885	15,794
New Jersey	205,109	204,768	1,299	78,205	1,279	430	113,842	6,953	1,197	103	228	1,232	341
Pennsylvania	428,306	427,838	1,244	153,690	5,276	1,070	234,829	26,339	3,636	220	327	1,207	468
EAST NORTH CENTRAL:													
Ohio	308,227	307,958	349	6,024	106,427	2,901	93,816	88,353	7,879	241	206	1,762	269
Indiana	111,782	111,718	78	635	41,599	2,155	7,786	52,678	5,739	98	69	881	64
Illinois	327,406	327,075	484	2,904	87,486	19,661	40,653	127,933	45,276	594	479	1,605	331
Michigan	167,191	166,439	322	2,830	39,840	5,147	53,315	49,190	14,284	279	229	1,003	752
Wisconsin	10,687	10,672	27	110	2,975	1,063	1,865	3,102	1,404	37	23	66	15
WEST NORTH CENTRAL:													
Minnesota	9,340	9,288	39	146	927	4,585	730	1,549	1,107	77	58	70	52
Iowa	17,330	17,322	13	91	938	11,037	1,229	2,302	1,485	61	28	138	8
Missouri	223,631	223,559	78	433	6,227	112,821	6,043	59,122	36,919	379	172	1,365	72
North Dakota	370	366	4	7	33	191	30	49	39	4	1	5	4
South Dakota	639	636		7	49	406	39	80	41	10	1	3	3
Nebraska	13,697	13,679	7	100	481	3,395	798	2,266	3,241	149	37	205	18
Kansas	66,249	66,190	41	207	1,280	36,109	2,398	9,500	15,619	332	95	609	59
SOUTH ATLANTIC:													
Delaware	32,515	32,507	61	1,539	68	30	30,539	242	87	5	11	25	8
Maryland	275,507	275,352	332	3,947	574	181	266,890	1,291	537	45	73	1,482	155
District of Columbia	131,611	131,498	485	2,902	882	352	122,134	2,512	1,032	78	73	1,048	113
Virginia	649,835	649,738	445	3,993	756	142	639,536	3,760	481	46	75	504	97
West Virginia	114,774	114,749	69	1,605	2,262	308	93,005	16,617	595	55	42	191	25
North Carolina	918,529	918,497	176	1,406	475	95	912,597	2,563	375	15	37	758	32
South Carolina	793,627	793,603	51	538	212	47	791,482	793	162	8	15	295	24
Georgia	1,070,925	1,070,881	148	844	896	158	1,046,363	20,259	1,017	38	61	1,097	44
Florida	421,481	421,311	183	1,033	791	194	394,220	20,907	2,118	41	71	1,753	170
EAST SOUTH CENTRAL:													
Kentucky	225,972	225,950	29	281	3,625	642	8,159	211,153	1,397	45	45	574	22
Tennessee	477,546	477,508	49	294	1,826	971	31,609	429,872	10,725	61	66	2,035	38
Alabama	944,566	944,516	50	393	1,086	320	37,175	901,541	2,725	61	55	1,110	50
Mississippi	1,009,622	1,009,574	22	133	956	721	8,918	970,932	26,284	41	41	1,526	48
WEST SOUTH CENTRAL:													
Arkansas	478,393	478,374	22	139	1,200	2,235	13,263	83,680	375,788	94	75	1,878	19
Louisiana	775,517	775,369	52	219	716	561	5,700	37,888	729,304	66	90	773	148
Oklahoma	172,131	172,069	18	119	727	3,983	4,180	15,283	146,602	202	136	819	62
Texas	854,498	854,351	56	293	790	1,730	7,883	15,147	825,923	306	205	2,018	147
MOUNTAIN:													
Montana	1,242	1,233	6	31	106	265	116	184	148	339	23	15	9
Idaho	653	646	2	7	37	105	57	85	162	167	21	3	7
Wyoming	1,242	1,240	3	12	90	322	107	204	209	273	12	8	2
Colorado	11,767	11,748	31	114	446	2,232	825	2,044	2,883	3,039	59	75	19
New Mexico	2,836	2,832	3	17	55	194	147	325	1,440	590	21	40	4
Arizona	10,696	10,646	23	150	296	619	979	1,361	5,656	1,306	192	64	50
Utah	1,096	1,090	6	10	60	164	88	149	259	327	15	12	6
Nevada	506	504		12	35	75	68	66	129	81	29	9	2
PACIFIC:													
Washington	6,673	6,565	40	147	561	996	794	919	955	304	1,741	108	108
Oregon	2,184	2,165	8	49	131	351	234	266	560	77	454	35	19
California	79,396	78,825	361	1,218	3,042	5,877	9,537	10,307	29,161	1,666	16,882	774	571

[1] Includes persons born in outlying possessions and American citizens born abroad or at sea.

TABLE 14.—NATIVE NEGRO POPULATION OF EACH DIVISION AND STATE, BY DIVISION AND STATE OF BIRTH: 1930—Continued

DIVISION AND STATE	NEGRO POPULATION BORN IN—													
	New England division						Middle Atlantic division			East North Central division				
	Maine	New Hampshire	Vermont	Massachusetts	Rhode Island	Connecticut	New York	New Jersey	Pennsylvania	Ohio	Indiana	Illinois	Michigan	Wisconsin
United States	**1,334**	**494**	**853**	**32,009**	**7,468**	**15,372**	**125,964**	**80,937**	**187,121**	**129,116**	**53,032**	**101,878**	**35,906**	**3,266**
GEOGRAPHIC DIVISIONS:														
New England	907	372	538	25,731	5,976	11,467	2,214	838	1,221	281	75	163	74	13
Middle Atlantic	245	64	210	4,034	1,037	2,776	115,876	75,646	163,388	6,747	1,287	2,483	998	114
East North Central	68	14	36	683	115	344	2,422	984	9,097	111,681	46,458	85,265	32,342	2,581
West North Central	12	4	16	104	16	30	301	111	579	1,401	1,198	6,638	471	227
South Atlantic	58	28	30	999	236	599	3,967	2,977	10,763	4,251	713	1,123	742	87
East South Central	12	3	1	83	15	36	268	124	709	2,438	1,980	2,510	497	68
West South Central	5	3	1	91	24	24	251	75	444	782	501	1,756	321	73
Mountain	2	-	5	38	9	20	97	44	212	338	206	471	80	30
Pacific	25	6	16	246	40	76	568	138	708	1,197	614	1,469	381	73
NEW ENGLAND:														
Maine	**659**	3	-	51	2	8	3	3	14	1	-	2	-	2
New Hampshire	4	**223**	26	64	-	9	17	5	9	4	7	13	-	-
Vermont	2	17	**347**	33	4	1	35	5	1	4	-	1	-	-
Massachusetts	211	116	119	**24,358**	545	732	851	362	646	143	52	97	53	6
Rhode Island	7	5	14	538	**5,242**	214	195	82	123	20	1	5	5	-
Connecticut	24	8	32	687	183	**10,503**	1,113	381	428	109	15	45	16	5
MIDDLE ATLANTIC:														
New York	140	42	169	2,830	710	1,932	**108,351**	6,354	8,310	2,545	556	1,402	498	73
New Jersey	42	10	25	569	172	481	5,149	**64,352**	8,704	682	160	292	134	11
Pennsylvania	63	12	16	635	155	363	2,376	4,940	**146,374**	3,520	571	789	366	30
EAST NORTH CENTRAL:														
Ohio	24	5	12	189	27	92	803	330	4,891	**99,479**	3,184	2,483	1,197	84
Indiana	9	1	2	38	8	20	95	37	503	2,296	**35,727**	2,962	559	55
Illinois	18	4	12	278	50	122	817	334	1,753	4,631	4,885	**76,069**	1,360	541
Michigan	16	4	10	161	23	108	673	276	1,881	5,050	2,473	3,027	**29,121**	169
Wisconsin	1	-	-	17	7	2	34	7	69	225	189	724	105	**1,732**
WEST NORTH CENTRAL:														
Minnesota	1	2	5	18	3	10	56	14	76	184	169	392	75	107
Iowa	1	1	1	9	-	1	24	6	61	98	99	683	32	26
Missouri	3	1	3	53	7	11	126	46	261	688	632	4,667	193	47
North Dakota	1	-	1	2	-	-	1	2	4	14	1	13	3	2
South Dakota	-	-	-	-	-	-	5	-	2	8	2	24	14	1
Nebraska	1	-	-	3	2	1	26	7	67	101	62	263	42	13
Kansas	5	-	6	19	4	7	63	36	108	308	233	596	112	31
SOUTH ATLANTIC:														
Delaware	1	-	2	29	5	24	93	282	1,064	32	16	11	5	4
Maryland	5	1	4	165	56	101	626	683	2,638	312	80	123	57	2
District of Columbia	22	6	9	254	72	122	756	513	1,633	439	117	233	83	10
Virginia	14	13	6	210	62	140	1,062	697	2,234	456	72	121	92	15
West Virginia	1	-	4	39	3	22	116	120	1,369	1,822	137	199	99	5
North Carolina	7	1	2	92	10	64	473	263	670	288	54	53	74	6
South Carolina	-	-	-	33	9	9	215	87	236	115	14	39	41	3
Georgia	1	3	3	72	8	61	274	132	438	433	109	180	154	20
Florida	7	4	-	105	11	56	352	200	481	354	114	164	137	22
EAST SOUTH CENTRAL:														
Kentucky	6	-	-	11	3	9	62	20	199	1,180	1,503	808	123	11
Tennessee	3	2	-	26	6	12	67	38	189	572	244	835	155	20
Alabama	3	1	-	26	5	15	94	54	245	465	133	322	149	17
Mississippi	-	-	1	20	1	-	45	12	76	221	100	545	70	20
WEST SOUTH CENTRAL:														
Arkansas	-	-	-	10	9	3	38	12	89	202	158	726	85	29
Louisiana	2	-	1	23	9	17	85	18	116	188	75	365	74	14
Oklahoma	-	1	-	14	3	-	33	10	76	178	125	346	70	8
Texas	3	2	-	44	3	4	95	35	163	214	143	319	92	22
MOUNTAIN:														
Montana	1	-	-	1	2	2	7	4	20	36	14	47	7	2
Idaho	-	-	-	1	-	1	2	1	4	13	7	15	2	-
Wyoming	-	-	-	2	-	1	6	1	5	35	17	31	3	4
Colorado	-	-	1	18	4	8	27	15	72	126	73	212	28	7
New Mexico	-	-	-	2	-	1	5	3	9	11	12	28	3	1
Arizona	1	-	4	11	3	4	43	18	89	98	61	100	24	13
Utah	-	-	-	3	-	3	2	1	7	12	13	25	8	2
Nevada	-	-	-	-	-	-	5	1	6	7	9	13	5	1
PACIFIC:														
Washington	7	-	1	18	4	10	55	10	82	174	100	224	45	18
Oregon	-	-	1	5	1	1	14	7	28	43	19	49	18	2
California	18	6	14	223	35	65	499	121	598	980	495	1,196	318	53

Table 14.—NATIVE NEGRO POPULATION OF EACH DIVISION AND STATE, BY DIVISION AND STATE OF BIRTH: 1930—Continued

DIVISION AND STATE	NEGRO POPULATION BORN IN— West North Central division							South Atlantic division								
	Minnesota	Iowa	Missouri	North Dakota	South Dakota	Nebraska	Kansas	Delaware	Maryland	District of Columbia	Virginia	West Virginia	North Carolina	South Carolina	Georgia	Florida
United States	**3,990**	**12,410**	**159,113**	**377**	**504**	**5,882**	**47,443**	**32,184**	**275,093**	**72,018**	**908,551**	**64,898**	**1,028,538**	**1,095,214**	**1,403,856**	**314,688**
GEOGRAPHIC DIVISIONS:																
New England	23	16	134	3	13	11	34	133	1,452	891	9,223	152	5,881	4,269	5,982	1,002
Middle Atlantic	136	293	1,916	51	27	165	553	9,242	43,076	9,446	171,693	5,684	84,268	100,179	84,685	22,475
East North Central	677	2,751	22,222	52	77	808	4,340	205	2,596	1,506	22,490	6,104	18,073	27,099	110,423	8,939
West North Central	2,643	8,191	121,165	158	288	3,949	35,153	20	367	267	2,377	296	1,456	1,446	4,262	776
South Atlantic	80	157	857	19	17	100	277	22,507	226,557	59,291	691,711	51,399	902,275	946,447	1,122,715	273,864
East South Central	58	152	2,070	12	13	80	269	24	289	145	5,993	801	8,138	7,754	57,456	5,261
West South Central	111	263	5,061	20	5	226	2,823	10	302	110	2,877	182	6,943	6,610	12,381	1,611
Mountain	51	194	1,953	30	25	190	1,533	6	116	91	598	87	316	277	762	134
Pacific	211	393	3,735	32	39	353	2,461	37	338	271	1,589	193	1,188	1,133	5,190	626
NEW ENGLAND:																
Maine	-----	-----	3	-----	-----	-----	-----	3	12	3	41	-----	19	13	9	3
New Hampshire	-----	-----	-----	-----	-----	1	2	1	12	10	68	-----	26	16	14	9
Vermont	1	-----	2	-----	-----	1	-----	1	10	3	19	3	10	10	5	1
Massachusetts	15	10	82	1	3	4	15	81	700	504	4,607	73	3,032	1,860	2,030	445
Rhode Island	-----	-----	-----	-----	1	-----	1	7	301	110	1,141	14	267	176	167	60
Connecticut	7	6	47	2	9	5	16	40	417	261	3,347	62	2,527	2,194	3,757	484
MIDDLE ATLANTIC:																
New York	83	138	1,010	34	12	82	282	847	8,133	3,929	58,919	1,048	33,961	41,866	23,776	9,598
New Jersey	22	35	243	9	5	14	102	2,529	9,473	1,741	36,635	613	19,010	16,450	22,380	5,011
Pennsylvania	31	120	663	8	10	69	169	5,866	25,470	3,776	76,139	4,023	31,297	41,863	38,529	7,866
EAST NORTH CENTRAL:																
Ohio	89	193	1,973	11	22	90	523	72	1,184	565	13,892	4,384	9,939	11,831	48,847	3,102
Indiana	63	171	1,481	2	4	68	366	13	99	70	971	181	1,110	669	4,350	323
Illinois	352	1,694	14,885	22	30	432	2,246	55	695	526	3,726	568	2,760	5,533	24,902	1,888
Michigan	116	393	3,414	13	20	177	1,014	63	586	329	3,711	943	4,155	8,921	31,054	3,553
Wisconsin	57	300	469	4	1	41	191	2	32	16	190	28	109	145	1,270	73
WEST NORTH CENTRAL:																
Minnesota	**2,384**	432	1,105	41	36	130	457	1	39	29	200	33	64	71	255	38
Iowa	67	**6,599**	3,500	8	26	189	648	1	34	14	638	49	134	88	220	51
Missouri	81	527	**106,728**	6	22	242	5,215	9	155	77	977	120	848	791	2,729	337
North Dakota	23	17	39	**94**	5	5	11	-----	1	2	6	3	1	7	9	1
South Dakota	23	47	104	-----	**175**	28	29	1	4	-----	10	2	1	-----	20	1
Nebraska	27	342	1,762	2	11	**3,123**	1,128	3	23	19	131	20	76	66	203	257
Kansas	38	227	7,927	7	13	232	**27,665**	5	111	126	415	69	332	423	826	91
SOUTH ATLANTIC:																
Delaware	-----	3	22	-----	-----	1	4	**21,311**	5,340	113	2,152	38	620	329	430	206
Maryland	7	26	110	1	3	8	26	906	**201,244**	3,562	37,090	949	12,616	7,593	2,248	682
District of Columbia	27	28	185	5	4	30	73	87	16,346	**52,513**	30,236	751	8,026	10,166	3,383	626
Virginia	3	17	68	3	4	7	40	95	2,311	2,347	**576,588**	2,058	44,354	8,711	2,479	593
West Virginia	6	61	168	2	2	14	55	16	548	222	31,401	**46,834**	8,304	2,441	2,905	334
North Carolina	11	7	51	1	-----	5	20	31	311	239	9,578	426	**808,298**	79,368	13,272	1,074
South Carolina	8	1	32	-----	-----	2	4	8	87	51	617	31	6,913	**776,058**	6,924	793
Georgia	11	6	103	-----	2	13	23	24	131	151	1,682	140	5,208	32,695	**996,411**	9,921
Florida	7	8	118	7	2	20	32	29	239	93	2,367	172	7,936	29,086	94,663	**259,635**
EAST SOUTH CENTRAL:																
Kentucky	9	48	479	3	5	22	76	1	68	37	1,965	456	1,005	916	3,390	321
Tennessee	23	42	798	2	2	15	89	10	81	54	1,985	141	3,492	3,403	21,886	557
Alabama	11	23	205	1	2	28	50	10	95	38	1,123	166	1,444	2,258	28,374	3,667
Mississippi	15	39	588	6	4	15	54	3	45	16	920	38	2,197	1,177	3,806	716
WEST SOUTH CENTRAL:																
Arkansas	20	56	1,934	7	1	33	184	5	51	26	704	38	3,336	3,926	4,987	190
Louisiana	16	38	417	3	-----	24	63	-----	110	26	815	42	1,117	725	2,060	805
Oklahoma	23	94	1,590	6	2	106	2,162	2	37	13	401	46	859	821	1,868	133
Texas	52	75	1,120	4	2	63	414	3	104	45	957	56	1,631	1,138	3,466	483
MOUNTAIN:																
Montana	21	18	137	19	5	10	55	-----	10	6	47	3	17	9	22	2
Idaho	4	4	51	-----	-----	7	39	-----	3	3	13	2	16	5	11	4
Wyoming	1	23	175	1	6	27	89	-----	4	5	37	7	10	6	27	11
Colorado	9	103	1,146	3	4	92	875	-----	36	24	267	37	96	74	253	38
New Mexico	4	10	74	-----	3	6	97	-----	2	3	32	6	22	21	56	5
Arizona	9	23	262	6	5	30	284	6	43	38	166	26	133	148	353	66
Utah	2	9	78	-----	2	11	62	-----	7	9	18	2	15	12	19	6
Nevada	1	4	30	1	-----	7	32	-----	11	3	18	4	7	2	21	2
PACIFIC:																
Washington	72	71	508	19	12	33	281	7	48	29	229	42	151	79	170	39
Oregon	8	18	193	-----	2	19	111	2	18	13	51	7	30	34	57	22
California	131	304	3,034	13	25	301	2,069	28	272	229	1,309	144	1,007	1,020	4,963	565

TABLE 14.—NATIVE NEGRO POPULATION OF EACH DIVISION AND STATE, BY DIVISION AND STATE OF BIRTH: 1930—Continued

DIVISION AND STATE	NEGRO POPULATION BORN IN—															
	East South Central division				West South Central division				Mountain division							
	Kentucky	Tennessee	Alabama	Mississippi	Arkansas	Louisiana	Oklahoma	Texas	Montana	Idaho	Wyoming	Colorado	New Mexico	Arizona	Utah	Nevada
United States	**292, 365**	**539, 556**	**1, 133, 771**	**1, 227, 757**	**449, 451**	**882. 024**	**115, 284**	**864, 210**	**937**	**372**	**596**	**6, 062**	**1, 293**	**2, 265**	**627**	**175**
GEOGRAPHIC DIVISIONS:																
New England	332	421	854	172	91	226	61	181	7	2	7	23	2	7	5	...
Middle Atlantic	5, 764	8, 193	26, 626	4, 613	1, 797	4, 148	779	3, 939	108	30	34	261	39	121	33	11
East North Central	76, 888	81, 082	86, 314	76, 972	29, 111	27, 983	5, 098	12, 390	115	44	91	681	117	140	49	12
West North Central	8, 493	21, 590	9, 044	35, 741	27, 622	8, 375	9, 863	12, 591	75	27	102	580	105	79	37	7
South Atlantic	4, 639	8, 899	50, 648	4, 758	887	2, 904	557	2, 056	55	11	22	126	29	75	13	...
East South Central	190, 406	391, 009	929, 666	1, 002, 417	15, 722	22, 419	711	2, 279	19	7	10	90	23	30	28	1
West South Central	3, 017	24, 124	26, 292	98, 565	369, 785	805, 262	92, 488	810, 082	27	34	22	349	91	107	30	8
Mountain	924	1, 263	1, 203	1, 028	1, 187	1, 747	2, 301	5, 651	345	144	252	3, 190	669	1, 156	308	58
Pacific	1, 902	2, 975	3, 124	3, 491	3, 249	8, 960	3, 426	15, 041	186	73	56	762	218	550	124	78
NEW ENGLAND:																
Maine	...	2	4	1	...	4	2	3	...	...	...	...	...	...	...	...
New Hampshire	4	10	8	9	6	1	2	1	...	...	1	...	...	...	...	...
Vermont	6	9	6	3	1	...	1	1	1	...	...	...	...	...	...	...
Massachusetts	184	210	378	97	54	128	24	103	2	1	3	19	1	5	3	...
Rhode Island	11	25	25	4	...	7	4	12	1	...	...	1	...	...	1	...
Connecticut	127	165	433	58	30	86	28	61	3	1	3	3	1	2	1	...
MIDDLE ATLANTIC:																
New York	2, 011	3, 051	5, 023	1, 819	766	2, 662	349	2, 053	63	23	15	128	15	49	18	3
New Jersey	553	870	5, 043	487	234	393	124	446	17	3	6	45	7	19	5	1
Pennsylvania	3, 200	4, 272	16, 560	2, 307	797	1, 093	306	1, 440	28	4	13	88	17	53	10	7
EAST NORTH CENTRAL:																
Ohio	27, 177	19, 222	34, 366	7, 588	3, 377	2, 096	739	1, 667	29	6	28	103	23	41	8	3
Indiana	25, 317	13, 728	6, 205	7, 428	2, 819	1, 630	436	854	12	5	12	49	8	9	2	1
Illinois	17, 280	34, 844	24, 958	50, 851	16, 425	19, 867	2, 315	6, 669	46	22	25	355	60	54	28	4
Michigan	6, 627	12, 478	20, 216	9, 869	5, 931	3, 988	1, 451	2, 914	21	11	24	152	23	34	10	4
Wisconsin	487	810	569	1, 236	559	402	157	286	7	...	2	22	3	2	1	...
WEST NORTH CENTRAL:																
Minnesota	465	439	314	331	277	224	214	392	26	1	4	29	7	4	5	1
Iowa	392	522	568	820	433	304	335	413	4	3	3	35	5	7	2	2
Missouri	4, 957	16, 836	5, 966	31, 363	21, 559	5, 680	3, 468	6, 212	23	16	31	226	30	34	50	4
North Dakota	15	17	6	11	8	13	3	15	1	...	...	1	1	1	...	...
South Dakota	26	21	12	21	8	10	7	16	...	...	4	6	...	...	...	...
Nebraska	325	486	840	615	730	441	717	1, 353	5	5	41	72	12	6	8	...
Kansas	2, 313	3, 269	1, 338	2, 580	4, 607	1, 703	5, 119	4, 190	16	2	19	211	50	27	7	...
SOUTH ATLANTIC:																
Delaware	34	34	146	28	7	21	18	41	...	...	...	1	1	3	...	...
Maryland	254	316	508	213	90	164	64	219	8	1	2	13	10	10	1	...
District of Columbia	386	613	874	639	136	312	86	498	8	4	3	33	4	24	2	...
Virginia	526	1, 507	1, 493	234	66	183	51	181	16	...	4	13	1	11	1	...
West Virginia	2, 467	2, 794	10, 560	796	126	211	107	151	3	1	7	26	9	7	2	...
North Carolina	196	821	1, 206	340	82	125	50	118	1	1	1	12	...	...	...	...
South Carolina	40	199	435	119	29	75	12	46	1	1	1	2	2	1	...	...
Georgia	346	1, 514	17, 587	812	173	480	68	296	11	1	3	11	2	8	2	...
Florida	390	1, 101	17, 839	1, 577	178	1, 333	101	506	7	2	1	15	...	11	5	...
EAST SOUTH CENTRAL:																
Kentucky	**185, 051**	16, 752	7, 589	1, 761	587	442	110	258	3	...	5	18	2	8	9	...
Tennessee	4, 297	**333, 704**	13, 551	48, 320	7, 412	2, 393	242	678	6	6	4	26	7	8	3	1
Alabama	545	4, 282	**883, 289**	13, 425	594	1, 485	183	463	5	1	1	26	11	3	14	...
Mississippi	513	6, 271	25, 237	**938, 911**	7, 129	18, 099	176	880	5	...	...	20	3	11	2	...
WEST SOUTH CENTRAL:																
Arkansas	877	16, 432	9, 142	57, 229	**340, 182**	28, 886	1, 554	5, 166	5	12	4	57	6	6	4	...
Louisiana	401	1, 047	5, 925	30, 515	8, 706	**710, 894**	447	9, 257	9	7	3	25	8	6	6	2
Oklahoma	957	3, 873	4, 903	5, 550	12, 935	7, 265	**85, 760**	40, 642	3	11	5	119	29	25	8	2
Texas	782	2, 772	6, 322	5, 271	7, 962	58, 217	4, 727	**755, 017**	10	4	10	148	48	70	12	4
MOUNTAIN:																
Montana	59	68	28	29	33	17	27	71	**299**	6	8	17	1	4	1	3
Idaho	14	37	20	14	22	29	27	84	8	**110**	2	17	3	3	23	1
Wyoming	59	55	56	34	32	34	50	93	6	1	**178**	78	3	1	6	...
Colorado	450	644	516	434	500	386	524	1, 473	13	5	42	**2, 892**	53	15	18	1
New Mexico	62	67	107	89	141	171	277	851	4	1	2	49	**515**	18	1	...
Arizona	227	330	422	382	402	1, 029	1, 330	2, 895	6	4	10	78	89	**1, 113**	3	3
Utah	37	44	36	32	49	45	53	112	7	7	9	46	4	1	**250**	3
Nevada	16	18	18	14	8	36	13	72	2	10	1	13	1	1	6	**47**
PACIFIC:																
Washington	250	281	197	191	147	218	131	459	87	31	16	117	18	18	14	3
Oregon	51	76	76	63	75	143	74	268	16	9	5	28	2	6	10	1
California	1, 601	2, 618	2, 851	3, 237	3, 027	8, 599	3, 221	14, 314	83	33	35	617	198	526	100	74

TABLE 14.—NATIVE NEGRO POPULATION OF EACH DIVISION AND STATE, BY DIVISION AND STATE OF BIRTH: 1930—Continued

DIVISION AND STATE	NEGRO POPULATION BORN IN—													American citizens born at sea	American citizens born abroad
	Pacific division			United States, State not reported	Outlying possessions										
	Washington	Oregon	California		Total	Alaska	American Samoa	Guam	Hawaii	Panama Canal Zone	Philippine Islands	Puerto Rico	Virgin Islands of the U. S.		
United States	**2,998**	**746**	**19,481**	**32,384**	**17,625**	**42**	**30**	**48**	**217**	**594**	**402**	**11,132**	**5,160**	**39**	**2,996**
GEOGRAPHIC DIVISIONS:															
New England	31	3	56	319	271	-	-	1	8	25	26	107	104	3	137
Middle Atlantic	595	32	490	5,324	15,863	5	-	13	44	426	135	10,389	4,851	12	728
East North Central	248	40	718	5,317	264	2	2	2	13	41	34	135	35	10	1,157
West North Central	80	24	288	2,395	61	4	2	-	7	4	22	17	5	-	155
South Atlantic	123	15	320	7,153	421	16	-	25	19	24	31	228	78	5	242
East South Central	24	7	176	5,245	97	-	9	-	8	7	12	49	12	-	61
West South Central	53	29	424	5,488	171	1	14	-	4	20	12	87	33	2	203
Mountain	69	25	278	226	52	3	1	1	8	3	24	9	3	-	47
Pacific	1,775	571	16,731	917	425	11	2	6	106	44	106	111	39	7	266
NEW ENGLAND:															
Maine	1	-	-	13	5	-	-	-	-	-	-	2	3	-	4
New Hampshire	-	-	1	9	3	-	-	-	-	1	-	2	-	-	-
Vermont	-	-	-	1	4	-	-	-	-	-	4	-	-	-	6
Massachusetts	16	3	37	155	150	-	-	1	7	21	20	53	48	2	103
Rhode Island	6	-	5	30	7	-	-	-	-	-	1	4	2	1	14
Connecticut	8	-	13	111	102	-	-	-	1	3	1	46	51	-	10
MIDDLE ATLANTIC:															
New York	264	19	279	2,885	15,305	1	-	12	22	385	82	10,145	4,658	6	483
New Jersey	145	8	75	1,232	247	3	-	-	6	11	18	96	113	1	93
Pennsylvania	186	5	136	1,207	311	1	-	1	16	30	35	148	80	5	152
EAST NORTH CENTRAL:															
Ohio	52	3	151	1,762	57	-	1	1	3	7	9	31	5	3	209
Indiana	20	-	49	881	22	1	-	-	3	-	4	8	6	2	40
Illinois	124	19	336	1,605	97	-	1	1	3	14	14	55	9	4	230
Michigan	49	15	165	1,003	85	1	-	-	4	20	7	38	15	1	666
Wisconsin	3	3	17	66	3	-	-	-	-	-	-	3	-	-	12
WEST NORTH CENTRAL:															
Minnesota	25	2	31	70	5	1	-	-	2	-	1	1	-	-	47
Iowa	9	-	19	138	2	1	-	-	1	-	-	-	-	-	6
Missouri	32	8	132	1,365	22	2	2	-	1	1	2	12	2	-	50
North Dakota	-	-	1	5	1	-	-	-	-	-	1	-	-	-	3
South Dakota	-	-	1	3	-	-	-	-	-	-	-	-	-	-	3
Nebraska	5	2	30	205	6	-	-	-	1	1	3	1	-	-	12
Kansas	9	12	74	609	25	-	-	-	2	2	15	3	3	-	34
SOUTH ATLANTIC:															
Delaware	6	-	5	25	5	-	-	-	1	1	-	3	-	-	3
Maryland	30	5	38	1,482	128	1	-	1	1	8	10	70	37	2	25
District of Columbia	15	3	55	1,048	74	13	-	2	7	1	11	30	10	-	39
Virginia	25	4	46	504	69	2	-	2	2	4	6	39	14	1	27
West Virginia	14	2	26	191	11	-	-	-	1	1	1	8	-	-	14
North Carolina	12	-	25	758	23	-	-	8	1	1	-	10	3	-	9
South Carolina	5	1	9	295	18	-	-	7	-	1	-	7	3	-	6
Georgia	7	-	54	1,097	31	-	-	2	4	2	-	20	3	-	13
Florida	9	-	62	1,753	62	-	-	3	2	5	3	41	8	2	106
EAST SOUTH CENTRAL:															
Kentucky	10	2	33	574	9	-	1	-	2	-	2	4	-	-	13
Tennessee	8	3	55	2,035	16	-	6	-	1	1	2	4	2	-	22
Alabama	4	1	50	1,110	41	-	2	-	2	4	5	24	4	-	9
Mississippi	2	1	38	1,526	31	-	-	-	3	2	3	17	6	-	17
WEST SOUTH CENTRAL:															
Arkansas	7	7	61	1,878	8	-	1	-	-	1	2	4	-	1	10
Louisiana	13	4	73	773	98	-	2	-	-	19	1	56	20	-	50
Oklahoma	15	9	112	819	9	-	1	-	1	-	3	3	1	-	53
Texas	18	9	178	2,018	56	1	10	-	3	-	6	24	12	1	90
MOUNTAIN:															
Montana	12	3	8	15	3	2	-	-	-	-	-	-	1	-	6
Idaho	8	5	8	3	3	1	-	-	-	-	-	2	-	-	4
Wyoming	7	1	4	8	1	-	-	-	-	-	-	1	-	-	1
Colorado	12	6	41	75	5	-	-	-	-	3	1	1	-	-	14
New Mexico	3	-	18	40	-	-	-	-	-	-	-	-	-	-	4
Arizona	18	7	167	64	36	-	1	1	6	-	22	5	1	-	14
Utah	2	2	11	12	4	-	-	-	2	-	1	-	1	-	2
Nevada	7	1	21	9	-	-	-	-	-	-	-	-	-	-	2
PACIFIC:															
Washington	1,480	102	159	108	31	5	-	-	6	-	12	7	1	3	74
Oregon	45	351	58	35	6	1	-	-	4	-	1	-	-	-	13
California	250	118	16,514	774	388	5	2	6	96	44	93	104	38	4	179

Table 15.—NEGRO POPULATION DISTRIBUTED AS BORN IN STATE OF RESIDENCE, IN OTHER STATES, OR IN FOREIGN COUNTRIES, FOR CITIES OF 50,000 OR MORE HAVING AT LEAST 5,000 NEGROES, 1930, WITH PERCENTAGES FOR 1930, 1920, AND 1910

[Percentages for 1920 or for 1910 not shown if the population of the city was under 50,000 or the number of Negroes under 5,000. An asterisk (*) indicates that the percentage was less than one-tenth of 1 percent]

CITY OF RESIDENCE	Negro population, 1930 [1]	NEGRO POPULATION BORN IN THE UNITED STATES AND WITH STATE OF BIRTH REPORTED								FOREIGN BORN			
		Born in State of residence				Born in other States							
		Number, 1930	Percent of total			Number, 1930	Percent of total			Number, 1930	Percent of total		
			1930	1920	1910		1930	1920	1910		1930	1920	1910
NEW ENGLAND DIVISION													
MASSACHUSETTS:													
Boston	20, 574	7, 754	37. 7	30. 2	29. 2	9, 322	45. 3	50. 7	57. 2	3, 287	16. 0	17. 6	12. 9
Cambridge	5, 419	2, 704	49. 9	43. 0	------	1, 519	28. 0	35. 3	------	1, 155	21. 3	20. 9	------
RHODE ISLAND:													
Providence	5, 473	2, 830	51. 7	42. 0	39. 2	1, 961	35. 8	42. 5	50. 3	652	11. 9	14. 8	9. 8
CONNECTICUT:													
Hartford	6, 510	1, 961	30. 1	------	------	4, 432	68. 1	------	------	81	1. 2	------	------
New Haven	5, 302	2, 303	43. 4	------	------	2, 563	48. 3	------	------	402	7. 6	------	------
MIDDLE ATLANTIC DIVISION													
NEW YORK:													
Buffalo	13, 563	2, 450	18. 1	------	------	10, 634	78. 4	------	------	361	2. 7	------	------
New York	327, 706	79, 264	24. 2	25. 7	29. 4	176, 272	53. 8	51. 3	56. 9	54, 754	16. 7	20. 0	12. 8
Bronx Borough	12, 930	4, 249	32. 9	41. 9	36. 0	6, 383	49. 4	40. 2	55. 0	1, 744	13. 5	12. 9	8. 4
Brooklyn Borough	68, 921	20, 332	29. 5	35. 3	38. 6	34, 064	49. 4	44. 2	49. 2	11, 266	16. 3	18. 7	11. 0
Manhattan Borough	224, 670	47, 642	21. 2	20. 9	23. 6	124, 087	55. 2	54. 4	61. 1	39, 833	17. 7	21. 4	14. 4
Queens Borough	18, 609	6, 000	32. 2	47. 6	56. 4	10, 602	57. 0	44. 3	40. 2	1, 700	9. 1	6. 5	3. 2
Richmond Borough	2, 576	1, 041	40. 4	46. 5	53. 0	1, 136	44. 1	39. 2	40. 7	211	8. 2	12. 7	5. 9
NEW JERSEY:													
Atlantic City	15, 611	3, 114	19. 9	17. 6	------	11, 895	76. 2	77. 7	------	519	3. 3	4. 1	------
Camden	11, 340	4, 052	35. 7	36. 3	41. 8	7, 172	63. 2	62. 6	57. 0	66	. 6	. 6	. 7
Jersey City	12, 575	3, 156	25. 1	23. 4	25. 2	9, 144	72. 7	73. 1	71. 8	208	1. 7	3. 0	2. 6
Newark	38, 880	9, 528	24. 5	28. 8	41. 5	28, 493	73. 3	68. 9	56. 3	458	1. 2	1. 8	1. 6
Trenton	8, 057	2, 580	32. 0	------	------	5, 319	66. 0	------	------	78	1. 0	------	------
PENNSYLVANIA:													
Chester	9, 245	2, 988	32. 3	31. 4	------	6, 225	67. 3	67. 8	------	20	. 2	. 6	------
Harrisburg	6, 382	2, 995	46. 9	46. 6	------	3, 343	52. 4	52. 3	------	35	. 5	. 6	------
Philadelphia	219, 599	64, 855	29. 5	29. 6	35. 1	151, 849	69. 1	68. 4	62. 9	2, 017	. 9	1. 5	1. 4
Pittsburgh	54, 983	18, 022	32. 8	29. 5	34. 4	36, 467	66. 3	69. 2	63. 6	277	. 5	. 8	1. 0
EAST NORTH CENTRAL DIVISION													
OHIO:													
Akron	11, 080	2, 133	19. 3	14. 0	------	8, 882	80. 2	84. 9	------	27	. 2	. 7	------
Cincinnati	47, 818	11, 776	24. 6	24. 4	28. 4	35, 654	74. 6	74. 9	69. 5	39	. 1	. 2	. 2
Cleveland	71, 899	15, 607	21. 7	16. 9	35. 7	55, 198	76. 8	81. 0	57. 8	471	. 7	1. 2	3. 5
Columbus	32, 774	12, 199	37. 2	38. 0	52. 6	20, 271	61. 9	60. 8	46. 4	50	. 2	. 3	. 3
Dayton	17, 077	5, 175	30. 3	32. 7	------	11, 834	69. 3	66. 5	------	32	. 2	. 4	------
Springfield	8, 249	3, 864	46. 8	46. 8	------	4, 363	52. 9	52. 2	------	12	. 1	. 1	------
Toledo	13, 260	2, 932	22. 1	24. 5	------	10, 094	76. 1	72. 1	------	79	. 6	1. 7	------
Youngstown	14, 552	3, 324	22. 8	16. 3	------	11, 108	76. 3	82. 4	------	50	. 3	. 6	------
INDIANA:													
East Chicago	5, 088	669	13. 1	------	------	4, 394	86. 4	------	------	8	. 2	------	------
Evansville	6, 514	2, 060	31. 6	29. 7	32. 1	4, 413	67. 7	69. 4	67. 6	7	. 1	. 1	(*)
Gary	17, 922	2, 254	12. 6	6. 0	------	15, 501	86. 5	92. 9	------	41	. 2	. 6	------
Indianapolis	43, 967	14, 425	32. 8	28. 3	33. 0	29, 968	65. 9	71. 0	66. 2	50	. 1	. 2	. 1
ILLINOIS:													
Chicago	233, 903	41, 693	17. 8	14. 9	19. 3	189, 643	81. 1	83. 2	77. 1	1, 338	. 6	. 9	1. 5
East St. Louis	11, 536	2, 818	24. 4	23. 0	32. 9	8, 630	74. 8	76. 1	66. 4	6	. 1	. 1	. 1
MICHIGAN:													
Detroit	120, 066	16, 881	14. 1	8. 4	32. 2	100, 806	84. 0	87. 2	44. 9	1, 445	1. 2	2. 8	15. 7
Flint	5, 725	888	15. 5	------	------	4, 627	80. 8	------	------	64	1. 1	------	------
WISCONSIN:													
Milwaukee	7, 501	768	10. 2	------	------	6, 653	88. 7	------	------	39	. 5	------	------
WEST NORTH CENTRAL DIVISION													
IOWA:													
Des Moines	5, 428	2, 248	41. 4	31. 3	------	3, 143	57. 9	67. 2	------	14	. 3	. 2	------
MISSOURI:													
Kansas City	38, 574	15, 668	40. 6	42. 5	54. 7	22, 415	58. 1	55. 0	42. 3	58	. 2	. 6	. 2
St. Louis	93, 580	30, 553	32. 6	36. 7	47. 3	62, 518	66. 8	62. 4	51. 4	95	. 1	. 1	. 3
NEBRASKA:													
Omaha	11, 123	2, 329	20. 9	13. 1	18. 2	8, 558	76. 9	82. 9	78. 3	40	. 4	. 9	. 9
KANSAS:													
Kansas City	19, 872	6, 130	30. 8	28. 1	32. 9	13, 588	68. 4	70. 8	65. 7	19	. 1	. 2	. 2
Topeka	5, 756	2, 930	50. 9	------	------	2, 782	48. 3	------	------	7	. 1	------	------
Wichita	5, 623	1, 685	30. 0	------	------	3, 785	67. 3	------	------	10	. 2	------	------

[1] Includes persons born in the United States, State of birth not reported; persons born in outlying possessions; and American citizens born abroad or at sea.

TABLE 15.—NEGRO POPULATION DISTRIBUTED AS BORN IN STATE OF RESIDENCE, IN OTHER STATES, OR IN FOREIGN COUNTRIES, FOR CITIES OF 50,000 OR MORE HAVING AT LEAST 5,000 NEGROES, 1930, WITH PERCENTAGES FOR 1930, 1920, AND 1910—Continued

CITY OF RESIDENCE	Negro population, 1930 [1]	NEGRO POPULATION BORN IN THE UNITED STATES AND WITH STATE OF BIRTH REPORTED: Born in State of residence: Number, 1930	Born in State of residence: Percent of total: 1930	1920	1910	Born in other States: Number, 1930	Born in other States: Percent of total: 1930	1920	1910	FOREIGN BORN: Number, 1930	FOREIGN BORN: Percent of total: 1930	1920	1910
SOUTH ATLANTIC DIVISION													
DELAWARE:													
Wilmington	12,080	5,933	49.1	46.9	56.2	6,076	50.3	51.9	43.3	53	0.4	0.3	0.2
MARYLAND:													
Baltimore	142,106	84,410	59.4	66.8	76.5	55,547	39.1	32.3	22.7	724	.5	.6	.4
DISTRICT OF COLUMBIA:													
Washington	132,068	52,513	39.8	42.3	42.8	77,937	59.0	56.7	56.2	457	.3	.3	.3
VIRGINIA:													
Norfolk	43,942	29,796	67.8	63.3	66.8	13,918	31.7	35.8	32.8	111	.3	.7	.
Richmond	52,988	43,522	82.1	86.3	91.9	9,364	17.7	12.0	7.9	37	.1	.1	.
Roanoke	12,368	10,016	81.0	86.6	--------	2,319	18.8	13.2	--------	8	.1	(*)	--------
WEST VIRGINIA:													
Charleston	6,734	3,573	53.1	--------	--------	3,141	46.6	--------	--------	6	.1	--------	--------
NORTH CAROLINA:													
Asheville	14,255	5,864	41.1	--------	--------	8,355	58.6	--------	--------	4	(*)	--------	--------
Charlotte	25,163	12,486	49.6	--------	--------	12,335	49.0	--------	--------	7	(*)	--------	--------
Durham	18,717	16,011	85.5	--------	--------	2,688	14.4	--------	--------	12	.1	--------	--------
Greensboro	14,050	10,567	75.2	--------	--------	3,451	24.6	--------	--------	11	.1	--------	--------
Winston-Salem	32,566	18,125	55.7	--------	--------	14,398	44.2	--------	--------	6	(*)	--------	--------
SOUTH CAROLINA:													
Charleston	28,062	27,242	97.1	96.7	98.0	792	2.8	3.0	1.9	16	.1	.2	.1
Columbia	19,519	18,704	95.8	--------	--------	644	3.3	--------	--------	4	(*)	--------	--------
GEORGIA:													
Atlanta	90,075	83,812	93.0	87.7	88.0	5,977	6.6	11.8	11.7	35	(*)	(*)	.1
Augusta	24,190	17,511	72.4	70.8	--------	6,624	27.4	28.7	--------	4	(*)	.1	--------
Macon	23,158	22,118	95.5	94.1	--------	977	4.2	5.7	--------	1	(*)	(*)	--------
Savannah	38,896	25,342	65.2	64.6	65.0	13,266	34.1	34.7	34.6	51	.1	.2	.3
FLORIDA:													
Jacksonville	48,196	21,225	44.0	47.8	45.8	26,645	55.3	50.0	53.4	190	.4	.5	.5
Miami	25,116	11,072	44.1	--------	--------	8,435	33.6	--------	--------	5,512	21.9	--------	--------
Tampa	21,172	12,009	56.7	60.2	--------	8,476	40.0	32.8	--------	631	3.0	5.8	--------
EAST SOUTH CENTRAL DIVISION													
KENTUCKY:													
Louisville	47,354	34,499	72.9	77.3	81.8	12,681	26.8	22.2	17.8	25	.1	.1	.1
TENNESSEE:													
Chattanooga	33,289	12,022	36.1	41.3	--------	21,177	63.6	58.2	--------	11	(*)	(*)	--------
Knoxville	17,093	9,400	55.0	67.9	--------	7,654	44.8	31.7	--------	8	(*)	.1	--------
Memphis	96,550	45,938	47.6	43.9	49.7	49,740	51.5	53.6	48.8	26	(*)	(*)	(*)
Nashville	42,836	38,528	89.9	91.2	91.6	3,966	9.3	8.4	8.2	20	(*)	.1	(*)
ALABAMA:													
Birmingham	99,077	83,847	84.6	83.8	75.7	15,013	15.2	15.6	23.7	18	(*)	.1	(*)
Mobile	24,514	21,448	87.5	87.1	87.7	2,850	11.6	11.6	10.8	119	.5	.6	.4
Montgomery	29,970	28,113	93.8	--------	--------	1,827	6.1	--------	--------	6	(*)	--------	--------
WEST SOUTH CENTRAL DIVISION													
ARKANSAS:													
Little Rock	19,698	13,927	70.7	62.6	--------	5,316	27.0	32.8	--------	8	(*)	.1	--------
LOUISIANA:													
New Orleans	129,632	116,597	89.9	87.4	85.6	12,043	9.3	11.1	13.6	666	.5	1.1	.4
Shreveport	27,219	23,657	86.9	--------	--------	3,465	12.7	--------	--------	10	(*)	--------	--------
OKLAHOMA:													
Oklahoma City	14,662	5,655	38.6	28.0	16.6	8,857	60.4	71.4	82.6	10	.1	.1	.2
Tulsa	15,203	5,891	38.7	30.1	--------	9,191	60.5	69.2	--------	12	.1	.2	--------
TEXAS:													
Austin	9,868	9,258	93.8	--------	--------	434	4.4	--------	--------	11	.1	--------	--------
Beaumont	18,551	7,650	41.2	--------	--------	10,861	58.5	--------	--------	14	.1	--------	--------
Dallas	38,742	33,708	87.0	82.0	79.4	4,927	12.7	16.4	19.8	20	.1	.1	.1
Fort Worth	22,234	19,799	89.0	85.0	81.0	2,217	10.0	13.2	17.0	33	.1	.3	.2
Galveston	13,226	8,967	67.8	--------	--------	4,159	31.4	--------	--------	65	.5	--------	--------
Houston	63,337	47,742	75.4	80.2	80.7	15,099	23.8	19.3	18.4	54	.1	.1	.3
Port Arthur	10,003	2,456	24.6	--------	--------	7,487	74.8	--------	--------	39	.4	--------	--------
San Antonio	17,978	16,557	92.1	88.8	86.0	1,330	7.4	10.2	12.4	41	.2	.3	.3
Waco	9,370	8,747	93.4	--------	--------	574	6.1	--------	--------	4	(*)	--------	--------
MOUNTAIN DIVISION													
COLORADO:													
Denver	7,204	1,703	23.6	19.7	17.9	5,414	75.2	77.6	78.8	32	.4	.6	.8
PACIFIC DIVISION													
CALIFORNIA:													
Los Angeles	38,894	6,701	17.2	15.6	13.8	31,337	80.6	82.0	83.4	525	1.3	1.1	1.4
Oakland	7,503	1,755	23.4	22.3	--------	5,322	70.9	72.0	--------	204	2.7	3.5	--------

[1] Includes persons born in the United States, State of birth not reported; persons born in outlying possessions; and American citizens born abroad or at sea.

TABLE 16.—NATIVE NEGRO POPULATION BY STATE OF BIRTH, FOR CITIES OF 50,000 OR MORE HAVING AT LEAST 5,000 NEGROES: 1930

NEGRO POPULATION BORN IN—

CITY OF RESIDENCE	Total native Negro population	New England division						Middle Atlantic division			East North Central division					W. N. Central division	
		Maine	New Hampshire	Vermont	Massachusetts	Rhode Island	Connecticut	New York	New Jersey	Pennsylvania	Ohio	Indiana	Illinois	Michigan	Wisconsin	Minnesota	Iowa
NEW ENGLAND DIVISION																	
MASSACHUSETTS:																	
Boston	17,287	121	26	19	7,754	213	214	326	176	348	79	32	58	21	3	8	8
Cambridge	4,264	14	27	15	2,704	19	46	71	24	60	10	2	7	7	1	----	1
RHODE ISLAND:																	
Providence	4,821	3	2	11	310	2,830	118	93	56	74	6	----	3	2	----	----	----
CONNECTICUT:																	
Hartford	6,429	----	1	3	112	9	1,961	100	56	61	27	----	7	6	----	1	1
New Haven	4,900	14	1	9	145	37	2,303	272	106	124	25	6	11	7	----	1	2
MIDDLE ATLANTIC DIVISION																	
NEW YORK:																	
Buffalo	13,202	----	----	2	55	8	20	2,450	74	434	374	86	111	53	10	9	23
New York	272,952	134	36	64	2,329	567	1,428	79,264	5,275	6,226	1,721	358	1,026	336	42	59	81
Bronx Borough	11,186	3	1	1	109	28	68	4,249	253	258	73	9	23	11	6	3	2
Brooklyn Borough	57,655	15	11	8	363	134	306	20,332	997	1,083	216	46	86	46	6	11	7
Manhattan Borough	184,837	109	22	46	1,729	372	940	47,642	3,647	4,470	1,340	283	871	254	25	41	69
Queens Borough	16,909	7	2	9	113	28	109	6,000	317	385	86	20	45	25	5	3	3
Richmond Borough	2,365	----	----	----	15	5	5	1,041	61	30	6	----	1	----	----	1	----
NEW JERSEY:																	
Atlantic City	15,092	----	1	1	51	17	42	218	3,114	1,545	69	23	29	20	1	6	7
Camden	11,274	1	1	----	15	15	20	63	4,052	894	26	6	3	3		3	1
Jersey City	12,367	6	----	6	68	17	46	551	3,156	210	61	18	39	14	----		1
Newark	38,422	4	1	1	95	35	90	693	9,528	650	150	21	54	36	1	1	10
Trenton	7,979	1	----	----	6	3	10	95	2,580	343	11	4	6	10	1	----	----
PENNSYLVANIA:																	
Chester	9,225	----	----	----	8	1	5	19	88	2,988	23	6	2	3	----	----	1
Harrisburg	6,347	----	----	----	6	3	2	34	30	2,995	51	5	6	8	1	----	1
Philadelphia	217,582	44	9	9	450	110	253	1,372	3,610	64,855	735	138	281	124	9	18	26
Pittsburgh	54,706	5	----	1	45	12	26	199	163	18,022	1,031	133	171	81	7	1	27
EAST NORTH CENTRAL DIVISION																	
OHIO																	
Akron	11,053	----	----	----	3	----	9	29	15	283	2,133	88	79	35	----	6	7
Cincinnati	47,779	4	2	1	19	1	6	71	31	152	11,776	461	220	81	8	8	12
Cleveland	71,428	8	----	3	90	10	28	335	110	1,339	15,607	714	669	304	25	32	50
Columbus	32,724	3	----	1	12	2	8	69	42	395	12,199	311	210	95	10	13	18
Dayton	17,045	1	----	----	6	1	5	22	11	115	5,175	364	100	51	3	2	10
Springfield	8,237	----	----	1	2	----	----	14	9	25	3,864	65	32	32	----	----	4
Toledo	13,181	3	1	----	12	1	8	51	14	145	2,932	255	451	228	10	7	25
Youngstown	14,502	1	----	----	7	----	1	53	20	653	3,324	75	61	40	----	4	9
INDIANA:																	
East Chicago	5,080	----	----	----	----	----	----	4	5	14	55	669	226	9	4	11	2
Evansville	6,507	----	1	----	----	----	----	3	2	6	33	2,060	106	2	1	1	2
Gary	17,881	1	----	2	8	2	3	14	7	204	159	2,254	644	84	16	22	72
Indianapolis	43,917	3	----	----	10	5	6	40	7	147	746	14,425	802	99	18	13	35
ILLINOIS:																	
Chicago	232,565	12	2	9	249	43	102	719	285	1,528	3,979	3,666	41,693	1,178	385	285	1,120
East St. Louis	11,530	----	1	----	1	----	----	2	5	11	36	26	2,818	10	4	3	11
MICHIGAN:																	
Detroit	118,621	7	2	8	124	13	86	486	207	1,378	3,322	1,259	1,747	16,881	67	58	212
Flint	5,661	----	----	----	3	1	----	12	8	46	166	115	111	888	11	8	23
WISCONSIN:																	
Milwaukee	7,462	1	----	----	8	2	1	19	6	58	163	130	532	52	768	37	246
WEST NORTH CENTRAL DIVISION																	
IOWA:																	
Des Moines	5,414	1	----	----	2	----	----	6	----	17	31	36	157	11	7	16	2,248
MISSOURI:																	
Kansas City	38,516	2	----	----	20	2	4	43	10	75	156	95	402	62	10	25	192
St. Louis	93,485	1	1	----	26	2	2	68	21	125	385	407	3,329	95	21	34	139
NEBRASKA:																	
Omaha	11,083	1	----	----	1	1	1	22	5	46	78	39	193	36	11	23	271
KANSAS:																	
Kansas City	19,853	1	----	1	3	1	1	7	3	14	48	57	174	22	9	20	68
Topeka	5,749	1	----	----	1	----	----	3	5	6	39	11	50	11	8	2	28
Wichita	5,613	----	----	----	----	----	----	7	1	13	23	21	57	4	1	1	9

TABLE 16.—NATIVE NEGRO POPULATION BY STATE OF BIRTH, FOR CITIES OF 50,000 OR MORE HAVING AT LEAST 5,000 NEGROES: 1930—Continued

CITY OF RESIDENCE	NEGRO POPULATION BORN IN—															
	West North Central division—Con.					South Atlantic division									E. S. Central division	
	Missouri	North Dakota	South Dakota	Nebraska	Kansas	Delaware	Maryland	District of Columbia	Virginia	West Virginia	North Carolina	South Carolina	Georgia	Florida	Kentucky	Tennessee
NEW ENGLAND DIVISION																
MASSACHUSETTS:																
Boston	41	1	-	1	9	44	387	304	2,394	46	1,512	968	1,035	270	94	93
Cambridge	14	-	-	-	-	7	53	41	383	4	392	132	103	19	15	15
RHODE ISLAND:																
Providence	-	-	1	-	-	3	146	54	612	5	201	99	74	35	6	17
CONNECTICUT:																
Hartford	5	-	-	1	-	3	47	57	463	5	302	196	2,594	168	11	35
New Haven	14	-	-	-	2	12	110	59	486	18	517	187	207	62	6	20
MIDDLE ATLANTIC DIVISION																
NEW YORK:																
Buffalo	177	-	2	4	31	11	165	73	1,128	64	1,035	1,970	1,283	265	294	773
New York	618	26	9	57	187	711	6,656	3,358	44,471	699	26,120	33,765	19,546	8,249	1,216	1,651
Bronx Borough	34	4	1	1	6	33	225	101	1,743	31	792	1,236	590	249	39	77
Brooklyn Borough	70	3	2	9	23	97	976	403	9,604	154	8,023	5,824	2,988	814	191	207
Manhattan Borough	477	18	6	43	150	535	5,034	2,661	30,490	468	15,658	23,850	14,483	6,831	874	1,263
Queens Borough	36	1	-	4	7	44	382	169	2,226	37	1,382	2,714	1,445	330	106	95
Richmond Borough	1	-	-	-	1	2	39	24	408	9	265	141	40	25	6	9
NEW JERSEY:																
Atlantic City	28	2	1	2	7	335	2,303	451	3,008	105	1,286	976	586	307	38	98
Camden	6	1	-	2	3	570	875	75	1,449	15	940	550	1,176	248	24	32
Jersey City	20	1	3	-	7	30	297	164	1,847	17	935	1,780	1,889	543	42	79
Newark	51	-	-	-	21	84	665	179	5,634	127	3,941	3,035	8,116	1,557	91	148
Trenton	10	-	-	-	1	52	172	50	955	20	547	1,309	1,307	219	20	36
PENNSYLVANIA:																
Chester	6	-	-	-	2	560	2,275	56	1,253	7	299	541	795	150	9	27
Harrisburg	3	-	-	-	6	17	391	57	1,209	174	255	327	473	76	17	33
Philadelphia	197	3	1	29	53	3,794	15,528	2,352	41,274	659	18,691	27,930	22,930	5,472	437	790
Pittsburgh	199	2	1	11	42	23	1,112	524	9,255	838	3,199	3,363	5,998	766	741	1,243
EAST NORTH CENTRAL DIVISION																
OHIO:																
Akron	61	-	-	8	36	2	60	18	449	135	267	321	2,617	327	386	517
Cincinnati	201	2	1	7	54	2	64	45	1,072	236	1,127	2,072	9,365	468	9,085	2,947
Cleveland	628	3	7	30	133	36	416	214	2,830	514	1,729	3,509	14,821	925	2,806	5,979
Columbus	136	-	8	8	55	4	92	47	3,409	1,060	2,310	1,471	4,774	206	1,660	1,444
Dayton	81	-	-	6	25	3	33	15	324	89	265	370	3,210	84	3,197	1,634
Springfield	19	-	-	-	2	-	27	3	194	40	200	37	1,376	16	1,065	558
Toledo	297	3	1	6	61	1	40	20	330	80	355	355	1,263	124	1,205	1,598
Youngstown	60	-	-	3	7	8	121	39	1,210	191	759	963	2,456	208	235	512
INDIANA:																
East Chicago	121	1	-	5	18	-	5	5	42	10	37	32	307	22	237	309
Evansville	40	-	-	1	5	-	3	1	20	2	15	9	56	12	2,993	886
Gary	439	-	2	22	154	2	29	20	229	32	204	215	1,079	104	825	1,956
Indianapolis	410	1	2	14	81	3	29	24	315	66	442	214	2,076	80	12,512	7,186
ILLINOIS:																
Chicago	7,685	14	16	340	1,808	45	556	449	2,756	447	2,116	4,039	21,969	1,646	10,594	23,485
East St. Louis	621	-	-	4	24	1	1	1	32	6	32	23	168	11	331	1,486
MICHIGAN:																
Detroit	2,315	9	12	105	587	44	426	248	2,854	686	3,164	7,403	25,400	2,610	4,672	8,864
Flint	142	-	1	4	55	-	14	6	125	39	130	178	630	66	165	365
WISCONSIN:																
Milwaukee	344	4	-	32	152	-	19	12	129	25	72	111	1,124	63	335	612
WEST NORTH CENTRAL DIVISION																
IOWA:																
DesMoines	1,225	-	1	28	230	-	11	3	264	17	45	24	78	11	116	143
MISSOURI:																
Kansas City	15,668	3	3	108	3,746	3	37	33	229	33	158	200	498	67	727	1,594
St. Louis	30,553	1	6	48	394	5	78	32	409	45	435	406	1,647	205	3,081	11,258
NEBRASKA:																
Omaha	1,363	2	5	2,329	813	2	15	14	100	15	56	48	171	242	261	401
KANSAS:																
Kansas City	2,961	4	3	43	6,130	1	15	9	80	12	95	135	320	25	409	917
Topeka	455	-	-	27	2,930	-	2	2	28	6	20	78	26	4	275	560
Wichita	394	-	-	14	1,685	-	1	4	21	1	29	24	68	8	105	206

TABLE 16.—NATIVE NEGRO POPULATION BY STATE OF BIRTH, FOR CITIES OF 50,000 OR MORE HAVING AT LEAST 5,000 NEGROES: 1930—Continued

CITY OF RESIDENCE	NEGRO POPULATION BORN IN— E. S. Central div.—Con.		West South Central division				Mountain division								Pacific division			Other native Negro[1]
	Alabama	Mississippi	Arkansas	Louisiana	Oklahoma	Texas	Montana	Idaho	Wyoming	Colorado	New Mexico	Arizona	Utah	Nevada	Washington	Oregon	California	
NEW ENGLAND DIVISION																		
MASSACHUSETTS:																		
Boston	177	56	37	80	13	66	------	1	1	7	------	3	3	------	7	2	18	211
Cambridge	14	6	3	3	2	6	------	------	------	------	------	------	------	------	1	------	2	41
RHODE ISLAND:																		
Providence	12	1	------	3	------	7	------	------	------	1	------	------	1	------	4	------	1	30
CONNECTICUT:																		
Hartford	113	12	9	16	4	5	1	------	------	------	------	------	------	------	1	------	------	36
New Haven	29	14	5	26	9	8	------	1	------	1	------	1	1	------	4	------	4	34
MIDDLE ATLANTIC DIVISION																		
NEW YORK:																		
Buffalo	969	482	195	186	40	194	3	1	1	7	1	1	2	------	10	------	8	118
New York	3,205	969	375	2,182	234	1,592	48	20	13	100	11	34	13	3	204	19	229	17,416
Bronx Borough	104	49	24	89	13	57	2	------	------	7	------	1	------	------	16	1	10	554
Brooklyn Borough	499	132	46	307	40	218	2	------	2	10	------	8	1	------	39	1	36	3,259
Manhattan Borough	2,430	736	282	1,656	164	1,253	35	20	10	78	10	25	11	3	133	16	166	13,108
Queens Borough	157	51	23	116	13	61	7	------	1	4	1	------	------	------	16	1	16	307
Richmond Borough	15	1	------	14	4	3	2	------	------	1	------	------	1	------	------	------	1	188
NEW JERSEY:																		
Atlantic City	118	25	20	29	15	46	------	------	1	5	1	------	1	------	62	2	7	83
Camden	69	19	5	14	10	19	2	1	------	4	------	------	------	------	10	------	2	50
Jersey City	290	30	17	35	6	52	4	1	1	1	1	1	------	------	10	------	4	67
Newark	2,601	80	44	88	25	105	6	------	------	8	3	1	2	------	12	1	26	401
Trenton	74	10	2	21	2	11	------	------	------	5	------	2	------	------	------	1	3	80
PENNSYLVANIA:																		
Chester	54	3	8	4	3	13	------	1	------	2	------	------	------	------	------	------	1	12
Harrisburg	87	16	6	14	5	24	1	------	------	1	------	1	------	------	1	------	2	9
Philadelphia	2,410	412	179	489	97	633	16	3	6	30	10	22	3	4	121	3	83	878
Pittsburgh	5,556	697	195	292	67	371	5	------	2	16	------	7	2	1	24	1	12	217
EAST NORTH CENTRAL DIVISION																		
OHIO:																		
Akron	2,445	231	119	99	101	113	------	------	------	3	2	1	------	------	------	2	8	38
Cincinnati	6,185	951	174	261	46	165	1	------	2	11	2	8	------	------	6	------	17	349
Cleveland	10,972	3,058	1,270	694	222	561	12	4	6	26	5	8	3	------	18	------	42	623
Columbus	1,616	273	140	126	52	146	3	------	2	10	4	6	------	------	3	------	17	254
Dayton	1,427	159	69	49	28	57	1	------	1	4	------	2	------	1	------	------	9	36
Springfield	547	35	24	9	4	23	------	------	------	------	------	------	------	------	------	------	------	10
Toledo	865	936	753	255	100	193	2	------	5	11	1	3	1	------	3	------	16	155
Youngstown	2,594	369	204	86	35	97	------	------	2	11	------	6	1	------	4	------	3	70
INDIANA:																		
East Chicago	1,090	1,147	303	251	34	75	1	------	2	7	------	------	------	------	1	------	2	17
Evansville	69	83	17	17	12	10	1	------	------	1	1	------	------	------	------	------	2	34
Gary	2,553	3,379	1,595	797	228	358	3	1	2	15	1	2	------	1	6	------	10	126
Indianapolis	1,096	1,582	383	219	53	204	1	2	4	12	2	3	1	------	6	------	14	524
ILLINOIS:																		
Chicago	21,247	38,356	12,165	17,811	1,907	5,760	35	18	21	281	45	43	22	4	97	18	286	1,229
East St. Louis	577	3,863	922	251	36	121	1	------	------	2	------	------	------	------	2	------	4	82
MICHIGAN:																		
Detroit	15,816	6,904	3,754	2,752	927	1,935	12	9	15	104	15	24	8	1	29	9	117	934
Flint	411	589	594	312	57	214	2	1	------	8	------	1	1	------	4	------	9	146
WISCONSIN:																		
Milwaukee	467	685	492	319	120	234	6	------	1	20	2	2	1	------	2	3	10	41
WEST NORTH CENTRAL DIVISION																		
IOWA:																		
Des Moines	209	64	111	34	92	122	1	------	2	14	4	2	------	------	2	------	6	23
MISSOURI:																		
Kansas City	723	1,528	3,784	1,564	2,268	3,756	10	3	12	129	16	17	10	4	11	3	40	433
St. Louis	4,094	19,627	10,450	3,153	602	1,726	7	4	9	46	8	10	3	------	16	2	55	414
NEBRASKA:																		
Omaha	794	553	636	392	620	1,192	4	4	28	50	5	6	6	------	4	2	26	196
KANSAS:																		
Kansas City	483	1,498	2,539	862	1,266	1,402	2	1	6	35	11	6	------	------	1	1	17	135
Topeka	77	142	239	88	336	190	2	------	2	36	7	------	1	------	2	1	11	37
Wichita	107	245	444	155	982	754	------	------	------	18	1	2	3	------	------	1	7	143

[1] Includes persons born in outlying possessions and American citizens born abroad or at sea.

TABLE 16.—NATIVE NEGRO POPULATION BY STATE OF BIRTH, FOR CITIES OF 50,000 OR MORE HAVING AT LEAST 5,000 NEGROES: 1930—Continued

CITY OF RESIDENCE	Total native Negro population	NEGRO POPULATION BORN IN—															
		New England division						Middle Atlantic division			East North Central division					W. N. Central division	
		Maine	New Hampshire	Vermont	Massachusetts	Rhode Island	Connecticut	New York	New Jersey	Pennsylvania	Ohio	Indiana	Illinois	Michigan	Wisconsin	Minnesota	Iowa
SOUTH ATLANTIC DIVISION																	
DELAWARE:																	
Wilmington	12,027	1	-	2	17	4	9	35	136	485	20	7	6	3	1	-	2
MARYLAND:																	
Baltimore	141,382	3	-	1	116	46	71	398	414	1,407	216	54	92	44	1	5	20
DISTRICT OF COLUMBIA:																	
Washington	131,611	22	6	9	254	72	122	756	513	1,633	439	117	233	83	10	27	28
VIRGINIA:																	
Norfolk	53,831	4	-	1	60	14	20	124	59	168	40	6	11	6	-	-	1
Richmond	52,951	-	5	-	18	7	17	157	90	223	56	12	15	11	4	-	1
Roanoke	12,360	-	-	-	5	-	2	11	10	72	38	5	2	8	-	-	-
WEST VIRGINIA:																	
Charleston	6,728	-	-	-	4	-	2	11	16	50	129	19	12	13	-	-	4
NORTH CAROLINA:																	
Asheville	14,251	-	-	-	3	1	2	11	5	39	32	5	7	7	1	1	2
Charlotte	25,156	-	-	-	4	-	2	18	8	47	13	1	4	8	-	-	-
Durham	18,705	-	-	-	3	-	1	20	14	21	28	3	5	3	-	2	-
Greensboro	14,039	-	-	-	11	2	7	27	7	29	14	2	1	2	1	2	-
Winston-Salem	32,560	1	-	-	3	-	5	29	14	44	47	8	4	8	1	2	1
SOUTH CAROLINA:																	
Charleston	28,046	-	-	-	5	-	-	50	16	15	9	1	5	1	-	-	-
Columbia	19,515	-	-	-	6	2	1	14	8	15	9	1	1	4	-	2	-
GEORGIA:																	
Atlanta	90,040	-	2	-	18	1	8	41	10	46	71	25	39	28	4	8	3
Augusta	24,186	-	-	1	3	1	1	21	6	22	10	4	10	5	2	-	2
Macon	23,157	-	-	-	2	-	7	12	3	15	11	6	3	9	1	-	-
Savannah	38,845	-	-	-	21	2	7	74	15	48	14	11	14	2	-	-	-
FLORIDA:																	
Jacksonville	48,006	-	1	-	20	-	7	103	38	87	42	16	27	21	4	-	-
Miami	19,604	-	-	-	6	-	4	47	21	41	37	5	20	3	4	-	-
Tampa	20,541	-	-	-	10	1	5	22	13	41	31	8	11	9	1	-	-
EAST SOUTH CENTRAL DIVISION																	
KENTUCKY:																	
Louisville	47,329	2	-	-	5	2	3	25	10	67	293	862	200	44	4	7	17
TENNESSEE:																	
Chattanooga	33,278	-	-	-	4	-	2	12	11	31	118	16	36	27	1	-	1
Knoxville	17,085	-	-	-	1	1	2	5	11	44	71	15	24	20	1	2	3
Memphis	96,524	-	-	-	3	3	3	19	5	26	123	38	254	26	7	13	18
Nashville	42,816	1	-	-	5	-	3	17	1	19	95	64	103	30	3	1	9
ALABAMA:																	
Birmingham	99,059	-	-	-	5	1	3	21	3	66	116	33	82	32	2	4	3
Mobile	24,395	1	-	-	2	-	-	9	1	18	20	9	27	4	4	-	1
Montgomery	29,964	-	1	-	-	-	-	9	2	14	25	-	15	12	-	1	4
WEST SOUTH CENTRAL DIVISION																	
ARKANSAS:																	
Little Rock	19,690	-	-	-	2	1	1	10	1	12	23	5	50	8	1	1	6
LOUISIANA:																	
New Orleans	128,966	1	-	-	14	6	6	58	11	59	81	27	182	34	7	5	11
Shreveport	27,209	-	-	-	1	-	1	3	-	4	6	2	16	4	-	-	1
OKLAHOMA:																	
Oklahoma City	14,652	-	-	-	1	-	-	8	3	10	24	21	32	8	1	7	12
Tulsa	15,191	-	1	-	3	-	-	5	-	13	33	18	41	9	-	1	10
TEXAS:																	
Austin	9,857	-	-	-	2	-	-	3	-	3	5	4	1	-	-	1	-
Beaumont	18,537	-	-	-	1	-	1	5	-	2	5	6	11	2	1	3	2
Dallas	38,722	-	-	-	2	-	1	11	2	14	15	7	27	14	1	9	2
Fort Worth	22,201	-	-	-	3	-	-	4	2	6	14	6	12	6	1	-	4
Galveston	13,161	-	-	-	1	-	-	9	2	10	8	7	18	6	1	-	1
Houston	63,283	-	1	-	4	1	1	15	3	30	36	17	45	10	-	7	16
Port Arthur	9,964	-	-	-	6	1	-	4	2	7	1	3	9	1	-	1	2
San Antonio	17,937	-	-	-	6	-	-	7	6	15	12	3	18	2	-	-	1
Waco	9,366	-	-	-	-	-	-	2	-	2	13	4	3	2	4	2	4
MOUNTAIN DIVISION																	
COLORADO:																	
Denver	7,172	-	-	-	12	1	7	22	11	53	84	48	129	23	3	7	61
PACIFIC DIVISION																	
CALIFORNIA:																	
Los Angeles	38,369	6	3	2	91	12	27	219	57	251	454	239	570	158	28	78	157
Oakland	7,299	2	-	4	20	5	6	46	8	50	73	43	124	29	4	8	28

TABLE 16.—NATIVE NEGRO POPULATION BY STATE OF BIRTH, FOR CITIES OF 50,000 OR MORE HAVING AT LEAST 5,000 NEGROES: 1930—Continued

CITY OF RESIDENCE	NEGRO POPULATION BORN IN—																
	West North Central division—Con.					South Atlantic division									E. S. Central division	
	Missouri	North Dakota	South Dakota	Nebraska	Kansas	Delaware	Maryland	District of Columbia	Virginia	West Virginia	North Carolina	South Carolina	Georgia	Florida	Kentucky	Tennessee
SOUTH ATLANTIC DIVISION																	
DELAWARE:																	
Wilmington	12			1		5,933	2,672	76	1,211	28	356	240	351	160	17	17
MARYLAND:																	
Baltimore	82	1	2	6	20	219	84,410	1,319	29,332	403	10,865	6,492	1,942	568	155	233
DISTRICT OF COLUMBIA:																	
Washington	185	5	4	30	73	87	16,346	52,513	30,236	751	8,026	10,166	3,383	626	386	613
VIRGINIA:																	
Norfolk	9		1		4	12	250	80	29,796	100	11,363	866	294	129	26	73
Richmond	10	1	2	3	2	7	154	97	43,522	123	4,285	3,207	449	103	41	67
Roanoke	1			1	1		21	25	10,016	236	1,063	359	188	23	14	127
WEST VIRGINIA:																	
Charleston	12		1	2	6	1	15	20	1,700	3,573	341	87	154	14	163	94
NORTH CAROLINA:																	
Asheville	3						5	18	117	9	5,864	7,104	577	78	14	160
Charlotte	4				1	1	24	33	147	18	12,486	10,811	897	83	12	49
Durham	2				5	1	14	9	391	18	16,011	1,758	242	37	13	22
Greensboro	3				2	1	16	20	316	17	10,567	2,306	401	63	11	28
Winston-Salem	5				1	8	12	24	1,047	73	18,125	12,034	719	96	13	84
SOUTH CAROLINA:																	
Charleston					1	1	9	8	49		142	27,242	298	101	5	14
Columbia	3						4	5	40	5	157	18,704	254	61	3	12
GEORGIA:																	
Atlanta	24		1	1	3	5	8	20	194	24	317	2,413	83,812	300	49	274
Augusta	5						6	3	69	1	94	6,105	17,511	86	8	27
Macon	8					2	5	3	43	7	42	98	22,118	103	7	31
Savannah	2			3			23	5	157	6	366	11,421	25,342	574	10	50
FLORIDA:																	
Jacksonville	16			9	6	5	30	24	284	10	799	6,888	16,686	21,225	35	130
Miami	7	1		1	4	2	30	4	135	14	310	1,098	5,747	11,072	32	94
Tampa	11				1	2	13	5	140	8	467	1,452	5,431	12,009	40	70
EAST SOUTH CENTRAL DIVISION																	
KENTUCKY:																	
Louisville	143	2	4	10	27		29	12	256	46	209	210	1,292	111	34,499	6,041
TENNESSEE:																	
Chattanooga	18			1	8	1	4	5	160	17	238	528	13,556	141	96	12,022
Knoxville	8			3	2	2	13	7	319	21	973	1,631	3,318	75	204	9,400
Memphis	370			6	32	1	23	20	260	13	473	261	1,161	88	388	45,938
Nashville	65	1	2	4	18	2	11	8	70	21	89	111	524	62	671	38,528
ALABAMA:																	
Birmingham	46			6	10	2	17	8	177	46	239	569	8,206	495	166	872
Mobile	13		1	4	5	1	11	2	76	2	74	77	296	325	22	64
Montgomery	13				2		8	6	49	6	61	74	992	199	23	56
WEST SOUTH CENTRAL DIVISION																	
ARKANSAS:																	
Little Rock	117	1		4	24	1		8	61	1	180	264	337	22	57	569
LOUISIANA:																	
New Orleans	96	1		10	11		44	16	255	10	116	145	334	239	147	283
Shreveport	27			1	10		5	3	25	3	35	29	106	29	10	52
OKLAHOMA:																	
Oklahoma City	184			16	216		5	4	31	4	90	71	183	9	117	455
Tulsa	279		1	22	320	1	9	4	40	12	76	100	134	20	101	424
TEXAS:																	
Austin	15				3		4	3	17		26	21	31	7	15	53
Beaumont	21			1	4		1	3	24	1	25	20	75	39	16	37
Dallas	126			9	47		3	3	59	3	72	50	234	17	87	286
Fort Worth	66		1	2	23		3	3	36	1	69	39	97	15	37	146
Galveston	24			5	7	1	7	4	34	1	33	22	54	17	17	32
Houston	109			7	35		13	3	99	6	160	92	293	79	63	210
Port Arthur	5				3		2		20	1	16	9	30	27	6	22
San Antonio	42		1	2	16		7	7	31	4	22	31	75	12	49	75
Waco	22			3	2		2		21		43	14	49	6	11	52
MOUNTAIN DIVISION																	
COLORADO:																	
Denver	753	3	1	62	570		23	21	120	12	47	37	123	22	260	349
PACIFIC DIVISION																	
CALIFORNIA:																	
Los Angeles	1,537	7	12	147	1,077	10	110	103	569	59	386	444	2,921	297	758	1,383
Oakland	260	1	1	39	173		28	17	117	18	93	84	203	32	111	194

TABLE 16.—NATIVE NEGRO POPULATION BY STATE OF BIRTH, FOR CITIES OF 50,000 OR MORE HAVING AT LEAST 5,000 NEGROES: 1930—Continued

CITY OF RESIDENCE	NEGRO POPULATION BORN IN— E. S. Central div.—Con.		West South Central division				Mountain division								Pacific division			Other native Negro[1]
	Alabama	Mississippi	Arkansas	Louisiana	Oklahoma	Texas	Montana	Idaho	Wyoming	Colorado	New Mexico	Arizona	Utah	Nevada	Washington	Oregon	California	
SOUTH ATLANTIC DIVISION																		
DELAWARE:																		
Wilmington	115	17	2	13	16	32	-	-	-	-	1	2	-	-	6	-	3	18
MARYLAND:																		
Baltimore	407	122	53	118	55	170	5	1	1	11	7	8	1	-	23	5	33	1,425
DISTRICT OF COLUMBIA:																		
Washington	874	639	136	312	86	498	8	4	3	33	4	24	2	-	15	3	55	1,161
VIRGINIA:																		
Norfolk	66	23	10	27	5	43	4	-	-	3	-	3	1	-	1	1	10	117
Richmond	95	28	10	22	3	28	2	-	1	1	-	1	-	-	-	1	5	65
Roanoke	62	16	1	17	1	6	1	-	-	2	-	-	-	-	-	-	1	25
WEST VIRGINIA:																		
Charleston	193	40	8	7	6	9	-	-	-	1	1	-	-	-	5	-	1	14
NORTH CAROLINA:																		
Asheville	110	17	5	7	1	8	-	-	1	-	-	-	-	-	2	-	3	32
Charlotte	97	25	11	10	-	4	-	-	-	1	-	-	-	-	1	-	1	335
Durham	42	13	4	5	5	4	-	-	-	1	-	-	-	-	-	-	2	6
Greensboro	112	15	9	15	-	10	-	-	-	1	-	-	-	-	-	-	-	21
Winston-Salem	71	17	6	8	6	4	-	-	-	2	-	-	-	-	-	-	1	37
SOUTH CAROLINA:																		
Charleston	37	6	1	11	-	5	-	-	-	-	-	-	-	-	-	1	1	12
Columbia	22	5	2	-	1	4	1	-	-	-	-	-	-	-	2	-	-	167
GEORGIA:																		
Atlanta	1,733	125	34	49	19	65	1	-	-	2	-	2	-	-	2	-	8	251
Augusta	86	15	5	9	4	9	1	-	1	-	-	1	-	-	-	-	1	51
Macon	520	18	4	3	1	6	-	-	-	1	-	-	-	-	-	-	6	62
Savannah	343	25	6	27	2	27	-	-	1	1	-	2	-	-	1	-	6	237
FLORIDA:																		
Jacksonville	1,106	88	13	72	13	51	2	1	1	2	-	1	-	-	1	-	6	136
Miami	621	49	13	54	7	16	2	-	-	-	-	1	-	-	-	-	5	97
Tampa	524	52	7	71	8	17	-	-	-	-	-	1	-	-	-	-	4	56
EAST SOUTH CENTRAL DIVISION																		
KENTUCKY:																		
Louisville	1,730	509	135	197	33	114	1	-	1	6	-	2	1	-	6	2	11	149
TENNESSEE:																		
Chattanooga	5,555	382	42	85	23	43	-	1	-	1	3	-	-	-	-	1	9	79
Knoxville	679	93	31	35	8	21	-	-	1	1	-	-	1	-	1	1	6	31
Memphis	2,819	35,301	5,734	1,773	109	334	3	-	-	4	1	4	-	-	4	1	19	846
Nashville	1,242	363	75	113	20	124	-	1	1	5	1	-	1	1	-	-	9	322
ALABAMA:																		
Birmingham	83,847	3,241	90	292	34	92	2	-	1	9	2	1	5	-	1	-	13	199
Mobile	21,448	1,416	18	294	5	37	-	-	-	2	-	-	-	-	-	1	8	97
Montgomery	28,113	131	12	50	6	53	-	-	-	1	-	-	-	-	-	-	2	24
WEST SOUTH CENTRAL DIVISION																		
ARKANSAS:																		
Little Rock	383	1,254	13,927	1,421	111	359	-	-	1	14	-	-	-	-	1	1	4	447
LOUISIANA:																		
New Orleans	1,607	7,382	176	116,597	30	581	2	2	1	3	2	2	3	-	6	2	35	326
Shreveport	148	329	513	23,657	73	2,011	2	3	-	1	2	1	1	-	1	-	7	87
OKLAHOMA:																		
Oklahoma City	434	510	727	593	5,655	5,023	-	2	-	30	2	6	1	-	2	-	15	140
Tulsa	321	533	1,828	939	5,891	3,855	1	1	3	14	3	4	-	1	2	1	8	109
TEXAS:																		
Austin	39	41	53	62	19	9,258	-	-	-	3	-	-	-	-	-	-	3	165
Beaumont	183	268	77	9,995	17	7,650	-	-	-	5	2	-	1	1	1	-	5	26
Dallas	360	268	536	2,164	432	33,708	1	1	1	25	1	6	3	3	3	1	21	87
Fort Worth	176	148	239	805	223	19,799	-	-	2	10	-	3	-	-	1	-	14	185
Galveston	124	138	97	3,402	62	8,967	1	-	-	7	-	4	1	-	-	-	2	35
Houston	564	629	404	11,880	203	47,742	1	-	-	12	3	11	1	-	2	1	33	442
Port Arthur	74	160	53	6,999	18	2,456	-	-	-	-	-	1	-	-	1	1	2	21
San Antonio	105	117	60	469	93	16,557	1	-	1	8	3	11	-	-	1	-	17	50
Waco	67	43	43	108	42	8,747	-	-	-	2	2	2	1	-	1	-	2	45
MOUNTAIN DIVISION																		
COLORADO:																		
Denver	220	249	346	269	274	1,064	8	5	31	1,703	23	13	11	1	9	3	24	55
PACIFIC DIVISION																		
CALIFORNIA:																		
Los Angeles	1,484	1,707	1,602	4,273	1,303	7,905	36	15	15	307	113	231	47	15	80	32	6,701	331
Oakland	200	284	143	1,277	101	1,290	8	4	10	54	6	23	14	17	43	27	1,755	222

[1] Includes persons born in outlying possessions and American citizens born abroad or at sea.

Table 17.—NATIVE NEGRO POPULATION BORN IN EACH STATE, DISTRIBUTED ACCORDING TO SELECTED STATES OF RESIDENCE: 1930

[These figures relate only to Negroes born in continental United States with the State of birth reported]

STATE	Number	Per-cent distri-bution
NEW ENGLAND		
MAINE, Negroes born in	1,334	100.0
Living in Maine	659	49.4
Living in other States	675	50.6
Massachusetts	211	15.8
New York	140	10.5
Pennsylvania	63	4.7
New Jersey	42	3.1
Connecticut	24	1.8
Ohio	24	1.8
District of Columbia	22	1.6
California	18	1.3
Illinois	18	1.3
Michigan	16	1.2
All other	97	7.3
NEW HAMPSHIRE, Negroes born in	494	100.0
Living in New Hampshire	223	45.1
Living in other States	271	54.9
Massachusetts	116	23.5
New York	42	8.5
Vermont	17	3.4
Virginia	13	2.6
Pennsylvania	12	2.4
New Jersey	10	2.0
All other	61	12.3
VERMONT, Negroes born in	853	100.0
Living in Vermont	347	40.7
Living in other States	506	59.3
New York	169	19.8
Massachusetts	119	14.0
Connecticut	32	3.8
New Hampshire	26	3.0
New Jersey	25	2.9
Pennsylvania	16	1.9
California	14	1.6
Rhode Island	14	1.6
Illinois	12	1.4
Ohio	12	1.4
Michigan	10	1.2
All other	57	6.7
MASSACHUSETTS, Negroes born in	32,009	100.0
Living in Massachusetts	24,358	76.1
Living in other States	7,651	23.9
New York	2,830	8.8
Connecticut	687	2.1
Pennsylvania	635	2.0
New Jersey	569	1.8
Rhode Island	538	1.7
Illinois	278	.9
District of Columbia	254	.8
California	223	.7
Virginia	210	.7
Ohio	189	.6
Maryland	165	.5
Michigan	161	.5
Florida	105	.3
All other	807	2.5
RHODE ISLAND, Negroes born in	7,468	100.0
Living in Rhode Island	5,242	70.2
Living in other States	2,226	29.8
New York	710	9.5
Massachusetts	545	7.3
Connecticut	183	2.5
New Jersey	172	2.3
Pennsylvania	155	2.1
District of Columbia	72	1.0
Virginia	62	.8
Maryland	56	.7
Illinois	50	.7
California	35	.5
All other	186	2.5
CONNECTICUT, Negroes born in	15,372	100.0
Living in Connecticut	10,503	68.3
Living in other States	4,869	31.7
New York	1,932	12.6
Massachusetts	732	4.8
New Jersey	481	3.1
Pennsylvania	363	2.4
Rhode Island	214	1.4
Virginia	140	.9
District of Columbia	122	.8
Illinois	122	.8
Michigan	108	.7
Maryland	101	.7
All other	554	3.6

STATE	Number	Per-cent distri-bution
MIDDLE ATLANTIC		
NEW YORK, Negores born in	125,964	100.0
Living in New York	108,351	86.0
Living in other States	17,613	14.0
New Jersey	5,149	4.1
Pennsylvania	2,376	1.9
Connecticut	1,113	.9
Virginia	1,062	.8
Massachusetts	851	.7
Illinois	817	.6
Ohio	803	.6
District of Columbia	756	.6
Michigan	673	.5
Maryland	626	.5
California	499	.4
North Carolina	473	.4
Florida	352	.3
All other	2,063	1.6
NEW JERSEY, Negroes born in	80,937	100.0
Living in New Jersey	64,352	79.5
Living in other States	16,585	20.5
New York	6,354	7.9
Pennsylvania	4,940	6.1
Virginia	697	.9
Maryland	683	.8
District of Columbia	513	.6
Connecticut	381	.5
Massachusetts	362	.4
Illinois	334	.4
Ohio	330	.4
Delaware	282	.3
Michigan	276	.3
North Carolina	263	.3
All other	1,170	1.4
PENNSYLVANIA, Negroes born in	187,121	100.0
Living in Pennsylvania	146,374	78.2
Living in other States	40,747	21.8
New Jersey	8,704	4.7
New York	8,310	4.4
Ohio	4,891	2.6
Maryland	2,638	1.4
Virginia	2,234	1.2
Michigan	1,881	1.0
Illinois	1,753	.9
District of Columbia	1,633	.9
West Virginia	1,369	.7
Delaware	1,064	.6
North Carolina	670	.4
Massachusetts	646	.3
California	598	.3
Indiana	503	.3
All other	3,853	2.1
EAST NORTH CENTRAL		
OHIO, Negroes born in	129,116	100.0
Living in Ohio	99,479	77.0
Living in other States	29,637	23.0
Michigan	5,050	3.9
Illinois	4,631	3.6
Pennsylvania	3,520	2.7
New York	2,545	2.0
Indiana	2,296	1.8
West Virginia	1,822	1.4
Kentucky	1,180	.9
California	980	.8
Missouri	688	.5
New Jersey	682	.5
Tennessee	572	.4
Alabama	465	.4
Virginia	456	.4
District of Columbia	439	.3
Georgia	433	.3
All other	3,878	3.0
INDIANA, Negroes born in	53,032	100.0
Living in Indiana	35,727	67.4
Living in other States	17,305	32.6
Illinois	4,885	9.2
Ohio	3,884	6.0
Michigan	2,473	4.7
Kentucky	1,503	2.8
Missouri	632	1.2
Pennsylvania	571	1.1
New York	556	1.0
California	495	.9
Tennessee	244	.5
Kansas	233	.4
All other	2,529	4.8

STATE	Number	Per-cent distri-bu-tion
EAST NORTH CENTRAL—Continued		
ILLINOIS, Negores born in	101,878	100.0
Living in Illinois	76,069	74.7
Living in other States	25,809	25.3
Missouri	4,667	4.6
Michigan	3,027	3.0
Indiana	2,962	2.9
Ohio	2,483	2.4
New York	1,402	1.4
California	1,196	1.2
Tennessee	835	.8
Kentucky	808	.8
Pennsylvania	789	.8
Arkansas	726	.7
Wisconsin	724	.7
Iowa	683	.7
Kansas	596	.6
Mississippi	545	.5
Minnesota	392	.4
Louisiana	365	.4
Oklahoma	346	.3
Alabama	322	.3
Texas	319	.3
All other	2,622	2.6
MICHIGAN, Negroes born in	35,906	100.0
Living in Michigan	29,121	81.1
Living in other States	6,785	18.9
Illinois	1,360	3.8
Ohio	1,197	3.3
Indiana	559	1.6
New York	498	1.4
Pennsylvania	366	1.0
California	318	.9
Missouri	193	.5
Tennessee	155	.4
Georgia	154	.4
Alabama	149	.4
Florida	137	.4
New Jersey	134	.4
Kentucky	123	.4
Kansas	112	.3
Wisconsin	105	.3
All other	1,225	3.4
WISCONSIN, Negroes born in	3,266	100.0
Living in Wisconsin	1,732	53.0
Living in other States	1,534	47.0
Illinois	541	16.6
Michigan	169	5.2
Minnesota	107	3.3
Ohio	84	2.6
New York	73	2.2
Indiana	55	1.7
California	53	1.6
Missouri	47	1.4
Kansas	31	.9
Pennsylvania	30	.9
Arkansas	29	.9
Iowa	26	.8
Florida	22	.7
Texas	22	.7
All other	245	7.5
WEST NORTH CENTRAL		
MINNESOTA, Negroes born in	3,990	100.0
Living in Minnesota	2,384	59.7
Living in other States	1,606	40.3
Illinois	342	8.8
California	131	3.3
Michigan	116	2.9
Ohio	89	2.2
New York	83	2.1
Missouri	81	2.0
Washington	72	1.8
Iowa	67	1.7
Indiana	63	1.6
Wisconsin	57	1.4
Texas	52	1.3
All other	443	11.1
IOWA, Negroes born in	12,410	100.0
Living in Iowa	6,599	53.2
Living in other States	5,811	46.8
Illinois	1,694	13.7
Missouri	527	4.2
Minnesota	432	3.5
Michigan	393	3.2
Nebraska	342	2.8
California	304	2.4
Wisconsin	300	2.4
Kansas	227	1.8
Ohio	193	1.6
Indiana	171	1.4
New York	138	1.1
Pennsylvania	120	1.0
Colorado	103	.8
All other	867	7.0

TABLE 17.—NATIVE NEGRO POPULATION BORN IN EACH STATE, DISTRIBUTED ACCORDING TO SELECTED STATES OF RESIDENCE: 1930—Continued

[These figures relate only to Negroes born in continental United States with the State of birth reported]

STATE	Number	Per cent distribution
WEST NORTH CENTRAL—Continued		
MISSOURI, Negroes born in	159, 113	100. 0
Living in Missouri	106 728	67. 1
Living in other States	52, 385	32. 9
Illinois	14 885	9. 4
Kansas	7, 927	5. 0
Iowa	3, 500	2. 2
Michigan	3 414	2. 1
California	3. 034	1. 9
Ohio	1, 973	1. 2
Arkansas	1, 934	1. 2
Nebraska	1, 762	1. 1
Oklahoma	1, 590	1. 0
Indiana	1, 481	. 9
Colorado	1, 146	. 7
Texas	1, 120	. 7
Minnesota	1, 105	. 7
New York	1, 010	. 6
Tennessee	798	. 5
All other	5, 706	3. 6
NORTH DAKOTA, Negroes born in	377	100. 0
Living in North Dakota	94	24. 9
Living in other States	283	75. 1
Minnesota	41	10. 9
New York	34	9. 0
Illinois	22	5. 8
Montana	19	5. 0
Washington	19	5. 0
California	13	3. 4
Michigan	13	3. 4
Ohio	11	2. 9
All other	111	29. 4
SOUTH DAKOTA, Negroes born in	504	100. 0
Living in South Dakota	175	34. 7
Living in other States	329	65. 3
Minnesota	36	7. 1
Illinois	30	6. 0
Iowa	26	5. 2
California	25	5. 0
Missouri	22	4. 4
Ohio	22	4. 4
Michigan	20	4. 0
Kansas	13	2. 6
All other	135	26. 8
NEBRASKA, Negroes born in	5, 882	100. 0
Living in Nebraska	3, 123	53. 1
Living in other States	2, 759	46. 9
Illinois	432	7. 3
California	301	5. 1
Missouri	242	4. 1
Kansas	232	3. 9
Iowa	189	3. 2
Michigan	177	3. 0
Minnesota	130	2. 2
Oklahoma	106	1. 8
Colorado	92	1. 6
Ohio	90	1. 5
New York	82	1. 4
Pennsylvania	69	1. 2
Indiana	68	1. 2
Texas	63	1. 1
All other	486	8. 3
KANSAS, Negroes born in	47, 443	100. 0
Living in Kansas	27, 665	58. 3
Living in other States	19, 778	41. 7
Missouri	5, 215	11. 0
Illinois	2, 246	4. 7
Oklahoma	2, 162	4. 6
California	2, 069	4. 4
Nebraska	1, 128	2. 4
Michigan	1, 014	2. 1
Colorado	875	1. 8
Iowa	648	1. 4
Ohio	523	1. 1
Minnesota	457	1. 0
Texas	414	. 9
Indiana	366	. 8
Arizona	284	. 6
New York	282	. 6
Washington	281	. 6
All other	1, 814	3. 8
SOUTH ATLANTIC		
DELAWARE, Negroes born in	32, 184	100. 0
Living in Delaware	21, 311	66. 2
Living in other States	10 873	33. 8
Pennsylvania	5, 866	18. 2
New Jersey	2, 529	7. 9
Maryland	906	2. 8
New York	847	2. 6
Virginia	95	. 3
District of Columbia	87	. 3
Massachusetts	81	. 3
Ohio	72	. 2
Michigan	63	. 2
Illinois	55	. 2
Connecticut	40	. 1
All other	232	. 7
MARYLAND, Negroes born in	275 093	100. 0
Living in Maryland	201, 244	73. 2
Living in other States	73, 849	26. 8
Pennsylvania	25, 470	9. 3
District of Columbia	16, 346	5. 9
New Jersey	9, 473	3. 4
New York	8, 133	3. 0
Delaware	5, 340	1. 9
Virginia	2, 311	. 8
Ohio	1, 184	. 4
Massachusetts	700	. 3
Illinois	695	. 3
Michigan	586	. 2
West Virginia	548	. 2
Connecticut	417	. 2
North Carolina	311	. 1
Rhode Island	301	. 1
All other	2, 034	. 7
DISTRICT OF COLUMBIA, Negroes born in	72, 018	100. 0
Living in the District of Columbia	52, 513	72. 9
Living elsewhere	19, 505	27. 1
New York	3, 929	5. 5
Pennsylvania	3, 776	5. 2
Maryland	3, 562	4. 9
Virginia	2, 347	3. 3
New Jersey	1, 741	2. 4
Ohio	565	. 8
Illinois	526	. 7
Massachusetts	504	. 7
Michigan	329	. 5
Connecticut	261	. 4
North Carolina	239	. 3
California	229	. 3
West Virginia	222	. 3
Georgia	151	. 2
Kansas	126	. 2
Delaware	113	. 2
Rhode Island	110	. 2
All other	775	1. 1
VIRGINIA, Negroes born in	908, 551	100. 0
Living in Virginia	576, 588	63. 5
Living in other States	331, 963	36. 5
Pennsylvania	76, 139	8. 4
New York	58, 919	6. 5
Maryland	37, 090	4. 1
New Jersey	36, 635	4. 0
West Virginia	31, 401	3. 5
District of Columbia	30, 236	3. 3
Ohio	13, 892	1. 5
North Carolina	9, 578	1. 1
Massachusetts	4, 607	. 5
Illinois	3, 726	. 4
Michigan	3. 711	. 4
Connecticut	3, 347	. 4
Florida	2, 367	. 3
Delaware	2, 152	. 2
Tennessee	1. 985	. 2
Kentucky	1, 965	. 2
Georgia	1, 682	. 2
California	1, 309	. 1
Rhode Island	1, 141	. 1
Alabama	1, 123	. 1
All other	8, 958	1. 0
WEST VIRGINIA, Negroes born in	64, 898	100. 0
Living in West Virginia	46, 834	72. 2
Living in other States	18, 064	27. 8
Ohio	4, 384	6. 8
Pennsylvania	4, 023	6. 2
Virginia	2, 058	3. 2
SOUTH ATLANTIC—Continued		
WEST VIRGINIA—Continued.		
Living in other States—Continued.		
New York	1, 048	1. 6
Maryland	949	1. 5
Michigan	943	1. 5
District of Columbia	751	1. 2
New Jersey	613	. 9
Illinois	568	. 9
Kentucky	456	. 7
North Carolina	426	. 7
Indiana	181	. 3
Florida	172	. 3
Alabama	166	. 3
California	144	. 2
Tennessee	141	. 2
Georgia	140	. 2
Missouri	120	. 2
All other	781	1. 2
NORTH CAROLINA, Negroes born in	1, 028, 538	100. 0
Living in North Carolina	808, 298	78. 6
Living in other States	220, 240	21. 4
Virginia	44, 354	4. 3
New York	33, 961	3. 3
Pennsylvania	31, 297	3. 0
New Jersey	19, 010	1. 8
Maryland	12, 616	1. 2
Ohio	9, 939	1. 0
West Virginia	8, 304	. 8
District of Columbia	8, 026	. 8
Florida	7, 936	. 8
South Carolina	6, 913	. 7
Georgia	5, 208	. 5
Michigan	4, 155	. 4
Tennessee	3, 492	. 3
Arkansas	3, 336	. 3
Massachusetts	3, 032	. 3
Illinois	2, 760	. 3
Connecticut	2, 527	. 2
Mississippi	2, 197	. 2
Texas	1, 631	. 2
Alabama	1, 444	. 1
All other	8, 102	. 8
SOUTH CAROLINA, Negroes born in	1, 095, 214	100. 0
Living in South Carolina	776, 058	70. 9
Living in other States	319, 156	29. 1
North Carolina	79, 368	7. 2
New York	41, 866	3. 8
Pennsylvania	41, 863	3. 8
Georgia	32, 695	3. 0
Florida	29, 086	2. 7
New Jersey	16, 450	1. 5
Ohio	11, 831	1. 1
District of Columbia	10, 166	. 9
Michigan	8, 921	. 8
Virginia	8, 711	. 8
Maryland	7, 593	. 7
Illinois	5, 533	. 5
Arkansas	3, 926	. 4
Tennessee	3, 403	. 3
West Virginia	2, 441	. 2
Alabama	2, 258	. 2
Connecticut	2, 194	. 2
Massachusetts	1, 860	. 2
All other	8, 991	. 8
GEORGIA, Negroes born in	1, 403, 856	100. 0
Living in Georgia	996, 411	71. 0
Living in other States	407, 445	29. 0
Florida	94, 663	6. 7
Ohio	48, 847	3. 5
Pennsylvania	38, 529	2. 7
Michigan	31, 054	2. 2
Alabama	28, 374	2. 0
Illinois	24, 902	1. 8
New York	23, 776	1. 7
New Jersey	22, 380	1. 6
Tennessee	21, 886	1. 6
North Carolina	13, 272	. 9
South Carolina	6, 924	. 5
Arkansas	4, 987	. 4
California	4, 963	. 4
Indiana	4, 350	. 3
Mississippi	3, 806	. 3
Connecticut	3, 757	. 3
Texas	3, 466	. 2
Kentucky	3, 390	. 2
District of Columbia	3, 383	. 2

TABLE 17.—NATIVE NEGRO POPULATION BORN IN EACH STATE, DISTRIBUTED ACCORDING TO SELECTED STATES OF RESIDENCE: 1930—Continued

[These figures relate only to Negroes born in continental United States with the State of birth reported]

STATE	Number	Per cent distribution
SOUTH ATLANTIC—Continued		
GEORGIA—Continued.		
Living in other States—Continued.		
West Virginia	2,905	0.2
Missouri	2,729	.2
Virginia	2,479	.2
Maryland	2,248	.2
Louisiana	2,060	.1
Massachusetts	2,030	.1
Oklahoma	1,868	.1
All other	4,417	.3
FLORIDA, Negroes born in	314,688	100.0
Living in Florida	259,635	82.5
Living in other States	55,053	17.5
Georgia	9,921	3.2
New York	9,598	3.1
Pennsylvania	7,866	2.5
New Jersey	5,011	1.6
Alabama	3,667	1.2
Michigan	3,553	1.1
Ohio	3,102	1.0
Illinois	1,888	.6
North Carolina	1,074	.3
Louisiana	805	.3
South Carolina	793	.3
Mississippi	716	.2
Maryland	682	.2
District of Columbia	626	.2
Virginia	593	.2
California	565	.2
Tennessee	557	.2
All other	4,036	1.3
EAST SOUTH CENTRAL		
KENTUCKY, Negroes born in	292,365	100.0
Living in Kentucky	185,051	63.3
Living in other States	107,314	36.7
Ohio	27,177	9.3
Indiana	25,317	8.7
Illinois	17,280	5.9
Michigan	6,627	2.3
Missouri	4,957	1.7
Tennessee	4,297	1.5
Pennsylvania	3,200	1.1
West Virginia	2,467	.8
Kansas	2,313	.8
New York	2,011	.7
California	1,601	.5
Oklahoma	957	.3
Arkansas	877	.3
Texas	782	.3
New Jersey	553	.2
Alabama	545	.2
Virginia	526	.2
Mississippi	513	.2
All other	5,314	1.8
TENNESSEE, Negroes born in	539,556	100.0
Living in Tennessee	363,704	67.4
Living in other States	175,852	32.6
Illinois	34,844	6.5
Ohio	19,222	3.6
Missouri	16,836	3.1
Kentucky	16,752	3.1
Arkansas	16,432	3.0
Indiana	13,728	2.5
Michigan	12,478	2.3
Mississippi	6,271	1.2
Alabama	4,282	.8
Pennsylvania	4,272	.8
Oklahoma	3,873	.7
Kansas	3,269	.6
New York	3,051	.6
West Virginia	2,794	.5
Texas	2,772	.5
California	2,618	.5
Georgia	1,514	.3
Virginia	1,507	.3
Florida	1,101	.2
Louisiana	1,047	.2
All other	7,189	1.3
ALABAMA, Negroes born in	1,133,771	100.0
Living in Alabama	883,289	77.9
Living in other States	250,482	22.1
Ohio	34,366	3.0
Mississippi	25,237	2.2
Illinois	24,958	2.2
Michigan	20,216	1.8
Florida	17,839	1.6
Georgia	17,587	1.6
Pennsylvania	16,560	1.5
EAST SOUTH CENTRAL—Continued		
ALABAMA—Continued.		
Living in other States—Continued.		
Tennessee	13,551	1.2
West Virginia	10,560	.9
Arkansas	9,142	.8
Kentucky	7,589	.7
Texas	6,322	.6
Indiana	6,205	.5
Missouri	5,966	.5
Louisiana	5,925	.5
New Jersey	5,043	.4
New York	5,023	.4
Oklahoma	4,903	.4
California	2,851	.3
Virginia	1,493	.1
Kansas	1,338	.1
All other	7,808	.7
MISSISSIPPI, Negroes born in	1,227,757	100.0
Living in Mississippi	938,911	76.5
Living in other States	288,846	23.5
Arkansas	57,229	4.7
Illinois	50,851	4.1
Tennessee	48,320	3.9
Missouri	31,363	2.6
Louisiana	30,515	2.5
Alabama	13,425	1.1
Michigan	9,869	.8
Ohio	7,588	.6
Indiana	7,428	.6
Oklahoma	5,550	.5
Texas	5,271	.4
California	3,237	.3
Kansas	2,580	.2
Pennsylvania	2,307	.2
New York	1,819	.1
Kentucky	1,761	.1
Florida	1,577	.1
All other	8,156	.7
WEST SOUTH CENTRAL		
ARKANSAS, Negroes born in	449,451	100.0
Living in Arkansas	340,182	75.7
Living in other States	109,269	24.3
Missouri	21,559	4.8
Illinois	16,425	3.7
Oklahoma	12,935	2.9
Louisiana	8,706	1.9
Texas	7,962	1.8
Tennessee	7,412	1.6
Mississippi	7,129	1.6
Michigan	5,931	1.3
Kansas	4,607	1.0
Ohio	3,377	.8
California	3,027	.7
Indiana	2,819	.6
Pennsylvania	797	.2
New York	766	.2
Nebraska	730	.2
Alabama	594	.1
Kentucky	587	.1
Wisconsin	559	.1
Colorado	500	.1
All other	2,847	.6
LOUISIANA, Negroes born in	882,024	100.0
Living in Louisiana	710,894	80.6
Living in other States	171,130	19.4
Texas	58,217	6.6
Arkansas	28,886	3.3
Illinois	19,867	2.3
Mississippi	18,099	2.1
California	8,599	1.0
Oklahoma	7,265	.8
Missouri	5,680	.6
Michigan	3,988	.5
New York	2,662	.3
Tennessee	2,393	.3
Ohio	2,096	.2
Kansas	1,703	.2
Indiana	1,630	.2
Alabama	1,485	.2
Florida	1,333	.2
Pennsylvania	1,093	.1
Arizona	1,029	.1
All other	5,105	.6
OKLAHOMA, Negroes born in	115,284	100.0
Living in Oklahoma	85,760	74.4
Living in other States	29,524	25.6
Kansas	5,119	4.4
Texas	4,727	4.1
WEST SOUTH CENTRAL—Continued		
OKLAHOMA—Continued.		
Living in other States—Continued.		
Missouri	3,468	3.0
California	3,221	2.8
Illinois	2,315	2.0
Arkansas	1,554	1.3
Michigan	1,451	1.3
Arizona	1,330	1.2
Ohio	739	.6
Nebraska	717	.6
Colorado	524	.5
Louisiana	447	.4
Indiana	436	.4
New York	349	.3
Iowa	335	.3
Pennsylvania	306	.3
All other	2,486	2.2
TEXAS, Negroes born in	864,210	100.0
Living in Texas	755,017	87.4
Living in other States	109,193	12.6
Oklahoma	40,642	4.7
California	14,314	1.7
Louisiana	9,257	1.1
Illinois	6,669	.8
Missouri	6,212	.7
Arkansas	5,166	.6
Kansas	4,190	.5
Michigan	2,914	.3
Arizona	2,895	.3
New York	2,053	.2
Ohio	1,667	.2
Colorado	1,473	.2
Pennsylvania	1,440	.2
Nebraska	1,353	.2
All other	8,948	1.0
MOUNTAIN		
MONTANA, Negroes born in	937	100.0
Living in Montana	299	31.9
Living in other States	638	68.1
Washington	87	9.3
California	83	8.9
New York	63	6.7
Illinois	46	4.9
Ohio	29	3.1
Pennsylvania	28	3.0
Minnesota	26	2.8
Missouri	23	2.5
Michigan	21	2.4
New Jersey	17	1.8
Kansas	16	1.7
Oregon	16	1.7
Virginia	16	1.7
All other	167	17.8
IDAHO, Negroes born in	72	100.0
Living in Idaho	110	29.6
Living in other States	262	70.4
California	33	8.9
Washington	31	8.3
New York	23	6.2
Illinois	22	5.9
Missouri	16	4.3
All other	137	36.8
WYOMING, Negroes born in	596	100.0
Living in Wyoming	178	29.9
Living in other States	418	70.1
Colorado	42	7.0
Nebraska	41	6.9
California	35	5.9
Missouri	31	5.2
Ohio	28	4.7
Illinois	25	4.2
Michigan	24	4.0
Kansas	19	3.2
Washington	16	2.7
New York	15	2.5
All other	142	23.8
COLORADO, Negroes born in	6,062	100.0
Living in Colorado	2,892	47.7
Living in other States	3,170	52.3
California	617	10.2
Illinois	355	5.9
Missouri	226	3.7
Kansas	211	3.5
Michigan	152	2.5
Texas	148	2.4
New York	128	2.1

TABLE 17.—NATIVE NEGRO POPULATION BORN IN EACH STATE, DISTRIBUTED ACCORDING TO SELECTED STATES OF RESIDENCE: 1930—Continued

[These figures relate only to Negroes born in continental United States with the State of birth reported]

STATE	Number	Per cent distribution
MOUNTAIN—Continued		
COLORADO—Continued.		
Living in other States—Continued.		
Oklahoma	119	2.0
Washington	117	1.9
Ohio	103	1.7
Pennsylvania	88	1.5
Arizona	78	1.3
Wyoming	78	1.3
Nebraska	72	1.2
Arkansas	57	.9
All other	621	10.2
NEW MEXICO, Negroes born in	1,293	100.0
Living in New Mexico	515	39.8
Living in other States	778	60.2
California	198	15.3
Arizona	89	6.9
Illinois	60	4.6
Colorado	53	4.1
Kansas	50	3.9
Texas	48	3.7
Missouri	30	2.3
Oklahoma	29	2.2
Michigan	23	1.8
Ohio	23	1.8
Washington	18	1.4
Pennsylvania	17	1.3
New York	15	1.2
All other	125	9.7
ARIZONA, Negroes born in	2,265	100.0
Living in Arizona	1,113	49.1
Living in other States	1,152	50.9
California	526	23.2
Texas	70	3.1
Illinois	54	2.4
Pennsylvania	53	2.3
New York	49	2.2
Ohio	41	1.8
Michigan	34	1.5
Missouri	34	1.5
Kansas	27	1.2
Oklahoma	25	1.1
District of Columbia	24	1.1
New Jersey	19	.8
New Mexico	18	.8
Washington	18	.8
Colorado	15	.7
All other	145	6.4
MOUNTAIN—Continued		
UTAH, Negroes born in	627	100.0
Living in Utah	250	39.9
Living in other States	377	60.1
California	100	15.9
Illinois	28	4.5
Idaho	23	3.7
Colorado	18	2.9
New York	18	2.9
Missouri	15	2.4
Alabama	14	2.2
Washington	14	2.2
Texas	12	1.9
All other	135	21.5
NEVADA, Negroes born in	175	100.0
Living in Nevada	47	26.9
Living in other States	128	73.1
California	74	42.3
Pennsylvania	7	4.0
All other	47	26.9
PACIFIC		
WASHINGTON, Negroes born in	2,998	100.0
Living in Washington	1,480	49.4
Living in other States	1,518	50.6
New York	264	8.8
California	250	8.3
Pennsylvania	186	6.2
New Jersey	145	4.8
Illinois	124	4.1
Ohio	52	1.7
Michigan	49	1.6
Oregon	45	1.5
Missouri	32	1.1
Maryland	30	1.0
Minnesota	25	.8
Virginia	25	.8
Indiana	20	.7
Arizona	18	.6
Texas	18	.6
Massachusetts	16	.5
District of Columbia	15	.5
Oklahoma	15	.5
All other	189	6.3
PACIFIC—Continued		
OREGON, Negroes born in	746	100.0
Living in Oregon	351	47.1
Living in other States	395	52.9
California	118	15.8
Washington	102	13.7
Illinois	19	2.5
New York	19	2.5
Michigan	15	2.0
Kansas	12	1.6
All other	110	14.7
CALIFORNIA, Negroes born in	19,481	100.0
Living in California	16,514	84.8
Living in other States	2,967	15.2
Illinois	336	1.7
New York	279	1.4
Texas	178	.9
Arizona	167	.9
Michigan	165	.8
Washington	159	.8
Ohio	151	.8
Pennsylvania	136	.7
Missouri	132	.7
Oklahoma	112	.6
New Jersey	75	.4
Kansas	74	.4
Louisiana	73	.3
Florida	62	.3
Arkansas	61	.4
Oregon	58	.3
District of Columbia	55	.3
Tennessee	55	.3
Georgia	54	.3
Alabama	50	.3
All other	535	2.7

TABLE 18.—NATIVE NEGRO POPULATION BY STATE OF RESIDENCE AND STATE OF BIRTH: 1930

[The figures relate only to Negroes born in continental United States with the State of birth reported]

STATE	Number	Per cent distribution
NEW ENGLAND		
MAINE, Negroes living in	871	100.0
Born in Maine	659	75.7
Born in other States	212	24.3
Massachusetts	51	5.9
Virginia	41	4.7
North Carolina	19	2.2
Pennsylvania	14	1.6
All other States	87	10.0
NEW HAMPSHIRE, Negroes living in	583	100.0
Born in New Hampshire	223	38.3
Born in other States	360	61.7
Virginia	68	11.7
Massachusetts	64	11.0
North Carolina	26	4.5
Vermont	26	4.5
New York	17	2.9
South Carolina	16	2.7
All other States	143	24.5
VERMONT, Negroes living in	544	100.0
Born in Vermont	347	63.8
Born in other States	197	36.2
New York	35	6.4
Massachusetts	33	6.1
Virginia	19	3.5
New Hampshire	17	3.1
Maryland	10	1.8
North Carolina	10	1.8
South Carolina	10	1.8
All other States	63	11.6
MASSACHUSETTS, Negroes living in	43,021	100.0
Born in Massachusetts	24,358	56.6
Born in other States	18,663	43.4
Virginia	4,607	10.7
North Carolina	3,032	7.0
Georgia	2,030	4.7
South Carolina	1,860	4.3
New York	851	2.0
Connecticut	732	1.7
Maryland	700	1.6
Pennsylvania	646	1.5
Rhode Island	545	1.3
District of Columbia	504	1.2
Florida	445	1.0
Alabama	378	.9
New Jersey	362	.8
Maine	211	.5
All other States	1,760	4.1
RHODE ISLAND, Negroes living in	8,798	100.0
Born in Rhode Island	5,242	59.6
Born in other States	3,556	40.4
Virginia	1,141	13.0
Massachusetts	538	6.1
Maryland	301	3.4
North Carolina	267	3.0
Connecticut	214	2.4
New York	195	2.2
South Carolina	176	2.0
Georgia	167	1.9
Pennsylvania	123	1.4
District of Columbia	110	1.3
New Jersey	82	.9
Florida	60	.7
All other States	182	2.1
CONNECTICUT, Negroes living in	27,753	100.0
Born in Connecticut	10,503	37.8
Born in other States	17,250	62.2
Georgia	3,757	13.5
Virginia	3,347	12.1
North Carolina	2,527	9.1
South Carolina	2,194	7.9
New York	1,113	4.0
Massachusetts	687	2.5
Florida	484	1.7
Alabama	433	1.6
Pennsylvania	428	1.5
Maryland	417	1.5
New Jersey	381	1.4
District of Columbia	261	.9
Rhode Island	183	.7
Tennessee	165	.6
Kentucky	127	.5
Ohio	109	.4
All other States	637	2.3
MIDDLE ATLANTIC		
NEW YORK, Negroes living in	336,240	100.0
Born in New York	108,351	32.2
Born in other States	227,889	67.8
Virginia	58,919	17.5
South Carolina	41,866	12.5
North Carolina	33,961	10.1
Georgia	23,776	7.1
Florida	9,598	2.9
Pennsylvania	8,310	2.5
Maryland	8,133	2.4
New Jersey	6,354	1.9
Alabama	5,023	1.5
District of Columbia	3,929	1.2
Tennessee	3,051	.9
Massachusetts	2,830	.8
Louisiana	2,662	.8
Ohio	2,545	.8
Texas	2,053	.6
Kentucky	2,011	.6
Connecticut	1,932	.6
Mississippi	1,819	.5
Illinois	1,402	.4
West Virginia	1,018	.3
Missouri	1,010	.3
All other States	5,657	1.7
NEW JERSEY, Negroes living in	203,536	100.0
Born in New Jersey	64,352	31.6
Born in other States	139,184	68.4
Virginia	36,635	18.0
Georgia	22,380	11.0
North Carolina	19,010	9.3
South Carolina	16,450	8.1
Maryland	9,473	4.7
Pennsylvania	8,704	4.3
New York	5,149	2.5
Alabama	5,043	2.5
Florida	5,011	2.5
Delaware	2,529	1.2
District of Columbia	1,741	.9
Tennessee	870	.4
Ohio	682	.3
West Virginia	613	.3
Massachusetts	569	.3
Kentucky	553	.3
All other States	3,772	1.9
PENNSYLVANIA, Negroes living in	426,631	100.0
Born in Pennsylvania	146,374	34.3
Born in other States	280,257	65.7
Virginia	76,139	17.8
South Carolina	41,863	9.8
Georgia	38,529	9.0
North Carolina	31,297	7.3
Maryland	25,470	6.0
Alabama	16,560	3.9
Florida	7,866	1.8
Delaware	5,866	1.4
New Jersey	4,940	1.2
Tennessee	4,272	1.0
West Virginia	4,023	.9
District of Columbia	3,776	.9
Ohio	3,520	.8
Kentucky	3,200	.8
New York	2,376	.6
Mississippi	2,307	.5
Texas	1,440	.3
Louisiana	1,093	.3
All other States	5,720	1.3
EAST NORTH CENTRAL		
OHIO, Negroes living in	306,196	100.0
Born in Ohio	99,479	32.5
Born in other States	206,717	67.5
Georgia	48,847	16.0
Alabama	34,366	11.2
Kentucky	27,177	8.9
Tennessee	19,222	6.3
Virginia	13,892	4.5
South Carolina	11,831	3.9
North Carolina	9,939	3.2
Mississippi	7,588	2.5
Pennsylvania	4,891	1.6
West Virginia	4,384	1.4
Arkansas	3,377	1.1
Indiana	3,184	1.0
Florida	3,102	1.0
Illinois	2,483	.8
Louisiana	2,096	.7
Missouri	1,973	.6
Texas	1,667	.5
Michigan	1,197	.4
Maryland	1,184	.4
All other States	4,317	1.4
EAST NORTH CENTRAL—Continued		
INDIANA, Negroes living in	110,837	100.0
Born in Indiana	35,727	32.2
Born in other States	75,110	67.8
Kentucky	25,317	22.8
Tennessee	13,728	12.4
Mississippi	7,428	6.7
Alabama	6,205	5.6
Georgia	4,350	3.9
Illinois	2,962	2.7
Arkansas	2,819	2.5
Ohio	2,296	2.1
Louisiana	1,630	1.5
Missouri	1,481	1.3
North Carolina	1,110	1.0
Virginia	971	.9
Texas	854	.8
South Carolina	669	.6
Michigan	559	.5
Pennsylvania	503	.5
Oklahoma	436	.4
Kansas	366	.3
Florida	323	.3
All other States	1,103	1.0
ILLINOIS, Negroes living in	325,470	100.0
Born in Illinois	76,069	23.4
Born in other States	249,401	76.6
Mississippi	50,851	15.6
Tennessee	34,844	10.7
Alabama	24,958	7.7
Georgia	24,902	7.7
Louisiana	19,867	6.1
Kentucky	17,280	5.3
Arkansas	16,425	5.0
Missouri	14,885	4.6
Texas	6,669	2.0
South Carolina	5,533	1.7
Indiana	4,885	1.5
Ohio	4,631	1.4
Virginia	3,726	1.1
North Carolina	2,760	.8
Oklahoma	2,315	.7
Kansas	2,246	.7
Florida	1,888	.6
Pennsylvania	1,753	.5
Iowa	1,694	.5
Michigan	1,360	.4
All other States	5,929	1.8
MICHIGAN, Negroes living in	165,436	100.0
Born in Michigan	29,121	17.6
Born in other States	136,315	82.4
Georgia	31,054	18.8
Alabama	20,216	12.2
Tennessee	12,478	7.5
Mississippi	9,869	6.0
South Carolina	8,921	5.4
Kentucky	6,627	4.0
Arkansas	5,931	3.6
Ohio	5,050	3.1
North Carolina	4,155	2.5
Louisiana	3,988	2.4
Virginia	3,711	2.2
Florida	3,553	2.1
Missouri	3,414	2.1
Illinois	3,027	1.8
Texas	2,914	1.8
Indiana	2,473	1.5
Pennsylvania	1,881	1.1
Oklahoma	1,451	.9
Kansas	1,014	.6
All other States	4,588	2.8
WISCONSIN, Negroes living in	10,606	100.0
Born in Wisconsin	1,732	16.3
Born in other States	8,874	83.7
Georgia	1,270	12.0
Mississippi	1,236	11.7
Tennessee	810	7.6
Illinois	724	6.8
Alabama	569	5.4
Arkansas	559	5.3
Kentucky	487	4.6
Missouri	469	4.4
Louisiana	402	3.8
Iowa	300	2.8
Texas	286	2.7
Ohio	225	2.1
Kansas	191	1.8
Virginia	190	1.8
Indiana	189	1.8
Oklahoma	157	1.5
South Carolina	145	1.4
North Carolina	109	1.0
Michigan	105	1.0
All other States	451	4.3

TABLE 18.—NATIVE NEGRO POPULATION BY STATE OF RESIDENCE AND STATE OF BIRTH: 1930—Continued.

[These figures relate only to Negroes born in continental United States with the State of birth reported]

STATE	Number	Per cent distribution
WEST NORTH CENTRAL		
MINNESOTA, Negroes living in	9,218	100.0
Born in Minnesota	2,384	25.9
Born in other States	6,834	74.1
Missouri	1,105	12.0
Kentucky	465	5.0
Kansas	457	5.0
Tennessee	439	4.8
Iowa	432	4.7
Illinois	392	4.3
Texas	392	4.3
Mississippi	331	3.6
Alabama	314	3.4
Arkansas	277	3.0
Georgia	255	2.8
Louisiana	224	2.4
Oklahoma	214	2.3
Virginia	200	2.2
Ohio	184	2.0
Indiana	169	1.8
Nebraska	130	1.4
Wisconsin	107	1.2
All other States	747	8.1
IOWA, Negroes living in	17,184	100.0
Born in Iowa	6,599	38.4
Born in other States	10,585	61.6
Missouri	3,500	20.4
Mississippi	820	4.8
Illinois	683	4.0
Kansas	648	3.8
Virginia	638	3.7
Alabama	568	3.3
Tennessee	522	3.0
Arkansas	433	2.5
Texas	413	2.4
Kentucky	392	2.3
Oklahoma	335	1.9
Louisiana	304	1.8
Georgia	220	1.3
Nebraska	189	1.1
North Carolina	134	.8
All other States	786	4.6
MISSOURI, Negroes living in	222,194	100.0
Born in Missouri	106,728	48.0
Born in other States	115,466	52.0
Mississippi	31,363	14.1
Arkansas	21,559	9.7
Tennessee	16,836	7.6
Texas	6,212	2.8
Alabama	5,966	2.7
Louisiana	5,680	2.6
Kansas	5,215	2.3
Kentucky	4,957	2.2
Illinois	4,667	2.1
Oklahoma	3,468	1.6
Georgia	2,729	1.2
Virginia	977	.4
North Carolina	848	.4
South Carolina	791	.4
Ohio	688	.3
Indiana	632	.3
Iowa	527	.2
Florida	337	.2
All other States	2,014	.9
NORTH DAKOTA, Negroes living in	361	100.0
Born in North Dakota	94	26.0
Born in other States	267	74.0
Missouri	39	10.8
Minnesota	23	6.4
Iowa	17	4.7
Tennessee	17	4.7
Kentucky	15	4.2
Texas	15	4.2
Ohio	14	3.9
Illinois	13	3.6
Louisiana	13	3.6
Kansas	11	3.0
Mississippi	11	3.0
All other States	79	21.9
SOUTH DAKOTA, Negroes living in	633	100.0
Born in South Dakota	175	27.6
Born in other States	458	72.4
Missouri	104	16.4
Iowa	47	7.4
Kansas	29	4.6
Nebraska	28	4.4
Kentucky	26	4.1
Illinois	24	3.8
Minnesota	23	3.6
Mississippi	21	3.3
WEST NORTH CENTRAL—Continued		
SOUTH DAKOTA—Continued.		
Born in other States—Continued.		
Tennessee	21	3.3
Georgia	20	3.2
Texas	16	2.5
Michigan	14	2.2
Alabama	12	1.9
Louisiana	10	1.6
Virginia	10	1.6
All other States	53	8.4
NEBRASKA, Negroes living in	13,474	100.0
Born in Nebraska	3,123	23.2
Born in other States	10,351	76.8
Missouri	1,762	13.1
Texas	1,353	10.0
Kansas	1,128	8.4
Alabama	840	6.2
Arkansas	730	5.4
Oklahoma	717	5.3
Mississippi	615	4.6
Tennessee	486	3.6
Louisiana	441	3.3
Iowa	342	2.5
Kentucky	325	2.4
Illinois	263	2.0
Florida	257	1.9
Georgia	203	1.5
Virginia	131	1.0
Ohio	101	.7
All other States	657	4.9
KANSAS, Negroes living in	65,581	100.0
Born in Kansas	27,665	42.2
Born in other States	37,916	57.8
Missouri	7,927	12.1
Oklahoma	5,119	7.8
Arkansas	4,607	7.0
Texas	4,190	6.4
Tennessee	3,269	5.0
Mississippi	2,580	3.9
Kentucky	2,313	3.5
Louisiana	1,703	2.6
Alabama	1,338	2.0
Georgia	826	1.3
Illinois	596	.9
South Carolina	423	.6
Virginia	415	.6
North Carolina	332	.5
Ohio	308	.5
Indiana	233	.4
Nebraska	232	.4
Iowa	227	.3
Colorado	211	.3
All other States	1,067	1.6
SOUTH ATLANTIC		
DELAWARE, Negroes living in	32,482	100.0
Born in Delaware	21,311	65.6
Born in other States	11,171	34.4
Maryland	5,340	16.4
Virginia	2,152	6.6
Pennsylvania	1,064	3.3
North Carolina	620	1.9
Georgia	430	1.3
South Carolina	329	1.0
New Jersey	282	.9
Florida	206	.6
Alabama	146	.4
District of Columbia	113	.3
New York	93	.3
All other States	396	1.2
MARYLAND, Negroes living in	273,870	100.0
Born in Maryland	201,244	73.5
Born in other States	72,626	26.5
Virginia	37,090	13.5
North Carolina	12,616	4.6
South Carolina	7,593	2.8
District of Columbia	3,562	1.3
Pennsylvania	2,638	1.0
Georgia	2,248	.8
West Virginia	949	.3
Delaware	906	.3
New Jersey	683	.2
Florida	682	.2
New York	626	.2
Alabama	508	.2
Tennessee	316	.1
Ohio	312	.1
Kentucky	254	.1
Texas	219	.1
Mississippi	213	.1
All other States	1,211	.4
SOUTH ATLANTIC—Continued		
DISTRICT OF COLUMBIA, Negroes living in	130,450	100.0
Born in District of Columbia	52,513	40.3
Born in other States	77,937	59.7
Virginia	30,236	23.2
Maryland	16,346	12.5
South Carolina	10,166	7.8
North Carolina	8,026	6.2
Georgia	3,383	2.6
Pennsylvania	1,633	1.3
Alabama	874	.7
New York	756	.6
West Virginia	751	.6
Mississippi	639	.5
Florida	626	.5
Tennessee	613	.5
New Jersey	513	.4
Texas	498	.4
Ohio	439	.3
Kentucky	386	.3
Louisiana	312	.2
Massachusetts	254	.2
Illinois	233	.2
All other States	1,253	1.0
VIRGINIA, Negroes living in	649,234	100.0
Born in Virginia	576,588	88.8
Born in other States	72,646	11.2
North Carolina	44,354	6.8
South Carolina	8,711	1.3
Georgia	2,479	.4
District of Columbia	2,347	.4
Maryland	2,311	.4
Pennsylvania	2,234	.3
West Virginia	2,058	.3
Tennessee	1,507	.2
Alabama	1,493	.2
New York	1,062	.2
New Jersey	697	.1
Florida	593	.1
Kentucky	526	.1
Ohio	456	.1
All other States	1,818	.3
WEST VIRGINIA, Negroes living in	114,558	100.0
Born in West Virginia	46,834	40.9
Born in other States	67,724	59.1
Virginia	31,401	27.4
Alabama	10,560	9.2
North Carolina	8,304	7.2
Georgia	2,905	2.5
Tennessee	2,794	2.4
Kentucky	2,467	2.2
South Carolina	2,441	2.1
Ohio	1,822	1.6
Pennsylvania	1,369	1.2
Mississippi	796	.7
Maryland	548	.5
Florida	334	.3
District of Columbia	222	.2
Louisiana	211	.2
Illinois	199	.2
Missouri	168	.1
All other States	1,183	1.0
NORTH CAROLINA, Negroes living in	917,739	100.0
Born in North Carolina	808,298	88.1
Born in other States	109,441	11.9
South Carolina	79,368	8.6
Georgia	13,272	1.4
Virginia	9,578	1.0
Alabama	1,206	.1
Florida	1,074	.1
Tennessee	821	.1
Pennsylvania	670	.1
New York	473	.1
All other States	2,979	.3
SOUTH CAROLINA, Negroes living in	793,308	100.0
Born in South Carolina	776,058	97.8
Born in other States	17,250	2.2
Georgia	6,924	.9
North Carolina	6,913	.9
Florida	793	.1
Virginia	617	.1
Alabama	435	.1
All other States	1,568	.2

TABLE 18.—NATIVE NEGRO POPULATION BY STATE OF RESIDENCE AND STATE OF BIRTH: 1930—Continued

[These figures relate only to Negroes born in continental United States with the State of birth reported]

STATE	Number	Per cent distribution
SOUTH ATLANTIC—Continued		
GEORGIA, Negroes living in	1,069,784	100.0
Born in Goergia	995,411	93.1
Born in other States	73,373	6.9
South Carolina	32,695	3.1
Alabama	17,587	1.6
Florida	9,921	.9
North Carolina	5,208	.5
Virginia	1,682	.2
Tennessee	1,514	.1
Mississippi	812	.1
All other States	3,954	.4
FLORIDA, Negroes living in	419,558	100.0
Born in Florida	259,635	61.9
Born in other States	159,923	38.1
Georgia	94,663	22.6
South Carolina	29,086	6.9
Alabama	17,839	4.3
North Carolina	7,936	1.9
Virginia	2,367	.6
Mississippi	1,577	.4
Louisiana	1,333	.3
Tennessee	1,101	.3
Texas	506	.1
Pennsylvania	481	.1
Kentucky	390	.1
Ohio	354	.1
New York	352	.1
Maryland	239	.1
All other States	1,699	.4
EAST SOUTH CENTRAL		
KENTUCKY, Negroes living in	225,376	100.0
Born in Kentucky	185,051	82.1
Born in other States	40,325	17.9
Tennessee	16,752	7.4
Alabama	7,589	3.4
Georgia	3,390	1.5
Virginia	1,965	.9
Mississippi	1,761	.8
Indiana	1,503	.7
Ohio	1,180	.5
North Carolina	1,005	.4
South Carolina	916	.4
Illinois	808	.4
Arkansas	587	.3
Missouri	479	.2
West Virginia	456	.2
Louisiana	442	.2
Florida	321	.1
Texas	258	.1
Pennsylvania	199	.1
Michigan	123	.1
All other States	591	.3
TENNESSEE, Negroes living in	475,473	100.0
Born in Tennessee	363,704	76.5
Born in other States	111,769	23.5
Mississippi	48,320	10.2
Georgia	21,886	4.6
Alabama	13,551	2.9
Arkansas	7,412	1.6
Kentucky	4,297	.9
North Carolina	3,492	.7
South Carolina	3,403	.7
Louisiana	2,393	.5
Virginia	1,985	.4
Illinois	835	.2
Missouri	798	.2
Texas	678	.1
Ohio	572	.1
Florida	557	.1
Indiana	244	.1
Oklahoma	242	.1
All other States	1,104	.2
ALABAMA, Negroes living in	943,406	100.0
Born in Alabama	883,289	93.6
Born in other States	60,117	6.4
Georgia	28,374	3.0
Mississippi	13,425	1.4
Tennessee	4,282	.5
Florida	3,667	.4
South Carolina	2,258	.2
Louisiana	1,485	.2
North Carolina	1,444	.2
Virginia	1,123	.1
Arkansas	594	.1
Kentucky	545	.1
All other States	2,920	.3

STATE	Number	Per cent distribution
EAST SOUTH CENTRAL—Continued		
MISSISSIPPI, Negroes living in	1,008,048	100.0
Born in Mississippi	938,911	93.1
Born in other States	69,137	6.9
Alabama	25,237	2.5
Louisiana	18,099	1.8
Arkansas	7,129	.7
Tennessee	6,271	.6
Georgia	3,806	.4
North Carolina	2,197	.2
South Carolina	1,177	.1
Virginia	920	.1
Texas	880	.1
Florida	716	.1
Missouri	588	.1
Illinois	545	.1
Kentucky	513	.1
All other States	1,059	.1
WEST SOUTH CENTRAL		
ARKANSAS, Negroes living in	476,496	100.0
Born in Arkansas	340,182	71.4
Born in other States	136,314	28.6
Mississippi	57,229	12.0
Louisiana	28,886	6.1
Tennessee	16,432	3.4
Alabama	9,142	1.9
Texas	5,166	1.1
Georgia	4,987	1.0
South Carolina	3,926	.8
North Carolina	3,336	.7
Missouri	1,934	.4
Oklahoma	1,554	.3
Kentucky	877	.2
Illinois	726	.2
Virginia	704	.1
All other States	1,415	.3
LOUISIANA, Negroes living in	774,596	100.0
Born in Louisiana	710,894	91.8
Born in other States	63,702	8.2
Mississippi	30,515	3.9
Texas	9,257	1.2
Arkansas	8,706	1.1
Alabama	5,925	.8
Georgia	2,060	.3
North Carolina	1,117	.1
Tennessee	1,047	.1
Virginia	815	.1
Florida	805	.1
South Carolina	725	.1
Oklahoma	447	.1
Missouri	417	.1
Kentucky	401	.1
All other States	1,465	.2
OKLAHOMA, Negroes living in	171,250	100.0
Born in Oklahoma	85,760	50.1
Born in other States	85,490	49.9
Texas	40,642	23.7
Arkansas	12,935	7.6
Louisiana	7,265	4.2
Mississippi	5,550	3.2
Alabama	4,903	2.9
Tennessee	3,873	2.3
Kansas	2,162	1.3
Georgia	1,868	1.1
Missouri	1,590	.9
Kentucky	957	.6
North Carolina	859	.5
South Carolina	821	.5
Virginia	401	.2
Illinois	346	.2
Ohio	178	.1
Florida	133	.1
Indiana	125	.1
Colorado	119	.1
California	112	.1
Nebraska	106	.1
All other States	545	.3
TEXAS, Negroes living in	852,333	100.0
Born in Texas	755,017	88.6
Born in other States	97,316	11.4
Louisiana	58,217	6.8
Arkansas	7,962	.9
Alabama	6,322	.7
Mississippi	5,271	.6
Oklahoma	4,727	.6
Georgia	3,466	.4
Tennessee	2,772	.3

STATE	Number	Per cent distribution
WEST SOUTH CENTRAL—Continued		
TEXAS—Continued.		
Born in other States—Continued.		
North Carolina	1,631	0.2
South Carolina	1,138	.1
Missouri	1,120	.1
Virginia	957	.1
Kentucky	782	.1
Florida	483	.1
All other States	2,468	.3
MOUNTAIN		
MONTANA, Negroes living in	1,218	100.0
Born in Montana	299	24.5
Born in other States	919	75.5
Missouri	137	11.2
Texas	71	5.8
Tennessee	68	5.6
Kentucky	59	4.8
Kansas	55	4.5
Illinois	47	3.9
Virginia	47	3.9
Ohio	36	3.0
Arkansas	33	2.7
Mississippi	29	2.4
Alabama	28	2.3
Oklahoma	27	2.2
All other States	282	23.2
IDAHO, Negroes living in	643	100.0
Born in Idaho	110	17.1
Born in other States	533	82.9
Texas	84	13.1
Missouri	51	7.9
Kansas	39	6.1
Tennessee	37	5.8
Louisiana	29	4.5
Oklahoma	27	4.2
Utah	23	3.6
Arkansas	22	3.4
Alabama	20	3.1
Colorado	17	2.6
All other States	184	28.6
WYOMING, Negroes living in	1,232	100.0
Born in Wyoming	178	14.4
Born in other States	1,054	85.6
Missouri	175	14.2
Texas	93	7.5
Kansas	89	7.2
Colorado	78	6.3
Kentucky	59	4.8
Alabama	56	4.5
Tennessee	55	4.5
Oklahoma	50	4.1
Virginia	37	3.0
Ohio	35	2.8
Louisiana	34	2.8
Mississippi	34	2.8
Arkansas	32	2.6
Illinois	31	2.5
Georgia	27	2.2
Nebraska	27	2.2
All other States	142	11.5
COLORADO, Negroes living in	11,673	100.0
Born in Colorado	2,892	24.8
Born in other States	8,781	75.2
Texas	1,473	12.6
Missouri	1,146	9.8
Kansas	875	7.5
Tennessee	644	5.5
Oklahoma	524	4.5
Alabama	516	4.4
Arkansas	500	4.3
Kentucky	450	3.9
Mississippi	434	3.7
Louisiana	386	3.3
Virginia	267	2.3
Georgia	253	2.2
Illinois	212	1.8
Ohio	126	1.1
All other States	975	8.4
NEW MEXICO, Negroes living in	2,792	100.0
Born in New Mexico	515	18.4
Born in other States	2,277	81.6
Texas	851	30.5
Oklahoma	277	9.9
Louisiana	171	6.1

TABLE 18.—NATIVE NEGRO POPULATION BY STATE OF RESIDENCE AND STATE OF BIRTH: 1930—Continued

[These figures relate only to Negroes born in continental United States with the State of birth reported]

STATE	Number	Per-cent distri-bution
MOUNTAIN—Continued		
NEW MEXICO—Continued.		
Born in other States—Continued.		
Arkansas	141	5.1
Alabama	107	3.8
Kansas	97	3.5
Mississippi	89	3.2
Missouri	74	2.7
Tennessee	67	2.4
Kentucky	62	2.2
All other States	341	12.2
ARIZONA, Negroes living in	10,582	100.0
Born in Arizona	1,113	10.5
Born in other States	9,469	89.5
Texas	2,895	27.4
Oklahoma	1,330	12.6
Louisiana	1,029	9.7
Alabama	422	4.0
Arkansas	402	3.8
Mississippi	382	3.6
Georgia	353	3.3
Tennessee	330	3.1
Kansas	284	2.7
Missouri	262	2.5
Kentucky	227	2.1
California	167	1.6
Virginia	166	1.6
South Carolina	148	1.4
North Carolina	133	1.3
Illinois	100	0.9
All other States	839	7.9
UTAH, Negroes living in	1,078	100.0
Born in Utah	250	23.2
Born in other States	828	76.8
Texas	112	10.4
Missouri	78	7.2
Kansas	62	5.8
Oklahoma	53	4.9
Arkansas	49	4.5
Colorado	46	4.3
Louisiana	45	4.2
Tennessee	44	4.1
Kentucky	37	3.4
Alabama	36	3.3
Mississippi	32	3.0
Illinois	25	2.3
Georgia	19	1.8
Virginia	18	1.7
All other States	172	16.0

STATE	Number	Per-cent distri-bution
MOUNTAIN—Continued		
NEVADA, Negroes living in	495	100.0
Born in Nevada	47	9.5
Born in other States	448	90.5
Texas	72	14.5
Louisiana	36	7.3
Kansas	32	6.5
Missouri	30	6.1
California	21	4.2
Georgia	21	4.2
Alabama	18	3.6
Tennessee	18	3.6
Virginia	18	3.6
Kentucky	16	3.2
Mississippi	14	2.8
Colorado	13	2.6
Illinois	13	2.6
Oklahoma	13	2.6
Maryland	11	2.2
Idaho	10	2.6
All other States	92	18.6
PACIFIC		
WASHINGTON, Negroes living in	6,457	100.0
Born in Washington	1,480	22.9
Born in other States	4,977	77.1
Missouri	508	7.9
Texas	459	7.1
Kansas	281	4.4
Tennessee	281	4.4
Kentucky	250	3.9
Virginia	229	3.5
Illinois	224	3.5
Louisiana	218	3.4
Alabama	197	3.1
Mississippi	191	3.0
Ohio	174	2.7
Georgia	170	2.6
California	159	2.5
North Carolina	151	2.3
Arkansas	147	2.3
Oklahoma	131	2.0
Colorado	117	1.8
Oregon	102	1.6
Indiana	100	1.5
All other States	888	13.8

STATE	Number	Per-cent distri-bu-tion
PACIFIC—Continued		
OREGON, Negroes living in	2,130	100.0
Born in Oregon	351	16.5
Born in other States	1,779	83.5
Texas	268	12.6
Missouri	193	9.1
Louisiana	143	6.7
Kansas	111	5.2
Alabama	76	3.6
Tennessee	76	3.6
Arkansas	75	3.5
Oklahoma	74	3.5
Mississippi	63	3.0
California	58	2.7
Georgia	57	2.7
Kentucky	51	2.4
Virginia	51	2.4
Illinois	49	2.3
Washington	45	2.1
Ohio	43	2.0
South Carolina	34	1.6
North Carolina	30	1.4
Colorado	28	1.3
Pennsylvania	28	1.3
All other States	226	10.6
CALIFORNIA, Negroes living in	78,051	100.0
Born in California	16,514	21.2
Born in other States	61,537	78.8
Texas	14,314	18.3
Louisiana	8,599	11.0
Georgia	4,963	6.4
Mississippi	3,237	4.1
Oklahoma	3,221	4.1
Missouri	3,034	3.9
Arkansas	3,027	3.9
Alabama	2,851	3.7
Tennessee	2,618	3.4
Kansas	2,069	2.7
Kentucky	1,601	2.1
Virginia	1,309	1.7
Illinois	1,196	1.5
South Carolina	1,020	1.3
North Carolina	1,007	1.3
Ohio	980	1.3
Colorado	617	.8
Pennsylvania	598	.8
Florida	565	.7
Arizona	526	.7
All other States	4,185	5.4

CHAPTER V.—URBANIZATION

Definition of terms used.—Urban population, as the term is used here, is, in general, that residing in cities or other incorporated places having 2,500 or more inhabitants, the remainder being classified as rural. In 1930, in addition, the population of townships or other political subdivisions (not incorporated) which had a population of 10,000 or more, and a population density of 1,000 or more per square mile, was regarded as urban.

The rural population has been divided into two groups, rural-farm and rural-nonfarm population. This classification has been made on the basis of whether or not the family was living on a farm. The rural-nonfarm population includes in the main persons living in small towns, villages, etc., both incorporated and unincorporated. The rural-nonfarm population includes also a considerable number of families living in wholly rural areas, but not on farms.

Urban and rural Negro population.—The Negro population is, in the main, rural. But in 1930, of the total Negro population, only 56.3 percent was rural, as compared with 66 percent in 1920, and 72.7 percent in 1910. These data indicate the increasing movement of Negroes from the rural areas to the urban centers, and if the trend continues it is probable that by 1940, the Negro, like the white population, will be predominantly urban. In 1930 the Negro population constituted 12.4 percent of the rural population of the United States, as compared with 10.4 percent in 1920. The Negroes in urban population formed only 7.5 percent of the total in 1930, as compared with 6.6 percent in 1920.

The general trend of the Negro movement has been from rural areas and small urban centers to cities of 100,000 or more inhabitants. Between 1920 and 1930, the Negro population of urban territory increased from 3,559,473 to 5,193,913, while that of rural areas decreased from 6,903,658 to 6,697,230. The Negro population of cities, with 100,000 or more inhabitants, increased approximately 1,200,000 during that same period.

In both decades, 1920 to 1930, and 1910 to 1920, the urban Negro population increased at a greater rate than the white population. The percentage of increase for the Negroes for the period 1920 to 1930 was 45.9 and for 1910 to 1920 was 32.6, as compared with 24.1 and 28.5, respectively, for the white population.

Rural and urban Negro population by sections and divisions.—A large part of the Negro population in the North and West was urban, while that of the South was rural. In 1930, the Negro population was 88.3 percent urban in the North and 82.5 percent in the West, as compared with 31.7 percent in the South.

There has been a steady increase from 1910 to 1930 in the percentage of the Negro urban population in the South Atlantic, the East South Central, and the West South Central divisions, in fact, in the South as a whole.

Although the total Negro population in the United States in 1930 was 43.7 percent urban, yet in only 15 States (1 in the North, 13 in the South, and 1 in the West) was the Negro population less than 50 percent urban, while the white population was 53 percent urban. There were 28 States (9 in the North, 13 in the South, and 6 in the West) with a white population that was less than 50 percent urban.

Urban, rural-farm, and rural-nonfarm Negro population.—In 1930, of the total Negro population in the United States, 39.4 percent was rural-farm, that is, living on farms or in incorporated places of less than 2,500 inhabitants and in territory outside of incorporated places. The Negroes in incorporated places of less than 2,500 inhabitants and in the territory outside of these places, but not living on farms, constituted 17 percent of the total Negro population in 1930.

In the South, the Negro population was approximately one-half rural-farm while in the North and West 2.7 and 5.1 percent, respectively, of the total Negro population was rural-farm. In the South 19.1 percent of the Negro population was rural-nonfarm in 1930.

Negro population in the largest cities.—There were 2,881,790 Negroes in the 93 cities having a total population of 100,000 or more in 1930. Seven cities, New York, Chicago, Philadelphia, Baltimore, Washington, New Orleans, and Detroit had more than 100,000 Negroes. Over one-third of the Negro population in the North was concentrated in the 4 northern cities having 100,000 or more Negroes. More than two-thirds of the Negro population in the North was in the cities with total population of 100,000 or more inhabitants. The Negro population represented more than 38 percent of the total in Birmingham and Memphis; over 33 percent in Atlanta, Jacksonville, and Norfolk; more than 25 percent in Washington, New Orleans, Richmond, Nashville, and Chattanooga; and more than 20 percent in Houston, Miami, and Tampa. In 1930, there were 80 cities in the United States with a Negro population of 10,000 or more.

In almost every southern city, the proportion of Negroes in the total population has been decreasing, while in the northern cities the proportion has been increasing.

TABLE 1.—NEGRO AND WHITE POPULATION, URBAN (BY CLASSES OF CITIES AND OTHER URBAN PLACES) AND RURAL, FOR THE UNITED STATES: 1930

AREA	POPULATION									
	All classes [1]		Negro		White [2]					
					Total		Native		Foreign born	
	1930	1920	1930	1920	1930	1920	1930	1920	1930	1920
	NUMBER									
United States	122,775,046	105,710,620	11,891,143	10,463,131	108,864,207	94,820,915	95,497,800	81,108,161	13,366,407	13,712,754
Urban territory [3]	68,954,823	54,304,603	5,193,913	3,559,473	62,836,605	50,620,084	52,109,746	40,263,101	10,726,859	10,356,983
Places of 2,500 to 10,000	10,614,746	9,591,747	726,574	667,848	9,692,504	8,903,499	8,831,361	7,823,402	861,143	1,080,097
Places of 10,000 to 25,000	9,097,200	6,942,742	627,851	480,778	8,383,915	6,450,414	7,363,200	5,465,029	1,020,715	985,385
Places of 25,000 to 100,000	12,917,141	10,340,788	957,698	726,271	11,781,664	9,594,234	10,075,800	7,847,635	1,705,864	1,746,599
Places of 100,000 to 500,000	15,497,194	11,060,025	1,533,613	958,378	13,719,573	10,073,615	11,769,442	8,172,626	1,950,131	1,900,989
Places of 500,000 and over	20,828,542	16,369,301	1,348,177	726,198	19,258,949	15,598,322	14,069,943	10,954,409	5,189,006	4,643,913
Rural territory	53,820,223	51,406,017	6,697,230	6,903,658	46,027,602	44,200,831	43,388,054	40,845,060	2,639,548	3,355,771
	PERCENT DISTRIBUTION BY AREA									
United States	100.0	100.0	100.0	100.0	100.0	100.0	100.0	100.0	100.0	100.0
Urban territory	56.2	51.4	43.7	34.0	57.7	53.4	54.6	49.6	80.3	75.5
Places of 2,500 to 10,000	8.6	9.1	6.1	6.4	8.9	9.4	9.2	9.6	6.4	7.9
Places of 10,000 to 25,000	7.4	6.6	5.3	4.6	7.7	6.8	7.7	6.7	7.6	7.2
Places of 25,000 to 100,000	10.5	9.8	8.1	6.9	10.8	10.1	10.6	9.7	12.8	12.7
Places of 100,000 to 500,000	12.6	10.5	12.9	9.2	12.6	10.6	12.3	10.1	14.6	13.9
Places of 500,000 and over	17.0	15.5	11.3	6.9	17.7	16.5	14.7	13.5	38.8	33.9
Rural territory	43.8	48.6	56.3	66.0	42.3	46.6	45.4	50.4	19.7	24.5
	PERCENT DISTRIBUTION BY RACIAL CLASS									
United States	100.0	100.0	9.7	9.9	88.7	89.7	77.8	76.7	10.9	13.0
Urban territory	100.0	100.0	7.5	6.6	91.1	93.2	75.6	74.1	15.6	19.1
Places of 2,500 to 10,000	100.0	100.0	6.8	7.0	91.3	92.8	83.2	81.6	8.1	11.3
Places of 10,000 to 25,000	100.0	100.0	6.9	6.9	92.2	92.9	80.9	78.7	11.2	14.2
Places of 25,000 to 100,000	100.0	100.0	7.4	7.0	91.2	92.8	78.0	75.9	13.2	16.9
Places of 100,000 to 500,000	100.0	100.0	9.9	8.7	88.5	91.1	75.9	73.9	12.6	17.2
Places of 500,000 and over	100.0	100.0	6.5	4.4	92.5	95.3	67.6	66.9	24.9	28.4
Rural territory	100.0	100.0	12.4	13.4	85.5	86.0	80.6	79.5	4.9	6.5

[1] Includes "other races."
[2] The white population in 1920 included 700,541 persons (estimated) who would have been classified as Mexicans in 1930.
[3] The number of places in urban territory is given as follows:

	1930	1920		1930	1920
Total	3,165	2,787	Places of 25,000 to 100,000	283	219
Places of 2,500 to 10,000	2,183	2,041	Places of 100,000 to 500,000	80	56
Places of 10,000 to 25,000	606	459	Places of 500,000 and over	13	12

Table 2.—Racial Composition of the Urban and Rural Population for the United States: 1930, 1920, and 1910

CLASS AND YEAR	POPULATION		PERCENT OF TOTAL POPULATION		PERCENT DISTRIBUTION	
	Urban	Rural	Urban	Rural	Urban	Rural
All Classes: [1]						
1930	68, 954, 823	53, 820, 223	56. 2	43. 8	100. 0	100. 0
1920	54, 304, 603	51, 406, 017	51. 4	48. 6	100. 0	100. 0
1910	42, 166, 120	49, 806, 146	45. 8	54. 2	100. 0	100. 0
Negro:						
1930	5, 193, 913	6, 697, 230	43. 7	56. 3	7. 5	12. 4
1920	3, 559, 473	6, 903, 658	34. 0	66. 0	6. 6	13. 4
1910	2, 684, 797	7, 142, 966	27. 3	72. 7	6. 4	14. 3
White:						
1930	62, 836, 605	46, 027, 602	57. 7	42. 3	91. 1	85. 5
1920 [2]	50, 620, 084	44, 200, 831	53. 4	46. 6	93. 2	86. 0
1910 [2]	39, 379, 294	42, 352, 663	48. 2	51. 8	93. 4	85. 0
Native:						
1930	52, 109, 746	43, 388, 054	54. 6	45. 4	75. 6	80. 6
1920	40, 263, 101	40, 845, 060	49. 6	50. 4	74. 1	79. 5
1910	29, 846, 561	38, 539, 851	43. 6	56. 4	70. 8	77. 4
Foreign born:						
1930	10, 726, 859	2, 639, 548	80. 3	19. 7	15. 6	4. 9
1920	10, 356, 983	3, 355, 771	75. 5	24. 5	19. 1	6. 5
1910	9, 532, 733	3, 812, 812	71. 4	28. 6	22. 6	7. 7

[1] Includes "Other races."
[2] The white population in 1920 and 1910 included 700,541 and 367,510 persons (estimated), respectively, who would have been classified as Mexicans in 1930.

Table 3.—Increase in Urban and Rural Population for the United States: 1910 to 1930

RACIAL CLASS AND DECADE	NUMBER		PERCENT INCREASE OR DECREASE—	
	Urban	Rural	Urban	Rural
All Classes:				
1920–30	14, 650, 220	2, 414, 206	27. 0	4. 7
1910–20	12, 138, 483	1, 599, 871	28. 8	3. 2
Negro:				
1920–30	1, 634, 440	−206, 428	45. 9	−3. 0
1910–20	874, 676	−239, 308	32. 6	−3. 4
White:[1]				
1920–30	12, 216, 521	1, 826, 771	24. 1	4. 1
1910–20	11, 240, 790	1, 848, 168	28. 5	4. 4
Native:				
1920–30	11, 846, 645	2, 542, 994	29. 4	6. 2
1910–20	10, 416, 540	2, 305, 209	34. 9	6. 0
Foreign born:				
1920–30	369, 876	−716, 223	3. 6	−21. 3
1910–20	824, 250	−457, 041	8. 6	−12. 0

[1] The white population in 1920 and 1910 included 700,541 and 367,510 persons (estimated), respectively, who would have been classified as Mexicans in 1930.

Table 4.—Percent, Urban and Rural, in the Negro Population, by Sections and Southern Divisions: 1930, 1920, and 1910

SECTION AND DIVISION	PERCENT URBAN			PERCENT RURAL		
	1930	**1920**	**1910**	**1930**	**1920**	**1910**
United States	**43. 7**	**34. 0**	**27. 3**	**56. 3**	**66. 0**	**72. 7**
The South	31. 7	25. 3	21. 2	68. 3	74. 7	78. 8
South Atlantic	33. 1	26. 5	22. 1	66. 9	73. 5	77. 9
East South Central	28. 6	22. 6	19. 2	71. 4	77. 4	80. 8
West South Central	32. 6	25. 9	22. 0	67. 4	74. 1	78. 0
The North	88. 3	84. 9	76. 9	11. 7	15. 1	23. 1
The West	82. 5	74. 0	78. 6	17. 5	26. 0	21. 4

Table 5.—PERCENT DISTRIBUTION OF NEGRO AND WHITE POPULATION, URBAN AND RURAL, AND NEGRO PERCENTAGE IN THE URBAN AND RURAL POPULATION, BY SECTIONS AND SOUTHERN DIVISIONS: 1930 AND 1920

SECTION AND DIVISION	PERCENT DISTRIBUTION										PERCENT NEGRO IN TOTAL POPULATION	
	Total population		Negro population		White population [1]							
					Total		Native		Foreign-born			
	1930	**1920**	**1930**	**1920**	**1930**	**1920**	**1930**	**1920**	**1930**	**1920**	**1930**	**1920**
URBAN												
United States	**100. 0**	**100. 0**	**100. 0**	**100. 0**	**100. 0**	**100. 0**	**100. 0**	**100. 0**	**100. 0**	**100. 0**	**7. 5**	**6. 6**
The South	18. 7	17. 1	57. 1	63. 2	15. 3	13. 9	17. 7	16. 3	3. 4	4. 7	23. 0	24. 2
South Atlantic	8. 3	8. 0	28. 2	32. 2	6. 7	6. 3	7. 7	7. 4	2. 1	2. 1	25. 7	26. 4
East South Central	4. 0	3. 7	14. 6	16. 1	3. 2	2. 8	3. 8	3. 4	. 4	. 5	27. 3	28. 6
West South Central	6. 4	5. 5	14. 3	15. 0	5. 3	4. 8	6. 2	5. 5	. 9	2. 1	16. 8	18. 0
The North	71. 1	74. 2	41. 0	35. 1	74. 5	77. 1	71. 8	74. 6	87. 6	86. 9	4. 3	3. 1
The West	10. 1	8. 6	1. 9	1. 6	10. 3	9. 0	10. 5	9. 1	9. 0	8. 4	1. 4	1. 2
RURAL												
United States	**100. 0**	**100. 0**	**100. 0**	**100. 0**	**100. 0**	**100. 0**	**100. 0**	**100. 0**	**100. 0**	**100. 0**	**12. 4**	**13. 4**
The South	46. 4	46. 3	95. 5	96. 5	39. 3	38. 7	41. 3	41. 0	6. 4	10. 6	25. 6	28. 0
South Atlantic	18. 8	18. 8	44. 2	46. 1	15. 5	14. 6	16. 2	15. 6	3. 1	2. 8	29. 3	33. 0
East South Central	13. 2	13. 4	28. 4	28. 3	11. 3	11. 2	12. 0	12. 0	. 6	. 7	26. 7	28. 3
West South Central	14. 4	14. 1	23. 0	22. 1	12. 5	12. 9	13. 1	13. 3	2. 7	7. 1	19. 8	21. 0
The North	44. 5	45. 5	4. 2	3. 2	51. 2	52. 2	49. 8	50. 7	75. 4	70. 9	1. 2	1. 0
The West	9. 1	8. 2	. 3	. 3	9. 5	9. 1	8. 9	8. 3	18. 2	18. 6	. 4	. 5

[1] Percent distribution of the white population per 1920 based upon figures which included Mexicans.

TABLE 6.—URBAN AND RURAL POPULATION, BY RACIAL CLASSES, BY SECTIONS, AND SOUTHERN DIVISIONS: 1930

RACIAL CLASS	United States	THE SOUTH: Total	THE SOUTH: South Atlantic division	THE SOUTH: East South Central division	THE SOUTH: West South Central division	The North	The West
URBAN POPULATION							
All classes [1]	68, 954, 823	12, 904, 248	5, 698, 122	2, 778, 687	4, 427, 439	49, 057, 772	6, 992, 803
Negro	5, 193, 913	2, 966, 325	1, 462, 904	759, 166	744, 255	2, 128, 329	99, 259
White	62, 836, 605	9, 594, 145	4, 231, 820	2. 018, 882	3, 343, 443	46, 800, 609	6, 441, 851
Native	52, 109, 746	9, 231, 423	4, 009, 090	1, 977, 070	3, 245, 263	37, 403, 036	5, 475, 287
Foreign born	10, 726, 859	362, 722	222, 730	41, 812	98, 180	9, 397, 573	966, 564
TOTAL RURAL POPULATION							
All classes [1]	53, 820, 223	24, 953, 385	10, 095, 467	7, 108, 527	7, 749, 391	23, 963, 419	4, 903, 419
Negro	6, 697, 230	6, 395, 252	2, 958, 484	1, 899, 072	1, 537, 696	280, 890	21, 088
White	46, 027, 602	18, 079, 734	7, 117, 464	5, 205, 732	5, 756, 538	23, 587, 758	4, 360, 110
Native	43, 388, 054	17, 910, 281	7, 035, 916	5, 189, 879	5, 684, 486	21, 598, 778	3, 878, 995
Foreign-born	2, 639, 548	169, 453	81, 548	15, 853	72, 052	1, 988, 980	481, 115
RURAL-FARM POPULATION [2]							
All classes [1]	30, 157, 513	16, 271, 330	5, 878, 956	5, 084, 435	5, 307, 939	11, 661, 452	2, 224, 731
Negro	4, 680, 523	4, 608, 786	1, 940, 501	1, 481, 742	1, 186, 543	65, 601	6, 136
White	24, 884, 834	11, 343, 125	3, 921, 849	3, 599. 723	3, 821, 553	11, 556, 489	1, 985, 220
Native	23, 800, 747	11. 274, 220	3, 905. 523	3. 593, 474	3, 775, 223	10, 762, 898	1, 763, 629
Foreign born	1, 084, 087	68, 905	16, 326	6, 249	46, 330	793, 591	221, 591
RURAL-NONFARM POPULATION [3]							
All classes [1]	23, 662. 710	8, 682, 055	4, 216, 511	2, 024, 092	2, 441. 452	12, 301, 967	2, 678, 688
Negro	2, 016, 707	1, 786, 466	1, 017, 983	417, 330	351, 153	215, 289	14, 952
White	21, 142, 768	6, 736, 609	3, 195, 615	1, 606, 009	1. 934, 985	12, 031, 269	2, 374, 890
Native	19, 587, 307	6, 636, 061	3, 130, 393	1, 596. 405	1, 909, 263	10, 835, 880	2. 115, 366
Foreign born	1, 555, 461	100, 548	65, 222	9, 604	25, 722	1, 195, 389	259, 524

RACIAL CLASS	United States	THE SOUTH: Total	THE SOUTH: South Atlantic division	THE SOUTH: East South Central division	THE SOUTH: West South Central division	The North	The West
PERCENT URBAN							
All classes [1]	56. 2	34. 1	36. 1	28. 1	36. 4	67. 2	58. 8
Negro	43. 7	31. 7	33. 1	28. 6	32. 6	88. 3	82. 5
White	57. 7	34. 7	37. 3	27. 9	36. 7	66. 5	59. 6
Native	54. 6	34. 0	36. 3	27. 6	36. 3	63. 4	58. 5
Foreign born	80. 3	68. 2	73. 2	72. 5	57. 7	82. 5	66. 8
PERCENT RURAL							
All classes [1]	43. 8	65. 9	63. 9	71. 9	63. 6	32. 8	41. 2
Negro	56. 3	68. 3	66. 9	71. 4	67. 4	11. 7	17. 5
White	42. 3	65. 3	62. 7	72. 1	63. 3	33. 5	40. 4
Native	45. 4	66. 0	63. 7	72. 4	63. 7	36. 6	41. 5
Foreign-born	19. 7	31. 8	26. 8	27. 5	42. 3	17. 5	33. 2
PERCENT RURAL-FARM							
All classes [1]	24. 6	43. 0	37. 2	51. 4	43. 6	16. 0	18. 7
Negro	39. 4	49. 2	43. 9	55. 7	52. 0	2. 7	5. 1
White	22. 9	41. 0	34. 6	49. 8	42. 0	16. 4	18. 4
Native	24. 9	41. 5	35. 4	50. 1	42. 3	18. 2	18. 9
Foreign born	8. 1	12. 9	5. 4	10. 8	27. 2	7. 0	15. 3
PERCENT RURAL-NONFARM							
All classes [1]	19. 3	22. 9	26. 7	20. 5	20. 0	16. 8	22. 5
Negro	17. 0	19. 1	23. 0	15. 7	15. 4	8. 9	12. 4
White	19. 4	24. 3	28. 2	22. 2	21. 3	17. 1	22. 0
Native	20. 5	24. 4	28. 3	22. 3	21. 4	18. 4	22. 6
Foreign born	11. 6	18. 9	21. 4	16. 7	15. 1	10. 5	17. 9

[1] Includes "Other races."
[2] The rural farm population as shown for 1930 comprises all persons living on farms in rural areas, that is in incorporated places of less than 2,500 inhabitants, and in territory outside of incorporated places.
[3] The rural-nonfarm population, sometimes termed the "village" population, includes, in general, all persons living outside cities or other incorporated places having 2,500 inhabitants or more who do not live on farms.

TABLE 7.—NEGRO AND WHITE POPULATION, URBAN AND RURAL, BY SECTIONS, DIVISIONS, AND STATES: 1930

SECTION, DIVISION, AND STATE	URBAN		RURAL		PERCENT URBAN	
	Negro	White	Negro	White	Negro	White
United States	**5, 193, 913**	**62, 836, 605**	**3, 697, 230**	**46, 027, 602**	**43. 7**	**57. 7**
The North	**2, 128, 329**	**46, 800, 609**	**280, 890**	**23, 587, 758**	**88. 3**	**66. 5**
The South	**2, 966, 325**	**9, 594, 145**	**6, 395, 252**	**18, 079, 734**	**31. 7**	**34. 7**
The West	**99, 259**	**6, 441, 851**	**21, 088**	**4, 360, 110**	**82. 5**	**59. 6**
GEOGRAPHIC DIVISIONS:						
New England	81, 443	6, 225, 108	12, 643	1, 840, 005	86. 6	77. 2
Middle Atlantic	939, 064	19, 426, 948	113, 835	5, 745, 156	89. 2	77. 2
East North Central	848, 627	15, 880, 308	81, 823	8, 397, 355	91. 2	65. 4
West North Central	259, 195	5, 268, 245	72, 589	7, 605, 242	78. 1	40. 9
South Atlantic	1, 462, 904	4, 231, 820	2, 958, 484	7, 117, 464	33. 1	37. 3
East South Central	759, 166	2, 018, 882	1, 899, 072	5, 205, 732	28. 6	27. 9
West South Central	744, 255	3, 343, 443	1, 537, 696	5, 756, 538	32. 6	36. 7
Mountain	21, 032	1, 353, 283	9, 193	1, 950, 303	69. 6	41. 0
Pacific	78, 227	5, 088, 568	11, 895	2, 409, 807	86. 8	67. 9
NEW ENGLAND:						
Maine	703	320, 296	393	474, 887	64. 1	40. 3
New Hampshire	594	272, 376	196	191, 974	75. 2	58. 7
Vermont	213	118, 510	355	240, 455	37. 5	33. 0
Massachusetts	46, 323	3, 781, 458	6, 042	411, 468	88. 5	90. 2
Rhode Island	9, 079	625, 856	834	51, 160	91. 6	92. 4
Connecticut	24, 531	1, 106, 612	4, 823	470, 061	83. 6	70. 2
MIDDLE ATLANTIC:						
New York	390, 499	10, 112, 383	22, 315	2, 037, 910	94. 6	83. 2
New Jersey	174, 985	3, 161, 384	33, 843	667, 825	83. 8	82. 6
Pennsylvania	373, 580	6, 153, 181	57, 677	3, 039, 421	86. 6	66. 9
EAST NORTH CENTRAL:						
Ohio	271, 972	4, 229, 930	37, 332	2, 101, 206	87. 9	66. 8
Indiana	103, 042	1, 682, 994	8, 940	1, 433, 142	92. 0	54. 0
Illinois	304, 036	5, 300, 343	24, 936	1, 966, 018	92. 4	72. 9
Michigan	159, 704	3, 126, 763	9, 749	1, 523, 408	94. 2	67. 2
Wisconsin	9, 873	1, 540, 278	866	1, 373, 581	91. 9	52. 9
WEST NORTH CENTRAL:						
Minnesota	9, 110	1, 245, 518	335	1, 293, 455	96. 5	49. 1
Iowa	15, 185	960, 517	2, 195	1, 487, 865	87. 4	39. 2
Missouri	169, 954	1, 683, 348	53, 886	1, 715, 539	75. 9	49. 5
North Dakota	216	112, 443	161	558, 800	57. 3	16. 8
South Dakota	337	129, 992	309	539, 461	52. 2	19. 4
WEST NORTH CENTRAL—Continued.						
Nebraska	13, 112	469, 679	640	884, 023	95. 3	34. 7
Kansas	51, 281	666, 748	15, 063	1, 126, 099	77. 3	37. 2
SOUTH ATLANTIC:						
Delaware	15, 037	108, 043	17, 565	97, 651	46. 1	52. 5
Maryland	159, 654	814, 348	116, 725	539, 822	57. 8	60. 1
District of Columbia	132, 068	353, 914	-	-	100. 0	100. 0
Virginia	213, 401	571, 656	436, 764	1, 198, 749	32. 8	32. 3
West Virginia	31, 224	460, 165	83, 669	1, 153, 769	27. 2	28. 5
North Carolina	246, 237	563, 478	672, 410	1, 671, 470	26. 8	25. 2
South Carolina	138, 354	232, 641	655, 327	711, 399	17. 4	24. 6
Georgia	316, 637	578, 550	754, 488	1, 258, 424	29. 6	31. 5
Florida	210, 292	549, 025	221, 536	486, 180	48. 7	53. 0
EAST SOUTH CENTRAL:						
Kentucky	116, 561	682, 356	109, 479	1, 706, 008	51. 6	28. 6
Tennessee	240, 168	656, 248	237, 478	1, 482, 371	50. 3	30. 7
Alabama	268, 450	475, 660	676, 384	1, 225, 115	28. 4	28. 0
Mississippi	133, 987	204, 618	875, 731	792, 238	13. 3	20. 5
WEST SOUTH CENTRAL:						
Arkansas	89, 162	293, 459	389, 301	1, 081, 447	18. 6	21. 3
Louisiana	257, 463	574, 249	518, 863	743, 911	33. 2	43. 6
Oklahoma	67, 801	736, 429	104, 397	1, 386, 995	39. 4	34. 7
Texas	329, 829	1, 739, 306	525, 135	2, 544, 185	38. 6	40. 6
MOUNTAIN:						
Montana	1, 027	178, 408	229	338, 919	81. 8	34. 5
Idaho	502	128, 002	166	309, 560	75. 1	29. 3
Wyoming	859	66, 610	391	147, 457	68. 7	31. 1
Colorado	10, 471	489, 947	1, 357	471, 170	88. 5	51. 0
New Mexico	1, 718	93, 171	1, 132	238, 584	60. 3	28. 1
Arizona	5, 147	102, 011	5, 602	162, 367	47. 9	38. 6
Utah	944	262, 427	164	233, 528	85. 2	52. 9
Nevada	364	32, 707	152	48, 718	70. 5	40. 2
PACIFIC:						
Washington	5, 818	862, 576	1, 022	658, 523	85. 1	56. 7
Oregon	1, 890	482, 374	344	454, 655	84. 6	51. 5
California	70, 519	3, 743, 618	10, 529	1, 296, 629	87. 0	74. 3

TABLE 8.—NEGRO POPULATION, URBAN AND RURAL, BY SECTIONS, DIVISIONS, AND STATES: 1930, 1920, AND 1910

SECTION, DIVISION, AND STATE	URBAN			RURAL			PERCENT						NEGRO PERCENTAGE OF TOTAL					
							•Urban			Rural			Urban			Rural		
	1930	1920	1910	1930	1920	1910	1930	1920	1910	1930	1920	1910	1930	1920	1910	1930	1920	1920
United States	5, 193, 913	3, 559, 473	2, 684, 797	6, 697, 230	6, 903, 658	7, 142, 966	43. 7	34. 0	27. 3	56. 3	66. 0	72. 7	7. 5	6. 6	6. 4	12. 4	13. 4	14. 3
The North	2, 128, 329	1, 250, 312	790, 534	280, 890	221, 997	237, 140	88. 3	84. 9	76. 9	11. 7	15. 1	23. 1	4. 3	3. 1	2. 5	1. 2	1. 0	1. 0
The South	2, 966, 325	2, 250, 969	1, 854, 455	6, 395, 252	6, 661, 262	6, 849, 972	31. 7	25. 3	21. 2	68. 2	74. 7	78. 8	23. 0	24. 2	28. 0	25. 6	28. 0	30. 3
The West	99, 259	58, 192	39, 608	21, 088	20, 399	10, 854	82. 5	74. 0	78. 6	17. 5	26. 0	21. 4	1. 4	1. 2	1. 2	. 4	. 5	. 3
GEOGRAPHIC DIVISIONS:																		
New England	81, 443	71, 416	56, 445	12, 643	7, 635	9, 861	86. 6	90. 3	85. 1	13. 4	9. 7	14. 9	1. 3	1. 2	1. 1	0. 7	0. 5	0. 6
Middle Atlantic	939, 064	517, 432	339, 246	113, 835	82, 751	78, 624	89. 2	86. 2	81. 2	10. 8	13. 8	18. 8	4. 6	3. 1	2. 5	1. 9	1. 5	1. 4
East North Central	848, 627	448, 873	230, 542	81, 823	65, 681	70, 294	91. 2	87. 2	76. 6	8. 8	12. 8	23. 4	5. 1	3. 4	2. 4	1. 0	. 8	. 8
West North Central	259, 195	212, 591	164, 301	72, 589	65, 930	78, 361	78. 1	76. 3	67. 7	21. 9	23. 7	32. 3	4. 7	4. 5	4. 2	. 9	. 8	1. 0
South Atlantic	1, 462, 904	1, 144, 371	909, 520	2, 958, 484	3, 180, 749	3, 202, 968	33. 1	26. 5	22. 1	66. 9	73. 5	77. 9	25. 7	26. 4	29. 4	29. 3	33. 0	35. 2
East South Central	759, 166	571, 316	509, 097	1, 899, 072	1, 952, 216	2, 143, 416	28. 6	22. 6	19. 2	71. 4	77. 4	80. 8	27. 3	28. 6	32. 3	26. 7	28. 3	31. 4
West South Central	744, 255	535, 282	435, 838	1, 537, 696	1, 528, 297	1, 548, 588	32. 6	25. 9	22. 0	67. 4	74. 1	78. 0	16. 8	18. 0	22. 3	19. 8	21. 0	22. 7
Mountain	21, 032	16, 678	15, 446	9, 193	14, 123	6, 021	69. 6	54. 1	72. 0	30. 4	45. 9	28. 0	1. 4	1. 4	1. 6	. 4	. 7	. 4
Pacific	78, 227	41, 514	24, 362	11, 895	6, 276	4, 833	86. 8	86. 9	83. 4	13. 2	13. 1	16. 6	1. 4	1. 2	1. 0	. 4	. 3	. 3
NEW ENGLAND:																		
Maine	703	766	792	393	544	571	64. 1	58. 5	58. 1	35. 9	41. 5	41. 9	0. 2	0. 3	0. 3	0. 1	0. 1	0. 1
New Hampshire	594	441	356	196	180	208	75. 2	71. 0	63. 1	24. 8	29. 0	36. 9	. 2	. 2	. 1	. 1	. 1	. 1
Vermont	213	220	326	355	352	1, 295	37. 5	38. 5	20. 1	62. 5	61. 5	79. 9	. 2	. 2	. 3	. 1	. 1	. 5
Massachusetts	46, 323	43, 624	35, 243	6, 042	1, 842	2, 812	88. 5	95. 9	92. 6	11. 5	4. 1	7. 4	1. 2	1. 2	1. 1	1. 4	. 9	1. 2
Rhode Island	9, 079	9, 710	9, 055	834	326	474	91. 6	96. 8	95. 0	8. 4	3. 2	5. 0	1. 4	1. 6	1. 7	1. 6	2. 1	2. 6
Connecticut	24, 531	16, 655	10, 673	4, 823	4, 391	4, 501	83. 6	79. 1	70. 3	16. 4	20. 9	29. 7	2. 2	1. 8	1. 5	1. 0	1. 0	1. 2
MIDDLE ATLANTIC:																		
New York	390, 499	185, 212	117, 486	22, 315	13, 271	16, 705	94. 6	93. 3	87. 6	5. 4	6. 7	12. 4	3. 7	2. 2	1. 6	1. 1	. 7	. 9
New Jersey	174, 985	92, 328	65, 427	33, 843	24, 804	24, 333	83. 8	78. 8	72. 9	16. 2	21. 2	27. 1	5. 2	3. 7	3. 4	4. 8	3. 6	3. 9
Pennsylvania	373, 580	239, 892	156, 333	57, 677	44, 676	37, 586	86. 6	84. 3	80. 6	13. 4	15. 7	19. 4	5. 7	4. 3	3. 4	1. 9	1. 4	1. 2
EAST NORTH CENTRAL:																		
Ohio	271, 972	155, 975	82, 282	37, 332	30, 212	29, 170	87. 9	83. 8	73. 8	12. 1	16. 2	26. 2	6. 0	4. 2	3. 1	1. 7	1. 5	1. 4
Indiana	103, 042	71, 813	48, 425	8, 940	8, 997	11, 895	92. 0	88. 9	80. 3	8. 0	11. 1	19. 7	5. 7	4. 8	4. 2	. 6	. 6	. 8
Illinois	304, 036	161, 728	85, 538	24, 936	20, 546	23, 511	92. 4	88. 7	78. 4	7. 6	11. 3	21. 6	5. 4	3. 7	2. 5	1. 2	1. 0	1. 1
Michigan	159, 704	55, 006	12, 156	9, 749	5, 076	4, 959	94. 2	91. 6	71. 0	5. 8	8. 4	29. 0	4. 8	2. 5	. 9	. 6	. 4	. 3
Wisconsin	9, 873	4, 351	2, 141	866	850	759	91. 9	83. 7	73. 8	8. 1	16. 3	26. 2	. 6	. 3	. 2	. 1	. 1	. 1
WEST NORTH CENTRAL:																		
Minnesota	9, 110	8, 250	6, 518	335	559	566	96. 5	93. 7	92. 0	3. 5	6. 3	8. 0	. 7	. 8	. 8	(1)	(1)	(1)
Iowa	15, 185	15, 345	9, 786	2, 195	3, 660	5, 187	87. 4	80. 7	65. 4	12. 6	19. 3	34. 6	1. 6	1. 8	1. 4	. 1	. 2	. 3
Missouri	169, 954	134, 167	104, 461	53, 886	44, 074	52, 990	75. 9	75. 3	66. 3	24. 1	24. 7	33. 7	9. 1	8. 5	7. 5	3. 0	2. 4	2. 8
North Dakota	216	272	306	161	195	311	57. 3	58. 2	49. 6	42. 7	41. 8	50. 4	. 2	. 3	. 5	(1)	(1)	. 1
South Dakota	337	340	412	309	492	405	52. 2	40. 9	50. 4	47. 8	59. 1	49. 6	. 3	. 3	. 5	. 1	. 1	. 1
Nebraska	13, 112	12, 121	6, 621	640	1, 121	1, 068	95. 3	91. 5	86. 1	4. 7	8. 5	13. 9	2. 7	3. 0	2. 1	. 1	. 1	. 1
Kansas	51, 281	42, 096	36, 196	15, 063	15, 829	17, 834	77. 3	72. 7	67. 0	22. 7	27. 3	33. 0	7. 0	6. 8	7. 3	1. 3	1. 4	1. 5
SOUTH ATLANTIC:																		
Delaware	15, 037	12, 992	11, 157	17, 565	17, 343	20, 024	46. 1	42. 8	35. 8	53. 9	57. 2	64. 2	12. 2	10. 8	11. 5	15. 2	17. 0	19. 0
Maryland	159, 654	124, 509	99, 230	116, 725	119, 970	133, 020	57. 8	50. 9	42. 7	42. 2	49. 1	57. 3	16. 4	14. 3	15. 1	17. 8	20. 7	20. 9
District of Columbia	132, 068	109, 966	94, 446	------	------	------	100. 0	100. 0	100. 0	------	------	------	27. 1	25. 1	28. 5	------	------	------
Virginia	213, 401	209, 134	158, 218	436, 764	480, 883	512, 878	32. 8	30. 3	23. 6	67. 2	69. 7	76. 4	27. 2	31. 0	33. 2	26. 7	29. 4	32. 4
West Virginia	31, 224	22, 484	15, 380	83, 669	63, 861	48, 793	27. 2	26. 0	24. 0	72. 8	74. 0	76. 0	6. 4	6. 1	6. 7	6. 8	5. 8	4. 9
North Carolina	246, 237	155, 165	115, 975	672, 410	608, 242	581, 868	26. 8	20. 3	16. 6	73. 2	79. 7	83. 4	30. 4	31. 6	36. 4	28. 5	29. 4	30. 8
South Carolina	138, 354	116, 489	101, 702	655, 327	748, 230	734, 141	17. 4	13. 5	12. 2	82. 6	86. 5	87. 8	37. 3	39. 6	45. 2	47. 9	53. 8	56. 9
Georgia	316, 637	273, 036	224, 826	754, 488	933, 329	952, 161	29. 6	22. 6	19. 1	70. 4	77. 4	80. 9	35. 4	37. 5	41. 7	37. 5	34. 1	46. 0
Florida	210, 292	120, 596	88, 586	221, 536	208, 891	220, 083	48. 7	36. 6	28. 7	51. 3	63. 4	71. 3	27. 7	33. 9	40. 4	31. 3	34. 1	41. 2
EAST SOUTH CENTRAL:																		
Kentucky	116, 561	105, 393	106, 631	109. 479	130, 545	155, 025	51. 6	44. 7	40. 8	48. 4	55. 3	59. 2	14. 6	16. 6	19. 2	6. 0	7. 3	8. 9
Tennessee	240, 168	170, 464	150, 506	237, 478	281, 294	322, 582	50. 3	37. 7	31. 8	49. 7	62. 3	68. 2	26. 8	27. 9	34. 1	13. 8	16. 3	18. 5
Alabama	268, 450	196, 833	156, 603	676, 384	703, 819	751, 679	28. 4	21. 9	17. 2	71. 6	78. 1	82. 8	36. 1	38. 6	42. 3	35. 6	38. 3	42. 5
Mississippi	133, 987	98, 626	95, 357	875, 731	836, 558	914, 130	13. 3	10. 5	9. 4	86. 7	89. 5	90. 6	39. 5	41. 1	46. 0	52. 4	54. 0	57. 5
WEST SOUTH CENTRAL:																		
Arkansas	89, 162	73, 592	59, 147	389, 301	398, 628	383, 744	18. 6	15. 6	13. 4	81. 4	84. 4	86. 6	23. 3	25. 3	29. 2	26. 5	27. 3	28. 0
Louisiana	257, 463	190, 413	160, 845	518, 863	509, 844	553, 029	33. 2	27. 2	22. 5	66. 8	72. 8	77. 5	30. 9	30. 3	32. 4	40. 9	43. 6	47. 7
Oklahoma	67, 801	47, 904	36, 982	104, 397	101, 504	100, 630	39. 4	32. 1	26. 9	60. 6	67. 9	73. 1	8. 3	8. 9	11. 6	6. 6	6. 8	7. 5
Texas	329, 829	223, 373	178, 864	525, 135	518, 321	511, 185	38. 6	30. 1	25. 9	61. 4	69. 9	74. 1	13. 8	14. 8	19. 1	15. 3	16. 5	17. 3
MOUNTAIN:																		
Montana	1, 027	1, 270	1, 455	229	388	379	81. 8	76. 6	79. 3	18. 2	23. 4	20. 7	. 6	. 7	1. 1	. 1	. 1	. 2
Idaho	502	645	426	166	275	225	75. 1	70. 1	65. 4	24. 9	29. 9	34. 6	. 4	. 5	. 6	. 1	. 1	. 1
Wyoming	859	833	1, 041	391	542	1, 194	68. 7	60. 6	46. 6	31. 3	39. 4	53. 4	1. 2	1. 5	2. 4	. 3	. 4	1. 2
Colorado	10, 471	9, 364	9, 359	1, 357	1, 954	2, 094	88. 5	82. 7	81. 7	11. 5	17. 3	18. 3	2. 0	2. 1	2. 3	. 3	. 4	. 5
New Mexico	1, 718	861	795	1, 132	4, 872	833	60. 3	15. 0	48. 8	39. 9	85. 0	51. 2	1. 6	1. 3	1. 7	. 4	1. 6	. 3
Arizona	5, 147	2, 631	1, 310	5, 602	5, 374	699	47. 9	32. 9	65. 2	52. 1	67. 1	34. 8	3. 4	2. 2	2. 1	2. 0	2. 5	. 5
Utah	944	1, 006	959	164	440	185	85. 2	69. 6	83. 8	14. 8	30. 4	16. 2	. 4	. 5	. 6	. 1	. 2	. 1
Nevada	364	68	101	152	278	412	70. 5	19. 7	19. 7	29. 5	80. 3	80. 3	1. 1	. 4	. 8	. 3	. 4	. 6
PACIFIC:																		
Washington	5, 818	5, 782	4, 699	1, 022	1, 101	1, 359	85. 1	84. 0	77. 6	14. 9	16. 0	22. 4	. 7	. 8	. 8	. 2	. 2	. 3
Oregon	1, 890	1, 844	1, 264	344	300	228	84. 6	86. 0	84. 7	15. 4	14. 0	15. 3	. 4	. 5	. 5	. 1	. 1	. 1
California	70, 519	33, 888	18, 399	10, 529	4, 875	3, 246	87. 0	87. 4	84. 0	13. 0	12. 6	15. 0	1. 7	1. 5	1. 3	. 7	. 4	. 4

[1] Less than 1/10 of 1 percent.

TABLE 9.—NEGRO AND WHITE POPULATION, FOR CITIES OF 100,000 INHABITANTS OR MORE: 1930

CITY	All classes [1]	Negro	WHITE			PERCENT OF ALL CLASSES	
			Total	Native	Foreign born	Negro	Foreign-born white
Total	**36,325,736**	**2,881,790**	**32,978,522**	**25,839,385**	**7,139,137**	**7.9**	**19.7**
New York, N. Y	6,930,446	327,706	6,587,225	4,293,825	2,293,400	4.7	33.1
Bronx Borough	1,265,258	12,930	1,251,747	774,405	477,342	1.0	37.7
Brooklyn Borough	2,560,401	68,921	2,488,448	1,619,678	868,770	2.7	33.9
Manhattan Borough	1,867,312	224,670	1,631,756	990,138	641,618	12.0	34.4
Queens Borough	1,079,129	18,609	1,059,680	793,530	266,150	1.7	24.7
Richmond Borough	158,346	2,576	155,594	116,074	39,520	1.6	25.0
Chicago, Ill	3,376,438	233,903	3,117,731	2,275,674	842,057	6.9	24.9
Philadelphia, Pa	1,950,961	219,599	1,728,457	1,359,833	368,624	11.3	18.9
Baltimore, Md	804,874	142,106	662,124	587,714	74,410	17.7	9.2
Washington, D. C	486,869	132,068	353,914	323,982	29,932	27.1	6.1
New Orleans, La	458,762	129,632	327,729	308,048	19,681	28.3	4.3
Detroit, Mich	1,568,662	120,066	1,440,141	1,040,860	399,281	7.7	25.5
Birmingham, Ala	259,678	99,077	160,551	154,684	5,867	38.2	2.3
Memphis, Tenn	253,143	96,550	156,528	151,266	5,262	38.1	2.1
St. Louis, Mo	821,960	93,580	726,879	646,493	80,386	11.4	9.8
Atlanta, Ga	270,366	90,075	180,247	175,520	4,727	33.3	1.7
Cleveland, Ohio	900,429	71,899	827,090	597,603	229,487	8.0	25.5
Houston, Tex	292,352	63,337	214,687	203,394	11,293	21.7	3.9
Pittsburgh, Pa	669,817	54,983	614,317	505,245	109,072	8.2	16.3
Richmond, Va	182,929	52,988	129,871	125,825	4,046	29.0	2.2
Jacksonville, Fla	129,549	48,196	81,320	76,967	4,353	37.2	3.4
Cincinnati, Ohio	451,160	47,818	403,112	368,277	34,835	10.6	7.7
Louisville, Ky	307,745	47,354	260,347	251,364	8,983	15.4	2.9
Indianapolis, Ind	364,161	43,967	320,064	306,324	13,740	12.1	3.8
Norfolk, Va	129,710	43,942	85,514	81,175	4,339	33.9	3.3
Nashville, Tenn	153,866	42,836	111,025	109,237	1,788	27.8	1.2
Los Angeles, Calif	1,238,048	38,894	1,073,584	891,736	181,848	3.1	14.7
Newark, N. J	442,337	38,880	402,596	287,392	115,204	8.8	26.0
Dallas, Tex	260,475	38,742	215,720	209,247	6,473	14.9	2.5
Kansas City, Mo	399,746	38,574	357,741	333,463	24,278	9.6	6.1
Chattanooga, Tenn	119,798	33,289	86,495	85,031	1,464	27.8	1.2
Columbus, Ohio	290,564	32,774	257,595	242,316	15,279	11.3	5.3
Miami, Fla	110,637	25,116	85,461	77,243	8,218	22.7	7.4
Fort Worth, Tex	163,447	22,234	137,197	134,279	2,918	13.6	1.8
Tampa, Fla	101,161	21,172	79,822	65,392	14,430	20.9	14.3
Boston, Mass	781,188	20,574	758,756	529,400	229,356	2.6	29.4
Kansas City, Kans	121,857	19,872	99,161	91,568	7,593	16.3	6.2
San Antonio, Tex	231,542	17,978	130,737	122,698	8,039	7.8	3.5
Gary, Ind	100,426	17,922	78,992	59,647	19,345	17.8	19.3
Knoxville, Tenn	105,802	17,093	88,705	87,881	824	16.2	.8
Dayton, Ohio	200,982	17,077	183,831	171,817	12,014	8.5	6.0
Tulsa, Okla	141,258	15,203	123,896	121,206	2,690	10.8	1.9
Oklahoma City, Okla	185,389	14,662	169,033	165,890	3,143	7.9	1.7
Youngstown, Ohio	170,002	14,552	155,108	122,170	32,938	8.6	19.4
Buffalo, N. Y	573,076	13,563	558,869	440,553	118,316	2.4	20.6
Toledo, Ohio	290,718	13,260	276,741	243,267	33,474	4.6	11.5
Jersey City, N. J	316,715	12,575	303,887	233,574	70,313	4.0	22.2
Wilmington, Del	106,597	12,080	94,459	81,867	12,592	11.3	11.8
Camden, N. J	118,700	11,340	107,283	88,668	18,615	9.6	15.7
Omaha, Nebr	214,006	11,123	201,657	172,869	28,788	5.2	13.5
Akron, Ohio	255,040	11,080	243,744	212,176	31,568	4.3	12.4
Trenton, N. J	123,356	8,057	115,236	88,479	26,757	6.5	21.7
Oakland, Calif	284,063	7,503	267,473	217,985	49,488	2.6	17.4
Milwaukee, Wis	578,249	7,501	568,807	459,424	109,383	1.3	18.9
Denver, Colo	287,861	7,204	272,977	241,742	31,235	2.5	10.9
Evansville, Ind	102,249	6,514	95,714	93,632	2,082	6.4	2.0
Hartford, Conn	164,072	6,510	157,467	112,939	44,528	4.0	27.1
Flint, Mich	156,492	5,725	150,023	129,089	20,934	3.7	13.4
Wichita, Kans	111,110	5,623	104,322	102,059	2,263	5.1	2.0
Providence, R. I	252,981	5,473	247,271	182,666	64,605	2.2	25.5
Des Moines, Iowa	142,559	5,428	136,724	127,414	9,310	3.8	6.5
Cambridge, Mass	113,643	5,419	108,046	75,716	32,330	4.8	28.4
New Haven, Conn	162,655	5,302	157,254	117,163	40,091	3.3	24.6
Elizabeth, N. J	114,589	4,761	109,732	80,576	29,156	4.2	25.4
Minneapolis, Minn	464,356	4,176	459,479	378,645	80,834	.9	17.4
St. Paul, Minn	271,606	4,001	266,645	222,502	44,143	1.5	16.3
San Francisco, Calif	634,394	3,803	594,969	441,583	153,386	.6	24.2
New Bedford, Mass	112,597	3,631	108,868	71,535	37,333	3.2	33.2
South Bend, Ind	104,193	3,431	100,689	86,669	14,020	3.3	13.5
Yonkers, N. Y	134,646	3,332	131,234	97,169	34,065	2.5	25.3
Bridgeport, Conn	146,716	3,314	143,325	102,566	40,759	2.3	27.8
Seattle, Wash	365,583	3,303	350,548	277,573	72,975	.9	20.0
Springfield, Mass	149,900	3,141	146,665	114,023	32,642	2.1	21.8
Peoria, Ill	104,969	3,037	101,735	94,999	6,736	2.9	6.4
Canton, Ohio	104,906	3,004	101,837	88,624	13,213	2.9	12.6
Paterson, N. J	138,513	2,952	135,424	92,815	42,609	2.1	30.8
Grand Rapids, Mich	168,592	2,795	165,555	138,315	27,240	1.7	16.2
San Diego, Calif	147,995	2,723	134,024	117,658	16,366	1.8	11.1
Rochester, N. Y	328,132	2,679	325,294	250,598	74,696	.8	22.8
Fort Wayne, Ind	114,946	2,360	112,505	106,776	5,729	2.1	5.0
Albany, N. Y	127,412	2,324	124,960	107,042	17,918	1.8	14.1
Reading, Pa	111,171	1,964	109,183	99,620	9,563	1.8	8.6
Syracuse, N. Y	209,326	1,899	207,174	172,164	35,010	.9	16.7
El Paso, Tex	102,421	1,855	41,965	39,121	2,844	1.8	2.8
Portland, Oreg	301,815	1,559	296,177	247,841	48,336	.5	16.0
Worcester, Mass	195,311	1,378	193,818	142,771	51,047	.7	26.1
Erie, Pa	115,967	1,214	114,686	97,445	17,241	1.0	14.9
Lynn, Mass	102,320	815	101,415	74,324	27,091	.8	26.5
Scranton, Pa	143,433	734	142,670	117,240	25,430	.5	17.7
Tacoma, Wash	106,817	730	104,559	84,763	19,796	.7	18.5
Salt Lake City, Utah	140,267	681	138,070	120,835	17,235	.5	12.3
Spokane, Wash	115,514	617	114,327	98,137	16,190	.5	14.0
Utica, N. Y	101,740	456	101,244	79,935	21,309	.4	20.9
Duluth, Minn	101,463	416	100,909	75,980	24,929	.4	24.6
Fall River, Mass	115,274	382	114,767	82,689	32,078	.3	27.8
Long Beach, Calif	142,032	353	139,176	125,921	13,255	.2	9.3
Somerville, Mass	103,908	274	103,585	74,040	29,545	.3	28.4
Lowell, Mass	100,234	126	100,052	73,923	26,129	.1	26.1

[1] Includes 465,424 "Other races."

Table 10.—CITIES HAVING A NEGRO POPULATION OF 10,000 OR MORE IN 1930, WITH COMPARATIVE FIGURES FOR 1920 AND 1910, AND PERCENT INCREASE IN WHITE POPULATION, 1910 TO 1930

CITY	NEGRO POPULATION										PERCENT INCREASE OR DECREASE (—) IN WHITE POPULATION	
				Increase or decrease (—)				Percent of total population				
	1930	1920	1910	1920 to 1930 Number	1920 to 1930 Percent	1910 to 1920 Number	1910 to 1920 Percent	1930	1920	1910	1920–1930[1]	1910–1920
New York, N. Y	327,706	152,467	91,709	175,239	114.9	60,758	66.3	4.7	2.7	1.9	20.7	16.9
Chicago, Ill	233,903	109,458	44,103	124,445	113.7	65,355	148.2	6.9	4.1	2.0	20.5	21.0
Philadelphia, Pa	219,599	134,229	84,459	85,370	63.6	49,770	58.9	11.3	7.4	5.5	2.4	15.4
Baltimore, Md	142,106	108,322	84,749	33,784	31.2	23,573	27.8	17.7	14.8	15.2	5.9	32.1
Washington, D. C	132,068	109,966	94,446	22,102	20.1	15,520	16.4	27.1	25.1	28.5	8.3	38.4
New Orleans, La	129,632	100,930	89,262	28,702	28.4	11,668	13.1	28.3	26.1	26.3	14.9	14.6
Detroit, Mich	120,066	40,838	5,741	79,228	194.0	35,097	611.3	7.7	4.1	1.2	51.4	107.0
Birmingham, Ala	99,077	70,230	52,305	28,847	41.1	17,925	34.3	38.2	39.3	39.4	47.9	35.1
Memphis, Tenn	96,550	61,181	52,441	35,369	57.8	8,740	16.7	38.1	37.7	40.0	54.8	28.7
St. Louis, Mo	93,580	69,854	43,960	23,726	34.0	25,894	58.9	11.4	9.0	6.4	3.5	9.4
Atlanta, Ga	90,075	62,796	51,902	27,279	43.4	10,894	21.0	33.3	31.3	33.5	30.8	34.0
Cleveland, Ohio	71,899	34,451	8,448	37,448	108.7	26,003	307.8	8.0	4.3	1.5	8.6	38.1
Houston, Tex	63,337	33,960	23,929	29,377	86.5	10,031	41.9	21.7	24.6	30.4	116.3	90.2
Pittsburgh, Pa	54,983	37,725	25,623	17,258	45.7	12,102	47.2	8.2	6.4	4.8	11.6	8.3
Richmond, Va	52,988	54,041	46,733	−1,053	−1.9	7,308	15.6	29.0	31.5	36.6	10.5	45.4
Jacksonville, Fla	48,196	41,520	29,293	6,676	16.1	12,227	41.7	37.2	45.3	50.8	62.7	76.4
Cincinnati, Ohio	47,818	30,079	19,639	17,739	59.0	10,440	53.2	10.6	7.5	5.4	8.6	7.9
Louisville, Ky	47,354	40,087	40,522	7,267	18.1	−435	−1.1	15.4	17.1	18.1	33.7	6.2
Indianapolis, Ind	43,967	34,678	21,816	9,289	26.8	12,862	59.0	12.1	11.0	9.3	14.5	31.9
Norfolk, Va	43,942	43,392	25,039	550	1.3	18,353	73.3	33.9	37.5	37.1	18.4	70.5
Nashville, Tenn	42,836	35,633	36,523	7,203	20.2	−890	−2.4	27.8	30.1	33.1	34.2	12.0
Savannah, Ga	38,896	39,179	33,246	−283	−.7	5,933	17.8	45.7	47.1	51.1	4.6	38.5
Los Angeles, Calif	38,894	15,579	7,599	23,315	149.7	7,980	105.0	3.1	2.7	2.4	107.6	79.1
Newark, N. J	38,880	16,977	9,475	21,903	129.0	7,502	79.2	8.8	4.1	2.7	1.4	17.6
Dallas, Tex	38,742	24,023	18,024	14,719	61.3	5,999	33.3	14.9	15.1	19.6	63.4	82.2
Kansas City, Mo	38,574	30,719	23,566	7,855	25.6	7,153	30.4	9.6	9.5	9.5	22.7	30.6
Chattanooga, Tenn	33,289	18,889	17,942	14,400	76.2	947	5.3	27.8	32.6	40.2	121.8	46.3
Columbus, Ohio	32,774	22,181	12,739	10,593	47.8	9,442	74.1	11.3	9.4	7.0	20.0	27.3
Winston-Salem, N. C	32,566	20,735	9,087	11,831	57.1	11,648	128.2	43.3	42.8	40.0	54.5	103.2
Montgomery, Ala	29,970	19,827	19,322	10,143	51.2	505	2.6	45.4	45.6	50.7	52.8	25.7
Charleston, S. C	28,062	32,326	31,056	−4,264	−13.2	1,270	4.1	45.1	47.6	52.8	−4.0	28.2
Shreveport, La	27,219	17,485	13,896	9,734	55.7	3,589	25.8	35.5	39.9	49.6	86.9	87.0
Charlotte, N. C	25,163	14,641	11,752	10,522	71.9	2,889	24.6	30.4	31.6	34.6	81.4	42.4
Miami, Fla	25,116	9,270	2,258	15,846	170.9	7,012	310.5	22.7	31.3	41.3	321.6	531.6
Mobile, Ala	24,514	23,906	22,763	608	2.5	1,143	5.0	35.9	39.3	44.2	18.3	28.2
Augusta, Ga	24,190	22,582	18,344	1,608	7.1	4,238	23.1	40.1	43.0	44.7	20.4	32.0
Macon, Ga	23,158	23,093	18,150	65	.3	4,943	27.2	43.0	43.6	44.6	2.6	32.8
Fort Worth, Tex	22,234	15,896	13,280	6,338	39.9	2,616	19.7	13.6	14.9	18.1	59.5	50.9
Tampa, Fla	21,172	11,531	8,951	9,641	83.6	2,580	28.8	20.9	22.3	23.7	99.5	39.1
Boston, Mass	20,574	16,350	13,564	4,224	25.8	2,786	20.5	2.6	2.2	2.0	3.9	11.4
Kansas City, Kans	19,872	14,405	9,286	5,467	38.0	5,119	55.1	16.3	14.2	11.3	17.6	18.8
Little Rock, Ark	19,698	17,477	14,539	2,221	12.7	2,938	20.2	24.1	26.8	31.6	30.0	51.8
Columbia, S. C	19,519	14,455	11,546	5,064	35.0	2,909	25.2	37.8	38.5	43.9	38.9	56.2
Jackson, Miss	19,423	9,936	10,554	9,487	95.5	−618	−5.9	40.2	43.5	49.6	124.0	20.3
Portsmouth, Va	18,849	23,245	11,617	−4,396	−18.9	11,628	100.1	41.2	42.7	35.9	−13.9	44.2
Durham, N. C	18,717	7,654	6,869	11,063	144.5	785	11.4	36.0	35.2	37.7	136.9	23.6
Beaumont, Tex	18,551	13,210	6,896	5,341	40.4	6,314	91.6	32.1	32.7	33.4	41.6	98.0
San Antonio, Tex	17,978	14,341	10,716	3,637	25.4	3,625	33.8	7.8	8.9	11.1	24.1	71.1
Gary, Ind	17,922	5,299	383	12,623	238.2	4,916	1,283.6	17.8	9.6	2.3	58.4	205.1
Knoxville, Tenn	17,093	11,302	7,638	5,791	51.2	3,664	48.0	16.2	14.5	21.0	33.4	131.7
Dayton, Ohio	17,077	9,025	4,842	8,052	89.2	4,183	86.4	8.5	5.9	4.2	28.1	28.5
Atlantic City, N. J	15,611	10,946	9,834	4,665	42.6	1,112	11.3	23.6	21.6	21.3	27.3	9.5
Tulsa, Okla	15,203	8,878	1,959	6,325	71.2	6,919	353.2	10.8	12.3	10.8	97.6	292.7
Oklahoma City, Okla	14,662	8,241	6,546	6,421	77.9	1,695	25.9	7.9	9.0	10.2	106.1	44.1
Youngstown, Ohio	14,552	6,662	1,936	7,890	118.4	4,726	244.1	8.6	5.0	2.4	23.6	62.9
Asheville, N. C	14,255	7,145	5,359	7,110	99.5	1,786	33.3	28.4	25.1	28.6	68.3	59.3
Columbus, Ga	14,157	9,093	7,644	5,064	55.7	1,449	19.0	32.8	29.2	37.2	31.5	70.7
Greensboro, N. C	14,050	5,973	5,710	8,077	135.2	263	4.6	26.2	30.1	35.9	184.6	36.4
Buffalo, N. Y	13,563	4,511	1,773	9,052	200.7	2,738	154.4	2.4	.9	.4	11.3	19.0
Newsport News, Va	13,281	14,077	7,259	−796	−5.7	6,818	93.9	38.6	39.5	35.9	−1.6	66.0
Toledo, Ohio	13,260	5,691	1,877	7,569	133.0	3,814	203.2	4.6	2.3	1.1	16.7	42.5
Galveston, Tex	13,226	9,888	8,036	3,338	33.8	1,852	23.0	25.0	22.3	21.7	8.0	18.8
Wilmington, N. C	13,106	13,461	12,107	−355	−2.6	1,354	11.2	40.6	40.3	47.0	−3.7	46.0
Lexington, Ky	12,759	12,450	11,011	309	2.5	1,439	13.1	27.9	30.0	31.4	13.4	20.8
Petersburg, Va	12,600	13,608	11,014	−1,008	−7.4	2,594	23.6	44.1	43.9	45.7	−8.2	32.7
Jersey City, N. J	12,575	8,000	5,960	4,575	57.2	2,040	34.2	4.0	2.7	2.2	4.8	10.8
Raleigh, N. C	12,575	8,544	7,372	4,031	47.2	1,172	15.9	33.6	35.0	38.4	56.2	34.0
Roanoke, Va	12,368	9,331	7,924	3,037	32.5	1,407	17.8	17.9	18.4	22.7	37.0	54.0
Wilmington, Del	12,080	10,746	9,081	1,334	12.4	1,665	18.3	11.3	9.8	10.4	−5.0	26.9
Vicksburg, Miss	11,915	9,148	12,053	2,767	30.2	−2,905	−24.1	51.9	50.6	57.9	23.5	1.9
Bessemer, Ala	11,691	10,561	6,210	1,130	10.7	4,351	70.1	56.4	56.6	57.2	11.3	74.5
East St. Louis, Ill	11,536	7,437	5,882	4,099	55.1	1,555	26.4	15.5	11.1	10.0	5.8	12.6
Meridian, Miss	11,352	8,343	9,321	3,009	36.1	−978	−10.5	35.5	35.7	40.0	36.9	7.8
Camden, N. J	11,340	8,500	6,076	2,840	33.4	2,424	39.9	9.6	7.3	6.4	−0.4	21.9
Omaha, Nebr	11,123	10,315	5,143	808	7.8	5,172	100.6	5.2	5.4	3.4	11.8	24.9
Akron, Ohio	11,080	5,580	657	5,500	98.6	4,923	749.3	4.3	2.7	1.0	20.2	196.4
Greenville, S. C	10,871	8,184	6,319	2,687	32.8	1,865	29.5	37.3	35.4	40.1	22.3	58.6
Baton Rouge, La	10,675	8,560	7,899	2,115	24.7	661	8.4	34.7	39.3	53.0	51.7	89.2
Monroe, La	10,112	5,540	5,320	4,572	82.5	220	4.1	38.9	43.7	52.1	122.2	46.0
Port Arthur, Tex	10,003	3,910	1,493	6,093	155.8	2,417	161.9	19.7	17.6	19.5	112.7	197.2

[1] The figures for the white population in 1920 for cities having 100,000 or more inhabitants and 100 or more Mexicans in 1930, were adjusted for (comparison with 1930 only) by deducting the estimated number of persons who would have been classified as Mexicans under the 1930 classification.

Table 11.—NEGRO POPULATION OF CITIES AND OTHER URBAN PLACES: 1930 AND 1920

[Places having no Negro population are omitted]

City or other urban place	Population: Total, 1930	Negro: 1930	Negro: 1920
Alabama			
Alabama City	8,544	473	242
Albertville	2,716	116	(1)
Alexander City	4,519	1,244	(1)
Andalusia	5,154	1,257	1,021
Anniston	22,345	7,161	5,834
Athens	4,238	853	776
Atmore	3,035	1,327	(1)
Attalla	4,585	1,200	1,017
Auburn	2,800	1,188	(1)
Bessemer	20,721	11,691	10,561
Birmingham	259,678	99,077	70,230
Brewton	2,818	1,314	1,376
Carbon Hill	2,519	633	729
Cullman	2,786	5	(1)
Decatur [2]	15,593	3,867	2,421
Demopolis	4,037	2,365	1,554
Dothan	16,046	6,194	4,290
Elba	2,523	745	(1)
Enterprise	3,702	1,005	708
Eufaula	5,208	2,273	2,657
Fairfield	11,059	6,393	2,290
Florala	2,580	772	854
Florence	11,729	2,751	2,329
Fort Payne	3,375	110	(1)
Gadsden	24,042	6,345	4,218
Greenville	3,985	1,983	1,885
Guntersville	2,826	441	(1)
Homewood	6,103	1,771	(1)
Huntsville	11,554	3,825	2,935
Jacksonville	2,840	517	(1)
Jasper	5,313	982	601
Lanett	5,204	878	939
Leeds	2,529	569	(1)
Mobile	68,202	24,514	23,906
Montgomery	66,079	29,970	19,827
Opelika	6,156	2,674	2,269
Opp	2,918	391	(1)
Ozark	3,103	1,188	879
Phenix City [3]	13,862	4,065	802
Piedmont	3,668	297	320
Prichard	4,580	2,059	(1)
Roanoke	4,373	691	502
Russellville	3,146	442	(1)
Selma	18,012	9,249	8,200
Sheffield	6,221	1,531	1,918
Sylacauga	4,115	978	(1)
Talladega	7,596	2,652	2,656
Tarrant City	7,341	852	(1)
Troy	6,814	3,115	2,854
Tuscaloosa	20,659	7,075	4,557
Tuscumbia	4,533	1,516	1,281
Tuskegee	3,314	2,288	(1)
Union Springs	2,875	1,578	2,772
Arizona			
Bisbee	8,023	83	76
Douglas	9,828	210	171
Flagstaff	3,891	100	33
Glendale	3,665	3	4
Globe	7,157	64	216
Jerome	4,933	23	44
Mesa	3,711	130	69
Miami	7,693	75	47
Nogales [4]	6,006	679	218
Phoenix	48,118	2,366	1,075
Prescott	5,517	148	167
Tucson	32,506	1,003	346
Winslow	3,917	65	37
Yuma	4,892	198	93
Arkansas			
Arkadelphia	3,380	575	766
Batesville	4,484	431	627
Benton	3,445	207	157
Blytheville	10,098	2,731	1,085
Brinkley	3,046	1,507	1,285
Camden	7,273	2,872	1,319
Clarksville	3,031	184	(1)
Conway	5,534	928	741
Crossett	2,811	1,172	1,052
De Queen	2,938	143	105
Dermott	2,942	1,625	(1)
El Dorado	16,421	3,836	1,004
Fayetteville	7,394	339	313
Fordyce	3,206	1,302	1,241
Forrest City	4,594	1,967	1,305
Fort Smith	31,429	3,467	3,584
Helena	8,316	4,420	4,863
Hope	6,008	1,986	1,412
Hot Springs	20,238	4,194	2,811
Jonesboro	10,326	1,316	1,362
Little Rock	81,679	19,698	17,477
McGehee	3,488	1,236	(1)
Magnolia	3,008	984	(1)
Malvern	5,115	1,084	951
Marianna	4,314	2,305	3,234
Arkansas—Continued			
Monticello	3,076	632	(1)
Morrilton	4,043	737	778
Newport	4,547	1,406	1,401
North Little Rock	19,418	6,097	4,851
Osceola	2,573	1,027	(1)
Paragould	5,966	20	28
Paris	3,234	42	(1)
Pine Bluff	20,760	6,163	6,403
Prescott	3,033	1,131	1,023
Russellville	5,628	488	464
Searcy	3,387	597	485
Smackover	2,544	457	(1)
Stamps	2,705	1,293	1,093
Stuttgart	4,927	1,179	1,177
Texarkana [5]	10,764	3,109	2,406
Trumann	2,995	66	17
Van Buren	5,182	578	541
Warren	2,523	319	(1)
West Helena	4,489	2,173	4,244
Wynne	3,505	1,139	1,017
California			
Alameda	35,033	294	217
Albany	8,569	2	(1)
Alhambra	29,472	96	44
Anaheim	10,995	25	17
Arcadia	5,216	9	(1)
Auburn	2,661	20	(1)
Azusa	4,808	6	(1)
Bakersfield	26,015	868	369
Banning	2,752	5	(1)
Bell	7,884	2	(1)
Belvedere township	33,023	13	(6)
Benicia	2,913	4	2
Berkeley	82,109	2,177	507
Beverly Hills	17,429	397	11
Brawley	10,439	194	98
Burbank	16,662	6	(7)
Burlingame	13,270	8	3
Calexico	6,299	161	315
Chico	7,961	43	72
Chino	3,118	4	(1)
Chula Vista	3,869	9	(1)
Claremont	2,719	3	(1)
Coalinga	2,851	1	1
Colton	8,014	17	25
Compton	12,516	1	(1)
Corona	7,018	23	10
Coronado	5,425	60	39
Daly City	7,838	20	22
Delano	2,632	39	(1)
Dinuba	2,968	5	2
Dunsmuir	2,610	34	9
El Centro	8,434	607	330
El Cerrito	3,870	2	(1)
Eureka	15,752	37	31
Exeter	2,685	2	(1)
Fort Bragg	3,022	2	4
Fresno	52,513	838	508
Fullerton	10,860	41	18
Gilroy	3,502	4	8
Gardena township	15,969	15	(6)
Glendale	62,736	38	22
Glendora	2,761	1	(1)
Grass Valley	3,817	1	2
Hanford	7,028	101	105
Hollister	3,757	34	33
Huntington Beach	3,690	6	(1)
Huntington Park	24,591	1	(7)
Inglewood	19,480	3	2
La Mesa	2,513	1	(1)
La Verne	2,860	2	(1)
Lindsay	3,878	3	5
Livermore	3,119	5	(1)
Long Beach	142,032	353	142
Los Angeles	1,238,048	38,894	15,579
Madera	4,665	105	55
Martinez	6,569	12	11
Marysville	5,763	163	185
Merced	7,066	189	31
Mill Valley	4,164	2	1
Modesto	13,842	170	94
Monrovia	10,890	461	133
Montebello	5,498	1	(1)
Monterey	9,141	66	42
Mountain View	3,308	3	(1)
Napa	6,437	9	15
National City	7,301	12	7
Needles	3,144	127	49
Oakland	284,063	7,503	5,489
Oceanside	3,508	4	(1)
Ontario	13,583	49	11
Orange	8,066	6	3
Oroville	3,698	45	40
Oxnard	6,285	34	74
Pacific Grove	5,558	73	56
California—Continued			
Palo Alto	13,652	188	59
Pasadena	76,086	3,015	1,094
Paso Robles	2,573	26	(1)
Petaluma	8,245	3	13
Piedmont	9,333	40	13
Pittsburg	9,610	149	75
Pomona	20,804	47	46
Porterville	5,303	37	18
Red Bluff	3,517	44	50
Redding	4,188	41	26
Redlands	14,177	154	77
Redondo Beach	9,347	17	11
Redwood City	8,926	67	19
Richmond	20,093	48	33
Riverside	29,696	604	505
Roseville	6,425	31	24
Sacramento	93,750	1,086	675
Salinas	10,263	55	26
San Anselmo	4,650	1	(1)
San Bernardino	37,481	518	269
San Bruno	3,610	12	(1)
San Buenaventura	11,603	52	21
San Diego	147,995	2,723	996
San Fernando	7,567	9	1
San Francisco	634,394	3,803	2,414
San Gabriel	7,224	16	11
Sanger	2,967	3	12
San Jose	57,651	240	191
San Leandro	11,455	4	1
San Luis Obispo	8,276	5	3
San Marino	3,730	59	(1)
San Mateo	13,444	189	55
San Rafael	8,022	8	7
Santa Anna	30,322	109	22
Santa Barbara	33,613	525	186
Santa Clara	6,302	4	10
Santa Cruz	14,395	35	28
Santa Monica	37,146	740	282
Santa Paula	7,452	11	4
Santa Rosa	10,636	19	12
Sausalito	3,667	7	3
Selma	3,047	2	2
Sierre Madre	3,550	5	(1)
South Gate	19,632	2	(1)
South Pasadena	13,730	35	22
South San Francisco	6,193	48	37
Stockton	47,963	433	336
Sunnyvale	3,094	5	(1)
Tracy	3,829	21	(1)
Tulare	6,207	166	15
Turlock	4,276	1	5
Ukiah	3,124	4	(1)
Upland	4,713	7	1
Vallejo	14,476	297	315
Visalia	7,263	52	53
Watsonville	8,344	17	11
Whittier	14,822	18	11
Willow Glen	4,167	1	(1)
Woodland	5,542	87	95
Yuba City	3,605	3	(1)
Colorado			
Alamosa	5,107	37	15
Boulder	11,223	121	128
Brighton	3,394	5	26
Canon City	5,938	151	117
Colorado Springs	33,237	965	1,009
Denver	287,861	7,204	6,075
Durango	5,400	18	35
Englewood	7,980	37	29
Fort Collins	11,489	12	7
Fort Morgan	4,423	2	6
Grand Junction	10,247	58	76
Greeley	12,203	20	18
La Junta	7,193	155	93
Lamar	4,233	38	16
Las Animas	2,517	13	(1)
Leadville	3,771	17	23
Longmont	6,029	2	14
Monte Vista	2,610	2	(1)
Montrose	3,566	4	6
Pueblo	50,096	1,305	1,395
Rocky Ford	3,426	14	32
Salida	5,065	18	15
Sterling	7,195	39	24
Trinidad	11,732	144	141
Walsenburg	5,503	90	43
Connecticut			
Ansonia city	19,898	1,082	532
Bridgeport city	146,716	3,314	2,228
Bristol city	28,451	108	61
Danbury city	22,261	203	175
Danielson borough	4,210	17	28
Derby city	10,788	77	91

See footnotes at end of table.

TABLE 11.—NEGRO POPULATION OF CITIES AND OTHER URBAN PLACES: 1930 AND 1920—Continued

[Places having no Negro population are omitted]

CITY OR OTHER URBAN PLACE	POPULATION		
	Total, 1930	Negro	
		1930	1920
CONNECTICUT—Contd.			
East Hartford town	17, 125	115	115
Greenwich borough	5, 981	118	175
Groton borough	4, 122	30	52
Hartford city	164, 072	6, 510	4, 199
Jewett City borough	4, 436	18	25
Meriden city	38, 481	125	148
Middletown city	24, 554	227	57
Naugatuck borough	14, 315	23	15
New Britain city	68, 128	359	303
New Haven city	162, 655	5, 302	4, 573
New London city	29, 640	765	508
Norwalk city	36, 019	871	631
Norwich city	23, 021	421	534
Putnam city	7, 318	77	62
Rockville city	7, 445	95	85
Shelton city	10, 113	46	31
Southington borough	5, 125	1	11
Stafford Springs borough	3, 492	4	10
Stamford city	46, 346	2, 138	874
Stratford town	19, 212	229	174
Torrington city	26, 040	167	104
Wallingford borough	11, 170	37	13
Waterbury city	99, 902	1, 660	951
West Hartford town	24, 941	126	72
West Haven town	25, 808	143	(8)
Willimantic city	12, 102	77	67
Winsted city	7, 883	46	72
DELAWARE			
Dover	4, 800	1, 113	1, 059
Milford	3, 719	740	569
New Castle	4, 131	572	618
Newark	3, 899	532	(1)
Wilmington	106, 597	12, 080	10, 746
DISTRICT OF COLUMBIA			
Washington	486, 869	132, 068	109, 966
FLORIDA			
Apalachicola	3, 150	1, 329	1, 440
Arcadia	4, 082	1, 169	705
Avon Park	3, 355	928	(1)
Bartow	5, 269	1, 715	1, 217
Bradentown	5, 986	1, 536	1, 001
Clearwater	7, 607	2, 012	(1)
Coral Gables	5, 697	441	(1)
Daytona Beach	16, 598	5, 426	(9)
De Funiak Springs	2, 636	573	(1)
De Land	5, 246	1, 515	1, 190
Eustis	2, 835	881	(1)
Fernandina	3, 023	1, 484	2, 824
Fort Lauderdale	8, 666	1, 994	(1)
Fort Myers	9, 082	2, 450	845
Fort Pierce	4, 803	1, 226	(1)
Gainesville	10, 465	4, 106	2, 937
Haines City	3, 037	861	(1)
Hialeah	2, 600	201	(1)
Hollywood	2, 869	263	(1)
Jacksonville	129, 549	48, 196	41, 520
Key West	12, 831	2, 274	4, 030
Kissimmee	3, 163	759	618
Lake City	4, 416	1, 301	1, 505
Lakeland	18, 554	3, 941	1, 557
Lake Wales	3, 401	921	(1)
Lake Worth	5, 940	115	(1)
Leesburg	4, 113	1, 421	(1)
Live Oak	2, 734	1, 038	1, 424
Manatee	3, 219	1, 180	(1)
Marianna	3, 372	1, 033	(1)
Melbourne	2, 677	939	(1)
Miami	110, 637	25, 116	9, 270
Miami Beach	6, 494	230	(1)
New Smyrna	4, 149	1, 249	(1)
Ocala	7, 281	2, 953	2, 050
Orlando	27, 330	7, 590	2, 552
Palatka	6, 500	3, 000	2, 634
Palmetto	3, 043	1, 174	(1)
Panama City	5, 402	978	(1)
Pensacola	31, 579	9, 583	10, 404
Perry	2, 744	1, 053	(1)
Plant City	6, 800	2, 091	1, 076
Pompano	2, 614	1, 487	(1)
Quincy	3, 788	1, 847	1, 880
River Junction	5, 624	1, 733	(1)
St. Augustine	12, 111	3, 293	1, 772
St. Petersburg	40, 425	7, 416	2, 433
Sanford	10, 100	4, 884	2, 491
Sarasota	8, 398	2, 169	(1)
Sebring	2, 912	680	(1)
South Jacksonville	5, 597	592	195
Tallahassee	10, 700	4, 401	2, 719
Tampa	101, 161	21, 172	11, 531
FLORIDA—Continued			
Tarpon Springs	3, 414	622	(1)
Wauchula	2, 574	15	(1)
West Palm Beach	26, 610	8, 999	3, 490
Winter Haven	7, 130	1, 556	(1)
Winter Park	3, 686	1, 181	(1)
GEORGIA			
Albany	14, 507	7, 394	6, 144
Americus	8, 760	4, 627	4, 629
Athens	18, 192	6, 378	6, 595
Atlanta	270, 366	90, 075	62, 796
Augusta	60, 342	24, 190	22, 582
Bainbridge	6, 141	2, 901	2, 220
Barnesville	3, 236	1, 124	1, 041
Brunswick	14, 022	6, 049	7, 120
Buford	3, 357	777	563
Cairo	3, 169	1, 286	(1)
Canton	2, 892	228	175
Carrollton	5, 052	1, 023	873
Cartersville	5, 250	1, 615	1, 499
Cedartown	8, 124	1, 400	890
Collegepark	6, 604	1, 613	904
Columbus	43, 131	14, 157	9, 093
Commerce	3, 002	419	(1)
Cordele	6, 880	3, 490	3, 254
Covington	3, 203	1, 219	1, 112
Cuthbert	3, 235	1, 963	1, 926
Dalton	8, 160	1, 028	744
Dawson	3, 827	2, 209	1, 946
Decatur	13, 276	2, 515	1, 266
Douglas	4, 206	1, 515	1, 122
Dublin	6, 681	2, 806	3, 443
Eastman	3, 022	1, 304	1, 090
East Point	9, 512	1, 569	865
East Thomaston	3, 061	2	(1)
Elberton	4, 650	1, 601	2, 403
Fitzgerald	6, 412	2, 260	2, 441
Fort Valley	4, 560	2, 408	1, 444
Gainesville	8, 624	2, 051	1, 512
Griffin	10, 321	3, 396	2, 614
Hapeville	4, 224	90	(1)
Lafayette	2, 811	304	(1)
La Grange	20, 131	5, 471	4, 576
Macon	53, 829	23, 158	23, 093
Manchester	3, 745	745	602
Marietta	7, 638	2, 247	1, 823
Milledgeville	5, 534	2, 719	2, 305
Millen	2, 527	1, 030	(1)
Monroe	3, 706	987	977
Moultrie	8, 027	3, 078	2, 808
Newman	6, 386	2, 359	3, 070
Pelham	2, 762	852	816
Porterdale	3, 002	104	109
Quitman	4, 149	1, 992	2, 039
Rockmart	3, 264	458	(1)
Rome	21, 843	4, 737	3, 328
Sandersville	3, 011	1, 556	1, 287
Savannah	85, 024	38, 896	39, 179
Statesboro	3, 996	1, 301	1, 228
Thomaston	4, 922	1, 997	895
Thomasville	11, 733	6, 074	4, 322
Tifton	3, 390	651	650
Toccoa	4, 602	1, 139	949
Trion	3, 289	30	(1)
Valdosta	13, 482	6, 265	5, 508
Vidalia	3, 585	1, 298	1, 035
Washington	3, 158	1, 766	2, 484
Waycross	15, 510	5, 956	9, 198
Waynesboro	3, 922	2, 239	1, 896
Winder	3, 283	546	649
IDAHO			
Boise	21, 544	81	63
Burley	3, 826	1	27
Caldwell	4, 974	1	4
Coeur d'Alene	8, 297	11	5
Idaho Falls	9, 429	47	44
Kellogg	4, 124	2	(7)
Lewiston	9, 403	31	32
Moscow	4, 476	1	6
Nampa	8, 206	10	32
Pocatello	16, 471	267	366
Rexburg	3, 048	1	2
St. Anthony	2, 778	14	8
Twin Falls	8, 787	30	35
Wallace	3, 634	4	8
Weiser	2, 724	1	1
ILLINOIS			
Abingdon	2, 771	6	13
Alton	30, 151	2, 714	1, 707
Anna	3, 436	2	1
Arlington Heights	4, 997	3	(1)
ILLINOIS—Continued			
Aurora	46, 589	936	627
Barrington	3, 213	2	(1)
Batavia	5, 045	108	60
Belleville	28, 425	178	180
Belvidere	8, 123	15	32
Berwyn	47, 027	8	1
Bloomington	30, 930	804	799
Blue Island	16, 534	9	8
Bradley	3, 048	9	(1)
Brookfield	10, 035	4	3
Bushnell	2, 850	7	14
Cairo	13, 532	4, 575	5, 000
Calumet City [10]	12, 298	24	28
Canton	11, 718	67	99
Carbondale	7, 528	1, 409	1, 109
Carlinville	4, 144	6	8
Carmi	2, 932	108	139
Centralia	12, 583	1, 108	990
Champaign	20, 348	1, 598	1, 234
Charleston	8, 012	15	30
Chester	3, 922	89	134
Chicago	3, 376, 438	233, 903	109, 458
Chicago Heights	22, 321	2, 198	731
Cicero	66, 602	5	4
Clinton	5, 920	41	98
Collinsville	9, 235	300	299
Crystal Lake	3, 732	4	(1)
Danville	36, 765	2, 565	2, 356
Decatur	57, 510	1, 947	1, 178
De Kalb	8, 545	8	17
Dixon	9, 908	125	104
Dolton	2, 923	37	(1)
Downers Grove	8, 977	17	11
Duquoin	7, 593	594	417
Dwight	2, 534	2	(1)
East Moline	10, 107	470	409
East Peoria	5, 027	5	(1)
East St. Louis	74, 347	11, 536	7, 437
Edwardsville	6, 235	419	365
Effingham	4, 978	5	(7)
Elgin	35, 929	310	116
Elmhurst	14, 055	13	5
Evanston	63, 338	4, 938	2, 522
Fairfield	3, 280	1	3
Forest Park	14, 555	1	(7)
Freeport	22, 045	380	338
Fulton	2, 656	1	(1)
Galena	3, 878	16	14
Galesburg	28, 830	891	848
Galva	2, 875	13	7
Geneseo	3, 406	9	14
Geneva	4, 607	169	(11)
Georgetown	3, 407	109	102
Glencoe	6, 295	313	324
Glen Ellyn	7, 680	36	23
Granite City	25, 130	5	7
Greenville	3, 233	31	44
Harrisburg	11, 625	532	441
Harvard	2, 988	2	7
Harvey	16, 374	405	171
Highland Park	12, 203	177	60
Hillsboro	4, 435	101	94
Hinsdale	6, 923	86	36
Homewood	3, 227	2	(1)
Hoopeston	5, 613	31	51
Jacksonville	17, 747	1, 053	1, 176
Jerseyville	4, 309	34	42
Joliet	42, 993	1, 309	701
Kankakee	20, 620	562	265
Kenilworth	2, 501	107	(1)
Kewanee	17, 093	278	166
La Grange	10, 103	350	176
La Grange Park	2, 939	6	(1)
Lake Forest	6, 554	228	138
Lawrenceville	6, 303	107	84
Libertyville	3, 791	2	(1)
Lincoln	12, 855	309	257
Litchfield	6, 612	114	117
Lockport	3, 383	32	39
Lombard	6, 197	2	(1)
Macomb	8, 509	114	112
Madison	7, 661	1, 013	647
Marion	9, 033	287	307
Marseilles	4, 292	4	1
Mattoon	14, 631	147	178
Maywood	25, 829	722	267
Melrose Park	10, 741	121	94
Mendota	4, 008	12	21
Metropolis	5, 573	613	741
Moline	32, 236	302	338
Monmouth	8, 666	418	480
Morris	5, 568	9	13
Mound City	2, 548	873	927
Mount Carmel	7, 132	3	5
Mount Vernon	12, 375	560	438

See footnotes at end of table.

Table 11.—NEGRO POPULATION OF CITIES AND OTHER URBAN PLACES: 1930 AND 1920—Continued

[Places having no Negro population are omitted]

CITY OR OTHER URBAN PLACE	POPULATION: Total, 1930	Negro: 1930	Negro: 1920
Illinois—Continued			
Murphysboro	8,182	749	1,107
Niles Center	5,007	2	(1)
Normal	6,768	99	183
North Chicago	8,466	521	90
Oak Park	63,982	143	169
Olney	6,140	2	2
Ottawa	15,094	130	62
Pana	5,835	2	3
Paris	8,781	253	284
Park Ridge	10,417	14	7
Paxton	2,892	3	8
Pekin	16,129	1	31
Peoria	104,969	3,037	2,130
Peoria Heights	3,279	9	(1)
Peru	9,121	1	2
Phoenix	3,033	457	(1)
Pinckneyville	3,046	2	9
Pontiac	8,272	481	290
Princeton	4,762	41	42
Quincy	39,241	1,145	1,210
River Forest	8,829	101	6
River Grove	2,741	1	(1)
Riverside	6,770	16	17
Rochelle	3,785	6	9
Rockford	85,864	1,110	490
Rock Island	37,953	680	754
St. Charles	5,377	43	20
Salem	4,420	1	6
Savanna	5,086	71	117
Shelbyville	3,491	15	52
Sparta	3,385	534	557
Springfield	71,864	3,324	2,769
Spring Valley	5,270	34	26
Steger	2,985	8	(1)
Sterling	10,012	45	43
Streator	14,728	142	199
Summit	6,548	493	30
Sycamore	4,021	128	120
Taylorville	7,316	85	52
Tuscola	2,569	26	55
Urbana	13,060	394	335
Venice	5,362	1,619	394
Virden	3,011	2	3
Washington Park	3,837	1	(1)
Watseka	3,144	38	43
Waukegan	33,499	1,017	351
Western Springs	3,894	17	(1)
Westville	3,901	77	70
Wheaton	7,258	129	48
Wilmette	15,233	192	75
Winnetka	12,166	256	74
Wood River	8,136	1	25
Woodstock	5,471	20	9
Zion	5,991	70	106
Indiana			
Alexandria	4,408	21	62
Anderson	39,804	1,387	912
Angola	2,665	10	4
Attica	3,700	1	5
Auburn	5,088	5	5
Bedford	13,208	101	55
Bloomington	18,227	519	479
Bluffton	5,074	2	3
Boonville	4,208	126	153
Brazil	8,744	304	276
Clinton	7,936	67	177
Columbus	9,935	146	172
Connersville	12,795	481	484
Crawfordsville	10,355	225	265
Crown Point	4,046	87	18
Dunkirk	2,583	75	55
East Chicago	54,784	5,088	1,424
Elkhart	32,949	539	308
Evansville	102,249	6,514	6,394
Fort Wayne	114,946	2,360	1,454
Frankfort	12,196	90	71
Franklin	5,682	243	285
Garrett	4,428	50	70
Gary	100,426	17,922	5,299
Goshen	10,397	2	3
Greencastle	4,613	200	131
Greenfield	4,188	18	35
Greensburg	5,702	8	25
Hammond	64,560	623	137
Hartford City	6,613	2	2
Hobart	5,787	4	16
Huntington	13,420	1	(7)
Indianapolis	364,161	43,967	34,678
Jeffersonville	11,946	1,296	1,413
Kokomo	32,843	1,143	876
Lafayette	26,240	426	378
La Porte	15,755	174	127
Lawrenceburg	4,072	54	31
Indiana—Continued			
Lebanon	6,445	84	70
Logansport	18,508	240	277
Madison	6,530	243	293
Marion	24,496	1,056	1,135
Martinsville	4,962	4	26
Michigan City	26,735	1,071	334
Mishawaka	28,630	51	23
Mitchell	3,226	113	99
Mount Vernon	5,035	455	426
Muncie	46,548	2,646	2,054
New Albany	25,819	1,292	1,446
New Castle	14,027	326	298
Noblesville	4,811	229	243
North Manchester	2,765	1	1
North Vernon	2,989	149	148
Oakland City	2,842	10	(1)
Peru	12,730	128	136
Petersburg	2,609	8	(1)
Portland	5,276	54	69
Princeton	7,505	340	415
Rensselaer	2,798	3	9
Richmond	32,493	2,139	1,494
Rochester	3,518	2	5
Rushville	5,709	161	213
Seymour	7,508	67	74
Shelbyville	10,618	345	331
South Bend	104,193	3,431	1,269
Sullivan	5,306	50	57
Tell City	4,873	27	47
Terre Haute	62,810	3,461	3,646
Union City [12]	3,084	10	38
Valparaiso	8,079	3	(7)
Vincennes	17,564	280	280
Wabash	8,840	124	149
Warsaw	5,730	39	34
Washington	9,070	90	122
West Lafayette	5,095	2	9
West Terre Haute	3,588	2	5
Winchester	4,487	25	23
Iowa			
Albia	4,425	77	84
Ames	10,261	54	40
Anamosa	3,579	58	66
Atlantic	5,585	20	23
Belle Plaine	3,239	3	6
Bettendorf	2,768	24	(1)
Boone	11,886	36	91
Burlington	26,755	377	322
Carroll	4,691	16	24
Cedar Falls	7,362	8	16
Cedar Rapids	56,097	746	677
Centerville	8,147	257	254
Chariton	5,365	40	43
Charles City	8,039	8	22
Cherokee	6,443	13	16
Clarinda	4,962	140	177
Clear Lake	3,066	1	4
Clinton	25,726	231	321
Council Bluffs	42,048	669	598
Cresco	3,069	1	1
Creston	8,615	31	40
Davenport	60,751	787	681
Decorah	4,581	9	2
Denison	3,905	6	3
Des Moines	142,559	5,428	5,512
Dubuque	41,679	88	73
Eldora	3,200	47	46
Estherville	4,940	8	38
Fairfield	6,619	59	84
Fort Dodge	21,895	298	373
Fort Madison	13,779	363	328
Glenwood	4,269	50	48
Grinnell	4,949	18	40
Hampton	3,473	10	13
Independence	3,691	2	1
Indianola	3,488	5	8
Iowa City	15,340	110	60
Iowa Falls	4,112	16	21
Jefferson	3,431	2	3
Keokuk	15,106	846	955
Knoxville	4,697	3	8
Marion	4,348	10	18
Marshalltown	17,373	338	250
Mason City	23,304	319	350
Missouri Valley	4,230	15	16
Mount Pleasant	3,743	87	166
Muscatine	16,778	57	102
Newton	11,560	37	49
Oelwein	7,794	33	45
Onawa town	2,538	36	(1)
Osage	2,964	2	5
Osceola	2,871	27	18
Oskaloosa	10,123	171	226
Ottumwa	28,075	424	521
Iowa—Continued			
Perry	5,881	109	121
Red Oak	5,778	54	32
Sac City	2,854	7	1
Sheldon	3,320	1	3
Shenandoah	6,502	10	24
Sioux City	79,183	1,064	1,139
Spencer	5,019	2	10
Tama	2,626	1	2
Valley Junction	4,280	134	34
Vinton	3,372	1	(7)
Washington	4,814	49	78
Waterloo	46,191	1,214	837
Waukon	2,526	5	(1)
Waverly	3,652	2	3
Webster City	7,024	11	4
Kansas			
Abilene	5,658	120	106
Anthony	2,947	69	55
Arkansas City	13,946	602	483
Atchison	13,024	1,517	1,497
Augusta	4,033	17	14
Baxter Springs	4,541	173	189
Beloit	3,502	2	5
Chanute	10,277	507	375
Cherryvale	4,251	160	227
Clay Center	4,386	51	97
Coffeyville	16,198	1,824	1,480
Columbus	3,235	33	57
Concordia	5,792	39	61
Council Grove	2,898	75	83
Dodge City	10,059	205	117
El Dorado	10,311	224	212
Emporia	14,067	564	483
Eureka	3,698	25	19
Fort Scott	10,763	729	822
Fredonia	3,446	34	12
Galena	4,736	144	168
Garden City	6,121	252	217
Garnett	2,768	87	(1)
Great Bend	5,548	280	254
Herington	4,519	77	40
Hiawatha	3,302	144	197
Hoisington	3,001	6	(1)
Holton	2,705	44	49
Horton	4,049	164	150
Humboldt	2,558	87	72
Hutchinson	27,085	954	1,016
Independence	12,782	1,104	781
Iola	7,160	329	411
Junction City	7,407	493	477
Kansas City	121,857	19,872	14,405
Kingman	2,752	25	(1)
Larned	3,532	100	90
Lawrence	13,726	1,437	1,466
Leavenworth	17,466	2,184	1,990
Liberal	5,294	3	2
Lyons	2,939	58	45
McPherson	6,147	3	(7)
Manhattan	10,136	332	289
Marysville	4,013	9	8
Neodesha	3,381	1	11
Newton	11,034	518	570
Norton	2,767	12	(1)
Olathe	3,656	269	219
Osawatomie	4,440	302	244
Ottawa	9,563	449	421
Paola	3,762	295	222
Parsons	14,903	1,277	1,338
Pittsburg	18,145	394	486
Pratt	6,322	254	302
Salina	20,155	532	641
Topeka	64,120	5,756	4,272
Wellington	7,405	185	222
Wichita	111,110	5,623	3,545
Winfield	9,398	256	262
Kentucky			
Ashland	29,074	936	489
Bellevue	8,497	4	13
Bowling Green	12,348	2,426	2,099
Catlettsburg	5,025	119	140
Central City	4,321	449	272
Clifton	3,080	6	(1)
Corbin	8,036	20	2
Covington	65,252	3,466	3,040
Cumberland	2,639	47	(1)
Cynthiana	4,386	659	698
Danville	6,729	1,789	1,357
Dayton	9,071	4	19
Earlington	3,309	1,279	1,414
Elizabethtown	2,590	329	349
Elsmere	2,917	218	(1)
Fort Thomas	10,008	38	22

See footnotes at end of table.

TABLE 11.—NEGRO POPULATION OF CITIES AND OTHER URBAN PLACES: 1930 AND 1920—Continued

[Places having no Negro population are omitted]

CITY OR OTHER URBAN PLACE	POPULATION Total, 1930	Negro 1930	Negro 1920
KENTUCKY—Continued			
Frankfort	11, 626	2, 205	2, 246
Franklin	3, 056	759	793
Fulton	3, 502	532	615
Georgetown	4, 229	1, 184	1, 204
Glasgow	5, 042	772	438
Harlan	4, 327	570	103
Harrodsburg	4, 029	853	965
Hazard	7, 021	810	568
Henderson	11, 668	2, 346	2, 968
Hopkinsville	10, 746	3, 980	3, 652
Irvine	3, 640	92	99
Jenkins	8, 465	1, 386	777
Lebanon	3, 248	626	725
Lexington	45, 736	12, 759	12, 450
Louisville	307, 745	47, 354	40, 087
Ludlow	6, 485	5	26
Madisonville	6, 908	1, 783	1, 531
Mayfield	8, 177	1, 147	1, 123
Maysville	6, 557	1, 180	1, 032
Middlesborough	10, 350	1, 021	1, 213
Morganfield	2, 551	454	528
Mount Sterling	4, 350	1, 036	1, 048
Murray	2, 891	532	(1)
Newport	29, 744	1, 231	864
Nicholasville	3, 128	709	696
Owensboro	22, 765	2, 509	2, 836
Paducah	33, 541	6, 744	5, 586
Paris	6, 204	1, 533	1, 599
Pikeville	3, 376	120	(1)
Pineville	3, 567	438	407
Princeton	4, 764	914	840
Providence	4, 742	1, 014	974
Richmond	6, 495	1, 896	1, 675
Russellville	3, 297	714	783
Shelbyville	4, 033	1, 123	1, 224
Somerset	5, 506	434	448
Winchester	8, 233	2, 007	2, 379
LOUISIANA			
Abbeville	4, 356	1, 115	1, 176
Alexandria	23, 025	9, 546	7, 863
Amite	2, 536	791	(1)
Bastrop	5, 121	1, 604	(1)
Baton Rouge	30, 729	10, 675	8, 560
Bogalusa	14, 029	4, 751	2, 605
Bossier City	4, 003	1, 374	(1)
Covington	3, 208	946	760
Crowley	7, 656	2, 583	2, 190
De Quincy	3, 589	820	(1)
De Ridder	3, 747	1, 255	790
Donaldsonville	3, 788	1, 394	1, 506
Eunice	3, 597	964	1, 013
Ferriday	2, 502	1, 501	(1)
Franklin	3, 271	1, 339	1, 391
Gretna	9, 584	2, 178	1, 969
Hammond	6, 072	2, 147	1, 279
Haynesville	2, 541	641	(1)
Homer	2, 909	1, 016	829
Houma	6, 531	1, 244	1, 380
Jackson	3, 966	1, 299	(1)
Jennings	4, 036	1, 146	1, 179
Lafayette	14, 635	5, 013	2, 999
Lake Charles	15, 791	5, 948	4, 472
Lake Providence	2, 867	1, 706	(1)
Leesville	3, 291	893	552
Mansfield	3, 837	1, 446	739
Merryville	2, 626	916	1, 135
Minden	5, 623	2, 034	2, 518
Monroe	26, 028	10, 112	5, 540
Morgan City	5, 985	1, 660	1, 930
Natchitoches	4, 547	1, 856	1, 505
New Iberia	8, 003	2, 545	2, 105
New Orleans	458, 762	129, 632	100, 930
Oakdale	3, 188	856	1, 320
Opelousas	6, 299	2, 858	2, 056
Pineville	3, 612	537	(1)
Plaquemine	5, 124	1, 931	2, 122
Ponchatoula	2, 898	1, 050	(1)
Rayne	3, 710	1, 216	1, 003
Ruston	4, 400	1, 201	961
Shreveport	76, 655	27, 219	17, 485
Slidell	2, 807	769	996
Tallulah	3, 332	1, 701	(1)
Thibodaux	4, 442	1, 226	1, 008
West Monroe	6, 566	986	(1)
Westwego	3, 987	513	(6)
Winnfield	3. 721	1, 310	879
MAINE			
Auburn	18, 571	11	7
Augusta	17, 198	30	34
Bangor	28, 749	228	208
Bath	9, 110	35	42
Belfast	4, 993	8	12
MAINE—Continued			
Brewer	6, 329	2	2
Brunswick	6, 144	19	27
Calais	5, 470	10	(7)
Eastport	3, 466	4	5
Fort Fairfield	2, 616	2	(1)
Gardiner	5, 609	8	15
Lewiston	34, 948	25	54
Old Town	7, 266	6	(7)
Portland	70, 810	268	300
Rockland	9, 075	32	29
Saco	7, 233	3	5
South Portland	13, 840	4	8
Waterville	15, 454	4	8
Westbrook	10, 807	4	(7)
MARYLAND			
Annapolis	12, 531	3, 218	2, 954
Baltimore	804, 874	142, 106	108, 322
Brunswick	3, 671	131	149
Cambridge	8, 544	2, 262	2, 306
Chestertown	2, 809	852	821
Crisfield	3, 850	928	1, 145
Cumberland	37, 747	1, 161	1, 433
Easton	4, 092	1, 021	904
Elkton	3, 331	410	387
Frederick	14, 434	1, 551	1, 236
Frostburg	5, 588	200	206
Hagerstown	30, 861	1, 517	1, 509
Havre de Grace	3, 985	639	806
Hyattsville	4, 264	199	220
Laurel	2, 532	243	(1)
Mount Rainier	3, 832	1	(1)
Pocomoke City	2, 609	638	(1)
Salisburytown	10, 997	1, 912	1, 619
Takoma Park	6, 415	351	221
Westernport	3, 440	9	21
Westminster	4, 463	305	250
MASSACHUSETTS			
Abington town	5, 872	5	14
Amesbury town	11, 899	19	17
Amherst town	5, 888	133	173
Andover town	9, 969	90	100
Arlington town	36, 094	64	41
Athol town	10, 677	23	1
Attleboro city	21, 769	84	118
Auburn town	6, 147	2	8
Ayer town	3, 060	21	17
Barnstable town	7, 271	484	148
Belmont town	21, 748	16	28
Beverly city	25, 086	47	60
Blackstone town	4, 674	2	17
Boston city	781, 188	20, 574	16, 350
Braintree town	15, 712	22	9
Bridgewater town	9, 055	155	71
Brockton city	63, 797	483	559
Brookline town	47, 490	298	349
Cambridge city	113, 643	5, 419	5, 334
Canton town	5, 816	75	45
Chelsea city	45, 816	293	373
Chicopee city	43, 930	17	10
Clinton town	12, 817	3	2
Concord town	7, 477	38	28
Dalton town	4, 220	47	39
Danvers town	12, 957	15	9
Dartmouth town	8, 778	154	55
Dedham town	15, 136	80	39
Dudley town	4, 265	10	14
Easthampton town	11, 323	1	(7)
Everett city	48, 424	1, 002	1, 129
Fairhaven town	10, 951	158	55
Fall River city	115, 274	382	315
Fitchburg city	4, 692	19	32
Framingham town	22, 210	162	174
Franklin town	7, 028	4	7
Gardner city	19, 399	18	25
Gloucester city	24, 204	3	6
Great Barrington town	5, 934	74	82
Greenfield town	15, 500	94	83
Haverhill city	48, 710	272	361
Hingham town	6, 657	76	73
Holyoke city	56, 537	132	146
Hopedale town	2, 973	1	(7)
Hudson town	8, 469	16	17
Ipswich town	5, 599	6	12
Lawrence city	85, 068	166	219
Lee town	4, 061	20	34
Lexington town	9, 467	34	29
Longmeadow town	4, 437	23	13
Leominster city	21, 810	87	95
Lowell city	100, 234	126	170
Lynn city	102, 320	815	812
Malden city	58, 036	632	531
MASSACHUSETTS—Contd.			
Mansfield town	6, 364	3	12
Marblehead town	8, 668	7	7
Marlborough city	15, 587	22	18
Medford city	59, 714	595	535
Melrose city	23, 170	68	105
Methuen town	21, 069	47	58
Middleborough town	8, 608	101	44
Millbury town	6, 957	3	1
Milford town	14, 741	13	3
Milton town	16, 434	54	32
Nantucket town	3, 678	279	112
Natick town	13, 589	31	19
Needham town	10, 845	19	17
New Bedford city	112, 597	3, 631	4, 998
Newburyport city	15, 084	100	126
Newton city	65, 276	630	561
North Adams city	21, 621	126	98
Northampton city	24, 381	67	67
North Andover town	6, 961	2	(7)
North Attleborough town	10, 197	36	50
Northbridge town	9, 713	7	7
Norwood town	15, 049	22	15
Palmer town	9, 577	39	42
Peabody city	21, 345	25	33
Pittsfield city	49, 677	529	398
Plymouth town	13, 042	224	153
Provincetown	3, 808	62	56
Quincy city	71, 983	34	27
Randolph town	6, 553	21	15
Reading town	9, 767	9	3
Revere city	35, 680	84	48
Rockland town	7, 524	28	26
Salem city	43, 353	101	130
Saugus town	14, 700	131	40
Somerset town	5, 398	6	4
Somerville city	103, 908	274	328
Southbridge town	14, 264	2	15
Spencer town	6, 272	16	5
Springfield city	149, 900	3, 141	2, 650
Stoneham town	10, 060	14	45
Stoughton town	8, 204	13	16
Swampscott town	10, 346	20	17
Taunton city	37, 355	372	345
Uxbridge town	6, 285	2	5
Wakefield town	16, 318	21	20
Walpole town	7, 273	16	12
Waltham city	39, 247	46	43
Ware town	7, 385	2	2
Watertown town	34, 913	14	34
Webster town	12, 992	1	15
Wellesley town	11, 439	48	36
Westfield city	19, 775	33	31
West Springfield town	16, 684	99	148
Weymouth town	20, 882	70	29
Whitman town	7, 638	43	41
Winchester town	12, 719	237	227
Winthrop town	16, 852	75	109
Woburn city	19, 434	284	286
Worcester city	195, 311	1, 378	1, 258
MICHIGAN			
Adrian	13, 064	126	135
Albion	8, 324	943	696
Allegon	3, 941	45	52
Alma	6, 734	20	13
Ann Arbor	26, 944	940	580
Battle Creek	43, 573	1, 795	1, 055
Bay City	47, 355	170	127
Belding	4, 140	3	6
Benton Harbor	15, 434	928	394
Berkley	5, 571	1	(1)
Big Rapids	4, 671	6	(7)
Birmingham	9, 539	104	8
Boyne City	2, 650	27	47
Buchanan	3, 922	19	5
Cadillac	9, 570	4	4
Charlotte	5, 307	6	11
Cheboygan	4, 923	4	10
Coldwater	6, 735	15	10
Dearborn	50, 358	43	1
Detroit	1, 568, 662	120, 066	40, 838
Dowagiac	5, 550	241	236
Durand	3, 081	5	8
East Grand Rapids	4, 024	17	(1)
East Lansing	4, 389	1	(1)
Eaton Rapids	2, 822	1	(1)
Ecorse	12, 716	1, 417	7
Escanaba	14, 524	17	18
Fenton	3, 171	2	1
Ferndale	20, 855	171	18
Flint	156, 492	5, 725	1, 701
Gladstone	5, 170	8	11
Grand Haven	8, 345	37	29
Grand Lodge	3, 572	4	2

See footnotes at end of table.

TABLE 11.—NEGRO POPULATION OF CITIES AND OTHER URBAN PLACES: 1930 AND 1920—Continued

[Places having no Negro population are omitted]

CITY OR OTHER URBAN PLACE	POPULATION		
	Total, 1930	Negro	
		1930	1920
MICHIGAN—Continued			
Grand Rapids	168,592	2,795	1,090
Greenville	4,730	26	16
Grosse Pointe	5,173	61	(1)
Grosse Pointe Farms	3,533	68	(1)
Grosse Pointe Park	11,174	102	(7)
Hamtramck	56,268	4,068	2,022
Hancock	5,795	2	(7)
Highland Park	52,959	1,171	358
Hillsdale	5,896	10	15
Holland	14,346	6	7
Houghton	3,757	1	1
Howell	3,615	17	19
Inkster	4,440	1,195	(1)
Ionia	6,562	8	7
Iron Mountain	11,652	5	(7)
Iron River	4,665	6	1
Ironwood	14,299	1	1
Ishpeming	9,238	1	(7)
Jackson	55,187	1,692	810
Kalamazoo	54,786	967	752
Kingsford	5,526	2	(1)
Lansing	78,397	1,409	698
Lapeer	5,008	50	27
Lincoln Park	12,336	3	(1)
Ludington	8,898	3	(7)
Manistee	8,078	1	(7)
Manistique	5,198	3	7
Marine City	3,462	10	(7)
Marquette	14,789	187	84
Marshall	5,019	36	12
Mason	2,575	24	(1)
Melvindale	4,053	2	(1)
Midland	8,038	11	12
Monroe	18,110	379	26
Mount Clemens	13,497	274	73
Mount Pleasant	5,211	2	3
Munising	3,956	11	10
Muskegon	41,390	596	182
Muskegon Heights	15,584	691	32
Niles	11,326	261	155
Otsego	3,245	2	13
Petoskey	5,740	33	14
Pleasant Ridge	2,885	28	(1)
Plymouth	4,484	8	2
Pontiac	64,928	2,553	619
Port Huron	31,361	933	500
River Rouge	17,314	2,145	150
Rochester	3,554	9	3
Roseville	6,836	302	(1)
Royal Oak	22,904	36	2
Saginaw	80,715	2,853	328
St. Clair	3,389	3	4
St. Clair Shores	6,745	77	(1)
St. Johns	3,929	2	4
St. Joseph	8,349	90	109
Sault Ste. Marie	13,755	23	49
South Haven	4,804	78	38
Sturgis	6,950	8	9
Three Rivers	6,863	91	31
Traverse City	12,539	38	28
Trenton	4,022	16	(1)
Wakefield	3,677	1	(7)
Wayne	3,423	3	(1)
Wyandotte	28,368	9	10
Ypsilanti	10,143	1,294	627
Zeeland	2,850	1	(1)
MINNESOTA			
Albert Lea	10,169	14	7
Alexandria	3,876	5	11
Anoka	4,851	18	35
Austin	12,276	10	25
Bayport	2,590	44	(1)
Bemidji	7,202	13	21
Blue Earth	2,884	1	2
Brainerd	10,221	2	3
Columbia Heights	5,613	4	3
Crookston	6,321	1	1
Duluth	101,463	416	495
East Grand Forks	2,922	1	(1)
Edina	3,138	20	(1)
Fairmont	5,521	3	4
Fairbault	12,767	12	13
Fergus Falls	9,389	77	77
Grand Rapids	3,206	2	(7)
Hastings	5,086	8	10
Hibbing village	15,666	7	2
Hopkins [13]	3,834	5	2
Hutchinson	3,406	3	2
International Falls	5,036	10	9
Luverne	2,644	7	1
Mankato	14,038	4	3
MINNESOTA—Continued			
Minneapolis	464,356	4,176	3,927
Montevideo	4,319	1	3
Moorhead	7,651	20	17
New Ulm	7,308	2	(7)
Northfield	4,153	2	14
North St. Paul	2,915	7	(1)
Owatonna	7,654	17	11
Red Wing	9,629	17	23
Redwood Falls	2,552	6	(1)
Richfield	3,344	4	(1)
Rochester	20,621	37	37
St. Cloud	21,000	36	50
St. Paul	271,606	4,001	3,376
St. Peter	4,811	42	17
Sauk Center	2,716	6	1
South St. Paul	10,009	2	3
Stillwater	7,173	3	4
Thief River Falls	4,268	3	1
Two Harbors	4,425	2	5
Virginia	11,963	15	13
Waseca	3,815	9	1
West St. Paul	4,463	2	(7)
Willmar	6,173	2	1
Winona	20,850	7	12
Worthington	3,878	4	(7)
MISSISSIPPI			
Aberdeen	3,925	1,773	2,121
Amory	3,214	979	872
Bay St. Louis	3,724	1,047	746
Belzoni	2,735	1,451	(1)
Biloxi	14,850	2,445	1,615
Brookhaven	5,288	1,988	1,983
Canton	4,725	2,619	1,726
Clarksdale	10,043	5,025	4,392
Cleveland	3,240	1,189	(1)
Columbia	4,833	1,988	789
Columbus	10,743	4,862	5,572
Corinth	6,220	1,599	1,617
Greenville	14,807	8,370	6,939
Greenwood	11,123	5,385	4,031
Grenada	4,349	1,906	1,571
Gulfport	12,547	3,158	1,955
Hattiesburg	18,601	6,811	4,937
Indianola	3,116	1,612	(1)
Jackson	48,282	19,423	9,936
Kosciusko	3,237	1,153	(1)
Laurel	18,017	6,838	5,038
Lexington	2,590	1,397	(1)
Louisville	3,013	1,064	(1)
McComb	10,057	2,013	1,734
Meridian	31,954	11,352	8,343
Natchez	13,422	7,159	6,801
New Albany	3,187	1,033	863
Oxford	2,890	902	(1)
Pascagoula	4,339	986	1,196
Pass Christian	3,004	1,437	(1)
Philadelphia	2,560	422	(1)
Picayune	4,698	1,827	(1)
Starkville	3,612	1,361	996
Tupelo	6,361	2,284	2,077
Vicksburg	22,943	11,915	9,148
Water Valley	3,738	1,205	1,275
West Point	4,677	2,121	1,796
Winona	2,607	1,123	1,198
Yazoo City	5,579	2,765	2,709
MISSOURI			
Bonne Terre	4,021	80	109
Boonville	6,435	933	815
Brentwood	2,819	335	(1)
Brookfield	6,428	257	195
Butler	2,706	143	164
Cameron	3,507	52	78
Cape Girardeau	16,227	968	790
Carrollton	4,058	293	388
Carthage	9,736	298	413
Caruthersville	4,781	1,105	1,156
Chaffee	2,902	4	3
Charleston	3,357	741	517
Chillicothe	8,177	358	382
Clayton	9,613	342	135
Clinton	5,744	312	341
Columbia	14,967	2,301	1,919
Crystal City	3,057	285	(1)
De Soto	5,069	236	272
Excelsior Springs	4,565	274	308
Farmington	3,001	155	156
Fayette	2,630	702	(1)
Ferguson	3,798	52	(1)
Festus	4,085	354	434
MISSOURI—Continued			
Fredericktown	2,954	149	172
Fulton	6,105	1,174	1,252
Hannibal	22,761	2,013	1,792
Higginsville	3,339	336	430
Independence	15,296	846	864
Jefferson City	21,596	2,164	1,977
Joplin	33,454	755	741
Kansas City	399,746	38,574	30,719
Kennett	4,128	94	63
Kirksville	8,293	113	105
Kirkwood	9,169	777	611
Lebanon	3,562	165	147
Lexington	4,595	787	966
Liberty	3,516	496	421
Louisiana	3,549	396	555
Macon	3,851	340	488
Maplewood	12,657	124	41
Marceline	3,555	82	75
Marshall	8,103	664	616
Maryville	5,217	84	121
Mexico	8,290	1,244	899
Moberly	13,772	1,024	821
Neosho	4,485	77	135
Nevada	7,448	73	73
North Kansas City	2,574	4	(1)
Perryville	2,964	1	(1)
Poplar Bluff	7,551	829	886
Richmond	4,129	414	529
Richmond Heights	9,150	695	(1)
Rolla	3,670	113	(1)
St. Charles	10,491	552	554
St. Joseph	80,935	4,055	4,209
St. Louis	821,960	93,580	69,854
Ste. Genevieve	2,662	72	(1)
Sedalia	20,806	2,106	2,062
Sikeston	5,676	448	90
Slater	3,478	459	485
Springfield	57,527	1,779	1,664
Trenton	6,992	80	118
University City	25,809	169	71
Warrensburg	5,146	315	336
Washington	5,918	72	75
Webb City	6,876	19	47
Webster Groves	16,487	975	442
West Plains	3,335	86	86
MONTANA			
Anaconda	12,494	101	92
Billings	16,380	142	130
Bozeman	6,855	19	40
Butte	39,532	163	214
Deer Lodge	3,510	26	37
Great Falls	28,822	209	202
Havre	6,372	36	59
Helena	11,803	131	220
Kalispell	6,094	36	37
Lewistown	5,358	15	77
Livingston	6,391	1	17
Miles City	7,175	35	41
Missoula	14,657	110	92
Roundup	2,577	1	(1)
Whitefish	2,803	2	2
NEBRASKA			
Alliance	6,669	203	136
Auburn	3,068	7	8
Aurora	2,715	3	9
Beatrice	10,297	82	80
Blair	2,791	3	3
Broken Bow	2,715	9	20
Chadron	4,606	5	12
Columbus	6,898	5	17
Fairbury	6,192	10	29
Falls City	5,787	51	32
Fremont	11,407	58	49
Gering	2,531	24	(7)
Grand Island	18,041	120	126
Hastings	15,490	70	81
Holdredge	3,263	4	5
Kearney	8,575	5	23
Lincoln	75,933	997	896
McCook	6,688	30	21
Nebraska City	7,230	61	57
Norfolk	10,717	27	35
North Platte	12,061	35	59
Omaha	214,006	11,123	10,315
Schuyler	2,588	8	7
Scottsbluff	8,465	62	62
Seward	2,737	1	(1)
Sidney	3,306	8	13
South Sioux City	3,927	72	(1)

See footnotes at end of table.

TABLE 11.—NEGRO POPULATION OF CITIES AND OTHER URBAN PLACES: 1930 AND 1920—Continued

[Places having no Negro population are omitted]

CITY OR OTHER URBAN PLACE	POPULATION: Total, 1930	POPULATION: Negro 1930	POPULATION: Negro 1920
NEBRASKA—Continued			
Superior	3, 044	3	8
Wahoo	2, 689	4	(1)
Wymore	2, 680	1	(7)
York	5, 712	21	17
NEVADA			
Elko	3, 217	65	(1)
Ely	3, 045	19	(1)
Las Vegas	5, 165	144	(1)
Reno	18, 529	123	65
Sparks	4, 508	13	3
NEW HAMPSHIRE			
Claremont town	12, 377	29	13
Concord city	25, 228	58	44
Dover city	13, 573	5	14
Exeter town	4, 872	3	3
Franklin city	6, 576	11	7
Keene city	13, 794	12	6
Laconia city	12, 471	9	16
Lebanon town	7, 073	6	8
Littleton town	4, 558	1	(7)
Manchester city	76, 834	26	62
Nashua city	31, 463	66	31
Newport town	4, 659	6	(7)
Portsmouth city	14, 495	361	163
Rochester city	10, 209	1	14
NEW JERSEY			
Asbury Park city	14, 981	3, 549	2, 824
Atlantic City	66, 198	15, 611	10, 946
Audubon	8, 904	15	14
Bayonne city	88, 979	2, 205	648
Belleville town	26, 974	1, 023	469
Belmar	3, 491	213	(1)
Bergenfield	8, 816	87	26
Bernardsville	3, 336	13	(1)
Beverly	2, 864	410	287
Bloomfield town	38, 077	881	646
Bogota	7, 341	7	3
Boonton	6, 866	204	46
Bordentown	4, 405	416	251
Bound Brook	7, 372	21	21
Bradley Beach	3, 306	9	(1)
Bridgeton city	15, 699	1, 526	1, 146
Burlington city	10, 844	1, 408	624
Caldwell	5, 144	143	118
Camden city	118, 700	11, 340	8, 500
Cape May	2, 637	483	484
Carlstadt	5, 425	3	54
Carteret borough	13, 339	386	63
Chatham	3, 869	31	(1)
Clementon	2, 605	12	(1)
Cliffside Park borough	15, 267	3	4
Clifton city	46, 875	117	47
Closter	2, 502	80	(1)
Collingswood borough	12, 723	12	15
Crawford township	11. 126	822	(6)
Dover town	10, 031	108	48
Dumont	5, 861	94	10
Dunellen	5, 148	36	33
East Newark	2, 686	18	97
East Orange city	68, 020	4, 880	2, 378
East Paterson	4, 779	14	(1)
East Rutherford	7, 080	263	246
Edgewater	4, 089	1	3
Egg Harbor	3, 478	443	183
Elizabeth city	114, 589	4, 761	1, 970
Englewood city	17, 805	2, 524	1, 138
Fairlawn	5, 990	26	(1)
Fairview	9, 067	7	(7)
Flemington	2, 729	23	41
Fort Lee	8, 759	9	2
Freehold	6, 894	592	341
Garfield city	29, 739	228	8
Glassboro	4, 799	762	(1)
Glen Ridge	7, 365	217	152
Glen Rock	4, 369	195	(1)
Gloucester city	13, 796	5	2
Guttenberg	6, 535	1	9
Hackensack city	24, 568	2, 530	1, 153
Hackettstown	3, 038	3	(7)
Haddonfield	8, 857	392	370
Haddon Heights	5, 394	8	17
Haledon	4, 812	15	19
Hammonton	7, 656	79	25
Harrisontown	15, 601	105	59
Hasbouck Heights	5, 658	2	12
Hawthorne borough	11, 868	11	17
Highland Park	8, 691	115	36
Hightstown	3, 012	237	198
Hillsdale	2, 959	40	(1)
Hillside township	17, 601	32	(6)
Hoboken city	59, 261	462	204
Irvington town	56, 733	118	104
Jersey City	316, 715	12, 575	8, 000
Kearnytown	40, 716	187	78
Keyport	4, 940	253	177
Lambertville	4, 518	145	119
Leonia	5, 350	122	64
Linden city [14]	21, 206	884	1
Lindenwold	2, 523	188	(1)
Little Ferry	4, 155	23	13
Lodi borough	11, 549	133	20
Long Branch city	18, 399	1, 609	1, 034
Lyndhurst township	17, 362	46	(6)
Madison	7, 481	567	403
Manville	5, 441	33	(1)
Maplewood township	21, 321	295	(6)
Margate City	2, 913	55	(1)
Maywood	3, 398	15	(1)
Merchantville	3, 592	37	43
Metuchen	5, 748	213	157
Middlesex	3, 504	35	(1)
Midland Park	3, 638	9	(1)
Milltown	2, 994	2	4
Millville city	14, 705	154	147
Montclair town	42, 017	6, 384	3, 461
Morristown town	15, 197	1, 377	897
Neptune township	10, 625	1, 869	(6)
Newark city	442, 337	38, 880	16, 971
New Brunswick city	34, 555	2, 086	1, 124
New Milford [15]	2, 556	15	(1)
Newton	5, 401	27	14
North Bergen township	40, 714	86	(6)
Northfield	2, 804	105	(1)
North Plainfield	9, 760	131	157
Nutley town	20, 572	484	172
Ocean City	5, 525	611	181
Orange city	35, 399	5, 027	3, 621
Palisades Park	7, 065	8	4
Palmyra [16]	4, 968	420	(1)
Paramus	2, 649	57	(1)
Passaic city	62, 959	1, 858	591
Paterson city	138, 513	2, 952	1, 551
Paulsboro	7, 121	679	190
Pennsgrove	5, 895	746	346
Pensauken township	16, 915	1, 405	(6)
Perth Amboy city	43, 516	939	492
Phillipsburg town	19, 255	31	31
Pitman	5, 411	60	27
Plainfield city	34, 422	3, 648	2, 445
Pleasantville city	11, 580	1, 992	973
Pompton Lakes	3, 104	17	(1)
Princeton	6, 992	1, 053	1, 017
Rahway city	16, 011	875	525
Ramsey	3, 258	41	(1)
Raritan	4, 751	4	(7)
Red Bank borough	11, 622	1, 596	930
Ridgefield	4, 671	3	(1)
Ridgefield Park village	10, 764	12	19
Ridgewood village	12, 188	399	196
Rockaway	3, 132	34	12
Roselle borough	13, 021	1, 538	417
Roselle Park	8, 969	72	53
Rutherford borough	14, 915	288	197
Salem	8, 047	1, 498	1, 260
Sayreville	8, 658	216	(6)
Secaucus	8, 950	62	38
Somerville	8, 255	559	431
South Amboy	8, 476	2	5
South Orange village	13, 630	665	340
South Plainfield	5, 047	38	(1)
South River borough	10, 759	197	8
Summit city	14, 556	1, 261	488
Teaneck township	16, 513	66	(6)
Tenafly	5, 669	42	43
Totowa	4, 600	45	(1)
Trenton city	123, 356	8, 057	4, 315
Union City	58, 659	38	21
Union township	16, 472	1, 633	(6)
Ventnor	6, 674	110	(1)
Verona	7, 161	225	90
Vineland	7, 556	324	229
Wallington	9, 063	232	11
Wanaque	3, 119	80	20
Washington	4, 410	100	79
Weehawken township	14, 807	58	(6)
West Caldwell	2, 911	33	(1)
Westfield town	15, 801	1, 019	632
West New York town	37, 107	173	92
West Orange town	24, 327	234	104
West Paterson	3, 101	14	(1)
Westville	3, 462	1	(1)
Westwood	4, 861	238	74
Wharton	3, 683	8	(7)
Wildwood	5, 330	530	239
Woodbury	8, 172	951	811
Woodbridge township	25, 266	494	(6)
Wood Ridge	5, 159	7	(1)
NEW MEXICO			
Alamogordo	3, 096	78	(1)
Albuquerque	26, 570	441	213
Carlsbad	3, 708	111	(1)
Clayton	2, 518	9	(1)
Clovis	8, 027	85	30
Deming	3, 377	20	49
Gallup	5, 992	118	54
Las Cruces	5, 811	206	54
Las Vegas city	4, 719	30	49
Las Vegas town	4, 378	6	18
Raton	6, 090	127	136
Roswell	11, 173	343	164
Santa Fe	11, 176	73	44
Silver City	3, 519	52	46
Tucumcari	4, 143	19	4
NEW YORK			
Albany	127, 412	2, 324	1, 239
Albion	4, 878	3	46
Amityville	4, 407	55	96
Amsterdam	34, 817	146	148
Auburn	36, 652	469	491
Babylon	4, 342	94	93
Ballston Spa	4, 591	4	6
Batavia	17, 375	40	30
Bath	4, 015	43	72
Beacon	11, 933	327	187
Binghamton	76, 662	722	623
Brockport	3, 511	4	2
Bronxville	6, 387	322	102
Buffalo	573, 076	13, 563	4, 511
Canajoharie	2, 519	17	(1)
Canandaigua	7, 541	37	67
Canastota	4, 235	14	19
Canton	2, 822	8	4
Carthage	4, 460	5	7
Catskill	5, 082	283	192
Cedarhurst	5, 065	147	75
Cobleskill	2, 594	42	(1)
Cohoes	23, 226	1	8
Cooperstown	2, 909	1	2
Corning	15, 777	91	86
Cortland	15, 043	26	23
Dannemora	3, 348	336	148
Depew	6, 536	224	8
Dobbs Ferry	5, 741	58	196
Dolgeville	3, 309	3	3
Dunkirk	17, 802	52	27
East Aurora	4, 815	12	10
East Rochester	6, 627	14	17
East Rockaway	4, 340	10	(1)
Ellenville	3, 280	20	27
Elmira	47, 397	830	555
Elmsford	2, 935	191	(1)
Endicott [17]	16, 231	24	10
Fairport	4, 604	4	7
Farmingdale	3, 373	1	(1)
Floral Park	10, 016	11	1
Fort Edward	3, 850	12	19
Fort Plain	2, 725	6	18
Frankfort	4, 203	4	29
Fredonia	5, 814	5	5
Freeport	15, 467	351	388
Fulton	12, 462	9	16
Garden City	7, 180	223	(1)
Geneva	16, 053	153	133
Glen Cove	11, 430	812	326
Glens Falls	18, 531	46	15
Gloversville	23, 099	178	207
Goshen	2, 891	181	213
Gouverneur	4, 015	1	(7)
Gowanda	3, 042	9	5
Granville	3, 483	1	1
Great Neck	4, 010	116	(1)
Greenport	3, 062	133	90
Hastings-on-Hudson	7, 097	30	5
Haverstraw	5, 621	274	187
Hempstead	12, 650	782	230
Herkimer	10, 446	10	22
Highland Falls	2, 910	222	124
Homer	3, 195	22	(1)
Hoosick Falls	4, 755	25	18
Hornell	16, 250	48	56
Hudson	12, 337	557	368
Hudson Falls	6, 449	13	16
Ilion	9, 890	2	12

See footnotes at end of table.

TABLE 11.—NEGRO POPULATION OF CITIES AND OTHER URBAN PLACES: 1930 AND 1920—Continued

[Places having no Negro population are omitted]

CITY OR OTHER URBAN PLACE	POPULATION Total, 1930	Negro 1930	Negro 1920
NEW YORK—Continued			
Irvington	3,067	49	41
Ithaca	20,708	637	453
Jamestown	45,155	296	191
Johnson City	13,567	4	(7)
Johnstown	10,801	62	77
Kenmore	16,482	11	(7)
Kingston	28,088	636	563
Lackawanna	23,948	2,051	269
Lake Placid	2,930	1	(1)
Lancaster	7,040	15	24
Larchmont	5,282	177	(1)
Lawrence	3,041	66	53
Le Roy	4,474	149	87
Liberty	3,427	13	(1)
Lindenhurst	4,040	6	(1)
Little Falls	11,105	10	22
Lockport	23,160	190	109
Long Beach	5,817	65	(1)
Lowville	3,424	13	(7)
Lynbrook	11,993	60	15
Lyons	3,956	9	17
Malone	8,657	16	9
Mamaroneck	11,766	454	260
Massena	10,637	21	48
Mechanicsville	7,924	38	40
Medina	6,071	13	23
Middletown	21,276	459	378
Mineola	8,155	28	20
Monticello	3,450	15	(1)
Mount Kisco	5,127	109	76
Mount Morris	3,238	17	17
Mount Vernon	61,499	3,608	1,345
Newark	7,649	22	29
Newburgh	31,275	894	632
New Rochelle	54,000	4,644	2,637
New York	6,930,446	327,706	152,467
Bronx Borough	1,265,258	12,930	4,803
Brooklyn	2,560,401	68,921	31,912
Manhattan	1,867,312	224,670	109,133
Queens	1,079,129	18,609	5,120
Richmond	158,346	2,576	1,499
Niagara Falls	75,460	906	509
North Pelham	4,890	150	(1)
Northport	2,528	35	(1)
North Tarrytown	7,417	399	255
North Tonawanda	19,019	3	3
Norwich	8,378	92	114
Nyack	5,392	568	315
Ogdensburg	16,915	20	36
Olean	21,790	296	238
Oneida	10,558	50	63
Oneonta	12,536	71	71
Ossining	15,241	1,107	443
Oswego	22,652	43	52
Owego	4,742	109	126
Palmyra	2,592	7	(1)
Patchogue	6,860	98	29
Peekskill	17,125	582	310
Pelham Manor	4,908	228	(1)
Penn Yan	5,329	55	60
Plattsburg	13,349	18	17
Pleasantville	4,540	67	42
Port Chester	22,662	873	204
Port Jervis	10,243	98	95
Poughkeepsie	40,288	1,101	850
Rensselaer	11,223	27	44
Rochester	328,132	2,679	1,579
Rockville Centre	13,718	608	147
Rome	32,338	367	170
Rye	8,712	433	295
Sag Harbor	2,773	57	85
Salamanca	9,577	26	17
Saranac Lake	8,020	45	33
Saratoga Springs	13,169	442	480
Saugerties	4,060	21	18
Scarsdale	9,690	462	168
Schenectady	95,692	618	388
Sea Cliff	3,456	60	(1)
Seneca Falls	6,443	20	27
Silver Creek	3,160	24	21
Solvay	7,986	3	9
Southampton	3,737	342	86
South Glens Falls	2,689	4	(1)
Spring Valley	3,948	74	63
Suffern	3,757	16	16
Syracuse	209,326	1,899	1,260
Tarrytown	6,841	312	268
Troy	72,763	606	579
Tuckahoe	6,138	560	112
Tupper Lake	5,271	2	1
Utica	101,740	456	354
Valley Stream	11,790	1	(1)
Walden	4,283	2	6
Walton	3,496	5	13
Wappingers Falls	3,336	11	13

CITY OR OTHER URBAN PLACE	POPULATION Total, 1930	Negro 1930	Negro 1920
NEW YORK—Continued			
Warsaw	3,477	25	15
Waterford	2,921	7	(7)
Waterloo	4,047	6	14
Watertown	32,205	85	94
Watervliet	16,083	45	102
Watkins Glen [18]	2,956	74	63
Waverly	5,662	26	25
Wellsville	5,674	50	87
Westfield	3,466	1	2
West Haverstraw	2,834	117	(1)
Whitehall	5,191	10	20
White Plains	35,830	2,150	995
Williston Park	4,427	7	(1)
Yonkers	134,646	3,332	1,940
Yorkville	3,406	9	(1)
NORTH CAROLINA			
Albemarle	3,493	60	25
Asheboro	5,021	802	450
Asheville	50,193	14,255	7,145
Beaufort	2,957	1,008	990
Belmont	4,121	395	228
Bessemer City	3,739	615	(1)
Burlington	9,737	636	556
Canton	5,117	96	104
Chapel Hill	2,699	891	(1)
Charlotte	82,675	25,163	14,641
Cherryville	2,756	141	(1)
Clinton	2,712	912	(1)
Concord	11,820	1,966	1,746
Dunn	4,558	1,873	765
Durham	52,037	18,717	7,654
Edenton	3,563	1,478	1,569
Elizabeth City	10,037	3,722	3,439
Fayetteville	13,049	5,357	3,376
Forest City	4,069	587	(1)
Gastonia	17,093	3,207	2,330
Goldsboro	14,985	6,868	4,882
Graham	2,972	336	(1)
Greensboro	53,569	14,050	5,973
Greenville	9,194	4,233	2,827
Hamlet	4,801	1,463	1,128
Henderson	6,345	2,843	2,056
Hendersonville	5,070	1,258	894
Hickory	7,363	1,696	1,043
High Point	36,745	7,229	2,900
Kings Mountain	5,632	685	420
Kinston	11,362	5,062	4,011
Laurinburg	3,312	1,258	1,041
Lenoir	6,532	1,303	868
Lexington	9,652	1,533	943
Lincolnton	3,781	524	534
Lumberton	4,140	1,123	656
Monroe	6,100	1,982	1,049
Mooresville	5,619	699	529
Morehead City	3,483	743	581
Morganton	6,001	1,018	623
Mount Airy	6,045	477	438
Mount Olive	2,685	1,054	(1)
New Bern	11,981	6,277	6,735
Newton	4,394	509	325
North Wilkesboro	3,668	426	(1)
Oxford	4,101	1,611	1,328
Raheigh	37,379	12,575	8,544
Reidsville	6,851	2,333	1,994
Roanoke Rapids	3,404	49	134
Rockingham	2,906	1,116	876
Rocky Mount	21,412	8,702	4,623
Roxboro	3,657	1,098	(1)
Salisbury	16,951	3,964	3,572
Sanford	4,253	1,070	791
Shelby	10,789	2,125	637
Smithfield	2,543	758	(1)
Southern Pines	2,524	860	(1)
Spencer	3,128	67	82
Spindale	3,066	43	(1)
Statesville	10,490	1,648	1,383
Tarboro	6,379	2,336	1,661
Thomasville	10,090	1,672	814
Wadesboro	3,124	1,197	971
Washington	7,035	3,170	2,877
Williamston	2,731	1,436	(1)
Wilmington	32,270	13,106	13,461
Wilson	12,613	6,205	5,208
Winston-Salem	75,274	32,566	20,735
NORTH DAKOTA			
Bismarck	11,090	45	41
Devils Lake	5,451	24	42
Dickinson	5,025	2	4
Fargo	28,619	35	42
Grafton	3,136	1	(7)
Grand Forks	17,112	18	27

CITY OR OTHER URBAN PLACE	POPULATION Total, 1930	Negro 1930	Negro 1920
NORTH DAKOTA—Contd.			
Jamestown	8,187	2	13
Mandan	5,037	9	13
Minot	16,099	70	65
Wahpeton	3,176	1	10
Williston	5,106	9	15
OHIO			
Akron	255,040	11,080	5,580
Alliance	23,047	937	419
Ashland	11,141	53	30
Ashtabula	23,301	204	153
Athens	7,252	159	228
Barberton	23,934	953	740
Barnesville	4,602	170	189
Bedford	6,814	17	5
Bellaire	13,327	565	411
Bellefontaine	9,543	362	367
Bellevue	6,256	10	18
Berea	5,697	175	17
Bexley	7,396	212	(1)
Bowling Green	6,688	42	31
Bridgeport	4,655	232	213
Bucyrus	10,027	80	52
Cadiz	2,597	345	(1)
Cambridge	16,129	439	344
Campbell [19]	14,673	1,858	597
Canton	104,906	3,004	1,283
Carey	2,722	1	(1)
Chagrin Falls	2,739	11	(1)
Chillicothe	18,340	1,275	961
Cincinnati	451,160	47,818	30,079
Circleville	7,369	374	357
Cleveland	900,429	71,899	34,451
Cleveland Heights	50,945	573	185
Clyde	3,159	6	7
Columbus	290,564	32,774	22,181
Conneaut	9,691	35	48
Coshocton	10,908	159	112
Crestline	4,425	167	121
Cuyahoga Falls	19,797	34	11
Dayton	200,982	17,077	9,025
Deer Park	2,642	1	(1)
Defiance	8,818	22	16
Delaware	8,675	442	400
Delphos	5,672	10	27
Dennison	4,529	75	81
Dover	9,716	239	179
East Cleveland	39,667	160	116
East Liverpool	23,329	508	338
East Palestine	5,215	54	35
Eaton	3,347	50	50
Elmwood Place	4,562	125	125
Elyria	25,633	1,052	539
Euclid	12,751	54	44
Fairport Harbor	4,972	2	12
Fairview	3,689	3	(1)
Findlay	19,363	219	227
Fostoria	12,790	347	169
Franklin	4,491	176	145
Fremont	13,422	256	144
Galion	7,674	1	5
Gallipolis	7,106	609	482
Garfield Heights	15,589	54	1
Geneva	3,791	34	61
Girard	9,859	223	24
Glouster	2,903	210	173
Grand View Heights	6,358	21	(1)
Greenfield	3,871	228	201
Greenville	7,036	19	22
Hamilton	52,176	1,958	1,328
Hillsboro	4,040	425	559
Hubbard	4,080	59	85
Ironton	16,621	928	846
Jackson	5,922	45	61
Kent	8,375	241	167
Kenton	7,069	126	149
Lakewood	70,509	103	100
Lancaster	18,716	182	200
Lebanon	3,222	280	296
Lima	42,287	1,422	1,243
Lisbon	3,405	50	77
Lockland	5,703	1,164	738
Logan	6,080	36	23
London	4,141	352	339
Lorain	44,512	966	552
Lowellville	2,550	76	(1)
Mansfield	33,525	910	249
Maple Heights	5,950	115	(1)
Marietta	14,285	286	246
Marion	31,084	387	239
Martins Ferry	14,524	276	245
Marysville	3,639	76	90
Massillon	26,400	1,219	624
Maumee	4,588	18	11
Mayfield Heights	2,612	16	(1)

See footnotes at end of table.

Table 11.—NEGRO POPULATION OF CITIES AND OTHER URBAN PLACES: 1930 AND 1920—Continued

[Places having no Negro population are omitted]

CITY OR OTHER URBAN PLACE	POPULATION: Total, 1930	POPULATION: Negro 1930	POPULATION: Negro 1920
Ohio—Continued			
Medina	4,071	95	77
Miamisburg	5,518	5	4
Middleport	3,505	138	193
Middletown	29,992	2,805	1,377
Minerva	2,675	9	(1)
Mingo Junction	5,030	257	138
Montpelier	3,677	7	5
Mount Healthy	3,530	23	(1)
Mount Vernon	9,370	357	367
Napoleon	4,545	2	2
Nelsonville	5,322	129	189
Newark	30,596	729	551
New Boston	5,931	20	35
Newcomerstown	4,265	220	5
New Lexington	3,901	4	(7)
New Philadelphia	12,365	99	18
Newton Falls	3,458	4	(1)
Niles	16,314	214	2
North Canton	2,648	10	(1)
North College Hill	4,139	1	(1)
North Olmsted	2,624	2	(1)
Norwalk	7,776	70	62
Norwood	33,411	40	95
Oakwood	6,494	78	(1)
Oberlin	4,292	956	666
Orrville	4,427	62	8
Oxford	2,588	312	(1)
Painesville	10,944	429	217
Parma	13,899	4	(1)
Perrysburg	3,182	12	(1)
Piqua	16,009	567	499
Pomeroy	3,563	182	166
Port Clinton	4,408	17	7
Portsmouth	42,560	1,891	1,160
Ravenna	8,019	254	211
Reading	5,723	59	77
Rittman	2,785	2	(1)
Rocky River	5,632	11	(1)
St. Bernard	7,487	3	2
St. Marys	5,433	37	40
Salem	10,622	195	188
Sandusky	24,622	883	571
Sebring	3,949	30	54
Shaker Heights village	17,783	367	49
Shelby	6,198	2	4
Sidney	9,301	146	144
South Euclid	4,399	28	(1)
Springfield	68,743	8,249	7,029
Steubenville	35,422	2,776	1,115
Struthers	11,249	636	245
Tiffin	16,428	48	61
Toledo	290,718	13,260	5,691
Toronto	7,044	114	17
Troy	8,675	550	448
Uhrichsville	6,437	81	77
Union City [20]	1,305	10	26
Upper Arlington	3,059	48	(1)
Upper Sandusky	3,889	3	5
Urbana	7,742	704	820
Van Wert	8,472	82	105
Wadsworth	5,930	112	95
Wapakoneta	5,378	1	2
Warren	41,062	2,548	702
Washington Court House	8,426	548	558
Wauseon	2,889	3	5
Wellston	5,319	19	21
Wellsville	7,956	473	541
Westerville	2,879	16	(1)
Willard	4,514	140	54
Willoughby	4,252	54	10
Wilmington	5,332	398	408
Wooster	10,742	121	99
Wyoming	3,767	707	(1)
Xenia	10,507	2,166	2,021
Youngstown	170,002	14,552	6,662
Zanesville	36,440	1,776	1,559
Oklahoma			
Ada	11,261	479	343
Altus	8,439	992	145
Anadarko	5,036	486	264
Ardmore	15,741	2,069	2,008
Bartlesville	14,763	610	526
Blackwell	9,521	5	1
Bristow	6,619	558	345
Chandler	2,717	357	(1)
Chickasha	14,099	1,625	1,183
Claremore	3,720	408	334
Cleveland	2,959	1	1
Clinton	7,512	434	49
Cushing	9,301	567	446
Drumwright	4,972	110	172
Duncan	8,363	312	76
Durant	7,463	2	4
Elk City	5,666	2	2
Oklahoma—Con.			
El Reno	9,384	533	487
Enid	26,399	763	474
Frederick	4,568	550	260
Guthrie	9,582	1,759	2,370
Hartshorne	3,587	396	377
Hobart	4,982	276	6
Holdenville	7,268	631	270
Hollis	2,914	145	(1)
Hominy	3,485	179	54
Hugo	5,272	797	693
Idabel	2,581	628	631
Kingfisher	2,726	310	(1)
Lawton	12,121	809	405
McAlester	11,804	1,348	1,529
Mangum	4,806	321	55
Maud	4,326	41	(1)
Muskogee	32,026	6,576	7,195
Nowata	3,531	513	515
Okemah	4,002	94	(1)
Oklahoma City	185,389	14,662	8,241
Okmulgee	17,097	3,213	3,359
Pauls Valley	4,235	340	320
Pawhuska	5,931	555	385
Pawnee	2,562	134	(1)
Perry	4,206	319	233
Ponca City	16,136	732	200
Poteau	3,169	198	113
Purcell	2,817	250	301
Sand Springs	6,674	710	413
Sapulpa	10,533	1,039	1,317
Sayre	3,157	9	(1)
Seminole	11,459	841	67
Shawnee	23,283	1,044	698
Stillwater	7,016	223	112
Sulphur	4,242	151	103
Tulsa	141,258	15,203	8,878
Vinita	4,263	415	328
Wagoner	2,994	497	543
Wewoka	10,401	1,575	449
Woodward	5,056	5	(7)
Oregon			
Albany	5,325	5	1
Ashland	4,544	2	15
Astoria	10,349	3	8
Baker	7,858	21	10
Bend	8,848	8	7
Burns	2,599	3	(1)
Coquille	2,732	2	(1)
Corvallis	7,585	7	15
Eugene	18,901	5	9
Hillsboro	3,039	3	(1)
Hood River	2,757	1	1
Klamath Falls	16,093	97	16
La Grande	8,050	39	15
Marshfield	5,287	21	23
Medford	11,007	5	5
Pendleton	6,621	46	71
Portland	301,815	1,559	1,556
Salem	26,266	58	63
The Dalles	5,883	5	8
Pennsylvania			
Abington township	18,648	1,334	(6)
Aliquippa borough [21]	27,116	2,592	5
Allentown city	92,563	357	176
Altoona city	82,054	696	888
Ambler	3,944	506	378
Ambridge borough	20,227	130	66
Apollo	3,406	49	76
Archbald	9,587	1	2
Arnold borough	10,575	27	55
Ashland	7,164	1	(7)
Aspinwall	4,263	22	21
Athens	4,372	40	29
Avalon	5,940	110	95
Bangor	5,824	2	7
Beaver	5,665	44	61
Beaver Falls city [22]	17,147	751	336
Bedford	2,953	117	(1)
Bellefonte	4,804	69	116
Bellvue borough	10,252	211	273
Bentleyville	3,609	120	81
Berwick borough	12,660	27	8
Bethlehem city	57,892	715	344
Birdsboro	3,542	10	(7)
Blairsville	5,296	201	118
Blakely	8,260	9	2
Bloomsburg	9,093	45	66
Boyertown	3,943	1	(7)
Brackenridge	6,250	349	114
Braddock borough	19,329	2,224	735
Bradford city	19,306	118	157
Pennsylvania—Con.			
Brentwood	5,381	1	(1)
Bridgeport	5,595	45	32
Bridgeville	3,939	81	17
Bristol borough	11,799	390	387
Brockway	2,690	3	(1)
Brookville	4,387	19	9
Brownsville	2,869	102	172
Burnham	3,089	5	15
Butler city	23,568	169	299
Camp Hill	3,111	4	(1)
Canonsburg borough	12,558	625	431
Carbondale	20,061	2	2
Carlisle borough	12,596	888	1,027
Carnegie borough	12,497	488	243
Castle Shannon	3,810	11	(1)
Centerville	6,467	61	49
Chambersburg borough	13,788	585	628
Charleroi borough	11,260	175	329
Cheltenham township	15,731	981	(1)
Chester city	59,164	9,245	7,125
Clairton city [23]	15,291	2,070	621
Clarks Summit	2,604	1	(1)
Clearfield	9,221	59	128
Clifton Heights	5,057	5	7
Coatesville city	14,582	2,222	1,881
Collingdale	7,857	10	15
Columbia borough	11,349	407	335
Connellsville city	13,290	417	516
Conshohocken borough	10,815	304	86
Coraopolis borough	10,724	878	349
Corry	7,152	13	12
Coudersport	2,740	9	7
Crafton	7,004	54	55
Curwensville	3,140	60	74
Dale	3,364	115	94
Danville	7,185	33	35
Darby	9,899	1,367	1,114
Derry	3,046	5	30
Donora borough	13,905	986	855
Dormont borough	13,190	7	6
Downingtown	4,548	345	368
Doylestown	4,577	65	102
Du Bois city	11,595	11	27
Dunmore borough	22,627	11	10
Duquesne city	21,396	1,817	817
East Conemaugh	4,979	137	246
East McKeesport	2,922	9	(1)
East Mauch Chunk	3,739	13	(7)
Easton city	34,468	514	283
East Pittsburgh	6,214	123	528
East Stroudsburg	6,099	30	51
Ebensburg	3,063	19	(4)
Edgewood	4,821	41	32
Elizabeth	2,939	248	191
Ellwood City borough	12,323	134	90
Emaus	6,419	2	(7)
Emporium	2,929	20	44
Emsworth	2,709	1	(1)
Ephrata	4,988	4	(7)
Erie city	115,967	1,214	749
Etna	7,493	4	8
Exeter	5,724	5	(7)
Farrell borough	14,359	1,606	1,349
Ford City	6,127	273	316
Forest Hills	4,549	7	(1)
Fountain Hill	4,568	15	(1)
Frackville	8,034	6	2
Franklin city	10,254	296	274
Freedom	3,227	132	65
Freeport	2,772	12	16
Gettysburg	5,584	207	237
Glassport	8,390	77	61
Glenolden	4,482	35	(1)
Greencastle	2,557	70	(1)
Greensburg city	16,508	360	330
Greenville	8,628	65	40
Grove City	6,156	10	14
Hamburg	3,637	1	1
Hanover borough	11,805	3	8
Hanover township	17,770	22	(1)
Harrisburg city	80,339	6,382	5,248
Hatboro	2,651	43	(1)
Haverford township	21,362	643	(6)
Hazleton city	36,765	2	22
Hellertown	3,851	4	10
Hollidaysburg	5,969	56	56
Homestead borough	20,141	3,367	1,814
Honesdale	5,490	1	5
Hummelstown	3,036	7	6
Huntingdon	7,558	115	136
Indiana	9,569	40	28
Ingram	3,866	29	12
Irwin	3,443	43	47
Jeannette borough	15,126	284	129
Jenkintown	4,797	308	250

See footnotes at end of table.

TABLE 11.—NEGRO POPULATION OF CITIES AND OTHER URBAN PLACES: 1930 AND 1920—Continued

[Places having no Negro population are omitted]

CITY OR OTHER URBAN PLACE	POPULATION: Total, 1930	Negro: 1930	Negro: 1920
PENNSYLVANIA—Con.			
Jersey Shore	5, 781	35	52
Johnstown city	66, 993	1, 444	1, 650
Kane	6, 232	44	94
Kennett Square	3, 091	438	(1)
Kingston borough [24]	21, 600	9	3
Kittanning	7, 808	83	68
Lancaster city	59, 949	1, 281	915
Lansdale	8, 379	27	10
Lansdowne	9, 542	348	223
Lansford	9, 632	1	4
Larksville	9, 322	37	18
Latrobe borough	10, 644	39	62
Lebanon city	25, 561	101	113
Leechburg	4, 489	41	35
Leetsdale	2, 774	149	(1)
Lehighton	6, 490	7	10
Lemoyne	4, 171	14	(1)
Lewisburg	3, 308	18	23
Lewistown borough	13, 357	95	102
Lititz	4, 368	9	3
Lock Haven	9, 668	43	72
Lower Merion township	35, 166	2, 919	(6)
McDonald	3, 281	307	231
McKeesport city	54, 632	1, 893	928
McKees Rocks borough	18, 116	488	114
Mahanoy City borough	14, 784	1	8
Marcus Hook	4, 867	211	143
Masontown	3, 873	82	(1)
Meadville city	16, 698	498	439
Mechanicsburg	5, 647	56	86
Media	5, 372	805	522
Meyersdale	3, 065	63	121
Middletown	6, 085	306	327
Midland	6, 007	771	309
Millvale	8, 166	10	5
Milton	8, 552	100	190
Monaca	4, 641	60	24
Monessen city	20, 268	1, 201	588
Monongahela City	8, 675	453	593
Montoursville	2, 710	7	(1)
Morrisville	5, 368	46	44
Mount Carmel borough	17, 967	1	2
Mount Joy	2, 716	56	(1)
Mount Lebanon township	13, 403	84	(6)
Mount Oliver	7, 071	6	(7)
Mount Penn	3, 017	3	(1)
Mount Pleasant	5, 869	141	133
Mount Union	4, 892	549	391
Munhall borough	12, 995	82	24
Nanticoke city	26, 043	14	30
Nanty-Glo	5, 598	3	2
Narberth	4, 669	69	49
New Brighton	9, 950	389	197
New Castle city	48, 674	1, 572	867
New Cumberland	4, 283	9	(1)
New Kensington borough	16, 762	680	357
Norristown borough	35, 853	2, 118	1, 507
North Bellevernon	3, 072	45	34
North Braddock borough	16, 782	488	393
North Charleroi	2, 879	22	(1)
North East	3, 670	15	19
Northumberland	4, 483	15	5
Norwood	3, 878	53	(1)
Oakmont	6, 027	215	105
Oil City	22, 075	209	226
Old Forge borough	12, 661	1	2
Olyphant borough	10, 743	9	21
Oxford	2, 606	228	(1)
Parnassus	6, 240	97	88
Pen Argyl	4, 310	17	18
Penbrook	3, 567	5	(1)
Perkasie	3, 463	1	2
Philadelphia city	1, 950, 961	219, 599	134, 229
Philipsburg	3, 600	47	58
Phoenixville borough	12, 029	268	181
Pittsburgh	669, 817	54, 983	37, 725
Pittston city	18, 246	4	12
Plains township	16, 044	7	(1)
Polk	3, 337	68	41
Port Carbon	3, 225	5	(7)
Port Vue	3, 510	38	55
Pottstown borough	19, 430	454	450
Pottsville city	24, 300	436	111
Prospect Park	4, 623	98	154
Punxsutawney	9, 266	4	9
Quakertown	4, 883	13	10
Rankin	7, 956	1, 556	873
Reading city	111, 171	1, 964	924
Ridgway	6, 313	3	8
Ridley Park	3, 356	52	(1)
Roaring Spring	2, 724	11	(1)
Rochester	7, 726	296	209
Royersford	3, 719	14	19
St. Clair	7, 296	7	8
St. Marys	7, 433	5	24
Sayre	7, 902	1	5
Scottdale	6, 714	96	174
Scranton city	143, 433	734	563
Sewickley	5, 599	713	570
Shamokin borough	20, 274	34	44
Sharon city	25, 908	506	701
Sharon Hill	3, 825	9	(1)
Sharpsburg	8, 642	203	316
Sharpsville	5, 194	123	82
Shenandoah borough	21, 782	19	20
Shillington	4, 401	1	(1)
Shippensburg	4, 345	101	194
Somerset	4, 395	47	29
South Brownsville	5, 314	535	338
South Connellsville	2, 516	38	(1)
Southwest Greensburg	3, 105	10	7
South Williamsport	6, 058	14	21
Spring City	2, 963	14	21
Springdale	4, 781	4	1
State College	4, 450	1	(1)
Steelton borough	13, 291	2, 532	1, 973
Stowe township	13, 368	69	(6)
Stroudsburg	5, 961	107	77
Sunbury city	15, 626	21	18
Susquehanna depot	3, 203	1	1
Swarthmore	3, 405	290	(1)
Swissvale borough	16, 029	514	298
Tamaqua borough	12, 936	10	13
Tarentum	9, 551	108	123
Titusville	8, 055	49	86
Towanda	4, 104	13	34
Trafford	4, 187	107	64
Turtle Creek borough	10, 690	18	24
Tyrone	9, 042	144	192
Uniontown city	19, 544	1, 107	1, 203
Upland	2, 500	82	(1)
Upper Darby township	46, 626	427	(6)
Vandergrift borough	11, 479	160	65
Verona	4, 376	167	182
Warren brough	14, 863	2	6
Washington city	24, 545	2, 029	1, 825
Waynesboro borough	10, 167	152	162
Waynesburg [25]	4, 915	116	98
Wellsboro	3, 643	24	37
Wesleyville	2, 854	26	(1)
West Chester borough	12, 325	2, 086	1, 831
West Conshohocken	2, 579	18	(1)
West Homestead	3, 552	210	84
Westmont	3, 388	16	(1)
West Newton	2, 953	96	44
West Pittston	7, 940	43	66
West Reading	4, 908	4	(7)
West View	6, 028	11	4
West York	5, 381	7	16
Wilkes-Barre city	86, 626	877	552
Wilkinsburg	29, 639	541	484
Williamsport city	45, 729	934	914
Wilmerding	6, 291	107	77
Wilson	8, 265	4	212
Windber	9, 205	17	6
Wyoming	4, 648	2	2
Wyomissing	3, 111	12	(1)
Yeadon	5, 430	115	(1)
York city	55, 254	2, 266	1, 416
RHODE ISLAND			
Barrington town	5, 162	6	10
Bristol town	11, 953	34	41
Burrillville town	7, 677	15	21
Central Falls	25, 898	4	92
Cranston	42, 911	244	204
Cumberland town	10, 304	3	1
East Greenwich town	3, 666	31	28
East Providence town	29, 995	764	615
Johnston town	9, 357	16	2
Lincoln town	10, 421	28	43
Newport	27, 612	1, 554	1, 607
North Providence town	11, 104	93	56
Pawtucket	77, 149	298	332
Providence	252, 981	5, 473	5, 655
Warren town	7, 974	29	75
Warwick town	23, 196	248	182
Westerly town	10, 997	138	228
West Warwick town	17, 696	10	11
Woonsocket	49, 376	91	70
SOUTH CAROLINA			
Abbeville	4, 414	1, 502	1, 763
Aiken	6, 033	3, 489	2, 286
Anderson	14, 383	3, 833	3, 030
Batesburg	2, 839	1, 041	1, 031
Beaufort	2, 776	1, 323	1, 557
Bennettsville	3, 667	1, 541	1, 302
Camden	5, 183	2, 457	1, 849
Charleston	62, 265	28, 062	32, 326
Cheraw	3, 573	1, 782	1, 635
Chester	5, 528	2, 159	2, 153
Clinton	5, 643	1, 261	1, 125
Clover	3, 111	315	(1)
Columbia	51, 581	19, 519	14, 455
Conway	3, 011	1, 290	(1)
Darlington	5, 556	2, 572	1, 941
Dillon	2, 731	931	(1)
Easley	4, 886	810	605
Eau Claire	2, 915	578	876
Florence	14, 774	6, 067	4, 714
Gaffney	6, 827	1, 580	1, 291
Georgetown	5, 082	2, 920	2, 907
Greenville	29, 154	10, 871	8, 184
Greenwood	11, 020	3, 512	2, 895
Hartsville	5, 067	1, 975	1, 164
Honea Path	2, 740	287	-------
Lancaster	3, 545	1, 196	1, 145
Laurens	5. 443	1, 963	1. 658
Marion	4, 921	2, 547	1, 853
Mullins	3, 158	1, 500	(1)
Newberry	7, 298	2, 304	2, 061
Orangeburg	8, 776	3, 952	3, 306
Rock Hill	11, 322	2, 410	1, 931
Spartanburg	28, 723	9, 826	8, 003
Summerville	2, 579	1, 055	930
Sumter	11, 780	5, 145	3, 869
Union	7, 419	2, 142	1, 813
Walterboro	2, 592	908	(1)
Whitmire	2, 763	375	(1)
Woodruff	3, 175	479	(1)
York [26]	2, 827	875	831
SOUTH DAKOTA			
Aberdeen	16, 465	8	21
Brookings	4, 376	6	11
Deadwood	2, 559	16	(1)
Hot Springs	2, 908	4	(1)
Huron	10, 946	68	56
Madison	4, 289	3	3
Mitchell	10, 942	62	15
Mobridge	3, 464	4	2
Pierre	3, 659	3	18
Rapid City	10, 404	11	15
Redfield	2, 664	1	(7)
Sioux Falls	33, 362	100	83
Watertown	10, 214	2	13
Yankton	6, 072	49	102
TENNESSEE			
Alcoa	5, 255	1, 587	1, 482
Athens	5, 385	639	460
Bristol [27]	12, 005	959	939
Brownsville	3, 204	1, 394	1, 390
Chattanooga	119, 798	33, 289	18, 889
Clarksville	9, 242	3, 409	3, 363
Cleveland	9, 136	1, 069	879
Columbia	7, 882	2, 507	1, 950
Cookeville	3, 738	17	(1)
Covington	3, 397	1, 249	1, 265
Dickson	2, 902	222	(1)
Dyersburg	8, 733	2, 695	2, 396
Elizabethton	8, 093	331	44
Erwin	3, 623	11	2
Etowah	4, 209	17	10
Fayetteville	3, 822	1, 150	1, 191
Franklin	3, 377	1, 352	1, 423
Gallatin	3, 050	971	969
Greeneville	5, 544	575	470
Harriman	4. 588	451	447
Humboldt	4. 613	1, 623	1, 450
Jackson	22, 172	7, 595	6, 299
Johnson City	25, 080	2, 335	1, 593
Kingsport	11, 914	595	454
Knoxville	105, 802	17, 093	11, 302
La Follette	2, 637	240	429
Lawrenceburg	3, 102	260	(1)
Lebanon	4, 656	1, 174	1, 187
Lenoir City	4, 470	8	10
Lewisburg	3, 112	531	559
Loudon	2, 578	125	(1)
McMinnville	3, 914	688	678
Martin	3, 300	737	371
Maryville	4, 958	363	291
Memphis	253, 143	96, 550	61, 181
Milan	3, 155	860	(1)
Morristown	7, 305	1, 141	963
Murfreesboro	7, 993	2, 185	1, 986
Nashville	153. 866	42, 836	35, 633
Newport	2, 989	227	220
Paris	8, 164	1, 984	1, 229

See footnotes at end of table.

TABLE 11.—NEGRO POPULATION OF CITIES AND OTHER URBAN PLACES: 1930 AND 1920—Continued

[Places having no Negro population are omitted]

CITY OR OTHER URBAN PLACE	POPULATION Total, 1930	Negro 1930	Negro 1920
TENNESSEE—Continued			
Pulaski	3,367	1,083	1,050
Rockwood	3,898	350	602
Shelbyville	5,010	1,187	685
Springfield	5,577	1,369	865
Trenton	2,892	1,029	934
Tullahoma	4,023	689	629
Union City	5,865	1,417	1,245
TEXAS			
Abilene	23,175	1,403	410
Alamo Heights	3,874	110	(1)
Alice	4,239	159	(1)
Alpine	3,495	27	(1)
Amarillo	43,132	1,600	316
Arlington	3,661	302	214
Athens	4,342	1,140	786
Austin	53,120	9,868	6,921
Ballinger	4,187	419	172
Bay City	4,070	915	704
Beaumont	57,732	18,551	13,210
Beeville	4,806	330	303
Belton	3,779	625	805
Big Spring	13,735	490	(7)
Bonham	5,655	908	916
Borger	6,532	122	(1)
Bowie	3,131	3	1
Brady	3,983	317	(1)
Breckenridge	7,569	426	(1)
Brenham	5,974	1,896	1,933
Brownsville	22,021	101	49
Brownwood	12,789	518	382
Bryan	7,814	2,599	2,180
Burkburnett	3,281	92	6
Cameron	4,565	1,066	1,102
Center	2,510	453	(1)
Childress	7,163	333	33
Cisco	6,027	253	110
Clarendon	2,756	124	(1)
Clarksville	2,952	910	1,020
Cleburne	11,539	867	957
Coleman	6,078	405	183
Colorado	4,671	414	(1)
Commerce	4,267	365	380
Corpus Christi	27,741	1,951	456
Corsicana	15,202	3,332	2,585
Cotulla	3,175	20	(1)
Crockett	4,441	1,772	1,200
Crystal City	6,609	8	(6)
Cuero	4,672	1,117	794
Dallas	260,475	38,742	24,023
Del Rio	11,693	216	182
Denison	13,850	2,621	3,056
Denton	9,587	789	691
Donna	4,103	21	(1)
Eagle Pass	5,059	18	64
Eastland	4,648	235	299
Edinburg	4,821	117	(1)
Electra	6,712	183	30
El Paso	102,421	1,855	1,330
Ennis	7,069	1,954	1,924
Floydada	2,637	54	(1)
Fort Stockton	2,695	19	(1)
Fort Worth	163,447	22,234	15,896
Freeport	3,162	183	(1)
Gainesville	8,915	926	1,089
Galveston	52,938	13,226	9,888
Gatesville	2,601	255	(1)
Georgetown	3,583	728	599
Gonzales	3,859	746	658
Goose Creek	5,208	122	(1)
Graham	4,981	156	(1)
Greenville	12,407	2,086	2,255
Harlingen	12,124	359	5
Haskell	2,632	169	(1)
Hearne	2,956	1,289	1,276
Henderson	2,932	1,006	(1)
Highland Park	8,422	1,311	(1)
Hillsboro	7,823	1,289	1,025
Houston	292,352	63,337	33,960
Huntsville	5,028	1,363	2,092
Jacksonville	6,748	1,611	688
Jasper	3,393	1,157	(1)
Kenedy	2,610	215	(1)
Kerrville	4,546	408	(1)
Kingsville	6,815	519	327
Lamesa	3,528	78	(1)
Lampasas	2,709	237	(1)
Laredo	32,618	72	41
Littlefield	3,218	122	(1)
Lockhart	4,367	605	537
Longview	5,036	1,737	1,797
Lubbock	20,520	1,100	63
Lufkin	7,311	1,349	765
Luling	5,970	942	(1)
McAllen	9,074	53	29
TEXAS—Continued			
McCamey	3,446	222	(1)
McKinney	7,307	767	783
Marfa	3,909	34	28
Marlin	5,338	1,676	1,449
Marshall	16,203	6,693	5,797
Mart	2,853	663	605
Memphis	4,257	239	1
Mercedes	6,608	84	10
Mexia	6,579	1,871	1,326
Midland	5,484	237	(1)
Mineola	3,304	856	(1)
Mineral Wells	5,986	600	677
Mission	5,120	56	(7)
Mount Pleasant	3,541	979	1,102
Nacogdoches	5,687	1,362	951
Navasota	5,128	2,483	2,493
New Braunfels	6,242	233	194
Olney	4,138	113	(1)
Orange	7,913	2,150	2,456
Paducah	2,802	221	(1)
Palestine	11,445	3,227	2,926
Pampa	10,470	267	(7)
Paris	15,649	3,265	3,573
Pearsall	2,536	55	(1)
Pecos	3,304	162	(1)
Pelly	3,452	661	(1)
Pittsburg	2,640	970	849
Plainview	8,834	241	5
Port Arthur	50,902	10,003	3,910
Quanah	4,464	211	66
Ranger	6,208	200	239
Robstown	4,183	162	(1)
Rusk	3,859	1,044	(1)
San Angelo	25,308	1,653	602
San Antonio	231,542	17,978	14,341
San Benito	10,753	179	36
San Marcos	5,134	645	739
Seguin	5,225	1,014	848
Seymour	2,626	91	(1)
Shamrock	3,780	77	(1)
Sherman	15,713	2,014	2,075
Slaton	3,876	212	(1)
Smithville	3,296	800	669
Snyder	3,008	27	(1)
South San Antonio	2,708	97	(1)
Stamford	4,095	293	176
Stephenville	3,944	128	172
Sulphur Springs	5,417	1,005	1,160
Sweetwater	10,848	539	177
Taylor	7,463	1,869	1,396
Teague	3,509	593	447
Temple	15,345	2,802	2,078
Terrell	8,795	2,239	2,194
Texarkana [28]	16,602	4,934	3,207
Texas City	3,534	468	336
Tyler	17,113	4,092	2,822
University Park	4,200	113	(1)
Uvalde	5,286	164	115
Vernon	9,137	744	197
Victoria	7,421	1,100	1,159
Waco	52,848	9,370	7,726
Waxahachie	8,042	1,913	1,864
Weatherford	4,912	220	245
Wellington	3,570	347	(1)
Weslaco	4,879	44	(1)
Wharton	2,691	513	(1)
Wichita Falls	43,690	4,312	2,217
Wink	3,963	212	(1)
Yoakum	5,656	896	1,026
UTAH			
Bingham Canyon	3,248	1	1
Helper	2,707	19	(1)
Ogden	40,272	224	265
Park City	4,281	10	4
Price	4,084	1	(1)
Provo	14,766	8	8
Salt Lake City	140,267	681	718
VERMONT			
Barre	11,307	9	3
Bennington	7,390	9	13
Brattleboro	8,709	4	8
Burlington	24,789	96	96
Montpelier	7,837	1	8
Newport	5,094	1	1
Proctor	2,515	1	(7)
Rutland	17,315	26	12
St. Albans	8,020	35	29
St. Johnsbury	7,920	4	2
Springfield	4,943	2	3
Windsor	3,689	4	6
Winooski	5,308	21	34
VIRGINIA			
Abingdon	2,877	527	637
Alexandria	24,149	4,912	4,112
Appalachia	3,595	136	(1)
Bedford	3,713	908	1,001
Big Stone Gap	3,908	480	435
Bluefield [29]	3,906	285	413
Bristol [30]	8,840	1,184	1,062
Buena Vista	4,002	264	356
Cape Charles	2,527	679	720
Charlottesville	15,245	4,083	2,947
Clifton Forge	6,839	1,175	1,000
Covington	6,538	1,114	1,136
Danville	22,247	5,519	5,678
Farmville	3,133	1,269	1,189
Franklin	2,930	1,351	(1)
Fredericksburg	6,819	1,218	1,193
Galax	2,544	148	(1)
Hampton	6,382	2,804	2,169
Harrisonburg	7,232	848	780
Hopewell	11,327	1,318	235
Lexington	3,752	1,076	940
Lynchburg	40,661	9,653	8,329
Marion	4,156	324	322
Martinsville	7,705	1,963	1,512
Newport News	34,417	13,281	14,077
Norfolk	129,710	43,942	43,392
Norton	3,077	397	393
Petersburg	28,564	12,600	13,608
Phoebus	2,956	869	942
Portsmouth	45,704	18,849	23,245
Pulaski	7,168	1,045	988
Radford	6,227	637	525
Richmond	182,929	52,988	54,041
Roanoke	69,206	12,368	9,331
Salem	4,833	683	618
Saltville	2,964	96	(1)
South Boston	4,841	1,726	1,892
South Norfolk	7,857	1,703	2,015
Staunton	11,990	1,805	1,774
Suffolk	10,271	3,806	3,616
Vinton	3,610	309	308
Waynesboro [31]	6,226	688	(1)
Williamsburg	3,778	854	(1)
Winchester	10,855	1,043	934
Wytheville	3,327	474	624
WASHINGTON			
Aberdeen	21,723	48	57
Anacortes	6,564	1	6
Bellingham	30,823	40	40
Bremerton	10,170	84	114
Centralia	8,058	8	13
Chehalis	4,907	5	7
Cle Elum	2,508	24	28
Dayton	2,528	1	2
Ellensburg	4,621	80	88
Everett	30,567	119	150
Hoquiam	12,766	15	6
Kelso	6,260	22	(1)
Longview	10,652	56	(1)
Mount Vernon	3,690	9	6
Olympia	11,733	7	5
Pasco	3,496	8	19
Port Angeles	10,188	54	87
Port Townsend	3,979	6	4
Pullman	3,322	4	(1)
Puyallup	7,094	4	4
Renton	4,062	1	(7)
Seattle	365,583	3,303	2,894
Sedro-Woolley	2,719	2	7
Snohomish	2,688	2	9
Spokane	115,514	617	727
Tacoma	106,817	730	898
Toppenish	2,774	41	30
Vancouver	15,766	19	20
Walla Walla	15,976	111	100
Wenatchee	11,627	67	31
Yakima	22,101	330	263
WEST VIRGINIA			
Beckley	9,357	1,599	700
Benwood	3,950	51	56
Bluefield [32]	19,339	3,363	2,718
Buckhannon	4,374	152	165
Charleston	60,408	6,734	4,502
Chester	3,701	2	11
Clarksburg	28,866	1,211	1,258
Dunbar	4,189	8	(1)
Elkins	7,345	282	307
Fairmont	23,159	1,929	848
Follansbee	4,841	8	(7)
Grafton	7,737	247	234
Hinton	6,654	755	253
Huntington	75,572	4,630	2,883

See footnotes at end of table.

TABLE 11.—NEGRO POPULATION OF CITIES AND OTHER URBAN PLACES: 1930 AND 1920—Continued

[Places having no Negro population are omitted]

CITY OR OTHER URBAN PLACE	POPULATION: Total, 1930	POPULATION: Negro 1930	POPULATION: Negro 1920
WEST VIRGINIA—Con.			
Kenova	3,680	10	(1)
Keyser	6,248	160	217
Logan	4,396	242	189
Mannington	3,261	83	41
Martinsburg	14,857	1,046	1,019
Montgomery	2,906	518	(1)
Morgantown	16,186	334	267
Moundsville	14,411	726	409
New Martinsville	2,814	5	(1)
Parkersburg	29,623	875	695
Point Pleasant	3,301	161	185
Princeton	6,955	408	393
Richwood	5,720	12	26
St. Albans	3,254	139	130
Shinnston	2,802	42	(1)
Sistersville	3,072	22	47
South Charleston	5,904	40	166
Welch	5,376	1,216	654
Wellsburg	6,398	303	88
Weston	8,646	95	242
Wheeling	61,659	2,192	1,623
Williamson	9,410	1,624	1,144
WISCONSIN			
Baraboo	5,545	19	27
Beaver Dam	9,867	1	2
WISCONSIN—Continued			
Beloit	23,611	836	834
Columbus	2,514	1	(1)
Delavan	3,301	40	42
Eau Claire	26,287	11	21
Edgerton	2,906	3	10
Fon du Lac	26,449	16	50
Green Bay	37,415	21	32
Janesville	21,628	31	22
Kaukauna	6,581	3	4
Kenosha	50,262	198	101
La Crosse	39,614	38	39
Lake Geneva	3,073	18	2
Madison	57,899	348	259
Manitowoc	22,963	2	7
Marinette	13,734	15	19
Menasha	9,062	8	1
Milwaukee	578,249	7,501	2,229
Monroe	5,015	1	(7)
Neenah	9,151	10	4
Oconto	5,030	1	1
Oshkosh	40,108	33	39
Portage	6,308	2	5
Racine	67,542	477	294
Rhinelander	8,019	2	1
Sheboygan Falls	2,934	1	(1)
Shorewood	13,479	2	(7)
Sparta	4,949	7	11
WISCONSIN—Continued			
Sturgeon Bay	4,983	1	7
Superior	36,113	51	107
Tomahawk	2,919	6	(7)
Viroqua	2,792	1	1
Watertown	10,613	2	5
Waukesha	17,176	84	49
Waupaca	3,131	1	1
Waupun	5,768	62	45
Wausau	23,758	5	3
Wauwatosa	21,194	6	7
West Allis	34,671	1	(7)
West Milwaukee	4,168	1	(1)
Whitefish Bay	5,362	5	(1)
Whitewater	3,465	1	1
WYOMING			
Casper	16,619	146	162
Cheyenne	17,361	305	343
Evanston	3,075	5	17
Green River	2,589	48	(1)
Laramie	8,609	109	46
Rawlins	4,868	94	95
Rock Springs	8,440	102	62
Sheridan	8,536	50	106

1 Data not available. Places were either unincorporated in 1920 or had less than 2,500 inhabitants.
2 Albany and Decatur cities and Fairview town consolidated as Decatur City in 1927, combined population in 1920, 12,404; Negro, 3,180.
3 Phenix city and Girard city consolidated as Phenix City in 1923, combined population in 1920, 10,374; Negro, 2,458.
4 Total population 1920 for Nogales corrected by inclusion of population (3,261) of Camp Stephen D. Little, erroneously returned as outside. Number of Negroes not available.
5 Combined population of Texarkana city, Miller County, Ark., and Texarkana city, Bowie County, Tex., 27,366; Negro, 8,043 in 1930, and 5,613 in 1920.
6 Data not available by color.
7 No Negro population.
8 Organized in 1921.
9 Daytona Beach, Daytona, and Seabreeze cities consolidated as Daytona Beach city in 1925. Negro population for Daytona 2,478, not available for Daytona Beach and Seabreeze.
10 Name changed from West Hammond in 1924.
11 Figures for Geneva city for 1920 corrected by inclusion of population (596) of State Training School for Girls erroneously enumerated as in Geneva township. Data not available for Negroes in this institution.
12 Combined population of Union city, Randolph County, Indiana, and Union city village, Darke County, Ohio, 4,389; Negro, 20 in 1930, and 64 in 1920.
13 Name changed from West Minneapolis in 1928.
14 Linden borough and Linden township consolidated as Linden city in 1925; combined Negro population for 1920 not available.
15 New Milford borough incorporated from Palisades township in 1922.
16 Palmyra township incorporated as a borough in 1923.
17 Union and Endicott villages consolidated as Endicott village in 1921; combined Negro population for 1920, 16.
18 Name changed from Watkins in 1926.
19 Name changed from East Youngstown in 1926.
20 Combined population of Union city village, Darke County, Ohio and Union city, Randolph County, Ind., 4,389; Negro, 20 in 1930, and 64 in 1920.
21 Aliquippa and Woodlawn boroughs consolidated as Aliquippa borough in 1928; combined Negro population in 1920, 978.
22 Beaver Falls and College Hill boroughs consolidated as Beaver Falls city in 1930; combined Negro population in 1920, 364.
23 Clairton, North Clairton, and Wilson boroughs consolidated as Clairton city in 1922; combined Negro population in 1920 not available for North Clairton and Wilson borough.
24 Dorranceton and Kingston boroughs consolidated as Kingston borough in 1922; combined Negro population in 1920, 10.
25 East Waynesburg and Waynesburg borough consolidated as Waynesburg borough in 1923; combined Negro population in 1920 not available for East Waynesburg, or Waynesburg borough.
26 Yorkville changed to York May 15, 1915.
27 Combined population of Bristol city, Sullivan County, Tenn., and Bristol city, Va., 20,845; Negro, 2,143 in 1930, and 2,001 in 1920.
28 Combined population of Texarkana city, Bowie County, Tex., and Texarkana city, Miller County, Ark., 26,366; Negro, 8,043 in 1930, and 5,613 in 1920.
29 Combined population of Bluefield town, Tazewell County, Va., and Bluefield city, Mercer County, W. Va., 23,245; Negro, 3,648 in 1930, and 3,131 in 1920.
30 Combined population of Bristol city Va., and Bristol city, Sullivan County, Tenn.: 20,845; Negro, 2,143 in 1930, and 2,001 in 1920.
31 Basic city and Waynesboro towns consolidated as Waynesboro town in 1923.
32 Combined population of Bluefield city, Mercer County, W. Va., and Bluefield town, Tazewell County, Va., 23,245; Negro, 3,648 in 1930, and 3,131 in 1920.

TABLE 12.—NEGRO POPULATION BY WARDS OR EQUIVALENT SUBDIVISIONS OF CITIES HAVING 50,000 OR MORE INHABITANTS OF WHOM AT LEAST 20,000 ARE NEGROES: 1930

[Percent not shown where less than one-tenth of 1 percent]

STATE, CITY, AND WARD OR EQUIVALENT SUBDIVISION	NEGRO POPULATION	
	Number	Percent of total population
ALABAMA		
Birmingham	99,077	38.2
(Not reported by wards)		
Mobile	24,514	35.9
Ward 1	1,959	45.7
Ward 2	80	4.3
Ward 3	181	9.7
Ward 4	675	12.5
Ward 5	1,274	34.8
Ward 6	3,590	46.7
Ward 7	13,804	85.2
Ward 8	289	2.6
Ward 9	1,362	23.5
Ward 10	1,167	15.3
Not located in wards	133	5.3
Montgomery	29,970	45.4
Ward 1	1,709	26.3
Ward 2	11,750	71.4
Ward 3	444	8.0
Ward 4	3,608	52.2
Ward 5	3,426	33.5
Ward 6	3,664	70.7
Ward 7	5,221	42.4
Ward 23	148	5.0
CALIFORNIA		
Los Angeles	38,894	3.1
Assembly district 51	64	0.1
Assembly district 54	38	.1
Assembly district 55	450	.4
Assembly district 56	275	.8
Assembly district 57	590	.5
Assembly district 58	849	.9
Assembly district 59	2,880	3.9
Assembly district 60	913	.8
Assembly district 61	830	1.0
Assembly district 62	27,227	35.6
Assembly district 63	114	.2
Assembly district 64	1,092	1.4
Assembly district 65	6	------
Assembly district 66	39	.1
Assembly district 67	27	------
Assembly district 72	3,500	3.3
DISTRICT OF COLUMBIA		
Washington	132,068	27.1
Tract 1	235	3.7
Tract 2	596	6.1
Tract 3	538	4.1
Tract 4	42	7.6
Tract 5	225	5.6
Tract 6	3,136	16.6
Tract 7	4,881	26.8
Tract 8	155	4.2
Tract 9	4,553	29.7
Tract 10	17,482	78.7
Tract 11	10,951	47.1
Tract 12	6,766	30.5
Tract 13	6,550	34.5
Tract 14	19,145	64.1
Tract 15	8,534	17.3
Tract 16	201	1.2
Tract 17	153	1.4
Tract 18	564	3.0
Tract 19	12	2.7
Tract 20	301	1.9
Tract 21	------	------
Tract 22	745	7.7
Tract 23	1,182	16.3
Tract 24	1,126	28.6
Tract 25	1,181	55.2
Tract 26	9,380	19.8
Tract 27	9,868	23.2
Tract 28	11,728	48.9
Tract 29	6,389	70.3
Tract 30	5,449	26.8
FLORIDA		
Jacksonville	48,196	37.2
Ward 1	21	0.4
Ward 2	3,966	46.4
Ward 3	1,405	35.9
FLORIDA—Continued		
Jacksonville—Con.		
Ward 4	583	15.5
Ward 5	4,830	75.5
Ward 6	6,474	51.5
Ward 7	7,183	79.5
Ward 8	7,735	79.9
Ward 9	2,366	36.0
Ward 10	572	3.8
Ward 11	3,776	43.9
Ward 12	1,781	27.0
Ward 13	5,632	35.6
Ward 14	1,596	24.8
Ward 15	276	2.6
Miami	25,116	22.7
(Not reported by wards.)		
Tampa	21,172	20.9
Ward 1	5,548	57.0
Ward 2	78	1.3
Ward 3	1,742	23.6
Ward 4	2,849	24.0
Ward 5	2,252	32.2
Ward 6	14	.2
Ward 7	2,735	26.8
Ward 8	1,880	34.9
Ward 9	3,621	22.6
Ward 10	433	5.3
Ward 11	10	.1
Ward 12	10	.2
GEORGIA		
Atlanta	90,075	33.3
Ward 1	24,286	95.4
Ward 2	7,584	31.0
Ward 3	11,774	35.0
Ward 4	19,482	60.7
Ward 5	5,589	29.0
Ward 6	6,870	42.1
Ward 7	3,523	15.4
Ward 8	1,214	5.8
Ward 9	916	4.5
Ward 10	5,717	30.8
Ward 11	2,770	17.8
Ward 12	95	1.2
Ward 13	255	2.0
Augusta	24,190	40.1
Ward 1	1,461	25.5
Ward 2	4,936	65.7
Ward 3	6,989	67.2
Ward 4	7,892	52.4
Ward 5	451	4.9
Ward 6	611	11.5
Ward 7	1,850	25.8
Macon	23,158	43.0
Ward 1	4,851	46.6
Ward 2	5,845	47.8
Ward 3	8,098	49.9
Ward 4	4,364	29.2
Savannah	38,896	45.7
ILLINOIS		
Chicago	233,903	6.9
Community area:		
Area 1	128	0.2
Area 2	46	.1
Area 3	531	.4
Area 4	11	------
Area 5	19	------
Area 6	198	.2
Area 7	143	.1
Area 8	4,231	5.3
Area 9	4	.1
Area 10	4	------
Arae 11	2	------
Area 12	2	------
Area 13	66	.6
Area 14	46	.1
Area 15	9	------
Area 16	37	.1
Area 17	3	------
ILLINOIS—Continued		
Chicago—Contd.		
Community area—Con.		
Area 18	5	.1
Area 19	4	------
Area 20	7	------
Area 21	4	------
Area 22	19	------
Area 23	43	.1
Area 24	841	.4
Area 25	132	.1
Area 26	46	.1
Area 27	1,848	2.9
Area 28	25,239	16.6
Area 29	374	.3
Area 30	679	.9
Area 31	5	------
Area 32	98	1.2
Area 33	2,474	23.8
Area 34	4,058	18.9
Area 35	44,644	88.8
Area 36	4,317	28.9
Area 37	1,093	7.6
Area 38	82,329	94.6
Area 39	185	.7
Area 40	40,460	91.9
Area 41	521	1.1
Area 42	8,578	13.0
Area 43	171	.2
Area 44	10	------
Area 45	4	------
Area 46	738	1.3
Area 47	------	------
Area 48	19	.3
Area 49	1,256	2.9
Area 50	------	------
Area 51	------	------
Area 52	------	------
Area 53	170	.6
Area 54	------	------
Area 55	------	------
Area 56	------	------
Area 57	6	.1
Area 58	41	.1
Area 59	3	------
Area 60	1	------
Area 61	79	.1
Area 62	------	------
Area 63	------	------
Area 64	------	------
Area 65	3	------
Area 66	6	------
Area 67	1,967	3.1
Area 68	1,126	1.3
Area 69	254	.4
Area 70	------	------
Area 71	17	------
Area 72	50	.4
Area 73	33	.2
Area 74	------	------
Area 75	4,466	35.0
INDIANA		
Indianapolis	43,967	12.1
Ward 1	7,002	17.7
Ward 2	4,446	22.2
Ward 3	5,594	35.8
Ward 4	9,585	12.4
Ward 5	6,898	67.6
Ward 6	2,355	37.2
Ward 7	592	5.6
Ward 8	1,021	7.3
Ward 9	556	1.1
Ward 10	2,210	6.2
Ward 11	359	3.2
Ward 12	772	11.6
Ward 13	383	1.7
Ward 14	520	3.4
Ward 15	1,674	5.9
KENTUCKY		
Louisville	47,354	15.4
Ward 1	1,219	4.3
Ward 2	612	1.6
Ward 3	4,760	22.2
Ward 4	3,856	19.4
Ward 5	2,730	11.6
Ward 6	1,510	7.0
Ward 7	6,566	36.7
KENTUCKY—Continued		
Louisville—Con.		
Ward 8	9,158	31.7
Ward 9	6,264	34.2
Ward 10	5,550	18.2
Ward 11	2,135	8.5
Ward 12	2,994	8.7
LOUISIANA		
New Orleans	129,632	28.3
Ward 1	3,872	27.3
Ward 2	8,310	53.0
Ward 3	10,072	26.1
Ward 4	6,178	28.5
Ward 5	8,589	30.9
Ward 6	2,908	18.6
Ward 7	17,737	38.0
Ward 8	1,736	6.4
Ward 9	6,916	17.2
Ward 10	9,247	39.9
Ward 11	17,457	50.5
Ward 12	9,837	29.3
Ward 13	6,404	23.3
Ward 14	4,022	11.9
Ward 15	6,098	31.2
Ward 16	4,430	28.0
Ward 17	5,819	25.3
Shreveport	27,219	35.5
(Not reported by wards.)		
MARYLAND		
Baltimore	142,106	17.7
Ward 1	116	0.4
Ward 2	229	1.3
Ward 3	2,637	20.1
Ward 4	4,489	40.2
Ward 5	6,913	57.7
Ward 6	4,387	15.1
Ward 7	8,258	26.4
Ward 8	1,792	4.2
Ward 9	1,220	3.0
Ward 10	6,476	35.3
Ward 11	7,026	41.7
Ward 12	4,498	11.9
Ward 13	4,055	10.5
Ward 14	15,392	68.5
Ward 15	9,795	13.9
Ward 16	17,387	39.2
Ward 17	14,559	88.4
Ward 18	9,384	55.1
Ward 19	7,237	33.9
Ward 20	738	1.7
Ward 21	2,779	16.2
Ward 22	4,940	45.5
Ward 23	2,632	19.2
Ward 24	28	.1
Ward 25	1,951	8.4
Ward 26	806	1.6
Ward 27	2,315	3.0
Ward 28	67	.4
MASSACHUSETTS		
Boston	20,574	2.6
Ward 1	190	0.3
Ward 2	201	.6
Ward 3	893	1.3
Ward 4	2,933	9.5
Ward 5	765	2.5
Ward 6	37	.1
Ward 7	6	------
Ward 8	996	3.1
Ward 9	10,100	33.3
Ward 10	268	0.9
Ward 11	476	1.6
Ward 12	2,954	8.2
Ward 13	31	.1
Ward 14	188	.3
Ward 15	17	.1
Ward 16	16	.1
Ward 17	62	.2
Ward 18	53	.1
Ward 19	30	.1
Ward 20	24	.1
Ward 21	96	.3
Ward 22	238	.8

TABLE 12.—NEGRO POPULATION BY WARDS OR EQUIVALENT SUBDIVISIONS OF CITIES HAVING 50,000 OR MORE INHABITANTS OF WHOM AT LEAST 20,000 ARE NEGROES: 1930—Continued

[Percent not shown where less than one-tenth of 1 percent]

STATE, CITY, AND WARD OR EQUIVALENT SUBDIVISION	NEGRO POPULATION: Number	NEGRO POPULATION: Percent of total population
MICHIGAN		
Detroit	120,066	7.7
Ward 1	6,069	9.1
Ward 2	486	1.4
Ward 3	18,180	54.6
Ward 4	222	.6
Ward 5	24,750	53.8
Ward 6	1,394	2.5
Ward 7	13,247	54.7
Ward 8	738	1.0
Ward 9	17,663	18.9
Ward 10	869	1.3
Ward 11	5,215	18.3
Ward 12	3,355	4.3
Ward 13	4,758	6.4
Ward 14	9,308	11.7
Ward 15	997	1.7
Ward 16	7,591	4.9
Ward 17	637	.9
Ward 18	1,358	1.7
Ward 19	952	1.6
Ward 20	1,197	1.8
Ward 21	1,048	.5
Ward 22	32	------
MISSOURI		
Kansas City	38,574	9.6
Ward 1	3,407	13.0
Ward 2	9,439	41.0
Ward 3	3,183	12.9
Ward 4	13,080	51.2
Ward 5	309	1.6
Ward 6	305	1.7
Ward 7	558	2.2
Ward 8	453	1.7
Ward 9	1,138	4.4
Ward 10	56	.2
Ward 11	3,520	15.5
Ward 12	845	3.1
Ward 13	208	.9
Ward 14	1,557	6.2
Ward 15	74	.2
Ward 16	442	1.5
St. Louis	93,580	11.4
Statistical area:		
Area 1	680	2.5
Area 2	2	------
Area 3	10	1
Area 4	83	6
Area 5	424	1.2
Area 6	271	.5
Area 7	13	------
Area 8	162	1.9
Area 9	317	1.3
Area 10	1,540	4.0
Area 11	22,352	43.1
Area 12	458	1.4
Area 13	593	3.7
Area 14	8	.1
Area 15	291	.7
Area 16	44	.1
Area 17	82	.2
Area 18	7,587	24.8
Area 19	1,597	5.8
Area 20	1,406	5.4
Area 21	32,655	73.1
Area 22	11,853	38.1
Area 23	1,150	1.9
Area 24	22	.1
Area 25	8,972	37.0
Area 26	1,008	2.6
NEW JERSEY		
Newark	38,880	8.8
Ward 1	1,415	5.4
Ward 2	2,159	18.3
Ward 3	11,947	44.9
Ward 4	1,053	15.5
Ward 5	1,076	6.0
Ward 6	2,320	10.9
Ward 7	4,349	30.7
Ward 8	2,142	5.5
Ward 9	2,076	3.4
Ward 10	1,660	8.2
Ward 11	1,121	4.1
Ward 12	413	1.9
Ward 13	313	.6
Ward 14	3,137	9.8

STATE, CITY, AND WARD OR EQUIVALENT SUBDIVISION	NEGRO POPULATION: Number	NEGRO POPULATION: Percent of total population
NEW JERSEY—Contd.		
Newark—Contd.		
Ward 15	2,663	19.3
Ward 16	1,036	2.3
NEW YORK		
New York City	327,706	4.7
Bronx Borough	12,930	1.0
Statistical area:		
Area B 1 A	1,951	1.9
Area B 1 B	1,449	1.1
Area B 2	528	.3
Area B 3 A	2,681	2.3
Area B 3 B	2,497	2.2
Area B 4	1,165	1.3
Area B 5	1,009	.4
Area B 6	171	4.2
Area B 7	483	.9
Area B 9 A	741	.6
Area B 9 B	255	.2
Brooklyn Borough	68,921	2.7
Statistical area:		
Area K 1	6,265	8.8
Area K 2 A	55	------
Area K 2 B	38	------
Area K 3	2,754	3.1
Area K 4 A	576	.3
Area K 4 B	184	.2
Area K 4 C	904	.5
Area K 5 A	1,716	2.1
Area K 5 B	265	.4
Aera K 6 A	1,212	.6
Area K 6 B	909	.5
Area K 7	13,001	12.0
Area K 8	5,157	3.2
Area K 9 A	18,375	12.4
Area K 9 B	8,160	8.0
Area K 9 C	2,615	3.6
Area K 10 A	604	.7
Area K 10 B	1,788	1.7
Area K 11 A	1,426	.9
Area K 11 B	76	.2
Area K 13 A	1,342	1.3
Area K 13 B	1,407	1.5
Area K 15	92	.2
Manhattan Borough	224,670	12.0
Statistical area:		
Area M 1 A	1,722	2.4
Area M 1 B	953	1.2
Area M 2 A	585	.6
Area M 2 B	151	.2
Area M 2 C	178	.2
Area M 3 A	1,767	2.4
Area M 3 B	4,723	5.8
Area M 4 A	374	.4
Area M 4 B	437	.6
Area M 5 A	3,893	4.3
Area M 5 B	8,528	4.5
Area M 6 A	742	.6
Area M 6 B	2,575	3.2
Area M 6 C	10,222	11.7
Area M 7	32,395	31.7
Area M 8 A	2,864	3.2
Area M 8 B	101,257	95.1
Area M 8 C	48,059	44.6
Area M 9 A	1,646	1.8
Area M 9 B	310	.4
Area M 10	1,489	8.4
Queens Borough	18,609	1.7
Statistical area:		
Area Q 1	457	0.2
Area Q 2 A	1,633	.9
Area Q 2 B	8,382	4.2
Area Q 3 A	3,100	1.5
Area Q 3 B	272	.2
Area Q 4	1,882	5.4
Area Q 5	2,883	2.3
Richmond Borough	2,576	1.6
Statistical area:		
Area R 1	2,161	2.0
Area R 2	415	.8

STATE, CITY, AND WARD OR EQUIVALENT SUBDIVISION	NEGRO POPULATION: Number	NEGRO POPULATION: Percent of total population
NORTH CAROLINA		
Charlotte	25,163	30.4
Ward 1	3,404	40.0
Ward 2	8,048	75.8
Ward 3	1,918	41.6
Ward 4	348	6.5
Ward 5	376	5.9
Ward 6	229	2.2
Ward 7	1,855	18.4
Ward 8	246	3.0
Ward 9	1,875	31.3
Ward 10	2,096	34.9
Ward 11	4,768	73.8
Winston-Salem	32,566	43.3
Ward 1	2,352	19.3
Ward 2	2,513	28.9
Ward 3	21,702	68.8
Salem ward	5,999	26.2
OHIO		
Cincinnati	47,818	10.6
Ward 1	809	4.4
Ward 2	1,096	3.4
Ward 3	3,455	19.6
Wrad 4	3,505	24.8
Ward 5	170	0.9
Ward 6	1,110	8.1
Ward 7	888	7.3
Ward 8	585	3.9
Ward 9	431	2.4
Ward 10	182	1.6
Ward 11	2	------
Ward 12	50	.3
Ward 13	1,134	3.1
Ward 14	985	7.1
Ward 15	5,977	50.0
Ward 16	9,641	78.1
Ward 17	6,082	51.0
Ward 18	7,632	71.8
Ward 19	184	1.2
Ward 20	167	.5
Ward 21	1,262	12.2
Ward 22	969	7.1
Ward 23	236	1.3
Ward 24	150	.6
Ward 25	494	2.8
Ward 26	622	3.4
Cleveland	71,899	8.0
Statistical area:		
Area 1	5	------
Area 2	416	1.9
Area 3	50	.2
Area 4	2	------
Area 5	10	.1
Area 6	425	1.5
Area 7	19	.1
Area 8	25	.1
Area 9	3	------
Area 10	1	------
Area 11	86	.7
Area 12	1	------
Area 13	10	.1
Area 14	864	2.7
Area 15	78	.3
Area 16	109	.5
Area 17	135	.6
Area 18	212	.9
Area 19	494	2.6
Area 20	10,913	42.1
Area 21	17,748	58.2
Area 22	5,778	26.3
Area 23	16,467	72.4
Area 24	11,265	70.2
Area 25	184	.6
Area 26	1,666	9.2
Area 27	1,305	5.2
Area 28	141	.5
Area 29	41	.3
Area 30	469	1.7
Area 31	132	.7
Area 32	223	.8
Area 33	379	1.5
Area 34	74	.4
Area 35	1,439	4.2
Area 36	390	2.0
Area 37	53	.4

STATE, CITY, AND WARD OR EQUIVALENT SUBDIVISION	NEGRO POPULATION: Number	NEGRO POPULATION: Percent of total population
OHIO		
Cleveland—Contd.		
Statistical area—Contd.		
Area 38	121	0.6
Area 39	84	.4
Area 40	82	.5
Columbus	32,774	11.3
Ward 1	903	4.5
Ward 2	235	1.8
Ward 3	298	1.8
Ward 4	988	7.0
Ward 5	406	2.6
Ward 6	6,093	51.2
Ward 7	8,322	72.5
Ward 8	2,328	15.6
Ward 9	343	3.2
Ward 10	669	3.2
Ward 11	1,137	5.1
Ward 12	2,676	17.5
Ward 13	4,421	41.5
Ward 14	1,843	13.4
Ward 15	10	.1
Ward 16	794	7.2
Ward 17	1,080	4.4
Ward 18	167	1.3
Ward 19	61	.3
PENNSYLVANIA		
Philadelphia	219,599	11.3
Ward 1	993	2.4
Ward 2	5,046	17.9
Ward 3	3,579	21.1
Ward 4	4,669	33.0
Ward 5	1,155	11.9
Ward 6	324	19.8
Ward 7	8,430	41.7
Ward 8	1,051	8.5
Ward 9	99	6.0
Ward 10	903	8.7
Ward 11	1,316	21.3
Ward 12	1,790	20.3
Ward 13	3,431	26.4
Ward 14	6,531	46.0
Ward 15	4,093	10.7
Ward 16	686	6.8
Ward 17	411	3.6
Ward 18	32	.1
Ward 19	1,267	3.0
Ward 20	14,849	35.9
Ward 21	1,032	2.6
Ward 22	9,580	9.1
Ward 23	1,449	2.9
Ward 24	13,041	23.7
Ward 25	588	1.3
Ward 26	5,486	8.9
Ward 27	2,889	13.0
Ward 28	6,413	12.7
Ward 29	6,615	21.9
Ward 30	19,537	70.3
Ward 31	17	.1
Ward 32	14,476	31.7
Ward 33	122	.2
Ward 34	15,400	16.0
Ward 35	877	1.5
Ward 36	16,322	29.8
Ward 37	1,611	8.0
Ward 38	2,857	3.8
Ward 39	2,393	2.9
Ward 40	7,341	6.8
Ward 41	2,208	5.4
Ward 42	926	.7
Ward 43	873	1.7
Ward 44	11,168	26.2
Ward 45	321	.8
Ward 46	1,442	1.7
Ward 47	13,766	40.9
Ward 48	184	.6
Pittsburgh	54,983	8.2
Ward 1	257	2.7
Ward 2	916	13.7
Ward 3	8,873	40.1
Ward 4	1,358	4.8
Ward 5	15,695	53.8
Ward 6	2,348	12.6
Ward 7	966	5.6
Ward 8	589	2.9
Ward 9	500	2.5
Ward 10	1,874	7.4

TABLE 12.—NEGRO POPULATION BY WARDS OR EQUIVALENT SUBDIVISIONS OF CITIES HAVING 50,000 OR MORE INHABITANTS OF WHOM AT LEAST 20,000 ARE NEGROES: 1930—Continued

[Percent not shown where less than one-tenth of 1 percent]

STATE, CITY, AND WARD OR EQUIVALENT SUBDIVISION	NEGRO POPULATION	
	Number	Percent of total population
PENNSYLVANIA—Con.		
Pittsburgh—Con.		
Ward 11	1,339	5.6
Ward 12	4,483	16.8
Ward 13	4,249	14.0
Ward 14	731	1.8
Ward 15	1,142	3.9
Ward 16	383	1.5
Ward 17	397	1.7
Ward 18	1,320	6.0
Ward 19	450	1.1
Ward 20	793	3.1
Ward 21	1,948	8.6
Ward 22	838	5.3
Ward 23	116	.7
Ward 24	29	.2
Ward 25	1,666	10.1
Ward 26	638	2.7
Ward 27	712	2.5
Ward 28	235	2.7
Ward 29	10	.1
Ward 30	15	.2
Ward 31	63	1.2
Ward 32	50	1.0
SOUTH CAROLINA		
Charleston	28,062	45.1
Ward 1	549	27.5
Ward 2	226	8.3
Ward 3	613	31.2
Ward 4	2,650	52.6
Ward 5	1,616	39.9
Ward 6	919	21.4
Ward 7	1,600	44.8
Ward 8	1,843	40.5
Ward 9	2,721	59.7
Ward 10	3,997	47.4
Ward 11	6,105	49.2
Ward 12	5,223	60.1
TENNESSEE		
Chattanooga	33,289	27.8
Ward 1	1,162	13.4
Ward 2	588	20.2
Ward 3	2,888	89.8
Ward 4	4,313	73.2
Ward 5	2,418	48.5
Ward 6	818	37.9
Ward 7	6,323	72.6
Ward 8	4,535	67.3
Ward 9	953	10.6
Ward 10	270	11.4
Ward 11	647	7.0
Ward 12	4,955	31.3
Ward 13	866	6.6
Ward 14	124	10.4
TENNESSEE—Con.		
Chattanooga—Con.		
Ward 15	126	3.2
Ward 16	75	13.1
Ward 17	508	4.8
Ward 18	854	15.6
Ward 19	866	16.2
Memphis	96,550	38.1
Ward 1	1,642	60.3
Ward 2	386	20.9
Ward 3	106	7.6
Ward 4	194	23.6
Ward 5	4,348	77.4
Ward 6	1,424	59.9
Ward 7	3,610	62.7
Ward 8	2,212	40.3
Ward 9	3,192	41.6
Ward 10	1,820	78.7
Ward 11	5,253	81.0
Ward 12	2,144	52.6
Ward 13	3,806	37.7
Ward 14	4,204	70.6
Ward 15	706	25.5
Ward 16	688	8.6
Ward 17	1,306	11.0
Ward 18	407	10.4
Ward 19	4,479	42.5
Ward 20	686	7.2
Ward 21	4,118	40.4
Ward 22	1,535	45.6
Ward 23	808	24.8
Ward 24	5,783	82.6
Ward 25	3,837	40.6
Ward 26	2,662	40.3
Ward 27	1,618	30.2
Ward 28	156	4.3
Ward 29	4,964	57.5
Ward 30	237	8.7
Ward 31	817	7.0
Ward 32	2,072	47.5
Ward 33	313	6.0
Ward 34	1,823	37.5
Ward 35	3,847	86.2
Ward 36	140	1.7
Ward 37	2,582	79.6
Ward 38	508	10.0
Ward 39	3,826	90.0
Ward 40	2,476	66.0
Ward 41	2,635	86.2
Ward 42	1,906	39.1
Ward 43	811	34.4
Ward 44	166	9.0
Ward 45	233	4.2
Ward 46	37	1.4
Ward 47	1,841	65.5
Ward 48	1,251	86.3
Ward 49	281	18.9
Ward 50	654	31.1
TENNESSEE—Con.		
Nashville	42,836	27.8
Ward 1	383	5.1
Ward 2	3,744	36.5
Ward 3	5,022	77.6
Ward 4	4,140	93.3
Ward 5	440	46.2
Ward 6	720	30.9
Ward 7	499	17.6
Ward 8	1,576	44.0
Ward 9	2,668	53.0
Ward 10	877	18.1
Ward 11	4,311	51.4
Ward 12	690	10.0
Ward 13	2,064	41.2
Ward 14	3,997	65.4
Ward 15	1,818	41.1
Ward 16	3,892	52.1
Ward 17	1,025	21.3
Ward 18	559	9.2
Ward 19	2,026	32.4
Ward 20	958	11.2
Ward 21	228	2.6
Ward 22	660	8.6
Ward 23	38	.6
Ward 24	84	1.1
Ward 25	3	.1
Ward 26	197	4.8
Ward 27	217	3.9
TEXAS		
Dallas	38,742	14.9
(Not reported by wards.)		
Fort Worth	22,234	13.6
Ward 1	1,677	58.1
Ward 2 N	277	8.3
Ward 2 S	48	3.1
Ward 3 E	3,601	74.3
Ward 3 W	77	9.0
Ward 4 E	26	1.5
Ward 4 W	528	21.5
Ward 5 E	972	37.4
Ward 5 W	393	15.7
Ward 6 C	365	10.5
Ward 6 E	727	21.7
Ward 6 W	466	22.9
Ward 7 NE	3,145	88.1
Ward 7 NW	1,156	36.4
Ward 7 S	5	.8
Ward 7 SE	1,557	22.4
Ward 7 SW	118	4.6
Ward 8 NE	119	4.3
Ward 8 NW	141	4.7
Ward 8 SE	131	4.0
Ward 8 SW	200	6.7
TEXAS—Con.		
Fort Worth—Con.		
Ward 9 E	552	28.1
Ward 9 W	151	6.2
Ward 10 C	140	5.6
Ward 10 N	203	10.1
Ward 10 S	68	1.5
Ward 11 E	46	1.2
Ward 11 NW	68	2.3
Ward 11 SW	13	.4
Ward 12 E	747	15.3
Ward 12 W	43	.9
Ward 13 C	10	.6
Ward 13 N	------	------
Ward 13 S	------	------
Ward 14	192	4.8
Ward 15 N	------	------
Ward 15 S	2	.2
Ward 16 E	263	4.6
Ward 16 W	1,311	26.3
Ward 17	241	6.4
Ward 18	8	.4
Ward 19 N	26	.6
Ward 19 S	500	15.2
Ward 20	21	.9
Ward 21 E	28	1.3
Ward 21 W	34	1.2
Ward 22	7	.1
Ward 23 E	32	.7
Ward 23 W	3	.2
Ward 24	954	24.3
Ward 25	751	24.5
Ward 26	9	3.4
Ward 27	54	2.1
Ward 28	1	.1
Ward 29	3	2.6
Not in wards	24	2.5
Houston	63,337	21.7
(Not reported by wards.)		
VIRGINIA		
Norfolk	43,942	33.9
(Not reported by wards.)		
Richmond	52,988	29.0
Clay ward	7,669	15.3
Jefferson ward	12,420	33.0
Lee ward	15,792	28.3
Madison ward	17,107	43.5

CHAPTER VI.—"THE BLACK BELT"

Diffusion of Negro population.—Some of the 11,891,143 Negro inhabitants of continental United States lived in every State and in 2,855, or 92.1 percent of all the counties, parishes, or other civil divisions of the States. Negroes inhabited the District of Columbia and every county in 18 States; all except 1 county in 7 States; all except 2 counties in Wyoming and Nevada; all except 3 in Arkansas and New Mexico; all except 4 in Oklahoma and Oregon; all except 6 in Indiana, Illinois, Kansas, and Washington, and all except 7 in Michigan, and 9 in Colorado.

Of the 2,855 counties or parishes having Negro inhabitants in 1930, there were 1,666 which had a total Negro population of less than 1,000. There were 1,189 counties, 967 in the South, 204 in the North, and 18 in the West, having a Negro population of 1,000 or more. There were 581 counties having 1,000 to 5,000 Negro inhabitants; 271 counties having 5,000 to 10,000; 266 counties having 10,000 to 25,000; 46 counties having 25,000 to 50,000; and 15 counties having a Negro population of 50,000 to 100,000. There were 10 counties, 6 in the South and 4 in the North, with a Negro population of 100,000 or more.

Area of relatively high proportion of Negroes.—The area made up of a number of counties in eastern Virginia and North Carolina; a belt of counties extending from the Atlantic coast through South Carolina, central Georgia, and Alabama; together with a portion of the lower Mississippi Valley, has a large proportion of Negroes in the total population and is generally known as the "Black Belt." In these counties, the proportion of Negroes in the total population was 50 percent or more.

Decrease in the number of counties and population in the "Black Belt."—In 1930 there were 191 counties in which the population was 50 percent or more Negro as compared with 221 in 1920, and 264 in 1910. The Negro population of these 191 counties in 1930 was 2,738,432, or 29.3 percent of the total Negro population of the South, as compared with 3,251,440 in 1920, 3,932,484 in 1910, and 4,057,619 in 1900. Since 1900 the Negro population of the "Black Belt" has decreased 1,319,187, or 32.4 percent. However, part of this decrease has been due to a decrease of the area included in the "Black Belt."

The total white population in the counties having 50 percent or more of Negro population was 1,595,564 in 1930, 1,815,245 in 1920, 2,094,964 in 1910, and 2,163,731 in 1900.

"Black Belt" counties, by States.—Georgia had 48 counties in 1930 in which the Negro population constituted 50 percent or more of the total; Mississippi, 35; South Carolina, 25; Virginia, 21; Alabama, 18; Louisiana, 16; Arkansas, 9; North Carolina, 9; Florida, 4; Texas, 4; and Tennessee, 2. There were no counties having 50 percent or more Negro population in 5 Southern States, Delaware, Maryland, West Virginia, Kentucky, and Oklahoma.

Southern counties by proportion of population Negro: 1930.—In 1930, of the 1,415 counties in the South, 604, or 42.7 percent, had a Negro population which constituted less than 12.5 percent of the total population. The Negro population constituted between 12.5 and 24.9 percent of the total population in 227 counties; between 25 and 49.9 percent in 393 counties; between 50 and 74.9 percent in 172 counties; and 75 percent or more in 19 counties. The counties having 75 percent or more Negroes were distributed as follows: Mississippi, 8; Alabama, 6; Georgia, 2; and 1 each in Virginia, Arkansas, and Louisiana.

TABLE 1.—NUMBER OF COUNTIES REPORTING NEGRO INHABITANTS, 1930, BY SECTIONS, DIVISIONS, AND STATES

DIVISION AND STATE	Total number of counties	COUNTIES REPORTING	
		Negro inhabitants	No Negro inhabitants
United States	[1] **3,100**	**2,855**	**245**
The North	**1,274**	**1,118**	**156**
The South	**1,415**	**1,395**	**20**
The West	**411**	**342**	**69**
GEOGRAPHIC DIVISIONS:			
New England	67	66	1
Middle Atlantic	150	149	1
East North Central	436	400	36
West North Central	621	503	118
South Atlantic	581	579	2
East South Central	364	364	----------
West South Central	470	452	18
Mountain	278	220	58
Pacific	133	122	11
NEW ENGLAND:			
Maine	16	16	----------
New Hampshire	10	10	----------
Vermont	14	13	1
Massachusetts	14	14	----------
Rhode Island	5	5	----------
Connecticut	8	8	----------
MIDDLE ATLANTIC:			
New York	62	62	----------
New Jersey	21	21	----------
Pennsylvania	67	66	1
EAST NORTH CENTRAL:			
Ohio	88	87	1
Indiana	92	86	6
Illinois	102	96	6
Michigan	83	76	7
Wisconsin	71	55	16
WEST NORTH CENTRAL:			
Minnesota	87	71	16
Iowa	99	87	12
Missouri	115	103	12
WEST NORTH CENTRAL—Continued.			
North Dakota	53	33	20
South Dakota	69	45	24
Nebraska	93	65	28
Kansas	105	99	6
SOUTH ATLANTIC:			
Delaware	3	3	----------
Maryland	24	24	----------
District of Columbia	1	1	----------
Virginia	124	124	----------
West Virginia	55	54	1
North Carolina	100	100	----------
South Carolina	46	46	----------
Georgia	161	160	1
Florida	67	67	----------
EAST SOUTH CENTRAL:			
Kentucky	120	120	----------
Tennessee	95	95	----------
Alabama	67	67	----------
Mississippi	82	82	----------
WEST SOUTH CENTRAL:			
Arkansas	75	72	3
Louisiana	64	64	----------
Oklahoma	77	73	4
Texas	254	243	11
MOUNTAIN:			
Montana	56	45	11
Idaho	44	30	14
Wyoming	24	22	2
Colorado	63	54	9
New Mexico	31	28	3
Arizona	14	13	1
Utah	29	13	16
Nevada	17	15	2
PACIFIC:			
Washington	39	33	6
Oregon	36	32	4
California	58	57	1

[1] Includes Baltimore city, St. Louis city, 24 independent cities in Virginia, and that part of Yellowstone National Park in Wyoming.

Table 2.—NUMBER OF COUNTIES IN WHICH THE NEGRO POPULATION WAS 50 PERCENT OR MORE OF THE TOTAL POPULATION, BY DIVISIONS, AND STATES: 1880 TO 1930

DIVISION AND STATE	1930	1920	1910	1900	1890	1880
The South	**191**	**221**	**264**	**286**	**282**	**300**
South Atlantic	107	130	156	165	156	168
East South Central	55	54	61	63	62	69
West South Central	29	37	47	58	64	63
SOUTH ATLANTIC:						
Maryland			1	2	2	3
Virginia	21	23	32	36	39	46
West Virginia						
North Carolina	9	12	14	18	16	22
South Carolina	25	32	33	30	26	25
SOUTH ATLANTIC—Continued.						
Georgia	48	58	66	67	63	63
Florida	4	5	10	12	10	9
EAST SOUTH CENTRAL:						
Tennessee	2	2	2	3	3	5
Alabama	18	18	21	22	20	24
Mississippi	35	34	38	38	39	40
WEST SOUTH CENTRAL:						
Arkansas	9	11	14	15	15	13
Louisiana	16	22	25	31	33	36
Texas	4	4	8	12	16	14

Table 3.—NUMBER AND AREA OF COUNTIES IN WHICH THE NEGRO POPULATION WAS 50 PERCENT OR MORE OF TOTAL POPULATION, BY DIVISIONS, AND STATES: 1930, 1920, AND 1910

DIVISION AND STATE	NUMBER OF COUNTIES					AREA OF COUNTIES IN SQUARE MILES							
	1930	1920	1910	Increase or decrease (−)		1930	1920	1910	Increase or decrease (−)		Percent of total area of specified section, division, or State		
				1920–30	1910–20				1920–30	1910–20	1930	1920	1910
The South	**191**	**221**	**264**	**−30**	**−43**	**105, 315**	**122, 532**	**147, 219**	**−17, 217**	**−24, 687**	**12. 0**	**14. 0**	**16. 8**
South Atlantic	107	130	156	−23	−26	50, 932	63, 883	76, 584	−12, 951	−12, 701	18. 9	23. 7	28. 5
East South Central	55	54	61	1	−7	36, 048	35, 598	40, 721	450	−5, 123	20. 1	19. 8	22. 7
West South Central	29	37	47	−8	−10	18, 335	23, 051	29, 914	−4, 716	−6, 863	4. 3	5. 4	7. 0
SOUTH ATLANTIC:													
Maryland			1		−1			464		−464			4. 7
Virginia	21	23	32	−2	−9	7, 650	7, 882	11, 375	−232	−3, 493	19. 0	19. 6	28. 3
North Carolina	9	12	14	−3	−2	4, 480	6, 019	6, 044	−1, 539	−25	9. 2	12. 3	12. 4
South Carolina	25	32	33	−7	−1	16, 452	20, 777	23, 316	−4, 325	−2, 539	53. 9	68. 1	76. 5
Georgia	48	58	66	−10	−8	19, 791	24, 999	27, 418	−5, 208	−2, 419	33. 7	42. 6	46. 7
Florida	4	5	10	−1	−5	2, 559	4, 206	7, 967	−1, 647	−3, 761	4. 7	7. 7	14. 5
EAST SOUTH CENTRAL:													
Tennessee	2	2	2			1, 126	1, 126	1, 126			2. 7	2. 7	2. 7
Alabama	18	18	21		−3	14, 432	14, 428	16, 678	4	−2, 250	28. 1	28. 1	32. 5
Mississippi	35	34	38	1	−4	20, 490	20, 044	22, 917	446	−2, 873	44. 2	43. 2	49. 4
WEST SOUTH CENTRAL:													
Arkansas	9	11	14	−2	−3	5, 934	7, 244	9, 556	−1, 310	−2, 312	11. 3	13. 8	18. 2
Louisiana	16	22	25	−6	−3	10, 224	13, 151	15, 207	−2, 927	−2, 056	22. 5	29. 0	33. 5
Texas	4	4	8		−4	2, 177	2, 656	5, 151	−479	−2, 495	. 8	1. 0	2. 0

Table 4.—COUNTIES CLASSIFIED ACCORDING TO NEGRO POPULATION, BY SECTIONS, AND SOUTHERN DIVISIONS: 1930

SECTION AND DIVISION	Total number of counties	Reporting no Negro population	REPORTING NEGRO POPULATION										
			Total	Under 1,000				1,000 or more						
				Total	Under 100	100 to 500	500 to 1,000	Total	1,000 to 5,000	5,000 to 10,000	10,000 to 25,000	25,000 to 50,000	50,000 to 100,000	100,000 and over
United States	**[1] 3, 100**	**245**	**2, 855**	**1, 666**	**1, 009**	**440**	**217**	**1, 189**	**581**	**271**	**266**	**46**	**15**	**10**
THE SOUTH	1, 415	20	1, 395	428	142	161	125	967	429	243	238	42	9	6
South Atlantic	581	2	579	102	23	40	39	477	215	120	117	19	3	3
East South Central	364		364	117	28	50	39	247	113	52	64	12	4	2
West South Central	470	18	452	209	91	71	47	243	101	71	57	11	2	1
THE NORTH	1, 274	156	1, 118	914	611	224	79	204	137	27	27	3	6	4
THE WEST	411	69	342	324	256	55	13	18	15	1	1	1		

[1] Includes Baltimore city, St. Louis city, 24 independent cities in Virginia, and that part of Yellowstone National Park in Wyoming.

TABLE 5.—NEGRO AND WHITE POPULATION OF COUNTIES IN WHICH THE NEGRO POPULATION WAS 50 PERCENT OR MORE OF TOTAL POPULATION, BY DIVISIONS, AND STATES: 1900 TO 1930

DIVISION AND STATE	NEGRO POPULATION								WHITE POPULATION							
	1930	1920	1910	1900	Percent of total Negro population of division or State				1930	1920	1910	1900	Percent of total white population of division or State			
					1930	1920	1910	1900					1930	1920	1910	1900
The South	**2,738,432**	**3,251,440**	**3,932,484**	**4,057,619**	**29.3**	**36.5**	**44.9**	**51.2**	**1,595,564**	**1,815,245**	**2,094,964**	**2,163,731**	**5.8**	**7.5**	**10.2**	**13.1**
South Atlantic	1,182,260	1,632,589	1,988,088	2,006,301	26.7	37.7	48.3	53.8	780,786	1,059,774	1,236,542	1,219,672	6.9	11.0	15.3	18.2
East South Central	1,120,122	1,076,831	1,277,080	1,325,226	42.1	42.7	48.1	53.0	546,754	444,976	498,985	546,196	7.6	7.0	8.7	10.8
West South Central	436,050	542,020	667,316	726,092	19.1	26.3	33.6	42.9	268,024	310,495	359,437	397,863	2.9	3.8	5.3	8.3
SOUTH ATLANTIC:																
Delaware	-	-	-	-	-	-	-	-	-	-	-	-	-	-	-	-
Maryland	-	-	8,572	14,791	-	-	3.7	6.3	-	-	7,813	13,094	-	-	0.7	1.4
District of Columbia	-	-	-	-	-	-	-	-	-	-	-	-	-	-	-	-
Virginia	156,537	167,895	271,097	286,733	24.1	24.3	40.4	43.4	116,847	123,669	201,575	202,027	6.6	7.6	14.5	16.9
West Virginia	-	-	-	-	-	-	-	-	-	-	-	-	-	-	-	-
North Carolina	149,592	176,441	166,520	198,237	16.3	23.1	23.9	31.7	108,292	136,295	123,841	152,251	4.8	7.6	8.3	12.0
South Carolina	446,435	622,779	699,471	662,991	56.2	72.0	83.7	84.7	279,645	377,719	403,227	342,669	29.6	46.1	59.4	61.4
Georgia	381,618	606,595	735,972	708,765	35.6	50.3	62.5	68.5	241,699	384,390	434,209	423,042	13.2	22.8	30.3	35.8
Florida	48,078	58,879	106,456	134,784	11.1	17.9	34.5	58.4	34,303	37,701	65,877	86,589	3.3	5.9	14.8	29.1
EAST SOUTH CENTRAL:																
Kentucky	-	-	-	-	-	-	-	-	-	-	-	-	-	-	-	-
Tennessee	38,322	40,485	40,412	123,535	8.0	9.0	8.5	25.7	16,632	16,399	15,742	84,882	.8	.9	.9	5.5
Alabama	380,863	386,293	487,399	505,576	40.3	42.9	53.7	61.1	195,641	171,286	198,572	205,486	11.5	11.8	16.2	20.5
Mississippi	700,937	650,053	749,269	696,115	69.4	69.5	74.2	76.7	334,481	257,291	284,671	255,828	33.6	30.1	36.2	39.9
WEST SOUTH CENTRAL:																
Arkansas	188,282	218,474	226,145	187,866	39.4	46.3	51.1	51.2	101,385	97,438	104,389	90,336	7.4	7.6	9.2	9.6
Louisiana	198,588	274,793	356,707	418,148	25.6	39.2	50.0	64.3	131,246	178,942	194,319	220,339	10.0	16.3	20.6	30.2
Oklahoma	-	-	-	-	-	-	-	-	-	-	-	-	-	-	-	-
Texas	49,180	48,753	84,464	120,078	5.8	6.6	12.2	19.3	35,393	34,115	60,729	87,188	.8	1.9	.9	3.6

TABLE 6.—SOUTHERN COUNTY AREAS CLASSIFIED ACCORDING TO SPECIFIC PERCENTAGE NEGRO IN THE POPULATION, BY DIVISIONS, AND STATES: 1930

DIVISION AND STATE	Total number of counties	NUMBER OF COUNTIES IN WHICH THE PERCENT OF NEGRO POPULATION WAS—					Total area in square miles	AREA IN SQUARE MILES OF COUNTIES IN WHICH THE PERCENT OF NEGRO POPULATION WAS—					Total land area	PERCENT DISTRIBUTION IN AREA OF DIVISION OR STATE IN WHICH THE PERCENT OF NEGRO POPULATION WAS—				
		Less than 12.5[1]	12.5 to 24.9	25 to 49.9	50 to 74.9	75 or more		Less than 12.5[1]	12.5 to 24.9	25 to 49.9	50 to 74.9	75 or more		Less than 12.5[1]	12.5 to 24.9	25 to 49.9	50 to 74.9	75 or more
The South	**1,415**	**604**	**227**	**393**	**172**	**19**	**878,328**	**415,510**	**130,834**	**226,669**	**93,918**	**11,397**	**100.0**	**47.3**	**14.9**	**25.8**	**10.7**	**1.3**
South Atlantic	581	149	96	229	104	3	269,073	61,249	46,348	110,544	49,462	1,470	100.0	22.8	17.2	41.1	18.4	0.5
East South Central	364	171	73	65	41	14	179,509	65,992	35,466	42,003	27,055	8,993	100.0	36.8	19.8	23.4	15.1	5.0
West South Central	470	284	58	99	27	2	429,746	288,269	49,020	74,122	17,401	934	100.0	67.1	11.4	17.2	4.0	.2
SOUTH ATLANTIC:																		
Delaware	3	1	2	-	-	-	1,965	435	1,530	-	-	-	100.0	22.1	77.9	-	-	-
Maryland	24	7	7	10	-	-	9,941	3,681	2,464	3,796	-	-	100.0	37.0	24.8	38.2	-	-
District of Columbia	1	-	-	1	-	-	62	-	-	62	-	-	100.0	-	-	100.0	-	-
Virginia	124	34	24	45	20	1	40,262	13,488	5,806	13,318	7,462	188	100.0	33.5	14.4	33.1	18.5	.5
West Virginia	55	51	4	-	-	-	24,022	22,014	2,008	-	-	-	100.0	91.6	8.4	-	-	-
North Carolina	100	29	17	45	9	-	48,740	12,278	8,565	23,417	4,480	-	100.0	25.2	17.6	48.0	9.2	-
South Carolina	46	-	4	17	25	-	30,495	-	3,098	10,945	16,452	-	100.0	-	10.2	35.9	53.9	-
Georgia	161	24	21	68	46	2	58,725	7,292	7,982	23,660	18,509	1,282	100.0	12.4	13.6	40.3	31.5	2.2
Florida	67	3	17	43	4	-	54,861	2,061	14,895	35,346	2,559	-	100.0	3.8	27.2	64.4	4.7	-
EAST SOUTH CENTRAL:																		
Kentucky	120	93	25	2	-	-	40,181	31,115	7,974	1,092	-	-	100.0	77.4	19.8	2.7	-	-
Tennessee	95	66	18	9	2	-	41,687	26,814	8,951	4,796	1,126	-	100.0	64.3	21.5	11.5	2.7	-
Alabama	67	10	16	23	12	6	51,279	7,106	11,493	18,248	10,030	4,402	100.0	13.9	22.4	35.6	19.6	8.6
Mississippi	82	2	14	31	27	8	46,362	957	7,048	17,867	15,899	4,591	100.0	2.1	15.2	38.5	34.3	9.9
WEST SOUTH CENTRAL:																		
Arkansas	75	37	8	21	8	1	52,525	25,987	5,621	14,983	5,352	582	100.0	49.5	10.7	28.5	10.2	1.1
Louisiana	64	1	12	35	15	1	45,409	1,501	9,802	23,882	9,872	352	100.0	3.3	21.6	52.6	21.7	.8
Oklahoma	77	69	6	2	-	-	69,414	62,581	5,645	1,188	-	-	100.0	90.2	8.1	1.7	-	-
Texas	254	177	32	41	4	-	262,398	198,200	27,952	34,069	2,177	-	100.0	75.5	10.7	13.0	.8	-

[1] Includes counties reporting no Negro population.

Table 7.—NEGRO POPULATION IN COUNTIES IN THE SOUTH CLASSIFIED ACCORDING TO PERCENT NEGRO, BY DIVISIONS, AND STATES: 1930, 1920, AND 1910

DIVISION, STATE, AND YEAR	Total	NEGRO POPULATION IN COUNTIES IN WHICH THE PERCENT NEGRO WAS—					Total	PERCENT OF THE TOTAL NEGRO POPULATION IN COUNTIES IN WHICH THE PERCENT NEGRO WAS—				
		Less than 12.5 [1]	12.5 to 24.9	25 to 49.9	50 to 74.9	75 or more		Less than 12.5 [1]	12.5 to 24.9	25 to 49.9	50 to 74.9	75 or more
The South:												
1930	**9,361,577**	**604,956**	**1,708,008**	**4,310,181**	**2,363,112**	**375,320**	**100.0**	**6.5**	**18.2**	**46.0**	**25.2**	**4.0**
1920	**8,912,231**	**516,972**	**1,269,519**	**3,874,300**	**2,546,955**	**704,485**	**100.0**	**5.8**	**14.2**	**43.5**	**28.6**	**7.9**
1910	**8,749,427**	**401,024**	**1,013,764**	**3,402,155**	**2,870,001**	**1,062,483**	**100.0**	**4.6**	**11.6**	**38.9**	**32.8**	**12.1**
SOUTH ATLANTIC:												
1930	4,421,388	211,770	741,217	2,286,141	1,149,316	32,944	100.0	4.8	16.8	51.7	26.0	0.7
1920	4,325,120	155,637	534,438	2,002,456	1,544,611	87,978	100.0	3.6	12.4	46.3	35.7	2.0
1910	4,112,488	119,336	385,290	1,619,774	1,800,468	187,620	100.0	2.9	9.4	39.4	43.8	4.6
EAST SOUTH CENTRAL:												
1930	2,658,238	157,668	456,866	923,582	817,461	302,661	100.0	5.9	17.2	34.7	30.8	11.4
1920	2,523,532	155,424	338,241	953,036	571,616	505,215	100.0	6.2	13.4	37.8	22.7	20.0
1910	2,652,513	131,209	347,831	896,393	571,531	705,549	100.0	4.9	13.1	33.8	21.5	26.6
WEST SOUTH CENTRAL:												
1930	2,281,951	235,518	509,925	1,100,458	396,335	39,715	100.0	10.3	22.3	48.2	17.4	1.7
1920	2,063,579	205,911	396,840	918,808	430,728	111,292	100.0	10.0	19.2	44.5	20.9	5.4
1910	1,984,426	150,479	280,643	885,988	498,002	169,314	100.0	7.6	14.1	44.6	25.1	8.5
SOUTH ATLANTIC:												
Delaware:												
1930	32,602	18,471	14,131	-----	-----	-----	100.0	56.7	43.3	-----	-----	-----
1920	30,335	16,325	14,010	-----	-----	-----	100.0	53.8	46.2	-----	-----	-----
1910	31,181	-----	31,181	-----	-----	-----	100.0	-----	100.0	-----	-----	-----
Maryland:												
1930	276,379	24,322	182,115	69,942	-----	-----	100.0	8.8	65.9	25.3	-----	-----
1920	244,479	22,617	135,562	86,300	-----	-----	100.0	9.3	55.4	35.3	-----	-----
1910	232,250	23,743	108,049	91,886	8,572	-----	100.0	10.2	46.5	39.6	3.7	-----
District of Columbia:												
1930	132,068	-----	-----	132,068	-----	-----	100.0	-----	-----	100.0	-----	-----
1920	109,966	-----	-----	109,966	-----	-----	100.0	-----	-----	100.0	-----	-----
1910	94,446	-----	-----	94,446	-----	-----	100.0	-----	-----	100.0	-----	-----
Virginia:												
1930	650,165	38,128	88,137	367,363	152,780	3,757	100.0	5.9	13.6	56.5	23.5	0.6
1920	690,017	28,223	59,590	434,309	164,292	3,603	100.0	4.1	8.6	62.9	23.8	.5
1910	671,096	23,358	61,753	314,888	271,097	-----	100.0	3.5	9.2	46.9	40.4	-----
West Virginia:												
1930	114,893	66,870	48,023	-----	-----	-----	100.0	58.2	41.8	-----	-----	-----
1920	86,345	42,716	43,629	-----	-----	-----	100.0	49.5	50.5	-----	-----	-----
1910	64,173	30,736	18,770	14,667	-----	-----	100.0	47.9	29.2	22.9	-----	-----
North Carolina:												
1930	918,647	41,827	160,277	566,951	149,592	-----	100.0	4.6	17.4	61.7	16.3	-----
1920	763,407	33,348	122,933	430,685	176,441	-----	100.0	4.4	16.1	56.4	23.1	-----
1910	697,843	29,001	87,104	415,218	166,520	-----	100.0	4.2	12.5	59.5	23.9	-----
South Carolina:												
1930	793,681	-----	48,361	298,885	446,435	-----	100.0	-----	6.1	37.7	56.2	-----
1920	864,719	-----	19,027	222,913	572,156	50,623	100.0	-----	2.2	25.8	66.2	5.9
1910	835,843	-----	12,098	124,274	619,748	79,723	100.0	-----	1.4	14.9	74.1	9.5
Georgia:												
1930	1,071,125	19,756	78,823	590,928	352,431	29,187	100.0	1.8	7.4	55.2	32.9	2.7
1920	1,206,365	11,163	83,173	505,434	572,843	33,752	100.0	.9	6.9	41.9	47.5	2.8
1910	1,176,987	11,304	39,944	389,767	655,915	80,057	100.0	1.0	3.4	33.1	55.7	6.8
Florida:												
1930	431,828	2,396	121,350	260,004	48,078	-----	100.0	.6	28.1	60.2	11.1	-----
1920	329,487	1,245	56,514	212,849	58,879	-----	100.0	.4	17.2	64.6	17.9	-----
1910	308,669	1,194	26,391	174,628	78,616	27,840	100.0	.4	8.5	56.6	25.5	9.0
EAST SOUTH CENTRAL:												
Kentucky:												
1930	226,040	71,962	142,374	11,704	-----	-----	100.0	31.8	63.0	5.2	-----	-----
1920	235,938	69,496	125,507	40,935	-----	-----	100.0	29.5	53.2	17.3	-----	-----
1910	261,656	58,799	153,160	49,697	-----	-----	100.0	22.5	58.5	19.0	-----	-----
Tennessee:												
1930	477,646	72,350	160,785	206,189	38,322	-----	100.0	15.1	33.7	43.2	8.0	-----
1920	451,758	72,083	92,739	246,451	40,485	-----	100.0	16.0	20.5	54.6	9.0	-----
1910	473,088	58,061	89,796	284,819	17,710	22,702	100.0	12.3	19.0	60.2	3.7	4.8
Alabama:												
1930	944,834	11,281	99,356	453,334	266,328	114,535	100.0	1.2	10.5	48.0	28.2	12.1
1920	900,652	11,861	82,926	419,572	200,930	185,363	100.0	1.3	9.2	46.6	22.3	20.6
1910	908,282	12,062	69,266	339,555	200,208	287,191	100.0	1.3	7.6	37.4	22.0	31.6
Mississippi:												
1930	1,009,718	2,075	54,351	252,355	512,811	188,126	100.0	.2	5.4	25.0	50.8	18.6
1920	935,184	1,984	37,069	246,078	330,201	319,852	100.0	.2	4.0	26.3	35.3	34.2
1910	1,009,487	2,287	35,609	222,322	353,613	395,656	100.0	.2	3.5	22.0	35.0	39.2
WEST SOUTH CENTRAL:												
Arkansas:												
1930	478,463	19,914	32,709	237,558	156,916	31,366	100.0	4.2	6.8	49.7	32.8	6.6
1920	472,220	22,900	28,931	201,915	156,267	62,207	100.0	4.8	6.1	42.8	33.1	13.2
1910	442,891	25,387	19,000	172,359	131,977	94,168	100.0	5.7	4.3	38.9	29.8	21.3
Louisiana:												
1930	776,326	578	53,905	523,255	190,239	8,349	100.0	.1	6.9	67.4	24.5	1.1
1920	700,257	-----	40,284	385,180	225,708	49,085	100.0	-----	5.8	55.0	32.2	7.0
1910	713,874	-----	51,260	305,907	281,561	75,146	100.0	-----	7.2	42.9	39.4	10.5
Oklahoma:												
1930	172,198	107,365	50,797	14,036	-----	-----	100.0	62.3	29.5	8.2	-----	-----
1920	149,408	79,552	54,146	15,710	-----	-----	100.0	53.2	36.2	10.5	-----	-----
1910	137,612	58,004	26,908	52,700	-----	-----	100.0	42.2	19.6	38.3	-----	-----
Texas:												
1930	854,964	107,661	372,514	325,609	49,180	-----	100.0	12.6	43.6	38.1	5.8	-----
1920	741,694	103,459	273,479	316,003	48,753	-----	100.0	13.9	36.9	42.6	6.6	-----
1910	690,049	67,088	183,475	355,022	84,464	-----	100.0	9.7	26.6	51.4	12.2	-----

[1] Includes counties reporting no Negro population.

TABLE 8.—NEGRO PERCENTAGE OF TOTAL POPULATION, NUMBER OF NEGROES PER SQUARE MILE, AND LAND AREA, BY SELECTED COUNTIES: 1930, 1920, AND 1910

[This table shows the ranking counties whose Negro population was 50 percent or more for each year]

COUNTIES	Percent of total population	Number per square mile	Land area in square miles
1930			
Lownds, Alae	85.8	26.6	739
Tunica, Miss	85.8	43.6	418
Greene, Ala	82.4	25.6	635
Macon, Ala	82.4	36.4	614
Issaquena, Miss	81.4	11.5	406
Crittenden, Ark	79.0	53.9	582
Sumter, Ala	78.9	23.4	908
Bullock, Ala	78.7	25.8	610
Noxubee, Miss	78.7	29.5	682
Madison, Miss	78.6	38.8	725
Lee, Ga	77.9	19.9	326
Burke, Ga	77.7	23.7	956
Wilcox, Ala	77.6	21.6	896
Coahoma, Miss	77.4	67.7	530
Charles City, Va	77.0	20.0	188
Leflore, Miss	76.4	71.5	572
West Feliciana, La	76.4	23.7	352
Holmes, Miss	76.3	39.1	751
Jefferson, Miss	75.8	21.4	507
East Carroll, La	74.8	28.2	420
Claiborne, Miss	74.4	18.5	489
Calhoun, S. C	74.3	31.7	391
Dallas, Ala	74.2	42.7	957
Bolivar, Miss	74.0	59.8	879
Hale, Ala	73.9	30.0	646
De Soto, Miss	73.8	39.5	475
Sharkey, Miss	73.8	24.3	422
Allendale, S. C	73.4	22.4	435
Fayette, Tenn	73.0	34.1	618
Perry, Ala	72.6	26.0	737
Marengo, Ala	72.3	27.3	966
Washington, Miss	72.0	54.1	723
Concordia, La	71.9	12.9	714
Clarendon, S. C	71.8	33.7	640
Hancock, Ga	71.5	17.6	530
Marshall, Miss	71.5	25.8	689
Russell, Ala	71.5	29.9	655
Tensas, La	71.5	17.1	632
Beaufort, S. C	71.4	22.2	702
Stewart, Ga	71.4	19.3	411
Terrell, Ga	71.0	40.3	322
Calhoun, Ga	70.3	26.2	284
Sunflower, Miss	70.3	69.2	674
Wilkinson, Miss	70.1	14.7	667
Harris, Ga	69.1	15.4	501
Quitman, Ga	69.1	18.3	144
Humphreys, Miss	68.9	41.7	408
Talbot, Ga	68.9	18.7	312
Quitman, Miss	68.6	43.9	395
Taliaferro, Ga	68.4	19.9	212
East Feliciana, La	68.1	25.6	464
Jefferson, Fla	68.0	17.2	530
Tallahatchie, Miss	68.0	38.5	629
Jasper, S. C	67.9	11.4	596
Liberty, Ga	67.9	10.2	543
Berkeley, S. C	67.7	12.5	1,203
Yazoo, Miss	67.7	27.9	905
Houston, Ga	67.6	17.2	443
Nansemond, Va	67.5	36.1	421
Sumter, S. C	67.5	48.5	638
Fairfield, S. C	67.4	22.2	706
Lee, S. C	67.4	39.7	409
McIntosh, Ga	67.3	8.2	470
St. Francis, Ark	67.3	35.8	628
Macon, Ga	67.2	33.7	332
Randolph, Ga	67.2	28.0	412
McCormick, S. C	67.1	20.0	385
Phillips, Ark	67.0	39.4	692
Williamsburg, S. C	66.9	26.5	882
Sussex, Va	66.2	15.5	515
Haywood, Tenn	66.1	33.9	508
Warren, Ga	65.7	18.2	404
Adams, Miss	65.5	36.2	426
Lee, Ark	65.4	29.0	601
Clay, Ga	65.3	22.3	203
Sumter, Ga	64.9	38.1	456
Lincoln, Ark	64.6	22.9	571
Madison, La	64.5	14.7	650
Georgetown, S. C	64.4	16.9	828
Bamberg, S. C	64.3	32.9	379
Jones, Ga	64.2	15.3	377
Peach, Ga	63.9	36.7	179
Desha, Ark	63.7	18.6	747
Twiggs, Ga	63.7	17.0	314
Orangeburg, S. C	63.6	35.9	1,131
Barnwell, S. C	63.5	25.8	522
Edgefield, S. C	63.5	23.7	518
Warren, N. C	63.5	34.9	425
Wilkes, Ga	63.3	22.0	458
West Baton Rouge, La	63.1	28.7	214
Columbia, Ga	63.0	15.8	350
Bossier, La	62.9	20.7	863
Panola, Miss	62.8	25.8	696
Northampton, N. C	62.7	33.8	504
Chicot, Ark	62.5	23.3	607
Marion, Tex	62.3	16.5	391
Putnam, Ga	62.3	14.4	361
Schley, Ga	62.1	21.6	154
De Soto, La	62.0	22.0	872
Clay, Miss	61.8	27.2	408
Baker, Ga	61.3	13.4	357
Southampton, Va	61.0	27.1	604
Jasper, Ga	60.9	16.3	321
Greensville, Va	60.7	26.5	307
Hoke, N. C	60.6	20.7	417
Dinwiddie, Va	60.5	21.6	517
Webster, Ga	60.4	10.1	302
Harrison, Tex	60.1	33.7	872
Surry, Va	60.1	15.3	278
Tate, Miss	60.1	26.6	400
Oktibbeha, Miss	59.5	24.9	457
Grenada, Miss	59.4	22.6	442
Camden, Ga	59.1	5.3	711
Dorchester, S. C	58.9	18.2	613
New Kent, Va	58.8	13.2	191
Hertford, N. C	58.7	30.2	341
Leon, Fla	58.7	19.3	715
Warren, Miss	58.4	36.5	572
Monroe, Ga	58.2	14.4	470
Jefferson, Ga	58.1	18.6	646
Pointe Coupee, La	58.1	21.2	576
Halifax, N. C	57.9	45.6	676
Jefferson, Ark	57.9	41.1	903
Cumberland, Va	57.8	14.9	293
Jenkins, Ga	57.8	21.8	342
Kemper, Miss	57.8	16.8	752
Lowndes, Miss	57.7	34.7	499
Morgan, Ga	57.6	18.5	390
Barbour, Ala	57.5	20.5	912
Dougherty, Ga	57.5	37.5	342
Morehouse, La	57.4	16.4	831
Carroll, Miss	57.0	18.1	624
Hampton, S. C	57.0	19.1	513
Edgecombe, N. C	56.9	53.6	509
Marlboro, S. C	56.9	34.7	519
Gadsden, Fla	56.8	31.4	540
Screven, Ga	56.7	14.6	794
Bertie, N. C	56.6	20.8	703
Washington, Ga	56.5	21.1	669
Marion, Ga	56.2	10.9	360
Brunswick, Va	56.1	20.6	557
Pulaski, Ga	56.1	19.6	258
Claiborne, La	55.9	23.2	778
Dooly, Ga	55.8	25.4	397
Monroe, Ark	55.7	19.1	603
Autauga, Ala	55.4	18.7	584
Crawford, Ga	55.3	12.2	319
Jefferson Davis, Miss	55.3	19.6	404
Kershaw, S. C	55.0	26.3	671
Choctaw, Ala	54.8	12.1	932
Marion, S. C	54.8	28.2	529
Essex, Va	54.7	14.8	258
Hinds, Miss	54.7	54.3	858
King and Queen, Va	54.6	13.0	320
Colleton, S. C	54.5	12.5	1,122
Rankin, Miss	54.5	14.0	791
St. Helena, La	54.3	11.0	420
Charleston, S. C	54.2	59.4	923
Northampton, Va	53.5	41.5	239
Scotland, N. C	53.5	30.9	349
Early, Ga	53.3	18.6	524
Amite, Miss	52.8	14.6	714
Brooks, Ga	52.8	21.9	514
Montgomery, Ala	52.8	64.8	805
Mecklenburg, Va	52.7	25.7	669
San Jacinto, Tex	52.7	8.5	602
James City, Va	52.6	12.5	163
Greene, Ga	52.5	15.9	416
Madison, Fla	52.5	10.6	774
Monroe, Ala	52.5	15.6	1,012
Clarke, Ala	52.4	11.2	1,216
Meriwether, Ga	52.4	23.7	496
Darlington, S. C	52.2	35.7	605
Lincoln, Ga	52.2	14.1	291
Anson, N. C	52.0	27.4	556
Gregg, Tex	52.0	26.3	312
Prince Edward, Va	52.0	21.2	356
Chester, S. C	51.7	27.8	592
Goochland, Va	51.7	14.3	287
Lee, Ala	51.7	30.6	608
Isle of Wight, Va	51.6	22.0	314
Amelia, Va	51.4	12.4	371
Powhatan, Va	51.4	11.6	273
Iberville, La	50.9	21.5	584
Natchitoches, La	50.9	15.2	1,289
McDuffie, Ga	50.7	15.9	287
Carolina, Va	50.6	14.6	529
Chickasaw, Miss	50.2	20.9	501
Mitchell, Ga	50.2	21.6	548
Richland, La	50.1	23.4	565
Decatur, Ga	50.0	20.3	583

TABLE 8.—NEGRO PERCENTAGE OF TOTAL POPULATION, NUMBER OF NEGROES PER SQUARE MILE, AND LAND AREA, BY SELECTED COUNTIES: 1930, 1920, AND 1910—Continued

[This table shows the ranking counties whose Negro population was 50 percent or more for each year]

1920

COUNTIES	Percent of total population	Number per square mile	Land area in square miles
Issaquena, Miss	90.8	17.0	406
Tunica, Miss	89.3	43.6	418
Lowndes, Ala	86.7	29.8	739
East Carroll, La	86.4	23.1	420
Tensas, La	85.3	16.3	632
Coahoma, Miss	84.8	66.4	530
Crittenden, Ark	84.1	42.4	582
Madison, La	83.7	13.9	650
Macon, Ala	83.2	31.9	614
Greene, Ala	83.0	23.7	635
Sharkey, Miss	83.0	27.9	422
West Feliciana, La	82.8	28.9	352
Bolivar, Miss	82.4	54.1	879
Lee, Ga	82.3	27.5	326
Humphreys, Miss	82.2	38.7	408
Bullock, Ala	81.5	33.9	610
Washington, Miss	81.5	57.6	723
Wilcox, Ala	80.5	27.9	896
Burke, Ga	80.3	25.9	956
Noxubee, Miss	79.3	27.6	682
Concordia, La	78.8	13.8	714
Beaufort, S. C	78.4	24.9	702
Leflore, Miss	78.0	50.8	572
Madison, Miss	78.0	31.5	725
Allendale, S. C	77.6	28.7	435
Sumter, Ala	77.6	21.8	908
Dallas, Ala	77.3	44.2	957
Lee, Ark	77.3	37.1	601
Holmes, Miss	77.2	35.5	751
Russell, Ala	76.3	32.0	655
Fairfield, S. C	76.1	29.3	706
Quitman, Miss	75.8	38.1	395
De Soto, Miss	75.7	38.8	475
Charles City, Va	75.2	19.2	188
Desha, Ark	75.2	20.4	747
Jefferson, Miss	75.0	23.6	507
Fayette, Tenn	74.7	38.1	618
McIntosh, Ga	74.3	8.1	470
Sunflower, Miss	74.2	51.0	674
Phillips, Ark	73.9	47.6	692
Wilkinson, Miss	73.9	17.0	667
Chicot, Ark	73.8	26.5	607
Claiborne, Miss	73.7	19.6	489
Hale, Ala	73.7	27.7	646
Berkeley, S. C	72.5	13.2	1,238
Jefferson, Fla	72.5	18.0	585
Marengo, Ala	72.4	27.0	966
Marshall, Miss	72.2	27.3	689
Jasper, S. C	72.1	11.9	596
Clarendon, S. C	72.0	35.7	704
Hancock, Ga	72.0	24.9	530
Perry, Ala	72.0	24.8	737
Talbot, Ga	71.7	25.6	312
Terrell, Ga	71.7	43.6	322
Yazoo, Miss	71.7	29.4	905
Stewart, Ga	71.5	21.0	411
Harris, Ga	71.1	22.4	501
Quitman, Ga	71.1	16.9	144
Jasper, Ga	71.0	36.2	321
Jones, Ga	70.9	24.9	377
Sumter, S. C	70.9	53.1	574
Bossier, La	70.6	18.2	863
Taliaferro, Ga	70.5	29.4	212
Columbia, Ga	70.4	23.6	350
St. Francis, Ark	70.4	31.8	628
Tallahatchie, Miss	70.4	40.2	629
Edgefield, S. C	69.6	31.8	524
Putnam, Ga	68.8	28.9	361
Adams, Miss	68.7	35.8	426
Calhoun, Ga	68.7	24.7	284
Calhoun, S. C	68.6	32.2	391
East Feliciana, La	68.6	25.9	464
Bamberg, S. C	68.5	38.3	375
McCormick, S. C	68.5	29.7	379

COUNTIES	Percent of total population	Number per square mile	Land area in square miles
Macon, Ga	68.1	32.6	369
Lincoln, Ark	68.0	22.3	571
Morehouse, La	68.0	15.8	831
Baker, Ga	67.7	15.7	357
Barnwell, S. C	67.5	29.9	522
West Baton Rouge, La	67.5	35.0	214
Leon, Fla	67.4	17.0	715
Lee, S. C	67.3	44.3	407
Clay, Ga	67.1	25.0	203
Sumter, Ga	67.0	43.6	456
Haywood, Tenn	66.8	33.4	508
Dougherty, Ga	66.6	39.1	342
Georgetown, S. C	66.6	17.5	828
Wilkes, Ga	66.5	35.1	458
Houston, Ga	66.1	24.8	585
Warren, Ga	66.1	19.4	404
Williamsburg, S. C	66.0	27.5	927
Orangeburg, S. C	65.8	37.8	1,131
Randolph, Ga	65.8	26.7	412
Sussex, Va	65.7	16.4	515
Jefferson, Ark	65.5	43.7	903
Lowndes, Miss	64.9	36.0	499
Morgan, Ga	64.0	33.0	390
Warren, N. C	64.0	32.5	425
Twiggs, Ga	63.9	21.2	314
Warren, Miss	63.9	37.3	572
Nansemond, Va	63.7	30.6	421
Panola, Miss	63.7	25.5	696
Monroe, Ga	63.4	21.9	584
Cumberland, Va	63.2	19.6	293
Gadsden, Fla	62.9	27.4	540
Hinds, Miss	62.6	41.6	858
Grenada, Miss	62.1	19.1	442
Pulaski, Ga	61.8	27.8	258
Harrison, Tex	61.7	30.8	872
Southampton, Va	61.4	28.0	604
Camden, Ga	61.3	6.0	711
Marion, Tex	61.2	17.1	391
Surry, Va	61.2	20.5	278
Hertford, N. C	61.1	29.2	341
Monroe, Ark	61.1	21.9	603
De Soto, La	61.0	20.5	872
Jenkins, Ga	60.9	25.5	342
Pointe Coupee, La	60.7	26.0	576
Barbour, Ala	60.6	21.3	912
Hampton, S. C	60.6	23.1	513
Dinwiddie, Va	60.3	20.9	518
Powhatan, Va	60.2	14.4	273
Clay, Miss	59.9	25.7	408
Montgomery, Ala	59.9	60.5	801
Dooly, Ga	59.8	30.9	397
Liberty, Ga	59.8	8.1	936
Northampton, N. C	59.6	27.4	504
Oktibbeha, Miss	59.6	22.0	457
Marlboro, S. C	59.3	37.9	519
Charleston, S. C	59.2	72.3	888
Halifax, N. C	59.2	38.3	676
Schley, Ga	59.1	20.1	154
Greene, Ga	59.0	26.9	416
Scotland, N. C	59.0	26.4	349
Tate, Miss	58.9	28.9	400
Dorchester, S. C	58.8	18.7	613
Edgecombe, N. C	58.8	43.9	509
Greensville, Va	58.8	22.2	307
Screven, Ga	58.8	17.4	794
Crawford, Ga	58.5	16.3	319
Early, Ga	58.4	21.2	524
Washington, Ga	58.3	24.5	669
Jefferson, Ga	58.2	20.4	646
Brooks, Ga	58.1	27.7	514
Colleton, S. C	58.1	15.4	1,126
Newberry, S. C	58.1	34.3	601
Kershaw, S. C	58.0	25.4	673
Chester, S. C	57.9	32.7	592

COUNTIES	Percent of total population	Number per square mile	Land area in square miles
New Kent, Va	57.8	13.7	191
Webster, Ga	57.7	10.2	302
Richland, La	57.5	21.2	565
Essex, Va	57.3	19.0	258
Iberville, La	57.3	26.3	584
Brunswick, Va	57.2	21.6	557
Lee, Ala	57.2	30.9	608
Abbeville, S. C	56.9	30.3	510
Bertie, N. C	56.8	19.4	703
Darlington, S. C	56.7	36.7	605
Oglethorpe, Ga	56.7	22.8	504
Autauga, Ala	56.6	18.3	584
Kemper, Miss	56.5	14.7	752
Carroll, Miss	55.9	18.2	624
Amelia, Va	55.8	14.7	371
Meriwether, Ga	55.8	29.4	496
Baldwin, Ga	55.7	35.9	307
Rankin, Miss	55.7	14.3	791
San Jacinto, Tex	55.6	9.1	602
Marion, S. C	55.4	24.9	529
Prince Edward, Va	55.4	23.0	356
Hoke, N. C	55.3	15.6	417
James City, Va	55.3	12.5	163
Choctaw, Ala	55.2	12.3	932
King and Queen, Va	55.2	15.8	320
Monroe, Ala	55.2	15.8	1,012
Mitchell, Ga	55.0	25.7	548
St. James, La	54.7	45.7	254
Goochland, Va	54.0	16.7	287
Marion, Ga	53.9	11.4	360
St. John the Baptist, La	53.9	27.8	231
Marion, Fla	53.8	7.8	1,647
Coweta, Ga	53.7	35.2	443
Northampton, Va	53.7	40.1	239
Natchitoches, La	53.6	16.1	1,289
Butts, Ga	53.4	32.4	203
McDuffie, Ga	53.3	21.4	287
Claiborne, La	53 1	19.0	778
Mecklenburg, Va	53.1	24.8	669
Woodruff, Ark	53.1	19.8	577
Jefferson Davis, Miss	52.9	16.7	404
Lincoln, Ga	52.9	17.7	291
Plaquemines, La	52.9	5.3	1,011
Greenwood, S. C	52.8	40.0	473
Clarke, Ala	52.7	11.4	1,216
Copiah, Miss	52.7	19.6	769
King William, Va	52.7	17.5	263
Saluda, S. C	52.7	26.7	435
Aiken, S. C	52.6	21.8	1,100
Worth, Ga	52.6	19.3	651
Anson, N. C	52.5	26.7	556
Walker, Tex	52.5	12.3	791
Craven, N. C	52.3	23.0	660
Thomas, Ga	52.2	32.6	530
Crisp, Ga	52.1	35.6	277
Decatur, Ga	51.9	20.0	823
East Baton Rouge, La	51.9	50.8	455
Laurens, S. C	51.9	32.0	690
Madison, Fla	51.4	11.8	719
Lancaster, Va	51.3	38.5	130
St. Landry, La	51.3	38.9	681
Dillon, S. C	51.2	27.5	471
Henry, Ga	51.1	32.2	324
Lowndes, Ga	51.0	28.4	476
Glynn, Ga	50.9	22.4	439
Pike, Ga	50.9	35.2	307
Caroline, Va	50.6	15.3	529
St. Charles, La	50.6	14.7	295
Greene, N. C	50.5	32.5	252
Middlesex, Va	50.5	28.2	146
Ouachita, Ark	50.5	14.2	733
Pitt, N. C	50.5	36.7	627
St. Helena, La	50.2	10.1	420

TABLE 8.—NEGRO PERCENTAGE OF TOTAL POPULATION, NUMBER OF NEGROES PER SQUARE MILE, AND LAND AREA, BY SELECTED COUNTIES: 1930, 1920, AND 1910—Continued

[This table shows the ranking counties whose Negro population was 50 percent or more for each year]

1910

COUNTIES	Percent of total population	Number per square mile	Land area in square miles
Issaquena, Miss	94.2	24.5	406
Tensas, La	91.5	24.7	632
Tunica, Miss	90.7	40.5	418
East Carroll, La	89.3	24.7	420
Sharkey, Miss	89.0	31.5	444
Coahoma, Miss	88.8	57.3	530
Madison, La	88.6	14.5	650
Lowndes, Ala	88.2	38.1	739
Bolivar, Miss	87.4	48.6	879
Beaufort, S. C	86.9	28.7	920
Greene, Ala	86.7	31.0	635
Lee, Ga	85.6	30.7	326
Washington, Miss	85.0	47.4	877
Crittenden, Ark	84.6	32.6	582
Macon, Ala	84.6	35.9	614
Leflore, Miss	84.4	53.5	572
Bullock, Ala	84.0	41.6	610
Noxubee, Miss	84.0	35.1	682
Concordia, La	83.6	16.7	714
Burke, Ga	82.4	23.5	956
West Feliciana, La	81.9	31.3	352
Wilcox, Ala	81.6	30.8	896
Dallas, Ala	81.5	45.5	957
Madison, Miss	81.5	37.7	725
Sumter, Ala	81.3	25.7	908
Sunflower, Miss	80.9	33.7	690
Chicot, Ark	80.4	29.1	607
Holmes, Miss	79.8	37.4	834
Desha, Ark	79.4	16.2	747
Hales, Ala	78.9	34.0	646
Phillips, Ark	78.6	38.1	692
Perry, Ala	78.5	33.2	737
Jefferson, Miss	78.4	28.2	507
Lee, Ark	78.4	31.6	601
Claiborne, Miss	78.2	27.8	489
Quitman, Ga	78.1	24.9	144
Russell, Ala	77.9	30.8	655
Berkeley, S. C	77.6	14.7	1,238
McIntosh, Ga	77.3	10.6	470
Marengo, Ala	77.3	31.9	966
Stewart, Ga	77.3	25.3	411
Bossier, La	77.0	19.4	863
Wilkinson, Miss	76.9	20.8	667
Calhoun, S. C	76.6	32.6	391
Quitman, Miss	76.5	22.4	395
Jefferson, Fla	76.2	22.4	585
Yazoo, Miss	76.1	34.2	1,038
De Soto, Miss	76.0	37.0	475
Fairfield, S. C	76.0	28.3	792
Leon, Fla	75.8	20.6	715
Terrell, Ga	75.5	51.6	322
Dougherty, Ga	75.1	35.2	342
Fayette, Tenn	75.0	36.7	618
Adams, Miss	74.8	44.4	426
Columbia, Ga	74.6	26.3	350
Hancock, Ga	74.4	26.9	530
Morehouse, La	74.4	16.8	831
Calhoun, Ga	73.8	29.4	284
Houston, Ga	73.6	29.7	585
Taliaferro, Ga	73.6	30.4	212
Clay, Ga	73.3	32.4	203
Putnam, Ga	73.3	28.2	361
Sumter, Ga	73.0	46.6	456
Sumter, S. C	73.0	49.0	574
West Baton Rouge, La	73.0	43.1	214
Clarendon, S. C	72.7	32.6	717
East Feliciana, La	72.5	31.3	464
Georgetown, S. C	72.3	19.5	828
Marshall, Miss	72.2	28.1	689
Barnwell, S. C	72.0	27.7	890
Harris, Ga	71.9	25.7	501
Baker, Ga	71.7	16.0	357
Charles City, Va	71.7	20.0	188
Warwick, Va	71.7	64.7	67
Jefferson, Ark	71.5	41.7	903
Hinds, Miss	71.3	52.9	858
Edgefield, S. C	71.1	28.7	700
Grenada, Miss	71.0	25.3	442
Lowndes, Miss	71.0	43.7	479
Jones, Ga	70.9	24.6	377
Wilkes, Ga	70.8	36.2	458
Macon, Ga	70.5	28.7	369
Talbot, Ga	70.4	26.4	312
Warren, Miss	69.9	45.8	572
Clay, Miss	69.8	34.6	408
Bamberg, S. C	69.4	34.7	371
Jasper, Ga	69.4	35.8	321
Tallahatchie, Miss	69.4	32.1	629
Chattachoochee, Ga	69.2	17.7	218
Montgomery, Ala	69.2	71.0	801
Randolph, Ga	68.9	31.5	412
Twiggs, Ga	68.9	23.6	314
St. Francis, Ark	68.8	24.7	628
Warren, Ga	68.6	20.1	404
Haywood, Tenn	68.4	34.9	508
Lee, S. C	68.1	42.4	407
Morgan, Ga	68.0	34.4	390
Webster, Ga	68.0	13.8	302
Panola, Miss	67.9	30.5	696
Pointe Coupee, La	67.8	29.8	576
Gadsden, Fla	67.4	27.7	540
Monroe, Ga	66.8	23.4	584
Camden, Ga	66.5	7.2	711
Richland, La	66.4	18.5	565
Lincoln, Ark	65.9	17.5	571
Cumberland, Va	65.8	20.7	293
Orangeburg, S. C	65.8	32.5	1,131
Sussex, Va	65.6	17.4	515
Warren, N. C	65.2	31.1	425
Chester, S. C	65.0	32.3	592
De Soto, La	64.8	20.6	872
Abbeville, S. C	64.7	33.2	678
Halifax, N. C	64.6	36.0	676
Liberty, Ga	64.6	8.9	936
Oktibbeha, Miss	64.4	27.7	457
Hampton, S. C	64.2	16.8	958
Marion, Tex	64.2	17.2	391
Newberry, S. C	63.7	36.7	601
Harrison, Tex	63.6	27.2	872
Jenkins, Ga	63.3	21.3	342
Charleston, S. C	63.2	81.8	685
Schley, Ga	63.1	21.4	154
Amelia, Va	63.0	14.8	371
Colleton, S. C	63.0	16.7	1,333
Fort Ben, Tex	62.9	14.4	792
Greene, Ga	62.9	28.0	416
Monroe, Ark	62.9	20.8	603
Barbour, Ala	62.5	22.4	912
Choctaw, Ala	62.2	12.3	932
Early, Ga	62.2	21.5	524
Glynn, Ga	62.2	22.3	439
Greensville, Va	62.2	24.1	307
Greenwood, S. C	62.2	41.9	508
Caddo, La	62.1	41.1	880
Dooly, Ga	61.9	32.1	397
Iberville, La	61.8	32.8	584
Surry, Va	61.8	21.6	278
East Baton Rouge, La	61.7	46.9	455
Washington, Ga	61.7	26.0	669
Williamsburg, S. C	61.7	23.1	1,006
Dorchester, S. C	61.4	17.9	613
Southampton, Va	61.2	26.6	604
Edgecombe, N. C	60.8	38.2	509
Marion, Fla	60.8	9.9	1,647
Dinwiddie, Va	60.7	18.1	518
Jefferson, Ga	60.7	18.0	720
Kershaw, S. C	60.7	24.4	673
Marlboro, S. C	60.7	36.5	519
Oglethorpe, Ga	60.7	22.5	504
Norfolk, Va	60.3	78.7	404
Screven, Ga	60.2	15.3	794
Baldwin, Ga	60.0	35.8	307
St. Charles, La	60.0	22.8	295
Lee, Ala	59.8	31.1	632
Claiborne, La	59.6	19.2	778
New Kent, Va	59.6	14.6	191
Powhatan, Va	59.6	13.3	273
Rankin, Miss	59.5	18.0	791
Lincoln, Ga	59.4	17.8	291
Prince Edward, Va	59.3	23.8	356
Crawford, Ga	59.2	15.4	319
Brooks, Ga	59.1	27.4	514
Brunswick, Va	59.1	20.4	557
Darlington, S. C	59.1	35.2	605
Pulaski, Ga	59.1	29.2	463
Hertford, N. C	58.9	26.7	341
Thomas, Ga	58.8	32.2	530
Troup, Ga	58.7	35.4	435
Bertie, N. C	58.6	19.2	703
Marion, Ga	58.6	14.9	360
Autauga, Ala	58.5	20.1	584
Meriwether, Ga	58.5	29.7	496
Northampton, N. C	58.5	25.9	504
Tate, Miss	58.5	28.8	400
Essex, Va	58.4	20.6	258
Woodruff, Ark	58.4	20.3	577
Carroll, Miss	58.2	21.6	624
McDuffie, Ga	58.0	20.9	287
Prince George, Va	58.0	15.5	294
Monroe, Ala	57.9	15.5	1,012
Nansemond, Va	57.8	36.7	423
Decatur, Ga	57.6	20.3	823
Kemper, Miss	57.5	15.5	752
St. James, La	57.2	51.8	254
Florence, S. C	57.0	33.5	607
King William, Va	56.8	18.5	263
St. John the Baptist, La	56.7	35.2	231
Goochland, Va	56.6	18.2	287
Mecklenburg, Va	56.6	24.5	669
Ouachita, Ark	56.6	16.8	733
Coweta, Ga	56.5	34.6	470
King and Queen, Va	56.1	16.8	320
Clarke, Ala	55.9	14.2	1,216
Graven, N. C	55.9	21.7	660
Northampton, Va	55.9	39.0	239
Natchitoches, La	55.8	15.8	1,289
Alachua, Fla	55.7	15.1	1,262
Chickasaw, Miss	55.7	25.4	501
Hernando, Fla	55.7	5.6	497
Copiah, Miss	55.6	26.0	669
Madison, Fla	55.6	13.1	719
Monroe, Miss	55.5	25.4	770
Waller, Tex	55.3	12.9	519
Chatham, Ga	55.2	118.9	370
Scotland, N. C	55.2	24.3	349
Gregg, Tex	55.0	24.9	312
Upson, Ga	54.9	22.1	317
Amite, Miss	54.8	17.6	714
Laurens, S. C	54.8	33.0	690
Ouachita, La	54.8	22.0	642
Plaquemines, La	54.7	6.8	1,005
Aiken, S. C	54.6	20.8	1,100
Nottaway, Va	54.6	23.7	310
Chowan, N. C	54.5	37.3	165
Red River, La	54.5	15.5	400
Marion, S. C	54.4	21.2	529
San Jacinto, Texas	54.4	8.6	602
Citrus, Fla	54.0	5.9	620
St. Mary, La	54.0	33.6	632
Drew, Ark	53.7	13.9	847
Richland, S. C	53.6	48.3	611
Saluda, S. C	53.4	25.7	435
Lunenburg, Va	53.3	15.8	430
Robertson, Texas	53.1	16.7	872
Butler, Ala	53.0	20.1	763
Lowndes, Ga	53.0	26.9	482
York, S. C	53.0	38.8	651
Butts, Ga	52.8	35.5	203
Charlotte, Va	52.8	16.8	496
Nassau, Fla	52.8	8.8	630
Caroline, Va	52.7	16.5	529
Lancaster, Va	52.7	39.5	130
Mitchell, Ga	52.7	21.3	548
Ashley, Ark	52.5	14.1	940
Crisp, Ga	52.5	31.0	277
Jefferson Davis, Miss	52.5	16.7	404
Middlesex, Va	52.4	31.8	146
Anson, N. C	52.3	24.0	556
Charles, Md	52.3	18.5	464
Lafayette, Ark	52.3	13.7	525
Pike, Ga	52.1	33.1	307
Walker, Texas	52.1	10.6	791
Putnam, Fla	52.0	9.0	752
Yalobusha, Miss	52.0	22.8	490
Chambers, Ala	51.8	31.7	588
Pickens, Ala	51.7	14.8	875
Union, S. C	51.7	31.4	492
Webster, La	51.6	16.3	609
Caswell, N. C	51.5	19.0	402
Vance, N. C	51.5	35.9	279
Newton, Ga	51.3	36.1	262
Wilkinson, Ga	51.2	10.9	472
Henry, Ga	51.1	31.4	324
Dillon, S. C	51.0	24.5	471
Spalding, Ga	51.0	48.1	209
Clarke, Ga	50.6	103.2	114
Perquimans, N. C	50.6	22.2	252
Princess Anne, Va	50.5	20.9	279
Montgomery, Miss	50.4	22.4	398
Isle of Wight, Va	50.3	23.9	314
Elbert, Ga	50.1	33.5	361
Pasquotank, N. C	50.1	37.5	223
Westmoreland, Va	50.1	18.5	252
Halifax, Va	50.0	24.6	814

TABLE 9.—PERCENT NEGRO AND NUMBER OF NEGROES PER 1,000 WHITES FOR THE COUNTIES HAVING A POPULATION OF 50 PERCENT OR MORE NEGRO, BY STATES: 1930 AND 1920

STATE AND COUNTY	NEGRO POPULATION: Percent of total population 1930	Percent of total population 1920	Per 1,000 whites 1930	Per 1,000 whites 1920
ALABAMA				
Autauga	55.4	56.6	1,241	1,302
Barbour	57.5	60.6	1,355	1,536
Bullock	78.7	81.5	3,696	4,411
Choctaw	54.8	55.2	1,211	1,231
Clarke	52.4	52.7	1,100	1,112
Dallas	74.2	77.3	2,872	3,400
Greene	82.4	83.0	4,671	4,868
Hale	73.9	73.7	2,833	2,800
Lee	51.7	57.2	1,069	1,338
Lowndes	85.8	86.7	6,048	6,494
Macon	82.4	83.2	4,667	4,969
Marengo	72.3	72.4	2,615	2,623
Monroe	52.5	55.2	1,108	1,237
Montgomery	52.8	59.9	1,121	1,397
Perry	72.6	72.0	2,650	2,566
Russell	71.5	76.3	2,503	3,215
Sumter	78.9	77.6	3,739	3,456
Wilcox	77.6	80.5	3,474	4,121
ARKANSAS				
Chicot	62.5	73.8	1,669	2,833
Crittenden	79.0	84.1	3,765	5,298
Desha	63.7	75.2	1,768	3,037
Jefferson	57.9	65.5	1,375	1,897
Lee	65.4	77.3	1,890	3,413
Lincoln	64.6	68.0	1,832	2,123
Monroe	55.7	61.1	1,257	1,574
Ouachita	43.4	50.5	769	1,019
Phillips	67.0	73.9	2,046	2,841
St. Francis	67.3	70.4	2,067	2,374
Woodruff	44.2	53.1	794	1,131
FLORIDA				
Gadsden	56.8	62.9	1,313	1,697
Jefferson	68.0	72.5	2,127	2,643
Leon	58.7	67.4	1,424	2,065
Madison	52.5	51.4	1,107	1,059
Marion	49.1	53.8	963	1,163
GEORGIA				
Baker	61.3	67.7	1,585	2,092
Baldwin	46.9	55.7	884	1,256
Brooks	52.8	58.1	1,118	1,384
Burke	77.7	80.3	3,479	4,088
Butts	48.0	53.4	924	1,148
Calhoun	70.3	68.7	2,363	2,190
Camden	59.1	61.3	1,444	1,585
Clay	65.3	67.1	1,881	2,043
Columbia	63.0	70.4	1,700	2,380
Coweta	43.1	53.7	757	1,160
Crawford	55.3	58.5	1,235	1,407
Crisp	48.3	52.1	933	1,086
Decatur	50.0	51.9	1,000	1,078
Dooly	55.8	59.8	1,264	1,490
Dougherty	57.5	66.6	1,351	1,998
Early	53.3	58.4	1,141	1,406
Glynn	42.8	50.9	747	1,036
Greene	52.5	59.0	1,107	1,441
Hancock	71.5	72.0	2,509	2,574
Harris	69.1	71.1	2,232	2,456
Henry	49.7	51.1	988	1,046
Houston	67.6	66.1	2,089	1,946
Jasper	60.9	71.0	1,560	2,449
Jefferson	58.1	58.2	1,387	1,391
Jenkins	57.8	60.9	1,371	1,555
Jones	64.2	70.9	1,795	2,432
Lee	77.9	82.3	3,534	4,659
Liberty	67.9	59.8	2,111	1,485
Lincoln	52.2	52.9	1,090	1,123
Lowndes	46.0	51.0	850	1,042
McDuffie	50.7	53.3	1,029	1,144
McIntosh	67.3	74.3	2,062	2,890
Macon	67.2	68.1	2,053	2,133
Marion	56.2	53.9	1,282	1,168
Meriwether	52.4	55.8	1,103	1,261
Mitchell	50.2	55.0	1,009	1,221
Monroe	58.2	63.4	1,390	1,731
Morgan	57.6	64.0	1,361	1,776
Oglethorpe	49.7	56.7	988	1,308
Peach	63.9	(1)	1,773	(1)
GEORGIA—Continued				
Pike	49.8	50.9	991	1,036
Pulaski	56.1	61.8	1,280	1,620
Putnam	62.3	68.8	1,652	2,204
Quitman	69.1	71.1	2,242	2,462
Randolph	67.2	65.8	2,054	1,928
Schley	62.1	59.1	1,638	1,445
Screven	56.7	58.8	1,308	1,428
Stewart	71.4	71.5	2,491	2,509
Sumter	64.9	67.0	1,848	2,031
Talbot	68.9	71.7	2,216	2,528
Taliaferro	68.4	70.5	2,165	2,386
Terrell	71.0	71.7	2,446	2,535
Thomas	48.6	52.2	946	1,094
Twiggs	63.7	63.9	1,757	1,772
Warren	65.7	66.1	1,919	1,952
Washington	56.5	58.3	1,297	1,397
Webster	60.4	57.7	1,524	1,362
Wilkes	63.3	66.5	1,723	1,983
Worth	45.4	52.6	831	1,109
LOUISIANA				
Bossier	62.9	70.6	1,703	2,407
Caliborne	55.9	53.1	1,267	1,131
Concordia	71.9	78.8	2,561	3,717
De Soto	62.0	61.0	1,636	1,563
East Baton Rouge	43.1	51.9	759	1,079
East Carroll	74.8	86.4	2,978	6,353
East Feliciana	68.1	68.6	2,133	2,190
Iberville	50.9	57.3	1,055	1,345
Madison	64.5	83.7	1,842	5,124
Morehouse	57.4	68.0	1,350	2,130
Natchitoches	50.9	53.6	1,074	1,156
Plaquemines	47.1	52.9	897	1,126
Pointe Coupee	58.1	60.7	1,388	1,542
Richland	50.1	57.5	1,004	1,353
St. Charles	34.7	50.6	531	1,025
St. Helena	54.3	50.2	1,188	1,007
St. James	49.2	54.7	975	1,206
St. John the Baptist	49.3	53.9	974	1,171
St. Landry	49.1	51.3	966	1,055
Tensas	71.5	85.3	2,522	5,830
West Baton Rouge	63.1	67.5	1,712	2,075
West Feliciana	76.4	82.8	3,251	4,814
MISSISSIPPI				
Adams	65.5	68.7	1,897	2,200
Amite	52.8	49.3	1,121	972
Bolivar	74.0	82.4	2,946	4,730
Carroll	57.0	55.9	1,328	1,266
Chickasaw	50.2	49.8	1,008	991
Claiborne	74.4	73.7	2,904	2,800
Clay	61.8	59.9	1,618	1,497
Coahoma	77.4	84.8	3,468	5,640
Copiah	49.4	52.7	976	1,113
De Soto	73.8	75.7	2,818	3,117
Grenada	59.4	62.1	1,466	1,637
Hinds	54.7	62.6	1,208	1,671
Holmes	76.3	77.2	3,222	3,380
Humphreys	68.9	82.2	2,271	4,628
Issaquena	81.4	90.8	4,383	9,850
Jefferson	75.8	75.0	3,139	2,999
Jefferson Davis	55.3	52.9	1,238	1,124
Kemper	57.8	56.5	1,392	1,316
Leflore	76.4	78.0	3,252	3,559
Lowndes	57.7	64.9	1,367	1,853
Madison	78.6	78.0	3,675	3,543
Marshall	71.5	72.2	2,505	2,594
Noxubee	78.7	79.3	3,705	3,833
Oktibbeha	59.5	59.6	1,466	1,474
Panola	62.8	63.7	1,688	1,759
Quitman	68.6	75.8	2,189	3,136
Rankin	54.5	55.7	1,198	1,260
Sharkey	73.8	83.0	2,847	4,926
Sunflower	70.3	74.2	2,385	2,886
Tallahatchie	68.0	70.4	2,135	2,388
Tate	60.1	58.9	1,509	1,434
Tunica	85.8	89.3	6,103	8,464
Warren	58.4	63.9	1,405	1,769
Washington	72.0	81.5	2,645	4,427
Wilkinson	70.1	73.9	2,347	2,825
Yazoo	67.7	71.7	2,094	2,531
NORTH CAROLINA				
Anson	52.0	52.5	1,081	1,103
Bertie	56.6	56.8	1,302	1,318
Craven	48.3	52.3	934	1,098
Edgecombe	56.9	58.8	1,321	1,428
Greene	47.9	50.5	921	1,020
Halifax	57.9	59.2	1,377	1,450
Hertford	58.7	61.1	1,423	1,570
Hoke	60.6	55.3	1,645	1,292
Northampton	62.7	59.6	1,684	1,477
Pitt	48.4	50.5	939	1,022
Scotland	53.5	59.0	1,225	1,520
Warren	63.5	64.0	1,743	1,778
SOUTH CAROLINA				
Abbeville	47.4	56.9	902	1,319
Aiken	45.4	52.6	832	1,111
Allendale	73.4	77.6	2,763	3,470
Bamberg	64.3	68.5	1,799	2,173
Barnwell	63.5	67.5	1,736	2,079
Beaufort	71.4	78.4	2,494	3,635
Berkeley	67.7	72.5	2,096	2,637
Calhoun	74.3	68.6	2,886	2,181
Charleston	54.2	59.2	1,186	1,456
Chester	51.7	57.9	1,072	1,376
Clarendon	71.8	72.0	2,545	2,569
Colleton	54.5	58.1	1,196	1,386
Darlington	52.2	56.7	1,091	1,312
Dillon	46.9	51.2	907	1,058
Dorchester	58.9	58.8	1,434	1,427
Edgefield	63.5	69.6	1,739	2,284
Fairfield	67.4	76.1	2,065	3,187
Georgetown	64.4	66.6	1,811	1,994
Greenwood	43.3	52.8	762	1,121
Hampton	57.0	60.6	1,323	1,538
Jasper	67.9	72.1	2,118	2,581
Kershaw	55.0	58.0	1,223	1,384
Laurens	42.1	51.9	726	1,081
Lee	67.4	67.3	2,070	2,057
McCormick	67.1	68.5	2,040	2,177
Marion	54.8	55.4	1,212	1,245
Marlboro	56.9	59.3	1,346	1,455
Newberry	46.6	58.1	872	1,384
Orangeburg	63.6	65.8	1,760	1,927
Saluda	48.6	52.7	946	1,113
Sumter	67.5	70.9	2,075	2,437
Williamsburg	66.9	66.0	2,017	1,945
TENNESSEE				
Fayette	73.0	74.7	2,706	2,951
Haywood	66.1	66.8	1,950	2,012
TEXAS				
Gregg	52.0	48.7	1,085	950
Harrison	60.1	61.7	1,510	1,608
Marion	62.3	61.2	1,649	1,581
San Jacinto	52.7	55.6	1,150	1,253
Walker	46.0	52.5	882	1,105
VIRGINIA				
Amelia	51.4	55.8	1,057	1,263
Brunswick	56.1	57.2	1,278	1,334
Caroline	50.6	50.6	1,031	1,025
Charles City	77.0	75.2	3,787	3,318
Cumberland	57.8	63.2	1,371	1,714
Dinwiddie	60.5	60.3	1,533	1,517
Essex	54.7	57.3	1,212	1,344
Goochland	51.7	54.0	1,072	1,172
Greenville	60.7	58.8	1,546	1,428
Isle of Wight	51.6	49.5	1,067	982
James City	52.6	55.3	1,112	1,239
King and Queen	54.6	55.2	1,207	1,232
King William	48.0	52.7	971	1,179
Lancaster	44.6	51.3	806	1,052
Mecklenburg	52.7	53.1	1,114	1,134
Middlesex	46.2	50.5	859	1,019
Nansemond	67.5	63.7	2,075	1,758
New Kent	58.8	57.8	1,437	1,396
Northampton	53.5	53.7	1,150	1,160
Powhatan	51.4	60.2	1,056	1,510
Prince Edward	52.0	55.4	1,082	1,243
Southampton	61.0	61.4	1,565	1,591
Surry	60.1	61.2	1,507	1,576
Sussex	66.2	65.7	1,956	1,914

[1] Organized from parts of Houston and Macon Counties in 1925.

CHAPTER VII.—SEX DISTRIBUTION

Ratios of Negro males to females.—An excess of females over males in the Negro population of the United States has appeared persistently in the census returns for the last 100 years. In 1930 there were 179,805 more females than males in the Negro population of the United States while there were 1,463,501 more males than females in the white population. The sex ratio, or the number of males per 100 females, for the Negro population in the United States was 97 in 1930 as compared with 102.7 for the white population. During the last 10 censuses the sex ratio for the Negro population has varied from 96.2 to 99.6.

Sex ratios by sections and divisions.—There was a deficiency of males in the Negro population in the South as a whole in 1930, and an excess in the Negro population in the North and West. Within the South itself the sex ratio was lowest in the South Atlantic division and highest in the West South Central division. During the period 1910 to 1930, the ratio of males to females in the Negro population decreased in the North, the West, and the South, as well as in all the divisions of the South.

Sex ratios in urban and rural areas.—The rural Negro population was predominantly male and the urban Negro population was predominantly female in 1930. The sex ratio for rural areas was 101.7 as compared with 91.3 for urban areas. A higher sex ratio existed for the Negro population in rural-nonfarm areas than in either the rural-farm or urban areas. The preponderance of females in the Negro population in urban areas is doubtless due primarily to the fact that cities afford more opportunities for gainful employment of women than do the rural districts.

The excess of females in the urban population was much greater in the South than in the North and West and, among the Southern divisions, in the South Atlantic division, in which the sex ratio was 85.7.

Sex ratios in the "Black Belt."—In the aggregate for the counties in which the population was 50 percent or more Negro in 1930, the proportion of males was smaller than it was in the aggregate for the other counties in the United States. In fact, in only two Southern States, Virginia and Tennessee, was there an excess of males over females in the counties having 50 percent or more Negro population. The difference in the sex ratios between counties in which Negroes constituted 50 percent or more of the population, and counties having a smaller proportion of Negroes, may be associated with the tendency of the Negroes to move out of the Black Belt. It would appear that this tendency was stronger among the males than among the females.

Sex ratios in cities.—The excess of females over males was not as great in the larger cities as it was in the smaller cities. The sex ratio in the cities of the South was decidedly lower than for cities of the North and West. The ratio of males to 100 females was lower in the South than in the North and West for cities having 10,000 or more Negro inhabitants in 1930. The sex ratio for the cities with 2,500 to 10,000 Negro inhabitants was 82.9 in the South and 98.6 in the North in 1930.

TABLE 1.—NEGRO POPULATION OF THE UNITED STATES, BY SEX: 1820 TO 1930

CENSUS YEAR	Total	Male	Female	EXCESS OF—		Males per 100 females	INCREASE OVER PRECEDING CENSUS			
				Males	Females		Males		Females	
							Number	Percent	Number	Percent
1930	11,891,143	5,855,669	6,035,474		179,805	97.0	646,233	12.4	781,779	14.9
1920	10,463,131	5,209,436	5,253,695		44,259	99.2	323,555	6.6	311,813	8.3
1910	9,827,763	4,885,881	4,941,882		56,001	98.9	499,334	11.4	494,435	11.1
1900	8,833,994	4,386,547	4,447,447		60,900	98.6	650,944	17.4	694,374	18.5
1890	7,488,676	3,735,603	3,753,073		17,470	99.5	482,488	14.8	425,395	12.8
1880	6,580,793	3,253,115	3,327,678		74,563	97.8	859,852	35.9	840,932	33.8
1870	4,880,009	2,393,263	2,486,746		93,483	96.2	176,519	8.0	261,660	11.8
1860	4,441,830	2,216,744	2,225,086		8,342	99.6	405,486	22.4	397,536	21.8
1850	3,638,808	1,811,258	1,827,550		16,292	99.1	378,270	26.4	386,890	26.9
1840	2,873,648	1,432,988	1,440,660		7,672	99.5	266,712	22.9	278,294	23.9
1830	2,328,642	1,166,276	1,162,366	3,910		100.3	265,480	25.5	291,506	33.5
1820	1,771,656	900,796	870,860	29,936		103.4				

TABLE 2.—POPULATION OF THE UNITED STATES BY SEX, COLOR, AND NATIVITY: 1930

COLOR AND NATIVITY	Male	Female	EXCESS OF—		Males per 100 females
			Males	Females	
All classes	**62,137,080**	**60,637,966**	**1,499,114**		**102.5**
Negro	5,855,669	6,035,474		179,805	97.0
White	55,163,854	53,700,353	1,463,501		102.7
Native	48,010,145	47,487,655	522,490		101.1
Native parentage	35,460,001	34,676,613	783,388		102.3
Mixed parentage	4,111,468	4,250,497		139,029	96.7
Foreign parentage	8,438,676	8,560,545		121,869	98.6
Foreign born	7,153,709	6,212,698	941,011		115.1
Mexican	758,674	663,859	94,815		114.3
Indian	170,350	162,047	8,303		105.1
Chinese	59,802	15,152	44,650		394.7
Japanese	81,771	57,063	24,708		143.3
Filipino	42,268	2,940	39,328		1,437.7
Hindu	2,860	270	2,590		1,059.3
Korean	1,223	637	586		192.0
All other	609	171	438		356.1

TABLE 3.—SEX RATIOS OF NEGRO AND WHITE POPULATION FOR THE UNITED STATES: 1820 TO 1930

CENSUS YEAR	MALES PER 100 FEMALES					
	Negro population	White population				
		Total	Native			Foreign born
			Total	Native parentage	Foreign or mixed parentage	
1930	97.0	102.7	101.1	102.3	98.0	115.1
1920	99.2	104.4	101.7	103.0	98.6	121.7
1910	98.9	106.6	102.7	104.0	99.5	129.2
1900	98.6	104.9	102.8	103.7	100.3	117.4
1890	99.5	105.4	102.9	103.5	101.0	118.7
1880	97.8	104.0	102.1	(1)	(1)	115.9
1870	96.2	102.8	100.6	(1)	(1)	115.3
1860	99.6	105.3	103.7	(1)	(1)	115.1
1850	99.1	105.2	103.1	(1)	(1)	123.8
1840	99.5	104.5	(1)	(1)	(1)	(1)
1830	100.3	103.8	(1)	(1)	(1)	(1)
1820	103.4	103.2	(1)	(1)	(1)	(1)

[1] No data available.

TABLE 4.—NEGRO POPULATION CLASSIFIED BY SEX, 1930; BY SEX RATIOS, 1900 TO 1930; AND SEX RATIOS FOR WHITE CLASSES, 1930; BY SECTIONS, AND SOUTHERN DIVISIONS

SECTION AND DIVISION	NEGRO POPULATION, 1930					MALES PER 100 FEMALES						
	Total	Male	Female	Excess of—		Negro population				White population, 1930		
				Males	Females	1930	1920	1910	1900	Total	Native	Foreign-born
United States	**11, 891, 143**	**5, 855, 669**	**6, 035, 474**	----------	**179, 805**	**97. 0**	**99. 2**	**98. 9**	**98. 6**	**102. 7**	**101. 1**	**115. 1**
THE SOUTH	9, 361, 577	4, 583, 591	4, 777, 986	----------	194, 395	95. 9	97. 8	98. 4	98. 2	102. 5	102. 0	130. 2
South Atlantic	4, 421, 388	2, 156, 531	2, 264, 857	----------	108, 326	95. 2	97. 3	97. 5	96. 9	101. 3	100. 7	127. 1
East South Central	2, 658, 238	1, 301, 552	1, 356, 686	----------	55, 134	95. 9	97. 2	98. 4	98. 9	101. 7	101. 5	137. 2
West South Central	2, 281, 951	1, 125, 508	1, 156, 443	----------	30, 935	97. 3	99, 5	100. 4	99. 9	104. 6	104. 1	133. 5
THE NORTH	2, 409, 219	1, 210, 707	1, 198, 512	12, 195	----------	101. 0	106. 1	101. 8	101. 7	102. 1	100. 2	112. 3
THE WEST	120, 347	61, 371	58, 976	2, 395	----------	104. 1	132. 0	120. 7	130. 6	107. 8	104. 3	133. 9

TABLE 5.—NEGRO AND WHITE POPULATION BY SEX, WITH THE NUMBER OF MALES PER 100 FEMALES, FOR CLASSES OF URBAN PLACES, BY DIVISIONS: 1930

DIVISION AND RACIAL CLASS	POPULATION OF PLACES HAVING IN 1930 A POPULATION OF —														
	500,000			100,000 to 500,000			25,000 to 100,000			10,000 to 25,000			2,500 to 10,000		
	Male	Female	Males per 100 females	Male	Female	Males per 100 females	Male	Female	Males per 100 females	Male	Female	Males per 100 females	Male	Female	Males per 100 females
United States:															
Negro	**665, 055**	**683, 122**	**97. 4**	**731, 916**	**801, 697**	**91. 3**	**447, 434**	**510, 264**	**87. 7**	**294, 719**	**333, 132**	**88. 5**	**340, 029**	**386, 545**	**88. 0**
White	**9, 666, 626**	**9, 592, 323**	**100. 8**	**6, 752, 300**	**6, 967, 273**	**96. 9**	**5, 805, 033**	**5, 976, 631**	**97. 1**	**4, 143, 851**	**4, 240, 064**	**97. 7**	**4, 794, 760**	**4, 897, 744**	**97. 9**
NEW ENGLAND:															
Negro	10, 223	10, 351	98. 8	17, 592	18, 173	96. 8	7, 679	8, 113	94. 7	3, 306	3, 136	105. 4	1, 489	1, 381	107. 8
White	371, 680	387, 076	96. 0	814, 054	868, 479	93. 7	943, 024	996, 756	94. 6	602, 319	633, 093	95. 1	299, 701	308, 926	97. 0
MIDDLE ATLANTIC:															
Negro	300, 477	315, 374	95. 3	46, 678	46, 489	100. 4	49, 223	52, 696	93. 4	42, 097	41, 582	101. 2	21, 650	22, 798	95. 0
White	4, 741, 835	4, 747, 033	99. 9	1, 207, 476	1, 223, 127	98. 7	1, 359, 863	1, 384, 928	98. 2	1, 197, 941	1, 213, 659	98. 7	1, 162, 723	1, 188, 363	97. 8
EAST NORTH CENTRAL:															
Negro	217, 941	215, 428	101. 2	114, 491	110, 825	103. 3	54, 549	51, 863	105. 2	22, 971	22, 891	100. 3	18, 849	18, 819	100. 2
White	3, 037, 040	2, 916, 729	104. 1	1, 366, 868	1, 380, 377	99. 0	1, 638, 124	1, 646, 894	99. 5	863, 913	875, 819	98. 6	1, 061, 955	1, 092, 589	97. 2
WEST NORTH CENTRAL:															
Negro	45, 832	47, 748	96. 0	43, 743	45, 470	96. 2	10, 088	10, 112	99. 8	15, 491	14, 983	103. 4	12, 951	12, 777	101. 4
White	354, 838	372, 041	95. 4	842, 374	884, 264	95. 3	392, 547	416, 240	94. 3	417, 272	436, 378	95. 6	566, 206	586, 085	69. 6
SOUTH ATLANTIC:															
Negro	70, 043	72, 063	97. 2	197, 547	228, 090	86. 6	192, 562	232, 437	82. 8	89, 935	108, 401	83. 0	124, 926	146, 900	85. 0
White	325, 327	336, 797	96. 6	530, 082	560, 526	94. 6	522, 032	555, 784	93. 9	256, 501	269, 872	95. 0	427, 434	447, 465	95. 5
EAST SOUTH CENTRAL:															
Negro	----------	----------	------	157, 468	178, 731	88. 1	51, 540	61, 190	84. 2	71, 243	85, 028	83. 8	70, 704	83, 262	84. 9
White	----------	----------	------	417, 769	445, 882	93. 7	161, 331	168, 742	95. 6	157, 001	164, 924	95. 2	243, 922	259, 311	94. 1
WEST SOUTH CENTRAL:															
Negro	----------	----------	------	142, 101	161, 542	88. 0	72, 871	84, 288	86. 5	46, 867	54, 283	86. 3	85, 210	97, 093	87. 8
White	----------	----------	------	672, 941	688, 023	97. 8	279, 516	282, 418	99. 0	241, 439	244, 806	98. 6	463, 598	470, 702	98. 5
MOUNTAIN:															
Negro	----------	----------	------	3, 740	4, 145	90. 2	3, 297	3, 379	97. 6	1, 129	1, 056	106. 9	2, 442	1, 844	132. 4
White	----------	----------	------	200, 077	210, 970	94. 8	134, 292	133, 354	100. 7	115, 270	115, 112	100. 1	227, 792	216, 416	105. 3
PACIFIC:															
Negro	20, 539	22, 158	92. 7	8, 556	8, 232	103. 9	5, 625	6, 186	90. 9	1, 680	1, 772	94. 8	1, 808	1, 671	108. 2
White	835, 906	832, 647	100. 4	700, 659	705, 625	99. 3	374, 304	391, 515	95. 6	292, 195	286, 401	102. 0	341, 429	327, 887	104. 1

TABLE 6.—NEGRO POPULATION, BY SEX, WITH THE NUMBER OF MALES PER 100 FEMALES, FOR CLASSES OF URBAN PLACES: 1930

SEX	NEGRO POPULATION						
	Urban						Rural
	Total	Places of 500,000 or more	Places of 100,000 to 500, 000	Places of 25,000 to 100,000	Places of 10,000 to 25,000	Places of 2,500 to 10,000	
Both sexes	5, 193, 913	1, 348, 177	1, 153, 613	957, 698	627, 851	726, 574	6, 697, 230
Male	2, 479, 158	665, 055	731, 916	447, 434	294, 719	340, 034	3, 376, 511
Female	2, 714, 755	683, 122	801, 697	510, 264	333, 132	386, 540	3, 320, 719
Excess:							
Of males	----------	----------	----------	----------	----------	----------	55, 792
Of females	235, 597	18, 067	69, 781	62, 830	38, 413	46, 506	----------
Males per 100 females	91. 3	97. 4	91. 3	87. 7	88. 5	88. 0	101. 7

TABLE 7.—SEX RATIOS BY CLASSES OF URBAN PLACES, FOR THE NEGRO AND WHITE POPULATION: 1930

RACIAL CLASS	MALES PER 100 FEMALES						
	Urban population						Rural population
	Total	Places of 500,000 or more	Places of 100,000 to 500,000	Places of 25,000 to 100,000	Places of 10,000 to 25,000	Places of 2,500 to 10,000	
Negro	91. 3	97. 4	91. 3	87. 7	88. 5	88. 0	101. 7
White	98. 4	100. 8	96. 9	97. 1	97. 7	97. 9	109. 0
Native	96. 0	97. 5	94. 7	95. 1	95. 9	96. 3	107. 6
Native parentage	97. 3	100. 0	96. 5	96. 4	96. 8	96. 8	107. 1
Foreign or mixed parentage	93. 7	95. 4	91. 1	92. 4	93. 7	94. 5	110. 7
Foreign-born	111. 0	110. 1	111. 2	110. 1	112. 3	115. 8	134. 0

TABLE 8.—SEX RATIOS OF URBAN AND RURAL POPULATION, BY RACIAL CLASSES: 1930 AND 1920

RACIAL CLASS	MALES PER 100 FEMALES							
	Urban population		Rural population					
			Total		Rural-farm		Rural-nonfarm	
	1930	1920	1930	1920	1930	1920	1930	1920
All classes	**98.1**	**100.4**	**108.3**	**108.0**	**111.0**	**109.1**	**105.0**	**106.5**
Negro	91.3	95.4	101.7	101.2	101.2	100.3	102.8	103.7
White	98.4	100.5	109.0	109.0	112.7	110.8	104.7	106.6
Native	96.0	96.9	107.6	106.7	111.6	109.5	102.9	102.7
Native parentage	97.3	98.6	107.1	106.3	110.4	108.5	103.0	102.8
Mixed parentage	91.9	92.5	107.7	107.2	116.4	113.1	99.7	100.1
Foreign parentage	94.5	95.0	112.7	110.4	122.6	117.2	104.2	103.4
Foreign born	111.0	115.9	134.0	141.8	139.4	136.2	130.4	146.2
Other races	124.7	276.9	123.2	126.6	120.3	121.9	126.6	134.7

TABLE 9.—NEGRO POPULATION AND SEX RATIOS OF COUNTIES HAVING 50 PERCENT OR MORE NEGROES AND COUNTIES HAVING LESS THAN 50 PERCENT NEGRO POPULATION, BY SECTIONS, SOUTHERN DIVISIONS, AND SOUTHERN STATES: 1930

SECTION, DIVISION, AND STATE	NEGRO POPULATION IN—				MALES PER 100 FEMALES IN NEGRO POPULATION IN—	
	Counties 50 percent or more Negro		Counties less than 50 percent Negro		Counties 50 per cent or more Negro	Counties less than 50 percent Negro
	Male	Female	Male	Female		
United States	**1,338,069**	**1,400,363**	**4,517,600**	**4,635,111**	**95.6**	**97.5**
THE SOUTH	1,338,069	1,400,363	3,245,522	3,377,623	95.6	96.1
South Atlantic	572,476	609,784	1,584,055	1,655,073	93.9	95.7
East South Central	548,749	571,373	752,803	785,313	96.0	95.9
West South Central	216,844	219,206	908,664	937,237	98.9	97.0
THE NORTH	------	------	1,210,707	1,198,512	------	101.0
THE WEST	------	------	61,371	58,976	------	104.1
SOUTH ATLANTIC:						
Delaware	------	------	16,983	15,619	------	108.7
Maryland	------	------	140,506	135,873	------	103.4
District of Columbia	------	------	62,225	69,843	------	89.1
Virginia	79,255	77,282	242,290	251,338	102.6	96.4
West Virginia	------	------	60,873	54,020	------	112.7
North Carolina	73,339	76,253	373,161	395,894	96.2	94.3
South Carolina	212,305	234,130	166,995	180,251	90.7	92.6
Georgia	184,291	197,327	329,160	360,347	93.4	91.3
Florida	23,286	24,792	191,862	191,888	93.9	100.0
EAST SOUTH CENTRAL:						
Kentucky	------	------	113,501	112,539	------	100.9
Tennessee	19,337	18,985	213,232	226,092	101.9	94.3
Alabama	182,919	197,944	274,225	289,746	92.4	94.6
Mississippi	346,493	354,444	151,845	156,936	97.8	96.8
WEST SOUTH CENTRAL:						
Arkansas	94,064	94,218	142,845	147,336	99.8	97.0
Louisiana	98,688	99,900	280,485	297,253	98.8	94.4
Oklahoma	------	------	86,818	85,380	------	101.7
Texas	24,092	25,088	398,516	407,268	96.0	97.9

TABLE 10.—SEX RATIOS OF NEGRO AND WHITE POPULATION, URBAN AND RURAL, BY SECTIONS, AND SOUTHERN DIVISIONS: 1930

SECTION AND DIVISION	MALES PER 100 FEMALES					
	Negro population	White population				
		Total	Native			Foreign born
			Total	Native parentage	Foreign or mixed parentage	
	URBAN POPULATION					
United States	**91.3**	**98.4**	**96.0**	**97.3**	**93.7**	**111.0**
THE SOUTH	86.2	96.0	95.1	95.5	91.2	122.3
South Atlantic	85.7	95.0	93.9	94.1	92.1	117.5
East South Central	86.0	94.3	93.7	94.3	85.8	129.4
West South Central	87.4	98.3	97.5	98.0	92.4	130.7
THE NORTH	98.7	98.7	96.1	97.7	94.0	109.5
THE WEST	96.8	100.1	96.7	98.9	92.1	121.2
	TOTAL RURAL POPULATION					
United States	**101.7**	**109.0**	**107.6**	**107.1**	**110.7**	**134.0**
THE SOUTH	100.8	106.1	105.8	105.6	112.2	149.2
South Atlantic	100.3	105.3	104.8	104.6	110.6	158.3
East South Central	100.2	104.8	104.6	104.6	108.8	160.6
West South Central	102.5	108.5	108.1	107.9	113.8	137.4
THE NORTH	120.3	109.2	107.7	107.0	109.7	126.6
THE WEST	147.0	120.5	116.0	116.2	115.6	164.3
	RURAL-FARM POPULATION					
United States	**101.2**	**112.7**	**111.6**	**110.4**	**120.0**	**139.4**
THE SOUTH	100.9	108.2	108.1	107.9	116.3	134.7
South Atlantic	100.1	107.2	107.1	107.1	115.6	134.0
East South Central	100.3	106.8	106.8	106.7	122.1	148.8
West South Central	103.1	110.6	110.4	110.1	115.7	133.2
THE NORTH	121.2	115.5	114.3	112.4	120.4	134.4
THE WEST	127.8	123.4	119.4	119.1	120.3	160.6
	RURAL-NONFARM POPULATION					
United States	**102.8**	**104.7**	**102.9**	**103.0**	**102.4**	**130.4**
THE SOUTH	100.5	102.7	102.0	101.8	108.2	160.2
South Atlantic	100.7	103.0	102.0	101.7	109.2	165.2
East South Central	100.1	100.3	100.0	100.0	99.3	168.9
West South Central	100.5	104.3	103.9	103.6	109.8	145.4
THE NORTH	120.0	103.4	101.5	101.9	100.4	121.6
THE WEST	155.9	118.1	113.2	113.8	111.3	167.5

Table 11.—NEGRO AND WHITE POPULATION, URBAN AND RURAL, BY SEX, WITH THE NUMBER OF MALES PER 100 FEMALES, BY DIVISIONS: 1930 AND 1920

DIVISION AND RACIAL CLASS	URBAN POPULATION						RURAL POPULATION					
	1930			1920			1930			1920		
	Male	Female	Males per 100 females	Male	Female	Males per 100 females	Male	Female	Males per 100 females	Male	Female	Males per 100 females
United States:												
Negro	**2,479,158**	**2,714,755**	**91.3**	**1,737,820**	**1,821,653**	**95.4**	**3,376,511**	**3,320,719**	**101.7**	**3,471,616**	**3,432,042**	**101.2**
White	**31,162,570**	**31,674,035**	**98.4**	**25,373,627**	**25,246,457**	**100.5**	**24,001,284**	**22,026,318**	**109.0**	**23,057,028**	**21,143,803**	**109.0**
New England:												
Negro	40,289	41,154	97.9	36,098	35,318	102.2	6,674	5,969	111.8	4,057	3,578	113.4
White	3,030,778	3,194,330	94.9	2,846,476	2,942,482	96.7	941,687	898,318	104.8	781,435	745,686	104.8
Middle Atlantic:												
Negro	460,125	478,939	96.1	257,592	259,840	99.1	60,701	53,134	114.2	43,555	39,196	111.1
White	9,669,838	9,757,110	99.1	8,054,951	8,086,704	99.6	2,970,996	2,774,160	107.1	2,835,537	2,664,648	106.4
East North Central:												
Negro	428,801	419,826	102.1	236,592	212,281	111.5	46,567	35,256	132.1	36,434	29,247	124.6
White	7,967,900	7,912,408	100.7	6,405,597	6,186,939	103.5	4,403,675	3,993,680	110.3	4,342,452	4,003,874	108.5
West North Central:												
Negro	128,105	131,090	97.7	108,127	104,464	103.5	39,445	33,144	119.0	35,635	30,295	117.6
White	2,573,237	2,695,008	95.5	2,246,069	2,264,529	99.2	3,994,028	3,611,214	110.6	4,047,675	3,667,114	110.4
South Atlantic:												
Negro	675,013	787,891	85.7	543,188	601,183	90.4	1,481,518	1,476,966	100.3	1,590,189	1,590,560	100.0
White	2,061,376	2,170,444	95.0	1,573,226	1,618,862	97.2	3,650,071	3,467,393	105.3	3,320,064	3,136,788	105.8
East South Central:												
Negro	350,955	408,211	86.0	269,319	301,997	89.2	950,597	948,475	100.2	974,476	977,740	99.7
White	980,023	1,038,859	94.3	695,478	727,082	95.7	2,663,383	2,542,349	104.8	2,531,034	2,413,953	104.9
West South Central:												
Negro	347,049	397,206	87.4	257,107	278,175	92.4	778,459	759,237	102.5	772,350	755,947	102.2
White	1,657,494	1,685,949	98.3	1,231,595	1,197,019	102.9	2,995,071	2,761,467	108.5	2,972,282	2,714,831	109.5
Mountain:												
Negro	10,613	10,419	101.9	8,536	8,142	104.8	5,699	3,494	163.1	11,190	2,933	381.5
White	677,431	675,852	100.2	609,590	581,285	104.9	1,059,276	891,027	118.9	1,108,119	913,905	121.3
Pacific:												
Negro	38,208	40,019	95.5	21,261	20,253	105.0	6,851	5,044	135.8	3,730	2,546	146.5
White	2,544,493	2,544,075	100.0	1,710,645	1,641,555	104.2	1,323,097	1,086,710	121.8	1,118,430	883,004	126.7

Table 12.—NEGRO POPULATION BY SEX, WITH NUMBER OF MALES PER 100 FEMALES, BY DIVISIONS, AND STATES: 1900 TO 1930

[Sex ratio not shown where number of females is less than 100]

DIVISION AND STATE	1930				1920		1910		1900		MALES PER 100 FEMALES			
	Male	Female	Excess of—		Male	Female	Male	Female	Male	Female	1930	1920	1910	1900
			Males	Females										
United States	5,855,669	6,035,474	--------	179,805	5,209,436	5,253,695	4,885,881	4,941,882	4,386,547	4,447,447	97.0	99.2	98.9	98.6
GEOGRAPHIC DIVISIONS:														
New England	46,963	47,123	--------	160	40,155	38,896	32,783	33,523	28,579	30,520	99.7	103.2	97.8	93.6
Middle Atlantic	520,826	532,073	--------	11,247	301,147	299,036	203,466	214,404	159,711	166,210	97.9	100.7	94.9	96.1
East North Central	475,368	455,082	20,286	--------	273,026	241,528	156,431	144,405	134,445	123,397	104.5	113.0	108.3	109.0
West North Central	167,550	164,234	3,316	--------	143,762	134,759	125,864	116,798	121,272	116,637	102.0	106.7	107.8	104.0
South Atlantic	2,156,531	2,264,837	--------	108,326	2,133,377	2,191,743	2,029,808	2,082,680	1,835,525	1,893,492	95.2	97.3	97.5	96.9
East South Central	1,301,552	1,356,686	--------	55,134	1,243,795	1,279,737	1,315,792	1,336,721	1,243,082	1,256,804	95.9	97.2	98.4	98.9
West South Central	1,125,508	1,156,443	--------	30,935	1,029,457	1,034,122	994,025	990,401	846,797	847,269	97.3	99.5	100.4	99.9
Mountain	16,312	13,913	2,399	--------	19,726	11,075	11,766	9,701	9,104	6,486	117.2	178.1	121.3	140.4
Pacific	45,059	45,063	--------	4	24,991	22,799	15,946	13,249	8,032	6,632	100.0	109.6	120.4	121.1
NEW ENGLAND:														
Maine	597	499	98	--------	716	594	700	663	670	649	119.6	120.5	105.6	103.2
New Hampshire	524	266	258	--------	333	288	288	276	327	335	197.0	115.6	104.3	97.6
Vermont	310	258	52	--------	320	252	1,173	448	454	372	120.2	127.0	261.8	122.0
Massachusetts	26,097	26,268	--------	171	22,912	22,554	18,748	19,307	15,591	16,383	99.3	101.6	97.1	95.2
Rhode Island	4,862	5,051	--------	189	5,096	4,940	4,645	4,884	4,290	4,802	96.3	103.2	95.1	89.3
Connecticut	14,573	14,781	--------	208	10,778	10,268	7,229	7,945	7,247	7,979	98.6	105.0	91.0	90.8
MIDDLE ATLANTIC:														
New York	199,485	213,329	--------	13,844	95,418	103,065	64,034	70,157	46,618	52,614	93.5	92.6	91.3	88.6
New Jersey	102,929	105,899	--------	2,970	57,432	59,700	43,602	46,158	33,745	36,099	97.2	96.2	94.5	93.5
Pennsylvania	218,412	212,845	5,567	--------	148,297	136,271	95,830	98,089	79,348	77,497	102.6	108.8	97.7	102.4
EAST NORTH CENTRAL:														
Ohio	159,128	150,176	8,952	--------	100,160	86,027	57,995	53,457	49,985	46,916	106.0	116.4	108.5	106.5
Indiana	57,068	54,914	2,154	--------	41,817	38,993	31,044	29,276	29,701	27,804	103.9	107.2	106.0	106.8
Illinois	164,425	164,547	--------	122	93,835	88,439	56,909	52,140	45,121	39,957	99.9	106.1	109.1	112.9
Michigan	88,936	80,517	8,419	--------	34,249	25,833	9,007	8,108	8,220	7,596	110.5	132.6	111.1	108.2
Wisconsin	5,811	4,928	883	--------	2,965	2,236	1,476	1,424	1,418	1,124	117.9	132.6	103.7	126.2
WEST NORTH CENTRAL:														
Minnesota	5,005	4,440	565	--------	4,851	3,958	4,183	2,901	2,836	2,123	112.7	122.6	144.2	133.6
Iowa	9,987	8,393	594	--------	10,121	8,884	8,120	6,853	6,875	5,818	107.1	113.9	118.2	118.7
Missouri	111,929	111,911	18	--------	90,991	87,250	80,489	76,963	81,206	80,028	100.0	104.3	104.6	101.5
North Dakota	243	134	109	--------	276	191	381	236	173	113	181.3	144.5	161.4	153.1
South Dakota	343	303	40	--------	475	357	468	349	272	193	113.2	133.1	134.1	140.9
Nebraska	7,063	6,689	374	--------	7,309	5,933	4,259	3,430	3,368	2,901	105.6	123.2	124.2	116.1
Kansas	33,980	32,364	1,616	--------	29,739	28,186	27,964	26,066	26,542	25,461	105.0	105.5	107.3	104.2
SOUTH ATLANTIC:														
Delaware	16,983	15,619	1,364	--------	15,655	14,680	16,011	15,170	15,616	15,081	108.7	106.6	105.5	103.5
Maryland	140,506	135,873	4,633	--------	123,453	121,026	114,749	117,501	115,617	119,447	103.4	102.0	97.7	96.8
District of Columbia	62,225	69,843	--------	7,618	50,855	59,111	42,615	51,831	38,348	48,354	89.1	86.0	82.2	79.3
Virginia	321,545	328,620	--------	7,075	342,536	347,481	330,542	340,554	323,459	337,263	97.8	98.6	97.1	95.9
West Virginia	60,873	54,020	6,853	--------	47,129	39,216	36,607	27,556	25,167	18,332	112.7	120.2	132.8	137.3
North Carolina	446,500	472,147	--------	25,647	373,965	389,442	339,581	358,262	303,624	320,845	94.6	96.0	94.8	94.6
South Carolina	379,300	414,381	--------	35,081	422,185	442,534	408,078	427,765	383,626	398,695	91.5	95.4	95.4	96.2
Georgia	513,451	557,674	--------	44,223	590,443	615,922	580,263	596,724	509,869	524,944	92.1	95.9	97.2	97.1
Florida	215,148	216,680	--------	1,532	167,156	162,331	161,362	147,307	120,199	110,531	99.3	103.0	109.5	108.7
EAST SOUTH CENTRAL:														
Kentucky	113,501	112,539	962	--------	118,548	117,390	131,492	130,164	142,073	142,633	100.9	101.0	101.0	99.6
Tennessee	232,569	245,077	--------	12,508	222,639	229,119	233,710	239,378	238,388	241,855	94.9	97.2	97.6	98.6
Alabama	457,144	487,690	--------	30,546	439,779	460,873	447,794	460,488	409,237	418,070	93.7	95.4	97.2	97.9
Mississippi	498,338	511,380	--------	13,042	462,829	472,355	502,796	506,691	453,384	454,246	97.4	98.0	99.2	99.8
WEST SOUTH CENTRAL:														
Arkansas	236,909	241,554	--------	4,645	236,895	235,325	223,323	219,568	185,342	181,514	98.1	100.7	101.7	102.1
Louisiana	379,173	397,153	--------	17,980	344,794	355,463	353,824	360,050	322,664	328,140	95.5	97.0	98.3	98.3
Oklahoma	86,818	85,380	1,438	--------	76,294	73,114	71,937	65,675	28,656	27,028	101.7	104.3	109.5	106.0
Texas	422,608	432,356	--------	9,748	371,474	370,220	344,941	345,108	310,135	310,587	97.7	100.3	100.0	99.9
MOUNTAIN:														
Montana	710	546	164	--------	962	696	1,058	776	912	611	130.0	138.2	136.3	149.3
Idaho	395	273	122	--------	585	335	398	253	166	127	144.7	174.6	157.3	130.7
Wyoming	699	551	148	--------	863	512	1,544	691	631	309	126.9	168.6	223.4	204.2
Colorado	5,739	6,089	--------	350	5,834	5,484	5,867	5,586	4,473	4,097	94.3	106.4	105.0	109.2
New Mexico	1,531	1,319	212	--------	4,593	1,140	891	737	1,023	587	116.1	402.9	120.9	174.3
Arizona	6,352	4,397	1,955	--------	5,859	2,146	1,054	955	1,363	485	144.5	273.0	110.4	281.0
Utah	609	499	110	--------	834	612	691	453	454	218	122.0	136.3	152.5	208.3
Nevada	277	239	38	--------	196	150	263	250	82	52	115.9	130.7	105.2	--------
PACIFIC:														
Washington	3,797	3,043	754	--------	3,957	2,926	3,736	2,322	1,589	925	124.8	135.2	160.9	171.8
Oregon	1,210	1,024	186	--------	1,197	947	907	585	677	428	118.2	126.4	155.0	158.2
California	40,052	40,996	--------	944	19,837	18,926	11,303	10,342	5,766	5,279	97.7	104.8	109.3	109.2

TABLE 13.—URBAN AND RURAL NEGRO POPULATION BY SEX, WITH NUMBER OF MALES PER 100 FEMALES, AND PERCENT URBAN, BY SECTIONS, DIVISIONS, AND STATES: 1930

[Sex ratio not shown where number of females is less than 100]

SECTION, DIVISION, AND STATE	URBAN POPULATION			RURAL POPULATION			MALES PER 100 FEMALES		PERCENT URBAN OF TOTAL POPULATION		
	Total	Male	Female	Total	Male	Female	Urban	Rural	Total	Male	Female
United States	5,193,913	2,479,158	2,714,755	6,697,230	3,376,511	3,320,719	91.3	101.7	43.7	42.3	45.0
The North	2,128,329	1,057,320	1,071,009	280,890	153,387	127,503	98.7	120.3	88.3	87.3	89.4
The South	2,966,325	1,373,017	1,593,308	6,395,252	3,210,574	3,184,678	86.2	100.8	31.7	30.0	33.3
The West	99,259	48,821	50,438	21,088	12,550	8,538	96.8	147.0	82.5	79.6	85.5
GEOGRAPHIC DIVISIONS:											
New England	81,443	40,289	41,154	12,643	6,674	5,969	97.9	111.8	86.6	85.8	87.3
Middle Atlantic	939,064	460,125	478,939	113,835	60,701	53,134	96.1	114.2	89.2	88.3	90.0
East North Central	848,627	428,801	419,826	81,823	46,567	35,256	102.1	132.1	91.2	90.2	92.3
West North Central	259,195	128,105	131,090	72,589	39,445	33,144	97.7	119.0	78.1	76.5	79.8
South Atlantic	1,462,904	675,013	787,891	2,958,484	1,481,518	1,476,966	85.7	100.3	33.1	31.3	34.8
East South Central	759,166	350,955	408,211	1,899,072	950,597	948,475	86.0	100.2	28.6	27.0	30.1
West South Central	744,255	347,049	397,206	1,537,696	778,459	759,237	87.4	102.5	32.6	30.8	34.3
Mountain	21,032	10,613	10,419	9,193	5,699	3,494	101.9	163.1	69.6	65.1	74.9
Pacific	78,227	38,208	40,019	11,895	6,851	5,044	95.5	135.8	86.8	84.8	88.8
NEW ENGLAND:											
Maine	703	363	340	393	234	159	106.8	147.2	64.1	60.8	68.1
New Hampshire	594	420	174	196	104	92	241.4		75.2	80.2	65.4
Vermont	213	114	99	355	196	159		123.3	37.5	36.8	38.4
Massachusetts	46,323	22,817	23,506	6,042	3,280	2,762	97.1	118.8	88.5	87.4	89.5
Rhode Island	9,079	4,428	4,651	834	434	400	95.2	108.5	91.6	91.1	92.1
Connecticut	24,531	12,147	12,384	4,823	2,426	2,397	98.1	101.2	83.6	83.4	83.8
MIDDLE ATLANTIC:											
New York	390,499	187,862	202,637	22,315	11,623	10,692	92.7	108.7	94.6	94.2	95.0
New Jersey	174,985	85,321	89,664	33,843	17,608	16,235	95.2	108.5	83.8	82.9	84.7
Pennsylvania	373,580	186,942	186,638	57,677	31,470	26,207	100.2	120.1	86.6	85.6	87.7
EAST NORTH CENTRAL:											
Ohio	271,972	138,224	133,748	37,332	20,904	16,428	103.3	127.2	87.9	86.9	89.1
Indiana	103,042	51,788	51,254	8,940	5,280	3,660	101.0	144.3	92.0	90.7	93.3
Illinois	304,036	150,386	153,650	24,936	14,039	10,897	97.9	128.8	92.4	91.5	93.4
Michigan	159,704	83,121	76,583	9,749	5,815	3,934	108.5	147.8	94.2	93.5	95.1
Wisconsin	9,873	5,282	4,591	866	529	337	115.1	157.0	91.9	90.9	93.2
WEST NORTH CENTRAL:											
Minnesota	9,110	4,816	4,294	335	189	146	112.2	129.5	95.6	96.2	96.7
Iowa	15,185	7,749	7,436	2,195	1,238	957	104.2	129.4	87.4	86.2	88.6
Missouri	169,954	83,527	86,427	53,886	28,402	25,484	96.6	111.5	75.9	74.6	77.2
North Dakota	216	133	83	161	110	51			57.3	54.7	61.9
South Dakota	337	171	166	309	172	137	103.0	125.5	52.2	49.9	54.8
Nebraska	13,112	6,675	6,437	640	388	252	103.7	154.0	95.3	94.5	96.2
Kansas	51,281	25,034	26,247	15,063	8,946	6,117	95.4	146.2	77.3	73.7	81.1
SOUTH ATLANTIC:											
Delaware	15,037	7,538	7,499	17,565	9,445	8,120	100.5	116.3	46.1	44.4	48.0
Maryland	159,654	78,421	81,233	116,725	62,085	54,640	96.5	113.6	57.8	55.8	59.8
District of Columbia	132,068	62,225	69,843				89.1		100.0	100.0	100.0
Virginia	213,401	99,273	114,128	436,764	222,272	214,492	87.0	103.6	32.8	30.9	34.7
West Virginia	31,224	15,586	15,638	83,669	45,287	38,382	99.7	118.0	27.2	25.6	28.9
North Carolina	246,237	112,494	133,743	672,410	334,006	338,404	84.1	98.7	26.8	25.2	28.3
South Carolina	138,354	60,319	78,035	655,327	318,981	336,346	77.3	94.8	17.4	15.9	18.8
Georgia	316,637	140,573	176,064	754,488	372,878	381,610	79.8	97.7	29.6	27.4	31.6
Florida	210,292	98,584	111,708	221,536	116,564	104,972	88.3	111.0	48.7	45.8	51.6
EAST SOUTH CENTRAL:											
Kentucky	116,561	56,086	60,475	109,479	57,415	52,064	92.7	110.3	51.6	49.4	53.7
Tennessee	240,168	111,505	128,663	237,478	121,064	116,414	86.7	104.0	50.3	47.9	52.5
Alabama	268,450	123,127	145,323	676,384	334,017	342,367	84.7	97.6	28.4	26.9	29.8
Mississippi	133,987	60,237	73,750	875,731	438,101	437,630	81.7	100.1	13.3	12.1	14.4
WEST SOUTH CENTRAL:											
Arkansas	89,162	40,844	48,318	389,301	196,065	193,236	84.5	101.5	18.6	17.2	20.0
Louisiana	257,463	118,439	139,024	518,863	260,734	258,129	85.2	101.0	33.2	31.2	35.0
Oklahoma	67,801	32,470	35,331	104,397	54,348	50,049	91.9	108.6	39.4	37.4	41.4
Texas	329,829	155,296	174,533	525,135	267,312	257,823	89.0	103.7	38.6	36.7	40.4
MOUNTAIN:											
Montana	1,027	556	471	229	154	75	118.0		81.8	78.3	86.3
Idaho	502	276	226	166	119	47	122.1		75.1	69.9	82.8
Wyoming	859	453	406	391	246	145	111.6	169.7	68.7	64.8	73.7
Colorado	10,471	4,965	5,506	1,357	774	583	90.2	132.8	88.5	86.5	90.4
New Mexico	1,718	872	846	1,132	659	473	103.1	139.3	60.3	57.0	64.1
Arizona	5,147	2,783	2,364	5,602	3,569	2,033	117.7	175.6	47.9	43.8	53.8
Utah	944	520	424	164	89	75	122.6		85.2	85.4	85.0
Nevada	364	188	176	152	89	63	106.8		70.5	67.9	73.6
PACIFIC:											
Washington	5,818	3,167	2,651	1,022	630	392	119.5	160.7	85.1	83.4	87.1
Oregon	1,890	993	897	344	217	127	110.7	170.9	84.6	82.1	87.6
California	70,519	34,048	36,471	10,529	6,004	4,525	93.4	132.7	87.0	85.0	89.0

TABLE 14.—NEGRO POPULATION, WITH NUMBER OF MALES PER 100 FEMALES, BY STATES, ARRANGED ACCORDING TO SEX RATIOS: 1930, 1920, 1910, AND 1900

STATE	1930		STATE	1920		STATE	1910		STATE	1900	
	Males per 100 females	Population		Males per 100 females	Population		Males per 100 females	Population		Males per 100 females	Population
United States	**97.0**	**11,891,143**	**United States**	**99.2**	**10,463,131**	**United States**	**98.9**	**9,827,763**	**United States**	**98.6**	**8,833,994**
District of Columbia	89.1	132,068	District of Columbia	86.0	109,966	District of Columbia	82.2	94,446	District of Columbia	79.3	86,702
South Carolina	91.5	793,681	New York	92.6	198,483	Connecticut	91.0	15,174	New York	88.6	99,232
Georgia	92.1	1,071,125	Alabama	95.4	900,652	New York	91.3	134,191	Rhode Island	89.3	9,092
New York	93.5	412,814	South Carolina	95.4	864,719	New Jersey	94.5	89,760	Connecticut	90.8	15,226
Alabama	93.7	944,834	Georgia	95.9	1,206,365	North Carolina	94.8	697,843	New Jersey	93.5	69,844
Colorado	94.3	11,828	North Carolina	96.0	763,407	Rhode Island	95.1	9,529	North Carolina	94.6	624,469
North Carolina	94.6	918,647	New Jersey	96.2	117,132	South Carolina	95.4	835,843	Massachusetts	95.2	31,974
Tennessee	94.9	477,646	Louisiana	97.0	700,257	Massachusetts	97.1	38,055	Virginia	95.9	660,722
Louisiana	95.5	776,326	Tennessee	97.2	451,758	Virginia	97.1	671,096	South Carolina	96.2	782,321
Rhode Island	96.3	9,913	Mississippi	98.0	935,184	Alabama	97.2	908,282	Maryland	96.8	235,064
New Jersey	97.2	208,828	Virginia	98.6	690,017	Georgia	97.2	1,176,987	Georgia	97.1	1,034,813
Mississippi	97.4	1,009,718	Texas	100.3	741,694	Tennessee	97.6	473,088	New Hampshire	97.6	662
California	97.7	81,048	Arkansas	100.7	472,220	Maryland	97.7	232,250	Alabama	97.9	827,307
Texas	97.7	854,964	Kentucky	101.0	235,938	Pennsylvania	97.7	193,919	Louisiana	98.3	650,804
Virginia	97.8	650,165	Massachusetts	101.6	45,466	Louisiana	98.3	713,874	Tennessee	98.6	480,243
Arkansas	98.1	478,463	Maryland	102.0	244,479	Mississippi	99.2	1,009,487	Kentucky	99.6	284,706
Connecticut	98.6	29,354	Florida	103.0	329,487	Texas	100.0	690,049	Mississippi	99.8	907,630
Florida	99.3	431,828	Rhode Island	103.2	10,036	Kentucky	101.0	261,656	Texas	99.9	620,722
Massachusetts	99.3	52,365	Missouri	104.3	178,241	Arkansas	101.7	442,891	Missouri	101.5	161,234
Illinois	99.9	328,972	Oklahoma	104.3	149,408	Wisconsin	103.7	2,900	Arkansas	102.1	366,856
Missouri	100.0	223,840	California	104.8	38,763	New Hampshire	104.3	564	Pennsylvania	102.4	156,845
Kentucky	100.9	226,040	Connecticut	105.0	21,046	Missouri	104.6	157,452	Maine	103.2	1,319
Oklahoma	101.7	172,198	Kansas	105.5	57,925	Colorado	105.0	11,453	Delaware	103.5	30,697
Pennsylvania	102.6	431,257	Illinois	106.1	182,274	Nevada	105.2	513	Kansas	104.2	52,003
Maryland	103.4	276,379	Colorado	106.4	11,318	Delaware	105.5	31,181	Oklahoma	106.0	55,684
Indiana	103.9	111,982	Delaware	106.6	30,335	Maine	105.6	1,363	Ohio	106.5	96,901
Kansas	105.0	66,344	Indiana	107.2	80,810	Indiana	106.0	60,320	Indiana	106.8	57,505
Nebraska	105.6	13,752	Pennsylvania	108.8	284,568	Kansas	107.3	54,030	Michigan	108.2	15,816
Ohio	106.0	309,304	Iowa	113.9	19,005	Ohio	108.5	111,452	Florida	108.7	230,730
Iowa	107.1	17,380	New Hampshire	115.6	621	Illinois	109.1	109,049	California	109.2	11,045
Delaware	108.7	32,602	Ohio	116.4	186,187	California	109.3	21,645	Colorado	109.2	8,570
Michigan	110.5	169,453	West Virginia	120.2	86,345	Florida	109.5	308,669	Illinois	112.9	85,078
Minnesota	112.7	9,445	Maine	120.5	1,310	Oklahoma	109.5	137,612	Nebraska	116.1	6,269
West Virginia	112.7	114,893	Minnesota	122.6	8,809	Arizona	110.4	2,009	Iowa	118.2	12,693
South Dakota	113.2	646	Nebraska	123.2	13,242	Michigan	111.1	17,115	Vermont	122.0	826
Nevada	115.9	516	Oregon	126.4	2,144	Iowa	118.5	14,973	Wisconsin	126.2	2,542
New Mexico	116.1	2,850	Vermont	127.0	572	New Mexico	120.9	1,628	Idaho	130.7	293
Wisconsin	117.9	10,739	Nevada	130.7	346	Nebraska	124.2	7,689	Minnesota	133.6	4,959
Oregon	118.2	2,234	Michigan	132.6	60,082	West Virginia	132.8	64,173	West Virginia	137.3	43,499
Maine	119.6	1,096	Wisconsin	132.6	5,201	South Dakota	134.1	817	South Dakota	140.9	465
Vermont	120.2	568	South Dakota	133.1	832	Montana	136.3	1,834	Montana	149.3	1,523
Utah	122.0	1,108	Washington	135.2	6,883	Minnesota	144.2	7,084	North Dakota	153.1	286
Washington	124.8	6,840	Utah	136.3	1,446	Utah	152.5	1,144	Nevada	(1)	134
Wyoming	126.9	1,250	Montana	138.2	1,658	Oregon	155.0	1,492	Oregon	158.2	1,105
Montana	130.0	1,256	North Dakota	144.5	467	Idaho	157.3	651	Washington	171.8	2,514
Arizona	144.5	10,749	Wyoming	168.6	1,375	Washington	160.9	6,058	New Mexico	174.3	1,610
Idaho	144.7	668	Idaho	174.6	920	North Dakota	161.4	617	Wyoming	204.2	940
North Dakota	181.3	377	Arizona	273.0	8,005	Wyoming	223.4	2,235	Utah	208.3	672
New Hampshire	197.0	790	New Mexico	402.9	5,730	Vermont	261.8	1,621	Arizona	281.0	1,848

[1] Number of females less than 100.

TABLE 15.—NEGRO POPULATION BY SEX, WITH MALES PER 100 FEMALES FOR THE 80 CITIES HAVING 10,000 OR MORE NEGRO INHABITANTS, 1930, 1920, AND 1910; AND MALES PER 100 FEMALES IN THE WHITE POPULATION: 1930

CITY	NEGRO POPULATION						MALES PER 100 FEMALES					
	1930		1920		1910		Negro population			White population, 1930		
	Male	Female	Male	Female	Male	Female	1930	1920	1910	Total	Native	Foreign-born
Total, all cities having 10,000 or more Negro inhabitants	**1,596,113**	**1,739,836**	**1,070,952**	**1,123,746**	**737,020**	**824,297**	**91.7**	**95.3**	**89.4**	**99.4**	**96.7**	**110.1**
Cities of the South	828,432	954,789	642,680	710,062	508,214	587,013	86.8	90.5	86.6	95.7	94.5	118.8
Cities of the North and West	767,681	785,047	428,272	413,694	228,806	237,284	97.8	103.5	96.4	100.3	97.3	109.7
CITIES OF THE SOUTH												
Asheville, N. C	6,379	7,876	3,135	4,010	2,363	2,996	81.0	78.2	78.9	87.2	86.8	104.4
Atlanta, Ga	39,923	50,152	28,993	33,803	23,219	28,683	79.6	85.8	81.0	93.3	91.6	124.1
Augusta, Ga	10,698	13,492	10,610	11,972	8,160	10,184	79.3	88.6	80.1	94.9	94.5	115.2
Baltimore, Md	70,043	72,063	52,889	55,433	39,054	45,695	97.2	95.4	85.5	96.6	95.2	108.3
Baton Rouge, La	4,682	5,993	3,775	4,785	3,430	4,469	78.1	78.9	76.8	94.4	93.5	129.1
Beaumont, Tex	8,967	9,584	6,597	6,613	3,276	3,620	93.6	99.8	90.5	102.7	101.5	137.2
Bessemer, Ala	5,593	6,098	5,370	5,191	3,176	3,034	91.7	103.4	104.7	97.2	96.5	122.3
Birmingham, Ala	46,582	52,495	34,160	36,070	25,662	26,643	88.7	94.7	96.3	97.5	96.5	124.8
Charleston, S. C	11,955	16,107	14,801	17,525	13,714	17,342	74.2	84.5	79.1	92.3	90.9	126.3
Charlotte, N. C	11,437	13,726	6,810	7,831	5,201	6,551	83.3	87.0	79.4	95.8	95.1	154.4
Chattanooga, Tenn	15,690	17,599	9,567	9,322	8,848	9,094	89.2	102.6	97.3	95.4	95.0	122.2
Columbia, S. C	8,484	11,035	6,630	7,825	5,226	6,320	76.9	84.7	82.7	93.8	93.1	144.9
Columbus, Ga	6,079	8,078	4,039	5,054	3,287	4,357	75.3	79.9	75.4	88.9	88.4	164.4
Dallas, Tex	18,101	20,641	11,828	12,195	8,680	9,344	87.7	97.0	92.9	94.5	93.7	124.1
Durham, N. C	8,616	10,101	3,637	4,017	3,106	3,763	85.3	90.5	82.5	92.5	92.1	140.7
Fort Worth, Tex	10,560	11,674	8,010	7,886	6,781	6,499	90.5	101.6	104.3	96.3	95.8	127.3
Galveston, Tex	6,402	6,824	5,027	4,861	3,881	4,155	93.8	103.4	93.4	112.0	106.4	160.5
Greenville, S. C	4,843	6,028	3,817	4,367	2,829	3,490	80.3	87.4	81.1	88.0	87.3	136.4
Greensboro, N. C	6,470	7,580	2,817	3,156	2,556	3,144	85.4	89.3	81.6	93.5	93.0	139.6
Houston, Tex	30,160	33,177	16,394	17,566	11,218	12,711	90.9	93.3	88.3	101.5	100.4	124.9
Jackson, Miss	9,140	10,283	4,403	5,533	4,752	5,802	88.9	79.6	81.9	91.9	91.0	190.4
Jacksonville, Fla	22,225	25,971	20,222	21,298	14,556	14,737	85.6	94.9	98.8	95.7	94.2	127.0
Knoxville, Tenn	8,131	8,962	5,434	5,868	3,600	4,038	90.7	92.6	89.2	93.4	93.2	119.1
Lexington, Ky	6,132	6,627	5,945	6,505	5,075	5,936	92.5	91.4	85.5	91.8	91.0	150.8
Little Rock, Ark	8,889	10,809	8,292	9,185	7,060	7,479	82.2	80.3	94.4	92.1	91.6	119.0
Louisville, Ky	22,742	24,612	19,094	20,993	19,602	20,920	92.4	91.0	93.7	92.8	92.2	109.7
Macon, Ga	10,274	12,884	10,867	12,226	8,305	9,845	79.7	88.9	84.4	89.6	89.1	125.2
Memphis, Tenn	44,859	51,691	28,935	32,246	25,259	27,182	86.8	89.7	92.9	93.6	92.7	124.5
Meridian, Miss	4,915	6,437	3,620	4,713	4,273	5,048	76.4	77.0	84.6	89.3	88.8	133.6
Miami, Fla	11,902	13,214	4,579	4,691	1,137	1,121	90.1	97.6	101.4	99.7	98.5	111.8
Mobile, Ala	11,051	13,463	11,102	12,804	10,344	12,419	82.1	86.7	83.3	97.8	94.8	187.9
Monroe, La	4,751	5,361	2,528	3,012	2,331	2,989	88.6	83.9	78.0	105.6	104.5	142.7
Montgomery, Ala	13,054	16,916	8,553	11,274	8,293	11,029	77.2	75.9	75.2	94.9	94.3	132.8
Nashville, Tenn	19,464	23,372	16,173	19,460	16,229	20,294	83.3	83.1	80.0	89.6	89.3	113.1
New Orleans, La	59,732	69,900	46,919	54,011	40,946	48,316	85.5	86.9	84.7	93.8	91.7	134.2
Newport News, Va	6,442	6,839	7,654	6,423	3,714	3,545	94.2	119.2	104.8	110.7	108.7	141.0
Norfolk, Va	20,790	23,152	21,794	21,598	11,887	13,152	89.8	100.9	90.4	106.3	105.0	131.8
Oklahoma City, Okla	7,171	7,491	4,151	4,090	3,534	3,012	95.7	101.5	117.3	102.8	102.2	139.7
Petersburg, Va	5,734	6,866	6,174	7,434	4,831	6,183	83.5	83.1	78.1	87.5	86.9	120.7
Port Arthur, Tex	4,934	5,069	2,030	1,880	968	525	97.3	108.0	184.4	114.1	111.2	219.1
Portsmouth, Va	8,941	9,908	11,635	11,610	5,542	6,075	90.2	100.2	91.2	108.1	108.0	111.6
Raleigh, N. C	5,817	6,758	4,180	4,364	3,275	4,097	86.1	95.8	79.9	93.8	93.3	138.3
Richmond, Va	24,354	28,634	24,696	29,345	21,472	25,261	85.1	84.2	85.0	89.4	88.7	115.7
Roanoke, Va	5,755	6,613	4,455	4,876	3,650	4,274	87.0	91.4	85.4	93.8	93.3	137.4
San Antonio, Tex	8,184	9,794	6,842	7,499	4,909	5,807	83.6	91.2	84.5	99.7	99.0	110.9
Savannah, Ga	17,315	21,581	18,566	20,613	15,218	18,028	80.2	90.1	84.4	92.8	91.3	125.5
Shreveport, La	12,223	14,996	8,176	9,309	6,226	7,670	81.5	87.8	81.2	96.3	95.6	123.3
Tampa, Fla	10,072	11,100	5,614	5,917	4,431	4,520	90.7	94.9	98.0	98.3	94.3	118.9
Tulsa, Okla	7,241	7,962	4,366	4,512	990	969	90.9	96.8	102.2	99.5	98.8	135.8
Vicksburg, Miss	5,225	6,690	3,869	5,279	5,231	6,822	78.1	73.3	76.7	92.1	90.6	140.8
Washington, D. C	62,225	69,843	50,855	59,111	42,615	51,831	89.1	86.0	82.2	91.4	89.8	109.6
Wilmington, Del	6,056	6,024	5,568	5,178	4,390	4,691	100.5	107.5	93.6	99.8	96.9	121.1
Wilmington, N. C	5,855	7,251	6,241	7,220	5,482	6,625	80.7	86.4	82.7	91.5	90.8	129.3
Winston-Salem, N. C	15,173	17,393	10,232	10,503	4,410	4,677	87.2	97.4	94.3	93.3	93.0	133.9
CITIES OF THE NORTH AND WEST												
Akron, Ohio	5,748	5,332	3,554	2,026	357	300	107.8	175.4	119.0	103.8	101.1	123.6
Atlantic City, N. J	7,527	8,084	5,251	5,695	4,851	4,983	93.1	92.2	97.4	89.6	87.1	100.2
Boston, Mass	10,223	10,351	8,295	8,055	6,664	6,900	98.8	103.0	96.6	96.0	96.8	94.2
Buffalo, N. Y	7,064	6,499	2,522	1,989	933	840	108.7	126.8	111.1	98.3	95.6	109.2
Camden, N. J	5,676	5,664	4,304	4,196	2,949	3,127	100.2	102.6	94.3	100.2	98.2	110.6
Chicago, Ill	115,488	118,415	55,943	53,515	22,685	21,418	97.5	104.5	105.9	102.5	98.0	115.9
Cincinnati, Ohio	23,914	23,904	15,145	14,934	9,905	9,734	100.0	101.4	101.8	93.6	92.5	105.9
Cleveland, Ohio	36,180	35,719	18,733	15,718	4,341	4,107	101.3	119.2	105.7	102.9	98.8	114.7
Columbus, Ohio	17,126	15,648	11,788	10,393	6,784	5,955	109.4	113.4	113.9	95.9	94.3	123.4
Dayton, Ohio	8,608	8,469	4,776	4,249	2,475	2,367	101.6	112.4	104.6	98.4	97.0	119.6
Detroit, Mich	62,239	57,827	23,605	17,233	2,985	2,756	107.6	137.0	108.3	109.9	104.7	124.6
East St. Louis, Ill	5,743	5,793	3,908	3,529	3,233	2,649	99.1	110.7	122.0	102.0	100.4	123.5
Gary, Ind	9,393	8,529	2,991	2,308	242	141	110.1	129.6	171.6	117.2	105.7	162.2
Indianapolis, Ind	21,263	22,704	17,378	17,300	10,803	11,013	93.7	100.5	98.1	94.2	93.4	113.8
Jersey City, N. J	6,229	6,346	4,099	3,901	3,020	2,940	98.2	105.1	102.7	101.3	99.0	109.2
Kansas City, Kans	9,628	10,244	7,130	7,275	4,622	4,664	94.0	98.0	99.1	100.6	99.1	120.0
Kansas City, Mo	18,599	19,975	15,472	15,247	11,885	11,681	93.1	101.5	101.7	94.7	93.1	119.2
Los Angeles, Calif	18,349	20,545	7,389	8,190	3,682	3,917	89.3	90.2	94.0	95.5	93.1	108.6
Newark, N. J	19,280	19,600	8,552	8,425	4,477	4,998	98.4	101.5	89.6	102.4	98.7	112.5
New York, N. Y	156,968	170,738	72,351	80,116	42,143	49,566	91.9	90.3	85.0	100.6	97.8	105.9
Bronx Borough	6,302	6,628	2,269	2,534	1,911	2,206	95.1	89.5	86.6	99.3	97.7	102.1
Brooklyn Borough	32,835	36,086	15,197	16,715	10,245	12,463	91.0	90.9	82.2	100.7	97.4	107.0
Manhattan Borough	108,229	116,441	51,912	57,221	28,024	32,510	92.9	90.7	86.2	101.5	98.3	106.8
Queens Borough	8,347	10,262	2,238	2,882	1,440	1,758	81.3	77.7	81.9	99.5	97.5	105.6
Richmond Borough	1,255	1,321	735	764	523	629	95.0	96.2	83.1	107.7	104.1	118.9
Omaha, Nebr.[1]	5,607	5,516	5,598	4,717	2,811	2,332	101.6	118.7	120.5	97.5	95.4	110.7
Philadelphia, Pa	108,483	111,116	67,132	67,097	39,431	45,028	97.6	100.1	87.6	98.4	97.1	103.3
Pittsburgh, Pa	27,962	27,021	19,913	17,812	13,351	12,272	103.5	111.8	108.8	98.1	95.5	111.2
St. Louis, Mo	45,832	47,748	35,359	34,495	22,168	21,792	96.0	102.5	101.7	95.4	93.1	115.5
Toledo, Ohio	6,967	6,293	3,184	2,507	937	940	110.7	127.0	99.7	102.7	100.0	124.8
Youngstown, Ohio	7,585	6,967	3,900	2,762	1,072	864	108.9	141.2	124.1	103.5	97.8	127.9

[1] Figures for 1910 include South Omaha.

Table 16.—NEGRO POPULATION BY SEX, WITH NUMBER OF MALES PER 100 FEMALES, FOR THE 183 CITIES AND URBAN PLACES HAVING 2,500 TO 10,000 NEGRO INHABITANTS: 1930

CITY	NEGRO POPULATION		
	Male	Female	Males per 100 females
Total, all cities having 2,500 to 10,000 Negro inhabitants	**396,371**	**452,963**	**87.5**
Cities of the South	266,072	321,100	82.9
Cities of the North	116,500	118,111	98.6
Cities of the West	13,799	13,752	100.3
CITIES OF THE SOUTH			
Aiken, S. C.	1,546	1,943	79.6
Albany, Ga.	3,140	4,254	73.8
Alexandria, La.	4,375	5,171	84.6
Alexandria, Va.	2,375	2,537	93.6
Americus, Ga.	1,969	2,658	74.1
Anderson, S. C.	1,674	2,159	77.5
Annapolis, Md.	1,486	1,732	85.8
Anniston, Ala.	3,319	3,842	86.4
Athens, Ga.	2,737	3,641	75.2
Austin, Tex.	4,318	5,550	77.8
Bainbridge, Ga.	1,281	1,620	79.1
Bluefield, W. Va.[1]	1,603	1,760	91.1
Blytheville, Ark.	1,291	1,440	89.7
Bogalusa, La.	2,392	2,359	101.4
Brunswick, Ga.	2,793	3,256	85.8
Bryan, Tex.	1,155	1,444	80.0
Camden, Ark.	1,300	1,572	82.7
Canton, Miss.	1,145	1,474	77.7
Charleston, W. Va.	3,191	3,543	90.1
Charlottesville, Va.	1,883	2,200	85.6
Clarksdale, Miss.	2,209	2,816	78.4
Clarksville, Tenn.	1,534	1,875	81.8
Columbia, Tenn.	1,086	1,421	76.4
Columbus, Miss.	2,084	2,778	75.0
Cordele, Ga.	1,526	1,964	77.7
Corsicana, Tex.	1,543	1,789	86.2
Covington, Ky.	1,739	1,727	100.7
Crowley, La.	1,182	1,401	84.4
Danville, Va.	2,363	3,156	74.9
Darlington, S. C.	1,139	1,433	79.5
Daytona Beach, Fla.	2,469	2,957	83.5
Decatur, Ala.	1,789	2,078	86.1
Decatur, Ga.	1,130	1,385	81.6
Denison, Tex.	1,225	1,396	87.8
Dothan, Ala.	2,932	3,262	89.9
Dublin, Ga.	1,202	1,604	74.9
Dyersburg, Tenn.	1,276	1,419	89.9
El Dorado, Ark.	1,675	2,161	77.5
Elizabeth City, N. C.	1,730	1,992	86.8
Fairfield, Ala.	3,131	3,262	96.0
Fayetteville, N. C.	2,382	2,975	80.1
Florence, Ala.	1,172	1,579	74.2
Florence, S. C.	2,605	3,462	75.2
Fort Smith, Ark.	1,621	1,846	87.8
Gadsden, Ala.	3,165	3,180	99.5
Gainesville, Fla.	1,931	2,175	88.8
Gastonia, N. C.	1,462	1,745	83.8
Georgetown, S. C.	1,295	1,625	79.7
Goldsboro, N. C.	3,122	3,746	83.3
Greenville, Miss.	3,880	4,490	86.4
Greenville, N. C.	1,840	2,393	76.9
Greenwood, Miss.	2,354	3,031	77.7
Greenwood, S. C.	1,514	1,998	75.8
Griffin, Ga.	1,507	1,889	79.8
Gulfport, Miss.	1,556	1,602	97.1
Hampton, Va.	1,307	1,497	87.3
Hattiesburg, Miss.	3,077	3,734	82.4
Helena, Ark.	1,941	2,479	78.3
CITIES OF THE SOUTH—con.			
Henderson, N. C.	1,292	1,551	83.3
High Point, N. C.	3,493	3,736	93.5
Hopkinsville, Ky.	1,786	2,194	81.4
Hot Springs, Ark.	1,864	2,330	80.0
Huntington, W. Va.	2,195	2,435	90.1
Huntsville, Ala.	1,674	2,151	77.8
Jackson, Tenn.	3,433	4,162	82.5
Kinston, N. C.	2,228	2,834	78.6
Lafayette, La.	2,293	2,720	84.3
La Grange, Ga.	2,494	2,977	83.8
Lake Charles, La.	2,744	3,204	85.6
Lakeland, Fla.	1,822	2,119	86.0
Laurel, Miss.	3,132	3,706	84.5
Lynchburg, Va.	4,164	5,489	75.9
Marion, S. C.	1,210	1,337	90.5
Marshall, Tex.	3,042	3,651	83.3
Milledgeville, Ga.	1,212	1,507	80.4
Moultrie, Ga.	1,410	1,668	84.5
Muskogee, Okla.	3,051	3,525	86.6
Natchez, Miss.	2,965	4,194	70.7
New Bern, N. C.	2,869	3,408	84.2
New Iberia, La.	1,184	1,361	87.0
North Little Rock, Ark.	2,894	3,203	90.4
Ocala, Fla.	1,325	1,628	81.4
Okmulgee, Okla.	1,449	1,764	82.1
Opelika, Ala.	1,165	1,509	77.2
Opelousas, La.	1,286	1,572	81.8
Orangeburg, S. C.	1,749	2,203	79.4
Orlando, Fla.	3,444	4,146	83.1
Owensboro, Ky.	1,196	1,313	91.1
Paducah, Ky.	3,207	3,537	90.7
Palatka, Fla.	1,434	1,566	91.6
Palestine, Tex.	1,420	1,807	78.6
Paris, Tex.	1,492	1,773	84.2
Pensacola, Fla.	4,379	5,204	84.1
Phenix City, Ala.	1,828	2,237	81.7
Pine Bluff, Ark.	2,659	3,504	75.9
Rocky Mount, N. C.	3,928	4,774	82.3
Rome, Ga.	2,212	2,525	87.6
St. Augustine, Fla.	1,473	1,820	80.9
St. Petersburg, Fla.	3,301	4,115	80.2
Salisbury, N. C.	1,837	2,127	86.4
Sanford, Fla.	2,412	2,472	97.6
Selma, Ala.	3,881	5,368	72.3
Spartanburg, S. C.	4,392	5,434	80.8
Suffolk, Va.	1,665	2,141	77.8
Sumter, S. C.	2,161	2,984	72.4
Talladega, Ala.	1,188	1,464	81.1
Tallahassee, Fla.	1,879	2,522	74.5
Temple, Tex.	1,352	1,450	93.2
Texarkana, Ark.	1,421	1,688	84.2
Texarkana, Tex.	2,224	2,710	82.1
Thomasville, Ga.	2,622	3,452	76.0
Troy, Ala.	1,405	1,710	82.2
Tuscaloosa, Ala.	3,147	3,928	80.1
Tyler, Tex.	1,839	2,253	81.6
Valdosta, Ga.	2,788	3,477	80.2
Waco, Tex.	4,381	4,989	87.8
Washington, N. C.	1,450	1,720	84.3
Waycross, Ga.	2,677	3,279	81.6
West Palm Beach, Fla.	4,317	4,682	92.2
Wichita Falls, Tex.	2,012	2,300	87.5
Wilson, N. C.	2,769	3,436	80.6
Yazoo City, Miss.	1,187	1,578	75.2
CITIES OF THE NORTH			
Alaquippa Borough, Pa.	1,414	1,178	120.0
Alton, Ill.	1,378	1,336	103.1
Asbury Park, N. J.	1,668	1,881	88.7
Bridgeport, Conn.	1,715	1,599	107.3
Cairo, Ill.	2,259	2,316	97.5
Cambridge, Mass.	2,600	2,819	92.2
Canton, Ohio	1,581	1,423	111.1
Chester, Pa.	4,774	4,471	106.8
Danville, Ill.	1,227	1,338	91.7
Des Moines, Iowa	2,661	2,767	96.2
East Chicago, Ind.	2,724	2,364	115.2
East Orange, N. J.	2,205	2,675	82.4
Elizabeth, N. J.	2,445	2,316	105.6
Englewood, N. J.	1,157	1,367	84.6
Evanston, Ill.	2,262	2,676	84.5
Evansville, Ind.	3,203	3,311	96.7
Flint, Mich.	3,036	2,689	112.9
Grand Rapids, Mich.	1,409	1,386	101.7
Hackensack, N. J.	1,221	1,309	93.3
Hamtramck, Mich.	2,087	1,981	105.4
Harrisburg, Pa.	3,198	3,184	100.4
Hartford, Conn.	3,144	3,366	93.4
Homestead Borough, Pa.	1,853	1,514	122.4
Lower Merion Township, Pa.	1,018	1,901	53.6
Middletown, Ohio	1,396	1,409	99.1
Milwaukee, Wis.	4,034	3,467	116.4
Minneapolis, Minn.	2,189	1,987	110.2
Montclair, N. J.	2,656	3,728	71.2
Mount Vernon, N. Y.	1,528	2,080	73.5
Muncie, Ind.	1,346	1,300	103.5
New Bedford, Mass.	1,851	1,780	104.0
New Haven, Conn.	2,626	2,676	98.1
New Rochelle, N. Y.	1,965	2,679	73.3
Orange, N. J.	2,373	2,654	89.4
Paterson, N. J.	1,441	1,511	95.4
Peoria, Ill.	1,649	1,388	118.8
Plainfield, N. J.	1,726	1,922	89.8
Pontiac, Mich.	1,380	1,173	117.6
Providence, R. I.	2,631	2,842	92.6
Rochester, N. Y.	1,308	1,371	95.4
Saginaw, Mich.	1,646	1,207	136.4
St. Joseph, Mo.	2,067	1,988	104.0
St. Paul, Minn.	2,086	1,915	108.9
South Bend, Ind.	1,775	1,656	107.2
Springfield, Ill.	1,643	1,681	97.7
Springfield, Mass.	1,574	1,567	100.4
Springfield, Ohio	4,151	4,098	101.3
Steelton Borough, Pa.	1,335	1,197	111.5
Steubenville, Ohio	1,513	1,263	119.8
Terre Haute, Ind.	1,695	1,766	96.0
Topeka, Kans.	2,760	2,996	92.1
Trenton, N. J.	4,231	3,826	110.6
Warren, Ohio	1,364	1,184	115.2
Wichita, Kans.	2,762	2,861	96.5
Yonkers, N. Y.	1,560	1,772	88.0
CITIES OF THE WEST			
Denver, Colo.	3,365	3,839	87.7
Oakland, Calif.	3,750	3,753	99.9
Pasadena, Calif.	1,353	1,662	81.4
San Diego, Calif.	1,324	1,399	94.6
San Francisco, Calif.	2,190	1,613	135.8
Seattle, Wash.	1,817	1,486	122.3

[1] The combined Negro population for Bluefield city, Mercer County, W. Va., and Bluefield town, Tazewell County, Va.: males 1,748; females 1,900; males per 100 emales, 92.

CHAPTER VIII.—AGE DISTRIBUTION

The age classification.—At every census, some attempt has been made to distribute the population by age. The age classification is based upon the age at the last birthday, that is, the age in completed years.

Apart from the abnormalities in age distribution due to immigration, there are some irregularities in the age distribution by single years which are due to errors in the census returns. Ages may be misstated, either intentionally or through ignorance of the true age on the part of the person giving the information. Where the age is not accurately known, there is a tendency to report it in multiples of 2 or 5, or even, in case of ages above 20, as a multiple of 10. There is also a tendency to concentrate on age 21 for men. In general, the degree of accuracy is greater for adults than for children. The errors at all ages are greatest for those classes of population in which the proportion of illiterates is the greatest. The returns also exaggerate the number of Negro and Indian centenarians. The age distribution of Negroes, if ages were accurately reported, would approximate that of native whites of white parentage, except that the younger groups would be relatively larger and the older groups smaller, because the life span of Negroes is shorter than that of whites. The number of Negroes in the age group under 5, as compared with that of 5 to 9, shows approximately the extent of the underenumeration of young Negro children, while the irregularities in the older age group are the results of the tendency to report ages in multiples of 2, 5, and 10.

In general, the age distribution for Negro males is more symmetrical and appears to be more accurate than that for females. The number of females in the age group 20 to 24 years was larger in 1930 than the expected survivorship from the age group 10 to 14 years as returned in 1920. This excess is undoubtedly due to the understatement of age. Prior censuses and censuses of other countries show similar age discrepancies that can be accounted for only by erroneous returns. The variation in the percent in each group as between males and females is probably the result of the understatement of age by Negro females. On the whole, the returns present a reasonably accurate age distribution, and, when greater accuracy is necessary, it is always possible to make adjustments for obvious inaccuracies.

Distribution by 5-year age groups.—About 53 percent of the Negro population in 1930 was less than 25 years of age, as compared with 46.9 percent for the white population. There was a greater percent of Negro population in each age group under 25 years than for the white population. The percent of the Negro population in each group over 45 years was less than for the white population. The migration of the Negroes to the North and West has affected the age distribution in those two sections. Hence, the percent of the Negro population in the lower age groups in those two sections was not so great as for the country as a whole. Over 52 percent of the Negro population was in the age group 24 or under in 1930. The proportion of the native white population falling into this group was practically the same as that for the Negro.

There was an increase from 1920 to 1930 in the number of Negroes in each 5-year age group, except for the group 100 years and over. Children 2 to 14 years of age constituted a smaller percent of the total Negro population in 1930 than in 1920. With the exception of the age group 20 to 24 years, the percent of the Negro population in each age was greater in 1930 than in 1920 for every age group from 15 to 45 years.

Median age.—The median age, or the age which divides a population into two equal groups, the number older being exactly equal to the number younger, was 23.4 years in 1930 as compared with 22.3 years in 1920 for the Negro population. The median age for the Negro population has been increasing at each census since 1850. In 1850 the median age was 17.3; in 1860, 17.7; in 1870, 18.5; in 1900, 19.4; and in 1910, 20.8. This increase in the median age has been due to two causes—first, an increase in the average length of life; and, second, a reduction in the birth rate, which has resulted in a decrease in the proportion of young people in the population.

The median age of male Negroes was the same as that for native white males in 1930. The median age for Negro females was lower than that for Negro males or for native white females.

Age by sex.—In 1930 the number of females in the Negro population was greater than the number of males for every age under 45 years, except for the ages 4, 10, 12, and 41. The males outnumbered the females for every age from 45 to 70 years, with the exception of the age 48.

The proportion of Negro males in the total Negro population was equal to or greater than that for the females of all ages under 14 years. A greater proportion of the female Negro population than of the male Negro population was in the age group 15 to 39 years. For each age group over 40 years, with the exception of the age group 90 to 94 years, the proportion of the Negro male population in that age group equals or exceeds the proportion for the female population.

Urban, rural-farm, and rural-nonfarm population.—Since there are important differences in age distribution between the urban and rural areas and between farm and nonfarm population, separate figures have been given for these three subdivisions of the population.

For persons in each age group under 20 years, the rural percentages were higher than the urban in the United States as a whole, and also in the South and North. There was a pronounced difference between urban and rural areas in the proportion of Negroes in the more active age and in the lower age groups. The opportunities to be found in urban communities have attracted large numbers of persons in the more active ages. In urban areas more than one-half of the Negro population fell into the age group of 25 years and over, while in the rural areas over 59 percent of the Negro population fell into the age class under 25 years.

In urban areas there was an excess of males in all age groups from 40 to 59 years. In rural-nonfarm areas the number of males exceeded the number of females in every age group from 25 to 74 years. In the rural-farm areas the males exceeded the females in all the age groups from 5 to 19 years and from 45 to 84 years.

Number of males per 100 females by age groups.—There were less than 100 males per 100 females in every age group under 45 years in the Negro population in 1930. For the age groups 45 to 74 years the ratio of males per 100 females was greater than 100. The number of males per 100 females in each age group over 75 years gradually declined to 45.9 for the age group 100 years and over.

Age distribution by color and nativity.—Table 2 shows the percent distribution by 5-year age periods for the 1930 population of the United States, classified by color, nativity, and parentage. The Negro population figures on which these percentages are based appear in table 7.

TABLE 1.—POPULATION BY 5-YEAR AGE PERIODS, BY COLOR, BY SECTIONS: 1930

AGE	Total	Negro	White	Other races	PERCENT DISTRIBUTION	
					Negro	White
	UNITED STATES					
All ages	**122,775,046**	**11,891,143**	**108,864,207**	**2,019,696**	**100.0**	**100.0**
Under 5 years	11,444,390	1,230,206	9,927,396	286,788	10.3	9.1
5 to 9 years	12,607,609	1,368,381	10,956,144	283,084	11.5	10.1
10 to 14 years	12,004,877	1,251,542	10,546,282	207,053	10.5	9.7
15 to 19 years	11,552,115	1,250,528	10,111,584	190,003	10.5	9.3
20 to 24 years	10,870,378	1,203,191	9,466,155	201,032	10.1	8.7
25 to 29 years	9,833,608	1,071,787	8,573,696	188,125	9.0	7.9
30 to 34 years	9,120,421	864,514	8,109,766	146,141	7.3	7.4
35 to 39 years	9,208,645	890,900	8,183,620	134,125	7.5	7.5
40 to 44 years	7,990,195	687,423	7,198,507	104,265	5.8	6.6
45 to 49 years	7,042,279	630,065	6,322,989	89,225	5.3	5.8
50 to 54 years	5,975,804	504,590	5,409,056	62,158	4.2	5.0
55 to 59 years	4,645,677	309,397	4,293,107	43,173	2.6	3.9
60 to 64 years	3,751,221	242,169	3,476,993	32,059	2.0	3.2
65 to 69 years	2,770,605	155,177	2,594,840	20,588	1.3	2.4
70 to 74 years	1,950,004	99,096	1,838,050	12,858	.8	1.7
75 to 79 years	1,106,390	58,711	1,039,862	7,817	.5	1.0
80 to 84 years	534,676	33,377	496,803	4,496	.3	.5
85 years and over	272,130	26,358	242,028	3,744	.2	.2
Unknown	94,022	13,731	77,329	2,962	.1	.1
	THE SOUTH					
All ages	**37,857,633**	**9,361,577**	**27,673,879**	**822,177**	**100.0**	**100.0**
Under 5 years	4,152,716	1,016,579	3,017,349	118,788	10.9	10.9
5 to 9 years	4,536,133	1,150,248	3,264,359	121,526	12.3	11.8
10 to 14 years	4,145,954	1,069,120	2,985,163	91,671	11.4	10.8
15 to 19 years	4,010,733	1,063,846	2,857,176	89,711	11.4	10.3
20 to 24 years	3,604,321	953,787	2,566,877	83,657	10.2	9.3
25 to 29 years	3,001,560	774,708	2,157,552	69,300	8.3	7.8
30 to 34 years	2,549,672	599,236	1,898,612	51,824	6.4	6.9
35 to 39 years	2,516,921	630,877	1,837,148	48,896	6.7	6.7
40 to 44 years	2,081,684	495,604	1,548,583	37,497	5.3	5.6
45 to 49 years	1,890,769	469,050	1,387,574	34,145	5.0	5.0
50 to 54 years	1,625,244	390,051	1,211,800	23,393	4.2	4.4
55 to 59 years	1,188,700	239,306	931,942	17,452	2.6	3.4
60 to 64 years	923,301	195,897	713,793	13,611	2.1	2.6
65 to 69 years	646,576	125,331	512,771	8,474	1.3	1.9
70 to 74 years	470,928	80,889	384,784	5,255	.9	1.4
75 to 79 years	276,285	47,731	225,424	3,130	.5	.8
80 to 84 years	136,002	27,799	106,334	1,869	.3	.4
85 years and over	72,795	22,076	49,307	1,412	.2	.2
Unknown	27,339	9,442	17,331	566	.1	.1

AGE	Total	Negro	White	Other races	PERCENT DISTRIBUTION	
					Negro	White
	THE NORTH					
All ages	**73,021,191**	**2,409,219**	**70,388,367**	**223,605**	**100.0**	**100.0**
Under 5 years	6,319,029	205,753	6,084,368	28,908	8.5	8.6
5 to 9 years	6,979,970	209,381	6,744,716	25,873	8.7	9.6
10 to 14 years	6,831,165	174,430	6,638,899	17,836	7.2	9.4
15 to 19 years	6,538,659	178,518	6,344,131	16,010	7.4	9.0
20 to 24 years	6,262,367	239,506	5,998,787	24,074	9.9	8.5
25 to 29 years	5,863,239	285,507	5,550,334	27,398	11.9	7.9
30 to 34 years	5,641,966	253,325	5,367,450	21,191	10.5	7.6
35 to 39 years	5,736,747	246,718	5,471,626	18,403	10.2	7.8
40 to 44 years	5,032,724	180,936	4,838,945	12,843	7.5	6.9
45 to 49 years	4,373,324	151,271	4,212,356	9,697	6.3	6.0
50 to 54 years	3,701,165	107,100	3,587,424	6,641	4.4	5.1
55 to 59 years	2,956,461	65,434	2,886,254	4,773	2.7	4.1
60 to 64 years	2,419,602	43,166	2,372,936	3,500	1.8	3.4
65 to 69 years	1,817,214	27,808	1,786,965	2,441	1.2	2.5
70 to 74 years	1,268,605	16,945	1,250,147	1,513	.7	1.8
75 to 79 years	714,740	10,285	703,409	1,046	.4	1.0
80 to 84 years	343,976	5,222	338,239	515	.2	.5
85 years and over	172,148	3,995	167,685	468	.2	.2
Unknown	48,090	3,919	43,696	475	.2	.1
	THE WEST					
All ages	**11,896,222**	**120,347**	**10,801,961**	**973,914**	**100.0**	**100.0**
Under 5 years	972,645	7,874	825,679	139,092	6.5	7.6
5 to 9 years	1,091,506	8,752	947,069	135,685	7.3	8.8
10 to 14 years	1,027,758	7,992	922,220	97,546	6.6	8.5
15 to 19 years	1,002,723	8,164	910,277	84,282	6.8	8.4
20 to 24 years	1,003,690	9,898	900,491	93,301	8.2	8.3
25 to 29 years	968,809	11,572	865,810	91,427	9.6	8.0
30 to 34 years	928,783	11,953	843,704	73,126	9.9	7.8
35 to 39 years	954,977	13,305	874,846	66,826	11.1	8.1
40 to 44 years	875,787	10,883	810,979	53,925	9.0	7.5
45 to 49 years	778,186	9,744	723,059	45,383	8.1	6.7
50 to 54 years	649,395	7,439	609,832	32,124	6.2	5.6
55 to 59 years	500,516	4,657	474,911	20,948	3.9	4.4
60 to 64 years	408,318	3,106	390,264	14,948	2.6	3.6
65 to 69 years	306,815	2,038	295,104	9,673	1.7	2.7
70 to 74 years	210,471	1,262	203,119	6,090	1.0	1.9
75 to 79 years	115,365	695	111,029	3,641	.6	1.0
80 to 84 years	54,698	356	52,230	2,112	.3	.5
85 years and over	27,187	287	25,036	1,864	.2	.2
Unknown	18,593	370	16,302	1,921	.3	.2

TABLE 2.—PERCENT DISTRIBUTION BY AGE FOR THE POPULATION OF THE UNITED STATES, BY COLOR AND NATIVITY: 1930

[Percent not shown where less than one-tenth of 1 percent]

AGE	Total population	Negro	NATIVE WHITE				Foreign-born white	Other races
			Total	Native parentage	Foreign parentage	Mixed parentage		
All ages	**100.0**	**100.0**	**100.0**	**100.0**	**100.0**	**100.0**	**100.0**	**100.0**
Under 5 years	9.3	10.3	10.4	11.3	6.6	10.0	.2	14.2
5 to 9 years	10.3	11.5	11.3	11.9	9.5	10.7	.9	14.0
10 to 14 years	9.8	10.5	10.9	10.7	11.8	10.4	1.1	10.3
15 to 19 years	9.4	10.5	10.2	9.9	11.9	9.9	2.4	9.4
20 to 24 years	8.9	10.1	9.2	9.1	9.9	9.1	5.0	10.0
25 to 29 years	8.0	9.0	7.9	7.9	7.9	8.3	7.6	9.3
30 to 34 years	7.4	7.3	7.2	7.0	7.6	7.9	9.3	7.2
35 to 39 years	7.5	7.5	6.9	6.7	7.3	7.6	12.2	6.6
40 to 44 years	6.5	5.8	5.8	5.6	5.9	6.5	12.7	5.2
45 to 49 years	5.7	5.3	5.0	4.9	4.9	5.6	11.7	4.4
50 to 54 years	4.9	4.2	4.3	4.2	4.5	4.6	9.9	3.1
55 to 59 years	3.8	2.6	3.4	3.3	4.0	3.4	7.7	2.1
60 to 64 years	3.1	2.0	2.7	2.6	3.2	2.4	6.8	1.6
65 to 69 years	2.3	1.3	2.0	1.9	2.4	1.6	5.3	1.0
70 to 74 years	1.6	.8	1.4	1.5	1.6	1.0	3.4	.6
75 to 79 years	.9	.5	.8	.9	.7	.5	2.0	.4
80 to 84 years	.4	.3	.4	.4	.2	.2	1.1	.2
85 years and over	.2	.2	.2	.2	.1	.1	.6	.2
Unknown	.1	.1	.1	.1	------	------	.1	.1

TABLE 3.—MEDIAN AGES, BY COLOR, NATIVITY, AND SEX, FOR THE UNITED STATES: 1930 AND 1920

COLOR AND NATIVITY	TOTAL		MALE		FEMALE	
	1930	**1920**	**1930**	**1920**	**1930**	**1920**
All classes	**26.4**	**25.2**	**26.7**	**25.8**	**26.1**	**24.7**
Negro	23.4	22.3	23.7	22.8	23.2	22.0
White [1]	26.9	25.6	27.2	26.1	26.7	25.1
Native	23.8	22.4	23.7	22.4	23.9	22.3
Native parentage	23.3	22.7	23.4	22.8	23.3	22.5
Foreign parentage	25.2	21.6	24.9	21.4	25.4	21.7
Mixed parentage	24.9	21.8	24.3	21.3	25.5	22.2
Foreign born	44.4	40.0	44.6	40.1	44.0	39.9
Mexican [1]	20.2	-------	21.6	-------	18.7	-------
Indian	19.6	19.7	20.0	20.4	19.1	19.0
Chinese	32.3	40.2	35.1	42.7	17.3	19.4
Japanese	24.5	30.2	29.7	34.1	15.9	24.0

[1] Mexicans included in white population for 1920.

TABLE 4.—URBAN, RURAL-FARM, AND RURAL-NONFARM NEGRO POPULATION, CLASSIFIED BY 5-YEAR AGE PERIODS, BY SECTIONS: 1930

AGE	Urban	RURAL			PERCENT DISTRIBUTION	
		Total	Rural-farm	Rural-nonfarm	Urban	Rural
	UNITED STATES					
All ages	**5,193,913**	**6,697,230**	**4,680,523**	**2,016,707**	**100.0**	**100.0**
Under 5 years	427,607	802,599	588,846	213,753	8.2	12.0
5 to 9 years	468,357	900,024	670,165	229,859	9.0	13.4
10 to 14 years	407,867	843,675	645,112	198,563	7.9	12.6
15 to 19 years	447,155	803,373	597,578	205,795	8.6	12.0
20 to 24 years	560,215	642,976	423,663	219,313	10.8	9.6
25 to 29 years	596,430	475,357	291,400	183,957	11.5	7.1
30 to 34 years	496,472	368,042	225,679	142,363	9.6	5.5
35 to 39 years	498,065	392,835	248,319	144,516	9.6	5.9
40 to 44 years	369,429	317,994	205,354	112,640	7.1	4.7
45 to 49 years	316,590	313,475	209,878	103,597	6.1	4.7
50 to 54 years	228,556	276,034	191,244	84,790	4.4	4.1
55 to 59 years	132,940	176,457	123,604	52,853	2.6	2.6
60 to 64 years	95,784	146,385	102,457	43,928	1.8	2.2
65 to 69 years	60,533	94,644	64,749	29,895	1.2	1.4
70 to 74 years	36,650	62,446	41,400	21,046	.7	.9
75 to 79 years	21,327	37,384	24,248	13,136	.4	.6
80 to 84 years	11,666	21,711	14,001	7,710	.4	.3
85 years and over	8,932	17,426	11,145	6,281	.2	.3
Unknown	9,338	4,393	1,681	2,712	.2	.1
	THE NORTH					
All ages	**2,128,329**	**280,890**	**65,301**	**215,289**	**100.0**	**100.0**
Under 5 years	179,197	26,556	6,746	19,810	8.4	9.5
5 to 9 years	180,831	28,550	7,346	21,204	8.5	10.2
10 to 14 years	148,084	26,346	7,322	19,024	7.0	9.4
15 to 19 years	152,777	25,741	6,979	18,762	7.2	9.2
20 to 24 years	215,385	24,121	5,423	18,698	10.1	8.6
25 to 29 years	262,175	23,332	4,102	19,230	12.3	8.3
30 to 34 years	231,322	21,993	3,682	18,311	10.9	7.8
35 to 39 years	224,596	22,122	4,222	17,900	10.6	7.9
40 to 44 years	162,434	18,502	3,889	14,613	7.6	6.6
45 to 49 years	134,231	17,040	3,848	13,192	6.3	6.1
50 to 54 years	92,926	14,174	3,442	10,732	4.4	5.0
55 to 59 years	55,264	10,170	2,642	7,528	2.6	3.6
60 to 64 years	35,578	7,588	2,149	5,439	1.7	2.7
65 to 69 years	22,362	5,446	1,538	3,908	1.1	1.9
70 to 74 years	13,156	3,789	1,031	2,758	.6	1.3
75 to 79 years	7,772	2,513	653	1,860	.4	.9
80 to 84 years	3,903	1,319	302	1,017	.2	.5
85 years and over	2,924	1,071	243	828	.1	.4
Unknown	3,402	517	42	475	.2	.2
	THE SOUTH					
All ages	**2,966,325**	**6,395,252**	**4,608,786**	**1,786,466**	**100.0**	**100.0**
Under 5 years	242,220	774,359	581,424	192,935	8.2	12.1
5 to 9 years	280,569	869,679	662,083	207,596	9.5	13.6
10 to 14 years	253,466	815,654	637,124	178,530	8.5	12.8
15 to 19 years	287,828	776,018	590,038	185,980	9.7	12.1
20 to 24 years	336,686	617,101	417,802	199,299	11.4	9.6
25 to 29 years	324,501	450,207	286,902	163,305	10.9	7.0
30 to 34 years	255,110	344,126	221,611	122,515	8.6	5.4
35 to 39 years	262,337	368,540	243,646	124,894	8.8	5.8
40 to 44 years	197,862	297,742	201,048	96,694	6.7	4.7
45 to 49 years	174,145	294,905	205,601	89,304	5.9	4.6
50 to 54 years	129,403	260,648	187,445	73,203	4.4	4.1
55 to 59 years	73,765	165,541	120,735	44,806	2.5	2.6
60 to 64 years	57,621	138,276	100,145	38,131	1.9	2.2
65 to 69 years	36,491	88,840	63,104	25,736	1.2	1.4
70 to 74 years	22,447	58,442	40,305	18,137	.8	.9
75 to 79 years	13,007	34,724	23,568	11,156	.4	.5
80 to 84 years	7,473	20,326	13,682	6,644	.3	.3
85 years and over	5,785	16,291	10,888	5,403	.2	.3
Unknown	5,609	3,833	1,635	2,198	.2	.1
	THE WEST					
All ages	**99,259**	**21,088**	**6,136**	**14,952**	**100.0**	**100.0**
Under 5 years	6,190	1,684	676	1,008	6.2	8.0
5 to 9 years	6,957	1,795	736	1,059	7.0	8.5
10 to 14 years	6,317	1,675	666	1,009	6.4	7.9
15 to 19 years	6,550	1,614	561	1,053	6.6	7.7
20 to 24 years	8,144	1,754	438	1,316	8.2	8.3
25 to 29 years	9,754	1,818	396	1,422	9.8	8.6
30 to 34 years	10,030	1,923	386	1,537	10.1	9.1
35 to 39 years	11,132	2,173	451	1,722	11.2	10.3
40 to 44 years	9,123	1,750	417	1,333	9.2	8.3
45 to 49 years	8,214	1,530	429	1,101	8.3	7.3
50 to 54 years	6,227	1,212	357	855	6.3	5.7
55 to 59 years	3,911	746	227	519	3.9	3.5
60 to 64 years	2,585	521	163	358	2.6	2.5
65 to 69 years	1,680	358	107	251	1.7	1.7
70 to 74 years	1,047	215	64	151	1.1	1.0
75 to 79 years	548	147	27	120	.6	.7
80 to 84 years	290	66	17	49	.3	.3
85 years and over	223	64	14	50	.2	.3
Unknown	327	43	4	39	.3	.2

TABLE 5.—POPULATION CLASSIFIED BY COLOR AND 5-YEAR AGE PERIODS, FOR THE UNITED STATES: 1930 AND 1920

[Percent not shown where less than one-tenth of 1 percent]

AGE	ALL CLASSES		NEGRO		WHITE		OTHER RACES		PERCENT DISTRIBUTION							
									All classes		Negro		White		Other races	
	1930	1920	1930	1920	1930	1920	1930	1920	1930	1920	1930	1920	1930	1920	1930	1920
All ages	**122,775,046**	**105,710,620**	**11,891,143**	**10,463,131**	**108,864,207**	**94,820,915**	**2,019,696**	**426,574**	**100.0**	**100.0**	**100.0**	**100.0**	**100.0**	**100.0**	**100.0**	**100.0**
Under 5 years	11,444,390	11,573,230	1,230,206	1,143,699	9,927,396	10,373,921	286,788	55,610	9.3	10.9	10.3	10.9	9.1	10.9	14.2	13.0
5 to 9 years	12,607,609	11,398,075	1,368,381	1,266,207	10,956,144	10,087,245	283,084	44,623	10.3	10.8	11.5	12.1	10.1	10.6	14.0	10.5
10 to 14 years	12,004,877	10,641,137	1,251,542	1,236,914	10,546,282	9,369,322	207,053	34,901	9.8	10.1	10.5	11.8	9.7	9.9	10.3	8.2
15 to 19 years	11,552,115	9,430,556	1,250,528	1,083,215	10,111,584	8,314,155	190,003	33,186	9.4	8.9	10.5	10.4	9.3	8.8	9.4	7.8
20 to 24 years	10,870,378	9,277,021	1,203,191	1,054,847	9,466,155	8,185,341	201,032	36,833	8.9	8.8	10.1	10.1	8.7	8.6	10.0	8.6
25 to 29 years	9,833,608	9,086,491	1,071,787	909,739	8,573,696	8,141,690	188,125	35,062	8.0	8.6	9.0	8.7	7.9	8.6	9.3	8.2
30 to 34 years	9,120,421	8,071,193	864,514	697,865	8,109,766	7,338,790	146,141	34,538	7.4	7.6	7.3	6.7	7.4	7.7	7.2	8.1
35 to 39 years	9,208,645	7,775,281	890,900	773,931	8,183,620	6,965,805	134,125	35,545	7.5	7.4	7.5	7.4	7.5	7.3	6.6	8.3
40 to 44 years	7,990,195	6,345,557	687,423	559,701	7,198,507	5,755,547	104,265	30,309	6.5	6.0	5.8	5.3	6.6	6.1	5.2	7.1
45 to 49 years	7,042,279	5,763,620	630,065	551,589	6,322,989	5,188,040	89,225	23,991	5.7	5.5	5.3	5.3	5.8	5.5	4.4	5.6
50 to 54 years	5,975,804	4,734,873	504,590	399,110	5,409,056	4,317,266	62,158	18,497	4.9	4.5	4.2	3.8	5.0	4.6	3.1	4.3
55 to 59 years	4,645,677	3,549,124	309,397	229,980	4,293,107	3,305,671	43,173	13,473	3.8	3.4	2.6	2.2	3.9	3.5	2.1	3.2
60 to 64 years	3,751,221	2,982,548	242,169	200,118	3,476,993	2,771,433	32,059	10,997	3.1	2.8	2.0	1.9	3.2	2.9	1.6	2.6
65 to 69 years	2,770,605	2,068,475	155,177	137,035	2,594,840	1,924,296	20,588	7,144	2.3	2.0	1.3	1.3	2.4	2.0	1.0	1.7
70 to 74 years	1,950,004	1,395,036	99,096	91,579	1,838,050	1,298,738	12,858	4,719	1.6	1.3	.8	.9	1.7	1.4	.6	1.1
75 to 79 years	1,106,390	856,560	58,711	52,352	1,039,862	801,678	7,817	2,530	.9	.8	.5	.5	1.0	.8	.4	.6
80 to 84 years	534,676	402,779	33,377	28,122	496,803	373,066	4,496	1,591	.4	.4	.3	.3	.5	.4	.2	.4
85 to 89 years	205,469	156,539	14,948	12,281	188,414	143,536	2,107	722	.2	.1	.1	.1	.2	.2	.1	.2
90 to 94 years	51,664	39,980	6,332	5,847	44,453	33,713	879	420	------	------	.1	.1	------	------	------	.1
95 to 99 years	11,033	9,579	2,611	2,562	7,981	6,831	441	186	------	------	------	------	------	------	------	------
100 years and over	3,964	4,267	2,467	2,935	1,180	1,168	317	164	------	------	------	------	------	------	------	------
Unknown	94,022	148,699	13,731	23,503	77,329	123,663	2,962	1,533	.1	.1	.1	.2	.1	.1	.1	.4

Table 6.—CUMULATIVE AGE OF THE POPULATION BY SINGLE YEARS UP TO 51 PERCENT, BY COLOR AND NATIVITY, FOR THE UNITED STATES: 1930

[Percent not shown where less than one-tenth of 1 percent]

AGE	ALL CLASSES [1]		NEGRO		NATIVE WHITE-NATIVE PARENTAGE		NATIVE WHITE-FOREIGN OR MIXED PARENTAGE		FOREIGN-BORN WHITE	
	Number	Percent	Number	Percent	Number	Percent	Number	Percent	Number	Percent
All known ages	**122, 681, 024**	**100. 0**	**11, 877, 412**	**100. 0**	**70, 079, 253**	**100. 0**	**25, 351, 042**	**100. 0**	**13, 356, 583**	**100. 0**
Under 1 year	2, 190, 791	1. 8	232, 378	2. 0	1, 549, 340	2. 2	345, 962	1. 4	1, 428	
1 year	4, 355, 356	3. 6	454, 914	3. 8	3, 074, 879	4. 4	704, 645	2. 8	4, 656	
2 years	6, 681, 372	5. 4	707, 499	6. 0	4, 687, 765	6. 7	1, 104, 008	4. 4	10, 110	0. 1
3 years	9, 075, 835	7. 4	971, 813	8. 2	6, 326, 637	9. 0	1, 528, 310	6. 0	17, 785	. 1
4 years	11, 444, 390	9. 3	1, 230, 206	10. 4	7, 939, 165	11. 3	1, 960, 443	7. 7	27, 788	. 2
5 years	13, 949, 640	11. 4	1, 503, 938	12. 7	9, 626, 673	13. 7	2, 432, 211	9. 6	39, 668	. 3
6 years	16, 464, 925	13. 4	1, 785, 654	15. 0	11, 295, 173	16. 1	2, 920, 767	11. 5	56, 597	. 4
7 years	18, 935, 084	15. 4	2, 056, 882	17. 3	12, 917, 963	18. 4	3, 415, 833	13. 5	81, 537	. 6
8 years	21, 539, 299	17. 6	2, 338, 363	19. 7	14, 621, 375	20. 9	3, 947, 872	15. 6	112, 968	. 8
9 years	24, 051, 999	19. 6	2, 598, 587	21. 9	16, 260, 203	23. 2	4, 473, 858	17. 6	149, 479	1. 1
10 years	26, 552, 647	21. 6	2, 874, 691	24. 2	17, 845, 747	25. 5	5, 025, 759	19. 8	185, 887	1. 4
11 years	28, 872, 041	23. 5	3, 096, 575	26. 1	19, 341, 122	27. 6	5, 561, 809	21. 9	212, 456	1. 6
12 years	31, 352, 164	25. 6	3, 360, 254	28. 3	20, 885, 422	29. 8	6, 164, 454	24. 3	238, 985	1. 8
13 years	33, 674, 491	27. 4	3, 596, 669	30. 3	22, 324, 776	31. 9	6, 747, 602	26. 6	265, 949	2. 0
14 years	36, 056, 876	29. 4	3, 850, 129	32. 4	23, 788, 555	33. 9	7, 344, 052	29. 0	297, 215	2. 2
15 years	38, 352, 575	31. 3	4, 090, 566	34. 4	25, 181, 472	35. 9	7, 931, 601	31. 3	335, 639	2. 5
16 years	40, 719, 890	33. 2	4, 348, 291	36. 6	26, 609, 967	38. 0	8, 523, 441	33. 6	386, 716	2. 9
17 years	43, 015, 712	35. 1	4, 593, 276	38. 7	27, 992, 891	39. 9	9, 089, 974	35. 9	451, 986	3. 4
18 years	45, 373, 546	37. 0	4, 862, 407	40. 9	29, 389, 949	41. 9	9, 660, 608	38. 1	532, 072	4. 0
19 years	47, 608, 991	38. 8	5, 100, 657	42. 9	30, 721, 058	43. 8	10, 198, 503	40. 2	621, 845	4. 7
20 years	49, 831, 422	40. 6	5, 359, 204	45. 1	32, 019, 848	45. 7	10, 715, 561	42. 3	728, 764	5. 5
21 years	52, 042, 453	42. 4	5, 587, 508	47. 0	33, 337, 366	47. 6	11, 229, 275	44. 3	845, 274	6. 3
22 years	54, 244, 984	44. 2	5, 836, 899	49. 1	34, 617, 695	49. 4	11, 730, 602	46. 3	974, 258	7. 3
23 years	56, 375, 775	46. 0	6, 071, 391	51. 1	35, 859, 587	51. 2	12, 199, 820	48. 1	1, 118, 379	8. 4
24 years	58, 479, 369	47. 7					12, 647, 159	49. 9	1, 283, 837	9. 6
25 years	60, 565, 784	49. 4					13, 080, 322	51. 6	1, 472, 171	11. 0
26 years	62, 551, 741	51. 0							1, 666, 239	12. 5
27 years									1, 864, 614	14. 0
28 years									2, 085, 781	15. 6
29 years									2, 304, 843	17. 3
30 years									2, 579, 239	19. 3
31 years									2, 765, 622	20. 7
32 years									3, 024, 542	22. 6
33 years									3, 280, 765	24. 6
34 years									3, 551, 673	26. 6
35 years									3, 891, 233	29. 1
36 years									4, 197, 873	31. 4
37 years									4, 492, 897	33. 6
38 years									4, 864, 245	36. 4
39 years									5, 183, 340	38. 8
40 years									5, 609, 608	42. 0
41 years									5, 864, 340	43. 9
42 years									6, 258, 198	46. 9
43 years									6, 569, 834	49. 2
44 years									6, 877, 516	51. 5

[1] Includes "Other races".

Table 7.—NEGRO POPULATION BY 5-YEAR AGE PERIODS, BY SEX, FOR THE UNITED STATES: 1930, 1920, AND 1910

[Percent not shown where less than 1/10 of 1 percent]

AGE	TOTAL			MALE			FEMALE			PERCENT DISTRIBUTION								
										Total			Male			Female		
	1930	1920	1910	1930	1920	1910	1930	1920	1910	1930	1920	1910	1930	1920	1910	1930	1920	1910
All ages	**11, 891, 143**	**10, 463, 131**	**9, 827, 763**	**5, 855, 669**	**5, 209, 436**	**4, 855, 881**	**6, 035, 474**	**5, 253, 695**	**4, 941, 882**	**100. 0**	**100. 0**	**100. 0**	**100. 0**	**100. 0**	**100. 0**	**100. 0**	**100. 0**	**10. 00**
Under 5 years	1, 230, 306	1, 143, 699	1, 263, 288	611, 231	568, 633	629, 320	618, 975	575, 066	633, 968	10. 3	10. 9	12. 9	10. 4	10. 9	12. 9	10. 3	10. 9	12. 8
Under 1 year	232, 378	227, 660	252, 386	115, 388	112, 660	125, 459	116, 990	115, 000	126, 927	2. 0	2. 2	2. 6	2. 0	2. 2	2. 6	1. 9	2. 2	2. 6
1 year	222, 536	210, 558	219, 240	110, 284	104, 664	109, 357	112, 252	105, 894	109, 883	1. 9	2. 0	2. 2	1. 9	2. 0	2. 2	1. 9	2. 0	2. 2
2 years	252, 585	225, 939	260, 037	125, 695	112, 265	130, 191	126, 890	113, 674	129, 845	2. 1	2. 2	2. 6	2. 1	2. 2	2. 7	2. 1	2. 2	2. 6
3 years	264, 314	240, 978	264, 547	130, 378	118, 573	130, 526	133, 936	122, 405	134, 021	2. 2	2. 3	2. 7	2. 2	2. 3	2. 7	2. 2	2. 3	2. 7
4 years	258, 393	238, 564	267, 078	129, 486	120, 471	133, 786	128, 907	118, 093	133, 292	2. 2	2. 3	2. 7	2. 2	2. 3	2. 7	2. 1	2. 2	42. 7
5 to 9 years	1, 368, 381	1, 266, 207	1, 246, 553	679, 748	631, 341	619, 175	688, 633	634, 866	627, 378	11. 5	12. 1	12. 7	11. 6	12. 1	12. 7	11. 4	12. 1	12. 7
10 to 14 years	1, 251, 542	1, 236, 914	1, 155, 266	623, 228	616, 251	578, 074	628, 314	620, 663	577, 192	10. 5	11. 8	11. 8	10. 6	11. 8	11. 8	10. 4	11. 8	11. 7
15 to 19 years	1, 250, 528	1, 083, 215	1, 060, 416	595, 646	513, 416	507, 945	654, 882	569, 799	552, 471	10. 5	10. 4	10. 8	10. 2	9. 9	10. 4	10. 9	10. 8	11. 2
20 to 24 years	1, 203, 191	1, 054, 847	1, 030, 795	553, 622	487, 169	482, 157	649, 569	567, 678	548, 638	10. 1	10. 1	10. 5	9. 5	9. 4	9. 9	10. 8	10. 8	11. 1
25 to 29 years	1, 071, 787	909, 739	881, 227	500, 520	424, 352	421, 805	571, 267	485, 387	459, 422	9. 0	8. 7	9. 0	8. 5	8. 1	8. 6	9. 5	9. 2	9. 3
30 to 34 years	864, 514	697, 865	668, 089	416, 869	331, 579	332, 163	447, 645	366, 286	335, 926	7. 3	6. 7	6. 8	7. 1	6. 4	6. 8	7. 4	7. 0	6. 8
35 to 39 years	890, 900	773, 931	633, 449	430, 472	383, 587	320, 450	460, 428	390, 344	312, 999	7. 5	7. 4	6. 4	7. 4	7. 4	6. 6	7. 6	7. 4	6. 3
40 to 44 years	687, 423	559, 701	455, 413	339, 329	275, 926	229, 680	348, 094	283, 775	225, 733	5. 8	5. 3	4. 6	5. 8	5. 3	4. 7	5. 8	5. 4	4. 6
45 to 49 years	630, 065	551, 589	385, 909	323, 162	320, 506	199, 928	306, 903	231, 083	185, 981	5. 3	5. 3	3. 9	5. 5	6. 2	4. 1	5. 1	4. 4	3. 8
50 to 54 years	504, 590	399, 110	326, 070	277, 532	227, 995	179, 387	227, 058	171, 115	146, 683	4. 2	3. 8	3. 3	4. 7	4. 4	3. 7	3. 8	3. 3	3. 0
55 to 59 years	309, 397	229, 980	209, 622	174, 367	129, 153	115, 090	135, 030	100, 827	94, 532	2. 6	2. 2	2. 1	3. 0	2. 5	2. 4	2. 2	1. 9	1. 9
60 to 64 years	242, 169	200, 118	186, 502	133, 349	112, 137	101, 149	108, 820	87, 981	85, 353	2. 0	1. 9	1. 9	2. 3	2. 2	2. 1	1. 8	1. 7	1. 7
65 to 69 years	155, 177	137, 035	123, 550	82, 843	76, 184	67, 956	72, 334	60, 851	55, 594	1. 3	1. 3	1. 3	1. 4	1. 5	1. 4	1. 2	1. 2	1. 1
70 to 74 years	99, 096	91, 579	78, 839	50, 896	47, 411	40, 584	48, 200	44, 168	38, 255	. 8	. 9	. 8	. 9	. 9	. 8	. 8	. 8	. 8
75 to 79 years	58, 711	52, 352	44, 018	29, 219	27, 172	22, 667	29, 492	25, 180	21, 351	. 5	. 5	. 4	. 5	. 5	. 5	. 5	. 5	. 4
80 to 84 years	33, 377	28, 122	25, 579	15, 343	13, 049	11, 696	18, 034	15, 073	13, 883	. 3	. 3	. 3	. 3	. 3	. 2	. 3	. 3	. 3
85 to 89 years	14, 948	12, 281	11, 166	6, 864	5, 620	5, 164	8, 084	6, 661	6, 002	. 1	. 1	. 1	. 1	. 1	. 1	. 1	. 1	. 1
90 to 94 years	6, 332	5, 847	5, 850	2, 516	2, 340	2, 394	3, 816	3, 507	3, 456	. 1	. 1	. 1	. 1			. 1	. 1	. 1
95 to 99 years	2, 611	2, 562	2, 447	1, 073	1, 087	1, 017	1, 538	1, 475	1, 430									
100 years and over	2, 467	2, 935	2, 675	776	1, 018	1, 004	1, 691	1, 917	1, 671									
Unknown	13, 731	23, 503	31, 040	7, 064	13, 510	17, 076	6, 667	9, 993	13, 964	. 1	. 2	. 3	. 1	. 3	. 3	. 1	. 2	. 3

Table 8.—CUMULATIVE POPULATION AND PERCENT DISTRIBUTION BY AGE GROUPS, BY COLOR, AND SEX, FOR THE UNITED STATES: 1930

[Percent not shown where less than 1/10 of 1 percent]

AGE	ALL CLASSES [1]			NEGRO			WHITE			PERCENT DISTRIBUTION								
										All classes			Negro			White		
	Total	Male	Female	Total	Male	Female	Total	Male	Female	Total	Male	Female	Total	Male	Female	Total	Male	Female
All known ages	**122, 681, 024**	**62, 085, 264**	**60, 595, 760**	**11, 877, 412**	**5, 848, 605**	**6, 028, 807**	**108, 786, 878**	**55, 121, 345**	**53, 665, 533**	**100. 0**	**100. 0**	**100. 0**	**100. 0**	**100. 0**	**100. 0**	**100. 0**	**100. 0**	**100. 0**
Under 5 years	11, 444, 390	5, 806, 174	5, 638, 216	1, 230, 206	611, 231	618, 975	9, 927, 396	5, 051, 131	4, 876, 265	9. 3	9. 4	9. 3	10. 4	10. 5	10. 3	9. 1	9. 2	9. 1
Under 10 years	24, 051, 999	12, 187, 282	11, 864, 717	2, 598, 587	1, 290, 979	1, 307, 608	20, 883, 540	10, 609, 730	10, 273, 810	19. 6	19. 6	19. 6	21. 9	22. 1	21. 7	19. 2	19. 2	19. 1
Under 15 years	36, 056, 876	18, 256, 059	17, 800, 817	3, 850, 129	1, 914, 207	1, 935, 922	31, 429, 822	15, 949, 698	15, 480, 124	29. 4	29. 4	29. 4	32. 4	32. 7	32. 1	28. 9	28. 9	28. 8
Under 20 years	47, 608, 991	24, 013, 884	23, 595, 107	5, 100, 657	2, 509, 853	2, 590, 804	41, 541, 406	21, 013, 673	20, 527, 733	38. 8	38. 7	38. 9	42. 9	42. 9	43. 0	38. 2	38. 1	38. 3
Under 25 years	58, 479, 369	29, 350, 699	29, 128, 670	6, 303, 848	3, 063, 475	3, 240, 373	51, 007, 561	25, 679, 689	25, 327, 872	47. 7	47. 3	48. 1	53. 1	52. 4	53. 7	46. 9	46. 6	47. 2
Under 30 years	68, 312, 977	34, 210, 879	34, 102, 098	7, 375, 635	3, 563, 995	3, 811, 640	59, 581, 257	29, 926, 646	29, 654, 611	55. 7	55. 1	56. 3	62. 1	60. 9	63. 2	54. 8	54. 3	55. 3
Under 35 years	77, 433, 398	38, 772, 665	38, 660, 733	8, 240, 149	3, 980, 864	4, 259, 285	67, 691, 023	33, 985, 825	33, 705, 198	63. 1	62. 5	63. 8	69. 4	68. 1	70. 6	62. 2	61. 7	62. 8
Under 40 years	86, 642, 043	43, 452, 525	43, 189, 518	9, 131, 049	4, 411, 336	4, 719, 713	75, 874, 643	38, 157, 031	37, 717, 612	70. 6	70. 0	71. 3	76. 9	75. 4	78. 3	69. 7	69. 2	70. 3
Under 45 years	94, 632, 238	47, 588, 984	47, 043, 254	9, 818, 472	4, 750, 665	5, 067, 807	83, 073, 150	41, 890, 622	41, 182, 528	77. 1	76. 7	77. 6	82. 7	81. 2	84. 1	76. 4	76. 0	76. 7
Under 50 years	101, 674, 517	51, 260, 908	50, 413, 609	10, 448, 537	5, 073, 827	5, 374, 710	89, 396, 139	45, 184, 401	44, 211, 738	82. 9	82. 6	83. 2	88. 0	86. 8	89. 2	82. 2	82. 0	82. 4
50 years and over	21, 006, 507	10, 824, 356	10, 182, 151	1, 428, 875	774, 778	654, 097	19, 390, 739	9, 936, 944	9, 453, 795	17. 1	17. 4	16. 8	12. 0	13. 2	10. 8	17. 8	18. 0	17. 6
55 years and over	15, 030, 703	7, 692, 711	7, 337, 992	924, 285	497, 246	427, 039	13, 981, 683	7, 121, 663	6, 860, 020	12. 3	12. 4	12. 1	7. 8	8. 5	7. 1	12. 9	12. 9	12. 8
60 years and over	10, 385, 026	5, 266, 719	5, 118, 307	614, 888	322, 879	292, 009	9, 688, 576	4, 896, 595	4, 791, 981	8. 5	8. 5	8. 4	5. 2	5. 5	4. 8	8. 9	8. 9	8. 9
65 years and over	6, 633, 805	3, 325, 211	3, 308, 594	372, 719	189, 530	183, 189	6, 211, 583	3, 107, 585	3, 103, 998	5. 4	5. 4	5. 5	3. 1	3. 2	3. 0	5. 7	5. 6	5. 8
70 years and over	3, 863, 200	1, 907, 399	1, 955, 801	217, 542	106, 687	110, 855	3, 616, 743	1, 784, 762	1, 831, 981	3. 1	3. 1	3. 2	1. 8	1. 8	1. 8	3. 3	3. 2	3. 4
75 years and over	1, 913, 196	915, 752	997, 444	118, 446	55, 791	62, 655	1, 778, 693	851, 414	927, 279	1. 6	1. 5	1. 6	1. 0	1. 0	1. 0	1. 6	1. 5	1. 7
80 years and over	806, 806	368, 148	438, 658	59, 735	26, 572	33, 163	738, 831	337, 488	401, 343	. 7	. 6	. 7	. 5	. 5	. 6	. 7	. 6	. 7
85 years and over	272, 130	117, 010	155, 120	26, 358	11, 229	15, 129	242, 028	104, 026	138, 002	. 2	. 2	. 3	. 2	. 2	. 3	. 2	. 2	. 3
90 years and over	66, 661	26, 117	40, 544	11, 410	4, 365	7, 045	53, 614	21, 038	32, 576	. 1	-----	. 1	. 1	. 1	. 1	-----	-----	. 1
95 years and over	14, 997	5, 686	9, 311	5, 078	1, 849	3, 229	9, 161	3, 504	5, 657	-----	-----	-----	-----	-----	. 1	-----	-----	-----
100 years and over	3, 964	1, 403	2, 561	2, 467	776	1, 691	1, 180	503	677	-----	-----	-----	-----	-----	-----	-----	-----	-----

[1] Includes 2,016,734 persons of known ages belonging to "Other races."

Table 9.—Negro Population Under and Over 25 Years of Age for the Urban, Rural-Farm, and Rural-Non-Farm Areas: 1930 and 1920

AREA	UNDER 25 YEARS		25 YEARS AND OVER [1]	
	1930	**1920**	**1930**	**1920**
	NUMBER			
Total	**6, 303, 848**	**5, 784, 882**	**5, 587, 295**	**4, 673, 249**
Urban	2, 311, 201	1, 578, 448	2, 882, 712	1, 981, 025
Rural	3, 992, 647	4, 206, 434	2, 704, 583	2, 697, 224
Rural-farm	2, 925, 364	3, 229, 324	1, 755, 159	1, 870, 639
Rural-nonfarm	1, 067, 283	977, 110	949, 424	826, 585
	PERCENT DISTRIBUTION			
Total	**100. 0**	**100. 0**	**100. 0**	**100. 0**
Urban	36. 7	27. 3	51. 6	42. 3
Rural	63. 3	72. 7	48. 4	57. 7
Rural-farm	46. 4	55. 8	31. 4	40. 0
Rural-nonfarm	16. 9	16. 9	17. 0	17. 7

[1] Includes "Age unknown."

Table 10.—Number of Males per 100 Females, by 5-Year Age Periods and by Color, for the United States: 1930 and 1920

[Ratio not shown where number of females is less than 100]

AGE	ALL CLASSES		NEGRO		WHITE [1]		OTHER RACES	
	1930	**1920**	**1930**	**1920**	**1930**	**1920**	**1930**	**1920**
All ages	**102. 5**	**104. 0**	**97. 0**	**99. 2**	**102. 7**	**104. 4**	**123. 9**	**156. 6**
Under 5 years	103. 0	102. 5	98. 7	98. 9	103. 6	102. 9	100. 6	102. 2
5 to 9 years	102. 5	101. 9	98. 7	99. 4	103. 0	102. 2	101. 7	101. 3
10 to 14 years	102. 2	101. 8	99. 2	99. 3	102. 6	102. 2	104. 0	105. 3
15 to 19 years	99. 4	98. 3	91. 0	90. 1	100. 3	99. 3	107. 0	126. 7
20 to 24 years	96. 4	95. 3	85. 2	85. 8	97. 2	96. 4	139. 7	137. 1
25 to 29 years	97. 7	99. 8	87. 6	87. 4	98. 2	101. 2	149. 4	126. 5
30 to 34 years	100. 1	104. 8	93. 1	90. 5	100. 2	106. 0	141. 9	197. 7
35 to 39 years	103. 3	110. 1	93. 5	98. 3	104. 0	111. 1	139. 8	251. 5
40 to 44 years	107. 3	107. 4	97. 5	97. 2	107. 8	107. 9	156. 0	274. 0
45 to 49 years	108. 9	117. 8	105. 3	138. 7	108. 7	115. 4	160. 6	291. 9
50 to 54 years	110. 1	115. 3	122. 2	133. 2	108. 5	113. 3	166. 5	306. 4
55 to 59 years	109. 3	112. 6	129. 1	128. 1	107. 6	111. 2	159. 8	318. 2
60 to 64 years	107. 3	112. 9	122. 5	127. 5	106. 0	111. 6	148. 3	272. 4
65 to 69 years	104. 8	109. 2	114. 5	125. 2	104. 0	107. 9	143. 9	212. 0
70 to 74 years	103. 5	102. 6	105. 6	107. 3	103. 2	102. 0	135. 7	170. 4
75 to 79 years	98. 0	96. 2	99. 1	107. 9	97. 7	95. 4	132. 8	125. 9
80 to 84 years	88. 6	85. 7	85. 1	86. 6	88. 7	85. 6	107. 9	98. 6
85 to 89 years	79. 3	79. 4	84. 9	84. 4	78. 7	78. 9	97. 7	91. 0
90 to 94 years	65. 4	69. 4	65. 9	66. 7	65. 1	69. 7	76. 5	83. 4
95 to 99 years	63. 5	67. 8	69. 8	73. 7	60. 3	65. 6	90. 1	69. 1
100 years and over	54. 8	57. 7	45. 9	53. 1	74. 3	66. 6	64. 2	------

[1] Mexicans included with "White" for 1920 and with "Other races" for 1930.

Table 11.—NEGRO POPULATION CLASSIFIED BY SEX AND SINGLE YEARS OF AGE, WITH THE NUMBER OF MALES PER 100 FEMALES: 1930 AND 1920

AGE	1930			1920			INCREASE OR DECREASE (—)			PERCENT INCREASE			MALES PER 100 FEMALES	
	Total	Male	Female	Total	Male	Female	Total	Male	Female	Total	Male	Female	**1930**	**1920**
All ages	**11, 891, 143**	**5, 855, 669**	**6, 035, 474**	**10, 463, 131**	**5, 209, 436**	**5, 253, 695**	**1, 428, 012**	**646, 233**	**781, 779**	**13. 6**	**12. 4**	**14. 9**	**97. 0**	**99. 2**
Under 1 year	232, 378	115, 388	116, 990	227, 660	112, 660	115, 000	4, 718	2, 728	1, 990	2. 1	2. 4	1. 7	98. 6	98. 0
1 year	222, 536	110, 284	112, 252	210, 558	104, 664	105, 894	11, 978	5, 620	6, 358	5. 7	5. 4	6. 0	98. 2	98. 8
2 years	252, 585	125, 695	126, 890	225, 939	112, 265	113, 674	26, 646	13, 430	13, 216	11. 8	12. 0	11. 6	99. 1	98. 8
3 years	264, 314	130, 378	133, 936	240, 978	118, 573	122, 405	23, 336	11, 805	11, 531	9. 7	10. 0	9. 4	97. 3	96. 9
4 years	258, 393	129, 486	128, 907	238, 564	120, 471	118, 093	19, 829	9, 015	10, 814	8. 3	7. 5	9. 2	100. 4	102. 0
5 years	273, 732	136, 447	137, 285	252, 847	126, 220	126, 627	20, 885	10, 227	10, 658	8. 3	8. 1	8. 4	99. 4	99. 7
6 years	281, 716	139, 265	142, 451	263, 756	130, 268	133, 488	17, 960	8, 997	8, 963	6. 8	6. 9	6. 7	97. 8	97. 6
7 years	271, 228	134, 403	136, 825	256, 445	127, 898	128, 547	14, 783	6, 505	8, 278	5. 8	5. 1	6. 4	98. 2	99. 5
8 years	281, 481	139, 759	141, 722	259, 690	129, 691	129, 999	21, 791	10, 068	11, 723	8. 4	7. 8	9. 0	98. 6	99. 8
9 years	260, 224	129, 874	130, 350	233, 469	117, 264	116, 205	26, 755	12, 610	14, 145	11. 5	10. 8	12. 2	99. 6	100. 9

TABLE 11.—NEGRO POPULATION CLASSIFIED BY SEX AND SINGLE YEARS OF AGE, WITH THE NUMBER OF MALES PER 100 FEMALES: 1930 AND 1920—Continued

AGE	1930			1920			INCREASE OR DECREASE (—)			PERCENT INCREASE			MALES PER 100 FEMALES	
	Total	Male	Female	Total	Male	Female	Total	Male	Female	Total	Male	Female	1930	1920
10 years	276, 104	138, 953	137, 151	263, 569	133, 104	130, 465	12, 535	5, 849	6, 686	4. 8	4. 4	5. 1	101. 3	102. 0
11 years	221, 884	110, 329	111, 555	217, 850	108, 849	109, 001	4, 034	1, 480	2, 554	1. 9	1. 4	2. 3	98. 9	99. 9
12 years	263, 679	132, 232	131, 447	274, 482	137, 689	136, 793	−10, 803	−5, 457	−5, 346	−3. 9	−4. 0	−3. 9	100. 6	100. 7
13 years	236, 415	116, 419	119, 996	233, 317	114, 550	118, 767	3, 098	1, 869	1, 229	1. 3	1. 6	1. 0	97. 0	96. 4
14 years	253, 460	125, 295	128, 165	247, 696	122, 059	125, 637	5, 764	3, 236	2, 528	2. 3	2. 7	2. 0	97. 8	97. 2
15 years	240, 437	117, 062	123, 375	214, 082	103, 063	111, 019	26, 355	13, 999	12, 356	12. 3	13. 6	11. 1	94. 9	92. 8
16 years	257, 725	123, 890	133, 835	225, 012	106, 028	118, 984	32, 713	17, 862	14, 851	14. 5	16. 8	12. 5	92. 6	89. 1
17 years	244, 985	120, 994	123, 991	205, 787	100, 059	105, 728	39, 198	20, 935	18, 263	19. 0	20. 9	17. 3	97. 6	94. 6
18 years	269, 131	123, 927	145, 204	229, 442	107, 218	122, 224	39, 689	16, 709	22, 980	17. 3	15. 6	18. 8	85. 3	87. 7
19 years	238, 250	109, 773	128, 477	208, 892	97, 048	111, 844	29, 358	12, 725	16, 633	14. 1	13. 1	14. 9	85. 4	86. 8
20 years	258, 547	110, 375	148, 172	210, 621	87, 789	122, 832	47, 926	22, 586	25, 340	22. 8	25. 7	20. 6	74. 5	71. 5
21 years	228, 304	113, 774	114, 530	200, 919	100, 001	100, 918	27, 385	13, 773	13, 612	13. 6	13. 8	13. 5	99. 3	99. 1
22 years	249, 391	115, 651	133, 740	224, 766	105, 414	119, 352	24, 625	10, 237	14, 388	11. 0	9. 7	12. 1	86. 5	88. 3
23 years	234, 492	107, 116	127, 376	209, 718	96, 854	112, 864	24, 774	10, 262	14, 512	11. 8	10. 6	12. 9	84. 1	85. 8
24 years	232, 457	106, 706	125, 751	208, 823	97, 111	111, 712	23, 634	9, 595	14, 039	11. 3	9. 9	12. 6	84. 9	86. 9
25 years	246, 247	112, 485	133, 762	218, 213	99, 348	118, 865	28, 034	13, 137	14, 897	12. 8	13. 2	12. 5	84. 1	83. 6
26 years	203, 611	92, 974	110, 637	186, 454	85, 079	101, 375	17, 157	7, 895	9, 262	9. 2	9. 3	9. 1	84. 0	83. 9
27 years	194, 922	92, 341	102, 581	172, 090	82, 241	89, 849	22, 832	10, 100	12, 732	13. 3	12. 3	14. 2	90. 0	91. 5
28 years	224, 824	105, 189	119, 635	191, 395	90, 327	101, 068	33, 429	14, 862	18, 567	17. 5	16. 5	18. 4	87. 9	89. 4
29 years	202, 183	97, 531	104, 652	141, 587	67, 357	74, 230	60, 596	30, 174	30, 422	42. 8	44. 8	41. 0	93. 2	90. 7
30 years	281, 746	135, 112	146, 634	215, 229	97, 320	117, 909	66, 517	37, 792	28, 725	30. 9	38. 8	24. 4	92. 1	82. 5
31 years	116, 444	57, 438	59, 006	99, 808	48, 377	51, 431	16, 636	9, 061	7, 575	16. 7	18. 7	14. 7	97. 3	94. 1
32 years	177, 640	85, 060	92, 580	137, 473	63, 499	73, 974	40, 167	21, 561	18, 606	29. 2	34. 0	25. 2	91. 9	85. 8
33 years	140, 590	67, 484	73, 106	117, 713	57, 278	60, 435	22, 877	10, 206	12, 671	19. 4	17. 8	21. 0	92. 3	94. 8
34 years	148, 094	71, 775	76, 319	127, 642	65, 105	62, 537	20, 452	6, 670	13, 782	16. 0	10. 2	22. 0	94. 0	104. 1
35 years	235, 883	116, 691	119, 192	202, 250	99, 798	102, 452	33, 633	16, 893	16, 740	16. 6	16. 9	16. 3	97. 9	97. 4
36 years	155, 019	73, 709	81, 310	139, 256	67, 995	71, 261	15, 763	5, 714	10, 049	11. 3	8. 4	14. 1	90. 7	95. 4
37 years	143, 709	69, 824	73, 885	128, 126	65, 340	62, 786	15, 583	4, 484	11, 099	12. 2	6. 9	17. 7	94. 5	104. 1
38 years	199, 174	94, 642	104, 532	172, 472	84, 917	87, 555	26, 702	9, 725	16, 977	15. 5	11. 5	19. 4	90. 5	97. 0
39 years	157, 115	75, 606	81, 509	131, 827	65, 537	66, 290	25, 288	10, 069	15, 219	19. 2	15. 4	23. 0	92. 8	98. 9
40 years	261, 039	127, 820	133, 219	218, 164	105, 684	112, 480	42, 875	22, 136	20, 739	19. 7	20. 9	18. 4	95. 9	94. 0
41 years	86, 211	44, 264	41, 947	74, 106	38, 327	35, 779	12, 105	5, 937	6, 168	16. 3	15. 5	17. 2	105. 5	107. 1
42 years	146, 701	72, 757	73, 944	112, 426	55, 650	56, 776	34, 275	17, 107	17, 168	30. 5	30. 7	30. 2	98. 4	98. 0
43 years	98, 900	48, 089	50, 811	79, 847	39, 446	40, 401	19, 053	8, 643	10, 410	23. 9	21. 9	25. 8	94. 6	97. 6
44 years	94, 572	46, 399	48, 173	75, 158	36, 819	38, 339	19, 414	9, 580	9, 834	25. 8	26. 0	25. 7	96. 3	96. 0
45 years	192, 073	99, 946	92, 127	156, 361	82, 384	73, 977	35, 712	17, 562	18, 150	22. 8	21. 3	24. 5	108. 5	111. 4
46 years	97, 077	49, 971	47, 106	91, 590	55, 251	36, 339	5, 487	−5, 280	10, 767	6. 0	−9. 6	29. 6	106. 1	152. 0
47 years	94, 389	49, 158	45, 231	95, 933	61, 227	34, 706	−1, 544	−12, 069	10, 525	−1. 6	−19. 7	30. 3	108. 7	176. 4
48 years	134, 805	66, 868	67, 937	116, 772	68, 554	48, 218	18, 033	−1, 686	19, 719	15. 4	−2. 5	40. 9	98. 4	142. 2
49 years	111, 721	57, 219	54, 502	90, 933	53, 090	37, 843	20, 788	4, 129	16, 659	22. 9	7. 8	44. 0	105. 0	140. 3
50 years	208, 328	109, 761	98, 567	160, 796	87, 460	73, 336	47, 532	22, 301	25, 231	29. 6	25. 5	34. 4	111. 4	119. 3
51 years	59, 703	34, 190	25, 513	49, 791	29, 968	19, 823	9, 912	4, 222	5, 690	19. 9	14. 1	28. 7	134. 0	151. 2
52 years	95, 976	54, 643	41, 333	74, 984	44, 699	30, 285	20, 992	9, 944	11, 048	28. 0	22. 2	36. 5	132. 2	147. 6
53 years	65, 962	37, 096	28, 866	53, 145	31, 355	21, 790	12, 817	5, 741	7, 076	24. 1	18. 3	32. 5	128. 5	143. 9
54 years	74, 621	41, 842	32, 779	60, 394	34, 513	25, 881	14, 227	7, 329	6, 898	23. 6	21. 2	26. 7	127. 6	133. 4
55 years	97, 247	54, 239	43, 008	73, 805	40, 652	33, 153	23, 442	13, 587	9, 855	31. 8	33. 4	29. 7	126. 1	122. 6
56 years	65, 235	37, 505	27, 730	49, 398	28, 410	20, 988	15, 837	9, 095	6, 742	32. 1	32. 0	32. 1	135. 3	135. 4
57 years	45, 654	26, 488	19, 166	33, 815	19, 661	14, 154	11, 839	6, 827	5, 012	35. 0	34. 7	35. 4	138. 2	138. 9
58 years	57, 952	31, 923	26, 029	42, 001	22, 945	19, 056	15, 951	8, 978	6, 973	38. 0	39. 1	36. 6	122. 6	120. 4
59 years	43, 309	24, 212	19, 097	30, 961	17, 485	13, 476	12, 348	6, 727	5, 621	39. 9	38. 5	41. 7	126. 8	129. 7
60 years	113, 757	60, 902	52, 855	97, 228	51, 597	45, 631	16, 529	9, 305	7, 224	17. 0	18. 0	15. 8	115. 2	113. 1
61 years	24, 205	13, 818	10, 387	21, 278	12, 587	8, 691	2, 927	1, 231	1, 696	13. 8	9. 8	19. 5	133. 0	144. 8
62 years	37, 399	21, 202	16, 197	29, 432	17, 333	12, 099	7, 967	3, 869	4, 098	27. 1	22. 3	33. 9	130. 9	143. 3
63 years	35, 443	19, 900	15, 543	27, 652	16, 329	11, 323	7, 791	3, 571	4, 220	28. 2	21. 9	37. 3	128. 0	144. 2
64 years	31, 365	17, 527	13, 838	24, 528	14, 291	10, 237	6, 837	3, 236	3, 601	27. 9	22. 6	35. 2	126. 7	139. 6
65 years	70, 261	36, 962	33, 299	60, 903	32, 536	28, 367	9, 358	4, 426	4, 932	15. 4	13. 6	17. 4	111. 0	114. 7
66 years	19, 164	10, 552	8, 612	18, 189	10, 753	7, 436	975	−201	1, 176	5. 4	−1. 9	15. 8	122. 5	144. 6
67 years	20, 269	11, 166	9, 103	18, 721	11, 061	7, 660	1, 548	105	1, 443	8. 3	. 9	18. 8	122. 7	144. 4
68 years	25, 596	13, 447	12, 149	22, 472	12, 365	10, 107	3, 124	1, 082	2, 042	13. 9	8. 8	20. 2	110. 7	122. 3
69 years	19, 887	10, 716	9, 171	16, 750	9, 469	7, 281	3, 137	1, 247	1, 890	18. 7	13. 2	26. 0	116. 8	130. 1
70 years	47, 941	22, 943	24, 998	45, 898	21, 972	23, 926	2, 043	971	1, 072	4. 5	4. 4	4. 5	91. 8	91. 8
71 years	10, 112	5, 530	4, 582	9, 701	5, 315	4, 386	411	215	196	4. 2	4. 0	4. 5	120. 7	121. 2
72 years	17, 074	9, 328	7, 746	14, 844	8, 205	6, 639	2, 230	1, 123	1, 107	15. 0	13. 6	16. 7	120. 4	123. 6
73 years	11, 987	6, 479	5, 508	10, 382	5, 821	4, 561	1, 605	658	947	15. 5	11. 3	20. 8	117. 6	127. 6
74 years	11, 982	6, 616	5, 366	10, 754	6, 098	4, 656	1, 228	518	710	11. 4	8. 5	15. 2	123. 3	131. 0
75 years	26, 409	12, 211	14, 198	24, 370	11, 873	12, 497	2, 039	338	1, 701	8. 4	2. 8	13. 6	86. 0	95. 0
76 years	10, 059	5, 380	4, 679	9, 265	5, 145	4, 120	794	235	559	8. 6	4. 6	13. 6	115. 0	124. 9
77 years	6, 413	3, 566	2, 847	5, 302	3, 015	2, 287	1, 111	551	560	21. 0	18. 3	24. 5	125. 3	131. 8
78 years	9, 611	4, 886	4, 725	8, 185	4, 326	3, 859	1, 426	560	866	17. 4	12. 9	22. 4	103. 4	112. 1
79 years	6, 219	3, 176	3, 043	5, 230	2, 813	2, 417	989	363	626	18. 9	12. 9	25. 9	104. 4	116. 4
80 years	17, 882	7, 474	10, 408	15, 931	6, 916	9, 015	1, 951	558	1, 393	12. 2	8. 1	15. 5	71. 8	76. 7
81 years	3, 498	1, 790	1, 708	2, 984	1, 519	1, 465	514	271	243	17. 2	17. 8	16. 6	104. 8	103. 7
82 years	4, 638	2, 330	2, 308	3, 501	1, 681	1, 821	1, 136	649	487	32. 4	38. 6	26. 7	101. 0	92. 3
83 years	3, 565	1, 837	1, 728	2, 698	1, 373	1, 325	867	464	403	32. 1	33. 8	30. 4	106. 3	103. 6
84 years	3, 794	1, 912	1, 882	3, 007	1, 560	1, 447	787	352	435	26. 2	22. 6	30. 1	101. 6	107. 8
85 years	6, 418	2, 662	3, 756	5, 301	2, 234	3, 067	1, 117	428	689	21. 1	19. 2	22. 5	70. 9	72. 8
86 years	2, 865	1, 444	1, 421	2, 095	1, 041	1, 054	770	403	367	36. 8	38. 7	34. 8	101. 6	98. 8
87 years	2, 274	1, 149	1, 125	1, 977	981	996	297	168	129	15. 0	17. 1	13. 0	102. 1	98. 5
88 years	1, 780	863	917	1, 470	689	781	310	174	136	21. 1	25. 3	17. 4	94. 1	88. 2
89 years	1, 611	746	865	1, 438	675	763	173	71	102	12. 0	10. 5	13. 4	86. 2	88. 5
90 years	2, 914	1, 475	2, 439	3, 637	1, 329	2, 308	277	146	131	7. 6	11. 0	5. 7	60. 5	57. 6
91 years	617	295	322	601	271	330	16	24	−8	2. 7	8. 9	−2. 4	91. 6	82. 1
92 years	731	299	432	665	289	376	66	10	56	9. 9	3. 5	14. 9	69. 2	76. 9
93 years	569	246	323	489	243	246	80	3	77	16. 4	1. 2	31. 3	76. 2	98. 8
94 years	501	201	300	455	208	247	46	−7	53	10. 1	−3. 4	21. 5	67. 0	84. 2
95 years	888	323	565	883	340	543	5	−17	22	. 6	−5. 0	4. 1	57. 2	62. 6
96 years	503	237	266	460	219	241	43	18	25	9. 3	8. 2	10. 4	89. 1	90. 9
97 years	397	182	215	344	146	198	53	36	17	15. 4	24. 7	8. 6	84. 7	73. 7
98 years	524	204	320	556	236	320	−32	−32	---	−5. 8	−13. 6	---	63. 8	73. 8
99 years	299	127	172	319	146	173	−20	−19	−1	−6. 3	−13. 0	−. 1	73. 8	84. 4
100 years and over	2, 467	776	1, 691	2, 935	1, 018	1, 917	−468	−242	−226	−15. 9	−11. 8	−11. 8	45. 9	53. 1
Unknown	13, 731	7, 064	6, 667	23, 503	13, 510	9, 993	−9, 772	−6, 446	−3, 326	−41. 6	−47. 7	−33. 3	106. 0	135. 2

TABLE 12.—URBAN, RURAL-FARM, AND RURAL-NONFARM POPULATION BY 5-YEAR AGE PERIODS, COLOR, AND SEX, FOR THE UNITED STATES: 1930 AND 1920

AREA, SEX, AND AGE	ALL CLASSES		NEGRO		WHITE		OTHER RACES	
	1930	1920	1930	1920	1930	1920	1930	1920
URBAN								
Total, all ages	**68, 954, 823**	**54, 304, 603**	**5, 193, 913**	**3, 559, 473**	**62, 836, 605**	**50, 620, 084**	**924, 305**	**125, 046**
Under 5 years	5, 626, 360	5, 275, 751	427, 607	268, 069	5, 074, 431	4, 995, 277	124, 322	12, 405
5 to 9 years	6, 211, 141	5, 050, 276	468, 357	291, 762	5, 621, 105	4, 751, 102	121, 679	7, 412
10 to 14 years	5, 949, 693	4, 664, 312	407, 867	291, 094	5, 455, 278	4, 368, 076	86, 548	5, 142
15 to 19 years	6, 015, 411	4, 445, 963	447, 155	310, 522	5. 486, 937	4, 127, 762	81, 319	7, 679
20 to 24 years	6, 420, 308	5, 102, 099	560, 215	417, 001	5, 764, 707	4, 672, 551	95, 386	12, 547
25 to 29 years	6, 171, 951	5, 319, 058	596, 430	414, 678	5, 479, 587	4, 891, 160	95, 934	13, 220
30 to 34 years	5, 773, 476	4, 726, 556	496, 472	326, 228	5, 202, 393	4, 386, 394	74, 611	13, 934
35 to 39 years	5, 773, 764	4, 453, 437	498, 065	353, 756	5, 208, 009	4, 085, 805	67, 690	13, 876
40 to 44 years	4, 932, 386	3, 602, 119	369, 429	251, 029	4, 511, 361	3, 339, 865	51, 596	11, 225
45 to 49 years	4, 222, 829	3, 190, 639	316, 590	222, 941	3, 863, 049	2, 959, 292	43, 190	8, 406
50 to 54 years	3, 491, 257	2, 613, 070	228, 556	150, 746	3, 234, 066	2, 455, 550	28, 635	6, 874
55 to 59 years	2, 656, 416	1, 895, 847	132, 940	82, 638	2, 504, 103	1, 808, 184	19, 373	5, 025
60 to 64 years	2, 120, 260	1, 528, 090	95, 784	65, 368	2, 010, 616	1, 459, 086	13, 860	3, 636
65 to 69 years	1, 527, 724	1, 000, 986	60, 533	42, 000	1, 458, 713	957, 304	8, 478	1, 682
70 to 74 years	1, 031, 232	660, 731	36, 650	27, 734	989, 824	632, 056	4, 758	941
75 to 79 years	563, 217	398, 637	21, 327	16, 179	539, 243	382, 188	2, 647	270
80 to 84 years	267, 715	185, 455	11, 666	7, 908	254, 628	177, 434	1, 421	113
85 to 89 years	102, 133		5, 282		96, 223		628	
90 to 94 years	25, 147	92, 742	2, 059	6, 421	22, 879	86, 255	209	66
95 to 99 years	5, 007		852		4, 012		143	
100 and over	1, 360		739		544		77	
Unknown	66, 036	98, 835	9, 338	13, 399	54, 897	84, 843	1, 801	593
Male, all ages	**34, 154, 760**	**27, 203, 312**	**2, 479, 158**	**1, 737, 820**	**31, 162, 570**	**25, 373, 627**	**513, 032**	**91, 865**
Under 5 years	2, 855, 018	2, 662, 585	212, 456	131, 798	2, 580, 231	2, 524, 316	62, 325	6, 471
5 to 9 years	3, 128, 686	2, 531, 575	229, 368	142, 780	2, 838, 298	2, 384, 915	61, 020	3, 880
10 to 14 years	2, 970, 019	2, 313, 652	195, 305	137, 844	2, 731, 149	2, 173, 033	43, 565	2, 775
15 to 19 years	2, 881, 288	2, 130, 053	195, 723	138, 893	2, 644, 165	1, 986, 143	41, 400	5, 017
20 to 24 years	3, 030, 032	2, 421, 604	240, 821	189, 209	2, 733, 702	2, 223, 982	55, 509	8, 413
25 to 29 years	2, 998, 048	2, 635, 308	271, 191	194, 089	2, 669, 001	2, 432, 562	57, 856	8, 657
30 to 34 years	2, 865. 528	2, 421, 943	239. 226	157, 923	2, 581, 974	2, 253, 410	44, 328	10, 610
35 to 39 years	2, 918, 120	2, 329, 406	242, 537	178, 973	2, 635, 619	2, 139, 010	39, 964	11, 423
40 to 44 years	2, 539, 994	1, 849, 460	185, 421	128, 227	2, 322, 735	1, 711, 739	31, 838	9, 494
45 to 49 years	2, 170, 686	1, 685, 492	162, 055	127, 634	1, 982, 403	1, 550, 422	26, 228	7, 436
50 to 54 years	1, 773, 324	1, 351, 300	120, 482	81, 905	1, 635, 241	1, 263, 086	17, 601	6, 309
55 to 59 years	1, 324, 757	961, 623	69, 921	42, 788	1, 243, 257	914, 123	11, 579	4, 712
60 to 64 years	1, 035, 328	765, 374	47, 738	32, 919	979, 540	729, 051	8, 050	3, 404
65 to 69 years	728, 128	484, 551	28, 505	20, 166	694, 767	462, 834	4, 856	1, 551
70 to 74 years	481, 805	306, 332	16, 563	12, 433	462, 473	293, 049	2, 769	850
75 to 79 years	252, 489	177, 802	9, 151	7, 389	241, 828	170, 188	1, 510	225
80 to 84 years	113, 321	77, 167	4, 630	3, 153	107, 973	73, 924	718	90
85 to 89 years	40, 948		2, 132		38, 553		263	
90 to 94 years	9, 013	35, 976	750	2, 280	8, 183	33, 651	80	45
95 to 99 years	1, 762		304		1, 396		62	
100 and over	462		206		232		24	
Unknown	36, 004	62, 109	4, 673	7, 417	29, 844	54, 189	1, 487	503
Female, all ages	**34, 800, 063**	**27, 101, 291**	**2, 714, 755**	**1, 821, 653**	**31, 674, 035**	**25, 246, 457**	**411, 273**	**33, 181**
Under 5 years	2, 771, 342	2, 613, 166	215, 151	136, 271	2, 494, 194	2, 470, 961	61, 997	5, 934
5 to 9 years	3, 082, 455	2, 518, 701	238, 989	148, 982	2, 782, 807	2, 366, 187	60, 659	3, 532
10 to 14 years	2, 979, 674	2, 350, 660	212, 562	153, 250	2, 724, 129	2, 195, 043	42, 983	2, 367
15 to 19 years	3, 134, 123	2, 315, 910	251, 432	171, 629	2, 842, 772	2, 141, 619	39, 919	2, 662
20 to 24 years	3, 390, 276	2, 680, 495	319, 394	227, 792	3, 031, 005	2, 448, 569	39, 877	4, 134
25 to 29 years	3, 173, 903	2, 683, 750	325, 239	220, 589	2, 810, 586	2, 458, 598	38, 078	4, 563
30 to 34 years	2, 907, 948	2, 304, 613	257, 246	168, 305	2, 620, 419	2, 132, 984	30, 283	3, 324
35 to 39 years	2, 855, 644	2, 124, 031	255, 528	174, 783	2, 572, 390	1, 946, 795	27, 726	2, 453
40 to 44 years	2, 392, 392	1, 752, 659	184, 008	122, 802	2, 188, 626	1, 628, 126	19, 758	1, 731
45 to 49 years	2, 052, 143	1, 505, 147	154, 535	95, 307	1, 880, 646	1, 408, 870	16, 962	970
50 to 54 years	1, 717, 933	1, 261, 770	108, 074	68, 841	1, 598, 825	1, 192, 364	11, 034	565
55 to 59 years	1, 331, 659	934, 224	63, 019	39, 850	1, 260, 846	894, 061	7, 794	311
60 to 64 years	1, 084, 932	762, 716	48, 046	32, 449	1, 031, 076	730, 035	5, 810	232
65 to 69 years	799, 596	516, 435	32, 028	21, 834	763, 946	494, 470	3, 622	131
70 to 74 years	549, 427	354, 399	20, 087	15, 301	527, 351	339, 007	1, 989	91
75 to 79 years	310, 728	220, 835	12, 176	8, 790	297, 415	212, 000	1, 137	45
80 to 84 years	154, 394	108, 288	7, 036	4, 755	146, 655	103, 510	703	23
85 to 89 years	61, 185		3, 150		57, 670		365	
90 to 94 years	16, 134	56, 766	1, 309	4, 141	14, 696	52, 604	129	21
95 to 99 years	3, 245		548		2, 616		81	
100 and over	898		533		312		53	
Unknown	30, 032	36, 726	4, 665	5, 982	25, 053	30, 654	314	90

TABLE 12.—URBAN, RURAL-FARM, AND RURAL-NONFARM POPULATION BY 5-YEAR AGE PERIODS, COLOR, AND SEX, FOR THE UNITED STATES: 1930 AND 1920—Continued

AREA, SEX, AND AGE	ALL CLASSES 1930	ALL CLASSES 1920	NEGRO 1930	NEGRO 1920	WHITE 1930	WHITE 1920	OTHER RACES 1930	OTHER RACES 1920
RURAL-FARM								
Total, all ages	**30, 157, 513**	**31, 358, 640**	**4, 680, 523**	**5, 099, 963**	**24, 884, 834**	**26, 072, 800**	**592, 156**	**185, 877**
Under 5 years	3, 341, 426	3, 980, 035	588, 846	681, 209	2, 665, 005	3, 270, 332	87, 575	28, 494
5 to 9 years	3, 779, 692	4, 109, 131	670, 165	767, 200	3, 018, 915	3, 317, 943	90, 612	23, 988
10 to 14 years	3, 740, 947	3, 975, 769	645, 112	752, 871	3, 026, 278	3, 203, 889	69, 557	19, 009
15 to 19 years	3, 420, 969	3, 265, 307	597, 578	592, 847	2, 759, 839	2, 656, 553	63, 552	15, 907
20 to 24 years	2, 434, 241	2, 485, 088	423, 663	435, 197	1, 955, 548	2, 035, 249	55, 030	14, 642
25 to 29 years	1, 819, 078	2, 129, 934	291, 400	325, 992	1, 482, 921	1, 790, 910	44, 757	13, 032
30 to 34 years	1, 671, 506	1, 880, 905	225, 679	248, 512	1, 410, 797	1, 620, 104	35, 030	12, 289
35 to 39 years	1, 787, 982	1, 905, 184	248, 319	288, 476	1, 506, 690	1, 603, 545	32, 973	13, 163
40 to 44 years	1, 644, 222	1, 600, 799	205, 354	214, 860	1, 411, 371	1, 374, 172	27, 497	11, 767
45 to 49 years	1, 561, 391	1, 537, 230	209, 878	236, 917	1, 326, 314	1, 290, 723	25, 199	9, 590
50 to 54 years	1, 397, 989	1, 265, 364	191, 244	180, 826	1, 187, 503	1, 077, 639	19, 242	6, 899
55 to 59 years	1, 109, 510	974, 876	123, 604	107, 444	972, 186	862, 538	13, 720	4, 894
60 to 64 years	887, 854	844, 305	102, 457	98, 957	775, 226	741, 283	10, 171	4, 065
65 to 69 years	647, 665	598, 940	64, 749	69, 064	576, 156	526, 872	6, 760	3, 004
70 to 74 years	457, 508	385, 452	41, 400	44, 523	411, 725	338, 858	4, 383	2, 071
75 to 79 years	258, 785	228, 233	24, 248	24, 506	231, 796	202, 555	2, 741	1, 172
80 to 84 years	123, 160	110, 283	14, 001	13, 782	107, 634	95, 723	1, 525	778
85 to 89 years	47, 245		6, 087		40, 395		763	
90 to 94 years	12, 846	63, 271	2, 798	11, 650	9, 733	50, 905	315	716
95 to 99 years	3, 163		1, 130		1, 890		143	
100 and over	1, 565		1, 130		310		125	
Unknown	8, 769	18, 534	1, 681	5, 130	6, 602	13, 007	486	397
Male, all ages	**15, 864, 375**	**16, 360, 059**	**2, 354, 445**	**2, 553, 234**	**13, 186, 577**	**13, 704, 724**	**323, 353**	**102, 101**
Under 5 years	1, 694, 915	2, 023, 960	292, 985	340, 598	1, 357, 880	1, 669, 067	44, 050	14, 295
5 to 9 years	1, 926, 056	2, 095, 453	336, 463	385, 875	1, 543, 534	1, 697, 598	46, 059	11, 980
10 to 14 years	1, 932, 699	2, 055, 953	329, 346	383, 180	1, 567, 300	1, 663, 077	36, 053	9, 696
15 to 19 years	1, 830, 526	1, 695, 156	301, 727	289, 148	1, 495, 161	1, 397, 626	33, 638	8, 382
20 to 24 years	1, 309, 335	1, 258, 105	204, 272	197, 634	1, 073, 805	1, 052, 939	31, 258	7, 532
25 to 29 years	932, 992	1, 066, 812	135, 841	145, 592	771, 651	915, 022	25, 500	6, 198
30 to 34 years	833, 180	943, 802	103, 852	111, 204	710, 062	825, 492	19, 266	7, 106
35 to 39 years	895, 665	978, 364	113, 332	134, 979	764, 564	835, 135	17, 769	8, 250
40 to 44 years	844, 484	825, 071	95, 265	99, 298	733, 172	718, 079	16, 047	7, 694
45 to 49 years	827, 932	853, 505	105, 737	137, 568	706, 488	709, 640	15, 707	6, 297
50 to 54 years	776, 855	715, 766	110, 150	107, 154	654, 263	604, 106	12, 442	4, 506
55 to 59 years	634, 462	558, 088	74, 602	64, 216	551, 005	490, 709	8, 855	3, 163
60 to 64 years	518, 615	496, 404	61, 992	60, 111	450, 123	433, 771	6, 500	2, 522
65 to 69 years	383, 662	354, 389	38, 742	42, 520	340, 692	310, 061	4, 228	1, 808
70 to 74 years	271, 900	221, 266	23, 700	25, 369	245, 620	194, 730	2, 580	1, 167
75 to 79 years	149, 467	122, 660	13, 508	13, 796	134, 350	108, 243	1, 609	621
80 to 84 years	66, 301	55, 091	7, 090	6, 800	58, 385	47, 938	826	353
85 to 89 years	22, 969		2, 986		19, 575		408	
90 to 94 years	5, 444	29, 555	1, 150	5, 242	4, 158	23, 997	136	316
95 to 99 years	1, 298		483		745		70	
100 and over	546		355		129		62	
Unknown	5, 072	10, 659	867	2, 950	3, 915	7, 494	290	215
Female, all ages	**14, 293, 138**	**14, 998, 581**	**2, 326, 078**	**2, 546, 729**	**11, 698, 257**	**12, 368, 076**	**268, 803**	**83, 776**
Under 5 years	1, 646, 511	1, 956, 075	295, 861	340, 611	1, 307, 125	1, 601, 265	43, 525	14, 199
5 to 9 years	1, 853, 636	2, 013, 678	333, 702	381, 325	1, 475, 381	1, 620, 345	44, 553	12, 008
10 to 14 years	1, 808, 248	1, 919, 816	315, 766	369, 691	1, 458, 978	1, 540, 812	33, 504	9, 313
15 to 19 years	1, 590, 443	1, 570, 151	295, 851	303, 699	1, 264, 678	1, 258, 927	29, 914	7, 525
20 to 24 years	1, 124, 906	1, 226, 983	219, 391	237, 563	881, 743	982, 310	23, 772	7, 110
25 to 29 years	886, 086	1, 063, 122	155, 559	180, 400	711, 270	875, 888	19, 257	6, 834
30 to 34 years	838, 326	937, 103	121, 827	137, 308	700, 735	794, 612	15, 764	5, 183
35 to 39 years	892, 317	926, 820	134, 987	153, 497	742, 126	768, 410	15, 204	4, 913
40 to 44 years	799, 738	775, 728	110, 089	115, 562	678, 199	656, 093	11, 450	4, 073
45 to 49 years	733, 459	683, 725	104, 141	99, 349	619, 826	581, 083	9, 492	3, 293
50 to 54 years	621, 134	549, 598	81, 094	73, 672	533, 240	473, 533	6, 800	2, 393
55 to 59 years	475, 048	416, 788	49, 002	43, 228	421, 181	371, 829	4, 865	1, 731
60 to 64 years	369, 239	347, 901	40, 465	38, 846	325, 103	307, 512	3, 671	1, 543
65 to 69 years	264, 003	244, 551	26, 007	26, 544	235, 464	216, 811	2, 532	1, 196
70 to 74 years	185, 608	164, 186	17, 700	19, 154	166, 105	144, 128	1, 803	904
75 to 79 years	109, 318	105, 573	10, 740	10, 710	97, 446	94, 312	1, 132	551
80 to 84 years	56, 859	55, 192	6, 911	6, 982	49, 249	47, 785	699	425
85 to 89 years	24, 276		3, 101		20, 820		355	
90 to 94 years	7, 402	33, 716	1, 648	6, 408	5, 575	26, 908	179	400
95 to 99 years	1, 865		647		1, 145		73	
100 and over	1, 019		775		181		63	
Unknown	3, 697	7, 875	814	2, 180	2, 687	5, 513	196	182

TABLE 12.—URBAN, RURAL-FARM, AND RURAL-NONFARM POPULATION BY 5-YEAR AGE PERIODS, COLOR, AND SEX, FOR THE UNITED STATES: 1930 AND 1920—Continued

AREA, SEX, AND AGE	ALL CLASSES		NEGRO		WHITE		OTHER RACES	
	1930	1920	1930	1920	1930	1920	1930	1920
RURAL-NONFARM								
Total, all ages	**23,662,710**	**20,047,377**	**2,016,707**	**1,803,695**	**21,142,768**	**18,128,031**	**503,235**	**115,651**
Under 5 years	2,476,604	2,317,444	213,753	194,421	2,187,960	2,108,312	74,891	14,711
5 to 9 years	2,616,776	2,238,668	229,859	207,245	2,316,124	2,018,200	70,793	13,223
10 to 14 years	2,314,237	2,001,056	198,563	192,949	2,064,726	1,797,357	50,948	10,750
15 to 19 years	2,115,735	1,719,286	205,795	179,846	1,864,808	1,529,840	45,132	9,600
20 to 24 years	2,015,829	1,689,834	219,313	202,649	1,745,900	1,477,541	50,616	9,644
25 to 29 years	1,842,579	1,637,499	183,957	169,069	1,611,188	1,459,620	47,434	8,810
30 to 34 years	1,675,439	1,463,732	142,363	123,125	1,496,576	1,332,292	36,500	8,315
35 to 39 years	1,646,899	1,416,660	144,516	131,699	1,468,921	1,276,455	33,462	8,506
40 to 44 years	1,413,587	1,142,639	112,640	93,812	1,275,775	1,041,510	25,172	7,317
45 to 49 years	1,258,059	1,035,751	103,597	91,731	1,133,626	938,025	20,836	5,995
50 to 54 years	1,086,558	856,439	84,790	67,538	987,487	784,177	14,281	4,724
55 to 59 years	879,751	678,401	52,853	39,898	816,818	634,949	10,080	3,554
60 to 64 years	743,107	610,153	43,928	35,793	691,151	571,064	8,028	3,296
65 to 69 years	595,216	468,549	29,895	25,971	559,971	440,120	5,350	2,458
70 to 74 years	461,264	348,853	21,046	19,322	436,501	327,824	3,717	1,707
75 to 79 years	284,388	229,690	13,136	11,667	268,823	216,935	2,429	1,088
80 to 84 years	143,801	107,041	7,710	6,432	134,541	99,909	1,550	700
85 to 89 years	56,091		3,579		51,796		716	
90 to 94 years	13,671	54,352	1,475	5,554	11,841	48,088	355	710
95 to 99 years	2,863		629		2,079		155	
100 and over	1,039		598		326		115	
Unknown	19,217	31,330	2,712	4,974	15,830	25,813	675	543
Male, all ages	**12,117,945**	**10,337,060**	**1,022,066**	**918,382**	**10,814,707**	**9,352,304**	**281,172**	**66,374**
Under 5 years	1,256,241	1,170,916	105,790	96,237	1,113,014	1,067,331	37,437	7,348
5 to 9 years	1,326,366	1,125,973	113,917	102,686	1,176,767	1,016,692	35,682	6,595
10 to 14 years	1,166,059	999,701	98,577	95,227	1,041,519	899,040	25,963	5,434
15 to 19 years	1,046,011	848,583	98,196	85,375	924,649	758,062	23,166	5,146
20 to 24 years	997,448	847,336	108,529	100,326	858,509	741,655	30,410	5,355
25 to 29 years	929,140	836,113	93,488	84,671	806,305	746,717	29,347	4,725
30 to 34 years	863,078	765,038	73,791	62,452	767,143	697,364	22,144	5,222
35 to 39 years	866,075	766,591	74,603	69,635	771,023	691,196	20,449	5,760
40 to 44 years	751,981	611,012	58,643	48,401	677,684	557,594	15,654	5,017
45 to 49 years	673,306	578,553	55,370	55,304	604,888	519,113	13,048	4,136
50 to 54 years	581,466	468,479	46,900	38,936	525,777	426,412	8,789	3,131
55 to 59 years	466,773	360,354	29,844	22,149	430,806	335,829	6,123	2,376
60 to 64 years	387,565	320,022	23,619	19,107	359,347	298,797	4,599	2,118
65 to 69 years	306,022	240,877	15,596	13,498	287,364	225,884	3,062	1,495
70 to 74 years	237,942	178,703	10,633	9,609	225,255	168,137	2,054	957
75 to 79 years	145,648	119,503	6,560	5,987	137,748	112,952	1,340	564
80 to 84 years	71,516	53,645	3,623	3,096	67,104	50,202	789	347
85 to 89 years	26,976		1,746		24,860		370	
90 to 94 years	5,974	25,554	616	2,543	5,193	22,685	165	326
95 to 99 years	1,223		286		860		77	
100 and over	395		215		142		38	
Unknown	10,740	20,107	1,524	3,143	8,750	16,642	466	322
Female, all ages	**11,544,765**	**9,710,317**	**994,641**	**885,313**	**10,328,061**	**8,775,727**	**222,063**	**49,277**
Under 5 years	1,220,363	1,146,528	107,963	98,184	1,074,946	1,040,981	37,454	7,363
5 to 9 years	1,290,410	1,112,695	115,942	104,559	1,139,357	1,001,508	35,111	6,628
10 to 14 years	1,148,178	1,001,355	99,986	97,722	1,023,207	898,317	24,985	5,316
15 to 19 years	1,069,724	870,703	107,599	94,471	940,159	771,778	21,966	4,454
20 to 24 years	1,018,381	842,498	110,784	102,323	887,391	735,886	20,206	4,289
25 to 29 years	913,439	801,386	90,469	84,398	804,883	712,903	18,087	4,085
30 to 34 years	812,361	698,694	68,572	60,673	729,433	634,928	14,356	3,093
35 to 39 years	780,824	650,069	69,913	62,064	697,898	585,259	13,013	2,746
40 to 44 years	661,606	531,627	53,997	45,411	598,091	483,916	9,518	2,300
45 to 49 years	584,753	457,198	48,227	36,427	528,738	418,912	7,788	1,859
50 to 54 years	505,092	387,960	37,890	28,602	461,710	357,765	5,492	1,593
55 to 59 years	412,978	318,047	23,009	17,749	386,012	299,120	3,957	1,178
60 to 64 years	355,542	290,131	20,309	16,686	331,804	272,267	3,429	1,178
65 to 69 years	289,194	227,672	14,299	12,473	272,607	214,236	2,288	963
70 to 74 years	223,322	170,150	10,413	9,713	211,246	159,687	1,663	750
75 to 79 years	138,740	110,187	6,576	5,680	131,075	103,983	1,089	524
80 to 84 years	72,285	53,396	4,087	3,336	67,437	49,707	761	353
85 to 89 years	29,115		1,833		26,936		346	
90 to 94 years	7,697	28,798	859	3,011	6,648	25,403	190	384
95 to 99 years	1,640		343		1,219		78	
100 and over	644		383		184		77	
Unknown	8,477	11,223	1,188	1,831	7,080	9,171	209	221

TABLE 13.—PERCENT DISTRIBUTION BY 5-YEAR AGE PERIODS, BY COLOR, AND SEX, FOR THE URBAN, RURAL-FARM, AND RURAL-NONFARM POPULATION OF THE UNITED STATES: 1930 AND 1920

[Percent not shown where less than 1/10 of 1 percent]

AREA AND AGE	ALL CLASSES						NEGRO				WHITE				OTHER RACES			
	Total		Male		Female		Male		Female		Male		Female		Male		Female	
	1930	1920	1930	1920	1930	1920	1930	1920	1930	1920	1930	1920	1930	1920	1930	1920	1930	1920
URBAN																		
All ages	100.0	100.0	100.0	100.0	100.0	100.0	100.0	100.0	100.0	100.0	100.0	100.0	100.0	100.0	100.0	100.0	100.0	100.0
Under 5 years	8.2	9.7	8.4	9.8	8.0	9.6	8.6	7.6	7.9	7.5	8.3	9.9	7.9	9.8	12.1	7.0	15.1	17.9
5 to 9 years	9.0	9.3	9.2	9.3	8.9	9.3	9.3	8.2	8.8	8.2	9.1	9.4	8.8	9.4	11.9	4.2	14.7	10.6
10 to 14 years	8.6	8.6	8.7	8.5	8.6	8.7	7.9	7.9	7.8	8.4	8.8	8.6	8.6	8.7	8.5	3.0	10.5	7.1
15 to 19 years	8.7	8.2	8.4	7.8	9.0	8.5	7.9	8.0	9.3	9.4	8.5	7.8	9.0	8.5	8.1	5.5	9.7	8.0
20 to 24 years	9.3	9.4	8.9	8.9	9.7	9.9	9.7	10.9	11.8	12.5	8.8	8.8	9.6	9.7	10.8	9.2	9.7	12.5
25 to 29 years	9.0	9.8	8.8	9.7	9.1	9.9	10.9	11.2	12.0	12.1	8.6	9.6	8.9	9.7	11.3	9.4	9.3	13.8
30 to 34 years	8.4	8.7	8.4	8.9	8.4	8 5	9.6	9.1	9.5	9.2	8.3	8.9	8.3	8.4	8.6	11.5	7.4	10.0
35 to 39 years	8.4	8.2	8.5	8.6	8.2	7.8	9.8	10.3	9.4	9.6	8.5	8.4	8.1	7.7	7.8	12.4	6.7	7.4
40 to 44 years	7.2	6.6	7.4	6.8	6.9	6.5	7.5	7.4	6.8	6.7	7.5	6.7	6.9	6.4	6.2	10.3	4.8	5.2
45 to 49 years	6.1	5.9	6.4	6.2	5.9	5.6	6.5	7.3	5.7	5.2	6.4	6.1	5.9	5.6	5.1	8.1	4.1	2.9
50 to 54 years	5.1	4.8	5.2	5.0	4.9	4.7	4.9	4.7	4.0	3.8	5.2	5.0	5.0	4.7	3.4	6.9	2.7	1.7
55 to 59 years	3.9	3.5	3.9	3.5	3.8	3.4	2.8	2.5	2.3	2.2	4.0	3.6	4.0	3.5	2.3	5.1	1.9	.9
60 to 64 years	3.1	2.8	3.0	2.8	3.1	2.8	1.9	1.9	1.8	1.8	3.1	2.9	3.3	2.9	1.6	3.7	1.4	.7
65 to 69 years	2.2	1.8	2.1	1.8	2.3	1.9	1.1	1.2	1.2	1.2	2.2	1.8	2.4	2.0	.9	1.7	.9	.4
70 to 74 years	1.5	1.2	1.4	1.1	1.6	1.3	.7	.7	.7	.8	1.5	1.2	1.7	1.3	.5	.9	.5	.3
75 to 79 years	.8	.7	.7	.7	.9	.8	.4	.4	.4	.5	.8	.7	.9	.8	.3	.2	.3	.1
80 to 84 years	.4	.3	.3	.3	.4	.4	.2	.2	.3	.3	.3	.3	.5	.4	.1	.1	.2	.1
85 years and over	.2	.2	.2	.1	.2	.2	.1	.1	.2	.2	.2	.1	.2	.2	.1	-------	.2	.1
Unknown	.1	.2	.1	.2	.1	.1	.2	.4	.2	.3	.1	.2	.1	.1	.3	.5	.1	.3
RURAL-FARM																		
All ages	100.0	100.0	100.0	100.0	100.0	100.0	100.0	100.0	100.0	100.0	100.0	100.0	100.0	100.0	100.0	100.0	100.0	100.0
Under 5 years	11.1	12.7	10.7	12.4	11.5	13.0	12.4	13.3	12.7	13.4	10.3	12.2	11.2	12.9	13.6	14.0	16.2	16.9
5 to 9 years	12.5	13.1	12.1	12.8	13.0	13.4	14.3	15.1	14.3	15.0	11.7	12.4	12.6	13.1	14.2	11.7	16.6	14.3
10 to 14 years	12.4	12.7	12.2	12.6	12.7	12.8	14.0	15.0	13.6	14.5	11.9	12.1	12.5	12.5	11.1	9.5	12.5	11.1
15 to 19 years	11.3	10.4	11.5	10.4	11.1	10.5	12.8	11.3	12.7	11.9	11.3	10.2	10.8	10.2	10.4	8.2	11.1	9.0
20 to 24 years	8.1	7.9	8.3	7.7	7.9	8.2	8.7	7.7	9.4	9.3	8.1	7.7	7.5	7.9	9.7	7.4	8.8	8.5
25 to 29 years	6.0	6.8	5.9	6.5	6.2	7.1	5.8	5.7	6.7	7.1	5.9	6.7	6.1	7.1	7.9	6.1	7.2	8.2
30 to 34 years	5.5	6.0	5.3	5.8	5.9	6.2	4.4	4.4	5.2	5.4	5.4	6.0	6.0	6.4	6.0	7.0	5.9	6.2
35 to 39 years	5.9	6.1	5.6	6.0	6.2	6.2	4.8	5.3	5.8	6.0	5.8	6.1	6.3	6.2	5.5	8.1	5.7	5.9
40 to 44 years	5.5	5.1	5.3	5.0	5.6	5.2	4.0	3.9	4.7	4.5	5.6	5.2	5.8	5.3	5.0	7.5	4.3	4.9
45 to 49 years	5.2	4.9	5.2	5.2	5.1	4.6	4.5	5.4	4.5	3.9	5.4	5.2	5.3	4.7	4.9	6.2	3.5	3.9
50 to 54 years	4.6	4.0	4.9	4.4	4.3	3.7	4.7	4.2	3.5	2.9	5.0	4.4	4.6	3.8	3.8	4.4	2.5	2.9
55 to 59 years	3.7	3.1	4.0	3.4	3.3	2.8	3.2	2.5	2.1	1.7	4.2	3.6	3.6	3.0	2.7	3.1	1.8	2.1
60 to 64 years	2.9	2.7	3.3	3.0	2.6	2.3	2.6	2.4	1.7	1.5	3.4	3.2	2.8	2.5	2.0	2.5	1.4	1.8
65 to 69 years	2.1	1.9	2.4	2.2	1.8	1.6	1.6	1.7	1.1	1.0	2.6	2.3	2.0	1.8	1.3	1.8	.9	1.4
70 to 74 years	1 5	1.2	1.7	1.4	1.3	1.1	1.0	1.0	.8	.8	1.9	1.4	1.4	1.2	.8	1.1	.7	1.1
75 to 79 years	.9	.7	.9	.7	.8	.7	.6	.5	.5	.4	1.0	.8	.8	.8	.5	.6	.4	.7
80 to 84 years	.4	.4	.4	.3	.4	.4	.3	.3	.3	.3	.4	.3	.4	.4	.3	.3	.3	.5
85 years and over	.2	.2	.2	.2	.2	.2	.2	.2	.3	.3	.2	.2	.2	.2	.2	.3	.2	.5
Unknown	-------	.1	-------	.1	-------	.1	-------	.1	-------	.1	-------	.1	-------	-------	.1	.2	.1	.2
RURAL-NONFARM																		
All ages	100.0	100.0	100.0	100.0	100.0	100.0	100.0	100.0	100.0	100.0	100.0	100.0	100.0	100.0	100.0	100.0	100.0	100.0
Under 5 years	10.5	11.6	10.4	11.3	10.6	11.8	10.4	10.5	10.9	11.1	10.3	11.4	10.4	11.9	13.3	11.1	16.9	14.9
5 to 9 years	11.1	11.2	10.9	10.9	11.2	11.5	11.1	11.2	11.7	11.8	10.9	10.9	11.0	11.4	12.7	9.9	15.8	13.5
10 to 14 years	9.8	10.0	9.6	9.7	9.9	10.3	9.6	10.4	10.1	11.0	9.6	9.6	9.9	10.2	9.2	8.2	11.3	10.8
15 to 19 years	8.9	8.6	8.6	8.2	9.3	9.0	9.6	9.3	10.8	10.7	8.5	8.1	9.1	8.8	8.2	7.8	9.9	9.0
20 to 24 years	8.5	8.4	8.2	8.2	8.8	8.7	10.6	10.9	11.1	11.6	7.9	7.9	8.6	8.4	10.8	8.1	9.1	8.7
25 to 29 years	7.8	8.2	7.7	8.1	7.9	8.3	9.1	9.2	9.1	9.5	7.5	8.0	7.8	8.1	10.4	7.1	8.1	8.3
30 to 34 years	7.1	7.3	7.1	7.4	7.0	7.2	7.2	6.8	6.9	6.9	7.1	7.5	7.1	7.2	7.9	7.9	6.5	6.3
35 to 39 years	7.0	7.1	7.1	7.4	6.8	6.7	7.3	7.6	7.0	7.0	7.1	7.4	6.8	6.7	7.3	8.7	5.9	5.6
40 to 44 years	6.0	5.7	6.2	5.9	5.7	5.5	5.7	5.3	5.4	5.1	6.3	6.0	5.8	5.5	5.6	7.6	4.3	4.7
45 to 49 years	5.3	5.2	5.6	5.6	5.1	4.7	5.4	6.0	4.8	4.1	5.6	5.6	5.1	4.8	4.6	6.2	3.5	3.8
50 to 54 years	4.6	4.3	4.8	4.5	4.4	4.0	4.6	4.2	3.8	3.2	4.9	4.6	4.5	4.1	3.1	4.7	2.5	3.2
55 to 59 years	3.7	3.4	3.9	3.5	3.6	3.3	2.9	2.4	2.3	2.0	4.0	3.6	3.7	3.4	2.2	3.6	1.8	2.4
60 to 64 years	3.1	3.0	3.2	3.1	3.1	3.0	2.3	2.1	2.0	1.9	3.3	3.2	3.2	3.1	1.6	3.2	1.5	2.4
65 to 69 years	2.5	2.3	2.5	2.3	2.5	2.3	1.5	1.5	1.4	1.4	2.7	2.4	2.6	2.4	1.1	2.3	1.0	2.0
70 to 74 years	1.9	1.7	2.0	1.7	1.9	1.8	1.0	1.0	1.0	1.1	2.1	1.8	2.0	1.8	.7	1.4	.7	1.5
75 to 79 years	1.2	1.1	1.2	1.2	1.2	1.1	.6	.7	.7	.6	1.3	1.2	1.3	1.2	.5	.8	.5	1.1
80 to 84 years	.6	.5	.6	.5	.6	.5	.4	.3	.4	.4	.6	.5	.7	.6	.3	.5	.3	.7
85 years and over	.3	.3	.3	.2	.3	.3	.3	.3	.3	.3	.3	.2	.3	.3	.2	.5	.3	.8
Unknown	.1	.2	.1	.2	.1	.1	.1	.3	.1	.2	.1	.2	.1	.1	.2	.5	.1	.4

139634

Table 14.—NEGRO POPULATION IN URBAN, RURAL-FARM, AND RURAL-NONFARM AREAS, BY SEX AND SINGLE YEARS OF AGE, AND BY SEX, FOR THE UNITED STATES: 1930

AGE	TOTAL			URBAN			RURAL								
							Total			Rural-farm			Rural-nonfarm		
	Total	Male	Female	Total	Male	Female	Total	Male	Female	Total	Male	Female	Total	Male	Female
All ages	11,891,143	5,855,669	6,035,474	5,193,913	2,479,158	2,714,755	6,697,230	3,376,511	3,320,719	4,680,523	2,354,445	2,326,078	2,016,707	1,022,066	994,641
Under 1 year	232,378	115,388	116,990	80,218	40,023	40,195	152,160	75,365	76,795	110,957	54,895	56,062	41,203	20,470	20,733
1 year	222,536	110,284	112,252	78,443	38,876	39,567	144,093	71,408	72,685	105,203	52,166	53,037	38,890	19,242	19,648
2 years	252,585	125,695	126,890	87,964	43,766	44,198	164,621	81,929	82,692	120,381	60,029	60,352	44,240	21,900	22,340
3 years	264,314	130,378	133,936	91,693	45,207	46,486	172,621	85,171	87,450	127,338	62,995	64,343	45,283	22,176	23,107
4 years	258,393	129,486	128,907	89,289	44,584	44,705	169,104	84,902	84,202	124,967	62,900	62,067	44,137	22,002	22,135
5 years	273,732	136,447	137,285	93,266	45,997	47,269	180,466	90,450	90,016	133,777	67,300	66,477	46,689	23,150	23,539
6 years	281,716	139,265	142,451	94,540	46,222	48,318	187,176	93,043	94,133	139,483	69,462	70,021	47,693	23,581	24,112
7 years	271,228	134,403	136,825	93,056	45,609	47,447	178,172	88,794	89,378	132,669	66,279	66,390	45,503	22,515	22,988
8 years	281,481	139,759	141,722	95,792	46,574	49,218	185,689	93,185	92,504	138,782	69,857	68,925	46,907	23,328	23,579
9 years	260,224	129,874	130,350	91,703	44,966	46,737	168,521	84,908	83,613	125,454	63,565	61,889	43,067	21,343	21,724
10 years	276,104	138,953	137,151	91,812	44,863	46,949	184,292	94,090	90,202	139,287	71,633	67,654	45,005	22,457	22,548
11 years	221,884	110,329	111,555	75,332	36,480	38,852	146,552	73,849	72,703	111,160	56,461	54,699	35,392	17,388	18,004
12 years	263,679	132,232	131,447	82,980	40,012	42,968	180,699	92,220	88,479	139,360	71,508	67,852	41,339	20,712	20,627
13 years	236,415	116,419	119,996	76,537	35,959	40,578	159,878	80,460	79,418	122,396	61,991	60,405	37,482	18,469	19,013
14 years	253,460	125,295	128,165	81,206	37,991	43,215	172,254	87,304	84,950	132,909	67,753	65,156	39,345	19,551	19,794
15 years	240,437	117,062	123,375	78,616	35,886	42,730	161,821	81,176	80,645	123,860	62,801	61,059	37,961	18,375	19,586
16 years	257,725	123,890	133,835	85,606	38,230	47,376	172,119	85,660	86,459	131,278	66,288	64,990	40,841	19,372	21,469
17 years	244,985	120,994	123,991	86,706	39,077	47,629	158,279	81,917	76,362	118,400	62,478	55,922	39,879	19,439	20,440
18 years	269,131	123,927	145,204	98,809	41,470	57,339	170,322	82,457	87,865	125,213	61,391	63,822	45,109	21,066	24,043
19 years	238,250	109,773	128,477	97,418	41,060	56,358	140,832	68,713	72,119	98,827	48,769	50,058	42,005	19,944	22,061
20 years	258,547	110,375	148,172	107,867	42,631	65,236	150,680	67,744	82,936	104,711	47,085	57,626	45,969	20,659	25,310
21 years	228,304	113,774	114,530	100,872	46,097	54,775	127,432	67,677	59,755	85,767	45,866	39,901	41,665	21,811	19,854
22 years	249,391	115,651	133,740	115,619	50,038	65,581	133,772	65,613	68,159	87,531	42,357	45,174	46,241	23,256	22,985
23 years	234,492	107,116	127,376	116,178	49,858	66,320	118,314	57,258	61,056	75,080	35,651	39,429	43,234	21,607	21,627
24 years	232,457	106,706	125,751	119,679	52,197	67,482	112,778	54,509	58,269	70,574	33,313	37,261	42,204	21,196	21,008
25 years	246,247	112,485	133,762	128,362	56,533	71,829	117,885	55,952	61,933	74,600	34,369	40,231	43,285	21,583	21,702
26 years	203,611	92,974	110,637	110,463	48,593	61,870	93,148	44,381	48,767	57,890	26,796	31,094	35,258	17,585	17,673
27 years	194,922	92,341	102,581	110,437	51,040	59,397	84,485	41,301	43,184	51,286	24,242	27,044	33,199	17,059	16,140
28 years	224,824	105,189	119,635	126,356	57,849	68,507	98,468	47,340	51,128	60,320	27,862	32,458	38,148	19,478	18,670
29 years	202,183	97,531	104,652	120,812	57,176	63,636	81,371	40,355	41,016	47,304	22,572	24,732	34,067	17,783	16,284
30 years	281,746	135,112	146,634	154,997	73,706	81,291	126,749	61,406	65,343	78,976	36,589	42,387	47,773	24,817	22,956
31 years	116,444	57,438	59,006	69,642	34,348	35,294	46,802	23,090	23,712	27,611	13,045	14,566	19,191	10,045	9,146
32 years	177,640	85,060	92,580	105,077	50,516	54,561	72,563	34,544	38,019	44,023	19,877	24,146	28,540	14,667	13,873
33 years	140,590	67,484	73,106	81,125	38,999	42,126	59,465	28,485	30,980	36,551	16,772	19,779	22,914	11,713	11,201
34 years	148,094	71,775	76,319	85,631	41,657	43,974	62,463	30,118	32,345	38,518	17,569	20,949	23,945	12,549	11,396
35 years	235,883	116,691	119,192	130,572	65,448	65,124	105,311	51,243	54,068	66,699	30,637	36,062	38,612	20,606	18,006
36 years	155,019	73,709	81,310	85,612	41,163	44,449	69,407	32,546	36,861	43,887	19,632	24,255	25,520	12,914	12,606
37 years	143,709	69,824	73,885	81,486	39,966	41,520	62,223	29,858	32,365	39,171	17,932	21,239	23,052	11,926	11,126
38 years	199,174	94,642	104,532	110,295	52,629	57,666	88,889	42,023	46,866	57,002	25,698	31,304	31,887	16,325	15,562
39 years	157,115	75,606	81,509	90,100	43,331	46,769	67,005	32,265	34,740	41,560	19,433	22,127	25,445	12,832	12,613
40 years	261,039	127,820	133,219	135,246	67,525	67,721	125,793	60,295	65,498	82,278	37,453	44,825	43,515	22,842	20,673
41 years	86,211	44,264	41,947	47,984	24,923	23,061	38,227	19,341	18,886	24,237	11,877	12,360	13,990	7,464	6,526
42 years	146,701	72,757	73,944	82,120	41,499	40,621	64,581	31,258	33,323	40,973	18,922	22,051	23,608	12,336	11,272
43 years	98,900	48,089	50,811	54,665	27,030	27,635	44,235	21,059	23,176	28,224	13,059	15,165	16,011	8,000	8,011
44 years	94,572	46,399	48,173	49,414	24,444	24,970	45,158	21,955	23,203	29,642	13,954	15,688	15,516	8,001	7,515
45 years	192,073	99,946	92,127	95,780	50,805	44,975	96,293	49,141	47,152	64,860	31,991	32,869	31,433	17,150	14,283
46 years	97,077	49,971	47,106	48,345	24,595	23,750	48,732	25,376	23,356	32,702	16,725	15,977	16,030	8,651	7,379
47 years	94,389	49,158	45,231	47,736	24,613	23,123	46,653	24,545	22,108	31,257	16,286	14,971	15,396	8,259	7,137
48 years	134,805	66,868	67,937	66,428	32,933	33,495	68,377	33,935	34,442	46,011	22,387	23,624	22,366	11,548	10,818
49 years	111,721	57,219	54,502	58,301	29,109	29,192	53,420	28,110	25,310	35,048	18,348	16,700	18,372	9,762	8,610
50 years	208,328	109,761	98,567	92,298	47,470	44,828	116,030	62,291	53,739	80,218	43,212	37,006	35,812	19,079	16,733
51 years	59,703	34,190	25,513	27,796	15,172	12,624	31,907	19,018	12,889	21,950	13,319	8,631	9,957	5,699	4,258
52 years	95,976	54,643	41,333	44,590	24,067	20,523	51,386	30,576	20,810	35,642	21,543	14,099	15,744	9,033	6,711
53 years	65,962	37,096	28,866	30,154	15,852	14,302	35,808	21,244	14,564	24,940	15,149	9,791	10,868	6,095	4,773
54 years	74,621	41,842	32,779	33,718	17,921	15,797	40,903	23,921	16,982	28,494	16,927	11,567	12,409	6,994	5,415
55 years	97,247	54,239	43,008	40,096	21,161	18,935	57,151	33,078	24,073	40,414	23,698	16,716	16,737	9,380	7,357
56 years	65,235	37,505	27,730	27,973	14,998	12,975	37,262	22,507	14,755	26,157	16,177	9,980	11,105	6,330	4,775
57 years	45,654	26,488	19,166	20,076	10,799	9,277	25,578	15,689	9,889	17,803	11,188	6,615	7,775	4,501	3,274
58 years	57,952	31,923	26,029	24,767	12,790	11,977	33,185	19,133	14,052	23,344	13,678	9,666	9,841	5,455	4,386
59 years	43,309	24,212	19,097	20,028	10,173	9,855	23,281	14,039	9,242	15,886	9,861	6,025	7,395	4,178	3,217
60 years	113,757	60,902	52,855	43,635	21,290	22,345	70,122	39,612	30,510	49,390	28,594	20,796	20,732	11,018	9,714
61 years	24,205	13,818	10,387	10,297	5,358	4,939	13,908	8,460	5,448	9,694	6,126	3,568	4,214	2,334	1,880
62 years	37,399	21,202	16,197	15,423	7,908	7,515	21,976	13,294	8,682	15,194	9,573	5,621	6,782	3,721	3,061
63 years	35,443	19,900	15,543	14,048	7,015	7,033	21,395	12,885	8,510	14,950	9,382	5,568	6,445	3,503	2,942
64 years	31,365	17,527	13,838	12,381	6,167	6,214	18,984	11,360	7,624	13,229	8,317	4,912	5,755	3,043	2,712
65 years	70,261	36,962	33,299	26,450	12,327	14,123	43,811	24,635	19,176	30,416	17,739	12,677	13,395	6,896	6,499
66 years	19,164	10,552	8,612	7,302	3,570	3,732	11,862	6,982	4,880	8,145	5,010	3,135	3,717	1,972	1,745
67 years	20,269	11,166	9,103	8,279	3,936	4,343	11,990	7,230	4,760	8,047	5,100	2,947	3,943	2,130	1,813
68 years	25,596	13,447	12,149	9,878	4,573	5,305	15,718	8,874	6,844	10,742	6,295	4,447	4,976	2,579	2,397
69 years	19,887	10,716	9,171	8,624	4,099	4,525	11,263	6,617	4,646	7,399	4,598	2,801	3,864	2,019	1,845
70 years	47,941	22,943	24,998	17,035	7,206	9,829	30,906	15,737	15,169	20,673	10,925	9,748	10,233	4,812	5,421
71 years	10,112	5,530	4,582	4,114	1,999	2,115	5,998	3,531	2,467	3,888	2,374	1,514	2,110	1,157	953
72 years	17,074	9,328	7,746	6,487	3,127	3,360	10,587	6,201	4,386	7,015	4,314	2,701	3,572	1,887	1,685
73 years	11,987	6,479	5,508	4,590	2,127	2,463	7,397	4,352	3,045	4,839	2,989	1,850	2,558	1,363	1,195
74 years	11,982	6,616	5,366	4,424	2,104	2,320	7,558	4,512	3,046	4,985	3,098	1,887	2,573	1,414	1,159
75 years	26,409	12,211	14,198	8,992	3,568	5,424	17,407	8,633	8,774	11,513	5,897	5,616	5,894	2,736	3,158
76 years	10,059	5,380	4,679	3,778	1,754	2,024	6,281	3,626	2,655	4,065	2,459	1,606	2,216	1,167	1,049
77 years	6,413	3,566	2,847	2,384	1,134	1,250	4,029	2,432	1,597	2,564	1,648	916	1,465	784	681
78 years	9,611	4,886	4,725	3,550	1,577	1,973	6,071	3,319	2,752	3,855	2,161	1,694	2,216	1,158	1,058
79 years	6,219	3,176	3,043	2,623	1,118	1,505	3,596	2,058	1,538	2,251	1,343	908	1,345	715	630
80 years	17,882	7,474	10,408	5,787	2,106	3,681	12,095	5,368	6,727	8,022	3,653	4,369	4,073	1,715	2,358
81 years	3,498	1,790	1,708	1,354	577	777	2,144	1,213	931	1,308	777	531	836	436	400
82 years	4,638	2,330	2,308	1,741	756	985	2,897	1,574	1,323	1,817	1,027	790	1,080	547	533
83 years	3,565	1,837	1,728	1,375	589	786	2,190	1,248	942	1,380	817	563	810	431	379
84 years	3,794	1,912	1,882	1,409	602	807	2,385	1,310	1,075	1,474	816	658	911	494	417
85 years	6,418	2,662	3,756	2,073	773	1,300	4,345	1,889	2,456	2,803	1,227	1,576	1,542	662	880
86 years	2,865	1,444	1,421	1,086	458	628	1,779	986	793	1,101	615	486	678	371	307
87 years	2,274	1,149	1,125	887	382	505	1,387	767	620	841	459	382	546	308	238
88 years	1,780	863	917	638	284	354	1,142	579	563	712	365	347	430	214	216
89 years	1,611	746	865	598	235	363	1,013	511	502	630	320	310	383	191	192
90 years	3,914	1,475	2,439	1,162	410	752	2,752	1,065	1,687	1,859	714	1,145	893	351	542
91 years	617	295	322	221	91	130	396	204	192	239	123	116	157	81	76
92 years	731	299	432	268	98	170	463	201	262	291	123	168	172	78	94
93 years	569	246	323	216	75	141	353	171	182	215	115	100	138	56	82
94 years	501	201	300	192	76	116	309	125	184	194	75	119	115	50	65
95 years	888	323	565	288	93	195	600	230	370	398	153	245	202	77	125
96 years	503	237	266	156	63	93	347	174	173	219	97	122	128	77	51
97 years	397	182	215	126	48	78	271	134	137	179	88	91	92	46	46
98 years	524	204	320	175	58	117	349	146	203	219	94	125	130	52	78
99 years	299	127	172	107	42	65	192	85	107	115	51	64	77	34	43
100 and over	2,467	776	1,691	739	206	533	1,728	570	1,158	1,130	355	775	598	215	383
Unknown	13,731	7,064	6,667	9,338	4,673	4,665	4,393	2,391	2,002	1,681	867	814	2,712	1,524	1,188

99576—35——7

TABLE 15.—NEGRO POPULATION CLASSIFIED BY 5-YEAR AGE PERIODS, BY DIVISIONS, AND STATES: 1930 AND 1920

[Percent not shown where less than 1/10 of 1 percent]

AGE PERIOD	UNITED STATES		NEW ENGLAND DIVISION		MIDDLE ATLANTIC DIVISION		EAST NORTH CENTRAL DIVISION		WEST NORTH CENTRAL DIVISION		SOUTH ATLANTIC DIVISION	
	1930	1920	1930	1920	1930	1920	1930	1920	1930	1920	1930	1920
All ages	**11, 891, 143**	**10, 463, 131**	**94, 086**	**79, 051**	**1, 052, 899**	**600, 183**	**930, 450**	**514, 554**	**331, 784**	**278, 521**	**4, 421, 388**	**4, 325, 120**
Under 5 years	1, 230, 206	1, 143, 699	8, 915	7, 415	93, 251	47, 306	78, 446	36, 991	25, 141	19, 689	490, 017	527, 394
5 to 9 years	1, 368, 381	1, 266, 207	9, 452	6, 365	91, 773	44, 846	80, 378	37, 434	27, 778	21, 555	567, 507	576, 032
10 to 14 years	1, 251, 542	1, 236, 914	8, 184	5, 920	74, 250	42, 370	66, 849	36, 095	25, 146	22, 367	529, 828	549, 327
15 to 19 years	1, 250, 528	1, 083, 215	7, 340	5, 745	77, 480	44, 555	67, 451	37, 914	26, 247	22, 333	521, 795	471, 573
20 to 24 years	1, 203, 191	1, 054, 847	7, 322	7, 818	111, 164	69, 331	91, 637	57, 944	29, 383	26, 661	444, 981	432, 646
25 to 29 years	1, 071, 787	909, 739	7, 911	8, 307	132, 852	73, 415	112, 929	64, 317	31, 815	29, 592	348, 820	341, 706
30 to 34 years	864, 514	697, 865	7, 948	7, 234	114, 472	61, 970	101, 232	52, 949	29, 673	25, 943	271, 640	255, 853
35 to 39 years	890, 900	773, 931	8, 399	7, 781	108, 151	66, 277	98, 513	56, 008	31, 655	27, 916	288, 155	286, 222
40 to 44 years	687, 423	559, 701	7, 010	6, 138	77, 467	46, 960	69, 968	38, 416	26, 491	21, 113	229, 900	210, 501
45 to 49 years	630, 065	551, 589	6, 522	5, 437	63, 096	39, 169	57, 705	34, 026	23, 948	19, 097	207, 302	202, 557
50 to 54 years	504, 590	399, 110	5, 205	3, 761	43, 924	25, 037	39, 689	22, 396	18, 282	13, 858	181, 281	157, 149
55 to 59 years	309, 397	229, 980	3, 479	2, 283	25, 538	13, 733	24, 335	13, 149	12, 082	8, 612	107, 864	89, 012
60 to 64 years	242, 169	200, 118	2, 497	1, 776	16, 185	9, 641	15, 837	9, 731	8, 647	6, 727	88, 723	82, 002
65 to 69 years	155, 177	137, 035	1, 644	1, 199	9, 923	6, 244	10, 206	6, 410	6, 035	4, 646	57, 650	56, 033
70 to 74 years	99, 096	91, 579	971	780	5, 755	3, 989	6, 425	4, 396	3, 794	3, 294	37, 814	37, 907
75 to 79 years	58, 711	52, 352	607	500	3, 313	2, 326	3, 827	2, 846	2, 538	2, 161	21, 505	20, 253
80 to 84 years	33, 377	28, 122	332	199	1, 603	1, 047	1, 876	1, 255	1, 411	1, 051	12, 153	10, 956
85 to 89 years	14, 948	12, 281	130	104	697	440	973	632	734	435	5, 200	4, 570
90 to 94 years	6, 332	5, 847	58	27	242	177	341	194	238	205	2, 253	2, 298
95 to 99 years	2, 611	2, 562	16	17	84	61	131	100	86	105	912	955
100 and over	2, 467	2, 935	10	9	66	63	118	94	71	92	855	1, 100
Unknown	13, 731	23, 503	133	236	1, 613	1, 226	1, 584	1, 257	589	1, 069	5, 233	9, 074
Percent	**100. 0**	**100. 0**	**100. 0**	**100. 0**	**100. 0**	**100. 0**	**100. 0**	**100. 0**	**100. 0**	**100. 0**	**100. 0**	**100. 0**
Under 5 years	10. 3	10. 9	9. 5	9. 4	8. 9	7. 9	8. 4	7. 2	7. 6	7. 1	11. 1	12. 2
5 to 9 years	11. 5	12. 1	10. 0	8. 1	8. 7	7. 5	8. 6	7. 3	8. 4	7. 7	12. 8	13. 3
10 to 14 years	10. 5	11. 8	8. 7	7. 5	7. 1	7. 1	7. 2	7. 0	7. 6	8. 0	12. 0	12. 7
15 to 19 years	10. 5	10. 4	7. 8	7. 3	7. 4	7. 4	7. 2	7. 4	7. 9	8. 0	11. 8	10. 9
20 to 24 years	10. 1	10. 1	7. 8	9. 9	10. 6	11. 6	9. 8	11. 3	8. 9	9. 6	10. 1	10. 0
25 to 29 years	9. 0	8. 7	8. 4	10. 5	12. 6	12. 2	12. 1	12. 5	9. 6	10. 6	7. 9	7. 9
30 to 34 years	7. 3	6. 7	8. 4	9. 2	10. 9	10. 3	10. 9	10. 3	8. 9	9. 3	6. 1	5. 9
35 to 39 years	7. 5	7. 4	8. 9	9. 8	10. 3	11. 0	10. 6	10. 9	9. 5	10. 0	6. 5	6. 6
40 to 44 years	5. 8	5. 3	7. 5	7. 8	7. 4	7. 8	7. 5	7. 5	8. 0	7. 6	5. 2	4. 9
45 to 49 years	5. 3	5. 3	6. 9	6. 9	6. 0	6. 5	6. 2	6. 6	7. 2	6. 9	4. 7	4. 7
50 to 54 years	4. 2	3. 8	5. 5	4. 8	4. 2	4. 2	4. 3	4. 4	5. 5	5. 0	4. 1	3. 6
55 to 59 years	2. 6	2. 2	3. 7	2. 9	2. 4	2. 3	2. 6	2. 6	3. 6	3. 1	2. 4	2. 1
60 to 64 years	2. 0	1. 9	2. 7	2. 2	1. 5	1. 6	1. 7	1. 9	2. 6	2. 4	2. 0	1. 9
65 to 69 years	1. 3	1. 3	1. 7	1. 5	. 9	. 1	1. 1	1. 2	1. 8	1. 7	1. 3	1. 3
70 to 74 years	. 8	. 9	1. 0	1. 0	. 5	. 7	. 7	. 9	1. 1	1. 2	. 9	. 9
75 to 79 years	. 5	. 5	. 6	. 6	. 3	. 4	. 4	. 6	. 8	. 8	. 5	. 5
80 to 84 years	. 3	. 3	. 4	. 3	. 2	. 2	. 2	. 2	. 4	. 4	. 3	. 3
85 and over	. 2	. 2	. 2	. 2	. 1	. 1	. 2	. 2	. 3	. 3	. 2	. 2
Unknown	. 1	. 2	. 1	. 3	. 2	. 2	. 2	. 2	. 2	. 4	. 1	. 2

AGE PERIOD	EAST SOUTH CENTRAL DIVISION		WEST SOUTH CENTRAL DIVISION		MOUNTAIN DIVISION		PACIFIC DIVISION		ALABAMA		ARIZONA	
	1930	1920	1930	1920	1930	1920	1930	1920	1930	1920	1930	1920
All ages	**2, 658, 238**	**2, 523, 532**	**2, 281, 951**	**2, 063, 579**	**30, 225**	**30, 801**	**90, 122**	**47, 790**	**944, 834**	**900, 652**	**10, 749**	**8, 005**
Under 5 years	288, 162	277, 670	238, 400	222, 582	2, 084	1, 540	5, 790	3, 112	107, 836	104, 155	793	333
5 to 9 years	317, 125	321, 148	265, 616	253, 977	2, 149	1, 520	6, 603	3, 330	117, 708	122, 493	831	303
10 to 14 years	294, 215	320, 568	245, 077	255, 596	2, 027	1, 485	5, 965	3, 186	108, 934	118, 268	727	263
15 to 19 years	296, 706	269, 917	245, 345	226, 382	2, 055	1, 733	6, 109	3, 063	109, 216	96, 998	788	338
20 to 24 years	270, 538	242, 842	238, 268	208, 509	2, 567	5, 008	7, 331	4, 088	97, 073	86, 094	1, 128	1, 856
25 to 29 years	220, 896	202, 326	204, 992	179, 893	2, 763	5, 223	8, 809	4, 960	77, 518	69, 766	1, 163	1, 899
30 to 34 years	167, 458	151, 527	160, 138	134, 222	2, 901	3, 277	9, 052	4, 890	55, 559	50, 445	1, 178	969
35 to 39 years	177, 034	172, 751	165, 688	148, 247	3, 340	3, 090	9, 965	5, 639	59, 120	58, 801	1, 295	721
40 to 44 years	137, 640	124, 216	128, 064	105, 627	2, 664	2, 334	8, 219	4, 396	45, 142	40, 546	901	499
45 to 49 years	139, 118	134, 874	122, 630	110, 666	2, 470	1, 998	7, 274	3, 765	54, 154	52, 064	747	359
50 to 54 years	117, 720	100, 065	91, 050	72, 822	1, 919	1, 323	5, 520	2, 699	37, 718	33, 619	489	194
55 to 59 years	73, 471	58, 496	57, 971	42, 297	1, 170	768	3, 487	1, 630	23, 164	18, 778	267	113
60 to 64 years	60, 362	52, 321	46, 812	36, 271	842	526	2, 264	1, 123	19, 674	17, 170	193	49
65 to 69 years	38, 621	36, 290	29, 060	25, 144	536	355	1, 502	714	12, 689	11, 795	105	43
70 to 74 years	25, 246	24, 395	17, 829	16, 171	330	205	932	442	8, 247	8, 200	58	18
75 to 79 years	15, 071	14, 235	11, 155	9, 639	184	134	511	258	4, 884	4, 555	33	21
80 to 84 years	9, 214	8, 002	6, 432	5, 409	87	66	269	137	3, 076	2, 757	15	6
85 to 89 years	3, 992	3, 489	3, 060	2, 504	41	32	131	75	1, 300	1, 116	7	----------
90 to 94 years	1, 775	1, 662	1, 359	1, 251	20	9	46	24	617	564	4	1
95 to 99 years	727	737	628	568	6	10	21	9	267	260	----------	1
100 and over	704	810	621	752	8	6	14	9	257	298	1	----------
Unknown	2, 443	5, 191	1, 766	5, 050	62	159	308	241	681	1, 910	26	19
Percent	**100. 0**	**100. 0**	**100. 0**	**100. 0**	**100. 0**	**100. 0**	**100. 0**	**100. 0**	**100. 0**	**100. 0**	**100. 0**	**100. 0**
Under 5 years	10. 8	11. 0	10. 4	10. 8	6. 9	5. 0	6. 4	6. 5	11. 4	11. 6	7. 4	4. 2
5 to 9 years	11. 9	12. 7	11. 6	12. 3	7. 1	4. 9	7. 3	7. 0	12. 5	13. 6	7. 7	3. 8
10 to 14 years	11. 1	12. 7	10. 7	12. 4	6. 7	4. 8	6. 6	6. 7	11. 5	13. 1	6. 8	3. 3
15 to 19 years	11. 2	10. 7	10. 8	11. 0	6. 8	5. 6	6. 8	6. 4	11. 6	10. 8	7. 3	4. 2
20 to 24 years	10. 2	9. 6	10. 4	10. 1	8. 5	16. 3	8. 1	8. 6	10. 3	9. 6	10. 5	23. 2
25 to 29 years	8. 3	8. 0	9. 0	8. 7	9. 1	17. 0	9. 8	10. 4	8. 2	7. 7	10. 8	23. 7
30 to 34 years	6. 3	6. 0	7. 0	6. 5	9. 6	10. 6	10. 0	10. 2	5. 9	5. 6	11. 0	12. 1
35 to 39 years	6. 7	6. 8	7. 3	7. 2	11. 1	10. 0	11. 1	11. 8	6. 3	6. 5	12. 0	9. 0
40 to 44 years	5. 2	4. 9	5. 6	5. 1	8. 8	7. 6	9. 1	9. 2	4. 8	4. 5	8. 4	6. 2
45 to 49 years	5. 2	5. 3	5. 4	5. 4	8. 2	6. 5	8. 1	7. 9	5. 7	5. 8	6. 9	4. 5
50 to 54 years	4. 4	4. 0	4. 0	3. 5	6. 3	4. 3	6. 1	5. 6	4. 0	3. 7	4. 5	2. 4
55 to 59 years	2. 8	2. 3	2. 5	2. 0	3. 9	2. 5	3. 9	3. 4	2. 5	2. 1	2. 5	1. 4
60 to 64 years	2. 3	2. 1	2. 1	1. 8	2. 8	1. 7	2. 5	2. 3	2. 1	1. 9	1. 8	. 6
65 to 69 years	1. 5	1. 4	1. 3	1. 2	1. 8	1. 2	1. 7	1. 5	1. 3	1. 3	1. 0	. 5
70 to 74 years	. 9	1. 0	. 8	. 8	1. 1	. 7	1. 0	. 9	. 9	. 9	. 5	. 2
75 to 79 years	. 6	. 6	. 5	. 5	. 6	. 4	. 6	. 5	. 5	. 5	. 3	. 3
80 to 84 years	. 3	. 3	. 3	. 3	. 3	. 2	. 3	. 3	. 3	. 3	. 1	. 1
85 and over	. 3	. 3	. 2	. 2	. 2	. 2	. 2	. 2	. 3	. 2	. 1	----------
Unknown	. 1	. 2	. 1	. 2	. 2	. 5	. 3	. 5	. 1	. 2	. 2	. 2

TABLE 15.—NEGRO POPULATION CLASSIFIED BY 5-YEAR AGE PERIODS, BY DIVISIONS, AND STATES: 1930 AND 1920—Continued

[See note at head of this table]

AGE PERIOD	ARKANSAS		CALIFORNIA		COLORADO		CONNECTICUT		DELAWARE		DISTRICT OF COLUMBIA	
	1930	1920	1930	1920	1930	1920	1930	1920	1930	1920	1930	1920
All ages	**478,463**	**472,220**	**81,048**	**38,763**	**11,828**	**11,318**	**29,354**	**21,046**	**32,602**	**30,335**	**132,068**	**109,966**
Under 5 years	49,957	51,274	5,283	2,596	773	693	2,969	1,873	2,787	2,776	10,006	7,774
5 to 9 years	55,233	57,543	6,028	2,776	775	716	2,900	1,732	3,248	2,961	10,838	8,410
10 to 14 years	52,911	59,434	5,422	2,663	757	780	2,347	1,658	2,985	3,010	9,484	8,432
15 to 19 years	52,545	52,308	5,565	2,562	783	848	2,316	1,634	2,985	2,893	10,675	9,703
20 to 24 years	49,256	46,624	6,711	3,399	892	970	2,669	2,275	2,988	3,033	14,406	12,550
25 to 29 years	40,164	40,184	8,168	4,080	995	1,111	3,017	2,258	2,819	2,628	14,989	12,095
30 to 34 years	31,431	29,342	8,312	3,959	1,049	1,027	2,632	1,873	2,477	2,089	12,360	9,762
35 to 39 years	33,161	33,346	9,052	4,500	1,224	1,255	2,669	1,985	2,715	2,318	12,154	11,022
40 to 44 years	26,153	23,655	7,309	3,441	1,025	1,015	2,116	1,559	2,137	1,973	9,563	8,502
45 to 49 years	27,917	28,486	6,381	2,971	1,077	932	1,721	1,403	1,937	1,864	8,920	7,650
50 to 54 years	21,509	17,868	4,733	2,116	851	700	1,410	995	1,804	1,483	6,944	4,989
55 to 59 years	13,400	10,180	2,926	1,252	567	394	863	572	1,139	1,009	4,001	2,690
60 to 64 years	9,931	8,099	1,935	924	383	312	708	437	931	791	2,785	2,353
65 to 69 years	6,115	5,684	1,270	594	292	186	440	314	704	573	1,942	1,436
70 to 74 years	3,874	3,467	811	348	186	121	244	185	417	372	1,123	1,076
75 to 79 years	2,255	1,955	453	212	96	75	159	144	270	210	613	554
80 to 84 years	1,304	998	227	107	46	38	88	49	135	91	357	283
85 to 89 years	622	469	112	62	19	19	41	29	67	29	172	139
90 to 94 years	254	215	40	19	7	6	13	7	22	15	51	49
95 to 99 years	108	101	19	8	6	5	4	3	12	5	25	16
100 and over	121	133	12	9	5	4	3	3	3	--------	8	13
Unknown	242	855	279	165	20	111	25	58	20	212	652	468
Percent	**100.0**	**100.0**	**100.0**	**100.0**	**100.0**	**100.0**	**100.0**	**100.0**	**100.0**	**100.0**	**100.0**	**100.0**
Under 5 years	10.4	10.9	6.5	6.7	6.5	6.1	10.1	8.9	8.5	9.2	7.6	7.1
5 to 9 years	11.5	12.2	7.4	7.2	6.6	6.3	9.9	8.2	10.0	9.8	8.2	7.6
10 to 14 years	11.1	12.6	6.7	6.9	6.4	6.9	8.0	7.9	9.2	9.9	7.2	7.7
15 to 19 years	11.0	11.1	6.9	6.6	6.6	7.5	7.9	7.8	9.2	9.5	8.1	8.8
20 to 24 years	10.3	9.9	8.3	8.8	7.5	8.6	9.1	10.8	9.2	10.0	10.9	11.4
25 to 29 years	8.4	8.5	10.1	10.5	8.4	9.8	10.3	10.7	8.6	8.7	11.3	11.0
30 to 34 years	6.6	6.2	10.3	10.2	8.9	9.1	9.0	8.9	7.6	6.9	9.4	8.9
35 to 39 years	6.9	7.1	11.2	11.6	10.3	11.1	9.1	9.4	8.3	7.6	9.2	10.0
40 to 44 years	5.5	5.0	9.0	8.9	8.7	9.0	7.2	7.4	6.6	6.5	7.2	7.7
45 to 49 years	5.8	6.0	7.9	7.7	9.1	8.2	5.9	6.7	5.9	6.1	6.8	7.0
50 to 54 years	4.5	3.8	5.8	5.5	7.2	6.2	4.8	4.7	5.5	4.9	5.3	4.5
55 to 59 years	2.8	2.2	3.6	3.2	4.8	3.5	2.9	2.7	3.5	3.3	3.0	2.4
60 to 64 years	2.1	1.7	2.4	2.4	3.2	2.8	2.4	2.1	2.9	2.6	2.1	2.1
65 to 69 years	1.3	1.2	1.6	1.5	2.5	1.6	1.5	1.5	2.2	1.9	1.5	1.3
70 to 74 years	.8	.7	1.0	.9	1.6	1.1	.8	.9	1.3	1.2	.9	1.0
75 to 79 years	.5	.4	.6	.5	.8	.7	.5	.7	.8	.7	.5	.5
80 to 84 years	.3	.2	.3	.3	.4	.3	.3	.2	.4	.3	.3	.3
85 and over	.2	.2	.2	.3	.3	.3	.2	.2	.3	.2	.2	.2
Unknown	.1	.2	.3	.4	.2	1.0	.1	.3	.1	.7	.5	.4

AGE PERIOD	FLORIDA		GEORGIA		IDAHO		ILLINOIS		INDIANA		IOWA	
	1930	1920	1930	1920	1930	1920	1930	1920	1930	1920	1930	1920
All ages	**431,828**	**329,487**	**1,071,125**	**1,206,365**	**668**	**920**	**328,972**	**182,274**	**111,982**	**80,810**	**17,380**	**19,005**
Under 5 years	40,441	33,264	116,016	145,332	30	55	25,378	12,333	9,142	5,922	1,391	1,550
5 to 9 years	45,450	37,774	134,026	161,906	39	51	25,760	12,736	9,967	6,527	1,563	1,553
10 to 14 years	42,116	37,116	131,393	159,704	35	48	22,111	12,516	8,477	6,374	1,408	1,492
15 to 19 years	43,355	33,408	134,216	135,056	40	52	23,363	12,969	8,746	6,582	1,414	1,518
20 to 24 years	48,402	33,896	112,334	121,625	40	78	33,264	19,575	10,184	8,399	1,363	1,786
25 to 29 years	45,950	29,672	82,252	95,914	45	114	41,279	22,821	11,583	8,735	1,352	2,032
30 to 34 years	34,403	23,665	61,392	68,616	68	105	36,531	19,513	10,802	7,464	1,361	1,714
35 to 39 years	34,832	26,898	66,898	76,102	84	125	35,905	21,136	10,841	8,011	1,516	1,795
40 to 44 years	26,752	19,222	51,337	53,058	83	66	25,862	14,797	8,393	5,822	1,327	1,371
45 to 49 years	23,856	19,534	45,526	52,270	56	77	21,756	12,676	7,324	5,257	1,291	1,273
50 to 54 years	17,203	12,729	49,591	48,147	49	65	14,686	7,967	5,799	4,017	1,061	977
55 to 59 years	10,208	6,886	26,412	24,428	31	33	8,765	4,468	3,838	2,438	787	605
60 to 64 years	7,566	5,301	23,612	23,201	27	18	5,697	3,243	2,[illegible]	1,855	566	469
65 to 69 years	4,850	3,553	14,496	15,065	16	17	3,594	2,021	1,754	1,306	392	323
70 to 74 years	2,760	2,316	9,443	9,963	6	5	2,126	1,375	1,140	830	246	200
75 to 79 years	1,577	1,301	5,652	5,316	13	6	1,237	869	668	570	157	132
80 to 84 years	883	733	3,115	3,115	3	2	585	408	311	252	84	67
85 to 89 years	393	314	1,369	1,322	2	--------	325	208	167	117	47	38
90 to 94 years	179	149	642	707	1	--------	115	66	57	34	10	11
95 to 99 years	77	68	258	295	--------	1	46	43	25	18	7	5
100 and over	100	86	264	424	--------	--------	46	47	16	18	5	4
Unknown	475	1,602	881	1,799	--------	2	541	487	309	262	32	90
Percent	**100.0**	**100.0**	**100.0**	**100.0**	**100.0**	**100.0**	**100.0**	**100.0**	**100.0**	**100.0**	**100.0**	**100.0**
Under 5 years	9.4	10.1	10.8	12.0	4.5	6.0	7.7	6.8	8.2	7.3	8.0	8.2
5 to 9 years	10.5	11.5	12.5	13.7	5.8	5.5	7.8	7.0	8.9	8.1	9.0	8.2
10 to 14 years	9.8	11.3	12.3	13.2	5.2	5.2	6.7	6.9	7.6	7.9	8.1	7.9
15 to 19 years	10.0	10.1	12.5	11.2	6.0	5.7	7.1	7.1	7.8	8.1	8.1	8.0
20 to 24 years	11.2	10.3	10.5	10.1	6.0	8.5	10.1	10.7	9.1	10.4	7.8	9.4
25 to 29 years	10.6	9.0	7.7	8.0	6.7	12.4	12.5	12.5	10.3	10.8	7.8	10.7
30 to 34 years	8.0	7.2	5.7	5.7	10.2	11.4	11.1	10.7	9.6	9.2	7.8	9.0
35 to 39 years	8.1	8.2	6.2	6.3	12.6	13.6	10.9	11.6	9.7	9.9	8.7	9.4
40 to 44 years	6.2	5.8	4.8	4.4	12.4	7.2	7.9	8.1	7.5	7.2	7.6	7.2
45 to 49 years	5.5	5.9	4.3	4.3	8.4	8.4	6.6	7.0	6.5	6.5	7.4	6.7
50 to 54 years	4.0	3.9	4.6	4.0	7.3	7.1	4.5	4.4	5.2	5.0	6.1	5.1
55 to 59 years	2.4	2.1	2.5	2.0	4.6	3.6	2.7	2.5	3.4	3.0	4.5	3.2
60 to 64 years	1.8	1.6	2.2	1.9	4.0	2.0	1.7	1.8	2.2	2.3	3.3	2.5
65 to 69 years	1.1	1.1	1.4	1.2	2.4	1.8	1.1	1.1	1.6	1.6	2.3	1.7
70 to 74 years	.6	.7	.9	.8	.9	.5	.6	.8	1.0	1.0	1.4	1.1
75 to 79 years	.4	.4	.5	.4	1.9	.7	.4	.5	.6	.7	.9	.7
80 to 84 years	.2	.2	.3	.3	.4	.2	.2	.2	.3	.3	.5	.4
85 and over	.2	.2	.2	.2	.4	.1	.2	.2	.2	.2	.4	.3
Unknown	.1	.5	.1	.1	--------	.2	.2	.3	.3	.3	.2	.5

TABLE 15.—NEGRO POPULATION CLASSIFIED BY 5-YEAR AGE PERIODS, BY DIVISIONS, AND STATES: 1930 AND 1920—Continued

[See note at head of this table]

AGE PERIOD	KANSAS		KENTUCKY		LOUISIANA		MAINE		MARYLAND		MASSACHUSETTS	
	1930	1920	1930	1920	1930	1920	1930	1920	1930	1920	1930	1920
All ages	**66,344**	**57,925**	**226,040**	**235,938**	**776,326**	**700,257**	**1,096**	**1,310**	**276,379**	**244,479**	**52,365**	**45,466**
Under 5 years	5,182	4,693	18,587	20,468	84,986	77,296	107	113	27,006	24,145	4,708	4,308
5 to 9 years	6,019	5,066	21,824	22,813	93,082	86,599	89	106	29,564	25,509	5,301	3,555
10 to 14 years	5,608	5,191	20,290	23,015	84,800	87,272	100	93	25,627	25,010	4,698	3,302
15 to 19 years	5,434	4,990	20,762	21,592	81,293	75,502	74	103	25,417	23,293	4,018	3,189
20 to 24 years	5,486	5,346	19,816	22,526	79,550	68,945	56	131	27,411	24,297	3,798	4,485
25 to 29 years	5,554	5,398	18,202	20,988	69,041	59,965	81	112	25,509	22,291	4,035	4,926
30 to 34 years	5,473	4,597	16,792	17,198	52,188	45,468	70	122	21,826	17,990	4,421	4,318
35 to 39 years	5,713	4,844	18,268	18,962	56,356	51,060	91	109	21,949	19,411	4,769	4,611
40 to 44 years	5,018	3,991	15,572	14,955	43,748	37,057	76	80	17,710	15,341	4,016	3,570
45 to 49 years	4,512	3,765	15,066	15,248	41,319	36,372	93	82	15,753	14,375	3,874	3,169
50 to 54 years	3,841	2,984	12,641	11,872	30,364	24,088	67	58	12,793	10,691	3,060	2,138
55 to 59 years	2,745	1,924	8,447	7,892	20,098	14,396	50	51	8,060	6,828	2,084	1,284
60 to 64 years	1,953	1,592	6,842	6,321	15,133	12,322	45	53	6,312	5,459	1,393	969
65 to 69 years	1,433	1,182	5,016	4,759	9,768	8,590	33	39	4,315	3,789	930	645
70 to 74 years	939	916	3,489	3,133	6,089	5,729	29	23	2,824	2,662	549	413
75 to 79 years	672	699	2,086	1,971	3,912	3,542	19	21	1,521	1,543	332	250
80 to 84 years	387	258	1,169	969	2,259	2,075	10	5	889	716	175	105
85 to 89 years	213	126	578	445	1,074	955	2	4	345	293	68	51
90 to 94 years	57	55	200	179	467	472	1	-------	123	98	31	17
95 to 99 years	23	30	84	80	238	204	-------	1	37	49	9	11
100 and over	24	29	51	60	211	234	1	1	31	27	4	5
Unknown	58	249	258	492	350	2,114	2	3	1,357	662	92	145
Percent	**100.0**	**100.0**	**100.0**	**100.0**	**100.0**	**100.0**	**100.0**	**100.0**	**100.0**	**100.0**	**100.0**	**100.0**
Under 5 years	7.8	8.1	8.2	8.7	10.9	11.0	9.8	8.6	9.8	9.9	9.0	9.5
5 to 9 years	9.1	8.7	9.7	9.7	12.0	12.4	8.1	8.1	10.7	10.4	10.1	7.8
10 to 14 years	8.5	9.0	9.0	9.8	10.9	12.5	9.1	7.1	9.3	10.2	9.0	7.3
15 to 19 years	8.2	8.6	9.2	9.2	10.5	10.8	6.8	7.9	9.2	9.5	7.7	7.0
20 to 24 years	8.3	9.2	8.8	9.5	10.2	9.8	5.1	10.0	9.9	9.9	7.3	9.9
25 to 29 years	8.4	9.3	8.1	8.9	8.9	8.6	7.4	8.5	9.2	9.1	7.7	10.8
30 to 34 years	8.2	7.9	7.4	7.3	6.7	6.5	6.4	9.3	7.9	7.4	8.4	9.5
35 to 39 years	8.6	8.4	8.1	8.0	7.3	7.3	8.3	8.3	7.9	7.9	9.1	10.1
40 to 44 years	7.6	6.9	6.9	6.3	5.6	5.3	6.9	6.1	6.4	6.3	7.7	7.9
45 to 49 years	6.8	6.5	6.7	6.5	5.3	5.2	8.5	6.3	5.7	5.9	7.4	7.0
50 to 54 years	5.8	5.2	5.6	5.0	3.9	3.4	6.1	4.4	4.6	4.4	5.8	4.7
55 to 59 years	4.1	3.3	3.7	3.3	2.6	2.1	4.6	3.9	2.9	2.8	4.0	2.8
60 to 64 years	2.9	2.7	3.0	2.7	1.9	1.8	4.1	4.0	2.3	2.2	2.7	2.1
65 to 69 years	2.2	2.0	2.2	2.0	1.3	1.2	3.0	3.0	1.6	1.5	1.8	1.4
70 to 74 years	1.4	1.6	1.5	1.3	.8	.8	2.6	1.8	1.0	1.1	1.0	.9
75 to 79 years	1.0	1.2	.9	.8	.5	.5	1.7	1.6	.6	.6	.6	.5
80 to 84 years	.6	.4	.5	.4	.3	.3	.9	.4	.3	.3	.3	.2
85 and over	.5	.4	.4	.3	.3	.3	.4	.5	.2	.2	.2	.2
Unknown	.1	.4	.1	.2	----------	.3	.2	.2	.5	.3	.2	.3

AGE PERIOD	MICHIGAN		MINNESOTA		MISSISSIPPI		MISSOURI		MONTANA		NEBRASKA	
	1930	1920	1930	1920	1930	1920	1930	1920	1930	1920	1930	1920
All ages	**169,453**	**60,082**	**9,445**	**8,809**	**1,009,718**	**935,184**	**223,840**	**178,241**	**1,256**	**1,658**	**13,752**	**13,242**
Under 5 years	15,231	4,141	615	522	117,435	107,394	16,830	11,956	66	109	1,046	878
5 to 9 years	14,732	3,748	675	511	127,225	124,163	18,346	13,424	62	99	1,101	875
10 to 14 years	11,387	3,336	612	492	116,839	126,861	16,518	14,194	90	89	930	879
15 to 19 years	10,888	4,096	614	496	114,893	103,682	17,735	14,302	58	82	962	940
20 to 24 years	17,731	8,608	650	793	104,361	89,183	20,665	17,174	78	107	1,122	1,463
25 to 29 years	24,305	9,540	732	1,074	82,827	72,519	22,690	19,358	100	138	1,404	1,619
30 to 34 years	21,514	7,136	883	965	61,499	54,403	20,559	17,059	97	159	1,314	1,480
35 to 39 years	19,101	6,757	1,036	1,127	64,084	62,351	21,855	18,395	123	205	1,457	1,615
40 to 44 years	12,054	3,975	889	877	49,903	45,067	17,926	13,685	115	185	1,240	1,085
45 to 49 years	9,050	3,346	870	749	45,539	44,280	16,080	12,323	115	149	1,116	895
50 to 54 years	5,420	2,018	653	462	42,163	33,597	11,854	8,810	119	111	803	563
55 to 59 years	3,121	1,175	475	281	26,931	19,692	7,576	5,415	82	79	455	338
60 to 64 years	1,920	779	286	186	22,483	18,904	5,503	4,205	62	58	307	240
65 to 69 years	1,188	549	215	112	13,507	12,751	3,766	2,863	34	41	207	141
70 to 74 years	672	351	95	66	8,608	8,365	2,386	2,011	29	20	109	87
75 to 79 years	472	219	72	36	5,219	4,811	1,546	1,229	11	10	83	60
80 to 84 years	222	97	34	28	3,216	2,833	866	667	8	5	38	30
85 to 89 years	95	46	16	9	1,400	1,249	431	244	4	3	24	15
90 to 94 years	37	15	9	4	625	623	152	132	1	----------	10	3
95 to 99 years	17	5	1	1	242	281	51	66	----------	2	4	1
100 and over	12	8	2	1	283	291	39	57	----------	1	1	1
Unknown	284	137	11	17	436	1,884	466	672	2	6	19	34
Percent	**100.0**	**100.0**	**100.00**	**100.0**	**100.0**	**100.0**	**100.0**	**100.0**	**100.0**	**100.0**	**100.0**	**100.0**
Under 5 years	9.0	6.9	6.5	5.9	11.6	11.5	7.5	6.7	5.3	6.6	7.6	6.6
5 to 9 years	8.7	6.2	7.1	5.8	12.6	13.3	8.2	7.5	4.9	6.0	8.0	6.6
10 to 14 years	6.7	5.6	6.5	5.6	11.6	13.6	7.4	8.0	7.2	5.4	6.8	6.6
15 to 19 years	6.4	6.8	6.5	5.6	11.4	11.1	7.9	8.0	4.6	4.9	7.0	7.1
20 to 24 years	10.5	14.3	6.9	9.0	10.3	9.5	9.2	9.6	6.2	6.5	8.2	11.0
25 to 29 years	14.3	15.9	7.8	12.2	8.2	7.8	10.1	10.9	8.0	8.3	10.2	12.2
30 to 34 years	12.7	11.9	9.3	11.0	6.1	5.8	9.2	9.6	7.7	9.6	9.6	11.2
35 to 39 years	11.3	11.2	11.0	12.8	6.3	6.7	9.8	10.3	9.8	12.4	10.6	12.2
40 to 44 years	7.1	6.6	9.4	10.0	4.9	4.8	8.0	7.7	9.2	11.2	9.0	8.2
45 to 49 years	5.3	5.6	9.2	8.5	4.5	4.7	7.2	6.9	9.2	9.0	8.1	6.8
50 to 54 years	3.2	3.4	6.9	5.2	4.2	3.6	5.3	4.9	9.5	6.7	5.8	4.3
55 to 59 years	1.8	2.0	5.0	3.2	2.7	2.1	3.4	3.0	6.5	4.8	3.3	2.6
60 to 64 years	1.1	1.3	3.0	2.1	2.2	2.0	2.5	2.4	4.9	3.5	2.2	1.8
65 to 69 years	.7	.9	2.3	1.3	1.3	1.4	1.7	1.6	2.7	2.5	1.5	1.1
70 to 74 years	.4	.6	1.0	.7	.9	.9	1.1	1.1	2.3	1.2	.8	.7
75 to 79 years	.3	.4	.8	.4	.5	.5	.7	.7	.9	.6	.6	.5
80 to 84 years	.1	.2	.4	.3	.3	.3	.4	.4	.6	.3	.3	.2
85 and over	.1	.1	.3	.2	.3	.3	.3	.3	.4	.4	.3	.2
Unknown	.2	.2	.1	.2	----------	.2	.2	.4	.2	.4	.1	.3

Table 15.—NEGRO POPULATION CLASSIFIED BY 5-YEAR AGE PERIODS, BY DIVISIONS, AND STATES: 1930 AND 1920—Continued

[See note at head of this table]

Age period	NEVADA 1930	NEVADA 1920	NEW HAMPSHIRE 1930	NEW HAMPSHIRE 1920	NEW JERSEY 1930	NEW JERSEY 1920	NEW MEXICO 1930	NEW MEXICO 1920	NEW YORK 1930	NEW YORK 1920	NORTH CAROLINA 1930	NORTH CAROLINA 1920
All ages	**516**	**346**	**790**	**621**	**208, 828**	**117, 132**	**2, 850**	**5, 733**	**412, 814**	**198, 483**	**918, 647**	**763, 407**
Under 5 years	21	15	48	72	19, 790	10, 171	249	181	34, 116	14, 726	114, 695	106, 460
5 to 9 years	23	18	45	59	19, 824	10, 260	273	190	31, 317	12, 454	130, 143	111, 405
10 to 14 years	13	12	48	60	16, 598	9, 578	249	153	24, 624	11, 637	117, 763	101, 046
15 to 19 years	15	20	63	36	16, 795	9, 370	259	234	27, 472	13, 129	115, 166	86, 608
20 to 24 years	29	22	86	48	21, 295	11, 682	236	1, 670	47, 974	24, 087	95, 004	74, 809
25 to 29 years	44	30	59	63	23, 424	12, 110	245	1, 591	59, 075	27, 600	69, 843	54, 272
30 to 34 years	50	38	71	45	19, 787	10, 619	223	672	49, 742	23, 577	51, 384	40, 037
35 to 39 years	62	46	84	64	19, 349	11, 858	295	341	45, 285	23, 489	51, 189	44, 011
40 to 44 years	71	35	76	43	14, 525	8, 944	221	253	31, 640	16, 087	40, 748	33. 335
45 to 49 years	57	49	86	32	12, 587	8, 109	183	181	24, 195	11, 919	37, 095	30, 909
50 to 54 years	45	19	49	19	9, 645	5, 470	181	95	15, 548	7, 774	32, 683	24, 988
55 to 59 years	34	15	32	18	5, 808	3, 182	83	59	8, 667	4, 230	20, 584	15, 435
60 to 64 years	21	8	11	18	3. 815	2, 184	74	35	5, 335	2, 993	15, 421	13, 899
65 to 69 years	13	11	17	12	2, 307	1, 471	30	32	3, 359	1, 927	10, 304	10, 247
70 to 74 years	8	3	5	5	1, 371	909	20	20	1, 851	1, 224	7, 306	6, 987
75 to 79 years	4	3	3	6	819	579	9	9	1, 093	701	4, 190	3, 767
80 to 84 years	----------	1	2	5	405	269	5	5	506	303	2, 351	1, 992
85 to 89 years	3	1	----------	1	168	96	3	5	223	122	1, 036	865
90 to 94 years	----------	----------	2	----------	67	34	5	1	67	55	439	443
95 to 99 years	----------	----------	----------	----------	27	15	----------	1	25	18	185	173
100 and over	1	----------	----------	----------	19	18	1	----------	17	16	180	182
Unknown	2	----------	3	15	403	204	6	5	683	415	938	1, 537
Percent	100. 0	100. 0	100. 0	100. 0	100. 0	100. 0	100. 0	100. 0	100. 0	100. 0	100. 0	100. 0
Under 5 years	4. 1	4. 3	6. 1	11. 6	9. 5	8. 7	8. 7	3. 2	8. 3	7. 4	12. 5	13. 9
5 to 9 years	4. 5	5. 2	5. 7	9. 5	9. 5	8. 8	9. 6	3. 3	7. 6	6. 3	14. 2	14. 6
10 to 14 years	2. 5	3. 5	6. 1	9. 7	7. 9	8. 2	8. 7	2. 7	6. 0	5. 9	12. 8	13. 2
15 to 19 years	2. 9	5. 8	8. 0	5. 8	8. 0	8. 0	9. 1	4. 1	6. 7	6. 6	12. 5	11. 3
20 to 24 years	5. 6	6. 4	10. 9	7. 7	10. 2	10. 0	8. 3	29. 1	11. 6	12. 1	10. 3	9. 8
25 to 29 years	8. 5	8. 7	7. 5	10. 1	11. 2	10. 3	8. 6	27. 8	14. 3	13. 9	7. 6	7. 1
30 to 34 years	9. 7	11. 0	9. 0	7. 2	9. 5	9. 1	7. 8	11. 7	12. 0	11. 9	5. 6	5. 2
35 to 39 years	12. 0	13. 3	10. 6	10. 3	9. 3	10. 1	10. 4	5. 9	11. 0	11. 8	5. 6	5. 8
40 to 44 years	13. 8	10. 1	9. 6	6. 9	7. 0	7. 6	7. 8	4. 4	7. 7	8. 1	4. 4	4. 4
45 to 49 years	11. 0	14. 2	10. 9	5. 2	6. 0	6. 9	6. 4	3. 2	5. 9	6. 0	4. 0	4. 0
50 to 54 years	8. 7	5. 5	6. 2	3. 1	4. 6	4. 7	6. 4	1. 7	3. 8	3. 9	3. 6	3. 3
55 to 59 years	6. 6	4. 3	4. 1	2. 9	2. 8	2. 7	2. 9	1. 0	2. 1	2. 1	2. 2	2. 0
60 to 64 years	4. 1	2. 3	1. 4	2. 9	1. 8	1. 9	2. 6	. 6	1. 3	1. 5	1. 7	1. 8
65 to 69 years	2. 5	3. 2	2. 2	1. 9	1. 1	1. 3	1. 1	. 6	. 8	1. 0	1. 1	1. 3
70 to 74 years	1. 6	. 9	. 6	. 8	. 7	. 8	. 7	. 3	. 4	. 6	. 8	. 9
75 to 79 years	. 8	. 9	. 4	1. 0	. 4	. 5	. 3	. 2	. 3	. 4	. 5	. 5
80 to 84 years	----------	. 3	. 3	. 8	. 2	. 2	. 2	. 1	. 1	. 2	. 3	. 3
85 and over	. 8	. 3	. 3	. 2	. 1	. 1	. 3	. 1	. 1	. 1	. 2	. 2
Unknown	. 4	----------	. 4	2. 4	. 2	. 2	. 2	. 1	. 2	. 2	. 1	. 2

AGE PERIOD	NORTH DAKOTA 1930	NORTH DAKOTA 1920	OHIO 1930	OHIO 1920	OKLAHOMA 1930	OKLAHOMA 1920	OREGON 1930	OREGON 1920	PENNSYLVANIA 1930	PENNSYLVANIA 1920	RHODE ISLAND 1930	RHODE ISLAND 1920
All ages	**377**	**467**	**309, 304**	**186, 187**	**172, 198**	**149, 408**	**2, 234**	**2, 144**	**431, 257**	**284, 568**	**9, 913**	**10, 036**
Under 5 years	30	20	27, 845	14, 227	17, 337	16, 214	107	117	39, 345	22, 409	1, 008	997
5 to 9 years	21	42	28, 959	14, 048	19, 792	18, 658	127	134	40, 632	22, 132	1, 069	847
10 to 14 years	15	41	24, 086	13, 494	18, 296	18, 684	122	129	33, 028	21, 155	938	752
15 to 19 years	26	24	23, 758	13, 897	18, 811	16, 518	128	118	33, 213	22, 056	807	732
20 to 24 years	32	25	29, 392	20, 814	17, 893	14, 547	161	150	41, 895	33, 562	674	844
25 to 29 years	31	42	34, 366	22, 568	15, 595	12, 493	175	188	50, 353	33, 705	690	915
30 to 34 years	32	48	31, 179	18, 245	12, 469	9, 670	198	223	44, 943	27, 774	718	841
35 to 39 years	34	60	31, 488	19, 530	12, 235	10, 875	267	300	43, 517	30, 930	745	957
40 to 44 years	40	48	22, 784	13, 431	9, 739	7, 626	255	231	31, 302	21, 929	696	833
45 to 49 years	37	43	18, 955	12, 407	8, 785	7, 595	224	196	26, 314	19, 141	705	721
50 to 54 years	32	27	13, 351	8, 169	7, 546	5, 854	168	147	18, 731	11, 793	586	522
55 to 59 years	19	15	8, 327	4, 940	4, 943	3, 454	129	89	11, 063	6, 321	427	331
60 to 64 years	12	15	5, 630	3, 770	3, 264	2, 485	65	44	7, 035	4, 464	323	280
65 to 69 years	7	9	3, 573	2, 467	2, 207	1, 797	55	26	4, 257	2, 846	212	178
70 to 74 years	6	5	2, 427	1, 793	1, 297	1, 153	20	24	2, 533	1, 856	134	148
75 to 79 years	2	----------	1, 420	1, 156	846	689	15	7	1, 401	1, 046	83	75
80 to 84 years	----------	----------	739	490	512	347	10	5	692	475	55	30
85 to 89 years	1	1	371	260	259	174	2	7	306	222	19	17
90 to 94 years	----------	----------	127	75	109	80	----------	2	108	88	9	3
95 to 99 years	----------	----------	42	33	44	36	----------	----------	32	28	3	2
100 and over	----------	----------	42	21	65	62	----------	----------	30	29	1	----------
Unknown	----------	2	433	352	154	397	6	7	527	607	11	11
Percent	100. 0	100. 0	100. 0	100. 0	100. 0	100. 0	100. 0	100. 0	100. 0	100. 0	100. 0	100. 0
Under 5 years	8. 0	4. 3	9. 0	7. 6	10. 1	10. 9	4. 8	5. 5	9. 1	7. 9	10. 2	9. 9
5 to 9 years	5. 6	9. 0	9. 4	7. 5	11. 5	12. 5	5. 7	6. 3	9. 4	7. 8	10. 8	8. 4
10 to 14 years	4. 0	8. 8	7. 8	7. 2	10. 6	12. 5	5. 5	6. 0	7. 7	7. 4	9. 5	7. 5
15 to 19 years	6. 9	5. 1	7. 7	7. 5	10. 9	11. 1	5. 7	5. 5	7. 7	7. 8	8. 1	7. 3
20 to 24 years	8. 5	5. 4	9. 5	11. 2	10. 4	9. 7	7. 2	7. 0	9. 7	11. 8	6. 8	8. 4
25 to 29 years	8. 2	9. 0	11. 1	12. 1	9. 1	8. 4	7. 8	8. 8	11. 7	11. 8	7. 0	9. 1
30 to 34 years	8. 5	10. 3	10. 1	9. 8	7. 2	6. 5	8. 9	10. 4	10. 4	9. 8	7. 2	8. 4
35 to 39 years	9. 0	12. 8	10 2	10. 5	7. 1	7. 3	12. 0	14. 0	10. 1	10. 9	7. 5	9. 5
40 to 44 years	10. 6	10. 3	7. 4	7. 2	5. 7	5. 1	11. 4	10. 8	7. 3	7. 7	7. 0	8. 3
45 to 49 years	9. 8	9. 2	6. 1	6. 7	5. 1	5. 1	10. 0	9. 1	6. 1	6. 7	7. 1	7. 2
50 to 54 years	8. 5	5. 8	4. 3	4. 4	4. 4	3. 9	7. 5	6. 9	4. 3	4. 1	5. 9	5. 2
55 to 59 years	5. 0	3. 2	2. 7	2. 7	2. 9	2. 3	5. 8	4. 2	2. 6	2. 2	4. 3	3. 3
60 to 64 years	3. 2	3. 2	1. 8	2. 0	1. 9	1. 7	2. 9	2. 1	1. 6	1. 6	3. 3	2. 8
65 to 69 years	1. 9	1. 9	1. 2	1. 3	1. 3	1. 2	2. 5	1. 2	1. 0	1. 0	2. 1	1. 8
70 to 74 years	1. 6	1. 1	. 8	1. 0	. 8	. 8	. 9	1. 1	. 6	. 7	1. 4	1. 5
75 to 79 years	. 5	----------	. 5	. 6	. 5	. 5	. 7	. 3	. 3	. 4	. 8	. 7
80 to 84 years	----------	----------	. 2	. 3	. 3	. 2	. 4	. 2	. 2	. 2	. 6	. 3
85 and over	. 3	. 2	. 2	. 2	. 3	. 2	. 1	. 4	. 1	. 1	. 3	. 2
Unknown	----------	. 4	. 1	. 2	. 1	. 3	. 3	. 3	. 1	. 2	. 1	. 1

TABLE 15.—NEGRO POPULATION CLASSIFIED BY 5-YEAR AGE PERIODS, BY DIVISIONS, AND STATES: 1930 AND 1920—Continued

[See note at head of this table]

AGE PERIOD	SOUTH CAROLINA		SOUTH DAKOTA		TENNESSEE		TEXAS		UTAH		VERMONT	
	1930	1920	1930	1920	1930	1920	1930	1920	1930	1920	1930	1920
All ages	793, 681	864, 719	646	832	477, 646	451, 758	854, 964	741, 694	1, 108	1, 446	568	572
Under 5 years	96, 300	117, 526	47	70	44, 304	45, 653	86, 120	77, 798	89	95	75	52
5 to 9 years	116, 296	128, 265	53	84	50, 368	51, 679	97, 509	91, 177	77	78	48	66
10 to 14 years	111, 123	123, 498	55	78	48, 152	52, 424	89, 070	90, 206	86	77	54	55
15 to 19 years	106, 429	99, 680	62	63	51, 835	47, 645	92, 696	82, 054	44	67	62	51
20 to 24 years	76, 652	85, 361	65	74	49, 288	45, 039	91, 569	78, 393	69	136	39	35
25 to 29 years	51, 299	61, 815	52	69	42, 349	39, 053	80, 192	67, 251	88	180	29	33
30 to 34 years	38, 969	45, 672	51	80	33, 608	29, 481	64, 050	49, 742	101	162	36	35
35 to 39 years	45, 019	51, 331	44	80	35, 562	32, 637	63, 936	52, 966	119	197	41	55
40 to 44 years	37, 000	37, 419	51	56	27, 023	23, 648	48, 424	37, 289	109	151	30	53
45 to 49 years	33, 038	36, 052	42	49	24, 359	23, 282	44, 609	38, 213	109	136	43	30
50 to 54 years	26, 944	24, 672	38	35	25, 198	20, 977	31, 631	25, 012	86	69	33	29
55 to 59 years	16, 401	13, 995	25	34	14, 929	12, 134	19, 530	14, 267	49	36	23	27
60 to 64 years	15, 555	15, 269	20	20	11, 363	9, 926	18, 484	13, 365	32	20	17	19
65 to 69 years	9, 620	10, 028	15	16	7, 409	6, 985	10, 970	9, 073	24	13	12	11
70 to 74 years	6, 129	6, 681	13	9	4, 902	4, 697	6, 569	5, 822	9	10	10	6
75 to 79 years	3, 285	3, 332	6	5	2, 882	2, 898	4, 142	3, 453	7	3	11	4
80 to 84 years	1, 866	1, 835	2	1	1, 753	1, 443	2, 357	1, 989	7	5	2	5
85 to 89 years	778	708	2	2	714	679	1, 095	906	1	2	----------	2
90 to 94 years	336	408	----------	----------	333	296	529	484	1	----------	2	----------
95 to 99 years	141	153	----------	2	134	116	238	227	----------	----------	----------	----------
100 and over	128	191	----------	----------	113	161	224	323	----------	----------	1	----------
Unknown	373	828	3	5	1, 068	905	1, 020	1, 684	1	9	----------	4
Percent	100. 0	100. 0	100. 0	100. 0	100. 0	100. 0	100. 0	100. 0	100. 0	100. 0	100. 0	100. 0
Under 5 years	12. 1	13. 6	7. 3	8. 4	9. 3	10. 1	10. 1	10. 5	8. 0	6. 6	13. 2	9. 1
5 to 9 years	14. 7	14. 8	8. 2	10. 1	10. 5	11. 4	11. 4	12. 3	6. 9	5. 4	8. 5	11. 5
10 to 14 years	14. 0	14. 3	8. 5	9. 4	10. 1	11. 6	10. 4	12. 2	7. 8	5. 3	9. 5	9. 6
15 to 19 years	13. 4	11. 5	9. 6	7. 6	10. 9	10. 5	10. 8	11. 1	4. 0	4. 6	10. 9	8. 9
20 to 24 years	9. 7	9. 9	10. 1	8. 9	10. 3	10. 0	10. 7	10. 6	6. 2	9. 4	6. 9	6. 1
25 to 29 years	6. 5	7. 1	8. 0	8. 3	8. 9	8. 6	9. 4	9. 1	7. 9	12. 4	5. 1	5. 8
30 to 34 years	4. 9	5. 3	7. 9	9. 6	7. 0	6. 5	7. 5	6. 7	9. 1	11. 2	6. 3	6. 1
35 to 39 years	5. 7	5. 9	6. 8	9. 6	7. 4	7. 2	7. 5	7. 1	10. 7	13. 6	7. 2	9. 6
40 to 44 years	4. 7	4. 3	7. 9	6. 7	5. 7	5. 2	5. 7	5. 0	9. 8	10. 4	5. 3	9. 3
45 to 49 years	4. 2	4. 2	6. 5	5. 9	5. 1	5. 2	5. 2	5. 2	9. 8	9. 4	7. 6	5. 2
50 to 54 years	3. 4	2. 9	5. 9	4. 2	5. 3	4. 6	3. 7	3. 4	7. 8	4. 8	5. 8	5. 1
55 to 59 years	2. 1	1. 6	3. 9	4. 1	3. 1	2. 7	2. 3	1. 9	4. 4	2. 5	4. 0	4. 7
60 to 64 years	2. 0	1. 8	3. 1	2. 4	2. 4	2. 2	2. 2	1. 8	2. 9	1. 4	3. 0	3. 3
65 to 69 years	1. 2	1. 2	2. 3	1. 9	1. 6	1. 5	1. 3	1. 2	2. 2	. 9	2. 1	1. 9
70 to 74 years	. 8	. 8	2. 0	1. 1	1. 0	1. 0	. 8	. 8	. 8	. 7	1. 8	1. 0
75 to 79 years	. 4	. 4	. 9	. 6	. 6	. 6	. 5	. 5	. 6	. 2	1. 9	. 7
80 to 84 years	. 2	. 2	. 3	. 1	. 4	. 3	. 3	. 3	. 6	. 3	. 4	. 9
85 and over	. 2	. 2	. 3	. 5	. 3	. 3	. 2	. 3	. 2	. 1	. 5	. 3
Unknown	----------	. 1	. 5	. 6	. 2	. 2	. 1	. 2	. 1	. 6	----------	. 7

AGE PERIOD	VIRGINIA		WASHINGTON		WEST VIRGINIA		WISCONSIN		WYOMING	
	1930	1920	1930	1920	1930	1920	1930	1920	1930	1920
All ages	650, 165	690, 017	6, 840	6, 883	114, 893	86, 345	10, 739	5, 201	1, 250	1, 375
Under 5 years	70, 662	81, 263	400	399	12, 104	8, 854	850	368	63	59
5 to 9 years	85, 074	88, 097	448	420	12, 868	8, 705	960	375	69	65
10 to 14 years	78, 893	83, 765	421	394	10, 444	7, 746	788	375	70	63
15 to 19 years	73, 443	72, 915	416	383	10, 109	8, 017	696	370	68	92
20 to 24 years	56, 567	66, 603	459	539	11, 217	10, 472	1, 066	548	95	169
25 to 29 years	44, 478	53, 515	466	692	11, 681	9, 504	1, 396	653	83	160
30 to 34 years	38, 283	40, 657	542	708	10, 546	7, 365	1, 206	591	135	145
35 to 39 years	43, 027	47, 273	646	839	10, 372	7, 856	1, 178	574	138	200
40 to 44 years	36, 655	36, 540	655	724	7, 998	5, 111	875	391	139	130
45 to 49 years	34, 802	35, 251	669	598	6, 375	4, 652	620	340	126	115
50 to 54 years	28, 955	26, 493	619	436	4, 364	2, 957	433	225	99	70
55 to 59 years	18, 520	16, 093	432	289	2, 539	1, 648	274	128	57	39
60 to 64 years	14, 853	14, 563	264	155	1, 688	1, 166	151	84	50	26
65 to 69 years	10, 339	10, 516	177	94	1, 080	826	97	67	22	12
70 to 74 years	7, 148	7, 356	101	70	664	494	60	47	14	8
75 to 79 years	4, 038	3, 999	43	39	359	231	30	32	11	7
80 to 84 years	2, 360	2, 047	32	25	197	144	19	8	3	4
85 to 89 years	944	830	17	6	96	70	15	1	2	2
90 to 94 years	426	397	6	3	35	32	5	4	1	1
95 to 99 years	164	185	2	1	13	11	1	1	----------	----------
100 and over	126	163	2	----------	15	14	2	----------	----------	1
Unknown	408	1, 496	23	69	129	470	17	19	5	7
Percent	100. 0	100. 0	100. 0	100. 0	100. 0	100. 0	100. 0	100. 0	100. 0	100. 0
Under 5 years	10. 9	11. 8	5. 8	5. 8	10. 5	10. 3	7. 9	7. 1	5. 0	4. 3
5 to 9 years	13. 1	12. 8	6. 5	6. 1	11. 2	10. 1	8. 9	7. 2	5. 5	4. 7
10 to 14 years	12. 1	12. 1	6. 2	5. 7	9. 1	9. 0	7. 3	7. 2	5. 6	4. 6
15 to 19 years	11. 3	10. 6	6. 1	5. 6	8. 8	9. 3	6. 5	7. 1	5. 4	6. 7
20 to 24 years	8. 7	9. 7	6. 7	7. 8	9. 8	12. 1	9. 9	10. 5	7. 6	12. 3
25 to 29 years	6. 8	7. 8	6. 8	10. 1	10. 2	11. 0	13. 0	12. 6	6. 6	11. 6
30 to 34 years	5. 9	5. 9	7. 9	10. 3	9. 2	8. 5	11. 2	11. 4	10. 8	10. 5
35 to 39 years	6. 6	6. 9	9. 4	12. 2	9. 0	9. 1	11. 0	11. 0	11. 0	14. 5
40 to 44 years	5. 6	5. 3	9. 6	10. 5	7. 0	5. 9	8. 1	7. 5	11. 1	9. 5
45 to 49 years	5. 4	5. 1	9. 8	8. 7	5. 5	5. 4	5. 8	6. 5	10. 1	8. 4
50 to 54 years	4. 5	3. 8	9. 0	6. 3	3. 8	3. 4	4. 0	4. 3	7. 9	5. 1
55 to 59 years	2. 8	2. 3	6. 3	4. 2	2. 2	1. 9	2. 6	2. 5	4. 6	2. 8
60 to 64 years	2. 3	2. 1	3. 9	2. 3	1. 5	1. 4	1. 4	1. 6	4. 0	1. 9
65 to 69 years	1. 6	1. 5	2. 6	1. 4	. 9	1. 0	. 9	1. 3	1. 8	. 9
70 to 74 years	1. 1	1. 1	1. 5	1. 0	. 6	. 6	. 6	. 9	1. 1	. 6
75 to 79 years	. 6	. 6	. 6	. 6	. 3	. 3	. 3	. 6	. 9	. 5
80 to 84 years	. 4	. 3	. 5	. 4	. 2	. 2	. 2	. 2	. 2	. 3
85 and over	. 3	. 2	. 4	. 1	. 1	. 1	. 2	. 1	. 2	. 3
Unknown	. 1	. 2	. 3	1. 0	. 1	. 5	. 2	. 4	. 4	. 5

Table 16.—NEGRO POPULATION CLASSIFIED BY 5-YEAR AGE PERIODS, AND SEX, AND BY DIVISIONS, AND STATES: 1930

[Percent not shown where less than 1/10 of 1 percent or where base is less than 100]

AGE PERIOD	UNITED STATES		NEW ENGLAND DIVISION		MIDDLE ATLANTIC DIVISION		EAST NORTH CENTRAL DIVISION		WEST NORTH CENTRAL DIVISION		SOUTH ATLANTIC DIVISION	
	Male	Female	Male	Female	Male	Female	Male	Female	Male	Female	Male	Female
All ages	**5,855,669**	**6,035,474**	**46,963**	**47,123**	**520,826**	**532,073**	**475,368**	**455,082**	**167,550**	**164,234**	**2,156,531**	**2,264,857**
Under 5 years	611,231	618,975	4,462	4,453	46,381	46,870	38,939	39,507	12,645	12,496	243,099	246,918
5 to 9 years	679,748	688,633	4,663	4,789	45,169	46,604	39,522	40,856	13,923	13,855	281,172	286,335
10 to 14 years	623,228	628,314	4,076	4,109	36,063	38,187	32,577	34,272	12,389	12,757	263,936	265,892
15 to 19 years	595,646	654,882	3,495	3,845	34,860	42,620	31,818	35,633	12,582	13,665	250,359	271,436
20 to 24 years	553,622	649,569	3,404	3,918	50,054	61,110	43,175	48,462	13,547	15,836	204,838	240,143
25 to 29 years	500,520	571,267	3,891	4,020	63,993	68,859	55,820	57,109	15,079	16,736	159,831	188,989
30 to 34 years	416,869	447,645	4,064	3,884	58,523	55,949	52,915	48,317	14,761	14,912	126,726	144,914
35 to 39 years	430,472	460,428	4,254	4,145	55,713	52,438	52,807	45,706	16,023	15,632	134,111	154,044
40 to 44 years	339,329	348,094	3,547	3,463	40,582	36,885	38,650	31,318	13,955	12,536	109,626	120,274
45 to 49 years	323,162	306,903	3,446	3,076	33,216	29,880	32,125	25,580	12,951	10,997	100,199	107,103
50 to 54 years	277,532	227,058	2,723	2,482	23,571	20,353	22,337	17,352	10,138	8,144	99,538	81,743
55 to 59 years	174,367	135,030	1,849	1,630	13,677	11,861	13,602	10,733	6,766	5,316	60,934	46,930
60 to 64 years	133,349	108,820	1,250	1,247	8,272	7,913	8,372	7,465	4,740	3,907	49,179	39,544
65 to 69 years	82,843	72,334	810	834	4,746	5,177	5,248	4,958	3,259	2,776	30,720	26,930
70 to 74 years	50,896	48,200	457	514	2,704	3,051	3,147	3,278	1,987	1,807	19,500	18,314
75 to 79 years	29,219	29,492	264	343	1,422	1,891	1,834	1,993	1,286	1,252	10,741	10,764
80 to 84 years	15,343	18,034	141	191	627	976	883	993	678	733	5,614	6,539
85 to 89 years	6,864	8,084	63	67	294	403	455	518	357	377	2,372	2,828
90 to 94 years	2,516	3,816	25	33	90	152	152	189	97	141	859	1,394
95 to 99 years	1,073	1,538	7	9	33	51	55	76	32	54	372	540
100 and over	776	1,691	4	6	17	49	32	86	29	42	251	604
Unknown	7,064	6,667	68	65	819	794	903	681	326	263	2,554	2,679
Percent	**100.0**	**100.0**	**100.0**	**100.0**	**100.0**	**100.0**	**100.0**	**100.0**	**100.0**	**100.0**	**100.0**	**100.0**
Under 5 years	10.4	10.3	9.5	9.4	8.9	8.8	8.2	8.7	7.5	7.6	11.3	10.9
5 to 9 years	11.6	11.4	9.9	10.2	8.7	8.8	8.3	9.0	8.3	8.4	13.0	12.6
10 to 14 years	10.6	10.4	8.7	8.7	6.9	7.2	6.9	7.5	7.4	7.8	12.2	11.7
15 to 19 years	10.2	10.9	7.4	8.2	6.7	8.0	6.7	7.8	7.5	8.3	11.6	12.0
20 to 24 years	9.5	10.8	7.2	8.3	9.6	11.5	9.1	10.6	8.1	9.6	9.5	10.6
25 to 29 years	8.5	9.5	8.3	8.5	12.3	12.9	11.7	12.5	9.0	10.2	7.4	8.3
30 to 34 years	7.1	7.4	8.7	8.2	11.2	10.5	11.1	10.6	8.8	9.1	5.9	6.4
35 to 39 years	7.4	7.6	9.1	8.8	10.7	9.9	11.1	10.0	9.6	9.5	6.2	6.8
40 to 44 years	5.8	5.8	7.6	7.3	7.8	6.9	8.1	6.9	8.3	7.6	5.1	5.3
45 to 49 years	5.5	5.1	7.3	6.5	6.4	5.6	6.8	5.6	7.7	6.7	4.6	4.7
50 to 54 years	4.7	3.8	5.8	5.3	4.5	3.8	4.7	3.8	6.1	5.0	4.6	3.6
55 to 59 years	3.0	2.2	3.9	3.5	2.6	2.2	2.9	2.4	4.0	3.2	2.8	2.1
60 to 64 years	2.3	1.8	2.7	2.6	1.6	1.5	1.8	1.6	2.8	2.4	2.3	1.7
65 to 69 years	1.4	1.2	1.7	1.8	.9	1.0	1.1	1.1	1.9	1.7	1.4	1.2
70 to 74 years	.9	.8	1.0	1.1	.5	.6	.7	.7	1.2	1.1	.9	.8
75 to 79 years	.5	.5	.6	.7	.3	.4	.4	.4	.8	.8	.5	.5
80 to 84 years	.3	.3	.3	.4	.1	.2	.2	.2	.4	.4	.3	.3
85 years and over	.2	.3	.2	.2	.1	.1	.1	.2	.3	.4	.2	.2

AGE PERIOD	EAST SOUTH CENTRAL DIVISION		WEST SOUTH CENTRAL DIVISION		MOUNTAIN DIVISION		PACIFIC DIVISION		ALABAMA		ARIZONA	
	Male	Female	Male	Female	Male	Female	Male	Female	Male	Female	Male	Female
All ages	**1,301,552**	**1,356,686**	**1,125,508**	**1,156,443**	**16,312**	**13,913**	**45,059**	**45,063**	**457,144**	**487,690**	**6,352**	**4,397**
Under 5 years	143,472	144,690	118,288	120,112	1,071	1,013	2,874	2,916	53,478	54,358	396	397
5 to 9 years	158,632	158,493	132,330	133,286	1,038	1,111	3,299	3,304	58,961	58,747	407	424
10 to 14 years	148,082	146,133	122,185	122,892	986	1,041	2,934	3,031	54,626	54,308	368	359
15 to 19 years	142,693	154,013	115,894	129,451	1,065	990	2,880	3,229	51,787	57,429	460	328
20 to 24 years	123,634	146,904	110,224	128,044	1,409	1,158	3,337	3,994	43,513	53,560	743	385
25 to 29 years	101,251	119,645	95,157	109,835	1,415	1,348	4,083	4,726	34,896	42,622	664	499
30 to 34 years	77,635	89,823	76,204	83,934	1,537	1,364	4,504	4,548	24,914	30,645	711	467
35 to 39 years	81,286	95,748	79,576	86,112	1,829	1,511	4,873	5,092	25,702	33,418	786	509
40 to 44 years	63,911	73,729	63,177	64,887	1,489	1,175	4,392	3,827	19,314	25,828	571	330
45 to 49 years	70,423	68,695	65,506	57,124	1,411	1,059	3,885	3,389	29,949	24,205	479	268
50 to 54 years	64,715	53,005	50,399	40,651	1,118	801	2,993	2,527	20,230	17,488	302	187
55 to 59 years	41,867	31,604	33,043	24,928	682	488	1,947	1,540	13,031	10,133	190	77
60 to 64 years	33,678	26,684	26,154	20,658	541	301	1,163	1,101	10,864	8,810	125	68
65 to 69 years	21,099	17,522	15,913	13,147	299	237	749	753	6,705	5,984	59	46
70 to 74 years	13,120	12,126	9,316	8,513	193	137	472	460	4,123	4,124	41	17
75 to 79 years	7,516	7,555	5,786	5,369	114	70	256	255	2,378	2,506	23	10
80 to 84 years	4,259	4,955	2,979	3,453	43	44	119	150	1,335	1,741	6	9
85 to 89 years	1,805	2,187	1,440	1,610	23	18	55	76	584	716	5	2
90 to 94 years	711	1,064	551	808	10	10	21	25	225	392	1	3
95 to 99 years	315	412	246	382	3	3	10	11	124	143	-	-
100 and over	225	479	209	412	5	3	4	10	74	183	1	-
Unknown	1,223	1,220	931	835	31	31	209	99	331	350	14	12
Percent	**100.0**	**100.0**	**100.0**	**100.0**	**100.0**	**100.0**	**100.0**	**100.0**	**100.0**	**100.0**	**100.0**	**100.0**
Under 5 years	11.0	10.7	10.5	10.4	6.6	7.3	6.4	6.5	11.7	11.1	6.2	9.0
5 to 9 years	12.2	11.7	11.8	11.5	6.4	8.0	7.3	7.3	12.9	12.0	6.4	9.6
10 to 14 years	11.4	10.8	10.9	10.6	6.0	7.5	6.5	6.7	11.9	11.1	5.8	8.2
15 to 19 years	11.0	11.4	10.3	11.2	6.5	7.1	6.4	7.2	11.3	11.8	7.2	7.5
20 to 24 years	9.5	10.8	9.8	11.1	8.6	8.3	7.4	8.9	9.5	11.0	11.7	8.8
25 to 29 years	7.8	8.8	8.5	9.5	8.7	9.7	9.1	10.5	7.6	8.7	10.5	11.3
30 to 34 years	6.0	6.6	6.8	7.3	9.4	9.8	10.0	10.1	5.4	6.3	11.2	10.6
35 to 39 years	6.2	7.1	7.1	7.4	11.2	10.9	10.8	11.3	5.6	6.9	12.4	11.6
40 to 44 years	4.9	5.4	5.6	5.6	9.1	8.4	9.7	8.5	4.2	5.3	9.0	7.5
45 to 49 years	5.4	5.1	5.8	4.9	8.7	7.6	8.6	7.5	6.6	5.0	7.5	6.1
50 to 54 years	5.0	3.9	4.5	3.5	6.9	5.8	6.6	5.6	4.4	3.6	4.8	4.3
55 to 59 years	3.2	2.3	2.9	2.2	4.2	3.5	4.3	3.4	2.9	2.1	3.0	1.8
60 to 64 years	2.6	2.0	2.3	1.8	3.3	2.2	2.6	2.4	2.4	1.8	2.0	1.5
65 to 69 years	1.6	1.3	1.4	1.1	1.8	1.7	1.7	1.7	1.5	1.2	.9	1.0
70 to 74 years	1.0	.9	.8	.7	1.2	1.0	1.0	1.0	.9	.8	.6	.4
75 to 79 years	.6	.6	.5	.5	.7	.5	.6	.6	.5	.5	.4	.2
80 to 84 years	.3	.4	.3	.3	.3	.3	.3	.3	.3	.4	.1	.2
85 years and over	.2	.3	.2	.3	.3	.2	.2	.3	.2	.3	.1	.1

TABLE 16.—NEGRO POPULATION CLASSIFIED BY 5-YEAR AGE PERIODS, AND SEX, AND BY DIVISIONS, AND STATES: 1930—Continued

[See note at head page of this table]

AGE PERIOD	ARKANSAS Male	ARKANSAS Female	CALIFORNIA Male	CALIFORNIA Female	COLORADO Male	COLORADO Female	CONNECTICUT Male	CONNECTICUT Female	DELAWARE Male	DELAWARE Female	DISTRICT OF COLUMBIA Male	DISTRICT OF COLUMBIA Female
All ages	**236, 909**	**241, 554**	**40, 052**	**40, 996**	**5, 739**	**6, 089**	**14, 573**	**14, 781**	**16, 983**	**15, 619**	**62, 225**	**69, 843**
Under 5 years	24, 660	25, 297	2, 635	2, 648	389	384	1, 459	1, 510	1, 391	1, 396	5, 036	4, 970
5 to 9 years	27, 496	27, 737	3, 030	2, 998	369	406	1, 426	1, 474	1, 622	1, 626	5, 314	5, 524
10 to 14 years	26, 514	26, 397	2, 638	2, 784	360	397	1, 122	1, 225	1, 485	1, 500	4, 432	5, 052
15 to 19 years	25, 017	27, 528	2, 615	2, 950	353	430	1, 091	1, 225	1, 503	1, 482	4, 757	5, 918
20 to 24 years	22, 831	26, 425	3, 033	3, 678	384	508	1, 184	1, 485	1, 573	1, 415	6, 472	7, 934
25 to 29 years	18, 545	21, 619	3, 730	4, 438	444	551	1, 521	1, 496	1, 478	1, 341	6, 994	7, 995
30 to 34 years	14, 510	16, 921	4, 101	4, 211	482	567	1, 392	1, 240	1, 283	1, 194	5, 889	6, 471
35 to 39 years	15, 351	17, 810	4, 379	4, 673	598	626	1, 351	1, 318	1, 453	1, 262	5, 797	6, 357
40 to 44 years	12, 284	13, 869	3, 866	3, 443	511	514	1, 076	1, 040	1, 150	987	4, 493	5, 070
45 to 49 years	15, 517	12, 400	3, 364	3, 017	547	530	892	829	1, 038	899	4, 247	4, 673
50 to 54 years	12, 174	9, 335	2, 516	2, 217	438	413	734	676	999	805	3, 433	3, 511
55 to 59 years	8, 035	5, 365	1, 589	1, 337	289	278	461	402	628	511	1, 966	2, 035
60 to 64 years	5, 782	4, 149	977	958	231	152	364	344	523	408	1, 274	1, 511
65 to 69 years	3, 503	2, 612	602	668	148	144	222	218	376	328	849	1, 093
70 to 74 years	2, 150	1, 724	399	412	95	91	119	125	215	202	508	615
75 to 79 years	1, 231	1, 024	216	237	54	42	74	85	137	133	231	382
80 to 84 years	634	670	98	129	19	27	39	49	63	72	117	240
85 to 89 years	335	287	49	63	10	9	20	21	35	32	69	103
90 to 94 years	107	147	17	23	3	4	8	5	8	14	16	35
95 to 99 years	48	60	8	11	3	3	1	3	7	5	9	16
100 and over	48	73	4	8	2	3	3	------	1	2	2	6
Unknown	137	105	186	93	10	10	14	11	15	5	320	332
Percent	**100. 0**	**100. 0**	**100. 0**	**100. 0**	**100. 0**	**100. 0**	**100. 0**	**100. 0**	**100. 0**	**100. 0**	**100. 0**	**100. 0**
Under 5 years	10. 4	10. 5	6. 6	6. 5	6. 8	6. 3	10. 0	10. 2	8. 2	8. 9	8. 1	7. 1
5 to 9 years	11. 6	11. 5	7. 6	7. 3	6. 4	6. 7	9. 8	10. 0	9. 6	10. 4	8. 5	7. 9
10 to 14 years	11. 2	10. 9	6. 6	6. 8	6. 3	6. 5	7. 7	8. 3	8. 7	9. 6	7. 1	7. 2
15 to 19 years	10. 6	11. 4	6. 5	7. 2	6. 2	7. 1	7. 5	8. 3	8. 9	9. 5	7. 6	8. 5
20 to 24 years	9. 6	10. 9	7. 6	9. 0	6. 7	8. 3	8. 1	10. 0	9. 3	9. 1	10. 4	11. 4
25 to 29 years	7. 8	8. 9	9. 3	10. 8	7. 7	9. 0	10. 4	10. 1	8. 7	8. 6	11. 2	11. 4
30 to 34 years	6. 1	7. 0	10. 2	10. 3	8. 4	9. 3	9. 6	8. 4	7. 6	7. 6	9. 5	9. 3
35 to 39 years	6. 5	7. 4	10. 9	11. 4	10. 4	10. 3	9. 3	8. 9	8. 6	8. 1	9. 3	9. 1
40 to 44 years	5. 2	5. 7	9. 7	8. 4	8. 9	8. 4	7. 4	7. 0	6. 8	6. 3	7. 2	7. 3
45 to 49 years	6. 5	5. 1	8. 4	7. 4	9. 5	8. 7	6. 1	5. 6	6. 1	5. 8	6. 8	6. 7
50 to 54 years	5. 1	3. 9	6. 3	5. 4	7. 6	6. 8	5. 0	4. 6	5. 9	5. 2	5. 5	5. 0
55 to 59 years	3. 4	2. 2	4. 0	3. 3	5. 0	4. 6	3. 2	2. 7	3. 7	3. 3	3. 2	2. 9
60 to 64 years	2. 4	1. 7	2. 4	2. 3	4. 0	2. 5	2. 5	2. 3	3. 1	2. 6	2. 0	2. 2
65 to 69 years	1. 5	1. 1	1. 5	1. 6	2. 6	2. 4	1. 5	1. 5	2. 2	2. 1	1. 4	1. 6
70 to 74 years	. 9	. 7	1. 0	1. 0	1. 7	1. 5	. 8	. 8	1. 3	1. 3	. 8	. 9
75 to 79 years	. 5	. 4	. 5	. 6	. 9	. 7	. 5	. 6	. 8	. 9	. 4	. 5
80 to 84 years	. 3	. 3	. 2	. 3	. 3	. 4	. 3	. 3	. 4	. 5	. 2	. 3
85 years and over	. 2	. 2	. 2	. 3	. 3	. 3	. 2	. 2	. 3	. 3	. 2	. 2

AGE PERIOD	FLORIDA Male	FLORIDA Female	GEORGIA Male	GEORGIA Female	IDAHO Male	IDAHO Female	ILLINOIS Male	ILLINOIS Female	INDIANA Male	INDIANA Female	IOWA Male	IOWA Female
All ages	**215, 148**	**216, 680**	**513, 451**	**557, 674**	**395**	**273**	**164, 427**	**164, 427**	**57, 068**	**54, 914**	**8, 987**	**8, 393**
Under 5 years	20, 095	20, 346	57, 436	58, 580	15	15	12, 611	12, 767	4, 578	4, 564	651	740
5 to 9 years	22, 324	23, 126	66, 258	67, 768	25	14	12, 622	13, 138	4, 971	4, 996	796	767
10 to 14 years	20, 862	21, 254	65, 689	65, 704	17	18	10, 665	11, 446	4, 150	4, 327	710	698
15 to 19 years	20, 002	23, 353	63, 755	70, 461	24	16	10, 898	12, 465	4, 208	4, 538	679	735
20 to 24 years	22, 145	26, 257	56, 174	62, 160	23	17	15, 108	18, 156	4, 862	5, 322	679	684
25 to 29 years	21, 785	24, 165	36, 286	45, 966	22	23	19, 890	21, 389	5, 649	5, 934	682	670
30 to 34 years	16, 793	17, 610	27, 084	34, 308	28	40	18, 562	17, 969	5, 580	5, 222	712	649
35 to 39 years	17, 182	17, 650	29, 093	37, 805	53	31	18, 606	17, 299	5, 664	5, 177	765	751
40 to 44 years	13, 947	12, 805	22, 126	29, 211	53	30	13, 888	11, 974	4, 510	3, 883	688	639
45 to 49 years	13, 217	10, 639	19, 165	26, 361	38	18	11, 762	9, 994	3, 865	3, 459	710	581
50 to 54 years	9, 975	7, 228	28, 908	20, 683	29	20	8, 076	6, 610	3, 221	2, 578	594	467
55 to 59 years	6, 291	3, 917	15, 290	11, 122	18	13	4, 771	3, 994	2, 132	1, 706	451	336
60 to 64 years	4, 444	3, 122	13, 611	10, 001	20	7	2, 905	2, 792	1, 332	1, 107	326	240
65 to 69 years	2, 775	2, 075	7, 932	6, 564	13	3	1, 755	1, 839	940	814	238	154
70 to 74 years	1, 463	1, 297	4, 873	4, 570	4	2	986	1, 140	603	537	137	109
75 to 79 years	830	747	2, 803	2, 849	9	4	553	684	331	337	83	74
80 to 84 years	422	461	1, 456	1, 659	3	------	249	336	159	152	41	43
85 to 89 years	196	197	637	732	1	1	144	181	88	79	17	30
90 to 94 years	77	102	259	383	------	1	52	63	23	34	4	6
95 to 99 years	32	45	104	154	------	------	21	25	9	16	4	3
100 and over	36	64	79	185	------	------	13	33	6	10	2	3
Unknown	255	220	433	448	------	------	288	253	187	122	18	14
Percent	**100. 0**	**100. 0**	**100. 0**	**100. 0**	**100. 0**	**100. 0**	**100. 0**	**100. 0**	**100. 0**	**100. 0**	**100. 0**	**100. 0**
Under 5 years	9. 3	9. 4	11. 2	10. 5	3. 8	5. 5	7. 7	7. 8	8. 0	8. 3	7. 2	8. 8
5 to 9 years	10. 4	10. 7	12. 9	12. 2	6. 3	5. 1	7. 7	8. 0	8. 7	9. 1	8. 9	9. 1
10 to 14 years	9. 7	9. 8	12. 8	11. 8	4. 3	6. 6	6. 5	7. 0	7. 3	7. 9	7. 9	8. 3
15 to 19 years	9. 3	10. 8	12. 4	12. 6	6. 1	5. 9	6. 6	7. 6	7. 4	8. 3	7. 6	8. 8
20 to 24 years	10. 3	12. 1	9. 8	11. 1	5. 8	6. 2	9. 2	11. 0	8. 5	9. 7	7. 6	8. 1
25 to 29 years	10. 1	11. 2	7. 1	8. 2	5. 6	8. 4	12. 1	13. 0	9. 9	10. 8	7. 6	8. 0
30 to 34 years	7. 8	8. 1	5. 3	6. 2	7. 1	14. 7	11. 3	10. 9	9. 8	9. 5	7. 9	7. 7
35 to 39 years	8. 0	8. 1	5. 7	6. 8	13. 4	11. 4	11. 3	10. 5	9. 9	9. 4	8. 5	8. 9
40 to 44 years	6. 5	5. 9	4. 3	5. 2	13. 4	11. 0	8. 4	7. 3	7. 9	7. 1	7. 7	7. 6
45 to 49 years	6. 1	4. 9	3. 7	4. 7	9. 6	6. 6	7. 2	6. 1	6. 8	6. 3	7. 9	6. 9
50 to 54 years	4. 6	3. 3	5. 6	3. 7	7. 3	7. 3	4. 9	4. 0	5. 6	4. 7	6. 6	5. 6
55 to 59 years	2. 9	1. 8	3. 0	2. 0	4. 6	4. 8	2. 9	2. 4	3. 7	3. 1	5. 0	4. 0
60 to 64 years	2. 1	1. 4	2. 7	1. 8	5. 1	2. 6	1. 8	1. 7	2. 3	2. 0	3. 6	2. 9
65 to 69 years	1. 3	1. 0	1. 5	1. 2	3. 3	1. 1	1. 1	1. 1	1. 6	1. 5	2. 6	1. 8
70 to 74 years	. 7	. 6	. 9	. 8	1. 0	. 7	. 6	. 7	1. 1	1. 0	1. 5	1. 3
75 to 79 years	. 4	. 3	. 5	. 5	2. 3	1. 5	. 3	. 4	. 6	. 6	. 9	. 9
80 to 84 years	. 2	. 2	. 3	. 3	. 8	------	. 2	. 2	. 3	. 3	. 5	. 5
85 years and over	. 2	. 2	. 2	. 3	. 3	. 7	. 1	. 2	. 2	. 3	. 3	. 5

TABLE 16.—NEGRO POPULATION CLASSIFIED BY 5-YEAR AGE PERIODS, AND SEX, AND BY DIVISIONS, AND STATES: 1930—Continued

[See note at head of this table]

AGE PERIOD	KANSAS		KENTUCKY		LOUISIANA		MAINE		MARYLAND		MASSACHUSETTS	
	Male	Female	Male	Female	Male	Female	Male	Female	Male	Female	Male	Female
All ages	**33, 980**	**32, 364**	**113, 501**	**112, 539**	**379, 173**	**397, 153**	**597**	**499**	**140, 506**	**135, 873**	**26, 097**	**26, 268**
Under 5 years	2, 612	2, 570	9, 370	9, 217	42, 202	42, 784	63	44	13, 484	13, 522	2, 388	2, 320
5 to 9 years	2, 963	3, 056	10, 936	10, 888	46, 313	46, 769	46	43	14, 449	15, 115	2, 620	2, 681
10 to 14 years	2, 756	2, 852	10, 030	10, 260	41, 980	42, 820	46	54	12, 622	13, 005	2, 387	2, 311
15 to 19 years	2, 631	2, 803	10, 201	10, 561	38, 192	43, 101	42	32	12, 554	12, 863	1, 949	2, 069
20 to 24 years	2, 714	2, 772	9, 648	10, 168	36, 546	43, 004	32	24	13, 841	13, 570	1, 772	2, 026
25 to 29 years	2, 775	2, 779	8, 789	9, 413	31, 806	37, 235	37	44	13, 065	12, 444	1, 913	2, 122
30 to 34 years	2, 886	2, 587	8, 179	8, 613	24, 535	27, 653	34	36	11, 218	10, 608	2, 216	2, 205
35 to 39 years	2, 998	2, 715	9, 162	9, 106	27, 002	29, 354	54	37	11, 373	10, 576	2, 385	2, 384
40 to 44 years	2, 626	2, 392	7, 875	7, 697	21, 791	21, 957	45	31	9, 223	8, 487	2, 000	2, 016
45 to 49 years	2, 339	2, 173	7, 701	7, 365	21, 383	19, 936	58	35	8, 244	7, 509	2, 049	1, 825
50 to 54 years	2, 114	1, 727	6, 781	5, 860	16, 233	14, 131	29	38	6, 903	5, 890	1, 619	1, 441
55 to 59 years	1, 552	1, 193	4, 587	3, 860	11, 099	8, 999	26	24	4, 364	3, 696	1, 113	971
60 to 64 years	1, 034	919	3, 595	3, 247	8, 177	6, 956	26	19	3, 372	2, 940	689	704
65 to 69 years	776	657	2, 678	2, 338	5, 078	4, 690	20	13	2, 271	2, 044	449	481
70 to 74 years	506	433	1, 888	1, 601	2, 965	3, 124	14	15	1, 465	1, 359	257	292
75 to 79 years	320	352	1, 020	1, 066	1, 901	2, 011	15	4	756	765	135	197
80 to 84 years	191	196	534	635	992	1, 267	8	2	393	496	66	109
85 to 89 years	112	101	260	318	458	616	1	1	157	188	30	38
90 to 94 years	24	33	78	122	183	284	--------	1	46	77	11	20
95 to 99 years	8	15	36	48	84	154	--------	--------	18	19	3	6
100 and over	10	14	18	33	63	148	--------	1	9	22	--------	4
Unknown	33	25	135	123	190	160	1	1	679	678	46	46
Percent	**100. 0**	**100. 0**	**100. 0**	**100. 0**	**100. 0**	**100. 0**	**100. 0**	**100. 0**	**100. 0**	**100. 0**	**100. 0**	**100. 0**
Under 5 years	7. 7	7. 9	8. 3	8. 2	11. 1	10. 8	10. 6	8. 8	9. 6	10. 0	9. 2	8. 8
5 to 9 years	8. 7	9. 4	9. 6	9. 7	12. 2	11. 8	7. 7	8. 6	10. 3	11. 1	10. 0	10. 2
10 to 14 years	8. 1	8. 8	8. 8	9. 1	11. 1	10. 8	7. 7	10. 8	9. 0	9. 6	9. 1	8. 8
15 to 19 years	7. 7	8. 7	9. 0	9. 4	10. 1	10. 9	7. 0	6. 4	8. 9	9. 5	7. 5	7. 9
20 to 24 years	8. 0	8. 6	8. 5	9. 0	9. 6	10. 8	5. 4	4. 8	9. 9	10. 0	6. 8	7. 7
25 to 29 years	8. 2	8. 6	7. 7	8. 4	8. 4	9. 4	6. 2	8. 8	9. 3	9. 2	7. 3	8. 1
30 to 34 years	8. 5	8. 0	7. 2	7. 7	6. 5	7. 0	5. 7	7. 2	8. 0	7. 8	8. 5	8. 4
34 to 39 years	8. 8	8. 4	8. 1	8. 1	7. 1	7. 4	9. 0	7. 4	8. 1	7. 8	9. 1	9. 1
40 to 44 years	7. 7	7. 4	6. 9	6. 8	5. 7	5. 5	7. 5	6. 2	6. 6	6. 2	7. 7	7. 7
45 to 49 years	6. 9	6. 7	6. 8	6. 5	5. 6	5. 0	9. 7	7. 0	5. 9	5. 5	7. 9	6. 9
50 to 54 years	6. 2	5. 3	6. 0	5. 2	4. 3	3. 6	4. 9	7. 6	4. 9	4. 3	6. 2	5. 5
55 to 59 years	4. 6	3. 7	4. 0	3. 4	2. 9	2. 3	4. 4	4. 8	3. 1	2. 7	4. 3	3. 7
60 to 64 years	3. 0	2. 8	3. 2	2. 9	2. 2	1. 8	4. 4	3. 8	2. 4	2. 2	2. 6	2. 7
65 to 69 years	2. 3	2. 0	2. 4	2. 1	1. 3	1. 2	3. 4	2. 6	1. 6	1. 5	1. 7	1. 8
70 to 74 years	1. 5	1. 3	1. 7	1. 4	. 8	. 8	2. 3	3. 0	1. 0	1. 0	1. 0	1. 1
75 to 79 years	. 9	1. 1	. 9	. 9	. 5	. 5	2. 5	. 8	. 5	. 6	. 5	. 7
80 to 84 years	. 6	. 6	. 5	. 6	. 3	. 3	1. 3	. 4	. 3	. 4	. 3	. 4
85 years and over	. 5	. 5	. 3	. 5	. 2	. 3	. 2	. 6	. 2	. 2	. 2	. 3

AGE PERIOD	MICHIGAN		MINNESOTA		MISSISSIPPI		MISSOURI		MONTANA		NEBRASKA	
	Male	Female	Male	Female	Male	Female	Male	Female	Male	Female	Male	Female
All ages	**88, 936**	**80, 517**	**5, 005**	**4, 440**	**498, 338**	**511, 380**	**111, 929**	**111, 911**	**710**	**546**	**7, 063**	**6, 689**
Under 5 years	7, 578	7, 653	320	295	58, 663	58, 772	8, 494	8, 336	38	28	531	515
5 to 9 years	7, 325	7, 407	332	343	63, 760	63, 465	9, 251	9, 095	28	34	546	555
10 to 14 years	5, 540	5, 847	320	292	59, 296	57, 543	8, 084	8, 434	43	47	484	446
15 to 19 years	5, 143	5, 745	282	332	55, 752	59, 141	8, 480	9, 255	32	26	455	507
20 to 24 years	8, 473	9, 258	311	339	48, 136	56, 225	9, 302	11, 363	42	36	503	619
25 to 29 years	12, 414	11, 891	379	353	38, 400	44, 427	10, 502	12, 188	51	49	692	712
30 to 34 years	11, 760	9, 754	472	411	28, 764	32, 735	9, 983	10, 576	48	49	661	653
35 to 39 years	10, 756	8, 345	540	496	29, 771	34, 313	10, 926	10, 929	62	61	744	713
40 to 44 years	7, 147	4, 907	499	390	24, 001	25, 902	9, 433	8, 493	75	40	659	581
45 to 49 years	5, 361	3, 689	483	387	21, 399	24, 140	8, 735	7, 345	65	50	630	486
50 to 54 years	3, 186	2, 234	394	259	23, 634	18, 529	6, 522	5, 332	69	50	467	336
55 to 59 years	1, 803	1, 318	276	199	15, 822	11, 109	4, 211	3, 365	53	29	247	208
60 to 64 years	1, 001	919	158	128	13, 067	9, 416	3, 022	2, 481	43	19	181	126
65 to 69 years	595	593	121	94	7, 742	5, 765	1, 995	1, 771	26	8	112	95
70 to 74 years	305	367	49	46	4, 577	4, 031	1, 225	1, 161	20	9	56	53
75 to 79 years	220	252	32	40	2, 704	2, 515	804	742	6	5	42	41
80 to 84 years	102	120	16	18	1, 542	1, 674	409	457	5	3	21	17
85 to 89 years	41	54	7	9	640	760	206	225	3	1	13	11
90 to 94 years	14	23	5	4	267	358	60	92	--------	1	4	6
95 to 99 years	6	11	--------	1	94	148	20	31	--------	--------	--------	4
100 and over	--------	12	1	1	92	191	15	24	--------	--------	1	--------
Unknown	166	118	8	3	215	221	250	216	1	1	14	5
Percent	**100. 0**	**100. 0**	**100. 0**	**100. 0**	**100. 0**	**100. 0**	**100. 0**	**100. 0**	**100. 0**	**100. 0**	**100. 0**	**100. 0**
Under 5 years	8. 5	9. 5	6. 4	6. 6	11. 8	11. 5	7. 6	7. 4	5. 4	5. 1	7. 5	7. 7
5 to 9 years	8. 2	9. 2	6. 6	7. 7	12. 8	12. 4	8. 3	8. 1	3. 9	6. 2	7. 7	8. 3
10 to 14 years	6. 2	7. 3	6. 4	6. 6	11. 9	11. 3	7. 2	7. 5	6. 1	8. 6	6. 9	6. 7
15 to 19 years	5. 8	7. 1	5. 6	7. 5	11. 2	11. 6	7. 6	8. 3	4. 5	4. 8	6. 4	7. 6
20 to 24 years	9. 5	11. 5	6. 2	7. 6	9. 7	11. 0	8. 3	10. 2	5. 9	6. 6	7. 1	9. 3
25 to 29 years	14. 0	14. 8	7. 6	8. 0	7. 7	8. 7	9. 4	10. 9	7. 2	9. 0	9. 8	10. 6
30 to 34 years	13. 2	12. 1	9. 4	9. 3	5. 8	6. 4	8. 9	9. 5	6. 8	9. 0	9. 4	9. 8
35 to 39 years	12. 1	10. 4	10. 8	11. 2	6. 0	6. 7	9. 8	9. 8	8. 7	11. 2	10. 5	10. 7
40 to 44 years	8. 0	6. 1	10. 0	8. 8	4. 8	5. 1	8. 4	7. 6	10. 6	7. 3	9. 3	8. 7
45 to 49 years	6. 0	4. 6	9. 7	8. 7	4. 3	4. 7	7. 8	6. 6	9. 2	9. 2	8. 9	7. 3
50 to 54 years	3. 6	2. 8	7. 9	5. 8	4. 7	3. 6	5. 8	4. 8	9. 7	9. 2	6. 6	5. 0
55 to 59 years	2. 0	1. 6	5. 5	4. 5	3. 2	2. 2	3. 8	3. 0	7. 5	5. 3	3. 5	3. 1
60 to 64 years	1. 1	1. 1	3. 2	2. 9	2. 6	1. 8	2. 7	2. 2	6. 1	3. 5	2. 6	1. 9
65 to 69 years	. 7	. 7	2. 4	2. 1	1. 6	1. 1	1. 8	1. 6	3. 7	1. 5	1. 6	1. 4
70 to 74 years	. 3	. 5	1. 0	1. 0	. 9	. 8	1. 1	1. 0	2. 8	1. 6	. 8	. 8
75 to 79 years	. 2	. 3	. 6	. 9	. 5	. 5	. 7	. 7	. 8	. 9	. 6	. 6
80 to 84 years	. 1	. 1	. 3	. 4	. 3	. 3	. 4	. 4	. 7	. 5	. 3	. 3
85 years and over	. 1	. 1	. 3	. 3	. 2	. 3	. 3	. 3	. 4	. 4	. 3	. 3

TABLE 16.—NEGRO POPULATION CLASSIFIED BY 5-YEAR AGE PERIODS, AND SEX, AND BY DIVISIONS, AND STATES: 1930—Continued

[See note at head of this table]

AGE PERIOD	NEVADA		NEW HAMPSHIRE		NEW JERSEY		NEW MEXICO		NEW YORK		NORTH CAROLINA	
	Male	Female	Male	Female	Male	Female	Male	Female	Male	Female	Male	Female
All ages	**277**	**239**	**524**	**266**	**102,929**	**105,899**	**1,531**	**1,319**	**199,485**	**213,329**	**446,500**	**472,147**
Under 5 years	10	11	20	28	9,904	9,886	140	109	16,923	17,193	57,040	57,655
5 to 9 years	11	12	23	22	9,788	10,036	131	142	15,327	15,990	64,644	65,499
10 to 14 years	5	8	24	24	8,143	8,455	119	100	11,886	12,738	58,815	58,948
15 to 19 years	6	9	35	28	7,664	9,131	132	127	11,993	15,479	55,846	59,320
20 to 24 years	15	14	61	25	9,817	11,478	116	120	21,024	26,950	43,601	51,403
25 to 29 years	19	25	40	19	11,156	12,268	121	124	27,994	31,081	31,595	38,248
30 to 34 years	30	20	62	9	10,014	9,773	114	109	24,978	24,764	23,827	27,557
35 to 39 years	31	31	61	23	9,748	9,601	144	151	22,916	22,369	23,472	27,717
40 to 44 years	37	34	53	23	7,367	7,158	121	100	16,119	15,521	18,940	21,808
45 to 49 years	37	20	66	20	6,466	6,121	110	73	12,303	11,892	17,519	19,576
50 to 54 years	26	19	32	17	5,074	4,571	122	59	7,949	7,599	17,583	15,100
55 to 59 years	19	15	21	11	3,123	2,685	53	30	4,338	4,329	11,643	8,941
60 to 64 years	14	7	7	4	1,982	1,833	54	20	2,519	2,816	8,242	7,179
65 to 69 years	7	6	10	7	1,147	1,160	18	12	1,388	1,971	5,449	4,855
70 to 74 years	4	4	4	1	690	681	16	4	760	1,091	3,779	3,527
75 to 79 years	4		1	2	364	455	6	3	428	665	2,169	2,021
80 to 84 years			2		159	246	4	1	191	315	1,127	1,224
85 to 89 years	1	2			69	99	3		92	131	476	560
90 to 94 years			1	1	29	38	5		18	49	164	275
95 to 99 years					7	20			10	15	72	113
100 and over	1				5	14	1		3	14	42	138
Unknown		2	1	2	213	190	1	5	326	357	455	483
Percent	**100.0**	**100.0**	**100.0**	**100.0**	**100.0**	**100.0**	**100.0**	**100.0**	**100.0**	**100.0**	**100.0**	**100.0**
Under 5 years	3.6	4.6	3.8	10.5	9.6	9.3	9.1	8.3	8.5	8.1	12.8	12.2
5 to 9 years	4.0	5.0	4.4	8.3	9.5	9.5	8.6	10.8	7.7	7.5	14.5	13.9
10 to 14 years	1.8	3.3	4.6	9.0	7.9	8.0	7.8	9.9	6.0	6.0	13.2	12.5
15 to 19 years	2.2	3.8	6.7	10.5	7.4	8.6	8.6	9.6	6.0	7.3	12.5	12.6
20 to 24 years	5 4	5.9	11.6	9.4	9.5	10.8	7.6	9.1	10.5	12.6	9.8	10.9
25 to 29 years	6.9	10.5	7.6	7.1	10.8	11.6	7.9	9.4	14.0	14.6	7.1	8.1
30 to 34 years	10.8	8.4	11.8	3.4	9.7	9.2	7.4	8.3	12.5	11.6	5.3	5.8
35 to 39 years	11.2	13.0	11.6	8.6	9.5	9.1	9.4	11.4	11.5	10.5	5.3	5.9
40 to 44 years	13.4	14.2	10.1	8.6	7.2	6.8	7.9	7.6	8.1	7.3	4.2	4.6
45 to 49 years	13.4	8.4	12.6	7.5	6.3	5.8	7.2	5.5	6.2	5.6	3.9	4.1
50 to 54 years	9.4	7.9	6.1	6.4	4.9	4.3	8.0	4.5	4.0	3.6	3.9	3.2
55 to 59 years	6.9	6.3	4.0	4.1	3.0	2.5	3.5	2.3	2.2	2.0	2.6	1.9
60 to 64 years	5.1	2.9	1.3	1.5	1.9	1.7	3.5	1.5	1.3	1.3	1.8	1.5
65 to 69 years	2.5	2.5	1.9	2.6	1.1	1.1	1.2	.9	.7	.9	1.2	1.0
70 to 74 years	1.4	1.7	.8	.4	.7	.6	1.0	.3	.4	.5	.8	.7
75 to 79 years	1.4		.2	.8	.4	.4	.4	.2	.2	.3	.5	.4
80 to 84 years			.4		.2	.2	.3	.1	.1	.1	.3	.3
85 years and over	.7	.8	.2	.4	.1	.2	.6		.1	.1	.2	.2

AGE PERIOD	NORTH DAKOTA		OHIO		OKLAHOMA		OREGON		PENNSYLVANIA		RHODE ISLAND	
	Male	Female	Male	Female	Male	Female	Male	Female	Male	Female	Male	Female
All ages	**243**	**134**	**159,128**	**150,176**	**86,818**	**85,380**	**1,210**	**1,024**	**218,412**	**212,845**	**4,862**	**5,051**
Under 5 years	20	10	13,766	14,079	8,595	8,742	44	63	19,554	19,791	494	514
5 to 9 years	13	8	14,133	14,826	9,908	9,884	54	73	20,054	20,578	525	544
10 to 14 years	10	5	11,827	12,259	9,122	9,174	61	61	16,034	16,994	474	464
15 to 19 years	19	7	11,240	12,518	9,099	9,712	60	68	15,203	18,010	355	452
20 to 24 years	9	23	14,199	15,193	8,321	9,572	75	86	19,213	22,682	331	343
25 to 29 years	19	12	17,135	17,231	7,421	8,174	95	80	24,843	25,510	356	334
30 to 34 years	15	17	16,335	14,844	6,083	6,386	109	89	23,531	21,412	338	380
35 to 39 years	25	9	17,084	14,404	6,064	6,171	148	119	23,049	20,468	380	365
40 to 44 years	24	16	12,565	10,219	4,887	4,852	147	108	17,096	14,206	354	342
45 to 49 years	28	9	10,755	8,200	4,579	4,206	130	94	14,447	11,867	357	348
50 to 54 years	25	7	7,583	5,768	4,594	2,952	105	63	10,548	8,183	290	296
55 to 59 years	14	5	4,722	3,615	3,095	1,848	84	45	6,216	4,847	211	216
60 to 64 years	8	4	3,060	2,570	1,973	1,291	35	30	3,771	3,264	153	170
65 to 69 years	6	1	1,908	1,665	1,281	926	30	25	2,211	2,046	102	110
70 to 74 years	6		1,224	1,203	755	542	10	10	1,254	1,279	59	75
75 to 79 years	1	1	713	707	478	368	10	5	630	771	32	51
80 to 84 years			362	377	259	253	7	3	277	415	26	29
85 to 89 years	1		173	198	127	132	2		133	173	12	7
90 to 94 years			61	66	55	54			43	65	3	6
95 to 99 years			18	24	23	21			16	16	3	
100 and over			13	29	22	43			9	21	1	
Unknown			252	181	77	77	4	2	280	247	6	5
Percent	**100.0**	**100.0**	**100.0**	**100.0**	**100.0**	**100.0**	**100.0**	**100.0**	**100.0**	**100.0**	**100.0**	**100.0**
Under 5 years	8.2	7.5	8.7	9.4	9.9	10.2	3.6	6.2	9.0	9.3	10.2	10.2
5 to 9 years	5.3	6.0	8.9	9.9	11.4	11.6	4.5	7.1	9.2	9.7	10.8	10.8
10 to 14 years	4.1	3.7	7.4	8.2	10.5	10.7	5.0	6.0	7.3	8.0	9.7	9.2
15 to 19 years	7.8	5.2	7.1	8.3	10.5	11.4	5.0	6.6	7.0	8.5	7.3	8.9
20 to 24 years	3.7	17.2	8.9	10.1	9.6	11.2	6.2	8.4	8.8	10.7	6.8	6.8
25 to 29 years	7.8	9.0	10.8	11.5	8.5	9.6	7.9	7.8	11.4	12.0	7.3	6.6
30 to 34 years	6.2	12.7	10.3	9.9	7.0	7.5	9.0	8.7	10.8	10.1	7.0	7.5
35 to 39 years	10.3	6.7	10.7	9.6	7.0	7.2	12.2	11.6	10.6	9.6	7.8	7.2
40 to 44 years	9.9	11.9	7.9	6.8	5.6	5.7	12.1	10.5	7.8	6.7	7.3	6.8
45 to 49 years	11.5	6.7	6.8	5.5	5.3	4.9	10.7	9.2	6.6	5.6	7.3	6.9
50 to 54 years	10.3	5.2	4.8	3.8	5.3	3.5	8.7	6.2	4.8	3.8	6.0	5.9
55 to 59 years	5.8	3.7	3.0	2.4	3.6	2.2	6.9	4.4	2.8	2.3	4.3	4.3
60 to 64 years	3.3	3.0	1.9	1.7	2.3	1.5	2.9	2.9	1.7	1.5	3.1	3.4
65 to 69 years	2.5	.7	1.2	1.1	1.5	1.1	2.5	2.4	1.0	1.0	2.1	2.2
70 to 74 years	2.5		.8	.8	.9	.6	.8	1.0	.6	.6	1.2	1.5
75 to 79 years	.4	.7	.4	.5	.6	.4	.8	.5	.3	.4	.7	1.0
80 to 84 years			.2	.3	.3	.3	.6	.3	.1	.2	.5	.6
85 years and over	.4		.2	.2	.3	.3	.2		.1	.1	.4	.3

TABLE 16.—NEGRO POPULATION CLASSIFIED BY 5-YEAR AGE PERIODS, AND SEX, AND BY DIVISIONS, AND STATES: 1930—Continued

[See note at head of this table]

AGE PERIOD	SOUTH CAROLINA		SOUTH DAKOTA		TENNESSEE		TEXAS		UTAH		VERMONT	
	Male	Female	Male	Female	Male	Female	Male	Female	Male	Female	Male	Female
All ages	**379,300**	**414,381**	**343**	**303**	**232,569**	**245,077**	**422,608**	**432,356**	**609**	**499**	**310**	**258**
Under 5 years	47,656	48,644	17	30	21,961	22,343	42,831	43,289	49	40	38	37
5 to 9 years	57,803	58,493	22	31	24,975	25,393	48,613	48,896	38	39	23	25
10 to 14 years	55,474	55,649	25	30	24,130	24,022	44,569	44,501	40	46	23	31
15 to 19 years	50,805	55,624	36	26	24,953	26,882	43,586	49,110	25	19	23	39
20 to 24 years	34,172	42,480	29	36	22,337	26,951	42,526	49,043	36	33	24	15
25 to 29 years	21,868	29,431	30	22	19,166	23,183	37,385	42,807	46	42	24	5
30 to 34 years	16,972	21,997	32	19	15,778	17,830	31,076	32,974	51	50	22	14
35 to 39 years	19,484	25,535	25	19	16,651	18,911	31,159	32,777	66	53	23	18
40 to 44 years	16,842	20,158	26	25	12,721	14,302	24,215	24,209	53	56	19	11
45 to 49 years	15,223	17,815	26	16	11,374	12,985	24,027	20,582	67	42	24	19
50 to 54 years	13,773	13,171	22	16	14,070	11,128	17,398	14,233	61	25	19	14
55 to 59 years	8,750	7,651	15	10	8,427	6,502	10,814	8,716	29	20	17	6
60 to 64 years	8,937	6,618	11	9	6,152	5,211	10,222	8,262	20	12	11	6
65 to 69 years	5,171	4,449	11	4	3,974	3,435	6,051	4,919	14	10	7	5
70 to 74 years	3,185	2,944	8	5	2,582	2,370	3,446	3,123	4	5	4	6
75 to 79 years	1,638	1,647	4	2	1,414	1,468	2,176	1,966	5	2	7	4
80 to 84 years	827	1,039	---	2	848	905	1,094	1,263	4	3	---	2
85 to 89 years	347	431	1	1	321	393	520	575	---	1	---	---
90 to 94 years	119	217	---	---	141	192	206	323	---	1	2	---
95 to 99 years	69	72	---	---	61	73	91	147	---	---	---	---
100 and over	40	88	---	---	41	72	76	148	---	---	---	1
Unknown	145	228	3	---	542	526	527	493	1	---	---	---
Percent	**100.0**	**100.0**	**100.0**	**100.0**	**100.0**	**100.0**	**100.0**	**100.0**	**100.0**	**100.0**	**100.0**	**100.0**
Under 5 years	12.6	11.7	5.0	9.9	9.4	9.1	10.1	10.0	8.0	8.0	12.3	14.3
5 to 9 years	15.2	14.1	6.4	10.2	10.7	10.4	11.5	11.3	6.2	7.8	7.4	9.7
10 to 14 years	14.6	13.4	7.3	9.9	10.4	9.8	10.5	10.3	6.6	9.2	7.4	12.0
15 to 19 years	13.4	13.4	10.5	8.6	10.7	11.0	10.3	11.4	4.1	3.8	7.4	15.1
20 to 24 years	9.0	10.3	8.5	11.9	9.6	11.0	10.1	11.3	5.9	6.6	7.7	5.8
25 to 29 years	5.8	7.1	8.7	7.3	8.2	9.5	8.8	9.9	7.6	8.4	7.7	1.9
30 to 34 years	4.5	5.3	9.3	6.3	6.8	7.3	7.4	7.6	8.4	10.0	7.1	5.4
35 to 39 years	5.1	6.2	7.3	6.3	7.2	7.7	7.4	7.6	10.8	10.6	7.4	7.0
40 to 44 years	4.4	4.9	7.6	8.3	5.5	5.8	5.7	5.6	8.7	11.2	6.1	4.3
45 to 49 years	4.0	4.3	7.6	5.3	4.9	5.3	5.7	4.8	11.0	8.4	7.7	7.4
50 to 54 years	3.6	3.2	6.4	5.3	6.0	4.5	4.1	3.3	10.0	5.0	6.1	5.4
55 to 59 years	2.3	1.8	4.4	3.3	3.6	2.7	2.6	2.0	4.8	4.0	5.5	2.3
60 to 64 years	2.4	1.6	3.2	3.0	2.6	2.1	2.4	1.9	3.3	2.4	3.5	2.3
65 to 69 years	1.4	1.1	3.2	1.3	1.7	1.4	1.4	1.1	2.3	2.0	2.3	1.9
70 to 74 years	.8	.7	2.3	1.7	1.1	1.0	.8	.7	.7	1.0	1.3	2.3
75 to 79 years	.4	.4	1.2	.7	.6	.6	.5	.5	.8	.4	2.3	1.6
80 to 84 years	.2	.3	---	.7	.4	.4	.3	.3	.7	.6	---	.8
85 years and over	.2	.2	.3	.3	.2	.3	.2	.3	---	.4	.6	.4

AGE PERIOD	VIRGINIA		WASHINGTON		WEST VIRGINIA		WISCONSIN		WYOMING	
	Male	Female	Male	Female	Male	Female	Male	Female	Male	Female
All ages	**321,545**	**328,620**	**3,797**	**3,043**	**60,873**	**54,020**	**5,811**	**4,928**	**699**	**551**
Under 5 years	34,973	35,689	195	205	5,988	6,116	406	444	34	29
5 to 9 years	42,429	42,645	215	233	6,329	6,539	471	489	29	40
10 to 14 years	39,430	39,463	235	186	5,127	5,317	395	393	34	36
15 to 19 years	36,432	37,011	205	211	4,705	5,404	329	367	33	35
20 to 24 years	27,327	29,240	229	230	5,533	5,684	533	533	50	45
25 to 29 years	20,715	23,763	258	208	6,045	5,636	732	664	48	35
30 to 34 years	17,860	20,423	294	248	5,800	4,746	678	528	73	62
35 to 39 years	20,297	22,730	346	300	5,960	4,412	697	481	89	49
40 to 44 years	18,102	18,553	379	276	4,803	3,195	540	335	68	71
45 to 49 years	17,622	17,180	391	278	3,924	2,451	382	238	68	58
50 to 54 years	15,328	13,627	372	247	2,636	1,728	271	162	71	28
55 to 59 years	10,358	8,162	274	158	1,644	895	174	100	31	26
60 to 64 years	7,773	7,080	151	113	1,003	685	74	77	34	16
65 to 69 years	5,274	5,065	117	60	623	457	50	47	14	8
70 to 74 years	3,651	3,497	63	38	361	303	29	31	9	5
75 to 79 years	2,009	2,029	30	13	168	191	17	13	7	4
80 to 84 years	1,113	1,247	14	18	96	101	11	8	2	1
85 to 89 years	420	524	4	13	35	61	9	6	---	2
90 to 94 years	157	269	4	2	13	22	2	3	1	---
95 to 99 years	56	108	2	---	5	8	1	---	---	---
100 and over	39	87	---	2	3	12	---	2	---	---
Unknown	180	228	19	4	72	57	10	7	4	1
Percent	**100.0**	**100.0**	**100.0**	**100.0**	**100.0**	**100.0**	**100.0**	**100.0**	**100.0**	**100.0**
Under 5 years	10.9	10.9	5.1	6.7	9.8	11.3	7.0	9.0	4.9	5.3
5 to 9 years	13.2	13.0	5.7	7.7	10.4	12.1	8.1	9.9	4.1	7.3
10 to 14 years	12.3	12.0	6.2	6.1	8.4	9.8	6.8	8.0	4.9	6.5
15 to 19 years	11.3	11.3	5.4	6.9	7.7	10.0	5.7	7.4	4.7	6.4
20 to 24 years	8.5	8.9	6.0	7.6	9.1	10.5	9.2	10.8	7.2	8.2
25 to 29 years	6.4	7.2	6.8	6.8	9.9	10.4	12.6	13.5	6.9	6.4
30 to 34 years	5.6	6.2	7.7	8.1	9.5	8.8	11.7	10.7	10.4	11.3
35 to 39 years	6.3	6.9	9.1	9.9	9.8	8.2	12.0	9.8	12.7	8.9
40 to 44 years	5.6	5.6	10.0	9.1	7.9	5.9	9.3	6.8	9.7	12.9
45 to 49 years	5.5	5.2	10.3	9.1	6.4	4.5	6.6	4.8	9.7	10.5
50 to 54 years	4.8	4.1	9.8	8.1	4.3	3.2	4.7	3.3	10.2	5.1
55 to 59 years	3.2	2.5	7.2	5.2	2.7	1.7	3.0	2.0	4.4	4.7
60 to 64 years	2.4	2.2	4.0	3.7	1.6	1.3	1.3	1.6	4.9	2.9
65 to 69 years	1.6	1.5	3.1	2.0	1.0	.8	.9	1.0	2.0	1.5
70 to 74 years	1.1	1.1	1.7	1.2	.6	.6	.5	.6	1.3	.9
75 to 79 years	.6	.6	.8	.4	.3	.4	.3	.3	1.0	.7
80 to 84 years	.3	.4	.4	.6	.2	.2	.2	.2	.3	.2
85 years and over	.2	.3	.3	.6	.1	.2	.2	.2	.1	.4

TABLE 17.—NEGRO POPULATION CLASSIFIED BY SINGLE YEARS OF AGE UP TO 29, BY SEX, AND BY STATES: 1930

AGE	ALABAMA		ARIZONA		ARKANSAS		CALIFORNIA		COLORADO		CONNECTICUT		DELAWARE		DISTRICT OF COLUMBIA		FLORIDA	
	Male	Female	Male	Female	Male	Female	Male	Female	Male	Female	Male	Female	Male	Female	Male	Female	Male	Female
Under 1 year	10,077	10,429	80	73	4,761	4,948	469	502	69	81	283	287	283	265	921	926	3,671	3,678
1 year	9,537	9,748	75	78	4,288	4,450	489	510	75	84	260	283	248	255	926	944	3,524	3,594
2 years	11,134	11,222	84	86	4,960	5,085	563	506	72	62	320	290	273	291	1,044	959	4,115	4,212
3 years	11,387	11,774	77	86	5,367	5,514	551	575	79	81	285	339	262	304	1,124	1,049	4,440	4,550
4 years	11,343	11,185	80	74	5,284	5,300	563	555	94	76	311	311	325	281	1,021	1,092	4,345	4,312
5 years	11,879	11,858	79	81	5,569	5,502	640	584	73	82	305	315	301	306	1,101	1,099	4,424	4,476
6 years	12,146	12,184	75	80	5,677	5,848	608	575	72	85	283	301	353	342	1,064	1,098	4,640	4,803
7 years	11,786	11,835	82	91	5,373	5,372	582	632	66	79	267	279	313	315	1,040	1,093	4,471	4,668
8 years	12,126	12,100	86	82	5,554	5,652	617	613	78	83	290	281	352	344	1,065	1,119	4,507	4,735
9 years	11,024	10,770	85	90	5,323	5,363	583	594	80	77	281	298	303	319	1,044	1,115	4,282	4,444
10 years	11,989	11,853	84	86	5,868	5,747	589	578	73	79	272	294	351	369	996	1,125	4,596	4,551
11 years	9,204	9,263	62	68	4,756	4,824	501	547	64	83	223	232	264	256	883	918	3,655	3,759
12 years	11,489	11,133	72	78	5,608	5,487	507	571	81	81	227	246	336	302	879	1,062	4,451	4,483
13 years	10,445	10,500	75	58	4,906	5,126	493	497	65	75	199	247	240	283	801	972	3,916	4,104
14 years	11,499	11,559	75	69	5,376	5,213	548	591	77	79	201	206	294	290	873	975	4,244	4,357
15 years	10,670	11,116	75	54	5,031	5,130	491	511	53	75	206	243	267	295	846	977	3,859	4,234
16 years	11,659	12,094	92	64	5,192	5,553	511	567	80	90	225	222	311	299	872	1,094	4,071	4,629
17 years	11,299	10,758	75	66	5,067	5,093	521	565	58	91	225	230	315	297	969	1,105	3,895	4,486
18 years	10,117	12,645	104	65	5,095	6,305	535	680	77	84	227	271	299	316	1,039	1,362	4,335	5,112
19 years	8,042	10,816	114	79	4,632	5,447	557	627	85	90	208	259	311	275	1,031	1,380	3,842	4,892
20 years	8,389	12,801	130	73	4,427	6,260	506	684	79	91	220	280	313	345	1,102	1,575	3,877	5,564
21 years	8,955	9,186	134	59	5,074	4,700	621	682	66	105	217	258	317	245	1,217	1,404	4,393	4,676
22 years	9,463	11,028	169	71	4,773	5,313	629	772	67	107	228	337	346	256	1,371	1,553	4,672	5,365
23 years	8,441	10,397	172	96	4,298	5,169	613	730	78	108	239	302	291	254	1,406	1,676	4,605	5,298
24 years	8,265	10,148	138	86	4,259	4,983	664	810	94	97	280	308	306	315	1,376	1,726	4,598	5,354
25 years	8,648	10,685	135	85	4,285	5,082	713	871	92	115	294	318	293	293	1,560	1,819	4,848	5,525
26 years	6,811	8,480	150	99	3,566	4,469	651	854	86	117	265	284	252	266	1,214	1,460	4,022	4,675
27 years	5,976	7,411	102	103	3,473	3,841	724	807	82	95	287	288	279	248	1,380	1,493	4,065	4,390
28 years	7,358	8,762	123	111	3,835	4,491	769	949	85	110	303	308	320	269	1,391	1,672	4,622	5,084
29 years	6,103	7,284	154	101	3,386	3,736	873	957	99	114	372	298	334	265	1,449	1,551	4,228	4,491

AGE	GEORGIA		IDAHO		ILLINOIS		INDIANA		IOWA		KANSAS		KENTUCKY		LOUISIANA		MAINE		MARYLAND	
	Male	Female	Male	Female	Male	Female	Male	Female	Male	Female	Male	Female	Male	Female	Male	Female	Male	Female	Male	Female
Under 1 year	10,890	11,152	3	2	2,486	2,443	836	818	119	139	463	479	1,751	1,749	7,993	8,096	10	11	2,523	2,523
1 year	10,109	10,397	4	3	2,355	2,366	836	832	125	124	475	460	1,652	1,631	7,604	7,754	8	5	2,493	2,490
2 years	11,939	12,123	1	2	2,596	2,567	973	948	132	142	556	541	1,940	1,945	8,627	8,648	14	10	2,747	2,811
3 years	12,123	12,542	5	3	2,579	2,733	942	1,002	138	162	569	554	1,958	1,935	9,050	9,369	16	5	2,907	2,872
4 years	12,375	12,366	2	5	2,595	2,658	991	964	137	173	549	536	2,069	1,957	8,928	8,917	15	13	2,814	2,826
5 years	12,792	13,048	4	2	2,557	2,781	1,017	981	131	146	607	591	2,166	2,128	9,126	9,311	10	6	2,873	2,965
6 years	13,713	14,143	3	7	2,500	2,653	1,006	984	162	168	569	591	2,263	2,201	9,695	9,906	5	9	2,985	3,043
7 years	13,093	13,468	7	-------	2,510	2,529	935	1,022	150	137	583	621	2,169	2,142	9,177	9,275	9	10	2,832	2,967
8 years	13,867	14,203	2	5	2,595	2,642	1,001	1,058	193	168	582	614	2,227	2,300	9,702	9,674	11	12	2,902	3,175
9 years	12,793	12,906	9	-------	2,460	2,533	1,012	951	160	148	622	639	2,111	2,116	8,613	8,603	11	6	2,857	2,965
10 years	14,218	13,998	3	5	2,470	2,672	922	960	160	133	593	604	2,121	2,151	9,542	9,397	15	14	2,960	2,903
11 years	11,227	11,081	2	3	2,087	2,182	758	849	130	131	541	541	1,812	1,911	7,356	7,583	10	7	2,371	2,418
12 years	14,118	14,000	4	3	2,045	2,167	863	859	142	139	557	512	2,049	2,042	9,049	8,940	7	14	2,511	2,669
13 years	12,641	12,836	2	4	1,977	2,184	760	831	137	132	520	588	1,899	1,990	7,793	8,210	6	8	2,419	2,475
14 years	13,485	13,789	6	3	2,086	2,241	847	828	141	163	545	607	2,149	2,166	8,240	8,600	8	11	2,361	2,540
15 years	12,567	13,460	3	5	1,974	2,116	815	786	128	150	523	582	1,918	2,009	7,738	8,136	6	7	2,274	2,411
16 years	13,182	14,631	4	2	2,082	2,343	867	889	139	141	520	533	2,144	2,207	7,833	8,889	10	8	2,576	2,512
17 years	12,571	13,473	3	-------	2,167	2,294	817	906	143	157	523	539	2,043	2,115	7,440	8,338	5	5	2,531	2,509
18 years	13,537	15,541	6	6	2,284	2,837	863	1,030	125	153	545	611	2,140	2,167	8,086	9,406	10	4	2,539	2,804
19 years	11,898	13,356	8	3	2,391	2,875	846	927	144	134	520	538	1,956	2,063	7,095	8,332	11	8	2,634	2,627
20 years	11,630	15,757	4	2	2,368	3,300	911	1,097	141	133	541	596	1,944	2,130	7,227	9,891	9	4	2,516	2,785
21 years	10,615	11,059	3	6	2,896	3,083	943	943	132	126	540	480	2,016	1,894	7,377	7,648	2	1	2,771	2,435
22 years	10,419	12,835	4	3	3,024	3,706	1,022	1,064	137	146	513	537	1,925	2,073	7,893	8,792	5	8	2,887	2,846
23 years	9,078	11,788	6	2	3,280	3,929	963	1,107	138	148	526	561	1,838	2,009	7,101	8,515	8	6	2,798	2,731
24 years	8,432	10,721	6	4	3,540	4,138	1,023	1,111	131	131	594	598	1,925	2,062	6,948	8,158	8	5	2,869	2,773
25 years	9,294	12,010	1	1	3,762	4,271	1,139	1,216	119	128	569	574	1,859	2,055	7,564	8,975	9	10	2,814	2,765
26 years	6,751	8,834	5	5	3,645	4,077	1,025	1,131	148	122	536	525	1,589	1,894	6,220	7,367	6	10	2,369	2,290
27 years	6,363	7,808	5	8	3,853	4,031	1,059	1,039	137	134	536	526	1,665	1,716	5,826	6,809	8	5	2,456	2,297
28 years	7,632	9,613	5	4	4,140	4,568	1,118	1,236	133	136	533	568	1,874	1,941	6,489	7,622	6	7	2,777	2,668
29 years	6,246	7,701	6	5	4,490	4,442	1,308	1,312	145	150	601	586	1,802	1,807	5,707	6,462	8	12	2,649	2,424

AGE	MASSACHUSETTS		MICHIGAN		MINNESOTA		MISSISSIPPI		MISSOURI		MONTANA		NEBRASKA		NEVADA		NEW HAMPSHIRE		NEW JERSEY	
	Male	Female	Male	Female	Male	Female	Male	Female	Male	Female	Male	Female	Male	Female	Male	Female	Male	Female	Male	Female
Under 1 year	437	422	1,506	1,462	54	52	10,974	10,948	1,644	1,612	6	6	110	107	4	4	6	4	1,975	1,970
1 year	423	456	1,341	1,371	59	61	10,455	10,383	1,587	1,554	9	7	91	97	1	1	3	3	1,865	1,847
2 years	478	472	1,575	1,562	69	54	11,921	11,987	1,664	1,728	4	6	117	103	2	4	4	10	2,029	1,983
3 years	510	496	1,623	1,709	76	63	12,999	13,187	1,776	1,799	10	3	118	111	2	-------	5	6	2,094	2,107
4 years	540	474	1,533	1,549	62	65	12,314	12,267	1,823	1,643	9	6	95	97	1	2	2	5	1,941	1,979
5 years	504	542	1,557	1,644	66	61	13,212	13,279	1,801	1,790	4	6	114	110	3	3	6	2	2,100	2,079
6 years	577	540	1,467	1,473	64	64	13,186	13,226	1,804	1,832	5	7	112	107	-------	5	5	3	1,912	2,004
7 years	519	523	1,380	1,450	59	75	12,589	12,451	1,891	1,884	1	10	102	104	3	1	5	7	1,962	1,958
8 years	495	551	1,513	1,487	73	77	13,091	12,909	1,855	1,823	7	7	103	126	4	1	4	4	1,917	2,078
9 years	525	525	1,408	1,353	70	66	11,682	11,600	1,900	1,766	11	4	115	108	1	2	3	6	1,897	1,917
10 years	539	495	1,300	1,387	65	60	13,589	12,706	1,826	1,855	10	7	100	86	3	2	2	5	1,913	1,898
11 years	463	460	1,084	1,124	73	64	10,155	10,088	1,490	1,532	10	11	95	71	-------	2	5	2	1,487	1,598
12 years	498	488	1,021	1,118	60	63	12,723	12,228	1,661	1,763	8	6	101	109	-------	3	7	5	1,693	1,710
13 years	436	429	1,018	1,098	57	48	10,772	10,682	1,561	1,596	6	13	95	85	1	1	5	6	1,442	1,580
14 years	451	439	1,117	1,120	65	57	12,057	11,839	1,546	1,688	9	10	93	95	1	-------	5	6	1,608	1,669
15 years	426	426	970	1,008	62	55	11,353	11,076	1,633	1,689	4	6	81	91	-------	3	8	6	1,410	1,593
16 years	395	400	1,024	1,047	56	72	12,224	12,203	1,697	1,774	9	4	102	97	3	1	3	5	1,559	1,770
17 years	400	379	953	1,139	39	69	12,149	10,759	1,743	1,720	3	6	103	83	1	2	10	5	1,504	1,772
18 years	373	445	1,034	1,208	60	60	11,268	13,970	1,700	2,076	9	7	88	123	2	1	6	6	1,609	2,016
19 years	355	419	1,162	1,343	65	76	8,758	11,133	1,707	1,996	7	3	81	113	-------	2	8	6	1,582	1,980
20 years	347	395	1,211	1,658	61	63	9,518	14,180	1,683	2,271	10	9	80	112	3	2	13	7	1,680	2,245
21 years	366	405	1,541	1,531	65	78	10,145	9,710	1,791	2,001	4	5	116	107	3	1	14	6	1,801	2,020
22 years	364	419	1,781	1,898	58	74	10,346	11,662	1,887	2,284	11	12	112	125	4	4	11	3	2,091	2,380
23 years	360	401	1,902	2,011	71	59	9,275	10,466	1,960	2,351	9	7	82	116	1	3	9	4	2,072	2,332
24 years	335	406	2,038	2,160	56	65	8,852	10,207	1,981	2,456	8	3	113	159	4	4	14	5	2,173	2,501
25 years	361	430	2,187	2,342	74	62	9,904	11,597	2,037	2,611	12	15	132	133	4	5	5	2	2,270	2,565
26 years	338	420	2,204	2,126	70	58	7,455	8,798	1,895	2,420	11	4	118	135	3	4	8	5	1,976	2,347
27 years	383	394	2,479	2,294	74	61	6,665	7,578	2,011	2,224	6	8	144	137	4	3	8	7	2,168	2,307
28 years	424	457	2,724	2,624	73	83	8,109	9,400	2,183	2,477	11	10	136	147	4	8	12	3	2,257	2,493
29 years	407	421	2,820	2,505	88	89	6,267	7,054	2,379	2,456	11	12	162	160	4	5	7	2	2,485	2,556

Table 17.—NEGRO POPULATION CLASSIFIED BY SINGLE YEARS OF AGE UP TO 29, BY SEX, AND BY STATES: 1930—Continued

AGE	NEW MEXICO		NEW YORK		NORTH CAROLINA		NORTH DAKOTA		OHIO		OKLAHOMA		OREGON		PENNSYLVANIA		RHODE ISLAND		SOUTH CAROLINA	
	Male	Female	Male	Female	Male	Female	Male	Female	Male	Female	Male	Female	Male	Female	Male	Female	Male	Female	Male	Female
Under 1 year	22	23	3, 246	3, 370	10, 779	10, 739	4	2	2, 687	2, 639	1, 636	1, 667	8	15	3, 663	3, 722	88	105	8, 692	9, 063
1 year	22	17	3, 386	3, 197	10, 331	10, 868	4	3	2, 528	2, 539	1, 553	1, 554	8	14	3, 662	3, 706	99	110	8, 477	8, 722
2 years	32	20	3, 526	3, 579	11, 563	11, 799	1	2	2, 790	2, 929	1, 791	1, 736	11	7	4, 126	4, 096	100	107	9, 875	10, 016
3 years	28	22	3, 447	3, 593	12, 213	12, 501	5	1	2, 945	3, 088	1, 761	1, 911	8	14	4, 144	4, 188	105	99	10, 224	10, 549
4 years	36	27	3, 318	3, 454	12, 154	11, 748	6	2	2, 816	2, 884	1, 854	1, 874	9	13	3, 959	4, 079	102	93	10, 388	10, 294
5 years	27	24	3, 303	3, 474	13, 438	13, 319	6	2	2, 915	3, 049	1, 868	1, 906	7	12	4, 144	4, 135	116	111	11, 416	11, 416
6 years	24	26	3, 135	3, 280	13, 346	13, 725	1	2	2, 831	2, 965	2, 035	2, 120	11	15	4, 011	4, 181	97	119	12, 040	12, 342
7 years	31	31	3, 067	3, 159	12, 425	12, 860	2	2	2, 747	2, 876	1, 963	1, 882	11	13	3, 930	4, 067	104	116	11, 311	11, 561
8 years	26	29	2, 976	3, 121	13, 271	13, 290	2	-------	2, 900	3, 092	2, 086	2, 042	13	9	4, 040	4, 141	108	102	12, 161	12, 424
9 years	23	32	2, 846	2, 956	12, 164	12, 305	2	2	2, 740	2, 844	1, 956	1, 934	12	24	3, 929	4, 054	100	96	10, 875	10, 750
10 years	27	28	2, 779	2, 915	12, 829	12, 692	3	1	2, 703	2, 791	2, 057	1, 977	16	12	3, 756	3, 869	90	97	12, 153	11, 919
11 years	21	21	2, 333	2, 461	10, 428	10, 453	-------	1	2, 234	2, 365	1, 701	1, 695	10	12	3, 081	3, 343	99	89	9, 097	9, 113
12 years	32	28	2, 411	2, 597	12, 521	12, 507	4	1	2, 411	2, 390	1, 947	1, 906	10	11	3, 262	3, 398	108	92	12, 660	12, 405
13 years	18	27	2, 103	2, 364	11, 105	11, 303	1	1	2, 215	2, 256	1, 621	1, 676	11	14	2, 888	3, 180	95	93	10, 275	10, 655
14 years	21	26	2, 260	2, 401	11, 932	11, 993	2	1	2, 264	2, 457	1, 796	1, 920	14	12	3, 047	3, 204	82	93	11, 289	11, 557
15 years	22	21	2, 127	2, 293	11, 234	11, 521	3	2	2, 082	2, 357	1, 734	1, 805	13	9	2, 766	3, 122	78	87	10, 201	10, 915
16 years	30	30	2, 035	2, 561	11, 617	12, 558	4	3	2, 199	2, 417	1, 852	1, 945	10	17	3, 085	3, 422	73	103	11, 025	12, 250
17 years	29	26	2, 260	2, 809	11, 468	11, 255	5	1	2, 275	2, 307	1, 857	1, 858	11	16	2, 951	3, 415	64	79	10, 059	10, 197
18 years	25	30	2, 613	3, 724	11, 724	12, 939	2	1	2, 242	2, 703	1, 890	2, 188	14	19	3, 095	4, 023	73	99	11, 023	12, 491
19 years	26	20	2, 958	4, 092	9, 803	11, 047	5	-------	2, 442	2, 734	1, 766	1, 916	12	7	3, 306	4, 028	67	84	8, 497	9, 771
20 years	28	24	3, 278	4, 941	9, 800	12, 105	4	3	2, 426	2, 939	1, 730	2, 070	13	20	3, 243	4, 441	77	62	8, 372	11, 373
21 years	33	28	3, 861	4, 543	9, 366	9, 466	-------	3	2, 778	2, 630	1, 770	1, 708	14	8	3, 590	3, 858	77	66	7, 747	7, 590
22 years	17	23	4, 329	5, 589	8, 949	10, 866	1	9	2, 930	3, 189	1, 683	1, 934	14	23	3, 964	4, 712	53	65	6, 993	8, 613
23 years	21	26	4, 573	5, 906	7, 910	9, 657	3	2	2, 869	3, 132	1, 553	1, 864	19	17	4, 064	4, 724	58	85	5, 780	7, 771
24 years	17	19	4, 983	5, 971	7, 576	9, 309	1	6	3, 196	3, 303	1, 585	1, 996	15	18	4, 352	4, 947	66	65	5, 280	7, 133
25 years	12	27	5, 454	6, 725	7, 563	9, 619	1	2	3, 294	3, 674	1, 566	1, 719	21	18	4, 740	5, 231	73	61	5, 913	7, 984
26 years	24	25	4, 973	5, 715	5, 989	7, 567	1	-------	2, 979	3, 164	1, 375	1, 633	10	13	4, 287	4, 703	67	80	3, 959	5, 668
27 years	18	18	5, 364	5, 799	5, 807	6, 716	3	5	3, 325	3, 166	1, 437	1, 576	19	12	4, 807	4, 787	66	52	3, 700	4, 904
28 years	33	28	5, 940	6, 663	6, 599	7, 861	10	1	3, 725	3, 616	1, 614	1, 713	25	16	5, 441	5, 541	81	68	4, 695	6, 250
29 years	34	26	6, 263	6, 179	5, 637	6, 485	4	4	3, 812	3, 611	1, 429	1, 533	20	21	5, 568	5, 248	69	73	3, 601	4, 625

AGE	SOUTH DAKOTA		TENNESSEE		TEXAS		UTAH		VERMONT		VIRGINIA		WASHINGTON		WEST VIRGINIA		WISCONSIN		WYOMING	
	Male	Female	Male	Female	Male	Female	Male	Female	Male	Female	Male	Female	Male	Female	Male	Female	Male	Female	Male	Female
Under 1 year	6	5	4, 212	4, 187	8, 149	8, 473	14	8	7	9	6, 467	6, 541	42	30	1, 181	1, 099	74	102	7	3
1 year	1	8	3, 814	3, 876	8, 039	8, 152	11	8	8	6	6, 160	6, 434	37	41	1, 143	1, 138	78	68	6	3
2 years	5	2	4, 423	4, 755	8, 836	8, 737	6	10	11	7	7, 275	7, 321	33	48	1, 255	1, 259	76	96	7	5
3 years	3	7	4, 676	4, 683	9, 003	9, 044	11	10	2	8	7, 385	7, 787	43	45	1, 206	1, 351	88	98	9	7
4 years	2	8	4, 836	4, 842	8, 804	8, 883	7	4	10	7	7, 686	7, 606	40	41	1, 203	1, 269	90	80	5	11
5 years	7	3	4, 768	4, 964	9, 565	9, 415	7	7	8	2	8, 387	8, 200	47	48	1, 296	1, 317	99	95	2	8
6 years	4	8	5, 075	5, 310	9, 630	9, 976	8	8	3	7	8, 590	8, 617	43	51	1, 331	1, 321	95	89	4	7
7 years	3	4	4, 936	4, 990	10, 027	10, 152	7	9	4	5	8, 571	8, 598	42	44	1, 180	1, 341	80	107	6	9
8 years	6	8	5, 226	5, 174	9, 934	10, 003	11	6	2	4	8, 744	8, 855	38	43	1, 292	1, 356	96	97	8	3
9 years	2	8	4, 970	4, 955	9, 457	9, 350	5	9	6	7	8, 137	8, 375	45	47	1, 230	1, 204	101	101	9	13
10 years	4	9	5, 260	5, 091	10, 044	9, 792	9	10	4	4	8, 700	8, 557	50	38	1, 211	1, 231	86	86	3	12
11 years	7	3	4, 277	4, 256	7, 957	7, 828	3	10	4	6	7, 214	7, 101	47	39	950	1, 069	90	77	8	5
12 years	3	7	5, 097	5, 067	9, 453	9, 255	9	11	5	8	8, 347	8, 319	44	36	1, 053	1, 049	80	74	8	5
13 years	7	4	4, 561	4, 538	8, 360	8, 498	6	8	5	5	7, 362	7, 594	43	34	975	995	72	88	9	5
14 years	4	7	4, 935	5, 070	8, 755	9, 128	13	7	5	8	7, 807	7, 892	51	39	938	973	67	68	6	9
15 years	7	4	4, 692	4, 956	8, 409	9, 276	5	3	2	6	7, 355	7, 608	41	35	852	1, 038	42	59	6	8
16 years	4	4	4, 975	5, 337	8, 893	10, 007	4	2	5	5	7, 611	7, 855	42	55	916	1, 045	65	74	3	5
17 years	11	6	5, 127	5, 141	8, 882	9, 375	2	2	5	10	7, 325	7, 363	41	41	976	1, 051	64	69	10	9
18 years	7	5	5, 350	6, 046	8, 998	10, 732	11	4	4	10	7, 599	7, 621	33	39	1, 037	1, 147	68	68	7	4
19 years	7	7	4, 809	5, 402	8, 404	9, 720	3	8	7	8	6, 542	6, 564	48	41	924	1, 123	90	97	7	9
20 years	4	5	4, 774	6, 239	8, 550	11, 382	3	3	6	4	5, 996	6, 877	52	42	993	1, 220	77	103	9	9
21 years	5	5	4, 526	4, 660	8, 839	8, 444	7	4	5	3	5, 816	5, 554	45	39	1, 047	966	103	95	10	6
22 years	5	12	4, 522	5, 643	8, 783	9, 984	10	9	5	2	5, 886	6, 062	43	43	1, 143	1, 185	104	93	5	11
23 years	7	6	4, 151	5, 205	8, 191	9, 559	5	8	4	2	4, 971	5, 537	44	57	1, 155	1, 118	107	119	11	5
24 years	8	8	4, 364	5, 204	8, 163	9, 674	11	9	4	4	4, 658	5, 210	45	49	1, 195	1, 195	142	123	15	14
25 years	7	6	4, 497	5, 575	8, 307	9, 697	9	10	4	1	4, 707	5, 510	36	48	1, 141	1, 159	146	129	10	7
26 years	6	5	3, 654	4, 624	7, 214	8, 390	11	5	6	1	3, 863	4, 489	46	38	991	1, 105	122	131	8	5
27 years	10	2	3, 380	3, 932	7, 073	8, 037	8	9	3	-------	3, 817	4, 324	48	33	1, 086	1, 015	145	122	7	10
28 years	3	4	4, 059	4, 870	7, 589	8, 823	6	9	6	-------	4, 324	5, 029	55	40	1, 368	1, 134	165	141	8	7
29 years	4	5	3, 576	4, 182	7, 202	7, 860	12	9	5	3	4, 004	4, 411	73	49	1, 459	1, 223	154	141	15	6

Table 18.—AGE BY SINGLE YEARS FROM 60 TO 79, FOR THE NEGRO POPULATION, BY SEX, FOR STATES HAVING AT LEAST 100,000 NEGROES: 1930

AGE	NEW YORK		NEW JERSEY		PENNSYLVANIA		OHIO		INDIANA		ILLINOIS		MICHIGAN		MISSOURI	
	Male	Female	Male	Female	Male	Female	Male	Female	Male	Female	Male	Female	Male	Female	Male	Female
All ages	199,485	213,329	102,929	105,899	218,412	212,845	159,128	150,176	57,068	54,914	164,425	164,547	88,936	80,517	111,929	111,911
60 years	1,002	1,246	813	778	1,570	1,425	1,172	976	515	394	1,149	1,103	386	344	1,183	986
61 years	301	310	239	208	457	373	399	310	192	146	374	352	122	104	380	297
62 years	465	467	341	302	664	550	540	462	230	187	490	472	179	165	542	433
63 years	420	426	311	300	589	482	489	408	204	189	480	450	170	169	512	413
64 years	331	367	278	245	491	434	460	414	191	191	412	415	144	137	405	352
65 years	565	763	454	474	905	867	694	616	339	321	690	702	218	238	793	656
66 years	175	269	160	127	286	241	268	237	126	98	240	236	91	71	285	257
67 years	218	303	174	168	295	320	294	249	139	137	281	298	106	98	279	252
68 years	204	333	193	215	394	325	358	269	163	125	282	312	104	98	351	333
69 years	226	303	166	176	331	293	294	294	173	133	262	291	76	88	287	273
70 years	268	484	294	301	507	541	439	499	229	201	359	471	115	146	475	510
71 years	110	135	98	72	170	149	163	142	89	78	129	161	46	47	146	116
72 years	150	179	128	136	260	251	257	199	115	105	205	183	57	77	252	210
73 years	116	156	104	86	141	179	173	189	70	76	155	169	37	46	163	154
74 years	116	137	66	86	176	159	192	174	100	77	138	156	50	51	189	171
75 years	146	234	128	181	245	309	238	262	92	133	176	280	66	97	283	307
76 years	82	135	76	73	134	146	145	137	71	68	115	116	54	38	150	121
77 years	58	82	52	64	84	87	99	92	49	33	73	88	36	31	103	91
78 years	78	108	66	78	102	129	135	120	70	56	99	115	38	54	150	130
79 years	64	106	42	59	65	100	96	96	49	47	90	85	26	32	118	93

AGE	MARYLAND		DIST. OF COLUMBIA		VIRGINIA		WEST VIRGINIA		NORTH CAROLINA		SOUTH CAROLINA		GEORGIA		FLORIDA	
	Male	Female	Male	Female	Male	Female	Male	Female	Male	Female	Male	Female	Male	Female	Male	Female
All ages	140,506	135,873	62,225	69,843	321,545	328,620	60,873	54,020	446,500	472,147	379,300	414,381	513,451	557,674	215,148	216,680
60 years	1,438	1,375	603	743	3,598	3,424	426	265	3,542	3,444	4,465	3,707	7,008	5,558	2,130	1,506
61 years	366	324	143	157	766	632	113	78	884	641	819	556	1,160	783	431	287
62 years	580	484	217	230	1,256	1,088	171	121	1,326	1,050	1,273	872	1,950	1,312	657	476
63 years	502	399	182	214	1,133	1,029	145	101	1,311	1,085	1,325	737	1,856	1,283	657	457
64 years	486	358	129	167	1,020	907	148	120	1,179	959	1,055	746	1,637	1,065	569	396
65 years	963	868	369	530	2,307	2,382	225	166	2,277	2,261	2,603	2,378	3,875	3,360	1,289	1,000
66 years	269	257	90	85	682	609	106	75	750	574	555	463	935	679	350	232
67 years	322	280	128	126	707	572	92	81	773	602	602	414	928	716	357	267
68 years	390	349	132	188	896	856	104	80	929	818	811	697	1,250	1,052	433	342
69 years	327	290	130	164	682	646	96	55	720	600	600	497	944	757	346	234
70 years	619	704	201	293	1,627	1,806	129	129	1,593	1,785	1,537	1,724	2,495	2,671	692	713
71 years	159	123	62	67	352	325	54	39	440	332	299	237	470	363	158	130
72 years	307	209	99	95	656	597	75	54	707	559	584	419	806	652	260	210
73 years	198	170	82	77	527	400	50	33	492	437	409	276	544	464	190	123
74 years	182	153	64	83	489	369	53	48	547	414	356	288	558	420	163	121
75 years	297	325	83	170	852	985	60	73	916	1,009	758	919	1,290	1,568	360	363
76 years	159	134	39	65	350	316	31	29	407	323	274	244	474	397	159	116
77 years	86	66	29	41	270	216	28	23	270	193	170	121	308	254	75	75
78 years	122	129	47	66	319	311	24	33	348	296	258	223	476	400	140	132
79 years	92	111	33	40	218	201	25	33	228	200	178	140	255	230	96	61

AGE	KENTUCKY		TENNESSEE		ALABAMA		MISSISSIPPI		ARKANSAS		LOUISIANA		OKLAHOMA		TEXAS	
	Male	Female	Male	Female	Male	Female	Male	Female	Male	Female	Male	Female	Male	Female	Male	Female
All ages	113,501	112,539	232,569	245,077	457,144	487,690	498,338	511,380	236,909	241,554	379,173	397,153	86,818	85,380	422,608	432,356
60 years	1,557	1,453	3,000	2,551	5,242	4,557	6,606	5,217	2,672	2,080	3,807	3,542	772	548	4,347	3,881
61 years	358	323	582	461	1,111	751	1,176	774	557	371	797	596	247	137	1,150	828
62 years	588	556	907	770	1,681	1,201	1,928	1,232	921	545	1,329	1,011	299	193	1,667	1,258
63 years	555	456	866	743	1,470	1,265	1,790	1,147	859	605	1,195	958	353	222	1,645	1,281
64 years	537	459	797	686	1,360	1,036	1,567	1,046	773	548	1,049	849	302	191	1,413	1,014
65 years	1,116	963	1,785	1,643	3,218	2,985	3,952	3,016	1,653	1,197	2,353	2,224	478	378	2,599	2,165
66 years	366	317	487	356	833	642	893	605	143	304	648	568	168	130	821	703
67 years	375	347	570	433	803	642	924	622	455	316	653	522	204	135	933	671
68 years	453	411	621	591	1,105	1,030	1,160	908	550	466	792	794	203	156	955	828
69 years	368	300	511	412	746	685	813	614	432	329	632	582	228	127	743	552
70 years	812	804	1,139	1,278	2,086	2,364	2,379	2,323	977	935	1,414	1,661	286	247	1,519	1,627
71 years	237	152	256	227	395	356	397	305	219	145	299	267	89	58	357	294
72 years	347	259	462	360	722	620	729	630	388	262	549	516	159	95	657	481
73 years	246	214	304	267	460	368	522	378	271	204	332	313	105	79	453	385
74 years	246	172	371	238	460	416	550	395	295	178	371	367	116	63	460	336
75 years	425	498	613	737	1,083	1,301	1,287	1,383	525	508	816	990	160	148	928	949
76 years	189	180	266	234	414	365	456	333	234	155	334	300	116	59	374	292
77 years	144	102	172	124	257	197	310	193	150	93	230	183	67	45	250	188
78 years	170	175	210	220	403	426	412	392	199	160	311	357	84	70	382	344
79 years	92	111	153	153	221	217	239	214	123	108	210	181	51	46	242	193

TABLE 19.—NEGRO POPULATION FOR THE URBAN, RURAL-FARM, AND RURAL-NONFARM AREAS, BY 5-YEAR AGE PERIODS, SEX, AND STATES: 1930

[Percent not shown where less than 1/10 of 1 percent or where base is less than 100]

STATE AND AGE	TOTAL		URBAN		RURAL						PERCENT DISTRIBUTION							
					Total		Rural-farm		Rural-nonfarm		Urban		Rural					
													Total		Rural-farm		Rural-nonfarm	
	Male	Female	Male	Female	Male	Female	Male	Female	Male	Female	Male	Female	Male	Female	Male	Female	Male	Female
MAINE																		
All ages	**597**	**499**	**363**	**340**	**234**	**159**	**67**	**48**	**167**	**111**	100.0	100.0	100.0	100.0			100.0	100.0
Under 5 years	63	44	41	30	22	14	7	7	15	7	11.3	8.8	9.4	8.8			9.0	6.3
5 to 9 years	46	43	32	26	14	17	5	6	9	11	8.8	7.6	6.0	10.7			5.4	9.9
10 to 14 years	46	54	25	34	21	20	9	7	12	13	6.9	10.0	9.0	12.6			7.2	11.7
15 to 19 years	42	32	26	25	16	7	4	2	12	5	7.2	7.4	6.8	4.4			7.2	4.5
20 to 24 years	32	24	19	15	13	9	6	3	7	6	5.2	4.4	5.6	5.7			4.2	5.4
25 to 29 years	37	44	22	36	15	8	5	4	10	4	6.1	10.6	6.4	5.0			6.0	3.6
30 to 34 years	34	36	23	23	11	13	1	2	10	11	6.3	6.8	4.7	8.2			6.0	9.9
35 to 39 years	54	37	28	26	26	11	9	4	17	7	7.7	7.6	11.1	6.9			10.2	6.3
40 to 44 years	45	31	28	22	17	9	3	3	14	6	7.7	6.5	7.3	5.7			8.4	5.4
45 to 49 years	58	35	36	23	22	12	3	2	19	10	9.9	6.8	9.4	7.5			11.4	9.0
50 to 54 years	29	38	20	28	9	10	1	1	8	9	5.5	8.2	3.8	6.3			4.8	8.1
55 to 59 years	26	24	15	18	11	6	4		7	6	4.1	5.3	4.7	3.8			4.2	5.4
60 to 64 years	26	19	15	12	11	7	1		10	7	4.1	3.5	4.7	4.4			6.0	6.3
65 to 69 years	20	13	12	8	8	5		2	8	3	3.3	2.4	3.4	3.1			4.8	2.7
70 to 74 years	14	15	9	8	5	7	3	2	2	5	2.5	2.4	2.1	4.4			1.2	4.5
75 to 79 years	15	4	8	2	7	2	4	1	3	1	2.2	.6	3.0	1.3			1.8	.9
80 to 84 years	8	2	4	2	4		1		3		1.1	.6	1.7				1.8	
85 and over	1	3		2	1	1		1	1			.6	.4	.6			.6	
Unknown	1	1			1	1	1	1					.4	.6				
NEW HAMPSHIRE																		
All ages	**524**	**266**	**420**	**174**	**104**	**92**	**23**	**24**	**81**	**68**	100.0	100.0	100.0					
Under 5 years	20	28	12	15	8	13	1	2	7	11	2.9	8.6	7.7					
5 to 9 years	23	22	9	12	14	10	1	4	13	6	2.1	6.9	13.5					
10 to 14 years	24	24	16	13	8	11	3	4	5	7	3.8	7.5	7.7					
15 to 19 years	35	28	23	20	12	8	4	1	8	7	5.5	11.5	11.5					
20 to 24 years	61	25	48	18	13	7	4	3	9	4	11.4	10.3	12.5					
25 to 29 years	40	19	36	14	4	5			4	5	8.6	8.0	3.8					
30 to 34 years	62	9	57	7	5	2		1	5	1	13.6	4.0	4.8					
35 to 39 years	61	23	56	17	5	6	1	1	4	5	13.3	9.8	4.8					
40 to 44 years	53	23	48	15	5	8	2	2	3	6	11.4	8.6	4.8					
45 to 49 years	66	20	56	13	10	7	3	3	7	4	13.3	7.5	9.6					
50 to 54 years	32	17	25	13	7	4	1	1	6	3	6.0	7.5	6.7					
55 to 59 years	21	11	14	7	7	4	2		5	4	3.3	4.0	6.7					
60 to 64 years	7	4	6	3	1	1			1	1	1.4	1.7	1.0					
65 to 69 years	10	7	8	4	2	3			2	3	1.9	2.3	1.9					
70 to 74 years	4	1	3	1	1				1		.7	.6	1.0					
75 to 79 years	1	2		1	1	1			1	1		.6	1.0					
80 to 84 years	2		2								.5							
85 and over	1	1	1	1							.2	.6						
Unknown	1	2			1	2	1	2					1.0					
VERMONT																		
All ages	**310**	**258**	**114**	**99**	**196**	**159**	**77**	**52**	**119**	**107**	100.0		100.0	100.0			100.0	100.0
Under 5 years	38	37	14	8	24	29	6	14	18	15	12.3		12.2	18.2			15.1	14.0
5 to 9 years	23	25	8	10	15	15	8	9	7	6	7.0		7.7	9.4			5.9	5.6
10 to 14 years	23	31	5	10	18	21	5	6	13	15	4.4		9.2	13.2			10.9	14.0
15 to 19 years	23	39	6	15	17	24	5	5	12	19	5.3		8.7	15.1			10.1	17.8
20 to 24 years	24	15	5	4	19	11	8		11	11	4.4		9.7	6.9			9.2	10.3
25 to 29 years	24	5	10	2	14	3	7	2	7	1	8.8		7.1	1.9			5.9	.9
30 to 34 years	22	14	7	8	15	6	8	3	7	3	6.1		7.7	3.8			5.9	2.8
35 to 39 years	23	18	14	10	9	8	7	2	2	6	12.3		4.6	5.0			1.7	5.6
40 to 44 years	19	11	11	4	8	7	1	1	7	6	9.6		4.1	4.4			5.9	5.6
45 to 49 years	24	19	11	10	13	9	7	2	6	7	9.6		6.6	5.7			5.0	6.5
50 to 54 years	19	14	8	4	11	10	5	5	6	5	7.0		5.6	6.3			5.0	4.7
55 to 59 years	17	6	7	2	10	4	2		8	4	6.1		5.1	2.5			6.7	3.7
60 to 64 years	11	6	3	2	8	4	2		6	4	2.6		4.1	2.5			5.0	3.7
65 to 69 years	7	5	1	2	6	3	1		5	3	.9		3.1	1.9			4.2	2.8
70 to 74 years	4	6	1	5	3	1	2	1	1		.9		1.5	.6			.8	
75 to 79 years	7	4	2	1	5	3	3	2	2	1	1.8		2.6	1.9			1.7	.9
80 to 84 years		2		2														
85 and over	2	1	1		1	1			1	1	.9		.5	.6			.8	.9
Unknown																		
MASSACHUSETTS																		
All ages	**26,097**	**26,268**	**22,817**	**23,506**	**3,280**	**2,762**	**260**	**157**	**3,020**	**2,605**	100.0	100.0	100.0	100.0	100.0	100.0	100.0	100.0
Under 5 years	2,388	2,320	2,036	2,006	352	314	22	16	330	298	8.9	8.5	10.7	11.4	8.5	10.2	10.9	11.4
5 to 9 years	2,620	2,681	2,235	2,286	385	395	17	21	368	374	9.8	9.7	11.7	14.3	6.5	13.4	12.2	14.4
10 to 14 years	2,387	2,311	1,978	1,964	409	347	30	17	379	330	8.7	8.4	12.5	12.6	11.5	10.8	12.5	12.7
15 to 19 years	1,949	2,069	1,650	1,790	299	279	23	19	276	260	7.2	7.6	9.1	10.1	8.8	12.1	9.1	10.0
20 to 24 years	1,772	2,026	1,595	1,803	177	223	12	10	165	213	7.0	7.7	5.4	8.1	4.6	6.4	5.5	8.2
25 to 29 years	1,913	2,122	1,744	1,977	169	145	13	9	156	136	7.6	8.4	5.2	5.2	5.0	5.7	5.2	5.2
30 to 34 years	2,216	2,205	2,034	2,064	182	141	17	8	165	133	8.9	8.8	5.5	5.1	6.5	5.1	5.5	5.1
35 to 39 years	2,385	2,384	2,127	2,178	258	206	29	20	229	186	9.3	9.3	7.9	7.5	11.2	12.7	7.6	7.1
40 to 44 years	2,000	2,016	1,774	1,842	226	174	17	6	209	168	7.8	7.8	6.9	6.3	6.5	3.8	6.9	6.4
45 to 49 years	2,049	1,825	1,794	1,676	255	149	14	9	241	140	7.9	7.1	7.8	5.4	5.4	5.7	8.0	5.4
50 to 54 years	1,619	1,441	1,401	1,326	218	115	20	12	198	103	6.1	5.6	6.6	4.2	7.7	7.6	6.6	4.0
55 to 59 years	1,113	971	951	888	162	83	22	1	140	82	4.2	3.8	4.9	3.0	8.5	.6	4.6	3.1
60 to 64 years	689	704	620	643	69	61	11	6	58	55	2.7	2.7	2.1	2.2	4.2	3.8	1.9	2.1
65 to 69 years	449	481	403	429	46	52	3		43	52	1.8	1.8	1.4	1.9	1.2		1.4	2.0
70 to 74 years	257	292	221	256	36	36	7	2	29	34	1.0	1.1	1.1	1.3	2.7	1.3	1.0	1.3
75 to 79 years	135	197	119	181	16	16	2	1	14	15	.5	.8	.5	.6	.8	.6	.5	.6
80 to 84 years	66	109	59	95	7	14			7	14	.3	.4	.2	.5			.2	.5
85 and over	44	68	36	59	8	9	1		7	9	.2	.3	.2	.3	.4		.2	.3
Unknown	46	46	40	43	6	3			6	3	.2	.2	.2	.1			.2	.1

TABLE 19.—NEGRO POPULATION FOR THE URBAN, RURAL-FARM, AND RURAL-NONFARM AREAS, BY 5-YEAR AGE PERIODS, SEX, AND STATES: 1930—Continued

[See note at head of this table]

STATE AND AGE	TOTAL		URBAN		RURAL						PERCENT DISTRIBUTION							
					Total		Rural-farm		Rural-nonfarm		Urban		Rural					
													Total		Rural-farm		Rural-nonfarm	
	Male	Female	Male	Female	Male	Female	Male	Female	Male	Female	Male	Female	Male	Female	Male	Female	Male	Female
RHODE ISLAND																		
All ages	4,862	5,051	4,428	4,651	434	400	55	38	379	362	100.0	100.0	100.0	100.0	------	------	100.0	100.0
Under 5 years	494	514	458	479	36	35	1	2	35	33	10.3	10.3	8.3	8.8	------	------	9.2	9.1
5 to 9 years	525	544	481	496	44	48	6	2	38	46	10.9	10.7	10.1	12.0	------	------	10.0	12.7
10 to 14 years	474	464	425	422	49	42	8	1	41	41	9.6	9.1	11.3	10.5	------	------	10.8	11.3
15 to 19 years	355	452	312	409	43	43	6	7	37	36	7.0	8.8	9.9	10.8	------	------	9.8	9.9
20 to 24 years	331	343	295	314	36	29	6	5	30	24	6.7	6.8	8.3	7.3	------	------	7.9	6.6
25 to 29 years	356	334	321	310	35	24	3	2	32	22	7.2	6.7	8.1	6.0	------	------	8.4	6.1
30 to 34 years	338	380	310	358	28	22	5	2	23	20	7.0	7.7	6.5	5.5	------	------	6.1	5.5
35 to 39 years	380	365	355	337	25	28	4	2	21	26	8.0	7.2	5.8	7.0	------	------	5.5	7.2
40 to 44 years	354	342	331	319	23	23	3	2	20	21	7.5	6.9	5.3	5.8	------	------	5.3	5.8
45 to 49 years	357	348	333	322	24	26	4	4	20	22	7.5	6.9	5.5	6.5	------	------	5.3	6.1
50 to 54 years	290	296	265	273	25	23	1	3	24	20	6.0	5.9	5.8	5.8	------	------	6.3	5.5
55 to 59 years	211	216	193	199	18	17	4	1	14	16	4.4	4.3	4.1	4.3	------	------	3.7	4.4
60 to 64 years	153	170	130	154	23	16	1	2	22	14	2.9	3.3	5.3	4.0	------	------	5.8	3.9
65 to 69 years	102	110	91	101	11	9	3	3	8	6	2.1	2.2	2.5	2.3	------	------	2.1	1.7
70 to 74 years	59	75	55	72	4	3	------	------	4	3	1.2	1.5	.9	.8	------	------	1.1	.8
75 to 79 years	32	51	28	47	4	4	------	------	4	4	.6	1.0	.9	1.0	------	------	1.1	1.1
80 to 84 years	26	29	22	26	4	3	------	------	4	3	.5	.6	.9	.8	------	------	1.1	.8
85 and over	19	13	18	9	1	4	------	------	1	4	.4	.2	.2	1.0	------	------	.3	1.1
Unknown	6	5	5	4	1	1	------	------	1	1	.1	.1	.2	.3	------	------	.3	.3
CONNECTICUT																		
All ages	14,573	14,781	12,147	12,384	2,426	2,397	184	148	2,242	2,249	100.0	100.0	100.0	100.0	100.0	100.0	100.0	100.0
Under 5 years	1,459	1,510	1,247	1,291	212	219	5	8	207	211	10.3	10.4	8.7	9.1	2.7	5.4	9.2	9.4
5 to 9 years	1,426	1,474	1,234	1,265	192	209	11	15	181	194	10.2	10.2	7.9	8.7	6.0	10.1	8.1	8.6
10 to 14 years	1,122	1,225	948	1,034	174	191	16	8	158	183	7.8	8.3	7.2	8.0	8.7	5.4	7.0	8.1
15 to 19 years	1,091	1,225	899	1,024	192	201	14	12	178	189	7.4	8.3	7.9	8.4	7.6	8.1	7.9	8.4
20 to 24 years	1,184	1,485	957	1,217	227	268	16	13	211	255	7.9	9.8	9.4	11.2	8.7	8.8	9.4	11.3
25 to 29 years	1,521	1,496	1,278	1,277	243	219	14	12	229	207	10.5	10.3	10.0	9.1	7.6	8.1	10.2	9.2
30 to 34 years	1,392	1,240	1,168	1,057	224	183	16	14	208	169	9.6	8.5	9.2	7.6	8.7	9.5	9.3	7.5
35 to 39 years	1,351	1,318	1,151	1,104	200	214	16	14	184	200	9.5	8.9	8.2	8.9	8.7	9.5	8.2	8.9
40 to 44 years	1,076	1,040	905	869	171	171	17	12	154	159	7.5	7.0	7.0	7.1	9.2	8.1	6.9	7.1
45 to 49 years	892	829	743	682	149	147	16	7	133	140	6.1	5.5	6.1	6.1	8.7	4.7	5.9	6.2
50 to 54 years	734	676	600	538	134	138	12	13	122	125	4.9	4.3	5.5	5.8	6.5	8.8	5.4	5.6
55 to 59 years	461	402	369	333	92	69	9	7	83	62	3.0	2.7	3.8	2.9	4.9	4.7	3.7	2.8
60 to 64 years	364	344	278	285	86	59	9	7	77	52	2.3	2.3	3.5	2.5	4.9	4.7	3.4	2.3
65 to 69 years	222	218	181	171	41	47	8	3	33	44	1.5	1.4	1.7	2.0	4.3	2.0	1.5	2.0
70 to 74 years	119	125	85	98	34	27	3	------	31	27	.7	.8	1.4	1.1	1.6	------	1.4	1.2
75 to 79 years	74	85	46	67	28	18	1	------	27	18	.4	.5	1.2	.8	.5	------	1.2	.8
80 to 84 years	39	49	26	39	13	10	1	2	12	8	.2	.3	.5	.4	.5	1.4	.5	.4
85 and over	32	29	21	23	11	6	------	1	11	5	.2	.2	.5	.3	------	.7	.5	.2
Unknown	14	11	11	10	3	1	------	------	3	1	.1	.1	.1	------	------	------	.1	------
NEW YORK																		
All ages	199,485	213,329	187,862	202,637	11,623	10,692	1,346	964	10,277	9,728	100.0	100.0	100.0	100.0	100.0	100.0	100.0	100.0
Under 5 years	16,923	17,193	15,922	16,158	1,001	1,035	113	108	888	927	8.5	8.0	8.6	9.7	8.4	11.2	8.6	9.5
5 to 9 years	15,327	15,990	14,313	15,016	1,014	974	111	119	903	855	7.6	7.4	8.7	9.1	8.2	12.3	8.8	8.8
10 to 14 years	11,886	12,738	11,012	11,846	874	892	109	110	765	782	5.9	5.8	7.5	8.3	8.1	11.4	7.4	8.0
15 to 19 years	11,993	15,479	11,060	14,536	933	943	170	89	763	854	5.9	7.2	8.0	8.8	12.6	9.2	7.4	8.8
20 to 24 years	21,024	26,950	19,805	25,819	1,219	1,131	138	88	1,081	1,043	10.5	12.7	10.5	10.6	10.3	9.1	10.5	10.7
25 to 29 years	27,994	31,081	26,758	29,968	1,236	1,113	126	65	1,110	1,048	14.2	14.8	10.6	10.4	9.4	6.7	10.8	10.8
30 to 34 years	24,978	24,764	23,869	23,784	1,109	980	74	70	1,035	910	12.7	11.7	9.5	9.2	5.5	7.3	10.1	9.4
35 to 39 years	22,916	22,369	21,869	21,480	1,047	889	91	57	956	832	11.6	10.6	9.0	8.3	6.8	5.9	9.3	8.6
40 to 44 years	16,119	15,521	15,289	14,810	830	711	88	61	742	650	8.1	7.3	7.1	6.6	6.5	6.3	7.2	6.7
45 to 49 years	12,303	11,892	11,604	11,257	699	635	84	66	615	569	6.2	5.6	6.0	5.9	6.2	6.8	6.0	5.8
50 to 54 years	7,949	7,599	7,424	7,154	525	445	84	50	441	395	4.0	3.5	4.5	4.2	6.2	5.2	4.3	4.1
55 to 59 years	4,338	4,329	3,971	4,025	367	304	44	18	323	286	2.1	2.0	3.2	2.8	3.3	1.9	3.1	2.9
60 to 64 years	2,519	2,816	2,267	2,609	252	207	38	25	214	182	1.2	1.3	2.2	1.9	2.8	2.6	2.1	1.9
65 to 69 years	1,388	1,971	1,199	1,798	189	173	24	14	165	159	.6	.9	1.6	1.6	1.8	1.5	1.6	1.6
70 to 74 years	760	1,091	624	999	136	92	26	11	110	81	.3	.5	1.2	.9	1.9	1.1	1.1	.8
75 to 79 years	428	665	343	581	85	84	12	9	73	75	.2	.3	.7	.8	.9	.9	.7	.8
80 to 84 years	191	315	150	284	41	31	4	1	37	30	.1	.1	.4	.3	.3	.1	.4	.3
85 and over	123	209	90	188	33	21	7	------	26	21	------	.1	.3	.2	.5	------	.3	.2
Unknown	326	357	293	325	33	32	3	3	30	29	.2	.2	.3	.3	.2	.3	.3	.3
NEW JERSEY																		
All ages	102,929	105,899	85,321	89,664	17,608	16,235	2,713	1,884	14,895	14,351	100.0	100.0	100.0	100.0	100.0	100.0	100.0	100.0
Under 5 years	9,904	9,886	8,155	8,208	1,749	1,678	238	247	1,511	1,431	9.6	9.2	9.9	10.3	8.8	13.1	10.1	10.0
5 to 9 years	9,788	10,036	7,999	8,225	1,789	1,811	270	244	1,519	1,567	9.4	9.2	10.2	11.2	10.0	13.0	10.2	10.9
10 to 14 years	8,143	8,455	6,512	6,859	1,631	1,596	223	224	1,408	1,372	7.6	7.6	9.3	9.8	8.2	11.9	9.5	9.6
15 to 19 years	7,664	9,131	6,079	7,600	1,585	1,531	298	192	1,287	1,339	7.1	8.5	9.0	9.4	11.0	10.2	8.6	9.3
20 to 24 years	9,817	11,478	8,246	9,981	1,571	1,497	324	160	1,247	1,337	9.7	11.1	8.9	9.2	11.9	8.5	8.4	9.3
25 to 29 years	11,156	12,268	9,747	10,912	1,409	1,356	221	132	1,188	1,224	11.4	12.2	8.0	8.4	8.1	7.0	8.0	8.5
30 to 34 years	10,014	9,773	8,655	8,571	1,359	1,202	188	112	1,171	1,090	10.1	9.6	7.7	7.4	6.9	5.9	7.9	7.6
35 to 39 years	9,748	9,601	8,428	8,373	1,320	1,228	193	134	1,127	1,094	9.9	9.3	7.5	7.6	7.1	7.1	7.6	7.6
40 to 44 years	7,367	7,158	6,194	6,133	1,173	1,025	181	122	992	903	7.3	6.8	6.7	6.3	6.7	6.5	6.7	6.3
45 to 49 years	6,466	6,121	5,354	5,139	1,112	982	165	84	947	898	6.3	5.7	6.3	6.0	6.1	4.5	6.4	6.3
50 to 54 years	5,074	4,571	4,057	3,762	1,017	809	148	81	869	728	4.8	4.2	5.8	5.0	5.5	4.3	5.8	5.1
55 to 59 years	3,123	2,685	2,441	2,182	682	503	100	53	582	450	2.9	2.4	3.9	3.1	3.7	2.8	3.9	3.1
60 to 64 years	1,982	1,833	1,515	1,453	467	380	71	44	396	336	1.8	1.6	2.7	2.3	2.6	2.3	2.7	2.3
65 to 69 years	1,147	1,160	861	944	286	216	44	17	242	199	1.0	1.1	1.6	1.3	1.6	.9	1.6	1.4
70 to 74 years	690	681	501	513	189	168	26	20	163	148	.6	.6	1.1	1.0	1.0	1.1	1.1	1.0
75 to 79 years	364	455	246	359	118	96	11	11	107	85	.3	.4	.7	.6	.4	.6	.7	.6
80 to 84 years	159	246	100	173	59	73	5	4	54	69	.1	.2	.3	.4	.2	.2	.4	.5
85 and over	110	171	72	123	38	48	4	1	34	47	.1	.1	.2	.3	.1	.1	.2	.3
Unknown	213	190	159	154	54	36	3	2	51	34	.2	.2	.3	.2	.1	.1	.3	.2

TABLE 19.—NEGRO POPULATION FOR THE URBAN, RURAL-FARM, AND RURAL-NONFARM AREAS, BY 5-YEAR AGE PERIODS, SEX, AND STATES: 1930—Continued

[See note at head of this table]

STATE AND AGE	TOTAL		URBAN		RURAL						PERCENT DISTRIBUTION							
					Total		Rural-farm		Rural-nonfarm		Urban		Rural					
													Total		Rural-farm		Rural-nonfarm	
	Male	Female	Male	Female	Male	Female	Male	Female	Male	Female	Male	Female	Male	Female	Male	Female	Male	Female
PENNSYLVANIA																		
All ages	**218,412**	**212,845**	**186,942**	**186,638**	**31,470**	**26,207**	**2,310**	**1,799**	**29,160**	**24,408**	100.0	100.0	100.0	100.0	100.0	100.0	100.0	100.0
Under 5 years	19,554	19,791	16,513	16,684	3,041	3,107	217	190	2,824	2,917	8.8	8.9	9.7	11.9	9.4	10.6	9.7	12.0
5 to 9 years	20,054	20,578	16,821	17,347	3,233	3,231	225	215	3,008	3,016	9.0	9.3	10.3	12.3	9.7	12.0	10.3	12.4
10 to 14 years	16,034	16,994	13,263	14,320	2,771	2,674	251	225	2,520	2,449	7.1	7.7	8.8	10.2	10.9	12.5	8.6	10.0
15 to 19 years	15,203	18,010	12,603	15,526	2,600	2,484	290	180	2,310	2,304	6.7	8.3	8.3	9.5	12.6	10.0	7.9	9.4
20 to 24 years	19,213	22,682	16,704	20,449	2,509	2,233	181	121	2,328	2,112	8.9	11.0	8.0	8.5	7.8	6.7	8.0	8.7
25 to 29 years	24,843	25,510	21,988	22,915	2,855	2,595	129	128	2,726	2,467	11.8	12.3	9.1	9.9	5.6	7.1	9.3	10.1
30 to 34 years	23,531	21,412	20,549	19,153	2,982	2,259	135	133	2,847	2,126	11.0	10.3	9.5	8.6	5.8	7.4	9.8	8.7
35 to 39 years	23,049	20,468	20,115	18,459	2,934	2,009	157	126	2,777	1,883	10.8	9.9	9.3	7.7	6.8	7.0	9.5	7.7
40 to 44 years	17,096	14,206	14,847	12,702	2,249	1,504	138	109	2,111	1,395	7.9	6.8	7.1	5.7	6.0	6.1	7.2	5.7
45 to 49 years	14,447	11,867	12,465	10,553	1,982	1,314	147	131	1,835	1,183	6.7	5.7	6.3	5.0	6.4	7.3	6.3	4.8
50 to 54 years	10,548	8,183	9,053	7,175	1,495	1,008	127	75	1,368	933	4.8	3.8	4.8	3.8	5.5	4.2	4.7	3.8
55 to 59 years	6,216	4,847	5,162	4,265	1,054	582	116	58	938	524	2.8	2.3	3.3	2.2	5.0	3.2	3.2	2.1
60 to 64 years	3,771	3,264	3,097	2,824	674	440	73	35	601	405	1.7	1.5	2.1	1.7	3.2	1.9	2.1	1.7
65 to 69 years	2,211	2,046	1,749	1,753	462	293	53	31	409	262	.9	.9	1.5	1.1	2.3	1.7	1.4	1.1
70 to 74 years	1,254	1,279	977	1,089	277	190	38	19	239	171	.5	.6	.9	.7	1.6	1.1	.8	.7
75 to 79 years	630	771	467	646	163	125	20	11	143	114	.2	.3	.5	.5	.9	.6	.5	.5
80 to 84 years	277	415	208	340	69	75	7	7	62	68	.1	.2	.2	.3	.3	.4	.2	.3
85 and over	201	275	146	230	55	45	4	4	51	41	.1	.1	.2	.2	.2	.2	.2	.2
Unknown	280	247	215	208	65	39	2	1	63	38	.1	.1	.2	.1	.1	.1	.2	.2
OHIO																		
All ages	**159,128**	**150,176**	**138,224**	**133,748**	**20,904**	**16,428**	**4,072**	**3,369**	**16,832**	**13,059**	100.0	100.0	100.0	100.0	100.0	100.0	100.0	100.0
Under 5 years	13,766	14,079	12,038	12,325	1,728	1,754	371	369	1,357	1,385	8.7	9.2	8.3	10.7	9.1	11.0	8.1	10.6
5 to 9 years	14,133	14,826	12,214	12,886	1,919	1,940	447	435	1,472	1,505	8.8	9.6	9.2	11.8	11.0	12.9	8.7	11.5
10 to 14 years	11,827	12,259	9,992	10,558	1,835	1,701	456	418	1,379	1,283	7.2	7.9	8.8	10.4	11.2	12.4	8.2	9.8
15 to 19 years	1,240	12,518	9,250	10,878	1,990	1,640	392	355	1,598	1,285	6.7	8.1	9.5	10.0	9.6	10.5	9.5	9.8
20 to 24 years	14,199	15,193	12,231	13,892	1,968	1,301	313	211	1,655	1,090	8.8	10.4	9.4	7.9	7.7	6.3	9.8	8.3
25 to 29 years	17,135	17,231	15,469	15,999	1,666	1,232	195	167	1,471	1,065	11.2	12.0	8.0	7.5	4.8	5.0	8.7	8.2
30 to 34 years	16,335	14,844	14,744	13,624	1,591	1,220	186	179	1,405	1,041	10.7	10.2	7.6	7.4	4.6	5.3	8.3	8.0
35 to 39 years	17,084	14,404	15,466	13,248	1,618	1,156	211	191	1,407	965	11.2	9.9	7.7	7.0	5.2	5.7	8.4	7.4
40 to 44 years	12,565	10,219	11,215	9,175	1,350	1,044	222	204	1,128	840	8.1	6.9	6.5	6.4	5.5	6.1	6.7	6.4
45 to 49 years	10,755	8,200	9,461	7,311	1,294	889	221	192	1,073	697	6.8	5.5	6.2	5.4	5.4	5.7	6.4	5.3
50 to 54 years	7,583	5,768	6,483	5,054	1,100	714	252	149	848	565	4.7	3.8	5.3	4.3	6.2	4.4	5.0	4.3
55 to 59 years	4,722	3,615	3,897	3,054	825	561	232	154	593	407	2.8	2.3	3.9	3.4	5.7	4.6	3.5	3.1
60 to 64 years	3,060	2,570	2,414	2,173	646	397	197	119	449	278	1.7	1.6	3.1	2.4	4.8	3.5	2.7	2.1
65 to 69 years	1,908	1,665	1,407	1,358	501	307	164	83	337	224	1.0	1.0	2.4	1.9	4.0	2.5	2.0	1.7
70 to 74 years	1,224	1,203	840	951	384	252	105	70	279	182	.6	.7	1.8	1.5	2.6	2.1	1.7	1.4
75 to 79 years	713	707	480	551	233	156	64	41	169	115	.3	.4	1.1	.9	1.6	1.2	1.0	.9
80 to 84 years	362	377	242	299	120	78	24	15	96	63	.2	.2	.6	.5	.6	.4	.6	.5
85 and over	265	317	172	245	93	72	20	16	73	56	.1	.2	.4	.4	.5	.5	.4	.4
Unknown	252	181	209	167	43	14	------	1	43	13	.2	.1	.2	.1	------	------	.3	.1
INDIANA																		
All ages	**57,068**	**54,914**	**51,788**	**51,254**	**5,280**	**3,660**	**1,427**	**1,107**	**3,853**	**2,553**	100.0	100.0	100.0	100.0	100.0	100.0	100.0	100.0
Under 5 years	4,578	4,564	4,254	4,267	324	297	122	96	202	201	8.2	8.3	6.1	8.1	8.5	8.7	5.2	7.9
5 to 9 years	4,971	4,996	4,598	4,629	373	367	139	122	234	245	8.9	9.0	7.1	10.0	9.7	11.0	6.1	9.6
10 to 14 years	4,150	4,327	3,766	3,987	384	340	127	126	257	214	7.3	7.8	7.3	9.3	8.9	11.4	6.7	8.4
15 to 19 years	4,208	4,538	3,713	4,187	495	351	138	100	357	251	7.2	8.2	9.4	9.6	9.7	9.0	9.3	9.8
20 to 24 years	4,862	5,322	4,372	5,071	490	251	94	61	396	190	8.4	9.9	9.3	6.9	6.6	5.5	10.3	7.4
25 to 29 years	5,649	5,934	5,160	5,687	489	247	71	70	418	177	10.0	11.1	9.3	6.7	5.0	6.3	10.8	6.9
30 to 34 years	5,580	5,222	5,186	4,982	394	240	67	54	327	186	10.0	9.7	7.5	6.6	4.7	4.9	8.5	7.3
35 to 39 years	5,664	5,177	5,244	4,898	420	279	76	78	344	201	10.1	9.6	8.0	7.6	5.3	7.0	8.9	7.9
40 to 44 years	4,510	3,883	4,177	3,639	333	244	83	72	250	172	8.1	7.1	6.3	6.7	5.8	6.5	6.5	6.7
45 to 49 years	3,865	3,459	3,549	3,202	316	257	80	80	236	177	6.9	6.2	6.0	7.0	5.6	7.2	6.1	6.9
50 to 54 years	3,221	2,578	2,887	2,354	334	224	102	78	232	146	5.6	4.6	6.3	6.1	7.1	7.0	6.0	5.7
55 to 59 years	2,132	1,706	1,866	1,537	266	169	92	61	174	108	3.6	3.0	5.0	4.6	6.4	5.5	4.5	4.2
60 to 64 years	1,332	1,107	1,153	988	179	119	66	31	113	88	2.2	1.9	3.4	3.3	4.6	2.8	2.9	3.4
65 to 69 years	940	814	764	719	176	95	69	29	107	66	1.5	1.4	3.3	2.6	4.8	2.6	2.8	2.6
70 to 74 years	603	537	475	454	128	83	46	23	82	60	.9	.9	2.4	2.3	3.2	2.1	2.1	2.4
75 to 79 years	331	337	249	288	82	49	32	14	50	35	.5	.6	1.6	1.3	2.2	1.3	1.3	1.4
80 to 84 years	159	152	117	130	42	22	12	6	30	16	.2	.3	.8	.6	.8	.5	.8	.6
85 and over	126	139	93	117	33	22	10	5	23	17	.2	.2	.6	.6	.7	.5	.6	.7
Unknown	187	122	165	118	22	4	1	1	21	3	.3	.2	.4	.1	.1	.1	.5	.1
ILLINOIS																		
All ages	**164,425**	**164,547**	**150,386**	**153,650**	**14,039**	**10,897**	**2,906**	**2,573**	**11,133**	**8,324**	100.0	100.0	100.0	100.0	100.0	100.0	100.0	100.0
Under 5 years	12,611	12,767	11,576	11,805	1,035	962	271	232	767	730	7.7	7.7	7.4	8.8	9.3	9.0	6.9	8.8
5 to 9 years	12,622	13,138	11,509	11,945	1,113	1,193	291	329	822	864	7.7	7.8	7.9	10.9	10.0	12.8	7.4	10.4
10 to 14 years	10,665	11,446	9,465	10,348	1,200	1,098	332	330	868	768	6.3	6.7	8.5	10.1	11.4	12.8	7.8	9.2
15 to 19 years	10,898	12,465	9,650	11,430	1,248	1,035	331	272	917	763	6.4	7.4	8.9	9.5	11.4	10.6	8.2	9.2
20 to 24 years	15,108	18,156	14,084	17,300	1,024	856	203	186	821	670	9.4	11.3	7.3	7.9	7.0	7.2	7.4	8.0
25 to 29 years	19,890	21,389	18,682	20,616	1,208	773	146	140	1,062	633	12.4	13.4	8.6	7.1	5.0	5.4	9.5	7.6
30 to 34 years	18,562	17,969	17,362	17,188	1,200	781	123	145	1,077	636	11.5	11.2	8.5	7.2	4.2	5.6	9.7	7.6
35 to 39 years	18,606	17,299	17,410	16,481	1,196	818	151	158	1,045	660	11.6	10.7	8.5	7.5	5.2	6.1	9.4	7.9
40 to 44 years	13,888	11,974	12,860	11,181	1,028	793	169	173	859	620	8.6	7.3	7.3	7.3	5.8	6.7	7.7	7.4
45 to 49 years	11,762	9,994	10,783	9,316	979	678	169	157	810	521	7.2	6.1	7.0	6.2	5.8	6.1	7.3	6.3
50 to 54 years	8,076	6,610	7,236	6,015	840	595	205	148	635	447	4.8	3.9	6.0	5.5	7.1	5.8	5.7	5.4
55 to 59 years	4,771	3,994	4,119	3,595	652	399	153	90	499	309	2.7	2.3	4.6	3.7	5.3	3.5	4.5	3.7
60 to 64 years	2,905	2,792	2,435	2,486	470	306	137	83	333	223	1.6	1.6	3.3	2.8	4.7	3.2	3.0	2.7
65 to 69 years	1,755	1,839	1,420	1,615	335	224	85	47	250	177	.9	1.1	2.4	2.1	2.9	1.8	2.2	2.1
70 to 74 years	986	1,140	765	1,000	221	140	64	35	157	105	.5	.7	1.6	1.3	2.2	1.4	1.4	1.3
75 to 79 years	553	684	417	568	136	116	39	20	97	96	.3	.4	1.0	1.1	1.3	.8	.9	1.2
80 to 84 years	249	336	190	274	59	62	19	12	40	50	.1	.2	.4	.6	.7	.5	.4	.6
85 and over	230	302	157	248	73	54	17	14	56	40	.1	.2	.5	.5	.6	.5	.5	.5
Unknown	288	253	266	239	22	14	1	2	21	12	.2	.2	.2	.1	------	.1	.2	.1

Table 19.—NEGRO POPULATION FOR THE URBAN, RURAL-FARM, AND RURAL-NONFARM AREAS, BY 5-YEAR AGE PERIODS, SEX, AND STATES: 1930—Continued

[See note at head of this table]

STATE AND AGE	TOTAL		URBAN		RURAL						PERCENT DISTRIBUTION							
					Total		Rural-farm		Rural-nonfarm		Urban		Rural					
													Total		Rural-farm		Rural-nonfarm	
	Male	Female	Male	Female	Male	Female	Male	Female	Male	Female	Male	Female	Male	Female	Male	Female	Male	Female
MICHIGAN																		
All ages	**88,936**	**80,517**	**83,121**	**76,583**	**5,815**	**3,934**	**1,305**	**1,059**	**4,510**	**2,875**	**100.0**	**100.0**	**100.0**	**100.0**	**100.0**	**100.0**	**100.0**	**100.0**
Under 5 years	7,578	7,653	7,254	7,297	324	356	93	93	231	263	8.7	9.5	5.6	9.0	7.1	8.8	5.1	9.1
5 to 9 years	7,325	7,407	6,943	7,025	382	382	116	128	266	254	8.4	9.2	6.6	9.7	8.9	12.1	5.9	8.8
10 to 14 years	5,540	5,847	5,164	5,483	376	364	141	127	235	237	6.2	7.2	6.5	9.3	10.8	12.0	5.2	8.2
15 to 19 years	5,143	5,745	4,760	5,431	383	314	130	83	253	231	5.7	7.1	6.6	8.0	10.0	7.8	5.6	8.0
20 to 24 years	8,473	9,258	7,914	8,987	559	271	78	53	481	218	9.5	11.7	9.6	6.9	6.0	5.0	10.7	7.6
25 to 29 years	12,414	11,891	11,747	11,566	667	325	55	54	612	271	14.1	15.1	11.5	8.3	4.2	5.1	13.6	9.4
30 to 34 years	11,760	9,754	11,137	9,386	623	368	56	50	567	318	13.4	12.3	10.7	9.4	4.3	4.7	12.6	11.1
35 to 39 years	10,756	8,345	10,233	8,001	523	344	69	79	454	265	12.3	10.4	9.0	8.7	5.3	7.5	10.1	9.2
40 to 44 years	7,147	4,907	6,694	4,646	453	261	76	64	377	197	8.1	6.1	7.8	6.6	5.8	6.0	8.4	6.9
45 to 49 years	5,361	3,689	4,952	3,421	409	268	82	86	327	182	6.0	4.5	7.0	6.8	6.3	8.1	7.3	6.3
50 to 54 years	3,186	2,234	2,871	2,028	315	206	104	65	211	141	3.5	2.6	5.4	5.2	8.0	6.1	4.7	4.9
55 to 59 years	1,803	1,318	1,548	1,182	255	136	90	54	165	82	1.9	1.5	4.4	3.5	6.9	5.1	3.7	2.9
60 to 64 years	1,001	919	809	800	192	119	70	44	122	75	1.0	1.0	3.3	3.0	5.4	4.2	2.7	2.6
65 to 69 years	595	593	435	511	160	82	79	32	81	50	.5	.7	2.8	2.1	6.1	3.0	1.8	1.7
70 to 74 years	305	367	228	307	77	60	30	21	47	39	.3	.4	1.3	1.5	2.3	2.0	1.0	1.4
75 to 79 years	220	252	156	213	64	39	22	13	42	26	.2	.3	1.1	1.0	1.7	1.2	.9	.9
80 to 84 years	102	120	72	99	30	21	11	8	19	13	.1	.1	.5	.5	.8	.8	.4	.5
85 and over	61	100	44	86	17	14	3	4	14	10	.1	.1	.3	.4	.2	.4	.3	.3
Unknown	166	118	160	114	6	4	------	1	6	3	.2	.1	.1	.1	------	.1	.1	.1
WISCONSIN																		
All ages	**5,811**	**4,928**	**5,282**	**4,591**	**529**	**337**	**226**	**151**	**303**	**186**	**100.0**	**100.0**	**100.0**	**100.0**	**100.0**	**100.0**	**100.0**	**100.0**
Under 5 years	406	444	363	402	43	42	28	25	15	17	6.9	8.8	8.1	12.5	12.4	16.6	5.0	9.1
5 to 9 years	471	489	428	433	43	56	33	26	10	30	8.1	9.4	8.1	16.6	14.6	17.2	3.3	16.1
10 to 14 years	395	393	362	356	33	37	23	26	10	11	6.9	7.8	6.2	11.0	10.2	17.2	3.3	5.9
15 to 19 years	329	367	288	344	41	23	22	11	19	12	5.5	7.5	7.8	6.8	9.7	7.3	6.3	6.5
20 to 24 years	533	533	473	502	60	31	21	8	39	23	9.0	10.9	11.3	9.2	9.3	5.3	12.9	12.4
25 to 29 years	732	664	687	637	45	27	14	8	31	19	13.0	13.9	8.5	8.0	6.2	5.3	10.2	10.2
30 to 34 years	678	528	637	499	41	29	10	9	31	20	12.1	10.9	7.8	8.6	4.4	6.0	10.2	10.8
35 to 39 years	697	481	648	458	49	23	13	9	36	14	12.3	10.0	9.3	6.8	5.8	6.0	11.9	8.5
40 to 44 years	540	335	497	317	43	18	15	8	28	10	9.4	6.9	8.1	5.3	6.6	5.3	9.2	5.4
45 to 49 years	382	238	347	227	35	11	10	6	25	5	6.6	4.9	6.6	3.3	4.4	4.0	8.3	2.7
50 to 54 years	271	162	239	153	32	9	12	6	20	3	4.5	3.3	6.0	2.7	5.3	4.0	6.6	1.6
55 to 59 years	174	100	148	85	26	15	11	6	15	9	2.8	1.9	4.9	4.5	4.9	4.0	5.0	4.8
60 to 64 years	74	77	60	66	14	11	4	2	10	9	1.1	1.4	2.6	3.3	1.8	1.3	3.3	4.8
65 to 69 years	50	47	43	46	7	1	4	1	3	------	.8	1.0	1.3	.3	1.8	.7	1.0	------
70 to 74 years	29	31	22	30	7	1	2	------	5	1	.4	.7	1.3	.3	.9	------	1.7	.5
75 to 79 years	17	13	14	12	3	1	2	------	1	1	.3	.3	.6	.3	.9	------	.3	.5
80 to 84 years	11	8	7	8	4	------	1	------	3	------	.1	.2	.8	------	.4	------	1.0	------
85 and over	12	11	9	9	3	2	1	------	2	2	.2	.2	.6	.6	.4	------	.7	1.1
Unknown	10	7	10	7	------	------	------	------	------	------	.2	.2	------	------	------	------	------	------
MINNESOTA																		
All ages	**5,005**	**4,440**	**4,816**	**4,294**	**189**	**146**	**105**	**88**	**84**	**58**	**100.0**	**100.0**	**100.0**	**100.0**	**100.0**	------	------	------
Under 5 years	320	295	308	284	12	11	7	6	5	5	6.4	6.6	6.3	7.5	6.7	------	------	------
5 to 9 years	332	343	318	326	14	17	8	13	6	4	6.6	7.6	7.4	11.6	7.6	------	------	------
10 to 14 years	320	292	306	269	14	23	11	14	3	9	6.4	6.3	7.4	15.8	10.5	------	------	------
15 to 19 years	282	332	263	310	19	22	14	15	5	7	5.5	7.2	10.1	15.1	13.3	------	------	------
20 to 24 years	311	339	302	334	9	5	5	4	4	1	6.3	7.8	4.8	3.4	4.8	------	------	------
25 to 29 years	379	353	365	346	14	7	11	5	3	2	7.6	8.1	7.4	4.8	10.5	------	------	------
30 to 34 years	472	411	462	401	10	10	6	5	4	5	9.6	9.3	5.3	6.8	5.7	------	------	------
35 to 39 years	540	496	524	486	16	10	4	2	12	8	10.9	11.3	8.5	6.8	3.8	------	------	------
40 to 44 years	499	390	489	382	10	8	3	2	7	6	10.2	8.9	5.3	5.5	2.9	------	------	------
45 to 49 years	483	387	466	379	17	8	6	6	11	2	9.7	8.8	9.0	5.5	5.7	------	------	------
50 to 54 years	394	259	381	254	13	5	7	2	6	3	7.9	5.9	6.9	3.4	6.7	------	------	------
55 to 59 years	276	199	268	190	8	9	7	6	1	3	5.6	4.4	4.2	6.2	6.7	------	------	------
60 to 64 years	158	128	149	122	9	6	4	3	5	3	3.1	2.8	4.8	4.1	3.8	------	------	------
65 to 69 years	121	94	112	94	9	------	3	------	6	------	2.3	2.2	4.8	------	2.9	------	------	------
70 to 74 years	49	46	42	45	7	1	4	1	3	------	.9	1.0	3.7	.7	3.8	------	------	------
75 to 79 years	32	40	29	38	3	2	1	2	2	------	.6	.9	1.6	1.4	1.0	------	------	------
80 to 84 years	16	18	13	16	3	2	2	2	1	------	.3	.4	1.6	1.4	1.9	------	------	------
85 and over	13	15	11	15	2	------	2	------	------	------	.2	.3	1.1	------	1.9	------	------	------
Unknown	8	3	8	3	------	------	------	------	------	------	.2	.1	------	------	------	------	------	------
IOWA																		
All ages	**8,987**	**8,393**	**7,749**	**7,436**	**1,238**	**957**	**319**	**253**	**919**	**704**	**100.0**	**100.0**	**100.0**	**100.0**	**100.0**	**100.0**	**100.0**	**100.0**
Under 5 years	651	740	575	648	76	92	23	36	53	56	7.4	8.7	6.1	9.6	7.2	14.2	5.8	8.0
5 to 9 years	796	767	697	675	99	92	33	21	66	71	9.0	9.1	8.0	9.6	10.3	8.3	7.2	10.1
10 to 14 years	710	698	616	613	94	85	24	19	70	66	7.9	8.2	7.6	8.9	7.5	7.5	7.6	9.4
15 to 19 years	679	735	591	643	88	92	27	22	61	70	7.6	8.6	7.1	9.6	8.5	8.7	6.6	9.9
20 to 24 years	679	684	585	625	94	59	27	18	67	41	7.5	8.4	7.6	6.2	8.5	7.1	7.3	5.8
25 to 29 years	682	670	602	601	80	69	20	13	60	56	7.8	8.1	6.5	7.2	6.3	5.1	6.5	8.0
30 to 34 years	712	649	616	600	96	49	19	11	77	38	7.9	8.1	7.8	5.1	6.0	4.3	8.4	5.4
35 to 39 years	765	751	699	677	66	74	15	16	51	58	9.0	9.1	5.3	7.7	4.7	6.3	5.5	8.2
40 to 44 years	688	639	617	576	71	63	11	9	60	54	8.0	7.7	5.7	6.6	3.4	3.6	6.5	7.7
45 to 49 years	710	581	609	519	101	62	20	13	81	49	7.9	7.0	8.2	6.5	6.3	5.1	8.8	7.0
50 to 54 years	594	467	510	411	84	56	21	20	63	36	6.6	5.5	6.8	5.9	6.6	7.9	6.9	5.1
55 to 59 years	451	336	381	290	70	46	21	15	49	31	4.9	3.9	5.7	4.8	6.6	5.9	5.3	4.4
60 to 64 years	326	240	246	204	80	36	30	11	50	25	3.2	2.7	6.5	3.8	9.4	4.3	5.4	3.6
65 to 69 years	238	154	185	136	53	18	11	7	42	11	2.4	1.8	4.3	1.9	3.4	2.8	4.6	1.6
70 to 74 years	137	109	102	86	35	23	7	11	28	12	1.3	1.2	2.8	2.4	2.2	4.3	3.0	1.7
75 to 79 years	83	74	56	59	27	15	5	4	22	11	.7	.8	2.2	1.0	1.6	1.6	2.4	1.6
80 to 84 years	41	43	30	32	11	11	3	3	8	8	.4	.4	.9	1.1	.9	1.2	.9	1.1
85 and over	27	42	16	32	11	10	2	4	9	6	.2	.4	.9	1.6	1.6	1.6	1.0	.9
Unknown	18	14	16	9	2	5	------	------	2	5	.2	.1	.2	.5	------	------	.2	.7

TABLE 19.—NEGRO POPULATION FOR THE URBAN, RURAL-FARM, AND RURAL-NONFARM AREAS, BY 5-YEAR AGE PERIODS, SEX, AND STATES: 1930—Continued

[See note at head of this table]

STATE AND AGE	TOTAL		URBAN		RURAL						PERCENT DISTRIBUTION							
					Total		Rural-farm		Rural-nonfarm		Urban		Rural					
													Total		Rural-farm		Rural-nonfarm	
	Male	Female	Male	Female	Male	Female	Male	Female	Male	Female	Male	Female	Male	Female	Male	Female	Male	Female
MISSOURI																		
All ages	**111,929**	**111,911**	**83,527**	**86,427**	**28,402**	**25,484**	**15,851**	**13,762**	**12,551**	**11,722**	**100.0**	**100.0**	**100.0**	**100.0**	**100.0**	**100.0**	**100.0**	**100.0**
Under 5 years	8,494	8,336	5,716	5,637	2,778	2,699	1,704	1,644	1,074	1,055	6.8	6.5	9.8	10.6	10.8	11.9	8.6	9.0
5 to 9 years	9,251	9,095	6,340	6,199	2,911	2,896	1,691	1,720	1,220	1,176	7.6	7.2	10.2	11.4	10.7	12.5	9.7	10.0
10 to 14 years	8,084	8,434	5,181	5,699	2,903	2,735	1,758	1,604	1,145	1,131	6.2	6.6	10.2	10.7	11.1	11.7	9.1	9.6
15 to 19 years	8,480	9,255	5,729	6,587	2,751	2,668	1,646	1,558	1,105	1,110	6.9	7.6	9.7	10.5	10.4	11.3	8.8	9.5
20 to 24 years	9,302	11,363	6,988	9,075	2,314	2,288	1,332	1,332	982	956	8.4	10.5	8.1	9.0	8.4	9.7	7.8	8.2
25 to 29 years	10,502	12,188	8,659	10,271	1,843	1,917	1,007	1,029	836	888	10.4	11.9	6.5	7.5	6.4	7.5	6.7	7.6
30 to 34 years	9,983	10,576	8,263	8,973	1,720	1,603	900	847	820	756	9.9	10.4	6.1	6.3	5.7	6.2	6.5	6.4
35 to 39 years	10,926	10,929	9,046	9,135	1,880	1,794	1,003	955	877	839	10.8	10.6	6.6	7.0	6.3	6.9	7.0	7.2
40 to 44 years	9,433	8,493	7,688	7,018	1,745	1,475	916	777	829	698	9.2	8.1	6.1	5.8	5.8	5.6	6.6	6.0
45 to 49 years	8,735	7,345	6,974	5,926	1,761	1,419	966	716	795	703	8.3	6.9	6.2	5.6	6.1	5.2	6.3	6.0
50 to 54 years	6,522	5,332	4,975	4,206	1,547	1,126	828	495	719	631	6.0	4.9	5.4	4.4	5.2	3.6	5.7	5.4
55 to 59 years	4,211	3,365	3,025	2,561	1,186	804	621	345	565	459	3.6	3.0	4.2	3.2	3.9	2.5	4.5	3.9
60 to 64 years	3,022	2,481	1,941	1,805	1,081	676	568	272	513	404	2.3	2.1	3.8	2.7	3.6	2.0	4.1	3.4
65 to 69 years	1,995	1,771	1,214	1,309	781	462	408	172	373	290	1.5	1.5	2.7	1.8	2.6	1.2	3.0	2.5
70 to 74 years	1,225	1,161	723	806	502	355	224	127	278	228	.9	.9	1.8	1.4	1.4	.9	2.2	1.9
75 to 79 years	804	742	443	510	361	232	160	77	201	155	.5	.6	1.3	.9	1.0	.6	1.6	1.3
80 to 84 years	409	457	233	299	176	158	72	47	104	111	.3	.3	.6	.6	.5	.3	.8	.9
85 and over	301	372	172	241	129	131	40	40	89	91	.2	.3	.5	.5	.3	.3	.7	.8
Unknown	250	216	217	170	33	46	7	5	26	41	.3	.2	.1	.2	------	------	.2	.3
NORTH DAKOTA																		
All ages	**243**	**134**	**133**	**83**	**110**	**51**	**53**	**25**	**57**	**26**	**100.0**	------	**100.0**	------	------	------	------	------
Under 5 years	20	10	10	------	10	10	7	7	3	3	7.5	------	9.1	------	------	------	------	------
5 to 9 years	13	8	5	2	8	6	5	3	3	3	3.8	------	7.3	------	------	------	------	------
10 to 14 years	10	5	2	4	8	1	5	1	3	------	1.5	------	7.3	------	------	------	------	------
15 to 19 years	19	7	11	1	8	6	4	3	4	3	8.3	------	7.3	------	------	------	------	------
20 to 24 years	9	23	2	16	7	7	3	5	4	2	1.5	------	6.4	------	------	------	------	------
25 to 29 years	19	12	16	10	3	2	2	------	1	2	12.0	------	2.7	------	------	------	------	------
30 to 34 years	15	17	10	11	5	6	2	2	3	4	7.5	------	4.5	------	------	------	------	------
35 to 39 years	25	9	15	7	10	2	2	2	8	------	11.3	------	9.1	------	------	------	------	------
40 to 44 years	24	16	17	13	7	3	3	------	4	3	12.8	------	6.4	------	------	------	------	------
45 to 49 years	28	9	15	8	13	1	6	1	7	------	11.3	------	11.8	------	------	------	------	------
50 to 54 years	25	7	15	5	10	2	5	------	5	2	11.3	------	9.1	------	------	------	------	------
55 to 59 years	14	5	8	4	6	1	3	------	3	1	6.0	------	5.5	------	------	------	------	------
60 to 64 years	8	4	3	------	5	4	2	1	3	3	2.3	------	4.5	------	------	------	------	------
65 to 69 years	6	1	2	1	4	------	2	------	2	------	1.5	------	3.6	------	------	------	------	------
70 to 74 years	6	------	1	------	5	------	2	------	3	------	.8	------	4.5	------	------	------	------	------
75 to 79 years	1	1	1	1	------	------	------	------	------	------	.8	------	------	------	------	------	------	------
80 to 84 years	------	------	------	------	------	------	------	------	------	------	------	------	------	------	------	------	------	------
85 and over	1	------	------	------	1	------	------	------	1	------	------	------	.9	------	------	------	------	------
Unknown	------	------	------	------	------	------	------	------	------	------	------	------	------	------	------	------	------	------
SOUTH DAKOTA																		
All ages	**343**	**303**	**171**	**166**	**172**	**137**	**127**	**105**	**45**	**32**	**100.0**	**100.0**	**100.0**	**100.0**	**100.0**	**100.0**	------	------
Under 5 years	17	30	9	15	8	15	8	15	------	------	5.3	9.0	4.7	10.9	6.3	14.3	------	------
5 to 9 years	22	31	9	12	13	19	11	15	2	4	5.3	7.2	7.6	13.9	8.7	14.3	------	------
10 to 14 years	25	30	8	11	17	19	14	14	3	5	4.7	6.6	9.9	13.9	11.0	13.3	------	------
15 to 19 years	36	26	15	9	21	17	20	12	1	5	8.8	5.4	12.2	12.4	15.7	11.4	------	------
20 to 24 years	29	36	17	24	12	12	11	11	1	1	9.9	14.5	7.0	8.8	8.7	10.5	------	------
25 to 29 years	30	22	19	16	11	6	7	5	4	1	11.1	9.6	6.4	4.4	5.5	4.8	------	------
30 to 34 years	32	19	19	10	13	9	7	5	6	4	11.1	6.0	7.6	6.6	5.5	4.8	------	------
35 to 39 years	25	19	12	13	13	6	4	4	9	2	7.0	7.8	7.6	4.4	3.1	3.8	------	------
40 to 44 years	26	25	12	13	14	12	12	10	2	2	7.0	7.8	8.1	8.8	9.4	9.5	------	------
45 to 49 years	26	16	14	9	12	7	7	3	5	4	8.2	5.4	7.0	5.1	5.5	2.9	------	------
50 to 54 years	22	16	11	12	11	4	10	3	1	1	6.4	7.2	6.4	2.9	7.9	2.9	------	------
55 to 59 years	15	10	8	4	7	6	3	4	4	2	4.7	2.4	4.1	4.4	2.4	3.8	------	------
60 to 64 years	11	9	6	8	5	1	4	1	1	------	3.5	4.8	2.9	.7	3.1	1.0	------	------
65 to 69 years	11	4	2	3	9	1	5	------	4	1	1.2	1.8	5.2	.7	3.9	------	------	------
70 to 74 years	8	5	4	4	4	1	2	1	2	------	2.3	2.4	2.3	.7	1.6	1.0	------	------
75 to 79 years	4	2	2	------	2	2	2	2	------	------	1.2	------	1.2	1.5	1.6	1.9	------	------
80 to 84 years	------	2	------	2	------	------	------	------	------	------	------	1.2	------	------	------	------	------	------
85 and over	1	1	1	1	------	------	------	------	------	------	.6	.6	------	------	------	------	------	------
Unknown	3	------	3	------	------	------	------	------	------	------	1.8	------	------	------	------	------	------	------
NEBRASKA																		
All ages	**7,063**	**6,689**	**6,675**	**6,437**	**388**	**252**	**110**	**67**	**278**	**185**	**100.0**	**100.0**	**100.0**	**100.0**	**100.0**	------	**100.0**	**100.0**
Under 5 years	531	515	520	499	11	16	6	7	5	9	7.8	7.8	2.8	6.3	5.5	------	1.8	4.9
5 to 9 years	546	555	525	530	21	25	5	9	16	16	7.9	8.2	5.4	9.9	4.5	------	5.8	8.6
10 to 14 years	484	446	452	424	32	22	16	11	16	11	6.8	6.6	8.2	8.7	14.5	------	5.8	5.9
15 to 19 years	455	507	411	467	44	40	29	12	15	28	6.2	7.3	11.3	15.9	26.4	------	5.4	15.1
20 to 24 years	503	619	474	606	29	13	10	3	19	10	7.1	9.4	7.5	5.2	9.1	------	6.8	5.4
25 to 29 years	692	712	652	695	40	17	3	3	37	14	9.8	10.8	10.3	6.7	2.7	------	13.3	7.6
30 to 34 years	661	653	626	634	35	19	4	2	31	17	9.4	9.8	9.0	7.5	3.6	------	11.2	9.2
35 to 39 years	744	713	714	693	30	20	2	4	28	16	10.7	10.8	7.7	7.9	1.8	------	10.1	8.6
40 to 44 years	659	581	622	561	37	20	2	4	35	16	9.3	8.7	9.5	7.9	1.8	------	12.6	8.6
45 to 49 years	630	486	601	471	29	15	5	4	24	11	9.0	7.3	7.5	6.0	4.5	------	8.6	5.9
50 to 54 years	467	336	440	321	27	15	11	2	16	13	6.6	5.0	7.0	6.0	10.0	------	5.8	7.0
55 to 59 years	247	208	231	200	16	8	5	2	11	6	3.5	3.1	4.1	3.2	4.5	------	4.0	3.2
60 to 64 years	181	126	169	117	12	9	4	1	8	8	2.5	1.8	3.1	3.6	3.6	------	2.9	4.3
65 to 69 years	112	95	102	91	10	4	5	1	5	3	1.5	1.4	2.6	1.6	4.5	------	1.8	1.6
70 to 74 years	56	53	52	48	4	5	1	1	3	4	.8	.7	1.0	2.0	.9	------	1.1	2.2
75 to 79 years	42	41	40	39	2	2	------	------	2	2	.6	.6	.5	.8	------	------	.7	1.1
80 to 84 years	21	17	15	15	6	2	1	1	5	1	.2	.2	1.5	.8	.9	------	1.8	.5
85 and over	18	21	15	21	3	------	1	------	2	------	.2	.3	.8	------	.9	------	.7	------
Unknown	14	5	14	5	------	------	------	------	------	------	.2	.1	------	------	------	------	------	------

TABLE 19.—NEGRO POPULATION FOR THE URBAN, RURAL-FARM, AND RURAL-NONFARM AREAS, BY 5-YEAR AGE PERIODS, SEX, AND STATES: 1930—Continued

[See note at head of this table]

STATE AND AGE	TOTAL		URBAN		RURAL						PERCENT DISTRIBUTION							
					Total		Rural-farm		Rural-nonfarm		Urban		Rural: Total		Rural: Rural-farm		Rural: Rural-nonfarm	
	Male	Female	Male	Female	Male	Female	Male	Female	Male	Female	Male	Female	Male	Female	Male	Female	Male	Female
KANSAS																		
All ages	**33,980**	**32,364**	**25,034**	**26,247**	**8,946**	**6,117**	**2,413**	**1,979**	**6,533**	**4,138**	**100.0**	**100.0**	**100.0**	**100.0**	**100.0**	**100.0**	**100.0**	**100.0**
Under 5 years	2,612	2,570	2,103	2,015	509	555	185	187	324	368	8.4	7.7	5.7	9.1	7.7	9.4	5.0	8.9
5 to 9 years	2,963	3,056	2,310	2,458	653	598	245	212	408	386	9.2	9.4	7.3	9.8	10.2	10.7	6.2	9.3
10 to 14 years	2,756	2,852	2,092	2,240	664	612	241	228	423	384	8.4	8.5	7.4	10.0	10.0	11.5	6.5	9.3
15 to 19 years	2,631	2,803	1,970	2,236	661	567	254	208	407	359	7.9	8.5	7.4	9.3	10.5	10.5	6.2	8.7
20 to 24 years	2,714	2,772	1,929	2,288	785	484	194	142	591	342	7.7	8.7	8.8	7.9	8.0	7.2	9.0	8.3
25 to 29 years	2,775	2,779	1,981	2,377	794	402	109	96	685	306	7.9	9.1	8.9	6.6	4.5	4.9	10.5	7.4
30 to 34 years	2,886	2,587	2,037	2,228	849	359	110	94	739	265	8.1	8.5	9.5	5.9	4.6	4.7	11.3	6.4
35 to 39 years	2,998	2,715	2,122	2,239	876	476	156	151	720	325	8.5	8.5	9.8	7.8	6.5	7.6	11.0	7.9
40 to 44 years	2,626	2,392	1,896	1,986	730	406	158	128	572	278	7.6	7.6	8.2	6.6	6.5	6.5	8.8	6.7
45 to 49 years	2,339	2,173	1,810	1,790	529	383	133	128	396	255	7.2	6.8	5.9	6.3	5.5	6.5	6.1	6.2
50 to 54 years	2,114	1,727	1,568	1,371	546	356	165	112	381	244	6.3	5.2	6.1	5.8	6.8	5.7	5.8	5.9
55 to 59 years	1,552	1,193	1,115	906	437	287	138	88	299	199	4.5	3.5	4.9	4.7	5.7	4.4	4.6	4.8
60 to 64 years	1,034	919	771	737	263	182	108	62	155	120	3.1	2.8	2.9	3.0	4.5	3.1	2.4	2.9
65 to 69 years	776	657	561	517	215	140	74	51	141	89	2.2	2.0	2.4	2.3	3.1	2.6	2.2	2.2
70 to 74 years	506	533	331	323	175	110	57	37	118	73	1.3	1.2	2.0	1.8	2.4	1.9	1.8	1.8
75 to 79 years	320	352	203	259	117	93	40	25	77	68	.8	1.0	1.3	1.5	1.7	1.3	1.2	1.6
80 to 84 years	191	196	130	148	61	48	23	8	38	40	.5	.6	.7	.8	1.0	.4	.6	1.0
85 and over	154	163	88	111	66	52	21	20	45	32	.4	.4	.7	.9	.9	1.0	.7	.8
Unknown	33	25	17	18	16	7	2	2	14	5	.1	.1	.2	.1	.1	.1	.2	.1
DELAWARE																		
All ages	**16,983**	**15,619**	**7,538**	**7,499**	**9,445**	**8,120**	**3,720**	**3,035**	**5,725**	**5,085**	**100.0**	**100.0**	**100.0**	**100.0**	**100.0**	**100.0**	**100.0**	**100.0**
Under 5 years	1,391	1,396	540	532	851	864	367	353	484	511	7.2	7.1	9.0	10.6	9.9	11.6	8.5	10.0
5 to 9 years	1,622	1,626	637	648	985	978	428	420	557	558	8.5	8.6	10.4	12.0	11.5	13.8	9.7	11.0
10 to 14 years	1,485	1,500	528	565	957	935	422	395	535	540	7.0	7.5	10.1	11.5	11.3	13.0	9.3	10.6
15 to 19 years	1,503	1,482	511	645	992	837	473	351	519	486	6.8	8.6	10.5	10.3	12.7	11.6	9.1	9.6
20 to 24 years	1,573	1,415	669	716	904	699	378	248	526	451	8.9	9.5	9.6	8.6	10.2	8.2	9.2	8.9
25 to 29 years	1,478	1,341	785	773	693	568	191	187	502	381	10.4	10.3	7.3	7.0	5.1	6.2	8.8	7.5
30 to 34 years	1,283	1,194	672	647	611	547	192	173	419	374	8.9	8.6	6.5	6.7	5.2	5.7	7.3	7.4
35 to 39 years	1,453	1,262	799	764	654	498	189	174	465	324	10.6	10.2	6.9	6.1	5.1	5.7	8.1	6.4
40 to 44 years	1,150	987	604	533	546	454	197	157	349	297	8.0	7.1	5.8	5.6	5.3	5.2	6.1	5.8
45 to 49 years	1,038	899	539	473	499	426	187	138	312	288	7.2	6.3	5.3	5.2	5.0	4.5	5.4	5.7
50 to 54 years	999	805	449	432	550	373	216	137	334	236	6.0	5.8	5.8	4.6	5.8	4.5	5.8	4.6
55 to 59 years	628	511	269	248	359	263	146	88	213	175	3.6	3.3	3.8	3.2	3.9	2.9	3.7	3.4
60 to 64 years	523	408	225	190	298	218	123	71	175	147	3.0	2.5	3.2	2.7	3.3	2.3	3.1	2.9
65 to 69 years	376	328	149	138	227	190	91	65	136	125	2.0	1.8	2.4	2.3	2.4	2.1	2.4	2.5
70 to 74 years	215	202	75	85	140	117	59	36	81	81	1.0	1.1	1.5	1.4	1.6	1.2	1.4	1.6
75 to 79 years	137	133	50	55	87	78	29	25	58	53	.7	.7	.9	1.0	.8	.8	1.0	1.0
80 to 84 years	63	72	19	31	44	41	17	10	27	31	.3	.4	.5	.5	.5	.3	.5	.6
85 and over	51	53	13	22	38	31	12	7	26	24	.2	.3	.4	.4	.3	.2	.5	.5
Unknown	15	5	5	2	10	3	3	—	7	3	.1	—	.1	—	.1	—	.1	.1
MARYLAND																		
All ages	**140,506**	**135,873**	**78,421**	**81,233**	**62,085**	**54,640**	**23,821**	**20,460**	**38,264**	**34,180**	**100.0**	**100.0**	**100.0**	**100.0**	**100.0**	**100.0**	**100.0**	**100.0**
Under 5 years	13,484	13,522	6,809	6,911	6,675	6,611	2,655	2,649	4,020	3,962	8.7	8.5	10.8	12.1	11.1	12.9	10.5	11.6
5 to 9 years	14,449	15,115	7,069	7,673	7,380	7,442	3,121	3,056	4,259	4,386	9.0	9.4	11.9	13.6	13.1	14.9	11.1	12.8
10 to 14 years	12,622	13,005	5,577	6,379	7,045	6,626	3,084	2,850	3,961	3,776	7.1	7.9	11.3	12.1	12.9	13.9	10.4	11.0
15 to 19 years	12,554	12,863	5,655	7,099	6,899	5,764	3,066	2,288	3,833	3,476	7.2	8.7	11.1	10.5	12.9	11.2	10.0	10.2
20 to 24 years	13,841	13,570	7,694	8,980	6,147	4,590	2,124	1,488	4,023	3,102	9.8	11.1	9.9	8.4	8.9	7.3	10.5	9.1
25 to 29 years	13,065	12,444	8,649	8,873	4,416	3,571	1,314	1,152	3,102	2,419	11.0	10.9	7.1	6.5	5.5	5.6	8.1	7.1
30 to 34 years	11,218	10,608	7,548	7,486	3,670	3,122	1,135	1,056	2,535	2,066	9.6	9.2	5.9	5.7	4.8	5.2	6.6	6.0
35 to 39 years	11,373	10,576	7,860	7,372	3,513	3,204	1,189	1,103	2,324	2,101	10.0	9.1	5.7	5.9	5.0	5.4	6.1	6.1
40 to 44 years	9,223	8,487	6,072	5,660	3,151	2,827	1,111	990	2,040	1,837	7.7	7.0	5.1	5.2	4.7	4.8	5.3	5.4
45 to 49 years	8,244	7,509	5,185	4,658	3,059	2,851	1,130	1,019	1,929	1,832	6.6	5.7	4.9	5.2	4.7	5.0	5.0	5.4
50 to 54 years	6,903	5,890	3,907	3,378	2,996	2,512	1,160	915	1,836	1,597	5.0	4.2	4.8	4.6	4.9	4.5	4.8	4.7
55 to 59 years	4,364	3,696	2,129	2,002	2,235	1,694	873	606	1,362	1,088	2.7	2.5	3.6	3.1	3.7	3.0	3.6	3.2
60 to 64 years	3,372	2,940	1,587	1,606	1,785	1,334	709	475	1,076	859	2.0	2.0	2.9	2.4	3.0	2.3	2.8	2.5
65 to 69 years	2,271	2,044	974	1,095	1,297	949	530	323	767	626	1.2	1.3	2.1	1.7	2.2	1.6	2.0	1.8
70 to 74 years	1,465	1,359	575	720	890	639	283	200	607	439	.7	.9	1.4	1.2	1.2	1.0	1.6	1.3
75 to 79 years	756	765	295	341	461	424	171	131	290	293	.4	.4	.7	.8	.7	.6	.8	.9
80 to 84 years	393	496	136	245	257	251	100	86	157	165	.2	.3	.4	.5	.4	.4	.4	.5
85 and over	230	306	103	147	127	159	46	59	81	100	.1	.2	.2	.3	.2	.3	.2	.3
Unknown	679	678	597	608	82	70	20	14	62	56	.8	.7	.1	.1	.1	.1	.2	.2
DISTRICT OF COLUMBIA																		
All ages	**62,225**	**69,843**	**62,225**	**69,843**	—	—	—	—	—	—	**100.0**	**100.0**	—	—	—	—	—	—
Under 5 years	5,036	4,970	5,036	4,970	—	—	—	—	—	—	8.1	7.1	—	—	—	—	—	—
5 to 9 years	5,314	5,524	5,314	5,524	—	—	—	—	—	—	8.5	7.9	—	—	—	—	—	—
10 to 14 years	4,432	5,052	4,432	5,052	—	—	—	—	—	—	7.1	7.2	—	—	—	—	—	—
15 to 19 years	4,757	5,918	4,757	5,918	—	—	—	—	—	—	7.6	8.5	—	—	—	—	—	—
20 to 24 years	6,472	7,934	6,472	7,934	—	—	—	—	—	—	10.4	11.4	—	—	—	—	—	—
25 to 29 years	6,994	7,995	6,994	7,995	—	—	—	—	—	—	11.2	11.4	—	—	—	—	—	—
30 to 34 years	5,889	6,471	5,889	6,471	—	—	—	—	—	—	9.5	9.3	—	—	—	—	—	—
35 to 39 years	5,797	6,357	5,797	6,357	—	—	—	—	—	—	9.3	9.1	—	—	—	—	—	—
40 to 44 years	4,493	5,070	4,493	5,070	—	—	—	—	—	—	7.2	7.3	—	—	—	—	—	—
45 to 49 years	4,247	4,673	4,247	4,673	—	—	—	—	—	—	6.8	6.7	—	—	—	—	—	—
50 to 54 years	3,433	3,511	3,433	3,511	—	—	—	—	—	—	5.5	5.0	—	—	—	—	—	—
55 to 59 years	1,966	2,035	1,966	2,035	—	—	—	—	—	—	3.2	2.9	—	—	—	—	—	—
60 to 64 years	1,274	1,511	1,274	1,511	—	—	—	—	—	—	2.0	2.2	—	—	—	—	—	—
65 to 69 years	849	1,093	849	1,093	—	—	—	—	—	—	1.4	1.6	—	—	—	—	—	—
70 to 74 years	508	615	508	615	—	—	—	—	—	—	.8	.9	—	—	—	—	—	—
75 to 79 years	231	382	231	382	—	—	—	—	—	—	.4	.5	—	—	—	—	—	—
80 to 84 years	117	240	117	240	—	—	—	—	—	—	.2	.3	—	—	—	—	—	—
85 and over	96	160	96	160	—	—	—	—	—	—	.2	.2	—	—	—	—	—	—
Unknown	320	332	320	332	—	—	—	—	—	—	.5	.5	—	—	—	—	—	—

TABLE 19.—NEGRO POPULATION FOR THE URBAN, RURAL-FARM, AND RURAL-NONFARM AREAS, BY 5-YEAR AGE PERIODS, SEX, AND STATES: 1930—Continued

[See note at head of this table]

STATE AND AGE	TOTAL		URBAN		RURAL						PERCENT DISTRIBUTION							
					Total		Rural-farm		Rural-nonfarm		Urban		Rural					
													Total		Rural-farm		Rural-nonfarm	
	Male	Female	Male	Female	Male	Female	Male	Female	Male	Female	Male	Female	Male	Female	Male	Female	Male	Female
VIRGINIA																		
All ages	321,545	328,620	99,273	114,128	222,272	214,492	132,913	126,054	89,359	88,438	100.0	100.0	100.0	100.0	100.0	100.0	100.0	100.0
Under 5 years	34,973	35,689	8,947	9,160	26,026	26,529	15,729	16,007	10,297	10,422	9.0	8.0	11.7	12.4	11.8	12.7	11.5	11.9
5 to 9 years	42,429	42,645	10,755	11,147	31,674	31,498	19,869	19,664	11,805	11,834	10.8	9.8	14.3	14.7	14.9	15.6	13.2	13.4
10 to 14 years	39,430	39,463	9,271	10,260	30,159	29,203	19,906	19,103	10,253	10,100	9.3	9.0	13.6	13.6	15.0	15.2	11.5	11.4
15 to 19 years	36,432	37,011	8,882	11,550	27,550	25,461	18,100	15,651	9,450	9,810	8.9	10.1	12.4	11.9	13.6	12.4	10.6	11.1
20 to 24 years	27,327	29,240	8,943	12,113	18,384	17,127	10,131	9,049	8,253	8,078	9.0	10.6	8.3	8.0	7.6	7.2	9.2	9.1
25 to 29 years	20,715	23,763	8,571	11,127	12,144	12,636	5,776	6,372	6,368	6,264	8.6	9.7	5.5	5.9	4.3	5.1	7.1	7.1
30 to 34 years	17,860	20,423	7,778	9,384	10,082	11,039	4,707	5,705	5,375	5,334	7.8	8.2	4.5	5.1	3.5	4.5	6.0	6.0
35 to 39 years	20,297	22,730	8,668	10,315	11,629	12,415	5,837	6,778	5,792	5,637	8.7	9.0	5.2	5.8	4.4	5.4	6.5	6.4
40 to 44 years	18,102	18,553	7,371	7,879	10,731	10,674	5,799	6,070	4,932	4,604	7.4	6.9	4.8	5.0	4.4	4.8	5.5	5.2
45 to 49 years	17,622	17,180	6,854	7,068	10,768	10,112	6,202	5,851	4,566	4,261	6.9	6.2	4.8	4.7	4.7	4.6	5.1	4.8
50 to 54 years	15,328	13,627	5,187	5,006	10,141	8,621	6,167	5,028	3,974	3,593	5.2	4.4	4.6	4.0	4.6	4.0	4.4	4.1
55 to 59 years	10,358	8,162	3,026	2,826	7,332	5,336	4,726	3,144	2,606	2,192	3.0	2.5	3.3	2.5	3.6	2.5	2.9	2.5
60 to 64 years	7,773	7,080	2,185	2,373	5,588	4,707	3,638	2,710	1,950	1,997	2.2	2.1	2.5	2.2	2.7	2.1	2.2	2.3
65 to 69 years	5,274	5,065	1,284	1,611	3,990	3,454	2,620	1,925	1,370	1,529	1.3	1.4	1.8	1.6	2.0	1.5	1.5	1.7
70 to 74 years	3,651	3,497	765	990	2,886	2,507	1,836	1,353	1,050	1,154	.8	.9	1.3	1.2	1.4	1.1	1.2	1.3
75 to 79 years	2,009	2,029	388	571	1,621	1,458	1,002	742	619	716	.4	.5	.7	.7	.8	.6	.7	.8
80 to 84 years	1,113	1,247	190	346	923	901	532	489	391	412	.2	.3	.4	.4	.4	.4	.4	.5
85 and over	672	988	119	274	553	714	303	372	250	342	.1	.2	.2	.3	.2	.3	.3	.4
Unknown	180	228	89	128	91	100	33	41	58	59	.1	.1	------	------	------	------	.1	.1
WEST VIRGINIA																		
All ages	60,873	54,020	15,586	15,638	45,287	38,382	2,019	1,796	43,268	36,586	100.0	100.0	100.0	100.0	100.0	100.0	100.0	100.0
Under 5 years	5,988	6,116	1,252	1,248	4,736	4,868	216	193	4,520	4,675	8.0	8.0	10.5	12.7	10.7	10.7	10.4	12.8
5 to 9 years	6,329	6,539	1,354	1,426	4,975	5,113	241	277	4,734	4,836	8.7	9.1	11.0	13.3	11.9	15.4	10.9	13.2
10 to 14 years	5,127	5,317	1,208	1,262	3,919	4,055	251	248	3,668	3,807	7.8	8.1	8.7	10.6	12.4	13.8	8.5	10.4
15 to 19 years	4,705	5,404	1,199	1,518	3,506	3,886	246	212	3,260	3,674	7.7	9.7	7.7	10.1	12.2	11.8	7.5	10.0
20 to 24 years	5,533	5,684	1,434	1,716	4,099	3,968	168	136	3,931	3,832	9.2	11.0	9.1	10.3	8.3	7.6	9.1	10.5
25 to 29 years	6,045	5,636	1,581	1,649	4,464	3,987	99	107	4,365	3,880	10.1	10.5	9.9	10.4	4.9	6.0	10.1	10.6
30 to 34 years	5,800	4,746	1,530	1,508	4,270	3,238	96	83	4,174	3,155	9.8	9.6	9.4	8.4	4.8	4.6	9.6	8.6
35 to 39 years	5,960	4,412	1,504	1,465	4,456	2,947	99	96	4,357	2,851	9.6	9.4	9.8	7.7	4.9	5.3	10.1	7.8
40 to 44 years	4,803	3,195	1,316	1,149	3,487	2,046	103	89	3,384	1,957	8.4	7.3	7.7	5.3	5.1	5.0	7.8	5.3
45 to 49 years	3,924	2,451	1,131	912	2,793	1,539	109	78	2,684	1,461	7.3	5.8	6.2	4.0	5.4	4.3	6.2	4.0
50 to 54 years	2,636	1,728	789	668	1,847	1,060	98	91	1,749	969	5.1	4.3	4.1	2.8	4.9	5.1	4.0	2.6
55 to 59 years	1,644	895	513	356	1,131	539	90	58	1,041	481	3.3	2.3	2.5	1.4	4.5	3.2	2.4	1.3
60 to 64 years	1,003	685	323	294	680	391	69	38	611	353	2.1	1.9	1.5	1.0	3.4	2.1	1.4	1.0
65 to 69 years	623	457	212	169	411	288	57	33	354	255	1.4	1.1	.9	.8	2.8	1.8	.8	.7
70 to 74 years	361	303	111	119	250	184	35	23	215	161	.7	.8	.6	.5	1.7	1.3	.5	.4
75 to 79 years	168	191	53	68	115	123	17	15	98	108	.3	.4	.3	.3	.8	.8	2	.3
80 to 84 years	96	101	33	47	63	54	13	9	50	45	.2	.3	.1	.1	.6	.5	.1	.1
85 and over	56	103	21	35	35	68	8	9	27	59	.1	.2	.1	.2	.4	.5	.1	.2
Unknown	72	57	22	29	50	28	4	1	46	27	.1	.2	.1	.1	.2	.1	.1	.1
NORTH CAROLINA																		
All ages	446,500	472,147	112,494	133,743	334,006	338,404	248,869	248,627	85,137	89,777	100.0	100.0	100.0	100.0	100.0	100.0	100.0	100.0
Under 5 years	57,040	57,655	11,569	11,551	45,471	46,104	34,585	35,174	10,886	10,930	10.3	8.6	13.6	13.6	13.9	14.1	12.8	12.2
5 to 9 years	64,644	65,499	13,053	13,918	51,591	51,581	39,970	39,735	11,621	11,846	11.6	10.4	15.4	15.2	16.1	16.0	13.6	13.2
10 to 14 years	58,815	58,948	11,416	12,382	47,399	46,566	37,830	36,536	9,569	10,030	10.1	9.3	14.2	13.8	15.2	14.7	11.2	11.2
15 to 19 years	55,846	59,320	11,692	15,540	44,154	43,780	34,522	33,384	9,632	10,396	10.4	11.6	13.2	12.9	13.9	13.4	11.3	11.6
20 to 24 years	43,601	51,403	12,828	18,280	30,773	33,123	21,518	22,862	9,255	10,261	11.4	13.7	9.2	9.8	8.6	9.2	10.9	11.4
25 to 29 years	31,595	38,248	11,435	15,269	20,160	22,979	12,797	15,308	7,363	7,671	10.2	11.4	6.0	6.8	5.1	6.2	8.6	8.5
30 to 34 years	23,827	27,557	8,879	10,498	14,948	17,059	9,798	11,725	5,150	5,334	7.9	7.8	4.5	5.0	3.9	4.7	6.0	5.9
35 to 39 years	23,472	27,717	8,358	10,053	15,114	17,664	10,311	12,445	4,803	5,219	7.4	7.5	4.5	5.2	4.1	5.0	5.6	5.8
40 to 44 years	18,940	21,808	6,287	7,277	12,653	14,531	8,872	10,264	3,781	4,267	5.6	5.4	3.8	4.3	3.6	4.1	4.4	4.8
45 to 49 years	17,519	19,576	5,105	6,214	12,414	13,362	9,122	9,471	3,292	3,891	4.5	4.6	3.7	3.9	3.7	3.8	3.9	4.3
50 to 54 years	17,583	15,100	4,546	4,472	13,037	10,628	9,777	7,456	3,260	3,172	4.0	3.3	3.9	3.1	3.9	3.0	3.8	3.5
55 to 59 years	11,643	8,941	2,568	2,553	9,075	6,388	7,025	4,503	2,050	1,885	2.3	1.9	2.7	1.9	2.8	1.8	2.4	2.1
60 to 64 years	8,242	7,179	1,888	2,065	6,354	5,114	4,776	3,510	1,578	1,604	1.7	1.5	1.9	1.5	1.9	1.4	1.9	1.8
65 to 69 years	5,449	4,855	1,123	1,354	4,326	3,501	3,286	2,354	1,040	1,147	1.0	1.0	1.3	1.0	1.3	.9	1.2	1.3
70 to 74 years	3,779	3,527	731	895	3,048	2,632	2,268	1,719	780	913	.6	.7	.9	.8	.9	.7	.9	1.0
75 to 79 years	2,169	2,021	388	536	1,781	1,485	1,280	958	501	527	.3	.4	.5	.4	.5	.4	.6	.6
80 to 84 years	1,127	1,224	222	306	905	918	613	589	292	329	.2	.2	.3	.3	.2	.2	.3	.4
85 and over	754	1,086	122	241	632	845	437	561	195	284	.1	.2	.2	.2	.2	.2	.2	.3
Unknown	455	483	284	339	171	144	82	73	89	71	.3	.3	.1	------	------	------	.1	.1
SOUTH CAROLINA																		
All ages	379,300	414,381	60,319	78,035	318,981	336,346	245,021	252,933	73,960	83,413	100.0	100.0	100.0	100.0	100.0	100.0	100.0	100.0
Under 5 years	47,656	48,644	6,019	6,384	41,637	42,260	32,109	32,454	9,528	9,806	10.0	8.2	13.1	12.6	13.1	12.8	12.9	11.8
5 to 9 years	57,803	58,493	7,533	7,967	50,270	50,526	39,674	39,753	10,596	10,773	12.5	10.2	15.8	15.0	16.2	15.7	14.3	12.9
10 to 14 years	55,474	55,649	6,756	7,679	48,718	47,970	39,697	38,588	9,021	9,382	11.2	9.8	15.3	14.3	16.2	15.3	12.2	11.2
15 to 19 years	50,805	55,624	6,787	9,699	44,018	45,925	35,474	35,560	8,544	10,365	11.3	12.4	13.8	13.7	14.5	14.1	11.6	12.4
20 to 24 years	34,172	42,480	6,297	10,034	27,875	32,446	19,451	22,314	8,424	10,132	10.4	12.9	8.7	9.7	7.9	8.8	11.4	12.1
25 to 29 years	21,868	29,431	5,284	8,013	16,584	21,418	10,774	14,685	5,810	6,733	8.8	10.3	5.2	6.4	4.4	5.8	7.9	8.1
30 to 34 years	16,972	21,997	4,148	5,657	12,824	16,340	8,859	11,629	3,965	4,711	6.9	7.2	4.0	4.9	3.6	4.6	5.4	5.6
35 to 39 years	19,484	25,535	4,407	6,201	15,077	19,334	10,923	14,164	4,154	5,170	7.3	7.9	4.7	5.7	4.5	5.6	5.6	6.2
40 to 44 years	16,842	20,158	3,477	4,707	13,365	15,451	10,011	11,380	3,354	4,071	5.8	6.0	4.2	4.6	4.1	4.5	4.5	4.9
45 to 49 years	15,223	17,815	2,909	3,781	12,314	14,034	9,529	10,504	2,785	3,530	4.8	4.8	3.9	4.2	3.9	4.2	3.8	4.2
50 to 54 years	13,773	13,171	2,409	2,719	11,364	10,452	8,889	7,651	2,475	2,801	4.0	3.5	3.6	3.1	3.6	3.0	3.3	3.4
55 to 59 years	8,750	7,651	1,354	1,557	7,396	6,094	5,965	4,447	1,431	1,647	2.2	2.0	2.3	1.8	2.4	1.8	1.9	2.0
60 to 64 years	8,937	6,618	1,328	1,371	7,609	5,247	6,089	3,742	1,520	1,505	2.2	1.8	2.4	1.6	2.5	1.5	2.1	1.8
65 to 69 years	5,171	4,449	728	973	4,443	3,476	3,474	2,387	969	1,089	1.2	1.2	1.4	1.0	1.4	.9	1.3	1.3
70 to 74 years	3,185	2,944	452	608	2,733	2,336	2,075	1,564	658	772	.7	.8	.9	.7	.8	.6	.9	.9
75 to 79 years	1,638	1,647	229	285	1,409	1,362	1,065	934	344	428	.4	.4	.4	.4	.4	.4	.5	.5
80 to 84 years	827	1,039	94	180	733	859	530	605	203	254	.2	.2	.2	.3	.2	.2	.3	.3
85 and over	575	808	65	129	510	679	360	478	150	201	.1	.2	.2	.2	.1	.2	.2	.2
Unknown	145	228	43	91	102	137	73	94	29	43	.1	.1	------	------	------	------	------	.1

TABLE 19.—NEGRO POPULATION FOR THE URBAN, RURAL-FARM, AND RURAL-NONFARM AREAS, BY 5-YEAR AGE PERIODS, SEX, AND STATES: 1930—Continued

[See note at head of this table]

STATE AND AGE	TOTAL		URBAN		RURAL						PERCENT DISTRIBUTION							
					Total		Rural-farm		Rural-nonfarm		Urban		Rural					
													Total		Rural-farm		Rural-nonfarm	
	Male	Female	Male	Female	Male	Female	Male	Female	Male	Female	Male	Female	Male	Female	Male	Female	Male	Female
GEORGIA																		
All ages	**513,451**	**557,674**	**140,573**	**176,064**	**372,878**	**381,610**	**275,790**	**279,974**	**97,088**	**101,636**	**100.0**	**100.0**	**100.0**	**100.0**	**100.0**	**100.0**	**100.0**	**100.0**
Under 5 years	57,436	58,580	12,498	12,762	44,938	45,818	34,533	35,118	10,405	10,700	8.9	7.2	12.1	12.0	12.5	12.5	10.7	10.5
5 to 9 years	66,258	67,768	15,107	15,697	51,151	52,071	40,285	40,696	10,866	11,375	10.7	8.9	13.7	13.6	14.6	14.5	11.2	11.2
10 to 14 years	65,689	65,704	14,201	15,931	51,488	49,773	41,607	39,784	9,881	9,989	10.1	9.0	13.8	13.0	15.1	14.2	10.2	9.8
15 to 19 years	63,755	70,461	14,490	20,207	49,265	50,254	38,847	38,153	10,418	12,101	10.3	11.5	13.2	13.2	14.1	13.6	10.7	11.9
20 to 24 years	50,174	62,160	14,958	23,086	35,216	39,074	23,625	26,486	11,591	12,588	10.6	13.1	9.4	10.2	8.6	9.5	11.9	12.4
25 to 29 years	36,286	45,966	13,588	19,734	22,698	26,232	13,837	17,242	8,861	8,990	9.7	11.2	6.1	6.9	5.0	6.2	9.1	8.8
30 to 34 years	27,084	34,308	10,557	14,055	16,527	20,253	10,363	13,694	6,164	6,559	7.5	8.0	4.4	5.3	3.8	4.9	6.3	6.5
35 to 39 years	29,093	37,805	11,264	15,234	17,829	22,571	11,602	15,635	6,227	6,936	8.0	8.7	4.8	5.9	4.2	5.6	6.4	6.8
40 to 44 years	22,126	29,211	8,655	11,038	13,471	18,173	8,959	12,862	4,512	5,311	6.2	6.3	3.6	4.8	3.2	4.6	4.6	5.2
45 to 49 years	19,165	26,361	7,366	9,400	11,799	16,961	7,973	12,186	3,826	4,775	5.2	5.3	3.2	4.4	2.9	4.4	3.9	4.7
50 to 54 years	28,908	20,683	7,450	6,833	21,458	13,850	16,366	9,867	5,092	3,983	5.3	3.9	5.8	3.6	5.9	3.5	5.2	3.9
55 to 59 years	15,290	11,122	3,620	3,584	11,670	7,538	8,889	5,368	2,781	2,170	2.6	2.0	3.1	2.0	3.2	1.9	2.9	2.1
60 to 64 years	13,611	10,001	2,934	3,188	10,677	6,813	8,174	4,650	2,503	2,163	2.1	1.8	2.9	1.8	3.0	1.7	2.6	2.1
65 to 69 years	7,932	6,564	1,686	2,051	6,246	4,513	4,729	3,100	1,517	1,413	1.2	1.2	1.7	1.2	1.7	1.1	1.6	1.4
70 to 74 years	4,873	4,570	994	1,348	3,879	3,222	2,820	2,131	1,059	1,091	.7	.8	1.0	.8	1.0	.8	1.1	1.1
75 to 79 years	2,803	2,849	567	837	2,236	2,012	1,593	1,366	643	646	.4	.5	.6	.5	.6	.5	.7	.6
80 to 84 years	1,456	1,659	264	472	1,192	1,187	847	790	345	397	.2	.3	.3	.3	.3	.3	.4	.4
85 and over	1,079	1,454	200	393	879	1,061	614	712	265	349	.1	.2	.2	.3	.2	.3	.3	.3
Unknown	433	448	174	214	259	234	127	134	132	100	.1	.1	.1	.1	------	------	.1	.1
FLORIDA																		
All ages	**215,148**	**216,680**	**98,584**	**111,708**	**116,564**	**104,972**	**38,611**	**36,858**	**77,953**	**68,114**	**100.0**	**100.0**	**100.0**	**100.0**	**100.0**	**100.0**	**100.0**	**100.0**
Under 5 years	20,095	20,346	8,651	8,831	11,444	11,515	4,192	4,145	7,252	7,370	8.8	7.9	9.8	11.0	10.9	11.2	9.3	10.8
5 to 9 years	22,324	23,126	9,664	10,153	12,660	12,973	4,913	4,908	7,747	8,065	9.8	9.1	10.9	12.4	12.7	13.3	9.9	11.8
10 to 14 years	20,862	21,254	8,648	9,422	12,214	11,832	5,355	5,008	6,859	6,824	8.8	8.4	10.5	11.3	13.9	13.6	8.8	10.0
15 to 19 years	20,002	23,353	8,234	11,308	11,768	12,045	4,819	4,675	6,949	7,370	8.4	10.1	10.1	11.5	12.5	12.7	8.9	10.8
20 to 24 years	22,145	26,257	10,084	14,266	12,061	11,991	3,245	3,517	8,816	8,474	10.2	12.8	10.3	11.4	8.4	9.5	11.3	12.4
25 to 29 years	21,785	24,165	11,371	14,441	10,414	9,724	2,332	2,416	8,082	7,308	11.5	12.9	8.9	9.3	6.0	6.6	10.4	10.7
30 to 34 years	16,793	17,610	9,105	10,586	7,688	7,024	1,747	1,920	5,941	5,104	9.2	9.5	6.6	6.7	4.5	5.2	7.6	7.5
35 to 39 years	17,182	17,650	9,162	10,306	8,020	7,344	1,863	2,222	6,157	5,122	9.3	9.2	6.9	7.0	4.8	6.0	7.9	7.5
40 to 44 years	13,947	12,805	7,059	7,198	6,888	5,607	1,724	1,901	5,164	3,706	7.2	6.4	5.9	5.3	4.5	5.2	6.6	5.4
45 to 49 years	13,217	10,639	6,165	5,755	7,052	4,884	2,103	1,819	4,949	3,065	6.3	5.2	6.0	4.7	5.4	4.9	6.3	4.5
50 to 54 years	9,975	7,228	4,328	3,692	5,647	3,536	1,714	1,425	3,933	2,111	4.4	3.3	4.8	3.4	4.4	3.9	5.0	3.1
55 to 59 years	6,291	3,917	2,406	1,919	3,885	1,998	1,624	861	2,261	1,137	2.4	1.7	3.3	1.9	4.2	2.3	2.9	1.7
60 to 64 years	4,444	3,122	1,650	1,469	2,794	1,653	1,132	750	1,662	903	1.7	1.3	2.4	1.6	2.9	2.0	2.1	1.3
65 to 69 years	2,775	2,075	984	945	1,791	1,130	818	513	973	617	1.0	.8	1.5	1.1	2.1	1.4	1.2	.9
70 to 74 years	1,463	1,297	485	592	978	705	479	316	499	389	.5	.5	.8	.7	1.2	.9	.6	.6
75 to 79 years	830	747	258	332	572	415	273	210	299	205	.3	.3	.5	.4	.7	.6	.4	.3
80 to 84 years	422	461	122	177	300	284	140	126	160	158	.1	.2	.3	.3	.4	.3	.2	.2
85 and over	341	408	100	189	241	219	106	108	135	111	.1	.2	.2	.2	.3	.3	.2	.2
Unknown	255	220	108	127	147	93	32	18	115	75	.1	.1	.1	.1	.1	------	.1	.1
KENTUCKY																		
All ages	**113,501**	**112,539**	**56,086**	**60,475**	**57,415**	**52,064**	**25,298**	**22,551**	**32,117**	**29,513**	**100.0**	**100.0**	**100.0**	**100.0**	**100.0**	**100.0**	**100.0**	**100.0**
Under 5 years	9,370	9,217	3,938	3,918	5,432	5,199	2,629	2,506	2,803	2,793	7.0	6.5	9.5	10.2	10.4	11.1	8.7	9.5
5 to 9 years	10,936	10,888	4,636	4,735	6,300	6,153	3,009	2,939	3,291	3,214	8.3	7.8	11.0	11.8	11.9	13.0	10.2	10.9
10 to 14 years	10,030	10,260	4,165	4,503	5,865	5,757	2,936	2,804	2,929	2,953	7.4	7.4	10.2	11.1	11.6	12.4	9.1	10.0
15 to 19 years	10,201	10,561	4,463	5,132	5,738	5,429	2,857	2,495	2,881	2,934	8.0	8.5	10.0	10.4	11.3	11.1	9.0	9.9
20 to 24 years	9,648	10,168	4,734	5,778	4,914	4,390	2,023	1,863	2,891	2,527	8.4	9.6	8.6	8.4	8.0	8.3	9.0	8.6
25 to 29 years	8,789	9,413	4,845	5,644	3,944	3,769	1,436	1,426	2,508	2,343	8.6	9.3	6.9	7.2	5.7	6.3	7.8	7.9
30 to 34 years	8,179	8,613	4,588	5,316	3,591	3,297	1,290	1,269	2,301	2,028	8.2	8.8	6.3	6.3	5.1	5.6	7.2	6.9
35 to 39 years	9,162	9,106	5,383	5,659	3,779	3,447	1,367	1,395	2,412	2,052	9.6	9.4	6.6	6.6	5.4	6.2	7.5	7.0
40 to 44 years	7,875	7,697	4,504	4,741	3,371	2,956	1,337	1,182	2,034	1,774	8.0	7.8	5.9	5.7	5.3	5.2	6.3	6.0
45 to 49 years	7,701	7,365	4,447	4,486	3,254	2,879	1,277	1,156	1,977	1,723	7.9	7.4	5.7	5.5	5.0	5.1	6.2	5.8
50 to 54 years	6,781	5,860	3,612	3,382	3,169	2,478	1,398	1,023	1,771	1,455	6.4	5.6	5.5	4.8	5.5	4.5	5.5	4.9
55 to 59 years	4,587	3,860	2,293	2,131	2,294	1,729	1,087	767	1,207	962	4.1	3.5	4.0	3.3	4.3	3.4	3.8	3.3
60 to 64 years	3,595	3,247	1,714	1,788	1,881	1,459	889	588	992	871	3.1	3.0	3.3	2.8	3.5	2.6	3.1	3.0
65 to 69 years	2,678	2,338	1,162	1,255	1,516	1,083	732	438	784	645	2.1	2.1	2.6	2.1	2.9	1.9	2.4	2.2
70 to 74 years	1,888	1,601	788	820	1,100	781	513	287	587	494	1.4	1.4	1.9	1.5	2.0	1.3	1.8	1.7
75 to 79 years	1,020	1,066	398	553	622	513	271	180	351	333	.7	.9	1.1	1.0	1.1	.8	1.1	1.1
80 to 84 years	534	635	206	318	328	317	135	114	193	203	.4	.5	.6	.6	.5	.5	.6	.7
85 and over	392	521	155	250	237	271	103	114	134	157	.3	.4	.4	.5	.4	.5	.4	.5
Unknown	135	123	55	66	80	57	9	5	71	52	.1	.1	.1	.1	------	------	.2	.2
TENNESSEE																		
All ages	**232,569**	**245,077**	**111,505**	**128,663**	**121,064**	**116,414**	**89,120**	**85,395**	**31,944**	**31,019**	**100.0**	**100.0**	**100.0**	**100.0**	**100.0**	**100.0**	**100.0**	**100.0**
Under 5 years	21,961	22,343	8,936	9,088	13,025	13,255	10,175	10,361	2,850	2,894	8.0	7.1	10.8	11.4	11.4	12.1	8.9	9.3
5 to 9 years	24,975	25,393	10,040	10,549	14,935	14,844	11,775	11,608	3,160	3,236	9.0	8.2	12.3	12.8	13.2	13.6	9.9	10.4
10 to 14 years	24,130	24,022	9,057	9,787	15,073	14,235	12,021	11,212	3,052	3,023	8.1	7.6	12.5	12.2	13.5	13.1	9.6	9.7
15 to 19 years	24,953	26,882	9,712	12,564	15,241	14,318	11,670	10,794	3,571	3,524	8.7	9.8	12.6	12.3	13.1	12.6	11.2	11.4
20 to 24 years	22,337	26,951	11,060	15,494	11,277	11,457	7,725	8,045	3,552	3,412	9.9	12.0	9.3	9.8	8.7	9.4	11.1	11.0
25 to 29 years	19,166	23,183	11,311	14,944	7,855	8,239	5,096	5,684	2,759	2,555	10.1	11.6	6.5	7.1	5.7	6.7	8.6	8.2
30 to 34 years	15,778	17,830	9,527	11,296	6,251	6,534	4,148	4,556	2,103	1,978	8.5	8.8	5.2	5.6	4.7	5.3	6.6	6.4
35 to 39 years	16,651	18,911	10,163	11,925	6,488	6,986	4,468	4,940	2,020	2,046	9.1	9.3	5.4	6.0	5.0	5.8	6.3	6.6
40 to 44 years	12,721	14,302	7,852	8,608	4,869	5,694	3,346	3,976	1,523	1,718	7.0	6.7	4.0	4.9	3.8	4.7	4.8	5.5
45 to 49 years	11,374	12,985	6,935	7,441	4,439	5,544	3,007	3,979	1,432	1,565	6.2	5.8	3.7	4.8	3.4	4.7	4.5	5.0
50 to 54 years	14,070	11,128	6,623	6,214	7,447	4,914	5,568	3,407	1,879	1,507	5.9	4.8	6.2	4.2	6.2	4.0	5.9	4.9
55 to 59 years	8,427	6,502	3,777	3,488	4,650	3,014	3,476	2,095	1,174	919	3.4	2.7	3.8	2.6	3.9	2.5	3.7	3.0
60 to 64 years	6,152	5,211	2,734	2,735	3,418	2,476	2,506	1,671	912	805	2.5	2.1	2.8	2.1	2.8	2.0	2.9	2.6
65 to 69 years	3,974	3,435	1,616	1,664	2,358	1,771	1,721	1,198	637	573	1.4	1.3	1.9	1.5	1.9	1.4	2.0	1.8
70 to 74 years	2,532	2,370	948	1,164	1,584	1,206	1,141	778	443	428	.9	.9	1.3	1.0	1.3	.9	1.4	1.4
75 to 79 years	1,414	1,468	492	700	922	768	624	475	298	293	.4	.5	.8	.7	.7	.6	.9	.9
80 to 84 years	848	905	291	425	557	480	383	330	174	150	.3	.3	.5	.4	.4	.4	.5	.5
85 and over	564	730	207	327	357	403	228	253	129	150	.2	.3	.3	.3	.3	.3	.4	.5
Unknown	542	526	224	250	318	276	42	33	276	243	.2	.2	.3	.2	------	------	.9	.8

Table 19.—NEGRO POPULATION FOR THE URBAN, RURAL-FARM, AND RURAL-NONFARM AREAS, BY 5-YEAR AGE PERIODS, SEX, AND STATES: 1930—Continued

[See note at head of this table]

STATE AND AGE	TOTAL		URBAN		RURAL						PERCENT DISTRIBUTION							
					Total		Rural-farm		Rural-nonfarm		Urban		Rural: Total		Rural: Rural-farm		Rural: Rural-nonfarm	
	Male	Female	Male	Female	Male	Female	Male	Female	Male	Female	Male	Female	Male	Female	Male	Female	Male	Female
ALABAMA																		
All ages	**457, 144**	**487, 690**	**123, 127**	**145, 323**	**334, 017**	**342, 367**	**244, 696**	**251, 846**	**89, 321**	**90, 521**	**100. 0**	**100. 0**	**100. 0**	**100. 0**	**100. 0**	**100. 0**	**100. 0**	**100. 0**
Under 5 years	53, 478	54, 358	11, 903	12, 017	41, 575	42, 341	31, 534	31, 939	10, 041	10, 402	9. 7	8. 3	12. 4	12. 4	12. 9	12. 7	11. 2	11. 5
5 to 9 years	58, 961	58, 747	12, 863	13, 610	46, 098	45, 137	35, 930	34, 984	10, 168	10, 153	10. 4	9. 4	13. 8	13. 2	14. 7	13. 9	11. 4	11. 2
10 to 14 years	54, 626	54, 308	11, 517	12, 256	43, 109	42, 052	35, 118	33, 583	7, 991	8, 469	9. 4	8. 4	12. 9	12. 3	14. 4	13. 3	8. 9	9. 4
15 to 19 years	51, 787	57, 429	11, 716	15, 815	40, 071	41, 614	31, 734	31, 795	8, 337	9, 819	9. 5	10. 9	12. 0	12. 2	13. 0	12. 6	9. 3	10. 8
20 to 24 years	43, 513	53, 560	12, 952	18, 673	30, 561	34, 887	20, 028	23, 392	10, 533	11, 495	10. 5	12. 8	9. 1	10. 2	8. 2	9. 3	11. 8	12. 7
25 to 29 years	34, 896	42, 622	12, 690	17, 169	22, 206	25, 453	13, 094	16, 207	9, 112	9, 246	10. 3	11. 8	6. 6	7. 4	5. 4	6. 4	10. 2	10. 2
30 to 34 years	24, 914	30, 645	9, 610	12, 182	15, 304	18, 463	8, 896	12, 098	6, 408	6, 365	7. 8	8. 4	4. 6	5. 4	3. 6	4. 8	7. 2	7. 0
35 to 39 years	25, 702	33, 418	10, 089	12, 474	15, 613	20, 944	9, 291	14, 492	6, 322	6, 452	8. 2	8. 6	4. 7	6. 1	3. 8	5. 8	7. 1	7. 1
40 to 44 years	19, 314	25, 828	7, 606	8, 822	11, 708	17, 006	7, 290	12, 463	4, 418	4, 543	6. 2	6. 1	3. 5	5. 0	3. 0	4. 9	4. 9	5. 0
45 to 49 years	29, 949	24, 205	8, 298	7, 761	21, 651	16, 444	o16, 000	12, 311	5, 651	4, 133	6. 7	5. 3	6. 5	4. 8	6. 5	4. 9	6. 3	4. 6
50 to 54 years	20, 230	17, 488	5, 510	5, 199	14, 720	12, 289	11, 116	9, 335	3, 604	2, 954	4. 5	3. 6	4. 4	3. 6	4. 5	3. 7	4. 0	3. 3
55 to 59 yaars	13, 031	10, 133	2, 975	2, 804	10, 056	7, 329	7, 874	5, 668	2, 182	1, 661	2. 4	1. 9	3. 0	2. 1	3. 2	2. 3	2. 4	1. 8
60 to 64 years	10, 864	8, 810	2, 340	2, 407	8, 524	6, 403	6, 772	4, 765	1, 752	1, 638	1. 9	1. 7	2. 6	1. 9	2. 8	1. 9	2. 0	1. 8
65 to 69 years	6, 705	5, 984	1, 325	1, 661	5, 380	4, 323	4, 318	3, 202	1, 062	1, 121	1. 1	1. 1	1. 6	1. 3	1. 8	1. 3	1. 2	1. 2
70 to 74 years	4, 123	4, 124	750	1, 013	3, 373	3, 111	2, 649	2, 289	724	822	. 6	. 7	1. 0	. 9	1. 1	. 9	. 8	. 9
75 to 79 years	2, 378	2, 506	418	579	1, 960	1, 927	1, 526	1, 423	434	504	. 3	. 4	. 6	6	. 6	. 6	. 5	. 6
80 to 84 years	1, 335	1, 741	241	407	1, 094	1, 334	816	947	278	387	. 2	. 3	. 3	. 4	. 3	. 4	. 3	. 4
85 and over	1, 007	1, 434	202	309	805	1, 125	581	839	224	286	. 2	. 2	. 2	. 3	. 2	. 3	. 3	. 3
Unknown	331	350	122	165	209	185	129	114	80	71	. 1	. 1	. 1	. 1	. 1	------	. 1	. 1
MISSISSIPPI																		
All ages	**498, 338**	**511, 380**	**60, 237**	**73, 750**	**438, 101**	**437, 630**	**382, 748**	**380, 088**	**55, 353**	**57, 542**	**100. 0**	**100. 0**	**100. 0**	**100. 0**	**100. 0**	**100. 0**	**100. 0**	**100. 0**
Under 5 years	58, 663	58, 772	5, 336	5, 569	53, 327	53, 203	47, 908	47, 724	5, 419	5, 482	8. 9	7. 6	12. 2	12. 2	12. 5	12. 6	9. 8	9. 5
5 to 9 years	63, 760	63, 465	6, 031	6, 299	57, 729	57, 166	52, 402	51, 534	5, 327	5, 632	10. 0	8. 5	13. 2	13. 1	13. 7	13. 6	9. 6	9. 8
10 to 14 years	59, 296	57, 543	5, 162	5, 718	54, 134	51, 825	49, 783	47, 166	4, 351	4, 659	8. 6	7. 8	12. 4	11. 8	13. 0	12. 4	7. 9	8. 1
15 to 19 years	55, 752	59, 141	5, 511	7, 594	50, 241	51, 547	45, 323	45, 685	4, 918	5, 862	9. 1	10. 3	11. 5	11. 8	11. 8	12. 0	8. 9	10. 2
20 to 24 years	48, 136	56, 225	6, 410	9, 659	41, 726	46, 566	34, 826	38, 921	6, 900	7, 645	10. 6	13. 1	9. 5	10. 6	9. 1	10. 2	12. 5	13. 3
25 to 29 years	38, 400	44, 427	6, 124	8, 917	32, 276	35, 510	26, 064	29, 107	6, 212	6, 403	10. 2	12. 1	7. 4	8. 1	6. 8	7. 7	11. 2	11. 1
30 to 34 years	28, 764	32, 735	4, 901	6, 201	23, 863	26, 534	19, 439	22, 244	4, 424	4, 290	8. 1	8. 4	5. 4	6. 1	5. 1	5. 9	8. 0	7. 5
35 to 39 years	29, 771	34, 313	5, 054	6, 518	24, 717	27, 795	20, 404	23, 459	4, 313	4, 336	8. 4	8. 8	5. 6	6. 4	5. 3	6. 2	7. 8	7. 5
40 to 44 years	24, 001	25, 902	3, 986	4, 512	20, 015	21, 390	16, 830	18, 220	3, 185	3, 170	6. 6	6. 1	4. 6	4. 9	4. 4	4. 8	5. 8	5. 5
45 to 49 years	21, 399	24, 140	3, 532	4, 003	17, 867	20, 137	15, 229	17, 346	2, 638	2, 791	5. 9	5. 4	4. 1	4. 6	4. 0	4. 6	4. 8	4. 9
50 to 54 years	23, 634	18, 529	2, 758	2, 846	20, 876	15, 683	18, 475	13, 524	2, 401	2, 159	4. 6	3. 9	4. 8	3. 6	4. 8	3. 6	4. 3	3. 8
55 to 59 years	15, 822	11, 109	1, 867	1, 711	13, 955	9, 398	12, 331	8, 090	1, 624	1, 308	3. 1	2. 3	3. 2	2. 1	3. 2	2. 1	2. 9	2. 3
60 to 64 years	13, 067	9, 416	1, 421	1, 493	11, 646	7, 923	10, 293	6, 609	1, 353	1, 314	2. 4	2. 0	2. 7	1. 8	2. 7	1. 7	2. 4	2. 3
65 to 69 years	7, 742	5, 765	874	994	6, 868	4, 771	5, 988	3, 928	880	843	1. 5	1. 3	1. 6	1. 1	1. 6	1. 0	1. 6	1. 5
70 to 74 years	4, 577	4, 031	525	697	4, 052	3, 334	3, 456	2, 652	596	682	. 9	. 9	. 9	. 8	. 9	. 7	1. 1	1. 2
75 to 79 years	2, 704	2, 515	333	460	2, 371	2, 055	2, 000	1, 645	371	410	. 6	. 6	. 5	. 5	. 5	. 4	. 7	. 7
80 to 84 years	1, 542	1, 674	183	268	1, 359	1, 406	1, 142	1, 114	217	292	. 3	. 4	. 3	. 3	. 3	. 3	. 4	. 5
85 and over	1, 093	1, 457	137	196	956	1, 261	780	1, 029	176	232	. 2	. 3	. 2	. 3	. 2	. 3	. 3	. 4
Unknown	215	221	92	95	123	126	75	94	48	32	. 2	. 1	------	------	------	------	. 1	. 1
ARKANSAS																		
All ages	**236, 909**	**241, 554**	**40, 844**	**48, 318**	**196, 065**	**193, 236**	**164, 399**	**160, 212**	**31, 666**	**33, 024**	**100. 0**	**100. 0**	**100. 0**	**100. 0**	**100. 0**	**100. 0**	**100. 0**	**100. 0**
Under 5 years	24, 660	25, 297	3, 108	3, 254	21, 552	22, 043	18, 752	19, 031	2, 800	3, 012	7. 6	6. 7	11. 0	11. 4	11. 4	11. 9	8. 8	9. 1
5 to 9 years	27, 496	27, 737	3, 678	3, 845	23, 818	23, 892	20, 736	20, 726	3, 082	3, 166	9. 0	8. 0	12. 1	12. 4	12. 6	12. 9	9. 7	9. 6
10 to 14 years	26, 514	26, 397	3, 529	3, 861	22, 985	22, 536	20, 242	19, 567	2, 743	2, 969	8. 6	8. 0	11. 7	11. 7	12. 3	12. 2	8. 7	9. 0
15 to 19 years	25, 017	27, 528	3, 637	4, 901	21, 380	22, 627	18, 583	19, 342	2, 797	3, 285	8. 9	10. 1	10. 9	11. 7	11. 3	12. 1	8. 8	9. 9
20 to 24 years	22, 831	26, 425	4, 047	5, 869	18, 784	20, 556	15, 440	16, 645	3, 344	3, 911	9. 9	12. 1	9. 6	10. 6	9. 4	10. 4	10. 6	11. 8
25 to 29 years	18, 545	21, 619	3, 910	5, 666	14, 635	15, 953	11, 503	12, 609	3, 132	3, 344	9. 6	11. 7	7. 5	8. 3	7. 0	7. 9	9. 9	10. 1
30 to 34 years	14, 510	16, 921	3, 377	4, 423	11, 133	12, 498	8, 667	9, 905	2, 466	2, 593	8. 3	9. 2	5. 7	6. 5	5. 3	6. 2	7. 8	7. 9
35 to 39 years	15, 351	17, 810	3, 585	4, 529	11, 766	13, 281	9, 183	10, 566	2, 583	2, 715	8. 8	9. 4	6. 0	6. 9	5. 6	8. 2	8. 2	8. 2
40 to 44 years	12, 284	13, 869	2, 880	3, 421	9, 404	10, 448	7, 517	8, 341	1, 887	2, 107	7. 1	7. 1	4. 8	5. 4	4. 6	5. 2	6. 0	6. 4
45 to 49 years	15, 517	12, 400	3, 182	2, 820	12, 335	9, 580	10, 052	7, 810	2, 283	1, 770	7. 8	5. 8	6. 3	5. 0	6. 1	4. 9	7. 2	5. 4
50 to 54 years	12, 174	9, 335	2, 232	2, 096	9, 942	7, 239	8, 350	5, 862	1, 592	1, 377	5. 5	4. 3	5. 1	3. 7	5. 1	3. 7	5. 0	4. 2
55 to 59 years	8, 035	5, 365	1, 273	1, 140	6, 762	4, 225	5, 781	3, 389	981	836	3. 1	2. 4	3. 4	2. 2	3. 5	2. 1	3. 1	2. 5
60 to 64 years	5, 782	4, 149	945	937	4, 837	3, 212	4, 080	2, 531	757	681	2. 3	1. 9	2. 5	1. 7	2. 5	1. 6	2. 4	2. 1
65 to 69 years	3, 503	2, 612	583	591	2, 920	2, 021	2, 434	1, 544	486	477	1. 4	1. 2	1. 5	1. 0	1. 5	1. 0	1. 5	1. 4
70 to 74 years	2, 150	1, 724	368	373	1, 782	1, 351	1, 484	1, 008	298	343	. 9	. 8	. 9	. 7	. 9	. 6	. 9	1. 0
75 to 79 years	1, 231	1, 024	238	272	993	752	805	557	188	195	. 6	. 6	. 5	. 4	. 5	. 3	. 6	. 6
80 to 84 years	634	670	115	158	519	512	408	396	111	116	. 3	. 3	. 3	. 3	. 2	. 2	. 4	. 4
85 and over	538	567	97	123	441	444	329	342	112	102	. 2	. 3	. 2	. 2	. 2	. 2	. 4	. 3
Unknown	137	105	60	39	77	66	53	41	24	25	. 1	. 1	------	------	------	------	. 1	. 1
LOUISIANA																		
All ages	**379, 173**	**397, 153**	**118, 429**	**139, 024**	**260, 734**	**258, 129**	**187, 132**	**185, 364**	**73, 602**	**72, 765**	**100. 0**	**100. 0**	**100. 0**	**100. 0**	**100. 0**	**100. 0**	**100. 0**	**100. 0**
Under 5 years	42, 202	42, 784	10, 926	11, 078	31, 276	31, 706	23, 672	23, 965	7, 604	7, 741	9. 2	8. 0	12. 0	12. 3	12. 6	12. 9	10. 3	10. 6
5 to 9 years	46, 313	46, 769	12, 116	12, 727	34, 197	34, 042	25, 976	25, 866	8, 221	8, 176	10. 2	9. 2	13. 1	13. 2	13. 9	14. 0	11. 2	11. 2
10 to 14 years	41, 980	42, 820	10, 138	11, 561	31, 842	31, 259	24, 783	24, 171	7, 059	7, 088	8. 6	8. 3	12. 2	12. 1	13. 2	13. 0	9. 6	9. 6
15 to 19 years	38, 192	43, 101	10, 225	13, 612	27, 967	29, 489	21, 441	21, 922	6, 526	7, 567	8. 6	9. 8	10. 7	11. 4	11. 5	11. 8	8. 9	10. 4
20 to 24 years	36, 546	43, 004	11, 925	16, 900	24, 621	26, 104	16, 824	18, 050	7, 797	8, 054	10. 1	12. 2	9. 4	10. 1	9. 0	9. 7	10. 6	11. 1
25 to 29 years	31, 806	37, 235	12, 631	16, 617	19, 175	20, 618	12, 283	13, 576	6, 892	7, 042	10. 7	12. 0	7. 4	8. 0	6. 6	7. 3	9. 4	9. 7
30 to 34 years	24, 535	27, 653	10, 131	12, 256	14, 404	15, 397	9, 058	10, 196	5, 346	5, 201	8. 6	8. 8	5. 5	6. 0	4. 8	5. 5	7. 3	7. 1
35 to 39 years	27, 002	29, 354	10, 859	12, 707	16, 143	16, 647	10, 347	11, 208	5, 796	5, 439	9. 2	9. 1	6. 2	6. 4	5. 5	6. 0	7. 9	7. 5
40 to 44 years	21, 791	21, 957	8, 486	8, 962	13, 305	12, 995	8, 686	8, 955	4, 619	4, 040	7. 2	6. 4	5. 1	5. 0	4. 6	4. 8	6. 3	5. 6
45 to 49 years	21, 383	19, 936	7, 774	7, 736	13, 609	12, 200	9, 209	8, 499	4, 400	3, 701	6. 6	5. 6	5. 2	4. 7	4. 9	4. 6	6. 0	5. 1
50 to 54 years	16, 233	14, 131	5, 181	5, 144	11, 052	8, 987	7, 940	6, 409	3, 112	2, 578	4. 4	3. 7	4. 2	3. 5	4. 2	3. 5	4. 2	3. 5
55 to 59 years	11, 099	8, 999	3, 260	3, 192	7, 839	5, 807	5, 771	4, 106	2, 068	1, 701	2. 8	2. 3	3. 0	2. 2	3. 1	2. 2	2. 8	2. 3
60 to 64 years	8, 177	6, 956	2, 014	2, 300	6, 163	4, 656	4, 611	3, 178	1, 552	1, 478	1. 7	1. 7	2. 4	1. 8	2. 5	1. 7	2. 1	2. 0
65 to 69 years	5, 078	4, 690	1, 168	1, 663	3, 910	3, 027	2, 873	1, 974	1, 037	1, 053	1. 0	1. 2	1. 5	1. 2	1. 5	1. 1	1. 4	1. 4
70 to 74 years	2, 965	3, 124	693	1, 081	2, 272	2, 043	1, 643	1, 321	629	722	. 6	. 8	. 9	. 8	. 9	. 7	. 9	1. 0
75 to 79 years	1, 901	2, 011	413	623	1, 488	1, 388	1, 030	859	458	529	. 3	. 4	. 6	. 5	. 6	. 5	. 6	. 7
80 to 84 years	992	1, 267	222	401	770	866	560	533	210	333	. 2	. 3	. 3	. 3	. 3	. 3	. 3	. 5
85 and over	788	1, 202	187	378	601	824	375	533	226	291	. 2	. 3	. 2	. 3	. 2	. 3	. 3	. 4
Unknown	190	160	90	86	100	74	50	43	50	31	. 1	. 1	------	------	------	------	. 1	------

TABLE 19.—NEGRO POPULATION FOR THE URBAN, RURAL-FARM, AND RURAL-NONFARM AREAS, BY 5-YEAR AGE PERIODS, SEX, AND STATES: 1930—Continued

[See note at head of this table]

STATE AND AGE	TOTAL		URBAN		RURAL						PERCENT DISTRIBUTION									
					Total		Rural-farm		Rural-nonfarm		Urban		Rural							
													Total		Rural-farm		Rural-nonfarm			
	Male	Female	Male	Female	Male	Female	Male	Female	Male	Female	Male	Female	Male	Female	Male	Female	Male	Female		
OKLAHOMA																				
All ages	**86,818**	**85,380**	**32,470**	**35,331**	**54,348**	**50,039**	**41,429**	**38,085**	**12,919**	**11,964**	**100.0**	**100.0**	**100.0**	**100.0**	**100.0**	**100.0**	**100.0**	**100.0**		
Under 5 years	8,595	8,742	2,575	2,560	6,020	6,182	4,842	5,003	1,178	1,179	7.9	7.2	11.1	12.4	11.7	13.1	9.1	9.9		
5 to 9 years	9,908	9,884	2,947	3,087	6,961	6,797	5,629	5,393	1,332	1,404	9.1	8.7	12.8	13.6	13.6	14.2	10.3	11.7		
10 to 14 years	9,122	9,174	2,527	2,803	6,595	6,371	5,375	5,137	1,220	1,234	7.8	7.9	12.1	12.7	13.0	13.5	9.4	10.3		
15 to 19 years	9,099	9,712	2,717	3,549	6,382	6,164	5,146	4,853	1,236	1,311	8.4	10.0	11.7	12.3	12.4	12.7	9.6	11.0		
20 to 24 years	8,321	9,572	3,413	4,776	4,908	4,796	3,563	3,543	1,345	1,253	10.5	13.5	9.0	9.6	8.6	9.3	10.4	10.5		
25 to 29 years	7,421	8,174	3,660	4,501	3,761	3,673	2,614	2,621	1,147	1,052	11.3	12.7	6.9	7.3	6.3	6.9	8.9	8.8		
30 to 34 years	6,083	6,386	3,057	3,469	3,026	2,917	2,097	2,137	929	780	9.4	9.8	5.6	5.8	5.1	5.6	7.2	6.5		
35 to 39 years	6,064	6,171	3,021	3,122	3,043	3,049	2,092	2,185	951	864	9.3	8.8	5.6	6.1	5.0	5.7	7.4	7.2		
40 to 44 years	4,887	4,852	2,303	2,229	2,584	2,623	1,862	1,956	722	667	7.1	6.3	4.8	5.2	4.5	5.1	5.6	5.6		
45 to 49 years	4,579	4,206	2,056	1,846	2,523	2,360	1,824	1,711	699	649	6.3	5.2	4.6	4.7	4.4	4.5	5.4	5.4		
50 to 54 years	4,594	2,952	1,627	1,194	2,967	1,758	2,281	1,275	686	483	5.0	3.4	5.5	3.5	5.5	3.3	5.3	4.0		
55 to 59 years	3,095	1,848	971	739	2,124	1,109	1,627	779	497	330	3.0	2.1	3.9	2.2	3.9	2.0	3.8	2.8		
60 to 64 years	1,973	1,291	640	524	1,333	767	979	523	354	244	2.0	1.5	2.5	1.5	2.4	1.4	2.7	2.0		
65 to 69 years	1,281	926	412	375	869	551	644	372	225	179	1.3	1.1	1.6	1.1	1.6	1.0	1.7	1.5		
70 to 74 years	755	542	228	187	527	355	373	224	154	131	.7	.5	1.0	.7	.9	.6	1.2	1.1		
75 to 79 years	478	368	140	154	338	214	222	138	116	76	.4	.4	.6	.4	.5	.4	.9	.6		
80 to 84 years	259	253	89	106	170	147	109	96	61	51	.3	.3	.3	.3	.3	.3	.5	.4		
85 and over	227	250	45	73	182	177	130	116	52	61	.1	.2	.3	.4	.3	.3	.4	.5		
Unknown	77	77	42	38	35	39	20	23	15	16	.1	.1	.1	.1	------	.1	.1	.1		
TEXAS																				
All ages	**422,608**	**432,356**	**155,296**	**174,533**	**267,312**	**257,823**	**209,468**	**200,454**	**57,844**	**57,369**	**100.0**	**100.0**	**100.0**	**100.0**	**100.0**	**100.0**	**100.0**	**100.0**		
Under 5 years	42,831	43,289	12,178	12,166	30,653	31,123	25,314	25,593	5,339	5,530	7.8	7.0	11.5	12.1	12.1	12.8	9.2	9.6		
5 to 9 years	48,613	48,896	14,105	14,662	34,508	34,234	28,437	28,129	6,071	6,105	9.1	8.4	12.9	13.3	13.6	14.0	10.5	10.6		
10 to 14 years	44,569	44,501	12,517	13,396	32,052	31,105	26,790	25,772	5,262	5,333	8.1	7.7	12.0	12.1	12.8	12.9	9.1	9.3		
15 to 19 years	43,586	49,110	13,181	17,809	30,405	31,301	25,294	25,283	5,111	6,018	8.5	10.2	11.4	12.1	12.1	12.6	8.8	10.5		
20 to 24 years	42,526	49,043	16,222	22,270	26,304	26,773	19,990	20,184	6,314	6,589	10.4	12.8	9.8	10.4	9.5	10.1	10.9	11.5		
25 to 29 years	37,385	42,807	17,393	22,347	19,992	20,460	14,270	14,723	5,722	5,737	11.2	12.8	7.5	7.9	6.8	7.3	9.9	10.0		
30 to 34 years	31,076	32,974	15,279	17,099	15,797	15,875	11,233	11,496	4,564	4,379	9.8	9.8	5.9	6.2	5.4	5.7	7.9	7.6		
35 to 39 years	31,159	32,777	14,923	16,440	16,236	16,337	11,717	11,902	4,519	4,435	9.6	9.4	6.1	6.3	5.6	5.9	7.8	7.7		
40 to 44 years	24,215	24,209	11,480	11,625	12,735	12,584	9,260	9,338	3,475	3,246	7.4	6.7	4.8	4.9	4.4	4.7	6.0	5.7		
45 to 49 years	24,027	20,582	10,085	9,308	13,942	11,274	10,365	8,405	3,577	2,869	6.5	5.3	5.2	4.4	4.9	4.2	6.2	5.0		
50 to 54 years	17,398	14,233	6,637	5,939	10,761	8,294	8,270	6,255	2,491	2,039	4.3	3.4	4.0	3.2	3.9	3.1	4.3	3.6		
55 to 59 years	10,814	8,716	3,793	3,420	7,021	5,296	5,478	4,003	1,543	1,293	2.4	2.0	2.6	2.1	2.6	2.0	2.7	2.3		
60 to 64 years	10,222	8,262	3,116	3,052	7,106	5,210	5,634	3,860	1,472	1,350	2.0	1.7	2.7	2.0	2.7	1.9	2.5	2.4		
65 to 69 years	6,051	4,919	1,816	1,914	4,235	3,005	3,308	2,125	927	880	1.2	1.1	1.6	1.2	1.6	1.1	1.6	1.5		
70 to 74 years	3,446	3,123	991	1,153	2,455	1,970	1,890	1,400	565	570	.6	.7	.9	.8	.9	.7	1.0	1.0		
75 to 79 years	2,176	1,966	643	725	1,533	1,241	1,157	845	376	396	.4	.4	.6	.5	.6	.4	.7	.7		
80 to 84 years	1,094	1,263	349	453	745	810	548	555	197	255	.2	.3	.3	.3	.3	.3	.3	.4		
85 and over	893	1,193	269	401	624	792	420	524	204	268	.2	.2	.2	.3	.2	.3	.4	.5		
Unknown	527	493	319	354	208	139	93	62	115	77	.2	.2	.1	.1	------	------	.2	.1		
MONTANA																				
All ages	**710**	**546**	**556**	**471**	**154**	**75**	**46**	**23**	**108**	**52**	**100.0**	**100.0**	**100.0**	------	------	------	**100.0**	------		
Under 5 years	38	28	35	24	3	4	2	2	1	2	6.3	5.1	1.9	------	------	------	.9	------		
5 to 9 years	28	34	24	30	4	4	2	1	2	3	4.3	6.4	2.6	------	------	------	1.9	------		
10 to 14 years	43	47	40	41	3	6	2	1	1	5	7.2	8.7	1.9	------	------	------	.9	------		
15 to 19 years	32	26	27	23	5	3	------	1	5	2	4.9	4.9	3.2	------	------	------	4.6	------		
20 to 24 years	42	36	34	29	8	7	2	2	6	5	6.1	6.2	5.2	------	------	------	5.6	------		
25 to 29 years	51	49	42	48	9	1	2	------	7	1	7.6	10.2	5.8	------	------	------	6.5	------		
30 to 34 years	48	49	38	42	10	7	4	2	6	5	6.8	8.9	6.5	------	------	------	5.6	------		
35 to 39 years	62	61	46	54	16	7	4	1	12	6	8.3	11.5	10.4	------	------	------	11.1	------		
40 to 44 years	75	40	59	29	16	11	2	5	14	6	10.6	6.2	10.4	------	------	------	13.0	------		
45 to 49 years	65	50	46	45	19	5	6	1	13	4	8.3	9.6	12.3	------	------	------	12.0	------		
50 to 54 years	69	50	57	45	12	5	6	1	6	4	10.3	9.6	7.8	------	------	------	5.6	------		
55 to 59 years	53	29	37	25	16	4	5	3	11	1	6.7	5.3	10.4	------	------	------	10.2	------		
60 to 64 years	43	19	35	16	8	3	1	2	7	1	6.3	3.4	5.2	------	------	------	6.5	------		
65 to 69 years	26	8	17	7	9	1	3	------	6	1	3.1	1.5	5.8	------	------	------	5.6	------		
70 to 74 years	20	9	11	6	9	3	3	------	6	3	2.0	1.3	5.8	------	------	------	5.6	------		
75 to 79 years	6	5	5	3	1	2	1	------	------	2	.9	.6	.6	------	------	------	------	------		
80 to 84 years	5	3	1	2	4	1	------	1	4	------	.2	.4	2.6	------	------	------	3.7	------		
85 and over	3	2	2	2	1	------	1	------	------	------	.4	.4	.6	------	------	------	------	------		
Unknown	1	1	------	------	1	1	------	------	1	1	------	------	.6	------	------	------	.9	------		
IDAHO																				
All ages	**395**	**273**	**276**	**226**	**119**	**47**	**46**	**24**	**73**	**23**	**100.0**	**100.0**	**100.0**	------	------	------	------	------		
Under 5 years	15	15	11	11	4	4	------	3	4	1	4.0	4.9	3.4	------	------	------	------	------		
5 to 9 years	25	14	17	12	8	2	3	------	5	2	6.2	5.3	6.7	------	------	------	------	------		
10 to 14 years	17	18	10	15	7	3	3	2	4	1	3.6	6.6	5.9	------	------	------	------	------		
15 to 19 years	24	16	16	12	8	4	6	1	2	3	5.8	5.3	6.7	------	------	------	------	------		
20 to 24 years	23	17	14	14	9	3	5	1	4	2	5.1	6.2	7.6	------	------	------	------	------		
25 to 29 years	22	23	11	23	11	------	3	------	8	------	4.0	10.2	9.2	------	------	------	------	------		
30 to 34 years	28	40	23	35	5	5	2	4	3	1	8.3	15.5	4.2	------	------	------	------	------		
35 to 39 years	53	31	35	26	18	5	4	3	14	2	12.7	11.5	15.1	------	------	------	------	------		
40 to 44 years	53	30	42	27	11	3	2	1	9	2	15.2	11.9	9.2	------	------	------	------	------		
45 to 49 years	38	18	27	12	11	6	5	2	6	4	9.8	5.3	9.2	------	------	------	------	------		
50 to 54 years	29	20	22	18	7	2	5	1	2	1	8.0	8.0	5.9	------	------	------	------	------		
55 to 59 years	18	13	15	9	3	4	1	4	2	------	5.4	4.0	2.5	------	------	------	------	------		
60 to 64 years	20	7	13	5	7	2	4	1	3	1	4.7	2.2	5.9	------	------	------	------	------		
65 to 69 years	13	3	10	3	3	------	1	------	2	------	3.6	1.3	2.5	------	------	------	------	------		
70 to 74 years	4	2	3	2	1	------	1	------	------	------	1.1	.9	.8	------	------	------	------	------		
75 to 79 years	9	4	6	2	3	2	1	------	2	2	2.2	.9	2.5	------	------	------	------	------		
80 to 84 years	3	------	------	------	3	------	------	------	3	------	------	------	2.5	------	------	------	------	------		
85 and over	1	2	1	------	------	2	------	1	------	1	.4	------	------	------	------	------	------	------		
Unknown	------	------	------	------	------	------	------	------	------	------	------	------	------	------	------	------	------	------		

TABLE 19.—NEGRO POPULATION FOR THE URBAN, RURAL-FARM, AND RURAL-NONFARM AREAS, BY 5-YEAR AGE PERIODS, SEX, AND STATES: 1930—Continued

[See note at head of this table]

STATE AND AGE	TOTAL		URBAN		RURAL						PERCENT DISTRIBUTION							
					Total		Rural-farm		Rural-nonfarm		Urban		Rural					
													Total		Rural-farm		Rural-nonfarm	
	Male	Female	Male	Female	Male	Female	Male	Female	Male	Female	Male	Female	Male	Female	Male	Female	Male	Female
WYOMING																		
All ages	699	551	453	406	246	145	42	22	204	123	100.0	100.0	100.0	100.0	------	------	100.0	100.0
Under 5 years	34	29	22	19	12	10	3	2	9	8	4.9	4.7	4.9	6.9	------	------	4.4	6.5
5 to 9 years	29	40	22	30	7	10	3	2	4	8	4.9	7.4	2.8	6.9	------	------	2.0	6.5
10 to 14 years	34	36	24	25	10	11	4	------	6	11	5.3	6.2	4.1	7.6	------	------	2.9	8.9
15 to 19 years	33	35	21	27	12	8	2	1	10	7	4.6	6.7	4.9	5.5	------	------	4.9	5.7
20 to 24 years	50	45	34	33	16	12	1	3	15	9	7.5	8.1	6.5	8.3	------	------	7.4	7.3
25 to 29 years	48	35	30	25	18	10	3	1	15	9	6.6	6.2	7.3	6.9	------	------	7.4	7.3
30 to 34 years	73	62	40	46	33	16	1	4	32	12	8.8	11.3	13.4	11.0	------	------	15.7	9.8
35 to 39 years	89	49	54	31	35	18	3	3	32	15	11.9	7.6	14.2	12.4	------	------	15.7	12.2
40 to 44 years	68	71	42	54	26	17	2	1	24	16	9.3	13.3	10.6	11.7	------	------	11.8	13.0
45 to 49 years	68	58	48	44	20	14	3	------	17	14	10.6	10.8	8.1	9.7	------	------	8.3	11.4
50 to 54 years	71	28	53	24	18	4	6	2	12	2	11.7	5.9	7.3	2.8	------	------	5.9	1.6
55 to 59 years	31	26	17	22	14	4	3	1	11	3	3.8	5.4	5.7	2.8	------	------	5.4	2.4
60 to 64 years	34	16	23	11	11	5	3	------	8	5	5.1	2.7	4.5	3.4	------	------	3.9	4.1
65 to 69 years	14	8	10	5	4	3	1	1	3	2	2.2	1.2	1.6	2.1	------	------	1.5	1.6
70 to 74 years	9	5	6	2	3	3	1	1	2	2	1.3	.5	1.2	2.1	------	------	1.0	1.6
75 to 79 years	7	4	2	4	5	------	2	------	3	------	.4	1.0	2.0	------	------	------	1.5	------
80 to 84 years	2	1	1	1	1	------	1	------	------	------	.2	.2	.4	------	------	------	------	------
85 and over	1	2	1	2	------	------	------	------	------	------	.2	.5	------	------	------	------	------	------
Unknown	4	1	3	1	1	------	------	------	1	------	.7	.2	.4	------	------	------	.5	------
COLORADO																		
All ages	5,739	6,089	4,965	5,506	774	583	186	174	588	409	100.0	100.0	100.0	100.0	100.0	100.0	100.0	100.0
Under 5 years	389	384	340	337	49	47	16	18	33	29	6.8	6.1	6.3	8.1	8.6	10.3	5.6	7.1
5 to 9 years	369	406	327	357	42	49	13	21	29	28	6.6	6.5	5.4	8.4	7.0	12.1	4.9	6.8
10 to 14 years	360	397	308	354	52	43	13	12	39	31	6.2	6.4	6.7	7.4	7.0	6.9	6.6	7.6
15 to 19 years	353	430	295	369	58	61	14	18	44	43	5.9	6.7	7.5	10.5	7.5	10.3	7.5	10.5
20 to 24 years	384	508	350	466	34	42	7	14	27	28	7.0	8.5	4.4	7.2	3.8	8.0	4.6	6.8
25 to 29 years	444	551	391	511	53	40	14	5	39	35	7.9	9.3	6.8	6.9	7.5	2.9	6.6	8.6
30 to 34 years	482	567	439	521	43	46	3	10	40	36	8.8	9.5	5.6	7.9	1.6	5.7	6.8	8.8
35 to 39 years	598	626	514	576	84	50	13	12	71	38	10.4	10.5	10.9	8.6	7.0	6.9	12.1	9.3
40 to 44 years	511	514	444	461	67	53	11	17	56	36	8.9	8.4	8.7	9.1	5.9	9.8	9.5	8.8
45 to 49 years	547	530	466	482	81	48	22	17	59	31	9.4	8.8	10.5	8.2	11.8	9.8	10.0	7.6
50 to 54 years	438	413	366	376	72	37	22	10	50	27	7.4	6.8	9.3	6.3	11.8	5.7	8.5	6.6
55 to 59 years	289	278	254	254	35	24	10	8	25	16	5.1	4.6	4.5	4.1	5.4	4.6	4.3	3.9
60 to 64 years	231	152	191	145	40	7	9	3	31	4	3.8	2.6	5.2	1.2	4.8	1.7	5.3	1.0
65 to 69 years	148	144	126	130	22	14	4	5	18	9	2.5	2.4	2.8	2.4	2.2	2.9	3.1	2.2
70 to 74 years	95	91	77	86	18	5	8	3	10	2	1.6	1.6	2.3	.9	4.3	1.7	1.7	.5
75 to 79 years	54	42	41	35	13	7	4	1	9	6	.8	.6	1.7	1.2	2.2	.6	1.5	1.5
80 to 84 years	19	27	16	24	3	3	------	------	3	3	.3	.4	.4	.5	------	------	.5	.7
85 and over	18	19	12	14	6	5	2	------	4	5	.2	.3	.8	.9	1.1	------	.7	1.2
Unknown	10	10	8	8	2	2	1	------	1	2	.2	.1	.3	.3	.5	------	.2	.6
NEW MEXICO																		
All ages	1,531	1,319	872	846	659	473	279	225	380	248	100.0	100.0	100.0	100.0	100.0	100.0	100.0	100.0
Under 5 years	140	109	77	60	63	49	35	27	28	22	8.8	7.1	9.6	10.4	12.5	12.0	7.4	8.9
5 to 9 years	131	142	62	76	69	66	38	34	31	32	7.1	9.0	10.5	14.0	13.6	15.1	8.2	12.9
10 to 14 years	119	130	58	72	61	58	33	40	28	18	6.7	8.5	9.3	12.3	11.8	17.8	7.4	7.3
15 to 19 years	132	127	66	85	66	42	39	22	27	20	7.6	10.0	10.0	8.9	14.0	9.8	7.1	8.1
20 to 24 years	116	120	65	81	51	39	17	16	34	23	7.5	9.6	7.7	8.2	6.1	7.1	8.9	9.3
25 to 29 years	121	124	78	87	43	37	12	11	31	26	8.9	10.3	6.5	7.8	4.3	4.9	8.2	10.5
30 to 34 years	114	109	78	70	36	39	11	17	25	22	8.9	8.3	5.5	8.2	3.9	7.6	6.6	8.9
35 to 39 years	144	151	83	96	61	55	16	24	45	31	9.5	11.3	9.3	11.6	5.7	10.7	11.8	12.5
40 to 44 years	121	100	74	75	47	25	20	9	27	16	8.5	8.9	7.1	5.3	7.2	4.0	7.1	6.5
45 to 49 years	110	73	57	48	53	25	18	13	35	12	6.5	5.7	8.0	5.3	6.5	5.8	9.2	4.8
50 to 54 years	122	59	77	43	45	16	19	6	26	10	8.8	5.1	6.8	3.4	6.8	2.7	6.8	4.0
55 to 59 years	53	30	35	21	18	9	9	3	9	6	4.0	2.5	2.7	1.9	3.2	1.3	2.4	2.4
60 to 64 years	54	20	33	15	21	5	3	2	18	3	3.8	1.8	3.2	1.1	1.1	.9	4.7	1.2
65 to 69 years	18	12	7	8	11	4	3	1	8	3	.8	.9	1.7	.8	1.1	.4	2.1	1.2
70 to 74 years	16	4	11	3	5	1	------	------	5	1	1.3	.4	.8	.2	------	------	1.3	.4
75 to 79 years	6	3	3	3	3	------	2	------	1	------	.3	.4	.5	------	.7	------	.3	------
80 to 84 years	4	1	3	1	1	------	1	------	------	------	.3	.1	.2	------	.4	------	------	------
85 and over	9	------	4	------	5	------	3	------	2	------	.5	------	.8	------	1.1	------	.5	------
Unknown	1	5	1	2	------	3	------	------	------	3	.1	.2	------	.6	------	------	------	1.2
ARIZONA																		
All ages	6,352	4,397	2,783	2,364	3,569	2,033	700	549	2,869	1,484	100.0	100.0	100.0	100.0	100.0	100.0	100.0	100.0
Under 5 years	396	397	168	181	228	216	78	75	150	141	6.0	7.7	6.4	10.6	11.1	13.7	5.2	9.5
5 to 9 years	407	424	189	187	218	237	82	72	136	165	6.8	7.9	6.1	11.7	11.7	13.1	4.7	11.1
10 to 14 years	368	359	153	158	215	201	72	52	143	149	5.5	6.7	6.0	9.9	10.3	9.5	5.0	10.0
15 to 19 years	460	328	185	157	275	171	68	47	207	124	6.6	6.6	7.7	8.4	9.7	8.6	7.2	8.4
20 to 24 years	743	385	257	229	486	156	50	36	436	120	9.2	9.7	13.6	7.7	7.1	6.6	15.2	8.1
25 to 29 years	664	499	283	288	381	211	44	63	337	148	10.2	12.2	10.7	10.4	6.3	11.5	11.7	10.0
30 to 34 years	711	467	327	265	384	202	35	49	349	153	11.7	11.2	10.8	9.9	5.0	8.9	12.2	10.3
35 to 39 years	786	509	345	291	441	218	59	52	382	166	12.4	12.3	12.4	10.7	8.4	9.5	13.3	11.2
40 to 44 years	571	330	272	203	299	127	48	31	251	96	9.8	8.6	8.4	6.2	6.9	5.6	8.7	6.5
45 to 49 years	479	268	230	148	249	120	55	37	194	83	8.3	6.3	7.0	5.9	7.9	6.7	6.8	5.6
50 to 54 years	302	187	143	106	159	81	44	15	115	66	5.1	4.5	4.5	4.0	6.3	2.7	4.0	4.4
55 to 59 years	190	77	93	44	97	33	27	3	70	30	3.3	1.9	2.7	1.6	3.9	.5	2.4	2.0
60 to 64 years	125	68	68	41	57	27	15	8	42	19	2.4	1.7	1.6	1.3	2.1	1.5	1.5	1.3
65 to 69 years	59	46	26	30	33	16	10	3	23	13	.9	1.3	.9	.8	1.4	.5	.8	.9
70 to 74 years	41	17	18	9	23	8	10	3	13	5	.6	.4	.6	.4	1.4	.5	.5	.3
75 to 79 years	23	10	9	8	14	2	2	2	12	------	.3	.3	.4	.1	.3	.4	.4	------
80 to 84 years	6	9	4	7	2	2	1	------	1	2	.1	.3	.1	.1	.1	------	------	.1
85 and over	7	5	3	3	4	2	------	------	4	2	.1	.1	.1	.1	------	------	.1	.1
Unknown	14	12	10	9	4	3	------	1	4	2	.4	.4	.1	.1	------	.2	.1	.1

TABLE 19.—NEGRO POPULATION FOR THE URBAN, RURAL-FARM, AND RURAL-NONFARM AREAS, BY 5-YEAR AGE PERIODS, SEX, AND STATES: 1930—Continued

[See note at head of this table]

STATE AND AGE	TOTAL Male	TOTAL Female	URBAN Male	URBAN Female	RURAL Total Male	RURAL Total Female	RURAL Rural-farm Male	RURAL Rural-farm Female	RURAL Rural-nonfarm Male	RURAL Rural-nonfarm Female	PERCENT DISTRIBUTION Urban Male	PERCENT DISTRIBUTION Urban Female	PERCENT DISTRIBUTION Rural Total Male	PERCENT DISTRIBUTION Rural Total Female	PERCENT DISTRIBUTION Rural-farm Male	PERCENT DISTRIBUTION Rural-farm Female	PERCENT DISTRIBUTION Rural-nonfarm Male	PERCENT DISTRIBUTION Rural-nonfarm Female
UTAH																		
All ages	**609**	**499**	**520**	**424**	**89**	**75**	**18**	**12**	**71**	**63**	**100.0**	**100.0**	-	-	-	-	-	-
Under 5 years	49	40	38	33	11	7	3	-	8	7	7.3	7.8	-	-	-	-	-	-
5 to 9 years	38	39	33	34	5	5	-	1	5	4	6.3	8.0	-	-	-	-	-	-
10 to 14 years	40	46	33	40	7	6	2	1	5	5	6.3	9.4	-	-	-	-	-	-
15 to 19 years	25	19	19	14	6	5	3	1	3	4	3.7	3.3	-	-	-	-	-	-
20 to 24 years	36	33	35	27	1	6	-	2	1	4	6.7	6.4	-	-	-	-	-	-
25 to 29 years	46	42	40	37	6	5	2	-	4	5	7.7	8.7	-	-	-	-	-	-
30 to 34 years	51	50	43	39	8	11	-	-	8	11	8.3	9.2	-	-	-	-	-	-
35 to 39 years	66	53	57	48	9	5	-	1	9	4	11.0	11.3	-	-	-	-	-	-
40 to 44 years	53	56	45	49	8	7	-	1	8	6	8.7	11.6	-	-	-	-	-	-
45 to 49 years	67	42	56	34	11	8	-	3	11	5	10.8	8.0	-	-	-	-	-	-
50 to 54 years	61	25	52	22	9	3	5	1	4	2	10.0	5.2	-	-	-	-	-	-
55 to 59 years	29	20	26	17	3	3	1	-	2	3	5.0	4.0	-	-	-	-	-	-
60 to 64 years	20	12	17	11	3	1	2	1	1	-	3.3	2.6	-	-	-	-	-	-
65 to 69 years	14	10	12	7	2	3	-	-	2	3	2.3	1.7	-	-	-	-	-	-
70 to 74 years	4	5	4	5	-	-	-	-	-	-	.8	1.2	-	-	-	-	-	-
75 to 79 years	5	2	5	2	-	-	-	-	-	-	1.0	.5	-	-	-	-	-	-
80 to 84 years	4	3	4	3	-	-	-	-	-	-	.8	.7	-	-	-	-	-	-
85 and over	-	2	-	2	-	-	-	-	-	-	-	.5	-	-	-	-	-	-
Unknown	1	-	1	-	-	-	-	-	-	-	.2	-	-	-	-	-	-	-
NEVADA																		
All ages	**277**	**239**	**188**	**176**	**89**	**63**	**11**	**6**	**78**	**57**	**100.0**	**100.0**	-	-	-	-	-	-
Under 5 years	10	11	9	9	1	2	-	-	1	2	4.8	5.1	-	-	-	-	-	-
5 to 9 years	11	12	7	7	4	5	-	-	4	5	3.7	4.0	-	-	-	-	-	-
10 to 14 years	5	8	3	4	2	4	-	1	2	3	1.6	2.3	-	-	-	-	-	-
15 to 19 years	6	9	3	6	3	3	-	-	3	3	1.6	3.4	-	-	-	-	-	-
20 to 24 years	15	14	5	11	10	3	2	-	8	3	2.7	6.3	-	-	-	-	-	-
25 to 29 years	19	25	14	17	5	8	-	-	5	8	7.4	9.7	-	-	-	-	-	-
30 to 34 years	30	20	24	17	6	3	-	-	6	3	12.8	9.7	-	-	-	-	-	-
35 to 39 years	31	31	22	21	9	10	-	2	9	8	11.7	11.9	-	-	-	-	-	-
40 to 44 years	37	34	30	28	7	6	-	1	7	5	16.0	15.9	-	-	-	-	-	-
45 to 49 years	37	20	25	18	12	2	3	-	9	2	13.3	10.2	-	-	-	-	-	-
50 to 54 years	26	19	17	12	9	7	2	1	7	6	9.0	6.8	-	-	-	-	-	-
55 to 59 years	19	15	11	12	8	3	2	-	6	3	5.9	6.8	-	-	-	-	-	-
60 to 64 years	14	7	7	4	7	3	1	1	6	2	3.7	2.3	-	-	-	-	-	-
65 to 69 years	7	6	4	4	3	2	-	-	3	2	2.1	2.3	-	-	-	-	-	-
70 to 74 years	4	4	4	3	-	1	-	-	-	1	2.1	1.7	-	-	-	-	-	-
75 to 79 years	4	-	2	-	2	-	-	-	2	-	1.1	-	-	-	-	-	-	-
80 to 84 years	-	-	-	-	-	-	-	-	-	-	-	-	-	-	-	-	-	-
85 and over	2	2	1	1	1	1	1	-	-	1	.5	.6	-	-	-	-	-	-
Unknown	-	-	-	-	-	-	-	-	-	-	-	-	-	-	-	-	-	-
WASHINGTON																		
All ages	**3,797**	**3,043**	**3,167**	**2,651**	**630**	**392**	**155**	**113**	**475**	**279**	**100.0**	**100.0**	**100.0**	**100.0**	**100.0**	**100.0**	**100.0**	**100.0**
Under 5 years	195	205	159	166	36	39	15	6	21	33	5.0	6.3	5.7	9.9	9.7	5.3	4.4	11.8
5 to 9 years	215	233	185	201	30	32	11	14	19	18	5.8	7.6	4.8	8.2	7.1	12.4	4.0	6.5
10 to 14 years	235	186	186	154	49	32	11	10	38	22	5.9	5.8	7.8	8.2	7.1	8.8	8.0	7.9
15 to 19 years	205	211	163	182	42	29	13	10	29	19	5.1	6.9	6.7	7.4	8.4	8.8	6.1	6.8
20 to 24 years	229	230	178	204	51	26	3	4	48	22	5.6	7.7	8.1	6.6	1.9	3.5	10.1	7.9
25 to 29 years	258	208	220	193	38	15	4	6	34	9	6.9	7.3	6.0	3.8	2.6	5.3	7.2	3.2
30 to 34 years	294	248	252	229	42	19	8	6	34	13	8.0	8.6	6.7	4.8	5.2	5.3	7.2	4.7
35 to 39 years	346	300	294	270	52	30	7	10	45	20	9.3	10.2	8.3	7.7	4.5	8.8	9.5	7.2
40 to 44 years	379	276	330	236	49	40	9	7	40	33	10.4	8.9	7.8	10.2	5.8	6.2	8.4	11.8
45 to 49 years	391	278	330	252	61	26	13	10	48	16	10.4	9.5	9.7	6.6	8.4	8.8	10.1	5.7
50 to 54 years	372	247	322	211	50	36	12	10	38	26	10.2	8.0	7.9	9.2	7.7	8.8	8.0	9.3
55 to 59 years	274	158	241	135	33	23	12	7	21	16	7.6	5.1	5.2	5.9	7.7	6.2	4.4	5.7
60 to 64 years	151	113	122	97	29	16	15	3	14	13	3.9	3.7	4.6	4.1	9.7	2.7	2.9	4.7
65 to 69 years	117	60	86	46	31	14	11	6	20	8	2.7	1.7	4.9	3.6	7.1	5.3	4.2	2.9
70 to 74 years	63	38	47	29	16	9	5	2	11	7	1.5	1.1	2.5	2.3	3.2	1.8	2.3	2.5
75 to 79 years	30	13	20	10	10	3	4	-	6	3	.6	.4	1.6	.8	3.6	-	1.3	1.1
80 to 84 years	14	18	8	17	6	1	2	-	4	1	.3	.6	1.0	.3	1.3	-	.8	.4
85 and over	10	17	7	15	3	2	-	2	3	-	.2	.6	.5	.5	-	1.8	.6	-
Unknown	19	4	17	4	2	-	-	-	2	-	.5	.2	.3	-	-	-	.4	-
OREGON																		
All ages	**1,210**	**1,024**	**993**	**897**	**217**	**127**	**27**	**17**	**190**	**110**	**100.0**	**100.0**	**100.0**	**100.0**	-	-	**100.0**	**100.0**
Under 5 years	44	63	36	49	8	14	-	-	8	14	3.6	5.5	3.7	11.0	-	-	4.2	12.7
5 to 9 years	54	73	41	63	13	10	1	-	12	10	4.1	7.0	6.0	7.9	-	-	6.3	9.1
10 to 14 years	61	61	47	51	14	10	1	1	13	9	4.7	5.7	6.5	7.9	-	-	6.8	8.2
15 to 19 years	60	68	55	60	5	8	-	-	5	8	5.5	6.7	2.3	6.3	-	-	2.6	7.3
20 to 24 years	75	86	58	73	17	13	2	1	15	12	5.8	8.1	7.8	10.2	-	-	7.9	10.9
25 to 29 years	95	80	66	69	29	11	1	2	28	9	6.6	7.7	13.4	8.7	-	-	14.7	8.2
30 to 34 years	109	89	94	75	15	14	-	-	15	14	9.5	8.4	6.9	11.0	-	-	7.9	12.7
35 to 39 years	148	119	115	103	33	16	5	1	28	15	11.6	11.5	15.2	12.6	-	-	14.7	13.6
40 to 44 years	147	108	129	100	18	8	2	2	16	6	13.0	11.1	8.3	6.3	-	-	8.4	5.5
45 to 49 years	130	94	110	88	20	6	2	3	18	3	11.1	9.8	9.2	4.7	-	-	9.5	2.7
50 to 54 years	105	63	90	54	15	9	4	4	11	5	9.1	6.0	6.9	7.1	-	-	5.8	4.5
55 to 59 years	84	45	74	41	10	4	4	1	6	3	7.5	4.6	4.6	3.1	-	-	3.2	2.7
60 to 64 years	35	30	25	29	10	1	2	1	8	-	2.5	3.2	4.6	.8	-	-	4.2	-
65 to 69 years	30	25	25	25	5	-	1	-	4	-	2.5	2.8	2.3	-	-	-	2.1	-
70 to 74 years	10	10	9	8	1	2	-	1	1	1	.9	.9	.5	1.6	-	-	.5	.9
75 to 79 years	10	5	8	4	2	1	1	-	1	1	.8	.4	.9	.8	-	-	.5	.9
80 to 84 years	7	3	6	3	1	-	1	-	-	-	.6	.3	.5	-	-	-	-	-
85 and over	2	-	1	-	1	-	-	-	1	-	.1	-	.5	-	-	-	.5	-
Unknown	4	2	4	2	-	-	-	-	-	-	.4	.2	-	-	-	-	-	-

TABLE 19.—NEGRO POPULATION FOR THE URBAN, RURAL-FARM, AND RURAL-NONFARM AREAS, BY 5-YEAR AGE PERIODS, SEX, AND STATES: 1930—Continued

[See note at head of this table]

STATE AND AGE	TOTAL		URBAN		RURAL						PERCENT DISTRIBUTION							
					Total		Rural-farm		Rural-nonfarm		Urban		Rural					
													Total		Rural-farm		Rural-nonfarm	
	Male	Female	Male	Female	Male	Female	Male	Female	Male	Female	Male	Female	Male	Female	Male	Female	Male	Female
CALIFORNIA																		
All ages	**40,052**	**40,996**	**34,048**	**36,471**	**6,004**	**4,525**	**1,932**	**1,529**	**4,072**	**2,996**	**100.0**	**100.0**	**100.0**	**100.0**	**100.0**	**100.0**	**100.0**	**100.0**
Under 5 years	2,635	2,648	2,216	2,190	419	458	186	205	233	253	6.5	6.0	7.0	10.1	9.6	13.4	5.7	8.4
5 to 9 years	3,030	2,998	2,531	2,522	499	476	237	201	262	275	7.4	6.9	8.3	10.5	12.3	13.1	6.4	9.2
10 to 14 years	2,638	2,784	2,204	2,337	434	447	203	202	231	245	6.5	6.4	7.2	9.9	10.5	13.2	5.7	8.2
15 to 19 years	2,615	2,950	2,195	2,570	420	380	166	149	254	231	6.4	7.0	7.0	8.4	8.6	9.7	6.2	7.7
20 to 24 years	3,033	3,678	2,604	3,343	429	335	138	132	291	203	7.6	9.2	7.1	7.4	7.1	8.6	7.1	6.8
25 to 29 years	3,730	4,438	3,251	4,030	479	408	118	105	361	303	9.5	11.0	8.0	9.0	6.1	6.9	8.9	10.1
30 to 34 years	4,101	4,211	3,521	3,812	580	399	129	101	451	298	10.3	10.5	9.7	8.8	6.7	6.6	11.1	9.9
35 to 39 years	4,379	4,673	3,800	4,251	579	422	126	105	453	317	11.2	11.7	9.6	9.3	6.5	6.9	11.1	10.6
40 to 44 years	3,866	3,443	3,312	3,092	554	351	145	101	409	250	9.7	8.5	9.2	7.8	7.5	6.6	10.0	8.3
45 to 49 years	3,364	3,017	2,873	2,775	491	242	144	72	347	170	8.4	7.6	8.2	5.3	7.5	4.7	8.5	5.7
50 to 54 years	2,516	2,217	2,136	1,981	380	236	119	62	261	174	6.3	5.4	6.3	5.2	6.2	4.1	6.4	5.8
55 to 59 years	1,589	1,337	1,321	1,207	268	130	86	37	182	93	3.9	3.3	4.5	2.9	4.5	2.4	4.5	3.1
60 to 64 years	977	958	799	878	178	80	63	23	115	57	2.3	2.4	3.0	1.8	3.3	1.5	2.8	1.9
65 to 69 years	602	668	485	607	117	61	40	17	77	44	1.4	1.7	1.9	1.3	2.1	1.1	1.9	1.5
70 to 74 years	399	412	325	379	74	33	19	7	55	26	1.0	1.0	1.2	.7	1.0	.5	1.4	.9
75 to 79 years	216	237	167	209	49	28	6	1	43	27	.5	.6	.8	.6	.3	.1	1.1	.9
80 to 84 years	98	129	74	115	24	14	5	5	19	9	.2	.3	.4	.3	.3	.3	.5	.3
85 and over	78	105	59	93	19	12	2	2	17	10	.2	.3	.3	.3	.1	.1	.4	.3
Unknown	186	93	175	80	11	13	-------	2	11	11	.5	.2	.2	.3	-------	.1	.3	.4

TABLE 20.—AGE DISTRIBUTION BY 5-YEAR AGE PERIODS WITH SINGLE YEARS UNDER 5, BY COLOR, AND SEX, FOR THE 80 CITIES HAVING 10,000 OR MORE NEGRO INHABITANTS: 1930

CITY AND AGE	ALL CLASSES			NEGRO			WHITE			OTHER RACES		
	Total	Male	Female	Total	Male	Female	Total	Male	Female	Total	Male	Female
ALABAMA												
Bessemer	**20,271**	**10,045**	**10,676**	**11,691**	**5,593**	**6,098**	**9,028**	**4,450**	**4,578**	**2**	**2**	-------
Under 5 years	1,956	1,009	947	1,096	566	530	860	443	417	-------	-------	-------
Under 1 year	377	182	195	204	95	109	173	87	86	-------	-------	-------
1 year 2 years 3 years 4 years	1,579	827	752	892	471	421	687	356	331	-------	-------	-------
5 to 9 years	2,076	971	1,105	1,136	516	620	940	455	485	-------	-------	-------
10 to 14 years	1,828	877	951	937	450	487	891	427	464	-------	-------	-------
15 to 19 years	1,960	913	1,047	1,049	473	576	910	439	471	1	1	-------
20 to 24 years	2,257	1,017	1,240	1,297	569	728	960	448	512	-------	-------	-------
25 to 29 years	2,329	1,092	1,237	1,485	675	810	844	417	427	-------	-------	-------
30 to 34 years	1,718	842	876	1,004	494	510	714	348	366	-------	-------	-------
35 to 39 years 40 to 44 years	3,156	1,542	1,614	1,927	926	1,001	1,229	616	613	-------	-------	-------
45 to 49 years 50 to 54 years	2,048	1,102	946	1,117	616	501	930	485	445	1	1	-------
55 to 59 years 60 to 64 years	831	415	416	392	188	204	439	227	212	-------	-------	-------
65 to 69 years 70 to 74 years	417	200	217	187	88	99	230	112	118	-------	-------	-------
75 years and over	132	59	73	55	28	27	77	31	46	-------	-------	-------
Unknown	13	6	7	9	4	5	4	2	2	-------	-------	-------
Birmingham	**259,678**	**125,855**	**133,823**	**99,077**	**46,582**	**52,495**	**160,551**	**79,240**	**81,311**	**50**	**33**	**17**
Under 5 years	22,746	11,587	11,159	8,717	4,369	4,348	14,026	7,218	6,808	3	-------	3
Under 1 year	4,389	2,263	2,126	1,657	817	840	2,732	1,446	1,286	-------	-------	-------
1 year	4,267	2,165	2,102	1,617	799	818	2,649	1,366	1,283	1	-------	1
2 years	4,605	2,329	2,276	1,730	840	890	2,873	1,489	1,384	2	-------	2
3 years	4,841	2,482	2,359	1,932	984	948	2,909	1,498	1,411	-------	-------	-------
4 years	4,644	2,348	2,296	1,781	929	852	2,863	1,419	1,444	-------	-------	-------
5 to 9 years	24,962	12,475	12,487	9,363	4,531	4,832	15,594	7,941	7,653	5	3	2
10 to 14 years	22,013	10,904	11,109	8,276	4,031	4,245	13,734	6,872	6,862	3	1	2
15 to 19 years	23,891	10,713	13,178	9,446	3,990	5,456	14,441	6,721	7,720	4	2	2
20 to 24 years	28,665	12,580	16,085	11,773	4,875	6,898	16,890	7,703	9,187	2	2	-------
25 to 29 years	29,264	13,489	15,775	12,479	5,455	7,024	16,778	8,029	8,749	7	5	2
30 to 34 years	23,626	11,362	12,264	9,223	4,282	4,941	14,399	7,077	7,322	4	3	1
35 to 39 years	22,776	11,261	11,515	9,351	4,466	4,885	13,420	6,793	6,627	5	2	3
40 to 44 years	17,001	8,775	8,226	6,319	3,240	3,079	10,676	5,529	5,147	6	6	-------
45 to 49 years	14,564	7,634	6,930	5,483	2,895	2,588	9,076	4,735	4,341	5	4	1
50 to 54 years	10,838	5,666	5,172	3,619	1,925	1,694	7,215	3,738	3,477	4	3	1
55 to 59 years	6,906	3,558	3,348	1,839	1,025	814	5,065	2,531	2,534	2	2	-------
60 to 64 years	4,923	2,484	2,439	1,312	661	651	3,611	1,823	1,788	-------	-------	-------
65 to 69 years	3,214	1,495	1,719	778	359	419	2,436	1,136	1,300	-------	-------	-------
70 to 74 years	2,099	965	1,134	457	211	246	1,642	754	888	-------	-------	-------
75 years and over	2,036	840	1,196	565	234	331	1,471	606	865	-------	-------	-------
Unknown	154	67	87	77	33	44	77	34	43	-------	-------	-------

TABLE 20.—AGE DISTRIBUTION BY 5-YEAR AGE PERIODS WITH SINGLE YEARS UNDER 5, BY COLOR, AND SEX, FOR THE 80 CITIES HAVING 10,000 OR MORE NEGRO INHABITANTS: 1930—Continued

CITY AND AGE	ALL CLASSES			NEGRO			WHITE			OTHER RACES		
	Total	Male	Female	Total	Male	Female	Total	Male	Female	Total	Male	Female
ALABAMA—continued												
Mobile	**68,202**	**32,666**	**35,536**	**24,514**	**11,051**	**13,463**	**43,606**	**21,557**	**22,049**	**82**	**58**	**24**
Under 5 years	5,595	2,795	2,800	2,016	978	1,038	3,573	1,816	1,757	6	1	5
Under 1 year	1,027	491	536	355	160	195	670	331	339	2	-	2
1 year	1,098	518	580	358	164	194	739	354	385	1	-	1
2 years	1,168	611	557	441	224	217	726	387	339	1	-	1
3 years	1,168	593	575	434	214	220	733	379	354	1	-	1
4 years	1,134	582	552	428	216	212	705	365	340	1	1	-
5 to 9 years	6,011	3,010	3,001	2,184	1,072	1,112	3,824	1,935	1,889	3	3	-
10 to 14 years	5,447	2,690	2,757	1,876	891	985	3,567	1,797	1,770	4	2	2
15 to 19 years	6,363	2,874	3,489	2,295	949	1,346	4,058	1,917	2,141	10	8	2
20 to 24 years	7,463	3,381	4,082	2,827	1,095	1,732	4,620	2,274	2,346	16	12	4
25 to 29 years	6,843	3,197	3,646	2,652	1,113	1,539	4,177	2,073	2,104	14	11	3
30 to 34 years	5,777	2,781	2,996	2,088	896	1,192	3,681	1,878	1,803	8	7	1
35 to 39 years	5,575	2,723	2,852	2,192	986	1,206	3,378	1,733	1,645	5	4	1
40 to 44 years	4,367	2,120	2,247	1,614	715	899	2,746	1,401	1,345	7	4	3
45 to 49 years	4,197	2,107	2,090	1,666	848	818	2,529	1,257	1,272	2	2	-
50 to 54 years	3,303	1,600	1,703	1,055	501	554	2,244	1,097	1,147	4	2	2
55 to 59 years	2,180	1,075	1,105	593	309	284	1,587	766	821	-	-	-
60 to 64 years	1,978	1,006	972	643	355	288	1,332	649	683	3	2	1
65 to 69 years	1,300	619	681	358	189	169	942	430	512	-	-	-
70 to 74 years	836	340	496	175	57	118	661	283	378	-	-	-
75 years and over	842	298	544	209	65	144	633	233	400	-	-	-
Unknown	125	50	75	71	32	39	54	18	36	-	-	-
Montgomery	**66,079**	**30,635**	**35,444**	**29,970**	**13,054**	**16,916**	**36,105**	**17,577**	**18,528**	**4**	**4**	-
Under 5 years	5,624	2,847	2,777	2,384	1,152	1,232	3,240	1,695	1,545	-	-	-
Under 1 year	1,069	566	503	455	243	212	614	323	291	-	-	-
1 year	1,002	494	508	419	195	224	583	299	284	-	-	-
2 years	1,223	612	611	507	239	268	716	373	343	-	-	-
3 years	1,194	587	607	524	243	281	670	344	326	-	-	-
4 years	1,136	588	548	479	232	247	657	356	301	-	-	-
5 to 9 years	6,310	3,135	3,175	2,859	1,370	1,489	3,451	1,765	1,686	-	-	-
10 to 14 years	5,669	2,837	2,832	2,600	1,243	1,357	3,069	1,594	1,475	-	-	-
15 to 19 years	6,468	2,870	3,598	3,301	1,388	1,913	3,167	1,482	1,685	-	-	-
20 to 24 years	7,395	3,040	4,355	3,628	1,438	2,190	3,767	1,602	2,165	-	-	-
25 to 29 years	6,713	2,907	3,806	3,105	1,219	1,886	3,606	1,686	1,920	2	2	-
30 to 34 years	5,481	2,424	3,057	2,289	902	1,387	3,192	1,522	1,670	-	-	-
35 to 39 years	5,401	2,510	2,891	2,468	1,011	1,457	2,932	1,498	1,434	1	1	-
40 to 44 years	4,356	2,045	2,311	2,010	880	1,130	2,346	1,165	1,181	-	-	-
45 to 49 years	3,981	1,946	2,035	1,911	908	1,003	2,069	1,037	1,032	1	1	-
50 to 54 years	2,983	1,497	1,486	1,306	651	655	1,677	846	831	-	-	-
55 to 59 years	1,854	910	944	607	279	328	1,247	631	616	-	-	-
60 to 64 years	1,464	718	746	551	257	294	913	461	452	-	-	-
65 to 69 years	997	417	580	359	133	226	638	284	354	-	-	-
70 to 74 years	665	254	411	253	97	156	412	157	255	-	-	-
75 years and over	671	268	403	308	122	186	363	146	217	-	-	-
Unknown	47	10	37	31	4	27	16	6	10	-	-	-
ARKANSAS												
Little Rock	**81,679**	**38,609**	**43,070**	**19,698**	**8,889**	**10,809**	**61,954**	**29,703**	**32,251**	**27**	**17**	**10**
Under 5 years	5,720	2,925	2,795	1,323	651	672	4,396	2,274	2,122	1	-	1
Under 1 year	1,045	531	514	261	123	138	784	408	376	-	-	-
1 year	1,040	527	513	236	117	119	804	410	394	-	-	-
2 years	1,180	601	579	283	126	157	897	475	422	-	-	-
3 years	1,214	643	571	261	142	119	952	501	451	1	-	1
4 years	1,241	623	618	282	143	139	959	480	479	-	-	-
5 to 9 years	6,643	3,354	3,289	1,528	760	768	5,109	2,592	2,517	6	2	4
10 to 14 years	6,333	3,172	3,161	1,459	712	747	4,873	2,459	2,414	1	1	-
15 to 19 years	7,171	3,214	3,957	1,723	711	1,012	5,447	2,503	2,944	1	-	1
20 to 24 years	8,937	3,775	5,162	2,219	909	1,310	6,715	2,863	3,852	3	3	-
25 to 29 years	8,337	3,666	4,671	2,142	824	1,318	6,189	2,837	3,352	6	5	1
30 to 34 years	7,242	3,215	4,027	1,849	766	1,083	5,392	2,448	2,944	1	1	-
35 to 39 years	7,216	3,436	3,780	1,919	863	1,056	5,292	2,570	2,722	5	3	2
40 to 44 years	5,893	2,881	3,012	1,529	700	829	4,362	2,180	2,182	2	1	1
45 to 49 years	5,214	2,649	2,565	1,338	667	671	3,876	1,982	1,894	-	-	-
50 to 54 years	4,178	2,064	2,114	1,008	502	506	3,170	1,562	1,608	-	-	-
55 to 59 years	2,893	1,430	1,463	537	277	260	2,355	1,152	1,203	1	1	-
60 to 64 years	2,291	1,126	1,165	442	216	226	1,849	910	939	-	-	-
65 to 69 years	1,478	735	743	280	143	137	1,198	592	606	-	-	-
70 to 74 years	1,006	474	532	161	71	90	845	403	442	-	-	-
75 years and over	1,077	456	621	234	114	120	843	342	501	-	-	-
Unknown	50	37	13	7	3	4	43	34	9	-	-	-
CALIFORNIA												
Los Angeles	**1,238,048**	**610,678**	**627,370**	**38,894**	**18,349**	**20,545**	**1,073,584**	**524,493**	**549,091**	**125,570**	**67,836**	**57,734**
Under 5 years	78,799	40,206	38,593	2,435	1,220	1,215	59,046	30,185	28,861	17,318	8,801	8,517
Under 1 year	15,103	7,718	7,385	461	225	236	11,169	5,733	5,436	3,473	1,760	1,713
1 year	14,863	7,648	7,215	456	224	232	11,128	5,729	5,399	3,279	1,695	1,584
2 years	15,751	7,987	7,764	480	256	224	11,877	6,026	5,851	3,394	1,705	1,689
3 years	16,382	8,415	7,967	512	248	264	12,168	6,283	5,885	3,702	1,884	1,818
4 years	16,700	8,438	8,262	526	267	259	12,704	6,414	6,290	3,470	1,757	1,713
5 to 9 years	86,569	43,375	43,194	2,808	1,420	1,388	67,033	33,621	33,412	16,728	8,334	8,394
10 to 14 years	77,634	38,819	38,815	2,505	1,208	1,297	63,663	31,922	31,741	11,466	5,689	5,777
15 to 19 years	84,516	40,698	43,818	2,643	1,211	1,432	71,743	34,414	37,329	10,130	5,073	5,057
20 to 24 years	109,221	53,055	56,166	3,455	1,488	1,967	93,165	44,499	48,666	12,601	7,068	5,533
25 to 29 years	122,836	61,529	61,307	4,326	1,926	2,400	104,630	51,599	53,031	13,880	8,004	5,876
30 to 34 years	116,783	58,782	58,001	4,145	1,966	2,179	101,765	50,688	51,077	10,873	6,128	4,745
35 to 39 years	114,695	57,399	57,296	4,563	2,083	2,480	100,889	50,168	50,721	9,243	5,148	4,095
40 to 44 years	101,434	51,952	49,482	3,455	1,739	1,716	90,690	45,774	44,916	7,289	4,439	2,850
45 to 49 years	89,528	45,328	44,200	2,995	1,445	1,550	80,492	40,180	40,312	6,041	3,703	2,338
50 to 54 years	75,022	36,845	38,177	2,107	1,060	1,047	69,010	33,447	35,563	3,905	2,338	1,567
55 to 59 years	57,188	27,051	30,137	1,257	635	622	53,426	25,039	28,387	2,505	1,377	1,128
60 to 64 years	45,603	20,786	24,817	833	394	489	43,130	19,604	23,526	1,590	788	802
65 to 69 years	33,493	15,013	18,480	564	218	346	31,944	14,333	17,611	985	462	523
70 to 74 years	22,724	10,339	12,385	336	160	176	21,890	9,933	11,957	498	246	252
75 years and over	21,306	9,145	12,161	381	155	226	20,450	8,784	11,666	475	206	269
Unknown	697	356	341	36	21	15	618	303	315	43	32	11

TABLE 20.—AGE DISTRIBUTION BY 5-YEAR AGE PERIODS WITH SINGLE YEARS UNDER 5, BY COLOR, AND SEX, FOR THE 80 CITIES HAVING 10,000 OR MORE NEGRO INHABITANTS: 1930—Continued

CITY AND AGE	ALL CLASSES			NEGRO			WHITE			OTHER RACES		
	Total	Male	Female	Total	Male	Female	Total	Male	Female	Total	Male	Female
DELAWARE												
Wilmington	**106,597**	**53,297**	**53,300**	**12,080**	**6,056**	**6,024**	**94,459**	**47,189**	**47,270**	**58**	**52**	**6**
Under 5 years	7,941	3,953	3,988	833	419	414	7,104	3,531	3,573	4	3	1
Under 1 year	1,470	710	760	147	69	78	1,322	640	682	1	1	-
1 year	1,502	755	747	146	77	69	1,356	678	678	-	-	-
2 years	1,602	795	807	174	83	91	1,427	712	715	1	-	1
3 years	1,659	843	816	176	86	90	1,483	757	726	-	-	-
4 years	1,708	850	858	190	104	86	1,516	744	772	2	2	-
5 to 9 years	9,458	4,748	4,710	957	480	477	8,498	4,267	4,231	3	1	2
10 to 14 years	9,818	4,835	4,983	826	380	446	8,992	4,455	4,537	-	-	-
15 to 19 years	9,239	4,496	4,743	886	381	505	8,350	4,112	4,238	3	3	-
20 to 24 years	9,805	4,896	4,909	1,141	544	597	8,658	4,346	4,312	6	6	-
25 to 29 years	9,062	4,619	4,443	1,369	686	683	7,680	3,921	3,759	13	12	1
30 to 34 years	8,759	4,425	4,334	1,134	583	551	7,620	3,837	3,783	5	5	-
35 to 39 years	9,074	4,696	4,378	1,312	684	628	7,755	4,005	3,750	7	7	-
40 to 44 years	7,688	3,963	3,725	948	508	440	6,731	3,448	3,283	9	7	2
45 to 49 years	6,468	3,369	3,099	802	435	367	5,663	2,931	2,732	3	3	-
50 to 54 years	5,590	2,802	2,788	694	356	338	4,896	2,446	2,450	-	-	-
55 to 59 years	4,058	1,975	2,083	404	206	198	3,652	1,767	1,885	2	2	-
60 to 64 years	3,606	1,746	1,860	316	169	147	3,289	1,576	1,713	1	1	-
65 to 69 years	2,522	1,237	1,285	197	105	92	2,324	1,131	1,193	1	1	-
70 to 74 years	1,762	790	972	117	60	57	1,645	730	915	-	-	-
75 years and over	1,677	692	985	138	56	82	1,538	635	903	1	1	-
Unknown	70	55	15	6	4	2	64	51	13	-	-	-
DISTRICT OF COLUMBIA												
Washington	**486,869**	**231,883**	**254,986**	**132,068**	**62,225**	**69,843**	**353,914**	**168,982**	**184,932**	**887**	**676**	**211**
Under 5 years	32,304	16,398	15,906	10,006	5,036	4,970	22,240	11,337	10,903	58	25	33
Under 1 year	6,136	3,136	3,000	1,847	921	926	4,275	2,207	2,068	14	8	6
1 year	6,185	3,087	3,098	1,870	926	944	4,305	2,158	2,147	10	3	7
2 years	6,509	3,330	3,179	2,003	1,044	959	4,494	2,278	2,216	12	8	4
3 years	6,788	3,478	3,310	2,173	1,124	1,049	4,606	2,351	2,255	9	3	6
4 years	6,686	3,367	3,319	2,113	1,021	1,092	4,560	2,343	2,217	13	3	10
5 to 9 years	35,624	17,797	17,827	10,838	5,314	5,524	24,721	12,449	12,272	65	34	31
10 to 14 years	32,712	16,015	16,697	9,484	4,432	5,052	23,181	11,559	11,622	47	24	23
15 to 19 years	35,806	16,899	18,907	10,675	4,757	5,918	25,080	12,105	12,975	51	37	14
20 to 24 years	48,387	22,909	25,478	14,406	6,472	7,934	33,865	16,344	17,521	116	93	23
25 to 29 years	48,120	23,401	24,719	14,989	6,994	7,995	32,991	16,290	16,701	140	117	23
30 to 34 years	45,095	21,411	23,684	12,360	5,889	6,471	32,612	15,421	17,191	123	101	22
35 to 39 years	43,587	20,724	22,863	12,154	5,797	6,357	31,328	14,842	16,486	105	85	20
40 to 44 years	36,326	17,314	19,012	9,563	4,493	5,070	26,708	12,776	13,932	55	45	10
45 to 49 years	32,574	15,277	17,297	8,920	4,247	4,673	23,615	10,996	12,619	39	34	5
50 to 54 years	28,732	13,653	15,079	6,944	3,433	3,511	21,766	10,199	11,567	22	21	1
55 to 59 years	21,609	10,038	11,571	4,001	1,966	2,035	17,578	8,045	9,533	30	27	3
60 to 64 years	16,958	7,761	9,197	2,785	1,274	1,511	14,161	6,476	7,685	12	11	1
65 to 69 years	11,712	5,194	6,518	1,942	849	1,093	9,756	4,332	5,424	14	13	1
70 to 74 years	7,694	3,297	4,397	1,123	508	615	6,566	2,784	3,782	5	5	-
75 years and over	7,847	2,980	4,867	1,226	444	782	6,618	2,534	4,084	3	2	1
Unknown	1,782	815	967	652	320	332	1,128	493	635	2	2	-
FLORIDA												
Jacksonville	**129,549**	**62,018**	**67,531**	**48,196**	**22,225**	**25,971**	**81,320**	**39,767**	**41,553**	**33**	**26**	**7**
Under 5 years	10,614	5,370	5,244	3,543	1,739	1,804	7,069	3,630	3,439	2	1	1
Under 1 year	1,910	989	921	618	310	308	1,291	679	612	1	-	1
1 year	1,964	980	984	622	291	331	1,342	689	653	-	-	-
2 years	2,149	1,087	1,062	713	357	356	1,436	730	706	-	-	-
3 years	2,376	1,169	1,207	842	404	438	1,533	764	769	1	1	-
4 years	2,215	1,145	1,070	748	377	371	1,467	768	699	-	-	-
5 to 9 years	11,478	5,636	5,842	4,231	2,066	2,165	7,245	3,569	3,676	2	1	1
10 to 14 years	10,768	5,304	5,464	3,973	1,883	2,090	6,793	3,420	3,373	2	1	1
15 to 19 years	11,211	4,927	6,284	4,360	1,813	2,547	6,849	3,113	3,736	2	1	1
20 to 24 years	13,708	5,758	7,950	5,705	2,236	3,469	8,002	3,521	4,481	1	1	-
25 to 29 years	14,282	6,497	7,785	6,194	2,666	3,528	8,086	3,829	4,257	2	2	-
30 to 34 years	11,977	5,728	6,249	4,631	2,133	2,498	7,345	3,594	3,751	1	1	-
35 to 39 years	12,014	5,878	6,136	4,802	2,238	2,564	7,209	3,638	3,571	3	2	1
40 to 44 years	9,143	4,661	4,482	3,506	1,718	1,788	5,632	2,940	2,692	5	3	2
45 to 49 years	7,633	3,901	3,732	2,850	1,485	1,365	4,781	2,414	2,367	2	2	-
50 to 54 years	5,815	3,076	2,739	1,834	983	851	3,975	2,087	1,888	6	6	-
55 to 59 years	3,753	1,942	1,811	912	486	426	2,839	1,454	1,385	2	2	-
60 to 64 years	2,805	1,355	1,450	687	342	345	2,116	1,011	1,105	2	2	-
65 to 69 years	1,770	825	945	442	215	227	1,327	609	718	1	1	-
70 to 74 years	1,211	544	667	230	102	128	981	442	539	-	-	-
75 years and over	1,267	567	700	260	105	155	1,007	462	545	-	-	-
Unknown	100	49	51	36	15	21	64	34	30	-	-	-
Miami	**110,637**	**54,629**	**56,008**	**25,116**	**11,902**	**13,214**	**85,461**	**42,675**	**42,786**	**60**	**52**	**8**
Under 5 years	9,323	4,793	4,530	2,639	1,339	1,300	6,681	3,454	3,227	3	-	3
Under 1 year	1,716	900	816	467	260	207	1,248	640	608	1	-	1
1 year	1,763	940	823	471	247	224	1,292	693	599	-	-	-
2 years	1,971	964	1,007	523	247	276	1,447	717	730	1	-	1
3 years	2,079	1,065	1,014	603	296	307	1,475	769	706	1	-	1
4 years	1,794	924	870	575	289	286	1,219	635	584	-	-	-
5 to 9 years	9,636	4,837	4,799	2,746	1,331	1,415	6,888	3,504	3,384	2	2	-
10 to 14 years	8,491	4,130	4,361	2,025	929	1,096	6,466	3,201	3,265	-	-	-
15 to 19 years	8,300	3,834	4,466	1,970	803	1,167	6,330	3,031	3,299	-	-	-
20 to 24 years	10,195	4,608	5,587	2,867	1,171	1,696	7,322	3,433	3,889	6	4	2
25 to 29 years	11,684	5,624	6,060	3,735	1,742	1,993	7,942	3,875	4,067	7	7	-
30 to 34 years	10,583	5,163	5,420	2,804	1,352	1,452	7,770	3,805	3,965	9	6	3
35 to 39 years	9,854	4,849	5,005	2,271	1,104	1,167	7,573	3,735	3,838	10	10	-
40 to 44 years	8,074	4,204	3,870	1,544	824	720	6,522	3,372	3,150	8	8	-
45 to 49 years	6,821	3,487	3,334	1,113	588	525	5,701	2,892	2,809	7	7	-
50 to 54 years	5,345	2,781	2,564	647	342	305	4,694	2,435	2,259	4	4	-
55 to 59 years	4,068	2,090	1,978	315	174	141	3,753	1,916	1,837	-	-	-
60 to 64 years	3,222	1,647	1,575	190	91	99	3,030	1,554	1,476	2	2	-
65 to 69 years	2,205	1,172	1,033	118	64	54	2,086	1,107	979	1	1	-
70 to 74 years	1,440	745	695	54	20	34	1,386	725	661	-	-	-
75 years and over	1,284	621	663	59	24	35	1,224	596	628	1	1	-
Unknown	112	44	68	19	4	15	93	40	53	-	-	-

TABLE 20.—AGE DISTRIBUTION BY 5-YEAR AGE PERIODS WITH SINGLE YEARS UNDER 5, BY COLOR, AND SEX, FOR THE 80 CITIES HAVING 10,000 OR MORE NEGRO INHABITANTS: 1930—Continued

CITY AND AGE	ALL CLASSES			NEGRO			WHITE			OTHER RACES		
	Total	Male	Female	Total	Male	Female	Total	Male	Female	Total	Male	Female
FLORIDA—continued												
Tampa	**101,161**	**49,747**	**51,414**	**21,172**	**10,072**	**11,100**	**79,822**	**39,574**	**40,248**	**167**	**101**	**66**
Under 5 years	8,403	4,281	4,122	1,636	831	805	6,756	3,443	3,313	11	7	4
Under 1 year	1,414	720	694	274	142	132	1,137	575	562	3	3	----
1 year	1,634	830	804	309	143	166	1,323	686	637	2	1	1
2 years	1,724	880	854	337	185	152	1,395	694	701	2	1	1
3 years	1,828	939	889	368	195	173	1,457	743	714	3	1	2
4 years	1,793	912	881	348	166	182	1,444	745	699	1	1	----
5 to 9 years	9,208	4,665	4,543	1,817	909	908	7,377	3,750	3,627	14	6	8
10 to 14 years	9,387	4,687	4,700	1,663	833	830	7,699	3,842	3,857	25	12	13
15 to 19 years	9,941	4,671	5,270	1,828	792	1,036	8,098	3,871	4,227	15	8	7
20 to 24 years	10,212	4,442	5,770	2,447	981	1,466	7,757	3,457	4,300	8	4	4
25 to 29 years	9,830	4,589	5,241	2,728	1,186	1,542	7,087	3,393	3,694	15	10	5
30 to 34 years	8,548	4,176	4,372	2,221	1,034	1,187	6,311	3,132	3,179	16	10	6
35 to 39 years	8,487	4,201	4,286	2,078	1,039	1,039	6,397	3,153	3,244	12	9	3
40 to 44 years	7,084	3,629	3,455	1,543	794	749	5,516	2,817	2,699	25	18	7
45 to 49 years	5,841	3,004	2,837	1,312	674	638	4,521	2,325	2,196	8	5	3
50 to 54 years	4,607	2,443	2,164	835	457	378	3,763	1,979	1,784	9	7	2
55 to 59 years	3,224	1,697	1,527	431	244	187	2,790	1,451	1,339	3	2	1
60 to 64 years	2,468	1,261	1,207	278	151	127	2,190	1,110	1,080	----	----	----
65 to 69 years	1,722	902	820	162	75	87	1,556	825	731	4	2	2
70 to 74 years	1,091	557	534	94	31	63	997	526	471	----	----	----
75 years and over	1,050	514	536	81	31	50	967	482	485	2	1	1
Unknown	58	28	30	18	10	8	40	18	22	----	----	----
GEORGIA												
Atlanta	**270,366**	**126,493**	**143,873**	**90,075**	**39,923**	**50,152**	**180,247**	**86,535**	**93,712**	**44**	**35**	**9**
Under 5 years	20,928	10,533	10,395	7,090	3,501	3,589	13,835	7,031	6,804	3	1	2
Under 1 year	4,031	2,012	1,989	1,318	651	667	2,712	1,391	1,321	1	----	1
1 year	3,818	1,914	1,904	1,173	562	611	2,644	1,351	1,293	1	1	----
2 years	4,275	2,114	2,161	1,551	759	792	2,724	1,355	1,369	----	----	----
3 years	4,501	2,254	2,247	1,515	758	757	2,985	1,496	1,489	1	----	1
4 years	4,303	2,209	2,094	1,533	771	762	2,770	1,438	1,332	----	----	----
5 to 9 years	24,270	12,084	12,186	8,314	4,120	4,194	15,952	7,961	7,991	4	3	1
10 to 14 years	23,189	11,269	11,920	8,499	4,017	4,482	14,688	7,250	7,438	2	2	----
15 to 19 years	25,495	11,544	13,951	9,578	3,993	5,585	15,912	7,547	8,365	5	4	1
20 to 24 years	30,980	13,437	17,543	10,857	4,280	6,577	20,123	9,157	10,966	----	----	----
25 to 29 years	29,185	13,058	16,127	10,336	4,235	6,101	18,847	8,822	10,025	2	1	1
30 to 34 years	24,277	11,268	13,009	7,843	3,330	4,513	16,433	7,938	8,495	1	----	1
35 to 39 years	23,265	11,043	12,222	7,982	3,501	4,481	15,273	7,535	7,738	10	7	3
40 to 44 years	17,653	8,312	9,341	5,741	2,555	3,186	11,907	5,752	6,155	5	5	----
45 to 49 years	15,053	7,168	7,885	4,753	2,109	2,644	10,297	5,056	5,241	3	3	----
50 to 54 years	12,431	6,089	6,342	3,636	1,829	1,807	8,792	4,257	4,535	3	3	----
55 to 59 years	8,137	3,908	4,229	1,826	909	917	6,309	2,997	3,312	2	2	----
60 to 64 years	5,997	2,853	3,144	1,446	671	775	4,548	2,179	2,369	3	3	----
65 to 69 years	3,903	1,680	2,223	912	396	516	2,991	1,284	1,707	----	----	----
70 to 74 years	2,647	1,086	1,561	553	223	330	2,093	862	1,231	1	1	----
75 years and over	2,665	1,012	1,653	635	227	408	2,030	785	1,245	----	----	----
Unknown	291	149	142	74	27	47	217	122	95	----	----	----
Macon	**53,829**	**24,767**	**29,062**	**23,158**	**10,274**	**12,884**	**30,664**	**14,489**	**16,175**	**7**	**4**	**3**
Under 5 years	4,330	2,180	2,150	1,896	945	951	2,433	1,234	1,199	1	1	----
Under 1 year	765	380	385	351	166	185	414	214	200	----	----	----
1 year	786	407	379	339	172	167	447	235	212	----	----	----
2 years	909	467	442	398	213	185	511	254	257	----	----	----
3 years	937	454	483	410	191	219	526	262	264	1	1	----
4 years	933	472	461	398	203	195	535	269	266	----	----	----
5 to 9 years	5,129	2,519	2,610	2,228	1,086	1,142	2,901	1,433	1,468	----	----	----
10 to 14 years	4,872	2,365	2,507	2,119	1,011	1,108	2,753	1,354	1,399	----	----	----
15 to 19 years	5,538	2,419	3,119	2,487	1,037	1,450	3,050	1,382	1,668	1	----	1
20 to 24 years	6,094	2,521	3,573	2,788	1,095	1,693	3,304	1,426	1,878	2	----	2
25 to 29 years	5,132	2,284	2,848	2,293	959	1,334	2,838	1,324	1,514	1	1	----
30 to 34 years	4,298	1,941	2,357	1,868	814	1,054	2,429	1,126	1,303	1	1	----
35 to 39 years	4,430	2,044	2,386	1,963	818	1,145	2,467	1,226	1,241	----	----	----
40 to 44 years	3,676	1,773	1,903	1,686	802	884	1,990	971	1,019	----	----	----
45 to 49 years	3,054	1,456	1,598	1,248	567	681	1,805	888	917	1	1	----
50 to 54 years	2,569	1,242	1,327	1,050	530	520	1,519	712	807	----	----	----
55 to 59 years	1,491	696	795	451	193	258	1,040	503	537	----	----	----
60 to 64 years	1,198	564	634	421	182	239	777	382	395	----	----	----
65 to 69 years	793	324	469	255	96	159	538	228	310	----	----	----
70 to 74 years	593	216	377	178	47	131	415	169	246	----	----	----
75 years and over	514	167	347	161	63	98	353	104	249	----	----	----
Unknown	118	56	62	66	29	37	52	27	25	----	----	----
Savannah	**85,024**	**39,540**	**45,484**	**38,896**	**17,315**	**21,581**	**46,069**	**22,180**	**23,889**	**59**	**45**	**14**
Under 5 years	6,327	3,133	3,194	2,660	1,295	1,365	3,663	1,835	1,828	4	3	1
Upder 1 year	1,211	569	642	516	230	286	694	338	356	1	1	----
1 year	1,168	595	573	483	234	249	685	361	324	----	----	----
2 years	1,264	591	673	516	238	278	747	352	395	1	1	----
3 years	1,300	650	650	553	278	275	746	371	375	1	1	----
4 years	1,384	728	656	592	315	277	791	413	378	1	----	1
5 to 9 years	7,468	3,618	3,850	3,246	1,522	1,724	4,220	2,095	2,125	2	1	1
10 to 14 years	6,995	3,239	3,756	2,964	1,301	1,663	4,028	1,937	2,091	3	1	2
15 to 19 years	7,781	3,396	4,385	3,528	1,366	2,162	4,243	2,024	2,219	10	6	4
20 to 24 years	9,681	4,101	5,580	4,982	1,903	3,079	4,693	2,192	2,501	6	6	----
25 to 29 years	9,120	3,962	5,158	4,933	2,003	2,930	4,183	1,955	2,228	4	4	----
30 to 34 years	7,459	3,493	3,966	3,605	1,656	1,949	3,848	1,832	2,016	6	5	1
35 to 39 years	7,876	3,727	4,149	4,113	1,888	2,225	3,759	1,836	1,923	4	3	1
40 to 44 years	5,735	2,811	2,924	2,672	1,298	1,374	3,061	1,511	1,550	2	2	----
45 to 49 years	5,087	2,559	2,528	2,335	1,200	1,135	2,749	1,357	1,392	3	2	1
50 to 54 years	3,775	1,958	1,817	1,499	779	720	2,276	1,179	1,097	----	----	----
55 to 59 years	2,581	1,274	1,307	843	441	402	1,732	829	903	6	4	2
60 to 64 years	2,041	944	1,097	620	282	338	1,416	658	758	5	4	1
65 to 69 years	1,343	601	742	392	171	221	949	428	521	2	2	----
70 to 74 years	850	379	471	215	94	121	634	284	350	1	1	----
75 years and over	826	304	522	236	86	150	589	217	372	1	1	----
Unknown	79	41	38	53	30	23	26	11	15	----	----	----

TABLE 20.—AGE DISTRIBUTION BY 5-YEAR AGE PERIODS WITH SINGLE YEARS UNDER 5, BY COLOR, AND SEX, FOR THE 80 CITIES HAVING 10,000 OR MORE NEGRO INHABITANTS: 1930—Continued

CITY AND AGE	ALL CLASSES			NEGRO			WHITE			OTHER RACES		
	Total	Male	Female	Total	Male	Female	Total	Male	Female	Total	Male	Female
GEORGIA—continued												
Augusta	**60, 342**	**28, 329**	**32, 013**	**24, 190**	**10, 698**	**13, 492**	**35, 997**	**17, 525**	**18, 472**	**155**	**106**	**49**
Under 5 years	4, 938	2, 448	2, 490	1, 775	869	906	3, 144	1, 572	1, 572	19	7	12
Under 1 year	907	443	464	316	157	159	588	284	304	3	2	1
1 year	916	466	450	325	153	172	587	313	274	4	-	4
2 years	1, 009	501	508	363	190	173	641	309	332	5	2	3
3 years	1, 065	539	626	374	184	190	686	353	333	5	2	3
4 years	1, 041	499	542	397	185	212	642	313	329	2	1	1
5 to 9 years	5, 824	2, 972	2, 852	2, 285	1, 123	1, 162	3, 522	1, 839	1, 683	17	10	7
10 to 14 years	5, 207	2, 502	2, 705	2, 149	979	1, 170	3, 043	1, 516	1, 527	15	7	8
15 to 19 years	5, 637	2, 481	3, 156	2, 458	1, 013	1, 445	3, 166	1, 457	1, 709	13	11	2
20 to 24 years	6, 577	2, 766	3, 811	2, 972	1, 201	1, 771	3, 591	1, 555	2, 036	14	10	4
25 to 29 years	6, 015	2, 654	3, 361	2, 662	1, 081	1, 581	3, 334	1, 561	1, 773	19	12	7
30 to 34 years	4, 953	2, 401	2, 552	1, 944	842	1, 102	2, 996	1, 550	1, 446	13	9	4
35 to 39 years	5, 214	2, 546	2, 668	2, 096	898	1, 198	3, 107	1, 640	1, 467	11	8	3
40 to 44 years	3, 993	1, 936	2, 057	1, 641	760	881	2, 345	1, 169	1, 176	7	7	-
45 to 49 years	3, 478	1, 708	1, 770	1, 473	701	772	1, 996	1, 000	996	9	7	2
50 to 54 years	2, 883	1, 450	1, 433	1, 023	506	517	1, 858	942	916	2	2	-
55 to 59 years	1, 841	880	961	547	242	305	1, 290	634	656	4	4	-
60 to 64 years	1, 485	660	825	494	212	282	984	441	543	7	7	-
65 to 69 years	1, 023	438	585	314	135	179	707	301	406	2	2	-
70 to 74 years	600	241	359	144	54	90	454	185	269	2	2	-
75 years and over	597	209	388	178	68	110	418	140	278	1	1	-
Unknown	77	37	40	35	14	21	42	23	19	-	-	-
Columbus	**43, 131**	**19, 717**	**23, 414**	**14, 157**	**6, 079**	**8, 078**	**28, 972**	**13, 637**	**15, 335**	**2**	**1**	**1**
Under 5 years	3, 863	1, 959	1, 904	1, 216	626	590	2, 647	1, 333	1, 314	-	-	-
Under 1 year	711	366	345	221	111	110	490	255	235	-	-	-
1 year	694	324	370	204	109	95	490	215	275	-	-	-
2 years	835	426	409	274	144	130	561	282	279	-	-	-
3 years	830	437	393	259	139	120	571	298	273	-	-	-
4 years	793	406	387	258	123	135	535	283	252	-	-	-
5 to 9 years	4, 456	2, 195	2, 261	1, 428	685	743	3, 028	1, 510	1, 518	-	-	-
10 to 14 years	3, 974	1, 909	2, 065	1, 356	622	734	2, 618	1, 287	1, 331	-	-	-
15 to 19 years	4, 472	1, 931	2, 541	1, 614	646	968	2, 858	1, 285	1, 573	-	-	-
20 to 24 years	4, 797	1, 904	2, 893	1, 823	689	1, 134	2, 974	1, 215	1, 759	-	-	-
25 to 29 years	4, 421	1, 942	2, 479	1, 587	626	961	2, 834	1, 316	1, 518	-	-	-
30 to 34 years	3, 411	1, 578	1, 833	988	423	565	2, 423	1, 155	1, 268	-	-	-
35 to 39 years	3, 427	1, 608	1, 819	1, 107	459	648	2, 320	1, 149	1, 171	-	-	-
40 to 44 years	2, 647	1, 218	1, 429	803	340	463	1, 844	878	966	-	-	-
45 to 49 years	2, 244	1, 074	1, 170	757	320	437	1, 487	754	723	-	-	-
50 to 54 years	1, 763	794	969	547	240	307	1, 215	553	662	1	1	-
55 to 59 years	1, 279	578	701	311	139	172	967	439	528	1	-	1
60 to 64 years	916	426	490	269	127	142	647	299	348	-	-	-
65 to 69 years	595	266	329	153	71	82	442	195	247	-	-	-
70 to 74 years	421	168	253	76	25	51	345	143	202	-	-	-
75 years and over	417	148	269	109	32	77	308	116	192	-	-	-
Unknown	28	19	9	13	9	4	15	10	5	-	-	-
ILLINOIS												
Chicago	**3, 376, 438**	**1, 710, 663**	**1, 665, 775**	**233, 903**	**115, 488**	**118, 415**	**3, 117, 731**	**1, 578, 244**	**1, 539, 487**	**24, 804**	**16, 931**	**7, 873**
Under 5 years	255, 359	129, 522	125, 837	17, 529	8, 731	8, 798	234, 641	119, 172	115, 469	3, 189	1, 619	1, 570
Under 1 year	50, 056	25, 373	24, 683	3, 452	1, 750	1, 703	45, 800	23, 217	22, 583	803	406	397
1 year	48, 836	24, 847	23, 989	3, 262	1, 630	1, 632	44, 928	22, 890	22, 038	646	327	319
2 years	51, 918	26, 393	25, 525	3, 587	1, 798	1, 789	47, 728	24, 283	23, 445	603	312	291
3 years	52, 835	26, 675	26, 160	3, 654	1, 781	1, 873	48, 588	24, 613	23, 975	593	281	312
4 years	51, 714	26, 234	25, 480	3, 573	1, 772	1, 801	47, 597	24, 169	23, 428	544	293	251
5 to 9 years	274, 457	138, 412	136, 045	17, 141	8, 342	8, 799	254, 934	128, 835	126, 099	2, 382	1, 235	1, 147
10 to 14 years	283, 726	142, 056	141, 670	14, 102	6, 668	7, 434	268, 423	134, 781	133, 642	1, 201	607	594
15 to 19 years	292, 575	141, 724	150, 851	15, 154	6, 880	8, 274	276, 092	134, 090	142, 002	1, 329	754	575
20 to 24 years	325, 183	156, 435	168, 748	24, 833	10, 965	13, 868	296, 355	142, 376	153, 979	3, 995	3, 094	901
25 to 29 years	329, 400	164, 473	164, 927	32, 439	15, 400	17, 039	292, 355	145, 517	146, 838	4, 606	3, 556	1, 050
30 to 34 years	309, 755	157, 155	152, 600	28, 305	14, 373	13, 932	278, 612	140, 621	137, 991	2, 838	2, 161	677
35 to 39 years	317, 225	164, 700	152, 525	27, 316	14, 103	13, 213	287, 732	148, 952	138, 780	2, 177	1, 645	532
40 to 44 years	265, 823	142, 829	122, 994	18, 762	10, 106	8, 656	245, 841	131, 769	114, 072	1, 220	954	266
45 to 49 years	212, 248	114, 678	97, 570	15, 391	8, 296	7, 095	196, 130	105, 866	90, 264	727	516	211
50 to 54 years	161, 533	85, 442	76, 091	9, 611	5, 253	4, 358	151, 471	79, 867	71, 604	451	322	129
55 to 59 years	117, 599	60, 580	57, 019	3, 464	2, 853	2, 611	111, 871	57, 548	54, 323	264	179	85
60 to 64 years	92, 990	46, 618	46, 372	3, 319	1, 589	1, 730	89, 497	44, 916	44, 581	174	113	61
65 to 69 years	64, 912	31, 784	33, 128	2, 034	898	1, 136	62, 775	30, 815	31, 960	103	71	32
70 to 74 years	38, 849	18, 664	20, 185	1, 099	447	652	37, 709	18, 192	19, 517	41	25	16
75 years and over	30, 690	13, 146	17, 544	1, 076	411	665	29, 574	12, 716	16, 858	40	19	21
Unknown	4, 114	2, 445	1, 669	328	173	155	3, 719	2, 211	1, 508	67	61	6
East St. Louis	**74, 347**	**37, 461**	**36, 886**	**11, 536**	**5, 743**	**5, 793**	**62, 769**	**31, 690**	**31, 079**	**42**	**28**	**14**
Under 5 years	6, 454	3, 241	3, 213	1, 163	575	588	5, 282	2, 660	2, 622	9	6	3
Under 1 year	1, 244	623	621	220	106	114	1, 024	517	507	-	-	-
1 year	1, 234	645	589	217	107	110	1, 015	537	478	2	1	1
2 years	1, 323	683	640	239	123	116	1, 081	557	524	3	3	-
3 years	1, 331	628	703	241	117	124	1, 088	510	578	2	1	1
4 years	1, 322	662	660	246	122	124	1, 074	539	535	2	1	1
5 to 9 years	6, 658	3, 436	3, 222	1, 128	530	598	5, 525	2, 904	2, 621	5	2	3
10 to 14 years	6, 481	3, 205	2, 276	973	469	504	5, 508	2, 736	2, 772	-	-	-
15 to 19 years	6, 716	3, 248	3, 468	981	458	523	5, 734	2, 790	2, 944	1	-	1
20 to 24 years	7, 091	3, 338	3, 753	1, 217	543	674	5, 872	2, 795	3, 077	2	-	2
25 to 29 years	6, 953	3, 360	3, 593	1, 324	607	717	5, 625	2, 749	2, 876	4	4	-
30 to 34 years	6, 365	3, 221	3, 144	1, 131	572	559	5, 226	2, 642	2, 584	8	7	1
35 to 39 years	6, 241	3, 169	3, 072	1, 125	588	537	5, 112	2, 579	2, 533	4	2	2
40 to 44 years	5, 514	2, 944	2, 570	798	454	344	4, 714	2, 488	2, 226	2	2	-
45 to 49 years	4, 559	2, 430	2, 129	622	361	261	3, 935	2, 068	1, 867	2	1	1
50 to 54 years	3, 760	1, 998	1, 762	470	260	210	3, 290	1, 738	1, 552	-	-	-
55 to 59 years	2, 672	1, 394	1, 278	219	136	83	2, 449	1, 255	1, 194	4	3	1
60 to 64 years	2, 028	1, 052	976	158	70	88	1, 870	982	888	-	-	-
65 to 69 years	1, 330	683	647	82	41	41	1, 247	641	606	1	1	-
70 to 74 years	750	372	378	49	25	24	701	347	354	-	-	-
75 years and over	673	305	368	56	29	27	617	276	341	-	-	-
Unknown	102	65	37	40	25	15	62	40	22	-	-	-

TABLE 20.—AGE DISTRIBUTION BY 5-YEAR AGE PERIODS WITH SINGLE YEARS UNDER 5, BY COLOR, AND SEX, FOR THE 80 CITIES HAVING 10,000 OR MORE NEGRO INHABITANTS 1930:—Continued

CITY AND AGE	ALL CLASSES			NEGRO			WHITE			OTHER RACES		
	Total	Male	Female	Total	Male	Female	Total	Male	Female	Total	Male	Female
INDIANA												
Gary	**100,426**	**54,593**	**45,833**	**17,922**	**9,393**	**8,529**	**78,992**	**42,622**	**36,370**	**3,512**	**2,578**	**934**
Under 5 years	9,496	4,866	4,630	1,672	860	812	7,464	3,832	3,632	360	174	186
Under 1 year	1,851	950	901	283	144	139	1,476	768	708	92	38	54
1 year	1,830	922	908	309	176	133	1,450	708	742	71	38	33
2 years	1,987	1,017	970	348	183	165	1,570	803	767	69	31	38
3 years	1,922	996	926	369	172	197	1,476	785	691	77	39	38
4 years	1,906	981	925	363	185	178	1,492	768	724	51	28	23
5 to 9 years	9,962	4,893	5,069	1,654	814	840	8,060	3,957	4,103	248	122	126
10 to 14 years	9,480	4,696	4,784	1,313	669	644	8,014	3,958	4,056	153	69	84
15 to 19 years	8,646	4,142	4,504	1,231	566	665	7,275	3,494	3,781	140	82	58
20 to 24 years	9,959	5,362	4,597	1,851	881	970	7,407	3,889	3,518	701	592	109
25 to 29 years	10,508	5,833	4,675	2,391	1,203	1,188	7,359	3,996	3,363	758	624	124
30 to 34 years	9,431	5,224	4,207	2,134	1,131	1,003	6,878	3,762	3,116	419	331	88
35 to 39 years	9,861	5,733	4,128	1,968	1,071	897	7,554	4,385	3,169	339	277	62
40 to 44 years	7,937	4,813	3,124	1,343	806	537	6,416	3,862	2,554	178	145	33
45 to 49 years	5,869	3,554	2,315	996	588	408	4,768	2,887	1,881	105	79	26
50 to 54 years	3,798	2,356	1,442	585	357	228	3,171	1,972	1,199	42	27	15
55 to 59 years	2,268	1,362	906	359	213	146	1,889	1,138	751	20	11	9
60 to 64 years	1,355	793	562	185	112	73	1,163	679	484	7	2	5
65 to 69 years	848	463	385	101	54	47	739	405	334	8	4	4
70 to 74 years	464	216	248	48	20	28	412	192	220	4	4	-
75 years and over	355	161	194	56	25	31	296	136	160	3	-	3
Unknown	189	126	63	35	23	12	127	78	49	27	25	2
Indianapolis	**364,161**	**176,647**	**187,514**	**43,967**	**21,263**	**22,704**	**320,064**	**155,282**	**164,782**	**130**	**102**	**28**
Under 5 years	27,649	13,818	13,831	3,457	1,701	1,756	24,183	12,112	12,071	9	5	4
Under 1 year	5,345	2,708	2,637	643	323	320	4,701	2,385	2,316	1	-	1
1 year	5,366	2,702	2,664	639	307	332	4,725	2,394	2,331	2	1	1
2 years	5,575	2,778	2,797	733	364	369	4,841	2,414	2,427	1	-	1
3 years	5,704	2,820	2,884	708	336	372	4,993	2,482	2,511	3	2	1
4 years	5,659	2,810	2,849	734	371	363	4,923	2,437	2,486	2	2	-
5 to 9 years	30,274	15,261	15,013	3,905	1,980	1,925	26,360	13,275	13,085	9	6	3
10 to 14 years	27,112	13,541	13,571	3,369	1,584	1,785	23,738	11,954	11,784	5	3	2
15 to 19 years	28,298	13,398	14,900	3,432	1,592	1,840	24,863	11,804	13,059	3	2	1
20 to 24 years	33,155	15,100	18,055	3,899	1,744	2,155	29,249	13,350	15,899	7	6	1
25 to 29 years	33,288	15,631	17,657	4,288	1,921	2,367	28,986	13,699	15,287	14	11	3
30 to 34 years	31,587	15,312	16,275	4,145	1,980	2,165	27,428	13,321	14,107	14	11	3
35 to 39 years	30,819	15,194	15,625	4,223	2,044	2,179	26,583	13,137	13,446	13	13	-
40 to 44 years	27,297	13,368	13,929	3,545	1,709	1,836	23,739	11,651	12,088	13	8	5
45 to 49 years	24,102	11,792	12,310	3,133	1,565	1,568	20,959	10,218	10,741	10	9	1
50 to 54 years	20,806	10,481	10,325	2,440	1,346	1,094	18,354	9,126	9,228	12	9	3
55 to 59 years	16,028	7,869	8,159	1,523	801	722	14,499	7,063	7,436	6	5	1
60 to 64 years	12,733	6,245	6,488	973	511	462	11,748	5,723	6,025	12	11	1
65 to 69 years	8,957	4,204	4,753	662	315	347	8,293	3,887	4,406	2	2	-
70 to 74 years	5,948	2,739	3,209	416	207	209	5,531	2,531	3,000	1	1	-
75 years and over	5,683	2,487	3,196	423	188	235	5,260	2,299	2,961	-	-	-
Unknown	425	207	218	134	75	59	291	132	159	-	-	-
KANSAS												
Kansas City	**121,857**	**60,867**	**60,990**	**19,872**	**9,628**	**10,244**	**99,161**	**49,721**	**49,440**	**2,824**	**1,518**	**1,306**
Under 5 years	10,649	5,534	5,115	1,632	837	795	8,532	4,467	4,065	485	230	255
Under 1 year	2,023	1,071	952	276	145	131	1,634	867	767	113	59	54
1 year	2,009	1,033	976	295	158	137	1,613	831	782	101	44	57
2 years	2,107	1,051	1,056	324	164	160	1,698	855	843	85	32	53
3 years	2,259	1,176	1,083	384	184	200	1,784	949	835	91	43	48
4 years	2,251	1,2 3	1,048	353	186	167	1,803	965	838	95	52	43
5 to 9 years	12,217	6,225	5,992	1,849	907	942	9,882	5,067	4,815	486	251	235
10 to 14 years	10,891	5,474	5,417	1,645	783	862	8,962	4,552	4,410	284	139	145
15 to 19 years	10,631	5,157	5,474	1,554	741	813	8,873	4,300	4,573	204	116	88
20 to 24 years	10,782	5,038	5,744	1,487	645	842	9,058	4,261	4,797	237	132	105
25 to 29 years	10,310	4,937	5,373	1,748	764	984	8,310	4,035	4,275	252	138	114
30 to 34 years	9,718	4,813	4,905	1,777	828	949	7,724	3,863	3,861	217	122	95
35 to 39 years	9,986	4,982	5,004	1,885	888	997	7,867	3,950	3,917	234	144	90
40 to 44 years	8,631	4,484	4,147	1,586	807	779	6,881	3,571	3,310	164	106	58
45 to 49 years	7,567	3,934	3,633	1,551	795	756	5,901	3,065	2,836	115	74	41
50 to 54 years	5,950	3,080	2,870	1,104	587	517	4,785	2,464	2,321	61	29	32
55 to 59 years	4,708	2,346	2,362	745	403	342	3,924	1,921	2,003	39	22	17
60 to 64 years	3,594	1,814	1,780	504	264	240	3,072	1,544	1,528	18	6	12
65 to 69 years	2,635	1,306	1,329	337	165	172	2,284	1,139	1,145	14	2	12
70 to 74 years	1,768	894	874	210	107	103	1,552	783	769	6	4	2
75 years and over	1,770	826	944	252	105	147	1,511	718	793	7	3	4
Unknown	50	23	27	6	2	4	43	21	22	1	-	1
KENTUCKY												
Lexington	**45,736**	**21,920**	**23,816**	**12,759**	**6,132**	**6,627**	**32,972**	**15,783**	**17,189**	**5**	**5**	-
Under 5 years	3,064	1,545	1,519	854	417	437	2,210	1,128	1,082	-	-	-
Under 1 year	592	298	294	170	85	85	422	213	209	-	-	-
1 year	558	306	252	142	76	66	416	230	186	-	-	-
2 years	643	328	315	182	94	88	461	234	227	-	-	-
3 years	625	288	337	187	86	101	438	202	236	-	-	-
4 years	646	325	321	173	76	97	473	249	224	-	-	-
5 to 9 years	3,665	1,852	1,813	1,015	517	498	2,650	1,335	1,315	-	-	-
10 to 14 years	3,377	1,650	1,727	916	422	494	2,461	1,228	1,233	-	-	-
15 to 19 years	3,683	1,737	1,946	993	463	530	2,689	1,273	1,416	1	1	-
20 to 24 years	4,233	1,938	2,295	1,112	516	596	3,121	1,422	1,699	-	-	-
25 to 29 years	3,850	1,831	2,019	1,085	500	585	2,736	1,329	1,434	2	2	-
30 to 34 years	3,733	1,740	1,993	1,094	481	613	2,638	1,258	1,380	1	1	-
35 to 39 years	3,912	1,874	2,038	1,259	585	674	2,653	1,289	1,364	-	-	-
40 to 44 years	3,417	1,676	1,741	1,071	544	527	2,345	1,131	1,214	1	1	-
45 to 49 years	3,227	1,537	1,690	998	522	476	2,229	1,015	1,214	-	-	-
50 to 54 years	2,773	1,361	1,412	808	420	388	1,965	941	1,024	-	-	-
55 to 59 years	2,093	1,010	1,083	517	252	265	1,576	758	818	-	-	-
60 to 64 years	1,751	841	910	397	202	195	1,354	639	715	-	-	-
65 to 69 years	1,263	588	675	279	140	139	984	448	536	-	-	-
70 to 74 years	817	383	434	174	85	89	643	298	345	-	-	-
75 years and over	861	355	506	186	66	120	675	289	386	-	-	-
Unknown	17	2	15	1	-	1	16	2	14	-	-	-

Table 20.—AGE DISTRIBUTION BY 5-YEAR AGE PERIODS WITH SINGLE YEARS UNDER 5, BY COLOR, AND SEX FOR THE 80 CITIES HAVING 10,000 OR MORE NEGRO INHABITANTS: 1930—Continued

CITY AND AGE	ALL CLASSES			NEGRO			WHITE			OTHER RACES		
	Total	Male	Female	Total	Male	Female	Total	Male	Female	Total	Male	Female
KANSAS—continued												
Louisville	**307,745**	**148,084**	**159,661**	**47,354**	**22,742**	**24,612**	**260,347**	**125,312**	**135,035**	**44**	**30**	**14**
Under 5 years	24,734	12,634	12,100	3,101	1,582	1,519	21,627	11,049	10,578	6	3	3
Under 1 year	4,781	2,451	2,330	574	295	279	4,206	2,155	2,051	1	1	----
1 year	4,718	2,407	2,311	582	280	302	4,134	2,125	2,009	2	2	----
2 years	5,128	2,608	2,520	665	343	322	4,463	2,265	2,198	----	----	----
3 years	4,985	2,506	2,479	623	313	310	4,360	2,193	2,167	2	----	2
4 years	5,122	2,662	2,460	657	351	306	4,464	2,311	2,153	1	----	1
5 to 9 years	26,350	13,276	13,074	3,536	1,767	1,769	22,812	11,509	11,303	2	----	2
10 to 14 years	23,565	11,654	11,911	3,197	1,561	1,636	20,367	10,092	10,275	1	1	----
15 to 19 years	25,124	11,803	13,321	3,533	1,583	1,950	21,590	10,220	11,370	1	----	1
20 to 24 years	29,329	13,180	16,149	4,341	1,854	2,487	24,981	11,321	13,660	7	5	2
25 to 29 years	28,582	13,511	15,071	4,682	2,174	2,508	23,889	11,328	12,561	11	9	2
30 to 34 years	26,304	12,745	13,559	4,583	2,145	2,438	21,716	10,595	11,121	5	5	----
35 to 39 years	25,547	12,621	12,926	4,968	2,416	2,552	20,575	10,202	10,373	4	3	1
40 to 44 years	21,303	10,327	10,976	3,932	1,915	2,017	17,369	8,410	8,959	2	2	----
45 to 49 years	19,478	9,516	9,962	3,734	1,893	1,841	15,740	7,621	8,119	4	2	2
50 to 54 years	16,763	8,159	8,604	2,824	1,470	1,354	13,938	6,689	7,249	1	----	1
55 to 59 years	12,912	6,245	6,667	1,665	880	785	11,247	5,365	5,882	----	----	----
60 to 64 years	10,311	4,876	5,435	1,294	628	666	9,017	4,248	4,769	----	----	----
65 to 69 years	7,419	3,364	4,055	815	390	425	6,604	2,974	3,630	----	----	----
70 to 74 years	5,128	2,257	2,871	497	233	264	4,631	2,024	2,607	----	----	----
75 years and over	4,617	1,819	2,798	587	218	369	4,030	1,601	2,429	----	----	----
Unknown	279	97	182	65	33	32	214	64	150	----	----	----
LOUISIANA												
Baton Rouge	**30,729**	**14,422**	**16,307**	**10,675**	**4,682**	**5,993**	**20,048**	**9,735**	**10,313**	**6**	**5**	**1**
Under 5 years	2,488	1,231	1,257	736	365	371	1,750	865	885	2	1	1
Under 1 year	456	222	234	131	57	74	324	165	159	1	----	1
1 year	474	243	231	143	73	70	331	170	161	----	----	----
2 years	485	239	246	149	79	70	335	159	176	1	1	----
3 years	525	264	261	157	87	70	368	177	191	----	----	----
4 years	548	263	285	156	69	87	392	194	198	----	----	----
5 to 9 years	2,729	1,366	1,363	916	451	465	1,813	915	898	----	----	----
10 to 14 years	2,500	1,173	1,327	878	407	471	1,622	766	856	----	----	----
15 to 19 years	2,853	1,196	1,657	1,064	424	640	1,789	772	1,017	----	----	----
20 to 24 years	3,677	1,599	2,078	1,321	501	820	2,355	1,097	1,258	1	1	----
25 to 29 years	3,573	1,624	1,949	1,298	520	778	2,274	1,103	1,171	1	1	----
30 to 34 years	2,704	1,303	1,401	892	372	520	1,810	929	881	2	2	----
35 to 39 years	2,625	1,302	1,323	989	435	554	1,636	867	769	----	----	----
40 to 44 years	2,023	1,036	987	705	334	371	1,318	702	616	----	----	----
45 to 49 years	1,677	815	862	662	316	346	1,015	499	516	----	----	----
50 to 54 years	1,242	613	629	422	198	224	820	415	405	----	----	----
55 to 59 years	909	443	466	274	137	137	635	306	329	----	----	----
60 to 64 years	626	282	344	203	95	108	423	187	236	----	----	----
65 to 69 years	443	181	262	127	52	75	316	129	187	----	----	----
70 to 74 years	300	129	171	81	37	44	219	92	127	----	----	----
75 years and over	358	128	230	106	38	68	252	90	162	----	----	----
Unknown	2	1	1	1	----	1	1	1	----	----	----	----
Monroe	**26,028**	**12,940**	**13,088**	**10,112**	**4,751**	**5,361**	**15,846**	**8,140**	**7,706**	**70**	**49**	**21**
Under 5 years	2,127	1,048	1,079	681	322	359	1,441	723	718	5	3	2
Under 1 year	396	193	203	124	61	63	272	132	140	----	----	----
1 year	410	205	205	128	57	71	281	148	133	1	----	1
2 years	406	210	196	133	71	62	271	138	133	2	1	1
3 years	470	223	247	140	57	83	330	166	164	----	----	----
4 years	445	217	228	156	76	80	287	139	148	2	2	----
5 to 9 years	2,259	1,187	1,072	760	386	374	1,490	794	696	9	7	2
10 to 14 years	1,996	990	1,006	750	349	401	1,242	640	602	4	1	3
15 to 19 years	2,270	1,020	1,250	920	408	512	1,344	608	736	6	4	2
20 to 24 years	3,350	1,473	1,877	1,484	647	837	1,861	823	1,038	5	3	2
25 to 29 years	3,227	1,555	1,672	1,437	639	798	1,781	909	872	9	7	2
30 to 34 years	2,501	1,261	1,240	951	439	512	1,545	819	726	5	3	2
35 to 39 years	2,339	1,216	1,123	946	451	495	1,383	757	626	10	8	2
40 to 44 years	1,792	970	822	713	369	344	1,077	600	477	2	1	1
45 to 49 years	1,437	812	625	581	308	273	852	501	351	4	3	1
50 to 54 years	960	551	409	350	202	148	607	348	259	3	1	2
55 to 59 years	606	314	292	184	78	106	420	234	186	2	2	----
60 to 64 years	440	225	215	123	63	60	314	159	155	3	3	----
65 to 69 years	316	142	174	83	33	50	230	106	124	3	3	----
70 to 74 years	193	79	114	51	21	30	142	58	84	----	----	----
75 years and over	194	87	107	83	29	54	111	58	53	----	----	----
Unknown	21	10	11	15	7	8	6	3	3	----	----	----
New Orleans	**458,762**	**219,250**	**239,512**	**129,632**	**59,732**	**69,900**	**327,729**	**158,659**	**169,070**	**1,401**	**859**	**542**
Under 5 years	38,588	19,577	19,011	11,518	5,773	5,745	26,961	13,749	13,212	109	55	54
Under 1 year	7,004	3,461	3,543	2,147	1,085	1,062	4,833	2,365	2,468	24	11	13
1 year	7,399	3,711	3,688	2,186	1,078	1,108	5,195	2,625	2,570	18	8	10
2 years	7,741	4,026	3,715	2,339	1,166	1,173	5,378	2,848	2,530	24	12	12
3 years	8,239	4,165	4,074	2,416	1,214	1,202	5,803	2,939	2,864	20	12	8
4 years	8,205	4,214	3,991	2,430	1,230	1,200	5,752	2,972	2,780	23	12	11
5 to 9 years	43,327	21,785	21,542	12,570	6,173	6,397	30,631	15,554	15,077	126	58	68
10 to 14 years	37,226	18,268	18,958	10,280	4,826	5,454	26,842	13,389	13,453	104	53	51
15 to 19 years	40,370	18,840	21,530	11,340	4,959	6,381	28,922	13,830	15,092	108	51	57
20 to 24 years	46,363	20,853	25,510	13,974	5,796	8,178	32,216	14,943	17,273	173	114	59
25 to 29 years	45,627	21,406	24,221	14,536	6,294	8,242	30,887	14,972	15,915	204	140	64
30 to 34 years	40,259	19,435	20,824	11,700	5,309	6,391	28,434	14,037	14,397	125	89	36
35 to 39 years	38,770	18,870	19,900	12,295	5,675	6,620	26,361	13,123	13,238	114	72	42
40 to 44 years	30,822	15,062	15,760	9,100	4,391	4,709	21,650	10,627	11,023	72	44	28
45 to 49 years	27,293	13,539	13,754	8,192	4,083	4,109	19,032	9,414	9,618	69	42	27
50 to 54 years	21,928	10,576	11,352	5,319	2,593	2,726	16,545	7,941	8,604	64	42	22
55 to 59 years	16,514	7,813	8,701	3,450	1,737	1,713	13,022	6,016	6,976	42	30	12
60 to 64 years	12,540	5,709	6,831	2,162	962	1,200	10,329	4,705	5,624	49	42	7
65 to 69 years	8,242	3,441	4,801	1,366	544	822	6,855	2,885	3,970	21	12	9
70 to 74 years	5,429	2,108	3,321	808	276	532	4,612	1,825	2,787	9	7	2
75 years and over	5,245	1,847	3,398	953	300	653	4,280	1,539	2,741	12	8	4
Unknown	219	121	98	69	41	28	150	80	70	----	----	----

TABLE 20.—AGE DISTRIBUTION BY 5-YEAR AGE PERIODS WITH SINGLE YEARS UNDER 5, BY COLOR, AND SEX FOR THE 80 CITIES HAVING 10,000 OR MORE NEGRO INHABITANTS: 1930—Continued

CITY AND AGE	ALL CLASSES			NEGRO			WHITE			OTHER RACES		
	Total	Male	Female	Total	Male	Female	Total	Male	Female	Total	Male	Female
LOUISIANA—continued												
Shreveport	**76, 655**	**36, 483**	**40, 172**	**27, 219**	**12, 223**	**14, 996**	**49, 293**	**24, 186**	**25, 107**	**143**	**74**	**69**
Under 5 years	6, 208	3, 180	3, 028	1, 930	970	960	4, 255	2, 199	2, 056	23	11	12
Under 1 year	1, 193	606	587	360	176	184	825	427	398	8	3	5
1 year	1, 108	551	557	348	179	169	755	370	385	5	2	3
2 years	1, 218	630	588	394	191	203	821	436	385	3	3	----
3 years	1, 339	697	642	399	199	200	934	495	439	6	3	3
4 years	1, 350	696	654	429	225	204	920	471	449	1	----	1
5 to 9 years	6, 948	3, 501	3, 447	2, 232	1, 109	1, 123	4, 695	2, 384	2, 311	21	8	13
10 to 14 years	6, 186	2, 993	3, 193	2, 196	987	1, 209	3, 976	2, 002	1, 974	14	4	10
15 to 19 years	6, 612	2, 890	3, 722	2, 451	952	1, 499	4, 151	1, 934	2, 217	10	4	6
20 to 24 years	8, 591	3, 518	5, 073	3, 301	1, 274	2, 027	5, 276	2, 236	3, 040	14	8	6
25 to 29 years	9, 022	4, 011	5, 011	3, 733	1, 572	2, 161	5, 273	2, 432	2, 841	16	7	9
30 to 34 years	7, 386	3, 505	3, 881	2, 656	1, 242	1, 414	4, 719	2, 253	2, 466	11	10	1
35 to 39 years	7, 086	3, 534	3, 552	2, 702	1, 231	1, 471	4, 373	2, 295	2, 078	11	8	3
40 to 44 years	5, 221	2, 675	2, 546	1, 852	889	963	3, 363	1, 784	1, 579	6	2	4
45 to 49 years	4, 240	2, 196	2, 044	1, 563	779	784	2, 674	1, 416	1, 258	3	1	2
50 to 54 years	3, 152	1, 630	1, 522	976	499	477	2, 170	1, 126	1, 044	6	5	1
55 to 59 years	2, 141	1, 115	1, 026	564	289	275	1, 576	825	751	1	1	----
60 to 64 years	1, 457	732	725	381	173	208	1, 073	557	516	3	2	1
65 to 69 years	908	376	532	253	90	163	654	285	369	1	1	----
70 to 74 years	706	306	400	187	73	114	518	233	285	1	----	1
75 years and over	741	299	442	221	88	133	518	209	309	2	2	----
Unknown	50	22	28	21	6	15	29	16	13	----	----	----
MARYLAND												
Baltimore	**804, 874**	**395, 888**	**408, 986**	**142, 106**	**70, 043**	**72, 063**	**662, 124**	**325, 327**	**336, 797**	**644**	**518**	**126**
Under 5 years	64, 474	32, 762	31, 712	12, 274	6, 099	6, 175	52, 146	26, 632	25, 514	54	31	23
Under 1 year	11, 807	5, 996	5, 811	2, 244	1, 138	1, 106	9, 552	4, 853	4, 699	11	5	6
1 year	12, 208	6, 161	6, 047	2, 252	1, 100	1, 152	9, 948	5, 055	4, 893	8	6	2
2 years	13, 236	6, 692	6, 544	2, 565	1, 269	1, 296	10, 656	5, 414	5, 242	15	9	6
3 years	13, 747	6, 936	6, 811	2, 656	1, 313	1, 343	11, 082	5, 618	5, 464	9	5	4
4 years	13, 476	6, 977	6, 499	2, 557	1, 279	1, 278	10, 908	5, 692	5, 216	11	6	5
5 to 9 years	73, 191	36, 518	36, 673	13, 053	6, 250	6, 803	60, 093	30, 245	29, 848	45	23	22
10 to 14 years	68, 648	34, 025	34, 623	10, 423	4, 824	5, 599	58, 201	29, 189	29, 012	24	12	12
15 to 19 years	67, 669	32, 798	34, 871	11, 076	4, 893	6, 183	56, 564	27, 886	28, 678	29	19	10
20 to 24 years	75, 455	36, 148	39, 307	14, 976	6, 967	8, 009	60, 407	29, 119	31, 288	72	62	10
25 to 29 years	72, 631	35, 996	36, 635	15, 972	7, 923	8, 049	56, 578	28, 005	28, 573	81	68	13
30 to 34 years	67, 589	33, 609	33, 980	13, 701	6, 905	6, 796	53, 811	26, 634	27, 177	77	70	7
35 to 39 years	67, 471	34, 058	33, 413	13, 869	7, 180	6, 689	53, 533	26, 823	26, 710	69	55	14
40 to 44 years	56, 987	28, 757	28, 230	10, 551	5, 526	5, 025	46, 389	23, 190	23, 199	47	41	6
45 to 49 years	49, 405	24, 697	24, 708	8, 830	4, 689	4, 141	40, 542	19, 978	20, 564	33	30	3
50 to 54 years	40, 856	20, 004	20, 852	6, 314	3, 384	2, 930	34, 494	16, 576	17, 918	48	44	4
55 to 59 years	30, 752	14, 956	15, 796	3, 511	1, 829	1, 682	27, 222	13, 108	14, 114	19	19	----
60 to 64 years	25, 291	11, 891	13, 400	2, 665	1, 331	1, 334	22, 606	10, 541	12, 065	20	19	1
65 to 69 years	18, 023	8, 181	9, 842	1, 678	799	879	16, 336	7, 374	8, 962	9	8	1
70 to 74 years	12, 248	5, 410	6, 838	1, 024	446	578	11, 218	4, 958	6, 260	6	6	----
75 years and over	10, 913	4, 451	6, 462	1, 001	410	591	9, 910	4, 039	5, 871	2	2	----
Unknown	3, 271	1, 627	1, 644	1, 188	588	600	2, 074	1, 030	1, 044	9	9	----
MASSACHUSETTS												
Boston	**781, 188**	**383, 454**	**397, 734**	**20, 574**	**10, 223**	**10, 351**	**758, 756**	**371, 680**	**387, 076**	**1, 858**	**1, 551**	**307**
Under 5 years	62, 374	31, 568	30, 806	1, 582	784	798	60, 669	30, 716	29, 953	123	68	55
Under 1 year	11, 704	5, 920	5, 784	278	135	143	11, 404	5, 770	5, 634	22	15	7
1 year	12, 209	6, 177	6, 032	320	149	171	11, 868	6, 018	5, 850	21	10	11
2 years	12, 831	6, 424	6, 407	326	156	170	12, 480	6, 257	6, 223	25	11	14
3 years	12, 906	6, 589	6, 317	334	169	165	12, 545	6, 403	6, 142	27	17	10
4 years	12, 724	6, 458	6, 266	324	175	149	12, 372	6, 268	6, 104	28	15	13
5 to 9 years	66, 229	33, 359	32, 870	1, 686	810	876	64, 415	32, 483	31, 932	128	66	62
10 to 14 years	64, 998	32, 359	32, 639	1, 423	715	708	63, 507	31, 602	31, 905	68	42	26
15 to 19 years	65, 965	32, 198	33, 767	1, 280	603	677	64, 591	31, 521	33, 070	94	74	20
20 to 24 years	70, 757	33, 057	37, 700	1, 554	738	816	69, 054	32, 196	36, 858	149	123	26
25 to 29 years	67, 585	32, 814	34, 771	1, 943	947	996	65, 448	31, 691	33, 757	194	176	18
30 to 34 years	62, 998	31, 242	31, 756	2, 064	1, 035	1, 029	60, 711	30, 013	30, 698	223	194	29
35 to 39 years	64, 115	32, 068	32, 047	2, 234	1, 114	1, 120	61, 676	30, 774	30, 902	205	180	25
40 to 44 years	55, 393	28, 351	27, 042	1, 803	916	887	53, 407	27, 276	26, 131	183	159	24
45 to 49 years	50, 178	25, 001	25, 177	1, 644	854	790	48, 384	24, 003	24, 381	150	144	6
50 to 54 years	43, 258	21, 265	21, 993	1, 248	652	596	41, 884	20, 495	21, 389	126	118	8
55 to 59 years	35, 696	17, 428	18, 268	798	437	361	34, 812	16, 907	17, 905	86	84	2
60 to 64 years	27, 720	13, 243	14, 477	523	265	258	27, 123	12, 906	14, 217	74	72	2
65 to 69 years	19, 602	9, 161	10, 441	325	157	168	19, 246	8, 974	10, 272	31	30	1
70 to 74 years	12, 120	5, 429	6, 691	185	89	96	11, 922	5, 328	6, 594	13	12	1
75 years and over	10, 915	4, 186	6, 729	227	77	150	10, 684	4, 105	6, 579	4	4	----
Unknown	1, 285	725	560	55	30	25	1, 223	690	533	7	5	2
MICHIGAN												
Detroit	**1, 568, 662**	**821, 920**	**746, 742**	**120, 066**	**62, 239**	**57, 827**	**1, 440, 141**	**753, 936**	**686, 205**	**8, 455**	**5, 745**	**2, 710**
Under 5 years	146, 610	74, 639	71, 971	10, 618	5, 314	5, 304	134, 938	68, 801	66, 137	1, 054	524	530
Under 1 year	28, 523	14, 516	14, 007	2, 062	1, 046	1, 016	26, 194	13, 342	12, 852	267	128	139
1 year	28, 183	14, 414	13, 769	1, 889	940	949	26, 079	13, 373	12, 706	215	101	114
2 years	29, 788	15, 007	14, 781	2, 183	1, 101	1, 082	27, 404	13, 793	13, 611	201	113	88
3 years	30, 711	15, 661	15, 050	2, 304	1, 121	1, 183	28, 206	14, 433	13, 773	201	107	94
4 years	29, 405	15, 041	14, 364	2, 180	1, 106	1, 074	27, 055	13, 860	13, 195	170	75	95
5 to 9 years	148, 173	74, 956	73, 217	10, 201	5, 146	5, 055	137, 161	69, 392	67, 769	811	418	393
10 to 14 years	133, 280	66, 409	66, 871	7, 728	3, 719	4, 009	125, 101	62, 460	62, 641	451	230	221
15 to 19 years	123, 082	59, 216	63, 866	7, 454	3, 409	4, 045	115, 164	55, 532	59, 632	464	275	189
20 to 24 years	151, 642	75, 248	76, 394	13, 078	6, 088	6, 990	137, 314	68, 214	69, 100	1, 250	946	304
25 to 29 years	170, 272	89, 944	80, 328	18, 473	9, 221	9, 252	150, 127	79, 395	70, 732	1, 672	1, 328	344
30 to 34 years	160, 573	87, 439	73, 134	16, 116	8, 686	7, 430	143, 419	77, 939	65, 480	1, 038	814	224
35 to 39 years	156, 526	88, 222	68, 304	14, 035	7, 854	6, 181	141, 753	79, 816	61, 937	738	552	186
40 to 44 years	119, 148	68, 655	50, 493	8, 515	5, 036	3, 479	110, 252	63, 346	46, 906	381	273	108
45 to 49 years	86, 582	49, 322	37, 260	6, 095	3, 601	2, 494	80, 223	45, 542	34, 681	264	179	85
50 to 54 years	60, 275	32, 695	27, 580	3, 402	1, 980	1, 422	56, 735	30, 625	26, 110	138	90	48
55 to 59 years	40, 251	20, 878	19, 373	1, 817	1, 017	800	38, 358	19, 811	18, 547	76	50	26
60 to 64 years	28, 891	14, 271	14, 620	1, 030	508	522	27, 811	13, 725	14, 086	50	38	12
65 to 69 years	19, 878	9, 401	10, 477	560	252	308	19, 277	9, 135	10, 142	41	14	27
70 to 74 years	12, 155	5, 568	6, 587	311	123	188	11, 832	5, 438	6, 394	12	7	5
75 years and over	10, 283	4, 400	5, 883	400	143	257	9, 873	4, 251	5, 622	10	6	4
Unknown	1, 041	657	384	233	142	91	803	514	289	5	1	4

Table 20.—AGE DISTRIBUTION BY 5-YEAR AGE PERIODS WITH SINGLE YEARS UNDER 5, BY COLOR, AND SEX FOR THE 80 CITIES HAVING 10,000 OR MORE NEGRO INHABITANTS: 1930—Continued

CITY AND AGE	ALL CLASSES			NEGRO			WHITE			OTHER RACES		
	Total	Male	Female	Total	Male	Female	Total	Male	Female	Total	Male	Female
MISSISSIPPI												
Jackson	**48,282**	**22,966**	**25,316**	**19,423**	**9,140**	**10,283**	**28,854**	**13,821**	**15,033**	**5**	**5**	
Under 5 years	3,919	1,956	1,963	1,616	814	802	2,303	1,142	1,161			
Under 1 year	751	374	377	315	165	150	436	209	227			
1 year	730	378	352	302	155	147	428	223	205			
2 years	776	387	389	336	162	174	440	225	215			
3 years	847	416	431	374	192	182	473	224	249			
4 years	815	401	414	289	140	149	526	261	265			
5 to 9 years	4,124	2,078	2,046	1,698	865	833	2,426	1,213	1,213			
10 to 14 years	3,517	1,740	1,777	1,448	689	759	2,069	1,051	1,018			
15 to 19 years	4,252	1,913	2,339	1,868	792	1,076	2,384	1,121	1,263			
20 to 24 years	6,282	2,639	3,643	2,727	1,170	1,557	3,554	1,468	2,086	1	1	
25 to 29 years	5,791	2,648	3,143	2,481	1,113	1,368	3,310	1,535	1,775			
30 to 34 years	4,528	2,247	2,281	1,762	880	882	2,766	1,367	1,399			
35 to 39 years	3,968	1,936	2,032	1,580	741	839	2,386	1,193	1,193	2	2	
40 to 44 years	3,058	1,576	1,482	1,196	599	597	1,861	976	885	1	1	
45 to 49 years	2,658	1,348	1,310	980	492	488	1,678	856	822			
50 to 54 years	2,068	1,032	1,036	753	380	373	1,315	652	663			
55 to 59 years	1,316	649	667	416	201	215	899	447	452	1	1	
60 to 64 years	993	457	536	330	155	175	663	302	361			
65 to 69 years	658	299	359	212	99	113	446	200	246			
70 to 74 years	493	191	302	131	56	75	362	135	227			
75 years and over	597	231	366	183	78	105	414	153	261			
Unknown	60	26	34	42	16	26	18	10	8			
Meridian	**31,954**	**14,634**	**17,320**	**11,352**	**4,915**	**6,437**	**20,602**	**9,719**	**10,883**			
Under 5 years	2,739	1,344	1,395	1,023	471	552	1,716	873	843			
Under 1 year	521	251	270	192	82	110	329	169	160			
1 year	520	261	259	196	84	112	324	177	147			
2 years	580	288	292	212	100	112	368	188	180			
3 years	615	301	314	229	109	120	386	192	194			
4 years	503	243	260	194	96	98	309	147	162			
5 to 9 years	3,034	1,483	1,551	1,143	579	564	1,891	904	987			
10 to 14 years	2,732	1,296	1,436	971	447	524	1,761	849	912			
15 to 19 years	3,176	1,396	1,780	1,225	507	718	1,951	889	1,062			
20 to 24 years	3,457	1,389	2,068	1,366	482	884	2,091	907	1,184			
25 to 29 years	3,017	1,301	1,716	1,193	452	741	1,824	849	975			
30 to 34 years	2,434	1,066	1,368	844	340	504	1,590	726	864			
35 to 39 years	2,523	1,118	1,405	929	399	530	1,594	719	875			
40 to 44 years	2,119	1,031	1,088	696	306	390	1,423	725	698			
45 to 49 years	1,880	907	973	654	314	340	1,226	593	633			
50 to 54 years	1,517	754	763	395	174	221	1,122	580	542			
55 to 59 years	1,046	492	554	241	100	141	805	392	413			
60 to 64 years	894	459	435	268	152	116	626	307	319			
65 to 69 years	584	272	313	189	91	98	395	180	215			
70 to 74 years	346	148	198	100	49	51	246	99	147			
75 years and over	427	166	261	110	50	60	317	116	201			
Unknown	29	13	16	5	2	3	24	11	13			
Vicksburg	**22,943**	**10,519**	**12,424**	**11,915**	**5,225**	**6,690**	**11,017**	**5,283**	**5,734**	**11**	**11**	
Under 5 years	1,677	837	840	791	389	402	886	448	438			
Under 1 year	310	151	159	154	67	87	156	84	72			
1 year 2 years 3 years 4 years	1,367	686	681	637	322	315	730	364	366			
5 to 9 years	1,979	951	1,028	975	460	515	1,004	491	513			
10 to 14 years	1,748	867	881	862	422	440	886	445	441			
15 to 19 years	1,935	848	1,087	995	413	582	940	435	505			
20 to 24 years	2,462	963	1,499	1,253	485	768	1,208	477	731	1	1	
25 to 29 years	2,405	1,028	1,377	1,330	518	812	1,073	508	565	2	2	
30 to 34 years	1,924	874	1,050	1,021	430	591	903	444	459			
35 to 39 years 40 to 44 years	3,659	1,730	1,929	2,010	892	1,118	1,648	837	811	1	1	
45 to 49 years 50 to 54 years	2,661	1,313	1,348	1,451	690	761	1,207	620	587	3	3	
55 to 59 years 60 to 64 years	1,396	660	736	658	301	357	735	356	379	3	3	
65 to 69 years 70 to 74 years	673	293	380	327	140	187	345	152	193	1	1	
75 years and over	384	134	250	208	68	140	176	66	110			
Unknown	40	21	19	34	17	17	6	4	2			
MISSOURI												
Kansas City	**399,746**	**194,542**	**205,204**	**38,574**	**18,599**	**19,975**	**357,741**	**173,960**	**183,781**	**3,431**	**1,983**	**1,448**
Under 5 years	26,128	13,202	12,926	2,154	1,086	1,068	23,454	11,873	11,581	520	243	277
Under 1 year	5,008	2,526	2,482	382	197	185	4,512	2,274	2,238	114	55	59
1 year	5,040	2,576	2,464	420	217	203	4,514	2,307	2,207	106	52	54
2 years	5,333	2,698	2,635	471	229	242	4,764	2,415	2,349	98	54	44
3 years	5,356	2,712	2,644	451	225	226	4,803	2,447	2,356	102	40	62
4 years	5,391	2,690	2,701	430	218	212	4,861	2,430	2,431	100	42	58
5 to 9 years	29,029	14,568	14,461	2,475	1,237	1,238	26,108	13,124	12,984	446	207	239
10 to 14 years	26,920	13,304	13,616	2,113	974	1,139	24,525	12,201	12,324	282	129	153
15 to 19 years	29,776	13,862	15,914	2,484	1,115	1,369	27,031	12,591	14,440	261	156	105
20 to 24 years	38,439	17,045	21,394	3,351	1,308	2,043	34,704	15,499	19,205	384	238	146
25 to 29 years	39,911	18,446	21,465	4,318	1,894	2,424	35,198	16,286	18,912	395	266	129
30 to 34 years	37,426	18,001	19,425	4,077	1,852	2,225	33,057	15,966	17,091	292	183	109
35 to 39 years	37,774	18,641	19,133	4,654	2,265	2,389	32,802	16,163	16,639	318	213	105
40 to 44 years	32,180	16,319	15,861	3,818	1,957	1,861	28,160	14,217	13,943	202	145	57
45 to 49 years	27,703	14,148	13,555	3,394	1,884	1,510	24,176	12,178	11,998	133	86	47
50 to 54 years	22,374	11,324	11,050	2,368	1,287	1,081	19,938	9,994	9,944	68	43	25
55 to 59 years	16,945	8,618	8,327	1,283	714	569	15,615	7,882	7,733	47	22	25
60 to 64 years	12,968	6,490	6,478	811	419	392	12,124	6,049	6,075	33	22	11
65 to 69 years	9,623	4,729	4,894	505	245	260	9,104	4,475	4,629	14	9	5
70 to 74 years	6,256	3,070	3,186	304	152	152	5,941	2,913	3,028	11	5	6
75 years and over	5,886	2,563	3,323	336	147	189	5,531	2,405	3,126	19	11	8
Unknown	408	212	196	129	63	66	273	144	129	6	5	1

TABLE 20.—AGE DISTRIBUTION BY 5-YEAR AGE PERIODS WITH SINGLE YEARS UNDER 5, BY COLOR, AND SEX FOR THE 80 CITIES HAVING 10,000 OR MORE NEGRO INHABITANTS: 1930—Continued

CITY AND AGE	ALL CLASSES			NEGRO			WHITE			OTHER RACES		
	Total	Male	Female	Total	Male	Female	Total	Male	Female	Total	Male	Female
MISSOURI—continued												
St. Louis	**821, 960**	**401, 706**	**420, 254**	**93, 580**	**45, 832**	**47, 748**	**726, 879**	**354, 838**	**372, 041**	**1, 501**	**1, 036**	**465**
Under 5 years	58, 483	29, 622	28, 861	6, 634	3, 335	3, 299	51, 672	26, 189	25, 483	177	98	79
Under 1 year	11, 255	5, 812	5, 443	1, 304	654	650	9, 913	5, 135	4, 778	38	23	15
1 year	11, 126	5, 664	5, 462	1, 222	619	603	9, 870	5, 029	4, 841	34	16	18
2 years	11, 959	6, 026	5, 933	1, 321	641	680	10, 605	5, 368	5, 237	33	17	16
3 years	12, 330	6, 148	6, 182	1, 438	706	732	10, 858	5, 421	5, 437	34	21	13
4 years	11, 813	5, 972	5, 841	1, 349	715	634	10, 426	5, 236	5, 190	38	21	17
5 to 9 years	62, 139	31, 456	30, 683	6, 988	3, 541	3, 447	55, 001	27, 835	27, 166	150	80	70
10 to 14 years	58, 507	29, 073	29, 434	5, 960	2, 822	3, 138	52, 451	26, 195	26, 256	96	56	40
15 to 19 years	67, 023	31, 885	35, 138	6, 683	3, 036	3, 647	60, 243	28, 781	31, 462	97	68	29
20 to 24 years	81, 199	37, 103	44, 096	9, 348	3, 991	5, 357	71, 692	33, 002	38, 690	159	110	49
25 to 29 years	80, 048	38, 209	41, 839	11, 389	5, 208	6, 181	68, 474	32, 862	35, 612	185	139	46
30 to 34 years	72, 106	35, 343	36, 763	10, 172	4, 927	5, 245	61, 792	30, 315	31, 477	142	101	41
35 to 39 years	71, 734	35, 283	36, 451	10, 302	5, 180	5, 122	61, 303	30, 019	31, 284	129	84	45
40 to 44 years	62, 632	31, 202	31, 430	7, 968	4, 247	3, 721	54, 557	26, 870	27, 687	107	85	22
45 to 49 years	54, 841	27, 603	27, 238	6, 747	3, 650	3, 097	48, 013	23, 888	24, 125	81	65	16
50 to 54 years	46, 278	23, 246	23, 032	4, 543	2, 493	2, 050	41, 672	20, 700	20, 972	63	53	10
55 to 59 years	35, 161	17, 630	17, 531	2, 702	1, 444	1, 258	32, 415	16, 151	16, 264	44	35	9
60 to 64 years	28, 173	13, 798	14, 375	1, 705	871	834	26, 429	12, 894	13, 535	39	33	6
65 to 69 years	19, 732	9, 364	10, 368	1, 040	483	557	18, 677	8, 867	9, 810	15	14	1
70 to 74 years	12, 488	5, 858	6, 630	627	267	360	11, 853	5, 584	6, 269	8	7	1
75 years and over	10, 934	4, 724	6, 210	681	288	393	10, 245	4, 429	5, 816	8	7	1
Unknown	482	307	175	91	49	42	390	257	133	1	1	
NEBRASKA												
Omaha	**214, 006**	**105, 896**	**108, 110**	**11, 123**	**5, 607**	**5, 516**	**201, 657**	**99, 540**	**102, 117**	**1, 226**	**749**	**477**
Under 5 years	17, 514	9, 056	8, 458	878	439	439	16, 456	8, 535	7, 921	180	82	98
Under 1 year	3, 445	1, 783	1, 662	173	85	88	3, 227	1, 680	1, 547	45	18	27
1 year	3, 371	1, 739	1, 632	164	81	83	3, 175	1, 644	1, 531	32	14	18
2 years	3, 506	1, 844	1, 662	192	98	94	3, 274	1, 725	1, 549	40	21	19
3 years	3, 604	1, 838	1, 766	185	93	92	3, 384	1, 729	1, 655	35	16	19
4 years	3, 588	1, 852	1, 736	164	82	82	3, 396	1, 757	1, 639	28	13	15
5 to 9 years	19, 071	9, 709	9, 362	893	446	447	18, 005	9, 178	8, 827	173	85	88
10 to 14 years	17, 212	8, 588	8, 624	724	377	347	16, 403	8, 171	8, 232	85	40	45
15 to 19 years	17, 768	8, 422	9, 346	736	343	393	16, 961	8, 045	8, 916	71	34	37
20 to 24 years	19, 357	8, 741	10, 616	919	397	522	18, 320	8, 261	10, 059	118	83	35
25 to 29 years	18, 545	8, 683	9, 862	1, 151	548	603	17, 231	8, 025	9, 205	163	110	53
30 to 34 years	18, 380	8, 913	9, 467	1, 105	539	566	17, 143	8, 287	8, 856	132	87	45
35 to 39 years	18, 784	9, 450	9, 334	1, 223	616	607	17, 444	8, 745	8, 699	117	89	28
40 to 44 years	16, 425	8, 483	7, 942	1, 012	532	480	15, 351	7, 903	7, 448	62	48	14
45 to 49 years	13, 610	7, 047	6, 563	931	522	409	12, 636	6, 493	6, 143	43	32	11
50 to 54 years	10, 642	5, 520	5, 122	619	355	264	9, 998	5, 149	4, 849	25	16	9
55 to 59 years	8, 045	3, 995	4, 050	346	181	165	7, 678	3, 799	3, 879	21	15	6
60 to 64 years	6, 649	3, 280	3, 369	229	132	97	6, 407	3, 138	3, 269	13	10	3
65 to 69 years	5, 231	2, 671	2, 560	158	83	75	5, 060	2, 577	2, 483	13	11	2
70 to 74 years	3, 427	1, 756	1, 671	75	37	38	3, 346	1, 714	1, 632	6	5	1
75 years and over	3, 131	1, 448	1, 683	107	48	59	3, 022	1, 399	1, 623	2	1	1
Unknown	215	134	81	17	12	5	196	121	75	2	1	1
NEW JERSEY												
Atlantic City	**66, 198**	**31, 449**	**34, 749**	**15, 611**	**7, 527**	**8, 084**	**50, 514**	**23, 866**	**26, 648**	**73**	**56**	**17**
Under 5 years	3, 907	1, 987	1, 920	942	471	471	2, 961	1, 515	1, 446	4	1	3
Under 1 year	705	355	350	176	80	96	529	275	254			
1 year	715	362	353	178	97	81	536	265	271	1		1
2 years	783	392	391	194	102	92	589	290	299			
3 years	858	438	420	203	100	103	655	338	317			
4 years	846	440	406	191	92	99	652	347	305	3	1	2
5 to 9 years	4, 612	2, 304	2, 308	1, 030	522	508	3, 575	1, 777	1, 798	7	5	2
10 to 14 years	4, 695	2, 327	2, 368	837	403	434	3, 853	1, 922	1, 931	5	2	3
15 to 19 years	5, 103	2, 369	2, 734	953	423	530	4, 147	1, 944	2, 203	3	2	1
20 to 24 years	5, 818	2, 663	3, 155	1, 489	660	829	4, 326	2, 000	2, 326	3	3	
25 to 29 years	5, 987	2, 733	3, 254	1, 867	842	1, 025	4, 114	1, 887	2, 227	6	4	2
30 to 34 years	5, 927	2, 856	3, 071	1, 721	850	871	4, 199	2, 001	2, 198	7	5	2
35 to 39 years	6, 322	2, 965	3, 357	1, 743	813	930	4, 573	2. 148	2, 425	6	4	2
40 to 44 years	5, 702	2, 764	2, 938	1, 561	750	811	4, 129	2, 003	2, 126	12	11	1
45 to 49 years	4, 969	2, 382	2, 587	1, 268	635	633	3, 695	1, 741	1, 954	6	6	
50 to 54 years	4, 160	1, 992	2, 168	956	521	435	3, 200	1, 467	1, 733	4	4	
55 to 59 years	2, 967	1, 393	1, 574	469	256	213	2, 492	1, 131	1, 361	6	6	
60 to 64 years	2, 361	1, 090	1, 271	328	176	152	2, 030	912	1, 118	3	2	1
65 to 69 years	1, 540	710	830	179	84	95	1, 360	625	735	1	1	
70 to 74 years	1, 058	488	570	107	50	57	951	438	513			
75 years and over	923	360	563	113	46	67	810	314	496			
Unknown	147	66	81	48	25	23	99	41	58			
Camden	**118, 700**	**59, 442**	**59, 258**	**11, 340**	**5, 676**	**5, 664**	**107, 283**	**53, 706**	**53, 577**	**77**	**60**	**17**
Under 5 years	10, 090	5, 010	5, 080	1, 139	562	577	8, 946	4, 446	4, 500	5	2	3
Under 1 year	1, 877	927	950	231	110	121	1, 646	817	829			
1 year	1, 777	856	921	188	89	99	1, 587	767	820	2		2
2 years	2, 159	1, 106	1, 053	230	120	110	1, 927	985	942	2	1	1
3 years	2, 163	1, 056	1, 107	262	123	139	1, 901	933	968			
4 years	2, 114	1, 065	1, 049	228	120	108	1, 885	944	941	1	1	
5 to 9 years	11, 723	5, 891	5, 832	1, 175	583	592	10, 543	5, 305	5, 238	5	3	2
10 to 14 years	12, 146	6, 088	6, 058	978	475	503	11, 162	5, 611	5, 551	6	2	4
15 to 19 years	11, 370	5, 471	5, 899	939	462	477	10, 427	5, 007	5, 420	4	2	2
20 to 24 years	10, 335	5, 031	5, 304	1, 016	452	564	9, 315	4, 575	4, 740	4	4	
25 to 29 years	9, 340	4, 630	4, 710	1, 151	570	581	8, 181	4, 054	4, 127	8	6	2
30 to 34 years	9, 211	4, 571	4, 640	1, 018	490	528	8, 183	4, 071	4, 112	10	10	
35 to 39 years	9, 941	5, 143	4, 798	1, 107	593	514	8, 824	4, 542	4, 282	10	8	2
40 to 44 years	8, 467	4, 438	4, 029	862	447	415	7, 600	3, 986	3, 614	5	5	
45 to 49 years	7, 039	3, 683	3, 356	650	346	304	6, 381	3, 330	3, 051	8	7	1
50 to 54 years	5, 787	2, 988	2, 799	482	268	214	5, 304	2, 719	2, 585	1	1	
55 to 59 years	4, 413	2, 233	2, 180	333	172	161	4, 076	2, 058	2, 018	4	3	1
60 to 64 years	3, 479	1, 709	1, 770	208	117	91	3, 267	1, 588	1, 679	4	4	
65 to 69 years	2, 437	1, 198	1, 239	127	57	70	2, 307	1, 138	1, 169	3	3	
70 to 74 years	1, 543	741	802	66	41	25	1, 477	700	777			
75 years and over	1, 331	593	738	77	36	41	1, 254	557	697			
Unknown	48	24	24	12	5	7	36	19	17			

Table 20.—AGE DISTRIBUTION BY 5-YEAR AGE PERIODS WITH SINGLE YEARS UNDER 5, BY COLOR, AND SEX FOR THE 80 CITIES HAVING 10,000 OR MORE NEGRO INHABITANTS: 1930—Continued

CITY AND AGE	ALL CLASSES			NEGRO			WHITE			OTHER RACES		
	Total	Male	Female	Total	Male	Female	Total	Male	Female	Total	Male	Female
NEW JERSEY—continued												
Jersey City	**316, 715**	**159, 315**	**157, 400**	**12, 575**	**6, 229**	**6, 346**	**303, 887**	**152, 890**	**150, 997**	**253**	**196**	**57**
Under 5 years	26, 295	13, 346	12, 949	1, 239	602	637	25, 037	12, 732	12, 305	19	12	7
Under 1 year	5, 102	2, 597	2, 505	271	128	143	4, 828	2, 467	2, 361	3	2	1
1 year	4, 812	2, 501	2, 302	244	129	115	4, 564	2, 379	2, 185	4	2	2
2 years	5, 291	2, 703	2, 588	256	128	128	5, 029	2, 570	2, 459	6	5	1
3 years	5, 621	2, 868	2, 753	253	114	139	5, 366	2, 753	2, 613	2	1	1
4 years	5, 469	2, 668	2, 801	215	103	112	5, 250	2, 563	2, 687	4	2	2
5 to 9 years	30, 071	15, 144	14, 927	1, 183	579	604	28, 870	14, 558	14, 312	18	7	11
10 to 14 years	30, 941	15, 426	15, 515	919	407	512	30, 014	15, 014	15, 000	8	5	3
15 to 19 years	29, 579	14, 544	15, 035	934	413	521	28, 637	14, 127	14, 510	8	4	4
20 to 24 years	29, 857	14, 799	15, 058	1, 398	669	729	28, 432	14, 107	14, 325	27	23	4
25 to 29 years	28, 365	14, 468	13, 897	1, 576	768	808	26, 758	13, 676	13, 082	31	24	7
30 to 34 years	26, 905	13, 653	13, 252	1, 263	674	589	25, 603	12, 949	12, 654	39	30	9
35 to 39 years	26, 279	13, 340	12, 939	1, 165	613	552	25, 095	12, 711	12, 384	19	16	3
40 to 44 years	22, 218	11, 676	10, 542	793	411	382	21, 401	11, 243	10, 158	24	22	2
45 to 49 years	18, 184	9, 426	8, 758	721	376	345	17, 449	9, 039	8, 410	14	11	3
50 to 54 years	15, 245	7, 815	7, 430	534	285	249	14, 690	7, 512	7, 178	21	18	3
55 to 59 years	11, 383	5, 668	5, 715	357	180	177	11, 011	5, 473	5, 538	15	15	-----
60 to 64 years	9, 003	4, 297	4, 706	240	119	121	8, 756	4, 171	4, 585	7	7	-----
65 to 69 years	5, 924	2, 865	3, 059	140	79	61	5, 782	2, 785	2, 997	2	1	1
70 to 74 years	3, 495	1, 630	1, 865	62	32	30	3, 433	1, 598	1, 835	-----	-----	-----
75 years and over	2, 834	1, 150	1, 684	44	18	26	2, 790	1, 132	1, 658	-----	-----	-----
Unknown	137	68	69	7	4	3	129	63	66	1	1	-----
Newark	**442, 337**	**223, 763**	**218, 574**	**38, 880**	**19, 280**	**19, 600**	**402, 596**	**203, 717**	**198, 879**	**861**	**766**	**95**
Under 5 years	36, 150	18, 303	17, 847	3, 821	1, 873	1, 948	32, 286	16, 407	15, 879	43	23	20
Under 1 year	6, 830	3, 439	3, 391	791	397	394	6, 028	3, 037	2, 991	11	5	6
1 year	6, 796	3, 438	3, 358	702	335	367	6, 087	3, 098	2, 989	7	5	2
2 years	7, 363	3, 681	3, 682	796	405	391	6, 559	3, 271	3, 288	8	5	3
3 years	7, 587	3, 916	3, 671	774	370	404	6, 802	3, 541	3, 261	11	5	6
4 years	7, 574	3, 829	3, 745	758	366	392	6, 810	3, 460	3, 350	6	3	3
5 to 9 years	41, 120	20, 737	20, 383	3, 735	1, 872	1, 863	37, 345	18, 842	18, 503	40	23	17
10 to 14 years	41, 089	20, 794	20, 295	2, 856	1, 345	1, 511	38, 223	19, 441	18, 782	10	8	2
15 to 19 years	41, 899	20, 468	21, 431	2, 948	1, 307	1, 641	38, 928	19, 141	19, 787	23	20	3
20 to 24 years	42, 888	20, 813	22, 075	4, 347	1, 942	2, 405	38, 483	18, 822	19, 661	58	49	9
25 to 29 years	40, 167	20, 307	19, 860	5, 273	2, 517	2, 756	34, 788	17, 701	17, 087	106	89	17
30 to 34 years	37, 693	19, 400	18, 293	4, 235	2, 199	2, 036	33, 317	17, 070	16, 247	141	131	10
35 to 39 years	37, 505	19, 443	18, 062	3, 991	2, 098	1, 893	33, 423	17, 261	16, 162	91	84	7
40 to 44 years	31, 060	16, 670	14, 390	2, 502	1, 352	1, 150	28, 462	15, 224	13, 238	96	94	2
45 to 49 years	26, 265	13, 839	12, 426	2, 087	1, 140	947	24, 103	12, 625	11, 478	75	74	1
50 to 54 years	20, 979	10, 867	10, 112	1, 331	742	589	19, 577	10, 058	9, 519	71	67	4
55 to 59 years	15, 389	7, 865	7, 524	721	403	318	14, 620	7, 414	7, 206	48	48	-----
60 to 64 years	12, 069	5, 927	6, 142	448	226	222	11, 588	5, 670	5, 918	33	31	2
65 to 69 years	8, 185	3, 966	4, 219	257	117	140	7, 916	3, 837	4, 079	12	12	-----
70 to 74 years	5, 241	2, 464	2, 777	145	75	70	5, 090	2, 383	2, 707	6	6	-----
75 years and over	4, 232	1, 678	2, 554	142	51	91	4, 083	1, 621	2, 462	7	6	1
Unknown	406	222	184	41	21	20	364	200	164	1	1	-----
NEW YORK												
Buffalo	**573, 076**	**284, 460**	**288, 616**	**13, 563**	**7, 064**	**6, 499**	**558, 869**	**277, 040**	**281, 829**	**644**	**356**	**288**
Under 5 years	47, 687	23, 923	23, 764	1, 287	624	663	46, 319	23, 261	23, 058	81	38	43
Under 1 year	9, 266	4, 640	4, 626	249	110	139	9, 004	4, 526	4, 478	13	4	9
1 year	9, 144	4, 680	4, 464	224	118	106	8, 903	4, 556	4, 347	17	6	11
2 years	9, 646	4, 812	4, 834	285	139	146	9, 347	4, 667	4, 680	14	6	8
3 years	9, 856	4, 923	4, 933	263	133	130	9, 567	4, 774	4, 793	26	16	10
4 years	9, 775	4, 868	4, 907	266	124	142	9, 498	4, 738	4, 760	11	6	5
5 to 9 years	51, 930	25, 973	25, 957	1, 123	543	580	50, 740	25, 403	25, 337	67	27	40
10 to 14 years	51, 842	25, 923	25, 919	873	429	444	50, 921	25, 478	25, 443	48	16	32
15 to 19 years	49, 636	24, 103	25, 533	834	364	470	48, 754	23, 720	25, 034	48	19	29
20 to 24 years	50, 118	23, 791	26, 327	1, 415	652	763	48, 638	23, 106	25, 532	65	33	32
25 to 29 years	48, 709	24, 061	24, 648	2, 058	1, 091	967	46, 563	22, 911	23, 652	88	59	29
30 to 34 years	48, 878	24, 175	24, 703	1, 872	1, 028	844	46, 935	23, 100	23, 835	71	47	24
35 to 39 years	49, 871	25, 636	24, 235	1, 630	919	711	48, 182	24, 683	23, 499	59	34	25
40 to 44 years	42, 764	22, 391	20, 373	925	566	359	41, 799	21, 799	20, 000	40	26	14
45 to 49 years	34, 757	17, 830	16, 927	652	389	263	34, 074	17, 419	16, 655	31	22	9
50 to 54 years	28, 507	14, 201	14, 306	350	196	154	28, 145	13, 997	14, 148	12	8	4
55 to 59 years	21, 734	10, 624	11, 110	219	113	106	21, 501	10, 498	11, 003	14	13	1
60 to 64 years	18, 222	8, 816	9, 406	142	65	77	18, 070	8, 744	9, 326	10	7	3
65 to 69 years	12, 894	6, 174	6, 720	78	38	40	12, 808	6, 131	6, 677	8	5	3
70 to 74 years	8, 440	3, 837	4, 603	46	19	27	8, 393	3, 817	4, 576	1	1	-----
75 years and over	6, 647	2, 790	3, 857	46	24	22	6, 600	2, 765	3, 835	1	1	-----
Unknown	440	212	228	13	4	9	427	208	219	-----	-----	-----
New York	**6, 930, 446**	**3, 472, 956**	**3, 457, 490**	**327, 706**	**156, 968**	**170, 738**	**6, 587, 225**	**3, 303, 198**	**3, 284, 027**	**15, 515**	**12, 790**	**2, 725**
Under 5 years	535, 600	272, 438	263, 162	26, 920	13, 431	13, 489	507, 846	258, 572	249, 274	834	435	399
Under 1 year	100, 398	51, 178	49, 220	5, 176	2, 569	2, 607	95, 035	48, 520	46, 515	187	89	98
1 year	101, 845	51, 630	50, 215	5, 195	2, 692	2, 503	96, 491	48, 862	47, 629	159	76	83
2 years	111, 268	56, 690	54, 578	5, 653	2, 825	2, 828	105, 432	53, 764	51, 668	183	101	82
3 years	111, 998	57, 081	54, 917	5, 605	2, 725	2, 880	106, 246	54, 273	51, 973	147	83	64
4 years	110, 091	55, 859	54, 232	5, 291	2, 620	2, 671	104, 642	53, 153	51, 489	158	86	72
5 to 9 years	577, 284	291, 782	285, 502	24, 365	11, 894	12, 471	552, 261	279, 553	272, 708	658	335	323
10 to 14 years	575, 300	290, 263	285, 037	18, 662	8, 987	9, 675	556, 262	281, 072	275, 190	376	204	172
15 to 19 years	599, 286	293, 740	305, 546	21, 120	9, 169	11, 951	577, 634	284, 228	293, 406	532	343	189
20 to 24 years	687, 417	327, 734	359, 683	38, 658	16, 664	21, 994	647, 298	309, 930	337, 368	1, 461	1, 140	321
25 to 29 years	695, 984	341, 448	354, 536	48, 661	22, 779	25, 882	644, 709	316, 465	328, 244	2, 614	2, 204	410
30 to 34 years	649, 576	327, 685	321, 891	40, 533	20, 121	20, 412	606, 387	305, 225	301, 162	2, 656	2, 339	317
35 to 39 years	621, 248	319, 859	301, 389	36, 924	18, 539	18, 385	582, 129	299, 348	282, 781	2, 195	1, 972	223
40 to 44 years	518, 588	272, 868	245, 720	25, 515	12, 909	12, 606	491, 344	258, 370	232, 974	1, 729	1, 589	140
45 to 49 years	422, 063	219, 600	202, 463	19, 057	9, 607	9, 450	401, 988	209, 049	192, 939	1, 018	944	74
50 to 54 years	340, 807	175, 346	165, 461	11, 922	6, 032	5, 890	328, 215	168, 712	159, 503	670	602	68
55 to 59 years	246, 277	123, 128	123, 149	6, 365	3, 155	3, 210	239, 551	119, 644	119, 907	361	329	32
60 to 64 years	190, 527	92, 494	98, 033	3, 767	1, 708	2, 059	186, 563	90, 610	95, 953	197	176	21
65 to 69 years	127, 356	60, 451	66, 905	2, 331	891	1, 440	124, 928	59, 480	65, 448	97	80	17
70 to 74 years	77, 327	35, 866	41, 461	1, 236	448	788	76, 054	35, 387	40, 667	37	31	6
75 years and over	59, 819	25, 243	34, 576	1, 184	400	784	58, 616	24, 828	33, 788	19	15	4
Unknown	5, 987	3, 011	2, 976	486	234	252	5, 440	2, 725	2, 715	61	52	9

TABLE 20.—AGE DISTRIBUTION BY 5-YEAR AGE PERIODS WITH SINGLE YEARS UNDER 5, BY COLOR, AND SEX FOR THE 80 CITIES HAVING 10,000 OR MORE NEGRO INHABITANTS: 1930—Continued

CITY AND AGE	ALL CLASSES			NEGRO			WHITE			OTHER RACES		
	Total	Male	Female	Total	Male	Female	Total	Male	Female	Total	Male	Female
NORTH CAROLINA												
Asheville	**50,193**	**23,124**	**27,069**	**14,255**	**6,379**	**7,876**	**35,933**	**16,740**	**19,193**	**5**	**5**	-
Under 5 years	4,455	2,201	2,254	1,238	588	650	3,217	1,613	1,604	-	-	-
Under 1 year	796	398	398	203	93	110	593	305	288	-	-	-
1 year	886	432	454	257	128	129	629	304	325	-	-	-
2 years	908	443	465	249	111	138	659	332	327	-	-	-
3 years	929	455	474	259	123	136	670	332	338	-	-	-
4 years	936	473	463	270	133	137	666	340	326	-	-	-
5 to 9 years	4,978	2,448	2,530	1,410	690	720	3,568	1,758	1,810	-	-	-
10 to 14 years	4,417	2,133	2,284	1,301	640	661	3,116	1,493	1,623	-	-	-
15 to 19 years	4,645	2,032	2,613	1,407	608	799	3,237	1,423	1,814	1	1	-
20 to 24 years	5,379	2,136	3,243	1,848	687	1,161	3,531	1,449	2,082	-	-	-
25 to 29 years	5,240	2,311	2,929	1,774	727	1,047	3,465	1,583	1,882	1	1	-
30 to 34 years	4,489	2,056	2,433	1,303	584	719	3,186	1,472	1,714	-	-	-
35 to 39 years	4,345	2,060	2,285	1,247	561	686	3,098	1,499	1,599	-		
40 to 44 years	3,273	1,567	1,706	887	410	477	2,384	1,155	1,229	2	2	-
45 to 49 years	2,611	1,189	1,422	633	290	343	1,977	898	1,079	1	1	-
50 to 54 years	2,191	1,058	1,133	486	248	238	1,705	810	895	-	-	-
55 to 59 years	1,388	662	726	243	124	119	1,145	538	607	-	-	-
60 to 64 years	1,092	534	558	201	104	97	891	430	461	-	-	-
65 to 69 years	704	306	398	113	48	65	591	258	333	-	-	-
70 to 74 years	472	224	248	75	33	42	397	191	206	-	-	-
75 years and over	474	194	280	74	31	43	400	163	237	-	-	-
Unknown	40	13	27	15	6	9	25	7	18	-	-	-
Charlotte	**82,675**	**39,583**	**43,092**	**25,183**	**11,437**	**13,726**	**57,490**	**28,128**	**29,362**	**22**	**18**	**4**
Under 5 years	7,832	4,002	3,830	2,140	1,064	1,076	5,689	2,937	2,752	3	1	2
Under 1 year	1,449	796	653	383	210	173	1,065	586	479	1	-	1
1 year	1,454	741	713	405	198	207	1,049	543	506	-	-	-
2 years	1,605	786	819	414	197	217	1,190	589	601	1	-	1
3 years	1,649	802	847	459	210	249	1,189	591	598	1	1	-
4 years	1,675	877	798	479	249	230	1,196	628	568	-	-	-
5 to 9 years	8,529	4,246	4,283	2,536	1,208	1,328	5,992	3,038	2,954	1	-	1
10 to 14 years	7,015	3,464	3,551	2,234	1,054	1,180	4,781	2,410	2,371	-	-	-
15 to 19 years	7,532	3,333	4,199	2,551	1,059	1,492	4,979	2,272	2,707	2	2	-
20 to 24 years	10,099	4,336	5,763	3,511	1,442	2,069	6,586	2,892	3,694	2	2	-
25 to 29 years	9,607	4,351	5,256	3,182	1,361	1,821	6,423	2,988	3,435	2	2	-
30 to 34 years	7,650	3,764	3,886	2,138	1,006	1,132	5,510	2,756	2,754	2	2	-
35 to 39 years	6,806	3,396	3,410	1,991	912	1,079	4,812	2,482	2,330	3	2	1
40 to 44 years	4,865	2,504	2,361	1,348	658	690	3,516	1,845	1,671	1	1	-
45 to 49 years	3,952	1,968	1,984	1,168	541	627	2,784	1,427	1,357	-	-	-
50 to 54 years	3,015	1,530	1,485	819	415	404	2,194	1,113	1,081	2	2	-
55 to 59 years	1,870	928	942	441	220	221	1,428	707	721	1	1	-
60 to 64 years	1,424	694	730	329	155	174	1,094	538	556	1	1	-
65 to 69 years	888	390	498	208	92	116	680	298	382	-	-	-
70 to 74 years	580	262	318	104	51	53	475	210	265	1	1	-
75 years and over	583	214	369	156	53	103	427	161	266	-	-	-
Unknown	428	201	227	307	146	161	120	54	66	1	1	-
Durham	**52,037**	**24,629**	**27,408**	**18,717**	**8,616**	**10,101**	**33,313**	**16,008**	**17,305**	**7**	**5**	**2**
Under 5 years	5,240	2,558	2,682	1,765	851	914	3,475	1,707	1,768	-	-	-
Under 1 year	961	477	484	332	158	174	629	319	310	-	-	-
1 year	1,022	516	506	344	160	184	678	356	322	-	-	-
2 years	1,059	512	547	367	190	177	692	322	370	-	-	-
3 years	1,145	548	597	380	180	200	765	368	397	-	-	-
4 years	1,053	505	548	342	163	179	711	342	369	-	-	-
5 to 9 years	5,580	2,799	2,781	1,932	953	979	3,648	1,846	1,802	-	-	-
10 to 14 years	4,671	2,308	2,363	1,689	842	847	2,982	1,466	1,516	-	-	-
15 to 19 years	5,357	2,348	3,009	2,029	831	1,198	3,328	1,517	1,811	-	-	-
20 to 24 years	6,409	2,774	3,635	2,600	1,060	1,540	3,806	1,712	2,094	3	2	1
25 to 29 years	5,657	2,589	3,068	2,294	995	1,299	3,362	1,593	1,769	1	1	-
30 to 34 years	4,483	2,224	2,259	1,619	787	832	2,862	1,435	1,427	2	2	-
35 to 39 years	3,834	1,870	1,964	1,468	696	772	2,366	1,174	1,192	-	-	-
40 to 44 years	2,875	1,439	1,436	969	476	493	1,906	963	943	-	-	-
45 to 49 years	2,428	1,147	1,281	828	407	421	1,600	740	860	-	-	-
50 to 54 years	1,936	914	1,022	563	269	294	1,373	645	728	-	-	-
55 to 59 years	1,232	605	627	328	161	167	904	444	460	-	-	-
60 to 64 years	975	465	510	276	139	137	699	326	373	-	-	-
65 to 69 years	570	245	325	146	59	87	424	186	238	-	-	-
70 to 74 years	416	189	227	93	39	54	323	150	173	-	-	-
75 years and over	327	129	198	89	34	55	237	95	142	1	-	1
Unknown	47	26	21	29	17	12	18	9	9	-	-	-
Greensboro	**53,569**	**25,566**	**28,003**	**14,050**	**6,470**	**7,580**	**39,515**	**19,092**	**20,423**	**4**	**4**	-
Under 5 years	5,424	2,781	2,643	1,244	627	617	4,180	2,154	2,026	-	-	-
Under 1 year	1,056	518	538	253	123	130	803	395	408	-	-	-
1 year	1,059	548	511	227	116	111	832	432	400	-	-	-
2 years	1,073	567	506	256	134	122	817	433	384	-	-	-
3 years	1,133	601	532	265	130	135	868	471	397	-	-	-
4 years	1,103	547	556	243	124	119	860	423	437	-	-	-
5 to 9 years	5,830	2,932	2,898	1,398	668	730	4,432	2,264	2,168	-	-	-
10 to 14 years	4,935	2,419	2,516	1,297	609	688	3,638	1,810	1,828	-	-	-
15 to 19 years	5,222	2,353	2,869	1,563	644	919	3,658	1,708	1,950	1	1	-
20 to 24 years	6,215	2,680	3,535	1,858	787	1,071	4,357	1,893	2,464	-	-	-
25 to 29 years	5,707	2,599	3,108	1,715	752	963	3,990	1,845	2,145	2	2	-
30 to 34 years	4,670	2,241	2,429	1,191	579	612	3,479	1,662	1,817	-	-	-
35 to 39 years	4,054	1,977	2,077	1,048	485	563	3,006	1,492	1,514	-	-	-
40 to 44 years	3,117	1,522	1,595	783	363	420	2,334	1,159	1,175	-	-	-
45 to 49 years	2,577	1,264	1,313	656	310	346	1,921	954	967	-	-	-
50 to 54 years	1,998	1,001	997	514	262	252	1,483	738	745	1	1	-
55 to 59 years	1,296	648	648	262	148	114	1,034	500	534	-	-	-
60 to 64 years	1,043	505	538	205	98	107	838	407	431	-	-	-
65 to 69 years	559	243	316	112	52	60	447	191	256	-	-	-
70 to 74 years	465	223	242	96	46	50	369	177	192	-	-	-
75 years and over	434	171	263	96	38	58	338	133	205	-	-	-
Unknown	23	7	16	12	2	10	11	5	6	-	-	-

TABLE 20.—AGE DISTRIBUTION BY 5-YEAR AGE PERIODS WITH SINGLE YEARS UNDER 5, BY COLOR, AND SEX FOR THE 80 CITIES HAVING 10,000 OR MORE NEGRO INHABITANTS: 1930—Continued

CITY AND AGE	ALL CLASSES			NEGRO			WHITE			OTHER RACES		
	Total	Male	Female	Total	Male	Female	Total	Male	Female	Total	Male	Female
NORTH CAROLINA—continued												
Raleigh	**37,379**	**17,827**	**19,552**	**12,575**	**5,817**	**6,758**	**24,794**	**12,003**	**12,791**	**10**	**7**	**3**
Under 5 years	2,949	1,490	1,459	1,042	531	511	1,907	959	948			
Under 1 year	499	254	245	164	86	78	335	168	167			
1 year	571	274	297	194	91	103	377	183	194			
2 years	585	295	290	221	113	108	364	182	182			
3 years	644	336	308	235	124	111	409	212	197			
4 years	650	331	319	228	117	111	422	214	208			
5 to 9 years	3,667	1,826	1,841	1,320	642	678	2,347	1,184	1,163			
10 to 14 years	3,252	1,616	1,636	1,204	572	632	2,048	1,044	1,004			
15 to 19 years	3,496	1,622	1,874	1,369	613	756	2,126	1,008	1,118	1	1	
20 to 24 years	4,084	1,773	2,311	1,581	667	914	2,502	1,106	1,396	1		1
25 to 29 years	3,985	1,798	2,187	1,381	604	777	2,603	1,193	1,410	1	1	
30 to 34 years	3,306	1,618	1,688	989	458	531	2,317	1,160	1,157			
35 to 39 years	3,114	1,563	1,551	956	464	492	2,156	1,097	1,059	2	2	
40 to 44 years	2,460	1,199	1,261	732	344	388	1,726	854	872	2	1	1
45 to 49 years	2,028	979	1,049	636	276	360	1,390	702	688	2	1	1
50 to 54 years	1,669	789	880	480	246	234	1,189	543	646			
55 to 59 years	1,106	523	583	266	128	138	839	394	445	1	1	
60 to 64 years	847	412	435	244	106	138	603	306	297			
65 to 69 years	581	245	336	156	73	83	425	172	253			
70 to 74 years	374	162	212	96	41	55	278	121	157			
75 years and over	445	205	240	122	51	71	323	154	169			
Unknown	16	7	9	1	1		15	6	9			
Wilmington	**32,270**	**15,013**	**17,257**	**13,106**	**5,855**	**7,251**	**19,159**	**9,156**	**10,003**	**5**	**2**	**3**
Under 5 years	2,961	1,481	1,480	1,215	620	595	1,745	861	884	1		1
Under 1 year	591	285	306	231	113	118	360	172	188			
1 year	554	273	281	243	110	133	311	163	148			
2 years	578	285	293	233	130	103	345	155	190			
3 years	593	309	284	243	125	118	350	184	166			
4 years	645	329	316	265	142	123	379	187	192	1		1
5 to 9 years	3,534	1,762	1,772	1,472	709	763	2,061	1,053	1,008	1		1
10 to 14 years	2,989	1,463	1,526	1,292	596	696	1,697	867	830			
15 to 19 years	3,212	1,422	1,790	1,381	578	803	1,830	843	987	1	1	
20 to 24 years	3,310	1,414	1,896	1,365	560	805	1,945	854	1,091			
25 to 29 years	2,828	1,278	1,550	1,160	496	664	1,668	782	886			
30 to 34 years	2,551	1,111	1,440	1,030	433	597	1,521	678	843			
35 to 39 years	2,589	1,188	1,401	1,110	470	640	1,477	717	760	2	1	1
40 to 44 years	2,049	983	1,066	842	378	464	1,207	605	602			
45 to 49 years	1,771	848	923	704	309	395	1,067	539	528			
50 to 54 years	1,500	743	757	583	285	298	917	458	459			
55 to 59 years	959	465	494	325	162	163	634	303	331			
60 to 64 years	746	342	404	236	110	126	510	232	278			
65 to 69 years	491	207	284	164	59	105	327	148	179			
70 to 74 years	374	161	213	105	46	59	269	115	154			
75 years and over	389	138	251	117	43	74	272	95	177			
Unknown	17	7	10	5	1	4	12	6	6			
Winston-Salem	**75,274**	**35,792**	**39,482**	**32,566**	**15,173**	**17,393**	**42,705**	**20,616**	**22,089**	**3**	**3**	
Under 5 years	7,656	3,913	3,743	2,915	1,472	1,443	4,741	2,441	2,300			
Under 1 year	1,403	717	686	500	250	250	903	467	436			
1 year	1,514	754	760	575	274	301	939	480	459			
2 years	1,540	787	753	576	274	302	964	513	451			
3 years	1,594	832	762	612	342	270	982	490	492			
4 years	1,605	823	782	652	332	320	953	491	462			
5 to 9 years	8,119	4,048	4,071	3,341	1,617	1,724	4,778	2,431	2,347			
10 to 14 years	6,650	3,264	3,386	2,796	1,341	1,455	3,854	1,923	1,931			
15 to 19 years	7,559	3,321	4,238	3,501	1,476	2,025	4,058	1,845	2,213			
20 to 24 years	9,504	3,998	5,506	4,680	1,931	2,749	4,824	2,067	2,757			
25 to 29 years	8,750	3,964	4,786	4,120	1,860	2,260	4,630	2,104	2,526			
30 to 34 years	6,908	3,381	3,527	3,113	1,517	1,596	3,795	1,864	1,931			
35 to 39 years	5,896	2,919	2,977	2,580	1,240	1,340	3,315	1,678	1,637	1	1	
40 to 44 years	4,051	2,052	1,999	1,730	839	891	2,321	1,213	1,108			
45 to 49 years	3,040	1,446	1,594	1,256	566	690	1,784	880	904			
50 to 54 years	2,509	1,273	1,236	1,028	554	474	1,481	719	762			
55 to 59 years	1,635	811	824	572	295	277	1,062	515	547	1	1	
60 to 64 years	1,236	582	654	425	208	217	810	373	437	1	1	
65 to 69 years	836	407	429	263	140	123	573	267	306			
70 to 74 years	468	222	246	119	63	56	349	159	190			
75 years and over	448	185	263	126	54	72	322	131	191			
Unknown	9	6	3	1		1	8	6	2			
OHIO												
Akron	**255,040**	**130,029**	**125,011**	**11,080**	**5,748**	**5,332**	**243,744**	**124,137**	**119,607**	**216**	**144**	**72**
Under 5 years	24,030	12,169	11,861	1,086	522	564	22,915	11,638	11,277	29	9	20
Under 1 year	4,599	2,383	2,216	202	96	106	4,388	2,284	2,104	9	3	6
1 year	4,559	2,309	2,250	190	101	89	4,361	2,204	2,157	8	4	4
2 years	4,897	2,503	2,394	231	124	107	4,662	2,379	2,283	4		4
3 years	5,034	2,480	2,554	225	99	126	4,804	2,380	2,424	5	1	4
4 years	4,941	2,494	2,447	238	102	136	4,700	2,391	2,309	3	1	2
5 to 9 years	26,547	12,191	13,356	1,168	555	613	25,343	12,618	12,725	36	18	18
10 to 14 years	22,521	11,173	11,348	852	408	444	21,651	10,754	10,897	18	11	7
15 to 19 years	20,355	9,593	10,762	865	386	479	19,482	9,203	10,279	8	4	4
20 to 24 years	25,787	12,394	13,393	1,148	565	583	24,622	11,814	12,808	17	15	2
25 to 29 years	26,113	13,254	12,859	1,471	731	740	24,618	12,505	12,113	24	18	6
30 to 34 years	24,970	13,149	11,821	1,267	690	577	23,683	12,447	11,236	20	12	8
35 to 39 years	23,726	12,999	10,727	1,204	712	492	22,495	12,265	10,230	27	22	5
40 to 44 years	17,925	9,925	8,000	709	421	288	17,207	9,496	7,711	9	8	1
45 to 49 years	13,544	7,480	6,064	557	335	222	12,976	7,134	5,842	11	11	
50 to 54 years	9,798	5,165	4,633	318	190	128	9,475	4,970	4,505	5	5	
55 to 59 years	6,814	3,474	3,340	179	112	67	6,629	3,356	3,273	6	6	
60 to 64 years	4,965	2,388	2,577	110	55	55	4,852	2,330	2,522	3	3	
65 to 69 years	3,519	1,664	1,855	71	31	40	3,446	1,632	1,814	2	1	1
70 to 74 years	2,321	1,073	1,248	30	11	19	2,291	1,062	1,229			
75 years and over	1,948	836	1,112	30	14	16	1,917	821	1,096	1	1	
Unknown	157	102	55	15	10	5	142	92	50			

TABLE 20.—AGE DISTRIBUTION BY 5-YEAR AGE PERIODS WITH SINGLE YEARS UNDER 5, BY COLOR, AND SEX FOR THE 80 CITIES HAVING 10,000 OR MORE NEGRO INHABITANTS: 1930—Continued

CITY AND AGE	ALL CLASSES			NEGRO			WHITE			OTHER RACES		
	Total	Male	Female	Total	Male	Female	Total	Male	Female	Total	Male	Female
OHIO—continued												
Cincinnati	**451,160**	**218,995**	**232,165**	**47,818**	**23,914**	**23,904**	**403,112**	**194,915**	**208,197**	**230**	**166**	**64**
Under 5 years	32,990	16,686	16,304	4,003	1,995	2,008	28,960	14,678	14,282	27	13	14
Under 1 year	6,448	3,283	3,165	739	356	383	5,703	2,923	2,780	6	4	2
1 year	6,367	3,287	3,080	730	370	360	5,632	2,915	2,717	5	2	3
2 years	6,753	3,368	3,385	829	411	418	5,920	2,957	2,963	4	-	4
3 years	6,773	3,360	3,413	864	414	450	5,902	2,942	2,960	7	4	3
4 years	6,649	3,388	3,261	841	444	397	5,803	2,941	2,862	5	3	2
5 to 9 years	34,541	17,337	17,204	4,094	2,009	2,085	30,422	15,315	15,107	25	13	12
10 to 14 years	32,238	16,206	16,032	3,450	1,630	1,820	28,780	14,570	14,210	8	6	2
15 to 19 years	35,154	16,698	18,456	3,486	1,552	1,934	31,658	15,139	16,519	10	7	3
20 to 24 years	42,316	19,944	22,372	5,068	2,347	2,721	37,227	17,581	19,646	21	16	5
25 to 29 years	40,714	19,651	21,063	5,856	2,839	3,017	34,828	16,787	18,041	30	25	5
30 to 34 years	37,800	18,523	19,277	4,849	2,453	2,396	32,923	16,050	16,873	28	20	8
35 to 39 years	38,977	19,407	19,570	5,041	2,658	2,383	33,905	16,726	17,179	31	23	8
40 to 44 years	33,768	16,784	16,984	3,723	1,984	1,739	30,029	14,787	15,242	16	13	3
45 to 49 years	29,916	14,610	15,306	2,957	1,610	1,347	26,948	12,990	13,958	11	10	1
50 to 54 years	25,923	12,631	13,292	2,139	1,170	969	23,772	11,451	12,321	12	10	2
55 to 59 years	20,364	9,852	10,512	1,201	686	515	19,161	9,164	9,997	2	2	-
60 to 64 years	16,867	7,904	8,963	842	443	399	16,019	7,456	8,563	6	5	1
65 to 69 years	12,846	5,804	7,042	472	232	240	12,372	5,570	6,802	2	2	-
70 to 74 years	8,816	3,847	4,969	294	136	158	8,522	3,711	4,811	-	-	-
75 years and over	7,665	3,000	4,665	286	140	146	7,378	2,859	4,519	1	1	-
Unknown	265	111	154	57	30	27	208	81	127	-	-	-
Cleveland	**900,429**	**456,856**	**443,573**	**71,899**	**36,180**	**35,719**	**827,090**	**419,541**	**407,549**	**1,440**	**1,135**	**305**
Under 5 years	70,538	35,784	34,754	6,458	3,186	3,272	63,942	32,525	31,417	138	73	65
Under 1 year	13,204	6,713	6,491	1,240	624	616	11,931	6,070	5,861	33	19	14
1 year	13,104	6,735	6,369	1,178	593	585	11,902	6,130	5,772	24	12	12
2 years	14,483	7,303	7,180	1,320	635	685	13,133	6,654	6,479	30	14	16
3 years	14,929	7,506	7,423	1,432	705	727	13,473	6,788	6,685	24	13	11
4 years	14,818	7,527	7,291	1,288	629	659	13,503	6,883	6,620	27	15	12
5 to 9 years	81,897	41,198	40,699	6,466	3,127	3,339	75,334	38,019	37,315	97	52	45
10 to 14 years	84,869	42,437	42,432	4,923	2,415	2,508	79,895	39,993	39,902	51	29	22
15 to 19 years	83,471	40,731	42,740	4,879	2,268	2,611	78,534	38,415	40,119	58	48	10
20 to 24 years	85,492	41,243	44,249	7,062	3,214	3,848	78,227	37,857	40,370	203	172	31
25 to 29 years	79,846	39,202	40,644	9,087	4,320	4,767	70,482	34,649	35,833	277	233	44
30 to 34 years	77,060	38,725	38,335	8,448	4,273	4,175	68,446	34,315	34,131	166	137	29
35 to 39 years	82,861	43,688	39,173	8,561	4,570	3,991	74,178	39,013	35,165	122	105	17
40 to 44 years	69,692	37,899	31,793	5,662	3,143	2,519	63,927	34,663	29,264	103	93	10
45 to 49 years	57,167	31,116	26,051	4,235	2,396	1,839	52,856	28,655	24,201	76	65	11
50 to 54 years	42,748	22,975	19,773	2,607	1,481	1,126	40,101	21,459	18,642	40	35	5
55 to 59 years	29,390	15,269	14,121	1,406	774	632	27,950	14,467	13,483	34	28	6
60 to 64 years	22,408	11,339	11,069	902	462	440	21,465	10,839	10,626	41	38	3
65 to 69 years	14,828	7,126	7,702	463	218	245	14,344	6,889	7,455	21	19	2
70 to 74 years	9,514	4,358	5,156	322	131	191	9,183	4,222	4,961	9	5	4
75 years and over	7,921	3,374	4,547	249	105	144	7,671	3,268	4,403	1	1	-
Unknown	727	392	335	169	97	72	555	293	262	3	2	1
Columbus	**290,564**	**143,359**	**147,205**	**32,774**	**17,126**	**15,648**	**257,595**	**126,070**	**131,525**	**195**	**163**	**32**
Under 5 years	22,142	11,169	10,973	2,612	1,302	1,310	19,521	9,862	9,659	9	5	4
Under 1 year	4,199	2,119	2,080	490	238	252	3,707	1,880	1,827	2	1	1
1 year	4,299	2,128	2,171	519	256	263	3,779	1,871	1,908	1	1	-
2 years	4,542	2,304	2,238	527	248	279	4,011	2,053	1,958	4	3	1
3 years	4,599	2,370	2,229	559	288	271	4,038	2,082	1,956	2	-	2
4 years	4,503	2,248	2,255	517	272	245	3,986	1,976	2,010	-	-	-
5 to 9 years	2,351	11,851	11,500	2,806	1,399	1,407	20,534	10,446	10,088	11	6	5
10 to 14 years	21,579	10,775	10,804	2,474	1,204	1,270	19,101	9,568	9,533	4	3	1
15 to 19 years	22,300	10,415	11,885	2,408	1,114	1,294	19,882	9,294	10,588	10	7	3
20 to 24 years	27,406	12,748	14,658	2,914	1,417	1,497	24,473	11,316	13,157	19	15	4
25 to 29 years	26,696	13,437	13,259	3,504	1,851	1,653	23,161	11,558	11,603	31	28	3
30 to 34 years	25,376	12,851	12,525	3,424	1,882	1,542	21,925	10,947	10,978	27	22	5
35 to 39 years	24,619	12,481	12,138	3,486	1,897	1,589	21,111	10,563	10,548	22	21	1
40 to 44 years	21,576	11,046	10,530	2,590	1,446	1,144	18,962	9,577	9,385	24	23	1
45 to 49 years	19,345	9,768	9,577	2,390	1,333	1,057	16,941	8,423	8,518	14	12	2
50 to 54 years	16,437	8,149	8,288	1,615	937	678	14,809	7,202	7,607	13	10	3
55 to 59 years	12,755	6,239	6,516	978	545	433	11,769	5,686	6,083	8	8	-
60 to 64 years	9,995	4,801	5,194	628	336	292	9,366	4,464	4,902	1	1	-
65 to 69 years	7,117	3,318	3,799	385	216	169	6,730	3,100	3,630	2	2	-
70 to 74 years	5,007	2,291	2,716	256	120	136	4,751	2,171	2,580	-	-	-
75 years and over	4,675	1,925	2,750	268	105	163	4,407	1,820	2,587	-	-	-
Unknown	188	95	93	36	22	14	152	73	79	-	-	-
Dayton	**200,982**	**99,822**	**101,160**	**17,077**	**8,608**	**8,469**	**183,831**	**91,157**	**92,674**	**74**	**57**	**17**
Under 5 years	15,860	8,062	7,798	1,576	754	822	14,281	7,307	6,974	3	1	2
Under 1 year	3,153	1,587	1,566	312	166	146	2,841	1,421	1,420	-	-	-
1 year	3,068	1,564	1,504	270	124	146	2,798	1,440	1,358	-	-	-
2 years	3,245	1,632	1,613	334	144	190	2,911	1,488	1,423	-	-	-
3 years	3,170	1,590	1,580	330	150	180	2,839	1,440	1,399	1	-	1
4 years	3,224	1,689	1,535	330	170	160	2,892	1,518	1,374	2	1	1
5 to 9 years	16,843	8,385	8,458	1,641	815	826	15,199	7,569	7,630	3	1	2
10 to 14 years	15,892	7,932	7,960	1,401	668	733	14,489	7,264	7,225	2	-	2
15 to 19 years	16,002	7,652	8,350	1,311	588	723	14,689	7,063	7,626	2	1	1
20 to 24 years	19,916	9,597	10,319	1,569	731	838	18,337	8,860	9,477	10	6	4
25 to 29 years	18,694	9,262	9,432	1,874	914	960	16,807	8,337	8,470	13	11	2
30 to 34 years	17,206	8,598	8,608	1,612	840	772	15,585	7,752	7,833	9	6	3
35 to 39 years	16,968	8,613	8,355	1,711	882	829	15,247	7,721	7,526	10	10	-
40 to 44 years	14,409	7,396	7,013	1,272	693	579	13,131	6,698	6,433	6	5	1
45 to 49 years	12,357	6,368	5,989	1,091	617	474	11,263	5,748	5,515	3	3	-
50 to 54 years	10,766	5,474	5,292	778	439	339	9,985	5,032	4,953	3	3	-
55 to 59 years	8,130	4,086	4,044	498	283	215	7,628	3,799	3,829	4	4	-
60 to 64 years	6,570	3,252	3,318	289	162	127	6,279	3,088	3,191	2	2	-
65 to 69 years	4,900	2,268	2,632	175	88	87	4,723	2,178	2,545	2	2	-
70 to 74 years	3,305	1,527	1,778	90	51	39	3,214	1,475	1,739	1	1	-
75 years and over	3,052	1,289	1,763	171	75	96	2,880	1,213	1,667	1	1	-
Unknown	112	61	51	18	8	10	94	53	41	-	-	-

TABLE 20.—AGE DISTRIBUTION BY 5-YEAR AGE PERIODS WITH SINGLE YEARS UNDER 5, BY COLOR, AND SEX FOR THE 80 CITIES HAVING 10,000 OR MORE NEGRO INHABITANTS: 1930—Continued

CITY AND AGE	ALL CLASSES			NEGRO			WHITE			OTHER RACES		
	Total	Male	Female	Total	Male	Female	Total	Male	Female	Total	Male	Female
OHIO—continued												
Toledo	**290, 718**	**147, 691**	**143, 027**	**13, 260**	**6, 967**	**6, 293**	**276, 741**	**140, 236**	**136, 505**	**717**	**488**	**229**
Under 5 years	23, 118	11, 714	11, 404	1, 115	549	566	21, 894	11, 104	10, 790	109	61	48
Under 1 year	4, 532	2, 311	2, 221	231	128	103	4, 284	2, 174	2, 110	17	9	8
1 year	4, 299	2, 176	2, 123	194	93	101	4, 087	2, 076	2, 011	18	7	11
2 years	4, 726	2, 391	2, 335	244	119	125	4, 455	2, 257	2, 198	27	15	12
3 years	4, 854	2, 406	2, 448	232	103	129	4, 598	2, 286	2, 312	24	17	7
4 years	4, 707	2, 430	2, 277	214	106	108	4, 470	2, 311	2, 159	23	13	10
5 to 9 years	24, 808	12, 461	12, 347	1, 109	535	574	23, 610	11, 874	11, 736	89	52	37
10 to 14 years	23, 207	11, 600	11, 607	830	432	398	22, 337	11, 149	11, 188	40	19	21
15 to 19 years	23, 455	11, 270	12, 185	843	374	469	22, 585	10, 875	11, 710	27	21	6
20 to 24 years	27, 419	13, 459	13, 960	1, 330	601	729	26, 014	12, 804	13, 210	75	54	21
25 to 29 years	26, 614	13, 634	12, 980	1, 671	842	829	24, 843	12, 718	12, 125	100	74	26
30 to 34 years	24, 984	13, 108	11, 876	1, 567	850	717	23, 333	12, 202	11, 131	84	56	28
35 to 39 years	25, 930	13, 783	12, 147	1, 556	870	686	24, 309	12, 863	11, 446	65	50	15
40 to 44 years	21, 533	11, 428	10, 105	1, 026	587	439	20, 455	10, 798	9, 657	52	43	9
45 to 49 years	18, 789	9, 881	8, 908	878	549	329	17, 875	9, 304	8, 571	36	28	8
50 to 54 years	15, 229	7, 880	7, 349	559	344	215	14, 657	7, 526	7, 131	13	10	3
55 to 59 years	11, 614	5, 853	5, 761	317	186	131	11, 284	5, 657	5, 627	13	10	3
60 to 64 years	9, 057	4, 502	4, 555	187	112	75	8, 865	4, 386	4, 479	5	4	1
65 to 69 years	6, 610	3, 244	3, 366	118	64	54	6, 485	3, 175	3, 310	7	5	2
70 to 74 years	4, 254	2, 049	2, 205	70	35	35	4, 184	2, 014	2, 170	-	-	-
75 years and over	4, 016	1, 778	3, 238	72	32	40	3, 943	1, 746	2, 197	1	-	1
Unknown	81	47	34	12	5	7	68	41	27	1	1	-
Youngstown	**170, 002**	**86, 739**	**83, 263**	**14, 552**	**7, 585**	**6, 967**	**155, 108**	**78, 898**	**76, 210**	**342**	**256**	**86**
Under 5 years	16, 069	7, 989	8, 080	1, 659	785	874	14, 371	7, 185	7, 186	39	19	20
Under 1 year	3, 023	1, 493	1, 530	331	172	159	2, 683	1, 319	1, 364	9	2	7
1 year	2, 932	1, 454	1, 478	298	138	160	2, 628	1, 315	1, 313	6	1	5
2 years	2, 231	1, 596	1, 635	343	155	188	2, 880	1, 437	1, 443	8	4	4
3 years	3, 453	1, 727	1, 726	365	164	201	3, 080	1, 555	1, 525	8	8	-
4 years	3, 430	1, 719	1, 711	322	156	166	3, 100	1, 559	1, 541	8	4	4
5 to 9 years	18, 382	9, 301	9, 081	1, 578	794	784	16, 772	8, 494	8, 278	32	13	19
10 to 14 years	17, 709	8, 909	8, 800	1, 120	532	588	16, 572	8, 363	8, 209	17	14	3
15 to 19 years	15, 586	7, 528	8, 058	999	451	548	14, 574	7, 069	7, 505	13	8	5
20 to 24 years	14, 810	7, 152	7, 658	1, 393	664	729	13, 378	6, 451	6, 927	39	37	2
25 to 29 years	14, 160	7, 050	7, 110	1, 857	941	916	12, 218	6, 041	6, 177	85	68	17
30 to 34 years	13, 558	6, 933	6, 625	1, 601	864	737	11, 919	6, 038	5, 881	38	31	7
35 to 39 years	14, 453	7, 712	6, 741	1, 510	861	649	12, 907	6, 822	6, 085	36	29	7
40 to 44 years	12, 483	6, 846	5, 637	983	593	390	11, 476	6, 233	5, 243	24	20	4
45 to 49 years	10, 304	5, 653	4, 651	774	470	304	9, 522	5, 176	4, 346	8	7	1
50 to 54 years	7, 809	4, 279	3, 530	478	286	192	7, 325	3, 988	3, 337	6	5	1
55 to 59 years	5, 360	2, 847	2, 513	255	147	108	5, 102	2, 697	2, 405	3	3	-
60 to 64 years	3, 763	1, 942	1, 821	137	76	61	3, 624	1, 864	1, 760	2	2	-
65 to 69 years	2, 539	1, 217	1, 322	87	51	36	2, 452	1, 166	1, 286	-	-	-
70 to 74 years	1, 568	754	814	47	31	16	1, 521	723	798	-	-	-
75 years and over	1, 386	596	790	58	28	30	1, 328	568	760	-	-	-
Unknown	63	31	32	16	11	5	47	20	27	-	-	-
OKLAHOMA												
Oklahoma City	**185, 389**	**93, 751**	**91, 638**	**14, 662**	**7, 171**	**7, 491**	**169, 033**	**85, 673**	**83, 360**	**1, 694**	**907**	**787**
Under 5 years	16, 250	8, 284	7, 966	1, 033	522	511	15, 007	7, 652	7, 355	210	110	100
Under 1 year	3, 249	1, 653	1, 596	199	106	93	3, 011	1, 522	1, 489	39	25	14
1 year	3, 305	1, 723	1, 582	183	90	93	3, 076	1, 612	1, 464	46	21	25
2 years	3, 167	1, 596	1, 571	223	109	114	2, 915	1, 472	1, 443	29	15	14
3 years	3, 287	1, 684	1, 603	217	106	111	3, 023	1, 555	1, 468	47	23	24
4 years	3, 242	1, 628	1, 614	211	111	100	2, 982	1, 491	1, 491	49	26	23
5 to 9 years	16, 416	8, 264	8, 152	1, 226	605	621	14, 961	7, 550	7, 411	229	109	120
10 to 14 years	13, 273	6, 541	6, 732	996	464	532	12, 121	6, 003	6, 118	156	74	82
15 to 19 years	15, 342	6, 765	8, 577	1, 287	554	733	13, 928	6, 159	7, 769	127	52	75
20 to 24 years	23, 222	10, 864	12, 358	2, 010	860	1, 150	21, 019	9, 922	11, 097	193	82	111
25 to 29 years	22, 001	10, 987	11, 014	2, 007	944	1, 063	19, 831	9, 963	9, 868	163	80	83
30 to 34 years	18, 235	9, 591	8, 644	1, 557	781	776	16, 527	8, 719	7, 808	151	91	60
35 to 39 years	15, 567	8, 296	7, 271	1, 359	689	670	14, 061	7, 507	6, 554	147	100	47
40 to 44 years	11, 956	6, 456	5, 500	1, 039	536	503	10, 828	5, 867	4, 961	89	53	36
45 to 49 years	9, 622	5, 158	4, 464	807	441	366	8, 743	4, 665	4, 078	72	52	20
50 to 54 years	7, 642	4, 193	3, 449	538	335	203	7, 045	3, 816	3, 229	59	42	17
55 to 59 years	5, 511	2, 978	2, 533	305	190	115	5, 178	2, 772	2, 406	28	16	12
60 to 64 years	3, 876	2, 035	1, 841	187	108	79	3, 661	1, 908	1, 753	28	19	9
65 to 69 years	2, 671	1, 416	1, 255	123	59	64	2, 526	1, 342	1, 184	22	15	7
70 to 74 years	1, 846	968	878	55	29	26	1, 779	930	849	12	9	3
75 years and over	1, 740	822	918	100	37	63	1, 634	783	851	6	2	4
Unknown	219	133	86	33	17	16	184	115	69	2	1	1
Tulsa	**141, 258**	**70, 114**	**71, 144**	**15, 203**	**7, 241**	**7, 962**	**123, 896**	**61, 778**	**62, 118**	**2, 159**	**1, 095**	**1, 064**
Under 5 years	12, 147	6, 175	5, 972	1, 034	514	520	10, 816	5, 511	5, 305	297	150	147
Under 1 year	2, 363	1, 224	1, 139	218	116	102	2, 096	1, 079	1, 017	49	29	20
1 year	2, 276	1, 137	1, 139	186	88	98	2, 038	1, 023	1, 015	52	26	26
2 years	2, 419	1, 222	1, 197	202	109	93	2, 158	1, 085	1, 073	59	28	31
3 years	2, 580	1, 296	1, 284	226	105	121	2, 285	1, 155	1, 130	69	36	33
4 years	2, 509	1, 296	1, 213	202	96	106	2, 239	1, 169	1, 070	68	31	37
5 to 9 years	13, 015	6, 526	6, 489	1, 101	539	562	11, 657	5, 867	5, 790	257	120	137
10 to 14 years	10, 706	5, 368	5, 338	966	469	497	9, 512	4, 777	4, 735	228	122	106
15 to 19 years	11, 199	5, 089	6, 110	1, 171	492	679	9, 808	4, 494	5, 314	220	103	117
20 to 24 years	15, 490	7, 026	8, 464	1, 945	791	1, 154	13, 319	6, 138	7, 181	226	97	129
25 to 29 years	16, 426	7, 622	8, 804	2, 317	1, 005	1, 312	13, 860	6, 486	7, 374	249	131	118
30 to 34 years	14, 708	7, 206	7, 502	1, 836	846	990	12, 676	6, 245	6, 431	196	115	81
35 to 39 years	13, 502	6, 921	6, 581	1, 657	851	806	11, 694	5, 986	5, 708	151	84	67
40 to 44 years	10, 145	5, 441	4, 704	1, 075	589	486	8, 950	4, 789	4, 161	120	63	57
45 to 49 years	7, 638	4, 151	3, 487	833	459	374	6, 727	3, 654	3, 073	78	38	40
50 to 54 years	5, 641	3, 104	2, 537	494	284	210	5, 091	2, 784	2, 307	56	36	20
55 to 59 years	3, 890	2, 044	1, 846	302	163	139	3, 552	1, 868	1, 684	36	13	23
60 to 64 years	2, 640	1, 391	1, 249	193	103	90	2, 424	1, 278	1, 146	23	10	13
65 to 69 years	1, 774	890	884	121	59	62	1, 643	826	817	10	5	5
70 to 74 years	1, 214	617	597	63	32	31	1, 145	581	564	6	4	2
75 years and over	1, 054	498	556	88	40	48	961	455	506	5	3	2
Unknown	69	45	24	7	5	2	61	39	22	1	1	-

TABLE 20.—AGE DISTRIBUTION BY 5-YEAR AGE PERIODS WITH SINGLE YEARS UNDER 5, BY COLOR, AND SEX FOR THE 80 CITIES HAVING 10,000 OR MORE NEGRO INHABITANTS: 1930—Continued

CITY AND AGE	ALL CLASSES			NEGRO			WHITE			OTHER RACES		
	Total	Male	Female	Total	Male	Female	Total	Male	Female	Total	Male	Female
PENNSYLVANIA												
Philadelphia	**1, 950, 961**	**968, 281**	**982, 680**	**219, 599**	**108, 483**	**111, 116**	**1, 728, 457**	**857, 403**	**871, 054**	**2, 905**	**2, 395**	**510**
Under 5 years	148, 409	75, 271	73, 138	18, 658	9, 311	9, 347	129, 548	65, 860	63, 688	203	100	103
Under 1 year	27, 614	13, 981	13, 633	3, 473	1, 773	1, 700	24, 093	12, 186	11, 907	48	22	26
1 year	27, 726	14, 141	13, 585	3, 404	1, 675	1, 729	24, 280	12, 441	11, 839	42	25	17
2 years	30, 658	15, 475	15, 183	3, 962	1, 972	1, 990	26, 657	13, 481	13, 176	39	22	17
3 years	31, 678	16, 099	15, 579	3, 994	2, 026	1, 968	27, 642	14, 057	13, 585	42	16	26
4 years	30, 733	15, 575	15, 158	3, 825	1, 865	1, 960	26, 876	13, 695	13, 181	32	15	17
5 to 9 years	168, 660	84, 935	83, 725	19, 300	9, 564	9, 736	149. 227	75, 315	73, 912	133	56	77
10 to 14 years	169, 323	84, 694	84, 629	15, 526	7, 485	8, 041	153, 703	77, 160	76, 543	94	49	45
15 to 19 years	169, 255	82, 678	86, 577	15, 908	7, 008	8, 900	153, 262	75, 615	77, 647	85	55	30
20 to 24 years	181, 832	87, 289	94, 543	22, 527	9, 812	12, 715	159, 061	77, 269	81, 792	244	208	36
25 to 29 years	174, 760	86, 243	88, 517	27, 726	13, 303	14, 423	146. 655	72, 597	74, 058	379	343	36
30 to 34 years	165, 287	83, 205	82, 082	24, 093	12, 182	11, 911	140, 753	70, 621	70, 132	441	402	39
35 to 39 years	167, 771	85, 210	82, 561	23, 642	12, 134	11, 508	143, 740	72, 730	71, 010	389	346	43
40 to 44 years	140, 258	72, 223	68, 035	16, 639	8, 911	7, 728	123, 295	63, 022	60, 273	324	290	34
45 to 49 years	119, 529	60, 702	58, 827	13, 485	7, 206	6, 279	105, 817	53, 290	52, 527	227	206	21
50 to 54 years	102, 587	51, 355	51, 232	9, 372	5, 177	4, 195	93, 059	46, 039	47, 020	156	139	17
55 to 59 years	79, 376	38, 730	40, 646	5, 275	2, 862	2, 413	73, 992	35, 773	38, 219	109	95	14
60 to 64 years	64, 098	30, 814	33, 284	3, 244	1, 616	1, 628	60, 783	29, 136	31, 647	71	62	9
65 to 69 years	44, 447	21, 039	23, 408	1, 855	910	945	42, 566	20, 107	22, 459	26	22	4
70 to 74 years	29, 014	13, 197	15, 817	1, 086	507	579	27, 917	12, 679	15, 238	11	11	-
75 years and over	25, 234	10, 173	15, 061	1, 029	388	641	24, 193	9, 775	14, 418	12	10	2
Unknown	1, 121	523	598	234	107	127	886	415	471	1	1	-
Pittsburgh	**669, 817**	**332, 576**	**337, 241**	**54, 983**	**27, 962**	**27, 021**	**614, 317**	**304, 194**	**310, 123**	**517**	**420**	**97**
Under 5 years	57, 090	29, 222	27, 868	4, 934	2, 448	2, 486	52, 120	26, 759	25, 361	36	15	21
Under 1 year	10, 765	5, 573	5, 192	912	444	468	9, 845	5, 124	4, 721	8	5	3
1 year	10, 906	5, 645	5, 261	939	478	461	9, 962	5, 166	4, 796	5	1	4
2 years	11, 593	5, 878	5, 715	1, 023	501	522	10, 565	5, 377	5, 188	5	-	5
3 years	11, 899	6, 121	5, 778	1, 013	514	499	10, 876	5, 602	5, 274	10	5	5
4 years	11, 927	6, 005	5, 922	1, 047	511	536	10, 872	5, 490	5, 382	8	4	4
5 to 9 years	62, 158	31, 171	30, 987	5, 035	2, 454	2, 581	57, 085	28, 694	28, 391	38	23	15
10 to 14 years	61, 915	30, 718	31, 197	4, 068	1, 962	2, 106	57, 833	28, 747	29, 086	14	9	5
15 to 19 years	62, 382	29, 950	32, 432	4, 043	1, 831	2, 212	58, 310	28, 093	30, 217	29	26	3
20 to 24 years	62, 497	29, 110	33, 387	5, 190	2, 357	2, 833	57, 246	26, 700	30, 546	61	53	8
25 to 29 years	57, 304	27, 765	29, 539	6, 362	3, 183	3, 179	50, 865	24, 514	26, 351	77	68	9
30 to 34 years	54, 388	27, 398	26, 990	6, 019	3, 188	2, 831	48, 291	24, 143	24, 148	78	67	11
35 to 39 years	54, 996	28, 066	26, 930	5, 757	3, 065	2, 692	49, 184	24, 955	24, 229	55	46	9
40 to 44 years	46, 867	24, 276	22, 591	4, 201	2, 283	1, 918	42, 624	21, 953	20, 671	42	40	2
45 to 49 years	41, 473	21, 423	20, 050	3, 566	2, 006	1, 560	37, 879	19, 396	18, 483	28	21	7
50 to 54 years	34, 316	17, 686	16, 630	2, 478	1, 414	1, 064	31, 817	16, 254	15, 563	21	18	3
55 to 59 years	25, 663	12, 815	12, 848	1, 430	802	628	24, 213	11, 996	12, 217	20	17	3
60 to 64 years	19, 679	9, 750	9, 929	837	463	374	18, 833	9, 278	9, 555	9	9	-
65 to 69 years	13, 618	6, 509	7, 109	492	258	234	13, 123	6, 248	6, 875	3	3	-
70 to 74 years	8, 359	3, 831	4, 528	293	135	158	8, 063	3, 693	4, 370	3	3	-
75 years and over	6, 844	2, 754	4, 090	246	101	145	6, 595	2, 651	3, 944	3	2	1
Unknown	268	132	136	32	12	20	236	120	116	-	-	-
SOUTH CAROLINA												
Charleston	**62, 264**	**28, 382**	**33, 883**	**28, 062**	**11, 955**	**16, 107**	**34, 177**	**16, 403**	**17, 774**	**26**	**24**	**2**
Under 5 years	5, 915	2, 937	2, 978	2, 768	1, 310	1, 458	3, 144	1, 624	1, 520	3	3	-
Under 1 year	1, 064	544	520	489	238	251	575	306	269	-	-	-
1 year	1, 111	522	589	545	242	303	565	279	286	1	1	-
2 years	1, 261	652	609	589	303	286	672	349	323	-	-	-
3 years	1, 222	623	599	572	274	298	650	349	301	-	-	-
4 years	1, 257	596	661	573	253	320	682	341	341	2	2	-
to 9 years	6, 461	3, 222	3, 239	3, 072	1, 516	1, 556	3, 387	1, 704	1, 683	2	2	-
10 to 14 years	5, 808	2, 820	2, 988	2, 663	1, 254	1, 409	3, 145	1, 566	1, 579	-	-	-
15 to 19 years	6, 031	2, 649	3, 382	2, 902	1, 144	1, 758	3, 128	1, 505	1, 623	1	-	1
20 to 24 years	6, 665	2, 715	3, 950	3, 352	1, 196	2, 156	3, 311	1, 517	1, 794	2	2	-
25 to 29 years	5, 838	2, 449	3, 389	2, 974	1, 120	1, 854	2, 862	1, 327	1, 535	2	2	-
30 to 34 years	4, 615	2, 106	2, 509	2, 120	863	1, 257	2, 493	1, 241	1, 252	2	2	-
35 to 39 years	5, 137	2, 336	2, 801	2, 470	1, 028	1, 442	2, 664	1, 305	1, 359	3	3	-
40 to 44 years	4, 027	1, 926	2, 101	1, 761	782	979	2, 264	1, 143	1, 121	2	1	1
45 to 49 years	3, 333	1, 573	1, 760	1, 390	622	768	1, 942	950	992	1	1	-
50 to 54 years	2, 668	1, 207	1, 461	943	416	527	1, 721	787	934	4	4	-
55 to 59 years	1, 852	851	1, 001	531	229	302	1, 321	622	699	-	-	-
60 to 64 years	1, 535	670	865	470	217	253	1, 063	451	612	2	2	-
65 to 69 years	1, 014	400	614	297	123	174	715	275	440	2	2	-
70 to 74 years	668	275	393	175	72	103	493	203	290	-	-	-
75 years and over	659	230	429	161	61	100	498	169	329	-	-	-
Unknown	39	16	23	13	2	11	26	14	12	-	-	-
Columbia	**51, 581**	**24, 005**	**27, 576**	**19, 519**	**8, 484**	**11, 035**	**32, 042**	**15, 507**	**16, 535**	**20**	**14**	**6**
Under 5 years	3, 959	1, 946	2, 013	1, 436	676	760	2, 520	1, 267	1, 253	3	3	-
Under 1 year	759	385	374	258	122	136	500	262	238	1	1	-
1 year	704	340	364	249	116	133	454	223	231	1	1	-
2 years	813	406	407	303	153	150	510	253	257	-	-	-
3 years	844	407	437	321	148	173	522	258	264	1	1	-
4 years	839	408	431	305	137	168	534	271	263	-	-	-
5 to 9 years	4, 829	2, 418	2, 411	1, 849	899	950	2, 978	1, 517	1, 461	2	2	-
10 to 14 years	4, 427	2, 150	2, 277	1, 806	824	982	2, 619	1, 326	1, 293	2	-	2
15 to 19 years	5, 090	2, 160	2, 930	2, 264	851	1, 413	2, 821	1, 306	1, 515	5	3	2
20 to 24 years	5, 937	2, 519	3, 418	2, 460	976	1, 484	3, 475	1, 542	1, 933	2	1	1
25 to 29 years	5, 205	2, 270	2, 935	2, 027	806	1, 221	3, 178	1, 464	1, 714	-	-	-
30 to 34 years	4, 488	2, 126	2, 362	1, 595	699	896	2, 891	1, 425	1, 466	2	2	-
35 to 39 years	4, 455	2, 154	2, 301	1, 664	730	934	2, 789	1, 422	1, 367	2	2	-
40 to 44 years	3, 504	1, 642	1, 862	1, 323	592	731	2, 181	1, 050	1, 131	-	-	-
45 to 49 years	2, 969	1, 435	1, 534	1, 026	456	570	1, 943	979	964	-	-	-
50 to 54 years	2, 454	1, 231	1, 223	814	404	410	1, 639	826	813	1	1	-
55 to 59 years	1, 515	756	759	407	205	202	1, 108	551	557	-	-	-
60 to 64 years	1, 095	554	541	343	177	166	752	377	375	-	-	-
65 to 69 years	678	275	403	215	81	134	462	194	268	1	-	1
70 to 74 years	494	206	288	145	58	87	349	148	201	-	-	-
75 years and over	436	148	288	106	36	70	330	112	218	-	-	-
Unknown	46	15	31	39	14	25	7	1	6	-	-	-

TABLE 20.—AGE DISTRIBUTION BY 5-YEAR AGE PERIODS WITH SINGLE YEARS UNDER 5, BY COLOR, AND SEX FOR THE 80 CITIES HAVING 10,000 OR MORE NEGRO INHABITANTS: 1930—Continued

CITY AND AGE	ALL CLASSES			NEGRO			WHITE			OTHER RACES		
	Total	Male	Female	Total	Male	Female	Total	Male	Female	Total	Male	Female
SOUTH CAROLINA—continued												
Greenville	**29,154**	**13,401**	**15,753**	**10,871**	**4,843**	**6,028**	**18,279**	**8,554**	**9,725**	**4**	**4**	-
Under 5 years	2,462	1,256	1,206	968	476	492	1,494	780	714	-	-	-
Under 1 year	445	238	207	190	98	92	255	140	115	-	-	-
1 year	421	198	223	168	78	90	253	120	133	-	-	-
2 years	504	262	242	200	94	106	304	168	136	-	-	-
3 years	541	264	277	212	97	115	329	167	162	-	-	-
4 years	551	294	257	198	109	89	353	185	168	-	-	-
5 to 9 years	2,961	1,473	1,488	1,153	583	570	1,808	890	918	-	-	-
10 to 14 years	2,659	1,280	1,379	1,044	485	559	1,615	795	820	-	-	-
15 to 19 years	2,910	1,296	1,614	1,267	568	699	1,643	728	915	-	-	-
20 to 24 years	3,483	1,387	2,096	1,425	536	889	2,058	851	1,207	-	-	-
25 to 29 years	2,993	1,262	1,731	1,165	484	681	1,828	778	1,050	-	-	-
30 to 34 years	2,437	1,112	1,325	889	395	494	1,548	717	831	-	-	-
35 to 39 years	2,414	1,130	1,284	876	386	490	1,538	744	794	-	-	-
40 to 44 years	1,741	787	954	568	225	343	1,173	562	611	-	-	-
45 to 49 years	1,487	694	793	466	190	276	1,021	504	517	-	-	-
50 to 54 years	1,250	642	608	375	202	173	874	439	435	1	1	-
55 to 59 years	742	360	382	198	92	106	544	268	276	-	-	-
60 to 64 years	595	294	301	179	98	81	415	195	220	1	1	-
65 to 69 years	380	168	212	88	43	45	290	123	167	2	2	-
70 to 74 years	296	130	166	77	31	46	219	99	120	-	-	-
75 years and over	281	107	174	83	30	53	198	77	121	-	-	-
Unknown	63	23	40	50	19	31	13	4	9	-	-	-
TENNESSEE												
Chattanooga	**119,798**	**57,932**	**61,866**	**33,289**	**15,690**	**17,599**	**86,495**	**42,230**	**44,265**	**14**	**12**	**2**
Under 5 years	10,594	5,377	5,217	2,618	1,266	1,352	7,976	4,111	3,865	-	-	-
Under 1 year	2,089	1,089	1,000	456	233	223	1,633	856	777	-	-	-
1 year	1,951	987	964	449	206	243	1,502	781	721	-	-	-
2 years	2,158	1,057	1,101	566	253	313	1,592	804	788	-	-	-
3 years	2,234	1,155	1,079	567	292	275	1,667	863	804	-	-	-
4 years	2,162	1,089	1,073	580	282	298	1,582	807	775	-	-	-
5 to 9 years	12,141	6,078	6,063	3,128	1,529	1,599	9,013	4,549	4,464	-	-	-
10 to 14 years	10,264	5,083	5,181	2,793	1,340	1,453	7,471	3,743	3,728	-	-	-
15 to 19 years	11,359	5,295	6,064	3,167	1,404	1,763	8,191	3,890	4,301	1	1	-
20 to 24 years	13,426	6,000	7,426	3,911	1,616	2,295	9,513	4,383	5,130	2	1	1
25 to 29 years	12,296	5,680	6,616	3,875	1,726	2,149	8,419	3,953	4,466	2	1	1
30 to 34 years	10,200	4,866	5,334	3,019	1,424	1,595	7,179	3,440	3,739	2	2	-
35 to 39 years	9,931	4,888	5,043	3,171	1,533	1,638	6,759	3,354	3,405	1	1	-
40 to 44 years	7,393	3,668	3,725	2,118	1,055	1,063	5,272	2,610	2,662	3	3	-
45 to 49 years	6,390	3,202	3,188	1,803	898	905	4,586	2,303	2,283	1	1	-
50 to 54 years	5,645	2,851	2,794	1,648	863	785	3,997	1,988	2,009	-	-	-
55 to 59 years	3,616	1,863	1,753	806	430	376	2,809	1,432	1,377	1	1	-
60 to 64 years	2,632	1,326	1,306	567	303	264	2,064	1,022	1,042	1	1	-
65 to 69 years	1,647	750	897	288	133	155	1,359	617	742	-	-	-
70 to 74 years	1,198	547	651	182	90	92	1,016	457	559	-	-	-
75 years and over	1,050	449	601	192	78	114	858	371	487	-	-	-
Unknown	16	9	7	3	2	1	13	7	6	-	-	-
Knoxville	**105,802**	**50,973**	**54,829**	**17,093**	**8,131**	**8,962**	**88,705**	**42,838**	**45,867**	**4**	**4**	-
Under 5 years	10,048	5,122	4,926	1,314	642	672	8,734	4,480	4,254	-	-	-
Under 1 year	2,012	1,034	978	245	119	126	1,767	915	852	-	-	-
1 year	1,956	1,007	949	247	129	118	1,709	878	831	-	-	-
2 years	2,004	1,019	985	254	125	129	1,750	894	856	-	-	-
3 years	2,000	1,049	951	267	140	127	1,733	909	824	-	-	-
4 years	2,076	1,013	1,063	301	129	172	1,775	884	891	-	-	-
5 to 9 years	10,360	5,185	5,175	1,469	689	780	8,891	4,496	4,395	-	-	-
10 to 14 years	9,306	4,590	4,716	1,436	717	719	7,870	3,873	3,997	-	-	-
15 to 19 years	10,219	4,813	5,406	1,660	771	889	8,559	4,042	4,517	-	-	-
20 to 24 years	11,861	5,255	6,606	2,089	909	1,180	9,771	4,345	5,426	1	1	-
25 to 29 years	10,519	4,787	5,732	1,904	836	1,068	8,613	3,949	4,664	2	2	-
30 to 34 years	8,676	4,231	4,445	1,477	711	766	7,199	3,520	3,679	-	-	-
35 to 39 years	8,032	3,858	4,174	1,519	747	772	6,513	3,111	3,402	-	-	-
40 to 44 years	6,547	3,199	3,348	1,141	534	607	5,406	2,665	2,741	-	-	-
45 to 49 years	5,509	2,715	2,794	944	470	474	4,565	2,245	2,320	-	-	-
50 to 54 years	4,953	2,538	2,415	809	435	374	4,144	2,103	2,041	-	-	-
55 to 59 years	3,440	1,691	1,749	481	264	217	2,959	1,427	1,532	-	-	-
60 to 64 years	2,514	1,235	1,279	308	152	156	2,205	1,082	1,123	1	1	-
65 to 69 years	1,620	768	852	201	97	104	1,419	671	748	-	-	-
70 to 74 years	1,064	500	564	133	57	76	931	443	488	-	-	-
75 years and over	972	403	569	132	57	75	840	346	494	-	-	-
Unknown	162	83	79	76	43	33	86	40	46	-	-	-
Memphis	**253,143**	**120,581**	**132,562**	**96,550**	**44,859**	**51,691**	**156,528**	**75,672**	**80,856**	**65**	**50**	**15**
Under 5 years	19,718	10,062	9,656	7,062	3,537	3,525	12,649	6,522	6,127	7	3	4
Under 1 year	3,743	1,974	1,769	1,337	671	666	2,405	1,302	1,103	1	1	-
1 year	3,558	1,840	1,718	1,208	615	593	2,349	1,224	1,125	1	1	-
2 years	4,054	2,029	2,025	1,488	732	756	2,565	1,297	1,268	1	-	1
3 years	4,217	2,138	2,079	1,501	763	738	2,715	1,374	1,341	1	1	-
4 years	4,146	2,081	2,065	1,528	756	772	2,615	1,325	1,290	3	-	3
5 to 9 years	21,071	10,479	10,592	7,489	3,686	3,803	13,579	6,790	6,789	3	3	-
10 to 14 years	18,317	8,968	9,349	6,511	3,087	3,424	11,805	5,880	5,925	1	1	-
15 to 19 years	20,917	9,201	11,716	7,918	3,276	4,642	12,994	5,920	7,074	5	5	-
20 to 24 years	27,780	11,950	15,830	10,847	4,482	6,365	16,931	7,466	9,465	2	2	-
25 to 29 years	27,994	12,504	15,490	11,987	5,087	6,900	16,003	7,415	8,588	4	2	2
30 to 34 years	23,153	10,964	12,189	9,208	4,219	4,989	13,936	6,738	7,198	9	7	2
35 to 39 years	23,110	11,148	11,962	9,780	4,525	5,255	13,323	6,617	6,706	7	6	1
40 to 44 years	18,146	9,119	9,027	7,187	3,595	3,592	10,953	5,519	5,434	6	5	1
45 to 49 years	15,268	7,676	7,592	6,042	3,017	3,025	9,217	4,653	4,564	9	6	3
50 to 54 years	12,829	6,604	6,225	4,863	2,598	2,265	7,957	3,998	3,959	9	8	1
55 to 59 years	8,462	4,219	4,243	2,694	1,415	1,279	5,768	2,804	2,964	-	-	-
60 to 64 years	6,312	3,094	3,218	2,003	986	1,017	4,309	2,108	2,201	-	-	-
65 to 69 years	4,056	1,972	2,084	1,143	581	562	2,911	1,389	1,522	2	2	-
70 to 74 years	2,616	1,163	1,453	701	301	400	1,915	862	1,053	-	-	-
75 years and over	2,758	1,159	1,599	843	338	505	1,915	821	1,094	-	-	-
Unknown	636	299	337	272	129	143	363	170	193	1	-	1

TABLE 20.—AGE DISTRIBUTION BY 5-YEAR AGE PERIODS WITH SINGLE YEARS UNDER 5, BY COLOR, AND SEX FOR THE 80 CITIES HAVING 10,000 OR MORE NEGRO INHABITANTS: 1930—Continued

CITY AND AGE	ALL CLASSES			NEGRO			WHITE			OTHER RACES		
	Total	Male	Female	Total	Male	Female	Total	Male	Female	Total	Male	Female
TENNESSEE—continued												
Nashville	**153,866**	**71,945**	**81,921**	**42,836**	**19,464**	**23,372**	**111,025**	**52,477**	**58,548**	**5**	**4**	**1**
Under 5 years	12,376	6,231	6,145	3,083	1,537	1,546	9,293	4,694	4,599			
Under 1 year	2,568	1,290	1,278	636	315	321	1,932	975	957			
1 year	2,342	1,213	1,129	536	278	258	1,806	935	871			
2 years	2,452	1,213	1,239	628	302	326	1,824	911	913			
3 years	2,501	1,247	1,254	636	308	328	1,865	939	926			
4 years	2,513	1,268	1,245	647	334	313	1,866	934	932			
5 to 9 years	13,794	6,830	6,964	3,681	1,759	1,922	10,113	5,071	5,042			
10 to 14 years	12,477	6,111	6,366	3,400	1,660	1,740	9,077	4,451	4,626			
15 to 19 years	14,014	6,446	7,568	4,067	1,784	2,283	9,947	4,662	5,285			
20 to 24 years	16,259	7,019	9,240	4,442	1,815	2,627	11,816	5,203	6,613	1	1	
25 to 29 years	14,716	6,512	8,204	4,355	1,846	2,509	10,359	4,664	5,695	2	2	
30 to 34 years	12,446	5,729	6,717	3,521	1,530	1,991	8,925	4,199	4,726			
35 to 39 years	12,302	5,658	6,644	3,724	1,593	2,131	8,577	4,065	4,512	1		1
40 to 44 years	9,857	4,613	5,244	2,872	1,297	1,575	6,985	3,316	3,669			
45 to 49 years	8,932	4,211	4,721	2,699	1,268	1,431	6,232	2,942	3,290	1	1	
50 to 54 years	8,670	4,170	4,500	2,681	1,304	1,377	5,989	2,866	3,123			
55 to 59 years	5,983	2,894	3,089	1,476	755	721	4,507	2,139	2,368			
60 to 64 years	4,646	2,227	2,419	1,155	574	581	3,491	1,653	1,838			
65 to 69 years	3,160	1,500	1,660	701	335	366	2,459	1,165	1,294			
70 to 74 years	2,132	948	1,184	461	216	245	1,671	732	939			
75 years and over	2,031	815	1,216	473	172	301	1,558	643	915			
Unknown	71	31	40	45	19	26	26	12	14			
TEXAS												
Beaumont	**57,732**	**28,844**	**28,888**	**18,551**	**8,967**	**9,584**	**38,507**	**19,512**	**18,995**	**674**	**365**	**309**
Under 5 years	5,233	2,649	2,584	1,690	832	858	3,456	1,764	1,692	87	53	34
Under 1 year	1,025	517	508	302	151	151	701	350	351	22	16	6
1 year	1,038	530	508	294	134	160	723	383	340	21	13	8
2 years	1,051	503	548	376	170	206	660	325	335	15	8	7
3 years	1,067	555	512	361	189	172	687	356	331	19	10	9
4 years	1,052	544	508	357	188	169	685	350	335	10	6	4
5 to 9 years	5,466	2,739	2,727	1,852	901	951	3,507	1,793	1,714	107	45	62
10 to 14 years	4,887	2,428	2,459	1,638	805	833	3,176	1,582	1,594	73	41	32
15 to 19 years	5,530	2,564	2,966	1,846	808	1,038	3,614	1,724	1,890	70	32	38
20 to 24 years	6,872	3,099	3,773	2,298	957	1,341	4,519	2,116	2,403	55	26	29
25 to 29 years	6,640	3,275	3,365	2,312	1,090	1,222	4,281	2,160	2,121	47	25	22
30 to 34 years	5,247	2,670	2,577	1,658	812	846	3,538	1,830	1,708	51	28	23
35 to 39 years	4,862	2,503	2,359	1,723	851	872	3,090	1,623	1,467	49	29	20
40 to 44 years	3,688	1,954	1,734	1,219	654	565	2,429	1,276	1,153	40	24	16
45 to 49 years	3,064	1,671	1,393	1,004	565	439	2,019	1,077	942	41	29	12
50 to 54 years	2,240	1,174	1,066	536	280	256	1,685	884	801	19	10	9
55 to 59 years	1,412	745	667	279	158	121	1,118	579	539	15	8	7
60 to 64 years	946	501	445	186	87	99	756	410	346	4	4	
65 to 69 years	700	371	329	151	87	64	541	278	263	8	6	2
70 to 74 years	422	235	187	52	23	29	365	208	157	5	4	1
75 years and over	421	207	214	86	45	41	333	161	172	2	1	1
Unknown	102	59	43	21	12	9	80	47	33	1		1
Dallas	**260,475**	**126,071**	**134,404**	**38,742**	**18,101**	**20,641**	**215,720**	**104,799**	**110,921**	**6,013**	**3,171**	**2,842**
Under 5 years	20,738	10,507	10,231	2,751	1,404	1,347	17,021	8,623	8,398	966	480	486
Under 1 year	3,967	2,033	1,934	496	243	253	3,253	1,676	1,577	218	114	104
1 year	3,947	2,069	1,878	550	303	247	3,219	1,672	1,547	178	94	84
2 years	4,165	2,087	2,078	548	282	266	3,419	1,712	1,707	198	93	105
3 years	4,308	2,138	2,170	556	276	280	3,560	1,775	1,785	192	87	105
4 years	4,351	2,180	2,171	601	300	301	3,570	1,788	1,782	180	92	88
5 to 9 years	22,826	11,367	11,459	3,070	1,495	1,575	18,890	9,442	9,448	866	430	436
10 to 14 years	19,392	9,667	9,725	2,726	1,315	1,411	16,101	8,086	8,015	565	266	299
15 to 19 years	21,659	9,903	11,756	3,263	1,326	1,937	17,843	8,297	9,546	553	280	273
20 to 24 years	28,903	12,880	16,023	4,510	1,756	2,754	23,774	10,780	12,994	619	344	275
25 to 29 years	30,387	13,930	16,457	5,177	2,243	2,934	24,613	11,365	13,248	597	322	275
30 to 34 years	26,028	12,714	13,314	4,320	2,057	2,263	21,268	10,398	10,870	440	259	181
35 to 39 years	23,667	11,827	11,840	3,897	1,900	1,997	19,299	9,659	9,640	471	268	203
40 to 44 years	18,189	9,327	8,862	2,973	1,446	1,527	14,930	7,726	7,204	286	155	131
45 to 49 years	14,270	7,181	7,089	2,352	1,239	1,113	11,651	5,789	5,862	267	153	114
50 to 54 years	11,029	5,595	5,434	1,459	792	667	9,454	4,744	4,710	116	59	57
55 to 59 years	7,790	3,858	3,932	769	410	359	6,923	3,389	3,534	98	59	39
60 to 64 years	5,828	2,815	3,013	601	323	278	5,156	2,447	2,709	71	45	26
65 to 69 years	3,931	1,825	2,106	357	182	175	3,534	1,624	1,910	40	19	21
70 to 74 years	2,799	1,285	1,514	210	92	118	2,568	1,180	1,388	21	13	8
75 years and over	2,673	1,206	1,467	245	87	158	2,401	1,105	1,296	27	14	13
Unknown	366	184	182	62	34	28	294	145	149	10	5	5
Fort Worth	**163,447**	**80,015**	**83,432**	**22,234**	**10,560**	**11,674**	**137,197**	**67,320**	**69,877**	**4,016**	**2,135**	**1,881**
Under 5 years	13,023	6,551	6,472	1,488	742	746	10,867	5,486	5,381	668	323	345
Under 1 year	2,374	1,187	1,187	283	151	132	1,951	959	992	140	77	63
1 year	2,445	1,242	1,203	296	149	147	2,029	1,038	991	120	55	65
2 years	2,644	1,324	1,320	285	142	143	2,235	1,128	1,107	124	54	70
3 years	2,782	1,391	1,391	332	156	176	2,305	1,160	1,145	145	75	70
4 years	2,778	1,407	1,371	292	144	148	2,347	1,201	1,146	139	62	77
5 to 9 years	15,269	7,671	7,598	1,841	875	966	12,825	6,473	6,352	603	323	280
10 to 14 years	13,417	6,671	6,746	1,729	821	908	11,252	5,623	5,629	436	227	209
15 to 19 years	14,041	6,512	7,529	1,831	811	1,020	11,886	5,538	6,348	324	163	161
20 to 24 years	16,876	7,580	9,296	2,441	1,026	1,415	14,071	6,340	7,731	364	214	150
25 to 29 years	16,698	7,696	9,002	2,732	1,197	1,535	13,657	6,341	7,316	309	158	151
30 to 34 years	15,242	7,334	7,908	2,398	1,121	1,277	12,496	6,040	6,456	348	173	175
35 to 39 years	14,574	7,261	7,313	2,361	1,113	1,248	11,896	5,973	5,923	317	175	142
40 to 44 years	11,518	5,963	5,555	1,794	946	848	9,514	4,886	4,628	210	131	79
45 to 49 years	9,529	5,002	4,527	1,436	773	663	7,900	4,120	3,780	193	109	84
50 to 54 years	7,320	3,897	3,423	803	461	342	6,437	3,385	3,052	80	51	29
55 to 59 years	5,300	2,660	2,640	460	247	213	4,782	2,380	2,402	58	33	25
60 to 64 years	3,915	1,970	1,945	342	175	167	3,525	1,771	1,754	48	24	24
65 to 69 years	2,625	1,308	1,317	217	99	118	2,380	1,195	1,185	28	14	14
70 to 74 years	1,876	895	981	127	50	77	1,730	833	897	19	12	7
75 years and over	1,831	833	998	156	69	87	1,666	761	905	9	3	6
Unknown	393	211	182	78	34	44	313	175	138	2	2	

TABLE 20.—AGE DISTRIBUTION BY 5-YEAR AGE PERIODS WITH SINGLE YEARS UNDER 5, BY COLOR, AND SEX FOR THE 80 CITIES HAVING 10,000 OR MORE NEGRO INHABITANTS: 1930—Continued

CITY AND AGE	ALL CLASSES			NEGRO			WHITE			OTHER RACES		
	Total	Male	Female	Total	Male	Female	Total	Male	Female	Total	Male	Female
TEXAS—continued												
Galveston	**52,938**	**27,495**	**25,443**	**13,226**	**6,402**	**6,824**	**37,060**	**19,575**	**17,485**	**2,652**	**1,518**	**1,134**
Under 5 years	4,102	2,053	2,049	945	467	478	2,771	1,410	1,361	386	176	210
Under 1 year	806	397	409	181	79	102	531	282	249	94	36	58
1 year	788	379	409	169	89	80	567	273	294	52	17	35
2 years	826	440	386	197	105	92	548	289	259	81	46	35
3 years	849	437	412	200	96	104	568	300	268	81	41	40
4 years	833	400	433	198	98	100	557	266	291	78	36	42
5 to 9 years	4,260	2,130	2,130	1,008	489	519	2,845	1,427	1,418	407	214	193
10 to 14 years	3,699	1,787	1,912	800	376	424	2,667	1,284	1,383	232	127	105
15 to 19 years	4,244	2,023	2,221	1,032	434	598	3,026	1,481	1,545	186	108	78
20 to 24 years	5,849	2,851	2,998	1,486	575	911	4,094	2,117	1,977	269	159	110
25 to 29 years	5,949	3,102	2,847	1,787	816	971	3,873	2,121	1,752	289	165	124
30 to 34 years	5,002	2,672	2,330	1,443	716	727	3,334	1,823	1,511	225	133	92
35 to 39 years	4,641	2,475	2,166	1,442	697	745	2,998	1,639	1,359	201	139	62
40 to 44 years	3,929	2,197	1,732	1,072	596	476	2,669	1,476	1,193	188	125	63
45 to 49 years	3,333	1,868	1,465	871	492	379	2,360	1,311	1,049	102	65	37
50 to 54 years	2,491	1,433	1,058	512	307	205	1,911	1,082	829	68	44	24
55 to 59 years	1,849	1,016	833	294	177	117	1,521	819	702	34	20	14
60 to 64 years	1,421	793	628	249	130	119	1,140	642	498	32	21	11
65 to 69 years	979	533	446	119	54	65	848	471	377	12	8	4
70 to 74 years	569	294	275	63	30	33	497	258	239	9	6	3
75 years and over	599	252	347	96	41	55	493	205	288	10	6	4
Unknown	22	16	6	7	5	2	13	9	4	2	2	----
Houston	**292,352**	**145,962**	**146,390**	**63,337**	**30,160**	**33,177**	**214,687**	**108,149**	**106,538**	**14,328**	**7,653**	**6,675**
Under 5 years	23,783	12,058	11,725	4,588	2,323	2,265	17,083	8,694	8,389	2,112	1,041	1,071
Under 1 year	4,504	2,262	2,242	876	449	427	3,218	1,603	1,615	410	210	200
1 year	4,629	2,254	2,375	869	419	450	3,319	1,639	1,680	441	196	245
2 years	4,883	2,502	2,381	983	491	492	3,468	1,789	1,679	432	222	210
3 years	4,906	2,534	2,372	930	498	432	3,530	1,823	1,707	446	213	233
4 years	4,861	2,506	2,355	930	466	464	3,548	1,840	1,708	383	200	183
5 to 9 years	25,495	12,784	12,711	5,101	2,499	2,652	18,322	9,309	9,013	2,072	1,026	1,046
10 to 14 years	21,525	10,671	10,854	4,312	2,049	2,263	15,916	7,954	7,962	1,297	668	629
15 to 19 years	25,033	11,559	13,474	5,443	2,249	3,194	18,400	8,732	9,668	1,190	578	612
20 to 24 years	34,343	16,014	18,329	8,059	3,429	4,630	24,740	11,735	13,005	1,544	850	694
25 to 29 years	34,850	16,953	17,897	8,766	3,929	4,837	24,444	12,103	12,341	1,640	921	719
30 to 34 years	29,147	14,901	14,246	6,932	3,372	3,560	20,956	10,800	10,156	1,259	729	530
35 to 39 years	26,163	13,633	12,530	6,416	3,203	3,213	18,673	9,787	8,886	1,074	643	431
40 to 44 years	19,813	10,568	9,245	4,367	2,277	2,090	14,736	7,867	6,869	710	424	286
45 to 49 years	16,133	8,599	7,534	3,529	1,882	1,647	12,022	6,392	5,630	582	325	257
50 to 54 years	11,922	6,182	5,740	2,205	1,200	1,005	9,381	4,808	4,573	336	174	162
55 to 59 years	7,955	4,144	3,811	1,222	665	557	6,544	3,376	3,168	189	103	86
60 to 64 years	6,146	3,085	3,061	921	456	465	5,094	2,560	2,534	131	69	62
65 to 69 years	3,976	1,954	2,022	495	233	262	3,413	1,693	1,720	68	28	40
70 to 74 years	2,683	1,278	1,405	286	129	157	2,361	1,126	1,235	36	23	13
75 years and over	2,622	1,188	1,434	373	170	203	2,198	994	1,204	51	24	27
Unknown	763	391	372	322	145	177	404	219	185	37	27	10
Port Arthur	**50,902**	**26,766**	**24,136**	**10,003**	**4,934**	**5,069**	**38,975**	**20,775**	**18,200**	**1,924**	**1,057**	**867**
Under 5 years	5,685	2,890	2,795	937	462	475	4,354	2,221	2,133	394	207	187
Under 1 year	1,143	598	545	160	75	85	888	475	413	95	48	47
1 year	1,120	563	557	191	96	95	854	430	424	75	37	38
2 years	1,041	531	510	183	93	90	792	403	389	66	35	31
3 years	1,230	622	608	213	105	108	930	464	466	87	53	34
4 years	1,151	576	575	190	93	97	890	449	441	71	34	37
5 to 9 years	5,685	2,859	2,826	1,052	498	554	4,300	2,184	2,116	333	177	156
10 to 14 years	4,185	2,100	2,085	889	436	453	3,107	1,570	1,537	189	94	95
15 to 19 years	4,217	1,937	2,280	907	363	544	3,190	1,514	1,676	120	60	60
20 to 24 years	6,328	3,182	3,146	1,244	558	686	4,898	2,521	2,377	186	103	83
25 to 29 years	6,509	3,385	3,124	1,432	655	777	4,892	2,633	2,259	185	97	88
30 to 34 years	5,202	2,897	2,305	1,005	511	494	4,032	2,283	1,749	165	103	62
35 to 39 years	4,273	2,479	1,794	998	535	463	3,139	1,854	1,285	136	90	46
40 to 44 years	2,864	1,618	1,246	601	353	248	2,203	1,225	978	60	40	20
45 to 49 years	2,113	1,302	811	381	243	138	1,649	1,013	636	83	46	37
50 to 54 years	1,465	853	612	256	154	102	1,186	683	503	23	16	7
55 to 59 years	892	498	394	123	72	51	748	417	331	21	9	12
60 to 64 years	574	308	266	76	43	33	481	255	226	17	10	7
65 to 69 years	400	208	192	39	20	19	358	187	171	3	1	2
70 to 74 years	260	133	127	24	11	13	233	120	113	3	2	1
75 years and over	218	95	123	29	15	14	184	79	105	5	1	4
Unknown	32	22	10	10	5	5	21	16	5	1	1	----
San Antonio	**231,542**	**113,676**	**117,866**	**17,978**	**8,184**	**9,794**	**130,737**	**65,275**	**65,462**	**82,827**	**40,217**	**42,610**
Under 5 years	21,084	10,531	10,553	1,098	536	562	9,030	4,594	4,436	10,956	5,401	5,555
Under 1 year	4,456	2,233	2,223	209	93	116	1,761	899	862	2,486	1,241	1,245
1 year	4,015	2,052	1,963	216	116	100	1,729	889	840	2,070	1,047	1,023
2 years	3,993	2,009	1,984	213	102	111	1,727	897	830	2,053	1,010	1,043
3 years	4,464	2,197	2,267	222	105	117	1,947	959	988	2,295	1,133	1,162
4 years	4,156	2,040	2,116	238	120	118	1,866	950	916	2,052	970	1,082
5 to 9 years	23,744	11,903	11,841	1,443	716	727	10,614	5,375	5,239	11,687	5,812	5,875
10 to 14 years	19,366	9,670	9,696	1,332	649	683	9,480	4,761	4,719	8,554	4,260	4,294
15 to 19 years	21,450	10,251	11,199	1,710	728	982	10,918	5,351	5,567	8,822	4,172	4,650
20 to 24 years	25,392	12,621	12,771	2,129	913	1,216	14,648	7,609	7,039	8,615	4,099	4,516
25 to 29 years	22,533	10,873	11,660	2,037	834	1,203	13,235	6,655	6,580	7,261	3,384	3,877
30 to 34 years	19,268	9,318	9,950	1,889	829	1,060	11,957	5,882	6,075	5,422	2,607	2,815
35 to 39 years	18,453	9,081	9,372	1,910	874	1,036	11,214	5,672	5,542	5,329	2,535	2,794
40 to 44 years	14,629	7,265	7,364	1,355	675	680	9,187	4,566	4,621	4,087	2,024	2,063
45 to 49 years	12,902	6,377	6,525	1,115	527	588	7,976	4,018	3,958	3,811	1,832	1,979
50 to 54 years	10,043	4,919	5,129	723	342	381	6,690	3,297	3,393	2,635	1,280	1,355
55 to 59 years	7,454	3,606	3,848	414	197	217	5,014	2,419	2,595	2,026	990	1,036
60 to 64 years	5,864	2,916	2,948	333	160	173	4,014	1,983	2,031	1,517	773	744
65 to 69 years	3,892	1,814	2,078	188	80	108	2,802	1,287	1,515	902	447	455
70 to 74 years	2,632	1,198	1,434	131	51	80	1,959	884	1,075	542	263	279
75 years and over	2,709	1,273	1,436	157	66	91	1,931	887	1,044	621	320	301
Unknown	122	60	62	14	7	7	68	35	33	40	18	22

TABLE 20.—AGE DISTRIBUTION BY 5-YEAR AGE PERIODS WITH SINGLE YEARS UNDER 5, BY COLOR, AND SEX FOR THE 80 CITIES HAVING 10,000 OR MORE NEGRO INHABITANTS: 1930—Continued

CITY AND AGE	ALL CLASSES			NEGRO			WHITE			OTHER RACES		
	Total	Male	Female	Total	Male	Female	Total	Male	Female	Total	Male	Female
VIRGINIA												
Newport News	**34,417**	**17,554**	**16,863**	**13,281**	**6,442**	**6,839**	**21,120**	**11,097**	**10,023**	**16**	**15**	**1**
Under 5 years	3,052	1,592	1,460	1,216	614	602	1,836	978	858			
Under 1 year	586	312	274	228	123	105	358	189	169			
1 year	558	267	291	214	94	120	344	173	171			
2 years	621	340	281	244	116	128	377	224	153			
3 years	661	342	319	264	142	122	397	200	197			
4 years	626	331	295	266	139	127	360	192	168			
5 to 9 years	3,322	1,610	1,712	1,366	668	698	1,956	942	1,014			
10 to 14 years	2,849	1,357	1,492	1,203	535	668	1,646	822	824			
15 to 19 years	3,222	1,563	1,659	1,246	548	698	1,976	1,015	961			
20 to 24 years	3,746	1,904	1,842	1,359	617	742	2,386	1,286	1,100	1	1	
25 to 29 years	3,445	1,742	1,703	1,306	608	698	2,138	1,133	1,005	1	1	
30 to 34 years	2,896	1,520	1,376	1,087	506	581	1,808	1,013	795	1	1	
35 to 39 years	2,740	1,400	1,340	1,203	570	633	1,534	827	707	3	3	
40 to 44 years	2,373	1,240	1,133	987	506	481	1,382	730	652	4	4	
45 to 49 years	2,189	1,184	1,005	961	534	427	1,228	650	578			
50 to 54 years	1,695	898	797	591	337	254	1,102	559	543	2	2	
55 to 59 years	1,116	632	484	291	166	125	823	464	359	2	2	
60 to 64 years	764	434	330	214	118	96	550	316	234			
65 to 69 years	464	238	226	120	59	61	342	178	164	2	1	1
70 to 74 years	279	123	156	68	27	41	211	96	115			
75 years and over	258	113	145	62	29	33	196	84	112			
Unknown	7	4	3	1		1	6	4	2			
Norfolk	**129,710**	**65,049**	**64,661**	**43,942**	**20,790**	**23,152**	**85,514**	**44,054**	**41,460**	**254**	**205**	**49**
Under 5 years	9,654	4,903	4,751	3,378	1,700	1,678	6,261	3,197	3,064	15	6	9
Under 1 year	1,817	920	897	616	315	301	1,200	605	595	1		1
1 year	1,707	865	842	579	281	298	1,126	583	543	2	1	1
2 years	2,063	1,030	1,033	740	358	382	1,319	671	648	4	1	3
3 years	2,048	1,056	992	718	361	357	1,325	692	633	5	3	2
4 years	2,019	1,032	987	725	385	340	1,291	646	645	3	1	2
5 to 9 years	11,833	6,022	5,811	4,171	2,085	2,086	7,636	3,927	3,709	26	10	16
10 to 14 years	10,594	5,168	5,426	3,737	1,769	1,968	6,844	3,391	3,453	13	8	5
15 to 19 years	12,248	6,556	5,692	3,849	1,716	2,133	8,378	4,826	3,552	21	14	7
20 to 24 years	13,099	6,622	6,477	4,359	1,858	2,501	8,727	4,751	3,976	13	13	
25 to 29 years	12,262	5,875	6,387	4,350	1,887	2,463	7,882	3,960	3,922	30	28	2
30 to 34 years	11,505	5,603	5,902	3,833	1,727	2,106	7,634	3,838	3,796	38	38	
35 to 39 years	11,678	5,786	5,892	4,290	2,002	2,288	7,355	3,758	3,597	33	26	7
40 to 44 years	9,519	4,830	4,689	3,522	1,743	1,779	5,981	3,072	2,909	16	15	1
45 to 49 years	8,072	4,165	3,907	3,019	1,555	1,464	5,041	2,599	2,442	12	11	1
50 to 54 years	6,345	3,210	3,135	2,138	1,122	1,016	4,194	2,075	2,119	13	13	
55 to 59 years	4,429	2,305	2,124	1,231	668	563	3,187	1,627	1,560	11	10	1
60 to 64 years	3,342	1,679	1,663	885	443	442	2,450	1,229	1,221	7	7	
65 to 69 years	2,166	1,053	1,113	502	237	265	1,663	815	848	1	1	
70 to 74 years	1,467	647	820	295	131	164	1,169	513	656	3	3	
75 years and over	1,347	557	790	294	108	186	1,051	447	604	2	2	
Unknown	150	68	82	89	39	50	61	29	32			
Petersburg	**28,564**	**13,185**	**15,379**	**12,600**	**5,734**	**6,866**	**15,962**	**7,449**	**8,513**	**2**	**2**	
Under 5 years	2,276	1,115	1,161	1,047	510	537	1,229	605	624			
Under 1 year	413	191	222	177	80	97	236	111	125			
1 year	383	193	190	174	86	88	209	107	102			
2 years	467	235	232	227	115	112	240	120	120			
3 years	463	223	240	220	101	119	243	122	121			
4 years	550	273	277	249	128	121	301	145	156			
5 to 9 years	2,987	1,425	1,562	1,375	655	720	1,612	770	842			
10 to 14 years	2,785	1,393	1,392	1,235	623	612	1,550	770	780			
15 to 19 years	2,814	1,281	1,533	1,270	552	718	1,544	729	815			
20 to 24 years	2,707	1,164	1,543	1,240	505	735	1,467	659	808			
25 to 29 years	2,383	1,049	1,334	1,167	493	674	1,216	556	660			
30 to 34 years	2,076	942	1,134	900	403	497	1,176	539	637			
35 to 39 years	2,265	1,035	1,230	1,030	457	573	1,235	578	657			
40 to 44 years	1,960	917	1,043	887	419	468	1,073	498	575			
45 to 49 years	1,732	814	918	771	375	396	961	439	522			
50 to 54 years	1,579	765	814	645	313	332	934	452	482			
55 to 59 years	946	461	485	306	153	153	639	307	332	1	1	
60 to 64 years	782	339	443	302	119	183	479	219	260	1	1	
65 to 69 years	480	193	287	162	56	106	318	137	181			
70 to 74 years	403	158	245	124	50	74	279	108	171			
75 years and over	386	132	254	137	50	87	249	82	167			
Unknown	3	2	1	2	1	1	1	1				
Portsmouth	**45,704**	**22,915**	**22,789**	**18,849**	**8,941**	**9,908**	**26,781**	**13,911**	**12,870**	**74**	**63**	**11**
Under 5 years	3,404	1,683	1,721	1,510	732	778	1,887	947	940	7	4	3
Under 1 year	594	296	298	247	123	124	346	173	173	1		1
1 year	616	301	315	246	117	129	368	183	185	2	1	1
2 years	689	350	339	326	160	166	362	189	173	1	1	
3 years	721	356	365	309	143	166	410	211	199	2	2	
4 years	784	380	404	382	189	193	401	191	210	1		1
5 to 9 years	4,461	2,235	2,226	2,067	987	1,080	2,389	1,244	1,145	5	4	1
10 to 14 years	4,165	2,071	2,094	1,780	854	926	2,384	1,217	1,167	1		1
15 to 19 years	4,399	2,280	2,119	1,649	758	891	2,748	1,521	1,227	2	1	1
20 to 24 years	4,710	2,401	2,309	1,775	776	999	2,929	1,619	1,310	6	6	
25 to 29 years	4,041	1,927	2,114	1,671	700	971	2,360	1,218	1,142	10	9	1
30 to 34 years	3,711	1,814	1,897	1,573	715	858	2,121	1,083	1,038	17	16	1
35 to 39 years	3,721	1,863	1,858	1,712	821	891	2,003	1,036	967	6	6	
40 to 44 years	3,154	1,593	1,561	1,380	687	693	1,770	903	867	4	3	1
45 to 49 years	2,911	1,448	1,463	1,279	628	651	1,623	813	810	9	7	2
50 to 54 years	2,464	1,320	1,144	976	538	438	1,487	781	706	1	1	
55 to 59 years	1,592	838	754	555	307	248	1,034	528	506	3	3	
60 to 64 years	1,243	647	596	421	205	216	819	439	380	3	3	
65 to 69 years	759	368	391	238	120	118	521	248	273			
70 to 74 years	517	246	271	135	68	67	382	178	204			
75 years and over	431	168	263	122	45	77	309	123	186			
Unknown	21	13	8	6		6	15	13	2			

TABLE 20.—AGE DISTRIBUTION BY 5-YEAR AGE PERIODS WITH SINGLE YEARS UNDER 5, BY COLOR, AND SEX FOR THE 80 CITIES HAVING 10,000 OR MORE NEGRO INHABITANTS: 1930—Continued

CITY AND AGE	ALL CLASSES			NEGRO			WHITE			OTHER RACES		
	Total	Male	Female	Total	Male	Female	Total	Male	Female	Total	Male	Female
VIRGINIA—continued												
Richmond	**182, 929**	**85, 715**	**97, 214**	**52, 988**	**24, 354**	**28, 634**	**129, 871**	**61, 306**	**68, 565**	**70**	**55**	**15**
Under 5 years	14, 075	7, 022	7, 053	4, 576	2, 217	2, 359	9, 490	4, 799	4, 691	9	6	3
Under 1 year	2, 629	1, 304	1, 325	811	394	417	1, 816	909	907	2	1	1
1 year	2, 731	1, 357	1, 374	855	403	452	1, 874	952	922	2	2	-
2 years	2, 789	1, 380	1, 409	927	458	469	1, 861	922	939	1	-	1
3 years	2, 959	1, 449	1, 510	998	471	527	1, 958	976	982	3	2	1
4 years	2, 967	1, 532	1, 435	985	491	494	1, 981	1, 040	941	1	1	-
5 to 9 years	16, 531	8, 195	8, 336	5, 389	2, 622	2, 767	11, 136	5, 569	5, 567	6	4	2
10 to 14 years	15, 250	7, 473	7, 777	4, 754	2, 285	2, 469	10, 495	5, 187	5, 308	1	1	-
15 to 19 years	16, 511	7, 377	9, 134	4, 904	2, 048	2, 856	11, 605	5, 327	6, 278	2	2	-
20 to 24 years	18, 452	8, 028	10, 424	5, 011	2, 090	2, 921	13, 433	5, 932	7, 501	8	6	2
25 to 29 years	17, 330	7, 906	9, 424	4, 988	2, 184	2, 804	12, 334	5, 718	6, 616	8	4	4
30 to 34 years	15, 619	7, 285	8, 334	4, 444	2, 001	2, 443	11, 165	5, 276	5, 889	10	8	2
35 to 39 years	15, 855	7, 573	8, 282	5, 041	2, 289	2, 752	10, 808	5, 278	5, 530	6	6	-
40 to 44 years	12, 700	6, 087	6, 613	3, 897	1, 857	2, 040	8, 799	4, 227	4, 572	4	3	1
45 to 49 years	11, 359	5, 476	5, 883	3, 586	1, 750	1, 836	7, 767	3, 721	4, 046	6	5	1
50 to 54 years	9, 231	4, 377	4, 854	2, 441	1, 200	1, 241	6, 787	3, 174	3, 613	3	3	-
55 to 59 years	6, 720	3, 196	3, 524	1, 391	704	687	5, 328	2, 491	2, 837	1	1	-
60 to 64 years	5, 091	2, 293	2, 798	987	461	526	4, 100	1, 828	2, 272	4	4	-
65 to 69 years	3, 397	1, 487	1, 910	703	296	407	2, 692	1, 189	1, 503	2	2	-
70 to 74 years	2, 405	1, 014	1, 391	428	199	229	1, 977	815	1, 162	-	-	-
75 years and over	2, 291	878	1, 413	396	130	266	1, 895	748	1, 147	-	-	-
Unknown	112	48	64	52	21	31	60	27	33	-	-	-
Roanoke	**69, 206**	**33, 271**	**35, 935**	**12, 368**	**5, 755**	**6, 613**	**56, 834**	**27, 513**	**29, 321**	**4**	**3**	**1**
Under 5 years	6, 414	3, 258	3, 156	1, 144	574	570	5, 270	2, 684	2, 586	-	-	-
Under 1 year	1, 174	623	551	199	106	93	975	517	458	-	-	-
1 year	1, 176	582	594	181	98	83	995	484	511	-	-	-
2 years	1, 331	656	675	246	115	131	1, 085	541	544	-	-	-
3 years	1, 353	676	677	239	111	128	1, 114	565	549	-	-	-
4 years	1, 380	721	659	279	144	135	1, 101	577	524	-	-	-
5 to 9 years	7, 063	3, 570	3, 493	1, 252	610	642	5, 811	2, 960	2, 851	-	-	-
10 to 14 years	6, 220	3, 036	3, 184	1, 151	547	604	5, 069	2, 489	2, 580	-	-	-
15 to 19 years	6, 600	3, 005	3, 595	1, 280	544	736	5, 320	2, 461	2, 859	-	-	-
20 to 24 years	7, 407	3, 103	4, 304	1, 305	532	773	6, 102	2, 571	3, 531	-	-	-
25 to 29 years	6, 846	3, 209	3, 637	1, 266	550	716	5, 579	2, 658	2, 921	1	1	-
30 to 34 years	6, 091	2, 983	3, 108	1, 126	551	575	4, 964	2, 432	2, 532	1	-	1
35 to 39 years	5, 509	2, 675	2, 834	1, 082	486	596	4, 426	2, 188	2, 238	1	1	-
40 to 44 years	4, 298	2, 192	2, 106	806	407	399	3, 492	1, 785	1, 707	-	-	-
45 to 49 years	3, 692	1, 889	1, 803	653	337	316	3, 038	1, 551	1, 487	1	1	-
50 to 54 years	2, 904	1, 449	1, 455	470	245	225	2, 434	1, 204	1, 230	-	-	-
55 to 59 years	2, 134	1, 048	1, 086	301	153	148	1, 833	895	938	-	-	-
60 to 64 years	1, 599	791	808	195	95	100	1, 404	696	708	-	-	-
65 to 69 years	974	477	497	127	51	76	847	426	421	-	-	-
70 to 74 years	710	303	407	76	26	50	634	277	357	-	-	-
75 years and over	699	258	441	121	42	79	578	216	362	-	-	-
Unknown	46	25	21	13	5	8	33	20	13	-	-	-

TABLE 21.—AGE DISTRIBUTION BY SINGLE YEARS UP TO 29, AND FROM 60 TO 79 YEARS, FOR THE NEGRO POPULATION, BY SEX, FOR THE 15 CITIES HAVING AT LEAST 50,000 NEGROES: 1930

AGE	ATLANTA		BALTIMORE		BIRMINGHAM		CHICAGO		CLEVELAND		DETROIT		HOUSTON		MEMPHIS	
	Male	Female	Male	Female	Male	Female	Male	Female	Male	Female	Male	Female	Male	Female	Male	Female
All ages	**39,923**	**50,152**	**70,043**	**72,063**	**46,582**	**52,495**	**115,488**	**118,415**	**36,180**	**35,719**	**62,239**	**57,827**	**30,160**	**33,177**	**44,859**	**51,691**
Up to 29 years	24,146	30,528	36,956	40,818	27,251	32,803	56,986	64,212	18,530	20,345	32,897	34,655	16,428	19,841	23,155	28,659
Under 1 year	651	667	1,138	1,106	817	840	1,750	1,703	624	616	1,046	1,016	449	427	671	666
1 year	562	611	1,100	1,152	799	818	1,630	1,632	593	585	940	949	419	450	615	593
2 years	759	792	1,269	1,296	840	890	1,798	1,789	635	685	1,101	1,082	491	492	732	756
3 years	758	757	1,313	1,343	984	948	1,781	1,873	705	727	1,121	1,183	498	432	763	738
4 years	771	762	1,279	1,278	929	852	1,772	1,801	629	659	1,106	1,074	466	464	756	772
5 years	761	773	1,280	1,357	909	895	1,699	1,931	649	718	1,103	1,128	471	530	701	739
6 years	775	832	1,268	1,373	943	979	1,626	1,774	638	671	1,038	1,028	484	535	727	788
7 years	841	793	1,245	1,320	915	960	1,707	1,685	632	655	975	974	493	526	764	770
8 years	867	921	1,215	1,432	891	1,024	1,695	1,744	617	692	1,033	997	551	539	746	762
9 years	876	875	1,242	1,321	873	974	1,615	1,665	591	603	997	928	450	522	748	744
10 years	940	990	1,250	1,277	962	964	1,565	1,708	539	619	892	962	467	520	735	795
11 years	724	745	920	1,051	715	760	1,372	1,445	492	457	752	765	394	398	556	611
12 years	791	969	975	1,192	799	819	1,252	1,417	495	488	776	779	404	456	632	683
13 years	768	887	873	1,009	763	825	1,233	1,408	436	450	647	756	388	421	557	618
14 years	794	891	806	1,070	792	877	1,246	1,456	453	494	752	747	396	468	607	717
15 years	786	910	810	1,081	761	941	1,223	1,296	395	470	628	665	358	518	582	700
16 years	776	1,073	945	1,154	818	1,077	1,239	1,482	427	494	672	721	393	582	566	801
17 years	779	1,070	954	1,178	806	1,047	1,390	1,521	485	472	634	798	469	593	654	873
18 years	859	1,288	1,069	1,362	813	1,216	1,449	1,928	453	569	716	866	512	718	746	1,144
19 years	793	1,249	1,115	1,408	792	1,175	1,579	2,047	508	606	759	995	517	783	728	1,124
20 years	872	1,567	1,108	1,562	818	1,408	1,576	2,442	521	699	868	1,229	581	922	788	1,329
21 years	852	1,016	1,275	1,371	873	1,207	2,048	2,290	602	668	1,089	1,141	577	766	796	1,037
22 years	921	1,380	1,476	1,665	1,038	1,400	2,186	2,836	662	803	1,269	1,456	714	908	936	1,302
23 years	829	1,339	1,518	1,642	1,069	1,402	2,427	3,032	641	782	1,370	1,510	751	986	919	1,320
24 years	806	1,275	1,590	1,769	1,077	1,481	2,728	3,268	788	896	1,492	1,654	806	1,048	1,043	1,377
25 years	986	1,474	1,676	1,783	1,214	1,544	2,822	3,383	860	991	1,622	1,826	799	1,011	1,109	1,533
26 years	716	1,156	1,369	1,447	964	1,331	2,814	3,254	727	886	1,643	1,658	764	899	966	1,390
27 years	776	1,066	1,482	1,483	1,006	1,308	2,986	3,227	814	862	1,818	1,794	692	913	929	1,208
28 years	911	1,280	1,724	1,730	1,189	1,439	3,278	3,651	1,004	1,028	2,026	2,033	862	1,049	1,099	1,494
29 years	846	1,125	1,672	1,606	1,082	1,402	3,500	3,524	915	1,000	2,112	1,941	812	965	984	1,275
60 to 79 years	1,426	1,838	2,806	3,069	1,346	1,466	3,175	3,863	871	940	972	1,151	915	972	2,026	2,218
60 years	365	457	646	685	308	295	641	680	189	177	221	214	196	222	504	540
61 years	46	46	134	145	67	78	215	227	53	50	58	53	56	45	112	81
62 years	93	93	198	203	118	101	269	299	79	74	86	91	68	91	134	140
63 years	87	102	192	167	93	83	262	278	79	73	79	87	71	58	127	153
64 years	80	77	161	134	75	94	202	246	62	66	64	77	65	49	109	103
65 years	198	249	374	407	172	196	376	449	90	105	113	138	94	117	287	272
66 years	36	49	80	96	39	43	129	139	31	35	37	32	30	41	62	53
67 years	45	66	100	112	38	53	141	176	28	24	41	48	42	38	75	82
68 years	64	65	125	137	65	66	121	191	40	43	36	50	37	35	94	93
69 years	53	87	120	127	45	61	131	181	29	38	25	40	30	31	63	62
70 years	115	182	193	300	88	119	167	277	56	82	52	82	66	78	153	232
71 years	20	33	50	44	23	32	58	95	18	18	14	24	12	16	31	40
72 years	33	43	91	104	41	47	92	107	26	37	24	31	24	18	52	52
73 years	29	34	59	68	33	23	77	98	17	32	14	20	12	28	36	43
74 years	26	33	53	62	26	25	53	75	14	22	19	31	15	17	29	33
75 years	61	124	80	129	54	70	82	143	18	23	29	60	37	47	61	118
76 years	22	22	51	48	21	19	49	49	9	10	17	20	18	8	37	36
77 years	16	22	32	18	11	10	36	41	11	9	14	11	15	9	15	15
78 years	26	30	34	45	16	30	34	63	13	12	17	28	16	12	26	40
79 years	11	19	33	38	13	21	40	49	9	10	12	14	11	12	19	30

TABLE 21.—AGE DISTRIBUTION BY SINGLE YEARS UP TO 29, AND FROM 60 TO 79 YEARS, FOR THE NEGRO POPULATION, BY SEX, FOR THE 15 CITIES HAVING AT LEAST 50,000 NEGROES: 1930—Continued

AGE	NEW ORLEANS		NEW YORK		PHILADELPHIA		PITTSBURGH		RICHMOND		ST. LOUIS		WASHINGTON	
	Male	Female	Male	Female	Male	Female	Male	Female	Male	Female	Male	Female	Male	Female
All ages	**59,732**	**69,900**	**156,968**	**170,738**	**108,483**	**111,116**	**27,962**	**27,021**	**24,354**	**28,634**	**45,832**	**47,748**	**62,225**	**69,843**
Up to 29 years	33,821	40,397	82,924	95,462	56,483	63,162	14,235	15,397	13,446	16,176	21,933	25,069	33,005	37,393
Under 1 year	1,085	1,062	2,569	2,607	1,773	1,700	444	468	394	417	654	650	921	926
1 year	1,078	1,108	2,692	2,503	1,675	1,729	478	461	403	452	619	603	926	944
2 years	1,166	1,173	2,825	2,828	1,972	1,990	501	522	458	469	641	680	1,044	959
3 years	1,214	1,202	2,725	2,880	2,026	1,968	514	499	471	527	706	732	1,124	1,049
4 years	1,230	1,200	2,620	2,671	1,865	1,960	511	536	491	494	715	634	1,021	1,092
5 years	1,203	1,254	2,606	2,734	1,955	1,918	531	508	504	510	743	711	1,101	1,099
6 years	1,322	1,342	2,444	2,569	1,848	2,003	480	532	538	519	678	663	1,064	1,098
7 years	1,242	1,327	2,382	2,476	1,932	1,930	488	526	527	559	717	707	1,040	1,093
8 years	1,223	1,301	2,280	2,418	1,943	1,996	508	510	524	594	711	689	1,065	1,119
9 years	1,183	1,173	2,182	2,274	1,886	1,889	447	505	529	585	692	677	1,044	1,115
10 years	1,075	1,148	2,091	2,238	1,798	1,864	450	517	494	571	656	715	996	1,125
11 years	864	979	1,758	1,886	1,456	1,608	356	404	440	465	532	571	883	918
12 years	982	1,061	1,811	1,963	1,529	1,583	406	396	502	496	594	624	879	1,062
13 years	898	1,103	1,608	1,789	1,345	1,517	347	391	428	447	538	604	801	972
14 years	1,007	1,163	1,719	1,799	1,357	1,469	403	398	421	490	502	624	873	975
15 years	938	1,094	1,572	1,753	1,295	1,485	353	374	375	478	591	612	846	977
16 years	979	1,258	1,566	1,900	1,379	1,636	364	430	407	590	566	672	872	1,094
17 years	996	1,274	1,742	2,111	1,349	1,675	360	435	400	543	592	687	969	1,105
18 years	1,024	1,360	2,024	2,931	1,411	2,075	358	464	452	637	600	857	1,039	1,362
19 years	1,022	1,395	2,265	3,256	1,574	2,079	396	509	414	608	687	819	1,031	1,380
20 years	1,030	1,705	2,567	3,994	1,555	2,418	401	521	399	601	665	989	1,102	1,575
21 years	1,046	1,407	3,081	3,626	1,814	2,149	441	509	414	542	751	880	1,217	1,404
22 years	1,191	1,653	3,441	4,509	2,102	2,673	473	592	451	623	812	1,100	1,371	1,553
23 years	1,296	1,728	3,619	4,905	2,059	2,678	500	579	394	589	878	1,169	1,406	1,676
24 years	1,233	1,685	3,947	4,960	2,282	2,797	542	632	432	566	885	1,219	1,376	1,726
25 years	1,315	1,781	4,478	5,620	2,573	3,007	579	622	442	646	962	1,318	1,560	1,819
26 years	1,183	1,547	4,032	4,714	2,266	2,622	559	634	387	510	918	1,231	1,214	1,460
27 years	1,184	1,558	4,341	4,838	2,598	2,769	622	597	407	516	997	1,119	1,380	1,493
28 years	1,314	1,730	4,831	5,584	2,998	3,146	680	664	469	592	1,130	1,274	1,391	1,672
29 years	1,298	1,626	5,097	5,126	2,868	2,879	743	662	479	540	1,201	1,239	1,449	1,551
60 to 79 years	1,941	2,859	3,298	4,716	3,259	3,494	909	846	1,022	1,296	1,778	1,944	2,862	3,601
60 years	381	517	731	962	727	771	203	155	212	247	373	338	603	743
61 years	127	126	187	214	196	166	53	40	63	50	128	106	143	157
62 years	176	218	313	321	250	248	80	80	87	89	168	140	217	230
63 years	138	170	275	308	225	232	75	51	41	81	109	134	182	214
64 years	140	169	202	254	218	211	52	48	58	59	93	116	129	167
65 years	248	333	379	567	393	426	128	108	132	197	210	218	369	530
66 years	67	121	124	189	106	103	28	33	45	44	63	56	90	85
67 years	81	116	128	222	119	133	35	32	35	39	60	80	128	126
68 years	79	120	122	229	169	154	36	27	39	75	87	111	132	188
69 years	69	132	138	233	123	129	31	34	45	52	63	92	130	164
70 years	113	232	154	360	218	269	55	69	84	110	111	157	201	293
71 years	36	63	67	92	69	65	14	11	24	40	33	34	62	67
72 years	61	98	97	128	92	109	40	33	40	41	50	73	99	95
73 years	39	70	64	110	65	72	9	24	27	17	33	44	82	77
74 years	27	69	66	98	63	64	17	21	24	21	40	52	64	83
75 years	57	121	80	160	85	139	28	37	28	63	65	75	83	170
76 years	31	43	54	87	46	69	7	10	12	18	25	36	39	65
77 years	30	35	34	40	30	37	5	4	5	16	20	27	29	41
78 years	26	66	46	69	43	53	7	14	10	22	22	26	47	66
79 years	15	40	37	73	22	44	6	15	11	15	25	29	33	40

CHAPTER IX.—MARITAL CONDITION

The marital inquiry.—The inquiry regarding marital condition was first made in the census of 1880, but the results were not tabulated; the earliest Federal census figures on the marital condition are, therefore, those for 1890.

The terms "single", "married", "widowed", and "divorced", refer to the marital status at the time the census was taken. A person who has been widowed or divorced, but has remarried, is reported as married, so that the returns for widowed and divorced persons do not represent the total number of persons now living, who have been widowed or divorced. Since it is probable that some divorced persons are reported as single, married, or widowed, census returns doubtless understate somewhat the actual number of divorced persons who have not remarried.

For a small number of persons marital condition was not reported. When under 18 years old such persons were classified as single, otherwise as "unknown." Where space will conveniently permit, the "unknown" are shown separately in the tables; from other tables they are omitted, since they have no particular significance, and form only two-tenths of 1 percent of the total male population 15 years old and over, and one-tenth of 1 percent of the female. They are always included in the totals on which the percentages single, married, widowed, and divorced are computed. The percentages would be practically the same, however, if they were based on the number of persons for whom marital condition was reported.

The number of persons under 15 years of age, who are married, widowed, or divorced, is naturally very small, comprising in 1930, 133 Negro males, and 1,027 Negro females. In most of the tables, therefore, statistics on the marital condition are presented only for persons 15 years of age and over, since the total population in this age group forms a more logical base for the computation of percentages single, married, etc., than would the aggregate population of all ages.

Marital condition and sex.—Of the total number of Negro males 15 years of age and over, 59.8 percent were married, 32.2 percent were single, 6.3 percent were widowed, and 1.4 percent were divorced. Of the Negro females 15 years old and over, 58.5 percent were married, 23.3 percent were single, 15.9 percent were widowed, and 2.2 percent were divorced.

In the Negro population of 15 years old and over, the excess of females over males amounted to 158,090 in 1930. Among single persons, the Negro males exceeded the Negro females by 317,144. The principal reason for this disparity in unmarried persons is in the tendency of men to marry at a later age than women.

There were at the same time almost three times as many widows as widowers in the Negro population in 1930. This excess of widows over widowers is due primarily to the greater longevity of women than of men. The excess is made still greater by the fact that men usually marry at later ages than women, so that even aside from the greater longevity of women, marriage is more likely to be broken by the death of the husband than by the death of the wife. The excess of widows over widowers is naturally correlative to the excess of single men over single women.

Marital condition and age.—Age composition is an important factor in the statistics of marital conditions. The proportion of Negro males married, in each age group, increased from 3.7 percent for males 15 to 19 years of age to 78.9 percent for males 45 to 49 years of age. For the age groups over 50 years of age the percent married gradually declined to approximately 51 percent for males 75 years old and over. The proportion of Negro females married, in each age group, increased from 20.5 percent for females 15 to 19 years of age to 75.2 percent for females 35 to 39 years of age. For the age groups over 40 years the proportion of females married decreases to 14.9 percent for those 75 years old and over. More than one-half of the Negro females 65 years old and over were widowed.

In the early age groups, the ratio of married to single is larger for females than for males, but the excess of females gradually decreases with each advance in age period, until in the old age periods, the ratio is reversed, and there are nearly twice as many married men as married women. Widows, on the other hand, outnumber widowers in all age groups. Single males exceed single females in all age groups, but in the older age periods, the excess of males is more than counterbalanced by the excess of widows over widowers.

The median age at marriage.—From tabulation by single years, it is possible to arrive at an approximation of the median age of first marriage. The true median age at first marriage could only be computed from tabulation of records of all first marriages in a given period. In the earlier years, however, nearly all marriages are first marriages, and the number of persons who are, or who have been, married increases rapidly with every year of age. In these ages, also, there are comparatively few deaths for persons who are, or who have been, married. Therefore, it may be assumed that the age at which exactly 50 percent of the persons enumerated are, or have been, married, and at which 50 percent remain single, will practically coincide with the median age at first marriage. The median age at first marriage of both Negro males and females is earlier than that for any other racial group, and approximately 2 years earlier than for native whites. The median age for Negro males was 2.8 years greater in 1930 than for Negro females.

Marital condition in urban, rural-farm, and rural-nonfarm areas.—Although the percentage of Negro males 15 years old and over who were married was higher in urban than in rural-farm areas in 1930, the percent married in each age group was greater in the rural-farm than in the urban areas. The percentage of Negro males 15 years old and over who were single was greater in rural-farm areas but the percentage decreased relatively much more in the rural-farm areas as the age increased.

The percent of Negro females 15 years old and over who were married, was greater in rural-farm areas than in urban areas.

TABLE 1.—MEDIAN AGE AT MARRIAGE, BY SEX, COLOR, AND NATIVITY, FOR THE UNITED STATES: 1930

COLOR AND NATIVITY	Male	Female
All classes	25.6	22.4
Negro	23.3	20.5
Native white	25.6	22.6
Native parentage	25.0	22.0
Foreign or mixed parentage	27.3	23.9
Foreign-born white	27.6	23.4

TABLE 2.—NUMBER AND INCREASE IN THE MARRIED AND DIVORCED IN THE NEGRO POPULATION 15 YEARS OLD AND OVER: 1900 TO 1930

SEX AND CENSUS YEAR	Married	Divorced	INCREASE: Married, Number	INCREASE: Married, Percent	INCREASE: Divorced, Number	INCREASE: Divorced, Percent
TOTAL:						
1930	4,755,965	144,581	666,377	16.3	74,021	104.9
1920	4,089,588	70,560	564,411	16.0	17,128	32.1
1910	3,525,177	53,432	658,474	23.0	20,373	61.6
1900	2,866,703	33,059				
MALES:						
1930	2,357,821	55,713	307,414	15.0	29,024	108.7
1920	2,050,407	26,689	301,179	17.2	6,543	32.5
1910	1,749,228	20,146	326,342	22.9	9,120	82.7
1900	1,422,886	11,026				
FEMALES:						
1930	2,398,144	88,868	358,963	17.6	44,997	102.6
1920	2,039,181	43,871	263,232	14.8	10,585	31.8
1910	1,775,949	33,286	332,132	23.0	11,253	51.1
1900	1,443,817	22,033				

TABLE 3.—RATIO OF MALES TO FEMALES OF THE NEGRO POPULATION 15 YEARS OLD AND OVER, 1890 TO 1930; BY URBAN, RURAL-FARM, RURAL-NONFARM, SECTIONS, AND SOUTHERN DIVISIONS, 1930

YEAR, AREA, SECTION, AND DIVISION	MALES PER 1,000 FEMALES: Total	Single	Married	Widowed	Divorced
1930	961	1,333	983	379	627
1920	991	1,339	1,006	395	608
1910	986	1,315	985	413	605
1900	979	1,286	986	365	500
1890	974	1,292	990	286	488
	1930				
Urban	899	1,267	960	315	562
Rural-farm	1,011	1,304	994	492	711
Rural-nonfarm	1,049	1,605	1,026	433	758
THE SOUTH	943	1,261	980	376	570
South Atlantic	934	1,206	974	351	563
East South Central	938	1,276	984	379	545
West South Central	965	1,375	986	422	598
THE NORTH	1,022	1,591	993	390	830
THE WEST	1,056	2,054	1,001	378	792

TABLE 4.—MARITAL CONDITION OF THE POPULATION 15 YEARS OLD AND OVER, BY SEX, AND RACIAL CLASSES, FOR THE UNITED STATES: 1910 TO 1930

RACIAL CLASS AND CENSUS YEAR	MALES 15 YEARS OLD AND OVER: Total	Single: Number	Single: Percent	Married: Number	Married: Percent	Widowed: Number	Widowed: Percent	Divorced	Unknown	FEMALES 15 YEARS OLD AND OVER: Total	Single: Number	Single: Percent	Married: Number	Married: Percent	Widowed: Number	Widowed: Percent	Divorced	Unknown
All classes:																		
1930	43,881,022	14,953,712	34.1	26,327,109	60.0	2,025,036	4.6	489,478	85,686	42,837,149	11,306,653	26.4	26,170,756	61.1	4,734,207	11.1	573,148	52,385
1920	36,920,663	12,967,565	35.1	21,849,266	59.2	1,758,308	4.8	235,284	110,240	35,177,515	9,616,902	27.3	21,318,933	60.6	3,917,625	11.1	273,304	50,751
1910	32,425,805	12,550,129	38.7	18,092,600	55.8	1,471,390	4.5	156,162	155,524	30,047,325	8,933,170	29.7	17,684,687	58.9	3,176,228	10.6	185,068	68,172
Negro:																		
1930	3,941,462	1,270,950	32.2	2,357,821	59.8	247,595	6.3	55,713	9,383	4,099,552	953,806	23.3	2,398,144	58.5	652,663	15.9	88,868	6,071
1920	3,393,211	1,104,877	32.6	2,050,407	60.4	200,734	5.9	26,689	10,504	3,423,100	825,258	24.1	2,039,181	59.6	507,961	14.8	43,871	6,829
1910	3,059,312	1,083,472	35.4	1,749,228	57.2	189,970	6.2	20,146	16,496	3,103,344	823,996	26.6	1,775,949	57.2	459,831	14.8	33,286	10,282
White:																		
1930	39,214,156	13,364,509	34.1	23,603,312	60.2	1,745,213	4.5	408,073	73,049	38,220,229	10,229,306	26.8	23,444,243	61.3	4,023,372	10.5	477,624	45,684
1920 [1]	33,335,586	11,782,665	35.3	19,698,113	59.1	1,549,164	4.6	207,663	97,981	31,654,841	8,772,732	27.7	19,210,238	60.7	3,399,662	10.7	228,565	43,644
1910 [1]	29,158,125	11,360,282	39.0	16,253,940	55.7	1,274,388	4.4	135,203	134,312	26,857,337	8,091,249	30.1	15,852,011	59.0	2,705,990	10.1	150,801	57,286
Other races:[2]																		
1930	725,403	318,253	43.9	365,976	50.5	32,228	4.4	5,692	3,254	517,368	123,541	23.9	328,369	63.5	58,172	11.2	6,656	630
1920	191,866	80,023	41.7	100,746	52.5	8,410	4.4	932	1,755	99,574	18,912	19.0	69,514	69.8	10,002	10.0	868	278
1910	208,368	106,375	51.1	89,432	42.9	7,032	3.4	813	4,716	86,644	17,925	20.7	57,727	65.5	10,407	12.0	981	604

[1] Includes Mexicans.
[2] Includes Mexicans (1930 only), Indians, Chinese, Japanese, Filipinos, and all other.

TABLE 5.—PERCENT DISTRIBUTION, BY MARITAL CONDITION, FOR THE POPULATION 15 YEARS OLD AND OVER, BY SEX, RACIAL CLASSES, AND 5-YEAR AGE PERIODS, FOR THE UNITED STATES: 1930

RACIAL CLASS AND AGE	MALES 15 YEARS OLD AND OVER: Single	Married	Widowed	Divorced	FEMALES 15 YEARS OLD AND OVER: Single	Married	Widowed	Divorced
All classes	**34.1**	**60.0**	**4.6**	**1.1**	**26.4**	**61.1**	**11.1**	**1.3**
15 to 19 years	98.0	1.7	(1)	(1)	86.8	12.6	.2	.2
20 to 24 years	70.8	28.1	.3	.4	46.0	51.6	1.0	1.1
25 to 29 years	36.7	61.3	.8	1.0	21.7	74.3	2.1	1.8
30 to 34 years	21.2	76.0	1.3	1.4	13.2	81.5	3.3	1.9
35 to 39 years	15.4	81.0	2.0	1.5	10.4	82.3	5.3	1.9
40 to 44 years	13.1	82.1	3.0	1.6	9.5	80.6	8.0	1.8
45 to 49 years	11.9	82.1	4.3	1.7	9.0	77.6	11.6	1.7
50 to 54 years	10.9	81.0	6.3	1.6	9.2	72.3	16.9	1.5
55 to 59 years	10.3	79.5	8.4	1.6	9.0	66.2	23.4	1.0
60 to 64 years	9.6	76.2	12.4	1.5	8.9	65.9	33.1	1.3
65 to 69 years	9.3	71.5	17.8	1.3	8.4	46.6	44.1	.8
70 to 74 years	8.6	64.7	25.4	1.1	8.4	35.0	55.9	.5
75 years and over	7.0	50.4	41.5	.8	7.3	18.2	73.9	.3
Negro	**32.2**	**59.8**	**6.3**	**1.4**	**23.3**	**58.5**	**15.9**	**2.2**
15 to 19 years	96.0	3.7	.1	.1	77.9	20.5	.9	.6
20 to 24 years	54.7	42.8	1.3	.9	33.1	60.4	4.1	2.3
25 to 29 years	27.7	67.9	2.5	1.6	15.9	73.5	7.4	3.1
30 to 34 years	19.0	75.1	3.7	2.0	9.9	76.0	10.8	3.2
35 to 39 years	14.1	78.7	4.9	2.1	6.9	75.2	14.9	2.9
40 to 44 years	11.7	78.9	7.1	2.1	5.8	71.2	20.4	2.6
45 to 49 years	8.9	80.2	8.8	1.9	4.6	67.9	25.2	2.1
50 to 54 years	7.2	79.6	11.4	1.7	4.5	60.3	33.4	1.8
55 to 59 years	6.4	78.6	13.3	1.6	4.0	55.1	39.2	1.5
60 to 64 years	5.5	74.8	18.1	1.5	4.0	43.7	51.0	1.1
65 to 69 years	5.3	69.9	23.4	1.3	3.8	35.9	59.2	.9
70 to 74 years	4.8	63.4	30.5	1.1	4.0	25.7	69.5	.5
75 years and over	4.8	51.5	42.5	.8	3.6	14.9	80.8	.3
White	**34.1**	**60.2**	**4.5**	**1.1**	**26.8**	**61.3**	**10.5**	**1.2**
15 to 19 years	98.3	1.5	(1)	(1)	88.1	11.5	.1	.2
20 to 24 years	72.6	26.5	.2	.4	48.0	50.3	.6	1.0
25 to 29 years	37.5	60.8	.6	1.0	22.6	74.3	1.3	1.6
30 to 34 years	21.2	76.3	1.0	1.3	13.7	82.0	2.4	1.8
35 to 39 years	15.3	81.4	1.7	1.5	10.9	83.0	4.2	1.8
40 to 44 years	13.2	82.5	2.6	1.6	10.0	81.6	6.6	1.7
45 to 49 years	12.1	82.4	3.8	1.6	9.5	78.6	10.1	1.6
50 to 54 years	11.2	81.3	5.8	1.6	9.6	73.5	15.4	1.5
55 to 59 years	10.6	79.7	8.0	1.6	9.4	67.0	22.3	1.2
60 to 64 years	10.2	76.3	11.9	1.5	9.2	57.8	31.9	1.0
65 to 69 years	9.5	71.6	17.4	1.3	8.7	47.2	43.1	.7
70 to 74 years	8.7	64.8	25.1	1.1	8.7	35.5	55.1	.5
75 years and over	7.1	50.4	41.4	.8	7.6	18.5	73.4	.3
Other races	**43.9**	**50.5**	**4.4**	**.8**	**23.9**	**63.5**	**11.2**	**1.3**
15 to 19 years	97.8	1.9	(1)	(1)	79.3	19.8	.4	.4
20 to 24 years	74.3	24.4	.5	.4	32.9	63.6	1.8	1.5
25 to 29 years	47.9	49.7	1.2	.8	13.1	81.6	3.3	1.8
30 to 34 years	31.3	65.1	2.3	1.0	7.3	85.7	5.3	1.6
35 to 39 years	22.8	72.4	3.4	1.1	5.3	85.0	8.1	1.5
40 to 44 years	18.9	74.4	5.2	1.1	4.4	80.1	14.0	1.5
45 to 49 years	15.5	76.2	7.0	1.1	3.8	74.2	20.5	1.4
50 to 54 years	14.9	74.0	9.7	1.2	4.0	66.0	28.6	1.3
55 to 59 years	12.9	73.3	12.4	1.1	3.3	58.5	37.0	1.0
60 to 64 years	12.5	68.7	17.4	1.1	3.4	46.5	48.8	1.0
65 to 69 years	12.6	64.2	21.8	1.0	3.5	39.0	56.1	1.1
70 to 74 years	13.6	57.6	27.3	.9	3.4	29.8	65.9	.7
75 years and over	11.6	48.1	39.0	.7	3.3	20.5	75.4	.3

[1] Less than 1/10 of 1 percent.

TABLE 6.—MARITAL CONDITION OF THE NEGRO POPULATION 15 TO 34 YEARS OLD, BY SEX, AND SINGLE YEARS OF AGE, FOR THE UNITED STATES: 1930

AGE	MALES									FEMALES								
	Total	Single		Married		Widowed		Divorced	Unknown	Total	Single		Married		Widowed		Divorced	Unknown
		Number	Percent	Number	Percent	Number	Percent				Number	Percent	Number	Percent	Number	Percent		
Negro population:																		
15 years	117,062	116,867	99.8	183	0.2	9	(1)	3	------	123,375	119,639	97.0	3,483	2.8	159	0.1	94	------
16 years	123,890	123,333	99.6	531	.4	17	(1)	9	------	133,835	121,941	91.1	11,070	8.3	519	.4	305	------
17 years	120,994	119,078	98.4	1,805	1.5	63	0.1	48	------	123,991	100,744	81.3	21,667	17.5	983	.8	597	------
18 years	123,927	117,147	94.5	6,166	5.0	193	.2	116	305	145,204	97,183	66.9	44,600	30.7	1,899	1.3	1,314	208
19 years	109,773	95,409	86.9	13,332	12.1	369	.3	265	398	128,477	70,557	54.9	53,421	41.6	2,585	2.0	1,688	226
20 years	110,375	84,044	76.1	24,652	22.3	756	.7	541	382	148,172	66,705	45.0	74,463	50.3	4,188	2.8	2,625	191
21 years	113,774	70,804	62.2	40,823	35.9	1,077	.9	733	337	114,530	43,088	37.6	65,036	56.8	3,814	3.3	2,406	186
22 years	115,651	60,592	52.4	52,045	45.0	1,561	1.3	1,107	346	133,740	42,720	31.9	82,200	61.5	5,427	4.1	3,201	192
23 years	107,116	46,804	43.7	57,080	53.3	1,745	1.6	1,183	304	127,376	33,721	26.5	83,945	65.9	6,079	4.8	3,477	154
24 years	106,706	40,312	37.8	62,572	58.6	2,075	1.9	1,449	298	125,751	28,663	22.8	86,430	68.7	6,963	5.5	3,541	154
25 years	112,485	38,720	34.4	69,310	61.6	2,473	2.2	1,650	332	133,762	27,692	20.7	93,220	69.7	8,654	6.5	4,013	183
26 years	92,974	27,862	30.0	61,205	65.8	2,218	2.4	1,466	223	110,637	19,051	17.2	80,597	72.8	7,366	6.7	3,511	112
27 years	92,341	25,246	27.3	63,106	68.3	2,275	2.5	1,466	248	102,581	15,497	15.1	76,305	74.4	7,525	7.3	3,138	116
28 years	105,189	25,907	24.6	74,349	70.7	2,914	2.8	1,768	251	119,635	16,315	13.6	89,892	75.1	9,508	7.9	3,790	130
29 years	97,531	21,053	21.6	71,899	73.7	2,717	2.8	1,670	192	104,652	12,077	11.5	79,844	76.3	9,292	8.9	3,326	113
30 years	135,112	30,207	22.4	97,250	72.0	4,852	3.6	2,538	265	146,634	18,908	12.9	107,044	73.0	15,626	10.7	4,845	211
31 years	57,438	11,117	19.4	43,147	75.1	1,923	3.3	1,123	128	59,006	5,506	9.3	45,861	77.7	5,689	9.6	1,881	69
32 years	85,060	15,738	18.5	64,301	75.6	3,149	3.7	1,683	189	92,580	8,563	9.2	70,744	76.4	10,210	11.0	2,962	101
33 years	67,484	11,162	16.5	52,262	77.4	2,539	3.8	1,400	121	73,106	5,602	7.7	57,032	78.0	8,178	11.2	2,224	70
34 years	71,775	10,991	15.3	56,314	78.5	2,809	3.9	1,493	168	76,319	5,626	7.4	59,716	78.2	8,559	11.2	2,351	67

[1] Less than 1/10 of 1 percent.

TABLE 7.—MARITAL CONDITION OF THE TOTAL POPULATION, BY SEX, AND RACIAL CLASSES, AND 5-YEAR AGE PERIODS, FOR THE UNITED STATES: 1930

RACIAL CLASS AND AGE	MALES						FEMALES					
	Total	Single	Married	Widowed	Divorced	Unknown	Total	Single	Married	Widowed	Divorced	Unknown
All classes	**62,137,080**	**33,208,947**	**26,327,870**	**2,025,078**	**489,499**	**85,686**	**60,637,966**	**29,102,964**	**26,174,997**	**4,734,374**	**573,246**	**52,385**
Under 15 years old	18,256,059	18,255,235	761	42	21	-------	17,800,817	17,796,311	4,241	167	98	-------
15 years old and over	43,881,021	14,953,712	26,327,109	2,025,036	489,478	85,686	42,837,149	11,306,653	26,170,756	4,734,207	573,148	52,385
15 to 19 years	5,757,825	5,645,359	100,362	1,513	1,348	9,243	5,794,290	5,032,174	731,967	12,337	12,371	5,441
20 to 24 years	5,336,815	3,779,443	1,500,493	17,657	21,900	17,322	5,533,563	2,547,057	2,857,665	56,375	62,464	10,002
25 to 29 years	4,860,180	1,785,413	2,977,004	39,013	50,229	8,521	4,973,428	1,079,923	3,697,645	102,041	89,124	4,695
30 to 34 years	4,561,786	965,945	3,468,176	59,493	62,669	5,503	4,558,635	603,048	3,715,648	148,571	88,219	3,149
35 to 39 years	4,679,860	718,396	3,792,614	93,204	70,765	4,881	4,528,785	472,053	3,725,680	240,604	87,533	2,915
40 to 44 years	4,136,459	543,309	3,396,838	125,677	66,415	4,220	3,853,736	367,077	3,106,901	306,958	70,117	2,683
45 to 49 years	3,671,924	435,252	3,013,521	158,561	60,850	3,740	3,370,355	303,864	2,616,213	391,342	56,446	2,490
50 to 54 years	3,131,645	341,611	2,537,625	198,486	50,621	3,302	2,844,159	260,602	2,057,326	481,334	42,428	2,469
55 to 59 years	2,425,992	251,017	1,929,201	204,742	38,220	2,812	2,219,685	199,569	1,469,931	520,158	27,898	2,129
60 to 64 years	1,941,508	191,488	1,478,550	240,520	28,279	2,671	1,809,713	160,619	1,029,354	599,644	17,983	2,113
65 to 69 years	1,417,812	131,451	1,013,226	252,072	18,783	2,280	1,352,793	114,186	630,293	596,224	10,204	1,886
70 to 74 years	991,647	84,851	641,628	251,970	11,157	2,041	958,357	80,918	334,963	536,003	4,830	1,643
75 years and over	915,752	64,315	461,683	379,638	7,431	2,685	997,444	73,312	181,944	736,807	2,859	2,522
Unknown	51,816	15,862	16,188	2,490	811	16,465	42,206	12,251	15,226	5,809	672	8,248
Negro	**5,855,669**	**3,185,005**	**2,357,954**	**247,610**	**55,717**	**9,383**	**6,035,474**	**2,888,607**	**2,399,171**	**652,721**	**88,904**	**6,071**
Under 15 years old	1,914,207	1,914,055	133	15	4	-------	1,935,922	1,934,801	1,027	58	36	-------
15 years old and over	3,941,462	1,270,950	2,357,821	247,595	55,713	9,383	4,099,552	953,806	2,398,144	652,663	88,868	6,071
15 to 19 years	595,646	571,834	22,017	651	441	703	654,882	510,064	134,241	6,145	3,998	434
20 to 24 years	553,622	302,556	237,172	7,214	5,013	1,667	649,569	214,897	392,074	26,471	15,250	877
25 to 29 years	500,520	138,788	339,869	12,597	8,020	1,246	571,267	90,632	419,858	42,345	17,778	654
30 to 34 years	416,869	79,215	313,274	15,272	8,237	871	447,645	44,205	340,397	48,262	14,263	518
35 to 39 years	430,472	60,682	338,705	21,263	9,050	772	460,428	31,702	346,217	68,496	13,544	469
40 to 44 years	339,329	39,703	267,772	24,088	7,119	647	348,094	20,061	247,700	70,935	8,971	427
45 to 49 years	323,162	28,760	259,149	28,402	6,300	551	306,903	14,142	208,459	77,347	6,584	371
50 to 54 years	277,532	19,891	220,934	31,733	4,586	388	227,058	10,167	136,804	75,792	3,976	319
55 to 59 years	174,367	11,078	137,017	23,200	2,803	269	135,030	5,341	74,453	52,964	2,055	217
60 to 64 years	133,349	7,335	99,687	24,137	1,965	225	108,820	4,393	47,569	55,455	1,200	203
65 to 69 years	82,843	4,364	57,881	19,371	1,090	137	72,334	2,716	26,001	42,825	651	141
70 to 74 years	50,896	2,454	32,278	15,500	553	111	48,200	1,916	12,411	33,478	261	134
75 years and over	55,791	2,677	28,757	23,728	459	170	62,655	2,281	9,311	50,614	212	237
Unknown	7,064	1,613	3,309	439	77	1,626	6,667	1,289	2,649	1,534	125	1,070
White	**55,163,854**	**29,313,557**	**23,603,919**	**1,745,239**	**428,090**	**73,049**	**53,700,353**	**25,706,178**	**23,447,330**	**4,023,477**	**477,684**	**45,684**
Under 15 years old	15,949,698	15,949,048	607	26	17	-------	15,480,124	15,476,872	3,087	105	60	-------
15 years old and over	39,214,156	13,364,509	23,603,312	1,745,213	428,073	73,049	38,220,229	10,229,306	23,444,243	4,023,372	477,624	45,684
15 to 19 years	5,063,975	4,977,503	76,465	833	861	8,313	5,047,609	4,449,325	579,504	5,832	8,028	4,920
20 to 24 years	4,666,016	3,389,842	1,234,723	9,882	16,387	15,182	4,800,139	2,304,549	2,412,268	28,387	45,931	9,004
25 to 29 years	4,246,957	1,592,650	2,581,163	25,045	41,278	6,821	4,326,739	979,382	3,216,233	57,175	69,974	3,975
30 to 34 years	4,059,179	859,861	3,099,125	42,246	53,591	4,356	4,050,587	554,453	3,323,466	97,089	72,978	2,601
35 to 39 years	4,171,206	639,880	3,397,317	69,273	60,864	3,872	4,012,414	437,404	3,331,898	167,550	73,153	2,409
40 to 44 years	3,733,591	491,575	3,081,779	98,256	58,595	3,386	3,464,916	345,230	2,826,591	230,337	60,528	2,230
45 to 49 years	3,293,779	397,943	2,712,488	126,327	53,964	3,057	3,029,210	288,425	2,382,342	306,961	49,392	2,090
50 to 54 years	2,815,281	315,948	2,287,972	162,975	45,583	2,803	2,593,775	249,506	1,905,135	398,865	38,157	2,112
55 to 59 years	2,225,068	236,505	1,772,722	178,255	35,121	2,465	2,068,039	193,675	1,385,758	461,044	25,682	1,880
60 to 64 years	1,789,010	181,762	1,365,713	213,058	26,098	2,379	1,687,983	155,781	975,776	537,884	16,654	1,888
65 to 69 years	1,322,823	125,560	947,545	230,050	17,566	2,102	1,272,017	111,177	600,998	548,662	9,458	1,722
70 to 74 years	933,348	81,389	605,085	234,449	10,535	1,890	904,702	78,816	320,929	498,930	4,529	1,498
75 years and over	851,414	60,645	428,812	352,576	6,908	2,473	927,279	70,781	171,097	680,529	2,621	2,251
Unknown	42,509	13,446	12,403	1,988	722	13,950	34,820	10,802	12,248	4,127	539	7,104

TABLE 7.—MARITAL CONDITION OF THE TOTAL POPULATION, BY SEX AND RACIAL CLASSES, AND 5-YEAR AGE PERIODS, FOR THE UNITED STATES: 1930—Continued

RACIAL CLASS AND AGE	MALES						FEMALES					
	Total	Single	Married	Widowed	Divorced	Unknown	Total	Single	Married	Widowed	Divorced	Unknown
Other races	**1,117,557**	**710,385**	**365,997**	**32,229**	**5,692**	**3,254**	**902,139**	**508,179**	**328,496**	**58,176**	**6,658**	**630**
Under 15 years old	392,154	392,132	21	1	-------	-------	384,771	384,638	127	4	2	-------
15 years old and over	725,403	318,253	365,976	32,228	5,692	3,254	517,368	123,541	328,369	58,172	6,656	630
15 to 19 years	98,204	96,022	1,880	29	46	227	91,799	72,785	18,222	360	345	87
20 to 24 years	117,177	87,045	28,598	561	500	473	83,855	27,611	53,323	1,517	1,283	121
25 to 29 years	112,703	53,975	55,972	1,371	931	454	75,422	9,909	61,554	2,521	1,372	66
30 to 34 years	85,738	26,869	55,777	1,975	841	276	60,403	4,390	51,785	3,220	978	30
35 to 39 years	78,182	17,834	56,592	2,668	851	237	55,943	2,947	47,565	4,558	836	37
40 to 44 years	63,539	12,031	47,287	3,333	701	187	40,726	1,786	32,610	5,686	618	26
45 to 49 years	54,983	8,549	41,884	3,832	586	132	34,242	1,297	25,412	7,034	470	29
50 to 54 years	38,832	5,772	28,719	3,778	452	111	23,326	929	15,387	6,677	295	38
55 to 59 years	26,557	3,434	19,462	3,287	296	78	16,616	553	9,720	6,150	161	32
60 to 64 years	19,149	2,391	13,150	3,325	216	67	12,910	445	6,009	6,305	129	22
65 to 69 years	12,146	1,527	7,800	2,651	127	41	8,442	293	3,294	4,737	95	23
70 to 74 years	7,403	1,008	4,265	2,021	69	40	5,455	186	1,623	3,595	40	11
75 years and over	8,547	993	4,114	3,334	64	42	7,510	250	1,536	5,664	26	34
Unknown	2,243	803	476	63	12	889	719	160	329	148	8	74

TABLE 8.—MARITAL CONDITION OF THE URBAN, RURAL-FARM, AND RURAL-NONFARM NEGRO POPULATION 15 YEARS OLD AND OVER, BY SEX, AND 5-YEAR AGE PERIODS, FOR THE UNITED STATES: 1930

AREA AND AGE	MALES 15 YEARS OLD AND OVER									FEMALES 15 YEARS OLD AND OVER								
	Total	Single		Married		Widowed		Divorced	Unknown	Total	Single		Married		Widowed		Divorced	Unknown
		Number	Per cent	Number	Per cent	Number	Per cent				Number	Per cent	Number	Per cent	Number	Per cent		
Urban	**1,842,029**	**576,114**	**31.3**	**1,112,731**	**60 4**	**118,454**	**6.4**	**30,809**	**3,921**	**2,048,053**	**454,635**	**22.2**	**1,158,802**	**56.6**	**376,331**	**18.4**	**54,790**	**3,495**
15 to 19 years	195,723	188,368	96.2	6,759	3.5	179	0.1	151	266	251,432	197,431	78.5	49,654	19.7	2,320	0.9	1,783	244
20 to 24 years	240,821	138,750	57.6	96,638	40.1	2,684	1.1	2,208	541	319,394	111,111	34.8	185,760	58.2	13,661	4.3	8,367	495
25 to 29 years	271,191	84,425	31.1	175,977	64.9	6,071	2.2	4,318	400	325,239	57,645	17.7	229,027	70.4	26,518	8.2	11,667	382
30 to 34 years	239,226	51,863	21.7	173,521	72.5	8,527	3.6	5,029	286	257,246	29,356	11.4	185,860	72.2	32,059	12.5	9,666	305
35 to 39 years	242,537	40,903	16.9	183,389	75.6	12,201	5.0	5,713	331	255,528	21,399	8.4	179,590	70.3	45,077	17.6	9,179	283
40 to 44 years	185,421	26,320	14.2	140,480	75.8	13,984	7.5	4,383	254	184,008	13,008	7.1	119,937	65.2	45,143	24.5	5,676	244
45 to 49 years	162,055	18,564	11.5	124,057	76.6	15,567	9.6	3,632	235	154,535	9,075	5.9	92,940	60.1	48,255	31.2	4,059	206
50 to 54 years	120,482	11,868	9.9	90,190	74.9	15,864	13.2	2,398	162	108,074	6,014	5.6	55,367	51.2	44,340	41.0	2,182	171
55 to 59 years	69,921	6,208	8.9	51,390	73.5	10,889	15.6	1,330	104	63,019	3,103	4.9	28,100	44.6	30,639	48.6	1,072	105
60 to 64 years	47,738	3,702	7.8	32,865	68.8	10,265	21.5	813	93	48,046	2,317	4.8	16,053	33.4	29,011	60.4	560	105
65 to 69 years	28,505	2,037	7.1	18,084	63.4	7,899	27.7	432	53	32,028	1,431	4.5	8,398	26.2	21,821	68.1	306	72
70 to 74 years	16,563	1,022	6.2	9,413	56.8	5,888	35.5	197	43	20,087	908	4.5	3,565	17.7	15,446	76.9	99	69
75 years and over	17,173	1,001	5.8	7,791	45.4	8,168	47.6	163	50	24,752	943	3.8	2,685	10.8	20,953	84.7	77	94
Unknown	4,673	1,083	23.2	2,177	46.6	268	5.7	42	1,103	4,665	894	19.2	1,866	40.0	1,088	23.3	97	720
Rural-farm	**1,395,651**	**460,114**	**33.0**	**841,149**	**60.3**	**79,452**	**5.7**	**13,800**	**1,136**	**1,380,749**	**352,961**	**25.6**	**845,806**	**61.3**	**161,530**	**11.7**	**19,421**	**1,031**
15 to 19 years	301,727	289,513	96.0	11,402	3.8	358	0.1	219	235	295,851	233,308	78.9	58,286	19.7	2,637	0.9	1,500	120
20 to 24 years	204,272	103,864	50.8	95,073	46.5	3,135	1.5	1,875	325	219,391	71,302	32.5	135,507	61.8	8,114	3.7	4,274	194
25 to 29 years	135,841	26,710	19.7	102,894	75.7	4,040	3.0	2,095	102	155,559	20,483	13.2	122,559	78.8	9,009	5.8	3,414	94
30 to 34 years	103,852	11,694	11.3	86,566	83.4	3,872	3.7	1,664	56	121,827	8,609	7.1	101,703	83.5	8,964	7.4	2,470	81
35 to 39 years	113,332	8,008	7.1	98,550	87.0	5,082	4.5	1,645	47	134,987	5,737	4.3	113,856	84.3	13,058	9.7	2,261	75
40 to 44 years	95,265	5,465	5.7	82,778	86.9	5,682	6.0	1,293	47	110,089	3,976	3.6	89,652	81.4	14,567	13.2	1,807	87
45 to 49 years	105,737	4,276	4.0	92,429	87.4	7,577	7.2	1,412	43	104,141	2,767	2.7	83,329	80.0	16,622	16.0	1,361	62
50 to 54 years	110,150	3,690	3.3	95,246	86.5	9,953	9.0	1,209	52	81,094	2,221	2.7	59,560	73.4	18,244	22.5	1,001	68
55 to 59 years	74,602	2,251	3.0	63,672	85.3	7,762	10.4	881	36	49,002	1,195	2.4	34,366	70.1	12,837	26.2	569	35
60 to 64 years	61,992	1,772	2.9	50,555	81.6	8,920	14.4	701	44	40,465	1,131	2.8	23,248	57.5	15,661	38.7	381	44
65 to 69 years	38,742	1,148	3.0	29,905	77.2	7,254	18.7	405	30	26,007	719	2.8	12,644	48.6	12,408	47.7	204	32
70 to 74 years	23,700	704	3.0	16,752	70.7	6,014	25.4	213	17	17,700	575	3.2	6,249	35.3	10,755	60.8	83	38
75 years and over	25,572	802	3.1	14,818	57.9	9,740	38.1	172	40	23,822	722	3.0	4,467	18.8	18,478	77.6	83	72
Unknown	867	217	25.0	509	58.7	63	7.3	16	62	814	216	26.5	380	46.7	176	21.6	13	29
Rural-nonfarm	**703,782**	**234,722**	**33.4**	**403,941**	**57.4**	**49,689**	**7.1**	**11,104**	**4,326**	**670,750**	**146,210**	**21.8**	**393,536**	**58.7**	**114,802**	**17.1**	**14,657**	**1,545**
15 to 19 years	98,196	93,953	95.7	3,856	3.9	114	0.1	71	202	107,599	79,325	73.7	26,301	24.4	1,188	1.1	715	70
20 to 24 years	108,529	59,942	55.2	45,461	41.9	1,395	1.3	930	801	110,784	32,484	29.3	70,807	63.9	4,696	4.2	2,609	188
25 to 29 years	93,488	27,653	29.6	60,998	65.2	2,486	2.7	1,607	744	90,469	12,504	13.8	68,272	75.5	6,818	7.5	2,697	178
30 to 34 years	73,791	15,658	21.2	53,187	72.1	2,873	3.9	1,544	529	68,572	6,240	9.1	52,834	77.0	7,239	10.6	2,127	132
35 to 39 years	74,603	11,771	15.8	56,766	76.1	3,980	5.3	1,692	394	69,913	4,566	6.5	52,771	75.5	10,361	14.8	2,104	111
40 to 44 years	58,643	7,918	13.5	44,514	75.9	4,422	7.5	1,443	346	53,997	3,077	5.7	38,111	70.6	11,225	20.8	1,488	96
45 to 49 years	55,370	5,920	10.7	42,663	77.1	5,258	9.5	1,256	273	48,227	2,300	4.8	32,190	66.7	12,470	25.9	1,164	103
50 to 54 years	46,900	4,333	9.2	35,498	75.7	5,916	12.6	979	174	37,890	1,932	5.1	21,877	57.7	13,208	34.9	793	80
55 to 59 years	29,844	2,619	8.8	21,955	73.6	4,549	15.2	592	129	23,009	1,043	4.5	11,987	52.1	9,488	41.2	414	77
60 to 64 years	23,619	1,861	7.9	16,267	68.9	4,952	21.0	451	88	20,309	945	4.7	8,268	40.7	10,783	53.1	259	54
65 to 69 years	15,596	1,179	7.6	9,892	63.4	4,218	27.0	253	54	14,299	566	4.0	4,959	34.7	8,596	60.1	141	37
70 to 74 years	10,633	728	6.8	6,113	57.5	3,598	33.9	143	51	10,413	433	4.2	2,597	24.9	7,277	69.9	79	27
75 years and over	13,046	874	6.7	6,148	47.1	5,820	44.6	124	80	14,081	616	4.4	2,159	15.3	11,183	79.4	52	71
Unknown	1,524	313	20.5	623	40.9	108	7.1	19	461	1,188	179	15.1	403	33.9	270	22.7	15	321

TABLE 9.—MARITAL CONDITION OF THE NEGRO POPULATION 15 YEARS OLD AND OVER, BY SEX, BY SECTIONS, DIVISIONS, AND STATES: 1930

SECTION, DIVISION, AND STATE	MALES 15 YEARS OLD AND OVER						FEMALES 15 YEARS OLD AND OVER					
	Total	Single	Married	Widowed	Divorced	Unknown	Total	Single	Married	Widowed	Divorced	Unknown
United States	**3,941,462**	**1,270,950**	**2,357,821**	**247,595**	**55,713**	**9,383**	**4,099,552**	**953,808**	**2,398,144**	**652,663**	**88,868**	**6,071**
The North	919,898	300,663	548,040	54,586	14,477	2,132	899,757	189,021	551,772	140,032	17,432	1,500
The South	2,972,395	954,074	1,782,255	189,714	39,363	6,984	3,153,235	756,892	1,818,884	503,911	69,076	4,472
The West	49,169	16,213	27,526	3,295	1,868	267	46,560	7,893	27,488	8,720	2,360	99
NEW ENGLAND	33,762	12,134	19,140	1,931	474	83	33,772	8,718	19,057	5,256	697	44
Maine	442	184	210	40	8	-------	358	116	188	38	15	1
New Hampshire	457	192	237	18	9	1	192	57	112	19	4	-------
Vermont	226	96	109	12	7	2	165	51	84	25	5	-------
Massachusetts	18,702	7,006	10,304	1,056	283	53	18,956	5,186	10,311	3,064	363	32
Rhode Island	3,369	1,199	1,855	250	59	6	3,529	923	1,855	624	125	2
Connecticut	10,566	3,457	6,425	555	108	21	10,572	2,385	6,507	1,486	185	9
MIDDLE ATLANTIC	393,213	135,809	234,880	19,020	2,419	1,085	400,412	97,399	240,697	57,591	3,789	936
New York	155,349	55,311	92,159	6,456	821	602	167,408	44,060	96,475	24,801	1,520	552
New Jersey	75,094	24,628	45,928	3,994	432	112	77,522	18,041	47,247	11,452	674	108
Pennsylvania	162,770	55,870	96,793	8,570	1,166	371	155,482	35,298	96,975	21,338	1,595	276
EAST NORTH CENTRAL	364,330	113,390	219,028	23,148	8,162	602	340,447	59,052	217,399	54,214	9,422	360
Ohio	119,402	37,361	71,922	7,535	2,440	144	109,012	19,662	70,599	15,863	2,811	77
Indiana	43,369	13,259	25,823	3,019	1,146	122	41,027	7,320	25,491	7,018	1,127	71
Illinois	128,527	39,768	76,887	8,799	2,866	207	127,196	22,349	77,865	23,112	3,722	148
Michigan	68,493	21,408	41,891	3,492	1,587	115	59,610	9,153	41,061	7,707	1,630	59
Wisconsin	4,539	1,594	2,505	303	123	14	3,602	568	2,383	514	132	5
WEST NORTH CENTRAL	128,593	39,330	74,992	10,487	3,422	362	125,126	23,852	74,619	22,971	3,524	160
Minnesota	4,033	1,304	2,261	283	178	7	3,510	596	2,141	642	126	5
Iowa	6,830	2,234	3,841	471	274	10	6,188	1,137	3,766	1,009	270	6
Missouri	86,100	26,201	50,784	7,221	1,698	196	86,046	16,788	50,988	16,176	1,976	118
North Dakota	200	95	70	21	13	1	111	22	68	17	4	-------
South Dakota	279	119	131	22	7	-------	212	48	125	30	9	-------
Nebraska	5,502	1,662	3,159	454	212	15	5,173	845	3,130	967	219	12
Kansas	25,649	7,715	14,746	2,015	1,040	133	23,886	4,416	14,401	4,130	920	19
SOUTH ATLANTIC	1,368,324	474,492	798,453	81,096	10,689	3,594	1,465,712	393,603	819,932	230,957	18,993	2,227
Delaware	12,485	4,971	6,485	880	96	53	11,097	3,024	6,424	1,544	82	23
Maryland	99,951	37,113	55,258	6,376	782	422	94,231	24,295	55,009	13,466	1,006	455
District of Columbia	47,443	15,925	28,212	2,714	342	250	54,297	14,058	29,942	9,556	530	211
Virginia	204,713	75,076	114,672	12,630	2,008	327	210,823	59,134	116,842	31,848	2,834	165
West Virginia	43,429	15,492	24,969	2,302	636	30	36,048	7,602	23,838	4,045	544	19
North Carolina	266,001	98,885	152,237	13,023	1,418	438	290,045	90,894	157,643	38,356	2,773	379
South Carolina	218,367	76,557	130,007	10,999	629	175	251,595	74,892	135,531	39,385	1,579	208
Georgia	324,068	103,281	196,041	21,538	2,786	422	365,622	90,080	201,168	67,516	6,530	328
Florida	151,867	47,192	90,572	10,634	1,992	1,477	151,954	29,624	93,535	25,241	3,115	439
EAST SOUTH CENTRAL	851,366	257,791	521,025	57,094	13,004	2,452	907,370	201,964	529,453	150,767	23,854	1,332
Kentucky	83,165	26,864	47,225	7,242	1,722	112	82,174	17,585	47,137	15,349	2,007	96
Tennessee	161,503	49,752	96,330	11,862	2,903	656	173,319	38,962	98,188	30,642	4,924	603
Alabama	290,079	91,027	176,191	18,544	3,912	405	320,277	77,161	179,650	55,127	8,000	339
Mississippi	316,619	90,148	201,279	19,446	4,467	1,279	331,600	68,256	204,478	49,649	8,923	294
WEST SOUTH CENTRAL	752,705	221,791	462,777	51,524	15,675	938	780,153	161,325	469,499	122,187	26,229	913
Arkansas	158,239	42,866	100,470	11,773	3,002	128	162,123	30,171	101,199	25,927	4,743	83
Louisiana	248,678	76,739	153,916	14,833	2,855	335	264,780	59,127	157,360	42,049	5,871	373
Oklahoma	59,193	17,969	34,965	4,637	1,506	116	57,580	11,879	35,096	8,553	1,972	80
Texas	286,595	84,217	173,426	20,281	8,312	359	295,670	60,148	175,844	45,658	13,643	377
MOUNTAIN	13,217	4,831	6,918	952	480	36	10,748	1,653	6,640	2,024	418	13
Montana	601	237	276	50	32	6	437	65	267	78	25	2
Idaho	338	118	168	35	16	1	226	27	162	27	10	-------
Wyoming	602	240	292	53	14	3	446	73	278	78	16	1
Colorado	4,621	1,240	2,757	438	173	13	4,902	798	2,778	1,135	185	6
New Mexico	1,141	364	661	75	40	1	938	158	618	128	32	2
Arizona	5,181	2,381	2,373	258	157	12	3,217	450	2,163	481	121	2
Utah	482	160	267	28	27	-------	374	42	251	63	18	-------
Nevada	251	91	124	15	21	-------	208	40	123	34	11	-------
PACIFIC	35,952	11,382	20,608	2,343	1,388	231	35,812	6,240	20,848	6,696	1,942	86
Washington	3,152	1,126	1,567	264	166	29	2,419	376	1,466	431	143	3
Oregon	1,051	367	551	85	47	1	827	134	512	142	38	1
California	31,749	9,889	18,490	1,994	1,175	201	32,566	5,730	18,870	6,123	1,761	82

Table 10.—PERCENT DISTRIBUTION BY MARITAL CONDITION OF THE NEGRO MALE POPULATION 15 YEARS OLD AND OVER, BY SECTIONS, DIVISIONS, AND STATES: 1900 TO 1930

SECTION, DIVISION, AND STATE	PERCENT SINGLE				PERCENT MARRIED				PERCENT WIDOWED				PERCENT DIVORCED			
	1930	1920	1910	1900	1930	1920	1910	1900	1930	1920	1910	1900	1930	1920	1910	1900
United States	**32.2**	**32.6**	**35.4**	**39.2**	**59.8**	**60.4**	**57.2**	**54.0**	**6.3**	**5.9**	**6.2**	**5.7**	**1.4**	**0.8**	**0.7**	**0.4**
The North	**32.7**	**35.6**	**39.2**	**44.4**	**59.6**	**57.2**	**52.7**	**48.2**	**5.9**	**5.8**	**6.6**	**6.1**	**1.6**	**1.0**	**.9**	**.6**
The South	**32.1**	**31.7**	**34.8**	**38.4**	**60.0**	**61.3**	**57.9**	**55.0**	**6.4**	**6.0**	**6.2**	**5.7**	**1.3**	**.7**	**.6**	**.4**
The West	**33.0**	**45.4**	**45.5**	**52.8**	**56.0**	**46.8**	**46.6**	**38.6**	**6.7**	**5.2**	**5.5**	**5.8**	**3.8**	**2.0**	**1.6**	**1.0**
New England	35.9	38.9	41.5	43.3	56.7	54.9	51.7	49.8	5.7	5.2	5.8	5.8	1.4	.7	.7	.4
Maine	41.6	43.2	45.1	44.5	47.5	47.0	44.9	46.6	9.0	8.0	8.3	5.6	1.8	1.1	1.6	1.3
New Hampshire	42.0	44.1	41.5	48.5	51.9	48.6	48.5	40.9	3.9	5.3	7.9	8.0	2.0	2.0	1.7	1.1
Vermont	42.5	46.4	72.6	47.4	48.2	47.2	23.5	43.4	5.3	4.7	2.6	5.5	3.1	1.7	1.3	.9
Massachusetts	37.5	39.3	41.7	44.3	55.1	54.9	51.9	49.5	5.6	4.7	5.3	5.0	1.5	.7	.6	.3
Rhode Island	35.6	40.1	40.0	41.6	55.1	52.6	53.0	51.7	7.4	6.3	5.9	5.8	1.8	.9	.9	.5
Connecticut	32.7	36.9	35.2	41.2	60.8	56.8	56.5	50.7	5.3	5.6	7.5	7.2	1.0	.6	.6	.5
Middle Atlantic	34.5	36.2	39.2	45.5	59.7	57.9	54.5	48.7	4.8	5.0	5.5	5.0	.6	.4	.3	.2
New York	35.6	36.6	41.1	45.5	59.3	57.7	53.3	49.1	4.2	4.5	4.9	4.8	.5	.3	.3	.2
New Jersey	32.8	32.9	37.2	41.9	61.2	60.6	56.8	51.5	5.3	5.8	5.4	4.9	.6	.4	.3	.2
Pennsylvania	34.3	37.2	38.8	47.0	59.5	57.0	54.3	47.2	5.3	5.1	6.0	5.1	.7	.4	.3	.2
East North Central	31.1	35.2	38.8	35.4	60.1	57.3	51.7	55.5	6.4	6.0	7.3	8.2	2.2	1.3	1.4	.9
Ohio	31.3	36.2	39.6	42.9	60.2	56.8	51.7	48.8	6.3	5.5	7.0	6.9	2.0	1.3	1.2	.7
Indiana	30.6	32.9	37.9	42.0	59.5	57.9	51.7	48.0	7.0	7.1	8.3	7.7	2.6	1.6	1.8	1.5
Illinois	30.9	34.1	38.6	46.0	59.8	57.7	51.7	45.8	6.8	6.7	7.2	6.6	2.2	1.2	1.4	.8
Michigan	31.3	37.5	36.8	41.7	61.2	56.9	53.5	49.5	5.1	4.2	7.0	7.4	2.3	1.2	1.8	.9
Wisconsin	35.1	39.7	43.9	50.7	55.2	52.5	45.6	41.1	6.7	5.3	7.4	6.5	2.7	1.9	2.2	.6
West North Central	30.6	34.3	39.0	43.8	58.3	56.5	51.4	48.0	8.2	7.3	7.5	6.8	2.7	1.6	1.3	.8
Minnesota	32.3	37.5	48.5	51.3	56.1	54.6	44.2	41.5	7.0	5.8	5.1	4.8	4.4	1.9	1.0	1.0
Iowa	32.7	33.7	37.8	43.3	56.2	56.7	51.8	47.7	6.9	7.1	7.4	6.5	4.0	2.0	2.3	1.5
Missouri	30.4	34.4	38.9	44.5	59.0	56.3	51.4	47.6	8.4	7.5	7.8	6.7	2.0	1.4	1.2	.7
North Dakota	47.5	48.7	57.4	59.8	35.0	39.3	32.3	28.0	10.5	7.1	4.5	10.6	6.5	2.2	1.5	.8
South Dakota	42.7	42.5	45.6	58.1	47.0	49.3	47.2	35.3	7.9	5.5	5.6	4.2	2.5	1.9	1.6	1.4
Nebraska	30.2	38.0	43.5	53.7	57.4	54.4	48.1	39.9	8.3	5.7	6.7	5.2	3.9	1.6	1.5	.7
Kansas	30.1	32.6	36.9	39.0	57.5	58.0	53.5	51.8	7.9	7.2	7.4	7.5	4.1	1.9	1.5	.8
South Atlantic	34.7	33.1	35.6	39.0	58.4	60.7	57.9	54.9	5.9	5.5	5.6	5.2	.8	.4	.4	.2
Delaware	39.8	38.0	41.0	43.2	51.9	54.2	51.0	49.3	7.0	6.8	7.2	6.3	.8	.4	.3	.2
Maryland	37.1	36.2	39.0	42.3	55.3	56.7	53.8	51.1	6.4	6.4	6.6	5.5	.8	.5	.3	.2
District of Columbia	33.6	34.3	37.7	41.0	59.5	58.6	55.6	52.5	5.7	6.1	5.8	6.1	.7	.5	.6	.3
Virginia	36.7	35.8	39.3	42.6	56.0	57.7	54.3	51.3	6.2	5.6	5.8	5.4	1.0	.5	.3	.2
West Virginia	35.7	39.5	48.1	53.9	57.5	54.5	45.7	39.1	5.3	4.5	4.9	4.3	1.5	.9	.7	.4
North Carolina	37.2	34.1	36.2	39.3	57.2	60.6	58.2	54.8	4.9	4.8	5.0	5.0	.5	.2	.2	.2
South Carolina	35.1	32.4	33.5	35.9	59.5	62.5	61.1	59.0	5.0	4.6	4.8	4.6	.3	.1	.1	.1
Georgia	31.9	29.9	32.3	35.8	60.5	63.6	60.9	57.9	6.6	5.8	5.9	5.3	.9	.5	.4	.3
Florida	31.1	31.9	35.6	41.7	59.6	60.0	54.9	51.5	7.0	6.9	6.1	5.5	1.3	.7	.9	.5
East South Central	30.3	30.2	33.7	38.2	61.2	62.2	58.5	54.8	6.7	6.4	6.6	6.1	1.5	.9	.8	.5
Kentucky	32.3	33.3	38.2	42.3	56.8	57.2	52.6	49.5	8.7	7.8	7.6	6.9	2.1	1.5	1.1	.7
Tennessee	30.8	30.8	35.0	40.2	59.6	60.7	56.4	52.2	7.3	7.3	7.3	6.5	1.8	1.0	.8	.4
Alabama	31.4	30.5	32.9	37.2	60.7	62.2	59.7	56.3	6.4	6.1	6.4	5.8	1.3	.8	.7	.5
Mississippi	28.5	28.7	32.2	36.6	63.6	64.5	60.3	56.9	6.1	5.9	6.2	5.8	1.4	.7	.8	.4
West South Central	29.5	30.8	34.5	37.4	61.5	61.4	57.4	55.2	6.8	6.2	6.7	6.2	2.1	1.2	.8	.6
Arkansas	27.1	28.5	32.6	36.7	63.5	63.5	58.1	55.0	7.4	6.6	7.8	7.2	1.9	1.2	.9	.6
Louisiana	30.9	31.4	35.4	36.8	61.9	62.3	57.8	56.8	6.0	5.5	5.8	5.8	1.1	.6	.4	.4
Oklahoma	30.4	31.1	35.4	37.0	59.1	59.8	55.5	54.8	7.8	7.2	7.5	6.9	2.5	1.4	1.0	.7
Texas	29.4	31.8	34.7	38.6	60.5	59.7	57.0	53.7	7.1	6.5	6.6	6.0	2.9	1.7	1.2	.9
Mountain	36.6	55.7	43.9	54.8	52.3	37.9	47.6	36.5	7.2	4.3	5.8	5.7	3.6	1.6	1.8	.9
Montana	39.4	42.8	49.8	63.4	45.9	48.5	43.1	28.9	8.3	5.3	4.5	5.6	5.3	3.2	1.6	.8
Idaho	34.9	47.0	51.1	61.8	49.7	45.2	40.6	34.7	10.4	6.2	4.9	3.5	4.7	1.2	2.9	
Wyoming	39.9	48.7	70.2	65.1	48.5	43.0	25.9	27.6	8.8	4.9	2.1	5.9	2.3	3.0	1.1	.7
Colorado	26.8	33.1	36.2	42.2	59.7	56.2	54.8	47.4	9.5	7.4	6.7	6.5	3.7	1.9	2.0	1.0
New Mexico	31.9	73.7	39.4	57.9	57.9	22.5	49.7	32.9	6.6	2.5	8.5	4.4	3.5	1.2	1.9	1.5
Arizona	46.0	67.8	37.8	73.0	45.8	28.2	52.5	20.8	5.0	2.7	6.5	4.6	3.0	1.2	1.9	.7
Utah	33.2	36.1	43.4	70.7	55.4	57.4	44.4	23.1	5.8	4.1	5.6	3.7	5.6	2.1	1.3	1.0
Nevada	36.3	40.1	44.5		49.4	50.3	44.5		6.0	5.6	8.8		8.4	1.1	2.1	
Pacific	31.7	36.6	46.6	50.3	57.3	54.4	45.9	41.2	6.5	6.0	5.3	5.9	3.9	2.3	1.4	1.0
Washington	35.7	40.6	54.5	58.4	49.7	48.6	38.8	33.9	8.4	6.5	3.8	5.3	5.3	3.1	1.5	1.0
Oregon	34.9	38.9	52.1	64.9	52.4	52.8	40.9	28.9	8.1	4.9	5.2	4.5	4.5	2.7	1.6	1.5
California	31.1	35.6	43.3	45.7	58.2	55.7	48.9	45.3	6.3	5.9	5.9	6.3	3.7	2.1	1.3	1.0

TABLE 11.—PERCENT DISTRIBUTION BY MARITAL CONDITION OF THE NEGRO FEMALE POPULATION 15 YEARS OLD AND OVER, BY SECTIONS, DIVISIONS, AND STATES: 1900 TO 1930

SECTION, DIVISION, AND STATE	PERCENT SINGLE				PERCENT MARRIED				PERCENT WIDOWED				PERCENT DIVORCED			
	1930	1920	1910	1900	1930	1920	1910	1900	1930	1920	1910	1900	1930	1920	1910	1900
United States	23.3	24.1	26.6	29.9	58.5	59.6	57.2	53.7	15.9	14.8	14.8	15.4	2.2	1.3	1.1	0.8
The North	21.0	22.2	27.6	32.5	61.3	60.9	54.7	50.3	15.6	15.5	16.2	16.1	1.9	1.2	1.1	.8
The South	24.0	24.5	26.4	29.5	57.7	59.3	57.6	54.1	16.0	14.7	14.6	15.3	2.2	1.3	1.1	.8
The West	17.0	17.1	23.0	26.5	59.0	61.7	56.6	53.0	18.7	18.1	17.3	18.0	5.1	2.9	2.6	1.9
NEW ENGLAND	25.8	27.1	32.1	35.7	56.4	55.3	50.0	46.8	15.6	16.4	16.8	16.3	2.1	1.0	.9	.7
Maine	32.4	33.7	38.8	35.9	52.5	51.2	43.8	46.0	10.6	13.5	14.9	17.1	4.2	1.6	2.2	.7
New Hampshire	29.7	27.9	39.8	46.4	58.3	59.0	46.0	37.2	9.9	8.2	12.3	13.9	2.1	4.4	.5	2.2
Vermont	30.9	29.5	26.3	37.6	50.9	53.0	62.2	46.5	15.2	15.7	9.1	14.7	3.0	1.8	2.5	1.2
Massachusetts	27.4	28.0	32.8	35.1	54.4	54.1	49.6	47.3	16.2	16.8	16.8	16.4	1.9	.9	.7	.5
Rhode Island	26.2	27.4	30.0	35.2	52.6	53.0	49.9	46.0	17.7	17.9	18.2	17.5	3.5	1.5	1.4	1.2
Connecticut	22.6	24.6	31.3	36.8	61.5	59.2	51.1	46.8	14.1	15.2	16.5	15.3	1.7	.9	1.1	.8
MIDDLE ATLANTIC	24.3	25.7	30.7	36.2	60.1	58.8	53.3	48.1	14.4	14.8	15.2	15.0	.9	.5	.5	.3
New York	26.3	28.8	32.3	38.1	57.6	54.8	50.6	44.7	14.8	15.6	16.3	16.6	.9	.5	.5	.4
New Jersey	23.3	25.3	29.5	34.7	60.9	58.5	55.2	49.8	14.8	15.6	14.7	14.4	.9	.5	.3	.3
Pennsylvania	22.7	23.5	30.1	35.6	62.4	62.1	54.5	49.7	13.7	13.8	14.6	14.1	1.0	.5	.5	.3
EAST NORTH CENTRAL	17.3	18.2	24.3	28.7	63.9	64.6	56.8	53.1	15.9	15.5	16.8	16.6	2.8	1.6	1.7	1.3
Ohio	18.0	18.9	26.5	30.5	64.8	65.9	56.5	52.9	14.6	13.6	15.3	15.3	2.6	1.5	1.4	1.0
Indiana	17.8	18.6	24.0	28.1	62.1	62.1	55.9	52.5	17.1	17.0	17.7	17.1	2.7	1.9	2.2	1.9
Illinois	17.6	18.3	22.2	26.8	61.2	62.0	57.7	53.6	18.2	18.1	17.9	18.0	2.9	1.6	1.7	1.3
Michigan	15.4	15.2	24.5	28.7	68.9	72.7	57.7	53.9	12.9	10.7	15.6	15.9	2.7	1.3	1.8	1.3
Wisconsin	15.8	19.7	32.5	33.6	66.2	65.8	50.0	49.9	14.3	11.7	15.0	14.6	3.7	2.5	2.4	1.8
WEST NORTH CENTRAL	19.1	20.1	24.6	29.8	59.6	60.6	56.2	51.6	18.4	17.1	17.2	17.1	2.8	2.0	1.7	1.1
Minnesota	17.0	17.0	27.5	29.3	61.0	65.2	56.9	53.7	18.3	15.5	13.8	14.6	3.6	2.1	1.3	1.9
Iowa	18.4	17.7	22.5	27.6	60.9	65.3	60.9	56.6	16.3	14.1	13.7	14.0	4.4	2.6	2.6	1.2
Missouri	19.5	20.8	24.7	30.4	59.3	59.3	54.9	50.3	18.8	17.9	18.3	18.0	2.3	1.8	1.6	1.1
North Dakota	19.8	22.1	30.3	-------	61.3	60.7	57.3	-------	15.3	15.7	8.6	-------	3.6	1.4	3.8	-------
South Dakota	22.6	22.1	30.2	25.6	59.0	62.1	58.0	58.9	14.2	14.0	10.3	14.0	4.2	1.3	1.5	1.6
Nebraska	16.3	15.5	23.4	33.9	60.5	67.5	59.2	48.2	18.7	14.3	15.2	16.3	4.2	2.5	2.0	1.2
Kansas	18.5	19.8	24.3	28.0	60.3	61.2	58.1	54.9	17.3	16.2	15.6	15.4	3.9	2.6	1.6	1.3
SOUTH ATLANTIC	26.9	26.2	28.2	31.3	55.9	58.6	56.9	53.5	15.8	14.4	14.0	14.4	1.3	.7	.6	.5
Delaware	27.3	27.0	30.8	32.3	57.9	58.6	54.6	53.2	13.9	13.5	13.9	13.9	.7	.4	.3	.2
Maryland	25.8	26.1	31.1	34.4	58.4	58.5	54.2	50.4	14.3	14.6	14.1	14.3	1.1	.6	.4	.3
District of Columbia	25.9	28.5	33.1	38.8	55.1	51.0	47.0	42.0	17.6	19.5	18.9	18.6	1.0	.7	.7	.6
Virginia	28.0	27.9	31.7	35.4	55.4	57.1	53.3	49.4	15.1	14.0	14.3	14.7	1.3	.7	.5	.3
West Virginia	21.1	20.9	25.4	31.8	66.1	67.1	62.2	54.7	11.2	10.6	11.1	12.4	1.5	1.0	1.1	.6
North Carolina	31.3	29.8	32.0	35.5	54.4	56.8	54.9	51.3	13.2	12.6	12.3	12.7	1.0	.4	.4	.3
South Carolina	29.8	28.1	27.9	29.5	53.9	57.9	57.8	56.6	15.7	13.5	13.8	13.4	.6	.4	.3	.3
Georgia	24.6	23.2	24.6	27.0	55.0	60.1	59.3	56.3	18.5	15.6	15.0	15.6	1.8	.9	.8	.8
Flordia	19.5	20.8	21.6	25.1	61.6	62.6	63.7	59.0	16.6	15.3	12.5	14.6	2.0	1.1	1.3	1.0
EAST SOUTH CENTRAL	22.3	23.4	25.0	28.6	58.4	59.2	57.8	54.0	16.6	15.6	15.5	16.2	2.6	1.6	1.4	1.0
Kentucky	21.4	22.7	27.4	30.8	57.4	57.5	53.9	50.1	18.7	17.8	16.8	17.6	2.4	1.9	1.6	1.2
Tennessee	22.5	22.9	25.9	29.9	56.7	58.6	55.5	51.4	17.7	16.6	16.8	17.3	2.8	1.8	1.5	1.0
Alabama	24.1	24.4	25.1	28.6	56.1	57.8	57.7	54.3	17.2	16.0	15.5	16.1	2.5	1.6	1.5	.9
Mississippi	20.6	22.9	23.8	27.2	61.7	61.5	60.2	56.5	15.0	14.0	14.3	15.2	2.7	1.4	1.3	.9
WEST SOUTH CENTRAL	20.7	22.6	24.7	26.9	60.2	60.9	58.8	55.7	15.7	14.2	14.6	15.9	3.4	2.1	1.5	1.3
Arkansas	18.6	20.6	22.9	25.5	62.4	63.5	60.9	57.5	16.0	13.8	14.4	15.7	2.9	2.0	1.4	1.1
Louisiana	22.3	24.1	25.9	26.9	59.4	59.9	57.5	55.8	15.9	14.4	15.3	16.3	2.2	1.3	.9	.9
Oklahoma	20.6	21.1	21.8	24.3	61.0	62.5	64.0	60.9	14.9	13.1	12.4	13.0	3.4	2.0	1.4	1.4
Texas	20.3	22.6	25.1	27.9	59.5	59.8	57.8	54.1	15.4	14.4	14.5	15.8	4.6	3.0	2.2	1.8
MOUNTAIN	15.4	15.7	22.5	25.7	61.8	64.2	56.6	53.7	18.8	17.2	17.5	17.6	3.9	2.7	2.9	2.1
Montana	14.9	15.6	26.0	27.0	61.1	63.0	57.4	49.3	17.8	18.1	13.1	20.8	5.7	3.3	3.5	2.7
Idaho	11.9	13.2	29.2	-------	71.7	71.1	54.1	-------	11.9	13.2	14.4	-------	4.4	2.6	1.4	-------
Wyoming	16.4	16.0	27.1	43.6	62.3	65.5	54.6	49.6	17.5	16.0	13.6	4.7	3.6	2.6	4.6	1.3
Colorado	16.3	17.9	21.2	24.8	56.7	58.8	57.2	53.4	23.2	20.0	18.7	18.7	3.8	3.1	2.5	2.0
New Mexico	16.8	13.2	20.6	22.0	65.9	73.2	58.7	58.8	13.6	11.8	17.3	17.1	3.4	1.2	3.3	2.1
Arizona	14.0	13.1	22.8	22.4	67.2	69.5	54.8	60.2	15.0	15.1	19.2	15.1	3.8	2.3	3.0	2.0
Utah	11.2	10.4	22.2	22.2	67.1	74.8	60.5	58.2	16.8	12.2	11.5	15.0	4.8	2.6	2.7	2.6
Nevada	19.2	20.2	23.9	-------	59.1	62.1	45.5	-------	16.3	13.7	24.4	-------	5.3	3.2	6.1	-------
PACIFIC	17.4	17.8	23.4	27.3	58.2	60.5	56.6	52.3	18.7	18.5	17.1	18.3	5.4	3.0	2.3	1.7
Washington	15.5	14.5	22.9	26.2	60.6	66.3	59.4	57.9	17.8	15.3	12.7	14.2	5.9	3.5	2.5	1.3
Oregon	16.2	14.9	20.0	40.0	61.9	67.9	59.2	41.2	17.2	13.1	18.0	16.5	4.6	4.0	2.7	2.3
California	17.6	18.4	23.7	26.4	57.9	59.2	55.8	52.3	18.8	19.3	18.1	19.3	5.4	2.9	2.3	1.8

TABLE 12.—MARITAL CONDITION OF THE NEGRO POPULATION 15 YEARS OLD AND OVER, BY SEX, AND 5-YEAR AGE PERIODS, BY DIVISIONS, AND STATES: 1930

[Percent not shown where less than 1/10 of 1 percent or where base is less than 100]

DIVISION OR STATE, AND AGE	MALES 15 YEARS OLD AND OVER									FEMALES 15 YEARS OLD AND OVER								
	Total	Single		Married		Widowed		Divorced	Unknown	Total	Single		Married		Widowed		Divorced	Unknown
		Number	Percent	Number	Percent	Number	Percent				Number	Percent	Number	Percent	Number	Percent		
NEW ENGLAND																		
Total	**33, 762**	**12, 134**	**35. 9**	**19, 140**	**56. 7**	**1, 931**	**5. 7**	**474**	**83**	**33, 772**	**8, 718**	**25. 8**	**19, 057**	**56. 4**	**5, 256**	**15. 6**	**697**	**44**
15 to 19 years	3, 495	3, 451	98. 7	42	1. 2	1	-----	-----	1	3, 845	3, 366	87. 5	471	12. 2	5	. 1	3	-----
20 to 24 years	3, 404	2, 420	71. 1	943	27. 7	17	. 5	11	13	3, 918	1, 840	47. 0	1, 989	50. 8	44	1. 1	38	7
25 to 29 years	3, 891	1, 634	42. 0	2, 176	55. 9	42	1. 1	33	6	4, 020	940	23. 4	2, 843	70. 7	146	3. 6	88	3
30 to 34 years	4, 064	1, 214	29. 9	2, 682	66. 0	96	2. 4	66	6	3, 884	584	15. 0	2, 898	74. 6	267	6. 9	132	3
35 to 39 years	4, 254	985	23. 2	3, 051	71. 7	143	3. 4	72	3	4, 145	489	11. 8	3, 098	74. 7	424	10. 2	129	5
40 to 44 years	3, 547	736	20. 7	2, 566	72. 3	157	4. 4	79	9	3, 463	380	11. 0	2, 399	69. 3	551	15. 9	128	5
45 to 49 years	3, 446	628	18. 2	2, 516	73. 0	229	6. 6	70	3	3, 076	307	10. 0	2, 043	66. 4	656	21. 3	68	2
50 to 54 years	2, 723	406	14. 9	1, 992	73. 2	254	9. 3	65	6	2, 482	286	11. 5	1, 467	59. 1	677	27. 3	50	2
55 to 59 years	1, 849	261	14. 1	1, 325	71. 7	227	12. 3	34	2	1, 630	158	9. 7	875	53. 7	562	34. 5	35	-----
60 to 64 years	1, 250	151	12. 1	876	70. 1	204	16. 3	19	-----	1, 247	153	12. 3	489	39. 2	591	47. 4	12	2
65 to 69 years	810	100	12. 3	519	64. 1	178	22. 0	11	2	834	80	9. 6	260	31. 2	484	58. 0	9	1
70 to 74 years	457	60	13. 1	232	50. 8	156	34. 1	8	1	514	63	12. 3	114	22. 2	335	65. 2	2	-----
75 and over	504	73	14. 5	200	39. 7	226	44. 8	4	1	649	54	8. 3	87	13. 4	505	77. 8	3	-----
Unknown	68	15	-----	20	-----	1	-----	2	30	65	18	-----	24	-----	9	-----	-----	14
MIDDLE ATLANTIC																		
Total	**393, 213**	**135, 809**	**34. 5**	**234, 880**	**59. 7**	**19, 020**	**4. 8**	**2, 419**	**1, 085**	**400, 412**	**97, 399**	**24. 3**	**240, 697**	**60. 1**	**57, 591**	**14. 4**	**3, 789**	**936**
15 to 19 years	34, 860	33, 915	97. 3	813	2. 3	12	-----	9	111	42, 620	34, 706	81. 4	7, 591	17. 8	157	. 4	68	98
20 to 24 years	50, 054	31, 622	63. 2	17, 875	35. 7	238	. 5	104	215	61, 110	23, 313	38. 1	36, 077	59. 0	1, 146	1. 9	402	172
25 to 29 years	63, 993	23, 463	36. 7	39, 356	61. 5	714	1. 1	287	173	68, 859	14, 880	21. 6	49, 738	72. 2	3, 355	4. 9	749	137
30 to 34 years	58, 523	15, 226	26. 0	41, 479	70. 9	1, 336	2. 3	396	86	55, 949	8, 197	14. 7	42, 171	75. 4	4, 739	8. 5	739	103
35 to 39 years	55, 713	11, 765	21. 1	41, 306	74. 1	2, 061	3. 7	506	75	52, 438	5, 934	11. 3	38, 543	73. 5	7, 176	13. 7	707	78
40 to 44 years	40, 582	7, 601	18. 7	30, 140	74. 3	2, 366	5. 8	390	85	36, 885	3, 635	9. 9	25, 230	68. 4	7, 470	20. 3	488	62
45 to 49 years	33, 216	5, 116	15. 4	25, 114	75. 6	2, 635	7. 9	287	64	29, 880	2, 604	8. 7	18, 896	63. 2	7, 987	26. 7	336	57
50 to 54 years	23, 571	3, 195	18. 6	17, 430	73. 9	2, 702	11. 5	201	43	20, 353	1, 651	8. 1	11, 084	54. 5	7, 424	36. 5	156	38
55 to 59 years	13, 677	1, 689	12. 3	9, 913	72. 5	1, 931	14. 1	121	23	11, 861	885	7. 5	5, 616	47. 3	5, 263	44. 4	79	18
60 to 64 years	8, 272	986	11. 9	5, 582	67. 5	1, 623	19. 6	58	23	7, 913	603	7. 6	2, 858	36. 1	4, 401	55. 6	32	19
65 to 69 years	4, 746	487	10. 3	2, 959	62. 3	1, 265	26. 7	25	10	5, 177	364	7. 0	1, 475	28. 5	3, 311	64. 0	16	11
70 to 74 years	2, 704	268	9. 9	1, 475	54. 5	930	34. 4	22	9	3, 051	195	6. 4	639	20. 9	2, 198	72. 0	10	9
75 and over	2, 483	223	9. 0	1, 088	43. 8	1, 152	46. 4	10	10	3, 522	224	6. 4	444	12. 6	2, 839	80. 6	3	12
Unknown	819	253	30. 9	350	42. 7	55	6. 7	3	158	794	208	26. 2	335	42. 2	125	15. 7	4	122
EAST NORTH CENTRAL																		
Total	**364, 330**	**113, 390**	**31. 1**	**219, 028**	**60. 1**	**23, 148**	**6. 4**	**8, 162**	**602**	**340, 447**	**59, 052**	**17. 3**	**217, 399**	**63. 9**	**54, 214**	**15. 9**	**9, 422**	**360**
15 to 19 years	31, 818	30, 815	96. 8	948	3. 0	13	-----	18	24	35, 633	26, 899	75. 5	8, 256	23. 2	269	. 8	188	21
20 to 24 years	43, 175	26, 152	60. 6	16, 212	37. 5	381	. 9	375	55	48, 462	13, 494	27. 8	31, 939	65. 9	1, 808	3. 7	1, 160	61
25 to 29 years	55, 820	18, 706	33. 5	34, 814	62. 4	1, 201	2. 2	1, 042	57	57, 109	7, 203	12. 6	43, 917	76. 9	3, 897	6. 8	2, 055	37
30 to 34 years	52, 915	12, 100	22. 9	37, 431	70. 7	1, 943	3. 7	1, 394	47	48, 317	3, 923	8. 1	37, 514	77. 6	5, 016	10. 4	1, 829	35
35 to 39 years	52, 807	9, 686	18. 3	38, 725	73. 3	2, 716	5. 1	1, 611	69	45, 706	2, 884	6. 3	34, 566	75. 6	6, 506	14. 2	1, 727	23
40 to 44 years	38, 650	5, 872	15. 2	28, 612	74. 0	2, 874	7. 4	1, 256	36	31, 318	1, 676	5. 4	22, 333	71. 3	6, 300	20. 1	993	16
45 to 49 years	32, 125	4, 067	12. 7	23, 846	74. 2	3, 132	9. 7	1, 045	35	25, 580	1, 134	4. 4	17, 054	66. 7	6, 670	26. 1	704	18
50 to 54 years	22, 337	2, 538	11. 4	16, 249	72. 7	2, 911	13. 0	620	19	17, 352	685	3. 9	10, 175	58. 6	6, 089	35. 1	387	16
55 to 59 years	13, 602	1, 441	10. 6	9, 696	71. 3	2, 076	15. 3	371	18	10, 733	362	3. 4	5, 394	50. 3	4, 762	44. 4	198	17
60 to 64 years	8, 372	797	9. 5	5, 608	67. 0	1, 746	20. 9	207	14	7, 465	270	3. 6	3, 084	41. 3	4, 008	53. 7	90	13
65 to 69 years	5, 248	462	8. 8	3, 248	61. 9	1, 420	27. 1	112	6	4, 958	176	3. 5	1, 625	32. 8	3, 110	62. 7	41	6
70 to 74 years	3, 147	254	8. 1	1, 725	54. 8	1, 105	35. 1	58	5	3, 278	124	3. 8	736	22. 5	2, 385	72. 8	26	7
75 and over	3, 411	272	8. 0	1, 496	43. 9	1, 590	46. 6	42	11	3, 855	122	3. 2	479	12. 4	3, 224	83. 6	14	16
Unknown	903	228	25. 2	418	46. 3	40	4. 4	11	206	681	100	14. 7	327	48. 0	170	25. 0	10	74
WEST NORTH CENTRAL																		
Total	**128, 593**	**39, 330**	**30. 6**	**74, 992**	**58. 3**	**10, 487**	**8. 2**	**3, 422**	**362**	**125, 126**	**23, 852**	**19. 1**	**74, 619**	**59. 6**	**22, 971**	**18. 4**	**3, 524**	**160**
15 to 19 years	12, 582	12, 145	96. 5	415	3. 3	9	. 1	7	6	13, 665	10, 641	77. 9	2, 824	20. 7	118	. 9	75	7
20 to 24 years	13, 547	8, 294	61. 2	4, 914	36. 3	144	1. 1	168	27	15, 836	5, 415	34. 2	9, 339	59. 0	635	4. 0	430	17
25 to 29 years	15, 079	5, 170	34. 3	9, 166	60. 8	349	2. 3	375	19	16, 736	2, 779	16. 6	12, 058	72. 0	1, 216	7. 3	669	14
30 to 34 years	14, 761	3, 594	24. 3	10, 066	68. 2	549	3. 7	504	48	14, 912	1, 607	10. 8	11, 085	74. 3	1, 601	10. 7	605	14
35 to 39 years	16, 023	2, 986	18. 6	11, 573	72. 2	858	5. 4	555	51	15, 632	1, 171	7. 5	11, 590	74. 1	2, 276	14. 6	587	8
40 to 44 years	13, 955	2, 300	16. 5	10, 030	71. 9	1, 088	7. 8	504	33	12, 536	728	5. 8	8, 936	71. 3	2, 458	19. 6	406	8
45 to 49 years	12, 951	1, 736	13. 4	9, 435	72. 9	1, 294	10. 0	463	23	10, 997	531	4. 8	7, 364	67. 0	2, 785	25. 3	309	8
50 to 54 years	10, 138	1, 205	11. 9	7, 240	71. 4	1, 344	13. 3	322	27	8, 144	364	4. 5	4, 920	60. 4	2, 654	32. 6	195	11
55 to 59 years	6, 766	754	11. 1	4, 743	70. 1	1, 044	15. 4	211	14	5, 316	205	3. 9	2, 827	53. 2	2, 152	40. 5	126	6
60 to 64 years	4, 740	382	8. 1	3, 162	66. 7	1, 060	22. 4	128	8	3, 907	124	3. 2	1, 690	43. 3	2, 042	52. 3	47	4
65 to 69 years	3, 259	300	9. 2	1, 934	59. 3	929	28. 5	89	7	2, 776	79	2. 8	1, 040	37. 5	1, 617	58. 2	37	3
70 to 74 years	1, 987	154	7. 8	1, 121	56. 4	611	33. 3	43	8	1, 807	73	4. 0	470	26. 0	1, 241	68. 7	18	5
75 and over	2, 479	209	8. 4	1, 088	43. 9	1, 124	45. 3	47	11	2, 599	92	3. 5	389	15. 0	2, 093	80. 5	11	14
Unknown	326	101	31. 0	105	32. 2	34	10. 4	6	80	263	43	16. 3	87	33. 1	83	31. 6	9	41
SOUTH ATLANTIC																		
Total	**1, 368, 324**	**474, 492**	**34. 7**	**798, 453**	**58. 4**	**81, 096**	**5. 9**	**10, 689**	**3, 594**	**1, 465, 712**	**393, 603**	**26. 9**	**819, 932**	**55. 9**	**230, 957**	**15. 8**	**18, 993**	**2, 227**
15 to 19 years	250, 359	241, 052	96. 3	8, 762	3. 5	194	. 1	106	245	271, 436	220, 063	81. 1	48, 432	17. 8	1, 874	. 7	904	163
20 to 24 years	204, 838	114, 064	55. 7	86, 947	42. 4	2, 101	1. 0	999	727	240, 143	90, 015	37. 5	137, 664	57. 3	8, 726	3. 6	3, 420	318
25 to 29 years	159, 831	43, 319	27. 1	110, 775	69. 3	3, 655	2. 3	1, 525	557	188, 989	33, 590	17. 8	137, 420	72. 7	14, 039	7. 4	3, 720	220
30 to 34 years	126, 726	22, 975	18. 1	97, 530	77. 0	4, 350	3. 4	1, 512	359	144, 914	15, 562	10. 7	110, 137	76. 0	16, 054	11. 1	2, 979	182
35 to 39 years	134, 111	17, 320	12. 9	108, 543	80. 9	6, 321	4. 7	1, 636	291	154, 044	10, 993	7. 1	116, 271	75. 5	23, 811	15. 5	2, 790	179
40 to 44 years	109, 626	11, 538	10. 5	88, 912	81. 1	7, 662	7. 0	1, 297	217	120, 274	7, 194	6. 0	85, 537	71. 1	25, 458	21. 2	1, 920	165
45 to 49 years	100, 199	8, 290	8. 3	81, 891	81. 7	8, 712	8. 7	1, 120	186	107, 103	5, 009	4. 7	73, 106	68. 3	27, 430	25. 6	1, 433	125
50 to 54 years	99, 538	6, 316	6. 3	81, 370	81. 7	10, 726	10. 8	996	130	81, 743	3, 981	4. 9	49, 143	60. 1	27, 626	33. 8	876	117
55 to 59 years	60, 934	3, 368	5. 5	49, 122	80. 6	7, 756	12. 7	587	101	469, 30	1, 981	4. 2	26, 212	55. 9	18, 255	38. 9	402	80
60 to 64 years	49, 179	2, 475	5. 0	37, 545	76. 3	8, 638	17. 6	444	77	39, 544	1, 765	4. 5	17, 133	43. 3	20, 312	51. 4	259	75
65 to 69 years	30, 720	1, 436	4. 7	22, 157	72. 1	6, 839	22. 3	236	52	269, 30	1, 126	4. 2	9, 703	36. 0	15, 907	59. 1	136	58
70 to 74 years	19, 500	868	4. 5	12, 802	65. 7	5, 666	29. 1	124	40	18, 314	809	4. 4	4, 689	25. 6	12, 704	69. 4	58	54
75 and over	20, 209	924	4. 6	10, 776	53. 3	8, 344	41. 3	91	74	22, 669	973	4. 3	3, 375	14. 9	18, 160	80. 1	60	101
Unknown	2, 554	547	21. 4	1, 321	51. 7	132	5. 2	16	538	2, 679	542	20. 2	1, 110	41. 4	601	22. 4	36	390

TABLE 12.—MARITAL CONDITION OF THE NEGRO POPULATION 15 YEARS OLD AND OVER, BY SEX, AND 5-YEAR AGE PERIODS, BY DIVISIONS, AND STATES: 1930—Continued

[See note at head of this table]

DIVISION OR STATE, AND AGE	MALES 15 YEARS OLD AND OVER									FEMALES 15 YEARS OLD AND OVER								
	Total	Single		Married		Widowed		Divorced	Unknown	Total	Single		Married		Widowed		Divorced	Unknown
		Number	Percent	Number	Percent	Number	Percent				Number	Percent	Number	Percent	Number	Percent		
EAST SOUTH CENTRAL																		
Total	**851, 366**	**257, 791**	**30. 3**	**521, 025**	**61. 2**	**57, 094**	**6. 7**	**13, 004**	**2, 452**	**907, 370**	**201, 964**	**22. 3**	**529, 453**	**58. 4**	**150, 767**	**16. 6**	**23, 854**	**1, 332**
15 to 19 years	142, 693	135, 714	95. 1	6, 361	4. 5	237	. 2	159	222	154, 013	115, 182	74. 8	35, 400	23. 0	1, 949	1. 3	1, 376	106
20 to 24 years	123, 634	60, 554	49. 0	58, 782	47. 5	2, 248	1. 8	1, 584	466	146, 904	44, 114	30. 0	90, 445	61. 6	7, 405	5. 0	4, 738	202
25 to 29 years	101, 251	22, 992	22. 7	72, 555	71. 7	3, 310	3. 3	2, 050	344	119, 645	17, 118	14. 3	87, 429	73. 1	10, 270	8. 6	4, 698	130
30 to 34 years	77, 635	11, 746	15. 1	60, 562	78. 0	3, 325	4. 3	1, 773	229	89, 823	7, 816	8. 7	67, 724	75. 4	10, 645	11. 9	3, 543	95
35 to 39 years	81, 286	8, 629	10. 6	66, 194	81. 4	4, 374	5. 4	1, 906	183	95, 748	5, 721	6. 0	72, 071	75. 3	14, 601	15. 2	3, 273	82
40 to 44 years	63, 911	5, 434	8. 5	52, 115	81. 5	4, 733	7. 4	1, 439	190	73, 729	3, 714	5. 0	52, 644	71. 4	15, 061	20. 4	2, 236	74
45 to 49 years	70, 423	4, 322	6. 1	58, 586	83. 2	6, 059	8. 6	1, 296	160	68, 695	2, 683	3. 9	47, 456	69. 1	16, 864	24. 5	1, 632	60
50 to 54 years	64, 715	3, 159	4. 9	53, 186	82. 2	7, 220	11. 2	1, 058	92	53, 005	1, 930	3. 6	32, 966	62. 2	16, 978	32. 0	1, 066	65
55 to 59 years	41, 867	1, 807	4. 3	34, 190	81. 7	5, 162	12. 3	648	60	31, 604	1, 056	3. 3	18, 289	57. 9	11, 647	36. 9	560	52
60 to 64 years	33, 678	1, 347	4. 0	26, 086	77. 5	5, 692	16. 9	499	54	26, 684	942	3. 5	12, 115	45. 4	13, 210	49. 5	369	48
65 to 69 years	21, 099	852	4. 0	15, 226	72. 2	4, 691	22. 2	295	35	17, 522	555	3. 2	6, 763	38. 6	9, 978	56. 9	194	32
70 to 74 years	13, 120	475	3. 6	8, 608	65. 6	3, 855	29. 4	150	32	12, 126	416	3. 4	3, 266	26. 9	8, 332	68. 7	74	38
75 and over	14, 831	533	3. 6	8, 019	54. 1	6, 101	41. 1	133	45	16, 652	517	3. 1	2, 502	15. 0	13, 519	81. 2	61	53
Unknown	1, 223	227	18. 6	555	45. 4	87	7. 1	14	340	1, 220	200	16. 4	383	31. 4	308	25. 2	34	295
WEST SOUTH CENTRAL																		
Total	**752, 705**	**221, 791**	**29. 5**	**462, 777**	**61. 5**	**51, 524**	**6. 8**	**15, 675**	**938**	**780, 153**	**161, 325**	**20. 7**	**469, 499**	**60. 2**	**122, 187**	**15. 7**	**26, 229**	**913**
15 to 19 years	115, 894	110, 905	95. 7	4, 583	4. 0	184	. 2	142	80	129, 451	95, 778	74. 0	30, 526	23. 6	1, 748	1. 4	1, 364	35
20 to 24 years	110, 224	456, 121	50. 9	50, 203	45. 5	2, 041	1. 9	1, 713	146	128, 044	34, 927	27. 3	81, 665	63. 8	6, 534	5. 1	4, 826	92
25 to 29 years	95, 157	21, 335	22. 4	67, 983	71. 4	3, 220	3. 4	2, 544	75	109, 835	13, 274	12. 1	82, 062	74. 7	8, 992	8. 2	5, 405	102
25 to 39 years	76, 204	10, 642	14. 0	59. 709	78. 4	3, 461	4. 5	2, 316	76	83, 934	5, 970	7. 1	64, 517	76. 9	9, 342	11. 1	4, 025	80
35 to 39 years	79, 576	7, 792	9. 8	64, 792	81. 4	4, 485	5. 6	2, 430	77	86, 112	4, 073	4. 7	65, 377	75. 9	12, 727	14. 8	3, 853	82
40 to 44 years	63, 177	5, 034	8. 0	51, 382	81. 3	4, 859	7. 7	1, 840	62	64, 887	2, 474	3. 8	47, 154	72. 7	12, 657	19. 5	2, 510	92
45 to 49 years	65, 506	3, 757	5. 7	53, 995	82. 4	5, 926	9. 0	1, 763	65	57, 124	1, 659	2. 9	39, 698	69. 5	13, 807	24. 2	1, 860	100
50 to 54 years	50, 399	2, 438	4. 8	40, 646	80. 6	6, 121	12. 1	1, 132	62	40, 651	1, 125	2. 8	25, 144	61. 9	13, 217	32. 5	1, 099	66
55 to 59 years	33, 043	1, 378	4. 2	26, 268	79. 5	4, 637	14. 0	715	45	24, 928	614	2. 5	14, 241	57. 1	9, 451	37. 9	580	42
60 to 64 years	26, 154	947	3. 6	19, 772	75. 6	4, 866	18. 6	526	43	20, 658	485	2. 3	9, 626	46. 6	10, 148	49. 1	358	41
65 to 69 years	15, 913	583	3. 7	11, 216	70. 5	3, 795	23. 8	296	23	13, 147	304	2. 3	4, 841	36. 8	7, 777	59. 2	196	29
70 to 74 years	9, 316	309	3. 3	5, 919	63. 5	2, 945	31. 6	127	16	8, 514	209	2. 5	2, 374	27. 9	5, 842	68. 6	68	20
75 and over	11, 211	351	3. 1	5, 825	52. 0	4, 905	43. 8	113	17	12, 034	276	2. 3	1, 928	16. 0	9, 732	80. 9	59	39
Unknown	931	199	21. 4	484	52. 0	79	8. 5	18	151	835	157	18. 8	346	41. 4	213	25. 5	26	93
MOUNTAIN																		
Total	**13, 217**	**4, 831**	**36. 6**	**6, 918**	**52. 3**	**952**	**7. 2**	**480**	**36**	**10, 748**	**1, 653**	**15. 4**	**6, 640**	**61. 8**	**2, 024**	**18. 8**	**418**	**13**
15 to 19 years	1, 065	1, 020	95. 8	39	3. 7	1	. 1		5	990	763	77. 1	217	21. 9	8	. 8	2	
20 to 24 years	1, 409	1, 052	74. 7	327	23. 2	9	. 6	19	2	1, 158	354	30. 6	707	61. 1	41	3. 5	55	1
25 to 29 years	1, 415	656	46. 4	693	49. 0	24	1. 7	42		1, 348	171	12. 7	1, 006	74. 6	106	7. 9	64	1
30 to 34 years	1, 537	553	36. 0	857	55. 8	62	4. 0	60	5	1, 364	99	7. 3	1, 038	76. 1	156	11. 4	69	2
35 to 39 years	1, 829	523	28. 6	1, 137	62. 2	78	4. 3	85	6	1, 511	84	5. 6	1, 127	74. 6	230	15. 2	68	2
40 to 44 years	1, 489	332	22. 3	988	66. 4	94	6. 3	72	3	1, 175	56	4. 8	845	71. 9	221	18. 8	52	1
45 to 49 years	1, 411	240	17. 0	976	69. 2	128	9. 1	64	3	1, 059	38	3. 6	725	68. 5	253	23. 9	42	1
50 to 54 years	1, 118	174	15. 6	755	67. 5	139	12. 4	47	3	801	38	4. 7	477	59. 6	253	31. 6	33	
55 to 59 years	682	99	14. 5	455	66. 7	93	13. 6	34	1	488	16	3. 3	241	49. 4	216	44. 3	15	
60 to 64 years	541	76	14. 0	335	61. 9	103	19. 0	26	1	301	8	2. 7	129	42. 9	156	51. 8	7	1
65 to 69 years	299	37	12. 4	175	58. 5	73	24. 4	12	2	237	6	2. 5	75	31. 6	149	62. 9	7	
70 to 74 years	193	25	13. 0	96	49. 7	60	31. 1	12		137	6	4. 4	21	15. 3	110	80. 3		
75 and over	198	37	18. 7	70	35. 4	86	43. 4	5		148	8	5. 4	20	13. 5	119	80. 4	1	
Unknown	31	7		15		2		2	5	31	6		12		6		3	4
PACIFIC																		
Total	**35, 952**	**11, 382**	**31. 7**	**20, 608**	**57. 3**	**2, 343**	**6. 5**	**1, 388**	**231**	**35, 812**	**6, 240**	**17. 4**	**20, 848**	**58. 2**	**6, 696**	**18. 7**	**1, 942**	**86**
15 to 19 years	2, 880	2, 817	97. 8	54	1. 9				9	3, 229	2, 666	82. 6	524	16. 2	17	. 5	18	4
20 to 24 years	3, 337	2, 277	68. 2	969	29. 0	35	1. 0	40	16	3, 994	1, 425	35. 7	2, 249	56. 3	132	3. 3	181	7
25 to 29 years	4, 083	1, 513	37. 1	2, 351	57. 6	82	2. 0	122	15	4, 726	677	14. 3	3, 385	71. 6	324	6. 9	330	10
30 to 34 years	4, 504	1, 165	25. 9	2, 958	65. 7	150	3. 3	216	15	4, 548	447	9. 8	3, 313	72. 8	442	9. 7	342	4
35 to 39 years	4, 873	996	20. 4	3, 384	69. 4	227	4. 7	249	17	5, 092	353	6. 9	3, 574	70. 2	745	14. 6	410	10
40 to 44 years	4, 392	856	19. 5	3, 027	68. 9	255	5. 8	242	12	3, 827	204	5. 3	2, 622	68. 5	759	19. 8	238	4
45 to 49 years	3, 885	604	15. 5	2, 790	71. 8	287	7. 4	192	12	3, 389	177	5. 2	2. 117	62. 5	895	26. 4	200	
50 to 54 years	2, 993	460	15. 4	2, 066	69. 0	316	10. 6	145	6	2, 527	107	4. 2	1, 428	56. 5	874	34. 6	114	4
55 to 59 years	1, 947	281	14. 4	1, 305	67. 0	274	14. 1	82	5	1, 540	64	4. 2	758	49. 2	656	42. 6	60	2
60 to 64 years	1, 163	174	15. 0	721	62. 0	205	17. 6	58	5	1, 101	43	3. 9	445	40. 4	587	53. 3	26	
65 to 69 years	749	107	14. 3	447	59. 7	181	24. 2	14		753	26	3. 5	219	29. 1	492	65. 3	15	1
70 to 74 years	472	41	8. 7	300	63. 6	122	25. 8	9		460	21	4. 6	102	22. 2	331	72. 0	5	1
75 and over	465	55	11. 8	195	41. 9	200	43. 0	14	1	527	15	2. 8	87	16. 5	423	80. 3		2
Unknown	209	36	17. 2	41	19. 6	9	4. 3	5	118	99	15		25		19		3	37
States																		
MAINE																		
Total	**442**	**184**	**41. 6**	**210**	**47. 5**	**40**	**9. 0**	**8**		**358**	**116**	**32. 4**	**188**	**52. 5**	**38**	**10. 6**	**15**	**1**
15 to 19 years	42	41		1						32	31		1					
20 to 24 years	32	29		3						24	15		8					1
25 to 29 years	37	20		17						44	13		29		1		1	
30 to 34 years	34	15		17				2		36	8		25				3	
35 to 39 years	54	22		27		4		1		37	10		20		4		3	
40 to 44 years	45	12		32		1				31	7		20		3		1	
45 to 49 years	58	18		34		4		2		35	6		25		2		2	
50 to 54 years	29	6		19		4				38	10		21		5		2	
55 to 59 years	26	8		15		3				24	5		13		4		2	
60 to 64 years	26	5		16		3		2		19	3		11		4		1	
65 to 69 years	20	2		13		4		1		13	2		5		6			
70 to 74 years	14	2		7		5				15	3		6		6			
75 and over	24	4		8		12				9	3		3		3			
Unknown	1			1						1			1					

TABLE 12.—MARITAL CONDITION OF THE NEGRO POPULATION 15 YEARS OLD AND OVER, BY SEX, AND 5-YEAR AGE PERIODS, BY DIVISIONS, AND STATES: 1930—Continued

[See note at head of this table]

DIVISION OR STATE, AND AGE	MALES 15 YEARS OLD AND OVER: Total	Single: Number	Single: Per cent	Married: Number	Married: Per cent	Widowed: Number	Widowed: Per cent	Divorced	Unknown	FEMALES 15 YEARS OLD AND OVER: Total	Single: Number	Single: Per cent	Married: Number	Married: Per cent	Widowed: Number	Widowed: Per cent	Divorced	Unknown
NEW HAMPSHIRE																		
Total	**457**	**192**	**42.0**	**237**	**51.9**	**18**	**3.9**	**9**	**1**	**192**	**57**	**29.7**	**112**	**58.3**	**19**	**9.9**	**4**	----
15 to 19 years	35	35	----	----	----	----	----	----	----	28	22	----	6	----	----	----	----	----
20 to 24 years	61	46	----	13	----	----	----	1	1	25	15	----	10	----	----	----	----	----
25 to 29 years	40	27	----	13	----	----	----	----	----	19	5	----	13	----	1	----	----	----
30 to 34 years	62	19	----	41	----	1	----	1	----	9	4	----	3	----	----	----	2	----
35 to 39 years	61	24	----	35	----	2	----	----	----	23	1	----	22	----	----	----	----	----
40 to 44 years	53	16	----	36	----	----	----	1	----	23	2	----	20	----	1	----	----	----
45 to 49 years	66	9	----	48	----	5	----	4	----	20	----	----	17	----	3	----	----	----
50 to 54 years	32	5	----	24	----	2	----	1	----	17	2	----	13	----	2	----	----	----
55 to 59 years	21	4	----	14	----	2	----	1	----	11	3	----	3	----	4	----	1	----
60 to 64 years	7	----	----	6	----	1	----	----	----	4	1	----	3	----	----	----	----	----
65 to 69 years	10	2	----	5	----	3	----	----	----	7	1	----	----	----	5	----	1	----
70 to 74 years	4	2	----	1	----	1	----	----	----	1	----	----	----	----	1	----	----	----
75 and over	4	3	----	----	----	1	----	----	----	3	----	----	1	----	2	----	----	----
Unknown	1	----	----	1	----	----	----	----	----	2	1	----	1	----	----	----	----	----
VERMONT																		
Total	**226**	**96**	**42.5**	**109**	**48.2**	**12**	**5.3**	**7**	**2**	**165**	**51**	**30.9**	**84**	**50.9**	**25**	**15.2**	**5**	----
15 to 19 years	23	23	----	----	----	----	----	----	----	39	32	----	7	----	----	----	----	----
20 to 24 years	24	22	----	2	----	----	----	----	----	15	6	----	9	----	----	----	----	----
25 to 29 years	24	14	----	10	----	----	----	----	----	5	----	----	5	----	----	----	----	----
30 to 34 years	22	8	----	12	----	----	----	1	1	14	3	----	10	----	1	----	----	----
35 to 39 years	23	6	----	14	----	1	----	2	----	18	2	----	14	----	1	----	1	----
40 to 44 years	19	6	----	11	----	----	----	2	----	11	2	----	9	----	----	----	----	----
45 to 49 years	24	4	----	18	----	1	----	1	----	19	5	----	8	----	4	----	2	----
50 to 54 years	19	3	----	13	----	2	----	----	1	14	----	----	12	----	1	----	1	----
55 to 59 years	17	3	----	10	----	3	----	1	----	6	----	----	4	----	2	----	----	----
60 to 64 years	11	4	----	7	----	----	----	----	----	6	----	----	4	----	1	----	1	----
65 to 69 years	7	----	----	5	----	2	----	----	----	5	----	----	----	----	5	----	----	----
70 to 74 years	4	----	----	3	----	1	----	----	----	6	----	----	2	----	4	----	----	----
75 and over	9	3	----	4	----	2	----	----	----	7	1	----	----	----	6	----	----	----
Unknown	----	----	----	----	----	----	----	----	----	----	----	----	----	----	----	----	----	----
MASSACHUSETTS																		
Total	**18,702**	**7,006**	**37.5**	**10,304**	**55.1**	**1,056**	**5.6**	**283**	**53**	**18,956**	**5,186**	**27.4**	**10,311**	**54.4**	**3,064**	**16.2**	**363**	**32**
15 to 19 years	1,949	1,931	99.1	17	.9	----	----	----	1	2,069	1,862	90.0	204	9.9	1	----	2	----
20 to 24 years	1,772	1,333	75.2	419	23.6	10	.6	6	4	2,026	1,083	53.5	900	44.4	21	1.0	17	5
25 to 29 years	1,913	937	49.0	933	48.8	20	1.0	20	3	2,122	605	28.5	1,404	66.2	73	3.4	39	1
30 to 34 years	2.216	717	32.4	1,400	63.2	58	2.6	37	4	2,205	390	17.7	1,588	72.0	159	7.2	65	3
35 to 39 years	2,385	615	25.8	1,637	68.6	80	3.4	51	2	2,384	316	13.3	1,752	73.5	232	9.7	80	4
40 to 44 years	2,000	435	21.8	1,419	71.0	87	4.4	52	7	2,016	244	12.1	1 388	68.8	309	15.3	71	4
45 to 49 years	2,049	394	19.2	1,491	72.8	127	6.2	34	3	1,825	197	10.8	1,212	66.4	385	21.1	29	2
50 to 54 years	1,619	255	15.8	1,178	72.8	143	8.8	41	2	1,441	171	11.9	837	58.1	404	28.0	27	2
55 to 59 years	1,113	165	14.8	795	71.4	133	11.9	18	2	971	96	9.9	495	51.0	357	36.8	23	----
60 to 64 years	689	94	13.6	472	68.5	113	16.4	10	----	704	88	12.5	266	37.8	345	49.0	4	1
65 to 69 years	449	58	12.9	286	63.7	98	21.8	6	1	481	53	11.0	148	30.8	278	57.8	2	----
70 to 74 years	257	29	11.3	137	53.3	85	33.1	6	----	292	38	13.0	56	19.2	196	67.1	2	----
75 and over	245	36	14.7	106	43.3	102	41.6	1	----	374	28	7.5	42	11.2	302	80.7	2	----
Unknown	46	7	----	14	----	----	----	1	24	46	15	----	19	----	2	----	----	10
RHODE ISLAND																		
Total	**3,369**	**1,199**	**35.6**	**1,855**	**55.1**	**250**	**7.4**	**59**	**6**	**3,529**	**923**	**26.2**	**1,855**	**52.6**	**624**	**17.7**	**125**	**2**
15 to 19 years	355	350	98.6	5	1.4	----	----	----	----	452	396	87.6	55	12.2	1	.2	----	----
20 to 24 years	331	242	73.1	85	25.7	2	.6	1	1	343	164	47.8	167	48.7	3	.9	9	----
25 to 29 years	356	144	40.4	205	57.6	4	1.1	2	1	334	71	21.3	240	71.9	7	2.1	15	1
30 to 34 years	338	115	34.0	203	60.1	13	3.8	7	----	380	51	13.4	279	73.4	23	6.1	27	----
35 to 39 years	380	91	23.9	273	71.8	13	3.4	3	----	365	38	10.4	266	72.9	46	12.6	15	----
40 to 44 years	354	67	18.9	255	72.0	23	6.5	8	1	342	30	8.8	238	69.6	52	15.2	22	----
45 to 49 years	357	62	17.4	255	71.4	25	7.0	15	----	348	41	11.8	224	64.4	66	19.0	17	----
50 to 54 years	290	48	16.6	197	67.9	32	11.0	12	1	296	49	16.6	160	54.1	76	25.7	11	----
55 to 59 years	211	28	13.3	153	72.5	25	11.8	5	----	216	28	13.0	110	50.9	76	35.2	2	----
60 to 64 years	153	20	13.1	107	69.9	24	15.7	2	----	170	27	15.9	51	30.0	88	51.8	4	----
65 to 69 years	102	15	14.7	59	57.8	27	26.5	1	----	110	9	8.2	38	34.5	60	54.5	2	1
70 to 74 years	59	7	----	30	----	20	----	2	----	75	9	----	15	----	51	----	----	----
75 and over	77	7	----	27	----	42	----	1	----	93	9	----	11	----	72	----	1	----
Unknown	6	3	----	1	----	----	----	----	2	5	1	----	1	----	3	----	----	----
CONNECTICUT																		
Total	**10,576**	**3,457**	**32.7**	**6,425**	**60.8**	**555**	**5.3**	**108**	**21**	**10,572**	**2,385**	**22.6**	**6,507**	**61.5**	**1,486**	**14.1**	**185**	**9**
15 to 19 years	1,091	1,071	98.2	19	1.7	1	.1	----	----	1,225	1,023	83.5	198	16.2	3	.2	1	----
20 to 24 years	1,184	748	63.2	421	35.6	5	.4	3	7	1,485	557	37.5	895	60.3	20	1.3	12	1
25 to 29 years	1,521	492	32.3	998	65.6	18	1.2	11	2	1,496	246	16.4	1,152	77.0	64	4.3	33	1
30 to 34 years	1,392	340	24.4	1,009	72.5	24	1.7	18	1	1,240	128	10.3	993	80.1	84	6.8	35	----
35 to 39 years	1,351	227	16.8	1,065	78.8	43	3.2	15	1	1,318	122	9.3	1,024	77.7	141	10.7	30	1
40 to 44 years	1,076	200	18.6	813	75.6	46	4.3	16	1	1,040	95	9.1	724	69.6	186	17.9	34	1
45 to 49 years	892	141	15.8	670	75.1	67	7.5	14	----	829	58	7.0	557	67.2	196	23.6	18	----
50 to 54 years	734	89	12.1	561	76.4	71	9.7	11	2	676	54	8.0	424	62.7	189	28.0	9	----
55 to 59 years	461	53	11.5	338	73.3	61	13.2	9	----	402	26	6.5	250	62.2	119	29.6	7	----
60 to 64 years	364	28	7.7	268	73.6	63	17.3	5	----	344	34	9.9	154	44.8	153	44.5	2	1
65 to 69 years	222	23	10.4	151	68.0	44	19.8	3	1	218	15	6.9	69	31.7	130	59.6	4	----
70 to 74 years	119	20	16.8	54	45.4	44	37.0	----	1	125	13	10.4	35	28.0	77	61.6	----	----
75 and over	145	20	13.8	55	37.9	67	46.2	2	1	163	13	8.0	30	18.4	120	73.6	----	----
Unknown	14	5	----	3	----	1	----	1	4	11	1	----	2	----	4	----	----	4

TABLE 12.—MARITAL CONDITION OF THE NEGRO POPULATION 15 YEARS OLD AND OVER, BY SEX, AND 5-YEAR AGE PERIODS, BY DIVISIONS, AND STATES: 1930—Continued

[See note at head of this table.]

DIVISION OR STATE, AND AGE	MALES 15 YEARS OLD AND OVER									FEMALES 15 YEARS OLD AND OVER								
	Total	Single		Married		Widowed		Divorced	Unknown	Total	Single		Married		Widowed		Divorced	Unknown
		Number	Per cent	Number	Per cent	Number	Per cent				Number	Per cent	Number	Per cent	Number	Per cent		
NEW YORK																		
Total	**155,349**	**55,311**	**35.6**	**92,159**	**59.3**	**6,456**	**4.2**	**821**	**602**	**167,408**	**44,060**	**26.3**	**96,475**	**57.6**	**24,801**	**14.8**	**1,520**	**552**
15 to 19 years	11,993	11,629	97.0	288	2.4	4	------	2	70	15,479	12,714	82.1	2,619	16.9	66	.4	22	58
20 to 24 years	21,024	13,517	64.3	7,230	34.4	104	.5	37	136	26,950	11,059	41.0	15,146	56.2	505	1.0	144	96
25 to 29 years	27,994	10,835	38.7	16,708	59.7	272	1.0	83	96	31,081	7,902	25.4	21,251	68.4	1,534	4.9	307	87
30 to 34 years	24,978	6,929	27.7	17,342	69.4	509	2.0	143	55	24,764	4,321	17.4	17,832	72.0	2,217	9.0	334	60
35 to 39 years	22,916	5,096	22.2	16,802	73.3	780	3.4	189	49	22,369	3,085	13.8	15,622	69.8	3,320	14.8	291	51
40 to 44 years	16,119	2,994	18.6	12,010	74.5	925	5.7	139	51	15,521	1,930	12.4	9,900	63.8	3,462	22.3	192	37
45 to 49 years	12,303	1,908	15.5	9,307	75.6	952	7.7	101	35	11,892	1,222	10.3	6,887	57.9	3,614	30.4	133	36
50 to 54 years	7,949	1,080	13.6	5,893	74.1	900	11.3	61	15	7,599	755	9.9	3,654	48.1	3,120	41.1	52	18
55 to 59 years	4,338	574	13.2	3,136	72.3	586	13.5	31	11	4,329	359	8.3	1,768	40.8	2,168	50.1	22	12
60 to 64 years	2,519	316	12.5	1,696	67.3	479	19.0	16	12	2,816	266	9.4	857	30.4	1,666	59.2	13	14
65 to 69 years	1,388	163	11.7	881	63.5	334	24.1	8	2	1,971	163	8.3	469	23.8	1,327	67.3	4	8
70 to 74 years	760	91	12.0	413	54.3	248	32.6	6	2	1,091	83	7.6	194	17.8	706	73.9	3	5
75 and over	742	78	10.5	313	42.2	344	46.4	3	4	1,189	96	8.1	137	11.5	946	79.6	1	9
Unknown	326	101	31.0	140	42.9	19	5.8	2	64	357	105	29.4	139	38.9	50	14.0	2	61
NEW JERSEY																		
Total	**75,094**	**24,628**	**32.8**	**45,928**	**61.2**	**3,994**	**5.3**	**432**	**112**	**77,522**	**18,041**	**23.3**	**47,247**	**60.9**	**11,452**	**14.8**	**674**	**108**
15 to 19 years	7,664	7,501	97.9	151	.2	3	------	1	8	9,131	7,508	82.2	1,580	17.3	23	.3	12	8
20 to 24 years	9,817	6,083	62.0	3,658	37.3	35	.4	18	23	11,478	4,179	36.4	6,983	60.8	225	2.0	73	18
25 to 29 years	11,156	3,650	32.7	7,288	65.3	141	1.3	64	13	12,268	2,373	19.3	9,147	74.6	586	4.8	147	15
30 to 34 years	10,014	2,280	22.8	7,465	74.5	211	2.1	51	7	9,773	1,211	12.4	7,589	77.7	850	8.7	113	10
35 to 39 years	9,748	1,734	17.8	7,497	76.9	418	4.3	94	5	9,601	904	9.4	7,297	76.0	1,280	13.3	109	11
40 to 44 years	7,367	1,177	16.0	5,675	77.0	435	5.9	72	8	7,158	578	8.1	5,169	72.2	1,308	18.3	96	7
45 to 49 years	6,466	858	13.3	5,054	78.2	512	7.9	40	2	6,121	466	7.6	4,073	66.5	1,517	24.8	60	5
50 to 54 years	5,074	606	11.9	3,867	76.2	553	10.9	43	5	4,571	313	6.8	2,618	57.3	1,599	35.0	35	6
55 to 59 years	3,123	310	9.9	2,337	74.8	449	14.4	27	------	2,685	190	7.1	1,373	51.1	1,101	41.0	20	1
60 to 64 years	1,982	188	9.5	1,398	70.5	386	19.5	9	1	1,833	115	6.3	716	39.1	999	54.5	3	------
65 to 69 years	1,147	90	7.8	750	65.4	300	26.2	5	2	1,160	71	6.1	363	31.3	722	62.2	4	------
70 to 74 years	690	50	7.2	386	55.9	250	36.2	4	------	681	42	6.2	152	22.3	485	71.2	2	------
75 and over	633	39	6.2	306	48.3	284	44.9	4	------	872	49	5.6	101	11.6	722	82.8	------	------
Unknown	213	62	29.1	96	45.1	17	8.0	------	38	190	42	22.1	86	45.3	35	18.4	------	27
PENNSYLVANIA																		
Total	**162,770**	**55,870**	**34.3**	**96,793**	**59.5**	**8,570**	**5.3**	**1,166**	**371**	**155,482**	**35,298**	**22.7**	**96,975**	**62.4**	**21,338**	**13.7**	**1,595**	**276**
15 to 19 years	15,203	14,785	97.3	374	2.5	5	------	6	33	18,010	14,484	80.4	3,392	18.8	68	.4	34	32
20 to 24 years	19,213	12,022	62.6	6,987	36.4	99	.5	49	56	22,682	8,075	35.6	13,948	61.5	416	1.8	185	58
25 to 29 years	24,843	8,978	36.1	15,360	61.8	301	1.2	140	64	25,510	4,605	18.1	19,340	75.8	1,235	4.8	295	35
30 to 34 years	23,531	6,017	25.6	16,672	70.9	616	2.6	202	24	21,412	2,665	12.4	16,750	78.2	1,672	7.8	292	33
35 to 39 years	23,049	4,935	21.4	17,007	73.8	863	3.7	223	21	20,468	1,945	9.5	15,624	76.3	2,576	12.6	307	16
40 to 44 years	17,096	3,430	20.1	12,455	72.9	1,006	5.9	179	26	14,206	1,127	7.9	10,161	71.5	2,700	19.0	200	18
45 to 49 years	14,447	2,350	16.3	10,753	74.4	1,171	8.1	146	27	11,867	916	7.7	7,936	66.9	2,856	24.1	143	16
50 to 54 years	10,548	1,509	14.3	7,670	72.7	1,249	11.8	97	23	8,183	583	7.1	4,812	58.8	2,705	33.1	69	14
55 to 59 years	6,216	805	13.0	4,440	71.4	896	14.4	63	12	4,847	336	6.9	2,475	51.1	1,994	41.1	37	5
60 to 64 years	3,771	482	12.8	2,488	66.0	758	20.1	33	10	3,264	222	6.8	1,285	39.4	1,736	53.2	16	5
65 to 69 years	2,211	234	10.6	1,328	60.1	631	28.5	12	6	2,046	130	6.4	643	31.4	1,262	61.7	8	3
70 to 74 years	1,254	127	10.1	676	53.9	432	34.4	12	7	1,279	70	5.5	293	22.9	907	70.9	5	4
75 and over	1,108	106	9.6	469	42.3	524	47.3	3	6	1,461	79	5.4	206	14.1	1,171	80.2	2	3
Unknown	280	90	32.1	114	40.7	19	6.8	1	56	247	61	24.7	110	44.5	40	16.2	2	34
OHIO																		
Total	**119,402**	**37,361**	**31.3**	**71,922**	**60.2**	**7,535**	**6.3**	**2,440**	**144**	**109,012**	**19,662**	**18.0**	**70,599**	**64.8**	**15,863**	**14.6**	**2,811**	**77**
15 to 19 years	11,240	10,905	97.0	320	2.8	2	------	7	6	12,518	9,645	77.0	2,758	22.0	72	.6	39	4
20 to 24 years	14,199	8,647	60.9	5,330	37.5	107	.8	105	10	15,193	4,344	28.6	10,006	65.9	458	3.0	370	15
25 to 29 years	17,135	5,440	31.7	11,013	64.3	384	2.2	284	14	17,231	2,017	11.7	13,594	78.9	1,008	5.8	608	4
30 to 34 years	16,335	3,641	22.3	11,802	72.2	524	3.2	359	9	14,844	1,093	7.4	11,887	80.1	1,350	9.1	506	8
35 to 39 years	17,084	3,106	18.2	12,662	74.1	824	4.8	478	14	14,404	868	6.0	11,212	77.8	1,832	12.7	490	2
40 to 44 years	12,565	1,897	15.1	9,413	74.9	849	6.8	398	8	10,219	541	5.3	7,623	74.6	1,760	17.2	214	1
45 to 49 years	10,755	1,388	12.9	7,993	74.3	1,049	9.8	316	9	8,200	427	5.2	5,621	68.5	1,925	23.5	223	4
50 to 54 years	7,583	935	12.3	5,484	72.3	953	12.6	206	5	5,768	251	4.4	3,558	61.7	1,805	31.3	150	4
55 yo 59 years	4,722	548	11.6	3,350	70.9	698	14.8	116	10	3,615	143	4.0	1,983	54.9	1,421	39.3	61	7
60 to 64 years	3,060	336	11.0	2,046	66.9	600	19.6	73	5	2,570	112	4.4	1,180	45.9	1,241	48.3	31	6
65 to 69 years	1,908	203	10.6	1,145	60.0	510	26.7	47	3	1,665	77	4.6	598	35.9	969	58.2	19	2
70 to 74 years	1,224	116	9.5	667	54.5	409	33.4	29	3	1,203	61	5.1	297	24.7	831	69.1	14	------
75 and over	1,340	128	9.6	581	43.4	613	45.7	16	2	1,401	54	3.9	193	13.8	1,146	81.8	3	5
Unknown	252	71	28.2	116	46.0	13	5.2	6	46	181	29	16.0	89	49.2	45	24.9	3	15
INDIANA																		
Total	**43,369**	**13,259**	**30.6**	**25,823**	**59.9**	**3,019**	**7.0**	**1,146**	**122**	**41,027**	**7,320**	**17.8**	**25,491**	**62.1**	**7,018**	**17.1**	**1,127**	**71**
15 to 19 years	4,208	4,067	96.6	132	3.1	1	------	2	6	4,538	3,464	76.3	1,005	22.1	36	.8	26	7
20 to 24 years	4,862	3,004	61.8	1,749	36.0	38	.8	60	11	5,322	1,633	30.7	3,305	62.1	220	4.1	144	20
25 to 29 years	5,649	1,938	34.3	3,458	61.2	109	1.9	139	5	5,934	818	13.8	4,466	75.3	409	6.9	235	6
30 to 34 years	5,580	1,234	22.1	3,943	70.7	209	3.7	184	10	5,222	446	8.5	3,976	76.1	571	10.9	224	5
35 to 39 years	5,664	1,006	17.8	4,133	73.0	282	5.0	229	14	5,177	318	6.1	3,944	76.2	722	13.9	193	------
40 to 44 years	4,510	698	15.5	3,309	73.4	333	7.4	163	7	3,883	233	6.0	2,795	72.0	752	19.4	100	3
45 to 49 years	3,865	495	12.8	2,865	74.1	350	9.1	148	7	3,459	131	3.8	2,427	70.2	814	23.5	84	3
50 to 54 years	3,221	317	9.8	2,441	75.8	376	11.7	85	2	2,578	112	4.3	1,575	61.1	828	32.1	61	2
55 to 59 years	2,132	190	8.9	1,574	73.8	308	14.4	57	3	1,706	58	3.4	944	55.3	673	39.4	31	------
60 to 64 years	1,332	110	8.3	933	70.0	250	18.8	37	2	1,107	26	2.3	507	45.8	558	50.4	15	1
65 to 69 years	940	71	7.6	612	65.1	234	24.9	22	1	814	21	2.6	289	35.5	499	61.3	5	------
70 to 74 years	603	44	7.3	319	52.9	230	38.1	9	1	537	20	3.7	130	24.2	380	70.8	3	4
75 and over	616	46	7.5	267	43.3	290	47.1	9	4	628	19	3.0	75	11.9	525	83.6	4	5
Unknown	187	39	20.9	88	47.1	9	4.8	2	49	122	21	17.2	53	43.4	31	25.4	2	15

TABLE 12.—MARITAL CONDITION OF THE NEGRO POPULATION 15 YEARS OLD AND OVER, BY SEX, AND 5-YEAR AGE PERIODS, BY DIVISIONS, AND STATES: 1930—Continued

[See note at head of this table]

DIVISION OR STATE, AND AGE	MALES 15 YEARS OLD AND OVER									FEMALES 15 YEARS OLD AND OVER								
	Total	Single		Married		Widowed		Divorced	Unknown	Total	Single		Married		Widowed		Divorced	Unknown
		Number	Percent	Number	Percent	Number	Percent				Number	Percent	Number	Percent	Number	Percent		
ILLINOIS																		
Total	**128, 527**	**39, 768**	**30. 9**	**76, 887**	**59. 8**	**8, 799**	**6. 8**	**2, 866**	**207**	**127, 196**	**22, 349**	**17. 6**	**77, 865**	**61. 2**	**23, 112**	**18. 2**	**3, 722**	**148**
15 to 19 years	10, 898	10, 519	96. 5	360	3. 3	8	. 1	7	4	12, 465	9, 389	75. 3	2, 861	23. 0	130	1. 0	76	9
20 to 24 years	15, 108	9, 088	60. 2	5, 707	37. 8	166	1. 1	132	15	18, 156	5, 255	28. 9	11, 607	63. 9	850	4. 7	430	14
25 to 29 years	19, 890	6, 867	34. 5	12, 165	61. 2	470	2. 4	371	17	21, 389	3, 123	14. 6	15, 724	73. 5	1, 709	8. 0	816	17
30 to 34 years	18, 562	4, 332	23. 3	12, 899	69. 5	781	4. 2	535	15	17, 969	1, 674	9. 3	13, 375	74. 4	2, 183	12. 1	723	14
35 to 39 years	18, 606	3, 515	18. 9	13, 468	72. 4	1, 046	5. 6	552	25	17, 299	1, 189	6. 9	12, 459	72. 0	2, 896	16. 7	741	14
40 to 44 years	13, 888	2, 077	15. 0	10, 191	73. 4	1, 157	8. 3	450	13	11, 974	678	5. 7	8, 100	67. 6	2, 784	23. 3	405	7
45 to 49 years	11, 762	1, 456	12. 4	8, 687	73. 9	1, 229	10. 4	381	9	9, 994	428	4. 3	6, 334	63. 4	2, 952	29. 5	272	8
50 to 54 years	8, 076	851	10. 5	5, 870	72. 7	1, 141	14. 1	203	11	6, 610	246	3. 7	3, 595	54. 4	2, 633	39. 8	130	6
55 to 59 years	4, 771	482	10. 1	3, 380	70. 8	783	16. 4	123	3	3, 994	124	3. 1	1, 785	44. 7	2, 007	50. 3	69	9
60 to 64 pears	2, 905	250	8. 6	1, 923	66. 2	666	22. 9	61	5	2, 792	85	3. 0	1, 013	36. 3	1, 655	59. 3	35	4
65 to 69 years	1, 755	128	7. 3	1, 091	62. 2	510	29. 1	26	---	1, 839	62	3. 4	535	29. 1	1, 226	66. 7	12	4
70 to 74 years	986	69	7. 0	553	56. 1	349	35. 4	14	1	1, 140	29	2. 5	225	19. 7	881	77. 3	3	2
75 and over	1, 032	70	6. 8	471	45. 6	477	46. 2	10	4	1, 322	31	2. 3	147	11. 1	1, 134	85. 8	5	5
Unknown	288	64	22. 2	122	42. 4	16	5. 6	1	85	253	36	14. 2	105	41. 5	72	28. 5	5	35
MICHIGAN																		
Total	**68, 493**	**21, 408**	**31. 3**	**41, 891**	**61. 2**	**3, 492**	**5. 1**	**1, 587**	**115**	**59, 610**	**9, 153**	**15. 4**	**41, 061**	**68. 9**	**7, 707**	**12. 9**	**1, 630**	**59**
15 to 19 years	5, 143	5, 004	97. 3	129	2. 5	2	---	2	6	5, 745	4, 134	72. 0	1, 538	26. 8	27	. 5	45	1
20 to 24 years	8, 473	5, 074	59. 9	3, 247	38. 3	61	. 7	77	14	9, 258	2, 153	23. 3	6, 630	71. 6	259	2. 8	204	12
25 to 29 years	12, 414	4, 174	33. 6	7, 764	62. 5	223	1. 8	232	21	11, 891	1, 168	9. 8	9, 636	81. 0	716	6. 0	361	10
30 to 34 years	11, 760	2, 701	23. 0	8, 347	71. 0	403	3. 4	296	13	9, 754	667	6. 8	7, 866	80. 6	865	8. 9	350	6
35 to 39 years	10, 756	1, 895	17. 6	7, 988	74. 3	527	4. 9	330	16	8, 345	478	5. 7	6, 570	78. 7	1, 006	12. 1	284	7
40 to 44 years	7, 147	1, 087	15. 2	5, 344	74. 8	484	6. 8	226	6	4, 907	214	4. 4	3, 576	72. 9	936	19. 1	178	3
45 to 49 years	5, 361	660	12. 3	4, 044	75. 4	461	8. 6	187	9	3, 689	138	3. 7	2, 508	68. 0	923	25. 0	117	3
50 to 54 years	3, 186	383	12. 0	2, 293	72. 0	401	12. 6	108	1	2, 234	71	3. 2	1, 339	59. 9	783	35. 0	38	3
55 to 59 years	1, 803	191	10. 6	1, 283	71. 2	261	14. 5	66	2	1, 318	33	2. 5	633	48. 0	616	46. 7	35	1
60 to 64 years	1, 001	92	9. 2	665	66. 4	209	20. 9	34	1	919	42	4. 6	356	38. 7	512	55. 7	7	2
65 to 69 years	595	50	8. 4	367	61. 7	161	27. 1	16	1	593	14	2. 4	192	32. 4	383	64. 6	4	---
70 to 74 years	305	24	7. 9	169	55. 4	107	35. 1	5	---	367	12	3. 3	79	21. 5	270	73. 6	5	1
75 and over	383	20	5. 2	165	43. 1	191	49. 9	6	1	472	17	3. 6	62	13. 1	390	82. 6	2	1
Unknown	166	53	31. 9	86	51. 8	1	. 6	2	24	118	12	10. 2	76	64. 4	21	17. 8	---	9
WISCONSIN																		
Total	**4, 539**	**1, 594**	**35. 1**	**2, 505**	**55, 2**	**303**	**6. 7**	**123**	**14**	**3, 602**	**568**	**15. 8**	**2, 383**	**66. 2**	**514**	**14. 3**	**132**	**5**
15 to 19 years	329	320	97. 3	7	2. 1	---	---	---	2	367	267	72. 8	94	25. 6	4	1. 1	2	---
20 to 24 years	533	339	63. 6	179	33. 6	9	1. 7	1	5	533	109	20. 5	391	73. 4	21	3. 9	12	---
25 to 29 years	732	287	39. 2	414	56. 6	15	2. 0	16	---	664	77	11. 6	497	74. 8	55	8. 3	35	---
30 to 34 years	678	192	28. 3	440	64. 9	26	3. 8	20	---	528	43	8. 1	410	77. 7	47	8. 9	26	2
35 to 39 years	697	164	23. 5	474	68. 0	37	5. 3	22	---	481	31	6. 4	381	79. 2	50	10. 4	19	---
40 to 44 years	540	113	20. 9	355	65. 7	51	9. 4	19	2	335	10	3. 0	239	71. 3	68	20. 3	16	2
45 to 49 years	382	68	17. 8	257	67. 3	43	11. 3	13	1	238	10	4. 2	164	68. 9	56	23. 5	8	---
50 to 54 years	271	52	19. 2	161	59. 4	40	14. 8	18	---	162	5	3. 1	108	66. 7	40	24. 7	8	1
55 to 59 years	174	30	17. 2	109	62. 6	26	14. 9	9	---	100	4	4. 0	49	49. 0	45	45. 0	2	---
60 to 64 years	74	9	---	41	---	21	---	2	1	77	5	---	28	---	42	---	2	---
65 to 69 years	50	10	---	33	---	5	---	1	1	47	2	---	11	---	33	---	1	---
70 to 74 years	29	1	---	17	---	10	---	1	---	31	2	---	5	---	23	---	1	---
75 and over	40	8	---	12	---	19	---	1	---	32	1	---	2	---	29	---	---	---
Unknown	10	1	---	6	---	1	---	---	2	7	2	---	4	---	1	---	---	---
MINNESOTA																		
Total	**4, 033**	**1, 304**	**32. 3**	**2, 261**	**56. 1**	**283**	**7. 0**	**178**	**7**	**3, 510**	**596**	**17. 0**	**2, 141**	**61. 0**	**642**	**18. 3**	**126**	**5**
15 to 19 years	282	276	97. 9	5	1. 8	---	---	---	1	332	284	85. 5	45	13. 6	1	. 3	2	---
20 to 24 years	311	219	70. 4	85	27. 3	1	. 3	6	---	339	136	40. 1	186	54. 9	6	1. 8	11	---
25 to 29 years	379	164	43. 3	195	51. 5	4	1. 1	15	1	353	43	12. 2	276	78. 2	13	3. 7	20	1
30 to 34 years	472	150	31. 8	284	60. 2	17	3. 6	20	1	411	39	9. 5	317	77. 1	41	10. 0	14	---
35 to 39 years	540	134	24. 8	366	67. 8	18	3. 3	22	---	496	24	4. 8	392	79. 0	54	10. 9	26	---
40 to 44 years	499	106	21. 2	331	66. 3	25	5. 0	36	1	390	17	4. 4	295	75. 6	59	15. 1	19	---
45 to 49 years	483	95	19. 7	326	67. 5	32	6. 6	30	---	387	17	4. 4	259	66. 9	93	24. 0	18	---
50 to 54 years	394	65	16. 5	256	65. 0	52	13. 2	20	1	259	13	5. 0	161	62. 2	78	30. 1	7	---
55 to 59 years	276	36	13. 0	204	73. 9	27	9. 8	8	1	199	8	4. 0	111	55. 8	72	36. 2	6	2
60 to 64 years	158	23	14. 6	97	61. 4	30	19. 0	8	---	128	5	3. 9	58	45. 3	63	49. 2	1	1
65 to 69 years	121	19	15. 7	70	57. 9	24	19. 8	7	1	94	4	---	28	---	60	---	1	1
70 to 74 years	49	4	---	24	---	18	---	3	---	46	3	---	5	---	38	---	---	---
75 and over	61	12	---	12	---	34	---	3	---	73	2	---	7	---	64	---	---	---
Unknown	8	1	---	6	---	1	---	---	---	3	1	---	1	---	---	---	1	---
IOWA																		
Total	**6, 830**	**2, 234**	**32. 7**	**3, 841**	**56. 2**	**471**	**6. 9**	**274**	**10**	**6, 188**	**1, 137**	**18. 4**	**3, 766**	**60. 9**	**1, 009**	**16. 3**	**270**	**6**
15 to 19 years	679	662	97. 5	16	2. 4	---	---	1	---	735	611	83. 1	113	15. 4	2	. 3	8	1
20 to 24 years	679	455	67. 0	211	31. 1	2	. 3	10	1	684	233	34. 1	402	58. 8	14	2. 0	35	---
25 to 29 years	682	250	36. 7	396	58. 1	6	. 9	29	1	670	85	12. 7	499	74. 5	41	6. 1	44	1
30 to 34 years	712	203	28. 5	450	63. 2	21	2. 9	37	1	649	43	6. 6	494	76. 1	61	9. 4	51	---
35 to 39 years	765	157	20. 5	542	70. 8	28	3. 7	38	---	751	39	5. 2	588	78. 3	83	11. 1	41	---
40 to 44 years	688	151	21. 9	464	67. 4	32	4. 7	41	---	639	32	5. 0	485	75. 9	95	14. 9	27	---
45 to 49 years	710	120	16. 9	508	71. 5	47	6. 6	35	---	581	30	5. 2	428	73. 7	100	17. 2	23	---
50 to 54 years	594	71	12. 0	423	71. 2	64	10. 8	36	---	467	23	4. 9	291	62. 3	127	27. 2	25	1
55 to 59 years	451	62	13. 7	320	71. 0	48	10. 6	20	1	336	15	4. 5	211	62. 8	104	31. 0	6	---
60 to 64 years	326	31	9. 5	216	66. 3	70	21. 5	9	---	240	6	2. 5	117	48. 8	113	47. 1	4	---
65 to 69 years	238	34	14. 3	139	58. 4	53	22. 3	10	2	154	8	5. 2	70	45. 5	73	47. 4	3	---
70 to 74 years	137	21	15. 3	76	55. 5	34	24. 8	5	1	109	2	1. 8	36	33. 0	68	62. 4	2	1
75 and over	151	10	6. 6	75	49. 7	64	42. 4	2	---	159	8	5. 0	27	17. 0	124	78. 0	---	---
Unknown	18	7	---	5	---	2	---	1	3	14	2	---	5	---	4	---	1	2

TABLE 12.—MARITAL CONDITION OF THE NEGRO POPULATION 15 YEARS OLD AND OVER, BY SEX, AND 5-YEAR AGE PERIODS, BY DIVISIONS, AND STATES: 1930—Continued

[See note at head of this table]

DIVISION OR STATE, AND AGE	MALES 15 YEARS OLD AND OVER									FEMALES 15 YEARS OLD AND OVER								
	Total	Single		Married		Widowed		Divorced	Unknown	Total	Single		Married		Widowed		Divorced	Unknown
		Number	Percent	Number	Percent	Number	Percent				Number	Percent	Number	Percent	Number	Percent		
MISSOURI																		
Total	**86,100**	**26,201**	**30.4**	**50,784**	**59.0**	**7,221**	**8.4**	**1,698**	**196**	**86,046**	**16,788**	**19.5**	**50,988**	**59.3**	**16,176**	**18.8**	**1,976**	**118**
15 to 19 years	8,480	8,144	96.0	321	3.8	7	.1	4	4	9,255	7,036	76.0	2,087	22.5	92	1.0	37	3
20 to 24 years	9,302	5,459	58.7	3.620	38.9	121	1.3	86	16	11,363	3,837	33.8	6,757	59.5	504	4.4	253	12
25 to 29 years	10,502	3,488	33.2	6,557	62.4	261	2.5	182	14	12,188	2,143	17.6	8,662	71.1	958	7.9	415	10
30 to 34 years	9,983	2,388	23.9	6,932	69.4	388	3.9	256	19	10,576	1,256	11.9	7,754	73.3	1,215	11.5	338	13
35 to 39 years	10,926	2,024	18.5	7,967	72.9	638	5.8	283	14	10,929	910	8.3	7,940	72.7	1,740	15.9	332	7
40 to 44 years	9,433	1,550	16.4	6,819	72.3	816	8.7	235	13	8,493	540	6.4	5,929	69.8	1,804	21.2	215	5
45 to 49 years	8,735	1,136	13.0	6,385	73.1	946	10.8	254	14	7,345	380	5.2	4,791	65.2	2,003	27.3	165	6
50 to 54 years	6,522	812	12.5	4,657	71.4	902	13.8	142	9	5,332	257	4.8	3,131	58.7	1,837	34.5	99	8
55 to 59 years	4,211	472	11.2	2,929	69.6	695	16.5	112	3	3,365	130	3.9	1,708	50.8	1,458	43.3	66	3
60 to 64 years	3,022	247	8.2	2,012	66.6	701	23.2	55	7	2,481	89	3.6	1,010	40.7	1,357	54.7	22	3
65 to 69 years	1,995	176	8.8	1,169	58.6	605	30.3	42	3	1,771	53	3.0	620	35.0	1,077	60.8	20	1
70 to 74 years	1,225	94	7.7	681	55.6	427	34.9	20	3	1,161	52	4.5	294	25.3	809	69.7	4	2
75 and over	1,514	139	9.2	661	43.7	689	45.5	23	2	1,571	70	4.5	237	15.1	1,250	79.6	7	7
Unknown	250	72	28.8	74	29.6	25	10.0	4	75	216	35	16.2	68	31.5	72	33.3	3	38
NORTH DAKOTA																		
Total	**200**	**95**	**47.5**	**70**	**35.0**	**21**	**10.5**	**13**	**1**	**111**	**22**	**19.8**	**68**	**61.3**	**17**	**15.3**	**4**	-
15 to 19 years	19	19	-	-	-	-	-	-	-	7	7	-	-	-	-	-	-	-
20 to 24 years	9	8	-	1	-	-	-	-	-	23	9	-	13	-	1	-	-	-
25 to 29 years	19	8	-	10	-	-	-	1	-	12	2	-	6	-	3	-	1	-
30 to 34 years	15	10	-	4	-	-	-	1	-	17	-	-	13	-	3	-	1	-
35 to 39 years	25	12	-	8	-	1	-	4	-	9	1	-	7	-	1	-	-	-
40 to 44 years	24	6	-	12	-	3	-	3	-	16	-	-	13	-	1	-	2	-
54 to 49 years	28	11	-	12	-	3	-	2	-	9	-	-	7	-	2	-	-	-
50 to 54 years	25	9	-	11	-	4	-	1	-	7	-	-	5	-	2	-	-	-
55 to 59 years	14	6	-	6	-	1	-	-	1	5	1	-	3	-	1	-	-	-
60 to 64 years	8	2	-	4	-	1	-	1	-	4	2	-	1	-	1	-	-	-
65 to 69 years	6	1	-	1	-	4	-	-	-	1	-	-	-	-	1	-	-	-
70 to 74 years	6	3	-	1	-	2	-	-	-	-	-	-	-	-	-	-	-	-
75 and over	2	-	-	-	-	2	-	-	-	1	-	-	-	-	1	-	-	-
Unknown	-	-	-	-	-	-	-	-	-	-	-	-	-	-	-	-	-	-
SOUTH DAKOTA																		
Total	**279**	**119**	**42.7**	**131**	**47.0**	**22**	**7.9**	**7**	-	**212**	**48**	**22.6**	**125**	**59.0**	**30**	**14.2**	**9**	-
15 to 19 years	36	36	-	-	-	-	-	-	-	26	23	-	3	-	-	-	-	-
20 to 24 years	29	25	-	4	-	-	-	-	-	36	14	-	21	-	-	-	1	-
25 to 29 years	30	13	-	15	-	1	-	1	-	22	5	-	15	-	1	-	1	-
30 to 34 years	32	11	-	20	-	-	-	1	-	19	2	-	15	-	-	-	2	-
35 to 39 years	25	7	-	18	-	-	-	-	-	19	-	-	17	-	1	-	1	-
40 to 44 years	26	6	-	17	-	2	-	1	-	25	2	-	17	-	4	-	2	-
45 to 49 years	26	6	-	15	-	4	-	1	-	16	-	-	10	-	5	-	1	-
50 to 54 years	22	5	-	12	-	2	-	3	-	16	1	-	10	-	5	-	-	-
55 to 59 years	15	3	-	10	-	2	-	-	-	10	1	-	6	-	2	-	1	-
60 to 64 years	11	1	-	7	-	3	-	-	-	9	-	-	4	-	5	-	-	-
65 to 69 years	11	4	-	2	-	5	-	-	-	4	-	-	3	-	1	-	-	-
70 to 74 years	8	2	-	4	-	2	-	-	-	5	-	-	4	-	1	-	-	-
75 and over	5	-	-	4	-	1	-	-	-	5	-	-	-	-	5	-	-	-
Unknown	3	-	-	3	-	-	-	-	-	-	-	-	-	-	-	-	-	-
NEBRASKA																		
Total	**5,502**	**1,662**	**30.2**	**3,159**	**57.4**	**454**	**8.3**	**212**	**15**	**5,173**	**845**	**16.3**	**3,130**	**60.5**	**967**	**18.7**	**219**	**12**
15 to 19 years	455	445	97.8	8	1.8	1	.2	-	1	507	395	77.9	104	20.5	4	.8	3	1
20 to 24 years	503	325	64.6	166	33.0	1	.2	7	4	619	185	29.9	383	61.9	19	3.1	28	4
25 to 29 years	692	257	37.1	394	56.9	18	2.6	23	-	712	100	14.0	515	72.3	58	8.1	37	2
30 to 34 years	661	151	22.8	456	69.0	28	4.2	24	2	653	49	7.5	493	75.5	67	10.3	44	-
35 to 39 years	744	147	19.8	519	69.8	39	5.2	39	-	713	39	5.5	529	74.2	116	16.3	29	-
40 to 44 years	659	114	17.3	447	67.8	55	8.3	40	3	581	31	5.3	391	67.3	120	20.7	37	2
45 to 49 years	630	97	15.4	438	69.5	63	10.0	28	4	486	19	3.9	303	62.3	140	28.8	23	1
50 to 54 years	467	49	10.5	316	67.7	79	16.9	23	-	336	9	2.7	204	60.7	117	34.8	5	1
55 to 59 years	247	29	11.7	170	68.8	38	15.4	10	-	208	9	4.3	103	49.5	88	42.3	8	-
60 to 64 years	181	12	6.6	114	63.0	46	25.4	9	-	126	3	2.4	40	31.7	80	63.5	3	-
65 to 69 years	112	8	7.1	59	52.7	37	33.0	8	-	95	2	-	42	-	51	-	-	-
70 to 74 years	56	6	-	35	-	15	-	-	-	53	2	-	7	-	41	-	2	1
75 and over	81	13	-	33	-	33	-	1	1	79	1	-	13	-	65	-	-	-
Unknown	14	9	-	4	-	1	-	-	-	5	1	-	3	-	1	-	-	-
KANSAS																		
Total	**25,649**	**7,715**	**30.1**	**14,746**	**57.5**	**2,015**	**7.9**	**1,040**	**133**	**23,886**	**4,416**	**18.5**	**14,401**	**60.3**	**4,130**	**17.3**	**920**	**19**
15 to 19 years	2,631	2,563	97.4	65	2.5	1	-	2	-	2,803	2,285	81.5	472	16.8	19	.7	25	2
20 to 24 years	2,714	1,803	66.4	827	30.5	19	.7	59	6	2,772	1,001	36.1	1,577	56.9	91	3.3	102	1
25 to 29 years	2,775	990	35.7	1,599	57.6	59	2.1	124	3	2,779	401	14.4	2,085	75.0	142	5.1	151	-
30 to 34 years	2,886	681	23.6	1,920	66.5	95	3.3	165	25	2,587	218	8.4	1,999	77.3	214	8.3	155	1
35 to 39 years	2,998	505	16.8	2,153	71.8	134	4.5	169	37	2,715	158	5.8	2,117	78.0	281	10.3	158	1
40 to 44 years	2,626	367	14.0	1,940	73.9	155	5.9	148	16	2,392	106	4.4	1,806	75.5	375	15.7	104	1
45 to 49 years	2,339	271	11.6	1,751	74.9	199	8.5	113	5	2,173	85	3.9	1,566	72.1	442	20.3	79	1
50 to 54 years	2,114	194	9.2	1,565	74.0	241	11.4	97	17	1,727	61	3.5	1,118	64.7	488	28.3	59	1
55 to 59 years	1,552	146	9.4	1,104	71.1	233	15.0	61	8	1,193	41	3.4	685	57.4	427	35.8	39	1
60 to 64 years	1,034	66	6.4	712	68.9	209	20.2	46	1	919	19	2.1	460	50.1	423	46.0	17	-
65 to 69 years	776	58	7.5	494	63.7	201	25.9	22	1	657	12	1.8	277	42.2	354	53.9	13	1
70 to 74 years	506	24	4.7	300	59.3	163	32.2	15	4	433	14	3.2	124	28.6	284	65.6	10	1
75 and over	665	35	5.3	303	45.6	301	45.3	18	8	711	11	1.5	105	14.8	584	82.1	4	7
Unknown	33	12	-	13	-	5	-	1	2	25	4	-	10	-	6	-	4	1

TABLE 12.—MARITAL CONDITION OF THE NEGRO POPULATION 15 YEARS OLD AND OVER, BY SEX, AND 5-YEAR AGE PERIODS, BY DIVISIONS, AND STATES: 1930—Continued

[See note at head of this table]

DIVISION OF STATE, AND AGE	MALES 15 YEARS OLD AND OVER									FEMALES 15 YEARS OLD AND OVER								
	Total	Single		Married		Widowed		Divorced	Unknown	Total	Single		Married		Widowed		Divorced	Unknown
		Number	Percent	Number	Percent	Number	Percent				Number	Percent	Number	Percent	Number	Percent		
DELAWARE																		
Total	**12,485**	**4,971**	**39.8**	**6,485**	**51.9**	**830**	**7.0**	**96**	**53**	**11,097**	**3,024**	**27.3**	**6,424**	**57.9**	**1,544**	**13.9**	**82**	**23**
15 to 19 years	1,503	1,473	98.0	27	1.8			1	2	1,482	1,278	86.2	200	13.5	1	.1	1	2
20 to 24 years	1,573	1,121	71.3	432	27.5	11	.7	2	7	1,415	657	46.4	725	51.2	19	1.3	14	
25 to 29 years	1,478	657	44.5	797	53.9	16	1.1	5	3	1,341	345	25.7	948	70.7	43	3.2	3	2
30 to 34 years	1,283	418	32.6	813	63.4	37	2.9	15		1,194	206	17.3	914	76.5	63	5.3	11	
35 to 39 years	1,453	412	28.4	965	66.4	54	3.7	18	4	1,262	178	14.1	961	76.1	109	8.6	13	1
40 to 44 years	1,150	272	23.7	797	69.3	67	5.8	13	1	987	118	12.0	726	73.6	128	13.0	13	2
45 to 49 years	1,038	209	20.1	738	71.1	78	7.5	13		899	82	9.1	644	71.6	158	17.6	13	2
50 to 54 years	999	155	15.5	698	69.9	135	13.5	10	1	805	51	6.3	532	66.1	215	26.7	7	
55 to 59 years	628	92	14.6	425	67.7	99	15.8	8	4	511	38	7.4	300	58.7	166	32.5	3	4
60 to 64 years	523	71	13.6	331	63.3	107	20.5	6	8	408	27	6.6	201	49.3	176	43.1	2	2
65 to 69 years	376	37	9.8	233	62.0	100	26.6	3	3	328	14	4.3	148	45.1	162	49.4	2	2
70 to 74 years	215	27	12.6	114	53.0	69	32.1	1	4	202	11	5.4	69	34.2	120	59.4		2
75 and over	251	23	9.2	107	42.6	107	42.6		14	258	19	7.4	52	20.2	183	70.9		4
Unknown	15	4		8				1	2	5			4		1			
MARYLAND																		
Total	**99,951**	**37,113**	**37.1**	**55,258**	**55.3**	**6,376**	**6.4**	**782**	**422**	**94,231**	**24,295**	**25.8**	**55,009**	**58.4**	**13,466**	**14.3**	**1,006**	**455**
15 to 19 years	12,554	12,253	97.6	269	2.1	3		7	22	12,863	10,794	83.9	2,010	15.6	23	.2	10	26
20 to 24 years	13,841	9,275	67.0	4,428	32.0	66	.5	25	47	13,570	5,680	41.9	7,552	55.7	206	1.5	98	34
25 to 29 years	13,065	5,016	38.4	7,743	59.3	185	1.4	89	32	12,444	2,654	21.3	9,095	73.1	522	4.2	154	19
30 to 34 years	11,218	3,030	27.0	7,755	69.1	297	2.6	111	25	10,608	1,460	13.8	8,166	77.0	780	7.4	184	18
35 to 39 years	11,373	2,395	21.1	8,365	73.6	447	3.9	147	19	10,576	1,160	11.0	8,069	76.3	1,150	10.9	174	23
40 to 44 years	9,223	1,644	17.8	6,827	74.0	615	6.7	116	21	8,487	773	9.1	6,158	72.6	1,403	16.5	137	16
45 to 49 years	8,244	1,270	15.4	6,102	74.0	764	9.3	95	13	7,509	541	7.2	5,158	68.7	1,676	22.3	114	20
50 to 54 years	6,903	846	12.3	5,058	73.3	894	13.0	90	15	5,890	407	6.9	3,666	62.2	1,734	29.4	66	17
55 to 59 years	4,364	466	10.7	3,184	73.0	658	15.1	47	9	3,696	224	6.1	2,103	56.9	1,327	35.9	29	13
60 to 64 years	3,372	323	9.6	2,290	67.9	724	21.5	28	7	2,940	204	6.9	1,356	46.1	1,341	45.6	20	19
65 to 69 years	2,271	205	9.0	1,460	64.3	587	25.8	16	3	2,044	118	5.8	800	39.1	1,105	54.1	7	14
70 to 74 years	1,465	119	8.1	840	57.3	493	33.7	5	8	1,359	70	5.2	364	26.8	899	66.2	7	19
75 and over	1,379	125	9.1	633	45.9	612	44.4	4	5	1,567	91	5.8	237	15.1	1,211	77.3	3	25
Unknown	679	146	21.5	304	44.8	31	4.6	2	196	678	119	17.6	275	40.6	89	13.1	3	192
DISTRICT OF COLUMBIA																		
Total	**47,443**	**15,925**	**33.6**	**28,212**	**59.5**	**2,714**	**5.7**	**342**	**250**	**54,297**	**14,058**	**25.9**	**29,942**	**55.1**	**9.556**	**17.6**	**530**	**211**
15 to 19 years	4,757	4,591	96.5	156	3.3	1		1	8	5,918	4,862	82.2	1,028	17.4	14	.2	2	12
20 to 24 years	6,472	3,983	61.5	2,432	37.6	22	.3	11	24	7,924	3,303	41.6	4,424	55.8	143	1.8	42	22
25 to 29 years	6,994	2,386	34.1	4,473	64.0	93	1.3	28	14	7,995	1,883	23.6	5,631	70.4	374	4.7	90	17
30 to 34 years	5,889	1,460	24.8	4,195	71.2	158	2.7	66	10	6,471	1,086	16.8	4,683	72.4	592	9.1	99	11
35 to 39 years	5,797	1,150	19.8	4,325	74.6	250	4.3	66	6	6,357	826	13.0	4,526	71.2	893	14.0	104	8
40 to 44 years	4,493	753	16.8	3,414	76.0	266	5.9	52	8	5,070	593	11.7	3,312	65.3	1,085	21.4	73	7
45 to 49 years	4,247	569	13.4	3,229	76.0	396	9.3	45	8	4,673	480	10.3	2,775	59.4	1,365	29.2	52	1
50 to 54 years	3,433	438	12.8	2,581	75.2	370	10.8	37	7	3,511	390	11.1	1,687	48.0	1,400	39.9	30	4
55 to 59 years	1,966	216	11.0	1,461	74.3	270	13.7	18	1	2,035	194	9.5	904	44.4	914	44.9	18	5
60 to 64 years	1,274	156	12.2	851	66.8	254	19.9	11	2	1,511	171	11.3	426	30.6	869	57.5	8	1
65 to 69 years	849	82	9.7	542	63.8	222	26.1	1	2	1,093	97	8.9	263	24.1	725	66.3	4	4
70 to 74 years	508	43	8.5	271	53.3	187	36.8	5	2	615	55	8.9	78	12.7	479	77.9	1	2
75 and over	444	45	10.1	178	40.1	218	49.1	1	2	782	61	7.8	63	8.1	655	83.8	2	1
Unknown	320	53	16.6	104	32.5	7	2.2		156	332	57	17.2	106	31.9	48	14.5	5	116
VIRGINIA																		
Total	**204,713**	**75,076**	**36.7**	**114,672**	**56.0**	**12,630**	**6.2**	**2,008**	**327**	**210,823**	**59,134**	**28.0**	**116,842**	**55.4**	**31,848**	**15.1**	**2,834**	**165**
15 to 19 years	36,432	35,749	98.1	644	1.8	6		7	26	37,011	32,090	86.7	4,704	12.7	116	.3	80	21
20 to 24 years	27,327	18,161	66.5	8,816	32.3	162	.6	119	69	29,240	12,893	44.1	15,318	52.4	618	2.1	382	29
25 to 29 years	20,715	6,991	33.7	13,050	63.0	367	1.8	244	63	23,763	5,021	21.1	16,973	71.4	1,232	5.2	523	14
30 to 34 years	17,860	3,865	21.6	13,181	73.8	508	2.8	271	35	20,423	2,559	12.5	15,692	76.8	1,680	8.2	484	8
35 to 39 years	20,297	3,150	15.5	15,917	78.4	866	4.3	321	43	22,730	1,897	8.3	17,619	77.5	2,743	12.1	458	13
40 to 44 years	18,102	2,264	12.5	14,408	79.6	1,141	6.3	271	18	18,553	1,334	7.2	13,874	74.8	3,016	16.3	319	10
45 to 49 years	17,622	1,664	9.4	14,218	80.7	1,485	8.4	242	13	17,180	985	5.7	12,152	70.7	3,784	22.0	241	18
50 to 54 years	15,328	1,271	8.3	12,180	79.5	1,662	10.8	203	12	13,627	810	5.9	8,762	64.3	3,867	28.4	177	11
55 to 59 years	10,358	693	6.7	8,280	79.9	1,240	12.0	138	7	8,162	413	5.1	4,829	59.2	2,843	34.8	69	8
60 to 64 years	7,773	499	6.4	5,808	74.7	1,381	17.8	84	1	7,080	385	5.4	3,318	46.9	3,319	46.9	53	5
65 to 69 years	5,274	323	6.1	3,733	70.8	1,165	22.1	48	5	5,065	290	5.7	1,876	37.0	2,863	56.5	31	5
70 to 74 years	3,651	197	5.4	2,350	64.4	1,070	29.3	30	4	3,497	186	5.3	978	28.0	2,321	66.4	8	4
75 and over	3,794	209	5.5	1,980	52.2	1,571	41.4	27	7	4,264	226	5.3	660	15.5	3,360	78.8	8	10
Unknown	180	40	22.2	107	59.4	6	3.3	3	24	228	45	19.7	87	38.2	86	37.7	1	9
WEST VIRGINIA																		
Total	**43,429**	**15,492**	**35.7**	**24,969**	**57.5**	**2,302**	**5.3**	**636**	**30**	**36,048**	**7,602**	**21.1**	**23,838**	**66.1**	**4,045**	**11.2**	**544**	**19**
15 to 19 years	4,705	4,612	98.0	86	1.8	2		3	2	5,404	4,085	75.6	1,273	23.6	21	.4	23	2
20 to 24 years	5,533	3,785	68.4	1,683	30.4	28	.5	31	6	5,684	1,748	30.8	3,712	65.3	136	2.4	88	
25 to 29 years	6,045	2,224	36.8	3,641	60.2	88	1.5	88	4	5,636	695	12.3	4,595	81.5	241	4.3	101	4
30 to 34 years	5,800	1,424	24.6	4,130	71.2	148	2.6	96	2	4,746	359	7.6	3,990	84.1	308	6.5	86	3
35 to 39 years	5,960	1,215	20.4	4,417	74.1	219	3.7	107	2	4,412	242	5.5	3,625	82.2	443	10.0	98	4
40 to 44 years	4,803	793	16.5	3,600	75.0	303	6.3	106	1	3,195	144	4.5	2,510	78.6	481	15.1	60	
45 to 49 years	3,924	548	14.0	2,965	75.6	318	8.1	91	2	2,451	104	4.2	1,843	75.2	469	19.1	35	
50 to 54 years	2,636	375	14.2	1,881	71.4	320	12.1	60		1,728	89	5.2	1,144	66.2	467	27.0	27	1
55 to 59 years	1,644	233	14.2	1,170	71.2	217	13.2	22	2	895	40	4.5	517	57.8	327	36.5	11	
60 to 64 years	1,003	118	11.8	677	67.5	196	19.5	11	1	685	30	4.4	304	44.4	347	50.7	3	1
65 to 69 years	623	73	11.7	364	58.4	173	27.8	13		457	17	3.7	171	37.4	262	57.3	6	1
70 to 74 years	361	38	10.5	185	51.2	134	37.1	4		303	17	5.6	73	24.1	209	69.0	4	
75 and over	320	31	9.7	133	41.6	150	46.9	4	2	395	21	5.3	55	13.9	317	80.3	1	1
Unknown	72	23		37		6			6	57	11		26		17		1	2

Table 12.—MARITAL CONDITION OF THE NEGRO POPULATION 15 YEARS OLD AND OVER, BY SEX, AND 5-YEAR AGE PERIODS, BY DIVISIONS, AND STATES: 1930—Continued

[See note at head of this table]

DIVISION OR STATE, AND AGE	MALES 15 YEARS OLD AND OVER									FEMALES 15 YEARS OLD AND OVER								
	Total	Single		Married		Widowed		Divorced	Unknown	Total	Single		Married		Widowed		Divorced	Unknown
		Number	Percent	Number	Percent	Number	Percent				Number	Percent	Number	Percent	Number	Percent		
NORTH CAROLINA																		
Total	**266,001**	**98,885**	**37.2**	**152,237**	**57.2**	**13,023**	**4.9**	**1,418**	**438**	**290,045**	**90,894**	**31.3**	**157,643**	**54.4**	**38,356**	**13.2**	**2,773**	**379**
15 to 19 years	55,846	54,364	97.3	1,390	2.5	23	------	15	54	59,320	50,543	85.2	8,469	14.3	207	0.3	77	24
20 to 24 years	43,601	25,480	58.4	17,518	40.2	339	.8	149	115	51,403	22,020	42.8	27,645	53.8	1,235	2.4	424	79
25 to 29 years	31,595	8,167	25.8	22,535	71.3	629	2.0	192	72	38,248	7,952	20.8	27,396	71.6	2,300	6.0	556	44
30 to 34 years	23,827	3,643	15.3	19,198	80.6	737	3.1	211	38	27,557	3,270	11.9	21,179	76.9	2,620	9.5	457	31
35 to 39 years	23,472	2,457	10.5	19,784	84.3	981	4.2	224	26	27,717	2,152	7.8	21,527	77.7	3,603	13.0	402	33
40 to 44 years	18,940	1,534	8.1	16,044	84.7	1,200	6.3	149	13	21,808	1,433	6.6	15,992	73.3	4,072	18.7	273	38
45 to 49 years	17,519	1,063	6.1	15,059	86.0	1,259	7.2	125	13	19,576	1,031	5.3	13,937	71.2	4,336	22.1	242	30
50 to 54 years	17,583	827	4.7	15,021	85.4	1,606	9.1	117	12	15,100	855	5.7	9,430	62.5	4,637	30.7	154	24
55 to 59 years	11,643	449	3.9	9,753	83.8	1,332	11.4	98	11	8,941	444	5.0	5,223	58.4	3,174	35.5	85	15
60 to 64 years	8,242	313	3.8	6,516	79.1	1,340	16.3	70	3	7,179	382	5.3	3,220	44.9	3,521	49.0	44	12
65 to 69 years	5,449	187	3.4	4,132	75.8	1,088	20.0	35	7	4,855	260	5.4	1,784	36.7	2,777	57.2	26	8
70 to 74 years	3,779	138	3.7	2,680	70.9	939	24.8	19	3	3,527	199	5.6	968	27.4	2,344	66.5	12	4
75 and over	4,050	164	4.0	2,342	57.8	1,526	37.7	11	7	4,331	240	5.5	655	15.1	3,412	78.8	11	13
Unknown	455	99	21.8	265	58.2	24	5.3	3	64	483	113	23.4	218	45.1	118	24.4	10	24
SOUTH CAROLINA																		
Total	**218,867**	**76,557**	**35.1**	**130,007**	**59.5**	**10,999**	**5.0**	**629**	**175**	**251,595**	**74,892**	**29.8**	**135,531**	**53.9**	**39,385**	**15.7**	**1,579**	**208**
15 to 19 years	50,805	48,965	96.4	1,779	3.5	27	.1	9	25	55,624	46,023	82.7	9,262	16.7	228	.4	89	22
20 to 24 years	34,172	16,735	49.0	17,000	49.7	296	.9	89	52	42,480	16,423	38.7	24,357	57.3	1,367	3.2	292	41
25 to 29 years	21,868	4,184	19.1	17,138	78.4	452	2.1	81	13	29,431	5,262	17.9	21,574	73.3	2,251	7.6	325	19
30 to 34 years	16,972	2,068	12.2	14,262	84.0	549	3.2	86	7	21,997	2,224	10.1	16,989	77.2	2,537	11.5	219	28
35 to 39 years	19,484	1,422	7.3	17,143	88.0	812	4.2	97	10	25,535	1,672	6.5	19,370	75.9	4,240	16.6	231	22
40 to 44 years	16,842	1,034	6.1	14,683	87.2	1,042	6.2	72	11	20,158	1,080	5.4	14,202	70.5	4,696	23.3	166	14
45 to 49 years	15,223	698	4.6	13,308	87.4	1,147	7.5	63	7	17,815	716	4.0	12,131	68.1	4,849	27.2	110	9
50 to 54 years	13,773	541	3.9	11,831	85.9	1,341	9.7	50	10	13,171	561	4.3	7,774	59.0	4,762	36.2	64	10
55 to 59 years	8,750	268	3.1	7,490	85.6	963	11.0	25	4	7,651	253	3.3	4,234	55.3	3,123	40.8	35	6
60 to 64 years	8,937	257	2.9	7,328	82.0	1,318	14.7	24	10	6,618	234	3.5	2,784	42.1	3,562	53.8	27	11
65 to 69 years	5,171	143	2.8	4,019	77.7	990	19.1	14	5	4,449	134	3.0	1,541	34.6	2,756	61.9	13	5
70 to 74 years	3,185	106	3.3	2,195	68.9	868	27.3	11	5	2,944	116	3.9	698	23.7	2,120	72.0	2	8
75 and over	3,040	97	3.2	1,746	57.4	1,184	38.9	7	6	3,494	131	3.7	513	14.7	2,838	81.2	5	7
Unknown	145	39	26.9	85	58.6	10	6.9	1	10	228	63	27.6	102	44.7	56	24.6	1	6
GEORGIA																		
Total	**324,068**	**103,281**	**31.9**	**196,041**	**60.5**	**21,539**	**6.6**	**2,786**	**422**	**365,622**	**90,080**	**24.6**	**201,168**	**55.0**	**67.516**	**18.5**	**6,530**	**328**
15 to19 years	63,755	59,863	93.9	3,667	5.8	109	.2	56	60	70,461	53,495	75.9	15,517	22.0	990	1.4	432	27
20 to 24 years	50,174	23,628	47.1	25,158	50.1	898	1.8	395	95	62,160	20.339	32.7	36,570	58.8	3,735	6.0	1,472	44
25 to 29 years	36,286	7,740	21.3	26,830	73.9	1,213	3.3	467	36	45,966	7,066	15.4	32,584	70.9	4,996	10.9	1,295	25
30 to 34 years	27,084	3.844	14.2	21,605	79.8	1,227	4.5	367	41	34,308	3,183	9.3	24,940	72.7	5,182	15.1	971	32
35 to 39 years	29,093	2,795	9.6	24,282	83.5	1,625	5.6	366	25	37,805	2,171	5.7	27,277	72.2	7,472	19.8	850	35
40 to 44 years	22,126	1,701	7.7	18,310	82.8	1,826	8.3	277	12	29,211	1,295	4.4	19,817	67.8	7,491	25.6	584	24
45 to 49 years	19,165	1,089	5.7	15,939	83.2	1,889	9.9	228	20	26,361	823	3.1	17,471	66.3	7,629	28.9	424	14
50 to 54 years	28,908	1,062	3.7	24,599	85.1	2,983	10.3	249	15	20,683	620	3.0	12,059	58.3	7,735	37.4	247	22
55 to 59 years	15,290	508	3.3	12,720	83.2	1,918	12.5	127	17	11,122	295	2.7	6,130	55.1	4,594	41.3	92	11
60 to 64 years	13,611	458	3.4	10,637	78.2	2,369	17.4	127	20	10,001	264	2.6	4,244	42.4	5,406	54.1	73	14
65 to 69 years	7,932	218	2.7	5,876	74.1	1,762	22.2	70	6	6,564	160	2.4	2,349	35.8	4,006	61.0	37	12
70 to 74 years	4,873	138	2.8	3,266	67.0	1,437	29.5	28	4	4,570	124	2.7	1,139	24.9	3,276	71.7	21	10
75 and over	5,338	158	3.0	2,887	54.1	2,248	42.1	26	19	5,962	159	2.7	870	14.6	4,881	81.9	23	29
Unknown	433	79	18.2	265	61.2	34	7.9	3	52	448	86	19.2	201	44.9	123	27.5	9	29
FLORIDA																		
Total	**151,867**	**47,192**	**31.1**	**90,572**	**59.6**	**10,634**	**7.0**	**1,992**	**1,477**	**151,954**	**29,624**	**19.5**	**93.535**	**61.6**	**25,241**	**16.6**	**3,115**	**439**
15 to 19 years	20,002	19,182	95.9	744	3.7	23	.1	7	46	23.353	16,893	72.3	5.969	25.6	274	1.2	190	27
20 to 24 years	22,145	11,896	53.7	9,480	42.8	279	1.3	178	312	26,257	6,952	26.5	17,361	66.1	1,267	4.8	608	69
25 to 29 years	21,785	5,954	27.3	14,568	66.9	612	2.8	331	320	24,165	2,712	11.2	18,624	77.1	2,080	8.6	673	76
30 to 34 years	16,793	3,223	19.2	12,391	73.8	689	4.1	289	201	17,610	1,215	6.9	13,584	77.1	2,292	13.0	468	51
35 to 39 years	17,182	2,324	13.5	13,345	77.7	1,067	6.2	290	156	17,650	695	3.9	13,297	75.3	3,158	17.9	460	40
40 to 44 years	13,947	1,543	11.1	10,829	77.6	1,202	8.6	241	132	12,805	424	3.3	8,946	69.9	3,086	24.1	295	54
45 to 49 years	13,217	1,180	8.9	10,333	78.2	1,376	10.4	218	110	10,639	247	2.3	6,995	65.7	3.164	29.7	202	31
50 to 54 years	9.975	801	8.0	7,521	75.4	1,415	14.2	180	58	7,228	198	2.7	4,089	56.6	2,809	38.9	104	28
55 to 59 years	6,291	443	7.0	4,639	73.7	1,059	16.8	104	46	3,917	80	2.0	1,972	50.3	1,787	45.6	60	18
60 to 64 years	4,444	280	6.3	3,107	69.9	949	21.4	83	25	3,122	68	2.2	1,244	39.8	1.771	56.7	29	10
65 to 69 years	2,775	168	6.1	1,798	64.8	752	27.1	36	21	2,075	36	1.7	771	37.2	1,251	60.3	10	7
70 to 74 years	1,463	62	4.2	901	61.6	469	32.1	21	10	1,297	31	2.4	322	24.8	936	72.2	3	5
75 and over	1,593	72	4.5	770	48.3	728	45.7	11	12	1,616	25	1.5	270	16.7	1,303	80.6	7	11
Unknown	255	64	25.1	146	57.3	14	5.5	3	28	220	48	21.8	91	41.4	63	28.6	6	12
KENTUCKY																		
Total	**83,165**	**26,864**	**32.3**	**47,225**	**56.8**	**7,242**	**8.7**	**1,722**	**112**	**82,174**	**17,585**	**21.4**	**47,137**	**57.4**	**15,349**	**18.7**	**2,007**	**96**
15 to 19 years	10,201	9,865	96.7	311	3.0	13	.1	7	5	10,561	8,444	80.0	1,948	18.4	91	.9	75	3
20 to 24 years	9,648	6,108	63.3	3,302	34.2	110	1.1	109	19	10,168	3,763	37.0	5,659	55.7	420	4.1	311	15
25 to 29 years	8,789	3,103	35.3	5,205	59.2	264	3.0	212	5	9,413	1,761	18.7	6,626	70.4	672	7.1	348	6
30 to 34 years	8,179	1,882	23.0	5,644	69.0	385	4.7	261	7	8,613	932	10.8	6,452	74.9	898	10.4	324	7
35 to 39 years	9,162	1,637	17.9	6,670	72.8	550	6.0	297	8	9,106	736	8.1	6,830	75.0	1,226	13.5	306	8
40 to 44 years	7,875	1,179	15.0	5,837	74.1	606	7.7	248	5	7,697	548	7.1	5,497	71.4	1,419	18.4	228	5
45 to 49 years	7,701	1,013	13.2	5,697	74.0	791	10.3	187	13	7,365	448	6.1	5,027	68.3	1,702	23.1	182	6
50 to 54 years	6,781	746	11.0	4,983	73.5	913	13.5	138	1	5,860	311	5.3	3,691	63.0	1,749	29.8	101	8
55 to 59 years	4,587	432	9.4	3,374	73.6	695	15.2	81	5	3,860	177	4.6	2,192	56.8	1,439	37.3	47	5
60 to 64 years	3,595	332	9.2	2,429	67.6	746	20.8	82	6	3,247	170	5.2	1,514	46.6	1,519	46.8	40	4
65 to 69 years	2,678	257	9.6	1,667	62.2	694	25.9	54	6	2,338	101	4.3	906	38.8	1,307	55.9	23	1
70 to 74 years	1,888	146	7.7	1,119	59.3	596	31.6	25	2	1,601	73	4.6	428	26.7	1,088	68.0	7	5
75 and over	1,946	146	7.5	916	47.1	857	44.0	18	9	2,222	108	4.9	319	14.4	1,778	80.0	9	8
Unknown	135	18	13.3	71	52.6	22	16.3	3	21	123	13	10.6	48	39.0	41	33.3	6	15

TABLE 12.—MARITAL CONDITION OF THE NEGRO POPULATION 15 YEARS OLD AND OVER, BY SEX, AND 5-YEAR AGE PERIODS, BY DIVISIONS, AND STATES: 1930—Continued

[See note at head of this table]

DIVISION OR STATE, AND AGE	MALES 15 YEARS OLD AND OVER									FEMALES 15 YEARS OLD AND OVER								
	Total	Single		Married		Widowed		Divorced	Unknown	Total	Single		Married		Widowed		Divorced	Unknown
		Number	Percent	Number	Percent	Number	Percent				Number	Percent	Number	Percent	Number	Percent		
TENNESSEE																		
Total	**161, 503**	**49, 752**	**30. 8**	**96, 330**	**59. 6**	**11, 862**	**7. 3**	**2, 903**	**656**	**173, 319**	**38, 962**	**22. 5**	**98, 188**	**56. 7**	**30, 642**	**17. 7**	**4, 924**	**603**
15 to 19 years	24, 953	23, 613	94. 6	1, 200	4. 8	44	. 2	33	63	26, 882	20, 641	76. 8	5, 667	21. 1	290	1. 1	244	40
20 to 24 years	22, 337	11, 979	53. 6	9, 538	42. 7	404	1. 8	325	91	26, 951	8, 997	33. 4	15, 639	58. 0	1, 336	5. 0	906	73
25 to 29 years	19, 166	5, 084	26. 5	12, 964	67. 6	601	3. 1	460	57	23, 183	3, 702	16. 0	16, 368	70. 6	2, 030	8. 8	1, 045	38
30 to 34 years	15, 778	2, 794	17. 7	11, 836	75. 0	696	4. 4	429	23	17, 830	1, 671	9. 4	13, 138	73. 7	2, 241	12. 6	749	31
35 to 39 years	16, 651	2, 044	12. 3	13, 126	78. 8	980	5. 9	469	32	18, 911	1, 295	6. 8	13, 786	72. 9	3, 070	16. 2	730	30
40 to 44 years	12, 721	1, 292	10. 2	10, 082	79. 3	1, 019	8. 0	307	21	14, 302	813	5. 7	9, 899	69. 2	3, 102	21. 7	468	20
45 to 49 years	11, 374	931	8. 2	8, 988	79. 0	1, 166	10. 3	257	32	12, 985	569	4. 4	8, 679	66. 8	3, 388	26. 1	325	24
50 to 54 years	14, 070	800	5. 7	11, 312	80. 4	1, 668	11. 9	272	18	11, 128	446	4. 0	6, 726	60. 4	3, 716	33. 4	216	24
55 to 59 years	8, 427	410	4. 9	6, 719	79. 7	1, 133	13. 4	152	13	6, 502	266	4. 1	3, 559	54. 7	2, 547	39. 2	110	20
60 to 64 years	6, 152	314	5. 1	4, 564	74. 2	1, 180	19. 2	78	16	5, 211	205	3. 9	2, 209	42. 4	2, 712	52. 0	65	20
65 to 69 years	3, 974	199	5. 0	2, 756	69. 4	956	24. 1	51	12	3, 435	122	3. 6	1, 291	37. 6	1, 975	57. 5	35	12
70 to 74 years	2, 532	98	3. 9	1, 597	63. 1	793	31. 3	28	16	2, 370	75	3. 2	644	27. 2	1, 621	68. 4	12	18
75 and over	2, 826	114	4. 0	1, 455	51. 5	1, 202	42. 5	37	18	3, 103	103	3. 3	450	14. 5	2, 524	81. 3	10	16
Unknown	542	80	14. 8	193	35. 6	20	3. 7	5	244	526	57	10. 8	133	25. 3	90	17. 1	9	237
ALABAMA																		
Total	**290, 079**	**91, 027**	**31. 4**	**176, 191**	**60. 7**	**18, 544**	**6. 4**	**3, 912**	**405**	**320, 277**	**77, 161**	**24. 1**	**179, 650**	**56. 1**	**55, 127**	**17. 2**	**8, 000**	**339**
15 to 19 years	51, 787	49, 812	96. 2	1, 776	3. 4	83	. 2	55	61	57, 429	44, 527	77. 5	11, 631	20. 3	766	1. 3	460	45
20 to 24 years	43, 513	21, 777	50. 0	20, 324	46. 7	801	1. 8	510	101	53, 560	17, 263	32. 2	31, 603	59. 0	2, 931	5. 5	1, 686	77
25 to 29 years	34, 896	7, 813	22. 4	25, 218	72. 3	1, 161	3. 3	639	65	42, 622	6, 424	15. 1	30, 480	71. 5	4, 060	9. 5	1, 615	43
30 to 34 years	24, 914	3, 734	15. 0	19, 563	78. 5	1, 074	4. 3	513	30	30, 645	2, 843	9. 3	22, 381	73. 0	4, 208	13. 7	1, 188	25
35 to 39 years	25, 702	2, 648	10. 3	21, 084	82. 0	1, 393	5. 4	545	32	33, 418	1, 985	5. 9	24, 689	73. 9	5, 646	16. 9	1, 077	21
40 to 44 years	19, 314	1, 553	8. 0	15, 777	81. 7	1, 537	8. 0	427	20	25, 828	1, 319	5. 1	18, 074	70. 0	5, 692	22. 0	717	26
45 to 49 years	29, 949	1, 410	4. 7	25, 695	85. 8	2, 382	8. 0	441	21	24, 205	902	3. 7	16, 339	67. 5	6, 444	26. 6	506	14
50 to 54 years	20, 230	873	4. 3	16, 827	83. 2	2, 245	11. 1	269	16	17, 488	674	3. 9	10, 487	60. 0	5, 971	34. 1	343	13
55 to 59 years	13, 031	491	3. 8	10, 825	83. 1	1, 515	11. 6	187	13	10, 133	339	3. 3	5, 718	56. 4	3, 885	38. 3	176	15
60 to 64 years	10, 864	358	3. 3	8, 559	78. 8	1, 775	16. 3	159	13	8, 810	302	3. 4	3, 968	45. 0	4, 405	50. 0	119	16
65 to 69 years	6, 705	206	3. 1	4, 930	73. 5	1, 474	22. 0	92	3	5, 984	184	3. 1	2, 236	37. 4	3, 496	58. 4	57	11
70 to 74 years	4, 123	109	2. 6	2, 814	68. 3	1, 158	28. 1	39	3	4, 124	148	3. 6	1, 091	26. 5	2, 849	69. 1	29	7
75 and over	4, 720	163	3. 5	2, 602	55. 1	1, 916	40. 6	31	8	5, 681	170	3. 0	826	14. 5	4, 658	82. 0	15	12
Unknown	331	80	24. 2	197	59. 5	30	9. 1	5	19	350	81	23. 1	127	36. 3	116	33. 1	12	14
MISSISSIPPI																		
Total	**316, 619**	**90, 148**	**28. 5**	**201, 279**	**63. 6**	**19, 446**	**6. 1**	**4, 467**	**1, 279**	**331, 600**	**68, 256**	**20. 6**	**204, 478**	**61. 7**	**49, 649**	**15. 0**	**8, 923**	**294**
15 to 19 years	55, 752	52, 424	94. 0	3, 074	5. 5	97	. 2	64	93	59, 141	41, 570	70. 3	16, 154	27. 3	802	1. 4	597	18
20 to 24 years	48, 136	20, 690	43. 0	25, 618	53. 2	933	1. 9	640	255	56, 225	14, 091	25. 1	37, 544	66. 8	2, 718	4. 8	1, 835	37
25 to 29 years	38, 400	6, 992	18. 2	29, 168	76. 0	1, 284	3. 3	739	217	44, 427	5, 231	11. 8	33, 955	76. 4	3, 508	7. 9	1, 690	43
30 to 34 years	28, 764	3, 336	11. 6	23, 519	81. 8	1, 170	4. 1	570	169	32, 735	2, 370	7. 2	25, 753	78. 7	3, 298	10. 1	1, 282	32
35 to 39 years	29, 771	2, 300	7. 7	25, 314	85. 0	1, 451	4. 9	595	111	34, 313	1, 705	5. 0	26, 766	78. 0	4, 659	13. 6	1, 160	23
40 to 44 years	24, 001	1, 410	5. 9	20, 419	85. 1	1, 571	6. 5	457	144	25, 902	1, 034	4. 0	19, 174	74. 0	4, 848	18. 7	823	23
45 to 49 years	21, 399	968	4. 5	18, 206	85. 1	1, 720	8. 0	411	94	24, 140	764	3. 2	17, 411	72. 1	5, 330	22. 1	619	16
50 to 54 years	23, 634	740	3. 1	20, 064	84. 9	2, 394	10. 1	379	57	18, 529	499	2. 7	12, 062	65. 1	5, 542	29. 9	406	20
55 to 59 years	15, 822	474	3. 0	13, 272	83. 9	1, 819	11. 5	228	29	11, 109	274	2. 5	6, 820	61. 4	3, 776	34. 0	227	12
60 to 64 years	13, 067	343	2. 6	10, 534	80. 6	1, 991	15. 2	180	19	9, 416	265	2. 8	4, 424	47. 0	4, 574	48. 6	145	8
65 to 69 years	7, 742	190	2. 5	5, 873	75. 9	1, 567	20. 2	98	14	5, 765	148	2. 6	2, 330	40. 4	3, 200	55. 5	79	8
70 to 74 years	4, 577	122	2. 7	3, 078	67. 2	1, 308	28. 6	58	11	4, 031	120	3. 0	1, 103	27. 4	2, 774	68. 8	26	8
75 and over	5, 339	110	2. 1	3, 046	57. 1	2, 126	39. 8	47	10	5, 646	136	2. 4	907	16. 1	4, 559	80. 7	27	17
Unknown	215	49	22. 8	94	43. 7	15	7. 0	1	56	221	49	22. 2	75	33. 9	61	27. 6	7	29
ARKANSAS																		
Total	**158, 239**	**42, 866**	**27. 1**	**100, 470**	**63. 5**	**11, 773**	**7. 4**	**3, 002**	**128**	**162, 123**	**30, 171**	**18. 6**	**101, 199**	**62. 4**	**25, 927**	**16. 0**	**4, 743**	**83**
15 to 19 years	25, 017	23, 810	95. 2	1, 098	4. 4	61	. 2	35	13	27, 528	19, 280	70. 0	7, 449	27. 1	498	1. 8	295	6
20 to 24 years	22, 831	10, 445	45. 7	11, 478	50. 3	512	2. 2	371	25	26, 425	6, 117	23. 1	17, 713	67. 0	1, 621	6. 1	960	14
25 to 29 years	18, 545	3, 474	18. 7	13, 817	74. 5	769	4. 1	480	5	21, 619	2, 126	9. 8	16, 560	76. 6	1, 946	9. 0	973	14
30 to 34 years	14, 510	1, 617	11. 1	11, 726	80. 8	769	5. 3	391	7	16, 921	970	5. 7	13, 345	78. 9	1, 936	11. 4	666	4
35 to 39 years	15, 351	1, 157	7. 5	12, 741	83. 0	1, 013	6. 6	433	7	17, 810	602	3. 4	13, 902	78. 1	2, 638	14. 8	662	6
40 to 44 years	12, 284	794	6. 5	10, 068	82. 0	1, 079	8. 8	336	7	13, 869	377	2. 7	10, 396	75. 0	2, 666	19. 2	427	3
45 to 49 years	15, 517	601	3. 9	13, 109	84. 5	1, 456	9. 4	346	5	12, 400	230	1. 9	8, 926	72. 0	2, 909	23. 5	329	6
50 to 54 years	12, 174	396	3. 3	10, 053	82. 6	1, 485	12. 2	234	6	9, 335	188	2. 0	5, 946	63. 7	2, 974	31. 9	224	3
55 to 59 years	8, 035	214	2. 7	6, 577	81. 9	1, 084	13. 5	156	4	5, 365	91	1. 7	3, 181	59. 3	1, 991	37. 1	99	3
60 to 64 years	5, 782	152	2. 6	4, 479	77. 5	1, 034	17. 9	113	4	4, 149	59	1. 4	1, 913	46. 1	2, 120	51. 1	52	5
65 to 69 years	3, 503	81	2. 3	2, 543	72. 6	825	23. 6	53	1	2, 612	39	1. 5	951	36. 4	1, 588	60. 8	32	2
70 to 74 years	2, 150	49	2. 3	1, 411	65. 6	660	30. 7	28	2	1, 724	26	1. 5	501	29. 1	1, 180	68. 4	16	1
75 and over	2, 403	57	2. 4	1, 311	54. 6	1, 012	42. 1	23	--------	2, 261	45	2. 0	381	16. 9	1, 828	80. 8	6	1
Unknown	137	19	13. 9	59	43. 1	14	10. 2	3	42	105	21	20. 0	35	33. 3	32	30. 5	2	15
LOUISIANA																		
Total	**248, 678**	**76, 739**	**30. 9**	**153, 916**	**61. 9**	**14, 833**	**6. 0**	**2, 855**	**335**	**264, 780**	**59, 127**	**22. 3**	**157, 360**	**59. 4**	**42, 049**	**15. 9**	**5, 871**	**373**
15 to 19 years	38, 192	36, 709	96. 1	1, 401	3. 7	33	. 1	25	24	43, 101	32, 668	75. 8	9, 697	22. 5	408	. 9	315	13
20 to 24 years	36, 546	19, 484	53. 3	16, 229	44. 4	440	1. 2	343	50	43, 004	13, 065	30. 4	27, 154	63. 1	1, 682	3. 9	1, 075	28
25 to 29 years	31, 806	7, 829	24. 6	22, 747	71. 5	732	2. 3	467	31	37, 235	5, 452	14. 6	27, 801	74. 7	2, 753	7. 4	1, 183	46
30 to 34 years	24, 535	3, 859	15. 7	19, 361	78. 9	872	3. 6	413	30	27, 653	2, 601	9. 4	21, 200	76. 7	2, 961	10. 7	848	43
35 to 39 years	27, 002	2, 994	11. 1	22, 369	82. 8	1, 186	4. 4	419	34	29, 354	1, 943	6. 6	22, 217	75. 7	4, 267	14. 5	884	43
40 to 44 years	21, 791	1, 925	8. 8	18, 145	83. 3	1, 350	6. 2	343	28	21, 957	1, 151	5. 2	15, 797	71. 9	4, 372	19. 9	591	46
45 to 49 years	21, 383	1, 508	7. 1	17, 858	83. 5	1, 676	7. 8	315	26	19, 936	780	3. 9	13, 610	68. 3	5, 061	25. 4	437	48
50 to 54 years	16, 233	971	6. 0	13, 233	81. 5	1, 791	11. 0	214	24	14, 131	537	3. 8	8, 551	60. 5	4, 770	33. 8	246	27
55 to 59 years	11, 099	575	5. 2	8, 915	80. 3	1, 463	13. 2	126	20	8, 999	297	3. 3	4, 999	55. 6	3, 539	39. 3	143	21
60 to 64 years	8, 177	350	4. 3	6, 200	75. 8	1, 518	18. 6	94	15	6, 956	245	3. 5	3, 075	44. 2	3, 539	50. 9	83	14
65 to 69 years	5, 078	226	4. 5	3, 609	71. 1	1, 179	23. 2	54	10	4, 690	133	2. 8	1, 664	35. 5	2, 844	60. 6	37	12
70 to 74 years	2, 965	138	4. 7	1, 882	63. 5	920	31. 0	20	5	3, 124	113	3. 6	830	26. 6	2, 166	69. 3	10	5
75 and over	3, 681	129	3. 5	1, 871	50. 8	1, 658	45. 0	18	5	4, 480	116	2. 6	705	15. 7	3, 637	81. 2	13	9
Unknown	190	42	22. 1	96	50. 5	15	7. 9	4	33	160	26	16. 3	60	37. 5	50	31. 3	6	18

TABLE 12.—MARITAL CONDITION OF THE NEGRO POPULATION 15 YEARS OLD AND OVER, BY SEX, AND 5-YEAR AGE PERIODS, BY DIVISIONS, AND STATES: 1930—Continued

[See note at head of this table]

DIVISION OR STATE, AND AGE	MALES 15 YEARS OLD AND OVER									FEMALES 15 YEARS OLD AND OVER								
	Total	Single		Married		Widowed		Divorced	Unknown	Total	Single		Married		Widowed		Divorced	Unknown
		Number	Percent	Number	Percent	Number	Percent				Number	Percent	Number	Percent	Number	Percent		
OKLAHOMA																		
Total	**59,193**	**17,969**	**30.4**	**34,965**	**59.1**	**4,637**	**7.8**	**1,506**	**116**	**57,580**	**11,879**	**20.6**	**35,096**	**61.0**	**8,553**	**14.9**	**1,972**	**80**
15 to 19 years	9,099	8,758	96.3	320	3.5	8	.1	7	6	9,712	7,330	75.5	2,189	22.5	119	1.2	72	2
20 to 24 years	8,321	4,576	55.0	3,440	41.3	155	1.9	131	19	9,572	2,746	28.7	5,974	62.4	491	5.1	355	6
25 to 29 years	7,421	1,816	24.5	5,039	67.9	309	4.2	247	10	8,174	908	11.1	6,098	74.6	737	9.0	424	7
30 to 34 years	6,083	901	14.8	4,649	76.4	310	5.1	213	10	6,386	355	5.6	4,955	77.6	730	11.4	339	7
35 to 39 years	6,064	659	10.9	4,742	78.2	401	6.6	258	4	6,171	228	3.7	4,672	75.7	961	15.6	304	6
40 to 44 years	4,887	375	7.7	3,874	79.3	451	9.2	181	6	4,852	112	2.3	3,637	75.0	919	18.9	178	6
45 to 49 years	4,579	309	6.7	3,627	79.2	477	10.4	156	10	4,206	71	1.7	3,072	73.0	913	21.7	145	5
50 to 54 years	4,594	230	5.0	3,588	78.1	639	13.9	131	6	2,952	38	1.3	1,944	65.9	885	30.0	78	7
55 to 59 years	3,095	138	4.5	2,391	77.3	488	15.8	71	7	1,848	22	1.2	1,106	59.8	673	36.4	42	5
60 to 64 years	1,973	87	4.4	1,411	71.5	406	20.6	56	13	1,291	15	1.2	670	51.9	589	45.6	15	2
65 to 69 years	1,281	51	4.0	874	68.2	323	25.2	30	3	926	19	2.1	385	41.6	507	54.8	13	2
70 to 74 years	755	20	2.6	487	64.5	229	30.3	17	2	542	10	1.8	184	33.9	343	63.3	3	2
75 and over	964	30	3.1	487	50.5	434	45.0	7	6	871	9	1.0	169	19.4	676	77.6	3	14
Unknown	77	19		36		7		1	14	77	16		41		10		1	9
TEXAS																		
Total	**286,595**	**84,217**	**29.4**	**173,426**	**60.5**	**20,281**	**7.1**	**8,312**	**359**	**295,670**	**60,148**	**20.3**	**175,844**	**59.5**	**45,658**	**15.4**	**13,643**	**377**
15 to 19 years	43,586	41,628	95.5	1,764	4.0	82	.2	75	37	49,110	36,500	74.3	11,191	22.8	723	1.5	682	14
20 to 24 years	42,526	21,616	50.8	19,056	44.8	934	2.2	868	52	49,043	12,999	26.5	30,824	62.9	2,740	5.6	2,436	44
25 to 29 years	37,385	8,216	22.0	26,380	70.6	1,410	3.8	1,350	29	42,807	4,788	11.2	31,603	73.8	3,556	8.3	2,825	35
30 to 34 years	31,076	4,265	13.7	23,973	77.1	1,510	4.9	1,299	29	32,974	2,044	6.2	25,017	75.9	3,715	11.3	2,172	26
35 to 39 years	31,159	2,982	9.6	24,940	80.0	1,885	6.0	1,320	32	32,777	1,300	4.0	24,586	75.0	4,861	14.8	2,003	27
40 to 44 years	24,215	1,940	8.0	19,295	79.7	1,979	8.2	980	21	24,209	434	3.4	17,324	71.6	4,700	19.4	1,314	37
45 to 49 years	24,027	1,339	5.6	19,401	80.7	2,317	9.6	946	24	20,582	578	2.8	14,090	68.5	4,924	23.9	949	41
50 to 54 years	17,398	841	4.8	13,772	79.2	2,206	12.7	553	26	14,233	362	2.5	8,703	61.1	4,588	32.2	551	29
55 to 59 years	10,814	451	4.2	8,385	77.5	1,602	14.8	362	14	8,716	204	2.3	4,955	56.8	3,248	37.3	296	13
60 to 64 years	10,222	358	3.5	7,682	75.2	1,908	18.7	263	11	8,262	166	2.0	3,968	48.0	3,900	47.2	208	20
65 to 69 years	6,051	225	3.7	4,190	69.2	1,468	24.3	159	9	4,919	113	2.3	1,841	37.4	2,838	57.7	114	13
70 to 74 years	3,446	102	3.0	2,139	62.1	1,136	33.0	62	7	3,123	60	1.9	859	27.5	2,153	68.9	39	12
75 and over	4,163	135	3.2	2,156	51.8	1.801	43.3	65	6	4,422	106	2.4	673	15.2	3,591	81.2	37	15
Unknown	527	119	22.6	293	55.6	43	8.2	10	62	493	94	19.1	210	42.6	121	24.5	17	51
MONTANA																		
Total	**601**	**237**	**39.4**	**276**	**45.9**	**50**	**8.3**	**32**	**6**	**437**	**65**	**14.9**	**267**	**61.1**	**78**	**17.8**	**25**	**2**
15 to 19 years	32	29		3						26	2		4					
20 to 24 years	42	27		12		1		1	1	36	9		23				4	
25 to 29 years	51	26		22		2		1		49	7		36		3		3	
30 to 34 years	48	21		21		1		4	1	49	8		32		5		3	1
35 to 39 years	62	23		38		1				61	8		41		6		6	
40 to 44 years	75	22		41		5		6	1	40	4		23		7		6	
45 to 49 years	65	20		37		2		5	1	50			41		7		1	1
50 to 54 years	69	23		35		5		6		50	2		38		9		1	
55 to 59 years	53	17		27		7		2		29	1		14		14			
60 to 64 years	43	11		22		6		4		19	1		9		8		1	
65 to 69 years	26	7		10		7		1	1	8	1		2		5			
70 to 74 years	20	5		6		7		2		9			1		8			
75 and over	14	6		2		6				10	1		3		6			
Unknown	1								1	1	1							
IDAHO																		
Total	**338**	**118**	**34.9**	**168**	**49.7**	**35**	**10.4**	**16**	**1**	**226**	**27**	**11.9**	**162**	**71.7**	**27**	**11.9**	**10**	
15 to 19 years	24	23		1						16	15				1			
20 to 24 years	23	18		5						17	4		12		1			
25 to 29 years	22	7		14				1		23	1		19		3			
30 to 34 years	28	8		19				1		40	2		33		3		2	
35 to 39 years	53	21		24		6		2		31	3		26				2	
40 to 44 years	53	10		36		5		1	1	30			24		2		4	
45 to 49 years	38	5		26		6		1		18			15		2		1	
50 to 54 years	29	7		16		4		2		20	1		15		3		1	
55 to 59 years	18	4		10		3		1		13			8		5			
60 to 64 years	20	6		7		5		2		7			4		3			
65 to 69 years	13	4		4		2		3		3			2		1			
70 to 74 years	4	1		1		2				2			1		1			
75 and over	13	4		5		2		2		6	1		3		2			
Unknown																		
WYOMING																		
Total	**602**	**240**	**39.9**	**292**	**48.5**	**53**	**8.8**	**14**	**3**	**446**	**73**	**16.4**	**278**	**62.3**	**78**	**17.5**	**16**	**1**
15 to 19 years	33	30		2					1	35	29		6					
20 to 24 years	50	35		12				2	1	45	16		26		1		2	
25 to 29 years	48	29		19						35	10		22		1		2	
30 to 34 years	73	38		31		2		2		62	3		44		11		4	
35 to 39 years	89	42		43		1		3		49	3		38		7		1	
40 to 44 years	68	19		41		7		1		71	6		51		11		2	1
45 to 49 years	68	13		48		7				58	5		45		6		2	
50 to 54 years	71	16		38		15		2		28			19		7		2	
55 to 59 years	31	5		21		4		1		26	1		12		12		1	
60 to 64 years	34	7		20		5		2		16			8		8			
65 to 69 years	14	1		9		4				8			5		3			
70 to 74 years	9			7		2				5			2		3			
75 and over	10	5				5				7					7			
Unknown	4			1		1		1	1	1					1			

Table 12.—MARITAL CONDITION OF THE NEGRO POPULATION 15 YEARS OLD AND OVER, BY SEX, AND 5-YEAR AGE PERIODS, BY DIVISIONS, AND STATES: 1930—Continued

[See note at head of this table]

DIVISION OR STATE, AND AGE	MALES 15 YEARS OLD AND OVER									FEMALES 15 YEARS OLD AND OVER								
	Total	Single		Married		Widowed		Divorced	Unknown	Total	Single		Married		Widowed		Divorced	Unknown
		Number	Per cent	Number	Per cent	Number	Per cent				Number	Per cent	Number	Per cent	Number	Per cent		
COLORADO																		
Total	4,621	1,240	26.8	2,757	59.7	438	9.5	173	13	4,902	798	16.3	2,778	56.7	1,135	23.2	185	6
15 to 19 years	353	335	94.9	16	4.5	1	.3		1	430	346	80.5	80	18.6	4	.9		
20 to 24 years	384	250	65.1	126	32.8	4	1.0	4		508	186	36.6	279	54.9	25	4.9	18	
25 to 29 years	444	160	36.0	259	58.3	10	2.3	15		551	94	17.1	370	67.2	52	9.4	34	1
30 to 34 years	482	120	24.9	313	64.9	29	6.0	18	2	567	42	7.4	430	75.8	66	11.6	28	1
35 to 39 years	598	106	17.7	418	69.9	29	4.8	41	4	626	33	5.3	450	71.9	115	18.4	26	2
40 to 44 years	511	76	14.9	366	71.6	45	8.8	24		514	29	5.6	352	68.5	113	22.0	20	
45 to 49 years	547	66	12.1	391	71.5	60	11.0	29	1	530	21	4.0	333	62.8	152	28.7	24	
50 to 54 years	438	45	10.3	320	73.1	57	13.0	14	2	413	21	5.1	218	52.8	154	37.3	20	
55 to 59 years	289	24	8.3	212	73.4	41	14.2	11	1	278	8	2.9	129	46.4	132	47.5	9	
60 to 64 years	231	25	10.8	150	64.9	47	20.3	8	1	152	3	2.0	65	42.8	81	53.3	3	
65 to 69 years	148	9	6.1	97	65.5	38	25.7	4		144	4	2.8	45	31.3	93	64.6	2	
70 to 74 years	95	9		45		37		4		91	6		12		73			
75 and over	91	13		38		39		1		88	3		12		72		1	
Unknown	10	2		6		1			1	10	2		3		3			2
NEW MEXICO																		
Total	1,141	364	31.9	661	57.9	75	6.6	40	1	938	158	16.8	618	65.9	128	13.6	32	2
15 to 19 years	132	128	97.0	4	3.0					127	99	78.0	25	19.7	2	1.6	1	
20 to 24 years	116	75	64.7	39	33.6			2		120	28	23.3	78	65.0	3	2.5	10	1
25 to 29 years	121	39	32.2	73	60.3	2	1.7	7		124	11	8.9	103	83.1	7	5.6	3	
30 to 34 years	114	26	22.8	82	71.9	3	2.6	3		109	5	4.6	86	78.9	12	11.0	6	
35 to 39 years	144	22	15.3	112	77.8	5	3.5	5		151	6	4.0	121	80.1	20	13.2	4	
40 to 44 years	121	20	16.5	89	73.6	7	5.8	5		100	3	3.0	73	73.0	22	22.0	2	
45 to 49 years	110	19	17.3	79	71.8	11	10.0	1		73	1		61		9		2	
50 to 54 years	122	18	14.8	83	68.0	13	10.7	8		59	2		40		13		4	
55 to 59 years	53	8		39		4		2		30	1		15		14			
60 to 64 years	54	6		34		10		4		20			8		12			
65 to 69 years	18	1		11		4		2		12	1		3		8			
70 to 74 years	16	1		12		2		1		4			2		2			
75 and over	19	1		4		14				4					4			
Unknown	1								1	5	1		3					1
ARIZONA																		
Total	5,181	2,381	46.0	2,373	45.8	258	5.0	157	12	3,217	450	14.0	2,163	67.2	481	15.0	121	2
15 to 19 years	460	446	97.0	11	2.4				3	328	233	71.0	93	28.4	1	.3	1	
20 to 24 years	743	612	82.4	120	16.2	4	.5	7		385	98	25.5	256	66.5	11	2.9	20	
25 to 29 years	664	360	54.2	278	41.9	10	1.5	16		499	37	7.4	406	81.4	40	8.0	16	
30 to 34 years	711	314	44.2	345	48.5	26	3.7	24	2	467	32	6.9	360	77.1	53	11.3	22	
35 to 39 years	786	279	35.5	444	56.5	33	4.2	28	2	509	21	4.1	386	75.8	74	14.5	28	
40 to 44 years	571	162	28.4	356	62.3	20	3.5	32	1	330	9	2.7	255	77.3	57	17.3	9	
45 to 49 years	479	99	20.7	325	67.8	37	7.7	17	1	268	5	1.9	193	72.0	61	22.8	9	
50 to 54 years	302	39	12.9	215	71.2	39	12.9	8	1	187	7	3.7	118	63.1	58	31.0	4	
55 to 59 years	190	31	16.3	117	61.6	28	14.7	14		77	2		45		27		3	
60 to 64 years	125	11	8.8	85	68.0	24	19.2	5		68	3		27		35		2	1
65 to 69 years	59	10		33		15			1	46			15		27		4	
70 to 74 years	41	8		21		8		4		17			3		14			
75 and over	36	6		15		14		1		24	2		1		21			
Unknown	14	4		8				1	1	12	1		5		2		3	1
UTAH																		
Total	482	160	33.2	267	55.4	28	5.8	27		374	42	11.2	251	67.1	63	16.8	18	
15 to 19 years	25	24		1						19	12		7					
20 to 24 years	36	24		10				2		33	8		24				1	
25 to 29 years	46	21		23				2		42	5		32				5	
30 to 34 years	51	20		26		1		4		50	5		39		4		2	
35 to 39 years	66	20		41		2		3		53	5		40		7		1	
40 to 44 years	53	15		36		1		1		56	1		45		4		6	
45 to 49 years	67	9		48		3		7		42	3		28		10		1	
50 to 54 years	61	16		37		4		4		25	1		19		5			
55 to 59 years	29	2		21		4		2		20	1		8		10		1	
60 to 64 years	20	4		10		5		1		12	1		6		4		1	
65 to 69 years	14	2		9		3				10			2		8			
70 to 74 years	4			3		1				5					5			
75 and over	9	2		2		4		1		7			1		6			
Unknown	1	1																
NEVADA																		
Total	251	91	36.3	124	49.4	15	6.0	21		208	40	19.2	123	59.1	34	16.3	11	
15 to 19 years	6	5		1						9	7		2					
20 to 24 years	15	11		3				1		14	5		9					
25 to 29 years	19	14		5						25	6		18				1	
30 to 34 years	30	6		20				4		20	2		14		2		2	
35 to 39 years	31	10		17		1		3		31	5		25		1			
40 to 44 years	37	8		23		4		2		34	4		22		5		3	
45 to 49 years	37	9		22		2		4		20	3		9		6		2	
50 to 54 years	26	10		11		2		3		19	4		10		4		1	
55 to 59 years	19	8		8		2		1		15	2		10		2		1	
60 to 64 years	14	6		7		1				7			2		5			
65 to 69 years	7	3		2				2		6			1		4		1	
70 to 74 years	4	1		1		1		1		4					4			
75 and over	6			4		2				2	1				1			
Unknown										2	1		1					

TABLE 12.—MARTIAL CONDITION OF THE NEGRO POPULATION 15 YEARS OLD AND OVER, BY SEX, AND 5-YEAR AGE PERIODS, BY DIVISIONS, AND STATES: 1930—Continued

[See note at head of this table]

DIVISION OR STATE, AND AGE	MALES 15 YEARS OLD AND OVER: Total	Single		Married		Widowed		Divorced	Unknown	FEMALES 15 YEARS OLD AND OVER: Total	Single		Married		Widowed		Divorced	Unknown
		Number	Per cent	Number	Per cent	Number	Per cent				Number	Per cent	Number	Per cent	Number	Per cent		
WASHINGTON																		
Total	**3,152**	**1,126**	**35.7**	**1,567**	**49.7**	**264**	**8.4**	**166**	**29**	**2,419**	**376**	**15.5**	**1,466**	**60.6**	**431**	**17.8**	**143**	**3**
15 to 19 years	205	200	97.6	4	2.0	------	------	------	1	211	184	87.2	25	11.8	------	------	2	------
20 to 24 years	229	172	75.1	48	21.0	1	.4	6	2	230	76	33.0	137	59.6	6	2.6	10	1
25 to 29 years	258	128	49.6	119	46.1	4	1.6	6	1	208	34	16.3	146	70.2	9	4.3	19	------
30 to 34 years	294	100	34.0	164	55.8	10	3.4	19	1	248	25	10.1	177	71.4	20	8.1	26	------
35 to 39 years	346	107	30.9	192	55.5	16	4.6	25	6	300	18	6.0	226	75.3	27	9.0	28	1
40 to 44 years	379	117	30.9	208	54.9	21	5.5	30	3	276	6	2.2	214	77.5	40	14.5	16	------
45 to 49 years	391	88	22.5	253	64.7	24	6.1	23	3	278	14	5.0	175	62.9	70	25.2	19	------
50 to 54 years	372	92	24.7	229	61.6	28	7.5	21	2	247	6	2.4	171	69.2	59	23.9	11	------
55 to 59 years	274	49	17.9	154	56.2	54	19.7	17	------	158	3	1.9	96	60.8	55	34.8	4	------
60 to 64 years	151	28	18.5	78	51.7	32	21.2	11	2	113	4	3.5	55	48.7	51	45.1	3	------
65 to 69 years	117	19	16.2	62	53.0	33	28.2	3	------	60	4	------	23	------	31	------	2	------
70 to 74 years	63	8	------	33	------	19	------	3	------	38	1	------	14	------	21	------	2	------
75 and over	54	13	------	18	------	22	------	1	------	48	------	------	6	------	42	------	------	------
Unknown	19	5	------	5	------	------	------	1	8	4	1	------	1	------	------	------	1	1
OREGON																		
Total	**1,051**	**367**	**34.9**	**551**	**52.4**	**85**	**8.1**	**47**	**1**	**827**	**134**	**16.2**	**512**	**61.9**	**142**	**17.2**	**38**	**1**
15 to 19 years	60	60	------	------	------	------	------	------	------	68	56	------	12	------	------	------	------	------
20 to 24 years	75	50	------	23	------	1	------	1	------	86	31	------	47	------	3	------	5	------
25 to 29 years	95	50	------	41	------	2	------	2	------	80	12	------	62	------	2	------	4	------
30 to 34 years	109	40	36.7	54	49.5	6	5.5	9	------	89	11	------	66	------	4	------	8	------
35 to 39 years	148	37	25.0	95	64.2	9	6.1	7	------	119	10	8.4	84	70.6	16	13.4	9	------
40 to 44 years	147	45	30.6	86	58.5	9	6.1	7	------	108	4	3.7	86	79.6	17	15.7	1	------
45 to 49 years	130	26	20.0	80	61.5	14	10.8	9	1	94	2	------	67	------	20	------	5	------
50 to 54 years	105	27	25.7	62	59.0	11	10.5	5	------	63	2	------	34	------	24	------	3	------
55 to 59 years	84	10	------	60	------	10	------	4	------	45	------	------	27	------	15	------	3	------
60 to 64 years	35	9	------	18	------	8	------	------	------	30	4	------	13	------	13	------	------	------
65 to 69 years	30	6	------	14	------	8	------	2	------	25	1	------	8	------	16	------	------	------
70 to 74 years	10	2	------	5	------	3	------	------	------	10	1	------	4	------	5	------	------	------
75 and over	19	4	------	11	------	3	------	1	------	8	------	------	1	------	6	------	------	1
Unknown	4	1	------	2	------	1	------	------	------	2	------	------	1	------	1	------	------	------
CALIFORNIA																		
Total	**31,749**	**9,889**	**31.1**	**18,490**	**58.2**	**1,994**	**6.3**	**1,175**	**201**	**32,566**	**5,730**	**17.6**	**18,870**	**57.9**	**6.123**	**18.8**	**1,761**	**82**
15 to 19 years	2,615	2,557	97.8	50	1.9	------	------	------	8	2,950	2,426	82.2	487	16.5	17	.6	16	4
20 to 24 years	3,033	2,055	67.8	898	29.6	33	1.1	33	14	3,678	1,318	35.8	2,065	56.1	123	3.3	166	6
25 to 29 years	3,730	1,335	35.8	2,191	58.7	76	2.0	114	14	4,438	631	14.2	3,177	71.6	313	7.1	307	10
30 to 34 years	4,101	1,025	25.0	2,740	66.8	134	3.3	188	14	4,211	411	9.8	3,070	72.9	418	9.9	308	4
35 to 39 years	4,379	852	19.5	3,097	70.7	202	4.6	217	11	4,673	325	7.0	3,264	69.8	702	15.0	373	9
40 to 44 years	3,866	694	18.0	2,733	70.7	225	5.8	205	9	3,443	194	5.6	2,322	67.4	702	20.4	221	4
45 to 49 years	3,364	490	14.6	2,457	73.0	249	7.4	160	8	3,017	161	5.3	1,875	62.1	805	26.7	176	------
50 to 54 years	2,516	341	13.6	1,775	70.5	277	11.0	119	4	2,217	99	4.5	1,223	55.2	791	35.7	100	4
55 to 59 years	1,589	222	14.0	1,091	68.7	210	13.2	61	5	1,337	61	4.6	635	47.5	586	43.8	53	2
60 to 64 years	977	137	14.0	625	64.0	165	16.9	47	3	958	35	3.7	377	39.4	523	54.6	23	------
65 to 69 years	602	82	13.6	371	61.6	140	23.3	9	------	668	21	3.1	188	28.1	445	66.6	13	1
70 to 74 years	399	31	7.8	262	65.7	100	25.1	6	------	412	19	4.6	84	20.4	305	74.0	3	1
75 and over	392	38	9.7	166	42.3	175	44.6	12	1	471	15	3.2	80	17.0	375	79.6	------	1
Unknown	186	30	16.1	34	18.3	8	4.3	4	110	93	14	------	23	------	18	------	2	36

Table 13.—MARITAL CONDITION OF THE NEGRO POPULATION 15 TO 34 YEARS OLD, BY SEX, AND SINGLE YEARS OF AGE, BY THE SOUTHERN DIVISIONS, AND STATES: 1930

[Percent not shown where less than 1/10 of 1 percent]

DIVISION OR STATE, AND AGE	MALES									FEMALES								
	Total	Single		Married		Widowed		Divorced	Unknown	Total	Single		Married		Widowed		Divorced	Unknown
		Number	Percent	Number	Percent	Number	Percent				Number	Percent	Number	Percent	Number	Percent		
The South																		
15 years	101,000	100,835	99.8	154	0.2	9	-----	2	-----	105,963	102,566	96.8	3,156	3.0	152	0.1	89	-----
16 years	106,953	106,432	99.5	495	.5	17	-----	9	-----	115,108	104,531	90.8	9,814	8.5	480	.4	283	-----
17 years	103,973	102,220	98.3	1,650	1.6	60	0.1	43	-----	105,173	84,951	80.8	18,768	17.8	904	.9	550	-----
18 years	106,076	99,942	94.2	5,595	5.3	188	.2	109	242	122,792	81,442	66.3	38,281	31.2	1,724	1.4	1,202	143
19 years	90,944	78,242	86.0	11,812	13.0	341	.4	244	305	105,864	57,533	54.3	44,339	41.9	2,311	2.2	1,520	161
20 years	91,158	68,174	74.8	21,493	23.6	695	.8	491	305	122,554	54,573	44.5	61,809	50.4	3,726	3.0	2,316	130
21 years	91,911	55,060	59.9	35,029	38.1	983	1.1	640	279	91,345	33,977	37.2	51,861	56.8	3,295	3.6	2,086	126
22 years	92,054	45,695	49.6	43,710	47.5	1,409	1.5	972	268	106,010	33,375	31.5	65,100	61.4	4,683	4.4	2,710	142
23 years	82,842	33,742	40.7	46,324	55.9	1,524	1.8	1,007	245	99,014	25,705	26.0	65,118	65.8	5,137	5.2	2,939	115
24 years	80,651	28,068	34.8	49,376	61.2	1,779	2.2	1,186	242	96,168	21,426	22.3	65,886	68.5	5,824	6.1	2,933	99
25 years	84,763	26,609	31.4	54,420	64.2	2,114	2.5	1,357	263	102,069	20,546	20.1	70,954	69.5	7,185	7.0	3,249	135
26 years	67,294	17,972	26.7	46,136	68.6	1,855	2.8	1,154	177	82,009	13,628	16.6	59,700	72.8	5,895	7.2	2,714	72
27 years	64,448	15,288	23.7	45,992	71.4	1,837	2.9	1,138	193	74,095	10,598	14.3	55,037	74.3	5,906	8.0	2,471	83
28 years	74,655	16,042	21.5	54,769	73.4	2,330	3.1	1,313	201	87,202	11,287	12.9	65,504	75.1	7,411	8.5	2,907	93
29 years	65,079	11,735	18.0	49,996	76.8	2,049	3.1	1,157	142	73,094	7,923	10.8	55,716	76.2	6,904	9.4	2,482	69
30 years	96,489	18,904	19.6	71,648	74.3	3,832	4.0	1,899	206	108,462	13,214	12.2	78,976	72.8	12,332	11.4	3,789	151
31 years	36,713	5,896	16.1	28,614	77.9	1,383	3.8	719	101	40,314	3,423	8.5	31,340	77.7	4,145	10.3	1,359	47
32 years	56,165	8,640	15.4	44,015	78.4	2,244	4.0	1,127	139	64,963	5,526	8.5	49,858	76.7	7,382	11.4	2,127	70
33 years	44,129	6,010	13.6	35,380	80.2	1,749	4.0	905	85	51,291	3,585	7.0	40,110	78.2	5,960	11.6	1,587	49
34 years	47,069	5,913	12.6	38,144	81.0	1,928	4.1	951	133	53,641	3,600	6.7	42,094	78.5	6,222	11.6	1,685	40
South Atlantic																		
15 years	49,455	49,373	99.8	80	.2	2	-----	-----	-----	52,459	51,147	97.5	1,239	2.4	56	.1	17	-----
16 years	52,181	51,975	99.6	202	.4	2	-----	2	-----	56,873	52,688	92.6	3,969	7.0	158	.3	58	-----
17 years	50,109	49,390	98.6	683	1.4	18	-----	18	-----	51,736	43,475	84.0	7,839	15.2	293	.6	129	-----
18 years	53,132	50,483	95.0	2,454	4.6	58	.1	32	105	59,333	42,328	71.3	16,038	27.0	588	1.0	302	77
19 years	45,482	39,831	87.6	5,343	11.7	114	.3	54	140	51,035	30,425	59.6	19,347	37.9	779	1.5	398	86
20 years	44,599	34,373	77.1	9,719	21.8	218	.5	125	164	57,601	28,720	49.9	26,881	46.7	1,338	2.3	597	65
21 years	43,289	27,168	62.8	15,489	35.8	317	.7	155	160	43,395	18,317	42.2	23,279	53.6	1,217	2.8	525	57
22 years	42,666	22,308	52.3	19,521	45.8	478	1.1	222	137	49,581	17,876	36.1	29,113	58.7	1,802	3.6	710	80
23 years	37,994	16,567	43.6	20,559	54.1	508	1.3	222	138	45,830	13,767	30.0	29,147	63.6	2,035	4.4	814	67
24 years	36,290	13,648	37.6	21,659	59.7	580	1.6	275	128	43,736	11,335	25.9	29,244	66.9	2,334	5.3	774	49
25 years	38,133	12,976	34.0	23,909	62.7	747	2.0	335	166	46,684	10,866	23.3	31,779	68.1	3,099	6.6	876	64
26 years	29,410	8,630	29.3	19,785	67.3	636	2.2	266	93	36,354	7,018	19.3	26,225	72.1	2,401	6.6	675	35
27 years	28,953	7,588	26.2	20,280	70.0	647	2.2	324	114	33,195	5,513	16.6	24,489	73.8	2,498	7.5	648	47
28 years	33,728	8,085	24.0	24,352	72.2	862	2.6	322	107	39,580	5,941	15.0	29,622	74.8	3,139	7.9	836	42
29 years	29,607	6,040	20.4	22,449	75.8	763	2.6	278	77	33,176	4,252	12.8	25,305	76.3	2,902	8.7	685	32
30 years	44,282	9,591	21.7	32,579	73.6	1,477	3.3	508	127	50,762	7,183	14.2	36,732	72.4	5,647	11.1	1,119	81
31 years	16,346	2,928	17.9	12,630	77.3	546	3.3	183	59	17,980	1,769	9.8	14,038	78.1	1,768	9.8	382	23
32 years	25,341	4,404	17.4	19,688	77.7	883	3.5	299	67	29,342	2,930	10.0	22,490	76.6	3,300	11.2	585	37
33 years	19,686	3,022	15.4	15,675	79.6	683	3.5	259	47	23,078	1,818	7.9	18,141	78.6	2,634	11.4	464	21
34 years	21,071	3,030	14.4	16,958	80.5	761	3.6	263	59	23,752	1,862	7.8	18,736	78.9	2,705	11.4	429	20
East South Central																		
15 years	28,633	28,586	99.8	41	.1	5	-----	1	-----	29,157	28,028	96.1	1,044	3.6	51	.2	34	-----
16 years	31,002	30,803	99.4	187	.6	8	-----	4	-----	31,841	28,379	89.1	3,164	9.9	173	.5	125	-----
17 years	30,618	29,967	97.9	614	2.0	29	.1	8	-----	28,773	22,383	77.8	5,859	20.4	322	1.1	209	-----
18 years	28,875	26,737	92.6	1,916	6.6	77	.3	44	101	34,828	21,641	62.1	12.090	34.7	604	1.7	445	48
19 years	23,565	19,621	83.3	3,603	15.3	118	.5	102	121	29,414	14,751	50.1	13,243	45.0	799	2.7	563	58
20 years	24,625	17,570	71.4	6,509	26.4	266	1.1	181	99	35,350	14,451	40.9	18,737	53.0	1,255	3.6	865	42
21 years	25,642	14,417	56.2	10,563	41.2	352	1.4	223	87	25,450	8,669	34.1	14,881	58.5	1,106	4.3	747	47
22 years	26,256	12,193	46.4	13,109	49.9	482	1.8	374	98	130,406	8,745	28.8	19,072	62.7	1,534	5.0	1,012	43
23 years	23,705	8,893	37.5	13,803	58.2	529	2.2	396	84	28,077	6,644	23.7	18,670	66.5	1,677	6.0	1,050	36
24 years	23,406	7,481	32.0	14,798	63.2	619	2.6	410	98	27,621	5,605	20.3	19,085	69.1	1,833	6.6	1,064	34
25 years	24,908	7,273	29.2	16,336	65.6	738	3.0	480	81	29,912	5,588	18.7	20,845	69.7	2,271	7.6	1,163	45
26 years	19,509	4,782	24.5	13,601	69.7	637	3.3	418	71	23,796	3,712	15.6	17,256	72.5	1,858	7.8	949	21
27 years	17,686	3,871	21.9	12,817	72.5	576	3.3	357	65	20,637	2,748	13.3	15,335	74.3	1,724	8.4	812	18
28 years	21,400	4,177	19.5	15,988	74.7	740	3.5	420	75	24,973	3,015	12.1	18,660	74.7	2,288	9.2	980	30
29 years	17,748	2,889	16.3	13,813	77.8	619	3.5	375	52	20,327	2,055	10.1	15,333	75.4	2,129	10.5	794	16
30 years	27,748	5,102	18.4	20,704	74.6	1,236	4.5	645	61	31,199	3,475	11.1	22,591	72.4	3,695	11.8	1,396	42
31 years	9,873	1,498	15.2	7,737	78.4	367	3.7	238	33	11,095	902	8.1	8,557	77.1	1,202	10.8	421	13
32 years	15,378	2,143	13.9	12,160	79.1	658	4.3	360	57	18,188	1,483	8.2	13,833	76.1	2,173	11.9	680	19
33 years	11,915	1,517	12.7	9,601	80.6	509	4.3	260	28	14,276	1,003	7.0	11,001	77.1	1,725	12.1	532	15
34 years	12,721	1,486	11.7	10,360	81.4	555	4.4	270	50	15,065	933	6.3	11,742	77.9	1,850	12.3	514	6
West South Central																		
15 years	22,912	22,876	99.8	33	.1	2	-----	1	-----	24,347	23,391	96.1	873	3.6	45	.2	38	-----
16 years	23,770	23,654	99.5	106	.4	7	-----	3	-----	26,394	23,464	88.9	2,681	10.2	149	.6	100	-----
17 years	23,246	22,863	98.4	353	1.5	13	.1	17	-----	24,664	19,093	77.4	5,070	20.6	289	1.2	212	-----
18 years	24,069	22,722	94.4	1,225	5.1	53	.2	33	36	28,631	17,473	61.0	10,153	35.5	532	1.9	455	18
19 years	21,897	18,790	85.8	2,866	13.1	109	.5	88	44	25,415	12,357	48.6	11,749	46.2	733	2.9	559	17
20 years	21,934	16,231	74.0	5,265	24.0	211	1.0	185	42	29,603	11,402	38.5	16,191	54.7	1,133	3.8	854	23
21 years	23,060	13,475	58.4	8,977	38.9	314	1.4	262	32	22,500	6,991	31.1	13,701	60.9	972	4.3	814	22
22 years	23,132	11,194	48.4	11,080	47.9	449	1.9	376	33	26,023	6,754	26.0	16,915	65.0	1,347	5.2	988	19
23 years	21,143	8,282	39.2	11,962	56.6	487	2.3	389	23	25,107	5,294	21.1	17,301	68.9	1,425	5.7	1,075	12
24 years	20,955	6,939	33.1	12,919	61.7	580	2.8	501	16	24,811	4,436	18.1	17,557	70.8	1,657	6.7	1,095	16
25 years	21,722	6,360	29.3	14,175	65.3	629	2.9	542	16	25,473	4,092	16.1	18,330	72.0	1,815	7.1	1,210	26
26 years	18,375	4,560	24.8	12,750	69.4	582	3.2	470	13	21,859	2,898	13.3	16,219	74.2	1,636	7.5	1,090	16
27 years	17,809	3,829	21.5	12,895	72.4	614	3.4	457	14	20,263	2,337	11.5	15,213	75.1	1,684	8.3	1,011	18
28 years	19,527	3,780	19.4	14,429	73.9	728	3.7	571	19	22,649	2,331	10.3	17,222	76.0	1,984	8.8	1,091	21
29 years	17,724	2,806	15.8	13,734	77.5	667	3.8	504	13	19,591	1,616	8.2	15,078	77.0	1,873	9.6	1,003	21
30 years	24,459	4,211	17.2	18,365	75.1	1,119	4.6	746	18	26,501	2,556	9.6	19,653	74.2	2,990	11.3	1,274	28
31 years	10,494	1,470	14.0	8,247	78.6	470	4.5	298	9	11,239	752	6.7	8,745	77.8	1,175	10.5	556	11
32 years	15,446	2,093	13.6	12,167	78.8	703	4.6	468	15	17,433	1,113	6.4	13,535	77.6	1,909	11.0	862	14
33 years	12,528	1,471	11.7	10,104	80.7	557	4.4	386	10	13,937	764	5.5	10,968	78.7	1,601	11.5	591	13
34 years	13,277	1,397	10.5	10,826	81.5	612	4.6	418	24	14,824	785	5.3	11,616	78.4	1,667	11.2	742	14

Table 13.—MARITAL CONDITION OF THE NEGRO POPULATION 15 TO 34 YEARS OLD, BY SEX, AND SINGLE YEARS OF AGE, BY THE SOUTHERN DIVISIONS, AND STATES: 1930—Continued

[Percent not shown where less than 1/10 of 1 percent]

DIVISION OR STATE, AND AGE	MALES									FEMALES								
	Total	Single		Married		Widowed		Divorced	Unknown	Total	Single		Married		Widowed		Divorced	Unknown
		Number	Percent	Number	Percent	Number	Percent				Number	Percent	Number	Percent	Number	Percent		
SOUTH ATLANTIC																		
DELAWARE																		
15 years	267	267	100.0	-	-	-	-	-	-	295	291	98.6	4	1.4	-	-	-	-
16 years	311	310	99.7	1	0.3	-	-	-	-	299	287	96.0	12	4.0	-	-	-	-
17 years	315	314	99.7	1	.3	-	-	-	-	297	261	87.9	36	12.1	-	-	-	-
18 years	299	286	95.7	10	3.3	-	-	1	2	316	255	80.7	59	18.7	1	0.3	-	1
19 years	311	296	95.2	15	4.8	-	-	-	-	275	184	66.9	89	32.4	-	-	1	1
20 years	313	273	87.2	37	11.8	1	0.3	-	2	345	210	60.9	130	37.7	4	1.2	1	-
21 years	317	238	75.1	75	23.7	3	.9	1	-	245	124	50.6	115	46.9	4	1.6	2	-
22 years	346	242	69.9	99	28.6	2	.6	1	2	256	127	49.6	124	48.4	3	1.2	2	-
23 years	291	185	63.6	102	35.1	2	.7	-	2	254	99	39.0	148	58.3	4	1.6	3	-
24 years	306	183	59.8	119	38.9	3	1.0	-	1	315	97	30.8	208	66.0	4	1.3	6	-
25 years	293	161	54.9	125	42.7	5	1.7	1	1	293	93	31.7	190	64.8	8	2.7	2	-
26 years	252	128	50.8	119	47.2	3	1.2	2	-	266	67	25.2	188	70.7	11	4.1	-	-
27 years	279	117	41.9	160	57.3	-	-	1	1	248	55	22.2	187	75.4	4	1.6	1	1
28 years	320	139	43.4	177	55.3	3	.9	1	-	269	74	27.5	186	69.1	9	3.3	-	-
29 years	334	112	33.5	216	64.7	5	1.5	-	1	265	56	21.1	197	74.3	11	4.2	-	1
30 years	425	174	40.9	243	57.2	7	1.6	1	-	348	78	22.4	247	71.0	19	5.5	4	-
31 years	152	48	31.6	97	63.8	5	3.3	2	-	156	23	14.7	124	79.5	7	4.5	2	-
32 years	283	83	29.3	194	68.6	5	1.8	1	-	281	56	19.9	214	76.2	10	3.6	1	-
33 years	201	53	26.4	135	67.2	9	4.5	4	-	195	21	10.8	157	80.5	16	8.2	1	-
34 years	222	60	27.0	144	64.9	11	5.0	7	-	214	28	13.1	172	80.4	11	5.1	3	-
MARYLAND																		
15 years	2,274	2,270	99.8	4	.2	-	-	-	-	2,411	2,376	98.5	34	1.4	1	-	-	-
16 years	2,576	2,570	99.8	6	.2	-	-	-	-	2,512	2,406	95.8	103	4.1	2	.1	1	-
17 years	2,531	2,506	99.0	24	.9	-	-	1	-	2,509	2,207	88.0	297	11.8	4	.2	1	-
18 years	2,539	2,472	97.4	59	2.3	-	-	1	7	2,804	2,129	75.9	654	23.3	4	.1	3	14
19 years	2,634	2,435	92.4	176	6.7	3	.1	5	15	2,627	1,676	63.8	922	35.1	12	.5	5	12
20 years	2,516	2,141	85.1	355	14.1	3	.1	1	16	2,785	1,496	53.7	1,250	44.9	20	.7	10	9
21 years	2,771	2,130	76.9	627	22.6	4	.1	1	9	2,435	1,194	49.0	1,195	49.1	24	1.0	16	6
22 years	2,887	1,928	66.8	932	32.3	11	.4	7	9	2,846	1,201	42.2	1,576	55.4	37	1.3	26	6
23 years	2,798	1,624	58.0	1,136	40.6	22	.8	11	5	2,731	974	35.7	1,677	61.4	52	1.9	23	5
24 years	2,869	1,452	50.6	1,378	48.0	26	.9	5	8	2,773	815	29.4	1,854	66.9	73	2.6	23	8
25 years	2,814	1,334	47.4	1,431	50.9	31	1.1	12	6	2,765	731	26.4	1,902	68.8	100	3.6	26	6
26 years	2,369	971	41.0	1,337	56.4	29	1.2	22	10	2,290	533	23.3	1,636	71.4	93	4.1	26	2
27 years	2,456	912	37.1	1,490	60.7	32	1.3	13	9	2,297	479	20.9	1,695	73.8	89	3.9	31	3
28 years	2,777	955	34.4	1,759	63.3	35	1.3	22	6	2,668	509	19.1	1,986	74.4	127	4.8	41	5
29 years	2,649	844	31.9	1,726	65.2	58	2.2	20	1	2,424	402	16.6	1,876	77.4	113	4.7	30	3
30 years	3,329	1,077	32.4	2,137	64.2	79	2.4	31	5	3,224	568	17.6	2,410	74.8	180	5.6	62	4
31 years	1,643	431	26.2	1,146	69.8	49	3.0	12	5	1,509	197	13.1	1,174	77.8	104	6.9	32	2
32 years	2,487	661	26.6	1,714	68.9	79	3.2	30	3	2,302	310	13.5	1,734	75.3	220	9.6	32	6
33 years	1,798	416	23.1	1,317	73.2	39	2.2	23	3	1,702	190	11.2	1,343	78.9	132	7.8	35	2
34 years	1,961	445	22.7	1,441	73.5	51	2.6	15	9	1,871	195	10.4	1,505	80.4	144	7.7	23	4
DISTRICT OF COLUMBIA																		
15 years	846	845	99.9	1	.1	-	-	-	-	977	958	98.1	17	1.7	2	.2	-	-
16 years	872	871	99.9	1	.1	-	-	-	-	1,094	1,045	95.5	46	4.2	2	.2	1	-
17 years	969	958	98.9	11	1.1	-	-	-	-	1,105	970	87.8	133	12.0	2	.2	-	-
18 years	1,039	994	95.7	40	3.8	-	-	-	5	1,362	1,025	75.3	330	24.2	1	.1	1	5
19 years	1,031	923	89.5	103	10.0	1	.1	1	3	1,380	864	62.6	502	36.4	7	.5	-	7
20 years	1,102	901	81.8	196	17.8	1	.1	-	4	1,575	863	54.8	689	43.7	16	1.0	3	4
21 years	1,217	857	70.4	349	28.7	5	.4	-	6	1,404	658	46.9	711	50.6	22	1.6	8	5
22 years	1,371	820	59.8	535	39.0	6	.4	4	6	1,553	626	40.3	888	57.2	29	1.9	5	5
23 years	1,406	758	53.9	635	45.2	6	.4	3	4	1,676	606	36.2	1,016	60.6	35	2.1	16	3
24 years	1,376	647	47.0	717	52.1	4	.3	4	4	1,726	550	31.9	1,120	64.9	41	2.4	10	5
25 years	1,560	675	43.3	860	55.1	18	1.2	5	2	1,819	538	29.6	1,185	65.1	71	3.9	20	5
26 years	1,214	441	36.3	753	62.0	12	1.0	5	3	1,460	385	26.4	1,015	69.5	44	3.0	10	6
27 years	1,380	435	31.5	919	66.6	19	1.4	3	4	1,493	328	22.0	1,079	72.3	74	5.0	11	1
28 years	1,391	452	32.5	912	65.6	20	1.4	4	3	1,672	366	21.9	1,184	70.8	90	5.4	30	2
29 years	1,449	383	26.4	1,029	71.0	24	1.7	11	2	1,551	266	17.2	1,168	75.3	95	6.1	19	3
30 years	1,784	552	30.9	1,169	65.5	41	2.3	18	4	2,014	420	20.9	1,410	70.0	157	7.8	24	3
31 years	845	184	21.8	627	74.2	22	2.6	12	-	919	146	15.9	682	74.2	72	7.8	16	3
32 years	1,249	305	24.4	889	71.2	40	3.2	13	2	1,381	221	16.0	990	71.7	150	10.9	18	2
33 years	1,011	217	21.5	758	75.0	23	2.3	10	3	1,106	145	13.1	835	75.5	101	9.1	23	2
34 years	1,000	202	20.2	752	75.2	32	3.2	13	1	1,051	154	14.7	766	72.9	112	10.7	18	1
VIRGINIA																		
15 years	7,355	7,346	99.9	9	.1	-	-	-	-	7,608	7,494	98.5	109	1.4	4	.1	1	-
16 years	7,611	7,594	99.8	17	.2	-	-	-	-	7,855	7,477	95.2	362	4.6	15	.2	1	-
17 years	7,325	7,277	99.3	45	.6	-	-	3	-	7,363	6,562	89.1	780	10.6	14	.2	7	-
18 years	7,599	7,423	97.7	163	2.1	2	-	2	9	7,621	6,041	79.3	1,519	19.9	27	.4	26	8
19 years	6,542	6,109	93.4	410	6.3	4	.1	2	17	6,564	4,516	68.8	1,934	29.5	56	.9	45	13
20 years	5,996	5,168	86.2	775	12.9	21	.4	12	20	6,877	4,079	59.3	2,669	38.8	62	.9	57	10
21 years	5,816	4,352	74.8	1,418	24.4	20	.3	11	15	5,554	2,757	49.6	2,641	47.6	81	1.5	71	4
22 years	5,886	3,744	63.6	2,072	35.2	39	.7	22	9	6,062	2,552	42.1	3,293	54.3	128	2.1	83	6
23 years	4,971	2,706	54.4	2,187	44.0	32	.6	29	17	5,537	1,944	35.1	3,355	60.6	157	2.8	76	5
24 years	4,658	2,191	47.0	2,364	50.8	50	1.1	45	8	5,210	1,561	30.0	3,360	64.5	190	3.6	95	4
25 years	4,707	1,979	42.0	2,594	55.1	74	1.6	40	20	5,510	1,530	27.8	3,607	65.5	252	4.6	115	6
26 years	3,863	1,465	37.9	2,286	59.2	53	1.4	54	5	4,489	1,006	22.4	3,194	71.2	199	4.4	90	-
27 years	3,817	1,254	32.9	2,443	64.0	69	1.8	41	10	4,324	852	19.7	3,128	72.3	229	5.3	112	3
28 years	4,324	1,289	29.8	2,864	66.2	85	2.0	69	17	5,029	934	18.6	3,690	73.4	291	5.8	109	5
29 years	4,004	1,004	25.1	2,863	71.5	86	2.1	40	11	4,411	699	15.8	3,354	76.0	261	5.9	97	-
30 years	5,731	1,531	26.7	3,963	69.2	135	2.4	96	6	6,651	1,131	17.0	4,802	72.2	560	8.4	153	5
31 years	2,334	466	20.0	1,752	75.1	73	3.1	36	7	2,528	311	12.3	1,990	78.7	164	6.5	62	1
32 years	3,719	791	21.3	2,769	74.5	104	2.8	42	13	4,260	503	11.8	3,312	77.7	346	8.1	98	1
33 years	2,914	538	18.5	2,230	76.5	89	3.1	53	4	3,451	307	8.9	2,766	80.2	285	8.3	92	1
34 years	3,162	539	17.0	2,467	78.0	107	3.4	44	5	3,533	307	8.7	2,822	79.9	325	9.2	79	-

Table 13.—MARITAL CONDITION OF THE NEGRO POPULATION 15 TO 34 YEARS OLD, BY SEX, AND SINGLE YEARS OF AGE, BY THE SOUTHERN DIVISIONS, AND STATES: 1930—Continued

[Percent not shown where less than 1/10 of 1 percent]

DIVISION OR STATE, AND AGE	MALES									FEMALES								
	Total	Single		Married		Widowed		Divorced	Unknown	Total	Single		Married		Widowed		Divorced	Unknown
		Number	Percent	Number	Percent	Number	Percent				Number	Percent	Number	Percent	Number	Percent		
SOUTH ATLANTIC—Con.																		
WEST VIRGINIA																		
15 years	852	848	99.5	4	0.5	----	----	----	----	1,038	991	95.5	45	4.3	----	----	2	----
16 years	916	913	99.7	3	.3	----	----	----	----	1,045	911	87.2	132	12.6	2	0.2	----	----
17 years	976	971	99.5	5	.5	----	----	----	----	1,051	829	78.9	219	20.8	----	----	3	----
18 years	1,037	1,015	97.9	19	1.8	----	----	2	1	1,147	753	65.4	378	33.0	5	.4	10	1
19 years	924	865	93.6	55	6.0	2	0.2	1	1	1,123	601	53.5	499	44.4	14	1.2	8	1
20 years	993	873	87.9	112	11.3	1	.1	4	3	1,220	569	46.6	617	50.6	20	1.6	14	----
21 years	1,047	822	78.5	219	20.9	4	.4	2	----	966	347	35.9	591	61.2	17	1.8	11	----
22 years	1,143	797	69.7	329	28.8	6	.5	9	2	1,185	344	29.0	795	67.1	29	2.4	17	----
23 years	1,155	657	56.9	483	41.8	7	.6	7	1	1,118	255	22.8	805	72.0	37	3.3	21	----
24 years	1,195	636	53.2	540	45.2	10	.8	9	----	1,195	233	19.5	904	75.6	33	2.8	25	----
25 years	1,141	504	44.2	610	53.5	12	1.1	14	1	1,159	191	16.5	903	77.9	46	4.0	18	1
26 years	991	413	41.7	560	56.5	9	.9	8	1	1,105	164	14.8	880	79.6	36	3.3	24	1
27 years	1,086	416	38.3	634	58.4	12	1.1	24	----	1,015	119	11.7	845	83.3	33	3.3	18	----
28 years	1,386	491	35.4	831	60.0	27	1.9	17	2	1,134	116	10.2	934	82.4	62	5.5	20	2
29 years	1,459	400	27.4	1,006	69.0	28	1.9	25	----	1,223	105	8.6	1,033	84.5	64	5.2	21	----
30 years	1,720	511	29.7	1,137	66.1	48	2.8	23	1	1,452	154	10.6	1,168	80.4	97	6.7	32	1
31 years	839	186	22.2	625	74.5	15	1.8	13	----	661	43	6.5	572	86.5	34	5.1	12	----
32 years	1,219	292	24.0	872	71.5	33	2.7	21	1	987	71	7.2	837	84.8	62	6.3	16	1
33 years	955	210	22.0	702	73.5	27	2.8	16	----	804	44	5.5	696	86.6	49	6.1	15	----
34 years	1,067	225	21.1	794	74.4	25	2.3	23	----	842	47	5.6	717	85.2	66	7.8	11	1
NORTH CAROLINA																		
15 years	11,234	11,216	99.8	17	.2	1	----	----	----	11,521	11,344	98.5	171	1.5	4	----	2	----
16 years	11,617	11,591	99.8	25	.2	1	----	----	----	12,558	12,007	95.6	531	4.2	19	.2	1	----
17 years	11,468	11,375	99.2	89	.8	1	----	3	----	11,255	9,984	88.7	1,231	10.9	23	.2	17	----
18 years	11,724	11,307	96.4	382	3.3	9	.1	2	24	12,939	10,001	77.3	2,839	21.9	67	.5	24	8
19 years	9,803	8,875	90.5	877	8.9	11	.1	10	30	11,047	7,207	65.2	3,697	33.5	94	.9	33	16
20 years	9,800	7,933	80.9	1,783	18.2	26	.3	23	35	12,105	6,749	55.8	5,125	42.3	149	1.2	74	8
21 years	9,366	6,254	66.8	3,016	32.2	37	.4	33	26	9,466	4,626	48.9	4,615	48.8	153	1.6	60	12
22 years	8,949	4,914	54.9	3,897	43.5	90	1.0	30	18	10,866	4,496	41.4	6,025	55.4	241	2.2	88	16
23 years	7,910	3,509	44.4	4,280	54.1	77	1.0	26	18	9,657	3,362	34.8	5,860	60.7	306	3.2	101	28
24 years	7,576	2,870	37.9	4,542	60.0	109	1.4	37	18	9,309	2,787	29.9	6,020	64.7	386	4.1	101	15
25 years	7,563	2,624	34.7	4,754	62.9	115	1.5	47	23	9,619	2,683	27.9	6,300	65.5	487	5.1	136	13
26 years	5,989	1,694	28.3	4,151	69.3	100	1.7	34	10	7,567	1,697	22.4	5,353	70.7	404	5.3	104	9
27 years	5,807	1,413	24.3	4,207	72.4	131	2.3	43	13	6,716	1,269	18.9	4,960	73.9	380	5.7	97	10
28 years	6,599	1,469	22.3	4,930	74.7	152	2.3	36	12	7,861	1,360	17.3	5,846	74.4	527	6.7	120	8
29 years	5,637	967	17.2	4,493	79.7	131	2.3	32	14	6,485	943	14.5	4,937	76.1	502	7.7	99	4
30 years	8,287	1,627	19.6	6,335	76.4	236	2.8	74	15	9,619	1,538	16.0	6,968	72.4	925	9.6	173	15
31 years	3,150	490	15.6	2,542	80.7	90	2.9	22	6	3,504	381	10.9	2,772	79.1	291	8.3	60	----
32 years	4,537	631	13.9	3,703	81.6	152	3.4	45	6	5,495	586	10.7	4,274	77.8	530	9.6	94	11
33 years	3,776	453	12.0	3,160	83.7	122	3.2	34	7	4,381	391	8.9	3,482	79.5	435	9.9	71	2
34 years	4,077	442	10.8	3,458	84.8	137	3.4	36	4	4,558	374	8.2	3,683	80.8	439	9.6	59	3
SOUTH CAROLINA																		
15 years	10,201	10,187	99.9	14	.1	----	----	----	----	10,915	10,715	98.2	196	1.8	3	----	1	----
16 years	11,025	10,995	99.7	30	.3	----	----	----	----	12,250	11,559	94.4	670	5.5	17	.1	4	----
17 years	10,059	9,915	98.6	140	1.4	3	----	1	----	10,197	8,823	86.5	1,326	13.0	35	.3	13	----
18 years	11,023	10,473	95.0	524	4.8	8	.1	4	14	12,491	9,009	72.1	3,357	26.9	79	.6	37	9
19 years	8,497	7,395	87.0	1,071	12.6	16	.2	4	11	9,771	5,917	60.6	3,713	38.0	94	1.0	34	13
20 years	8,372	6,223	74.3	2,089	25.0	35	.4	9	16	11,373	5,755	50.6	5,348	47.0	211	1.9	45	14
21 years	7,747	4,162	53.7	3,512	45.3	43	.6	16	14	7,590	3,192	42.1	4,166	54.9	174	2.3	52	6
22 years	6,993	2,966	42.4	2,936	56.3	61	.9	24	6	8,613	3,160	36.7	5,107	59.3	271	3.1	60	15
23 years	5,780	1,925	33.3	3,752	64.9	75	1.3	20	8	7,771	2,371	30.5	4,990	64.2	332	4.3	74	4
24 years	5,280	1,459	27.6	3,711	70.3	82	1.6	20	8	7,133	1,945	27.3	4,746	66.5	379	5.3	61	2
25 years	5,913	1,469	24.8	4,302	72.8	117	2.0	19	6	7,984	1,882	23.6	5,469	68.5	538	6.7	89	6
26 years	3,959	805	20.3	3,051	77.1	85	2.1	13	5	5,668	1,108	19.5	4,103	72.4	390	6.9	66	1
27 years	3,700	631	17.1	2,979	80.5	71	1.9	18	1	4,904	843	17.2	3,612	73.7	394	8.0	51	4
28 years	4,695	805	17.1	3,755	80.0	117	2.5	17	1	6,250	888	14.2	4,784	76.5	501	8.0	72	5
29 years	3,601	474	13.2	3,051	84.7	62	1.7	14	----	4,625	541	11.7	3,606	78.0	428	9.3	47	3
30 years	6,807	1,040	15.3	5,493	80.7	236	3.5	35	3	8,620	1,181	13.7	6,299	73.1	1,019	11.8	105	16
31 years	1,878	244	13.0	1,560	83.1	64	3.4	9	1	2,345	213	9.1	1,852	79.0	253	10.8	23	4
32 years	3,241	334	10.3	2,790	86.1	100	3.1	17	----	4,282	375	8.8	3,373	78.8	490	11.4	38	6
33 years	2,433	236	9.7	2,108	86.6	75	3.1	12	2	3,330	243	7.3	2,685	80.6	380	11.4	21	1
34 years	2,613	214	8.2	2,311	88.4	74	2.8	13	1	3,420	212	6.2	2,780	81.3	395	11.5	32	1
GEORGIA																		
15 years	12,567	12,545	99.8	21	.2	1	----	----	----	13,460	12,951	96.2	467	3.5	34	.3	8	----
16 years	13,182	13,083	99.2	97	.7	1	----	1	----	14,631	12,982	88.7	1,527	10.4	84	.6	38	----
17 years	12,571	12,241	97.4	309	2.5	11	.1	10	----	13,473	10,526	78.1	2,716	20.2	171	1.3	60	----
18 years	13,537	12,392	91.5	1,060	7.8	33	.2	16	36	15,541	9,991	64.3	5,063	32.6	322	2.1	148	17
19 years	11,898	9,602	80.7	2,180	18.3	63	.5	29	24	13,356	7,045	52.7	5,744	43.0	379	2.8	178	10
20 years	11,630	7,883	67.8	3,552	30.5	112	1.0	59	24	15,757	6,877	43.6	7,954	50.5	643	4.1	274	9
21 years	10,615	5,625	53.0	4,747	44.7	159	1.5	62	22	11,059	4,015	36.3	6,260	56.6	557	5.0	218	9
22 years	10,419	4,463	42.8	5,631	54.0	209	2.0	95	21	12,835	3,967	30.9	7,726	60.2	821	6.4	312	9
23 years	9,078	3,178	35.0	5,590	61.6	212	2.3	83	15	11,788	3,097	26.3	7,505	63.7	815	6.9	360	11
24 years	8,432	2,479	29.4	5,638	66.9	206	2.4	96	13	10,721	2,383	22.2	7,125	66.5	899	8.4	308	6
25 years	9,294	2,565	27.6	6,326	68.1	282	3.0	111	10	12,010	2,392	19.9	8,102	67.5	1,178	9.8	328	10
26 years	6,751	1,546	22.9	4,904	72.6	214	3.2	81	6	8,834	1,498	17.0	6,229	70.5	881	10.0	222	4
27 years	6,363	1,314	20.7	4,734	74.4	202	3.2	104	9	7,808	1,090	14.0	5,615	71.9	881	11.3	217	5
28 years	7,632	1,368	17.9	5,884	77.1	283	3.7	90	7	9,613	1,200	12.5	7,026	73.1	1,091	11.3	293	3
29 years	6,246	947	15.2	4,982	79.8	232	3.7	81	4	7,701	886	11.5	5,612	72.9	965	12.5	235	3
30 years	10,368	1,777	17.1	7,968	76.9	467	4.5	134	22	12,944	1,577	12.2	8,980	69.4	1,955	15.1	416	16
31 years	3,156	432	13.7	2,554	80.9	137	4.3	33	----	4,020	304	7.6	3,045	75.7	561	14.0	107	3
32 years	5,298	716	13.5	4,263	80.5	230	4.3	82	7	6,716	581	8.7	4,924	73.3	1,014	15.1	194	3
33 years	4,020	451	11.2	3,312	82.4	187	4.7	64	6	5,232	337	6.4	3,917	74.9	842	16.1	131	5
34 years	4,242	468	11.0	3,508	82.7	206	4.9	54	6	5,396	384	7.1	4,074	75.5	810	15.0	123	5

TABLE 13.—MARITAL CONDITION OF THE NEGRO POPULATION 15 TO 34 YEARS OLD, BY SEX, AND SINGLE YEARS OF AGE, BY THE SOUTHERN DIVISIONS, AND STATES: 1930—Continued

[Percent not shown where less than 1/10 of 1 percent]

DIVISION OR STATE, AND AGE	MALES									FEMALES								
	Total	Single		Married		Widowed		Divorced	Unknown	Total	Single		Married		Widowed		Divorced	Unknown
		Number	Percent	Number	Percent	Number	Percent				Number	Percent	Number	Percent	Number	Percent		
SOUTH ATLANTIC—Con.																		
FLORIDA																		
15 years	3,859	3,849	99.7	10	0.3					4,234	4,027	95.1	196	4.6	8	0.2	3	
16 years	4,071	4,048	99.4	22	.5			1		4,629	4,014	86.7	586	12.7	17	.4	12	
17 years	3,895	3,833	98.4	59	1.5	3	0.1			4,486	3,313	73.9	1,101	24.5	44	1.0	28	
18 years	4,335	4,121	95.1	197	4.5	6	.1	4	7	5,112	3,124	61.1	1,839	36.0	82	1.6	53	14
19 years	3,842	3,331	86.7	456	11.9	14	.4	2	39	4,892	2,415	49.4	2,247	45.9	123	2.5	94	13
20 years	3,877	2,978	76.8	820	21.2	18	.5	17	44	5,564	2,122	38.1	3,099	55.7	213	3.8	119	11
21 years	4,393	2,728	62.1	1,526	34.7	42	1.0	29	68	4,676	1,404	30.0	2,985	63.8	185	4.0	87	15
22 years	4,672	2,434	52.1	2,090	44.7	54	1.2	30	64	5,365	1,403	26.2	3,579	66.7	243	4.5	117	23
23 years	4,605	2,025	44.0	2,394	52.0	75	1.6	43	68	5,298	1,059	20.0	3,791	71.6	297	5.6	140	11
24 years	4,598	1,731	37.6	2,650	57.6	90	2.0	59	68	5,354	964	18.0	3,907	73.0	329	6.1	145	9
25 years	4,848	1,665	34.3	2,907	60.0	93	1.9	86	97	5,525	826	15.0	4,121	74.6	419	7.6	142	17
26 years	4,022	1,167	29.0	2,624	65.2	131	3.3	47	53	4,675	560	12.0	3,627	77.6	343	7.3	133	12
27 years	4,065	1,096	27.0	2,714	66.8	111	2.7	77	67	4,390	478	10.9	3,368	76.7	414	9.4	110	20
28 years	4,622	1,117	24.2	3,240	70.1	140	3.0	66	59	5,084	494	9.7	3,986	78.4	441	8.7	151	12
29 years	4,228	909	21.5	3,083	72.9	137	3.2	55	44	4,491	354	7.9	3,522	78.4	463	10.3	137	15
30 years	5,831	1,302	22.3	4,134	70.9	228	3.9	96	71	5,890	536	9.1	4,448	75.5	735	12.5	150	21
31 years	2,349	447	19.0	1,727	73.5	91	3.9	44	40	2,338	151	6.5	1,827	78.1	282	12.1	68	10
32 years	3,308	591	17.9	2,494	75.4	140	4.2	48	35	3,638	227	6.2	2,832	77.8	478	13.1	94	7
33 years	2,578	448	17.4	1,953	75.8	112	4.3	43	22	2,877	140	4.9	2,260	78.6	394	13.7	75	8
34 years	2,727	435	16.0	2,083	76.4	118	4.3	58	33	2,867	161	5.6	2,217	77.3	403	14.1	81	5
EAST SOUTH CENTRAL																		
KENTUCKY																		
15 years	1,918	1,913	99.7	5	.3					2,009	1,939	96.5	64	3.2	6	.3		
16 years	2,144	2,134	99.5	10	.5					2,207	1,982	89.8	211	9.6	8	.4	6	
17 years	2,043	2,013	98.5	25	1.2	5	.2			2,115	1,712	80.9	374	17.7	15	.7	14	
18 years	2,140	2,049	95.7	83	3.9	6	.3	1	1	2,167	1,568	72.4	545	25.1	29	1.3	23	2
19 years	1,956	1,756	89.8	188	9.6	2	.1	6	4	2,063	1,243	60.3	754	36.5	33	1.6	32	1
20 years	1,944	1,581	81.3	330	17.0	21	1.1	10	2	2,130	1,047	49.2	972	45.6	61	2.9	47	3
21 years	2,016	1,448	71.8	539	26.7	10	.5	12	7	1,894	794	41.9	978	51.6	65	3.4	52	5
22 years	1,925	1,232	64.0	646	33.6	18	.9	27	2	2,073	775	37.4	1,169	56.4	73	3.5	54	2
23 years	1,838	985	53.6	810	44.1	21	1.1	20	2	2,009	584	29.1	1,252	62.3	102	5.1	68	3
24 years	1,925	862	44.8	977	50.8	40	2.1	40	6	2,062	563	27.3	1,288	62.5	119	5.8	90	2
25 years	1,859	835	44.9	926	49.8	50	2.7	47	1	2,055	501	24.4	1,346	65.5	121	5.9	85	2
26 years	1,589	625	39.3	892	56.1	43	2.7	28	1	1,894	398	21.0	1,299	68.6	129	6.8	66	2
27 years	1,665	574	34.5	989	59.4	56	3.4	45	1	1,716	309	18.0	1,230	71.7	115	6.7	61	1
28 years	1,874	572	30.5	1,191	63.6	60	3.2	49	2	1,941	303	15.6	1,411	72.7	153	7.9	73	1
29 years	1,802	497	27.6	1,207	67.0	55	3.1	43		1,807	250	13.8	1,340	74.2	154	8.5	63	
30 years	2,491	711	28.5	1,586	63.7	109	4.4	84	1	2,523	344	13.6	1,839	72.9	243	9.6	94	3
31 years	1,159	261	22.5	805	69.5	56	4.8	34	3	1,216	113	9.3	934	76.8	114	9.4	54	1
32 years	1,663	345	20.7	1,179	70.9	78	4.7	60	1	1,822	206	11.3	1,355	74.4	191	10.5	67	3
33 years	1,382	293	21.2	975	70.5	70	5.1	44		1,469	135	9.2	1,112	75.7	166	11.3	56	
34 years	1,484	272	18.3	1,099	74.1	72	4.9	39	2	1,583	134	8.5	1,212	76.6	184	11.6	53	
TENNESSEE																		
15 years	4,692	4,683	99.8	8	.2	1				4,956	4,797	96.8	145	2.9	8	.2	6	
16 years	4,975	4,950	99.5	24	.5			1		5,337	4,867	91.2	428	8.0	23	.4	19	
17 years	5,127	5,018	97.9	102	2.0	7	.1			5,141	4,133	80.4	927	18.0	51	1.0	30	
18 years	5,350	4,975	93.0	320	6.0	13	.2	12	30	6,046	3,955	65.4	1,906	31.5	80	1.3	85	20
19 years	4,809	3,987	82.9	746	15.5	23	.5	20	33	5,402	2,889	53.5	2,261	41.9	128	2.4	104	20
20 years	4,774	3,449	72.2	1,192	25.0	55	1.2	45	33	6,239	2,803	44.9	3,078	49.3	203	3.3	138	17
21 years	4,526	2,805	62.0	1,603	35.4	59	1.3	42	17	4,660	1,750	37.6	2,561	55.0	206	4.4	125	18
22 years	4,522	2,352	52.0	2,006	44.4	71	1.6	77	16	5,643	1,864	33.0	3,295	58.4	277	4.9	193	14
23 years	4,151	1,763	42.5	2,188	52.7	104	2.5	83	13	5,205	1,398	26.9	3,270	62.8	299	5.7	225	13
24 years	4,364	1,610	36.9	2,549	58.4	115	2.6	78	12	5,204	1,182	22.7	3,435	66.0	351	6.7	225	11
25 years	4,497	1,536	34.2	2,704	60.1	133	3.0	104	20	5,575	1,134	20.3	3,757	67.4	419	7.5	250	15
26 years	3,654	1,019	27.9	2,410	66.0	115	3.1	102	8	4,624	768	16.6	3,271	70.7	378	8.2	202	5
27 years	3,380	854	25.3	2,333	69.0	105	3.1	77	11	3,932	629	16.0	2,809	71.4	316	8.0	173	5
28 years	4,059	979	24.1	2,867	70.6	123	3.0	80	10	4,870	688	14.1	3,471	71.3	467	9.6	235	9
29 years	3,576	696	19.5	2,650	74.1	125	3.5	97	8	4,182	483	11.5	3,060	73.2	450	10.8	185	4
30 years	5,427	1,179	21.7	3,846	70.9	242	4.5	151	9	5,824	700	12.0	4,137	71.0	699	12.0	274	14
31 years	2,020	387	19.2	1,507	74.6	75	3.7	51		2,283	210	9.2	1,708	74.8	260	11.4	99	6
32 years	3,207	525	16.4	2,431	75.8	147	4.6	95	9	3,681	340	9.2	2,740	74.4	456	12.4	141	4
33 years	2,469	326	13.2	1,963	79.5	114	4.6	65	1	2,958	208	7.0	2,219	75.0	400	13.5	125	6
34 years	2,655	377	14.2	2,089	78.7	118	4.4	67	4	3,084	213	6.9	2,334	75.7	426	13.8	110	1
ALABAMA																		
15 years	10,670	10,659	99.9	10	.1	1				11,116	10,781	97.0	311	2.8	13	.1	11	
16 years	11,659	11,592	99.4	62	.5	2		3		12,094	11,011	91.0	980	8.1	61	.5	42	
17 years	11,299	11,107	98.3	182	1.6	7	.1	3		10,758	8,741	81.3	1,841	17.1	117	1.1	59	
18 years	10,117	9,505	94.0	535	5.3	29	.3	13	35	12,645	8,252	65.3	3,995	31.6	249	2.0	130	19
19 years	8,042	6,949	86.4	987	12.3	44	.5	36	26	10,816	5,742	53.1	4,504	41.6	326	3.0	218	26
20 years	8,389	6,229	74.3	2,002	23.9	82	1.0	47	29	12,801	5,684	44.4	6,308	49.3	478	3.7	316	15
21 years	8,955	5,245	58.6	3,495	39.0	131	1.5	74	10	9,186	3,377	36.8	5,094	55.5	431	4.7	263	21
22 years	9,463	4,478	47.3	4,665	49.3	174	1.8	119	27	11,028	3,384	30.7	6,661	60.4	612	5.5	353	18
23 years	8,441	3,208	38.0	4,901	58.1	181	2.1	132	19	10,397	2,583	24.8	6,777	65.2	653	6.3	375	9
24 years	8,265	2,617	31.7	5,261	63.7	233	2.8	138	16	10,148	2,235	22.0	6,763	66.6	757	7.5	379	14
25 years	8,648	2,535	29.3	5,694	65.8	255	2.9	147	17	10,685	2,154	20.2	7,213	67.5	907	8.5	396	15
26 years	6,811	1,672	24.5	4,778	70.2	224	3.3	123	14	8,480	1,405	16.6	6,027	71.1	710	8.4	332	6
27 years	5,976	1,269	21.2	4,384	73.4	202	3.4	106	15	7,411	1,004	13.5	5,407	73.0	700	9.4	293	7
28 years	7,358	1,396	19.0	5,547	75.4	267	3.6	137	11	8,762	1,116	12.7	6,432	73.4	891	10.2	314	9
29 years	6,103	941	15.4	4,815	78.9	213	3.5	126	8	7,284	745	10.2	5,401	74.1	852	11.7	280	6
30 years	9,095	1,693	18.6	6,798	74.7	423	4.7	171	10	10,707	1,314	12.3	7,407	69.2	1,485	13.9	490	11
31 years	3,169	462	14.6	2,513	79.3	107	3.4	80	7	3,751	323	8.6	2,808	74.9	478	12.7	141	1
32 years	4,847	670	13.8	3,860	79.6	214	4.4	99	4	6,253	500	8.0	4,654	74.4	873	14.0	221	5
33 years	3,738	464	12.4	3,041	81.4	153	4.1	75	5	4,886	373	7.6	3,666	75.0	672	13.8	171	4
34 years	4,065	445	10.9	3,351	82.4	177	4.4	88	4	5,048	333	6.6	3,846	76.2	700	13.9	165	4

Table 13.—MARITAL CONDITION OF THE NEGRO POPULATION 15 TO 34 YEARS OLD, BY SEX, AND SINGLE YEARS OF AGE, BY THE SOUTHERN DIVISIONS, AND STATES: 1930—Continued

[Percent not shown where less than 1/10 of 1 percent]

DIVISION OR STATE, AND AGE	MALES									FEMALES								
	Total	Single		Married		Widowed		Divorced	Unknown	Total	Single		Married		Widowed		Divorced	Unknown
		Number	Percent	Number	Percent	Number	Percent				Number	Percent	Number	Percent	Number	Percent		
East South Central—Continued																		
MISSISSIPPI																		
15 years	11, 353	11, 331	99. 8	18	0. 2	3	------	1	------	11, 076	10, 511	94. 9	524	4. 7	24	0. 2	17	------
16 years	12, 224	12, 127	99. 2	91	. 7	6	------	------	------	12, 203	10, 519	86. 2	1, 545	12. 7	81	. 7	58	------
17 years	12, 149	11, 829	97. 4	305	2. 5	10	0. 1	5	------	10, 759	7, 797	72. 5	2, 717	25. 3	139	1. 3	106	------
18 years	11, 268	10, 208	90. 6	978	8. 7	29	. 3	18	35	13, 970	7, 866	56. 3	5, 644	40. 4	246	1. 8	207	7
19 years	8, 758	6, 929	79. 1	1, 682	19. 2	49	. 6	40	58	11, 133	4, 877	43. 8	5, 724	51. 4	312	2. 8	209	11
20 years	9, 518	6, 311	66. 3	2, 985	31. 4	108	1. 1	79	35	14, 180	4, 917	34. 7	8, 379	59. 1	513	3. 6	364	7
21 years	10, 145	4, 919	48. 5	4, 926	48. 6	152	1. 5	95	53	9, 710	2, 748	28. 3	6, 248	64. 3	404	4. 2	307	3
22 years	10, 346	4, 131	39. 9	5, 792	56. 0	219	2. 1	151	53	11, 662	2, 722	23. 3	7, 947	68. 1	572	4. 9	412	9
23 years	9, 275	2, 937	31. 7	5, 904	63. 7	223	2. 4	161	50	10, 466	2, 079	19. 9	7, 371	70. 4	623	6. 0	382	11
24 years	8, 852	2, 392	27. 0	6, 011	67. 9	231	2. 6	154	64	10, 207	1, 625	15. 9	7, 599	74. 4	606	5. 9	370	7
25 years	9, 904	2, 367	23. 9	7, 012	70. 8	300	3. 0	182	43	11, 597	1, 799	15. 5	8, 529	73. 5	824	7. 1	432	13
26 years	7, 455	1, 466	19. 7	5, 521	74. 1	255	3. 4	165	48	8, 798	1, 141	13. 0	6, 659	75. 7	641	7. 3	349	8
27 years	6, 665	1, 174	17. 6	5, 111	76. 7	213	3. 2	129	38	7, 578	806	10. 6	5, 889	77. 7	593	7. 8	285	5
28 years	8, 109	1, 230	15. 2	6, 383	78. 7	290	3. 6	154	52	9, 400	908	9. 7	7, 346	78. 1	777	8. 3	358	11
29 years	6, 267	755	12. 0	5, 141	82. 0	226	3. 6	109	36	7, 054	577	8. 2	5, 532	78. 4	673	9. 5	266	6
30 years	10, 735	1, 519	14. 1	8, 474	78. 9	462	4. 3	239	41	12, 145	1, 117	9. 2	9, 208	75. 8	1, 268	10. 4	538	14
31 years	3, 525	388	11. 0	2, 912	82. 6	129	3. 7	73	23	3, 845	256	6. 7	3, 107	80. 8	350	9. 1	127	5
32 years	5, 661	603	10. 7	4, 690	82. 8	219	3. 9	106	43	6, 432	437	6. 8	5, 084	79. 0	653	10. 2	251	7
33 years	4, 326	434	10. 0	3, 622	83. 7	172	4. 0	76	22	4, 963	287	5. 8	4, 004	80. 7	487	9. 8	180	5
34 years	4, 517	392	8. 7	3, 821	84. 6	188	4. 2	76	40	5, 350	273	5. 1	4, 350	81. 3	540	10. 1	186	1
West South Central																		
ARKANSAS																		
15 years	5, 031	5, 019	99. 8	12	. 2	------	------	------	------	5, 130	4, 890	95. 3	216	4. 2	12	. 2	12	------
16 years	5, 192	5, 173	99. 6	18	. 3	------	------	1	------	5, 553	4, 826	86. 9	662	11. 9	43	. 8	22	------
17 years	5, 067	4, 977	98. 2	83	1. 6	5	. 1	2	------	5, 093	3, 806	74. 7	1, 160	22. 8	78	1. 5	49	------
18 years	5, 095	4, 775	93. 7	287	5. 6	19	. 4	8	6	6, 305	3, 450	54. 7	2, 607	41. 3	145	2. 3	101	2
19 years	4, 632	3, 866	83. 5	698	15. 1	37	. 8	24	7	5, 447	2, 308	42. 4	2, 804	51. 5	220	4. 0	111	4
20 years	4, 427	3, 175	71. 7	1, 140	25. 8	66	1. 5	39	7	6, 260	2, 098	33. 5	3, 704	59. 2	290	4. 6	163	5
21 years	5, 074	2, 617	51. 6	2, 314	45. 6	76	1. 5	64	3	4, 700	1, 245	26. 5	3, 068	65. 3	230	4. 9	153	4
22 years	4, 773	2, 002	41. 9	2, 566	53. 8	122	2. 6	79	4	5, 313	1, 128	21. 2	3, 665	69. 0	333	6. 3	186	1
23 years	4, 298	1, 451	33. 8	2, 637	61. 4	120	2. 8	82	8	5, 169	942	18. 2	3, 639	70. 4	364	7. 0	221	3
24 years	4, 259	1, 200	28. 2	2, 821	66. 2	128	3. 0	107	3	4, 983	704	14. 1	3, 637	73. 0	404	8. 1	237	1
25 years	4, 285	1, 074	25. 1	2, 968	69. 3	144	3. 4	97	2	5, 082	639	12. 6	3, 805	74. 9	402	7. 9	230	6
26 years	3, 566	734	20. 6	2, 578	72. 3	155	4. 3	98	1	4, 469	506	11. 3	3, 345	74. 8	406	9. 1	209	3
27 years	3, 473	619	17. 8	2, 602	74. 9	152	4. 4	100	------	3, 841	368	9. 6	2, 950	76. 8	339	8. 8	182	2
28 years	3, 835	617	16. 1	2, 959	77. 2	162	4. 2	96	1	4, 491	381	8. 5	3, 503	78. 0	422	9. 4	183	2
29 years	3, 386	430	12. 7	2, 710	80. 0	156	4. 6	89	1	3, 736	232	6. 2	2, 957	79. 1	377	10. 1	169	1
30 years	4, 939	708	14. 3	3, 806	77. 1	276	5. 6	147	2	5, 407	432	8. 0	4, 125	76. 3	647	12. 0	200	3
31 years	1, 873	195	10. 4	1, 546	82. 5	79	4. 2	53	------	2, 127	112	5. 3	1, 672	78. 6	239	11. 2	104	------
32 years	2, 868	309	10. 8	2, 326	81. 1	161	5. 6	72	------	3, 531	190	5. 4	2, 811	79. 6	373	10. 6	157	------
33 years	2, 352	203	8. 6	1, 964	83. 5	126	5. 4	59	------	2, 870	109	3. 8	2, 327	81. 1	342	11. 9	92	------
34 years	2, 478	202	8. 2	2, 084	84. 1	127	5. 1	60	5	2, 986	127	4. 3	2, 410	80. 7	335	11. 2	113	1
LOUISIANA																		
15 years	7, 738	7, 731	99. 9	6	. 1	------	------	1	------	8, 136	7, 807	96. 0	305	3. 7	13	. 2	11	------
16 years	7, 833	7, 800	99. 6	32	. 4	1	------	------	------	8, 889	7, 913	89. 0	916	10. 3	35	. 4	25	------
17 years	7, 440	7, 324	98. 4	109	1. 5	1	------	6	------	8, 338	6, 493	77. 9	1, 737	20. 8	63	. 8	45	------
18 years	8, 086	7, 666	94. 8	396	4. 9	10	. 1	4	10	9, 406	6, 084	64. 7	3, 078	32. 7	129	1. 4	108	7
19 years	7, 095	6, 188	87. 2	858	12. 1	21	. 3	14	14	8, 332	4, 371	52. 5	3, 661	43. 9	168	2. 0	126	6
20 years	7, 227	5, 455	75. 5	1, 673	23. 1	45	. 6	40	14	9, 891	4, 103	41. 5	5, 301	53. 6	294	3. 0	186	7
21 years	7, 377	4, 492	60. 9	2, 761	37. 4	60	. 8	49	15	7, 648	2, 616	34. 2	4, 579	59. 9	248	3. 2	196	9
22 years	7, 893	4, 064	51. 5	3, 638	46. 1	101	1. 3	79	11	8, 792	2, 592	29. 5	5, 609	63. 8	347	3. 9	238	6
23 years	7, 101	2, 969	41. 8	3, 949	55. 6	104	1. 5	76	3	8, 515	2, 010	23. 6	5, 908	69. 4	352	4. 1	242	3
24 years	6, 948	2, 504	36. 0	4, 208	60. 6	130	1. 9	99	7	8, 158	1, 744	21. 4	5, 757	70. 6	441	5. 4	213	3
25 years	7, 564	2, 360	31. 2	4, 944	65. 4	158	2. 1	96	6	8, 975	1, 687	18. 8	6, 460	72. 0	555	6. 2	264	9
26 years	6, 220	1, 656	26. 6	4, 343	69. 8	123	2. 0	93	5	7, 367	1, 183	16. 1	5, 459	74. 1	468	6. 4	249	8
27 years	5, 826	1, 388	23. 8	4, 206	72. 2	131	2. 2	93	8	6, 809	953	14. 0	5, 098	74. 9	529	7. 8	223	6
28 years	6, 489	1, 378	21. 2	4, 820	74. 3	185	2. 9	98	8	7, 622	960	12. 6	5, 815	76. 3	600	7. 9	233	14
29 years	5, 707	1, 047	18. 3	4, 434	77. 7	135	2. 4	87	4	6, 462	669	10. 4	4, 969	76. 9	601	9. 3	214	9
30 years	8, 082	1, 489	18. 4	6, 135	75. 9	305	3. 8	144	9	9, 029	1, 108	12. 3	6, 666	73. 8	952	10. 5	289	14
31 years	3, 360	543	16. 2	2, 630	78. 3	122	3. 6	62	3	3, 526	313	8. 9	2, 748	77. 9	349	9. 9	110	6
32 years	4, 932	790	16. 0	3, 891	78. 9	158	3. 2	84	9	5, 631	489	8. 7	4, 340	77. 1	622	11. 0	169	11
33 years	4, 011	544	13. 6	3, 262	81. 3	144	3. 6	57	4	4, 677	343	7. 3	3, 688	78. 9	514	11. 0	127	5
34 years	4, 150	493	11. 9	3, 443	83. 0	143	3. 4	66	5	4, 790	348	7. 3	3, 758	78. 5	524	10. 9	153	7
OKLAHOMA																		
15 years	1, 734	1, 732	99. 9	2	. 1	------	------	------	------	1, 805	1, 739	96. 3	61	3. 4	4	. 2	1	------
16 years	1, 852	1, 846	99. 7	5	. 3	1	------	------	------	1, 945	1, 750	90. 0	181	9. 3	7	. 4	7	------
17 years	1, 857	1, 827	98. 4	26	1. 4	2	. 1	2	------	1, 858	1, 480	79. 7	345	18. 6	19	1. 0	14	------
18 years	1, 890	1, 798	95. 1	88	4. 7	------	------	3	1	2, 188	1, 389	63. 5	740	33. 8	37	1. 7	20	2
19 years	1, 766	1, 555	88. 1	199	11. 3	5	. 3	2	5	1, 916	972	50. 7	862	45. 0	52	2. 7	30	------
20 years	1, 730	1, 345	77. 7	364	21. 0	6	. 3	13	2	2, 070	844	40. 8	1, 100	53. 1	72	3. 5	52	2
21 years	1, 770	1, 116	63. 1	598	33. 8	30	1. 7	20	6	1, 708	573	33. 5	1, 008	59. 0	67	3. 9	60	------
22 years	1, 683	875	52. 0	738	43. 9	36	2. 1	28	6	1, 934	537	27. 8	1, 213	62. 7	103	5. 3	79	2
23 years	1, 553	672	43. 3	824	53. 1	31	2. 0	22	4	1, 864	404	21. 7	1, 269	68. 1	116	6. 2	75	------
24 years	1, 585	568	35. 8	916	57. 8	52	3. 3	48	1	1, 996	388	19. 4	1, 384	69. 3	133	6. 7	89	2
25 years	1, 566	522	33. 3	938	59. 9	60	3. 8	45	1	1, 719	274	15. 9	1, 219	70. 9	136	7. 9	88	2
26 years	1, 375	364	26. 5	924	67. 2	51	3. 7	34	2	1, 633	209	12. 8	1, 218	74. 6	118	7. 2	88	------
27 years	1, 437	335	23. 3	994	69. 2	61	4. 2	47	------	1, 576	159	10. 1	1, 182	75. 0	151	9. 6	83	1
28 years	1, 614	344	21. 3	1, 133	70. 2	69	4. 3	63	5	1, 713	153	8. 9	1, 285	75. 0	190	11. 1	83	2
29 years	1, 429	251	17. 6	1, 050	73. 5	68	4. 8	58	2	1, 533	113	7. 4	1, 194	77. 9	142	9. 3	82	2
30 years	1, 781	342	19. 2	1, 297	72. 8	82	4. 6	57	3	1, 873	155	8. 3	1, 396	74. 5	224	12. 0	97	1
31 years	913	142	15. 6	681	74. 6	62	6. 8	26	2	958	55	5. 7	754	78. 7	102	10. 6	46	1
32 years	1, 214	168	13. 8	949	78. 2	54	4. 4	42	1	1, 371	56	4. 1	1, 087	79. 3	143	10. 4	85	------
33 years	999	121	12. 1	783	78. 4	45	4. 5	48	2	1, 064	45	4. 2	847	79. 6	131	12. 3	39	2
34 years	1, 176	128	10. 9	939	79. 8	67	5. 7	40	2	1, 120	44	3. 9	871	77. 8	130	11. 6	72	3

TABLE 13.—MARITAL CONDITION OF THE NEGRO POPULATION 15 TO 34 YEARS OLD, BY SEX, AND SINGLE YEARS OF AGE, BY THE SOUTHERN DIVISIONS, AND STATES: 1930—Continued

[Percent not shown where less than 1/10 of 1 percent]

DIVISION OR STATE, AND AGE	MALES									FEMALES								
	Total	Single		Married		Widowed		Divorced	Unknown	Total	Single		Married		Widowed		Divorced	Unknown
		Number	Percent	Number	Percent	Number	Percent				Number	Percent	Number	Percent	Number	Percent		
WEST SOUTH CENTRAL—Continued																		
TEXAS																		
15 years	8,409	8,394	99.8	13	0.2	2				9,276	8,955	96.5	291	3.1	16	0.2	14	
16 years	8,893	8,835	99.3	51	.6	5	0.1	2		10,007	8,975	89.7	922	9.2	64	.6	46	
17 years	8,882	8,735	98.3	135	1.5	5	.1	7		9,375	7,314	78.0	1,828	19.5	129	1.4	104	
18 years	8,998	8,483	94.3	454	5.0	24	.3	18	19	10,732	6,550	61.0	3,728	34.7	221	2.1	226	7
19 years	8,404	7,181	85.4	1,111	13.2	46	.5	48	18	9,720	4,706	48.4	4,422	45.5	293	3.0	292	7
20 years	8,550	6,256	73.2	2,088	24.4	94	1.1	93	19	11,382	4,357	38.3	6,086	53.5	477	4.2	453	9
21 years	8,839	5,250	59.4	3,304	37.4	148	1.7	129	8	8,444	2,557	30.3	5,046	59.8	427	5.1	405	9
22 years	8,783	4,253	48.4	4,138	47.1	190	2.2	190	12	9,984	2,497	25.0	6,428	64.4	564	5.6	485	10
23 years	8,191	3,190	38.9	4,552	55.6	232	2.8	209	8	9,559	1,938	20.3	6,485	67.8	593	6.2	537	6
24 years	8,163	2,667	32.7	4,974	60.9	270	3.3	247	5	9,674	1,650	17.1	6,779	70.1	679	7.0	556	10
25 years	8,307	2,404	28.9	5,325	64.1	267	3.2	304	7	9,697	1,492	15.4	6,846	70.6	722	7.4	628	9
26 years	7,214	1,806	25.0	4,905	68.0	253	3.5	245	5	8,390	1,000	11.9	6,197	73.9	644	7.7	544	5
27 years	7,073	1,487	21.0	5,093	72.0	270	3.8	217	6	8,037	857	10.7	5,983	74.4	665	8.3	523	9
28 years	7,589	1,441	19.0	5,517	72.7	312	4.1	314	5	8,823	837	9.5	6,619	75.0	772	8.7	592	3
29 years	7,202	1,078	15.0	5,540	76.9	308	4.3	270	6	7,860	602	7.7	5,958	75.8	753	9.6	538	9
30 years	9,657	1,672	17.3	7,127	73.8	456	4.7	398	4	10,192	861	8.4	7,466	73.3	1,167	11.5	688	10
31 years	4,348	590	13.6	3,390	78.0	207	4.8	157	4	4,628	272	5.9	3,571	77.2	485	10.5	296	4
32 years	6,432	826	12.8	5,001	77.8	330	5.1	270	5	6,900	378	5.5	5,297	76.8	771	11.2	451	3
33 years	5,166	603	11.7	4,095	79.3	242	4.7	222	4	5,326	267	5.0	4,106	77.1	614	11.5	333	6
34 years	5,473	574	10.5	4,360	79.7	275	5.0	252	12	5,928	266	4.5	4,577	77.2	678	11.4	404	3

TABLE 14.—MARITAL CONDITION OF THE URBAN, RURAL-FARM, AND RURAL-NONFARM NEGRO POPULATION 15 YEARS OLD AND OVER, BY SEX, AND 5-YEAR AGE PERIODS, BY GEOGRAPHIC DIVISIONS: 1930

AREA AND AGE	MALES 15 YEARS OLD AND OVER				FEMALES 15 YEARS OLD AND OVER				MALES 15 YEARS OLD AND OVER				FEMALES 15 YEARS OLD AND OVER			
	Total	Single	Married	Widowed or divorced	Total	Single	Married	Widowed or divorced	Total	Single	Married	Widowed or divorced	Total	Single	Married	Widowed or divorced
	NEW ENGLAND								MIDDLE ATLANTIC							
Urban	**29,085**	**10,211**	**16,735**	**2,063**	**29,753**	**7,503**	**16,794**	**5,414**	**349,615**	**119,782**	**210,534**	**18,431**	**364,276**	**88,991**	**217,474**	**56,999**
15 to 19 years	2,916	2,876	39		3,283	2,871	406	6	29,742	28,895	739	18	37,662	30,683	6,675	214
20 to 24 years	2,919	2,033	852	23	3,371	1,571	1,718	75	44,755	28,047	16,229	315	56,249	21,540	33,097	1,470
25 to 34 years	7,010	2,483	4,298	218	7,133	1,364	5,171	592	111,566	35,146	73,762	2,458	115,303	21,789	84,204	9,104
35 to 44 years	6,828	1,466	4,943	407	6,743	739	4,865	1,130	86,742	17,413	64,462	4,731	81,957	8,968	57,865	14,995
45 to 54 years	5,292	843	3,911	530	4,908	511	3,056	1,337	49,957	7,247	37,543	5,074	45,040	3,862	26,247	14,850
55 to 64 years	2,601	325	1,876	399	2,546	267	1,175	1,102	18,453	2,162	13,130	3,124	17,358	1,302	7,086	8,936
65 and over	1,463	173	803	483	1,712	165	383	1,163	7,733	671	4,382	2,666	10,020	661	2,020	7,317
Rural-farm	**505**	**248**	**213**	**44**	**318**	**97**	**188**	**33**	**4,612**	**2,115**	**2,148**	**339**	**2,965**	**750**	**1,934**	**276**
15 to 19 years	56	56			46	39	7		758	751	6		461	402	59	
20 to 24 years	52	48	3	1	34	20	14		643	502	137	4	369	160	208	
25 to 34 years	89	49	39	1	59	14	41	4	873	352	495	20	640	91	531	16
35 to 44 years	109	41	63	5	69	11	54	4	848	217	575	56	609	32	527	50
45 to 54 years	87	24	52	11	62	7	49	6	755	161	508	85	487	30	392	64
55 to 64 years	67	19	39	9	24	3	14	7	442	80	288	74	233	15	161	57
65 and over	43	11	15	17	21	2	7	12	285	51	135	98	160	19	52	89
Rural-nonfarm	**4,172**	**1,675**	**2,192**	**298**	**3,701**	**1,118**	**2,075**	**506**	**38,986**	**13,912**	**22,198**	**2,669**	**33,171**	**7,658**	**21,289**	**4,105**
15 to 19 years	523	519	3	1	516	456	58	2	4,360	4,269	68	3	4,497	3,621	857	11
20 to 24 years	433	339	88	4	513	249	257	7	4,656	3,073	1,509	23	4,492	1,613	2,772	78
25 to 34 years	856	316	521	18	712	146	529	37	10,077	3,191	6,578	255	8,865	1,197	7,174	462
35 to 44 years	864	214	611	39	796	119	578	98	8,075	1,736	6,409	536	6,757	569	5,381	796
45 to 54 years	790	167	545	77	588	75	405	108	6,075	903	4,493	666	4,706	363	3,341	989
55 to 64 years	431	68	286	76	307	41	175	91	3,054	433	2,077	535	2,183	171	1,227	782
65 and over	265	49	133	83	264	30	71	163	1,915	256	1,005	640	1,570	103	486	971
	EAST NORTH CENTRAL								WEST NORTH CENTRAL							
Urban	**328,875**	**99,730**	**201,065**	**27,611**	**316,080**	**54,064**	**201,755**	**59,941**	**100,003**	**29,554**	**59,619**	**10,613**	**102,530**	**19,328**	**60,081**	**22,980**
15 to 19 years	27,661	26,740	872	28	32,270	24,113	7,710	427	8,990	8,659	314	11	10,253	8,022	2,082	144
20 to 24 years	39,074	23,211	15,113	703	45,752	12,569	30,276	2,849	10,297	6,224	3,836	220	12,968	4,531	7,485	937
25 to 34 years	100,811	27,686	67,932	5,106	100,184	10,555	77,152	12,407	24,327	6,986	15,893	1,413	27,173	3,936	19,487	3,723
35 to 44 years	84,444	13,954	62,594	7,813	72,044	4,269	52,798	14,942	24,473	4,184	17,753	2,506	23,799	1,673	16,897	5,213
45 to 54 years	48,808	5,634	36,209	6,927	39,081	1,636	24,310	13,105	18,389	2,259	13,334	2,766	15,682	732	9,645	5,286
55 to 64 years	18,449	1,694	12,985	3,752	15,966	519	7,024	8,400	8,321	787	5,742	1,779	7,148	237	3,200	3,701
65 and over	8,818	602	4,968	3,237	10,138	310	2,171	7,639	4,931	374	2,662	1,886	5,202	161	1,221	3,908
Rural-farm	**6,946**	**2,561**	**3,666**	**704**	**5,377**	**1,206**	**3,554**	**610**	**12,971**	**4,161**	**7,528**	**1,270**	**10,493**	**2,023**	**7,384**	**1,082**
15 to 19 years	1,013	998	13		821	715	105	1	1,994	1,934	57	3	1,830	1,334	468	27
20 to 24 years	709	561	143	2	519	219	280	19	1,582	897	649	32	1,515	365	1,085	63
25 to 34 years	923	359	516	47	876	125	714	37	2,207	502	1,604	97	2,117	131	1,861	125
35 to 44 years	1,085	225	788	68	1,036	54	910	71	2,291	310	1,797	181	2,064	89	1,798	177
45 to 54 years	1,237	185	904	146	967	41	805	121	2,190	250	1,665	275	1,505	40	1,270	195
55 to 64 years	1,052	125	767	157	644	22	508	113	1,518	145	1,068	305	811	29	612	170
65 and over	925	107	535	283	509	27	231	247	1,180	119	684	376	644	31	289	323
Rural-nonfarm	**28,509**	**11,099**	**14,297**	**2,995**	**18,990**	**3,782**	**12,090**	**3,085**	**15,619**	**5,615**	**7,845**	**2,026**	**12,103**	**2,501**	**7,154**	**2,433**
15 to 19 years	3,144	3,077	63	3	2,542	2,071	441	29	1,598	1,552	44	2	1,582	1,285	274	22
20 to 24 years	3,392	2,380	956	51	2,191	706	1,383	100	1,668	1,173	429	60	1,353	519	769	65
25 to 34 years	7,001	2,761	3,797	427	4,366	446	3,565	353	3,306	1,276	1,735	267	2,358	319	1,795	243
35 to 44 years	5,928	1,379	3,955	576	3,944	237	3,191	513	3,214	792	2,053	318	2,305	137	1,831	337
45 to 54 years	4,417	786	2,982	635	2,884	142	2,114	624	2,510	432	1,676	382	1,954	123	1,369	462
55 to 64 years	2,473	419	1,552	491	1,588	91	946	545	1,667	204	1,095	359	1,264	63	705	496
65 and over	2,063	279	966	807	1,444	85	438	914	1,614	170	797	631	1,236	52	389	786

TABLE 14.—MARITAL CONDITION OF THE URBAN, RURAL-FARM, AND RURAL-NONFARM NEGRO POPULATION 15 YEARS OLD AND OVER, BY SEX, AND 5-YEAR AGE PERIODS, BY GEOGRAPHIC DIVISIONS, 1930—Continued

AREA AND AGE	MALES 15 YEARS OLD AND OVER				FEMALES 15 YEARS OLD AND OVER				MALES 15 YEARS OLD AND OVER				FEMALES 15 YEARS OLD AND OVER			
	Total	Single	Married	Widowed or divorced	Total	Single	Married	Widowed or divorced	Total	Single	Married	Widowed or divorced	Total	Single	Married	Widowed or divorced
	SOUTH ATLANTIC								EAST SOUTH CENTRAL							
Urban	**481, 169**	**155, 476**	**288, 468**	**36, 025**	**582, 457**	**148, 143**	**308, 894**	**124, 237**	**257, 371**	**76, 397**	**155, 781**	**24, 766**	**310, 162**	**68, 104**	**164, 071**	**77, 515**
15 to 19 years	62, 207	59, 821	2, 249	87	83, 484	67, 392	15, 016	1, 007	31, 402	29, 957	1, 294	91	41, 105	31, 419	8, 547	1, 093
20 to 24 years	69, 379	39, 066	29, 096	1, 063	97, 125	37, 644	53, 493	5, 860	35, 156	18, 898	15, 038	1, 140	49, 604	16, 733	27, 756	5, 020
25 to 34 years	124, 364	31, 360	87, 844	4, 985	154, 166	25, 800	106, 810	21, 368	63, 596	15, 028	44, 408	4, 078	81, 669	11, 816	54, 981	14, 783
35 to 44 years	103, 153	14, 789	80, 031	8, 165	118, 578	9, 738	78, 103	30, 560	54, 637	7, 000	42, 181	5, 398	63, 259	4, 615	40, 833	17, 746
45 to 54 years	71, 999	6, 855	55, 687	9, 336	73, 645	4, 488	39, 289	29, 752	41, 715	3, 560	32, 157	5, 959	41, 332	2, 110	22, 238	16, 933
55 to 64 years	31, 245	2, 266	22, 745	6, 173	31, 147	1, 648	11, 580	17, 851	19, 121	1, 239	13, 995	3, 865	18, 557	803	6, 942	10, 782
65 and over	17, 180	985	10, 002	6, 136	22, 442	1, 074	3, 859	17, 415	11, 251	611	6, 427	4, 187	14, 060	522	2, 572	10, 925
Rural-farm	**549, 725**	**203, 342**	**315, 447**	**30, 483**	**552, 623**	**166, 909**	**319, 580**	**65, 658**	**446, 642**	**135, 274**	**279, 636**	**31, 356**	**451, 523**	**104, 374**	**281, 096**	**65, 707**
15 to 19 years	135, 547	130, 927	4, 370	147	130, 274	109, 288	19, 895	1, 040	91, 584	87, 071	4, 188	245	90, 769	68, 372	20, 707	1, 641
20 to 24 years	80, 640	45, 290	34, 015	1, 197	86, 100	34, 738	47, 890	3, 378	64, 602	29, 205	33, 328	1, 957	72, 221	20, 630	46, 570	4, 954
25 to 34 years	84, 017	15, 517	65, 559	2, 880	103, 454	13, 778	82, 193	7, 403	79, 463	11, 205	63, 962	4, 248	92, 591	9, 031	74, 194	9, 312
35 to 44 years	78, 789	5, 580	69, 059	4, 123	96, 330	4, 577	80, 175	11, 499	64, 333	3, 617	56, 250	4, 435	80, 127	3, 178	65, 440	11, 456
45 to 54 years	80, 742	3, 201	71, 031	6, 478	73, 636	2, 325	57, 156	14, 094	72, 070	2, 210	63, 136	6, 695	62, 081	1, 679	47, 078	13, 286
55 to 64 years	54, 048	1, 663	45, 803	6, 554	35, 021	1, 109	22, 557	11, 316	45, 228	1, 137	38, 159	5, 905	30, 253	773	19, 207	10, 247
65 and over	35, 568	1, 081	25, 372	9, 079	27, 433	1, 005	9, 528	16, 839	29, 107	753	20, 476	7, 848	23, 235	628	7, 799	14, 757
Rural-nonfarm	**337, 430**	**115, 674**	**194, 538**	**25, 277**	**330, 632**	**78, 551**	**191, 458**	**60, 055**	**147, 353**	**46, 120**	**85, 608**	**13, 976**	**145, 685**	**29, 486**	**84, 286**	**31, 399**
15 to 19 years	52, 605	50, 304	2, 143	66	57, 678	43, 383	13, 521	731	19, 707	18, 686	879	60	22, 139	15, 391	6, 146	591
20 to 24 years	54, 819	29, 708	23, 836	840	56, 918	17, 633	36, 281	2, 908	23, 876	12, 451	10, 416	735	25, 079	6, 751	16, 119	2, 169
25 to 34 years	78, 176	19, 417	54, 902	3, 177	76, 283	9, 578	58, 554	8, 021	35, 827	8, 505	24, 747	2, 132	35, 208	4, 087	25, 978	5, 061
35 to 44 years	61, 795	8, 489	48, 365	4, 628	59, 410	3, 872	43, 530	11, 920	26, 227	3, 446	19, 878	2, 619	26, 091	1, 642	18, 442	5, 969
45 to 54 years	46, 996	4, 550	36, 543	5, 740	41, 565	2, 177	25, 804	13, 519	21, 353	1, 711	16, 479	2, 979	18, 287	824	11, 106	6, 321
55 to 64 years	24, 820	1, 914	18, 119	4, 698	20, 306	989	9, 208	10, 061	11, 196	778	8, 122	2, 231	9, 478	422	4, 255	4, 757
65 and over	17, 681	1, 162	10, 361	6, 085	18, 038	829	4, 380	12, 771	8, 692	496	4, 950	3, 190	9, 005	338	2, 160	6, 476

AREA AND AGE	MALES 15 YEARS OLD AND OVER				FEMALES 15 YEARS OLD AND OVER				MALES 15 YEARS OLD AND OVER				FEMALES 15 YEARS OLD AND OVER			
	Total	Single	Married	Widowed or divorced	Total	Single	Married	Widowed or divorced	Total	Single	Married	Widowed or divorced	Total	Single	Married	Widowed or divorced
	WEST SOUTH CENTRAL								MOUNTAIN							
Urban	**256, 705**	**72, 903**	**157, 753**	**25, 616**	**302, 206**	**61, 587**	**166, 305**	**73,871**	**8, 603**	**2, 684**	**4, 904**	**993**	**8, 303**	**1, 262**	**4, 929**	**2, 101**
15 to 19 years	29, 760	28, 464	1, 177	94	39, 870	30, 043	8, 641	1, 176	632	599	28	1	693	543	143	7
20 to 24 years	35, 607	18, 794	15, 416	1, 344	49, 815	14, 917	29, 412	5, 442	794	547	228	19	890	281	527	81
25 to 34 years	69, 438	14, 730	49, 592	5, 048	86, 378	10, 466	59, 577	16, 249	1, 901	649	1, 109	139	2, 071	226	1, 512	331
35 to 44 years	57, 537	6, 441	44, 843	6, 187	63, 035	3, 785	41, 199	17, 971	2, 164	450	1, 476	233	2, 069	112	1, 457	497
45 to 54 years	38, 774	2, 918	30, 003	5, 801	36, 083	1, 430	19, 481	15, 101	1, 742	266	1, 208	264	1, 477	63	902	511
55 to 64 years	16, 012	992	11, 463	3, 522	15, 304	526	5, 795	8, 942	875	111	587	175	652	19	294	339
65 and over	9, 066	461	5, 003	3, 578	11, 204	320	1, 987	8, 854	472	56	257	159	429	13	89	327
Rural-farm	**371, 880**	**111, 571**	**231, 224**	**28, 821**	**355, 762**	**77, 293**	**230, 859**	**47, 418**	**921**	**314**	**507**	**96**	**668**	**117**	**485**	**66**
15 to 19 years	70, 464	67, 472	2, 761	182	71, 400	52, 956	17, 000	1, 425	132	130	2		91	74	16	1
20 to 24 years	55, 817	27, 208	26, 730	1, 811	58, 422	15, 107	39, 320	3, 966	84	47	33	4	74	27	45	2
25 to 34 years	71, 725	10, 296	57, 037	4, 356	77, 263	5, 899	64, 385	6, 940	136	47	85	3	166	8	147	11
35 to 44 years	60, 664	3, 383	52, 455	4, 798	64, 451	1, 760	54, 258	8, 404	184	35	135	13	164	5	144	15
45 to 54 years	58, 291	1, 855	50, 010	6, 397	46, 226	860	35, 905	9, 431	221	31	156	33	110	2	99	9
55 to 64 years	33, 961	802	27, 932	5, 205	22, 369	373	14, 480	7, 503	96	12	65	19	40	1	25	14
65 and over	20, 742	503	14, 176	6, 045	15, 462	303	5, 428	9, 706	67	12	30	24	22		8	14
Rural-nonfarm	**124, 120**	**37, 317**	**73, 800**	**12, 762**	**122, 185**	**22, 445**	**72, 335**	**27, 127**	**3, 693**	**1, 833**	**1, 507**	**343**	**1, 777**	**274**	**1, 226**	**275**
15 to 19 years	15, 670	14, 969	645	50	18, 181	12, 779	4, 885	511	301	291	9		206	146	58	2
20 to 24 years	18, 800	10, 119	8, 057	599	19, 807	4, 903	12, 933	1, 952	531	458	66	5	194	46	135	13
25 to 34 years	30, 198	6, 951	21, 063	2, 137	30, 128	2, 879	22, 617	4, 575	915	513	356	46	475	36	385	53
35 to 44 years	24, 552	3, 002	18, 876	2, 629	23, 513	1, 002	17, 074	5, 372	970	370	514	83	453	23	371	59
45 to 54 years	18, 840	1, 422	14, 628	2, 744	15, 466	494	9, 456	5, 451	566	117	367	81	273	11	201	61
55 to 64 years	9, 224	531	6, 645	2, 017	7, 913	200	3, 592	4, 092	252	52	138	62	97	4	51	41
65 and over	6, 632	279	3, 781	2, 558	7, 028	166	1, 728	5, 114	151	31	54	65	71	7	19	45

AREA AND AGE	MALES 15 YEARS OLD AND OVER				FEMALES 15 YEARS OLD AND OVER			
	Total	Single	Married	Widowed or divorced	Total	Single	Married	Widowed or divorced
	PACIFIC							
Urban	**30, 603**	**9, 377**	**17, 872**	**3, 145**	**32, 286**	**5, 653**	**18, 499**	**8, 063**
15 to 19 years	2, 413	2, 357	47		2, 812	2, 345	434	29
20 to 24 years	2, 840	1, 930	830	65	3, 620	1, 325	1, 996	294
25 to 34 years	7, 404	2, 220	4, 660	500	8, 408	1, 049	5, 993	1, 353
35 to 44 years	7, 980	1, 526	5, 586	841	8, 052	508	5, 510	2, 021
45 to 54 years	5, 861	850	4, 195	804	5, 361	257	3, 139	1, 961
55 to 64 years	2, 582	334	1, 732	508	2, 387	99	1, 057	1, 229
65 and over	1, 327	127	784	415	1, 560	56	346	1, 154
Rural-farm	**1, 449**	**528**	**780**	**139**	**1, 020**	**192**	**726**	**101**
15 to 19 years	179	174	5		159	128	29	2
20 to 24 years	143	106	35	2	137	36	95	6
25 to 34 years	260	77	163	19	220	15	196	9
35 to 44 years	294	65	206	23	226	7	202	17
	PACIFIC—Continued							
Rural-farm—Continued								
45 to 54 years	294	49	213	31	161	4	135	22
55 to 64 years	182	40	106	36	72	1	50	21
65 and over	97	17	52	28	43	1	18	24
Rural-nonfarm	**3, 900**	**1, 477**	**1, 956**	**447**	**2, 506**	**395**	**1, 623**	**474**
15 to 19 years	288	286	2		258	193	61	4
20 to 24 years	354	241	104	8	237	64	158	13
25 to 34 years	923	381	486	51	646	60	509	76
35 to 44 years	991	261	619	109	641	42	484	114
45 to 54 years	723	165	448	105	394	23	271	100
55 to 64 years	346	81	188	75	182	7	96	79
65 and over	262	59	106	97	137	5	44	88

TABLE 15.—PERCENT MARRIED IN THE URBAN, RURAL-FARM, AND RURAL-NONFARM NEGRO POPULATION 15 YEARS OLD AND OVER, BY SEX, AND 5-YEAR AGE PERIODS, BY GEOGRAPHIC DIVISIONS: 1930

[Percent not shown where base is less than 100]

AREA AND AGE	NEW ENGLAND		MIDDLE ATLANTIC		EAST NORTH CENTRAL		WEST NORTH CENTRAL		SOUTH ATLANTIC		EAST SOUTH CENTRAL		WEST SOUTH CENTRAL		MOUNTAIN		PACIFIC	
	Male	Female	Male	Female	Male	Female	Male	Female	Male	Female	Male	Female	Male	Female	Male	Female	Male	Female
Urban	**57.5**	**56.4**	**60.2**	**59.7**	**61.1**	**63.8**	**59.6**	**58.6**	**60.0**	**53.0**	**60.5**	**52.9**	**61.5**	**55.0**	**57.0**	**59.4**	**58.4**	**57.3**
15 to 19 years	1.3	12.4	2.5	17.7	3.2	23.9	3.5	20.3	3.6	18.0	4.1	20.8	4.0	21.7	4.4	20.6	1.9	15.4
20 to 24 years	29.2	51.0	36.3	58.8	38.7	66.2	37.3	57.7	41.9	55.1	42.8	56.0	43.3	59.0	28.7	59.2	29.2	55.1
25 to 34 years	61.3	72.5	66.1	73.0	67.4	77.0	65.3	71.7	70.6	69.3	69.8	67.3	71.4	69.0	58.3	73.0	62.9	71.3
35 to 44 years	72.4	72.1	74.3	70.6	74.1	73.3	72.5	71.0	77.6	65.9	77.2	64.5	77.9	65.4	68.2	70.4	70.0	68.4
45 to 54 years	73.9	62.3	75.2	58.3	74.2	62.2	72.5	61.5	77.3	53.3	77.1	53.8	77.4	54.0	69.3	61.1	71.6	58.6
55 to 64 years	72.1	46.2	71.2	40.8	70.4	44.0	69.0	44.8	72.8	37.2	73.2	37.4	71.6	37.9	67.1	45.1	67.1	44.3
65 and over	54.9	22.4	56.7	20.2	56.3	21.4	54.0	23.0	58.2	17.2	57.1	18.3	55.2	17.7	54.4	20.7	59.1	22.2
Rural-farm	**42.2**	**59.1**	**46.6**	**65.2**	**52.8**	**66.1**	**58.0**	**70.4**	**57.4**	**57.8**	**62.6**	**62.3**	**62.2**	**64.9**	**55.0**	**72.6**	**53.8**	**71.2**
15 to 19 years	...	...	.8	12.8	1.3	12.8	2.9	25.6	3.2	15.3	4.6	22.8	3.9	23.8	1.5	...	2.8	18.2
20 to 24 years	...	...	21.3	56.4	20.2	53.9	41.0	71.6	42.2	55.6	51.6	64.5	47.9	67.3	...	...	24.5	69.3
25 to 34 years	...	...	56.7	83.0	55.9	81.5	72.7	87.9	78.0	79.4	80.5	80.1	79.5	83.3	62.5	88.6	62.7	89.1
35 to 44 years	57.8	...	67.8	86.5	72.6	87.8	78.4	87.1	87.7	83.2	87.4	81.7	86.5	84.2	73.4	87.8	70.1	89.4
45 to 54 years	...	...	67.3	80.5	73.1	83.2	76.0	84.4	88.0	77.6	87.6	75.8	85.8	77.7	70.6	90.0	72.4	83.9
55 to 64 years	...	...	65.2	69.1	72.9	78.9	70.4	75.5	84.7	64.4	84.4	63.5	82.2	64.7	...	...	58.2	...
65 and over	...	...	47.4	32.5	57.8	45.4	58.0	44.9	71.3	34.7	70.3	33.6	68.3	35.1	...	...	...	...
Rural-nonfarm	**52.5**	**56.1**	**56.9**	**64.2**	**50.1**	**63.7**	**50.2**	**59.1**	**57.7**	**57.9**	**58.1**	**57.9**	**59.5**	**59.2**	**40.8**	**69.0**	**50.2**	**64.8**
15 to 19 years	.6	11.2	1.6	19.1	2.0	17.3	2.8	17.3	4.1	23.4	4.5	27.8	4.1	26.9	3.0	28.2	.7	23.6
20 to 24 years	20.3	50.1	32.4	61.7	28.2	63.1	25.7	56.8	43.5	63.7	43.6	64.3	42.9	65.3	12.4	69.6	29.4	66.7
25 to 34 years	60.9	74.3	65.3	80.9	54.2	81.7	52.5	76.1	70.2	76.8	69.1	73.8	69.7	75.1	38.9	81.1	52.7	78.8
35 to 44 years	70.7	72.6	73.6	79.6	66.7	80.9	63.9	79.4	78.3	73.3	75.8	70.7	76.9	72.6	53.0	81.9	62.5	75.5
45 to 54 years	69.0	68.9	74.0	71.0	67.5	73.3	66.8	70.1	77.8	62.1	77.2	60.7	77.6	61.1	64.8	73.6	62.0	68.8
55 to 64 years	66.4	57.0	68.0	56.2	62.8	59.6	65.7	55.8	73.0	45.3	72.5	44.9	72.0	45.4	54.8	...	54.3	52.7
65 and over	50.2	26.9	52.5	31.0	46.8	30.3	49.4	31.5	58.6	24.3	56.9	24.0	57.0	24.6	35.8	...	40.5	32.1

TABLE 16.—MARITAL CONDITION OF THE NEGRO POPULATION 15 YEARS OLD AND OVER, BY SEX, AND 5-YEAR AGE PERIODS, FOR CITIES HAVING 10,000 OR MORE NEGRO INHABITANTS: 1930

CITY AND AGE	MALES 15 YEARS OLD AND OVER									FEMALES 15 YEARS OLD AND OVER								
	Total	Single		Married		Widowed		Divorced	Unknown	Total	Single		Married		Widowed		Divorced	Unknown
		Number	Percent	Number	Percent	Number	Percent				Number	Percent	Number	Percent	Number	Percent		
AKRON, OHIO																		
Total	**4,263**	**1,352**	**31.7**	**2,597**	**60.9**	**214**	**5.0**	**86**	**14**	**3,711**	**635**	**17.1**	**2,557**	**68.9**	**425**	**11.5**	**89**	**5**
15 to 19 years	386	376	97.4	9	2.3	...	...	...	1	479	354	73.9	118	24.6	4	.8	2	1
20 to 24 years	565	340	60.2	217	38.4	3	.5	5	...	583	149	25.6	399	68.4	16	2.7	17	2
25 to 34 years	1,421	348	24.5	1,005	70.7	33	2.3	30	5	1,317	84	6.4	1,107	84.1	89	6.8	35	2
35 to 44 years	1,133	179	15.8	850	75.0	67	5.9	35	2	780	36	4.6	613	78.6	112	14.4	19	...
45 to 54 years	525	80	15.2	363	69.1	67	12.8	13	2	350	5	1.4	246	70.3	88	25.1	11	...
55 to 64 years	167	23	13.8	113	67.7	27	16.2	3	1	122	6	4.9	57	46.7	56	45.9	3	...
65 years and over	56	5	...	34	...	17	...	...	...	75	1	...	14	...	58	...	2	...
ASHEVILLE, N. C.																		
Total	**4,461**	**1,371**	**30.7**	**2,807**	**62.9**	**247**	**5.5**	**32**	**4**	**5,845**	**1,545**	**26.4**	**3,194**	**54.6**	**1,033**	**17.7**	**70**	**3**
15 to 19 years	608	591	97.2	15	2.5	2	.3	...	...	799	679	85.0	119	14.9	1	.1	...	...
20 to 24 years	687	378	55.0	302	44.0	3	.4	3	1	1,161	463	39.9	660	56.8	32	2.8	6	...
25 to 34 years	1,311	252	19.2	1,007	76.8	38	2.9	14	...	1,766	271	15.3	1,279	72.4	187	10.6	28	1
35 to 44 years	971	97	10.0	801	82.5	63	6.5	9	1	1,163	84	7.2	746	64.1	307	26.4	26	...
45 to 54 years	538	37	6.9	436	81.0	61	11.3	4	...	581	29	5.0	284	48.9	260	44.8	7	1
55 to 64 years	228	11	4.8	173	75.9	42	18.4	1	1	216	10	4.6	81	37.5	123	56.9	1	1
65 years and over	112	3	2.7	69	61.6	38	33.9	1	1	150	6	4.0	23	15.3	119	79.3	2	...
ATLANTA, GA.																		
Total	**28,285**	**8,598**	**30.4**	**17,377**	**61.4**	**1,955**	**6.9**	**334**	**21**	**37,887**	**9,275**	**24.5**	**18,654**	**49.2**	**8,769**	**23.1**	**1,169**	**20**
15 to 19 years	3,993	3,783	94.7	188	4.7	7	.2	11	4	5,585	4,410	79.0	1,053	18.9	61	1.1	61	...
20 to 24 years	4,280	2,233	52.2	1,946	45.5	66	1.5	34	1	6,577	2,485	37.8	3,405	51.8	431	6.6	253	3
25 to 34 years	7,565	1,591	21.0	5,604	74.1	242	3.2	122	6	10,614	1,617	15.2	6,862	64.7	1,661	15.6	470	4
35 to 44 years	6,056	663	10.9	4,838	79.9	459	7.6	93	3	7,667	503	6.6	4,560	59.5	2,318	30.2	280	6
45 to 54 years	3,938	235	6.0	3,095	78.6	553	14.0	54	1	4,451	165	3.7	2,053	46.1	2,148	48.3	83	2
55 to 64 years	1,580	65	4.1	1,188	75.2	313	19.8	14	...	1,692	49	2.9	535	31.6	1,093	64.6	15	...
65 years and over	846	22	2.6	502	59.3	313	37.0	6	3	1,254	32	2.6	173	13.8	1,040	82.9	5	4
ATLANTIC CITY, N. J.																		
Total	**6,131**	**2,142**	**34.9**	**3,510**	**57.3**	**425**	**6.9**	**44**	**10**	**6,671**	**1,589**	**23.8**	**3,670**	**55.0**	**1,345**	**20.2**	**55**	**12**
15 to 19 years	423	412	97.4	11	2.6	...	...	...	...	530	438	82.6	89	16.8	3	.6	...	...
20 to 24 years	660	430	65.2	226	34.2	2	.3	2	...	829	350	42.2	462	55.7	13	1.6	4	...
25 to 34 years	1,692	616	36.4	1,039	61.4	27	1.6	8	2	1,896	418	22.0	1,295	68.3	155	8.2	23	5
35 to 44 years	1,563	386	24.7	1,070	68.5	87	5.6	19	1	1,741	235	13.5	1,114	64.0	370	21.3	22	...
45 to 54 years	1,156	208	18.0	796	68.9	142	12.3	9	1	1,068	103	9.6	521	48.8	437	40.9	6	1
55 to 64 years	432	71	16.4	266	61.6	89	20.6	6	...	365	29	7.9	132	36.2	204	55.9	...	...
65 years and over	180	13	7.2	90	50.0	76	42.2	...	1	219	11	5.0	48	21.9	160	73.1	...	...

TABLE 16.—MARITAL CONDITION OF THE NEGRO POPULATION 15 YEARS OLD AND OVER, BY SEX, AND 5-YEAR AGE PERIODS, FOR CITIES HAVING 10,000 OR MORE NEGRO INHABITANTS: 1930—Continued

CITY AND AGE	MALES 15 YEARS OLD AND OVER									FEMALES 15 YEARS OLD AND OVER								
	Total	Single		Married		Widowed		Divorced	Unknown	Total	Single		Married		Widowed		Divorced	Unknown
		Number	Per cent	Number	Per cent	Number	Per cent				Number	Per cent	Number	Per cent	Number	Per cent		
AUGUSTA, GA.																		
Total	7,727	2,151	27.8	4,788	62.0	693	9.0	91	4	10,254	2,356	23.0	5,024	49.0	2,657	25.9	207	10
15 to 19 years	1,013	971	95.9	38	3.8	2	.2	1	1	1,445	1,119	77.4	296	20.5	21	1.5	8	1
20 to 24 years	1,201	583	48.5	572	47.6	29	2.4	15	2	1,771	626	35.3	963	54.4	144	8.1	37	1
25 to 34 years	1,923	339	17.6	1,449	75.4	114	5.9	21	----	2,683	389	14.5	1,726	64.3	487	18.2	80	1
35 to 44 years	1,658	149	9.0	1,339	80.8	147	8.9	23	----	2,079	122	5.9	1,228	59.1	661	31.8	65	3
45 to 54 years	1,207	70	5.8	946	78.4	170	14.1	21	----	1,289	62	4.8	599	46.5	613	47.6	13	2
55 to 64 years	454	33	7.3	300	66.1	113	24.9	8	----	587	28	4.8	145	24.7	411	70.0	3	----
65 years and over	257	5	1.9	134	52.1	115	44.7	2	1	379	8	2.1	58	15.3	312	82.3	1	----
BALTIMORE, MD.																		
Total	52,870	18,440	34.9	30,327	57.4	3,291	6.2	502	310	53,486	13,295	24.9	30,657	57.3	8,447	15.8	710	377
15 to 19 years	4,893	4,719	96.4	160	3.3	3	.1	4	7	6,183	5,000	80.9	1,138	18.4	17	.3	9	19
20 to 24 years	6,967	4,272	61.3	2,609	37.4	39	.6	20	27	8,009	3,176	39.7	4,588	57.3	146	1.8	81	18
25 to 34 years	14,828	4,799	32.4	9,557	64.5	298	2.0	138	36	14,845	2,688	18.1	10,905	73.5	975	6.6	250	27
35 to 44 years	12,706	2,732	21.5	9,077	71.4	692	5.4	182	23	11,714	1,338	11.4	8,167	69.7	1,946	16.6	230	33
45 to 54 years	8,073	1,272	15.8	5,662	70.1	1,003	12.4	118	18	7,071	603	8.5	4,011	56.7	2,318	32.8	111	28
55 to 64 years	3,160	364	11.5	2,126	67.3	634	20.1	26	10	3,016	241	8.0	1,213	40.2	1,521	50.4	22	19
65 years and over	1,655	158	9.5	877	53.0	598	36.1	12	10	2,048	145	7.1	393	19.2	1,456	71.1	4	50
BATON ROUGE, LA.																		
Total	3,459	1,102	31.9	2,102	60.8	177	5.1	74	4	4,686	1,265	27.0	2,234	47.7	935	20.0	251	1
15 to 19 years	424	410	96.7	11	2.6	----	----	1	2	640	526	82.2	104	16.3	4	.6	6	----
20 to 24 years	501	275	54.9	209	41.7	3	.6	14	----	820	315	38.4	408	49.8	41	5.0	56	----
25 to 34 years	892	245	27.5	598	67.0	27	3.0	22	----	1,298	255	19.6	789	60.8	151	11.6	103	----
35 to 44 years	769	94	12.2	619	80.5	31	4.0	24	1	925	116	12.5	546	59.0	196	21.2	66	1
45 to 54 years	514	45	8.8	423	82.3	37	7.2	9	----	570	32	5.6	281	49.3	243	42.6	14	----
55 to 64 years	232	21	9.1	174	75.0	34	14.7	2	1	245	15	6.1	79	32.2	147	60.0	4	----
65 years and over	127	12	9.4	68	53.5	45	35.4	2	----	187	6	3.2	27	14.4	152	81.3	2	----
BEAUMONT, TEX.																		
Total	6,429	1,762	27.4	3,922	61.0	463	7.2	275	7	6,942	1,244	17.9	4,064	58.5	1,146	16.5	487	1
15 to 19 years	808	779	96.4	22	2.7	4	.5	1	2	1,038	774	74.6	229	22.1	15	1.4	20	----
20 to 24 years	957	467	48.8	429	44.8	30	3.1	28	3	1,341	284	21.2	853	63.6	95	7.1	109	----
25 to 34 years	1,902	331	17.4	1,375	72.3	114	6.0	82	----	2,068	125	6.0	1,524	73.7	235	11.4	184	----
35 to 44 years	1,505	116	7.7	1,173	77.9	119	7.9	96	1	1,437	43	3.0	969	67.4	311	21.6	114	----
45 to 54 years	845	45	5.3	665	78.7	85	10.1	49	1	695	13	1.9	372	53.5	264	38.0	46	----
55 to 64 years	245	11	4.5	178	72.7	42	17.1	14	----	220	4	1.8	80	36.4	126	57.3	9	1
65 years and over	155	9	5.8	74	47.7	68	43.9	4	----	134	----	----	30	22.4	100	74.6	4	----
BESSEMER,[1] ALA.																		
Total	4,060	1,255	30.9	2,379	58.6	380	9.4	44	3	4,461	926	20.8	2,403	53.9	1,066	23.9	65	1
BIRMINGHAM, ALA.																		
Total	33,651	9,834	29.2	20,633	61.3	2,520	7.5	609	55	39,070	8,014	20.5	21,522	55.2	8,205	21.0	1,245	54
15 to 19 years	3,990	3,839	96.2	114	2.9	11	.3	7	19	5,456	4,109	75.3	1,130	20.7	124	2.3	84	9
20 to 24 years	4,875	2,598	53.3	2,068	42.4	124	2.5	73	12	6,898	1,984	28.8	4,128	59.8	514	7.5	255	17
25 to 34 years	9,737	2,037	20.9	7,071	72.6	433	4.4	186	10	11,965	1,319	11.0	8,393	70.1	1,716	14.3	525	12
35 to 44 years	7,706	871	11.3	6,028	78.2	611	7.9	191	5	7,964	396	5.0	5,143	64.6	2,152	27.0	269	4
45 to 54 years	4,820	320	6.6	3,741	77.6	651	13.5	105	3	4,282	157	3.7	2,146	50.1	1,889	44.1	84	6
55 to 64 years	1,686	121	7.2	1,174	69.6	353	20.9	36	2	1,465	35	2.4	468	31.9	940	64.2	19	3
65 years and over	804	42	5.2	417	51.9	332	41.3	10	3	996	10	1.0	133	13.4	843	84.6	7	3
BOSTON, MASS.																		
Total	7,914	3,021	38.2	4,246	53.7	477	6.0	131	39	7,969	2,049	25.7	4,306	54.0	1,417	17.8	175	22
15 to 19 years	603	593	98.3	9	1.5	----	----	----	1	677	603	89.1	73	10.8	----	----	1	----
20 to 24 years	738	544	73.7	189	25.6	3	.4	1	1	816	418	51.2	379	46.4	9	1.1	5	5
25 to 34 years	1,982	842	42.5	1,061	53.5	47	2.4	25	7	2,025	476	23.5	1,387	68.5	117	5.8	42	3
35 to 44 years	2,030	567	27.9	1,319	65.0	83	4.1	52	9	2,007	276	13.8	1,356	67.6	296	14.7	76	3
45 to 54 years	1,506	303	20.1	1,034	68.7	130	8.6	39	----	1,386	170	12.3	775	55.9	408	29.4	31	2
55 to 64 years	702	116	16.5	458	65.2	117	16.7	10	1	619	58	9.4	250	40.4	295	47.7	16	----
65 years and over	323	51	15.8	172	53.3	97	30.0	3	----	414	40	9.7	79	19.1	291	70.3	4	----
BUFFALO, N. Y.																		
Total	5,468	2,000	36.6	3,222	58.9	202	3.7	43	1	4,812	852	17.7	3,268	67.9	612	12.7	76	4
15 to 19 years	364	354	97.3	10	2.7	----	----	----	----	470	368	78.3	95	20.2	3	.6	4	----
20 to 24 years	652	420	64.4	223	34.2	5	.8	3	1	763	199	26.1	540	70.8	14	1.8	10	----
25 to 34 years	2,119	727	34.3	1,343	63.4	30	1.4	19	----	1,811	170	9.4	1,463	80.8	138	7.6	39	1
35 to 44 years	1,485	343	23.1	1,071	72.1	61	4.1	10	----	1,070	71	6.6	822	76.8	163	15.2	14	----
45 to 54 years	585	115	19.7	413	70.6	49	8.4	8	----	417	21	5.0	254	60.9	136	32.6	6	----
55 to 64 years	178	32	18.0	117	65.7	27	15.2	2	----	183	15	8.2	67	36.6	98	53.6	3	----
65 years and over	81	8	----	42	----	30	----	1	----	89	6	----	23	----	60	----	----	----
CAMDEN, N. J.																		
Total	4,056	1,333	32.9	2,431	59.9	270	6.7	15	7	3,992	922	23.1	2,478	62.1	563	14.1	24	5
15 to 19 years	462	461	99.8	1	.2	----	----	----	----	477	386	80.9	90	18.9	----	----	1	----
20 to 24 years	452	260	57.5	187	41.1	1	.2	1	3	564	205	36.3	345	61.2	10	1.8	4	----
25 to 34 years	1,060	309	29.2	726	68.5	21	2.0	3	1	1,109	208	18.8	840	75.7	55	5.0	6	----
35 to 44 years	1,040	192	18.5	769	73.9	72	6.9	6	1	929	66	7.1	726	78.1	125	13.5	11	1
45 to 54 years	614	75	12.2	466	75.9	71	11.6	2	----	518	38	7.3	314	60.6	163	31.5	2	1
55 to 64 years	289	22	7.6	206	71.3	58	20.1	3	----	252	10	4.0	126	50.0	116	46.0	----	----
65 years and over	134	12	9.0	75	56.0	47	35.1	----	----	136	6	4.4	37	27.2	93	68.4	----	----

[1] Not shown by age group for cities less than 25,000 in population.

TABLE 16.—MARITAL CONDITION OF THE NEGRO POPULATION 15 YEARS OLD AND OVER, BY SEX, AND 5-YEAR AGE PERIODS, FOR CITIES HAVING 10,000 OR MORE NEGRO INHABITANTS: 1930—Continued

CITY AND AGE	MALES 15 YEARS OLD AND OVER: Total	Single: Number	Single: Per cent	Married: Number	Married: Per cent	Widowed: Number	Widowed: Per cent	Divorced	Unknown	FEMALES 15 YEARS OLD AND OVER: Total	Single: Number	Single: Per cent	Married: Number	Married: Per cent	Widowed: Number	Widowed: Per cent	Divorced	Unknown
CHARLESTON, S. C.																		
Total	7,875	2,252	28.6	5,069	64.4	474	6.0	74	6	11,684	3,103	26.6	5,593	47.9	2,735	23.4	247	6
15 to 19 years	1,144	1,105	96.6	38	3.3	----	----	----	1	1,758	1,378	78.4	364	20.7	6	.3	10	----
20 to 24 years	1,196	486	40.6	695	58.1	5	.4	8	2	2,156	760	35.3	1,230	57.1	126	5.8	37	3
25 to 34 years	1,983	310	15.6	1,602	80.8	41	2.1	29	1	3,111	554	17.8	1,988	63.9	473	15.2	95	1
35 to 44 years	1,810	203	11.2	1,468	81.1	120	6.6	19	----	2,421	221	9.1	1,289	53.2	837	34.6	73	1
45 to 54 years	1,038	92	8.9	810	78.0	122	11.8	14	----	1,295	103	8.0	515	39.8	652	50.3	24	1
55 to 64 years	446	36	8.1	308	69.1	98	22.0	4	----	555	50	9.0	148	26.7	353	63.6	4	
65 years and over	256	20	7.8	146	57.0	88	34.4	----	2	377	30	8.0	57	15.1	286	75.9	4	----
CHARLOTTE, N. C.																		
Total	8,111	2,446	30.2	5,005	61.7	544	6.7	45	71	10,142	2,683	26.5	5,407	53.3	1,913	18.9	106	33
15 to 19 years	1,059	1,020	96.3	37	3.5	----	----	----	2	1,492	1,183	79.3	294	19.7	9	.6	3	3
20 to 24 years	1,442	689	47.8	712	49.4	17	1.2	5	19	2,069	747	36.1	1,212	58.6	83	4.0	16	11
25 to 34 years	2,367	486	20.5	1,764	74.5	84	3.5	15	18	2,953	527	17.8	1,961	66.4	409	13.9	44	12
35 to 44 years	1,570	168	10.7	1,238	78.9	138	8.8	15	11	1,769	132	7.5	1,152	65.1	456	25.8	29	----
45 to 54 years	956	49	5.1	761	79.6	135	14.1	6	5	1,031	43	4.2	516	50.0	461	44.7	10	1
55 to 64 years	375	13	3.5	273	72.8	82	21.9	4	3	395	9	2.3	134	33.9	251	63.5	1	----
65 years and over	196	4	2.0	113	57.7	78	39.8	----	1	272	11	4.0	44	16.2	216	79.4	1	----
CHATTANOOGA, TENN.																		
Total	11,555	3,297	28.5	7,182	62.2	878	7.6	189	9	13,195	2,596	19.7	7,565	57.3	2,618	19.8	411	5
15 to 19 years	1,404	1,335	95.1	67	4.8	----	----	----	2	1,763	1,308	74.2	418	23.7	20	1.1	17	----
20 to 24 years	1,616	849	52.5	722	44.7	24	1.5	19	2	2,295	676	29.5	1,404	61.2	139	6.1	76	----
25 to 34 years	3,150	688	21.8	2,287	72.6	105	3.3	68	2	3,744	396	10.6	2,753	73.5	428	11.4	166	1
35 to 44 years	2,588	276	10.7	2,061	79.6	199	7.7	50	2	2,701	143	5.3	1,825	67.6	623	23.1	108	2
45 to 54 years	1,761	114	6.5	1,334	75.8	268	15.2	44	1	1,690	43	2.5	872	51.6	737	43.6	37	1
55 to 64 years	733	28	3.8	548	74.8	151	20.6	6	----	640	17	2.7	233	36.4	384	60.0	5	1
65 years and over	301	7	2.3	161	53.5	131	43.5	2	----	361	13	3.6	59	16.3	287	79.5	2	----
CHICAGO, ILL.																		
Total	91,747	27,750	30.2	55,674	60.7	6,317	6.9	1,884	122	93,384	15,687	16.8	57,076	61.1	17,732	19.0	2,794	95
15 to 19 years	6,880	6,618	96.2	252	3.7	6	.1	3	1	8,274	6,083	73.5	2,036	24.6	93	1.1	56	6
20 to 24 years	10,965	6,513	59.4	4,220	38.5	129	1.2	94	9	13,868	3,882	28.0	8,936	64.4	713	5.1	328	9
25 to 34 years	29,773	8,512	28.6	19,587	65.8	1,016	3.4	632	26	30,971	3,710	12.0	22,731	73.4	3,289	10.6	1,216	25
35 to 44 years	24,209	4,122	17.0	17,587	72.6	1,775	7.3	700	25	21,869	1,386	6.3	14,959	68.4	4,666	21.3	844	14
45 to 54 years	13,549	1,470	10.8	9,996	73.8	1,733	12.8	344	6	11,453	446	3.9	6,453	56.3	4,274	37.3	272	8
55 to 64 years	4,442	374	8.4	3,005	67.6	963	21.7	97	3	4,341	116	2.7	1,517	34.9	2,635	60.7	64	9
65 years and over	1,756	106	6.0	954	54.3	683	38.9	13	----	2,453	52	2.1	372	15.2	2,013	82.1	10	6
CINCINNATI, OHIO																		
Total	18,280	5,522	30.2	11,430	62.5	1,083	5.9	235	10	17,991	3,236	18.0	11,664	64.8	2,743	15.2	342	6
15 to 19 years	1,552	1,497	96.5	53	3.4	----	----	2	----	1,934	1,426	73.7	485	25.1	18	.9	5	----
20 to 24 years	2,347	1,326	56.5	985	42.0	22	.9	14	----	2,721	737	27.1	1,842	67.7	90	3.3	50	2
25 to 34 years	5,292	1,355	25.6	3,756	71.0	122	2.3	58	1	5,413	562	10.4	4,308	79.6	398	7.4	144	1
35 to 44 years	4,642	782	16.8	3,526	76.0	243	5.2	87	4	4,122	290	7.0	3,071	74.5	678	16.4	83	----
45 to 54 years	2,780	372	13.4	2,029	73.0	317	11.4	60	2	2,316	133	5.7	1,414	61.1	722	31.2	47	----
55 to 64 years	1,129	135	12.0	790	70.0	194	17.2	9	1	914	47	5.1	408	44.6	448	49.0	8	3
65 years and over	508	47	9.3	270	53.1	185	36.4	5	1	544	37	6.8	119	21.9	383	70.4	5	----
CLEVELAND, OHIO																		
Total	27,452	8,271	30.1	16,967	61.8	1,636	6.0	552	26	26,600	4,537	17.1	17,073	64.2	4,226	15.9	743	21
15 to 19 years	2,268	2,205	97.2	59	2.6	----	----	1	3	2,611	1,983	75.9	602	23.1	16	.6	8	2
20 to 24 years	3,214	1,911	59.5	1,251	38.9	27	.8	22	3	3,848	1,055	27.4	2,560	66.5	134	3.5	97	2
25 to 34 years	8,593	2,299	26.8	5,859	68.2	272	3.2	159	4	8,942	941	10.5	6,812	76.2	852	9.5	331	6
35 to 44 years	7,713	1,235	16.0	5,779	74.9	468	6.1	225	6	6,510	372	5.7	4,758	73.1	1,165	17.9	215	----
45 to 54 years	3,877	439	11.3	2,893	74.6	444	11.5	99	2	2,965	133	4.5	1,770	59.7	982	33.1	78	2
55 to 64 years	1,236	102	8.3	849	68.7	249	20.1	34	2	1,072	23	2.1	439	41.0	595	55.5	11	4
65 years and over	454	45	9.9	229	50.4	171	37.7	9	----	580	16	2.8	95	16.4	464	80.0	3	2
COLUMBIA, S. C.																		
Total	6,085	2,084	34.2	3,596	59.1	365	6.0	26	14	8,343	2,434	29.2	4,114	49.3	1,674	20.1	115	6
15 to 19 years	851	807	94.8	44	5.2	----	----	----	----	1,413	1,097	77.6	302	21.4	7	.5	6	1
20 to 24 years	976	501	51.3	470	48.2	2	.2	3	----	1,484	602	40.6	797	53.7	61	4.1	23	1
25 to 34 years	1,505	414	27.5	1,049	69.7	35	2.3	7	----	2,117	429	20.3	1,376	65.0	262	12.4	49	1
35 to 44 years	1,322	204	15.4	1,011	76.5	93	7.0	12	2	1,665	188	11.3	990	59.5	466	28.0	21	----
45 to 54 years	860	111	12.9	643	74.8	101	11.7	2	3	980	82	8.4	487	49.7	399	40.7	11	1
55 to 64 years	382	36	9.4	262	68.6	81	21.2	1	2	368	23	6.3	104	28.3	236	64.1	4	1
65 years and over	175	8	4.6	111	63.4	53	30.3	1	2	291	10	3.4	49	16.8	230	79.0	1	1
COLUMBUS, GA.																		
Total	4,146	1,188	28.7	2,614	63.0	332	8.0	12	----	6,011	1,429	23.8	2,900	48.2	1,643	27.3	35	4
15 to 19 years	646	602	93.2	43	6.7	1	.2	----	----	968	734	75.8	207	21.4	25	2.6	2	----
20 to 24 years	689	314	45.6	346	50.2	24	3.5	5	----	1,134	356	31.4	621	54.8	145	12.8	12	----
25 to 34 years	1,049	184	17.5	808	77.0	54	5.1	3	----	1,526	219	14.4	976	64.0	317	20.8	12	2
35 to 44 years	799	58	7.3	652	81.6	87	10.9	2	----	1,111	69	6.2	645	58.1	392	35.3	5	----
45 to 54 years	560	19	3.4	471	84.1	69	12.3	1	----	744	33	4.4	342	46.0	365	49.1	3	1
55 to 64 years	266	8	3.0	210	78.9	47	17.7	1	----	314	11	3.5	82	26.1	220	70.1	1	----
65 years and over	128	3	2.3	76	59.4	49	38.3	----	----	210	7	3.3	24	11.4	179	85.2	----	----

TABLE 16.—MARITAL CONDITION OF THE NEGRO POPULATION 15 YEARS OLD AND OVER, BY SEX, AND 5-YEAR AGE PERIODS, FOR CITIES HAVING 10,000 OR MORE NEGRO INHABITANST: 1930—Continued

CITY AND AGE	MALES 15 YEARS OLD AND OVER: Total	Single: Number	Single: Per cent	Married: Number	Married: Per cent	Widowed: Number	Widowed: Per cent	Divorced	Unknown	FEMALES 15 YEARS OLD AND OVER: Total	Single: Number	Single: Per cent	Married: Number	Married: Per cent	Widowed: Number	Widowed: Per cent	Divorced	Unknown
COLUMBUS, OHIO																		
Total	**13, 221**	**-3, 889**	**29. 4**	**8, 135**	**61. 5**	**821**	**6. 2**	**365**	**11**	**11, 661**	**2, 006**	**17. 2**	**7, 542**	**64. 7**	**1, 665**	**14. 3**	**443**	**5**
15 to 19 years	1, 114	1, 054	94. 6	56	5. 0	------	------	3	1	1, 294	1, 014	78. 4	268	20. 7	2	. 2	9	1
20 to 24 years	1, 417	845	59. 6	541	38. 2	12	. 8	15	4	1, 497	431	28. 8	986	65. 9	26	1. 7	53	1
25 to 34 years	3, 733	1, 034	27. 7	2, 518	67. 5	75	2. 0	105	1	3, 195	296	9. 3	2, 565	80. 3	169	5. 3	165	------
35 to 44 years	3, 343	572	17. 1	2, 471	73. 9	171	5. 1	129	------	2, 733	149	5. 5	2, 105	77. 0	343	12. 6	136	------
45 to 54 years	2, 270	262	11. 5	1, 669	73. 5	261	11. 5	77	1	1, 735	76	4. 4	1, 151	66. 3	442	25. 5	65	1
55 to 64 years	881	81	9. 2	628	71. 3	146	16. 6	26	------	725	21	2. 9	366	50. 5	323	44. 6	15	------
65 years and over	441	33	7. 5	247	56. 0	152	34. 5	8	1	468	17	3. 6	94	20. 1	357	76. 3	------	------
DALLAS, TEX.																		
Total	**13, 887**	**3, 431**	**24. 7**	**8, 774**	**63. 2**	**1, 196**	**8. 6**	**473**	**13**	**16, 308**	**2, 701**	**16. 6**	**9, 263**	**56. 8**	**3, 236**	**19. 8**	**1, 092**	**16**
15 to 19 years	1, 326	1, 244	93. 8	77	5. 8	4	. 3	1	------	1, 937	1, 340	69. 2	513	26. 5	41	2. 1	42	1
20 to 24 years	1, 756	809	46. 1	866	49. 3	44	2. 5	35	2	2, 754	676	24. 5	1, 689	61. 3	198	7. 2	189	2
25 to 34 years	4, 300	839	19. 5	3, 077	71. 6	213	5. 0	170	1	5, 197	467	9. 0	3, 581	68. 9	704	13. 5	445	------
35 to 44 years	3, 346	335	10. 0	2, 556	76. 4	299	8. 9	156	------	3, 524	139	3. 9	2, 245	63. 7	849	24. 1	287	4
45 to 54 years	2, 031	143	7. 0	1, 494	73. 6	318	15. 7	75	1	1, 780	49	2. 8	885	49. 7	748	42. 0	96	2
55 to 64 years	733	39	5. 3	476	64. 9	190	25. 9	27	1	637	15	2. 4	261	41. 0	340	53. 4	21	------
65 years and over	361	18	5. 0	211	58. 4	122	33. 8	9	1	451	11	2. 4	79	17. 5	349	77. 4	11	1
DAYTON, OHIO																		
Total	**6, 371**	**1, 873**	**29. 4**	**3, 910**	**61. 4**	**424**	**6. 7**	**155**	**9**	**6, 088**	**1, 088**	**17. 9**	**3, 912**	**64. 3**	**910**	**14. 9**	**171**	**7**
15 to 19 years	588	563	95. 7	25	4. 3	------	------	------	------	723	565	78. 1	151	20. 9	5	. 7	2	------
20 to 24 years	731	415	56. 8	305	41. 7	5	. 7	6	------	838	242	28. 9	542	64. 7	33	3. 9	21	------
25 to 34 years	1, 754	479	27. 3	1, 176	67. 0	54	3. 1	44	1	1, 732	159	9. 2	1, 365	78. 8	141	8. 1	65	2
35 to 44 years	1, 575	252	16. 0	1, 164	73. 9	95	6. 0	64	------	1, 408	81	5. 8	1, 058	75. 1	214	15. 2	54	1
45 to 54 years	1, 056	95	9. 0	801	75. 9	127	12. 0	31	2	813	24	3. 0	569	70. 0	197	24. 2	23	------
55 to 64 years	445	49	11. 0	314	70. 6	73	16. 4	9	------	342	12	3. 5	166	48. 5	160	46. 8	4	------
65 years and over	214	19	8. 9	122	57. 0	70	32. 7	1	2	222	2	. 9	59	26. 6	159	71. 6	1	1
DETROIT, MICH.																		
Total	**48, 060**	**14, 605**	**30. 4**	**30, 135**	**62. 7**	**2, 298**	**4. 8**	**957**	**65**	**43, 459**	**6, 688**	**15. 4**	**29, 878**	**68. 7**	**5, 760**	**13. 3**	**1, 096**	**37**
15 to 19 years	3, 409	3, 304	96. 9	100	2. 9	1	------	1	3	4, 045	2, 861	70. 7	1, 135	28. 1	19	. 5	30	------
20 to 24 years	6, 088	3, 580	58. 8	2, 410	39. 6	42	. 7	49	7	6, 990	1, 624	23. 2	5, 004	71. 6	212	3. 0	146	4
25 to 34 years	17, 907	4, 880	27. 3	12, 218	68. 2	445	2. 5	343	21	16, 682	1, 472	8. 8	13, 402	80. 3	1, 288	7. 7	506	14
35 to 44 years	12, 890	2, 012	15. 6	9, 759	75. 7	734	5. 7	372	13	9, 660	546	5. 7	7, 257	75. 1	1, 548	16. 0	300	9
45 to 54 years	5, 581	628	11. 3	4, 196	75. 2	607	10. 9	148	2	3, 916	131	3. 3	2, 417	61. 7	1, 272	32. 5	92	4
55 to 64 years	1, 525	121	7. 9	1, 098	72. 0	266	17. 4	38	2	1, 322	33	2. 5	481	36. 4	788	59. 6	19	1
65 years and over	518	32	6. 2	279	53. 9	202	39. 0	5	------	753	12	1. 6	121	16. 1	617	81. 9	3	------
DURHAM, N. C.																		
Total	**5, 970**	**2, 031**	**34. 0**	**3, 556**	**59. 6**	**288**	**4. 8**	**94**	**1**	**7, 361**	**2, 186**	**29. 7**	**3, 923**	**53. 3**	**1, 084**	**14. 7**	**167**	**1**
15 to 19 years	831	801	96. 4	28	3. 4	------	------	2	------	1, 198	1, 013	84. 6	179	14. 9	3	. 3	3	------
20 to 24 years	1, 060	609	57. 5	429	40. 5	8	. 8	14	------	1, 540	635	41. 2	846	54. 9	36	2. 3	23	------
25 to 34 years	1, 782	415	23. 3	1, 297	72. 8	40	2. 2	30	------	2, 131	399	18. 7	1, 481	69. 5	179	8. 4	72	------
35 to 44 years	1, 172	138	11. 8	925	78. 9	75	6. 4	33	1	1, 265	83	6. 6	861	68. 1	279	22. 1	42	------
45 to 54 years	676	43	6. 4	553	81. 8	67	9. 9	13	------	715	35	4. 9	397	55. 5	262	36. 6	21	------
55 to 64 years	300	14	4. 7	233	77. 7	53	17. 7	------	------	304	12	3. 9	124	40. 8	165	54. 3	3	------
65 years and over	132	6	4. 5	79	59. 8	45	34. 1	2	------	196	7	3. 6	29	14. 8	157	80. 1	2	1
EAST ST. LOUIS, ILL.																		
Total	**4, 169**	**1, 163**	**27. 9**	**2, 631**	**63. 1**	**335**	**8. 0**	**34**	**6**	**4, 103**	**739**	**18. 0**	**2, 605**	**63. 5**	**699**	**17. 0**	**49**	**11**
15 to 19 years	458	436	95. 2	22	4. 8	------	------	------	------	523	368	70. 4	137	26. 2	14	2. 7	3	1
20 to 24 years	543	283	52. 1	245	45. 1	11	2. 0	4	------	674	165	24. 5	444	65. 9	52	7. 7	13	------
25 to 34 years	1, 179	248	21. 0	866	73. 5	57	4. 8	8	------	1, 276	132	10. 3	993	77. 8	133	10. 4	16	2
35 to 44 years	1, 042	117	11. 2	812	77. 9	95	9. 1	16	2	881	47	5. 3	647	73. 4	170	19. 3	16	1
45 to 54 years	621	48	7. 7	477	76. 8	91	14. 7	5	------	471	13	2. 8	295	62. 6	162	34. 4	1	------
55 to 64 years	206	14	6. 8	156	75. 7	35	17. 0	1	------	171	6	3. 5	68	39. 8	96	56. 1	------	1
65 years and over	95	7	------	42	------	46	------	------	------	92	3	------	19	------	70	------	------	------
FORT WORTH, TEX.																		
Total	**8, 122**	**1. 938**	**23. 9**	**5, 234**	**64. 4**	**662**	**8. 2**	**272**	**16**	**9, 054**	**1, 390**	**15. 4**	**5, 468**	**60. 4**	**1, 740**	**19. 2**	**434**	**22**
15 to 19 years	811	764	94. 2	43	5. 3	3	. 4	1	------	1, 020	702	68. 8	277	27. 2	22	2. 2	18	1
20 to 24 years	1, 026	509	49. 6	482	47. 0	23	2. 2	12	------	1, 415	355	25. 1	913	64. 5	91	6. 4	55	1
25 to 34 years	2, 318	407	17. 6	1, 703	73. 5	101	4. 4	103	4	2, 812	238	8. 5	2, 051	72. 9	344	12. 2	174	5
35 to 44 years	2, 059	164	8. 0	1, 624	78. 9	178	8. 6	89	4	2, 096	52	2. 5	1, 470	70. 1	450	21. 5	122	2
45 to 54 years	1, 234	53	4. 3	962	78. 0	166	13. 5	53	------	1, 005	19	1. 9	552	54. 9	383	38. 1	49	2
55 to 64 years	422	20	4. 7	298	70. 6	94	22. 3	10	------	380	9	2. 4	144	37. 9	214	56. 3	13	------
65 years and over	218	15	6. 9	106	48. 6	93	42. 7	4	------	282	6	2. 1	44	15. 6	226	80. 1	3	3
GALVESTON, TEX.																		
Total	**5, 070**	**1, 370**	**27. 0**	**3, 011**	**59. 4**	**311**	**6. 1**	**372**	**6**	**5, 403**	**950**	**17. 6**	**3, 088**	**57. 2**	**847**	**15. 7**	**509**	**9**
15 to 19 years	434	413	95. 2	18	4. 1	------	------	3	------	598	437	73. 1	140	23. 4	5	. 8	16	------
20 to 24 years	575	309	53. 7	239	41. 6	2	. 3	23	2	911	243	26. 7	551	60. 5	34	3. 7	80	3
25 to 34 years	1, 532	341	22. 3	1, 034	67. 5	39	2. 5	118	------	1, 698	146	8. 6	1, 196	70. 4	134	7. 9	221	1
35 to 44 years	1, 293	193	14. 9	905	70. 0	66	5. 1	127	2	1, 221	70	5. 7	794	65. 0	216	17. 7	140	1
45 to 54 years	799	76	9. 5	566	70. 8	87	10. 9	69	1	584	31	5. 3	309	52. 9	200	34. 2	43	1
55 to 64 years	307	28	9. 1	185	60. 3	68	22. 1	26	------	236	18	7. 6	75	31. 8	132	55. 9	9	2
65 years and over	125	8	6. 4	61	48. 8	49	39. 2	6	1	153	4	2. 6	22	14. 4	126	82. 4	------	1

TABLE 16.—MARITAL CONDITION OF THE NEGRO POPULATION 15 YEARS OLD AND OVER, BY SEX, AND 5-YEAR AGE PERIODS, FOR CITIES HAVING 10,000 OR MORE NEGRO INHABITANTS: 1930—Continued

MALES 15 YEARS OLD AND OVER

CITY AND AGE	Total	Single: Number	Single: Percent	Married: Number	Married: Percent	Widowed: Number	Widowed: Percent	Divorced	Unknown
GARY, IND.									
Total	**7,050**	**2,071**	**29.4**	**4,470**	**63.4**	**384**	**5.4**	**118**	**7**
15 to 19 years	566	551	97.3	14	2.5	------	------	1	------
20 to 24 years	881	524	59.5	342	38.8	10	1.1	4	1
25 to 34 years	2,334	615	26.3	1,618	69.3	71	3.0	28	2
35 to 44 years	1,877	278	14.8	1,438	76.6	112	6.0	49	------
45 to 54 years	945	78	8.3	745	78.8	96	10.2	26	------
55 to 64 years	325	17	5.2	236	72.6	62	19.1	9	1
65 years and over	99	5	------	62	------	31	------	1	------
GREENSBORO, N. C.									
Total	**4,566**	**1,652**	**36.2**	**2,643**	**57.9**	**245**	**5.4**	**23**	**3**
15 to 19 years	644	627	97.4	15	2.3	1	.2	1	------
20 to 24 years	787	500	63.5	279	35.5	6	.8	2	------
25 to 34 years	1,331	345	25.9	938	70.5	39	2.9	9	------
35 to 44 years	848	121	14.3	673	79.4	46	5.4	6	2
45 to 54 years	572	41	7.2	473	82.7	55	9.6	2	1
55 to 64 years	246	11	4.5	184	74.8	49	19.9	2	------
65 years and over	136	6	4.4	80	58.8	49	36.0	1	------
GREENVILLE, S. C.									
Total	**3,299**	**966**	**29.3**	**2,072**	**62.8**	**248**	**7.5**	**8**	**5**
15 to 19 years	568	535	94.2	29	5.1	2	.4	------	2
20 to 24 years	536	209	39.0	316	59.0	8	1.5	2	1
25 to 34 years	879	132	15.0	699	79.5	46	5.2	2	------
35 to 44 years	611	57	9.3	494	80.9	59	9.7	1	------
45 to 54 years	392	17	4.3	313	79.8	59	15.1	2	1
55 to 64 years	190	5	2.6	145	76.3	40	21.1	------	------
65 years and over	104	6	5.8	63	60.6	33	31.7	1	1
HOUSTON, TEX.									
Total	**23,339**	**6,305**	**27.0**	**14,374**	**61.6**	**1,698**	**7.3**	**917**	**45**
15 to 19 years	2,249	2,145	95.4	92	4.1	3	.1	6	3
20 to 24 years	3,429	1,792	52.3	1,479	43.1	67	2.0	85	6
35 to 34 years	7,301	1,466	20.1	5,174	70.9	295	4.0	357	9
35 to 44 years	5,480	588	10.7	4,189	76.4	407	7.4	288	8
45 to 54 years	3,082	210	6.8	2,316	75.1	413	13.4	143	------
55 to 64 years	1,121	55	4.9	769	68.6	271	24.2	25	1
65 years and over	532	16	3.0	266	50.0	238	44.7	12	------
INDIANAPOLIS, IND.									
Total	**15,998**	**4,462**	**27.9**	**9,922**	**62.0**	**1,213**	**7.6**	**359**	**42**
15 to 19 years	1,592	1,515	95.2	75	4.7	------	------	1	1
20 to 24 years	1,744	1,038	59.5	672	38.5	15	.9	18	1
25 to 34 years	3,901	970	24.9	2,690	69.0	132	3.4	105	4
35 to 44 years	3,753	534	14.2	2,851	76.0	256	6.8	110	2
45 to 54 years	2,911	271	9.3	2,224	76.4	329	11.3	81	6
55 to 64 years	1,312	85	6.5	968	73.8	223	17.0	34	2
65 years and over	710	38	5.4	407	57.3	256	36.1	9	------
JACKSON, MISS.									
Total	**6,772**	**2,113**	**31.2**	**4,152**	**61.3**	**357**	**5.3**	**112**	**37**
15 to 19 years	792	727	91.8	64	8.1	1	.1	------	------
20 to 24 years	1,170	581	49.7	570	48.7	7	.6	11	1
25 to 34 years	1,993	508	25.5	1,404	70.4	32	1.6	44	5
35 to 44 years	1,340	172	12.8	1,043	77.8	86	6.4	35	4
45 to 54 years	872	84	9.6	675	77.4	94	10.8	15	4
55 to 64 years	356	25	7.0	265	74.4	58	16.3	3	5
65 to years and over	233	15	6.4	130	55.8	78	33.5	4	6
JACKSONVILLE, FLA.									
Total	**16,537**	**4,509**	**27.3**	**10,555**	**63.8**	**1,273**	**7.7**	**186**	**14**
15 to 19 years	1,813	1,744	96.2	66	3.6	1	.1	------	2
20 to 24 years	2,236	1,162	52.0	1,034	46.2	27	1.2	12	1
25 to 34 years	4,799	973	20.3	3,600	75.0	164	3.4	58	4
35 to 44 years	3,956	395	10.0	3,161	79.9	339	8.6	57	4
45 to 54 years	2,468	180	7.3	1,901	77.0	349	14.1	36	2
55 to 64 years	828	37	4.5	567	68.5	204	24.6	20	------
65 years and over	422	16	3.8	214	50.7	189	44.8	3	------
JERSEY CITY, N. J.									
Total	**4,641**	**1,541**	**33.2**	**2,860**	**61.6**	**209**	**4.5**	**29**	**2**
15 to 19 years	413	403	97.6	10	2.4	------	------	------	------
20 to 24 years	669	390	58.3	275	41.1	3	.4	1	------
25 to 34 years	1,442	420	29.1	988	68.5	22	1.5	11	1
35 to 44 years	1,024	203	19.8	762	74.4	46	4.5	13	------
45 to 54 years	661	86	13.0	515	77.9	57	8.6	3	------
55 to 64 years	299	30	10.0	224	74.9	44	14.7	1	------
65 years and over	129	7	5.4	86	66.7	36	27.9	------	------

FEMALES 15 YEARS OLD AND OVER

CITY AND AGE	Total	Single: Number	Single: Percent	Married: Number	Married: Percent	Widowed: Number	Widowed: Percent	Divorced	Unknown
GARY, IND.									
Total	**6,233**	**906**	**14.5**	**4,355**	**69.9**	**864**	**13.9**	**106**	**2**
15 to 19 years	665	478	71.9	178	26.8	6	.9	3	------
20 to 24 years	970	204	21.0	698	72.0	49	5.1	19	------
25 to 34 years	2,191	166	7.6	1,801	82.2	176	8.0	48	------
35 to 44 years	1,434	42	2.9	1,142	79.6	226	15.8	24	------
45 to 54 years	636	10	1.6	419	65.9	196	30.8	10	1
55 to 64 years	219	5	2.3	84	38.4	128	58.4	2	------
65 years and over	106	1	.9	27	25.5	77	72.6	------	1
GREENSBORO, N. C.									
Total	**5,545**	**1,652**	**29.8**	**2,895**	**52.2**	**934**	**16.8**	**61**	**3**
15 to 19 years	919	755	82.2	152	16.5	10	1.1	2	------
20 to 24 years	1,071	479	44.7	543	50.7	39	3.6	9	1
25 to 34 years	1,575	291	18.5	1,086	69.0	170	10.8	26	2
35 to 44 years	983	69	7.0	665	67.7	234	23.8	15	------
45 to 54 years	598	40	6.7	334	55.9	218	36.5	6	------
55 to 64 years	221	9	4.1	90	40.7	119	53.8	3	------
65 years and over	168	8	4.8	23	13.7	137	81.5	------	------
GREENVILLE, S. C.									
Total	**4,407**	**1,077**	**24.4**	**2,399**	**54.4**	**915**	**20.8**	**8**	**8**
15 to 19 years	699	522	74.7	167	23.9	9	1.3	------	1
20 to 24 years	889	291	32.7	562	63.2	33	3.7	1	2
25 to 34 years	1,175	166	14.1	833	70.9	172	14.6	4	------
35 to 44 years	833	52	6.2	539	64.7	237	28.5	2	3
45 to 54 years	449	26	5.8	206	45.9	216	48.1	1	------
55 to 64 years	187	4	2.1	58	31.0	125	66.8	------	------
65 years and over	144	8	5.6	16	11.1	120	83.3	------	------
HOUSTON, TEX.									
Total	**25,997**	**4,634**	**17.8**	**14,984**	**57.6**	**4,678**	**18.0**	**1,667**	**34**
15 to 19 years	3,194	2,324	72.8	756	23.7	52	1.6	61	1
20 to 24 years	4,630	1,118	24.1	2,969	64.1	259	5.6	275	9
35 to 34 years	8,397	806	9.6	5,851	69.7	1,013	12.1	723	4
35 to 44 years	5,303	233	4.4	3,466	65.4	1,189	22.4	412	3
45 to 54 years	2,652	78	2.9	1,422	53.6	1,006	37.9	142	4
55 to 64 years	1,022	22	2.2	348	34.1	609	59.6	42	1
65 years and over	622	6	1.0	84	13.5	521	83.8	8	3
INDIANAPOLIS, IND.									
Total	**17,238**	**3,077**	**17.9**	**10,227**	**59.3**	**3,467**	**20.1**	**439**	**28**
15 to 19 years	1,840	1,394	75.8	411	22.3	21	1.1	12	2
20 to 24 years	2,155	710	32.9	1,276	59.2	115	5.3	49	5
25 to 34 years	4,532	555	12.2	3,289	72.6	496	10.9	188	4
35 to 44 years	4,015	257	6.4	2,827	70.4	806	20.1	124	1
45 to 54 years	2,662	101	3.8	1,674	62.9	834	31.3	49	4
55 to 64 years	1,184	29	2.4	562	47.5	578	48.8	14	1
65 years and over	791	20	2.5	160	20.2	607	76.7	3	1
JACKSON, MISS.									
Total	**7,889**	**1,808**	**22.9**	**4,591**	**58.2**	**1,150**	**14.6**	**290**	**50**
15 to 19 years	1,076	736	68.5	324	30.1	4	.4	11	------
20 to 24 years	1,557	509	32.7	947	60.8	40	2.6	60	1
25 to 34 years	2,250	345	15.3	1,596	70.9	193	8.6	107	9
35 to 44 years	1,436	119	8.3	991	69.0	253	17.6	66	7
45 to 54 years	861	60	7.0	494	57.4	269	31.2	34	4
55 to 64 years	390	18	4.6	176	45.1	185	47.4	8	3
65 to years and over	293	18	6.1	61	20.8	204	69.6	4	6
JACKSONVILLE, FLA.									
Total	**19,912**	**3,732**	**18.7**	**11,601**	**58.3**	**4,120**	**20.7**	**449**	**10**
15 to 19 years	2,547	1,933	75.9	557	21.9	27	1.1	30	------
20 to 24 years	3,469	937	27.0	2,250	64.9	201	5.8	76	5
25 to 34 years	6,026	606	10.1	4,502	74.7	757	12.6	159	2
35 to 44 years	4,352	174	4.0	2,860	65.7	1,188	27.3	129	1
45 to 54 years	2,216	56	2.5	1,096	49.5	1,021	46.1	43	------
55 to 64 years	771	16	2.1	246	31.9	498	64.6	11	------
65 years and over	510	7	1.4	78	15.3	424	83.1	1	------
JERSEY CITY, N. J.									
Total	**4,593**	**903**	**19.7**	**2,936**	**63.9**	**713**	**15.5**	**38**	**3**
15 to 19 years	521	397	76.2	120	23.0	3	.6	1	------
20 to 24 years	729	219	30.0	487	66.8	19	2.6	4	------
25 to 34 years	1,397	183	13.1	1,092	78.2	104	7.4	18	------
35 to 44 years	934	61	6.5	718	76.9	144	15.4	10	1
45 to 54 years	594	25	4.2	362	60.9	201	33.8	5	1
55 to 64 years	298	13	4.4	137	46.0	148	49.7	------	------
65 years and over	117	4	3.4	19	16.2	94	80.3	------	------

TABLE 16.—MARITAL CONDITION OF THE NEGRO POPULATION 15 YEARS OLD AND OVER, BY SEX, AND 5-YEAR AGE PERIODS, FOR CITIES HAVING 10,000 OR MORE NEGRO INHABITANTS: 1930—Continued

CITY AND AGE	MALES 15 YEARS OLD AND OVER									FEMALES 15 YEARS OLD AND OVER								
	Total	Single		Married		Widowed		Divorced	Unknown	Total	Single		Married		Widowed		Divorced	Unknown
		Number	Per cent	Number	Per cent	Number	Per cent				Number	Per cent	Number	Per cent	Number	Per cent		
KANSAS CITY, KANS.																		
Total	**7,101**	**1,628**	**22.9**	**4,702**	**66.2**	**529**	**7.4**	**235**	**7**	**7,645**	**1,227**	**16.0**	**4,809**	**62.9**	**1,296**	**17.0**	**312**	**1**
15 to 19 years	741	716	96.6	23	3.1	1	.1	1	-------	813	665	81.8	137	16.9	6	.7	5	-------
20 to 24 years	645	383	59.4	251	38.9	3	.5	8	-------	842	261	31.0	523	62.1	23	2.7	35	-------
25 to 34 years	1,592	291	18.3	1,194	75.0	50	3.1	55	2	1,933	188	9.7	1,509	78.1	127	6.6	109	-------
35 to 44 years	1,695	137	8.1	1,385	81.7	96	5.7	75	2	1,776	64	3.6	1,375	77.4	242	13.6	95	-------
45 to 54 years	1,382	64	4.6	1,133	82.0	127	9.2	56	2	1,273	33	2.6	863	67.8	333	26.2	44	-------
55 to 64 years	667	30	4.5	483	72.4	123	18.4	31	-------	582	11	1.9	290	49.8	263	45.2	18	-------
65 years and over	377	7	1.9	232	61.5	129	34.2	9	-------	422	5	1.2	112	26.5	299	70.9	6	-------
KANSAS CITY, MO.																		
Total	**15,302**	**4,345**	**28.4**	**9,111**	**59.5**	**1,425**	**9.3**	**380**	**41**	**16,530**	**3,028**	**18.3**	**9,215**	**55.7**	**3,729**	**22.6**	**527**	**31**
15 to 19 years	1,115	1,068	95.8	44	3.9	1	.1	-------	2	1,369	1,052	76.8	281	20.5	20	1.5	16	-------
20 to 24 years	1,308	768	58.7	499	38.1	20	1.5	17	4	2,043	752	36.8	1,087	53.2	129	6.3	71	4
25 to 34 years	3,746	1,105	29.5	2,396	64.0	143	3.8	93	9	4,649	730	15.7	3,153	67.8	546	11.7	210	10
35 to 44 years	4,222	773	18.3	2,961	70.1	364	8.6	118	6	4,250	327	7.7	2,797	65.8	982	23.1	140	4
45 to 54 years	3,171	424	13.4	2,217	69.9	432	13.6	92	6	2,591	110	4.2	1,421	54.8	993	38.3	65	2
55 to 64 years	1,133	139	12.3	710	62.7	243	21.4	39	2	961	29	3.0	346	36.0	568	59.1	18	-------
65 years and over	544	47	8.6	264	48.5	214	39.3	18	1	601	18	3.0	109	18.1	469	78.0	5	-------
KNOXVILLE, TENN.																		
Total	**6,083**	**2,004**	**32.9**	**3,640**	**59.8**	**342**	**5.6**	**79**	**18**	**6,791**	**1,605**	**23.6**	**3,790**	**55.8**	**1,190**	**17.5**	**183**	**23**
15 to 19 years	771	735	95.3	34	4.4	-------	-------	-------	2	889	697	78.4	183	20.6	3	.3	4	2
20 to 24 years	909	510	56.1	380	41.8	6	.7	8	5	1,180	434	36.8	672	56.9	32	2.7	36	6
25 to 34 years	1,547	428	27.7	1,072	69.3	25	1.6	20	2	1,834	279	15.2	1,323	72.1	161	8.8	67	4
35 to 44 years	1,281	190	14.8	1,001	78.1	61	4.8	28	1	1,379	118	8.6	937	67.9	277	20.1	46	1
45 to 54 years	905	84	9.3	713	78.8	88	9.7	17	3	848	42	5.0	478	56.4	302	35.6	24	2
55 to 64 years	416	29	7.0	290	69.7	90	21.6	5	2	373	23	6.2	140	37.5	207	55.5	2	1
65 years and over	211	20	9.5	124	58.8	66	31.3	1	-------	255	9	3.5	46	18.0	194	76.1	4	2
LEXINGTON, KY.																		
Total	**4,776**	**1,563**	**32.7**	**2,708**	**56.7**	**388**	**8.1**	**114**	**3**	**5,198**	**1,076**	**20.7**	**2,813**	**54.1**	**1,141**	**22.0**	**167**	**1**
15 to 19 years	463	443	95.7	19	4.1	-------	-------	1	-------	530	438	82.6	81	15.3	4	.8	6	1
20 to 24 years	516	308	59.7	192	37.2	4	.8	12	-------	596	217	36.4	339	56.9	22	3.7	18	-------
25 to 34 years	981	320	32.6	591	60.2	37	3.8	31	2	1,198	195	16.3	836	69.8	111	9.3	56	-------
35 to 44 years	1,129	237	21.0	784	69.4	76	6.7	32	-------	1,201	113	9.4	821	68.4	220	18.3	47	-------
45 to 54 years	942	154	16.3	666	70.7	103	10.9	19	-------	864	69	8.0	480	55.6	284	32.9	31	-------
55 to 64 years	454	66	14.5	308	67.8	69	15.2	11	-------	460	26	5.7	198	43.0	229	49.8	7	-------
65 years and over	291	35	12.0	148	50.9	99	34.0	8	1	348	18	5.2	58	16.7	270	77.6	2	-------
LITTLE ROCK, ARK.																		
Total	**6,766**	**1,842**	**27.2**	**4,146**	**61.3**	**585**	**8.6**	**187**	**6**	**8,622**	**1,810**	**21.0**	**4,367**	**50.6**	**1,934**	**22.4**	**508**	**3**
15 to 19 years	711	688	96.8	20	2.8	2	.3	1	-------	1,012	790	78.1	199	19.7	9	.9	14	-------
20 to 24 years	909	478	52.6	386	42.5	25	2.8	20	-------	1,310	448	34.2	697	53.2	82	6.3	83	-------
25 to 34 years	1,590	340	21.4	1,131	71.1	69	4.3	48	2	2,401	343	14.3	1,518	63.2	324	13.5	216	-------
35 to 44 years	1,563	203	13.0	1,167	74.7	132	8.4	60	1	1,885	139	7.4	1,132	60.1	479	25.4	135	-------
45 to 54 years	1,169	91	7.8	895	76.6	141	12.1	40	2	1,177	61	5.2	587	49.9	481	40.9	48	-------
55 to 64 years	493	31	6.3	357	72.4	89	18.1	16	-------	486	21	4.3	172	35.4	286	58.8	7	-------
65 years and over	328	11	3.4	189	57.6	127	38.7	1	-------	347	8	2.3	62	17.9	272	78.4	4	1
LOS ANGELES, CALIF.																		
Total	**14,501**	**4,193**	**28.9**	**8,897**	**61.4**	**877**	**6.0**	**522**	**12**	**16,645**	**2,889**	**17.4**	**9,463**	**56.9**	**3,343**	**20.1**	**939**	**1**
15 to 19 years	1,211	1,187	98.0	23	1.9	-------	-------	-------	1	1,432	1,182	82.5	235	16.4	9	.6	6	-------
20 to 24 years	1,488	974	65.5	474	31.9	23	1.5	17	-------	1,967	711	36.1	1,081	55.0	79	4.0	96	-------
25 to 34 years	3,892	1,065	27.4	2,571	66.1	95	2.4	158	3	4,579	554	12.1	3,275	71.5	414	9.0	333	3
35 to 44 years	3,822	601	15.7	2,828	74.0	214	5.6	178	1	4,196	260	6.2	2,796	66.6	809	19.3	328	3
45 to 54 years	2,505	255	10.2	1,894	75.6	241	9.6	115	-------	2,597	123	4.7	1,461	56.3	871	33.5	142	-------
55 to 64 years	1,029	88	8.6	767	74.5	129	12.5	45	-------	1,111	40	3.6	451	40.6	593	53.4	26	1
65 years and over	533	20	3.8	333	62.5	172	32.3	7	1	748	17	2.3	157	21.0	564	75.4	8	2
LOUISVILLE, KY.																		
Total	**17,832**	**5,254**	**29.5**	**10,401**	**58.3**	**1,687**	**9.5**	**473**	**17**	**19,688**	**3,997**	**20.3**	**10,662**	**54.2**	**4,398**	**22.3**	**619**	**12**
15 to 19 years	1,583	1,520	96.0	58	3.7	4	.3	1	-------	1,950	1,560	80.0	359	18.4	15	.8	16	-------
20 to 24 years	1,854	1,094	59.0	721	38.9	12	.6	24	3	2,487	904	36.3	1,374	55.2	121	4.9	85	3
25 to 34 years	4,319	1,260	29.2	2,731	63.2	192	4.4	133	3	4,946	800	16.2	3,370	68.1	550	11.1	225	1
35 to 44 years	4,331	747	17.2	3,077	71.0	323	7.5	180	4	4,569	392	8.6	2,999	65.6	986	21.6	189	3
45 to 54 years	3,363	435	12.9	2,338	69.5	498	14.8	90	2	3,195	225	7.0	1,782	55.8	1,104	34.6	82	2
55 to 64 years	1,508	135	9.0	1,002	66.4	336	22.3	32	3	1,451	71	4.9	591	40.7	774	53.3	14	1
65 years and over	841	62	7.4	449	53.4	317	37.7	13	-------	1,058	42	4.0	173	16.4	837	79.1	6	-------
MACON, GA.																		
Total	**7,232**	**2,057**	**28.4**	**4,547**	**62.9**	**506**	**7.0**	**113**	**9**	**9,683**	**2,222**	**22.9**	**4,853**	**50.1**	**2,284**	**23.6**	**301**	**23**
15 to 19 years	1,037	997	96.1	36	3.5	3	.3	1	-------	1,450	1,124	77.5	287	19.8	23	1.6	16	-------
20 to 24 years	1,095	537	49.0	518	47.3	25	2.3	15	-------	1,693	579	34.2	913	53.9	123	7.3	75	3
25 to 34 years	1,773	295	16.6	1,380	77.8	65	3.7	33	-------	2,388	309	12.9	1,614	67.6	356	14.9	107	2
35 to 44 years	1,620	139	8.6	1,318	81.4	121	7.5	40	2	2,029	132	6.5	1,229	60.6	587	28.9	74	7
45 to 54 years	1,097	60	5.5	882	80.4	140	12.8	15	-------	1,201	52	4.3	570	47.5	551	45.9	26	2
55 to 64 years	375	21	5.6	255	68.0	91	24.3	8	-------	497	13	2.6	161	32.4	320	64.4	2	1
65 years and over	206	4	1.9	141	68.4	60	29.1	1	-------	388	9	2.3	62	16.0	314	80.9	1	2

TABLE 16.—MARITAL CONDITION OF THE NEGRO POPULATION 15 YEARS OLD AND OVER, BY SEX, AND 5-YEAR AGE PERIODS, FOR CITIES HAVING 10,000 OR MORE NEGRO INHABITANTS: 1930—Continued

CITY AND AGE	MALES 15 YEARS OLD AND OVER									FEMALES 15 YEARS OLD AND OVER								
	Total	Single		Married		Widowed		Divorced	Unknown	Total	Single		Married		Widowed		Divorced	Unknown
		Number	Percent	Number	Percent	Number	Percent				Number	Percent	Number	Percent	Number	Percent		
MEMPHIS, TENN.																		
Total	**34, 549**	**9, 535**	**27. 6**	**21, 427**	**62. 0**	**2, 758**	**8. 0**	**694**	**135**	**40, 939**	**8, 097**	**19. 8**	**22, 488**	**54. 9**	**8, 874**	**21. 7**	**1, 358**	**122**
15 to 19 years	3, 276	3, 100	94. 6	143	4. 4	4	-----	7	22	4, 642	3, 365	72. 5	1, 131	24. 4	84	1. 8	51	11
20 to 24 years	4, 482	2, 340	52. 2	1, 965	43. 8	83	1. 9	66	28	6, 365	1, 970	31. 0	3, 758	59. 0	394	6. 2	222	21
25 to 34 years	9, 306	2, 216	23. 8	6, 472	69. 5	361	3. 9	230	27	11, 889	1, 686	14. 2	8, 116	68. 3	1, 523	12. 8	542	22
35 to 44 years	8, 120	1, 074	13. 2	6, 194	76. 3	613	7. 5	216	23	8, 847	649	7. 3	5, 664	64. 0	2, 171	24. 5	348	15
45 to 54 years	5, 615	520	9. 3	4, 224	75. 2	743	13. 2	116	12	5, 290	259	4. 9	2, 744	51. 9	2, 129	40. 2	144	14
55 to 64 years	2, 401	169	7. 0	1, 716	71. 5	477	19. 9	35	4	2, 296	92	4. 0	786	34. 2	1, 375	59. 9	34	9
65 years and over	1, 220	82	6. 7	637	52. 2	472	38. 7	22	7	1, 467	55	3. 7	221	15. 1	1, 166	79. 5	11	14
MERIDIAN, MISS.																		
Total	**3, 418**	**967**	**28. 3**	**2, 141**	**62. 6**	**245**	**7. 2**	**61**	**4**	**4, 797**	**1, 157**	**24. 1**	**2, 379**	**49. 6**	**1, 068**	**22. 3**	**186**	**7**
15 to 19 years	507	475	93. 7	29	5. 7	-----	-----	1	2	718	535	74. 5	169	23. 5	6	. 8	8	-----
20 to 24 years	482	222	46. 1	247	51. 2	6	1. 2	7	-----	884	348	39. 4	462	52. 3	34	3. 8	39	1
25 to 34 years	792	163	20. 6	582	73. 5	22	2. 8	25	-----	1, 245	189	15. 2	797	64. 0	175	14. 1	83	1
35 to 44 years	705	62	8. 8	580	82. 3	48	6. 8	15	-----	920	56	6. 1	556	60. 4	273	29. 7	34	1
45 to 54 years	488	32	6. 6	391	80. 1	58	11. 9	6	1	561	17	3. 0	266	47. 4	260	46. 3	16	2
55 to 64 years	252	8	3. 2	193	76. 6	47	18. 7	4	-----	257	6	2. 3	98	38. 1	147	57. 2	5	1
65 years and over	190	5	2. 6	118	62. 1	64	33. 7	3	-----	209	5	2. 4	31	14. 8	172	82. 3	1	-----
MIAMI, FLA.																		
Total	**8, 303**	**2, 331**	**28. 1**	**5, 443**	**65. 6**	**434**	**5. 2**	**93**	**2**	**9, 403**	**1, 731**	**18. 4**	**6, 043**	**64. 3**	**1, 411**	**15. 0**	**217**	**1**
15 to 19 years	803	774	96. 4	28	3. 5	1	. 1	-----	-----	1, 167	858	73. 5	292	25. 0	12	1. 0	5	-----
20 to 24 years	1, 171	623	53. 2	534	45. 6	7	. 6	6	1	1, 696	445	26. 2	1, 142	67. 3	66	3. 9	43	-----
25 to 34 years	3, 094	669	21. 6	2, 309	74. 6	62	2. 0	53	1	3, 445	316	9. 2	2, 662	77. 3	356	10. 3	111	-----
35 to 44 years	1, 928	184	9. 5	1, 584	82. 2	146	7. 6	14	-----	1, 887	79	4. 2	1, 379	73. 1	387	20. 5	42	-----
45 to 54 years	930	55	5. 9	741	79. 7	118	12. 7	16	-----	830	19	2. 3	454	54. 7	344	41. 4	13	-----
55 to 64 years	265	18	6. 8	185	69. 8	59	22. 3	3	-----	240	5	2. 1	82	34. 2	152	63. 3	1	-----
65 years and over	108	7	6. 5	60	55. 6	40	37. 0	1	-----	123	5	4. 1	26	21. 1	90	73. 2	2	-----
MOBILE, ALA.																		
Total	**8, 110**	**2, 461**	**30. 3**	**4, 904**	**60. 5**	**607**	**7. 5**	**125**	**13**	**10, 328**	**2, 410**	**23. 3**	**5, 330**	**51. 6**	**2, 277**	**22. 0**	**293**	**18**
15 to 19 years	949	906	95. 5	42	4. 4	1	. 1	-----	-----	1, 346	1, 040	77. 3	278	20. 7	18	1. 3	8	2
20 to 24 years	1, 095	594	54. 2	474	43. 3	15	1. 4	8	4	1, 732	592	34. 2	1, 006	58. 1	79	4. 6	51	4
25 to 34 years	2, 009	475	23. 6	1, 428	71. 1	64	3. 2	37	5	2, 731	455	16. 7	1, 830	67. 0	341	12. 5	101	4
35 to 44 years	1, 701	246	14. 5	1, 294	76. 1	116	6. 8	45	-----	2, 105	175	8. 3	1, 303	61. 9	539	25. 6	87	1
45 to 54 years	1, 349	152	11. 3	1, 033	76. 6	141	10. 5	22	1	1, 372	90	6. 6	666	48. 5	579	42. 2	34	3
55 to 64 years	664	60	9. 0	455	68. 5	138	20. 8	10	1	572	29	5. 1	181	31. 6	352	61. 5	10	-----
65 years and over	311	18	5. 8	163	52. 4	128	41. 2	1	1	431	19	4. 4	53	12. 3	355	82. 4	2	2
MONROE, LA.																		
Total	**3, 694**	**1, 116**	**30. 2**	**2, 288**	**61. 9**	**262**	**7. 1**	**27**	**1**	**4, 227**	**753**	**17. 8**	**2, 504**	**59. 2**	**884**	**20. 9**	**86**	-----
15 to 19 years	408	393	96. 3	14	3. 4	1	. 2	-----	-----	512	349	68. 2	143	27. 9	15	2. 9	5	-----
20 to 24 years	647	362	56. 0	272	42. 0	11	1. 7	2	-----	837	222	26. 5	555	66. 3	47	5. 6	13	-----
25 to 34 years	1, 078	251	23. 3	775	71. 9	46	4. 3	6	-----	1, 310	136	10. 4	968	73. 9	175	13. 4	31	-----
35 to 44 years	820	82	10. 0	664	81. 0	60	7. 3	13	1	839	34	4. 1	554	66. 0	228	27. 2	23	-----
45 to 54 years	510	22	4. 3	407	79. 8	76	14. 9	5	-----	421	8	1. 9	198	47. 0	202	48. 0	13	-----
55 to 64 years	141	4	2. 8	104	73. 8	32	22. 7	1	-----	166	3	1. 8	63	38. 0	99	59. 6	1	-----
65 years and over	83	1	-----	46	-----	36	-----	-----	-----	134	1	. 7	18	13. 4	115	85. 8	-----	-----
MONTGOMERY, ALA.																		
Total	**9, 289**	**2, 876**	**31. 0**	**5, 647**	**60. 8**	**603**	**6. 5**	**153**	**10**	**12, 838**	**3, 178**	**24. 8**	**6, 135**	**47. 8**	**3, 060**	**23. 8**	**439**	**26**
15 to 19 years	1, 388	1, 322	95. 2	62	4. 5	1	. 1	2	1	1, 913	1, 507	78. 8	364	19. 0	18	. 9	18	6
20 to 24 years	1, 438	771	53. 6	626	43. 5	22	1. 5	15	4	2, 190	821	37. 5	1, 132	51. 7	137	6. 3	90	10
25 to 34 years	2, 121	454	21. 4	1, 559	73. 5	57	2. 7	51	-----	3, 273	548	16. 7	2, 076	63. 4	481	14. 7	161	7
35 to 44 years	1, 891	196	10. 4	1, 525	80. 6	122	6. 5	47	1	2, 587	189	7. 3	1, 509	58. 3	766	29. 6	122	1
45 to 54 years	1, 559	95	6. 1	1, 278	82. 0	162	10. 4	21	3	1, 658	72	4. 3	788	47. 5	764	46. 1	34	-----
55 to 64 years	536	13	2. 4	402	75. 0	111	20. 7	10	-----	622	20	3. 2	171	27. 5	420	67. 5	10	1
65 years and over	352	23	6. 5	193	54. 8	128	36. 4	7	1	568	13	2. 3	86	15. 1	468	82. 4	1	-----
NASHVILLE, TENN.																		
Total	**14, 508**	**4, 231**	**29. 2**	**8, 781**	**60. 5**	**1, 144**	**7. 9**	**333**	**19**	**18, 164**	**4, 167**	**22. 9**	**9, 196**	**50. 6**	**3, 997**	**22. 0**	**788**	**16**
15 to 19 years	1, 784	1, 704	95. 5	73	4. 1	5	. 3	2	-----	2, 283	1, 835	80. 4	405	17. 7	15	. 7	27	1
20 to 24 years	1, 815	1, 000	55. 1	740	40. 8	35	1. 9	35	5	2, 627	980	37. 3	1, 368	52. 1	141	5. 4	138	-----
25 to 34 years	3, 376	826	24. 5	2, 317	68. 6	117	3. 5	109	7	4, 500	763	17. 0	2, 853	63. 4	570	12. 7	309	5
35 to 44 years	2, 890	352	12. 2	2, 240	77. 5	199	6. 9	96	3	3, 706	298	8. 0	2, 340	63. 1	863	23. 3	204	1
45 to 54 years	2, 572	223	8. 7	1, 977	76. 9	312	12. 1	59	1	2, 808	178	6. 3	1, 555	55. 4	998	35. 5	73	4
55 to 64 years	1, 329	87	6. 5	998	75. 1	221	16. 6	22	1	1, 302	61	4. 7	500	38. 4	711	54. 6	29	1
65 years and over	723	34	4. 7	424	58. 6	254	35. 1	10	1	912	47	5. 2	164	18. 0	692	75. 9	7	2
NEWARK, N. J.																		
Total	**14, 190**	**4, 459**	**31. 4**	**9, 024**	**63. 6**	**615**	**4. 3**	**69**	**23**	**14, 278**	**2, 793**	**19. 6**	**9, 317**	**65. 3**	**2, 016**	**14. 1**	**140**	**12**
15 to 19 years	1, 307	1, 261	96. 5	42	3. 2	1	. 1	1	2	1, 641	1, 265	77. 1	362	22. 1	8	. 5	5	1
20 to 24 years	1, 942	1, 082	55. 7	839	43. 2	9	. 5	6	6	2, 405	673	28. 0	1, 641	68. 2	66	2. 7	23	2
25 to 34 years	4, 716	1, 226	26. 0	3, 385	71. 8	77	1. 6	21	7	4, 792	570	11. 9	3, 791	79. 1	372	7. 8	57	2
35 to 44 years	3, 450	553	16. 0	2, 690	78. 0	179	5. 2	25	3	3, 043	175	5. 8	2, 280	74. 9	552	18. 1	33	3
45 to 54 years	1, 882	265	14. 1	1, 449	77. 0	158	8. 4	10	-----	1, 536	76	4. 9	948	61. 7	493	32. 1	17	2
55 to 64 years	629	51	8. 1	470	74. 7	105	16. 7	3	-----	540	16	3. 0	230	42. 6	290	53. 7	4	-----
65 years and over	243	15	6. 2	140	57. 6	85	35. 0	3	-----	301	15	5. 0	54	17. 9	231	76. 7	1	-----

TABLE 16.—MARITAL CONDITION OF THE NEGRO POPULATION 15 YEARS OLD AND OVER, BY SEX, AND 5-YEAR AGE PERIODS, FOR CITIES HAVING 10,000 OR MORE NEGRO INHABITANTS: 1930—Continued

CITY AND AGE	MALES 15 YEARS OLD AND OVER									FEMALES 15 YEARS OLD AND OVER								
	Total	Single		Married		Widowed		Divorced	Unknown	Total	Single		Married		Widowed		Divorced	Unknown
		Number	Percent	Number	Percent	Number	Percent				Number	Percent	Number	Percent	Number	Percent		
NEW ORLEANS, LA.																		
Total	**42,960**	**13,141**	**30.6**	**27,075**	**63.0**	**2,272**	**5.3**	**436**	**36**	**52,304**	**12,167**	**23.3**	**29,084**	**55.6**	**10,019**	**19.2**	**1,007**	**27**
15 to 19 years	4,959	4,732	95.4	213	4.3	6	.1	4	4	6,381	4,883	76.5	1,407	22.0	49	.8	41	1
20 to 24 years	5,796	3,172	54.7	2,519	43.5	48	.8	48	9	8,178	2,865	35.0	4,895	59.9	255	3.1	160	3
25 to 34 years	11,603	2,787	24.0	8,399	72.4	261	2.2	151	5	14,633	2,438	16.7	10,459	71.5	1,339	9.2	387	10
35 to 44 years	10,066	1,355	13.5	8,109	80.6	468	4.6	129	5	11,329	1,153	10.2	7,475	66.0	2,422	21.4	273	6
45 to 54 years	6,676	725	10.9	5,284	79.1	594	8.9	71	2	6,835	497	7.3	3,588	52.5	2,637	38.6	110	3
55 to 64 years	2,699	254	9.4	1,923	71.2	496	18.4	25	1	2,913	210	7.2	929	31.9	1,740	59.7	32	2
65 years and over	1,120	105	9.4	607	54.2	398	35.5	8	2	2,007	117	5.8	319	15.9	1,567	78.1	4	-------
NEWPORT NEWS, VA.																		
Total	**4,625**	**1,572**	**34.0**	**2,608**	**56.4**	**354**	**7.7**	**89**	**2**	**4,871**	**1,147**	**23.5**	**2,634**	**55.1**	**909**	**18.7**	**129**	**2**
15 to 19 years	548	533	97.3	15	2.7	-------	-------	-------	-------	698	572	81.9	116	16.6	5	.7	5	-------
20 to 24 years	617	398	64.5	215	34.8	1	.2	2	1	742	298	40.2	396	53.4	28	3.8	18	2
25 to 34 years	1,114	335	30.1	723	64.9	28	2.5	28	-------	1,279	197	15.4	887	69.4	144	11.3	51	-------
35 to 44 years	1,076	179	16.6	773	71.8	96	8.9	27	1	1,114	53	4.8	779	69.9	243	21.8	39	-------
45 to 54 years	871	88	10.1	621	71.3	133	15.3	29	-------	681	21	3.1	401	58.9	248	36.4	11	-------
55 to 64 years	284	29	10.2	199	70.1	54	19.0	2	-------	221	3	1.4	87	39.4	127	57.5	4	-------
65 years and over	115	10	8.7	62	53.9	42	36.5	1	-------	135	3	2.2	18	13.3	113	83.7	1	-------
NEW YORK, N. Y.																		
Total	**122,656**	**43,283**	**35.3**	**73,447**	**59.9**	**4,944**	**4.0**	**584**	**398**	**135,103**	**35,960**	**26.6**	**77,279**	**57.2**	**20,295**	**15.0**	**1,155**	**414**
15 to 19 years	9,169	8,903	97.1	218	2.4	3	-------	1	44	11,951	9,820	82.2	2,013	16.8	54	.5	16	48
20 to 24 years	16,664	10,753	64.5	5,724	34.3	86	.5	25	76	21,994	9,118	41.5	12,282	55.8	425	1.9	110	59
25 to 34 years	42,900	14,431	33.6	27,599	64.3	613	1.4	162	95	46,294	10,534	22.8	31,983	69.1	3,169	6.8	490	118
35 to 44 years	31,448	6,261	19.9	23,460	74.6	1,401	4.5	255	71	30,991	4,178	13.5	20,614	66.5	5,748	18.5	378	73
45 to 54 years	15,639	2,160	13.8	11,853	75.8	1,479	9.5	106	41	15,340	1,542	10.1	8,012	52.2	5,612	36.6	131	43
55 to 64 years	4,863	545	11.2	3,493	71.8	778	16.0	28	19	5,269	446	8.5	1,800	34.2	2,976	56.5	25	22
65 years and over	1,739	161	9.3	998	57.4	571	32.8	5	4	3,012	242	8.0	476	15.8	2,280	75.7	4	10
Bronx Borough																		
Total	**4,479**	**1,359**	**30.3**	**2,944**	**65.7**	**154**	**3.4**	**14**	**8**	**4,799**	**1,319**	**27.5**	**2,881**	**60.0**	**558**	**11.6**	**30**	**11**
15 to 19 years	370	363	98.1	6	1.6	-------	-------	-------	1	598	539	90.1	54	9.0	2	.3	2	1
20 to 24 years	550	368	66.9	176	32.0	3	.5	1	2	785	375	47.8	397	50.6	8	1.0	3	2
25 to 34 years	1,423	382	26.8	1,026	72.1	11	.8	4	-------	1,470	252	17.1	1,139	77.5	61	4.1	13	5
35 to 44 years	1,131	148	13.1	942	83.3	36	3.2	5	-------	993	82	8.3	774	77.9	127	12.8	9	1
45 to 54 years	653	63	9.6	545	83.5	42	6.4	2	1	595	39	6.6	396	66.6	157	26.4	3	-------
55 to 64 years	227	20	8.8	178	78.4	27	11.9	2	-------	207	16	7.7	82	39.6	109	52.7	-------	-------
65 years and over	110	10	9.1	65	59.1	35	31.8	-------	-------	132	9	6.8	30	22.7	93	70.5	-------	-------
Brooklyn Borough																		
Total	**24,330**	**7,827**	**32.2**	**15,455**	**63.5**	**851**	**3.5**	**99**	**98**	**27,259**	**6,961**	**25.5**	**16,149**	**59.2**	**3,851**	**14.1**	**202**	**96**
15 to 19 years	2,026	1,960	96.7	53	2.6	-------	-------	-------	13	2,795	2,293	82.0	469	16.8	15	.5	4	14
20 to 24 years	3,615	2,223	61.5	1,349	37.3	13	.4	6	24	4,816	1,869	38.8	2,826	58.7	81	1.7	30	10
25 to 34 years	8,259	2,268	27.5	5,853	70.9	85	1.0	26	27	8,864	1,705	19.2	6,506	73.4	555	6.3	72	26
35 to 44 years	5,759	889	15.4	4,623	80.3	195	3.4	42	10	5,729	649	11.3	3,995	69.7	999	17.4	70	16
45 to 54 years	3,063	332	10.8	2,439	79.6	270	8.8	17	5	3,113	274	8.8	1,725	55.4	1,084	34.8	20	10
55 to 64 years	1,097	92	8.4	852	77.7	145	13.2	6	2	1,157	94	8.1	462	39.9	592	51.2	5	4
65 years and over	441	41	9.3	256	58.0	142	32.2	2	-------	719	63	8.8	135	18.8	519	72.2	1	1
Manhattan Borough																		
Total	**86,903**	**32,155**	**37.0**	**50,377**	**58.0**	**3,652**	**4.2**	**440**	**279**	**94,430**	**25,500**	**27.0**	**53,159**	**56.3**	**14,626**	**15.5**	**849**	**296**
15 to 19 years	6,155	5,978	97.1	146	2.4	2	-------	1	28	7,667	6,224	81.2	1,366	17.8	35	.5	9	33
20 to 24 years	11,599	7,622	65.7	3,846	33.2	67	.6	16	48	15,036	6,295	41.9	8,315	55.3	314	2.1	68	44
25 to 34 years	31,212	11,346	36.4	19,191	61.5	488	1.6	123	64	33,396	8,080	24.2	22,450	67.2	2,399	-------	383	84
35 to 44 years	22,847	5,017	22.0	16,464	72.1	1,112	4.9	193	61	22,299	3,251	14.6	14,411	64.6	4,309	19.3	274	54
45 to 54 years	10,852	1,671	15.4	7,971	73.5	1,093	10.1	83	34	10,537	1,139	10.8	5,234	49.7	4,036	38.3	95	33
55 to 64 years	3,123	389	12.5	2,146	68.7	552	17.7	20	16	3,460	307	8.9	1,073	31.0	2,047	59.2	17	16
65 years and over	987	92	9.3	561	56.8	328	33.2	2	4	1,885	150	8.0	262	13.9	1,463	77.6	2	8
Queens Borough																		
Total	**6,034**	**1,609**	**26.7**	**4,161**	**69.0**	**230**	**3.8**	**26**	**8**	**7,686**	**1,893**	**24.6**	**4,562**	**59.4**	**1,159**	**15.1**	**65**	**7**
15 to 19 years	545	531	97.4	12	2.2	1	.2	-------	1	790	678	85.8	109	13.8	2	.3	1	-------
20 to 24 years	792	466	58.8	320	40.4	2	.3	2	2	1,222	518	42.4	673	55.1	21	1.7	8	2
25 to 34 years	1,736	344	19.8	1,358	78.2	24	1.4	9	1	2,273	411	18.1	1,698	74.7	144	6.3	19	1
35 to 44 years	1,514	163	10.8	1,290	85.2	50	3.3	11	-------	1,761	164	9.3	1,290	73.3	284	16.1	21	2
45 to 54 years	926	65	7.0	792	85.5	65	7.0	3	1	969	75	7.7	577	59.5	305	31.5	12	-------
55 to 64 years	352	32	9.1	283	80.4	37	10.5	-------	-------	407	25	6.1	165	40.5	212	52.1	3	2
65 years and over	149	6	4.0	93	62.4	49	32.9	1	-------	248	17	6.9	40	16.1	190	76.6	1	-------
Richmond Borough																		
Total	**910**	**333**	**36.6**	**510**	**56.0**	**57**	**6.3**	**5**	**5**	**929**	**287**	**30.9**	**528**	**56.8**	**101**	**10.9**	**9**	**4**
15 to 19 years	73	71	-------	1	-------	-------	-------	-------	1	101	86	85.1	15	14.9	-------	-------	-------	-------
20 to 24 years	108	74	68.5	33	30.6	1	.9	-------	-------	135	61	45.2	71	52.6	1	.7	1	1
25 to 34 years	270	91	33.7	171	63.3	5	1.9	-------	3	291	86	39.6	190	65.3	10	3.4	3	2
35 to 44 years	197	44	22.3	141	71.6	8	4.1	4	-------	209	32	15.3	144	68.9	29	13.9	4	-------
45 to 54 years	145	29	20.0	106	73.1	9	6.2	1	-------	126	15	11.9	80	63.5	30	23.8	1	-------
55 to 64 years	64	12	-------	34	-------	17	-------	-------	1	38	4	-------	18	-------	16	-------	-------	-------
65 years and over	52	12	-------	23	-------	17	-------	-------	-------	28	3	-------	9	-------	15	-------	-------	1

TABLE 16.—MARITAL CONTITION OF THE NEGRO POPULATION 15 YEARS OLD AND OVER, BY SEX, AND 5-YEAR AGE PERIODS FOR CITIES HAVING 10,000 OR MORE NEGRO INHABITANTS: 1930—Continued

CITY AND AGE	MALES 15 YEARS OLD AND OVER									FEMALES 15 YEARS OLD AND OVER								
	Total	Single		Married		Widowed		Divorced	Unknown	Total	Single		Married		Widowed		Divorced	Unknown
		Number	Percent	Number	Percent	Number	Percent				Number	Percent	Number	Percent	Number	Percent		
NORFOLK, VA.																		
Total	**15,236**	**5,149**	**33.8**	**8,950**	**58.7**	**959**	**6.3**	**163**	**15**	**17,420**	**4,354**	**25.0**	**9,633**	**55.3**	**3,178**	**18.2**	**246**	**9**
15 to 19 years	1,716	1,662	96.9	52	3.0	1	.1	-	1	2,133	1,795	84.2	329	15.4	4	.2	5	-
20 to 24 years	1,858	1,183	63.7	653	35.1	11	.6	9	2	2,501	1,053	42.1	1,340	53.6	75	3.0	32	1
25 to 34 years	3,614	1,113	30.8	2,369	65.6	82	2.3	48	2	4,569	896	19.6	3,176	69.5	401	8.8	94	2
35 to 44 years	3,745	717	19.1	2,740	73.2	230	6.1	57	1	4,067	402	9.9	2,799	68.8	793	19.5	72	1
45 to 54 years	2,677	336	12.6	1,999	74.7	310	11.6	30	2	2,480	137	5.5	1,440	58.1	872	35.2	31	-
55 to 64 years	1,111	93	8.4	823	74.1	178	16.0	17	-	1,005	41	4.1	426	42.4	528	52.5	10	-
65 years and over	476	38	8.0	291	61.1	144	30.3	2	1	615	21	3.4	106	17.2	485	78.9	2	1
OKLAHOMA CITY, OKLA.																		
Total	**5,580**	**1,507**	**27.0**	**3,481**	**62.4**	**358**	**6.4**	**188**	**46**	**5,827**	**1,063**	**18.2**	**3,522**	**60.4**	**918**	**15.8**	**294**	**30**
15 to 19 years	554	527	95.1	25	4.5	-	-	-	2	733	510	69.6	206	28.1	10	1.4	6	1
20 to 24 years	860	457	53.1	368	42.8	12	1.4	18	5	1,150	319	27.7	723	62.9	57	5.0	47	4
25 to 34 years	1,725	323	18.7	1,280	74.2	55	3.2	57	10	1,839	156	8.5	1,346	73.2	199	10.8	135	3
35 to 44 years	1,225	124	10.1	953	77.8	80	6.5	68	-	1,173	53	4.5	797	67.9	242	20.6	79	2
45 to 54 years	776	55	7.1	570	73.5	110	14.2	33	8	569	19	3.3	339	59.6	185	32.5	23	3
55 to 64 years	298	10	3.4	211	70.8	59	19.8	10	8	194	2	1.0	75	38.7	112	57.7	3	2
65 years and over	125	6	4.8	68	54.4	41	32.8	2	8	153	2	1.3	29	19.0	110	71.9	-	12
OMAHA, NEBR.																		
Total	**4,345**	**1,246**	**28.7**	**2,545**	**58.6**	**375**	**8.6**	**166**	**13**	**4,283**	**663**	**15.5**	**2,575**	**60.1**	**848**	**19.8**	**185**	**12**
15 to 19 years	343	334	97.4	7	2.0	1	.3	-	1	393	297	75.6	89	22.6	3	.8	3	1
20 to 24 years	397	241	60.7	145	36.5	-	-	7	4	522	148	28.4	326	62.5	18	3.4	26	4
25 to 34 years	1,087	316	29.1	695	63.9	42	3.9	33	1	1,169	125	10.7	858	73.4	116	9.9	68	2
35 to 44 years	1,148	195	17.0	805	70.1	79	6.9	67	2	1,087	59	5.4	752	69.2	219	20.1	55	2
45 to 54 years	877	110	12.5	603	68.8	122	13.9	38	4	673	22	3.3	396	58.8	231	34.3	22	2
55 to 64 years	313	28	8.9	200	63.9	71	22.7	14	-	262	9	3.4	103	39.3	140	53.4	10	-
65 years and over	168	13	7.7	87	51.8	60	35.7	7	1	172	2	1.2	48	27.9	120	69.8	1	1
PETERSBURG, VA.																		
Total	**3,946**	**1,337**	**33.9**	**2,327**	**59.0**	**260**	**6.6**	**19**	**3**	**4,997**	**1,383**	**27.7**	**2,466**	**49.3**	**1,072**	**21.5**	**70**	**6**
15 to 19 years	552	537	97.3	15	2.7	-	-	-	-	718	612	85.2	102	14.2	3	.4	-	1
20 to 24 years	505	333	65.9	167	33.1	3	.6	1	1	735	341	46.4	344	46.8	37	5.0	12	1
25 to 34 years	896	248	27.7	619	69.1	25	2.8	3	1	1,171	240	20.5	778	66.4	123	10.5	27	3
35 to 44 years	876	136	15.5	675	77.1	58	6.6	6	1	1,041	102	9.8	686	65.9	232	22.3	21	-
45 to 54 years	688	54	7.8	550	79.9	79	11.5	5	-	728	44	6.0	400	54.9	277	38.0	7	-
55 to 64 years	272	19	7.0	206	75.7	43	15.8	4	-	336	28	8.3	113	33.6	192	57.1	2	1
65 years and over	156	10	6.4	94	60.3	52	33.3	-	-	267	15	5.6	43	16.1	208	77.9	1	-
PHILADELPHIA, PA.																		
Total	**82.123**	**27,428**	**33.4**	**50,037**	**60.9**	**4,068**	**5.0**	**458**	**132**	**83,992**	**20,124**	**24.0**	**51,046**	**60.8**	**11,952**	**14.2**	**754**	**116**
15 to 19 years	7,008	6,801	97.1	184	2.6	3	-	3	17	8,900	7,287	81.9	1,551	17.4	34	.4	13	15
20 to 24 years	9,812	5,974	60.9	3,752	38.2	51	.5	23	12	12,715	4,850	38.1	7,559	59.4	219	1.7	69	18
25 to 34 years	25,485	7,696	30.2	17,140	67.3	483	1.9	136	30	26,334	4,668	17.7	19,621	74.5	1,723	6.5	295	27
35 to 44 years	21,045	4,305	20.5	15,615	74.2	954	4.5	156	15	19,236	1,913	9.9	13,888	72.2	3,168	16.5	245	22
45 to 54 years	12,383	1,896	15.3	9,191	74.2	1,184	9.6	93	19	10,474	898	8.6	6,260	59.8	3,206	30.6	101	9
55 to 64 years	4,478	564	12.6	3,130	69.9	740	16.5	37	7	4,041	322	8.0	1,659	41.1	2,030	50.2	26	4
65 years and over	1,805	161	8.9	984	54.5	648	35.9	9	3	2,165	147	6.8	463	21.4	1,549	71.5	5	1
PITTSBURGH, PA.																		
Total	**21,098**	**7,167**	**34.0**	**12,596**	**59.7**	**1,106**	**5.2**	**202**	**27**	**19,848**	**3,955**	**19.9**	**12,622**	**63.6**	**2,983**	**15.0**	**276**	**12**
15 to 19 years	1,831	1,778	97.1	50	2.7	1	.1	1	1	2,212	1,761	79.6	428	19.3	15	.7	6	2
20 to 24 years	2,357	1,503	63.8	819	34.7	26	1.1	3	6	2,833	904	31.9	1,806	63.7	79	2.8	43	1
25 to 34 years	6,371	1,992	31.3	4,164	65.4	138	2.2	71	6	6,010	773	12.9	4,672	77.7	457	7.6	107	1
35 to 44 years	5,348	1,177	22.0	3,848	72.0	252	4.7	67	4	4,610	305	6.6	3,437	74.6	789	17.1	76	3
45 to 54 years	3,420	526	15.4	2,538	74.2	305	8.9	45	6	2,624	151	5.8	1,687	64.3	753	28.7	31	2
55 to 64 years	1,265	149	11.8	903	71.4	198	15.7	14	1	1,002	37	3.7	475	47.4	480	47.9	9	1
65 years and over	494	40	8.1	267	54.0	185	37.4	1	1	537	23	4.3	107	19.9	405	75.4	2	-
PORT ARTHUR, TEX.																		
Total	**3,538**	**966**	**27.3**	**2,323**	**65.7**	**132**	**3.7**	**117**	-	**3,587**	**587**	**16.4**	**2,388**	**66.6**	**387**	**10.8**	**225**	-
15 to 19 years	363	350	96.4	12	3.3	1	.3	-	-	544	376	69.1	157	28.9	-	-	11	-
20 to 24 years	558	309	55.4	240	43.0	2	.4	7	-	686	110	16.0	515	75.1	18	2.6	43	-
25 to 34 years	1,166	193	16.6	903	77.4	17	1.5	53	-	1,271	80	6.3	1,006	79.2	93	7.3	92	-
35 to 44 years	888	75	8.4	743	83.7	35	3.9	35	-	711	15	2.1	530	74.5	106	14.9	60	-
45 to 54 years	397	28	7.1	318	80.1	32	8.1	19	-	240	4	1.7	146	60.8	78	32.5	12	-
55 to 64 years	115	7	6.1	81	70.4	24	20.9	3	-	84	-	-	27	-	51	-	6	-
65 years and over	46	3	-	23	-	20	-	-	-	46	1	-	5	-	40	-	-	-
PORTSMOUTH, VA.																		
Total	**6,368**	**2,080**	**32.7**	**3,649**	**57.3**	**519**	**8.2**	**79**	**41**	**7,124**	**1,679**	**23.6**	**3,740**	**52.5**	**1,531**	**21.5**	**173**	**1**
15 to 19 years	758	735	97.0	22	2.9	-	-	-	1	891	743	83.4	141	15.8	2	.2	5	-
20 to 24 years	776	489	63.0	276	35.6	4	.5	6	1	999	420	42.0	523	52.4	34	3.4	21	1
25 to 34 years	1,415	409	28.9	919	64.9	56	4.0	15	16	1,829	306	16.7	1,204	65.8	251	13.7	68	-
35 to 44 years	1,508	253	16.8	1,097	72.7	110	7.3	26	22	1,584	128	8.1	1,036	65.4	376	23.7	44	-
45 to 54 years	1,166	139	11.9	851	73.0	153	13.1	23	-	1,089	57	5.2	603	55.4	401	36.8	28	-
55 to 64 years	512	40	7.8	358	69.9	109	21.3	4	1	464	19	4.1	183	39.4	257	55.4	5	-
65 years and over	233	15	6.4	126	54.1	87	37.3	5	-	262	5	1.9	49	18.7	206	78.6	2	-

TABLE 16.—MARITAL CONDITION OF THE NEGRO POPULATION 15 YEARS OLD AND OVER, BY SEX, AND 5-YEAR AGE PERIODS, FOR CITIES HAVING 10,000 OR MORE NEGRO INHABITANTS: 1930—Continued

CITY AND AGE	MALES 15 YEARS OLD AND OVER									FEMALES 15 YEARS OLD AND OVER								
	Total	Single		Married		Widowed		Divorced	Unknown	Total	Single		Married		Widowed		Divorced	Unknown
		Number	Per cent	Number	Per cent	Number	Per cent				Number	Per cent	Number	Per cent	Number	Per cent		
RALEIGH, N. C.																		
Total	**4,072**	**1,506**	**37.0**	**2,254**	**55.4**	**286**	**7.0**	**23**	**3**	**4,937**	**1,552**	**31.4**	**2,337**	**47.3**	**999**	**20.2**	**47**	**2**
15 to 19 years	613	597	97.4	15	2.4	-	-	-	1	756	661	87.4	93	12.3	-	-	2	-
20 to 24 years	667	450	67.5	209	31.3	4	.6	3	1	914	458	50.1	403	44.1	50	5.5	2	1
25 to 34 years	1,062	298	28.1	712	67.0	45	4.2	7	-	1,308	274	20.9	849	64.9	168	12.8	16	1
35 to 44 years	808	104	12.9	636	78.7	64	7.9	4	-	880	87	9.9	558	63.4	221	25.1	14	-
45 to 54 years	522	50	9.6	405	77.6	61	11.7	6	-	594	46	7.7	296	49.8	242	40.7	10	-
55 to 64 years	234	6	2.6	174	74.4	52	22.2	2	-	276	13	4.7	106	38.4	155	56.2	2	-
65 years and over	165	1	.6	103	62.4	60	36.4	1	-	209	13	6.2	32	15.3	163	78.0	1	-
RICHMOND, VA.																		
Total	**17,230**	**5,194**	**30.1**	**10,665**	**61.9**	**1,116**	**6.5**	**248**	**7**	**21,039**	**5,465**	**26.0**	**11,090**	**52.7**	**4,075**	**19.4**	**405**	**4**
15 to 19 years	2,048	1,995	97.4	53	2.6	-	-	-	-	2,856	2,426	84.9	409	14.3	13	.5	8	-
20 to 24 years	2,090	1,227	58.7	831	39.8	16	.8	15	1	2,921	1,252	42.9	1,551	53.1	75	2.6	41	2
25 to 34 years	4,185	1,010	24.1	2,996	71.6	109	2.6	68	2	5,247	944	18.0	3,707	70.6	453	8.6	143	-
35 to 44 years	4,146	575	13.9	3,264	78.7	212	5.1	94	1	4,792	459	9.6	3,208	66.9	994	20.7	130	1
45 to 54 years	2,950	263	8.9	2,300	78.0	339	11.5	48	-	3,077	243	7.9	1,644	53.4	1,122	36.5	68	-
55 to 64 years	1,165	85	7.3	856	73.5	204	17.5	20	-	1,213	69	5.7	445	36.7	689	56.8	10	-
65 years and over	625	34	5.4	352	56.3	236	37.8	3	-	902	64	7.1	116	12.9	716	79.4	5	1
ROANOKE, VA.																		
Total	**4,024**	**1,318**	**32.8**	**2,429**	**60.4**	**216**	**5.4**	**60**	**1**	**4,797**	**1,329**	**27.7**	**2,530**	**52.7**	**820**	**17.1**	**112**	**6**
15 to 19 years	544	534	98.2	10	1.8	-	-	-	-	736	627	85.2	97	13.2	5	.7	6	1
20 to 24 years	532	317	59.6	203	38.2	6	1.1	5	1	773	321	41.5	406	52.5	24	3.1	20	2
25 to 34 years	1,101	305	27.7	760	69.0	22	2.0	14	-	1,291	261	20.2	866	67.1	122	9.5	42	-
35 to 44 years	893	102	11.4	726	81.3	46	5.2	19	-	995	68	6.8	719	72.3	176	17.7	31	1
45 to 54 years	582	43	7.4	465	79.9	58	10.0	16	-	541	30	5.5	310	57.3	190	35.1	10	1
55 to 64 years	248	15	6.0	192	77.4	37	14.9	4	-	248	11	4.4	98	39.5	137	55.2	2	-
65 years and over	119	2	1.7	69	58.0	47	39.5	1	-	205	10	4.9	31	15.1	162	79.0	1	1
ST. LOUIS, MO.																		
Total	**36,134**	**10,902**	**30.2**	**22,140**	**61.3**	**2,563**	**7.1**	**499**	**30**	**37,864**	**7,362**	**19.4**	**22,600**	**59.7**	**7,160**	**18.9**	**716**	**26**
15 to 19 years	3,036	2,888	95.1	142	4.7	3	.1	3	-	3,647	2,745	75.3	863	23.7	32	.9	6	1
20 to 24 years	3,991	2,285	57.3	1,637	41.0	45	1.1	23	1	5,357	1,729	32.3	3,298	61.6	239	4.5	88	3
25 to 34 years	10,135	2,946	29.1	6,768	66.8	277	2.7	141	3	11,426	1,772	15.5	8,246	72.2	1,119	9.8	285	4
35 to 44 years	9,427	1,659	17.6	6,947	73.7	637	6.8	177	7	8,843	720	8.1	6,154	69.6	1,735	19.6	229	5
45 to 54 years	6,143	783	12.7	4,505	73.3	740	12.0	112	3	5,147	271	5.3	3,029	58.8	1,765	34.3	79	3
55 to 64 years	2,315	227	9.8	1,615	69.8	441	19.0	31	1	2,092	71	3.4	787	37.6	1,211	57.9	23	-
63 years and over	1,038	96	9.2	509	49.0	420	40.5	12	1	1,317	42	3.2	212	16.1	1,048	79.6	6	9
SAN ANTONIO, TEX.																		
Total	**6,283**	**1,781**	**28.3**	**3,893**	**62.0**	**376**	**6.0**	**232**	**1**	**7,822**	**1,570**	**20.1**	**4,095**	**52.4**	**1,620**	**20.7**	**535**	**2**
15 to 19 years	728	695	95.5	30	4.1	1	.1	2	-	982	767	78.1	189	19.2	11	1.1	15	-
20 to 24 years	913	471	51.6	403	44.1	14	1.5	25	-	1,216	372	30.6	698	57.4	62	5.1	84	-
25 to 34 years	1,663	337	20.3	1,192	71.7	46	2.8	88	-	2,263	261	11.5	1,490	65.8	306	13.5	206	-
35 to 44 years	1,549	167	10.8	1,224	79.0	84	5.4	74	-	1,716	101	5.9	1,059	61.7	404	23.5	152	-
45 to 54 years	869	66	7.6	681	78.4	91	10.5	31	-	969	44	4.5	500	51.6	372	38.4	53	-
55 to 64 years	357	21	5.9	261	73.1	66	18.5	9	-	390	14	3.6	117	30.0	242	62.1	16	1
65 years and over	197	19	9.6	101	51.3	74	37.6	3	-	279	9	3.2	42	15.1	220	78.9	8	-
SAVANNAH, GA.																		
Total	**13,197**	**4,068**	**30.8**	**7,990**	**60.5**	**1,010**	**7.7**	**115**	**14**	**16,829**	**4,279**	**25.4**	**8,465**	**50.3**	**3,817**	**22.7**	**260**	**8**
15 to 19 years	1,366	1,307	95.7	58	4.2	-	-	-	1	2,162	1,703	78.8	438	20.3	14	0.6	7	-
20 to 24 years	1,903	1,048	55.1	828	43.5	16	.8	7	4	3,079	1,205	39.1	1,698	55.1	141	4.6	35	-
25 to 34 years	3,659	933	25.5	2,562	70.0	128	3.5	31	5	4,879	911	18.7	3,146	64.5	710	14.6	108	4
35 to 44 years	3,186	494	15.5	2,383	74.8	263	8.3	46	-	3,599	292	8.1	2,135	59.3	1,100	30.6	70	2
45 to 54 years	1,979	197	10.0	1,488	75.2	269	13.6	24	1	1,855	104	5.6	786	42.4	935	50.4	30	-
55 to 64 years	723	61	8.4	472	65.3	184	25.4	6	-	740	38	5.1	182	24.6	514	69.5	6	-
65 years and over	351	19	5.4	182	51.9	149	42.5	1	-	492	26	5.3	69	14.0	395	80.3	2	-
SHREVEPORT, LA.																		
Total	**9,157**	**2,581**	**28.2**	**5,778**	**63.1**	**639**	**7.0**	**157**	**2**	**11,704**	**2,552**	**21.8**	**6,157**	**52.6**	**2,563**	**21.9**	**423**	**9**
15 to 19 years	952	907	95.3	42	4.4	2	.2	-	1	1,499	1,148	76.6	298	19.9	36	2.4	16	1
20 to 24 years	1,274	656	51.5	566	44.4	33	2.6	19	-	2,027	654	32.3	1,153	56.9	148	7.3	71	1
25 to 34 years	2,814	629	22.4	2,025	72.0	99	3.5	61	-	3,575	525	14.7	2,352	65.8	521	14.6	175	2
35 to 44 years	2,120	259	12.2	1,663	78.4	156	7.4	42	-	2,434	166	6.8	1,512	62.1	650	26.7	103	3
45 to 54 years	1,278	87	6.8	1,017	79.6	149	11.7	25	-	1,261	33	2.6	634	50.3	545	43.2	47	2
55 to 64 years	462	26	5.6	327	70.8	101	21.9	7	1	483	15	3.1	144	29.8	317	65.6	7	-
65 years and over	251	16	6.4	134	53.4	98	39.0	3	-	410	8	2.0	59	14.4	340	82.9	3	-
TAMPA, FLA.																		
Total	**7,499**	**2,313**	**30.8**	**4,489**	**59.9**	**543**	**7.2**	**148**	**6**	**8,557**	**1,604**	**18.7**	**5,002**	**58.5**	**1,665**	**19.5**	**285**	**1**
15 to 19 years	792	764	96.5	26	3.3	-	-	1	1	1,036	755	72.9	256	24.7	11	1.1	14	-
20 to 24 years	981	561	57.2	392	40.0	18	1.8	8	2	1,466	416	28.4	933	63.6	64	4.4	53	-
25 to 34 years	2,220	553	24.9	1,542	69.5	76	3.4	49	-	2,729	305	11.2	2,010	73.7	311	11.4	103	-
35 to 44 years	1,833	262	14.3	1,371	74.8	145	7.9	53	2	1,788	80	4.5	1,157	64.7	474	26.5	77	-
45 to 54 years	1,131	124	11.0	825	72.9	156	13.8	25	1	1,016	36	3.5	515	50.7	436	42.9	28	1
55 to 64 years	395	36	9.1	252	63.8	100	25.3	7	-	314	8	2.5	96	30.6	203	64.6	7	-
65 years and over	137	11	8.0	73	53.3	48	35.0	5	-	200	3	1.5	31	15.5	163	81.5	3	-

TABLE 16.—MARITAL CONDITION OF THE NEGRO POPULATION 15 YEARS OLD AND OVER, BY SEX, AND 5-YEAR AGE PERIODS, FOR CITIES HAVING 10,000 OR MORE NEGRO INHABITANTS: 1930—Continued

CITY AND AGE	MALES 15 YEARS OLD AND OVER									FEMALES 15 YEARS OLD AND OVER								
	Total	Single		Married		Widowed		Divorced	Unknown	Total	Single		Married		Widowed		Divorced	Unknown
		Number	Per cent	Number	Per cent	Number	Per cent				Number	Per cent	Number	Per cent	Number	Per cent		
TOLEDO, OHIO																		
Total	5,451	1,536	28.2	3,378	62.0	427	7.8	106	4	4,755	668	14.0	3,267	68.7	744	15.6	73	3
15 to 19 years	374	357	95.5	15	4.0	2	.5	-	-	469	310	66.1	149	31.8	8	1.7	2	-
20 to 24 years	601	325	54.1	267	44.4	4	.7	5	-	729	154	21.1	515	70.6	46	6.3	14	-
25 to 34 years	1,692	441	26.1	1,150	68.0	77	4.6	23	1	1,546	124	8.0	1,243	80.4	149	9.6	30	-
35 to 44 years	1,457	267	18.3	1,019	69.9	133	9.1	36	2	1,125	56	5.0	854	75.9	196	17.4	19	-
45 to 54 years	893	106	11.9	644	72.1	110	12.3	33	-	544	16	2.9	372	68.4	150	27.6	6	-
55 to 64 years	298	29	9.7	204	68.5	58	19.5	6	1	206	5	2.4	101	49.0	99	48.1	-	1
65 years and over	131	9	6.9	77	58.8	42	32.1	3	-	129	2	1.6	30	23.3	93	72.1	2	2
TULSA, OKLA.																		
Total	5,719	1,365	23.9	3,576	62.5	559	9.8	214	5	6,383	1,058	16.6	3,704	58.0	1,262	19.8	358	1
15 to 19 years	492	463	94.1	26	5.3	1	.2	2	-	679	454	66.9	199	29.3	21	3.1	5	-
20 to 24 years	791	394	49.8	364	46.0	19	2.4	13	1	1,154	287	24.9	731	63.3	85	7.4	51	-
25 to 34 years	1,851	341	18.4	1,320	71.3	108	5.8	79	3	2,302	241	10.5	1,574	68.4	320	13.9	167	-
35 to 44 years	1,440	109	7.6	1,100	76.4	159	11.0	72	-	1,292	55	4.3	790	61.1	345	26.7	101	1
45 to 54 years	743	44	5.9	526	70.8	133	17.9	40	-	584	15	2.6	304	52.1	236	40.4	29	-
55 to 64 years	266	11	4.1	178	66.9	71	26.7	6	-	229	3	1.3	82	35.8	142	62.0	2	-
65 years and over	131	1	.8	61	46.6	67	51.1	2	-	141	2	1.4	24	17.0	112	79.4	3	-
VICKSBURG, MISS.[1]																		
Total	3,954	1,057	26.7	2,565	64.9	255	6.4	74	3	5,333	1,063	19.9	2,787	52.3	1,213	22.7	264	6
WASHINGTON, D. C.																		
Total	47,443	15,925	33.6	23,212	59.5	2,714	5.7	342	250	54,297	14,058	25.9	29,942	55.1	9,556	17.6	530	211
15 to 19 years	4,757	4,591	96.5	156	3.3	1	-	1	8	5,918	4,862	82.2	1,028	17.4	14	.2	2	12
20 to 24 years	6,472	3,983	61.5	2,432	37.6	22	.3	11	24	7,934	3,303	41.6	4,424	55.8	143	1.8	42	22
25 to 34 years	12,883	3,846	29.9	8,668	67.3	251	1.9	94	24	14,466	2,969	20.5	10,314	71.3	966	6.7	189	28
35 to 44 years	10,290	1,903	18.5	7,739	75.2	516	5.0	118	14	11,427	1,419	12.4	7,838	68.6	1,978	17.3	177	15
45 to 54 years	7,680	1,007	13.1	5,810	75.7	766	10.0	82	15	8,184	870	10.6	4,462	54.5	2,765	33.8	82	5
55 to 64 years	3,240	372	11.5	2,312	71.4	524	16.2	29	3	3,546	365	10.3	1,366	38.5	1,783	50.3	26	6
65 years and over	1,801	170	9.4	991	55.0	627	34.8	7	6	2,490	213	8.6	404	16.2	1,859	74.7	7	7
WILMINGTON, DEL.																		
Total	4,777	1,864	39.0	2,548	53.3	324	6.8	31	10	4,687	1,293	27.6	2,622	55.9	733	15.6	37	2
15 to 19 years	381	369	96.9	10	2.6	-	-	1	1	505	442	87.5	60	11.9	1	.2	1	1
20 to 24 years	544	375	68.9	163	30.0	3	.6	-	3	597	257	43.0	325	54.4	10	1.7	5	-
25 to 34 years	1,269	519	40.9	715	56.3	25	2.0	8	2	1,234	313	25.4	851	69.0	62	5.0	8	-
35 to 44 years	1,192	349	29.3	775	65.0	51	4.3	15	2	1,068	168	15.7	750	70.2	139	13.0	11	-
45 to 54 years	791	165	20.9	535	67.6	87	11.0	4	-	705	74	10.5	425	60.3	195	27.7	11	-
55 to 64 years	375	65	17.3	230	61.3	77	20.5	2	1	345	28	8.1	151	43.8	164	47.5	1	1
65 years and over	221	20	9.0	119	53.8	81	36.7	1	-	231	11	4.8	58	25.1	162	70.1	-	-
WILMINGTON, N. C.																		
Total	3,930	1,419	36.1	2,256	57.4	240	6.1	13	2	5,197	1,565	30.1	2,513	48.4	1,076	20.7	40	3
15 to 19 years	578	572	99.0	6	1.0	-	-	-	-	803	687	85.6	115	14.3	1	.1	-	-
20 to 24 years	560	347	62.0	210	37.5	3	.5	-	-	805	391	48.6	392	48.7	21	2.6	1	-
25 to 34 years	929	290	31.2	613	66.0	20	2.2	4	2	1,261	285	22.6	831	65.9	124	9.8	20	1
35 to 44 years	848	134	15.8	653	77.0	55	6.5	6	-	1,104	114	10.3	705	63.9	271	24.5	12	2
45 to 54 years	594	55	9.3	480	80.8	56	9.4	3	-	693	54	7.8	342	49.4	294	42.4	3	-
55 to 64 years	272	11	4.0	207	76.1	54	19.9	-	-	289	20	6.9	97	33.6	168	58.1	4	-
65 years and over	148	9	6.1	87	58.8	52	35.1	-	-	238	13	5.5	30	12.6	195	81.9	-	-
WINSTON-SALEM, N. C.																		
Total	10,743	3,886	36.2	6,254	58.2	563	5.2	39	1	12,771	3,717	29.1	6,943	54.4	2,040	16.0	66	5
15 to 19 years	1,476	1,433	97.1	42	2.8	-	-	1	-	2,025	1,659	81.9	354	17.5	9	.4	3	-
20 to 24 years	1,931	1,115	57.7	799	41.4	14	.7	3	-	2,749	1,131	41.1	1,518	55.2	89	3.2	8	3
25 to 34 years	3,377	862	25.5	2,404	71.2	96	2.8	14	1	3,856	700	18.2	2,661	69.0	463	12.0	32	-
35 to 44 years	2,079	310	14.9	1,610	77.4	148	7.1	11	-	2,231	155	6.9	1,502	67.3	559	25.1	14	1
45 to 54 years	1,120	111	9.9	870	77.7	131	11.7	8	-	1,164	47	4.0	652	56.0	457	39.3	7	1
55 to 64 years	503	41	8.2	366	72.8	94	18.7	2	-	494	16	3.2	208	42.1	268	54.3	2	-
65 years and over	257	14	5.4	163	63.4	80	31.1	-	-	251	8	3.2	48	19.1	195	77.7	-	-
YOUNGSTOWN, OHIO																		
Total	5,474	1,638	29.9	3,401	62.1	332	6.1	99	4	4,721	709	15.0	3,327	70.5	601	12.7	82	2
15 to 19 years	451	438	97.1	13	2.9	-	-	-	-	548	402	73.4	143	26.1	1	.2	2	-
20 to 24 years	664	390	58.7	258	38.9	10	1.5	6	-	729	144	19.8	542	74.3	26	3.6	17	-
25 to 34 years	1,805	466	25.8	1,259	69.8	50	2.8	29	1	1,653	104	6.3	1,384	83.7	131	7.9	33	1
35 to 44 years	1,454	218	15.0	1,110	76.3	91	6.3	35	-	1,039	35	3.4	851	81.9	136	13.1	17	-
45 to 54 years	756	87	11.5	559	73.9	86	11.4	22	2	496	17	3.4	316	63.7	153	30.8	10	-
55 to 64 years	223	28	12.6	145	65.0	47	21.1	3	-	169	6	3.6	72	42.6	89	52.7	2	-
65 years and over	110	8	7.3	51	46.4	47	42.7	4	-	82	-	-	17	-	65	-	-	-

[1] Not shown by age group for cities less than 25,000 in population.

TABLE 17.—PERCENT DISTRIBUTION BY MARITAL CONDITION OF THE NEGRO POPULATION 15 YEARS OLD AND OVER, BY SEX, FOR CITIES HAVING 10,000 OR MORE NEGRO INHABITANTS: 1930 AND 1920

[Percent not available in 1920 for cities under 25,000 population at that census]

CITY	MALES 15 YEARS OLD AND OVER								FEMALES 15 YEARS OLD AND OVER							
	Single		Married		Widowed		Divorced		Single		Married		Widowed		Divorced	
	1930	1920	1930	1920	1930	1920	1930	1920	1930	1920	1930	1920	1930	1920	1930	1920
Akron, Ohio	31.7	48.1	60.9	47.5	5.0	3.5	2.0	0.8	17.1	15.7	68.9	74.2	11.5	8.7	2.4	1.4
Asheville, N. C	30.7	29.1	62.9	63.5	5.5	6.0	.7	.6	26.4	29.2	54.6	50.4	17.7	18.2	1.2	1.3
Atlanta, Ga	30.4	29.7	61.4	62.6	6.9	7.4	1.2	.2	24.5	20.3	49.2	55.0	23.1	24.1	3.1	.5
Atlantic City, N. J	34.9	34.4	57.3	58.3	6.9	7.0	.7	.2	23.8	25.2	55.0	54.1	20.2	20.2	.8	.5
Augusta, Ga	27.8	29.7	62.0	61.9	9.0	7.8	1.2	.4	23.0	21.5	49.0	55.5	25.9	21.8	2.0	1.1
Baltimore, Md	34.9	34.7	57.4	58.2	6.2	6.3	.9	.7	24.9	25.9	57.3	56.4	15.8	16.8	1.3	.8
Baton Rouge, La	31.9	--------	60.8	--------	5.1	--------	2.1	--------	27.0	--------	47.7	--------	20.0	--------	5.4	--------
Beaumont, Tex	27.4	31.3	61.0	60.6	7.2	6.0	4.3	2.1	17.9	18.5	58.5	62.7	16.5	14.3	7.0	4.6
Bessemer, Ala	30.9	--------	58.6	--------	9.4	--------	1.1	--------	20.8	--------	53.9	--------	23.9	--------	1.5	--------
Birmingham, Ala	29.2	29.2	61.3	62.7	7.5	6.8	1.8	1.1	20.5	18.6	55.2	60.5	21.0	18.5	3.2	2.3
Boston, Mass	38.2	39.4	53.7	53.5	6.0	5.2	1.7	.9	25.7	25.8	54.0	53.7	17.8	19.3	2.2	.8
Buffalo, N. Y	36.6	41.2	58.9	53.7	3.7	3.8	.8	.5	17.7	18.3	67.9	67.5	12.7	12.8	1.6	1.0
Camden, N. J	32.9	31.2	59.9	61.3	6.7	7.0	.4	.2	23.1	20.9	62.1	62.8	14.1	15.8	.6	.3
Charleston, S. C	28.6	29.7	64.4	64.1	6.0	5.8	.9	.2	26.6	24.5	47.9	53.8	23.4	21.1	2.1	.4
Charlotte, N. C	30.2	30.9	61.7	62.0	6.7	6.9	.6	.1	26.5	26.1	53.3	53.9	18.9	19.5	1.0	.3
Chattanooga, Tenn	28.5	33.4	62.2	58.2	7.6	6.9	1.6	1.4	19.7	19.1	57.3	61.2	19.8	18.2	3.1	1.5
Chicago, Ill	30.2	34.4	60.7	58.1	6.9	6.3	2.1	1.0	16.8	17.6	61.1	61.8	19.0	18.9	3.0	1.6
Cincinnati, Ohio	30.2	32.4	62.5	60.7	5.9	5.8	1.3	.9	18.0	19.5	64.8	62.8	15.2	16.3	1.9	1.3
Cleveland, Ohio	30.1	35.6	61.8	59.2	6.0	4.0	2.0	.9	17.1	16.2	64.2	70.1	15.9	12.4	2.8	1.2
Columbia, S. C	34.2	35.8	59.1	58.5	6.0	5.2	.4	.4	29.2	26.3	49.3	52.1	20.1	20.2	1.4	1.3
Columbus, Ga	28.7	31.3	63.0	61.7	8.0	6.4	.3	.6	23.8	23.5	48.2	52.4	27.3	23.1	.6	1.0
Columbus, Ohio	29.4	35.1	61.5	57.8	6.2	5.2	2.8	1.6	17.2	19.5	64.7	64.6	14.3	13.8	3.8	2.1
Dallas, Tex	24.7	30.7	63.2	57.4	8.6	9.2	3.4	2.7	16.6	15.8	56.8	59.2	19.8	20.3	6.7	4.6
Dayton, Ohio	29.4	33.7	61.4	58.1	6.7	5.6	2.4	2.5	17.9	16.4	64.3	67.3	14.9	13.8	2.8	2.4
Detroit, Mich	30.4	38.3	62.7	57.1	4.8	3.6	2.0	1.0	15.4	14.5	68.7	74.2	13.3	10.0	2.5	1.2
Durham, N. C	34.0	--------	59.6	--------	4.8	--------	1.6	--------	29.7	--------	53.3	--------	14.7	--------	2.3	--------
East St. Louis, Ill	27.9	31.4	63.1	60.1	8.0	7.7	.8	.8	18.0	16.7	63.5	69.3	17.0	12.7	1.2	1.2
Fort Worth, Tex	23.9	33.6	64.4	58.8	8.2	5.3	3.3	1.8	15.4	19.9	60.4	60.7	19.2	15.9	4.8	3.3
Galveston, Tex	27.0	36.0	59.4	53.5	6.1	6.3	7.3	3.8	17.6	19.5	57.2	56.0	15.7	18.4	9.4	6.0
Gary, Ind	29.4	36.4	63.4	58.9	5.4	3.8	1.7	.8	14.5	13.5	69.9	75.0	13.9	10.2	1.7	1.3
Greensboro, N. C	36.2	--------	57.9	--------	5.4	--------	.5	--------	29.8	--------	52.2	--------	16.8	--------	1.1	--------
Greenville, S. C	29.3	--------	62.8	--------	7.5	--------	.2	--------	24.4	--------	54.4	--------	20.8	--------	.2	--------
Houston, Tex	27.0	29.0	61.6	60.2	7.3	7.2	3.9	3.4	17.8	18.0	57.6	59.3	18.0	17.1	6.4	5.4
Indianapolis, Ind	27.9	29.7	62.0	61.0	7.6	7.2	2.2	1.5	17.9	17.5	59.3	61.7	20.1	18.3	2.5	1.8
Jackson, Miss	31.2	--------	16.3	--------	5.3	--------	1.7	--------	22.9	--------	58.2	--------	14.6	--------	3.7	--------
Jacksonville, Fla	27.3	28.9	63.8	63.3	7.7	7.2	1.1	.5	18.7	18.5	58.3	63.2	20.7	17.4	2.3	.9
Jersey City, N. J	33.2	33.5	61.6	61.3	4.5	4.9	.6	.3	19.7	20.0	63.9	63.8	15.5	15.4	.8	.6
Kansas City, Kans	22.9	26.6	66.2	64.2	7.4	6.5	3.3	2.6	16.0	16.1	62.9	64.2	17.0	17.2	4.1	2.5
Kansas City, Mo	28.4	33.8	59.5	56.4	9.3	7.6	2.5	1.9	18.3	20.1	55.7	58.1	22.6	19.0	3.2	2.7
Knoxville, Tenn	32.9	30.7	59.8	61.3	5.6	7.0	1.3	.9	23.6	22.9	55.8	58.5	17.5	17.1	2.7	1.5
Lexington, Ky	32.7	32.3	56.7	57.9	8.1	7.7	2.4	1.7	20.7	22.2	54.1	53.3	22.0	22.3	3.2	2.0
Little Rock, Ark	27.2	30.8	61.3	58.8	8.6	7.5	2.8	2.4	21.0	20.3	50.6	55.2	22.4	20.2	5.9	3.8
Los Angeles, Calif	28.9	29.9	61.4	61.8	6.0	6.2	3.6	1.9	17.4	18.1	56.9	58.0	20.1	20.8	5.6	3.1
Louisville, Ky	29.5	33.3	58.3	56.8	9.5	7.5	2.7	2.3	20.3	22.1	54.2	52.5	22.3	22.3	3.1	3.0
Macon, Ga	28.4	27.3	62.9	66.3	7.0	5.7	1.6	.6	22.9	17.5	50.1	59.5	23.6	22.0	3.1	.9
Memphis, Tenn	27.6	30.5	62.0	60.1	8.0	7.9	2.0	1.2	19.8	19.7	54.9	56.0	21.7	21.7	3.3	2.5
Meridian, Miss	28.3	--------	62.6	--------	7.2	--------	1.8	--------	24.1	--------	49.6	--------	22.3	--------	3.9	--------
Miami, Fla	28.1	34.2	65.6	59.8	5.2	3.8	1.1	1.9	18.4	21.8	64.3	61.6	15.0	13.6	2.3	2.9
Mobile, Ala	30.3	29.1	60.5	62.0	7.5	6.8	1.5	1.9	23.3	20.8	51.6	54.5	22.0	21.4	2.8	3.2
Monroe, La	30.2	--------	61.9	--------	7.1	--------	.7	--------	17.8	--------	59.2	--------	20.9	--------	2.0	--------
Montgomery, Ala	31.0	27.0	60.8	64.4	6.5	7.1	1.6	1.5	24.8	23.0	47.8	49.4	23.8	24.1	3.4	3.6
Nashville, Tenn	29.2	27.6	60.5	61.4	7.9	8.9	2.3	1.9	22.9	22.3	50.6	51.3	22.0	23.3	4.3	3.0
Newark, N. J	31.4	31.1	63.6	62.8	4.3	5.0	.5	.7	19.6	21.0	65.3	64.3	14.1	14.1	1.0	.5
New Orleans, La	30.6	33.3	63.0	60.6	5.3	5.2	1.0	.6	23.3	24.7	55.6	53.7	19.2	20.1	1.9	1.2
Newport News, Va	34.0	44.0	56.4	52.2	7.7	3.2	1.9	.4	23.5	23.5	55.1	64.4	18.7	11.1	2.6	1.0
New York, N. Y	35.3	36.0	59.9	58.4	4.0	4.1	.5	.3	26.6	29.0	57.2	54.6	15.0	15.6	.9	.5
Bronx Borough	30.3	30.9	65.7	62.2	3.4	6.5	.3	.2	27.5	32.7	60.0	51.9	11.6	15.0	.6	.3
Brooklyn Borough	32.2	35.2	63.5	59.5	3.5	4.4	.4	.3	25.5	28.9	59.2	54.3	14.1	15.8	.7	.6
Manhattan Borough	37.0	36.6	58.0	57.8	4.2	3.9	.5	.2	27.0	28.8	56.3	55.0	15.5	15.6	.9	.5
Queens Borough	26.7	30.5	69.0	64.2	3.8	4.8	.4	.2	24.6	29.9	59.4	51.6	15.1	17.5	.8	.5
Richmond Borough	36.6	41.5	56.0	51.6	6.3	4.6	.5	.5	30.9	35.5	56.8	53.7	10.9	9.9	1.0	.7
Norfolk, Va	33.8	36.2	58.7	57.2	6.3	5.8	1.1	.8	25.0	24.1	55.3	59.2	18.2	15.6	1.4	1.1
Oklahoma City, Okla	27.0	31.6	62.4	58.5	6.4	7.8	3.4	2.0	18.2	19.8	60.4	60.4	15.8	16.5	5.0	3.2
Omaha, Nebr	28.7	36.0	58.6	56.4	8.6	5.7	3.8	1.7	15.5	14.9	60.1	67.9	19.8	14.6	4.3	2.5
Petersburg, Va	33.9	32.7	59.0	60.9	6.6	6.0	.5	.4	27.7	30.2	49.3	51.6	21.5	17.5	1.4	.6
Philadelphia, Pa	33.4	34.5	60.9	60.1	5.0	5.0	.6	.3	24.0	24.2	60.8	60.7	14.2	14.6	.9	.4
Pittsburgh, Pa	34.0	35.3	59.7	59.1	5.2	5.0	1.0	.3	19.9	19.6	63.6	66.1	15.0	13.6	1.4	.7
Port Arthur, Tex	27.3	--------	65.7	--------	3.7	--------	3.3	--------	16.4	--------	66.6	--------	10.8	--------	6.3	--------
Portsmouth, Va	32.7	35.1	57.3	57.6	8.2	6.8	1.2	.5	23.6	21.5	52.5	59.8	21.5	18.0	2.4	.7
Raleigh, N. C	37.0	--------	55.4	--------	7.0	--------	.6	--------	31.4	--------	47.3	--------	20.2	--------	1.0	--------
Richmond, Va	30.1	32.2	61.9	60.3	6.5	5.6	1.4	.7	26.0	29.0	52.7	50.9	19.4	18.0	1.9	1.1
Roanoke, Va	32.8	33.5	60.4	61.2	5.4	4.6	1.5	.7	27.7	28.8	52.7	53.9	17.1	15.7	2.3	1.4
St. Louis, Mo	30.2	34.7	61.3	57.7	7.1	6.5	1.4	1.0	19.4	19.4	59.7	60.3	18.9	18.7	1.9	1.3
San Antonio, Tex	28.3	29.8	62.0	62.0	6.0	5.4	3.7	2.7	20.1	20.1	52.4	56.3	20.7	18.7	6.8	4.9
Savannah, Ga	30.8	30.8	60.5	63.0	7.7	5.6	.9	.5	25.4	22.7	50.3	59.7	22.7	17.0	1.5	.6
Shreveport, La	28.2	30.2	63.1	61.6	7.0	7.0	1.7	.9	21.8	20.2	52.6	55.4	21.9	21.5	3.6	2.8
Tampa, Fla	30.8	36.1	59.9	55.1	7.2	7.2	2.0	1.3	18.7	21.1	58.5	55.5	19.5	21.1	3.3	2.3
Toledo, Ohio	28.2	37.2	62.0	57.0	7.8	4.1	1.9	1.7	14.0	16.9	68.7	70.0	15.6	11.8	1.5	1.3
Tulsa, Okla	23.9	29.7	62.5	61.7	9.8	6.4	3.7	2.1	16.6	23.1	58.0	59.8	19.8	13.7	5.6	3.3
Vicksburg, Miss	26.7	--------	64.9	--------	6.4	--------	1.9	--------	19.9	--------	52.3	--------	22.7	--------	5.0	--------
Washington, D. C	33.6	34.3	59.5	58.6	5.7	6.1	.7	.5	25.9	28.5	55.1	51.0	17.6	19.5	1.0	.7
Wilmington, Del	39.0	39.9	53.3	52.2	6.8	7.2	.6	.4	27.6	28.2	55.9	55.4	15.6	15.7	.8	.6
Wilmington, N. C	36.1	32.8	57.4	60.4	6.1	6.0	.3	.3	30.1	25.4	48.4	52.7	20.7	20.7	.8	.9
Winston-Salem, N. C	36.2	41.2	58.2	53.6	5.2	4.9	.4	.3	29.1	29.9	54.4	54.5	16.0	15.0	.5	5
Youngstown, Ohio	29.9	40.9	62.1	53.2	6.1	4.4	1.8	.7	15.0	15.8	70.5	73.3	12.7	9.8	1.7	[illegible]

Table 18.—MARITAL CONDITION OF THE NEGRO POPULATION 15 YEARS OLD AND OVER, BY SEX, FOR CITIES HAVING 5,000 TO 10,000 NEGRO INHABITANTS: 1930

CITY	MALES 15 YEARS OLD AND OVER						FEMALES 15 YEARS OLD AND OVER					
	Total	Single	Married	Widowed	Divorced	Unknown	Total	Single	Married	Widowed	Divorced	Unknown
Albany, Ga.	2,181	556	1,415	142	63	5	3,280	616	1,617	779	265	3
Alexandria, La.	3,106	944	1,917	213	28	4	3,777	845	2,053	759	118	2
Anniston, Ala.	2,277	651	1,406	176	44	--------	2,731	614	1,452	581	84	--------
Athens, Ga.	1,848	594	1,088	155	11	--------	2,672	777	1,157	716	22	--------
Austin, Tex.	3,159	879	1,854	224	127	75	4,307	938	2,056	831	348	134
Brunswick, Ga.	2,098	583	1,308	169	34	4	2,506	540	1,414	513	36	3
Cambridge, Mass.	1,736	588	1,029	92	26	1	2,005	546	1,104	326	29	--------
Charleston, W. Va.	2,431	892	1,362	148	29	--------	2,717	681	1,526	437	73	--------
Chester, Pa.	3,592	1,426	1,914	188	33	31	3,187	764	1,958	409	44	12
Clarksdale, Miss.	1,750	380	1,197	162	10	1	2,297	440	1,345	479	32	1
Danville, Va.	1,588	424	1,029	112	16	7	2,332	626	1,115	553	30	8
Daytona Beach, Fla.	1,754	489	1,111	130	24	--------	2,245	491	1,230	481	42	1
Denver, Colo.	2,730	674	1,694	255	102	5	3,133	488	1,746	778	116	5
Des Moines, Iowa	1,913	510	1,187	143	72	1	2,049	340	1,216	389	104	--------
Dothan, Ala.	1,845	665	1,010	113	51	6	2,223	598	1,037	429	156	3
East Chicago, Ind.	2,051	660	1,271	71	45	4	1,702	235	1,227	192	47	1
Evansville, Ind.	2,576	944	1,362	210	57	3	2,634	680	1,397	484	67	6
Fairfield, Ala.	2,152	655	1,345	99	53	--------	2,264	470	1,390	321	83	--------
Fayetteville, N. C.	1,567	596	883	75	11	2	2,146	754	975	384	29	4
Flint, Mich.	2,321	727	1,458	77	57	2	1,894	227	1,427	181	58	1
Florence, S. C.	1,681	493	1,085	78	25	--------	2,437	661	1,216	493	66	1
Gadsden, Ala.	2,214	675	1,293	137	108	1	2,251	442	1,290	390	128	1
Goldsboro, N. C.	2,040	694	1,220	109	17	--------	2,552	661	1,334	532	25	--------
Greenville, Miss.	2,996	993	1,807	143	47	6	3,602	1,035	1,950	558	53	6
Greenwood, Miss.	1,776	457	1,216	94	8	1	2,397	488	1,392	455	60	2
Harrisburg, Pa.	2,412	823	1,426	149	12	2	2,336	529	1,457	326	22	2
Hartford, Conn.	2,172	648	1,386	105	28	5	2,321	459	1,461	349	48	4
Hattiesburg, Miss.	2,091	507	1,375	114	94	1	2,701	509	1,537	403	251	1
High Point, N. C.	2,482	927	1,426	117	11	1	2,659	784	1,513	337	24	1
Jackson, Tenn.	2,528	759	1,528	211	30	--------	3,167	706	1,613	762	81	5
Kinston, N. C.	1,481	498	843	101	38	1	2,016	566	902	426	120	2
Lafayette, La.	1,468	551	828	83	6	--------	1,807	543	908	317	38	1
La Grange, Ga.	1,661	530	939	189	3	--------	2,116	547	988	565	15	1
Lake Charles, La.	1,836	491	1,158	109	77	1	2,210	479	1,238	312	181	--------
Laurel, Miss.	2,192	532	1,444	193	23	--------	2,684	472	1,582	575	55	--------
Lynchburg, Va.	2,854	924	1,682	205	43	--------	4,077	1,288	1,834	876	73	6
Marshall, Tex.	2,133	647	1,286	148	52	--------	2,679	611	1,314	614	140	--------
Milwaukee, Wis.	3,156	1,060	1,798	215	78	5	2,548	353	1,740	365	88	2
Montclair, N. J.	1,988	521	1,378	69	19	1	2,980	930	1,558	451	40	1
Muskogee, Okla.	2,213	588	1,379	168	73	5	2,678	556	1,452	521	146	3
Natchez, Miss.	2,147	639	1,341	133	30	4	3,270	858	1,638	651	122	1
New Bern, N. C.	1,939	674	1,083	162	19	1	2,467	616	1,211	604	35	1
New Haven, Conn.	1,935	617	1,174	119	23	2	1,957	404	1,204	305	42	2
North Little Rock, Ark.	2,119	638	1,267	189	18	7	2,324	455	1,319	516	32	2
Oakland, Calif.	3,050	956	1,724	159	155	56	3,019	510	1,735	574	181	19
Orange, N. J.	1,682	584	1,032	59	7	--------	1,996	528	1,104	342	21	1
Orlando, Fla.	2,468	664	1,609	156	33	6	3,073	601	1,782	579	84	27
Paducah, Ky.	2,502	812	1,397	265	25	3	2,767	618	1,390	704	52	3
Pensacola, Fla.	3,208	923	2,009	222	51	3	3,965	851	2,195	795	114	10
Pine Bluff, Ark.	1,986	491	1,267	167	61	--------	2,738	517	1,398	646	177	--------
Providence, R. I.	1,827	621	1,029	146	27	4	1,970	508	1,016	372	73	1
Rocky Mount, N. C.	2,549	808	1,568	164	8	1	3,214	877	1,683	625	22	7
St. Petersburg, Fla.	2,296	701	1,492	95	8	--------	3,039	711	1,690	574	63	1
Selma, Ala.	2,671	802	1,610	231	27	1	4,126	1,099	1,748	1,184	94	1
Spartansburg, S. C.	2,920	964	1,783	164	6	3	3,823	1,071	1,962	766	18	6
Springfield, Ohio	3,036	865	1,901	200	61	9	2,910	523	1,908	424	49	6
Sumter, S. C.	1,417	422	939	47	9	--------	2,112	539	1,127	422	24	--------
Thomasville, Ga.	1,806	557	1,099	123	27	--------	2,588	633	1,195	675	85	--------
Topeka, Kans.	2,047	520	1,258	164	105	--------	2,280	438	1,318	389	134	1
Trenton, N. J.	3,062	1,029	1,807	203	20	3	2,580	640	1,548	371	14	7
Tuscaloosa, Ala.	2,253	708	1,341	176	24	4	2,929	721	1,392	761	47	8
Valdosta, Ga.	1,971	601	1,209	125	35	1	2,585	541	1,343	582	119	--------
Waco, Tex.	3,200	909	1,864	261	163	3	3,823	798	1,900	771	350	4
Waycross, Ga.	1,746	465	1,149	116	12	4	2,328	531	1,256	495	44	2
West Palm Beach, Fla.	3,262	918	2,116	198	23	7	3,594	647	2,327	569	46	5
Wichita, Kans.	2,054	530	1,284	156	84	--------	2,118	373	1,271	395	79	--------
Wilson, N. C.	1,808	658	1,000	104	46	--------	2,418	730	1,065	478	138	7

TABLE 19.—MARITAL CONDITION OF THE NEGRO POPULATION 15 YEARS OLD AND OVER, BY SEX, FOR CITIES AND OTHER URBAN PLACES HAVING LESS THAN 5,000 NEGRO INHABITANTS: 1930

[Cities having less than 100 Negro inhabitants, omitted]

CITY	MALES 15 YEARS OLD AND OVER						FEMALES 15 YEARS OLD AND OVER					
	Total	Single	Married	Widowed	Divorced	Unknown	Total	Single	Married	Widowed	Divorced	Unknown
Abbeville, La.	342	120	186	29	6	1	399	116	199	71	13	----
Abbeville, S. C.	407	134	239	33	1	----	626	197	268	158	3	----
Aberdeen, Miss.	570	172	318	43	37	----	771	188	339	153	91	----
Abilene, Kans.	44	18	22	3	1	----	46	13	20	11	2	----
Abilene, Tex.	525	108	380	20	17	----	568	81	399	59	29	----
Abingdon, Va.	177	61	100	16	----	----	203	65	99	39	----	----
Abington, Pa.	438	131	282	23	2	----	498	123	299	72	3	1
Ada, Okla.	161	36	109	5	11	----	179	21	114	24	19	1
Adrian, Mich.	48	10	28	5	5	----	47	7	28	7	5	----
Aiken, S. C.	1,061	338	650	73	----	----	1,412	382	735	292	3	----
Alabama City, Ala.	163	58	92	12	1	----	172	43	91	37	1	----
Alameda, Calif.	85	31	50	2	2	----	106	25	57	14	10	----
Alamo Heights, Tex.	33	14	14	1	4	----	71	18	28	8	17	----
Albany, N. Y.	971	359	559	46	6	1	923	203	584	129	7	----
Albertville, Ala.	36	9	22	5	----	----	55	17	23	15	----	----
Albion, Mich.	323	94	203	13	9	4	311	65	198	36	8	4
Albuquerque, N. Mex.	167	46	109	6	6	----	159	18	107	28	6	----
Alcoa, Tenn.	602	170	401	29	1	1	499	75	379	43	2	----
Alexander City, Ala.	350	113	213	21	3	----	486	136	220	129	1	----
Alexandria, Va.	1,704	655	961	62	26	----	1,793	453	991	308	41	----
Alice, Tex.	54	16	34	4	----	----	61	21	32	8	----	----
Aliquippa Borough, Pa.	1,032	345	651	30	5	1	781	113	591	74	3	----
Allentown, Pa.	153	56	87	7	3	----	120	18	85	14	3	----
Alliance, Nebr.	73	24	43	2	4	----	65	14	41	6	4	----
Alliance, Ohio	332	102	212	14	4	----	307	47	208	43	9	----
Alton, Ill.	1,032	298	656	59	19	----	945	157	645	116	27	----
Altoona, Pa.	258	98	140	15	5	----	239	44	134	55	6	----
Altus, Okla.	361	110	216	30	3	2	363	57	213	71	21	1
Amarillo, Tex.	702	269	401	19	12	1	669	152	387	97	30	3
Ambler, Pa.	199	77	106	13	3	----	164	38	109	16	1	----
Ambridge, Pa.	54	16	37	1	----	----	41	6	34	1	----	----
Americus, Ga.	1,306	384	784	123	15	----	1,962	482	810	611	58	1
Amherst, Mass.	41	13	25	3	----	----	58	20	24	14	----	----
Amite, La.	252	94	128	17	13	----	283	69	125	65	24	----
Amory, Miss.	301	69	229	3	----	----	379	58	295	26	----	----
Amsterdam, N. Y.	45	14	28	3	----	----	51	15	30	6	----	----
Anaconda, Mont.	45	17	25	2	1	----	32	5	23	3	1	----
Anadarko, Okla.	176	79	90	5	2	----	166	33	96	35	2	----
Anderson, Ind.	512	140	324	23	25	----	480	82	330	49	19	----
Anderson, S. C.	1,100	351	662	85	----	2	1,564	445	821	292	1	5
Andalusia, Ala.	350	117	213	14	6	----	498	138	238	89	33	----
Ann Arbor, Mich.	370	130	204	22	14	----	361	66	221	53	21	----
Annapolis, Md.	1,090	356	640	72	17	5	1,291	336	704	217	32	2
Ansonia, Conn.	419	147	246	20	2	4	318	56	228	34	----	----
Apalachicola, Fla.	452	142	271	36	3	----	516	110	296	105	5	----
Appalachia, Va.	49	13	33	2	1	----	43	10	28	5	----	----
Arcadia, Fla.	413	128	263	21	1	----	424	71	282	67	3	1
Ardmore, Okla.	664	187	410	48	19	----	857	179	444	159	75	----
Arkadelphia, Ark.	192	53	116	15	8	----	231	51	123	41	15	1
Arkansas City, Kans.	203	42	140	12	9	----	211	24	147	33	6	1
Arlington, Tex.	93	22	53	18	----	----	108	22	61	23	1	1
Asbury Park, N. J.	1,309	404	776	111	7	11	1,519	320	843	329	18	9
Ashboro, N. C.	243	113	123	6	1	----	294	120	130	37	6	1
Ashland, Ky.	355	106	214	24	11	----	335	60	220	45	10	----
Ashtabula, Ohio	95	35	53	4	3	----	67	4	51	9	3	----
Atchison, Kans.	591	174	323	67	25	2	591	120	321	124	26	----
Athens, Ala.	241	66	157	11	7	----	374	108	181	73	12	----
Athens, Ohio	59	20	32	5	2	----	73	23	35	13	2	----
Athens, Tenn.	185	53	116	12	4	----	210	47	116	36	11	----
Athens, Tex.	367	108	214	43	2	----	417	74	211	122	10	----
Atmore, Ala.	411	147	227	37	----	----	508	141	247	119	1	----
Attalla, Ala.	395	118	234	37	5	1	413	80	252	73	8	----
Auburn, Ala.	328	114	193	18	3	----	470	157	202	94	17	----
Auburn, N. Y.	233	109	108	13	3	----	135	37	71	24	3	----
Aurora, Ill.	374	143	203	19	8	1	360	72	215	60	12	1
Avalon, Pa.	30	5	22	3	----	----	39	6	27	5	1	----
Avon Park, Fla.	349	86	211	29	23	----	325	40	209	61	15	----
Bainbridge, Ga.	909	319	493	93	4	----	1,222	322	494	398	6	2
Bakersfield, Calif.	332	87	202	29	14	----	329	56	199	67	7	----
Ballinger, Tex.	147	39	96	9	3	----	155	28	90	25	11	1
Bangor, Maine	75	25	43	5	2	----	73	23	39	6	5	----
Barberton, Ohio	361	120	218	18	5	----	285	40	209	29	7	----
Barnesville, Ga.	309	86	193	30	----	----	452	97	263	91	1	----
Barnesville, Ohio	62	27	30	4	1	----	58	15	32	10	1	----
Barnstable, Mass.	175	77	88	6	4	----	123	29	82	10	2	----
Bartlesville, Okla.	233	67	144	11	11	----	250	53	151	31	14	1
Bartow, Fla.	564	159	354	51	----	----	619	130	351	137	1	----
Bossier City, La.	423	165	220	29	9	----	485	152	238	73	22	----
Bastrop, La.	567	155	359	45	8	----	660	145	366	115	33	1
Batavia, Ill.	38	7	29	2	----	----	42	5	31	5	1	----
Batesburg, S. C.	291	93	181	16	1	----	399	125	196	68	9	1
Batesville, Ark.	170	47	102	16	4	1	191	40	105	35	11	----
Battle Creek, Mich.	685	243	394	27	20	1	664	120	411	103	29	1
Baxter Springs, Kans.	63	16	38	1	7	1	81	13	41	23	4	----
Bay City, Mich.	78	26	45	4	3	----	62	18	39	2	3	----
Bay City, Tex.	320	97	190	8	24	1	368	81	197	43	47	----
Bayonne, N. J.	769	249	481	36	3	----	756	170	486	96	4	----
Bay St. Louis, Miss.	317	122	171	13	10	1	395	111	181	88	11	4
Beacon, N. Y.	157	78	73	6	----	----	100	20	68	11	1	----
Beaufort, N. C.	314	127	169	16	2	----	345	110	170	54	11	----

TABLE 19.—MARITAL CONDITION OF THE NEGRO POPULATION 15 YEARS OLD AND OVER, BY SEX, FOR CITIES AND OTHER URBAN PLACES HAVING LESS THAN 5,000 NEGRO INHABITANTS: 1930—Continued

[Cities having less than 100 Negro inhabitants, omitted]

CITY	MALES 15 YEARS OLD AND OVER						FEMALES 15 YEARS OLD AND OVER					
	Total	Single	Married	Widowed	Divorced	Unknown	Total	Single	Married	Widowed	Divorced	Unknown
Beaufort, S. C	351	103	221	26	1	-	593	174	242	160	17	-
Beaver Falls, Pa	251	72	156	12	11	-	243	38	160	42	3	-
Beckley, W. Va	549	190	317	29	13	-	556	142	309	86	19	-
Bedford, Ind	34	5	23	2	4	-	38	7	24	5	2	-
Bedford, Pa	47	16	26	4	1	-	47	14	23	9	1	-
Bedford, Va	284	96	150	30	7	1	359	113	155	81	10	-
Beeville, Tex	104	37	61	4	2	-	128	35	70	20	3	-
Bellaire, Ohio	197	61	122	13	1	-	189	31	129	26	3	-
Bellefontaine, Ohio	124	37	73	11	3	-	136	30	78	22	6	-
Belleville, Ill	96	41	50	4	1	-	58	12	31	12	3	-
Belleville, N. J	345	111	222	12	-	-	346	78	236	31	1	-
Bellevue, Pa	76	28	42	6	-	-	86	21	48	17	-	-
Belmar, N. J	74	25	42	7	-	-	98	21	56	21	-	-
Belmont, N. C	115	41	71	3	-	-	139	45	73	20	1	-
Beloit, Wis	291	78	194	12	6	1	300	59	202	25	14	-
Belton, Tex	220	81	120	16	3	-	218	55	121	38	4	-
Belzoni, Miss	492	151	294	41	5	1	614	128	328	130	26	2
Bennettsville, S. C	416	136	252	27	1	-	622	189	298	134	-	1
Bentleyville, Pa	45	17	25	3	-	-	35	7	26	2	-	-
Benton, Ark	76	18	55	2	1	-	85	11	59	11	4	-
Benton Harbor, Mich	382	104	238	25	15	-	322	36	222	50	14	-
Berea, Ohio	59	18	37	2	2	-	51	14	31	4	2	-
Berkeley, Calif	791	193	542	29	25	2	908	163	561	133	46	5
Bessemer City, N. C	182	69	101	12	-	-	216	61	112	41	2	-
Bethlehem, Pa	257	86	148	14	2	7	234	37	150	40	5	2
Beverly, N. J	140	50	80	9	1	-	135	25	85	25	-	-
Beverly Hills, Calif	101	23	73	2	3	-	292	76	122	54	40	-
Bexley, Ohio	43	11	32	-	-	-	154	58	67	17	12	-
Big Spring, Tex	222	63	141	7	10	1	187	22	138	11	16	-
Big Stone Gap, Va	218	91	111	11	5	-	145	40	83	22	-	-
Billings, Mont	68	25	35	3	5	-	55	6	37	10	2	-
Biloxi, Miss	774	214	494	53	13	-	1,021	190	558	242	31	-
Binghamton, N. Y	267	98	146	17	5	1	279	61	150	65	3	-
Birmingham, Mich	20	3	15	2	-	-	83	26	44	9	4	-
Blairsville, Pa	60	18	39	3	-	-	61	16	40	5	-	-
Bloomfield, N. J	291	81	195	15	-	-	340	85	202	47	6	-
Bloomington, Ill	318	117	168	22	11	-	290	60	172	49	9	-
Bloomington, Ind	173	50	113	7	3	-	202	49	116	30	6	1
Bluefield, Va	93	36	56	1	-	-	91	17	59	15	-	-
Bluefield, W. Va	1,117	401	648	58	9	1	1,269	378	705	169	16	1
Blytheville, Ark	951	233	590	95	33	-	1,106	197	634	222	52	1
Bogalusa, La	1,809	657	997	144	11	-	1,726	370	1,024	308	24	-
Bonham, Tex	336	78	219	33	3	3	359	47	217	78	16	1
Boonton, N. J	74	18	54	2	-	-	78	17	54	7	-	-
Boonville, Ind	47	14	31	2	-	-	45	6	33	6	-	-
Boonville, Mo	422	201	168	32	10	11	299	60	167	56	15	1
Bordentown, N. J	155	61	83	9	2	-	120	24	78	18	-	-
Borger, Tex	49	9	34	-	4	2	48	5	35	7	1	-
Boulder, Colo	48	15	28	4	1	-	52	12	26	12	2	-
Bowling Green, Ky	791	238	452	77	23	1	1,034	261	479	253	41	-
Brackenridge, Pa	125	41	76	6	1	1	88	18	69	1	-	-
Braddock, Pa	896	366	488	29	13	-	699	119	487	87	5	1
Bradentown, Fla	540	167	288	63	22	-	585	109	292	163	21	-
Bradford, Pa	47	23	23	-	1	-	49	9	26	13	1	-
Brady, Tex	104	23	71	8	2	-	116	14	77	17	8	-
Brawley, Calif	71	28	40	2	1	-	76	7	52	15	2	-
Brazil, Ind	128	46	70	10	2	-	100	18	67	15	-	-
Breckenridge, Tex	143	44	88	5	6	-	184	37	106	26	15	-
Brenham, Tex	619	187	357	48	27	-	833	188	388	202	54	1
Brentwood, Mo	122	37	76	7	2	-	117	29	75	10	3	-
Brewton, Ala	396	119	225	52	-	-	534	116	230	187	1	-
Bridgeport, Conn	1,279	407	794	57	17	4	1,143	204	764	156	18	1
Bridgeport, Ohio	93	32	53	5	3	-	86	19	53	14	-	-
Bridgeton, N. J	550	205	313	32	-	-	528	127	322	77	2	-
Bridgewater, Mass	114	85	20	8	-	1	29	17	8	3	1	-
Brinkley, Ark	557	162	316	50	28	1	624	108	317	131	66	2
Bristol, Conn	42	15	25	-	2	-	32	9	23	-	-	-
Bristol, Pa	128	44	76	7	-	1	128	26	78	23	1	-
Bristol, Tenn	321	82	217	15	7	-	387	91	223	68	5	-
Bristol, Va	420	141	249	20	9	1	472	114	258	80	19	1
Bristow, Okla	192	53	119	12	8	-	229	41	139	36	13	-
Brockton, Mass	159	62	86	9	2	-	170	46	95	25	4	-
Bronxville, N. Y	54	13	38	3	-	-	268	106	100	54	8	-
Brookfield, Mo	101	30	59	9	3	-	93	17	58	16	2	-
Brookhaven, Miss	564	152	355	45	12	-	816	181	432	161	42	-
Brookline, Mass	65	26	38	1	-	-	212	118	59	30	4	1
Brownsville, Pa	38	10	27	-	1	-	41	10	25	5	1	-
Brownsville, Tenn	427	125	262	26	14	-	591	146	299	122	23	1
Brownsville, Tex	46	11	28	3	4	-	44	5	30	8	1	-
Bronwood, Texas	182	50	106	24	2	-	219	35	104	66	14	-
Brunswick, Md	44	18	24	2	-	-	34	8	22	4	-	-
Bryan, Tex	853	229	484	109	30	1	1,122	218	491	351	62	-
Buckhannan, W. Va	48	19	25	4	-	-	52	21	24	7	-	-
Buena Vista, Va	82	29	48	3	2	-	107	33	54	18	2	-
Buford, Ga	218	64	144	9	1	-	265	70	152	42	1	-
Burlington, Iowa	187	63	88	22	12	2	130	17	83	25	5	-
Burlington, N. J	509	177	303	24	4	1	471	100	310	56	2	3
Burlington, N. C	188	71	108	7	2	-	261	101	124	28	7	1
Butler, Mo	46	20	23	1	1	1	45	5	23	13	4	-
Butler, Pa	63	22	37	2	2	-	55	11	37	6	1	-
Butte, Mont	78	29	31	11	6	1	67	6	38	12	10	1
Cadiz, Ohio	103	40	57	4	2	-	111	27	61	20	3	-

TABLE 19.—MARITAL CONDITION OF THE NEGRO POPULATION 15 YEARS OLD AND OVER, BY SEX, FOR CITIES AND OTHER URBAN PLACES HAVING LESS THAN 5,000 NEGRO INHABITANTS: 1930—Continued

[Cities having less than 100 Negro inhabitants, omitted]

CITY	MALES 15 YEARS OLD AND OVER						FEMALES 15 YEARS OLD AND OVER					
	Total	Single	Married	Widowed	Divorced	Unknown	Total	Single	Married	Widowed	Divorced	Unknown
Cairo, Ga	405	124	257	18	6	-	461	108	261	73	18	1
Cairo, Ill	1,748	601	989	108	47	3	1,792	414	1,021	303	52	2
Caldwell, N. J	40	10	27	3	-	-	70	24	40	6	-	-
Calexico, Calif	73	25	44	4	-	-	62	10	37	15	-	-
Cambridge, Md	865	326	464	62	12	1	896	254	477	156	9	-
Cambridge, Ohio	152	53	89	8	2	-	147	33	88	19	7	-
Camden, Ark	934	272	558	78	26	-	1,149	253	599	240	57	-
Camden, S. C	659	251	380	26	-	2	944	270	491	175	5	3
Cameron, Tex	347	119	196	24	7	1	419	104	196	108	11	-
Campbell, Ohio	697	221	436	31	9	-	612	98	434	65	15	-
Canon City, Colo	111	46	46	9	10	-	28	1	20	5	2	-
Canonsburg, Pa	240	76	151	12	1	-	208	46	137	23	2	-
Canton, Ga	81	24	47	8	2	-	85	20	47	9	9	-
Canton, Miss	834	231	527	57	19	-	1,092	248	534	257	50	3
Canton, Ohio	1,215	400	750	43	22	-	1,009	175	694	114	25	1
Cape Charles, Va	243	89	134	20	-	-	263	61	137	60	5	-
Cape Girardeau, Mo	353	118	195	37	3	-	360	79	192	81	7	1
Cape May, N. J	187	60	111	15	1	-	188	39	101	47	1	-
Carbondale, Ill	477	144	293	33	7	-	528	112	304	99	13	-
Carbon Hill, Ala	202	65	114	23	-	-	217	44	120	51	1	1
Carlisle, Pa	290	108	165	16	1	-	340	99	175	57	9	-
Carlsbad, N. Mex	40	10	28	1	1	-	52	12	31	7	2	-
Carmi, Ill	39	12	22	4	1	-	38	12	21	5	-	-
Carnegie, Pa	184	63	110	6	5	-	153	26	110	13	4	-
Carrollton, Ga	292	78	186	26	1	1	404	105	201	97	1	-
Carrollton, Mo	119	28	67	13	11	-	121	26	66	22	7	-
Carteret, N. J	201	102	91	7	1	-	88	5	72	11	-	-
Cartersville, Ga	486	133	303	41	9	-	630	159	316	140	14	1
Carthage, Mo	120	36	72	8	4	-	119	24	73	12	10	-
Caruthersville, Mo	395	95	236	59	5	-	453	79	241	115	18	-
Casper, Wyo	65	18	40	2	4	1	61	6	37	12	5	1
Catlettsburg, Ky	43	16	25	1	1	-	38	3	22	12	1	-
Catskill, N. Y	120	33	80	7	-	-	105	19	65	21	-	-
Cedarhurst, N. Y	28	8	17	2	1	-	109	48	38	21	2	-
Cedar Rapids, Iowa	292	83	177	13	19	-	272	47	176	33	16	-
Cedartown, Ga	424	127	272	21	4	-	537	119	315	97	6	-
Center, Tex	136	37	75	18	6	-	180	49	77	42	12	-
Centerville, Iowa	94	27	57	9	1	-	93	25	59	9	-	-
Central City, Ky	159	45	106	6	2	-	185	37	116	28	4	-
Centralia, Ill	352	80	252	17	3	-	389	67	265	51	5	1
Chambersburg, Pa	207	85	110	12	-	-	210	59	102	49	-	-
Champaign, Ill	549	145	350	35	19	-	607	102	377	107	21	-
Chandler, Ohio	120	51	59	6	4	-	140	50	60	27	3	-
Chanute, Kans	193	69	112	10	2	-	174	40	105	24	5	-
Chapel Hill, N. C	265	90	164	11	-	-	332	107	169	53	1	2
Charleroi, Pa	64	18	35	10	1	-	60	11	38	10	1	-
Charleston, Mo	263	76	153	27	7	-	287	58	154	61	14	-
Charlottesville, Va	1,283	421	765	63	32	2	1,590	465	817	271	36	1
Chelsea, Mass	117	43	59	13	1	1	89	21	45	22	1	-
Cheltenham, Pa	305	93	200	10	-	2	437	158	222	52	3	2
Cheraw, S. C	491	147	313	31	-	-	679	183	366	128	2	-
Cherryvale, Kans	84	34	31	11	8	-	49	13	22	11	3	-
Cherryville, N. C	38	10	27	1	-	-	46	9	31	6	-	-
Chester, S. C	593	198	359	35	-	1	909	272	447	188	-	2
Chestertown, Md	285	103	153	29	-	-	317	92	161	62	2	-
Cheyenne, Wyo	119	26	79	11	3	-	131	19	82	26	4	-
Chicago Heights, Ill	861	293	504	39	23	2	744	107	496	126	15	-
Chickasha, Okla	565	137	326	99	2	1	584	118	333	126	7	-
Childress, Tex	117	28	81	5	3	-	139	16	86	26	11	-
Chillicothe, Mo	139	32	86	17	2	2	143	20	83	39	1	-
Chillicothe, Ohio	431	136	254	27	14	-	417	90	256	59	12	-
Circleville, Ohio	134	40	75	13	6	-	122	23	72	15	12	-
Cisco, Tex	93	22	66	5	-	-	113	23	67	18	5	-
Clairton, Pa	901	295	562	33	11	-	561	49	466	38	8	-
Claremore, Okla	144	42	87	13	1	1	153	29	84	37	3	-
Clarendon, Tex	43	13	27	3	-	-	44	9	26	9	-	-
Clarinda, Iowa	50	13	29	5	3	-	53	11	27	11	4	-
Clarksburg, W. Va	461	177	256	23	5	-	479	130	269	73	7	-
Clarksville, Ark	62	11	45	6	-	-	69	7	45	15	2	-
Clarksville, Tenn	1,130	328	651	73	77	1	1,443	339	659	293	151	1
Clarksville, Tex	296	80	175	34	7	-	387	88	176	107	16	-
Clayton, Mo	123	41	68	7	7	-	179	58	72	42	7	-
Clearwater, Fla	695	246	394	30	24	1	744	148	425	98	72	1
Cleburne, Tex	304	92	184	24	4	-	346	75	188	70	13	-
Cleveland, Miss	448	201	216	25	6	-	523	176	228	101	17	1
Cleveland, Tenn	334	103	202	20	9	-	388	89	223	51	25	-
Cleveland Heights, Ohio	141	18	117	2	4	-	405	139	162	65	39	-
Clifton, N. J	44	15	27	2	-	-	35	7	24	4	-	-
Clifton Forge, Va	397	137	232	24	4	-	449	120	244	76	9	-
Clinton, Iowa	86	24	49	7	6	-	91	12	53	25	1	-
Clinton, Mo	142	60	64	10	6	2	114	22	58	30	3	1
Clinton, N. C	240	70	151	14	5	-	339	118	167	53	1	-
Clinton, Okla	162	65	88	6	3	-	139	34	86	11	8	-
Clinton, S. C	365	108	217	38	2	-	495	157	241	95	2	-
Clover, S. C	91	43	42	5	1	-	126	41	56	28	1	-
Coatesville, Pa	843	282	508	49	4	-	695	130	470	88	7	-
Coffeyville, Kans	670	192	387	73	17	1	661	128	386	124	22	1
Coleman, Tex	145	48	73	22	2	-	150	34	77	35	3	1
College Park, Ga	473	143	297	23	10	-	604	161	324	98	21	-
Collinsville, Ill	100	32	64	4	-	-	106	24	62	20	-	-

Table 19.—MARITAL CONDITION OF THE NEGRO POPULATION 15 YEARS OLD AND OVER, BY SEX, FOR CITIES AND OTHER URBAN PLACES HAVING LESS THAN 5,000 NEGRO INHABITANTS: 1930—Continued

[Cities having less than 100 Negro inhabitants, omitted]

CITY	MALES 15 YEARS OLD AND OVER						FEMALES 15 YEARS OLD AND OVER					
	Total	Single	Married	Widowed	Divorced	Unknown	Total	Single	Married	Widowed	Divorced	Unknown
Colorado, Tex	150	55	70	21	4	-	149	35	77	30	7	-
Colorado Springs, Colo	320	94	189	26	10	1	442	87	208	125	22	-
Columbia, Miss	757	270	438	47	2	-	751	174	426	148	3	-
Columbia, Miss	801	257	451	82	1	10	937	233	476	214	8	6
Columbia, Pa	179	82	77	17	3	-	122	24	77	20	1	-
Columbia, Tenn	789	211	463	81	34	-	1,089	236	500	296	57	-
Columbus, Ind	56	18	32	5	1	-	51	12	32	7	-	-
Columbus, Miss	1,443	381	934	89	39	-	2,101	455	1,014	476	155	1
Commerce, Ga	106	28	63	15	-	-	150	41	66	43	-	-
Commerce, Tex	116	31	68	17	-	-	141	38	71	32	-	-
Concord, N. C	597	226	329	40	1	1	723	266	332	125	-	-
Connellsville, Pa	155	59	79	15	2	-	145	33	81	29	2	-
Connersville, Ind	176	50	113	9	4	-	169	24	118	22	5	-
Conshohocken, Pa	98	28	59	2	-	9	106	22	63	12	2	7
Conway, Ark	281	76	163	39	3	-	359	78	166	106	9	-
Conway, S. C	384	162	204	11	7	-	443	142	213	62	26	-
Coral Gables, Fla	136	36	96	4	-	-	198	50	120	25	3	-
Coraopolis Borough, Pa	357	116	221	18	2	-	284	40	215	26	3	-
Cordele, Ga	1,056	259	656	140	1	-	1,492	292	664	532	3	1
Corinth, Miss	516	155	322	27	12	-	677	165	378	103	31	-
Corpus Christi, Tex	719	219	450	20	24	6	758	153	482	107	16	-
Corsicana, Tex	1,134	271	706	91	66	-	1,371	222	722	293	134	-
Coshocton, Ohio	55	21	27	6	1	-	58	18	33	6	1	-
Council Bluffs, Iowa	246	44	166	18	17	1	255	39	159	40	17	-
Covington, Ga	354	103	212	30	9	-	490	126	217	96	51	-
Covington, Ky	1,388	432	852	70	32	2	1,405	254	856	255	39	1
Covington, La	295	78	190	23	4	-	367	83	208	66	10	-
Covington, Tenn	463	137	238	72	16	-	512	78	228	181	25	-
Covington, Va	365	112	226	20	7	-	375	76	237	48	14	-
Cranford, N. J	283	92	170	18	3	-	341	106	183	46	5	1
Cranston, R. I	128	76	43	6	2	1	95	42	32	17	3	1
Crawfordsville, Ind	70	21	41	8	-	-	85	22	42	19	2	-
Crestline, Ohio	61	13	43	5	-	-	52	6	39	5	2	-
Crisfield, Md	297	92	183	19	3	-	345	110	195	32	7	1
Crockett, Tex	615	229	313	44	27	2	660	161	334	115	46	4
Crossett, Ark	456	110	282	44	20	-	399	65	283	39	12	-
Crowley, La	771	231	500	38	1	1	980	239	581	154	5	1
Crystal City, Mo	115	48	58	5	4	-	98	22	59	13	4	-
Cuero, Tex	363	97	221	27	16	2	465	106	223	90	45	1
Cumberland, Md	396	126	230	33	7	-	399	104	225	59	10	1
Cushing, Okla	200	47	120	30	3	-	201	36	117	46	2	-
Cuthbert, Ga	639	195	378	58	7	1	825	202	384	221	18	-
Cynthiana, Ky	252	78	136	35	3	-	259	44	146	64	4	1
Dale, Pa	42	16	24	2	-	-	35	8	18	9	-	-
Dalton, Ga	299	86	191	22	-	-	371	76	215	77	3	-
Danbury, Conn	68	20	45	2	1	-	81	17	48	13	3	-
Dannemora, N. Y	336	212	112	8	4	-	-	-	-	-	-	-
Danville, Ill	903	283	545	56	15	4	962	181	570	186	25	-
Danville, Ky	681	255	373	49	2	2	757	188	380	175	12	2
Darby, Pa	442	111	292	26	2	11	500	110	296	83	2	9
Darlington, S. C	709	241	435	32	1	-	1,014	305	470	237	2	-
Dartmouth, Mass	46	19	27	-	-	-	31	7	23	1	-	-
Davenport, Iowa	317	123	164	15	15	-	274	42	182	40	10	-
Dawson, Ga	666	186	418	60	2	-	906	189	445	260	12	-
Decatur, Ala	1,267	313	808	103	37	6	1,529	266	839	291	125	8
Decatur, Ga	736	253	423	50	7	3	988	254	434	278	20	2
Decatur, Ill	704	177	461	47	19	-	686	118	474	82	12	-
De Funiak Springs, Fla	155	45	98	2	9	1	238	55	107	46	30	-
De Land, Fla	508	158	304	35	11	-	567	126	316	106	18	1
Delaware, Ohio	160	48	95	13	4	-	165	37	98	26	4	-
Del Rio, Tex	68	17	42	6	3	-	83	16	45	19	2	1
Demopolis, Ala	773	223	427	118	4	1	1,020	215	432	362	9	2
Denison, Tex	930	269	535	95	29	2	1,092	214	569	261	47	1
Denton, Tex	271	78	165	23	5	-	307	63	166	69	8	1
Depew, N. Y	122	55	65	2	-	-	66	5	54	7	-	-
De Queen, Ark	42	12	24	5	1	-	49	9	30	10	-	-
De Quincy, La	285	81	180	18	6	-	291	45	191	47	8	-
De Ridder, La	408	135	257	12	4	-	493	128	297	60	8	-
Dermott, Ark	554	103	377	37	35	2	665	82	408	113	62	-
De Soto, Mo	76	29	40	6	1	-	86	19	43	23	1	-
Dickson, Tenn	92	29	50	11	2	-	90	25	48	16	1	-
Dillon, S. C	232	66	152	11	1	2	381	148	169	57	6	1
Dixon, Ill	61	25	28	4	3	1	40	5	26	7	2	-
Dodge City, Kans	85	27	49	8	1	-	79	17	47	11	4	-
Donaldsonville, La	417	147	232	36	2	-	546	152	239	135	20	-
Donora, Pa	341	104	224	8	4	1	291	57	209	23	2	-
Douglas, Ga	525	196	274	42	12	1	563	146	309	100	7	1
Douglas, Ariz	79	22	47	5	5	-	89	9	53	20	7	-
Dover, Del	403	161	200	35	6	1	422	126	224	66	6	-
Dover, N. J	45	14	29	2	-	-	38	9	24	5	-	-
Dover, Ohio	93	33	53	2	5	-	74	16	52	5	1	-
Dowagiac, Mich	84	27	49	7	1	-	79	13	46	19	1	-
Downingtown, Pa	128	49	72	7	-	-	107	20	67	20	-	-
Drumright, Okla	45	10	24	1	10	-	41	9	20	6	6	-
Dublin, Ga	795	239	506	47	2	1	1,191	316	575	293	7	-
Duluth, Minn	162	44	97	10	10	1	164	20	92	37	15	-
Duncan, Okla	109	27	70	5	7	-	123	25	70	9	19	-
Dunn, N. C	540	201	319	20	-	-	657	223	327	104	3	-
Duquesne, Pa	706	258	420	20	6	2	518	85	388	36	7	2
Duquoin, Ill	196	59	107	21	9	-	231	48	123	49	11	-

TABLE 19.—MARITAL CONDITION OF THE NEGRO POPULATION 15 YEARS OLD AND OVER, BY SEX, FOR CITIES AND OTHER URBAN PLACES HAVING LESS THAN 5,000 NEGRO INHABITANTS: 1930—Continued

[Cities having less than 100 Negro inhabitants, omitted]

CITY	MALES 15 YEARS OLD AND OVER						FEMALES 15 YEARS OLD AND OVER					
	Total	Single	Married	Widowed	Divorced	Unknown	Total	Single	Married	Widowed	Divorced	Unknown
Dyersburg, Tenn.	956	341	500	110	3	2	1,080	263	516	286	13	2
Earlington, Ky.	475	120	274	77	4	-	453	85	266	101	1	-
Easley, S. C.	212	57	143	12	-	-	287	83	153	50	1	-
East Cleveland, Ohio	50	10	35	3	2	-	102	44	42	13	3	-
East Conemaugh, Pa.	45	5	37	3	-	-	37	1	34	2	-	-
East Hartford, Conn.	32	13	18	1	-	-	43	14	21	8	-	-
Eastland, Tex.	83	12	66	4	-	1	113	15	74	18	6	-
East Liverpool, Ohio	172	49	107	14	2	-	167	30	112	21	4	-
Eastman, Ga.	376	85	243	43	5	-	501	104	240	130	27	-
East Moline, Ill.	162	45	106	7	4	-	150	27	111	11	1	-
Easton, Md.	369	135	208	26	-	-	400	120	204	75	1	-
Easton, Pa.	204	77	112	11	4	-	172	36	108	27	-	1
East Orange, N. J.	1,624	463	1,089	59	12	1	2,087	566	1,176	326	18	1
East Pittsburgh, Pa.	52	21	27	3	-	1	35	5	23	7	-	-
East Point, Ga.	462	126	267	57	10	2	559	121	277	147	14	-
East Providence, R. I.	233	71	149	11	2	-	250	67	149	29	5	-
East Rutherford, N. J.	87	26	58	3	-	-	97	21	64	12	-	-
Eau Claire, S. C.	150	50	89	11	-	-	195	63	93	37	1	1
Ecorse, Mich.	474	114	343	13	4	-	422	53	328	39	2	-
Edenton, N. C.	413	119	257	36	1	-	565	154	287	121	3	-
Edinburg, Tex.	45	13	28	1	3	-	48	9	27	5	7	-
Edwardsville, Ill.	152	49	92	7	3	1	148	40	91	16	1	-
Egg Harbor, N. J.	150	39	100	10	1	-	161	33	103	25	-	-
Elba, Ala.	218	72	117	28	1	-	240	43	114	81	2	-
Elberton, Ga.	485	169	273	37	5	1	619	189	283	135	12	-
El Centro, Calif.	248	75	154	8	11	-	196	29	140	19	8	-
El Dorado, Ark.	1,225	282	754	133	29	27	1,640	318	796	432	86	8
El Dorado, Kans.	73	19	48	5	-	1	68	7	47	12	2	-
Electra, Tex.	74	16	52	4	2	-	77	4	62	4	7	-
Elgin, Ill.	163	61	79	13	10	-	104	10	63	23	8	-
Elizabeth, N. J.	1,731	552	1,103	68	7	1	1,617	307	1,118	180	9	3
Elizabeth, Pa.	90	33	48	9	-	-	86	21	53	12	-	-
Elizabeth City, N. C.	1,137	388	648	94	7	-	1,405	428	685	282	10	-
Elizabethton, Tenn.	111	34	70	6	1	-	105	23	66	13	3	-
Elizabethtown, Ky.	97	32	57	7	1	-	140	32	62	41	4	1
Elkhart, Ind.	196	43	134	8	11	-	200	29	137	28	6	-
Elkins, W. Va.	84	29	52	2	1	-	95	30	53	9	2	1
Elkton, Md.	160	57	81	20	2	-	152	55	74	20	3	-
Ellwood City, Pa.	47	13	30	3	-	1	51	15	29	6	1	-
Elmira, N. Y.	395	204	175	14	2	-	241	42	155	43	-	1
Elmsford, N. Y.	67	20	43	4	-	-	68	17	43	8	-	-
Elmwood Place, Ohio	48	11	35	2	-	-	45	9	28	8	-	-
El Paso, Tex.	741	199	465	48	29	-	738	108	473	128	28	1
El Reno, Okla.	212	59	118	17	17	1	207	42	113	30	22	-
Elsmere, Ky.	81	24	50	7	-	-	77	12	50	14	1	-
Elyria, Ohio	435	139	253	21	21	1	369	54	247	49	19	-
Emporia, Kans.	197	63	111	13	10	-	222	52	112	44	14	-
Englewood, N. J.	835	230	571	33	1	-	1,044	259	623	156	5	1
Ennis, Tex.	646	170	380	74	22	-	801	145	406	183	67	-
Enterprise, Ala.	309	81	188	40	-	-	379	85	190	104	-	-
Erie, Pa.	492	161	297	28	6	-	404	57	283	57	7	-
Eufaula, Ala.	622	198	364	49	11	-	969	225	389	315	40	-
Enid, Okla.	281	72	173	18	17	1	301	64	176	47	14	-
Eunice, La.	303	118	174	11	-	-	341	99	173	60	9	-
Eustis, Fla.	309	86	189	21	11	2	331	59	204	57	11	-
Evanston, Ill.	1,679	421	1,123	70	49	16	2,103	467	1,208	324	98	6
Everett, Mass.	353	131	202	17	3	-	385	107	205	65	7	1
Everett, Wash.	46	16	24	4	2	-	50	9	28	11	2	-
Excelsior Springs, Mo.	105	29	64	8	4	-	119	26	70	17	6	-
Fairhaven, Mass.	50	19	30	-	1	-	45	10	28	7	-	-
Fairmont, W. Va.	733	196	473	46	17	1	648	101	456	80	11	-
Fall River, Mass.	152	59	83	8	2	-	126	26	68	32	-	-
Farmington, Mo.	49	15	29	4	1	-	57	9	31	16	1	-
Farmville, Va.	400	132	249	16	3	-	502	138	268	87	9	-
Farrell, Pa.	615	200	378	22	15	-	477	72	367	36	2	-
Fayette, Mo.	261	107	122	30	1	1	279	82	119	77	1	-
Fayetteville, Ark.	110	22	70	15	2	1	130	25	70	30	4	1
Fayetteville, Tenn.	349	113	207	23	6	-	462	129	229	87	17	-
Fernandina, Fla.	487	169	266	50	2	-	623	132	326	157	8	-
Ferndale, Mich.	54	12	35	6	1	-	45	8	34	3	-	-
Ferriday, La.	546	169	320	23	33	1	604	128	323	113	37	3
Festus, Mo.	122	38	77	7	-	-	124	26	76	19	3	-
Findlay, Ohio	72	21	43	7	1	-	83	22	45	15	1	-
Fitzgerald, Ga.	642	148	445	39	10	-	914	143	555	179	37	-
Flagstaff, Ariz.	39	15	22	2	-	-	38	5	23	9	1	-
Florence, Ala.	807	239	487	66	15	-	1,151	268	573	273	37	-
Florala, Ala.	255	77	152	25	1	-	298	64	159	74	1	-
Ford City, Pa.	106	26	69	8	3	-	84	8	66	10	-	-
Fordyce, Ark.	414	96	270	44	4	-	504	97	273	124	10	-
Forest City, N. C.	149	40	105	4	-	-	203	59	116	28	-	-
Forrest City, Ark.	658	175	414	61	8	-	851	184	441	210	16	-
Fort Dodge, Iowa	97	25	64	6	2	-	118	26	66	15	11	-
Fort Lauderdale, Fla.	660	207	410	34	8	1	709	161	430	106	12	-
Fort Madison, Iowa	204	77	100	12	14	1	94	14	64	16	-	-
Fort Myers, Fla.	944	275	615	40	11	3	934	179	644	100	11	-
Fort Payne, Ala.	33	9	19	5	-	-	49	12	20	12	4	1
Fort Pierce, Fla.	421	146	246	16	-	13	417	87	244	74	6	6
Fort Scott, Kans.	268	80	144	36	7	1	269	59	150	54	6	-
Fort Smith, Ark.	1,218	337	741	114	25	1	1,437	306	828	259	44	-
Fort Valley, Ga.	722	256	417	39	10	-	981	345	423	180	30	3

TABLE 19.—MARITAL CONDITION OF THE NEGRO POPULATION 15 YEARS OLD AND OVER, BY SEX, FOR CITIES AND OTHER URBAN PLACES HAVING LESS THAN 5,000 NEGRO INHABITANTS: 1930—Continued

[Cities having less than 100 Negro inhabitants, omitted]

CITY	MALES 15 YEARS OLD AND OVER						FEMALES 15 YEARS OLD AND OVER					
	Total	Single	Married	Widowed	Divorced	Unknown	Total	Single	Married	Widowed	Divorced	Unknown
Fort Wayne, Ind	934	302	532	72	27	1	816	125	537	119	34	1
Fostoria, Ohio	137	48	73	12	3	1	102	13	76	10	1	2
Framingham, Mass	45	17	21	4	3	-	60	18	33	5	4	-
Frankfort, Ky	1,183	513	577	70	23	-	695	195	302	166	31	1
Franklin, Ind	92	34	52	5	1	-	90	21	50	16	3	-
Franklin, Ky	265	95	145	21	4	-	297	64	151	76	6	-
Franklin, La	407	126	236	37	8	-	536	164	239	114	18	1
Franklin, Ohio	61	16	41	3	1	-	59	10	42	7	-	-
Franklin, Pa	97	25	61	9	2	-	110	27	63	20	-	-
Franklin, Tenn	453	130	260	45	18	-	544	119	279	119	26	1
Franklin, V	418	146	253	18	1	-	526	155	294	70	6	1
Frederick, Md	521	175	303	35	8	-	622	189	304	108	21	-
Frederick, Okla	195	57	121	7	10	-	192	26	124	24	18	-
Fredericksburg, Va	371	133	209	28	1	-	480	165	224	79	12	-
Fredericktown, Mo	43	14	22	5	2	-	54	20	25	9	-	-
Freedom, Pa	44	9	31	4	-	-	40	9	26	5	-	-
Freehold, N. J	217	95	108	12	2	-	194	56	113	25	-	-
Freeport, Ill	138	41	86	9	2	-	129	18	86	23	2	-
Freeport, N. Y	101	24	75	2	-	-	155	35	93	25	1	1
Freeport, Tex	55	16	36	3	-	-	79	19	47	4	9	-
Fremont, Ohio	97	37	55	4	1	-	92	21	59	8	4	-
Fresno, Calif	325	103	190	23	8	1	310	57	184	50	19	-
Frostburg, Md	63	22	30	10	1	-	63	16	37	10	-	-
Fulton, Ky	156	40	88	27	1	-	226	57	89	74	6	-
Fulton, Mo	473	177	200	39	7	50	466	107	233	92	10	24
Gaffney, S. C	468	124	315	29	-	-	596	155	328	113	-	-
Gainesville, Fla	1,399	477	825	82	15	-	1,695	401	899	340	54	1
Gainesville, Ga	593	191	350	51	-	1	804	235	383	178	4	4
Gainesville, Tex	336	90	198	40	8	-	358	72	196	77	13	-
Galax, Va	47	16	30	-	1	-	63	19	34	9	1	-
Galena, Kans	49	11	30	6	2	-	65	11	36	15	2	1
Galesburg, Ill	346	94	205	32	15	-	368	71	215	75	7	-
Gallatin, Tenn	321	95	173	45	8	-	416	116	175	101	24	-
Gallipolis, Ohio	241	114	102	15	10	-	221	78	94	41	8	-
Gallup, N. Mex	45	15	27	1	1	1	49	12	28	7	1	1
Garden City, Kans	103	34	55	12	2	-	85	13	52	17	3	-
Garden City, N. Y	49	18	26	4	1	-	171	75	65	25	6	-
Garfield, N. J	64	9	53	2	-	-	59	4	49	6	-	-
Gastonia, N. C	998	312	631	54	1	-	1,297	379	738	179	1	-
Geneva, Ill	16	6	8	2	-	-	135	118	10	6	1	-
Geneva, N. Y	46	15	28	3	-	-	52	14	30	7	1	-
Georgetown, Ill	30	4	23	3	-	-	37	11	23	3	-	-
Georgetown, Ky	456	136	250	58	12	-	467	89	276	95	7	-
Georgetown, S. C	786	260	478	47	-	1	1,069	301	513	255	-	-
Georgetown, Tex	262	88	151	12	11	-	252	48	145	49	10	-
Gettysburg, Pa	75	28	34	11	2	-	67	12	38	17	-	-
Girard, Ohio	94	28	58	6	2	-	64	6	54	3	1	-
Glasgow, Ky	249	78	141	26	4	-	319	74	151	81	13	-
Glassboro, N. J	257	66	180	11	-	-	241	39	177	25	-	-
Glencoe, Ill	89	24	58	4	3	-	189	36	84	49	20	-
Glen Cove, N. Y	320	103	199	16	1	1	271	49	189	33	-	-
Glen Ridge, N. J	31	8	20	2	1	-	174	89	55	27	2	1
Glen Rock, N. J	65	17	44	3	1	-	87	23	48	13	3	-
Glouster, Ohio	93	37	46	8	2	-	58	9	43	6	-	-
Gloversville, N. Y	62	15	40	6	1	-	78	15	47	13	3	-
Gonzales, Tex	240	65	148	15	12	-	297	83	150	47	16	1
Goose Creek, Tex	59	17	27	7	8	-	31	4	20	5	2	-
Goshen, N. Y	70	22	36	10	1	1	56	11	33	10	2	-
Grafton, W. Va	78	26	48	4	-	-	86	20	53	12	1	-
Graham, N. C	107	44	60	1	2	-	119	41	66	10	2	-
Graham, Tex	76	15	55	5	1	-	67	11	46	6	4	-
Grand Island, Nebr	51	18	29	3	1	-	46	13	25	6	2	-
Grand Rapids, Mich	1,080	306	692	51	30	1	1,035	160	703	131	40	1
Great Bend, Kans	95	30	49	8	8	-	89	16	55	15	3	-
Great Falls, Mont	88	31	49	4	4	-	75	12	47	15	1	-
Great Neck, N. Y	44	11	32	1	-	-	53	15	33	5	-	-
Greencastle, Ind	75	26	38	11	-	-	77	17	42	18	-	-
Greenfield, Ohio	83	17	55	7	4	-	84	16	55	11	2	-
Greenpark, N. Y	47	14	31	2	-	-	43	10	26	7	-	-
Greensburg, Pa	138	45	83	6	4	-	124	25	81	17	1	-
Greenville, Ala	527	154	319	37	17	-	806	189	363	191	63	-
Greenville, N. C	1,150	354	718	70	7	1	1,710	495	820	364	28	3
Greenville, Tenn	181	54	108	15	4	-	225	64	112	43	6	-
Greenville, Tex	663	194	397	52	20	-	779	161	418	145	55	-
Greenwich, Conn	36	8	25	1	2	-	67	25	31	10	1	-
Greenwood, S. C	1,039	345	618	69	6	1	1,467	464	657	331	14	1
Grenada, Miss	628	163	390	39	28	8	812	146	428	147	91	-
Gretna, La	706	193	453	44	11	5	799	135	471	164	26	3
Griffin, Ga	1,001	312	577	93	19	-	1,413	330	619	411	53	-
Grosse Pointe Park, Mich	25	5	18	-	2	-	77	19	27	18	12	1
Gulfport, Miss	1,124	361	675	48	25	15	1,226	241	745	172	67	1
Guntersville, Ala	140	57	73	8	2	-	145	38	77	22	5	3
Guthrie, Okla	555	153	326	67	6	3	655	158	332	156	8	1
Hackensack, N. J	893	275	575	37	3	3	949	204	609	130	5	1
Haddonfield, N. J	124	54	63	6	1	-	168	52	88	25	3	-
Hagerstown, Md	557	219	274	54	10	-	639	190	301	133	14	1
Haines City, Fla	312	73	203	33	2	1	326	52	206	62	6	-
Hamilton, Ohio	755	231	428	64	30	2	675	118	425	109	23	-
Hamlet, N. C	436	125	277	31	3	-	574	171	298	100	5	-
Hammond, Ind	257	78	155	11	12	1	208	26	158	17	7	-

TABLE 19.—MARITAL CONDITION OF THE NEGRO POPULATION 15 YEARS OLD AND OVER, BY SEX, FOR CITIES AND OTHER URBAN PLACES HAVING LESS THAN 5,000 NEGRO INHABITANTS: 1930—Continued

[Cities having less than 100 Negro inhabitants, omitted]

CITY	MALES 15 YEARS OLD AND OVER						FEMALES 15 YEARS OLD AND OVER					
	Total	Single	Married	Widowed	Divorced	Unknown	Total	Single	Married	Widowed	Divorced	Unknown
Hammond, La.	731	266	411	51	3	-	761	185	413	156	7	-
Hampton, Va.	957	294	580	78	5	-	1,169	299	617	218	35	-
Hamtramck, Mich.	1,437	394	959	64	20	-	1,355	212	958	150	35	-
Hanford, Calif.	40	15	21	3	1	-	38	5	21	10	2	-
Hannibal, Mo.	772	276	380	88	28	-	761	154	388	179	40	-
Harlan, Ky.	199	65	117	13	4	-	207	42	130	31	4	-
Harlingen, Tex.	159	54	86	14	5	-	132	26	78	21	7	-
Harrisburg, Ill.	193	49	119	18	7	-	184	27	119	29	9	-
Harrison, N. J.	40	11	25	4	-	-	40	12	22	6	-	-
Harrisonburg, Va.	264	90	158	14	2	-	313	95	168	49	1	-
Harriman, Tenn.	128	48	71	7	2	-	173	46	81	41	5	-
Harrodsburg, Ky.	293	89	171	32	1	-	333	77	182	68	6	-
Hartshorne, Okla.	143	37	88	18	-	-	140	30	84	25	1	-
Hartsville, S. C.	575	196	342	37	-	-	739	235	377	126	1	-
Harvey, Ill.	132	44	85	3	-	-	145	30	90	23	2	-
Haskell, Tex.	61	12	44	2	3	-	61	13	39	6	3	-
Haverford twp., Pa.	185	54	126	5	-	-	319	116	155	40	3	5
Haverhill, Mass.	105	41	51	10	3	-	109	30	50	28	1	-
Haverstraw, N. Y.	121	53	64	3	1	-	84	22	57	5	-	-
Havre de Grace, Md.	211	50	138	21	1	1	247	43	139	63	2	-
Haynesville, La.	222	58	150	10	4	-	261	39	166	40	16	-
Hazard, Ky.	306	107	165	24	10	-	241	35	173	27	6	-
Hearne, Tex.	394	92	261	39	2	-	519	90	279	131	19	-
Helena, Ark.	1,541	451	924	154	12	-	2,054	430	994	607	22	1
Helena, Mont.	51	15	29	6	1	-	52	8	28	12	4	-
Hempstead, N. Y.	288	64	215	5	4	-	330	66	213	47	4	-
Henderson, Ky.	839	259	480	82	18	-	976	206	509	235	26	-
Henderson, N. C.	830	305	480	34	10	1	1,084	340	513	205	26	-
Henderson, Tex.	313	94	181	26	12	-	386	93	188	54	49	2
Hendersonville, N. C.	380	129	225	11	11	4	483	130	242	87	22	2
Hialeah, Fla.	77	32	42	3	-	-	68	14	41	12	1	-
Hiawatha, Kans.	51	19	28	3	1	-	54	17	29	8	-	-
Hickory, N. C.	529	189	316	22	2	-	640	210	328	100	1	1
Higginsville, Mo.	144	43	83	13	5	-	120	21	73	22	4	-
Highland Falls, N. Y.	89	11	72	6	-	-	93	14	72	7	-	-
Highland Park, Ill.	51	10	39	1	1	-	118	26	62	18	12	-
Highland Park, Mich.	430	136	267	16	11	-	416	66	274	51	24	1
Highland Park, N. J.	35	11	22	2	-	-	43	10	28	4	1	-
Highland Park, Tex.	446	76	340	23	7	-	827	148	462	142	72	3
Hightstown, N. J.	78	18	53	5	1	1	76	15	53	8	-	-
Hillsboro, Ill.	28	6	17	5	-	-	27	4	18	5	-	-
Hillsboro, Ohio	150	35	89	18	8	-	164	36	83	31	14	-
Hillsboro, Tex.	426	146	227	39	14	-	487	102	251	107	26	1
Hinton, W. Va.	264	90	154	16	4	-	277	55	167	53	2	-
Hobart, Okla.	101	31	52	5	13	-	88	17	50	12	9	-
Hoboken, N. J.	190	69	111	8	2	-	152	20	117	11	4	-
Holdenville, Okla.	210	61	120	18	11	-	250	58	118	57	17	-
Hollis, Okla.	52	11	39	2	-	-	59	7	42	8	2	-
Hollywood, Fla.	92	18	69	5	-	-	92	9	68	11	4	-
Holyoke, Mass.	47	20	27	-	-	-	51	17	27	7	-	-
Homer, La.	311	120	171	16	4	-	436	133	202	63	38	-
Homestead, Pa.	1,461	658	734	51	17	1	1,076	196	728	131	19	2
Homewood, Ala.	565	197	325	30	10	3	698	172	336	138	52	-
Hominy, Okla.	52	7	36	6	3	-	72	5	43	17	6	1
Honea Path, S. C.	91	32	57	2	-	-	120	46	65	9	-	-
Hope, Ark.	601	190	359	50	1	1	801	192	389	204	15	1
Hopewell, Va.	551	222	293	32	3	1	421	102	270	44	4	1
Hopkinsville, Ky.	1,339	384	754	161	40	-	1,740	411	787	468	74	-
Horton, Kans.	57	15	35	6	1	-	49	12	33	4	-	-
Hot Springs, Ark.	1,509	427	894	165	23	-	1,922	394	929	534	62	3
Houma, La.	387	120	239	24	4	-	484	94	272	111	7	-
Hudson, N. Y.	217	86	115	14	2	-	205	58	120	26	1	-
Hugo, Okla.	291	96	154	34	6	1	292	57	149	75	10	1
Humboldt, Kans.	27	10	16	-	1	-	30	7	17	4	2	-
Humboldt, Tenn.	543	168	330	37	7	1	651	124	367	153	7	-
Huntingdon, Pa.	41	16	21	3	1	-	44	15	18	11	-	-
Huntington, W. Va.	1,650	536	963	113	36	2	1,845	446	1,044	299	55	1
Huntsville, Ala.	1,203	324	736	121	22	-	1,667	321	761	501	83	1
Huntsville, Tex.	563	162	340	35	26	-	480	124	244	79	33	-
Hutchinson, Kans.	404	162	203	27	12	-	299	55	180	53	10	1
Hyattsville, Md.	71	29	36	6	-	-	75	20	39	16	-	-
Idabel, Okla.	204	66	113	21	4	-	262	58	111	78	15	-
Independence, Kans.	390	94	246	32	18	-	412	67	255	57	33	-
Independence, Mo.	293	66	186	23	18	-	325	48	197	68	12	-
Indianola, Miss.	527	147	313	66	1	-	664	146	325	184	9	-
Inkster, Mich.	370	73	285	9	3	-	357	42	291	23	1	-
Iola, Kans.	112	20	73	11	8	-	132	22	80	24	6	-
Iowa City, Iowa	52	23	25	1	3	-	34	6	22	5	1	-
Ironton, Ohio	339	122	190	20	7	-	312	62	177	56	17	-
Irvington, N. J.	40	7	31	2	-	-	57	21	35	1	-	-
Ithaca, N. Y.	257	76	159	20	1	1	260	52	154	53	1	-
Jackson, La.	563	293	215	27	3	25	666	199	351	86	5	25
Jackson, Mich.	799	286	404	63	46	-	504	82	323	71	28	-
Jacksonville, Ala.	148	39	87	21	1	-	186	53	89	40	4	-
Jacksonville, Ill.	418	173	200	31	8	6	413	93	230	80	10	-
Jacksonville, Tex.	566	180	14	56	16	-	619	132	307	140	40	-
Jamestown, N. Y.	107	34	68	3	1	1	108	21	70	15	2	-
Jasper, Ala.	327	94	198	8	26	1	381	67	200	40	74	-
Jasper, Tex.	389	128	228	23	10	-	402	109	229	47	17	-
Jeannette, Pa.	79	21	54	3	1	-	78	10	54	14	-	-

TABLE 19.—MARITAL CONDITION OF THE NEGRO POPULATION 15 YEARS OLD AND OVER, BY SEX, FOR CITIES AND OTHER URBAN PLACES HAVING LESS THAN 5,000 NEGRO INHABITANTS: 1930—Continued

[Cities having less than 100 Negro inhabitants, omitted]

CITY	MALES 15 YEARS OLD AND OVER						FEMALES 15 YEARS OLD AND OVER					
	Total	Single	Married	Widowed	Divorced	Unknown	Total	Single	Married	Widowed	Divorced	Unknown
Jefferson City, Mo	1,542	682	632	145	70	13	422	102	214	95	6	5
Jeffersonville, Ind	460	146	258	32	23	1	511	91	269	110	40	1
Jenkins, Ky	505	153	318	29	4	1	416	55	321	37	3	
Jenkintown, Pa	108	43	57	7		1	150	43	73	30	4	
Jennings, La	332	97	209	19	5	2	384	96	212	71	4	1
Johnson City, Tenn	880	283	508	55	34		821	190	432	165	33	1
Johnstown, Pa	492	166	300	20	5	1	450	75	309	61	4	1
Joliet, Ill	573	235	303	29	6		450	69	304	59	18	
Jonesboro, Ark	420	78	293	31	18		514	69	298	99	48	
Joplin, Mo	278	80	177	10	8	3	310	48	190	65	5	2
Junction City, Kans	176	40	124	10	2		205	31	135	30	9	
Kalamazoo, Mich	387	114	231	17	21	4	351	59	234	40	16	2
Kankakee, Ill	194	69	115	7	2	1	196	35	129	23	9	
Kearney, N. J	63	18	42	3			77	19	48	10		
Kenedy, Tex	70	21	41	5	3		76	13	47	14	2	
Kenilworth, Ill	30	2	26	1	1		77	20	40	11	6	
Kennett Square, Pa	166	53	95	18			145	31	93	21		
Kenosha, Wis	86	25	50	6	4	1	68	6	48	13	1	
Kent, Ohio	87	19	63	5			82	10	60	11	1	
Kenton, Ohio	49	10	29	8	2		49	13	29	5	2	
Keokuk, Iowa	328	108	187	17	16		337	69	187	64	17	
Kerrville, Tex	140	33	92	2	11	2	157	20	101	21	15	
Kewannee, Ill	110	32	71	7			97	12	76	6	3	
Keyport, N. J	85	25	52	8			88	28	49	10		1
Keyser, W. Va	61	24	31	4	2		56	13	33	8	2	
Key West, Fla	668	215	374	57	22		837	186	395	191	65	
Kingfisher, Okla	105	42	46	14	3		113	34	46	31	2	
Kings Mountain, N. C	174	55	112	5	2		234	56	134	40	4	
Kingsport, Tenn	211	76	117	16	2		199	54	119	24	2	
Kingston, N. Y	255	110	131	12	1	1	216	50	139	25	2	
Kingsville, Tex	223	51	142	7	23		192	31	114	19	28	
Kirksville, Mo	34	8	21	5			52	14	25	11	2	
Kirkwood, Mo	272	58	176	24	14		297	54	186	51	6	
Kissimmee, Fla	273	86	154	27	5	1	276	47	165	59	5	
Kokomo, Ind	418	116	273	10	19		403	55	274	54	19	1
Kosciusko, Miss	381	107	241	30	1	2	446	91	249	81	24	1
Lackawanna, N. Y	952	380	524	33	12	3	549	52	454	35	8	
Lafayette, Ga	99	39	52	7	1		101	31	55	15		
Lafayette, Ind	165	54	83	16	12		154	36	80	30	8	
La Follette, Tenn	78	27	40	10	1		79	22	42	13	2	
La Grange, Ill	115	33	79	2	1		156	30	88	30	8	
La Junta, Colo	67	18	42	6	1		59	7	39	13		
Lake City, Fla	410	133	254	17	4	2	535	137	275	115	7	1
Lake Forest, Ill	75	20	52	2	1		102	24	58	14	6	
Lakeland, Fla	1,345	378	838	80	47	2	1,546	316	906	258	65	1
Lake Providence, La	612	188	369	48	7		776	158	424	172	22	
Lake Wales, Fla	344	99	218	24	3		321	46	223	52		
Lakewood, Ohio	19	2	14	2	1		79	24	37	14	4	
Lake Worth, Fla	35	6	27	2			37	3	26	6	2	
Lambertville, N. J	47	18	22	7			44	6	25	12	1	
Lampasas, Tex	81	22	45	6	8		92	20	45	18	9	
Lancaster, Ohio	76	20	41	13	2		75	14	42	15	4	
Lancaster, Pa	525	230	258	31	6		438	108	253	70	7	
Lancaster, S. C	326	101	212	13			446	132	235	78	1	
Lanett, Ala	260	83	162	15			354	79	178	85	12	
Lansdowne, Pa	86	20	60	2	4		188	78	74	30	6	
Lansing, Mich	556	224	295	20	17		456	75	298	61	22	
La Porte, Ind	71	19	46	3	3		54	7	44	1	2	
Laramie, Wyo	53	32	18	3			45	8	28	7	2	
Larchmont, N. Y	33	10	23				137	61	52	18	5	1
Las Cruces, N. Mex	60	15	37	6	2		70	16	40	8	5	1
Las Vegas, Nev	62	19	38	1	4		56	7	38	10	1	
Laurel, Md	71	22	43	6			79	27	47	5		
Laurens, S. C	574	162	377	23	12		778	227	389	122	39	1
Laurinburg, N. C	362	125	214	15	6	2	485	151	224	87	22	1
Lawrence, Kans	536	170	301	52	13		620	158	306	138	18	
Lawrence, Mass	58	23	30	2	3		42	10	28	2	2	
Lawrenceburg, Tenn	80	26	51	2	1		107	32	57	15	3	
Lawrenceville, Ill	36	9	26		1		36	7	26	2	1	
Lawton, Okla	293	83	178	20	12		324	52	192	47	33	
Leavenworth, Kans	779	214	482	64	19		898	171	510	188	28	1
Lebanon, Ky	178	66	100	11	1		252	69	112	68	3	
Lebanon, Mo	63	22	36	3	2		67	10	38	16	3	
Lebanon, Ohio	100	38	53	9			97	27	50	18	2	
Lebanon, Pa	55	27	20	7	1		33	10	17	6		
Lebanon, Tenn	381	106	228	35	12		480	120	229	99	31	1
Leeds, Ala	179	67	106	5	1		185	46	115	21	3	
Leesburg, Fla	448	151	270	22	5		487	99	315	60	13	
Leesville, La	321	109	175	32	5		351	77	186	70	17	1
Leetsdale, Pa	57	20	30	5	2		41	7	27	7		
Lenoir, N. C	404	149	223	15		17	443	128	240	70	3	2
Leonia, N. J	36	10	24	1		1	56	15	34	6	1	
Le Roy, N. Y	37	11	25	1			52	16	28	8		
Lewisburg, Tenn	153	47	91	11	4		210	66	96	41	7	
Lexington, Miss	405	102	271	27	5		562	133	313	87	29	
Lexington, Mo	317	105	188	21	3		317	63	186	67	1	
Lexington, N. C	483	171	287	24	1		571	168	302	100		1
Lexington, Va	337	115	194	23	4	1	420	128	195	86	11	
Liberty, Mo	186	58	102	16	10		175	35	101	34	5	
Lima, Ohio	523	165	318	32	8		526	101	329	85	11	

Table 19.—MARITAL CONDITION OF THE NEGRO POPULATION 15 YEARS OLD AND OVER, BY SEX, FOR CITIES AND OTHER URBAN PLACES HAVING LESS THAN 5,000 NEGRO INHABITANTS: 1930—Continued

[Cities having less than 100 Negro inhabitants, omitted]

CITY	MALES 15 YEARS OLD AND OVER						FEMALES 15 YEARS OLD AND OVER					
	Total	Single	Married	Widowed	Divorced	Unknown	Total	Single	Married	Widowed	Divorced	Unknown
Lincoln, Ill	128	85	39	4	—	—	94	42	40	11	1	—
Lincoln, Nebr	394	117	233	31	13	—	366	71	230	49	16	—
Lincolnton, N. C	146	44	90	11	1	—	216	77	97	40	1	1
Linden, N. J	358	131	215	8	3	1	267	47	190	26	3	1
Lindenwold, N. J	61	19	40	2	—	—	57	7	39	11	—	—
Litchfield, Ill	41	9	27	5	—	—	36	3	28	5	—	—
Littlefield, Tex	62	28	30	2	2	—	38	4	27	3	3	1
Live Oak, Fla	322	90	212	14	4	2	422	92	230	87	13	—
Lockhart, Tex	228	80	131	16	—	1	236	40	132	56	8	—
Lockland, Ohio	453	126	294	25	8	—	437	60	303	68	6	—
Lockport, N. Y	77	25	50	2	—	—	71	21	46	4	—	—
Logan, W. Va	99	39	54	3	3	—	89	24	55	6	4	—
Loganport, Ind	88	29	53	5	1	—	91	13	61	15	2	—
Lodi, N. J	57	18	38	1	—	—	39	3	32	4	—	—
London, Ohio	123	34	71	17	1	—	116	28	64	19	4	1
Long Beach, Calif	148	40	92	9	7	—	152	26	96	23	7	—
Long Branch, N. J	599	191	356	51	—	1	629	116	378	134	1	—
Longview, Tex	549	140	346	48	15	—	727	116	378	167	66	—
Lorain, Ohio	362	130	210	13	9	—	306	38	206	42	20	—
Lower Merion township, Pa	829	258	529	29	7	6	1,674	587	796	262	27	2
Loudon, Tenn	38	15	20	2	1	—	50	17	17	11	5	—
Louisiana, Mo	150	39	89	19	3	—	173	33	94	38	8	—
Louisville, Miss	363	117	229	16	1	—	390	68	258	50	14	—
Lowell, Mass	45	14	27	4	—	—	45	17	24	4	—	—
Lubbock, Tex	415	103	265	38	8	1	430	62	292	48	28	—
Lufkin, Tex	459	138	280	26	15	—	534	89	309	76	59	1
Luling, Tex	327	121	173	14	19	—	381	99	184	51	47	—
Lumberton, N. C	314	120	181	13	—	—	443	190	190	58	5	—
Lynn, Mass	251	74	157	17	3	—	297	87	158	50	2	—
McAlester, Okla	461	128	260	68	4	1	516	107	263	137	9	—
McCamey, Tex	92	24	50	18	—	—	71	3	45	23	—	—
McComb, Miss	616	187	362	62	5	—	833	196	367	252	17	1
McDonald, Pa	112	34	68	10	—	—	104	21	73	10	—	—
McGehee, Ark	442	128	274	37	3	—	544	112	279	149	4	—
McKeesport, Pa	718	241	451	17	7	2	631	109	444	68	10	—
McKees Rocks, Pa	221	117	102	2	—	—	154	38	104	9	3	—
McKinney, Tex	287	89	152	30	12	4	302	62	154	69	13	4
McMinnville, Tenn	236	76	136	18	6	—	259	52	147	48	12	—
Macomb, Ill	40	11	26	3	—	—	36	7	26	2	1	—
Macon, Mo	126	39	69	15	3	—	148	35	67	42	4	—
Madera, Calif	37	9	27	1	—	—	35	6	27	1	1	—
Madison, Ill	382	132	221	23	4	2	351	62	226	57	6	—
Madison, Ind	95	36	50	4	5	—	90	23	48	14	5	—
Madison, N. J	193	53	128	11	—	1	251	71	140	36	3	1
Madison, Wis	131	46	71	8	6	—	130	25	70	27	8	—
Madisonville, Ky	672	186	417	65	3	1	746	142	420	170	13	1
Magnolia, Ark	293	79	170	17	26	1	405	112	175	79	38	1
Malden, Mass	216	77	122	15	2	—	249	74	133	39	3	—
Malvern, Ark	351	102	222	25	2	—	393	66	237	77	13	—
Mamaroneck, N. Y	158	45	104	7	—	2	191	54	106	31	—	—
Manatee, Fla	411	134	220	47	10	—	410	90	225	73	22	—
Manchester, Ga	228	78	123	27	—	—	285	77	129	76	3	—
Mangum, Okla	111	19	74	9	9	—	112	16	70	14	12	—
Manhattan, Kans	109	32	63	10	3	1	111	21	65	20	2	3
Mansfield, La	415	118	256	36	5	—	586	147	270	119	50	—
Mansfield, Ohio	362	149	199	10	4	—	306	59	192	43	11	1
Maple Heights, Ohio	35	8	26	1	—	—	32	5	23	4	—	—
Maplewood, Mo	34	8	25	—	1	—	41	9	25	7	—	—
Maplewood, N. J	41	13	25	2	1	—	227	112	80	28	6	1
Marcus Hook, Pa	99	41	47	9	2	—	73	16	49	7	1	—
Marianna, Ark	770	188	488	83	11	—	968	149	516	280	23	—
Marianna, Fla	331	105	194	27	5	—	460	121	218	110	11	—
Marietta, Ga	690	208	421	56	5	—	898	202	475	199	22	—
Marietta, Ohio	93	25	62	4	2	—	105	24	64	13	4	—
Marion, Ill	95	24	55	10	6	—	100	13	58	23	6	—
Marion, Ind	388	122	228	30	8	—	386	80	230	69	6	1
Marion, Ohio	149	50	80	16	3	—	130	19	88	18	5	—
Marion, S. C	783	288	445	33	17	—	880	230	486	133	31	—
Marion, Va	109	53	49	6	1	—	122	46	54	21	—	1
Marlin, Tex	539	161	305	51	22	—	697	143	311	157	85	1
Marquette, Mich	182	90	58	15	19	—	5	1	4	—	—	—
Marshall, Mo	251	79	143	16	11	2	284	64	146	51	21	2
Marshall, Tex	2,133	647	1,286	148	52	—	2,679	611	1,314	614	140	—
Marshalltown, Iowa	117	28	78	8	3	—	115	17	78	16	4	—
Mart, Tex	224	73	132	15	4	—	257	51	149	48	9	—
Martin, Tenn	229	49	147	25	8	—	275	46	162	50	17	—
Martinsburg, W. Va	382	158	189	29	5	1	395	128	208	53	2	4
Martins Ferry, Ohio	111	35	66	10	—	—	90	17	63	7	3	—
Martinsville, Va	618	235	339	41	3	—	718	249	346	118	5	—
Marysville, Calif	64	25	23	11	5	—	56	13	27	12	4	—
Marysville, Tenn	131	49	74	5	3	—	134	29	75	24	6	—
Mason City, Iowa	114	24	78	8	4	—	119	20	79	16	4	—
Massillon, Ohio	452	138	279	24	10	1	431	77	286	64	3	1
Mattoon, Ill	55	16	33	5	1	—	49	8	32	8	1	—
Mayfield, Ky	390	124	223	33	10	—	466	112	231	105	16	2
Maysville, Ky	412	135	228	25	23	1	454	95	232	97	30	—
Maywood, Ill	253	60	177	8	4	4	277	43	189	34	11	—
Meadville, Pa	184	56	110	15	1	2	171	33	107	27	2	2
Medford, Mass	187	58	120	6	3	—	220	65	119	35	—	1
Media, Pa	335	133	182	15	4	1	268	66	159	42	1	—

Table 19.—MARITAL CONDITION OF THE NEGRO POPULATION 15 YEARS OLD AND OVER, BY SEX, FOR CITIES AND OTHER URBAN PLACES HAVING LESS THAN 5,000 NEGRO INHABITANTS: 1930—Continued

[Cities having less than 100 Negro inhabitants, omitted]

CITY	MALES 15 YEARS OLD AND OVER						FEMALES 15 YEARS OLD AND OVER					
	Total	Single	Married	Widowed	Divorced	Unknown	Total	Single	Married	Widowed	Divorced	Unknown
Melbourne, Fla	336	107	212	13	4		325	53	211	58	3	
Melrose Park, Ill	44	11	30	2	1		40	4	28	5	3	
Memphis, Tex	89	22	59	4	4		92	10	62	10	10	
Merced, Calif	88	28	45	12	3		72	6	49	11	6	
Meriden, Conn	47	22	20	5			35	9	20	4	2	
Merryville, La	345	91	226	17	11		307	48	236	19	4	
Mesa, Ariz	41	19	20	2			37	12	17	6	2	
Metropolis, Ill	223	590	132	30	2		251	49	144	52	6	
Metuchen, N. J	68	17	45	6			70	13	42	11	4	
Mexia, Tex	573	152	353	57	11		803	206	383	163	51	
Mexico, Mo	445	137	257	41	10		462	114	275	65	6	2
Miami Beach, Fla	83	22	57	1	3		146	42	70	23	11	
Michigan City, Ind	745	258	349	64	74		208	40	137	26	5	
Middleboro, Mass	37	13	21	3			23	4	17	2		
Middleport, Ohio	50	18	23	8	1		58	19	19	17	2	1
Middlesborough, Ky	330	105	202	17	6		355	69	210	67	9	
Middletown, Conn	73	29	41	2	1		105	45	46	11	3	
Middletown, N. Y	156	69	79	6	2		200	56	103	36	4	1
Middletown, Ohio	950	274	628	28	19	1	925	171	632	99	23	
Middletown, Pa	106	48	49	8	1		91	16	62	11	2	
Midland, Pa	302	106	179	10	7		250	43	166	30	11	
Midland, Tex	86	28	50	6	1	1	91	14	55	12	10	
Milan, Tenn	298	88	170	32	8		326	69	176	77	3	1
Milford, Del	264	111	128	25			255	67	135	51		2
Milledgeville, Ga	781	226	494	58	3		1, 102	261	522	306	13	
Millen, Ga	357	95	229	27	2	4	415	97	195	116		7
Millville, N. J	51	15	30	6			55	17	31	6	1	
Milton, Pa	42	18	20	4			33	8	21	2	2	
Minden, La	645	190	415	28	12		860	218	480	128	30	4
Mineola, Tex	277	79	163	20	15		331	62	183	53	33	
Mineral Wells, Tex	209	52	131	13	13		255	34	147	49	25	
Mingo Junction, Ohio	95	28	60	6	1		72	9	56	6	1	
Minneapolis, Minn	1, 760	540	1, 031	122	65	2	1, 581	250	997	284	48	2
Missoula, Mont	45	16	24	1	4		38	7	20	10	1	
Mitchell, Ind	34	5	25	2	2		41	10	25	6		
Moberly, Mo	385	99	226	44	16		428	90	247	73	18	
Modesto, Calif	65	20	35	6	4		56	11	33	6	6	
Moline, Ill	120	29	80	8	3		120	18	83	18		1
Monessen, Pa	471	167	281	13	8	2	360	45	278	30	7	
Monmouth, Ill	157	53	84	19	1		158	28	96	29	5	
Monongahela City, Pa	156	39	100	13		4	160	35	100	20	2	3
Monroe, Ga	316	85	193	24	14		385	95	200	71	19	
Monroe, Mich	189	96	92		1		114	16	83	13	2	
Monroe, N. C	592	201	358	23	9	1	756	227	370	135	24	
Monrovia, Calif	156	37	103	15	1		187	36	104	38	9	
Montgomery, W. Va	199	68	105	23	3		219	54	112	49	4	
Monticello, Ark	225	70	127	14	14		273	49	136	58	30	
Mooresville, N. C	204	69	122	12	1		267	81	137	43	6	
Morgan City, La	537	149	324	61	3		616	128	351	127	10	
Morganfield, Ky	157	44	87	18	7	1	182	35	97	45	4	1
Morganton, N. C	284	101	175	8			364	123	180	53	8	
Morgantown, W. Va	143	48	88	5	2		117	36	75	6		
Morehead City, N. C	219	91	117	8	3		250	79	132	34	3	2
Morrilton, Ark	219	73	119	22	4	1	285	66	132	85	2	
Morristown, N. J	514	167	317	18	12		519	131	308	73	7	
Morristown, Tenn	339	123	204	12			486	199	211	73	3	
Moultrie, Ga	933	327	545	58	2	1	1, 145	309	601	224	10	1
Mound City, Ill	292	76	179	29	8		338	65	179	76	18	
Moundsville, W. Va	611	284	262	46	19		93	14	69	10		
Mount Airy, N. C	125	36	82	6	1		204	76	95	31	2	
Mount Clemens, Mich	96	35	56	4	1		107	19	63	19	6	
Mount Kisco, N. Y	39	10	28	1			48	14	29	5		
Mount Olive, N. C	293	115	163	14		1	382	139	186	54	3	
Mount Pleasant, Pa	56	26	28	2			42	6	30	6		
Mount Pleasant, Tex	343	124	200	15	4		369	80	213	62	14	
Mount Sterling, Ky	345	120	194	26	5		402	86	209	98	9	
Mount Union, Pa	216	85	119	11	1		153	34	108	11		
Mount Vernon, Ill	211	66	126	16	2	1	208	45	128	30	4	1
Mount Vernon, Ind	160	42	90	25	3		166	32	93	36	5	
Mount Vernon, N. Y	1, 137	337	756	36	4	4	1, 623	456	871	274	14	8
Mount Vernon, Ohio	127	44	71	9	3		124	22	74	25	1	2
Mullins, S. C	412	151	251	9	1		561	176	286	95	3	1
Muncie, Ind	1, 021	293	637	50	41		966	150	629	128	59	
Murfreesboro, Tenn	702	195	442	51	14		957	266	479	179	32	1
Murphysboro, Ill	286	97	161	21	7		287	72	159	49	6	1
Murray, Ky	186	57	120	8	1		210	49	116	40	2	3
Muskegon, Mich	293	107	161	17	8		213	31	148	29	5	
Muskegon Heights, Mich	312	105	175	19	13		214	34	153	22	5	
Nacogdoches, Tex	427	108	257	42	19	1	540	121	272	101	46	
Nantucket, Mass	99	36	58	5			70	13	51	5	1	
Natchitoches, La	510	155	311	37	7		801	197	350	232	22	
Navasota, Tex	789	256	428	71	34		1, 010	282	457	189	82	
Needles, Calif	45	12	31	2			45	9	31	5		
Nelsonville, Ohio	54	26	20	5	3		40	12	22	5	1	
Neptune, N. J	639	190	405	43	1		691	111	430	149	1	
New Albany, Ind	483	134	294	34	19	2	482	81	300	85	16	
New Albany, Miss	333	93	218	22			433	88	236	94	15	
Newark, Del	183	72	99	10	2		187	60	101	26		
Newark, Ohio	280	83	165	20	12		260	47	171	32	10	
New Bedford, Mass	1, 092	409	641	31	9	2	1, 062	263	625	150	24	

Table 19.—MARITAL CONDITION OF THE NEGRO POPULATION 15 YEARS OLD AND OVER, BY SEX, FOR CITIES AND OTHER URBAN PLACES HAVING LESS THAN 5,000 NEGRO INHABITANTS: 1930—Continued

[Cities having less than 100 Negro inhabitants, omitted]

CITY	MALES 15 YEARS OLD AND OVER						FEMALES 15 YEARS OLD AND OVER					
	Total	Single	Married	Widowed	Divorced	Unknown	Total	Single	Married	Widowed	Divorced	Unknown
Newberry, S. C	704	225	437	41	1		929	248	450	224	7	
New Braunfels, Tex	83	21	57		5		93	12	59	17	5	
New Brighton, Pa	132	45	78	9			145	38	81	22	4	
New Britain, Conn	130	49	78	3			112	21	81	9	1	
New Brunswick, N. J	752	240	464	37	8	3	713	141	467	92	8	5
Newburgh, N. Y	339	125	187	23	2	2	329	77	196	52	4	
Newburyport, Mass	44	16	24	4			42	11	22	9		
New Castle, Del	206	77	112	15	2		203	53	114	39	6	
New Castle, Ind	108	27	69	8	4		113	19	69	20	5	
New Castle, Pa	587	199	345	32	10	1	529	95	345	72	17	
Newcomerstown, Ohio	84	29	47	5	3		76	15	49	7	5	
New Iberia, La	802	304	415	74	8	1	960	294	443	208	14	1
New Kensington, Pa	271	110	129	29	2	1	203	25	139	36	2	1
New London, Conn	290	97	182	9	2		284	68	173	40	3	
Newman, Ga	717	222	428	52	14	1	929	255	437	182	54	1
Newport, Ark	603	130	386	58	29		543	80	308	95	60	
Newport, Ky	500	195	275	19	11		468	105	276	70	17	
Newport, R. I	503	148	295	46	14		612	133	321	131	27	
Newport, Tenn	79	31	46	2			78	28	43	7		
New Rochelle, N. Y	1,470	445	963	39	4	19	2,083	598	1,094	330	26	35
New Smyrna, Fla	436	110	305	17	4		446	67	306	65	7	1
Newton, Kans	183	52	116	9	6		173	23	113	32	5	
Newton, Mass	168	47	110	5	5	1	319	145	118	45	11	
Newton, N. C	161	69	86	5		1	176	69	82	25		
Niagara Falls, N. Y	371	126	222	19	4		311	45	214	46	6	
Nicholasville, Ky	254	72	146	29	7		285	63	152	63	7	
Niles, Mich	106	33	63	7	3		92	12	65	11	4	
Niles, Ohio	86	39	45	2			59	10	43	6		
Noblesville, Ind	97	30	54	10	3		83	14	55	11	3	
Nogales, Ariz	489	301	149	15	24		104	10	81	11	2	
Norristown, Pa	788	296	440	42	6	4	736	190	432	94	14	6
North Adams, Mass	48	17	24	6	1		37	6	24	6	1	
North Braddock, Pa	163	46	111	6			159	29	108	22		
North Chicago, Ill	176	28	141	7			185	20	139	23	3	
Northfield, N. J	55	26	18	10		1	49	13	21	15		
North Pelham, N. Y	49	10	37	1		1	74	24	41	9		
North Plainfield, N. J	32	9	20	3			66	26	29	11		
North Tarrytown, N. Y	133	46	75	4	1	7	160	40	82	29	2	7
North Vernon, Ind	48	17	26	5			53	12	27	13	1	
North Wilkesboro, N. C	12	34	73	5			152	51	81	17	3	
Norton, Va	137	50	66	13	8		125	25	71	21	8	
Norwalk, Conn	333	96	213	22	1	1	339	74	208	50	7	
Norwich, Conn	138	48	79	10		1	145	36	80	29		
Nowata, Okla	165	60	85	15	5		192	57	87	45	3	
Nutley, N. J	152	33	108	11			201	55	110	32	4	
Nyack, N. Y	224	66	143	13	2		235	56	136	36	1	6
Oakdale, La	272	69	182	16	5		340	59	193	67	21	
Oakmont, Pa	65	18	41	5	1		75	22	45	8		
Oak Park Village, Ill	38	13	24		1		93	31	36	15	11	
Oberlin, Ohio	331	104	208	16	3		356	69	212	63	12	
Ocala, Fla	989	261	615	105	5	3	1,214	255	691	246	19	3
Ocean City, N. J	209	63	133	11	2		247	57	148	41	1	
Ogden, Utah	100	33	58	3	6		75	5	58	10	2	
Oil City, Pa	76	27	44	4	1		69	17	40	12		
Okmulgee, Okla	1,032	314	598	89	31		1,292	312	628	293	57	2
Olathe, Kans	92	24	52	12	4		91	19	54	14	4	
Olean, N. Y	119	45	62	12			94	15	61	17	1	
Olney, Tex	46	7	38	1			49	4	36	5	4	
Opelika, Ala	761	230	462	59	9	1	1,110	294	466	321	27	2
Opelousas, La	840	290	489	51	6	4	1,062	311	506	214	29	2
Opp, Ala	111	29	58	20	4		165	39	62	59	5	
Orange, Tex	689	177	464	30	18		810	145	500	118	46	1
Orangeburg, S. C	1,177	454	679	38	5	1	1,588	486	738	332	32	
Osawatomie, Kans	110	30	71	3	6		98	12	71	8	7	
Osceola, Ark	382	87	245	40	9	1	431	70	245	96	20	
Oskaloosa, Iowa	69	19	41	7	2		61	12	34	14	1	
Ossining, N. Y	640	284	312	35	8	1	260	76	148	35	1	
Ottawa, Ill	51	20	28	1	2		49	12	29	7	1	
Ottawa, Kans	167	54	102	8	3		164	36	99	25	4	
Ottumwa, Iowa	171	64	86	16	5		147	23	91	27	6	
Owego, N. Y	43	14	22	7			39	6	26	6	1	
Owensboro, Ky	933	291	526	93	22	1	1,051	250	547	235	18	1
Oxford, Miss	303	108	176	12	7		387	107	192	75	13	
Oxford, N. C	474	176	271	23	4		627	196	308	116	7	
Oxford, Ohio	105	31	63	11			115	27	65	22	1	
Oxford, Pa	81	29	48	3	1		82	18	51	11	1	1
Ozark, Ala	361	102	207	43	9		440	115	214	104	7	
Paducah, Tex	78	20	54	2	2		85	16	59	6	4	
Painesville, Ohio	184	55	106	17	5	1	136	12	101	17	6	
Palatka, Fla	1,053	326	638	81	6	2	1,146	219	651	258	18	
Palestine, Tex	1,022	307	561	139	14	1	1,369	326	615	374	54	
Palmetto, Fla	419	107	299	13			396	63	296	37		
Palmyra, N. J	132	36	92	4			137	31	92	14		
Palto Alto, Calif	76	21	48	6	1		85	13	50	16	6	
Pampa, Tex	135	31	96	4	4		107	13	87	2	5	
Panama City, Fla	330	104	192	33	1		379	94	190	91	4	
Paola, Kans	107	30	62	10	5		94	14	59	17	4	
Paris, Ill	90	25	54	7	4		95	23	52	19	1	
Paris, Ky	576	188	330	44	14		617	126	332	138	21	
Paris, Tenn	634	187	382	57	6	2	745	173	392	165	13	2

TABLE 19.—MARITAL CONDITION OF THE NEGRO POPULATION 15 YEARS OLD AND OVER, BY SEX, FOR CITIES AND OTHER URBAN PLACES HAVING LESS THAN 5,000 NEGRO INHABITANTS: 1930—Continued

[Cities having less than 100 Negro inhabitants, omitted]

CITY	MALES 15 YEARS OLD AND OVER						FEMALES 15 YEARS OLD AND OVER					
	Total	Single	Married	Widowed	Divorced	Unknown	Total	Single	Married	Widowed	Divorced	Unknown
Paris, Tex	1,094	308	665	83	38	-	1,326	255	719	278	73	1
Parkersburg, W. Va	350	116	207	20	7	-	332	74	180	72	6	-
Parsons, Kans	448	118	268	51	11	-	486	93	282	90	21	-
Porterdale, Ga	26	9	14	1	2	-	56	33	15	5	3	-
Pasadena, Calif	1,021	277	670	55	19	-	1,323	295	682	298	48	-
Pascagoula, Miss	313	110	178	17	7	1	344	85	176	63	20	-
Passaic, N. J	638	181	430	22	5	-	692	161	429	94	8	-
Pass Christian, Miss	427	120	273	26	8	-	543	131	298	95	19	-
Paterson, N. J	1,062	344	656	54	8	-	1,138	258	681	185	13	1
Paulsboro, N. J	267	98	154	13	2	-	194	38	144	11	1	-
Pauls Valley, Okla	129	43	72	10	4	-	113	19	68	20	6	-
Pawhuska, Okla	206	35	143	18	10	-	235	29	153	31	21	1
Pawnee, Okla	47	10	33	2	2	-	49	10	34	3	2	-
Pawtucket, R. I	100	40	56	3	1	-	95	31	54	6	4	-
Pecos, Tex	55	11	41	2	1	-	52	4	39	8	1	-
Peekskill, N. Y	198	78	114	6	-	-	233	95	112	25	1	-
Pelham, Ga	224	54	155	12	3	-	338	67	188	65	18	-
Pelham Manor, N. Y	38	4	33	1	-	-	179	83	70	22	2	2
Pelly, Tex	263	68	190	5	-	-	235	24	196	15	-	-
Pennsgrove, N. J	283	104	158	18	3	-	241	61	152	22	6	-
Pensauken Township, N. J	468	135	302	29	1	1	454	80	317	55	1	1
Peoria, Ill	1,276	589	540	56	89	2	1,072	319	535	155	62	1
Perry, Fla	379	111	248	18	2	-	423	83	275	61	4	-
Perry, Iowa	35	12	21	2	-	-	39	8	22	8	1	-
Perry, Okla	126	42	66	11	6	1	108	15	61	26	5	1
Perth Amboy, N. J	360	104	239	17	-	-	280	39	213	26	2	-
Peru, Ind	59	18	32	5	4	-	47	9	31	7	-	-
Phenix City, Ala	1,126	265	789	66	5	1	1,519	311	826	366	14	2
Philadelphia, Miss	142	27	105	4	6	-	173	29	103	20	20	1
Phoebus, Va	305	110	170	24	1	-	385	93	172	106	13	1
Phoenix, Ariz	961	295	556	63	41	6	935	124	581	176	54	-
Phoenix, Ill	177	45	111	19	2	-	149	16	113	18	2	-
Phoenixville, Pa	102	47	48	4	2	1	82	14	46	18	3	1
Picayune, Miss	743	229	405	108	1	-	661	93	405	154	9	-
Piedmont, Ala	71	18	47	3	3	-	112	36	51	21	4	-
Pikeville, Ky	50	18	26	3	3	-	42	9	23	6	4	-
Pineville, Ky	134	38	92	3	-	1	155	39	90	23	3	-
Pineville, La	159	36	105	13	5	-	200	37	111	38	14	-
Piqua, Ohio	208	69	118	16	5	-	200	36	120	38	6	-
Pittsburg, Calif	78	30	39	8	1	-	48	5	38	4	1	-
Pittsburg, Kans	138	41	79	13	5	-	156	33	80	38	5	-
Pittsburg, Tex	306	84	194	22	6	-	358	58	206	77	17	-
Pittsfield, Mass	192	62	117	13	-	-	184	46	114	22	2	-
Plainfield, N. J	1,209	360	793	51	4	1	1,408	338	834	220	14	2
Plainview, Tex	111	32	62	10	7	-	95	6	66	20	3	-
Plant City, Fla	700	234	413	52	1	-	739	153	429	155	2	-
Plaquemine, La	657	173	395	76	12	1	810	157	397	216	40	-
Pleasantville, N. J	657	160	447	43	4	3	721	121	476	121	2	1
Plymouth, Mass	91	40	44	5	2	-	58	16	33	6	3	-
Pocatello, Idaho	123	31	75	13	4	-	104	12	75	12	5	-
Pocomoke City, Md	233	69	141	21	-	2	238	54	148	32	3	1
Point Pleasant, W. Va	61	21	30	9	1	-	60	13	36	10	1	-
Pomeroy, Ohio	58	18	32	8	-	-	61	17	30	13	1	-
Pompano, Fla	523	180	321	19	3	-	452	93	324	32	3	-
Ponca City, Okla	296	70	200	14	12	-	293	48	186	37	21	1
Ponchatoula, La	334	112	188	18	14	2	375	88	194	46	45	2
Pontiac, Ill	439	346	90	1	2	-	29	8	14	7	-	-
Pontiac, Mich	1,092	348	640	63	40	1	850	110	616	95	26	3
Poplar Bluff, Mo	277	68	167	36	6	-	344	66	170	97	11	-
Port Chester, N. Y	399	150	234	13	1	1	271	53	178	39	1	-
Port Huron, Mich	339	99	214	22	4	-	305	47	196	55	7	-
Portland, Maine	109	39	59	10	1	-	92	26	50	12	4	-
Portland, Oreg	692	217	382	59	34	-	625	109	378	108	29	1
Portsmouth, N. H	271	107	148	10	5	1	62	17	34	9	2	-
Portsmouth, Ohio	789	276	460	32	20	1	603	99	427	65	12	-
Poteau, Okla	58	6	43	4	5	-	70	11	41	12	6	-
Pottstown, Pa	167	62	89	15	1	-	149	35	95	18	-	1
Pottsville, Pa	186	72	101	12	1	-	121	21	86	14	-	-
Poughkeepsie, N. Y	381	119	236	22	4	-	407	104	236	60	5	2
Pratt, Kans	91	25	54	5	7	-	83	16	56	6	5	-
Prescott, Ariz	53	20	30	3	-	-	58	9	31	16	2	-
Prescott, Ark	368	111	221	32	4	-	463	126	224	102	11	-
Prichard, Ala	618	159	393	62	3	1	757	143	400	201	13	-
Princeton, Ind	131	44	69	9	9	-	131	27	70	24	10	-
Princeton, Ky	326	112	185	29	-	-	379	109	189	81	-	-
Princeton, N. J	397	125	234	23	3	12	413	95	247	65	3	3
Princeton, W. Va	170	67	82	17	4	-	135	30	83	20	2	-
Providence, Ky	398	90	261	30	17	-	386	55	263	55	13	-
Pueblo, Colo	497	128	299	47	17	6	536	86	317	108	25	-
Pulaski, Tenn	359	121	188	38	12	-	456	120	188	124	23	1
Pulaski, Va	328	107	192	25	4	-	379	114	201	62	2	-
Purcell, Okla	91	31	49	8	3	-	80	15	45	16	3	1
Quanah, Tex	77	15	55	6	1	-	88	11	61	7	9	-
Quincy, Fla	585	152	358	73	2	-	753	131	364	253	5	-
Quincy, Ill	436	124	248	43	21	-	435	70	257	93	15	-
Quitman, Ga	587	165	369	51	2	-	758	163	397	190	6	2
Racine, Wis	213	65	132	10	6	-	181	28	123	25	4	1
Radford, Va	183	51	113	14	5	-	202	51	115	34	2	-
Rahway, N. J	315	94	206	15	-	-	297	50	205	41	1	-
Ranger, Tex	79	18	48	6	7	-	74	11	51	7	5	-

TABLE 19.—MARITAL CONDITION OF THE NEGRO POPULATION 15 YEARS OLD AND OVER, BY SEX, FOR CITIES AND OTHER URBAN PLACES HAVING LESS THAN 5,000 NEGRO INHABITANTS: 1930—Continued

[Cities having less than 100 Negro inhabitants, omitted]

CITY	MALES 15 YEARS OLD AND OVER						FEMALES 15 YEARS OLD AND OVER					
	Total	Single	Married	Widowed	Divorced	Unknown	Total	Single	Married	Widowed	Divorced	Unknown
Rankin, Pa	617	227	354	31	5	-	489	68	351	58	12	-
Raton, N. Mex	50	14	30	1	5	-	51	11	29	10	1	-
Ravenna, Ohio	85	27	53	4	1	-	86	15	57	12	2	-
Rayne, La	352	114	219	18	-	1	419	112	231	69	6	1
Reading, Pa	855	299	504	39	4	9	663	125	470	58	8	2
Red Bank, N. J	567	190	325	44	8	-	595	149	350	88	8	-
Redlands, Calif	59	19	32	6	2	-	65	12	36	16	1	-
Reedsville, N. C	749	307	393	37	10	2	964	353	426	150	33	2
Reno, Nev	65	19	34	4	8	-	50	10	29	7	4	-
Richmond, Ind	769	222	477	50	20	-	751	136	472	115	28	-
Richmond, Ky	626	266	316	39	5	-	762	278	329	134	20	1
Richmond, Mo	168	44	102	20	2	-	164	29	103	30	2	-
Richmond Heights, Mo	226	41	175	9	1	-	247	41	176	21	9	-
Ridgewood, N. J	87	11	69	6	1	-	282	117	118	42	5	-
River Forest, Ill	30	10	18	-	2	-	53	12	26	12	3	-
River Junction, Fla	872	360	249	80	13	170	774	162	286	151	7	168
River Rouge, Mich	757	219	494	27	16	1	653	71	494	66	22	-
Riverside, Calif	188	66	108	10	3	1	217	53	117	40	6	1
Roanoke, Ala	193	56	114	13	10	-	280	78	124	49	29	-
Robstown, Tex	55	19	33	3	-	-	49	13	31	5	-	-
Rochester, N. Y	998	323	607	58	8	2	1,087	230	667	183	5	2
Rochester, Pa	82	18	61	3	-	-	91	17	66	8	-	-
Rockford, Ill	426	117	280	22	6	1	394	55	273	51	15	-
Rock Hill, S. C	666	222	404	39	1	-	1,020	301	489	225	4	1
Rockingham, N. C	325	122	184	18	1	-	480	178	207	88	5	2
Rock Island, Ill	294	79	170	34	11	-	235	31	155	43	6	-
Rockmart, Ga	143	37	95	11	-	-	169	32	110	27	-	-
Rock Springs, Wyo	41	9	29	3	-	-	32	3	25	4	-	-
Rockville Center, N. Y	188	61	125	2	-	-	302	103	163	34	-	2
Rockwood, Tenn	112	31	65	12	4	-	123	26	72	22	3	-
Rolla, Mo	43	14	26	3	-	-	38	8	25	4	1	-
Rome, Ga	1,562	447	962	136	17	-	1,834	392	1,034	378	29	1
Rome, N. Y	143	75	59	5	4	-	142	76	58	8	-	-
Roselle, N. J	526	152	346	22	5	1	502	99	347	52	3	1
Roseville, Mich	117	25	81	9	2	-	103	12	80	9	2	-
Roswell, N. Mex	137	58	71	7	1	-	125	23	80	18	4	-
Roxboro, N. C	315	118	174	23	-	-	414	175	189	47	2	1
Rushville, Ind	61	23	35	1	2	-	64	16	36	11	1	-
Rusk, Tex	483	266	148	47	22	-	464	134	190	90	50	-
Russellville, Ala	143	45	84	12	1	1	157	32	95	28	1	1
Russellville, Ark	146	24	98	22	2	-	179	37	99	37	6	-
Russellville, Ky	230	80	123	20	7	-	303	77	123	83	20	-
Ruston, La	367	109	218	37	2	1	489	113	245	113	17	1
Rutherford, N. J	99	27	71	1	-	-	146	40	80	24	2	-
Rye, N. Y	108	31	73	4	-	-	179	64	87	24	4	-
Sacramento, Calif	417	147	224	33	13	-	429	87	238	74	30	-
Saginaw, Mich	1,384	415	769	163	27	10	924	105	707	100	11	1
St. Albans, W. Va	50	18	29	1	2	-	55	17	29	7	2	-
St. Augustine, Fla	1,058	341	647	58	10	2	1,393	335	752	275	31	-
St. Charles, Mo	217	84	107	19	7	-	199	50	118	31	-	-
St. Joseph, Mo	1,648	531	899	129	82	7	1,613	334	891	302	79	7
St. Paul, Minn	1,685	519	961	114	89	2	1,521	253	921	291	53	3
Salem, Mass	41	20	20	1	-	-	41	12	18	11	-	-
Salem, N. J	592	294	277	20	1	-	522	148	284	87	2	1
Salem, Ohio	69	26	36	4	3	-	74	19	37	15	3	-
Salem, Va	208	55	136	16	1	-	265	72	142	49	2	-
Salina, Kans	187	34	131	11	10	1	209	44	130	28	7	-
Salisbury, Md	644	244	375	24	-	1	741	211	397	130	3	-
Salisbury, N. C	1,250	445	738	64	3	-	1,566	465	819	263	18	1
Salt Lake City, Utah	297	99	161	18	19	-	230	26	142	48	14	-
San Angelo, Tex	624	145	419	38	22	-	693	92	415	143	43	-
San Bernardino, Calif	221	56	138	9	18	-	208	32	131	36	9	-
San Benito, Tex	77	16	48	5	6	2	68	14	43	7	4	-
Sandersville, Ga	441	98	316	26	1	-	671	158	377	132	4	-
San Diego, Calif	1,012	237	637	85	52	1	1,092	163	660	214	55	-
Sand Springs, Okla	272	73	152	30	17	-	252	46	147	48	11	-
Sandusky, Ohio	299	90	190	13	5	1	287	49	187	40	11	-
Sanford, Fla	1,698	465	1,110	95	28	-	1,804	350	1,176	243	34	1
Sanford, N. C	303	99	184	20	-	-	396	119	209	62	6	-
San Francisco, Calif	1,961	823	854	101	87	96	1,400	261	764	247	101	27
San Jose, Calif	91	25	53	8	5	-	103	26	56	16	5	-
San Marcos, Tex	208	70	119	16	3	-	282	75	130	68	9	-
San Mateo, Calif	71	15	49	5	2	-	82	9	53	15	5	-
Santa Ana, Calif	44	9	30	3	2	-	40	2	32	6	-	-
Santa Barbara, Calif	198	42	138	14	4	-	239	38	142	48	11	-
Santa Monica, Calif	248	89	146	8	4	1	325	72	166	76	11	-
Sapulpa, Okla	322	72	212	27	11	-	387	60	226	75	26	-
Sarasota, Fla	847	275	490	65	14	3	773	131	512	116	11	3
Saratoga Springs, N. Y	170	56	90	23	1	-	200	40	100	57	3	-
Saugus, Mass	41	10	27	3	1	-	47	7	29	11	-	-
Sayreville, N. J	82	30	50	2	-	-	63	14	48	1	-	-
Scarsdale, N. Y	97	23	73	1	-	-	357	151	162	36	8	-
Schenectady, N. Y	289	140	133	13	2	1	219	49	135	33	2	-
Scranton, Pa	312	120	163	22	5	2	270	49	157	60	4	-
Searcy, Ark	187	48	103	21	14	1	220	50	101	45	23	1
Seattle, Wash	1,560	559	778	122	79	22	1,218	183	741	222	70	2
Sebring, Fla	254	74	161	15	4	-	223	41	156	21	5	-
Sedalia, Mo	756	218	418	76	44	-	876	191	454	186	45	-
Seguin, Tex	339	96	213	24	5	1	400	85	230	64	19	2
Seminole, Okla	326	127	168	21	10	-	351	91	193	40	26	1

Table 19.—MARITAL CONDITION OF THE NEGRO POPULATION 15 YEARS OLD AND OVER, BY SEX, FOR CITIES AND OTHER URBAN PLACES HAVING LESS THAN 5,000 NEGRO INHABITANTS: 1930—Continued

[Cities having less than 100 Negro inhabitants, omitted]

CITY	MALES 15 YEARS OLD AND OVER						FEMALES 15 YEARS OLD AND OVER					
	Total	Single	Married	Widowed	Divorced	Unknown	Total	Single	Married	Widowed	Divorced	Unknown
Sewickley, Pa	280	100	163	14	3	-	267	58	165	40	3	1
Shaker Heights, Ohio	63	18	44	-	1	-	302	136	84	55	27	-
Sharon, Pa	175	55	109	9	2	-	162	31	113	13	5	-
Sharpsburg, Pa	81	37	39	5	-	-	66	12	38	16	-	-
Sharpsville, Pa	42	13	27	2	-	-	36	9	25	2	-	-
Shawnee, Okla	389	127	234	18	10	-	394	70	242	65	16	1
Sheffield, Ala	500	152	296	42	10	-	628	126	336	147	19	-
Shelby, N. C	632	218	368	35	11	-	773	251	379	116	27	-
Shelbyville, Ind	131	33	83	14	1	-	131	29	88	11	2	1
Shelbyville, Ky	416	136	230	34	16	-	465	105	220	101	38	1
Shelbyville, Tenn	384	111	237	30	6	-	479	111	241	112	14	1
Sherman, Tex	682	138	452	68	24	-	871	153	474	193	51	-
Shippensburg, Pa	36	14	18	4	-	-	43	14	21	8	-	-
Sidney, Ohio	48	9	30	7	2	-	45	6	33	5	1	-
Sikeston, Mo	177	48	113	11	5	-	171	17	115	36	3	-
Sioux City, Iowa	458	164	269	10	14	1	398	83	254	44	13	4
Sioux Falls, S. D	42	13	24	4	1	-	43	6	24	9	4	-
Slater, Mo	169	53	85	24	7	-	185	60	91	29	5	-
Slaton, Tex	80	14	52	13	1	-	79	3	57	18	1	-
Slidell, La	265	92	146	25	2	-	269	62	144	62	1	-
Smackover, Ark	153	38	106	7	2	-	183	22	107	46	8	-
Smithfield, N. C	209	79	119	11	-	-	308	111	134	60	3	-
Smithville, Tex	246	64	147	22	13	-	329	71	151	87	20	-
Somerset, Ky	139	33	99	5	2	-	186	42	101	37	6	-
Somerville, Mass	109	39	66	2	1	1	100	16	63	18	3	-
Somerville, N. J	202	67	129	6	-	-	199	40	134	23	2	-
Southampton, N. Y	107	34	73	-	-	-	125	33	83	8	1	-
South Bend, Ind	1,364	364	890	63	46	1	1,204	173	878	130	23	-
South Boston, Va	491	165	285	29	12	-	667	190	319	124	33	1
South Brownsville, Pa	205	74	111	17	2	1	178	33	125	19	1	-
Southern Pines, N. C	252	90	150	11	1	-	295	86	157	44	8	-
South Jacksonville, Fla	196	55	128	10	2	1	214	52	125	35	1	1
South Norfolk, Va	539	142	364	33	-	-	638	160	362	113	3	-
South Orange, N. J	179	45	128	3	3	-	383	126	204	48	5	-
South River, N. J	77	28	49	-	-	-	51	-	47	4	-	-
Sparta, Ill	184	44	121	15	4	-	187	44	117	24	1	1
Spokane, Wash	253	79	138	18	14	4	239	36	129	55	19	-
Springfield, Ill	1,229	346	732	93	54	4	1,272	231	766	221	50	4
Springfield, Mass	1,157	373	696	69	17	2	1,177	247	711	193	25	1
Springfield, Mo	654	181	382	79	10	2	701	141	387	156	17	-
Springfield, Tenn	447	129	268	41	5	4	545	137	296	89	21	2
Stamford, Conn	733	208	500	20	4	1	809	160	533	107	9	-
Stamford, Tex	88	22	60	5	-	1	114	22	77	8	7	-
Stamps, Ark	441	77	294	29	41	-	529	87	332	58	50	2
Starkville, Miss	386	122	215	35	11	3	554	138	230	117	65	4
Statesboro, Ga	398	147	208	30	1	12	483	152	213	118	-	-
Statesville, N. C	520	179	295	30	16	-	669	215	321	117	16	-
Staunton, Va	576	189	346	35	6	-	747	220	370	137	19	1
Steelton, Pa	973	365	562	41	5	-	842	169	559	108	5	1
Stephenville, Tex	51	14	32	5	-	-	54	11	31	11	1	-
Steubenville, Ohio	1,152	403	664	58	27	-	952	154	647	120	29	2
Stillwater, Okla	76	16	49	10	1	-	77	17	52	7	1	-
Stockton, Calif	209	90	85	16	11	7	163	18	97	32	14	2
Stratford, Conn	67	22	42	3	-	-	78	17	43	16	2	-
Streator, Ill	53	18	29	4	2	-	57	16	33	7	1	-
Stroudsburg, Pa	55	23	24	7	1	-	34	7	16	8	3	-
Struthers, Ohio	215	51	151	12	1	-	206	32	153	21	-	-
Stuttgart, Ark	425	110	272	28	15	-	470	66	289	78	37	-
Suffolk, Va	1,108	371	649	75	11	2	1,567	480	760	299	25	3
Sulphur, Okla	52	18	25	8	1	-	64	13	24	26	1	-
Sulphur Springs, Tex	320	86	194	30	10	-	381	92	194	79	16	-
Summerville, S. C	291	88	183	20	-	-	406	124	183	99	-	-
Summit, Ill	192	51	127	10	4	-	168	20	132	16	-	-
Summit, N. J	404	139	250	10	4	1	642	212	322	97	9	2
Swarthmore, Pa	96	25	67	3	1	-	158	49	86	20	3	-
Sweetwater, Tex	204	72	121	10	1	-	202	38	123	34	7	-
Swissvale, Pa	186	54	123	9	-	-	167	27	125	14	1	-
Sycamore, Ill	43	12	29	1	1	-	39	8	27	4	-	-
Sylacauga, Ala	287	101	169	12	4	1	368	99	180	81	7	1
Syracuse, N. Y	774	302	437	29	5	1	662	122	436	92	12	-
Tacoma, Wash	303	88	173	21	19	2	269	45	161	47	16	-
Talladega, Ala	796	266	473	54	3	-	1,054	293	510	208	43	-
Tallahassee, Fla	1,307	385	834	61	11	16	1,873	439	961	411	44	18
Tallulah, La	668	240	387	41	-	-	703	140	390	171	2	-
Tarboro, N. C	655	210	401	38	5	1	876	262	445	154	15	-
Tarentum, Pa	46	9	29	8	-	-	34	3	27	4	-	-
Tarpon Springs, Fla	223	85	114	18	6	-	251	53	133	58	7	-
Tarrant, Ala	272	69	193	8	2	-	264	42	189	27	6	-
Taunton, Mass	109	42	63	4	-	-	109	27	62	16	4	-
Taylor, Tex	629	181	344	50	54	-	707	141	358	107	100	1
Teague, Tex	179	45	126	7	1	-	242	45	144	34	19	-
Temple, Tex	972	282	537	100	51	2	1,087	210	551	228	98	-
Terre Haute, Ind	1,300	338	770	129	39	24	1,349	247	758	273	50	21
Terrell, Tex	735	225	399	91	19	1	909	177	432	257	38	5
Terrytown, N. Y	115	35	70	7	1	2	126	38	70	18	-	-
Texarkana, Ark	1,058	328	651	72	7	-	1,295	285	661	319	23	2
Texarkana, Tex	1,597	409	1,034	113	39	2	2,049	385	1,139	417	106	2
Texas City, Tex	168	48	107	8	5	-	171	21	117	16	17	-
Thibodaux, La	358	110	220	26	2	-	456	108	238	100	10	-
Thomaston, Ga	650	197	411	34	6	2	769	172	489	98	9	1

TABLE 19.—MARITAL CONDITION OF THE NEGRO POPULATION 15 YEARS OLD AND OVER, BY SEX, FOR CITIES AND OTHER URBAN PLACES HAVING LESS THAN 5,000 NEGRO INHABITANTS: 1930—Continued

[Cities having less than 100 Negro inhabitants, omitted]

CITY	MALES 15 YEARS OLD AND OVER						FEMALES 15 YEARS OLD AND OVER					
	Total	Single	Married	Widowed	Divorced	Unknown	Total	Single	Married	Widowed	Divorced	Unknown
Thomasville, N. C	537	207	301	23	3	3	534	145	301	72	12	4
Tifton, Ga	209	48	117	44			270	46	120	104		
Toccoa, Ga	324	119	174	31			401	106	178	114	3	
Takoma Park, Md	122	38	71	13			123	39	71	13		
Toronto, Ohio	43	18	22	2	1		32	5	19	8		
Torrington, Conn	62	18	39	3	1	1	53	10	34	9		
Trafford, Pa	39	12	23	3	1		34	7	20	7		
Trenton, Tenn	366	120	195	51			420	101	201	118		
Trinidad, Colo	52	18	30	3	1		50	8	32	9	1	
Troy, Ala	954	313	553	39	49		1,293	347	580	238	128	
Troy, N. Y	260	112	125	16	1	6	220	58	114	39	3	6
Troy, Ohio	220	71	129	14	6		189	44	119	19	7	
Tuckahoe, N. Y	178	37	129	8	2	2	231	57	146	20	6	2
Tulare, Calif	77	31	37	6	3		52	9	34	7	2	
Tullahoma, Tenn	230	71	137	13	9		285	67	138	58	21	1
Tupelo, Miss	715	236	420	33	26		981	256	435	208	81	1
Tuscon, Ariz	400	143	231	14	12		392	65	255	57	14	1
Tuscumbia, Ala	459	135	287	32	5		612	162	294	131	23	2
Tuskegee, Ala	723	259	394	61	9		983	310	401	245	27	
Tyler, Tex	1,355	382	826	102	45		1,704	389	859	336	120	
Tyrone, Pa	50	15	33	2			54	15	34	5		
Union, N. J	542	171	342	22	6	1	577	126	352	96	3	
Union, S. C	615	200	372	41	2		879	280	393	201	5	
Union City, Tenn	471	133	272	62	4		583	114	291	174	4	
Union Springs, Ala	441	146	251	42	2		688	201	271	194	22	
Uniontown, Pa	422	157	238	24	3		399	97	236	56	10	
University City, Mo	43	16	19	5	3		118	39	37	29	12	1
University Park, Tex	40	7	28	3	2		67	16	41	3	7	
Upper Darby, Pa	74	19	52	2	1		282	134	108	28	11	1
Urbana, Ill	138	38	91	5	4		148	28	90	29		1
Urbana, Ohio	273	87	159	20	7		256	48	167	35	6	
Utica, N. Y	197	67	113	11	6		176	37	111	26	2	
Uvalde, Tex	49	19	28	2			64	21	32	8	3	
Vallejo, Calif	126	39	74	9	4		117	16	82	16	3	
Valley Junction, Iowa	51	13	34	3	1		48	3	33	8	4	
Van Buren, Ark	201	60	125	13	3		215	49	129	30	7	
Vandergrift, Pa	53	15	36	1	1		48	7	34	7		
Venice, Ill	618	165	413	36	4		548	57	407	78	6	
Ventnor, N. J	24	7	14	3			84	34	28	22		
Vernon, Tex	258	55	171	27	5		291	43	181	54	12	1
Verona, N. J	61	35	24	2			84	30	37	16	1	
Verona, Pa	59	20	36	3			59	11	34	14		
Victoria, Tex	384	138	198	30	17	1	490	140	213	109	28	
Vidalia, Ga	385	105	263	16	1		514	138	295	80		1
Vincennes, Ind	105	29	61	9	6		107	21	56	22	8	
Vineland, N. J	95	25	61	8	1		127	34	75	17	1	
Vinita, Okla	132	49	70	12	1		151	45	71	34	1	
Vinton, Va	95	23	58	8	1		105	29	59	17		
Wabash, Ind	44	12	29	2	1		42	7	27	6	2	
Wadesboro, N. C	300	102	172	17	3	6	483	162	211	95	5	10
Wadsworth, Ohio	39	16	22		1		44	11	23	10		
Wagoner, Okla	170	37	105	28			179	23	107	49		
Walla Walla, Wash	78	36	23	16	3		19	6	11	2		
Wallington, N. J	76	26	49	1			68	12	51	5		
Walterboro, S. C	238	75	156	7			356	95	186	75		
Warren, Ark	113	32	67	11	3		152	39	66	37	10	
Warren, Ohio	971	294	609	51	16	1	804	98	584	99	23	
Warrensburg, Mo	131	37	76	16	2		132	20	79	30	3	
Warwick, R. I	96	37	51	5	3		81	18	53	6	4	
Washington, Ga	530	147	331	44	7	1	741	185	364	166	24	2
Washington, N. J	42	10	28	4			33	5	24	4		
Washington, N. C	993	399	533	57	4		1,221	380	566	256	18	1
Washington, Pa	774	253	452	54	15		706	150	443	101	12	
Washington Court House, Ohio	198	56	122	13	7		207	39	128	38	2	
Waterbury, Conn	604	203	369	26	6		542	110	372	50	10	
Waterloo, Iowa	440	160	253	18	9		396	79	258	45	14	
Water Valley, Miss	354	98	224	26	4	2	467	89	240	92	27	19
Waukegan, Ill	411	115	259	26	10	1	340	48	243	46	3	
Waxahachie, Tex	653	181	372	90	10		753	148	379	214	12	
Waynesboro, Ga	697	198	446	39	14		1,004	209	472	282	41	
Waynesboro, Pa	53	19	30	4			62	20	30	12		
Waynesboro, Va	249	101	128	17	3		252	79	132	38	3	
Waynesburg, Pa	45	22	22	1			41	8	24	8	1	
Weatherford, Tex	68	22	38	5	3		84	12	42	26	4	
Webster Groves, Mo	303	71	193	25	14		418	95	214	77	32	
Welch, W. Va	461	184	248	23	6		438	111	250	65	12	
Wellington, Kans	64	14	43	6	1		75	16	46	11	2	
Wellington, Tex	130	34	85	6	4	1	133	15	94	20	4	
Wellsburg, W. Va	121	37	82	1	1		106	15	76	14	1	
Wellsville, Ohio	151	48	87	12	4		158	43	88	22	5	
West Chester, Pa	771	270	427	57	9	8	777	208	420	138	7	4
Westerly, R. I	54	16	28	7	3		45	13	28	3	1	
Westfield, N. J	338	97	218	18	4	1	451	154	243	41	9	4
West Hartford, Conn	29	5	21	3			87	47	26	9	4	1
West Haven, Conn	42	11	26	5			50	15	24	11		
West Haverstraw, N. Y	53	23	20	10			30	4	22	3	1	
West Helena, Ark	867	361	481	20	5		826	179	496	137	14	
West Homestead, Pa	79	27	47	5			72	19	50	2	1	
Westminister, Md	93	29	59	5			119	33	65	20	1	
West Monroe, La	371	88	250	27	6		395	52	260	70	13	

Table 19.—MARITAL CONDITION OF THE NEGRO POPULATION 15 YEARS OLD AND OVER, BY SEX, FOR CITIES AND OTHER URBAN PLACES HAVING LESS THAN 5,000 NEGRO INHABITANTS: 1930—Continued

[Cities having less than 100 Negro inhabitants, omitted]

CITY	MALES 15 YEARS OLD AND OVER						FEMALES 15 YEARS OLD AND OVER					
	Total	Single	Married	Widowed	Divorced	Unknown	Total	Single	Married	Widowed	Divorced	Unknown
West New York, N. J.	64	25	36	3	----	----	75	26	34	10	4	1
West Orange, N. J.	69	24	43	2	----	----	124	49	53	18	4	----
West Point, Miss.	595	139	389	45	22	----	898	197	444	193	64	----
Westwego, La.	178	52	102	11	3	10	183	44	102	20	5	12
Westwood, N. J.	71	21	46	4	----	----	80	20	52	8	----	----
Wewoka, Okla.	547	186	308	28	25	----	621	158	337	100	26	----
Wharton, Tex.	182	43	104	20	15	----	232	37	118	40	37	----
Wheaton, Ill.	43	13	27	2	1	----	48	12	26	5	2	3
Wheeling, W. Va.	862	277	523	51	11	----	855	164	518	148	25	----
White Plains, N. Y.	747	230	489	18	2	8	953	272	538	126	8	9
Whitmire, S. C.	102	41	54	7	----	----	134	50	61	23	----	----
Wichita Falls, Tex.	1,542	349	1,044	106	43	----	1,808	247	1,130	308	123	----
Wildwood, N. J.	180	46	120	14	----	----	217	37	125	51	4	----
Wilkes-Barre, Pa.	356	119	223	10	3	1	321	58	216	45	2	----
Wilkinsburg Borough, Pa.	188	70	105	12	1	----	187	40	111	32	3	1
Willard, Ohio	59	32	27	----	----	----	36	8	25	2	1	----
Williamsburg, Va.	305	117	162	24	2	----	326	110	158	51	7	----
Williamson, W. Va.	642	258	334	38	12	----	584	155	336	77	16	----
Williamsport, Pa.	308	88	190	26	4	----	356	84	192	69	11	----
Williamston, N. C.	392	99	269	18	6	----	502	137	278	79	8	----
Wilmerding, Pa.	42	14	27	----	1	----	37	3	30	4	----	----
Wilmette, Ill.	46	13	30	1	2	----	142	38	49	41	13	1
Wilmington, Ohio	158	48	87	17	6	----	141	32	83	19	7	----
Winchester, Ky.	785	261	431	75	18	----	807	152	443	179	32	1
Winchester, Mass.	64	22	37	5	----	----	108	47	40	17	4	----
Winchester, Va.	347	131	197	16	3	----	405	132	207	61	5	----
Winder, Ga.	171	57	102	9	3	----	220	58	108	45	9	----
Winfield, Kans.	88	21	55	8	4	----	103	26	56	17	4	----
Wink, Tex.	90	37	44	5	4	----	73	18	39	16	----	----
Winnetka, Ill.	56	10	45	----	----	1	199	63	86	34	16	----
Winnfield, La.	485	119	323	23	20	----	483	74	331	55	23	----
Winona, Miss.	370	108	221	27	14	----	449	120	240	62	27	----
Winter Haven, Fla.	525	164	317	37	7	----	588	123	333	115	17	----
Winter Park, Fla.	377	97	253	19	8	----	449	76	294	70	9	----
Woburn, Mass.	103	36	58	6	3	----	108	29	54	20	5	----
Woodbridge, N. J.	266	142	117	7	----	----	100	18	75	6	1	----
Woodbury, N. J.	323	109	195	19	----	----	329	79	196	54	----	----
Woodruff, S. C.	125	54	69	2	----	----	182	72	79	31	----	----
Wooster, Ohio	42	7	33	2	----	----	39	3	34	2	----	----
Worcester, Mass.	453	146	266	34	6	1	517	142	279	81	14	1
Wynne, Ark.	382	116	242	22	2	----	478	129	255	91	3	----
Wyoming, Ohio	248	57	181	5	5	----	282	52	186	36	7	1
Wytheville, Va.	140	48	83	9	----	----	186	44	94	40	7	1
Xenia, Ohio	735	199	435	69	32	----	848	189	444	184	31	----
Yakima, Wash.	127	35	69	13	10	----	119	18	75	20	6	----
Yazoo, Miss.	871	286	531	42	11	1	1,231	330	548	293	58	2
Yeadon, Pa.	37	4	30	2	----	1	49	13	33	3	----	----
Yoakun, Tex.	276	78	179	10	9	----	391	82	188	78	42	1
Yonkers, N. Y.	1,171	360	754	41	6	10	1,375	341	832	182	11	9
York, Pa.	773	245	473	49	6	----	775	168	474	124	9	----
York, S. C.	250	87	150	11	----	2	360	111	163	84	2	----
Ypsilanti, Mich.	459	103	290	37	29	----	405	39	282	59	25	----
Yuma, Ariz.	83	21	49	8	5	----	73	12	51	4	6	----
Zanesville, Ohio	673	212	394	60	7	----	637	141	387	97	12	----

CHAPTER X—FERTILITY

PROPORTION OF CHILDREN TO WOMEN OF CHILDBEARING AGE

Fertility relates to the ratio of children under 5 years of age to the number of women of child-bearing age.

Children under 5 years of age per 1,000 women.—The number of Negro children under 5 years of age per 1,000 females 15 to 44 years of age decreased from 429 to 393 during the decade 1920 to 1930. Comparative data for 1920, 1910, and 1900 indicate even greater changes in the proportion of children, showing a total decrease during the 30 years of 189 children per 1,000 females, as compared with a decrease of 122 for white children. In the North, there was a decline in the proportion of Negro children from 317 in 1900 to 295 in 1930; in the South, from 619 to 423; and in the West, from 269 to 239. In the United States as a whole, there was an increase during the 20 years, 1910 to 1930, of 696,696 Negro females, 15 to 44 years of age, and a decrease of 33,082 children under 5 years of age.

In 1900 there were 14 States, all in the South, in which the proportion of children to 1,000 females ranged from 500 in Delaware to 712 in South Carolina. At the census of 1910, the number of such States had been reduced to 10. By 1920 only 2 States, North Carolina and South Carolina, reported ratios of 500 or more children to females. In 1930, North Carolina was the only State in which the proportion of children to 1,000 females was greater than 500. New Hampshire, Maine, and Vermont have been omitted in considering these ratios for each year, due to their inappreciable Negro population. Among the States having, in 1930, 5,000 or more females 15 to 44 years old, California had the lowest ratio—226 children per 1,000 females; followed by New York with 251; the District of Columbia, 252; Illinois, 256; and Missouri, 268. In all of these States the ratio was considerably below the general average of 393 for the United States. However, the ratio of children to females showed an increase in 1930 as compared with 1920 in 26 States and the District of Columbia. Significant were the increases reported by such industrial States as Massachusetts, New York, New Jersey, Maryland, Pennsylvania, Ohio, Indiana, Illinois, and Michigan.

Children under 5 years of age per 1,000 women, in urban, rural-farm, and rural-nonfarm areas.—In 1930, the number of children under 5 years of age per 1,000 women, 15 to 44 years of age, was 268 in urban areas as compared with 567 in rural-farm and 426 in rural-nonfarm areas. The difference in the ratio between the urban and rural areas is more marked in the South than in either the North or West.

Children under 5 years of age per 1,000 married women.—The number of Negro children under 5 years of age per 1,000 married women 15 years old and over, declined from 561 to 513 during the period, 1920 to 1930. Since 1910, the number of Negro children under 5 years of age per 1,000 married women has decreased 198.

TABLE 1.—NUMBER, INCREASE, AND PROPORTION OF NEGRO AND WHITE WOMEN 15 TO 44 YEARS OF AGE, AND OF CHILDREN 10 YEARS OF AGE, UNDER 5, AND UNDER 1, FOR THE UNITED STATES: 1900 TO 1930

CENSUS YEAR AND DECADE	TOTAL POPULATION		WOMEN 15 TO 44 YEARS OF AGE		CHILDREN					
					Under 10 years of age		Under 5 years of age		Under 1 year of age	
	Negro	White [1]	Negro	White [1]	Negro	White [1]	Negro	White [1]	Negro	White [1]
	NUMBER									
1930	11,891,143	108,864,207	3,131,885	25,702,404	2,598,587	20,883,540	1,230,206	9,927,396	232,378	1,896,730
1920	10,463,131	94,820,915	2,663,269	22,017,601	2,409,906	20,461,166	1,143,699	10,373,921	227,660	2,017,767
1910	9,827,763	81,731,957	2,435,189	19,270,619	2,509,841	17,798,087	1,263,288	9,322,914	252,386	1,955,605
1900	8,833,994	66,809,196	2,087,324	15,576,952	2,418,413	15,558,278	1,215,655	7,919,952	244,510	1,665,007
	PERCENT IN EACH GROUP									
1930	100.0	100.0	26.3	23.6	21.9	19.2	10.3	9.1	2.0	1.7
1920	100.0	100.0	25.5	23.2	23.0	21.6	10.9	10.9	2.2	2.1
1910	100.0	100.0	24.8	23.6	25.5	21.8	12.9	11.4	2.6	2.4
1900	100.0	100.0	23.6	23.3	27.4	23.3	13.8	11.9	2.8	2.5
	INCREASE OR DECREASE (—)									
1920-30	1,428,012	14,043,292	468,616	3,684,803	188,681	422,374	86,507	−446,525	4,718	−121,037
1910-20	635,368	13,088,958	228,080	2,746,982	−99,935	2,663,079	−119,589	1,051,007	−24,726	62,162
1900-10	993,769	14,922,761	347,865	3,693,667	91,428	2,239,809	47,633	1,402,962	7,876	290,598
	PERCENT INCREASE OR DECREASE (—)									
1920-30	13.6	14.8	17.6	16.7	7.8	2.1	7.6	−4.3	2.1	−6.0
1910-20	6.5	16.0	9.4	14.3	−4.0	15.0	−9.5	11.3	−9.8	3.2
1900-10	11.2	22.3	16.7	23.7	3.8	14.4	3.9	17.7	3.2	17.5

[1] Includes Mexicans prior to 1930.

TABLE 2.—NUMBER OF CHILDREN UNDER 5 YEARS PER 1,000 WOMEN 15 TO 44 YEARS OF AGE, BY COLOR, SECTIONS, AND SOUTHERN DIVISIONS: 1900 TO 1930

SECTION, DIVISION, AND RACIAL CLASS	1930	1920	1910	1900	INCREASE OR DECREASE (−) 1920–1930	1910–1920	1900–1910
UNITED STATES							
Negro	393	429	519	582	−36	−90	−63
White [1]	386	471	484	508	−85	−13	−24
Other races	703	737	721	679	−34	16	42
THE SOUTH							
Negro	423	463	554	619	−40	−91	−65
White [1]	468	547	617	633	−79	−70	−16
Other races	644	748	906	795	−104	−158	111
SOUTH ATLANTIC:							
Negro	438	496	577	630	−58	−81	−53
White [1]	464	547	589	595	−83	−42	−6
Other races	738	872	860	629	−134	12	231
EAST SOUTH CENTRAL:							
Negro	424	442	535	598	−18	−93	−63
White [1]	506	568	626	630	−62	−58	−4
Other races	688	729	940	716	−41	−211	224
WEST SOUTH CENTRAL:							
Negro	396	422	532	627	−26	−110	−95
White [1]	443	531	644	692	−88	−113	−48
Other races	641	721	911	817	−80	−190	94
THE NORTH							
Negro	295	263	282	317	32	−19	−35
White [1]	364	449	442	470	−85	7	−28
Other races	796	685	645	678	111	40	−33
THE WEST							
Negro	239	236	231	269	3	5	−38
White [1]	326	423	434	477	−97	−11	−43
Other races	742	748	645	600	−6	103	45

[1] Includes Mexicans prior to 1930.

TABLE 3.—NEGRO AND WHITE WOMEN 15 TO 44 YEARS OF AGE AND CHILDREN UNDER 5 YEARS WITH NUMBER OF CHILDREN PER 1,000 WOMEN, FOR URBAN, RURAL-FARM, AND RURAL-NONFARM AREAS, BY SECTIONS: 1930

SECTION AND AREA	WOMEN 15 TO 44 YEARS OF AGE		CHILDREN UNDER 5 YEARS OF AGE		CHILDREN UNDER 5 YEARS PER 1,000 WOMEN 15 TO 44 YEARS OF AGE	
	Negro	White	Negro	White	Negro	White
UNITED STATES						
Urban	1,592,847	16,065,798	427,607	5,074,431	268	316
Rural	1,539,038	9,636,606	802,599	4,852,965	521	504
Rural-farm	1,037,704	4,978,751	588,846	2,665,005	567	535
Rural-nonfarm	501,334	4,657,855	213,753	2,187,960	426	470
THE SOUTH						
Urban	928,088	2,552,570	242,220	833,229	261	326
Rural	1,473,837	3,901,225	774,359	2,184,120	525	560
Rural-farm	1,023,402	2,337,472	581,424	1,364,575	568	584
Rural-nonfarm	450,435	1,563,753	192,935	819,545	428	524
THE NORTH						
Urban	636,144	11,880,182	179,197	3,818,598	282	321
Rural	60,854	4,835,152	26,556	2,265,770	436	469
Rural-farm	13,065	2,258,768	6,746	1,115,915	516	494
Rural-nonfarm	47,789	2,576,384	19,810	1,149,855	415	446
THE WEST						
Urban	28,615	1,633,046	6,190	422,604	216	259
Rural	4,347	900,229	1,684	403,075	387	448
Rural-farm	1,237	382,511	676	184,515	546	482
Rural-nonfarm	3,110	517,718	1,008	218,560	324	422

TABLE 4.—NEGRO WOMEN 15 TO 44 YEARS OF AGE, AND NEGRO CHILDREN UNDER 5 YEARS, WITH NUMBER OF NEGRO AND WHITE CHILDREN PER 1,000 WOMEN: 1900 TO 1930

CENSUS YEAR	Negro women 15 to 44 years of age	Negro children under 5 years of age	CHILDREN UNDER 5 YEARS PER 1,000 WOMEN 15 TO 44 YEARS OF AGE: Number, Negro	Number, White	Excess of Negro over white	Decrease, Negro	Decrease, White	Excess over 1930, Negro	Excess over 1930, White
1930	3,131,885	1,230,206	393	386	7	36	85	------	------
1920	2,663,269	1,143,699	429	471	[1] 42	90	13	36	85
1910	2,435,189	1,263,288	519	484	35	63	24	126	98
1900	2,087,324	1,215,655	582	508	74	------	------	189	122

[1] Excess of white over Negro.

TABLE 5.—NEGRO AND WHITE WOMEN 15 TO 44 YEARS OF AGE, AND CHILDREN UNDER 5 YEARS, BY NATIVITY, WITH NUMBER PER 1,000 WOMEN: 1930

COLOR AND NATIVITY	POPULATION, 1930: Women 15 to 44 years of age	Children under 5 years of age	CHILDREN UNDER 5 YEARS PER 1,000 WOMEN 15 TO 44 YEARS OF AGE: 1930	1920	Decrease 1920 to 1930
All classes	**29,242,437**	**11,444,390**	**391**	**467**	**76**
Negro	3,131,885	1,230,206	393	429	36
White	25,702,404	9,927,396	386	471	85
Native white	22,618,172	9,899,608	438	557	119
Native parentage	16,161,435	7,939,165	491	556	65
Foreign or mixed parentage	6,456,737	1,960,443	304	557	253
Foreign-born white	3,084,232	27,788	9	13	4
Mexican	305,870	214,773	702	(1)	------
Indian	68,598	46,680	680	683	3
Other races	33,680	25,335	752	836	84

[1] Included with white in 1920.

TABLE 6.—NEGRO AND WHITE MARRIED WOMEN 15 YEARS OF AGE AND OVER, AND CHILDREN UNDER 5 YEARS, WITH NUMBER OF CHILDREN PER 1,000 WOMEN, BY SECTIONS: 1910 TO 1930

SECTION AND CENSUS YEAR	MARRIED WOMEN 15 YEARS OF AGE AND OVER		CHILDREN UNDER 5 YEARS OF AGE		CHILDREN UNDER 5 YEARS PER 1,000 MARRIED WOMEN 15 YEARS OF AGE AND OVER	
	Negro	White	Negro	White	Negro	White
UNITED STATES						
1930	2,398,144	23,444,243	1,230,206	9,927,396	513	423
1920	2,039,181	19,210,238	1,143,699	10,373,921	561	540
1910	1,775,949	15,852,011	1,263,288	9,322,914	711	588
THE SOUTH						
1930	1,818,884	5,767,893	1,016,579	3,017,349	559	523
1920	1,689,904	4,665,303	1,027,646	2,994,503	608	642
1910	1,554,357	3,821,383	1,176,331	2,860,467	757	749
THE NORTH						
1930	551,772	15,242,232	205,753	6,084,368	373	399
1920	332,816	12,759,255	111,401	6,548,259	335	513
1910	211,347	10,782,530	83,729	5,816,524	396	539
THE WEST						
1930	27,488	2,434,118	7,874	825,679	286	339
1920	16,461	1,785,680	4,652	831,159	283	465
1910	10,245	1,248,098	3,228	645,923	315	518

Table 7.—NUMBER OF NEGRO AND WHITE CHILDREN UNDER 5 YEARS PER 1,000 WOMEN 15 TO 44 YEARS OF AGE, BY SOUTHERN DIVISIONS, AND STATES: 1900 TO 1930

DIVISION, STATE, AND RACIAL CLASS	1930	1920	1910	1900	INCREASE OR DECREASE (−)		
					1920–30	1910–20	1900–16
SOUTH ATLANTIC							
DELAWARE:							
Negro	363	381	415	500	−18	−34	−85
White	353	458	422	446	−105	36	−24
MARYLAND:							
Negro	394	391	443	483	3	−52	−40
White	372	432	431	461	−60	1	−30
DISTRICT OF COLUMBIA:							
Negro	252	222	234	254	30	−12	−20
White	235	228	299	302	7	−71	−3
VIRGINIA:							
Negro	466	493	545	594	−27	−52	−49
White	461	540	577	591	−79	−37	−14
WEST VIRGINIA:							
Negro	416	409	463	514	7	−54	−51
White	550	631	638	649	−81	−7	−11
NORTH CAROLINA:							
Negro	507	596	661	674	−89	−65	−13
White	530	636	675	677	−106	−39	−2
SOUTH CAROLINA:							
Negro	493	568	654	712	−75	−86	−58
White	495	601	647	630	−106	−46	17
GEORGIA:							
Negro	414	485	592	663	−71	−107	−71
White	461	565	647	642	−104	−82	5
FLORIDA:							
Negro	332	383	486	599	−51	−103	−113
White	413	500	600	639	−87	−100	−39

DIVISION, STATE, AND RACIAL CLASS	1930	1920	1910	1900	INCREASE OR DECREASE (−)		
					1920–30	1910–20	1900–16
EAST SOUTH CENTRAL							
KENTUCKY:							
Negro	335	343	381	454	−8	−38	−73
White	522	562	583	601	−40	−21	−18
TENNESSEE:							
Negro	346	391	468	544	−45	−77	−76
White	477	547	609	615	−70	−62	−6
ALABAMA:							
Negro	443	468	561	624	−25	−93	−63
White	522	604	691	680	−82	−87	11
MISSISSIPPI:							
Negro	465	468	588	652	−3	−120	−64
White	506	568	677	675	−62	−9	2
WEST SOUTH CENTRAL							
ARKANSAS:							
Negro	402	426	529	611	−24	−103	−82
White	511	608	700	689	−97	−92	11
LOUISIANA:							
Negro	420	432	527	620	−12	−95	−93
White	456	515	612	652	−59	−97	−40
OKLAHOMA:							
Negro	386	438	572	658	−52	−134	−86
White	466	558	664	722	−92	−106	−58
TEXAS:							
Negro	373	406	532	642	−33	−126	−110
White	407	500	625	698	−93	−125	−73

TABLE 8.—NEGRO AND WHITE WOMEN 15 TO 44 YEARS OF AGE, CHILDREN UNDER 5 YEARS, AND NUMBER OF CHILDREN PER 1,000 WOMEN, BY DIVISIONS, AND STATES: 1930 AND 1920

[Children per 1,000 women not shown where base is less than 100]

DIVISION AND STATE	WOMEN 15 TO 44 YEARS OF AGE				CHILDREN UNDER 5 YEARS OF AGE				CHILDREN UNDER 5 PER 1,000 WOMEN 15 TO 44 YEARS OF AGE					
	Negro		White		Negro		White		Negro		White		Increase or decrease (−) 1920–30	
	1930	1920	1930	1920[1]	1930	1920	1930	1920[1]	1930	1920	1930	1920[1]	Negro	White[1]
United States	**3,131,885**	**2,663,269**	**25,702,404**	**22,017,601**	**1,230,206**	**1,143,699**	**9,927,396**	**10,373,921**	**393**	**429**	**386**	**471**	**−36**	**−85**
GEOGRAPHIC DIVISIONS:														
New England	23,275	21,108	1,899,813	1,734,977	8,915	7,415	680,321	745,273	383	351	358	430	32	−72
Middle Atlantic	317,861	182,939	6,140,080	5,173,535	93,251	47,306	2,118,758	2,305,998	293	259	345	446	34	−101
East North Central	266,545	144,246	5,712,978	4,854,556	78,446	36,991	2,118,764	2,180,743	294	256	371	449	38	−78
West North Central	89,317	75,581	2,962,463	2,814,701	25,141	19,689	1,166,525	1,316,245	281	261	394	468	20	−74
South Atlantic	1,119,800	1,062,848	2,633,006	2,194,342	490,017	527,394	1,221,643	1,199,524	438	496	464	547	−58	−83
East South Central	679,862	628,839	1,648,498	1,426,127	288,162	277,670	834,129	810,201	424	442	506	568	−18	−62
West South Central	602,263	528,011	2,172,291	1,853,979	238,400	222,582	961,577	984,778	396	422	443	531	−26	−88
Mountain	7,546	6,636	742,709	713,555	2,084	1,540	325,009	383,287	276	232	438	537	44	−99
Pacific	25,416	13,061	1,790,566	1,251,829	5,790	3,112	500,670	447,872	228	238	280	358	−10	−78
NEW ENGLAND:														
Maine	204	306	168,746	166,544	107	113	74,806	74,917	525	369	443	450	156	−7
New Hampshire	127	127	101,046	98,138	48	72	39,294	41,316	378	567	389	421	−189	−32
Vermont	102	118	74,661	74,796	75	52	33,150	34,487	735	441	444	461	294	−17
Massachusetts	12,822	12,470	1,013,210	930,542	4,708	4,308	344,605	381,284	367	345	340	410	22	−70
Rhode Island	2,216	2,464	163,446	144,318	1,008	997	58,581	61,338	455	405	358	425	50	−67
Connecticut	7,804	5,623	378,704	320,639	2,969	1,873	129,885	151,931	380	333	343	474	47	−131
MIDDLE ATLANTIC:														
New York	136,164	67,188	3,064,202	2,522,447	34,116	14,726	953,331	994,584	251	219	311	394	32	−83
New Jersey	59,409	33,940	941,160	727,887	19,790	10,171	309,662	328,481	333	300	329	451	33	−122
Pennsylvania	122,288	81,811	2,134,718	1,923,201	39,345	22,409	855,765	982,933	322	274	401	511	48	−110
EAST NORTH CENTRAL:														
Ohio	84,409	50,018	1,480,130	1,289,972	27,845	14,227	544,568	571,861	330	284	368	443	46	−75
Indiana	30,076	21,910	703,001	649,096	9,142	5,922	274,618	283,247	304	270	391	436	34	−45
Illinois	99,252	54,271	1,792,182	1,513,891	25,378	12,333	585,645	642,616	256	227	327	424	29	−97
Michigan	49,900	16,709	1,075,214	808,571	15,231	4,141	445,235	399,700	305	248	414	494	57	−80
Wisconsin	2,908	1,338	662,451	593,026	850	368	268,698	283,319	292	275	406	478	17	−72
WEST NORTH CENTRAL:														
Minnesota	2,321	2,421	591,227	547,226	615	522	228,025	259,487	265	216	386	474	49	−88
Iowa	4,128	4,843	550,207	548,048	1,391	1,550	217,991	249,267	337	320	376	455	17	−59
Missouri	62,804	49,999	803,107	761,866	16,830	11,956	288,099	315,916	268	239	359	415	29	−56
North Dakota	84	102	146,933	137,601	30	20	74,259	89,964	--------	196	505	654	--------	−149
South Dakota	147	169	149,342	137,672	47	70	68,095	77,431	320	414	456	562	−94	−106
Nebraska	3,785	3,707	313,861	293,743	1,046	878	127,622	141,831	276	237	407	483	39	−76
Kansas	16,048	14,340	407,786	388,545	5,182	4,693	162,434	182,349	323	327	398	469	−4	−71
SOUTH ATLANTIC:														
Delaware	7,681	7,283	46,727	44,021	2,787	2,776	16,492	20,152	363	381	353	458	−18	−105
Maryland	68,548	61,777	316,357	284,332	27,006	24,145	117,544	122,844	394	391	372	432	3	−60
District of Columbia	39,745	35,055	94,806	99,385	10,006	7,774	22,240	22,632	252	222	235	228	30	7
Virginia	151,720	164,978	404,117	362,720	70,662	81,263	186,341	195,765	466	493	461	540	−27	−79
West Virginia	29,077	21,662	354,698	296,481	12,104	8,854	194,935	187,071	416	409	550	631	7	−81
North Carolina	226,053	178,722	516,478	393,422	114,695	106,460	273,807	250,294	507	596	530	636	−89	−106
South Carolina	195,225	206,813	219,692	184,526	96,300	117,526	108,642	110,992	493	568	495	601	−75	−106
Georgia	279,911	299,681	434,970	385,626	116,016	145,332	200,353	217,864	414	485	461	565	−71	−104
Florida	121,840	86,877	245,161	143,829	40,441	33,264	101,289	71,910	332	383	413	500	−51	−87
EAST SOUTH CENTRAL:														
Kentucky	55,558	59,610	525,148	482,330	18,587	20,468	274,257	271,143	335	343	522	562	−8	−40
Tennessee	128,059	116,858	498,329	429,518	44,304	45,653	237,483	235,079	346	391	477	547	−45	−70
Alabama	243,502	222,670	394,837	323,084	107,836	104,155	205,960	195,290	443	468	522	604	−25	−82
Mississippi	252,743	229,701	230,184	191,195	117,435	107,394	116,429	108,689	465	468	506	568	−3	−62
WEST SOUTH CENTRAL:														
Arkansas	124,172	120,425	310,288	278,693	49,957	51,274	158,614	169,520	402	426	511	608	−24	−97
Louisiana	202,304	179,057	316,743	255,811	84,986	77,296	144,541	131,745	420	432	456	515	−12	−59
Oklahoma	44,867	37,035	500,048	408,006	17,337	16,214	232,821	227,798	386	438	466	558	−52	−92
Texas	230,920	191,494	1,045,212	911,469	86,120	77,798	425,601	455,715	373	406	407	500	−33	−93
MOUNTAIN:														
Montana	261	382	112,353	119,013	66	109	46,518	65,500	253	285	414	550	−32	−136
Idaho	157	192	94,243	91,145	30	55	45,010	53,832	191	286	478	591	−95	−113
Wyoming	297	335	47,795	41,798	63	59	20,917	22,099	212	176	438	529	36	−91
Colorado	3,196	3,112	222,403	210,407	773	693	84,371	95,639	242	223	379	455	19	−76
New Mexico	731	747	74,819	73,043	249	181	39,904	43,773	341	242	533	599	99	−66
Arizona	2,518	1,390	62,647	66,418	793	333	24,495	35,764	315	240	391	538	75	−147
Utah	253	391	111,363	97,208	89	95	57,698	60,517	352	243	518	623	109	−105
Nevada	133	87	17,086	14,523	21	15	6,096	6,163	158	--------	357	424	--------	−67
PACIFIC:														
Washington	1,473	1,686	351,201	302,579	400	399	110,514	121,807	272	237	315	403	35	−88
Oregon	550	541	216,759	177,289	107	117	67,200	69,885	195	216	310	394	−21	−84
California	23,393	10,834	1,222,606	771,961	5,283	2,596	322,956	256,180	226	240	264	332	−14	−68

[1] Includes Mexican.

TABLE 9.—NEGRO WOMEN 15 TO 44 YEARS OF AGE, NEGRO CHILDREN UNDER 5 YEARS, AND NUMBER OF NEGRO CHILDREN PER 1,000 WOMEN, FOR URBAN, RURAL-FARM, AND RURAL-NONFARM AREAS, BY SECTIONS, DIVISIONS, AND STATES: 1930

[Children per 1,000 women not shown where base is less than 100]

SECTION, DIVISION, AND STATE	WOMEN 15 TO 44 YEARS OF AGE					CHILDREN UNDER 5 YEARS OF AGE					CHILDREN UNDER 5 PER 1,000 WOMEN 15 TO 44 YEARS OF AGE				
			Rural					Rural					Rural		
	Total	Urban	Total	Rural-farm	Rural-nonfarm	Total	Urban	Total	Rural-farm	Rural-non-farm	Total	Urban	Total	Rural-farm	Rural-non-farm
United States	3,131,885	1,592,847	1,539,038	1,037,704	501,334	1,230,206	427,607	802,599	588,846	213,753	393	268	521	567	426
The North	696,998	636,144	60,854	13,065	47,789	205,753	179,197	26,556	6,746	19,810	295	282	436	516	415
The South	2,401,925	928,088	1,473,837	1,023,402	450,435	1,016,579	242,220	774,359	581,424	192,935	423	261	525	568	428
The West	32,962	28,615	4,347	1,237	3,110	7,874	6,190	1,684	676	1,008	239	216	387	546	324
NEW ENGLAND	23,275	20,530	2,745	208	2,537	8,915	7,637	1,278	91	1,187	383	372	466	438	468
Maine	204	147	57	18	39	107	71	36	14	22	525	483	---	---	---
New Hampshire	127	91	36	8	28	48	27	21	3	18	378	---	---	---	---
Vermont	102	43	59	13	46	75	22	53	20	33	735	---	---	---	---
Massachusetts	12,822	11,654	1,168	72	1,096	4,708	4,042	666	38	628	367	347	570	---	573
Rhode Island	2,216	2,047	169	20	149	1,008	937	71	3	68	455	458	420	---	456
Connecticut	7,804	6,548	1,256	77	1,179	2,969	2,538	431	13	418	380	388	343	---	355
MIDDLE ATLANTIC	317,861	291,171	26,690	2,079	24,611	93,251	81,640	11,611	1,113	10,498	293	280	435	535	427
New York	136,164	130,397	5,767	430	5,337	34,116	32,080	2,036	221	1,815	251	246	353	514	340
New Jersey	59,409	51,570	7,839	852	6,987	19,790	16,363	3,427	485	2,942	333	317	437	569	421
Pennsylvania	122,288	109,204	13,084	797	12,287	39,345	33,197	6,148	407	5,741	322	304	470	511	467
EAST NORTH CENTRAL	266,545	250,250	16,295	3,252	13,043	78,446	71,581	6,865	1,700	5,165	294	286	421	523	396
Ohio	84,409	76,816	7,593	1,307	6,286	27,845	24,363	3,482	740	2,742	330	317	459	566	436
Indiana	30,076	28,464	1,612	435	1,177	9,142	8,521	621	218	403	304	299	385	501	342
Illinois	99,252	94,196	5,056	1,074	3,982	25,378	23,381	1,997	503	1,494	256	248	395	468	375
Michigan	49,900	48,017	1,883	383	1,500	15,231	14,551	680	186	494	305	303	361	486	329
Wisconsin	2,908	2,757	151	53	98	850	765	85	53	32	292	277	563	---	---
WEST NORTH CENTRAL	89,317	74,193	15,124	7,526	7,598	25,141	18,339	6,802	3,842	2,960	281	247	450	510	390
Minnesota	2,321	2,259	62	33	29	615	592	23	13	10	265	262	---	---	---
Iowa	4,128	3,722	406	89	317	1,391	1,223	168	59	109	337	329	414	---	344
Missouri	62,804	51,059	11,745	6,498	5,247	16,830	11,353	5,477	3,348	2,129	268	222	466	515	406
North Dakota	84	58	26	12	14	30	10	20	14	6	---	---	---	---	---
South Dakota	147	85	62	47	15	47	24	23	23	---	320	---	---	---	---
Nebraska	3,785	3,656	129	28	101	1,046	1,019	27	13	14	276	279	209	---	139
Kansas	16,048	13,354	2,694	819	1,875	5,182	4,118	1,064	372	692	323	308	395	454	369
SOUTH ATLANTIC	1,119,800	453,353	666,447	416,158	250,289	490,017	123,670	366,347	250,479	115,868	438	273	550	602	463
Delaware	7,681	4,078	3,603	1,290	2,313	2,787	1,072	1,715	720	995	363	263	476	558	430
Maryland	68,548	45,470	23,078	8,077	15,001	27,006	13,720	13,286	5,304	7,982	394	302	576	657	532
District of Columbia	39,745	39,745	---	---	---	10,006	10,006	---	---	---	252	252	---	---	---
Virginia	151,720	62,368	89,352	49,625	39,727	70,662	18,107	52,555	31,736	20,819	466	290	588	640	524
West Virginia	29,077	9,005	20,072	723	19,349	12,104	2,500	9,604	409	9,195	416	278	478	566	475
North Carolina	226,053	76,917	149,136	105,988	43,148	114,695	23,120	91,575	69,759	21,816	507	301	614	658	506
South Carolina	195,225	44,311	150,914	109,732	41,182	96,300	12,403	83,897	64,563	19,334	493	280	556	588	469
Georgia	279,911	103,354	176,557	124,072	52,485	116,016	25,260	90,756	69,651	21,105	414	244	514	561	402
Florida	121,840	68,105	53,735	16,651	37,084	40,441	17,482	22,959	8,337	14,622	332	257	427	501	394
EAST SOUTH CENTRAL	679,862	235,637	444,225	335,708	108,517	288,162	60,705	227,457	184,773	42,684	424	258	512	550	393
Kentucky	55,558	32,270	23,288	9,630	13,658	18,587	7,856	10,731	5,135	5,596	335	243	461	533	410
Tennessee	128,059	74,831	53,228	37,995	15,233	44,304	18,024	26,280	20,536	5,744	346	241	494	540	377
Alabama	243,502	85,135	158,367	110,447	47,920	107,836	23,920	83,916	63,473	20,443	443	281	530	575	427
Mississippi	252,743	43,401	209,342	177,636	31,706	117,435	10,905	106,530	95,629	10,901	465	251	509	538	344
WEST SOUTH CENTRAL	602,263	239,098	363,165	271,536	91,629	238,400	57,845	180,555	146,172	34,383	396	242	497	538	375
Arkansas	124,172	28,809	95,363	77,408	17,955	49,957	6,362	43,595	37,783	5,812	402	221	457	488	324
Louisiana	202,304	81,054	121,250	83,907	37,343	84,986	22,004	62,982	47,637	15,345	420	271	519	568	411
Oklahoma	44,867	21,645	23,222	17,295	5,927	17,337	5,135	12,202	9,845	2,357	386	237	525	569	398
Texas	230,920	107,590	123,330	92,926	30,404	86,120	24,344	61,776	50,907	10,869	373	226	501	548	357
MOUNTAIN	7,546	5,723	1,823	495	1,328	2,084	1,374	710	264	446	276	240	389	533	336
Montana	261	225	36	11	25	66	59	7	4	3	253	262	---	---	---
Idaho	157	137	20	10	10	30	22	8	3	5	191	161	---	---	---
Wyoming	297	216	81	13	68	63	41	22	5	17	212	190	---	---	---
Colorado	3,196	2,904	292	76	216	773	677	96	34	62	242	233	329	---	287
New Mexico	731	494	237	99	138	249	137	112	62	50	341	277	473	---	362
Arizona	2,518	1,433	1,085	278	807	793	349	444	153	291	315	244	409	550	361
Utah	253	214	39	5	34	89	71	18	3	15	352	332	---	---	---
Nevada	133	100	33	3	30	21	18	3	---	3	158	180	---	---	---
PACIFIC	25,416	22,892	2,524	742	1,782	5,790	4,816	974	412	562	228	210	386	555	315
Washington	1,473	1,314	159	43	116	400	325	75	21	54	272	247	472	---	466
Oregon	550	480	70	6	64	107	85	22	---	22	195	177	---	---	---
California	23,393	21,098	2,295	693	1,602	5,283	4,406	877	391	486	226	209	382	564	303

TABLE 10.—NEGRO AND WHITE WOMEN 15 TO 44 YEARS OF AGE, CHILDREN UNDER 5 YEARS, AND NUMBER OF CHILDREN PER 1,000 WOMEN, IN THE 65 CITIES OF 50,000 OR MORE INHABITANTS HAVING IN 1930 A NEGRO POPULATION OF 10,000 OR MORE: 1930 AND 1920

CITY	WOMEN 15 TO 44 YEARS OF AGE				CHILDREN UNDER 5 YEARS OF AGE				CHILDREN UNDER 5 PER 1,000 WOMEN 15 TO 44 YEARS OF AGE					
	Negro		White		Negro		White		Negro		White		Increase or decrease (—) 1920–30	
	1930	1920	1930	1920 [1]	1930	1920	1930	1920 [1]	1930	1920	1930	1920 [1]	Negro	White [1]
Akron, Ohio	3,159	1,421	64,377	48,420	1,086	306	22,915	20,572	344	215	356	425	129	−69
Asheville, N. C	4,889	2,369	10,320	5,944	1,238	679	3,217	2,211	253	287	312	372	−34	−60
Atlanta, Ga	30,443	21,088	51,744	39,481	7,090	4,544	13,835	12,589	233	215	267	319	18	−52
Atlantic City, N. J	4,996	3,722	13,505	10,364	942	591	2,961	3,153	189	159	219	304	30	−85
Augusta, Ga	7,978	7,327	9,607	8,029	1,775	1,527	3,144	2,728	222	208	327	340	14	−13
Baltimore, Md	40,751	33,224	165,625	158,300	12,274	8,366	52,146	60,981	301	252	315	385	49	−70
Beaumont, Tex	5,884	4,215	10,742	7,136	1,690	1,085	3,456	2,784	287	257	322	390	30	−68
Birmingham, Ala	32,283	22,127	44,752	29,411	8,717	5,617	14,026	10,901	270	254	313	371	16	−58
Boston, Mass	5,525	4,895	191,416	185,637	1,582	1,212	60,669	69,573	286	248	317	375	38	−58
Buffalo, N. Y	4,114	1,345	141,552	127,202	1,287	277	46,319	51,802	313	206	327	407	107	−80
Camden, N. J	3,079	2,323	26,295	25,815	1,139	750	8,946	12,208	370	323	340	473	47	−133
Charleston, S. C	9,446	10,514	8,684	9,008	2,768	2,761	3,144	3,512	293	263	362	390	30	−28
Charlotte, N. C	8,283	4,605	16,591	8,674	2,140	1,358	5,689	3,695	258	295	343	426	−37	−83
Chattanooga, Tenn	10,503	5,972	23,703	11,035	2,618	1,253	7,976	3,235	249	210	336	293	39	43
Chicago, Ill	74,982	35,574	833,662	666,698	17,529	6,404	234,641	265,943	234	180	281	399	54	−118
Cincinnati, Ohio	14,190	9,183	103,500	96,394	4,003	1,995	28,960	28,736	282	217	280	298	65	−18
Cleveland, Ohio	21,911	10,540	214,882	190,317	6,458	2,371	63,942	86,050	295	225	298	452	70	−154
Columbia, S. C	6,679	4,879	9,126	6,599	1,436	1,071	2,520	2,181	215	220	276	331	−5	−55
Columbus, Ohio	8,719	6,266	66,259	56,056	2,612	1,638	19,521	17,671	300	261	295	315	39	−20
Dallas, Tex	13,412	7,954	63,502	39,393	2,751	1,458	17,021	11,340	205	183	268	288	22	−20
Dayton, Ohio	4,701	2,513	47,365	36,407	1,576	704	14,281	13,320	335	280	302	366	55	−64
Detroit, Mich	37,377	12,212	373,787	236,514	10,618	2,482	134,938	109,603	284	203	361	463	81	−102
Durham, N. C	6,134	2,371	9,236	4,038	1,765	676	3,475	1,482	288	285	376	367	3	9
East St. Louis, Ill	3,354	2,108	16,240	14,716	1,163	669	5,282	5,921	347	317	325	402	30	−77
Fort Worth, Tex	7,343	5,268	38,402	24,433	1,438	1,009	10,867	7,529	203	192	283	308	11	−25
Galveston, Tex	4,428	3,160	9,337	8,419	945	573	2,771	2,988	213	181	297	355	32	−58
Gary, Ind	5,260	1,502	19,501	10,882	1,672	378	7,464	6,914	318	252	383	635	66	−252
Greensboro, N. C	4,548	1,760	11,065	3,972	1,244	561	4,180	1,478	274	319	378	372	−45	6
Houston, Tex	21,524	11,294	60,925	29,029	4,588	2,067	17,083	8,990	213	183	280	310	30	−30
Indianapolis, Ind	12,542	10,174	83,886	74,283	3,457	2,480	24,183	23,023	276	244	288	310	32	−22
Jacksonville, Fla	16,394	13,522	22,488	13,909	3,543	3,067	7,069	4,922	216	227	314	354	−11	−40
Jersey City, N. J	3,581	2,247	77,113	71,887	1,239	677	25,037	32,697	346	301	325	455	45	−130
Kansas City, Kans	5,364	4,038	24,733	21,160	1,632	1,120	8,532	9,072	304	277	345	429	27	−84
Kansas City, Mo	12,311	10,123	100,230	82,009	2,154	1,462	23,454	22,529	175	144	234	275	31	−41
Knoxville, Tenn	5,282	3,421	24,429	18,121	1,314	801	8,734	6,985	249	234	358	385	15	−27
Little Rock, Ark	6,608	5,721	17,996	13,568	1,323	1,186	4,396	4,087	200	207	244	301	−7	−57
Los Angeles, Calif	12,174	4,897	285,740	144,359	2,435	988	59,046	34,910	200	202	207	242	−2	−35
Louisville, Ky	13,952	12,542	68,044	51,855	3,101	2,353	21,627	15,718	222	188	318	303	34	15
Macon, Ga	7,560	7,425	8,623	8,201	1,896	1,563	2,433	2,779	251	211	282	339	40	−57
Memphis, Tenn	31,743	20,744	44,465	28,421	7,062	3,630	12,649	8,427	222	175	284	297	47	−13
Miami, Fla	8,195	2,920	22,208	5,162	2,639	1,103	6,681	1,811	322	378	301	351	−56	−50
Mobile, Ala	7,914	7,610	11,384	9,678	2,016	1,796	3,573	3,425	255	236	314	354	19	−40
Montgomery, Ala	9,963	6,621	10,055	6,525	2,384	1,433	3,240	2,170	239	216	322	333	23	−11
Nashville, Tenn	13,116	11,241	30,500	22,752	3,083	2,424	9,293	7,205	235	216	305	317	19	−12
Newark, N. J	11,881	5,233	102,182	98,812	3,821	1,467	32,286	43,086	322	280	316	436	42	−120
New Orleans, La	40,521	31,871	86,938	74,305	11,518	7,798	26,961	24,564	284	245	310	331	39	−21
New York, N. Y	111,230	54,348	1,775,935	1,431,670	26,920	11,147	507,846	549,402	242	205	286	384	37	−98
Norfolk, Va	13,270	13,536	21,752	18,899	3,378	3,271	6,261	6,388	255	242	288	338	13	−50
Oklahoma City, Okla	4,895	2,618	48,057	23,376	1,033	561	15,007	6,898	211	214	312	295	−3	17
Omaha, Nebr	3,171	3,031	53,184	46,813	878	652	16,456	15,846	277	215	309	338	62	−29
Philadelphia, Pa	67,185	42,959	434,912	420,350	18,658	9,769	129,548	168,828	278	227	298	402	51	−104
Pittsburgh, Pa	15,665	10,949	156,162	138,240	4,934	2,732	52,120	59,262	315	250	334	429	65	−95
Port Arthur, Tex	3,212	1,212	10,324	4,614	937	416	4,354	2,003	292	343	422	434	−51	−12
Richmond, Va	15,816	17,341	36,386	32,754	4,576	4,587	9,490	10,981	289	265	261	335	24	−74
Roanoke, Va	3,795	2,906	15,788	11,006	1,144	903	5,270	4,707	301	311	334	428	−10	−94
St. Louis, Mo	29,273	21,793	196,212	190,118	6,634	4,143	51,672	54,541	227	190	263	287	37	−24
San Antonio, Tex	6,177	4,720	35,424	38,994	1,098	965	9,030	13,819	178	204	255	354	−26	−99
Savannah, Ga	13,719	13,347	12,437	11,684	2,660	2,584	3,663	4,405	194	194	295	377	------	−82
Shreveport, La	9,535	5,899	14,221	7,306	1,930	1,210	4,255	2,223	202	205	299	304	−3	−5
Tampa, Fla	7,019	3,853	21,343	9,976	1,636	788	6,756	4,326	233	205	317	434	28	−117
Toledo, Ohio	3,869	1,667	69,279	59,767	1,115	346	21,894	22,390	288	208	316	375	80	−59
Tulsa, Okla	5,427	2,840	36,169	18,040	1,034	730	10,816	5,610	191	257	299	311	−66	−12
Washington, D. C	39,745	35,055	94,806	99,385	10,006	7,774	22,240	22,632	252	222	235	228	30	7
Wilmington, Del	3,404	3,010	23,125	24,095	833	679	7,104	10,861	245	226	307	451	19	−144
Winston-Salem, N. C	10,861	6,764	12,172	7,618	2,915	1,695	4,741	3,115	268	251	390	409	17	−19
Youngstown, Ohio	3,969	1,848	37,818	29,953	1,659	443	14,371	16,030	418	240	380	535	178	−155

[1] Includes Mexicans.

TABLE 11.—NEGRO WOMEN 15 TO 44 YEARS OF AGE, AND NEGRO CHILDREN UNDER 5 YEARS, WITH NUMBER OF NEGRO CHILDREN PER 1,000 WOMEN IN THE 147 CITIES HAVING 5,000 OR MORE NEGRO INHABITANTS: 1930

CITY	Women 15 to 44 years of age	CHILDREN UNDER 5 YEARS	
		Number	Per 1,000 women 15 to 44 years of age
ALABAMA			
Anniston	2,152	710	330
Bessemer	3,625	1,096	302
Birmingham	32,283	8,717	270
Dothan	1,840	648	352
Fairfield	1,923	683	355
Gadsden	1,864	600	322
Mobile	7,914	2,016	255
Montgomery	9,963	2,384	239
Selma	3,097	795	257
Tuscaloosa	2,331	641	275
ARKANSAS			
Little Rock	6,608	1,323	200
North Little Rock	1,822	526	289
Pine Bluff	2,066	419	203
CALIFORNIA			
Los Angeles	12,174	2,435	200
Oakland	2,124	417	196
COLORADO			
Denver	2,086	464	222
CONNECTICUT			
Hartford	1,778	691	389
New Haven	1,317	483	367
DELAWARE			
Wilmington	3,404	833	245
DISTRICT OF COLUMBIA			
Washington	39,745	10,006	252
FLORIDA			
Daytona Beach	1,795	425	237
Jacksonville	16,394	3,543	216
Miami	8,195	2,639	322
Orlando	2,554	649	254
Pensacola	3,039	760	250
St. Petersburg	2,561	616	241
Tampa	7,019	1,636	233
West Palm Beach	3,076	720	234
GEORGIA			
Albany	2,499	581	232
Athens	1,987	514	259
Atlanta	30,443	7,090	233
Augusta	7,978	1,775	222
Brunswick	1,964	428	218
Columbus	4,739	1,216	257
La Grange	1,726	535	310
Macon	7,560	1,896	251
Savannah	13,719	2,660	194
Thomasville	1,896	433	228
Valdosta	2,008	484	241
Waycross	1,849	528	286
ILLINOIS			
Chicago	74,982	17,529	234
East St. Louis	3,354	1,163	347
INDIANA			
East Chicago	1,494	526	352
Evansville	1,888	399	211
Gary	5,260	1,672	318
Indianapolis	12,542	3,457	276
IOWA			
Des Moines	1,407	483	343
KANSAS			
Kansas City	5,364	1,632	304
Topeka	1,481	452	305
Wichita	1,658	450	271
KENTUCKY			
Lexington	3,525	854	242
Louisville	13,952	3,101	222
Paducah	1,902	417	219
LOUISIANA			
Alexandria	2,993	819	274
Baton Rouge	3,683	736	200
Lafayette	1,381	545	395
Lake Charles	1,727	621	360
Monroe	3,498	681	195
New Orleans	40,521	11,518	284
Shreveport	9,535	1,930	202
MARYLAND			
Baltimore	40,751	12,274	301
MASSACHUSETTS			
Boston	5,525	1,582	286
Cambridge	1,342	497	370
MICHIGAN			
Detroit	37,377	10,618	284
Flint	1,599	574	359
MISSISSIPPI			
Clarksdale	1,881	256	136
Greenville	2,693	550	204
Greenwood	1,960	378	193
Hattiesburg	2,213	659	298
Jackson	6,319	1,616	256
Laurel	2,261	681	301
Meridian	3,767	1,023	272
Natchez	2,310	489	212
Vicksburg	3,871	791	204
MISSOURI			
Kansas City	12,311	2,154	175
St. Louis	29,273	6,634	227
NEBRASKA			
Omaha	3,171	878	277
NEW JERSEY			
Atlantic City	4,996	942	189
Camden	3,079	1,139	370
Jersey City	3,581	1,239	346
Montclair	2,350	563	240
Newark	11,881	3,821	322
Orange	1,478	469	317
Trenton	2,094	880	420
NEW YORK			
Buffalo	4,114	1,287	313
New York	111,230	26,920	242
NORTH CAROLINA			
Asheville	4,889	1,238	253
Charlotte	8,283	2,140	258
Durham	6,134	1,765	288
Fayetteville	1,721	567	329
Goldsboro	1,998	719	360
Greensboro	4,548	1,244	274
High Point	2,316	722	312
Kinston	1,538	489	318
NORTH CAROLINA—con.			
New Bern	1,791	583	326
Raleigh	3,858	1,042	270
Rocky Mount	2,593	891	344
Wilmington	3,973	1,215	306
Wilson	1,928	603	313
Winston-Salem	10,861	2,915	268
OHIO			
Akron	3,159	1,086	344
Cincinnati	14,190	4,003	282
Cleveland	21,911	6,458	295
Columbus	8,719	2,612	300
Dayton	4,701	1,576	335
Springfield	2,014	729	362
Toledo	3,869	1,115	288
Youngstown	3,969	1,659	418
OKLAHOMA			
Muskogee	1,991	490	246
Oklahoma City	4,895	1,033	211
Tulsa	5,427	1,034	191
PENNSYLVANIA			
Chester	2,485	842	339
Harrisburg	1,730	522	302
Philadelphia	67,185	18,658	278
Pittsburgh	15,665	4,934	315
RHODE ISLAND			
Providence	1,237	569	460
SOUTH CAROLINA			
Charleston	9,446	2,768	293
Columbia	6,679	1,436	215
Florence	1,996	496	248
Greenville	3,596	968	269
Spartanburg	3,086	921	298
Sumter	1,682	428	254
TENNESSEE			
Chattanooga	10,503	2,618	249
Jackson	2,384	539	226
Knoxville	5,282	1,314	249
Memphis	31,743	7,062	222
Nashville	13,116	3,083	235
TEXAS			
Austin	3,070	750	244
Beaumont	5,884	1,690	287
Dallas	13,412	2,751	205
Fort Worth	7,343	1,488	203
Galveston	4,428	945	213
Houston	21,524	4,588	213
Marshall	2,129	577	271
Port Arthur	3,212	937	292
San Antonio	6,177	1,098	178
Waco	2,922	688	235
VIRGINIA			
Danville	1,713	525	306
Lynchburg	2,861	831	290
Newport News	3,833	1,216	317
Norfolk	13,270	3,378	255
Petersburg	3,665	1,047	286
Portsmouth	5,303	1,510	285
Richmond	15,816	4,576	289
Roanoke	3,795	1,144	301
WEST VIRGINIA			
Charleston	2,099	509	242
WISCONSIN			
Milwaukee	2,109	574	272

CHAPTER XI—SCHOOL ATTENDANCE

The school attendance inquiry.—The statistics of school attendance obtained in the census of 1930 are based upon the answer to a question on the Population Schedule as to whether the person enumerated had attended school or college at any time between September 1, 1929, and the census date, April 1, 1930. If the person had attended any kind of school, college, or other educational institution at any time within the period in question, an affirmative answer was to be made. The total number of persons returned as attending school is therefore larger than the number who were in attendance at any one time between September 1, 1929, and April 1, 1930.

In 1920 the question was asked in practically the same form, though since the census date was January 1 (instead of Apr. 1) the period covered was somewhat less and the returns may have been somewhat smaller than they would have been if the inquiry had been made in April. It is believed, however, that the difference is very small and that the figures for 1930 are fairly comparable with those for 1920 and for the earlier censuses, except possibly those for 1890 and 1900. At these two censuses the enumerators were required to ascertain not only the fact of school attendance but also the number of months of attendance. In some instances the person from whom the enumerator obtained his information would not know the number of months of school attendance, even though he knew the child had attended school. In a few of these cases the enumerator probably made no report at all with respect to school attendance. The returns for 1890 and 1900 are therefore doubtless less complete than those for the subsequent censuses and perhaps less complete than those for earlier censuses. In the censuses prior to 1890, and also in 1910, as well as 1920, the general form of the inquiry on school attendance was the same as in 1930.

The ages of compulsory school attendance vary in different States, beginning at 6 years in 2 States, 7 years in 29 States and the District of Columbia, and at 8 years in 17 States. The main body of pupils in the elementary school (grades 1 to 8) are included in group 7 to 13 years of age, hence, statistics are presented in more detail in this chapter for this group than for the others.

In a total Negro population of 11,891,143, there were 2,553,151 persons, constituting 21.5 percent of the total population, who had attended school sometime between September 1, 1929, and April 1, 1930. Comparing the different classes of the population, the proportion in school, with the exception of the foreign born, does not vary greatly from the average for all classes combined (22.8 percent); of the Negroes, 21.5 percent; of the white, 22.9 percent; and of the foreign born white, 3.8 percent, were attending school. Of course, these comparisons are for the total population, infants, adults, as well as children of school age. In the following discussion the figures for population and school attendance are limited to the school age periods.

Increase in school attendance.—Between 1920 and 1930 the number of Negroes between 5 and 20 years of age attending school increased by 447,042, and the number not attending school decreased by 115,001. Considered by age periods, the number of Negroes in school, 5 and 6 years of age, increased 33,512; the number 7 to 13 years of age, 249,581; the number 14 and 15 years of age, 68,147; the number 16 and 17 years of age, 63,888; and the number 18 to 20 years of age, 31,914. However, part of the increase in each of these age groups represents a growth of population and a part to improved conditions and greater interest in education.

School attendance by single years of age.—In 1930 the largest numbers reported as attending school were those for 10 years of age, while the highest percentage was for those for 11 years of age. The percent attending school increased from 12.7, for children 5 years of age, to 92.2 for those 11 years of age, and then decreased to 6.6 percent for those 20 years of age.

School attendance by sex.—There was an excess of females over males attending school in 1930 at every age from 5 to 20 years, due partly to an excess of 111,004 females over males between the ages of 5 and 20 years.

School attendance in urban and rural areas.—The percent attending school was greater in urban than in rural areas. The percentages for the United States were, for children 7 to 20 years of age, 67 for urban, and 63, for rural areas; for children 7 to 13 years of age, 94.2 in the urban, and 83.8 in the rural areas; for children 14 and 15 years of age, 83.7 in the urban, and 75.3 in rural areas; for 16 and 17 years, 49.2 in urban, and 44.8 in rural areas; and for 18 to 20 years, 13.9 for urban, and 12.9 for rural areas.

School attendance by sections, divisions, and States.—In 1930 the percent of the Negro children 5 to 20 years of age attending school was 75.1 in the West, 68.2 in the North, and 58.5 in the South. By years of age, the greatest difference in percent attending school between the South and the North and West was for the ages 5, 6, 7, 15, 16, and 17.

There were 3 States, all in the South, reporting less than 60 percent of the Negro children 7 to 20 years of age attending school in 1930; 20 States, 11 in the South, 7 in the North, and 2 in the West, reporting between 60 and 70 percent; and the District of Columbia and 25 States, 14 in the North, 9 in the West, and 2 in the South, reporting 70 percent or more of the Negro children 7 to 20 years of age, attending school.

School attendance in cities.—The divergencies shown in the percent of the Negroes 7 to 20 years of age attending school, between various cities, indicate that a number of factors affect school attendance. These factors cannot be summed up into any general statement, since the statistics for each city represent conditions existing in that city, and perhaps not elsewhere.

In Northern cities, generally, the percentage of Negroes attending school was higher than the percentage in Southern cities.

School attendance and gainful employment.—The main purpose in presenting the data on school attendance and gainful employment is to show the number of Negroes who were neither attending school nor engaged in a gainful occupation.

In 1930 there were 56,081 male Negroes, between the ages of 10 to 15 years; 26,531 Negroes, 16 and 17 years of age; 28,821 between the ages of 18 and 20, and 18,554 between the ages of 21 and 24 years who were neither gainfully occupied nor attending school.

Over 80 percent of the male Negroes, 10 to 15 years of age, over 60 percent of those 16 to 20 years of age, and over 50 percent of those 21 to 24 years of age, who were neither gainfully employed nor attending school were in rural areas.

There were 61,594 Negro females, between 10 and 15 years of age; 48,219, 16 and 17 years of age; 72,985, between the ages of 18 and 20, and 47,567 between 21 and 24 years of age who were neither married nor gainfully occupied nor attending school in 1930.

More than two-thirds of the Negro females 10 to 24 years of age who were neither married nor gainfully employed nor attending school in 1930 were in rural areas.

TABLE 1.—SCHOOL ATTENDANCE, BY COLOR, AND NATIVITY, FOR THE UNITED STATES: 1930

COLOR AND NATIVITY	Total	ATTENDING SCHOOL: Number	ATTENDING SCHOOL: Percent	PERCENT DISTRIBUTION: Total population	PERCENT DISTRIBUTION: Population attending school
All classes	122,775,046	27,947,009	22.8	100.0	100.0
Negro	11,891,143	2,553,151	21.5	9.7	9.1
White	108,864,207	24,973,932	22.9	88.7	89.4
Native	95,497,800	24,460,860	25.6	77.8	87.5
Native parentage	70,136,614	17,918,875	25.5	57.1	64.1
Foreign or mixed parentage	25,361,186	6,541,985	25.8	20.7	23.4
Foreign born	13,366,407	513,072	3.8	10.9	1.8
Other races [1]	2,019,696	419,926	20.8	1.6	1.5

[1] Includes Mexican, Indian, Chinese, Japanese, Filipino, Hindu, Korean, and all other.

TABLE 2.—SCHOOL ATTENDANCE OF THE NEGRO AND WHITE POPULATION OF THE UNITED STATES, BY AGE PERIODS: 1930

AGE	NUMBER: Negro	NUMBER: White	PERCENT DISTRIBUTION: Negro	PERCENT DISTRIBUTION: White
All ages	2,553,151	24,973,932	100.0	100.0
Under 7 years	181,312	2,017,553	7.1	8.1
Under 5 years	4,813	56,374	.2	.2
5 years	34,748	458,629	1.4	1.8
6 years	141,751	1,502,550	5.6	6.0
7 to 20 years	2,300,812	22,007,950	90.1	88.1
7 to 13 years	1,580,624	14,547,737	61.9	58.3
14 and 15 years	385,502	3,716,963	15.1	14.9
16 and 17 years	232,648	2,405,061	9.1	9.6
18 to 20 years	102,038	1,338,189	4.0	5.4
21 years old and over	71,027	948,429	2.8	3.8

TABLE 3.—NEGRO SCHOOL ATTENDANCE, BY SINGLE YEARS OF AGE FROM 5 TO 20, BY SEX, AND PERCENT OF NEGROES AND WHITES IN SCHOOL, FOR THE UNITED STATES: 1930

AGE	NEGRO						PERCENT ATTENDING SCHOOL					
	Total		Male		Female		Negro			White		
	Attending school	Not attending school	Attending school	Not attending school	Attending school	Not attending school	Both sexes	Male	Female	Both sexes	Male	Female
5 to 20 years	2,477,311	1,651,687	1,193,775	815,222	1,283,536	836,465	60.0	59.4	60.5	71.5	71.7	71.2
5 years	34,748	238,984	16,274	120,173	18,474	118,811	12.7	11.9	13.5	21.1	20.6	21.7
6 years	141,751	139,965	67,735	71,530	74,016	68,435	50.3	48.6	52.0	69.1	68.3	69.9
7 to 13 years	1,580,624	230,391	778,899	123,070	801,725	107,321	87.3	86.4	88.2	96.6	96.5	96.7
7 years	207,248	63,980	101,153	33,250	106,095	30,730	76.4	75.3	77.5	91.6	91.4	91.9
8 years	238,002	43,479	117,194	22,565	120,808	20,914	84.6	83.9	85.2	95.7	95.6	95.8
9 years	229,466	30,758	113,588	16,286	115,878	14,472	88.2	87.5	88.9	96.7	96.6	96.8
10 years	251,219	24,885	125,543	13,410	125,676	11,475	91.0	90.3	91.6	98.1	98.0	98.2
11 years	204,479	17,405	100,879	9,450	103,600	7,955	92.2	91.4	92.9	98.2	98.2	98.3
12 years	239,453	24,226	118,545	13,687	120,908	10,539	90.8	89.6	92.0	98.1	98.0	98.2
13 years	210,757	25,658	101,997	14,422	108,760	11,236	89.1	87.6	90.6	97.6	97.5	97.6
14 and 15 years	385,502	108,395	182,559	59,798	202,943	48,597	78.1	75.3	80.7	90.4	90.8	90.1
14 years	210,308	43,152	101,039	24,256	109,269	18,896	83.0	80.6	85.3	94.3	94.6	94.1
15 years	175,194	65,243	81,520	35,542	93,674	29,701	72.9	69.6	75.9	86.4	86.8	85.9
16 and 17 years	232,648	270,062	104,560	140,324	128,088	129,738	46.3	42.7	49.7	58.9	58.4	59.3
16 years	142,654	115,071	64,056	59,834	78,598	55,237	55.4	51.7	58.7	68.0	67.7	62.8
17 years	89,994	154,991	40,504	80,490	49,490	74,501	36.7	33.5	39.9	49.5	48.9	50.1
18 to 20 years	102,038	663,890	43,748	300,327	58,290	363,563	13.3	12.7	13.8	22.6	23.7	21.5
18 years	55,931	213,200	23,771	100,156	32,160	113,044	20.8	19.2	22.1	32.2	32.7	31.7
19 years	29,168	209,082	12,793	96,980	16,375	112,102	12.2	11.7	12.7	20.8	21.9	19.7
20 years	16,939	241,608	7,184	103,191	9,755	138,417	6.6	6.5	6.6	14.1	15.7	12.6

TABLE 4.—SCHOOL ATTENDANCE OF NEGROES BY SINGLE YEARS OF AGE FROM 5 TO 20, BY SEX, FOR THE UNITED STATES: 1930, 1920, AND 1910

AGE	TOTAL						MALE						FEMALE					
	Number			Percent			Number			Percent			Number			Percent		
	1930	1920	1910	1930	1920	1910	1930	1920	1910	1930	1920	1910	1930	1920	1910	1930	1920	1910
5 to 20 years	2,477,311	2,030,269	1,644,75	60.0	53.5	44.7	1,193,775	69,063	771,537	59.4	52.4	42.9	1,283,536	1,061,203	373,172	60.5	54.5	46.4
5 years	34,748	29,760	25,060	12.7	11.8	9.8	16,274	14,122	11,774	11.9	11.2	9.3	18,474	15,638	13,286	13.5	12.3	10.3
6 years	141,751	113,227	78,124	50.3	42.9	29.7	67,735	54,306	37,051	48.6	41.7	28.5	74,016	58,921	41,073	52.0	44.1	30.9
7 years	207,248	166,457	120,104	76.4	64.9	47.7	101,153	81,807	58,270	75.3	64.0	46.3	106,095	84,650	61,834	77.5	65.9	49.2
8 years	238,002	188,743	146,186	84.6	72.7	57.9	117,194	93,447	70,609	83.9	72.1	56.5	120,808	95,296	75,577	85.2	73.3	59.3
9 years	229,466	179,845	144,540	88.2	77.0	64.6	113,588	89,558	71,232	87.5	76.4	63.7	115,878	90,287	73,308	88.9	77.7	65.4
10 years	251,219	210,888	169,155	91.0	80.0	69.8	125,543	105,328	83,575	90.3	79.1	68.0	125,676	105,560	85,580	91.6	80.9	71.5
11 years	204,479	178,834	141,723	92.2	82.1	72.7	100,879	88,166	68,730	91.4	81.0	70.8	103,600	90,668	72,993	92.9	83.2	74.5
12 years	239,453	221,168	183,267	90.8	80.6	70.1	118,545	108,801	88,619	89.6	79.0	67.5	120,908	112,367	94,648	92.0	82.1	72.8
13 years	210,757	185,108	151,816	89.1	79.3	68.4	101,997	88,592	71,574	87.6	77.3	64.9	108,760	96,516	80,242	90.6	81.3	71.9
14 years	210,308	181,761	146,034	83.0	73.4	62.3	101,039	85,701	66,988	80.6	70.2	57.4	109,269	96,060	79,046	85.3	76.5	67.0
15 years	175,194	135,594	111,860	72.9	63.3	53.9	81,520	60,524	49,221	69.6	58.7	48.3	93,674	75,070	62,639	75.9	67.6	59.3
16 years	142,654	106,045	93,055	55.4	47.1	41.5	64,056	44,260	38,600	51.7	41.7	36.2	78,598	61,785	54,455	58.7	51.9	46.3
17 years	89,994	62,715	59,090	36.7	30.5	29.0	40,504	26,105	24,727	33.5	26.1	24.7	49,490	36,610	34,363	39.9	34.6	33.1
18 years	55,931	39,748	41,507	20.8	17.3	17.9	23,771	15,842	16,613	19.2	14.8	15.3	32,160	23,906	24,894	22.1	19.6	20.2
19 years	29,168	20,615	21,110	12.2	9.9	10.9	12,793	8,631	8,964	11.7	8.9	9.9	16,375	11,984	12,146	12.7	10.7	11.9
20 years	16,939	9,761	12,128	6.6	4.6	5.6	7,184	3,876	5,040	6.5	4.4	5.4	9,755	5,885	7,088	6.6	4.8	5.8

99576—35——14

TABLE 5.—NEGRO POPULATION FROM 5 TO 20 YEARS OF AGE, ATTENDING AND NOT ATTENDING SCHOOL AND PERCENTAGES FOR NEGROES AND WHITES, BY SEX AND AGE PERIODS: 1930 AND 1920

[A minus sign (—) denotes decrease]

AGE AND CENSUS YEAR	NEGRO						PERCENT ATTENDING SCHOOL						PERCENT NOT ATTENDING SCHOOL					
	Attending school			Not attending school			Negro			White			Negro			White		
	Total	Male	Female	Total	Male	Female	Total	Male	Female	Total	Male	Female	Total	Male	Female	Total	Male	Female
5 to 20 years:																		
1930	2,477,311	1,193,775	1,283,536	1,651,687	815,222	836,465	60.0	59.4	60.5	71.5	71.7	71.2	40.0	40.6	39.5	28.5	28.3	28.8
1920	2,030,269	969,066	1,061,203	1,766,688	879,731	886,957	53.5	52.4	54.5	65.7	65.6	65.9	46.5	47.6	45.5	34.3	34.4	34.1
Increase, 1920–30	447,042	224,709	222,333	−115,001	−64,509	−50,492	6.5	7.0	6.0	5.8	6.1	5.3	−6.5	−7.0	−6.0	−5.8	−6.1	−5.3
5 and 6 years:																		
1930	176,499	84,009	92,490	378,949	191,703	187,246	31.8	30.5	33.1	45.1	44.4	45.9	68.2	69.5	66.9	54.9	55.6	54.1
1920	142,987	68,428	74,559	373,616	188,060	185,556	27.7	26.7	28.7	42.7	42.2	43.3	72.3	73.3	71.3	57.3	57.8	56.7
Increase, 1920–30	33,512	15,581	17,931	5,333	3,643	1,690	4.1	3.8	4.4	2.4	2.2	2.6	−4.1	−3.8	−4.4	−2.4	−2.2	−2.6
7 to 13 years:																		
1930	1,580,624	778,899	801,725	230,391	123,070	107,321	87.3	86.4	88.2	96.6	96.5	96.7	12.7	13.6	11.8	3.4	3.5	3.3
1920	1,331,043	655,699	675,344	407,779	213,346	194,433	76.5	75.5	77.6	92.5	92.4	92.6	23.5	24.5	22.4	7.5	7.6	7.4
Increase, 1920–30	249,581	123,200	126,381	−177,388	−90,276	−87,112	10.8	10.9	10.6	4.1	4.1	4.1	−10.8	−10.9	−10.6	−4.1	−4.1	−4.1
14 and 15 years:																		
1930	385,502	182,559	202,943	108,395	59,798	48,597	78.1	75.3	80.7	90.4	90.8	90.1	21.9	24.7	19.3	9.6	9.2	9.9
1920	317,355	146,225	171,130	144,423	78,897	65,526	68.7	65.0	72.3	81.5	81.4	81.6	31.3	35.0	27.7	18.5	18.6	18.4
Increase, 1920–30	68,147	36,334	31,813	−36,028	−19,099	−16,929	9.4	10.3	8.4	8.9	9.4	8.5	−9.4	−10.3	−8.4	−8.9	−9.4	−8.5
16 and 17 years:																		
1930	232,648	104,560	128,088	270,062	140,324	129,738	46.3	42.7	49.7	58.9	58.4	59.3	53.7	57.3	50.3	41.1	41.6	40.7
1920	168,760	70,365	98,395	262,039	135,722	126,317	39.2	34.1	43.8	43.4	41.0	45.7	60.8	65.9	56.2	56.6	59.0	54.3
Increase, 1920–30	63,888	34,195	29,693	8,023	4,602	3,421	7.1	8.6	5.9	15.5	17.4	13.6	−7.1	−8.6	−5.9	−15.5	−17.4	−13.6
18 to 20 years:																		
1930	102,038	43,748	58,290	663,890	300,327	363,563	13.3	12.7	13.8	22.6	23.7	21.5	86.7	87.3	86.2	77.4	76.3	78.5
1920	70,124	28,349	41,775	578,831	263,706	315,125	10.8	9.7	11.7	15.2	15.4	15.1	89.2	90.3	88.3	84.8	84.6	84.9
Increase, 1920–30	31,914	15,399	16,515	85,059	36,621	48,438	2.5	3.0	2.1	7.4	8.3	6.4	−2.5	−3.0	−2.1	−7.4	−8.3	−6.4

TABLE 6.—PERCENT OF INCREASE IN NEGRO POPULATION 5 TO 20 YEARS AND IN NUMBER ATTENDING SCHOOL, BY AGE PERIODS, FOR THE UNITED STATES: 1910 TO 1930

[A minus sign (—) denotes decrease]

AGE PERIOD	1920 to 1930		1910 to 1920	
	Total	Attending school	Total	Attending school
5 to 20 years	**8.7**	**22.0**	**3.2**	**23.4**
5 and 6 years	7.5	23.4	−.4	38.6
7 to 13 years	4.2	18.8	5.5	26.0
14 and 15 years	7.0	21.5	4.5	23.1
16 and 17 years	16.7	37.9	.6	10.9
18 to 20 years	18.0	45.5	1.4	−6.2

TABLE 7.—NEGRO CHILDREN 7 TO 15 YEARS OF AGE ATTENDING SCHOOL RANKED BY NUMBER AND PERCENT, WITH THE PERCENTAGE OF WHITE CHILDREN ATTENDING SCHOOL, IN CITIES HAVING 50,000 OR MORE NEGRO INHABITANTS: 1930

CITY	Rank by number attending school	Number attending school	CITY	Rank by percent attending school	PERCENT ATTENDING SCHOOL: Negro	White	Excess of white over Negro
New York, N. Y	1	34,527	Cleveland, Ohio	1	97.0	98.3	1.3
Philadelphia, Pa	2	28,424	Chicago, Ill	2	96.1	96.9	.8
Chicago, Ill	3	25,694	New York, N. Y	3	95.9	96.9	1.0
Baltimore, Md	4	18,598	Washington, D. C	4	95.9	97.7	1.8
New Orleans, La	5	17,955	Philadelphia, Pa	5	95.3	96.6	1.3
Washington, D. C	6	17,047	Pittsburgh, Pa	6	94.3	96.9	2.6
Detroit, Mich	7	14,468	St. Louis, Mo	7	94.2	94.9	.7
Birmingham, Ala	8	14,368	Houston, Tex	8	93.2	95.1	1.9
Atlanta, Ga	9	13,308	Baltimore, Md	9	92.6	94.1	1.5
Memphis, Tenn	10	11,378	Memphis, Tenn	10	92.3	97.1	4.8
St. Louis, Mo	11	10,692	Birmingham, Ala	11	92.0	97.1	5.1
Cleveland, Ohio	12	9,286	Richmond, Va	12	91.3	97.0	5.7
Richmond, Va	13	8,149	Detroit, Mich	13	90.9	97.8	6.9
Houston, Tex	14	7,706	New Orleans, La	14	90.9	94.3	3.4
Pittsburgh, Pa	15	7,339	Atlanta, Ga	15	86.6	95.2	8.6

TABLE 8.—THE NUMBER AND PERCENT ATTENDING SCHOOL FOR NEGROES AND WHITES FROM 5 TO 20 YEARS, BY GEOGRAPHIC DIVISIONS, AND SECTIONS: 1930

SECTION AND DIVISION	NEGRO			WHITE, ATTENDING SCHOOL		PERCENT DISTRIBUTION ATTENDING SCHOOL	
	Total	Attending school: Number	Percent	Number	Percent	Negro	White
United States	**4,128,998**	**2,477,311**	**60.0**	**23,969,129**	**71.5**	**100.0**	**100.0**
THE SOUTH	3,496,926	2,044,259	58.5	6,444,977	66.9	82.5	26.9
South Atlantic	1,721,330	983,407	57.1	2,611,374	66.4	39.7	10.9
East South Central	968,021	575,630	59.5	1,714,073	66.6	23.2	7.2
West South Central	807,575	485,222	60.1	2,119,530	67.7	19.6	8.8
THE NORTH	605,368	412,996	68.2	15,251,156	72.8	16.7	63.6
New England	26,401	19,262	73.0	1,733,928	73.7	.8	7.2
Middle Atlantic	263,331	174,159	66.1	5,339,867	71.5	7.0	22.3
East North Central	230,768	161,661	70.1	5,250,511	73.4	6.5	21.9
West North Central	84,868	57,914	68.2	2,926,850	73.7	2.3	12.2
THE WEST	26,704	20,056	75.1	2,272,996	76.9	.8	9.5
Mountain	6,710	4,650	69.3	796,412	74.7	.2	3.3
Pacific	19 994	15,406	77.1	1,476,584	78.1	.6	6.2

Table 9.—NEGRO AND WHITE POPULATION FROM 5 TO 20 YEARS OF AGE ATTENDING SCHOOL AND NOT ATTENDING SCHOOL, BY AGE PERIODS, FOR THE UNITED STATES: 1930 AND 1920

AGE	NUMBER		INCREASE OR DECREASE (—), 1920–30		AGE	NUMBER		INCREASE OR DECREASE (—), 1920–30	
	1930	1920	Number	Percent		1930	1920	Number	Percent
	NEGRO					WHITE			
5 to 20 years of age	4,128,998	3,796,957	332,041	8.7	5 to 20 years of age	33,536,777	29,333,533	4,203,244	14.3
Attending school	2,477,311	2,030,269	447,042	22.0	Attending school	23,969,129	19,278,528	4,690,601	24.3
Not attending school	1,651,687	1,766,688	−115,001	−6.5	Not attending school	9,567,648	10,055,005	−487,357	−41.8
5 and 6 years of age	555,448	516,603	38,845	7.5	5 and 6 years of age	4,345,141	4,149,665	195,476	4.7
Attending school	176,499	142,987	33,512	23.4	Attending school	1,961,179	1,773,939	187,240	10.6
Not attending school	378,949	373,616	5,333	1.4	Not attending school	2,383,962	2,375,726	8,236	.3
7 to 13 years of age	1,811,015	1,738,822	72,193	4.2	7 to 13 years of age	15,065,790	13,515,118	1,550,672	11.5
Attending school	1,580,624	1,331,043	249,581	18.8	Attending school	14,547,737	12,499,436	2,048,301	16.4
Not attending school	230,391	407,779	−177,388	−43.5	Not attending school	518,053	1,015,682	−497,629	−49.0
14 and 15 years of age	493,897	461,778	32,119	7.0	14 and 15 years of age	4,110,385	3,432,889	677,496	19.7
Attending school	385,502	317,355	68,147	21.5	Attending school	3,716,963	2,797,409	919,554	32.9
Not attending school	108,395	144,423	−36,028	−24.9	Not attending school	393,422	635,480	−242,058	−38.1
16 and 17 years of age	502,710	430,799	71,911	16.7	16 and 17 years of age	4,086,139	3,384,559	701,580	20.7
Attending school	232,648	168,760	63,888	37.9	Attending school	2,405,061	1,468,476	936,585	63.8
Not attending school	270,062	262,039	8,023	3.1	Not attending school	1,681,078	1,916,083	−235,005	−12.3
18 to 20 years of age	765,928	648,955	116,973	18.0	18 to 20 years of age	5,929,322	4,851,302	1,078,020	22.2
Attending school	102,038	70,124	31,914	45.5	Attending school	1,338,189	739,268	598,921	81.0
Not attending school	663,890	578,831	85,059	14.7	Not attending school	4,591,133	4,112,034	479,099	11.7

Table 10.—SCHOOL ATTENDANCE OF NEGRO AND WHITE POPULATION FROM 5 TO 20 YEARS, BY AGE PERIODS, AND SECTIONS: 1930 AND 1920

AGE	NEGRO PERSONS ATTENDING SCHOOL						WHITE PERSONS ATTENDING SCHOOL					
	1930		1920		Increase, 1920-30		1930		1920		Increase, 1920-30	
	Number	Percent distribution	Number	Percent distribution	Number	Percent	Number	Percent distribution	Number	Percent distribution	Number	Percent
	UNITED STATES											
5 to 20 years	2,477,311	100.0	2,030,269	100.0	447,042	22.0	23,969,129	100.0	19,278,528	100.0	4,690,601	24.3
5 and 6 years	176,499	7.1	142,987	7.0	33,512	23.4	1,961,179	8.2	1,773,939	9.2	187,240	10.6
7 to 13 years	1,580,624	63.8	1,331,043	65.6	249,581	18.8	14,547,737	60.7	12,499,436	64.8	2,048,301	16.4
14 and 15 years	385,502	15.6	317,355	15.6	68,147	21.5	3,716,963	15.5	2,797,409	14.5	919,554	32.9
16 and 17 years	232,648	9.4	168,760	8.3	63,888	37.9	2,405,061	10.0	1,468,476	7.6	936,585	63.8
18 to 20 years	102,038	4.1	70,124	3.5	31,914	45.5	1,338,189	5.6	739,268	3.8	598,921	81.0
	THE SOUTH											
5 to 20 years	2,044,259	100.0	1,803,363	100.0	240,896	13.4	6,444,977	100.0	5,437,416	100.0	1,007,561	18.5
5 and 6 years	129,607	6.3	120,621	6.7	8,986	7.4	381,116	5.9	363,396	6.7	17,720	4.9
7 to 13 years	1,314,235	64.3	1,183,595	65.6	130,640	11.0	4,062,204	63.0	3,532,969	65.0	529,235	15.0
14 and 15 years	322,421	15.8	283,225	15.7	39,196	13.8	981,142	15.2	825,722	15.2	155,420	18.8
16 and 17 years	193,778	9.5	152,885	8.5	40,893	26.7	650,847	10.1	483,901	8.9	166,946	34.5
18 to 20 years	84,218	4.1	63,037	3.5	21,181	33.6	369,668	5.7	231,428	4.3	138,240	59.7
	THE NORTH											
5 to 20 years	412,996	100.0	216,683	100.0	196,313	90.6	15,251,156	100.0	12,175,884	100.0	3,075,272	25.3
5 and 6 years	44,744	10.8	21,329	9.8	23,415	109.8	1,397,270	9.2	1,264,446	10.4	132,824	10.5
7 to 13 years	255,177	61.8	141,224	65.2	113,953	80.7	9,199,458	60.3	7,928,160	65.1	1,271,298	16.0
14 and 15 years	60,132	14.6	32,572	15.0	27,560	84.6	2,388,626	15.7	1,727,802	14.2	660,824	38.2
16 and 17 years	36,479	8.8	14,957	6.9	21,522	143.9	1,475,716	9.7	834,042	6.8	641,674	76.9
18 to 20 years	16,464	4.0	6,601	3.0	9,863	149.4	790,086	5.2	421,434	3.5	368,652	87.5
	THE WEST											
5 to 20 years	20,056	100.0	10,223	100.0	9,833	96.2	2,272,996	100.0	1,665,228	100.0	607,768	36.5
5 and 6 years	2,148	10.7	1,037	10.1	1,111	107.1	182,793	8.0	146,097	8.8	36,696	25.1
7 to 13 years	11,212	55.9	6,224	60.9	4,988	80.1	1,286,075	56.6	1,038,307	62.4	247,768	23.9
14 and 15 years	2,949	14.7	1,558	15.2	1,391	89.3	347,195	15.3	243,885	14.6	103,310	42.4
16 and 17 years	2,391	11.9	918	9.0	1,473	160.5	278,498	12.3	150,533	9.0	127,965	85.0
18 to 20 years	1,356	6.8	486	4.8	870	179.0	178,435	7.8	86,406	5.2	92,029	106.5

TABLE 11.—SCHOOL ATTENDANCE OF THE NEGRO POPULATION BY AGE PERIODS AND SEX, FOR THE URBAN, RURAL-FARM, AND RURAL-NONFARM AREAS OF THE UNITED STATES: 1930

AREA AND SEX	Total number attending school	PERSONS 7 TO 13 YEARS: Total number	PERSONS 7 TO 13 YEARS: Attending school: Number	PERSONS 7 TO 13 YEARS: Attending school: Percent	PERSONS 14 AND 15 YEARS: Total number	PERSONS 14 AND 15 YEARS: Attending school: Number	PERSONS 14 AND 15 YEARS: Attending school: Percent	PERSONS 16 AND 17 YEARS: Total number	PERSONS 16 AND 17 YEARS: Attending school: Number	PERSONS 16 AND 17 YEARS: Attending school: Percent	PERSONS 18 TO 20 YEARS: Total number	PERSONS 18 TO 20 YEARS: Attending school: Number	PERSONS 18 TO 20 YEARS: Attending school: Percent	OTHERS ATTENDING SCHOOL: Under 5 years	OTHERS ATTENDING SCHOOL: 5 years	OTHERS ATTENDING SCHOOL: 6 years	OTHERS ATTENDING SCHOOL: 21 years and over
United States	2, 553, 151	1, 811, 015	1, 580, 624	87. 3	493, 897	385, 502	78. 1	502, 710	232, 648	46. 3	765, 928	102, 038	13. 3	4, 813	34, 748	141, 751	71, 027
Urban:																	
Total	954, 641	607, 212	571, 918	94. 2	159, 822	133, 839	83. 7	172, 312	84, 703	49. 2	304, 094	42, 396	13. 9	3, 005	20, 384	63, 487	34, 909
Male	450, 830	294, 463	276, 174	93. 8	73, 877	61, 390	83. 1	77, 307	37, 040	47. 9	125, 161	18, 462	14. 8	1, 432	9, 558	30, 302	16, 472
Female	503, 811	312, 749	295, 744	94. 6	85, 945	72, 449	84. 3	95, 005	47, 663	50. 2	178, 933	23, 934	13. 4	1, 573	10, 826	33, 185	18, 437
Rural:																	
Total	1, 598, 510	1, 203, 803	1, 008, 706	83. 8	334, 075	251, 663	75. 3	330, 398	147, 945	44. 8	461, 834	59, 642	12. 9	1, 808	14, 364	78, 264	36, 118
Male	779, 788	607, 506	502, 725	82. 8	168, 480	121, 169	71. 9	167, 577	67, 520	40. 3	218, 914	25, 286	11. 6	880	6, 716	37, 433	18, 059
Female	818, 722	596, 297	505, 981	84. 9	165, 595	130, 494	78. 8	162, 821	80, 425	49. 4	242, 920	34, 356	14. 1	928	7, 648	40, 831	18, 059
Rural-farm:																	
Total	1, 199, 774	909, 108	753, 583	82. 9	256, 769	194, 447	75. 7	249, 678	115, 884	46. 4	328, 751	45, 051	13. 7	1, 271	10, 243	55, 618	23, 677
Male	587, 716	461, 294	377, 614	81. 9	130, 554	93, 945	72. 0	128, 766	53, 437	41. 5	157, 245	18, 954	12. 1	617	4, 857	26, 745	11, 547
Female	612, 058	447, 814	375, 969	84. 0	126, 215	100, 502	79. 6	120, 912	62, 447	51. 6	171, 506	26, 097	15. 2	654	5, 386	28, 873	12, 130
Rural-nonfarm:																	
Total	398, 736	294, 695	255, 123	86. 6	77, 306	57, 216	74. 0	80, 720	32, 061	39. 7	133, 083	14, 591	11. 0	537	4, 121	22, 646	12, 441
Male	192, 072	146, 212	125, 111	85. 6	37, 926	27, 224	71. 8	38, 811	14, 083	36. 3	61, 669	6, 332	10. 3	263	1, 859	10, 688	6, 512
Female	206, 664	148, 483	130, 012	87. 6	39, 380	29, 992	76. 2	41, 909	17, 978	42. 9	71, 414	8, 259	11. 6	274	2, 262	11, 958	5, 929

TABLE 12.—SCHOOL ATTENDANCE OF NEGRO POPULATION FROM 7 TO 20 YEARS, BY AGE PERIODS, IN URBAN AND RURAL COMMUNITIES, BY SECTIONS, AND SOUTHERN DIVISIONS: 1930

SECTION, DIVISION, AND AGE PERIOD	NUMBER: Urban: Attending school	NUMBER: Urban: Not attending school	NUMBER: Rural: Attending school	NUMBER: Rural: Not attending school	PERCENT ATTENDING SCHOOL: Urban	PERCENT ATTENDING SCHOOL: Rural
United States						
7 to 20 years	832, 856	410, 584	1, 467, 956	862, 154	67. 0	63. 0
7 to 13 years	571, 918	35, 294	1, 008, 706	195, 097	94. 2	83. 8
14 and 15 years	133, 839	25, 983	251, 663	82, 412	83. 7	75. 3
16 and 17 years	84, 703	87, 609	147, 945	182, 453	49. 2	44. 8
18 to 20 years	42, 396	261, 698	59, 642	402, 192	13. 9	12. 9
THE SOUTH						
7 to 20 years	502, 292	276, 568	1, 412, 360	839, 042	64. 5	62. 7
7 to 13 years	343, 885	27, 516	970, 350	192, 972	92. 6	83. 4
14 and 15 years	80, 278	21, 626	242, 143	80, 897	78. 8	75. 0
16 and 17 years	51, 218	60, 670	142, 560	176, 759	45. 8	44. 6
18 to 20 years	26, 911	166, 756	57, 307	388, 414	13. 9	12. 9
SOUTH ATLANTIC:						
7 to 20 years	253, 996	144, 271	667, 907	425, 486	63. 8	61. 1
7 to 13 years	177, 645	14, 933	471, 266	96, 232	92. 2	83. 0
14 and 15 years	39, 161	12, 279	112, 063	46, 000	76. 1	70. 9
16 and 17 years	23, 951	32, 366	60, 399	94, 183	42. 5	39. 1
18 to 20 years	13, 239	84, 693	24, 179	189, 071	13. 5	11. 3
EAST SOUTH CENTRAL:						
7 to 20 years	124, 003	69. 211	411, 349	233, 613	64. 2	63. 8
7 to 13 years	83, 914	6, 564	275, 311	54, 432	92. 7	83. 5
14 and 15 years	20, 501	5, 246	73, 122	20, 195	79. 6	78. 4
16 and 17 years	13, 106	15, 276	45, 568	48, 284	46. 2	48. 6
18 to 20 years	6, 482	42, 125	17, 348	110, 702	13. 3	13. 5
WEST SOUTH CETNRAL:						
7 to 20 years	124, 293	63, 086	333, 104	179, 943	66. 3	64. 9
7 to 13 years	82, 326	6, 019	223, 773	42, 308	93. 2	84. 1
14 and 15 years	20, 616	4, 101	56, 958	14, 702	83. 4	79. 5
16 and 17 years	14, 161	13, 028	36, 593	34, 292	52. 1	51. 6
18 to 20 years	7, 190	39, 938	15, 780	88, 641	15. 3	15. 1
THE NORTH						
7 to 20 years	316, 033	129, 992	52, 219	21, 809	70. 9	70. 5
7 to 13 years	219, 113	7, 499	36, 064	2, 007	96. 7	94. 7
14 and 15 years	51, 175	4, 259	8, 957	1, 453	92. 3	86. 0
16 and 17 years	31, 472	26, 405	5, 007	5, 416	54. 4	48. 0
18 to 20 years	14, 273	91, 829	2, 191	12, 933	13. 5	14. 5
THE WEST						
7 to 20 years	14, 531	4, 024	3, 377	1, 303	78. 3	72. 2
7 to 13 years	8, 920	279	2, 292	118	97. 0	95. 1
14 and 15 years	2, 386	98	563	62	96. 1	90. 1
16 and 17 years	2, 013	534	378	278	79. 0	57. 6
18 to 20 years	1, 212	3, 113	144	845	28. 0	14. 6

TABLE 13.—SCHOOL ATTENDANCE OF NEGRO CHILDREN 7 TO 15 YEARS OF AGE IN CITIES HAVING 25,000 OR MORE NEGRO INHABITANTS: 1930

CITY	Total	ATTENDING SCHOOL: Number	ATTENDING SCHOOL: Percent	Number not attending school
New York, N. Y	35, 999	34, 527	95. 9	1, 472
Philadelphia, Pa	29, 832	28, 424	95. 3	1, 408
Chicago, Ill	26, 732	25, 694	96. 1	1, 038
Baltimore, Md	20, 089	18, 598	92. 6	1, 491
New Orleans, La	19, 761	17, 955	90. 9	1, 806
Washington, D. C	17, 783	17, 047	95. 9	736
Detroit, Mich	15, 925	14, 468	90. 9	1, 457
Birmingham, Ala	15, 615	14, 368	92. 0	1, 247
Atlanta, Ga	15, 368	13, 308	86. 6	2, 060
Memphis, Tenn	12, 327	11, 378	92. 3	949
St. Louis, Mo	11, 356	10, 692	94. 2	664
Cleveland, Ohio	9, 578	9, 286	97. 0	292
Richmond, Va	8, 925	8, 149	91. 3	776
Houston, Tex	8, 269	7, 706	93. 2	563
Pittsburgh, Pa	7, 779	7, 339	94. 3	440
Jacksonville, Fla	7, 320	6, 646	90. 8	674
Norfolk, Va	6, 869	6, 242	90. 9	627
Cincinnati, Ohio	6, 495	6, 239	96. 1	256
Nashville, Tenn	6, 380	5, 728	89. 8	652
Indianapolis, Ind	6, 339	6, 110	96. 4	229
Louisville, Ky	5, 974	5, 655	94. 7	319
Newark, N. J	5, 550	5, 278	95. 1	272
Savannah, Ga	5, 458	4, 560	83. 5	898
Winston-Salem, N. C	5, 322	4, 817	90. 5	505
Chattanooga, Tenn	5, 219	4, 815	92. 3	404
Dallas, Tex	5, 110	4, 615	90. 3	495
Charleston, S. C	4, 977	4, 315	86. 7	662
Montgomery, Ala	4, 897	4, 348	88. 8	549
Los Angeles, Calif	4, 647	4, 516	97. 2	131
Columbus, Ohio	4, 609	4, 425	96. 0	184
Charlotte, N. C	4, 195	3, 685	87. 8	510
Kansas City, Mo	4, 089	3, 822	93. 5	267
Shreveport, La	3, 977	3, 729	93. 8	248
Miami, Fla	3, 931	3, 689	93. 8	242

Table 14.—SCHOOL ATTENDANCE OF NEGRO AND WHITE POPULATION BY SINGLE YEARS OF AGE FROM 5 TO 20, BY SECTIONS: 1930

AGE	NEGRO				WHITE, ATTENDING SCHOOL						WHITE, NOT ATTENDING SCHOOL					
	Total	Attending school		Not attending school	Native parentage		Foreign or mixed parentage		Foreign born		Native parentage		Foreign or mixed parentage		Foreign born	
		Number	Percent		Number	Percent	Number	Percent	Number	Percent	Number	Percent	Number	Percent	Number	Percent
United States	**4,128,998**	**2,477,311**	**60.0**	**1,651,687**	**17,288,107**	**71.8**	**6,291,273**	**71.9**	**389,749**	**55.6**	**6,792,576**	**28.2**	**2,463,845**	**28.1**	**311,227**	**44.4**
THE SOUTH																
5 years	228,690	21,229	9.3	207,461	46,327	7.3	2,787	13.7	69	18.3	588,313	92.7	17,507	86.3	308	81.7
6 years	237,974	108,378	43.4	129,596	318,423	50.1	13,176	60.6	334	63.9	316,777	49.9	8,569	39.4	189	36.1
7 years	228,227	167,364	73.3	60,863	513,043	83.8	19,384	89.0	568	87.7	99,124	16.2	2,401	11.0	80	12.3
8 years	237,462	195,903	82.5	41,559	596,266	92.0	22,664	95.6	823	95.4	51,729	8.0	1,055	4.4	40	4.6
9 years	217,895	188,734	86.6	29,161	584,071	94.1	22,217	96.6	951	96.4	36,336	5.9	792	3.4	36	3.6
10 years	234,543	210,578	89.8	23,965	593,520	96.2	23,524	98.3	1,043	97.5	23,132	3.8	411	1.7	27	2.5
11 years	186,923	170,259	91.1	16,664	540,847	96.5	22,083	98.5	801	98.6	19,667	3.5	342	1.5	11	1.4
12 years	227,145	203,690	89.7	23,455	557,458	96.0	24,381	98.4	811	97.4	23,133	4.0	399	1.6	22	2.6
13 years	202,528	177,707	87.7	24,821	513,577	95.0	23,328	97.5	844	96.2	26,884	5.0	592	2.5	33	3.8
14 years	217,981	176,594	81.0	41,387	505,041	89.8	23,098	92.3	972	94.2	57,201	10.2	1,921	7.7	60	5.8
15 years	206,963	145,827	70.1	61,136	430,762	80.1	20,205	81.6	1,064	84.8	107,140	19.9	4,560	18.4	190	15.2
16 years	222,061	118,928	53.6	103,133	360,709	63.8	16,428	62.4	1,223	66.5	204,558	36.2	9,881	37.6	615	33.5
17 years	209,146	74,850	35.8	134,296	259,994	47.5	11,407	45.4	1,086	50.8	287,871	52.5	13,719	54.6	1,053	49.2
18 years	228,868	46,744	20.4	182,124	177,108	32.0	7,816	30.2	856	32.5	376,106	68.0	18,062	69.8	1,777	67.5
19 years	196,808	23,741	11.9	173,067	107,471	20.8	5,098	20.8	586	21.2	408,264	79.2	19,395	79.2	2,172	78 8
20 years	213,712	13,733	6.4	199,979	66,913	13.2	3,363	13.9	457	14.1	438,601	86.8	20,756	86.1	2,777	85.9
THE NORTH																
5 years	43,292	12,753	29.5	30,539	235,199	25.9	127,091	30.8	3,306	31.8	674,127	74.1	285,505	69.2	7,102	68.2
6 years	42,023	31,991	76.1	10.032	686,548	77.1	333,388	78.2	11,738	79.6	203,471	22.9	92,821	21.8	3,011	20.4
7 years	41,244	38,270	92.8	2,974	825,336	95.0	411,489	95.1	20,481	94.9	43,418	5.0	21,061	4.9	1,108	5.1
8 years	42,248	40,409	95.6	1,839	879,121	97.1	451,457	97.4	26,247	96.6	26,026	2.9	12,273	2.6	918	3.4
9 years	40,574	39,036	96.2	1,538	851,330	97.7	449,687	97.9	30,679	97.2	20,065	2.3	9,830	2.1	883	2.8
10 years	39,837	38,946	97.8	891	819,500	98.8	477,847	98.9	30.691	98.5	10,173	1.2	5,221	1.1	481	1.5
11 years	33,432	32,719	97.9	713	790,794	98.8	465,615	99.0	21,654	98.4	9,310	1.2	4,804	1.0	353	1.6
12 years	34,926	34,177	97.9	749	815,894	98.8	524,868	98.9	21,548	98.4	9,980	1.2	5,624	1.1	341	1.6
13 years	32,422	31,620	97.5	802	757,892	98.4	505,641	98.6	21,687	98.4	12,041	1.6	7,008	1.4	358	1.6
14 years	33,813	32,097	94.9	1,716	740,157	95.9	500,419	95.8	24,577	96.1	31,294	4.1	22,140	4.2	987	3.9
15 years	32,031	28,035	87.5	3,996	651,190	89.2	443,926	86.6	28,357	89.0	78,933	10.8	68,964	13.4	3,502	11.0
16 years	34,039	22,392	65.8	11,647	522,583	71.0	324,976	63.1	27,384	63.7	213,518	29.0	190,078	36.9	15,636	36.3
17 years	34,261	14,087	41.1	20,174	377,381	53.0	202,146	41.0	21,246	37.8	334,752	47.0	290,757	59.0	35,016	62.2
18 years	38,501	8,469	22.0	30.032	248,027	34.7	123,342	25.0	14,628	21.1	467,421	65.3	370,312	75.0	54,699	78.9
19 years	39,686	5,014	12.6	34,672	152,969	22.1	76,453	16.5	10,829	13.9	539,790	77.9	388,035	83.5	67,281	86.1
20 years	43,039	2,981	6.9	40,058	102,495	15.2	52,558	11.8	8,785	9.4	570,852	84.8	393,131	88.2	85,148	90.6
THE WEST																
5 years	1,750	766	43.8	984	33,796	23.5	9,753	25.1	301	27.5	109,746	76.5	29,125	74.9	794	72.5
6 years	1,719	1,382	80.4	337	106,523	74.3	31,112	76.6	1,308	78.9	36,758	25.7	9,490	23.4	349	21.1
7 years	1,757	1,614	91.9	143	132,787	93.6	38,256	93.9	2,502	92.6	9,082	6.4	2,475	6.1	201	7.4
8 years	1,771	1,690	95.4	81	145,690	97.0	43,445	97.4	3,301	97.0	4,580	3.0	1,145	2.6	102	3.0
9 years	1,755	1,696	96.6	59	143,482	97.6	42,589	93.0	3,871	97.7	3,544	2.4	871	2.0	91	2.3
10 years	1,724	1,695	98.3	29	137,653	98.9	44,443	99.0	4,102	98.5	1,566	1.1	455	1.0	64	1.5
11 years	1,529	1,501	98.2	28	133,294	98.9	42,798	99.1	3,711	99.0	1,463	1.1	408	.9	39	1.0
12 years	1,608	1,586	98.6	22	136,234	98.8	46,931	99.1	3,774	99.1	1,601	1.2	442	.9	33	.9
13 years	1,465	1,430	97.6	35	127,197	98.6	46,027	98.8	3,988	98.7	1,763	1.4	552	1.2	54	1.3
14 years	1,666	1,617	97.1	49	126,691	97.4	47,591	97.4	4,557	97.6	3,395	2.6	1,278	2.6	113	2.4
15 years	1,443	1,332	92.3	111	116,980	93.7	46,335	92.9	5,038	94.9	7,912	6.3	3,559	7.1	273	5.1
16 years	1,625	1,334	82.1	291	107,433	84.5	41,703	82.6	5,225	84.0	19,694	15.5	8,774	17.4	994	16.0
17 years	1,578	1,057	67.0	521	86,488	70.4	32,998	68.0	4,651	67.7	36,438	29.6	15,506	32.0	2,218	32.3
18 years	1,762	718	40.7	1,044	61,511	47.9	22,605	44.2	3,323	40.9	66,885	52.1	28,497	55.8	4,803	59.1
19 years	1,756	413	23.5	1,343	38,370	31.3	13,730	28.1	2,167	24.3	84,245	68.7	35,184	71.9	6,738	75.7
20 years	1,796	225	12.5	1,571	26,032	21.7	9,092	19.2	1,605	16.5	93,897	78.3	38,158	80.8	8,147	83.5

TABLE 15.—SCHOOL ATTENDANCE OF THE NEGRO POPULATION FROM 7 TO 20 YEARS OF AGE, BY SECTIONS, DIVISIONS, AND STATES, 1930, 1920, AND 1910, AND BY AGE PERIODS: 1930

[Percent not shown where base is less than 100]

DIVISION OR STATE	1930			ATTENDING SCHOOL, 1920		ATTENDING SCHOOL, 1910		SCHOOL ATTENDANCE BY AGE PERIODS, 1930							
	Total number	Attending school						7 to 13 years old		14 and 15 years old		16 and 17 years old		18 to 20 years old	
		Number	Percent	Number	Percent	Number	Percent	Number	Percent	Number	Percent	Number	Percent	Number	Percent
United States	**3,573,550**	**2,300,812**	**64.4**	**1,887,282**	**57.5**	**1,541,575**	**48.8**	**1,580,624**	**87.3**	**385,502**	**78.1**	**232,648**	**46.3**	**102,038**	**13.3**
The North	520,053	368,252	70.8	195,354	62.9	137,479	59.5	255,177	96.4	60,132	91.3	36,479	53.4	16,464	13.6
The South	3,030,262	1,914,652	63.2	1,682,742	56.9	1,398,379	47.9	1,314,235	85.6	322,421	75.9	193,778	44.9	84,218	13.2
The West	23,235	17,908	77.1	9,186	66.8	5,717	61.2	11,212	96.6	2,949	94.9	2,391	74.6	1,356	25.5
NEW ENGLAND	22,525	16,942	75.2	11,167	66.8	9,461	65.3	11,947	97.6	2,747	91.1	1,481	51.6	767	17.5
Maine	246	206	83.7	176	63.3	213	62.5	135	96.4	31	-----	23	-----	17	-----
New Hampshire	160	106	66.3	93	69.4	74	55.6	63	-----	22	-----	11	-----	10	-----
Vermont	154	104	67.5	101	68.2	120	51.1	66	-----	18	-----	15	-----	5	-----
Massachusetts	12,596	9,781	77.7	6,420	68.9	5,410	66.1	6,768	97.4	1,600	91.8	911	57.9	502	21.5
Rhode Island	2,510	1,879	74.9	1,338	63.3	1,320	62.6	1,354	97.5	314	92.4	149	46.7	62	13.4
Connecticut	6,859	4,866	70.9	3,039	64.3	2,324	66.9	3,561	97.9	762	89.0	372	41.2	171	11.7
MIDDLE ATLANTIC	225,573	155,344	68.9	77,076	61.6	51,124	57.6	109,888	96.3	25,165	91.5	14,283	49.0	6,008	11.0
New York	78,440	53,041	67.6	21,267	58.9	14,159	55.6	36,807	96.6	8,472	93.3	5,353	55.4	2,409	11.1
New Jersey	49,047	34,086	69.5	17,471	64.4	11,938	58.7	24,286	97.0	5,545	88.3	2,971	45.0	1,284	11.6
Pennsylvania	98,086	68,217	69.5	38,338	61.8	25,027	58.4	48,795	95.8	11,148	91.8	5,959	46.3	2,315	10.5
EAST NORTH CENTRAL	198,010	143,951	72.7	67,374	63.5	41,742	61.3	98,341	97.0	23,580	93.2	15,154	58.3	6,876	15.2
Ohio	70,408	52,252	74.2	25,618	65.0	16,242	62.2	35,493	97.1	8,630	94.2	5,618	61.1	2,511	16.2
Indiana	25,210	18,284	72.5	11,604	63.2	9,136	62.5	12,400	97.0	3,066	93.6	1,921	55.2	897	15.8
Illinois	66,411	47,109	70.9	23,008	63.4	13,617	58.9	31,985	96.8	7,670	91.1	4,939	55.6	2,515	15.7
Michigan	33,735	24,575	72.8	6,445	58.4	2,375	63.9	17,252	97.2	3,991	94.7	2,464	59.2	868	11.4
Wisconsin	2,246	1,731	77.1	699	65.5	372	62.8	1,211	98.1	223	94.5	212	77.9	85	16.9
WEST NORTH CENTRAL	73,945	52,015	70.3	39,737	63.6	35,152	58.7	35,001	94.6	8,640	86.2	5,561	54.1	2,813	16.9
Minnesota	1,770	1,371	77.5	969	68.2	741	65.7	896	98.5	225	94.1	148	62.7	102	26.5
Iowa	4,052	3,109	76.7	2,897	67.5	2,269	63.4	2,014	97.8	549	94.3	358	61.7	188	22.7
Missouri	49,326	33,137	67.2	24,118	60.7	21,531	55.3	22,722	93.1	5,458	83.3	3,413	49.2	1,544	13.5
North Dakota	58	38	-----	67	-----	56	-----	20	-----	6	-----	7	-----	5	-----
South Dakota	157	121	77.1	131	63.6	117	67.2	72	-----	20	-----	19	-----	10	-----
Nebraska	2,742	2,087	76.1	1,630	63.4	874	61.1	1,378	98.4	340	94.4	252	65.5	117	19.6
Kansas	15,840	12,152	76.7	9,925	69.8	9,564	65.6	7,899	97.3	2,042	90.5	1,364	64.5	847	25.3
SOUTH ATLANTIC	1,491,660	921,903	61.8	845,820	58.4	672,549	48.6	648,911	85.4	151,224	72.2	84,350	40.0	37,418	12.0
Delaware	8,574	5,807	67.7	5,498	66.5	5,544	59.0	4,119	94.8	968	84.5	516	42.2	204	11.0
Maryland	74,043	47,472	64.1	39,789	58.5	36,503	53.8	35,937	93.5	7,102	74.1	3,163	31.2	1,270	8.0
District of Columbia	29,312	20,929	71.4	15,375	60.4	13,147	59.5	13,638	96.6	3,409	92.9	2,292	56.7	1,590	21.2
Virginia	216,489	141,093	65.2	131,284	59.1	111,337	49.5	99,417	86.8	23,486	76.6	12,767	42.3	5,423	13.2
West Virginia	30,369	21,861	72.0	13,922	61.4	9,169	53.5	15,080	93.5	3,279	86.3	2,103	52.7	1,399	21.7
North Carolina	331,149	218,320	65.9	171,379	64.2	135,297	56.0	151,122	88.8	35,885	76.9	21,408	45.6	9,905	14.7
South Carolina	306,379	182,791	59.7	203,028	64.1	144,803	47.5	125,377	79.7	30,923	70.3	18,301	42.0	8,190	13.3
Georgia	373,326	211,638	56.7	212,041	50.7	174,871	43.3	153,347	83.1	34,378	64.5	17,197	31.9	6,716	8.2
Florida	122,019	71,992	59.0	53,504	53.6	41,878	45.0	50,874	83.9	11,794	70.6	6,603	38.7	2,721	9.9
EAST SOUTH CENTRAL	838,176	535,352	63.9	461,566	55.5	425,687	48.7	359,225	85.5	93,623	78.6	58,674	48.0	23,830	13.5
Kentucky	58,192	39,361	67.6	39,133	62.7	42,081	55.0	26,450	91.1	6,702	81.3	4,193	49.3	2,016	16.3
Tennessee	141,251	91,268	64.6	75,324	53.9	73,980	48.8	60,824	88.9	15,876	80.8	10,036	48.8	4,532	13.9
Alabama	308,981	186,883	60.5	166,943	54.6	128,850	42.6	125,450	80.7	33,439	74.6	20,282	44.3	7,712	12.3
Mississippi	329,752	217,840	66.1	180,166	55.8	180,776	52.7	146,501	87.6	37,606	81.2	24,163	51.0	9,570	13.9
WEST SOUTH CENTRAL	700,426	457,397	65.3	375,356	55.5	300,143	45.5	306,099	86.4	77,574	80.5	50,754	51.8	22,970	15.2
Arkansas	148,780	99,989	67.2	84,729	54.7	73,287	49.9	65,441	87.3	17,216	83.0	11,839	56.6	5,493	17.1
Louisiana	238,255	147,048	61.7	103,598	45.4	69,992	29.9	102,152	83.1	24,007	73.2	14,078	43.3	6,811	13.6
Oklahoma	52,770	37,976	72.0	30,387	61.6	29,208	65.1	24,173	91.4	6,379	87.9	4,789	63.8	2,635	22.8
Texas	260,621	172,384	66.1	156,642	64.2	127,656	54.4	114,333	87.9	29,972	84.3	20,048	54.0	8,031	13.9
MOUNTAIN	5,882	4,221	71.8	2,867	60.1	2,373	61.3	2,800	95.3	677	89.8	472	58.6	272	19.6
Montana	207	160	77.3	171	70.4	176	62.2	108	97.3	26	-----	19	-----	7	-----
Idaho	104	76	73.1	97	65.1	47	-----	49	-----	16	-----	4	-----	7	-----
Wyoming	204	154	75.5	114	52.1	132	49.6	103	100.0	25	-----	14	-----	12	-----
Colorado	2,173	1,624	74.7	1,524	68.0	1,452	63.3	1,029	96.7	260	91.5	197	61.8	138	27.3
New Mexico	732	526	71.9	298	44.4	200	60.2	353	94.4	81	-----	63	54.8	29	19.0
Arizona	2,234	1,501	67.2	490	49.5	234	61.1	1,028	93.5	239	87.5	165	55.6	69	12.2
Utah	183	150	82.0	145	67.8	105	57.7	109	96.5	26	-----	6	-----	9	-----
Nevada	45	30	-----	28	-----	27	-----	21	-----	4	-----	4	-----	1	-----
PACIFIC	17,353	13,687	78.9	6,319	70.3	3,344	61.0	8,412	97.0	2,272	96.5	1,919	80.1	1,084	27.6
Washington	1,190	928	78.0	785	70.7	498	57.7	569	96.4	159	95.8	139	77.7	61	23.9
Oregon	365	285	78.1	254	72.2	95	52.8	172	96.6	47	-----	40	-----	26	-----
California	15,798	12,474	79.0	5,280	70.2	2,751	62.0	7,671	97.1	2,066	96.5	1,740	80.4	997	27.8

TABLE 16.—SCHOOL ATTENDANCE OF THE NEGRO POPULATION BY SINGLE YEARS OF AGE FROM 5 TO 20, BY STATES: 1930

[Percent not shown where base is less than 100]

AGE	NEW ENGLAND DIVISION								MIDDLE ATLANTIC DIVISION									
	Maine		New Hampshire		Vermont		Massachusetts		Rhode Island		Connecticut		New York		New Jersey		Pennsylvania	
	Number attending school	Percent	Number attending school	Percent	Number attending school	Percent	Number attending school	Percent	Number attending school	Percent	Number attending school	Percent	Number attending school	Percent	Number attending school	Percent	Number attending school	Percent
Single years:																		
5 years	8	-----	1	-----	4	-----	411	39.3	63	27.8	304	49.0	1,833	27.0	1,887	45.2	1,427	17.2
6 years	12	-----	5	-----	8	-----	864	77.4	155	71.8	485	83.0	4,906	76.5	3,236	82.6	5,526	67.5
7 years	17	-----	10	-----	7	-----	993	95.3	211	95.9	521	95.4	5,844	93.9	3,683	94.0	7,114	89.0
8 years	22	-----	7	-----	6	-----	1,006	96.2	200	95.2	556	97.4	5,841	95.8	3,844	96.2	7,810	95.5
9 years	16	-----	9	-----	13	-----	1,010	96.2	190	96.9	569	98.3	5,574	96.1	3,714	97.4	7,679	96.2
10 years	29	-----	7	-----	8	-----	1,019	98.5	183	97.9	561	99.1	5,579	98.0	3,717	97.5	7,471	98.0
11 years	17	-----	7	-----	9	-----	911	98.7	188	100.0	449	98.7	4,688	97.8	3,024	98.0	6,276	97.7
12 years	21	-----	12	-----	13	-----	971	98.5	195	97.5	464	98.1	4,902	97.9	3,349	98.4	6,533	98.1
13 years	13	-----	11	-----	10	-----	858	99.2	187	99.5	441	98.9	4,379	98.0	2,955	97.8	5,912	97.4
14 years	19	-----	11	-----	13	-----	854	96.0	171	97.7	383	94.1	4,471	95.9	3,066	93.6	5,965	95.4
15 years	12	-----	11	-----	5	-----	746	87.6	143	86.7	379	84.4	4,001	90.5	2,479	82.6	5,183	88.0
16 years	15	-----	7	-----	10	-----	536	67.4	100	56.8	227	50.8	3,324	72.3	1,856	55.8	3,833	58.9
17 years	8	-----	4	-----	5	-----	375	48.1	49	34.3	145	31.9	2,029	40.0	1,115	34.0	2,126	33.4
18 years	7	-----	5	-----	4	-----	257	31.4	34	19.8	95	19.1	1,201	19.0	673	18.6	1,252	17.6
19 years	8	-----	2	-----	-----	-----	157	20.3	18	11.9	51	10.9	739	10.5	388	10.9	682	9.3
20 years	2	-----	3	-----	1	-----	88	11.9	10	7.2	25	5.0	469	5.7	223	5.7	381	5.0

AGE	EAST NORTH CENTRAL DIVISION										PACIFIC DIVISION					
	Ohio		Indiana		Illinois		Michigan		Wisconsin		Washington		Oregon		California	
	Number attending school	Percent	Number attending school	Percent	Number attending school	Percent	Number attending school	Percent	Number attending school	Percent	Number attending school	Percent	Number attending school	Percent	Number attending school	Percent
Single years:																
5 years	1,298	21.8	327	16.4	1,622	30.4	1,668	52.1	107	55.2	7	-----	4	-----	632	51.6
6 years	4,468	77.1	1,528	76.8	4,026	78.1	2,520	85.7	146	79.3	63	-----	16	-----	997	84.3
7 years	5,305	94.3	1,837	93.9	4,733	93.9	2,687	94.9	175	93.6	75	-----	22	-----	1,130	93.1
8 years	5,758	96.1	1,983	96.3	5,021	95.9	2,897	96.6	188	97.4	77	-----	21	-----	1,183	96.2
9 years	5,414	97.0	1,896	96.6	4,818	96.5	2,664	96.5	198	98.0	90	-----	36	-----	1,139	96.8
10 years	5,383	98.0	1,843	97.9	5,030	97.8	2,644	98.4	171	99.4	86	-----	27	-----	1,151	98.6
11 years	4,538	98.7	1,585	98.6	4,188	98.1	2,165	98.1	166	99.4	84	-----	22	-----	1,032	98.5
12 years	4,714	98.2	1,693	98.3	4,134	98.1	2,106	98.5	154	100.0	80	-----	20	-----	1,064	98.7
13 years	4,381	98.0	1,563	98.2	4,061	97.6	2,089	98.7	159	99.4	77	-----	24	-----	972	98.2
14 years	4,548	96.3	1,610	96.1	4,124	95.3	2,178	97.4	131	97.0	89	-----	26	-----	1,115	97.9
15 years	4,082	92.0	1,456	90.9	3,546	86.7	1,813	91.7	92	91.1	70	-----	21	-----	951	94.9
16 years	3,425	74.2	1,176	67.0	2,947	66.6	1,531	73.9	121	87.1	77	-----	25	-----	946	87.8
17 years	2,193	47.9	745	43.2	1,992	44.7	933	44.6	91	68.4	62	-----	15	-----	794	73.1
18 years	1,254	25.4	463	24.5	1,254	24.5	454	20.2	44	32.4	34	-----	15	-----	530	43.6
19 years	768	14.8	269	15.2	791	15.0	276	11.0	27	14.4	16	-----	7	-----	306	25.8
20 years	489	9.1	165	8.2	470	8.3	138	4.8	14	7.8	11	-----	4	-----	161	13.5

AGE	WEST NORTH CENTRAL DIVISION													
	Minnesota		Iowa		Missouri		North Dakota		South Dakota		Nebraska		Kansas	
	Number attending school	Percent	Number attending school	Percent	Number attending school	Percent	Number attending school	Percent	Number attending school	Percent	Number attending school	Percent	Number attending school	Percent
Single years:														
5 years	77	60.6	164	59.2	1,036	28.8	1	-----	3	-----	158	70.5	354	29.5
6 years	123	96.1	294	89.1	2,571	70.7	1	-----	8	-----	204	93.2	906	78.1
7 years	130	97.0	277	96.5	3,361	89.0	3	-----	7	-----	201	97.6	1,154	95.8
8 years	149	99.3	355	98.3	3,369	91.6	2	-----	14	-----	226	98.7	1,155	96.6
9 years	134	98.5	298	96.8	3,392	92.5	3	-----	8	-----	217	97.3	1,220	96.7
10 years	123	98.4	286	97.6	3,512	95.4	4	-----	13	-----	184	98.9	1,179	98.5
11 years	137	100.0	259	99.2	2,875	95.1	1	-----	10	-----	164	98.8	1,062	98.2
12 years	121	98.4	274	97.5	3,251	94.9	5	-----	9	-----	210	100.0	1,046	97.8
13 years	102	97.1	265	98.5	2,962	93.8	2	-----	11	-----	176	97.8	1,083	97.7
14 years	120	98.4	294	96.7	2,860	88.4	1	-----	10	-----	185	98.4	1,083	94.0
15 years	105	89.7	255	91.7	2,598	78.2	5	-----	10	-----	155	90.1	959	86.8
16 years	91	71.1	199	71.1	2,058	59.3	4	-----	7	-----	152	76.4	773	73.4
17 years	57	52.8	159	53.0	1,355	39.1	3	-----	12	-----	100	53.8	591	55.6
18 years	45	37.5	91	32.7	837	22.2	1	-----	2	-----	66	31.3	430	37.2
19 years	39	27.7	61	21.9	450	12.2	3	-----	6	-----	22	11.3	257	24.3
20 years	18	14.5	36	13.1	257	6.5	1	-----	2	-----	29	15.1	160	14.1

TABLE 16.—SCHOOL ATTENDANCE OF THE NEGRO POPULATION BY SINGLE YEARS OF AGE FROM 5 TO 20, BY STATES: 1930—Continued

[Percent not shown where base is less than 100]

AGE	SOUTH ATLANTIC DIVISION																	
	Delaware		Maryland		District of Columbia		Virginia		West Virginia		North Carolina		South Carolina		Georgia		Florida	
	Number attending school	Percent	Number attending school	Percent	Number attending school	Percent	Number attending school	Percent	Number attending school	Percent	Number attending school	Percent	Number attending school	Percent	Number attending school	Percent	Number attending school	Percent
Single years:																		
5 years	47	7.7	600	10.3	737	33.5	564	3.4	234	9.0	1,067	4.0	1,205	5.3	2,119	8.2	1,291	14.5
6 years	407	58.6	3,240	53.7	1,608	74.4	5,667	32.9	1,417	53.4	13,395	49.5	9,012	37.0	13,795	49.5	5,099	54.0
7 years	554	88.2	4,988	86.0	1,977	92.7	12,283	71.5	2,145	85.1	20,090	79.5	14,612	63.9	19,431	73.2	6,969	76.3
8 years	653	93.8	5,641	92.8	2,092	95.8	14,807	84.1	2,452	92.6	23,145	87.1	18,316	74.5	22,831	81.3	7,553	81.7
9 years	583	93.7	5,525	94.9	2,077	96.2	14,754	89.4	2,288	94.0	21,899	89.5	17,325	80.1	21,894	85.2	7,407	84.9
10 years	706	98.1	5,652	96.4	2,088	98.4	15,744	91.2	2,339	95.8	23,504	92.1	20,498	85.2	24,682	87.5	8,008	87.5
11 years	502	96.5	4,626	96.6	1,768	98.2	13,238	92.5	1,950	96.6	19,405	92.9	15,819	86.9	19,760	88.6	6,518	87.9
12 years	622	97.5	4,965	95.8	1,903	98.0	15,216	91.3	2,025	96.3	22,978	91.8	21,335	85.1	24,078	85.6	7,690	86.1
13 years	499	95.4	4,540	92.8	1,733	97.7	13,375	89.4	1,881	95.5	20,101	89.7	17,472	83.5	20,671	81.1	6,729	83.9
14 years	536	91.8	4,061	82.9	1,769	95.7	12,952	82.5	1,733	90.7	19,822	82.9	17,148	75.1	19,450	71.3	6,559	76.3
15 years	432	76.9	3,041	64.9	1,640	90.0	10,534	70.4	1,546	81.8	16,063	70.6	13,775	65.2	14,928	57.4	5,235	64.7
16 years	329	53.9	2,033	40.0	1,344	68.4	7,880	51.0	1,233	62.9	13,129	54.3	11,486	49.3	10,905	39.2	4,135	47.5
17 years	187	30.6	1,130	22.4	948	45.7	4,887	33.3	870	42.9	8,279	36.4	6,815	33.6	6,292	24.2	2,468	29.4
18 years	112	18.2	680	12.7	693	28.9	2,953	19.4	631	28.9	5,480	22.2	4,640	19.7	3,664	12.6	1,506	15.9
19 years	62	10.6	368	7.0	498	20.7	1,580	12.1	434	21.2	2,808	13.5	2,239	12.3	1,888	7.5	794	9.1
20 years	30	4.6	222	4.2	399	14.9	890	6.9	334	15.1	1,617	7.4	1,311	6.6	1,164	4.3	421	4.5

AGE	EAST SOUTH CENTRAL DIVISION								WEST SOUTH CENTRAL DIVISION							
	Kentucky		Tennessee		Alabama		Mississippi		Arkansas		Louisiana		Oklahoma		Texas	
	Number attending school	Percent	Number attending school	Percent	Number attending school	Percent	Number attending school	Percent	Number attending school	Percent	Number attending school	Percent	Number attending school	Percent	Number attending school	Percent
Single years:																
5 years	406	9.5	642	6.6	1,120	4.7	6,848	25.9	618	5.6	1,900	10.3	672	17.8	1,159	6.1
6 years	2,474	55.4	5,030	48.4	8,191	33.7	15,567	58.9	6,109	53.0	9,126	46.6	2,816	67.8	5,425	27.7
6 years	3,611	83.7	7,756	78.1	15,226	64.5	19,338	77.2	8,237	76.7	13,057	70.8	3,242	84.3	13,848	68.6
8 years	4,055	89.6	8,976	86.3	18,405	76.0	21,682	83.4	9,333	83.3	15,410	79.5	3,677	89.1	16,875	84.6
9 years	3,884	91.9	8,931	90.0	17,783	81.6	20,300	87.2	9,296	87.0	14,392	83.6	3,544	91.1	16,852	89.6
10 years	4,007	93.8	9,557	92.3	20,439	85.7	23,934	91.0	10,556	90.9	16,570	87.5	3,778	93.7	18,516	93.3
11 years	3,483	93.6	7,943	93.1	16,248	88.0	18,785	92.8	8,798	91.8	13,250	88.7	3,238	95.3	14,928	94.6
12 years	3,826	93.5	9,382	92.3	19,593	86.6	22,997	92.2	10,122	91.2	15,758	87.6	3,609	93.7	17,591	94.0
13 years	3,584	92.2	8,279	91.0	17,756	84.8	19,465	90.7	9,099	90.7	13,715	85.7	3,085	93.6	15,723	93.3
14 years	3,715	86.1	8,551	85.5	18,202	78.9	20,455	85.6	9,132	86.2	13,368	79.0	3,363	90.5	15,778	88.2
15 years	2,987	76.1	7,325	75.9	15,237	69.9	17,151	76.5	8,084	79.6	10,639	67.0	3,016	85.2	14,194	80.3
16 years	2,521	57.9	6,085	59.0	12,499	52.6	14,867	60.9	7,019	65.3	8,594	51.4	2,757	72.6	12,112	64.1
17 years	1,672	40.2	3,951	38.5	7,783	35.3	9,296	40.6	4,820	47.4	5,484	34.8	2,032	54.7	7,936	43.5
18 years	1,063	24.7	2,471	21.7	4,414	19.4	5,783	22.9	3,124	27.4	3,640	20.8	1,418	34.8	4,472	22.7
19 years	590	14.7	1,320	12.9	2,086	11.1	2,487	12.5	1,591	15.8	1,919	12.4	774	21.0	2,303	12.7
20 years	363	8.9	741	6.7	1,212	5.7	1,300	5.5	778	7.3	1,252	7.3	443	11.7	1,256	6.3

AGE	MOUNTAIN DIVISION															
	Montana		Idaho		Wyoming		Colorado		New Mexico		Arizona		Utah		Nevada	
	Number attending school	Percent	Number attending school	Percent	Number attending school	Percent	Number attending school	Percent	Number attending school	Percent	Number attending school	Percent	Number attending school	Percent	Number attending school	Percent
Single years:																
5 years	2	-----	-----	-----	-----	-----	73	47.1	13	-----	31	19.4	2	-----	2	-----
6 years	10	-----	3	-----	10	-----	125	79.6	33	-----	110	71.0	12	-----	3	-----
7 years	10	-----	7	-----	15	-----	135	93.1	55	-----	147	85.0	15	-----	3	-----
8 years	14	-----	7	-----	11	-----	151	93.8	53	-----	155	92.3	15	-----	3	-----
9 years	15	-----	9	-----	22	-----	155	98.7	50	-----	163	93.1	14	-----	3	-----
10 years	17	-----	8	-----	15	-----	149	98.0	52	-----	166	97.6	19	-----	5	-----
11 years	20	-----	5	-----	13	-----	145	98.6	41	-----	124	95.4	13	-----	2	-----
12 years	14	-----	7	-----	13	-----	158	97.5	59	-----	148	98.7	20	-----	3	-----
13 years	18	-----	6	-----	14	-----	136	97.1	43	-----	125	94.0	13	-----	2	-----
14 years	19	-----	8	-----	14	-----	150	96.2	46	-----	131	91.0	18	-----	1	-----
15 years	7	-----	8	-----	11	-----	110	85.9	35	-----	108	83.7	8	-----	3	-----
16 years	12	-----	4	-----	6	-----	116	68.2	36	-----	104	66.7	5	-----	3	-----
17 years	7	-----	-----	-----	8	-----	81	54.4	27	-----	61	43.3	1	-----	1	-----
18 years	2	-----	5	-----	5	-----	67	41.6	14	-----	42	24.9	4	-----		-----
19 years	2	-----	1	-----	4	-----	43	24.6	11	-----	19	9.8	4	-----	-----	-----
20 years	3	-----	1	-----	3	-----	28	16.5	4	-----	8	3.9	1	-----	1	-----

Table 17.—SCHOOL ATTEDANCE OF NEGRO POPULATION, BY AGE PERIODS, AND SEX, FOR URBAN, RURAL-FARM, AND RURAL-NONFARM AREAS, BY STATES: 1930

[Percent not shown where base is less than 100]

STATE AND AREA	PERSONS 7 TO 13 YEARS OLD				PERSONS 14 AND 15 YEARS OLD				PERSONS 16 AND 17 YEARS OLD				PERSONS 18 TO 20 YEARS OLD			
	Male		Female		Male		Female		Male		Female		Male		Female	
	Number	Percent	Number	Percent	Number	Percent	Number	Percent	Number	Percent	Number	Percent	Number	Percent	Number	Percent
MAINE:																
Urban	41		42		8		13		9		8		8		4	
Rural-farm	12		8		2		3		1				1		2	
Rural-nonfarm	13		19		3		2		3		2		1		1	
NEW HAMPSHIRE:																
Urban	16		18		5		5		5		3		4		3	
Rural-farm	2		7		3		1				1					
Rural-nonfarm	12		8		4		4		1		1		2		1	
VERMONT:																
Urban	6		13		1		5		2		4				1	
Rural-farm	9		8		1		3		3				2			
Rural-nonfarm	13		17		5		3		2		4				2	
MASSACHUSETTS:																
Urban	2,843	97.5	2,868	97.1	671	93.8	712	94.1	415	61.4	422	62.9	235	25.3	245	22.1
Rural-farm	32		23		11		6		6		2					
Rural-nonfarm	516	98.1	486	98.2	123	81.5	77	76.2	31	29.8	35	34.3	7	5.1	15	10.6
RHODE ISLAND:																
Urban	630	98.1	610	97.6	128	94.1	149	91.4	52	41.9	81	50.9	32	16.7	26	11.3
Rural-farm	6		3		2		1				2				1	
Rural-nonfarm	51		54		18		16		3		11		2		1	
CONNECTICUT:																
Urban	1,468	97.9	1,557	98.1	316	90.8	343	90.5	161	42.9	157	41.5	59	11.3	75	11.1
Rural-farm	19		17		2		1		2		3		2			
Rural-nonfarm	232	96.3	268	98.2	45		55		23		26		21	16.7	14	10.7
NEW YORK:																
Urban	16,687	96.8	17,628	96.6	3,842	94.8	4,048	92.5	2,321	58.7	2,743	55.1	1,010	12.3	1,311	10.8
Rural-farm	145	98.0	157	96.9	48		29		16		18		4	3.8	3	
Rural-nonfarm	1,073	95.6	1,117	96.1	257	90.5	248	86.7	103	37.1	152	43.2	33	6.4	48	8.9
NEW JERSEY:																
Urban	9,666	97.0	10,037	97.0	2,155	91.7	2,366	88.6	1,117	47.0	1,337	46.1	530	13.3	560	10.5
Rural-farm	334	95.4	315	97.8	69		63		31	22.3	41		3	1.7	15	
Rural-nonfarm	1,933	97.0	2,001	96.8	457	78.7	435	84.8	198	36.1	247	44.6	78	11.0	98	12.2
PENNSYLVANIA:																
Urban	19,919	95.8	21,070	95.8	4,464	93.6	4,859	91.1	2,328	47.0	2,654	45.6	879	10.8	1,033	9.3
Rural-farm	314	96.0	290	93.2	100	90.1	78		47	38.8	30		14	9.2	15	
Rural-nonfarm	3,618	96.1	3,584	95.4	853	91.4	794	87.6	481	50.2	419	44.8	240	17.6	134	9.9
OHIO:																
Urban	14,910	97.1	15,609	97.0	3,436	95.4	3,864	93.7	2,303	62.4	2,452	60.2	934	15.9	973	13.1
Rural-farm	610	97.8	595	97.4	170	94.4	147	92.5	92	55.4	90	63.4	40	19.0	41	22.0
Rural-nonfarm	1,907	96.8	1,862	97.8	521	92.0	492	92.3	395	63.9	286	56.2	362	34.9	161	21.0
INDIANA:																
Urban	5,549	97.0	5,878	97.4	1,409	94.6	1,379	92.5	853	57.3	876	52.9	380	16.5	419	14.7
Rural-farm	184	96.3	161	97.6	41		46		35		26		18		11	
Rural-nonfarm	320	93.8	308	94.2	124	94.7	67		73	55.7	58		42	17.2	27	18.4
ILLINOIS:																
Urban	14,103	96.9	14,848	96.9	3,246	92.5	3,532	90.8	2,092	56.2	2,351	55.6	1,185	18.5	1,151	13.6
Rural-farm	391	94.2	458	95.2	121	81.8	122	88.4	64	47.8	54	50.0	16	9.5	24	17.1
Rural-nonfarm	1,127	96.5	1,058	96.3	362	90.3	287	86.7	225	57.4	153	50.8	76	16.4	63	14.7
MICHIGAN:																
Urban	7,977	97.4	8,292	97.4	1,866	95.7	1,867	94.1	1,165	63.3	1,157	56.6	459	14.7	359	8.9
Rural-farm	171	95.5	170	94.4	51		41		26		19		13		5	
Rural-nonfarm	340	95.5	302	94.4	72		94		37		60	57.1	18	8.5	14	10.3
WISCONSIN:																
Urban	538	98.7	555	97.9	95		108	95.6	101	88.6	100	74.6	42	20.4	37	14.7
Rural-farm	41		34		4		9		1		3					
Rural-nonfarm	15		28		5		2		5		2		6			
MINNESOTA:																
Urban	433	98.4	415	98.6	110	92.4	103	97.2	54		84	65.6	50	28.4	50	26.3
Rural-farm	12		23		3		3		4		4				1	
Rural-nonfarm	5		8		3		3				2				1	
IOWA:																
Urban	917	97.7	851	98.2	223	96.1	251	95.1	158	64.2	156	59.1	97	27.0	74	19.5
Rural-farm	38		24		12		10		3		8		2		2	
Rural-nonfarm	90		94		17		36		15		18		4		9	
MISSOURI:																
Urban	7,694	95.1	7,879	95.7	1,722	85.9	1,993	85.6	1,179	51.4	1,244	50.9	543	15.2	697	14.9
Rural-farm	2,021	83.9	2,053	86.7	531	75.6	462	75.7	281	40.7	304	49.4	81	9.1	89	9.3
Rural-nonfarm	1,565	92.8	1,510	93.4	404	85.4	346	78.6	215	47.4	190	43.9	58	9.4	76	11.0
NORTH DAKOTA:																
Urban	4		3		2		1		3		1		3			
Rural-farm	5		2		1		1									
Rural-nonfarm	4		2				1		2		1		2			
SOUTH DAKOTA:																
Urban	10		16		2		4		4		2		3		3	
Rural-farm	16		19		7		5		6		4				3	
Rural-nonfarm	4		7		1		1				3				1	
NEBRASKA:																
Urban	659	98.4	646	98.3	147	94.8	167	94.9	114	61.6	118	71.1	42	18.2	62	19.0
Rural-farm	16		15		9		3		10		4		6		3	
Rural-nonfarm	25		17		7		7		3		3		1		3	
KANSAS:																
Urban	2,998	97.1	3,210	97.5	720	90.3	838	92.4	492	61.7	594	70.3	306	25.9	389	27.6
Rural-farm	317	95.8	301	98.4	92	90.2	90	89.1	49	45.4	60		26	17.6	24	22.0
Rural-nonfarm	563	97.2	510	97.9	134	79.3	168	92.8	79	57.7	90	64.3	61	21.9	41	18.2
DELAWARE:																
Urban	800	97.4	798	95.9	160	93.6	194	89.4	113	55.1	142	53.2	40	11.1	50	11.0
Rural-farm	541	92.6	529	93.5	130	77.4	117	77.5	49	23.2	44	29.3	11	4.0	13	6.7
Rural-nonfarm	709	94.0	742	93.9	195	87.8	172	79.3	112	53.3	56	31.3	66	22.8	24	8.3
MARYLAND:																
Urban	8,385	95.0	9,326	95.5	1,570	81.9	1,945	78.6	805	36.3	1,034	38.6	316	8.5	509	10.3
Rural-farm	3,960	90.5	3,801	91.8	781	64.4	731	68.1	258	19.7	251	26.4	61	3.8	104	8.7
Rural-nonfarm	5,228	92.6	5,237	92.4	1,110	73.8	965	68.8	411	26.0	404	29.0	121	5.1	159	7.6
DISTRICT OF COLUMBIA:																
Urban	6,465	96.4	7,173	96.9	1,620	94.2	1,789	91.6	1,062	57.7	1,230	55.9	711	22.4	879	20.4
VIRGINIA:																
Urban	12,926	92.4	14,159	93.6	2,743	81.0	3,186	80.8	1,493	43.3	2,198	47.6	837	15.0	1,223	16.0
Rural-farm	23,092	83.0	23,151	85.4	5,665	71.5	6,046	80.2	2,730	35.7	3,348	50.3	772	8.5	1,213	15.9
Rural-nonfarm	12,918	84.6	13,171	86.9	2,792	72.4	3,054	75.9	1,311	34.2	1,687	42.8	565	10.3	813	14.0

Table 17.—SCHOOL ATTENDANCE OF NEGRO POPULATION, BY AGE PERIODS, AND SEX, FOR URBAN, RURAL-FARM, AND RURAL-NONFARM AREAS, BY STATES: 1930—Continued

[Percent not shown where base is less than 100]

STATE AND AREA	PERSONS 7 TO 13 YEARS OLD				PERSONS 14 AND 15 YEARS OLD				PERSONS 16 AND 17 YEARS OLD				PERSONS 18 TO 20 YEARS OLD			
	Male		Female		Male		Female		Male		Female		Male		Female	
	Number	Percent	Number	Percent	Number	Percent	Number	Percent	Number	Percent	Number	Percent	Number	Percent	Number	Percent
WEST VIRGINIA:																
Urban	1,712	95.6	1,807	95.2	399	91.3	465	88.2	275	57.8	367	63.3	199	25.3	277	28.0
Rural-farm	267	76.5	299	81.5	64	-----	79	72.5	25	-----	40	-----	14	9.0	22	21.0
Rural-nonfarm	5,369	93.4	5,626	94.1	1,104	87.8	1,168	84.9	648	49.0	748	52.2	354	17.6	533	22.2
NORTH CAROLINA:																
Urban	15,728	93.0	17,157	94.0	3,247	73.2	3,902	76.8	1,740	36.9	2,643	44.6	969	13.2	1,590	14.4
Rural-farm	46,049	86.1	45,935	87.9	10,893	72.6	11,951	82.5	5,848	40.1	7,736	55.9	2,093	11.6	3,614	19.8
Rural-nonfarm	12,789	89.1	13,464	90.4	2,728	73.3	3,164	80.0	1,443	38.1	1,998	49.2	610	10.2	1,029	15.2
SOUTH CAROLINA:																
Urban	8,841	88.4	9,906	90.9	1,687	66.8	2,425	74.2	1,043	38.7	1,688	45.6	625	14.9	913	13.6
Rural-farm	42,131	76.6	43,202	79.9	10,349	66.2	11,964	76.9	5,402	35.9	7,649	51.8	2,169	11.8	3,378	17.2
Rural-nonfarm:	10,178	75.1	11,119	80.4	1,926	58.0	2,572	70.6	916	27.2	1,603	40.3	387	7.2	718	9.9
GEORGIA:																
Urban	17,810	86.0	19,759	89.0	3,402	62.0	4,831	70.9	1,858	32.6	2,981	39.1	1,058	11.6	1,564	10.8
Rural-farm	45,578	80.1	46,241	83.3	9,527	57.1	11,795	72.3	3,932	24.5	6,200	39.1	1,236	5.9	1,966	9.0
Rural-nonfarm	11,575	80.8	12,384	93.9	2,154	55.3	2,669	64.8	803	20.2	1,423	30.7	347	5.0	545	6.6
FLORIDA:																
Urban	11,967	93.8	12,926	94.6	2,547	78.4	3,049	79.3	1,339	41.9	1,940	45.6	601	11.6	878	11.0
Rural-farm	5,363	75.1	5,284	76.9	1,419	64.9	1,471	71.1	733	35.3	911	46.4	220	9.0	413	15.8
Rural-nonfarm	7,446	74.6	7,888	77.3	1,546	57.9	1,762	65.8	739	27.4	941	32.5	252	5.7	357	7.1
KENTUCKY:																
Urban	5,713	94.6	6,106	95.7	1,436	83.9	1,639	86.3	899	49.9	1,118	54.5	495	17.9	599	18.0
Rural-farm	3,469	84.4	3,403	84.9	862	72.4	865	80.1	496	41.1	533	50.9	163	10.5	249	18.3
Rural-nonfarm	3,854	90.8	3,905	91.5	939	80.6	961	80.4	514	43.6	633	51.8	211	12.3	299	18.0
TENNESSEE:																
Urban	12,441	92.7	13,256	93.9	2,877	81.6	3,390	83.3	1,673	43.8	2,330	49.7	805	12.8	1,243	13.6
Rural-farm	13,989	84.4	13,537	86.1	3,708	77.3	3,861	81.9	2,290	46.6	2,333	53.4	778	12.2	970	15.6
Rural-nonfarm	3,824	88.1	3,777	89.0	1,008	77.2	1,032	83.3	646	47.1	764	54.0	294	13.0	442	18.8
ALABAMA:																
Urban	15,222	90.5	16,381	92.1	3,426	74.6	4,318	79.6	1,957	40.5	2,929	47.8	828	11.8	1,372	12.5
Rural-farm	36,530	74.7	36,341	77.2	10,227	70.6	10,711	77.3	6,069	41.1	6,664	51.3	1,770	12.4	2,720	14.8
Rural-nonfarm	10,166	82.5	10,810	85.7	2,228	71.9	2,529	74.5	1,145	34.1	1,518	40.6	416	7.9	606	8.7
MISSISSIPPI:																
Urban	7,049	91.9	7,746	93.8	1,420	69.7	1,995	80.2	920	40.0	1,280	46.2	460	13.4	680	12.0
Rural-farm	60,463	86.0	59,083	87.7	15,755	80.1	15,769	84.8	10,311	51.2	9,942	55.1	3,452	15.1	4,184	14.4
Rural-nonfarm	5,853	88.5	6,307	90.0	1,216	71.4	1,451	79.4	706	36.1	1,004	46.5	318	9.9	476	10.6
ARKANSAS:																
Urban	4,640	93.0	5,082	94.1	1,133	82.4	1,377	86.2	826	55.1	1,072	57.9	462	20.6	578	16.4
Rural-farm	24,149	85.1	24,033	86.0	6,474	81.0	6,416	84.3	4,328	56.6	4,396	58.3	1,942	19.1	1,943	16.0
Rural-nonfarm	3,656	90.7	3,881	91.5	859	82.6	957	84.7	573	51.6	644	51.4	256	14.7	312	13.2
LOUISIANA:																
Urban	14,148	92.5	15,471	93.1	3,052	76.6	3,802	78.9	1,731	42.7	2,400	45.1	856	13.4	1,182	12.4
Rural-farm	27,307	77.3	27,407	79.3	6,541	69.5	6,888	74.5	3,700	42.2	4,342	48.5	1,676	14.3	2,120	16.1
Rural-nonfarm	8,863	83.5	8,956	85.3	1,730	67.1	1,994	72.4	764	31.2	1,141	38.7	456	10.6	521	10.5
OKLAHOMA:																
Urban	3,630	94.6	3,802	95.1	826	88.1	1,084	90.9	682	62.6	804	62.0	438	24.0	505	19.4
Rural-farm	6,883	89.3	6,491	89.7	1,802	85.9	1,825	88.0	1,344	63.4	1,302	65.6	648	23.0	663	24.1
Rural-nonfarm	1,640	91.7	1,727	92.2	427	86.6	415	90.4	317	63.7	340	65.3	211	28.4	170	20.8
TEXAS:																
Urban	17,292	92.7	18,261	93.3	4,128	84.9	5,214	87.6	2,754	52.1	3,892	57.4	1,374	16.3	1,795	14.2
Rural-farm	32,673	84.5	32,082	85.8	8,343	80.9	8,798	85.6	5,178	49.6	6,019	58.4	1,693	11.9	2,259	15.0
Rural-nonfarm	6,948	87.8	7,077	89.2	1,663	83.7	1,826	83.8	1,015	49.6	1,190	52.0	412	12.4	498	12.0
MONTANA:																
Urban	46	-----	48	-----	10	-----	13	-----	11	-----	7	-----	3	-----	3	-----
Rural-farm	4	-----	2	-----	-----	-----	-----	-----	-----	-----	-----	-----	-----	-----	-----	-----
Rural-nonfarm	3	-----	5	-----	1	-----	2	-----	1	-----	-----	-----	1	-----	-----	-----
IDAHO:																
Urban	19	-----	17	-----	5	-----	5	-----	2	-----	2	-----	3	-----	2	-----
Rural-farm	3	-----	2	-----	3	-----	1	-----	-----	-----	-----	-----	-----	-----	-----	-----
Rural-nonfarm	7	-----	1	-----	1	-----	1	-----	-----	-----	-----	-----	-----	-----	1	-----
WYOMING:																
Urban	37	-----	39	-----	8	-----	9	-----	3	-----	7	-----	1	-----	9	-----
Rural-farm	4	-----	1	-----	2	-----	-----	-----	-----	-----	-----	-----	-----	-----	-----	-----
Rural-nonfarm	10	-----	12	-----	1	-----	5	-----	3	-----	1	-----	2	-----	-----	-----
COLORADO:																
Urban	424	96.6	476	96.2	100	93.5	120	92.3	74	62.7	95	62.5	59	28.0	64	26.7
Rural-farm	19	-----	24	-----	6	-----	5	-----	2	-----	5	-----	4	-----	2	-----
Rural-nonfarm	48	-----	38	-----	13	-----	16	-----	10	-----	11	-----	6	-----	3	-----
NEW MEXICO:																
Urban	91	-----	99	95.2	14	-----	28	-----	17	-----	22	-----	8	-----	11	-----
Rural-farm	47	-----	55	-----	15	-----	8	-----	8	-----	7	-----	3	-----	3	-----
Rural-nonfarm	31	-----	30	-----	9	-----	7	-----	4	-----	5	-----	2	-----	2	-----
ARIZONA:																
Urban	225	95.3	241	95.3	54	-----	52	-----	44	-----	39	-----	28	22.0	13	-----
Rural-farm	95	91.3	78	-----	20	-----	15	-----	17	-----	8	-----	4	-----	6	-----
Rural-nonfarm	191	92.7	198	93.4	55	-----	43	-----	26	-----	31	-----	9	4.9	9	-----
UTAH:																
Urban	42	-----	53	-----	14	-----	7	-----	3	-----	1	-----	5	-----	3	-----
Rural-farm	-----	-----	2	-----	2	-----	1	-----	1	-----	-----	-----	-----	-----	-----	-----
Rural-nonfarm	5	-----	7	-----	-----	-----	2	-----	1	-----	-----	-----	-----	-----	1	-----
NEVADA:																
Urban	6	-----	6	-----	-----	-----	3	-----	1	-----	-----	-----	-----	-----	-----	-----
Rural-farm	-----	-----	1	-----	-----	-----	-----	-----	-----	-----	-----	-----	-----	-----	-----	-----
Rural-nonfarm	4	-----	4	-----	1	-----	-----	-----	2	-----	1	-----	1	-----	-----	-----
WASHINGTON:																
Urban	239	96.0	228	95.4	67	-----	57	-----	48	-----	65	-----	24	21.8	26	25.0
Rural-farm	18	-----	20	-----	4	-----	2	-----	2	-----	5	-----	1	-----	2	-----
Rural-nonfarm	42	-----	22	-----	19	-----	10	-----	10	-----	9	-----	6	-----	2	-----
OREGON:																
Urban	62	-----	82	-----	23	-----	18	-----	15	-----	19	-----	14	-----	12	-----
Rural-farm	1	-----	1	-----	-----	-----	-----	-----	-----	-----	-----	-----	-----	-----	-----	-----
Rural-nonfarm	15	-----	11	-----	3	-----	3	-----	2	-----	4	-----	-----	-----	-----	-----
CALIFORNIA:																
Urban	3,146	97.0	3,294	97.5	854	98.0	925	96.8	724	85.7	814	83.1	442	32.1	481	27.3
Rural-farm	284	95.6	281	97.9	73	-----	59	-----	37	-----	39	-----	16	-----	14	-----
Rural-nonfarm	313	94.3	353	96.4	81	-----	74	-----	67	54.0	59	-----	15	11.2	29	19.9

Table 18.—SCHOOL ATTENDANCE OF NEGRO AND WHITE POPULATION BY AGE PERIODS, BY SECTIONS, DIVISIONS, AND STATES: 1930

[Percent not shown where base is less than 100]

DIVISION OR STATE AND RACIAL CLASS	Total number of persons attending school	PERSONS 7 TO 13 YEARS OLD			PERSONS 14 AND 15 YEARS OLD			PERSONS 16 AND 17 YEARS OLD			PERSONS 18 TO 20 YEARS OLD			OTHERS ATTENDING SCHOOL			
		Total number	Attending school: Number	Attending school: Per cent	Total number	Attending school: Number	Attending school: Per cent	Total number	Attending school: Number	Attending school: Per cent	Total number	Attending school: Number	Attending school: Per cent	Under 5 years old	5 years old	6 years old	21 years and over
United States:																	
Negro	2,553,151	1,811,015	1,580,624	87.3	493,897	385,502	78.1	502,710	232,648	46.3	765,928	102,038	13.3	4,813	34,748	141,751	71,027
White	24,973,932	15,065,790	14,547,737	96.6	4,110,385	3,716,963	90.4	4,086,139	2,405,061	58.9	5,929,322	1,338,189	22.6	56,374	458,629	1,502,550	948,429
THE NORTH:																	
Negro	430,796	264,683	255,177	96.4	65,844	60,132	91.3	68,300	36,479	53.4	121,226	16,464	13.6	1,588	12,795	31,991	16,212
White	15,888,164	9,400,734	9,199,458	97.9	2,594,446	2,388,626	92.1	2,555,473	1,475,716	57.7	3,726,755	790,086	21.2	42,806	365,553	1,031,674	594,202
THE SOUTH:																	
Negro	2,100,626	1,534,723	1,314,235	85.6	424,944	322,421	75.9	431,207	193,778	44.9	639,388	94,218	13.2	3,090	21,229	108,378	53,277
White	6,648,937	4,348,450	4,062,204	93.4	1,152,214	981,142	85.2	1,168,544	650,847	55.7	1,657,578	369,668	22.3	7,606	49,183	331,933	196,354
THE WEST:																	
Negro	21,729	11,609	11,212	96.6	3,109	2,949	94.9	3,203	2,391	74.6	5,314	1,356	25.5	135	766	1,382	1,538
White	2,436,831	1,316,606	1,286,075	97.7	363,725	347,195	95.5	362,122	278,498	76.9	544,989	178,435	32.7	5,962	43,850	138,943	157,873
NEW ENGLAND:																	
Negro	20,227	12,246	11,947	97.6	3,016	2,747	91.1	2,871	1,481	51.6	4,392	767	17.5	156	791	1,529	809
White	1,813,315	1,063,639	1,044,246	98.2	291,695	265,038	90.9	286,640	157,489	54.9	411,823	92,192	22.4	8,440	52,283	122,680	70,947
MAINE:																	
Negro	230	140	135	96.4	32	31	-----	28	23	-----	46	17	-----	2	8	12	2
White	180,391	106,978	104,828	98.0	28,589	26,218	91.7	27,849	16,660	59.8	39,351	9,110	23.2	627	6,099	12,955	3,894
NEW HAMPSHIRE:																	
Negro	116	66	63	-----	25	22	-----	23	11	-----	46	10	-----	1	1	5	3
White	98,255	59,958	58,702	97.9	16,219	15,160	93.5	15,739	8,732	55.5	22,592	5,008	22.2	398	1,707	5,801	2,747
VERMONT:																	
Negro	119	69	66	-----	21	18	-----	25	15	-----	39	5	-----	-----	4	8	3
White	76,315	47,850	46,546	97.3	13,052	11,829	90.6	12,726	7,093	55.7	18,345	3,910	21.3	87	716	4,394	1,740
MASSACHUSETTS:																	
Negro	11,732	6,946	6,768	97.4	1,742	1,600	91.8	1,574	911	57.9	2,334	502	21.5	106	411	864	570
White	950,210	538,819	529,703	98.3	149,345	138,697	92.9	145,949	86,791	59.5	211,281	52,935	25.1	5,081	26,669	64,001	46,333
RHODE ISLAND:																	
Negro	2,158	1,389	1,354	97.5	340	314	92.4	319	149	46.7	462	62	13.4	6	63	155	55
White	147,542	91,666	89,902	98.1	24,229	21,282	87.8	25,061	10,110	40.3	36,300	6,182	17.0	574	3,887	10,491	5,114
CONNECTICUT:																	
Negro	5,872	3,636	3,561	97.9	856	762	89.0	902	372	41.2	1,465	171	11.7	41	304	485	176
White	360,602	218,368	214,565	98.3	60,261	51,852	86.0	59,316	28,103	47.4	83,954	15,047	17.9	1,673	13,205	25,038	11,119
MIDDLE ATLANTIC:																	
Negro	181,295	114,076	109,888	96.3	27,500	25,165	91.5	29,143	14,283	49.0	54,854	6,008	11.0	782	5,147	13,668	6,354
White	5,563,034	3,345,845	3,267,711	97.7	922,146	852,362	92.4	911,438	486,783	53.4	1,350,031	256,216	19.0	17,029	120,228	356,567	206,138
NEW YORK:																	
Negro	63,163	38,088	36,807	96.6	9,081	8,472	93.3	9,665	5,353	55.4	21,606	2,409	11.1	265	1,833	4,906	3,118
White	2,570,265	1,484,895	1,451,373	97.7	411,740	386,860	94.0	409,953	244,012	59.5	640,532	132,708	20.7	8,874	67,748	165,428	113,262
NEW JERSEY:																	
Negro	40,601	25,050	24,286	97.0	6,280	5,545	88.3	6,605	2,971	45.0	11,112	1,284	11.6	233	1,887	3,236	1,159
White	865,780	516,018	506,264	98.1	141,527	129,064	91.2	140,980	67,212	47.7	203,064	34,911	17.2	4,613	33,679	60,838	29,199
PENNSYLVANIA:																	
Negro	77,531	50,938	48,795	95.8	12,139	11,148	91.8	12,873	5,959	46.3	22,136	2,315	10.5	284	1,427	5,526	2,077
White	2,126,989	1,344,935	1,310,074	97.4	368,879	336,438	91.2	360,505	175,559	48.7	506,435	88,597	17.5	3,542	18,801	130,301	63,677
EAST NORTH CENTRAL:																	
Negro	169,419	101,374	98,341	97.0	25,304	23,580	93.2	25,998	15,154	58.3	45,334	6,876	15.2	522	5,022	12,688	7,236
White	5,474,857	3,211,498	3,145,424	97.9	888,043	830,755	93.5	866,588	540,038	62.3	1,261,149	269,558	21.4	12,932	114,952	349,784	211,414
OHIO:																	
Negro	60,644	36,564	35,493	97.1	9,160	8,630	94.2	9,198	5,618	61.1	15,486	2,511	16.2	102	1,298	4,468	2,524
White	1,435,768	839,890	822,566	97.9	228,790	221,352	96.7	221,484	150,646	68.0	325,986	75,475	23.2	1,557	17,043	89,516	57,613
INDIANA:																	
Negro	21,201	12,781	12,400	97.0	3,276	3,066	93.6	3,479	1,921	55.2	5,674	897	15.8	48	327	1,528	1,014
White	685,844	413,035	404,053	97.8	113,022	108,414	95.9	111,101	69,644	62.7	160,862	35,244	21.9	749	6,890	40,331	20,519
ILLINOIS:																	
Negro	55,613	33,053	31,985	96.8	8,417	7,670	91.1	8,886	4,939	55.6	16,055	2,515	15.7	249	1,622	4,026	2,607
White	1,561,525	919,826	899,541	97.8	262,411	242,554	92.4	262,855	150,430	57.2	384,962	77,469	20.1	3,803	23,364	96,907	67,457
MICHIGAN:																	
Negro	29,880	17,741	17,252	97.2	4,215	3,991	94.7	4,163	2,464	59.2	7,616	868	11.4	92	1,668	2,520	1,025
White	1,100,569	638,276	626,604	98.2	170,018	160,192	94.2	162,437	100,415	61.8	235,702	48,312	20.5	2,722	45,318	77,229	39,777
WISCONSIN:																	
Negro	2,081	1,235	1,211	98.1	236	223	94.5	272	212	77.9	503	85	16.9	31	107	146	66
White	691,151	400,471	392,660	98.0	113,802	98,243	86.3	108,711	68,903	63.4	153,637	33,058	21.5	4,101	22,337	45,801	26,048
WEST NORTH CENTRAL:																	
Negro	59,855	36,987	35,001	94.6	10,024	8,640	86.2	10,288	5,561	54.1	16,646	2,813	16.9	128	1,793	4,106	1,813
White	3,036,958	1,779,749	1,742,077	97.9	492,562	440,471	89.4	490,807	291,406	59.4	703,752	172,120	24.5	4,405	78,133	202,643	105,703
MINNESOTA:																	
Negro	1,673	910	896	98.5	239	225	94.1	236	148	62.7	385	102	26.5	2	77	123	100
White	611,978	355,437	348,767	98.1	99,614	90,804	91.2	96,353	54,996	57.1	136,530	33,411	24.5	903	16,740	39,717	26,640
IOWA:																	
Negro	3,663	2,060	2,014	97.8	582	549	94.3	580	358	61.7	830	188	22.7	11	164	294	85
White	585,226	333,020	327,519	98.3	92,426	83,003	89.8	89,932	57,467	63.9	128,731	32,327	25.1	1,042	23,416	42,735	17,717
MISSOURI:																	
Negro	37,907	24,403	22,722	93.1	6,556	5,458	83.3	6,934	3,413	49.2	11,433	1,544	13.5	82	1,036	2,571	1,081
White	718,602	437,946	424,895	97.0	122,476	105,116	85.8	125,364	64,913	51.8	181,975	37,216	20.5	1,000	13,554	47,120	24,788
NORTH DAKOTA:																	
Negro	41	22	20	-----	8	6	-----	13	7	-----	15	5	-----	-----	1	1	1
White	178,919	109,569	106,815	97.5	30,965	27,346	88.3	30,319	17,702	58.4	42,357	10,642	25.1	150	1,186	10,086	4,992
SOUTH DAKOTA:																	
Negro	138	75	72	-----	22	20	-----	25	19	-----	35	10	-----	-----	3	7	7
White	171,175	103,760	101,587	97.9	27,823	24,694	88.8	27,196	17,036	62.6	38,918	10,792	27.7	174	1,477	10,681	4,734
NEBRASKA:																	
Negro	2,541	1,400	1,378	98.4	360	340	94.4	385	252	65.5	597	117	19.6	9	158	204	83
White	340,097	191,938	188,950	98.4	52,282	47,667	91.2	53,032	33,542	63.2	76,404	18,919	24.8	724	14,194	24,680	11,421
KANSAS:																	
Negro	13,892	8,117	7,899	97.3	2,257	2,042	90.5	2,115	1,364	64.5	3,351	847	25.3	24	354	906	456
White	430,961	248,079	243,544	98.2	66,976	61,841	92.3	68,611	45,750	66.7	98,837	28,813	29.2	412	7,566	27,624	15,411

TABLE 18.—SCHOOL ATTENDANCE OF NEGRO AND WHITE POPULATION BY AGE PERIODS, BY SECTIONS, DIVISIONS, AND STATES: 1930—Continued

[Percent not shown where base is less than 100]

DIVISION OR STATE AND RACIAL CLASS	Total number of persons attending school	PERSONS 7 TO 13 YEARS OLD			PERSONS 14 AND 15 YEARS OLD			PERSONS 16 AND 17 YEARS OLD			PERSONS 18 TO 20 YEARS OLD			OTHERS ATTENDING SCHOOL			
		Total number	Attending school		Total number	Attending school		Total number	Attending school		Total number	Attending school		Under 5 years old	5 years old	6 years old	21 years and over
			Number	Per cent		Number	Per cent		Number	Per cent		Number	Per cent				
SOUTH ATLANTIC:																	
Negro	1,008,655	760,076	648,911	85.4	209,503	151,224	72.2	210,899	84,350	40.0	311,182	37,418	12.0	1,396	7,864	53,640	23,852
White	2,695,051	1,782,550	1,676,602	94.1	469,672	388,562	82.7	473,058	243,856	51.5	670,215	139,727	20.8	2,978	18,963	143,664	80,699
DELAWARE:																	
Negro	6,559	4,347	4,119	94.8	1,146	968	84.5	1,222	516	42.2	1,859	204	11.0	18	47	407	280
White	43,764	27,599	26,903	97.5	7,276	6,733	92.5	7,347	3,937	53.6	10,830	2,099	19.4	52	197	2,507	1,336
MARYLAND:																	
Negro	52,566	38,424	35,937	93.5	9,586	7,102	74.1	10,128	3,163	31.2	15,905	1,270	8.0	102	600	3,240	1,152
White	282,623	182,733	177,155	96.9	48,397	39,608	81.8	48,698	21,661	44.5	71,451	12,844	18.0	378	2,573	16,887	11,517
DISTRICT OF COLUMBIA																	
Negro	25,627	14,112	13,638	96.6	3,671	3,409	92.9	4,040	2,292	56.7	7,489	1,590	21.2	84	737	1,608	2,269
White	70,129	33,627	32,966	98.0	9,036	8,727	96.6	9,302	6,739	72.4	17,472	5,830	33.4	143	1,933	4,080	9,711
VIRGINIA:																	
Negro	149,836	114,474	99,417	86.8	30,662	23,486	76.6	30,154	12,767	42.3	41,199	5,423	13.2	115	564	5,667	2,397
White	404,355	276,144	254,927	92.3	73,143	60,924	83.3	74,297	37,693	50.7	106,106	21,281	20.1	321	2,317	16,021	10,871
WEST VIRGINIA:																	
Negro	24,473	16,136	15,080	93.5	3,801	3,279	86.3	3,988	2,103	52.7	6,444	1,399	21.7	42	234	1,417	919
White	401,713	269,097	253,268	94.1	68,425	59,017	86.3	68,199	33,875	49.7	94,437	19,055	20.2	398	2,626	22,175	11,299
NORTH CAROLINA:																	
Negro	236,036	170,153	151,122	88.8	46,680	35,885	76.9	46,898	21,408	45.6	67,418	9,905	14.7	202	1,067	13,395	3,052
White	571,523	384,326	365,089	95.0	101,275	81,285	80.3	100,915	51,444	51.0	138,131	29,567	21.4	502	1,909	30,312	11,415
SOUTH CAROLINA:																	
Negro	199,514	157,359	125,377	79.7	43,962	30,923	70.3	43,531	18,301	42.0	61,527	8,190	13.3	205	1,205	9,012	6,301
White	243,878	164,216	152,648	93.0	42,495	32,907	77.4	43,130	22,158	51.4	60,660	13,993	23.1	261	1,157	13,089	7,665
GEORGIA:																	
Negro	234,249	184,449	153,347	83.1	53,301	34,378	64.5	53,857	17,197	31.9	81,719	6,716	8.2	359	2,119	13,795	6,338
White	444,460	299,633	275,631	92.0	80,666	64,353	79.8	82,161	42,060	51.2	117,078	21,726	18.6	585	4,303	25,267	10,535
FLORIDA:																	
Negro	79,795	60,622	50,874	83.9	16,694	11,794	70.6	17,081	6,603	38.7	27,622	2,721	9.9	269	1,291	5,099	1,144
White	232,606	145,175	138,015	95.1	38,959	35,008	89.9	39,009	24,289	62.3	54,050	13,332	24.7	338	1,948	13,326	6,350
EAST SOUTH CENTRAL:																	
Negro	587,277	420,221	359,225	85.5	119,064	93,623	78.6	122,234	58,674	48.0	176,657	23,830	13.5	897	9,016	31,262	10,750
White	1,763,708	1,166,718	1,078,765	92.5	306,382	263,023	85.8	311,431	171,633	55.1	431,099	96,981	22.5	2,145	15,096	88,572	47,490
KENTUCKY:																	
Negro	43,565	29,041	26,450	91.1	8,242	6,702	81.3	8,509	4,193	49.3	12,400	2,016	16.3	41	406	2,474	1,283
White	552,602	382,195	348,697	91.2	99,431	82,154	82.6	97,109	47,746	49.2	133,816	25,860	19.3	738	3,528	28,018	15,861
TENNESSEE:																	
Negro	99,657	68,398	60,824	88.9	19,653	15,876	80.8	20,580	10,036	48.8	32,620	4,532	13.9	138	642	5,030	2,579
White	507,376	338,127	311,894	92.2	88,718	76,468	86.2	92,371	50,003	54.1	131,780	28,192	21.4	501	2,785	23,960	13,573
ALABAMA:																	
Negro	200,428	155,517	125,450	80.7	44,844	33,439	74.6	45,810	20,282	44.3	62,810	7,712	12.3	182	1,120	8,191	4,052
White	424,894	284,053	263,569	92.8	75,220	65,710	87.4	77,657	43,354	55.8	103,728	22,236	21.4	407	1,322	18,035	10,261
MISSISSIPPI:																	
Negro	243,627	167,265	146,501	87.6	46,325	37,606	81.2	47,335	24,163	51.0	68,827	9,570	13.9	536	6,848	15,567	2,836
White	278,836	162,343	154,605	95.2	43,013	38,694	90.0	44,294	30,530	68.9	61,775	20,693	33.5	499	7,461	18,559	7,795
WEST SOUTH CENTRAL:																	
Negro	504,694	354,426	306,099	86.4	96,377	77,574	80.5	98,074	50,754	51.8	151,549	22,970	15.2	797	4,349	23,476	18,675
White	2,190,178	1,399,182	1,306,837	93.4	376,160	329,554	87.6	384,055	235,358	61.3	556,264	132,960	23.9	2,483	15,124	99,697	68,165
Arkansas:																	
Negro	108,528	74,959	65,441	87.3	20,750	17,216	83.0	20,905	11,839	56.6	32,166	5,493	17.1	98	618	6,109	1,714
White	351,034	228,392	209,536	91.7	61,423	52,559	85.6	61,440	37,152	60.5	85,255	21,069	24.8	378	1,828	20,070	8,442
Louisiana:																	
Negro	170,695	122,914	102,152	83.1	32,804	24,007	73.2	32,500	14,078	43.3	50,037	6,811	13.6	350	1,900	9,126	12,271
White	316,818	206,967	192,969	93.2	54,543	44,387	81.4	54,823	29,210	53.3	79,425	16,313	20.5	601	3,943	18,919	10,476
Oklahoma:																	
Negro	42,626	26,443	24,173	91.4	7,255	6,379	87.9	7,512	4,789	63.8	11,560	2,635	22.8	97	672	2,816	1,065
White	540,827	333,461	316,191	94.8	87,429	77,909	89.1	89,779	56,706	63.2	130,981	33,964	25.9	622	5,059	33,344	17,032
Texas:																	
Negro	182,845	130,110	114,333	87.9	35,568	29,972	84.3	37,157	20,048	54.0	57,786	8,031	13.9	252	1,159	5,425	3,625
White	981,499	630,360	588,141	93.3	172,765	154,699	89.5	178,013	112,290	63.1	260,603	61,614	23.6	882	4,294	27,364	32,215
MOUNTAIN:																	
Negro	4,881	2,937	2,800	95.3	754	677	89.8	806	472	58.6	1,385	272	19.6	11	123	306	220
White	830,226	486,246	473,676	97.4	130,161	121,067	93.0	127,345	88,422	69.4	182,664	54,811	30.0	1,135	10,062	48,374	32,679
Montana:																	
Negro	176	111	108	97.3	29	26	-----	22	19	-----	45	7	-----	-----	2	10	4
White	126,283	75,261	73,595	97.8	20,745	19,308	93.1	19,772	13,464	68.1	27,287	8,185	30.0	119	796	6,929	3,887
Idaho:																	
Negro	81	49	49	-----	17	16	-----	9	4	-----	29	7	-----	-----	-----	3	2
White	116,579	69,167	67,781	98.0	18,712	17,618	94.2	18,043	13,057	72.4	24,927	8,216	33.0	71	283	5,901	3,652
Wyoming:																	
Negro	167	103	103	100.0	29	25	-----	27	14	-----	45	12	-----	-----	-----	10	3
White	51,280	30,228	29,747	98.4	7,900	7,374	93.3	7,738	5,340	69.0	11,803	3,186	27.0	49	614	3,306	1,664
Colorado:																	
Negro	1,955	1,064	1,029	96.7	284	260	91.5	319	197	61.8	506	138	27.3	7	73	125	126
White	227,100	130,038	126,684	97.4	35,427	32,273	91.1	35,619	23,154	65.0	51,769	15,395	29.7	421	3,781	13,821	11,571
New Mexico:																	
Negro	583	374	353	94.4	90	81	-----	115	63	54.8	153	29	19.0	-----	13	33	11
White	85,132	53,275	50,458	94.7	13,514	11,980	88.6	13,611	8,320	61.1	19,389	4,761	24.1	219	1,698	5,570	2,216
Arizona:																	
Negro	1,711	1,099	1,028	93.5	273	239	87.5	297	165	55.6	565	69	12.2	4	31	110	65
White	62,155	35,516	34,482	97.1	9,231	8,592	93.1	9,300	6,283	67.6	13,796	4,075	29.5	130	1,381	3,969	3,243
Utah:																	
Negro	172	113	109	96.5	28	23	-----	10	6	-----	32	9	-----	-----	2	12	8
White	145,287	83,382	81,864	98.2	22,140	21,548	97.3	20,821	16,914	81.2	29,986	9,868	32.9	106	1,258	7,875	5,854
Nevada:																	
Negro	36	24	21	-----	4	4	-----	7	4	-----	10	1	-----	-----	2	3	1
White	16,410	9,379	9,065	96.7	2,492	2,374	95.3	2,441	1,890	77.4	3,707	1,215	32.8	20	251	1,003	592
PACIFIC:																	
Negro	16,848	8,672	8,412	97.0	2,355	2,272	96.5	2,397	1,919	80.1	3,929	1,084	27.6	124	643	1,076	1,318
White	1,606,605	830,360	812,399	97.8	233,564	226,128	96.8	234,777	190,076	81.0	362,325	123,624	34.1	4,827	33,788	90,569	125,194
Washington:																	
Negro	1,071	590	569	96.4	166	159	95.8	179	139	77.7	255	61	23.9	1	7	63	72
White	339,658	188,575	184,448	97.8	53,978	51,621	95.6	53,748	41,348	76.9	79,004	26,591	33.7	277	1,625	16,402	17,346
Oregon:																	
Negro	330	178	172	96.6	48	47	-----	54	40	-----	85	26	-----	-----	4	16	25
White	207,095	114,421	111,813	97.7	32,495	30,729	94.6	33,086	24,075	72.8	48,577	16,174	33.3	175	919	10,589	12,621
California:																	
Negro	15,447	7,904	7,671	97.1	2,141	2,066	96.5	2,164	1,740	80.4	3,589	997	27.8	123	632	997	1,221
White	1,059,852	527,364	516,138	97.9	147,091	143,778	97.7	147,943	124,653	84.3	234,744	80,859	34.4	4,375	31,244	63,578	95,227

Table 19.—SCHOOL ATTENDANCE OF NEGRO POPULATION BY AGE PERIODS, AND SEX, FOR CITIES OF 500,000 OR MORE INHABITANTS: 1930

[Percent not shown where base is less than 100]

CITY AND SEX	Total number attending school	PERSONS 7 TO 13 YEARS OLD: Total number	PERSONS 7 TO 13 YEARS OLD: Attending school: Number	PERSONS 7 TO 13 YEARS OLD: Attending school: Percent	PERSONS 14 AND 15 YEARS OLD: Total number	PERSONS 14 AND 15 YEARS OLD: Attending school: Number	PERSONS 14 AND 15 YEARS OLD: Attending school: Percent	PERSONS 16 AND 17 YEARS OLD: Total number	PERSONS 16 AND 17 YEARS OLD: Attending school: Number	PERSONS 16 AND 17 YEARS OLD: Attending school: Percent	PERSONS 18 TO 20 YEARS OLD: Total number	PERSONS 18 TO 20 YEARS OLD: Attending school: Number	PERSONS 18 TO 20 YEARS OLD: Attending school: Percent	OTHERS ATTENDING SCHOOL: 5 years Under	OTHERS ATTENDING SCHOOL: 5 years old	OTHERS ATTENDING SCHOOL: 6 years old	OTHERS ATTENDING SCHOOL: 21 years and over
BALTIMORE, MD.																	
Both sexes	23, 742	16, 322	15, 574	95. 4	3, 767	3, 024	80. 3	4, 231	1, 597	37. 7	7, 624	741	9. 7	70	424	1, 548	764
Male	10, 952	7, 720	7, 344	95. 1	1, 616	1, 337	82. 7	1, 899	690	36. 3	3, 292	281	8. 5	32	208	723	337
Female	12, 790	8, 602	8, 230	95. 7	2, 151	1, 687	78. 4	2, 332	907	38. 9	4, 332	460	10. 6	38	216	825	427
BOSTON, MASS.																	
Both sexes	3, 907	2, 122	2, 049	96. 6	560	518	92. 5	506	337	66. 6	785	171	21. 8	80	198	312	242
Male	1, 900	1, 042	1, 006	96. 5	276	255	92. 4	243	155	63. 8	351	79	22. 5	44	86	151	124
Female	2, 007	1, 080	1, 043	96. 6	284	263	92. 6	263	182	69. 2	434	92	21. 2	36	112	161	118
BUFFALO, N. Y.																	
Both sexes	2, 252	1, 374	1, 341	97. 6	336	319	94. 9	299	182	60. 9	575	58	10. 1	18	104	169	61
Male	1, 092	695	681	98. 0	168	161	95. 8	112	75	67. 0	241	32	13. 3	4	39	66	34
Female	1, 160	679	660	97. 2	168	158	94. 0	187	107	57. 2	334	26	7. 8	14	65	103	27
CHICAGO, ILL.																	
Both sexes	36, 962	21, 511	20, 831	96. 8	5, 221	4, 863	93. 1	5, 632	3, 203	56. 9	11, 021	1, 673	15. 2	226	1, 372	2, 770	2, 024
Male	17, 870	10, 439	10, 101	96. 8	2, 469	2, 314	93. 7	2, 629	1, 493	56. 8	4, 604	792	17. 2	110	641	1, 315	1, 104
Female	19, 092	11, 072	10, 730	96. 9	2, 752	2, 549	92. 6	3, 003	1, 710	56. 9	6, 417	881	13. 7	116	731	1, 455	920
CLEVELAND, OHIO																	
Both sexes	13, 051	7, 766	7, 557	97. 3	1, 812	1, 729	95. 4	1, 878	1, 132	60. 3	3, 356	383	11. 4	26	583	1, 152	489
Male	6, 365	3, 802	3, 705	97. 4	848	817	96. 3	912	558	61. 2	1, 482	188	12. 7	14	273	559	251
Female	6, 686	3, 964	3, 852	97. 2	964	912	94. 6	966	574	59. 4	1, 847	195	10. 4	12	310	593	238
DETROIT, MICH.																	
Both sexes	20, 589	12, 133	11, 813	97. 4	2, 792	2, 655	95. 1	2, 825	1, 664	58. 9	5, 433	593	10. 9	66	1, 179	1, 782	837
Male	10, 255	5, 972	5, 814	97. 4	1, 380	1, 326	96. 1	1, 306	806	61. 7	2, 343	329	14. 0	37	553	903	487
Female	10, 334	6, 161	5, 999	97. 4	1, 412	1, 329	94. 1	1, 519	858	56. 5	3, 090	264	8. 5	29	626	879	350
LOS ANGELES, CALIF.																	
Both sexes	7, 597	3, 661	3, 559	97. 2	986	957	97. 1	1, 025	886	86. 4	1, 760	529	30. 1	81	361	481	743
Male	3, 632	1, 798	1, 742	96. 9	473	461	97. 5	455	409	89. 9	777	255	32. 8	42	178	253	292
Female	3, 965	1, 863	1, 817	97. 5	513	496	96. 7	570	477	83. 7	983	274	27. 9	39	183	228	451
MILWAUKEE, WIS.																	
Both sexes	1, 458	866	850	98. 2	157	150	95. 5	173	136	78. 6	355	56	15. 8	26	87	107	46
Male	734	426	420	98. 6	72	69	------	77	68	------	163	33	20. 2	11	49	56	28
Female	724	440	430	97. 7	85	81	------	96	68	------	192	23	12. 0	15	38	51	18
NEW YORK, N. Y.																	
Both sexes	48, 409	29, 156	28, 111	96. 4	6, 843	6, 416	93. 8	7, 319	4, 156	56. 8	17, 046	1, 951	11. 4	185	1, 263	3, 815	2, 512
Male	23, 265	14, 112	13, 610	96. 4	3, 291	3, 124	94. 9	3, 308	1, 940	58. 6	6, 865	844	12. 3	96	609	1, 843	1, 199
Female	25, 144	15, 044	14, 501	96. 4	3, 552	3, 292	92. 7	4, 011	2, 216	55. 2	10, 181	1, 107	10. 9	89	654	1, 972	1, 313
Bronx Borough																	
Both sexes	2, 615	1, 612	1, 576	97. 8	340	319	93. 8	343	184	53. 6	717	104	14. 5	11	63	206	152
Male	1, 252	821	801	97. 6	167	161	96. 4	143	83	58. 0	253	33	13. 0	4	36	101	33
Female	1, 363	791	775	98. 0	173	158	91. 3	200	101	50. 5	464	71	15. 3	7	27	105	119
Brooklyn Borough																	
Both sexes	11, 226	6, 928	6, 725	97. 1	1, 593	1, 445	90. 7	1, 684	855	50. 8	3, 843	390	10. 1	62	336	959	454
Male	5, 437	3, 409	3, 312	97. 2	732	678	92. 6	755	402	53. 2	1, 490	145	9. 7	31	163	475	231
Female	5, 789	3, 519	3, 413	97. 0	861	767	89. 1	929	453	48. 8	2, 353	245	10. 4	31	173	484	223
Manhattan Borough																	
Both sexes	30, 592	18, 050	17, 303	95. 9	4, 346	4, 126	94. 9	4, 749	2, 821	59. 4	11, 389	1, 330	11. 7	104	768	2, 323	1, 817
Male	14, 717	8, 679	8, 321	95. 9	2, 124	2, 034	95. 8	2, 180	1, 328	60. 9	4, 715	614	13. 0	55	362	1, 106	897
Female	15, 875	9, 371	8, 982	95. 8	2, 222	2, 092	94. 1	2, 569	1, 493	58. 1	6, 674	716	10. 7	49	406	1, 217	920
Queens Borough																	
Both sexes	3, 476	2, 221	2, 172	97. 8	501	471	94. 0	480	256	53. 3	975	119	12. 2	7	84	292	75
Male	1, 631	1, 049	1, 025	97. 7	240	226	94. 2	199	110	55. 3	363	52	14. 3	5	42	139	32
Female	1, 845	1, 172	1, 147	97. 9	261	245	93. 9	281	146	52. 0	612	67	10. 9	2	42	153	43
Richmond Borough																	
Both sexes	500	345	335	97. 1	63	55	------	63	40	------	122	8	6. 6	1	12	35	14
Male	228	154	151	98. 1	28	25	------	31	17	------	44	------	------	1	6	22	6
Female	272	191	184	96. 3	35	30	------	32	23	------	78	8	------	------	6	13	8
PHILADELPHIA, PA.																	
Both sexes	36, 559	24, 276	23, 257	95. 8	5, 556	5, 167	93. 0	6, 039	2, 605	43. 1	11, 112	880	7. 9	145	894	2, 742	869
Male	17, 676	11, 889	11, 387	95. 8	2, 652	2, 502	94. 3	2, 728	1, 214	44. 5	4, 540	365	8. 0	74	427	1, 282	425
Female	18, 883	12, 387	11, 870	95. 8	2, 904	2, 665	91. 8	3, 311	1, 391	42. 0	6, 572	515	7. 8	71	467	1, 460	444
PITTSBURGH, PA.																	
Both sexes	10, 201	6, 251	5, 950	95. 2	1, 528	1, 389	90. 9	1, 589	776	48. 8	2, 649	326	12. 3	99	333	792	536
Male	4, 978	3, 002	2, 864	95. 4	756	693	91. 7	724	359	49. 6	1, 155	159	13. 8	44	166	372	321
Female	5, 223	3, 249	3, 086	95. 0	772	696	90. 2	865	417	48. 2	1, 494	167	11. 2	55	167	420	215
ST. LOUIS, MO.																	
Both sexes	14, 962	9, 027	8, 689	96. 3	2, 329	2, 003	86. 0	2, 517	1, 211	48. 1	4, 617	642	13. 9	48	660	1, 096	613
Male	7, 146	4, 440	4, 259	95. 9	1, 093	939	85. 9	1, 158	556	48. 0	1, 952	264	13. 5	20	308	552	248
Female	7, 816	4, 587	4, 430	96. 6	1, 236	1, 064	86. 1	1, 359	655	48 2	2, 665	378	14. 2	28	352	544	365
SAN FRANCISCO, CALIF.																	
Both sexes	386	205	195	95. 1	48	47	------	56	42	------	133	26	19. 5	------	18	23	35
Male	191	104	97	93. 3	27	27	------	26	16	------	71	12	------	------	10	9	20
Female	195	101	98	97. 0	21	20	------	30	26	------	62	14	------	------	8	14	15

Table 20.—SCHOOL ATTENDANCE OF NEGRO POPULATION 5 TO 20 YEARS OF AGE BY SINGLE YEARS, FOR CITIES OF 500,000 OR MORE INHABITANTS: 1930 AND 1920

[Percent not shown where base is less than 100]

CITY AND AGE	1930		1920	
	Number	Percent	Number	Percent
Baltimore, Md.:				
5 years	424	16.1	244	15.3
6 years	1,548	58.6	965	60.2
7 years	2,287	89.2	1,374	83.6
8 years	2,499	94.4	1,541	92.9
9 years	2,471	96.4	1,498	95.8
10 years	2,476	98.0	1,522	96.9
11 years	1,921	97.5	1,389	96.4
12 years	2,114	97.6	1,475	97.2
13 years	1,806	96.0	1,416	94.1
14 years	1,655	88.2	1,179	81.9
15 years	1,369	72.4	762	56.4
16 years	1,019	48.5	510	33.1
17 years	578	27.1	304	19.3
18 years	384	15.8	184	9.9
19 years	217	8.6	174	8.1
20 years	140	5.2	94	4.3
Boston, Mass.:				
5 years	198	60.0	100	48.5
6 years	312	86.9	146	82.0
7 years	306	95.6	194	90.7
8 years	312	96.3	172	94.5
9 years	336	95.2	183	93.4
10 years	304	96.5	183	97.3
11 years	253	97.7	183	97.3
12 years	290	96.7	174	97.8
13 years	248	98.8	164	95.3
14 years	283	95.0	149	94.3
15 years	235	89.7	129	86.6
16 years	204	80.6	106	59.6
17 years	133	52.6	59	34.1
18 years	96	37.8	42	20.0
19 years	44	17.1	39	16.8
20 years	31	11.4	22	8.8
Buffalo, N. Y.:				
5 years	104	43.2	15	-----
6 years	169	77.5	38	-----
7 years	196	94.2	45	-----
8 years	236	98.7	55	-----
9 years	211	97.2	40	-----
10 years	190	98.4	47	-----
11 years	177	98.9	38	-----
12 years	165	97.1	40	-----
13 years	166	98.8	37	-----
14 years	159	97.5	40	-----
15 years	160	92.5	26	-----
16 years	108	77.1	16	-----
17 years	74	46.5	11	-----
18 years	32	18.0	17	-----
19 years	20	10.9	1	-----
20 years	6	2.8	3	-----
Chicago, Ill.:				
5 years	1,372	37.8	433	35.2
6 years	2,770	81.5	931	73.2
7 years	3,180	93.8	1,046	86.5
8 years	3,292	95.7	1,117	90.7
9 years	3,161	96.4	1,059	92.1
10 years	3,214	98.2	1,197	93.9
11 years	2,763	98.1	1,115	93.5
12 years	2,662	98.2	1,184	95.6
13 years	2,599	98.4	1,080	92.7
14 years	2,624	97.1	1,132	89.9
15 years	2,239	88.9	829	74.1
16 years	1,876	68.9	594	51.0
17 years	1,327	45.6	352	27.5
18 years	817	24.2	230	14.6
19 years	553	15.3	129	7.0
20 years	303	7.5	76	3.8
Cleveland, Ohio:				
5 years	583	42.6	129	29.9
6 years	1,152	88.0	322	76.3
7 years	1,230	95.6	411	93.8
8 years	1,264	96.6	401	94.8
9 years	1,158	97.0	357	96.0
10 years	1,134	97.9	447	96.3
11 years	939	98.9	362	97.1
12 years	966	98.3	439	97.3
13 years	866	97.7	375	98.4
14 years	922	97.4	363	94.3
15 years	807	93.3	286	85.4
16 years	686	74.5	181	54.0
17 years	446	46.6	103	25.5
18 years	217	21.2	80	14.0
19 years	114	10.2	67	9.4
20 years	52	4.3	42	5.4
Detroit, Mich.:				
5 years	1,179	52.8	148	37.1
6 years	1,782	86.3	386	82.5
7 years	1,845	94.7	422	92.3
8 years	1,963	96.7	426	94.0
9 years	1,864	96.8	395	96.3
10 years	1,824	98.4	407	95.8
11 years	1,494	98.5	386	97.2
12 years	1,436	98.7	371	96.1
13 years	1,387	98.9	351	97.8
14 years	1,466	97.8	317	93.2
15 years	1,189	92.0	264	81.5
16 years	1,042	74.8	167	44.3
17 years	622	43.4	83	18.0
18 years	307	19.4	54	7.8
19 years	188	10.7	29	3.5
20 years	98	4.7	27	2.7
Los Angeles, Calif.:				
5 years	361	62.0	116	55.0
6 years	481	89.1	187	87.0
7 years	554	94.7	212	91.0
8 years	532	95.9	189	92.6
9 years	524	96.0	196	96.1
10 years	531	98.9	183	94.3
11 years	495	98.6	211	95.5
12 years	491	98.6	203	93.5
13 years	432	98.6	217	96.9
14 years	521	98.3	221	95.3
15 years	436	95.6	195	91.5
16 years	467	92.3	151	66.5
17 years	419	80.7	83	45.6
18 years	272	46.7	63	27.8
19 years	170	29.3	36	15.5
20 years	87	14.5	25	10.4
Milwaukee, Wis.:				
5 years	87	66.9	11	-----
6 years	107	81.7	23	-----
7 years	126	93.3	26	-----
8 years	136	97.1	25	-----
9 years	139	98.6	30	-----
10 years	119	99.2	29	-----
11 years	128	100.0	28	-----
12 years	111	100.0	26	-----
13 years	91	-----	24	-----
14 years	94	-----	17	-----
15 years	56	-----	20	-----
16 years	80	-----	6	-----
17 years	56	-----	9	-----
18 years	30	-----	6	-----
19 years	19	14.6	2	-----
20 years	7	5.4	1	-----
New York, N. Y.:				
5 years	1,263	23.7	430	22.8
6 years	3,815	76.1	1,168	66.5
7 years	4,545	93.6	1,559	86.9
8 years	4,482	95.4	1,548	92.0
9 years	4,266	95.7	1,576	91.9
10 years	4,237	97.9	1,612	95.4
11 years	3,560	97.7	1,480	95.4
12 years	3,691	97.8	1,613	95.1
13 years	3,330	98.0	1,375	94.0
14 years	3,396	96.5	1,411	90.4
15 years	3,020	90.8	1,040	75.4
16 years	2,579	74.4	653	41.5
17 years	1,577	40.9	334	19.0
18 years	959	19.4	176	8.0
19 years	611	11.1	130	4.8
20 years	381	5.8	102	3.2
Bronx Borough:				
5 years	63	24.0	22	-----
6 years	206	76.3	76	74.5
7 years	251	97.3	105	91.3
8 years	236	97.1	87	-----
9 years	250	95.8	133	94.3
10 years	233	98.7	94	-----
11 years	197	98.0	99	94.3
12 years	221	99.5	90	-----
13 years	188	98.4	65	-----
14 years	181	98.4	73	-----
15 years	138	88.5	44	-----
16 years	117	73.1	28	-----
17 years	67	36.6	17	-----
18 years	45	19.5	3	-----
19 years	27	11.3	4	-----
20 years	32	12.9	5	-----
Brooklyn Borough:				
5 years	336	25.0	118	26.3
6 years	959	75.8	255	63.8
7 years	1,152	94.2	397	85.0
8 years	1,097	96.7	366	91.0
9 years	1,040	97.7	374	90.8
10 years	1,007	98.2	392	95.1
11 years	858	97.7	346	94.8
12 years	820	97.9	382	94.3
13 years	751	98.3	340	92.4
14 years	766	95.3	319	88.6
15 years	679	86.1	245	74.2
16 years	519	68.0	134	36.5
17 years	336	36.5	78	17.9
18 years	201	17.7	37	7.5
19 years	122	10.1	33	6.1
20 years	67	4.5	31	4.4
Manhattan Borough:				
5 years	768	23.2	246	19.9
6 years	2,323	75.8	765	66.2
7 years	2,747	92.7	958	87.2
8 years	2,746	94.5	994	92.0
9 years	2,602	94.7	970	92.0
10 years	2,631	97.6	1,026	95.4
11 years	2,163	97.4	955	95.9
12 years	2,328	97.7	1,036	95.2
13 years	2,086	97.8	868	94.6
14 years	2,161	96.9	939	91.0
15 years	1,965	92.9	681	75.2
16 years	1,753	76.7	445	43.0
17 years	1,068	43.4	222	19.1
18 years	645	19.9	127	8.3
19 years	432	11.6	89	4.6
20 years	253	5.7	63	2.8
Queens Borough:				
5 years	84	22.6	40	-----
6 years	292	79.3	54	-----
7 years	338	95.5	76	-----
8 years	351	97.2	76	-----
9 years	321	97.9	75	-----
10 years	318	98.8	82	-----
11 years	293	99.7	66	-----
12 years	284	97.3	79	-----
13 years	267	98.9	82	-----
14 years	259	97.4	68	-----
15 years	212	90.2	58	-----
16 years	165	72.1	43	-----
17 years	91	36.3	14	-----
18 years	63	20.7	9	-----
19 years	27	8.6	4	-----
20 years	29	8.2	2	-----
Richmond Borough:				
5 years	12	-----	4	-----
6 years	35	-----	18	-----
7 years	57	-----	23	-----
8 years	52	-----	25	-----
9 years	53	-----	24	-----
10 years	48	-----	18	-----
11 years	49	-----	14	-----
12 years	38	-----	26	-----
13 years	38	-----	20	-----
14 years	29	-----	12	-----
15 years	26	-----	12	-----
16 years	25	-----	3	-----
17 years	15	-----	3	-----
18 years	5	-----	-----	-----
19 years	3	-----	-----	-----
20 years	-----	-----	1	-----
Philadelphia, Pa.:				
5 years	894	23.1	467	25.1
6 years	2,742	71.2	1,314	67.2
7 years	3,469	89.8	1,634	85.4
8 years	3,740	94.9	1,720	91.3
9 years	3,620	95.9	1,649	92.2
10 years	3,595	98.2	1,698	95.2
11 years	2,991	97.6	1,590	95.3
12 years	3,054	98.1	1,775	96.2
13 years	2,788	97.4	1,550	94.6
14 years	2,708	95.8	1,536	92.6
15 years	2,459	90.1	1,119	79.0
16 years	1,721	57.1	718	41.9
17 years	884	29.2	339	19.3
18 years	468	13.4	186	9.2
19 years	255	7.0	140	5.5
20 years	157	4.0	74	2.8
Pittsburgh, Pa:				
5 years	333	32.1	160	29.9
6 years	792	78.3	446	76.8
7 years	900	88.8	499	91.6
8 years	969	95.2	565	93.9
9 years	908	95.4	527	94.6
10 years	933	96.5	567	96.8
11 years	740	97.4	527	98.1
12 years	783	97.6	583	97.0
13 years	717	97.2	545	95.3
14 years	763	95.3	498	91.7
15 years	626	86.1	375	78.3
16 years	504	63.5	265	50.5
17 years	272	34.2	134	27.5
18 years	170	20.7	83	14.6
19 years	106	11.7	50	7.9
20 years	50	5.4	21	3.0
St. Louis, Mo.:				
5 years	660	45.4	332	39.1
6 years	1,096	81.7	654	75.9
7 years	1,326	93.1	810	89.0
8 years	1,329	94.9	861	91.2
9 years	1,319	96.3	840	92.2
10 years	1,334	97.3	979	96.2
11 years	1,080	97.9	889	96.7
12 years	1,193	97.9	931	96.6
13 years	1,108	97.0	883	94.1
14 years	1,043	92.6	807	86.9
15 years	960	79.8	604	69.7
16 years	732	59.1	421	44.9
17 years	479	37.5	202	22.2
18 years	328	22.5	147	13.9
19 years	212	14.1	101	8.5
20 years	102	6.2	42	3.7
San Francisco, Calif.:				
5 years	18	-----	3	-----
6 years	23	-----	17	-----
7 years	26	-----	19	-----
8 years	38	-----	18	-----
9 years	33	-----	21	-----
10 years	26	-----	23	-----
11 years	26	-----	14	-----
12 years	27	-----	23	-----
13 years	19	-----	17	-----
14 years	27	-----	18	-----
15 years	20	-----	18	-----
16 years	18	-----	13	-----
17 years	24	-----	7	-----
18 years	17	-----	2	-----
19 years	7	-----	2	-----
20 years	2	-----	2	-----

TABLE 21.—NEGRO POPULATION, ATTENDING AND NOT ATTENDING SCHOOL, BY AGE PERIODS, FOR CITIES OF 25,000 OR MORE INHABITANTS WHICH HAD A NEGRO POPULATION OF 1,000 OR MORE: 1930

STATE AND CITY	Total population	NEGRO — Total — Number	NEGRO — Total — Percent of total population	7 to 20 years old — Attending school — Number	7 to 20 years old — Attending school — Percent	7 to 20 years old — Not attending school	7 to 13 years old — Attending school — Number	7 to 13 years old — Attending school — Percent	7 to 13 years old — Not attending school	14 to 17 years old — Attending school — Number	14 to 17 years old — Attending school — Percent	14 to 17 years old — Not attending school	18 to 20 years old — Attending school — Number	18 to 20 years old — Attending school — Percent	18 to 20 years old — Not attending school
ALABAMA:															
Birmingham	259,678	99,077	38.2	16,948	66.2	8,637	11,616	94.9	628	4,599	64.6	2,520	733	11.8	5,489
Mobile	68,202	24,514	35.9	3,640	60.5	2,377	2,538	91.2	246	993	59.7	669	109	6.9	1,462
Montgomery	66,079	29,970	45.4	5,435	64.6	2,977	3,396	90.5	357	1,625	66.2	830	414	18.8	1,790
ARIZONA:															
Phoenix	48,118	2,366	4.9	342	70.7	142	230	93.9	15	99	76.2	31	13	11.9	96
Tucson	32,506	1,003	3.1	135	77.6	39	95	97.9	2	29	72.5	11	11	29.7	26
ARKANSAS:															
Fort Smith	31,429	3,467	11.0	638	70.7	265	385	97.7	9	214	72.1	83	39	18.4	173
Little Rock	81,679	19,698	24.1	3,150	69.6	1,378	2,009	97.1	60	889	71.9	348	252	20.6	970
CALIFORNIA:															
Berkeley	82,109	2,177	2.7	354	79.7	90	208	95.4	10	111	91.7	10	35	33.3	70
Los Angeles	1,238,048	38,894	3.1	5,931	79.8	1,501	3,559	97.2	102	1,843	91.6	168	529	30.1	1,231
Oakland	284,063	7,503	2.6	1,165	80.7	278	688	98.3	12	371	91.8	33	106	31.3	233
Pasadena	76,086	3,015	4.0	545	83.1	111	313	98.1	6	182	91.0	18	50	36.5	87
Sacramento	93,750	1,086	1.2	184	86.0	30	112	97.4	3	56	93.3	4	16	41.0	23
San Diego	147,995	2,723	1.8	413	81.9	91	276	97.9	6	118	92.9	9	19	20.0	76
San Francisco	634,394	3,803	.6	310	70.1	132	195	95.1	10	89	85.6	15	26	19.5	107
COLORADO:															
Denver	287,861	7,204	2.5	906	72.5	344	570	95.0	30	268	78.1	75	68	22.1	239
Pueblo	50,096	1,305	2.6	208	78.2	58	140	97.2	4	46	70.8	19	22	38.6	35
CONNECTICUT:															
Bridgeport	146,716	3,314	2.3	490	68.8	222	366	97.1	11	113	61.7	70	11	7.2	141
Hartford	164,072	6,510	4.0	1,219	73.8	433	901	99.3	6	286	69.9	123	32	9.5	304
New Haven	162,655	5,302	3.3	879	74.2	305	634	98.3	11	207	66.3	105	38	16.7	189
Stamford	46,346	2,138	4.6	324	67.2	158	237	96.0	10	74	56.9	56	13	12.4	92
Waterbury	99,902	1,660	1.7	260	70.5	109	195	97.5	5	56	62.9	33	9	11.3	71
DELAWARE:															
Wilmington	106,597	12,080	11.3	1,710	68.1	801	1,176	96.6	41	463	72.3	177	71	10.9	583
DISTRICT OF COLUMBIA:															
Washington	486,869	132,068	27.1	20,929	71.4	8,383	13,638	96.6	474	5,701	73.9	2,010	1,590	21.2	5,899
FLORIDA:															
Jacksonville	129,549	48,196	37.2	7,845	65.4	4,159	5,379	92.9	409	2,086	64.5	1,146	380	12.7	2,604
Miami	110,637	25,116	22.7	4,076	67.5	1,963	3,123	97.4	84	845	58.0	611	108	7.8	1,268
Orlando	27,330	7,590	27.8	1,239	61.8	767	905	93.5	63	304	56.0	239	30	6.1	465
Pensacola	31,579	9,583	30.3	1,604	67.1	786	1,102	93.9	72	409	67.7	195	93	15.2	519
St. Petersburg	40,425	7,416	18.3	1,390	67.8	661	1,019	97.9	22	332	61.6	207	39	8.3	432
Tampa	101,161	21,172	20.9	3,174	63.6	1,818	2,273	94.7	128	781	57.7	573	120	9.7	1,117
West Palm Beach	26,610	8,999	33.8	1,336	68.6	612	953	97.6	23	341	67.4	165	42	9.0	424
GEORGIA:															
Atlanta	270,366	90,075	33.3	15,937	62.0	9,752	10,896	90.9	1,091	4,057	57.3	3,022	984	14.9	5,639
Augusta	60,342	24,190	40.1	3,916	59.2	2,697	2,742	88.3	362	970	54.0	825	204	11.9	1,510
Columbus	43,131	14,157	32.8	2,309	54.7	1,909	1,669	85.9	275	516	44.6	641	124	11.1	993
Macon	53,829	23,158	43.0	3,498	53.2	3,074	2,539	84.5	467	846	46.0	994	113	6.5	1,613
Savannah	85,024	38,896	45.7	5,258	56.0	4,137	3,753	87.0	562	1,271	52.2	1,166	234	8.9	2,409
ILLINOIS:															
Alton	30,151	2,714	9.0	444	71.2	180	342	97.7	8	94	67.6	45	8	5.9	127
Chicago	3,376,438	233,903	6.9	30,570	70.5	12,815	20,831	96.8	680	8,066	74.3	2,787	1,673	15.2	9,348
Danville	36,765	2,565	7.0	467	69.7	203	327	94.5	19	121	61.1	77	19	15.1	107
Decatur	57,510	1,947	3.4	341	69.6	149	242	97.2	7	90	67.2	44	9	8.4	98
East St. Louis	74,347	11,536	15.5	2,034	71.4	815	1,423	97.6	35	527	73.0	195	84	12.6	585
Evanston	63,338	4,938	7.8	758	70.0	325	492	94.3	30	213	74.0	75	53	19.4	220
Joliet	42,993	1,309	3.0	164	62.6	98	121	93.8	8	34	66.7	17	9	11.0	73
Peoria	104,969	3,037	2.9	505	69.5	222	340	97.1	10	143	74.5	49	22	11.9	163
Quincy	39,241	1,145	2.9	170	75.2	56	123	99.2	1	44	77.2	13	3	6.7	42
Rockford	85,864	1,110	1.3	203	81.5	46	146	98.0	3	49	77.8	14	8	21.6	29
Springfield	71,864	3,324	4.6	542	73.2	198	372	98.9	4	150	69.1	67	20	13.6	127
Waukegan	33,499	1,017	3.0	167	79.5	43	117	100.0	-------	39	86.7	6	11	22.9	37
INDIANA:															
Anderson	39,804	1,387	3.5	236	70.2	100	172	97.7	4	55	64.7	30	9	12.0	66
East Chicago	54,784	5,088	9.3	754	71.8	296	510	95.3	25	216	79.1	57	28	11.6	214
Evansville	102,249	6,514	6.4	951	69.8	411	609	98.4	10	288	72.7	108	54	15.6	293
Fort Wayne	114,946	2,360	2.1	378	74.4	130	278	95.5	13	86	71.1	35	14	14.6	82
Gary	100,426	17,922	17.8	2,876	74.4	991	1,965	95.7	88	794	81.5	180	117	13.9	723
Indianapolis	364,161	43,967	12.1	7,166	71.9	2,803	4,910	97.4	130	1,922	71.8	755	334	14.8	1,918
Kokomo	32,843	1,143	3.5	203	76.6	62	144	96.6	5	51	71.8	20	8	17.8	37
Michigan City	26,735	1,071	4.0	66	60.6	43	49	96.1	2	14	48.3	15	3	10.3	26
Muncie	46,548	2,646	5.7	457	73.9	161	301	99.0	3	135	82.3	29	21	14.0	129
New Albany	25,819	1,292	5.0	212	68.8	96	161	98.8	2	43	58.1	31	8	11.3	63
Richmond	32,493	2,139	6.6	406	72.1	157	276	97.5	7	112	65.9	58	18	16.4	92
South Bend	104,193	3,431	3.3	536	72.4	204	388	99.0	4	126	71.6	50	22	12.8	150
Terre Haute	62,810	3,461	5.5	640	75.4	209	424	99.5	2	166	76.9	50	50	24.2	157
IOWA:															
Des Moines	142,559	5,428	3.8	1,004	77.5	292	677	97.8	15	270	77.4	79	57	22.4	198
Sioux City	79,183	1,064	1.3	134	66.7	67	93	97.9	2	36	67.9	17	5	9.4	48
Waterloo	46,191	1,214	2.6	257	78.8	69	178	99.4	1	68	79.1	18	11	18.0	50
KANSAS:															
Kansas City	121,857	19,872	16.3	3,662	79.2	963	2,393	97.0	73	1,008	78.9	270	261	29.6	620
Topeka	64,120	5,756	9.0	1,011	75.7	325	662	97.8	15	296	77.7	85	53	19.1	225
Wichita	111,110	5,623	5.1	1,048	76.9	315	686	98.4	11	290	82.4	62	72	22.9	242
KENTUCKY:															
Covington	65,252	3,466	5.3	447	69.7	194	295	96.1	12	125	72 3	48	27	16.8	134
Lexington	45,736	12,759	27.9	1,758	65.8	915	1,188	93.5	83	479	61.6	299	91	14.6	533
Louisville	307,745	47,354	15.4	6,645	68.7	3,027	4,499	96.9	145	1,825	66.6	917	321	14.0	1,965
Newport	29,744	1,231	4.1	185	67.8	88	131	97.8	3	50	68.5	23	4	6.1	62
Paducah	33,541	6,744	20.1	1,124	70.7	466	724	96.4	27	309	69.6	135	91	23.0	304
LOUISIANA:															
Baton Rouge	30,729	10,675	34.7	1,777	64.3	986	1,152	92.6	92	490	63.6	280	135	18.0	614
Monroe	26,028	10,112	38.9	1,467	61.5	919	973	94.3	59	424	62.9	250	70	10.3	610
New Orleans	458,762	129,632	28.3	20,881	65.7	10,923	14,618	94.0	941	5,303	60.9	3,406	960	12.7	6,576
Shreveport	76,655	27,219	35.5	4,487	68.0	2,108	2,964	96.3	114	1,276	68.5	588	247	14.9	1,406

Table 21.—Negro Population, Attending and Not Attending School, by Age Periods, for Cities of 25,000 or More Inhabitants Which Had a Negro Population of 1,000 or More: 1930—Continued

State and city	Total population	Negro: Total		Negro: 7 to 20 years old			Negro: 7 to 13 years old			Negro: 14 to 17 years old			Negro: 18 to 20 years old		
		Number	Percent of total population	Attending school: Number	Attending school: Percent	Not attending school	Attending school: Number	Attending school: Percent	Not attending school	Attending school: Number	Attending school: Percent	Not attending school	Attending school: Number	Attending school: Percent	Not attending school
Maryland:															
Baltimore	804, 874	142, 106	17. 7	20, 936	65. 5	11, 008	15, 574	95. 4	748	4, 621	57. 8	3, 377	741	9. 7	6, 883
Cumberland	37, 747	1, 161	3. 1	239	74. 5	82	184	93. 9	12	51	67. 1	25	4	8. 2	45
Hagerstown	30, 861	1, 517	4. 9	237	63. 7	135	165	97. 1	5	60	54. 1	51	12	13. 2	79
Massachusetts:															
Boston	781, 188	20, 574	2. 6	3, 075	77. 4	898	2, 049	96. 6	73	855	80. 2	211	171	21. 8	614
Cambridge	113, 643	5, 419	4. 8	1, 192	83. 1	243	805	98. 2	15	311	85. 9	51	76	30. 0	177
Everett	48, 424	1, 002	2. 1	219	82. 3	47	136	98. 6	2	61	85. 9	10	22	38. 6	35
New Bedford	112, 597	3, 631	3. 2	850	77. 3	250	667	94. 1	42	159	67. 1	78	24	15. 6	130
Springfield	149, 900	3, 141	2. 1	541	78. 2	151	344	98. 9	4	154	81. 9	34	43	27. 6	113
Worcester	195, 311	1, 378	. 7	278	79. 4	72	189	99. 0	2	75	75. 8	24	14	23. 3	46
Michigan:															
Battle Creek	43, 573	1, 795	4. 1	340	80. 4	83	203	98. 1	4	113	89. 0	14	24	27. 0	65
Detroit	1, 568, 662	120, 066	7. 7	16, 725	72. 1	6, 458	11, 813	97. 4	320	4, 319	76. 9	1, 298	593	10. 9	4, 840
Flint	156, 492	5, 725	3. 7	860	76. 5	264	603	99. 2	5	225	84. 0	43	32	12. 9	216
Grand Rapids	168, 592	2, 795	1. 7	447	75. 6	144	299	99. 0	3	119	80. 4	29	29	20. 6	112
Hamtramck	56, 268	4, 068	7. 2	738	75. 5	240	512	95. 7	23	201	75. 6	65	25	14. 1	152
Highland Park	52, 959	1, 171	2. 2	197	75. 5	64	134	99. 3	1	54	80. 6	13	9	15. 3	50
Jackson	55, 187	1, 692	3. 1	239	74. 2	83	178	100. 0	-	59	80. 8	14	2	2. 8	69
Lansing	78, 397	1, 409	1. 8	334	80. 5	81	187	95. 9	8	135	88. 8	17	12	17. 6	56
Pontiac	64, 928	2, 553	3. 9	338	73. 2	124	231	97. 9	5	95	81. 2	22	12	11. 0	97
Saginaw	80, 715	2, 853	3. 5	273	61. 6	170	203	84. 6	37	60	62. 5	36	10	9. 3	97
Minnesota:															
Minneapolis	464, 356	4, 176	. 9	588	80. 5	142	391	99. 2	3	156	83. 4	31	41	27. 5	108
St. Paul	271, 606	4, 001	1. 5	573	74. 9	192	374	97. 7	9	155	76. 4	48	44	24. 6	135
Mississippi:															
Jackson	48, 282	19, 423	40. 2	3, 078	63. 4	1, 779	2, 090	96. 0	87	769	62. 6	460	219	15. 1	1, 232
Meridian	31, 954	11, 352	35. 5	1, 908	60. 2	1, 264	1, 308	91. 4	123	476	53. 2	418	124	14. 6	723
Missouri:															
Kansas City	399, 746	38, 574	9. 6	4, 601	68. 0	2, 161	3, 063	94. 9	164	1, 283	69. 9	553	255	15. 0	1, 444
St. Joseph	80, 935	4, 055	5. 0	580	71. 6	230	377	96. 2	15	161	72. 5	61	42	21. 4	154
St. Louis	821, 960	93, 580	11. 4	12, 545	67. 8	5, 945	8, 689	96. 3	338	3, 214	66. 3	1, 632	642	13. 9	3, 975
Springfield	57, 527	1, 779	3. 1	307	74. 9	103	195	97. 0	6	88	75. 2	29	24	26. 1	68
Nebraska:															
Omaha	214, 006	11, 123	5. 2	1, 620	75. 2	533	1, 098	98. 4	18	447	80. 1	111	75	15. 7	404
New Jersey:															
Atlantic City	66, 198	15, 611	23. 6	1, 923	72. 6	725	1, 285	98. 5	20	518	76. 4	160	120	18. 0	545
Bayonne	88, 979	2, 205	2. 5	411	72. 2	158	293	100. 0	-	108	70. 6	45	10	8. 1	113
Belleville	26, 974	1, 023	3. 8	205	71. 9	80	145	96. 7	5	52	67. 5	25	8	13. 8	50
Camden	118, 700	11, 340	9. 6	1, 846	66. 7	921	1, 321	91. 0	131	462	63. 5	265	63	10. 7	525
East Orange	68, 020	4, 880	7. 2	770	70. 9	316	502	96. 5	18	226	77. 4	66	42	15. 3	232
Elizabeth	114, 589	4, 761	4. 2	707	69. 2	314	521	96. 5	19	156	65. 8	81	30	12. 3	214
Jersey City	316, 715	12, 575	4. 0	1, 915	68. 1	896	1, 397	96. 5	50	448	65. 3	238	70	10. 3	608
Montclair	42, 017	6, 384	15. 2	904	71. 0	369	550	97. 5	14	278	79. 7	71	76	21. 1	284
Newark	442, 337	38, 880	8. 8	5, 794	65. 9	2, 999	4, 362	96. 4	163	1, 313	61. 3	830	119	5. 6	2, 006
New Brunswick	34, 555	2, 086	6. 0	339	67. 0	167	257	94. 5	15	75	60. 5	49	7	6. 4	103
Orange	35, 399	5, 027	14. 2	856	71. 3	344	597	96. 3	23	224	69. 3	99	35	13. 6	222
Passaic	62, 959	1, 858	3. 0	286	65. 9	148	210	98. 1	4	70	69. 3	31	6	5. 0	113
Paterson	138, 513	2, 952	2. 1	411	64. 8	223	319	98. 8	4	82	56. 6	63	10	6. 0	156
Plainfield	34, 422	3, 648	10. 6	623	73. 2	228	457	97. 9	10	143	71. 1	58	23	12. 6	160
Trenton	123, 356	8, 057	6. 5	1, 424	72. 1	551	985	97. 4	26	386	69. 5	169	53	13. 0	356
New York:															
Albany	127, 412	2, 324	1. 8	270	65. 2	144	186	93. 9	12	65	65. 7	34	19	16. 2	98
Buffalo	573, 076	13, 563	2. 4	1, 900	73. 5	684	1, 341	97. 6	33	501	78. 9	134	58	10. 1	517
Mount Vernon	61, 499	3, 608	5. 9	531	63. 7	302	387	98. 7	5	126	69. 2	56	18	6. 9	241
New Rochelle	54, 000	4, 644	8. 6	650	68. 6	297	443	96. 9	14	168	79. 2	44	39	14. 0	239
New York	6, 930, 446	327, 706	4. 7	40, 634	67. 3	19, 730	28, 111	96. 4	1, 045	10, 572	74. 7	3, 590	1, 951	11. 4	15, 095
Bronx Borough	1, 265, 258	12, 930	1. 0	2, 183	72. 5	829	1, 576	97. 8	36	503	73. 6	180	104	14. 5	613
Brooklyn Borough	2, 560, 401	68, 921	2. 7	9, 415	67. 0	4, 633	6, 725	97. 1	203	2, 300	70. 2	977	390	10. 1	3, 453
Manhattan Borough	1, 867, 312	224, 670	12. 0	25, 580	66. 4	12, 954	17, 303	95. 9	747	6, 947	76. 4	2, 148	1, 330	11. 7	10, 059
Queens Borough	1, 079, 129	18, 609	1. 7	3, 018	72. 3	1, 159	2, 172	97. 8	49	727	74. 1	254	119	12. 2	856
Richmond Borough	158, 346	2, 576	1. 6	438	73. 9	155	335	97. 1	10	95	75. 4	31	8	6. 6	114
Poughkeepsie	40, 288	1, 101	2. 7	195	72. 0	76	130	97. 7	3	56	73. 7	20	9	14. 5	53
Rochester	328, 132	2, 679	. 8	392	76. 3	122	281	99. 3	2	90	81. 1	21	21	17. 5	99
Syracuse	209, 326	1, 899	. 9	293	75. 7	94	202	99. 5	1	73	77. 7	21	18	20. 0	72
White Plains	35, 830	2, 150	6. 0	249	58. 6	176	173	95. 6	8	68	66. 7	34	8	5. 6	134
Yonkers	134, 646	3, 332	2. 5	509	71. 3	205	335	99. 1	3	145	78. 0	41	29	15. 3	161
North Carolina:															
Asheville	50, 193	14, 255	28. 4	2, 636	67. 1	1, 295	1, 843	96. 6	65	661	63. 1	387	132	13. 5	843
Charlotte	82, 675	25, 163	30. 4	4, 120	58. 7	2, 897	3, 088	93. 6	211	899	47. 8	983	133	7. 2	1, 703
Durham	52, 037	18, 717	36. 0	3, 364	62. 6	2, 014	2, 415	96. 3	94	771	55. 2	625	178	12. 1	1, 295
Greensboro	53, 569	14, 050	26. 2	2, 667	65. 6	1, 401	1, 757	95. 0	93	694	60. 9	445	216	20. 0	863
High Point	36, 745	7, 229	19. 7	1, 234	59. 0	859	897	93. 7	60	281	54. 8	232	56	9. 0	567
Raleigh	37, 379	12, 575	33. 6	2, 603	69. 6	1, 136	1, 693	95. 9	73	686	64. 7	374	224	24. 5	689
Wilmington	32, 270	13, 106	40. 6	2, 617	68. 4	1, 209	1, 785	93. 3	129	693	64. 4	383	139	16. 6	697
Winston-Salem	75, 274	32, 566	43. 3	5, 337	57. 7	3, 915	4, 040	95. 8	177	1, 131	47. 5	1, 248	166	6. 3	2, 490
Ohio:															
Akron	255, 040	11, 080	4. 3	1, 964	74. 9	658	1, 353	97. 3	38	536	82. 1	117	75	13. 0	503
Canton	104, 906	3, 004	2. 9	419	66. 8	208	287	94. 4	17	117	74. 1	41	15	9. 1	150
Cincinnati	451, 160	47, 818	10. 6	7, 220	70. 4	3, 036	4, 991	96. 7	169	1, 943	72. 8	725	286	11. 8	2, 142
Cleveland	900, 429	71, 899	8. 0	10, 801	72. 9	4, 011	7, 557	97. 3	209	2, 861	77. 5	829	383	11. 4	2, 973
Columbus	290, 564	32, 774	11. 3	5, 332	75. 2	1, 754	3, 532	96. 5	129	1, 514	79. 9	382	286	18. 7	1, 243
Dayton	200, 982	17, 077	8. 5	2, 971	75. 1	983	2, 047	97. 2	58	793	77. 4	231	131	15. 9	694
Elyria	25, 633	1, 052	4. 1	158	68. 7	72	105	100. 0	-	45	75. 0	15	8	12. 3	57
Hamilton	52, 176	1, 958	3. 8	304	63. 6	174	204	95. 3	10	86	59. 7	58	14	11. 7	106
Lima	42, 287	1, 422	3. 4	289	82. 3	62	181	97. 3	5	87	89. 7	10	21	30. 9	47
Massillon	26, 400	1, 219	4. 6	241	74. 6	82	161	95. 3	8	78	80. 4	19	2	3. 5	55
Middleton	29, 992	2, 805	9. 4	635	79. 0	169	424	97. 5	11	181	81. 9	40	30	20. 3	118
Portsmouth	42, 560	1, 891	4. 4	306	74. 3	106	218	97. 3	6	78	76. 5	24	10	11. 6	76
Springfield	68, 743	8, 249	12. 0	1, 634	77. 0	488	1, 105	98. 7	15	459	82. 7	96	70	15. 7	377
Steubenville	35, 422	2, 776	7. 8	434	71. 9	170	294	97. 7	7	119	71. 3	48	21	15. 4	115
Toledo	290, 718	13, 260	4. 6	1, 837	72. 3	704	1, 271	95. 8	56	477	79. 2	125	89	14. 5	523
Warren	41, 062	2, 548	6. 2	440	75. 7	141	325	97. 6	8	96	72. 7	36	19	16. 4	97

TABLE 21.—NEGRO POPULATION, ATTENDING AND NOT ATTENDING SCHOOL, BY AGE PERIODS, FOR CITIES OF 25,000 OR MORE INHABITANTS WHICH HAD A NEGRO POPULATION OF 1,000 OR MORE: 1930—Continued

STATE AND CITY	Total population	NEGRO														
		Total		7 to 20 years old			7 to 13 years old			14 to 17 years old			18 to 20 years old			
		Number	Percent of total population	Attending school		Not attending school	Attending school		Not attending school	Attending school		Not attending school	Attending school		Not attending school	
				Number	Percent		Number	Percent		Number	Percent		Number	Percent		
OHIO—Continued.																
Youngstown	170,002	14,552	8.6	2,508	76.4	774	1,762	96.5	64	680	82.8	141	66	10.4	569	
Zanesville	36,440	1,776	4.9	328	72.1	127	207	97.6	5	97	75.2	32	24	21.1	90	
OKLAHOMA:																
Muskogee	32,026	6,576	20.5	1,370	77.2	405	803	98.2	15	445	82.1	97	122	29.4	293	
Oklahoma City	185,389	14,662	7.9	2,186	65.2	1,165	1,437	95.8	63	586	66.6	294	163	16.8	808	
Tulsa	141,258	15,203	10.8	2,161	69.0	972	1,396	97.4	37	607	76.6	185	158	17.4	750	
OREGON:																
Portland	301,815	1,559	.5	211	79.6	54	123	97.6	3	65	83.3	13	23	37.7	38	
PENNSYLVANIA:																
Aliquippa	27,116	2,592	9.6	439	68.8	199	338	98.0	7	93	67.4	45	8	5.2	147	
Chester	59,164	9,245	15.6	1,492	69.4	657	1,099	97.2	32	345	64.1	193	48	10.0	432	
Erie	115,967	1,214	1.0	175	70.3	74	121	93.1	9	51	71.8	20	3	6.3	45	
Harrisburg	80,339	6,382	7.9	1,110	73.9	393	733	97.6	18	306	74.6	104	71	20.8	271	
Johnstown	66,993	1,444	2.2	268	72.8	100	213	98.6	3	53	55.8	42	2	3.5	55	
Lancaster	59,949	1,281	2.1	209	68.3	97	158	97.5	4	41	56.2	32	10	14.1	61	
Lower Merion Township	35,166	2,919	8.3	279	56.3	217	169	90.4	18	87	72.5	33	23	12.2	166	
McKeesport	54,632	1,893	3.5	286	65.4	151	201	94.8	11	76	66.1	39	9	8.2	101	
New Castle	48,674	1.572	3.2	295	75.1	98	209	97.2	6	77	72.6	29	9	12.5	63	
Norristown	35,853	2,118	5.9	365	66.8	181	253	96.9	8	100	70.4	42	12	8.4	131	
Philadelphia	1,950,961	219,599	11.3	31,909	67.9	15,074	23,257	95.8	1,019	7,772	67.0	3,823	880	7.9	10,232	
Pittsburgh	669,817	54,983	8.2	8,441	70.2	3,576	5,950	95.2	301	2,165	69.5	952	326	12.3	2,323	
Reading	111,171	1,964	1.8	264	63.2	154	184	93.9	12	70	68.0	33	10	8.4	109	
York	55,254	2,266	4.1	404	71.0	165	293	96.4	11	104	68.9	47	7	6.1	107	
RHODE ISLAND:																
Newport	27,612	1,554	5.6	295	80.2	73	215	99.5	1	63	79.7	16	17	23.3	56	
Providence	252,981	5,473	2.2	1,014	74.6	346	731	97.2	21	256	68.8	116	27	11.4	209	
SOUTH CAROLINA:																
Charleston	62,265	28,062	45.1	4,943	61.5	3,099	3,598	90.1	397	1,154	55.5	927	191	9.7	1,775	
Columbia	51,581	19,519	37.8	3,428	59.3	2,356	2,329	90.4	247	857	54.1	728	242	14.9	1,381	
Greenville	28,154	10,871	37.3	1,867	55.9	1,470	1,404	91.1	137	401	44.4	503	62	7.0	830	
Spartanburg	28,723	9,826	34.2	1,931	60.1	1,280	1,401	93.2	102	448	50.1	446	82	10.1	732	
TENNESSEE:																
Chattanooga	119,798	33,289	27.8	5,616	65.1	3,011	3,940	94.8	216	1,407	61.7	872	269	12.3	1,923	
Johnson City	25,080	2,335	9.3	383	61.9	236	274	85.9	45	92	58.6	65	17	11.9	126	
Knoxville	105,802	17,093	16.2	2,871	65.5	1,513	1,966	96.2	78	767	63.5	441	138	12.2	994	
Memphis	253,143	96,550	38.1	13,388	63.5	7,692	9,180	94.4	541	3,560	64.7	1,940	648	11.1	5,211	
Nashville	153,866	42,836	27.8	6,908	64.7	3,772	4,538	91.2	437	1,944	65.5	1,026	426	15.6	2,309	
TEXAS:																
Amarillo	43,132	1,600	3.7	113	39.4	174	74	73.3	27	34	43.6	44	5	4.6	103	
Austin	53,120	9,868	18.6	1,796	72.3	688	1,119	96.7	38	503	74.5	172	174	26.7	478	
Beaumont	57,732	18,551	32.1	3,363	67.6	1,614	2,242	93.9	146	930	68.3	432	191	15.6	1,036	
Corpus Christi	27,741	1,951	7.0	251	55.7	200	202	86.7	31	44	44.0	56	5	4.2	113	
Dallas	260,475	38,742	14.9	5,439	62.3	3,293	3,695	92.5	300	1,517	64.0	854	227	9.6	2,139	
El Paso	102,421	1,855	1.8	251	71.3	101	166	94.3	10	70	73.7	25	15	18.5	66	
Fort Worth	163,447	22,234	13.6	3,544	68.4	1,638	2,415	95.8	107	979	70.7	406	150	11.8	1,125	
Galveston	52,938	13,226	25.0	1,844	67.8	874	1,193	95.8	52	554	73.4	201	97	13.5	621	
Houston	292,352	63,337	21.7	9,356	65.2	4,983	6,190	94.8	339	2,602	68.9	1,175	564	14.0	3,469	
Port Arthur	50,902	10,003	19.7	1,824	68.7	830	1,323	96.4	50	438	64.9	237	63	10.4	543	
San Angelo	25,308	1,653	6.5	179	57.2	134	122	81.9	27	45	60.0	30	12	13.5	77	
San Antonio	231,542	17,978	7.8	2,849	65.8	1,478	1,858	95.2	93	862	69.0	388	129	11.5	997	
Waco	52,848	9,370	17.7	1,809	71.1	737	1,096	93.4	77	584	75.2	193	129	21.6	467	
Wichita Falls	43,690	4,312	9.9	634	65.5	334	420	94.0	27	190	68.3	88	24	9.9	219	
VIRGINIA:																
Lynchburg	40,661	9,653	23.7	1,873	65.7	976	1,227	93.2	90	522	64.0	293	124	17.3	593	
Newport News	34,417	13,281	38.6	2,424	67.9	1,147	1,731	94.4	102	568	63.5	326	125	14.8	719	
Norfolk	129,710	43,942	33.9	7,412	67.6	3,557	5,121	92.5	415	1,886	65.9	977	405	15.8	2,165	
Petersburg	28,564	12,600	44.1	2,309	64.1	1,294	1,591	87.7	223	572	60.9	368	146	17.2	703	
Portsmouth	45,704	18,849	41.2	3,549	69.8	1,537	2,607	94.1	163	784	61.9	483	158	15.1	891	
Richmond	182,929	52,988	29.0	9,449	67.6	4,527	6,724	93.9	437	2,264	61.1	1,440	461	14.8	2,650	
Roanoke	69,206	12,368	17.9	2,372	68.8	1,075	1,579	95.5	75	648	65.4	343	145	18.1	657	
WASHINGTON:																
Seattle	365,583	3,303	.9	375	74.1	131	224	94.5	13	126	85.1	22	25	20.7	96	
WEST VIRGINIA:																
Charleston	60,408	6,734	11.1	1,157	72.8	433	733	96.4	27	311	77.2	92	113	26.5	314	
Clarksburg	28,866	1,211	4.2	227	79.1	60	132	98.5	2	70	79.5	18	25	38.5	40	
Huntington	75,572	4,630	6.1	752	71.8	295	513	94.1	32	192	71.1	78	47	20.3	185	
Wheeling	61,659	2,192	3.6	316	69.0	142	205	95.8	9	86	68.3	40	25	21.2	93	
WISCONSIN:																
Milwaukee	578,249	7,501	1.3	1,192	76.9	359	850	98.2	16	286	86.7	44	56	15.8	299	

Table 22.—SCHOOL ATTENDANCE FOR THE NEGRO POPULATION, 10 TO 24 YEARS OLD, BY SEX, AGE, AND OCCUPATIONAL STATUS FOR URBAN, RURAL-FARM, AND RURAL-NONFARM AREAS: 1930

AGE	MALES							FEMALES										
	Total number	Gainfully occupied		Not gainfully occupied			Total attending school	Total number	Gainfully occupied			Not gainfully occupied, not married			Not gainfully occupied, married			Total attending school
		Total	Attending school	Total	Attending school	Not attending school			Total	Attending school	Married	Total	Attending school	Not attending school	Total	Attending school	Not attending school	
10 to 24 years	**1,772,496**	**1,008,433**	**155,659**	**764,063**	**634,076**	**129,987**	**789,735**	**1,932,765**	**584,371**	**107,832**	**157,519**	**978,571**	**748,206**	**230,365**	**369,823**	**4,651**	**365,172**	**860,689**
10 to 15 years	740,290	150,050	95,364	590,240	534,159	56,081	629,523	751,689	90,007	64,954	958	658,130	596,536	61,594	3,552	397	3,155	661,887
10 to 13 years	497,933	66,323	50,664	431,610	396,300	35,310	446,964	500,149	41,878	34,844	17	458,126	424,053	34,073	145	47	98	458,944
14 years	125,295	37,311	22,777	87,984	78,262	9,722	101,039	128,165	21,842	15,327	195	105,653	93,836	11,817	670	106	564	109,269
15 years	117,062	46,416	21,923	70,646	59,597	11,049	81,520	123,375	26,287	14,783	746	94,351	78,647	15,704	2,737	244	2,493	93,674
16 and 17 years	244,884	149,853	36,060	95,031	68,500	26,531	104,560	257,826	81,719	24,472	7,433	150,803	102,584	48,219	25,304	1,032	24,272	128,088
16 years	123,890	67,499	20,981	56,391	43,075	13,316	64,056	133,835	38,284	14,482	2,421	86,902	63,619	23,283	8,649	497	8,152	78,598
17 years	120,994	82,554	15,079	38,640	25,425	13,215	40,504	123,991	43,435	9,990	5,012	63,901	38,965	24,936	16,655	535	16,120	49,490
18 to 20 years	344,075	289,461	17,955	54,614	25,793	28,821	43,748	421,853	180,274	13,471	47,055	116,150	43,165	72,985	125,429	1,654	123,775	58,290
18 years	123,927	97,715	9,718	26,212	14,053	12,159	25,771	145,204	58,275	6,950	11,066	53,395	24,523	28,872	33,534	687	32,847	32,160
19 years	109,773	93,108	5,192	16,665	6,701	9,054	12,795	128,477	55,267	3,832	14,435	34,224	12,042	22,182	38,986	501	38,485	16,375
20 years	110,375	98,638	3,045	11,737	4,139	7,598	7,184	148,172	66,732	2,689	21,554	28,531	6,600	21,931	52,909	466	52,443	9,755
21 to 24 years	443,247	419,069	6,280	24,178	5,624	18,554	11,904	501,397	232,371	4,935	102,073	53,488	5,921	47,567	215,538	1,568	213,970	12,424
	URBAN																	
10 to 24 years	**631,849**	**334,315**	**16,908**	**297,534**	**256,607**	**40,927**	**273,515**	**783,388**	**267,887**	**12,871**	**89,154**	**368,993**	**299,000**	**69,993**	**146,508**	**1,697**	**144,811**	**313,568**
10 to 15 years	231,191	13,759	5,026	217,432	206,816	10,616	211,842	255,292	9,639	3,182	266	244,672	232,318	12,354	981	127	854	235,627
10 to 13 years	157,314	3,176	1,804	154,138	148,648	5,490	150,452	169,347	1,938	1,064	7	167,368	162,097	5,271	41	17	24	163,178
14 years	37,991	3,755	1,427	34,236	32,106	2,130	33,533	43,215	2,558	897	43	40,500	37,736	2,764	157	35	122	38,668
15 years	35,886	6,828	1,795	29,058	26,062	2,996	27,857	42,730	5,143	1,221	216	36,804	32,485	4,319	783	75	708	33,781
16 and 17 years	77,307	35,496	4,769	41,811	32,271	9,540	37,040	95,005	27,532	3,290	2,605	59,274	44,058	15,216	8,199	315	7,884	47,663
16 years	38,230	13,881	2,447	24,349	19,778	4,571	22,225	47,376	10,960	1,692	748	33,816	26,681	7,135	2,600	155	2,445	28,528
17 years	39,077	21,615	2,322	17,462	12,493	4,969	14,815	47,629	16,572	1,598	1,857	25,458	17,377	8,081	5,599	160	5,439	19,135
18 to 20 years	125,161	99,340	4,368	25,821	14,094	11,727	18,462	178,933	89,163	3,670	23,202	44,239	19,658	24,581	45,531	606	44,925	23,934
18 years	41,470	29,419	1,952	12,051	7,334	4,717	9,286	57,339	25,630	1,507	4,644	20,446	10,914	9,532	11,263	234	11,029	12,655
19 years	41,060	32,850	1,412	8,210	4,347	3,863	5,759	56,358	28,240	1,138	7,217	13,391	5,681	7,710	14,727	211	14,516	7,030
20 years	42,631	37,071	1,004	5,560	2,413	3,147	3,417	65,236	35,293	1,025	11,341	10,402	3,063	7,339	19,541	161	19,380	4,249
21 to 24 years	198,190	185,720	2,745	12,470	3,426	9,044	6,171	254,158	141,553	2,729	63,081	20,808	2,966	17,842	91,797	649	91,148	6,344
	RURAL-FARM																	
10 to 24 years	**835,345**	**506,385**	**127,429**	**328,960**	**268,562**	**60,398**	**395,991**	**831,008**	**242,726**	**88,458**	**47,655**	**441,624**	**325,506**	**116,118**	**146,658**	**2,132**	**144,526**	**416,096**
10 to 15 years	392,147	122,537	84,732	269,610	235,480	34,130	320,212	376,825	73,662	58,632	581	301,494	264,498	36,996	1,669	191	1,478	323,321
10 to 13 years	261,593	58,947	46,487	202,646	179,780	22,866	226,267	250,610	37,851	32,455	8	212,693	190,344	22,349	66	20	46	222,819
14 years	67,753	29,818	19,821	37,935	32,380	5,555	52,201	65,156	17,507	13,599	132	47,335	40,730	6,605	314	46	268	54,375
15 years	62,801	33,772	18,424	29,029	23,320	5,709	41,744	61,059	18,304	12,578	441	41,466	33,424	8,042	1,289	125	1,164	46,127
16 and 17 years	128,766	92,385	28,397	36,381	25,040	11,341	53,437	120,912	43,855	19,539	3,866	65,834	42,411	23,425	11,223	497	10,726	62,447
16 years	66,288	44,152	16,866	22,136	16,250	5,886	33,116	64,990	22,716	11,848	1,368	38,318	26,881	11,437	3,956	233	3,723	38,962
17 years	62,478	48,233	11,531	14,245	8,790	5,455	20,321	55,922	21,139	7,691	2,498	27,516	15,530	11,986	7,267	264	7,003	23,485
18 to 20 years	157,245	139,305	11,776	17,940	7,178	10,762	18,954	171,506	66,335	8,672	17,547	51,433	16,625	34,808	53,738	800	52,938	26,097
18 years	61,391	52,106	6,862	9,285	4,388	4,897	11,250	63,822	24,767	4,895	4,959	23,693	9,776	13,917	15,362	345	15,017	15,016
19 years	48,769	43,642	3,243	5,127	1,904	3,233	5,147	50,058	19,466	2,373	5,234	14,680	4,422	10,258	15,912	217	15,695	7,012
20 years	47,085	43,557	1,671	3,528	886	2,642	2,557	57,626	22,102	1,404	7,354	13,060	2,427	10,633	22,464	238	22,226	4,069
21 to 24 years	157,187	152,158	2,524	5,029	864	4,165	3,388	161,765	58,874	1,615	25,661	22,863	1,972	20,891	80,028	644	79,384	4,231
	RURAL-NONFARM																	
10 to 24 years	**305,302**	**167,733**	**11,322**	**137,569**	**108,907**	**28,662**	**120,229**	**318,369**	**73,758**	**6,503**	**20,710**	**167,954**	**123,700**	**44,254**	**76,657**	**822**	**75,835**	**131,025**
10 to 15 years	116,952	13,754	5,606	103,198	91,863	11,335	97,469	119,572	6,706	3,140	111	111,964	99,720	12,244	902	79	823	102,939
10 to 13 years	79,026	4,200	2,373	74,826	67,872	6,954	70,245	80,192	2,089	1,325	2	78,065	71,612	6,453	38	10	28	72,947
14 years	19,551	3,738	1,529	15,813	13,776	2,037	15,305	19,794	1,777	831	20	17,818	15,370	2,448	199	25	174	16,226
15 years	18,375	5,816	1,704	12,559	10,215	2,344	11,919	19,586	2,840	984	89	16,081	12,738	3,343	665	44	621	13,766
16 and 17 years	38,811	21,972	2,894	16,839	11,189	5,650	14,083	41,909	10,332	1,643	962	25,695	16,115	9,580	5,882	220	5,662	17,978
16 years	19,372	9,466	1,668	9,906	7,047	2,859	8,715	21,469	4,608	942	305	14,768	10,057	4,711	2,093	109	1,984	11,108
17 years	19,439	12,506	1,226	6,933	4,142	2,791	5,368	20,440	5,724	701	657	10,927	6,058	4,869	3,789	111	3,678	6,870
18 to 20 years	61,669	50,816	1,811	10,853	4,521	6,332	6,332	71,414	24,776	1,129	6,506	20,478	6,882	13,596	26,160	248	25,912	8,259
18 years	21,066	16,190	904	4,876	2,331	2,545	3,235	24,043	7,878	548	1,463	9,256	3,833	5,423	6,909	108	6,801	4,489
19 years	19,944	16,616	537	3,328	1,350	1,978	1,887	22,061	7,561	321	1,984	6,153	1,939	4,214	8,347	73	8,274	2,333
20 years	20,659	18,010	370	2,649	840	1,809	1,210	25,310	9,337	260	2,859	5,069	1,110	3,959	10,904	67	10,837	1,437
21 to 24 years	87,870	81,191	1,011	6,679	1,334	5,345	2,345	85,474	31,944	591	13,331	9,817	983	8,834	43,713	275	43,438	1,849

TABLE 23.—SCHOOL ATTENDANCE FOR THE NEGRO POPULATION 10 TO 24 YEARS OLD, BY SEX, AGE, AND OCCUPATIONAL STATUS, FOR THE SOUTHERN STATES: 1930

STATE AND AGE	MALES							FEMALES										
	Total number	Gainfully occupied		Not gainfully occupied			Total attending school	Total number	Gainfully occupied			Not gainfully occupied, not married			Not gainfully occupied, married			Total attending school
		Total	Attending school	Total	Attending school	Not att. school			Total	Attending school	Married	Total	Attending school	Not att. school	Total	Attending school	Not att. school	
SOUTH ATLANTIC																		
DELAWARE																		
10 to 15 years	1,752	97	45	1,655	1,600	55	1,645	1,795	53	19	1	1,738	1,631	107	4	2	2	1,652
16 and 17 years	626	304	25	322	249	73	274	596	144	19	8	412	219	193	40	4	36	242
18 to 20 years	923	753	30	170	87	83	117	936	389	11	56	325	75	250	222	1	221	87
21 to 24 years	1,260	1,189	46	71	20	51	66	1,070	494	12	187	168	12	156	408	1	407	25
MARYLAND																		
10 to 15 years	14,896	1,192	440	13,704	12,795	909	13,235	15,416	597	135	5	14,780	13,508	1,272	39	7	32	13,650
16 and 17 years	5,107	3,094	200	2,013	1,274	739	1,474	5,021	1,507	118	82	3,196	1,561	1,635	318	10	308	1,689
18 to 20 years	7,689	6,710	122	979	376	603	498	8,216	3,773	131	825	2,442	625	1,817	2,001	16	1,985	772
21 to 24 years	11,325	10,794	90	531	99	432	189	10,785	5,633	108	2,355	1,205	104	1,101	3,947	21	3,926	233
DISTRICT OF COLUMBIA																		
10 to 15 years	5,278	161	121	5,117	4,985	132	5,106	6,029	107	63	3	5,905	5,728	177	17	4	13	5,795
16 and 17 years	1,841	696	141	1,145	921	224	1,062	2,199	542	112	32	1,510	1,115	395	147	3	144	1,230
18 to 20 years	3,172	2,435	244	737	467	270	711	4,317	2,158	225	588	1,226	626	600	933	28	905	879
21 to 24 years	5,370	4,917	264	453	200	253	464	6,359	3,911	240	1,810	523	153	370	1,935	28	1,897	421
VIRGINIA																		
10 to 15 years	46,785	4,884	2,074	41,901	37,577	4,324	39,651	47,071	1,752	727	11	45,185	40,664	4,521	134	17	117	41,408
16 and 17 years	14,936	8,490	1,125	6,446	4,409	2,037	5,534	15,218	3,548	422	182	10,800	6,786	4,014	960	25	935	7,233
18 to 21 years	20,137	16,515	489	3,622	1,685	1,937	2,174	21,062	7,678	341	1,331	8,503	2,875	5,628	4,791	33	4,758	3,249
21 to 24 years	21,331	19,704	132	1,627	389	1,238	521	22,363	9,507	171	3,460	3,667	415	3,252	9,189	39	9,150	625
WEST VIRGINIA																		
10 to 15 years	5,979	178	111	5,801	5,479	322	5,590	6,355	76	23	4	6,229	5,856	373	50	5	45	5,884
16 and 17 years	1,892	699	106	1,193	842	351	948	2,096	200	37	11	1,556	1,102	454	340	16	324	1,155
18 to 20 years	2,954	2,131	96	823	471	352	567	3,490	640	47	134	1,490	768	722	1,360	17	1,343	832
21 to 24 years	4,540	4,057	52	483	206	277	258	4,464	1,078	47	393	684	154	530	2,702	18	2,684	219
NORTH CAROLINA																		
10 to 15 years	70,049	14,205	8,791	55,844	50,623	5,221	59,414	70,469	7,599	5,419	55	62,699	57,026	5,673	171	14	157	62,459
16 and 17 years	23,085	14,826	3,367	8,259	5,664	2,595	9,031	23,813	7,319	2,217	364	15,096	10,120	4,976	1,398	40	1,358	12,377
18 to 20 years	31,327	26,386	1,486	4,941	2,186	2,755	3,672	36,091	14,788	1,247	2,929	12,571	4,917	7,654	8,732	69	8,663	6,233
21 to 24 years	33,801	31,753	256	2,048	421	1,627	677	39,298	17,642	279	6,619	5,755	694	5,061	15,901	63	15,838	1,036
SOUTH CAROLINA																		
10 to 15 years	65,675	19,865	12,157	45,810	38,602	7,208	50,759	66,564	12,643	8,953	82	53,749	46,322	7,427	172	13	159	55,288
16 and 17 years	21,084	15,760	3,949	5,324	3,412	1,912	7,361	22,447	9,729	3,528	644	11,366	7,365	4,001	1,352	47	1,305	10,940
18 to 20 years	27,892	24,877	1,949	3,015	1,232	1,783	3,181	33,635	16,901	1,842	4,153	8,469	3,017	5,452	8,265	150	8,115	5,009
21 to 24 years	25,800	24,814	585	986	239	747	824	31,107	15,774	427	6,950	3,274	323	2,951	12,059	165	11,894	915
GEORGIA																		
10 to 15 years	78,256	21,942	10,851	45,314	47,740	8,574	58,591	79,164	10,817	6,502	145	67,890	58,434	9,456	347	42	415	64,978
16 and 17 years	25,753	19,700	3,161	6,053	3,432	2,621	6,593	28,104	10,782	2,409	1,094	14,173	8,088	6,088	3,149	110	3,039	10,604
18 to 20 years	37,065	33,420	1,499	3,645	1,142	2,503	2,641	44,654	21,060	1,127	5,863	10,696	2,789	7,907	12,898	159	12,739	4,075
21 to 24 years	38,544	36,839	562	1,705	259	1,446	821	46,403	23,280	371	10,213	4,720	319	4,401	18,403	163	18,240	853
FLORIDA																		
10 to 15 years	24,721	4,608	2,089	20,113	17,581	2,532	19,670	25,488	2,442	1,273	48	22,816	19,774	3,042	230	22	208	21,069
16 and 17 years	7,966	5,140	838	2,826	1,973	853	2,811	9,115	2,848	579	361	4,941	3,176	1,765	1,326	37	1,289	3,792
18 to 20 years	12,054	10,384	360	1,670	713	957	1,073	15,568	6,983	294	2,374	3,774	1,327	2,447	4,811	27	4,784	1,648
21 to 24 years	18,268	17,105	89	1,163	178	985	267	20,693	10,407	94	5,788	1,810	146	1,664	8,476	30	8,446	270
E. SOUTH CENTRAL																		
KENTUCKY																		
10 to 15 years	11,948	1,010	515	10,938	10,049	889	10,564	12,269	331	177	13	11,862	10,856	1,006	76	5	71	11,038
16 and 17 years	4,187	2,038	373	2,149	1,536	613	1,909	4,322	677	122	80	3,140	2,142	998	505	20	485	2,284
18 to 20 years	6,040	4,690	216	1,350	653	697	869	6,360	1,998	108	470	2,561	1,023	1,538	1,801	16	1,785	1,147
21 to 24 years	7,704	7,005	90	699	188	511	278	8,038	3,300	72	1,302	1,353	166	1,187	3,385	19	3,366	257
TENNESSEE																		
10 to 15 years	28,822	4,831	3,228	23,991	21,899	2,092	25,127	28,978	2,699	2,001	36	26,121	23,891	2,230	158	18	140	25,910
16 and 17 years	10,102	5,757	1,469	4,345	3,140	1,205	4,609	10,478	2,689	761	277	6,711	4,628	2,083	1,078	38	1,040	5,427
18 to 20 years	14,933	12,306	715	2,627	1,162	1,465	1,877	17,687	6,855	450	1,851	5,438	2,147	3,291	5,394	58	5,336	2,655
21 to 24 years	17,563	16,491	189	1,072	280	792	469	20,712	9,437	185	3,957	2,671	312	2,359	8,604	45	8,559	542
ALABAMA																		
10 to 15 years	65,296	19,999	13,124	45,297	39,373	5,924	52,497	65,424	13,514	9,936	97	51,598	45,010	6,588	312	32	280	54,978
16 and 17 years	22,958	16,019	4,396	6,939	4,775	2,164	9,171	22,852	9,008	3,295	668	11,691	7,744	3,947	2,153	72	2,081	11,111
18 to 20 years	26,548	23,236	1,511	3,312	1,503	1,809	3,014	36,262	16,512	1,535	3,977	8,920	3,036	5,884	10,830	127	10,703	4,698
21 to 24 years	35,124	33,749	369	1,375	263	1,112	632	40,759	18,796	364	7,542	4,210	392	3,818	17,753	111	17,642	867
MISSISSIPPI																		
10 to 15 years	70,649	27,616	21,870	43,033	39,374	3,659	61,244	68,619	19,617	16,654	229	48,574	44,844	3,730	428	45	383	61,543
16 and 17 years	24,373	17,836	6,944	6,537	4,993	1,544	11,937	22,962	10,473	4,789	1,559	9,786	7,325	2,461	2,703	112	2,591	12,226
18 to 20 years	29,544	26,288	2,543	3,256	1,687	1,569	4,230	39,283	18,697	1,956	6,884	7,723	3,258	4,465	12,863	126	12,737	5,340
21 to 24 years	38,618	37,502	342	1,116	205	911	547	42,045	20,461	278	10,812	3,231	271	2,960	18,353	75	18,278	624

TABLE 23.—SCHOOL ATTENDANCE FOR THE NEGRO POPULATION 10 TO 24 YEARS OLD, BY SEX, AGE, AND OCCUPATIONAL STATUS, FOR THE SOUTHERN STATES: 1930—Continued

STATE AND AGE	MALES							FEMALES										
	Total number	Gainfully occupied		Not gainfully occupied			Total attending school	Total number	Gainfully occupied			Not gainfully occupied, not married			Not gainfully occupied, married			Total attending school
		Total	Attending school	Total	Attending school	Not att. school			Total	Attending school	Married	Total	Attending school	Not att. school	Total	Attending school	Not att. school	
W. SOUTH CENTRAL																		
ARKANSAS																		
10 to 15 years	31,545	6,967	5,410	24,578	22,213	2,365	27,623	31,527	4,103	3,458	35	27,184	24,673	2,511	240	37	203	28,168
16 and 17 years	10,259	5,796	2,384	4,463	3,343	1,120	5,727	10,646	2,768	1,418	237	6,293	4,590	1,703	1,585	104	1,481	6,112
18 to 20 years	14,154	11,309	1,341	2,845	1,319	1,526	2,660	18,012	5,375	784	1,423	4,945	1,927	3,018	7,692	122	7,570	2,833
21 to 24 years	18,404	17,369	202	1,035	175	860	377	20,165	6,381	154	2,638	2,413	184	2,229	11,371	45	11,326	383
LOUISIANA																		
10 to 15 years	49,718	10,368	6,197	39,350	34,282	5,068	40,479	50,956	6,605	4,449	66	44,021	38,336	5,685	330	36	294	42,821
16 and 17 years	15,273	9,765	2,360	5,508	3,835	1,673	6,195	17,227	5,588	1,590	572	9,558	6,165	3,393	2,081	128	1,953	7,883
18 to 20 years	22,408	19,249	1,586	3,159	1,402	1,757	2,988	27,629	11,036	964	3,051	7,604	2,603	5,001	8,989	256	8,733	3,823
21 to 24 years	29,319	28,026	965	1,293	296	997	1,261	33,113	13,647	519	6,103	3,716	362	3,354	15,750	318	15,432	1,199
OKLAHOMA																		
10 to 15 years	10,856	841	580	10,015	9,337	678	9,917	10,979	291	217	4	10,620	9,944	676	68	11	57	10,172
16 and 17 years	3,709	1,463	518	2,246	1,825	421	2,343	3,803	451	124	72	2,898	2,302	596	454	20	434	2,446
18 to 20 years	5,386	3,820	412	1,566	885	681	1,297	6,174	1,652	101	526	2,346	1,194	1,152	2,176	43	2,133	1,338
21 to 24 years	6,591	6,026	107	565	131	434	238	7,502	2,986	73	1,376	1,018	145	873	3,498	23	3,475	241
TEXAS																		
10 to 15 years	52,978	8,835	6,408	44,143	41,136	3,007	47,544	53,777	5,301	4,294	74	48,178	44,859	3,319	298	33	265	49,186
16 and 17 years	17,775	9,857	2,753	7,918	6,194	1,724	8,947	19,382	4,796	1,776	542	12,378	9,243	3,135	2,208	82	2,126	11,100
18 to 20 years	25,952	21,718	1,315	4,234	2,164	2,070	3,479	31,834	11,803	848	3,417	9,212	3,583	5,629	10,819	121	10,698	4,552
21 to 24 years	33,976	32,473	314	1,503	342	1,161	656	37,661	16,309	305	7,536	4,150	488	3,662	17,202	88	17,114	881

CHAPTER XII.—ILLITERACY

The illiteracy classification.—The Census Bureau defines as "illiterate" any person 10 years of age or over who is not able to read and write either in English or in some other language. The classification is based on the answers given to the enumerator in response to the question "Whether able to read and write." No specific test of ability to read and write was prescribed, but the enumerators were instructed not to return the answer "Yes" (which would classify the person as literate) simple because the person was able to write his or her name.

Statistics of illiteracy were first obtained for the entire population 10 years old and over in 1870. In the several censuses prior to 1930, two questions have been asked, namely, "Whether able to read" and "Whether able to write", and illiteracy has been defined as inability to write, "regardless of ability to read." As a matter of fact, the figures for illiterates presented in most of the tables in the Reports of the 1920 Census represent persons who were unable both to read and write, since every person tabulated as able to write was also counted as able to read. The earlier statistics are therefore strictly comparable with the 1930 figures obtained through the use of the consolidated question.

It should be noted that ability to read and write cannot be defined precisely as to cover all cases with certainty. A person may know the alphabet and a small number of printed words and yet not be able to read in a true sense; or he may be able to write his name or other disconnected words, but wholly unable to express his thoughts in writing in any satisfactory fashion. In general, the illiterate population, as shown by the census, may be assumed to comprise only those persons who have had no education whatever.

Color and nativity.—The variations in the proportion of illiterates in the several color and nativity classes reflect the education opportunities, past and present, which have been open to them in the different sections of the United States, and in the case of the foreign born in the countries from which they have come.

The decidedly higher percentage of illiteracy for the native whites of native parentage than for the native whites of foreign or mixed parentage results largely from the fact that a much larger proportion of the former class is found in the rural communities, where school attendance has been less general than in the cities. Further, most of the rural native whites of foreign or mixed parentage live in States where educational facilities, even in the country, are relatively good. In order to make a fair comparison between any two elements of the population, therefore, in regard to illiteracy, the statistics for individual cities and for urban and rural areas in individual States should be examined.

There has been a rapid decrease in Negro illiteracy during the 60 years. In 1930, the illiterates constituted 16.3 percent of the Negroes 10 years old and over, as compared with 22.9 percent in 1920, 30.4 percent in 1910, 44.5 percent in 1900, 57.1 percent in 1890, 70 percent in 1880, and 81.4 percent in 1870. There were 1,513,892 Negro illiterates 10 years old and over in 1930, 1,842,161 in 1920, 2,227,731 in 1910, 2,853,194 in 1900, 3,042,668 in 1890, 3,220,878 in 1880, and 2,789,689 in 1870.

Illiteracy by sex.—The percentage illiterate among Negro males 10 years old and over was 17.6 as compared with 15.1 for females. The proportion illiterate among Negro females was smaller than for males in 1930 for each group up to 45 years of age. For the age groups 45 to 54 years and 65 years and over, the percentage illiterate among the males was considerably less than among the females.

Illiteracy by age.—The results of the extension of educational opportunities from decade to decade are brought out clearly by the statistics of illiteracy for the various age periods. The illiteracy shown for persons in each age period measures the lack of educational advantages during the childhood and youth of that age group. If school facilities should make no further growth from now on, there would nevertheless be a gradual reduction in illiteracy for several decades to come, as the older and more illiterate population died out; and the general level of illiteracy would gradually approach that found at present in the younger age groups. The improvement in educational facilities can be seen by making a comparison of the percentages of illiteracy for the age groups 10 to 14, and 15 to 19, as shown by the census figures for 1900, 1910, 1920, and 1930.

In 1930, there was a gradual increase in the percentage of illiteracy with each advancing age group. There was a decrease between 1920 and 1930 in the percentage of illiteracy in each age group. It is interesting to note that as regards the individuals composing, respectively, the several age groups, the percentage illiterate among the survivors has decreased from census to census. For example, the persons who were 15 to 24 years of age in 1910, so far as they were living at succeeding censuses, were 25 to 34 years of age in 1920, and 35 to 44 years of age in 1930. The percentage illiterate for this group of Negroes decreased from 22 in 1910 to 17.9 in 1920 and 16.8 in 1930. In general, the proportion illiterate decreased in each decade among the survivors, both male and female, for each age group.

Illiteracy by sections, geographic divisions, and States.—In illiteracy, as in every other phase of Negro life in the United States, chief interest centers about conditions in the South. Of the 1,513,892 Negro illiterates, 10 years old and over, in the United States in 1930, 1,416,417, or 93.6 percent, were in the South. The percentage illiterate for Negroes in 1930 was 19.7 in the South as compared with 4.7 in the North and 3.3 in the West. The percentage illiterate in the Negro population 10 years of age and over in the South decreased from 33.3 in 1910 to 26.0 in 1920, and to 19.7 in 1930. Comparing the three Southern divisions, the highest percentage of illiteracy was in the East South Central division and the lowest in the West South Central.

There were 5 States in which the proportion of the Negro illiterates 10 years old and over was greater than 20 percent, 5 States in which the percent was between 15 and 20, and 5 States in which the percent was between 10 and 15. All of the 15 States having 10 percent or more illiterate were in the South. Between 1920 and 1930, the percentage illiterate in the Negro population in the 15 States having 10 percent or more illiterate in 1930 decreased.

Illiteracy in counties and cities.—In 1930 there were 213 counties, all in the South, in which 25 percent or more of the Negro population 10 years old and over was illiterate. The counties were distributed by States as follows: Alabama, 38; Georgia, 34; Louisiana, 29; South Carolina, 27; Mississippi, 21; Florida, 19; Virginia, 18; North Carolina, 12; Kentucky, 6; Tennessee, 4; Texas, 2; Maryland, 2; and Arkansas, 1.

In 1930, 16 out of the 80 cities having 10,000 or more Negro inhabitants reported a percentage of illiteracy of the Negro population 10 years old and over greater than that for the United States as a whole.

Urban and rural illiteracy.—Among the Negroes, the proportion illiterate in the rural-farm population exceeds that in the rural-nonfarm and the urban population. In 1930, of the 1,513,892 Negro illiterates, 794,866 were in rural-farm areas, 323,177 were in rural-nonfarm areas, and 395,849 in urban areas, the percentage illiteracy being 23.2 in the rural-farm, 20.5 in the rural-nonfarm, and 9.2 in the urban population, 10 years of age and over.

TABLE 1.—ILLITERACY IN THE POPULATION 10 YEARS OLD AND OVER, BY COLOR, AND NATIVITY, FOR THE UNITED STATES: 1930 AND 1920

COLOR AND NATIVITY	1930 [1]			1920 [1]		
	Total number	Illiterate		Total number	Illiterate	
		Number	Percent		Number	Percent
All classes	**98,723,047**	**4,283,753**	**4.3**	**82,739,315**	**4,931,905**	**6.0**
Negro	9,292,556	1,513,892	16.3	8,053,225	1,842,161	22.9
White	87,980,667	2,407,218	2.7	74,359,749	3,006,312	4.0
Native	74,763,739	1,103,134	1.5	60,861,863	1,242,572	2.0
Native parentage	53,876,411	986,469	1.8	44,077,564	1,109,875	2.5
For. or mixed par.	20,887,328	116,665	.6	16,784,299	132,697	.8
Foreign born	13,216,928	1,304,084	9.9	13,497,886	1,763,740	13.1
Other races	1,449,824	362,643	25.0	326,341	83,432	25.6

[1] Mexicans, with a relatively high percentage of illiteracy (27.5 in 1930), are included with "Other races" in the figures for 1930 and with the white population in 1920.

TABLE 2.—ILLITERACY IN THE URBAN, RURAL-FARM, AND RURAL-NONFARM NEGRO POPULATION 10 YEARS OLD AND OVER, BY AGE GROUPS, BY SECTIONS: 1930

AGE	URBAN ILLITERATE		RURAL-FARM ILLITERATE		RURAL-NONFARM ILLITERATE	
	Number	Percent	Number	Percent	Number	Percent
United States						
10 years and over [1]	**395,849**	**9.2**	**794,866**	**23.2**	**323,177**	**20.5**
10 to 14 years	4,746	1.2	50,157	7.8	11,335	5.7
15 to 24 years	42,178	4.2	160,037	15.7	55,246	13.0
25 to 34 years	72,899	6.7	119,881	23.2	58,246	17.8
35 to 44 years	82,453	9.5	124,903	27.5	57,185	22.2
45 to 54 years	80,223	14.7	138,833	34.6	55,586	29.5
55 to 64 years	52,488	22.9	99,749	44.1	37,692	38.9
65 years and over	59,555	42.8	100,747	64.8	47,204	60.5
THE SOUTH						
10 years and over [1]	**321,664**	**13.2**	**788,339**	**23.4**	**306,414**	**22.1**
10 to 14 years	4,427	1.7	49,999	7.8	11,146	6.2
15 to 24 years	37,733	6.0	159,271	15.8	54,101	14.0
25 to 34 years	60,297	10.4	119,006	23.4	55,929	19.6
35 to 44 years	66,727	14.5	123,798	27.8	54,113	24.4
45 to 54 years	64,507	21.3	137,637	35.0	52,173	32.1
55 to 64 years	41,410	31.5	98,736	44.7	35,153	42.4
65 years and over	45,577	53.5	99,344	65.6	43,235	64.5
THE NORTH						
10 years and over [1]	**71,873**	**4.1**	**6,276**	**12.2**	**15,885**	**9.1**
10 to 14 years	305	.2	156	2.1	182	1.0
15 to 24 years	4,360	1.2	747	6.0	1,074	2.9
25 to 34 years	12,389	2.5	852	10.9	2,210	5.9
35 to 44 years	15,375	4.0	1,058	13.0	2,872	8.8
45 to 54 years	15,300	6.7	1,128	15.5	3,223	13.5
55 to 64 years	10,637	11.7	968	20.2	2,420	18.7
65 years and over	13,196	26.3	1,356	36.0	3,789	36.5
THE WEST						
10 years and over [1]	**2,312**	**2.7**	**251**	**5.3**	**878**	**6.8**
10 to 14 years	14	.2	2	.3	7	.7
15 to 24 years	85	.6	19	1.9	71	3.0
25 to 34 years	213	1.1	23	2.9	107	3.6
35 to 44 years	351	1.7	47	5.4	200	6.5
45 to 54 years	416	2.9	68	8.7	190	9.7
55 to 64 years	441	6.8	45	11.5	119	13.6
65 years and over	782	20.6	47	20.5	180	29.0

[1] Includes persons of unknown age.

TABLE 3.—ILLITERACY IN THE POPULATION 10 YEARS OLD AND OVER, BY COLOR, AND AGE GROUPS, FOR THE UNITED STATES: 1930 AND 1920

AGE	1930			1920		
	Total number	Illiterate		Total number	Illiterate	
		Number	Percent		Number	Percent
All classes						
10 years and over	**98,723,047**	**4,283,753**	**4.3**	**82,739,315**	**4,931,905**	**6.0**
10 to 14 years	12,004,877	140,440	1.2	10,641,137	246,360	2.3
15 to 19 years	11,552,115	221,942	1.9	9,430,556	283,316	3.0
20 to 24 years	10,870,378	294,360	2.7	9,277,021	392,853	4.2
25 to 34 years	18,954,029	618,266	3.3	17,157,684	961,200	5.6
35 to 44 years	17,198,840	887,955	5.2	14,120,838	988,961	7.0
45 to 54 years	13,018,083	864,433	6.6	10,498,493	857,776	8.2
55 to 64 years	8,396,898	606,811	7.2	6,531,672	594,573	.91
65 years and over	6,633,805	642,966	9.7	4,933,215	591,385	12.0
Unknown	94,022	6,580	7.0	148,699	15,481	10.4
NEGRO						
10 years and over	**9,292,556**	**1,513,892**	**16.3**	**8,053,225**	**1,842,161**	**22.9**
10 to 14 years	1,251,542	66,238	5.3	1,236,914	140,892	11.4
15 to 19 years	1,250,528	111,111	8.9	1,083,215	152,998	14.1
20 to 24 years	1,203,191	146,350	12.2	1,054,847	179,124	17.0
25 to 34 years	1,936,301	251,026	13.0	1,607,604	287,063	17.9
35 to 44 years	1,578,323	264,541	16.8	1,333,632	310,538	23.3
45 to 54 years	1,134,655	274,642	24.2	950,699	323,924	34.1
55 to 64 years	551,566	189,929	34.4	430,098	212,682	49.4
65 years and over	372,719	207,506	55.7	332,713	227,310	68.3
Unknown	13,731	2,549	18.6	23,503	7,630	32.5
WHITE						
10 years and over	**87,980,667**	**2,407,218**	**2.7**	**74,359,749**	**3,006,312**	**4.0**
10 to 14 years	10,546,282	53,693	.5	9,369,322	100,643	1.1
15 to 19 years	10,111,584	81,995	.8	8,314,155	125,495	1.5
20 to 24 years	9,466,155	107,533	1.1	8,185,341	207,649	2.5
25 to 34 years	16,683,462	287,948	1.7	15,480,480	660,706	4.3
35 to 44 years	15,382,127	551,464	3.6	12,721,352	662,629	5.2
45 to 54 years	11,732,045	534,738	4.6	9,505,306	518,918	5.5
55 to 64 years	7,770,100	382,047	4.9	6,077,104	370,421	6.1
65 years and over	6,211,583	404,534	6.5	4,583,026	352,525	7.7
Unknown	77,329	3,266	4.2	123,663	7,326	5.9
OTHER RACES [1]						
10 years and over	**1,449,824**	**362,643**	**25.0**	**326,341**	**83,432**	**25.6**
10 to 14 years	207,053	20,509	9.9	34,901	4,825	13.8
15 to 19 years	190,003	28,836	15.2	33,186	4,823	14.5
20 to 24 years	201,032	40,477	20.1	36,833	6,080	16.5
25 to 34 years	334,266	79,292	23.7	69,600	13,431	19.3
35 to 44 years	238,390	71,950	30.2	65,854	15,794	24.0
45 to 54 years	151,383	55,053	36.4	42,488	14,934	35.1
55 to 64 years	75,232	34,835	46.3	24,470	11,470	46.9
65 years and over	49,503	30,926	62.5	17,476	11,550	66.1
Unknown	2,962	765	25.8	1,533	525	34.2

[1] Mexicans, with a relatively high percentage of illiteracy (27.5 in 1930) are included with "Other races" in the figures for 1930 and with the white population in 1920.

Table 4.—ILLITERACY IN THE POPULATION 10 YEARS OLD AND OVER, BY COLOR, NATIVITY, AND SEX, FOR THE UNITED STATES: 1870 TO 1930

[Percent not shown where base is less than 100]

CENSUS YEAR, COLOR, AND NATIVITY	TOTAL 10 YEARS OLD AND OVER			MALE			FEMALE		
	Total number	Illiterate		Total number	Illiterate		Total number	Illiterate	
		Number	Percent		Number	Percent		Number	Percent
1930									
All classes	98,723,047	4,283,753	4.3	49,949,798	2,198,293	4.4	48,773,249	2,095,460	4.3
Negro	9,292,556	1,513,892	16.3	4,564,690	801,949	17.6	4,727,866	711,943	15.1
White	87,980,667	2,407,218	2.7	44,554,124	1,214,025	2.7	43,426,543	1,193,193	2.7
Native	74,763,739	1,103,134	1.5	37,475,901	640,048	1.7	37,287,838	463,086	1.2
Native parentage	53,876,411	986,469	1.8	27,188,095	577,312	2.1	26,688,316	409,157	1.5
Foreign or mixed parentage	20,887,328	116,665	.6	10,287,806	62,736	.6	10,599,522	53,929	.5
Foreign born	13,216,928	1,304,084	9.9	7,078,223	573,977	8.1	6,138,705	730,107	11.9
Other races	1,449,824	362,643	25.0	830,984	182,319	21.9	618,840	180,324	29.1
Mexican	1,002,241	275,470	27.5	547,863	134,234	24.5	454,378	141,236	31.1
Indian	238,981	61,517	25.7	123,469	29,630	24.0	115,512	31,887	27.6
Chinese	63,392	12,912	20.4	53,650	10,735	20.0	9,742	2,177	22.3
Japanese	97,273	8,932	9.2	60,580	4,231	7.0	36,693	4,701	12.8
Filipino	42,964	2,834	6.6	41,128	2,589	6.3	1,836	245	13.3
Hindu	2,833	753	26.6	2,697	741	27.5	136	12	8.8
Korean	1,446	184	12.7	1,029	120	11.7	417	64	15.3
All other	694	41	5.9	568	39	6.9	126	2	1.6
1920 [1]									
All classes	82,739,315	4,931,905	6.0	42,289,969	2,540,209	6.0	40,449,346	2,391,696	5.9
Negro	8,053,225	1,842,161	22.9	4,009,462	942,368	23.5	4,043,763	899,793	22.3
White	74,359,749	3,006,312	4.0	38,070,736	1,551,529	4.1	36,289,013	1,454,783	4.0
Native	60,861,863	1,242,572	2.0	30,651,045	684,707	2.2	30,210,818	557,865	1.8
Native parentage	44,077,564	1,109,875	2.5	22,361,495	614,612	2.7	21,716,069	495,263	2.3
Foreign or mixed parentage	16,784,299	132,697	.8	8,289,550	70,095	.8	8,494,749	62,602	.7
Foreign born	13,497,886	1,763,740	13.1	7,419,691	866,822	11.7	6,078,195	896,918	14.8
Other races	326,341	83,432	25.6	209,771	46,312	22.1	116,570	37,120	31.8
Indian	176,925	61,730	34.9	91,546	30,010	32.8	85,379	31,720	37.2
Chinese	56,230	11,262	20.0	51,041	10,064	19.7	5,189	1,198	23.1
Japanese	84,238	9,276	11.0	58,806	5,145	8.7	25,432	4,131	16.2
Filipino	5,380	288	5.4	5,110	254	5.0	270	34	12.6
Hindu	2,460	791	32.2	2,382	785	33.0	78	6	--------
Korean	973	79	8.1	787	51	6.5	186	28	15.1
All other	135	6	4.4	99	3	--------	36	3	--------
1910									
All classes	71,580,270	5,516,163	7.7	37,027,558	2,814,950	7.6	34,552,712	2,701,213	7.8
Negro	7,317,922	2,227,731	30.4	3,673,386	1,096,000	30.1	3,680,536	1,131,731	30.7
White	63,933,870	3,184,633	5.0	33,164,229	1,662,505	5.0	30,769,641	1,522,128	4.9
Native	50,989,341	1,534,272	3.0	25,843,033	796,055	3.1	25,146,308	738,217	2.9
Native parentage	37,081,278	1,378,884	3.7	18,933,751	715,926	3.8	18,147,527	662,958	3.7
Foreign or mixed parentage	13,908,063	155,388	1.1	6,909,282	80,129	1.2	6,998,781	75,259	1.1
Foreign born	12,944,529	1,650,361	12.7	7,321,196	866,450	11.8	5,623,333	783,911	13.9
Other races	328,478	103,799	31.6	225,943	56,445	25.0	102,535	47,354	46.2
Indian	188,758	85,445	45.3	96,582	40,104	41.5	92,176	45,341	49.2
Chinese	68,924	10,891	15.8	65,479	9,849	15.0	3,445	1,042	30.2
Japanese	67,661	6,213	9.2	60,809	5,247	8.6	6,852	966	14.1
Filipino	145	52	35.9	136	51	37.5	9	1	--------
Hindu	2,540	1,142	45.0	2,523	1,141	45.2	17	1	--------
Korean	443	56	12.6	411	53	12.9	32	3	--------
All other	7	--------	--------	3	--------	--------	4	--------	--------
1900									
All classes	57,949,824	6,180,069	10.7	29,703,440	3,011,224	10.1	28,246,384	3,168,845	11.2
Negro	6,415,581	2,853,194	44.5	3,181,650	1,371,432	43.1	3,233,931	1,481,762	45.8
White	51,250,918	3,200,746	6.2	26,327,931	1,567,153	6.0	24,922,987	1,633,593	6.6
Native	41,236,662	1,913,611	4.6	20,912,940	955,517	4.6	20,323,722	958,094	4.7
Native parentage	30,310,261	1,734,764	5.7	15,452,855	862,175	5.6	14,857,406	872,589	5.9
Foreign or mixed parentage	10,926,401	178,847	1.6	5,460,085	93,342	1.7	5,466,316	85,505	1.6
Foreign born	10,014,256	1,287,135	12.9	5,414,991	611,636	11.3	4,599,265	675,499	14.7
Other races	283,325	126,129	44.5	193,859	72,639	37.5	89,466	53,490	59.8
Indian	171,552	96,347	56.2	86,504	45,376	52.5	85,048	50,971	59.9
Chinese	87,682	25,396	29.0	84,141	23,052	27.4	3,541	2,344	66.2
Japanese	24,091	4,386	18.2	23,214	4,211	18.1	877	175	20.0
1890 [2]									
All classes	47,413,559	6,324,702	13.3	24,352,659	3,008,222	12.4	23,060 900	3,316,480	14.4
Negro	5,328,972	3,042,668	57.1	2,646,171	1,438,923	54.4	2,682,801	1,603,745	59.8
White	41,931,074	3,212,574	7.7	21,578,245	1,517,722	7.0	20,352,829	1,694,852	8.3
Native	33,144,187	2,065,003	6.2	16,796,497	978,408	5.8	16,347,690	1,086,595	6.6
Native parentage	25,375,766	1,890,723	7.5	12,901,102	888,415	6.9	12,474,664	1,002,308	8.0
Foreign or mixed parentage	7,768,421	174,280	2.2	3,895,395	89,993	2.3	3,873,026	84,287	2.2
Foreign born	8,786,887	1,147,571	13.1	4,781,748	539,314	11.3	4,005,139	608,257	15.2
Other races	153,513	69,460	45.2	128,243	51,577	40.2	25,270	17,883	70.8
1880									
All classes	36,761,607	6,239,958	17.0	18,735,980	2,966,421	15.8	18,025,627	3,273,537	18.2
Negro and other races	4,601,207	3,220,878	70.0	2,310,730	1,555,616	67.3	2,290,477	1,665,262	72.7
White	32,160,400	3,019,080	9.4	16,425,250	1,410,805	8.6	15,735,150	1,608,275	10.2
Native	25,785,789	2,255,460	8.7	--------	--------	--------	--------	--------	--------
Foreign born	6,374,611	763,620	12.0	--------	--------	--------	--------	--------	--------
1870									
All classes	28,228,945	5,658,144	20.0	14,258,866	2,603,888	18.3	13,970,079	3,054,256	21.9
Negro	3,428,757	2,789,689	81.4	1,664,656	1,342,347	80.6	1,764,101	1,447,342	82.0
White	24,717,870	2,851,911	11.5	12,526,487	1,250,970	10.0	12,191,383	1,600,941	13.1
Other races	82,318	16,544	20.1	67,723	10,571	15.6	14,595	5,973	40.9

[1] Mexicans classified separately for the first time in 1930; included for the most part with whites of foreign birth or parentage in 1920 and 1910.
[2] Figures for 1890 are exclusive of persons in Indian Territory and on Indian reservations, areas specially enumerated, but for which illiteracy statistics are not available.

Table 5.—ILLITERACY IN THE POPULATION 21 YEARS OLD AND OVER, BY COLOR, NATIVITY, AND SEX, FOR THE UNITED STATES: 1900 TO 1930

CENSUS YEAR, COLOR, AND NATIVITY	TOTAL 21 YEARS OLD AND OVER			MALE			FEMALE		
	Total number	Illiterate		Total number	Illiterate		Total number	Illiterate	
		Number	Per cent		Number	Per cent		Number	Per cent
1930									
All classes	**72,943,624**	**3,863,215**	**5.3**	**37,056,757**	**1,942,729**	**5.2**	**35,886,867**	**1,920,486**	**5.4**
Negro	6,531,939	1,306,650	20.0	3,235,441	672,234	20.8	3,296,498	634,416	19.2
White	65,400,034	2,251,470	3.4	33,216,074	1,116,497	3.4	32,183,960	1,134,973	3.5
Native	52,762,391	954,968	1.8	26,418,580	545,849	2.1	26,343,811	409,119	1.6
Native parentage	38,116,766	855,318	2.2	19,257,937	492,322	2.6	18,858,829	362,996	1.9
Foreign or mixed parentage	14,645,625	99,650	.7	7,160,643	53,527	.7	7,484,982	46,123	.6
Foreign born	12,637,643	1,296,502	10.3	6,797,494	570,648	8.4	5,840,149	725,854	12.4
Other races [1]	1,011,651	305,095	30.2	605,242	153,998	25.4	406,409	151,097	37.2
1920 [2]									
All classes	**60,886,520**	**4,333,111**	**7.1**	**31,403,370**	**2,192,368**	**7.0**	**29,483,150**	**2,140,743**	**7.3**
Negro	5,522,475	1,512,987	27.4	2,792,006	748,229	26.8	2,730,469	764,758	28.0
White	55,113,461	2,747,814	5.0	28,442,400	1,403,609	4.9	26,671,061	1,344,205	5.0
Native	42,614,741	1,040,669	2.4	21,513,948	563,546	2.6	21,100,793	477,123	2.3
Native parentage	31,007,257	938,311	3.0	15,805,063	509,343	3.2	15,202,194	428,968	2.8
Foreign or mixed parentage	11,607,484	102,358	.9	5,708,835	54,203	.9	5,898,599	48,155	.8
Foreign born	12,498,720	1,707,145	13.7	6,928,452	840,063	12.1	5,570,268	867,082	15.5
Other races	250,584	72,310	28.9	168,964	40,530	24.0	81,620	31,780	38.9
1910 [2]									
All classes	**51,554,905**	**4,570,017**	**8.9**	**26,999,151**	**2,273,603**	**8.4**	**24,555,754**	**2,296,414**	**9.4**
Negro	4,886,615	1,742,648	35.7	2,458,873	819,135	33.3	2,427,742	923,513	38.0
White	46,416,750	2,739,838	5.9	24,357,514	1,406,364	5.8	22,059,236	1,333,474	6.0
Native	34,762,825	1,232,345	3.5	17,710,697	617,733	3.5	17,052,128	614,612	3.6
Native parentage	25,696,212	1,113,427	4.3	13,211,731	557,042	4.2	12,484,481	556,385	4.5
Foreign or mixed parentage	9,066,613	118,918	1.3	4,498,966	60,691	1.3	4,567,647	58,227	1.3
Foreign born	11,653,925	1,507,493	12.9	6,646,817	788,631	11.9	5,007,108	718,862	14.4
Other races	251,540	87,531	34.8	182,764	48,104	26.3	68,776	39,427	57.3
1900									
All classes	**40,782,007**	**4,881,026**	**12.0**	**21,134,299**	**2,288,470**	**10.8**	**19,647,708**	**2,592,556**	**13.2**
Negro	4,119,152	2,131,028	51.7	2,060,302	976,610	47.4	2,058,850	1,154,418	56.1
White	36,447,297	2,644,240	7.3	18,918,697	1,249,897	6.6	17,528,600	1,394,343	8.0
Native	27,478,882	1,455,083	5.3	14,014,427	687,581	4.9	13,464,455	767,502	5.7
Native parentage	20,607,766	1,318,529	6.4	10,569,743	618,606	5.9	10,038,023	699,923	7.0
Foreign or mixed parentage	6,871,116	136,554	2.0	3,444,684	68,975	2.0	3,426,432	67,579	2.0
Foreign born	8,968,415	1,189,157	13.3	4,904,270	562,316	11.5	4,064,145	626,841	15.4
Other races	215,558	105,758	49.1	155,300	61,963	39.9	60,258	43,795	72.7

[1] Includes Mexicans who were classified for the most part with whites of foreign birth or parentage in 1920 and 1910.
[2] Mexicans included with the white population in 1920 and 1910.

Table 6.—ILLITERACY IN THE NEGRO AND FOREIGN-BORN WHITE POPULATION 10 YEARS OLD AND OVER, WITH COUNTRY OF BIRTH, FOR THE UNITED STATES: 1930

RACIAL CLASS AND COUNTRY OF BIRTH	Total number	ILLITERATE	
		Number	Per-cent
Negro, total	**9,292,556**	**1,513,892**	**16.3**
Foreign-born white, total	13,216,928	1,304,084	9.9
COUNTRY OF BIRTH			
Azores	35,325	13,042	36.9
Portugal	69,535	24,109	34.7
Italy	1,769,705	447,831	25.3
Syria	56,870	14,345	25.2
Lithuania	193,196	47,344	24.5
Poland	1,262,892	239,651	19.0
Albania	8,683	1,579	18.2
Yugoslavia	210,141	32,774	15.6
Armenia	31,990	4,805	15.0
Turkey	48,467	6,851	14.1
Spain	57,957	8,132	14.0
Greece	173,531	23,630	13.6
Czechoslovakia	487,794	63,145	12.9
Mexico	22,684	2,662	11.7
Russia	1,150,441	130,302	11.3
Bulgaria	9,325	1,006	10.8
Austria	369,192	38,370	10.4
Canada-French	360,724	35,760	9.9
Hungary	272,977	26,761	9.8
Rumania	145,037	14,275	9.8
South America	28,852	1,978	6.9
Latvia	20,536	1,402	6.8
Cuba	15,079	993	6.6
Belgium	63,577	4,086	6.4
Finland	142,060	8,963	6.3
France	133,857	5,074	3.8
Germany	1,589,249	50,197	3.2
Netherlands	131,439	3,939	3.0
Switzerland	112,240	2,707	2.4
Norway	345,231	6,743	2.0
Australia	12,533	215	1.7
Luxemburg	9,023	148	1.6
Irish Free State	741,213	10,850	1.5
Sweden	592,291	9,011	1.5
Wales	59,315	856	1.4
Northern Ireland	177,319	2,188	1.2
Denmark	178,212	1,766	1.0
Newfoundland	23,297	198	.8
Canada-Other	872,987	4,908	.6
England	800,657	4,870	.6
Scotland	344,182	1,161	.3
All other countries	87,313	5,457	6.2

TABLE 7.—ILLITERACY IN THE POPULATION 10 YEARS OLD AND OVER, BY COLOR AND NATIVITY, BY SECTIONS, AND SOUTHERN DIVISIONS: 1930, 1920, AND 1910.

CENSUS YEAR, COLOR, AND NATIVITY	United States	THE SOUTH: Total	South Atlantic division	East South Central division	West South Central division	THE NORTH	THE WEST
	NUMBER ILLITERATE						
1930							
Negro	1,513,892	1,416,417	662,055	452,082	302,280	94,034	3,441
White:							
Native	1,103,134	767,180	314,583	270,130	182,467	291,994	43,960
Foreign born	1,304,084	51,524	31,328	4,238	15,958	1,180,152	72,408
1920							
Negro	1,842,161	1,751,658	812,842	536,583	402,233	87,133	3,370
White:							
Native	1,242,572	892,865	356,785	301,651	234,429	295,731	53,976
Foreign born	1,763,740	174,939	39,757	6,457	128,725	1,446,809	141,992
1910							
Negro	2,227,731	2,133,961	969,432	681,507	483,022	90,659	3,111
White:							
Native	1,534,272	1,079,583	433,809	381,230	264,544	398,496	56,193
Foreign born	1,650,361	130,823	37,934	8,215	84,674	1,398,943	120,595
	PERCENT ILLITERATE						
1930							
Negro	16.3	19.7	19.7	22.0	17.0	4.7	3.3
White:							
Native	1.5	3.7	3.7	5.0	2.6	.6	.6
Foreign born	9.9	9.8	10.4	7.4	9.4	10.5	5.1
1920							
Negro	22.9	26.0	25.2	27.9	25.3	7.0	4.9
White:							
Native	2.0	5.2	5.1	6.4	4.1	.8	1.0
Foreign born	13.1	21.5	12.8	9.1	29.9	12.9	9.8
1910							
Negro	30.4	33.3	32.5	34.8	33.1	10.5	7.0
White:							
Native	3.0	7.5	7.6	9.2	5.8	1.2	1.4
Foreign born	12.7	18.8	13.5	9.7	25.6	12.7	9.5
Negro:							
1930	16.3	19.7	19.7	22.0	17.0	4.7	3.3
1920	22.9	26.0	25.2	27.9	25.3	7.0	4.9
1910	30.4	33.3	32.5	34.8	33.1	10.5	7.0
White:							
Native:							
1930	1.5	3.7	3.7	5.0	2.6	.6	.6
1920	2.0	5.2	5.1	6.4	4.1	.8	1.0
1910	3.0	7.5	7.6	9.2	5.8	1.2	1.4
Foreign born:							
1930	9.9	9.8	10.4	7.4	9.4	10.5	5.1
1920	13.1	21.5	12.8	9.1	29.9	12.9	9.8
1910	12.7	18.8	13.5	9.7	25.6	12.7	9.5

TABLE 8.—ILLITERACY IN THE NEGRO POPULATION 10 YEARS OLD AND OVER, BY SECTIONS, AND SOUTHERN DIVISIONS: 1930, 1920, AND 1910

[A minus sign (−) denotes decrease; a plus sign (+) denotes increase]

CENSUS YEAR, SECTION, AND DIVISION	Total number	ILLITERATE: Number	ILLITERATE: Percent	Decennial increase in population	Decennial decrease in number illiterate
United States					
1930	9,292,556	1,513,892	16.3	1,239,331	328,269
1920	8,053,225	1,842,161	22.9	735,303	385,570
1910	7,317,922	2,227,731	30.4	902,341	625,463
THE SOUTH:					
1930	7,194,750	1,416,417	19.7	461,322	335,241
1920	6,733,428	1,751,658	26.0	324,889	382,303
1910	6,408,539	2,133,961	33.3	743,564	583,645
SOUTH ATLANTIC DIVISION:					
1930	3,363,864	662,055	19.7	142,170	150,787
1920	3,221,694	812,842	25.2	234,758	156,590
1910	2,986,936	969,432	32.5	331,103	280,847
EAST SOUTH CENTRAL DIVISION:					
1930	2,052,951	452,082	22.0	128,237	84,501
1920	1,924,714	536,583	27.9	−36,184	144,924
1910	1,960,898	681,507	34.8	158,070	206,331
WEST SOUTH CENTRAL DIVISION:					
1930	1,777,935	302,280	17.0	190,915	99,953
1920	1,587,020	402,233	25.3	126,315	80,789
1910	1,460,705	483,022	33.1	254,391	96,467
THE NORTH:					
1930	1,994,085	94,034	4.7	743,377	+6,901
1920	1,250,708	87,133	7.0	385,655	3,526
1910	865,053	90,659	10.5	140,309	41,530
THE WEST:					
1930	103,721	3,441	3.3	34,632	+71
1920	69,089	3,370	4.9	24,759	+259
1910	44,330	3,111	7.0	18,468	288

TABLE 9.—INCREASE IN NEGRO POPULATION AND DECREASE IN NUMBER ILLITERATE, BY SEX, BY SECTIONS, AND SOUTHERN DIVISIONS: 1920 TO 1930

[A plus sign (+) denotes increase]

SECTION AND DIVISION	INCREASE IN POPULATION 10 YEARS OLD AND OVER 1920–1930: Male	Female	DECREASE IN ILLITERATE 1920–1930: Male	Female
United States	555,228	684,103	140,419	187,850
THE SOUTH	186,254	275,068	144,895	190,346
South Atlantic	47,391	94,779	64,110	86,677
East South Central	55,502	72,735	34,577	49,924
West South Central	83,361	107,554	46,208	53,745
THE NORTH	355,849	387,528	+4,584	+2,317
THE WEST	13,125	21,507	108	+179

TABLE 10.—ILLITERACY IN THE NEGRO AND WHITE POPULATION 21 YEARS OLD AND OVER, BY SECTIONS, AND SOUTHERN DIVISIONS: 1930

SECTION AND DIVISION	NEGRO: Total number	NEGRO: Illiterate: Number	NEGRO: Illiterate: Percent	WHITE: Total number	WHITE: Illiterate: Number	WHITE: Illiterate: Percent
United States	6,531 939	1,306,650	20.0	65,400,034	2,251,470	3.4
THE SOUTH	4,848,072	1,212,258	25.0	15,016,965	711,862	4.7
South Atlantic	2,210,041	552,521	25.0	6,194,770	303,343	4.9
East South Central	1,402,055	392,519	28.0	3,816,222	235,387	6.2
West South Central	1,235,976	267,218	21.6	5,005,973	173,132	3.5
THE NORTH	1,598,098	91,052	5.7	43,363,284	1,429,140	3.3
THE WEST	85,769	3,340	3.9	7,019,785	110,468	1.6

TABLE 11.—INCREASE IN NEGRO POPULATION, AND DECREASE IN NEGRO ILLITERATES FOR THE UNITED STATES IN EACH AGE GROUP: 1910 TO 1930

AGE PERIOD	1920–1930: Increase [1] in population	1920–1930: Decrease in number illiterate	1910–1920: Increase [1] in population	1910–1920: Decrease [2] in number illiterate
10 years and over	1,239,331	328,269	735,303	385,570
10 to 14 years	14,628	74,654	81,648	77,663
15 to 19 years	167,313	41,887	22,799	61,862
20 to 24 years	148,344	32,774	24,052	66,736
25 to 34 years	328,697	36,037	58,288	93,679
35 to 44 years	244,691	45,997	244,770	41,320
45 to 54 years	183,956	49,282	238,720	11,006
55 to 64 years	121,468	22,753	33,974	36,902
65 years and over	40,006	19,804	38,589	+8,055
Unknown	−9,772	5,081	−7,537	4,457

[1] A minus (−) sign denotes a decrease.
[2] A plus (+) sign denotes an increase.

Table 12.—ILLITERACY IN THE NEGRO POPULATION, BY AGE GROUPS, BY SECTIONS, AND SOUTHERN DIVISIONS: 1930

AGE	THE SOUTH												THE NORTH			THE WEST		
	Total number	Illiterate		South Atlantic division			East South Central division			West South Central division			Total number	Illiterate		Total number	Illiterate	
		Number	Percent	Total Number	Illiterate Number	Illiterate Percent	Total Number	Illiterate Number	Illiterate Percent	Total Number	Illiterate Number	Illiterate Percent		Number	Percent		Number	Percent
10 years and over	**7, 194, 750**	**1, 416, 417**	**19. 7**	**3, 363, 864**	**662, 055**	**19. 7**	**2, 052, 951**	**452, 082**	**22. 0**	**1, 777, 935**	**302, 280**	**17.0**	**1, 994, 085**	**94, 034**	**4. 7**	**103, 721**	**3, 441**	**3. 3**
10 to 14 years	1, 069, 120	65, 572	6. 1	529, 828	35, 337	6. 7	294, 215	18, 569	6. 3	245, 077	11, 666	4. 8	174, 430	643	. 4	7, 992	23	. 3
15 to 24 years	2, 017, 633	251, 105	12. 4	966, 776	129, 630	13. 4	567, 244	76, 115	13. 4	483, 613	45, 360	9. 4	418, 024	6, 181	1. 5	18, 062	175	1. 0
25 to 34 years	1, 373, 944	235, 232	17. 1	620, 460	109, 306	17. 6	388, 354	75, 151	19. 1	365, 130	51, 775	14. 2	538, 832	15, 451	2. 9	23, 525	343	1. 5
35 to 44 years	1, 126, 481	244, 638	21. 7	518, 055	112, 110	21. 6	314, 674	76, 980	24. 5	293, 752	55, 548	18. 9	427, 654	19, 305	4. 5	24, 188	598	2. 5
45 to 54 years	859, 101	254, 317	29. 6	388, 583	113, 391	29. 2	256, 838	84, 470	32. 9	213, 680	56, 456	26. 4	258, 371	19, 651	7. 6	17, 183	674	3. 9
55 to 64 years	435, 203	175, 299	40. 3	196, 587	77, 375	39. 4	133, 833	58, 830	44. 0	104. 783	39, 094	37. 3	108, 600	14, 025	12. 9	7, 763	605	7. 8
65 years and over	303, 826	188, 156	61. 9	138, 342	83, 789	60. 6	95, 350	62, 410	65. 5	70, 134	41, 957	59. 8	64, 255	18, 341	28. 5	4, 638	1, 009	21. 8
Unknown	9, 442	2, 098	22. 2	5, 233	1, 117	21. 3	2, 443	557	22. 8	1, 766	424	24. 0	3, 919	437	11. 2	370	14	3. 8

Table 13.—ILLITERACY OF NEGRO CHILDREN 10 TO 14 YEARS OF AGE, AND PERCENT OF ILLITERACY OF NEGRO AND WHITE CHILDREN, BY STATES: 1930

[Ranked as to percent illiterate in the Negro population. Percent not shown where base is less than 100]

STATE	CHILDREN 10 TO 14 YEARS OF AGE						
	Negro, 1930		Percent illiterate				
			Negro		White, 1930		
	Total	Illiterate	1930	1920	Native parentage	Foreign or mixed parentage	Foreign born
United States	**1, 251, 542**	**66, 238**	**5. 3**	**11. 4**	**0. 6**	**0. 2**	**0. 3**
South Carolina	111, 123	11, 753	10. 6	9. 0	2. 0	. 5	--------
Alabama	108, 934	10, 203	9. 4	15. 8	1. 6	. 3	--------
Florida	42, 116	3, 314	7. 9	13. 3	1. 0	. 3	. 2
Louisiana	84, 800	6, 553	7. 7	25. 4	2. 2	. 9	1. 9
Georgia	131, 393	9, 248	7. 0	15. 2	1. 6	. 1	--------
North Carolina	117, 763	6, 325	5. 4	7. 9	1. 1	. 2	. 8
Mississippi	116, 839	6, 042	5. 2	15. 5	1. 0	1. 4	--------
Virginia	78, 893	4, 130	5. 2	9. 8	1. 9	. 3	--------
Arkansas	52, 911	2, 291	4. 3	13. 3	1. 6	. 6	--------
Tennessee	48, 152	1, 813	3. 8	13. 7	1. 8	. 1	--------
Texas	89, 070	2, 438	2. 7	4. 5	. 5	. 8	2. 9
Kentucky	20, 290	511	2. 5	4. 0	2. 3	. 4	2. 1
Oklahoma	18, 296	384	2. 1	5. 1	. 7	. 3	--------
West Virginia	10, 444	158	1. 5	2. 2	1. 1	. 2	. 5
Maryland	25, 627	371	1. 4	5. 9	. 4	. 3	. 4
Missouri	16, 518	217	1. 3	3. 6	. 4	. 2	. 2
New Mexico	249	3	1. 2	3. 3	1. 2	. 6	--------
Maine	100	1	1. 0	------	. 4	. 3	. 2
Oregon	122	1	. 8	------	. 2	. 2	. 3
Arizona	727	5	. 7	. 4	. 2	. 4	--------
Delaware	2, 985	21	. 7	1. 6	. 3	. 1	--------
Iowa	1, 408	9	. 6	. 5	. 2	. 2	. 1
Colorado	757	3	. 4	1. 0	. 2	. 2	. 3
Ohio	24, 086	88	. 4	. 5	. 2	. 2	. 3
Connecticut	2, 347	6	. 3	. 3	. 1	. 1	. 3
New Jersey	16, 598	58	0. 3	0. 5	0. 2	0. 2	0. 3
New York	24, 624	63	. 3	. 4	. 2	. 2	. 3
Wisconsin	788	2	. 3	. 3	. 2	. 2	. 4
California	5, 422	9	. 2	. 6	. 1	. 2	. 2
District of Columbia	9, 484	17	. 2	. 4	. 1	. 1	--------
Illinois	22, 111	53	. 2	. 5	. 2	. 2	. 2
Indiana	8, 477	19	. 2	. 4	. 2	. 1	. 1
Michigan	11, 387	28	. 2	. 2	. 1	. 1	. 1
Pennsylvania	33, 028	81	. 2	. 5	. 2	. 2	. 3
Washington	421	1	. 2	. 3	. 2	. 3	. 1
Kansas	5, 608	8	. 1	. 4	. 2	. 2	--------
Massachusetts	4, 698	7	. 1	. 4	. 2	. 2	. 2
Nebraska	930	1	. 1	. 3	. 2	. 2	. 2
Idaho	35	--------	------	------	. 1	. 1	. 3
Minnesota	612	--------	------	. 2	. 2	. 2	. 2
Montana	90	1	------	------	. 1	. 1	. 3
Nevada	13	--------	------	------	. 1	. 3	--------
New Hampshire	48	--------	------	------	. 3	. 2	. 2
North Dakota	15	1	------	------	. 2	. 3	. 4
Rhode Island	938	--------	------	. 4	. 2	. 2	. 1
South Dakota	55	--------	------	------	. 2	. 2	--------
Utah	86	--------	------	------	. 1	. 2	--------
Vermont	54	1	------	------	. 3	. 4	. 2
Wyoming	70	--------	------	------	. 2	. 1	3. 1

TABLE 14.—ILLITERACY IN NEGRO POPULATION AND PERCENT ILLITERACY IN NEGRO AND WHITE POPULATION, BY SEX, AND AGE GROUPS, BY SECTIONS: 1930

AGE	NEGRO POPULATION: Total: Total number	Total: Illiterate: Number	Total: Illiterate: Percent	Male: Total number	Male: Illiterate: Number	Male: Illiterate: Percent	Female: Total number	Female: Illiterate: Number	Female: Illiterate: Percent	PERCENT WHITE POPULATION ILLITERATE: Total	Male	Female
UNITED STATES												
10 years and over [1]	**9,292,556**	**1,513,892**	**16.3**	**4,564,690**	**801,949**	**17.6**	**4,727,866**	**711,943**	**15.1**	**2.7**	**2.7**	**2.7**
10 to 14 years	1,251,542	66,238	5.3	623,228	39,766	6.4	628,314	26,472	4.2	.5	.6	.4
15 to 24 years	2,453,719	257,461	10.5	1,149,268	160,566	14.0	1,304,451	96,895	7.4	1.0	1.2	.7
25 to 34 years	1,936,301	251,026	13.0	917,389	140,221	15.3	1,018,912	110,805	10.9	1.7	1.7	1.7
35 to 44 years	1,578,323	264,541	16.8	769,801	133,047	17.3	808,522	131,494	16.3	3.6	3.4	3.8
45 to 54 years	1,134,655	274,642	24.2	600,694	139,161	23.2	533,961	135,481	25.4	4.6	4.5	4.6
55 to 64 years	551,566	189,929	34.4	307,716	95,468	31.0	243,850	94,461	38.7	4.9	4.8	5.1
65 years and over	372,719	207,506	55.7	189,530	92,630	48.9	183,189	114,876	62.7	6.5	6.0	7.0
THE SOUTH												
10 years and over [1]	**7,194,750**	**1,416,417**	**19.7**	**3,506,598**	**750,595**	**21.4**	**3,688,152**	**665,822**	**18.1**	**3.8**	**4.4**	**3.3**
10 to 14 years	1,069,120	65,572	6.1	534,203	39,396	7.4	534,917	26,176	4.9	1.3	1.5	1.0
15 to 24 years	2,017,633	251,105	12.4	947,642	156,873	16.6	1,069,991	94,232	8.8	2.2	3.1	1.4
25 to 34 years	1,373,944	235,232	17.1	636,804	130,707	20.5	737,140	104,525	14.2	2.9	3.7	2.2
35 to 44 years	1,126,481	244,638	21.7	531,687	121,555	22.9	594,794	123,083	20.7	4.1	4.7	3.6
45 to 54 years	859,101	254,317	29.6	450,780	128,222	28.4	408,321	126,095	30.9	5.7	6.2	5.0
55 to 64 years	435,203	175,299	40.3	244,855	88,425	36.1	190,348	86,874	45.6	7.1	7.3	6.8
65 years and over	303,826	188,156	61.9	155,919	84,510	54.2	147,907	103,646	70.1	10.6	10.1	11.2
THE NORTH												
10 years and over [1]	**1,994,085**	**94,034**	**4.7**	**1,005,003**	**49,720**	**4.9**	**989,082**	**44,314**	**4.5**	**2.6**	**2.4**	**2.8**
10 to 14 years	174,430	643	.4	85,105	358	.4	89,325	285	.3	.2	.2	.2
15 to 24 years	418,024	6,181	1.5	192,935	3,587	1.9	225,089	2,594	1.2	.5	.5	.5
25 to 34 years	538,832	15,451	2.9	269,046	9,328	3.5	269,786	6,123	2.3	1.4	1.2	1.7
35 to 44 years	427,654	19,305	4.5	225,531	11,169	5.0	202,123	8,136	4.0	3.7	3.3	4.3
45 to 54 years	258,371	19,651	7.6	140,507	10,601	7.5	117,864	9,050	7.7	4.6	4.4	4.9
55 to 64 years	108,600	14,025	12.9	58,528	6,773	11.6	50,072	7,252	14.5	4.7	4.4	5.0
65 years and over	64,255	18,341	28.5	31,235	7,727	24.7	33,020	10,614	32.1	5.8	5.4	6.3
THE WEST												
10 years and over [1]	**103,721**	**3,441**	**3.3**	**53,089**	**1,634**	**3.1**	**50,632**	**1,807**	**3.6**	**1.3**	**1.2**	**1.4**
10 to 14 years	7,992	23	.3	3,920	12	.3	4,072	11	.3	.2	.2	.2
15 to 24 years	18,062	175	1.0	8,691	106	1.2	9,371	69	.7	.4	.4	.4
25 to 34 years	23,525	343	1.5	11,539	186	1.6	11,986	157	1.3	.8	.8	.9
35 to 44 years	24,188	598	2.5	12,583	323	2.6	11,605	275	2.4	1.5	1.4	1.7
45 to 54 years	17,183	674	3.9	9,407	338	3.6	7,776	336	4.3	1.9	1.8	2.1
55 to 64 years	7,763	605	7.8	4,333	270	6.2	3,430	335	9.8	2.3	2.0	2.5
65 years and over	4,638	1,009	21.8	2,376	393	16.5	2,262	616	27.2	3.0	2.7	3.4

[1] Includes persons of unknown age.

TABLE 15.—ILLITERACY IN THE NEGRO POPULATION 10 YEARS OLD AND OVER, BY SEX, BY SECTIONS, AND SOUTHERN DIVISIONS: 1930, 1920, AND 1910

[A plus sign (+) denotes increase]

CENSUS YEAR	THE SOUTH: Total	Male	Female	South Atlantic division: Total	Male	Female	East South Central division: Total	Male	Female	West South Central division: Total	Male	Female	THE NORTH: Total	Male	Female	THE WEST: Total	Male	Female
NUMBER ILLITERATE																		
1930	1,416,417	750,595	665,822	662,055	353,459	303,596	452,082	240,348	211,734	302,280	156,788	145,492	94,034	49,720	44,314	3,441	1,634	1,807
1920	1,751,658	895,490	856,168	812,842	417,569	395,273	536,583	274,925	261,658	402,233	202,996	199,237	87,133	45,136	41,997	3,370	1,742	1,628
1910	2,133,961	1,051,239	1,082,722	969,432	477,107	492,325	681,507	337,893	343,614	483,022	236,239	246,783	90,659	43,255	47,404	3,111	1,506	1,605
PERCENT ILLITERATE																		
1930	19.7	21.4	18.1	19.7	21.7	17.8	22.0	24.0	20.1	17.0	17.9	16.1	4.7	4.9	4.5	3.3	3.1	3.6
1920	26.0	27.0	25.1	25.2	26.3	24.1	27.9	29.1	26.7	25.3	25.6	25.0	7.0	7.0	7.0	4.9	4.4	5.6
1910	33.3	33.1	33.5	32.5	32.4	32.5	34.8	34.8	34.7	33.1	32.2	33.9	10.5	9.9	11.1	7.0	6.1	8.2
DECREASE IN NUMBER ILLITERATE																		
1930	335,241	144,895	190,346	150,787	64,110	86,677	84,501	34,577	49,924	99,953	46,208	53,745	+6,901	+4,584	+2,317	+71	108	+179
1920	382,303	155,749	226,554	156,590	59,538	97,052	144,924	62,968	81,956	80,789	33,243	47,546	3,526	+1,881	5,407	+259	+236	+23
1910	583,645	255,070	328,575	280,847	122,053	158,794	206,331	92,091	114,240	96,467	40,926	55,541	41,530	20,124	21,406	288	238	50

Table 16.—Illiteracy in the Negro Population 10 Years Old and Over, by Sex, and Age Groups, for the United States: 1900 to 1930

Age and census year	Illiterate					
	Number			Percent		
	Total	Male	Female	Total	Male	Female
10 years and over:						
1930	1,513,892	801,949	711,943	16.3	17.6	15.1
1920	1,842,161	942,368	899,793	22.9	23.5	22.3
1910	2,227,731	1,096,000	1,131,731	30.4	30.1	30.7
1900	2,853,194	1,371,432	1,481,762	44.5	43.1	45.8
10 to 14 years:						
1930	66,238	39,766	26,472	5.3	6.4	4.2
1920	140,892	81,944	58,948	11.4	13.3	9.5
1910	218,555	125,616	92,939	18.9	21.7	16.1
1900	328,992	183,540	145,452	30.1	33.5	26.8
15 to 19 years:						
1930	111,111	72,986	38,125	8.9	12.3	5.8
1920	152,998	94,455	58,543	14.1	18.4	10.3
1910	214,860	126,459	88,401	20.3	24.9	16.0
1900	312,094	173,891	138,203	31.8	36.7	27.2
20 to 24 years:						
1930	146,350	87,580	58,770	12.2	15.8	9.0
1920	179,124	96,895	82,229	17.0	19.9	14.5
1910	245,860	126,970	118,890	23.9	26.3	21.7
1900	340,516	165,085	175,431	35.1	36.0	34.4
25 to 34 years:						
1930	251,026	140,221	110,805	13.0	15.3	10.9
1920	287,063	143,515	143,548	17.9	19.0	16.9
1910	380,742	183,993	196,749	24.6	24.4	24.7
1900	496,180	222,516	273,664	39.3	35.7	42.8
35 to 44 years:						
1930	264,541	133,047	131,494	16.8	17.3	16.3
1920	310,538	144,961	165,577	23.3	22.0	24.6
1910	351,858	152,132	199,726	32.3	27.7	37.1
1900	437,503	177,199	260,304	52.0	43.0	60.6
45 to 54 years:						
1930	274,642	139,161	135,481	24.2	23.2	25.4
1920	323,924	164,954	158,970	34.1	30.1	38.5
1910	334,930	147,542	187,388	47.0	38.9	56.3
1900	420,438	191,883	228,555	68.1	59.3	77.8
55 to 64 years:						
1930	189,929	95,468	94,461	34.4	31.0	38.7
1920	212,682	103,407	109,275	49.4	42.9	57.9
1910	249,584	120,046	129,538	63.0	55.5	72.0
1900	267,312	134,535	132,777	78.4	73.4	84.3
65 and over:						
1930	207,506	92,630	114,876	55.7	48.9	62.7
1920	227,310	108,473	118,837	68.3	62.4	74.8
1910	219,255	107,877	111,378	74.5	70.7	78.6
1900	223,124	111,158	111,966	85.4	83.6	87.2
Unknown:						
1930	2,549	1,090	1,459	18.6	15.4	21.9
1920	7,630	3,764	3,866	32.5	27.9	38.7
1910	12,087	5,365	6,722	38.9	31.4	48.1
1900	27,035	11,625	15,410	55.4	46.2	65.1

Table 17.—Illiteracy in the Negro Population 10 Years Old and Over, by Sex, by Sections, and Divisions: 1930

Section and division	Total male	Total female	Illiterate			
			Number		Percent	
			Male	Female	Male	Female
United States	**4,564,690**	**4,727,866**	**801,949**	**711,943**	**17.6**	**15.1**
The South	3,506,598	3,688,152	750,595	665,822	21.4	18.1
South Atlantic	1,632,260	1,731,604	353,459	308,596	21.7	17.8
East South Central	999,448	1,053,503	240,348	211,734	24.0	20.1
West South Central	874,890	903,045	156,788	145,492	17.9	16.1
The North	1,005,003	989,082	49,720	44,314	4.9	4.5
New England	37,838	37,881	2,211	1,976	5.8	5.2
Middle Atlantic	429,276	438,599	16,861	15,362	3.9	3.5
East North Central	396,907	374,719	19,576	16,878	4.9	4.5
West North Central	140,982	137,883	11,072	10,098	7.9	7.3
The West	53,089	50,632	1,634	1,807	3.1	3.6
Mountain	14,203	11,789	552	518	3.9	4.4
Pacific	38,886	38,843	1,082	1,289	2.8	3.3

Table 18.—Percent Illiterate in Negro Population 10 Years Old and Over, 1930, 1920, and 1910, and in Native and Foreign-Born White Population, by States: 1930

[Ranked as to percent illiterate in the Negro population, 1930]

State	Negro population			White population, 1930		
				Native white		Foreign born
	1930	1920	1910	Native parentage	Foreign or mixed parentage	
United States	**16.3**	**22.9**	**30.4**	**1.8**	**0.6**	**9.9**
South Carolina	26.9	29.3	38.7	5.2	.9	5.7
Alabama	26.2	31.3	40.1	4.9	1.4	8.5
Louisiana	23.3	38.5	48.4	7.8	2.7	19.2
Mississippi	23.2	29.3	35.6	2.7	1.8	12.6
North Carolina	20.6	24.5	31.9	5.7	1.2	5.2
Georgia	19.9	29.1	36.5	3.4	.7	4.0
Virginia	19.2	23.5	30.0	5.0	.8	7.4
Florida	18.8	21.5	25.5	2.0	.8	5.4
Arkansas	16.1	21.8	26.4	3.5	1.9	6.6
Kentucky	15.4	21.0	27.6	5.9	1.0	5.8
Tennessee	14.9	22.4	27.3	5.4	1.1	5.8
Texas	13.4	17.8	24.6	1.4	2.1	7.3
Delaware	13.2	19.1	25.6	1.4	.5	14.3
Maryland	11.4	18.2	23.4	1.4	.9	12.2
West Virginia	11.3	15.3	20.3	3.8	1.1	19.2
Oklahoma	9.3	12.4	17.7	1.8	.9	5.6
Missouri	8.8	12.1	17.4	1.6	.8	7.5
Rhode Island	8.1	10.2	9.5	.5	.9	14.3
Ohio	6.4	8.1	11.1	.8	.5	11.6
Indiana	6.0	9.5	13.7	1.0	.8	10.1
New Mexico	6.0	4.3	14.2	8.2	1.5	6.8
Kansas	5.9	8.8	12.0	.5	.6	5.9
Iowa	5.4	8.1	10.3	.5	.4	3.6
Massachusetts	5.4	6.8	8.1	.3	.5	10.7
New Jersey	5.1	6.1	9.9	.5	.5	12.9
Connecticut	4.9	6.2	6.3	.3	.4	14.6
Vermont	4.9	6.2	4.8	1.0	2.0	7.2
Maine	4.8	5.9	8.0	1.4	2.1	8.5
Montana	4.6	6.0	7.0	.3	.3	4.3
Wisconsin	4.4	4.1	4.5	.4	.8	7.8
Idaho	4.2	5.4	6.4	.4	.4	4.0
Pennsylvania	4.2	6.1	9.1	.6	.5	15.4
Wyoming	4.2	5.3	5.0	.3	.3	4.2
District of Columbia	4.1	8.6	13.5	.2	.2	4.8
Arizona	4.0	4.6	7.2	.5	.5	3.6
Colorado	3.9	6.2	8.6	1.0	.4	8.6
Nebraska	3.9	4.8	7.2	.4	.4	6.0
New Hampshire	3.9	6.7	10.6	.6	1.1	9.6
Illinois	3.6	6.7	10.5	.7	.4	9.0
North Dakota	3.4	4.0	4.8	.3	.5	4.4
Utah	3.2	4.6	4.8	.3	.3	3.6
California	3.1	4.7	7.1	.3	.3	5.7
Michigan	3.0	4.2	5.7	.5	.6	6.7
Washington	2.9	4.0	4.3	.3	.3	2.9
New York	2.5	2.9	5.0	.6	.4	10.8
Oregon	2.5	4.7	3.4	.3	.3	3.6
South Dakota	2.2	5.2	5.5	.3	.5	3.7
Minnesota	2.0	3.1	3.4	.3	.5	4.3
Nevada	1.5	5.1	5.5	.2	.3	7.5

Table 19.—Illiteracy per 1,000 Population (Negro and White), 10 Years Old and Over, by Sections, and Southern Divisions: 1930, 1920, and 1910

Census year	United States	The South				The North	The West
		Total	South Atlantic division	East South Central division	West South Central division		
NEGRO							
1930	163	197	197	220	170	47	33
1920	229	260	252	279	253	70	49
1910	304	333	325	348	331	105	70
Decrease: **1910–30**	141	136	128	128	161	58	37
WHITE							
1930	27	38	39	50	28	26	13
1920	40	59	54	65	59	35	28
1910	50	80	78	92	72	41	33
Decrease: **1910–30**	23	42	39	42	44	15	20

Table 20.—Ratios of Illiteracy in the Negro and White Population 10 Years Old and Over, by Age Groups, for the United States: 1930, 1920, and 1910

Census year	10 years old and over [1]	10 to 14 years	15 to 19 years	20 to 24 years	25 to 34 years	35 to 44 years	45 to 54 years	55 to 64 years	65 years and over
	NEGRO								
	Illiteracy per 1,000 population of age specified								
1930	163	53	89	122	130	168	242	344	557
1920	229	114	141	170	179	233	341	494	683
1910	304	189	203	239	246	323	470	630	745
	DECREASE IN ILLITERACY PER 1,000 POPULATION								
1910-30	141	136	114	117	116	155	228	286	188
1920-30	66	61	52	48	49	65	99	150	126
1910-20	75	75	62	69	67	90	129	136	62
	WHITE								
	Illiteracy per 1,000 population of age specified								
1930	27	5	8	11	17	36	46	49	65
1920	40	11	15	25	43	52	55	61	77
1910	50	18	28	46	52	54	63	74	94
	Decrease in illiteracy per 1,000 population								
1910-30	23	13	20	35	35	18	17	25	29
1920-30	13	6	7	14	26	16	9	12	12
1910-20	10	7	13	21	9	2	8	13	17

[1] Includes persons of unknown ages.

Table 21.—Illiteracy in the Negro and White Population 10 Years Old and Over in the 15 Cities Having Over 50,000 Negro Inhabitants: 1930

City	Total Negro population	Negro: Total number	Negro: Illiterate: Number	Negro: Illiterate: Percent	White: Total number	White: Illiterate: Number	White: Illiterate: Percent
New York, N. Y	327, 706	276, 421	5, 722	2. 1	5, 527, 118	255, 533	4. 6
Chicago, Ill	233, 903	199, 233	4, 319	2. 2	2, 628, 156	82, 997	3. 2
Philadelphia, Pa	219, 599	181, 641	5, 432	3. 0	1, 449, 682	37, 266	2. 6
Baltimore, Md	142, 106	116, 779	8, 194	7. 0	549, 885	12, 588	2. 3
Washington, D. C	132, 068	111, 224	4, 591	4. 1	306, 953	1, 944	. 6
New Orleans, La	129, 632	105, 544	14, 107	13. 4	270, 137	6, 212	2. 3
Detroit, Mich	120, 066	99, 247	2, 688	2. 7	1, 168, 042	25, 353	2. 2
Birmingham, Ala	99, 077	80, 997	11, 875	14. 7	130, 931	1, 300	1. 0
Memphis, Tenn	96, 550	81, 999	6, 681	8. 1	130, 300	722	. 6
St. Louis, Mo	93, 580	79, 958	4, 133	5. 2	620, 206	8, 002	1. 3
Atlanta, Ga	90, 075	74, 671	7, 801	10. 4	150, 460	1, 478	1. 0
Cleveland, Ohio	71, 899	58, 975	2, 595	4. 4	687, 814	28, 685	4. 2
Houston, Tex	63, 337	53, 648	3, 792	7. 1	179, 282	1, 375	. 8
Pittsburgh, Pa	54, 983	45, 014	1, 555	3. 5	505, 112	12, 654	2. 5
Richmond, Va	52, 988	43, 023	5, 389	12. 5	109, 245	976	. 9

Table 22.—PERCENT ILLITERATE IN THE NEGRO POPULATION 10 YEARS OLD AND OVER, BY SEX, AND AGE GROUPS, BY SECTIONS, AND SOUTHERN DIVISIONS: 1930 AND 1920

Age and census year	United States: Total	United States: Male	United States: Female	The South: Total	The South: Male	The South: Female	South Atlantic division: Total	South Atlantic division: Male	South Atlantic division: Female	East South Central division: Total	East South Central division: Male	East South Central division: Female	West South Central division: Total	West South Central division: Male	West South Central division: Female	The North: Total	The North: Male	The North: Female	The West: Total	The West: Male	The West: Female
10 years old and over: [1]																					
1930	16. 3	17. 6	15. 1	19. 7	21. 4	18. 1	19. 7	21. 7	17. 8	22. 0	24. 0	20. 1	17. 0	17. 9	16. 1	4. 7	4. 9	4. 5	3. 3	3. 1	3. 6
1920	22. 9	23. 5	22. 3	26. 0	27. 0	25. 1	25. 2	26. 3	24. 1	27. 9	29. 1	26. 7	25. 3	25. 6	25. 0	7. 0	7. 0	7. 0	4. 9	4. 4	5. 6
10 to 14 years:																					
1930	5. 3	6. 4	4. 2	6. 1	7. 4	4. 9	6. 7	8. 2	5. 2	6. 3	7. 5	5. 1	4. 8	5. 5	4. 1	. 4	. 4	. 3	. 3	. 3	. 3
1920	11. 4	13. 3	9. 5	12. 4	14. 5	10. 4	10. 6	12. 7	8. 6	14. 5	16. 8	12. 1	13. 7	15. 4	12. 1	. 9	1. 0	. 7	. 8	1. 1	. 5
15 to 24 years:																					
1930	10. 5	14. 0	7. 4	12. 4	16. 6	8. 8	13. 4	18. 1	9. 2	13. 4	17. 8	9. 6	9. 4	12. 0	7. 1	1. 5	1. 9	1. 2	1. 0	1. 2	. 7
1920	15. 5	19. 1	12. 4	17. 6	21. 7	13. 9	17. 6	22. 0	13. 7	17. 9	22. 4	14. 0	17. 2	20. 4	14. 4	2. 4	3. 1	1. 7	2. 0	2. 7	1. 1
25 to 34 years:																					
1930	13. 0	15. 3	10. 9	17. 1	20. 5	14. 2	17. 6	21. 2	14. 6	19. 1	23. 3	15. 5	14. 2	16. 5	12. 1	2. 9	3. 5	2. 3	1. 5	1. 6	1. 3
1920	17. 9	19. 0	16. 9	21. 7	23. 9	20. 2	21. 3	23. 2	19. 7	23. 1	25. 2	21. 3	20. 8	21. 9	19. 9	3. 8	4. 3	3. 2	2. 6	2. 9	2. 2
35 to 44 years:																					
1930	16. 8	17. 3	16. 3	21. 7	22. 9	20. 7	21. 6	22. 8	20. 6	24. 5	26. 0	23. 1	18. 9	19. 8	18. 1	4. 5	5. 0	4. 0	2. 5	2. 6	2. 4
1920	23. 3	22. 0	24. 6	28. 0	26. 9	29. 1	27. 7	26. 6	28. 7	29. 5	28. 7	30. 3	27. 0	25. 5	28. 4	6. 0	6. 1	5. 9	3. 6	3. 6	3. 6
45 to 54 years:																					
1930	24. 2	23. 2	25. 4	29. 6	28. 4	30. 9	29. 3	28. 2	30. 3	32. 9	32. 1	33. 7	26. 4	24. 6	28. 5	7. 6	7. 5	7. 7	3. 9	3. 6	4. 3
1920	34. 1	30. 1	38. 5	39. 1	34. 5	45. 4	38. 6	34. 2	44. 3	41. 1	36. 9	46. 9	37. 6	32. 0	45. 8	11. 5	10. 6	12. 7	6. 9	5. 4	9. 1
55 to 64 years:																					
1930	34. 4	31. 0	38. 7	40. 3	36. 1	45. 6	39. 4	35. 4	44. 4	44. 0	40. 0	49. 1	37. 3	32. 5	43. 6	12. 9	11. 6	14. 5	7. 8	6. 2	9. 8
1920	49. 4	42. 9	57. 9	55. 0	47. 5	64. 6	54. 0	46. 7	63. 2	57. 1	49. 9	66. 5	54. 2	46. 1	64. 9	21. 4	18. 1	25. 3	13. 3	9. 8	18. 0
65 years and over:																					
1930	55. 7	48. 9	62. 7	61. 9	54. 2	70. 1	60. 6	53. 2	68. 2	65. 5	58. 2	73. 2	59. 8	50. 8	69. 6	28. 5	24. 7	32. 1	21. 8	16. 5	27. 2
1920	68. 3	62. 4	74. 8	73. 3	67. 0	80. 3	72. 3	66. 2	79. 1	74. 9	68. 8	81. 7	72. 9	66. 0	80. 9	39. 1	34. 1	44. 0	30. 9	23. 5	39. 9

[1] Includes persons of unknown age.

Table 23.—PERCENT ILLITERATE IN THE NEGRO, NATIVE WHITE, AND FOREIGN-BORN WHITE POPULATION 10 YEARS OLD AND OVER, BY AGE GROUPS, BY SECTIONS, AND SOUTHERN DIVISIONS: 1930 AND 1920

Age	The South: Negro	The South: Native white	The South: Foreign-born white	South Atlantic division: Negro	South Atlantic division: Native white	South Atlantic division: Foreign-born white	East South Central division: Negro	East South Central division: Native white	East South Central division: Foreign-born white	West South Central division: Negro	West South Central division: Native white	West South Central division: Foreign-born white	The North: Negro	The North: Native white	The North: Foreign-born white	The West: Negro	The West: Native white	The West: Foreign-born white
10 years and over: [1]																		
1930	19. 7	3. 7	9. 8	19. 7	3. 7	10. 4	22. 0	5. 0	7. 4	17. 0	2. 6	9. 4	4. 7	0. 6	10. 5	3. 3	0. 6	5. 1
1920	26. 0	5. 2	21. 5	25. 2	5. 1	12. 8	27. 9	6. 4	9. 1	25. 3	4. 1	29. 9	7. 0	. 8	12. 9	4. 9	1. 0	9. 8
10 to 14 years:																		
1930	6. 1	1. 3	. 8	6. 7	1. 2	. 3	6. 3	1. 8	. 7	4. 8	1. 0	2. 2	. 4	. 2	. 2	. 3	. 2	. 2
1920	12. 4	2. 5	26. 6	10. 6	2. 0	1. 5	14. 5	2. 6	3. 5	13. 7	3. 0	34. 3	. 9	. 2	. 9	. 8	. 4	6. 1
15 to 24 years:																		
1930	12. 4	2. 2	2. 5	13. 4	2. 2	2. 5	13. 4	3. 1	1. 8	9. 4	1. 6	2. 7	1. 5	. 4	2. 3	1. 0	. 4	1. 4
1920	17. 6	3. 4	24. 5	17. 6	3. 3	8. 2	17. 9	3. 8	7. 4	17. 2	3. 2	33. 4	2. 4	. 4	7. 7	2. 0	. 8	11. 4
25 to 34 years:																		
1930	17. 1	2. 9	5. 6	17. 6	2. 9	6. 2	19. 1	3. 8	4. 6	14. 2	2. 2	4. 6	2. 9	. 4	5. 9	1. 5	. 4	3. 7
1920	21. 7	4. 1	22. 7	21. 3	3. 9	15. 2	23. 1	5. 3	11. 3	20. 8	3. 5	31. 0	3. 8	. 5	15. 0	2. 6	. 8	11. 8
35 to 44 years:																		
1930	21. 7	3. 9	10. 5	21. 6	3. 9	11. 7	24. 5	5. 2	8. 8	18. 9	2. 9	8. 3	4. 5	. 6	12. 0	2. 5	. 6	5. 5
1920	28. 0	5. 5	21. 5	27. 7	5. 5	14. 8	29. 5	6. 9	10. 4	27. 0	4. 3	29. 5	6. 0	. 8	14. 7	3. 6	. 9	10. 3
45 to 54 years:																		
1930	29. 6	5. 4	11. 4	29. 2	5. 4	12. 9	32. 9	7. 2	8. 5	26. 4	3. 9	9. 7	7. 6	. 8	13. 0	3. 9	. 7	5. 8
1920	39. 1	7. 5	19. 9	38. 6	7. 4	12. 8	41. 1	10. 0	8. 7	37. 6	5. 4	27. 8	11. 5	1. 1	12. 9	6. 9	1. 3	8. 8
55 to 64 years:																		
1930	40. 3	6. 8	11. 1	39. 4	6. 8	12. 0	44. 0	9. 2	7. 9	37. 3	4. 8	11. 0	12. 9	1. 2	12. 5	7. 8	1. 0	5. 6
1920	55. 0	10. 2	18. 9	54. 0	10. 4	11. 6	57. 1	13. 2	7. 7	54. 2	7. 1	26. 8	21. 4	1. 8	12. 0	13. 3	1. 8	7. 5
65 years and over:																		
1930	61. 9	10. 5	12. 0	60. 6	10. 7	12. 1	65. 5	13. 7	7. 7	59. 8	7. 3	13. 3	28. 5	2. 3	13. 2	21. 8	1. 6	6. 1
1920	73. 3	13. 1	17. 6	72. 3	13. 5	11. 1	74. 9	16. 3	8. 4	72. 9	9. 0	25. 2	39. 1	2. 9	12. 7	30. 9	2. 5	8. 7

[1] Includes persons of unknown age.

TABLE 24.—ILLITERACY IN NEGRO POPULATION 10 YEARS OLD AND OVER, AND PERCENT ILLITERATE IN THE NEGRO AND WHITE POPULATION, IN THE URBAN, RURAL-FARM, AND RURAL-NONFARM AREAS, BY SECTIONS, AND DIVISIONS: 1930

SECTION AND DIVISION	NEGRO POPULATION								PERCENT ILLITERATE								
					Illiterate				Negro population			White population					
												Native			Foreign born		
	Total	Urban	Rural-farm	Rural-nonfarm	Total	Urban	Rural-farm	Rural-nonfarm	Urban	Rural-farm	Rural-nonfarm	Urban	Rural-farm	Rural-nonfarm	Urban	Rural-farm	Rural-nonfarm
United States	**9,292,556**	**4,297,949**	**3,421,512**	**1,573,095**	**1,513,892**	**395,849**	**794,866**	**323,177**	**9.2**	**23.2**	**20.5**	**0.5**	**3.1**	**2.1**	**10.0**	**7.8**	**10.4**
The South	**7,194,750**	**2,443,536**	**3,365,279**	**1,385,935**	**1,416,417**	**321,664**	**788,339**	**306,414**	**13.2**	**23.4**	**22.1**	**1.2**	**5.6**	**4.1**	**8.9**	**11.3**	**11.9**
The North	**1,994,085**	**1,768,301**	**51,509**	**174,275**	**94,034**	**71,873**	**6,276**	**15,885**	**4.1**	**12.2**	**9.1**	**.4**	**.9**	**1.1**	**10.6**	**7.7**	**11.2**
The West	**103,721**	**86,112**	**4,724**	**12,885**	**3,441**	**2,312**	**251**	**878**	**2.7**	**5.3**	**6.8**	**.3**	**.9**	**1.2**	**4.2**	**7.4**	**6.2**
THE SOUTH																	
South Atlantic	3,363,864	1,194,595	1,393,012	776,257	662,055	157,917	329,032	175,106	13.2	23.6	22.6	1.3	6.0	4.2	9.8	8.9	12.8
East South Central	2,052,951	629,698	1,092,788	330,465	452,082	93,019	281,750	77,313	14.8	25.8	23.4	1.6	6.8	5.3	6.6	10.4	9.1
West South Central	1,777,935	619,243	879,479	279,213	302,280	70,728	177,557	53,995	11.4	20.2	19.3	1.0	4.0	2.9	7.8	12.3	10.5
THE NORTH																	
New England	75,719	65,712	937	9,070	4,187	3,089	85	1,013	4.7	9.1	11.2	.4	1.4	1.2	11.6	12.4	11.3
Middle Atlantic	867,875	777,703	8,719	81,453	32,223	25,644	674	5,905	3.3	7.7	7.2	.4	.8	1.0	11.9	14.5	15.2
East North Central	771,626	704,436	14,429	52,761	36,454	30,204	1,202	5,038	4.3	8.4	9.5	.4	.9	1.3	8.8	8.2	9.4
West North Central	278,865	220,450	27,424	30,991	21,170	12,936	4,305	3,929	5.9	15.7	12.7	.4	.9	1.1	5.6	4.0	4.8
THE WEST																	
Mountain	25,992	18,244	1,827	5,921	1,070	622	85	363	3.4	4.7	6.1	.6	1.5	2.0	4.9	5.9	6.5
Pacific	77,729	67,868	2,897	6,964	2,371	1,690	166	515	2.5	5.7	7.4	.2	.4	.6	4.1	8.1	6.1

TABLE 25.—COUNTIES IN WHICH 25 PERCENT OR MORE OF THE NEGRO POPULATION 10 YEARS OLD AND OVER IS ILLITERATE: 1930

[Counties having less than 1,000 Negro inhabitants 10 years old and over are omitted]

STATE AND COUNTY	ILLITERATE Number	ILLITERATE Percent
ALABAMA		
Autauga	2,922	36.2
Baldwin	1,395	27.4
Barbour	5,345	39.1
Bibb	1,478	28.8
Bullock	3,160	26.7
Butler	3,474	32.4
Chambers	3,583	27.1
Choctaw	2,422	28.8
Clarke	2,643	26.2
Coffee	1,620	32.3
Conecuh	2,426	30.2
Coosa	974	29.2
Crenshaw	1,606	30.4
Dale	1,001	25.4
Dallas	10,533	33.7
Elmore	3,377	32.3
Escambia	1,688	25.7
Geneva	800	27.7
Greene	5,234	42.4
Hale	4,411	30.5
Henry	3,085	39.9
Houston	2,835	28.0
Jackson	553	27.2
Lee	4,463	32.9
Limestone	2,564	34.3
Lowndes	5,095	35.0
Marengo	6,377	32.0
Marshall	331	33.4
Monroe	2,942	25.8
Montgomery	10,535	25.4
Perry	4,254	30.3
Pickens	3,040	34.6
Pike	3,609	32.9
Russell	4,872	34.7
Sumter	5,073	32.5
Tallapoosa	1,942	27.1
Washington	1,670	33.4
Wilcox	5,198	36.2
ARKANSAS		
Chicot	2,940	25.7
FLORIDA		
Baker	414	29.6
Bay	656	28.0
Calhoun	385	37.5
De Soto	311	25.4
Gadsden	4,445	34.0
Gulf	228	27.0
Hamilton	1,224	42.0
Hendry	329	27.2
Highlands	559	25.4
Jackson	3,327	34.8
Jefferson	2,182	31.5
Leon	2,841	27.0
Liberty	454	42.2
Madison	2,326	37.8
Okaloosa	238	29.8
Okeechobee	260	26.0
FLORIDA—continued		
Pasco	375	26.0
Suwannee	1,095	26.5
Taylor	1,536	36.4
GEORGIA		
Bacon	212	26.9
Baker	922	26.6
Bleckley	1,035	41.5
Brooks	2,170	26.2
Burke	5,082	29.5
Charlton	225	29.6
Clinch	609	25.3
Dodge	1,808	30.5
Dooly	2,052	27.4
Dougherty	2,713	26.1
Early	2,132	29.0
Emanuel	1,865	26.9
Grady	1,300	26.2
Houston	1,589	28.4
Jeff Davis	319	26.3
Johnson	1,479	40.4
Laurens	3,450	34.1
Lee	1,625	33.0
McDuffie	1,006	28.4
Macon	2,451	29.3
Marion	768	26.8
Miller	738	32.7
Mitchell	2,426	27.7
Oconee	459	25.9
Oglethorpe	1,282	27.1
Peach	1,471	29.1
Pulaski	997	26.0
Putnam	1,208	30.7
Screven	2,323	27.4
Sumter	3,427	25.7
Telfair	916	25.0
Toombs	956	26.0
Twiggs	999	27.1
Wilkinson	1,085	28.2
KENTUCKY		
Hart	276	26.3
Henry	253	26.9
Jessamine	449	28.2
Marion	325	29.2
Simpson	409	29.3
Washington	269	26.8
LOUISIANA		
Acadia	2,513	42.5
Ascension	1,386	25.6
Assumption	1,503	32.4
Avoyelles	1,899	26.1
Calcasieu	2,383	25.8
Catahoula	1,125	31.4
Concordia	1,999	27.1
Evangeline	2,074	52.8
Iberia	2,968	36.7
Iberville	2,853	28.7
Jefferson	1,554	25.4
LOUISIANA—continued		
Jefferson Davis	1,425	41.0
Lafayette	5,824	61.7
Lafourche	1,193	30.0
Morehouse	2,750	25.6
Natchitoches	4,945	34.0
Plaquemines	1,427	44.2
Pointe Coupee	3,507	37.5
Red River	1,991	35.4
Richland	2,951	28.8
Saint Charles	874	27.1
Saint James	1,501	26.1
Saint John the Baptist	1,582	29.9
Saint Landry	8,659	41.6
Saint Martin	2,545	46.9
Tensas	2,632	30.8
Terrebonne	1,828	30.1
Vermilion	1,414	44.2
West Baton Rouge	1,255	26.3
MARYLAND		
Charles	1,443	27.6
St. Marys	1,058	26.5
MISSISSIPPI		
Adams	3,689	29.9
Bolivar	11,276	27.1
Franklin	1,236	34.3
Holmes	6,136	28.3
Humphreys	3,538	27.1
Issaquena	1,259	34.0
Jefferson	2,496	30.5
Kemper	2,393	26.2
Madison	5,500	26.6
Marion	1,484	26.1
Panola	3,421	25.3
Pearl River	1,322	32.4
Perry	527	25.6
Simpson	1,412	27.5
Smith	632	25.0
Tallahatchie	4,595	25.1
Tate	2,039	25.4
Tunica	3,758	25.8
Washington	9,446	30.0
Wilkinson	1,924	26.9
Winston	1,496	25.9
NORTH CAROLINA		
Anson	2,850	26.5
Beaufort	3,169	31.4
Edgecombe	5,814	29.7
Greene	1,766	27.8
Hyde	705	29.1
Martin	2,073	27.2
Northampton	2,975	25.0
Person	1,735	29.2
Pitt	4,855	25.8
Scotland	2,426	31.4
Stokes	459	26.9
Wilson	3,715	26.6
SOUTH CAROLINA		
Abbeville	2,151	25.9
Aiken	4,365	26.7
Allendale	3,287	46.1
Bamberg	2,277	25.7
Barnwell	3,097	31.5
Beaufort	3,837	32.4
Berkeley	2,934	27.2
Charleston	12,729	30.4
Cherokee	1,790	29.1
Chesterfield	2,441	27.4
Clarendon	5,385	35.4
Colleton	2,900	28.8
Darlington	4,929	31.5
Dillon	2,478	29.2
Dorchester	2,436	30.1
Fairfield	3,865	34.8
Georgetown	4,075	40.0
Hampton	3,091	42.6
Jasper	1,690	34.6
Kershaw	3,140	25.3
Laurens	3,766	28.6
Lee	3,968	35.0
Marion	3,482	32.3
Marlboro	3,901	30.4
Orangeburg	7,433	25.5
Sumter	5,934	26.7
Williamsburg	4,039	25.3
TENNESSEE		
Coffee	274	26.0
Hickman	312	36.5
Lake	811	26.4
Trousdale	272	27.7
TEXAS		
Liberty	947	25.2
Rockwall	368	25.3
VIRGINIA		
Amherst	1,188	28.7
Buckingham	1,215	29.3
Charlotte	1,514	32.3
Cumberland	1,007	32.5
Dinwiddie	2,892	32.8
Franklin	721	26.3
Greensville	1,815	31.8
Henry	1,079	25.0
King William	729	25.4
Lancaster	785	26.1
Nelson	811	25.1
Patrick	322	33.3
Pittsylvania	3,801	25.9
Prince Edward	1,409	25.7
Rappahannock	376	26.5
Richmond	608	31.1
Sussex	1,927	32.8
Wise	717	28.7

TABLE 26.—ILLITERACY IN THE NEGRO AND WHITE POPULATION 10 YEARS OLD AND OVER IN THE 80 CITIES HAVING 10,000 OR MORE NEGRO INHABITANTS: 1930

CITY	Total Negro population	NEGRO			WHITE		
		Total number	Illiterate		Total number	Illiterate	
			Number	Percent		Number	Percent
ALABAMA							
Bessemer	11, 691	9, 459	1, 988	21. 0	7, 228	135	1. 9
Birmingham	99, 077	80, 997	11, 875	14. 7	130, 931	1, 300	1. 0
Mobile	24, 514	20, 314	3, 779	18. 6	36, 209	259	. 7
Montgomery	29, 970	24, 727	4, 928	19. 9	29, 414	140	6. 5
ARKANSAS							
Little Rock	19, 698	16, 847	1, 619	9. 6	52, 449	1, 049	2. 0
CALIFORNIA							
Los Angeles	38, 894	33, 651	774	2. 3	947, 505	6, 270	. 7
DELAWARE							
Wilmington	12, 080	10, 290	855	8. 3	78, 857	2, 162	2. 7
DISTRICT OF COLUMBIA							
Washington	132, 068	111, 224	4, 591	4. 1	306, 953	1, 944	. 6
FLORIDA							
Jacksonville	48, 196	40, 422	4, 116	10. 2	67, 006	520	. 8
Miami	25, 116	19, 731	2, 034	10. 3	71, 892	282	. 4
Tampa	21, 172	17, 719	1, 769	10. 0	65, 689	2, 094	3. 2
GEORGIA							
Atlanta	90, 075	74, 671	7, 801	10. 4	150, 460	1, 478	1. 0
Augusta	24, 190	20, 130	2, 822	14. 0	29, 331	532	1. 8
Columbus	14, 157	11, 513	1, 785	15. 5	23, 297	700	3. 0
Macon	23, 158	19, 034	2, 802	14. 7	25, 330	327	1. 3
Savannah	38, 896	32, 990	5, 602	17. 0	38, 186	188	. 5
ILLINOIS							
Chicago	233, 903	199, 233	4, 319	2. 2	2, 628, 156	82, 997	3. 2
East St. Louis	11, 536	9, 245	551	6. 0	51, 962	692	1. 3
INDIANA							
Gary	17, 922	14, 596	475	3. 3	63, 468	3, 157	5. 0
Indianapolis	43, 967	36, 605	2, 078	5. 7	269, 521	1, 721	. 6
KANSAS							
Kansas City	19, 872	16, 391	808	4. 9	80, 747	1, 215	1. 5
KENTUCKY							
Lexington	12, 759	10, 890	1, 431	13. 1	28, 112	357	1. 3
Louisville	47, 354	40, 717	3, 612	8. 9	215, 908	2, 120	1. 0
LOUISIANA							
Baton Rouge	10, 675	9, 023	1, 417	15. 7	16, 485	188	1. 1
Monroe	10, 112	8, 671	1, 459	16. 8	12, 915	131	1. 0
New Orleans	129, 632	105, 544	14, 107	13. 4	270, 137	6, 212	2. 3
Shreveport	27, 219	23, 057	2, 434	10. 6	40, 343	242	. 6
MARYLAND							
Baltimore	142, 106	116, 779	8, 194	7. 0	549, 885	12, 588	2. 3
MASSACHUSETTS							
Boston	20, 574	17, 306	321	1. 9	633, 672	20, 309	3. 2
MICHIGAN							
Detroit	120, 066	99, 247	2, 688	2. 7	1, 168, 042	25, 353	2. 2
MISSISSIPPI							
Jackson	19, 423	16, 109	3, 003	18. 6	24, 125	219	. 9
Meridian	11, 352	9, 186	1, 916	20. 9	16, 995	422	2. 5
Vicksburg	11, 915	10, 149	1, 788	17. 6	9, 127	83	. 9
MISSOURI							
Kansas City	38, 574	33, 945	1, 508	4. 4	308, 179	3, 204	1. 0
St. Louis	93, 580	79, 958	4, 133	5. 2	620, 206	8, 002	1. 3
NEBRASKA							
Omaha	11, 123	9, 352	350	3. 7	167, 196	2, 676	1. 6
NEW JERSEY							
Atlantic City	15, 611	13, 639	254	1. 9	43, 978	750	1. 7
Camden	11, 340	9, 026	402	4. 5	87, 794	3, 982	4. 5
Jersey City	12, 575	10, 153	256	2. 5	249, 980	10, 131	4. 1
Newark	38, 880	31, 324	1, 896	6. 1	332, 965	16, 681	5. 0
NEW YORK							
Buffalo	13, 563	11, 153	291	2. 6	461, 810	11, 083	2. 4
New York	327, 706	276, 421	5, 722	2. 1	5, 527, 118	255, 533	4. 6
NORTH CAROLINA							
Asheville	14, 255	11, 607	1, 080	9. 3	29, 148	419	1. 4
Charlotte	25, 163	20, 487	4, 095	20. 0	45, 809	714	1. 6
Durham	18, 717	15, 020	1, 972	13. 1	26, 190	723	2. 8
Greensboro	14, 050	11, 408	1, 265	11. 1	30, 903	650	2. 1
Raleigh	12, 575	10, 213	1, 666	16. 3	20, 540	461	2. 2
Wilmington	13, 106	10, 419	1, 860	17. 9	15, 353	248	1. 6
Winston-Salem	32, 566	26, 310	3, 826	14. 5	33, 186	927	2. 8
OHIO							
Akron	11, 080	8, 826	564	6. 4	195, 486	3, 456	1. 8
Cincinnati	47, 818	39, 721	2, 701	6. 8	343, 730	3, 204	. 9
Cleveland	71, 899	58, 975	2, 595	4. 4	687, 814	28, 685	4. 2
Columbus	32, 774	27, 356	2, 118	7. 7	217, 540	2, 774	1. 3
Dayton	17, 077	13, 860	875	6. 3	154, 351	1, 466	. 9
Toledo	13, 260	11, 036	606	5. 5	231, 237	3, 908	1. 7
Youngstown	14, 552	11, 315	719	6. 4	123, 965	5, 294	4. 3
OKLAHOMA							
Oklahoma City	14, 662	12, 403	550	4. 4	139, 065	538	. 4
Tulsa	15, 203	13, 068	394	3. 0	101, 423	377	. 4
PENNSYLVANIA							
Philadelphia	219, 599	181, 641	5, 432	3. 0	1, 449, 682	37, 266	2. 6
Pittsburgh	54, 983	45, 014	1, 555	3. 5	505, 112	12, 654	2. 5
SOUTH CAROLINA							
Charleston	28, 062	22, 222	5, 123	23. 1	27, 646	342	1. 2
Columbia	19, 519	16, 234	3, 600	22. 2	26, 544	624	2. 4
Greenville	10, 871	8, 750	1, 682	19. 2	14, 977	210	1. 4
TENNESSEE							
Chattanooga	33, 289	27, 543	3, 193	11. 6	69, 506	1, 331	1. 9
Knoxville	17, 093	14, 310	1, 329	9. 3	71, 080	2, 214	3. 1
Memphis	96, 550	81, 999	6, 681	8. 1	130, 300	722	. 6
Nashville	42, 836	36, 072	3, 555	9. 9	91, 619	998	1. 1
TEXAS							
Beaumont	18, 551	15, 009	2, 908	19. 4	31, 544	573	1. 8
Dallas	38, 742	32, 921	2, 183	6. 6	179, 809	1, 119	. 6
Fort Worth	22, 234	18, 905	1, 305	6. 9	113, 505	623	. 5
Galveston	13, 226	11, 273	953	8. 5	31, 444	338	1. 1
Houston	63, 337	53, 648	3, 792	7. 1	179, 282	1, 375	. 8
Port Arthur	10, 003	8, 014	1, 691	21. 1	30, 321	1, 217	4. 0
San Antonio	17, 978	15, 437	816	5. 3	111, 093	691	. 6
VIRGINIA							
Newport News	13, 281	10, 699	1, 119	10. 5	17, 328	205	1. 2
Norfolk	43, 942	36, 393	4, 135	11. 4	71, 617	831	1. 2
Petersburg	12, 600	10, 178	1, 671	16. 4	13, 121	243	1. 9
Portsmouth	18, 849	15, 272	2, 467	16. 2	22, 505	234	1. 0
Richmond	52, 988	43, 023	5, 389	12. 5	109, 245	976	. 9
Roanoke	12, 368	9, 972	1, 251	12. 5	45, 753	717	1. 6

TABLE 27.—ILLITERACY IN THE POPULATION 10 YEARS OLD AND OVER, BY COLOR, AND NATIVITY, BY SECTIONS, DIVISIONS, AND STATES: 1930

SECTION, DIVISION, AND STATE	ALL CLASSES, 10 YEARS OLD AND OVER			NEGRO			NATIVE WHITE—NATIVE PARENTAGE			NATIVE WHITE—FOREIGN OR MIXED PARENTAGE			FOREIGN-BORN WHITE		
	Total number	Illiterate		Total number	Illiterate		Total number	Illiterate		Total number	Illiterate		Total number	Illiterate	
		Number	Per-cent		Number	Per-cent		Number	Per-cent		Number	Per-cent		Number	Per-cent
United States	98, 723, 047	4, 283, 753	4. 3	9, 292, 556	1, 513, 892	16. 3	53, 876, 411	986, 469	1. 8	20, 887, 328	116, 665	0. 6	13, 216, 928	1, 304, 084	9. 9
The North	59, 722, 192	1, 600, 630	2. 7	1, 994, 085	94, 034	4. 7	28, 878, 967	199, 103	. 7	17, 423, 694	92, 891	. 5	11, 256, 622	1, 180, 152	10. 5
The South	29, 168, 784	2, 416, 175	8. 3	7, 194, 750	1, 416, 417	19. 7	19, 653, 355	750, 719	3. 8	1, 210, 870	16, 461	1. 4	527, 946	51, 524	9. 8
The West	9, 832, 071	266, 948	2. 7	103, 721	3, 441	3. 3	5, 344, 089	36, 647	. 7	2, 252, 764	7, 313	. 3	1, 432, 360	72, 408	5. 1
NEW ENGLAND	6, 707, 717	245, 270	3. 7	75, 719	4, 187	5. 5	2, 426, 051	14, 080	. 6	2, 388, 014	16, 049	. 7	1, 811, 951	210, 046	11. 6
Maine	642, 659	17, 172	2. 7	900	43	4. 8	405, 763	5, 745	1. 4	136, 817	2, 872	2. 1	98, 310	8, 393	8. 5
New Hampshire	382, 400	10, 231	2. 7	697	27	3. 9	188, 364	1, 155	. 6	111, 717	1, 211	1. 1	81, 496	7, 820	9. 6
Vermont	291, 614	6, 299	2. 2	445	22	4. 9	184, 029	1, 921	1. 0	65, 382	1, 340	2. 0	41, 695	3, 005	7. 2
Massachusetts	3, 509, 317	124, 158	3. 5	42, 356	2, 303	5. 4	1, 081, 327	3, 247	. 3	1, 339, 077	6, 405	. 5	1, 042, 889	111, 568	10. 7
Rhode Island	560, 253	27, 536	4. 9	7, 836	635	8. 2	155, 058	741	. 5	227, 909	1, 991	. 9	168, 975	24, 124	14. 3
Connecticut	1, 321, 474	59, 874	4. 5	23, 485	1, 157	4. 9	411, 510	1, 271	. 3	507, 112	2, 230	. 4	378, 586	55, 136	14. 6
MIDDLE ATLANTIC	21, 575, 741	757, 228	3. 5	867, 875	32, 223	3. 7	8, 882, 572	52, 050	. 6	6, 588, 731	30, 693	. 5	5, 206, 049	636, 479	12. 2
New York	10, 513, 933	388, 883	3. 7	347, 381	8, 604	2. 5	3, 487, 903	19, 712	. 6	3, 506, 583	14, 942	. 4	3, 150, 593	341, 345	10. 8
New Jersey	3, 330, 748	128, 022	3. 8	169, 214	8, 711	5. 1	1, 215, 349	6, 336	. 5	1, 109, 603	5, 236	. 5	833, 727	107, 192	12. 9
Pennsylvania	7, 731, 060	240, 323	3. 1	351, 280	14, 908	4. 2	4, 179, 320	26, 002	. 6	1, 972, 545	10, 515	. 5	1, 221, 729	187, 942	15. 4
EAST NORTH CENTRAL	20, 674, 201	442, 064	2. 1	771, 626	36, 454	4. 7	11, 127, 295	79, 697	. 7	5, 523, 505	30, 587	. 6	3, 183, 971	281, 645	8. 8
Ohio	5, 434, 261	123, 804	2. 3	252, 500	16, 213	6. 4	3, 409, 567	26, 588	. 8	1, 129, 731	5, 799	. 5	637, 535	74, 131	11. 6
Indiana	2, 638, 556	43, 721	1. 7	92, 873	5, 605	6. 0	2, 074, 526	19, 974	1. 0	329, 041	2, 536	. 8	133, 889	13, 536	10. 1
Illinois	6, 333, 046	153, 507	2. 4	277, 834	10, 044	3. 6	2, 894, 330	20, 559	. 7	1, 927, 218	7, 725	. 4	1, 206, 896	108, 984	9. 0
Michigan	3, 891, 914	76, 800	2. 0	139, 490	4, 201	3. 0	1, 749, 814	8, 102	. 5	1, 163, 116	6, 688	. 6	822, 302	55, 034	6. 7
Wisconsin	2, 376, 424	44, 232	1. 9	8, 929	391	4. 4	999, 058	4, 474	. 4	974, 399	7, 839	. 8	383, 349	29, 960	7. 8
WEST NORTH CENTRAL	10, 764, 533	156, 068	1. 4	278, 865	21, 170	7. 6	6, 443, 049	53, 276	. 8	2, 923, 444	15, 562	. 5	1, 054, 651	51, 982	4. 9
Minnesota	2, 076, 201	26, 302	1. 3	8, 155	160	2. 0	749, 956	2, 489	. 3	920, 427	4, 755	. 5	386, 654	16, 759	4. 3
Iowa	2, 007, 699	15, 879	. 8	14, 426	777	5. 4	1, 287, 834	5, 805	. 5	536, 941	2, 372	. 4	165, 045	5, 932	3. 6
Missouri	2, 984, 368	67, 905	2. 3	188, 664	16, 532	8. 8	2, 207, 328	35, 824	1. 6	435, 029	3, 428	. 8	148, 460	11, 183	7. 5
North Dakota	527, 000	7, 814	1. 5	326	11	3. 4	162, 873	477	. 3	252, 612	1, 286	. 5	104, 703	4, 649	4. 4
South Dakota	543, 564	6, 763	1. 2	546	12	2. 2	260, 453	706	. 3	200, 633	933	. 5	65, 422	2, 422	3. 7
Nebraska	1, 106, 139	12, 725	1. 2	11, 605	450	3. 9	644, 021	2, 362	. 4	328, 392	1, 400	. 4	114, 896	6, 924	6. 0
Kansas	1, 519, 562	18, 680	1. 2	55, 143	3, 228	5. 9	1, 130, 584	5, 613	. 5	249, 410	1, 388	. 6	69, 471	4, 113	5. 9
SOUTH ATLANTIC	12, 171, 945	1, 012, 523	8. 3	3, 363, 864	662, 055	19. 7	7, 970, 015	310, 381	3. 9	520, 335	4, 202	. 8	301, 423	31, 328	10. 4
Delaware	196, 776	7, 805	4. 0	26, 567	3, 496	13. 2	126, 685	1, 775	1. 4	26, 686	121	. 5	16, 761	2, 392	14. 3
Maryland	1, 324, 241	49, 910	3. 8	219, 809	25, 073	11. 4	823, 262	11, 561	1. 4	185, 935	1, 641	. 9	94, 392	11, 539	12. 2
District of Columbia	418, 941	6, 611	1. 6	111, 224	4, 591	4. 1	223, 849	439	. 2	53, 445	94	. 2	29, 659	1, 411	4. 8
Virginia	1, 872, 838	162, 588	8. 7	494, 429	95, 148	19. 2	1, 308, 282	65, 114	5. 0	45, 514	368	. 8	23, 617	1, 738	7. 4
West Virginia	1, 301, 752	62, 492	4. 8	89, 921	10, 173	11. 3	1, 088, 214	41, 657	3. 8	72, 313	819	1. 1	51, 007	9, 788	19. 2
North Carolina	2, 352, 014	236, 261	10. 0	673, 809	139, 105	20. 6	1, 644, 224	93, 205	5. 7	14, 028	167	1. 2	8, 663	450	5. 2
South Carolina	1, 292, 939	192, 878	14. 9	581, 085	156, 065	26. 9	694, 683	36, 143	5. 2	11, 188	103	. 9	5, 239	297	5. 7
Georgia	2, 238, 192	210, 736	9. 4	821, 083	163, 237	19. 9	1, 376, 840	46, 707	3. 4	26, 109	191	. 7	13, 822	554	4. 0
Florida	1, 174, 252	83, 242	7. 1	345, 937	65, 167	18. 8	683, 976	13, 780	2. 0	85, 117	698	. 8	58, 263	3, 159	5. 4
EAST SOUTH CENTRAL	7, 560, 382	727, 861	9. 6	2, 052, 951	452, 082	22. 0	5, 270, 886	268, 052	5. 1	176, 022	2, 078	1. 2	57, 287	4, 238	7. 4
Kentucky	2, 005, 492	131, 545	6. 6	185, 629	28, 553	15. 4	1, 707, 149	100, 763	5. 9	90, 846	932	1. 0	21, 722	1, 267	5. 8
Tennessee	2, 028, 109	145, 460	7. 2	382, 974	57, 251	14. 9	1, 597, 782	87, 025	5. 4	34, 174	381	1. 1	12, 945	754	5. 8
Alabama	2, 000, 653	251, 095	12. 6	719, 290	188, 673	26. 2	1, 232, 304	60, 512	4. 9	32, 974	447	1. 4	15, 615	1, 335	8. 5
Mississippi	1, 526, 128	199, 761	13. 1	765, 058	177, 605	23. 2	733, 651	19, 752	2. 7	18, 028	318	1. 8	7, 005	882	12. 6
WEST SOUTH CENTRAL	9, 436, 457	675, 791	7. 2	1, 777, 935	302, 280	17. 0	6, 412, 454	172, 286	2. 7	514, 513	10, 181	2. 0	169, 236	15, 958	9. 4
Arkansas	1, 419, 945	96, 818	6. 8	373, 273	60, 102	16. 1	1, 003, 629	35, 280	3. 5	32, 092	610	1. 9	10, 118	666	6. 6
Louisiana	1, 622, 868	219, 750	13. 5	598, 258	139, 393	23. 3	887, 914	69, 288	7. 8	96, 876	2, 615	2. 7	34, 712	6, 677	19. 2
Oklahoma	1, 845, 657	51, 102	2. 8	135, 069	12, 560	9. 3	1, 519, 969	26, 941	1. 8	93, 072	855	. 9	26, 642	1, 479	5. 6
Texas	4, 547, 987	308, 121	6. 8	671, 335	90, 225	13. 4	3, 000, 942	40, 777	1. 4	292, 473	6, 101	2. 1	97, 764	7, 136	7. 3
MOUNTAIN	2, 909, 644	120, 866	4. 2	25, 992	1, 070	4. 1	1, 727, 104	26, 730	1. 5	612, 674	2, 316	. 4	285, 935	15, 962	5. 6
Montana	434, 351	7, 303	1. 7	1, 128	52	4. 6	211, 971	536	. 3	134, 993	396	. 3	72, 405	3, 085	4. 3
Idaho	349, 148	3, 743	1. 1	599	25	4. 2	236, 823	873	. 4	76, 389	278	. 4	30, 188	1, 198	4. 0
Wyoming	178, 973	2, 895	1. 6	1, 118	47	4. 2	112, 565	283	. 3	38, 382	98	. 3	19, 536	811	4. 2
Colorado	835, 341	23, 141	2. 8	10, 280	403	3. 9	520, 669	5, 095	1. 0	177, 009	712	. 4	85, 092	7, 331	8. 6
New Mexico	314, 370	41, 845	13. 3	2, 328	140	6. 0	225, 095	18, 468	8. 2	17, 540	265	1. 5	7, 755	530	6. 8
Airzona	335, 029	33, 969	10. 1	9, 125	366	4. 0	164, 848	785	. 5	33, 009	175	. 5	15, 410	551	3. 6
Utah	386, 347	4, 640	1. 2	942	30	3. 2	217, 325	608	. 3	116, 954	344	. 3	43, 348	1, 547	3. 6
Nevada	76, 085	3, 330	4. 4	472	7	1. 5	37, 808	82	. 2	18, 398	48	. 3	12, 201	909	7. 5
PACIFIC	6, 922, 427	146, 082	2. 1	77, 729	2, 371	3. 1	3, 616, 985	9, 917	. 3	1, 640, 090	4, 997	. 3	1, 146, 425	56, 446	4. 9
Washington	1, 312, 529	13, 458	1. 0	5, 992	174	2. 9	693, 200	2, 020	. 3	345, 929	1, 011	. 3	240, 846	7, 103	2. 9
Oregon	803, 408	17, 814	1. 0	2, 000	49	2. 5	508, 895	1, 505	. 3	176, 999	538	. 3	104, 276	3, 743	3. 6
California	4, 806, 490	124, 810	2. 6	69, 737	2, 148	3. 1	2, 414, 890	6, 392	. 3	1, 117, 162	3, 448	. 3	801, 303	45, 600	5. 7

TABLE 28.—PERCENT ILLITERATE IN THE POPULATION 10 YEARS OLD AND OVER, BY SEX, COLOR, AND NATIVITY, BY SECTIONS, DIVISIONS, AND STATES: 1930, 1920, AND 1910

SECTION, DIVISION, AND STATE	ALL CLASSES, 10 YEARS OLD AND OVER									NEGRO			NATIVE WHITE—NATIVE PARENTAGE			NATIVE WHITE—FOREIGN OR MIXED PARENTAGE			FOREIGN-BORN WHITE		
	Total			Male			Female														
	1930	1920	1910	1930	1920	1910	1930	1920	1910	1930	1920	1910	1930	1920	1910	1930	1920	1910	1930	1920	1910
United States	4.3	6.0	7.7	4.4	6.0	7.6	4.3	5.9	7.8	16.3	22.9	30.4	1.8	2.5	3.7	0.6	0.8	1.1	9.9	13.1	12.7
The North	2.7	3.6	4.3	2.5	3.7	4.3	2.9	3.7	4.8	4.7	7.0	10.5	.7	.9	1.4	.5	.6	.9	10.5	12.9	12.7
The South	8.3	11.4	15.6	9.0	11.8	15.4	7.6	10.9	15.8	19.7	26.0	33.3	3.8	5.3	7.7	1.4	3.7	4.3	9.8	21.5	18.8
The West	2.7	3.6	4.4	2.6	3.5	4.4	2.9	3.6	4.4	3.3	4.9	7.0	.7	1.2	1.7	.3	.6	.8	5.1	9.8	9.5
NEW ENGLAND	3.7	4.9	5.3	3.4	4.8	5.3	3.9	5.0	5.2	5.5	7.1	7.8	.6	.6	.7	.7	.8	1.3	11.6	14.0	13.8
Maine	2.7	3.3	4.1	3.2	3.9	4.9	2.1	2.5	3.2	4.8	5.9	8.0	1.4	1.3	1.4	2.1	2.9	4.5	8.5	11.1	13.7
New Hampshire	2.7	4.4	4.6	2.8	4.5	5.2	2.5	4.2	4.1	3.9	6.7	10.6	.6	.6	.8	1.1	1.1	2.1	9.6	15.4	14.5
Vermont	2.2	3.0	3.7	2.6	3.6	4.4	1.7	2.4	3.1	4.9	6.2	4.8	1.0	1.1	1.2	2.0	2.8	4.0	7.2	11.3	13.1
Massachusetts	3.5	4.7	5.2	3.1	4.5	5.0	3.9	4.9	5.3	5.4	6.8	8.1	.3	.3	.4	.5	.5	.7	10.7	12.8	12.7
Rhode Island	4.9	6.5	7.7	4.4	6.0	7.4	5.4	7.0	8.0	8.1	10.2	9.5	.5	.5	.7	.9	.9	1.8	14.3	16.5	17.3
Connecticut	4.5	6.2	6.0	3.9	5.8	5.7	5.1	6.6	6.3	4.9	6.2	6.3	.3	.4	.5	.4	.4	.8	14.6	17.0	15.4
MIDDLE ATLANTIC	3.5	4.9	5.7	3.1	4.7	5.6	3.9	5.1	5.7	3.7	5.0	7.9	.6	.7	1.2	.5	.5	.8	12.2	15.7	15.8
New York	3.7	5.1	5.5	3.1	4.5	5.0	4.3	5.6	5.9	2.5	2.9	5.0	.6	.6	.8	.4	.5	.7	10.8	14.2	13.7
New Jersey	3.8	5.1	5.6	3.5	4.9	5.5	4.2	5.3	5.7	5.1	6.1	9.9	.5	.7	1.1	.5	.4	.7	12.9	15.3	14.7
Pennsylvania	3.1	4.6	5.9	2.9	4.7	6.4	3.3	4.5	5.4	4.2	6.1	9.1	.6	.8	1.4	.5	.6	1.1	15.4	18.9	20.1
EAST NORTH CENTRAL	2.1	2.9	3.4	2.1	3.0	3.5	2.2	2.8	3.3	4.7	7.3	11.0	.7	1.0	1.7	.6	.6	.9	8.8	10.8	10.1
Ohio	2.3	2.8	3.2	2.3	3.0	3.5	2.2	2.6	3.0	6.4	8.1	11.1	.8	1.0	1.7	.5	.6	.9	11.6	12.6	11.5
Indiana	1.7	2.2	3.1	1.8	2.4	3.2	1.5	2.0	2.9	6.0	9.5	13.7	1.0	1.4	2.2	.8	1.0	1.4	10.1	11.8	11.7
Illinois	2.4	3.4	3.7	2.3	3.3	3.7	2.6	3.4	3.8	3.6	6.7	10.5	.7	1.1	1.7	.4	.4	.6	9.0	11.0	10.1
Michigan	2.0	3.0	3.3	1.9	3.1	3.6	2.1	2.9	3.1	3.0	4.2	5.7	.5	.6	1.0	.6	.7	1.2	6.7	9.9	9.3
Wisconsin	1.9	2.4	3.2	1.8	2.5	3.1	1.9	2.4	3.2	4.4	4.1	4.5	.4	.5	.6	.8	.8	1.0	7.8	8.4	8.7
WEST NORTH CENTRAL	1.4	2.0	2.9	1.5	2.0	2.9	1.4	1.9	2.9	7.6	10.5	14.9	.8	1.1	1.7	.5	.5	.7	4.9	6.4	7.6
Minnesota	1.3	1.8	3.0	1.2	1.8	2.9	1.3	1.9	3.1	2.0	3.1	3.4	.3	.4	.4	.5	.5	.6	4.3	5.4	7.6
Iowa	.8	1.1	1.7	.8	1.2	1.7	.7	1.0	1.7	5.4	8.1	10.3	.5	.5	.9	.4	.4	.6	3.6	4.9	6.3
Missouri	2.3	3.0	4.3	2.6	3.3	4.4	2.0	2.8	4.2	8.8	12.1	17.4	1.6	2.2	3.4	.8	.9	1.2	7.5	9.6	10.1
North Dakota	1.5	2.1	3.1	1.4	1.9	2.8	1.6	2.4	3.5	3.4	4.0	4.8	.3	.3	.3	.5	.5	.7	4.4	5.6	6.3
South Dakota	1.2	1.7	2.9	1.1	1.5	2.5	1.4	1.9	3.3	2.2	5.2	5.5	.3	.3	.3	.5	.5	.4	3.7	4.7	5.0
Nebraska	1.2	1.4	1.9	1.1	1.3	1.9	1.2	1.4	2.0	3.9	4.8	7.2	.4	.4	.6	.4	.4	.5	6.0	6.4	7.1
Kansas	1.2	1.6	2.2	1.3	1.7	2.3	1.2	1.6	2.1	5.9	8.8	12.0	.5	.6	.8	.6	.5	.8	5.9	10.5	10.5
SOUTH ATLANTIC	8.3	11.5	16.0	9.2	12.1	16.0	7.5	11.0	16.1	19.7	25.2	32.5	3.9	5.4	8.0	.8	.9	1.2	10.4	12.8	13.5
Delaware	4.0	5.9	8.1	4.2	6.2	8.4	3.8	5.5	7.8	13.2	19.1	25.6	1.4	2.0	3.3	.5	.6	.9	14.3	17.3	19.8
Maryland	3.8	5.6	7.2	4.1	5.7	7.2	3.5	5.4	7.1	11.4	18.2	23.4	1.4	2.0	3.0	.9	.9	1.0	12.2	13.4	11.9
District of Columbia	1.6	2.8	4.9	1.4	2.5	4.1	1.7	3.0	5.7	4.1	8.6	13.5	.2	.3	.6	.2	.2	.4	4.8	6.1	8.2
Virginia	8.7	11.2	15.2	10.0	12.1	15.7	7.4	10.2	14.6	19.2	23.5	30.0	5.0	6.1	8.2	.8	1.0	1.2	7.4	7.1	9.2
West Virginia	4.8	6.4	8.3	5.5	7.2	8.8	4.1	5.6	7.7	11.3	15.3	20.3	3.8	4.8	6.7	1.1	1.5	2.0	19.2	24.0	23.9
North Carolina	10.0	13.1	18.5	11.2	13.7	18.2	8.9	12.5	18.7	20.6	24.5	31.9	5.7	8.2	12.3	1.2	1.9	3.0	5.2	6.8	8.3
South Carolina	14.9	18.1	25.7	15.8	18.3	25.0	14.1	17.9	26.3	26.9	29.3	38.7	5.2	6.6	10.5	.9	1.0	1.4	5.7	6.2	6.8
Georgia	9.4	15.3	20.7	10.6	16.2	20.9	8.3	14.4	20.5	19.9	29.1	36.5	3.4	5.5	8.0	.7	1.1	1.6	4.0	5.4	6.0
Florida	7.1	9.6	13.8	7.7	9.6	13.2	6.5	9.5	14.4	18.8	21.5	25.5	2.0	3.1	5.2	.8	1.1	2.2	5.4	6.3	10.5
EAST SOUTH CENTRAL	9.6	12.7	17.4	10.8	13.3	17.4	8.5	12.0	17.3	22.0	27.9	34.8	5.1	6.6	9.6	1.2	1.5	1.7	7.4	9.1	9.7
Kentucky	6.6	8.4	12.1	7.7	9.3	12.6	5.4	7.6	11.6	15.4	21.0	27.6	5.9	7.3	10.7	1.0	1.3	1.5	5.8	7.3	8.3
Tennessee	7.2	10.3	13.6	8.4	11.2	13.8	6.0	9.5	13.4	14.9	22.4	27.3	5.4	7.4	9.9	1.1	1.5	1.8	5.8	8.3	8.3
Alabama	12.6	16.1	22.9	13.5	16.4	22.5	11.6	15.8	23.3	26.2	31.3	40.1	4.9	6.4	10.1	1.4	1.7	2.3	8.5	10.9	11.3
Mississippi	13.1	17.2	22.4	14.4	18.1	22.4	11.8	16.3	22.5	23.2	29.3	35.6	2.7	3.6	5.3	1.8	2.3	2.2	12.6	13.3	15.1
WEST SOUTH CENTRAL	7.2	10.0	13.2	7.3	10.0	12.7	7.0	10.0	13.3	17.0	25.3	33.1	2.7	3.9	5.6	2.0	6.6	7.7	9.4	29.9	25.6
Arkansas	6.8	9.4	12.6	7.4	9.6	12.1	6.2	9.1	13.1	16.1	21.8	26.4	3.5	4.6	7.1	1.9	2.0	2.8	6.6	8.3	8.9
Louisiana	13.5	21.9	29.0	13.6	21.6	28.0	13.5	22.2	30.1	23.3	38.5	48.4	7.8	11.4	15.0	2.7	3.5	3.6	19.2	21.9	24.0
Oklahoma	2.8	3.8	5.6	3.2	4.1	5.5	2.4	3.4	5.8	9.3	12.4	17.7	1.8	2.4	3.5	.9	1.2	1.3	5.6	14.0	9.8
Texas	6.8	8.3	9.9	6.8	8.5	9.8	6.8	8.2	10.1	13.4	17.8	24.6	1.4	2.2	3.3	2.1	9.4	11.6	7.3	33.8	30.0
MOUNTAIN	4.2	5.2	6.9	3.7	4.7	6.3	4.6	5.7	7.5	4.1	5.3	8.0	1.5	2.4	3.6	.4	1.0	1.2	5.6	12.7	12.5
Montana	1.7	2.3	4.8	1.7	2.3	5.2	1.7	2.3	4.0	4.6	6.0	7.0	.3	.3	.3	.3	.3	.4	4.3	5.6	9.4
Idaho	1.1	1.5	2.2	1.2	1.7	2.6	1.0	1.3	1.6	4.2	5.4	6.4	.4	.3	.4	.4	.3	.3	4.0	6.5	6.9
Wyoming	1.6	2.1	3.3	1.7	2.5	3.7	1.6	1.5	2.5	4.2	5.3	5.0	.3	.4	.3	.3	.3	.4	4.2	9.0	9.7
Colorado	2.8	3.2	3.7	2.5	2.9	3.6	3.1	3.6	3.8	3.9	6.2	8.6	1.0	1.7	2.0	.4	.6	.5	8.6	12.4	11.3
New Mexico	13.3	15.6	20.2	11.2	12.7	15.9	15.7	18.9	25.4	6.0	4.3	14.2	8.2	11.9	15.5	1.5	8.2	8.9	6.8	27.1	31.0
Arizona	10.1	15.3	20.9	9.0	13.9	19.2	11.4	17.1	23.5	4.0	4.6	7.2	.5	1.3	2.3	.5	4.6	8.4	3.6	27.5	31.5
Utah	1.2	1.9	2.5	1.3	2.1	2.7	1.1	1.6	2.2	3.2	4.6	4.8	.3	.3	.4	.3	.3	.4	3.6	6.3	5.9
Nevada	4.4	5.9	6.7	4.3	5.8	6.1	4.5	6.2	8.0	1.5	5.1	5.5	.2	.4	.4	.3	.2	.5	7.5	8.5	7.6
PACIFIC	2.1	2.7	3.0	2.1	2.8	3.3	2.1	2.5	2.5	3.1	4.6	6.3	.3	.4	.4	.3	.4	.5	4.9	8.6	8.0
Washington	1.0	1.7	2.0	1.0	1.7	2.1	1.0	1.6	1.8	2.9	4.0	4.3	.3	.3	.3	.3	.3	.3	2.9	4.7	4.8
Oregon	1.0	1.5	1.9	1.0	1.6	2.2	.9	1.3	1.4	2.5	4.7	3.4	.3	.4	.4	.3	.3	.4	3.6	5.1	6.1
California	2.6	3.3	3.7	2.6	3.5	4.2	2.6	3.1	3.1	3.1	4.7	7.1	.3	.4	.5	.3	.5	.6	5.7	10.5	10.0

TABLE 29.—ILLITERACY IN THE POPULATION 21 YEARS OLD AND OVER, BY COLOR, AND NATIVITY, BY DIVISIONS, AND STATES: 1930

SECTION, DIVISION, AND STATE	ALL CLASSES, 21 YEARS OLD AND OVER			NEGRO			NATIVE WHITE—NATIVE PARENTAGE			NATIVE WHITE—FOREIGN OR MIXED PARENTAGE			FOREIGN-BORN WHITE		
	Total number	Illiterate: Number	Illiterate: Per cent	Total number	Illiterate: Number	Illiterate: Per cent	Total number	Illiterate: Number	Illiterate: Per cent	Total number	Illiterate: Number	Illiterate: Per cent	Total number	Illiterate: Number	Illiterate: Per cent
United States	72, 943, 624	3, 863, 215	5. 3	6, 531, 939	1, 306, 650	20. 0	38, 116, 766	855, 318	2. 2	14, 645, 625	99, 650	0. 7	12, 637, 643	1, 296, 502	10. 3
The North	45, 092, 514	1, 552, 730	3. 4	1, 598, 098	91, 052	5. 7	20, 622, 021	176, 970	. 9	11, 979, 829	78, 884	. 7	10, 761, 434	1, 173, 286	10. 9
The South	20, 246, 959	2, 062, 864	10. 2	4, 848, 072	1, 212, 258	25. 0	13, 567, 398	645, 936	4. 8	940, 101	14, 691	1. 6	509, 466	51, 235	10. 1
The West	7, 604, 151	247, 621	3. 3	85, 769	3, 340	3. 9	3, 927, 347	32, 412	. 8	1, 725, 695	6, 075	. 4	1, 366, 743	71, 981	5. 3
NEW ENGLAND	5, 095, 074	239, 810	4. 7	58, 770	4, 104	7. 0	1, 802, 649	12, 146	. 7	1, 506, 908	13, 634	. 9	1, 721, 714	209, 046	12. 1
Maine	487, 125	16, 092	3. 3	713	40	5. 6	305, 668	4, 978	1. 6	89, 222	2, 646	3. 0	90, 891	8, 316	9. 1
New Hampshire	294, 055	9, 928	3. 4	566	24	4. 2	143, 751	1, 016	. 7	72, 671	1, 089	1. 5	76, 969	7, 782	10. 1
Vermont	220, 428	6, 013	2. 7	319	19	6. 0	135, 869	1, 741	1. 3	46, 802	1, 278	2. 7	37, 387	2, 964	7. 9
Massachusetts	2, 686, 487	121, 925	4. 5	32, 898	2, 263	6. 9	799, 584	2, 697	. 3	856, 456	5, 173	. 6	994, 411	111, 174	11. 2
Rhode Island	421, 197	26, 989	6. 4	5, 952	626	10. 5	111, 803	625	. 6	142, 588	1, 702	1. 2	160, 448	23, 993	15. 0
Connecticut	985, 782	58, 863	6. 0	18, 322	1, 132	6. 2	305, 974	1, 089	. 4	299, 169	1, 746	. 6	361, 608	54, 817	15. 2
MIDDLE ATLANTIC	16, 311, 742	738, 166	4. 5	696, 317	30, 948	4. 4	6, 496, 649	45, 486	. 7	4, 131, 762	23, 978	. 6	4, 960, 816	632, 172	12. 7
New York	8, 142, 851	379, 180	4. 7	287, 066	8, 113	2. 8	2, 590, 409	16, 770	. 6	2, 256, 655	11, 629	. 5	2, 990, 101	338, 529	11. 3
New Jersey	2, 512, 112	124, 932	5. 0	131, 896	8, 369	6. 3	892, 354	5, 652	. 6	688, 766	3, 919	. 6	796, 522	106, 464	13. 4
Pennsylvania	5, 656, 779	234, 054	4. 1	277, 355	14, 466	5. 2	3, 013, 886	23, 064	. 8	1, 186, 341	8, 430	. 7	1, 173, 693	187, 179	15. 9
EAST NORTH CENTRAL	15, 685, 265	428, 457	2. 7	621, 236	35, 675	5. 7	7, 931, 955	72, 273	. 9	4, 029, 715	27, 282	. 7	3, 047, 877	280, 308	9. 2
Ohio	4, 132, 251	119, 251	2. 9	199, 291	15, 857	8. 0	2, 508, 593	24, 160	1. 0	809, 635	4, 907	. 6	610, 549	73, 789	12. 1
Indiana	2, 003, 019	42, 047	2. 1	73, 642	5, 504	7. 5	1, 530, 279	18, 663	1. 2	262, 895	2, 421	. 9	129, 034	13, 475	10. 4
Illinois	4, 841, 768	149, 504	3. 1	226, 692	9, 818	4. 3	2, 052, 821	18, 871	. 9	1, 377, 258	6, 600	. 5	1, 162, 700	108, 418	9. 3
Michigan	2, 939, 409	74, 573	2. 5	114, 346	4, 113	3. 6	1, 230, 274	7, 048	. 6	808, 846	6, 023	. 7	772, 426	54, 776	7. 1
Wisconsin	1, 768, 818	42, 601	2. 4	7, 265	383	5. 3	609, 988	3, 531	. 6	771, 081	7, 331	1. 0	373, 168	29, 850	8. 0
WEST NORTH CENTRAL	8, 000, 433	146, 297	1. 8	221, 775	20, 325	9. 2	4, 390, 768	47, 065	1. 1	2, 311, 444	13, 990	. 6	1, 031, 527	51, 760	5. 0
Minnesota	1, 537, 983	24, 971	1. 6	6, 805	158	2. 3	443, 190	1, 923	. 4	702, 263	4, 206	. 6	378, 450	16, 702	4. 4
Iowa	1, 506, 129	14, 790	1. 0	11, 330	757	6. 7	879, 401	5, 014	. 6	451, 209	2, 206	. 5	161, 712	5, 886	3. 6
Missouri	2, 269, 657	63, 575	2. 8	150, 457	15, 763	10. 5	1, 599, 699	32, 504	2. 0	371, 677	3, 283	. 9	144, 076	11, 133	7. 7
North Dakota	358, 182	7, 160	2. 0	278	10	3. 6	88, 418	303	. 3	162, 953	966	. 6	102, 308	4, 629	4. 5
South Dakota	385, 808	6, 316	1. 6	420	12	2. 9	157, 113	513	. 3	152, 903	817	. 5	64, 174	2, 413	3. 8
Nebraska	812, 450	11, 996	1. 5	9, 521	442	4. 6	424, 077	1, 948	. 5	261, 382	1, 222	. 5	112, 444	6, 894	6. 1
Kansas	1, 130, 224	17, 489	1. 5	42, 964	3, 183	7. 4	798, 870	4, 860	. 6	209, 057	1, 290	. 6	68, 363	4, 103	6. 0
SOUTH ATLANTIC	8, 415, 339	859, 341	10. 2	2, 210, 041	552, 521	25. 0	5, 527, 515	268, 476	4. 9	377, 996	3, 719	1. 0	289, 259	31, 148	10. 8
Delaware	148, 792	7, 520	5. 1	19, 939	3, 359	16. 8	95, 674	1, 660	1. 7	17, 011	98	. 6	16, 097	2, 382	14. 8
Maryland	996, 928	46, 912	4. 7	163, 464	23, 311	14. 3	603, 368	10, 547	1. 7	138, 180	1, 478	1. 1	91, 178	11, 483	12. 6
District of Columbia	341, 465	6, 456	1. 9	88, 388	4, 489	5. 1	180, 871	405	. 2	43, 065	86	. 2	28, 495	1, 403	4. 9
Virginia	1, 300, 893	140, 450	10. 8	329, 220	82, 893	25. 2	914, 297	55, 355	6. 1	33, 910	308	. 9	22, 745	1, 730	7. 6
West Virginia	900, 987	56, 853	6. 3	67, 155	9, 697	14. 4	742, 035	36, 675	4. 9	42, 858	702	1. 6	48, 688	9, 725	20. 0
North Carolina	1, 542, 125	202, 223	13. 1	418, 975	116, 226	27. 7	1, 097, 596	82, 865	7. 5	10, 613	158	1. 5	8, 290	443	5. 3
South Carolina	819, 384	152, 312	18. 6	343, 788	121, 270	25. 3	461, 513	30, 458	6. 6	8, 582	93	1. 1	5, 022	295	5. 9
Georgia	1, 498, 567	175, 072	11. 7	528, 087	135, 392	25. 6	936, 386	38, 898	4. 2	20, 508	184	. 9	13, 324	552	4. 1
Florida	866, 198	71, 543	8. 3	251, 025	55, 884	22. 3	495, 775	11, 613	2. 3	63, 269	612	1. 0	55, 420	3, 135	5. 7
EAST SOUTH CENTRAL	5, 220, 526	628, 891	12. 0	1, 402, 055	392, 519	28. 0	3, 611, 664	229, 226	6. 3	148, 981	1, 941	1. 3	55, 577	4, 220	7. 6
Kentucky	1, 422, 434	114, 905	8. 1	140, 503	27, 065	19. 3	1, 178, 736	85, 653	7. 3	81, 878	900	1. 1	21, 196	1, 259	5. 9
Tennessee	1, 418, 144	126, 924	9. 0	271, 974	51, 310	18. 9	1, 105, 162	74, 454	6. 7	28, 329	366	1. 3	12, 496	752	6. 0
Alabama	1, 348, 401	213, 924	15. 9	479, 950	159, 909	33. 3	828, 303	52, 186	6. 3	24, 725	410	1. 7	15, 135	1, 335	8. 8
Mississippi	1, 031, 547	173, 138	16. 8	509, 628	154, 235	30. 3	499, 463	16, 933	3. 4	14, 049	265	1. 9	6, 750	874	12. 9
WEST SOUTH CENTRAL	6, 611, 094	574, 632	8. 7	1, 235, 976	267, 218	21. 6	4, 428, 219	148, 234	3. 3	413, 124	9, 031	2. 2	164, 630	15, 867	9. 6
Arkansas	968, 231	84, 197	8. 7	257, 130	53, 357	20. 8	674, 293	29, 474	4. 4	26, 265	571	2. 2	9, 951	664	6. 7
Louisiana	1, 134, 852	191, 249	16. 9	415, 047	120, 469	29. 0	606, 427	60, 459	10. 0	76, 158	2, 286	3. 0	33, 771	6, 663	19. 7
Oklahoma	1, 287, 131	45, 087	3. 5	94, 162	11, 552	12. 3	1, 045, 674	23, 246	2. 2	76, 971	797	1. 0	26, 030	1, 471	5. 7
Texas	3, 220, 880	254, 099	7. 9	469, 637	81, 840	17. 4	2, 101, 825	35, 055	1. 7	233, 730	5, 377	2. 3	94, 878	7, 069	7. 5
MOUNTAIN	2, 108, 221	107, 404	5. 1	21, 431	1, 019	4. 8	1, 176, 650	24, 028	2. 0	459, 557	1, 962	. 4	276, 394	15, 869	5. 7
Montana	318, 611	6, 989	2. 2	961	51	5. 3	143, 251	459	. 3	95, 017	321	. 3	69, 656	3, 066	4. 4
Idaho	246, 770	3, 520	1. 4	518	24	4. 6	153, 673	736	. 5	59, 487	244	. 4	29, 184	1, 194	4. 1
Wyoming	132, 954	2, 643	2. 0	962	47	4. 9	79, 185	214	. 3	28, 353	81	. 3	18, 845	795	4. 2
Colorado	623, 523	21, 608	3. 5	8, 570	393	4. 6	373, 373	4, 617	1. 2	130, 916	601	. 5	82, 760	7, 310	8. 8
New Mexico	216, 956	36, 306	16. 7	1, 768	123	7. 0	154, 415	16, 820	10. 9	13, 278	240	1. 8	7, 539	528	7. 0
Arizona	244, 115	28, 992	11. 9	7, 407	344	4. 6	120, 568	669	. 6	26, 122	149	. 6	14, 795	541	3. 7
Utah	264, 498	4, 155	1. 6	806	30	3. 7	123, 783	451	. 4	92, 080	285	. 3	41, 716	1, 535	3. 7
Nevada	60, 794	3, 191	5. 2	439	7	1. 6	28, 402	62	. 2	14, 304	41	. 3	11, 899	900	7. 6
PACIFIC	5, 495, 930	140, 217	2. 6	64, 338	2, 321	3. 6	2, 750, 697	8, 384	. 3	1, 266, 138	4, 113	. 3	1, 090, 349	56, 112	5. 1
Washington	1, 010, 167	12, 634	1. 3	5, 061	169	3. 3	500, 774	1, 568	. 3	256, 610	792	. 3	228, 263	7, 064	3. 1
Oregon	621, 375	7, 371	1. 2	1, 717	48	2. 8	373, 570	1, 223	. 3	138, 177	445	. 3	99, 264	3, 717	3. 7
California	3, 864, 388	120, 212	3. 1	57, 560	2, 104	3. 7	1, 876, 353	5, 593	. 3	871, 351	[illegible], 876	. 3	762, 822	45, 331	5. 9

TABLE 30.—ILLITERACY IN THE NEGRO POPULATION 10 YEARS OLD AND OVER, BY SEX, BY SECTIONS, DIVISIONS, AND STATES: 1930

SECTION, DIVISION, AND STATE	NUMBER ILLITERATE: Total 1930	Total 1920	Total 1910	Male 1930	Male 1920	Male 1910	Female 1930	Female 1920	Female 1910	PERCENT ILLITERATE: Total 1930	Total 1920	Total 1910	Male 1930	Male 1920	Male 1910	Female 1930	Female 1920	Female 1910
United States	1,513,892	1,842,161	2,227,731	801,949	942,368	1,096,000	711,943	899,793	1,131,731	16.3	22.9	30.4	17.6	23.5	30.1	15.1	22.3	30.7
The North	94,034	87,133	90,659	49,720	45,136	43,255	44,314	41,997	47,404	4.7	7.0	10.5	4.9	7.0	9.9	4.5	7.0	11.1
The South	1,416,417	1,751,658	2,133,961	750,595	895,490	1,051,239	665,822	856,168	1,082,722	19.7	26.0	33.3	21.4	27.0	33.1	18.1	25.1	33.5
The West	3,441	3,370	3,111	1,634	1,742	1,506	1,807	1,628	1,605	3.3	4.9	7.0	3.1	4.4	6.1	3.6	5.6	8.2
NEW ENGLAND	4,187	4,607	4,341	2,211	2,537	2,107	1,976	2,070	2,234	5.5	7.1	7.8	5.8	7.6	7.7	5.2	6.5	8.0
Maine	43	64	93	27	43	56	16	21	37	4.8	5.9	8.0	5.5	7.2	9.2	3.9	4.3	6.7
New Hampshire	27	33	51	21	20	30	6	13	21	3.9	6.7	10.6	4.4	7.3	12.1	2.8	6.0	9.0
Vermont	22	28	69	18	16	41	4	12	28	4.9	6.2	4.8	7.2	6.0	3.8	2.0	6.4	7.8
Massachusetts	2,303	2,565	2,584	1,152	1,300	1,286	1,151	1,265	1,298	5.4	6.8	8.1	5.5	6.8	8.2	5.4	6.8	8.1
Rhode Island	635	839	752	320	491	370	315	348	382	8.1	10.2	9.5	8.3	11.7	9.6	7.9	8.7	9.4
Connecticut	1,157	1,078	792	673	667	324	484	411	468	4.9	6.2	6.3	5.8	7.4	5.4	4.1	4.9	7.1
MIDDLE ATLANTIC	32,223	25,587	27,811	16,861	13,052	12,573	15,362	12,535	15,238	3.7	5.0	7.9	3.9	5.1	7.4	3.5	5.0	8.4
New York	8,604	5,032	5,768	4,035	2,202	2,433	4,569	2,830	3,335	2.5	2.9	5.0	2.4	2.7	4.4	2.5	3.2	5.5
New Jersey	8,711	5,910	7,405	4,651	2,875	3,296	4,060	3,035	4,109	5.1	6.1	9.9	5.6	6.1	9.1	4.7	6.2	10.7
Pennsylvania	14,908	14,645	14,638	8,175	7,975	6,844	6,733	6,670	7,794	4.2	6.1	9.1	4.6	6.3	8.6	3.9	5.9	9.6
EAST NORTH CENTRAL	36,454	32,052	28,071	19,576	16,989	13,897	16,878	15,063	14,174	4.7	7.3	11.0	4.9	7.2	10.4	4.5	7.4	11.7
Ohio	16,213	12,715	10,460	9,185	7,141	5,370	7,028	5,574	5,090	6.4	8.1	11.1	7.0	8.3	10.9	5.8	7.8	11.4
Indiana	5,605	6,476	6,959	2,967	3,312	3,403	2,638	3,164	3,556	6.0	9.5	13.7	6.2	9.3	13.0	5.8	9.7	14.6
Illinois	10,044	10,476	9,713	4,955	5,138	4,652	5,089	5,338	5,061	3.6	6.7	10.5	3.6	6.3	9.5	3.7	7.0	11.5
Michigan	4,201	2,203	826	2,244	1,293	411	1,957	910	415	3.0	4.2	5.7	3.0	4.3	5.3	3.0	4.2	6.1
Wisconsin	391	182	113	225	105	61	166	77	52	4.4	4.1	4.5	4.6	4.1	4.7	4.2	4.1	4.3
WEST NORTH CENTRAL	21,170	24,887	30,436	11,072	12,558	14,678	10,098	12,329	15,758	7.6	10.5	14.9	7.9	10.2	13.8	7.3	10.8	16.2
Minnesota	160	241	215	78	119	126	82	122	89	2.0	3.1	3.4	1.8	2.7	3.3	2.2	3.5	3.5
Iowa	777	1,288	1,272	439	705	662	338	578	610	5.4	8.1	10.3	5.8	8.2	9.7	4.9	7.9	11.0
Missouri	16,532	18,528	23,062	8,710	9,392	11,161	7,822	9,136	11,901	8.8	12.1	17.4	9.2	12.0	16.4	8.3	12.3	18.5
North Dakota	11	16	26	11	9	16	------	7	10	3.4	4.0	4.8	5.2	3.7	4.6	------	4.3	5.1
South Dakota	12	35	38	7	21	24	5	14	14	2.2	5.2	5.5	2.3	5.2	5.9	2.1	5.2	4.8
Nebraska	450	556	482	213	285	233	237	271	249	3.9	4.8	7.2	3.6	4.4	6.2	4.2	5.4	8.4
Kansas	3,228	4,228	5,341	1,614	2,027	2,456	1,614	2,201	2,885	5.9	8.8	12.0	5.7	8.1	10.5	6.0	9.5	13.6
SOUTH ATLANTIC	662,055	812,842	969,432	353,459	417,569	477,107	308,596	395,273	492,325	19.7	25.2	32.5	21.7	26.3	32.4	17.8	24.1	32.5
Delaware	3,496	4,700	6,345	1,919	2,523	3,220	1,577	2,177	3,125	13.2	19.1	25.6	13.7	19.6	25.0	12.5	18.6	26.3
Maryland	25,073	35,404	42,289	13,868	18,165	20,852	11,205	17,239	21,437	11.4	18.2	23.4	12.3	18.4	23.3	10.4	18.0	23.5
District of Columbia	4,591	8,053	10,814	1,973	3,169	4,015	2,618	4,884	6,799	4.1	8.6	13.5	3.8	7.4	11.3	4.4	9.6	15.3
Virginia	95,148	122,322	148,950	52,355	64,709	75,162	42,793	57,613	73,788	19.2	23.5	30.0	21.4	25.0	30.8	17.1	22.0	29.2
West Virginia	10,173	10,513	10,347	6,357	6,494	6,405	3,816	4,019	3,942	11.3	15.3	20.3	13.1	16.9	21.3	9.2	13.3	18.9
North Carolina	139,105	133,674	156,303	75,252	68,144	75,674	63,853	65,530	80,629	20.6	24.5	31.9	23.2	25.7	32.0	18.3	23.4	31.8
South Carolina	156,065	181,422	226,242	78,689	89,574	106,994	77,376	91,848	119,248	26.9	29.3	38.7	28.7	29.9	37.9	25.2	28.8	39.5
Georgia	163,237	261,115	308,639	87,694	135,897	154,466	75,543	125,218	154,173	19.9	29.1	36.5	22.5	31.2	37.2	17.5	27.2	35.8
Florida	65,167	55,639	59,503	35,352	28,894	30,319	29,815	26,745	29,184	18.8	21.5	25.5	20.5	21.9	24.4	17.2	21.1	26.6
EAST SOUTH CENTRAL	452,082	536,583	681,507	240,348	274,925	337,893	211,734	261,658	343,614	22.0	27.9	34.8	24.0	29.1	34.8	20.1	26.7	34.7
Kentucky	28,553	40,548	57,900	15,754	21,687	29,906	12,799	18,861	27,994	15.4	21.0	27.6	16.9	22.3	28.3	13.8	19.7	26.9
Tennessee	57,251	79,532	98,541	31,148	41,408	49,382	26,103	38,124	49,159	14.9	22.4	27.3	16.8	23.8	27.8	13.2	21.1	26.9
Alabama	188,673	210,690	265,628	97,416	104,639	129,385	91,257	106,051	136,243	26.2	31.3	40.1	28.3	32.0	39.7	24.4	30.5	40.5
Mississippi	177,605	205,813	259,438	96,030	107,191	129,220	81,575	98,622	130,218	23.2	29.3	35.6	25.5	31.0	35.7	21.0	27.6	35.6
WEST SOUTH CENTRAL	302,280	402,233	483,022	156,788	202,996	236,239	145,492	199,237	246,783	17.0	25.3	33.1	17.9	25.6	32.2	16.1	25.0	33.9
Arkansas	60,102	79,245	86,398	31,546	40,202	42,233	28,556	39,043	44,165	16.1	21.8	26.4	17.1	22.0	25.7	15.1	21.6	27.4
Louisiana	139,393	206,730	254,148	69,628	101,673	122,625	69,765	105,057	131,523	23.3	38.5	48.4	24.0	38.7	47.2	22.7	38.4	49.5
Oklahoma	12,560	14,205	17,858	6,824	7,368	8,802	5,736	6,837	9,056	9.3	12.4	17.7	10.0	12.5	16.4	8.6	12.3	19.1
Texas	90,225	102,053	124,618	48,790	53,753	62,579	41,435	48,300	62,039	13.4	17.8	24.6	14.7	18.7	24.7	12.2	16.9	24.5
MOUNTAIN	1,070	1,457	1,497	552	897	754	518	560	743	4.1	5.3	8.0	3.9	4.9	7.2	4.4	5.9	9.0
Montana	52	87	114	25	55	75	27	32	39	4.6	6.0	7.0	3.9	6.5	7.8	5.6	5.3	5.8
Idaho	25	44	37	14	37	18	11	7	19	4.2	5.4	6.4	3.9	7.0	4.9	4.5	2.4	8.9
Wyoming	47	66	102	23	42	53	24	24	49	4.2	5.3	5.0	3.6	5.2	3.7	5.0	5.4	8.4
Colorado	403	619	856	203	314	396	200	305	460	3.9	6.2	8.6	4.1	6.1	7.7	3.8	6.4	9.5
New Mexico	140	228	191	79	152	101	61	76	90	6.0	4.3	14.2	6.3	3.5	13.2	5.7	7.9	15.6
Arizona	366	338	122	191	257	68	175	81	54	4.0	4.6	7.2	3.4	4.6	7.6	4.9	4.5	6.8
Utah	30	59	49	15	29	28	15	30	21	3.2	4.6	4.8	2.9	3.9	4.4	3.6	5.7	5.4
Nevada	7	16	26	2	11	15	5	5	11	1.5	5.1	5.5	0.8	6.0	6.1	2.3	3.8	4.9
PACIFIC	2,371	1,913	1,614	1,082	845	752	1,289	1,068	862	3.1	4.6	6.3	2.8	3.9	5.3	3.3	5.5	7.6
Washington	174	245	239	89	131	126	85	114	113	2.9	4.0	4.3	2.6	3.7	3.6	3.3	4.5	5.5
Oregon	49	89	46	29	50	25	20	39	21	2.5	4.7	3.4	2.6	4.6	3.0	2.3	4.8	4.0
California	2,148	1,579	1,329	964	664	601	1,184	915	728	3.1	4.7	7.1	2.8	3.9	6.1	3.3	5.6	8.2

TABLE 31.—ILLITERACY IN THE NEGRO POPULATION 10 YEARS OLD AND OVER, BY SEX, AND BY AGE GROUPS, BY SECTIONS, DIVISIONS, AND STATES: 1930

[Percent not shown where base is less than 100]

SECTION, DIVISION, AND STATE	10 YEARS OLD AND OVER [1]									10 TO 14 YEARS			15 TO 24 YEARS		
	Total			Male			Female								
	Total number	Illiterate		Total number	Illiterate		Total number	Illiterate		Total number	Illiterate		Total number	Illiterate	
		Number	Percent		Number	Percent		Number	Percent		Number	Percent		Number	Percent
United States	**9, 292, 556**	**1, 513, 892**	**16. 3**	**4, 564, 690**	**801, 949**	**17. 6**	**4, 727, 866**	**711, 943**	**15. 1**	**1, 251, 542**	**66, 238**	**15. 3**	**2, 453, 719**	**257, 461**	**10. 5**
The North	**1, 994, 085**	**94, 034**	**4. 7**	**1, 005, 003**	**49, 720**	**4. 9**	**989, 082**	**44, 314**	**4. 5**	**174, 430**	**643**	**. 4**	**418, 024**	**6, 181**	**1. 5**
The South	**7, 194, 750**	**1, 416, 417**	**19. 7**	**3, 506, 598**	**750, 595**	**21. 4**	**3, 688, 152**	**665, 822**	**18. 1**	**1, 069, 120**	**65, 572**	**6. 1**	**2, 017, 633**	**251, 105**	**12. 4**
The West	**103, 721**	**3, 441**	**3. 3**	**53, 089**	**1, 634**	**3. 1**	**50, 632**	**1, 807**	**3. 6**	**7, 992**	**23**	**. 3**	**18, 062**	**175**	**1. 0**
NEW ENGLAND	75, 719	4, 187	5. 5	37, 838	2, 211	5. 8	37, 881	1, 976	5. 2	8, 185	15	. 2	14, 662	173	1. 2
Maine	900	43	4. 8	488	27	5. 5	412	16	3. 9	100	1	1. 0	130	3	2. 3
New Hampshire	697	27	3. 9	481	21	4. 4	216	6	2. 8	48	-----	-----	149	3	2. 0
Vermont	445	22	4. 9	249	18	7. 2	196	4	2. 0	54	1	-----	101	2	2. 0
Massachusetts	42, 356	2, 303	5. 4	21, 089	1, 152	5. 5	21, 267	1, 151	5. 4	4, 698	7	. 1	7, 816	68	. 9
Rhode Island	7, 836	635	8. 1	3, 843	320	8. 3	3, 993	315	7. 9	938	-----	-----	1, 481	22	1. 5
Connecticut	23, 485	1, 157	4. 9	11, 688	673	5. 8	11, 797	484	4. 1	2, 347	6	. 3	4, 985	75	1. 5
MIDDLE ATLANTIC	867, 875	32, 223	3. 7	429, 276	16, 861	3. 9	438, 599	15, 362	3. 5	74, 250	202	. 3	188, 644	2, 973	1. 6
New York	347, 381	8, 604	2. 5	167, 235	4, 035	2. 4	180, 146	4, 569	2. 5	24, 624	63	. 3	75, 446	1, 147	1. 5
New Jersey	169, 214	8, 711	5. 1	83, 237	4, 651	5. 6	85, 977	4, 060	4. 7	16, 598	58	. 3	38, 090	787	2. 1
Pennsylvania	351, 280	14, 908	4. 2	178, 804	8, 175	4. 6	172, 476	6, 733	3. 9	33, 028	81	. 2	75, 108	1, 039	1. 4
EAST NORTH CENTRAL	771, 626	36, 454	4. 7	396, 907	19, 576	4. 9	374, 719	16, 878	4. 5	66, 849	190	. 3	159, 088	1, 727	1. 1
Ohio	252, 500	16, 213	6. 4	131, 229	9, 185	7. 0	121, 271	7, 028	5. 8	24, 086	88	. 4	53, 150	808	1. 5
Indiana	92, 873	5, 605	6. 0	47, 519	2, 967	6. 2	45, 354	2, 638	5. 8	8, 477	19	. 2	18, 930	226	1. 2
Illinois	277, 834	10, 044	3. 6	139, 192	4, 955	3. 6	138, 642	5, 089	3. 7	22, 111	53	. 2	56, 627	444	. 8
Michigan	139, 490	4, 201	3. 0	74, 033	2, 244	3. 0	65, 457	1, 957	3. 0	11, 387	28	. 2	28, 619	227	. 8
Wisconsin	8, 929	391	4. 4	4, 934	225	4. 6	3, 995	166	4. 2	788	2	. 3	1, 762	22	1. 2
WEST NORTH CENTRAL	278, 865	21, 170	7. 6	140, 982	11, 072	7. 9	137, 883	10, 098	7. 3	25, 146	236	. 9	55, 630	1, 308	2. 4
Minnesota	8, 155	160	2. 0	4, 353	78	1. 8	3, 802	82	2. 2	612	-----	-----	1, 264	4	. 3
Iowa	14, 426	777	5. 4	7, 540	439	5. 8	6, 886	338	4. 9	1, 408	9	. 6	2, 777	24	. 9
Missouri	188, 664	16, 532	8. 8	94, 184	8, 710	9. 2	94, 480	7, 822	8. 3	16, 518	217	1. 3	38, 400	1, 162	3. 0
North Dakota	326	11	3. 4	210	11	5. 2	116	-----	-----	15	1	-----	58	-----	-----
South Dakota	546	12	2. 2	304	7	2. 3	242	5	2. 1	55	-----	-----	127	-----	-----
Nebraska	11, 605	450	3. 9	5, 986	213	3. 6	5, 619	237	4. 2	930	1	. 1	2, 084	16	. 8
Kansas	55, 143	3, 228	5. 9	28, 405	1, 614	5. 7	26, 738	1, 614	6. 0	5, 608	8	. 1	10, 920	102	. 9
SOUTH ATLANTIC	3, 363, 864	662, 055	19. 7	1, 632, 260	353, 459	21. 7	1, 731, 604	308, 596	17. 8	529, 828	35, 337	6. 7	966, 776	129, 630	13. 4
Delaware	26, 567	3, 496	13. 2	13, 970	1, 919	13. 7	12, 597	1, 577	12. 5	2, 985	21	. 7	5, 973	258	4. 3
Maryland	219, 809	25, 073	11. 4	112, 573	13, 868	12. 3	107, 236	11, 205	10. 4	25, 627	371	1. 4	52, 828	2, 874	5. 4
District of Columbia	111, 224	4, 591	4. 1	51, 875	1, 973	3. 8	59, 349	2, 618	4. 4	9, 484	17	. 2	25, 081	278	1. 1
Virginia	494, 429	95, 148	19. 2	244, 143	52, 355	21. 4	250, 286	42, 793	17. 1	78, 893	4, 130	5. 2	130, 010	14, 433	11. 1
West Virginia	89, 921	10, 173	11. 3	48, 556	6, 357	13. 1	41, 365	3, 816	9. 2	10, 444	158	1. 5	21, 326	846	4. 0
North Carolina	673, 809	139, 105	20. 6	324, 816	75, 252	23. 2	348, 993	63, 853	18. 3	117, 763	6, 325	5. 4	210, 170	29, 528	14. 0
South Carolina	581, 085	156, 065	26. 9	273, 841	78, 689	28. 7	307, 244	77, 376	25. 2	111, 123	11, 753	10. 6	183, 081	37, 888	20. 7
Georgia	821, 083	163, 237	19. 9	389, 757	87, 694	22. 5	431, 326	75, 543	17. 5	131, 393	9, 248	7. 0	246, 550	31, 746	12. 9
Florida	345, 937	65, 167	18. 8	172, 729	35, 352	20. 5	173, 208	29, 815	17. 2	42, 116	3, 314	7. 9	91, 757	11, 779	12. 8
EAST SOUTH CENTRAL	2, 052, 951	452, 082	22. 0	999, 448	240, 348	24. 0	1, 053, 503	211, 734	20. 1	294, 215	18, 569	6. 3	567, 244	76, 115	13. 4
Kentucky	185, 629	28, 553	15. 4	93, 195	15, 754	16. 9	92, 434	12, 799	13. 8	20, 290	511	2. 5	40, 578	1, 919	4. 7
Tennessee	382, 974	57, 251	14. 9	185, 633	31, 148	16. 8	197, 341	26, 103	13. 2	48, 152	1, 813	3. 8	101, 123	7, 920	7. 8
Alabama	719, 290	188, 673	26. 2	344, 705	97, 416	28. 3	374, 585	91, 257	24. 4	108, 934	10, 203	9. 4	206, 289	33, 482	16. 2
Mississippi	765, 058	177, 605	23. 2	375, 915	96, 030	25. 5	389, 143	81, 575	21. 0	116, 839	6, 042	5. 2	219, 254	32, 794	15. 0
WEST SOUTH CENTRAL	1, 777, 935	302, 280	17. 0	874, 890	156, 788	17. 9	903, 045	145, 492	16. 1	245, 077	11, 666	4. 8	483, 613	45, 360	9. 4
Arkansas	373, 273	60, 102	16. 1	184, 753	31, 546	17. 1	188, 520	28, 556	15. 1	52, 911	2, 291	4. 3	101, 801	8, 700	8. 5
Louisiana	598, 258	139, 393	23. 3	290, 658	69, 628	24. 0	307, 600	69, 765	22. 7	84, 800	6, 553	7. 7	160, 843	23, 624	14. 7
Oklahoma	135, 069	12, 560	9. 3	68, 315	6, 824	10. 0	66, 754	5, 736	8. 6	18, 296	384	2. 1	36, 704	1, 272	3. 5
Texas	671, 335	90, 225	13. 4	331, 164	48, 790	14. 7	340, 171	41, 435	12. 2	89, 070	2, 438	2. 7	184, 265	11, 764	6. 4
MOUNTAIN	25, 992	1, 070	4. 1	14, 203	552	3. 9	11, 789	518	4. 4	2, 027	12	. 6	4, 622	75	1. 6
Montana	1, 128	52	4. 6	644	25	3. 9	484	27	5. 6	90	1	-----	136	-----	-----
Idaho	599	25	4. 2	355	14	3. 9	244	11	4. 5	35	-----	-----	80	3	-----
Wyoming	1, 118	47	4. 2	636	23	3. 6	482	24	5. 0	70	-----	-----	163	1	. 6
Colorado	10, 280	403	3. 9	4, 981	203	4. 1	5, 299	200	3. 8	757	3	. 4	1, 675	21	1. 3
New Mexico	2, 328	140	6. 0	1, 260	79	6. 3	1, 068	61	5. 7	249	3	1. 2	495	20	4. 0
Arizona	9, 125	366	4. 0	5, 549	191	3. 4	3, 576	175	4. 9	727	5	. 7	1, 916	30	1. 6
Utah	942	30	3. 2	522	15	2. 9	420	15	3. 6	86	-----	-----	113	-----	-----
Nevada	472	7	1. 5	256	2	0. 8	216	5	2. 3	13	-----	-----	44	-----	-----
PACIFIC	77, 729	2, 371	3. 1	38, 886	1, 082	2. 8	38, 843	1, 289	3. 3	5, 965	11	. 2	13, 440	100	. 7
Washington	5, 992	174	2. 9	3, 387	89	2. 6	2, 605	85	3. 3	421	1	. 2	875	10	1. 1
Oregon	2, 000	49	2. 5	1, 112	29	2. 6	888	20	2. 3	122	1	. 8	289	. 2	. 7
California	69, 737	2, 148	3. 1	34, 387	964	2. 8	35, 350	1, 184	3. 3	5, 422	9	. 2	12, 276	88	. 7

[1] Includes persons of unknown age.

TABLE 31.—ILLITERACY IN THE NEGRO POPULATION 10 YEARS OLD AND OVER, BY SEX, AND BY AGE GROUPS, BY SECTIONS, DIVISIONS, AND STATES: 1930—Continued

[Percent not shown where base is less than 100]

SECTION, DIVISION, AND STATE	25 TO 34 YEARS			35 TO 44 YEARS			45 TO 54 YEARS			55 TO 64 YEARS			65 YEARS AND OVER			21 YEARS AND OVER		
	Total number	Illiterate		Total number	Illiterate		Total number	Illiterate		Total number	Illiterate		Total number	Illiterate		Total number	Illiterate	
		Number	Percent		Number	Percent		Number	Percent		Number	Percent		Number	Percent		Number	Percent
United States	1,936,301	251,026	13.0	1,578,323	264,541	16.8	1,134,655	274,642	24.2	551,566	189,929	34.4	372,719	207,506	55.7	6,531,939	1,306,650	20.0
The North	538,832	15,451	2.9	427,654	19,305	4.5	258,371	19,651	7.6	108,600	14,025	12.9	64,255	18,341	28.5	1,598,098	91,052	5.7
The South	1,373,944	235,232	17.7	1,126,481	244,638	21.7	859,101	254,317	29.6	435,203	175,299	40.3	303,826	188,156	61.9	4,848,072	1,212,258	25.0
The West	23,525	343	1.5	24,188	598	2.5	17,183	674	3.9	7,763	605	7.8	4,638	1,009	21.8	85,769	3,340	3.9
NEW ENGLAND	15,859	616	3.9	15,409	1,151	7.5	11,727	1,042	8.9	5,976	587	9.8	3,768	593	15.7	58,770	4,104	7.0
Maine	151	7	4.6	167	3	1.8	160	10	6.3	95	3	------	95	16	------	713	40	5.6
New Hampshire	130	1	.8	160	8	5.0	135	7	5.2	43	2	------	29	6	------	566	24	4.2
Vermont	65	------	------	71	2	------	76	7	------	40	5	------	38	5	------	319	19	6.0
Massachusetts	8,456	271	3.2	8,785	661	7.5	6,934	645	9.3	3,477	331	9.5	2,098	314	15.0	32,898	2,263	6.9
Rhode Island	1,408	101	7.2	1,441	174	12.1	1,291	145	11.2	750	98	13.1	516	93	18.0	5,952	626	10.5
Connecticut	5,649	236	4.2	4,785	303	6.3	3,131	228	7.3	1,571	148	9.4	992	159	16.0	18,322	1,132	6.2
MIDDLE ATLANTIC	247,324	6,736	2.7	185,618	7,260	3.9	107,020	6,455	6.0	41,723	3,984	9.5	21,683	4,474	20.6	696,317	30,948	4.4
New York	108,817	2,073	1.9	76,925	1,845	2.4	39,743	1,502	3.8	14,002	857	6.1	7,141	1,080	15.1	287,066	8,113	2.8
New Jersey	43,211	1,624	3.8	33,874	1,903	5.6	22,232	1,784	8.0	9,623	1,179	12.3	5,183	1,321	25.5	131,896	8,369	6.3
Pennsylvania	95,296	3,039	3.2	74,819	3,512	4.7	45,045	3,169	7.0	18,098	1,948	10.8	9,359	2,073	22.1	277,355	14,466	5.2
E. N. CENTRAL	214,161	5,744	2.7	168,481	7,496	4.4	97,394	8,032	8.2	40,172	5,784	14.4	23,897	7,289	30.5	621,236	35,675	5.7
Ohio	65,545	2,975	4.5	54,272	3,704	6.8	32,306	3,631	11.2	13,967	2,282	16.3	8,741	2,658	30.4	199,291	15,857	8.0
Indiana	22,385	616	2.8	19,234	917	4.8	13,123	1,205	9.2	6,277	1,070	17.0	4,138	1,516	36.6	73,642	5,504	7.5
Illinois	77,810	1,297	1.7	61,767	1,807	2.9	36,442	2,144	5.9	14,462	1,801	12.5	8,074	2,424	30.0	226,692	9,818	4.3
Michigan	45,819	804	1.8	31,155	978	3.1	14,470	953	6.6	5,041	574	11.4	2,715	623	22.9	114,346	4,113	3.6
Wisconsin	2,602	52	2.0	2,053	90	4.4	1,053	99	9.4	425	57	13.4	229	68	29.7	7,265	383	5.3
W. N. CENTRAL	61,488	2,355	3.8	58,146	3,398	5.8	42,230	4,122	9.8	20,729	3,670	17.7	14,907	5,985	40.1	221,775	20,325	9.2
Minnesota	1,615	12	.7	1,925	21	1.1	1,523	34	2.2	761	24	3.2	444	63	14.2	6,805	158	2.3
Iowa	2,713	52	1.9	2,843	104	3.7	2,352	154	6.5	1,353	161	11.9	948	267	28.2	11,330	757	6.7
Missouri	43,249	2,013	4.7	39,781	2,822	7.1	27,934	3,292	11.8	13,079	2,784	21.3	9,237	4,161	45.0	150,457	15,763	10.5
North Dakota	63	------	------	74	2	------	69	5	------	31	2	------	16	1	------	278	10	3.6
South Dakota	103	1	1.0	95	3	------	80	4	------	45	1	------	38	3	------	420	12	2.9
Nebraska	2,718	47	1.7	2,697	77	2.9	1,919	113	5.9	762	69	9.1	476	126	26.5	9,521	442	4.6
Kansas	11,027	230	2.1	10,731	369	3.4	8,353	520	6.2	4,698	629	13.4	3,748	1,364	36.4	42,964	3,183	7.4
S. ATLANTIC	620,460	109,306	17.6	518,055	112,110	21.6	388,583	113,391	29.2	196,587	77,375	39.4	138,342	83,789	60.6	2,210,041	552,521	25.0
Delaware	5,296	400	7.6	4,852	600	12.4	3,741	784	21.0	2,070	629	30.4	1,630	800	49.1	19,939	3,359	16.8
Maryland	47,335	3,698	7.8	39,659	4,385	11.1	28,546	5,013	17.6	14,372	3,832	26.7	10,085	4,784	47.4	163,464	23,311	14.3
District of Columbia	27,349	621	2.3	21,717	764	3.5	15,864	1,053	6.6	6,786	757	11.2	4,291	1,079	25.1	88,388	4,489	5.1
Virginia	82,761	13,568	16.4	79,682	16,470	20.7	63,757	17,803	27.9	33,373	12,699	38.1	25,545	15,894	62.2	329,220	82,893	25.2
West Virginia	22,227	2,154	9.7	18,370	2,634	14.3	10,739	2,062	19.2	4,227	1,141	27.0	2,459	1,151	46.8	67,155	9,697	14.4
North Carolina	121,227	24,636	20.3	91,937	22,679	24.7	69,778	23,324	33.4	36,005	15,727	43.7	25,991	16,629	64.0	418,975	116,226	27.7
South Carolina	90,268	25,988	28.8	82,019	27,050	33.0	59,982	23,486	39.2	31,956	15,088	47.2	22,283	14,686	65.9	343,788	121,270	35.3
Georgia	143,644	25,260	17.6	118,235	24,856	21.0	95,117	28,383	29.8	50,024	20,944	41.9	35,239	22,517	63.9	528,087	135,392	25.6
Florida	80,353	12,981	16.2	61,584	12,672	20.6	41,059	11,483	28.0	17,774	6,558	36.9	10,819	6,249	57.8	251,025	55,884	22.3
E. S. CENTRAL	388,354	74,151	19.1	314,674	76,980	24.5	256,838	84,470	32.9	133,833	58,830	44.0	95,350	62,410	65.5	1,402,055	392,519	28.0
Kentucky	34,994	3,022	8.6	33,840	4,355	12.9	27,707	5,807	21.0	15,289	5,374	35.1	12,673	7,457	58.8	140,503	27,065	19.3
Tennessee	75,957	8,247	10.9	62,585	9,181	14.7	49,557	11,045	22.3	26,292	8,665	33.0	18,240	10,260	56.3	271,974	51,310	18.9
Alabama	133,077	30,614	23.0	104,262	31,780	30.5	91,872	37,093	40.4	42,838	22,526	52.6	31,337	22,756	72.6	479,950	159,909	33.3
Mississippi	144,326	32,268	22.4	113,987	31,664	27.8	87,702	30,525	34.8	49,414	22,265	45.1	33,100	21,937	66.3	509,628	154,235	30.3
W. S. CENTRAL	365,130	51,775	14.2	293,752	55,548	18.9	213,680	56,456	26.4	104,783	39,094	37.3	70,134	41,957	59.8	1,235,976	267,218	21.6
Arkansas	71,595	9,477	13.2	59,314	10,573	17.8	49,426	12,530	25.4	23,331	8,196	35.1	14,653	8,278	56.5	257,130	53,357	20.8
Louisiana	121,229	25,801	21.3	100,104	26,736	26.7	71,683	25,001	34.9	35,231	16,078	45.6	24,018	15,473	64.4	415,047	120,469	29.0
Oklahoma	28,064	1,602	5.7	21,974	2,086	9.5	16,331	2,540	15.6	8,207	2,017	24.6	5,339	2,635	49.4	94,162	11,552	12.3
Texas	144,242	14,895	10.3	112,360	16,153	14.4	76,240	16,385	21.5	38,014	12,803	33.7	26,124	15,571	59.6	469,637	81,840	17.4
MOUNTAIN	5,667	116	2.0	6,004	214	3.6	4,389	221	5.0	2,012	184	9.1	1,212	245	20.2	21,431	1,019	4.8
Montana	197	2	1.0	238	4	1.7	234	15	6.4	144	14	9.7	87	16	------	961	51	5.3
Idaho	113	2	1.8	167	9	5.4	105	5	4.8	58	4	------	41	2	------	518	24	4.6
Wyoming	218	4	1.8	277	16	5.8	225	11	4.9	107	11	10.3	53	4	------	962	47	4.9
Colorado	2,044	29	1.4	2,249	58	2.6	1,928	77	4.0	950	79	8.3	657	134	20.4	8,570	393	4.6
New Mexico	468	17	3.6	516	31	6.0	364	26	7.1	157	15	9.6	73	27	------	1,768	123	7.0
Arizona	2,341	61	2.6	2,196	90	4.1	1,236	81	6.6	460	51	11.1	223	48	21.5	7,407	344	4.6
Utah	189	1	------	228	5	2.2	195	5	2.6	81	6	------	49	13	------	806	30	3.7
Nevada	94	------	------	133	1	.8	102	1	1.0	55	4	------	29	1	------	439	7	1.6
PACIFIC	17,861	227	1.3	18,184	384	2.1	12,794	453	3.5	5,751	421	7.3	3,426	764	22.3	64,338	2,321	3.6
Washington	1,008	9	.9	1,301	20	1.5	1,288	32	2.5	696	38	5.5	380	64	16.8	5,061	169	3.3
Oregon	373	4	1.1	522	11	2.1	392	6	1.5	194	9	4.6	102	16	15.7	1,717	48	2.8
California	16,480	214	1.3	16,361	353	2.2	11,114	415	3.7	4,861	374	7.7	2,944	684	23.2	57,560	2,104	3.7

TABLE 32.—ILLITERACY IN THE POPULATION 10 YEARS OLD AND OVER, BY AGE GROUPS, COLOR, AND NATIVITY, BY DIVISIONS, AND STATES: 1930

[Percent not shown where base is less than 100. "Total" includes unknown and "Other races"]

DIVISION, STATE, COLOR, AND NATIVITY	TOTAL 10 YEARS OLD AND OVER		10 TO 14 YEARS		15 TO 24 YEARS		25 TO 34 YEARS		35 TO 44 YEARS		45 TO 54 YEARS		55 TO 64 YEARS		65 YEARS AND OVER	
	Number illiterate	Percent illiterate	Number illiterate	Percent illiterate	Number illiterate	Percent illiterate	Number illiterate	Percent illiterate	Number illiterate	Percent illiterate	Number illiterate	Percent illiterate	Number illiterate	Percent illiterate	Number illiterate	Percent illiterate
United States																
All classes	**4, 283, 753**	**4. 3**	**140, 440**	**1. 2**	**516, 302**	**2. 3**	**618, 266**	**3. 3**	**887, 955**	**5. 2**	**864, 433**	**6. 6**	**606, 811**	**7. 2**	**642, 966**	**9. 7**
Negro	1, 513, 892	16. 3	66, 238	5. 3	257, 461	10. 5	251, 026	13. 0	264, 541	16. 8	274, 642	24. 2	189, 929	34. 4	207, 506	55. 7
Native white	1, 103, 134	1. 5	53, 323	. 5	167, 330	. 9	159, 068	1. 1	176, 926	1. 5	185, 902	2. 1	157, 254	2. 7	201, 198	4. 4
Foreign-born white	1, 304, 084	9. 9	370	. 3	22, 198	2. 2	128, 880	5. 7	374, 538	11. 3	348, 836	12. 1	224, 793	11. 6	203, 336	12. 3
NEW ENGLAND																
All classes	245, 270	3. 7	1, 472	. 2	8, 345	. 6	25, 602	2. 1	69, 016	5. 8	60, 848	6. 4	42, 275	6. 2	37, 522	6. 8
Negro	4, 187	5. 5	15	. 2	173	1. 2	616	3. 9	1, 151	7. 5	1, 042	8. 9	587	9. 8	593	15. 7
Native white	30, 129	. 6	1, 401	. 1	5, 087	. 4	4, 357	. 5	4, 827	. 7	4, 787	. 9	4, 556	1. 1	5, 046	1. 5
Foreign-born white	210, 046	11. 6	50	. 2	3, 014	2. 1	20, 455	6. 8	62, 811	13. 7	54, 820	13. 6	36, 984	13. 1	31, 800	16. 1
MAINE																
All classes	17, 172	2. 7	247	. 3	1, 534	1. 2	2, 024	1. 9	3, 250	3. 2	3, 494	3. 9	3, 058	4. 2	3, 549	5. 1
Negro	43	4. 8	1	1. 0	3	2. 3	7	4. 6	3	1. 8	10	6. 3	3		16	
Native white	8, 617	1. 6	237	. 3	1, 310	1. 1	1, 285	1. 4	1, 587	2. 0	1, 512	2. 2	1, 265	2. 2	1, 412	2. 5
Foreign-born white	8, 393	8. 5	5	. 2	212	2. 3	722	4. 6	1, 643	7. 9	1, 949	9. 3	1, 767	11. 0	2, 088	16. 7
NEW HAMPSHIRE																
All classes	10, 231	2. 7	89	. 2	426	. 6	880	1. 4	2, 249	3. 6	2, 258	4. 1	1, 991	4. 5	2, 314	5. 6
Negro	27	3. 9			3	2. 0	1	. 8	8	5. 0	7	5. 2	2		6	
Native white	2, 366	. 8	86	. 2	312	. 5	308	. 6	381	. 9	410	1. 1	394	1. 3	462	1. 5
Foreign-born white	7, 820	9. 6	3	. 2	109	1. 8	569	4. 7	1, 853	10. 1	1, 839	10. 1	1, 592	11. 2	1, 844	17. 0
VERMONT																
All classes	6, 299	2. 2	102	. 3	346	. 6	578	1. 2	1, 060	2. 3	1, 254	3. 0	1, 226	3. 8	1, 730	5. 5
Negro	22	4. 9	1		2	2. 0			2		7		5		5	
Native white	3, 261	1. 3	98	. 3	263	. 5	346	. 8	414	1. 1	604	1. 9	685	2. 6	849	3. 3
Foreign-born white	3, 005	7. 2	3	. 2	81	1. 7	227	3. 4	642	7. 5	641	7. 6	536	9. 1	874	15. 6
MASSACHUSETTS																
All classes	124, 158	3. 5	662	. 2	3, 393	. 5	12, 629	2. 0	36, 039	5. 7	31, 764	6. 4	21, 149	5. 9	18, 433	6. 7
Negro	2, 303	5. 4	7	. 1	68	. 9	271	3. 2	661	7. 5	645	9. 3	331	9. 5	314	15. 0
Native white	9, 652	. 4	627	. 2	1, 963	. 3	1, 453	. 3	1, 448	. 4	1, 357	. 5	1, 292	. 7	1, 478	. 9
Foreign-born white	111, 568	10. 7	26	. 2	1, 318	1. 6	10, 770	6. 2	33, 757	12. 9	29, 618	12. 6	19, 421	11. 8	16, 609	14. 6
RHODE ISLAND																
All classes	27, 536	4. 9	149	. 2	846	. 7	2, 987	2. 9	7, 475	7. 6	6, 789	8. 6	5, 029	9. 1	4, 249	10. 6
Negro	635	8. 1			22	1. 5	101	7. 2	174	12. 1	145	11. 2	98	13. 1	93	18. 0
Native white	2, 732	. 7	147	. 2	438	. 4	409	. 6	458	. 8	448	1. 1	463	1. 7	366	1. 8
Foreign-born white	24, 124	14. 3	2	. 1	379	2. 8	2, 471	8. 8	6, 835	16. 6	6, 186	16. 2	4, 462	16. 4	3, 782	20. 4
CONNECTICUT																
All classes	59, 874	4. 5	223	. 1	1, 800	. 6	6, 504	2. 7	18, 943	7. 8	15, 289	8. 5	9, 822	8. 0	7, 247	7. 8
Negro	1, 157	4. 9	6	. 3	75	1. 5	236	4. 2	303	6. 3	228	7. 3	148	9. 4	159	16. 0
Native white	3, 501	. 4	206	. 1	801	. 3	556	. 3	539	. 4	456	. 5	457	. 7	479	. 9
Foreign-born white	55, 136	14. 6	11	. 3	915	3. 3	5, 696	8. 8	18, 081	16. 9	14, 587	17. 4	9, 206	17. 0	6, 603	18. 1
MIDDLE ATLANTIC																
All classes	757, 228	3. 5	5, 079	. 2	30, 672	. 7	88, 589	2. 1	208, 711	5. 2	194, 423	6. 7	125, 279	6. 7	103, 496	7. 5
Negro	32, 223	3. 7	202	. 3	2, 973	1. 6	6, 736	2. 7	7, 260	3. 9	6, 455	6. 0	3, 984	9. 5	4, 474	20. 6
Native white	82, 743	. 5	4, 699	. 2	14, 890	. 4	12, 719	. 4	12, 210	. 5	11, 357	. 7	10, 684	. 9	15, 816	1. 8
Foreign-born white	636, 479	12. 2	167	. 3	12, 250	2. 8	67, 421	6. 5	187, 493	13. 2	175, 599	15. 8	110, 175	16. 5	82, 950	18. 0
NEW YORK																
All classes	388, 883	3. 7	2, 388	. 2	16, 771	. 8	48, 107	2. 2	101, 483	5. 1	96, 619	6. 7	66, 579	7. 3	56, 480	8. 5
Negro	8, 604	2. 5	63	. 3	1, 147	1. 5	2, 073	1. 9	1, 845	2. 4	1, 502	3. 8	857	6. 1	1, 080	15. 1
Native white	34, 654	. 5	2, 215	. 2	7, 180	. 4	5, 908	. 4	4, 967	. 5	4, 517	. 6	4, 060	. 8	5, 640	1. 4
Foreign-born white	341, 345	10. 8	106	. 3	8, 065	2. 7	38, 948	5. 7	93, 279	11. 2	89, 849	14. 0	61, 351	15. 9	49, 539	18. 5
NEW JERSEY																
All classes	128, 022	3. 8	798	. 2	5, 214	. 7	15, 891	2. 4	37, 855	6. 0	32, 595	7. 2	19, 653	7. 0	15, 826	7. 9
Negro	8, 711	5. 1	58	. 3	787	2. 1	1, 624	3. 8	1, 903	5. 6	1, 784	8. 0	1, 179	12. 3	1, 321	25. 5
Native white	11, 572	. 5	710	. 2	2, 282	. 4	1, 894	. 4	1, 857	. 5	1, 499	. 6	1, 315	. 8	1, 959	1. 6
Foreign-born white	107, 192	12. 9	29	. 3	2, 091	3. 2	12, 185	7. 7	33, 961	14. 6	29, 208	15. 9	17, 106	15. 5	12, 534	16. 6
PENNSYLVANIA																
All classes	240, 323	3. 1	1, 893	. 2	8, 687	. 5	24, 591	1. 7	69, 373	5. 1	65, 209	6. 3	39, 047	5. 8	31, 190	6. 1
Negro	14, 908	4. 2	81	. 2	1, 039	1. 4	3, 039	3. 2	3, 512	4. 7	3, 169	7. 0	1, 948	10. 8	2, 073	22. 1
Native white	36, 517	. 6	1, 774	. 2	5, 428	. 3	4, 917	. 4	5, 386	. 6	5, 341	. 8	5, 309	1. 1	8, 217	2. 2
Foreign-born white	187, 942	15. 4	32	. 3	2, 094	2. 6	16, 288	8. 1	60, 253	17. 1	56, 542	19. 5	31, 718	18. 7	20, 877	17. 7
EAST NORTH CENTRAL																
All classes	442, 064	2. 1	4, 385	. 2	20, 255	. 5	48, 899	1. 2	109, 730	2. 9	101, 870	3. 7	69, 699	3. 8	86, 031	5. 7
Negro	36, 454	4. 7	190	. 3	1, 727	1. 1	5, 744	2. 7	7, 496	4. 4	8, 032	8. 2	5, 784	14. 4	7, 289	30. 5
Native white	110, 284	. 7	4, 030	. 2	11, 972	. 3	12, 283	. 4	15, 567	. 6	17, 574	. 9	18, 249	1. 4	30, 014	2. 8
Foreign-born white	281, 645	8. 8	68	. 2	4, 156	1. 8	26, 100	4. 9	83, 653	10. 3	74, 727	11. 0	44, 762	9. 9	47, 825	11. 0
OHIO																
All classes	123, 804	2. 3	1, 439	. 2	5, 684	. 5	14, 638	1. 4	32, 474	3. 3	29, 452	3. 9	18, 887	3. 8	21, 003	5. 1
Negro	16, 213	6. 4	88	. 4	808	1. 5	2, 975	4. 5	3, 704	6. 8	3, 631	11. 2	2, 282	16. 3	2, 658	30. 4
Native white	32, 387	. 7	1, 322	. 2	3, 620	. 3	3, 584	. 4	4, 279	. 6	5, 008	. 9	5, 325	1. 3	9, 136	2. 7
Foreign-born white	74, 131	11. 6	22	. 3	1, 061	2. 3	7, 661	7. 0	24, 248	13. 6	20, 686	14. 6	11, 230	13. 5	9, 178	12. 6

TABLE 32.—ILLITERACY IN THE POPULATION 10 YEARS OLD AND OVER, BY AGE GROUPS, COLOR, AND NATIVITY, BY DIVISIONS, AND STATES: 1930—Continued

[Percent not shown where base is less than 100. "Total" includes unknown and "Other races"]

DIVISION, STATE, COLOR, AND NATIVITY	TOTAL 10 YEARS OLD AND OVER		10 TO 14 YEARS		15 TO 24 YEARS		25 TO 34 YEARS		35 TO 44 YEARS		45 TO 54 YEARS		55 TO 64 YEARS		65 YEARS AND OVER	
	Number illiterate	Percent illiterate	Number illiterate	Percent illiterate	Number illiterate	Percent illiterate	Number illiterate	Percent illiterate	Number illiterate	Percent illiterate	Number illiterate	Percent illiterate	Number illiterate	Percent illiterate	Number illiterate	Percent illiterate
INDIANA																
All classes	43,721	1.7	568	0.2	2,487	0.5	4,647	1.0	8,274	1.8	8,561	2.3	7,312	2.8	11,730	5.0
Negro	5,605	6.0	19	.2	226	1.2	616	2.8	917	4.8	1,205	9.2	1,070	17.0	1,516	36.6
Native white	22,510	.9	542	.2	1,624	.3	1,862	.4	2,618	.7	3,650	1.1	4,166	1.7	7,993	3.9
Foreign-born white	13,536	10.1	1	.1	205	2.5	1,311	6.5	4,284	12.5	3,518	12.1	2,006	10.3	2,188	10.4
ILLINOIS																
All classes	153,507	2.4	1,106	.2	6,631	.5	17,339	1.4	40,242	3.4	36,988	4.3	24,154	4.4	26,427	6.3
Negro	10,044	3.6	53	.2	444	.8	1,297	1.7	1,807	2.9	2,144	5.9	1,801	12.5	2,424	30.0
Native white	28,284	.6	1,010	.2	3,225	.3	3,379	.3	4,068	.5	4,249	.8	4,419	1.2	7,623	2.9
Foreign born white	108,984	9.0	17	.2	1,725	2.0	10,213	5.0	32,857	10.4	29,984	11.3	17,679	10.1	16,287	10.8
MICHIGAN																
All classes	76,800	2.0	649	.1	3,548	.4	8,772	1.1	20,503	2.8	17,701	3.6	11,499	3.7	13,984	5.5
Negro	4,201	3.0	28	.2	227	.8	804	1.8	978	3.1	953	6.6	574	11.4	623	22.9
Native white	14,790	.5	569	.1	2,067	.3	1,954	.3	2,449	.5	2,521	.8	2,258	1.1	2,889	1.9
Foreign-born white	55,034	6.7	19	.1	833	1.1	5,195	3.3	16,490	7.7	13,884	8.6	8,397	8.3	10,176	10.4
WISCONSIN																
All classes	44,232	1.9	623	.2	1,905	.4	3,503	.8	8,237	2.0	9,168	2.9	7,847	3.7	12,887	6.7
Negro	391	4.4	2	.3	22	1.2	52	2.0	90	4.4	99	9.4	57	13.4	68	29.7
Native white	12,313	.6	587	.2	1,436	.3	1,504	.4	2,153	.6	2,146	1.0	2,081	1.5	2,373	2.4
Foreign-born white	29,960	7.8	9	.4	332	1.8	1,720	4.1	5,774	8.0	6,655	7.9	5,450	7.5	9,996	10.9
WEST NORTH CENTRAL																
All classes	156,068	1.4	3,416	.3	12,152	.5	16,331	.8	25,897	1.4	28,837	2.0	26,098	2.6	42,959	4.9
Negro	21,170	7.6	236	.9	1,308	2.4	2,355	3.8	3,398	5.8	4,122	9.8	3,670	17.7	5,985	40.1
Native white	68,838	.7	2,871	.2	8,535	.4	8,279	.5	10,251	.6	11,322	1.0	10,744	1.4	16,627	2.8
Foreign-born white	51,982	4.9	11	.2	621	1.5	2,771	2.9	9,406	5.0	11,334	4.8	9,943	4.5	17,851	6.6
MINNESOTA																
All classes	26,302	1.3	513	.2	1,482	.3	1,968	.5	4,255	1.2	4,873	1.8	4,673	2.5	8,476	5.2
Negro	160	2.0	-----	-----	4	.3	12	.7	21	1.1	34	2.2	24	3.2	63	14.2
Native white	7,244	.4	456	.2	1,125	.3	1,065	.3	1,284	.4	1,180	.7	1,031	1.0	1,059	1.6
Foreign-born white	16,759	4.3	5	.2	139	1.0	584	1.8	2,570	3.6	3,339	3.7	3,267	4.0	6,844	7.0
IOWA																
All classes	15,879	.8	423	.2	1,206	.3	1,663	.5	2,560	.8	2,731	1.0	2,423	1.2	4,814	2.6
Negro	777	5.4	9	.6	24	.9	52	1.9	104	3.7	154	6.5	161	11.9	267	28.2
Native white	8,177	.4	401	.2	931	.2	974	.3	1,136	.4	1,325	.6	1,257	.8	2,113	1.6
Foreign-born white	5,932	3.6	1	.1	122	2.0	334	2.4	1,006	3.9	1,107	3.3	946	2.7	2,407	4.8
MISSOURI																
All classes	67,905	2.3	1,330	.4	5,702	.9	7,429	1.3	11,359	2.2	13,169	3.2	11,539	4.0	17,207	7.0
Negro	16,532	8.8	217	1.3	1,162	3.0	2,013	4.7	2,822	7.1	3,292	11.8	2,784	21.3	4,161	45.0
Native white	39,252	1.5	1,105	.4	4,270	.7	4,269	.9	5,534	1.2	6,648	1.9	6,682	2.7	10,661	5.2
Foreign-born white	11,183	7.5	2	.2	140	1.7	869	4.4	2,736	9.4	3,085	9.5	2,006	7.5	2,341	7.4
NORTH DAKOTA																
All classes	7,814	1.5	280	.4	623	.5	829	.9	1,266	1.5	1,439	2.2	1,300	3.3	2,070	6.8
Negro	11	3.4	1	-----	-----	-----	-----	-----	2	-----	5	-----	2	-----	1	-----
Native white	1,763	.4	207	.3	425	.3	348	.4	312	.5	209	.6	127	.7	134	1.4
Foreign-born white	4,649	4.4	2	.4	56	1.4	298	2.7	801	3.9	1,063	4.0	932	4.4	1,492	7.4
SOUTH DAKOTA																
All classes	6,763	1.2	199	.3	441	.3	533	.5	877	.9	1,095	1.6	1,311	3.1	2,277	6.2
Negro	12	2.2	-----	-----	-----	-----	1	1.0	3	-----	4	-----	1	-----	3	-----
Native white	1,639	.4	133	.2	294	.2	288	.3	355	.5	241	.5	149	.6	163	.9
Foreign-born white	2,422	3.7	-----	-----	31	1.3	118	2.1	356	3.1	445	3.0	509	3.6	960	5.9
NEBRASKA																
All classes	12,725	1.2	271	.2	879	.3	1,437	.7	2,366	1.2	2,480	1.8	2,094	2.2	3,171	3.7
Negro	450	3.9	1	.1	16	.8	47	1.7	77	2.9	113	5.9	69	9.1	126	26.5
Native white	3,762	1.4	239	.2	557	.2	530	.3	619	.4	632	.6	485	.7	680	1.3
Foreign-born white	6,924	6.0	1	.2	96	2.1	380	3.7	1,300	7.1	1,499	6.2	1,409	5.6	2,233	7.0
KANSAS																
All classes	18,680	1.2	400	.2	1,818	.5	2,472	.9	3,214	1.3	3,050	1.5	2,758	1.9	4,944	3.8
Negro	3,228	5.9	8	.1	102	.9	230	2.1	369	3.4	520	6.2	629	13.4	1,364	36.4
Native white	7,001	.5	330	.2	933	.3	805	.3	1,011	.4	1,087	.6	1,013	.8	1,817	1.8
Foreign-born white	4,113	5.9	-----	-----	37	1.8	188	3.6	637	6.4	796	5.8	874	5.5	1,574	7.1
SOUTH ATLANTIC																
All classes	1,012,523	8.3	50,827	2.9	179,490	5.7	159,311	7.0	173,049	9.0	177,738	12.1	127,382	14.3	143,265	20.9
Negro	662,055	19.7	35,337	6.7	129,630	13.4	109,306	17.6	112,110	21.6	113,391	29.2	77,375	39.4	83,089	60.6
Native white	314,583	3.7	15,045	1.2	48,340	2.2	46,049	2.9	50,962	3.9	55,028	5.4	44,251	6.8	54,616	10.7
Foreign-born white	31,328	10.4	9	.3	501	2.5	3,165	6.2	9,224	11.7	8,647	12.9	5,322	12.0	4,402	12.1
DELAWARE																
All classes	7,805	4.0	67	.3	455	1.1	807	2.2	1,621	4.7	1,786	6.6	1,356	7.3	1,708	10.2
Negro	3,496	13.2	21	.7	258	4.3	400	7.6	600	12.4	784	21.0	629	30.4	800	49.1
Native white	1,896	1.2	46	.2	161	.5	148	.5	235	1.0	334	1.7	334	2.4	637	4.8
Foreign-born white	2,392	14.3	-----	-----	36	3.0	256	8.9	774	16.6	664	18.4	393	16.4	269	14.6
MARYLAND																
All classes	49,910	3.8	808	.5	4,394	1.5	6,316	2.5	9,282	4.0	10,240	5.8	8,389	7.1	10,290	11.1
Negro	25,073	11.4	371	1.4	2,874	5.4	3,698	7.8	4,385	11.1	5,013	17.6	3,832	26.7	4,784	47.4
Native white	13,202	1.3	434	.3	1,363	.6	1,615	.8	2,051	1.2	2,225	1.7	2,153	2.4	3,324	4.7
Foreign-born white	11,539	12.2	3	.4	146	2.4	981	6.3	2,818	12.2	2,986	14.2	2,393	15.9	2,174	17.2

TABLE 32.—ILLITERACY IN THE POPULATION 10 YEARS OLD AND OVER, BY AGE GROUPS, COLOR, AND NATIVITY, BY DIVISIONS, AND STATES: 1930—Continued

[Percent not shown where base is less than 100. "Total" includes unknown and "Other races"]

DIVISION, STATE, COLOR, AND NATIVITY	TOTAL 10 YEARS OLD AND OVER		10 TO 14 YEARS		15 TO 24 YEARS		25 TO 34 YEARS		35 TO 44 YEARS		45 TO 54 YEARS		55 TO 64 YEARS		65 YEARS AND OVER	
	Number illiterate	Percent illiterate	Number illiterate	Percent illiterate	Number illiterate	Percent illiterate	Number illiterate	Percent illiterate	Number illiterate	Percent illiterate	Number illiterate	Percent illiterate	Number illiterate	Percent illiterate	Number illiterate	Percent illiterate
DISTRICT OF COLUMBIA																
All classes	6,611	1.6	36	0.1	378	0.4	877	0.9	1,234	1.5	1,501	2.4	1,102	2.9	1,449	5.3
Negro	4,591	4.1	17	.2	278	1.1	621	2.3	764	3.5	1,053	6.6	757	11.2	1,079	25.1
Native white	533	.2	19	.1	60	.1	75	.1	103	.2	76	.2	75	.3	121	.6
Foreign-born white	1,411	4.8	-------	-------	33	1.5	153	2.7	354	4.8	361	5.8	258	6.1	244	7.0
VIRGINIA																
All classes	162,588	8.7	7,681	2.8	25,506	5.4	23,386	7.0	27,290	9.3	29,489	12.5	21,880	14.8	27,158	23.3
Negro	95,148	19.2	4,130	5.2	14,433	11.1	13,568	16.4	16,470	20.7	17,803	27.9	12,699	38.1	15,894	62.2
Native white	65,482	4.8	3,524	1.9	11,002	3.2	9,646	3.9	10,357	5.0	11,167	6.7	8,813	7.9	10,928	12.4
Foreign-born white	1,738	7.4	-------	-------	34	2.3	142	3.8	430	7.3	485	8.9	338	9.0	307	10.3
WEST VIRGINIA																
All classes	62,492	4.8	1,953	1.0	7,269	2.2	9,173	3.7	13,196	6.4	12,662	8.1	8,448	8.9	9,721	13.3
Negro	10,173	11.3	158	1.5	846	4.0	2,154	9.7	2,634	14.3	2,062	19.2	1,141	27.0	1,151	46.8
Native white	42,476	3.7	1,792	1.0	6,266	2.1	5,863	2.7	6,805	4.0	7,547	5.7	6,200	7.2	7,965	11.8
Foreign-born white	9,788	19.2	3	.5	149	4.3	1,141	12.2	3,737	21.6	3,046	25.1	1,104	22.5	603	18.2
NORTH CAROLINA																
All classes	236,261	10.0	9,583	2.5	43,663	6.6	39,200	9.0	39,026	11.4	41,473	16.1	29,623	19.8	33,354	28.8
Negro	139,105	20.6	6,325	5.4	29,528	14.0	24,636	20.3	22,679	24.7	23,324	33.4	15,727	43.7	16,629	64.0
Native white	93,372	5.6	2,943	1.1	13,336	3.0	13,930	4.5	15,673	6.4	17,563	9.5	13,521	12.1	16,330	18.5
Foreign-born white	450	5.2	1	.8	19	3.4	85	4.9	141	6.0	84	4.8	62	5.0	55	6.2
SOUTH CAROLINA																
All classes	192,878	14.9	13,955	6.3	44,078	11.7	31,970	14.6	33,857	17.7	29,871	20.8	19,772	24.6	19,234	33.6
Negro	156,065	26.9	11,753	10.6	37,888	20.7	25,988	28.8	27,050	23.0	23,486	39.2	15,088	47.2	14,686	65.9
Native white	36,246	5.1	2,170	1.9	6,109	3.1	5,907	4.6	6,677	6.2	6,285	7.6	4,610	9.7	4,474	13.1
Foreign-born white	297	5.7	-------	-------	11	3.0	40	4.5	88	6.2	63	5.8	48	6.2	47	7.4
GEORGIA																
All classes	210,736	9.4	12,452	3.7	39,435	6.3	31,990	7.9	31,831	9.4	36,180	13.7	27,707	18.2	30,816	27.2
Negro	163,237	19.9	9,248	7.0	31,746	12.9	25,260	17.6	24,856	21.0	28,383	29.8	20,944	41.9	22,517	63.9
Native white	46,898	3.3	3,203	1.5	7,676	2.0	6,672	2.6	6,844	3.2	7,636	4.6	6,641	6.6	8,184	10.7
Foreign-born white	554	4.0	-------	-------	10	1.1	50	2.1	123	3.6	151	4.9	113	5.3	107	6.0
FLORIDA																
All classes	83,242	7.1	4,292	3.0	14,312	5.2	15,592	6.5	15,712	7.8	14,536	9.7	9,105	9.9	9,535	13.4
Negro	65,167	18.8	3,314	7.9	11,779	12.8	12,981	16.2	12,672	20.6	11,483	28.0	6,558	36.9	6,249	57.8
Native white	14,478	1.9	914	.9	2,367	1.3	2,193	1.5	2,217	1.7	2,195	2.3	1,904	2.9	2,663	5.2
Foreign-born white	3,159	5.4	2	.2	63	1.6	317	3.6	759	5.7	807	6.3	613	6.2	596	6.9
EAST SOUTH CENTRAL																
All classes	727,861	9.6	32,934	3.0	119,761	6.0	112,781	8.1	121,411	10.5	133,084	14.3	98,485	17.5	108,562	24.8
Negro	452,082	22.0	18,569	6.3	76,115	13.4	74,151	19.1	76,980	24.5	84,470	32.9	58,830	44.0	62,410	65.5
Native white	270,130	5.0	14,176	1.8	43,206	3.1	37,982	3.8	43,172	5.2	47,392	7.2	38,766	9.2	45,165	13.7
Foreign-born white	4,238	7.4	3	.7	55	1.8	358	4.6	1,038	8.8	1,063	8.5	802	7.9	904	7.7
KENTUCKY																
All classes	131,545	6.6	6,415	2.3	17,956	3.7	17,300	4.8	21,275	6.7	22,927	9.0	20,484	11.9	24,898	17.5
Negro	28,553	15.4	511	2.5	1,919	4.7	3,022	8.6	4,355	12.9	5,807	21.0	5,374	35.1	7,457	58.8
Native white	101,695	5.7	5,901	2.3	16,015	3.7	14,169	4.4	16,587	5.9	16,844	7.6	14,918	9.8	17,090	13.8
Foreign-born white	1,267	5.8	3	2.1	18	1.9	97	3.8	326	8.3	271	6.1	190	4.8	351	6.2
TENNESSEE																
All classes	145,460	7.2	6,006	2.1	22,595	4.3	20,155	5.4	23,292	7.4	26,785	10.6	21,652	13.7	24,790	20.8
Negro	57,251	14.9	1,813	3.8	7,920	7.8	8,247	10.9	9,181	14.7	11,045	22.3	8,665	33.0	10,260	56.3
Native white	87,406	5.4	4,191	1.8	14,657	3.5	11,849	4.0	13,922	5.6	15,557	7.8	12,825	9.9	14,341	14.6
Foreign-born white	754	5.8	-------	-------	9	1.2	50	2.6	179	6.3	175	6.3	154	7.1	186	7.9
ALABAMA																
All classes	251,095	12.6	13,233	4.4	42,783	7.7	39,661	10.6	41,690	14.1	49,219	20.1	31,102	24.0	33,155	33.4
Negro	188,673	26.2	10,203	9.4	33,482	16.2	30,614	23.0	31,780	30.5	37,093	40.4	22,526	52.6	22,756	72.6
Native white	60,959	4.8	3,015	1.6	9,254	2.7	8,921	3.7	9,547	5.1	11,727	7.9	8,292	9.9	10,171	15.6
Foreign-born white	1,335	8.5	-------	-------	11	1.3	103	5.1	342	10.1	381	10.2	274	10.0	218	8.4
MISSISSIPPI																
All classes	199,761	13.1	7,280	3.2	36,427	8.6	35,665	12.5	35,154	15.3	34,153	19.1	25,247	24.0	25,719	33.2
Negro	177,605	23.2	6,042	5.2	32,794	15.0	32,268	22.4	31,664	27.8	30,525	34.8	22,265	45.1	21,937	66.3
Native white	20,070	2.7	1,069	1.0	3,280	1.6	3,043	2.2	3,116	2.7	3,262	3.7	2,731	5.0	3,563	8.3
Foreign-born white	882	12.6	-------	-------	17	4.2	103	9.2	191	11.9	236	15.5	184	15.7	149	13.3
WEST SOUTH CENTRAL																
All classes	675,791	7.2	36,389	2.8	117,286	4.7	118,801	6.3	120,875	7.9	115,442	10.4	41,432	12.4	84,741	17.6
Negro	302,280	17.0	11,666	4.8	45,360	9.4	51,775	14.2	55,548	18.9	56,456	26.4	39,094	37.3	41,957	59.8
Native white	182,467	2.6	9,205	1.0	28,984	1.6	30,685	2.2	32,301	2.9	31,494	3.9	23,565	4.8	26,085	7.3
Foreign-born white	15,958	9.4	23	2.2	232	2.7	926	4.6	2,710	8.3	3,625	9.7	3,708	11.0	4,728	13.3
ARKANSAS																
All classes	96,818	6.8	4,796	2.3	14,484	3.8	14,318	5.5	16,152	7.4	18,879	10.7	13,440	13.0	14,660	19.4
Negro	60,102	16.1	2,291	4.3	8,700	8.5	9,477	13.2	10,573	17.8	12,530	25.4	8,196	35.1	8,278	56.5
Native white	35,890	3.5	2,493	1.6	5,745	2.1	4,759	2.6	5,408	3.5	6,162	5.0	5,098	6.6	6,195	10.6
Foreign-born white	666	6.6	-------	-------	7	2.1	47	5.0	140	8.2	161	6.9	129	5.7	181	7.3
LOUISIANA																
All classes	219,750	13.5	9,690	4.3	36,065	8.5	40,565	12.4	41,921	15.8	39,545	20.5	26,650	24.5	25,155	33.2
Negro	139,393	23.3	6,553	7.7	23,624	14.7	25,801	21.3	26,736	26.7	25,001	34.9	16,078	45.6	15,473	64.4
Native white	71,903	7.3	2,969	2.1	11,974	4.6	13,988	7.0	13,655	8.7	12,626	11.2	8,821	13.2	7,840	17.2
Foreign-born white	6,677	19.2	5	1.9	54	3.2	387	8.2	1,227	15.9	1,675	21.1	1,612	25.8	1,716	28.2

Table 32.—ILLITERACY IN THE POPULATION 10 YEARS OLD AND OVER, BY AGE GROUPS, COLOR, AND NATIVITY, BY DIVISIONS, AND STATES: 1930—Continued

[Percent not shown where base is less than 100. "Total" includes unknown and "Other races"]

DIVISION, STATE, COLOR, AND NATIVITY	TOTAL 10 YEARS OLD AND OVER		10 TO 14 YEARS		15 TO 24 YEARS		25 TO 34 YEARS		35 TO 44 YEARS		45 TO 54 YEARS		55 TO 64 YEARS		65 YEARS AND OVER	
	Number illiterate	Percent illiterate	Number illiterate	Percent illiterate	Number illiterate	Percent illiterate	Number illiterate	Percent illiterate	Number illiterate	Percent illiterate	Number illiterate	Percent illiterate	Number illiterate	Percent illiterate	Number illiterate	Percent illiterate
OKLAHOMA																
All classes	51,102	2.8	2,342	0.9	6,600	1.4	6,904	1.9	8,931	3.0	9,612	4.5	7,391	5.5	9,256	9.6
Negro	12,560	9.3	384	2.1	1,272	3.5	1,602	5.7	2,086	9.5	2,540	15.6	2,017	24.6	2,635	49.4
Native white	27,796	1.7	1,487	.7	3,858	.9	3,777	1.2	4,926	1.9	5,076	2.8	3,884	3.4	4,768	5.8
Foreign-born white	1,479	5.6			19	1.7	76	2.6	245	5.0	327	5.6	325	5.8	485	8.0
TEXAS																
All classes	308,121	6.8	19,561	3.3	60,137	5.1	57,014	6.1	53,871	7.2	47,406	8.9	33,951	10.9	35,670	15.3
Negro	90,225	13.4	2,438	2.7	11,764	6.4	14,895	10.3	16,153	14.4	16,385	21.5	12,803	33.7	15,571	59.6
Native white	46,878	1.4	2,256	.5	7,407	.9	8,161	1.2	8,312	1.5	7,630	2.0	5,762	2.5	7,282	28.6
Foreign-born white	7,136	7.3	18	2.9	152	2.9	416	3.6	1,098	6.0	1,462	6.9	1,642	8.4	2,346	11.3
MOUNTAIN																
All classes	120,866	4.2	4,578	1.2	16,836	2.5	21,424	4.0	24,185	4.7	21,023	5.5	16,201	6.8	16,344	9.1
Negro	1,070	4.1	12	.6	75	1.6	116	2.0	214	3.6	221	5.0	184	9.1	245	20.2
Native white	29,046	1.2	923	.3	3,894	.7	4,556	1.0	5,263	1.3	4,701	1.7	4,559	2.7	5,049	4.2
Foreign-born white	15,962	5.6	8	.4	270	1.7	1,380	4.0	4,009	6.2	4,338	6.2	3,008	5.9	2,930	6.1
MONTANA																
All classes	7,303	1.7	134	.2	432	.5	848	1.2	1,303	1.6	1,430	2.3	1,442	3.9	1,695	6.3
Negro	52	4.6	1				2	1.0	4	1.7	15	6.4	14	9.7	16	
Native white	932	.3	73	.1	126	.1	117	.2	146	.2	135	.3	129	.6	204	1.3
Foreign-born white	3,085	4.3	2	.3	63	1.4	263	3.4	706	4.0	829	4.3	621	4.9	596	6.0
IDAHO																
All classes	3,743	1.1	82	.2	276	.3	520	.9	754	1.3	658	1.4	607	2.0	810	3.6
Negro	25	4.2			3		2	1.8	9	5.4	5	4.8	4		2	
Native white	1,151	.4	64	.1	174	.2	188	.3	170	.3	171	.4	144	.6	216	1.3
Foreign-born white	1,198	4.0	1	.3	16	1.0	138	4.2	360	5.7	261	3.6	204	3.5	211	3.7
WYOMING																
All clases	2,895	1.6	75	.3	366	.9	577	1.6	712	2.0	521	2.2	314	2.5	326	3.7
Negro	47	4.2			1	.6	4	1.8	16	5.8	11	4.9	11	10.3	4	
Native white	381	.3	33	.2	83	.2	57	.2	63	.2	53	.3	41	.4	48	.8
Foreign-born white	811	4.2	4	3.1	23	1.9	76	2.7	255	4.7	211	4.3	116	4.1	125	5.4
COLORADO																
All classes	23,141	2.8	394	.4	2,357	1.3	3,647	2.4	5,132	3.5	4,791	4.1	3,509	4.5	3,266	5.3
Negro	403	3.9	3	.4	21	1.3	29	1.4	58	2.6	77	4.0	79	8.3	134	20.4
Native white	5,807	.8	174	.2	786	.5	922	.7	1,056	.9	969	1.1	847	1.4	1,034	2.3
Foreign-born white	7,331	8.6	1	.3	81	1.9	460	4.7	1,584	9.1	2,178	10.5	1,609	9.7	1,414	8.9
NEW MEXICO																
All classes	41,845	13.3	1,880	4.1	6,703	8.3	7,523	12.5	7,813	15.2	6,703	18.9	5,605	24.4	5,559	33.0
Negro	140	6.0	3	1.2	20	4.0	17	3.6	31	6.0	26	7.1	15	9.6	27	
Native white	18,733	7.7	412	1.2	2,378	3.8	2,948	6.3	3,494	8.8	4,094	11.3	3,149	17.5	3,232	25.2
Foreign-born white	530	6.8			11	2.6	65	5.5	179	8.9	135	7.6	75	6.0	65	6.1
ARIZONA																
All classes	33,969	10.1	1,789	4.2	5,824	7.2	6,918	9.7	6,653	11.1	5,478	13.2	3,760	16.4	3,463	22.0
Negro	366	4.0	5	.7	30	1.6	61	2.6	90	4.1	81	6.6	51	11.1	48	21.5
Native white	960	.5	62	.3	125	.3	167	.4	183	.5	146	.6	125	.9	134	1.4
Foreign-born white	551	3.6			16	1.6	65	2.8	142	3.6	146	3.9	93	3.9	89	5.0
UTAH																
All classes	4,660	1.2	185	.3	645	.7	817	1.1	1,047	1.7	766	1.7	469	1.7	686	3.0
Negro	30	3.2					1	.5	5	2.2	5	2.6	6		13	
Native white	952	.3	95	.2	199	.2	138	.2	132	.3	114	.3	104	.5	161	1.3
Foreign-born white	1,547	3.6			27	1.1	145	2.7	478	5.5	358	4.0	187	2.5	350	3.5
NEVADA																
All classes	3,330	4.4	39	.6	233	1.6	574	3.8	771	5.1	676	5.4	495	6.8	539	11.2
Negro	7	1.5							1	.8	1	1.0	4		1	
Native white	130	.2	10	.2	23	.2	19	.2	19	.2	19	.2	20	.4	20	.7
Foreign-born white	909	7.5			33	5.8	168	8.1	305	9.0	220	7.4	103	6.0	80	5.8
PACIFIC																
All classes	146,082	2.1	1,360	.2	11,505	.9	26,528	2.0	35,081	2.7	31,168	3.0	19,960	3.0	20,046	3.7
Negro	2,371	3.1	11	.2	100	.7	227	1.3	384	2.1	453	3.5	421	7.3	764	22.3
Native white	14,914	.3	973	.2	2,422	.2	2,158	.2	2,373	.2	2,247	.3	1,880	.4	2,770	.8
Foreign-born white	56,446	4.9	31	.2	1,099	1.4	6,304	3.6	14,194	5.4	14,683	5.6	10,089	5.6	9,946	6.1
WASHINGTON																
All classes	13,458	1.0	348	.3	878	.3	1,421	.6	2,587	1.1	2,996	1.5	2,285	1.8	2,853	2.8
Negro	174	2.9	1	.2	10	1.1	9	.9	20	1.5	32	2.5	38	5.5	64	16.8
Native white	3,031	.3	311	.2	570	.2	409	.2	410	.2	418	.3	365	.4	536	.9
Foreign-born white	7,103	2.9	5	.1	121	.7	504	1.6	1,528	2.9	1,913	3.3	1,419	3.4	1,596	4.3
OREGON																
All classes	7,814	1.0	161	.2	609	.4	1,013	.7	1,528	1.0	1,645	1.4	1,187	1.5	1,647	2.4
Negro	49	2.5	1	.8	2	.7	4	1.1	11	2.1	6	1.5	9	4.6	16	15.7
Native white	2,043	.3	148	.2	370	.2	276	.2	278	.2	280	.3	264	.4	413	.9
Foreign-born white	3,743	3.6	5	.3	70	1.0	310	2.4	873	3.9	1,031	4.3	642	3.5	808	4.5
CALIFORNIA																
All classes	124,810	2.6	851	.2	10,018	1.1	24,094	2.5	30,966	3.3	26,527	3.7	16,488	3.6	15,546	4.2
Negro	2,148	3.1	9	.2	88	.7	214	1.3	353	2.2	415	3.7	374	7.7	684	23.2
Native white	9,840	.3	514	.1	1,482	.2	1,473	.2	1,685	.3	1,549	.3	1,251	.4	1,821	.7
Foreign-born white	45,600	5.7	21	.2	908	1.6	5,490	4.2	11,793	6.2	11,739	6.6	8,028	6.6	7,542	7.0

TABLE 33.—ILLITERACY IN THE URBAN, RURAL-FARM, AND RURAL-NONFARM NEGRO POPULATION 10 YEARS OLD AND OVER, 1930, AND IN CITIES OF 25,000 OR MORE INHABITANTS AND SMALL CITIES AND COUNTRY DISTRICTS, BY SECTIONS, DIVISIONS, AND STATES: 1930 AND 1920

DIVISION OR STATE	TOTAL, 1930		URBAN 1930		RURAL, 1930				CITIES OF 25,000 OR MORE POPULATION				SMALLER CITIES AND COUNTRY DISTRICTS			
					Rural-farm		Rural-nonfarm		1930		1920		1930		1920	
	Number illiterate	Per-cent illiter-ate	Number illiterate	Per-cent illiter-ate	Number illiterate	Per-cent illiter-ate	Number illiterate	Per-cent illiter-ate	Number illiterate	Per-cent illiter-ate	Number illiterate	Per-cent illiter-ate	Number illiterate	Per-cent illiter-ate	Number illiterate	Per-cent illiter-ate
United States	**1,513,892**	**16.3**	**395,849**	**9.2**	**794,866**	**23.2**	**323,177**	**20.5**	**236,590**	**7.4**	**223,321**	**10.9**	**1,277,302**	**20.9**	**1,618,840**	**27.0**
The North	**94,034**	**4.7**	**71,873**	**4.1**	**6,276**	**12.2**	**15,885**	**9.1**	**56,937**	**3.7**	**49,078**	**5.5**	**37,097**	**8.2**	**38,055**	**10.6**
The South	**1,416,417**	**19.7**	**321,664**	**13.2**	**788,339**	**23.4**	**306,414**	**22.1**	**177,811**	**11.3**	**172,648**	**15.3**	**1,238,606**	**22.1**	**1,579,010**	**28.2**
The West	**3,441**	**3.3**	**2,312**	**2.7**	**251**	**5.3**	**878**	**6.8**	**1,842**	**2.5**	**1,595**	**4.0**	**1,599**	**5.5**	**1,775**	**6.0**
NEW ENGLAND	4,187	5.5	3,089	4.7	85	9.1	1,013	11.2	2,612	4.5	3,295	6.5	1,575	8.9	1,312	9.1
Maine	43	4.8	27	4.7	2	------	14	5.9	22	5.3	20	4.3	21	4.3	44	7.0
New Hampshire	27	3.9	20	3.7	1	------	6	5.4	16	11.7	10	13.9	11	2.0	23	5.5
Vermont	22	4.9	7	4.0	4	------	11	6.1	------	------	------	------	22	4.9	28	6.2
Massachusetts	2,303	5.4	1,437	3.8	64	18.8	802	18.8	1,158	3.4	1,855	5.9	1,145	13.6	710	12.0
Rhode Island	635	8.1	590	8.2	3	------	42	7.1	549	8.3	675	10.3	86	7.2	164	10.0
Connecticut	1,157	4.9	1,008	5.2	11	3.8	138	3.7	867	5.1	735	6.1	290	4.4	343	6.3
MIDDLE ATLANTIC	32,223	3.7	25,644	3.3	674	7.7	5,905	7.2	20,113	3.0	14,962	4.0	12,110	6.2	10,625	8.0
New York	8,604	2.5	7,609	2.3	120	6.5	875	5.3	6,802	2.2	3,530	2.3	1,802	5.0	1,502	7.2
New Jersey	8,711	5.1	6,624	4.7	331	9.2	1,756	7.6	4,441	4.4	2,822	5.0	4,270	6.3	3,088	7.7
Pennsylvania	14,908	4.2	11,411	3.7	223	6.8	3,274	7.8	8,870	3.4	8,610	5.1	6,038	6.6	6,035	8.4
EAST NORTH CENTRAL	36,454	4.7	30,204	4.3	1,212	8.4	5,038	9.5	25,917	4.1	20,868	6.4	10,537	7.8	11,184	10.0
Ohio	16,213	6.4	13,473	6.1	417	7.2	2,323	9.6	11,973	6.1	8,726	7.7	4,240	7.7	3,989	8.9
Indiana	5,605	6.0	4,928	5.8	151	7.3	526	9.5	4,387	5.6	4,514	8.9	1,218	8.2	1,962	11.2
Illinois	10,044	3.6	7,663	3.0	550	12.6	1,831	11.2	5,929	2.6	5,744	4.9	4,115	9.0	4,732	11.7
Michigan	4,201	3.0	3,797	2.9	87	4.5	317	5.0	3,352	2.8	1,787	4.0	849	4.8	416	5.7
Wisconsin	391	4.4	343	4.2	7	2.6	41	9.8	276	3.8	97	3.6	115	7.0	85	4.9
WEST NORTH CENTRAL	21,170	7.6	12,936	5.9	4,305	15.7	3,929	12.7	8,295	4.8	9,953	7.2	12,875	12.2	14,934	15.0
Minnesota	160	2.0	148	1.9	7	4.4	5	4.1	110	1.5	197	2.8	50	6.8	44	5.2
Iowa	777	5.4	587	4.7	31	6.8	159	11.5	398	4.4	494	6.2	379	7.1	789	10.0
Missouri	16,532	8.8	9,467	6.5	4,064	17.8	3,001	15.2	6,079	5.1	7,446	7.9	10,453	15.2	11,082	19.0
North Dakota	11	3.4	4	2.0	3	------	4	------	3	------	------	------	8	2.7	16	4.0
South Dakota	12	2.2	7	2.4	3	1.6	2	------	------	------	2	------	12	2.6	33	5.5
Nebraska	450	3.9	405	3.7	5	3.3	40	9.6	370	3.6	445	4.6	80	5.6	111	6.4
Kansas	3,228	5.9	2,318	5.5	192	5.4	718	7.8	1,335	5.0	1,369	7.4	1,893	6.6	2,859	9.7
SOUTH ATLANTIC	662,055	19.7	157,917	13.2	329,032	23.6	175,106	22.6	92,463	11.3	95,413	15.3	569,592	22.4	717,429	27.6
Delaware	3,496	13.2	1,169	9.2	908	17.5	1,419	16.3	855	8.3	1,473	15.7	2,641	16.2	3,227	21.2
Maryland	25,073	11.4	10,101	7.7	6,235	19.0	8,737	15.7	8,435	7.1	12,134	12.9	16,638	16.5	23,270	23.2
District of Columbia	4,591	4.1	4,591	4.1	------	------	------	------	4,591	4.1	8,053	8.6	------	------	------	------
Virginia	95,148	19.2	24,071	13.9	41,368	22.0	29,709	22.3	17,480	13.1	22,744	16.5	77,668	21.5	99,578	26.0
West Virginia	10,173	11.3	1,939	7.5	507	17.6	7,727	12.6	841	6.4	753	8.5	9,332	12.2	9,760	16.3
North Carolina	139,105	20.6	32,423	16.5	79,761	22.9	26,921	20.8	16,537	14.9	8,875	19.4	122,568	21.8	124,799	25.0
South Carolina	156,065	26.9	22,836	20.7	96,122	27.2	37,107	31.8	11,814	21.5	7,545	19.5	144,251	27.4	173,877	30.0
Georgia	163,237	19.9	39,231	15.1	89,530	22.1	34,476	22.2	20,812	13.1	26,876	20.2	142,425	21.5	234,239	30.7
Florida	65,167	18.8	21,556	12.5	14,601	25.5	29,010	25.1	11,098	10.5	6,960	11.4	54,069	22.5	48,679	24.6
EAST SOUTH CENTRAL	452,082	22.0	93,019	14.8	281,750	25.8	77,313	23.4	46,693	12.4	45,018	17.8	405,389	24.2	491,565	29.4
Kentucky	28,553	15.4	12,364	12.4	6,916	18.8	9,273	18.7	6,150	9.9	8,207	16.6	22,403	18.2	32,341	22.6
Tennessee	57,251	14.9	21,142	10.5	26,252	20.1	9,857	19.4	15,042	9.3	17,430	15.9	42,209	19.1	62,102	25.3
Alabama	188,673	26.2	38,817	17.8	112,595	31.1	37,261	26.8	20,582	16.3	19,381	20.5	168,091	28.3	191,309	33.0
Mississippi	177,605	23.2	20,696	18.7	135,987	24.1	20,922	23.0	4,919	19.4	------	------	172,686	23.3	205,813	29.3
WEST SOUTH CENTRAL	302,280	17.0	70,728	11.4	177,557	20.2	53,995	19.3	38,655	10.0	32,217	12.9	263,625	18.9	370,016	27.6
Arkansas	60,102	16.1	7,501	10.0	44,323	18.1	8,278	15.7	2,317	10.3	2,048	11.3	57,785	16.5	77,197	22.4
Louisiana	139,393	23.3	33,162	15.7	78,731	28.8	27,500	24.0	19,417	13.3	16,607	16.7	119,976	26.5	190,123	43.5
Oklahoma	12,560	9.3	3,494	6.2	6,542	11.2	2,524	12.8	1,359	4.3	1,337	6.6	11,201	10.8	12,868	13.6
Texas	90,225	13.4	26,571	9.6	47,961	15.9	15,693	17.0	15,562	8.4	12,225	11.0	74,663	15.4	89,828	19.5
MOUNTAIN	1,070	4.1	622	3.4	85	4.7	363	6.1	377	3.0	452	4.7	693	5.2	1,005	5.5
Montana	52	4.6	30	3.3	10	------	12	7.9	6	1.8	10	5.2	46	5.8	77	6.1
Idaho	25	4.2	16	3.5	3	------	6	------	------	------	------	------	25	4.2	44	5.4
Wyoming	47	4.2	41	5.4	1	------	5	1.7	------	------	------	------	47	4.2	66	5.3
Colorado	403	3.9	291	3.2	12	4.1	100	11.4	262	3.2	396	5.3	141	7.0	223	9.3
New Mexico	140	6.0	76	5.3	24	6.5	40	7.8	9	2.5	------	------	131	6.7	228	4.3
Arizona	366	4.0	137	3.1	35	3.7	194	5.2	79	2.7	25	2.7	287	4.6	313	4.9
Utah	30	3.2	25	3.1	------	------	5	4.5	21	2.7	21	2.4	9	5.3	38	9.7
Nevada	7	1.5	6	1.8	------	------	1	.8	------	------	------	------	7	1.5	16	5.1
PACIFIC	2,371	3.1	1,690	2.5	166	5.7	515	7.4	1,465	2.4	1,143	3.8	906	5.7	770	6.8
Washington	174	2.9	120	2.3	15	6.8	39	5.9	89	2.1	108	2.6	85	4.8	137	7.3
Oregon	49	2.5	40	2.4	3	------	6	2.3	28	1.9	69	5.0	21	3.8	20	3.9
California	2,148	3.1	1,530	2.5	148	5.6	470	7.8	1,348	2.4	966	3.9	800	5.9	613	6.9

TABLE 34.—ILLITERACY IN THE URBAN, RURAL-FARM, AND RURAL-NONFARM POPULATION 10 YEARS OLD AND OVER, BY COLOR, AND NATIVITY, 1930; AND PERCENT ILLITERACY IN THE URBAN AND RURAL, 1920, BY SECTIONS AND DIVISIONS

["All classes" includes "Other races"]

SECTION, DIVISION, AND RACE	URBAN				RURAL				RURAL-FARM			RURAL-NONFARM		
	Total number	Illiterate			Total number	Illiterate			Total number	Illiterate		Total number	Illiterate	
		Number	Percent			Number	Percent			Number	Percent		Number	Percent
			1930	1920			1930	1920						
United States														
All classes	**57, 117, 322**	**1, 800, 604**	**3. 2**	**4. 4**	**41, 605, 725**	**2, 483, 149**	**6. 0**	**7. 7**	**23, 036, 395**	**1, 583, 030**	**6. 9**	**18, 569, 330**	**900, 119**	**4. 8**
Negro	4, 297, 949	395, 849	9. 2	13. 4	4, 994, 607	1, 118, 043	22. 4	28. 5	3, 421, 512	794, 866	23. 2	1, 573, 095	323, 177	20. 5
Native white	41, 540, 771	223, 596	. 5	. 7	33, 222, 968	879, 538	2. 6	3. 4	18, 123, 567	559, 624	3. 1	15, 099, 401	319, 914	2. 1
Foreign-born white	10, 600, 298	1, 058, 845	10. 0	13. 0	2, 616, 630	245, 239	9. 4	13. 3	1, 077, 347	84, 477	7. 8	1, 539, 283	160, 762	10. 4
THE SOUTH														
All classes	10, 537, 190	500, 170	4. 7	6. 6	18, 631, 594	1, 916, 005	10. 3	13. 4	12, 054, 464	1, 357, 023	11. 3	6, 577, 130	558, 982	8. 5
Negro	2, 443, 536	321, 664	13. 2	17. 8	4, 751, 214	1, 094, 753	23. 0	29. 2	3, 365, 279	788, 339	23. 4	1, 385, 935	306, 414	22. 1
Native white	7, 484, 007	92, 662	1. 2	1. 7	13, 380, 218	674, 518	5. 0	6. 6	8, 400, 633	471, 198	5. 6	4, 979, 585	203, 320	4. 1
Foreign-born white	359, 685	31, 919	8. 9	16. 1	168, 261	19, 605	11. 7	29. 1	68, 618	7, 758	11. 3	99, 643	11, 847	11. 9
THE NORTH														
All classes	40, 638, 616	1, 198, 666	2. 9	4. 2	19, 083, 576	401, 964	2. 1	2. 6	9, 228, 851	147, 627	1. 6	9, 854, 725	254, 337	2. 6
Negro	1, 768, 301	71, 873	4. 1	6. 1	225, 784	22, 161	9. 8	11. 9	51, 509	6, 276	12. 2	174, 275	15, 885	9. 1
Native white	29, 485, 204	119, 426	. 4	. 5	16, 817, 457	172, 568	1. 0	1. 2	8, 360, 155	75, 599	. 9	8, 457, 302	96, 969	1. 1
Foreign-born white	9, 284, 781	986, 677	10. 6	13. 4	1, 971, 841	193, 475	9. 8	11. 0	788, 802	60, 510	7. 7	1, 183, 039	132, 965	11. 2
THE WEST														
All classes	5, 941, 516	101, 768	1. 7	2. 2	3, 890, 555	165, 180	4. 2	5. 2	1, 753, 080	78, 380	4. 5	2, 137, 475	86, 800	4. 1
Negro	86, 112	2, 312	2. 7	4. 3	17, 609	1, 129	6. 4	6. 6	4, 724	251	5. 3	12, 885	878	6. 8
Native white	4, 571, 560	11, 508	. 3	. 4	3, 025, 293	32, 452	1. 1	1. 7	1, 362, 779	12, 827	. 9	1, 662, 514	19, 625	1. 2
Foreign-born white	955, 832	40, 249	4. 2	7. 6	476, 528	32, 159	6. 7	13. 0	219, 927	16, 209	7. 4	256, 601	15, 950	6. 2
SOUTH ATLANTIC														
All classes	4, 659, 868	220, 729	4. 7	6. 4	7, 512, 077	791, 794	10. 5	14. 1	4, 339, 029	510, 088	11. 8	3, 173, 048	281, 706	8. 9
Negro	1, 194, 595	157, 917	13. 2	17. 2	2, 169, 269	504, 138	23. 2	28. 6	1, 393, 012	329, 032	23. 6	776, 257	175, 106	22. 6
Native white	3, 241, 619	40, 818	1. 3	1. 7	5, 248, 731	273, 765	5. 2	6. 9	2, 918, 599	176, 213	6. 0	2, 330, 132	97, 552	4. 2
Foreign-born white	220, 743	21, 604	9. 8	11. 2	80, 680	9, 724	12. 1	16. 4	16, 188	1, 437	8. 9	64, 492	8, 287	12. 8
EAST SOUTH CENTRAL														
All classes	2, 271, 272	121, 549	5. 4	7. 7	5, 289, 110	606, 312	11. 5	14. 3	3, 762, 936	464, 784	12. 4	1, 526, 174	141, 528	9. 3
Negro	629, 698	93, 019	14. 8	20. 6	1, 423, 253	359, 063	25. 2	30. 3	1, 092, 788	281, 750	25. 8	330, 465	77, 313	23. 4
Native white	1, 599, 519	25, 701	1. 6	2. 1	3, 847, 389	244, 429	6. 4	7. 8	2, 661, 807	181, 204	6. 8	1, 185, 582	63, 225	5. 3
Foreign-born white	41, 525	2, 721	6. 6	8. 4	15, 762	1, 517	9. 6	10. 5	6, 222	646	10. 4	9, 540	871	9. 1
WEST SOUTH CENTRAL														
All classes	3, 606, 050	157, 892	4. 4	6. 1	5, 830, 407	517, 899	8. 9	11. 8	3, 952, 499	382, 151	9. 7	1, 877, 908	135, 748	7. 2
Negro	619, 243	70, 728	11. 4	16. 1	1, 158, 692	231, 552	20. 0	29. 0	879, 479	177, 557	20. 2	279, 213	53, 995	19. 3
Native white	2, 642, 869	26, 143	1. 0	1. 5	4, 284, 098	156, 324	3. 6	5. 3	2, 820, 227	113, 781	4. 0	1, 463, 871	42, 543	2. 9
Foreign-born white	97, 417	7, 594	7. 8	23. 1	71, 819	8, 364	11. 6	36. 3	46, 208	5, 675	12. 3	25, 611	2, 689	10. 5
NEW ENGLAND														
All classes	5, 198, 807	198, 234	3. 8	5. 2	1, 508, 910	47, 036	3. 1	3. 6	408, 323	12, 718	3. 1	1, 100, 587	34, 318	3. 1
Negro	65, 712	3, 089	4. 7	6. 9	10, 007	1, 098	11. 0	9. 0	937	85	9. 1	9, 070	1, 013	11. 2
Native white	3, 581, 850	14, 901	. 4	. 5	1, 232, 215	15, 228	1. 2	1. 3	344, 341	4, 825	1. 4	887, 874	10, 403	1. 2
Foreign-born white	1, 546, 629	179, 423	11. 6	14. 0	265, 322	30, 623	11. 5	13. 7	62, 927	7, 798	12. 4	202, 395	22, 825	11. 3
MIDDLE ATLANTIC														
All classes	16, 910, 848	621, 593	3. 7	5. 2	4, 664, 893	135, 635	2. 9	4. 0	1, 349, 274	28, 985	2. 1	3, 315, 619	106, 650	3. 2
Negro	777, 703	25, 644	3. 3	4. 4	90, 172	6, 579	7. 3	9. 0	8, 719	674	7. 7	81, 453	5, 905	7. 2
Native white	11, 499, 936	44, 380	. 4	. 4	3, 971, 367	38, 363	1. 0	1. 2	1, 216, 043	10, 272	. 8	2, 755, 324	28, 091	1. 0
Foreign-born white	4, 608, 076	546, 551	11. 9	15. 1	597, 973	89, 928	15. 0	18. 9	122, 896	17, 782	14. 5	475, 077	72, 146	15. 2
EAST NORTH CENTRAL														
All classes	13, 885, 105	315, 746	2. 3	3. 3	6, 789, 096	126, 318	1. 9	2. 2	3, 550, 164	53, 308	1. 5	3, 238, 932	73, 010	2. 3
Negro	704, 436	30, 204	4. 3	6. 8	67, 190	6, 250	9. 3	10. 8	14, 429	1, 212	8. 4	52, 761	5, 038	9. 5
Native white	10, 499, 618	42, 609	. 4	. 6	6, 151, 182	67, 675	1. 1	1. 3	3, 274, 129	30, 279	. 9	2, 877, 053	37, 396	1. 3
Foreign-born white	2, 630, 222	232, 547	8. 8	11. 3	553, 749	49, 098	8. 9	8. 8	257, 810	21, 196	8. 2	295, 939	27, 902	9. 4
WEST NORTH CENTRAL														
All classes	4, 643, 856	63, 093	1. 4	2. 0	6, 120, 677	92, 975	1. 5	1. 9	3, 921, 090	52, 616	1. 3	2, 199, 587	40, 359	1. 8
Negro	220, 450	12, 936	5. 9	8. 6	58, 415	8, 234	14. 1	16. 9	27, 424	4, 305	15. 7	30, 991	3, 929	12. 7
Native white	3, 903, 800	17, 536	. 4	. 6	5, 462, 693	51, 302	. 9	1. 1	3, 525, 642	30, 223	. 9	1, 937, 051	21, 079	1. 1
Foreign-born white	499, 854	28, 156	5. 6	7. 5	554, 797	23, 826	4. 3	5. 5	345, 169	13, 734	4. 0	209, 628	10, 092	4. 8
MOUNTAIN														
All classes	1, 193, 585	22, 478	1. 9	2. 6	1, 716, 059	98, 388	5. 7	6. 8	854, 816	50, 083	5. 9	861, 243	48, 305	5. 6
Negro	18, 244	622	3. 4	4. 8	7, 748	448	5. 8	5. 8	1, 827	85	4. 7	5, 921	363	6. 1
Native white	981, 337	5, 444	. 6	. 8	1, 358, 441	23, 602	1. 7	2. 8	693, 447	10, 373	1. 5	664, 994	13, 229	2. 0
Foreign-born white	134, 309	6, 522	4. 9	9. 7	151, 626	9, 440	6. 2	14. 8	71, 029	4, 185	5. 9	80, 597	5, 255	6. 5
PACIFIC														
All classes	4, 747, 931	79, 290	1. 7	2. 1	2, 174, 496	66, 792	3. 1	3. 7	898, 264	28, 297	3. 2	1, 276, 232	38, 495	3. 0
Negro	67, 868	1, 690	2. 5	4. 1	9, 861	681	6. 9	8. 5	2, 897	166	5. 7	6, 964	515	7. 4
Native white	3, 590, 223	6, 064	. 2	. 3	1, 666, 852	8, 850	. 5	. 6	669, 332	2, 454	. 4	997, 520	6, 396	. 6
Foreign-born white	821, 523	33, 727	4. 1	7. 0	324, 902	22, 719	7. 0	11. 6	148, 898	12, 024	8. 1	176, 004	10, 695	6. 1

TABLE 35.—ILLITERACY IN THE POPULATION 10 YEARS OLD AND OVER, BY COLOR, AND NATIVITY, FOR CITIES OF 100,000 OR MORE: 1930 AND 1920

[Cities having less than 1,000 Negro population are omitted]

CITY	ALL CLASSES: Total number, 1930	ALL CLASSES: Illiterate: Number, 1930	ALL CLASSES: Illiterate: Percent 1930	ALL CLASSES: Illiterate: Percent 1920	NEGRO: Total number, 1930	NEGRO: Illiterate: Number, 1930	NEGRO: Illiterate: Percent 1930	NEGRO: Illiterate: Percent 1920	NATIVE WHITE: Total number, 1930	NATIVE WHITE: Illiterate: Number, 1930	NATIVE WHITE: Illiterate: Percent 1930	NATIVE WHITE: Illiterate: Percent 1920	FOREIGN-BORN WHITE: Total number, 1930	FOREIGN-BORN WHITE: Illiterate: Number, 1930	FOREIGN-BORN WHITE: Illiterate: Percent 1930	FOREIGN-BORN WHITE: Illiterate: Percent 1920	OTHER RACES, 1930: Total number	OTHER RACES, 1930: Number illiterate
Akron, Ohio	204,463	4,043	2.0	3.5	8,826	564	6.4	5.5	164,333	353	0.2	0.2	31,153	3,103	10.0	14.6	151	23
Albany, N. Y	109,409	1,495	1.4	3.0	2,017	51	2.5	3.8	89,595	229	.3	.4	17,699	1,205	6.8	14.8	98	10
Atlanta, Ga	225,168	9,283	4.1	6.6	74,671	7,801	10.4	17.8	145,766	1,267	.9	1.2	4,694	211	4.5	4.8	37	4
Baltimore, Md	667,209	20,862	3.1	4.4	116,779	8,194	7.0	12.9	475,975	2,714	.6	.6	73,910	9,874	13.4	14.0	545	80
Birmingham, Ala	211,970	13,182	6.2	8.4	80,997	11,875	14.7	18.4	125,098	602	.5	.7	5,833	698	12.0	15.6	42	7
Boston, Mass	652,585	20,969	3.2	4.0	17,306	321	1.9	2.2	406,745	630	.2	.1	226,927	19,679	8.7	9.9	1,607	339
Bridgeport, Conn	120,997	5,575	4.6	6.9	2,651	154	5.8	9.0	77,934	184	.2	.2	40,336	5,229	13.0	16.2	76	8
Buffalo, N. Y	473,459	11,404	2.4	4.2	11,153	291	2.6	2.8	345,550	722	.2	.3	116,260	10,361	8.9	13.5	496	30
Cambridge, Mass	94,267	2,969	3.1	3.1	4,257	57	1.3	2.5	58,040	80	.1	.1	31,814	2,816	8.9	8.1	156	16
Camden, N. J	96,887	4,396	4.5	5.0	9,026	402	4.5	9.4	69,375	305	.4	.6	18,419	3,677	20.0	17.6	67	12
Canton, Ohio	85,338	3,077	3.6	4.0	2,444	237	9.7	6.5	69,778	210	.3	.4	13,063	2,610	20.0	17.7	53	20
Chattanooga, Tenn	97,063	4,526	4.7	5.9	27,543	3,193	11.6	13.8	68,062	1,276	1.9	1.8	1,444	55	3.8	5.2	14	2
Chicago, Ill	2,846,622	91,474	3.2	4.6	199,233	4,319	2.2	3.9	1,794,570	3,707	.2	.2	833,586	79,290	9.5	11.6	19,233	4,158
Cincinnati, Ohio	383,629	5,943	1.5	2.0	39,721	2,701	6.8	10.9	309,224	1,049	.3	.4	34,506	2,155	6.2	6.7	178	38
Cleveland, Ohio	747,994	31,500	4.2	5.3	58,975	2,595	4.4	5.2	460,745	1,315	.3	.2	227,069	27,370	12.1	13.1	1,205	220
Columbus, Ohio	245,071	4,932	2.0	2.8	27,356	2,118	7.7	8.4	202,413	1,440	.7	1.4	15,127	1,334	8.8	11.3	175	40
Dallas, Tex	216,911	4,953	2.3	3.2	32,921	2,183	6.6	11.3	173,372	787	.5	.5	6,437	332	5.2	16.4	4,181	1,651
Dayton, Ohio	168,279	2,343	1.4	1.9	13,860	875	6.3	9.4	142,478	730	.5	.4	11,873	736	6.2	9.3	68	2
Denver, Colo	245,033	3,362	1.4	1.9	6,286	150	2.4	4.1	202,349	502	.2	.4	31,115	1,839	5.9	8.9	5,283	871
Des Moines, Iowa	119,186	832	.7	1.3	4,422	171	3.9	6.1	105,253	220	.2	.3	9,250	391	4.2	7.2	261	50
Detroit, Mich	1,273,879	28,743	2.3	3.8	99,247	2,688	2.7	3.9	779,534	1,450	.2	.2	388,508	23,903	6.2	9.7	6,590	702
Elizabeth, N. J	94,061	4,611	4.9	6.4	3,687	205	5.6	9.7	61,620	169	.3	.3	28,668	4,228	14.7	15.7	86	9
El Paso, Tex	79,700	6,360	8.0	8.5	1,591	63	4.0	2.7	32,703	61	.2	1.0	2,764	50	1.8	16.0	42,642	6,186
Evansville, Ind	84,846	1,491	1.8	2.6	5,648	489	8.7	14.6	77,109	908	1.2	1.4	2,073	94	4.5	5.2	16	-------
Flint, Mich	123,439	1,803	1.5	2.0	4,614	110	2.4	6.8	97,977	270	.3	.3	20,286	1,325	6.5	7.9	562	98
Fort Wayne, Ind	95,229	762	.8	2.3	1,928	89	4.6	8.8	87,579	285	.3	1.7	5,662	364	6.4	6.8	60	24
Fort Worth, Tex	135,155	2,916	2.2	3.9	18,905	1,305	6.9	7.5	110,605	460	.4	.6	2,900	163	5.6	30.1	2,745	988
Gary, Ind	80,968	4,626	5.7	7.5	14,596	475	3.3	8.2	44,404	104	.2	.3	19,064	3,053	16.0	16.6	2,904	994
Grand Rapids, Mich	138,793	2,271	1.6	3.8	2,309	62	2.7	1.9	109,314	237	.2	.2	26,985	1,955	7.2	12.4	185	17
Hartford, Conn	136,269	6,381	4.7	5.1	5,068	377	7.4	7.6	87,193	165	.2	.1	43,934	5,822	13.3	13.2	74	17
Houston, Tex	243,074	7,074	2.9	5.4	53,648	3,792	7.1	10.8	168,091	665	.4	.6	11,191	710	6.3	22.6	10,144	1,907
Indianapolis, Ind	306,238	3,812	1.2	2.1	36,605	2,078	5.7	8.3	255,886	1,038	.4	.7	13,635	683	5.0	8.3	112	13
Jacksonville, Fla	107,457	4,639	4.3	5.5	40,422	4,116	10.2	10.8	62,680	289	.5	.6	4,326	231	5.3	3.7	29	3
Jersey City, N. J	260,349	10,450	4.0	4.3	10,153	256	2.5	3.9	180,537	523	.3	.2	69,443	9,608	13.8	12.5	216	63
Kansas City, Kans	98,991	2,590	2.6	3.7	16,391	808	4.9	8.0	73,182	390	.5	.8	7,565	825	10.9	13.9	1,853	567
Kansas City, Mo	344,589	5,146	1.5	2.0	33,945	1,508	4.4	6.1	284,031	705	.2	.3	24,148	2,499	10.3	11.5	2,465	434
Knoxville, Tenn	85,394	3,545	4.2	6.3	14,310	1,329	9.3	13.7	70,261	2,174	3.1	5.0	819	40	4.9	4.4	4	2
Los Angeles, Calif	1,072,680	18,500	1.7	2.0	33,651	774	2.3	4.3	767,768	901	.1	.2	179,737	5,369	3.0	7.3	91,524	11,456
Louisville, Ky	256,661	5,734	2.2	4.0	40,717	3,612	8.9	14.9	206,966	1,703	.8	1.2	8,942	417	4.7	7.5	36	2
Memphis, Tenn	212,354	7,417	3.5	6.7	81,999	6,681	8.1	15.6	125,071	356	.3	.5	5,229	366	7.0	9.4	55	14
Miami, Fla	91,678	2,321	2.5	3.4	19,731	2,034	10.3	10.2	63,823	142	.2	.1	8,069	140	1.7	2.2	55	5
Milwaukee, Wis	482,289	10,056	2.1	3.0	6,250	232	3.7	3.1	366,421	788	.2	.2	108,106	8,806	8.1	9.6	1,512	230
Minneapolis, Minn	391,494	3,150	.8	1.2	3,591	60	1.7	3.5	306,953	642	.2	.1	80,368	2,387	3.0	3.9	582	61
Nashville, Tenn	127,696	4,553	3.6	7.2	36,072	3,555	9.9	18.4	89,851	925	1.0	2.0	1,768	73	4.1	7.4	5	-------
Newark, N. J	365,067	18,674	5.1	6.0	31,324	1,896	6.1	4.5	219,130	962	.4	.3	113,835	15,719	13.8	15.9	778	97
New Bedford, Mass	92,499	8,167	8.8	12.1	2,607	487	18.7	25.2	52,694	362	.7	.7	37,119	7,317	19.7	21.7	79	1
New Haven, Conn	134,441	6,390	4.8	6.3	4,316	136	3.2	4.0	90,231	154	.2	.2	39,809	6,092	15.3	17.2	85	8
New Orleans, La	376,847	20,475	5.4	5.9	105,544	14,107	13.4	15.7	250,616	3,327	1.3	1.0	19,521	2,885	14.8	13.9	1,166	156
New York, N. Y	5,817,562	264,606	4.5	6.2	276,421	5,722	2.1	2.1	3,261,099	13,008	.4	.3	2,266,019	242,525	10.7	13.8	14,023	3,351
Bronx Borough	1,053,665	41,694	4.0	4.5	10,312	133	1.3	1.6	570,875	1,170	.2	.1	471,983	40,311	8.5	9.7	495	80
Brooklyn Borough	2,115,311	110,323	5.2	6.1	55,898	1,553	2.8	2.9	1,197,960	4,406	.4	.2	858,801	103,932	12.1	14.5	2,652	432
Manhattan Broough	1,626,216	88,202	5.4	7.5	192,995	3,611	1.9	1.8	788,997	6,245	.8	.4	634,256	75,657	11.9	14.9	9,968	2,689
Queens Borough	893,376	20,222	2.3	3.3	15,164	383	2.5	3.4	615,401	962	.2	.2	262,066	18,763	7.2	10.5	745	114
Richmond Borough	128,994	4,165	3.2	4.0	2,052	42	2.0	2.7	87,866	225	.3	.3	38,913	3,862	9.9	11.2	163	36
Norfolk, Va	108,223	5,001	4.6	6.3	36,393	4,135	11.4	13.9	67,300	460	.7	1.1	4,317	371	8.6	6.0	213	35
Oakland, Calif	244,548	4,857	2.0	2.5	6,576	140	2.1	2.5	182,150	478	.3	.2	48,984	3,423	7.0	7.8	6,838	816
Oklahoma City, Okla	152,723	1,259	.8	1.5	12,403	550	4.4	5.8	135,936	464	.3	.4	3,129	74	2.4	12.9	1,255	171
Omaha, Nebr	177,421	3,203	1.8	2.5	9,352	350	3.7	4.5	138,563	290	.2	.2	28,633	2,386	8.3	9.5	873	177
Paterson, N. J	116,069	7,250	6.2	6.3	2,390	131	5.5	3.7	71,414	345	.5	.4	42,132	6,713	15.9	14.7	133	61
Peoria, Ill	89,193	440	.5	1.8	2,613	72	2.8	8.5	79,753	145	.2	.4	6,687	190	2.8	10.2	140	33
Philadelphia, Pa	1,633,892	42,942	2.6	4.0	181,641	5,432	3.0	4.6	1,084,258	2,363	.2	.3	365,424	34,903	9.6	12.8	2,569	244
Pittsburgh, Pa	550,569	14,284	2.6	4.3	45,014	1,555	3.5	5.2	396,985	1,009	.3	.3	108,127	11,645	10.8	14.9	443	75
Portland, Oreg	263,436	2,934	1.1	1.7	1,397	22	1.6	5.0	210,937	306	.1	.2	47,766	2,060	4.3	5.8	3,286	546
Providence, R. I	208,565	10,393	5.0	5.9	4,315	381	8.8	11.4	140,003	517	.4	.4	64,044	9,470	14.8	15.3	203	25
Reading, Pa	93,535	2,954	3.2	3.5	1,655	111	6.7	4.0	82,394	456	.6	.8	9,465	2,382	25.2	25.6	21	5
Richmond, Va	152,323	6,380	4.2	5.6	43,023	5,389	12.5	14.9	105,223	707	.7	1.0	4,022	269	6.7	7.8	55	15
Rochester, N. Y	278,113	10,216	3.7	4.5	2,273	32	1.4	1.9	202,059	348	.2	.2	73,632	9,826	13.3	15.0	149	10
St. Louis, Mo	701,338	12,331	1.8	2.7	79,958	4,133	5.2	8.2	540,421	1,655	.3	.5	79,785	6,347	8.0	10.1	1,174	196
St. Paul, Minn	226,353	2,520	1.1	1.6	3,478	43	1.2	2.2	178,255	311	.2	.2	43,928	2,078	4.7	5.3	692	88
San Antonio, Tex	186,714	14,462	7.7	11.4	15.437	816	5.3	7.1	103,131	445	.4	3.3	7,962	246	3.1	33.1	60,184	12,955
San Diego, Calif	126,300	1,084	.9	1.6	2,289	71	3.1	5.6	99,757	111	.1	.3	16,212	310	1.9	6.2	8,042	592
San Francisco, Calif	564,470	8,943	1.6	1.9	3,488	55	1.6	3.1	379,910	627	.2	.2	151,899	5,594	3.7	4.8	29,173	2,667
Seattle, Wash	317,553	2,524	.8	1.5	2,940	49	1.7	1.9	233,884	210	.1	.1	71,828	1,365	1.9	3.6	8,901	900
South Bend, Ind	84,664	1,605	1.9	3.6	2,814	159	5.7	3.6	67,870	158	.2	.5	13,910	1,281	9.2	13.0	70	7
Springfield, Mass	124,989	2,632	2.1	3.7	2,573	67	2.6	5.2	90,076	252	.3	.4	32,255	2,301	7.1	11.5	85	12
Syracuse, N. Y	175,453	4,364	2.5	4.0	1,569	70	4.5	3.6	139,174	266	.2	.4	34,491	4,001	11.6	16.2	219	27
Tampa, Fla	83,550	3,867	4.6	5.3	17,719	1,769	10.0	9.6	51,483	390	.8	.9	14,206	1,704	12.0	10.1	142	4
Toledo, Ohio	242,792	4,694	1.9	2.5	11,036	606	5.5	5.0	198,047	689	.3	.4	33,190	3,219	9.7	10.6	519	180
Trenton, N. J	101,971	4,944	4.8	6.9	6,309	514	8.1	6.9	69,057	370	.5	.4	26,548	4,041	15.2	20.2	57	19
Tulsa, Okla	116,096	837	.7	1.1	13,068	394	3.0	6.1	98,761	325	.3	.3	2,662	52	2.0	3.2	1,605	66
Washington, D. C	418,941	6,611	1.6	2.8	111,224	4,591	4.1	8.6	277,294	533	.2	.3	29,659	1,411	4.8	6.1	764	76
Wichita, Kans	92,210	645	.7	1.0	4,642	187	4.0	4.4	84,575	201	.2	.2	2,247	82	3.6	11.8	746	175
Wilmington, Del	89,198	3,034	3.4	5.5	10,290	855	8.3	15.7	66,347	226	.3	.5	12,510	1,936	15.5	19.2	51	17
Worcester, Mass	161,492	5,311	3.3	4.7	1,096	26	2.4	2.6	109,767	312	.3	.3	50,528	4,966	9.8	12.3	101	7
Yonkers, N. Y	111,081	3,331	3.0	5.5	2,765	105	3.8	3.5	74,742	154	.2	.2	33,506	3,066	9.2	16.4	68	6
Youngstown, Ohio	135,551	6,069	4.5	5.7	11,315	719	6.4	5.5	91,449	235	.3	.2	32,516	5,059	15.6	16.0	271	56

CHAPTER XIII.—FAMILIES

The family classification.—The decennial population census in the past has been mainly a compilation of statistics in which the individual person has been the unit. All recent censuses, however, have recognized the family as a unit to the extent of inquiring whether the home in which the family lives is owned or rented; and the schedules have shown the composition of the family by recording for each person his or her relationship to the head of the family—whether that of wife, son, granddaughter, mother-in-law, lodger, servant, or other relationship.

The term "family", as used in the tabulaton of results of the 1930 census, is limited in the main to what might be called private families, excluding the institutions and hotel or boarding-house groups which have been counted as families in prior censuses. Therefore a family may be defined as, in general, a group of persons related either by blood or by marriage or adoption, who live together as one household, usually sharing the same table. Single persons living alone were counted as families, as also were a few small groups of unrelated persons sharing the same living accommodations as "partners." Households reporting more than 10 lodgers were classified as boarding or lodging households, rather than as families. Two or more related persons occupying permanent quarters in a hotel were counted as a private family rather than as a part of the hotel group.

Since a home is defined as the living quarters occupied by a family, the number of homes is always the same as the number of families. In the classification by tenure a home was counted as owned if it was owned wholly or in part by any related member of the family. A home was counted as rented if it was not owned by any member of the family, even though no specific cash rental was paid. Living accommodations received as part of the man's salary or wages, or occupied free under any other conditions were thus counted as rented.

The value of the home, as reported in the census of 1930, was the approximate current market value of the home and referred to only nonfarm homes. The monthly rental was secured for each nonfarm family returned as occupying rented quarters. If the rent was not paid by the month then the equivalent monthly rental or approximate rental value for a month was to be reported.

The statistics relating to radio sets, showing the number of families having a radio set, did not represent the total number of radio sets in existence or used, since one family may have had two or more sets and since there were a considerable number of sets in use in nonfamily or nonhome establishments.

Size of families.—In 1930, of the 2,803,756 Negro families, 12.1 percent were comprised of 1 person, 26.4 percent of 2 persons, 17.9 percent of 3 persons, 12.9 percent of 4 persons, 9.5 percent of 5 persons, and 21.3 percent of 6 or more persons. The median size of the Negro family was 3.15 persons as compared with 3.34 for native-white families. The median size of the family in the South exceeded the median size for Negro families in the North and West.

Families classified by number of children.—There were no children under 10 years in 1,655,217, or 59 percent, of the Negro families reported at the census of 1930, 1 child under 10 years of age in 467,575, or 16.7 percent, of all Negro families, and 2 children under 10 years of age in 288,572, or 10.3 percent, of the Negro families. Of the 2,803,756 Negro families, there were 1,151,361, or 41.1 percent, in which there were no children under 21 years of age and 530,461, or 18.9 percent, in which there was 1 child under 21 years per family.

Families with lodgers.—In 1930, 84.8 percent of the Negro families had no lodgers, 8.7 percent had 1 lodger, 3.5 percent had 2 lodgers, and 2.9 percent had 3 or more lodgers.

Age of head of the family.—The age classification presented here is limited to those families with a man head. Hence, this classification applies to 80.7 percent of all Negro families. Of all the Negro families having a man head, 8.9 percent were under 25 years of age, 24.9 percent were 25 to 34 years of age, 25.8 percent were 35 to 44 years, 22.2 percent were 45 to 54 years, 11.6 percent were 55 to 64 years, and 6.4 percent were 65 years old and over.

Ownership of homes.—In 1930 of the 2,803,756 Negro homes, 669,645 or 23.9 percent were owned, and 2,050,217 or 73.1 percent were rented. Of the total number of homes, 65 percent were nonfarm homes and 35 percent were farm homes. Of the nonfarm homes, 26.4 percent were owned and 70.8 percent were rented, while 19.3 percent of the farm homes were owned and 77.4 percent rented. Between 1900 and 1930 the number of homes owned increased 296,195 or 79.3 percent, while the number of homes rented increased 714,941 or 53.5 percent. In the West, 37 percent of the Negro families owned their homes in 1930; in the South, 24.4 percent; and in the North, 21.1 percent.

Value of owned nonfarm homes and monthly rentals of rented nonfarm homes.—In 1930, of the 480,324 Negro-owned nonfarm homes, 39.3 percent had a value under $1,000; 13.8 percent, a value of $1,000 to $1,499; 8.8 percent, a value of $1,500 to $1,999; 12.4 percent, a value of $2,000 to $2,999; 12.4 percent, a value of $3,000 to $4,999; and 10.8 percent, a value of $5,000 or more.

The median value of Negro-owned nonfarm homes was $1,341 in 1930. In the South, 48.5 percent of the nonfarm homes, as compared with 14.8 percent in the North and 9.3 percent in the West, had a value under $1,000.

Of the 1,290,697 Negro-rented nonfarm homes, 37.2 percent had a monthly rental of less than $10, 18.7 percent a rental of $10 to $14, 10.4 percent a rental of $15 to $19, 14.6 percent a rental of $20 to $29, 11.6 percent a rental of $30 to $49, and 4.7 percent a rental of $50 or more per month in 1930. The median monthly rental of rented nonfarm homes was $13.04. In the South, 53.5 percent of the rented nonfarm homes, as compared with 9.1 percent in the West and 6.4 percent in the North, had a monthly rental under $10.

Employment status of homemaker.—A "homemaker" was defined as that woman member of the family who was responsible for the care of the home and family. (Hired housekeepers were not counted as homemakers.) In 1930, 62.5 percent of the Negro homemakers were not gainfully employed. Of those gainfully employed, 47.6 percent were gainfully employed as servants, waitresses, etc.; 19.5 percent were gainfully employed at home in agricultural occupations; 14.4 percent in other occupations at home; 7.4 percent were employed as industrial workers; and 11.1 percent were employed in other occupations. Homemakers returned as engaged in agricultural occupations at home consist in part of women operating their own farms and in part of women on the farm on which they live without wages.

Families having radio sets.—In 1930, 7.5 percent of all Negro families had a radio set. More than 14 percent of urban families had radio sets as compared with 0.3 percent for rural-farm families and 3 percent for rural-nonfarm families. A much larger percent of the Negro families in the North and West than in the South had radio sets in 1930.

Number of gainful workers per family.—Of all Negro families, 3.1 percent had no gainful workers, 54.7 percent had 1 gainful worker, 27.1 percent had 2 gainful workers, 8.9 percent had 3 gainful workers, and 6.3 percent had 4 or more gainful workers in 1930.

TABLE 1.—FAMILIES BY COLOR, AND NATIVITY OF HEAD, WITH TOTAL POPULATION, BY COLOR, AND NATIVITY, FOR THE UNITED STATES: 1930

COLOR AND NATIVITY	FAMILIES		POPULATION	
	Number	Percent	Number	Percent
All classes	**29, 904, 663**	**100. 0**	**122, 775, 046**	**100. 0**
Negro	2, 803, 756	9. 4	11, 891, 143	9. 7
White	26, 705, 294	89. 3	108, 864, 207	88. 7
Native	20, 968, 803	70. 1	95, 497, 800	77. 8
Native parentage	15, 507, 993	51. 9	70, 136, 614	57. 1
Foreign or mixed parentage	5, 460, 810	18. 3	25, 361, 186	20. 7
Foreign-born	5, 736, 491	19. 2	13, 366, 407	10. 9
Other races	395, 613	1. 3	2, 019, 696	1. 6

TABLE 2.—NONFARM AND FARM HOMES OF NEGRO FAMILIES, FOR THE UNITED STATES: 1930, 1920, AND 1910

CLASS OF HOME	NUMBER			PERCENT DISTRIBUTION		
	1930	1920	1910	1930	1920	1910
All homes	**2, 803, 756**	**2, 430, 828**	**2, 173, 018**	**100. 0**	**100. 0**	**100. 0**
Farm homes	981, 038	(1)	877, 648	35. 0	(1)	40. 4
Nonfarm homes	1, 822, 718	(1)	1, 295, 370	65. 0	(1)	59. 6

1 Data not available.

TABLE 3.—NONFARM HOMES OF NEGRO FAMILIES, BY VALUE OF MONTHLY RENTAL, FOR THE UNITED STATES: 1930

[Percent not shown where less than 1/10 of 1 percent]

VALUE OF OWNED NONFARM HOMES	Number	Percent distribution	MONTHLY RENTALS OF NONFARM HOMES	Number	Percent distribution
Owned nonfarm homes	**480, 324**	**100. 0**	**Rented nonfarm homes**	**1, 290, 697**	**100. 0**
Value under $1,000	188, 795	39. 3	Rental under $10	479, 539	37. 2
$1,000 to $1,499	66, 516	13. 8	$10 to $14	241, 898	18. 7
$1,500 to $1,999	42, 337	8. 8	$15 to $19	133, 854	10. 4
$2,000 to $2,999	59, 404	12. 4	$20 to $29	188, 079	14. 6
$3,000 to $4,999	59, 377	12. 4	$30 to $49	149, 096	11. 6
$5,000 to $7,499	31, 839	6. 6	$50 to $74	49, 353	3. 8
$7,500 to $9,999	10, 108	2. 1	$75 to $99	8, 838	. 7
$10,000 to $14,999	6, 676	1. 4	$100 to $149	1, 949	. 2
$15,000 to $19,999	1, 897	. 4	$150 to $199	452	------
$20,000 and over	1, 289	. 3	$200 and over	147	------
Not reported	12, 086	2. 5	Not reported	37, 492	2. 9

TABLE 4.—NEGRO FAMILIES, BY SIZE, FOR THE UNITED STATES: 1930

SIZE OF FAMILY	TOTAL		OWNERS	
	Number	Percent distribution	Number	Percent distribution
All families	**2, 803, 756**	**100. 0**	**669, 645**	**100. 0**
Families comprising—				
1 person	338, 114	12. 1	67, 834	10. 1
2 persons	739, 812	26. 4	169, 281	25. 3
3 persons	500, 990	17. 9	121, 553	18. 2
4 persons	361, 880	12. 9	88, 300	13. 2
5 persons	265, 136	9. 5	65, 368	9. 8
6 persons	193, 720	6. 9	49, 263	7. 4
7 persons	141, 149	5. 0	36, 840	5. 5
8 persons	99, 800	3. 6	26, 484	4. 0
9 persons	67, 607	2. 4	18, 316	2. 7
10 persons	43, 573	1. 6	11, 853	1. 8
11 persons	25, 411	. 9	7, 086	1. 1
12 or more persons	26, 564	. 9	7, 467	1. 1

TABLE 5.—FAMILIES HAVING MAN HEAD, CLASSIFIED BY AGE, COLOR, AND NATIVITY OF HEAD, FOR THE UNITED STATES: 1930

AGE OF MAN HEAD	NEGRO FAMILIES		NATIVE-WHITE FAMILIES		FOREIGN-BORN WHITE FAMILIES	
	Number	Percent distribution	Number	Percent distribution	Number	Percent distribution
All families having man head	**2, 262, 443**	**100. 0**	**18, 474, 735**	**100. 0**	**5, 019, 418**	**100. 0**
Under 25 years	201, 896	8. 9	986, 844	5. 3	49, 178	1. 0
25 to 34 years	563, 314	24. 9	4, 535, 328	24. 5	678, 714	13. 5
35 to 44 years	584, 294	25. 8	4, 927, 974	26. 7	1, 470, 252	29. 3
45 to 54 years	501, 944	22. 2	3, 829, 210	20. 7	1, 340, 291	26. 7
55 to 64 years	262, 624	11. 6	2, 518, 550	13. 6	865, 038	17. 2
65 to 74 years	107, 925	4. 8	1, 283, 987	6. 9	475, 291	9. 5
75 years and over	36, 996	1. 6	380, 490	2. 1	138, 607	2. 8
Unknown	3, 450	. 2	12, 352	. 1	2, 047	(1)

1 Less than 1/10 of 1 percent.

TABLE 6.—TENURE OF HOMES, BY COLOR OF HEAD OF FAMILY, FOR THE UNITED STATES: 1930, 1920, AND 1900

[Figures for 1930 and 1900 represent private-family homes alone; those for 1920 include the premises occupied by the small number of institutions and other quasi-family groups which were counted as families in that year]

COLOR AND CENSUS YEAR	All home	OWNED		RENTED		TENURE UNKNOWN	
		Number	Percent	Number	Percent	Number	Percent
ALL FAMILIES							
1930	29, 904, 663	14, 002, 074	46. 8	15, 319, 817	51. 2	582, 772	1. 9
1920	24, 351, 676	10, 866, 960	44. 6	12, 943, 598	53. 2	541, 118	2. 2
1900	15, 963, 965	7, 205, 212	45. 1	8, 223, 775	51. 5	534, 978	3. 4
NEGRO FAMILIES							
1930	2, 803, 756	669, 645	23. 9	2, 050, 217	73. 1	83, 894	3. 0
1920	2, 430, 828	542, 654	22. 3	1, 799, 694	74. 0	88, 480	3. 6
1900	1, 833, 759	373, 350	20. 4	1, 335, 276	72. 8	125, 003	6. 8
WHITE FAMILIES							
1930	26, 705, 294	13, 224, 389	49. 5	13, 004, 800	48, 7	476, 105	1. 8
1920	21, 825, 654	10, 286, 267	47. 1	11, 092, 896	50. 8	446, 491	2. 0
1900	14, 063, 791	6, 788, 069	48. 3	6, 871, 037	48. 9	404, 685	2. 9
OTHER FAMILIES							
1930	395, 613	108, 040	27. 3	264, 800	66. 9	22, 773	5. 8
1920	95, 194	38, 039	40. 0	51, 008	53. 6	6, 147	6. 5
1900	66, 415	43, 693	65. 8	17, 462	26. 3	5, 260	7. 9
	INCREASE OR DECREASE (—)						
ALL FAMILIES							
1900–1930	13, 940, 698	6, 796, 862	94. 3	7, 096, 042	86. 3	47, 794	8. 9
1920–30	5, 552, 987	3, 135, 114	28. 8	2, 376, 219	18. 4	41, 654	7. 7
1900–1920	8, 387, 711	3, 661, 748	50. 8	4, 719, 823	57. 4	6, 140	1. 1
NEGRO FAMILIES							
1900–1930	969, 997	296, 195	79. 3	714, 941	53. 5	−41. 139	−32. 9
1920–30	372, 938	126, 991	23. 4	250, 523	13. 9	−4, 586	−5. 2
1900–1920	597, 069	169, 204	45. 3	464, 418	34. 8	−36, 553	−29. 2
WHITE FAMILIES							
1900–1930	12, 641, 503	6, 436, 320	94. 8	6, 133, 763	89. 3	71, 420	17. 6
1920–30	4, 879, 640	2, 938, 122	28. 6	1, 911, 904	17. 2	29, 614	6. 6
1900–1920	7, 761, 863	3, 498, 198	51. 5	4, 221, 859	61. 4	41, 806	10. 3
OTHER FAMILIES							
1900–1930	329, 198	64, 347	147. 3	247, 338	1, 416. 4	17, 513	332. 9
1920–30	300, 419	70, 001	184. 0	213, 792	419. 1	16, 626	270. 5
1900–1920	28, 779	−5, 654	−12. 9	33, 546	192. 1	887	16. 9

TABLE 7.—FAMILIES CLASSIFIED BY NUMBER OF CHILDREN UNDER 10 AND UNDER 21 YEARS OLD, BY COLOR, AND NATIVITY OF HEAD, FOR THE UNITED STATES: 1930

NUMBER OF CHILDREN	NEGRO		NATIVE WHITE		FOREIGN-BORN WHITE	
	Number	Percent distribution	Number	Percent distribution	Number	Percent distribution
All families	**2, 803, 756**	**100. 0**	**20, 968, 803**	**100. 0**	**5, 736, 491**	**100. 0**
Families having—						
No children under 10	1, 655, 217	59. 0	12, 216, 802	58. 3	3, 544, 030	61. 8
1 child under 10	467, 575	16. 7	4, 164, 091	19. 9	1, 045, 547	18. 2
2 children under 10	288, 572	10. 3	2, 542, 041	12. 1	636, 073	11. 1
3 children under 10	190, 380	6. 8	1, 243, 766	5. 9	305, 503	5. 3
4 children under 10	121, 107	4. 3	560, 506	2. 7	138, 653	2. 4
5 children under 10	58, 180	2. 1	188, 425	. 9	50, 993	. 9
6 or more	22, 725	. 8	53, 172	. 3	15, 692	. 3
Families having—						
No children under 21	1, 151, 361	41. 1	8, 197, 010	39. 1	2, 132, 426	37. 2
1 child under 21	530, 461	18. 9	4, 558, 971	21. 7	1, 072, 289	18. 7
2 children under 21	356, 826	12. 7	3, 485, 729	16. 6	944, 760	16. 5
3 children under 21	249, 984	8. 9	2, 067, 053	9. 9	641, 636	11. 2
4 children under 21	177, 914	6. 3	1, 198, 678	5. 7	401, 049	7. 0
5 children under 21	125, 794	4. 5	686, 256	3. 3	240, 403	4. 2
6 or more	211, 416	7. 5	775, 106	3. 7	303, 928	5. 3

TABLE 8.—FAMILIES CLASSIFIED ACCORDING TO NUMBER OF GAINFUL WORKERS, BY COLOR, AND NATIVITY OF HEAD, FOR THE UNITED STATES: 1930

NUMBER OF GAINFUL WORKERS	NEGRO		NATIVE WHITE		FOREIGN-BORN WHITE	
	Number	Percent distribution	Number	Percent distribution	Number	Percent distribution
All families	**2, 803, 756**	**100. 0**	**20, 968, 803**	**100. 0**	**5, 736, 491**	**100. 0**
Families having—						
No gainful workers	86, 227	3. 1	1, 327, 676	6. 3	371, 311	6. 5
1 gainful worker	1, 532, 551	54. 7	13, 659, 468	65. 1	3, 116, 525	54. 3
2 gainful workers	758, 898	27. 1	4, 201, 458	20. 0	1, 288, 825	22. 5
3 gainful workers	250, 634	8. 9	1, 263, 185	6. 0	599, 778	10. 5
4 or more	175, 446	6. 3	517, 016	2. 5	360, 052	6. 3

TABLE 9.—FAMILIES CLASSIFIED ACCORDING TO NUMBER OF LODGERS, BY COLOR, AND NATIVITY OF HEAD, AND BY TENURE, FOR THE UNITED STATES: 1930

[Percent not shown where less than 1/10 of 1 percent]

NUMBER OF LODGERS AND TENURE	NEGRO FAMILIES		NATIVE-WHITE FAMILIES		FOREIGN-BORN WHITE FAMILIES	
	Number	Percent distribution	Number	Percent distribution	Number	Percent distribution
All families	**2, 803, 756**	**100. 0**	**20, 968, 803**	**100. 0**	**5, 736, 491**	**100. 0**
Families having—						
No lodgers	2, 378, 529	84. 8	19, 083, 472	91. 0	5, 149, 264	89. 8
1 lodger	245, 163	8. 7	1, 284, 797	6. 1	376, 613	6. 6
2 lodgers	97, 853	3. 5	340, 078	1. 6	115, 691	2. 0
3 lodgers	39, 790	1. 4	123, 812	. 6	44, 563	. 8
4 lodgers	19, 689	. 7	58, 108	. 3	20, 944	. 4
5 lodgers	9, 950	. 4	30, 547	. 1	10, 776	. 2
6 lodgers	5, 681	. 2	18, 244	. 1	6, 659	. 1
7 lodgres	3, 164	. 1	11, 715	. 1	4, 426	. 1
8 lodgers	1, 943	. 1	7, 993	--------	3, 182	. 1
9 lodgers	1, 213	--------	5, 717	--------	2, 511	--------
10 lodgers	781	--------	4, 320	--------	1, 862	--------
Owner families	669, 645	100. 0	10, 255, 682	100. 0	2, 968, 707	100. 0
Families having—						
No lodgers	584, 856	87. 3	9, 366, 136	91. 3	2, 690, 961	90. 6
1 lodger	49, 952	7. 5	621, 394	6. 1	181, 997	6. 1
2 lodgers	18, 894	2. 8	159, 636	1. 6	53, 911	1. 8
3 lodgers	7, 558	1. 1	55, 264	. 5	20, 266	. 7
4 lodgers	3, 830	. 6	24, 814	. 2	9, 424	. 3
5 lodgers	1, 883	. 3	12, 214	. 1	4, 760	. 2
6 or more lodgers	2, 672	. 4	16, 224	. 2	7, 388	. 2
Tenant families	2, 050, 217	100. 0	10, 314, 500	100. 0	2, 690, 300	100. 0
Families having—						
No lodgers	1, 720, 835	83. 9	9, 361, 841	90. 8	2, 391, 054	88. 9
1 lodger	188, 576	9. 2	636, 554	6. 2	188, 736	7. 0
2 lodgers	76, 590	3. 7	172, 838	1. 7	59, 855	2. 2
3 lodgers	31, 245	1. 5	65, 204	. 6	23, 408	. 9
4 lodgers	15, 376	. 7	31, 399	. 3	11, 060	. 4
5 lodgers	7, 842	. 4	17, 216	. 2	5, 703	. 2
6 or more lodgers	9, 753	. 5	29, 448	. 3	10, 485	. 4
Tenure unknown	83, 894	100. 0	398, 621	100. 0	77, 484	100. 0
Families having—						
No lodgers	72, 838	86. 8	355, 495	89. 2	67, 250	86. 8
1 lodger	6, 635	7. 9	26, 849	6. 7	5, 880	7. 6
2 lodgers	2, 369	2. 8	7, 604	1. 9	1, 925	2. 5
3 lodgers	987	1. 2	3, 344	. 8	889	1. 1
4 lodgers	483	. 6	1, 895	. 5	460	. 6
5 lodgers	225	. 3	1, 117	. 3	313	. 4
6 or more lodgers	357	. 4	2, 317	. 6	767	1. 0

TABLE 10.—FAMILIES WITH HOMEMAKER, BY COLOR, AND NATIVITY OF HEAD, AND EMPLOYMENT STATUS OF HOMEMAKER, FOR THE UNITED STATES: 1930

EMPLOYMENT STATUS OF HOMEMAKER	NEGRO		NATIVE WHITE		FOREIGN-BORN WHITE	
	Number	Percent distribution	Number	Percent distribution	Number	Percent distribution
Families having homemaker	**2, 601, 254**	**100. 0**	**20, 052, 869**	**100. 0**	**5, 404, 476**	**100. 0**
Not gainfully employed	1, 624, 814	62. 5	17, 698, 711	88. 3	4, 852, 931	89. 8
Gainfully employed	976, 440	37. 5	2, 354, 158	11. 7	551, 545	10. 2
Gainfully employed homemakers	976, 440	100. 0	2, 354, 158	100. 0	551, 545	100. 0
Employed at home	331, 225	33. 9	357, 413	15. 2	59, 289	10. 7
Agricultural occupations	190, 268	19. 5	180, 285	7. 7	21, 643	3. 9
Other occupations at home	140, 957	14. 4	177, 128	7. 5	37, 646	6. 8
Employed away from home	642, 369	65. 8	1, 992, 100	84. 6	491, 501	89. 1
Professional workers	23, 117	2. 4	328, 346	13. 9	35, 189	6. 4
Office workers	4, 157	. 4	443, 088	18. 8	53, 053	9. 6
Industrial workers	72, 538	7. 4	470, 287	20. 0	187, 022	33. 9
Servants, waitresses, etc	464, 608	47. 6	352, 449	15. 0	130, 318	23. 6
Saleswomen	3, 531	. 4	224, 326	9. 5	42, 387	7. 7
Other occupations away from home	74, 418	7. 6	173, 604	7. 4	43, 532	7. 9
Employed, place not specified	2, 846	. 3	4, 645	. 2	755	. 1

TABLE 11.—PERCENT OF HOMES OWNED BY NEGRO FAMILIES, BY SECTIONS: 1930, 1920, AND 1910

SECTION	ALL HOMES			FARM HOMES			NONFARM HOMES		
	1930	1920	1910	1930	1920	1910	1930	1920	1910
United States	**23. 9**	**22. 8**	**22. 5**	**19. 3**	(1)	**25. 1**	**26. 4**	(1)	**20. 7**
THE SOUTH	24. 4	22. 6	22. 4	19. 1	(1)	24. 6	28. 6	(1)	20. 7
THE NORTH	21. 1	20. 0	22. 3	33. 2	(1)	62. 6	20. 8	(1)	20. 1
THE WEST	37. 0	32. 8	32. 6	30. 9	(1)	77. 4	37. 3	(1)	30. 7

[1] Data not available.

TABLE 12.—MEDIAN SIZE OF URBAN, RURAL-FARM, AND RURAL-NONFARM NEGRO FAMILIES, BY DIVISIONS, AND STATES: 1930

[Median not shown where number of families is less than 100]

DIVISION AND STATE	Total	Urban	Rural-farm	Rural-nonfarm
United States	**3. 15**	**2. 70**	**4. 05**	**2. 96**
NEW ENGLAND	2. 77	2. 73	3. 02	3. 08
Maine	2. 86	2. 76	--------	--------
New Hampshire	2. 42	--------	--------	--------
Vermont	2. 35	--------	--------	--------
Massachusetts	2. 79	2. 75	--------	3. 27
Rhode Island	2. 56	2. 53	--------	3. 12
Connecticut	2. 81	2. 79	--------	2. 92
MIDDLE ATLANTIC	2. 79	2. 76	3. 49	3. 01
New York	2. 63	2. 62	3. 29	2. 83
New Jersey	2. 92	2. 89	3. 72	3. 03
Pennsylvania	2. 88	2. 86	3. 42	3. 05
EAST NORTH CENTRAL	2. 75	2. 74	3. 30	2. 76
Ohio	2. 80	2. 78	3. 45	2. 93
Indiana	2. 68	2. 68	3. 20	2. 52
Illinois	2. 67	2. 66	3. 35	2. 65
Michigan	2. 89	2. 91	2. 75	2. 55
Wisconsin	2. 52	2. 52	--------	--------
WEST NORTH CENTRAL	2. 50	2. 45	3. 20	2. 57
Minnesota	2. 34	2. 34	--------	--------
Iowa	2. 52	2. 56	2. 40	2. 30
Missouri	2. 48	2. 41	3. 24	2. 63
North Dakota	1. 56	--------	--------	--------
South Dakota	2. 57	--------	--------	--------
Nebraska	2. 41	2. 41	--------	--------
Kansas	2. 66	2. 65	3. 04	2. 51
SOUTH ATLANTIC	3. 48	2. 83	4. 69	3. 18
Delaware	2. 83	2. 47	4. 11	2. 84
Maryland	3. 12	2. 79	4. 47	3. 45
District of Columbia	2. 84	2. 84	--------	--------
Virginia	3. 55	2. 81	4. 82	3. 55
West Virginia	3. 08	2. 90	4. 53	3. 11
North Carolina	4. 18	3. 15	5. 29	3. 74
South Carolina	3. 95	2. 86	4. 86	3. 27
Georgia	3. 34	2. 72	4. 24	2. 94
Florida	2. 78	2. 69	3. 76	2. 55

TABLE 12.—MEDIAN SIZE OF URBAN, RURAL-FARM, AND RURAL-NONFARM NEGRO FAMILIES, BY DIVISIONS, AND STATES: 1930—Continued

[Median not shown where number of families is less than 100]

DIVISION AND STATE	Total	Urban	Rural-farm	Rural-nonfarm
EAST SOUTH CENTRAL	3.16	2.58	3.74	2.79
Kentucky	2.69	2.41	3.65	2.88
Tennessee	2.98	2.53	4.02	2.96
Alabama	3.33	2.80	4.06	2.93
Mississippi	3.20	2.47	3.51	2.46
WEST SOUTH CENTRAL	3.11	2.65	3.67	2.72
Arkansas	3.04	2.50	3.36	2.50
Louisiana	3.16	2.77	3.74	2.84
Oklahoma	3.13	2.60	4.00	2.79
Texas	3.09	2.61	3.86	2.68
MOUNTAIN	2.18	2.18	2.66	2.07
Montana	1.72	1.83		
Idaho	1.90	1.95		
Wyoming	1.85	1.94		1.47
Colorado	2.26	2.29	2.21	1.94
New Mexico	2.28	2.26	3.61	2.02
Arizona	2.22	2.12	2.85	2.28
Utah	2.12	2.13		
Nevada	1.50	1.61		
PACIFIC	2.32	2.32	2.74	2.19
Washington	2.12	2.12		2.06
Oregon	2.03	2.07		
California	2.35	2.35	2.85	2.21

TABLE 13.—NEGRO FAMILIES HAVING RADIO SET, IN URBAN, RURAL-FARM, AND RURAL-NONFARM AREAS: 1930

AREA	Total number of families	FAMILIES HAVING RADIO SET	
		Number	Percent
All families	2,803,756	209,779	7.5
Urban families	1,328,170	191,790	14.4
Urban farm families	2,385	80	3.4
Rural-farm families	978,653	3,327	.3
Rural-nonfarm families	496,933	14,662	3.0
All farm families	981,038	3,407	.3

TABLE 14.—FARM AND NONFARM HOMES OF NEGRO FAMILIES, BY SECTIONS: 1930

SECTION AND CENSUS YEAR	NUMBER			PERCENT DISTRIBUTION		
	All homes	Farm homes	Nonfarm homes	All homes	Farm homes	Nonfarm homes
United States:						
1930	2,803,756	981,038	1,822,718	100.0	100.0	100.0
1920	2,430,828	(1)	(1)	100.0	(1)	(1)
1910	2,173,018	877,648	1,295,370	100.0	100.0	100.0
THE SOUTH:						
1930	2,193,357	964,494	1,228,863	78.2	98.3	67.4
1920	2,047,809	(1)	(1)	84.2	(1)	(1)
1910	1,917,391	864,688	1,052,703	88.2	98.5	81.3
THE NORTH:						
1930	576,328	15,000	561,328	20.6	1.5	30.8
1920	362,694	(1)	(1)	14.9	(1)	(1)
1910	242,920	12,437	230,483	11.2	1.4	17.8
THE WEST:						
1930	34,071	1,544	32,527	1.2	.2	1.8
1920	20,325	(1)	(1)	.8	(1)	(1)
1910	12,707	523	12,184	.6	.1	.9

[1] Data not available.

TABLE 15.—FAMILIES BY TENURE, BY COLOR, AND NATIVITY OF HEAD, WITH TOTAL POPULATION BY COLOR, AND NATIVITY, FOR THE UNITED STATES: 1930

AREA AND COLOR AND NATIVITY	ALL FAMILIES		OWNER FAMILIES		TENANT FAMILIES		TENURE UNKNOWN		PERCENT OF TOTAL (FAMILIES)			POPULATION	
	Number	Percent distribution	Number	Percent distribution	Number	Percent distribution	Number	Percent distribution	Owner families	Tenant families	Tenure unknown	Number	Percent distribution
All families	**29,904,663**	**100.0**	**14,002,074**	**100.0**	**15,319,817**	**100.0**	**582,772**	**100.0**	**46.8**	**51.2**	**1.9**	**122,775,046**	**100.0**
Negro	2,803,756	9.4	669,645	4.8	2,050,217	13.4	83,894	14.4	23.9	73.1	3.0	11,891,143	9.7
White	26,705,294	89.3	13,224,389	94.4	13,004,800	84.9	476,105	81.7	49.5	48.7	1.8	108,864,207	88.7
Native	20,968,803	70.1	10,255,682	73.2	10,314,500	67.3	398,621	68.4	48.9	49.2	1.9	95,497,800	77.8
Foreign-born	5,736,491	19.2	2,968,707	21.2	2,690,300	17.6	77,484	13.3	51.8	46.9	1.4	13,366,407	10.9
Other races	395,613	1.3	108,040	.8	264,800	1.7	22,773	3.9	27.3	66.9	5.8	2,019,696	1.6
Urban	17,372,524	100.0	7,432,554	100.0	9,681,359	100.0	258,611	100.0	42.8	55.7	1.5	68,954,823	100.0
Negro	1,328,170	7.6	315,584	4.2	978,799	10.1	33,787	13.1	23.8	73.7	2.5	5,193,913	7.5
White	15,858,158	91.3	7,074,031	95.2	8,565,849	88.5	218,278	84.4	44.6	54.0	1.4	62,836,605	91.1
Native	11,322,555	65.2	4,941,762	66.5	6,213,093	64.2	167,700	64.8	43.6	54.9	1.5	52,109,746	75.6
Foreign-born	4,535,603	26.1	2,132,269	28.7	2,352,736	24.3	50,578	19.6	47.0	51.9	1.1	10,726,859	15.6
Other races	186,196	1.1	42,939	.6	136,711	1.4	6,546	2.5	23.1	73.4	3.5	924,305	1.3
Rural-farm	6,604,637	100.0	3,452,102	100.0	2,952,717	100.0	199,818	100.0	52.3	44.7	3.0	30,157,513	100.0
Negro	978,653	14.8	188,574	5.5	758,014	25.7	32,065	16.0	19.3	77.5	3.3	4,680,523	15.5
White	5,517,637	83.5	3,231,951	93.6	2,125,854	72.0	159,832	80.0	58.6	38.5	2.9	24,884,834	82.5
Native	5,006,748	75.8	2,840,831	82.3	2,022,067	68.5	143,850	72.0	56.7	40.4	2.9	23,800,747	78.9
Foreign-born	510,889	7.7	391,120	11.3	103,787	3.5	15,982	8.0	76.6	20.3	3.1	1,084,087	3.6
Other races	108,347	1.6	31,577	.9	68,849	2.3	7,921	4.0	29.1	63.5	7.3	592,156	2.0
Rural-nonfarm	5,927,502	100.0	3,117,418	100.0	2,685,741	100.0	124,343	100.0	52.6	45.3	2.1	23,662,710	100.0
Negro	496,933	8.4	165,487	5.3	313,404	11.7	18,042	14.5	33.3	63.1	3.6	2,016,707	8.5
White	5,329,499	89.9	2,918,407	93.6	2,313,097	86.1	97,995	78.8	54.8	43.4	1.8	21,142,768	89.4
Native	4,639,500	78.3	2,473,089	79.3	2,079,340	77.4	87,071	70.0	53.3	44.8	1.9	19,587,307	82.8
Foreign-born	689,999	11.6	445,318	14.3	233,757	8.7	10,924	8.8	64.5	33.9	1.6	1,555,461	6.6
Other races	101,070	1.7	33,524	1.1	59,240	2.2	8,306	6.7	33.2	58.6	8.2	503,235	2.1

Table 16.—TENURE OF FARM AND NONFARM HOMES OF NEGRO FAMILIES, FOR THE UNITED STATES: 1930, 1920, 1910, AND 1900

[Figures for 1930 and 1900 represent private-family homes alone; those for 1920 and 1910 include the premises occupied by the small number of institutions and other quasi-family groups which were counted as families in the respective censuses]

TENURE	1930		1920		1910		1900		INCREASE OR DECREASE (—)							
									1900 to 1930		1920 to 1930		1910 to 1920		1900 to 1910	
	Number	Percent distribution	Number	Percent distribution	Number	Percent distribution	Number	Percent distribution	Number	Percent	Number	Percent	Number	Percent	Number	Percent
All homes	**2,803,756**	**100.0**	**2,430,828**	**100.0**	**2,173,018**	**100.0**	**1,833,759**	**100.0**	**969,997**	**52.9**	**372,928**	**15.3**	**257,810**	**11.9**	**339,259**	**18.5**
Owned	669,645	23.9	542,654	22.3	488,699	22.5	373,450	20.4	296,195	79.3	126,991	23.4	53,955	11.0	115,249	30.9
Rented	2,050,217	73.1	1,799,694	74.0	1,603,719	73.8	1,335,276	72.8	714,941	53.5	250,523	13.9	195,975	12.2	268,443	20.1
Tenure unknown	83,894	3.0	88,480	3.6	80,600	3.7	125,033	6.8	−41,139	−32.9	−4,586	−5.2	7,880	9.8	−44,433	−35.5
Farm homes	981,038	100.0	(1)	(1)	877,648	100.0	758,463	100.0	222,575	29.3	(1)	(1)	(1)	(1)	119,185	15.7
Owned	189,321	19.3	(1)	(1)	220,698	25.1	191,143	25.2	−1,822	−1.0	(1)	(1)	(1)	(1)	29,555	15.5
Rented	759,520	77.4	(1)	(1)	653,768	74.5	560,005	73.8	199,515	35.6	(1)	(1)	(1)	(1)	93,763	16.7
Tenure unknown	32,197	3.3	(1)	(1)	3,182	.4	7,315	1.0	24,882	340.2	(1)	(1)	(1)	(1)	−4,133	−56.5
Nonfarm homes	1,822,718	100.0	(1)	(1)	1,295,370	100.0	1,075,296	100.0	747,422	69.5	(1)	(1)	(1)	(1)	220,074	20.5
Owned	480,324	26.4	(1)	(1)	268,001	20.7	182,307	17.0	298,017	163.5	(1)	(1)	(1)	(1)	85,694	47.0
Rented	1,290,697	70.8	(1)	(1)	949,951	73.3	775,271	72.1	515,426	66.5	(1)	(1)	(1)	(1)	174,680	22.5
Tenure unknown	51,697	2.8	(1)	(1)	77,418	6.0	117,718	10.9	−66,021	−56.1	(1)	(1)	(1)	(1)	−40,300	−34.2

[1] Data not available.

Table 17.—FAMILIES CLASSIFIED BY SEX OF HEAD, BY COLOR, AND NATIVITY, FOR THE UNITED STATES: 1930

AREA AND SEX	ALL CLASSES		NEGRO		NATIVE WHITE		FOREIGN-BORN WHITE		OTHER RACES	
	Number	Percent distribution	Number	Percent distribution	Number	Percent distribution	Number	Percent distribution	Number	Percent distribution
All families	**29,904,663**	**100.0**	**2,803,756**	**100.0**	**20,968,803**	**100.0**	**5,736,491**	**100.0**	**395,613**	**100.0**
Man head	26,111,761	87.3	2,262,443	80.7	18,474,735	88.1	5,019,418	87.5	355,165	89.8
Woman head	3,792,902	12.7	541,313	19.3	2,494,068	11.9	717,073	12.5	40,448	10.2
Urban families	17,372,524	100.0	1,328,170	100.0	11,322,555	100.0	4,535,603	100.0	186,196	100.0
Man head	14,720,340	84.7	992,802	74.7	9,629,721	85.0	3,936,357	86.8	161,460	86.7
Woman head	2,652,184	15.3	335,368	25.3	1,692,834	15.0	599,246	13.2	24,736	13.3
Rural-farm families	6,604,637	100.0	978,653	100.0	5,006,748	100.0	510,889	100.0	108,347	100.0
Man head	6,218,390	94.2	875,335	89.4	4,760,733	95.1	479,291	93.8	103,031	95.1
Woman head	386,247	5.8	103,318	10.6	246,015	4.9	31,598	6.2	5,316	4.9
Rural-nonfarm families	5,927,502	100.0	496,933	100.0	4,639,500	100.0	689,999	100.0	101,070	100.0
Man head	5,173,031	87.3	394,306	79.3	4,084,281	88.0	603,770	87.5	90,674	89.7
Woman head	754,471	12.7	102,627	20.7	555,219	12.0	86,229	12.5	10,396	10.3

Table 18.—PERCENT OF HOMES OWNED AND RENTED, BY COLOR, AND NATIVITY OF HEAD OF FAMILY, FOR THE UNITED STATES: 1930, 1920, 1910, AND 1900

CLASS AND TENURE	NEGRO				NATIVE WHITE [1]			FOREIGN-BORN WHITE [1]			OTHER RACES [1]		
	1930	1920	1910	1900	1930	1920	1900	1930	1920	1900	1930	1920	1900
All homes	**100.0**	**100.0**	**100.0**	**100.0**	**100.0**	**100.0**	**100.0**	**100.0**	**100.0**	**100.0**	**100.0**	**100.0**	**100.0**
Owned	23.9	22.3	22.5	20.4	48.9	48.4	49.6	51.8	43.2	44.8	27.3	40.0	65.8
Rented	73.1	74.0	73.8	72.8	49.2	49.4	47.5	46.9	55.1	52.4	66.9	53.6	26.3
Tenure unknown	3.0	3.6	3.7	6.8	1.9	2.2	2.9	1.4	1.7	2.8	5.8	6.5	7.9
Farm homes	100.0	100.0	100.0	100.0	100.0	100.0	100.0	100.0	100.0	100.0	100.0	100.0	100.0
Owned	19.3	(2)	25.1	25.2	56.9	(2)	67.7	76.7	(2)	80.8	29.1	(2)	90.8
Rented	77.4	(2)	74.5	73.8	40.2	(2)	31.6	20.2	(2)	18.6	63.6	(2)	7.2
Tenure unknown	3.3	(2)	.4	1.0	2.9	(2)	.7	3.1	(2)	.6	7.3	(2)	2.0
Nonfarm homes	100.0	100.0	100.0	100.0	100.0	100.0	100.0	100.0	100.0	100.0	100.0	100.0	100.0
Owned	26.4	(2)	20.7	17.0	46.4	(2)	37.3	49.2	(2)	35.5	26.6	(2)	50.2
Rented	70.8	(2)	73.3	72.1	52.0	(2)	58.2	49.6	(2)	61.2	68.2	(2)	38.2
Tenure unknown	2.8	(2)	6.0	10.9	1.6	(2)	4.4	1.2	(2)	3.3	5.2	(2)	11.6

[1] Data not available for 1910.

[2] Data not available.

TABLE 19.—FAMILIES BY COLOR, AND NATIVITY OF HEAD, WITH TOTAL POPULATION BY COLOR, AND NATIVITY, FOR THE UNITED STATES: 1930, 1920, 1900, AND 1890

[The family figures for 1930 and 1900 represent private families only; those for 1920 and 1890 include the small number of institutions and other quasi-family groups which were counted as families in those years]

COLOR AND NATIVITY	FAMILIES								POPULATION							
	1930		1920		1900		1890		1930		1920		1900		1890	
	Number	Percent	Number	Percent	Number	Percent	Number	Percent	Number	Percent	Number	Percent	Number	Percent	Number	Percent
All classes	**26,904,663**	**100.0**	**24,351,676**	**100.0**	**15,963,965**	**100.0**	**12,690,152**	**100.0**	**122,775,046**	**100.0**	**105,710,620**	**100.0**	**75,994,575**	**100.0**	**[1] 62,622,250**	**100.0**
Negro	2,803,756	9.4	2,430,828	10.0	1,833,759	11.5	1,410,769	11.1	11,891,143	9.7	10,463,131	9.9	8,833,994	11.6	7,470,040	11.9
White	26,705,294	89.3	21,825,654	89.6	14,063,791	88.1	11,255,169	88.7	108,864,207	88.7	94,820,915	89.7	66,809,196	87.9	54,983,890	87.8
Native	20,968,803	70.1	16,407,983	67.4	10,206,500	63.9	8,021,434	63.2	95,497,800	77.8	81,108,161	76.7	56,595,379	74.5	45,862,023	73.2
Foreign born	5,736,491	19.2	5,417,679	22.2	3,857,291	24.2	3,233,735	25.5	13,366,407	10.9	13,712,754	13.0	10,213,817	13.4	9,121,867	14.6
Other races [2]	395,613	1.3	95,194	.4	66,415	.4	24,214	.2	2,019,696	1.6	426,574	.4	351,385	.5	168,320	.3

[1] Exclusive of 325,464 persons specially enumerated in Indian Territory and on Indian reservations, for whom family data are not available.
[2] Figures for 1930 include Mexicans, who were for the most part classified as white at earlier censuses.

TABLE 20.—NEGRO FAMILIES CLASSIFIED BY NUMBER OF CHILDREN UNDER 10 YEARS OLD, BY TENURE, URBAN, RURAL-FARM, AND RURAL-NONFARM FAMILIES, FOR THE UNITED STATES: 1930

NUMBER OF CHILDREN UNDER 10 YEARS OLD	ALL FAMILIES				URBAN FAMILIES			RURAL-FARM FAMILIES			RURAL-NONFARM FAMILIES		
	Total	Owners	Tenants	Tenure unknown	Total	Owners	Tenants	Total	Owners	Tenants	Total	Owners	Tenants
All families	**2,803,756**	**669,645**	**2,050,217**	**83,894**	**1,328,170**	**315,584**	**978,799**	**978,653**	**188,574**	**758,014**	**496,933**	**165,487**	**313,404**
Families having—													
No children under 10	1,655,217	427,901	1,172,711	54,605	899,677	222,109	652,640	459,532	100,986	340,924	296,008	104,806	179,147
1 child under 10	467,575	102,509	351,504	13,562	200,955	44,595	151,570	183,017	32,411	144,717	83,603	25,503	55,217
2 children under 10	288,572	58,807	222,372	7,393	111,205	23,247	85,636	126,234	20,614	102,075	51,133	14,946	34,661
3 children under 10	190,380	38,523	147,504	4,353	63,687	13,579	49,035	93,475	15,014	76,063	33,218	9,930	22,406
4 children under 10	121,107	25,063	93,582	2,462	33,811	7,578	25,769	66,748	11,127	54,077	20,548	6,358	13,736
5 children under 10	58,180	12,127	44,960	1,093	13,942	3,290	10,483	35,171	5,985	28,437	9,067	2,852	6,040
6 or more	22,725	4,715	17,584	426	4,893	1,186	3,666	14,476	2,437	11,721	3,356	1,092	2,197
	Percent distribution												
All families	**100.0**	**100.0**	**100.0**	**100.0**	**100.0**	**100.0**	**100.0**	**100.0**	**100.0**	**100.0**	**100.0**	**100.0**	**100.0**
Families having—													
No children under 10	59.0	63.9	57.2	65.1	67.7	70.4	66.7	47.0	53.6	45.0	59.6	63.3	57.2
1 child under 10	16.7	15.3	17.1	16.2	15.1	14.1	15.5	18.7	17.2	19.1	16.8	15.4	17.6
2 children under 10	10.3	8.8	10.8	8.8	8.4	7.4	8.7	12.9	10.9	13.5	10.3	9.0	11.1
3 children under 10	6.8	5.8	7.2	5.2	4.8	4.3	5.0	9.6	8.0	10.0	6.7	6.0	7.1
4 children under 10	4.3	3.7	4.6	2.9	2.5	2.4	2.6	6.8	5.9	7.1	4.1	3.8	4.4
5 children under 10	2.1	1.8	2.2	1.3	1.0	1.0	1.1	3.6	3.2	3.8	1.8	1.7	1.9
6 or more	.8	.7	.9	.5	.4	.4	.4	1.5	1.3	1.5	.7	.7	.7

Table 21.—Negro Families Having Radio Set, by Sections, Divisions, and States: 1930

SECTION, DIVISION, AND STATE	NEGRO FAMILIES			Percent of all families having radio set
	Total number	Having radio set		
		Number	Percent	
United States	**2, 803, 756**	**209, 779**	**7. 5**	**40. 3**
The North	**576, 328**	**151, 633**	**26. 3**	**51. 1**
The South	**2, 193, 357**	**47, 443**	**2. 2**	**16. 4**
The West	**34, 071**	**10, 703**	**31. 4**	**44. 0**
New England	22, 864	7, 639	33. 4	53. 8
Maine	259	72	27. 8	39. 2
New Hampshire	117	32	27. 4	44. 4
Vermont	135	37	27. 4	44. 6
Massachusetts	12, 637	4, 352	34. 4	57. 6
Rhode Island	2, 542	821	32. 3	57. 1
Connecticut	7, 174	2, 325	32. 4	54. 7
Middle Atlantic	243, 371	72, 427	29. 8	55. 3
New York	95, 621	36, 817	38. 5	57. 9
New Jersey	48, 636	14, 288	29. 4	63. 4
Pennsylvania	99, 114	21, 322	21. 5	48. 1
East North Central	222, 240	58, 116	26. 2	50. 2
Ohio	75, 709	14, 123	18. 7	47. 7
Indiana	28, 771	5, 330	18. 5	41. 6
Illinois	78, 737	27, 490	34. 9	55. 6
Michigan	36, 500	10, 295	28. 2	50. 6
Wisconsin	2, 523	878	34. 8	51. 0
West North Central	87, 853	13, 451	15. 3	43. 1
Minnesota	2, 592	1, 047	40. 4	47. 3
Iowa	4, 571	1, 005	22. 0	48. 5
Missouri	59, 016	7, 813	13. 2	37. 4
North Dakota	120	34	28. 3	40. 9
South Dakota	166	45	27. 1	44. 2
Nebraska	3, 700	841	22. 7	47. 9
Kansas	17, 688	2, 666	15. 1	38. 9
South Atlantic	974, 592	28, 320	2. 9	19. 0
Delaware	7, 682	955	12. 4	45. 9
Maryland	61, 160	6, 975	11. 4	42. 9
District of Columbia	29, 995	7, 562	25. 2	53. 9
Virginia	140, 726	4, 914	3. 5	18. 2
West Virginia	26, 274	2, 016	7. 7	23. 3
North Carolina	180, 128	2, 313	1. 3	11. 2
South Carolina	168, 324	790	. 5	7. 6
Georgia	249, 942	1, 615	. 6	9. 9
Florida	110, 361	1, 180	1. 1	15. 4

Table 21.—Negro Families Having Radio Set, by Sections, Divisions, and States: 1930—Continued

SECTION, DIVISION, AND STATE	NEGRO FAMILIES			Percent of all families having radio set
	Total number	Having radio set		
		Number	Percent	
East South Central	653, 847	9, 222	1. 4	12. 3
Kentucky	60, 672	3, 355	5. 5	18. 3
Tennessee	120, 402	3, 242	2. 7	14. 3
Alabama	222, 533	1, 974	. 9	9. 5
Mississippi	250, 240	651	. 3	5. 4
West South Central	564, 918	9, 901	1. 8	16. 5
Arkansas	123, 009	1, 030	. 8	9. 1
Louisiana	190, 876	2, 142	1. 1	11. 2
Oklahoma	40, 238	1, 199	3. 0	21. 6
Texas	210, 795	5, 530	2. 6	18. 6
Mountain	8, 743	1, 337	15. 3	30. 9
Montana	458	74	16. 2	31. 9
Idaho	229	43	18. 8	30. 3
Wyoming	418	72	17. 2	34. 1
Colorado	3, 538	794	22. 4	37. 8
New Mexico	799	56	7. 0	11. 5
Arizona	2, 776	170	6. 1	18. 1
Utah	331	96	29. 0	41. 1
Nevada	194	32	16. 5	30. 6
Pacific	25, 328	9, 366	37. 0	49. 2
Washington	2, 059	568	27. 6	42. 3
Oregon	674	254	37. 7	43. 5
California	22, 595	8, 544	37. 8	52. 0

Table 22.—Median Size of Family, and Median Value or Rental of Nonfarm Homes, by Color, and Nativity of Head, for the United States: 1930

COLOR AND NATIVITY OF HEAD	Median size of family	Median value of owned non-farm homes	Median monthly rental of rented non-farm homes
All classes	**3. 40**	**$4, 778**	**$27. 15**
Negro	3. 15	1, 341	13. 04
Native white	3. 34	4, 766	27. 92
Foreign-born white	3. 74	5, 576	33. 00
Other races	4. 13	(1)	12. 28

[1] Less than $1,000.

Table 23.—FAMILIES HAVING SERVANTS LIVING IN THE HOME, BUT NO LODGERS, BY COLOR, AND NATIVITY OF HEAD, FOR THE UNITED STATES: 1930

[Families designated as "having servants" include only those reporting servants living in the home and no lodgers. This combination was obtained as a byproduct of the tabulation by number of lodgers, but the mechanical restrictions were such that it was not possible to obtain data for families having both servants and lodgers]

COLOR AND NATIVITY AND TENURE	TOTAL FAMILIES			URBAN FAMILIES			RURAL-FARM FAMILIES			RURAL-NONFARM FAMILIES		
	Total number	Having servants living in home		Total number	Having servants living in home		Total number	Having servants living in home		Total number	Having servants living in home	
		Number	Percent		Number	Percent		Number	Percent		Number	Percent
All families	29, 904, 663	523, 922	1. 8	17, 372, 524	376, 104	2. 2	6, 604, 637	57, 919	0. 9	5, 927, 502	89, 899	1. 5
Negro	2, 803. 756	8, 553	. 3	1, 328, 170	3, 239	. 2	978, 653	2, 969	. 3	496, 933	2, 345	. 5
White	26, 705, 294	513, 842	1. 9	15, 858, 158	371, 980	2. 3	5, 517, 637	54, 655	1. 0	5, 329, 499	87, 207	1. 6
Native	20, 968, 803	438, 345	2. 1	11, 322, 555	309, 724	2. 7	5, 006, 748	49, 877	1. 0	4, 639, 500	78, 744	1. 7
Foreign born	5, 736, 491	75, 497	1. 3	4, 535, 603	62, 256	1. 4	510, 889	4, 778	. 9	689. 999	8, 463	1. 2
Other races	395, 613	1, 527	. 4	186, 196	885	. 5	108, 347	295	. 3	101, 070	347	. 3
Owner families	14, 002, 074	354, 136	2. 5	7, 432, 554	250, 388	3. 4	3, 452, 102	41, 239	1. 2	3, 117, 418	62, 509	2. 0
Negro	669, 645	2, 236	. 3	315, 584	1, 022	. 3	188, 574	645	. 3	165, 487	569	. 3
White	13, 224, 389	351. 200	2. 7	7, 074, 031	248, 978	3. 5	3, 231, 951	40. 445	1. 3	2, 918, 407	61, 777	2. 1
Native	10, 255, 682	304, 452	3. 0	4, 941, 762	211, 482	4. 3	2, 840. 831	36, 825	1. 3	2, 473, 089	56, 145	2. 3
Foreign born	2, 968. 707	46, 748	1. 6	2, 132, 269	37, 496	1. 8	391, 120	3. 620	. 9	445. 318	5, 632	1. 3
Other races	108, 040	700	. 6	42, 939	388	. 9	31, 577	149	. 5	33, 524	163	. 5
Tenant families	15, 319, 817	162, 393	1. 1	9, 681, 359	121, 523	1. 3	2, 952, 717	15. 055	. 5	2, 685, 741	25, 815	1. 0
Negro	2, 050, 217	6, 049	. 3	978, 799	2, 140	. 2	758, 014	2, 215	. 3	313, 404	1, 694	. 5
White	13, 004, 800	155, 575	1. 2	8, 565, 849	118, 907	1. 4	2, 125, 854	12, 710	. 6	2, 313, 097	23, 958	1. 0
Native	10, 314, 500	127, 958	1. 2	6, 213, 093	94, 872	1. 5	2, 022, 067	11, 726	. 6	2, 079, 340	21, 360	1. 0
Foreign born	2, 690, 300	27, 617	1. 0	2, 352, 756	24, 035	1. 0	103, 787	984	. 9	233, 757	2, 598	1. 1
Other races	264, 800	769	. 3	136, 711	476	. 3	68, 849	130	. 2	59, 240	163	. 3

TABLE 24.—NEGRO HOME OWNERS, BY SECTIONS, DIVISIONS, AND STATES: 1930 AND 1920

[Minus sign (−) denotes decrease. Percent not shown where base is less than 100]

SECTION, DIVISION, AND STATE	NUMBER OF HOMES (ALL TENURES)		ALL OWNED HOMES						Percent increase of Negro population
	1930	1920	1930		1920		Increase		
			Number	Percent	Number	Percent	Number	Percent	
United States	2,803,756	2,430,328	669,645	23.9	542,654	22.3	126,991	23.4	13.6
The North	576,328	362,694	121,595	21.1	72,632	20.0	48,963	67.4	63.6
The South	2,193,357	2,047,809	535,433	24.4	463,358	22.6	72,075	15.6	5.0
The West	34,071	20,325	12,617	37.0	6,664	32.8	5,953	89.3	53.1
NEW ENGLAND	22,864	19,374	5,355	23.4	3,358	17.3	1,997	59.5	19.0
Maine	259	287	129	49.8	132	46.0	−3	−2.3	−16.3
New Hampshire	117	127	39	33.3	37	29.1	2		27.2
Vermont	135	130	48	35.6	46	35.4	2		−.7
Massachusetts	12,637	11,222	3,453	27.3	1,980	17.6	1,473	74.4	15.2
Rhode Island	2,542	2,587	599	23.6	404	15.6	195	48.3	−1.2
Connecticut	7,174	5,021	1,087	15.2	759	15.1	328	43.2	39.5
MIDDLE ATLANTIC	243,371	140,494	37,932	15.6	19,122	13.6	18,810	98.4	75.4
New York	95,621	46,975	7,920	8.3	3,375	7.2	4,545	134.7	108.0
New Jersey	48,636	28,091	11,329	23.3	5,598	19.9	5,731	102.4	78.3
Pennsylvania	99,114	65,428	18,683	18.9	10,149	15.5	8,534	84.1	51.5
EAST NORTH CENTRAL	222,240	127,765	51,077	23.0	28,395	22.2	22,682	79.9	80.8
Ohio	75,709	47,083	17,928	23.7	11,326	24.1	6,602	58.3	66.1
Indiana	28,771	21,581	8,614	29.9	5,521	25.6	3,093	56.0	38.6
Illinois	78,737	44,800	15,321	19.5	8,156	18.2	7,165	87.8	80.5
Michigan	36,500	13,011	8,830	24.2	3,119	24.0	5,711	183.1	182.0
Wisconsin	2,523	1,290	384	15.2	273	21.2	111	40.7	106.5
WEST NORTH CENTRAL	87,853	75,061	27,231	31.0	21,757	29.0	5,474	25.2	19.1
Minnesota	2,592	2,487	855	33.0	659	26.5	196	29.7	7.2
Iowa	4,571	5,108	1,918	42.0	1,698	33.2	220	13.0	−8.6
Missouri	59,016	47,881	13,374	22.7	10,301	21.5	3,073	29.8	25.6
North Dakota	120	147	28	23.3	42	28.6	−14		−19.3
South Dakota	166	243	77	46.4	106	43.6	−29	−27.4	−22.4
Nebraska	3,700	3,426	1,253	33.9	878	25.6	375	42.7	3.9
Kansas	17,688	15,769	9,726	55.0	8,073	51.2	1,653	20.5	14.5
SOUTH ATLANTIC	974,592	955,772	249,762	25.6	227,403	23.8	22,359	9.8	2.2
Delaware	7,682	6,886	2,017	26.3	1,597	23.2	420	26.3	7.5
Maryland	61,160	54,786	16,056	26.3	13,401	24.5	2,655	19.8	13.0
District of Columbia	29,995	24,929	7,316	24.4	3,435	13.8	3,881	113.0	20.1
Virginia	140,726	148,362	61,294	43.6	61,227	41.3	67	.1	−5.8
West Virginia	26,274	20,774	4,900	18.6	3,557	17.1	1,343	37.8	33.1
North Carolina	180,128	154,799	50,948	28.3	45,126	29.2	5,822	12.9	20.3
South Carolina	168,324	184,671	35,753	21.2	36,488	19.8	−735	−2.0	−8.2
Georgia	249,942	276,406	41,318	16.5	40,196	14.5	1,122	2.8	−11.2
Florida	110,361	84,159	30,160	27.3	22,376	26.6	7,784	34.8	31.1
EAST SOUTH CENTRAL	653,847	606,384	142,608	21.8	119,159	19.7	23,449	19.7	5.3
Kentucky	60,672	62,691	21,398	35.3	19,366	30.9	2,032	10.5	−4.2
Tennessee	120,402	111,407	33,655	28.0	28,060	25.2	5,595	19.9	5.7
Alabama	222,533	208,593	44,650	20.1	35,364	17.0	9,286	26.3	4.9
Mississippi	250,240	223,693	42,905	17.1	36,369	16.3	6,536	18.0	8.0
WEST SOUTH CENTRAL	564,918	485,653	143,063	25.3	116,796	24.0	26,267	22.5	10.6
Arkansas	123,009	114,457	27,722	22.5	27,143	23.7	579	2.1	1.3
Louisiana	190,876	165,329	39,457	20.7	28,832	17.4	10,625	36.9	10.9
Oklahoma	40,238	33,551	12,615	31.4	11,403	34.0	1,212	10.6	15.3
Texas	210,795	172,316	63,269	30.0	49,418	28.7	13,851	28.0	15.3
MOUNTAIN	8,743	7,299	3,131	35.8	2,179	29.9	952	43.7	1.9—
Montana	458	601	169	36.9	216	35.9	−47	−21.8	−24.2
Idaho	229	294	80	34.9	93	31.6	−13		−27.4
Wyoming	418	449	122	29.2	95	21.2	27		−9.1
Colorado	3,538	3,233	1,503	42.5	1,116	34.5	387	34.7	4.5
New Mexico	799	820	298	37.3	236	28.8	62	26.3	−50.3
Arizona	2,776	1,338	775	27.9	311	23.2	464	149.2	34.3
Utah	331	435	114	34.4	70	16.1	44		−23.4
Nevada	194	129	70	36.1	42	32.6	28		49.1
PACIFIC	25,328	13,026	9,486	37.5	4,485	34.4	5,001	111.5	88.9
Washington	2,059	1,888	934	45.4	740	39.2	194	26.2	−.6
Oregon	674	608	269	39.9	222	36.5	47	21.2	4.2
California	22,595	10,530	8,283	36.7	3,523	33.5	4,760	135.1	109.1

TABLE 25.—POPULATION, NUMBER OF OWNED HOMES, AND NUMBER OF PERSONS PER HOME, BY COLOR, SECTIONS, DIVISIONS, AND STATES: 1930 AND 1920

[A plus sign (+) indicates an increase]

SECTION, DIVISION, AND STATE	POPULATION				NUMBER OF OWNED HOMES				PERSONS PER OWNED HOME				DECREASE IN PERSONS PER OWNED HOME	
	1930		1920		1930		1920		1930		1920			
	Negro	White	Negro	White	Negro	White	Negro	White	Negro	White	Negro	White	Negro	White
United States	**11, 891, 143**	**108, 864, 207**	**10, 463, 131**	**94, 820, 915**	**669, 645**	**13, 224, 389**	**542, 654**	**10, 286, 267**	**18**	**8**	**19**	**9**	**1**	**1**
The North	**2, 409, 219**	**70, 383, 367**	**1, 472, 309**	**62, 122, 168**	**121, 595**	**8, 764, 890**	**72, 632**	**6, 721, 345**	**20**	**8**	**20**	**9**		**1**
The South	**9, 361, 577**	**27, 673, 879**	**8, 912, 231**	**24, 132, 214**	**535, 433**	**2, 932, 135**	**463, 358**	**2, 485, 497**	**17**	**9**	**19**	**10**	**2**	**1**
The West	**120, 347**	**10, 801, 961**	**78, 591**	**8, 566, 533**	**12, 617**	**1, 527, 364**	**6, 664**	**1, 079, 425**	**10**	**7**	**12**	**8**	**2**	**1**
NEW ENGLAND	94, 086	8, 065, 113	79, 051	7, 316, 079	5, 355	909, 703	3, 358	664, 670	18	9	24	11	6	2
Maine	1, 096	795, 183	1, 310	765, 695	129	119, 627	132	108, 549	8	7	10	7	2	
New Hampshire	790	464, 350	621	442, 331	39	64, 774	37	52, 740	20	7	17	8	+3	1
Vermont	568	358, 965	572	351, 817	48	52, 762	46	48, 322	12	7	12	7		
Massachusetts	52, 365	4, 192, 926	45, 466	3, 803, 524	3, 453	435, 613	1, 980	299, 155	15	10	23	13	8	3
Rhode Island	9, 913	677, 016	10, 036	593, 980	599	66, 837	404	41, 508	17	10	25	14	8	4
Connecticut	29, 354	1, 576, 673	21, 046	1, 358, 732	1, 087	170, 090	759	114, 396	27	9	28	12	1	3
MIDDLE ATLANTIC	1, 052, 899	25, 172, 104	600, 183	21, 641, 840	37, 932	2, 784, 641	19, 122	1, 843, 785	28	9	31	12	3	3
New York	412, 814	12, 150, 293	198, 483	10, 172, 027	7, 920	1, 146, 052	3, 375	734, 273	52	11	59	14	7	3
New Jersey	208, 828	3, 829, 209	117, 132	3, 037, 087	11, 329	459, 072	5, 598	266, 276	18	8	21	11	3	3
Pennsylvania	431, 257	9, 192, 602	284, 568	8, 432, 726	18, 683	1, 179, 517	10, 149	843, 236	23	8	28	10	5	2
EAST NORTH CENTRAL	930, 450	24, 277, 663	514, 554	20, 938, 862	51, 077	3, 341, 529	28, 395	2, 613, 587	18	7	18	8		1
Ohio	309, 304	6, 331, 136	186, 187	5, 571, 893	17, 928	894, 277	11, 326	707, 733	17	7	16	8	+1	1
Indiana	111, 982	3, 116, 136	80, 810	2, 849, 071	8, 614	465, 503	5, 521	389, 855	13	7	15	7	2	
Illinois	328, 972	7, 266, 361	182, 274	6, 299, 333	15, 321	867, 417	8, 156	650, 051	21	8	22	10	1	2
Michigan	169, 453	4, 650, 171	60, 082	3, 601, 627	8, 830	675, 817	3, 119	495, 768	19	7	19	7		
Wisconsin	10, 739	2, 913, 859	5, 201	2, 616, 938	384	438, 515	273	370, 180	28	7	19	7	+9	
WEST NORTH CENTRAL	331, 784	12, 873, 487	278, 521	12, 225, 387	27, 231	1, 729, 017	21, 757	1, 599, 303	12	7	13	8	1	1
Minnesota	9, 445	2, 538, 973	8, 809	2, 368, 936	855	347, 795	659	310, 508	11	7	13	8	2	1
Iowa	17, 380	2, 448, 382	19, 005	2, 384, 181	1, 918	338, 618	1, 698	330, 751	9	7	11	7	2	
Missouri	223, 840	3, 398, 887	178, 241	3, 225, 044	13, 374	446, 327	10, 301	391, 344	17	8	17	8		
North Dakota	377	671, 243	467	639, 954	28	80, 489	42	83, 861	13	8	11	8	+2	
South Dakota	646	669, 453	832	619, 147	77	79, 620	106	81, 779	8	8	8	8		
Nebraska	13, 752	1, 353, 702	13, 242	1, 279, 219	1, 253	179, 714	878	167, 852	11	8	15	8	4	
Kansas	66, 344	1, 792, 847	57, 925	1, 708, 906	9, 726	256, 454	8, 073	233, 208	7	7	7	7		
SOUTH ATLANTIC	4, 421, 388	11, 349, 284	4, 325, 120	9, 648, 940	249, 762	1, 215, 383	227, 403	992, 711	18	9	19	10	1	1
Delaware	32, 602	205, 694	30, 335	192, 615	2, 017	28, 168	1, 597	21, 230	16	7	19	9	3	2
Maryland	276, 379	1, 354, 170	244, 479	1, 204, 737	16, 056	192, 432	13, 401	145, 833	17	7	18	8	1	1
District of Columbia	132, 068	353, 914	109, 966	326, 860	7, 316	39, 874	3, 435	25, 059	18	9	32	13	14	4
Virginia	650, 165	1, 770, 405	690, 017	1, 617, 909	61, 294	210, 835	61, 227	180, 755	11	8	11	9		1
West Virginia	114, 893	1, 613, 934	86, 345	1, 377, 235	4, 900	163, 633	3, 557	137, 802	23	10	24	10	1	
North Carolina	918, 647	2, 234, 948	763, 407	1, 783, 779	50, 948	228, 087	45, 126	189, 933	18	10	17	9	+1	+1
South Carolina	793, 681	944, 040	864, 719	818, 538	35, 753	75, 470	36, 488	71, 660	22	13	24	11	2	+2
Georgia	1, 071, 125	1, 836, 974	1, 206, 365	1, 689, 114	41, 318	153, 126	40, 196	147, 982	26	12	30	11	4	+1
Florida	431, 828	1, 035, 205	329, 487	638, 153	30, 160	123, 758	22, 376	72, 457	14	8	15	9	1	1
EAST SOUTH CENTRAL	2, 658, 238	7, 224, 614	2, 523, 532	6, 367, 547	142, 608	782, 193	119, 159	703, 838	19	9	21	9	2	
Kentucky	226, 040	2, 388, 364	235, 938	2, 180, 560	21, 398	284, 881	19, 366	256, 621	11	8	12	8	1	
Tennessee	477, 646	2, 138, 619	451, 758	1, 885, 993	33, 655	236, 584	28, 060	213, 805	14	9	16	9	2	
Alabama	944, 834	1, 700, 775	900, 652	1, 447, 032	44, 650	153, 788	35, 364	136, 961	21	11	25	11	4	
Mississippi	1, 099, 718	996, 856	935, 184	853, 962	42, 905	106, 940	36, 369	96, 451	24	9	26	9	2	
WEST SOUTH CENTRAL	2, 281, 951	9, 099, 981	2, 063, 579	8, 115, 727	143, 063	934, 559	116, 796	788, 948	16	10	18	10	2	
Arkansas	478, 463	1, 374, 906	472, 220	1, 279, 757	27, 722	141, 008	27, 143	144, 095	17	10	17	9		+1
Louisiana	776, 326	1, 318, 160	700, 257	1, 096, 611	39, 457	125, 892	28, 832	97, 504	20	10	24	11	4	1
Oklahoma	172, 198	2, 123, 424	149, 408	1, 821, 194	12, 615	203, 990	11, 403	175, 024	14	10	13	10	+1	
Texas	854, 964	4, 283, 491	741, 694	3, 918, 165	63, 269	463, 669	49, 418	372, 325	14	9	15	11	1	2
MOUNTAIN	30, 225	3, 303, 586	30, 801	3, 212, 899	3, 131	436, 277	2, 179	414, 438	10	8	14	8	4	
Montana	1, 256	517, 327	1, 658	534, 260	169	69, 359	216	79, 637	7	7	8	7	1	
Idaho	668	437, 562	920	425, 668	80	58, 781	93	58, 460	8	7	10	7	2	
Wyoming	1, 250	214, 067	1, 375	190, 146	122	25, 934	95	23, 698	10	8	14	8	4	
Colorado	11, 828	961, 117	11, 318	924, 103	1, 503	127, 689	1, 116	115, 312	8	8	10	8	2	
New Mexico	2, 850	331, 755	5, 733	334, 673	298	44, 304	236	44, 884	10	7	24	7	14	
Arizona	10, 749	264, 378	8, 005	291, 449	775	30, 750	311	26, 486	14	9	26	11	12	2
Utah	1, 108	495, 955	1, 446	441, 901	114	68, 873	70	56, 999	10	7	21	8	11	1
Nevada	516	81, 425	346	70, 699	70	10, 587	42	8, 962	7	8	8	8	1	
PACIFIC	90, 122	7, 498, 375	47, 790	5, 353, 634	9, 486	1, 091, 087	4, 485	664, 987	10	7	11	8	1	1
Washington	6, 840	1, 521, 099	6, 883	1, 319, 777	934	242, 354	740	180, 948	7	6	9	7	2	1
Oregon	2, 234	937, 029	2, 144	769, 146	269	153, 130	222	107, 866	8	6	10	7	2	1
California	81, 048	5, 040, 247	38, 763	3, 264, 711	8, 283	695, 603	3, 523	376, 173	10	7	11	9	1	2

TABLE 26.—HOMES OF NEGRO FAMILIES BY TENURE, BY SECTIONS, DIVISIONS, AND STATES, 1930 AND 1920; WITH PERCENT OF TOTAL FOR 1930, 1920, AND 1910

SECTION, DIVISION, AND STATES	NUMBER OF HOMES								PERCENT OF TOTAL								
	Total		Owned		Rented		Tenure unknown		Owned			Rented			Tenure unknown		
	1930	1920	1930	1920	1930	1920	1930	1920	1930	1920	1910	1930	1920	1910	1930	1920	1910
United States	2,803,756	2,430,828	669,645	542,654	2,050,217	1,799,694	83,894	88,480	23.9	22.3	22.5	73.1	74.0	73.8	3.0	3.6	3.7
The North	576,328	362,694	121,595	72,632	439,971	280,261	14,762	9,801	21.1	20.0	22.3	76.3	77.3	74.1	2.6	2.7	3.6
The South	2,193,357	2,047,809	535,433	463,358	1,589,930	1,506,493	67,994	77,958	24.4	22.6	22.4	72.5	73.6	73.8	3.1	3.8	3.7
The West	34,071	20,325	12,617	6,664	20,316	12,940	1,138	721	37.0	32.8	32.6	59.6	63.7	63.9	3.3	3.5	3.5
NEW ENGLAND	22,864	19,374	5,355	3,358	17,014	15,640	495	376	23.4	17.3	17.2	74.4	80.7	80.9	2.2	1.9	2.0
Maine	259	287	129	132	121	148	9	7	49.8	46.0	42.9	46.7	51.6	53.1	3.5	2.4	4.1
New Hampshire	117	127	39	37	65	85	13	5	33.3	29.1	30.6	55.6	66.9	66.1	11.1	3.9	3.3
Vermont	135	130	48	46	83	78	4	6	35.6	35.4	20.4	61.5	60.0	77.9	3.0	4.6	1.8
Massachusetts	12,637	11,222	3,453	1,980	8,864	9,068	320	174	27.3	17.6	16.2	70.1	80.8	82.0	2.5	1.6	1.8
Rhode Island	2,542	2,587	599	404	1,902	2,119	41	64	23.6	15.6	15.2	74.8	81.9	82.7	1.6	2.5	2.1
Connecticut	7,174	5,021	1,087	759	5,979	4,142	108	120	15.2	15.1	18.1	83.3	82.5	79.9	1.5	2.4	2.0
MIDDLE ATLANTIC	243,371	140,494	37,932	19,122	199,287	118,074	6,152	3,298	15.6	13.6	12.6	81.9	84.0	82.7	2.5	2.3	4.7
New York	95,621	46,975	7,920	3,375	85,991	42,843	1,710	757	8.3	7.2	7.8	89.9	91.2	89.3	1.8	1.6	2.9
New Jersey	48,636	28,091	11,329	5,598	36,171	21,758	1,136	735	23.3	19.9	18.6	74.4	77.5	77.7	2.3	2.6	3.7
Pennsylvania	99,114	65,428	18,683	10,149	77,125	53,473	3,306	1,806	18.9	15.5	13.3	77.8	81.7	80.2	3.3	2.8	6.4
EAST NORTH CENTRAL	222,240	127,765	51,077	28,395	165,832	95,966	5,331	3,404	23.0	22.2	27.6	74.6	75.1	70.1	2.4	2.7	2.2
Ohio	75,709	47,083	17,928	11,326	56,079	34,799	1,702	958	23.7	24.1	30.1	74.1	73.9	67.7	2.2	2.0	2.2
Indiana	28,771	21,581	8,614	5,521	19,408	15,209	749	851	29.9	25.6	26.4	67.5	70.5	71.8	2.6	3.9	1.8
Illinois	78,737	44,800	15,321	8,156	61,921	35,362	1,495	1,282	19.5	18.2	23.0	78.6	78.9	74.4	1.9	2.9	2.6
Michigan	36,500	13,011	8,830	3,119	26,432	9,612	1,238	280	24.2	24.0	44.0	72.4	73.9	54.2	3.4	2.2	1.8
Wisconsin	2,523	1,290	384	273	1,992	984	147	33	15.2	21.2	25.6	79.0	76.3	71.8	5.8	2.6	2.7
WEST NORTH CENTRAL	87,853	75,061	27,231	21,757	57,838	50,581	2,784	2,723	31.0	29.0	32.1	65.8	67.4	63.7	3.2	3.6	4.2
Minnesota	2,592	2,487	855	659	1,669	1,729	68	99	33.0	26.5	24.7	64.4	69.5	69.4	2.6	4.0	5.9
Iowa	4,571	5,108	1,918	1,698	2,528	3,185	125	225	42.0	33.2	29.9	55.3	62.4	68.3	2.7	4.4	1.8
Missouri	59,016	47,881	13,374	10,301	43,571	35,825	2,071	1,755	22.7	21.5	26.6	73.8	74.8	68.7	3.5	3.7	4.7
North Dakota	120	147	28	42	83	97	9	8	23.3	28.6	35.6	69.2	66.0	51.4	7.5	5.4	13.0
South Dakota	166	243	77	106	87	119	2	18	46.4	43.6	45.1	52.4	49.0	46.5	1.2	7.4	8.4
Nebraska	3,700	3,426	1,253	878	2,327	2,400	120	148	33.9	25.6	24.1	62.9	70.1	70.9	3.2	4.3	5.0
Kansas	17,688	15,769	9,726	8,073	7,573	7,226	389	470	55.0	51.2	49.6	42.8	45.8	47.3	2.2	3.0	3.1
SOUTH ATLANTIC	974,592	955,772	249,762	227,403	696,573	692,572	28,257	35,797	25.6	23.8	23.6	71.5	72.5	72.7	2.9	3.7	3.7
Delaware	7,682	6,886	2,017	1,597	5,491	5,091	174	198	26.3	23.2	23.2	71.5	73.9	72.1	2.3	2.9	4.7
Maryland	61,160	54,786	16,056	13,401	43,332	40,015	1,772	1,370	26.3	24.5	25.6	70.9	73.0	69.5	2.9	2.5	4.9
District of Columbia	29,995	24,929	7,316	3,435	21,413	20,791	1,266	703	24.4	13.8	10.8	71.4	83.4	85.4	4.2	2.8	3.8
Virginia	140,726	148,362	61,294	61,227	76,498	83,873	2,934	3,262	43.6	41.3	41.3	54.4	56.5	55.9	2.1	2.2	2.8
West Virginia	26,274	20,774	4,900	3,557	20,681	16,546	693	671	18.6	17.1	19.3	78.7	79.6	77.1	2.6	3.2	3.6
North Carolina	180,128	154,799	50,948	45,126	123,882	103,861	5,298	5,812	28.3	29.2	28.7	68.8	67.1	68.1	2.9	3.8	3.2
South Carolina	168,324	184,671	35,753	36,488	129,447	140,153	3,124	8,030	21.2	19.8	18.5	76.9	75.9	77.6	1.9	4.3	3.9
Georgia	249,942	276,406	41,318	40,196	199,433	225,101	9,191	11,109	16.5	14.5	14.7	79.8	81.4	81.9	3.7	4.0	3.4
Florida	110,361	84,159	30,160	22,376	76,396	57,141	3,805	4,642	27.3	26.6	27.7	69.2	67.9	65.9	3.4	5.5	6.4
EAST SOUTH CENTRAL	653,847	606,384	142,608	119,159	494,142	465,518	17,097	21,707	21.8	19.7	19.8	75.6	76.8	76.8	2.6	3.6	3.4
Kentucky	60,672	62,691	21,398	19,366	37,766	41,476	1,508	1,849	35.3	30.9	31.8	62.2	66.2	64.9	2.5	2.9	3.3
Tennessee	120,402	111,407	33,655	28,060	82,515	79,871	4,232	3,476	28.0	25.2	25.3	68.5	71.7	72.1	3.5	3.1	2.5
Alabama	222,533	208,593	44,650	35,364	172,448	164,524	5,435	8,705	20.1	17.0	16.4	77.5	78.9	79.3	2.4	4.2	4.3
Mississippi	250,240	223,693	42,905	36,369	201,413	179,647	5,922	7,677	17.1	16.3	16.9	80.5	80.3	79.9	2.4	3.4	3.1
WEST SOUTH CENTRAL	564,918	485,653	143,063	116,796	399,215	438,403	22,640	20,454	25.3	24.0	23.9	70.7	71.7	72.1	4.0	4.2	4.0
Arkansas	123,009	114,457	27,722	27,143	87,803	83,095	7,484	4,219	22.5	23.7	24.6	71.4	72.6	70.8	6.1	3.7	4.7
Louisiana	190,876	165,329	39,457	28,832	145,608	128,830	5,811	7,667	20.7	17.4	17.1	76.3	77.9	79.0	3.0	4.6	3.9
Oklahoma	40,238	33,551	12,615	11,403	25,862	20,037	1,761	2,111	31.4	34.0	35.3	64.3	59.7	60.4	4.4	6.3	4.3
Texas	210,795	172,316	63,269	49,418	139,942	116,441	7,584	6,457	30.0	28.7	28.5	66.4	67.6	67.7	3.6	3.7	3.8
MOUNTAIN	8,743	7,299	3,131	2,179	5,258	4,838	354	282	35.8	29.9	28.1	60.1	66.3	67.7	4.0	3.9	4.2
Montana	458	601	169	216	268	345	21	40	36.9	35.9	32.8	58.5	57.4	60.5	4.6	6.7	6.7
Idaho	229	294	80	93	142	183	7	18	34.9	31.6	28.7	62.0	62.2	59.9	3.1	6.1	11.4
Wyoming	418	449	122	95	277	334	19	20	29.2	21.2	18.4	66.3	74.4	76.8	4.5	4.5	4.8
Colorado	3,538	3,233	1,503	1,116	1,899	2,038	136	79	42.5	34.5	27.6	53.7	63.0	69.5	3.8	2.4	2.9
New Mexico	799	820	298	236	473	553	28	31	37.3	28.8	30.3	59.2	67.4	67.7	3.5	3.8	2.0
Arizona	2,776	1,338	775	311	1,868	952	133	75	27.9	23.2	30.7	67.3	71.2	64.5	4.8	5.6	4.8
Utah	331	435	114	70	210	354	7	11	34.4	16.1	21.3	63.4	81.4	64.2	2.1	2.5	14.6
Nevada	194	129	70	42	121	79	3	8	36.1	32.6	35.7	62.4	61.2	62.9	1.5	6.2	1.4
PACIFIC	25,328	13,026	9,486	4,485	15,058	8,102	784	439	37.5	34.4	36.2	59.5	62.2	60.8	3.1	3.4	3.0
Washington	2,059	1,888	934	740	1,056	1,075	69	73	45.4	39.2	32.1	51.3	56.9	63.0	3.4	3.9	4.9
Oregon	674	608	269	222	376	375	29	11	39.9	36.5	28.2	55.8	61.7	62.5	4.3	1.8	9.2
California	22,595	10,530	8,283	3,523	13,626	6,652	686	355	36.7	33.5	37.8	60.3	63.2	60.2	3.0	3.4	2.1

TABLE 27.—URBAN, RURAL-FARM, AND RURAL-NONFARM HOMES OF NEGRO FAMILIES, BY TENURE, BY SECTIONS, DIVISIONS, AND STATES: 1930

SECTION, DIVISION, AND STATE	URBAN HOMES					RURAL-FARM HOMES					RURAL-NONFARM HOMES				
	Total	Owned		Rented	Tenure unknown	Total	Owned		Rented	Tenure unknown	Total	Owned		Rented	Tenure unknown
		Number	Per cent				Number	Per cent				Number	Per cent		
United States	1,328,170	315,584	23.8	978,799	33,787	978,653	188,574	19.3	758,014	32,065	496,933	165,487	33.3	313,404	18,042
The North	514,187	96,187	18.7	405,052	12,948	14,744	4,868	33.0	9,373	503	47,397	20,540	43.3	25,546	1,311
The South	785,189	208,698	20.6	556,560	19,931	962,401	183,245	19.0	747,666	31,490	445,767	143,490	32.2	285,704	16,573
The West	28,794	10,699	37.2	17,187	908	1,508	461	30.6	975	72	3,769	1,457	38.7	2,154	158
NEW ENGLAND	20,299	4,003	19.7	15,868	428	211	129	61.1	76	6	2,354	1,223	52.0	1,070	61
Maine	174	71	40.8	97	6	20	17	85.0	3	----------	65	41	63.1	21	3
New Hampshire	86	24	27.9	50	12	6	4	66.7	2	----------	25	11	44.0	13	1
Vermont	63	17	27.0	45	1	24	17	70.8	6	1	48	14	29.2	32	2
Massachusetts	11,382	2,657	23.3	8,436	289	95	54	56.8	39	2	1,160	742	64.0	389	29
Rhode Island	2,366	517	21.9	1,814	35	14	8	57.1	5	1	162	74	45.7	83	5
Connecticut	6,228	717	11.5	5,426	85	52	29	55.8	21	2	894	341	38.1	532	21
MIDDLE ATLANTIC	219,382	29,930	13.6	184,017	5,435	2,002	693	34.6	1,223	86	21,987	7,309	33.2	14,047	631
New York	91,281	6,577	7.2	83,149	1,555	447	128	28.6	297	22	3,893	1,215	31.2	2,545	133
New Jersey	41,379	7,879	19.0	32,607	893	796	301	37.8	466	29	6,461	3,149	48.7	3,098	214
Pennsylvania	86,722	15,474	17.8	68,261	2,987	759	264	34.8	460	35	11,633	2,945	25.3	8,404	284
EAST NORTH CENTRAL	204,357	41,951	20.5	157,535	4,871	4,180	2,150	51.4	1,918	112	13,703	6,976	50.9	6,379	348
Ohio	67,397	13,677	20.3	52,181	1,539	1,660	899	54.2	725	36	6,652	3,352	50.4	3,173	127
Indiana	26,861	7,658	28.5	18,511	692	592	293	49.5	272	27	1,318	663	50.3	625	30
Illinois	73,136	12,733	17.4	59,089	1,314	1,260	498	39.5	732	30	4,341	2,090	48.1	2,100	151
Michigan	34,571	7,584	21.9	25,803	1,184	601	412	68.6	173	16	1,328	834	62.8	456	38
Wisconsin	2,392	299	12.5	1,951	142	67	48	71.6	16	3	64	37	57.8	25	2
WEST NORTH CENTRAL	70,149	20,303	28.9	47,632	2,214	8,351	1,896	22.7	6,156	299	9,353	5,032	53.8	4,050	271
Minnesota	2,520	816	32.4	1,641	63	28	17	60.7	8	3	44	22	50.0	20	2
Iowa	4,045	1,726	42.7	2,207	112	130	75	57.7	50	5	396	117	29.5	271	8
Missouri	45,408	8,632	19.0	35,129	1,647	7,059	1,216	17.2	5,589	254	6,549	3,526	53.8	2,853	170
North Dakota	85	18	21.2	64	3	13	6	46.2	5	2	22	4	18.2	14	4
South Dakota	90	41	45.6	48	1	49	26	53.1	22	1	27	10	37.0	17	----------
Nebraska	3,599	1,214	33.7	2,273	112	29	12	41.4	15	2	72	27	37.5	39	6
Kansas	14,402	7,856	54.5	6,270	276	1,043	544	52.2	467	32	2,243	1,326	59.1	836	81
SOUTH ATLANTIC	368,826	88,679	24.0	271,588	8,559	364,268	85,008	23.3	268,240	11,020	241,498	76,075	31.5	156,745	8,678
Delaware	3,878	703	18.1	3,095	80	1,268	408	32.2	826	34	2,536	906	35.7	1,570	60
Maryland	37,731	5,073	13.4	31,457	1,201	8,016	3,405	42.5	4,412	199	15,413	7,578	49.2	7,463	372
District of Columbia	29,995	7,316	24.4	21,413	1,266	----------	----------	-----	----------	----------	----------	----------	-----	----------	----------
Virginia	54,779	15,758	28.8	38,303	718	47,408	26,180	55.2	20,118	1,110	38,539	19,356	50.2	18,077	1,106
West Virginia	7,193	2,214	30.8	4,709	270	688	401	58.3	264	23	18,393	2,285	12.4	15,708	400
North Carolina	57,501	16,212	28.2	40,263	1,026	85,455	20,337	23.8	62,327	2,791	37,172	14,399	38.7	21,292	1,481
South Carolina	36,807	8,572	23.3	27,608	627	92,663	17,010	18.4	74,072	1,581	38,854	10,171	26.2	27,767	916
Georgia	86,578	18,012	20.8	66,797	1,769	112,467	11,276	10.0	96,433	4,758	50,897	12,030	23.6	36,203	2,664
Florida	54,364	14,819	27.3	37,943	1,602	16,303	5,991	36.7	9,788	524	39,694	9,350	23.6	28,665	1,679
EAST SOUTH CENTRAL	214,280	58,032	27.1	151,176	5,072	330,252	51,662	15.6	270,474	8,116	109,315	32,914	30.1	72,492	3,909
Kentucky	34,399	9,883	28.7	23,869	647	10,583	4,355	41.2	5,809	419	15,690	7,160	45.6	8,088	442
Tennessee	68,401	18,952	27.7	47,232	2,217	36,913	8,301	22.5	27,185	1,427	15,088	6,402	42.4	8,098	588
Alabama	72,190	17,951	24.9	52,956	1,283	104,136	16,507	15.9	85,174	2,455	46,207	10,192	22.1	34,318	1,697
Mississippi	39,290	11,246	28.6	27,119	925	178,620	22,499	12.6	152,306	3,815	32,330	9,160	28.3	21,988	1,186
WEST SOUTH CENTRAL	202,083	61,987	30.7	133,796	6,300	267,881	46,575	17.4	208,952	12,354	94,954	34,501	36.3	56,467	3,982
Arkansas	25,462	8,891	34.9	15,819	752	78,722	11,479	14.6	61,367	5,876	18,825	7,352	39.1	10,617	856
Louisiana	69,395	15,826	22.8	52,014	1,555	82,916	10,890	13.1	69,177	2,849	38,565	12,741	33.0	24,417	1,407
Oklahoma	17,386	6,604	38.0	10,081	701	16,671	3,464	20.8	12,481	726	6,181	2,547	41.2	3,300	334
Texas	89,840	30,666	34.1	55,882	3,292	89,572	20,742	23.2	65,927	2,903	31,383	11,861	37.8	18,133	1,389
MOUNTAIN	6,444	2,406	37.3	3,796	242	589	190	32.3	364	35	1,710	535	31.3	1,098	77
Montana	368	137	37.2	215	16	24	13	54.2	9	2	66	19	28.8	44	3
Idaho	185	64	34.6	116	5	22	5	22.7	15	2	22	11	50.0	11	----------
Wyoming	284	86	30.3	190	8	16	11	68.8	5	----------	118	25	21.2	82	11
Colorado	3,131	1,368	43.7	1,646	117	100	52	52.0	39	9	307	83	27.0	214	10
New Mexico	495	196	39.6	286	13	106	52	49.1	53	1	198	50	25.3	134	14
Arizona	1,562	407	26.1	1,078	77	310	49	15.8	240	21	904	319	35.3	550	35
Utah	276	103	37.3	168	5	6	5	83.3	1	----------	49	6	12.2	41	2
Nevada	143	45	31.5	97	1	5	3	60.0	2	----------	46	22	47.8	22	2
PACIFIC	22,350	8,293	37.1	13,391	666	919	271	29.5	611	37	2,059	922	44.8	1,056	81
Washington	1,788	761	42.6	970	57	84	64	76.2	18	2	187	109	58.3	68	10
Oregon	567	236	41.6	309	22	13	9	69.2	4	----------	94	24	25.5	63	7
California	19,995	7,296	36.5	12,112	587	822	198	24.1	589	35	1,778	789	44.4	925	64

Table 28.—HOMES OF NEGRO FAMILIES BY TENURE, BY SECTIONS, DIVISIONS, AND STATES: 1930, 1920, 1910, AND 1900

[Figures for 1930 and 1900 represent private-family homes alone; those for 1920 and 1910 include the premises occupied by the small number of institutions and other quasi-family groups which were counted as families in the respective censuses]

AREA AND TENURE	1930 Number	1930 Percent distribution	1920 Number	1920 Percent distribution	1910 Number	1910 Percent distribution	1900 Number	1900 Percent distribution	INCREASE OR DECREASE (—) 1900 to 1930 Number	1900 to 1930 Per-cent	1920 to 1930 Number	1920 to 1930 Per-cent	1910 to 1920 Number	1910 to 1920 Per-cent	1900 to 1910 Number	1900 to 1910 Per-cent
United States																
All homes	2,803,756	100.0	2,430,828	100.0	2,173,018	100.0	1,833,759	100.0	969,997	52.9	372,928	15.3	257,810	11.9	339,259	18.5
Owned	669,645	23.9	542,654	22.3	488,699	22.5	373,450	20.4	296,195	79.3	126,991	23.4	53,955	11.0	115,249	30.9
Rented	2,050,217	73.1	1,799,694	74.0	1,603,719	73.8	1,335,276	72.8	714,941	53.5	250,523	13.9	195,975	12.2	268,443	20.1
Tenure unknown	83,894	3.0	88,480	3.6	80,600	3.7	125,033	6.8	—41,139	—32.9	—4,586	—5.2	7,880	9.8	—44,433	—35.5
THE NORTH																
All homes	576,328	100.0	362,694	100.0	242,920	100.0	189,770	100.0	386,558	203.7	213,634	58.9	119,774	49.3	53,150	28.0
Owned	121,595	21.1	72,632	20.0	54,109	22.3	44,041	23.2	77,554	176.1	48,963	67.4	18,523	34.2	10,068	22.0
Rented	439,971	76.3	280,261	77.3	179,949	74.1	136,183	71.8	303,788	223.1	159,710	57.0	100,312	55.7	43,766	32.1
Tenure unknown	14,762	2.6	9,801	2.7	8,862	3.6	9,546	5.0	5,216	54.6	4,961	50.6	939	10.6	—684	—72
THE SOUTH																
All homes	2,193,357	100.0	2,047,809	100.0	1,917,391	100.0	1,637,024	100.0	556,333	34.0	145,548	7.1	130,418	6.8	280,367	17.1
Owned	535,433	24.4	463,358	22.6	430,449	22.4	327,537	20.0	207,896	63.5	72,075	15.6	32,909	7.6	102,912	31.4
Rented	1,589,930	72.5	1,506,493	73.6	1,415,651	73.8	1,194,549	73.0	395,381	33.1	83,437	5.5	90,842	6.4	221,102	17.5
Tenure unknown	67,994	3.1	77,958	3.8	71,291	3.7	114,938	7.0	—46,944	—40.8	—9,964	—12.8	6,667	9.4	—43,647	—38.0
THE WEST																
All homes	34,071	100.0	20,325	100.0	12,707	100.0	6,965	100.0	27,106	389.2	13,746	67.6	7,618	60.0	5,742	82.4
Owned	12,617	37.0	6,664	32.8	4,141	32.6	1,872	26.9	10,745	574.0	5,953	89.3	2,523	60.9	2,269	121.2
Rented	20,316	59.6	12,940	63.7	8,119	63.9	4,544	65.2	15,772	347.1	7,376	57.0	4,821	59.4	3,575	78.7
Tenure unknown	1,138	3.3	721	3.5	447	3.5	549	7.9	589	107.3	417	57.8	274	61.3	—102	—18.6
NEW ENGLAND:																
All homes	22,864	100.0	19,374	100.0	15,214	100.0	12,873	100.0	9,991	77.6	3,490	18.0	4,160	27.3	2,341	18.2
Owned	5,355	23.4	3,358	17.3	2,615	17.2	2,215	17.2	3,140	141.8	1,997	59.5	743	28.4	400	18.1
Rented	17,014	74.4	15,640	80.7	12,302	80.9	9,941	77.2	7,073	71.1	1,374	8.8	3,338	27.1	2,361	23.8
Tenure unknown	495	2.2	376	1.9	297	2.0	717	5.6	—222	—31.0	119	31.6	7.9	26.6	—420	—58.6
MAINE																
All homes	259	100.0	287	100.0	294	100.0	292	100.0	—33	—11.3	—28	—9.8	—7	—2.4	2	.7
Owned	129	49.8	132	46.0	126	42.9	121	41.4	8	6.6	—3	—2.3	6	4.8	5	4.1
Rented	121	46.7	148	51.6	156	53.1	156	53.4	—35	—22.4	—27	—18.2	—8	—5.1	------	------
Tenure unknown	9	3.5	7	2.4	12	4.1	15	5.1	—6	—40.0	2	28.6	—5	—41.7	—3	—20.0
NEW HAMPSHIRE																
All homes	117	100.0	127	100.0	121	100.0	124	100.0	—7	—5.6	—10	—7.9	6	5.0	—3	—2.4
Owned	39	33.3	37	29.1	37	30.6	33	26.6	6	18.2	2	5.4	------	------	4	12.1
Rented	65	55.6	85	66.9	80	66.1	85	68.5	—20	—23.5	—20	—23.5	5	6.3	—5	—5.9
Tenure unknown	13	11.1	5	3.9	4	3.3	6	4.8	7	116.7	8	160.0	1	25.0	—2	—33.3
VERMONT																
All homes	135	100.0	130	100.0	226	100.0	154	100.0	—19	—12.3	5	3.8	—96	—42.5	72	46.8
Owned	48	35.6	46	35.4	46	20.4	49	31.8	—1	—2.0	2	4.3	------	------	—3	—6.1
Rented	83	61.5	78	60.0	176	77.9	97	63.0	—14	—14.4	5	6.4	—98	—55.7	79	81.4
Tenure unknown	4	3.0	6	4.6	4	1.8	8	5.2	—4	—50.0	—2	—33.3	2	50.0	—4	—50.0
MASSACHUSETTS																
All homes	12,637	100.0	11,222	100.0	8,705	100.0	6,880	100.0	5,757	83.7	1,415	12.6	2,517	28.9	1,825	26.5
Owned	3,453	27.3	1,980	17.6	1,412	16.2	1,094	15.9	2,359	215.6	1,473	74.4	568	40.2	318	29.1
Rented	8,864	70.1	9,068	80.8	7,136	82.0	5,347	77.7	3,517	65.8	—204	—2.2	1,932	27.1	1,789	33.5
Tenure unknown	320	2.5	174	1.6	157	1.8	439	6.4	—119	—27.1	146	83.9	17	10.8	—282	—64.2
RHODE ISLAND																
All homes	2,542	100.0	2,587	100.0	2,353	100.0	2,120	100.0	422	19.9	—45	—1.7	234	9.9	233	11.0
Owned	599	23.6	404	15.6	358	15.2	319	15.0	280	87.8	195	48.3	46	12.8	39	12.2
Rented	1,902	74.8	2,119	81.9	1,946	82.7	1,684	79.4	218	13.0	—217	—10.2	173	8.9	262	15.6
Tenure unknown	41	1.6	64	2.5	49	2.1	117	5.5	—76	—65.0	—23	—35.9	15	30.6	—68	—58.1
CONNECTICUT																
All homes	7,174	100.0	5,021	100.0	3,515	100.0	3,303	100.0	3,871	117.2	2,153	42.9	1,506	42.8	212	6.4
Owned	1,087	15.2	759	15.1	636	18.1	599	18.1	488	81.5	328	43.2	123	19.3	37	6.2
Rented	5,979	83.3	4,142	82.5	2,808	79.9	2,572	77.9	3,407	132.5	1,837	44.4	1,334	47.5	236	9.2
Tenure unknown	108	1.5	120	2.4	71	2.0	132	4.0	—24	—18.2	—12	—10.0	49	69.0	—61	—46.2
MIDDLE ATLANTIC:																
All homes	243,371	100.0	140,494	100.0	93,370	100.0	65,965	100.0	177,406	268.9	102,877	73.2	47,124	50.5	27,405	41.5
Owned	37,932	15.6	19,122	13.6	11,736	12.6	8,779	13.3	29,153	332.1	18,810	98.4	7,386	62.9	2,957	33.7
Rented	199,287	81.9	118,074	84.0	77,263	82.7	53,576	81.2	145,711	272.4	81,213	68.8	40,811	52.8	23,687	44.2
Tenure unknown	6,152	2.5	3,298	2.3	4,371	4.7	3,610	5.5	2,542	70.4	2,854	86.5	—1,073	—24.5	761	21.1
NEW YORK																
All homes	95,621	100.0	46,975	100.0	31,434	100.0	20,982	100.0	74,639	355.7	48,646	103.6	15,541	49.4	10,452	49.8
Owned	7,920	8.3	3,375	7.2	2,437	7.8	2,213	10.5	5,707	257.9	4,545	134.7	938	38.5	224	10.1
Rented	85,991	89.9	42,843	91.2	28,070	89.3	17,784	84.8	68,207	383.5	43,148	100.7	14,773	52.6	10,286	57.8
Tenure unknown	1,710	1.8	757	1.6	927	2.9	985	4.7	725	73.6	953	125.9	—170	—18.3	—58	—5.9
NEW JERSEY																
All homes	48,636	100.0	28,091	100.0	19,825	100.0	13,934	100.0	34,702	249.0	20,545	73.1	8,266	41.7	5,891	42.3
Owned	11,329	23.3	5,598	19.9	3,682	18.6	2,588	18.6	8,741	337.8	5,731	102.4	1,916	52.0	1,094	42.3
Rented	36,171	74.4	21,758	77.5	15,406	77.7	10,571	75.9	25,600	242.2	14,413	66.2	6,352	41.2	4,835	45.7
Tenure unknown	1,136	2.3	735	2.6	737	3.7	775	5.6	361	46.6	401	54.6	—2	—0.3	—38	—4.9
PENNSYLVANIA																
All homes	99,114	100.0	65,428	100.0	42,111	100.0	31,049	100.0	68,065	219.2	33,686	51.5	23,317	55.4	11,062	35.6
Owned	18,683	18.9	10,149	15.5	5,617	13.3	3,978	12.8	14,705	369.7	8,534	84.1	4,532	80.7	1,639	41.2
Rented	77,125	77.8	53,473	81.7	33,787	80.2	25,221	81.2	51,904	205.8	23,652	44.2	19,686	58.3	8,566	34.0
Tenure unknown	3,306	3.3	1,806	2.8	2,707	6.4	1,850	6.0	1,456	78.7	1,500	83.1	—901	—33.3	857	46.3

TABLE 28.—HOMES OF NEGRO FAMILIES BY TENURE, BY SECTIONS, DIVISIONS, AND STATES: 1930, 1920, 1910, AND 1900—Continued

[Figures for 1930 and 1900 represent private-family homes alone; those for 1920 and 1910 include the premises occupied by the small number of institutions and other quasi-family groups which were counted as families in the respective censuses]

AREA AND TENURE	1930		1920		1910		1900		INCREASE OR DECREASE (—)							
									1900 to 1930		1920 to 1930		1910 to 1920		1900 to 1910	
	Number	Per-cent distri-bution	Number	Per-cent distri-bution	Number	Per-cent distri-bution	Number	Per-cent distri-bution	Number	Per-cent	Number	Per-cent	Number	Per-cent	Number	Per-cent
EAST NORTH CENTRAL:																
All homes	222,240	100.0	127,765	100.0	74,654	100.0	58,738	100.0	163,502	278.4	94,475	73.9	53,111	71.1	15,916	27.1
Owned	51,077	23.0	28,395	22.2	20,620	27.6	16,661	28.4	34,416	206.6	22,682	79.9	7,775	37.7	3,959	23.8
Rented	165,832	74.6	95,966	75.1	52,364	70.1	39,403	67.1	126,429	320.9	69,866	72.8	43,602	83.3	12,961	32.9
Tenure unknown	5,331	2.4	3,404	2.7	1,670	2.2	2,674	4.6	2,657	99.4	1,927	56.6	1,734	103.8	−1,004	−37.5
OHIO																
All homes	75,709	100.0	47,083	100.0	28,135	100.0	22,420	100.0	53,289	237.7	28,626	60.8	18,948	67.3	5,715	25.5
Owned	17,928	23.7	11,326	24.1	8,467	30.1	6,927	30.9	11,001	158.8	6,602	58.3	2,859	33.8	1,540	22.2
Rented	56,079	74.1	34,799	73.9	19,051	67.7	14,589	65.1	41,490	284.4	21,280	61.2	15,748	82.7	4,462	30.6
Tenure unknown	1,702	2.2	958	2.0	617	2.2	904	4.0	798	88.3	744	77.7	341	55.3	−287	−31.7
INDIANA																
All homes	28,771	100.0	21,581	100.0	15,302	100.0	12,756	100.0	16,015	125.5	7,190	33.3	6,279	41.0	2,546	20.0
Owned	8,614	29.9	5,521	25.6	4,036	26.4	3,515	27.6	5,099	145.1	3,093	56.0	1,485	36.8	521	14.8
Rented	19,408	67.5	15,209	70.5	10,990	71.8	8,599	67.4	10,809	125.7	4,199	27.6	4,219	38.4	2,391	27.8
Tenure unknown	749	2.6	851	3.9	276	1.8	642	5.0	107	16.7	−102	−12.0	575	208.3	−366	−57.0
ILLINOIS																
All homes	78,737	100.0	44,800	100.0	26,149	100.0	19,240	100.0	59,497	309.2	33,937	75.8	18,651	71.3	6,909	35.9
Owned	15,321	19.5	8,156	18.2	6,012	23.0	4,479	23.3	10,842	242.1	7,165	87.8	2,144	35.7	1,533	34.2
Rented	61,921	78.6	35,362	78.9	19,455	74.4	13,810	71.8	48,111	348.4	26,559	75.1	15,907	81.8	5,645	40.9
Tenure unknown	1,495	1.9	1,282	2.9	682	2.6	951	4.9	544	57.2	213	16.6	600	88.0	−269	−28.3
MICHIGAN																
All homes	36,500	100.0	13,011	100.0	4,391	100.0	3,706	100.0	32,794	884.9	23,489	180.5	8,620	196.3	685	18.5
Owned	8,830	24.2	3,119	24.0	1,932	44.0	1,573	42.4	7,257	461.3	5,711	183.1	1,187	61.4	359	22.8
Rented	26,432	72.4	9,612	73.9	2,382	54.2	1,980	53.4	24,452	1,234.9	16,820	175.0	7,230	303.5	402	20.3
Tenure unknown	1,238	3.4	280	2.2	77	1.8	153	4.1	1,085	709.2	958	342.1	203	263.6	−76	−49.7
WISCONSIN																
All homes	2,523	100.0	1,290	100.0	677	100.0	616	100.0	1,907	309.6	1,233	95.6	613	90.5	61	9.9
Owned	384	15.2	273	21.2	173	25.6	167	27.1	217	129.9	111	40.7	100	57.8	6	3.6
Rented	1,992	79.0	984	76.3	486	71.8	425	69.0	1,567	368.7	1,008	102.4	498	102.5	61	14.4
Tenure unknown	147	5.8	33	2.6	18	2.7	24	3.9	123	512.5	114	345.5	15	83.3	−6	−25.0
WEST NORTH CENTRAL:																
All homes	87,853	100.0	75,061	100.0	59,682	100.0	52,194	100.0	35,659	68.3	12,792	17.0	15,379	25.8	7,488	14.3
Owned	27,231	31.0	21,757	29.0	19,138	32.1	16,386	31.4	10,845	66.2	5,474	25.2	2,619	13.7	2,752	16.8
Rented	57,838	65.8	50,581	67.4	38,020	63.7	33,263	63.7	24,575	73.9	7,257	14.3	12,561	33.0	4,757	14.3
Tenure unknown	2,784	3.2	2,723	3.6	2,524	4.2	2,545	4.9	239	9.4	61	2.2	199	7.9	−21	−.8
MINNESOTA																
All homes	2,592	100.0	2,487	100.0	1,685	100.0	1,084	100.0	1,508	139.1	105	4.2	802	47.6	601	55.4
Owned	855	33.0	659	26.5	416	24.7	140	12.9	715	510.7	196	29.7	243	58.4	276	197.1
Rented	1,669	64.4	1,729	69.5	1,169	69.4	859	79.2	810	94.3	−60	−3.5	560	47.9	310	36.1
Tenure unknown	68	2.6	99	4.0	100	5.9	85	7.8	−17	−20.0	−31	−31.3	−1	−1.0	15	17.6
IOWA																
All homes	4,571	100.0	5,108	100.0	3,807	100.0	2,915	100.0	1,656	56.8	−537	−10.5	1,301	34.2	892	30.6
Owned	1,918	42.0	1,698	33.2	1,138	29.9	900	30.9	1,018	113.1	220	13.0	560	49.2	238	26.4
Rented	2,528	55.3	3,185	62.4	2,599	68.3	1,892	64.9	636	33.6	−657	−20.6	586	22.5	707	37.4
Tenure unknown	125	2.7	225	4.4	70	1.8	123	4.2	2	1.6	−100	−44.4	155	221.4	−53	−43.1
MISSOURI																
All homes	59,016	100.0	47,881	100.0	38,134	100.0	34,779	100.0	24,237	69.7	11,135	23.3	9,747	25.6	3,355	9.6
Owned	13,374	22.7	10,301	21.5	10,130	26.6	9,535	27.4	3,839	40.3	3,073	29.8	171	1.7	595	6.2
Rented	43,571	73.8	35,825	74.8	26,206	68.7	23,629	67.9	19,942	84.4	7,746	21.6	9,619	36.7	2,577	10.9
Tenure unknown	2,071	3.5	1,755	3.7	1,798	4.7	1,615	4.6	456	28.2	316	18.0	−43	−2.4	183	11.3
NORTH DAKOTA																
All homes	120	100.0	147	100.0	146	100.0	67	100.0	53	79.1	−27	−18.4	1	.7	79	117.9
Owned	28	23.3	42	28.6	52	35.6	26	38.8	2	7.7	−14	−33.3	−10	−19.2	26	100.0
Rented	83	69.2	97	66.0	75	51.4	36	53.7	47	130.6	−14	−14.4	22	29.3	39	108.3
Tenure unknown	9	7.5	8	5.4	19	13.0	5	7.5	4	80.0	1	12.5	−11	−57.9	14	280.0
SOUTH DAKOTA																
All homes	166	100.0	243	100.0	215	100.0	107	100.0	59	55.1	−77	−31.7	28	13.0	108	100.9
Owned	77	46.4	106	43.6	97	45.1	46	43.0	31	67.4	−29	−27.4	9	9.3	51	110.9
Rented	87	52.4	119	49.0	100	46.5	51	47.7	36	70.6	−32	−26.9	19	19.0	49	96.1
Tenure unknown	2	1.2	18	7.4	18	8.4	10	9.3	−8	−80.0	−16	−88.9			8	80.0
NEBRASKA																
All homes	3,700	100.0	3,426	100.0	1,885	100.0	1,263	100.0	2,437	193.0	274	8.0	1,541	81.8	622	49.2
Owned	1,253	33.9	878	25.6	454	24.1	250	19.8	1,003	401.2	375	42.7	424	93.4	204	81.6
Rented	2,327	62.9	2,400	70.1	1,337	70.9	935	74.0	1,392	148.9	−73	−3.0	1,063	79.5	402	43.0
Tenure	120	3.2	148	4.3	94	5.0	78	6.2	42	53.8	−28	−18.9	54	57.4	16	20.5
KANSAS																
All homes	17,688	100.0	15,769	100.0	13,810	100.0	11,979	100.0	5,709	47.7	1,919	12.2	1,959	14.2	1,831	15.3
Owned	9,726	55.0	8,073	51.2	6,851	49.6	5,489	45.8	4,237	77.2	1,653	20.5	1,222	17.8	1,362	24.8
Rented	7,573	42.8	7,226	45.8	6,534	47.3	5,861	48.9	1,712	29.2	347	4.8	692	10.6	673	11.5
Tenure unknown	389	2.2	470	3.0	425	3.1	629	5.3	−240	−38.2	−81	−17.2	45	10.6	−204	−32.4
SOUTH ATLANTIC:																
All homes	974,592	100.0	955,772	100.1	882,647	100.0	761,105	100.0	213,487	28.0	18,820	2.0	73,125	8.3	121,542	16.0
Owned	249,762	25.6	227,403	23.8	208,247	23.6	159,595	21.0	90,167	56.5	22,359	9.8	19,156	9.2	48,652	30.5
Rented	696,573	71.5	692,572	72.5	641,368	72.7	545,240	71.6	151,333	27.8	4,001	.6	51,204	8.0	96,128	17.6
Tenure unknown	28,257	2.9	35,797	3.7	33,032	3.7	56,270	7.4	−28,013	−49.8	−7,540	−21.1	2,765	8.4	−23,238	−41.3
DELAWARE																
All homes	7,682	100.0	6,886	100.0	6,476	100.0	6,014	100.0	1,668	27.7	796	11.6	410	6.3	462	7.7
Owned	2,017	26.3	1,597	23.2	1,501	23.2	1,297	21.6	720	55.5	420	26.3	96	6.4	204	15.7
Rented	5,491	71.5	5,091	73.9	4,669	72.1	4,271	71.0	1,220	28.6	400	7.9	422	9.0	398	9.3
Tenure unknown	174	2.3	198	2.9	306	4.7	446	7.4	−272	−61.0	−24	−12.1	−108	−35.3	−140	−31.4

Table 28.—HOMES OF NEGRO FAMILIES BY TENURE, BY SECTIONS, DIVISIONS, AND STATES: 1930, 1920, 1910, AND 1900—Continued

[Figures for 1930 and 1900 represent private-family homes alone; those for 1920 and 1910 include the premises occupied by the small number of institutions and other quasi-family groups which were counted as families in the respective censuses]

AREA AND TENURE	1930		1920		1910		1900		INCREASE OR DECREASE (−)							
									1900 to 1930		1920 to 1930		1910 to 1920		1900 to 1910	
	Number	Percent distribution	Number	Percent distribution	Number	Percent distribution	Number	Percent distribution	Number	Percent	Number	Percent	Number	Percent	Number	Percent
MARYLAND																
All homes	61,160	100.0	54,786	100.0	47,177	100.0	45,310	100.0	15,850	35.0	6,374	11.6	7,609	16.1	1,867	4.1
Owned	16,056	26.3	13,401	24.5	12,068	25.6	10,401	23.0	5,655	54.5	2,655	19.8	1,333	11.0	1,667	16.0
Rented	43,332	70.9	40,015	73.0	32,774	69.5	30,826	68.0	12,506	40.6	3,317	8.3	7,241	22.1	1,948	6.3
Tenure unknown	1,772	2.9	1,370	2.5	2,335	4.9	4,083	9.0	−2,311	−56.6	402	29.3	−96.5	−41.3	−1,748	−42.8
DISTRICT OF COLUMBIA																
All homes	29,995	100.0	24,929	100.0	19,246	100.0	17,269	100.0	12,726	73.7	5,066	20.3	5,683	29.5	1,977	11.4
Owned	7,316	24.4	3,435	13.8	2,072	10.8	1,964	11.4	5,352	272.5	3,881	113.0	1,363	65.8	108	5.5
Rented	21,413	71.4	20,791	83.4	16,437	85.4	14,721	85.2	6,692	45.5	622	3.0	4,354	26.5	1,716	11.7
Tenure unknown	1,266	4.2	703	2.8	737	3.8	584	3.4	682	116.8	563	80.1	−34	−4.6	153	26.2
VIRGINIA																
All homes	140,726	100.0	148,362	100.0	137,771	100.0	128,530	100.0	12,196	9.5	−7,636	−5.1	10,591	7.7	9,241	7.2
Owned	61,294	43.6	61,227	41.3	56,933	41.3	46,268	36.0	15,026	32.5	67	.1	4,294	7.5	10,665	23.1
Rented	76,498	54.4	83,873	56.5	77,048	55.9	75,895	59.0	603	.8	−7,375	−8.8	6,825	8.9	1,153	1.5
Tenure unknown	2,934	2.1	3,262	2.2	3,790	2.8	6,367	5.0	−3,433	−53.9	−328	−10.1	−528	−13.9	−2,577	−40.5
WEST VIRGINIA																
All homes	26,274	100.0	20,774	100.0	14,197	100.0	8,248	100.0	18,026	218.5	5,500	26.5	6,577	46.3	5,949	72.1
Owned	4,900	18.6	3,557	17.1	2,743	19.3	1,983	24.0	2,917	147.1	1,343	37.8	814	29.7	760	38.3
Rented	20,681	78.7	16,546	79.6	10,942	77.1	5,888	71.4	14,793	251.2	4,135	25.0	5,604	51.2	5,054	85.8
Tenure unknown	693	2.6	671	3.2	512	3.6	377	4.6	316	83.8	22	3.3	159	31.1	135	35.8
NORTH CAROLINA																
All homes	180,128	100.0	154,799	100.0	139,713	100.0	122,208	100.0	57,920	47.4	25,329	16.4	15,086	10.8	17,505	14.3
Owned	50,948	28.3	45,126	29.2	40,118	28.7	29,019	23.7	21,929	75.6	5,822	12.9	5,008	12.5	11,099	38.2
Rented	123,882	68.8	103,861	67.1	95,148	68.1	85,681	70.1	38,201	44.6	20,021	19.3	8,713	9.2	9,467	11.0
Tenure unknown	5,298	2.9	5,812	3.8	4,447	3.2	7,508	6.1	−2,210	−29.4	−514	−8.8	1,365	30.7	−3,061	−40.8
SOUTH CAROLINA																
All homes	168,324	100.0	184,671	100.0	179,490	100.0	160,521	100.0	7,803	4.9	−16,347	−8.9	5,181	2.9	18,969	11.8
Owned	35,753	21.2	36,488	19.8	33,161	18.5	26,870	16.7	8,883	33.1	−735	−2.0	3,327	10.0	6,291	23.4
Rented	129,447	76.9	140,153	75.9	139,240	77.6	121,178	75.5	8,269	6.8	−10,706	−7.6	913	.7	18,062	14.9
Tenure unknown	3,124	1.9	8,030	4.3	7,089	3.9	12,473	7.8	−9,349	−75.0	−4,906	−61.1	941	13.3	−5,384	−43.2
GEORGIA																
All homes	249,942	100.0	276,406	100.0	263,183	100.0	221,254	100.0	28,688	13.0	−26,464	−9.6	13,223	5.0	41,929	19.0
Owned	41,318	16.5	40,196	14.5	38,735	14.7	26,636	12.0	14,682	55.1	1,122	2.8	1,461	3.8	12,099	45.4
Rented	199,433	79.8	225,101	81.4	215,459	81.9	174,251	78.8	25,182	14.5	−25,668	−11.4	9,642	4.5	41,208	23.6
Tenure unknown	9,191	3.7	11,109	4.0	8,989	3.4	20,367	9.2	−11,176	−54.9	−1,918	−17.3	2,120	23.6	−11,378	−55.9
FLORIDA																
All homes	110,361	100.0	84,159	100.0	75,394	100.0	51,751	100.0	58,610	113.3	26,202	31.1	8,765	11.6	23,643	45.7
Owned	30,160	27.3	22,376	26.6	20,916	27.7	15,157	29.3	15,003	99.0	7,784	34.8	1,460	7.0	5,759	38.0
Rented	76,396	69.2	57,141	67.9	49,651	65.9	32,529	62.9	43,867	134.9	19,255	33.7	7,490	15.1	17,122	52.6
Tenure unknown	3,805	3.4	4,642	5.5	4,827	6.4	4,065	7.9	−260	−6.4	−837	−18.0	−185	−3.8	762	18.7
East South Central:																
All homes	653,847	100.0	606,384	100.0	603,322	100.0	527,908	100.0	125,939	23.9	47,463	7.8	3,062	.5	75,414	14.3
Owned	142,608	21.8	119,159	19.7	119,291	19.8	91,320	17.3	51,288	56.2	23,449	19.7	−132	−.1	27,971	30.6
Rented	494,142	75.6	465,518	76.8	463,236	76.8	401,441	76.0	92,701	23.1	28,624	6.1	2,282	.5	61,795	15.4
Tenure unknown	17,097	2.6	21,707	3.6	20,795	3.4	35,147	6.7	−18,050	−51.4	−4,610	−21.2	912	4.4	−14,352	−40.8
KENTUCKY																
All homes	60,672	100.0	62,691	100.0	62,216	100.0	60,311	100.0	361	.6	−2,019	−3.2	475	.8	1,905	3.2
Owned	21,398	35.3	19,366	30.9	19,774	31.8	17,906	29.7	3,492	19.5	2,032	10.5	−408	−2.1	1,868	10.4
Rented	37,766	62.2	41,476	66.2	40,364	64.9	39,154	64.9	−1,388	−3.5	−3,710	−8.9	1,112	2.8	1,210	3.1
Tenure unknown	1,508	2.5	1,849	2.9	2,078	3.3	3,251	5.4	−1,743	−53.6	−341	−18.4	−229	−11.0	−1,173	−36.1
TENNESSEE																
All homes	120,402	100.0	111,407	100.0	106,558	100.0	96,427	100.0	23,975	24.9	8,995	8.1	4,849	4.6	10,131	10.5
Owned	33,655	28.0	28,060	25.2	27,012	25.3	21,023	21.8	12,632	60.1	5,595	19.9	1,048	3.9	5,989	28.5
Rented	82,515	68.5	79,871	71.7	76,833	72.1	69,911	72.5	12,604	18.0	2,644	3.3	3,038	4.0	6,922	9.9
Tenure unknown	4,232	3.5	3,476	3.1	2,713	2.5	5,493	5.7	−1,261	−23.0	756	21.7	763	28.1	−2,780	−50.6
ALABAMA																
All homes	222,533	100.0	208,593	100.0	206,884	100.0	178,365	100.0	44,168	24.8	13,940	6.7	1,709	.8	28,519	16.0
Owned	44,650	20.1	35,364	17.0	33,941	16.4	23,536	13.2	21,114	89.7	9,286	26.3	1,423	4.2	10,405	44.2
Rented	172,448	77.5	164,524	78.9	164,024	79.3	142,819	80.1	29,629	20.7	7,924	4.8	500	.3	21,205	14.8
Tenure unknown	5,435	2.4	8,705	4.2	8,919	4.3	12,010	6.7	−6,575	−54.7	−3,270	−37.6	−214	−2.4	−3,091	−25.7
MISSISSIPPI																
All homes	250,240	100.0	223,693	100.0	227,664	100.0	192,805	100.0	57,435	29.8	26,547	11.9	−3,971	−1.7	34,859	18.1
Owned	42,905	17.1	36,369	16.3	38,564	16.9	28,855	15.0	14,050	48.7	6,536	18.0	−2,195	−5.7	9,709	33.6
Rented	201,413	80.5	179,647	80.3	182,015	79.9	149,557	77.6	51,856	34.7	21,766	12.1	−2,368	−1.3	32,458	21.7
Tenure unknown	5,922	2.4	7,677	3.4	7,085	3.1	14,393	7.5	−8,471	−58.9	−1,755	−22.9	592	8.4	−7,308	−50.8
West South Central:																
All homes	564,918	100.0	485,653	100.0	431,422	100.0	348,011	100.0	216,907	62.3	79,265	16.3	54,231	12.6	83,411	24.0
Owned	143,063	25.3	116,796	24.0	102,911	23.9	76,622	22.0	66,441	86.7	26,267	22.5	13,885	13.5	26,289	34.3
Rented	399,215	70.7	348,403	71.7	311,047	72.1	247,868	71.2	151,347	61.1	50,812	14.6	37,356	12.0	63,179	25.5
Tenure unknown	22,640	4.0	20,454	4.2	17,464	4.0	23,521	6.8	−881	−3.7	2,186	10.7	2,990	17.1	−6,057	−25.8
ARKANSAS																
All homes	123,009	100.0	114,457	100.0	97,787	100.0	76,803	100.0	46,206	60.2	8,552	7.5	16,670	17.0	20,984	27.3
Owned	27,722	22.5	27,143	23.7	24,018	24.6	16,838	21.9	10,884	64.6	579	2.1	3,125	13.0	7,180	42.6
Rented	87,803	71.4	83,095	72.6	69,202	70.8	54,324	70.7	33,479	61.6	4,708	5.7	13,893	20.1	14,878	27.4
Tenure unknown	7,484	6.1	4,219	3.7	4,567	4.7	5,641	7.3	1,843	32.7	3,265	77.4	−348	−7.6	−1,074	−19.0
LOUISIANA																
All homes	190,876	100.0	165,329	100.0	159,350	100.0	140,264	100.0	50,612	36.1	25,547	15.5	5,979	3.8	19,086	13.6
Owned	39,457	20.7	28,832	17.4	27,237	17.1	20,453	14.6	19,004	92.9	10,625	36.9	1,595	5.9	6,784	33.2
Rented	145,608	76.3	128,830	77.9	125,926	79.0	108,702	77.5	36,906	34.0	16,778	13.0	2,904	2.3	17,224	15.8
Tenure unknown	5,811	3.0	7,667	4.6	6,187	3.9	11,109	7.9	−5,298	−47.7	−1,856	−24.2	1,480	23.9	−4,922	−44.3

TABLE 28.—HOMES OF NEGRO FAMILIES BY TENURE, BY SECTIONS, DIVISIONS, AND STATES: 1930, 1920, 1910, AND 1900—Continued

[Figures for 1930 and 1900 represent private-family homes alone; those for 1920 and 1910 include the premises occupied by the small number of institutions and other quasi-family groups which were counted as families in the respective censuses]

AREA AND TENURE	1930		1920		1910		1900		INCREASE OR DECREASE (−)							
									1900 to 1930		1920 to 1930		1910 to 1920		1900 to 1910	
	Number	Per-cent distri-bution	Number	Per-cent distri-bution	Number	Per-cent distri-bution	Number	Per-cent distri-bution	Number	Per-cent	Number	Per-cent	Number	Per-cent	Number	Per-cent
OKLAHOMA																
All homes	40,238	100.0	33,551	100.0	28,395	100.0	11,526	100.0	28,712	249.1	6,687	19.9	5,156	18.2	16,869	146.4
Owned	12,615	31.4	11,403	34.0	10,018	35.3	6,039	52.4	6,576	108.9	1,212	10.6	1,385	13.8	3,979	65.9
Rented	25,862	64.3	20,037	59.7	17,144	60.4	4,939	42.9	20,923	423.6	5,825	29.1	2,893	16.9	12,205	247.1
Tenure unknown	1,761	4.4	2,111	6.3	1,233	4.3	548	4.8	1,213	221.4	−350	−16.6	878	71.2	685	125.0
TEXAS																
All homes	210,795	100.0	172,316	100.0	145,890	100.0	119,418	100.0	91,377	76.5	38,479	22.3	26,426	18.1	26,472	22.2
Owned	63,269	30.0	49,418	28.7	41,638	28.5	33,292	27.9	29,977	90.0	13,851	28.0	7,780	18.7	8,346	25.1
Rented	139,942	66.4	116,441	67.6	98,775	67.7	79,903	66.9	60,039	75.1	23,501	20.2	17,666	17.9	18,872	23.6
Tenure unknown	7,584	3.6	6,457	3.7	5,477	3.8	6,223	5.2	1,361	21.9	1,127	17.5	980	17.9	−746	−12.0
MOUNTAIN:																
All homes	8,743	100.0	7,299	100.0	5,658	100.0	3,547	100.0	5,196	146.5	1,444	19.8	1,641	29.0	2,111	59.5
Owned	3,131	35.8	2,179	29.9	1,589	28.1	801	22.6	2,330	290.9	952	43.7	590	37.1	788	98.4
Rented	5,258	60.1	4,838	66.3	3,831	67.7	2,440	68.8	2,818	115.5	420	8.7	1,007	26.3	1,391	57.0
Tenure unknown	354	4.0	282	3.9	238	4.2	306	8.6	48	15.7	72	25.5	44	18.5	−68	−22.2
MONTANA																
All homes	458	100.0	601	100.0	555	100.0	393	100.0	65	16.5	−143	−23.8	46	8.3	162	41.2
Owned	169	36.9	216	35.9	182	32.8	75	19.1	94	125.3	−47	−21.8	34	18.7	107	142.7
Rented	268	58.5	345	57.4	336	60.5	280	71.2	−12	−4.3	−77	−22.3	9	2.7	56	20.0
Tenure unknown	21	4.6	40	6.7	37	6.7	38	9.7	−17	−44.7	−19	−47.5	3	8.1	−1	−2.6
IDAHO																
All homes	229	100.0	294	100.0	167	100.0	81	100.0	148	182.7	−65	−22.1	127	76.0	86	106.2
Owned	80	34.9	93	31.6	48	28.7	36	44.4	44	122.2	−13	−14.0	45	93.8	12	33.3
Rented	142	62.0	183	62.2	100	59.9	39	48.1	103	264.1	−41	−22.4	83	83.0	61	156.4
Tenure unknown	7	3.1	18	6.1	19	11.4	6	7.4	1	16.7	−11	−61.1	−1	−5.3	13	216.7
WYOMING																
All homes	418	100.0	449	100.0	375	100.0	160	100.0	258	161.3	−31	−6.9	74	19.7	215	134.4
Owned	122	29.2	95	21.2	69	18.4	32	20.0	90	281.3	27	28.4	26	37.7	37	115.6
Rented	277	66.3	334	74.4	288	76.8	116	72.5	161	138.8	−57	−17.1	46	16.0	172	148.3
Tenure unknown	19	4.5	20	4.5	18	4.8	12	7.5	7	58.3	−1	−5.0	2	11.1	6	50.0
COLORADO																
All homes	3,538	100.0	3,233	100.0	3,079	100.0	2,052	100.0	1,486	72.4	305	9.4	154	5.0	1,027	50.0
Owned	1,503	42.5	1,116	34.5	849	27.6	467	22.8	1,036	221.8	387	34.7	267	31.4	382	81.8
Rented	1,899	53.7	2,038	63.0	2,141	69.5	1,493	72.8	406	27.2	−139	−6.8	−103	−4.8	648	43.4
Tenure unknown	136	3.8	79	2.4	89	2.9	92	4.5	44	47.8	57	72.2	−10	−11.2	−3	−3.3
NEW MEXICO																
All homes	799	100.0	820	100.0	449	100.0	381	100.0	418	109.7	−21	−2.6	371	82.6	68	17.8
Owned	298	37.3	236	28.8	136	30.3	69	18.1	229	331.9	62	26.3	100	73.5	67	97.1
Rented	473	59.2	553	67.4	304	67.7	265	69.6	208	78.5	−80	−14.5	249	81.9	39	14.7
Tenure unknown	28	3.5	31	3.8	9	2.0	47	12.3	−19	−40.4	−3	−9.7	22	244.4	−38	−80.9
ARIZONA																
All homes	2,776	100.0	1,338	100.0	583	100.0	309	100.0	2,467	798.4	1,438	107.5	755	129.5	274	88.7
Owned	775	27.9	311	23.2	179	30.7	85	27.5	690	811.8	464	149.2	132	73.7	94	110.6
Rented	1,868	67.3	952	71.2	376	64.5	137	44.3	1,731	1,263.5	916	96.2	576	153.2	239	174.5
Tenure unknown	133	4.8	75	5.6	28	4.8	87	28.2	46	52.9	58	77.3	47	167.9	−59	−67.8
UTAH																
All homes	331	100.0	435	100.0	240	100.0	119	100.0	212	178.2	−104	−23.9	195	81.3	121	101.7
Owned	114	34.4	70	16.1	51	21.3	19	16.0	95	500.0	44	62.9	19	37.3	32	168.4
Rented	210	63.4	354	81.4	154	64.2	85	71.4	125	147.1	−144	−40.7	200	129.9	69	81.2
Tenure unknown	7	2.1	11	2.5	35	14.6	15	12.6	−8	−53.3	−4	−36.4	−24	−68.6	20	133.3
NEVADA																
All homes	194	100.0	129	100.0	210	100.0	52	100.0	142	273.1	65	50.4	−81	−38.6	158	303.8
Owned	70	36.1	42	32.6	75	35.7	18	34.6	52	288.9	28	66.7	−33	−44.0	57	316.7
Rented	121	62.4	79	61.2	132	62.9	25	48.1	96	384.0	42	53.2	−53	−40.2	107	428.0
Tenure unknown	3	1.5	8	6.2	3	1.4	9	17.3	−6	−66.7	−5	−62.5	5	166.7	−6	−66.7
PACIFIC:																
All homes	25,328	100.0	13,026	100.0	7,049	100.0	3,418	100.0	21,910	641.0	12,302	94.4	5,977	84.8	3,631	106.2
Ownded	9,486	37.5	4,485	34.4	2,552	36.2	1,071	31.3	8,415	785.7	5,001	111.5	1,933	75.7	1,481	138.3
Rented	15,058	59.5	8,102	62.2	4,288	60.8	2,104	61.6	12,954	615.7	6,956	85.9	3,814	88.9	2,184	103.8
Tenure unknown	784	3.1	439	3.4	209	3.0	243	7.1	541	222.6	345	78.6	230	110.0	−34	−14.0
WASHINGTON																
All homes	2,059	100.0	1,888	100.0	1,356	100.0	566	100.0	1,493	263.8	171	9.1	532	39.2	790	139.6
Owned	934	45.4	740	39.2	435	32.1	161	28.4	773	480.1	194	26.2	305	70.1	274	170.2
Rented	1,056	51.3	1,075	56.9	854	63.0	356	62.9	700	196.6	−19	−1.8	221	25.9	498	139.9
Tenure unknown	69	3.4	73	3.9	67	4.9	49	8.7	20	40.8	−4	−5.5	6	9.0	18	36.7
OREGON																
All homes	674	100.0	608	100.0	347	100.0	191	100.0	483	252.9	66	10.9	261	75.2	156	81.7
Owned	269	39.9	222	36.5	98	28.2	49	25.7	220	449.0	47	21.2	124	126.5	49	100.0
Rented	376	55.8	375	61.7	217	62.5	120	62.8	256	213.3	1	.3	158	72.8	97	80.8
Tenure unknown	29	4.3	11	1.8	32	9.2	22	11.5	7	31.8	18	163.6	−21	−65.6	10	45.5
CALIFORNIA																
All homes	22,595	100.0	10,530	100.0	5,346	100.0	2,661	100.0	19,934	749.1	12,065	114.6	5,184	97.0	2,685	100.9
Owned	8,283	36.7	3,523	33.5	2,019	37.8	861	32.4	7,422	862.0	4,760	135.1	1,504	74.5	1,158	134.5
Rented	13,626	60.3	6,652	63.2	3,217	60.2	1,628	61.2	11,998	737.0	6,974	104.8	3,435	106.8	1,589	97.6
Tenure unknown	686	3.0	355	3.4	110	2.1	172	6.5	514	298.8	331	93.2	245	222.7	−62	−36.0

Table 29.—OWNED NONFARM HOMES OF NEGRO FAMILIES, BY VALUE, WITH MEDIAN VALUE, BY SECTIONS, DIVISIONS, AND STATES: 1930

[Median not shown where number of families reporting value is less than 100]

SECTION, DIVISION, AND STATE	All owned nonfarm homes	NUMBER OF HOMES WITH VALUE											Median value
		Under $1,000	$1,000 to $1,499	$1,500 to $1,999	$2,000 to $2,999	$3,000 to $4,999	$5,000 to $7,499	$7,500 to $9,999	$10,000 to $14,999	$15,000 to $19,999	$20,000 and over	Not reported	
United States	**480,324**	**188,795**	**66,516**	**42,337**	**59,404**	**59,377**	**31,839**	**10,108**	**6,676**	**1,897**	**1,289**	**12,086**	**$1,341**
The North	**116,608**	**17,271**	**10,856**	**9,514**	**17,391**	**26,897**	**18,845**	**6,565**	**4,523**	**1,349**	**961**	**2,436**	**3,153**
The South	**351,576**	**170,392**	**54,791**	**32,012**	**40,061**	**28,684**	**10,648**	**3,097**	**1,847**	**455**	**267**	**9,322**	**1,007**
The West	**12,140**	**1,132**	**869**	**811**	**1,952**	**3,796**	**2,346**	**446**	**306**	**93**	**61**	**328**	**3,602**
NEW ENGLAND	5,204	275	278	342	747	1,502	1,208	394	272	56	23	107	4,207
Maine	111	21	15	20	23	18	9	3				2	1,963
New Hampshire	35	2	6	7	8	8	3					1	
Vermont	31	4			9	11	4	3					
Massachusetts	3,381	164	178	212	496	967	810	264	165	33	15	77	4,245
Rhode Island	588	31	29	46	103	211	116	27	18	2	1	4	3,787
Connecticut	1,058	53	50	57	108	287	266	97	89	21	7	23	4,739
MIDDLE ATLANTIC	37,210	2,104	1,991	2,023	4,749	9,989	8,808	3,077	2,345	809	497	818	4,467
New York	7,787	260	257	219	452	1,164	2,036	1,179	1,175	550	295	200	6,770
New Jersey	11,012	867	763	669	1,468	2,559	2,370	944	800	179	134	259	4,258
Pennsylvania	18,411	977	971	1,135	2,829	6,266	4,402	954	370	80	68	359	3,994
EAST NORTH CENTRAL	48,887	6,607	4,631	4,381	8,103	11,629	7,337	2,676	1,647	444	400	1,032	3,035
Ohio	17,005	2,224	1,586	1,572	3,077	4,802	2,464	652	254	62	44	268	2,971
Indiana	8,317	1,317	1,029	1,067	1,751	2,074	659	106	68	15	14	217	2,364
Illinois	14,814	2,581	1,556	1,173	2,043	2,409	2,177	956	921	295	302	401	2,928
Michigan	8,415	455	435	545	1,166	2,261	1,977	941	394	70	37	134	4,362
Wisconsin	336	30	25	24	66	83	60	21	10	2	3	12	3,410
WEST NORTH CENTRAL	25,307	8,285	3,956	2,768	3,792	3,777	1,492	418	259	40	41	479	1,531
Minnesota	837	37	28	46	94	354	234	25	8	1	1	9	4,181
Iowa	1,840	411	369	303	395	285	48	7	2			20	1,715
Missouri	12,152	4,225	1,674	1,001	1,490	1,841	984	357	234	34	35	277	1,519
North Dakota	22	5	3	5	3	4	2						
South Dakota	51	16	7	5	11	5	4	1				2	
Nebraska	1,237	102	141	185	355	357	61	7	3	1	1	24	2,503
Kansas	9,168	3,489	1,734	1,223	1,444	931	159	21	12	4	4	147	1,295
SOUTH ATLANTIC	164,566	75,174	25,498	14,304	18,689	14,983	7,029	2,310	1,433	304	166	4,676	1,094
Delaware	1,607	568	274	177	193	224	102	11	4	1	1	52	1,382
Maryland	12,648	4,239	1,548	954	1,499	2,433	1,336	174	82	15	2	366	1,686
District of Columbia	7,314	47	135	166	487	1,413	2,246	1,438	899	167	73	243	6,433
Virginia	35,100	14,143	6,262	3,564	5,036	3,564	1,043	152	95	26	13	1,202	1,224
West Virginia	4,496	1,111	638	500	847	742	355	75	54	14	16	144	1,927
North Carolina	30,571	13,573	5,492	3,300	3,826	2,348	800	207	128	22	20	855	1,117
South Carolina	18,697	11,842	2,739	1,246	1,428	723	217	65	24	11	4	398	[1]
Georgia	29,988	17,077	4,600	2,244	2,782	1,958	452	93	70	18	8	686	[1]
Florida	24,145	12,574	3,810	2,153	2,591	1,578	478	95	77	30	29	730	[1]
EAST SOUTH CENTRAL	90,768	44,995	15,205	9,266	10,567	6,281	1,633	338	156	68	31	2,228	[1]
Kentucky	17,028	9,276	2,246	1,404	1,627	1,399	469	74	31	13	8	481	[1]
Tennessee	25,335	9,667	4,694	3,363	3,717	2,518	582	134	57	20	9	574	1,289
Alabama	28,068	12,642	5,247	3,143	3,970	1,833	460	99	47	19	10	598	1,104
Mississippi	20,337	13,410	3,018	1,356	1,253	531	122	31	21	16	4	575	[1]
WEST SOUTH CENTRAL	96,242	50,223	14,088	8,442	10,805	7,420	1,986	449	258	83	70	2,418	[1]
Arkansas	16,223	9,272	2,760	1,420	1,379	685	175	32	24	7	3	466	[1]
Louisiana	28,487	15,447	3,844	2,245	2,946	2,385	779	186	75	30	18	531	[1]
Oklahoma	9,115	5,007	1,364	715	881	601	202	57	27	12	10	239	[1]
Texas	42,417	20,497	6,120	4,062	5,599	3,749	830	174	132	34	38	1,182	1,010
MOUNTAIN	2,937	643	397	320	563	702	187	20	18	2	4	81	2,121
Montana	155	38	24	19	39	19	10	1	2			3	1,868
Idaho	74	15	7	14	22	12						4	
Wyoming	110	30	13	12	20	23	7	2	1			2	1,958
Colorado	1,450	224	198	167	306	416	91	7	7	1		33	2,391
New Mexico	246	91	35	25	38	38	12	1		1		5	1,421
Arizona	726	213	107	67	106	138	47	8	7		4	29	1,713
Utah	109	7	4	12	25	46	11		1			3	3,217
Nevada	67	25	9	4	7	10	9	1				2	
PACIFIC	9,203	489	472	491	1,389	3,094	2,159	426	288	91	57	247	4,058
Washington	868	88	84	90	215	281	68	7	10	1		24	2,744
Oregon	259	22	16	18	44	114	33	7	2			3	3,491
California	8,076	379	372	383	1,130	2,699	2,058	412	276	90	57	220	4,233

[1] Less than $1,000.

Table 30.—PERCENT DISTRIBUTION OF NONFARM HOMES OF NEGRO FAMILIES, BY VALUE OR MONTHLY RENTAL, BY SECTIONS, AND STATES: 1930

[Percent not shown where less than 1/10 of 1 percent]

VALUE OR MONTHLY RENTALS	United States	The North	The South	The West	New England: Maine	New Hampshire	Vermont	Massachusetts	Rhode Island	Connecticut	Middle Atlantic: New York	New Jersey	Pennsylvania	East North Central: Ohio	Indiana	Illinois	Michigan	Wisconsin
Owned nonfarm homes	100.0	100.0	100.0	100.0	100.0	100.0	100.0	100.0	100.0	100.0	100.00	100.0	100.0	100.0	100.0	100.0	100.0	100.0
Value under $1,000	39.3	14.8	48.5	9.3	18.9	5.7	12.9	4.9	5.3	5.0	3.3	7.9	5.3	13.1	15.8	17.4	5.4	8.9
$1,000 to $1,499	13.8	9.3	15.6	7.2	13.5	17.1		5.3	4.9	4.7	3.3	6.9	5.3	9.3	12.4	10.5	5.2	7.4
$1,500 to $1,999	8.8	8.2	9.1	6.7	18.0	20.0		6.3	7.8	5.4	2.8	6.1	6.2	9.2	12.8	7.9	6.5	7.1
$2,000 to $2,999	12.4	14.9	11.4	16.1	20.7	22.9	29.0	14.7	17.5	10.2	5.8	13.3	15.4	18.1	21.1	13.8	13.9	19.6
$3,000 to $4,999	12.4	23.1	8.2	31.3	16.2	22.9	35.5	28.6	35.9	27.1	14.9	23.2	34.0	28.2	24.9	16.3	26.9	24.7
$5,000 to $7,499	6.6	16.2	3.0	19.3	8.1	8.6	12.9	24.0	19.7	25.1	26.1	21.5	23.9	14.5	7.9	14.7	23.5	17.9
$7,500 to $9,999	2.1	5.6	.9	3.7	2.7		9.7	7.8	4.6	9.2	15.1	8.6	5.2	3.8	1.3	6.5	11.2	6.3
$10,000 to $14,999	1.4	3.9	.5	2.5				4.9	3.1	8.4	15.1	7.3	2.0	1.5	.8	6.2	4.7	3.0
$15,000 to $19,999	.4	1.2	.1	.8				1.0	.3	2.0	7.1	1.6	.4	.4	.2	2.0	.8	.6
$20,000 and over	.3	.8	.1	.5				.4	.2	.7	3.8	1.2	.4	.3	.2	2.0	.4	.9
Not reported	2.5	2.1	2.7	2.7	1.8	2.9		2.3	.7	2.2	2.6	2.4	1.9	1.6	2.6	2.7	1.6	3.6
Rented nonfarm homes	100.0	100.0	100.0	100.0	100.0	100.0	100.0	100.0	100.0	100.0	100.0	100.0	100.0	100.0	100.0	100.0	100.0	100.0
Rental under $10	37.2	6.4	53.5	9.1	16.9	15.9	32.5	3.2	9.5	3.3	1.3	4.0	7.3	6.2	9.7	5.7	1.2	2.2
$10 to $14	18.7	10.5	23.0	14.2	23.7	25.4	18.2	9.7	31.3	15.1	3.2	8.1	10.2	13.5	22.6	8.8	3.2	8.1
$15 to $19	10.4	13.1	8.9	14.4	23.7	20.6	14.3	14.0	25.2	22.7	6.8	13.7	12.6	18.8	23.7	10.3	6.5	13.8
$20 to $29	14.6	27.5	7.5	34.5	23.7	27.0	27.3	37.4	27.5	41.3	19.7	34.1	30.7	35.8	30.0	22.0	28.5	39.4
$30 to $49	11.6	27.5	3.2	21.5	8.5	3.2	6.5	27.7	5.6	15.0	35.2	31.5	32.7	21.9	11.4	24.7	45.6	32.4
$50 to $74	3.8	10.2	.6	1.1	.8			4.7	.3	1.2	23.1	5.3	4.4	2.1	.8	20.7	12.4	2.6
$75 to $99	.7	1.9	.1	.2	.8			.6	.1	.2	5.0	.4	.4	.2	.1	4.9	1.0	.3
$100 to $149	.2	.4		.1				.1		.1	1.3	.2	.1	.1		.6	.2	.5
$150 to $199		.1									.4						.1	
$200 and over											.1							.1
Not reported	2.9	2.3	3.2	4.9	1.7	7.9	1.3	2.7	.5	1.2	3.9	2.5	1.6	1.3	1.8	2.1	1.4	1.1

VALUE OR MONTHLY RENTAL	West North Central: Minnesota	Iowa	Missouri	North Dakota	South Dakota	Nebraska	Kansas	South Atlantic: Delaware	Maryland	District of Columbia	Virginia	West Virginia	North Carolina	South Carolina	Georgia	Florida
Owned nonfarm homes	100.0	100.0	100.0	100.0	100.0	100.0	100.0	100.0	100.0	100.0	100.0	100.0	100.0	100.0	100.0	100.0
Value under $1,000	4.4	22.3	34.8	22.7	31.4	8.2	38.1	35.3	33.5	0.6	40.3	24.7	44.4	63.3	56.9	52.1
$1,000 to $1,499	3.3	20.1	13.8	13.6	13.7	11.4	18.9	17.1	12.2	1.8	17.8	14.2	18.0	14.6	15.3	15.8
$1,500 to $1,999	5.5	16.5	8.2	22.7	9.8	15.0	13.3	11.0	7.5	2.3	10.2	11.1	10.8	6.7	7.5	8.9
$2,000 to $2,999	11.2	21.5	12.3	13.6	21.6	28.7	15.8	12.0	11.9	6.7	14.3	18.8	12.5	7.6	9.3	10.7
$3,000 to $4,999	42.1	15.5	15.1	18.2	9.8	28.9	10.2	13.9	19.2	19.3	10.2	16.5	7.7	3.9	6.5	6.5
$5,000 to $7,499	28.0	2.6	8.1	9.1	7.8	4.9	1.7	6.3	10.6	30.7	3.0	7.9	2.6	1.2	1.5	2.0
$7,500 to $9,999	3.0	.4	2.9		2.0	.6	.2	.7	1.4	19.7	.4	1.7	.7	.3	.3	.4
$10,000 to $14,999	1.0	.1	1.9			.2	.1	.2	.6	12.3	.3	1.2	.4	.1	.2	.3
$15,000 to $19,999	.1		.3			.1		.1	.1	2.3	.1	.3	.1	.1	.1	.1
$20,000 and over	.1		.3			.1		.1		1.0		.4	.1			.1
Not reported	1.1	1.1	2.3		3.9	1.9	1.6	3.2	2.9	3.3	3.4	3.2	2.8	2.1	2.3	3.0
Rented nonfarm homes	100.0	100.0	100.0	100.0	100.0	100.0	100.0	100.0	100.0	100.0	100.0	100.0	100.0	100.0	100.0	100.0
Rental under $10	4.3	20.4	17.4	9.0	24.6	10.2	31.4	32.0	20.4	1.8	44.6	61.0	45.1	79.2	67.9	54.1
$10 to $14	16.0	29.5	19.0	21.8	21.5	25.5	34.6	15.0	14.6	8.8	31.1	17.2	32.9	13.1	19.0	25.2
$15 to $19	22.3	23.9	17.6	23.1	18.5	27.3	18.5	10.3	12.0	14.4	12.7	7.6	9.8	3.1	5.6	7.6
$20 to $29	35.6	20.1	25.1	16.7	24.6	28.6	10.3	23.1	25.2	24.3	7.7	9.7	7.5	1.6	2.9	7.2
$30 to $49	16.5	4.0	15.3	20.5	4.6	5.4	1.7	15.3	21.6	32.0	1.6	2.9	1.5	.3	.6	1.8
$50 to $74	1.2	.2	3.2	2.6		.1	.2	1.1	2.5	12.0	.1	.3	.1	.1	.1	.2
$75 to $99	.1		.3						.1	1.1		.1				
$100 to $149			.1			.1				.1						
$150 to $199																
$200 and over																
Not reported	4.1	1.9	2.0	6.4	6.2	2.8	3.2	3.1	3.5	5.6	2.2	1.3	2.9	2.6	3.9	3.7

VALUE OR MONTHLY RENTAL	East South Central: Kentucky	Tennessee	Alabama	Mississippi	West South Central: Arkansas	Louisiana	Oklahoma	Texas	Mountain: Montana	Idaho	Wyoming	Colorado	New Mexico	Arizona	Utah	Nevada	Pacific: Washington	Oregon	California
Owned nonfarm homes	100.0	100.0	100.0	100.0	100.0	100.0	100.0	100.0	100.0	100.0	100.0	100.0	100.0	100.00	100.0	100.0	100.0	100.0	100.0
Value under $1,000	54.5	38.2	45.0	65.9	57.2	54.2	54.9	48.3	24.5	20.3	27.3	15.4	37.0	29.3	6.4	37.3	10.1	8.5	4.7
$1,000 to $1,499	13.2	18.5	18.7	14.8	17.0	13.5	15.0	14.4	15.5	9.5	11.8	13.7	14.2	14.7	3.7	13.4	9.7	6.2	4.6
$1,500 to $1,999	8.2	13.3	11.2	6.7	8.8	7.9	7.8	9.6	12.3	18.9	10.9	11.5	10.2	9.2	11.0	6.0	10.4	6.9	4.7
$2,000 to $2,999	9.6	14.7	14.1	6.2	8.5	10.3	9.7	13.2	25.2	29.7	18.2	21.1	15.4	14.6	22.9	10.4	24.8	17.0	14.0
$3,000 to $4,999	8.2	9.9	6.5	2.6	4.2	8.4	6.6	8.8	12.3	16.2	20.9	28.7	15.4	19.0	42.2	14.9	32.4	44.0	33.4
$5,000 to $7,499	2.8	2.3	1.6	.6	1.1	2.7	2.2	2.0	6.5		6.4	6.3	4.9	6.5	10.1	13.4	7.8	12.7	25.5
$7,500 to $9,999	.4	.5	.4	.2	.2	.7	.6	.4	.6		1.8	.5	.4	1.1		1.5	.8	2.7	5.1
$10,000 to $14,999	.2	.2	.2	.1	.1	.3	.3	.3	1.3		.9	.5		1.0	.9		1.2	.8	3.4
$15,000 to $19,999	.1	.1	.1	.1		.1	.1	.1				.1	.4				.1		1.1
$20,000 and over						.1	.1	.1						.6					.7
Not reported	2.8	2.3	2.1	2.8	2.9	1.9	2.6	2.8	1.9	5.4	1.8	2.3	2.0	4.0	2.8	3.0	2.8	1.2	2.7
Rented nonfarm homes	100.0	100.0	100.0	100.0	100.0	100.0	100.0	100.0	100.0	100.0	100.0	100.0	100.0	100.0	100.0	100.0	100.0	100.0	100.0
Rental under $10	46.4	47.3	66.6	71.2	67.8	47.8	42.2	42.8	20.1	14.2	18.8	13.1	34.6	23.6	19.6	19.3	10.3	16.1	4.9
$10 to $14	26.4	31.9	22.3	20.0	19.8	22.7	23.8	26.7	22.4	37.0	35.7	25.0	27.7	29.2	26.3	28.6	16.9	15.9	8.9
$15 to $19	12.0	11.1	4.9	3.3	4.4	14.8	12.9	12.6	19.3	27.6	21.0	20.5	16.0	15.0	19.6	16.0	19.3	19.9	12.4
$20 to $29	10.1	6.1	2.0	1.6	2.3	10.1	12.7	11.2	20.5	12.6	15.1	30.5	15.0	17.9	23.9	21.0	32.3	36.6	39.0
$30 to $49	2.5	1.5	.6	.4	.5	2.1	3.5	2.3	13.1	3.9	5.9	7.2	3.8	5.7	8.6	13.4	14.8	10.5	27.9
$50 to $74	.3	.2	.1	.1	.1	.3	.5	.3	2.3	.8		.3	.5	.7			1.0	.3	1.4
$75 to $99							.1	.1	.4		.4	.1	.2	.1			.2		.2
$100 to $149							.1		.4			.1		.2	.5		.2		.1
$150 to $199															.5		.2		
$200 and over																			
Not reported	2.3	1.9	3.5	3.3	5.0	2.1	4.2	4.1	1.5	3.9	3.3	3.2	2.1	7.6	1.0	1.7	4.9	.8	5.2

TABLE 31.—RENTED NONFARM HOMES OF NEGRO FAMILIES BY MONTHLY RENTAL, WITH MEDIAN RENTALS, BY SECTIONS, DIVISIONS, AND STATES: 1930

[Median not shown where number of families reporting rental is less than 100]

SECTION, DIVISION, AND STATE	All rented nonfarm homes	NUMBER OF HOMES WITH MONTHLY RENTAL—											Median rental
		Under $10	$10 to $14	$15 to $19	$20 to $29	$30 to $49	$50 to $74	$75 to $99	$100 to $149	$150 to $199	$200 and over	Not reported	
United States	1,290,697	479,539	247,898	133,854	188,079	149,096	49,353	8,838	1,949	452	147	37,492	$13.04
The North	430,466	27,708	45,374	56,358	118,214	118,362	44,105	8,299	1,805	416	121	9,704	26.85
The South	840,908	450,070	193,779	74,712	63,204	26,578	5,034	504	124	31	26	26,846	(1)
The West	19,323	1,761	2,745	2,784	6,661	4,156	214	35	20	5	---	942	22.85
NEW ENGLAND	16,934	713	2,412	3,116	6,347	3,459	489	63	9	---	1	325	23.25
Maine	118	20	28	28	28	10	1	1	---	---	---	2	16.79
New Hampshire	63	10	16	13	17	2	---	---	---	---	---	5	---
Vermont	77	25	14	11	21	5	---	---	---	---	---	1	---
Massachusetts	8,823	282	858	1,237	3,301	2,440	412	49	6	---	---	238	25.80
Rhode Island	1,896	181	594	477	522	106	6	1	---	---	---	9	16.77
Connecticut	5,957	195	902	1,350	2,458	896	70	12	3	---	1	70	22.02
MIDDLE ATLANTIC	198,018	8,151	13,493	20,392	52,543	66,423	25,069	4,733	1,297	358	90	5,469	30.51
New York	85,686	1,095	2,740	5,856	16,870	30,124	19,791	4,293	1,136	333	80	3,368	39.69
New Jersey	35,686	1,424	2,907	4,904	12,175	11,227	1,897	152	74	14	4	908	26.70
Pennsylvania	76,646	5,632	7,846	9,632	23,498	25,072	3,381	288	87	11	6	1,193	26.22
EAST NORTH CENTRAL	163,872	9,172	18,190	23,229	47,302	42,023	17,281	3,388	473	56	29	2,729	26.34
Ohio	55,324	3,443	7,493	10,416	19,824	12,119	1,138	128	54	6	3	700	23.01
Indiana	19,133	1,849	4,317	4,541	5,734	2,172	153	19	7	4	2	335	18.56
Illinois	61,181	3,508	5,375	6,301	13,489	15,112	12,691	2,984	363	26	17	1,315	31.67
Michigan	26,258	328	845	1,698	7,477	11,980	3,248	251	48	20	6	357	34.34
Wisconsin	1,976	44	160	273	778	640	51	6	1	---	1	22	26.41
WEST NORTH CENTRAL	51,642	9,672	11,279	9,621	12,022	6,457	1,266	115	26	2	1	1,181	17.22
Minnesota	1,661	71	265	371	591	274	19	2	---	---	---	68	21.51
Iowa	2,478	506	731	592	498	98	6	---	---	---	---	47	14.85
Missouri	37,953	6,606	7,205	6,684	9,515	5,822	1,223	110	22	2	1	763	18.58
North Dakota	78	7	17	18	13	16	2	---	---	---	---	5	---
South Dakota	65	16	14	12	16	3	---	---	---	---	---	4	---
Nebraska	2,304	234	588	628	659	124	3	1	2	---	---	65	17.37
Kansas	7,103	2,232	2,459	1,316	730	120	13	2	2	---	---	229	12.45
SOUTH ATLANTIC	427,735	224,612	93,029	35,440	35,742	20,391	4,099	363	65	18	14	13,962	(1)
Delaware	4,662	1,491	701	480	1,077	714	50	2	2	---	1	144	15.70
Maryland	38,918	7,929	5,665	4,684	9,825	8,406	990	47	9	2	2	1,359	20.51
District of Columbia	21,409	393	1,874	3,091	5,197	6,846	2,559	229	21	6	1	1,192	29.14
Virginia	56,346	25,106	17,546	7,149	4,322	909	67	6	4	1	---	1,236	10.70
West Virginia	20,416	12,445	3,511	1,542	1,977	590	67	14	5	---	---	265	(1)
North Carolina	61,457	27,741	20,207	6,037	4,636	901	92	22	9	4	1	1,807	10.52
South Carolina	55,239	43,746	7,243	1,687	881	186	30	4	---	---	1	1,461	(1)
Georgia	102,743	69,734	19,512	5,727	3,012	615	85	11	8	4	6	4,029	(1)
Florida	66,545	36,027	16,770	5,043	4,815	1,224	159	28	7	1	2	2,469	(1)
EAST SOUTH CENTRAL	223,366	133,864	55,332	15,857	9,176	2,286	351	45	21	7	1	6,426	(1)
Kentucky	31,949	14,837	8,441	3,820	3,238	799	109	11	6	1	---	687	10.47
Tennessee	55,283	26,142	17,622	6,141	3,395	804	111	15	8		---	1,044	10.28
Alabama	87,112	58,002	19,445	4,257	1,761	494	73	14	4	5	1	3,056	(1)
Mississippi	49,022	34,883	9,824	1,639	782	189	58	5	3	---	---	1,639	(1)
WEST SOUTH CENTRAL	189,807	91,594	45,418	23,415	18,286	3,901	584	96	38	6	11	6,458	10.01
Arkansas	26,400	17,899	5,224	1,166	595	138	38	7	1	2	3	1,327	(1)
Louisiana	76,297	36,502	17,317	11,267	7,722	1,632	234	36	15	2	2	1,568	10.25
Oklahoma	13,342	5,628	3,177	1,723	1,697	461	69	13	9	---	2	563	11.20
Texas	73,768	31,565	19,700	9,259	8,272	1,670	243	40	13	2	4	3,000	10.97
MOUNTAIN	4,892	958	1,347	896	1,106	332	27	6	6	1	---	213	15.19
Montana	259	52	58	50	53	34	6	1	1	---	---	4	16.75
Idaho	127	18	47	35	16	5	1	---	---	---	---	5	14.57
Wyoming	272	51	97	57	41	16	---	1	---	---	---	9	14.15
Colorado	1,859	244	464	382	567	134	6	2	1	---	---	59	17.51
New Mexico	419	145	116	67	63	16	2	1	---	---	---	9	12.59
Arizona	1,628	384	476	245	291	93	12	1	3	---	---	123	13.87
Utah	209	41	55	41	50	18	---	---	1	1	---	2	15.91
Nevada	119	23	34	19	25	16	---	---	---	---	---	2	15.39
PACIFIC	14,431	803	1,398	1,888	5,555	3,824	187	29	14	4	---	729	24.97
Washington	1,037	107	175	200	335	153	10	2	2	2	---	51	20.33
Oregon	372	60	59	74	136	39	1	---	---	---	---	3	19.43
California	13,022	636	1,164	1,614	5,084	3,632	176	27	12	2	---	675	25.43

[1] Less than $10.

TABLE 32.—NEGRO FAMILIES CLASSIFIED BY NUMBER OF CHILDREN UNDER 10 YEARS OLD, BY SECTIONS, DIVISIONS, AND STATES: 1930

[Percent not shown where less than 1/10 of 1 percent]

SECTION, DIVISION, AND STATE	All families	FAMILIES HAVING SPECIFIED NUMBER OF CHILDREN UNDER 10 YEARS OLD							PERCENT OF ALL FAMILIES						
		None	1	2	3	4	5	6 or more	None	1	2	3	4	5	6 or more
United States	**2,803,756**	**1,655,217**	**467,575**	**288,572**	**190,380**	**121,107**	**58,180**	**22,725**	**59.0**	**16.7**	**10.3**	**6.8**	**4.3**	**2.1**	**0.8**
The North	**576,328**	**389,364**	**82,797**	**48,509**	**29,236**	**16,338**	**7,367**	**2,717**	**67.6**	**14.4**	**8.4**	**5.1**	**2.8**	**1.3**	**.5**
The South	**2,193,357**	**1,239,876**	**380,878**	**237,951**	**159,991**	**104,179**	**50,577**	**19,905**	**56.5**	**17.4**	**10.8**	**7.3**	**4.7**	**2.3**	**.9**
The West	**34,071**	**25,977**	**3,900**	**2,112**	**1,153**	**590**	**236**	**103**	**76.2**	**11.4**	**6.2**	**3.4**	**1.7**	**.7**	**.3**
NEW ENGLAND	22,864	15,133	3,073	1,999	1,378	767	362	152	66.2	13.4	8.7	6.0	3.4	1.6	.7
Maine	259	171	40	21	16	6	5	-	66.0	15.4	8.1	6.2	2.3	1.9	-
New Hampshire	117	85	18	8	2	3	1	-	72.6	15.4	6.8	1.7	2.6	.9	-
Vermont	135	99	14	8	7	4	2	1	73.3	10.4	5.9	5.2	3.0	1.5	.7
Massachusetts	12,637	8,462	1,620	1,094	744	441	195	81	67.0	12.8	8.7	5.9	3.5	1.5	.6
Rhode Island	2,542	1,710	311	216	153	78	54	20	67.3	12.2	8.5	6.0	3.1	2.1	.8
Connecticut	7,174	4,606	1,070	652	456	235	105	50	64.2	14.9	9.1	6.4	3.3	1.5	.7
MIDDLE ATLANTIC	243,371	160,563	36,394	21,856	13,011	7,140	3,180	1,227	66.0	15.0	9.0	5.3	2.9	1.3	.5
New York	95,621	65,401	14,180	8,327	4,469	2,068	855	321	68.4	14.8	8.7	4.7	2.2	.9	.3
New Jersey	48,636	31,140	7,416	4,449	2,813	1,728	798	292	64.0	15.2	9.1	5.8	3.6	1.6	.6
Pennsylvania	99,114	64,022	14,798	9,080	5,729	3,344	1,527	614	64.6	14.9	9.2	5.8	3.4	1.5	.6
EAST NORTH CENTRAL	222,240	150,717	31,725	18,358	11,119	6,418	2,857	1,046	67.8	14.3	8.3	5.0	2.9	1.3	.5
Ohio	75,709	50,185	10,942	6,548	4,176	2,380	1,080	398	66.3	14.5	8.6	5.5	3.1	1.4	.5
Indiana	28,771	19,986	3,954	2,164	1,376	809	345	137	69.5	13.7	7.5	4.8	2.8	1.2	.5
Illinois	78,737	55,174	10,877	6,172	3,405	1,951	850	308	70.1	13.8	7.8	4.3	2.5	1.1	.4
Michigan	36,500	23,625	5,590	3,287	2,051	1,204	547	196	64.7	15.3	9.0	5.6	3.3	1.5	.5
Wisconsin	2,523	1,747	362	187	111	74	35	7	69.2	14.3	7.4	4.4	2.9	1.4	.3
WEST NORTH CENTRAL	87,853	62,951	11,605	6,296	3,728	2,013	968	292	71.7	13.2	7.2	4.2	2.3	1.1	.3
Minnesota	2,592	1,975	321	144	81	39	22	10	76.2	12.4	5.6	3.1	1.5	.8	.4
Iowa	4,571	3,239	605	333	207	110	55	22	70.9	13.2	7.3	4.5	2.4	1.2	.5
Missouri	59,016	42,431	7,753	4,193	2,465	1,348	637	189	71.9	13.1	7.1	4.2	2.3	1.1	.3
North Dakota	120	103	8	6	3	-	-	-	85.8	6.7	5.0	2.5	-	-	-
South Dakota	166	128	13	10	7	4	3	1	77.1	7.8	6.0	4.2	2.4	1.8	.6
Nebraska	3,700	2,688	480	261	153	70	36	12	72.6	13.0	7.1	4.1	1.9	1.0	.3
Kansas	17,688	12,387	2,425	1,349	812	442	215	58	70.0	13.7	7.6	4.6	2.5	1.2	.3
SOUTH ATLANTIC	974,592	522,135	173,210	112,130	78,443	52,205	25,911	10,558	53.6	17.8	11.5	8.0	5.4	2.7	1.1
Delaware	7,682	5,005	1,134	678	427	267	125	46	65.2	14.8	8.8	5.6	3.5	1.6	.6
Maryland	61,160	37,539	9,278	5,681	4,088	2,581	1,345	648	61.4	15.2	9.3	6.7	4.2	2.2	1.1
District of Columbia	29,995	20,630	4,253	2,428	1,442	777	327	138	68.8	14.2	8.1	4.8	2.6	1.1	.5
Virginia	140,726	76,556	23,444	15,415	11,316	8,033	4,202	1,760	54.4	16.7	11.0	8.0	5.7	3.0	1.3
West Virginia	26,274	15,565	4,235	2,678	1,754	1,273	544	225	59.2	16.1	10.2	6.7	4.8	2.1	.9
North Carolina	180,128	81,067	33,934	24,236	18,276	13,019	6,786	2,810	45.0	18.8	13.5	10.1	7.2	3.8	1.6
South Carolina	168,324	78,089	33,015	22,510	16,178	11,003	5,430	2,099	46.4	19.6	13.4	9.6	6.5	3.2	1.2
Georgia	249,942	137,675	45,917	28,206	18,690	11,601	5,601	2,252	55.1	18.4	11.3	7.5	4.6	2.2	.9
Florida	110,361	70,009	18,000	10,298	6,272	3,651	1,551	580	63.4	16.3	9.3	5.7	3.3	1.4	.5
EAST SOUTH CENTRAL	653,847	382,288	111,432	68,159	44,179	28,621	13,806	5,362	58.5	17.0	10.4	6.8	4.4	2.1	.8
Kentucky	60,672	41,945	8,146	4,768	3,012	1,794	730	277	69.1	13.4	7.9	5.0	3.0	1.2	.5
Tennessee	120,402	76,149	19,312	11,286	6,969	4,237	1,811	638	63.2	16.0	9.4	5.8	3.5	1.5	.5
Alabama	222,533	123,163	39,556	24,808	16,571	10,952	5,352	2,131	55.3	17.8	11.1	7.4	4.9	2.4	1.0
Mississippi	250,240	141,031	44,418	27,297	17,627	11,638	5,913	2,316	56.4	17.8	10.9	7.0	4.7	2.4	.9
WEST SOUTH CENTRAL	564,918	335,453	96,236	57,662	37,369	23,353	10,860	3,985	59.4	17.0	10.2	6.6	4.1	1.9	.7
Arkansas	123,009	73,674	21,391	12,516	7,827	4,684	2,194	723	59.9	17.4	10.2	6.4	3.8	1.8	.6
Louisiana	190,876	110,637	33,020	20,076	13,304	8,529	3,883	1,427	58.0	17.3	10.5	7.0	4.5	2.0	.7
Oklahoma	40,238	23,855	6,654	4,131	2,704	1,719	840	335	59.3	16.5	10.3	6.7	4.3	2.1	.8
Texas	210,795	127,287	35,171	20,939	13,534	8,421	3,943	1,500	60.4	16.7	9.9	6.4	4.0	1.9	.7
MOUNTAIN	8,743	6,739	943	509	297	151	69	35	77.1	10.8	5.8	3.4	1.7	.8	.4
Montana	458	391	39	14	6	6	2	-	85.4	8.5	3.1	1.3	1.3	.4	-
Idaho	229	194	17	11	3	3	1	-	84.7	7.4	4.8	1.3	1.3	.4	-
Wyoming	418	354	34	9	10	9	2	-	84.7	8.1	2.2	2.4	2.2	.5	-
Colorado	3,538	2,790	356	206	108	43	24	11	78.9	10.1	5.8	3.1	1.2	.7	.3
New Mexico	799	571	95	57	35	22	13	6	71.5	11.9	7.1	4.4	2.8	1.6	.8
Arizona	2,776	2,014	354	179	124	62	27	16	72.6	12.8	6.4	4.5	2.2	1.0	.6
Utah	331	255	31	28	11	4	-	2	77.0	9.4	8.5	3.3	1.2	-	.6
Nevada	194	170	17	5	-	2	-	-	87.6	8.8	2.6	-	1.0	-	-
PACIFIC	25,328	19,238	2,957	1,603	856	439	167	68	76.0	11.7	6.3	3.4	1.7	.7	.3
Washington	2,059	1,633	222	102	56	26	14	6	79.3	10.8	5.0	2.7	1.3	.7	.3
Oregon	674	555	68	27	14	9	1	-	82.3	10.1	4.0	2.1	1.3	.1	-
California	22,595	17,050	2,667	1,474	786	404	152	62	75.5	11.8	6.5	3.5	1.8	.7	.3

TABLE 33.—NEGRO FAMILIES CLASSIFIED ACCORDING TO THE NUMBER OF GAINFUL WORKERS, BY SECTIONS, DIVISIONS, AND STATES: 1930

SECTION, DIVISION, AND STATE	ALL FAMILIES HAVING SPECIFIED NUMBER OF GAINFUL WORKERS						FARM FAMILIES HAVING SPECIFIED NUMBER OF GAINFUL WORKERS						NONFARM FAMILIES HAVING SPECIFIED NUMBER OF GAINFUL WORKERS					
	Total	None	1	2	3	4 or more	Total	None	1	2	3	4 or more	Total	None	1	2	3	4 or more
United States	**2,803,756**	**86,227**	**1,532,551**	**758,898**	**250,634**	**175,446**	**978,653**	**8,454**	**529,888**	**235,833**	**102,619**	**101,859**	**1,825,103**	**77,773**	**1,002,663**	**523,065**	**148,015**	**73,587**
The North	576,328	23,128	329,916	159,061	43,826	20,397	14,744	261	10,205	2,902	935	441	561,584	22,867	319,711	156,159	42,891	19,956
The South	2,193,357	60,961	1,181,401	591,573	205,018	154,404	962,401	8,159	518,535	232,699	101,616	101,392	1,230,956	52,802	662,866	358,874	103,402	53,012
The West	34,071	2,138	21,234	8,264	1,790	645	1,508	34	1,148	232	68	26	32,563	2,104	20,086	8,032	1,722	619
NEW ENGLAND	22,864	1,120	13,299	5,921	1,737	787	211	1	141	44	15	10	22,653	1,119	13,158	5,877	1,722	777
Maine	259	7	167	62	20	3	20	......	12	8	......	......	239	7	155	54	20	3
New Hampshire	117	15	71	22	6	3	6	......	3	2	......	1	111	15	68	20	6	2
Vermont	135	11	88	23	6	7	24	......	15	4	1	4	111	11	73	19	5	3
Massachusetts	12,637	634	7,435	3,157	991	420	95	......	73	15	5	2	12,542	634	7,362	3,142	986	418
Rhode Island	2,542	138	1,493	623	183	105	14	......	6	5	2	1	2,528	138	1,487	618	181	104
Connecticut	7,174	315	4,045	2,034	531	249	52	1	32	10	7	2	7,122	314	4,013	2,024	524	247
MIDDLE ATLANTIC	243,371	7,920	134,775	70,334	20,258	10,084	2,002	25	1,293	451	156	77	241,369	7,895	133,482	69,883	20,102	10,007
New York	95,621	2,710	51,103	29,528	8,248	4,032	447	9	274	112	30	22	95,174	2,701	50,829	29,416	8,218	4,010
New Jersey	48,636	1,641	26,042	14,393	4,390	2,170	796	8	517	171	68	32	47,840	1,633	25,525	14,222	4,322	2,138
Pennsylvania	99,114	3,569	57,630	26,413	7,620	3,882	759	8	502	168	58	23	98,355	3,561	57,128	26,245	7,562	3,856
EAST NORTH CENTRAL	222,240	9,621	129,683	59,800	16,013	7,123	4,180	122	2,809	856	265	128	218,060	9,499	126,874	58,944	15,748	6,995
Ohio	75,709	3,271	44,823	20,114	5,277	2,224	1,660	50	1,103	344	115	48	74,049	3,221	43,720	19,770	5,162	2,179
Indiana	28,771	1,298	17,427	7,364	1,922	760	592	19	391	131	35	16	28,179	1,279	17,036	7,233	1,887	744
Illinois	78,737	3,471	43,507	22,530	6,211	3,018	1,260	23	841	274	77	45	77,477	3,448	42,666	22,256	6,134	2,973
Michigan	36,500	1,439	22,315	9,212	2,461	1,073	601	30	432	97	29	13	35,899	1,409	21,883	9,115	2,432	1,060
Wisconsin	2,523	142	1,611	580	142	48	67	......	42	10	9	6	2,456	142	1,569	570	133	42
WEST NORTH CENTRAL	87,853	4,467	52,159	23,006	5,818	2,403	8,351	113	5,962	1,551	499	226	79,502	4,354	46,197	21,455	5,319	2,177
Minnesota	2,592	140	1,719	565	122	46	28	1	17	6	3	1	2,564	139	1,702	559	119	45
Iowa	4,571	318	2,928	997	250	78	130	5	91	24	7	3	4,441	313	2,837	973	243	75
Missouri	59,016	2,665	34,435	15,959	4,175	1,782	7,059	78	5,074	1,300	416	191	51,957	2,587	29,361	14,659	3,759	1,591
North Dakota	120	13	90	13	4	......	13	......	10	2	1	......	107	13	80	11	3	......
South Dakota	166	5	106	39	12	4	49	......	35	8	3	3	117	5	71	31	9	1
Nebraska	3,700	172	2,203	1,010	231	84	29	......	19	7	2	1	3,671	172	2,184	1,003	229	83
Kansas	17,688	1,154	10,678	4,423	1,024	409	1,043	29	716	204	67	27	16,645	1,125	9,962	4,219	957	382
SOUTH ATLANTIC	974,592	29,824	499,035	271,474	98,988	75,271	364,268	4,225	183,461	89,226	43,116	44,240	610,324	25,599	315,574	182,248	55,872	31,031
Delaware	7,682	348	4,302	2,050	641	341	1,268	17	720	346	122	63	6,414	331	3,582	1,704	519	278
Maryland	61,160	2,049	30,220	18,503	6,426	3,962	8,016	117	4,332	2,066	929	572	53,144	1,932	25,888	16,437	5,497	3,390
District of Columbia	29,995	981	13,619	10,177	3,313	1,905	......	......	......	......	......	......	29,995	981	13,619	10,177	3,313	1,905
Virginia	140,726	6,477	77,107	36,824	12,924	7,394	47,408	913	27,044	11,273	4,885	3,293	93,318	5,564	50,063	25,551	8,039	4,101
West Virginia	26,274	1,028	18,623	4,847	1,271	505	688	19	381	176	72	40	25,586	1,009	18,242	4,671	1,199	465
North Carolina	180,128	5,087	91,958	48,282	19,026	15,775	85,455	869	44,839	19,298	9,849	10,600	94,673	4,218	47,119	28,984	9,177	5,175
South Carolina	168,324	4,250	79,060	47,030	19,235	18,749	92,663	849	40,741	23,861	12,285	14,927	75,661	3,401	38,319	23,169	6,950	3,822
Georgia	249,942	6,047	124,016	72,052	27,008	20,819	112,467	1,178	56,739	28,288	13,278	12,984	137,475	4,869	67,277	43,764	13,730	7,835
Florida	110,361	3,557	60,130	31,709	9,144	5,821	16,303	263	8,665	3,918	1,696	1,761	94,058	3,294	51,465	27,791	7,448	4,060
EAST SOUTH CENTRAL	653,847	16,394	347,939	177,868	61,620	50,026	330,252	1,995	165,791	87,466	36,680	38,320	323,595	14,399	182,148	90,402	24,940	11,706
Kentucky	60,672	3,175	34,063	16,527	4,735	2,172	10,583	186	6,782	2,346	849	420	50,089	2,989	27,281	14,181	3,886	1,752
Tennessee	120,402	4,066	66,822	33,137	10,178	6,199	36,913	286	21,483	8,516	3,512	3,116	83,489	3,780	45,339	24,621	6,666	3,083
Alabama	222,533	5,300	118,607	58,033	21,868	18,725	104,136	835	50,321	26,239	12,513	14,228	118,397	4,465	68,286	31,794	9,355	4,497
Mississippi	250,240	3,853	128,447	70,171	24,839	22,930	178,620	688	87,205	50,365	19,806	20,556	71,620	3,165	41,242	19,806	5,033	2,374
WEST SOUTH CENTRAL	564,918	14,743	334,427	142,231	44,410	29,107	267,881	1,939	169,283	56,007	21,820	18,832	297,037	12,804	165,144	86,224	22,590	10,275
Arkansas	123,009	2,827	80,958	25,543	7,995	5,686	78,722	471	53,317	14,872	5,432	4,630	44,287	2,356	27,641	10,671	2,563	1,056
Louisiana	190,876	5,070	107,846	49,811	16,672	11,477	82,916	612	48,324	19,285	7,701	6,994	107,960	4,458	59,522	30,526	8,971	4,483
Oklahoma	40,238	1,553	25,173	9,878	2,460	1,174	16,671	223	11,858	3,034	983	573	23,567	1,330	13,315	6,844	1,477	601
Texas	210,795	5,293	120,450	56,999	17,283	10,770	89,572	633	55,784	18,816	7,704	6,635	121,223	4,660	64,666	38,183	9,579	4,135
MOUNTAIN	8,743	638	5,800	1,806	381	118	589	13	452	87	29	8	8,154	625	5,348	1,719	352	110
Montana	458	39	340	65	12	2	24	......	21	1	2	......	434	39	319	64	10	2
Idaho	229	18	172	30	8	1	22	1	13	5	3	......	207	17	159	25	5	1
Wyoming	418	32	306	65	11	4	16	1	8	4	2	1	402	31	298	61	9	3
Colorado	3,538	237	2,200	846	201	54	100	4	77	14	4	1	3,438	233	2,123	832	197	53
New Mexico	799	41	572	142	31	13	106	2	85	12	4	3	693	39	487	130	27	10
Arizona	2,776	236	1,831	565	102	42	310	5	241	49	12	3	2,466	231	1,590	516	90	39
Utah	331	22	228	67	13	1	6	......	2	2	2	......	325	22	226	65	11	1
Nevada	194	13	151	26	3	1	5	......	5	......	......	......	189	13	146	26	3	1
PACIFIC	25,328	1,500	15,434	6,458	1,409	527	919	21	696	145	39	18	24,409	1,479	14,738	6,313	1,370	506
Washington	2,059	153	1,424	380	84	18	84	4	64	15	......	1	1,975	149	1,360	365	84	17
Oregon	674	22	477	138	32	5	13	......	10	2	1	......	661	22	467	136	31	5
California	22,595	1,325	13,533	5,940	1,293	504	822	17	622	128	38	17	21,773	1,308	12,911	5,812	1,255	487

TABLE 34.—NEGRO FAMILIES BY SIZE, BY SECTIONS, DIVISIONS, AND STATES: 1930

SECTION, DIVISION, AND STATE	All families	FAMILIES COMPRISING—												PERCENT OF ALL FAMILIES					
		1 person	2 persons	3 persons	4 persons	5 persons	6 persons	7 persons	8 persons	9 persons	10 persons	11 persons	12 or more persons	1 person	2 persons	3 persons	4 persons	5 persons	6 or more persons
United States	**2,803,756**	**338,114**	**739,812**	**500,990**	**361,880**	**265,136**	**193,720**	**141,149**	**99,800**	**67,607**	**43,573**	**25,411**	**26,564**	**12.1**	**26.4**	**17.9**	**12.9**	**9.5**	**21.3**
The North	**576,328**	**80,084**	**183,678**	**106,563**	**72,550**	**48,937**	**32,724**	**21,127**	**13,119**	**7,958**	**4,574**	**2,406**	**2,608**	**13.9**	**31.9**	**18.5**	**12.6**	**8.5**	**14.7**
The South	**2,193,357**	**250,264**	**544,285**	**388,738**	**285,962**	**214,024**	**159,692**	**119,257**	**86,176**	**59,351**	**38,841**	**22,905**	**23,862**	**11.4**	**24.8**	**17.7**	**13.0**	**9.8**	**23.3**
The West	**34,071**	**7,766**	**11,849**	**5,689**	**3,368**	**2,175**	**1,304**	**765**	**505**	**298**	**158**	**100**	**94**	**22.8**	**34.8**	**16.7**	**9.9**	**6.4**	**9.5**
NEW ENGLAND	22,864	4,125	6,296	3,775	2,782	2,081	1,417	914	595	412	219	121	127	18.0	27.5	16.5	12.2	9.1	16.6
Maine	259	58	57	40	39	30	12	6	9	1	5	1	1	22.4	22.0	15.4	15.1	11.6	13.5
New Hampshire	117	28	33	20	13	7	4	6	3		2		1	23.9	28.2	17.1	11.1	6.0	13.7
Vermont	135	41	31	17	12	14	6	4	3	2	3	1	1	30.4	23.0	12.6	8.9	10.4	14.8
Massachusetts	12,637	2,276	3,455	2,032	1,555	1,154	816	523	329	234	120	72	71	18.0	27.3	16.1	12.3	9.1	17.1
Rhode Island	2,542	575	672	381	264	203	150	111	69	50	29	20	18	22.6	26.4	15.0	10.4	8.0	17.6
Connecticut	7,174	1,147	2,048	1,285	899	673	429	264	182	125	60	27	35	16.0	28.5	17.9	12.5	9.4	15.6
MIDDLE ATLANTIC	243,371	33,350	75,345	45,101	31,416	21,615	14,277	9,212	5,631	3,405	1,898	995	1,126	13.7	31.0	18.5	12.9	8.9	15.0
New York	95,621	15,118	30,440	17,909	12,375	8,053	5,109	3,019	1,647	950	498	223	280	15.8	31.8	18.7	12.9	8.4	12.3
New Jersey	48,636	6,528	14,025	8,930	6,349	4,406	3,030	2,131	1,369	846	475	281	266	13.4	28.8	18.4	13.1	9.1	17.3
Pennsylvania	99,114	11,704	30,880	18,262	12,692	9,156	6,138	4,062	2,615	1,609	925	491	580	11.8	31.3	18.4	12.8	9.2	16.6
EAST NORTH CENTRAL	222,240	28,349	72,272	41,609	28,109	18,806	12,744	8,237	5,172	3,089	1,861	945	1,047	12.8	32.5	18.7	12.6	8.5	14.9
Ohio	75,709	9,829	23,749	14,171	9,562	6,514	4,528	2,910	1,915	1,116	696	355	364	13.0	31.4	18.7	12.6	8.6	15.7
Indiana	28,771	4,065	9,329	5,365	3,543	2,394	1,563	1,022	626	402	249	99	114	14.1	32.4	18.6	12.3	8.3	14.2
Illinois	78,737	10,414	26,513	14,501	9,815	6,402	4,293	2,795	1,700	1,004	601	322	377	13.2	33.7	18.4	12.5	8.1	14.1
Michigan	36,500	3,671	11,799	7,104	4,875	3,316	2,246	1,428	875	544	299	162	181	10.1	32.3	19.5	13.4	9.1	15.7
Wisconsin	2,523	370	882	468	314	180	114	82	56	23	16	7	11	14.7	35.0	18.5	12.4	7.1	12.2
WEST NORTH CENTRAL	87,853	14,260	29,765	16,078	10,243	6,435	4,286	2,764	1,721	1,052	596	345	308	16.2	33.9	18.3	11.7	7.3	12.6
Minnesota	2,592	508	940	464	275	158	113	59	37	14	11	4	9	19.6	36.3	17.9	10.6	6.1	9.5
Iowa	4,571	840	1,432	788	555	360	243	144	81	56	36	18	18	18.4	31.3	17.2	12.1	7.9	13.0
Missouri	59,016	9,554	20,289	10,741	6,846	4,219	2,798	1,859	1,137	715	410	236	212	16.2	34.4	18.2	11.6	7.1	12.5
North Dakota	120	58	34	13	8	1	4			1	1			48.3	28.3	10.8	6.7	0.8	5.0
South Dakota	166	40	41	27	18	16	11	4	3	2	3		1	24.1	24.7	16.3	10.8	9.6	14.5
Nebraska	3,700	662	1,311	683	369	274	170	102	52	38	19	11	9	17.9	35.4	18.5	10.0	7.4	10.8
Kansas	17,688	2,598	5,718	3,362	2,172	1,407	947	596	411	226	116	76	59	14.7	32.3	19.0	12.3	8.0	13.7
SOUTH ATLANTIC	974,592	108,819	218,114	164,463	126,628	98,596	76,547	59,333	44,040	31,150	20,792	12,454	13,656	11.2	22.4	16.9	13.0	10.1	26.5
Delaware	7,682	1,274	2,141	1,308	916	639	463	335	237	155	100	61	53	16.6	27.9	17.0	11.9	8.3	18.3
Maryland	61,160	8,214	15,983	10,323	7,436	5,648	4,205	3,178	2,288	1,519	1,008	597	761	13.4	26.1	16.9	12.2	9.2	22.2
District of Columbia	29,995	4,124	8,973	5,648	3,875	2,636	1,748	1,111	785	439	288	159	209	13.7	29.9	18.8	12.9	8.8	15.8
Virginia	140,726	16,600	29,890	23,056	17,576	14,125	11,333	9,078	6,822	4,932	3,213	1,936	2,165	11.8	21.2	16.4	12.5	10.0	28.1
West Virginia	26,274	3,542	6,865	4,738	3,442	2,435	1,809	1,264	889	555	354	198	183	13.5	26.1	18.0	13.1	9.3	20.0
North Carolina	180,128	13,412	31,732	28,306	24,375	20,294	16,914	13,797	10,783	7,981	5,380	3,331	3,823	7.4	17.6	15.7	13.5	11.3	34.4
South Carolina	168,324	15,285	31,290	27,345	22,744	18,628	15,060	12,109	9,205	6,558	4,553	2,760	2,787	9.1	18.6	16.2	13.5	11.1	31.5
Georgia	249,942	27,744	60,124	44,180	32,817	24,817	18,543	14,020	10,120	7,112	4,724	2,786	2,955	11.1	24.1	17.7	13.1	9.9	24.1
Florida	110,361	18,624	31,116	19,559	13,447	9,374	6,472	4,441	2,911	1,899	1,172	626	720	16.9	28.2	17.7	12.2	8.5	16.5
EAST SOUTH CENTRAL	653,847	76,011	172,381	119,791	85,413	62,321	45,195	32,756	22,870	15,547	9,907	5,882	5,773	11.6	26.4	18.3	13.1	9.5	21.1
Kentucky	60,672	1,071	18,176	10,939	7,200	4,861	3,321	2,342	1,575	1,002	583	295	307	16.6	30.0	18.0	11.9	8.0	15.5
Tennessee	120,402	15,533	33,825	22,359	15,367	11,015	7,679	5,474	3,710	2,383	1,487	809	761	12.9	28.1	18.6	12.8	9.1	18.5
Alabama	222,533	24,053	53,783	40,398	29,510	22,448	16,534	12,110	8,712	6,145	3,854	2,463	2,523	10.8	24.2	18.2	13.3	10.1	23.5
Mississippi	250,240	26,354	66,597	46,095	33,336	23,997	17,661	12,830	8,873	6,017	3,983	2,315	2,182	10.5	26.6	18.4	13.3	9.6	21.5
WEST SOUTH CENTRAL	564,918	65,434	153,790	104,484	73,921	53,107	37,950	27,168	19,266	12,654	8,142	4,569	4,433	11.6	27.2	18.5	13.1	9.4	20.2
Arkansas	123,009	13,841	35,111	23,249	16,180	11,297	7,957	5,706	3,924	2,455	1,570	892	827	11.3	28.5	18.9	13.2	9.2	19.0
Louisiana	190,876	22,042	50,031	35,274	25,233	18,016	13,125	9,467	6,801	4,687	3,004	1,611	1,585	11.5	26.2	18.5	13.2	9.4	21.1
Oklahoma	40,238	4,646	11,018	7,028	5,167	3,795	2,760	1,987	1,457	996	665	341	378	11.5	27.4	17.5	12.8	9.4	21.3
Texas	210,795	24,905	57,630	38,933	27,341	19,999	14,108	10,008	7,084	4,516	2,903	1,725	1,643	11.8	27.3	18.5	13.0	9.5	19.9
MOUNTAIN	8,743	2,310	3,045	1,317	755	518	294	186	127	79	35	25	32	26.4	34.8	15.1	8.9	5.9	8.9
Montana	458	199	139	48	33	13	13	5	1	3	1		3	43.4	30.3	10.5	7.2	2.8	5.7
Idaho	229	81	83	32	12	10	5	2	2	1			1	35.4	36.2	14.0	5.2	4.4	4.8
Wyoming	418	161	136	62	15	15	14	5	4	5		1		38.5	32.5	14.8	3.6	3.6	6.9
Colorado	3,538	792	1,284	598	369	230	114	76	35	14	12	7	7	22.4	36.3	16.9	10.4	6.5	7.5
New Mexico	799	188	272	117	58	51	35	21	23	19	5	6	4	23.5	34.0	14.6	7.3	6.4	14.1
Arizona	2,776	701	951	393	255	178	98	70	55	33	16	10	16	25.3	34.3	14.2	9.2	6.4	10.7
Utah	331	91	120	45	27	18	12	5	7	3	1	1	1	27.5	36.3	13.6	8.2	5.4	9.1
Nevada	194	97	60	22	6	3	3	2		1				50.0	30.9	11.3	3.1	1.5	3.1
PACIFIC	25,328	5,456	8,804	4,372	2,593	1,657	1,010	579	378	219	123	75	62	21.5	34.8	17.3	10.2	6.5	9.7
Washington	2,059	587	711	311	183	111	64	39	30	11	6	4	2	28.5	34.5	15.1	8.9	5.4	7.6
Oregon	674	207	243	98	50	30	23	14	5	2		2		30.7	36.1	14.5	7.4	4.5	6.8
California	22,595	4,662	7,850	3,963	2,360	1,516	923	526	343	206	117	69	60	20.6	34.7	17.5	10.4	6.7	9.9

TABLE 35.—FAMILIES CLASSIFIED BY SEX, AGE, COLOR, AND NATIVITY OF HEAD, BY TENURE, FOR THE UNITED STATES: 1930

[The age classification was limited to families with a man reported as head. Percent not shown where less than 1/10 of 1 percent]

AREA, TENURE, AND AGE OF MAN HEAD	NUMBER OF FAMILIES					PERCENT DISTRIBUTION				
	All classes	Negro	Native white	Foreign-born white	Other races	All classes	Negro	Native white	Foreign-born white	Other races
TOTAL										
All families	**29,904,663**	**2,803,756**	**20,968,803**	**5,736,491**	**395,613**	-----	-----	-----	-----	-----
Man head, all ages	26,111,761	2,262,443	18,474,735	5,019,418	355,165	100.0	100.0	100.0	100.0	100.0
Under 25 years	1,266,056	201,896	986,844	49,178	28,138	4.8	8.9	5.3	1.0	7.9
25 to 34 years	5,878,711	563,314	4,535,328	678,714	101,355	22.5	24.9	24.5	13.5	28.5
35 to 44 years	7,082,391	584,294	4,927,974	1,470,252	99,871	27.1	25.8	26.7	29.3	28.1
45 to 54 years	5,743,244	501,944	3,829,210	1,340,291	71,799	22.0	22.2	20.7	26.7	20.2
55 to 64 years	3,680,822	262,624	2,518,550	865,038	34,610	14.1	11.6	13.6	17.2	9.7
65 to 74 years	1,880,969	107,925	1,283,987	475,291	13,766	7.2	4.8	6.9	9.5	3.9
75 years and over	561,223	36,996	380,490	138,607	5,130	2.1	1.6	2.1	2.8	1.4
Unknown	18,345	3,450	12,352	2,047	496	.1	.2	.1	-----	.1
Woman head, all ages	3,792,902	541,313	2,494,068	717,073	40,448	-----	-----	-----	-----	-----
Owner families	14,002,074	669,645	10,255,682	2,968,707	108,040	-----	-----	-----	-----	-----
Man head, all ages	12,179,477	534,458	8,944,053	2,606,730	94,236	100.0	100.0	100.0	100.0	100.0
Under 25 years	130,869	9,647	113,379	4,404	3,439	1.1	1.8	1.3	.2	3.6
25 to 34 years	1,516,341	64,407	1,279,977	153,291	18,666	12.4	12.1	14.3	5.9	19.8
35 to 44 years	3,142,403	129,496	2,327,569	659,178	26,160	25.8	24.2	26.0	25.3	27.8
45 to 54 years	3,201,077	159,543	2,250,355	768,592	22,587	26.3	29.9	25.2	29.5	24.0
55 to 64 years	2,396,679	102,872	1,710,106	569,871	13,830	19.7	19.2	19.1	21.9	14.7
65 to 74 years	1,361,618	49,471	961,517	344,028	6,602	11.2	9.3	10.8	13.2	7.0
75 years and over	424,288	18,265	296,737	106,471	2,815	3.5	3.4	3.3	4.1	3.0
Unknown	6,202	757	4,413	895	137	.1	.1	-----	-----	.1
Woman head, all ages	1,822,597	135,187	1,311,629	361,977	13,804	-----	-----	-----	-----	-----
Tenant families	15,319,817	2,050,217	10,314,500	2,690,300	264,800	-----	-----	-----	-----	-----
Man head, all ages	13,440,817	1,661,789	9,190,728	2,347,736	240,564	100.0	100.0	100.0	100.0	100.0
Under 25 years	1,079,013	182,036	831,819	43,024	22,134	8.0	11.0	9.1	1.8	9.2
25 to 34 years	4,228,955	480,068	3,158,712	513,897	76,278	31.5	28.9	34.4	21.9	31.7
35 to 44 years	3,827,742	439,869	2,524,783	794,412	68,678	28.5	26.5	27.5	33.8	28.5
45 to 54 years	2,455,682	330,686	1,522,314	556,917	45,765	18.3	19.9	16.6	23.7	19.0
55 to 64 years	1,226,722	153,485	769,816	284,343	19,078	9.1	9.2	8.4	12.1	7.9
65 to 74 years	487,637	55,704	301,157	124,394	6,382	3.6	3.4	3.3	5.3	2.7
75 years and over	126,015	17,552	76,737	29,764	1,962	.9	1.1	.8	1.3	.8
Unknown	9,051	2,389	5,390	985	287	.1	.1	.1	-----	.1
Woman head, all ages	1,879,000	388,428	1,123,772	342,564	24,236	-----	-----	-----	-----	-----
Tenure unknown	582,772	83,894	398,621	77,484	22,773	-----	-----	-----	-----	-----
Man head, all ages	491,467	66,196	339,954	64,952	20,365	100.0	100.0	100.0	100.0	100.0
Under 25 years	56,174	10,213	41,646	1,750	2,565	11.4	15.4	12.3	2.7	12.6
25 to 34 years	133,415	18,839	96,639	11,526	6,411	27.1	28.5	28.4	17.7	31.5
35 to 44 years	112,246	14,929	75,622	16,662	5,033	22.8	22.6	22.2	25.7	24.7
45 to 54 years	86,485	11,715	56,541	14,782	3,447	17.6	17.7	16.6	22.8	16.9
55 to 64 years	57,421	6,267	38,628	10,824	1,702	11.7	9.5	11.4	16.7	8.4
65 to 74 years	31,714	2,750	21,313	6,869	782	6.5	4.2	6.3	10.6	3.8
75 years and over	10,920	1,179	7,016	2,372	353	2.2	1.8	2.1	3.7	1.7
Unknown	3,092	304	2,549	167	72	.6	.5	.7	.3	.4
Woman head, all ages	91,305	17,698	58,667	12,532	2,408	-----	-----	-----	-----	-----
URBAN										
All families	17,372,524	1,328,170	11,322,555	4,535,603	186,196	-----	-----	-----	-----	-----
Man head, all ages	14,720,340	992,802	9,629,721	3,936,357	161,460	100.0	100.0	100.0	100.0	100.0
Under 25 years	612,201	64,638	493,710	42,041	11,812	4.2	6.5	5.1	1.1	7.3
25 to 34 years	3,500,898	278,244	2,585,143	588,762	48,749	23.8	28.0	26.8	15.0	30.2
35 to 44 years	4,269,793	298,213	2,704,584	1,218,852	48,144	29.0	30.0	28.1	31.0	29.8
45 to 54 years	3,242,018	216,414	1,943,869	1,049,670	32,065	22.0	21.8	20.2	26.7	19.9
55 to 64 years	1,929,481	90,984	1,192,146	632,312	14,039	13.1	9.2	12.4	16.1	8.7
65 to 74 years	908,497	32,256	552,470	318,820	4,951	6.2	3.2	5.7	8.1	3.1
75 years and over	245,156	9,856	149,540	84,287	1,473	1.7	1.0	1.6	2.1	.9
Unknown	12,296	2,197	8,259	1,613	227	.1	.2	.1	-----	.1
Woman head, all ages	2,652,184	335,368	1,692,834	599,246	24,736	-----	-----	-----	-----	-----
Owner families	7,432,554	315,584	4,941,762	2,132,269	42,939	-----	-----	-----	-----	-----
Man head, all ages	6,340,615	244,917	4,195,771	1,862,954	36,973	100.0	100.0	100.0	100.0	100.0
Under 25 years	51,908	3,616	44,144	3,030	1,118	.8	1.5	1.1	.2	3.0
25 to 34 years	812,282	33,031	651,835	119,888	7,528	12.8	13.5	15.5	6.4	20.4
35 to 44 years	1,794,017	69,044	1,198,722	514,706	11,545	28.3	28.2	28.6	27.6	31.2
45 to 54 years	1,717,639	76,091	1,065,812	566,361	9,375	27.1	31.1	25.4	30.4	25.4
55 to 64 years	1,179,603	41,055	746,823	386,915	4,810	18.6	16.8	17.8	20.8	13.0
65 to 74 years	609,761	16,435	379,462	211,938	1,926	9.6	6.7	9.0	11.4	5.2
75 years and over	172,052	5,218	103,715	59,494	625	2.7	2.1	2.5	3.2	1.7
Unknown	3,353	427	2,258	622	46	.1	.2	.1	-----	.1
Woman head, all ages	1,091,939	70,667	745,991	269,315	5,966	-----	-----	-----	-----	-----
Tenant families	9,681,359	978,799	6,213,093	2,352,756	136,711	-----	-----	-----	-----	-----
Man head, all ages	8,175,315	722,789	5,301,257	2,032,382	118,887	100.0	100.0	100.0	100.0	100.0
Under 25 years	538,567	57,896	432,940	37,700	10,031	6.6	8.0	8.2	1.9	8.4
25 to 34 years	2,627,099	236,732	1,891,131	460,006	39,230	32.1	32.8	35.7	22.6	33.0
35 to 44 years	2,425,944	222,537	1,475,783	692,474	35,150	29.7	30.8	27.8	34.1	29.6
45 to 54 years	1,490,323	136,238	857,901	474,363	21,821	18.2	18.8	16.2	23.3	18.4
55 to 64 years	729,030	48,223	432,340	239,622	8,845	8.9	6.7	8.2	11.8	7.4
65 to 74 years	288,066	15,201	166,414	103,575	2,876	3.5	2.1	3.1	5.1	2.4
75 years and over	69,722	4,413	40,740	23,783	786	.9	.6	.8	1.2	.7
Unknown	6,564	1,549	4,008	859	148	.1	.2	.1	-----	.1
Woman head, all ages	1,506,044	256,010	911,836	320,374	17,824	-----	-----	-----	-----	-----

Table 35.—FAMILIES CLASSIFIED BY SEX, AGE, COLOR, AND NATIVITY OF HEAD, BY TENURE, FOR THE UNITED STATES: 1930—Continued

[The age classification was limited to families with a man reported as head. Percent not shown where less than 1/10 of 1 percent]

AREA, TENURE, AND AGE OF MAN HEAD	NUMBER OF FAMILIES					PERCENT DISTRIBUTION				
	All classes	Negro	Native white	Foreign-born white	Other races	All classes	Negro	Native white	Foreign-born white	Other races
RURAL-FARM										
All families	6, 604, 637	978, 653	5, 006, 748	510, 889	108, 347					
Man head, all ages	6, 218, 390	875, 335	4, 760, 733	479, 291	103, 031	100. 0	100. 0	100. 0	100. 0	100. 0
Under 25 years	357, 550	96, 944	250, 251	2, 095	8, 260	5. 7	11. 1	5. 3	. 4	8. 0
25 to 34 years	1, 170, 855	186, 019	931, 656	27, 492	25, 688	18. 8	21. 3	19. 6	5. 7	24. 9
35 to 44 years	1, 505, 640	188, 555	1, 194, 789	95, 717	26, 579	24. 2	21. 5	25. 1	20. 0	25. 8
45 to 54 years	1, 453, 453	202, 714	1, 091, 550	136, 006	23, 183	23. 4	23. 2	22. 9	28. 4	22. 5
55 to 64 years	1, 037, 230	127, 655	775, 793	121, 476	12, 306	16. 7	14. 6	16. 3	25. 3	11. 9
65 to 74 years	541, 442	54, 814	406, 053	75, 534	5, 041	8. 7	6. 3	8. 5	15. 8	4. 9
75 years and over	149, 761	18, 058	109, 005	20, 850	1, 848	2. 4	2. 1	2. 3	4. 4	1. 8
Unknown	2, 459	576	1, 636	121	126		. 1			. 1
Woman head, all ages	386, 247	103, 318	246, 015	31, 598	5, 316					
Owner families	3, 452, 102	188, 574	2, 840, 831	391, 120	31, 577					
Man head, all ages	3, 208, 522	164, 218	2, 652, 005	363, 548	28, 751	100. 0	100. 0	100. 0	100. 0	100. 0
Under 25 years	36, 793	2, 788	32, 479	420	1, 106	1. 1	1. 7	1. 2	. 1	3. 8
25 to 34 years	318, 083	14, 119	288, 210	10, 659	5, 095	9. 9	8. 6	10. 9	2. 9	17. 7
35 to 44 years	716, 616	30, 617	618, 095	61, 115	6, 789	22. 3	18. 6	23. 3	16. 8	23. 6
45 to 54 years	868, 783	48, 040	709, 720	104, 166	6, 857	27. 1	29. 3	26. 8	28. 7	23. 8
55 to 64 years	726, 645	39, 300	579, 964	102, 277	5, 104	22. 6	23. 9	21. 9	28. 1	17. 8
65 to 74 years	420, 864	21, 285	330, 567	66, 401	2, 611	13. 1	13. 0	12. 5	18. 3	9. 1
75 years and over	119, 535	7, 949	92, 029	18, 423	1, 134	3. 7	4. 8	3. 5	5. 1	3. 9
Unknown	1, 203	120	941	87	55		. 1			. 2
Woman head, all ages	243, 580	24, 356	188, 826	27, 572	2, 826					
Tenant families	2, 952, 717	758, 014	2, 022, 067	103, 787	68, 849					
Man head, all ages	2, 826, 550	683, 799	1, 974, 777	101, 050	66, 924	100. 0	100. 0	100. 0	100. 0	100. 0
Under 25 years	300, 873	89, 604	203, 526	1, 497	6, 246	10. 6	13. 1	10. 3	1. 5	9. 3
25 to 34 years	810, 147	165, 400	610, 689	15, 553	18, 505	28. 7	24. 2	30. 9	15. 4	27. 7
35 to 44 years	748, 304	152, 498	545, 996	31, 798	18, 012	26. 5	22. 3	27. 6	31. 5	26. 9
45 to 54 years	548, 714	149, 265	356, 422	28, 075	14, 952	19. 4	21. 8	18. 0	27. 8	22. 3
55 to 64 years	285, 139	85, 010	177, 946	15, 705	6, 478	10. 1	12. 4	9. 0	15. 5	9. 7
65 to 74 years	106, 536	32, 039	65, 643	6, 757	2, 097	3. 8	4. 7	3. 3	6. 7	3. 1
75 years and over	25, 821	9, 556	14, 050	1, 637	578	. 9	1. 4	. 7	1. 7	. 9
Unknown	1, 016	427	505	28	56		. 1			. 1
Woman head, all ages	126, 167	74, 215	47, 290	2, 737	1, 925					
RURAL-NONFARM										
All families	5, 927, 502	496, 933	4, 639, 500	689, 999	101, 070					
Man head, all ages	5, 173, 031	394, 306	4, 084, 281	603, 770	90, 674	100. 0	100. 0	100. 0	100. 0	100. 0
Under 25 years	296, 305	40, 314	242, 883	5, 042	8, 066	5. 7	10. 2	5. 9	. 8	8. 9
25 to 34 years	1, 206, 958	99, 051	1, 018, 529	62, 460	26, 918	23. 3	25. 1	24. 9	10. 3	29. 7
35 to 44 years	1, 306, 958	97, 526	1, 028, 601	155, 683	25, 148	25. 3	24. 7	25. 2	25. 8	27. 7
45 to 54 years	1, 047, 773	82, 816	793, 791	154, 615	16, 551	20. 3	21. 0	19. 4	25. 6	18. 3
55 to 64 years	714, 111	43, 985	550, 611	111, 250	8, 265	13. 8	11. 2	13. 5	18. 4	9. 1
65 to 74 years	431, 030	20, 855	325, 464	80, 937	3, 774	8. 3	5. 3	8. 0	13. 4	4. 2
75 years and over	166, 306	9, 082	121, 945	33, 470	1, 809	3. 2	2. 3	3. 0	5. 5	2. 0
Unknown	3, 590	677	2, 457	313	143	. 1	. 2	. 1	. 1	. 2
Woman head, all ages	754, 471	102, 627	555, 219	86, 229	10, 396					
Owner families	3, 117, 418	165, 487	2, 473, 089	445, 318	33, 524					
Man head, all ages	2, 630, 340	125, 323	2, 096, 277	380, 228	28, 512	100. 0	100. 0	100. 0	100. 0	100. 0
Under 25 years	42, 168	3, 243	36, 756	954	1, 215	1. 6	2. 6	1. 8	. 3	4. 3
25 to 34 years	385, 976	17, 257	339, 932	22, 744	6, 043	14. 7	13. 8	16. 2	6. 0	21. 2
35 to 44 years	631, 770	29, 835	510, 752	83, 357	7, 826	24. 0	23. 8	24. 4	21. 9	27. 4
45 to 54 years	614, 655	35, 412	474, 823	98, 065	6, 355	23. 4	28. 3	22. 7	25. 8	22. 3
55 to 64 years	490, 431	22, 517	383, 319	80, 679	3, 916	18. 6	18. 0	18. 3	21. 2	13. 7
65 to 74 years	330, 993	11, 751	251, 488	65, 689	2, 065	12. 6	9. 4	12. 0	17. 3	7. 2
75 years and over	132, 701	5, 098	97, 993	28, 554	1, 056	5. 0	4. 1	4. 7	7. 5	3. 7
Unknown	1, 646	210	1, 214	186	36	. 1	. 2	. 1		. 1
Woman head, all ages	487, 078	40, 164	376, 812	65, 090	5, 012					
Tenant families	2, 685, 741	313, 404	2, 079, 340	233, 757	59, 240					
Man head, all ages	2, 438, 952	255, 201	1, 914, 694	214, 304	54, 753	100. 0	100. 0	100. 0	100. 0	100. 0
Under 25 years	239, 573	34, 536	195, 353	3, 827	5, 857	9. 8	13. 5	10. 2	1. 8	10. 7
25 to 34 years	791, 709	77, 936	656, 892	38, 338	18, 543	32. 5	30. 5	34. 3	17. 9	33. 9
35 to 44 years	653, 494	64, 834	503, 004	70, 140	15, 516	26. 8	25. 4	26. 3	32. 7	28. 3
45 to 54 years	416, 645	45, 183	307, 991	54, 479	8, 992	17. 1	17. 7	16. 1	25. 4	16. 4
55 to 64 years	212, 553	20, 252	159, 530	29, 016	3, 755	8. 7	7. 9	8. 3	13. 5	6. 9
65 to 74 years	93, 035	8, 464	69, 100	14, 062	1, 409	3. 8	3. 3	3. 6	6. 6	2. 6
75 years and over	30, 472	3, 583	21, 947	4, 344	598	1. 2	1. 4	1. 1	2. 0	1. 1
Unknown	1, 471	413	877	98	83		. 2			. 2
Woman head, all ages	246, 789	58, 203	164, 646	19, 453	4, 487					

Table 36.—NUMBER OF NEGRO FAMILIES FOR CITIES OF 100,000 OR MORE INHABITANTS: 1930 AND 1920

[Figures for 1930 represent private families only; those for 1920 include the small number of institutions and other quasi-family groups which were counted as families in that year]

CITY	NEGRO FAMILIES				CITY	NEGRO FAMILIES			
	1930	1920	Increase or decrease (−)			1930	1920	Increase or decrease (−)	
			Number	Percent				Number	Percent
Akron, Ohio	2, 471	1, 066	1, 405	131. 8	Canton, Ohio	719	281	438	155. 9
Albany, N. Y	628	306	322	105. 2	Chattanooga, Tenn	8, 848	5, 418	3, 430	63. 3
Atlanta, Ga	23, 450	18, 080	5, 370	29. 7	Chicago, Ill	55, 137	25, 684	29, 453	114. 7
Baltimore, Md	33, 102	26, 411	6, 691	25. 3	Cincinnati, Ohio	12, 634	8, 866	3, 768	42. 5
Birmingham, Ala	26, 429	19, 126	7, 303	38. 2	Cleveland, Ohio	17, 525	8, 155	9, 370	114. 9
Boston, Mass	5, 339	4, 403	936	21. 3	Columbus, Ohio	7, 995	5, 614	2, 381	42. 4
Bridgeport, Conn	900	576	324	56. 3	Dallas, Tex	10, 698	6, 374	4, 324	67. 8
Buffalo, N. Y	3, 241	1, 112	2, 129	191. 5	Dayton, Ohio	4, 342	2, 204	2, 138	97. 0
Cambridge, Mass	1, 305	1, 363	−58	−4. 3	Denver, Colo	2, 155	1, 618	537	33. 2
Camden, N. J	2, 710	2, 189	521	23. 8	Des Moines, Iowa	1, 487	1, 462	25	1. 7

Table 36.—NUMBER OF NEGRO FAMILIES FOR CITIES OF 100,000 OR MORE INHABITANTS: 1930 AND 1920—Con.

[See note at head of this table]

CITY	NEGRO FAMILIES			
	1930	1920	Increase or decrease (−)	
			Number	Percent
Detroit, Mich	25, 656	8, 357	17, 299	207. 0
Duluth, Minn	129	155	−26	−16. 8
Elizabeth, N. J	1, 120	427	693	162. 3
El Paso, Tex	567	380	187	49. 2
Erie, Pa	291	175	116	66. 3
Evansville, Ind	1, 720	1, 774	−54	−3. 0
Fall River, Mass	109	99	10	10. 1
Flint, Mich	1, 333	324	1, 009	311. 4
Fort Wayne, Ind	560	358	202	56. 4
Fort Worth, Tex	6, 239	4, 104	2, 135	52. 0
Gary, Ind	4, 336	1, 433	2, 903	202. 6
Grand Rapids, Mich	665	301	364	120. 9
Hartford, Conn	1, 675	980	695	70. 9
Houston, Tex	16, 966	9, 536	7, 430	77. 9
Indianapolis, Ind	11, 903	9, 388	2, 515	26. 8
Jacksonville, Fla	12, 179	11, 170	1, 009	9. 0
Jersey City, N. J	3, 075	1, 980	1, 095	55. 3
Kansas City, Kans	5, 631	4, 109	1, 522	37. 0
Kansas City, Mo	11, 436	8, 736	2, 700	30. 9
Knoxville, Tenn	4, 161	3, 021	1, 140	37. 7
Long Beach, Calif	106	47	59	125. 5
Los Angeles, Calif	11, 164	4, 368	6, 796	155. 6
Louisville, Ky	13, 909	12, 546	1, 363	10. 9
Lowell, Mass	31	41	−10	−24. 4
Lynn, Mass	212	211	1	. 5
Memphis, Tenn	29, 507	19, 132	10, 375	54. 2
Miami, Fla	6, 216	2, 351	3, 865	164. 4
Milwaukee, Wis	1, 810	599	1, 211	202. 2
Minneapolis, Minn	1, 199	1, 128	71	6. 3
Nashville, Tenn	12, 177	10, 923	1, 254	11. 5
Newark, N. J	9, 676	4, 277	5, 399	126. 2
New Bedford, Mass	818	1, 098	−280	−25. 5
New Haven, Conn	1, 460	1, 213	247	20. 4
New Orleans, La	34, 461	24, 942	9, 519	38. 2
New York, N. Y	77, 077	36, 063	41, 014	113. 7
Bronx Borough	2, 883	975	1, 908	195. 7
Brooklyn Borough	17, 016	7, 791	9, 225	118. 4
Manhattan Borough	52, 387	25, 807	26, 580	103. 0
Queens Borough	4, 237	1, 173	3, 064	261. 2
Richmond Borough	554	317	237	74. 8
Norfolk, Va	11, 488	11, 060	428	3. 9
Oakland, Calif	2, 122	1, 336	786	58. 8
Oklahoma City, Okla	3, 510	2, 052	1, 458	71. 1
Omaha, Nebr	3, 046	2, 648	398	15. 0
Paterson, N. J	757	425	332	78. 1
Peoria, Ill	626	606	20	3. 3
Philadelphia, Pa	50, 997	30, 995	20, 002	64. 5
Pittsburgh, Pa	12, 831	9, 039	3, 792	42. 0
Portland, Oreg	467	441	26	5. 9
Providence, R. I	1, 522	1, 565	−43	−2. 7
Reading, Pa	483	214	269	125. 7
Richmond, Va	13, 679	13, 307	372	2. 8
Rochester, N. Y	693	394	299	75. 9
St. Louis, Mo	23, 548	18, 573	4, 975	26. 8
St. Paul, Minn	1, 110	959	151	15. 7
Salt Lake City, Utah	200	221	−21	−9. 5
San Antonio, Tex	4, 847	3, 670	1, 177	32. 1
San Diego, Calif	829	324	505	155. 9
San Francisco, Calif	988	583	405	69. 5
Scranton, Pa	202	149	53	35. 6
Seattle, Wash	1, 005	760	245	32. 2
Somerville, Mass	68	79	−11	−13. 9
South Bend, Ind	807	302	505	167. 2
Spokane, Wash	204	216	−12	−5. 6
Springfield, Mass	851	666	185	27. 8
Syracuse, N. Y	488	344	144	41. 9
Tacoma, Wash	221	244	−23	−9. 4
Tampa, Fla	5, 369	3, 181	2, 188	68. 8
Toledo, Ohio	3, 198	1, 357	1, 841	135. 7
Trenton, N. J	1, 582	878	704	80. 2
Tulsa, Okla	3, 745	1, 972	1, 773	89. 9
Utica, N. Y	132	96	36	37. 5
Washington, D. C	29, 995	24, 929	5, 066	20. 3
Wichita, Kans	1, 415	934	481	51. 5
Wilmington, Del	3, 081	2, 527	554	21. 9
Worcester, Mass	313	304	9	3. 0
Yonkers, N. Y	790	476	314	66. 0
Youngstown, Ohio	3, 526	1, 574	1, 952	124. 0

Table 37.—MEDIAN SIZE OF NEGRO FAMILIES, BY TENURE, FOR CITIES OF 100,000 OR MORE INHABITANTS: 1930

[Median not shown where number of families is less than 100]

CITY	All families	Owner	Tenant
Akron, Ohio	3. 02	3. 79	2. 92
Albany, N. Y	2. 31	----	2. 29
Atlanta, Ga	2. 79	3. 07	2. 75
Baltimore, Md	2. 80	3. 24	2. 75
Birmingham, Ala	2. 80	3. 30	2. 70
Boston, Mass	2. 45	2. 74	2. 43
Bridgeport, Conn	2. 50	2. 42	2. 56
Buffalo, N. Y	2. 69	2. 49	2. 75
Cambridge, Mass	3. 16	3. 36	3. 11
Camden, N. J	2. 91	2. 90	2. 97
Canton, Ohio	2. 77	----	2. 71
Chattanooga, Tenn	2. 73	3. 02	2. 68
Chicago, Ill	2. 65	2. 99	2. 61
Cincinnati, Ohio	2. 59	3. 00	2. 56
Cleveland, Ohio	2. 76	3. 16	2. 73
Columbus, Ohio	2. 73	2. 95	2. 66
Dallas, Tex	2. 47	2. 83	2. 41
Dayton, Ohio	2. 81	3. 12	2. 69
Denver, Colo	2. 28	2. 34	2. 25
Des Moines, Iowa	2. 63	2. 74	2. 60
Detroit, Mich	2. 91	3. 37	2. 85
Duluth, Minn	2. 12	----	----
Elizabeth, N. J	3. 17	3. 29	3. 19
El Paso, Tex	2. 26	2. 38	2. 22
Erie, Pa	2. 85	----	2. 80
Evansville, Ind	2. 44	2. 58	2. 44
Fall River, Mass	2. 18	----	----
Flint, Mich	2. 75	3. 17	2. 51
Fort Wayne, Ind	2. 72	2. 80	2. 67
Fort Worth, Tex	2. 50	2. 77	2. 46
Gary, Ind	2. 86	3. 12	2. 79
Grand Rapids, Mich	2. 90	3. 05	2. 80
Hartford, Conn	3. 06	----	3. 07
Houston, Tex	2. 61	2. 99	2. 48
Indianapolis, Ind	2. 59	2. 79	2. 55
Jacksonville, Fla	2. 73	2. 90	2. 72
Jersey City, N. J	3. 00	3. 08	2. 99
Kansas City, Kans	2. 74	2. 79	2. 70
Kansas City, Mo	2. 23	2. 43	2. 22
Knoxville, Tenn	2. 88	3. 06	2. 81
Long Beach, Calif	2. 24	----	----
Los Angeles, Calif	2. 38	2. 67	2. 28
Louisville, Ky	2. 35	2. 71	2. 29
Lowell, Mass	----	----	----
Lynn, Mass	2. 93	----	3. 07
Memphis, Tenn	2. 38	2. 78	2. 30
Miami, Fla	2. 71	3. 38	2. 57
Milwaukee, Wis	2. 54	2. 96	2. 53
Minneapolis, Minn	2. 31	2. 60	2. 24
Nashville, Tenn	2. 56	2. 83	2. 47
Newark, N. J	2. 85	3. 03	2. 85
New Bedford, Mass	3. 66	3. 55	3. 81
New Haven, Conn	2. 47	2. 70	2. 45
New Orleans, La	2. 81	3. 42	2. 73
New York, N. Y	2. 61	3. 10	2. 59
Bronx Borough	3. 11	2. 97	3. 15
Brooklyn Borough	2. 84	3. 27	2. 83
Manhattan Borough	2. 48	2. 78	2. 48
Queens Borough	2. 92	3. 12	2. 83
Richmond Borough	2. 90	3. 14	2. 93
Norfolk, Va	2. 64	3. 22	2. 48
Oakland, Calif	2. 35	2. 67	2. 23
Oklahoma City, Okla	2. 61	3. 16	2. 51
Omaha, Nebr	2. 42	2. 65	2. 36
Paterson, N. J	2. 85	----	2. 85
Peoria, Ill	2. 53	2. 67	2. 51
Philadelphia, Pa	2. 79	2. 92	2. 79
Pittsburgh, Pa	2. 89	3. 19	2. 86
Portland, Oreg	2. 14	2. 27	2. 06
Providence, R. I	2. 44	2. 84	2. 40
Reading, Pa	2. 52	----	2. 49
Richmond, Va	2. 74	3. 06	2. 66
Rochester, N. Y	2. 46	2. 50	2. 46
St. Louis, Mo	2. 51	2. 97	2. 49
St. Paul, Minn	2. 39	2. 58	2. 29
Salt Lake City, Utah	2. 16	----	2. 03
San Antonio, Tex	2. 63	2. 82	2. 54
San Diego, Calif	2. 24	2. 34	2. 16
San Francisco, Calif	1. 98	2. 48	1. 92
Scranton, Pa	2. 34	----	2. 31
Seattle, Wash	2. 13	2. 31	2. 02
Somerville, Mass	----	----	----
South Bend, Ind	2. 89	3. 03	2. 90
Spokane, Wash	2. 24	2. 42	----
Springfield, Mass	2. 73	3. 13	2. 59
Syracuse, N. Y	2. 45	----	2. 45
Tacoma, Wash	2. 18	2. 42	2. 00
Tampa, Fla	2. 53	2. 74	2. 51
Toledo, Ohio	2. 59	2. 99	2. 50
Trenton, N. J	3. 43	3. 16	3. 51
Tulsa, Okla	2. 44	2. 83	2. 37
Utica, N. Y	2. 19	----	2. 14
Washington, D. C	2. 84	3. 11	2. 76
Wichita, Kans	2. 79	2. 98	2. 63
Wilmington, Del	2. 45	2. 81	2. 42
Worcester, Mass	3. 23	----	3. 23
Yonkers, N. Y	2. 73	2. 74	2. 77
Youngstown, Ohio	2. 95	3. 21	2. 88

TABLE 38.—HOMES OF NEGRO FAMILIES BY TENURE, FOR CITIES HAVING 10,000 OR MORE NEGRO INHABITANTS: 1930

STATE AND CITY	All homes	OWNED		RENTED		TENURE UNKNOWN	
		Number	Percent	Number	Percent	Number	Percent
ALABAMA							
Bessemer	3,307	713	21.6	2,547	77.0	47	1.4
Birmingham	26,429	4,709	17.8	21,213	80.3	507	1.9
Mobile	6,711	1,389	20.7	5,154	76.8	168	2.5
Montgomery	8,613	2,222	25.8	6,264	72.7	127	1.5
ARKANSAS							
Little Rock	5,140	1,752	34.1	3,246	63.2	142	2.8
CALIFORNIA							
Los Angeles	11,164	3,747	33.6	7,136	63.9	281	2.5
DELAWARE							
Wilmington	3,081	407	13.2	2,605	84.6	69	2.2
DISTRICT OF COLUMBIA							
Washington	29,995	7,316	24.4	21,413	71.4	1,266	4.2
FLORIDA							
Jacksonville	12,179	2.687	22.1	8,973	73.7	519	4.3
Miami	6,216	1,099	17.7	5,015	80.7	102	1.6
Tampa	5,369	830	15.5	4,397	81.9	142	2.6
GEORGIA							
Atlanta	23,450	3,654	15.6	19,530	83.3	266	1.1
Augusta	6,865	1,269	18.5	5,363	78.1	233	3.4
Columbus	3,686	634	17.2	2,945	79.9	107	2.9
Macon	6,691	1,227	18.3	5,315	79.4	149	2.2
Savannah	11,592	1,180	10.2	10,135	87.4	277	2.4
ILLINOIS							
Chicago	55,137	5,767	10.5	48,601	88.1	769	1.4
East St. Louis	3,009	875	29.1	1,965	65.3	169	5.6
INDIANA							
Gary	4,336	882	20.3	3,325	76.7	129	3.0
Indianapolis	11,903	2,887	24.3	8,713	73.2	303	2.5
KANSAS							
Kansas City	5,631	2,898	51.5	2,607	46.3	126	2.2
KENTUCKY							
Lexington	3,883	1,032	26.6	2,783	71.7	68	1.8
Louisville	13,909	2,790	20.1	10,892	78.3	227	1.6
LOUISIANA							
Baton Rouge	2,956	990	33.5	1,878	63.5	88	3.0
Monroe	2,976	590	19.8	2,343	78.7	43	1.4
New Orleans	34,461	4,566	13.2	29,093	84.4	802	2.3
Shreveport	7,818	2,274	29.1	5,418	69.3	126	1.6
MARYLAND							
Baltimore	33,102	3,793	11.5	28,182	85.1	1,127	3.4
MASSACHUSETTS							
Boston	5,339	727	13.6	4,431	83.0	181	3.4
MICHIGAN							
Detroit	25,656	3,841	15.0	20,775	81.0	1,040	4.1
MISSISSIPPI							
Jackson	4.797	1,200	25.0	3,442	71.8	155	3.2
Meridian	3,392	910	26.8	2,440	71.9	42	1.2
Vicksburg	4,165	1,058	25.4	3,037	72.9	70	1.7
MISSOURI							
Kansas City	11,436	1,825	16.0	9,044	79.1	567	5.0
St. Louis	23,548	2,198	9.3	20,546	87.3	804	3.4
NEBRASKA							
Omaha	3,046	977	32.1	1,987	65.2	82	2.7
NEW JERSEY							
Atlantic City	3,910	507	13.0	3,303	84.5	100	2.6
Camden	2,710	536	19.8	2,068	76.3	106	3.9
Jersey City	3,075	476	15.5	2,558	83.2	41	1.3
Newark	9,676	494	5.1	9,013	93.1	169	1.7
NEW YORK							
Buffalo	3,241	215	6.6	2,887	89.1	139	4.3
New York	77,077	4,280	5.6	71,687	93.0	1,110	1.4
Bronx Borough	2,883	162	5.6	2,575	89.3	146	5.1
Brooklyn Borough	17,016	1,511	8.9	14,929	87.7	566	3.4
Manhattan Borough	52,387	954	1.8	51,166	97.7	267	.5
Queens Borough	4,237	1,551	36.6	2,583	61.0	103	2.4
Richmond Borough	554	102	18.4	434	78.3	18	3.2
NORTH CAROLINA							
Asheville	3,205	902	28.1	2,261	70.5	42	1.3
Charlotte	6,407	1,122	17.5	5,111	79.8	174	2.7
Durham	4,188	910	21.7	3,162	75.5	116	2.8
Greensboro	3,053	946	31.0	2,019	66.1	88	2.9
Raleigh	2,735	926	33.9	1,790	65.5	19	.7
Wilmington	3,414	1,165	34.1	2,202	64.5	47.	1.4
Winston-Salem	8,180	1,268	15.5	6,889	84.2	23	.3
OHIO							
Akron	2,471	462	18.7	1,906	77.1	103	4.2
Cincinnati	12,634	1,126	8.9	11,244	89.0	264	2.1
Cleveland	17,525	1,451	8.3	15,634	89.2	440	2.5
Columbus	7,995	1,939	24.3	5,901	73.8	155	1.9
Dayton	4,342	1,280	29.5	2,945	67.8	117	2.7
Toledo	3,198	686	21.5	2,417	75.6	95	3.0
Youngstown	3,526	698	19.8	2,785	79.0	43	1.2
OKLAHOMA							
Oklahoma City	3,510	959	27.3	2,303	65.6	248	7.1
Tulsa	3,745	1,197	32.0	2,413	64.4	135	3.6
PENNSYLVANIA							
Philadelphia	50,997	7,830	15.4	41,145	80.7	2,022	4.0
Pittsburgh	12,831	2,121	16.5	10,358	80.7	352	2.7
SOUTH CAROLINA							
Charleston	8,869	904	10.2	7,767	87.6	198	2.2
Columbia	4,488	891	19.9	3,481	77.6	116	2.6
Greenville	2,981	417	14.0	2,487	83.4	77	2.6
TENNESSEE							
Chattanooga	8,848	1,406	15.9	7,261	82.1	181	2.0
Knoxville	4,161	1,286	30.9	2,727	65.5	148	3.6
Memphis	29,507	7,564	25.6	20,561	69.7	1,382	4.7
Nashville	12,177	3,469	28.5	8,456	69.4	252	2.1
TEXAS							
Beaumont	4,863	1,338	27.5	3,302	68.0	223	4.6
Dallas	10,698	2,659	24.9	7,460	69.7	579	5.4
Fort Worth	6,239	1,852	29.7	4,056	65.0	331	5.3
Galveston	3,756	508	13.5	3,189	84.9	59	1.6
Houston	16,966	5,331	31.4	11,118	65.5	517	3.0
Port Arthur	2,705	650	24.0	1,934	71.5	121	4.5
San Antonio	4,847	2,006	41.4	2,698	55.7	143	3.0
VIRGINIA							
Newport News	3,513	807	23.0	2,673	76.1	33	.9
Norfolk	11,488	2,453	21.4	8,870	77.2	165	1.4
Petersburg	3,472	825	23.8	2,584	74.4	63	1.8
Portsmouth	5,096	1,496	29.4	3,569	70.0	31	.6
Richmond	13,679	2,773	20.3	10,798	78.9	108	.8
Roanoke	2,806	1,082	38.6	1,700	60.6	24	.9

Table 39.—POPULATION, NUMBER OF OWNED HOMES, AND NUMBER OF PERSONS PER HOME, BY COLOR, FOR CITIES AND OTHER URBAN PLACES HAVING 10,000 OR MORE INHABITANTS: 1930

[Cities or other urban places having less than 100 Negro-owned homes are omitted]

CITY OR OTHER URBAN PLACE	POPULATION		NUMBER OF OWNED HOMES		PERSONS PER OWNED HOME	
	Negro	White	Negro	White	Negro	White
ALABAMA						
Anniston	7,161	15,182	544	1,136	13	13
Bessemer	11,691	9,028	713	966	16	9
Birmingham	99,077	160,551	4,709	16,867	21	10
Decatur	3,867	11,726	382	1,246	10	9
Dothan	6,194	9,852	317	899	20	11
Fairfield	6,393	4,666	650	440	10	11
Florence	2,751	8,978	351	904	8	10
Gadsden	6,345	17,696	343	1,284	18	14
Huntsville	3,825	7,729	441	687	9	11
Mobile	24,514	43,606	1,389	4,521	18	10
Montgomery	29,970	36,105	2,222	3,486	13	10
Phenix City	4,065	9,797	329	751	12	13
Selma	9,249	8,763	853	801	11	11
Tuscaloosa	7,075	13,583	548	973	13	14
ARIZONA						
Phoenix	2,366	37,857	181	3,875	13	10
ARKANSAS						
Blytheville	2,731	7,367	189	627	14	12
El Dorado	3,836	12,566	398	1,248	10	10
Fort Smith	3,467	27,915	304	3,211	11	9
Hot Springs	4,194	16,032	544	1,598	8	10
Jonesboro	1,316	9,008	164	1,070	8	8
Little Rock	19,698	61,954	1,752	6,776	11	9
North Little Rock	6,097	13,301	699	1,412	9	9
Pine Bluff	6,163	14,593	583	1,574	11	9
Texarkana	3,109	7,639	393	1,158	8	7
CALIFORNIA						
Berkeley	2,177	77,508	370	12,037	6	6
Fresno	838	46,844	132	6,987	6	7
Los Angeles	38,894	1,073,584	3,747	127,852	10	8
Oakland	7,503	267,473	752	39,437	10	7
Pasadena	3,015	69,143	406	11,091	7	6
Riverside	604	24,623	111	4,366	5	6
Sacramento	1,086	85,262	110	11,171	10	8
San Diego	2,723	134,024	374	20,577	7	7
San Francisco	3,803	594,969	134	56,663	28	11
COLORADO						
Colorado Springs	965	31,828	173	5,152	6	6
Denver	7,204	272,977	827	34,616	9	8
Pueblo	1,305	45,131	226	6,152	6	7
CONNECTICUT						
Bridgeport	3,314	143,325	111	10,444	30	14
New Haven	5,302	157,254	163	12,017	33	13
DELAWARE						
Wilmington	12,080	94,459	407	11,127	30	8
DISTRICT OF COLUMBIA						
Washington	132,068	353,914	7,316	39,874	18	9
FLORIDA						
Daytona Beach	5,426	11,161	666	1,606	8	7
Gainesville	4,106	6,355	421	689	10	9
Jacksonville	48,196	81,320	2,687	7,833	18	10
Key West	2,274	10,548	155	976	15	11
Lakeland	3,941	14,610	354	1,695	11	9
Miami	25,116	85,461	1,099	8,931	23	10
Orlando	7,590	19,735	599	2,642	13	7
Pensacola	9,583	21,965	771	2,046	12	11
St. Augustine	3,293	8,812	336	1,091	10	8
St. Petersburg	7,416	32,972	413	5,826	18	6
Sanford	4,884	5,216	429	634	11	8
Tallahassee	4,401	6,292	509	629	9	10
Tampa	21,172	79,822	830	8,066	26	10
West Palm Beach	8,999	17,596	582	1,905	15	9
GEORGIA						
Albany	7,394	7,112	414	584	18	12
Athens	6,378	11,813	548	961	12	12
Atlanta	90,075	180,247	3,654	16,021	25	11
Augusta	24,190	35,997	1,269	2,707	19	13
Brunswick	6,049	7,972	453	628	13	13
Columbus	14,157	28,972	634	1,822	22	16
Griffin	3,396	6,923	193	508	18	14
La Grange	5,471	14,658	226	529	24	28
Macon	23,158	30,664	1,227	2,317	19	13
Rome	4,737	17,097	405	1,436	12	12
Savannah	38,896	46,069	1,180	3,385	33	14
Thomasville	6,074	5,659	821	633	7	9
Valdosta	6,265	7,217	549	645	11	11
Waycross	5,956	9,554	704	839	8	11
ILLINOIS						
Alton	2,714	27,321	302	3,663	9	7
Aurora	936	45,348	129	7,476	7	6
Cairo	4,575	8,948	267	1,032	17	9
Centralia	1,108	11,466	154	1,923	7	6
Champaign	1,598	18,738	201	2,804	8	7
Chicago	233,903	3,117,731	5,767	255,906	41	12
Danville	2,565	34,173	305	5,210	8	7
Decatur	1,947	55,545	231	8,430	8	7
East St. Louis	11,536	62,769	875	7,001	13	9
Evanston	4,938	58,338	350	5,904	14	10
Galesburg	891	27,671	152	4,692	6	6
Jacksonville	1,053	16,693	167	1,955	6	9
Peoria	3,037	101,735	144	12,971	21	8
Quincy	1,145	38,062	133	5,429	9	7
Springfield	3,324	68,517	442	9,607	8	7
INDIANA						
Anderson	1,387	38,406	200	5,380	7	7
East Chicago	5,088	44,308	177	3,879	29	11
Evansville	6,514	95,714	397	11,798	16	8
Fort Wayne	2,360	112,505	161	16,738	15	7
Gary	17,922	78,992	882	8,263	20	10
Indianapolis	43,967	320,064	2,887	38,175	15	8
Jeffersonville	1,296	10,650	156	1,419	8	8
Kokomo	1,143	31,692	117	3,945	10	8
Marion	1,056	23,409	185	3,277	6	7
Muncie	2,646	43,870	325	5,978	8	7
New Albany	1,292	24,527	173	3,498	7	7
Richmond	2,139	30,336	236	4,036	9	8
South Bend	3,431	100,689	234	14,810	15	7
Terre Haute	3,461	59,322	395	7,916	9	7
IOWA						
Des Moines	5,428	136,724	567	18,750	10	7
Keokuk	846	14,250	130	2,238	7	6
Waterloo	1,214	44,894	148	6,135	8	7
KANSAS						
Atchison	1,517	11,378	286	1,702	5	7
Coffeyville	1,824	14,079	289	1,802	6	8
Fort Scott	729	10,105	138	1,488	5	7
Hutchinson	954	25,732	137	3,587	7	7
Independence	1,104	11,558	152	1,714	7	7
Kansas City	19,872	99,161	2,898	14,231	7	7
Lawrence	1,437	12,178	313	2,073	5	6
Leavenworth	2,184	15,241	388	2,720	6	6
Parsons	1,277	13,372	196	1,808	7	7
Topeka	5,756	56,602	925	8,779	6	6
Wichita	5,623	104,322	654	13,408	9	8
KENTUCKY						
Bowling Green	2,426	9,916	303	1,278	8	8
Covington	3,466	61,770	243	7,925	14	8
Frankfort	2,205	9,413	162	770	14	12
Henderson	2,346	9,322	282	1,143	8	8
Hopkinsville	3,980	6,766	475	828	8	8
Lexington	12,759	32,972	1,032	3,266	12	10
Louisville	47,354	260,347	2,790	30,097	17	9
Middlesborough	1,021	9,329	129	981	8	10
Owensboro	2,509	20,256	235	2,087	11	10
Paducah	6,744	26,795	560	2,690	12	10
LOUISIANA						
Alexandria	9,546	13,476	586	1,443	16	9
Baton Rouge	10,675	20,048	990	1,792	11	11
Bogalusa	4,751	9,275	260	749	18	12
Lafayette	5,013	9,615	634	1,277	8	8
Lake Charles	5,948	9,830	647	1,262	9	8
Monroe	10,112	15,846	590	1,540	17	10
New Orleans	129,632	327,729	4,566	25,959	28	13
Shreveport	27,219	49,293	2,274	5,643	12	9
MARYLAND						
Annapolis	3,218	9,125	186	714	17	13
Baltimore	142,106	662,124	3,793	93,684	37	7
Salisbury	1,912	9,077	160	1,335	12	7
MASSACHUSETTS						
Boston	20,574	758,756	727	45,271	28	17
Cambridge	5,419	108,046	327	6,149	17	18
Everett City	1,002	47,395	132	4,433	8	11
New Bedford	3,631	108,868	205	9,256	18	12
Springfield	3,141	146,665	163	13,075	19	11
MICHIGAN						
Ann Arbor	940	25,934	105	4,416	9	6
Battle Creek	1,795	41,696	220	6,455	8	6
Detroit	120,066	1,440,141	3,841	149,158	31	10
Ecorse	1,417	11,280	209	1,276	7	9
Flint	5,725	150,023	466	22,038	12	7
Grand Rapids	2,795	165,555	233	25,669	12	6
Hamtramck	4,068	52,111	169	5,261	24	10
Jackson	1,692	53,343	158	8,411	11	6
Kalamazoo	967	53,749	115	7,894	8	7
Lansing	1,409	76,939	156	11,633	9	7
Pontiac	2,553	61,529	199	7,579	13	8
River Rouge	2,145	15,116	283	1,675	8	9
Saginaw	2,853	75,743	137	12,695	21	6
Ypsilanti	1,294	8,830	219	1,545	6	6
MINNESOTA						
Minneapolis	4,176	459,479	308	54,066	14	8
St. Paul	4,001	266,645	413	33,922	10	8
MISSISSIPPI						
Biloxi	2,445	12,393	245	1,283	10	10
Clarksdale	5,025	5,010	325	468	15	11
Columbus	4,862	5,878	458	642	11	9
Greenville	8,370	6,348	804	601	10	11
Greenwood	5,385	5,738	328	603	16	10
Gulfport	3,158	9,385	298	1,052	11	9
Hattiesburg	6,811	11,779	664	1,446	10	8
Jackson	19,423	28,854	1,200	2,832	16	10
Laurel	6,838	11,175	492	1,229	14	9
McComb	2,013	8,039	188	1,020	11	8
Meridian	11,352	20,602	910	2,303	12	9
Natchez	7,159	6,255	532	609	13	10
Vicksburg	11,915	11,017	1,058	1,120	11	10

Table 39.—POPULATION, NUMBER OF OWNED HOMES, AND NUMBER OF PERSONS PER HOME, BY COLOR, FOR CITIES AND OTHER URBAN PLACES HAVING 10,000 OR MORE INHABITANTS: 1930—Continued

CITY OR OTHER URBAN PLACE	POPULATION		NUMBER OF OWNED HOMES		PERSONS PER OWNED HOME	
	Negro	White	Negro	White	Negro	White
MISSOURI						
Columbia	2,301	12,661	243	1,905	9	7
Hannibal	2,013	20.743	212	2,682	9	8
Independence	846	14,137	146	2,116	6	7
Jefferson City	2,164	19.407	137	2,147	16	9
Joplin	755	32,562	101	4,791	7	7
Kansas City	38,574	357,741	1,825	40,475	21	9
Moberly	1,024	12,748	119	2,005	9	6
St. Joseph	4.055	76,424	280	8,260	14	9
St. Louis	93,580	726,879	2,198	64,982	43	11
Sedalia	2,106	18,649	336	2,632	6	7
Springfield	1,779	55,740	264	7,885	7	7
Webster Groves	975	15,509	157	2,979	6	5
NEBRASKA						
Lincoln	997	74,634	116	10,546	9	7
Omaha	11,123	201,657	977	26,883	11	8
NEW JERSEY						
Asbury Park	3,549	11,412	255	1,471	14	8
Atlantic City	15,611	50,514	507	3,684	31	14
Bridgeton	1,526	14,166	113	2,277	14	6
Burlington	1,408	9.433	107	1,460	13	6
Camden	11,340	107,283	536	13,051	21	8
East Orange	4,880	63.087	293	6,476	17	10
Elizabeth	4,761	109,732	101	10,150	47	11
Englewood	2,524	15,263	208	2,198	12	7
Hackensack	2,530	22.000	168	3.045	15	7
Jersey City	12,575	303,887	476	17,738	26	17
Long Branch	1,609	16,778	118	2,604	14	6
Montclair	6,384	35.588	306	5,439	21	7
Neptune township	1,869	8,753	201	1,545	9	6
Newark	38,880	402.596	494	26,242	79	15
Orange	5,027	30,353	215	2,828	23	11
Pensauken township	1,405	15.509	163	2,567	9	6
Plainfield	3,648	30.744	239	4,063	15	8
Pleasantville	1,992	9,569	352	1,662	6	6
Red Bank	1,596	10.013	148	1,462	11	7
Trenton	8,057	115,236	242	14,298	33	8
Union township	1,633	14,836	178	2,616	9	6
NEW YORK						
Buffalo	13,563	558.869	215	59,347	63	9
New Rochelle	4,644	49.264	190	5,378	24	15
New York	327,706	6,587,225	4,280	344,418	77	19
Bronx Borough	12,930	1,251,747	162	33,806	80	37
Brooklyn Borough	68,921	2,488,448	1,511	156,527	46	16
Manhattan Borough	224,670	1,631,756	954	10,725	236	152
Queens Borough	18,609	1,059,680	1,551	124,356	12	9
Richmond Borough	2,576	155,594	102	19,004	25	8
Rochester	2,679	325,294	148	42,362	18	8
Yonkers	3,332	131,234	116	10,147	29	13
NORTH CAROLINA						
Asheville	14,255	35,933	902	3,534	16	10
Charlotte	25,163	57,490	1,122	5,072	22	11
Concord	1,966	9,853	219	994	9	10
Durham	18,717	33,313	910	2,440	21	14
Elizabeth City	3,722	6,314	313	748	12	8
Fayetteville	5,357	7,685	376	725	14	11
Gastonia	3,207	13,886	235	774	14	18
Goldsboro	6,868	8,117	393	712	17	11
Greensboro	14,050	39,515	946	3,244	15	12
High Point	7,229	29,503	430	2,555	17	12
Kinston	5,062	6,298	331	584	15	11
New Bern	6,277	5,703	487	537	13	11
Raleigh	12,575	24,794	926	1,993	14	12
Rocky Mount	8,702	12,704	605	1,112	14	11
Salisbury	3,964	12,981	332	1,289	12	10
Shelby	2,125	8,664	147	731	14	12
Statesville	1,648	8,842	159	1,028	10	9
Thomasville	1,672	8,418	136	758	12	11
Wilmington	13,106	19,159	1,165	1,869	11	10
Wilson	6,205	6,407	316	631	20	10
Winston-Salem	32,566	42,705	1,268	3,968	26	11
OHIO						
Akron	11,080	243,744	462	31,262	24	8
Chillicothe	1,275	17,063	144	2.446	9	7
Cincinnati	47,818	403,112	1,126	44,124	42	9
Cleveland	71,899	827,090	1,451	79,692	50	10
Columbus	32,774	257,595	1,939	30,423	17	8
Dayton	17,077	183,831	1,280	23,725	13	8
Hamilton	1,958	50,204	144	6,884	14	7
Ironton	928	15.692	138	2,115	7	7
Lima	1,422	40,848	163	5,071	9	8
Middletown	2,805	27,186	211	2,950	13	9
Portsmouth	1,891	40,658	140	4,752	14	9
Springfield	8,249	60,461	818	7,630	10	8
Toledo	13,260	276,741	686	36,400	19	8
Warren	2,548	38,493	122	5,167	21	7
Xenia	2,166	8,337	390	1,259	6	7
Youngstown	14,552	155,108	698	19,488	21	8
Zanesville	1,776	34,659	239	5,333	7	6
OKLAHOMA						
Ardmore	2,069	13,296	283	1,546	7	9
Chickasha	1,625	12,403	226	1,599	7	8
Enid	763	25,376	119	3,571	6	7
McAlester	1,348	9,771	189	1,291	7	8
Muskogee	6,576	24,063	850	2,768	8	9
Oklahoma City	14,662	169,033	959	16,698	15	10
Okmulgee	3,213	13,044	416	1,474	8	9
Sapulpa	1,039	9,181	137	1,049	8	9
Shawnee	1,044	21,763	103	2,582	10	8
Tulsa	15,203	123,896	1,197	12,556	13	10
Wewoka	1,575	8,709	156	622	10	14
OREGON						
Portland	1,559	296,177	199	46,629	8	6
PENNSYLVANIA						
Abington township	1,334	17,304	163	3,346	8	5
Aliquippa	2,592	24,516	131	2,225	20	11
Chester	9,245	49,870	412	5,662	22	9
Harrisburg	6,382	73,922	349	9,774	18	8
Lower Merion township	2,919	32,212	130	4,611	22	7
Norristown	2,118	33,720	126	4,507	17	7
Philadelphia	219,599	1,728,457	7,830	224,783	28	8
Pittsburgh	54,983	614,317	2,121	60,204	26	10
Steelton	2,532	10,711	181	1,277	14	8
Uniontown	1,107	18,428	105	2,256	11	8
Washington	2,029	22,505	163	2,768	12	8
West Chester	2,086	10,230	192	1,521	11	7
Williamsport	934	44,786	108	5,497	9	8
York	2,266	52,978	106	7,455	21	7
RHODE ISLAND						
East Providence	764	29.209	108	4,166	7	7
Newport	1,554	26,019	120	2,776	13	9
Providence	5,473	247,271	194	19,539	28	13
SOUTH CAROLINA						
Anderson	3,833	10,550	290	940	13	11
Charleston	28,062	34,177	904	2,579	31	13
Columbia	19,519	32,042	891	2,604	22	12
Florence	6,067	8,706	493	792	12	11
Greenville	10,871	18,279	417	1,745	26	10
Greenwood	3,512	7,508	220	519	16	14
Rock Hill	2,410	8,895	172	636	14	13
Spartanburg	9,826	18,892	630	1,607	16	12
Sumpter	5,145	6,634	341	631	15	11
TENNESSEE						
Bristol	959	11,045	155	1,370	6	8
Chattanooga	33,289	86,495	1,406	8,233	24	11
Jackson	7,595	14,575	567	1,787	13	8
Johnson City	2,335	22,734	233	1,973	10	12
Knoxville	17,093	88,705	1,286	8,575	13	10
Memphis	96,550	156,528	7,564	17,400	13	9
Nashville	42,836	111,025	3,469	11,319	12	10
TEXAS						
Austin	9,868	38,209	1,179	4,535	8	8
Beaumont	18,551	38,507	1,338	3,868	14	10
Cleburne	867	10,615	125	1,428	7	7
Corsicana	3,332	11,585	398	1,400	8	8
Dallas	38,742	215,720	2,659	22,289	15	10
Denison	2,621	11,172	436	1,525	6	7
El Paso	1,855	41,965	173	4,595	11	9
Fort Worth	22,234	137,197	1,852	17,153	12	8
Galveston	13,226	37,060	508	4,105	26	9
Greenville	2,086	10,260	220	1,423	9	7
Houston	63,337	214,687	5,331	23,678	12	9
Marshall	6,693	9,459	944	1,221	7	8
Palestine	3,227	8,142	373	970	9	8
Paris	3,265	12,362	322	1,474	10	8
Port Arthur	10,003	38,975	650	4,164	15	9
San Angelo	1,653	20,949	136	2,562	12	8
San Antonio	17,978	130,737	2,006	16,075	9	8
Sherman	2,014	13,589	313	1,840	6	7
Temple	2,802	11,915	247	1,521	11	8
Texarkana	4,934	11,649	597	1,593	8	7
Tyler	4,092	12,980	466	1,455	9	9
Waco	9,370	41,771	845	4,459	11	9
Wichita Falls	4,312	38,643	350	4,159	12	9
VIRGINIA						
Alexandria	4,912	19,230	453	2,330	11	8
Bristol	1,184	7,653	157	820	8	9
Charlottesville	4,083	11,158	497	1,314	8	8
Danville	5,519	16,722	560	1,775	10	9
Lynchburg	9,653	31,007	965	3,159	10	10
Newport News	13,281	21,120	807	1,963	16	11
Norfolk	43,942	85,514	2,453	8,037	18	11
Petersburg	12,600	15,962	825	1,329	15	12
Portsmouth	18,849	26,781	1,496	2,610	13	10
Richmond	52,988	129,871	2,773	12,032	19	11
Roanoke	12,368	56,834	1,082	6,270	11	9
Staunton	1,805	10,175	189	966	10	11
Suffolk	3,806	6,461	279	713	14	9
Winchester	1,043	9,811	102	1,166	10	8
WASHINGTON						
Seattle	3,303	350,548	390	49,909	8	7
Spokane	617	114,327	129	18,184	5	6
Tacoma	730	104,559	108	18,410	7	6
WEST VIRGINIA						
Bluefield	3,363	15,974	348	1,771	10	9
Charleston	6,734	53,644	413	4,532	16	12
Clarksburg	1,211	27,654	111	3,083	11	9
Huntington	4,630	70,925	293	6,829	16	10
Parkersburg	875	28,745	103	3,519	8	8
Wheeling	2,192	59,450	110	6,671	20	9
WISCONSIN						
Milwaukee	7,501	568,807	100	60,566	75	9

TABLE 40.—OWNED NONFARM HOMES OF NEGRO FAMILIES BY VALUE, WITH MEDIAN VALUE, FOR CITIES OF 100,000 OR MORE INHABITANTS: 1930

[Median not shown where number of families reporting value is less than 100]

CITY	All owned nonfarm homes	NUMBER OF HOMES WITH VALUE—											Median value
		Under $1,000	$1,000 to $1,499	$1,500 to $1,999	$2,000 to $2,999	$3,000 to $4,999	$5,000 to $7,499	$7,500 to $9,999	$10,000 to $14,999	$15,000 to $19,999	$20,000 and over	Not reported	
Akron, Ohio	462	10	5	17	61	251	101	8	-	3	-	6	$4,076
Albany, N. Y	62	1	1	2	6	14	21	8	4	-	2	3	-
Atlanta, Ga	3,653	452	526	371	845	1,069	269	49	39	9	3	21	2,553
Baltimore, Md	3,793	32	115	110	453	1,630	1,099	139	56	10	2	147	4,366
Birmingham, Ala	4,705	599	740	749	1,276	917	285	46	25	3	6	59	2,184
Boston, Mass	726	-	8	19	66	140	261	118	73	16	8	17	6,164
Bridgeport, Conn	111	11	3	6	14	33	34	3	3	1	1	2	4,242
Buffalo, N. Y	215	1	-	1	9	57	82	34	22	3	2	4	6,143
Cambridge, Mass	327	1	4	11	22	100	107	41	29	10	-	2	5,572
Camden, N. J	536	11	24	38	113	258	59	6	11	1	2	13	3,585
Canton, Ohio	78	-	1	9	20	33	13	2	-	-	-	-	-
Chattanooga, Tenn	1,406	124	174	203	392	339	116	26	14	3	1	14	2,497
Chicago, Ill	5,765	49	92	84	407	1,251	1,682	818	722	245	269	146	6,377
Cincinnati, Ohio	1,126	30	49	59	153	339	271	106	52	19	11	37	4,496
Cleveland, Ohio	1,451	7	13	12	63	283	592	307	114	21	10	29	6,406
Columbus, Ohio	1,939	28	57	115	317	843	463	75	24	3	3	11	4,060
Dallas, Tex	2,658	264	431	383	653	641	129	32	23	8	9	85	2,319
Dayton, Ohio	1,280	20	45	71	229	624	241	25	11	3	3	8	3,869
Denver, Colo	827	31	65	75	187	356	81	6	5	1	-	20	3,256
Des Moines, Iowa	566	112	117	110	121	82	18	2	-	-	-	4	1,736
Detroit, Mich	3,841	26	52	52	208	819	1,347	832	346	65	33	61	6,360
Duluth, Minn	51	-	5	4	8	21	9	3	-	1	-	-	-
Elizabeth, N. J	101	-	-	1	2	31	35	13	12	2	3	2	-
El Paso, Tex	173	8	19	23	48	60	13	1	-	-	-	1	2,750
Erie, Pa	58	-	1	1	7	30	14	1	2	2	-	-	-
Evansville, Ind	397	50	43	82	109	79	8	1	3	1	-	21	2,119
Fall River, Mass	10	1	-	-	-	6	3	-	-	-	-	-	-
Flint, Mich	466	7	12	15	67	190	136	13	8	-	-	18	4,295
Fort Wayne, Ind	161	4	9	19	37	65	20	-	2	-	-	5	3,277
Fort Worth, Tex	1,852	498	351	309	386	207	43	3	5	1	1	48	1,586
Gary, Ind	882	35	42	41	157	313	177	46	35	8	10	18	4,003
Grand Rapids, Mich	233	8	11	19	51	76	53	10	4	-	-	1	3,711
Hartford, Conn	91	-	-	-	2	6	16	17	34	8	1	7	-
Houston, Tex	5,330	470	569	665	1,664	1,357	299	55	66	16	20	149	2,533
Indianapolis, Ind	2,886	134	230	426	699	994	285	35	15	-	2	66	2,887
Jacksonville, Fla	2,687	509	498	434	592	385	118	30	14	14	10	83	1,840
Jersey City, N. J	476	-	1	3	9	87	161	101	75	16	11	12	7,050
Kansas City, Kans	2,897	693	575	515	588	405	76	10	6	1	2	26	1,663
Kansas City, Mo	1,825	60	133	147	424	677	259	57	24	4	7	33	3,390
Knoxville, Tenn	1,285	185	185	227	329	253	51	10	5	1	-	39	2,079
Long Beach, Calif	32	-	-	1	5	8	5	4	7	1	1	-	-
Los Angeles, Calif	3,746	24	70	107	357	1,177	1,290	298	192	69	43	119	5,152
Louisville, Ky	2,790	266	306	352	677	797	282	49	20	6	5	30	2,674
Lowell, Mass	6	1	1	1	1	2	-	-	-	-	-	-	-
Lynn, Mass	48	-	3	5	10	14	14	1	1	-	-	-	-
Memphis, Tenn	7,556	1,191	1,640	1,570	1,544	1,144	219	46	22	8	5	167	1,775
Miami, Fla	1,099	166	192	113	225	296	59	14	14	-	6	14	2,318
Milwaukee, Wis	100	-	1	3	7	30	28	17	8	2	1	3	-
Minneapolis, Minn	308	9	11	13	31	116	111	9	4	-	1	3	4,526
Nashville, Tenn	3,469	549	814	628	779	468	129	36	12	3	1	50	1,776
Newark, N. J	492	-	-	2	23	110	156	73	71	22	13	22	6,603
New Bedford, Mass	205	-	9	18	52	76	27	10	6	-	-	7	3,526
New Haven, Conn	163	-	1	-	5	45	60	26	20	4	1	1	6,250
New Orleans, La	4,563	463	557	516	916	1,351	504	132	57	22	13	32	2,796
New York, N. Y	4,278	5	11	10	41	376	1,276	902	893	431	228	105	8,519
Bronx Borough	162	-	-	-	5	12	39	30	53	18	4	1	9,542
Brooklyn Borough	1,511	1	3	1	9	109	336	396	485	105	28	38	9,252
Manhattan Borough	954	1	2	3	3	33	226	45	185	262	178	16	14,216
Queens Borough	1,551	2	3	4	19	190	645	422	163	45	18	40	7,083
Richmond Borough	100	1	3	2	5	32	30	9	7	1	-	10	-
Norfolk, Va	2,452	139	326	337	809	667	133	9	7	5	-	20	2,512
Oakland, Calif	752	11	18	19	114	318	206	21	13	3	1	28	4,258
Oklahoma City, Okla	959	101	124	134	213	253	78	17	12	1	2	24	2,509
Omaha, Nebr	975	56	103	147	287	306	52	5	1	-	-	18	2,601
Paterson, N. J	69	-	-	-	6	14	25	10	10	1	-	3	-
Peoria, Ill	144	3	8	19	35	55	19	-	-	-	1	4	3,182
Philadelphia, Pa	7,829	35	97	231	915	3,089	2,637	477	147	27	35	139	4,662
Pittsburgh, Pa	2,121	14	66	72	257	630	649	265	113	28	8	19	5,046
Portland, Oreg	198	9	7	13	32	98	30	5	1	-	-	3	3,745
Providence, R. I	194	4	4	12	39	70	43	10	8	1	-	3	4,043
Reading, Pa	83	1	-	8	20	36	14	1	2	-	-	1	-
Richmond, Va	2,772	286	410.	411	715	654	221	32	18	2	3	20	2,376
Rochester, N. Y	148	8	2	1	11	34	53	20	8	6	2	3	5,778
St. Louis, Mo	2,198	44	62	80	229	647	586	271	200	26	25	28	5,098
St. Paul, Minn	413	18	8	20	46	194	112	10	2	-	-	3	4,165
Salt Lake City, Utah	78	5	3	7	18	32	10	-	1	-	-	2	-
San Antonio, Tex	2,006	293	336	367	529	365	60	13	6	2	2	33	1,987
San Diego, Calif	374	8	25	29	109	151	39	8	4	1	-	-	3,212
San Francisco, Calif	134	1	2	5	13	35	38	16	17	2	-	5	5,559
Scranton, Pa	13	-	-	-	2	-	4	3	3	1	-	-	-
Seattle, Wash	390	17	16	29	79	175	49	6	9	1	-	9	3,556
Somerville, Mass	37	-	-	1	-	8	12	11	5	-	-	-	-
South Bend, Ind	234	5	10	28	42	102	38	4	2	2	-	1	3,618
Spokane, Wash	129	10	13	16	44	42	-	-	1	-	-	3	2,545
Springfield, Mass	163	1	1	4	9	46	64	15	14	-	-	9	5,625
Syracuse, N. Y	30	-	1	1	1	4	11	5	4	-	1	2	-
Tacoma, Wash	107	8	11	18	36	25	7	-	-	-	-	2	2,431
Tampa, Fla	830	120	129	149	256	138	24	1	3	4	3	3	2,061
Toledo, Ohio	683	12	16	29	97	316	185	15	5	3	3	2	4,180
Trenton, N. J	242	2	7	13	61	118	28	3	2	1	2	5	3,602
Tulsa, Okla	1,197	212	278	201	247	144	63	19	7	7	4	15	1,751
Utica, N. Y	6	-	-	-	1	-	4	-	1	-	-	-	-
Washington, D. C	7,314	47	135	166	487	1,413	2,246	1,438	899	167	73	243	6,433
Wichita, Kans	653	107	105	128	176	120	8	5	-	1	-	3	1,941
Wilmington, Del	407	11	12	26	79	167	91	9	3	1	1	7	3,862
Worcester, Mass	57	-	1	1	3	21	15	11	3	-	2	-	-
Yonkers, N. Y	116	-	-	1	1	18	52	17	17	8	2	-	6,827
Youngstown, Ohio	698	24	55	51	161	277	111	15	2	-	-	2	3,412

TABLE 41.—RENTED NONFARM HOMES OF NEGRO FAMILIES BY MONTHLY RENTAL, WITH MEDIAN RENTAL, FOR CITIES OF 100,000 OR MORE INHABITANTS: 1930

[Median not shown where number of families reporting rental is less than 100]

CITY	All rented nonfarm homes	NUMBER OF HOMES WITH MONTHLY RENTAL—											Median rental
		Under $10	$10 to $14	$15 to $19	$20 to $29	$30 to $49	$50 to $74	$75 to $99	$100 to $149	$150 to $199	$200 and over	Not reported	
Akron, Ohio	1,904	35	187	283	788	546	29	6	2	-	-	28	$25.49
Albany, N. Y	542	15	76	118	205	98	16	4	1	1	-	8	22.83
Atlanta, Ga	19,509	5,436	7,906	3,585	1,939	475	42	8	1	1	-	116	12.69
Baltimore, Md	28,180	1,582	3,520	3,700	9,146	8,225	978	45	6	2	-	976	25.25
Birmingham, Ala	21,204	7,218	9,428	2,799	1,172	377	37	6	1	2	-	164	11.75
Boston, Mass	4,431	19	206	463	1,538	1,613	365	44	6	-	-	177	29.36
Bridgeport, Conn	773	25	170	273	253	47	2	-	-	-	-	3	18.48
Buffalo, N. Y	2,887	15	70	346	1,331	1,040	35	2	6	1	1	40	27.46
Cambridge, Mass	964	1	23	106	390	408	24	3	-	-	-	9	28.94
Camden, N. J	2,068	36	216	515	924	314	9	-	1	-	-	53	22.60
Canton, Ohio	617	11	84	140	303	71	4	-	-	-	-	4	22.36
Chattanooga, Tenn	7,260	1,313	3,098	1,489	1,074	228	18	3	-	-	-	37	13.71
Chicago, Ill	48,600	372	1,891	3,768	11,552	14,268	12,421	2,956	348	24	14	986	38.72
Cincinnati, Ohio	11,243	527	2,000	2,951	3,365	1,847	310	54	29	1	1	158	20.19
Cleveland, Ohio	15,634	162	786	1,797	6,680	5,338	584	49	15	2	1	220	27.43
Columbus, Ohio	5,897	136	608	1,267	2,432	1,372	41	4	-	-	-	37	23.78
Dallas, Tex	7,453	753	2,337	1,732	1,713	473	36	1	3	-	-	405	16.25
Dayton, Ohio	2,945	51	288	461	1,461	637	22	1	1	-	1	22	24.53
Denver, Colo	1,237	54	216	270	529	125	5	2	-	-	-	36	21.14
Des Moines, Iowa	880	146	268	212	197	42	1	-	-	-	-	14	15.45
Detroit, Mich	20,774	62	286	854	5,399	10,541	3,082	239	43	17	4	247	36.95
Duluth, Minn	76	4	14	18	25	13	1	1	-	-	-	-	-
Elizabeth, N. J	976	7	93	269	402	175	14	2	1	-	-	13	22.80
El Paso, Tex	381	122	121	65	56	7	3	-	-	1	-	6	12.71
Erie, Pa	226	5	23	53	88	51	5	1	-	-	-	-	23.64
Evansville, Ind	1,262	149	365	357	321	46	1	1	-	-	-	22	16.48
Fall River, Mass	98	9	31	14	37	6	1	-	-	-	-	-	-
Flint, Mich	848	10	50	78	357	284	35	1	1	1	-	31	27.58
Fort Wayne, Ind	393	15	49	90	195	39	1	1	1	-	-	2	22.13
Fort Worth, Tex	4,055	742	1,793	789	552	37	4	1	-	-	-	137	13.39
Gary, Ind	3,324	47	211	536	1,608	732	59	4	2	2	-	123	25.02
Grand Rapids, Mich	420	10	41	74	212	72	4	-	-	-	-	7	23.84
Hartford, Conn	1,574	4	91	346	867	224	12	4	1	-	-	25	23.85
Houston, Tex	11,106	716	2,936	2,660	3,844	644	85	20	3	1	-	197	18.39
Indianapolis, Ind	8,713	606	2,224	2,477	2,333	919	60	7	2	1	-	84	18.00
Jacksonville, Fla	8,973	1,128	3,226	1,675	2,141	642	45	5	2	-	1	108	15.23
Jersey City, N. J	2,558	18	109	216	787	992	198	7	4	-	-	227	30.72
Kansas City, Kans	2,607	494	1,013	657	347	67	4	-	-	-	-	25	13.93
Kansas City, Mo	9,037	714	1,752	1,790	2,931	1,472	112	12	1	1	1	251	20.47
Knoxville, Tenn	2,726	312	1,063	617	530	133	20	1	1	-	-	49	14.83
Long Beach, Calif	73	-	3	10	40	17	3	-	-	-	-	-	-
Los Angeles, Calif	7,130	46	293	722	2,984	2,569	107	12	4	1	-	392	27.73
Louisville, Ky	10,892	2,503	3,142	2,334	2,125	573	81	7	3	1	-	123	14.59
Lowell, Mass	24	2	9	5	7	1	-	-	-	-	-	-	-
Lynn, Mass	157	1	10	23	100	22	-	-	-	-	-	1	24.40
Memphis, Tenn	20,527	8,005	8,299	2,501	1,030	327	49	9	3	1	-	303	11.27
Miami, Fla	5,015	516	3,158	682	488	114	18	6	2	-	1	30	13.13
Milwaukee, Wis	1,581	21	95	187	629	585	48	6	1	-	1	8	27.69
Minneapolis, Minn	847	24	135	201	279	143	11	1	-	-	-	53	21.33
Nashville, Tenn	8,453	3,655	2,851	1,205	584	84	14	-	1	-	-	59	10.95
Newark, N. J	9,010	40	359	962	3,796	3,290	281	47	27	6	-	202	28.02
New Bedford, Mass	579	35	189	156	168	28	1	-	-	-	-	2	17.07
New Haven, Conn	1,278	16	184	227	561	260	13	7	1	-	-	9	23.70
New Orleans, La	29,088	4,110	7,729	8,790	6,724	1,402	188	29	12	1	-	103	16.51
New York, N. Y	71,683	189	1,229	3,834	12,394	26,358	19,000	4,161	1,077	326	76	3,039	42.65
Bronx Borough	2,575	22	53	107	608	1,006	334	18	2	-	-	425	35.67
Brooklyn Borough	14,926	73	479	1,404	5,053	5,515	1,546	182	145	5	1	523	30.70
Manhattan Borough	51,166	72	614	2,183	6,108	18,441	16,474	3,932	922	320	74	2,026	46.91
Queens Borough	2,582	12	50	76	446	1,271	639	28	8	1	-	51	40.72
Richmond Borough	434	10	33	6	179	125	7	1	-	-	1	14	25.75
Norfolk, Va	8,843	1,282	4,120	1,853	1,280	231	13	1	-	-	-	63	13.77
Oakland, Calif	1,275	25	112	183	617	258	9	3	1	-	-	67	24.60
Oklahoma City, Okla	2,302	285	578	544	587	193	20	2	-	-	-	93	17.22
Omaha, Nebr	1,981	183	474	548	610	110	3	1	2	-	-	50	17.81
Paterson, N. J	670	10	71	153	227	178	8	-	-	-	-	23	23.94
Peoria, Ill	454	35	106	137	96	54	6	4	2	-	-	14	17.88
Philadelphia, Pa	41,139	405	2,281	3,627	13,526	18,098	2,311	157	40	5	5	684	30.43
Pittsburgh, Pa	10,358	116	635	1,159	3,303	4,040	849	96	36	4	-	120	29.72
Portland, Oreg	257	8	36	63	118	29	1	-	-	-	-	2	21.74
Providence, R. I	1,303	103	403	331	378	78	3	1	-	-	-	6	17.15
Reading, Pa	376	9	47	57	162	90	3	1	1	-	-	6	24.44
Richmond, Va	10,797	2,556	4,077	2,319	1,332	459	18	-	2	-	-	34	13.47
Rochester, N. Y	529	4	39	63	192	216	9	2	-	1	-	3	28.18
St. Louis, Mo	20,546	1,169	3,220	4,197	6,237	4,262	1,090	91	21	-	-	259	22.50
St. Paul, Minn	682	28	105	142	274	116	4	-	-	-	-	13	22.17
Salt Lake City, Utah	117	5	28	31	36	13	-	-	1	1	-	2	18.95
San Antonio, Tex	2,697	497	975	644	403	46	6	1	-	-	-	125	14.05
San Diego, Calif	435	24	43	89	234	35	3	-	1	-	-	6	22.50
San Francisco, Calif	801	7	40	60	253	323	31	7	2	1	-	77	30.12
Scranton, Pa	181	-	11	18	85	53	7	2	1	-	-	4	27.00
Seattle, Wash	592	23	61	94	253	128	4	2	-	2	-	25	24.17
Somerville, Mass	31	-	1	1	4	25	-	-	-	-	-	-	-
South Bend, Ind	552	17	45	104	234	128	8	1	1	-	-	14	24.40
Spokane, Wash	68	7	17	18	16	3	-	-	-	-	-	7	-
Springfield, Mass	681	9	58	107	403	90	8	-	-	-	-	6	24.06
Syracuse, N. Y	448	2	24	82	217	107	9	2	-	-	1	4	25.25
Tacoma, Wash	107	7	20	45	27	3	-	-	-	-	-	5	17.67
Tampa, Fla	4,397	627	1,655	1,069	823	141	16	1	-	-	-	65	14.65
Toledo, Ohio	2,403	22	102	247	990	954	58	4	3	1	-	22	28.28
Trenton, N. J	1,300	16	98	285	671	206	10	-	-	1	-	13	23.64
Tulsa, Okla	2,411	217	623	600	711	169	33	6	8	-	1	43	17.87
Utica, N. Y	124	4	30	37	42	10	1	-	-	-	-	-	18.78
Washington, D. C	21,409	393	1,874	3,091	5,197	6,846	2,559	229	21	6	1	1,192	29.14
Wichita, Kans	751	131	211	204	183	14	5	-	-	-	-	3	15.78
Wilmington, Del	2,604	71	332	392	1,023	705	38	-	1	-	-	42	24.75
Worcester, Mass	247	-	25	46	142	32	1	-	-	-	-	1	23.66
Yonkers, N. Y	654	3	21	48	229	288	37	9	6	-	-	13	31.35
Youngstown, Ohio	2,785	114	440	564	1,136	506	15	2	-	1	-	7	22.39

TABLE 42.—MEDIAN VALUE OR RENTAL OF NONFARM HOMES OWNED OR RENTED BY NEGRO FAMILIES, FOR CITIES HAVING 10,000 OR MORE NEGRO INHABITANTS: 1930

[Figures represent median value of owned nonfarm homes, and median monthly rental of rented nonfarm homes. Median not shown where number of families reporting value is less than 100]

STATE AND CITY	Median value	Median rental
ALABAMA		
Bessemer	$1,730	(1)
Birmingham	2,184	$11.75
Mobile	1,359	11.65
Montgomery	1,282	(1)
ARKANSAS		
Little Rock	1,867	12.04
CALIFORNIA		
Los Angeles	5,152	27.73
DELAWARE		
Wilmington	3,862	24.75
DISTRICT OF COLUMBIA		
Washington	6,433	29.14
FLORIDA		
Jacksonville	1,840	15.23
Miami	2,318	13.13
Tampa	2,061	14.65
GEORGIA		
Atlanta	2,553	12.69
Augusta	1,217	(1)
Columbus	1,510	10.85
Macon	1,406	(1)
Savannah	2,133	10.04
ILLINOIS		
Chicago	6,377	38.72
East St. Louis	1,650	15.32
INDIANA		
Gary	$4,003	$25.00
Indianapolis	2,887	18.00
KANSAS		
Kansas City	1,663	13.93
KENTUCKY		
Lexington	1,519	14.57
Louisville	2,674	14.59
LOUISIANA		
Baton Rouge	1,936	12.85
Monroe	1,689	11.99
New Orleans	2,796	16.51
Shreveport	1,886	13.68
MARYLAND		
Baltimore	4,366	25.25
MASSACHUSETTS		
Boston	6,164	29.36
MICHIGAN		
Detroit	6,360	36.95
MISSISSIPPI		
Jackson	1,820	13.06
Meridian	(2)	(1)
Vicksburg	1,119	(1)
MISSOURI		
Kansas City	3,390	20.47
St. Louis	5,098	22.50
NEBRASKA		
Omaha	$2,601	$17.81
NEW JERSEY		
Atlantic City	7,279	39.07
Camden	3,585	22.60
Jersey City	7,050	30.72
Newark	6,603	28.02
NEW YORK		
Buffalo	6,143	27.46
New York	8,519	42.65
Bronx Borough	9,542	35.67
Brooklyn Borough	9,252	30.70
Manhattan Borough	14,216	46.91
Queens Borough	7,083	40.72
Richmond Borough	-------	25.75
NORTH CAROLINA		
Asheville	2,687	16.48
Charlotte	2,786	12.99
Durham	2,382	15.25
Greensboro	2,277	16.80
Raleigh	1,735	14.48
Wilmington	1,433	10.36
Winston-Salem	2,772	12.77
OHIO		
Akron	4,076	25.49
Cincinnati	4,496	20.19
Cleveland	6,406	27.43
Columbus	4,060	23.78
Dayton	3,869	24.53
Toledo	4,180	28.28
Youngstown	3,412	22.39
OKLAHOMA		
Oklahoma City	$2,509	$17.22
Tulsa	1,751	17.87
PENNSYLVANIA		
Philadelphia	4,662	30.43
Pittsburgh	5,046	29.72
SOUTH CAROLINA		
Charleston	1,704	(1)
Columbia	1,464	10.81
Greenville	1,606	(1)
TENNESSEE		
Chattanooga	2,497	13.71
Knoxville	2,079	14.83
Memphis	1,775	11.27
Nashville	1,776	10.95
TEXAS		
Beaumont	1,709	13.17
Dallas	2,319	16.25
Fort Worth	1,586	13.39
Galveston	2,648	16.08
Houston	2,533	18.39
Port Authur	1,827	12.11
San Antonio	1,987	14.05
VIRGINIA		
Newport News	1,809	12.15
Norfolk	2,512	13.77
Petersburg	1,182	11.06
Portsmouth	1,448	12.82
Richmond	2,376	13.47
Roanoke	2,686	14.59

[1] Less than $10. [2] Less than $1,000.

TABLE 43.—PERCENT DISTRIBUTION OF NONFARM HOMES OF NEGRO FAMILIES, BY VALUE OR MONTHLY RENTAL, FOR CITIES OF 100,000 OR MORE INHABITANTS: 1930

[Percent not shown where less than 1/10 of 1 percent]

VALUE OR MONTHLY RENTAL	Akron, Ohio	Albany, N. Y.	Atlanta, Ga.	Baltimore, Md.	Birmingham, Ala.	Boston, Mass.	Bridgeport, Conn.	Buffalo, N. Y.	Cambridge, Mass.	Camden, N. J.	Canton, Ohio	Chattanooga, Tenn.	Chicago, Ill.	Cincinnati, Ohio	Cleveland, Ohio	Columbus, Ohio	Dallas, Tex.	Dayton, Ohio	Denver, Colo.	Des Moines, Iowa
Owned nonfarm homes	100.0	100.0	100.0	100.0	100.0	100.0	100.0	100.0	100.0	100.0	100.0	100.0	100.0	100.0	100.0	100.0	100.0	100.0	100.0	100.0
Value under $1,000	2.2	1.6	12.4	.8	12.7	------	9.9	.5	.3	2.1	------	8.8	.8	2.7	.5	1.4	9.9	1.6	3.7	19.8
$1,000 to $1,499	1.1	1.6	14.4	3.0	15.7	1.1	2.7	------	1.2	4.5	1.3	12.4	1.6	4.4	.9	2.9	16.2	3.5	7.9	20.7
$1,500 to $1,999	3.7	3.2	10.2	2.9	15.9	2.6	5.4	.5	3.4	7.1	11.5	14.4	1.5	5.2	.8	5.9	14.4	5.5	9.1	19.4
$2,000 to $2,999	13.2	9.7	23.1	11.9	27.1	9.1	12.6	4.2	6.7	21.1	25.6	27.9	7.1	13.6	4.3	16.3	24.6	17.9	22.6	21.4
$3,000 to $4.999	54.3	22.6	29.3	43.0	19.5	19.3	29.7	26.5	30.6	48.1	42.3	24.1	21.7	30.1	19.5	43.5	24.1	48.8	43.0	14.5
$5,000 to $7,499	21.9	33.9	7.4	29.0	6.1	36.0	30.6	38.1	32.7	11.0	16.7	8.3	29.2	24.1	40.8	23.9	4.9	18.8	9.8	3.2
$7,500 to $9,999	1.7	12.9	1.3	3.7	1.0	16.3	2.7	15.8	12.5	1.1	2.6	1.8	14.2	9.4	21.2	3.9	1.2	2.0	.7	.4
$10,000 to $14,999	------	6.5	1.1	1.5	.5	10.1	2.7	10.2	8.9	2.1	------	1.0	12.5	4.6	7.9	1.2	.9	.9	.6	------
$15,000 to $19,999	.6	------	.2	.3	.1	2.2	.9	1.4	3.1	.2	------	.2	4.2	1.7	1.4	.2	.3	.2	.1	------
$20,000 and over	------	3.2	.1	.1	.1	1.1	.9	.9	------	.4	------	.1	4.7	1.0	.7	.2	.3	.2	------	------
Not reported	1.3	4.8	.6	3.9	1.3	2.3	1.8	1.9	.6	2.4	------	1.0	2.5	3.3	2.0	.6	3.2	.6	2.4	.7
Rented nonfarm homes	100.0	100.0	100.0	100.0	100.0	100.0	100.0	100.0	100.0	100.0	100.0	100.0	100.0	100.0	100.0	100.0	100.0	100.0	100.0	100.0
Rental under $10	1.8	2.8	27.9	5.6	34.0	.4	3.2	.5	1	1.7	1.8	18.1	.8	4.7	1.0	2.3	10.1	1.7	4.4	16.6
$10 to $14	9.8	14.0	40.5	12.5	44.5	4.6	22.0	2.4	2.4	10.4	13.6	42.7	3.9	17.8	5.0	10.3	31.4	9.8	17.5	30.5
$15 to $19	14.9	21.8	18.4	13.1	13.2	10.4	35.3	12.0	11.0	24.9	22.7	20.5	7.8	26.2	11.5	21.5	23.2	15.7	21.8	24.1
$20 to $29	41.4	37.8	9.9	32.5	5.5	34.7	32.7	46.1	40.5	44.7	49.1	14.8	23.8	29.9	42.7	41.2	23.0	49.6	42.8	22.4
$30 to $49	28.7	18.1	2.4	29.2	1.8	36.4	6.1	36.0	42.3	15.2	11.5	3.1	29.4	16.4	34.1	23.3	6.3	21.6	10.1	4.8
$50 to $74	1.5	3.0	.2	3.5	.2	8.2	.3	1.2	2.5	.4	.6	.2	25.6	2.8	3.7	.7	.5	.7	.4	.1
$75 to $99	.3	.7	------	.2	------	1.0	------	.1	.3	------	------	------	6.1	.5	.3	.1	------	------	.2	------
$100 to $149	.1	.2	------	------	------	.1	------	.2	------	------	------	------	.7	.3	.1	------	------	------	------	------
$150 to $199	------	.2	------	------	------	------	------	------	------	------	------	------	------	------	------	------	------	------	------	------
$200 and over	------	------	------	------	------	------	------	------	------	------	------	------	------	------	------	------	------	------	------	------
Not reported	1.5	1.5	.6	3.5	.8	4.0	.4	1.4	.9	2.6	.6	.5	2.0	1.4	1.4	6	5.4	.7	2.9	1.6

TABLE 43.—PERCENT DISTRIBUTION OF NONFARM HOMES OF NEGRO FAMILIES, BY VALUE OR MONTHLY RENTAL, FOR CITIES OF 100,000 OR MORE INHABITANTS: 1930—Continued

[Percent not shown where less than 1/10 of 1 percent]

VALUE OR MONTHLY RENTAL	Detroit, Mich.	Duluth, Minn.	Elizabeth, N. J.	El Paso, Tex.	Erie, Pa.	Evansville, Ind.	Fall River, Mass.	Flint, Mich.	Fort Wayne, Ind.	Fort Worth, Tex.	Gary, Ind.	Grand Rapids, Mich.	Hartford, Conn.	Houston, Tex.	Indianapolis, Ind.	Jacksonville, Fla.	Jersey City, N. J.	Kansas City, Kans.	Kansas City, Mo.	Knoxville, Tenn.
Owned nonfarm homes	100.0	100.0	100.0	100.0	100.0	100.0	100.0	100.0	100.0	100.0	100.0	100.0	100.0	100.0	100.0	100.0	100.0	100.0	100.0	100.0
Value under $1,000	.7	-----	-----	4.6	-----	12.6	10.0	1.5	2.5	26.9	4.0	3.4	-----	8.8	4.6	18.9	-----	23.9	3.3	14.4
$1,000 to $1,499	1.4	9.8	-----	11.0	1.7	10.8	-----	2.6	5.6	19.0	4.8	4.7	-----	10.7	8.0	18.5	.2	19.8	7.3	14.4
$1,500 to $1,999	1.4	7.8	1.0	13.3	1.7	20.7	-----	3.2	11.8	16.7	4.6	8.2	-----	12.5	14.8	16.2	.6	17.8	8.1	17.7
$2,000 to $2,999	5.4	15.7	2.0	27.7	12.1	27.5	-----	14.4	23.0	20.8	17.8	21.9	2.2	31.2	24.2	22.0	1.9	20.3	23.2	25.6
$3,000 to $4,999	21.3	41.2	30.7	34.7	51.7	19.9	60.0	40.8	40.4	11.2	35.5	32.6	6.6	25.5	34.4	14.3	18.3	14.0	37.1	19.7
$5,000 to $7,499	35.1	17.6	34.7	7.5	24.1	2.0	30.0	29.2	12.4	2.3	20.1	22.7	17.6	5.6	9.9	4.4	33.8	2.6	14.2	4.0
$7,500 to $9,999	21.7	5.9	12.9	.6	1.7	.3	-----	2.8	-----	.2	5.2	4.3	18.7	1.0	1.2	1.1	21.2	.3	3.1	.8
$10,000 to $14,999	9.0	-----	11.9	-----	3.4	.8	-----	1.7	1.2	.3	4.0	1.7	37.4	1.2	.5	.5	15.8	.2	1.3	.4
$15,000 to $19,999	1.7	2.0	2.0	-----	3.4	.3	-----	-----	-----	.1	.9	-----	8.8	.3	-----	.5	3.4	-----	.2	.1
$20,000 and over	.9	-----	3.0	-----	-----	-----	-----	-----	-----	.1	1.1	-----	1.1	.1	.4	.4	2.3	.1	.4	-----
Not reported	1.6	-----	2.0	.6	-----	5.3	-----	3.9	3.1	2.6	2.0	.4	7.7	2.8	2.3	3.1	2.5	.9	1.8	3.0
Rented nonfarm homes	100.0	100.0	100.0	100.0	100.0	100.0	100.0	100.0	100.0	100.0	100.0	100.0	100.0	100.0	100.0	100.0	100.0	100.0	100.0	100.0
Rental under $10	.3	5.3	.7	32.0	2.2	11.8	9.2	1.2	3.8	18.3	1.4	2.4	.3	6.4	7.0	12.6	.7	18.9	7.9	11.4
$10 to $14	1.4	18.4	9.5	31.8	10.2	28.9	31.6	5.9	12.5	44.2	6.4	9.8	5.8	26.4	25.5	36.0	4.3	38.9	19.4	39.0
$15 to $19	4.1	23.7	27.6	17.1	23.5	28.3	14.3	9.2	22.9	19.5	16.1	17.6	22.0	24.0	28.4	18.7	8.4	25.2	19.8	22.6
$20 to $29	26.0	32.9	41.2	14.7	38.9	25.4	37.8	42.1	49.6	13.6	48.4	50.5	55.1	34.6	26.8	23.9	30.8	13.3	32.4	19.4
$30 to $49	50.7	17.1	17.9	1.8	22.6	3.6	6.1	33.5	9.9	.9	22.0	17.1	14.2	5.8	10.5	7.2	38.8	2.6	16.3	4.9
$50 to $74	14.8	1.3	1.4	.8	2.2	.1	1.0	4.1	.3	.1	1.8	1.0	.8	.8	.7	.5	7.7	.2	1.2	.7
$75 to $99	1.2	1.3	.2	-----	.4	.1	-----	.1	.3	-----	.1	-----	.3	.2	.1	.1	.3	-----	.1	-----
$100 to $149	.2	-----	.1	-----	-----	-----	-----	.1	.3	-----	.1	-----	.1	-----	-----	-----	.2	-----	-----	-----
$150 to $199	.1	-----	-----	.3	-----	-----	-----	.1	-----	-----	.1	-----	-----	-----	-----	-----	-----	-----	-----	-----
$200 and over	-----	-----	-----	-----	-----	-----	-----	-----	-----	-----	-----	-----	-----	-----	-----	-----	-----	-----	-----	-----
Not reported	1.2	-----	1.3	1.6	-----	1.7	-----	3.7	.5	3.4	3.7	1.7	1.6	1.8	1.0	1.2	8.9	1.0	2.8	1.8

VALUE OR MONTHLY RENTAL	Long Beach, Calif.	Los Angeles, Calif.	Louisville, Ky.	Lowell, Mass.	Lynn, Mass.	Memphis, Tenn.	Miami, Fla.	Milwaukee, Wis.	Minneapolis, Minn.	Nashville, Tenn.	Newark, N. J.	New Bedford, Mass.	New Haven, Conn.	New Orleans, La.	New York, N.Y.	Bronx Borough	Brooklyn Borough	Manhattan Borough	Queens Borough	Richmond Borough
Owned nonfarm homes	100.0	100.0	100.0	100.0	100.0	100.0	100.0	100.0	100.0	100.0	100.0	100.0	100.0	100.0	100.0	100.0	100.0	100.0	100.0	100.0
Value under $1,000	-----	.6	9.5	16.7	-----	15.8	15.1	-----	2.9	15.8	-----	-----	-----	10.1	.1	-----	.1	.1	.1	1.0
$1,000 to $1,499	-----	1.9	11.0	16.7	6.3	21.7	17.5	1.0	3.6	23.5	-----	4.4	.6	12.2	.3	-----	.2	.2	.2	3.0
$1,500 to $1,999	3.1	2.9	12.6	16.7	10.4	20.8	10.3	3.0	4.2	18.1	.4	8.8	-----	11.3	.2	-----	.1	.3	.3	2.0
$2,000 to $2,999	15.6	9.5	24.3	16.7	20.8	20.4	20.5	7.0	10.1	22.5	4.7	25.4	3.1	20.1	1.0	3.1	.6	.3	1.2	5.0
$3,000 to $4,999	25.0	31.4	28.6	33.3	29.2	15.1	26.9	30.0	37.7	13.5	22.4	37.1	27.6	29.6	8.8	7.4	7.2	3.5	12.3	32.0
$5,000 to $7,499	15.6	34.4	10.1	-----	29.2	2.9	5.4	28.0	36.0	3.7	31.7	13.2	36.8	11.0	29.8	24.1	22.2	23.7	41.6	30.0
$7,500 to $9,999	12.5	8.0	1.8	-----	2.1	.6	1.3	17.0	2.9	1.0	14.8	4.9	16.0	2.9	21.1	18.5	26.2	4.7	27.2	9.0
$10,000 to $14,999	21.9	5.1	.7	-----	2.1	.3	1.3	8.0	1.3	.3	14.4	2.9	12.3	1.2	20.9	32.7	32.1	19.4	10.5	7.0
$15,000 to $19,999	3.1	1.8	.2	-----	-----	.1	-----	2.0	-----	.1	4.5	-----	2.5	.5	10.1	11.1	6.9	27.5	2.9	1.0
$20,000 and over	3.1	1.1	.2	-----	-----	.1	.5	1.0	.3	-----	2.6	-----	.6	.3	5.3	2.5	1.9	18.7	1.2	-----
Not reported	-----	3.2	1.1	-----	-----	2.2	1.3	3.0	1.0	1.4	4.5	3.4	.6	.7	2.5	.6	2.5	1.7	2.6	10.0
Rented nonfarm homes	100.0	100.0	100.0	100.0	100.0	100.0	100.0	100.0	100.0	100.0	100.0	100.0	100.0	100.0	100.0	100.0	100.0	100.0	100.0	100.0
Rental under $10	-----	.6	23.0	8.3	.6	39.0	10.3	1.3	2.8	43.2	.4	6.0	1.3	14.1	.3	.9	.5	.1	.5	2.3
$10 to $14	4.1	4.1	28.8	37.5	6.4	40.4	63.0	6.0	15.9	33.7	4.0	32.6	14.4	26.6	1.7	2.1	3.2	1.2	1.9	7.6
$15 to $19	13.7	10.1	21.4	20.8	14.6	12.2	13.6	11.8	23.7	14.3	10.7	26.9	17.8	30.2	5.3	4.2	9.4	4.3	2.9	14.7
$20 to $29	54.8	41.9	19.5	29.2	63.7	5.0	9.7	39.8	32.9	6.9	42.1	29.0	43.9	23.1	17.3	23.6	33.9	11.9	17.3	41.2
$30 to $49	23.3	36.0	5.3	4.2	14.0	1.6	2.3	37.0	16.9	1.0	36.5	4.8	20.3	4.8	36.8	39.1	36.9	36.0	49.2	28.8
$50 to $74	4.1	1.5	.7	-----	-----	.2	.4	3.0	1.3	.2	3.1	.2	1.0	.6	26.5	13.0	10.4	32.2	24.7	1.6
$75 to $99	-----	.2	.1	-----	-----	-----	.1	.4	.1	-----	.5	-----	.5	.1	5.8	.7	1.2	7.7	1.1	.2
$100 to $149	-----	.1	-----	-----	-----	-----	-----	.1	-----	-----	.3	-----	.1	-----	1.5	.1	1.0	1.8	.3	-----
$150 to $199	-----	-----	-----	-----	-----	-----	-----	-----	-----	-----	.1	-----	-----	-----	.5	-----	-----	.6	-----	-----
$200 and over	-----	-----	-----	-----	-----	-----	-----	.1	-----	-----	-----	-----	-----	-----	.1	-----	-----	.1	-----	.2
Not reported	-----	5.5	1.1	-----	.6	1.5	.6	.5	6.3	.7	2.2	.3	.7	.4	4.2	16.5	3.5	4.0	2.0	3.2

VALUE OR MONTHLY RENTAL	Norfolk, Va.	Oakland, Calif.	Oklahoma City, Okla.	Omaha, Nebr.	Paterson, N. J.	Peoria, Ill.	Philadelphia, Pa.	Pittsburgh, Pa.	Portland, Oreg.	Providence, R. I.	Reading, Pa.	Richmond, Va.	Rochester, N. Y.	St. Louis, Mo.	St. Paul, Minn.	Salt Lake City, Utah	San Antonio, Tex.	San Diego, Calif.	San Francisco, Calif.
Owned nonfarm homes	100.0	100.00	100.0	100.0	100.0	100.0	100.0	100.0	100.0	100.0	100.0	100.0	100.0	100.0	100.0	100.0	100.0	100.0	100.0
Value under $1,000	5.7	1.5	10.5	5.7	-----	2.1	.4	.7	4.5	2.1	1.2	10.3	5.4	2.0	4.4	6.4	14.6	2.1	.7
$1,000 to $1,499	13.3	2.4	12.9	10.6	-----	5.6	1.2	3.1	3.5	2.1	-----	14.8	1.4	2.8	1.9	3.8	16.7	6.7	1.5
$1,500 to $1,999	13.7	2.5	14.0	15.1	-----	13.2	3.0	3.4	6.6	6.2	9.6	14.8	.7	3.6	4.8	9.0	18.3	7.8	3.7
$2,000 to $2,999	33.0	15.2	22.2	29.4	8.7	24.3	11.7	12.1	16.7	20.1	24.1	25.8	7.4	10.4	11.1	23.1	26.4	29.1	9.7
$3,000 to $4,999	27.2	42.3	26.4	31.4	20.3	38.2	39.5	29.7	49.5	36.1	43.4	23.6	23.0	29.4	47.0	41.0	18.2	40.4	26.1
$5,000 to $7,499	5.4	27.4	8.1	5.3	36.2	13.2	33.7	30.6	15.2	22.2	16.9	8.0	35.8	26.7	27.1	12.8	3.0	10.4	28.4
$7,500 to $9,999	.4	2.8	1.8	.5	14.5	-----	6.1	12.5	2.5	5.2	1.2	1.2	13.5	12.3	2.4	-----	.6	2.1	11.9
$10,000 to $14,999	.3	1.7	1.3	.1	14.5	-----	1.9	5.3	.5	4.1	2.4	.6	5.4	9.1	.5	1.3	.3	1.1	12.7
$15,000 to $19,999	.2	.4	.1	-----	1.4	-----	.3	1.3	-----	.5	-----	.1	4.1	1.2	-----	-----	.1	.3	1.5
$20,000 and over	-----	.1	.2	-----	-----	.7	.4	.4	-----	-----	-----	.1	1.4	1.1	-----	-----	.1	-----	-----
Not reported	.8	3.7	2.5	1.8	4.3	2.8	1.8	.9	1.5	1.5	1.2	.7	2.0	1.3	.7	2.6	1.6	-----	3.7
Rented nonfarm homes	100.0	100.0	100.0	100.0	100.0	100.0	100.0	100.0	100.0	100.0	100.0	100.0	100.0	100.0	100.0	100.0	100.0	100.0	100.0
Rental under $10	14.5	2.0	12.4	9.2	1.5	7.7	1.0	1.1	3.1	7.9	2.4	23.7	.8	5.7	4.1	4.3	18.4	5.5	.9
$10 to $14	46.6	8.8	25.1	23.9	10.6	23.3	5.5	6.1	14.0	30.9	12.5	37.8	7.4	15.7	15.4	23.9	36.2	9.9	5.0
$15 to $19	21.0	14.4	23.6	27.7	22.8	30.2	8.8	11.2	24.5	25.4	15.2	21.5	11.9	20.4	20.8	26.5	23.9	20.5	7.5
$20 to $29	14.5	48.4	25.5	30.8	33.9	21.1	32.9	31.9	45.9	29.0	43.1	12.3	36.3	30.4	40.2	30.8	14.9	53.8	31.6
$30 to $49	2.6	20.2	8.4	5.6	26.6	11.9	44.0	39.0	11.3	6.0	23.9	4.3	40.8	20.7	17.0	11.1	1.7	8.0	40.3
$50 to $74	.1	.7	.9	.2	1.2	1.3	5.6	8.2	.4	.2	.8	.2	1.7	5.3	.6	-----	.2	.7	3.9
$75 to $99	-----	.2	.1	.1	-----	.9	.4	.9	-----	.1	.3	-----	.4	.4	-----	-----	-----	-----	.9
$100 to $149	-----	.1	-----	.1	-----	.4	.1	.3	-----	-----	.3	-----	-----	.1	-----	.9	-----	.2	.2
$150 to $199	-----	-----	-----	-----	-----	-----	-----	-----	-----	-----	-----	-----	.2	-----	-----	.9	-----	-----	.1
$200 and over	-----	-----	-----	-----	-----	-----	-----	-----	-----	-----	-----	-----	-----	-----	-----	-----	-----	-----	-----
Not reported	.7	5.3	4.0	2.5	3.4	3.1	1.7	1.2	.8	.5	1.6	.3	.6	1.3	1.9	1.7	4.6	1.4	9.6

TABLE 43.—PERCENT DISTRIBUTION OF NONFARM HOMES OF NEGRO FAMILIES, BY VALUE OR MONTHLY RENTAL, FOR CITIES OF 100,000 OR MORE INHABITANTS: 1930—Continued

[Percent not shown where less than 1/10 of 1 percent]

VALUE OF MONTHLY RENTAL	Scranton, Pa.	Seattle, Wash.	Somerville, Mass.	South Bend, Ind.	Spokane, Wash.	Springfield, Mass.	Syracuse, N. Y.	Tacoma, Wash.	Tampa, Fla.	Toledo, Ohio.	Trenton, N. J.	Tulsa, Okla.	Utica, N. Y.	Washington, D. C.	Wichita, Kans.	Wilmington, Del.	Worcester, Mass.	Yonkers, N. Y.	Youngstown, Ohio
Owned nonfarm homes	100.0	100.0	100.0	100.0	100.0	100.0	100.0	100.0	100.0	100.0	100.0	100.0	100.0	100.0	100.0	100.0	100.0	100.0	100.0
Value under $1,000	------	4.4	------	2.1	7.8	.6	------	7.5	14.5	1.8	.8	17.7	------	.6	16.4	2.7	------	------	3.4
$1,000 to $1,499	------	4.1	------	4.3	10.1	.6	3.3	10.3	15.5	2.3	2.9	23.2	------	1.8	16.1	2.9	1.8	------	7.9
$1,500 to $1,999	------	7.4	2.7	12.0	12.4	2.5	3.3	16.8	18.0	4.2	5.4	16.8	------	2.3	19.6	6.4	1.8	.9	7.3
$2,000 to $2,999	15.4	20.3	------	17.9	34.1	5.5	3.3	33.6	30.8	14.2	25.2	20.6	16.7	6.7	27.0	19.4	5.3	.9	23.1
$3,000 to $4,999	------	44.9	21.6	43.6	32.6	28.2	13.3	23.4	16.6	46.3	48.8	12.0	------	19.3	18.4	41.0	36.8	15.5	39.7
$5,000 to $7,499	30.8	12.6	32.4	16.2	------	39.3	36.7	6.5	2.9	27.1	11.6	5.3	66.7	30.7	1.2	22.4	26.3	44.8	15.9
$7,500 to $9,999	23.1	1.5	29.7	1.7	------	9.2	16.7	------	.1	2.2	1.2	1.6	------	20.0	.8	2.2	19.3	14.7	2.1
$10,000 to $14,999	23.1	2.3	13.5	.9	.8	8.6	13.3	------	.4	.7	.8	.6	16.7	12.3	------	.7	5.3	14.7	.3
$15,000 to $19,999	7.7	.3	------	.9	------	------	------	------	.5	.4	.4	.6	------	2.3	.2	.2	------	6.9	------
$20,000 and over	------	------	------	------	------	------	3.3	------	.4	.4	.8	.3	------	1.0	------	.2	3.5	1.7	------
Not reported	------	2.3	------	.4	2.3	5.5	6.7	1.9	.4	.3	2.1	1.3	------	3.3	.5	1.7	------	------	.3
Rented nonfarm homes	100.0	100.0	100.0	100.0	100.0	100.0	100.0	100.0	100.0	100.0	100.0	100.0	100.0	100.0	100.0	100.0	100.0	100.0	100.0
Rental under $10	------	3.9	------	3.1	10.3	1.3	.4	6.5	14.3	.9	1.2	9.0	3.2	1.8	17.4	2.7	------	.5	4.1
$10 to $14	6.1	10.3	3.2	8.2	25.0	8.5	5.4	18.7	37.6	4.2	7.5	25.8	24.2	8.8	28.1	12.7	10.1	3.2	15.8
$15 to $19	9.9	15.9	3.2	18.8	26.5	15.7	18.3	42.1	24.3	10.3	21.9	24.9	29.8	14.4	27.2	15.1	18.6	7.3	20.3
$20 to $29	47.0	42.7	12.9	42.4	23.5	59.2	48.4	25.2	18.7	41.2	51.6	29.5	33.9	24.3	24.4	39.3	57.5	35.0	40.8
$30 to $49	29.3	21.6	80.6	23.2	4.4	13.2	23.9	2.8	3.2	39.7	15.8	7.0	8.1	32.0	1.9	27.1	13.0	44.0	18.2
$50 to $74	3.9	.7	------	1.4	------	1.2	2.0	------	.4	2.4	.8	1.4	.8	12.0	.7	1.5	.4	5.7	.5
$75 to $99	1.1	.3	------	.2	------	------	.4	------	------	.2	------	.2	------	1.1	------	------	------	1.4	.1
$100 to $149	.6	------	------	.2	------	------	------	------	------	.1	------	.3	------	.1	------	------	------	.9	------
$150 to $199	------	.3	------	------	------	------	------	------	------	------	.1	------	------	------	------	------	------	------	------
$200 and over	------	------	------	------	------	------	.2	------	------	------	------	------	------	------	------	------	------	------	------
Not reported	2.2	4.2	------	2.5	10.3	.9	.9	4.7	1.5	.9	1.0	1.8	------	5.6	.4	1.6	.4	2.0	.3

TABLE 44.—NEGRO FAMILIES, BY NUMBER OF GAINFUL WORKERS, FOR CITIES OF 100,000 OR MORE INHABITANTS: 1930

CITY	All families	FAMILIES BY NUMBER OF GAINFUL WORKERS: None		1		2 or more	
		Number	Percent	Number	Percent	Number	Percent
Akron, Ohio	2,471	73	3.0	1,601	64.8	797	32.3
Albany, N. Y	628	45	7.2	389	61.9	194	30.9
Atlanta, Ga	23,450	680	2.9	10,308	44.0	12,462	53.1
Baltimore, Md	33,102	956	2.9	15,399	46.5	16,747	50.6
Birmingham, Ala	26,429	777	2.9	15,097	57.1	10,555	39.9
Boston, Mass	5,339	254	4.8	3,099	58.0	1,986	37.2
Bridgeport, Conn	900	42	4.7	549	61.0	309	34.3
Buffalo, N. Y	3,241	172	5.3	2,024	62.4	1,045	32.2
Cambridge, Mass	1,305	53	4.1	735	56.3	517	39.6
Camden, N. J	2,710	118	4.4	1,503	55.5	1,089	40.2
Canton, Ohio	719	38	5.3	498	69.3	183	25.5
Chattanooga, Tenn	8,848	395	4.5	4,772	53.9	3,681	41.6
Chicago, Ill	55,137	1,914	3.5	28,729	52.1	24,494	44.4
Cincinnati, Ohio	12,634	397	3.1	7,139	56.5	5,098	40.4
Cleveland, Ohio	17,525	623	3.6	9,912	56.6	6,990	39.9
Columbus, Ohio	7,995	271	3.4	4,290	53.7	3,434	43.0
Dallas, Tex	10,698	224	2.1	4,911	45.9	5,563	52.0
Dayton, Ohio	4,342	184	4.2	2,365	54.5	1,793	41.3
Denver, Colo	2,155	126	5.8	1,265	58.7	764	35.5
Des Moines, Iowa	1,487	78	5.2	944	63.5	465	31.3
Detroit, Mich	25,656	918	3.6	15,194	59.2	9,544	37.2
Duluth, Minn	129	12	9.3	86	66.7	31	24.0
Elizabeth, N. J	1,120	37	3.3	665	59.4	418	37.3
El Paso, Tex	567	22	3.9	324	57.1	221	39.0
Erie, Pa	291	12	4.1	192	66.0	87	29.9
Evansville, Ind	1,720	115	6.7	1,060	61.6	545	31.7
Fall River, Mass	109	3	2.8	72	66.1	34	31.2
Flint, Mich	1,333	46	3.5	973	73.0	314	23.6
Fort Wayne, Ind	560	27	4.8	363	64.8	170	30.4
Fort Worth, Tex	6,239	222	3.6	3,169	50.8	2,848	45.6
Gary, Ind	4,336	175	4.0	3,047	70.3	1,114	25.7
Grand Rapids, Mich	665	38	5.7	377	56.7	250	37.6
Hartford, Conn	1,675	59	3.5	831	49.6	785	46.9
Houston, Tex	16,966	559	3.3	8,420	49.6	7,987	47.1
Indianapolis, Ind	11,903	393	3.3	6,679	56.1	4,831	40.6
Jacksonville, Fla	12,179	511	4.2	6,208	51.0	5,460	44.8
Jersey City, N. J	3,075	89	2.9	1,680	54.6	1,306	42.5
Kansas City, Kans	5,631	266	4.7	3,370	59.8	1,995	35.4
Kansas City, Mo	11,436	556	4.9	6,628	58.0	4,252	37.2
Knoxville, Tenn	4,161	181	4.3	1,957	47.0	2,023	48.6
Long Beach, Calif	106	6	5.7	50	47.2	50	47.2
Los Angeles, Calif	11,164	597	5.3	6,345	56.8	4,222	37.8
Louisville, Ky	13,909	526	3.8	7,204	51.8	6,179	44.4
Lowell, Mass	31	3	9.7	19	61.3	9	29.0
Lynn, Mass	212	20	9.4	116	54.7	76	35.8
Memphis, Tenn	29,507	1,155	3.9	17,098	57.9	11,254	38.1
Miami, Fla	6,216	87	1.4	2,402	38.6	3,727	60.0
Milwaukee, Wis	1,810	91	5.0	1,160	64.1	559	30.9
Minneapolis, Minn	1,199	52	4.3	800	66.7	347	28.9
Nashville, Tenn	12,177	499	4.1	6,308	51.8	5,370	44.1
Newark, N. J	9,676	298	3.1	5,030	52.0	4,348	44.9
New Bedford, Mass	818	81	9.9	498	60.9	239	29.2
New Haven, Conn	1,460	63	4.3	859	58.8	538	36.8
New Orleans, La	34,461	919	2.7	17,266	50.1	16,276	47.2
New York, N. Y	77,077	1,914	2.5	40,653	52.7	34,510	44.8
Bronx Borough	2,883	63	2.2	1,658	57.5	1,162	40.3
Brooklyn Borough	17,016	534	3.1	9,443	55.5	7,039	41.4
Manhattan Borough	52,387	1,203	2.3	27,054	51.6	24,130	46.1
Queens Borough	4,237	92	2.2	2,144	50.6	2,001	47.2
Richmond Borough	554	22	4.0	354	63.9	178	32.1
Norfolk, Va	11,488	415	3.6	5,982	52.1	5,091	44.3
Oakland, Calif	2,122	179	8.4	1,290	60.8	653	30.8
Oklahoma City, Okla	3,510	82	2.3	1,697	48.3	1,731	49.3
Omaha, Nebr	3,046	132	4.3	1,799	59.1	1,115	36.6
Paterson, N. J	757	20	2.6	371	49.0	366	48.3
Peoria, Ill	626	12	1.9	379	60.5	235	37.5
Philadelphia, Pa	50,997	1,423	2.8	26,511	52.0	23,063	45.2
Pittsburgh, Pa	12,831	487	3.8	7,940	61.9	4,404	34.3
Portland, Oreg	467	18	3.9	311	66.6	138	29.6
Providence, R. I	1,522	71	4.7	914	60.1	537	35.3
Reading. Pa	483	19	3.9	291	60.2	173	35.8
Richmond, Va	13,679	567	4.1	7,164	52.4	5,948	43.5
Rochester, N. Y	693	24	3.5	396	57.1	273	39.4
St. Louis, Mo	23,548	795	3.4	13,328	56.6	9,425	40.0
St. Paul, Minn	1,110	63	5.7	733	66.0	314	28.3
Salt Lake City, Utah	200	15	7.5	126	63.0	59	29.5
San Antonio, Tex	4,847	161	3.3	2,259	46.6	2,427	50.1
San Diego, Calif	829	52	6.3	479	57.8	298	35.9
San Francisco, Calif	988	67	6.8	642	65.0	279	28.2
Scranton, Pa	202	20	9.9	131	64.9	51	25.2
Seattle, Wash	1,005	59	5.9	695	69.2	251	25.0
Somerville, Mass	68	------	------	43	63.2	25	36.8
South Bend, Ind	807	21	2.6	503	62.3	283	35.1
Spokane, Wash	204	11	5.4	146	71.6	47	23.0
Springfield, Mass	851	31	3.6	489	57.5	331	38.9
Syracuse, N. Y	488	24	4.9	305	62.5	159	32.6
Tacoma, Wash	221	15	6.8	157	71.0	49	22.2
Tampa, Fla	5,369	181	3.4	2,533	47.2	2,655	49.5
Toledo, Ohio	3,198	122	3.8	2,002	62.6	1,074	33.6
Trenton, N. J	1,582	69	4.4	942	59.5	571	36.1
Tulsa, Okla	3,745	100	2.7	1,777	47.4	1,868	49.9
Utica, N. Y	132	7	5.3	79	59.8	46	34.8
Washington, D. C	29,995	981	3.3	13,619	45.4	15,395	51.3
Wichita, Kans	1,415	36	2.5	754	53.3	625	44.2
Wilmington, Del	3,081	147	4.8	1,697	55.1	1,237	40.1
Worcester, Mass	313	13	4.2	175	55.9	125	39.9
Yonkers, N. Y	790	21	2.7	399	50.5	370	46.8
Youngstown, Ohio	3,526	167	4.7	2,531	71.8	828	23.5

Table 45.—NUMBER AND PERCENT OF NEGRO OWNER AND TENANT FAMILIES HAVING 1 OR MORE LODGERS, FOR CITIES OF 100,000 OR MORE INHABITANTS: 1930

CITY	OWNER FAMILIES			TENANT FAMILIES		
	Total number	With lodgers		Total number	With lodgers	
		Number	Percent		Number	Percent
Akron, Ohio	462	113	24.5	1,906	574	30.1
Albany, N. Y	62	30	48.4	542	165	30.4
Atlanta, Ga	3,654	747	20.4	19,530	3,670	18.8
Baltimore, Md	3,793	1,294	34.1	28,182	9,219	32.7
Birmingham, Ala	4,709	774	16.4	21,213	4,089	19.3
Boston, Mass	727	299	41.1	4,431	1,021	23.0
Bridgeport, Conn	111	21	18.9	773	164	21.2
Buffalo, N. Y	215	57	26.5	2,887	1,103	38.2
Cambridge, Mass	327	76	23.2	964	141	14.6
Camden, N. J	536	143	26.7	2,068	604	29.2
Canton, Ohio	78	17	21.8	617	201	32.6
Chattanooga, Tenn	1,406	246	17.5	7,261	1,505	20.7
Chicago, Ill	5,767	2,048	35.5	48,601	17,795	36.6
Cincinnati, Ohio	1,126	205	18.2	11,244	2,354	20.9
Cleveland, Ohio	1,451	544	37.5	15,634	4,802	30.7
Columbus, Ohio	1,939	415	21.4	5,901	1,542	26.1
Dallas, Tex	2,659	491	18.5	7,460	1,833	24.6
Dayton, Ohio	1,280	266	20.8	2,945	733	24.9
Denver, Colo	827	195	23.6	1,237	269	21.7
Des Moines, Iowa	567	83	14.6	880	151	17.2
Detroit, Mich	3,841	1,402	36.5	20,775	9,216	44.4
Duluth, Minn	51	7	13.7	76	12	15.8
Elizabeth, N. J	101	23	22.8	976	226	23.2
El Paso, Tex	173	32	18.5	381	53	13.9
Erie, Pa	58	12	20.7	226	57	25.2
Evansville, Ind	397	91	22.9	1,262	391	31.0
Fall River, Mass	10	5	50.0	98	16	8.1
Flint, Mich	466	196	42.1	848	300	35.4
Fort Wayne, Ind	161	48	29.8	393	136	34.6
Fort Worth, Tex	1,852	332	17.9	4,056	802	19.8
Gary, Ind	882	224	25.4	3,325	1,048	31.5
Grand Rapids, Mich	233	57	24.5	420	129	30.7
Hartford, Conn	91	15	16.5	1,574	238	15.1
Houston, Tex	5,331	806	15.1	11,118	3,100	27.9
Indianapolis, Ind	2,887	484	16.8	8,713	1,713	19.7
Jacksonville, Fla	2,687	474	17.6	8,973	2,963	33.0
Jersey City, N. J	476	142	29.8	2,558	587	22.9
Kansas City, Kans	2,898	391	13.5	2,607	384	14.7
Kansas City, Mo	1,825	542	29.7	9,044	2,247	24.8
Knoxville, Tenn	1,286	222	17.3	2,727	741	27.2
Long Beach, Calif	32	12	37.5	73	17	23.3
Los Angeles, Calif	3,747	778	20.8	7,136	1,536	21.5
Louisville, Ky	2,790	464	16.6	10,892	2,347	21.5
Lowell, Mass	6	—	—	24	6	25.0
Lynn, Mass	48	6	12.5	157	22	14.0
Memphis, Tenn	7,564	1,015	13.4	20,561	3,869	18.8
Miami, Fla	1,099	265	24.1	5,015	1,337	26.7
Milwaukee, Wis	100	39	39.0	1,581	598	37.8
Minneapolis, Minn	308	75	24.4	847	207	24.4
Nashville, Tenn	3,469	470	13.5	8,456	1,395	16.5
Newark, N. J	494	155	31.4	9,013	2,368	26.3
New Bedford, Mass	205	25	12.2	579	73	12.6
New Haven, Conn	163	41	25.2	1,278	246	19.2
New Orleans, La	4,566	465	10.2	29,093	4,722	16.2
New York, N. Y	4,280	1,602	37.4	71,687	24,994	34.9
Bronx Borough	162	25	15.4	2,575	428	16.6
Brooklyn Borough	1,511	506	33.5	14,929	3,400	22.8
Manhattan Borough	954	613	64.3	51,166	20,384	39.8
Queens Borough	1,551	443	28.6	2,583	677	28.4
Richmond Borough	102	15	14.7	434	105	24.2
Norfolk, Va	2,453	508	20.7	8,870	2,349	26.5
Oakland, Calif	752	196	26.1	1,276	334	26.2
Oklahoma City, Okla	959	239	24.9	2,303	587	25.5
Omaha, Nebr	977	254	26.0	1,987	490	24.7
Paterson, N. J	69	14	20.2	670	134	20.0
Peoria, Ill	144	44	30.6	454	182	40.1
Philadelphia, Pa	7,830	2,696	34.4	41,145	13,603	33.1
Pittsburgh, Pa	2,121	591	27.9	10,358	3,019	29.1
Portland, Oreg	199	36	18.1	257	69	26.8
Providence, R. I	194	23	11.9	1,303	202	15.5
Reading, Pa	83	27	32.5	376	132	35.1
Richmond, Va	2,773	422	15.2	10,798	2,063	19.1
Rochester, N. Y	148	43	29.1	530	129	24.3
St. Louis, Mo	2,198	727	33.1	20,546	5,979	29.1
St. Paul, Minn	413	113	27.4	682	194	28.4
Salt Lake City, Utah	78	21	26.9	117	27	23.1
San Antonio, Tex	2,006	336	16.7	2,698	508	18.8
San Diego, Calif	374	59	15.8	435	83	19.1
San Francisco, Calif	134	27	20.1	801	237	29.6
Scranton, Pa	13	3	23.1	181	71	39.2
Seattle, Wash	390	78	20.0	592	142	24.0
Somerville, Mass	37	6	16.2	31	3	9.7
South Bend, Ind	234	44	18.8	552	150	27.2
Spokane, Wash	129	10	7.8	68	16	23.5
Springfield, Mass	163	33	20.2	681	107	15.7
Syracuse, N. Y	30	8	26.7	448	132	29.5
Tacoma, Wash	108	8	7.4	108	26	24.1
Tampa, Fla	830	233	28.1	4,397	1,518	34.5
Toledo, Ohio	686	222	32.3	2,417	884	36.6
Trenton, N. J	242	55	22.7	1,301	372	28.6
Tulsa, Okla	1,197	326	27.2	2,413	541	22.4
Utica, N. Y	6	2	33.3	124	43	34.7
Washington, D. C	7,316	2,573	35.2	21,413	7,087	33.1
Wichita, Kans	654	139	21.3	752	182	24.2
Wilmington, Del	407	132	32.4	2,605	930	35.7
Worcester, Mass	57	9	15.8	247	38	15.4
Yonkers, N. Y	116	28	24.1	654	143	21.9
Youngstown, Ohio	698	136	19.5	2,785	746	26.8

Table 46.—NEGRO FAMILIES HAVING RADIO SET, FOR CITIES OF 100,000 OR MORE INHABITANTS: 1930

[Percent not shown where base is less than 100]

CITY	NEGRO FAMILIES			Percent of all families having radio set
	Total number	Having radio set		
		Number	Percent	
Akron, Ohio	2,471	461	18.7	52.3
Albany, N. Y	628	130	20.7	56.0
Atlanta, Ga	23,450	740	3.2	26.0
Baltimore, Md	33,102	5,176	15.6	49.0
Birmingham, Ala	26,429	795	3.0	26.7
Boston, Mass	5,339	1,853	34.7	56.2
Bridgeport, Conn	900	330	36.7	58.5
Buffalo, N. Y	3,241	985	30.4	54.9
Cambridge, Mass	1,305	587	45.0	55.1
Camden, N. J	2,710	597	22.0	53.3
Canton, Ohio	719	75	10.4	50.7
Chattanooga, Tenn	8,848	342	3.9	23.1
Chicago, Ill	55,137	23,487	42.6	63.2
Cincinnati, Ohio	12,634	1,408	11.1	48.7
Cleveland, Ohio	17,525	4,003	22.8	48.1
Columbus, Ohio	7,995	1,672	20.9	49.7
Dallas, Tex	10,698	1,127	10.5	40.3
Dayton, Ohio	4,342	959	22.1	55.4
Denver, Colo	2,155	557	25.8	50.8
Des Moines, Iowa	1,487	335	22.5	51.5
Detroit, Mich	25,656	7,595	29.6	58.0
Duluth, Minn	129	48	37.2	49.9
Elizabeth, N. J	1,120	230	20.5	60.5
El Paso, Tex	567	56	9.9	19.1
Erie, Pa	291	78	26.8	51.4
Evansville, Ind	1,720	88	5.1	33.8
Fall River, Mass	109	38	34.9	44.5
Flint, Mich	1,333	317	23.8	52.3
Fort Wayne, Ind	560	153	27.3	61.2
Fort Worth, Tex	6,239	418	6.7	34.5
Gary, Ind	4,336	897	20.7	46.4
Grand Rapids, Mich	665	203	30.5	49.4
Hartford, Conn	1,675	426	25.4	51.4
Houston, Tex	16,966	1,089	6.4	31.9
Indianapolis, Ind	11,903	2,007	16.9	47.1
Jacksonville, Fla	12,179	428	3.5	24.7
Jersey City, N. J	3,075	1,215	39.5	63.2
Kansas City, Kans	5,631	869	15.4	41.8
Kansas City, Mo	11,436	1,729	15.1	48.9
Knoxville, Tenn	4,161	224	5.4	24.6
Long Beach, Calif	106	46	43.4	57.8
Los Angeles, Calif	11,164	5,136	46.0	58.8
Louisville, Ky	13,909	1,251	9.0	33.5
Lowell, Mass	31	4	---	40.3
Lynn, Mass	212	94	44.3	64.3
Memphis, Tenn	29,507	1,087	3.7	26.2
Miami, Fla	6,216	184	3.0	24.5
Milwaukee, Wis	1,810	593	32.8	62.8
Minneapolis, Minn	1,199	475	39.6	59.5
Nashville, Tenn	12,177	861	7.1	28.2
Newark, N. J	9,676	2,280	23.6	54.5
New Bedford, Mass	818	122	14.9	37.2
New Haven, Conn	1,460	603	41.3	54.2
New Orleans, La	34,461	1,154	3.3	21.0
New York, N. Y	77,077	30,917	40.1	59.2
Bronx Borough	2,883	1,275	44.2	64.9
Brooklyn Borough	17,016	5,628	33.1	59.4
Manhattan Borough	52,387	21,630	41.3	44.9
Queens Borough	4,237	2,163	51.1	75.0
Richmond Borough	554	221	39.9	67.4
Norfolk, Va	11,488	799	7.0	32.3
Oakland, Calif	2,122	759	35.8	57.9
Oklahoma City, Okla	3,510	319	9.1	36.5
Omaha, Nebr	3,046	693	22.8	52.6
Paterson, N. J	757	230	30.4	60.3
Peoria, Ill	626	184	29.4	54.7
Philadelphia, Pa	50,997	11,875	23.3	56.3
Pittsburgh, Pa	12,831	2,658	20.7	52.3
Portland, Oreg	467	226	48.4	57.7
Providence, R. I	1,522	459	30.2	55.1
Reading, Pa	483	104	21.5	56.2
Richmond, Va	13,679	969	7.1	33.7
Rochester, N. Y	693	238	34.3	55.7
St. Louis, Mo	23,548	4,361	18.5	50.2
St. Paul, Minn	1,110	488	44.0	59.5
Salt Lake City, Utah	200	64	32.0	54.3
San Antonio, Tex	4,847	463	9.6	26.1
San Diego, Calif	829	259	31.2	51.2
San Francisco, Calif	988	327	33.1	48.7
Scranton, Pa	202	32	15.8	39.2
Seattle, Wash	1,005	340	33.8	52.3
Somerville, Mass	68	44	---	64.1
South Bend, Ind	807	204	25.3	52.3
Spokane, Wash	204	57	27.9	47.9
Springfield, Mass	851	311	36.5	61.1
Syracuse, N. Y	488	154	31.6	56.1
Tacoma, Wash	221	66	29.9	48.5
Tampa, Fla	5,369	43	.8	14.7
Toledo, Ohio	3,198	949	29.7	61.3
Trenton, N. J	1,582	372	23.5	55.7
Tulsa, Okla	3,745	228	6.1	39.6
Utica, N. Y	132	47	35.6	48.5
Washington, D. C	29,995	7,562	25.2	53.9
Wichita, Kans	1,415	170	12.0	37.7
Wilmington, Del	3,081	570	18.5	53.6
Worcester, Mass	313	117	37.4	59.9
Yonkers, N. Y	790	299	37.8	64.8
Youngstown, Ohio	3,526	376	10.7	45.8

CHAPTER XIV.—OCCUPATIONS

The classification by occupation.—The census of 1930 sought to secure a definite statement of the occupation of each person engaged in gainful labor. The term gainful worker, in census usage, includes all persons who usually follow a gainful occupation, although they may not have been employed at the time the census was taken. It does not include women doing housework in their own homes without wages and having no other employment, nor children working at home, merely at general household work, chores, or at odd times at other work. The occupations returned for children under 10 years old were not compiled, hence all data presented in this chapter refer to gainful workers 10 years old and over.

The occupation classifications used in the census of 1930 differ somewhat from those used in the census of 1920. It has been necessary, for comparison, to assign a few of the occupational groups, as determined in the census of 1920, to general divisions of occupation different from those under which they were presented in 1920. Furthermore, in 1930, an occupational designation returned by the enumerators occasionally was assigned to an occupational group different from that under which it was classified in 1920. Since modifications of this kind in the initial classification of individual cases may be reflected in the 1930 figures, it is evident that a small increase or decrease in the number of workers shown in an occupation may be due to a difference in classification. The same is true, for the same reason, in regard to a small increase or decrease from 1910 to 1920.

Number of Negroes gainfully employed.—Of the 9,292,556 Negroes 10 years old and over, 5,503,535 were gainfully occupied in 1930. Of the Negro population, 59.2 percent were gainfully occupied in 1930 as compared with 47 percent for the native white population and 56.1 percent for the foreign-born white population.

More than 80 percent of the total male Negro population 10 years old and over were gainfully occupied in 1930, as compared with 73.4 percent for the male native white population, and over 38 percent of the female Negro population 10 years old and over as compared with 20.5 percent for the female native white population.

Number of Negroes gainfully occupied by sections.—In 1930, 58.5 percent of the Negroes, 45.6 percent of the native white, and 56.9 percent of the foreign-born white population 10 years old and over in the South were gainfully occupied; 61.6 percent of the Negroes, 47.4 percent of the native white, and 55.8 percent of the foreign-born white in the North; and 62.4 percent of the Negroes, 48.8 percent of the native white, and 58.1 percent of the foreign-born white population 10 years old and over in the West. Although increases were reported in 1930 over 1920 in the number of persons in each section who were gainfully occupied, the ratio of those occupied to the total population of persons 10 years old and over decreased in the South from 49.6 percent to 49.1 percent, in the North from from 50.5 percent to 49.5 percent, and in the West from 51.1 percent to 50.5 percent.

Proportion of the gainfully occupied Negroes in the various occupation groups.—Of the 5,505,535 gainful Negro workers shown in the 1930 census, 36.1 percent were occupied in agriculture; 28.6 percent in domestic and personal service; 18.6 percent in manufacturing and mechanical industries; 7.2 percent in transportation and communication; 3.3 percent in trade; 2.5 percent in professional service; 1.4 percent in the extraction of minerals, and the remaining 2.2 percent in public service, clerical occupations, and in forestry and fishing.

Since 1910 there has been a marked decrease in the proportion of gainful Negro workers occupied in agriculture and a marked increase in those occupied in domestic and personal service.

Negroes gainfully occupied by occupation groups by sections.—The Negro gainful workers in the North and West were largely occupied in domestic and personal service and in the manufacturing and mechanical industries, while those in the South were occupied largely in agriculture and in domestic and personal service.

Distribution of Negro gainful workers in the various occupation groups by sex.—In 1930, 40.7 percent of the male Negro gainful workers were occupied in agriculture; 25.2 percent in manufacturing and mechanical industries; 11.6 percent in domestic and personal service, and 10.8 percent in transportation and communication. The female Negro gainful workers were occupied in the main in domestic and personal service and in agriculture.

Distribution by occupation groups per 1,000 Negroes gainfully occupied.—A larger proportion of the Negro gainful workers than of the native white and foreign born white gainful workers were occupied in agriculture. In 1930 there were in agriculture, 361 Negroes per 1,000 gainfully occupied as compared with 214 native whites and 91 foreign-born whites. In domestic and personal service there were 287 Negroes per 1,000 gainfully occupied Negroes as compared with 66 for native white and 127 for foreign-born white.

Occupations in which Negroes predominate.—The Negro gainful workers exceeded those of all other classes in 10 occupations in 1930. Of the 911,943 persons engaged in these occupations, 72 percent were Negroes. The Negro workers in these occupations constituted 11.9 percent of the Negroes 10 years old and over reported as gainfully occupied in 1930. Over 75 percent of the launderers and laundresses (not in laundries) were Negroes and more than 68 percent of the cooks (other than in hotels, restaurants, and boarding houses) were Negroes in 1930.

Negro inhabitants per professional person.—In 1930 there was 1 Negro clergyman for every 475 Negro inhabitants, 1 college professor or college president for every 5,541 inhabitants, 1 dentist for every 6,707 inhabitants, 1 lawyer or judge or justice for every 9,536 inhabitants, 1 musician or teacher of music for every 1,124 inhabitants, 1 physician or surgeon for every 3,125 inhabitants, 1 school teacher for every 218 inhabitants, and 1 trained nurse for every 2,076 inhabitants.

Age of Negro gainful workers in 1930.—The percentage of Negroes gainfully occupied is of the total Negro population by ages as follows: 10 to 13 years, 10.8; 14 years, 23.3; 15 years, 30.2; 16 years, 41; 17 years, 51.3; 18 and 19 years, 60; 20 to 24 years, 67.9; 25 to 29 years, 70.1; 30 to 34 years, 71; 35 to 39 years, 71.6; 40 to 44 years, 72.2; 45 to 49 years, 72.7; 50 to 54 years, 73.7; 55 to 59 years, 72.4; 60 to 64 years, 68.2; 65 to 69 years, 62; 70 to 74 years, 50.6; 75 years and over, 32.5

The percentage of the male Negro gainful workers occupied by age groups were as follows: 10 to 13 years, 13.3; 14 years, 29.8; 15 years, 39.7; 16 years, 54.5; 17 years, 68.1; 18 and 19 years, 81.7; 20 to 24 years, 93.5; 25 to 29 years, 96.6; 30 to 34 years, 96.9; 35 to 39 years, 97.1; 40 to 44 years, 97.2; 45 to 49 years, 97.2; 50 to 54 years, 96.7; 55 to 59 years, 95.6; 60 to 64 years, 92.6; 65 to 69 years, 87.7; 70 to 74 years, 76.2; and 75 years and over, 54.2. The corresponding percentages for female Negro gainful workers were: 10 to 13 years, 8.4; 14 years, 17.0; 15 years, 21.3; 16 years, 28.6: 17 years, 35; 18 and 19 years, 41.5; 20 to 24 years, 46; 25 to 29 years, 46.9; 30 to 34 years, 46.9; 35 to 39 years, 47.7; 40 to 44 years, 47.8; 45 to 49 years, 46.9; 50 to 54 years, 45.5; 55 to 59 years, 42.3; 60 to 64 years, 38.3; 65 to 69 years, 32.5; 70 to 74 years, 23.5; and 75 years and over, 13.2

Over 75 percent of the male Negro gainful workers from 10 to 17 years of age were occupied in agriculture. Fully 66 percent of the male Negro gainful workers between 10 and 19 years of age, and about 59 percent of those over 60 years of age, were occupied in agriculture.

The female Negro gainful workers between 10 and 17 years of age were occupied in the main in agriculture, while a large portion of the female Negro gainful workers over 17 years of age were occupied in personal and domestic service. The percentages of female workers in each age group, who are occupied in domestic and personal service decrease with each age group over 29, while the corresponding age groups occupied in agriculture increase.

Number of Negro children 10 to 15 years old gainfully employed.—Of the 740,290 male Negroes 10 to 15 years old in the United States there were 150,000, or 20.3 percent, reported as gainfully occupied in 1930. Of the 751,689 female Negroes 10 to 15 years old, 90,007, or 12 percent, were reported as gainfully occupied. Over 98 percent of the Negro children 10 to 15 years old gainfully occupied in 1930 were in the South.

TABLE 1.—NUMBER AND PROPORTION OF PERSONS 10 YEARS OLD AND OVER GAINFULLY OCCUPIED, BY COLOR, NATIVITY, AND SEX, FOR THE UNITED STATES: 1930, 1920, AND 1910

[Percent not shown where less than 1/10 of 1 percent, or where base is less than 100]

CLASS OF POPULATION	TOTAL			MALE			FEMALE			PERCENT DISTRIBUTION OF GAINFULLY OCCUPIED		
	Total number	Gainfully occupied		Total number	Gainfully occupied		Total number	Gainfully occupied		Total	Male	Female
		Number	Percent		Number	Percent		Number	Percent			
1930	**98,723,047**	**48,829,920**	**49.5**	**49,949,798**	**38,077,804**	**76.2**	**48,773,249**	**10,752,116**	**22,0**	**100.0**	**100.0**	**100.0**
Negro	9,292,556	5,503,535	59.2	4,564,690	3,662,893	80.2	4,727,866	1,840,642	38.9	11.3	9.6	17.1
Native white	74,763,739	35,173,370	47.0	37,475,901	27,511,862	73.4	37,287,838	7,661,508	20.5	72.0	72.3	71.3
Foreign-born white	13,216,928	7,411,127	56.1	7,078,223	6,255,071	88.4	6,138,705	1,156,056	18.8	15.2	16.4	10.8
Other races	1,449,824	741,888	51.2	830,984	647,978	78.0	618,840	93,910	15.2	1.5	1.7	.9
Mexican [1]	1,002,241	498,765	49.8	547,863	431,677	78.8	454,378	67,088	14.8	1.0	1.1	.6
Indian	238,981	98,148	41.1	123,469	80,306	65.0	115,512	17,842	15.4	.2	.2	.2
Chinese	63,392	47,106	74.3	53,650	45,547	84.9	9,742	1,559	16.0	.1	.1	—
Japanese	97,273	54,230	55.8	60,580	47,489	78.4	36,693	6,741	18.4	.1	.1	.1
Filipino	42,964	39,615	92.2	41,128	39,073	95.0	1,836	542	29.5	.1	.1	—
All other	4,973	4,024	80.9	4,294	3,886	90.5	679	138	20.3	—	—	—
1920	**82,739,315**	**41,614,248**	**50.3**	**42,289,969**	**33,064,737**	**78.2**	**40,449,346**	**8,549,511**	**21.1**	**100.0**	**100.0**	**100.0**
Negro	8,053,225	4,824,151	59.9	4,009,462	3,252,862	81.1	4,043,763	1,571,289	38.9	11.6	9.8	18.4
Native white [1]	60,861,863	28,869,463	47.4	30,651,045	23,025,680	75.1	30,210,818	5,843,783	19.3	69.4	69.6	68.4
Foreign-born white [1]	13,497,886	7,746,460	57.4	7,419,691	6,627,997	89.3	6,078,195	1,118,463	18.4	18.6	20.0	13.1
Other races	326,341	174,174	53.4	209,771	158,198	75.4	116,570	15,976	13.7	.4	.5	.2
Indian	176,925	63,326	35.8	91,546	53,478	58.4	85,379	9,848	11.5	.2	.2	.1
Chinese	56,230	45,614	81.1	51,041	44,882	87.9	5,189	732	14.1	.1	.1	—
Japanese	84,238	57,903	68.7	58,806	52,614	89.5	25,432	5,289	20.8	.1	.2	.1
All other	8,948	7,331	81.9	8,378	7,224	86.2	570	107	18.8	—	—	—
1910	**71,580,270**	**38,167,336**	**53.3**	**37,027,558**	**30,091,564**	**81.3**	**34,552,712**	**8,075,772**	**23.4**	**100.0**	**100.0**	**100.0**
Negro	7,317,922	5,192,535	71.0	3,637,386	3,178,554	87.4	3,680,536	2,013,981	54.7	13.6	10.6	24.9
Native white [1]	50,989,341	24,962,554	49.0	25,843,033	20,141,636	77.9	25,146,308	4,820,918	19.2	65.4	66.9	59.7
Foreign-born white [1]	12,944,529	7,811,502	60.3	7,321,196	6,588,711	90.0	5,623,333	1,222,791	21.7	20.5	21.9	15.1
Other races	328,478	200,745	61.1	225,943	182,663	80.8	102,535	18,082	17.6	.5	.6	.2
Indian	188,758	73,916	39.2	96,582	59,206	61.3	92,176	14,710	16.0	.2	.2	.2
Chinese	68,924	123,811 (Chinese and Japanese)	90.6 (Chinese and Japanese)	65,479	120,460 (Chinese and Japanese)	95.4 (Chinese and Japanese)	3,445	3,351 (Chinese and Japanese)	32.5 (Chinese and Japanese)	.3 (Chinese and Japanese)	.4 (Chinese and Japanese)	—
Japanese	67,661			60,809			6,852					
All other	3,135	3,018	96.3	3,073	2,997	97.5	62	21	—	—	—	—

[1] In 1920 and in 1910 Mexicans were included for the most part in the white population.

TABLE 2.—NUMBER AND PROPORTION OF PERSONS GAINFULLY OCCUPIED, BY SEX, FOR THE UNITED STATES: 1900 TO 1930

SEX AND CENSUS YEAR	Total population	Population 10 years old and over	PERSONS 10 YEARS OLD AND OVER GAINFULLY OCCUPIED		
			Number	Percent of total population	Percent of population 10 years old and over
TOTAL					
1930	122,775,046	98,723,047	48,829,920	39.8	49.5
1920	105,710,620	82,739,315	41,614,248	39.4	50.3
1910	91,972,266	71,580,270	38,167,336	41.5	53.3
1900	75,994,575	57,949,824	29,073,233	38.3	50.2
MALE					
1930	62,137,080	49,949,798	38,077,804	61.3	76.2
1920	53,900,431	42,289,969	33,064,737	61.3	78.2
1910	47,332,277	37,027,558	30,091,564	63.6	81.3
1900	38,816,448	29,703,440	23,753,836	61.2	80.0
FEMALE					
1930	60,637,966	48,773,249	10,752,116	17.7	22.0
1920	51,810,189	40,449,346	8,549,511	16.5	21.1
1910	44,639,989	34,552,712	8,075,772	18.1	23.4
1900	37,178,127	28,246,384	5,319,397	14.3	18.8

TABLE 3.—NUMBER AND PROPORTION OF NEGROES GAINFULLY OCCUPIED, BY SEX, FOR THE UNITED STATES: 1910 TO 1930

SEX AND CENSUS YEAR	POPULATION		PERSONS 10 YEARS OLD AND OVER GAINFULLY OCCUPIED		
	Total	10 years old and over	Number	Percent of total population	Percent of population 10 years old and over
TOTAL					
1930	11,891,143	9,292,556	5,503,535	46.3	59.2
1920	10,463,131	8,053,225	4,824,151	46.1	59.9
1910	9,827,763	7,317,922	5,192,535	52.8	71.0
MALE					
1930	5,855,669	4,564,690	3,662,893	62.6	80.2
1920	5,209,436	4,009,462	3,252,862	62.4	81.1
1910	4,885,881	3,637,386	3,178,554	65.1	87.4
FEMALE					
1930	6,035,474	4,727,866	1,840,642	30.5	38.9
1920	5,253,695	4,043,763	1,571,289	29.9	38.9
1910	4,941,882	3,680,536	2,013,981	40.8	54.7

Table 4.—NUMBER AND PROPORTION OF PERSONS 10 YEARS OLD AND OVER GAINFULLY OCCUPIED, BY COLOR, NATIVITY, AND SEX, BY SECTIONS: 1930 AND 1920

CLASS OF POPULATION	TOTAL			MALE			FEMALE			PERCENT DISTRIBUTION OF GAINFULLY OCCUPIED		
	Total number	Gainfully occupied		Total number	Gainfully occupied		Total number	Gainfully occupied				
		Number	Percent		Number	Percent		Number	Percent	Total	Male	Female
	THE SOUTH											
1930	**29, 168, 784**	**14, 310, 217**	**49. 1**	**14, 624, 017**	**11, 147, 292**	**76. 2**	**14, 544, 767**	**3, 162, 925**	**21. 7**	**100. 0**	**100. 0**	**100. 0**
Negro	7, 194, 750	4, 210, 163	58. 5	3, 506, 598	2, 790, 120	79. 6	3, 688, 152	1, 420, 043	38. 5	29. 4	25. 0	44. 9
Native white	20, 864, 225	9, 521, 762	45. 6	10, 515, 369	7, 864, 076	74. 8	10, 348, 856	1, 657, 686	16. 0	66. 5	70. 5	52. 4
Foreign-born white	527, 946	300, 195	56. 9	298, 860	260, 006	87. 0	229, 086	40, 189	17. 5	2. 1	2. 3	1. 3
Other races [1]	581, 863	278, 097	47. 8	303, 190	233, 090	76. 9	278, 673	45, 007	16. 2	1. 9	2. 1	1. 4
1920	**24, 930, 212**	**12, 367, 091**	**49. 6**	**12, 631, 002**	**9, 753, 727**	**77. 2**	**12, 299, 210**	**2, 613, 364**	**21. 2**	**100. 0**	**100. 0**	**100. 0**
Negro	6, 733, 428	3, 969, 144	58. 9	3, 320, 344	2, 654, 917	80. 0	3, 413, 084	1, 314, 227	38. 5	32. 1	27. 2	50. 3
Native white	17, 326, 889	7, 903, 995	45. 6	8, 809, 398	6, 664, 304	75. 6	8, 517, 491	1, 239, 691	14. 6	63. 9	68. 3	47. 4
Foreign-born white	812, 649	472, 208	58. 1	470, 172	415, 191	88. 3	342, 477	57, 017	16. 6	3. 8	4. 3	2. 2
Other races [1]	57, 246	21, 744	38. 0	31, 088	19, 315	62. 1	26, 158	2, 429	9. 3	. 2	. 2	. 1
	THE NORTH											
1930	**59, 722, 192**	**29, 549, 871**	**49. 5**	**30, 155, 263**	**22, 961, 102**	**76. 1**	**29, 566, 929**	**6, 588, 769**	**22. 3**	**100. 0**	**100. 0**	**100. 0**
Negro	1, 994, 085	1, 228, 670	61. 6	1, 005, 003	829, 353	82. 5	989, 082	399, 317	40. 4	4. 2	3. 6	6. 1
Native white	46, 302, 661	21, 943, 512	47. 4	23, 078, 577	16, 755, 601	72. 6	23, 224, 084	5, 187, 911	22. 3	74. 3	73. 0	78. 7
Foreign-born white	11, 256, 622	6, 279, 199	55. 8	5, 958, 416	5, 283, 750	88. 7	5, 298, 206	995, 449	18. 8	21. 2	23. 0	15. 1
Other races [1]	168, 824	98, 490	58. 3	113, 267	92, 398	81. 6	55, 557	6, 092	11. 0	. 3	. 4	. 1
1920	**50, 632, 869**	**25, 578, 453**	**50. 5**	**25, 780, 163**	**20, 253, 565**	**78. 6**	**24, 852, 706**	**5, 324, 888**	**21. 4**	**100. 0**	**100. 0**	**100. 0**
Negro	1, 250, 708	807, 343	64. 6	649, 154	561, 774	86. 5	601, 554	245, 569	40. 8	3. 2	2. 8	4. 6
Native white	38, 074, 208	18, 326, 750	48. 1	19, 003, 721	14, 215, 814	74. 8	19, 070, 487	4, 110, 936	21. 6	71. 6	70. 2	77. 2
Foreign-born white	11, 238, 397	6, 408, 617	57. 0	6, 081, 256	5, 442, 379	89. 5	5, 157, 141	966, 238	18. 7	25. 1	26. 9	18. 1
Other races [1]	69, 556	35, 743	51. 4	46, 032	33, 598	73. 0	23, 524	2, 145	9. 1	. 1	. 2	(2)
	THE WEST											
1930	**9, 832, 071**	**4, 969, 832**	**50. 5**	**5, 170, 518**	**3, 969, 410**	**76. 8**	**4, 661, 553**	**1, 000, 422**	**21. 5**	**100. 0**	**100. 0**	**100. 0**
Negro	103, 721	64, 702	62. 4	53, 089	43, 420	81. 8	50, 632	21, 282	42. 0	1. 3	1. 1	2. 1
Native white	7, 596, 853	3, 708, 096	48. 8	3, 881, 955	2, 892, 185	74. 5	3, 714, 898	815, 911	22. 0	74. 6	72. 9	81. 6
Foreign-born white	1, 432, 360	831, 733	58. 1	820, 947	711, 315	86. 6	611, 413	120, 418	19. 7	16. 7	17. 9	12. 0
Other races [1]	699, 137	365, 301	52. 3	414, 527	322, 490	77. 8	284, 610	42, 811	15. 0	7. 4	8. 1	4. 3
1920	**7, 176, 234**	**3, 668, 704**	**51. 1**	**3, 878, 804**	**3, 057, 445**	**78. 8**	**3, 297, 430**	**611, 259**	**18. 5**	**100. 0**	**100. 0**	**100. 0**
Negro	69, 089	47, 664	69. 0	39, 964	36, 171	90. 5	29, 125	11, 493	39. 5	1. 3	1. 2	1. 9
Native white	5, 460, 766	2, 638, 718	48. 3	2, 837, 926	2, 145, 562	75. 6	2, 622, 840	493, 156	18. 8	71. 9	70. 2	80. 7
Foreign-born white	1, 446, 840	865, 365	59. 8	868, 263	770, 427	88. 7	578, 577	95, 208	16. 5	23. 6	25. 2	15. 6
Other races [1]	199, 539	116, 687	58. 5	132, 651	105, 285	79. 4	66, 888	11, 402	17. 0	3. 2	3. 4	1. 9

[1] Comprises Mexicans, Indians, Chinese, Japanese, Filipinos, Hindus, Koreans, Hawaiians, etc., in 1930. In 1920 Mexicans were included for the most part in the white population.
[2] Less than 1/10 of 1 percent.

Table 5.—Gainful Workers 10 Years Old and Over, by General Divisions of Occupations, by Color, and Nativity, per 1,000 Population, for the United States: 1930

OCCUPATION	DISTRIBUTION PER 1,000 GAINFULLY OCCUPIED		
	Negro	Native white	Foreign-born white
Total	**1, 000**	**1, 000**	**1, 000**
Agriculture	361	214	91
Domestic and personal service	287	66	127
Manufacturing and mechanical industries	186	275	441
Transportation, etc	72	82	66
Trade	33	137	127
Professional service	25	79	44
Extraction of minerals	14	19	31
Public service (not elsewhere classified)	9	19	16
Clerical occupations	7	104	41
Forestry and fishing	6	5	6

Table 6.—Gainful Workers 10 Years Old and Over, by Occupations in Which Negroes Predominated, in the United States: 1930

OCCUPATION	Total, all classes	NEGRO			
		Total	Male	Female	Percent of all classes
Bootblacks	18, 784	9, 499	9, 481	18	50. 6
Cooks, other than in hotels, restaurants, and boarding houses	321, 722	220, 538	17, 478	203, 060	68. 5
Laborers, cigar and tobacco factories	20, 581	12, 254	8, 863	3, 391	59. 5
Laborers, fertilizer factories	18, 243	15, 347	15, 268	79	84. 1
Laborers, turpentine farms and distilleries	37, 620	30, 849	30, 577	272	82. 0
Launderers and laundresses (not in laundry)	361, 033	271, 083	1, 985	269, 098	75. 1
Midwives	3, 566	1, 787	--------	1, 787	50. 1
Operatives, fertilizer factories	1, 538	1, 039	1, 000	39	67. 6
Operatives, turpentine farms and distilleries	1, 368	726	721	5	53. 1
Porters, except in stores	127, 488	93, 744	93, 714	30	73. 5

TABLE 7.—GAINFUL WORKERS 10 YEARS OLD AND OVER, BY COLOR, NATIVITY, AND GENERAL DIVISIONS OF OCCUPATIONS, FOR THE UNITED STATES: 1930, 1920, AND 1910

GENERAL DIVISION OF OCCUPATIONS	TOTAL		NEGRO		NATIVE WHITE		FOREIGN-BORN WHITE		OTHER RACES [1]		PERCENT OF TOTAL			
	Number	Per-cent distri-bution	Number	Per-cent distri-bution	Number	Per-cent distri-bution	Number	Per-cent distri-bution	Number	Per-cent distri-bution	Negro	Native white	For-eign-born white	Other races
1930—All occupations	**48, 829, 920**	**100. 0**	**5, 503, 535**	**100. 0**	**35, 173, 370**	**100. 0**	**7, 411, 127**	**100. 0**	**741, 888**	**100. 0**	**11. 3**	**72. 0**	**15. 2**	**1. 5**
Agriculture	10, 471, 998	21. 4	1, 987, 839	36. 1	7, 518, 519	21. 4	673, 662	9. 1	291, 978	39. 4	19. 0	71. 8	6. 4	2. 8
Forestry and fishing	250, 469	. 5	31, 732	. 6	167, 077	. 5	44, 846	. 6	6, 814	. 9	12. 7	66. 7	17. 9	2. 7
Extraction of minerals	984, 323	2. 0	74, 972	1. 4	658, 267	1. 9	232, 121	3. 1	18, 963	2. 6	7. 6	66. 9	23. 6	1. 9
Manufacturing and mechanical industries	14, 110, 652	28. 9	1, 024, 656	18. 6	9, 663, 796	27. 5	3, 265, 381	44. 1	156, 819	21. 1	7. 3	68. 5	23. 1	1. 1
Transportation and communication	3, 843, 147	7. 9	397, 645	7. 2	2, 876, 682	8. 2	488, 303	6. 6	80, 517	10. 9	10. 3	74. 9	12. 7	2. 1
Trade	6, 081, 467	12. 5	183, 809	3. 3	4, 835, 498	13. 7	1, 012, 605	13. 7	49, 555	6. 7	3. 0	79. 5	16. 7	. 8
Public service (not elsewhere classified)	856, 205	1. 8	50, 203	. 9	678, 578	1. 9	120, 775	1. 6	6, 649	. 9	5. 9	79. 3	14. 1	. 8
Professional service	3, 253, 884	6. 7	135, 925	2. 5	2, 775, 453	7. 9	328, 745	4. 4	13, 761	1. 9	4. 2	85. 3	10. 1	. 4
Domestic and personal service	4, 952, 451	10. 1	1, 576, 205	28. 6	2, 327, 821	6. 6	940, 904	12. 7	107, 521	14. 5	31. 8	47. 0	19. 0	2. 2
Clerical occupations	4, 025, 324	8. 2	40, 549	. 7	3, 671, 679	10. 4	303, 785	4. 1	9, 311	1. 3	1. 0	91. 2	7. 5	. 2
1920—All occupations	**41, 614, 248**	**100. 0**	**4, 824, 151**	**100. 0**	**28, 869, 463**	**100. 0**	**7, 746, 460**	**100. 0**	**174, 174**	**100. 0**	**11. 6**	**69. 4**	**18. 6**	**. 4**
Agriculture	10, 665, 812	25. 6	2, 133, 135	44. 2	7, 595, 074	26. 3	865, 752	11. 2	71, 851	41. 3	20. 0	71. 2	8. 1	. 7
Forestry and fishing	270, 214	. 6	31, 375	. 7	168, 438	. 6	65, 802	. 8	4, 599	2. 6	11. 6	62. 3	24. 4	1. 7
Extraction of minerals	1, 090, 223	2. 6	73, 229	1. 5	637, 934	2. 2	377, 138	4. 9	1, 922	1. 1	6. 7	58. 5	34. 6	. 2
Manufacturing and mechanical industries	12, 831, 879	30. 8	901, 181	18. 7	8, 274, 144	28. 7	3, 633, 914	46. 9	22, 640	13. 0	7. 0	64. 5	28. 3	. 2
Transportation and communication	3, 096, 829	7. 4	312, 538	6. 5	2, 227, 024	7. 7	549, 269	7. 1	7, 998	4. 6	10. 1	71. 9	17. 7	. 3
Trade	4, 257, 684	10. 2	141, 119	2. 9	3, 240, 479	11. 2	862, 365	11. 1	13, 721	7. 9	3. 3	76. 1	20. 3	. 3
Public service (not elsewhere classified)	738, 525	1. 8	50, 436	1. 0	560, 231	1. 9	125, 723	1. 6	2, 135	1. 2	6. 8	75. 9	17. 0	. 3
Professional service	2, 171, 251	5. 2	81, 771	1. 7	1, 847, 442	6. 4	238, 875	3. 1	3, 163	1. 8	3. 8	85. 1	11. 0	. 1
Domestic and personal service	3, 379, 995	8. 1	1, 063, 008	22. 0	1, 510, 796	5. 2	762, 280	9. 8	43, 911	25. 2	31. 4	44. 7	22. 6	1. 3
Clerical occupations	3, 111, 836	7. 5	36, 359	. 8	2, 807, 901	9. 7	265, 342	3. 4	2, 234	1. 3	1. 2	90. 2	8. 5	. 1
1910—All occupations	**38, 167, 336**	**100. 0**	**5, 192, 535**	**100. 0**	**24, 962, 554**	**100. 0**	**7, 811, 502**	**100. 0**	**200, 745**	**100. 0**	**13. 6**	**65. 4**	**20. 5**	**. 5**
Agriculture	12, 388, 309	32. 5	2, 834, 969	54. 6	8, 433, 130	33. 8	1, 039, 760	13. 3	80, 450	40. 1	22. 9	68. 1	8. 4	. 6
Forestry and fishing	241, 806	. 6	33, 776	. 7	146, 719	. 6	57, 137	. 7	4, 174	2. 1	14. 0	60. 7	23. 6	1. 7
Extraction of minerals	965, 169	2. 5	61, 129	1. 2	438, 448	1. 8	463, 036	5. 9	2, 556	1. 3	6. 3	45. 4	48. 0	. 3
Manufacturing and mechanical industries	10, 656, 545	27. 9	655, 906	12. 6	6, 582, 277	26. 4	3, 389, 379	43. 4	28, 983	14. 4	6. 2	61. 8	31. 8	. 3
Transportation and communication	2, 665, 269	7. 0	256, 098	4. 9	1, 703, 338	6. 8	694, 215	8. 9	11, 618	5. 8	9. 6	63. 9	26. 0	. 4
Trade	3, 633, 265	9. 5	119, 775	2. 3	2, 725, 426	10. 9	774, 575	9. 9	13, 489	6. 7	3. 3	75. 0	21. 3	. 4
Public service (not elsewhere classified)	431, 442	1. 1	22, 229	. 4	310, 323	1. 2	97, 969	1. 3	921	. 5	5. 2	71. 9	22. 7	. 2
Professional service	1, 711, 275	4. 5	68, 350	1. 3	1, 434, 560	5. 7	205, 550	2. 6	2, 815	1. 4	4. 0	83. 8	12. 0	. 2
Domestic and personal service	3, 755, 798	9. 8	1, 121, 251	21. 6	1, 661, 140	6. 7	919, 022	11. 8	54, 385	27. 1	29. 9	44. 2	24. 5	1. 4
Clerical occupations	1, 718, 458	4. 5	19, 052	. 4	1, 527, 193	6. 1	170, 859	2. 2	1, 354	. 7	1. 1	88. 9	9. 9	. 1

[1] Comprises Mexicans, Indians, Chinese, Japanese, Filipinos, Hindus, Koreans, Hawaiians, etc. In 1920 and 1910 Mexicans were included for the most part in the white population.

TABLE 8.—GAINFUL WORKERS 10 YEARS OLD AND OVER, BY COLOR, NATIVITY, SEX, AND GENERAL DIVISIONS OF OCCUPATIONS, FOR THE UNITED STATES: 1930

[Percent not shown where less than 1/10 of 1 percent]

SEX AND GENERAL DIVISION OF OCCUPATIONS	TOTAL		NEGRO		NATIVE WHITE		FOREIGN-BORN WHITE		OTHER RACES [1]		PERCENT OF TOTAL			
	Number	Percent distri-bution	Number	Percent distri-bution	Number	Percent distri-bution	Number	Percent distri-bution	Number	Percent distri-bution	Negro	Native white	Foreign born white	Other races [1]
Total—All occupations	**48, 829, 920**	**100. 0**	**5, 503, 535**	**100. 0**	**35, 173, 370**	**100. 0**	**7, 411, 127**	**100. 0**	**741. 888**	**100. 0**	**11. 3**	**72. 0**	**15. 2**	**1. 5**
Agriculture	10, 471, 998	21. 4	1, 987, 839	36. 1	7. 518, 519	21. 4	673, 662	9. 1	291, 978	39. 4	19. 0	71. 8	6. 4	2. 8
Forestry and fishing	250, 469	. 5	31, 732	. 6	167. 077	. 5	44, 846	. 6	6, 814	. 9	12. 7	66. 7	17. 9	2. 7
Extraction of minerals	984, 323	2. 0	74, 972	1. 4	658, 267	1. 9	232, 121	3. 1	18, 963	2. 6	7. 6	66. 9	23. 6	1. 9
Manufacturing and mechanical industries	14, 110, 652	28. 9	1, 024, 656	18. 6	9, 663, 796	27. 5	3, 265, 381	44. 1	156, 819	21. 1	7. 3	68. 5	23. 1	1. 1
Transportation and communication	3, 843, 147	7. 9	397. 645	7. 2	2, 876, 682	8. 2	488, 303	6. 6	80, 517	10. 9	10. 3	74. 9	12. 7	2. 1
Trade	6, 081, 467	12. 5	183, 809	3. 3	4, 835, 498	13. 7	1, 012, 605	13. 7	49, 555	6. 7	3. 0	79. 5	16. 7	. 8
Public service (not elsewhere classified)	856, 205	1. 8	50, 203	. 9	678. 578	1. 9	120, 775	1. 6	6, 649	. 9	5. 9	79. 3	14. 1	. 8
Professional service	3, 253, 884	6. 7	135, 925	2. 5	2, 775, 453	7. 9	328, 745	4. 4	13, 761	1. 9	4. 2	85. 3	10. 1	. 4
Domestic and personal service	4, 952, 451	10. 1	1, 576, 205	28. 6	2, 327, 821	6. 6	940, 904	12. 7	107, 521	14. 5	31. 8	47. 0	19. 0	2. 2
Clerical occupations	4, 025, 324	8. 2	40, 549	. 7	3, 671, 679	10. 4	303, 785	4. 1	9, 311	1. 3	1. 0	91. 2	7. 5	. 2
Male—All occupations	**38, 077, 804**	**100. 0**	**3, 662, 893**	**100. 0**	**27, 511, 862**	**100. 0**	**6, 255, 071**	**100. 0**	**647, 978**	**100. 0**	**9. 6**	**72. 3**	**16. 4**	**1. 7**
Agriculture	9, 562, 059	25. 1	1, 492. 555	40. 7	7, 151, 291	26. 0	647, 249	10. 3	270, 964	41. 8	15. 6	74. 8	6. 8	2. 8
Forestry and fishing	250, 140	. 7	31, 652	. 9	166, 883	. 6	44, 837	. 7	6, 768	1. 0	12. 7	66. 7	17. 9	2. 7
Extraction of minerals	983, 564	2. 6	74, 919	2. 0	657, 654	2. 4	232, 042	3. 7	18, 949	2. 9	7. 6	66. 9	23. 6	1. 9
Manufacturing and mechanical industries	12, 224, 345	32. 1	923. 586	25. 2	8. 212. 540	29. 9	2, 951, 751	47. 2	136, 468	21. 1	7. 6	67. 2	24. 1	1. 1
Transportation and communication	3, 561, 943	9. 4	395, 437	10. 8	2, 610, 354	9. 5	476, 095	7. 6	80, 057	12. 4	11. 1	73. 3	13. 4	2. 2
Trade	5, 118, 787	13. 4	169, 241	4. 6	4, 004, 558	14. 6	903, 042	14. 4	41, 946	6. 5	3. 3	78. 2	17. 6	. 8
Public service (not elsewhere classified)	838, 622	2. 2	49, 273	1. 3	662, 974	2. 4	119, 795	1. 9	6, 580	1. 0	5. 9	79. 1	14. 3	. 8
Professional service	1, 727, 650	4. 5	72, 898	2. 0	1, 419, 063	5. 2	225, 397	3. 6	10, 292	1. 6	4. 2	82. 1	13. 0	. 6
Domestic and personal service	1, 772, 200	4. 7	423, 645	11. 6	813, 780	3. 0	465, 465	7. 4	69, 310	10. 7	23. 9	45. 9	26. 3	3. 9
Clerical occupations	2, 038, 494	5. 4	29, 687	. 8	1, 812, 765	6. 6	189, 398	3. 0	6, 644	1. 0	1. 5	88. 9	9. 3	. 3
Female—All occupations	**10, 752, 116**	**100. 0**	**1, 840, 642**	**100. 0**	**7, 661, 508**	**100. 0**	**1, 156, 056**	**100. 0**	**93, 910**	**100. 0**	**17. 1**	**71. 3**	**10. 8**	**. 3**
Agriculture	909, 939	8. 5	495. 284	26. 9	367, 228	4. 8	26, 413	2. 3	21, 014	22. 5	54. 4	40. 4	2. 9	2. 9
Forestry and fishing	329	--------	80	--------	194	--------	9	--------	46	--------	24. 3	59. 0	2. 7	14. 0
Extraction of minerals	759	--------	53	--------	613	--------	79	--------	14	--------	7. 0	80. 8	10. 4	1. 8
Manufacturing and mechanical industries	1, 886, 307	17. 5	101, 070	5. 5	1, 451, 256	18. 9	313, 630	27. 1	20. 351	21. 7	5. 4	76. 9	16. 6	1. 1
Transportation and communication	281, 204	2. 6	2, 208	. 1	266, 328	3. 5	12, 208	1. 1	460	. 5	. 8	94. 7	4. 3	. 2
Trade	962. 680	9. 0	14, 568	. 8	830, 940	10. 8	109, 563	9. 5	7, 609	8. 1	1. 5	86. 3	11. 4	. 8
Public service (not elsewhere classified)	17, 583	. 2	930	. 1	15, 604	. 2	980	. 1	69	. 1	5. 3	88. 7	5. 6	. 4
Professional service	1, 526, 234	14. 2	63, 027	3. 4	1, 356, 390	17. 7	103, 348	8. 9	3, 469	3. 7	4. 1	88. 9	6. 8	. 2
Domestic and personal service	3, 180, 251	29. 6	1, 152, 560	62. 6	1, 514, 041	19. 8	475, 439	41. 4	38, 211	40. 7	36. 2	47. 6	14. 9	1. 2
Clerical occupations	1, 986, 830	18. 5	10, 862	. 6	1, 858, 914	24. 3	114, 387	9. 9	2, 667	2. 8	. 5	93. 6	5. 8	. 1

[1] Comprises Mexicans, Indians, Chinese, Japanese, Filipinos, Hindus, Koreans, Hawaiians, etc.

TABLE 9.—NUMBER AND PERCENT DISTRIBUTION OF GAINFUL WORKERS 10 YEARS OLD AND OVER, BY COLOR, AND NATIVITY, BY SECTIONS: 1930

GENERAL DIVISION OF OCCUPATIONS	TOTAL		NEGRO		NATIVE WHITE		FOREIGN-BORN WHITE		OTHER RACES [1]		PERCENT OF TOTAL			
	Number	Percent distribution	Number	Percent distribution	Number	Percent distribution	Number	Percent distribution	Number	Percent distribution	Negro	Native white	Foreign-born white	Other races [1]
	UNITED STATES													
All occupations	48, 829, 920	100. 0	5, 503, 535	100. 0	35, 173, 370	100. 0	7, 411, 127	100. 0	741, 888	100. 0	11. 3	72. 0	15. 2	1. 5
Agriculture	10, 471, 998	21. 4	1, 987, 839	36. 1	7, 518, 519	21. 4	673, 662	9. 1	291, 978	39. 4	19. 0	71. 8	6. 4	2. 8
Forestry and fishing	250, 469	. 5	31, 732	. 6	167, 077	. 5	44, 846	. 6	6, 814	. 9	12. 7	66. 7	17. 9	2. 7
Extraction of minerals	984, 323	2. 0	74, 972	1. 4	658, 267	1. 9	232, 121	3. 1	18, 963	2. 6	7. 6	66. 9	23. 6	1. 9
Manufacturing and mechanical industries	14, 110, 652	28. 9	1, 024, 656	18. 6	9, 663, 796	27. 5	3, 265, 381	44. 1	156, 819	21. 1	7. 3	68. 5	23. 1	1. 1
Transportation and communication	3, 843, 147	7. 9	397, 645	7. 2	2, 876, 682	8. 2	488, 303	6. 6	80, 517	10. 9	10. 3	74. 9	12. 7	2. 1
Trade	6, 081, 467	12. 5	183, 809	3. 3	4, 835, 498	13. 7	1, 012, 605	13. 7	49, 555	6. 7	3. 0	79. 5	16. 7	. 3
Public service (not elsewhere classified)	856, 205	1. 8	50, 203	. 9	678, 578	1. 9	120, 775	1. 6	6, 649	. 9	5. 9	79. 3	14. 1	. 8
Professional service	3, 253, 884	6. 7	135, 925	2. 5	2, 775, 453	7. 9	328, 745	4. 4	13, 761	1. 9	4. 2	85. 3	10. 1	. 4
Domestic and personal service	4, 952, 451	10. 1	1, 576, 205	28. 6	2, 327, 821	6. 6	940, 904	12. 7	107, 521	14. 5	31. 8	47. 0	19. 0	2. 2
Clerical occupations	4, 025, 324	8. 2	40, 549	. 7	3, 671, 679	10. 4	303, 785	4. 1	9, 311	1. 3	1. 0	91. 2	7. 5	. 2
	THE NORTH													
All occupations	29, 549, 871	100. 0	1, 228, 670	100. 0	21, 943, 512	100. 0	6, 279, 199	100. 0	98, 490	100. 0	4. 2	74. 3	21. 2	0. 3
Agriculture	3, 943, 198	13. 3	38, 816	3. 2	3, 415, 620	15. 6	475, 150	7. 6	13, 612	13. 8	1. 0	86. 6	12. 0	. 3
Forestry and fishing	72, 355	. 2	478	(2)	50, 906	. 2	19, 672	. 3	1, 299	1. 3	. 7	70. 4	27. 2	1. 8
Extraction of minerals	516, 593	1. 7	14, 364	1. 2	319, 621	1. 5	182, 006	2. 9	602	. 6	2. 8	61. 9	35. 2	. 1
Manufacturing and mechanical industries	10, 065, 768	34. 1	375, 083	30. 5	6, 730, 939	30. 7	2, 928, 430	46. 6	30, 656	31. 1	3. 7	66. 9	29. 1	. 3
Transportation and communication	2, 478, 876	8. 4	130, 711	10. 6	1, 916, 761	8. 7	414, 639	6. 6	16, 657	16. 9	5. 3	77. 3	16. 7	. 7
Trade	3, 982, 800	13. 5	64, 159	5. 2	3, 074, 609	14. 0	839, 963	13. 4	4, 069	4. 1	1. 6	77. 2	21. 1	. 1
Public service (not elsewhere classified)	526, 523	1. 8	18, 319	1. 5	406, 249	1. 9	100, 796	1. 6	1, 159	1. 2	3. 5	77. 2	19. 1	. 2
Professional service	2, 104, 244	7. 1	36, 551	3. 0	1, 803, 300	8. 2	261, 878	4. 2	2, 515	2. 6	1. 7	85. 7	12. 4	. 1
Domestic and personal service	2, 926, 899	9. 9	524, 989	42. 7	1, 573, 954	7. 2	801, 696	12. 8	26, 260	26. 7	17. 9	53. 8	27. 4	. 9
Clerical occupations	2, 933, 383	9. 9	25, 200	2. 1	2, 651, 553	12. 1	254, 969	4. 1	1, 661	1. 7	. 9	90. 4	8. 7	. 1
	THE SOUTH													
All occupations	14, 310, 217	100. 0	4, 210, 163	100. 0	9, 521, 762	100. 0	300, 195	100. 0	278, 097	100. 0	29. 4	66. 5	2. 1	1. 9
Agriculture	5, 581, 438	39. 0	1, 945, 210	46. 2	3, 462, 362	36. 4	40, 130	13. 4	133, 736	48. 1	34. 9	62. 0	. 7	2. 4
Forestry and fishing	102, 152	. 7	31, 155	. 7	67, 886	. 7	1, 624	. 5	1, 487	. 5	30. 5	66. 5	1. 6	1. 5
Extraction of minerals	339, 266	2. 4	60, 025	1. 4	257, 065	2. 7	18, 626	6. 2	3, 550	1. 3	17. 7	75. 8	5. 5	1. 0
Manufacturing and mechanical industries	2, 858, 258	20. 0	639, 844	15. 2	2, 077, 400	21. 8	88, 867	29. 6	52, 147	18. 8	22. 4	72. 7	3. 1	1. 8
Transportation and communication	944, 863	6. 6	261, 069	6. 2	644, 032	6. 8	14, 886	5. 0	24, 876	8. 9	27. 6	68. 2	1. 6	2. 6
Trade	1, 355, 153	9. 5	117, 062	2. 8	1, 154, 027	12. 1	63, 922	21. 3	20, 142	7. 2	8. 6	85. 2	4. 7	1. 5
Public service (note lsewhere classified)	221, 148	1. 5	28, 860	. 7	182, 821	1. 9	6, 631	2. 2	2, 836	1. 0	13. 1	82. 7	3. 0	1. 3
Professional service	728, 564	5. 1	96, 832	2. 3	605, 708	6. 4	21, 385	7. 1	4, 639	1. 7	13. 3	83. 1	2. 9	. 6
Domestic and personal service	1, 503, 305	10. 5	1, 015, 776	24. 1	423, 850	4. 5	32, 541	10. 8	31, 138	11. 2	67. 6	28. 2	2. 2	2. 1
Clerical occupations	676, 070	4. 7	14, 330	. 3	646, 611	6. 8	11, 583	3. 9	3, 546	1. 3	2. 1	95. 6	1. 7	. 5
	THE WEST													
All occupations	4, 969, 832	100. 0	64, 702	100. 0	3, 708, 096	100. 0	831, 733	100. 0	365, 301	1. 3	1. 3	74. 6	16. 7	7. 4
Agriculture	947, 362	19. 1	3, 813	5. 9	640, 537	17. 3	158, 382	19. 0	144, 630	39. 6	. 4	67. 6	16. 7	15. 3
Forestry and fishing	75, 962	1. 5	99	. 2	48, 285	1. 3	23, 550	2. 8	4, 028	1. 1	. 1	63. 6	31. 0	5. 3
Extraction of minerals	128, 464	2. 6	583	. 9	81, 581	2. 2	31, 489	3. 8	14, 811	4. 1	. 5	63. 5	24. 5	11. 5
Manufacturing and mechanical industries	1, 187, 286	23. 9	9, 729	15. 0	855, 457	23. 1	248, 084	29. 8	74, 016	20. 3	. 8	72. 1	20. 9	6. 2
Transportation and communication	419, 516	8. 4	5, 865	9. 1	315, 889	8. 5	58, 778	7. 1	38, 984	10. 7	1. 4	75. 3	14. 0	9. 3
Trade	743, 514	15. 0	2, 588	4. 0	606, 862	16. 4	108, 720	13. 1	25, 344	6. 9	. 3	81. 6	14. 6	3. 4
Public service (not elsewhere classified)	108, 534	2. 2	3, 024	4. 7	89, 508	2. 4	13, 348	1. 6	2, 654	. 7	2. 8	82. 5	12. 3	2. 4
Professional service	421, 076	8. 5	2, 542	3. 9	366, 445	9. 9	45, 482	5. 5	6, 607	1. 8	. 6	87. 0	10. 8	1. 6
Domestic and personal service	522, 247	10. 5	35, 440	54. 8	330, 017	8. 9	106, 667	12. 8	50, 123	13. 7	6. 8	63. 2	20. 4	9. 6
Clerical occupations	415, 871	8. 4	1, 019	1. 6	373, 515	10. 1	37, 233	4. 5	4, 104	1. 1	. 2	89. 8	9. 0	1. 0

[1] Comprises Mexicans, Indians, Chinese, Japanese, Filipinos, Hindus, Koreans, Hawaiians, etc.
[2] Less than 1/10 of 1 percent.

TABLE 10.—OCCUPATIONAL GAINS AND LOSSES MADE BY NEGROES IN THE MANUFACTURING AND MECHANICAL INDUSTRIES, FOR THE UNITED STATES: 1920 TO 1930

[Data for 1920 have been made comparable with those for 1930 by excluding those occupations which were classified in "Manufacturing and mechanical industries" group in 1920 but transferred to other groups in 1930; similarly, certain occupations classified in other groups in 1920 but included in the "Manufacturing and mechanical industries" in 1930 have been included in 1920 data]

[Percent not shown where base is less than 100]

OCCUPATION	1930	1920	INCREASE OR DECREASE (—) Number	INCREASE OR DECREASE (—) Percent
Manufacturing and mechanical industries	**1,024,656**	**[1] 901,181**	**123,475**	**13.7**
Apprentices to building and hand trades	643	1,267	—624	—49.3
Apprentices, other (except to building and hand trades)	448	[2] 1,052	—604	—57.4
Bakers	4,527	3,164	1,363	43.1
Blacksmiths, forgemen, and hammermen	5,682	8,886	—3,204	—36.1
Boilermakers	1,030	1,398	—368	—26.3
Brick and stone masons and tile layers	11,701	10,609	1,092	10.3
Builders and building contractors	2,570	1,454	1,116	76.8
Cabinetmakers	479	456	23	5.0
Carpenters	32,413	34,243	—1,830	—5.3
Compositors, linotypers, and typesetters	2,101	1,540	561	36.4
Coopers	1,849	2,191	—342	—15.6
Dressmakers and seamstresses (not in factory)	20,439	26,973	—6,534	—24.2
Dyers	510	298	212	71.1
Electricians	1,913	1,342	571	42.5
Electrotypers, stereotypers, and lithographers	48	78	—30	------
Engineers (stationary), cranemen, hoistmen, etc.				
Engravers	5,236	6,353	—1,117	—17.6
Filers, grinders, buffers, and polishers (metal)	29	45	—16	------
Firemen (except locomotive and fire department)	1,607	936	671	71.7
	18,265	23,153	—4,888	—21.1
Foremen and overseers (manufacturing)	2,653	[3] 3,444	—791	—23.0
Furnace men, smelter men, heaters, puddlers, etc	3,091	3,236	—145	—4.5
Glass blowers	34	45	—11	------
Jewelers, watchmakers, goldsmiths, and silversmiths	275	524	—249	—47.5
Loom fixers	9	29	—20	------
Machinists, millwrights, and toolmakers	8,218	10,286	—2,068	—20.1
Managers and officials (manufacturing)	337	177	160	90.4
Manufacturers	1,046	[4] 401	645	160.8
Mechanics (not otherwise specified)	26,710	([5])	------	------
Millers (grain, flour, feed, etc.)	240	367	—127	—34.6
Milliners and millinery dealers	451	590	—139	—23.6
Molders, founders, and casters (metal)	8,346	6,634	1,712	25.8
Oilers of machinery	1,073	1,027	46	4.5
Painters, glaziers, varnishers, enamelers, etc	18,293	9,432	8,861	93.9
Paper hangers	2,154	954	1,200	125.8
Pattern and model makers	54	48	6	------
Piano and organ tuners	80	77	3	------
Plasterers and cement finishers	13,465	7,082	6,383	90.1
Plumbers and gas and steam fitters	4,729	3,516	1,213	34.5
Pressmen and plate printers (printing)	189	101	88	87.1
Rollers and roll hands (metal)	1,224	736	488	66.3
Roofers and slaters	1,044	609	435	71.4
Sawyers	3,449	2,755	694	25.2
Shoemakers and cobblers (not in factory)	4,150	4,707	—557	—11.8
Skilled occupations (not elsewhere classified)	149	161	—12	—7.5
Stonecutters	328	280	48	17.1
Structural iron workers (building)	348	196	152	77.6
Tailors and tailoresses	7,505	6,892	613	8.9
Tinsmiths and coppersmiths	887	970	—83	—8.6
Upholsterers	915	648	267	41.2
Operatives (not otherwise specified):				
Building industry	685	345	340	98.6
Chemical and allied industries	4,368	3,155	1,213	38.4
Cigar and tobacco factories	20,721	19,849	872	4.4
Clay, glass, and stone industries	3,516	3,551	—35	—1.0
Clothing industries	22,216	13,888	8,328	60.0
Food and allied industries	17,834	16,515	1,319	8.0
Iron and steel, machinery, and vehicle industries	23,922	23,616	306	1.3
Metal industries (except iron and steel)	1,241	1,234	7	.6
Leather industries	2,004	2,907	—903	—31.1
Lumber and furniture industries	10,241	9,598	643	6.7
Paper, printing, and allied industries	2,866	2,704	162	6.0
Textile industries	7,238	7,687	—449	—5.8
Miscellaneous manufacturing industries	18,066	} 20,148	11,765	58.4
Not specified industries and services	13,847			
Laborers (not otherwise specified):				
Building, general, and not specified laborers	224,136	148,051	76,085	51.4
Chemical and allied industries	37,724	27,706	10,018	36.2
Cigar and tobacco factories	12,254	21,334	—9,080	—42.6
Clay, glass, and stone industries	22,399	18,753	3,646	19.4
Clothing industries	1,809	1,407	402	28.6
Food and allied industries	26,760	29,316	—2,556	—8.7
Iron and steel, machinery, and vehicle industries	107,739	105,641	2,098	2.0
Metal industries (except iron and steel)	5,293	3,996	1,297	32.5
Leather industries	2,705	3,391	—686	—20.2
Lumber and furniture industries	112,056	106,276	5,780	5.4
Paper, printing, and allied industries	6,276	4,318	1,958	45.3
Textile industries	15,022	17,047	—2,025	—11.9
Miscellaneous manufacturing industries	78,782	[6] 88,096	—9,314	—10.6

[1] Includes 9,290 Negroes omitted in detail because not comparable with 1930.
[2] Excludes "architects', designers', and draftsmen's apprentices."
[3] Includes "Farm foremen, turpentine farms."
[4] Includes "Farmers, turpentine farms."
[5] Comparable figures for 1920 not available.
[6] Includes "Farm laborers (turpentine farms)."

TABLE 11.—AVERAGE NUMBER OF NEGROES TO EACH NEGRO REPORTED IN THE PRINCIPAL PROFESSIONAL OCCUPATIONS, BY DIVISIONS, AND STATES: 1930

SECTION, DIVISION, AND STATE	Clergyman	College president and professor [1]	Dentist	Lawyer, judge, and justice	Musician and teacher of music	Physician and surgeon	Teacher (school)	Trained nurse
United States	**475**	**5,541**	**6,707**	**9,536**	**1,124**	**3,125**	**218**	**2,076**
The North	**423**	**12,747**	**2,605**	**3,141**	**392**	**1,582**	**403**	**1,231**
The South	**495**	**4,796**	**11,731**	**21,472**	**2,446**	**4,286**	**194**	**2,567**
The West	**289**	**24,069**	**2,407**	**2,735**	**196**	**1,228**	**665**	**971**
NEW ENGLAND	493	8,553	1,568	2,002	389	1,447	765	1,960
Maine	274	------	------	------	------	------	548	------
New Hampshire	------	------	------	------	790	------	395	------
Vermont	------	------	------	------	284	------	------	------
Massachusetts	513	5,818	1,247	1,378	315	1,114	595	1,496
Rhode Island	431	9,913	1,983	3,304	413	2,478	901	3,304
Connecticut	473	29,354	2,258	4,892	599	2,097	1,468	2,935
MIDDLE ATLANTIC	495	30,968	2,543	5,484	339	2,013	518	970
New York	641	21,727	2,517	3,440	193	1,966	592	536
New Jersey	390	26,104	2,861	9,079	604	1,952	401	1,848
Pennsylvania	455	61,608	2,436	8,801	699	2,093	529	2,124
EAST NORTH CENTRAL	405	11,929	2,689	2,231	466	1,387	457	1,865
Ohio	368	4,419	3,222	3,256	566	2,035	589	3,915
Indiana	318	55,991	3,199	1,806	704	1,400	192	2,800
Illinois	449	82,243	2,069	1,713	385	994	414	1,241
Michigan	486	84,727	3,389	2,648	480	1,678	1,334	1,584
Wisconsin	447	------	1,790	2,685	128	1,534	2,148	1,342
WEST NORTH CENTRAL	307	5,027	3,160	2,989	416	1,257	186	1,024
Minnesota	315	4,723	1,574	787	109	1,889	1,349	945
Iowa	241	8,690	2,897	2,173	435	2,173	1,931	4,345
Missouri	338	5,460	3,109	4,070	499	1,131	165	842
North Dakota	------	------	------	------	54	------	377	------
South Dakota	129	------	------	------	108	------	215	------
Nebraska	299	13,752	1,965	1,719	162	1,250	3,438	2,750
Kansas	251	3,317	4,739	2,369	539	1,580	165	1,701
SOUTH ATLANTIC	500	4,187	10,428	15,962	2,793	4,191	181	1,947
Delaware	329	1,918	5,434	16,301	1,254	2,508	167	4,075
Maryland	507	9,213	8,129	8,375	940	2,764	178	1,738
District of Columbia	484	1,390	1,834	1,348	572	691	101	763
Virginia	554	4,364	10,320	11,020	2,839	3,964	168	1,826
West Virginia	358	1,883	5,222	5,745	1,596	1,715	117	2,445
North Carolina	583	3,734	13,510	34,024	4,459	5,602	164	2,469
South Carolina	620	4,535	14,698	61,052	10,872	11,846	213	2,756
Georgia	513	6,086	17,852	71,408	5,052	5,550	212	1,800
Florida	290	4,036	9,596	43,183	1,799	4,498	208	1,582
EAST SOUTH CENTRAL	536	5,960	14,686	43,578	3,102	4,365	219	2,967
Kentucky	311	5,796	6,109	9,042	911	1,752	140	2,628
Tennessee	409	4,975	6,824	18,371	1,873	1,630	172	1,737
Alabama	572	6,797	20,996	236,209	4,478	8,145	227	2,304
Mississippi	717	5,870	34,818	168,286	7,061	14,221	281	8,078
WEST SOUTH CENTRAL	445	5,071	11,824	23,285	1,645	4,388	194	4,754
Arkansas	538	6,645	15,949	29,904	3,148	4,691	242	4,234
Louisiana	599	9,953	17,252	97,041	1,756	7,255	265	4,913
Oklahoma	272	4,783	9,567	3,249	946	1,656	103	3,743
Texas	370	3,239	8,550	40,713	1,399	4,130	165	5,245
MOUNTAIN	250	7,556	3,778	10,075	236	1,119	364	2,015
Montana	179	------	------	------	179	------	628	------
Idaho	223	------	------	------	334	668	------	------
Wyoming	179	------	------	------	156	------	1,250	------
Colorado	269	2,957	2,957	5,914	150	910	1,075	2,366
New Mexico	219	------	1,425	------	570	950	317	1,425
Arizona	256	------	5,375	10,749	448	1,075	182	1,792
Utah	369	------	------	------	554	------	------	554
Nevada	258	------	------	------	516	------	516	------
PACIFIC	305	90,122	2,146	2,198	185	1,269	920	827
Washington	297	------	2,280	2,280	114	2,280	6,840	1,710
Oregon	447	------	2,234	745	186	2,234	2,234	2,234
California	304	81,048	2,133	2,316	195	1,210	844	779

[1] Probably includes some teachers in schools below collegiate rank.

TABLE 12.—NUMBER OF NEGROES ENGAGED IN PRINCIPAL PROFESSIONS, BY SECTIONS, DIVISIONS, AND STATES: 1930

SECTION, DIVISION, AND STATE [1]	Total Negro population	NUMBER OF—							
		Clergymen	College presidents and professors [2]	Dentists	Lawyers, judges, and justices	Musicians and teachers of music	Physicians and surgeons	Teachers (school)	Trained nurses
United States	11, 891, 143	25, 034	2, 146	1, 773	1, 247	10, 583	3, 805	54, 439	5, 728
The North	2, 409, 219	5, 694	139	925	767	6, 141	1, 523	5, 972	1, 957
The South	9, 361, 577	18, 924	1, 952	798	436	3, 827	2, 184	48, 286	3, 647
The West	120, 347	416	5	50	44	615	98	181	124
NEW ENGLAND	94, 086	191	11	60	47	242	65	123	48
Maine	1, 096	4	—	—	—	—	—	2	—
New Hampshire	790	—	—	—	—	1	—	2	—
Vermont	568	—	—	—	—	2	—	—	—
Massachusetts	52, 365	102	9	42	38	166	47	88	35
Rhode Island	9, 913	23	1	5	3	24	4	11	3
Connecticut	29, 354	62	1	13	6	49	14	20	10
MIDDLE ATLANTIC	1, 052, 899	2, 126	34	414	192	3, 106	523	2, 034	1, 086
New York	412, 814	644	19	164	120	2, 143	210	697	770
New Jersey	208, 828	535	8	73	23	346	107	521	113
Pennsylvania	431, 257	947	7	177	49	617	206	816	203
EAST NORTH CENTRAL	930, 450	2, 297	78	346	417	1, 996	671	2, 035	499
Ohio	309, 304	840	70	96	95	546	152	525	79
Indiana	111, 982	352	2	35	62	159	80	583	40
Illinois	328, 972	732	4	159	192	854	331	795	265
Michigan	169, 453	349	2	50	64	353	101	127	107
Wisconsin	10, 739	24	—	6	4	84	7	5	8
WEST NORTH CENTRAL	331, 784	1, 080	66	105	111	797	264	1, 780	324
Minnesota	9, 445	30	2	6	12	87	5	7	10
Iowa	17, 380	72	2	6	8	40	8	9	4
Missouri	223, 840	663	41	72	55	449	198	1, 354	266
North Dakota	377	—	—	—	—	7	—	1	—
South Dakota	646	5	—	—	—	6	—	3	—
Nebraska	13, 752	46	1	7	8	85	11	4	5
Kansas	66, 344	264	20	14	28	123	42	402	39
SOUTH ATLANTIC	4, 421, 388	8, 842	1, 056	424	277	1, 583	1, 055	24, 375	2, 271
Delaware	32, 602	99	17	6	2	26	13	195	8
Maryland	276, 379	545	30	34	33	294	100	1, 555	159
District of Columbia	132, 068	273	95	72	98	231	191	1, 303	173
Virginia	650, 165	1, 173	149	63	59	229	164	3, 866	356
West Virginia	114, 893	321	61	22	20	72	67	985	47
North Carolina	918, 647	1, 575	246	68	27	206	164	5, 607	372
South Carolina	793, 681	1, 281	175	54	13	73	67	3, 727	288
Georgia	1, 071, 125	2, 087	176	60	15	212	193	5, 061	595
Florida	431, 828	1, 488	107	45	10	240	96	2, 076	273
EAST SOUTH CENTRAL	2, 658, 238	4, 957	446	181	61	857	609	12, 159	896
Kentucky	226, 040	727	39	37	25	248	129	1, 615	86
Tennessee	477, 646	1, 169	96	70	26	255	293	2, 782	275
Alabama	944, 834	1, 653	139	45	4	211	116	4, 170	410
Mississippi	1, 009, 718	1, 408	172	29	6	143	71	3, 592	125
WEST SOUTH CENTRAL	2, 281, 951	5, 125	450	193	98	1, 387	520	11, 752	480
Arkansas	478, 463	889	72	30	16	152	102	1, 974	113
Louisiana	776, 326	1, 295	78	45	8	442	107	2, 932	158
Oklahoma	172, 198	633	36	18	53	182	104	1, 667	46
Texas	854, 964	2, 308	264	100	21	611	207	5, 179	163
MOUNTAIN	30, 225	121	4	8	3	128	27	83	15
Montana	1, 256	7	—	—	—	7	—	2	—
Idaho	668	3	—	—	—	2	1	—	—
Wyoming	1, 250	7	—	—	—	8	—	1	—
Colorado	11, 828	44	4	4	2	79	13	11	5
New Mexico	2, 850	13	—	2	—	5	3	9	2
Arizona	10, 749	42	—	2	1	24	10	59	6
Utah	1, 108	3	—	—	—	2	—	—	2
Nevada	516	2	—	—	—	1	—	1	—
PACIFIC	90, 122	295	1	42	41	487	71	98	109
Washington	6, 840	23	—	3	3	60	3	1	4
Oregon	2, 234	5	—	1	3	12	1	1	1
California	81, 048	267	1	38	35	415	67	96	104

[1] States include small numbers of professional persons included in other census reports in "all other."
[2] Probably includes some teachers in schools below collegiate rank.

TABLE 13.—NEGROES IN PROPRIETARY, OFFICIAL, MANAGERIAL, AND SUPERVISORY PURSUITS (INCLUDING FOREMEN AND OVERSEERS) IN EACH INDUSTRY OR SERVICE GROUP BY SEX, FOR THE UNITED STATES: 1930

[Industries and occupations having no Negroes in a proprietary, official, or supervisory capacity are omitted]

INDUSTRY AND OCCUPATION	Total	Male	Female
United States	**949,234**	**849,064**	**100,170**
AGRICULTURE			
Agriculture	875,329	798,886	76,443
Farmers (owners and tenants)	873,653	797,231	76,422
Farm managers and foremen	1,676	1,655	21
FORESTRY AND FISHING			
Forestry	158	158	
Owners and proprietors, log and timber camps	61	61	
Managers and officials, log and timber camps	5	5	
Foremen, log and timber camps	92	92	
EXTRACTION AND MINERALS			
Coal mines	73	73	
Owners, operators, and proprietors	2	2	
Managers and officials	3	3	
Foremen and overseers	68	68	
Iron mines	8	8	
Foremen and overseers	8	8	
Other specified mines	6	6	
Managers and officials	1	1	
Foremen and overseers	5	5	
Not specified mines	2	2	
Owners, operators, and proprietors	1	1	
Foremen and overseers	1	1	
Quarries	59	59	
Owners, operators, and proprietors	4	4	
Managers and officials	5	5	
Foremen and overseers	50	50	
Oil wells and gas wells [1]	14	13	1
Owners, operators, and proprietors	5	4	1
Foremen and overseers	9	9	
Salt wells and works	3	3	
Foremen and overseers	3	3	
MANUFACTURING AND MECHANICAL INDUSTRIES			
Building industry	2,747	2,742	5
Builders and building contractors	2,410	2,406	4
Owners, operators, and proprietors	26	26	
Managers and officials	29	29	
Foremen and overseers	282	281	1
CHEMICAL AND ALLIED INDUSTRIES			
Charcoal and coke works	15	15	
Owners, operators, and proprietors	1	1	
Foremen and overseers	14	14	
Explosives, ammunition, and fireworks factories	1	1	
Foremen and overseers	1	1	
Fertilizer factories	59	59	
Owners, operators, and proprietors	1	1	
Managers and officials	1	1	
Foremen and overseers	57	57	
Gas works [1]	23	23	
Managers and officials	1	1	
Foremen and overseers	22	22	
Paint and varnish factories	16	16	
Owners, operators, and proprietors	1	1	
Managers and officials	1	1	
Foremen and overseers	14	14	
Petroleum refineries	19	19	
Foremen and overseers	19	19	
Rayon factories	1	1	
Foremen and overseers	1	1	
Soap factories	3	3	
Owners, operators, and proprietors	1	1	
Foremen and overseers	2	2	
Other chemical factories	115	107	8
Owners, operators, and proprietors	38	34	4
Managers and officials	7	7	
Foremen and overseers	70	66	4
Cigar and tobacco factories	88	76	12
Owners, operators, and proprietors	18	17	1
Managers and officials	1	1	
Foremen and overseers	69	58	11
CLAY, GLASS, AND STONE INDUSTRIES			
Brick, tile, and terra-cotta factories	55	55	
Owners, operators, and proprietors	2	2	
Managers and officials	3	3	
Foremen and overseers	50	50	
CLAY, GLASS, AND STONE INDUSTRIES—Con.			
Glass factories	16	16	
Owners, operators, and proprietors	1	1	
Foremen and overseers	15	15	
Lime, cement and artificial stone factories	61	61	
Owners, operators, and proprietors	16	16	
Managers and officials	2	2	
Foremen and overseers	43	43	
Marble and stone yards	5	5	
Owners, operators, and proprietors	1	1	
Foremen and overseers	4	4	
Potteries	5	5	
Foremen and overseers	5	5	
CLOTHING INDUSTRIES			
Corset factories	1	1	
Managers and officials	1	1	
Glove factories	1		1
Foremen and overseers	1		1
Hat factories (felt)	4	3	1
Owners, operators, and proprietors	2	2	
Foremen and overseers	2	1	1
Shirt, collar, and cuff factories	18	8	10
Foremen and overseers	18	8	10
Suit, coat, and overall factories	370	353	17
Owners, operators, and proprietors	341	330	11
Managers and officials	20	18	2
Foremen and overseers	9	5	4
Other clothing factories	66	13	53
Owners, operators, and proprietors	5	2	3
Managers and officials	5	5	
Foremen and overseers	56	6	50
FOOD AND ALLIED INDUSTRIES			
Bakeries	70	57	13
Owners, operators, and proprietors	28	24	4
Managers and officials	5	5	
Foremen and overseers	37	28	9
Butter, cheese, and condensed milk factories [2]	11	10	1
Owners, operators, and proprietors	1	1	
Foremen and overseers	10	9	1
Candy factories	17	10	7
Owners, operators, and proprietors	6	6	
Managers and officials	2	1	1
Foremen and overseers	9	3	6
Fish curing and packing	18	18	
Owners, operators, and proprietors	1	1	
Managers and officials	2	2	
Foremen and overseers	15	15	
Flour and grain mills	25	25	
Owners, operators, and proprietors	3	3	
Managers and officials	4	4	
Foremen and overseers	18	18	
Fruit and vegetable canning, etc	19	14	5
Managers and officials	4	4	
Foremen and overseers	15	10	5
Slaughter and packing houses [3]	55	52	3
Owners, operators, and proprietors	4	4	
Managers and officials	4	4	
Foremen and overseers	47	44	3
Sugar factories and refineries	19	19	
Foremen and overseers	19	19	
Other food factories	48	34	14
Owners, operators, and proprietors	14	13	1
Managers and officials	5	5	
Foremen and overseers	29	16	13
Liquor and beverage factories	26	26	
Owners, operators, and proprietors	8	8	
Managers and officials	7	7	
Foremen and overseers	11	11	
IRON AND STEEL, MACHINERY, AND VEHICLE INDUSTRIES			
Agricultural implement factories	7	7	
Foremen and overseers	7	7	
Automobile factories	93	93	
Owners, operators, and proprietors	3	3	
Managers and officials	3	3	
Foremen and overseers	87	87	

See footnotes at end of table.

Table 13.—NEGROES IN PROPRIETARY, OFFICIAL, MANAGERIAL, AND SUPERVISORY PURSUITS (INCLUDING FOREMEN AND OVERSEERS) IN EACH INDUSTRY OR SERVICE GROUP BY SEX, FOR THE UNITED STATES: 1930—Continued.

[Industries and occupations having no Negroes in a proprietary, official, or supervisory capacity are omitted]

INDUSTRY AND OCCUPATION	Total	Male	Female
IRON AND STEEL, MACHINERY, AND VEHICLE INDUSTRIES—Continued			
Automobile factories—Continued.			
Automobile repair shops	183	183	-
Owners, operators, and prorpietors	156	156	-
Managers and officials	14	14	-
Foremen and overseers	13	13	-
Blast furnaces and steel rolling mills [4]	190	189	1
Owners, operators, and proprietors	1	1	-
Managers and officials	4	4	-
Foreman and overseers	185	184	1
Car and railroad shops [5]	56	55	1
Foremen and overseers	56	55	1
Ship and boat building	22	22	-
Owners, operators, and proprietors	1	1	-
Foremen and overseers	21	21	-
Wagon and carriage factories	2	2	-
Managers and officials	1	1	-
Foremen and overseers	1	1	-
Other iron and steel and machinery factories [6]	202	200	2
Owners, operators, and proprietors	14	14	-
Managers and officials	6	6	-
Foremen and overseers	182	180	2
Not specified metal industries	60	60	-
Managers and officials	2	2	-
Foremen and overseers	58	58	-
METAL INDUSTRIES (EXCEPT IRON AND STEEL)			
Brass mills	9	9	-
Foremen and overseers	9	9	-
Copper factories	4	4	-
Foremen and overseers	4	4	-
Jewelry factories	2	2	-
Managers and officials	1	1	-
Foremen and overseers	1	1	-
Lead and zinc factories	3	3	-
Foremen and overseers	3	3	-
Tinware, enamelware, etc., factories	22	20	2
Owners, operators, and proprietors	4	4	-
Foremen and overseers	18	16	2
Other metal factories	7	6	1
Owners, operators, and proprietors	1	1	-
Managers and officials	1	1	-
Foremen and overseers	5	4	1
LEATHER INDUSTRIES			
Harness and saddle factories	1	1	-
Owners, operators, and proprietors	1	1	-
Leather belt, leather goods, etc., factories	6	4	2
Owners, operators, and proprietors	1	1	-
Foremen and overseers	5	3	2
Shoe factories	7	7	-
Owners, operators, and proprietors	1	1	-
Managers and officials	2	2	-
Foremen and overseers	4	4	-
Tanneries	19	16	3
Owners, operators, and proprietors	1	1	-
Managers and officials	1	1	-
Foremen and overseers	17	14	3
Trunk, suitcase, and bag factories	2	2	-
Foremen and overseers	2	2	-
LUMBER AND FURNITURE INDUSTRIES			
Furniture factories	51	47	4
Owners, operators, and proprietors	24	22	2
Managers and officials	4	4	-
Foremen and overseers	23	21	2
Saw and planing mills [7]	265	264	1
Owners, operators, and proprietors	47	47	-
Managers and officials	20	20	-
Foremen and overseers	198	197	1
Other woodworking factories	47	45	2
Owners, operators, and proprietors	6	6	-
Foremen and overseers	41	39	2
PAPER, PRINTING, AND ALLIED INDUSTRIES			
Blank book, envelope, tag, paper bag, etc., factories	5	4	1
Owners, operators, and proprietors	1	1	-
Managers and officials	1	1	-
Foremen and overseers	3	2	1

INDUSTRY AND OCCUPATION	Total	Male	Female
PAPER, PRINTING, AND ALLIED INDUSTRIES—Con.			
Paper and pulp mills	55	50	5
Managers and officials	4	4	-
Foremen and overseers	51	46	5
Paper box factories	3	2	1
Foremen and overseers	3	2	1
Printing, publishing, and engraving	235	219	16
Owners, operators, and proprietors	132	129	3
Managers and officials	59	49	10
Foremen and overseers	44	41	3
TEXTILE INDUSTRIES			
Carpet mills	5	3	2
Owners, operators, and proprietors	3	3	-
Foremen and overseers	2	-	2
Cotton mills	29	27	2
Owners, operators, and proprietors	1	1	-
Foremen and overseers	28	26	2
Hemp, jute, and linen mills	2	2	-
Foremen and overseers	2	2	-
Knitting mills	6	3	3
Foremen and overseers	6	3	3
Lace and embroidery mills	1	-	1
Foremen and overseers	1	-	1
Rope and cordage factories	3	3	-
Foremen and overseers	3	3	-
Sail, awning, and tent factories	2	2	-
Owners, operators, and proprietors	2	2	-
Silk mills	8	6	2
Managers and officials	1	1	-
Foremen and overseers	7	5	2
Textile dyeing, finishing, and printing mills	5	5	-
Foremen and overseers	5	5	-
Woolen and worsted mills	7	5	2
Foremen and overseers	7	5	2
Other and not specified textile mills	30	28	2
Owners, operators, and proprietors	2	2	-
Foremen and overseers	28	26	2
MISCELLANEOUS MANUFACTURING INDUSTRIES			
Broom and brush factories	14	14	-
Owners, operators, and proprietors	14	14	-
Button factories	3	-	3
Foremen and overseers	3	-	3
Electric light and power plants	35	35	-
Owners, operators, and proprietors	1	1	-
Managers and officials	1	1	-
Foremen and overseers	33	33	-
Electrical machinery and supply factories	27	24	3
Owners, operators, and proprietors	5	5	-
Managers and officials	1	1	-
Foremen and overseers	21	18	3
Rubber factories	10	9	1
Owners, operators, and proprietors	3	3	-
Foremen and overseers	7	6	1
Straw factories	1	1	-
Foremen and overseers	1	1	-
Turpentine farms and distilleries	202	202	-
Owners, operators, and proprietors	9	9	-
Managers and officials	3	3	-
Foremen and overseers	190	190	-
Other miscellaneous manufacturing industries	200	171	29
Owners, operators, and proprietors	49	45	4
Managers and officials	18	15	3
Foremen and officials	133	111	22
Other not specified manufacturing industries	176	145	31
Owners, operators, and proprietors	37	35	2
Managers and officials	21	19	2
Foremen and overseers	118	91	27
TRANSPORTATION AND COMMUNICATION			
Air transportation [8]	1	1	-
Foremen and overseers	1	1	-
Construction and maintenance of roads, streets, sewers, and bridges	362	362	-
Contractors, builders, and proprietors	130	130	-
Managers and officials	2	2	-
Foremen and overseers	230	230	-

See footnotes at end of table

Table 13.—NEGROES IN PROPRIETARY, OFFICIAL, MANAGERIAL, AND SUPERVISORY PURSUITS (INCLUDING FOREMEN AND OVERSEERS) IN EACH INDUSTRY OR SERVICE GROUP BY SEX, FOR THE UNITED STATES: 1930—Continued

[Professional pursuits and industries and occupations having no Negroes in a proprietary, official, or supervisory capacity are omitted]

INDUSTRY AND OCCUPATION	Total	Male	Female
TRANSPORTATION AND COMMUNICATION—Con.			
Express companies	25	25	---
Owners, operators, and proprietors	13	13	---
Managers and officials	4	4	---
Foremen and overseers	8	8	---
Garages, greasing stations, and automobile laundries	891	885	6
Owners, operators, and proprietors	424	420	4
Managers and officials	222	221	1
Foremen and overseers	245	244	1
Livery stables	75	75	---
Owners, operators, and proprietors	13	13	---
Managers and officials	10	10	---
Foremen and overseers	52	52	---
Pipe lines	4	4	---
Builders and building contractors	1	1	---
Foremen and overseers	3	3	---
Postal service	103	61	42
Managers and officials	6	6	---
Foremen and overseers	19	19	---
Postmasters	78	36	42
Radio broadcasting and transmitting	4	4	---
Announcers, directors, managers, and officials	4	4	---
Steam railroads [5]	885	877	8
Builders and building contractors	4	4	---
Conductors	35	35	---
Officials and superintendents	15	15	---
Foremen and overseers	831	823	8
Street railroads [5]	46	45	1
Builders and building contractors	1	1	---
Foremen and overseers	45	44	1
Telegraph and telephone	9	9	---
Builders and building contractors	2	2	---
Managers and officials	2	2	---
Foremen and overseers	5	5	---
Truck, transfer, and cab companies	1,916	1,891	25
Owners and proprietors	1,726	1,704	22
Managers and officials	152	149	3
Foremen and overseers	38	38	---
Water transportation	310	310	---
Builders and building contractors	1	1	---
Captains, masters, mates, and pilots	203	203	---
Managers and officials	2	2	---
Foremen and overseers	104	104	---
Other and not specified transportation and communication	5	5	---
Owners, operators, and proprietors	1	1	---
Managers and officials	1	1	---
Foremen and overseers	3	3	---
TRADE			
Advertising agencies	3	3	---
Managers and officials	2	2	---
Foremen and overseers	1	1	---
Banking and brokerage	270	252	18
Bankers and bank officials	80	68	12
Commercial brokers and commission men	21	21	---
Loan brokers and pawnbrokers	36	36	---
Stock brokers	95	90	5
Brokers not specified and promoters	35	34	1
Foremen and overseers	3	3	---
TRADE—Continued			
Grain elevators	14	14	---
Foremen and overseers	14	14	---
Insurance	511	499	12
Managers and officials	511	499	12
Real estate	21	20	1
Managers and officials	21	20	1
Stockyards [3]	15	15	---
Foremen and overseers	15	15	---
Warehouses and cold-storage plants	59	59	---
Owners, operators, and proprietors	10	10	---
Managers and officials	8	8	---
Foremen and overseers	41	41	---
WHOLESALE AND RETAIL TRADE			
Automobile agencies, stores, and filling stations	470	442	28
Retail dealers, automobiles and accessories	111	108	3
Retail dealers, gasoline and oil-filling stations	359	334	25
Wholesale and retail trade (except automobiles)	31,479	27,205	4,274
Wholesale dealers, importers, and exporters	130	129	1
Retail dealers	27,743	23,922	3,821
Employment office keepers	287	114	173
Undertakers	2,946	2,691	255
Floorwalkers and foremen in stores	373	349	24
Other and not specified trades	51	47	4
Owners, operators, and proprietors	42	38	4
Managers and officials	8	8	---
Foremen and overseers	1	1	---
PUBLIC SERVICE (NOT ELSEWHERE CLASSIFIED)			
Public service (not elsewhere classified)	987	862	125
Officials and inspectors (United States)	187	181	6
Officials and inspectors (State)	16	15	1
Officials and inspectors (county)	45	35	10
Officials and inspectors (city)	218	201	17
Detectives	157	151	6
Marshals and constables	80	80	---
Probation and truant officers	160	76	84
Sheriffs	124	123	1
DOMESTIC AND PERSONAL SERVICE			
Hotels, restaurants, boarding houses, etc	26,354	7,709	18,645
Boarding- and lodging-house keepers	13,109	997	12,112
Hotel keepers and managers	1,064	741	323
Housekeepers and stewards	1,638	606	1,032
Restaurant, cafe, and lunch-room keepers	10,543	5,365	5,178
Laundries	500	325	175
Owners and proprietors [9]	247	184	63
Managers and officials	88	55	33
Foremen and overseers	165	86	79
Cleaning, dyeing, and pressing shops	1,754	1,671	83
Owners and proprietors	1,464	1,398	66
Managers and officials	270	261	9
Foremen and overseers	20	12	8
NOT SPECIFIED INDUSTRIES AND SERVICES			
Not specified industries and services	137	131	6
Builders and building contractors	12	12	---
Owners, operators, and proprietors	7	4	3
Managers and officials	65	63	2
Foremen and overseers	53	52	1

[1] Doubtless some overlapping between persons engaged in the production and distribution of natural gas and artificial gas; also those working at petroleum refineries or pipe lines and those at oil wells.
[2] In some cases it was difficult to distinguish, from the enumerators' returns, persons working in butter, cheese, and condensed-milk factories from persons working for milk distributing companies or persons working on dairy farms.
[3] Sometimes it was impossible, from the enumerators' returns, to distinguish between workers in stockyards and workers in slaughter and packing houses.
[4] Includes tin-plate mills. Doubtless some overlapping between workers in blast furnaces and steel rolling mills and workers in iron manufacturing establishments.
[5] Sometimes it was impossible, from the enumerators' returns, to distinguish between workers in car and railroad shops and workers on steam and street railroads.
[6] Includes iron foundries.
[7] Includes box factories (wood).
[8] Sometimes it was impossible, from the enumerators' returns, to distinguish between workers at airports and workers in airplane factories.
[9] Some owners of hand laundries probably are included with laundry operatives.

TABLE 14.—NUMBER OF GAINFULLY OCCUPIED NEGRO WOMEN 15 YEARS OLD AND OVER, BY MARITAL CONDITION, WITH A DISTRIBUTION OF THE SINGLE AND UNKNOWN AND OF THE MARRIED BY AGE, BY SECTIONS, DIVISIONS, AND STATES: 1930

SECTION, DIVISION, AND STATE	TOTAL			GAINFULLY OCCUPIED											
	Total number	Gainfully occupied		Single and unknown					Married						Widowed and divorced
		Total	Percent	Total	15 to 19 years	20 to 24 years	25 to 44 years	45 years and over (including unknown)	Total	15 to 19 years	20 to 24 years	25 to 34 years	35 to 44 years	45 years and over (including unknown)	
United States	**4,099,552**	**1,776,922**	**43.3**	**499,934**	**181,773**	**144,773**	**145,669**	**27,719**	**795,032**	**33,680**	**123,627**	**273,031**	**212,733**	**151,961**	**481,956**
The North	899,757	398,774	44.3	113,439	23,659	33,441	47,652	8,687	189,885	4,142	25,716	74,323	54,492	31,212	95,450
The South	3,153,235	1,356,890	43.0	382,425	157,452	110,113	96,250	18,610	595,259	29,403	96,980	195,192	155,035	118,649	379,206
The West	46,560	21,258	45.7	4,070	662	1,219	1,767	422	9,888	135	931	3,516	3,206	2,100	7,300
NEW ENGLAND	33,772	15,423	45.7	5,337	1,128	1,378	2,026	805	6,499	101	594	2,066	2,053	1,685	3,587
Maine	358	147	41.1	68	7	13	29	19	53		1	19	12	21	26
New Hampshire	192	72	37.5	29	6	9	9	5	32		1	1	17	13	11
Vermont	165	53	32.1	19	9	4	4	2	16		2	3	5	6	18
Massachusetts	18,956	8,470	44.7	3,155	555	769	1,333	498	3,290	36	257	975	1,090	932	2,025
Rhode Island	3,529	1,665	47.2	572	154	128	164	126	632	16	41	178	193	204	461
Connecticut	10,572	5,016	47.4	1,494	397	455	487	155	2,476	49	292	890	736	509	1,046
MIDDLE ATLANTIC	400,412	200,162	50.0	66,705	13,634	19,270	28,730	5,071	94,088	1,975	13,641	37,727	26,554	14,191	39,369
New York	167,408	95,687	57.2	33,450	5,502	9,665	15,842	2,441	44,172	867	6,709	18,638	12,370	5,588	18,065
New Jersey	77,522	38,530	49.7	11,817	3,060	3,394	4,408	955	18,970	408	2,617	7,018	5,435	3,492	7,743
Pennsylvania	155,482	65,945	42.4	21,438	5,072	6,210	8,480	1,675	30,946	700	4,315	12,071	8,749	5,111	13,561
EAST NORTH CENTRAL	340,447	132,104	38.8	29,545	6,389	9,254	12,044	1,858	66,021	1,517	8,909	26,715	18,857	10,023	36,538
Ohio	109,012	40,350	37.0	9,140	2,169	2,873	3,396	702	20,723	454	2,560	7,971	6,138	3,600	10,487
Indiana	41,027	14,636	35.7	3,353	742	1,015	1,333	263	6,746	165	771	2,233	2,063	1,514	4,537
Illinois	127,196	55,793	43.9	12,233	2,421	3,785	5,335	692	27,446	662	3,994	11,488	7,595	3,707	16,114
Michigan	59,610	20,139	33.8	4,571	1,002	1,513	1,870	186	10,506	225	1,494	4,780	2,874	1,133	5,062
Wisconsin	3,602	1,186	32.9	248	55	68	110	15	600	11	90	243	187	69	338
WEST NORTH CENTRAL	125,126	51,085	40.8	11,852	2,508	3,539	4,852	953	23,277	549	2,572	7,815	7,028	5,313	15,956
Minnesota	3,510	1,246	35.5	286	58	95	98	35	521	9	44	160	174	134	439
Iowa	6,188	2,002	32.4	425	111	143	124	47	898	24	84	252	311	227	679
Missouri	86,046	37,167	43.2	8,924	1,843	2,597	3,796	688	16,913	428	1,971	5,860	4,996	3,658	11,330
North Dakota	111	44	39.6	9		6	2	1	22		5	4	8	5	13
South Dakota	212	67	31.6	15	3	6	6		32	1	3	6	13	9	20
Nebraska	5,173	2,266	43.8	438	95	124	184	35	1,076	21	100	349	384	222	752
Kansas	23,886	8,293	34.7	1,755	398	568	642	147	3,815	66	365	1,184	1,142	1,058	2,723
SOUTH ATLANTIC	1,465,712	652,267	44.5	202,264	81,344	59,343	51,314	10,263	286,165	12,971	46,113	94,887	76,109	56,085	163,838
Delaware	11,097	4,693	42.3	1,609	366	421	664	158	2,181	30	222	682	622	625	903
Maryland	94,231	44,253	47.0	13,813	3,745	4,030	4,775	1,263	21,598	512	2,754	7,272	6,159	4,901	8,842
District of Columbia	54,297	31,263	57.6	9,053	1,559	2,525	3,851	1,118	15,460	331	2,102	5,649	4,418	2,960	6,750
Virginia	210,823	76,016	36.1	25,236	8,178	7,564	7,617	1,877	31,490	906	4,073	9,721	9,317	7,473	19,290
West Virginia	36,048	8,629	23.9	2,458	537	770	970	181	4,061	86	454	1,429	1,235	857	2,110
North Carolina	290,045	114,849	39.6	43,702	17,092	13,735	10,811	2,064	46,076	1,965	7,990	15,913	11,675	8,533	25,071
South Carolina	251,595	121,388	48.2	42,262	21,299	11,464	8,062	1,437	50,479	3,070	8,744	15,492	13,086	10,087	28,647
Georgia	365,622	175,690	48.1	48,706	22,425	14,067	10,567	1,647	74,444	4,426	12,859	23,411	19,028	14,720	52,540
Florida	151,954	75,486	49.7	15,425	6,143	4,767	3,997	518	40,376	1,645	6,915	15,318	10,569	5,929	19,685
EAST SOUTH CENTRAL	907,370	406,734	44.8	108,742	47,372	29,578	26,325	5,467	179,423	10,320	29,346	55,007	45,330	39,420	118,569
Kentucky	82,174	33,304	40.5	7,460	1,696	2,065	2,821	878	15,378	348	1,514	4,261	4,593	4,662	10,466
Tennessee	173,319	73,525	42.4	18,634	6,060	5,689	5,701	1,184	31,943	1,334	4,779	10,359	8,467	7,004	22,948
Alabama	320,277	142,526	44.5	43,069	19,390	11,973	9,783	1,923	56,256	2,940	9,318	17,244	14,310	12,444	43,201
Mississippi	331,600	157,379	47.5	39,579	20,226	9,851	8,020	1,482	75,846	5,698	13,735	23,143	17,960	15,310	41,954
WEST SOUTH CENTRAL	780,153	297,889	38.2	71,419	28,736	21,192	18,611	2,880	129,671	6,112	21,521	45,298	33,596	23,144	96,799
Arkansas	162,123	51,374	31.7	12,229	5,734	3,409	2,685	401	19,747	1,087	3,237	6,309	5,109	4,005	19,398
Louisiana	264,780	106,682	40.3	29,423	11,638	8,283	8,155	1,347	46,713	2,228	7,546	15,750	12,295	8,894	30,546
Oklahoma	57,580	19,489	33.8	3,819	1,076	1,490	1,146	107	9,062	356	1,621	3,455	2,296	1,334	6,608
Texas	295,670	120,344	40.7	25,948	10,288	8,010	6,625	1,025	54,149	2,441	9,117	19,784	13,896	8,911	40,247
MOUNTAIN	10,748	4,455	41.4	782	157	205	329	91	2,075	38	171	707	654	505	1,598
Montana	437	167	38.2	33	3	5	20	5	70	1	3	20	13	33	64
Idaho	226	62	27.4	10	3	1	5	1	30		2	9	11	8	22
Wyoming	446	159	35.7	29	3	8	14	4	79		4	15	26	34	51
Colorado	4,902	2,226	45.4	406	82	108	168	48	928	20	80	294	286	248	892
New Mexico	938	342	36.5	57	16	17	18	6	177	2	22	60	52	41	108
Arizona	3,217	1,279	39.8	192	45	54	77	16	699	13	55	284	231	116	388
Utah	374	122	32.6	28	3	8	13	4	51	1	5	13	18	14	43
Nevada	208	98	47.1	27	2	4	14	7	41	1		12	17	11	30
PACIFIC	35,812	16,803	46.9	3,288	505	1,014	1,438	331	7,813	97	760	2,809	2,552	1,595	5,702
Washington	2,419	911	37.7	160	38	45	52	25	381	7	43	91	118	122	370
Oregon	827	382	46.2	68	14	17	29	8	179		15	43	68	53	135
California	32,566	15,510	47.6	3,060	453	952	1,357	298	7,253	90	702	2,675	2,366	1,420	5,197

TABLE 15.—NUMBER AND PROPORTION OF WOMEN 15 YEARS OLD AND OVER GAINFULLY OCCUPIED, BY COLOR, NATIVITY, AND MARITAL CONDITION, FOR THE UNITED STATES: 1930

CLASS OF POPULATION	TOTAL			SINGLE AND UNKNOWN			MARRIED			WIDOWED AND DIVORCED			PERCENT OF TOTAL GAINFULLY OCCUPIED		
	Total number	Gainfully occupied		Total number	Gainfully occupied		Total number	Gainfully occupied		Total number	Gainfully occupied		Single and unknown	Married	Widowed and divorced
		Number	Percent		Number	Percent		Number	Percent		Number	Percent			
All classes	**42,837,149**	**10,632,227**	**24.8**	**11,359,038**	**5,734,825**	**50.5**	**26,170,756**	**3,071,302**	**11.7**	**5,307,355**	**1,826,100**	**34.4**	**53.9**	**28.9**	**17.2**
Negro	4,099,552	1,776,922	43.3	959,877	499,934	52.1	2,398,144	795,032	33.2	741,531	481,956	65.0	28.1	44.7	27.1
Native white	32,155,087	7,608,789	23.7	9,498,027	4,622,496	48.7	19,200,906	1,883,872	9.8	3,456,154	1,102,421	31.9	60.8	24.8	14.5
Foreign-born white	6,065,142	1,155,717	19.1	776,963	573,431	73.8	4,243,337	361,427	8.5	1,044,842	220,859	21.1	49.6	31.3	19.1
Other races [1]	517,368	90,799	17.6	124,171	38,964	31.4	328,369	30,971	9.4	64,828	20,864	32.2	42.9	34.1	23.0

[1] Comprises Mexicans, Indians, Chinese, Japanese, Filipinos, Hindus, Koreans, Hawaiians, etc.

TABLE 16.—PERCENT OF NEGRO WOMEN 15 YEARS OLD AND OVER GAINFULLY OCCUPIED, BY MARITAL CONDITION, FOR CITIES OF 100,000 OR MORE INHABITANTS: 1930

[Percent not shown where base is less than 100]

CITY	Total	Single and unknown	Married	Widowed and divorced
Akron, Ohio	30.8	46.1	21.8	56.4
Albany, N. Y	46.8	67.0	36.6	60.3
Atlanta, Ga	63.6	64.2	56.5	76.6
Baltimore, Md	55.8	65.7	48.0	66.9
Birmingham, Ala	46.1	54.8	33.3	67.7
Boston, Mass	50.5	65.4	37.8	65.5
Bridgeport, Conn	40.0	58.5	30.2	60.9
Buffalo, N. Y	33.6	55.5	24.1	51.7
Cambridge, Mass	41.5	60.3	28.3	54.1
Camden, N. J	43.2	61.4	33.1	57.6
Canton, Ohio	22.4	31.3	17.6	35.3
Chattanooga, Tenn	47.0	51.3	37.8	66.3
Chicago, Ill	47.5	59.6	38.9	62.4
Cincinnati, Ohio	44.1	53.6	36.7	61.9
Cleveland, Ohio	41.2	53.6	32.3	60.3
Columbus, Ohio	43.5	48.2	37.2	61.3
Dallas, Tex	63.4	59.0	57.1	79.6
Dayton, Ohio	42.0	48.9	35.5	58.6
Denver, Colo	51.3	57.2	38.9	72.3
Des Moines, Iowa	38.0	39.7	27.3	63.1
Detroit, Mich	35.4	52.7	26.9	55.1
Duluth, Minn	39.6	-----	-----	-----
Elizabeth, N. J	37.9	60.0	29.6	50.8
El Paso, Tex	49.2	54.1	40.6	71.8
Erie, Pa	28.0	-----	19.8	-----
Evansville, Ind	40.4	52.9	28.3	55.4
Fall River, Mass	53.2	-----	-----	-----
Flint, Mich	24.9	43.4	16.5	57.3
Fort Wayne, Ind	33.1	46.0	23.5	56.2
Fort Worth, Tex	55.1	52.8	49.9	69.7
Gary, Ind	20.0	31.4	12.6	42.5
Grand Rapids, Mich	39.0	50.9	32.4	55.0
Hartford, Conn	51.4	61.8	45.2	62.2
Houston, Tex	55.3	55.8	47.4	73.4
Indianapolis, Ind	44.6	51.7	35.1	63.5
Jacksonville, Fla	53.4	52.6	47.7	68.5
Jersey City, N. J	43.3	66.4	31.8	60.6
Kansas City, Kans	36.8	44.8	28.4	55.8
Kansas City, Mo	52.5	63.5	40.9	69.8
Knoxville, Tenn	52.7	57.6	45.3	67.4
Long Beach, Calif	63.8	-----	-----	-----
Los Angeles, Calif	50.7	56.3	41.6	67.3
Louisville, Ky	54.3	58.7	45.9	68.3
Lowell, Mass	-----	-----	-----	-----
Lynn, Mass	38.0	-----	31.0	-----
Memphis, Tenn	49.4	57.5	38.2	67.4
Miami, Fla	78.5	69.2	78.9	87.0
Milwaukee, Wis	33.0	45.1	25.3	53.2
Minneapolis, Minn	39.1	58.3	27.1	60.5
Nashville, Tenn	53.7	57.2	43.5	70.3
Newark, N. J	50.1	69.7	41.2	63.0
New Bedford, Mass	32.8	55.1	22.6	35.6
New Haven, Conn	45.8	56.4	36.7	64.8
New Orleans, La	52.4	61.6	43.2	66.6
New York, N. Y	58.6	77.0	46.9	69.7
Bronx Borough	48.4	75.1	33.9	59.4
Brooklyn Borough	50.7	73.8	37.2	64.0
Manhattan Borough	62.0	78.5	51.0	72.1
Queens Borough	53.9	72.1	43.4	64.7
Richmond Borough	40.2	61.2	24.8	58.2
Norfolk, Va	54.7	59.7	48.0	67.4
Oakland, Calif	39.9	45.2	30.4	58.3
Oklahoma City, Okla	57.0	56.5	50.5	76.3
Omaha, Nebr	44.8	53.9	34.6	64.1
Paterson, N. J	56.6	78.4	45.4	66.7
Peoria, Ill	54.2	74.1	35.7	70.5
Philadelphia, Pa	50.8	69.6	40.0	64.5
Pittsburgh, Pa	34.8	52.2	23.7	56.8
Portland, Oreg	48.0	53.6	35.7	77.4
Providence, R. I	49.9	64.6	36.2	64.3
Reading, Pa	36.0	52.0	28.7	-----
Richmond, Va	53.6	62.0	44.3	66.4
Rochester, N. Y	49.7	68.1	40.3	60.1
St. Louis, Mo	46.0	57.9	36.2	62.9
St. Paul, Minn	32.7	43.4	22.4	52.6
Salt Lake City, Utah	38.7	-----	24.6	-----
San Antonio, Tex	58.0	56.0	50.1	74.4
San Diego, Calif	53.1	51.5	45.9	71.7
San Francisco, Calif	55.1	68.1	41.9	73.6
Scranton, Pa	31.9	-----	21.7	-----
Seattle, Wash	40.0	44.9	28.5	66.1
Somerville, Mass	32.0	-----	-----	-----
South Bend, Ind	34.7	53.2	28.2	51.0
Spokane, Wash	41.4	-----	27.1	-----
Springfield, Mass	46.2	63.3	35.2	62.8
Syracuse, N. Y	39.1	57.4	30.7	52.9
Tacoma, Wash	36.8	-----	21.1	-----
Tampa, Fla	63.0	62.2	58.1	76.1
Toledo, Ohio	35.0	47.2	26.7	58.3
Trenton, N. J	36.9	56.3	25.7	49.1
Tulsa, Okla	63.0	60.9	57.1	77.9
Utica, N. Y	51.1	-----	44.1	-----
Washington, D. C	57.6	63.4	51.6	66.9
Wichita, Kans	46.9	49.6	37.4	70.3
Wilmington, Del	51.6	65.7	41.8	61.3
Worcester, Mass	42.6	48.3	38.0	-----
Yonkers, N. Y	58.8	75.7	48.7	72.0
Youngstown, Ohio	20.2	30.5	13.0	44.8

TABLE 17.—PERCENT OF NEGRO CHILDREN 10 TO 15 YEARS OLD, GAINFULLY OCCUPIED, BY SEX, FOR CITIES OF 100,000 OR MORE INHABITANTS: 1930

[Percent not shown where base is less than 100]

CITY	Total	Male	Female
Akron, Ohio	0.8	0.8	0.8
Albany, N. Y	1.4	-----	-----
Atlanta, Ga	10.8	15.1	6.9
Baltimore, Md	4.2	3.9	4.4
Birmingham, Ala	5.0	6.7	3.4
Boston, Mass	1.2	1.8	.7
Bridgeport, Conn	1.8	3.2	.7
Buffalo, N. Y	1.1	.6	1.7
Cambridge, Mass	.2	-----	.3
Camden, N. J	1.9	2.1	1.7
Canton, Ohio	1.5	-----	1.2
Chattanooga, Tenn	4.5	5.9	3.2
Chicago, Ill	1.5	2.0	1.0
Cincinnati, Ohio	1.1	1.8	.6
Cleveland, Ohio	1.4	2.0	.8
Columbus, Ohio	1.3	1.7	.9
Dallas, Tex	4.8	7.0	2.9
Dayton, Ohio	1.5	2.3	.8
Denver, Colo	2.4	3.1	1.9
Des Moines, Iowa	.6	1.1	-----
Detroit, Mich	1.0	1.2	.8
Duluth, Minn	-----	-----	-----
Elizabeth, N. J	2.8	3.0	2.6
El Paso, Tex	4.6	-----	-----
Erie, Pa	-----	-----	-----
Evansville, Ind	2.9	4.1	1.8
Fall River, Mass	-----	-----	-----
Flint, Mich	.2	.4	-----
Fort Wayne, Ind	-----	-----	-----
Fort Worth, Tex	2.9	3.0	2.9
Gary, Ind	.5	.9	-----
Grand Rapids, Mich	1.3	.9	1.7
Hartford, Conn	1.0	1.8	.3
Houston, Tex	4.4	6.1	2.8
Indianapolis, Ind	1.6	2.2	1.0
Jacksonville, Fla	4.0	5.0	3.2
Jersey City, N. J	1.5	1.7	1.3
Kansas City, Kans	2.4	3.2	1.7
Kansas City, Mo	2.4	4.2	.9
Knoxville, Tenn	4.2	5.9	2.5
Long Beach, Calif	-----	-----	-----
Los Angeles, Calif	.8	.9	.8
Louisville, Ky	3.1	3.9	2.4
Lynn, Mass	-----	-----	-----
Memphis, Tenn	3.3	4.6	2.2
Miami, Fla	5.4	4.4	6.2
Milwaukee, Wis	.2	.3	-----
Minneapolis, Minn	2.3	3.1	1.4
Nashville, Tenn	5.0	7.0	3.1
Newark, N. J	2.5	2.4	2.5
New Bedford, Mass	1.2	.8	1.6
New Haven, Conn	2.4	3.5	1.4
New Orleans, La	5.4	6.7	4.2
New York, N. Y	1.1	1.1	1.1
Bronx Borough	.9	.7	1.2
Brooklyn Borough	1.3	1.3	1.3
Manhattan Borough	1.0	1.0	1.0
Queens Borough	1.4	1.3	1.6
Richmond Borough	-----	-----	-----
Norfolk, Va	3.3	4.4	2.4
Oakland, Calif	1.4	1.8	1.0
Oklahoma City, Okla	4.0	5.9	2.4
Omaha, Nebr	1.1	.9	1.2
Paterson, N. J	2.8	-----	5.0
Peoria, Ill	.7	-----	1.4
Philadelphia, Pa	1.2	1.2	1.1
Pittsburgh, Pa	1.1	1.3	.9
Portland, Oreg	-----	-----	-----
Providence, R. I	1.6	1.4	1.9
Reading, Pa	4.2	-----	-----
Richmond, Va	3.4	3.8	3.1
Rochester, N. Y	-----	-----	-----
St. Louis, Mo	3.3	4.4	2.3
St. Paul, Minn	.6	1.2	-----
Salt Lake City, Utah	-----	-----	-----
San Antonio, Tex	3.3	5.0	1.7
San Diego, Calif	.9	-----	.8
San Francisco, Calif	.7	-----	-----
Scranton, Pa	-----	-----	-----
Seattle, Wash	2.1	-----	-----
Somerville, Mass	-----	-----	-----
South Bend, Ind	.7	.7	.7
Spokane, Wash	-----	-----	-----
Springfield, Mass	1.4	1.3	1.5
Syracuse, N. Y	1.3	-----	-----
Tacoma, Wash	-----	-----	-----
Tampa, Fla	4.4	5.0	3.9
Toledo, Ohio	1.0	1.4	.6
Trenton, N. J	5.8	.6	9.9
Tulsa, Okla	1.7	2.3	1.2
Utica, N. Y	-----	-----	-----
Washington, D. C	2.4	3.1	1.8
Wichita, Kans	.7	1.2	.3
Wilmington, Del	1.9	1.8	1.9
Worcester, Mass	.7	-----	-----
Yonkers, N. Y	.8	1.6	-----
Youngstown, Ohio	.5	1.0	.1

TABLE 18.—PERCENT OF NEGRO WOMEN 15 YEARS OLD AND OVER, GAINFULLY OCCUPIED, BY MARITAL CONDITION, BY SECTIONS, DIVISIONS, AND STATES: 1930

[Percent not shown where base is less than 100]

SECTION, DIVISION, AND STATE	Total	Single and unknown	Married	Widowed and divorced
United States	43.3	52.1	33.2	65.0
The North	44.3	59.5	34.4	60.6
The South	43.0	50.2	32.7	66.2
The West	45.7	50.9	36.0	65.9
NEW ENGLAND	45.7	60.9	34.1	60.3
Maine	41.1	58.1	28.2	---
New Hampshire	37.5	---	28.6	---
Vermont	32.1	---	---	---
Massachusetts	44.7	60.5	31.9	59.1
Rhode Island	47.2	61.8	34.1	61.5
Connecticut	47.4	62.4	38.1	62.6
MIDDLE ATLANTIC	50.0	67.8	39.1	64.1
New York	57.2	75.0	45.8	68.6
New Jersey	49.7	65.1	40.2	63.9
Pennsylvania	42.4	60.3	31.9	59.1
EAST NORTH CENTRAL	38.8	49.7	30.4	57.4
Ohio	37.0	46.3	29.4	56.2
Indiana	35.7	45.4	26.5	55.7
Illinois	43.9	54.4	35.2	60.1
Michigan	33.8	49.6	25.6	54.2
Wisconsin	32.9	43.3	25.2	52.3
WEST NORTH CENTRAL	40.8	49.4	31.2	60.2
Minnesota	35.5	47.6	24.3	57.2
Iowa	32.4	37.2	23.8	53.1
Missouri	43.2	52.8	33.2	62.4
North Dakota	39.6	---	---	---
South Dakota	31.6	---	25.6	---
Nebraska	43.8	51.1	34.4	63.4
Kansas	34.7	39.6	26.5	53.9
SOUTH ATLANTIC	44.5	51.1	34.9	65.5
Delaware	42.3	52.8	34.0	55.5
Maryland	47.0	55.8	39.3	61.1
SOUTH ATLANTIC—Continued				
District of Columbia	57.6	63.4	51.6	66.9
Virginia	36.1	42.6	27.0	55.6
West Virginia	23.9	32.3	17.0	46.0
North Carolina	39.6	47.9	29.2	61.0
South Carolina	48.2	56.3	37.2	69.9
Georgia	48.1	53.9	37.0	71.0
Florida	49.7	51.3	43.2	69.4
EAST SOUTH CENTRAL	44.8	53.5	33.9	67.9
Kentucky	40.5	42.2	32.6	60.3
Tennessee	42.4	47.1	32.5	64.5
Alabama	44.5	55.6	31.3	68.4
Mississippi	47.5	57.7	37.1	71.6
WEST SOUTH CENTRAL	38.2	[illegible]4.0	27.6	65.2
Arkansas	31.7	40.4	19.5	63.2
Louisiana	40.3	49.5	29.7	63.7
Oklahoma	33.8	31.9	25.8	62.8
Texas	40.7	42.9	30.8	67.9
MOUNTAIN	41.4	46.9	31.3	65.4
Montana	38.2	---	26.2	62.1
Idaho	27.4	---	18.5	---
Wyoming	35.7	---	28.4	---
Colorado	45.4	50.5	33.4	67.6
New Mexico	36.5	35.6	28.6	67.5
Arizona	39.8	42.5	32.3	64.5
Utah	32.6	---	20.3	---
Nevada	47.1	---	33.3	---
PACIFIC	46.9	52.0	37.5	66.0
Washington	37.7	42.2	26.0	64.5
Oregon	46.2	50.4	35.0	75.0
California	47.6	52.6	38.4	65.9

TABLE 19.—NUMBER AND PROPORTION OF NEGRO CHILDREN 10 TO 15 YEARS OLD GAINFULLY OCCUPIED, BY SEX, FOR SECTIONS, DIVISIONS, AND STATES: 1930

[Percent not shown where base is less than 100]

SECTION, DIVISION, AND STATE	MALE			FEMALE		
	Total number	Gainfully occupied		Total number	Gainfully occupied	
		Number	Percent		Number	Percent
United States	740,290	150,050	20.3	751,689	90,007	12.0
The North	100,454	2,337	2.3	106,007	1,414	1.3
The South	635,203	147,599	23.2	640,880	88,547	13.8
The West	4,633	114	2.5	4,802	46	1.0
NEW ENGLAND	4,802	82	1.7	4,884	65	1.3
Maine	52	1	---	61	1	---
New Hampshire	32	---	---	30	1	---
Vermont	25	---	---	37	---	---
Massachusetts	2,813	40	1.4	2,737	33	1.2
Rhode Island	552	7	1.3	551	9	1.6
Connecticut	1,328	34	2.6	1,468	21	1.4
MIDDLE ATLANTIC	42,366	675	1.6	45,195	679	1.5
New York	14,013	152	1.1	15,031	176	1.2
New Jersey	9,553	270	2.8	10,048	268	2.7
Pennsylvania	18,800	253	1.3	20,116	235	1.2
EAST NORTH CENTRAL	38,460	809	2.1	40,598	334	.8
Ohio	13,909	324	2.3	14,616	104	.7
Indiana	4,965	97	2.0	5,113	36	.7
Illinois	12,639	296	2.3	13,562	143	1.1
Michigan	6,510	88	1.4	6,855	51	.7
Wisconsin	437	4	.9	452	---	---
WEST NORTH CENTRAL	14,826	771	5.2	15,330	336	2.2
Minnesota	382	8	2.1	347	2	.6
Iowa	838	28	3.3	848	7	.8
Missouri	9,717	616	6.3	10,123	281	2.8
North Dakota	13	---	---	7	---	---
South Dakota	32	3	---	34	---	---
Nebraska	565	16	2.8	537	8	1.5
Kansas	3,279	100	3.0	3,434	38	1.1
SOUTH ATLANTIC	313,391	67,132	21.4	318,351	36,086	11.3
Delaware	1,752	97	5.5	1,795	53	3.0
Maryland	14,896	1,192	8.0	15,416	597	3.9
SOUTH ATLANTIC—Con.						
District of Columbia	5,278	161	3.1	6,029	107	1.8
Virginia	46,785	4,884	10.4	47,071	1,752	3.7
West Virginia	5,979	178	3.0	6,355	76	1.2
North Carolina	70,049	14,205	20.3	70,469	7,599	10.8
South Carolina	65,675	19,865	30.2	66,564	12,643	19.0
Georgia	78,256	21,942	28.0	79,164	10,817	13.7
Florida	24,721	4,608	18.6	25,488	2,442	9.6
EAST SOUTH CENTRAL	176,715	53,456	30.2	175,290	36,161	20.6
Kentucky	11,948	1,010	8.5	12,269	331	2.7
Tennessee	28,822	4,831	16.8	28,978	2,699	9.3
Alabama	65,296	19,999	30.6	65,424	13,514	20.7
Mississippi	70,649	27,616	39.1	68,619	19,617	28.6
WEST SOUTH CENTRAL	145,097	27,011	18.6	147,239	16,300	11.1
Arkansas	31,545	6,967	22.1	31,527	4,103	13.0
Louisiana	49,718	10,368	20.9	50,956	6,605	13.0
Oklahoma	10,856	841	7.7	10,979	291	2.7
Texas	52,978	8,835	16.7	53,777	5,301	9.9
MOUNTAIN	1,154	50	4.3	1,216	16	1.3
Montana	47	1	---	53	1	---
Idaho	20	4	---	23	1	---
Wyoming	40	3	---	44	1	---
Colorado	413	22	5.3	472	7	1.5
New Mexico	141	6	4.3	151	2	1.3
Arizona	443	14	3.2	413	4	1.0
Utah	45	---	---	49	---	---
Nevada	5	---	---	11	---	---
PACIFIC	3,479	64	1.8	3,586	30	.8
Washington	276	9	3.3	221	2	.9
Oregon	74	3	---	70	1	---
California	3,129	52	1.7	3,295	27	.8

TABLE 20.—NUMBER OF NEGROES 10 YEARS OLD AND OVER GAINFULLY OCCUPIED, 1930, WITH PERCENT GAINFULLY OCCUPIED, 1930, 1920, AND 1910, BY SEX, BY SECTIONS, DIVISIONS, AND STATES

SECTION, DIVISION, AND STATE	TOTAL, 1930			MALE, 1930			FEMALE, 1930			PERCENT GAINFULLY OCCUPIED			
	Total number	Gainfully occupied		Total number	Gainfully occupied		Total number	Gainfully occupied		Male		Female	
		Number	Percent		Number	Percent		Number	Percent	1920	1910	1920	1910
United States	**9,292,556**	**5,503,535**	**59.2**	**4,564,690**	**3,662,893**	**80.2**	**4,727,866**	**1,840,642**	**38.9**	**81.1**	**87.4**	**38.9**	**54.7**
The North	**1,994,085**	**1,228,670**	**61.6**	**1,005,003**	**829,353**	**82.5**	**989,082**	**399,317**	**40.4**	**86.5**	**85.6**	**40.8**	**45.6**
The South	**7,194,750**	**4,210,163**	**58.5**	**3,506,598**	**2,790,120**	**79.6**	**3,688,152**	**1,420,043**	**38.5**	**80.0**	**87.6**	**38.5**	**56.0**
The West	**103,721**	**64,702**	**62.4**	**53,089**	**43,420**	**81.8**	**50,632**	**21,282**	**42.0**	**90.5**	**88.4**	**39.5**	**43.4**
NEW ENGLAND	75,719	45,129	59.6	37,838	29,686	78.5	37,881	15,443	40.8	82.6	86.2	44.2	49.8
Maine	900	530	56.7	488	363	74.4	412	147	35.7	86.7	96.9	36.3	37.1
New Hampshire	697	493	70.7	481	421	87.5	216	72	33.3	85.1	96.8	34.0	54.9
Vermont	445	247	55.5	249	194	77.9	196	53	27.0	89.5	93.8	36.9	34.5
Massachusetts	42,356	24,666	58.2	21,089	16,187	76.8	21,267	8,479	39.9	86.1	86.3	43.8	49.9
Rhode Island	7,836	4,693	59.9	3,843	3,023	78.7	3,993	1,670	41.8	85.6	87.2	43.9	50.5
Connecticut	23,485	14,520	61.8	11,688	9,498	81.3	11,797	5,022	42.6	86.7	82.3	46.0	50.7
MIDDLE ATLANTIC	867,875	560,738	64.6	429,276	360,329	83.9	438,599	200,409	45.7	86.8	86.9	46.4	52.3
New York	347,381	239,305	68.9	167,235	143,554	85.8	180,146	95,751	53.2	88.5	89.2	55.3	47.3
New Jersey	169,214	107,114	63.3	83,237	68,487	82.3	85,977	38,627	44.9	84.5	85.4	44.1	52.1
Pennsylvania	351,280	214,319	61.0	178,804	148,288	82.9	172,476	66,031	38.3	86.6	86.0	40.4	48.7
EAST NORTH CENTRAL	771,626	457,245	59.3	396,907	325,016	81.9	374,719	132,229	35.3	87.2	85.0	35.7	38.7
Ohio	252,500	145,379	57.6	131,229	104,982	80.0	121,271	40,397	33.3	86.6	83.7	34.2	39.4
Indiana	92,873	53,332	57.4	47,519	38,683	81.4	45,354	14,649	32.3	85.8	83.5	35.7	39.1
Illinois	277,834	171,073	61.6	139,192	115,236	82.8	138,642	55,837	40.3	87.1	86.9	38.5	39.0
Michigan	139,490	82,249	59.0	74,033	62,089	83.9	65,457	20,160	30.8	91.0	84.3	30.7	31.2
Wisconsin	8,929	5,212	58.4	4,934	4,026	81.6	3,995	1,186	29.7	89.5	93.5	32.7	37.4
WEST NORTH CENTRAL	278,865	165,558	59.4	140,982	114,322	81.1	137,883	51,236	37.2	84.7	84.2	36.8	40.3
Minnesota	8,155	4,809	59.0	4,353	3,562	81.8	3,802	1,247	32.8	93.1	90.7	36.6	36.5
Iowa	14,426	7,931	55.0	7,540	5,927	78.6	6,886	2,004	29.1	85.6	85.8	31.4	32.0
Missouri	188,664	114,825	60.9	94,184	77,530	82.3	94,480	37,295	39.5	85.1	85.1	40.0	44.8
North Dakota	326	219	67.2	210	175	83.3	116	44	37.9	100.0	88.8	27.8	43.4
South Dakota	546	308	56.4	304	241	79.3	242	67	27.7	88.0	83.4	34.7	31.1
Nebraska	11,605	7,179	61.9	5,986	4,910	82.0	5,619	2,269	40.4	86.6	89.7	37.2	39.5
Kansas	55,143	30,287	54.9	28,405	21,977	77.4	26,736	8,310	31.1	80.8	79.2	28.4	29.6
SOUTH ATLANTIC	3,363,864	1,951,791	58.0	1,632,260	1,275,378	78.1	1,731,604	676,413	39.1	79.4	87.1	39.0	54.6
Delaware	26,567	15,887	59.8	13,970	11,172	80.0	12,597	4,715	37.4	80.2	81.6	39.2	44.7
Maryland	219,809	136,014	61.9	112,573	91,537	81.3	107,236	44,477	41.5	82.5	84.5	43.3	49.6
District of Columbia	111,224	73,122	65.7	51,875	41,811	80.6	59,349	31,311	52.8	83.4	81.4	56.3	60.1
Virginia	494,429	258,066	52.2	244,143	181,064	74.2	250,286	77,002	30.8	77.4	84.1	29.5	40.7
West Vrirginia	89,921	47,207	52.5	48,556	38,547	79.4	41,365	8,660	20.9	83.8	88.3	19.8	30.5
North Carolina	673,809	365,544	54.3	324,816	245,479	75.6	348,993	120,065	34.4	76.5	88.5	34.4	55.7
South Carolina	581,085	343,476	59.1	273,841	213,167	77.8	307,244	130,309	42.4	78.5	88.7	45.5	66.8
Georgia	821,083	494,384	60.2	389,757	311,550	79.9	431,326	182,834	42.4	80.6	88.2	40.8	57.8
Florida	345,937	218,091	63.0	172,729	141,051	81.7	173,208	77,040	44.5	82.0	86.6	39.8	45.7
EAST SOUTH CENTRAL	2,052,951	1,250,026	60.9	999,448	816,059	81.7	1,053,503	433,967	41.2	81.2	89.2	40.8	61.0
Kentucky	185,629	106,572	57.4	93,195	73,098	78.4	92,434	33,474	36.2	81.5	84.2	38.1	44.6
Tennessee	382,974	222,693	58.1	185,633	147,237	79.3	197,341	75,456	38.2	80.8	86.8	37.8	50.4
Alabama	719,290	432,349	60.1	344,705	279,829	81.2	374,585	152,520	40.7	81.6	90.6	41.6	63.7
Mississippi	765,058	488,412	63.8	375,915	315,895	84.0	389,143	172,517	44.3	81.0	90.6	42.1	68.5
WEST SOUTH CENTRAL	1,777,935	1,008,346	56.7	874,890	698,683	79.9	903,045	309,663	34.3	79.6	86.6	34.8	52.0
Arkansas	373,273	201,948	54.1	184,753	147,538	79.9	188,520	54,410	28.9	81.1	89.3	33.3	57.9
Louisiana	598,258	345,389	57.7	290,658	233,907	80.5	307,600	111,482	36.2	79.9	85.5	35.6	48.4
Oklahoma	135,069	71,254	52.8	68,315	51,578	75.5	66,754	19,676	29.5	75.8	83.4	27.7	37.2
Texas	671,335	389,755	58.1	331,164	265,660	80.2	340,171	124,095	36.5	79.1	86.7	36.4	54.9
MOUNTAIN	25,992	16,204	62.3	14,203	11,741	82.7	11,789	4,463	37.9	92.7	87.2	38.0	45.0
Montana	1,128	695	61.6	644	528	82.0	484	167	34.5	94.3	85.0	34.2	46.6
Idaho	599	368	61.4	355	305	85.9	244	63	25.8	87.6	92.0	27.8	49.5
Wyoming	1,118	696	62.3	636	536	84.3	482	160	33.2	87.5	96.4	46.5	48.6
Colorado	10,280	6,220	60.5	4,981	3,991	80.1	5,299	2,229	42.1	85.6	85.1	40.2	44.1
New Mexico	2,328	1,355	58.2	1,260	1,012	80.3	1,068	343	32.1	96.8	87.7	31.5	42.7
Arizona	9,125	5,986	65.6	5,549	4,705	84.8	3,576	1,281	35.8	96.3	83.3	37.2	50.3
Utah	942	550	58.4	522	428	82.0	420	122	29.0	95.5	87.5	29.6	34.4
Nevada	472	334	70.8	256	236	92.2	216	98	45.4	98.4	91.9	58.5	52.9
PACIFIC	77,729	48,498	62.4	38,886	31,679	81.5	38,843	16,819	43.3	88.7	89.3	40.2	42.2
Washington	5,992	3,672	61.3	3,387	2,761	81.5	2,605	911	35.0	91.4	89.3	36.4	38.0
Oregon	2,000	1,331	66.6	1,112	948	85.3	888	383	43.1	96.0	96.7	39.0	44.1
California	69,737	43,495	62.4	34,387	27,970	81.3	35,350	15,525	43.9	87.7	88.6	40.8	43.1

TABLE 21.—NUMBER AND PROPORTION OF NEGROES 10 YEARS OLD AND OVER GAINFULLY OCCUPIED, BY SEX, AND MARITAL CONDITION OF FEMALES 15 YEARS OLD AND OVER, FOR CITIES OF 100,000 OR MORE INHABITANTS: 1930

[Cities having less than 100 gainfully occupied are omitted]

CITY	10 YEARS OLD AND OVER						CHILDREN 10 TO 15 YEARS OLD				FEMALES 15 YEARS OLD AND OVER				
	Males			Females			Total number	Gainfully occupied			Total number	Gainfully occupied			
	Total number	Gainfully occupied: Number	Gainfully occupied: Percent	Total number	Gainfully occupied: Number	Gainfully occupied: Percent		Total	Male	Female		Total	Single and unknown	Married	Widowed and divorced
Akron, Ohio	4, 671	3, 885	83. 2	4, 155	1, 144	27. 5	998	8	4	4	3, 711	1, 143	295	558	290
Albany, N. Y	1, 026	914	89. 1	991	432	43. 6	144	2	1	1	923	432	136	214	82
Atlanta, Ga	32, 302	26, 332	81. 5	42, 369	24, 285	57. 3	10, 195	1, 099	726	373	37, 887	24, 114	5, 965	10, 538	7, 611
Baltimore, Md	57, 694	48, 952	84. 8	59, 085	29, 934	50. 7	12, 314	512	218	294	53, 486	29, 838	8, 989	14, 725	6, 124
Birmingham, Ala	37, 682	30, 932	82. 1	43, 315	18, 067	41. 7	9, 978	498	320	178	39, 070	18, 002	4, 420	7, 182	6, 400
Boston, Mass	8, 629	7, 033	81. 5	8, 677	4, 027	46. 4	1, 685	21	15	6	7, 969	4, 025	1, 354	1, 629	1, 042
Bridgeport, Conn	1, 382	1, 173	84. 9	1, 269	457	36. 0	272	5	4	1	1, 143	457	120	231	106
Buffalo, N. Y	5, 897	5, 093	86. 4	5, 256	1, 621	30. 8	1, 046	12	3	9	4, 812	1, 619	475	788	356
Cambridge, Mass	2, 014	1, 485	73. 7	2, 243	833	37. 1	617	1	------	1	2, 005	833	329	312	192
Camden, N. J	4, 531	3, 618	79. 8	4, 495	1, 733	38. 6	1, 160	22	12	10	3, 992	1, 726	569	819	338
Canton, Ohio	1, 298	1, 057	81. 4	1, 146	228	19. 9	259	4	2	2	1, 009	226	55	122	49
Chattanooga, Tenn	12, 895	10, 524	81. 6	14, 648	6, 226	42. 5	3, 317	150	94	56	13, 195	6, 203	1, 334	2, 862	2, 007
Chicago, Ill	98, 415	85, 046	86. 4	100, 818	44, 421	44. 1	16, 621	243	156	87	93, 384	44, 397	9, 409	22, 181	12, 807
Cincinnati, Ohio	19, 910	16, 565	83. 2	19, 811	7, 933	40. 0	4, 091	46	34	12	17, 991	7, 927	1, 737	4, 279	1, 911
Cleveland, Ohio	29, 867	25, 203	84. 4	29, 108	10, 967	37. 7	5, 788	79	56	23	26, 600	10, 957	2, 442	5, 519	2, 996
Columbus, Ohio	14, 425	11, 531	79. 9	12, 931	5, 080	39. 3	2, 913	37	24	13	11, 661	5, 072	970	2, 809	1, 239
Dallas, Tex	15, 202	12, 893	84. 8	17, 719	10, 359	58. 5	3, 266	158	109	49	16, 308	10, 337	1, 603	5, 289	3, 445
Dayton, Ohio	7, 039	5, 733	81. 4	6, 821	2, 559	37. 5	1, 647	25	18	7	6, 088	2, 556	536	1, 387	633
Denver, Colo	2, 927	2, 472	84. 5	3, 359	1, 610	47. 9	492	12	7	5	3, 133	1, 608	282	680	646
Des Moines, Iowa	2, 139	1, 674	78. 3	2, 283	778	34. 1	540	3	3	------	2, 049	778	135	332	311
Detroit, Mich	51, 779	44, 916	86. 7	47, 468	15, 381	32. 4	9, 021	88	50	38	43, 459	15, 365	3, 545	8, 042	3, 778
Duluth, Minn	170	158	92. 9	176	65	36. 9	22	------	------	------	164	65	10	20	35
Elizabeth, N. J	1, 905	1, 615	84. 8	1, 782	616	34. 6	397	11	6	5	1, 617	613	186	331	96
El Paso, Tex	807	693	85. 9	784	366	46. 7	130	6	3	3	738	363	59	192	112
Erie, Pa	538	450	83. 6	448	113	25. 2	99	------	------	------	404	113	24	56	33
Evansville, Ind	2, 787	2, 228	79. 9	2, 861	1, 066	37. 3	546	16	11	5	2, 634	1, 063	363	395	305
Fall River, Mass	172	144	83. 7	145	67	46. 2	44	------	------	------	126	67	18	24	25
Flint, Mich	2, 516	2, 146	85. 3	2, 098	471	22. 4	469	1	1	------	1, 894	471	99	235	137
Fort Wayne, Ind	1, 016	829	81. 6	912	270	29. 6	208	------	------	------	816	270	58	126	86
Fort Worth, Tex	8, 943	7, 441	83. 2	9, 962	5, 001	50. 2	2, 054	60	29	31	9, 054	4, 991	746	2, 729	1, 516
Gary, Ind	7, 719	6, 495	84. 1	6, 877	1, 245	18. 1	1, 550	7	7	------	6, 233	1, 245	285	548	412
Grand Rapids, Mich	1, 178	966	82. 0	1, 131	405	35. 8	237	3	1	2	1, 035	404	82	228	94
Hartford, Conn	2, 454	1, 997	81. 4	2, 614	1, 194	45. 7	680	7	6	1	2, 321	1, 194	286	661	247
Houston, Tex	25, 388	21, 543	84. 9	28, 260	14, 395	50. 9	5, 188	227	148	79	25, 997	14, 367	2, 604	7, 104	4, 659
Indianapolis, Ind	17, 582	14, 370	81. 7	19, 023	7, 687	40. 4	3, 996	63	42	21	17, 238	7, 680	1, 605	3, 594	2, 481
Jacksonville, Fla	18, 420	14, 718	79. 9	22, 002	10, 676	48. 5	4, 703	190	109	81	19, 912	10, 633	1, 968	5, 534	3, 131
Jersey City, N. J	5, 048	4, 322	85. 6	5, 105	1, 993	39. 0	1, 076	16	8	8	4, 593	1, 990	602	933	455
Kansas City, Kans	7, 884	6, 291	79. 8	8, 507	2, 822	33. 2	1, 985	48	30	18	7, 645	2, 814	550	1, 367	897
Kansas City, Mo	16, 276	14, 167	87. 0	17, 669	8, 681	49. 1	2, 536	61	49	12	16, 530	8, 677	1, 943	3, 765	2, 969
Knoxville, Tenn	6, 800	5, 454	80. 2	7, 510	3, 588	47. 8	1, 729	72	50	22	6, 791	3, 578	937	1, 715	926
Long Beach, Calif	154	142	92. 2	165	97	58. 8	21	------	------	------	152	97	13	61	23
Los Angeles, Calif	15, 709	12, 901	82. 1	17, 942	8, 454	47. 1	2, 961	25	13	12	16, 645	8, 447	1, 632	3, 934	2, 881
Louisville, Ky	19, 393	16, 387	84. 5	21, 324	10, 699	50. 2	3, 848	119	72	47	19, 688	10, 683	2, 355	4, 899	3, 429
Lynn, Mass	292	222	76. 0	339	114	33. 6	94	3	1	2	297	113	43	49	21
Memphis, Tenn	37, 636	31, 773	84. 4	44, 363	20, 251	45. 6	7, 793	258	168	90	40, 939	20, 214	4, 724	8, 598	6, 89
Miami, Fla	9, 232	7, 802	84. 5	10, 499	7, 416	70. 6	2, 374	128	47	81	9, 403	7, 382	1, 198	4, 768	1, 416
Milwaukee, Wis	3, 420	2, 797	81. 8	2, 830	841	29. 7	607	1	1	------	2, 548	841	160	440	241
Minneapolis, Minn	1, 889	1, 610	85. 2	1, 702	619	36. 4	306	7	5	2	1, 581	618	147	270	201
Nashville, Tenn	16, 168	13, 092	81. 0	19, 904	9, 786	49. 2	4, 100	203	138	65	18, 164	9, 758	2, 392	4, 004	3, 362
Newark, N. J	15, 535	13, 308	85. 7	15, 789	7, 159	45. 3	3, 346	82	37	45	14, 278	7, 149	1, 954	3, 836	1, 359
New Bedford, Mass	1, 324	944	71. 3	1, 283	351	27. 4	506	6	2	4	1, 062	348	145	141	62
New Haven, Conn	2, 131	1, 731	81. 2	2, 185	897	41. 1	506	12	8	4	1, 957	896	229	442	225
New Orleans, La	47, 786	39, 512	82. 7	57, 758	27, 531	47. 7	12, 312	664	387	277	52, 304	27, 413	7, 508	12, 564	7, 341
New York, N. Y	131, 643	114, 552	87. 0	144, 778	79, 221	54. 7	21, 987	241	112	129	135, 103	79, 177	28, 006	36, 217	14, 954
Bronx Borough	5, 016	3, 689	73. 5	5, 296	2, 327	43. 9	1, 190	11	4	7	4, 799	2, 325	999	977	349
Brooklyn Borough	26, 418	22, 614	85. 6	29, 480	13, 825	46. 9	5, 098	68	33	35	27, 259	13, 816	5, 207	6, 014	2, 595
Manhattan Borough	92, 501	81, 912	88. 6	100, 494	58, 552	58. 3	13, 778	138	65	73	94, 430	58, 523	20, 253	27, 116	11, 154
Queens Borough	6, 709	5, 568	83. 0	8, 455	4, 144	49. 0	1, 679	24	10	14	7, 686	4, 140	1, 369	1, 979	792
Richmond Borough	999	769	77. 0	1, 053	373	35. 4	242	------	------	------	929	373	178	131	64
Norfolk, Va	17, 005	13, 661	80. 3	19, 388	9, 559	49. 3	4, 373	146	91	55	17, 420	9, 535	2, 604	4, 624	2, 307
Oakland, Calif	3, 291	2, 656	80. 7	3, 285	1, 208	36. 8	591	8	5	3	3, 019	1, 206	239	527	440
Oklahoma City, Okla	6, 044	4, 964	82. 1	6, 359	3, 326	52. 3	1, 183	47	32	15	5, 827	3, 322	617	1, 780	925
Omaha, Nebr	4, 722	3, 892	82. 4	4, 630	1, 919	41. 4	855	9	4	5	4, 283	1, 918	364	892	662
Paterson, N. J	1, 148	993	86. 5	1, 242	644	51. 9	216	6	------	6	1, 138	644	203	309	132
Peoria, Ill	1, 421	1, 179	83. 0	1, 192	582	48. 8	306	2	------	2	1, 072	581	237	191	153
Philadelphia, Pa	89, 608	76, 161	85. 0	92, 033	42, 729	46. 4	18, 256	211	106	105	83, 992	42, 692	14, 081	20, 419	8, 192
Pittsburgh, Pa	23, 060	19, 198	83. 3	21, 954	6, 923	31. 5	4, 795	52	30	22	19, 848	6, 917	2, 069	2, 997	1, 851
Portland, Oreg	730	626	85. 8	667	300	45. 0	99	3	3	------	625	300	59	135	106
Providence, R. I	2, 073	1, 664	80. 3	2, 242	988	44. 1	607	10	4	6	1, 970	983	329	368	286
Reading, Pa	925	769	83. 1	730	240	32. 9	165	7	4	3	663	239	66	135	38
Richmond, Va	19, 515	15, 348	78. 6	23, 508	11, 319	48. 1	5, 607	193	101	92	21, 039	11, 281	3, 389	4, 918	2, 974
Rochester, N. Y	1, 093	893	81. 7	1, 180	540	45. 8	216	------	------	------	1, 087	540	158	269	113
St. Louis, Mo	38, 956	33, 110	85. 0	41, 002	17, 436	42. 5	7, 163	239	151	88	37, 864	17, 414	4, 279	8, 181	4, 954
St. Paul, Minn	1, 830	1, 522	83. 2	1, 648	498	30. 2	320	2	2	------	1, 521	498	111	206	181
Salt Lake City, Utah	320	258	80. 6	260	89	34. 2	59	------	------	------	230	89	19	35	35
San Antonio, Tex	6, 932	5, 717	82. 5	8, 505	4, 542	53. 4	1, 639	54	40	14	7, 822	4, 536	881	2, 051	1, 604
San Diego, Calif	1, 094	916	83. 7	1, 195	580	48. 5	218	2	1	1	1, 092	580	84	303	193
San Francisco, Calif	2, 026	1, 747	86. 2	1, 462	772	52. 8	147	1	1	------	1, 400	772	196	320	256
Scranton, Pa	340	283	83. 2	295	86	29. 2	64	------	------	------	270	86	27	34	25
Seattle, Wash	1, 645	1, 405	85. 4	1, 295	487	37. 6	191	4	2	2	1, 218	487	83	211	193
Somerville, Mass	118	95	80. 5	114	32	28. 1	26	------	------	------	100	32	8	11	13
South Bend, Ind	1, 480	1, 259	85. 1	1, 334	418	31. 3	286	2	1	1	1, 204	418	92	248	78
Spokane, Wash	282	231	81. 9	257	99	38. 5	57	1	1	------	239	99	13	35	51
Springfield, Mass	1, 279	1, 032	80. 7	1, 294	544	42. 0	284	4	2	2	1, 177	544	157	250	137
Syracuse, N. Y	844	691	81. 9	725	259	35. 7	157	2	2	------	662	259	70	134	55
Tacoma, Wash	328	291	88. 7	294	99	33. 7	57	2	2	------	269	99	23	34	42
Tampa, Fla	8, 332	6, 821	81. 9	9, 387	5, 406	57. 6	1, 959	87	49	38	8, 557	5, 389	999	2, 907	1, 483
Toledo, Ohio	5, 883	5, 049	85. 8	5, 153	1, 667	32. 4	976	10	7	3	4, 755	1, 666	317	873	476
Trenton, N. J	3, 365	2, 434	72. 3	2, 944	974	33. 1	808	47	2	45	2, 580	951	364	398	189
Tulsa, Okla	6, 188	5, 273	85. 2	6, 880	4, 026	58. 5	1, 153	20	13	7	6, 383	4, 022	645	2, 115	1, 262
Utica, N. Y	210	180	85. 7	194	90	46. 4	39	------	------	------	176	90	24	49	17
Washington, D. C	51, 875	41, 811	80. 6	59, 349	31, 311	52. 8	11, 307	268	161	107	54, 297	31, 263	9, 053	15, 460	6, 750
Wichita, Kans	2, 273	1, 855	81. 6	2, 369	993	41. 9	566	4	3	1	2, 118	993	185	475	333
Wilmington, Del	5, 157	4, 431	85. 9	5, 133	2, 425	47. 2	965	18	8	10	4, 687	2, 420	851	1, 097	472
Worcester, Mass	510	392	76. 9	586	220	37. 5	147	1	1	------	517	220	69	106	45
Yonkers, N. Y	1, 279	1, 079	84. 4	1, 486	809	54. 4	258	2	2	------	1, 375	809	265	405	139
Youngstown, Ohio	6, 006	4, 901	81. 6	5, 309	955	18. 0	1, 326	7	6	1	4, 721	954	217	431	306

TABLE 22.—NUMBER OF NEGROES 10 YEARS OLD AND OVER GAINFULLY OCCUPIED, FOR CITIES HAVING 25,000 TO 100,000 INHABITANTS: 1930

[Cities having less than 100 gainfully occupied are omitted]

CITY	Total	Male	Female
ALABAMA			
Mobile	13,147	7,354	5,793
Montgomery	16,246	8,331	7,915
ARIZONA			
Phoenix	1,267	819	448
Tuscon	558	352	206
ARKANSAS			
Fort Smith	1,548	985	563
Little Rock	10,725	5,822	4,903
Texarkana [1]	1,482	907	575
CALIFORNIA			
Alameda	112	70	42
Bakersfield	462	301	161
Berkeley	1,099	707	392
Fresno	386	278	108
Pasadena	1,636	899	737
Riverside	230	151	79
Sacramento	556	378	178
San Bernardino	246	181	65
San Jose	133	82	51
Santa Barbara	321	184	137
Santa Monica	394	210	184
Stockton	249	169	80
COLORADO			
Colorado Springs	511	277	234
Pueblo	575	404	171
CONNECTICUT			
New Britain	153	118	35
New London	386	264	122
Norwalk	503	313	190
Stamford	1,154	682	472
Waterbury	772	562	210
FLORIDA			
Orlando	4,519	2,340	2,179
Pensacola	5,265	2,958	2,307
St. Petersburg	4,362	2,112	2,250
West Palm Beach	5,340	3,009	2,331
GEORGIA			
Augusta	13,815	7,177	6,638
Columbus	8,049	3,859	4,190
Macon	12,924	6,729	6,195
Savannah	22,336	12,531	9,805
ILLINOIS			
Alton	1,293	958	335
Aurora	463	330	133
Bloomington	392	285	107
Danville	1,015	737	278
Decatur	873	656	217
East St. Louis	5,054	3,752	1,302
Elgin	164	122	42
Evanston	2,888	1,524	1,364
Galesburg	428	295	133
Joliet	630	512	118
Maywood	381	231	150
Moline	154	110	44
Oak Park	113	38	75
Quincy	609	393	216
Rockford	500	381	119
Rock Island	335	260	75
Springfield	1,610	1,101	509
Waukegan	494	368	126
INDIANA			
Anderson	643	454	189
East Chicago	2,224	1,909	315
Elkhart	226	178	48
Hammond	295	244	51
Kokomo	512	380	132
Lafayette	205	145	60
Michigan City	756	703	53
Muncie	1,140	879	261
New Albany	621	423	198
Richmond	905	700	205
Terre Haute	1,623	1,130	493
IOWA			
Burlington	230	171	59
Cedar Rapids	339	258	81
Clinton	120	77	43
Council Bluffs	326	223	103
Davenport	411	293	118
Ottumwa	191	138	53
Sioux City	532	422	110
Waterloo	446	374	72
KANSAS			
Hutchinson	369	262	107
Topeka	2,611	1,789	822
KENTUCKY			
Ashland	449	306	143
Covington	1,855	1,270	585
KENTUCKY—con.			
Lexington	7,047	4,149	2,898
Newport	564	389	175
Paducah	3,763	2,212	1,551
LOUISIANA			
Baton Rouge	5,814	3,154	2,660
Monroe	5,771	3,483	2,288
Shreveport	15,718	8,450	7,268
MAINE			
Portland	139	97	42
MARYLAND			
Cumberland	533	353	180
Hagerstown	868	492	376
MASSACHUSETTS			
Brockton	211	135	76
Brookline town	255	63	192
Chelsea	137	106	31
Everett	432	305	127
Haverhill	133	81	52
Malden	286	186	100
Medford	224	166	58
Newton	402	158	244
Pittsfield	223	157	66
Taunton	111	86	25
MICHIGAN			
Ann Arbor	539	331	208
Battle Creek	865	597	268
Hamtramck	1,628	1,312	316
Highland Park	525	383	142
Jackson	811	627	184
Kalamazoo	447	314	133
Lansing	615	453	162
Muskegon	325	277	48
Pontiac	1,307	1,003	304
Port Huron	363	295	68
Saginaw	1,577	1,307	270
MISSISSIPPI			
Jackson	9,610	5,784	3,826
Meridian	6,172	3,235	2,937
MISSOURI			
Joplin	395	252	143
St. Joseph	2,157	1,378	779
Springfield	842	539	303
University City	143	43	100
MONTANA			
Great Falls	112	85	27
NEBRASKA			
Lincoln	513	354	159
NEW JERSEY			
Atlantic City	10,046	5,730	4,316
Bayonne	1,002	716	286
Belleville	469	314	155
Bloomfield	463	276	187
East Orange	2,729	1,522	1,207
Hoboken	227	181	46
Montclair	3,760	1,840	1,920
New Brunswick	997	698	299
Orange	2,584	1,537	1,047
Passaic	953	610	343
Perth Amboy	396	327	69
Plainfield	1,879	1,104	775
Woodbridge township	287	258	29
NEW MEXICO			
Albuquerque	212	152	60
NEW YORK			
Auburn	262	184	78
Binghamton	344	218	126
Elmira	313	215	98
Jamestown	131	89	42
Kingston	312	225	87
Mount Vernon	2,223	1,052	1,171
Newburgh	452	301	151
New Rochelle	2,834	1,347	1,487
Niagara Falls	480	355	125
Poughkeepsie	572	355	217
Rome	116	105	11
Schenectady	341	262	79
Troy	358	247	111
White Plains	1,361	702	659
NORTH CAROLINA			
Asheville	7,554	3,991	3,563
Charlotte	13,689	7,457	6,232
Durham	10,520	5,515	5,005
NORTH CAROLINA—con.			
Greensboro	7,036	3,988	3,048
High Point	3,827	2,290	1,537
Raleigh	6,260	3,409	2,851
Wilmington	6,498	3,503	2,995
Winston-Salem	18,424	9,887	8,537
OHIO			
Cleveland Heights	491	136	355
East Cleveland	118	42	76
Elyria	502	392	110
Hamilton	886	660	226
Lima	631	456	175
Lorain	396	318	78
Mansfield	438	340	98
Marion	182	132	50
Massillon	504	400	104
Middletown	1,103	842	261
Newark	337	238	99
Portsmouth	863	692	171
Springfield	3,636	2,657	979
Steubenville	1,310	1,065	245
Warren	1,035	892	143
Zanesville	811	580	231
OKLAHOMA			
Enid	396	242	154
Muskogee	2,925	1,835	1,090
PENNSYLVANIA			
Aliquippa	1,088	963	125
Allentown	173	135	38
Altoona	301	227	74
Bethlehem	311	238	73
Chester	4,357	3,240	1,117
Easton	263	193	70
Harrisburg	3,151	2,170	981
Johnstown	515	446	69
Lancaster	661	452	209
Lower Merion township	2,136	760	1,376
McKeesport	755	657	98
New Castle	623	496	127
Norristown	827	602	225
Sharon	193	162	31
Upper Darby township	298	69	229
Wilkes-Barre	388	329	59
Wilkinsburg	237	165	72
Williamsport	411	272	139
York	1,024	694	330
RHODE ISLAND			
Cranston	155	97	58
East Providence town	298	207	91
Newport	750	450	300
Pawtucket	120	90	30
SOUTH CAROLINA			
Charleston	14,320	7,185	7,135
Columbia	9,379	4,717	4,662
Greenville	6,364	3,097	3,267
Spartanburg	4,830	2,615	2,215
TENNESSEE			
Johnson City	983	570	413
TEXAS			
Amarillo	1,156	672	484
Austin	4,990	2,577	2,413
Beaumont	9,309	5,917	3,392
Corpus Christi	1,072	693	379
Galveston	8,017	4,784	3,233
Port Arthur	4,808	3,268	1,540
San Angelo	1,022	580	442
Texarkana [1]	2,426	1,449	977
Waco	4,850	2,829	2,021
Wichita Falls	2,602	1,422	1,180
UTAH			
Ogden	118	96	22
VIRGINIA			
Lynchburg	4,625	2,407	2,218
Newport News	6,026	4,203	1,823
Petersburg	6,622	3,513	3,109
Portsmouth	8,751	5,482	3,269
Roanoke	5,760	3,563	2,197
WEST VIRGINIA			
Charleston	3,596	2,135	1,461
Clarksburg	574	392	182
Huntington	2,303	1,432	871
Parkersburg	473	320	153
Wheeling	1,228	791	437
WISCONSIN			
Madison	168	114	54
Racine	240	188	52

[1] The inclusion of Texarkana, Ark., and Texarkana, Tex., in this table for cities of 25,000 to 100,000 is based upon the combined population (27,366 in 1930) of the 2 cities.

Table 23.—NEGRO MALES AND FEMALES 10 YEARS OLD AND OVER GAINFULLY OCCUPIED, BY STATES: 1930

OCCUPATION	United States			ALABAMA		ARIZONA		ARKANSAS		CALIFORNIA		COLORADO	
	Total	Male [1]	Female [1]	Male	Female	Male	Female	Male	Female	Male	Female	Male	Female
POPULATION 10 YEARS OLD AND OVER	9,292,556	4,564,690	4,727,866	344,705	374,585	5,549	3,576	184,753	188,520	34,387	35,350	4,981	5,299
GAINFUL WORKERS													
All occupations	**5,503,535**	**3,662,893**	**1,840,642**	**279,829**	**152,520**	**4,705**	**1,281**	**147,538**	**54,410**	**27,970**	**15,525**	**3,991**	**2,229**
Agriculture	1,987,839	1,492,555	495,284	150,807	70,994	687	43	104,563	27,171	2,323	72	160	8
Farmers (owners and tenants) [2]	873,653	797,231	76,422	82,300	11,039	102	4	72,860	7,002	447	18	72	4
Farm managers and foremen	1,676	1,655	21	130	-	4	-	71	10	23	-	-	-
Farm laborers	1,112,510	693,669	418,841	68,377	59,955	581	39	31,632	20,159	1,853	54	88	4
Wage workers	539,307	419,193	120,114	31,704	14,222	572	39	15,648	4,214	1,816	50	80	4
Unpaid family workers	573,203	274,476	298,727	36,673	45,733	9	-	15,984	15,945	37	4	8	-
Bakers	4,527	3,919	608	235	-	3	-	44	-	33	-	7	-
Barbers, hairdressers, and manicurists	34,263	21,447	12,816	871	415	98	20	484	224	358	276	37	39
Blacksmiths	5,274	5,274	-	485	-	5	-	241	-	29	-	4	-
Brakemen, steam railroad	3,347	3,347	-	348	-	5	-	116	-	5	-	7	-
Builders and building contractors	2,570	2,566	4	72	-	2	-	51	-	50	-	6	-
Carpenters	32,413	32,406	7	2,396	-	27	-	941	-	369	-	37	-
Chauffeurs and truck and tractor drivers	108,412	108,241	171	4,947	-	73	-	1,478	-	1,777	-	92	-
Cleaning, dyeing, and pressing shop workers	15,773	12,573	3,200	1,042	-	-	-	370	-	102	-	-	-
Clergyman	25,034	24,540	494	1,635	-	42	-	877	-	253	-	43	-
Clerks (except "Clerks" in stores)	25,185	20,255	4,930	384	84	14	5	131	56	426	94	53	22
Dealers, retail [3]	28,213	24,364	3,849	1,100	299	19	4	501	121	346	40	37	4
Delivery men, bakeries and stores [4]	25,299	25,277	22	2,101	-	5	-	599	-	56	-	8	-
Draymen, teamsters, and carriage drivers [5]	19,566	19,549	17	1,692	-	5	-	510	-	101	-	35	-
Elevator tenders	16,889	12,446	4,443	-	-	-	-	-	-	194	-	-	-
Engineers (stationary)	3,612	3,612	-	145	-	5	-	61	-	54	-	8	-
Firemen, except locomotive and fire department	18,265	18,265	-	1,405	-	11	-	341	-	45	-	18	-
Firemen, locomotive	4,642	4,642	-	661	-	3	-	31	-	5	-	4	-
Fishermen and oystermen	7,162	7,106	56	-	-	-	-	36	-	4	-	-	-
Furnace men, smelter men, heaters, puddlers, etc	3,091	3,091	-	287	-	-	-	-	-	-	-	16	-
Guards, watchmen, and doorkeepers	6,111	6,039	72	282	-	12	-	124	-	121	-	21	-
Insurance agents, managers, and officials	6,797	5,699	1,098	314	-	9	-	183	-	61	9	9	-
Janitors and sextons	78,415	72,382	6,033	2,272	-	239	-	702	-	2,996	-	493	62
Laborers, porters, and helpers in stores	62,829	61,601	1,228	3,288	-	70	-	1,332	-	585	-	139	-
Laborers (not otherwise specified):													
Automobile factories	16,450	16,289	161	-	-	-	-	-	-	-	-	-	-
Blast furnaces and steel rolling mills [6]	38,915	38,709	206	4,748	-	-	-	-	-	34	-	88	-
Brick, tile, and terra-cotta factories	12,180	12,095	85	-	-	-	-	-	-	-	-	-	-
Building construction, laborers and helpers	95,618	95,587	31	2,155	-	62	-	762	-	779	-	109	-
Car and railroad shops	9,226	9,130	96	1,018	-	-	-	-	-	-	-	-	-
Cigar and tobacco factories	12,254	8,863	3,391	-	-	-	-	-	-	-	-	-	-
Coal yards and lumber yards	18,998	18,983	15	-	-	-	-	-	-	70	-	-	-
Cotton mills	11,156	9,106	2,050	1,064	391	-	-	-	-	-	-	-	-
Domestic and personal service	22,934	21,650	1,284	-	-	-	-	-	-	91	-	-	-
Fertilizer factories	15,347	15,268	79	1,425	-	-	-	-	-	-	-	-	-
Garage	23,854	23,750	104	600	-	75	-	262	-	532	-	71	-
General and not specified in manufactures	128,518	123,898	4,620	4,164	-	161	-	2,599	-	1,198	-	114	-
Lime, cement, and artificial-stone factories	6,041	6,016	25	-	-	-	-	-	-	57	-	-	-
Petroleum refineries	7,863	7,828	35	-	-	-	-	-	-	11	-	-	-
Public service	34,924	34,422	502	1,468	-	104	-	428	-	688	-	22	-
Road and street	59,115	59,082	33	3,827	-	20	-	1,131	-	487	-	19	-
Saw and planing mills [7]	96,527	95,198	1,329	9,963	-	53	-	6,644	-	257	-	2	-
Slaughter and packing houses	9,332	8,854	478	-	-	-	-	-	-	-	-	-	-
Steam railroads	97,992	96,865	1,127	6,145	-	70	-	3,798	-	445	-	110	-
Street railroads	4,693	4,601	92	-	-	-	-	-	-	-	-	-	-
Truck, transfer, and cab companies	7,055	7,019	36	-	-	-	-	-	-	-	-	-	-
Laundry operatives [8]	58,080	10,534	47,546	-	2,095	-	21	-	613	59	212	13	11
Longshoremen and stevedores	25,444	25,434	10	1,383	-	-	-	-	-	91	-	-	-
Lumbermen, raftsmen, and woodchoppers	24,470	24,446	24	1,753	-	21	-	1,299	-	15	-	13	-
Machinists	7,647	7,647	-	449	-	25	-	130	-	137	-	5	-
Mail carriers	6,312	6,293	19	233	-	1	-	142	-	188	-	24	-
Masons, brick and stone, and tile layers	11,701	11,701	-	869	-	1	-	151	-	105	-	10	-
Mechanics, automobile factories, garages, and repair shops	21,088	21,086	2	720	-	36	-	403	-	442	-	37	-
Messengers, errand, and office boys and girls [9]	7,621	7,243	378	133	-	1	-	19	-	74	-	17	-
Molders, founders, and casters, iron	5,232	5,232	-	715	-	-	-	-	-	26	-	-	-
Musicians and teachers of music	10,583	7,747	2,836	110	101	18	6	107	45	296	119	60	19
Operatives (not otherwise specified):													
Automobile factories	3,245	3,154	91	-	-	-	-	-	-	-	-	-	-
Blast furnaces and steel rolling mills [6]	6,861	6,763	98	1,057	-	-	-	-	-	-	-	30	-
Car and railroad shops	3,670	3,644	26	444	-	2	-	185	-	35	-	3	-
Cigar and tobacco factories	20,721	5,745	14,976	-	-	-	-	-	-	-	-	-	-
Coal mines	57,315	57,291	24	12,742	-	-	-	91	-	-	-	267	-
Iron mines	3,448	3,448	-	3,345	-	-	-	-	-	-	-	-	-
Saw and planing mills [7]	6,548	6,309	239	690	-	-	-	435	-	27	-	-	-
Slaughter and packing houses	7,167	6,286	881	-	-	-	-	-	-	-	-	-	-
Suit, coat, and overall factories	5,672	3,812	1,860	-	-	-	-	-	-	-	-	-	-
Quarries	9,541	9,522	19	-	-	-	-	-	-	-	-	-	-
Painters, glaziers, and varnishers (building)	15,677	15,668	9	695	-	6	-	160	-	197	-	18	-
Physicians and surgeons	3,805	3,713	92	114	-	10	-	102	-	65	2	11	2
Plasterers and cement finishers	13,465	13,464	1	670	-	7	-	154	-	246	-	30	-
Plumbers and gas and steam fitters	4,729	4,729	-	454	-	7	-	146	-	46	-	6	-
Porters (except in stores)	93,744	93,714	30	2,064	-	214	-	1,262	-	2,197	-	561	-
Sailors and deck hands	6,659	6,656	3	-	-	-	-	-	-	105	-	-	-
Salesmen and saleswomen	13,550	9,172	4,378	399	272	12	2	181	91	151	74	79	8
Sawyers	3,449	3,445	4	393	-	-	-	237	-	16	-	-	-
Servants	836,928	109,586	727,342	3,989	40,364	216	788	1,810	14,068	2,243	10,862	273	1,504
Shoemakers and cobblers (not in factory)	4,150	4,129	21	313	-	4	-	98	-	53	-	9	-
Switchmen and flagmen, steam railroad	2,571	2,554	17	458	-	-	-	31	-	8	-	11	-
Tailors and tailoresses	7,505	6,953	552	175	-	12	-	90	-	117	-	21	3
Teachers (school)	54,439	8,767	45,672	599	3,571	11	48	442	1,532	21	75	-	11
Waiters	57,378	39,750	17,628	841	549	84	19	451	287	1,556	338	181	34
All other	828,600	402,847	425,753	30,676	33,385	2,138	325	10,072	10,202	4,512	3,352	543	502

See footnotes at end of table.

TABLE 23.—NEGRO MALES AND FEMALES 10 YEARS OLD AND OVER GAINFULLY OCCUPIED, BY STATES: 1930—Continued

OCCUPATION	CONNECTICUT		DELAWARE		DISTRICT OF COLUMBIA		FLORIDA		GEORGIA		IDAHO		ILLINOIS	
	Male	Female	Male	Female	Male	Female	Male	Female	Male	Female	Male	Female	Male	Female
POPULATION 10 YEARS AND OVER	11, 688	11, 797	13, 970	12, 597	51, 875	59, 349	172, 729	173, 208	389, 757	431, 326	355	244	139, 192	138, 642
GAINFUL WORKERS														
All occupations	**9, 498**	**5, 022**	**11, 172**	**4, 715**	**41, 811**	**31, 311**	**141, 051**	**77, 040**	**311, 550**	**182, 834**	**305**	**63**	**115, 236**	**55, 837**
Agriculture	444	11	3, 535	123	282	6	43, 729	12, 440	166, 678	59, 610	40		2, 580	188
Farmers (owners and tenants) [2]	36	2	784	24	41	1	9, 837	1, 247	79, 471	6, 498	18		865	40
Farm managers and foremen	6		8			1	140		186	4			8	
Farm laborers	402	9	2, 743	99	241	4	33, 752	11, 193	87, 021	53, 108	22		1, 707	148
Wage workers	401	9	2, 584	79	236	3	30, 178	8, 001	54, 123	21, 321	19		1, 565	126
Unpaid family workers	1		159	20	5	1	3, 574	3, 192	32, 898	31, 787	3		142	22
Bakers	7		5		97		262		305				206	49
Barbers, hairdressers, and manicurists	61	37	42	40	621	489	703	386	1, 168	425	6		1, 160	1, 212
Blacksmiths	10		3		25		173		462		1		112	
Brakemen, steam railroad			2		5		114		376				23	
Builders and building contractors	7		6		56		34		89		1		220	
Carpenters	68		50		315		1, 723		3, 301		3		924	
Chauffeurs and truck and tractor drivers	722		424		3, 957		4, 109		6, 640		3		3, 939	
Cleaning, dyeing, and pressing shop workers					161		956		1, 299				532	219
Clergymen	60		99		269		1, 453		2, 056		3		698	
Clerks (except "Clerks" in stores)	114	15	18	6	1, 149	650	234	78	440	158			3, 267	682
Dealers, retail [3]	43	8	73	7	591	52	1, 382	276	1, 681	449	1		1, 729	154
Delivery men, bakeries and stores [4]	67		31		652		1, 163		3, 851				529	
Draymen, teamsters, and carriage drivers [5]	90				237		626		1, 602				690	
Elevator tenders					834	204							537	
Engineers (stationary)	28		9		123		83		118		1		245	
Firemen, except locomotive and fire department	68		90		359		606		1, 387				830	
Firemen, locomotive	5		7		10		558		878		1		75	
Fishermen and oystermen			16				929							
Furnace men, smelter men, heaters, puddlers, etc													300	
Guards, watchmen, and doorkeepers	27		17		229		151		217		1		525	
Insurance agents, managers, and officials	6		5		82		312		605				578	67
Janitors and sextons	568		326		2, 080		1, 672		3, 022		55		5, 024	306
Laborers, porters, and helpers in stores	186		115		1, 596		2, 538		4, 335		3		3, 997	
Laborers (not otherwise specified:)														
Blast furnaces and steel rolling mills [6]	256		212										2, 738	
Building construction, laborers and helpers	587		812		3, 768		2, 054		3, 280		1		3, 752	
Car and railroad shops			121											
Coal yards and lumber yards	270		172		382				1, 327				1, 855	
Cotton mills									2, 299	791				
Domestic and personal service	93				265		1, 750		1, 659					
Fertilizer factories									2, 693					
Garage	127				267		740		698		6		2, 227	
General and not specified in manufactures	455		767		1, 709		8, 688		6, 310		15		4, 526	
Public service	73		219		2, 862		1, 451		2, 352		1		940	
Road and street	156		329		915		2, 402		4, 745				837	
Saw and planing mills [7]	7		164				9, 219		9, 691		1		629	
Slaughter and packing houses													2, 386	
Steam railroads	230		387		636		5, 732		7, 464		35		3, 441	
Laundry operatives [8]	44	202		23	317	1, 592		2, 140		3, 051		1	1, 589	5, 226
Longshoremen and stevedores							1, 882		1, 554					
Lumbermen, raftsmen, and woodchoppers	4		35				4, 078		2, 552				90	
Machinists	34		36		125		145		497				535	
Mail carriers	37		11		214		169		427				675	
Masons, brick and stone, and tile layers	42		16		243		395		1, 247		1		285	
Mechanics, automobile factories, garages, and repair shops	123		36		358		745		888		3		1, 911	
Messengers, errand, and office boys and girls [9]	47		13		1, 552	41	85		210				446	33
Molders, founders, and casters, iron	36		13										918	
Musicians and teachers of music	33	16	17	9	141	90	166	74	122	90		2	614	240
Operatives (not otherwise specified):														
Blast furnaces and steel rolling mills [6]	43												335	
Car and railroad shops	1		8				200		355				229	
Cigar and tobacco factories				3			469	672						
Coal mines													1, 242	
Saw and planing mills [7]							406		718					
Slaughter and packing houses													2, 157	394
Suit, coat, and overall factories										95			551	159
Quarries									1, 426					
Painters, glaziers, and varnishers (building)	86		27		276		482		1, 431		2		1, 464	
Physicians and surgeons	14		13		182	9	96		190		1		311	20
Plasterers and cement finishers	14		29		409		485		1, 050		2		562	
Plumbers and gas and steam fitters	14		14		100		106		356				282	
Porters (except in stores)					1, 650		2, 204		3, 046				10, 290	
Sailors and deck hands			15				178							
Salesmen and saleswomen	37	12	21	4	159	74	515	207	497	346		1	781	600
Sawyers							361		385					
Servants	645	3, 092	376	3, 110	3, 377	18, 072	4, 793	31, 325	6, 344	57, 856	19	32	5, 513	27, 652
Shoemakers and cobblers (not in factory)	6		10		96		196		441		1		175	
Switchmen and flagmen, steam railroad	2		20				163		247				78	
Tailors and tailoresses	35		13		208	38	292		316				711	69
Teachers (school)	2	18	26	169	214	1, 089	247	1, 829	501	4, 560			122	673
Waiters	255	75	74	50	1, 397	907	1, 083	539	1, 613	742	5	2	3, 387	1, 238
All other	3, 109	1, 536	2, 293	1, 171	6, 259	7, 998	25, 564	27, 074	42, 112	54, 661	93	25	27, 932	16, 656

See footnotes at end of table.

TABLE 23.—NEGRO MALES AND FEMALES 10 YEARS OLD AND OVER GAINFULLY OCCUPIED, BY STATES: 1930—Continued

OCCUPATION	INDIANA		IOWA		KANSAS		KENTUCKY		LOUISIANA		MAINE		MARYLAND	
	Male	Female	Male	Female	Male	Female	Male	Female	Male	Female	Male	Female	Male	Female
POPULATION 10 YEARS OLD AND OVER	47, 519	45, 354	7, 540	6, 886	28, 405	26, 738	93, 195	92, 434	290, 658	307, 600	488	412	112, 573	107, 236
GAINFUL WORKERS														
All occupations	**38, 683**	**14, 649**	**5, 927**	**2, 004**	**21, 977**	**8, 310**	**73, 098**	**33, 474**	**233, 907**	**111, 482**	**363**	**147**	**91, 537**	**44, 477**
Agriculture	1, 475	24	253	20	2, 066	76	21, 868	730	120, 224	38, 810	37	1	20, 956	826
Farmers (owners and tenants)[2]	441	14	116	14	975	39	8, 925	303	67, 015	6, 441	18	—	4, 710	155
Farm managers and foremen	4	—	—	—	6	—	25	—	108	—	—	—	94	—
Farm laborers	1, 030	10	137	6	1, 085	37	12, 918	427	53, 101	32, 369	19	1	16, 152	671
Wage workers	996	8	120	5	969	27	11, 361	191	34, 146	10, 498	19	1	15, 112	601
Unpaid family workers	34	2	17	1	116	10	1, 557	236	18, 955	21, 871	—	—	1, 040	70
Bakers	34	8	5	—	16	—	60	—	322	—	—	—	99	—
Barbers, hairdressers, and manicurists	522	286	75	27	198	104	556	230	811	559	6	5	487	303
Blacksmiths	47	—	7	—	46	—	150	—	419	—	1	—	59	—
Brakemen, steam railroad	8	—	9	—	26	—	86	—	385	—	1	—	10	—
Builders and building contractors	90	—	14	—	23	—	73	—	78	—	—	—	69	—
Carpenters	254	—	27	—	250	—	589	—	2, 759	—	2	—	571	—
Chauffeurs and truck and tractor drivers	1, 492	—	133	—	530	—	2, 226	—	5, 629	—	24	—	4, 394	—
Cleaning, dyeing, and pressing shop workers	—	21	—	—	46	—	266	—	1, 277	—	—	—	—	—
Clergymen	339	13	71	—	257	7	711	—	1, 279	—	4	—	529	—
Clerks (except "clerks" in stores)	188	83	43	22	213	41	142	69	391	104	4	2	474	92
Dealers, retail [3]	305	40	35	4	212	47	543	54	1, 395	223	4	—	911	119
Delivery men, bakeries and stores [4]	211	—	15	—	91	—	584	—	1, 879	—	1	—	562	—
Draymen, teamsters, and carriage drivers [5]	264	—	61	—	176	—	734	—	1, 217	—	7	—	504	—
Engineers (stationary)	51	—	20	—	28	—	71	—	171	—	1	—	85	—
Firemen, except locomotive and fire department	262	—	51	—	153	—	316	—	822	—	2	—	667	—
Firemen, locomotive	21	—	6	—	8	—	25	—	314	—	—	—	15	—
Fishermen and oystermen	—	—	—	—	—	—	—	—	372	—	10	—	1, 246	—
Guards, watchmen, and doorkeepers	104	—	16	—	60	—	95	—	333	—	1	—	125	—
Insurance agents, managers, and officials	50	29	3	—	22	—	186	—	623	97	1	—	101	—
Janitors and sextons	2, 341	141	514	45	1, 269	—	2, 315	—	999	—	16	—	2, 034	217
Laborers, porters, and helpers in stores	778	—	150	—	586	—	1, 473	—	3, 493	—	3	—	2, 360	—
Laborers (not otherwise specified):														
Automobile factories	377	2	—	—	—	—	—	—	—	—	—	—	—	—
Blast furnaces and steel rolling mills [6]	4, 447	—	—	—	—	—	279	—	—	—	—	—	3, 887	—
Brick, tile and terra-cotta factories	212	—	32	—	—	—	143	—	—	—	—	—	—	—
Building construction, laborers and helpers	1, 972	—	157	—	748	—	2, 239	—	2, 942	—	12	—	5, 353	—
Car and railroad shops	259	—	—	—	—	—	—	—	—	—	—	—	—	—
Cigar and tobacco factories	—	—	—	—	—	—	1, 181	316	—	—	—	—	—	—
Coal yards and lumber yards	413	—	19	—	146	—	—	—	1, 029	—	4	—	939	—
Domestic and personal service	—	—	—	—	—	—	—	—	1, 468	—	4	—	—	—
Fertilizer factories	—	—	—	—	—	—	—	—	—	—	—	—	1, 164	—
Garage	596	—	175	—	299	—	480	—	734	—	6	—	445	—
General and not specified in manufactures	2, 270	—	469	—	2, 326	—	3, 687	—	6, 489	—	33	—	5, 772	—
Lime, cement, and artificial stone factories	—	—	52	—	231	—	—	—	—	—	—	—	—	—
Petroleum refineries	5	—	—	—	53	—	—	—	1, 915	—	—	—	—	—
Public service	496	—	176	—	276	—	964	—	1, 622	—	5	—	1, 236	—
Road and street	549	—	123	—	276	—	1, 077	—	4, 937	—	2	—	2, 314	—
Saw and planing mills [7]	102	—	4	—	14	—	437	—	12, 343	—	1	—	755	—
Slaughter and packing houses	—	—	235	10	1, 051	—	—	—	—	—	—	—	—	—
Steam railroads	931	—	279	—	1, 827	—	3, 414	—	7, 686	—	16	—	1, 923	—
Laundry operatives [8]	—	360	—	15	—	488	—	608	—	1, 915	—	3	230	1, 243
Longshoremen and stevedores	—	—	—	—	—	—	—	—	3, 953	—	6	—	2, 334	—
Lumbermen, raftsmen, and woodchoppers	6	—	2	—	2	—	31	—	3, 262	—	8	—	321	—
Machinists	135	—	19	—	59	—	144	—	227	—	3	—	133	—
Mail carriers	96	—	9	—	64	—	128	—	288	—	—	—	144	—
Masons, brick and stone, and tile layers	98	—	10	—	110	—	317	—	741	—	1	—	138	—
Mechanics, automobile factories, garages, and repair shops	305	—	64	—	162	—	451	—	768	—	5	—	431	—
Messenger, errand, and office boys and girls [9]	65	4	7	—	25	—	74	—	195	—	1	—	264	—
Molders, founders, and casters, iron	293	—	31	—	—	—	—	—	—	—	—	—	118	—
Musicians and teachers of music	97	62	32	8	93	30	192	56	368	74	—	—	231	63
Operatives (not otherwise specified):														
Automobile factories	67	2	—	—	—	—	—	—	—	—	—	—	—	—
Blast furnaces and steel rolling mills [6]	527	—	—	—	—	—	40	—	—	—	—	—	632	—
Car and railroad shops	47	—	41	—	114	—	94	—	183	—	—	—	21	—
Cigar and tobacco factories	—	130	—	—	—	—	712	1, 325	—	222	—	—	—	28
Coal mines	314	—	485	—	277	—	7, 346	—	—	—	—	—	21	—
Saw and planing mills [7]	—	—	—	—	—	—	—	—	921	—	—	—	—	—
Slaughter and packing houses	—	—	122	9	421	59	—	—	—	—	—	—	62	—
Suit, coat, and overall factories	—	18	—	2	—	8	—	4	—	340	—	1	453	193
Quarries	56	—	—	—	—	—	507	—	—	—	2	—	381	—
Painters, glaziers, and varnishers (building)	191	—	30	—	84	—	241	—	813	—	4	—	298	—
Physicians and surgeons	77	3	8	—	42	—	128	—	107	—	—	—	100	—
Plasterers and cement finishers	239	—	39	—	158	—	452	—	848	—	1	—	305	—
Plumbers and gas and steam fitters	68	—	7	—	43	—	113	—	183	—	1	—	71	—
Porters (except in stores)	—	—	—	—	1, 326	—	2, 085	—	3, 890	—	—	—	1, 812	—
Sailors and deck hands	—	—	—	—	—	—	—	—	1, 183	—	1	—	564	—
Salesmen and saleswomen	134	84	19	10	52	31	142	86	438	174	2	—	209	70
Sawyers	7	—	—	—	—	—	21	—	299	—	—	—	—	—
Servants	1, 460	8, 587	258	1, 333	816	4, 784	2, 914	16, 550	3, 482	38, 883	35	69	3, 934	27, 142
Shoemakers and cobblers (not in factory)	54	—	11	—	34	—	73	—	222	—	1	—	102	—
Switchmen and flagmen, steam railroad	38	—	5	—	25	—	46	—	93	—	—	—	49	—
Tailors and tailoresses	92	11	12	—	40	—	92	5	160	—	—	—	212	13
Teachers (school)	122	461	1	8	81	321	326	1, 289	387	2, 545	—	2	324	1, 231
Waiters	742	258	67	27	227	66	965	257	916	556	6	2	2, 035	795
All other	11, 888	4, 022	1, 419	464	4, 199	2, 248	8, 494	11, 895	23, 623	26, 980	78	62	15, 562	12, 142

See footnotes at end of table.

TABLE 23.—NEGRO MALES AND FEMALES 10 YEARS OLD AND OVER GAINFULLY OCCUPIED, BY STATES: 1930—Continued

OCCUPATION	MASSACHUSETTS Male	MASSACHUSETTS Female	MICHIGAN Male	MICHIGAN Female	MINNESOTA Male	MINNESOTA Female	MISSISSIPPI Male	MISSISSIPPI Female	MISSOURI Male	MISSOURI Female	MONTANA Male	MONTANA Female	NEBRASKA Male	NEBRASKA Female
POPULATION 10 YEARS OLD AND OVER	21,089	21,267	74,033	65,457	4,353	3,802	375,915	389,143	94,184	94,480	644	484	5,986	5,619
GAINFUL WORKERS														
All occupations	**16,187**	**8,479**	**62,089**	**20,160**	**3,562**	**1,247**	**315,895**	**172,517**	**77,530**	**37,295**	**528**	**167**	**4,910**	**2,269**
Agriculture	1,088	77	1,177	32	72	5	243,406	119,242	12,684	759	50	1	103	4
Farmers (owners and tenants) [2]	89	5	448	23	27	2	161,274	19,601	5,653	226	22	1	49	3
Farm managers and foremen	16		5		2		113		18				2	
Farm laborers	983	72	724	9	43	3	82,019	99,641	7,013	533	28		52	1
Wage workers	973	71	678	8	35	1	27,011	12,323	6,237	298	27		44	1
Unpaid family workers	10	1	46	1	8	2	55,008	87,318	776	235	1		8	
Bakers	53		65		5		164		43				3	
Barbers, hairdressers, and manicurists	117	106	564	387	100	45	664	244	646	509	13	8	47	53
Blacksmiths	19		27		1		499		68		1		1	
Brakemen, steam railroad	5		9		2		216		19					
Builders and building contractors	18		100		4		77		79		1		5	
Carpenters	153		604		9		1,913		468		1		20	
Chauffeurs and truck and tractor drivers	803		2,855		60		2,783		3,618		7		182	
Cleaning, dyeing, and pressing shop workers				77			763		228	34				
Clergymen	99		337		30		1,392		649		7		45	
Clerks (except "clerks" in stores)	454	112	565	184	67	30	134	54	699	215	3	2	30	41
Dealers, retail [3]	145	19	733	89	32	2	718	205	814	78	4	1	45	5
Delivery men, bakeries and stores [4]	71		246		6		1,035		519		1		39	
Draymen, teamsters, and carriage drivers [5]	88		220		7		1,125		910		2		24	
Engineers (stationary)	92		94		12		94		55		6		14	
Firemen, except locomotive and fire department	168		261		15		935		480		3		25	
Firemen, locomotive	11		25		2		457		26				1	
Fishermen and oystermen	27						145							
Furnace men, smelter men, heaters, puddlers, etc			315											
Guards, watchmen, and doorkeepers	78		170		13		236		234		1		15	
Insurance agents, managers, and officials	19		64	14	3		214		200	24			3	
Janitors and sextons	1,033		2,836	263	265		997		4,606		91		410	
Laborers, porters, and helpers in stores	342		1,157		98		2,503		2,655		8		121	
Laborers (not otherwise specified):														
Automobile factories			13,025	96										
Blast furnaces and steel rolling mills [6]			524						800					
Brick, tile, and terra-cotta factories									1,017					
Building construction, laborers and helpers	519		4,697		29		1,138		3,985		5		152	
Car and railroad shops														
Cigar and tobacco factories														
Coal yards and lumber yards	164		399		7		776		774				17	
Cotton mills	77													
Domestic and personal service							990							
Fertilizer factories														
Garage	107		988		84		465		868		10		122	
General and not specified in manufactures	651		1,331		112		3,675		4,548		35		317	
Lime, cement, and artificial stone factories														
Petroleum refineries														
Public service	149		1,027		18		1,019		492		5		31	
Road and street	191		1,169		52		2,246		1,158		4		52	
Saw and planing mills [7]	10		38		3		12,139		106					
Slaughter and packing houses					56				986				646	
Steam railroads	272		405		55		5,818		3,251		27		132	
Truck, transfer, and cab companies														
Laundry operatives [8]	86	322		1,238		11		1,065		2,130		1		44
Longshoremen and stevedores	255													
Lumbermen, raftsmen, and woodchoppers	13		18		1		2,911		30		1		1	
Machinists	127		795		6		171		151		2		9	
Mail carriers	56		197		21		124		123				10	
Masons, brick and stone, and tile layers	91		353		7		402		165		2		11	
Mechanics, automobile factories, garages, and repair shops	211		1,042		53		640		687		6		32	
Messenger, errand, and office boys and girls [9]	66		49		13		57		254				15	
Molders, founders, and casters, iron	13		584		2				173					
Musicians and teachers of music	105	61	270	83	72	15	100	43	329	120	6	1	68	17
Operatives (not otherwise specified):														
Automobile factories			2,518	30					18					
Blast furnaces and steel rolling mills [6]	2													
Car and railroad shops	16		32		1		142		124				3	
Cigar and tobacco factories				37						212				
Coal mines									657		1			
Iron mines			1											
Saw and planing mills [7]							642							
Slaughter and packing houses					97				703				258	16
Suit, coat, and overall factories		33								34				
Quarries									736					
Painters, glaziers, and varnishers (building)	223		466		30		392		238		3		41	
Physicians and surgeons	46	1	100		5		69		196				11	
Plasterers and cement finishers	25		622		15		264		271		1		31	
Plumbers and gas and steam fitters	23		123		2		241		90		1		8	
Porters (except in stores)	1,300						1,550		5,628					
Sailors and deck hands	173													
Salesmen and saleswomen	88	37	292	151	19	13	274	188	281	117	6	1	11	8
Sawyers							413							
Servants	1,251	4,531	1,675	12,123	229	652	2,936	26,696	3,279	18,450	35	86	300	1,483
Shoemakers and cobblers (not in factory)	29		76		7		192		58		1		3	
Switchmen and flagmen, steam railroad	9		23		1		72		31		4		2	
Tailors and tailoresses	94	11	280	42	13		73		182	13	1		12	
Teachers (school)	9	79	11	116		7	507	3,085	326	1,028		2		4
Waiters	818	182	752	600	490	55	536	402	1,402	603	25	2	284	64
All other	4,035	2,908	15,783	4,598	1,259	412	14,451	21,293	13,713	12,969	148	62	1,198	530

See footnotes at end of table.

Table 23.—NEGRO MALES AND FEMALES 10 YEARS OLD AND OVER GAINFULLY OCCUPIED, BY STATES: 1930—Continued

OCCUPATION	NEVADA		NEW HAMPSHIRE		NEW JERSEY		NEW MEXICO		NEW YORK		NORTH CAROLINA		NORTH DAKOTA		OHIO	
	Male	Female	Male	Female	Male	Female	Male	Female	Male	Female	Male	Female	Male	Female	Male	Female
POPULATION, 10 YEARS OLD AND OVER	256	216	481	216	83, 237	85, 977	1, 260	1, 068	167, 235	180, 146	324, 816	348, 993	210	116	131, 229	121, 271
GAINFUL WORKERS																
All occupations	**236**	**98**	**421**	**72**	**63, 487**	**38, 627**	**1, 012**	**343**	**143, 554**	**95, 751**	**245, 479**	**120, 065**	**175**	**44**	**104, 982**	**40, 397**
Agriculture	11	1	23	1	5, 143	149	188	3	2, 214	44	139, 268	38, 988	34	3	3, 738	81
Farmers (owners and tenants) [2]	4	1	5	-	537	13	76	3	197	10	69, 795	4, 749	11	1	1, 207	47
Farm managers and foremen	-	-	-	-	25	-	-	-	11	-	90	-	-	-	20	-
Farm laborers	7	-	18	1	4, 581	136	112	-	2, 006	34	69, 383	34, 239	23	2	2, 511	34
Wage workers	7	-	17	1	4, 507	129	96	-	1, 984	32	38, 755	10, 575	22	-	2, 403	31
Unpaid family workers	-	-	1	-	74	7	16	-	22	2	30, 628	23, 664	1	2	108	3
Bakers	1	-	2	-	112	-	2	-	313	-	235	-	-	-	64	40
Barbers, hairdressers, and manicurists	5	-	1	-	574	443	21	2	1, 211	1, 497	1, 276	271	6	1	1, 386	814
Blacksmiths	-	-	2	-	50	-	5	-	97	-	415	-	-	-	92	-
Brakemen, steam railroad	-	-	-	-	11	-	2	-	13	-	168	-	2	-	20	-
Builders and building contractors	-	-	-	-	156	-	-	-	158	-	79	-	-	-	205	-
Carpenters	1	-	2	-	786	-	8	-	1, 715	-	1, 889	-	-	-	817	-
Chauffeurs and truck and tractor drivers	2	-	8	-	5, 279	-	11	-	10, 366	-	4, 637	-	3	-	5, 410	-
Cleaning, dyeing, and pressing shop workers	-	-	-	-	-	-	-	-	282	-	1, 115	-	-	-	331	100
Clergymen	2	-	-	-	527	-	13	-	623	-	1, 547	-	-	-	809	-
Clerks (except "clerks" in stores)	2	-	4	-	702	122	1	-	5, 192	728	252	129	-	-	1, 015	213
Dealers, retail [3]	3	-	3	-	679	106	4	2	1, 041	89	1, 159	200	3	5	1, 026	100
Delivery men, bakeries, and stores [4]	-	-	1	-	660	-	1	-	717	-	1, 997	-	-	-	350	-
Draymen, teamsters, and carriage drivers [5]	1	-	1	-	494	-	3	-	479	-	1, 000	-	2	-	618	-
Elevator tenders	-	-	-	-	-	-	-	-	5, 785	-	-	-	-	-	-	-
Engineers (stationary)	1	-	-	-	153	-	3	-	519	-	87	-	1	-	208	-
Firemen, except locomotive and fire department	1	-	1	-	478	-	9	-	1, 769	-	1, 243	-	1	-	764	-
Firemen, locomotive	-	-	-	-	26	-	-	-	41	-	406	-	-	-	65	-
Fishermen and oystermen	-	-	-	-	39	-	-	-	-	-	753	-	-	-	-	-
Furnace men, smelter men, heaters, puddlers, etc	-	-	-	-	-	-	-	-	-	-	-	-	-	-	411	-
Guards, watchmen, and doorkeepers	-	-	1	-	282	-	3	-	624	-	189	-	-	-	341	-
Insurance agents, managers and officials	-	-	-	-	103	-	-	-	169	12	249	-	-	-	231	39
Janitors and sextons	26	-	5	-	1, 445	-	67	-	4, 104	849	3, 165	-	15	-	4, 902	438
Laborers, porters, and helpers in stores	-	-	1	-	1, 345	-	7	-	4, 346	-	2, 159	-	-	-	2, 373	-
Laborers (not otherwise specified):																
Automobile factories	-	-	-	-	-	-	-	-	-	-	-	-	-	-	469	-
Blast furnaces and steel rolling mills [6]	-	-	-	-	491	-	-	-	1, 320	-	-	-	-	-	6, 759	-
Brick, tile, and terra-cotta factories	-	-	-	-	473	-	-	-	-	-	-	-	-	-	83	-
Building construction, laborers and helpers	2	-	4	-	5, 094	-	7	-	5, 254	-	3, 931	-	2	-	8, 813	-
Car and railroad shops	-	-	-	-	-	-	-	-	-	-	-	-	-	-	-	-
Cigar and tobacco factories	-	-	-	-	-	-	-	-	-	-	4, 166	1, 291	-	-	-	-
Coal yards and lumber yards	-	-	-	-	1, 019	-	-	-	1, 396	-	1, 057	-	-	-	648	-
Cotton mills	-	-	-	-	-	-	-	-	-	-	2, 218	224	-	-	-	-
Domestic and personal service	-	-	3	-	572	-	-	-	1, 295	-	-	-	-	-	-	-
Fertilizer factories	-	-	-	-	-	-	-	-	-	-	2, 610	-	-	-	-	-
Garage	6	-	1	-	807	-	32	-	2, 537	-	788	-	6	-	1, 564	-
General and not specified in manufactures	33	-	16	-	4, 732	-	40	-	4, 602	-	7, 312	-	12	-	5, 039	-
Lime, cement, and artificial stone factories	-	-	-	-	-	-	-	-	-	-	-	-	-	-	-	-
Petroleum refineries	-	-	-	-	338	-	-	-	-	-	-	-	-	-	-	-
Public service	-	-	4	-	1, 281	-	14	-	1, 325	-	1, 343	-	-	-	1, 995	-
Road and street	1	-	1	-	2, 020	-	35	-	1, 702	-	4, 449	-	-	-	3, 239	-
Saw and planing mills [7]	1	-	2	-	54	-	22	-	15	-	8, 510	-	-	-	95	-
Slaughter and packing houses	-	-	-	-	-	-	-	-	-	-	-	-	-	-	-	-
Steam railroads	21	-	2	-	1, 558	-	18	-	2, 273	-	4, 311	-	2	-	4, 158	-
Street railroads	-	-	-	-	-	-	-	-	1, 289	-	-	-	-	-	-	-
Trucks, transfer, and cab companies	-	-	-	-	-	-	-	-	903	-	-	-	-	-	-	-
Laundry operatives [8]	-	5	-	2	551	1, 638	-	1	1, 877	6, 731	-	2, 774	-	-	-	1, 277
Longshoremen and stevedores	-	-	-	-	542	-	-	-	3, 357	-	-	-	-	-	-	-
Lumbermen, raftsmen, and woodchoppers	-	-	2	-	36	-	3	-	16	-	2, 472	-	-	-	17	-
Machinists	5	-	5	-	248	-	7	-	505	-	275	-	-	-	427	-
Mail carriers	-	-	-	-	201	-	5	-	687	-	92	-	-	-	308	-
Masons, brick and stone, and tile layers	-	-	-	-	508	-	1	-	647	-	1, 278	-	-	-	434	-
Mechanics, automobile factories, garages, and repair shops	1	-	4	-	914	-	11	-	2, 121	-	808	-	-	-	1, 124	-
Messenger, errand, and office boys and girls [9]	-	-	1	-	202	-	1	-	1, 686	73	134	-	-	-	194	-
Molders, founders, and casters, iron	-	-	-	-	188	-	-	-	164	-	-	-	-	-	804	-
Musicians and teachers of music	-	1	1	-	239	107	2	3	1, 733	410	156	50	7	-	387	159
Operatives (not otherwise specified):																
Automobile factories	-	-	-	-	35	-	-	-	43	-	-	-	-	-	80	7
Blast furnaces and steel rolling mills [6]	-	-	-	-	150	-	-	-	213	-	-	-	-	-	1, 447	-
Car and railroad shops	-	-	-	-	13	-	4	-	30	-	140	-	-	-	111	-
Cigar and tobacco factories	-	-	-	-	-	324	-	-	400	54	2, 449	7, 143	-	-	-	373
Coal mines	-	-	-	-	-	-	73	-	-	-	-	-	1	-	1, 261	-
Iron mines	-	-	-	-	-	-	-	-	-	-	-	-	-	-	-	-
Saw and planing mills [7]	-	-	-	-	-	-	-	-	-	-	554	-	-	-	-	-
Slaughter and packing houses	-	-	-	-	-	-	-	-	-	-	-	-	-	-	-	-
Suit, coat, and overall factories	-	-	-	-	167	116	-	-	628	195	-	-	-	-	-	26
Quarries	-	-	-	-	-	-	-	-	71	-	-	-	-	-	184	-
Painters, glaziers, and varnishers (building)	1	-	1	-	699	-	5	-	2, 096	-	805	-	4	-	692	-
Physicians and surgeons	-	-	-	-	104	-	3	-	201	9	163	-	-	-	149	-
Plasterers and cement finishers	1	-	-	-	281	-	3	-	432	-	983	-	2	-	1, 187	-
Plumbers and gas and steam fitters	-	-	2	-	123	-	2	-	219	-	233	-	1	-	205	-
Porters (except in stores)	-	-	-	-	1, 978	-	-	-	15, 727	-	-	-	-	-	4, 435	-
Sailors and deck hands	-	-	-	-	71	-	-	-	1, 175	-	-	-	-	-	-	-
Salesmen and saleswomen	1	-	2	-	282	89	1	-	785	268	457	181	-	2	444	210
Sawyers	-	-	-	-	-	-	-	-	-	-	262	-	-	-	-	-
Servants	17	74	79	38	4, 649	24, 924	106	221	9, 856	57, 411	5, 596	39, 844	8	9	4, 207	24, 140
Shoemakers and cobblers (not in factory)	-	-	-	-	65	-	3	-	149	-	346	-	-	-	137	-
Switchmen and flagmen, steam railroad	-	-	-	-	103	-	-	-	145	-	107	-	-	-	46	-
Tailors and tailoresses	1	-	-	-	345	-	1	-	1, 075	36	186	-	1	-	270	15
Teachers (school)	-	1	-	2	79	442	4	5	126	571	888	4, 719	-	1	85	440
Waiters	2	1	138	1	1, 731	967	7	8	5, 175	2, 068	1, 130	366	-	3	1, 904	704
All other	87	15	98	28	16, 500	9, 200	254	98	26, 526	24, 703	21, 982	23, 885	62	20	25, 657	11, 221

See footnotes at end of table.

TABLE 23.—NEGRO MALES AND FEMALES 10 YEARS OLD AND OVER GAINFULLY OCCUPIED, BY STATES: 1930—Continued

OCCUPATION	OKLAHOMA		OREGON		PENNSYLVANIA		RHODE ISLAND		SOUTH CAROLINA		SOUTH DAKOTA		TENNESSEE	
	Male	Female	Male	Female	Male	Female	Male	Female	Male	Female	Male	Female	Male	Female
POPULATION 10 YEARS OLD AND OVER	68,315	66,754	1,112	888	178,804	172,476	3,843	3,993	273,841	307,244	304	242	185,633	197,341
GAINFUL WORKERS														
All occupations	**51,578**	**19,676**	**948**	**383**	**148,288**	**66,031**	**3,023**	**1,670**	**213,167**	**130,309**	**241**	**67**	**147,237**	**75,456**
Agriculture	25,648	2,324	37	3	3,718	43	155	4	141,525	70,767	83	2	57,369	12,422
Farmers (owners and tenants) [2]	14,650	838	10	1	523	11	10	1	66,857	7,303	45	1	32,713	2,190
Farm managers and foremen	40	1	-	-	32	-	-	-	164	-	-	-	51	1
Farm laborers	10,958	1,485	27	2	3,163	32	145	3	74,504	63,464	38	1	24,605	10,231
Wage workers	8,037	637	27	2	3,121	31	145	3	40,499	24,334	25	-	14,989	2,143
Unpaid family workers	2,921	848	-	-	42	1	-	-	34,005	39,130	13	1	9,616	8,088
Bakers	37	-	2	-	311	41	5	-	148	-	-	-	185	-
Barbers, hairdressers, and manicurists	370	196	12	2	1,491	899	26	19	625	140	7	16	865	569
Blacksmiths	50	-	-	-	161	-	1	-	366	-	-	-	306	-
Brakemen, steam railroad	9	-	1	-	48	-	-	-	152	-	-	-	135	-
Builders and building contractors	31	-	1	-	212	-	6	-	39	-	-	-	123	-
Carpenters	301	-	1	-	1,387	-	25	-	2,391	-	-	-	1,688	-
Chauffeurs and truck and tractor drivers	609	-	21	-	8,745	-	243	-	3,071	-	4	-	4,863	-
Cleaning, dyeing, and pressing shop workers	-	-	-	-	-	-	-	-	588	-	-	-	706	-
Clergymen	628	-	5	-	910	-	22	-	1,268	-	5	-	1,155	-
Clerks (except "clerks" in stores)	62	25	16	6	1,906	291	36	9	114	36	-	1	341	157
Dealers, retail [3]	411	95	5	1	1,535	142	28	4	751	173	3	-	1,140	140
Delivery men, bakeries, and stores [4]	108	-	-	-	895	-	36	-	1,598	-	-	-	1,503	-
Draymen, teamsters, and carriage drivers [5]	173	-	-	-	1,297	-	61	-	771	-	-	-	1,170	-
Elevator tenders	-	-	-	-	-	-	-	-	-	-	-	-	-	-
Engineers (stationary)	47	-	2	-	428	-	9	-	100	-	-	-	73	-
Firemen, except locomotive and fire-department	26	-	1	-	1,127	-	16	-	1,001	-	-	-	852	-
Firemen, locomotive	3	-	-	-	54	-	1	-	321	-	-	-	270	-
Fishermen and oystermen	-	-	1	-	-	-	16	-	-	-	-	-	-	-
Furnace men, smelter men, heaters, puddlers, etc	-	-	-	-	450	-	-	-	-	-	-	-	-	-
Guards, watchmen, and doorkeepers	33	-	-	-	586	-	15	-	142	-	-	-	170	-
Insurance agents, managers, and officials	49	-	-	-	153	-	2	-	94	-	-	-	186	33
Janitors and sextons	1,121	-	89	-	5,635	408	177	-	1,251	-	15	-	2,672	-
Laborers, porters, and helpers in stores	1,143	-	19	-	3,294	-	63	-	1,550	-	2	-	3,630	-
Laborers (not otherwise specified):														
Automobile factories	-	-	-	-	89	-	-	-	-	-	-	-	1,365	-
Blast furnaces and steel rolling mills [6]	-	-	-	-	10,102	-	-	-	-	-	-	-	-	-
Brick, tile, and terra-cotta factories	-	-	-	-	1,132	-	-	-	-	-	-	-	-	-
Building construction, laborers, and helpers	1,310	-	6	-	15,596	-	206	-	1,607	-	2	-	2,685	-
Car and railroad shops	-	-	-	-	160	-	-	-	-	-	-	-	-	-
Cigar and tobacco factories	-	-	-	-	-	-	-	-	-	-	-	-	674	357
Coal yards and lumber yards	-	-	1	-	1,200	-	118	-	-	-	-	-	1,137	-
Cotton mills	-	-	-	-	-	-	7	-	2,386	261	-	-	147	-
Domestic and personal service	-	-	-	-	629	-	-	-	-	-	-	-	1,121	-
Fertilizer factories	-	-	-	-	-	-	-	-	1,879	-	-	-	-	-
Garage	503	-	8	-	1,957	-	19	-	267	-	8	-	826	-
General and not specified in manufactures	3,629	-	35	-	6,153	-	135	-	4,830	-	22	-	5,198	-
Lime, cement, and artificial stone factories	-	-	-	-	439	-	-	-	-	-	-	-	404	-
Petroleum refineries	38	-	-	-	1,160	-	-	-	-	-	-	-	-	-
Public service	519	-	12	-	2,852	-	37	-	1,180	-	2	-	1,492	-
Road and street	680	-	7	-	3,022	-	67	-	3,754	-	-	-	3,282	-
Saw and planing mills [7]	367	-	34	-	124	-	1	-	8,734	-	1	-	2,732	-
Slaughter and packing houses	-	-	-	-	-	-	-	-	-	-	-	-	-	-
Steam railroads	1,266	-	65	-	4,164	-	56	-	3,891	-	7	-	4,943	-
Street railroads	-	-	-	-	-	-	-	-	-	-	-	-	-	-
Truck, transfer, and cab companies	-	-	-	-	-	-	-	-	-	-	-	-	-	-
Laundry operatives [8]	-	113	-	5	846	2,574	9	44	-	1,093	-	-	325	2,539
Longshoremen and stevedores	-	-	-	-	2,252	-	-	-	-	-	-	-	-	-
Lumbermen, raftsmen, and woodchoppers	86	-	23	-	20	-	9	-	1,997	-	-	-	376	-
Machinists	63	-	3	-	537	-	13	-	252	-	-	-	370	-
Mail carriers	34	-	1	-	538	-	8	-	94	-	1	-	235	-
Masons, brick and stone, and tile layers	48	-	1	-	422	-	17	-	842	-	-	-	902	-
Mechanics, automobile factories, garages, and repair shops	362	-	6	-	1,620	-	45	-	516	-	5	-	668	-
Messenger, errand, and office boys and girls [9]	38	-	1	-	701	53	10	-	105	-	-	-	149	-
Molders, founders, and casters, iron	-	-	-	-	248	-	4	-	-	-	-	-	542	-
Musicians and teachers of music	141	41	7	5	426	191	15	9	41	32	4	2	173	82
Operatives (not otherwise specified):														
Automobile factories	-	-	-	-	34	-	-	-	-	-	-	-	-	-
Blast furnaces and steel rolling mills [6]	-	-	-	-	1,749	-	-	-	-	-	-	-	-	-
Car and railroad shops	16	-	-	-	72	-	-	-	59	-	-	-	191	-
Cigar and tobacco factories	-	-	-	-	123	832	-	-	-	-	-	-	-	167
Coal mines	391	-	-	-	7,574	-	-	-	-	-	-	-	578	-
Iron mines	-	-	-	-	-	-	-	-	-	-	-	-	-	-
Saw and planing mills [7]	-	-	4	-	-	-	-	-	621	-	-	-	201	-
Slaughter and packing houses	-	-	-	-	-	-	-	-	-	-	-	-	-	-
Suit, coat, and overall factories	-	-	-	-	302	286	-	-	-	-	-	-	-	8
Quarries	-	-	-	-	481	-	-	-	-	-	-	-	637	-
Painters, glaziers, and varnishers (building)	104	-	1	-	634	-	30	-	1,007	-	1	-	491	-
Physicians and surgeons	103	-	1	-	195	11	4	-	64	-	-	-	285	-
Plasterers and cement finishers	75	-	-	-	1,350	-	5	-	412	-	2	-	708	-
Plumbers and gas and steam fitters	59	-	-	-	256	-	4	-	181	-	1	-	349	-
Porters (except in stores)	1,752	-	-	-	4,592	-	-	-	-	-	-	-	-	-
Sailors and deck hands	-	-	-	-	-	-	-	-	-	-	-	-	-	-
Salesmen and saleswomen	125	63	3	1	557	152	10	8	249	109	1	1	318	155
Sawyers	-	-	1	-	-	-	-	-	236	-	-	-	168	-
Servants	2,053	11,042	81	244	7,465	43,474	215	977	2,981	29,325	4	29	5,195	32,932
Shoemakers and cobblers (not in factory)	58	-	1	-	127	-	4	-	275	-	2	-	157	-
Switchmen and flagmen, steam railroad	9	-	-	-	57	-	-	-	86	-	-	-	238	-
Tailors and tailoresses	89	-	3	2	537	38	3	-	163	-	-	-	139	-
Teachers (school)	415	1,252	-	1	148	668	1	10	466	3,261	2	1	517	2,265
Waiters	379	157	96	11	2,667	1,875	57	30	488	205	2	-	1,307	610
All other	6,007	4,368	334	102	28,636	14,053	971	556	15,638	24,907	55	15	26,610	23,020

See footnotes at end of table.

TABLE 23.—NEGRO MALES AND FEMALES 10 YEARS OLD AND OVER GAINFULLY OCCUPIED, BY STATES: 1930—Continued

OCCUPATION	TEXAS		UTAH		VERMONT		VIRGINIA		WASHINGTON		WEST VIRGINIA		WISCONSIN		WYOMING	
	Male	Female	Male	Female	Male	Female	Male	Female	Male	Female	Male	Female	Male	Female	Male	Female
POPULATION, 10 YEARS OLD AND OVER	331,164	340,171	522	420	249	196	244,143	250,286	3,387	2,605	48,556	41,365	4,934	3,995	636	482
GAINFUL WORKERS																
All occupations	**265,660**	**124,095**	**428**	**122**	**194**	**53**	**181,064**	**77,002**	**2,761**	**911**	**38,547**	**8,660**	**4,026**	**1,186**	**536**	**160**
Agriculture	135,992	30,971	9	1	53	1	74,102	8,126	120	13	1,655	53	146	5	37	6
Farmers (owners and tenants) [2]	80,120	5,999	5	—	14	1	33,306	2,508	55	8	421	26	60	4	15	1
Farm managers and foremen	99	1	—	—	—	—	140	3	2	—	8	—	—	—	1	—
Farm laborers	55,773	24,971	4	1	39	—	40,656	5,615	63	5	1,226	27	86	1	21	5
Wage workers	34,419	6,423	4	1	36	—	32,230	3,652	59	3	1,078	13	62	1	17	2
Unpaid family workers	21,354	18,548	—	—	3	—	8,426	1,963	4	2	148	14	24	—	4	3
Bakers	141	—	1	—	—	—	265	—	5	—	15	—	1	2	1	—
Barbers, hairdressers, and manicurists	1,510	1,097	5	—	3	—	1,183	255	63	26	343	109	40	26	9	5
Blacksmiths	341	—	1	—	1	—	426	—	2	—	58	—	4	—	1	—
Brakemen, steam railroad	469	—	1	—	—	—	429	—	1	—	108	—	1	—	—	—
Builders and building contractors	196	—	1	—	—	—	111	—	4	—	15	—	2	—	2	—
Carpenters	1,753	—	2	—	2	—	1,698	—	20	—	128	—	17	—	1	—
Chauffeurs and truck and tractor drivers	6,459	—	7	—	3	—	4,827	—	44	—	651	—	75	—	6	—
Cleaning, dyeing, and pressing shop workers	479	—	—	—	—	—	—	—	—	2	—	9	—	—	—	—
Clergymen	2,270	—	3	—	—	—	1,153	—	20	—	313	—	24	—	6	—
Clerks (except "clerks" in stores)	486	107	4	—	2	—	393	169	20	11	56	16	14	9	—	—
Dealers, retail [3]	1,323	238	4	1	—	—	1,636	224	42	4	134	18	29	6	6	1
Delivery men, bakeries, and stores [4]	1,472	—	—	—	—	—	1,530	—	2	—	71	—	13	—	1	—
Draymen, teamsters, and carriage drivers [5]	1,523	—	1	—	—	—	867	—	6	—	97	—	5	—	2	—
Elevator tenders	—	—	—	—	—	—	—	—	—	5	—	—	—	—	—	—
Engineers (stationary)	141	—	—	—	—	—	101	—	9	—	50	—	5	—	1	—
Firemen, except locomotive and fire department	381	—	2	—	—	—	1,131	—	11	—	106	—	23	—	2	—
Firemen, locomotive	61	—	1	—	—	—	211	—	2	—	26	—	5	—	—	—
Fishermen and oystermen	—	—	—	—	—	—	2,327	—	4	—	—	—	—	—	—	—
Furnace men, smelter men, heaters, puddlers, etc.	—	—	—	—	—	—	—	—	—	—	159	—	—	—	—	—
Guards, watchmen, and doorkeepers	194	—	1	—	—	—	164	—	14	—	64	—	8	—	—	—
Insurance agents, managers, and officials	432	59	—	—	—	—	338	—	2	—	38	5	—	—	—	—
Janitors and sextons	3,747	—	35	—	6	—	3,015	—	320	16	1,226	112	116	6	53	—
Laborers, porters, and helpers in stores	5,085	—	2	—	—	—	2,355	—	33	—	158	—	121	—	4	—
Laborers (not otherwise specified):																
Automobile factories	—	—	—	—	—	—	—	—	—	—	—	—	30	—	—	—
Blast furnaces and steel rolling mills [6]	—	—	—	—	—	—	—	—	—	—	219	—	—	—	—	—
Brick, tile, and terra-cotta factories	—	—	—	—	—	—	—	—	—	—	—	—	—	—	—	—
Building construction, laborers and helpers	5,587	—	—	—	3	—	2,833	—	36	—	356	—	117	—	7	—
Car and railroad shops	—	—	—	—	—	—	—	—	—	—	243	—	—	—	—	—
Cigar and tobacco factories	—	—	—	—	—	—	2,106	942	—	—	—	—	—	—	—	—
Coal yards and lumber yards	—	—	—	—	1	—	—	—	2	—	—	—	21	—	—	—
Cotton mills	—	—	—	—	—	—	—	—	—	—	—	—	—	—	—	—
Domestic and personal service	4,053	—	—	—	—	—	—	—	—	—	—	—	—	—	—	—
Fertilizer factories	—	—	—	—	—	—	1,994	—	—	—	—	—	—	—	—	—
Garage	2,453	—	5	—	5	—	524	—	45	—	162	—	185	—	3	—
General and not specified in manufactures	12,236	—	15	—	35	—	6,099	—	145	—	992	—	126	—	41	—
Lime, cement, and artificial stone factories	—	—	—	—	—	—	—	—	—	—	—	—	—	—	—	—
Petroleum refineries	3,288	—	—	—	—	—	—	—	—	—	—	—	—	—	1	—
Public service	1,845	—	3	—	5	—	2,149	—	58	—	104	—	78	—	—	—
Road and street	3,290	—	1	—	6	—	4,100	—	36	—	291	—	79	—	2	—
Saw and planing mills [7]	5,545	—	—	—	—	—	6,296	—	17	—	41	—	14	—	1	—
Slaughter and packing houses	—	—	—	—	—	—	—	—	—	—	—	—	—	—	—	—
Steam railroads	6,683	—	22	—	5	—	6,859	—	96	—	1,741	—	82	—	113	—
Street railroads	—	—	—	—	—	—	—	—	—	—	—	—	—	—	—	—
Truck, transfer, and cab companies	—	—	—	—	—	—	—	—	—	—	—	—	—	—	—	—
Laundry operatives [8]	463	2,177	—	1	—	1	—	1,788	17	6	—	114	—	26	—	4
Longshoremen and stevedores	2,739	—	—	—	—	—	2,930	—	82	—	—	—	—	—	—	—
Lumbermen, raftsmen, and woodchoppers	1,398	—	—	—	—	—	1,491	—	12	—	17	—	3	—	—	—
Machinists	443	—	—	—	—	—	283	—	9	—	87	—	7	—	9	—
Mail carriers	241	—	4	—	1	—	426	—	8	—	28	—	—	—	—	—
Masons, brick and stone, and tile layers	223	—	—	—	2	—	418	—	2	—	129	—	13	—	3	—
Mechanics, automobile factories, garages, and repair shops	1,499	—	2	—	4	—	598	—	33	—	141	—	44	—	1	—
Messenger, errand, and office boys and girls [9]	88	—	1	—	—	—	216	—	7	—	23	—	4	—	—	—
Molders, founders, and casters, iron	—	—	—	—	—	—	—	—	4	—	—	—	72	—	—	—
Musicians and teachers of music	423	188	2	—	2	—	168	61	48	12	49	23	72	12	4	4
Operatives (not otherwise specified):																
Automobile factories	—	—	—	—	—	—	—	—	—	—	—	—	6	—	—	—
Blast furnaces and steel rolling mills [6]	—	—	—	—	—	—	—	—	—	—	118	—	—	—	—	—
Car and railroad shops	489	—	3	—	—	—	144	—	—	—	80	—	1	—	3	—
Cigar and tobacco factories	—	—	—	—	—	—	1,051	3,043	—	—	—	—	—	—	—	—
Coal mines	—	—	30	—	—	—	1,511	—	23	—	22,089	—	—	—	42	—
Iron mines	—	—	—	—	—	—	—	—	—	—	—	—	—	—	—	—
Saw and planing mills [7]	—	—	—	—	—	—	—	—	—	—	—	—	17	—	—	—
Slaughter and packing houses	—	—	—	—	—	—	—	—	—	—	—	—	—	—	—	—
Suit, coat, and overall factories	—	49	—	—	—	—	—	50	—	—	—	1	—	1	—	—
Quarries	—	—	—	—	2	—	667	—	—	—	244	—	—	—	—	—
Painters, glaziers and varnishers (building)	490	—	—	—	1	—	554	—	25	—	97	—	31	—	1	—
Physicians and surgeons	205	—	—	—	—	—	163	—	3	—	65	—	7	—	—	—
Plasterers and cement finishers	216	—	1	—	—	—	743	—	10	—	109	—	13	—	2	—
Plumbers and gas and steam fitters	340	—	—	—	2	—	196	—	1	—	49	—	1	—	—	—
Porters (except in stores)	7,733	—	—	—	—	—	1,658	—	—	—	—	—	—	—	—	—
Sailors and deck hands	—	—	—	—	—	—	377	—	10	—	—	—	—	10	—	—
Salesmen and saleswomen	572	233	2	—	1	—	467	194	17	1	68	40	8	—	3	—
Sawyers	—	—	—	—	—	—	288	—	1	—	2	—	—	—	—	—
Servants	7,998	51,130	40	74	11	31	5,235	35,003	231	528	1,231	5,138	102	572	24	88
Shoemakers and cobblers (not in factory)	129	—	1	—	—	—	350	—	11	—	47	—	1	—	1	—
Switchmen and flagmen, steam railroads	135	—	—	—	—	—	165	—	3	—	37	—	—	—	—	—
Tailors and tailoresses	407	—	1	—	—	—	185	—	17	2	243	—	32	3	2	—
Teachers (school)	1,025	4,154	—	—	—	—	474	3,392	—	1	257	728	1	4	—	1
Waiters	1,870	873	69	3	1	—	1,896	898	230	25	362	123	43	45	4	6
All other	27,099	32,819	146	42	37	20	27,188	22,857	778	259	3,355	2,171	2,107	459	137	45

[1] Data are included in these columns which are not shown separately in certain States, but are included in the "All other" item.
[2] The difference between agricultural statistics of the census of occupations and those of the census of agriculture is largely due to the fact that every farm operator is listed as a farmer in the latter, while in the former, he is listed under his principal occupation.
[3] Includes, also, managers and superintendents of retail stores.
[4] Some deliverymen probably were returned and classified as chauffeurs, and others as teamsters or truck drivers.
[5] Teamsters in agriculture, forestry, and the extraction of minerals are classified with the other workers in those industries, respectively; drivers for bakeries and stores are classified as deliverymen in trade; and drivers for laundries are classified as deliverymen in domestic and personal service.
[6] Includes tin-plate mills.
[7] Includes box factories (wood).
[8] Some owners of hand laundries are probably included with laundry operatives.
[9] Except telegraph messengers.

TABLE 24.—NEGRO GAINFUL WORKERS 10 YEARS OLD AND OVER, BY

[Of the 534 occupations and occupation groups of the census classification

	OCCUPATION	10 YEARS OLD AND OVER			10 TO 17 YEARS		18 AND 19 YEARS		20 TO 24 YEARS		25 TO 29 YEARS		30 TO 34 YEARS	
		Total	Male	Female	Male	Female	Male	Female	Male	Female	Male	Female	Male	Female
1	POPULATION 10 YEARS OLD AND OVER	9,292,556	4,564,690	4,727,866	985,174	1,009,515	233,700	273,681	553,622	649,569	500,520	571,267	416,869	447,645
	GAINFUL WORKERS													
2	**All occupations**	**5,503,535**	**3,662,893**	**1,840,642**	**299,903**	**171,726**	**190,823**	**113,542**	**517,707**	**299,103**	**483,423**	**267,688**	**403,804**	**210,157**
3	**Agriculture**	**1,987,839**	**1,492,555**	**495,284**	**227,624**	**118,239**	**99,328**	**42,228**	**202,698**	**73,872**	**142,671**	**47,320**	**111,515**	**36,221**
4	Farmers (owners and tenants)	873,653	797,231	76,422	-	-	12,719	-	80,666	3,150	86,618	4,694	76,064	6,233
5	Farm managers and foremen	1,676	1,655	21	-	-	17	-	68	-	105	-	131	1
6	Farm laborers	1,112,510	693,669	418,841	227,624	118,239	86,592	42,228	121,964	70,722	55,948	42,626	35,320	29,987
7	Wage workers	539,307	419,193	120,114	51,932	16,080	41,684	10,400	84,535	21,840	48,644	14,720	32,589	10,725
8	Unpaid family workers	573,203	274,476	298,727	175,692	102,159	44,908	31,828	37,429	48,882	7,304	27,906	2,731	19,262
9	**Forestry and fishing**	**31,732**	**31,652**	**80**	**1,262**	**10**	**1,560**	**9**	**5,242**	**11**	**4,563**	**8**	**3,545**	**6**
10	Fishermen and oystermen	7,162	7,106	56	285	4	333	5	941	7	799	6	643	3
11	Foresters, forest rangers, and timber cruisers	34	34	-	-	-	-	-	6	-	2	-	4	-
12	Owners and managers of log and timber camps	66	66	-	-	-	-	-	-	-	2	-	8	-
13	Owners and proprietors	61	61	-	-	-	-	-	-	-	2	-	7	-
14	Managers and officials	5	5	-	-	-	-	-	-	-	-	-	1	-
15	Lumbermen, raftsmen, and woodchoppers	24,470	24,446	24	977	6	1,227	4	4,295	4	3,760	2	2,890	3
16	Foremen	92	92	-	-	-	-	-	1	-	8	-	11	-
17	Inspectors, scalers, and surveyors	32	32	-	-	-	-	-	7	-	2	-	3	-
18	Teamsters and haulers	1,917	1,917	-	63	-	92	-	352	-	331	-	273	-
19	Other lumbermen, raftsmen, and woodchoppers.	22,429	22,405	24	915	6	1,135	4	3,925	4	3,419	2	2,603	3
20	**Extraction of minerals**	**74,972**	**74,919**	**53**	**1,508**	**3**	**2,854**	**3**	**10,063**	**9**	**11,851**	**15**	**10,937**	**9**
21	Operators, managers, and officials	21	20	1	-	-	-	-	-	-	1	-	2	-
22	Operators	12	11	1	-	-	-	-	-	-	-	-	1	-
23	Managers and officials	9	9	-	-	-	-	-	-	-	1	-	1	-
24	Foremen, overseers, and inspectors	170	170	-	-	-	1	-	7	-	9	-	12	-
25	Foremen and overseers	144	144	-	-	-	1	-	4	-	6	-	11	-
26	Inspectors	26	26	-	-	-	-	-	3	-	3	-	1	-
27	Coal mine operatives	57,315	57,291	24	948	1	1,931	2	7,131	4	8,985	7	8,697	3
28	Other operatives in extraction of minerals	17,466	17,438	28	560	2	922	1	2,925	5	2,856	8	2,226	6
29	Copper mine operatives	25	25	-	-	-	1	-	3	-	3	-	2	-
30	Gold and silver mine operatives	17	17	-	-	-	-	-	2	-	2	-	3	-
31	Iron mine operatives	3,448	3,448	-	46	-	162	-	555	-	704	-	505	-
32	Lead and zinc mine operatives	75	75	-	-	-	2	-	8	-	9	-	14	-
33	Other specified mine operatives	2,286	2,281	5	113	1	144	-	383	1	331	1	260	1
34	Not specified mine operatives	631	630	1	8	-	26	1	90	-	93	-	85	-
35	Quarry operatives	9,541	9,522	19	361	1	535	-	1,641	3	1,440	6	1,122	4
36	Oil and gas well operatives	1,129	1,129	-	20	-	30	-	192	-	231	-	191	-
37	Salt well and works operatives	314	311	3	12	-	22	-	51	1	43	1	44	1
38	**Manufacturing and mechanical industries.**	**1,024,656**	**923,586**	**101,070**	**27,038**	**5,151**	**37,808**	**6,683**	**133,581**	**18,444**	**146,155**	**17,466**	**125,820**	**14,123**
39	Apprentices to building and hand trades	643	643	-	492	-	41	-	48	-	18	-	10	-
40	Blacksmiths' apprentices	35	35	-	30	-	1	-	1	-	1	-	-	-
41	Boilermakers' apprentices	4	4	-	1	-	-	-	-	-	-	-	-	-
42	Carpenters' apprentices	111	111	-	79	-	11	-	12	-	3	-	2	-
43	Electricians' apprentices	22	22	-	19	-	-	-	1	-	1	-	-	-
44	Machinists' apprentices [1]	81	81	-	64	-	5	-	6	-	-	-	2	-
45	Plumbers' apprentices	42	42	-	19	-	4	-	1	-	6	-	4	-
46	Tinsmiths' and coppersmiths' apprentices	14	14	-	11	-	1	-	2	-	-	-	-	-
47	Apprentices to other building and hand trades.	334	334	-	269	-	19	-	25	-	7	-	2	-
48	Apprentices (except to building and hand trades).	448	366	82	257	60	36	7	46	8	17	2	4	2
49	Dressmakers' and milliners' apprentices	63	-	63	-	56	-	3	-	4	-	-	-	-
50	Jewelers', watchmakers', goldsmiths', and silversmiths' apprentices.	5	4	1	3	-	-	-	1	1	-	-	-	-
51	Printers' and bookbinders' apprentices	62	52	10	25	2	8	1	13	2	4	2	1	2
52	Other apprentices in manufacturing	318	310	8	229	2	28	3	32	1	13	-	3	-
53	Bakers	4,527	3,919	608	69	-	213	23	800	95	807	115	623	96
54	Blacksmiths, forgemen, and hammermen	5,682	5,682	-	-	-	27	-	248	-	372	-	554	-
55	Blacksmiths	5,274	5,274	-	-	-	24	-	201	-	299	-	477	-
56	Forgemen and hammermen	408	408	-	-	-	3	-	47	-	73	-	77	-
57	Boilermakers	1,030	1,030	-	-	-	8	-	53	-	91	-	155	-
58	Brick and stone masons and tile layers	11,701	11,701	-	-	-	166	-	855	-	1,252	-	1,262	-
59	Builders and building contractors	2,570	2,566	4	-	-	4	-	51	-	133	-	215	-
60	Cabinetmakers	479	479	-	-	-	6	-	45	-	62	-	62	-
61	Carpenters	32,413	32,406	7	99	-	359	-	1,712	2	2,306	-	2,848	2
62	Compositors, linotypers, and typesetters	2,101	1,903	198	26	1	81	7	288	45	324	37	307	47
63	Coopers	1,849	1,849	-	25	-	65	-	216	-	260	-	226	-
64	Dressmakers and seamstresses (not in factory)	20,439	6	20,433	-	69	-	292	1	1,478	-	2,712	-	3,203
65	Dyers	510	488	22	18	-	40	1	90	6	77	7	56	2
66	Electricians	1,913	1,913	-	-	-	50	-	231	-	347	-	377	-
67	Electrotypers, stereotypers, and lithographers	48	48	-	-	-	1	-	9	-	11	-	6	-
68	Electrotypers and stereotypers	29	29	-	-	-	1	-	4	-	5	-	5	-
69	Lithographers	19	19	-	-	-	-	-	5	-	6	-	1	-

See footnotes at end of table.

OCCUPATION, AGE, AND SEX, FOR THE UNITED STATES: 1930

those occupations in which there were no Negro workers are omitted]

35 TO 39 YEARS		40 TO 44 YEARS		45 TO 49 YEARS		50 TO 54 YEARS		55 TO 59 YEARS		60 TO 64 YEARS		65 TO 69 YEARS		70 TO 74 YEARS		75 YEARS AND OVER		UNKNOWN		
Male	Female	Male	Female	Male	Female	Male	Female	Male	Female	Male	Female	Male	Female	Male	Fe-male	Male	Fe-male	Male	Fe-male	
430,472	460,428	339,329	348,094	323,162	306,903	277,532	227,058	174,367	135,030	133,349	108,820	82,843	72,334	50,896	48,200	55,791	62,655	7,064	6,667	1
418,037	**219,586**	**329,762**	**166,355**	**314,200**	**144,001**	**268,330**	**103,328**	**166,770**	**57,173**	**123,515**	**41,711**	**72,646**	**23,513**	**38,786**	**11,328**	**30,228**	**8,278**	**4,959**	**3,143**	2
123,144	**41,161**	**104,612**	**34,747**	**117,226**	**33,214**	**122,125**	**26,453**	**83,253**	**15,361**	**69,138**	**12,535**	**42,883**	**7,187**	**24,807**	**3,695**	**20,605**	**2,803**	**926**	**248**	3
90,517	10,202	78,629	10,679	91,160	11,444	96,159	10,612	65,734	6,536	53,479	5,865	32,397	3,443	17,967	1,945	14,641	1,566	481	53	4
194	2	193	1	245	6	230	2	164	2	144	1	80	2	37	1	47	2	------	1	5
32,433	30,957	25,790	24,067	25,821	21,821	25,736	15,839	17,355	8,823	15,515	6,669	10,406	3,742	6,803	1,749	5,917	1,235	445	194	6
30,880	11,320	24,853	9,436	25,140	8,313	25,131	6,722	16,899	3,661	14,916	3,246	9,942	1,904	6,317	947	5,332	702	399	98	7
1,553	19,637	937	14,631	681	13,451	605	9,117	456	5,162	599	3,423	464	1,838	486	802	585	533	46	96	8
3,819	**6**	**3,168**	**11**	**2,881**	**4**	**2,341**	**6**	**1,391**	**2**	**877**	**3**	**485**	**1**	**268**	------	**196**	**1**	**54**	**2**	9
779	5	679	9	759	4	672	6	462	2	325	1	146	1	113	------	72	1	8	2	10
5	------	4	------	6	------	1	------	2	------	------	------	1	------	1	------	2	------	------	------	11
9	------	13	------	9	------	14	------	6	------	4	------	------	------	1	------	------	------	------	------	12
7	------	12	------	9	------	14	------	6	------	3	------	------	------	1	------	------	------	------	------	13
2	------	1	------	------	------	------	------	------	------	1	------	------	------	------	------	------	------	------	------	14
3,026	1	2,382	2	2,107	------	1,654	------	921	------	548	2	338	------	153	------	122	------	46	------	15
17	------	18	------	18	------	3	------	7	------	4	------	3	------	1	------	1	------	------	------	16
2	------	7	------	3	------	5	------	1	------	1	------	1	------	------	------	------	------	------	------	17
253	------	192	------	153	------	107	------	48	------	33	------	6	------	5	------	3	------	6	------	18
2,754	1	2,165	2	1,933	------	1,539	------	865	------	510	2	328	------	147	------	118	------	40	------	19
11,379	**9**	**8,625**	**2**	**7,451**	**2**	**4,894**	------	**2,687**	**1**	**1,466**	------	**719**	------	**255**	------	**135**	------	**95**	------	20
3	------	1	------	1	------	3	------	4	1	1	------	1	------	2	------	1	------	------	------	21
1	------	------	------	1	------	1	------	4	1	------	------	------	------	2	------	1	------	------	------	22
2	------	1	------	------	------	2	------	------	------	1	------	1	------	------	------	------	------	------	------	23
20	------	20	------	32	------	29	------	15	------	12	------	10	------	2	------	1	------	------	------	24
16	------	16	------	27	------	26	------	14	------	11	------	9	------	2	------	1	------	------	------	25
4	------	4	------	5	------	3	------	1	------	1	------	1	------	------	------	------	------	------	------	26
9,142	5	6,899	1	5,924	1	3,711	------	2,022	------	1,062	------	509	------	167	------	86	------	77	------	27
2,214	4	1,705	1	1,494	1	1,151	------	646	------	391	------	199	------	84	------	47	------	18	------	28
5	------	5	------	4	------	1	------	1	------	------	------	------	------	------	------	------	------	------	------	29
------	------	------	------	3	------	1	------	2	------	1	------	2	------	------	------	1	------	------	------	30
533	------	383	------	283	------	136	------	63	------	43	------	20	------	7	------	7	------	1	------	31
15	------	7	------	8	------	6	------	4	------	2	------	------	------	------	------	------	------	------	------	32
255	------	218	1	188	------	173	------	98	------	64	------	25	------	19	------	9	------	1	------	33
81	------	66	------	65	------	55	------	28	------	21	------	7	------	------	------	4	------	1	------	34
1,108	4	888	------	820	1	718	------	423	------	242	------	137	------	51	------	24	------	12	------	35
170	------	105	------	92	------	45	------	22	------	15	------	6	------	5	------	2	------	3	------	36
47	------	33	------	31	------	15	------	5	------	3	------	2	------	2	------	------	------	------	------	37
128,519	**13,732**	**96,874**	**9,131**	**84,788**	**6,795**	**62,031**	**4,265**	**34,639**	**2,284**	**22,580**	**1,431**	**12,238**	**732**	**5,757**	**326**	**3,839**	**245**	**1,919**	**262**	38
15	------	9	------	8	------	1	------	1	------	------	------	------	------	------	------	------	------	------	------	39
2	------	------	------	------	------	------	------	------	------	------	------	------	------	------	------	------	------	------	------	40
2	------	------	------	1	------	------	------	------	------	------	------	------	------	------	------	------	------	------	------	41
1	------	2	------	1	------	------	------	------	------	------	------	------	------	------	------	------	------	------	------	42
1	------	------	------	------	------	------	------	------	------	------	------	------	------	------	------	------	------	------	------	43
1	------	1	------	2	------	------	------	------	------	------	------	------	------	------	------	------	------	------	------	44
2	------	3	------	2	------	1	------	------	------	------	------	------	------	------	------	------	------	------	------	45
------	------	------	------	------	------	------	------	------	------	------	------	------	------	------	------	------	------	------	------	46
6	------	3	------	2	------	------	------	1	------	------	------	------	------	------	------	------	------	------	------	47
2	2	2	------	------	1	------	------	1	------	------	------	1	------	------	------	------	------	------	------	48
------	------	------	------	------	------	------	------	------	------	------	------	------	------	------	------	------	------	------	------	49
------	------	------	------	------	------	------	------	------	------	------	------	------	------	------	------	------	------	------	------	50
------	1	1	------	------	------	------	------	------	------	------	------	------	------	------	------	------	------	------	------	51
2	1	1	------	------	1	------	------	1	------	------	------	1	------	------	------	------	------	------	------	52
528	99	348	57	231	50	146	35	86	19	39	11	18	3	3	3	3	1	5	1	53
804	------	812	------	874	------	721	------	474	------	351	------	219	------	137	------	75	------	14	------	54
724	------	750	------	843	------	703	------	466	------	345	------	217	------	137	------	75	------	13	------	55
80	------	62	------	31	------	18	------	8	------	6	------	2	------	------	------	------	------	1	------	56
205	------	190	------	171	------	82	------	44	------	24	------	4	------	1	------	1	------	1	------	57
1,631	------	1,650	------	1,584	------	1,338	------	848	------	535	------	371	------	127	------	65	------	17	------	58
367	------	392	3	482	------	392	------	242	------	148	------	86	------	40	1	12	------	2	------	59
80	------	62	------	48	------	64	------	16	------	17	------	7	------	7	------	2	------	1	------	60
4,251	------	4,511	2	4,829	------	4,548	------	2,747	1	2,113	------	1,131	------	565	------	338	------	49	------	61
260	26	191	15	160	7	123	6	65	3	44	2	24	1	7	1	1	------	2	------	62
260	------	217	------	189	------	174	------	106	------	61	------	27	------	14	------	7	------	2	------	63
2	3,958	------	2,920	2	2,408	------	1,516	------	883	1	514	------	278	------	104	------	79	------	19	64
72	2	49	3	30	1	26	------	16	------	9	------	3	------	------	------	1	------	1	------	65
339	------	235	------	154	------	100	------	38	------	25	------	10	------	2	------	2	------	3	------	66
8	------	3	------	3	------	2	------	1	------	4	------	------	------	------	------	------	------	------	------	67
2	------	2	------	3	------	2	------	1	------	4	------	------	------	------	------	------	------	------	------	68
6	------	1	------	------	------	------	------	------	------	------	------	------	------	------	------	------	------	------	------	69

Table 24.—NEGRO GAINFUL WORKERS 10 YEARS OLD AND OVER, BY

[See note at

	OCCUPATION	10 YEARS OLD AND OVER			10 TO 17 YEARS		18 AND 19 YEARS		20 TO 24 YEARS		25 TO 29 YEARS		30 TO 34 YEARS	
		Total	Male	Female	Male	Female	Male	Female	Male	Female	Male	Female	Male	Female
	Manufacturing and mechanical industries—Continued.													
1	Engineers (stationary), cranemen, hoistmen, etc.	5,236	5,236	-	8	-	49	-	350	-	632	-	688	-
2	Engineers (stationary)	3,612	3,612	-	4	-	27	-	153	-	305	-	401	-
3	Cranemen, derrickmen, hoistmen, etc	1,624	1,624	-	4	-	22	-	197	-	327	-	287	-
4	Engravers	29	27	2	-	-	-	-	5	1	6	-	2	-
5	Filers, grinders, buffers, and polishers (metal)	1,607	1,574	33	11	3	49	1	215	5	321	9	242	5
6	Buffers and polishers	255	236	19	3	2	14	1	42	5	39	5	26	4
7	Filers	189	188	1	1	-	2	-	17	-	26	-	21	-
8	Grinders	1,163	1,150	13	7	1	33	-	156	-	256	4	195	1
9	Firemen (except locomotive and fire department).	18,265	18,265	-	49	-	163	-	1,137	-	2,148	-	2,528	-
10	Foremen and overseers (manufacturing)	2,653	2,436	217	2	3	21	8	96	35	231	32	318	42
11	Furnace men, smelter men, heaters, puddlers, etc.	3,091	3,091	-	13	-	43	-	302	-	535	-	558	-
12	Furnace men, smelter men, and pourers	2,446	2,446	-	10	-	34	-	242	-	415	-	448	-
13	Heaters	521	521	-	3	-	7	-	48	-	102	-	91	-
14	Puddlers	124	124	-	-	-	2	-	12	-	18	-	19	-
15	Glass blowers	34	34	-	-	-	3	-	7	-	3	-	4	-
16	Jewelers, watchmakers, goldsmiths, and silversmiths.	275	261	14	-	-	2	4	23	4	22	1	30	2
17	Goldsmiths and silversmiths	28	28						2	-	1	-	5	-
18	Jewelers and lapidaries (factory)	26	17	9	-	-	-	4	3	3	1	1	6	-
19	Jewelers and watchmakers (not in factory)	221	216	5	-	-	2	-	18	1	20	-	19	2
20	Loom fixers	9	9	-	-	-	-	-	3	-	1	-	-	-
21	Machinists, millwrights, and toolmakers	8,218	8,218	-	-	-	147	-	999	-	1,569	-	1,419	-
22	Machinists	7,647	7,647	-	-	-	142	-	958	-	1,476	-	1,341	-
23	Millwrights	435	435	-	-	-	-	-	24	-	65	-	53	-
24	Toolmakers and die setters and sinkers	136	136	-	-	-	5	-	17	-	28	-	25	-
25	Managers and officials (manufacturing)	337	317	20	-	-	4	-	11	1	29	3	42	5
26	Manufacturers	1,046	1,008	38	-	-	2	-	31	1	95	3	144	6
27	Mechanics (n. o. s.[2])	26,710	26,708	2	-	-	924	-	4,889	2	6,534	-	5,210	-
28	Air transportation	11	11	-	-	-	1	-	2	-	3	-	4	-
29	Automobile factories, garages, and repair shops.	21,088	21,086	2	-	-	793	-	4,144	2	5,541	-	4,239	-
30	Railroads and car shops	739	739	-	-	-	6	-	60	-	93	-	140	-
31	Other industries	4,872	4,872	-	-	-	124	-	683	-	897	-	827	-
32	Millers (grain, flour, feed, etc.)	240	238	2	-	-	3	-	17	-	25	-	23	-
33	Milliners and millinery dealers	451	10	441	-	-	-	27	1	104	5	93	2	72
34	Molders, founders, and casters (metal)	8,346	8,346	-	-	-	90	-	783	-	1,623	-	1,802	-
35	Brass molders, founders, and casters	277	277	-	-	-	2	-	34	-	45	-	52	-
36	Iron molders, founders, and casters	5,232	5,232	-	-	-	57	-	514	-	1,046	-	1,111	-
37	Other molders, founders, and casters	2,837	2,837	-	-	-	31	-	235	-	532	-	639	-
38	Oilers of machinery	1,073	1,072	1	4	-	27	-	112	-	190	-	179	-
39	Painters, glaziers, varnishers, enamelers, etc	18,293	18,152	141	130	9	400	13	1,859	36	2,461	31	2,538	16
40	Enamelers, lacquerers, and japanners	67	61	6	2	-	-	2	8	-	12	3	17	-
41	Painters, glaziers, and varnishers (building).	15,677	15,668	9	88	-	315	1	1,456	2	1,973	2	2,112	1
42	Painters, glaziers, and varnishers (factory).	2,549	2,423	126	40	9	85	10	395	34	476	26	409	15
43	Paper hangers	2,154	2,126	28	-	-	44	1	198	1	257	1	283	2
44	Pattern and model makers	54	53	1	-	-	1	-	5	-	8	-	5	1
45	Piano and organ tuners	80	80	-	-	-	-	-	5	-	5	-	9	-
46	Plasterers and cement finishers	13,465	13,464	1	-	-	146	-	921	-	1,588	-	1,825	-
47	Cement finishers	3,178	3,178	-	-	-	26	-	135	-	329	-	432	-
48	Plasterers	10,287	10,286	1	-	-	120	-	786	-	1,259	-	1,393	-
49	Plumbers and gas and steam fitters	4,729	4,729	-	-	-	42	-	327	-	562	-	629	-
50	Pressmen and plate printers (printing)	189	189	-	-	-	12	-	29	-	41	-	19	-
51	Rollers and roll hands (metal)	1,224	1,224	-	-	-	29	-	192	-	332	-	235	-
52	Roofers and slaters	1,044	1,044	-	-	-	29	-	109	-	145	-	172	-
53	Sawyers	3,449	3,445	4	-	-	138	-	567	-	590	1	498	2
54	Shoemakers and cobblers (not in factory)	4,150	4,129	21	187	-	232	-	534	3	463	4	406	3
55	Skilled occupations (not elsewhere classified)	149	147	2	-	-	5	1	15	-	25	-	28	-
56	Stonecutters	328	328	-	-	-	3	-	22	-	54	-	36	-
57	Structural iron workers (building)	348	348	-	-	-	7	-	25	-	58	-	63	-
58	Tailors and tailoresses	7,505	6,953	552	29	4	122	16	678	55	1,157	115	1,353	109
59	Tinsmiths and coppersmiths	887	887	-	-	-	16	-	91	-	106	-	106	-
60	Coppersmiths	37	37	-	-	-	-	-	4	-	4	-	3	-
61	Tinsmiths and sheet-metal workers	850	850	-	-	-	16	-	87	-	102	-	103	-
62	Upholsterers	915	867	48	9	-	26	1	94	8	114	7	104	8
	Operatives (n. o. s.[3]):													
63	Building industry	685	683	2	5	-	24	-	65	-	109	-	106	1
64	Chemical and allied industries	4,368	4,004	364	115	24	145	26	610	86	679	68	601	57
65	Charcoal and coke works	341	329	12	5	1	5	-	37	2	57	2	59	2
66	Explosives, ammunition, and fireworks factories.	78	66	12	1	1	2	-	3	5	4	1	6	2
67	Fertilizer factories	1,039	1,000	39	66	2	70	-	211	9	174	5	108	5
68	Gas works	306	306	-	5	-	1	-	28	-	34	-	37	-
69	Paint and varnish factories	330	305	25	5	3	6	5	46	2	52	7	69	3
70	Petroleum refineries	557	548	9	3	-	9	-	74	-	106	4	97	-
71	Rayon factories	94	76	18	1	1	7	2	16	4	11	3	5	3
72	Soap factories	151	126	25	4	-	3	3	20	5	18	10	21	4
73	Other chemical factories	1,472	1,248	224	25	16	42	16	175	59	223	36	199	38

See footnotes at end of table.

OCCUPATION, AGE, AND SEX, FOR THE UNITED STATES: 1930—Continued

[See head of table]

35 TO 39 YEARS		40 TO 44 YEARS		45 TO 49 YEARS		50 TO 54 YEARS		55 TO 59 YEARS		60 TO 64 YEARS		65 TO 69 YEARS		70 TO 74 YEARS		75 YEARS AND OVER		UNKNOWN		
Male	Female	Male	Female	Male	Female	Male	Female	Male	Female	Male	Female	Male	Female	Male	Female	Male	Female	Male	Female	
781	-	805	-	741	-	551	-	326	-	164	-	91	-	31	-	17	-	2	-	1
486	-	614	-	584	-	453	-	297	-	151	-	87	-	31	-	17	-	2	-	2
295	-	191	-	157	-	98	-	29	-	13	-	4	-	-	-	-	-	-	-	3
5	-	3	-	3	1	2	-	-	-	1	-	-	-	-	-	-	-	-	-	4
281	3	178	-	128	3	71	1	39	2	21	1	9	-	3	-	6	-	-	-	5
31	-	27	-	21	1	10	-	11	1	5	-	3	-	-	-	4	-	-	-	6
31	1	29	-	21	-	19	-	9	-	7	-	3	-	1	-	1	-	-	-	7
219	2	122	-	86	2	42	1	19	1	9	1	3	-	2	-	1	-	-	-	8
3,166	-	2,579	-	2,612	-	1,917	-	993	-	556	-	240	-	102	-	47	-	28	-	9
404	44	389	21	365	18	308	10	164	2	71	1	48	-	7	-	8	-	4	1	10
568	-	390	-	313	-	197	-	105	-	40	-	16	-	6	-	2	-	3	-	11
445	-	295	-	247	-	166	-	89	-	35	-	12	-	6	-	1	-	1	-	12
107	-	76	-	49	-	23	-	10	-	3	-	-	-	-	-	-	-	2	-	13
16	-	19	-	17	-	8	-	6	-	2	-	4	-	-	-	1	-	-	-	14
5	-	5	-	1	-	4	-	1	-	-	-	1	-	-	-	-	-	-	-	15
32	-	33	1	41	1	27	-	23	-	11	-	9	1	4	-	4	-	-	-	16
5	-	5	-	5	-	2	-	2	-	-	-	1	-	-	-	-	-	-	-	17
3	-	1	1	1	-	-	-	1	-	-	-	-	-	-	-	1	-	-	-	18
24	-	27	-	35	1	25	-	20	-	11	-	8	1	4	-	3	-	-	-	19
1	-	1	-	-	-	1	-	2	-	-	-	-	-	-	-	-	-	-	-	20
1,505	-	958	-	751	-	471	-	217	-	108	-	45	-	12	-	5	-	12	-	21
1,377	-	871	-	680	-	433	-	201	-	101	-	40	-	11	-	5	-	11	-	22
103	-	70	-	59	-	35	-	14	-	7	-	3	-	1	-	-	-	1	-	23
25	-	17	-	12	-	3	-	2	-	-	-	2	-	-	-	-	-	-	-	24
49	4	61	3	39	2	25	2	29	-	15	-	10	-	-	-	2	-	1	-	25
190	8	186	9	132	3	110	3	44	1	40	2	16	-	11	2	6	-	1	-	26
4,223	-	2,268	-	1,370	-	681	-	326	-	143	-	69	-	16	-	21	-	34	-	27
-	-	1	-	-	-	-	-	-	-	-	-	-	-	-	-	-	-	-	-	28
3,294	-	1,598	-	874	-	358	-	144	-	43	-	20	-	2	-	7	-	29	-	29
143	-	122	-	79	-	52	-	28	-	10	-	6	-	-	-	-	-	-	-	30
786	-	547	-	417	-	271	-	154	-	90	-	43	-	14	-	14	-	5	-	31
35	-	24	-	22	1	24	-	24	1	12	-	15	-	7	-	7	-	-	-	32
-	72	2	31	-	22	-	12	-	5	-	1	-	1	-	-	-	-	-	1	33
1,768	-	1,040	-	685	-	322	-	138	-	58	-	17	-	4	-	2	-	14	-	34
57	-	35	-	30	-	12	-	8	-	2	-	-	-	-	-	-	-	-	-	35
1,092	-	647	-	427	-	195	-	87	-	33	-	13	-	-	-	2	-	8	-	36
619	-	358	-	228	-	115	-	43	-	23	-	4	-	4	-	-	-	6	-	37
162	-	128	-	116	-	73	-	49	1	16	-	9	-	2	-	3	-	2	-	38
2,973	20	2,392	9	2,174	3	1,475	2	792	1	506	-	269	-	98	-	65	-	20	1	39
7	1	5	-	6	-	1	-	1	-	1	-	1	-	-	-	-	-	-	-	40
2,594	2	2,157	1	1,965	-	1,363	-	746	-	474	-	250	-	94	-	63	-	18	-	41
372	17	230	8	203	3	111	2	45	1	31	-	18	-	4	-	2	-	2	1	42
343	4	316	5	266	4	192	5	104	-	54	3	48	-	14	-	7	1	-	1	43
9	-	4	-	9	-	5	-	3	-	2	-	2	-	-	-	-	-	-	-	44
6	-	15	-	19	-	15	-	2	-	4	-	-	-	-	-	-	-	-	-	45
2,244	1	2,007	-	1,877	-	1,272	-	730	-	436	-	241	-	88	-	61	-	28	-	46
585	-	566	-	499	-	328	-	145	-	71	-	41	-	11	-	6	-	4	-	47
1,659	1	1,441	-	1,378	-	944	-	585	-	365	-	200	-	77	-	55	-	24	-	48
763	-	707	-	664	-	486	-	244	-	175	-	71	-	32	-	20	-	7	-	49
32	-	20	-	14	-	11	-	3	-	4	-	3	-	-	-	-	-	1	-	50
183	-	96	-	81	-	50	-	18	-	3	-	4	-	-	-	1	-	-	-	51
168	-	128	-	119	-	84	-	46	-	28	-	13	-	2	-	1	-	-	-	52
483	1	383	-	326	-	225	-	113	-	75	-	28	-	10	-	4	-	5	-	53
466	4	403	2	446	1	343	2	223	2	168	-	128	-	64	-	62	-	4	-	54
24	-	17	1	19	-	8	-	5	-	1	-	-	-	-	-	-	-	-	-	55
40	-	34	-	39	-	40	-	24	-	19	-	8	-	3	-	4	-	2	-	56
67	-	45	-	40	-	25	-	12	-	4	-	2	-	-	-	-	-	-	-	57
1,534	117	1,009	56	588	43	270	20	107	8	59	3	24	3	9	1	3	1	11	1	58
134	-	125	-	110	-	81	-	51	-	38	-	17	-	5	-	7	-	-	-	59
8	-	4	-	6	-	4	-	2	-	-	-	1	-	1	-	-	-	-	-	60
126	-	121	-	104	-	77	-	49	-	38	-	16	-	4	-	7	-	-	-	61
98	9	113	4	110	3	73	3	47	4	35	1	26	-	14	-	3	-	1	-	62
110	-	96	1	79	-	41	-	23	-	14	-	5	-	4	-	1	-	1	-	63
650	32	434	32	315	19	227	7	111	2	70	6	18	1	16	3	9	-	4	1	64
62	3	33	2	34	-	9	-	14	-	5	-	4	-	-	-	3	-	2	-	65
8	2	11	1	10	-	14	-	6	-	1	-	-	-	-	-	-	-	-	-	66
120	2	82	7	64	4	59	2	18	1	20	-	3	-	4	2	1	-	-	-	67
70	-	49	-	35	-	25	-	10	-	10	-	-	-	1	-	-	-	1	-	68
44	3	31	-	21	2	15	-	10	-	3	-	3	-	-	-	-	-	-	-	69
102	-	72	1	45	2	23	-	11	-	4	1	-	-	2	1	-	-	-	-	70
11	2	4	2	7	-	5	1	5	-	3	-	-	-	-	-	1	-	-	-	71
17	1	18	-	9	1	6	1	4	-	3	-	1	-	2	-	-	-	-	-	72
216	19	134	19	90	10	71	3	33	1	21	5	7	1	7	-	4	-	1	1	73

TABLE 24.—NEGRO GAINFUL WORKERS 10 YEARS OLD AND OVER, BY

[See note at

	OCCUPATION	10 YEARS OLD AND OVER			10 TO 17 YEARS		18 AND 19 YEARS		20 TO 24 YEARS		25 TO 29 YEARS		30 TO 34 YEARS	
		Total	Male	Female	Male	Female	Male	Female	Male	Female	Male	Female	Male	Female
	Manufacturing and mechanical industries—Continued.													
	Operatives (n. o. s.)—Continued.													
1	Cigar and tobacco factories	20,721	5,745	14,976	260	865	298	1,225	885	3,228	878	2,864	779	2,001
2	Clay, glass, and stone industries	3,516	3,099	417	80	28	110	36	415	108	489	88	450	42
3	Brick, tile, and terra-cotta factories	1,007	986	21	24	3	37	1	144	5	181	3	137	-------
4	Glass factories	1,114	776	338	41	20	46	31	121	93	99	71	104	35
5	Lime, cement, and artificial stone factories.	949	927	22	8	1	17	-------	115	2	157	5	163	4
6	Marble and stone yards	215	215	-------	2	-------	4	-------	13	-------	20	-------	20	-------
7	Potteries	231	195	36	5	4	6	4	22	8	32	9	26	3
8	Clothing industries	22,216	6,581	15,635	231	628	476	1,193	1,679	3,520	1,526	3,376	1,098	2,555
9	Corset factories	55	3	52	-------	-------	-------	4	-------	9	-------	12	1	4
10	Glove factories	248	16	232	3	9	4	35	3	78	4	53	-------	24
11	Hat factories (felt)	459	294	165	15	8	38	18	105	43	45	36	34	19
12	Shirt, collar, and cuff factories	1,539	560	979	20	78	44	101	145	224	103	202	100	147
13	Suit, coat, and overall factories	5,672	3,812	1,860	127	99	256	139	942	443	907	381	654	295
14	Other clothing factories	14,243	1,896	12,347	66	434	134	896	484	2,723	467	2,692	309	2,066
15	Food and allied industries	17,834	11,129	6,705	529	539	491	491	1,644	1,285	2,020	1,117	1,712	923
16	Bakeries	856	670	186	122	27	63	10	177	41	111	34	66	23
17	Butter, cheese, and condensed milk factories.	179	157	22	6	1	4	1	30	5	32	1	20	4
18	Candy factories	1,111	655	456	33	35	43	50	141	122	132	72	97	58
19	Fish curing and packing	1,872	868	1,004	77	71	43	59	96	145	103	122	75	126
20	Flour and grain mills	468	453	15	9	-------	15	-------	56	3	66	2	65	4
21	Fruit and vegetable canning, etc	979	284	695	32	62	30	62	59	155	36	113	25	82
22	Slaughter and packing houses	7,167	6,286	881	74	20	140	31	745	139	1,226	181	1,171	177
23	Sugar factories and refineries	300	280	20	10	-------	12	-------	37	1	56	3	43	1
24	Other food factories	4,127	768	3,359	54	317	50	273	128	659	141	577	85	439
25	Liquor and beverage industries	775	708	67	112	6	91	5	175	15	117	12	65	9
26	Iron and steel, machinery, and vehicle industries.	23,922	23,255	667	311	38	574	63	2,922	150	4,292	114	3,986	106
27	Agricultural implement factories	108	104	4	1	-------	4	-------	9	-------	18	1	14	1
28	Automobile factories	3,245	3,154	91	16	3	62	13	415	14	715	15	652	19
29	Automobile repair shops	617	612	5	32	1	39	1	134	1	153	-------	84	1
30	Blast furnaces and steel rolling mills [3]	6,861	6,763	98	45	3	153	8	902	26	1,339	17	1,255	18
31	Car and railroad shops	3,670	3,644	26	16	1	23	1	271	2	482	3	555	5
32	Ship and boat building	1,857	1,855	2	36	-------	81	-------	239		256	-------	277	-------
33	Wagon and carriage factories	27	25	2	-------	-------	2	1	5	-------	4	-------	3	-------
34	Other iron and steel and machinery factories.[4]	6,047	5,651	396	148	27	168	37	760	96	1,062	75	886	55
35	Not specified metal industries	1,490	1,447	43	17	3	42	2	187	10	263	3	260	7
36	Metal industries (except iron and steel)	1,241	978	263	21	20	44	24	161	89	190	52	183	26
37	Brass mills	270	252	18	4	2	8	-------	31	4	58	6	50	1
38	Clock and watch factories	28	16	12	1	1	-------	2	3	4	2	2	3	-------
39	Copper factories	83	82	1	1	-------	-------	-------	8	1	18	-------	15	-------
40	Gold and silver factories	30	24	6	1	-------	4	-------	3	4	5	-------	2	1
41	Jewelry factories	53	18	35	-------	6	2	8	4	15	3	3	2	1
42	Lead and zinc factories	68	64	4	-------	-------	4	-------	9	-------	10	2	10	-------
43	Tinware, enamelware, etc., factories	480	345	135	11	9	10	12	60	43	63	29	76	17
44	Other metal factories	229	177	52	3	2	16	2	43	18	31	10	25	6
45	Leather industries	2,004	1,615	389	67	24	93	47	257	84	278	70	212	59
46	Harness and saddle factories	70	67	3	1	-------	2	-------	2	1	10	1	4	1
47	Leather belt, leather goods, etc., factories.	213	96	117	6	13	11	18	21	27	19	29	16	15
48	Shoe factories	845	678	167	43	5	49	23	123	29	111	21	71	30
49	Tanneries	810	733	77	14	3	30	5	101	18	131	15	117	10
50	Trunk, suitcase, and bag factories	66	41	25	3	3	1	1	10	9	7	4	4	3
51	Lumber and furniture industries	10,241	9,416	825	525	79	530	64	1,806	213	1,590	141	1,122	88
52	Furniture factories	1,878	1,616	262	73	9	84	22	278	69	240	59	168	30
53	Piano and organ factories	59	59	-------	-------	-------	1	-------	7	-------	6	-------	3	-------
54	Saw and planing mills [5]	6,548	6,309	239	357	29	343	18	1,267	67	1,109	36	793	20
55	Other woodworking factories	1,756	1,432	324	95	41	102	24	254	77	235	46	158	38
56	Paper, printing, and allied industries	2,866	1,771	1,095	87	53	93	68	279	164	272	207	268	182
57	Blank book, envelop, tag, paper bag, etc., factories.	144	77	67	2	2	7	6	16	22	9	12	18	9
58	Paper and pulp mills	1,385	821	564	23	43	38	46	125	86	145	110	134	77
59	Paper box factories	127	76	51	7	4	6	4	16	12	19	16	10	5
60	Printing, publishing, and engraving	1,210	797	413	55	4	42	12	122	44	99	69	106	91
	Textile industries:													
61	Cotton mills	2,805	2,124	681	89	45	136	65	382	151	317	122	240	76
62	Knitting mills	884	238	646	16	61	23	88	53	180	43	113	38	79
63	Silk mills	330	105	225	8	24	11	21	21	57	14	35	25	34
64	Textile dyeing, finishing, and printing mills.	223	153	80	5	2	7	2	33	14	21	19	26	18
65	Woolen and worsted mills	234	111	123	1	12	8	17	20	14	17	19	15	17
66	Other textile mills	2,752	1,242	1,510	37	123	72	120	240	350	228	293	190	188
67	Carpet mills	234	166	68	8	5	10	2	29	13	25	8	22	4
68	Hemp, jute, and linen mills	113	61	52	-------	4	2	4	16	7	14	8	9	11
69	Lace and embroidery mills	111	10	101	-------	2	1	9	2	28	2	23	1	18
70	Rope and cordage factories	224	178	46	1	2	6	2	19	12	34	11	26	10
71	Sail, awning, and tent factories	63	48	15	-------	-------	1	-------	6	2	7	6	7	2
72	Other and not specified textile mills	2,007	779	1,228	28	110	52	103	168	288	146	237	125	143
73	Miscellaneous manufacturing industries	18,066	11,255	6,811	408	398	507	597	1,816	1,610	1,888	1,404	1,735	955
74	Broom and brush factories	414	341	73	11	5	13	3	41	23	40	15	46	11
75	Button factories	121	30	91	1	6	3	14	9	23	2	13	7	16
76	Electric light and power plants	696	696	-------	7	-------	12	-------	85	-------	99	-------	109	-------
77	Electrical machinery and supply factories.	577	473	104	12	7	27	14	65	30	82	27	85	11
78	Rubber factories	1,145	1,096	49	20	7	35	8	156	11	242	11	237	6

See footnotes at end of table.

OCCUPATION, AGE, AND SEX, FOR THE UNITED STATES: 1930—Continued

head of table]

35 TO 39 YEARS		40 TO 44 YEARS		45 TO 49 YEARS		50 TO 54 YEARS		55 TO 59 YEARS		60 TO 64 YEARS		65 TO 69 YEARS		70 TO 74 YEARS		75 YEARS AND OVER		UNKNOWN		
Male	Female	Male	Female	Male	Female	Male	Female	Male	Female	Male	Female	Male	Female	Male	Female	Male	Female	Male	Female	
721	1,774	539	1,155	486	795	382	523	221	234	171	170	69	81	33	30	18	16	5	15	1
463	52	386	29	281	18	184	6	129	2	60	6	29		12		5	1	6	1	2
158	2	105	2	66	2	64	2	40	1	12		11		5				2		3
105	39	90	24	77	14	39	3	31	1	13	6	7		1				2	1	4
149	5	122	3	84	2	43		33		21		8		2		4		1		5
26		36		34		29		19		5		3		2		1		1		6
25	6	33		20		9	1	6		9				2			1			7
767	2,050	427	1,096	207	655	103	293	38	142	9	70	6	22	4	9	1	5	9	21	8
2	11		4		4		2		2											9
	17		10		2	2	1		3											10
16	25	18	10	7	5	7	1	5		2								2		11
69	117	40	55	22	31	8	10	5	9	2	2	1	1	1	1				1	12
474	215	250	134	114	70	60	42	15	22	2	10	3	4	3		1	1	4	5	13
206	1,665	119	883	64	543	26	237	13	106	3	58	2	17		8		4	3	15	14
1,664	876	1,087	522	835	413	529	268	287	128	180	82	82	29	36	13	21	6	12	13	15
47	22	29	9	19	12	16	3	10		2	3	3	1	3	1	2				16
20	6	17		15		5	3	4		1	1	2				1				17
67	51	64	20	31	14	21	23	9	3	8	7	4	1	4		1				18
91	144	83	97	80	94	80	59	50	39	48	27	26	14	9	4	7	1		2	19
74	1	58	1	49	1	31	1	13		7	2	5		2		1		2		20
42	72	24	56	10	42	9	22	10	14	5	12	1	2	1					1	21
1,122	152	683	84	537	53	298	23	155	15	81	2	24	1	14	2	7		9	1	22
49	5	23	5	17	2	15	2	6	1	5		6				1				23
91	411	73	249	57	192	39	130	22	55	18	28	8	10	1	6	1	4		9	24
61	12	33	1	20	3	15	2	8	1	5		3		2			1	1		25
3,913	73	2,663	57	2,221	26	1,268	19	585	11	307	3	120	3	38		24		31	4	26
17		11	1	11	1	10		5		3		1								27
585	7	336	7	216	7	87	2	47	2	14		4	1	1				4	1	28
68		46		33		12	1	6		4						1				29
1,151	7	742	10	596	5	334		143	2	53	2	24		8		7		11		30
672	5	556	5	496	2	307	1	150		72		36	1	5				3		31
273		217		212		138		52	1	42		19		5		3		5		32
3		1		3	1	3		1												33
889	45	591	28	528	9	306	14	143	6	103	1	32	1	17		11		7	2	34
255	9	163	6	126	1	71	1	38		16		4		2		2		1	1	35
141	24	87	12	66	7	38	3	30	3	6	2	4	1	2		1		4		36
35	3	23	2	18		12		5		4		1		1				2		37
	3	2		1		3										1				38
19		8		7		2		3		1										39
2		3		1		1		2	1											40
4	1			2		1							1							41
14	2	5		1		4		6						1						42
45	8	34	7	25	5	11	1	7	2		2	2						1		43
22	7	12	3	11	2	4	2	7		1		1						1		44
229	43	143	31	120	14	100	11	46	2	25		23	1	9	1	9		4	2	45
5		11		7		9		3		8		2		2		1				46
10	6	3	7	4	1	2		3				1							1	47
92	24	55	17	54	8	37	7	22	1	4		7	1	4		4		2	1	48
116	9	68	6	55	5	49	4	18	1	13		13		3	1	3		2		49
6	4	6	1			3										1				50
1,133	92	817	54	745	38	492	21	253	10	185	9	101	5	54	4	53	5	10	2	51
182	27	154	18	157	10	89	5	65	3	58	3	25	2	26	2	15	2	2	1	52
7		12		10		6		2		2		1		1		1				53
771	24	534	18	489	9	333	8	144	3	91	2	52	1	11	1	9	2	6	1	54
173	41	117	18	89	19	64	8	42	4	34	4	23	2	16	1	28	1	2		55
227	171	174	85	158	84	92	49	48	19	41	7	18	2	6		6		2	4	56
7	7	8		3	5	3	1	3	2	1	1									57
107	76	82	35	81	49	47	25	11	10	17	4	2	2	5		4			1	58
4	3	7	3	4	1		2	2	1	1										59
109	85	77	47	70	29	42	21	32	6	22	2	16		1		2		2	3	60
298	73	205	61	169	36	134	26	59	15	48	6	21	2	14	1	11	1	1	1	61
24	56	19	21	7	20	7	18	5	3	2	3		2	1	2					62
9	17	7	15	4	14	1	4	4	1	1	1				2					63
15	16	17	6	16	3	5		3		4								1		64
13	16	8	15	8	6	13	4	2	1	2	2	2		2						65
152	155	96	103	90	68	55	39	46	23	20	14	5	11	5	3	4	14	2	6	66
20	14	14	5	9	8	8	5	11	2	4	1	1		2		1	1	2		67
9	9	6	3	3	5	1										1	1			68
1	9		6	1	3	1	1	1	1				1							69
34	6	17	1	19	1	8	1	7		4		1		1		1				70
6	1	4	2	6		6	1	3		2	1									71
82	116	55	86	52	51	31	31	24	20	10	12	3	10	2	3	1	12		6	72
1,568	802	1,071	464	847	287	639	147	343	78	236	27	115	13	42	5	23	5	17	19	73
44	6	49	6	35	1	23		13		14	1	10				2	2			74
3	12	1	5	3	1	1	1													75
127		96		67		55		19		10		5		1		1		3		76
74	4	50	4	36	4	20	2	13	1	8				1						77
197		95	2	48	1	34	2	21	1	5		4						2		78

TABLE 24.—NEGRO GAINFUL WORKERS 10 YEARS OLD AND OVER, BY

[See note at

	OCCUPATION	10 YEARS OLD AND OVER			10 TO 17 YEARS		18 AND 19 YEARS		20 TO 24 YEARS		25 TO 29 YEARS		30 TO 34 YEARS	
		Total	Male	Female	Male	Female	Male	Female	Male	Female	Male	Female	Male	Female
	Manufacturing and mechanical industries—Continued.													
	Operatives (n. o. s.)—Continued.													
	Miscellaneous manufacturing industries—Continued.													
1	Straw factories	13	5	8	-	-	-	-	2	2	2	4	-	1
2	Turpentine farms and distilleries	726	721	5	31	1	19	1	76	-	70	2	52	-
3	Other miscellaneous manufacturing industries.	6, 735	4, 573	2, 162	184	134	217	184	751	467	741	400	682	307
4	Other not specified manufacturing industries.	7, 639	3, 320	4, 319	142	238	181	373	631	1, 054	610	932	517	603
5	Not specified industries and services	13, 847	10, 375	3, 472	524	201	765	279	1, 871	720	1, 502	585	1, 238	372
	Laborers (n. o. s.)[2]:													
6	Building, general, and not specified laborers.	224, 136	219, 485	4, 651	6, 018	228	8, 316	242	26, 770	615	29, 907	548	27, 416	513
7	Laborers and helpers, building construction.	95, 618	95, 587	31	1, 326	-	2, 521	3	10, 603	7	14, 247	6	13, 648	3
8	General and not specified laborers	128, 518	123, 898	4, 620	4, 692	228	5, 795	239	16, 167	608	15, 660	542	13, 768	510
9	Chemical and allied industries	37, 724	37, 391	333	1, 133	27	1, 750	25	6, 420	67	6, 745	63	5, 282	50
10	Charcoal and coke works	1, 428	1, 419	9	30	1	39	-	156	1	282	1	222	1
11	Explosives, ammunition, and fire works factories.	345	335	10	15	-	6	2	56	3	59	2	44	1
12	Fertilizer factories	15, 347	15, 268	79	804	8	1, 053	5	3, 154	15	2, 647	13	1, 886	14
13	Gas works	4, 324	4, 319	5	37	-	107	1	472	-	698	2	618	-
14	Paint and varnish factories	756	739	17	11	3	21	2	108	2	151	4	112	2
15	Petroleum refineries	7, 863	7, 828	35	77	3	231	4	1, 277	8	1, 555	7	1, 292	3
16	Rayon factories	675	663	12	19	-	37	-	127	1	118	2	84	3
17	Soap factories	350	338	12	5	1	16	1	58	2	64	2	48	3
18	Other chemical factories	6, 636	6, 482	154	135	11	240	10	1, 012	35	1, 171	30	976	23
19	Cigar and tobacco factories	12, 254	8, 863	3, 391	337	201	499	263	1, 528	684	1, 459	559	1, 133	398
20	Clay, glass, and stone industries	22, 399	22, 108	291	600	14	994	23	3, 378	55	3, 704	52	3, 068	42
21	Brick, tile, and terra-cotta factories	12, 180	12, 095	85	348	4	571	4	1, 969	10	2, 110	16	1, 682	12
22	Glass factories	2, 475	2, 313	162	79	7	153	15	378	35	338	32	323	24
23	Lime, cement, and artificial stone factories.	6, 041	6, 016	25	122	-	195	-	803	6	1, 004	2	834	4
24	Marble and stone yards	1, 007	1, 007	-	25	-	38	-	125	-	150	-	135	-
25	Potteries	696	677	19	26	3	37	2	103	4	102	2	94	2
26	Clothing industries	1, 809	1, 439	370	83	30	167	38	360	101	291	70	184	43
27	Corset factories	5	4	1	-	-	-	-	2	-	1	1	-	-
28	Glove factories	27	21	6	1	-	2	-	5	-	1	2	3	2
29	Hat factories (felt)	88	81	7	4	1	14	2	29	-	6	3	8	-
30	Shirt, collar, and cuff factories	606	539	67	8	9	52	9	168	14	128	7	67	10
31	Suit, coat, and overall factories	480	446	34	36	2	42	1	97	9	93	5	58	5
32	Other clothing factories	603	348	255	34	18	57	26	59	78	62	52	48	26
33	Food and allied industries	26, 760	22, 422	4, 338	1, 092	450	1, 173	378	3, 680	850	3, 810	685	3, 123	528
34	Bakeries	1, 533	1, 445	88	133	5	108	9	275	19	266	18	192	10
35	Butter, cheese, and condensed milk factories.	534	516	18	35	1	28	2	95	2	80	4	71	1
36	Candy factories	523	375	148	27	21	38	18	79	39	66	23	46	16
37	Fish curing and packing	2, 011	1, 227	784	89	71	88	60	182	153	146	111	135	86
38	Flour and grain mills	2, 442	2, 417	25	67	2	75	1	360	4	400	6	317	3
39	Fruit and vegetable canning, etc	1, 488	1, 052	436	84	49	80	38	188	87	140	91	121	49
40	Slaughter and packing houses	9, 332	8, 854	478	124	14	273	22	1, 212	72	1, 619	106	1, 474	89
41	Sugar factories and refineries	2, 662	2, 553	109	80	5	118	4	435	11	448	15	327	18
42	Other food factories	4, 637	2, 441	2, 196	122	279	127	219	464	451	448	302	330	245
43	Liquor and beverage industries	1, 598	1, 542	56	331	3	238	5	390	12	197	9	110	11
44	Iron and steel, machinery, and vehicle industries.	107, 739	106, 802	937	1, 166	52	3, 070	63	16, 115	164	20, 586	194	17, 660	127
45	Agricultural implement factories	585	579	6	15	-	15	1	92	1	104	1	68	3
46	Automobile factories	16, 450	16, 289	161	99	10	379	6	2, 404	29	3, 424	38	3, 172	25
47	Automobile repair shops	2, 659	2, 644	15	116	1	202	2	751	1	631	3	364	3
48	Blast furnaces and steel rolling mills [3]	38, 915	38, 709	206	328	4	1, 066	13	6, 101	33	7, 736	40	6, 591	26
49	Car and railroad shops	9, 226	9, 130	96	59	5	184	6	1, 085	9	1, 379	15	1, 322	8
50	Ship and boat building	4, 566	4, 549	17	92	-	203	2	681	4	761	5	571	2
51	Wagon and carriage factories	153	153	-	6	-	8	-	21	-	20	-	22	-
52	Other iron and steel and machinery factories.[4]	23, 033	22, 716	317	353	23	725	25	3, 408	59	4, 223	70	3, 464	41
53	Not specified metal industries	12, 152	12, 033	119	98	9	288	8	1, 572	28	2, 308	22	2, 086	19
54	Metal industries (except iron and steel)	5, 293	5, 216	77	72	4	176	8	857	21	1, 108	12	905	11
55	Brass mills	1, 435	1, 419	16	8	1	42	3	209	2	309	3	256	2
56	Clock and watch factories	11	11	-	1	-	-	-	3	-	3	-	-	-
57	Copper factories	868	868	-	5	-	19	-	114	-	219	-	181	-
58	Gold and silver factories	11	8	3	-	-	1	-	1	2	1	-	2	1
59	Jewelry factories	8	8	-	-	-	-	-	-	-	1	-	3	-
60	Lead and zinc factories	663	660	3	8	-	17	-	108	2	136	-	116	-
61	Tinware, enamelware, etc., factories	1, 116	1, 073	43	26	2	66	5	199	12	215	7	168	6
62	Other metal factories	1, 181	1, 169	12	24	1	31	-	223	3	224	2	179	2
63	Leather industries	2, 705	2, 601	104	84	6	125	6	409	19	449	26	371	14
64	Harness and saddle factories	61	52	9	1	-	2	-	9	5	11	-	8	1
65	Leather belt, leather goods, etc., factories.	181	170	11	3	-	8	1	23	2	30	3	26	1
66	Shoe factories	623	591	32	52	2	58	3	122	7	83	6	74	5
67	Tanneries	1, 749	1, 699	50	25	4	55	2	241	4	311	17	253	7
68	Trunk, suitcase, and bag factories	91	89	2	3	-	2	-	14	1	14	-	10	-
69	Lumber and furniture industries	112, 056	109, 685	2, 371	6, 430	287	7, 942	224	23, 309	540	18, 794	388	12, 989	243
70	Furniture factories	3, 354	3, 148	206	249	12	273	19	623	60	512	43	326	28
71	Piano and organ factories	60	59	1	-	-	2	-	4	-	5	-	7	-
72	Saw and planing mills [5]	96, 527	95, 198	1, 329	5, 415	179	6, 881	127	20, 299	305	16, 322	207	11, 292	114
73	Other woodworking factories	12, 115	11, 280	835	766	96	786	78	2, 383	175	1, 955	138	1, 364	101

See footnotes at end of table.

OCCUPATION, AGE, AND SEX, FOR THE UNITED STATES: 1930—Continued

head of table]

35 TO 39 YEARS		40 TO 44 YEARS		45 TO 49 YEARS		50 TO 54 YEARS		55 TO 59 YEARS		60 TO 64 YEARS		65 TO 69 YEARS		70 TO 74 YEARS		75 YEARS AND OVER		UNKNOWN		
Male	Female	Male	Female	Male	Female	Male	Female	Male	Female	Male	Female	Male	Female	Male	Female	Male	Female	Male	Female	
1	1	---	---	---	---	---	---	---	---	---	---	---	---	---	---	---	---	---	---	1
77	---	72	---	73	---	100	1	62	---	53	---	25	---	8	---	2	---	1	---	2
615	313	431	156	363	89	253	61	153	29	104	6	42	4	17	4	14	3	6	5	3
430	466	277	291	222	191	153	80	62	47	42	20	29	9	15	1	4	---	5	14	4
1,161	350	825	284	724	196	579	157	362	92	273	65	168	34	96	25	88	19	199	93	5
29,360	550	23,726	449	22,299	427	17,501	374	10,744	236	7,602	202	4,670	130	2,579	67	1,920	56	657	14	6
14,904	6	11,759	1	10,760	1	7,508	2	4,083	2	2,273	---	1,099	---	444	---	222	---	190	---	7
14,456	544	11,967	448	11,539	426	9,993	372	6,661	234	5,329	202	3,571	130	2,135	67	1,698	56	467	14	8
5,289	41	3,626	24	3,093	16	2,011	6	1,003	6	576	3	276	4	94	---	32	1	61	---	9
222	---	146	---	128	3	85	---	53	1	30	---	16	1	5	---	2	---	3	---	10
50	---	37	2	24	---	16	---	18	---	7	---	1	---	1	---	---	---	1	---	11
1,817	7	1,281	2	1,097	6	758	2	365	3	220	2	109	1	40	---	12	1	25	---	12
681	1	495	---	474	---	354	---	173	---	115	---	58	1	20	---	6	---	11	---	13
125	1	81	1	57	---	40	---	13	2	12	---	4	---	4	---	---	---	---	---	14
1,290	4	840	4	638	1	322	---	165	---	74	1	44	---	12	---	4	---	7	---	15
92	2	66	1	56	1	39	1	12	---	10	---	1	1	1	---	---	---	1	---	16
57	1	30	2	26	---	20	---	7	---	5	---	2	---	---	---	---	---	---	---	17
955	25	650	12	593	5	377	3	197	---	103	---	41	---	11	---	8	---	13	---	18
1,118	412	743	302	707	241	560	147	314	68	219	62	128	29	71	16	43	8	4	1	19
3,026	38	2,226	21	1,986	21	1,387	10	825	7	497	1	242	3	81	1	50	1	44	2	20
1,637	15	1,153	6	1,022	6	711	2	409	3	257	1	132	2	44	---	28	1	22	1	21
282	17	237	12	193	10	152	5	74	3	52	---	24	1	11	1	10	---	7	---	22
867	3	660	3	611	2	421	3	257	1	144	---	59	---	18	---	9	---	12	1	23
147	---	108	---	97	---	73	---	52	---	28	---	18	---	7	---	2	---	2	---	24
93	3	68	---	63	3	30	---	33	---	16	---	9	---	1	---	1	---	1	---	25
144	31	73	25	54	15	40	9	15	7	16	---	7	---	2	1	2	---	1	---	26
---	---	---	---	---	---	---	---	---	---	1	---	---	---	---	---	---	---	---	---	27
5	1	2	1	---	---	1	---	---	---	1	---	---	---	---	---	---	---	---	---	28
8	---	4	---	3	---	4	---	1	1	---	---	---	---	---	---	---	---	---	---	29
48	3	30	8	15	1	12	4	4	2	4	---	2	---	1	---	---	---	---	---	30
52	2	19	3	19	3	14	4	4	---	7	---	1	---	1	---	2	---	1	---	31
31	25	18	13	17	11	9	1	6	4	3	---	4	---	---	1	---	---	---	---	32
3,141	508	2,119	341	1,785	235	1,174	173	609	102	392	46	179	19	75	11	40	6	30	6	33
189	9	89	12	78	4	55	---	28	1	17	1	5	---	7	---	2	---	1	---	34
66	2	52	3	38	1	24	1	9	1	7	---	7	---	3	---	---	---	1	---	35
43	8	32	9	13	5	18	4	5	3	8	2	---	---	---	---	---	---	---	---	36
142	115	122	55	103	48	104	37	46	26	33	12	20	5	9	2	5	1	3	2	37
355	2	262	5	232	1	160	---	79	1	55	---	25	---	13	---	11	---	6	---	38
132	42	99	28	81	22	50	17	34	10	25	2	9	1	5	---	4	---	---	---	39
1,427	76	960	48	779	25	485	16	250	9	151	---	53	---	19	---	12	---	16	1	40
363	19	241	12	240	11	134	4	77	5	43	3	30	1	12	1	3	---	2	---	41
321	227	199	166	178	116	115	93	63	45	43	26	22	12	5	8	3	5	1	2	42
103	8	63	3	43	2	29	1	18	1	10	---	8	---	2	---	---	---	---	1	43
16,793	121	11,577	92	8,992	56	5,491	33	2,763	19	1,423	5	636	1	210	2	116	4	204	4	44
86	---	60	---	63	---	42	---	13	---	11	---	3	---	---	---	7	---	---	---	45
2,814	24	1,695	17	1,204	9	598	3	282	---	120	---	46	---	10	---	3	---	39	---	46
255	2	136	1	94	1	54	---	27	1	9	---	---	---	1	---	1	---	3	---	47
6,092	30	4,115	28	3,125	12	1,856	10	910	5	431	1	179	1	69	1	25	1	85	1	48
1,472	15	1,157	13	1,006	9	678	9	366	2	236	2	125	---	34	---	18	1	9	2	49
671	---	514	1	434	---	294	1	149	1	98	---	47	---	16	1	9	---	9	---	50
18	---	13	---	16	---	12	---	6	---	5	---	3	---	---	---	1	---	2	---	51
3,446	38	2,493	24	1,983	19	1,320	6	679	9	359	---	149	---	52	---	37	2	25	1	52
1,939	12	1,394	8	1,067	6	637	4	331	1	154	2	84	---	28	---	15	---	32	---	53
797	8	498	5	379	4	223	3	103	---	46	1	23	---	7	---	9	---	13	---	54
223	2	149	2	106	---	59	1	28	---	17	---	6	---	4	---	3	---	---	---	55
1	---	1	---	1	---	---	---	1	---	---	---	---	---	---	---	---	---	---	---	56
131	---	99	---	51	---	27	---	11	---	7	---	2	---	---	---	2	---	---	---	57
---	---	1	---	1	---	1	---	---	---	---	---	---	---	---	---	---	---	---	---	58
2	---	1	---	---	---	1	---	---	---	---	---	---	---	---	---	---	---	---	---	59
115	1	66	---	49	---	25	---	12	---	5	---	1	---	---	---	---	---	2	---	60
141	3	86	3	82	3	43	1	23	---	11	1	6	---	3	---	4	---	---	---	61
184	2	95	---	89	1	67	1	28	---	6	---	8	---	---	---	---	---	11	---	62
334	16	269	12	202	3	145	1	98	---	55	1	33	---	11	---	6	---	10	---	63
3	1	8	2	1	---	3	---	2	---	1	---	1	---	1	---	1	---	---	---	64
21	3	19	1	13	---	17	---	8	---	2	---	---	---	---	---	---	---	---	---	65
59	5	41	3	33	1	33	---	13	---	10	---	7	---	2	---	2	---	2	---	66
241	7	191	6	143	1	87	1	72	---	41	1	21	---	7	---	3	---	8	---	67
10	---	10	---	12	1	5	---	3	---	1	---	4	---	1	---	---	---	---	---	68
12,466	243	8,953	179	7,574	111	5,380	78	2,675	29	1,706	28	795	9	331	4	192	3	149	5	69
301	17	245	10	216	5	167	6	97	2	66	2	42	1	24	---	6	---	1	1	70
13	1	11	---	5	---	6	---	2	---	2	---	1	---	1	---	---	---	---	---	71
10,901	137	7,814	105	6,603	66	4,656	45	2,317	17	1,478	14	658	5	268	2	161	3	133	3	72
1,251	88	883	64	750	40	551	27	259	10	160	12	94	3	38	2	25	---	15	1	73

TABLE 24.—NEGRO GAINFUL WORKERS 10 YEARS OLD AND OVER, BY

[See note at

	OCCUPATION	10 YEARS OLD AND OVER			10 TO 17 YEARS		18 AND 19 YEARS		20 TO 24 YEARS		25 TO 29 YEARS		30 TO 34 YEARS	
		Total	Male	Female	Male	Female	Male	Female	Male	Female	Male	Female	Male	Female
	Manufacturing and mechanical industries—Continued.													
	Laborers (n. o. s.)—Continued.													
1	Paper, printing, and allied industries	6, 276	5, 960	316	148	24	271	27	1, 060	61	1, 112	54	894	48
2	Blank book, envelop, tag, paper bag, etc., factories.	184	163	21	4	1	6	2	29	3	31	4	30	3
3	Paper and pulp mills	4, 970	4, 711	259	92	19	211	23	850	54	892	44	718	40
4	Paper box factories	109	101	8	8	1	6	2	18	1	25	1	19	
5	Printing, publishing, and engraving	1, 013	985	28	44	3	48		163	3	164	5	126	5
	Textile industries:													
6	Cotton mills	11, 156	9, 106	2, 050	500	166	766	194	2, 030	428	1, 461	298	951	247
7	Knitting mills	442	312	130	6	8	19	8	67	22	50	27	44	9
8	Silk mills	385	320	65	16	6	12	8	59	13	52	7	39	6
9	Textile dyeing, finishing, and printing mills.	492	480	12	14		21		95	4	84	2	68	1
10	Woolen and worsted mills	259	210	49	7	2	6	1	35	12	41	9	32	6
11	Other textile mills	2, 288	1, 804	484	70	40	103	43	345	145	378	79	264	54
12	Carpet mills	216	204	12	8	1	14	2	43	3	46	1	31	2
13	Hemp, jute, and linen mills	90	65	25	2	3	7	1	16	5	4	6	12	5
14	Lace and embroidery mills	3	3								1			
15	Rope and cordage factories	249	231	18	6	1	9	1	41	6	60	3	32	3
16	Sail, awning, and tent factories	36	34	2					5		8		8	1
17	Other and not specified textile mills	1, 694	1, 267	427	54	35	73	39	240	131	259	69	181	43
18	Miscellaneous manufacturing industries	78, 782	75, 489	3, 293	4, 515	293	4, 115	304	12, 560	730	11, 759	533	9, 169	379
19	Broom and brush factories	274	251	23	59	1	17	2	46	9	32	3	30	3
20	Button factories	23	18	5	1		1		7	3	2	2	4	
21	Electric light and power plants	4, 852	4, 850	2	75		181		671	2	771		699	
22	Electrical machinery and supply factories.	1, 302	1, 275	27	18		46		214	11	232	5	201	4
23	Rubber factories	1, 550	1, 520	30	26	2	63	5	217	4	346	5	312	4
24	Straw factories	8	7	1			1	1	3					
25	Turpentine farms and distilleries	30, 849	30, 577	272	3, 008	48	1, 964	22	5, 012	41	4, 010	36	2, 837	29
26	Other miscellaneous manufacturing industries.	22, 438	21, 634	804	762	62	1, 066	66	3, 777	159	3, 642	128	2, 974	89
27	Other not specified manufacturing industries.	17, 486	15, 357	2, 129	566	180	776	208	2, 613	501	2, 724	354	2, 112	250
28	**Transportation and communication**	**397, 645**	**395, 437**	**2, 208**	**7, 395**	**59**	**14, 444**	**123**	**62, 443**	**368**	**71, 575**	**374**	**59, 355**	**347**
	Water transportation (selected occupations):													
29	Boatmen, canal men, and lock keepers	282	282		4		7		36		24		40	
30	Captains, masters, mates, and pilots	203	203				1		11		13		21	
31	Longshoremen and stevedores	25, 444	25, 434	10	146		434	1	2, 249	2	3, 724		3, 768	1
32	Sailors and deck hands	6, 659	6, 656	3	110		228		1, 202		1, 246		966	
	Road and street transportation (selected occupations):													
33	Bus conductors	2	2						1					
34	Chauffeurs and truck and tractor drivers	108, 412	108, 241	171	1, 954	2	4, 289	17	19, 382	36	24, 175	27	19, 403	26
35	Draymen, teamsters, and carriage drivers [6]	19, 566	19, 549	17	477		550		1, 932	3	2, 156	1	2, 013	4
36	Garage owners, managers, and officials	646	641	5			4		40		108		129	
37	Garage owners and proprietors	424	420	4			3		16		62	1	76	
38	Garage managers and officials	222	221	1			1		24		46		53	
39	Garage laborers	23, 854	23, 750	104	883	4	1, 438	12	5, 734	26	6, 140	23	3, 794	13
40	Hostlers and stable hands	1, 590	1, 590		83		71		194		185		143	
41	Laborers, truck, transfer, and cab companies.	7, 055	7, 019	36	353	1	418	3	1, 077	7	1, 149	7	964	8
42	Laborers, road and street	59, 115	59, 082	33	1, 749	3	3, 275	6	10, 941	5	9, 992	4	7, 493	3
43	Road, street, etc., building and repairing	56, 286	56, 254	32	1, 719	3	3, 241	6	10, 734	5	9, 652	4	7, 167	3
44	Street cleaning	2, 829	2, 828	1	30		34		207		340		326	
45	Owners and managers, truck, transfer, and cab companies.	1, 878	1, 853	25			7		45		147	2	202	3
46	Owners and proprietors	1, 726	1, 704	22			6		39		136	2	184	3
47	Managers and officials	152	149	3			1		6		11		18	
	Railroad transportation (selected occupation):													
48	Baggagemen and freight agents	436	436				3		31		45		65	
49	Baggagemen	430	430				3		31		44		65	
50	Freight agents	6	6								1			
51	Boiler washers and engine hostlers	3, 813	3, 813		6		29		288		483		512	
52	Brakemen, steam railroad	3, 347	3, 347				6		155		332		430	
53	Conductors, steam railroad	35	35						2		4		3	
54	Conductors, street railroad	11	11				1				2		2	
55	Foremen and overseers	876	867	9					28		71	2	92	2
56	Steam railroad	831	823	8					28		67	2	89	2
57	Street railroad	45	44	1							4		3	
58	Laborers (includes construction laborers)	102, 685	101, 466	1, 219	1, 102	26	3, 090	38	16, 111	158	17, 389	204	14, 538	198
59	Steam railroad	97, 992	96, 865	1, 127	1, 076	25	3, 021	33	15, 598	152	16, 626	192	13, 830	177
60	Street railroad	4, 693	4, 601	92	26	1	69	5	513	6	763	12	708	21
61	Locomotive engineers	114	114				1		3		17		16	
62	Locomotive firemen	4, 642	4, 642				15		166		431		646	
63	Motormen	72	72						6		10		13	
64	Steam railroad	21	21						3		3		7	
65	Street railroad	51	51						3		7		6	
66	Officials and superintendents, steam railroad.	15	15										3	

See footnotes at end of table.

OCCUPATION, AGE, AND SEX, FOR THE UNITED STATES: 1930—Continued

head of table]

35 TO 39 YEARS		40 TO 44 YEARS		45 TO 49 YEARS		50 TO 54 YEARS		55 TO 59 YEARS		60 TO 64 YEARS		65 TO 69 YEARS		70 TO 74 YEARS		75 YEARS AND OVER		UNKNOWN		
Male	Female	Male	Female	Male	Female	Male	Female	Male	Female	Male	Female	Male	Female	Male	Female	Male	Female	Male	Female	
789	36	561	32	457	17	299	9	178	7	97		55		22		12	1	6		1
25	4	12	1	9		11	2	4	1	1		1								2
624	28	446	27	362	13	224	5	147	5	73		39		20		8	1	5		3
11	1	5	1	3	1	4		1								1				4
129	3	98	3	83	3	60	2	26	1	23		15		2		3		1		5
910	240	655	180	544	134	547	72	289	38	223	27	117	9	63	4	34	3	16	10	6
41	16	30	10	16	10	12	13	8	4	8	2	8	1	2		1				7
52	11	26	7	27	3	16	4	9		6		4		1		1				8
60	2	54		29	2	27	1	12		6		6				3		1		9
29	5	17	5	17	4	10	2	5	1	6		1	1	2	1	2				10
219	44	128	31	119	26	96	7	39	4	19	3	15	4	6		1	2	2	2	11
24	1	15	1	8	1	9		3		1				2						12
8	2	9	1	1	1	3		2				1	1							13
				2																14
27	1	16		18	2	7		11	1	1		3								15
1		3	1	4		3		1		1										16
159	40	85	28	86	22	74	7	22	3	16	3	11	3	4		1	2	2	2	17
9,127	364	6,957	231	6,145	199	5,067	111	2,666	57	1,791	38	877	28	379	9	226	6	136	11	18
27	3	9		13	1	9	1	4		4								1		19
2																1				20
725		549		477		342		178		92		40		30		9		11		21
205	3	114	3	104		61		46		17	1	9		2		3		3		22
217	3	118	3	102	3	67	1	27		11		7		3		1		3		23
2																		1		24
3,016	33	2,609	19	2,486	19	2,488	11	1,326	6	968	6	468	1	204		126	1	55		25
2,847	84	2,039	65	1,752	59	1,287	31	641	20	440	18	232	13	92	6	50	2	33	2	26
2,086	238	1,519	141	1,211	117	813	67	444	31	259	13	121	14	48	3	36	3	29	9	27
57,497	323	40,829	226	33,614	185	22,751	98	12,074	47	7,112	27	3,452	14	1,385	7	864	9	667	1	28
48		29		31		27		16		10		9		1						29
35		21		32		24		14		18		5		5		3				30
4,434	2	3,647		3,130	2	1,925	1	1,041	1	544		241		66		42		43		31
890	2	696		569		357	1	172		118		39		18		18		27		32
				1																33
16,272	25	9,518	18	6,503	12	3,681	6	1,576	2	790		338		116		77		167		34
2,334	3	2,209		2,297		2,046	1	1,342	1	975	3	606	1	342		236		34		35
130	2	91		68	2	47		12		9		1				1		1		36
95	1	64		51	2	36		7		7		1				1		1		37
35	1	27		17		11		5		2										38
2,797	9	1,357	5	824	10	433	1	169		59	1	46		18		11		37		39
191		154		158		140		108		77		45		20		19		2		40
894	5	617	3	596	1	430	1	222		149		67		42		29		12		41
7,282	4	5,369	2	4,692	4	3,596	1	2,067	1	1,321		704		316		193		92		42
6,959	4	5,058	1	4,369	4	3,310	1	1,872	1	1,133		584		236		140		80		43
323		311	1	323		286		195		188		120		80		53		12		44
272	2	294	9	312	5	236	1	143	1	97	1	63		24		8		3	1	45
251	2	271	6	286	5	217	1	131	1	92	1	59		21		8		3	1	46
21		23	3	26		19		12		5		4		3						47
82		60		65		40		26		12		4		1				2		48
80		59		64		39		26		12		4		1				2		49
2		1		1		1														50
698		598		520		363		179		90		31		6		3		7		51
662		632		556		321		139		72		25		5		1		11		52
6		7		3		4		1		2		3								53
4		1				1														54
135	2	134	2	154	1	125		68		37		19		1		2		1		55
131	2	128	1	145	1	118		63		33		17		1		2		1		56
4		6	1	9		7		5		4		2								57
14,972	203	11,200	140	9,582	116	6,556	61	3,468	33	1,976	17	888	9	265	7	140	9	189		58
14,224	184	10,681	130	9,043	110	6,207	57	3,286	28	1,873	16	840	7	245	7	136	9	179		59
748	19	519	10	539	6	349	4	182	5	103	1	48	2	20		4		10		60
17		14		16		14		9		4		2				1				61
961		877		708		455		221		105		42		8		3		4		62
21		5		9		2		4		1				1						63
7								1												64
14		5		9		2		3		1				1						65
1		2		1		1		4		1		2								66

TABLE 24.—NEGRO GAINFUL WORKERS 10 YEARS OLD AND OVER, BY

[See note at

	OCCUPATION	10 YEARS OLD AND OVER			10 TO 17 YEARS		18 AND 19 YEARS		20 TO 24 YEARS		25 TO 29 YEARS		30 TO 34 YEARS	
		Total	Male	Female	Male	Female	Male	Female	Male	Female	Male	Female	Male	Female
	Transportation and communication—Continued.													
	Railroad transportation (selected occupations)—Continued.													
1	Switchmen, flagmen, and yardmen	3, 446	3, 429	17	1	-	25	-	176	1	356	-	397	2
2	Switchmen and flagmen, steam railroad	2, 571	2, 554	17	-	-	16	-	113	1	243	-	275	2
3	Switchmen and flagmen, street railroad	52	52	-	-	-	-	-	2	-	7	-	3	-
4	Yardmen, steam railroad	823	823	-	1	-	9	-	61	-	106	-	119	-
5	Ticket and station agents	13	13	-	-	-	-	-	1	-	-	-	1	-
	Express, post, radio, telegraph, and telephone (selected occupations):													
6	Agents, express companies	6	5	1	-	-	-	1	-	-	1	-	-	-
7	Express messengers and railway mail clerks.	725	725	-	-	-	3	-	20	-	40	-	115	-
8	Express messengers	38	38	-	-	-	-	-	1	-	-	-	9	-
9	Railway mail clerks	687	687	-	-	-	3	-	19	-	40	-	106	-
10	Mail carriers	6, 312	6, 293	19	55	1	96	-	572	4	902	2	1, 214	3
11	Postmasters	78	36	42	-	-	-	-	3	4	3	2	2	4
12	Radio operators	8	8	-	-	-	-	-	3	-	2	-	1	-
13	Telegraph and telephone linemen	309	309	-	6	-	11	-	50	-	52	-	41	-
14	Telegraph messengers	178	177	1	67	-	37	1	33	-	11	-	4	-
15	Telegraph operators	44	36	8	1	-	-	2	4	3	1	2	5	1
16	Telephone operators	587	256	331	5	13	20	30	68	93	46	75	33	56
	Other transportation and communication pursuits:													
17	Apprentices	189	187	2	161	-	2	2	12	-	4	-	1	-
18	Steam railroad	15	15	-	-	-	-	-	7	-	2	-	-	-
19	Telegraph and telephone	1	1	-	1	-	-	-	-	-	-	-	-	-
20	Other transportation and communication.	173	171	2	160	-	2	2	5	-	2	-	1	-
21	Aviators	9	9	-	-	-	-	-	2	-	3	-	1	-
22	Foremen and overseers (n. o. s.)[2]	708	707	1	-	-	3	-	32	-	79	-	106	-
23	Air transportation	1	1	-	-	-	-	-	-	-	-	-	-	-
24	Garages, greasing stations, and automobile laundries.	245	244	1	-	-	2	-	25	-	55	-	55	-
25	Road, street, etc., building and repairing.	230	230	-	-	-	1	-	2	-	16	-	28	-
26	Telegraph and telephone	5	5	-	-	-	-	-	-	-	-	-	-	-
27	Other transportation and communication.	227	227	-	-	-	-	-	5	-	8	-	23	-
28	Inspectors	204	203	1	-	-	1	-	9	-	21	-	32	-
29	Steam railroad	172	172	-	-	-	1	-	8	-	17	-	29	-
30	Street railroad	10	10	-	-	-	-	-	-	-	1	-	3	-
31	Telegraph and telephone	2	1	1	-	-	-	-	-	-	-	-	-	-
32	Other transportation and communication.	20	20	-	-	-	-	-	1	-	3	-	-	-
33	Laborers (n. o. s.)[2]	8, 452	8, 424	28	147	4	253	2	1, 185	5	1, 441	3	1, 295	5
34	Air transportation	291	285	6	6	2	17	-	58	2	45	-	40	-
35	Express companies	1, 097	1, 096	1	23	-	34	-	131	-	172	-	197	1
36	Pipe lines	1, 030	1, 029	1	23	-	39	-	188	-	200	-	140	1
37	Telegraph and telephone	1, 357	1, 351	6	27	1	44	-	225	-	239	1	214	1
38	Water transportation [7]	2, 927	2, 926	1	64	-	100	-	418	1	517	-	418	-
39	Other transportation and communication.	1, 750	1, 737	13	4	1	19	2	165	2	268	2	286	2
40	Proprietors, managers, and officials (n. o. s.).[3]	54	54	-	-	-	-	-	-	-	2	-	7	-
41	Telegraph and telephone	2	2	-	-	-	-	-	-	-	-	-	-	-
42	Other transportation and communication.	52	52	-	-	-	-	-	-	-	2	-	7	-
43	Other occupations	5, 571	5, 446	125	85	5	126	8	639	21	768	19	844	18
44	Road, street, etc., building and repairing	383	382	1	6	1	12	-	57	-	52	-	52	-
45	Steam railroad	3, 381	3, 312	69	36	2	48	2	283	14	394	11	474	10
46	Street railroad	441	437	4	2	-	9	-	36	1	58	-	71	-
47	Other transportation and communication.	1, 366	1, 315	51	41	2	57	6	263	6	264	8	247	8
48	**Trade**	**183, 809**	**169, 241**	**14, 568**	**14, 646**	**371**	**10, 430**	**639**	**24, 576**	**1, 857**	**23, 441**	**1, 968**	**19, 385**	**1, 894**
49	Advertising agents	94	86	8	1	-	1	-	10	2	16	5	21	-
50	Apprentices, wholesale and retail trade	54	50	4	14	-	7	2	16	1	8	1	1	-
51	Bankers, brokers, and money lenders	267	249	18	-	-	1	-	10	4	22	2	31	3
52	Bankers and bank officials	80	68	12	-	-	-	-	3	4	9	2	10	2
53	Commercial brokers and commission men	21	21	-	-	-	-	-	1	-	-	-	2	-
54	Loan brokers and pawnbrokers	36	36	-	-	-	1	-	1	-	3	-	4	-
55	Stock brokers	95	90	5	-	-	-	-	5	-	7	-	9	-
56	Brokers not specified and promoters	35	34	1	-	-	-	-	-	-	3	-	6	1
57	"Clerks" in stores [8]	4, 911	3, 262	1, 649	379	79	385	141	659	361	482	252	337	222
58	Commercial travelers	534	444	90	-	-	12	-	35	7	46	12	56	9
59	Decorators, drapers, and window dressers	292	135	157	2	2	7	4	23	18	29	23	19	21
60	Deliverymen [9]	25, 299	25, 277	22	7, 314	4	3, 202	4	4, 245	8	2, 967	3	2, 044	2
61	Bakeries	230	230	-	60	-	27	-	36	-	38	-	21	-
62	Stores	25, 069	25, 047	22	7, 254	4	3, 175	4	4, 209	8	2, 929	3	2, 023	2
63	Floorwalkers, foremen, and overseers	448	424	24	-	-	1	2	15	3	30	7	54	2
64	Floorwalkers and foremen in stores	373	349	24	-	-	1	2	11	3	25	7	43	2
65	Foremen, warehouses, stockyards, etc	75	75	-	-	-	-	-	4	-	5	-	11	-
66	Inspectors, gaugers, and samplers	573	527	46	-	-	4	2	39	11	54	11	61	9

See footnotes at end of table.

OCCUPATION, AGE, AND SEX, FOR THE UNITED STATES: 1930—Continued

head of table]

35 TO 39 YEARS		40 TO 44 YEARS		45 TO 49 YEARS		50 TO 54 YEARS		55 TO 59 YEARS		60 TO 64 YEARS		65 TO 69 YEARS		70 TO 74 YEARS		75 YEARS AND OVER		UNKNOWN		
Male	Female	Male	Female	Male	Female	Male	Female	Male	Female	Male	Female	Male	Female	Male	Female	Male	Female	Male	Female	
572	3	531	3	508	5	367	2	229	1	150		67		28		16		6		1
427	3	401	3	395	5	287	2	182	1	121		55		20		14		5		2
5		6		9		10		6		2				2						3
140		124		104		70		41		27		12		6		2		1		4
1		1		3		2		2		2										5
2		1		1																6
137		130		124		86		48		16		6								7
2		13		7		1		3		1		1								8
135		117		117		85		45		15		5								9
1, 190	3	789	1	573		423	2	219	2	146	1	52		31		23		8		10
5	7	3	9	4	5	5	9	4		2	1	2	1	3						11
1		1																		12
43		47		29		15		8		5				1				1		13
2		5		6		3		3		4						2				14
11		6		4		3		1												15
27	33	17	11	23	10	8	6	7	1	2	1		2							16
5		1														1				17
4		1														1				18
																				19
1																				20
3																				21
119		104	1	105		67		49		23		15		5						22
		1																		23
44		25	1	21		7		3		4		2		1						24
31		38		41		29		25		13		4		2						25
2		1		2																26
42		39		41		31		21		6		9		2						27
35	1	27		25		25		18		5		4		1						28
27		23		21		21		17		4		3		1						29
2		2		1		1		1												30
	1																			31
6		2		3		3				1		1								32
1, 310	4	948	3	786	1	512		284		151	1	58		25		18		11		33
29	2	29		24		18		7		6		4		2						34
187		128		106		59		32		15		6		3		2		1		35
133		104		85		48		35		18		10		2		3		1		36
180	1	147	1	111		87		42		23	1	3		4		1		4		37
455		321		287		158		90		55		23		10		8		2		38
326	1	219	2	173	1	142		78		34		12		4		4		3		39
8		5		9		9		3		5		3				3				40
1				1																41
7		5		8		9		3		5		3				3				42
888	13	681	19	587	11	402	5	198	4	124	1	65	1	16		14		9		43
58		41		34		31		18		9		7		3		1		1		44
589	11	478	9	429	6	288	3	140		86	1	42		9		8		8		45
80		53	2	51	1	38		23		12		3				1				46
161	2	109	8	73	4	45	2	17	4	17		13	1	4		4				47
19, 794	**2, 257**	**15, 710**	**1, 766**	**14, 477**	**1, 616**	**11, 254**	**1, 009**	**6, 633**	**598**	**4, 338**	**296**	**2, 422**	**175**	**1, 103**	**61**	**786**	**37**	**246**	**24**	48
9		10	1	5		6		4		1		2								49
1				3																50
44	3	38	3	33	1	30	1	14		9	1	12		4		1				51
6	2	9	1	9		7		5		4	1	4		1		1				52
4		4		1		3		3				2		1						53
10		3		1		5		2		3		2		1						54
18	1	12	2	17	1	14	1	3		1		3		1						55
6		10		5		1		1		1		1								56
290	213	215	138	177	103	133	73	96	39	44	19	23	6	23		12		7	3	57
81	18	50	16	65	12	40	12	26	1	16	1	8	1	5		2		2	1	58
14	24	14	11	13	18	6	15	5	10	2	5	1	3		2		1			59
1, 838	1	1, 212		1, 013		664		356		196		119		39		41		27		60
15		8		11		8		1		3				1		1				61
1, 823	1	1, 204		1, 002		656		355		193		119		38		40		27		62
60	2	71	4	59	2	57		39	2	22		9		5		1		1		63
50	2	56	4	51	2	42		34	2	21		8		5		1		1		64
10		15		8		15		5		1		1								65
81	6	71	4	80	2	62		34	1	21		14		5		1				66

TABLE 24.—NEGRO GAINFUL WORKERS 10 YEARS OLD AND OVER, BY

[See note at

	OCCUPATION	10 YEARS OLD AND OVER			10 TO 17 YEARS		18 AND 19 YEARS		20 TO 24 YEARS		25 TO 29 YEARS		30 TO 34 YEARS	
		Total	Male	Female	Male	Female	Male	Female	Male	Female	Male	Female	Male	Female
	Trade—Continued.													
1	Insurance agents, managers, and officials	6,797	5,699	1,098	-	-	44	28	446	123	698	151	850	163
2	Insurance agents	6,286	5,200	1,086	-	-	44	28	430	122	659	149	775	162
3	Managers and officials, insurance companies.	511	499	12	-	-	-	-	16	1	39	2	75	1
4	Laborers in coal and lumber yards, warehouses, etc.	26,308	26,239	69	735	4	881	6	3,299	12	3,949	12	3,435	8
5	Coal yards and lumber yards	18,998	18,983	15	592	-	657	2	2,275	4	2,701	4	2,406	1
6	Grain elevators	692	692	-	8	-	19	-	80	-	100	-	101	-
7	Stockyards	1,982	1,982	-	20	-	50	-	245	-	377	-	321	-
8	Warehouses	4,081	4,033	48	100	4	136	3	618	7	699	7	538	7
9	Other and not specified trade	555	549	6	15	-	19	1	81	1	72	1	69	-
10	Laborers, porters, and helpers in stores	62,829	61,601	1,228	4,339	80	4,613	92	12,160	225	10,517	210	7,485	142
11	Newsboys	1,460	1,442	18	973	5	145	1	100	1	39	2	28	1
12	Proprietors, managers, and officials (n. o. s.[2])	357	180	177	-	-	-	1	3	7	10	11	17	17
13	Employment office keepers	287	114	173	-	-	-	1	-	7	6	11	9	16
14	Proprietors, etc., advertising agencies	2	2	-	-	-	-	-	-	-	-	-	-	-
15	Proprietors, etc., warehouses	18	18	-	-	-	-	-	-	-	-	-	1	-
16	Other proprietors, managers, and officials	50	46	4	-	-	-	-	3	-	4	-	7	1
17	Real estate agents and officials	4,050	3,577	473	-	-	10	2	97	23	259	53	445	70
18	Managers and officials, real estate companies.	21	20	1	-	-	-	-	2	-	3	-	1	-
19	Real estate agents	4,029	3,557	472	-	-	10	2	95	23	256	53	444	70
20	Retail dealers [10]	28,213	24,364	3,849	153	8	325	42	1,190	105	1,957	356	2,475	482
21	Automobiles and accessories	111	108	3	-	-	1	-	4	-	15	-	22	-
22	Books, music, news, and stationery	417	369	48	12	-	14	1	35	1	28	7	43	5
23	Buyers and shippers of livestock and other farm products.	149	149	-	-	-	4	-	9	-	5	-	8	-
24	Candy and confectionery	1,333	903	430	2	-	3	4	37	30	60	49	116	58
25	Cigars and tobacco	320	292	28	-	-	2	1	9	1	26	8	41	4
26	Coal and wood	1,853	1,793	60	-	-	15	1	54	5	127	2	152	6
27	Department stores	18	18	-	-	-	1	-	1	-	2	-	-	-
28	Dry goods, clothing, and boots and shoes	527	410	117	-	-	4	-	15	1	37	8	38	16
29	Drugs and medicines (including druggists and pharmacists).	1,482	1,314	168	-	-	7	2	87	29	218	38	241	34
30	5- and 10-cent and variety stores	37	30	7	-	-	-	-	3	-	5	1	6	-
31	Flour and feed	45	42	3	-	-	-	-	-	-	5	-	2	-
32	Food (except groceries and hucksters' goods).	3,496	3,329	167	38	-	98	3	383	12	399	20	432	23
33	Furniture, carpets, and rugs	250	228	22	-	-	1	-	3	1	8	2	15	2
34	Gasoline and oil filling stations	359	334	25	-	-	3	1	31	3	38	2	56	4
35	General stores	807	659	148	-	-	1	1	9	2	29	6	46	15
36	Groceries	7,547	5,739	1,808	5	1	23	11	98	62	265	133	475	229
37	Hardware, implements, and wagons	54	50	4	-	-	1	-	1	1	2	1	4	-
38	Hucksters and peddlers	4,356	3,944	412	96	7	110	14	236	27	313	22	373	37
39	Ice	775	772	3	-	-	8	-	39	-	69	-	80	1
40	Jewelry	88	87	1	-	-	-	-	2	-	4	1	7	-
41	Junk and rags	2,445	2,389	56	-	-	24	1	89	4	180	4	190	4
42	Lumber	183	183	-	-	-	-	-	2	-	13	-	16	-
43	Opticians	44	44	-	-	-	-	-	2	-	1	-	3	-
44	Other specified dealers	582	468	114	-	-	4	1	20	6	53	9	49	20
45	Not specified dealers	935	710	225	-	-	1	1	21	10	55	23	60	24
46	Salesmen and saleswomen	13,550	9,172	4,378	546	136	572	235	1,438	657	1,388	649	1,129	583
47	Auctioneers	11	11	-	-	-	-	-	1	-	-	-	2	-
48	Canvassers	1,187	475	712	12	12	11	17	40	43	49	86	52	79
49	Demonstrators	210	73	137	2	2	4	6	12	33	15	21	10	26
50	Sales agents	48	27	21	-	-	2	1	1	-	1	1	1	3
51	Salesmen and saleswomen	12,094	8,586	3,508	532	122	555	211	1,384	581	1,323	541	1,064	475
52	Undertakers	2,946	2,691	255	-	-	38	2	249	16	381	29	378	30
53	Wholesale dealers, importers, and exporters	130	129	1	-	-	-	-	4	-	17	-	14	-
54	Other pursuits in trade	4,697	3,693	1,004	190	53	182	75	538	183	572	199	505	130
55	Advertising agencies	137	134	3	4	-	7	-	19	1	22	-	18	1
56	Grain elevators	89	81	8	2	2	1	-	12	1	12	2	15	-
57	Stockyards	75	73	2	-	-	2	-	2	1	12	-	13	-
58	Warehouses and cold-storage plants	450	336	114	7	4	8	11	32	26	48	17	53	13
	Wholesale trade, and retail trade (except automobile):													
59	Fruit and vegetable graders and packers	216	172	44	11	6	16	6	27	12	28	5	20	2
60	Meat cutters	574	569	5	15	-	32	-	77	1	83	1	66	-
61	Other occupations	2,859	2,045	814	131	40	92	58	295	139	317	169	281	110
62	Other trade industries	297	283	14	20	1	24	-	74	2	50	5	39	4
63	**Public service (not elsewhere classified)**	**50,203**	**49,273**	**930**	**674**	**16**	**1,160**	**26**	**5,335**	**80**	**6,737**	**100**	**6,621**	**135**
64	Firemen, fire department	520	520	-	-	-	-	-	21	-	66	-	107	-
65	Guards, watchmen, and doorkeepers	6,111	6,039	72	11	-	45	-	237	4	457	7	467	7
66	Laborers, public service	34,924	34,422	502	643	16	905	26	3,858	62	4,904	62	4,645	61
67	Garbage men and scavengers	2,543	2,538	5	33	-	53	-	266	1	358	-	324	1
68	Other laborers	32,381	31,884	497	610	16	852	26	3,592	61	4,546	62	4,321	60
69	Marshals, sheriffs, detectives, etc	521	430	91	-	-	-	-	8	-	23	7	61	13
70	Detectives	157	151	6	-	-	-	-	3	-	10	1	25	-
71	Marshals and constables	80	80	-	-	-	-	-	2	-	6	-	9	-
72	Probation and truant officers	160	76	84	-	-	-	-	2	-	5	6	13	13
73	Sheriffs	124	123	1	-	-	-	-	1	-	2	-	14	-
74	Officials and inspectors (city and county)	263	236	27	-	-	-	-	5	1	15	5	16	5
75	Officials and inspectors (city)	218	201	17	-	-	-	-	4	-	12	4	15	3
76	Officials and inspectors (county)	45	35	10	-	-	-	-	1	1	3	1	1	2

See footnotes at end of table.

OCCUPATION, AGE, AND SEX, FOR THE UNITED STATES: 1930—Continued

head of table]

35 TO 39 YEARS		40 TO 44 YEARS		45 TO 49 YEARS		50 TO 54 YEARS		55 TO 59 YEARS		60 TO 64 YEARS		65 TO 69 YEARS		70 TO 74 YEARS		75 YEARS AND OVER		UNKNOWN		
Male	Female	Male	Female	Male	Female	Male	Female	Male	Female	Male	Female	Male	Female	Male	Female	Male	Female	Male	Female	
912	229	831	166	735	123	592	75	284	26	177	12	82	1	24	-	14	-	10	1	1
808	226	754	165	657	122	522	74	264	25	161	11	79	1	23	-	14	-	10	1	2
104	3	77	1	78	1	70	1	20	1	16	1	3	-	1	-	-	-	-	-	3
3,616	10	3,000	6	2,727	7	2,059	2	1,139	1	737	-	378	-	148	-	93	1	43	-	4
2,605	1	2,175	1	1,976	2	1,602	-	893	-	570	-	305	-	115	-	77	-	34	-	5
83	-	92	-	90	-	59	-	30	-	17	-	6	-	6	-	1	-	-	-	6
318	-	221	-	201	-	110	-	54	-	37	-	19	-	6	-	2	-	1	-	7
529	8	450	4	399	4	256	2	133	1	103	-	38	-	16	-	10	1	8	-	8
81	1	62	1	61	1	32	-	29	-	10	-	10	-	5	-	3	-	-	-	9
6,935	144	4,852	109	4,159	94	2,919	51	1,539	38	991	19	568	14	250	3	185	4	89	3	10
35	-	22	2	22	2	25	2	19	-	18	1	6	-	5	-	3	1	2	-	11
24	34	20	34	24	33	32	18	20	8	18	6	6	3	3	5	3	-	-	-	12
17	33	15	34	16	31	16	18	13	8	14	6	5	3	1	5	2	-	-	-	13
-	-	1	-	1	-	-	-	-	-	-	-	-	-	-	-	-	-	-	-	14
-	-	1	-	2	-	9	-	2	-	1	-	-	-	1	-	1	-	-	-	15
7	1	3	-	5	2	7	-	5	-	3	-	1	-	1	-	-	-	-	-	16
551	77	564	86	585	59	442	48	278	29	180	18	99	4	37	1	23	2	7	1	17
-	-	2	-	5	-	3	-	3	1	-	-	-	-	1	-	-	-	-	-	18
551	77	562	86	580	59	439	48	275	28	180	18	99	4	36	1	23	2	7	1	19
3,257	645	3,193	562	3,387	623	3,093	399	2,113	265	1,495	138	883	94	460	36	344	21	39	3	20
17	1	18	1	13	1	9	-	4	-	3	-	1	-	-	-	-	-	1	-	21
50	8	52	9	45	5	32	3	17	3	20	2	5	3	7	1	9	-	-	-	22
18	-	12	-	22	-	26	-	12	-	16	-	4	-	5	-	7	-	1	-	23
148	82	142	55	139	70	98	32	76	30	35	11	28	6	11	2	7	1	1	-	24
54	5	57	2	41	4	26	-	11	1	11	1	10	1	3	-	-	-	1	-	25
240	10	262	9	302	11	246	6	164	3	111	3	66	3	30	-	20	1	4	-	26
4	-	1	-	4	-	2	-	1	-	1	-	1	-	-	-	-	-	-	-	27
63	27	58	16	64	23	42	11	31	8	29	3	18	2	7	1	4	1	-	-	28
273	25	186	14	143	18	78	4	36	1	25	1	7	1	5	1	3	-	5	-	29
4	-	3	-	5	-	-	2	2	3	2	1	-	-	-	-	-	-	-	-	30
6	1	8	-	8	1	5	1	1	-	4	-	-	-	-	-	2	-	1	-	31
467	29	390	22	384	22	293	16	197	9	129	5	65	4	33	1	15	1	6	-	32
24	3	35	4	38	4	33	3	27	1	22	1	13	-	6	-	3	-	-	1	33
49	4	37	7	41	3	30	-	22	1	12	-	6	-	5	-	3	-	1	-	34
65	19	69	22	80	38	128	18	82	12	73	11	57	4	12	-	7	-	1	-	35
673	306	742	308	873	296	877	193	697	142	502	65	276	38	151	16	80	6	2	2	36
7	-	8	1	5	-	7	-	8	-	2	1	1	-	1	-	2	-	1	-	37
517	65	521	47	488	60	499	61	280	29	205	18	125	13	94	8	78	4	9	-	38
114	-	123	1	129	1	102	-	58	-	30	-	13	-	5	-	2	-	-	-	39
14	-	14	-	10	-	14	-	13	-	7	-	1	-	-	-	1	-	-	-	40
254	2	278	8	336	7	361	10	243	4	159	2	132	2	59	2	81	6	3	-	41
19	-	22	-	32	-	27	-	22	-	14	-	9	-	5	-	2	-	-	-	42
14	-	8	-	5	-	5	-	3	-	1	-	1	-	-	-	1	-	-	-	43
57	22	55	8	79	21	60	8	43	7	29	3	9	6	5	3	5	-	-	-	44
106	36	92	28	101	38	93	31	63	11	53	10	35	11	16	1	12	1	2	-	45
1,096	673	829	490	754	423	553	261	374	143	243	63	134	41	65	12	41	4	10	8	46
1	-	1	-	1	-	1	-	2	-	1	-	1	-	-	-	-	-	-	-	47
45	141	56	105	55	90	47	58	42	39	34	20	14	14	12	3	5	1	1	4	48
7	19	5	16	7	6	7	5	-	-	2	1	-	-	1	-	1	1	-	1	49
6	7	4	3	4	3	3	1	2	1	2	1	-	-	-	-	1	-	-	-	50
1,037	506	763	366	687	324	495	197	328	103	204	41	119	27	52	9	34	2	9	3	51
435	47	340	40	322	49	269	15	131	15	94	5	26	3	13	1	12	1	3	2	52
15	-	20	1	20	-	16	-	10	-	10	-	3	-	-	-	-	-	-	-	53
500	131	358	93	294	65	256	37	152	20	64	8	49	5	17	1	10	2	6	2	54
27	-	12	-	9	1	8	-	6	-	2	-	-	-	-	-	-	-	-	-	55
10	-	3	1	14	2	7	-	1	-	2	-	2	-	-	-	-	-	-	-	56
15	-	13	1	10	-	3	-	2	-	1	-	-	-	-	-	-	-	-	-	57
50	20	42	9	29	7	36	5	19	2	7	-	2	-	2	-	1	-	-	-	58
21	4	19	4	12	1	8	1	6	-	2	2	2	1	-	-	-	-	-	-	59
82	-	68	1	41	1	56	1	30	-	9	-	5	-	3	-	1	-	1	-	60
268	107	186	77	163	53	132	30	81	17	39	6	35	4	12	1	8	1	5	2	61
27	-	15	-	16	-	6	-	7	1	2	-	3	-	-	-	-	1	-	-	62
6,807	144	5,590	115	5,040	120	4,351	91	2,840	51	1,985	25	1,134	14	563	6	341	4	95	3	63
95	-	87	-	56	-	38	-	29	-	11	-	7	-	1	-	-	-	2	-	64
626	9	674	12	765	11	827	11	643	3	559	3	372	3	206	2	137	-	13	-	65
4,754	65	3,874	49	3,514	55	2,965	48	1,846	32	1,256	10	680	9	326	3	183	3	68	1	66
340	-	296	1	247	-	246	1	128	-	112	-	61	-	38	-	32	1	4	-	67
4,414	65	3,578	48	3,267	55	2,719	47	1,718	32	1,144	10	619	9	288	3	152	2	64	1	68
82	14	55	17	73	16	45	10	36	7	32	4	6	1	4	1	4	-	1	1	69
38	2	22	-	27	-	12	2	3	-	9	1	1	-	-	-	1	-	-	-	70
10	-	7	-	18	-	8	-	10	-	7	-	1	-	1	-	1	-	-	-	71
17	11	11	17	5	16	6	8	9	7	4	3	1	1	2	1	-	-	1	1	72
17	1	15	-	23	-	19	-	14	-	12	-	3	-	1	-	2	-	-	-	73
36	1	36	4	34	7	38	3	32	1	17	-	5	-	1	-	-	-	1	-	74
29	1	29	3	32	5	31	1	27	-	15	-	5	-	1	-	-	-	1	-	75
7	-	7	1	2	2	7	2	5	1	2	-	-	-	-	-	-	-	-	-	76

TABLE 24.—NEGRO GAINFUL WORKERS 10 YEARS OLD AND OVER, BY

[See note at

	OCCUPATION	10 YEARS OLD AND OVER			10 TO 17 YEARS		18 AND 19 YEARS		20 TO 24 YEARS		25 TO 29 YEARS		30 TO 34 YEARS	
		Total	Male	Female	Male	Female	Male	Female	Male	Female	Male	Female	Male	Female
	Public service (not elsewhere classified)—Continued.													
1	Officials and inspectors (State and United States.)	203	196	7					6	2	8	1	27	1
2	Officials and inspectors (State)	16	15	1					1		1		1	
3	Officials and inspectors (United States)	187	181	6					5	2	7	1	26	1
4	Policemen	1, 297	1, 264	33					19		124	1	219	5
5	Soldiers, sailors, and marines [11]	4, 601	4, 601		13		164		1, 022		939		872	
6	Other public service pursuits	1, 763	1, 565	198	7		46		159	11	201	17	207	43
7	**Professional service**	**135, 925**	**72, 898**	**63, 027**	**2, 654**	**595**	**2, 161**	**2, 993**	**6, 935**	**8, 057**	**7, 993**	**13, 178**	**7, 922**	**8, 102**
8	Actors and showmen	4, 130	2, 732	1, 398	89	64	168	161	668	531	585	331	413	157
9	Actors	2, 626	1, 327	1, 299	54	61	74	143	275	501	288	310	212	143
10	Showmen	1, 504	1, 405	99	35.	3	94	18	393	30	297	21	201	14
11	Architects	63	63						2		6		11	
12	Artists, sculptors, and teachers of art	430	230	200	4	1	7	6	45	51	37	41	39	15
13	Authors, editors, and reporters	425	341	84			2	3	37	11	57	12	39	13
14	Authors	49	41	8					6	2	7	2	5	1
15	Editors and reporters	376	300	76			2	3	31	9	50	10	34	12
16	Chemists, assayers, and metallurgists	361	347	14			4		31	2	69	4	56	2
17	Clergymen	25, 034	24, 540	494					225	14	694	30	1, 577	56
18	College presidents and professors [12]	2, 146	1, 126	1, 020					137	270	251	303	193	138
19	Dentists	1, 773	1, 746	27					40	1	212	5	483	6
20	Designers, draftsmen, and inventors	217	119	98			3	3	19	27	23	29	17	14
21	Designers	117	20	97			2	3	5	27	4	28	1	14
22	Draftsmen	83	82	1			1		14		19	1	15	
23	Inventors	17	17										1	
24	Lawyers, judges, and justices	1, 247	1, 223	24					31		93	3	195	7
25	Musicians and teachers of music	10, 583	7, 747	2, 836	107	55	340	114	1, 699	513	1, 769	523	1, 228	466
26	Osteopaths	19	14	5							2	1	1	1
27	Photographers	545	460	85	3	1	11	4	39	18	51	13	78	23
28	Physicians and surgeons	3, 805	3, 713	92					22	1	251	9	477	16
29	Teachers	54, 683	8, 955	45, 728	20	319	92	2, 009	1, 086	14, 017	1, 576	10, 053	1, 137	5, 834
30	Teachers (athletics, dancing, etc.)	244	188	56	1		3	9	26	17	40	17	29	7
31	Teachers (school)	54, 439	8, 767	45, 672	19	319	89	2, 000	1, 060	14, 000	1, 536	10, 036	1, 108	5, 827
32	Technical engineers	351	351						19		42		64	
33	Civil engineers and surveyors	160	160						8		22		23	
34	Electrical engineers	119	119						7		15		26	
35	Mechanical engineers [13]	70	70						4		5		15	
36	Mining engineers [14]	2	2											
37	Trained nurses	5, 728	147	5, 581	1	39	6	458	33	1, 730	26	1, 017	14	685
38	Veterinary surgeons	134	133	1					8		12		14	
39	Other professional pursuits	1, 810	529	1, 281			4	13	36	180	70	205	71	176
40	County agents, farm demonstrators, etc	226	136	90					2	9	13	16	14	17
41	Librarians	210	30	180				3		42	5	32	6	31
42	Social and welfare workers	1, 038	211	827			3	5	31	99	34	116	28	104
43	Other occupations	336	152	184			1	5	3	30	18	41	23	24
44	Semiprofessional and recreational pursuits	6, 343	4, 625	1, 718	80	2	83	7	271	109	418	153	523	189
45	Abstracters, notaries, and justices of peace	57	34	23					1	1	2	1	2	3
46	Architects', designers', and draftsmen's apprentices.	6	3	3	1	2	1	1	1					
47	Apprentices to other professional persons	16	15	1	4		5		4		1	1	1	
48	Billiard room, dance hall, skating rink, etc., keepers.	1, 935	1, 914	21			12		107		199	2	273	7
49	Chirpractors	184	142	42					3	2	8	5	14	5
50	Directors, managers, and officials, motion-picture production.	5	5								1		1	
51	Healers (not elsewhere classified)	901	518	383					7	19	29	32	49	40
52	Keepers of charitable and penal institutions.	202	96	106					2	4	6	3	10	10
53	Keepers of pleasure resorts, race tracks, etc.	109	99	10					5	2	8	1	4	3
54	Officials of lodges, societies, etc	451	287	164			1	1	5	12	12	18	15	16
55	Radio announcers, directors, managers, and officials.	4	4				1		2					
56	Religious workers	1, 196	434	762	8		16	2	14	49	28	64	40	74
57	Technicians and laboratory assistants	196	151	45			2	2	26	12	19	10	24	10
58	Theatrical owners, managers, and officials	166	155	11			2		15	1	17	1	24	2
59	Other occupants	915	768	147	67		43	1	79	7	88	15	66	19
60	Attendants and helpers, professional service	16, 098	13, 757	2, 341	2, 350	114	1, 441	215	2, 487	582	1, 749	446	1, 292	304
61	Attendants, pool rooms, bowling alleys, golf clubs, etc.	4, 120	4, 049	71	1, 724	3	752	8	735	24	305	17	177	15
62	Dentists' assistants and attendants	270	37	233	5	7	9	12	4	53	6	49	2	47
63	Helpers, motion-picture production	14	12	2					5	1	2			
64	Laborers, professional service	4, 147	3, 906	241	179	9	205	22	671	55	593	35	486	19
65	Laborers, recreation and amusement	4, 442	4, 349	93	328	8	357	10	791	17	612	13	470	6
66	Librarians' assistants and attendants	15	12	3					1	1	3		2	1
67	Physicians' and surgeons' attendants	1, 039	106	933	18	35	17	98	15	247	11	216	8	125
68	Stage hands and circus helpers	104	90	14	13	1	10	3	23	1	22	2	7	2
69	Theater ushers	409	285	124	42	9	43	14	74	50	44	20	23	16
70	Other attendants and helpers	1, 538	911	627	41	42	48	48	168	133	151	94	117	73
71	**Domestic and personal service**	**1, 576, 205**	**423, 645**	**1, 152, 560**	**15, 477**	**47, 022**	**19, 673**	**60, 017**	**63, 006**	**183, 247**	**64, 087**	**184, 772**	**54, 355**	**147, 806**
72	Barbers, haridressers, and manicurists	34, 263	21, 447	12, 816	205	95	342	228	1, 680	1, 279	2, 357	2, 406	2, 478	2, 557
73	Boarding and lodging house keepers	13, 109	997	12, 112			7	107	27	684	77	1, 444	91	1, 753
74	Bootblacks	9, 499	9, 481	18	2, 117	5	1, 596	2	2, 146	2	1, 087	2	656	3
75	Charwomen and cleaners	16, 117	4, 622	11, 495	114	286	164	478	602	1, 381	712	1, 643	576	1, 468

See footnotes at end of table.

OCCUPATION, AGE, AND SEX, FOR THE UNITED STATES: 1930—Continued

head of table]

35 TO 39 YEARS		40 TO 44 YEARS		45 TO 49 YEARS		50 TO 54 YEARS		55 TO 59 YEARS		60 TO 64 YEARS		65 TO 69 YEARS		70 TO 74 YEARS		75 YEARS AND OVER		UNKNOWN		
Male	Female	Male	Female	Male	Female	Male	Female	Male	Female	Male	Female	Male	Female	Male	Female	Male	Female	Male	Female	
30	2	33	1	34		27		16		8		3		4						1
3	1	1		1		2		2		1		1		1						2
27	1	32	1	33		25		14		7		2		3						3
250	9	212	7	167	6	135	5	88		29		13		7		1				4
740		436		227		114		53		9		4		2		3		3		5
194	44	183	25	170	25	162	14	9 7	8	64	8	44	1	12		12	1	1	1	6
8,900	**7,187**	**8,268**	**4,695**	**8,566**	**3,699**	**7,514**	**2,257**	**4,752**	**1,175**	**3,466**	**572**	**1,970**	**256**	**1,034**	**83**	**634**	**50**	**129**	**128**	7
304	84	180	34	121	17	95	6	38	2	24	2	9		12		6	1	20	8	8
174	77	98	31	59	17	46	6	17	2	7		1		3				19	8	9
130	7	82	3	62		49		21		17	2	8		9		6	1	1		10
12		10		9		10		3												11
34	32	21	19	20	22	12	5	6	3	3	3		2	1				1		12
41	15	36	7	33	10	39	9	21	3	18	1	9		4		4		1		13
5		4		6		3	2	2	1	3										14
36	15	32	7	27	10	36	7	19	2	15	1	9		4		4		1		15
68	2	39	1	35		23	1	6	1	8		3		4		1			1	16
2,887	81	3,583	84	4,277	81	4,092	67	2,662	38	2,114	22	1,265	9	691	4	429	7	44	1	17
148	106	96	65	92	51	70	39	55	28	33	11	31	5	13		6		1	4	18
419	5	269	6	153	3	91	1	56		12		6		2		1		2		19
15	12	12	4	5	3	11	4	7	2	4		2		1						20
2	12	3	4		3		4	2	2	1										21
13		7		3		5		3		1		1								22
		2		2		6		2		2		1		1						23
218	6	147	5	141	2	140	1	96		76		46		25		13		2		24
955	443	656	279	454	204	275	118	133	69	74	22	22	18	16	4	10	5	9	3	25
2	1	4	1	1	1	2		1				1								26
85	12	75	6	47	2	35	2	19	2	14	1	1		1		1			1	27
571	16	638	9	650	11	470	8	275	13	204	6	93	3	31		21		10		28
1,070	5,142	863	3,219	920	2,412	819	1,446	581	696	413	318	221	119	104	42	44	15	9	87	29
26	3	19	1	24	1	9		4		4			1	1		2				30
1,044	5,139	844	3,218	896	2,411	810	1,446	577	696	409	318	221	118	103	42	42	15	9	87	31
55		45		51		34		26		8		3		4						32
22		19		27		16		15		4		2		2						33
25		11		15		12		5		3										34
8		14		9		6		6		1				2						35
		1										1								36
21	558	13	380	10	311	11	190	5	99	1	64	5	34	1	8		1		7	37
17	1	15		21		11		13		8		7		3		4				38
89	184	82	156	66	147	42	97	34	65	18	28	10	17	6	3	1	3		7	39
36	17	28	11	17	11	10	6	10	1	3		2		1					2	40
5	20	3	19	4	11	3	9	2	7		3	1	1	1	1				1	41
28	120	28	111	23	103	13	77	9	47	6	22	6	15	2	1		3		4	42
20	27	23	15	22	22	16	5	13	10	9	3	1	1	2	1	1				43
705	247	640	268	629	297	551	196	317	116	197	66	99	37	66	15	41	12	5	4	44
3	8	5	6			9	3	2	1	6		2		2						45
																				46
																				47
351	4	300	3	256	1	215	3	105	1	52		27		10		5		2		48
29	8	29	9	22	4	21	6	6	3	2		6		2						49
				2						1										50
69	52	59	62	73	68	83	45	46	30	54	15	16	12	16	4	16	2	1	2	51
8	13	13	16	19	22	11	13	14	8	5	7	2	3	3	4	3	2		1	52
23	1	12	2	18		7	1	9		7		4		1		1				53
27	24	39	21	63	33	60	19	24	10	18	6	15	3	8	1					54
						1														55
51	107	44	113	68	149	52	89	44	52	30	34	15	17	13	6	10	6	1	3	56
31	3	27	3	11	3	6	2	3		1		1								57
22	2	22	3	18	1	17		12		5		1	1							58
91	25	90	30	79	16	69	15	52	11	16	4	10	1	11		6	2	1	1	59
1,184	240	844	152	831	125	681	67	398	38	237	28	137	12	49	7	52	6	25	5	60
130	2	85	1	60		43		19		13		3						3	1	61
3	32	2	14	2	12	4	4		3											62
		1	1	2						1				1						63
454	31	332	19	325	16	275	13	157	4	100	10	66	4	23	2	32	1	8	1	64
442	11	333	5	357	7	285	10	174	1	98	3	54	2	22		13		13		65
		1		3	1	2														66
16	83	7	47	3	44	5	14	3	11	1	8	2	2				3			67
5	1	2	3	1		2	1	3		2										68
17	4	15	8	10		8		2	1	2	1	3	1	1		1				69
117	76	66	54	68	45	57	25	40	18	20	6	9	3	2	5	6	2	1	3	70
54,091	**153,651**	**42,984**	**115,012**	**37,583**	**97,925**	**29,061**	**68,942**	**17,415**	**37,547**	**11,881**	**26,771**	**6,992**	**15,124**	**3,495**	**7,142**	**2,752**	**5,123**	**793**	**2,459**	71
3,045	2,767	2,816	1,530	2,701	1,086	2,264	501	1,516	203	1,029	74	546	37	265	21	154	10	49	22	72
121	2,165	118	1,765	148	1,637	143	1,109	87	629	76	381	43	237	32	111	24	78	3	21	73
525	2	437	1	321		242		143	1	104		60		16		20		11		74
607	1,703	515	1,365	445	1,280	356	836	202	482	150	297	97	136	41	61	35	40	6	39	75

TABLE 24.—NEGRO GAINFUL WORKERS 10 YEARS OLD AND OVER, BY

[See note at

	OCCUPATION	10 YEARS OLD AND OVER			10 TO 17 YEARS		18 AND 19 YEARS		20 TO 24 YEARS		25 TO 29 YEARS		30 TO 34 YEARS	
		Total	Male	Female	Male	Female	Male	Female	Male	Female	Male	Female	Male	Female
	Domestic and personal service—Contd.													
1	Cleaning, dyeing, and pressing shop workers	15,773	12,573	3,200	595	75	829	168	2,659	617	2,478	781	1,915	567
2	Owners and proprietors	1,464	1,398	66	-------	-------	9	-------	68	3	173	13	240	9
3	Managers and officials	270	261	9	-------	-------	1	-------	16	-------	34	1	45	3
4	Foremen and overseers	20	12	8	-------	-------	-------	-------	-------	1	1	1	3	1
5	Laborers	1,388	1,241	147	102	6	112	7	335	32	246	35	164	26
6	Other operatives	12,631	9,661	2,970	493	69	707	161	2,240	581	2,024	731	1,463	528
7	Elevator tenders	16,889	12,446	4,443	444	163	1,114	515	3,059	1,561	2,477	1,068	1,636	509
8	Hotel keepers and managers	1,064	741	323	-------	-------	3	-------	18	10	45	19	76	43
9	Housekeepers and stewards	19,865	2,046	17,819	-------	-------	33	618	157	2,315	230	2,516	273	2,309
10	Hotels, restaurants, boarding houses, etc	1,638	606	1,032	-------	-------	10	16	47	79	61	122	61	158
11	Other housekeepers and stewards	18,227	1,440	16,787	-------	-------	23	602	110	2,236	169	2,394	212	2,151
12	Janitors and sextons	78,415	72,382	6,033	847	57	1,530	114	5,857	472	7,525	665	8,056	740
13	Laborers, domestic and personal service	22,934	21,650	1,284	1,270	65	1,016	74	2,658	192	2,492	186	2,085	165
14	Launderers and laundresses (not in laundry)	271,083	1,985	269,098	98	4,815	75	6,861	204	24,319	224	31,075	207	30,702
15	Laundry owners, managers, and officials [15]	335	239	96	-------	-------	1	-------	5	4	17	8	31	9
16	Owners and proprietors	247	184	63	-------	-------	1	-------	1	1	11	2	26	6
17	Managers and officials	88	55	33	-------	-------	-------	-------	4	3	6	6	5	3
18	Laundry operatives [15]	58,080	10,534	47,546	471	1,934	638	3,090	2,011	9,588	2,215	9,514	1,699	6,697
19	Deliverymen [9]	504	503	1	48	1	38	-------	89	-------	89	-------	67	-------
20	Foremen and overseers	165	86	79	-------	-------	1	-------	5	11	21	16	17	13
21	Laborers	5,288	2,785	2,503	152	142	190	180	514	535	599	444	396	316
22	Other operatives	52,123	7,160	44,963	271	1,791	409	2,910	1,403	9,042	1,506	9,054	1,219	6,368
23	Midwives and nurses (not trained)	18,052	2,207	15,845	-------	-------	127	1,394	557	2,442	434	1,566	326	1,109
24	Midwives	1,787	-------	1,787	-------	-------	-------	-------	-------	7	-------	18	-------	27
25	Nurses (not trained)	16,265	2,207	14,058	-------	-------	127	1,394	557	2,435	434	1,548	326	1,082
26	Porters (except in stores)	93,744	93,714	30	2,406	2	4,191	3	15,414	6	16,239	5	13,543	3
27	Domestic and personal service	40,367	40,355	12	1,535	1	2,566	1	8,447	2	7,692	3	5,638	-------
28	Professional service	2,930	2,928	2	72	-------	205	-------	671	-------	531	-------	384	1
29	Steam railroad	25,585	25,584	1	95	-------	246	-------	2,084	-------	3,672	-------	3,868	-------
30	Other porters (except in stores)	24,862	24,847	15	704	1	1,174	2	4,212	4	4,344	2	3,653	2
31	Restaurant, cafe, and lunch-room keepers	10,543	5,365	5,178	-------	-------	17	17	152	192	394	540	596	705
	Servants:													
32	Cooks	279,621	47,617	232,004	301	3,273	1,436	11,818	6,727	41,598	8,300	41,038	7,083	31,530
33	Hotels, restaurants, boarding houses, etc.	59,083	30,139	28,944	190	253	951	1,015	4,482	4,002	5,484	4,947	4,593	4,308
34	Other cooks	220,538	17,478	203,060	111	3,020	485	10,803	2,245	37,596	2,816	36,091	2,490	27,222
35	Other servants	557,307	61,969	495,338	5,645	35,342	4,602	32,843	11,815	91,503	9,762	86,108	7,150	64,576
36	Hotels, restaurants, boarding houses, etc.	63,215	23,573	39,642	2,170	1,529	2,721	2,168	6,549	7,960	4,413	8,713	2,610	6,391
37	Other domestic and personal service	494,092	38,396	455,696	3,475	33,813	1,881	30,675	5,266	83,543	5,349	77,395	4,540	58,185
38	Waiters	57,378	39,750	17,628	953	908	1,920	1,684	7,137	5,060	6,843	4,161	5,670	2,338
39	Other pursuits	2,134	1,880	254	11	2	32	3	121	22	179	27	208	23
40	Cemetery keepers	352	346	6	-------	-------	4	-------	19	-------	15	-------	20	1
41	Hunters, trappers, and guides	235	235	-------	3	-------	12	-------	19	-------	38	-------	22	-------
42	Other occupations	1,547	1,299	248	8	2	16	3	83	22	126	27	166	22
43	**Clerical occupations**	**40,549**	**29,687**	**10,862**	**1,625**	**260**	**1,405**	**821**	**3,828**	**3,158**	**4,350**	**2,487**	**4,349**	**1,514**
44	Agents, collectors, and credit men	1,527	1,182	345	4	1	27	8	94	35	148	41	150	53
45	Agents (not elsewhere classified)	518	355	163	3	-------	9	4	20	10	38	15	44	28
46	Collectors	965	797	168	1	1	17	3	70	21	108	23	103	23
47	Credit men	6	4	2	-------	-------	-------	-------	2	-------	1	-------	-------	1
48	Purchasing agents (except for railroads)	38	26	12	-------	-------	1	1	2	4	1	3	3	1
49	Bookkeepers, cashiers, and accountants	2,731	747	1,984	11	46	28	150	90	595	145	443	124	285
50	Accountants and auditors	168	154	14	-------	-------	1	1	13	2	18	3	34	4
51	Bookkeepers and cashiers	2,563	593	1,970	11	46	27	149	77	593	127	440	90	281
52	Clerks (except "clerks" in stores)	25,185	20,255	4,930	254	125	510	305	2,592	1,221	3,349	1,050	3,378	741
53	Office-appliance operators	245	131	114	2	-------	5	1	17	13	19	12	16	24
54	Shipping clerks	4,208	4,077	131	47	3	144	5	712	30	769	36	666	25
55	Weighers	498	462	36	4	1	9	4	65	9	71	6	61	7
56	Other clerks	20,234	15,585	4,649	201	121	352	295	1,798	1,169	2,490	996	2,635	685
57	Messenger, errand, and office boys and girls [16]	7,621	7,243	378	1,355	43	825	56	1,004	100	652	62	657	47
58	Stenographers and typists	3,485	260	3,225	1	45	15	302	48	1,207	56	891	40	388

[1] Many of the machinists' apprentices probably are machine tenders.
[2] Not otherwise specified.
[3] Includes tin-plate mills.
[4] Includes iron foundries.
[5] Includes box factories (wood).
[6] Teamsters in agriculture, forestry, and the extraction of minerals are classified with the other workers in those industries, respectively; drivers for bakeries and stores are classified as deliverymen in trade; and drivers for laundries are classified as deliverymen in domestic and personal service.
[7] Most of these are construcing canals, docks, harbors, etc.
[8] Includes only persons specifically returned as "clerks" in stores. Many of these probably are "salesmen and saleswomen."

OCCUPATION, AGE, AND SEX, FOR THE UNITED STATES: 1930—Continued

head of table]

35 TO 39 YEARS		40 TO 44 YEARS		45 TO 49 YEARS		50 TO 54 YEARS		55 TO 59 YEARS		60 TO 64 YEARS		65 TO 69 YEARS		70 TO 74 YEARS		75 YEARS AND OVER		UNKNOWN		
Male	Female	Male	Female	Male	Female	Male	Female	Male	Female	Male	Female	Male	Female	Male	Female	Male	Female	Male	Female	
1,756	503	1,052	246	653	128	356	56	148	21	70	16	23	7	13	5	10	3	16	7	1
319	22	219	3	182	8	107	4	45	1	21	1	8	1	1	1	1	-	5	-	2
61	1	54	3	26	1	15	-	4	-	3	-	1	-	1	-	-	-	-	-	3
3	1	3	1	-	1	-	-	1	1	1	-	-	-	-	1	-	-	-	-	4
129	17	54	11	43	5	28	3	12	3	9	-	2	1	2	-	1	-	2	1	5
1,244	462	722	228	402	113	206	49	86	16	36	15	12	5	9	3	8	3	9	6	6
1,235	337	855	158	629	72	424	34	255	13	162	6	77	3	41	-	23	-	14	4	7
120	65	120	65	129	46	98	30	66	18	27	12	23	12	11	1	3	1	2	1	8
275	2,510	293	2,061	273	1,838	198	1,412	140	841	94	624	42	388	20	200	12	157	6	30	9
73	187	92	145	73	105	62	99	60	55	32	30	20	28	8	6	5	2	2	-	10
202	2,323	201	1,916	200	1,733	136	1,313	80	786	62	594	22	360	12	194	7	155	4	30	11
9,439	934	8,898	833	8,962	796	7,919	588	5,093	360	3,767	234	2,323	143	1,217	57	815	31	134	9	12
2,208	162	1,911	127	1,926	96	1,829	90	1,233	36	1,184	32	796	21	492	23	502	12	48	3	13
246	38,976	211	34,434	223	33,076	169	25,786	99	15,110	108	11,542	67	6,633	22	3,156	27	2,149	5	464	14
43	19	41	24	34	11	28	10	17	4	9	3	7	3	5	1	1	-	-	-	15
34	11	30	17	25	9	24	8	12	3	8	2	6	3	5	1	1	-	-	-	16
9	8	11	7	9	2	4	2	5	1	1	1	1	-	-	-	-	-	-	-	17
1,462	6,225	833	3,959	557	2,932	322	1,785	167	836	75	496	41	239	15	96	15	61	13	94	18
77	-	44	-	18	-	16	-	7	-	4	-	4	-	1	-	1	-	-	-	19
12	18	10	8	7	5	5	4	3	2	3	-	1	2	1	-	-	-	-	-	20
354	305	225	202	149	157	109	98	50	61	23	41	12	15	3	4	7	2	2	1	21
1,019	5,902	554	3,749	383	2,770	192	1,683	107	773	45	455	24	222	10	92	7	59	11	93	22
259	1,305	149	1,304	128	1,562	86	1,560	52	1,152	36	1,000	26	707	12	393	10	326	5	25	23
-	59	-	142	-	227	-	281	-	264	-	286	-	202	-	138	-	134	-	2	24
259	1,246	149	1,162	128	1,335	86	1,279	52	888	36	714	26	505	12	255	10	192	5	23	25
13,177	2	9,541	2	7,868	4	5,387	2	2,902	1	1,611	-	809	-	298	-	166	-	162	-	26
4,984	1	3,356	2	2,506	-	1,675	1	935	1	518	-	252	-	106	-	77	-	68	-	27
319	-	252	-	185	1	145	-	69	-	42	-	25	-	9	-	9	-	10	-	28
4,466	1	3,559	-	3,157	-	2,262	-	1,114	-	613	-	314	-	70	-	18	-	46	-	29
3,408	-	2,374	-	2,020	3	1,305	1	784	-	438	-	218	-	113	-	62	-	38	-	30
857	1,065	876	900	843	782	745	491	429	268	242	130	123	58	53	16	26	6	12	8	31
6,941	31,913	5,239	23,241	4,565	18,747	3,218	12,940	1,807	6,536	1,021	4,521	558	2,489	197	1,067	143	756	81	537	32
4,441	4,718	3,212	3,508	2,755	2,751	1,911	1,738	1,006	839	586	452	314	243	94	66	69	45	51	59	33
2,500	27,195	2,027	19,733	1,810	15,996	1,307	11,202	801	5,697	435	4,069	244	2,246	103	1,001	74	711	30	478	34
6,204	61,226	4,534	42,118	3,671	33,303	2,890	21,465	1,801	10,935	1,407	7,352	1,021	3,985	634	1,925	681	1,486	152	1,166	35
1,872	5,451	1,140	3,313	802	2,068	545	1,046	304	440	197	272	110	115	53	53	39	41	48	82	36
4,332	55,775	3,394	38,805	2,869	31,240	2,345	20,419	1,497	10,495	1,210	7,080	911	3,870	581	1,872	642	1,445	104	1,084	37
5,293	1,723	4,310	844	3,276	486	2,170	228	1,114	90	616	41	253	22	75	8	48	6	72	29	38
278	49	235	44	231	38	217	19	144	11	92	10	57	4	36	1	37	1	2	-	39
22	1	29	2	46	1	36	1	48	-	33	-	31	-	20	-	23	-	-	-	40
28	-	20	-	20	-	27	-	14	-	16	-	8	-	6	-	2	-	-	-	41
228	48	186	42	165	37	154	18	82	11	43	10	18	4	10	1	12	1	2	-	42
4,087	**1,116**	**3,102**	**650**	**2,574**	**451**	**2,008**	**207**	**1,086**	**107**	**672**	**51**	**351**	**10**	**139**	**8**	**76**	**6**	**35**	**16**	43
183	60	142	64	142	37	113	21	82	12	49	8	30	2	11	1	7	2	-	-	44
57	30	41	35	46	15	39	10	30	7	16	4	8	2	3	1	1	2	-	-	45
122	29	98	28	93	21	69	10	49	5	33	4	21	-	8	-	5	-	-	-	46
-	-	-	-	-	-	-	1	-	-	-	-	-	-	-	-	1	-	-	-	47
4	1	3	1	3	1	5	-	3	-	-	-	1	-	-	-	-	-	-	-	48
105	215	72	126	72	72	41	28	24	16	13	5	15	-	7	1	-	-	-	2	49
27	2	18	-	19	-	14	1	2	1	6	-	-	-	2	-	-	-	-	-	50
78	213	54	126	53	72	27	27	22	15	7	5	15	-	5	1	-	-	-	2	51
3,148	599	2,370	351	1,850	273	1,409	135	683	73	404	33	188	5	64	4	32	2	24	13	52
20	18	17	20	14	14	9	5	4	5	4	1	2	-	1	-	1	-	-	1	53
585	15	396	5	312	7	233	-	117	2	54	3	29	-	6	-	4	-	3	-	54
70	2	56	3	48	2	41	-	18	2	9	-	4	-	5	-	1	-	-	-	55
2,473	564	1,901	323	1,476	250	1,126	130	544	64	337	29	153	5	52	4	26	2	21	12	56
626	24	490	19	491	15	429	3	290	3	202	4	117	-	57	-	37	1	11	1	57
25	218	28	90	19	54	16	20	7	3	4	1	1	3	-	2	-	1	-	-	58

[9] Some deliverymen probably were returned and classified as chauffeurs, and others as teamsters or truck drivers.
[10] Includes also managers and superintendents of retail stores.
[11] Includes only those resident in continental United States at date of enumeration.
[12] Probably includes some teachers in schools below collegiate rank.
[13] Includes also all technical engineers not elsewhere classified.
[14] Includes also chemical and metallurgical engineers.
[15] Some owners of hand laundries probably are included with laundry operatives.
[16] Except telegraph messengers.

TABLE 25.—GAINFULLY OCCUPIED NEGRO WOMEN 15 YEARS OLD AND OVER, BY OCCUPATION AND MARITAL CONDITION, WITH A DISTRIBUTION OF THE SINGLE AND UNKNOWN AND OF THE MARRIED BY AGE, FOR THE UNITED STATES: 1930

OCCUPATION	Total	SINGLE AND UNKNOWN					MARRIED						Widowed and divorced
		Total	15 to 19 years	20 to 24 years	25 to 44 years	45 years and over (incl. unkn.)	Total	15 to 19 years	20 to 24 years	25 to 34 years	35 to 44 years	45 years and over (incl. unkn.)	
All occupations	**1,776,922**	**499,934**	**181,773**	**144,773**	**145,669**	**27,719**	**795,032**	**33,680**	**123,627**	**273,031**	**212,733**	**151,961**	**481,956**
Agriculture	**438,851**	**143,914**	**86,809**	**33,210**	**19,706**	**4,189**	**184,449**	**14,764**	**32,774**	**51,575**	**44,072**	**41,264**	**110,488**
Farmers (owners and tenants)	76,422	5,667		976	2,995	1,696	11,934		884	2,711	3,787	4,552	58,821
Farm managers and foremen	21	1				1	2					2	18
Farm laborers	362,408	138,246	86,809	32,234	16,711	2,492	172,513	14,764	31,890	48,864	40,285	36,710	51,649
Wage workers	114,817	34,464	16,074	9,374	7,450	1,566	45,711	4,250	9,429	13,367	10,075	8,590	34,642
Unpaid family workers	247,591	103,782	70,735	22,860	9,261	926	126,802	10,514	22,461	35,497	30,210	28,120	17,007
Forestry and fishing	**78**	**26**	**14**	**6**	**5**	**1**	**31**	**3**	**3**	**8**	**10**	**7**	**21**
Fishermen and oystermen	56	16	8	3	4	1	24	1	3	5	8	7	16
Lumbermen, raftsmen, and woodshoppers	22	10	6	3	1		7	2		3	2		5
Extraction of minerals	**52**	**9**	**4**	**3**	**2**		**29**	**1**	**5**	**15**	**8**		**14**
Operators	1												1
Coal mine operatives	24	4	2	2			16	1	2	8	5		4
Other operatives in extraction of minerals	27	5	2	1	2		13		3	7	3		9
Other specified mine operatives	5	1	1										4
Not specified mine operatives	1	1	1										
Quarry operatives	18	3		1	2		11		2	6	3		4
Salt well and works operatives	3						2		1	1			1
Manufacturing and mechanical industries	**100,497**	**29,119**	**9,156**	**8,887**	**9,588**	**1,488**	**48,065**	**1,874**	**8,077**	**18,682**	**12,849**	**6,583**	**23,313**
Apprentices (except to building and hand trades)	70	58	51	6	1		8	3	1	1	2	1	4
Dressmakers' and milliners' apprentices	51	47	44	3			3	2	1				1
Jewelers', watchmakers', goldsmiths', and silversmiths' apprentices	1	1		1									
Printers' and bookbinders' apprentices	10	6	3	2	1		2			1	1		2
Other apprentices in manufacturing	8	4	4				3	1			1	1	1
Bakers	608	139	14	49	64	12	304	8	38	121	84	53	165
Builders and building contractors	4	1			1		1				1		2
Carpenters	7	3		2	1		3			2	1		1
Compositors, linotypers, and typesetters	198	76	8	29	36	3	91		14	43	24	10	31
Dressmakers and seamstresses (not in factory)	20,433	3,419	272	764	1,815	568	10,496	78	561	3,452	3,964	2,441	6,518
Dyers	22	5	1	3	1		13		3	7	2	1	4
Engravers	2	1		1									1
Filers, grinders, buffers, and polishers (metal)	33	12	3	4	5		11	1	1	5	1	3	10
Buffers and polishers	18	10	2	4	4		6	1	1	3		1	2
Filers	1												1
Grinders	14	2	1		1		5			2	1	2	7
Forewomen and overseers (manufacturing)	217	57	9	21	26	1	116	2	12	50	34	18	44
Jewelers, watchmakers, goldsmiths, and silversmiths	14	8	3	4	1		4	1		2		1	2
Jewelers and lapidaries (factory)	9	7	3	3	1		1	1					1
Jewelers and watchmakers (not in factory)	5	1		1			3			2		1	1
Managers and officials (manufacturing)	20	3			3		14		1	6	5	2	3
Manufacturers	38	4			3	1	17		1	3	9	4	17
Mechanics (n. o. s.)[1], automobile factories, garages, and repair shops	2						1		1				1
Millers (grain, flour, feed, etc.)	2												2
Milliners and millinery dealers	441	160	25	61	69	5	212	2	39	86	65	20	69
Oilers of machinery	1												1
Painters, glaziers, varnishers, enamelers, etc	141	37	15	12	9	1	83	6	23	27	23	4	21
Enamelers, lacquerers, and japanners	6	1	1				3	1		2			2
Painters, glaziers, and varnishers (building)	9	2	1	1			5		1	1	3		2
Painters, glaziers, and varnishers (factory)	126	34	13	11	9	1	75	5	22	24	20	4	17
Paper hangers	28	2			1	1	16	1	1	2	6	6	10
Pattern and model makers	1						1			1			
Plasterers	1						1				1		
Sawyers	4						3			2	1		1
Shoemakers and cobblers (not in factory)	21	2		1	1		11		2	5	3	1	8
Skilled occupations (not elsewhere classified)	2	1	1										1
Tailoresses	552	126	18	32	65	11	314	2	23	147	104	38	112
Upholsterers	48	12	1	2	7	2	27		4	13	4	6	9
Operatives (n. o. s.)[1]:													
Building industry	2						2			1	1		
Chemical and allied industries	362	116	37	41	35	3	176	11	41	74	33	17	70
Charcoal and coke works	12	3	1		2		4		2	1	1		5
Explosives, ammunition, and fireworks factories	12	2	1	1			7		3	2	2		3
Fertilizer factories	39	12	2	6	4		15		3	7	3	2	12
Paint and varnish factories	25	10	5	2	3		12	3		6	1	2	3
Petroleum refineries	9	1			1		6			4		2	2
Rayon factories	18	6	2	2	2		12	1	2	4	4	1	
Soap factories	25	8	3	3	1	1	10		2	7		1	7
Other chemical factories	222	74	23	27	22	2	110	7	29	43	22	9	38
Cigar and tobacco factories	14,924	4,438	1,654	1,433	1,232	119	7,411	356	1,592	3,038	1,676	749	3,075
Clay, glass, and stone industries	415	136	51	51	31	3	202	11	40	80	52	19	77
Brick, tile, and terra-cotta factories	21	9	4	3	2		9		2	2	3	2	3
Glass factories	336	111	39	44	25	3	160	10	33	62	40	15	65
Lime, cement, and artificial stone factories	22	3		1	2		16	1	1	7	5	2	3
Potteries	36	13	8	3	2		17		4	9	4		6

See footnotes at end of table.

TABLE 25.—GAINFULLY OCCUPIED NEGRO WOMEN 15 YEARS OLD AND OVER, BY OCCUPATION AND MARITAL CONDITION, WITH A DISTRIBUTION OF THE SINGLE AND UNKNOWN AND OF THE MARRIED BY AGE, FOR THE UNITED STATES: 1930—Continued

OCCUPATION	Total	SINGLE AND UNKNOWN: Total	SINGLE AND UNKNOWN: 15 to 19 years	SINGLE AND UNKNOWN: 20 to 24 years	SINGLE AND UNKNOWN: 25 to 44 years	SINGLE AND UNKNOWN: 45 years and over (incl. unkn.)	MARRIED: Total	MARRIED: 15 to 19 years	MARRIED: 20 to 24 years	MARRIED: 25 to 34 years	MARRIED: 35 to 44 years	MARRIED: 45 years and over (incl. unkn.)	Widowed and divorced
Manufacturing and mechanical industries—Continued.													
Operatives (n. o. s.)—Continued.													
Clothing industries	15,604	5,853	1,537	1,929	2,214	173	7,347	234	1,436	3,417	1,776	484	2,404
Corset factories	52	21	4	7	9	1	24		2	10	8	4	7
Glove factories	232	94	36	32	26		105	7	38	42	14	4	33
Hat factories (felt)	165	63	20	23	20		83	6	18	33	23	3	19
Shirt, collar, and cuff factories	977	371	153	110	101	7	477	22	105	216	106	28	129
Suit, coat, and overall factories	1,859	650	208	225	206	11	873	28	189	404	192	60	336
Other clothing factories	12,319	4,654	1,116	1,532	1,852	154	5,785	171	1,084	2,712	1,433	385	1,880
Food and allied industries	6,639	1,778	753	490	493	42	3,341	184	627	1,278	827	425	1,520
Bakeries	186	77	37	20	19	1	78		18	35	18	7	31
Butter, cheese, and condensed milk factories	22	11	2	3	5	1	7		1	3	1	2	4
Candy factories	455	190	70	68	47	5	190	13	42	71	44	20	75
Fish curing and packing	992	219	97	51	61	10	540	19	80	165	155	121	233
Flour and grain mills	15	4		1	2	1	4		1	2	1		7
Fruit and vegetable canning, etc	692	186	97	51	35	3	343	22	77	137	72	35	163
Slaughter and packing houses	878	158	31	42	77	8	495	13	74	227	135	46	225
Sugar factories and refineries	20	5			5		9		1	1	6	1	6
Other food factories	3,312	905	412	249	231	13	1,642	114	324	628	388	188	765
Liquor and beverage industries	67	23	7	5	11		33	3	9	9	7	5	11
Iron and steel, machinery, and vehicle industries	661	206	78	68	54	6	319	15	67	129	76	32	136
Agricultural implement factories	4	1			1		2			1	1		1
Automobile factories	90	22	8	7	6	1	52	6	4	23	12	7	16
Automobile repair shops	4	1	1				2			1		1	1
Blast furnaces and steel rolling mills [2]	98	28	8	11	9		58	3	12	25	12	6	12
Car and railroad shops	25	3	1		2		16		2	7	6	1	6
Ship and boat building	2	1		1			1					1	
Wagon and carriage factories	2	1	1										1
Other iron and steel and machinery factories [3]	394	137	55	43	36	3	172	6	45	67	39	15	85
Not specified metal industries	42	12	4	6		2	16		4	5	6	1	14
Metal industries (except iron and steel)	262	114	39	49	24	2	113	4	35	48	20	6	35
Brass mills	18	3	2		1		13		3	6	4		2
Clock and watch factories	12	8	3	4	1		3			1	2		1
Copper factories	1						1		1				
Gold and silver factories	6	2		2			3		2	1			1
Jewelry factories	35	21	12	8		1	9	2	5	2			5
Lead and zinc factories	4	1			1		3			1	2		
Tinware, enamelware, etc., factories	134	65	18	26	20	1	52	2	15	23	8	4	17
Other metal factories	52	14	4	9	1		29		9	14	4	2	9
Leather industries	388	161	62	45	47	7	172	7	33	69	52	11	55
Harness and saddle factories	3						3		1	2			
Leather belt, leather goods, etc., factories	117	61	29	19	12	1	44	2	8	25	9		12
Shoe factories	166	67	22	13	28	4	72	5	13	21	28	5	27
Tanneries	77	27	7	11	7	2	37		7	14	10	6	13
Trunk, suitcase, and bag factories	25	6	4	2			16		4	7	5		3
Lumber and furniture industries	813	271	108	95	61	7	357	18	98	132	71	38	185
Furniture factories	262	87	23	33	29	2	116	7	31	50	16	12	59
Saw and planing mills [4]	233	70	30	27	12	1	92	7	32	25	22	6	71
Other woodworking factories	318	114	55	35	20	4	149	4	35	57	33	20	55
Paper, printing, and allied industries	1,094	332	97	84	127	24	557	21	65	241	152	78	205
Blank book, envelope, tag, paper bag, etc., factories	67	21	6	12	2	1	34	2	8	15	5	4	12
Paper and pulp mills	563	170	75	39	49	7	275	12	38	120	60	45	118
Paper box factories	51	25	7	8	10		16	1	3	8	3	1	10
Printing, publishing, and engraving	413	116	9	25	66	16	232	6	16	98	84	28	65
Textile industries—													
Cotton mills	674	186	82	58	42	4	317	18	69	122	68	40	171
Knitting mills	642	289	130	96	61	2	256	15	68	115	38	20	97
Silk mills	221	94	34	34	23	3	95	5	22	42	21	5	32
Textile dyeing, finishing, and printing mills	80	26	4	9	13		40		4	20	15	1	14
Woolen and worsted mills	123	47	27	7	8	5	52	2	6	24	18	2	24
Other textile mills	1,491	512	188	168	143	13	651	35	155	266	138	57	328
Carpet mills	68	23	6	9	6	2	30	1	4	8	12	5	15
Hemp, jute, and linen mills	50	18	5	4	9		20	1	3	8	4	4	12
Lace and embroidery mills	101	40	11	13	15	1	48		13	23	9	3	13
Rope and cordage factories	46	12	4	3	5		26		8	14	3	1	8
Sail, awning, and tent factories	15	3			3		8		2	4	2		4
Other and not specified textile mills	1,211	416	162	139	105	10	519	33	125	209	108	44	276
Miscellaneous manufacturing industries	6,788	2,446	804	812	752	78	3,217	152	695	1,433	706	231	1,125
Broom and brush factories	72	24	5	12	5	2	36	2	10	14	9	1	12
Button factories	91	35	16	10	9		47	4	12	18	12	1	9
Electrical machinery and supply factories	104	54	19	21	12	2	36	2	8	22	3	1	14
Rubber factories	47	21	9	7	5		20	4	4	11		1	6
Straw factories	8	3		1	2		5		1	4			
Turpentine farms and distilleries	5	3	2		1								2
Other miscellaneous manufacturing industries	2,155	706	262	208	211	25	1,052	41	230	445	258	78	397
Other not specified manufacturing industries	4,306	1,600	491	553	507	49	2,021	99	430	919	424	149	685
Not specified industries and services	3,443	1,177	360	353	345	119	1,508	76	313	522	346	251	758

See footnotes at end of table.

TABLE 25.—GAINFULLY OCCUPIED NEGRO WOMEN 15 YEARS OLD AND OVER, BY OCCUPATION AND MARITAL CONDITION, WITH A DISTRIBUTION OF THE SINGLE AND UNKNOWN AND OF THE MARRIED BY AGE, FOR THE UNITED STATES: 1930—Continued

OCCUPATION	Total	SINGLE AND UNKNOWN					MARRIED						Wid-owed and di-vorced
		Total	15 to 19 years	20 to 24 years	25 to 44 years	45 years and over (incl. unkn.)	Total	15 to 19 years	20 to 24 years	25 to 34 years	35 to 44 years	45 years and over (incl. unkn.)	
Manufacturing and mechanical industries—Continued.													
Laborers (n. o. s.[1]):													
Building, general, and not specified laborers	4, 594	1, 098	331	296	359	112	1, 715	71	238	535	448	423	1, 781
Laborers and helpers, building construction	31	14	3	6	4	1	12		1	5	5	1	5
General and not specified laborers	4, 563	1, 084	328	290	355	111	1, 703	71	237	530	443	422	1, 776
Chemical and allied industries	331	97	34	27	31	5	161	11	37	65	37	11	73
Charcoal and coke works	9	1			1		5	1	1	1		2	3
Explosives, ammunition, and fireworks factories	10	2		1	1		5	1	2		2		3
Fertilizer factories	78	30	10	8	11	1	28	1	7	14	3	3	20
Gas works	5	1			1		3	1		1	1		1
Paint and varnish factories	17	6	4		1	1	7		2	4	1		4
Petroleum refineries	34	14	4	3	6	1	15	1	5	6	3		5
Rayon factories	12						10		1	4	3	2	2
Soap factories	12	3	2	1			8		1	5	2		1
Other chemical factories	154	40	14	14	10	2	80	6	18	30	22	4	34
Cigar and tobacco factories	3, 372	960	356	310	259	35	1, 570	75	318	537	396	244	842
Clay, glass, and stone industries	289	89	25	24	36	4	142	9	23	53	35	22	58
Brick, tile, and terra-cotta factories	83	30	4	7	17	2	40	4	3	13	12	8	13
Glass factories	162	42	16	12	13	1	80	5	16	35	17	7	40
Lime, cement, and artificial stone factories	25	4		3	1		16		2	5	4	5	5
Potteries	19	13	5	2	5	1	6		2		2	2	
Clothing industries	370	134	55	48	25	6	172	12	44	68	32	16	64
Corset factories	1	1			1								
Glove factories	6	1			1		4			2	2		1
Hat factories (felt)	7	4	2		2		3	1		1		1	
Shirt, collar, and cuff factories	67	34	16	9	6	3	19	2	4	9	2	2	14
Suit, coat, and overall factories	34	8	3	4	1		18		3	6	4	5	8
Other clothing factories	255	86	34	35	14	3	128	9	37	50	24	8	41
Food and allied industries	4, 274	1, 293	597	367	298	31	2, 058	146	387	771	503	251	923
Bakeries	88	36	13	11	11	1	38	1	7	15	14	1	14
Butter, cheese, and condensed milk factories	18	4	2	1	1		11	1		4	4	2	3
Candy factories	147	74	34	24	14	2	42	4	9	19	6	4	31
Fish curing and packing	771	212	91	67	51	3	411	27	73	131	121	59	148
Flour and grain mills	24	3	1		1	1	15	1	3	7	3	1	6
Fruit and vegetable canning, etc	431	117	61	32	22	2	223	17	44	97	42	23	91
Slaughter and packing houses	474	94	16	33	44	1	265	15	33	123	67	27	115
Sugar factories and refineries	106	16	1	5	9	1	56	4	5	20	18	9	34
Other food factories	2, 159	719	371	189	139	20	966	75	206	339	223	123	474
Liquor and beverage industries	56	18	7	5	6		31	1	7	16	5	2	7
Iron and steel, machinery, and vehicle industries	929	252	76	71	96	9	493	27	76	212	131	47	184
Agricultural implement factories	6	1			1		5	1	1	3			
Automobile factories	159	45	7	11	26	1	87	5	16	41	22	3	27
Automobile repair shops	15	3	3				7		1	4		2	5
Blast furnaces and steel rolling mills [2]	206	51	11	14	22	4	120	5	15	45	42	13	35
Car and railroad shops	94	19	8	3	8		41	1	5	16	12	7	34
Ship and boat building	17	7	1	2	3	1	7	1	1	4	1		3
Other iron and steel and machinery factories [3]	315	94	35	30	27	2	159	10	23	74	38	14	62
Not specified metal industries	117	32	11	11	9	1	67	4	14	25	16	8	18
Metal industries (except iron and steel)	77	26	10	12	4		29	2	5	10	9	3	22
Brass mills	16	5	3	1	1		5	1		1	3		6
Gold and silver factories	3	2		2			1			1			
Lead and zinc factories	3	1		1			2		1		1		
Tinware, enamelware, etc., factories	43	14	6	6	2		16	1	3	6	3	3	13
Other metal factories	12	4	1	2	1		5		1	2	2		3
Leather industries	104	34	11	11	12		48	1	4	24	15	4	22
Harness and saddle factories	9	2		2			3				3		4
Leather belt, leather goods, etc., factories	11	4	1	2	1		7			4	3		
Shoe factories	32	15	4	4	7		11	1	3	5	2		6
Tanneries	50	12	6	2	4		26		1	15	7	3	12
Trunk, suitcase, and bag factories	2	1		1			1					1	
Lumber and furniture industries	2, 301	824	356	258	190	20	961	72	220	335	213	121	516
Furniture factories	206	80	26	32	21	1	78	5	19	37	11	6	48
Piano and organ factories	1						1				1		
Saw and planing mills [4]	1, 274	462	201	143	105	13	546	45	131	168	123	79	266
Other woodworking factories	820	282	129	83	64	6	336	22	70	130	78	36	202
Paper, printing, and allied industries	316	78	38	24	13	3	173	11	30	77	36	19	65
Blank book, envelope, tag, paper bag, etc., factories	21	3	1	2			15	1	1	7	4	2	3
Paper and pulp mills	259	61	31	19	9	2	142	10	28	65	27	12	56
Paper box factories	8	4	3		1		2		1			1	2
Printing, publishing, and engraving	28	10	3	3	3	1	14			5	5	4	4
Textile industries:													
Cotton mills	2, 028	591	266	189	125	11	866	61	195	318	181	111	571
Knitting mills	130	39	14	11	11	3	57	2	9	17	18	11	34
Silk mills	65	25	11	5	9		34	3	8	8	11	4	6
Textile dyeing, finishing, and printing mills	12	5		4	1		5			1	2	2	2
Woolen and worsted mills	49	14	3	5	6		26		7	9	7	3	9
Other textile mills	479	156	63	64	27	2	208	13	64	78	35	18	115
Carpet mills	12	7	2	2	3		5	1	1		2	1	
Hemp, jute, and linen mills	24	6	3	2	1		11		3	6	1	1	7
Rope and cordage factories	18	8	2	4	2		8		2	4	1	1	2
Sail, awning, and tent factories	2						2			1	1		
Other and not specified textile mills	423	135	56	56	21	2	182	12	58	67	30	15	106

See footnotes at end of table.

TABLE 25.—GAINFULLY OCCUPIED NEGRO WOMEN 15 YEARS OLD AND OVER, BY OCCUPATION AND MARITAL CONDITION, WITH A DISTRIBUTION OF THE SINGLE AND UNKNOWN AND OF THE MARRIED BY AGE, FOR THE UNITED STATES: 1930—Continued

OCCUPATION	Total	SINGLE AND UNKNOWN: Total	SINGLE AND UNKNOWN: 15 to 19 years	SINGLE AND UNKNOWN: 20 to 24 years	SINGLE AND UNKNOWN: 25 to 44 years	SINGLE AND UNKNOWN: 45 years and over (incl. unkn.)	MARRIED: Total	MARRIED: 15 to 19 years	MARRIED: 20 to 24 years	MARRIED: 25 to 34 years	MARRIED: 35 to 44 years	MARRIED: 45 years and over (incl. unkn.)	Widowed and divorced
Manufacturing and mechanical industries—Con.													
Laborers (n. o. s.)—Continued													
Miscellaneous manufacturing industries	3,241	1,096	444	348	272	32	1,467	90	321	538	320	198	678
Broom and brush factories	23	11	2	7	2		8	1	1	3	2	1	4
Button factories	5	3		2	1		1			1			1
Electric light and power plants	2	2		2									
Electrical machinery and supply factories	27	9		5	4		17		6	6	4	1	1
Rubber factories	29	6	3	1	1	1	17	3	2	6	4	2	6
Straw factories	1	1	1										
Turpentine farms and distilleries	258	68	43	13	10	2	150	12	26	52	32	28	40
Other miscellaneous manufacturing industries	790	223	94	63	57	9	348	17	75	122	80	54	219
Other not specified manufacturing industries	2,106	773	301	255	197	20	926	57	211	348	198	112	407
Transportation and communication	**2,203**	**554**	**128**	**180**	**215**	**31**	**1,117**	**42**	**165**	**435**	**307**	**168**	**532**
Water transportation (selected occupations):													
Longshoremen and stevedores	10	2		1		1	6	1	1	1	2	1	2
Sailors and deck hands	3						1				1		2
Road and street transportation (selected occupations):													
Chauffeurs and truck and tractor drivers	171	67	15	20	27	5	84	4	15	33	24	8	20
Draymen, teamsters, and carriage drivers[5]	17	4		2	2		5		1	2	2		8
Garage owners, managers, and officials	5	1				1	1					1	3
Garage owners and proprietors	4	1				1	1					1	2
Garage managers and officials	1												1
Garage laborers	103	32	11	11	9	1	49	3	12	23	5	6	22
Laborers, truck, transfer, and cab companies	36	9	3	3	2	1	18	1	3	9	4	1	9
Laborers, road and street	32	10	6	1	2	1	15	2	3	5	3	2	7
Road, street, etc., building and repairing	31	9	6	1	1	1	15	2	3	5	3	2	7
Street cleaning	1	1			1								
Owners and managers, truck, transfer, and cab companies	25	3			2	1	5			3	1	1	17
Owners and poprietors	22	3			2	1	5			3	1	1	14
Managers and officials	3												3
Railroad transportation (selected occupations):													
Forewomen and overseers	9	1			1		6			3	2	1	2
Steam railroad	8						6			3	2	1	2
Street rilaroad	1	1			1								
Laborers (includes construction laborers)	1,217	224	40	59	107	18	657	19	87	243	202	106	336
Steam railroad	1,125	204	37	56	95	16	614	17	84	224	188	101	307
Street railroad	92	20	3	3	12	2	43	2	3	19	14	5	29
Switchmen and flagmen, steam railroads	17	3		1	2		8			1	2	5	6
Express, post, radio, telegraph, and telephone (selected occupations):													
Agents, express companies	1	1	1										
Mail carriers	19	5		3	2		9	1		4	1	3	5
Postmistresses	42	4		3	1		31		1	5	14	11	7
Telegraph messengers	1						1	1					
Telegraph operators	8	5	1	3	1		2	1		1			1
Telephone operators	330	147	35	64	47	1	136	5	27	72	22	10	47
Other transportation and communication pursuits:													
Apprentices, other transportation and communication	2	2	2										
Forewomen and overseers, garages, greasing stations, and automobile laundries	1						1				1		
Inspectors, telegraph and telephone	1	1			1								
Laborers (n. o. s.[1])	28	7	6	1			12		3	6	2	1	9
Air transportation	6	2	2				2		2				2
Express companies	1						1			1			
Pipe lines	1						1			1			
Telegraph and telephone	6	1	1				2			1	1		3
Water transportation	1	1		1									
Other transportation and communication	13	3	3				6		1	3	1	1	4
Other occupations	125	26	8	8	9	1	70	4	12	24	19	11	29
Road, street, etc., building and repairing	1	1	1										
Steam railroad	69	13	3	5	5		42	1	8	15	12	6	14
Street railroad	4						1		1				3
Other transportation and communication	51	12	4	3	4	1	27	3	3	9	7	5	12
Trade	**14,522**	**3,020**	**776**	**961**	**1,081**	**202**	**7,752**	**151**	**772**	**2,381**	**2,529**	**1,919**	**3,750**
Advertising agents	8	4		1	3		2		1	1			2
Apprentices, wholesale and retail trade	4	4	2	1	1								
Bankers, brokers, and money lenders	18	8		3	4	1	5			1	3	1	5
Bankers and bank officials	12	7		3	3	1	3			1	2		2
Stock brokers	5						2				1	1	3
Brokers not specified and promoters	1	1			1								

See footnotes at end of table.

TABLE 25.—GAINFULLY OCCUPIED NEGRO WOMEN 15 YEARS OLD AND OVER, BY OCCUPATION AND MARITAL CONDITION, WITH A DISTRIBUTION OF THE SINGLE AND UNKNOWN AND OF THE MARRIED BY AGE, FOR THE UNITED STATES: 1930—Continued

OCCUPATION	Total	SINGLE AND UNKNOWN					MARRIED						Widowed and divorced
		Total	15 to 19 years	20 to 24 years	25 to 44 years	45 years and over (incl. unkn.)	Total	15 to 19 years	20 to 24 years	25 to 34 years	35 to 44 years	45 years and over (incl. unkn.)	
Trade—Continued.													
"Clerks" in stores [6]	1,644	570	184	223	147	16	859	23	120	291	252	173	215
Commercial travelers	90	15		3	10	2	48		3	10	22	13	27
Decorators, drapers, and window dressers	157	29	6	10	10	3	84		7	31	26	20	44
Deliverymen, stores [7]	22	14	7	6	1		5		2	3			3
Floorwalkers and forewomen in stores	24	6	2	1	2	1	11		1	4	4	2	7
Inspectors, gaugers, and samplers	46	9	1	4	4		25		5	12	6	2	12
Insurance agents, managers, and officials	1,098	224	22	75	111	16	553	5	39	176	224	109	321
Insurance agents	1,086	221	22	74	109	16	547	5	39	175	221	107	318
Managers and officials, insurance companies	12	3		1	2		6			1	3	2	3
Laborers in coal and lumber yards, warehouses, etc	68	24	8	4	10	2	19		4	6	5	4	25
Coal yards and lumber yards	15	6	2	3	1		7			4	1	2	2
Warehouses	47	15	5	1	7	2	11		3	2	4	2	21
Other and not specified trade	6	3	1		2		1		1				2
Laborers, porters, and helpers in stores	1,209	328	117	94	106	11	629	30	114	213	161	111	252
Newsgirls	16	5	3	1	1		7	1		1	2	3	4
Proprietors, managers, and officials (n. o. s.[1])	177	15	1	4	7	3	106		3	20	44	39	56
Employment office keepers	173	15	1	4	7	3	104		3	19	44	38	54
Other proprietors, managers, and officials	4						2			1		1	2
Real estate agents and officials	473	48	2	6	28	12	262		12	79	104	67	163
Managers and officials, real estate companies	1												1
Real estate agents	472	48	2	6	28	12	262		12	79	104	67	162
Retail dealers [8]	3,847	358	32	73	180	73	2,219	16	107	555	794	747	1,270
Automobiles and accessories	3												3
Books, music, news, and stationery	48	7	1		4	2	29		1	9	10	9	12
Candy and confectionery	430	36	3	6	18	9	259	1	19	73	99	67	135
Cigars and tobacco	28	4	1	1	2		11			6	3	2	13
Coal and wood	60	6	1		4	1	31		4	4	14	9	23
Dry goods, clothing, and boots and shoes	117	14			9	5	63		1	10	27	25	40
Drugs and medicines (including druggists and pharmacists)	168	61	2	23	35	1	75		5	35	23	12	32
5 and 10 cent and variety stores	7	1				1	4			1		3	2
Flour and feed	3						1				1		2
Food (except groceries and hucksters' goods)	167	22	2	6	9	5	96	1	4	30	30	31	49
Furniture, carpets, and rugs	22	2			1	1	11		1	1	4	5	9
Gasoline and oil filling stations	25	4	1	1	2		17		2	5	9	1	4
General stores	148	12		1	5	6	79	1	1	11	22	44	57
Groceries	1,808	101	7	17	51	26	1,133	5	42	272	435	379	574
Hardware, implements, and wagons	4						4		1	1	1	1	
Hucksters and peddlers	410	56	12	12	23	9	177	7	13	34	55	68	177
Ice	3						1					1	2
Jewelry	1						1			1			
Junk and rags	56	5	1		2	2	20		3	6	4	7	31
Other specified dealers	114	12	1	4	5	2	64		2	20	19	23	38
Not specified dealers	225	15		2	10	3	143	1	8	36	38	60	67
Saleswomen	4,365	1,054	292	354	356	52	2,289	50	265	738	712	524	1,022
Canvassers	710	84	16	21	36	11	357	8	19	92	138	100	269
Demonstrators	137	43	7	17	18	1	68		14	28	18	8	26
Sales agents	21	4			1	3	10	1		3	6		7
Saleswomen	3,497	923	269	316	301	37	1,854	41	232	615	550	416	720
Undertakers	255	27	2	7	15	3	138		8	38	48	44	90
Wholesale dealers, importers, and exporters	1												1
Other pursuits in trade	1,000	278	95	91	85	7	491	26	81	202	122	60	231
Advertising agencies	3						3		1	1		1	
Grain elevators	8	3	2	1			4			1	1	2	1
Stockyards	2	1		1									1
Warehouses and cold storage plants	114	27	11	10	5	1	64	4	14	22	16	8	23
Wholesale trade, and retail trade (except automobile):													
Fruit and vegetable graders and packers	42	15	9	5		1	15	1	5	5	3	1	12
Meat cutters	5						3				1	2	2
Other occupations	813	230	73	73	79	5	394	21	60	166	101	46	189
Other trade industries	13	2		1	1		8		1	7			3
Public service (not elsewhere classified)	**926**	**208**	**30**	**41**	**104**	**33**	**469**	**6**	**31**	**129**	**153**	**150**	**249**
Guards, watchmen, and doorkeepers	72	7		2	2	3	36		1	9	9	17	29
Laborers, public service	498	126	30	29	49	18	241	6	27	72	64	72	131
Garbage men and scavengers	5												5
Other laborers	493	126	30	29	49	18	241	6	27	72	64	72	126
Marshals, sheriffs, detectives, etc	91	14			11	3	50			8	22	20	27
Detectives	6	1			1		4			1	1	2	1
Probation and truant officers	84	13			10	3	45			7	20	18	26
Sheriffs	1						1				1		
Officials and inspectors (city and county)	27	5		1	3	1	17			4	5	8	5
Officials and inspectors (city)	17	2			2		12			3	4	5	3
Officials and inspectors (county)	10	3		1	1	1	5			1	1	3	2
Officials and inspectors (State and United States)	7	2		1	1		2				2		3
Officials and inspectors (State)	1						1				1		
Officials and inspectors (United States)	6	2		1	1		1				1		3
Policewomen	33	3			3		22			3	10	9	8
Other public service pursuits	198	51		8	35	8	101		3	33	41	24	46

See footnotes at end of table.

TABLE 25.—GAINFULLY OCCUPIED NEGRO WOMEN 15 YEARS OLD AND OVER, BY OCCUPATION AND MARITAL CONDITION, WITH A DISTRIBUTION OF THE SINGLE AND UNKNOWN AND OF THE MARRIED BY AGE, FOR THE UNITED STATES: 1930—Continued

OCCUPATION	Total	SINGLE AND UNKNOWN					MARRIED						Widowed and divorced
		Total	15 to 19 years	20 to 24 years	25 to 44 years	45 years and over (incl. unkn.)	Total	15 to 19 years	20 to 24 years	25 to 34 years	35 to 44 years	45 years and over (incl. unkn.)	
Professional service	**63,008**	**31,721**	**3,215**	**14,443**	**12,684**	**1,379**	**23,575**	**316**	**3,187**	**9,097**	**7,008**	**3,967**	**7,712**
Actresses and showwomen	1,396	612	155	276	174	7	633	64	219	256	77	17	151
Actresses	1,297	574	144	258	165	7	583	55	208	234	69	17	140
Showwomen	99	38	11	18	9	-	50	9	11	22	8	-	11
Artists, sculptors, and teachers of art	200	79	6	37	32	4	86	1	12	27	27	19	35
Authors, editors, and reporters	84	17	2	6	6	3	47	-	5	14	18	10	20
Authors	8	3	-	1	-	2	2	-	1	1	-	-	3
Editors and reporters	76	14	2	5	6	1	45	-	4	13	18	10	17
Chemists, assayers, and metallurgists	14	5	-	2	2	1	6	-	-	3	3	-	3
Clergymen	494	50	-	6	35	9	273	-	7	50	99	117	171
College presidents and professors [9]	1,020	639	-	242	360	37	292	-	26	122	86	58	86
Dentists	27	10	-	1	9	-	14	-	-	6	5	3	3
Designers, draftsmen, and inventors	98	38	3	21	14	-	42	-	5	23	12	2	18
Designers	97	37	3	21	13	-	42	-	5	23	12	2	18
Draftsmen	1	1	-	-	1	-	-	-	-	-	-	-	-
Lawyers, judges, and justices	24	8	-	-	8	-	13	-	-	3	9	1	3
Musicians and teachers of music	2,831	903	136	313	391	63	1,391	26	158	544	440	223	537
Osteopaths	5	2	-	-	1	1	1	-	-	1	-	-	2
Photographers	85	26	4	10	9	3	42	1	5	24	9	3	17
Physicians and surgeons	92	13	-	-	10	3	51	-	1	19	13	18	28
Teachers	45,728	24,340	2,138	11,466	9,755	981	16,897	169	2,305	6,688	5,084	2,651	4,491
Teachers (athletics, dancing, etc.)	56	28	7	10	11	-	24	2	7	13	2	-	4
Teachers (school)	45,672	24,312	2,131	11,456	9,744	981	16,873	167	2,298	6,675	5,082	2,651	4,487
Trained nurses	5,581	3,174	472	1,501	1,105	96	1,572	22	190	632	445	283	835
Veterinary surgeons	1	-	-	-	-	-	1	-	-	-	1	-	-
Other professional pursuits	1,281	462	9	134	272	47	533	4	39	154	184	152	286
County agents, farm demonstrators, etc	90	38	-	9	25	4	37	-	-	12	19	6	15
Librarians	180	83	3	31	41	8	65	-	8	27	22	8	32
Social and welfare workers	827	276	4	77	163	32	351	1	18	92	122	118	200
Other occupations	184	65	2	17	43	3	80	3	13	23	21	20	39
Semiprofessional and recreational pursuits	1,718	369	8	79	196	86	753	1	25	157	277	293	596
Abstracters, notaries, and justices of peace	23	3	-	-	2	1	16	-	-	3	11	2	4
Architects', designers', and draftsmen's apprentices	3	3	3	-	-	-	-	-	-	-	-	-	-
Apprentices to other professional persons	1	-	-	-	-	-	1	-	-	1	-	-	-
Billiard room, dance hall, skating rink, etc., keepers	21	3	-	-	3	-	10	-	-	4	3	3	8
Chiropractors	42	14	-	2	9	3	14	-	-	2	9	3	14
Healers (not elsewhere classified)	383	66	-	14	33	19	186	-	3	35	67	81	131
Keepers of charitable and penal institutions	106	24	-	2	15	7	27	-	2	3	10	12	55
Keepers of pleasure resorts, race tracks, etc	10	1	-	1	-	-	5	-	1	3	1	-	4
Officials of lodges, societies, etc	164	23	1	7	12	3	81	-	5	14	24	38	60
Religious workers	762	190	2	41	99	48	322	-	7	65	119	131	250
Technicians and laboratory assistants	45	20	2	8	9	1	18	-	4	9	2	3	7
Theatrical owners, managers, and officials	11	3	-	1	2	-	7	-	-	2	4	1	1
Other occupations	147	19	-	3	12	4	66	1	3	16	27	19	62
Attendants and helpers, professional service	2,329	974	282	349	305	38	928	28	190	374	219	117	427
Attendants, pool rooms, bowling alleys, golf clubs, etc	71	37	9	15	12	1	29	2	9	17	1	-	5
Dentists' assistants and attendants	233	100	19	35	43	3	103	-	14	51	30	8	30
Helpers, motion picture production	2	1	-	1	-	-	1	-	-	-	1	-	-
Laborers, professional service	240	90	27	29	26	8	100	3	21	26	29	21	50
Laborers, recreation and amusement	93	30	16	6	6	2	45	2	9	13	10	11	18
Librarians' assistants and attendants	3	1	-	1	-	-	2	-	-	1	-	1	-
Physicians' and surgeons' attendants	929	427	111	156	147	13	334	11	73	159	64	27	168
Stage hands and circus helpers	14	4	4	-	-	-	9	-	1	3	4	1	1
Theater ushers	122	64	18	32	14	-	44	3	17	16	7	1	14
Other attendants and helpers	622	220	78	74	57	11	261	7	46	88	73	47	141
Domestic and personal service	**1,145,937**	**286,021**	**80,706**	**84,790**	**100,273**	**20,252**	**525,510**	**16,404**	**77,839**	**188,885**	**144,873**	**97,509**	**334,406**
Barbers, hairdressers, and manicurists	12,804	2,351	262	619	1,332	138	7,097	42	524	2,904	2,577	1,050	3,356
Boarding and lodging house keepers	12,112	792	14	93	511	174	6,566	86	519	2,143	2,166	1,652	4,754
Bootblacks	18	8	6	1	1	-	5	1	-	2	1	1	5
Charwomen and cleaners	11,495	2,114	590	546	739	239	6,134	149	707	2,062	1,866	1,350	3,247
Cleaning, dyeing, and pressing shop workers	3,194	808	179	264	348	17	1,751	49	288	848	454	112	635
Owners and proprietors	66	6	-	1	5	-	38	-	2	16	13	7	22
Managers and officials	9	1	-	-	1	-	5	-	-	3	2	-	3
Forewomen and overseers	8	-	-	-	-	-	5	-	1	2	1	1	3
Laborers	146	35	7	11	15	2	80	4	17	35	16	8	31
Other operatives	2,965	766	172	252	327	15	1,623	45	268	792	422	96	576
Elevator tenders	4,439	1,912	542	843	516	11	1,910	121	586	848	289	66	617
Hotel keepers and managers	323	30	-	3	20	7	159	-	4	37	72	46	134
Housekeepers and stewardesses	17,819	3,974	429	1,084	1,826	635	7,002	151	907	2,389	2,088	1,467	6,843
Hotels, restaurants, boarding houses, etc	1,032	150	5	30	96	19	450	8	36	153	144	109	432
Other housekeepers and stewardesses	16,787	3,824	424	1,054	1,730	616	6,552	143	871	2,236	1,944	1,358	6,411
Janitors and sextons	6,033	690	124	169	277	120	3,360	41	264	1,002	1,106	947	1,983
Laborers, domestic and personal service	1,272	338	103	102	103	30	549	21	73	210	144	101	385
Laundresses (not in laundry)	268,500	32,554	7,587	8,003	12,775	4,189	138,195	2,819	12,790	39,318	43,185	40,083	97,751

See footnotes at end of table.

TABLE 25.—GAINFULLY OCCUPIED NEGRO WOMEN 15 YEARS OLD AND OVER, BY OCCUPATION AND MARITAL CONDITION, WITH A DISTRIBUTION OF THE SINGLE AND UNKNOWN AND OF THE MARRIED BY AGE, FOR THE UNITED STATES: 1930—Continued

OCCUPATON	Total	SINGLE AND UNKNOWN					MARRIED						Widowed and divorced
		Total	15 to 19 years	20 to 24 years	25 to 44 years	45 years and over (incl. unkn.)	Total	15 to 19 years	20 to 24 years	25 to 34 years	35 to 44 years	45 years and over (incl. unkn.)	
Domestic and personal service—Continued.													
Laundry owners, managers, and officials [10]	96	7		1	3	3	57		3	12	25	17	32
Owners and proprietors	63	4			1	3	39		1	7	18	13	20
Managers and officials	33	3		1	2		18		2	5	7	4	12
Laundry operatives [10]	47,391	12,659	3,771	4,090	4,312	486	23,397	960	4,573	9,659	5,617	2,588	11,335
Deliverymen [11]	1	1	1										
Forewomen and overseers	79	11		4	7		53		5	20	20	8	15
Laborers	2,483	715	243	239	209	24	1,093	44	219	421	266	143	675
Other operatives	44,828	11,932	3,527	3,847	4,096	462	22,251	916	4,349	9,218	5,331	2,437	10,645
Midwives and nurses (not trained)	15,845	4,075	1,131	1,456	1,114	374	6,019	211	742	1,273	1,407	2,386	5,751
Midwives	1,787	47		3	17	27	795		4	33	133	625	945
Nurses (not trained)	14,058	4,028	1,131	1,453	1,097	347	5,224	211	738	1,240	1,274	1,761	4,806
Porters (except in stores)	30	12	4	3	5		9	1	2	3	1	2	9
Domestic and personal service	12	5	2		3		3		2	1			4
Professional service	2						2			1		1	
Steam railroad	1						1				1		
Other porters (except in stores)	15	7	2	3	2		3	1		1		1	5
Restaurant, café, and lunch room keepers	5,178	424	10	45	281	88	3,058	7	115	836	1,220	880	1,696
Servants:													
Cooks	232,004	56,785	11,240	18,893	22,302	4,350	100,810	3,093	16,906	38,116	26,947	15,748	74,409
Hotels, restaurants, boarding houses, etc	28,944	5,616	876	1,625	2,686	429	14,076	313	1,773	5,164	4,314	2,512	9,252
Other cooks	203,060	51,169	10,364	17,268	19,616	3,921	86,734	2,780	15,133	32,952	22,633	13,236	65,157
Other servants	489,577	159,464	52,707	45,970	51,525	9,262	211,699	8,225	36,868	83,813	54,220	28,573	118,414
Hotels, restaurants, boarding houses, etc	39,433	10,550	2,665	3,422	4,077	386	19,274	687	3,583	8,789	4,617	1,598	9,609
Other domestic and personal service	450,144	148,914	50,042	42,548	47,448	8,876	192,425	7,538	33,285	75,024	49,603	26,975	108,805
Waiters	17,554	6,984	2,004	2,592	2,266	122	7,607	426	1,960	3,378	1,433	410	2,963
Other pursuits	253	40	3	13	17	7	126	1	8	32	55	30	87
Cemetery keepers	6	1			1		3			1	2		2
Other occupations	247	39	3	13	16	7	123	1	8	31	53	30	85
Clerical occupations	10,848	5,342	935	2,252	2,011	144	4,035	119	774	1,824	924	394	1,471
Agents, collectors, and credit women	345	58	7	17	25	9	173	2	16	52	65	38	114
Agents (not elsewhere classified)	163	23	2	1	12	8	84	2	8	25	32	17	56
Collectors	168	31	4	13	13	1	82		7	23	32	20	55
Credit women	2						1			1			1
Purchasing agents (except for railroads)	12	4	1	3			6		1	3	1	1	2
Bookkeepers, cashiers, and accountants	1,983	923	163	399	340	21	782	27	162	332	199	62	278
Accountants and auditors	14	5	1	1	3		4		1	2	1		5
Bookkeepers and cashiers	1,969	918	162	398	337	21	778	27	161	330	198	62	273
Clerks (except "clerks" in stores)	4,926	2,199	373	851	884	91	2,025	48	322	912	499	244	702
Office appliance operators	114	28	1	9	14	4	66		4	22	27	13	20
Shipping clerks	131	45	3	21	20	1	68	5	7	35	15	6	18
Weighers	36	7	4	2	1		18	1	6	9	1	1	11
Other clerks	4,645	2,119	365	819	849	86	1,873	42	305	846	456	224	653
Messenger, errand, and office girls [12]	369	202	82	72	43	5	125	8	26	56	24	11	42
Stenographers and typists	3,225	1,960	310	913	719	18	930	34	248	472	137	39	335

[1] Not otherwise specified.
[2] Includes tin-plate mills.
[3] Includes iron foundries.
[4] Includes box factories (wood).
[5] Teamsters in agriculture, forestry, and the extraction of minerals are classified with the other workers in those industries, respectively; drivers for bakeries and stores are classified as deliverymen in trade; and drivers for laundries are classified as deliverymen in domestic and personal service.
[6] Includes only persons specifically returned as "clerks" in stores. Many of these probably are "saleswomen."
[7] Some deliverymen probably were returned and classified as chauffeurs, and others as teamsters or truck drivers.
[8] Includes, also, managers and superintendents of retail stores.
[9] Probably includes some teachers in schools below collegiate rank.
[10] Some owners of hand laundries probably are included with laundry operatives.
[11] Some deliverymen probably were returned and classified as chauffeurs.
[12] Except telegraph messengers.

TABLE 26.—NEGRO GAINFUL WORKERS 10 YEARS OLD AND OVER, BY SEX, AND AGE, BY SECTIONS, DIVISIONS, AND STATES: 1930

SECTION, DIVISION, AND STATE	10 YEARS OLD AND OVER			10 TO 17 YEARS		18 AND 19 YEARS		20 TO 24 YEARS		25 TO 29 YEARS		30 TO 34 YEARS		35 TO 39 YEARS	
	Total	Male	Female	Male	Female	Male	Female	Male	Female	Male	Female	Male	Female	Male	Female
United States	5, 503, 535	3, 662, 893	1, 840, 642	299, 903	171, 726	190, 823	113, 542	517, 707	299, 103	483, 423	267, 688	403, 804	210, 157	418, 037	219, 586
The North	1, 228, 670	829, 353	399, 317	14, 541	9, 959	25, 615	18, 844	101, 507	63, 304	133, 351	70, 824	125, 817	58, 693	124, 608	57, 312
The South	4, 210, 163	2, 790, 120	1, 420, 043	284, 839	161, 526	164, 088	94, 094	411, 952	233, 337	344, 856	193, 738	272, 228	148, 395	287, 067	158, 775
The West	64, 702	43, 420	21, 282	523	241	1, 120	604	4, 248	2, 462	5, 216	3, 126	5, 759	3, 069	6, 362	3, 499
NEW ENGLAND	45, 129	29, 686	15, 443	641	477	933	776	3, 038	2, 030	3, 654	1, 984	3, 885	1, 891	4, 071	2, 002
Maine	510	363	147	3	3	7	4	27	14	35	23	32	15	47	18
New Hampshire	493	421	72	6	3	10	3	57	10	39	4	62	6	60	10
Vermont	247	194	53	3	3	9	6	21	6	23	-------	20	5	22	6
Massachusetts	24, 666	16, 187	8, 479	309	214	468	387	1, 544	1, 055	1, 758	1, 063	2, 106	1, 045	2, 256	1, 122
Rhode Island	4, 693	3, 023	1, 670	75	74	106	102	295	176	346	157	331	184	375	179
Connecticut	14, 520	9, 498	5, 022	245	180	333	274	1, 094	769	1, 453	737	1, 334	636	1, 311	667
MIDDLE ATLANTIC	560, 738	360, 329	200, 409	6, 132	5, 490	11, 850	10, 491	47, 016	34, 132	61, 969	36, 902	57, 096	29, 163	54, 358	27, 911
New York	239, 305	143, 554	95, 751	1, 764	1, 822	4, 415	4, 666	19, 851	16, 934	27, 135	19, 158	24, 373	14, 568	22, 381	13, 668
New Jersey	107, 114	68, 487	38, 627	1, 705	1, 525	2, 472	2, 063	9, 236	6, 238	10, 805	6, 348	9, 793	5, 199	9, 520	5, 103
Pennsylvania	214, 319	148, 288	66, 031	2, 663	2, 143	4, 963	3, 762	17, 929	10, 960	24, 029	11, 396	22, 930	9, 396	22, 457	9, 140
EAST NORTH CENTRAL	457, 245	325, 016	132, 229	4, 818	2, 700	9, 197	5, 571	39, 141	20, 257	53, 235	24, 299	50, 657	20, 744	50, 805	20, 190
Ohio	145, 379	104, 982	40, 397	1, 725	864	3, 101	1, 870	12, 583	5, 994	16, 196	6, 903	15, 536	6, 009	16, 316	6, 162
Indiana	53, 332	38, 683	14, 649	641	358	1, 183	589	4, 451	1, 996	5, 475	2, 171	5, 414	2, 042	5, 494	2, 122
Illinois	171, 073	115, 236	55, 837	1, 777	1, 056	3, 241	2, 178	13, 750	8, 751	19, 025	10, 771	17, 752	8, 907	17, 940	8, 546
Michigan	82, 249	62, 089	20, 160	647	405	1, 561	882	7, 872	3, 336	11, 834	4, 220	11, 310	3, 574	10, 411	3, 164
Wisconsin	5, 212	4, 026	1, 186	28	17	111	52	485	180	705	234	645	212	644	196
WEST NORTH CENTRAL	165, 558	114, 322	51, 236	2, 950	1, 292	3, 635	2, 006	12, 312	6, 885	14, 493	7, 639	14, 179	6, 895	15, 374	7, 209
Minnesota	4, 809	3, 562	1, 247	46	25	86	43	271	151	346	128	435	166	509	181
Iowa	7, 931	5, 927	2, 004	132	54	173	90	607	255	652	229	675	252	736	278
Missouri	114, 825	77, 530	37, 295	2, 206	1, 003	2, 567	1, 458	8, 557	5, 131	10, 134	5, 780	9, 645	5, 127	10, 551	5, 278
North Dakota	219	175	44	3	-------	3	-------	7	12	18	6	15	4	23	5
South Dakota	308	241	67	8	-------	11	4	21	10	29	8	32	7	22	6
Nebraska	7, 179	4, 910	2, 269	91	39	125	83	458	256	660	342	634	296	721	386
Kansas	30, 287	21, 977	8, 310	464	171	670	328	2, 391	1, 070	2, 654	1, 146	2, 743	1, 043	2, 812	1, 075
SOUTH ATLANTIC	1, 951, 791	1, 275, 378	676, 413	135, 841	72, 615	83, 383	47, 582	191, 400	114, 604	153, 742	92, 180	122, 324	70, 463	130, 062	75, 796
Delaware	15, 887	11, 172	4, 715	401	197	468	222	1, 474	661	1, 416	655	1, 243	545	1, 412	598
Maryland	136, 014	91, 537	44, 477	4, 286	2, 104	4, 416	2, 396	13, 088	7, 010	12, 682	6, 365	10, 917	5, 453	11, 107	5, 630
District of Columbia	73, 122	41, 811	31, 311	857	649	1, 525	1, 299	5, 827	4, 770	6, 653	5, 092	5, 647	4, 158	5, 598	4, 242
Virginia	258, 066	181, 064	77, 002	13, 374	5, 210	11, 294	4, 962	24, 925	12, 313	19, 632	9, 870	17, 028	8, 201	19, 443	9, 263
West Virginia	47, 207	38, 547	8, 660	877	276	1, 342	390	4, 846	1, 328	5, 801	1, 370	5, 601	1, 182	5, 810	1, 226
North Carolina	365, 544	245, 479	120, 065	29, 031	14, 918	17, 680	9, 528	40, 459	22, 902	30, 446	17, 053	23, 087	11, 855	22, 833	11, 825
South Carolina	343, 476	213, 167	130, 309	35, 625	22, 372	17, 142	11, 140	32, 549	21, 535	21, 282	14, 820	16, 506	11, 110	19, 080	12, 786
Georgia	494, 384	311, 550	182, 834	41, 642	21, 599	22, 607	13, 334	47, 652	31, 006	35, 023	23, 866	26, 208	18, 061	28, 172	20, 198
Florida	218, 091	141, 051	77, 040	9, 748	5, 290	6, 909	4, 311	20, 580	13, 079	20, 807	13, 089	16, 087	9, 898	16, 607	10, 028
EAST SOUTH CENTRAL	1, 250, 026	816, 059	433, 967	95, 106	59, 008	44, 096	28, 033	117, 171	68, 023	98, 584	55, 464	75, 535	42, 460	79, 281	46, 171
Kentucky	106, 572	73, 098	33, 474	3, 048	1, 008	3, 056	1, 268	8, 639	4, 030	8, 239	4, 018	7, 752	3, 838	8, 789	4, 248
Tennessee	222, 693	147, 237	75, 456	10, 588	5, 388	8, 052	4, 248	20, 745	12, 044	18, 481	10, 720	15, 250	8, 512	16, 135	9, 113
Alabama	432, 349	279, 829	152, 520	36, 018	22, 522	15, 558	10, 550	41, 427	24, 758	34, 090	19, 182	24, 171	14, 298	24, 957	15, 631
Mississippi	488, 412	315, 895	172, 517	45, 452	30, 090	17, 430	11, 967	46, 360	27, 191	37, 774	21, 544	28, 362	15, 812	29, 400	17, 179
WEST SOUTH CENTRAL	1, 008, 346	698, 683	309, 663	53, 892	29, 903	36, 609	18, 479	103, 381	50, 710	92, 530	46, 094	74, 369	35, 472	77, 724	36, 808
Arkansas	201, 948	147, 538	54, 410	12, 763	6, 871	7, 463	3, 410	21, 215	8, 346	17, 950	7, 053	14, 124	5, 549	14, 973	5, 990
Louisiana	345, 389	233, 907	111, 482	20, 133	12, 193	12, 681	6, 902	34, 594	17, 781	30, 923	15, 828	23, 915	12, 044	26, 340	13, 020
Oklahoma	71, 254	51, 578	19, 676	2, 304	742	2, 429	974	7, 417	3, 664	7, 102	3, 450	5, 861	2, 674	5, 839	2, 548
Texas	389, 755	265, 660	124, 095	18, 692	10, 097	14, 036	7, 193	40, 155	20, 919	36, 555	19, 763	30, 469	15, 205	30, 572	15, 250
MOUNTAIN	16, 204	11, 741	4, 463	192	78	358	130	1, 288	448	1, 327	612	1, 445	617	1, 691	690
Montana	695	528	167	2	1	14	3	33	10	44	24	48	18	60	22
Idaho	368	305	63	6	1	10	3	22	4	22	5	27	11	48	8
Wyoming	696	536	160	7	2	11	2	43	13	43	11	67	22	84	20
Colorado	6, 220	3, 991	2, 229	64	39	98	69	340	226	394	281	436	270	534	311
New Mexico	1, 355	1, 012	343	29	12	42	7	105	49	116	46	107	48	130	58
Arizona	5, 986	4, 705	1, 281	83	21	173	41	703	128	648	221	685	219	745	236
Utah	550	428	122	1	2	8	2	28	14	42	13	48	16	60	20
Nevada	334	236	98	-------	-------	2	3	14	4	18	11	27	13	30	15
PACIFIC	48, 498	31, 679	16, 819	331	163	762	474	2, 960	2, 014	3, 889	2, 514	4, 314	2, 452	4, 671	2, 809
Washington	3, 672	2, 761	911	29	16	57	30	196	100	233	73	273	108	317	115
Oregon	1, 331	948	383	9	7	14	8	66	40	91	37	105	41	140	59
California	43, 495	27, 970	15, 525	293	140	691	436	2, 698	1, 874	3, 565	2, 404	3, 936	2, 303	4, 214	2, 635

TABLE 26.—NEGRO GAINFUL WORKERS 10 YEARS OLD AND OVER, BY SEX, AND AGE, BY SECTIONS, DIVISIONS, AND STATES: 1930

SECTION, DIVISION, AND STATE	40 TO 44 YEARS		45 TO 49 YEARS		50 TO 54 YEARS		55 TO 59 YEARS		60 TO 64 YEARS		65 TO 69 YEARS		70 TO 74 YEARS		75 YEARS AND OVER		UNKNOWN	
	Male	Female	Male	Female	Male	Female	Male	Female	Male	Female	Male	Female	Male	Female	Male	Female	Male	Female
United States	**329,762**	**166,355**	**314,200**	**144,011**	**268,330**	**103,328**	**166,770**	**57,173**	**123,515**	**41,711**	**72,646**	**23,513**	**38,786**	**11,328**	**30,228**	**8,278**	**4,959**	**3,143**
The North	**93,534**	**40,789**	**79,029**	**32,908**	**56,052**	**21,246**	**33,524**	**11,735**	**20,051**	**6,772**	**11,346**	**3,577**	**5,343**	**1,501**	**3,539**	**982**	**1,496**	**871**
The South	**230,584**	**123,043**	**230,104**	**108,837**	**208,417**	**80,490**	**130,826**	**44,544**	**101,959**	**34,448**	**60,433**	**19,643**	**33,015**	**9,719**	**26,424**	**7,235**	**3,328**	**2,219**
The West	**5,644**	**2,523**	**5,067**	**2,266**	**3,861**	**1,592**	**2,420**	**894**	**1,505**	**491**	**867**	**293**	**428**	**108**	**265**	**61**	**135**	**53**
NEW ENGLAND	3,414	1,741	3,318	1,531	2,600	1,200	1,723	738	1,144	524	684	292	313	128	228	96	40	33
Maine	36	15	54	15	27	16	23	10	26	7	18	2	9	3	18	1	1	1
New Hampshire	53	10	65	5	32	12	20	5	6	-	6	1	3	-	1	2	1	1
Vermont	17	4	23	8	19	4	13	4	9	3	6	2	4	2	5	-	-	-
Massachusetts	1,914	976	1,960	880	1,538	702	1,031	432	626	298	378	162	171	64	105	56	23	23
Rhode Island	346	179	353	182	285	154	206	103	144	85	89	49	40	27	30	16	2	3
Connecticut	1,048	557	863	441	699	312	430	184	333	131	187	76	86	32	69	21	13	5
MIDDLE ATLANTIC	39,466	19,655	32,291	15,586	22,649	9,885	12,918	5,298	7,393	2,961	3,828	1,563	1,759	588	1,011	353	593	431
New York	15,662	9,369	11,925	6,990	7,611	4,187	4,075	2,127	2,231	1,114	1,125	604	480	206	300	129	226	209
New Jersey	7,173	3,869	6,305	3,251	4,890	2,251	2,969	1,279	1,800	716	927	417	473	165	266	94	153	109
Pennsylvania	16,631	6,417	14,061	5,345	10,148	3,347	5,874	1,892	3,362	1,131	1,776	542	806	217	445	130	214	113
EAST NORTH CENTRAL	37,247	13,629	30,946	10,717	21,173	6,636	12,587	3,582	7,273	1,959	4,143	959	1,927	416	1,220	266	647	304
Ohio	12,060	4,244	10,321	3,406	7,186	2,262	4,344	1,246	2,658	713	1,522	363	747	173	495	112	192	76
Indiana	4,400	1,651	3,765	1,406	3,089	1,015	2,030	593	1,196	335	785	177	405	84	229	52	126	58
Illinois	13,410	5,772	11,339	4,511	7,622	2,614	4,411	1,370	2,512	715	1,339	325	577	131	363	80	178	110
Michigan	6,872	1,848	5,158	1,319	3,022	702	1,650	342	846	178	457	89	181	25	125	19	143	57
Wisconsin	505	114	363	75	254	43	152	31	61	18	40	5	17	3	8	3	8	3
WEST NORTH CENTRAL	13,407	5,764	12,474	5,074	9,630	3,525	6,296	2,117	4,241	1,328	2,691	763	1,344	369	1,080	267	216	103
Minnesota	480	158	463	165	375	100	259	66	146	30	97	24	28	5	15	4	6	1
Iowa	652	245	676	198	568	158	419	110	284	69	196	35	79	18	61	9	17	4
Missouri	9,108	4,097	8,448	3,572	6,231	2,443	3,971	1,407	2,723	937	1,680	523	854	269	699	186	156	84
North Dakota	22	6	26	5	25	4	14	1	8	1	5	-	4	-	2	-	-	-
South Dakota	26	12	25	7	22	6	14	4	10	2	9	-	6	1	3	-	3	-
Nebraska	628	297	606	233	443	156	225	94	156	33	86	30	29	14	41	9	7	1
Kansas	2,491	949	2,230	894	1,966	658	1,394	435	914	25	618	151	344	62	259	59	27	13
SOUTH ATLANTIC	106,328	59,194	96,912	51,574	96,156	38,311	58,348	20,447	45,698	15,739	27,104	9,030	15,034	4,404	11,193	3,088	1,853	1,386
Delaware	1,115	446	1,009	441	957	380	599	220	467	153	318	120	165	42	115	33	13	2
Maryland	8,944	4,446	8,045	3,887	6,638	2,853	4,169	1,625	3,068	1,147	1,955	682	1,064	335	683	201	475	343
District of Columbia	4,306	3,296	4,051	3,023	3,203	2,131	1,803	1,154	1,109	714	648	386	281	136	153	98	150	163
Virginia	17,423	7,344	17,026	6,875	14,686	5,081	9,790	2,839	7,092	2,276	4,526	1,387	2,691	742	1,993	527	141	112
West Virginia	4,641	958	3,811	740	2,490	562	1,539	252	872	172	492	91	221	56	135	31	69	26
North Carolina	18,473	9,244	17,053	8,042	17,056	6,137	11,220	3,403	7,686	2,425	4,872	1,384	2,934	640	2,311	467	338	242
South Carolina	16,457	10,467	14,922	9,153	13,408	6,780	8,479	3,758	8,519	3,056	4,735	1,804	2,584	828	1,779	576	100	124
Georgia	21,505	15,708	18,257	13,679	28,180	10,629	14,830	5,335	12,856	4,448	7,185	2,491	3,966	1,302	3,112	940	355	238
Florida	13,464	7,285	12,738	5,734	9,538	3,758	5,919	1,861	4,029	1,348	2,373	685	1,128	323	912	215	212	136
EAST SOUTH CENTRAL	62,451	36,259	68,998	33,504	63,211	25,606	40,619	14,547	31,748	11,535	19,062	6,668	10,601	3,495	8,797	2,691	799	503
Kentucky	7,535	3,775	7,349	3,637	6,480	2,812	4,295	1,763	3,212	1,358	2,264	853	1,400	450	947	356	93	60
Tennessee	12,359	7,011	11,057	6,134	13,656	5,115	8,125	2,805	5,658	2,023	3,476	1,135	1,866	593	1,524	450	265	165
Alabama	18,847	12,378	29,452	11,556	19,747	8,393	12,658	4,631	10,278	3,885	6,064	2,352	3,403	1,230	2,875	981	284	173
Mississippi	23,710	13,095	21,140	12,177	23,328	9,286	15,541	5,348	12,600	4,269	7,258	2,328	3,932	1,222	3,451	904	157	105
WEST SOUTH CENTRAL	61,805	27,590	64,194	23,759	49,050	16,573	31,859	9,550	24,513	7,174	14,267	3,945	7,380	1,820	6,434	1,456	676	330
Arkansas	12,035	4,865	15,266	4,345	11,902	3,446	7,822	1,838	5,501	1,346	3,206	718	1,784	345	1,446	246	88	42
Louisiana	21,307	9,792	20,894	8,768	15,741	6,134	10,684	3,641	7,609	2,551	4,545	1,495	2,319	706	2,062	561	160	65
Oklahoma	4,724	1,891	4,445	1,527	4,447	936	2,959	598	1,794	314	1,113	202	567	66	517	65	60	25
Texas	23,739	11,042	23,589	9,119	16,960	6,057	10,394	3,473	9,609	2,963	5,403	1,529	2,710	703	2,409	584	368	198
MOUNTAIN	1,422	521	1,339	487	1,052	376	634	228	484	116	254	95	141	37	90	17	24	11
Montana	66	20	61	18	67	20	49	13	40	7	20	6	16	3	7	2	1	-
Idaho	48	11	37	7	28	6	16	5	19	1	11	1	3	-	8	-	-	-
Wyoming	65	28	64	28	66	14	30	10	31	5	12	3	6	2	4	-	3	-
Colorado	487	253	519	270	414	219	271	133	204	60	125	59	63	26	35	11	7	2
New Mexico	119	35	107	28	117	24	49	19	49	9	16	5	13	1	13	-	-	2
Arizona	550	143	452	109	274	76	172	33	111	26	49	16	32	2	15	4	13	6
Utah	52	15	63	15	60	7	29	9	16	4	14	2	4	3	3	-	-	-
Nevada	35	16	36	12	26	10	18	6	14	4	7	3	4	-	5	-	-	1
PACIFIC	4,222	2,002	3,728	1,779	2,809	1,216	1,786	666	1,021	375	613	198	287	71	175	44	111	42
Washington	360	107	370	123	356	93	253	64	134	45	101	19	45	7	25	9	12	2
Oregon	142	52	125	51	98	38	80	25	32	11	24	11	9	2	9	-	4	1
California	3,720	1,843	3,233	1,605	2,355	1,085	1,453	577	855	319	488	168	233	62	141	35	95	39

TABLE 27.—NEGROES 10 YEARS OLD AND OVER IN EACH INDUSTRY OR SERVICE GROUP, BY OCCUPATION, AND SEX, FOR THE UNITED STATES: 1930

[Occupations in which there are no Negroes are omitted]

INDUSTRY AND OCCUPATION	Total	Male	Female
AGRICULTURE			
Agriculture	1,988,221	1,492,926	495,295
Farmers (owners and tenants) [1]	873,653	797,231	76,422
Farm managers and foremen	1,676	1,655	21
Bookkeepers and cashiers	9	2	7
Clerks	9	8	1
Messenger, errand, and office boys and girls	1	1	
Salesmen and saleswomen	3	3	
Shipping clerks	1	1	
Stenographers and typists	5	2	3
Blacksmiths	218	218	
Brick and stone masons	1	1	
Carpenters	32	32	
Coopers	2	2	
Cranemen, derrickmen, hoistmen, etc	1	1	
Electricians	4	4	
Engineers (stationary)	16	16	
Machinists	2	2	
Mechanics (not otherwise specified)	28	28	
Other skilled trades	1	1	
Chauffeurs and truck and tractor drivers	16	16	
Farm laborers (wage workers)	539,307	419,193	120,114
Farm laborers (unpaid family workers)	573,203	274,476	298,727
Guards and watchmen	16	16	
Janitors	10	10	
All other occupations	7	7	
FORESTRY AND FISHING			
Fishing	7,178	7,122	56
Fishermen and oystermen	7,162	7,106	56
Clerks	1	1	
Other clerical pursuits	1	1	
Engineers (stationary)	2	2	
Mechanics (not otherwise specified)	2	2	
Other skilled trades	1	1	
Chauffeurs and truck and tractor drivers	6	6	
Guards and watchmen	2	2	
All other occupations	1	1	
Forestry	25,644	25,327	317
Owners and proprietors, log and timber camps	61	61	
Managers and officials, log and timber camps	5	5	
Foremen, log and timber camps	92	92	
Foresters, forest rangers, and timber cruisers	34	34	
Civil engineers and surveyors	1	1	
Other professional pursuits	1	1	
Agents (not elsewhere classified)	1	1	
Bookkeepers and cashiers	2	2	
Clerks	5	5	
Messenger, errand, and office boys and girls	1	1	
Purchasing agents	1	1	
Shipping clerks	1	1	
Stenographers and typists	1	1	
Blacksmiths	12	12	
Carpenters	6	6	
Cranemen, derrickmen, hoistmen, etc	10	10	
Engineers (stationary)	22	22	
Machinists	6	6	
Mechanics (not otherwise specified)	6	6	
Chauffeurs and truck and tractor drivers	500	500	
Inspectors, scalers, and surveyors	32	32	
Oilers of machinery	2	2	
Saw filers	25	25	
Teamsters and haulers	1,917	1,917	
Other lumbermen, raftsmen, and woodchoppers	22,429	22,405	24
Cooks	436	152	284
Guards and watchmen	18	18	
Housekeepers and stewards	4		4
Waiters	6	2	4
All other occupations	7	6	1
EXTRACTION OF MINERALS			
Coal mines	58,060	58,027	33
Owners, operators, and proprietors	2	2	
Managers and officials	3	3	
Foremen and overseers	68	68	
Civil engineers and surveyors	2	2	
Mining engineers	1	1	
Trained nurses	2		2
Agents (not elsewhere classified)	1		1
Bookkeepers and cashiers	1		1
Clerks	14	13	1
Messenger, errand, and office boys and girls	6	6	
Office appliance operators	1		1
Shipping clerks	1	1	
Weighers [2]	6	6	
Blacksmiths	58	58	
Boilermakers	1	1	
Brick and stone masons	10	10	
Carpenters	18	18	
Cranemen, derrickmen, hoistmen, etc	10	10	
Electricians	36	36	
Engineers (stationary)	102	102	
Machinists	117	117	
Mechanics (not otherwise specified)	22	22	
Painters, glaziers, and varnishers (building)	7	7	
Plumbers and gas and steam fitters	9	9	
Chauffeurs and truck and tractor drivers	84	84	

INDUSTRY AND OCCUPATION	Total	Male	Female
EXTRACTION OF MINERALS—Continued			
Coal mines—Continued.			
Firemen	77	77	
Guards and watchmen	19	19	
Inspectors	16	16	
Janitors	37	34	3
Oilers of machinery	6	6	
Operatives	57,315	57,291	24
Policemen	1	1	
All other occupations	7	7	
Copper mines	33	33	
Clerks	2	2	
Mechanics (not otherwise specified)	1	1	
Plumbers and gas and steam fitters	1	1	
Guards and watchmen	1	1	
Janitors	3	3	
Operatives	25	25	
Gold and silver mines	17	17	
Operatives	17	17	
Iron mines	3,560	3,560	
Foremen and overseers	8	8	
Electrical engineers	1	1	
Clerks	3	3	
Other clerical pursuits	2	2	
Blacksmiths	19	19	
Boilermakers	1	1	
Brick and stone masons	2	2	
Carpenters	11	11	
Cranemen, derrickmen, hoistmen, etc	2	2	
Engineers (stationary)	2	2	
Machinists	1	1	
Plumbers and gas and steam fitters	3	3	
Chauffeurs and truck and tractor drivers	3	3	
Firemen	47	47	
Guards and watchmen	2	2	
Inspectors	1	1	
Janitors	1	1	
Oilers of machinery	1	1	
Operatives	3,448	3,448	
All other occupations	2	2	
Lead and zinc mines	80	80	
Chauffeurs and truck and tractor drivers	2	2	
Operatives	75	75	
All other occupations	3	3	
Other specified mines	2,377	2,371	6
Managers and officials	1	1	
Foremen and overseers	5	5	
Blacksmiths	2	2	
Brick and stone masons	1	1	
Carpenters	4	4	
Cranemen, derrickmen, hoistmen, etc	4	4	
Electricians	1	1	
Engineers (stationary)	3	3	
Machinists	1	1	
Mechanics (not otherwise specified)	2	2	
Painters, glaziers, and varnishers (building)	1	1	
Plumbers and gas and steam fitters	1	1	
Other skilled trades	2	2	
Chauffeurs and truck and tractor drivers	16	16	
Firemen	23	23	
Guards and watchmen	7	7	
Inspectors	3	3	
Oilers of machinery	3	3	
Operatives	2,286	2,281	5
All other occupations	11	10	1
Not specified mines	669	668	1
Owners, operators, and proprietors	1	1	
Foremen and overseers	1	1	
Clerks	4	4	
Messenger, errand, and office boys and girls	1	1	
Blacksmiths	2	2	
Carpenters	2	2	
Electricians	1	1	
Engineers (stationary)	6	6	
Machinists	1	1	
Mechanics (not otherwise specified)	2	2	
Chauffeurs and truck and tractor drivers	6	6	
Firemen	5	5	
Guards and watchmen	3	3	
Janitors	1	1	
Operatives	631	630	1
All other occupations	2	2	
Quarries	10,369	10,348	21
Owners, operators, and proprietors	4	4	
Managers and officials	5	5	
Foremen and overseers	50	50	
Bookkeepers and cashiers	2	1	1
Clerks	7	7	
Messenger, errand, and office boys and girls	2	2	
Salesmen and saleswomen	1	1	
Shipping clerks	4	4	
Stenographers and typists	1		1
Weighers	3	3	

See footnotes at end of table.

Table 27.—NEGROES 10 YEARS OLD AND OVER IN EACH INDUSTRY OR SERVICE GROUP, BY OCCUPATION, AND SEX, FOR THE UNITED STATES: 1930—Continued

[Occupations in which there are no Negroes are omitted]

INDUSTRY AND OCCUPATION	Total	Male	Female
EXTRACTION OF MINERALS—Continued			
Quarries—Continued.			
Blacksmiths	30	30	
Boilermakers	1	1	
Brick and stone masons	26	26	
Carpenters	14	14	
Cranemen, derrickmen, hoistmen, etc	30	30	
Electricians	5	5	
Engineers (stationary)	45	45	
Machinists	14	14	
Mechanics (not otherwise specified)	11	11	
Painters, glaziers, and varnishers (building)	1	1	
Plumbers and gas and steam fitters	3	3	
Stonecutters	66	66	
Other skilled trades	1	1	
Chauffeurs and truck and tractor drivers	333	333	
Firemen	86	86	
Guards and watchmen	35	35	
Inspectors	5	5	
Janitors	3	3	
Oilers of machinery	9	9	
Operatives	9,541	9,522	19
All other occupations	31	31	
Oil wells and gas wells [3]	1,410	1,408	2
Owners, operators, and proprietors	5	4	1
Foremen and overseers	9	9	
Chemists, assayers, and metallurgists	1	1	
Agents (not elsewhere classified)	1	1	
Clerks	9	9	
Office appliance operators	1	1	
Shipping clerks	1	1	
Blacksmiths	9	9	
Boilermakers	3	3	
Carpenters	2	2	
Cement finishers	1	1	
Engineers (stationary)	25	25	
Machinists	1	1	
Mechanics (not otherwise specified)	8	8	
Painters, glaziers, and varnishers (building)	1	1	
Plumbers and gas and steam fitters	12	12	
Chauffeurs and truck and tractor drivers	133	133	
Firemen	5	5	
Guards and watchmen	5	5	
Inspectors	1	1	
Janitors	26	25	1
Operatives	1,129	1,129	
All other occupations	22	22	
Salt wells and works	348	345	3
Foremen and overseers	3	3	
Clerks	4	4	
Weighers	2	2	
Carpenters	1	1	
Coopers	1	1	
Engineers (stationary)	4	4	
Machinists	1	1	
Mechanics (not otherwise specified)	1	1	
Other skilled trades	1	1	
Chauffeurs and truck and tractor drivers	5	5	
Firemen	1	1	
Guards, watchmen, and doorkeepers	2	2	
Janitors	2	2	
Operatives	314	311	3
All other occupations	6	6	
MANUFACTURING AND MECHANICAL INDUSTRIES			
Building industry	181,423	181,173	250
Builders and building contractors	2,410	2,406	4
Owners, operators, and proprietors	26	26	
Managers and officials	29	29	
Foremen and overseers	282	281	1
Chemists	1	1	
Civil Engineers and surveyors	29	29	
Designers	1	1	
Draftsmen	11	11	
Electrical engineers	12	12	
Mechanical engineers [4]	6	6	
Accountants and auditors	4	3	1
Advertising agents	1	1	
Bookkeepers and cashiers	37	7	30
Canvassers	1		1
Clerks	80	53	27
Collectors	3	3	
Messengers, errand, and office boys and girls	18	15	3
Office appliance operators	4	4	
Shipping clerks	6	6	
Stenographers and typists	27	3	24
Weighers	1	1	
Blacksmiths	41	41	
Boilermakers	5	5	
Brick and stone masons and tile layers	10,887	10,887	
Cabinetmakers	15	15	
Carpenters	29,928	29,922	6
Cement finishers	2,578	2,578	
Coopers	1	1	
Coppersmiths	3	3	
Cranemen, derrickmen, hoistmen, etc	182	182	
MANUFACTURING AND MECHANICAL INDUSTRIES—Con.			
Building industry—Continued.			
Electricians	793	793	
Engineers	219	219	
Forgemen and hammermen	3	3	
Machinists	53	53	
Mechanics (not otherwise specified)	395	395	
Millwrights	1	1	
Painters, glaziers, and varnishers (building)	15,245	15,236	9
Paper hangers	2,154	2,126	28
Pattern and model makers	5	5	
Plasterers	10,287	10,286	1
Plumbers and gas and steam fitters	3,375	3,375	
Roofers and slaters	1,044	1,044	
Sawyers	1	1	
Stonecutters	29	29	
Structural iron workers	292	292	
Tinsmiths and sheet metal workers	513	513	
Other skilled trades	4	4	
Apprentices:			
Carpenters	99	99	
Electricians	8	8	
Machinists	1	1	
Plumbers	36	36	
Tinsmiths, and coppersmiths	10	10	
Apprentices to other building and hand trades	302	302	
Charwomen and cleaners	54	8	46
Chauffeurs and truck and tractor drivers	2,376	2,376	
Cooks	101	70	31
Draymen and teamsters	626	625	1
Elevator tenders	7	7	
Firemen	127	127	
Guards, watchmen, and doorkeepers	202	202	
Janitors	55	54	1
Laborers	95,618	95,587	31
Oilers of machinery	9	9	
Operatives	685	683	2
Policemen	1	1	
Porters	58	58	
Waiters	3	2	1
All other occupations	3	1	2
CHEMICAL AND ALLIED INDUSTRIES			
Charcoal and coke works	2,190	2,168	22
Owners, operators, and proprietors	1	1	
Foremen and overseers	14	14	
Chemists	1	1	
Mechanical engineers [4]	1	1	
Clerks	3	3	
Salesmen and saleswomen	2	2	
Shipping clerks	1	1	
Other clerical pursuits	1	1	
Boilermakers	1	1	
Brick and stone masons	5	5	
Cranemen, derrickmen, hoistmen, etc	4	4	
Electricians	1	1	
Engineers (stationary)	5	5	
Machinists	14	14	
Mechanics (not otherwise specified)	1	1	
Plumbers and gas and steam fitters	1	1	
Other skilled trades	1	1	
Chauffeurs and truck and tractor drivers	30	30	
Draymen and teamsters	7	7	
Firemen	29	29	
Furnace men	268	268	
Guards, watchmen, and doorkeepers	5	5	
Janitors	16	15	1
Laborers	1,428	1,419	9
Oilers of machinery	4	4	
Operatives	341	329	12
All other occupations	5	5	
Explosives, ammunition, and fireworks factories	476	451	25
Foremen and overseers	1	1	
Chemists	2	2	
Clerks	3	3	
Stenographers and typists	2		2
Electricians	1	1	
Engineers (stationary)	1	1	
Machinists	1	1	
Mechanics (not otherwise specified)	8	8	
Plumbers and gas and steam fitters	2	2	
Other skilled trades	2	2	
Chauffeurs and truck and tractor drivers	5	5	
Draymen and teamsters	7	7	
Firemen	5	5	
Guards, watchmen, and doorkeepers	2	2	
Janitors	6	6	
Laborers	345	335	10
Operatives	78	66	12
All other occupations	5	4	1
Fertilizer factories	17,020	16,900	120
Owners, operators, and proprietors	1	1	
Managers and officials	1	1	
Foremen and overseers	57	57	
Chemists	5	5	
Other professional pursuits	1	1	

See footnotes at end of table.

Table 27.—NEGROES 10 YEARS OLD AND OVER IN EACH INDUSTRY OR SERVICE GROUP, BY OCCUPATION, AND SEX, FOR THE UNITED STATES: 1930—Continued

[Occupations in which there are no Negroes are omitted]

INDUSTRY AND OCCUPATION	Total	Male	Female
MANUFACTURING AND MECHANICAL INDUSTRIES—Continued			
CHEMICAL AND ALLIED INDUSTRIES—continued			
Fertilizer factories—Continued.			
Bookkeepers and cashiers	1	1	-------
Clerks	14	13	1
Messenger, errand, and office boys and girls	10	10	-------
Salesmen and saleswomen	3	3	-------
Shipping clerks	7	7	-------
Stenographers and typists	2	1	1
Weighers	28	28	-------
Blacksmiths	8	8	-------
Carpenters	13	13	-------
Compositors, linotypers, and typesetters	17	17	-------
Cranemen, derrickmen, hoistmen, etc	5	5	-------
Electricians	3	3	-------
Engineers (stationary)	14	14	-------
Machinists	25	25	-------
Mechanics (not otherwise specified)	25	25	-------
Millwrights	9	9	-------
Other skilled trades	3	3	-------
Chauffeurs and truck and tractor drivers	191	191	-------
Draymen and teamsters	43	43	-------
Firemen	75	75	-------
Guards, watchmen, and doorkeepers	27	27	-------
Janitors	16	16	-------
Laborers	15, 347	15, 268	79
Oilers of machinery	11	11	-------
Operatives	1, 039	1, 000	39
All other occupations	19	19	-------
Gas works [3]	5, 973	5, 769	24
Managers and officials	1	1	-------
Foremen and overseers	22	22	-------
Chemists	2	2	-------
Civil engineers and surveyors	1	1	-------
Mechanical engineers [4]	1	1	-------
Accountants and auditors	1	1	-------
Bookkeepers and cashiers	1	1	-------
Clerks	48	46	2
Messenger, errand, and office boys and girls	21	20	1
Salesmen and saleswomen	3	3	-------
Shipping clerks	1	1	-------
Weighers	1	1	-------
Blacksmiths	7	7	-------
Boilermakers	3	3	-------
Brick and stone masons and tile layers	5	5	-------
Carpenters	1	1	-------
Cranemen, derrickmen, hoistmen, etc	2	2	-------
Electricians	5	5	-------
Engineers (stationary)	22	22	-------
Forgemen and hammermen	2	2	-------
Machinists	14	14	-------
Mechanics (not otherwise specified)	38	38	-------
Millwrights	1	1	-------
Plumbers and gas and steam fitters	188	188	-------
Other skilled trades	1	1	-------
Apprentices:			
Plumber	1	1	-------
Charwomen and cleaners	6	1	5
Chauffeurs and truck and tractor drivers	99	99	-------
Draymen and teamsters	10	10	-------
Elevator tenders	10	10	-------
Firemen	249	249	-------
Guards, watchmen, and doorkeepers	36	36	-------
Janitors	156	145	11
Laborers	4, 324	4, 319	5
Oilers of machinery	7	7	-------
Operatives	306	306	-------
Painters, glaziers, and varnishers (factory)	5	5	-------
Porters	181	181	-------
All other occupations	11	11	-------
Paint and varnish factories	1, 400	1, 349	51
Owners, operators, and proprietors	1	1	-------
Managers and officials	1	1	-------
Foremen and overseers	14	14	-------
Chemists	7	7	-------
Bookkeepers and cashiers	1	-------	1
Clerks	9	8	1
Messenger, errand, and office boys and girls	3	3	-------
Salesmen and saleswomen	1	1	-------
Shipping clerks	19	19	-------
Weighers	1	1	-------
Carpenters	1	1	-------
Compositors, linotypers, and typesetters	2	1	1
Coopers	1	1	-------
Electricians	1	1	-------
Engineers (stationary)	1	1	-------
Machinists	6	6	-------
Mechanics (not otherwise specified)	4	4	-------
Painters, glaziers, and varnishers (building)	7	7	-------
Chauffeurs and truck and tractor drivers	71	71	-------
Draymen and teamsters	3	3	-------
Elevator tenders	1	1	-------
Firemen	20	20	-------
Guards, watchmen, and doorkeepers	10	10	-------
Janitors	33	31	2
Laborers	756	739	17
Operatives	330	305	25
Painters, glaziers, and varnishers (factory) [5]	27	25	2
Porters	64	64	-------
All other occupations	5	3	2
MANUFACTURING AND MECHANICAL INDUSTRIES—Continued			
CHEMICAL AND ALLIED INDUSTRIES—continued			
Petroleum refineries	9, 433	9, 386	47
Foremen and overseers	19	19	-------
Chemists	6	6	-------
Lawyers	1	1	-------
Accountants and auditors	1	1	-------
Agents (not elsewhere classified)	2	1	1
Clerks	19	19	-------
Messenger, errand, and office boys and girls	31	31	-------
Salesmen and saleswomen	1	1	-------
Shipping clerks	11	11	-------
Weighers	2	2	-------
Blacksmiths	7	7	-------
Boilermakers	26	26	-------
Brick and stone masons and tile layers	55	55	-------
Carpenters	20	20	-------
Cement finishers	2	2	-------
Coopers	19	19	-------
Cranemen, derrickmen, hoistmen, etc	3	3	-------
Electricians	3	3	-------
Engineers (stationary)	13	13	-------
Machinists	17	17	-------
Mechanics (not otherwise specified)	37	37	-------
Millwrights	1	1	-------
Painters, glaziers, and varnishers (building)	9	9	-------
Plumbers and gas and steam fitters	45	45	-------
Skilled occupations (not elsewhere classified)	14	14	-------
Toolmakers and die setters and sinkers	1	1	-------
Charwomen and cleaners	2	1	1
Chauffeurs and truck and tractor drivers	153	153	-------
Draymen and teamsters	107	107	-------
Firemen	81	81	-------
Guards, watchmen, and doorkeepers	25	25	-------
Housekeepers and stewards	1	1	-------
Janitors	95	94	1
Laborers	7, 863	7, 828	35
Oilers of machinery	17	17	-------
Operatives	557	548	9
Painters, glaziers, and varnishers (factory)	27	27	-------
Porters	140	140	-------
Rayon factories	899	867	32
Foremen and overseers	1	1	-------
Clerks	1	1	-------
Brick and stone masons and tile layers	29	29	-------
Carpenters	1	1	-------
Cement finishers	1	1	-------
Electricians	1	1	-------
Engineers (stationary)	1	1	-------
Plumbers and gas and steam fitters	1	1	-------
Chauffeurs and truck and tractor drivers	6	6	-------
Draymen and teamsters	2	2	-------
Firemen	8	8	-------
Guards, watchmen, and doorkeepers	1	1	-------
Janitors	69	68	1
Laborers	675	663	12
Operatives	94	76	18
All other occupations	8	7	1
Soap factories	644	591	53
Owners, operators, and proprietors	1	1	-------
Foremen and overseers	2	2	-------
Chemists	6	6	-------
Agents (not elsewhere classified)	2	1	1
Bookkeepers and cashiers	3	2	1
Canvassers	9	3	6
Clerks	4	3	1
Commercial travelers	5	3	2
Messenger, errand, and office boys and girls	2	1	1
Salesmen and saleswomen	5	3	2
Shipping clerks	10	10	-------
Stenographer and typist	1	-------	1
Engineers (stationary)	3	3	-------
Machinists	4	4	-------
Mechanics (not otherwise specified)	1	1	-------
Millwrights	1	1	-------
Chauffeurs and truck and tractor drivers	15	15	-------
Draymen and teamsters	3	3	-------
Elevator tenders	5	5	-------
Firemen	12	12	-------
Guards, watchmen, and doorkeepers	2	2	-------
Janitors	19	18	1
Laborers	350	338	12
Oilers of machinery	1	1	-------
Operatives	151	126	25
Painters, glaziers, and varnishers (factory)	1	1	-------
Porters	26	26	-------
Other chemical factories	10, 069	9, 530	539
Owners, operators, and proprietors	38	34	4
Managers and officials	7	7	-------
Foremen and overseers	70	66	4
Chemists	163	158	5
Electrical engineers	2	2	-------
Lawyers	1	1	-------
Agents (not elsewhere classified)	36	15	21
Bookkeepers and cashiers	11	3	8
Canvassers	36	9	27
Clerks	86	70	16
Collectors	4	4	-------
Commercial travelers	47	31	16

See footnotes at end of table.

TABLE 27.—NEGROES 10 YEARS OLD AND OVER IN EACH INDUSTRY OR SERVICE GROUP, BY OCCUPATION, AND SEX, FOR THE UNITED STATES: 1930—Continued

[Occupations in which there are no Negroes are omitted]

INDUSTRY AND OCCUPATION	Total	Male	Female
MANUFACTURING AND MECHANICAL INDUSTRIES—Continued			
CHEMICAL AND ALLIED INDUSTRIES—continued			
Other chemical factories—Continued.			
Messenger, errand, and office boys and girls	39	36	3
Purchasing agents	2	2	
Sales agents	3	3	
Salesmen and saleswomen	58	39	19
Shipping clerks	93	88	5
Stenographers and typists	15	1	14
Weighers	6	5	1
Blacksmiths	4	4	
Boilermakers	1	1	
Brick and stone masons and tile layers	4	4	
Cabinetmakers	1	1	
Carpenters	7	7	
Cement finishers	2	2	
Compositors, linotypers, and typesetters	4	4	
Coopers	5	5	
Cranemen, derrickmen, hoistmen, etc	9	9	
Electricians	4	4	
Engineers (stationary)	39	39	
Machinists	44	44	
Mechanics (not otherwise specified)	34	34	
Millwrights	8	8	
Painters, glaziers, and varnishers (building)	1	1	
Plumbers and gas and steam fitters	9	9	
Tinsmiths and sheet-metal workers	3	3	
Other skilled trades	1	1	
Apprentices	2	2	
Charwomen and cleaners	8	2	6
Chauffeurs and truck and tractor drivers	224	224	
Draymen and teamsters	57	57	
Elevator tenders	25	22	3
Firemen	226	226	
Guards, watchmen, and doorkeepers	45	44	1
Housekeepers and stewards	1		1
Janitors	158	153	5
Laborers	6,636	6,482	154
Oilers of machinery	8	8	
Operatives	1,472	1,248	224
Painters, glaziers, and varnishers (factory)	16	14	2
Policemen	1	1	
Porters	293	293	
Cigar and tobacco factories	34,301	15,789	18,512
Owners, operators, and proprietors	18	17	1
Managers and officials	1	1	
Foremen and overseers	69	58	11
Trained nurses	3		3
Bookkeepers and cashiers	2		2
Clerks	60	33	27
Commercial travelers	4	4	
Messenger, errand, and office boys and girls	18	18	
Sales agents	1	1	
Salesmen and saleswomen	11	11	
Shipping clerks	87	68	19
Stenographers and typists	2		2
Weighers	22	13	9
Blacksmiths	3	3	
Carpenters	12	12	
Coopers	162	162	
Engineers (stationary)	12	12	
Machinists	64	64	
Mechanics (not otherwise specified)	20	20	
Plumbers and gas and steam fitters	1	1	
Tinsmiths and sheet-metal workers	1	1	
Other skilled trades	7	7	
Apprentices	3	1	2
Charwomen and cleaners	37	1	36
Chauffeurs and truck and tractor drivers	176	176	
Draymen and teamsters	19	19	
Elevator tenders	72	72	
Firemen	116	116	
Guards, watchmen, and doorkeepers	30	28	2
Janitors	135	105	30
Laborers	12,254	8,863	3,391
Oilers of machinery	14	14	
Operatives	20,721	5,745	14,976
Painters, glaziers, and varnishers (factory)	3	3	
Porters	140	140	
All other occupations	1		1
CLAY, GLASS, AND STONE INDUSTRIES			
Brick, tile, and terra cotta factories	14,356	14,245	111
Owners, operators, and proprietors	2	2	
Managers and officials	3	3	
Foremen and overseers	50	50	
Clerks	6	5	1
Messenger, errand, and office boys and girls	8	8	
Office appliance operators	1		1
Shipping clerks	6	6	
Stenographers and typists	1	1	
Other clerical pursuits	1	1	
Blacksmiths	14	14	
Brick and stone masons and tile layers	99	99	
Carpenters	6	6	
Cranemen, derrickmen, hoistmen, etc	12	12	
Electricians	2	2	
Engineers (stationary)	18	18	
Machinists	31	31	
Mechanics (not otherwise specified)	17	17	
Millwrights	1	1	
Painters, glaziers, and varnishers (building)	3	3	

INDUSTRY AND OCCUPATION	Total	Male	Female
MANUFACTURING AND MECHANICAL INDUSTRIES—Continued			
CLAY, GLASS, AND STONE INDUSTRIES—continued			
Brick, tile, and terra cotta factories—Continued.			
Plumbers and gas and steam fitters	1	1	
Apprentices	1	1	
Chauffeurs and truck and tractor drivers	302	302	
Draymen and teamsters	99	99	
Firemen	399	399	
Guards, watchmen, and doorkeepers	40	40	
Janitors	25	25	
Laborers	12,180	12,095	85
Oilers of machinery	7	7	
Operatives	1,007	986	21
Painters, glaziers, and varnishers (factory)	2	2	
All other occupations	12	9	3
Glass factories	3,997	3,487	510
Owners, operators, and proprietors	1	1	
Foremen and overseers	15	15	
Chemists	1	1	
Designers	1	1	
Electrical engineers	1	1	
Clerks	8	6	2
Commercial travelers	1	1	
Messenger, errand, and office boys and girls	6	6	
Salesmen and saleswomen	1	1	
Shipping clerks	18	18	
Stenographers and typists	1		1
Weighers	1	1	
Blacksmiths	2	2	
Boilermakers	2	2	
Brick and stone masons and tile layers	2	2	
Carpenters	3	3	
Coopers	1	1	
Cranemen, derrickmen, hoistmen, etc	4	4	
Electricians	3	3	
Engineers (stationary)	2	2	
Engravers	2	2	
Glass blowers	33	33	
Machinists	29	29	
Mechanics (not otherwise specified)	1	1	
Plumbers and gas and steam fitters	1	1	
Apprentices	1	1	
Chauffeurs and truck and tractor drivers	68	68	
Draymen and teamsters	12	12	
Firemen	49	49	
Guards, watchmen, and doorkeepers	15	15	
Janitors	66	60	6
Laborers	2,475	2,313	162
Oilers of machinery	8	8	
Operatives	1,114	776	338
Painters, glaziers, and varnishers, (factory)	2	2	
Porters	46	46	
All other occupations	1		1
Lime, cement, and artificial stone factories	7,867	7,813	54
Owners, operators, and proprietors	16	16	
Managers and officials	2	2	
Foremen and overseers	43	43	
Chemists	3	3	
Designers	1	1	
Clerks	10	10	
Commercial travelers	3	3	
Messenger, errand, and office boys and girls	6	3	3
Salesmen and saleswomen	1	1	
Shipping clerks	1	1	
Stenographers and typists	2		2
Weighers	6	6	
Blacksmiths	1	1	
Boilermakers	2	2	
Brick and stone masons and tile layers	12	12	
Carpenters	5	5	
Cement finishers	68	68	
Coopers	6	6	
Cranemen, derrickmen, hoistmen, etc	10	10	
Engineers (stationary)	26	26	
Machinists	24	24	
Mechanics (not otherwise specified)	31	31	
Millwrights	4	4	
Painters, glaziers, and varnishers (building)	1	1	
Pattern and model makers	1	1	
Plumbers and gas and steam fitters	1	1	
Other skilled trades	1	1	
Chauffeurs and truck and tractor drivers	315	315	
Draymen and teamsters	54	54	
Elevator tenders	4	4	
Firemen	112	112	
Guards, watchmen, and doorkeepers	45	45	
Janitors	32	30	2
Laborers	6,041	6,016	25
Oilers of machinery	13	13	
Operatives	949	927	22
Painterts, glaziers, and varnishers (factory)	1	1	
All other occupations	14	14	
Marble and stone yards	1,669	1,665	4
Owners, operators, and proprietors	1	1	
Foremen and overseers	4	4	
Clerks	3	2	1
Messenger, errand, and office boys and girls	1	1	
Salesmen and saleswomen	1	1	
Shipping clerks	2	2	
Other clerical pursuits	1	1	
Blacksmiths	4	4	

See footnotes at end of table.

TABLE 27.—NEGROES 10 YEARS OLD AND OVER IN EACH INDUSTRY OR SERVICE GROUP, BY OCCUPATION, AND SEX, FOR THE UNITED STATES: 1930—Continued

[Occupations is which there are no Negroes are omitted]

INDUSTRY AND OCCUPATION	Total	Male	Female
MANUFACTURING AND MECHANICAL INDUSTRIES—Continued			
CLAY, GLASS, AND STONE INDUSTRIES—continued			
Marble and stone yards—Continued.			
Brick and stone masons and tile layers	54	54	---
Cranemen, derrickmen, hoistmen, etc	9	9	---
Engineers (stationary)	1	1	---
Machinists	6	6	---
Mechanics (not otherwise specified)	7	7	---
Millwrights	1	1	---
Plumbers and gas and steam fitters	1	1	---
Sawyers	6	6	---
Stone cutters	225	225	---
Toolmakers and die setters and sinkers	1	1	---
Other skilled trades	1	1	---
Apprentices	2	2	---
Chauffeurs and truck and tractor drivers	74	74	---
Draymen and teamseters	12	12	---
Firemen	7	7	---
Guards, watchmen, and doorkeepers	2	2	---
Janitors	10	10	---
Laborers	1,007	1,007	---
Operatives	215	215	---
All other occupations	11	8	3
Potteries	1,001	939	62
Foremen and overseers	5	5	---
Clerks	4	2	2
Salesmen and saleswomen	1	---	1
Shipping clerks	4	4	---
Brick and stone masons and tile layers	4	4	---
Carpenters	2	2	---
Engineers (stationary)	2	2	---
Machinists	2	2	---
Mechanics (not otherwise specified)	3	3	---
Plumbers and gas and steam fitters	3	3	---
Chauffeurs and truck and tractor drivers	12	12	---
Draymen and teamsters	5	5	---
Guards, watchmen, and doorkeepers	5	5	---
Janitors	15	12	3
Laborers	696	677	19
Operatives	231	195	36
Painters, glaziers, and varnishers (factory)	1	---	1
All other occupations	6	6	---
CLOTHING INDUSTRIES			
Corset factories	96	29	67
Managers and officials	1	1	---
Designers	1	---	1
Agents (not elsewhere classified)	2	---	2
Canvassers	1	---	1
Clerks	2	---	2
Messenger, errand, and office boys and girls	1	---	1
Purchasing agents	1	---	1
Salesmen and saleswomen	3	1	2
Shipping clerks	5	4	1
Mechanics (not otherwise specified)	2	2	---
Other skilled trades	1	1	---
Firemen	3	3	---
Guards, watchmen, and doorkeepers	1	1	---
Janitors	2	2	---
Laborers	5	4	1
Operatives	55	3	52
All other occupations	10	7	3
Glove factories	297	53	244
Foremen and overseers	1	---	1
Bookkeepers and cashiers	1	---	1
Clerks	3	---	3
Shipping clerks	4	4	---
Mechanics (not otherwise specified)	1	1	---
Chauffeurs and truck and tractor drivers	2	2	---
Janitors	1	---	1
Laborers	27	21	6
Operatives	248	16	232
All other occupations	9	9	---
Hat factories (felt)	842	654	188
Owners, operators, and proprietors	2	2	---
Foremen and overseers	2	1	1
Designers	2	---	2
Bookkeepers and cashiers	2	1	1
Clerks	12	9	3
Commercial travelers	1	1	---
Messenger, errand, and office boys and girls	28	26	2
Office appliance operators	1	---	1
Purchasing agents	2	---	2
Salesmen and saleswomen	3	3	---
Shipping clerks	55	54	1
Engineers (stationary)	3	3	---
Machinists	3	3	---
Mechanics (not otherwise specified)	1	1	---
Painters, glaziers, and varnishers (building)	1	1	---
Chauffeurs and truck and tractor drivers	8	8	---
Dyers	5	5	---
Elevator tenders	8	8	---
Firemen	13	13	---
Guards, watchmen, and doorkeepers	2	2	---
Janitors	15	15	---
Laborers	88	81	7
Operatives	459	294	165
Porters	120	120	---
All other occupations	6	3	3
MANUFACTURING AND MECHANICAL INDUSTRIES—Continued			
CLOTHING INDUSTRIES—continued			
Shirt, collar, and cuff factories	2,327	1,253	1,074
Foremen and overseers	18	8	10
Bookkeepers and cashiers	1	---	1
Clerks	18	14	4
Messenger, errand, and office boys and girls	10	10	---
Salesmen and saleswomen	3	---	3
Shipping clerks	13	12	1
Stenographers and typists	2	---	2
Other clerical pursuits	1	1	---
Carpenters	1	1	---
Electricians	1	1	---
Engineers (stationary)	1	1	---
Machinists	3	3	---
Mechanics (not otherwise specified)	2	2	---
Chauffeurs and truck and tractor drivers	5	5	---
Elevator tenders	4	3	1
Firemen	1	1	---
Guards, watchmen, and doorkeepers	4	4	---
Janitors	19	15	4
Laborers	606	539	67
Operatives	1,539	560	979
Porters	71	71	---
All other occupations	4	2	2
Suit, coat, and overall factories	15,075	12,552	2,523
Owners, operators, and proprietors	341	330	11
Managers and officials	20	18	2
Foremen and overseers	9	5	4
Designers	1	---	1
Photographers	1	1	---
Agents (not elsewhere classified)	6	5	1
Bookkeepers and cashiers	16	3	13
Canvassers	5	5	---
Clerks	57	41	16
Collectors	1	1	---
Commercial travelers	9	9	---
Messenger, errand, and office boys and girls	160	150	10
Salesmen and saleswomen	24	22	2
Shipping clerks	100	100	---
Stenographers and typists	3	---	3
Carpenters	1	1	---
Electricians	1	1	---
Engineers (stationary)	1	1	---
Machinists	5	5	---
Mechanics (not otherwise specified)	2	2	---
Pattern and model makers	1	1	---
Tailors and tailoresses	7,505	6,953	552
Apprentices	36	33	3
Charwomen and cleaners	8	3	5
Chauffeurs and truck and tractor drivers	124	124	---
Draymen and teamsters	3	3	---
Dyers	2	2	---
Elevator tenders	11	9	2
Firemen	7	7	---
Guards, watchmen, and doorkeepers	10	10	---
Janitors	48	45	3
Laborers	480	446	34
Operatives	5,672	3,812	1,860
Porters	405	404	1
Other clothing factories	16,769	3,864	12,905
Owners, operators, and proprietors	5	2	3
Managers and officials	5	5	---
Foremen and overseers	56	6	50
Designers	49	7	42
Draftsmen	2	2	---
Accountants and auditors	1	1	---
Agents (not elsewhere classified)	14	4	10
Bookkeepers and cashiers	10	4	6
Canvassers	6	3	3
Clerks	146	59	87
Collectors	1	---	1
Commercial travelers	9	9	---
Messenger, errand, and office boys and girls	191	165	26
Purchasing agents	1	---	1
Salesmen and saleswomen	29	20	9
Shipping clerks	409	395	14
Stenographers and typists	6	---	6
Compositors, linotypers, and typesetters	1	1	---
Electricians	1	1	---
Engineers (stationary)	4	4	---
Machinists	12	12	---
Mechanics (not otherwise specified)	3	3	---
Painters, glaziers, and varnishers (building)	1	1	---
Other skilled trades	1	1	---
Apprentices:			
Designers and draftmen	1	---	1
Machinists	1	1	---
Other	1	1	---
Charwomen	23	1	22
Chauffeurs and truck and tractor drivers	46	46	---
Draymen and teamsters	1	1	---
Dyers	9	9	---
Elevator tenders	59	51	8
Firemen	14	14	---
Guards, watchmen, and doorkeepers	24	24	---
Janitors	89	76	13
Laborers	603	348	255
Operatives	14,243	1,896	12,347
Porters	690	690	---
All other occupations	2	1	1

See footnotes at end of table.

TABLE 27.—NEGROES 10 YEARS OLD AND OVER IN EACH INDUSTRY OR SERVICE GROUP, BY OCCUPATION, AND SEX, FOR THE UNITED STATES: 1930—Continued

[Occupations in which there are no Negroes are omitted]

INDUSTRY AND OCCUPATION	Total	Male	Female
MANUFACTURING AND MECHANICAL INDUSTRIES—Continued			
FOOD AND ALLIED INDUSTRIES			
Bakeries	9,242	8,259	983
Owners, operators, and proprietors	28	24	4
Managers and officials	5	5	-
Foremen and overseers	37	28	9
Electrical engineers	1	1	-
Agents (not elsewhere classified)	1	-	1
Bookkeepers and cashiers	2	1	1
Clerks	64	46	18
Collectors	1	1	-
Commercial travelers	14	12	2
Credit men	1	1	-
Messenger, errand, and office boys and girls	9	9	-
Salesmen and saleswomen	9	4	5
Shipping clerks	31	30	1
Stenographers and typists	4	-	4
Weighers	6	5	1
Carpenters	6	6	-
Electricians	2	2	-
Engineers (stationary)	17	17	-
Machinists	8	8	-
Mechanics (not otherwise specified)	41	41	-
Apprentices	40	40	-
Bakers	4,527	3,919	608
Charwomen and cleaners	45	7	38
Chauffeurs and truck and tractor drivers [6]	186	186	-
Deliverymen [6]	230	230	-
Draymen and teamsters [6]	11	11	-
Elevator tenders	26	25	1
Firemen	135	135	-
Guards, watchmen, and doorkeepers	10	10	-
Housekeepers and stewards	4	-	4
Janitors	396	384	12
Laborers	1,533	1,445	88
Operatives	856	670	186
Painters, glaziers, and varnishers (factory)	3	3	-
Porters	953	953	-
Butter, cheese, and condensed milk factories [7]	983	940	43
Owners, operators, and proprietors	1	1	-
Foremen and overseers	10	9	1
Electrical engineers	1	1	-
Canvassers	1	1	-
Clerks	11	10	1
Messenger, errand, and office boys and girls	1	1	-
Purchasing agents	1	-	1
Salesmen and saleswomen	2	2	-
Shipping clerks	4	4	-
Blacksmiths	4	4	-
Engineers (stationary)	6	6	-
Machinists	4	4	-
Mechanics (not otherwise specified)	5	5	-
Other skilled trades	2	2	-
Chauffeurs and truck and tractor drivers	82	82	-
Draymen and teamsters	8	8	-
Elevator tenders	2	2	-
Firemen	28	28	-
Guards, watchmen, and doorkeepers	5	5	-
Janitors	38	38	-
Laborers	534	516	18
Oilers of machinery	1	1	-
Operatives	179	157	22
Painters, glaziers, and varnishers (factory)	1	1	-
Porters	52	52	-
Candy factories	2,199	1,566	633
Owners, operators, and proprietors	6	6	-
Managers and officials	2	1	1
Foremen and overseers	9	3	6
Designers	1	1	-
Bookkeepers and cashiers	3	1	2
Canvassers	1	1	-
Clerks	29	26	3
Commercial travelers	5	5	-
Messenger, errand, and office boys and girls	8	8	-
Office appliance operators	1	-	1
Salesmen and saleswomen	3	2	1
Shipping clerks	25	25	-
Stenographers and typists	1	-	1
Engineers (stationary)	5	5	-
Machinists	6	6	-
Mechanics (not otherwise specified)	2	2	-
Plumbers and gas and steam fitters	1	1	-
Other skilled trades	2	2	-
Apprentices	1	1	-
Charwomen and cleaners	3	-	3
Chauffeurs and truck and tractor drivers	116	116	-
Draymen and teamsters	5	5	-
Elevator tenders	7	6	1
Firemen	28	28	-
Guards, watchmen, and doorkeepers	8	8	-
Janitors	41	32	9
Laborers	523	375	148
Operatives	1,111	655	456
Painters, glaziers, and varnishers (factory)	1	-	1
Porters	244	244	-
All other occupations	1	1	-
Fish curing and packing	3,964	2,170	1,794
Owners, operators, and proprietors	1	1	-
Managers and officials	2	2	-
Foremen and overseers	15	15	-
Messenger, errand, and office boys and girls	2	2	-
Weighers	2	-	2
MANUFACTURING AND MECHANICAL INDUSTRIES—Continued			
FOOD AND ALLIED INDUSTRIES—continued			
Fish curing and packing—Continued.			
Blacksmiths	1	1	-
Coopers	1	1	-
Electricians	1	1	-
Engineers (stationary)	5	5	-
Machinists	2	2	-
Mechanics (not otherwise specified)	1	1	-
Chauffeurs and truck and tractor drivers	18	17	1
Firemen	18	18	-
Guards, watchmen, and doorkeepers	4	4	-
Laborers	2,011	1,227	784
Operatives	1,872	868	1,004
All other occupations	8	5	3
Flour and grain mills	3,777	3,728	49
Owners, operators, and proprietors	3	3	-
Managers and officials	4	4	-
Foremen and overseers	18	18	-
Electrical engineers	1	1	-
Mechanical engineers	1	1	-
Bookkeepers and cashiers	1	1	-
Clerks	9	9	-
Commercial travelers	1	-	1
Messenger, errand, and office boys and girls	4	3	1
Salesmen and saleswomen	2	1	1
Shipping clerks	4	4	-
Stenographers and typists	1	1	-
Weighers	16	16	-
Carpenters	1	1	-
Coopers	1	1	-
Cranemen, derrickmen, hoistmen, etc	1	1	-
Engineers (stationary)	12	12	-
Machinists	25	25	-
Mechanics (not otherwise specified)	5	5	-
Millers	238	236	2
Millwrights	4	4	-
Painters, glaziers, and varnishers (building)	1	1	-
Plumbers and gas and steam fitters	1	1	-
Chauffeurs and truck and tractor drivers	286	285	1
Draymen and teamsters	51	51	-
Elevator tenders	7	7	-
Firemen	58	58	-
Guards, watchmen, and doorkeepers	13	13	-
Janitors	27	24	3
Laborers	2,442	2,417	25
Oilers of machinery	10	10	-
Operatives	468	453	15
Porters	61	61	-
Fruit and vegetable canning, etc	2,703	1,558	1,145
Managers and officials	4	4	-
Foremen and overseers	15	10	5
Chemists	1	1	-
Agents (not elsewhere classified)	1	1	-
Bookkeepers and cashiers	1	1	-
Clerks	8	6	2
Messenger, errand, and office boys and girls	1	1	-
Shipping clerks	9	9	-
Weighers	1	-	1
Coopers	3	3	-
Electricians	1	1	-
Engineers (stationary)	6	6	-
Machinists	11	11	-
Mechanics (not otherwise specified)	3	3	-
Other skilled trades	1	1	-
Chauffeurs and truck and tractor drivers	47	46	1
Draymen and teamsters	10	10	-
Elevator tenders	3	3	-
Firemen	30	30	-
Guards, watchmen, and doorkeepers	1	1	-
Housekeepers and stewards	2	2	-
Janitors	37	35	2
Laborers	1,488	1,052	436
Operatives	979	284	695
Porters	36	36	-
All other occupations	4	1	3
Slaughter and packing houses [8]	18,426	17,028	1,398
Owners, operators, and proprietors	4	4	-
Managers and officials	4	4	-
Foremen and overseers	47	44	3
Chemists	1	1	-
Bookkeepers and cashiers	4	3	1
Canvassers	1	1	-
Clerks	77	70	7
Collectors	1	1	-
Commercial travelers	1	1	-
Messenger, errand, and office boys and girls	5	5	-
Purchasing agents	1	1	-
Salesmen and saleswomen	11	11	-
Shipping clerks	74	73	1
Stenographers and typists	2	-	2
Weighers	35	31	4
Blacksmiths	2	2	-
Boilermakers	5	5	-
Brick and stone masons and tile layers	2	2	-
Carpenters	15	15	-
Coopers	66	66	-
Cranemen, derrickmen, hoistmen, etc	4	4	-
Electricians	6	6	-
Engineers (stationary)	28	28	-

See footnotes at end of table.

TABLE 27.—NEGROES 10 YEARS OLD AND OVER IN EACH INDUSTRY OR SERVICE GROUP, BY OCCUPATION, AND SEX, FOR THE UNITED STATES: 1930—Continued

[Occupations in which there are no Negroes are omitted]

INDUSTRY AND OCCUPATION	Total	Male	Female
MANUFACTURING AND MECHANICAL INDUSTRIES—Continued			
FOOD AND ALLIED INDUSTRIES—continued			
Slaughter and packing houses—Continued.			
Machinists	45	45	
Mechanics (not otherwise specified)	26	26	
Millwrights	5	5	
Painters, glaziers, and varnishers (building)	1	1	
Plumbers and gas and steam fitters	14	14	
Other skilled trades	1	1	
Apprentices	1	1	
Chauffeurs and truck and tractor drivers	587	587	
Draymen and teamsters	56	56	
Elevator tenders	65	65	
Firemen	166	166	
Guards, watchmen, and doorkeepers	34	33	1
Housekeepers and stewards	5	1	4
Janitors	282	273	9
Laborers	9,332	8,854	478
Oilers of machinery	8	8	
Operatives	7,167	6,286	881
Painters, glaziers, and varnishers (factory)	12	10	2
Porters	219	218	1
All other occupations	4		4
Sugar factories and refineries	3,280	3,148	132
Foremen and overseers	19	19	
Mechanical engineers	3	3	
Clerks	5	5	
Messenger, errand, and office boys and girls	1	1	
Salesmen and saleswomen	1	1	
Shipping clerks	7	7	
Stenographers and typists	1		1
Weighers	18	18	
Blacksmiths	6	6	
Brick and stone masons and tile layers	7	7	
Carpenters	4	4	
Coopers	18	18	
Electricians	1	1	
Engineers (stationary)	17	17	
Machinists	26	26	
Mechanics (not otherwise specified)	16	16	
Millwrights	1	1	
Plumbers and gas and steam fitters	5	5	
Chauffeurs and truck and tractor drivers	30	30	
Draymen and teamsters	5	5	
Elevator tenders	4	4	
Firemen	40	40	
Guards, watchmen, and doorkeepers	21	21	
Janitors	9	9	
Laborers	2,662	2,553	109
Oilers of machinery	10	10	
Operatives	300	280	20
Painters, glaziers, and varnishers (factory)	1	1	
Porters	38	38	
All other occupations	4	2	2
Other food factories	9,593	4,001	5,592
Owners, operators, and proprietors	14	13	1
Managers and officials	5	5	
Foremen and overseers	29	16	13
Chemists	3	3	
Agents (not elsewhere classified)	2	2	
Bookkeepers and cashiers	3	1	2
Canvassers	4	2	2
Clerks	19	14	5
Commercial travelers	4	4	
Messenger, errand, and office boys and girls	6	6	
Sales agents	1		1
Salesmen and saleswomen	15	12	3
Shipping clerks	19	19	
Stenographers	2		2
Weighers	9	6	3
Blacksmiths	1	1	
Carpenters	6	6	
Coopers	4	4	
Cranemen, derrickmen, hoistmen, etc.	1	1	
Electricians	2	2	
Engineers (stationary)	14	14	
Machinists	24	24	
Mechanics (not elsewhere classified)	14	14	
Millers	2	2	
Millwrights	2	2	
Painters, glaziers, and varnishers (building)	1	1	
Plumbers and gas and steam fitters	1	1	
Apprentices	1	1	
Chauffeurs and truck and tractor drivers	283	283	
Draymen and teamsters	33	33	
Elevator tenders	19	19	
Firemen	81	81	
Guards, watchmen, and doorkeepers	14	14	
Janitors	78	74	4
Laborers	4,637	2,441	2,196
Oilers of machinery	3	3	
Operatives	4,127	768	3,359
Porters	109	109	
All other occupations	1		1
Liquor and beverage industries	3,185	3,045	140
Owners, operators, and proprietors	8	8	
Managers and officials	7	7	
Foremen and overseers	11	11	
Chemists	1	1	
Advertising agents	1	1	
Bookkeepers and cashiers	5		5
Clerks	10	5	5
Commercial travelers	2	2	
MANUFACTURING AND MECHANICAL INDUSTRIES—Continued			
FOOD AND ALLIED INDUSTRIES—continued			
Liquor and beverage industries—Continued.			
Messenger, errand, and office boys and girls	11	11	
Salesmen and saleswomen	8	7	7
Shipping clerks	1	1	
Stenographers and typists	2		2
Weighers	1		1
Coopers	5	5	
Engineers (stationary)	5	5	
Machinists	17	17	
Mechanics (not otherwise specified)	12	12	
Apprentices	1	1	
Chauffeurs and truck and tractor drivers	533	533	
Draymen and teamsters	35	35	
Elevator tenders	1	1	
Firemen	31	31	
Guards, watchmen, and doorkeepers	6	6	
Janitors	24	21	3
Laborers	1,598	1,542	56
Oilers of machinery	2	2	
Operatives	775	708	67
Porters	71	71	
All other occupations	1	1	
IRON AND STEEL, MACHINERY, AND VEHICLE INDUSTRIES			
Agricultural implement factories	1,092	1,080	12
Foremen and overseers	7	7	
Chemists	1	1	
Agents (not elsewhere classified)	1	1	
Clerks	9	9	
Messenger, errand, and office boys and girls	1	1	
Office appliance operators	1	1	
Shipping clerks	9	8	1
Stenographers and typists	1	1	
Weighers	3	3	
Blacksmiths	5	5	
Boilermakers	1	1	
Carpenters	2	2	
Cranemen, derrickmen, hoistmen, etc.	4	4	
Electricians	2	2	
Engineers (stationary)	1	1	
Machinists	22	22	
Mechanics (not otherwise specified)	12	12	
Millwrights	3	3	
Iron molders, founders, and casters	117	117	
All other molders, founders, and casters	2	2	
Pattern and model makers	1	1	
Sawyers	1	1	
Apprentices	1	1	
Buffers and polishers (metal)	7	7	
Chauffeurs and truck and tractor drivers	16	16	
Draymen and teamsters	8	8	
Elevator tenders	3	3	
Firemen	9	9	
Furnace men, smelter men, and pourers	13	13	
Grinders (metal)	31	31	
Guards, watchmen, and doorkeepers	3	3	
Heaters	1	1	
Janitors	59	58	1
Laborers	585	579	6
Oilers of machinery	1	1	
Operatives	108	104	4
Painters, glaziers, and varnishers (factory)	24	24	
Porters	17	17	
Automobile factories	25,895	25,598	297
Owners, operators, and proprietors	3	3	
Managers and officials	3	3	
Foremen and overseers	87	87	
Chemists, assayers, and metallurgists	2	2	
Draftsmen	7	7	
Electrical engineers	1	1	
Mechanical engineers	1	1	
Accountants and auditors	1	1	
Agents (not elsewhere classified)	3	3	
Bookkeepers and cashiers	5	2	3
Clerks	106	103	3
Commercial travelers	3	3	
Messenger, errand, and office boys and girls	11	11	
Salesmen and saleswomen	8	8	
Shipping clerks	72	72	
Stenographers and typists	2	1	1
Weighers	5	5	
Blacksmiths	29	29	
Boilermakers	6	6	
Brick and stone masons and tile layers	8	8	
Cabinetmakers	1	1	
Carpenters	55	55	
Cement finishers	9	9	
Coopers	1	1	
Coppersmiths	1	1	
Cranemen, derrickmen, hoistmen, etc.	56	56	
Electricians	75	75	
Engineers (stationary)	21	21	
Forgemen and hammermen	175	175	
Machinists	958	958	
Mechanics (not otherwise specified)	811	811	
Millwrights	102	102	
Iron molders, founders, and casters	210	210	
Other molders, founders, and casters	27	27	
Painters, glaziers, and varnishers (building)	6	6	
Pattern and model makers	5	5	
Plumbers and gas and steam fitters	19	19	

See footnotes at end of table.

TABLE 27.—NEGROES 10 YEARS OLD AND OVER IN EACH INDUSTRY OR SERVICE GROUP, BY OCCUPATION, AND SEX, FOR THE UNITED STATES: 1930—Continued

[Occupations in which there are no Negroes are omitted]

INDUSTRY AND OCCUPATION	Total	Male	Female
MANUFACTURING AND MECHANICAL INDUSTRIES—Continued			
IRON AND STEEL, MACHINERY, AND VEHICLE INDUSTRIES—continued			
Automobile factories—Continued.			
Rollers and roll hands	5	5	
Sawyers	51	51	
Skilled occupations (not elsewhere classified)	14	14	
Tinsmiths and sheet metal workers	10	10	
Toolmakers and die setters and sinkers	62	62	
Upholsterers	60	54	6
Apprentices:			
Electricians	1	1	
Machinists	9	9	
Other apprentices	15	15	
Buffers and polishers (metal)	74	74	
Charwomen and cleaners	14	11	3
Chauffeurs and truck and tractor drivers	315	315	
Draymen and teamsters	16	16	
Elevator tenders	19	14	5
Enamelers, lacquerers, and japanners	6	6	
Filers (metal)	20	20	
Firemen	114	114	
Furnace men, smelter men, and pourers	71	71	
Grinders (metal)	225	223	2
Guards, watchmen, and doorkeepers	74	74	
Heaters	73	73	
Housekeepers and stewards	1		1
Janitors	1,126	1,111	15
Laborers	16,450	16,289	161
Oilers of machinery	28	28	
Operatives	3,245	3,154	91
Painters, glaziers, and varnishers (factory)	526	520	6
Policemen	1	1	
Porters	375	375	
Automobile repair shops	12,793	12,752	41
Owners, operators, and proprietors	156	156	
Managers and officials	14	14	
Foremen and overseers	13	13	
Bookkeepers and cashiers	11	1	10
Clerks	9	7	2
Messenger, errand, and office boys and girls	4	4	
Salesmen and saleswomen	4	4	
Stenographers and typists	2		2
Blacksmiths	12	12	
Cabinetmakers	1	1	
Carpenters	1	1	
Electricians	15	15	
Engineers (stationary)	2	2	
Forgemen and hammermen	2	2	
Machinists	711	711	
Mechanics (not otherwise specified)	7,677	7,677	
Painters, glaziers, and varnishers (building)	5	5	
Tinsmiths and sheet metal workers	1	1	
Upholsterers	8	8	
Other skilled trades	1	1	
Apprentices:			
Machinists	13	13	
Other apprentices	118	117	1
Buffers and polishers (metal)	1	1	
Chauffeurs and truck and tractor drivers	198	198	
Firemen	1	1	
Guards, watchmen, and doorkeepers	16	16	
Janitors	48	48	
Laborers	2,659	2,644	15
Oilers of machinery	5	5	
Operatives	617	612	5
Painters, glaziers, and varnishers (factory)	326	322	4
Porters	138	138	
All other occupations	4	2	2
Blast furnaces and steel rolling mills [9]	52,956	52,625	331
Owners, operators, and proprietors	1	1	
Managers and officials	4	4	
Foremen and overseers	185	184	1
Chemists, assayers, and metallurgists	9	9	
Civil engineers and surveyors	3	3	
Draftsmen	2	2	
Mechanical engineers	3	3	
Social and welfare workers	5	3	2
Trained nurses	1		1
Bookkeepers and cashiers	4	3	1
Clerks	86	85	1
Commercial travelers	1	1	
Messenger, errand, and office boys and girls	41	41	
Office appliance operators	1	1	
Salesmen and saleswomen	1	1	
Shipping clerks	120	120	
Stenographers and typists	4		4
Weighers	30	30	
Blacksmiths	73	73	
Boilermakers	40	40	
Brick and stone masons and tile layers	195	195	
Cabinetmakers	1	1	
Carpenters	39	39	
Cement finishers	8	8	
Coopers	6	6	
Cranemen, derrickmen, hoistmen, etc	454	454	
Electricians	38	38	
Engineers (stationary)	110	110	
Engravers	1	1	
Forgemen and hammermen	43	43	
Blast furnaces and steel rolling mills—Continued.			
Machinists	303	303	
Mechanics (not otherwise specified)	111	111	
Millwrights	50	50	
Brass molders, founders, and casters (metal)	1	1	
Iron molders, founders, and casters	518	518	
Painters, glaziers, and varnishers (building)	10	10	
Pattern and model makers	3	3	
Plumbers and gas and steam fitters	61	61	
Rollers and roll hands	1,080	1,080	
Sawyers	13	13	
Skilled occupations (not elsewhere classified)	39	38	1
Tinsmiths and sheet-metal workers	9	9	
Toolmakers and die setters and sinkers	7	7	
Other skilled trades	1	1	
Apprentices:			
Electricians	1	1	
Other apprentices	7	7	
Buffers and polishers (metal)	20	20	
Charwomen and cleaners	8	5	3
Chauffeurs and truck and tractor drivers	326	326	
Draymen and teamsters	44	44	
Elevator tenders	8	8	
Enamelers, lacquerers, and japanners	1	1	
Filers (metal)	4	4	
Firemen	625	625	
Furnace men, smelter men, and pourers	927	927	
Grinders (metal)	207	206	1
Guards, watchmen, and doorkeepers	70	70	
Heaters	320	320	
Housekeepers and stewards	2	2	
Janitors	529	517	12
Laborers	38,915	38,709	206
Oilers of machinery	119	119	
Operatives	6,861	6,763	98
Painters, glaziers, and varnishers (factory)	70	70	
Policemen	2	2	
Porters	99	99	
Puddlers	76	76	
Car and railroad shops [10]	16,279	16,148	131
Foremen and overseers	56	55	1
Electrical engineers	1	1	
Bookkeepers and cashiers	1	1	
Clerks	93	93	
Messenger, errand, and office boys and girls	30	29	1
Office appliance operators	1	1	
Salesmen and saleswomen	1	1	
Shipping clerks	7	7	
Stenographers and typists	1	1	
Weighers	4	4	
Blacksmiths	251	251	
Boilermakers	351	351	
Brick and stone masons and tile layers	8	8	
Cabinetmakers	15	15	
Carpenters	348	348	
Coopers	5	5	
Coppersmiths	9	9	
Cranemen, derrickmen, hoistmen, etc	34	34	
Electricians	36	36	
Engineers (stationary)	25	25	
Forgemen and hammermen	25	25	
Machinists	601	601	
Mechanics (not elsewhere specified)	288	288	
Millwrights	1	1	
Brass molders, founders, and casters	1	1	
Iron molders, founders, and casters	91	91	
Other molders, founders, and casters	2	2	
Painters, glaziers, and varnishers (building)	4	4	
Plumbers and gas and steam fitters	68	68	
Rollers and roll hands	8	8	
Sawyers	1	1	
Tinsmiths and sheet metal workers	23	23	
Toolmakers and die setters and sinkers	2	2	
Upholsterers	38	38	
Other skilled trades	1	1	
Apprentices:			
Blacksmiths	2	2	
Carpenters	1	1	
Machinists	2	2	
Plumbers	1	1	
Other apprentices	13	13	
Buffers and polishers (metal)	7	6	1
Charwomen and cleaners	3	2	1
Chauffeurs and truck and tractor drivers	22	22	
Draymen and teamsters	4	4	
Filers (metal)	2	2	
Firemen (except locomotive)	220	220	
Furnace men, smelter men, and pourers	18	18	
Grinders (metal)	8	8	
Guards, watchmen, and doorkeepers	30	30	
Heaters	12	12	
Janitors	142	137	5
Laborers	9,226	9,130	96
Oilers of machinery	148	148	
Operatives	3,670	3,644	26
Painters, glaziers, and varnishers (factory)	219	219	
Porters	96	96	
All other occupations	2	2	

See footnotes at end of table.

TABLE 27.—NEGROES 10 YEARS OLD AND OVER IN EACH INDUSTRY OR SERVICE GROUP, BY OCCUPATION, AND SEX, FOR THE UNITED STATES: 1930—Continued

[Occupations in which there are no Negroes are omitted]

INDUSTRY AND OCCUPATION	Total	Male	Female
MANUFACTURING AND MECHANICAL INDUSTRIES—Continued			
IRON AND STEEL, MACHINERY, AND VEHICLE INDUSTRIES—continued			
Ship and boat building	7,628	7,605	23
Owners, operators, and proprietors	1	1	--------
Foremen and overseers	21	21	--------
Bookkeepers and cashiers	2	2	--------
Clerks	32	32	--------
Commercial travelers	1	1	--------
Messenger, errand, and office boys and girls	7	7	--------
Office appliance operators	2	2	--------
Shipping clerks	5	5	--------
Weighers	4	4	--------
Other clerical pursuits	1	1	--------
Blacksmiths	65	65	--------
Boilermakers	38	38	--------
Brick and stone masons and tile layers	6	6	--------
Cabinetmakers	1	1	--------
Carpenters	350	349	1
Cement finishers	8	8	--------
Compositors, linotypers, and typesetters	2	2	--------
Coopers	8	8	--------
Coppersmiths	2	2	--------
Cranemen, derrickmen, hoistmen, etc	19	19	--------
Electricians	2	2	--------
Engineers (stationary)	15	15	--------
Forgemen and hammermen	4	4	--------
Machinists	51	51	--------
Mechanics (not otherwise specified)	67	67	--------
Millwrights	1	1	--------
Iron molders, founders, and casters	19	19	--------
All other molders, founders, and casters	3	3	--------
Painters, glaziers, and varnishers (building)	13	13	--------
Pattern and model makers	4	4	--------
Plumbers and gas and steam fitters	29	29	--------
Sawyers	2	2	--------
Tinsmiths and sheet-metal workers	2	2	--------
Toolmakers and die setters and sinkers	1	1	--------
Apprentices:			
Designers and draftsmen	1	1	--------
Carpenters	2	2	--------
Tinsmiths and coppersmiths	1	1	--------
Other apprentices	6	6	--------
Buffers and polishers (metal)	1	1	--------
Chauffeurs and truck and tractor drivers	51	51	--------
Draymen and teamsters	15	15	--------
Firemen	57	57	--------
Furnace men, smelter men, and pourers	1	1	--------
Grinders (metal)	2	2	--------
Guards, watchmen, and doorkeepers	19	19	--------
Heaters	19	19	--------
Janitors	53	53	--------
Laborers	4,566	4,549	17
Oilers of machinery	7	7	--------
Operatives	1,857	1,855	2
Painters, glaziers, and varnishers (factory)	155	154	1
Policemen	1	1	--------
Porters	19	19	--------
All other occupations	7	5	2
Wagon and carriage factories	288	286	2
Managers and officials	1	1	--------
Foremen and overseers	1	1	--------
Clerks	2	2	--------
Blacksmiths	35	35	--------
Carpenters	4	4	--------
Machinists	2	2	--------
Mechanics (not otherwise specified)	16	16	--------
Millwrights	1	1	--------
Iron molders, founders, and casters	3	3	--------
Painters, glaziers, and varnishers (building)	1	1	--------
Sawyers	2	2	--------
Other skilled trades	1	1	--------
Chauffeurs and truck and tractor drivers	7	7	--------
Draymen and teamsters	8	8	--------
Firemen	4	4	--------
Guards, watchmen, and doorkeepers	4	4	--------
Laborers	153	153	--------
Operatives	27	25	2
Painters, glaziers, and varnishers (factory)	7	7	--------
All other occupations	9	9	--------
Other iron and steel and machinery factories [11]	41,618	40,833	785
Owners, operators, and proprietors	14	14	--------
Managers and officials	6	6	--------
Foremen and overseers	182	180	2
Civil engineers and surveyors	2	2	--------
Draftsmen	16	16	--------
Mechanical engineers [4]	6	6	--------
Social and welfare workers	3	2	1
Trained nurses	1	--------	1
Advertising agents	1	1	--------
Agents (not elsewhere classified)	9	7	2
Bookkeepers and cashiers	9	6	3
Canvassers	1	1	--------
Clerks	142	137	5
Commercial travelers	3	3	--------
Messenger, errand, and office boys and girls	48	47	1
Office appliance operators	5	5	--------
Purchasing agents	1	1	--------
Sales agents	1	1	--------
Salesmen and saleswomen	4	4	--------
Shipping clerks	173	171	2
MANUFACTURING AND MECHANICAL INDUSTRIES—Continued			
IRON AND STEEL, MACHINERY, AND VEHICLE INDUSTRIES—continued			
Other iron and steel and machinery factories—Con.			
Stenographers and typists	11	3	8
Weighers	22	22	--------
Blacksmiths	1,409	1,409	--------
Boilermakers	232	232	--------
Brick and stone masons and tile layers	31	31	--------
Cabinetmakers	3	3	--------
Carpenters	50	50	--------
Cement finishers	6	6	--------
Compositors, linotypers, and typesetters	2	2	--------
Coopers	3	3	--------
Coppersmiths	1	1	--------
Cranemen, derrickmen, hoistment, etc	230	230	--------
Electricians	25	25	--------
Engineers (stationary)	74	74	--------
Forgemen and hammermen	111	111	--------
Machinists	922	922	--------
Mechanics (not otherwise specified)	676	676	--------
Millwrights	28	28	--------
Brass molders, founders, and casters	2	2	--------
Iron molders, founders, and casters	4,201	4,201	--------
Other molders, founders, and casters	15	15	--------
Painters, glaziers, and varnishers (building)	4	4	--------
Pattern and model makers	10	10	--------
Plumbers and gas and steam fitters	90	90	--------
Rollers and roll hands	38	38	--------
Sawyers	10	10	--------
Skilled occupations (not elsewhere classified)	27	27	--------
Tinsmiths and sheet-metal workers	21	21	--------
Toolmakers and die setters and sinkers	26	26	--------
Upholsterers	2	1	1
Apprentices:			
Blacksmiths	21	21	--------
Boiler makers	3	3	--------
Machinists	15	15	--------
Other apprentices	25	25	--------
Buffers and polishers	63	60	3
Charwomen and cleaners	19	13	6
Chauffeurs and truck and tractor drivers	585	585	--------
Draymen and teamsters	64	64	--------
Elevator tenders	31	27	4
Enamelers, lacquerers, and japanners	13	13	--------
Filers	20	20	--------
Firemen	473	473	--------
Furnace men, smelter men, and pourers	564	564	--------
Grinders	400	395	5
Guards, watchmen, and doorkeepers	115	115	--------
Heaters	51	51	--------
Housekeepers and stewards	2	--------	2
Janitors	602	581	21
Laborers	23,033	22,716	317
Oilers of machinery	45	45	--------
Oilers of machinery	45	45	--------
Operatives	6,047	5,651	396
Painters, glaziers, and varnishers (factory)	142	137	5
Policemen	3	3	--------
Porters	356	356	--------
Puddlers	17	17	--------
Not specified metal industries	18,064	17,882	182
Managers and officials	2	2	--------
Foremen and overseers	58	58	--------
Chemists, assayers, and metallurgists	7	7	--------
Draftsmen	1	1	--------
Bookkeepers and cashiers	2	--------	2
Clerks	20	18	2
Commercial travelers	1	--------	1
Messenger, errand, and office boys and girls	4	4	--------
Salesmen and saleswomen	1	1	--------
Shipping clerks	39	39	--------
Weighers	10	10	--------
Blacksmiths	21	21	--------
Boilermakers	19	19	--------
Brick and stone masons and tile layers	13	13	--------
Carpenters	12	12	--------
Compositors, linotypers, and typesetters	1	1	--------
Coopers	3	3	--------
Cranemen, derrickmen, hoistmen, etc	72	72	--------
Electricians	2	2	--------
Engineers (stationary)	10	10	--------
Forgemen and hammermen	26	26	--------
Machinists	109	109	--------
Mechanics (not otherwise specified)	56	56	--------
Millwrights	13	13	--------
Iron molders, founders, and casters	36	36	--------
Other molders, founders and casters	2,621	2,621	--------
Painters, glaziers, and varnishers (building)	8	8	--------
Pattern and model makers	8	8	--------
Plumbers and gas and steam fitters	16	16	--------
Rollers and roll hands	19	19	--------
Skilled occupation (not elsewhere classified)	11	10	1
Tinsmiths and sheet-metal workers	11	11	--------
Toolmakers and die setters and sinkers	2	2	--------
Machinists' apprentices	2	2	--------
Other apprentices	12	12	--------
Buffers and polishers	25	22	3
Chauffeurs and truck and tractor drivers	189	189	--------
Draymen and teamsters	15	15	--------
Elevator tenders	5	5	--------

See footnotes at end of table.

TABLE 27.—NEGROES 10 YEARS OLD AND OVER IN EACH INDUSTRY OR SERVICE GROUP, BY OCCUPATION, AND SEX, FOR THE UNITED STATES: 1930—Continued

[Occupations in which there are no Negroes are omitted]

INDUSTRY AND OCCUPATION	Total	Male	Female
MANUFACTURING AND MECHANICAL INDUSTRIES—Continued			
IRON AND STEEL, MACHINERY, AND VEHICLE INDUSTRIES—continued			
Not specified metal industries—Continued.			
Enamelers, lacquerers, and japanners	4	4	-
Filer	1	1	-
Firemen	186	186	-
Furnace men, smelter men, and pourers	289	289	-
Grinders	216	211	5
Guards, watchmen, and doorkeepers	39	39	-
Heaters	23	23	-
Janitors	92	88	4
Laborers	12,152	12,033	119
Oilers of machinery	2	2	-
Operatives	1,490	1,447	43
Painters, glaziers, and varnishers (factory)	14	13	1
Porters	48	48	-
Puddlers	24	24	-
All other occupations	2	1	1
Metal industries (except iron and steel)	-	-	-
Brass mills	2,388	2,348	40
Foremen and overseers	9	9	-
Draftsmen	1	1	-
Bookkeepers and cashiers	1	1	-
Clerks	15	15	-
Messenger, errand, and office boys and girls	1	1	-
Shipping clerks	8	7	1
Weighers	2	2	-
Carpenters	1	1	-
Compositors, linotypers, and typesetters	1	1	-
Cranemen, derrickmen, hoistmen, etc	9	9	-
Engineers (stationary)	2	2	-
Machinists	24	24	-
Mechanics (not otherwise specified)	9	9	-
Millwrights	1	1	-
Molders, founders, and casters	273	273	-
Plumbers and gas and steamfitters	2	2	-
Rollers and roll hands	47	47	-
Sawyers	2	2	-
Tinsmiths and sheet-metal workers	4	4	-
Machinists' apprentices	1	1	-
Buffers and polishers	15	13	2
Chauffeurs and truck and tractor drivers	32	32	-
Draymen and teamsters	1	1	-
Elevator tenders	3	2	1
Enamelers, lacquerers, and japanners	1	1	-
Filers	12	11	1
Firemen	27	27	-
Furnace men, smelter men, and pourers	73	73	-
Grinders	26	26	-
Guards, watchmen, and doorkeepers	7	7	-
Heaters	6	6	-
Janitors	31	31	-
Laborers	1,435	1,419	16
Oilers of machinery	2	2	-
Operatives	270	252	18
Painters, glaziers, and varnishers (factory)	2	2	-
Porters	29	29	-
All other occupations	3	2	1
Clock and watch factories	60	45	15
Clerks	3	1	2
Messenger, errand, and office boys and girls	1	1	-
Shipping clerks	3	3	-
Engineers (stationary)	1	1	-
Mechanics (not otherwise specified)	3	3	-
Apprentices	1	-	1
Chauffeurs and truck and tractor drivers	1	1	-
Firemen	1	1	-
Guards, watchmen, and doorkeepers	1	1	-
Janitors	4	4	-
Laborers	11	11	-
Operatives	28	16	12
All other occupations	2	2	-
Copper factories	1,108	1,106	2
Foremen and overseers	4	4	-
Clerks	10	10	-
Messenger, errand, and office boys and girls	2	2	-
Carpenters	2	2	-
Coppersmiths	5	5	-
Cranemen, derrickmen, hoistmen, etc	5	5	-
Engravers	1	1	-
Forgemen and hammermen	2	2	-
Machinists	11	11	-
Mechanics (not otherwise specified)	1	1	-
Millwrights	1	1	-
Iron molders, founders, and casters	3	3	-
All other molders, founders, and casters	15	15	-
Painters, glaziers, and varnishers (building)	1	1	-
Rollers and roll hands	12	12	-
Skilled occupations (not elsewhere classified)	3	3	-
Tinsmiths and sheet-metal workers	4	4	-
Other skilled trades	1	1	-
Buffers and polishers	3	3	-
Chauffeurs and truck and tractor drivers	4	4	-
Draymen and teamsters	1	1	-
Firemen	19	19	-
Furnace men, smelter men, and pourers	27	27	-
Grinders	1	1	-
Guards, watchmen, and doorkeepers	3	3	-
Janitors	8	7	1
Laborers	868	868	-

INDUSTRY AND OCCUPATION	Total	Male	Female
MANUFACTURING AND MECHANICAL INDUSTRIES—Continued			
IRON AND STEEL, MACHINERY, AND VEHICLE INDUSTRIES—continued			
Copper factories—Continued.			
Operatives	83	82	1
Painters, glaziers, and varnishers (factory)	1	1	-
All other occupations	7	7	-
Gold and silver factories	86	74	12
Chemists, assayers, and metallurgists	1	1	-
Clerks	2	1	1
Messenger, errand, and office boys and girls	4	4	-
Shipping clerks	1	1	-
Engravers	1	1	-
Goldsmiths and silversmiths	13	13	-
Machinists	1	1	-
Buffers and polishers	9	7	2
Chauffeurs and truck and tractor drivers	2	2	-
Firemen	1	1	-
Guards, watchmen, and doorkeepers	2	2	-
Heaters	1	1	-
Janitors	1	1	-
Laborers	11	8	3
Operatives	30	24	6
All other occupations	6	6	-
Jewelry factories	196	143	53
Managers and officials	1	1	-
Foremen and overseers	1	1	-
Designers	1	1	-
Clerks	4	2	2
Commercial travelers	3	3	-
Messenger, errand, and office boys and girls	17	17	-
Salesmen and saleswomen	2	2	-
Shipping clerks	16	16	-
Stenographers and typists	1	-	1
Other clerical pursuits	1	1	-
Engravers	4	4	-
Goldsmiths and silversmiths	8	8	-
Jewelers and lapidaries (factory)	23	14	9
Mechanics (not otherwise specified)	1	1	-
Other skilled trades	1	1	-
Jewelers, watchmakers', goldsmiths', and silversmiths' apprentices	2	2	-
Buffers and polishers	10	6	4
Chauffeurs and truck and tractor drivers	3	3	-
Enamelers, lacquerers, and japanners	2	-	2
Firemen	1	1	-
Guards, watchmen, and doorkeepers	3	3	-
Heaters	1	1	-
Janitors	1	1	-
Laborers	8	8	-
Operatives	53	18	35
Porters	28	28	-
Lead and zinc factories	944	936	8
Foremen and overseers	3	3	-
Clerks	3	3	-
Messenger, errand, and office boys and girls	1	1	-
Shipping clerks	2	2	-
Brick and stone masons and tile layers	1	1	-
Cranemen, derrickmen, hoistmen, etc	2	2	-
Electricians	1	1	-
Engineers (stationary)	4	4	-
Machinists	2	2	-
Mechanics (not otherwise specified)	2	2	-
Molders, founders, and casters	14	14	-
Skilled occupations (not elsewhere classified)	4	4	-
Chauffeurs and truck and tractor drivers	6	6	-
Firemen	26	26	-
Furnace men, smelter men, and pourers	119	119	-
Grinders	1	1	-
Guards and doorkeepers	1	-	1
Janitors	11	11	-
Laborers	663	660	3
Oilers of machinery	1	1	-
Operatives	68	64	4
All other occupations	9	9	-
Tinware, enamelware, etc., factories	2,088	1,894	194
Owners, operators, and proprietors	4	4	-
Foremen and overseers	18	16	2
Designers	1	-	1
Bookkeepers and cashiers	2	-	2
Clerks	8	7	1
Messenger, errand, and office boys and girls	1	-	1
Salesmen and saleswomen	1	1	-
Shipping clerks	7	7	-
Stenographers and typists	1	-	1
Brick and stone masons and tile layers	1	1	-
Carpenters	1	1	-
Compositors, linotypers, and typesetters	2	2	-
Coopers	1	1	-
Engineers (stationary)	3	3	-
Machinists	11	11	-
Mechanics (not otherwise specified)	8	8	-
Millwrights	2	2	-
Moulders, founders, and casters	44	44	-
Pattern and model makers	1	1	-
Plumbers and gas and steam fitters	4	4	-
Rollers and roll hands	12	12	-
Tinsmiths and sheet metal workers	132	132	-
Toolmakers and die setters and sinkers	2	2	-
Other skilled trades	1	1	-
Tinsmiths' and coppersmiths' apprentices	1	1	-

See footnotes at end of table.

TABLE 27.—NEGROES 10 YEARS OLD AND OVER IN EACH INDUSTRY OR SERVICE GROUP, BY OCCUPATION, AND SEX, FOR THE UNITED STATES: 1930—Continued

[Occupations in which there are no Negroes are omitted]

INDUSTRY AND OCCUPATION	Total	Male	Female
MANUFACTURING AND MECHANICAL INDUSTRIES—Continued			
IRON AND STEEL, MACHINERY, AND VEHICLE INDUSTRIES—continued			
Tinware, enamelware, etc., factories—Continued.			
Buffers and polishers	1	1	--------
Chauffeurs and truck and tractor drivers	49	49	--------
Draymen and teamsters	3	3	--------
Elevator tenders	2	1	1
Enamelers, lacquerers, and japanners	32	30	2
Firemen	22	22	--------
Furnace men, smelter men, and pourers	18	18	--------
Grinders	15	15	--------
Guards, watchmen, and doorkeepers	6	6	--------
Heaters	2	2	--------
Janitors	24	22	2
Laborers	1,116	1,073	43
Operatives	480	345	135
Painters, glaziers, and varnishers (factory)	12	10	2
Porters	36	36	--------
All other occupations	1	--------	1
Other metal factories	1,655	1,579	76
Owners, operators, and proprietors	1	1	--------
Managers and officials	1	1	--------
Foremen and overseers	5	4	1
Chemists, assayers, and metallurgists	2	2	--------
Designers	2	--------	2
Accountants and auditors	1	1	--------
Clerks	4	4	--------
Salesmen and saleswomen	1	1	--------
Shipping clerks	12	11	1
Stenographers and typists	1	--------	1
Weighers	2	2	--------
Carpenters	1	1	--------
Cranemen. derrickmen, hoistmen, etc	3	3	--------
Electricians	2	2	--------
Engineers (stationary)	2	2	--------
Machinists	7	7	--------
Mechanics (not otherwise specified)	4	4	--------
Iron molders. founders, and casters	2	2	--------
All other molders, founders, and casters	40	40	--------
Rollers and roll hands	3	3	--------
Sawyers	1	1	--------
Tinsmiths and sheet metal workers	1	1	--------
Apprentices	2	2	--------
Buffers and polishers	11	10	1
Chauffeurs and truck and tractor drivers	18	18	--------
Elevator tenders	1	1	--------
Firemen	16	16	--------
Furnace men. smelter men, and pourers	20	20	--------
Grinders	7	7	--------
Guards, watchmen, and doorkeepers	3	3	--------
Janitors	29	27	2
Laborers	1,181	1,169	12
Oilers of machinery	1	1	--------
Operatives	229	177	52
Painters. glaziers, and varnishers (factory)	10	6	4
Porters	23	23	--------
Puddlers	3	3	--------
All other occupations	3	3	--------
LEATHER INDUSTRIES			
Harness and saddle factories	150	138	12
Owners, operators, and proprietors	1	1	--------
Clerks	1	1	--------
Machinists	1	1	--------
Laborers	61	52	9
Operatives	70	67	3
All other occupations	16	16	--------
Leather belt, leather goods, etc., factories	501	366	135
Owners, operators, and proprietors	1	1	--------
Foremen and overseers	5	3	2
Chemists	1	1	--------
Other professional pursuits	1	1	--------
Bookkeepers and cashiers	1	--------	1
Clerks	4	3	1
Messenger, errand, and office boys and girls	3	3	--------
Salesmen and saleswomen	1	--------	1
Shipping clerks	23	23	--------
Stenographers and typists	1	--------	1
Machinists	6	6	--------
Mechanics (not otherwise specified)	3	3	--------
Toolmakers and die setters and sinkers	1	1	--------
Other skilled trades	2	2	--------
Chauffeurs and truck and tractor drivers	12	12	--------
Dyers	3	3	--------
Firemen	5	5	--------
Guards, watchmen, and doorkeepers	3	3	--------
Janitors	6	6	--------
Laborers	181	170	11
Operatives	213	96	117
Porters	21	21	--------
All other occupations	4	3	1
Shoe factories	2,159	1,938	221
Owners, operators, and proprietors	1	1	--------
Managers and officials	2	2	--------
Foremen and overseers	4	4	--------
Designers	2	2	--------
Agents (not elsewhere classified)	3	3	--------
Bookkeepers and cashiers	3	1	2
MANUFACTURING AND MECHANICAL INDUSTRIES—Continued			
LEATHER INDUSTRIES—continued			
Shoe factories—Continued.			
Clerks	22	19	3
Commercial travelers	5	5	--------
Messenger, errand, and office boys and girls	21	20	1
Salesmen and saleswomen	8	7	1
Shipping clerks	31	31	--------
Stenographers and typists	2	--------	2
Engineers (stationary)	3	3	--------
Machinists	5	5	--------
Mechanics (not otherwise specified)	12	12	--------
Pattern and model makers	1	1	--------
Plumbers and gas and steam fitters	1	1	--------
Apprentices	3	3	--------
Charwomen and cleaners	4	--------	4
Chauffeurs and truck and tractor drivers	27	27	--------
Draymen and teamsters	1	1	--------
Dyers	16	13	3
Elevator tenders	16	15	1
Firemen	15	15	--------
Guards, watchmen, and doorkeepers	9	9	--------
Janitors	81	78	3
Laborers	623	591	32
Operatives	845	678	167
Painters, glaziers, and varnishers (factory)	1	--------	1
Porters	391	391	--------
All other occupations	1	--------	1
Tanneries	2,765	2,630	135
Owners, operators, and proprietors	1	1	--------
Managers and officials	1	1	--------
Foremen and overseers	17	14	3
Clerks	7	6	1
Messenger, errand, and office boys and girls	4	4	--------
Salesmen and saleswomen	1	1	--------
Shipping clerks	18	18	--------
Weighers	2	2	--------
Blacksmiths	1	1	--------
Cranemen, derrickmen, hoistmen, etc	1	1	--------
Engineers (stationary)	2	2	--------
Machinists	15	15	--------
Mechanics (not otherwise specified)	5	5	--------
Millwrights	1	1	--------
Other skilled trades	4	4	--------
Chauffeurs and truck and tractor drivers	12	12	--------
Draymen and teamsters	9	9	--------
Dyers	10	10	--------
Elevator tenders	1	1	--------
Firemen	43	43	--------
Guards, watchmen, and doorkeepers	5	5	--------
Janitors	18	18	--------
Laborers	1,749	1,699	50
Operatives	810	733	77
Painters, glaziers, and varnishers (factory)	10	6	4
Porters	18	18	--------
Trunk, suitcase, and bag factories	230	201	29
Foremen and overseers	2	2	--------
Clerks	3	3	--------
Commercial travelers	1	1	--------
Shipping clerks	6	6	--------
Cabinetmakers	1	1	--------
Machinists	1	1	--------
Mechanics (not otherwise specified)	1	1	--------
Painters, glaziers, and varnishers (building)	1	1	--------
Sawyers	2	2	--------
Other skilled trades	2	2	--------
Chauffeurs and truck and tractor drivers	13	13	--------
Firemen	7	7	--------
Laborers	91	89	2
Operatives	66	41	25
Painters, glaziers, and varnishers (factory)	3	2	1
Porters	21	21	--------
All other occupations	9	8	1
LUMBER AND FURNITURE INDUSTRIES			
Furniture factories	7,934	7,324	610
Owners, operatives, and proprietors	24	22	2
Managers and officials	4	4	--------
Foremen and overseers	23	21	2
Agents (not elsewhere classified)	3	2	1
Bookkeepers and cashiers	2	--------	2
Clerks	31	28	3
Commercial travelers	2	2	--------
Messenger, errand, and office boys and girls	8	8	--------
Office appliance operators	1	1	--------
Salesmen and saleswomen	5	5	--------
Shipping clerks	46	45	1
Stenographers and typists	7	1	6
Weighers	1	1	--------
Blacksmiths	5	5	--------
Cabinetmakers	390	390	--------
Carpenters	109	109	--------
Coopers	1	1	--------
Engineers (stationary)	6	6	--------
Machinists	27	27	--------
Mechanics (not otherwise specified)	32	32	--------
Painters, glaziers, and varnishers (building)	4	4	--------
Plumbers and gas and steam fitters	1	1	--------
Sawyers	23	22	1

See footnotes at end of table.

TABLE 27.—NEGROES 10 YEARS OLD AND OVER IN EACH INDUSTRY OR SERVICE GROUP, BY OCCUPATION, AND SEX, FOR THE UNITED STATES: 1930—Continued

[Occupations in which there are no Negroes are omitted]

INDUSTRY AND OCCUPATION	Total	Male	Female
MANUFACTURING AND MECHANICAL INDUSTRIES—Continued			
LUMBER AND FURNITURE INDUSTRIES—continued			
Furniture factories—Continued.			
Skilled occupations (not elsewhere classified)	3	3	--------
Tinsmiths and sheet-metal workers	1	1	--------
Upholsters	717	686	31
Apprentices:			
Carpenters	2	2	--------
Machinists	1	1	--------
Other apprentices	10	10	--------
Buffers and polishers (metal)	1	1	--------
Charwomen and cleaners	9	1	8
Chauffeurs and truck and tractor drivers	378	378	--------
Draymen and teamsters	44	44	--------
Elevator tenders	24	17	7
Enamelers, lacquerers, and japanners	2	1	1
Firemen	148	148	--------
Guards, watchmen, and doorkeepers	50	50	--------
Janitors	100	87	13
Laborers	3, 354	3, 148	206
Operatives	1, 878	1, 616	262
Painters, glaziers, and varnishers (factory)	299	236	63
Porters	157	156	1
All other occupations	1	1	--------
Piano and organ factories	200	195	5
Agents (not elsewhere classified)	2	2	--------
Clerks	3	3	--------
Collectors	2	2	--------
Messengers, errand, and office boy and girls	2	2	--------
Shipping clerks	3	3	--------
Cabinetmakers	2	2	--------
Electricians	1	1	--------
Engineers (stationary)	2	2	--------
Mechanics (not elsewhere specified)	2	2	--------
Piano and organ tuners (factory)	2	2	--------
Other skilled trades	2	2	--------
Chauffeurs and truck and tractor drivers	17	17	--------
Draymen and teamsters	2	2	--------
Elevator tenders	4	2	2
Firemen	2	2	--------
Guards, watchmen, and doorkeepers	1	1	--------
Janitors	12	12	--------
Laborers	60	59	1
Operatives	59	59	--------
Painters, glaziers, and varnishers (factory)	4	3	1
Porters	15	15	--------
All other occupations	1	--------	1
Saw and planing mills [12]	113, 862	112, 264	1, 598
Owners, operators, and proprietors	47	47	--------
Managers and officials	20	20	--------
Foremen and overseers	198	197	1
Draftsmen	1	1	--------
Electrical engineers	1	1	--------
Lawyers	2	2	--------
Mechanical engineers	2	2	--------
Agents (not elsewhere classified)	6	6	--------
Clerks	142	133	9
Collectors	1	1	--------
Commercial travelers	1	1	--------
Messenger, errand, and office boys and girls	13	13	--------
Purchasing agents	1	1	--------
Salesmen and saleswomen	4	4	--------
Shipping clerks	26	26	--------
Stenographers and typists	2	1	1
Weighers	2	2	--------
Blacksmiths	101	101	--------
Boilermakers	3	3	--------
Brick and stone masons and tile layers	14	14	--------
Cabinetmakers	5	5	--------
Carpenters	184	184	--------
Compositors, linotypers, and typesetters	2	2	--------
Coopers	9	9	--------
Cranemen, derrickmen, hoistmen, etc	31	31	--------
Electricians	6	6	--------
Engineers (stationary)	124	124	--------
Machinists	221	221	--------
Mechanics (not otherwise specified)	70	70	--------
Millwrights	94	94	--------
Painters, glaziers, and varnishers (building)	4	4	--------
Plumbers and gas and steam fitters	26	26	--------
Sawyers	2, 955	2, 952	3
Skilled occupations (not elsewhere classified)	2	2	--------
Toolmakers and die setters and sinkers	2	2	--------
Other skilled trades	1	1	--------
Apprentices:			
Carpenters	1	1	--------
Machinists	3	3	--------
Other apprentices	2	2	--------
Chauffeurs and truck and tractor drivers	1, 627	1, 626	1
Draymen and teamsters	1, 479	1, 478	1
Elevator tenders	3	3	--------
Firemen	2, 606	2, 606	--------
Grinders (metal)	1	1	--------
Guards, watchmen, and doorkeepers	389	388	1
Janitors	63	55	8
Laborers	96, 527	95, 198	1, 329
Oilers of machinery	99	99	--------
Operatives	6, 548	6, 309	239
MANUFACTURING AND MECHANICAL INDUSTRIES—Continued			
LUMBER AND FURNITURE INDUSTRIES—continued			
Saw and planing mills—Continued.			
Painters, glaziers, and varnishers (factory)	67	67	--------
Porters	44	44	--------
Saw filers	72	72	--------
All other occupations	8	3	5
Other woodworking factories	16, 607	15, 431	1, 176
Owners, operators, and proprietors	6	6	--------
Foremen and overseers	41	39	2
Agents (not elsewhere classified)	1	1	--------
Bookkeepers and cashiers	3	1	2
Clerks	26	21	5
Messenger, errand, and office boys and girls	6	6	--------
Office-appliance operators	1	1	--------
Purchasing agents	1	1	--------
Salesmen and saleswomen	2	1	1
Shipping clerks	8	8	--------
Stenographers and typists	1	1	--------
Blacksmiths	8	8	--------
Cabinetmakers	11	11	--------
Carpenters	65	65	--------
Compositors, linotypers, and typesetters	2	2	--------
Coopers	1, 218	1, 218	--------
Coppersmiths	1	1	--------
Cranemen, derrickmen, hoistmen, etc	29	29	--------
Electricians	2	2	--------
Engineers (stationary)	23	23	--------
Machinists	50	50	--------
Mechanics (not otherwise specified)	23	23	--------
Millwrights	12	12	--------
Painters, glaziers, and varnishers (building)	1	1	--------
Pattern and model makers	2	2	--------
Plumbers and gas and steam fitters	1	1	--------
Sawyers	271	271	--------
Skilled occupations (not elsewhere classified)	5	5	--------
Toolmakers and die setters and sinkers	1	1	--------
Other skilled trades	2	2	--------
Apprentices:			
Machinists	1	1	--------
Other apprentices	14	14	--------
Chauffeurs and truck and tractor drivers	161	161	--------
Draymen and teamsters	66	66	--------
Firemen	490	490	--------
Guards, watchmen, and doorkeepers	78	77	1
Janitors	48	46	2
Laborers	12, 115	11, 280	835
Oilers of machinery	3	3	--------
Operatives	1, 756	1, 432	324
Painters, glaziers, and varnishers (factory)	16	14	2
Porters	26	26	--------
Saw filers	7	7	--------
All other occupations	3	1	2
PAPER, PRINTING, AND ALLIED INDUSTRIES			
Blank book, envelop, tag, paper bag, etc., factories	490	394	96
Owners, operators, and proprietors	1	1	--------
Managers and officials	1	1	--------
Foremen and overseers	3	2	1
Bookkeepers and cashiers	1	--------	1
Clerks	19	16	3
Messenger, errand, and office boys and girls	8	7	1
Office-appliance operators	1	1	--------
Salesmen and saleswomen	2	2	--------
Shipping clerks	16	16	--------
Stenographers and typists	1	--------	1
Compositors, linotypers, and typesetters	6	5	1
Electricians	1	1	--------
Engineers (stationary)	1	1	--------
Machinists	2	2	--------
Pressmen and plate printers	2	2	--------
Chauffeurs and truck and tractor drivers	30	30	--------
Draymen and teamsters	6	6	--------
Elevator tenders	3	3	--------
Firemen	5	5	--------
Guards, watchmen, and doorkeepers	4	4	--------
Janitors	21	21	--------
Laborers	184	163	21
Operatives	144	77	67
Painters, glaziers, and varnishers (factory)	1	1	--------
Porters	26	26	--------
All other occupations	1	1	--------
Paper and pulp mills	7, 539	6, 693	846
Managers and officials	4	4	--------
Foremen and overseers	51	46	5
Chemists	1	1	--------
Accountants and auditors	2	2	--------
Agents (not elsewhere classified)	1	1	--------
Bookkeepers and cashiers	1	--------	1
Clerks	44	38	6
Commercial travelers	2	2	--------
Messenger, errand, and office boys and girls	15	15	--------
Purchasing agents	2	2	--------
Shipping clerks	33	33	--------
Stenographers and typists	3	--------	3
Weighers	9	9	--------
Blacksmiths	4	4	--------

See footnotes at end of table.

TABLE 27.—NEGROES 10 YAERS OLD AND OVER IN EACH INDUSTRY OR SERVICE GROUP, BY OCCUPATION, AND SEX, FOR THE UNITED STATES: 1930—Continued

[Occupations in which there are no Negroes are omitted]

INDUSTRY AND OCCUPATION	Total	Male	Female
MANUFACTURING AND MECHANICAL INDUSTRIES—Continued			
PAPER, PRINTING, AND ALLIED INDUSTRIES—contd.			
Paper and pulp mills—Continued.			
Boilermakers	6	6	-------
Brick and stone masons and tile layers	4	4	-------
Carpenters	7	7	-------
Compositors, linotypers, and typesetters	3	3	-------
Cranemen, derrickmen, hoistmen, etc	3	3	-------
Electricians	1	1	-------
Engineers (stationary)	16	16	-------
Machinists	30	30	-------
Mechanics (not otherwise specified)	14	14	-------
Millwrights	5	5	-------
Plumbers and gas and steam fitters	6	6	-------
Sawyers	6	6	-------
Charwomen and cleaners	7	2	5
Chauffeurs and truck and tractor drivers	251	250	1
Draymen and teamsters	53	53	-------
Elevator tenders	14	14	-------
Firemen	262	262	-------
Guards, watchmen, and doorkeepers	26	26	-------
Housekeepers and stewards	1	1	-------
Janitors	109	107	2
Laborers	4,970	4,711	259
Oilers of machinery	16	16	-------
Operatives	1,385	821	564
Porters	172	172	-------
Paper box factories	315	252	63
Foremen and overseers	3	2	1
Clerks	4	2	2
Shipping clerks	3	3	-------
Compositors, linotypers, and typesetters	5	4	1
Engineers (stationary)	1	1	-------
Machinists	4	4	-------
Mechanics (not otherwise specified)	1	1	-------
Toolmakers and die setters and sinkers	1	1	-------
Chauffeurs and truck and tractor drivers	21	21	-------
Draymen and teamsters	4	4	-------
Elevator tenders	1	1	-------
Firemen	5	5	-------
Guards, watchmen, and doorkeepers	2	2	-------
Janitors	8	8	-------
Laborers	109	101	8
Operatives	127	76	51
Porters	16	16	-------
Printing, publishing, and engraving	8,289	7,246	1,043
Owners, operators, and proprietors	132	129	3
Managers and officials	59	49	10
Foremen and overseers	44	41	3
Draftsmen	1	1	-------
Lawyers	1	1	-------
Mechanical engineers	1	1	-------
Photographers	2	2	-------
Accountants and auditors	3	3	-------
Advertising agents	30	27	3
Agents (not elsewhere classified)	9	5	4
Bookkeepers and cashiers	60	11	49
Canvassers	71	47	24
Clerks	300	195	105
Collectors	10	7	3
Commercial travelers	1	1	-------
Messenger, errand, and office boys and girls	177	172	5
Office appliance operators	15	12	3
Sales agents	1	-------	1
Salesmen and saleswomen	11	10	1
Shipping clerks	134	131	3
Stenographers and typists	133	7	126
Weighers	2	2	-------
Cabinetmakers	1	1	-------
Carpenters	4	4	-------
Compositors, linotypers, and typesetters	1,957	1,765	192
Electricians	2	2	-------
Electrotypers and stereotypers	29	29	-------
Engineers (stationary)	16	16	-------
Engravers	16	14	2
Lithographers	19	19	-------
Machinists	24	24	-------
Mechanics (not otherwise specified)	17	17	-------
Molders, founders, and casters (metal)	2	2	-------
Painters, glaziers, and varnishers (building)	1	1	-------
Plumbers and gas and steam fitters	1	1	-------
Pressmen and plate printers	187	187	-------
Toolmakers and die setters and sinkers	1	1	-------
Other skilled trades	4	4	-------
Apprentices:			
Printers and bookbinders	62	52	10
Other apprentices	2	1	1
Charwomen and cleaners	22	2	20
Chauffeurs and truck and tractor drivers	381	381	-------
Draymen and teamsters	17	17	-------
Elevator tenders	64	51	13
Firemen	33	33	-------
Guards, watchmen, and doorkeepers	40	40	-------
Housekeepers and stewards	8	2	6
Janitors	653	639	14
Laborers	1,013	985	28
Oilers of machinery	3	3	-------
Operatives	1,210	797	413
Painters, glaziers, and varnishers (factory)	2	2	-------
Porters	1,301	1,300	1
MANUFACTURING AND MECHANICAL INDUSTRIES—Continued			
TEXTILE INDUSTRIES			
Carpet mills	518	430	88
Owners, operators, and proprietors	3	3	-------
Foremen and overseers	2	-------	2
Designers	2	-------	2
Bookkeepers and cashiers	1	-------	1
Clerks	4	4	-------
Salesmen and saleswomen	1	1	-------
Shipping clerks	3	3	-------
Stenographers and typists	1	-------	1
Carpenters	1	1	-------
Engineers (stationary)	2	2	-------
Machinists	3	3	-------
Mechanics (not otherwise specified)	1	1	-------
Painters, glaziers, and varnishers (building)	1	1	-------
Tinsmiths and sheet-metal workers	1	1	-------
Chauffeurs and truck and tractor drivers	8	8	-------
Dyers	4	2	2
Elevator tenders	1	1	-------
Firemen	2	2	-------
Guards, watchmen, and doorkeepers	2	2	-------
Janitors	8	8	-------
Laborers	216	204	12
Operatives	234	166	68
Porters	15	5	-------
All other occupations	2	2	-------
Cotton mills	16,312	13,373	2,939
Owners, operators, and proprietors	1	1	-------
Foremen and overseers	28	26	2
Trained nurses	3	-------	3
Agents (not elsewhere classified)	1	-------	1
Bookkeepers and cashiers	1	-------	1
Clerks	12	10	2
Messenger, errand, and office boys and girls	19	19	-------
Shipping clerks	16	16	-------
Weighers	25	25	-------
Other clerical pursuits	1	-------	1
Blacksmiths	6	6	-------
Boilermakers	1	1	-------
Brick and stone masons and tile layers	17	17	-------
Carpenters	24	24	-------
Cranemen, derrickmen, hoistmen, etc	1	1	-------
Electricians	2	2	-------
Engineers (stationary)	14	14	-------
Loom fixers	3	3	-------
Machinists	74	74	-------
Mechanics (not otherwise specified)	29	29	-------
Painters, glaziers, and varnishers (building)	32	32	-------
Plumbers and gas and steam fitters	42	42	-------
Sawyers	2	2	-------
Other skilled trades	1	1	-------
Machinists' apprentices	2	2	-------
Charwomen and cleaners	182	47	135
Chauffeurs and truck and tractor drivers	480	480	-------
Draymen and teamsters	144	144	-------
Dyers	204	204	-------
Elevator tenders	11	8	3
Firemen	616	616	-------
Guards, watchmen, and doorkeepers	47	47	-------
Housekeepers and stewards	1	-------	1
Janitors	220	161	59
Laborers	11,156	9,106	2,050
Oilers of machinery	28	28	-------
Operatives	2,805	2,124	681
Porters	61	61	-------
Hemp, jute, and linen mills	236	156	80
Foremen and overseers	2	2	-------
Clerks	2	1	1
Commercial travelers	1	-------	1
Messenger, errand, and office boys and girls	1	1	-------
Shipping clerks	3	3	-------
Weighers	2	2	-------
Loom fixers	2	2	-------
Machinists	1	1	-------
Mechanics (not otherwise specified)	2	2	-------
Other skilled trades	1	1	-------
Chauffeurs and truck and tractor drivers	3	3	-------
Firemen	7	7	-------
Guards, watchmen, and doorkeepers	1	1	-------
Laborers	90	65	25
Operatives	113	61	52
All other occupations	5	4	1
Knitting mills	1,669	866	803
Foremen and overseers	6	3	3
Agents (not elsewhere classified)	3	1	2
Bookkeepers and cashiers	1	-------	1
Canvassers	4	1	3
Clerks	14	9	5
Commercial travelers	5	4	1
Messenger, errand, and office boys and girls	4	4	-------
Salesmen and saleswomen	14	12	2
Shipping clerks	14	13	1
Stenographers and typists	1	-------	1
Engineers (stationary)	4	4	-------
Machinists	11	11	-------
Mechanics (not otherwise specified)	2	2	-------
Plumbers and gas and steam fitters	2	2	-------
Charwomen and cleaners	1	-------	1
Chauffeurs and truck and tractor drivers	21	21	-------
Dyers	56	56	-------

See footnotes at end of table.

TABLE 27.—NEGROES 10 YEARS OLD AND OVER IN EACH INDUSTRY OR SERVICE GROUP, BY OCCUPATION, AND SEX, FOR THE UNITED STATES: 1930—Continued

[Occupations in which there are no Negroes are omitted]

INDUSTRY AND OCCUPATION	Total	Male	Female
MANUFACTURERS AND MECHANICAL INDUSTRIES—Continued			
TEXTILE INDUSTRIES—continued			
Knitting mills—Continued.			
Elevator tenders	2	2	-
Firemen	60	60	-
Guards, watchmen, and doorkeepers	15	15	-
Janitors	62	57	5
Laborers	442	312	130
Oilers of machinery	1	1	-
Operatives	884	238	646
Porters	35	34	1
All other occupations	5	4	1
Lace and embroidery mills	136	25	111
Foremen and overseers	1	-	1
Designers	3	-	3
Clerks	5	1	4
Messenger, errand, and office boys and girls	3	1	2
Shipping clerks	1	1	-
Dyers	2	2	-
Guards, watchmen, and doorkeepers	1	1	-
Laborers	3	3	-
Operatives	111	10	101
All other occupations	6	6	-
Rope and cordage factories	527	462	65
Foremen and overseers	3	3	-
Professional pursuits	1	1	-
Clerks	2	1	1
Messenger, errand, and office boys and girls	1	1	-
Shipping clerks	3	3	-
Weighers	2	2	-
Machinists	13	13	-
Painters, glaziers, and varnishers (building)	1	1	-
Other skilled trades	1	1	-
Chauffeurs and truck and tractor drivers	7	7	-
Guards, watchmen, and doorkeepers	1	1	-
Janitors	6	6	-
Laborers	249	231	18
Oilers of machinery	6	6	-
Operatives	224	178	46
All other occupations	7	7	-
Sail, awning, and tent factories	132	113	19
Owners, operators, and proprietors	2	2	-
Canvassers	1	1	-
Clerks	1	-	1
Shipping clerks	2	2	-
Mechanics (not otherwise specified)	2	2	-
Chauffeurs and truck and tractor drivers	14	14	-
Laborers	36	34	2
Operatives	63	48	15
All other occupations	11	10	1
Silk mills	954	648	306
Managers and officials	1	1	-
Foremen and overseers	7	5	2
Chemists	1	1	-
Designers	1	-	1
Agents (not elsewhere classified)	2	-	2
Bookkeepers and cashiers	3	2	1
Clerks	9	8	1
Messenger, errand, and office boys and girls	10	10	-
Salesmen and saleswomen	4	2	2
Shipping clerks	23	23	-
Brick and stone masons and tile layers	1	1	-
Cabinetmakers	1	1	-
Carpenters	1	1	-
Electricians	1	1	-
Engineers (stationary)	3	3	-
Loom fixers	2	2	-
Machinists	3	3	-
Mechanics (not otherwise specified)	1	1	-
Painters, glaziers, and varnishers (building)	2	2	-
Other skilled trades	1	1	-
Charwomen and cleaners	2	1	1
Chauffeurs and truck and tractor drivers	13	13	-
Draymen and teamsters	1	1	-
Dyers	23	22	1
Elevator tenders	2	1	1
Firemen	23	23	-
Guards, watchmen, and doorkeepers	13	13	-
Janitors	58	55	3
Laborers	383	320	65
Operatives	330	105	225
Porters	26	26	-
All other occupations	1	-	1
Textile dyeing, finishing, and printing mills	948	847	101
Foremen and overseers	5	5	-
Bookkeepers and cashiers	2	-	2
Clerks	10	9	1
Messenger, errand, and office boys and girls	2	2	-
Shipping clerks	2	2	-
Stenographers and typists	1	-	1
Weighers	2	2	-
Carpenters	1	1	-
Coopers	1	1	-
Engineers (stationary)	4	4	-
Machinists	8	8	-
Mechanics (not otherwise specified)	4	4	-
MANUFACTURING AND MECHANICAL INDUSTRIES—Continued			
TEXTILE INDUSTRIES—continued			
Textile dyeing, finishing, nd printing mills—Contd.			
Painters, glaziers, and varnishers (building)	1	1	-
Plumbers and gas and steam fitters	1	1	-
Chauffeurs and truck and tractor drivers	14	14	-
Draymen and teamsters	3	3	-
Dyers	102	97	5
Firemen	33	33	-
Guards, watchmen, and doorkeepers	2	2	-
Janitors	14	14	-
Laborers	492	480	12
Operatives	233	153	80
Porters	11	11	-
Woolen and worsted mills	612	433	179
Foremen and overseers	7	5	2
Clerks	4	3	1
Messenger, errand, and office boys and girls	4	4	-
Shipping clerks	6	6	-
Weighers	1	1	-
Engineers (stationary)	3	3	-
Loom fixers	2	2	-
Machinists	9	9	-
Mechanics (not otherwise specified)	2	2	-
Millwrights	2	2	-
Plumbers and gas and steam fitters	1	1	-
Other skilled trades	2	2	-
Apprentices	1	1	-
Charwomen and cleaners	6	2	4
Chauffeurs and truck and tractor drivers	12	12	-
Draymen and teamsters	1	1	-
Dyers	7	7	-
Elevator tenders	1	1	-
Firemen	11	11	-
Guards, watchmen, and doorkeepers	9	9	-
Janitors	13	13	-
Laborers	259	210	49
Oilers of machinery	1	1	-
Operatives	234	111	123
Porters	14	14	-
Other and not specified textile mills	4, 158	2, 462	1, 696
Owners, operators, and proprietors	2	2	-
Foremen and overseers	28	26	2
Chemists	1	1	-
Designers	5	-	5
Agents (not elsewhere classified)	2	2	-
Bookkeepers and cashiers	2	-	2
Clerks	30	20	10
Commercial travelers	1	1	-
Messenger, errand, and office boys and girls	19	15	4
Salesmen and saleswomen	1	1	-
Shipping clerks	44	43	1
Stenographers and typists	1	-	1
Weighers	3	2	1
Carpenters	6	6	-
Compositors, linotypers, and typesetters	3	3	-
Cranemen, derrickmen, hoistmen, etc	1	1	-
Electricians	1	1	-
Engineers (stationary)	6	6	-
Machinists	19	19	-
Mechanics (not otherwise specified)	11	11	-
Plumbers and gas and steam fitters	3	3	-
Upholsters	3	3	-
Charwomen and cleaners	6	1	5
Chauffeurs and truck and tractor drivers	60	60	-
Draymen and teamsters	12	12	-
Dyers	12	12	-
Elevator tenders	1	1	-
Firemen	38	38	-
Guards, watchmen, and doorkeepers	15	15	-
Janitors	51	43	8
Laborers	1, 694	1, 267	427
Oilers of machinery	4	4	-
Operatives	2, 007	779	1, 228
Porters	65	64	1
All other occupations	1	-	1
MISCELLANEOUS MANUFACTURING INDUSTRIES			
Broom and brush factories	766	666	100
Owners, operators, and proprietors	14	14	-
Bookkeepers and cashiers	1	-	1
Canvassers	1	1	-
Clerks	1	1	-
Commercial travelers	3	3	-
Messenger, errand, and office boys and girls	1	1	-
Salesmen and saleswomen	6	6	-
Shipping clerks	1	1	-
Weighers	1	-	1
Mechanics (not otherwise specified)	3	3	-
Sawyers	1	1	-
Toolmakers and die setters and sinkers	2	2	-
Apprentices	1	-	1
Chauffeurs and truck and tractor drivers	11	11	-
Firemen	2	2	-
Janitors	10	10	-
Laborers	274	251	23
Operatives	414	341	73
Painters, glaziers, and varnishers (factory)	4	4	-
All other occupations	15	14	1

See footnotes at end of table.

Table 27.—NEGROES 10 YEARS OLD AND OVER IN EACH INDUSTRY OR SERVICE GROUP, BY OCCUPATION, AND SEX, FOR THE UNITED STATES: 1930—Continued

[Occupations in which there are no Negroes are omitted]

INDUSTRY AND OCCUPATION	Total	Male	Female
Manufacturing and Mechanical Industries—Continued			
MISCELLANEOUS MANUFACTURING INDUSTRIES—con.			
Button factories	168	64	104
Foremen and overseers	3		3
Clerks	1		1
Commercial travelers	1	1	
Messenger, errand, and office boys and girls	4	3	1
Shipping clerks	3	2	1
Machinists	1	1	
Chauffeurs and truck and tractor drivers	1	1	
Dyers	2	2	
Laborers	23	18	5
Operatives	121	30	91
Painters, glaziers, and varnishers (factory)	1		1
All other occupations	7	5	1
Electric light and power plants	7,655	7,598	57
Owners, operators, and proprietors	1	1	
Managers and officials	1	1	
Foremen and overseers	33	33	
Chemists	3	3	
Civil engineers and surveyors	3	3	
Electrical engineers	17	17	
Mechanical engineers	1	1	
Agents (not elsewhere classified)	2	2	
Bookkeepers and cashiers	3	3	
Canvassers	5	5	
Clerks	44	41	3
Collectors	1	1	
Messenger, errand, and office boys and girls	23	23	
Office appliance operators	1		1
Salesmen and saleswomen	2	2	
Shipping clerks	8	6	2
Stenographers and typists	5	2	3
Other clerical pursuits	3	3	
Blacksmiths	6	6	
Boilermakers	10	10	
Brick and stone masons and tile layers	4	4	
Carpenters	11	11	
Cement finishers	1	1	
Cranemen, derrickmen, hoistmen, etc	10	10	
Electricians	253	253	
Engineers (stationary)	74	74	
Machinists	33	33	
Mechanics (not otherwise specified)	74	74	
Painters, glaziers, and varnishers (building)	3	3	
Plumbers and gas and steam fitters	35	35	
Apprentices:			
Electricians	2	2	
Other apprentices	2	2	
Charwomen and cleaners	24	4	20
Chauffeurs and truck and tractor drivers	184	184	
Draymen and teamsters	15	15	
Elevator tenders	24	12	12
Firemen	431	431	
Guards, watchmen, and doorkeepers	45	44	1
Housekeepers and stewards	3	1	2
Janitors	399	388	11
Laborers	4,852	4,850	2
Oilers of machinery	40	40	
Operatives	696	696	
Painters, glaziers, and varnishers (factory)	5	5	
Porters	263	263	
Electrical machinery and supplies factories	3,095	2,919	176
Owners, operators, and proprietors	5	5	
Managers and officials	1	1	
Foremen and overseers	21	18	3
Chemists	1	1	
Draftsmen	3	2	1
Electrical engineers	8	8	
Mechanical engineers [4]	1	1	
Photographers	1	1	
Agents (not elsewhere classified)	3	3	
Bookkeepers and cashiers	4	1	3
Clerks	60	50	10
Collectors	2	2	
Commercial travelers	1	1	
Messenger, errand, and office boys and girls	16	15	1
Sales men and saleswomen	12	12	
Shipping clerks	65	65	
Stenographers and typists	3		3
Weighers	4	4	
Blacksmiths	2	2	
Brick and stone masons and tile layers	3	3	
Cabinetmakers	2	2	
Carpenters	5	5	
Compositors, linotypers, and typesetters	1	1	
Coppersmiths	1	1	
Cranemen, derrickmen, hoistmen, etc	21	21	
Electricians	169	169	
Engineers (stationary)	18	18	
Glass blowers	1	1	
Machinists	47	47	
Mechanics (not otherwise specified)	81	81	
Iron molders, founders, and casters	1	1	
Other molders, founders, and casters	44	44	
Plumbers and gas and steam fitters	6	6	
Toolmakers and die setters and sinkers	1	1	
Apprentices:			
Electricians	4	4	
Machinists	1	1	
Other apprentices	10	10	
Manufacturing and Mechanical Industries—Continued			
MISCELLANEOUS MANUFACTURING INDUSTRIES—con.			
Electrical machinery and supplies factories—Contd.			
Buffers and polishers (metal)	4	2	2
Charwomen and cleaners	11	1	10
Chauffeurs and truck and tractor drivers	105	105	
Draymen and teamsters	4	4	
Elevator tenders	13	12	1
Filers (metal)	1	1	
Firemen	39	39	
Furnace men, smelter men, and pourers	3	3	
Grinders (metal)	4	3	1
Guards, watchmen, and doorkeepers	17	17	
Heaters (metal)	1	1	
Housekeepers and stewards	3	1	2
Janitors	177	171	6
Laborers	1,302	1,275	27
Oilers of machinery	12	12	
Operatives	577	473	104
Painters, glaziers, and varnishers (factory)	18	16	2
Porters	175	175	
Independent hand trades	27,530	6,565	20,965
Blacksmiths	2,052	2,052	
Cabinetmakers	4	4	
Carpenters	5	5	
Coppersmiths	1	1	
Goldsmiths and silversmiths	2	2	
Jewelers and watchmakers (not in factory)	221	216	5
Mechanics (not otherwise specified)	9	9	
Piano and organ tuners	78	78	
Shoemakers and cobblers (not in factory)	4,150	4,129	21
Tinsmiths and sheeet-metal workers	40	40	
Upholsters	5	3	2
Other skilled trades	1	1	
Apprentices:			
Blacksmiths	9	9	
Dressmakers and milliners	63		63
Dressmakers and seamstresses (not in factory)	20,439	6	20,433
Milliners and millinery dealers	451	10	441
Rubber factories	3,492	3,403	89
Owners, operators, and proprietors	3	3	
Foremen and overseers	7	6	1
Bookkeepers and cashiers	1	1	
Clerks	18	18	
Commercial travelers	4	4	
Messenger, errand, and office boys and girls	2	2	
Sales agents	1	1	
Salesmen and saleswomen	3	2	1
Shipping clerks	25	25	
Stenographers and typists	3		3
Weighers	6	6	
Blacksmiths	3	3	
Brick and stone masons and tile layers	1	1	
Carpenters	1	1	
Cranemen, derrickmen, hoistmen, etc	1	1	
Electricians	3	3	
Engineers (stationary)	4	4	
Machinists	24	24	
Mechanics (not otherwise specified)	29	29	
Plumbers and gas and steam fitters	4	4	
Machinists' apprentices	1	1	
Charwomen and cleaner	1		1
Chauffeurs and truck and tractor drivers	97	99	
Draymen and teamsters	3	3	
Elevator tenders	48	47	1
Firemen	40	40	
Guards, watchmen, and doorkeepers	13	13	
Janitors	363	360	3
Laborers	1,550	1,520	30
Operatives	1,145	1,096	49
Painters, glaziers, and varnishers (factory)	10	10	
Porters	78	78	
Straw factories	30	20	10
Foremen and overseers	1	1	
Machinists	1	1	
Laborers	8	7	1
Operatives	13	5	8
All other occupations	7	6	1
Turpentine farms and distilleries	32,683	32,402	281
Owners, operators, and proprietors	9	9	
Managers and officials	3	3	
Foremen and overseers	190	190	
Clerks	4	3	1
Shipping clerks	2	2	
Other clerical pursuits	7	7	
Blacksmiths	7	7	
Carpenters	4	4	
Coopers	162	162	
Mechanics (not otherwise specified)	10	10	
Millwrights	1	1	
Other skilled trades	10	10	
Chauffeurs and truck and tractor drivers	236	236	
Draymen and teamsters	409	409	
Firemen	26	26	
Guards, watchmen, and doorkeepers	16	15	1
Laborers	30,849	30,577	272
Operatives	726	721	5
All other occupations	12	10	2

See footnotes at end of table.

TABLE 27.—NEGROES 10 YEARS OLD AND OVER IN EACH INDUSTRY OR SERVICE GROUP, BY OCCUPATION, AND SEX, FOR THE UNITED STATES: 1930—Continued

[Occupations in which there are no Negroes are omitted]

INDUSTRY AND OCCUPATION	Total	Male	Female
MANUFACTURING AND MECHANICAL INDUSTRIES—Continued			
MISCELLANEOUS MANUFACTURING INDUSTRIES—con.			
Other miscellaneous manufacturing industries	34,394	31,255	3,139
Owners operators, and proprietors	49	45	4
Managers and officials	18	15	3
Foremen and overseers	133	111	22
Chemists	4	4	-------
Civil engineers and surveyors	1	1	-------
Designers	25	1	24
Electrical engineers	3	3	-------
Mechanical engineers [4]	2	2	-------
Photographers	2	2	-------
Trained nurses	1	-------	1
Advertising agents	1	1	-------
Agents (not elsewhere classified)	10	7	3
Bookkeepers and cashiers	13	4	9
Canvassers	11	3	8
Clerks	112	97	15
Collectors	2	1	1
Commercial travelers	7	7	-------
Messenger, errand, and office boys and girls	54	51	3
Office appliance operators	1	1	-------
Sales agents	1	-------	1
Salesmen and saleswomen	88	85	3
Shipping clerks	137	131	6
Stenographers and typists	7	1	6
Weighers	38	37	1
Blacksmiths	23	23	-------
Boilermakers	2	2	-------
Brick and stone masons and tile layers	3	3	-------
Cabinetmakers	3	3	-------
Carpenters	31	31	-------
Compositors, linotypers, and typesetters	7	5	2
Coopers	10	10	-------
Cranemen, derrickmen, hoistmen, etc	12	12	-------
Electricians	9	9	-------
Engineers (stationary)	249	249	-------
Machinists	189	189	-------
Mechanics (not otherwise specified)	133	133	-------
Millwrights	45	45	-------
Iron molders, founders, and casters	1	1	-------
Other molders, founders, and casters	1	1	-------
Painters, glaziers, and varnishers (building)	6	6	-------
Pattern and model makers	2	1	1
Plumbers and gas and steam fitters	13	13	-------
Sawyers	3	3	-------
Skilled occupations (not elsewhere classified)	3	3	-------
Tinsmiths and sheet-metal workers	7	7	-------
Toolmakers and die setters and sinkers	1	1	-------
Upholsterers	21	20	1
Apprentices:			
Machinists	1	1	-------
Other apprentices	5	5	-------
Buffers and polishers (metal)	1	1	-------
Charwomen and cleaners	17	5	12
Chauffeurs and truck and tractor drivers	1,615	1,614	1
Draymen and teamsters	387	387	-------
Dyers	28	20	8
Elevator tenders	8	5	3
Filers (metal)	22	22	-------
Firemen	784	784	-------
Furnace men, smelter men, and pourers (metal)	3	3	-------
Grinders (metal)	5	5	-------
Guards, watchmen, and doorkeepers	209	206	3
Housekeepers and stewards	1	-------	1
Janitors	172	151	21
Laborers	22,438	21,634	804
Oilers of machinery	82	82	-------
Operatives	6,735	4,573	2,162
Painters, glaziers, and varnishers (factory)	39	29	10
Policemen	1	1	-------
Porters	346	346	-------
All other occupations	1	1	-------
Other not specified manufacturing industries	31,600	24,887	6,713
Owners, operators, and proprietors	37	35	2
Managers and officials	21	19	2
Foremen and overseers	118	91	27
Chemists	15	15	-------
Civil engineers and surveyors	2	2	-------
Designers	8	2	6
Draftsmen	3	3	-------
Electrical engineers	2	2	-------
Mechanical engineers	3	3	-------
Photographers	1	1	-------
Social and welfare workers	1	1	-------
Trained nurses	2	-------	2
Accountants and auditors	2	2	-------
Agents (not elsewhere classified)	9	3	6
Bookkeepers and cashiers	17	4	13
Canvassers	10	2	8
Clerks	196	152	44
Collectors	2	2	-------
Commercial travelers	4	1	3
Messenger, errand, and office boys and girls	111	105	6
Purchasing agents	1	1	-------
Salesmen and saleswomen	23	14	9
Shipping clerks	288	283	5
Stenographers and typists	20	5	15
Weighers	5	5	-------
Blacksmiths	41	41	-------

See footnotes at end of table.

INDUSTRY AND OCCUPATION	Total	Male	Female
MANUFACTURING AND MECHANICAL INDUSTRIES—Continued			
MISCELLANEOUS MANUFACTURING INDUSTRIES—con.			
Other not specified manufacturing industries—Con.			
Boilermakers	17	17	-------
Brick and stone masons and tile layers	3	3	-------
Cabinet makers	11	11	-------
Carpenters	91	91	-------
Cement finishers	2	2	-------
Compositors, linotypers, and typesetters	25	25	-------
Coopers	34	34	-------
Coppersmiths	2	2	-------
Cranemen, derrickmen, hoistmen, etc	21	21	-------
Electricians	30	30	-------
Engineers (stationary)	101	101	-------
Engravers	1	1	-------
Forgemen and hammermen	6	6	-------
Jewelers and lapidaries (factory)	2	2	-------
Machinists	303	303	-------
Mechanics (not otherwise specified)	488	488	-------
Millwrights	20	20	-------
Iron molders, founders, and casters	20	20	-------
Other molders, founders, and casters	5	5	-------
Painters, glaziers, and varnishers (building)	3	3	-------
Pattern and model makers	7	7	-------
Plumbers and gas and steam fitters	41	41	-------
Sawyers	34	34	-------
Skilled occupations (not elsewhere classified)	2	2	-------
Stone cutters	1	1	-------
Tinsmiths and sheet-metal workers	16	16	-------
Toolmakers and die setters and sinkers	10	10	-------
Upholsterers	15	14	1
Apprentices:			
Machinists	4	4	-------
Other apprentices	19	18	1
Charwomen and cleaners	49	8	41
Chauffeurs and truck and tractor drivers	537	537	-------
Draymen and teamsters	96	96	-------
Dyers	15	12	3
Elevator tenders	166	150	16
Enamelers, lacquerers, and japanners	5	4	1
Firemen	644	644	-------
Furnace men, smelter men, and pourers (metal)	21	21	-------
Grinders (metal)	11	11	-------
Guards, watchmen, and doorkeepers	275	274	1
Housekeepers and stewards	10	2	8
Janitors	645	611	34
Laborers	17,486	15,357	2,129
Oilers of machinery	16	15	1
Operatives	7,639	3,320	4,319
Painters, glaziers, and varnishers (factory)	103	95	8
Porters	1,602	1,600	2
All other occupations	4	4	-------
TRANSPORTATION AND COMMUNICATION			
Air transportation [13]	436	430	6
Foremen and overseers	1	1	-------
Clerks	1	1	-------
Messenger, errand, and office boys and girls	3	3	-------
Aviators	9	9	-------
Carpenters	2	2	-------
Mechanics (not otherwise specified)	11	11	-------
Other skilled trades	2	2	-------
Apprentices	2	2	-------
Chauffeurs and truck and tractor drivers	7	7	-------
Firemen	2	2	-------
Guards, watchmen, and doorkeepers	9	9	-------
Housekeepers and stewards	1	1	-------
Janitors	49	49	-------
Laborers	291	285	6
Operatives	17	17	-------
Porters	29	29	-------
Construction and maintenance of roads, streets, sewers, and bridges	64,243	63,895	348
Contractors, builders, and proprietors	130	130	-------
Managers and officials	2	2	-------
Foremen and overseers	230	230	-------
Civil engineers and surveyors	20	20	-------
Draftsmen	2	2	-------
Agents (not elsewhere classified)	1	1	-------
Bookkeepers and cashiers	1	1	-------
Clerks	14	13	1
Commercial travelers	1	1	-------
Messenger, errand, and office boys and girls	2	2	-------
Office-appliance operators	1	1	-------
Stenographers and typists	4	3	1
Weighers	2	2	-------
Blacksmiths	44	44	-------
Brick and stone masons and tile layers	100	100	-------
Carpenters	97	97	-------
Cement finishers	447	447	-------
Cranemen, derrickmen, hoistmen, etc	40	40	-------
Electricians	5	5	-------
Engineers (stationary)	87	87	-------
Machinists	22	22	-------
Mechanics (not otherwise specified)	49	49	-------
Painters, glaziers, and varnishers (building)	9	9	-------
Plumbers and gas and steam fitters	40	40	-------
Structural iron workers	18	18	-------
Apprentices	2	2	-------

TABLE 27.—NEGROES 10 YEARS OLD AND OVER IN EACH INDUSTRY OR SERVICE GROUP, BY OCCUPATION, AND SEX, FOR THE UNITED STATES: 1930—Continued

[Occupations in which there are no Negroes are omitted]

INDUSTRY AND OCCUPATION	Total	Male	Female
TRANSPORTATION AND COMMUNICATION—Contd.			
Construction and maintenance of roads, streets sewers, and bridges—Continued.			
Chauffeurs and truck and tractor drivers	1,453	1,451	2
Cooks	544	236	308
Draymen and teamsters	1,200	1,200	-------
Firemen	40	40	-------
Guards and watchmen	69	69	-------
Inspectors	13	13	-------
Janitors	16	16	-------
Laborers, road, street, etc., building and repairing	56,286	56,254	32
Laborers, street cleaning	2,829	2,828	1
Oilers of machinery	7	7	-------
Porters	18	18	-------
Waiters	13	11	2
All other occupations	385	384	1
Express companies	2,904	2,872	32
Owners, operators, and proprietors	13	13	-------
Managers and officials	4	4	-------
Foremen and overseers	8	8	-------
Accountants and auditors	1	1	-------
Agents, express companies	6	5	1
Bookkeepers and cashiers	6	1	5
Clerks	58	50	8
Express messengers	38	38	-------
Messenger, errand, and office boys and girls	10	9	1
Shipping clerks	7	7	-------
Stenographers and typists	5	1	4
Weighers	1	1	-------
Blacksmiths	1	1	-------
Carpenters	3	3	-------
Mechanics (not otherwise specified)	13	13	-------
Chauffeurs and truck and tractor drivers	751	751	-------
Draymen and teamsters	470	470	-------
Elevator tenders	2	1	1
Guards, watchmen, and doorkeepers	8	8	-------
Inspectors	1	1	-------
Janitors	55	47	8
Laborers	1,097	1,096	1
Operatives (not otherwise specified)	52	50	2
Porters	292	292	-------
All other occupations	2	1	1
Garages, greasing stations, and automobile laundries	44,466	44,274	192
Owners, operators, and proprietors	424	420	4
Managers and officials	222	221	1
Foremen and overseers	245	244	1
Mechanical engineers	1	1	-------
Other professional pursuits	1	1	-------
Accountants and auditors	1	1	-------
Advertising agents	1	1	-------
Bookkeepers and cashiers	32	10	22
Clerks	71	63	8
Collectors	1	1	-------
Messenger, errand, and office boys and girls	7	6	1
Salesmen and saleswomen	104	102	2
Shipping clerks	1	1	-------
Stenographers and typists	4	-------	4
Blacksmiths	11	11	-------
Carpenters	5	5	-------
Electricians	7	7	-------
Engineers (stationary)	4	4	-------
Machinists	1,145	1,145	-------
Mechanics (not otherwise specified)	12,600	12,598	2
Millwrights	1	1	-------
Painters, glaziers, and varnishers (building)	12	12	-------
Plumbers and gas and steam fitters	1	1	-------
Tinsmiths and sheet metal workers	1	1	-------
Upholsterers	3	3	-------
Other skilled trades	2	2	-------
Apprentices	188	186	2
Charwomen and cleaners	19	5	14
Chauffeurs and truck and tractor drivers	1,217	1,214	3
Draymen and teamsters	4	4	-------
Elevator tenders	18	15	3
Firemen	23	23	-------
Guards, watchmen, and doorkeepers	423	423	-------
Janitors	604	595	9
Laborers	23,854	23,750	104
Oilers of machinery	30	30	-------
Operatives	755	746	9
Painters, glaziers, and varnishers (factory)	129	129	-------
Porters	2,290	2,289	1
All other occupations	5	3	2
Livery stables	1,836	1,832	4
Owners, operators, and proprietors	13	13	-------
Managers and officials	10	10	-------
Foremen and overseers	52	52	-------
Clerks	1	-------	1
Salesmen and saleswomen	1	1	-------
Stenographers and typists	3	1	2
Blacksmiths	14	14	-------
Chauffeurs and truck and tractor drivers	7	7	-------
Draymen, teasmsters, and carriage drivers	89	89	-------
Guards and watchmen	25	25	-------
Hostlers and stable hands	1,590	1,590	-------
Janitors	10	10	-------
Porters	10	10	-------
All other occupations	11	10	1
TRANSPORTATION AND COMMUNICATION—Contd.			
Pipe lines	1,122	1,121	1
Builders and building contractors	1	1	-------
Foremen and overseers	3	3	-------
Clerks	2	2	-------
Stenographers and typists	1	1	-------
Blacksmiths	1	1	-------
Mechanics (not otherwise specified)	2	2	-------
Painters, glaziers, and varnishers (building)	1	1	-------
Plumbers and gas and steam fitters	20	20	-------
Chauffeurs and truck and tractor drivers	6	6	-------
Draymen and teamsters	10	10	-------
Firemen	1	1	-------
Laborers	1,030	1,029	1
Oilers of machinery	2	2	-------
Operatives	39	39	-------
Painters, glaziers, and varnishers (except building)	1	1	-------
All other occupations	2	2	-------
Postal Service	17,669	17,084	585
Managers and officials	6	6	-------
Foremen and overseers	19	19	-------
Postmasters	78	36	42
Other professional pursuits	1	1	-------
Accountants and auditors	1	1	-------
Agents (not elsewhere classified)	1	1	-------
Bookkeepers and cashiers	4	4	-------
Clerks	6,852	6,612	240
Mail carriers	6,312	6,293	19
Messenger, errand, and office boys and girls	114	112	2
Office appliance operators	3	-------	3
Railway mail clerks	687	687	-------
Shipping clerks	2	2	-------
Stenographers and typists	5	-------	5
Weighers	1	1	-------
Other clerical pursuits	4	4	-------
Carpenters	2	2	-------
Compositors, linotypers, and typesetters	3	3	-------
Electricians	1	1	-------
Engineers (stationary)	3	3	-------
Machinists	5	5	-------
Mechanics (not otherwise specified)	39	39	-------
Other skilled trades	5	5	-------
Charwomen and cleaners	157	11	146
Chauffeurs and truck and tractor drivers	236	236	-------
Draymen, teamsters, and carriage drivers	10	10	-------
Elevator tenders	61	58	3
Firemen	49	49	-------
Guards, watchmen, and doorkeepers	46	46	-------
Inspectors	1	1	-------
Janitors	1,131	1,031	100
Laborers	1,452	1,445	7
Operatives	104	90	14
Porters	269	269	-------
All other occupations	5	1	4
Radio broadcasting and transmitting	60	60	-------
Announcers, directors, managers, and officials	4	4	-------
Clerks	1	1	-------
Messenger, errand, and office boys and girls	2	2	-------
Stenographers and typists	1	1	-------
Electricians	1	1	-------
Mechanics (not otherwise specified)	2	2	-------
Janitors	9	9	-------
Laborers	19	19	-------
Operatives	4	4	-------
Radio operators	8	8	-------
All other occupations	9	9	-------
Steam railroads [10]	162,630	160,796	1,834
Builders and building contractors	4	4	-------
Conductors	35	35	-------
Officials and superintendents	15	15	-------
Foremen and overseers	831	823	8
Chemists	3	3	-------
Civil engineers and surveyors	4	4	-------
Electrical engineers	3	3	-------
Lawyers	1	1	-------
Mechanical engineers	1	1	-------
Social and welfare workers	3	2	1
Accountants and auditors	4	4	-------
Agents (not elsewhere classified)	33	32	1
Baggagemen	427	427	-------
Bookkeepers and cashiers	11	8	3
Clerks	961	937	24
Collectors	1	1	-------
Freight agents	6	6	-------
Messenger, errand, and office boys and girls	307	305	2
Office appliance operators	8	7	1
Salesmen and saleswomen	8	7	1
Shipping clerks	67	65	2
Stenographers and typists	13	10	3
Ticket and station agents	13	13	-------
Weighers	13	13	-------
Blacksmiths	180	180	-------
Boilermakers	231	231	-------
Brick and stone masons and tile layers	21	21	-------
Cabinetmakers	3	3	-------
Carpenters	397	397	-------
Cement finishers	4	4	-------
Coopers	31	31	-------

See footnotes at end of table.

TABLE 27.—NEGROES 10 YEARS OLD AND OVER IN EACH INDUSTRY OR SERVICE GROUP, BY OCCUPATION, AND SEX, FOR THE UNITED STATES: 1930—Continued

[Occupations in which there are no Negroes are omitted]

INDUSTRY AND OCCUPATION	Total	Male	Female
TRANSPORTATION AND COMMUNICATION—Contd.			
Steam railroads—Continued.			
Coppersmiths	3	3	----
Cranemen, derrickmen, hoistmen, etc	57	57	----
Electricians	63	63	----
Engineers (stationary) [14]	193	193	----
Foregmen and hammermen	6	6	----
Locomotive engineers [14]	114	114	----
Locomotive firemen [14]	4, 642	4, 642	----
Machinists	600	600	----
Mechanics (not otherwise specified)	375	375	----
Millwrights	1	1	----
Iron molders, founders, and casters	5	5	----
Other molders, founders, and casters	2	2	----
Painters, glaziers, and varnishers (building)	17	17	----
Plumbers and gas and steam fitters	78	78	----
Sawyers	1	1	----
Structural iron workers (building)	34	34	----
Tinsmiths and sheet metal workers	13	13	----
Toolmakers and die setters and sinkers	3	3	----
Upholsterers	15	13	2
Other skilled trades	1	1	----
Apprentices:			
Carpenters	1	1	----
Electricians	1	1	----
Machinists	4	4	----
Other apprentices	15	15	----
Boiler washers and engine hostlers	3, 813	3, 813	----
Brakemen	3, 347	3, 347	----
Charwomen and cleaners	138	63	75
Chauffeurs and truck and tractor drivers	365	365	----
Cooks	5, 397	5, 151	246
Draymen and teamsters	125	125	----
Elevator tenders	96	82	14
Firemen (except locomotive) [14]	265	265	----
Guards, watchmen, and doorkeepers	128	128	----
Heaters	5	5	----
Housekeepers and stewards	252	178	74
Inspectors	172	172	----
Janitors	1, 618	1, 519	99
Laborers	97, 992	96, 865	1, 127
Motormen	21	21	----
Painters, glaziers, and varnishers (factory)	182	180	2
Policemen	4	4	----
Porters	25, 585	25, 584	1
Switchmen and flagmen	2, 571	2, 554	17
Waiters	6, 466	6, 404	62
Yardmen	823	823	----
All other occupations	3, 382	3, 313	69
Street railroads [14]	6, 668	6, 546	122
Builders and building contractors	1	1	----
Foremen and overseers	45	44	1
Civil engineers and surveyors	4	4	----
Electrical engineers	1	1	----
Agents (not elsewhere classified)	6	6	----
Baggagemen	3	3	----
Bookkeepers and cashiers	1	1	----
Clerks	32	30	2
Messenger, errand, and office boys and girls	20	19	1
Shipping clerks	2	1	1
Stenographers and typists	4	2	2
Other clerical pursuits	1	1	----
Blacksmiths	3	3	----
Boilermakers	1	1	----
Brick and stone masons and tile layers	6	6	----
Carpenters	21	21	----
Cement finishers	2	2	----
Cranemen, derrickmen, hoistmen, etc	2	2	----
Electricians	31	31	----
Engineers (stationary)	18	18	----
Machinists	18	18	----
Mechanics (not otherwise specified)	76	76	----
Moulders, founders, and casters (metal)	1	1	----
Painters, glaziers, and varnishers (building)	1	1	----
Plumbers and gas and steam fitters	4	4	----
Structural iron workers (building)	1	1	----
Upholsterers	1	1	----
Charwomen and cleaners	6	1	5
Chauffeurs and truck and tractor drivers	31	31	----
Conductors	11	11	----
Cooks	7	7	----
Draymen, teamsters, and carriage drivers	8	8	----
Elevator tenders	26	25	1
Firemen	38	38	----
Guards, watchmen, and doorkeepers	8	8	----
Inspectors	10	10	----
Janitors	142	134	8
Laborers	4, 693	4, 601	92
Motormen	51	51	----
Oilers of machinery	24	24	----
Painters, glaziers, and varnishers (factory)	10	10	----
Porters	795	795	----
Switchmen and flagmen	52	52	----
All other occupations	450	441	9
Telegraph and telephone	3, 995	3, 478	517
Builders and building contractors	2	2	----
Managers and officials	2	2	----
Foremen and overseers	5	5	----
Civil engineers and surveyors	1	1	----
Accountants and auditors	1	1	----
Bookkeeper and cashiers	1	----	1
TRANSPORTATION AND COMMUNICATION—Contd.			
Telegraph and telephone—Continued.			
Canvassers	2	2	----
Clerks	34	27	7
Messenger, errand, and office boys and girls	17	16	1
Office appliance operators	2	1	1
Shipping clerks	4	4	----
Stenographers and typists	1	----	1
Telegraph messengers	178	177	1
Telegraph operators	44	36	8
Telephone operators	587	256	331
Blacksmiths	1	1	----
Brick and stone masons and tile layers	16	16	----
Carpenters	2	2	----
Electricians	11	11	----
Engineers (stationary)	2	2	----
Machinists	6	6	----
Mechanics (not otherwise specified)	15	15	----
Plumbers and gas and steam fitters	2	2	----
Telegraph and telephone linemen	309	309	----
Other skilled trades	2	2	----
Apprentices	1	1	----
Charwomen and cleaners	35	4	31
Chauffeurs and truck and tractor drivers	26	26	----
Draymen, teamsters, and carriage drivers	5	5	----
Elevator tenders	34	22	12
Firemen	4	4	----
Guards, watchmen, and doorkeepers	6	6	----
Housekeepers and stewards	11	1	10
Inspectors	2	1	1
Janitors	835	738	97
Laborers	1, 357	1, 351	6
Operatives	58	49	9
Porters	373	373	----
All other occupations	1	1	----
Truck, transfer, and cab companies	41, 152	40, 904	248
Owners and proprietors	1, 726	1, 704	22
Managers and officials	152	149	3
Foremen and overseers	38	38	----
Accountants and auditors	1	1	----
Advertising agents	1	1	----
Agents (not elsewhere classified)	5	5	----
Bookkeepers and cashiers	45	11	34
Canvassers	1	----	1
Clerks	100	61	39
Collectors	2	1	1
Messenger, errand, and office boys and girls	22	13	9
Salesmen and saleswomen	3	3	----
Shipping clerks	9	8	1
Stenographers and typists	13	3	10
Weighers	4	4	----
Blacksmiths	10	10	----
Carpenters	2	2	----
Cranemen, derrickmen, hoistmen, etc	1	1	----
Electricians	4	4	----
Engineers (stationary)	3	3	----
Machinists	19	19	----
Mechanics (not otherwise specified)	126	126	----
Painters, glaziers, and varnishers (building)	2	2	----
Upholsterers	1	1	----
Other skilled trades	2	2	----
Bus conductors	2	2	----
Charwomen and cleaners	26	2	24
Chauffeurs and truck and tractor drivers	22, 986	22, 942	44
Draymen, teamsters, and carriage drivers	8, 040	8, 034	6
Elevator tenders	5	5	----
Firemen	9	9	----
Guards, watchmen, and doorkeepers	17	17	----
Housekeepers and stewards	6	3	3
Inspectors	2	2	----
Janitors	82	80	2
Laborers	7, 055	7, 019	36
Oilers of machinery	2	2	----
Operatives	201	189	12
Painters, glaziers, and varnishers (factory)	9	9	----
Porters	418	417	1
Water transportation	45, 287	44, 959	328
Builders and building contractors	1	1	----
Captains, masters, mates, and pilots	203	203	----
Managers and officials	2	2	----
Foremen and overseers	104	104	----
Civil engineers and surveyors	1	1	----
Electrical engineers	1	1	----
Accountants and auditors	1	1	----
Agents (not elsewhere classified)	8	7	1
Bookkeepers and cashiers	9	9	----
Clerks	120	118	2
Messenger, errand, and office boys and girls	41	41	----
Office-appliance operators	1	----	1
Salesmen and saleswomen	1	1	----
Shipping clerks	10	10	----
Stenographers and typists	4	3	1
Weighers	15	15	----
Blacksmiths	15	15	----
Boilermakers	4	4	----
Brick and stone masons and tile layers	3	3	----
Carpenters	75	75	----
Compositors, linotypers, and typesetters	19	19	----
Coopers	19	19	----
Cranemen, derrickmen, hoistmen, etc	34	34	----
Electricians	6	6	----

See footnotes at end of table.

TABLE 27.—NEGROES 10 YEARS OLD AND OVER IN EACH INDUSTRY OR SERVICE GROUP, BY OCCUPATION, AND SEX, FOR THE UNITED STATES: 1930—Continued

[Occupations in which there are no Negroes are omitted]

INDUSTRY AND OCCUPATION	Total	Male	Female
TRANSPORTATION AND COMMUNICATION—Contd.			
Water transportation—Continued.			
Engineers (stationary)	182	182	-------
Machinists	23	23	-------
Mechanics (not otherwise specified)	24	24	-------
Millwrights	1	1	-------
Painters, glaziers, and varnishers (building)	8	8	-------
Plumbers and gas and steam fitters	9	9	-------
Other skilled trades	4	4	-------
Boatmen, canal men, and lock keepers	282	282	-------
Charwomen and cleaners	13	6	7
Chauffeurs and truck and tractor drivers	130	130	-------
Cooks	2,506	2,315	191
Draymen and teamsters	74	74	-------
Elevator tenders	3	3	-------
Firemen	1,500	1,500	-------
Guards, watchmen, and doorkeepers	144	143	1
Housekeepers and stewards	898	811	87
Inspectors	2	2	-------
Janitors	55	52	3
Laborers	2,927	2,926	1
Longshoremen and stevedores	25,444	25,434	10
Oilers of machinery	102	102	-------
Operatives	109	105	4
Painters, glaziers, and varnishers (factory) [15]	5	5	-------
Porters	436	436	-------
Sailors and deck hands	6,659	6,656	3
Waiters	3,050	3,034	16
Other and not specified transportation and communication	398	388	10
Owners, operators, and proprietors	1	1	-------
Managers and officials	1	1	-------
Foremen and overseers	3	3	-------
Draftsmen	1	1	-------
Clerks	23	22	1
Messenger, errand, and office boys and girls	6	6	-------
Shipping clerks	2	2	-------
Stenographers and typists	1	-------	1
Carpenters	1	1	-------
Cranemen, derrickmen, hoistmen, etc	1	1	-------
Engineers (stationary)	2	2	-------
Machinists	1	1	-------
Painters, glaziers, and varnishers (building)	1	1	-------
Chauffeurs and truck and tractor drivers	21	21	-------
Draymen, teamsters, and carriage drivers	9	9	-------
Firemen	1	1	-------
Guards, watchmen, and doorkeepers	1	1	-------
Inspectors	1	1	-------
Laborers	279	273	6
Operatives	18	18	-------
Porters	15	15	-------
All other occupations	9	7	2
TRADE			
Advertising agencies	340	319	21
Managers and officials	2	2	-------
Foremen and overseers	1	1	-------
Advertising agents	39	36	3
Agents (not elsewhere classified)	1	1	-------
Canvassers	1	1	-------
Clerks	15	8	7
Messenger, errand, and office boys and girls	6	6	-------
Shipping clerks	6	6	-------
Stenographers and typists	7	1	6
Carpenters	4	4	-------
Compositors, linotypers, and typesetters	3	3	-------
Mechanics (not otherwise specified)	5	5	-------
Painters, glaziers, and varnishers (building)	1	1	-------
Chauffeurs and truck and tractor drivers	13	13	-------
Draymen and teamsters	1	1	-------
Guards, watchmen, and doorkeepers	2	2	-------
Janitors	5	4	1
Laborers	65	65	-------
Porters	25	25	-------
All other occupations	138	134	4
Banking and brokerage	9,283	8,534	749
Bankers and bank officials	80	68	12
Commercial brokers and commission men	21	21	-------
Loan brokers and pawnbrokers	36	36	-------
Stock brokers	95	90	5
Brokers not specified and promoters	35	34	1
Foremen and overseers	3	3	-------
Accountants and auditors	13	13	-------
Agents (not elsewhere classified)	41	40	1
Bookkeepers and cashiers	89	38	51
Canvassers	2	2	-------
Clerks	479	401	78
Collectors	11	9	2
Commercial travelers	2	2	-------
Messenger, errand, and office boys and girls	1,023	1,016	7
Office appliance operators	3	3	-------
Purchasing agents	2	2	-------
Salesmen and saleswomen	2	2	-------
Shipping clerks	13	13	-------
Stenographers and typists	67	6	61
Weighers	1	1	-------
Carpenters	4	4	-------
Compositors, linotypers, and typesetters	2	2	-------

INDUSTRY AND OCCUPATION	Total	Male	Female
TRADE—Continued			
Banking and brokerage—Continued.			
Electricians	5	5	-------
Engineers (stationary)	10	10	-------
Mechanics (not otherwise specified)	7	7	-------
Painters, glaziers, and varnishers (building)	2	2	-------
Other skilled trades	1	1	-------
Charwomen and cleaners	130	12	118
Chauffeurs and truck and tractor drivers	111	111	-------
Draymen, teamsters, and carriage drivers	6	6	-------
Elevator tenders	398	255	143
Firemen	45	45	-------
Guards, watchmen, and doorkeepers [16]	196	195	1
Housekeepers and stewards	20	3	17
Janitors	3,766	3,524	242
Laborers	299	294	5
Operatives (not otherwise specified)	37	32	5
Policemen	32	32	-------
Porters	2,194	2,194	-------
Grain elevators	909	900	9
Foremen and overseers	14	14	-------
Clerks	7	6	1
Shipping clerks	4	4	-------
Weighers	3	3	-------
Cranemen, derrickmen, hoistmen, etc	3	3	-------
Engineers (stationary)	2	2	-------
Machinists	3	3	-------
Mechanics (not otherwise specified)	2	2	-------
Millwrights	1	1	-------
Other skilled trades	2	2	-------
Chauffeurs and truck and tractor drivers	40	40	-------
Draymen and teamsters	17	17	-------
Firemen	6	6	-------
Guards, watchmen, and doorkeepers	7	7	-------
Inspectors	1	1	-------
Janitors	4	4	-------
Laborers	692	692	-------
All other occupations	101	93	8
Insurance	9,939	7,211	2,728
Managers and officials	511	499	12
Lawyers	3	2	1
Social and welfare workers	1	1	-------
Trained nurses	18	-------	18
Accountants and auditors	40	36	4
Agents:			
Insurance agents	6,286	5,200	1,086
Purchasing agents	2	2	-------
Agents (not elsewhere classified)	8	6	2
Bookkeepers and cashiers	314	61	253
Canvassers	1	1	-------
Clerks	793	259	534
Collectors	679	548	131
Commercial travelers	2	2	-------
Messenger, errand, and office boys and girls	127	118	9
Office appliance operators	8	4	4
Shipping clerks	7	7	-------
Stenographers and typists	652	16	636
Carpenters	1	1	-------
Compositors, linotypers, and typesetters	4	4	-------
Engineers (stationary)	2	2	-------
Machinists	1	1	-------
Mechanics (not otherwise specified)	2	2	-------
Charwomen and cleaners	13	3	10
Chauffeurs and truck and tractor drivers	12	12	-------
Elevator tenders	27	21	6
Firemen	5	5	-------
Guards, watchmen, and doorkeepers	5	4	1
Housekeepers and stewards	4	1	3
Janitors	211	196	15
Laborers	35	34	1
Operatives (not otherwise specified)	12	10	2
Porters	153	153	-------
Real estate	5,211	4,266	945
Managers and officials	21	20	1
Civil engineers and surveyors	1	1	-------
Lawyers	6	6	-------
Mechanical engineers	1	1	-------
Accountants and auditors	3	3	-------
Agents:			
Real estate agents	4,029	3,557	472
Agents (not elsewhere classified)	3	2	1
Bookkeepers and cashiers	101	19	82
Clerks	183	96	87
Collectors	77	70	7
Messenger, errand, and office boys and girls	36	30	6
Stenographers and typists	270	9	261
Compositors, linotypers, and typesetters	1	1	-------
Engineers (stationary)	11	11	-------
Machinists	1	1	-------
Mechanics (not otherwise specified)	17	17	-------
Charwomen and cleaners	13	3	10
Chauffeurs and truck and tractor drivers	56	56	-------
Draymen and teamsters	4	4	-------
Elevator tenders	12	9	3
Firemen	4	4	-------
Guards, watchmen, and doorkeepers	24	24	-------

See footnotes at end of table.

TABLE 27.—NEGROES 10 YEARS OLD AND OVER IN EACH INDUSTRY OR SERVICE GROUP, BY OCCUPATION, AND SEX, FOR THE UNITED STATES: 1930—Continued

[Occupations in which there are no Negroes are omitted]

INDUSTRY AND OCCUPATION	Total	Male	Female
TRADE—Continued			
Real estate—Continued.			
Housekeepers and stewards	1		1
Janitors	199	186	13
Porters	136	135	1
All other occupations	1	1	
Stockyards [5]	2,288	2,280	8
Foremen and overseers	15	15	
Agents (not elsewhere classified)	1	1	
Clerks	8	8	
Messenger, errand, and office boys and girls	3	3	
Purchasing agents	1	1	
Salesmen and saleswomen	7	7	
Shipping clerks	10	10	
Weighers	6	4	2
Carpenters	1	1	
Electricians	1	1	
Engineers (stationary)	1	1	
Machinists	7	7	
Mechanics (not otherwise specified)	9	9	
Millwrights	1	1	
Painters, glaziers, and varnishers (building)	2	2	
Plumbers and gas and steam fitters	10	10	
Other skilled trades	3	3	
Chauffeurs and truck and tractor drivers	27	27	
Draymen and teamsters	4	4	
Elevator tenders	12	12	
Firemen	18	18	
Guards, watchmen, and doorkeepers	9	9	
Inspectors	12	11	1
Janitors	39	36	3
Laborers	1,982	1,982	
Policemen	1	1	
Porters	22	22	
All other occupations	76	74	2
Warehouses and cold-storage plants	6,376	6,182	194
Owners, operators, and proprietors	10	10	
Managers and officials	8	8	
Foremen and overseers	41	41	
Electrical engineers	1	1	
Agents (not elsewhere classified)	1	1	
Bookkeepers and cashiers	1	1	
Clerks	136	124	12
Messenger, errand, and office boys and girls	7	7	
Salesmen and saleswomen	6	6	
Shipping clerks	62	62	
Stenographers and typists	5	1	4
Weighers	17	16	1
Blacksmiths	1	1	
Cabinetmakers	1	1	
Carpenters	8	8	
Coopers	14	14	
Cranemen, derrickmen, hoistmen, etc	2	2	
Electricians	1	1	
Engineers (stationary)	10	10	
Machinists	2	2	
Mechanics (not otherwise specified)	4	4	
Millwrights	2	2	
Painters, glaziers, and varnishers (building)	2	2	
Plumbers and gas and steam fitters	1	1	
Tinsmiths and sheet-metal workers	1	1	
Chauffeurs and truck and tractor drivers	704	704	
Draymen and teamsters	98	98	
Elevator tenders	34	32	2
Firemen	23	23	
Guards, watchmen, and doorkeepers	102	100	2
Inspectors	101	98	3
Janitors	115	111	4
Laborers	4,081	4,033	48
Painters, glaziers, and varnishers (factory)	2	2	
Porters	317	316	1
All other occupations	455	338	117
WHOLESALE AND RETAIL TRADE			
Automobile agencies, stores, and filling stations	12,111	11,990	121
Retail dealers, automobiles and accessories	111	108	3
Retail dealers, gasoline and oil filling stations	359	334	25
Accountants and auditors	1	1	
Advertising agents	1	1	
Agents (not elsewhere classified)	3	3	
Bookkeepers and cashiers	14	2	12
Canvassers	1	1	
Clerks	65	58	7
Collectors	1	1	
Messenger, errand, and office boys and girls	17	16	1
Sales agents	1	1	
Salesmen and saleswomen	1,725	1,687	38
Shipping clerks	12	12	
Stenographers and typists	4		4
Carpenters	1	1	
Electricians	2	2	
Engineers (stationary)	1	1	
Machinists	34	34	
Mechanics (not otherwise specified)	517	517	
Painters, glaziers, and varnishers (building)	1	1	
Plumbers and gas and steam fitters	2	2	
Apprentices	2	2	
Charwomen and cleaners	12	8	4
TRADE—Continued			
WHOLESALE AND RETAIL TRADE—continued			
Automobile agencies, stores, and filling stations—Con.			
Chauffeurs and truck and tractor drivers	476	476	
Draymen and teamsters	7	7	
Elevator tenders	8	8	
Firemen	2	2	
Guards, watchmen, and doorkeepers	54	54	
Inspectors	2	2	
Janitors	305	301	4
Laborers	8,131	8,113	18
Oilers of machinery	10	10	
Operatives	220	215	5
Painters, glaziers, and varnishers (factory)	9	9	
Wholesale and retail trade (except automobiles)	192,261	176,161	16,100
Wholesale dealers, importers, and exporters	130	129	1
Retail dealers:			
Books, music, news, and stationary	417	369	48
Buyers and shippers of livestock and other farm products	149	149	
Candy and confectionery	1,333	903	430
Cigars and tobacco	320	292	28
Coal and wood	1,853	1,793	60
Department stores	18	18	
Dry goods, clothing, and boots and shoes	527	410	117
Drugs and medicines (including druggists and pharmacists)	1,482	1,314	168
Five and ten cent and variety stores	37	30	7
Flour and feed	45	42	3
Food (except groceries and hucksters' goods)	3,496	3,329	167
Furniture, carpets, and rugs	250	228	22
General stores	807	659	148
Groceries	7,547	5,739	1,808
Hardware, implements, and wagons	54	50	4
Hucksters and peddlers	4,356	3,944	412
Ice	775	772	3
Jewelry	88	87	1
Junk and rags	2,445	2,389	56
Lumber	183	183	
Opticians	44	44	
Other specified dealers	582	468	114
Not specified dealers	935	710	225
Employment-office keepers	287	114	173
Undertakers	2,946	2,691	255
Floorwalkers and foremen in stores	373	349	24
Chemists	22	21	1
Designers	3	1	2
Electrical engineer	4	4	
Lawyers	2	2	
Mechanical engineers	2	2	
Photographers	7	6	1
Social and welfare workers	3	1	2
Trained nurses	4	1	3
Accountants and auditors	5	4	1
Advertising agents	5	4	1
Agents (not elsewhere classified)	98	45	53
Auctioneers	11	11	
Bookkeepers and cashiers	458	78	380
Canvassers	933	325	608
"Clerks" in stores [17]	4,911	3,262	1,649
Clerks (except "clerks" in stores)	2,125	1,193	932
Collectors	106	96	10
Commercial travelers	357	295	62
Credit men	2	1	1
Demonstrators	210	73	137
Messenger, errand, and office boys and girls [18]	1,673	1,547	126
Office-appliance operators	12	10	2
Purchasing agents	2	2	
Sales agents	35	19	16
Salesmen and saleswomen	9,624	6,316	3,308
Shipping clerks	1,237	1,195	42
Stenographers and typists	219	16	203
Weighers	40	36	4
Blacksmiths	13	13	
Boilermakers	1	1	
Brick and stonemasons and tile layers	15	15	
Carpenters	100	100	
Compositors, linotypers, and typesetters	10	9	1
Coopers	5	5	
Coppersmiths	5	5	
Cranemen, derrickmen, hoistmen, etc	34	34	
Electricians	61	61	
Engineers (stationary)	64	64	
Engravers	3	3	
Machinists	42	42	
Mechanics (not otherwise specified)	478	478	
Painters, glaziers, and varnishers (building)	89	89	
Plumbers and gas and steam fitters	46	46	
Sawyers	38	38	
Tinsmiths and sheet-metal workers	22	22	
Toolmakers and die setters and sinkers	1	1	
Other skilled trades	2	2	
Apprentices:			
Electricians	2	2	
Jewelers', watchmakers', goldsmiths', and silversmiths'	2	2	
Other apprentices	55	51	4
Charwomen and cleaners	482	170	312
Chauffeurs and truck and tractor drivers [6]	21,421	21,412	9
Decorators, drapers, and window dressers	292	135	157
Deliverymen [6]	25,069	25,047	22

See footnotes at end of table.

TABLE 27.—NEGROES 10 YEARS OLD AND OVER IN EACH INDUSTRY OR SERVICE GROUP, BY OCCUPATION, AND SEX, FOR THE UNITED STATES: 1930—Continued

[Occupations in which there are no Negroes are omitted]

INDUSTRY AND OCCUPATION	Total	Male	Female
TRADE—Continued			
WHOLESALE AND RETAIL TRADE—Continued			
Wholesale and retail trade (except automobiles)—Continued.			
Draymen, teamsters, and carriage drivers [6]	2,179	2,177	2
Elevator tenders	2,534	1,283	1,251
Firemen	258	258	-------
Fruit and vegetable graders and packers	216	172	44
Guards, watchmen, and doorkeepers	629	619	10
Housekeepers and stewards	100	13	87
Inspectors	316	276	40
Janitors	5,491	5,210	281
Laborers, coal yards and lumber yards	18,998	18,983	15
Laborers, porters, and helpers in stores	54,698	53,488	1,210
Meat cutters	574	569	5
Newsboys	1,460	1,442	18
Oilers of machinery	2	2	-------
Painters, glaziers, and varnishers (factory)	4	4	-------
Policemen	2	2	-------
All other occupations	2,859	2,045	814
Other and not specified trades	767	618	149
Owners, operators, and proprietors	42	38	4
Managers and officials	8	8	-------
Foremen and overseers	1	1	-------
Civil engineers and surveyors	1	1	-------
Lawyers	1	1	-------
Accountants and auditors [19]	16	15	1
Agents (not elsewhere classified)	23	13	10
Bookkeepers and cashiers	8	1	7
Canvassers	3	2	1
Clerks	52	28	24
Collectors	13	9	4
Messenger, errand, and office boys and girls	22	22	-------
Office-appliance operators	2	1	1
Purchasing agents	6	1	5
Sales agents	1	-------	1
Salesmen and saleswomen	2	1	1
Shipping clerks	9	9	-------
Stenographers and typists [20]	88	6	82
Weighers	2	2	-------
Carpenters	1	1	-------
Electricians	1	1	-------
Mechanics (not otherwise specified)	2	2	-------
Other skilled trades	1	1	-------
Chauffeurs and truck and tractor drivers	17	17	-------
Draymen, teamsters, and carriage drivers	28	28	-------
Guards, watchmen, and doorkeepers	1	1	-------
Inspectors	141	139	2
Janitors	29	27	2
Laborers	156	156	-------
Operatives	28	26	2
Porters	58	58	-------
All other occupations	4	2	2
PUBLIC SERVICE (NOT ELSEWHERE CLASSIFIED)			
Public service (not elsewhere classified) [21]	62,483	58,962	3,521
Officials and inspectors (United States)	187	181	6
Officials and inspectors (State)	16	15	1
Officials and inspectors (county)	45	35	10
Officials and inspectors (city)	218	201	17
Detectives	157	151	6
Marshals and constables	80	80	-------
Probation and truant officers	160	76	84
Sheriffs	124	123	1
Builders and building contractors	9	9	-------
Firemen (fire department)	520	520	-------
Guards, watchmen, and doorkeepers	510	497	
Garbage men and scavangers	2,543	2,538	13
Other laborers	32,381	31,884	45
Policemen	1,224	1,192	97
Soldiers, sailors, and marines	4,601	4,601	32
Other public-service pursuits	1,763	1,565	198
Chemists, assayers, and metallurgists	22	20	2
Civil engineers and surveyors	46	46	-------
Draftsmen	10	10	-------
Electrical engineers	5	5	-------
Lawyers, judges, and justices	49	49	-------
Mechanical engineers	2	2	-------
Mining engineers	1	1	-------
Photographers	9	9	-------
Social and welfare workers	66	9	57
Trained nurses	100	3	97
Accountants and auditors	11	11	-------
Agents (not elsewhere classified)	40	30	10
Bookkeepers and cashiers	40	33	7
Clerks	2,193	1,669	524
Messenger, errand, and office boys and girls	1,984	1,946	38
Office appliance operators	131	48	83
Shipping clerks	19	19	-------
Stenographers and typists	205	49	156
Weighers	18	18	-------
Other clerical pursuits	11	10	1
Blacksmiths	42	42	-------
Boiler makers	8	8	-------
Cabinetmakers	1	1	-------
Carpenters	103	103	-------
Coopers	5	5	-------
Cranemen, derrickmen, hoistmen, etc	6	6	-------
Electricians	60	60	-------
PUBLIC SERVICE (NOT ELSEWHERE CLASSIFIED)—Continued			
Public service (not elsewhere classified—Continued.			
Engineers (stationary)	179	179	-------
Machinists	57	57	-------
Mechanics (not otherwise specified)	150	150	-------
Painters, glaziers, and varnishers (building)	49	49	-------
Plumbers and gas and steam fitters	336	336	-------
Structural iron workers (building)	3	3	-------
Upholsterers	2	2	-------
Other skilled trades	11	11	-------
Charwomen and cleaners	1,397	408	989
Chauffeurs and truck and tractor drivers	2,654	2,654	-------
Cooks	880	546	334
Draymen, teamsters, and carriage drivers	1,215	1,214	1
Elevator tenders	312	257	55
Firemen (except fire department)	685	685	-------
Housekeepers and stewards	92	24	68
Janitors	3,372	3,187	185
Oilers of macinery	33	33	-------
Porters	873	873	-------
Waiters	458	414	44
PROFESSIONAL SERVICE			
Professional service (except recreation and amusement	138,263	71,784	66,479
PROFESSIONAL PURSUITS			
Architects	63	63	-------
Artists, sculptors, and teachers of art	430	230	200
Authors	49	41	8
Chemists, assayers, and metallurgists	50	44	6
Civil engineers and surveyors	33	33	-------
Clergymen	25,034	24,540	494
College presidents and professors	2,146	1,126	1,020
County agents, farm and demonstrator, etc	226	136	90
Dentists	1,773	1,746	27
Designers	4	-------	4
Draftsmen	19	19	-------
Editors and reporters	376	300	76
Electrical engineers	36	36	-------
Inventors	17	17	-------
Lawyers	1,175	1,152	23
Librarians	210	30	180
Mechanical engineers [4]	23	23	-------
Osteopaths	19	14	5
Photographers	503	425	78
Physicians and surgeons	3,805	3,713	92
Social and welfare workers	949	188	761
Teachers (athletics, dancing, etc.)	244	188	56
Teachers (school)	54,439	8,767	45,672
Trained nurses	5,587	142	5,445
Veterinary surgeons	134	133	1
Other professional occupations	336	152	184
SEMIPROFESSIONAL PURSUITS			
Abstracters, notaries, and justices of peace	57	34	23
Architects', designers', and draftsmen's apprentices	1	1	-------
Apprentices to other professional persons	16	15	1
Chiropractors	184	142	42
Healers (not elsewhere classified)	901	518	383
Keepers of charitable and penal institutions	202	96	106
Officials of lodges, societies, etc	451	287	164
Religious workers	1,196	434	762
Technicians and laboratory assistants	196	151	45
Other semiprofessional occupations	43	28	15
ATTENDANTS AND HELPERS			
Dentists' assistants and attendants	270	37	233
Librarians' assistants and attendants	15	12	3
Laborers	4,147	3,906	241
Physicians' and surgeons' attendants	1,039	106	933
Porters	2,930	2,928	2
Other attendants and helpers	1,447	880	567
OTHER OCCUPATIONS			
Accountants and auditors	34	29	5
Advertising agents	4	4	-------
Agents (not elsewhere classified)	13	8	5
Bookkeepers and cashiers	304	62	242
Canvassers	7	3	4
Clerks	1,196	401	795
Collectors	10	7	3
Commercial travelers	1	1	-------
Credit men	1	-------	1
Messenger, errand, and office boys and girls	222	184	38
Office appliance operators	6	6	-------
Purchasing agents	3	2	1
Shipping clerks	20	19	1
Stenographers and typists	971	53	918
Blacksmiths	10	10	-------
Cabinetmakers	3	3	-------
Compositors, linotypers, and typesetters	10	10	-------
Engineers (stationary)	169	169	-------

See footnotes at end of table.

Table 27.—NEGROES 10 YEARS OLD AND OVER IN EACH INDUSTRY OR SERVICE GROUP, BY OCCUPATION, AND SEX, FOR THE UNITED STATES: 1930—Continued

[Occupations in which there are no Negroes are omitted]

INDUSTRY AND OCCUPATION	Total	Male	Female
PROFESSIONAL SERVICE—Continued			
OTHER OCCUPATIONS—continued			
Professional service—Continued.			
Machinists	6	6	-
Mechanics (not otherwise specified)	36	56	-
Toolmakers and die setters and sinkers	1	1	-
Upholsterers	2	1	1
Other skilled trades	1	1	-
Charwomen and cleaners	749	142	607
Chauffeurs and truck and tractor drivers	585	581	4
Cooks	4, 565	1, 712	2, 853
Draymen, teamsters, and carriage drivers	43	43	-
Elevator tenders	368	230	138
Firemen	707	707	-
Guards, watchmen, and doorkeepers	216	201	15
Housekeepers and stewards	516	64	452
Janitors and sextons	14, 960	13, 345	1, 615
Oilers of machinery	6	6	-
Policemen	7	7	-
Waiters	1, 715	876	839
All other occupations	1	1	-
Recreation and amusement	35, 110	29, 476	5, 634
Billiard room, dance hall, skating rink, etc., keepers	1, 935	1, 914	21
Directors, managers, and officials, motion picture production	5	5	-
Keepers of pleasure resorts, race tracks, etc	109	99	10
Theatrical owners, managers, and officials	166	155	11
Actors	2, 626	1, 327	1, 299
Electrical engineers	1	1	-
Musicians and teachers of music	10, 583	7, 747	2, 836
Photographers	14	11	3
Showmen	1, 504	1, 405	99
Social and welfare workers	1	1	-
Trained nurses	1	-	1
Advertising agents	4	4	-
Agents (not elsewhere classified)	11	10	1
Bookkeepers and cashiers	319	34	285
Clerks	239	178	61
Commercial travelers	2	2	-
Messenger, errand, and office boys and girls	34	34	-
Office appliance operators	1	1	-
Salesmen and saleswomen	17	16	1
Shipping clerks	11	11	-
Stenographers and typists	13	1	12
Blacksmiths	10	10	-
Compositors, linotypers, andtype setters	1	1	-
Electricians	32	32	-
Engineers (stationary)	23	23	-
Machinists	5	5	-
Mechanics (not otherwise specified)	25	25	-
Toolmakers and die setters and sinkers	2	2	-
Attendants, pool rooms, bowling alleys, golf clubs, etc	4, 120	4, 049	71
Charwomen and cleaners	230	50	180
Chauffeurs and truck and tractor drivers	57	57	-
Cooks	143	83	60
Draymen, teamsters, and carriage drivers	22	22	-
Elevator tenders	47	25	22
Firemen	43	43	-
Guards, watchmen, and doorkeepers	116	115	1
Helpers, motion picture production	14	12	2
Housekeepers and stewards	115	39	76
Janitors	2, 281	2, 134	147
Laborers, recreation and amusement	4, 442	4, 349	93
Policemen	6	6	-
Porters	4, 181	4, 179	2
Stage hands and circus helpers	104	90	14
Theater ushers	409	285	124
Waiters	123	113	10
Other attendants and helpers, recreation and amusement	91	31	60
Other recreational occupations	872	740	132
DOMESTIC AND PERSONAL SERVICE			
Hotels, restaurants, boarding houses, etc	228, 166	122, 273	105, 893
Boarding and lodging house keepers	13, 109	997	12, 112
Hotel keepers and managers	1, 064	741	323
Housekeepers and stewards	1, 638	606	1, 032
Restaurant, cafe, and lunch room keepers	10, 543	5, 365	5, 178
Chemists	1	1	-
Civil engineers and surveyors	1	1	-
Electrical engineers	7	7	-
Mechanical engineers	1	1	-
Trained nurses	3	1	2
Other professional pursuits	1	1	-
Accountants and auditors	7	6	1
Advertising agents	2	1	1
Agents (not elsewhere classified)	4	2	2
Bookkeepers and cashiers	268	79	189
Canvassers	2	2	-
Clerks	745	526	219
Credit men	1	1	-
Messenger, errand, and office boys and girls	122	111	11
Office appliance operators	2	1	1
Purchasing agents	2	2	-
Salesmen and saleswomen	153	85	68
Shipping clerks	18	17	1
DOMESTIC AND PERSONAL SERVICE—Continued			
Hotels, restaurants, boarding houses, etc.—Contd.			
Stenographers and typists	30	10	20
Weighers	2	2	-
Blacksmiths	2	2	-
Boilermakers	1	1	-
Carpenters	10	10	-
Electricians	15	15	-
Engineers (stationary)	149	149	-
Machinists	10	10	-
Mechanics (not otherwise specified)	32	32	-
Painters, glaziers, and varnishers (building)	18	18	-
Plumbers and gas and steam fitters	9	9	-
Upholsterers	2	2	-
Other skilled trades	3	3	-
Charwomen and cleaners	517	139	378
Chauffeurs and truck and tractor drivers	335	335	-
Draymen, teamsters, and carriage drivers	14	14	-
Elevator tenders	2, 531	1, 492	1, 039
Firemen	636	636	-
Guards, watchmen, and doorkeepers	129	128	1
Janitors	3, 374	3, 225	149
Laborers	3, 591	3, 214	377
Launderers and laundresses	984	100	885
Oilers of machinery	6	6	-
Policemen	1	1	-
Porters	22, 192	22, 185	7
Servants:			
Cooks	59, 083	30, 139	28, 944
Other servants	63, 215	23, 573	39, 642
Waiters	43, 581	28, 269	15, 312
Domestic and personal service (not elsewhere classified)	1, 173, 984	192, 421	981, 563
Electrical engineers	2	2	-
Other professional pursuits	5	2	3
Accountants and auditors	1	-	1
Agents (not elsewhere classified)	34	31	3
Bookkeepers and cashiers	46	7	39
Clerks	104	68	36
Collectors	1	-	1
Messenger, errand, and office boys and girls	84	75	9
Purchasing agents	1	-	1
Stenographers and typists	14	-	14
Blacksmiths	4	4	-
Carpenters	12	12	-
Electricians	12	12	-
Engineers (stationary)	291	291	-
Machinists	3	3	-
Mechanics (not otherwise specified)	50	50	-
Painters, glaziers, and varnishers (building)	6	6	-
Plumbers and gas and steam fitters	5	5	-
Other skilled trades	10	10	-
Barbers, hairdressers, and manicurists	34, 363	21, 447	12, 816
Bootblacks	9, 499	9, 481	18
Cemetery keepers	352	346	6
Charwomen and cleaners	11, 272	3, 324	7, 948
Chauffeurs and truck and tractor drivers	32, 402	32, 316	86
Draymen, teamsters, and carriage drivers	59	59	-
Elevator tenders	8, 162	6, 892	1, 270
Firemen	1, 506	1, 506	-
Guards, watchmen, and doorkeepers	288	282	6
Housekeepers and stewards	16, 108	269	15, 839
Hunters, trappers, and guides	235	235	-
Janitors and sextons	30, 102	27, 553	2, 549
Laborers	19, 343	18, 436	907
Launderers and laundresses	270, 099	1, 885	268, 214
Midwives	1, 787	-	1, 787
Nurses (not trained)	16, 265	2, 207	14, 058
Policemen	3	3	-
Porters	18, 175	18, 170	5
Servants:			
Cooks	205, 801	7, 145	198, 656
Other servants	494, 092	38, 396	455, 696
Waiters	1, 899	577	1, 322
All other occupations	1, 587	1, 314	273
Laundries	60, 610	12, 768	47, 842
Owners and proprietors [22]	247	184	63
Managers and officials	88	55	33
Foremen and overseers	165	86	79
Mechanical engineers	2	2	-
Agents (not elsewhere classified)	2	2	-
Bookkeepers and cashiers	22	3	19
Canvassers	30	26	4
Clerks	169	45	124
Collectors	1	1	-
Messenger, errand, and office boys and girls	37	31	6
Shipping clerks	11	10	1
Stenographers and typists	6	-	6
Weighers	12	8	4
Carpenters	5	5	-
Electricians	3	3	-
Engineers (stationary)	142	142	-
Machinists	52	52	-
Mechanics (not otherwise specified)	47	47	-
Millwrights	2	2	-
Tinsmiths and sheet-metal workers	2	2	-
Charwomen and cleaners	20	2	18
Chauffeurs and truck and tractor drivers [6]	321	320	1
Deliverymen [6]	504	503	1
Draymen, teamsters, and carriage drivers	9	9	-

See footnotes at end of table.

Table 27.—NEGROES 10 YEARS OLD AND OVER IN EACH INDUSTRY OR SERVICE GROUP, BY OCCUPATION, AND SEX, FOR THE UNITED STATES: 1930—Continued

[Occupations in which there are no Negroes are omitted]

INDUSTRY AND OCCUPATION	Total	Male	Female
DOMESTIC AND PERSONAL SERVICE—Continued			
Laundries—Continued.			
Elevator tenders	28	26	2
Firemen	471	471	-------
Guards, watchmen, and doorkeepers	117	117	-------
House keepers and stewards	2	-------	2
Janitors	185	173	12
Laborers	5, 288	2, 785	2, 503
Oilers of machinery	3	3	-------
Operatives (not otherwise specified)[22]	52, 123	7, 160	44, 963
Porters	489	489	-------
All other occupations	5	4	1
Cleaning, dyeing, and pressing shops	16, 630	13, 340	3, 290
Owners and proprietors	1, 464	1, 398	66
Managers and officials	270	261	9
Foremen and overseers	20	12	8
Chemists	6	6	-------
Other professional pursuits	1	1	-------
Agents (not elsewhere classified)	1	1	-------
Bookkeepers and cashiers	29	-------	29
Canvassers	16	15	1
Clerks	60	23	37
Collectors	1	1	-------
Messenger, errand, and office boys and girls	33	30	3
Salesmen and saleswomen	2	-------	2
Shipping clerks	15	8	7
Stenographers and typists	4	2	2
Other clerical pursuits	1	1	-------
Electricians	1	1	-------
Engineers (stationary)	9	9	-------
Machinists	6	6	-------
Mechanics (not otherwise specified)	10	10	-------
Plumbers and gas and steam fitters	3	3	-------
Other skilled trades	1	1	-------
Charwomen and cleaners	11	7	4
Chauffeurs and truck and tractor drivers	212	210	2
Draymen, teamsters, and carriage drivers	1	1	-------
Firemen	60	60	-------
Guards, watchmen, and doorkeepers	32	31	1
Janitors	45	43	2
Laborers	1, 388	1, 241	147
Operatives (not otherwise specified)	12, 631	9, 661	2, 970
Porters	296	296	-------
All other occupations	1	1	-------
NOT SPECIFIED INDUSTRIES AND SERVICES			
Not specified industries and services	158, 882	148, 967	9, 915
Builders and building contractors	12	12	-------
Owners, operators, and proprietors	7	4	3
Managers and officials	65	63	2
Foremen and overseers	53	52	1
Chemists, assayers, and metallurgists	3	3	-------
Civil engineers and surveyors	3	3	-------
Designers	1	-------	1
Draftsmen	3	3	-------
Electrical engineers	4	4	-------
Mechanical engineers [4]	5	5	-------
Social and welfare workers	3	-------	3
Trained nurses	2	-------	2
Accountants and auditors	11	11	-------
Advertising agents	1	1	-------
Agents (not elsewhere classified)	42	27	15
NOT SPECIFIED INDUSTRIES AND SERVICE—Contd.			
Not specified industries and services—Continued.			
Bookkeepers and cashiers	164	51	113
Canvassers	16	7	9
Clerks	826	485	341
Collectors	19	16	3
Commercial travelers	10	9	1
Messenger, errand, and office boys and girls	319	290	29
Office appliance operators	16	10	6
Purchasing agents	4	4	-------
Salesmen and saleswomen	3	1	2
Shipping clerks	144	139	5
Stenographers and typists	571	31	540
Weighers	3	3	-------
Blacksmiths	296	296	-------
Boilermakers	4	4	-------
Brick and stone masons and tile layers	10	10	-------
Cabinetmakers	1	1	-------
Carpenters	17	17	-------
Cement finishers	19	19	-------
Compositors, linotypers, and typesetters	1	1	-------
Coopers	13	13	-------
Cranemen, derrickmen, hoistmen, etc	113	113	-------
Electricians	31	31	-------
Engineers (stationary)	379	379	-------
Forgemen and hammermen	1	1	-------
Goldsmiths and silversmiths	4	4	-------
Machinists	50	50	-------
Mechanics (not otherwise specified)	321	321	-------
Millwrights	2	2	-------
Iron molders, founders, and casters	1	1	-------
All other molders, founders, and casters	1	1	-------
Painters, glaziers, and varnishers (building)	58	58	-------
Pattern and model makers	1	1	-------
Plumbers and gas and steam fitters	9	9	-------
Sawyers	7	7	-------
Skilled occupations (not elsewhere classified)	1	1	-------
Stonecutters	7	7	-------
Tinsmiths and sheet metal workers	6	6	-------
Tool makers and die setters and sinkers	1	1	-------
Upholsterers	8	8	-------
Apprentices:			
Electricians	1	1	-------
Other apprentices	1	1	-------
Buffers and polishers (metal)	1	1	-------
Charwomen and cleaners	232	114	118
Chauffeurs and truck and tractor drivers	5, 997	5, 964	13
Cooks	158	61	97
Draymen and teamsters	1, 521	1, 515	6
Dyers	2	2	-------
Elevator tenders	1, 326	937	389
Filers (metal)	2	2	-------
Firemen	1, 269	1, 269	-------
General and not specified laborers	128, 518	123, 898	4, 620
Grinders (metal)	1	1	-------
Guards, watchmen, and doorkeepers	340	338	2
Housekeepers and stewards	15	3	12
Janitors	1, 122	1, 028	94
Oilers of machinery	14	14	-------
Operatives (not otherwise specified)	13, 847	10, 375	3, 472
Painters, glaziers, and varnishers (factory)	2	2	-------
Policemen	2	2	-------
Porters	797	797	-------
Waiters	62	46	16

1 The difference between agricultural statistics of the Census of Occupations and those of the Census of Agriculture is largely due to the fact that every farm operator is listed as a farmer in the latter, while in the former, he is listed under his principal occupation.

2 Does not include "check weighers."

3 Doubtless some overlapping between persons engaged in the production and distribution of natural gas and artificial gas; also those working at petroleum refineries or pipe lines and those at oil wells.

4 Includes, also, all technical engineers not elsewhere classified.

5 Some of these probably are working in paint shops rather than in paint factories.

6 Some deliverymen doubtless were returned and classified as chauffeurs, and others as teamsters or truck drivers.

7 In some cases it was difficult from the enumerators' returns to distinguish persons working in butter, cheese, and condensed-milk factories from persons working for milk distributing companies or persons working on dairy farms.

8 Sometimes it was impossible from the enumerators' returns to distinguish between workers in stockyards and workers in slaughter and packing houses.

9 Includes tin-plate mills. Doubtless some overlapping between workers in blast furnaces and steel rolling mills and workers in iron manufacturing establishments.

10 In some cases it was difficult to distinguish between workers in car and railroad shops and workers on steam and street railroads.

11 Includes iron foundries.

12 Includes box factories (wood).

13 Sometimes it was impossible from the enumerators returns to distinguish between workers at airports and workers in airplane factories.

14 Doubtless there is considerable overlapping between locomotive engineers and stationary engineers, and between locomotive firemen and firemen of stationary boilers.

15 Probably painters of boats and ships.

16 May include some vault custodians.

17 Includes only persons specifically returned as "clerks" in stores. Many of these probably are "salesmen and saleswomen."

18 Includes bundle and cash boys and girls.

19 Includes accountants and auditors for accounting and auditing companies.

20 Includes public stenographers.

21 Public service, as here presented, does not as a rule include those public employees who, occupationally, can be better classified elsewhere—public school teachers, postal employees, etc.

22 Some owners of hand laundries probably are included with laundry operatives.

VITAL STATISTICS, BIRTHS AND INFANT MORTALITY

GROWTH OF REGISTRATION AREA FOR BIRTHS: 1915 TO 1930

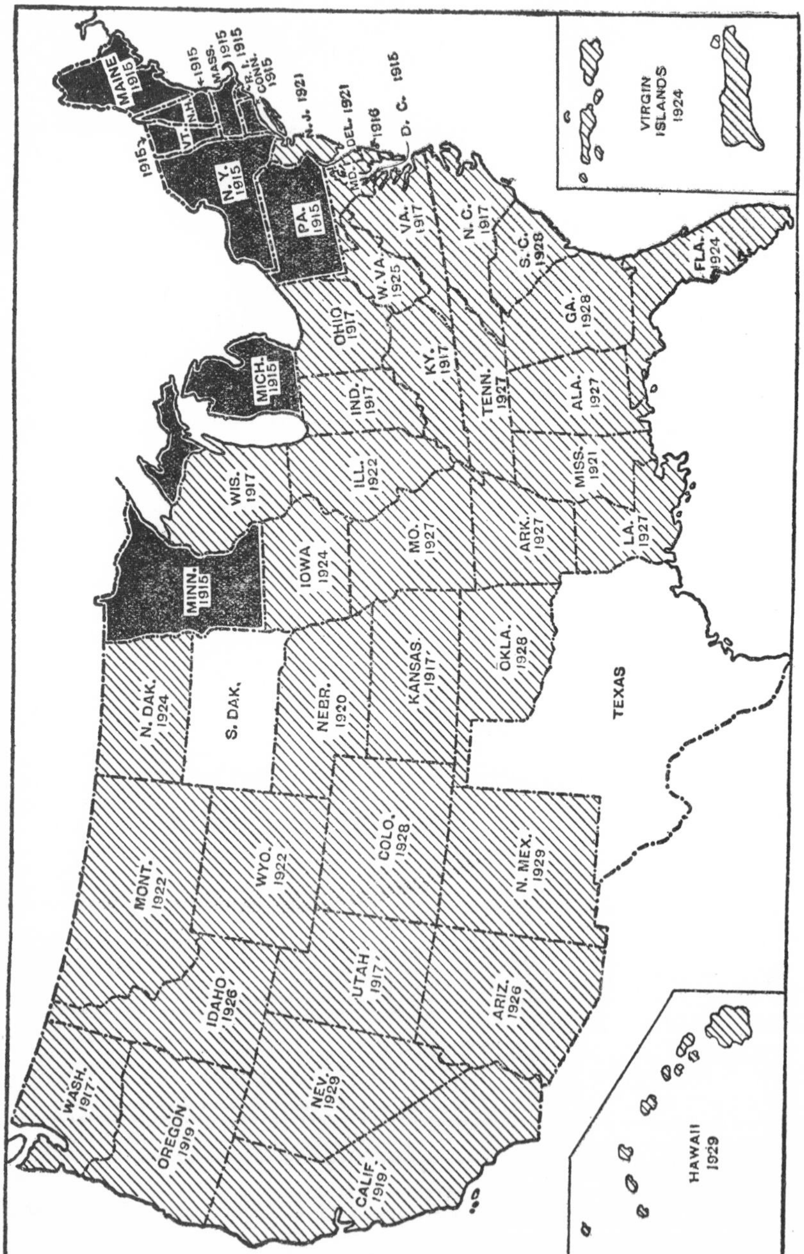

ORIGINAL REGISTRATION STATES, 1915 STATES ADDED SINCE 1915 STATES NOT IN REGISTRATION AREA

CHAPTER XV.—VITAL STATISTICS, BIRTHS AND INFANT MORTALITY

The registration area and classification of births.—The statistics given here were compiled by the Bureau of the Census from data on transcripts of birth, death, and stillbirth certificates received from the registration areas.

The birth registration area was established in 1915 and the report at that time included data for only 10 States and the District of Columbia. In 1920 the birth registration area comprised 23 States and the District of Columbia, having approximately 59.8 percent of the total population of the United States and about 37.5 percent of the total Negro population. In 1930 and 1931 the birth registration area embraced 46 States and the District of Columbia (all States except Texas and South Dakota) and was estimated to contain 94.7 percent of the total population and about 92.8 percent of the Negro population.

The classification of births and deaths by race distinguishes white, Negro, Indian, Chinese, Japanese, and "other races" which includes Mexicans, so far as reported as such. The term "colored", as used in many of the tables in this chapter, includes the nonwhite population for which data by race were not separately reported by States, or if reported, were considered by the Bureau to be too deficient to justify a presentation by racial designations such as Negro, Indian, Chinese, etc. However, 14 of the 23 tables in this chapter relate to the Negro and other colored population, while 9 relate to the colored population as a whole. Only States in which Negroes constitute 55 percent or more of the total "colored" population have been included in the tables relating to the colored population, except in tables 9, 11, 12, and 13 which relate to the entire registration area. The 15 omitted States had a combined Negro population, in 1930, of only 142,004, or 1.2 percent of the total Negro population of the United States, a number too small to affect materially the Negro-birth or infant mortality figures.

Ratio of births to deaths.—For the Negro population, births outnumbered deaths in 23 States and in the District of Columbia in 1930. The greatest excesses in 1930 were 9.8, 9.6, 9.1, and 9.1 for Mississippi, North Carolina, South Carolina, and Alabama, respectively.

In 1930 Kentucky, Oklahoma, and Tennessee, and in 1920 Kentucky were the only Southern States in the registration area where Negro deaths exceeded Negro births. It is probable that the excess of deaths over births in these States was largely, if not wholly, due to the failure of colored parents to register births. There were 239,275 Negro livebirths in the registration area in 1930 and this represents a birth rate of 21.7 per 1,000 enumerated Negro population. Total Negro deaths, exclusive of stillbirths, in 1930 numbered 182,009, and represented a death rate of 16.5 per 1,000 Negro population.

In 1930 there were 239,275 Negro births reported in the birth registration area and there were 234,203, or 5,072 less, in 1931. Male births outnumbered female in both 1931 and 1930 in the area as a whole, but for both years there was an excess of female over male births in several States.

The States with the highest birth rates in 1930 were South Carolina, Connecticut, North Carolina, Mississippi, Alabama, and Virginia.

Births by age of mother.—In 1930, 31.1 percent of the colored births in the 31 States selected from those in the registration area were by mothers 20 to 24 years of age, 22 percent by mothers 15 to 19 years of age, 20 percent by mothers of 25 to 29 years of age, 12.5 percent by mothers 30 to 34 years of age. 8.6 percent by mothers 35 to 39 years of age, 2.6 percent by mothers 40 to 44 years of age, 0.6 percent by mothers 10 to 14 years of age, and 2.6 percent by mothers 45 years of age or over, and those whose ages were unknown or not stated.

Percent of children living to those ever born.—The percent of children living, out of the total ever born to Negro women who bore children, was 88.3 in 1931, as compared with 88.2 in 1930, 87.9 in 1929, 87.5 in 1928, and 86.7 in 1927. The percent of children living out of the total number ever born to white women who bore children in 1931 was 91.8.

Average number of children ever born to Negro women.—The average number of children born to Negro women who bore children in 1931 was 3.6, as compared with 3 percent for white women.

Illegitimate births.—The ratio of illegitimate Negro births to 1,000 total Negro births was 143.4 in 1930 and 153.9 in 1931. The ratio was higher in both years for female than for male births. The ratios were highest in Maryland, Deleware, Alabama, North Carolina, South Carolina, and the District of Columbia. Around 74 percent of the Negro illegitimate births in 1931 and 1930 were by mothers under 25 years of age. The greatest number of illegitimate births was by mothers 15 to 19 years of age.

Birth rates in cities and rural districts.—In 1931 birth rates for the colored population in rural districts equaled or exceeded birth rates for colored in cities in 17 of the 31 States selected from those in the registration area. These 17 States included all the Southern States except Louisiana. The death rate was higher than the birth rate in the cities in 15 of these 31 States. In rural districts the death rate exceeded the birth rate in 13 States, all of which, except Kentucky, were in the North and West.

Births per 100 deaths in cities having 25,000 or more Negro inhabitants.—In 15 cities in 1931 and 17 cities in 1930, out of a total of 31 cities, the colored deaths outnumbered the births. For Kansas City, Mo., Savannah, Ga., and Chattanooga, Tenn., in 1931 the colored births per 100 deaths were 64, 66, and 67, respectively. In all the cities having 100,000 or more Negro inhabitants (New York, Chicago, Philadelphia, Baltimore, Washington, New Orleans, and Detroit) the number of colored births equaled or exceeded colored deaths, while among the cities having 50,000 to 100,000 Negro inhabitants, Atlanta, Memphis, and St. Louis were the only ones to report an excess of colored deaths over births.

Stillbirths.—The number of Negro stillbirths per 100 Negro live births was 7.6 in 1931 and 8.3 in 1930. The number of stillbirths per 100 live births was greater in cities and incorporated places than in rural districts in both 1930 and 1931.

Infant mortality.—The number of deaths of Negro children under 1 year of age per 1,000 Negro live births was 92.7 in 1931 and 99.5 in 1930 as compared with 56.7 and 59.6, respectively, for white children. The number of deaths of all colored children under 1 year of age per 1,000 live births was highest in 1931 in Iowa, Delaware, Kentucky, Maryland, and Pennsylvania.

Deaths under 1 year of age by cause.—The percentages of the total Negro deaths under 1 year of age by cause in 1931 were as follows: Premature births, 20.3 percent; diarrhea and enteritis, 10.4 percent; bronchopneumonia, 9.9 percent; lobar and unspecified pneumonia, 5.6 percent; congenital debility, icterus, and sclerema, 5 percent; syphilis, 3.6 percent; injury at birth, 3.5 percent; unknown or ill-defined diseases, 18 percent; and other causes, 23.7 percent.

Table 1.—NEGRO BIRTHS AND DEATHS (EXCLUSIVE OF STILLBIRTHS) IN REGISTRATION AREA: 1930 AND 1920

AREA AND YEAR		Enumerated Negro population	Births	Deaths	Rate per 1,000 Negro population	
					Births	Deaths
Birth registration area	**1930**	**11, 035, 533**	**239, 275**	**182, 009**	**21. 7**	**16. 5**
	1920	**3, 922, 084**	**103, 796**	**72, 411**	**26. 5**	**18. 5**
Alabama	1930	944, 834	22, 969	14, 407	24. 3	15. 2
	1920	900, 652	([1])	([1])	([1])	([1])
Arizona	1930	10, 749	131	206	12. 2	19. 2
	1920	8, 005	([1])	([1])	([1])	([1])
Arkansas	1930	478, 463	9, 077	6, 461	19. 0	13. 5
	1920	472, 220	([1])	([1])	([1])	([1])
California	1930	81, 048	1, 003	1, 157	12. 4	14. 3
	1920	38, 763	657	779	16. 9	20. 1
Colorado	1930	11, 828	136	302	11. 5	25. 5
	1920	11, 318	([1])	([1])	([1])	([1])
Connecticut	1930	29, 354	728	513	24. 8	17. 5
	1920	21, 046	554	491	26. 3	23. 3
Delaware	1930	32, 602	723	706	22. 2	21. 7
	1920	30, 335	([1])	([1])	([1])	([1])
District of Columbia	1930	132, 068	3, 036	2, 780	23. 0	21. 0
	1920	109, 966	2, 498	2, 289	22. 7	20. 8
Florida	1930	431, 828	8, 385	7, 166	19. 4	16. 6
	1920	329, 487	([1])	([1])	([1])	([1])
Georgia	1930	1, 071, 125	23, 392	17, 182	21. 8	16. 0
	1920	1, 206, 365	([1])	([1])	([1])	([1])
Idaho	1930	668	8	13	12. 0	19. 5
	1920	920	([1])	([1])	([1])	([1])
Illinois	1930	328, 972	5, 917	5, 824	18. 0	17. 7
	1920	182, 274	([1])	([1])	([1])	([1])
Indiana	1930	111, 982	1, 977	2, 185	17. 7	19. 5
	1920	80, 810	1, 503	1, 802	18. 6	22. 3
Iowa	1930	17, 380	277	298	15. 9	17. 1
	1920	19, 005	([1])	([1])	([1])	([1])
Kansas	1930	66, 344	999	1, 082	15. 1	16. 3
	1920	57, 925	1, 003	1, 189	17. 3	20. 5
Kentucky	1930	226, 040	3, 376	4, 748	14. 9	21. 0
	1920	235, 938	4, 137	4, 560	17. 5	19. 3
Louisiana	1930	776, 326	16, 668	12, 036	21. 5	15. 5
	1920	700, 257	([1])	([1])	([1])	([1])
Maine	1930	1, 096	15	18	13. 7	16. 4
	1920	1, 310	6	31	4. 6	23. 7
Maryland	1930	276, 379	6, 401	5, 251	23. 2	19. 0
	1920	244, 479	6, 753	5, 198	27. 6	21. 3
Massachusetts	1930	52, 365	961	834	18. 4	15. 9
	1920	45, 466	1, 234	993	27. 1	21. 8
Michigan	1930	169, 453	3, 468	2, 786	20. 5	16. 4
	1920	60, 082	1, 324	1, 529	22. 0	25. 4
Minnesota	1930	9, 445	114	196	12. 1	20. 8
	1920	8, 809	129	188	14. 6	21. 3
Mississippi	1930	1, 009, 718	24, 804	14, 910	24. 6	14. 8
	1920	935, 184	([1])	([1])	([1])	([1])
Missouri	1930	223, 840	3, 688	4, 604	16. 5	20. 6
	1920	178, 241	([1])	([1])	([1])	([1])
Montana	1930	1, 256	16	28	12. 7	22. 3
	1920	1, 658	([1])	([1])	([1])	([1])
Nebraska	1930	13, 752	235	255	17. 1	18. 5
	1920	13, 242	185	228	14. 0	17. 2
Nevada	1930	516	6	14	11. 6	27. 1
	1920	346	([1])	([1])	([1])	([1])
New Hampshire	1930	790	9	7	11. 4	8. 9
	1920	621	6	11	9. 7	17. 7
New Jersey	1930	208, 828	4, 955	3, 519	23. 7	16. 9
	1920	117, 132	([1])	([1])	([1])	([1])
New Mexico	1930	2, 850	25	59	8. 8	20. 7
	1920	5, 733	([1])	([1])	([1])	([1])
New York	1930	412, 814	8, 872	6, 841	21. 5	16. 6
	1920	198, 483	4, 791	3, 938	24. 1	19. 8
North Carolina	1930	918, 647	22, 785	13, 976	24. 8	15. 2
	1920	763, 407	23, 954	12, 315	31. 4	16. 1
North Dakota	1930	377	1	5	2. 7	13. 3
	1920	467	([1])	([1])	([1])	([1])
Ohio	1930	309, 304	5, 931	5, 803	19. 2	18. 8
	1920	186, 187	3, 889	4, 010	20. 9	21. 5
Oklahoma	1930	172, 198	1, 582	2, 242	9. 2	13. 0
	1920	149, 408	([1])	([1])	([1])	([1])
Oregon	1930	2, 234	24	55	10. 7	24. 6
	1920	2, 144	28	33	13. 1	15. 4
Pennsylvania	1930	431, 257	9, 443	7, 459	21. 9	17. 3
	1920	284, 568	6, 478	6, 065	22. 8	21. 3
Rhode Island	1930	9, 913	239	219	24. 1	22. 1
	1920	10, 036	([1])	([1])	([1])	([1])
South Carolina	1930	793, 681	20, 396	13, 160	25. 7	16. 6
	1920	864, 719	23, 946	14, 338	27. 7	16. 6
Tennessee	1930	477, 646	8, 105	8, 744	17. 0	18. 3
	1920	451, 758	([1])	([1])	([1])	([1])
Utah	1930	1, 108	15	23	13. 5	20. 8
	1920	1, 446	29	29	20. 1	20. 1
Vermont	1930	568	11	8	19. 4	14. 1
	1920	572	1	6	1. 7	10. 5
Virginia	1930	650, 165	15, 689	11, 699	24. 1	18. 0
	1920	690, 017	20, 515	12, 130	29. 7	17. 6
Washington	1930	6, 840	62	144	9. 1	21. 1
	1920	6, 883	89	143	12. 9	20. 8
West Virginia	1930	114, 893	2, 454	1, 854	21. 4	16. 1
	1920	86, 345	([1])	([1])	([1])	([1])
Wisconsin	1930	10, 739	154	201	14. 3	18. 7
	1920	5, 201	87	116	16. 7	22. 3
Wyoming	1930	1, 250	13	29	10. 4	23. 2
	1920	1, 375	([1])	([1])	([1])	([1])

[1] Not in birth registration area, 1920.

TABLE 2.—TOTAL NUMBER OF NEGRO BIRTHS (EXCLUSIVE OF STILLBIRTHS), BY SEX AND LEGITIMACY, IN REGISTRATION AREA IN CONTINENTAL UNITED STATES:[1] 1931 AND 1930

AREA AND SEX	1931 Total	1931 Legitimate	1931 Illegitimate	1930 Total	1930 Legitimate	1930 Illegitimate
Registration area [1]	**234, 203**	**198, 486**	**35, 717**	**239, 275**	**205, 255**	**34, 020**
Male	**118, 862**	**100, 944**	**17, 918**	**121, 495**	**104, 391**	**17, 104**
Female	**115, 341**	**97, 542**	**17, 799**	**117, 780**	**100, 864**	**16, 916**
ALABAMA	22, 904	18, 472	4, 432	22, 969	18, 809	4, 160
Male	11, 603	9, 330	2, 273	11, 590	9, 497	2, 093
Female	11, 301	9, 142	2, 159	11, 379	9, 312	2, 067
ARIZONA	132	125	7	131	120	11
Male	73	71	2	59	53	6
Female	59	54	5	72	67	5
ARKANSAS	9, 447	8, 187	1, 260	9, 077	8, 058	1, 019
Male	4, 863	4, 237	626	4, 594	4, 090	504
Female	4, 584	3, 950	634	4, 483	3, 968	515
COLORADO	120	106	14	136	122	14
Male	69	60	9	63	54	9
Female	51	46	5	73	68	5
CONNECTICUT	677	619	58	728	667	61
Male	349	315	34	370	333	37
Female	328	304	24	358	334	24
DELAWARE	684	542	142	723	571	152
Male	363	303	60	368	294	74
Female	321	239	82	355	277	78
DISTRICT OF COLUMBIA	2, 965	2, 433	532	3, 036	2, 475	561
Male	1, 515	1, 239	276	1, 592	1, 307	285
Female	1, 450	1, 194	256	1, 444	1, 168	276
FLORIDA	8, 360	7, 069	1, 291	8, 385	7, 180	1, 205
Male	4, 238	3, 594	644	4, 290	3, 686	604
Female	4, 122	3, 475	647	4, 095	3, 494	601
GEORGIA	24, 254	20, 429	3, 825	23, 392	19, 840	3, 552
Male	12, 405	10, 513	1, 892	11, 821	10, 044	1, 777
Female	11, 849	9, 916	1, 933	11, 571	9, 796	1, 775
IDAHO	5	5	--------	8	8	--------
Male	1	1	--------	4	4	--------
Female	4	4	--------	4	4	--------
ILLINOIS	5, 455	4, 882	573	5, 917	5, 416	501
Male	2, 795	2, 485	310	3, 021	2, 757	264
Female	2, 660	2, 397	263	2, 896	2, 659	237
INDIANA	1, 851	1, 698	153	1, 977	1, 786	191
Male	944	864	80	957	867	90
Female	907	834	73	1, 020	919	101
IOWA	242	222	20	277	252	25
Male	122	115	7	136	121	15
Female	120	107	13	141	131	10
KANSAS	927	827	100	999	893	106
Male	469	415	54	518	472	46
Female	458	412	46	481	421	60
KENTUCKY	3, 251	2, 953	298	3, 376	3, 040	336
Male	1, 609	1, 455	154	1, 688	1, 524	164
Female	1, 642	1, 498	144	1, 688	1, 516	172
LOUISIANA	16, 986	14, 213	2, 773	16, 668	14, 140	2, 528
Male	8, 538	7, 077	1, 461	8, 425	7, 137	1, 288
Female	8, 448	7, 136	1, 312	8, 243	7, 003	1, 240
MAINE	21	18	3	15	15	--------
Male	11	10	1	10	10	--------
Female	10	8	2	5	5	--------
MARYLAND	6, 213	4, 804	1, 409	6, 401	5, 044	1, 357
Male	3, 104	2, 369	735	3, 145	2, 492	653
Female	3, 109	2, 435	674	3, 256	2, 552	704
MICHIGAN	3, 228	2, 988	240	3, 468	3, 226	242
Male	1, 620	1, 506	114	1, 761	1, 635	126
Female	1, 608	1, 482	126	1, 707	1, 591	116
MINNESOTA	99	84	15	114	104	10
Male	44	38	6	62	58	4
Female	55	46	9	52	46	6
MISSISSIPPI	23, 470	20, 189	3, 281	24, 804	21, 726	3, 078
Male	12, 009	10, 379	1, 630	12, 738	11, 202	1, 536
Female	11, 461	9, 810	1, 651	12, 066	10, 524	1, 542
MISSOURI	3, 580	3, 056	524	3, 688	3, 191	497
Male	1, 838	1, 585	253	1, 899	1, 634	265
Female	1, 742	1, 471	271	1, 789	1, 557	232
MONTANA	19	18	1	16	15	1
Male	6	6	--------	9	8	1
Female	13	12	1	7	7	--------
NEBRASKA	229	213	16	235	206	29
Male	115	105	10	114	97	17
Female	114	108	6	121	109	12
NEVADA	7	6	1	6	6	--------
Male	5	4	1	4	4	--------
Female	2	2	--------	2	2	--------
NEW HAMPSHIRE	6	6	--------	9	8	1
Male	3	3	--------	3	3	--------
Female	3	3	--------	6	5	1
NEW JERSEY	4, 680	4, 223	457	4, 955	4, 505	450
Male	2, 336	2, 087	249	2, 524	2, 302	222
Female	2, 344	2, 136	208	2, 431	2, 203	228
NEW MEXICO	42	40	2	25	25	--------
Male	24	23	1	14	14	--------
Female	18	17	1	11	11	--------
NEW YORK	8, 655	8, 064	591	8, 872	8, 313	559
Male	4, 365	4, 084	281	4, 506	4, 233	273
Female	4, 290	3, 980	310	4, 366	4, 080	286
NORTH CAROLINA	22, 316	18, 214	4, 102	22, 785	18, 758	4, 027
Male	11, 412	9, 359	2, 053	11, 607	9, 519	2, 088
Female	10, 904	8, 855	2, 049	11, 178	9, 239	1, 939
NORTH DAKOTA	3	1	2	1	1	--------
Male	1	1	--------	--------	--------	--------
Female	2	--------	2	1	1	--------
OHIO	5, 025	4, 457	568	5, 931	5, 441	490
Male	2, 526	2, 251	275	3, 070	2, 829	241
Female	2, 499	2, 206	293	2, 861	2, 612	249
OKLAHOMA	1, 812	1, 641	171	1, 582	1, 480	102
Male	934	857	77	827	773	54
Female	878	784	94	755	707	48
OREGON	18	18	--------	24	23	1
Male	8	8	--------	9	8	1
Female	10	10	--------	15	15	--------
PENNSYLVANIA	8, 650	7, 506	1, 144	9, 443	8, 270	1, 173
Male	4, 470	3, 860	610	4, 777	4, 179	598
Female	4, 180	3, 646	534	4, 666	4, 091	575
RHODE ISLAND	200	175	25	239	221	18
Male	101	89	12	110	103	7
Female	99	86	13	129	118	11
SOUTH CAROLINA	20, 254	16, 555	3, 699	20, 396	16, 758	3, 638
Male	10, 162	8, 412	1, 750	10, 360	8, 570	1, 790
Female	10, 092	8, 143	1, 949	10, 036	8, 188	1, 848
TENNESSEE	7, 890	6, 762	1, 128	8, 105	7, 019	1, 086
Male	3, 983	3, 412	571	4, 219	3, 654	565
Female	3, 907	3, 350	557	3, 886	3, 365	521
UTAH	17	16	1	15	13	2
Male	10	9	1	8	7	1
Female	7	7	--------	7	6	1
VERMONT	3	3	--------	11	10	1
Male	1	1	--------	6	6	--------
Female	2	2	--------	5	4	1
VIRGINIA	14, 954	12, 365	2, 589	15, 689	13, 104	2, 585
Male	7, 578	6, 305	1, 273	7, 849	6, 573	1, 276
Female	7, 376	6, 060	1, 316	7, 840	6, 531	1, 309
WASHINGTON	67	61	6	62	58	4
Male	39	36	3	36	34	2
Female	28	25	3	26	24	2
WEST VIRGINIA	2, 169	1, 923	246	2, 454	2, 215	239
Male	1, 064	943	121	1, 269	1, 145	124
Female	1, 105	980	125	1, 185	1, 070	115
WISCONSIN	172	155	17	154	147	7
Male	84	75	9	81	77	4
Female	88	80	8	73	70	3
WYOMING	8	7	1	13	12	1
Male	3	3	--------	6	6	--------
Female	5	4	1	7	6	1

[1] Exclusive of California and Massachusetts. These States do not require a statement concerning legitimacy of child.

TABLE 3.—PERCENT OF CHILDREN LIVING TO THOSE EVER BORN IN REGISTRATION AREA,[1] BY COLOR, AND NATIVITY OF MOTHER: 1927 TO 1931

COLOR AND NATIVITY OF MOTHER	1931	1930	1929	1928	1927
Total	91.1	91.0	90.7	90.5	90.1
Colored	87.7	87.9	87.8	87.5	86.8
Negro	88.3	88.2	87.9	87.5	86.7
Other colored	83.6	85.2	87.5	87.5	88.2
White	91.8	91.5	91.1	91.0	90.6
Native	92.1	92.0	91.8	91.7	91.4
Foreign-born	89.4	88.5	87.9	87.8	87.3
Unknown	91.8	92.1	92.2	90.6	90.1

[1] Exclusive of Delaware, Maine, Massachusetts, New Hampshire, and Rhode Island in 1927; exclusive of Colorado, Maine, Massachusetts, New Hampshire, and Rhode Island in other years.

TABLE 4.—AVERAGE NUMBER OF CHILDREN EVER BORN TO WOMEN WHO BORE CHILDREN IN 1931 AND 1930, BY AGE, AND COLOR OF MOTHER, IN THE REGISTRATION AREA IN CONTINENTAL UNITED STATES [1]

COLOR AND YEAR		All ages	Under 20	20 to 24	25 to 29	30 to 34	35 to 39	40 to 44	45 to 49	50 and over	Unknown
Total	1931	3.1	1.3	1.9	2.9	4.2	5.8	7.4	9.0	7.3	2.6
	1930	3.1	1.3	1.9	2.9	4.2	5.8	7.5	9.0	7.5	2.5
Colored	1931	3.7	1.3	2.5	4.2	5.9	7.5	9.1	10.0	7.7	2.4
	1930	3.7	1.3	2.5	4.2	5.9	7.5	9.2	10.2	8.2	2.3
Negro	1931	3.6	1.3	2.5	4.2	5.9	7.5	9.2	10.1	8.0	2.3
	1930	3.6	1.3	2.5	4.2	5.9	7.6	9.3	10.3	8.4	2.2
Other colored	1931	4.2	1.4	2.5	4.2	5.9	7.5	8.6	9.3	6.6	3.8
	1930	4.0	1.3	2.4	4.0	5.4	6.8	8.2	8.8	7.5	3.5
White	1931	3.0	1.2	1.9	2.8	4.0	5.5	7.3	8.8	7.2	2.9
	1930	3.1	1.2	1.9	2.8	4.0	5.6	7.3	8.8	7.2	2.8

[1] Exclusive of Colorado, Maine, Massachusetts, New Hampshire, and Rhode Island.

TABLE 5.—NUMBER OF ILLEGITIMATE BIRTHS (EXCLUSIVE OF STILLBIRTHS) IN THE REGISTRATION AREA OF CONTINENTAL UNITED STATES,[1] WITH RATIOS TO 1,000 TOTAL BIRTHS, BY AGE, COLOR, AND NATIVITY OF MOTHER: 1931 AND 1930

COLOR, NATIVITY OF MOTHER, AND YEAR		NUMBER										RATIO									
		All ages	10 to 14 years	15 to 19 years	20 to 24 years	25 to 29 years	30 to 34 years	35 to 39 years	40 to 44 years	45 years and over	Unknown	All ages	10 to 14 years	15 to 19 years	20 to 24 years	25 to 29 years	30 to 34 years	35 to 39 years	40 to 44 years	45 years and over	Unknown
Total	**1931**	**69,403**	**1,478**	**30,866**	**18,950**	**6,382**	**3,071**	**1,967**	**611**	**91**	**5,987**	**35.4**	**615.3**	**129.0**	**32.7**	**12.9**	**9.3**	**9.3**	**8.6**	**12.9**	**222.1**
	1930	**66,991**	**1,620**	**30,191**	**18,052**	**5,888**	**2,765**	**1,820**	**582**	**112**	**5,961**	**32.7**	**595.4**	**119.4**	**29.8**	**11.6**	**8.0**	**8.2**	**7.8**	**15.3**	**220.9**
Colored	1931	36,418	966	15,879	8,549	3,401	1,781	1,099	325	58	4,360	147.5	725.8	299.7	112.6	67.5	55.7	51.4	50.3	58.2	793.9
	1930	34,647	1,085	15,311	7,921	3,080	1,582	1,026	307	75	4,260	138.2	713.8	281.3	102.3	61.0	50.0	47.0	46.1	70.1	757.3
Negro	1931	35,717	956	15,630	8,344	3,322	1,739	1,074	316	56	4,280	153.9	730.9	306.5	116.3	71.1	59.0	54.5	53.2	62.5	811.1
	1930	34,020	1,079	15,118	7,724	2,995	1,546	997	301	73	4,187	143.4	715.0	286.7	104.9	63.3	52.5	49.2	48.6	73.3	801.6
Other colored	1931	701	10	249	205	79	42	25	9	2	80	47.2	434.8	125.1	49.4	21.7	16.9	14.6	17.3	19.8	372.1
	1930	627	6	193	197	85	36	29	6	2	73	47.0	545.5	113.1	51.7	27.0	16.5	18.8	12.7	27.0	181.6
White	1931	32,985	512	14,987	10,401	2,981	1,290	868	286	33	1,627	19.2	478.1	80.5	20.6	6.7	4.3	4.6	4.4	5.5	75.8
	1930	32,344	535	14,880	10,131	2,808	1,183	794	275	37	1,701	18.0	445.5	75.0	19.2	6.2	3.7	4.0	4.1	5.9	79.6
Native	1931	30,942	497	14,572	9,831	2,725	1,156	751	249	29	1,132	20.3	470.2	80.6	20.9	7.0	4.6	4.9	4.9	6.4	63.4
	1930	29,984	526	14,407	9,467	2,534	1,050	677	228	26	1,069	19.1	442.8	75.3	19.5	6.4	4.0	4.2	4.4	5.6	61.0
Foreign born	1931	1,358	6	312	521	237	124	109	35	4	10	7.1	600.0	60.5	15.5	4.6	2.7	3.1	2.5	2.7	3.4
	1930	1,602	6	404	621	261	128	111	46	10	15	7.2	600.0	60.0	15.1	4.4	2.4	2.7	2.9	6.2	4.9
Unknown	1931	685	9	103	49	19	10	8	2	------	485	320.7	([2])	351.5	125.6	57.8	43.3	47.6	35.1	-------	741.6
	1930	758	3	69	43	13	5	6	1	1	617	396.7	100.0	371.0	124.6	54.4	27.8	50.4	15.2	200.0	803.4

[1] Exclusive of California and Massachusetts. These States do not require a statement concerning legitimacy of child. [2] Rate not computed.

TABLE 6.—PERCENT DISTRIBUTION OF ILLEGITIMATE BIRTHS BY AGE, COLOR, AND NATIVITY OF MOTHER, IN THE REGISTRATION AREA OF CONTINENTAL UNITED STATES:[1] 1931 AND 1930

COLOR, NATIVITY OF MOTHER, AND YEAR		All ages	10 to 14 years	15 to 19 years	20 to 24 years	25 to 29 years	30 to 34 years	35 to 39 years	40 to 44 years	45 years and over	Unknown
Total	**1931**	**100.0**	**2.1**	**44.5**	**27.3**	**9.2**	**4.4**	**2.8**	**0.9**	**0.1**	**8.6**
	1930	**100.0**	**2.4**	**45.1**	**26.9**	**8.8**	**4.1**	**2.7**	**.9**	**.2**	**8.9**
Colored	1931	100.0	2.7	43.6	23.5	9.3	4.9	3.0	.9	.2	12.0
	1930	100.0	3.1	44.2	22.9	8.9	4.6	3.0	.9	.2	12.3
Negro	1931	100.0	2.7	43.8	23.3	9.3	4.9	3.0	.9	.2	12.0
	1930	100.0	3.2	44.4	22.7	8.8	4.5	2.9	.9	.2	12.3
Other colored	1931	100.0	1.4	35.5	29.2	11.3	6.0	3.6	1.3	.3	11.4
	1930	100.0	1.0	30.8	31.4	13.6	5.7	4.6	1.0	.3	11.6
White	1931	100.0	1.6	45.4	31.5	9.0	3.9	2.6	.9	.1	4.9
	1930	100.0	1.7	46.0	31.3	8.7	3.7	2.5	.9	.1	5.3
Native	1931	100.0	1.6	47.1	31.8	8.8	3.7	2.4	.8	.1	3.7
	1930	100.0	1.8	48.0	31.6	8.5	3.5	2.3	.8	.1	3.6
Foreign born	1931	100.0	.4	23.0	38.4	17.5	9.1	8.0	2.6	.3	.7
	1930	100.0	.4	25.2	38.8	16.3	8.0	6.9	2.9	.6	.9
Unknown	1931	100.0	1.3	15.0	7.2	2.8	1.5	1.2	.3	------------	70.8
	1930	100.0	.4	9.1	5.7	1.7	.7	.8	.1	.1	81.4

[1] Exclusive of California and Massachusetts. These States do not require a statement concerning legitimacy of child.

TABLE 7.—RATIO OF NEGRO ILLEGITIMATE BIRTHS TO 1,000 TOTAL NEGRO BIRTHS, BY SEX, IN REGISTRATION AREA IN CONTINENTAL UNITED STATES[1]: 1931 AND 1930

AREA AND SEX	ILLEGITIMATE BIRTHS			
	Number		Ratio	
	1931	1930	1931	1930
Registration area [1]	35,717	34,020	153.9	143.4
Male	17,918	17,104	152.1	141.8
Female	17,799	16,916	155.8	144.8
ALABAMA	4,432	4,160	193.5	181.1
Male	2,273	2,093	195.9	180.6
Female	2,159	2,067	191.0	181.7
ARIZONA	7	11	53.0	84.0
Male	2	6	27.4	101.7
Female	5	5	84.7	69.4
ARKANSAS	1,260	1,019	133.4	112.3
Male	626	504	128.7	109.7
Female	634	515	138.3	114.9
COLORADO	14	14	116.7	102.9
Male	9	9	103.4	142.9
Female	5	5	98.0	68.5
CONNECTICUT	58	61	85.7	83.8
Male	34	37	97.4	100.0
Female	24	24	73.2	67.0
DELAWARE	142	152	207.6	210.2
Male	60	74	165.3	201.1
Female	82	78	255.5	219.7
DISTRICT OF COLUMBIA	532	561	179.4	184.8
Male	276	285	182.2	179.0
Female	256	276	176.6	191.1
FLORIDA	1,291	1,205	154.4	143.7
Male	644	604	152.0	140.8
Female	647	601	157.0	146.8
GEORGIA	3,825	3,552	157.7	151.8
Male	1,892	1,777	152.5	150.3
Female	1,933	1,775	163.1	153.4
ILLINOIS	573	501	105.0	84.7
Male	310	264	110.9	87.4
Female	263	237	98.9	81.8
INDIANA	153	191	82.7	96.6
Male	80	90	84.7	94.0
Female	73	101	80.5	99.0
IOWA	20	25	82.6	90.3
Male	7	15	57.4	110.3
Female	13	10	108.3	70.9
KANSAS	100	106	107.9	106.1
Male	54	46	115.1	88.8
Female	46	60	100.4	124.7
KENTUCKY	298	336	91.7	99.5
Male	154	164	95.7	97.2
Female	144	172	87.7	101.9
LOUISIANA	2,773	2,528	163.3	151.7
Male	1,461	1,288	171.1	152.9
Female	1,312	1,240	155.3	150.4
MAINE	3	----------	142.9	----------
Male	1	----------	90.9	----------
Female	2	----------	200.0	----------
MARYLAND	1,409	1,357	226.8	212.0
Male	735	653	236.8	207.6
Female	674	704	216.8	216.2
MICHIGAN	240	242	74.3	69.8
Male	114	126	70.4	71.6
Female	126	116	78.4	68.0
MINNESOTA	15	10	151.5	87.7
Male	6	4	136.4	64.5
Female	9	6	163.6	115.4
MISSISSIPPI	3,281	3,078	139.8	124.1
Male	1,630	1,536	135.7	120.6
Female	1,651	1,542	144.1	127.8
MISSOURI	524	497	146.4	134.8
Male	253	265	137.6	139.5
Female	271	232	155.6	129.7
MONTANA	1	1	52.6	62.5
Male	----------	1	----------	111.1
Female	1	----------	76.9	----------
NEBRASKA	16	29	69.9	123.4
Male	10	17	87.0	149.1
Female	6	12	52.6	99.2
NEVADA	1	----------	142.9	----------
Male	1	----------	200.0	----------
Female	----------	----------	----------	----------
NEW HAMPSHIRE	----------	1	----------	111.1
Male	----------	----------	----------	----------
Female	----------	1	----------	166.7
NEW JERSEY	457	450	97.6	90.8
Male	249	222	106.6	88.0
Female	208	228	88.7	93.8
NEW MEXICO	2	----------	47.6	----------
Male	1	----------	41.7	----------
Female	1	----------	55.6	----------
NEW YORK	591	559	68.3	63.0
Male	281	273	64.4	60.6
Female	310	286	72.3	65.5
NORTH CAROLINA	4,102	4,027	183.8	176.7
Male	2,053	2,088	179.9	179.9
Female	2,049	1,939	187.9	173.5
NORTH DAKOTA	2	----------	666.7	----------
Male	----------	----------	----------	----------
Female	2	----------	1,000.0	----------
OHIO	568	490	113.0	82.6
Male	275	241	108.9	78.5
Female	293	249	117.2	87.0
OKLAHOMA	171	102	94.4	64.5
Male	77	54	82.4	65.3
Female	94	48	107.1	63.6
OREGON	----------	1	----------	41.7
Male	----------	1	----------	111.1
Female	----------	----------	----------	----------
PENNSYLVANIA	1,144	1,173	132.3	124.2
Male	610	598	136.5	125.2
Female	534	575	127.8	123.2
RHODE ISLAND	25	18	125.0	75.3
Male	12	7	118.8	63.6
Female	13	11	131.3	85.3
SOUTH CAROLINA	3,699	3,638	182.6	178.4
Male	1,750	1,790	172.2	172.8
Female	1,949	1,848	193.1	184.1
TENNESSEE	1,128	1,086	143.0	134.0
Male	571	565	143.4	133.9
Female	557	521	142.6	134.1
UTAH	1	2	58.8	133.3
Male	1	1	100.0	125.0
Female	----------	1	----------	142.9
VERMONT	----------	1	----------	90.9
Male	----------	----------	----------	----------
Female	----------	1	----------	200.0
VIRGINIA	2,589	2,585	173.1	164.8
Male	1,273	1,276	168.0	162.6
Female	1,316	1,309	178.4	167.0
WASHINGTON	6	4	89.6	64.5
Male	3	2	76.9	55.6
Female	3	2	107.1	76.9
WEST VIRGINIA	246	239	113.4	97.4
Male	121	124	113.7	97.7
Female	125	115	113.1	97.0
WISCONSIN	17	7	98.8	45.5
Male	9	4	107.1	49.4
Female	8	3	90.9	41.1
WYOMING	1	1	125.0	76.9
Male	----------	----------	----------	----------
Female	1	1	200.0	142.9

[1] Exclusive of California and Massachusetts. These States do not require a statement concerning legitimacy of child.

TABLE 8.—NUMBER OF COLORED[1] AND WHITE BIRTHS (EXCLUSIVE OF STILLBIRTHS) PER 100 DEATHS IN THE BIRTH REGISTRATION CITIES HAVING 25,000 OR MORE NEGRO INHABITANTS: 1931 AND 1930

CITY	1931		1930	
	Colored	White	Colored	White
Atlanta, Ga	87	163	86	166
Baltimore, Md	108	128	116	139
Birmingham, Ala	105	190	111	189
Charleston, S. C	86	155	94	156
Charlotte, N. C	86	218	94	219
Chattanooga, Tenn	67	170	59	175
Chicago, Ill	119	151	117	171
Cincinnati, Ohio	80	122	92	131
Cleveland, Ohio	100	170	117	190
Columbus, Ohio	104	123	100	123
Detroit, Mich	133	228	133	238
Indianapolis, Ind	102	137	98	138
Jacksonville, Fla	81	175	75	175
Kansas City, Mo	64	128	67	134
Louisville, Ky	71	141	66	152
Memphis, Tenn	80	140	79	146
Miami, Fla	136	144	151	170
Montgomery, Ala	89	160	79	145
Nashville, Tenn	90	151	84	173
Newark, N. J	165	191	145	194
New Orleans, La	100	134	96	130
New York, N. Y	119	151	130	166
Bronx Borough	129	168	107	185
Brooklyn Borough	149	176	167	196
Manhattan Borough	116	122	126	133
Queens Borough	82	153	103	171
Richmond Borough	22	127	30	132
Norfolk, Va	87	166	83	175
Philadelphia, Pa	129	135	137	148
Pittsburgh, Pa	104	157	119	167
Richmond, Va	102	133	106	148
St. Louis, Mo	84	119	95	133
Savannah, Ga	66	152	68	146
Shreveport, La	90	135	72	140
Washington, D. C	101	133	109	138
Winston-Salem, N. C	116	259	109	231

[1] Includes Negro, and other nonwhite races.

TABLE 9.—DEATHS (EXCLUSIVE OF STILLBIRTHS) FOR CERTAIN SUBDIVISIONS OF THE FIRST YEAR OF LIFE, BY SEX, AND COLOR, IN THE BIRTH REGISTRATION AREA IN CONTINENTAL UNITED STATES: 1931 AND 1930

AGE, SEX, AND YEAR		Total	Negro	Other colored	White
Under 1 year	1931	130,134	21,716	3,565	104,853
	1930	142,413	23,812	2,517	116,084
Male	1931	74,056	12,047	1,965	60,044
	1930	80,744	13,187	1,346	66,211
Female	1931	56,078	9,669	1,600	44,809
	1930	61,669	10,625	1,171	49,873
Under 1 day	1931	31,786	3,944	377	27,465
	1930	33,062	4,027	275	28,760
Male	1931	18,474	2,214	214	16,046
	1930	19,048	2,224	151	16,673
Female	1931	13,312	1,730	163	11,419
	1930	14,014	1,803	124	12,087
1 day	1931	8,400	1,270	127	7,003
	1930	9,158	1,406	75	7,677
Male	1931	4,852	711	81	4,060
	1930	5,266	805	41	4,420
Female	1931	3,548	559	46	2,943
	1930	3,892	601	34	3,257
2 days	1931	5,806	829	103	4,874
	1930	6,415	938	76	5,401
Male	1931	3,514	484	62	2,968
	1930	3,867	539	43	3,285
Female	1931	2,292	345	41	1,906
	1930	2,548	399	33	2,116
3 to 6 days	1931	9,966	1,612	221	8,133
	1930	11,287	1,808	178	9,301
Male	1931	5,835	951	134	4,750
	1930	6,520	1,065	99	5,356
Female	1931	4,131	661	87	3,383
	1930	4,767	743	79	3,945
1 week	1931	7,695	1,383	164	6,148
	1930	8,539	1,493	144	6,902
Male	1931	4,296	742	94	3,460
	1930	4,764	810	87	3,867
Female	1931	3,399	641	70	2,688
	1930	3,775	683	57	3,035
2 weeks	1931	5,149	888	118	4,143
	1930	5,533	951	78	4,504
Male	1931	2,931	482	70	2,379
	1930	3,032	484	46	2,502
Female	1931	2,218	406	48	1,764
	1930	2,501	467	32	2,002
3 weeks but under 1 month	1931	4,290	699	140	3,451
	1930	4,663	770	72	3,821
Male	1931	2,398	392	76	1,930
	1930	2,633	417	29	2,187
Female	1931	1,892	307	64	1,521
	1930	2,030	353	43	1,634
Under 1 month	1931	73,092	10,625	1,250	61,217
	1930	78,657	11,393	898	66,366
Male	1931	42,300	5,976	731	35,593
	1930	45,130	6,344	496	38,290
Female	1931	30,792	4,649	519	25,624
	1930	33,527	5,049	402	28,076
1 month	1931	10,632	1,967	333	8,332
	1930	11,614	2,121	232	9,261
Male	1931	6,098	1,066	183	4,849
	1930	6,627	1,156	129	5,342
Female	1931	4,534	901	150	3,483
	1930	4,987	965	103	3,919

AGE, SEX, AND YEAR		Total	Negro	Other colored	White
2 months	1931	8,419	1,597	310	6,512
	1930	9,167	1,679	193	7,295
Male	1931	4,824	863	178	3,783
	1930	5,177	926	100	4,151
Female	1931	3,595	734	132	2,729
	1930	3,990	753	93	3,144
3 months	1931	6,566	1,283	313	4,970
	1930	7,720	1,530	203	5,987
Male	1931	3,615	724	165	2,726
	1930	4,374	844	111	3,419
Female	1931	2,951	559	148	2,244
	1930	3,346	686	92	2,568
4 months	1931	5,562	1,173	264	4,125
	1930	6,278	1,293	169	4,816
Male	1931	3,106	652	146	2,308
	1930	3,521	754	89	2,678
Female	1931	2,456	521	118	1,817
	1930	2,757	539	80	2,138
5 months	1931	4,734	988	221	3,525
	1930	5,358	1,115	140	4,103
Male	1931	2,592	537	121	1,934
	1930	3,017	614	74	2,329
Female	1931	2,142	451	100	1,591
	1930	2,341	501	66	1,774
6 months	1931	4,463	909	190	3,364
	1930	5,153	1,096	146	3,911
Male	1931	2,474	504	102	1,868
	1930	2,867	604	75	2,188
Female	1931	1,989	405	88	1,496
	1930	2,286	492	71	1,723
7 months	1931	3,845	747	157	2,941
	1930	4,354	884	124	3,346
Male	1931	2,134	421	87	1,626
	1930	2,434	471	62	1,901
Female	1931	1,711	326	70	1,315
	1930	1,920	413	62	1,445
8 months	1931	3,699	737	155	2,807
	1930	4,054	792	113	3,149
Male	1931	2,044	400	75	1,569
	1930	2,193	422	52	1,719
Female	1931	1,655	337	80	1,238
	1930	1,861	370	61	1,430
9 months	1931	3,324	620	122	2,582
	1930	3,651	706	112	2,833
Male	1931	1,802	340	59	1,403
	1930	1,993	371	71	1,551
Female	1931	1,522	280	63	1,179
	1930	1,658	335	41	1,282
10 months	1931	2,871	538	125	2,208
	1930	3,220	583	95	2,542
Male	1931	1,529	279	52	1,198
	1930	1,690	327	45	1,318
Female	1931	1,342	259	73	1,010
	1930	1,530	256	50	1,224
11 months	1931	2,927	532	125	2,270
	1930	3,187	620	92	2,475
Male	1931	1,538	285	66	1,187
	1930	1,721	354	42	1,325
Female	1931	1,389	247	59	1,083
	1930	1,466	266	50	1,150

TABLE 10.—MOTHERS OF NEGRO CHILDREN BORN IN 1930 HAVING SPECIFIED NUMBER OF CHILDREN EVER BORN, WITH THE AVERAGE NUMBER LIVING AND THE PERCENT OF MOTHERS HAVING SPECIFIED NUMBER LIVING, IN THE REGISTRATION AREA IN CONTINENTAL UNITED STATES:[1] 1930

[Percents are shown in *italics* when the number of mothers having specified number of children living is less than 5]

MOTHER AND NUMBER OF CHILDREN	Number of mothers	Average number of children living	PERCENT OF MOTHERS HAVING SPECIFIED NUMBER OR MORE OF CHILDREN LIVING																		
			1	2	3	4	5	6	7	8	9	10	11	12	13	14	15	16	17	18	19
Negro mothers having born—																					
1 child	70,545	1.0	100.0	------	------	------	------	------	------	------	------	------	------	------	------	------	------	------	------	------	------
2 children	41,950	1.9	100.0	86.1	------	------	------	------	------	------	------	------	------	------	------	------	------	------	------	------	------
3 children	29,735	2.7	100.0	96.1	77.1	------	------	------	------	------	------	------	------	------	------	------	------	------	------	------	------
4 children	22,473	3.6	100.0	98.3	90.7	68.7	------	------	------	------	------	------	------	------	------	------	------	------	------	------	------
5 children	17,519	4.4	100.0	98.9	95.5	86.0	61.7	------	------	------	------	------	------	------	------	------	------	------	------	------	------
6 children	13,656	5.3	100.0	99.4	97.7	92.6	80.6	56.0	------	------	------	------	------	------	------	------	------	------	------	------	------
7 children	10,268	6.0	100.0	99.7	98.5	95.5	88.4	73.6	49.0	------	------	------	------	------	------	------	------	------	------	------	------
8 children	8,152	6.8	100.0	99.7	99.0	96.9	92.3	84.5	68.2	44.0	------	------	------	------	------	------	------	------	------	------	------
9 children	5,869	7.6	100.0	99.9	99.3	98.2	95.3	89.4	80.4	62.8	38.5	------	------	------	------	------	------	------	------	------	------
10 children	4,612	8.4	100.0	99.9	99.4	98.6	96.7	92.5	84.8	74.0	54.8	34.3	------	------	------	------	------	------	------	------	------
11 children	2,920	9.0	100.0	100.0	99.7	98.9	97.2	94.0	88.4	80.4	68.1	48.6	28.5	------	------	------	------	------	------	------	------
12 children	2,106	9.6	100.0	99.9	99.7	98.8	97.7	95.5	91.2	84.3	73.7	59.0	40.9	24.0	------	------	------	------	------	------	------
13 children	1,334	10.4	100.0	99.9	99.6	99.1	98.4	96.3	93.6	87.9	81.0	70.4	54.6	36.1	19.7	------	------	------	------	------	------
14 children	824	10.6	100.0	100.0	99.5	99.0	98.7	97.0	93.3	86.9	80.8	70.3	55.5	41.6	26.1	15.3	------	------	------	------	------
15 children	465	11.5	100.0	100.0	100.0	99.6	99.1	98.3	96.8	93.3	85.2	80.0	69.0	56.1	39.6	23.4	14.0	------	------	------	------
16 children	232	11.5	100.0	100.0	99.6	99.1	98.3	95.3	92.2	90.1	81.5	74.6	62.9	54.7	42.7	28.9	16.8	10.3	------	------	------
17 children	122	11.8	100.0	100.0	99.2	99.2	98.4	96.7	95.1	91.8	84.4	73.8	62.3	54.1	45.1	33.6	23.0	15.6	10.7	------	------
18 children	48	11.8	100.0	100.0	100.0	97.9	97.9	93.8	89.6	87.5	81.3	70.8	60.4	52.1	45.8	37.5	27.1	16.7	10.4	*6.3*	------
19 children	32	12.9	100.0	100.0	100.0	100.0	100.0	100.0	100.0	93.8	93.8	84.4	68.8	62.5	50.0	43.8	31.3	21.9	18.8	*12.5*	*12.5*
20 children	21	12.0	100.0	100.0	100.0	100.0	100.0	100.0	95.2	95.2	95.2	76.2	71.4	42.9	33.3	28.6	*19.0*	*19.0*	*19.0*	*4.8*	*4.8*
21 children	12	11.2	100.0	100.0	100.0	100.0	100.0	100.0	100.0	91.7	75.0	75.0	50.0	41.7	*25.0*	*16.7*	*16.7*	*16.7*	*8.3*	------	------
22 children	6	12.8	100.0	100.0	100.0	100.0	100.0	100.0	100.0	100.0	100.0	100.0	100.0	*66.7*	*50.0*	*33.3*	*33.3*	------	------	------	------
23 children	2	10.0	*100.0*	*100.0*	*100.0*	*100.0*	*100.0*	*100.0*	*100.0*	*100.0*	*50.0*	*50.0*	*50.0*	*50.0*	------	------	------	------	------	------	------
24 children	3	15.0	*100.0*	*100.0*	*100.0*	*100.0*	*100.0*	*100.0*	*100.0*	*100.0*	*100.0*	*100.0*	*100.0*	*100.0*	*100.0*	*100.0*	*66.7*	*33.3*	------	------	------
25 children	3	13.0	*100.0*	*100.0*	*100.0*	*100.0*	*100.0*	*100.0*	*100.0*	*100.0*	*100.0*	*100.0*	*100.0*	*100.0*	*66.7*	*33.3*	------	------	------	------	------
27 children	1	21.0	*100.0*	*100.0*	*100.0*	*100.0*	*100.0*	*100.0*	*100.0*	*100.0*	*100.0*	*100.0*	*100.0*	*100.0*	*100.0*	*100.0*	*100.0*	*100.0*	*100.0*	*100.0*	*100.0*

[1] Exclusive of Colorado, Maine, Massachusetts, New Hampshire, and Rhode Island.

TABLE 11.—INFANT MORTALITY RATE (DEATHS[1] UNDER 1 YEAR OF AGE PER 1,000 LIVE BIRTHS) IN THE BIRTH REGISTRATION AREA IN CONTINENTAL UNITED STATES: 1931 AND 1930

AGE, SEX, AND YEAR		Total	Negro	Other colored	White
Under 1 year	1931	61.6	92.7	117.8	56.7
	1930	64.6	99.5	141.1	59.6
Male	1931	68.3	101.4	127.3	63.2
	1930	71.3	108.5	146.4	66.1
Female	1931	54.5	83.8	107.9	49.9
	1930	57.5	90.2	135.4	52.7
Under 1 day	1931	15.0	16.8	12.5	14.9
	1930	15.0	16.8	15.4	14.8
Male	1931	17.0	18.6	13.9	16.9
	1930	16.8	18.3	16.4	16.7
Female	1931	12.9	15.0	11.0	12.7
	1930	13.1	15.3	14.3	12.8
1 day	1931	4.0	5.4	4.2	3.8
	1930	4.2	5.9	4.2	3.9
Male	1931	4.5	6.0	5.2	4.3
	1930	4.7	6.6	4.5	4.4
Female	1931	3.5	4.8	3.1	3.3
	1930	3.6	5.1	3.9	3.4
2 days	1931	2.7	3.5	3.4	2.6
	1930	2.9	3.9	4.3	2.8
Male	1931	3.2	4.1	4.0	3.1
	1930	3.4	4.4	4.7	3.3
Female	1931	2.2	3.0	2.8	2.1
	1930	2.4	3.4	3.8	2.2
3 to 6 days	1931	4.7	6.9	7.3	4.4
	1930	5.1	7.6	10.0	4.8
Male	1931	5.4	8.0	8.7	5.0
	1930	5.8	8.8	10.8	5.3
Female	1931	4.0	5.7	5.9	3.8
	1930	4.4	6.3	9.1	4.2
1 week	1931	3.6	5.9	5.4	3.3
	1930	3.9	6.2	8.1	3.5
Male	1931	4.0	6.2	6.1	3.6
	1930	4.2	6.7	9.5	3.9
Female	1931	3.3	5.6	4.7	3.0
	1930	3.5	5.8	6.6	3.2
2 weeks	1931	2.4	3.8	3.9	2.2
	1930	2.5	4.0	4.4	2.3
Male	1931	2.7	4.1	4.5	2.5
	1930	2.7	4.0	5.0	2.5
Female	1931	2.2	3.5	3.2	2.0
	1930	2.3	4.0	3.7	2.1
3 weeks but under 1 month	1931	2.0	3.0	4.6	1.9
	1930	2.1	3.2	4.0	2.0
Male	1931	2.2	3.3	4.9	2.0
	1930	2.3	3.4	3.2	2.2
Female	1931	1.8	2.7	4.3	1.7
	1930	1.9	3.0	5.0	1.7
Under 1 month	1931	34.6	45.4	41.3	33.1
	1930	35.7	47.6	50.3	34.1
Male	1931	39.0	50.3	47.4	37.5
	1930	39.9	52.2	54.0	38.2
Female	1931	29.9	40.3	35.0	28.5
	1930	31.3	42.9	46.5	29.7
1 month	1931	5.0	8.4	11.0	4.5
	1930	5.3	8.9	13.0	4.8
Male	1931	5.6	9.0	11.9	5.1
	1930	5.9	9.5	14.0	5.3
Female	1931	4.4	7.8	10.1	3.9
	1930	4.7	8.2	11.9	4.1
2 months	1931	4.0	6.8	10.2	3.5
	1930	4.2	7.0	10.8	3.7
Male	1931	4.4	7.3	11.5	4.0
	1930	4.6	7.6	10.9	4.1
Female	1931	3.5	6.4	8.9	3.0
	1930	3.7	6.4	10.8	3.3
3 months	1931	3.1	5.5	10.3	2.7
	1930	3.5	6.4	11.4	3.1
Male	1931	3.3	6.1	10.7	2.9
	1930	3.9	6.9	12.1	3.4
Female	1931	2.9	4.8	10.0	2.5
	1930	3.1	5.8	10.6	2.7
4 months	1931	2.6	5.0	8.7	2.2
	1930	2.8	5.4	9.5	2.5
Male	1931	2.9	5.5	9.5	2.4
	1930	3.1	6.2	9.7	2.7
Female	1931	2.4	4.5	8.0	2.0
	1930	2.6	4.6	9.2	2.3
5 months	1931	2.2	4.2	7.3	1.9
	1930	2.4	4.7	7.8	2.1
Male	1931	2.4	4.5	7.8	2.0
	1930	2.7	5.1	8.1	2.3
Female	1931	2.1	3.9	6.7	1.8
	1930	2.2	4.3	7.6	1.9
6 months	1931	2.1	3.9	6.3	1.8
	1930	2.3	4.6	8.2	2.0
Male	1931	2.3	4.2	6.6	2.0
	1930	2.5	5.0	8.2	2.2
Female	1931	1.9	3.5	5.9	1.7
	1930	2.1	4.2	8.2	1.8
7 months	1931	1.8	3.2	5.2	1.6
	1930	2.0	3.7	6.9	1.7
Male	1931	2.0	3.5	5.6	1.7
	1930	2.2	3.9	6.7	1.9
Female	1931	1.7	2.8	4.7	1.5
	1930	1.8	3.5	7.2	1.5
8 months	1931	1.8	3.1	5.1	1.5
	1930	1.8	3.3	6.3	1.6
Male	1931	1.9	3.4	4.9	1.7
	1930	1.9	3.5	5.7	1.7
Female	1931	1.6	2.9	5.4	1.4
	1930	1.7	3.1	7.1	1.5
9 months	1931	1.6	2.6	4.0	1.4
	1930	1.7	3.0	6.3	1.5
Male	1931	1.7	2.9	3.8	1.5
	1930	1.8	3.1	7.7	1.5
Female	1931	1.5	2.4	4.2	1.3
	1930	1.5	2.8	4.7	1.4
10 months	1931	1.4	2.3	4.1	1.2
	1930	1.5	2.4	5.3	1.3
Male	1931	1.4	2.3	3.4	1.3
	1930	1.5	2.7	4.9	1.3
Female	1931	1.3	2.2	4.9	1.1
	1930	1.4	2.2	5.8	1.3
11 months	1931	1.4	2.3	4.1	1.2
	1930	1.4	2.6	5.2	1.3
Male	1931	1.4	2.4	4.3	1.2
	1930	1.5	2.9	4.6	1.3
Female	1931	1.4	2.1	4.0	1.2
	1930	1.4	2.3	5.8	1.2

[1] Exclusive of stillbirths.

TABLE 12.—DEATHS UNDER 1 YEAR OF AGE (EXCLUSIVE OF STILLBIRTHS) FROM IMPORTANT CAUSES, BY COLOR, IN THE BIRTH REGISTRATION AREA IN CONTINENTAL UNITED STATES: 1931 AND 1930

Detailed international list no.	CAUSE OF DEATH AND YEAR		Total	Negro	Other colored	White
	All causes	**1931**	**130,134**	**21,716**	**3,565**	**104,853**
		1930	**142,413**	**23,812**	**2,517**	**116,084**
7	Measles	1931	753	67	54	632
		1930	816	87	46	683
8	Scarlet fever	1931	113	9	2	102
		1930	111	7	-------	104
9	Whooping-cough	1931	2,633	496	113	2,024
		1930	3,378	650	88	2,640
10	Diphtheria	1931	393	81	5	307
		1930	458	88	5	365
11	Influenza	1931	3,800	723	132	2,945
		1930	2,924	590	64	2,270
13	Dysentery	1931	620	177	32	411
		1930	853	218	35	600
15	Erysipelas	1931	635	32	14	589
		1930	708	29	13	666
18	Epidemic cerebrospinal meningitis	1931	366	41	9	316
		1930	476	60	6	410
22	Tetanus	1931	127	66	1	60
		1930	136	64	3	69
23	Tuberculosis of the respiratory system	1931	358	103	35	220
		1930	421	135	30	256
24	Tuberculosis of the meninges, etc	1931	377	54	24	299
		1930	444	54	20	370
25–32	Other forms of tuberculosis	1931	184	47	15	122
		1930	196	41	13	142
34	Syphilis	1931	1,738	774	68	896
		1930	1,810	831	42	937
86	Convulsions	1931	710	179	12	519
		1930	913	246	11	656
106	Bronchitis	1931	773	141	13	619
		1930	941	188	11	742
107	Bronchopneumonia	1931	13,461	2,149	556	10,756
		1930	14,142	2,343	363	11,436
108, 109	Lobar and unspecified pneumonia	1931	5,062	1,221	197	3,644
		1930	5,427	1,238	148	4,041
117, 118	Diseases of the stomach	1931	588	153	24	411
		1930	766	180	26	560
119	Diarrhea and enteritis	1931	14,024	2,266	797	10,961
		1930	17,292	2,686	502	14,104
122b	Intestinal obstruction	1931	906	103	19	784
		1930	892	96	19	777
157	Congenital malformations	1931	11,494	557	139	10,798
		1930	11,749	530	62	11,157
158, 161 b, c	Congenital debility, icterus, sclerema	1931	5,283	1,088	185	4,010
		1930	5,584	1,175	113	4,296
159	Premature birth	1931	33,772	4,418	503	28,851
		1930	36,756	4,787	346	31,623
160	Injury at birth	0931	10,048	769	97	9,182
		1930	10,626	778	75	9,773
161 a, d	Other diseases of early infancy	1931	4,160	536	91	3,533
		1930	4,873	684	80	4,109
172–198, 201–214	External causes	1931	2,070	395	79	1,596
		1930	2,343	463	61	1,819
199, 200	Unknown or ill-defined diseases	1931	7,875	3,917	176	3,782
		1930	8,804	4,304	207	4,293
	All other causes	1931	7,811	1,154	173	6,484
		1930	8,574	1,260	128	7,186

TABLE 13.—INFANT MORTALITY RATE (DEATHS[1] UNDER 1 YEAR OF AGE PER 1,000 LIVE BIRTHS) FROM IMPORTANT CAUSE, IN THE BIRTH REGISTRATION AREA IN CONTINENTAL UNITED STATES: 1931 AND 1930

[Rates in *italics* are based on less than 5 deaths]

Detailed international list no.	CAUSE OF DEATH AND YEAR	Total	Negro	Other colored	White
	All causes 1931	**61.6**	**92.7**	**117.8**	**56.7**
	1930	64.6	99.5	141.1	59.6
7	Measles 1931	0.4	0.3	1.8	0.4
	1930	.4	.4	2.6	.4
8	Scarlet fever 1931	.1	(2)	*.1*	.1
	1930	.1	(2)	------	.1
9	Whooping-cough 1931	1.2	2.1	3.7	1.1
	1930	1.5	2.7	4.9	1.4
10	Diphtheria 1931	.2	.3	.2	.2
	1930	.2	.4	.3	.2
11	Influenza 1931	1.8	3.1	4.4	1.6
	1930	1.3	2.5	3.6	1.2
13	Dysentery 1931	.3	.8	1.1	.2
	1930	.4	.9	2.0	.3
15	Erysipelas 1931	.3	.1	.5	.3
	1930	.3	.1	.7	.3
18	Epidemic cerebrospinal meningitis 1931	.2	.2	.3	.2
	1930	.2	.3	.3	.2
22	Tetanus 1931	.1	.3	(2)	(2)
	1930	.1	.3	*.2*	(2)
23	Tuberculosis of the respiratory system 1931	.2	.4	1.2	.1
	1930	.2	.6	1.7	.1
24	Tuberculosis of the meninges, etc 1931	.2	.2	.8	.2
	1930	.2	.2	1.1	.2
25 to 32	Other forms of tuberculosis 1931	.1	.2	.5	.1
	1930	.1	.2	.7	.1
34	Syphilis 1931	.8	3.3	2.2	.5
	1930	.8	3.5	2.4	.5
86	Convlusions 1931	.3	.8	.4	.3
	1930	.4	1.0	.6	.3
106	Bronchitis 1931	0.4	0.6	0.4	0.3
	1930	.4	.8	.6	.4
107	Bronchopneumonia 1931	6.4	9.2	18.4	5.8
	1930	6.4	9.8	20.3	5.9
108, 109	Lobar and unspecified pneumonia 1931	2.4	5.2	6.5	2.0
	1930	2.5	5.2	8.3	2.1
117, 118	Diseases of the stomach 1931	.3	.7	.8	.2
	1930	.3	.8	1.5	.3
119	Diarrhea and enteritis 1931	6.6	9.7	26.3	5.9
	1930	7.8	11.2	28.1	7.2
122b	Intestinal obstruction 1931	.4	.4	.6	.4
	1930	.4	.4	1.1	.4
157	Congenital malformations 1931	5.4	2.4	4.6	5.8
	1930	5.3	2.2	3.5	5.7
158, 161 b, c	Congenita debility, icterus, sclerema 1931	2.5	4.6	6.1	2.2
	1930	2.5	4.9	6.3	2.2
159	Premature birth 1931	16.0	18.9	16.6	15.6
	1930	16.7	20.0	19.4	16.2
160	Injury at birth 1931	4.8	3.3	3.2	5.0
	1930	4.8	3.3	4.2	5.0
161 a, b	Other diseases of early infancy 1931	2.0	2.3	3.0	1.9
	1930	2.2	2.9	4.5	2.1
172–198, 201–214	External causes 1931	1.0	1.7	2.6	.9
	1930	1.1	1.9	3.4	.9
199, 200	Unknown or ill-defined diseases 1931	3.7	16.7	5.8	2.0
	1930	4.0	18.0	11.6	2.5
	All other causes 1931	3.7	4.9	5.7	3.2
	1930	3.9	5.3	7.1	3.7

[1] Exclusive of stillbirths.

[2] Less than 1/10 of 1 per 1,000 births.

TABLE 14.—NEGRO BIRTHS (EXCLUSIVE OF STILLBIRTHS), BY SEX, IN REGISTRATION CITIES, INCORPORATED PLACES, AND RURAL DISTRICTS: 1931 AND 1930

["Cities" includes municipalities of 10,000 inhabitants or more in 1930 and in some States certain towns and townships having populations of 10,000 or more with a population density of 1,000 or more per square mile; "Incorporated places" includes minor cities with populations from 2,500 to 10,000 in 1930; the remainder of the State is included in "Rural"]

AREA AND YEAR	Total	Male	Female	Percent distribution of total births
Registration area in continental United States 1931	**234,203**	**118,862**	**115,341**	100.0
1930	239,275	121,495	117,780	100.0
Cities 1931	81,398	41,435	39,963	34.8
1930	85,037	43,155	41,882	35.5
Incorporated places 1931	15,039	7,568	7,471	6.4
1930	16,809	8,472	8,337	7.0
Rural 1931	137,766	69,859	67,907	58.8
1930	137,429	69,868	67,561	57.4
ALABAMA 1931	22,904	11,603	11,301	100.0
1930	22,969	11,590	11,379	100.0
Cities 1931	4,288	2,153	2,135	18.7
1930	4,453	2,288	2,165	19.4
Incorporated places 1931	1,214	613	601	5.3
1930	1,273	623	650	5.5
Rural 1931	17,402	8,837	8,565	76.0
1930	17,243	8,679	8,564	75.1
ARIZONA 1931	132	73	59	100.0
1930	131	59	72	100.0
Cities 1931	77	41	36	58.3
1930	75	33	42	57.3
Incorporated places 1931	28	17	11	21.2
1930	32	14	18	24.4
Rural 1931	27	15	12	20.5
1930	24	12	12	18.3
ARKANSAS 1931	9,447	4,863	4,584	100.0
1930	9.077	4,594	4,483	100.0
Cities 1931	725	366	359	7.7
1930	758	403	355	8.4
Incorporated places 1931	658	331	327	7.0
1930	765	388	377	8.4
Rural 1931	8,064	4,166	3,898	85.4
1930	7,554	3,803	3,751	83.2
CALIFORNIA 1931	1,152	556	596	100.0
1930	1,003	500	503	100.0
Cities 1931	929	457	472	80.6
1930	811	412	399	80.9
Incorporated places 1931	53	25	28	4.6
1930	58	27	31	5.8
Rural 1931	170	74	96	14.8
1930	134	61	73	13.4
COLORADO 1931	120	69	51	100.0
1930	136	63	73	100.0
Cities 1931	98	61	37	81.7
1930	113	52	61	83.1
Incorporated places 1931	5	1	4	4.2
1930	6	5	1	4.4
Rural 1931	17	7	10	14.2
1930	17	6	11	12.5
CONNECTICUT 1931	677	349	328	100.0
1930	728	370	358	100.0
Cities 1931	619	316	303	91.4
1930	666	336	330	91.5
Incorporated places 1931	21	11	10	3.1
1930	14	7	7	1.9
Rural 1931	37	22	15	5.5
1930	48	27	21	6.6
DELAWARE 1931	684	363	321	100.0
1930	723	368	355	100.0
Cities 1931	228	114	114	33.3
1930	240	129	111	33.2
Incorporated places 1931	79	44	35	11.5
1930	62	30	32	8.6
Rural 1931	377	205	172	55.1
1930	421	209	212	58.2
DISTRICT OF COLUMBIA 1931	2,965	1,515	1,450	100.0
1930	3,036	1,592	1,444	100.0
FLORIDA 1931	8,360	4,238	4,122	100.0
1930	8,385	4,290	4,095	100.0
Cities 1931	2,716	1,396	1,320	32.5
1930	2,740	1,435	1,305	32.7
Incorporated places 1931	1,167	596	571	14.0
1930	1,167	565	602	13.9
Rural 1931	4,477	2,246	2,231	53.6
1930	4,478	2,290	2,188	53.4
GEORGIA 1931	24,254	12,405	11,849	100.0
1930	23,392	11,821	11,571	100.0
Cities 1931	4,994	2,591	2,403	20.6
1930	5,027	2,526	2,501	21.5
Incorporated places 1931	2,668	1,315	1,353	11.0
1930	2,352	1,197	1,155	10.1
Rural 1931	16,592	8,499	8,093	68.4
1930	16,013	8,098	7,915	68.5
IDAHO 1931	5	1	4	100.0
1930	8	4	4	100.0
Cities 1931	5	1	4	100.0
1930	7	4	3	87.5
Incorporated places 1931	------	------	------	------
1930	1	------	1	12.5
Rural 1931	------	------	------	------
1930	------	------	------	------
ILLINOIS 1931	5,455	2,795	2,660	100.0
1930	5,917	3,021	2,896	100.0
Cities 1931	5,013	2,577	2,436	91.9
1930	5,489	2,810	2,679	92.8
Incorporated places 1931	154	72	82	2.8
1930	166	86	80	2.8
Rural 1931	288	146	142	5.3
1930	262	125	137	4.4

TABLE 14.—NEGRO BIRTHS (EXCLUSIVE OF STILLBIRTHS), BY SEX, IN REGISTRATION CITIES, INCORPORATED PLACES, AND RURAL DISTRICTS: 1931 AND 1930—Continued

[See note at head of this table]

AREA AND YEAR		Total	Male	Female	Percent distribution of total births
INDIANA	1931	1,851	944	907	100.0
	1930	1,977	957	1,020	100.0
Cities	1931	1,737	892	845	93.8
	1930	1,820	877	943	92.1
Incorporated places	1931	37	15	22	2.0
	1930	44	23	21	2.2
Rural	1931	77	37	40	4.2
	1930	113	57	56	5.7
IOWA	1931	242	122	120	100.0
	1930	277	136	141	100.0
Cities	1931	206	106	100	85.1
	1930	232	115	117	83.8
Incorporated places	1931	15	9	6	6.2
	1930	19	10	9	6.9
Rural	1931	21	7	14	8.7
	1930	26	11	15	9.4
KANSAS	1931	927	469	458	100.0
	1930	999	518	481	100.0
Cities	1931	665	342	323	71.7
	1930	730	371	359	73.1
Incorporated places	1931	86	35	51	9.3
	1930	89	46	43	8.9
Rural	1931	176	92	84	19.0
	1930	180	101	79	18.0
KENTUCKY	1931	3,251	1,609	1,642	100.0
	1930	3,376	1,688	1,688	100.0
Cities	1931	1,204	602	602	37.0
	1930	1,247	636	611	36.9
Incorporated places	1931	377	195	182	11.6
	1930	484	248	236	14.3
Rural	1931	1,670	812	858	51.4
	1930	1,645	804	841	48.7
LOUISIANA	1931	16,986	8,538	8,448	100.0
	1930	16,668	8,425	8,243	100.0
Cities	1931	4,750	2,406	2,344	28.0
	1930	4,652	2,317	2,335	27.9
Incorporated places	1931	1,578	813	765	9.3
	1930	1,754	910	844	10.5
Rural	1931	10,658	5,319	5,339	62.7
	1930	10,262	5,198	5,064	61.6
MAINE	1931	21	11	10	100.0
	1930	15	10	5	100.0
Cities	1931	11	6	5	52.4
	1930	9	5	4	60.0
Incorporated places	1931	3	2	1	14.3
	1930				
Rural	1931	7	3	4	33.3
	1930	6	5	1	40.0
MARYLAND	1931	6,213	3,104	3,109	100.0
	1930	6,401	3,145	3,256	100.0
Cities	1931	3,384	1,684	1,700	54.5
	1930	3,490	1,699	1,791	54.5
Incorporated places	1931	245	130	115	3.9
	1930	238	106	132	3.7
Rural	1931	2,584	1,290	1,294	41.6
	1930	2,673	1,340	1,333	41.8
MASSACHUSETTS	1931	984	494	490	100.0
	1930	961	476	485	100.0
Cities	1931	861	428	433	87.5
	1930	834	406	428	86.8
Incorporated places	1931	35	18	17	3.6
	1930	35	16	19	3.6
Rural	1931	88	48	40	8.9
	1930	92	54	38	9.6
MICHIGAN	1931	3,228	1,620	1,608	100.0
	1930	3,468	1,761	1,707	100.0
Cities	1931	2,978	1,488	1,490	92.3
	1930	3,208	1,631	1,577	92.5
Incorporated places	1931	100	51	49	3.1
	1930	100	50	50	2.9
Rural	1931	150	81	69	4.6
	1930	160	80	80	4.6
MINNESOTA	1931	99	44	55	100.0
	1930	114	62	52	100.0
Cities	1931	89	41	48	89.9
	1930	103	57	46	90.4
Incorporated places	1931	5	2	3	5.1
	1930	6	2	4	5.3
Rural	1931	5	1	4	5.1
	1930	5	3	2	4.4
MISSISSIPPI	1931	23,470	12,009	11,461	100.0
	1930	24,804	12,738	12,066	100.0
Cities	1931	1,969	1,000	969	8.4
	1930	2,242	1,136	1,106	9.0
Incorporated places	1931	1,472	753	719	6.3
	1930	2,913	1,442	1,471	11.7
Rural	1931	20,029	10,256	9,773	85.3
	1930	19,649	10,160	9,489	79.2
MISSOURI	1931	3,580	1,838	1,742	100.0
	1930	3,688	1,899	1,789	100.0
Cities	1931	2,523	1,298	1,225	70.5
	1930	2,683	1,363	1,320	72.7
Incorporated places	1931	245	113	132	6.8
	1930	226	127	99	6.1
Rural	1931	812	427	385	22.7
	1930	779	409	370	21.1
MONTANA	1931	19	6	13	100.0
	1930	16	9	7	100.0
Cities	1931	16	5	11	84.2
	1930	9	4	5	56.3
Incorporated places	1931	2		2	10.5
	1930	5	4	1	31.3
Rural	1931	1	1		5.3
	1930	2	1	1	12.5
NEBRASKA	1931	229	115	114	100.0
	1930	235	114	121	100.0
Cities	1931	214	105	109	93.4
	1930	217	104	113	92.3
Incorporated places	1931	7	6	1	3.1
	1930	8	2	6	3.4
Rural	1931	8	4	4	3.5
	1930	10	8	2	4.3
NEVADA	1931	7	5	2	100.0
	1930	6	4	2	100.0
Cities	1931	2	2		28.6
	1930	1	1		16.7
Incorporated places	1931	3	2	1	42.9
	1930	3	1	2	50.0
Rural	1931	2	1	1	28.6
	1930	2	2		33.3
NEW HAMPSHIRE	1931	6	3	3	100.0
	1930	9	3	6	100.0
Cities	1931	4	2	2	66.7
	1930	6		6	66.7
Incorporated places	1931				
	1930				
Rural	1931	2	1	1	33.3
	1930	3			33.3
NEW JERSEY	1931	4,680	2,336	2,344	100.0
	1930	4,955	2,524	2,431	100.0
Cities	1931	3,760	1,878	1,882	80.3
	1930	3,932	1,980	1,952	79.4
Incorporated places	1931	343	173	170	7.3
	1930	446	239	207	9.0
Rural	1931	577	285	292	12.3
	1930	577	305	272	11.6
NEW MEXICO	1931	42	24	18	100.0
	1930	25	14	11	100.0
Cities	1931	7	2	5	16.7
	1930	8	6	2	32.0
Incorporated places	1931	18	11	7	42.9
	1930	10	4	6	40.0
Rural	1931	17	11	6	40.5
	1930	7	4	3	28.0
NEW YORK	1931	8,655	4,365	4,290	100.0
	1930	8,872	4,506	4,366	100.0
Cities	1931	8,036	4,045	3,991	92.8
	1930	8,254	4,205	4,049	93.0
Incorporated places	1931	170	78	92	2.0
	1930	176	84	92	2.0
Rural	1931	449	242	207	5.2
	1930	442	217	225	5.0
NORTH CAROLINA	1931	22,316	11,412	10,904	100.0
	1930	22,785	11,607	11,178	100.0
Cities	1931	3,895	2,052	1,843	17.5
	1930	4,074	2,119	1,955	17.9
Incorporated places	1931	1,044	498	546	4.7
	1930	984	507	477	4.3
Rural	1931	17,377	8,862	8,515	77.9
	1930	17,727	8,981	8,746	77.8
NORTH DAKOTA	1931	3	1	2	100.0
	1930	1		1	100.0
Cities	1931	1	1		33.3
	1930				
Incorporated places	1931	1		1	33.3
	1930				
Rural	1931	1		1	33.3
	1930	1		1	100.0
OHIO	1931	5,025	2,526	2,499	100.0
	1930	5,931	3,070	2,861	100.0
Cities	1931	4,481	2,257	2,224	89.2
	1930	5,128	2,639	2,489	86.5
Incorporated places	1931	196	104	92	3.9
	1930	266	134	132	4.5
Rural	1931	348	165	183	6.9
	1930	537	297	240	9.1
OKLAHOMA	1931	1,812	934	878	100.0
	1930	1,582	827	755	100.0
Cities	1931	650	333	317	35.9
	1930	558	281	277	35.3
Incorporated places	1931	312	168	144	17.2
	1930	262	135	127	16.6
Rural	1931	850	433	417	46.9
	1930	762	411	351	48.2

TABLE 14.—NEGRO BIRTHS (EXCLUSIVE OF STILLBIRTHS), BY SEX, IN REGISTRATION CITIES, INCORPORATED PLACES, AND RURAL DISTRICTS: 1931 AND 1930—Continued

[See note at head of this table]

AREA AND YEAR		Total	Male	Female	Percent distribution of total births
OREGON	1931	18	8	10	100.0
	1930	24	9	15	100.0
Cities	1931	13	4	9	72.2
	1930	17	6	11	70.8
Incorporated places	1931	4	3	1	22.2
	1930	2	----	2	8.3
Rural	1931	1	1	----	5.6
	1930	5	3	2	20.8
PENNSYLVANIA	1931	8,650	4,470	4,180	100.0
	1930	9,443	4,777	4,666	100.0
Cities	1931	7,571	3,911	3,660	87.5
	1930	8,081	4,108	3,973	85.6
Incorporated places	1931	289	135	154	3.3
	1930	387	185	202	4.1
Rural	1931	790	424	366	9.1
	1930	975	484	491	10.3
RHODE ISLAND	1931	200	101	99	100.0
	1930	239	110	129	100.0
Cities	1931	182	88	94	91.0
	1930	221	98	123	92.5
Incorporated places	1931	1	1	----	.5
	1930	2	2	----	.8
Rural	1931	17	12	5	8.5
	1930	16	10	6	6.7
SOUTH CAROLINA	1931	20,254	10,162	10,092	100.0
	1930	20,396	10,360	10,036	100.0
Cities	1931	2,035	1,061	974	10.0
	1930	2,071	1,013	1,058	10.2
Incorporated places	1931	1,018	510	508	5.0
	1930	1,016	514	502	5.0
Rural	1931	17,201	8,591	8,610	84.9
	1930	17,309	8,833	8,476	84.9
TENNESSEE	1931	7,890	3,983	3,907	100.0
	1930	8,105	4,219	3,886	100.0
Cities	1931	3,352	1,685	1,667	42.5
	1930	3,497	1,810	1,687	43.1
Incorporated places	1931	635	341	294	8.0
	1930	625	337	288	7.7
Rural	1931	3,903	1,957	1,946	49.5
	1930	3,983	2,072	1,911	49.1
UTAH	1931	17	10	7	100.0
	1930	15	8	7	100.0
Cities	1931	16	10	6	94.1
	1930	13	7	6	86.7
Incorporated places	1931	----	----	----	----
	1930	1	----	1	6.7
Rural	1931	1	----	1	5.9
	1930	1	1	----	6.7
VERMONT	1931	3	1	2	100.0
	1930	11	6	5	100.0
Cities	1931	2	----	2	66.7
	1930	6	3	3	54.5
Incorporated places	1931	----	----	----	----
	1930	----	----	----	----
Rural	1931	1	1	----	33.3
	1930	5	3	2	45.5
VIRGINIA	1931	14,954	7,578	7,376	100.0
	1930	15,689	7,849	7,840	100.0
Cities	1931	3,627	1,845	1,782	24.3
	1930	3,717	1,833	1,884	23.7
Incorporated places	1931	604	300	304	4.0
	1930	639	320	319	4.1
Rural	1931	10,723	5,433	5,290	71.7
	1930	11,333	5,696	5,637	72.2
WASHINGTON	1931	67	39	28	100.0
	1930	62	36	26	100.0
Cities	1931	58	34	24	86.6
	1930	57	33	24	91.9
Incorporated places	1931	2	2	----	3.0
	1930	1	----	1	1.6
Rural	1931	7	3	4	10.4
	1930	4	3	1	6.5
WEST VIRGINIA	1931	2,169	1,064	1,105	100.0
	1930	2,454	1,269	1,185	100.0
Cities	1931	346	190	156	16.0
	1930	403	219	184	16.4
Incorporated places	1931	143	74	69	6.6
	1930	167	79	88	6.8
Rural	1931	1,680	800	880	77.5
	1930	1,884	971	913	76.8
WISCONSIN	1931	172	84	88	100.0
	1930	154	81	73	100.0
Cities	1931	93	44	49	54.1
	1930	99	51	48	64.3
Incorporated places	1931	----	----	----	----
	1930	1	1	----	.6
Rural	1931	79	40	39	45.9
	1930	54	29	25	35.1
WYOMING	1931	8	3	5	100.0
	1930	13	6	7	100.0
Cities	1931	3	----	3	37.5
	1930	3	2	1	23.1
Incorporated places	1931	2	1	1	25.0
	1930	4	2	2	30.8
Rural	1931	3	2	1	37.5
	1930	6	2	4	46.2

TABLE 15.—NEGRO STILLBIRTHS, BY SEX, IN REGISTRATION CITIES, INCORPORATED PLACES, AND RURAL DISTRICTS: 1931 AND 1930

["Cities" includes municipalities of 10,000 inhabitants or more in 1930 and in some States certain towns and townships having populations of 10,000 or more with a population density of 1,000 or more per square mile; "Incorporated places" includes minor cities with populations from 2,500 to 10,000 in 1930; the remainder of the State is included in "Rural"]

AREA AND YEAR		Total	Male	Female	Sex unknown	Per 100 live births
Registration area in continental United States	**1931**	**17,884**	**10,060**	**7,503**	**321**	**7.6**
	1930	**19,743**	**11,115**	**8,291**	**337**	**8.3**
Cities	1931	6,822	3,726	2,960	136	8.4
	1930	7,631	4,229	3,283	119	9.0
Incorporated places	1931	1,261	711	535	15	8.4
	1930	1,571	881	667	23	9.3
Rural	1931	9,801	5,623	4,008	170	1.0
	1930	10,541	6,005	4,341	195	7.7
ALABAMA	1931	1,701	955	733	13	7.4
	1930	1,878	1,085	769	24	8.2
Cities	1931	358	190	166	2	8.3
	1930	431	238	192	1	9.7
Incorporated places	1931	110	59	51	----	9.1
	1930	124	73	50	1	9.7
Rural	1931	1,233	706	516	11	7.1
	1930	1,323	774	527	22	7.7
ARIZONA	1931	11	6	5	----	8.3
	1930	9	6	3	----	6.9
Cities	1931	7	5	2	----	9.1
	1930	5	4	1	----	6.7
Incorporated places	1931	1	----	1	----	3.6
	1930	1	1	----	----	3.1
Rural	1931	3	1	2	----	11.1
	1930	3	1	2	----	12.5
ARKANSAS	1931	661	376	268	17	7.0
	1930	752	410	317	25	8.3
Cities	1931	82	45	37	----	11.3
	1930	93	44	47	2	12.3
Incorporated places	1931	40	26	14	----	6.1
	1930	67	37	29	1	8.8
Rural	1931	539	305	217	17	6.7
	1930	592	329	241	22	7.8
CALIFORNIA	1931	52	36	16	----	4.5
	1930	49	28	21	----	4.9
Cities	1931	45	31	14	----	4.8
	1930	40	26	14	----	4.9
Incorporated places	1931	2	2	----	----	3.8
	1930	1	----	1	----	1.7
Rural	1931	5	3	2	----	2.9
	1930	8	2	6	----	6.0
COLORADO	1931	8	5	2	1	6.7
	1930	10	6	4	----	7.4
Cities	1931	5	3	1	1	5.1
	1930	9	5	4	----	8.0
Incorporated places	1931	----	----	----	----	----
	1930	----	----	----	----	----
Rural	1931	3	2	1	----	17.6
	1930	1	1	----	----	5.9
CONNECTICUT	1931	35	20	15	----	5.2
	1930	36	23	12	1	4.9
Cities	1931	34	19	15	----	5.5
	1930	31	20	10	1	4.7
Incorporated places	1931	1	1	----	----	4.8
	1930	1	1	----	----	7.1
Rural	1931	----	----	----	----	----
	1930	4	2	2	----	8.3
DELAWARE	1931	41	26	15	----	6.0
	1930	57	33	23	1	7.9
Cities	1931	14	12	2	----	6.1
	1930	34	19	15	----	14.2
Incorporated places	1931	6	4	2	----	7.6
	1930	5	2	2	1	8.1
Rural	1931	21	10	11	----	5.6
	1930	18	12	6	----	4.3
DISTRICT OF COLUMBIA	1931	221	126	93	2	7.5
	1930	242	141	100	1	8.0
City	1931	221	126	93	2	7.5
	1930	242	141	100	1	8.0

TABLE 15.—NEGRO STILLBIRTHS, BY SEX, IN REGISTRATION CITIES, INCORPORATED PLACES, AND RURAL DISTRICTS: 1931 AND 1930—Continued

[See note at head of this table]

AREA AND YEAR	Total	Male	Female	Sex unknown	Per 100 live births
FLORIDA 1931	833	418	392	23	10.0
1930	1,006	562	415	29	12.0
Cities 1931	324	174	149	1	11.9
1930	373	215	154	4	13.6
Incorporated places 1931	104	55	48	1	8.9
1930	143	72	67	4	12.3
Rural 1931	405	189	195	21	9.0
1930	490	275	194	21	10.9
GEORGIA 1931	2,255	1,287	953	15	9.3
1930	2,339	1,340	992	7	10.0
Cities 1931	604	316	288	—	12.1
1930	584	317	266	1	11.6
Incorporated places 1931	237	140	96	1	8.9
1930	282	157	123	2	12.0
Rural 1931	1,414	831	569	14	8.5
1930	1,473	866	603	4	9.2
IDAHO 1931	—	—	—	—	—
1930	1	—	1	—	12.5
Cities 1931	—	—	—	—	—
1930	1	—	1	—	14.3
Incorporated places 1931	—	—	—	—	—
1930	—	—	—	—	—
Rural 1931	—	—	—	—	—
1930	—	—	—	—	—
ILLINOIS 1931	355	185	142	28	6.5
1930	383	216	155	12	6.5
Cities 1931	319	164	127	28	6.4
1930	353	203	138	12	6.4
Incorporated places 1931	13	8	5	—	8.4
1930	12	6	6	—	7.2
Rural 1931	23	13	10	—	8.0
1930	18	7	11	—	6.9
INDIANA 1931	111	62	49	—	6.0
1930	114	58	56	—	5.8
Cities 1931	101	57	44	—	5.8
1930	106	52	54	—	5.8
Incorporated places 1931	2	1	1	—	5.4
1930	3	3	—	—	6.8
Rural 1931	8	4	4	—	10.4
1930	5	3	2	—	4.4
IOWA 1931	13	4	9	—	5.4
1930	22	13	9	—	7.9
Cities 1931	11	3	8	—	5.3
1930	21	13	8	—	9.1
Incorporated places 1931	—	—	—	—	—
1930	1	—	1	—	5.3
Rural 1931	2	1	1	—	9.5
1930	—	—	—	—	—
KANSAS 1931	67	37	29	1	7.2
1930	75	37	36	2	7.5
Cities 1931	56	31	24	1	8.4
1930	56	31	24	1	7.7
Incorporated places 1931	6	3	3	—	7.0
1930	6	3	3	—	6.7
Rural 1931	5	3	2	—	2.8
1930	13	3	9	1	7.2
KENTUCKY 1931	258	129	128	1	7.9
1930	243	133	109	1	7.2
Cities 1931	89	46	43	—	7.4
1930	110	54	56	—	8.8
Incorporated places 1931	51	27	24	—	13.5
1930	31	17	14	—	6.4
Rural 1931	118	56	61	1	7.1
1930	102	62	39	1	6.2
LOUISIANA 1931	1,198	681	510	7	7.1
1930	1,256	698	552	6	7.5
Cities 1931	311	157	153	1	6.5
1930	343	187	155	1	7.4
Incorporated places 1931	134	80	53	1	8.5
1930	149	82	67	—	8.5
Rural 1931	753	444	304	5	7.1
1930	764	429	330	5	7.4
MARYLAND 1931	632	360	220	52	10.2
1930	739	406	290	43	11.5
Cities 1931	340	190	116	34	10.0
1930	404	222	161	21	11.6
Incorporated places 1931	22	11	8	3	9.0
1930	41	22	16	3	17.2
Rural 1931	270	159	96	15	10.4
1930	294	162	113	19	11.0
MASSACHUSETTS 1931	62	40	22	—	6.3
1930	58	33	25	—	6.0
Cities 1931	57	37	20	—	6.6
1930	51	30	21	—	6.1
Incorporated places 1931	2	2	—	—	5.7
1930	3	1	2	—	8.6
Rural 1931	3	1	2	—	3.4
1930	4	2	2	—	4.3
MICHIGAN 1931	186	105	80	1	5.8
1930	205	107	97	1	5.9
Cities 1931	167	94	73	—	5.6
1930	192	101	90	1	6.0
Incorporated places 1931	6	4	1	1	6.0
1930	6	3	3	—	6.0
Rural 1931	13	7	6	—	8.7
1930	7	3	4	—	4.4
MINNESOTA 1931	9	6	3	—	9.1
1930	8	6	2	—	7.0
Cities 1931	9	6	3	—	10.1
1930	8	6	2	—	7.8
Incorporated places 1931	—	—	—	—	—
1930	—	—	—	—	—
Rural 1931	—	—	—	—	—
1930	—	—	—	—	—
MISSISSIPPI 1931	1,419	793	580	46	6.0
1930	1,687	915	733	39	6.8
Cities 1931	212	121	89	2	10.8
1930	259	131	125	3	11.6
Incorporated places 1931	48	23	21	4	3.3
1930	207	113	90	4	7.1
Rural 1931	1,159	649	470	40	5.8
1930	1,221	671	518	32	6.2
MISSOURI 1931	327	179	128	20	9.1
1930	363	173	153	37	9.8
Cities 1931	240	127	95	18	9.5
1930	283	130	121	32	10.5
Incorporated places 1931	24	12	11	1	9.8
1930	20	11	8	1	8.8
Rural 1931	63	40	22	1	7.8
1930	60	32	24	4	7.7
MONTANA 1931	2	2	—	—	10.5
1930	—	—	—	—	—
Cities 1931	2	2	—	—	12.5
1930	—	—	—	—	—
Incorporated places 1931	—	—	—	—	—
1930	—	—	—	—	—
Rural 1931	—	—	—	—	—
1930	—	—	—	—	—
NEBRASKA 1931	7	6	1	—	3.1
1930	14	11	3	—	6.0
Cities 1931	6	5	1	—	2.8
1930	13	11	2	—	6.0
Incorporated places 1931	1	1	—	—	14.3
1930	—	—	—	—	—
Rural 1931	—	—	—	—	—
1930	1	—	1	—	10.0
NEVADA 1931	—	—	—	—	—
1930	1	—	1	—	16.7
Cities 1931	—	—	—	—	—
1930	—	—	—	—	—
Incorporated places 1931	—	—	—	—	—
1930	—	—	—	—	—
Rural 1931	—	—	—	—	—
1930	1	—	1	—	50.0
NEW JERSEY 1931	264	132	130	2	5.6
1930	332	189	137	6	6.7
Cities 1931	217	106	110	1	5.8
1930	287	161	121	5	7.3
Incorporated places 1931	23	14	9	—	6.7
1930	20	13	6	1	4.5
Rural 1931	24	12	11	1	4.2
1930	25	15	10	—	4.3
NEW MEXICO 1931	1	—	1	—	2.4
1930	3	1	2	—	12.0
Cities 1931	—	—	—	—	—
1930	1	—	1	—	12.5
Incorporated places 1931	—	—	—	—	—
1930	1	—	1	—	10.0
Rural 1931	1	—	1	—	5.9
1930	1	1	—	—	14.3
NEW YORK 1931	702	393	275	34	8.1
1930	738	407	309	22	8.3
Cities 1931	673	375	264	34	8.4
1930	709	393	294	22	8.6
Incorporated places 1931	10	9	1	—	5.9
1930	4	3	1	—	2.3
Rural 1931	19	9	10	—	4.2
1930	25	11	14	—	5.7
NORTH CAROLINA 1931	1,727	975	723	29	7.7
1930	1,914	1,097	782	35	8.4
Cities 1931	453	231	218	4	11.6
1930	527	307	215	5	12.9
Incorporated places 1931	109	57	51	1	10.4
1930	116	63	51	2	11.8
Rural 1931	1,165	687	454	24	6.7
1930	1,271	727	516	28	7.2
OHIO 1931	295	166	128	1	5.9
1930	395	220	174	1	6.7
Cities 1931	265	149	116	—	5.9
1930	354	196	158	—	6.9
Incorporated places 1931	10	6	3	1	5.1
1930	5	5	—	—	1.9
Rural 1931	20	11	9	—	5.7
1930	36	19	16	1	6.7
OKLAHOMA 1931	100	53	47	—	5.5
1930	117	69	47	1	7.4
Cities 1931	43	28	15	—	6.6
1930	52	26	25	1	9.3
Incorporated places 1931	26	13	13	—	8.3
1930	16	10	6	—	6.1
Rural 1931	31	12	19	—	3.6
1930	49	33	16	—	6.4

TABLE 15.—NEGRO STILLBIRTHS, BY SEX, IN REGISTRATION CITIES, INCORPORATED PLACES, AND RURAL DISTRICTS: 1931 AND 1930—Continued

[See note at head of this table]

AREA AND YEAR		Total	Male	Female	Sex unknown	Per 100 live births
OREGON	1931	3	3	-------	-------	16.7
	1930	3	3	-------	-------	12.5
Cities	1931	3	3	-------	-------	23.1
	1930	1	1	-------	-------	5.9
Incorporated places	1931	-------	-------	-------	-------	-------
	1930	1	1	-------	-------	50.0
Rural	1931	-------	-------	-------	-------	-------
	1930	1	1	-------	-------	20.0
PENNSYLVANIA	1931	531	305	222	4	6.1
	1930	568	328	236	4	6.0
Cities	1931	467	269	195	3	6.2
	1930	483	279	203	1	6.0
Incorporated places	1931	24	14	10	-------	8.3
	1930	23	14	9	-------	5.9
Rural	1931	40	22	17	1	5.1
	1930	62	35	24	3	6.4
RHODE ISLAND	1931	12	5	7	-------	6.0
	1930	10	6	4	-------	4.2
Cities	1931	11	4	7	-------	6.0
	1930	10	6	4	-------	4.5
Incorporated places	1931	-------	-------	-------	-------	-------
	1930	-------	-------	-------	-------	-------
Rural	1931	1	1	-------	-------	5.9
	1930	-------	-------	-------	-------	-------
SOUTH CAROLINA	1931	1,798	1,057	741	-------	8.9
	1930	1,930	1,122	808	-------	9.5
Cities	1931	287	157	130	-------	14.1
	1930	332	192	140	-------	16.0
Incorporated places	1931	110	61	49	-------	10.8
	1930	138	84	54	-------	13.6
Rural	1931	1,401	839	562	-------	8.1
	1930	1,460	846	614	-------	8.4
TENNESSEE	1931	658	373	283	2	8.3
	1930	809	468	333	8	10.0
Cities	1931	350	203	147	-------	10.4
	1930	401	232	167	2	11.5
Incorporated places	1931	52	28	24	-------	8.2
	1930	76	42	32	2	12.2
Rural	1931	256	142	112	2	6.6
	1930	332	194	134	4	8.3
UTAH	1931	-------	-------	-------	-------	-------
	1930	1	-------	1	-------	6.7
Cities	1931	-------	-------	-------	-------	-------
	1930	1	-------	1	-------	7.7
Incorporated places	1931	-------	-------	-------	-------	-------
	1930	-------	-------	-------	-------	-------
Rural	1931	-------	-------	-------	-------	-------
	1930	-------	-------	-------	-------	-------
VIRGINIA	1931	1,172	657	493	22	7.8
	1930	1,219	676	512	31	7.8
Cities	1931	393	214	175	4	10.8
	1930	394	215	177	2	10.6
Incorporated places	1931	69	40	28	1	11.4
	1930	52	32	19	1	8.1
Rural	1931	710	403	290	17	6.6
	1930	773	429	316	28	6.8
WASHINGTON	1931	6	3	3	-------	9.0
	1930	5	-------	5	-------	8.1
Cities	1931	4	2	2	-------	6.9
	1930	4	-------	4	-------	7.0
Incorporated places	1931	-------	-------	-------	-------	-------
	1930	1	-------	1	-------	100.0
Rural	1931	2	1	1	-------	28.6
	1930	-------	-------	-------	-------	-------
WEST VIRGINIA	1931	143	90	53	-------	6.6
	1930	144	83	61	-------	5.9
Cities	1931	38	23	15	-------	11.0
	1930	27	17	10	-------	6.7
Incorporated places	1931	18	10	8	-------	12.6
	1930	15	10	5	-------	9.0
Rural	1931	87	57	30	-------	5.2
	1930	102	56	46	-------	5.4
WISCONSIN	1931	8	4	4	-------	4.7
	1930	8	6	2	-------	5.2
Cities	1931	4	1	3	-------	4.3
	1930	6	4	2	-------	6.1
Incorporated places	1931	-------	-------	-------	-------	-------
	1930	-------	-------	-------	-------	-------
Rural	1931	4	3	1	-------	5.1
	1930	2	2	-------	-------	3.7

TABLE 16.—COMPARISON OF BIRTH AND DEATH RATES FOR COLORED[1] AND WHITE POPULATION IN SELECTED REGISTRATION STATES: 1927 TO 1931

["Rural" includes incorporated places]

AREA	RATE PER 1,000 POPULATION									
	Births (exclusive of stillbirths)					Deaths (exclusive of stillbirths)				
	1931	1930	1929	1928	1927	1931	1930	1929	1928	1927
SELECTED REGISTRATION STATES[2]										
ALABAMA	23.5	24.0	24.0	24.5	26.3	10.7	11.5	12.4	12.3	10.5
Colored	24.1	24.3	23.5	23.9	25.2	14.0	15.2	16.2	16.2	13.7
White	23.2	23.9	24.2	24.8	26.9	8.8	9.4	10.2	10.0	8.7
Cities	19.6	20.6	21.1	21.8	24.6	14.7	15.5	16.7	16.8	15.5
Colored	18.8	19.9	20.4	21.3	23.7	19.0	20.2	21.2	21.4	19.9
White	20.1	21.0	21.4	22.1	25.2	12.1	12.6	13.8	13.8	12.8
Rural	24.6	25.0	24.7	25.1	26.7	9.5	10.3	11.3	11.2	9.4
Colored	25.8	25.6	24.3	24.6	25.6	12.5	13.7	14.9	14.9	12.2
White	24.0	24.7	24.9	25.4	27.2	7.9	8.5	9.4	9.2	7.9
ARKANSAS	22.0	22.1	20.2	20.8	22.1	9.6	10.2	10.5	10.9	10.0
Colored	19.7	18.9	17.8	17.8	18.6	11.9	13.5	13.8	14.3	13.4
White	22.8	23.2	21.0	21.9	23.3	8.8	9.1	9.4	9.7	8.8
Cities	15.9	17.7	18.1	19.1	20.2	16.7	18.3	19.2	20.5	20.5
Colored	14.0	15.0	15.8	17.0	18.7	23.0	26.4	29.5	31.7	29.7
White	16.5	18.5	18.8	19.7	20.7	14.8	15.9	16.1	17.1	17.8
Rural	22.9	22.7	20.4	20.9	22.3	8.6	9.1	9.7	10.0	9.0
Colored	20.4	19.4	18.0	17.8	18.6	10.5	11.9	12.4	12.9	12.0
White	23.8	23.9	21.3	22.1	23.6	7.9	8.1	8.7	8.9	8.0
CONNECTICUT	15.7	17.2	17.1	18.0	18.7	10.6	10.7	11.5	11.4	10.8
Colored	22.2	24.5	24.6	23.6	24.9	16.9	17.4	17.7	17.4	17.6
White	15.6	17.0	17.0	17.9	18.6	10.5	10.6	11.4	11.3	10.7
Cities	18.6	20.3	19.9	20.6	21.4	11.2	11.2	11.9	11.8	11.2
Colored	24.8	27.0	26.1	25.3	42.0	17.8	17.5	17.6	17.7	28.4
White	18.5	20.2	19.7	20.5	21.1	11.0	11.1	11.8	11.7	10.9
Rural	9.8	10.7	9.4	10.6	11.3	9.5	9.7	10.3	10.4	9.9
Colored	10.4	12.4	15.1	13.1	5.1	13.0	17.3	18.6	15.5	4.9
White	9.7	10.7	9.4	10.6	11.5	9.4	9.6	10.2	10.3	10.1
DELAWARE	17.7	18.7	18.1	18.3	18.2	13.8	13.6	13.2	13.6	12.8
Colored	20.8	22.1	22.3	21.9	22.0	21.1	21.4	19.9	18.4	18.8
White	17.2	18.2	17.4	17.7	17.6	12.6	12.4	12.1	12.8	11.9
Cities	20.6	21.6	20.2	20.0	19.6	13.9	14.6	13.4	14.2	13.6
Colored	18.8	19.9	20.1	19.3	19.7	20.9	23.1	21.9	21.4	21.5
White	20.9	21.8	20.3	20.1	19.6	13.0	13.6	12.3	13.3	12.6
Rural	15.3	16.4	16.3	16.8	17.0	13.7	12.8	13.1	13.1	12.2
Colored	21.9	23.3	23.6	23.4	23.3	21.1	20.4	18.8	16.7	17.2
White	14.0	15.1	14.9	15.6	15.8	12.3	11.4	12.0	12.4	11.2
DISTRICT OF COLUMBIA	19.0	19.2	18.4	18.7	19.1	15.8	15.1	15.4	15.1	14.7
Colored	22.1	23.0	22.2	21.8	22.3	22.0	21.0	21.7	21.4	21.1
White	17.9	17.8	17.0	17.5	17.9	13.4	12.9	13.0	12.8	12.4
FLORIDA	18.0	18.2	18.8	21.5	25.6	12.0	12.3	12.7	13.7	13.6
Colored	19.0	19.3	20.1	22.0	25.4	16.0	16.5	17.1	18.2	17.9
White	17.5	17.8	18.2	21.3	25.7	10.4	10.6	10.8	1.7	11.7
SELECTED REGISTRATION STATES—Continued										
FLORIDA—Continued.										
Cities	17.5	18.5	18.4	20.5	23.8	13.7	14.0	13.0	13.2	13.5
Colored	17.0	17.4	19.2	20.1	23.3	18.1	18.7	18.7	19.4	20.6
White	17.7	18.9	18.2	20.7	24.0	12.0	12.2	10.9	10.9	11.0
Rural	18.2	18.1	18.9	22.0	26.4	11.0	11.3	12.6	13.9	13.6
Colored	20.2	20.3	20.5	22.8	26.2	14.8	15.3	16.6	17.7	16.8
White	17.4	17.1	18.2	21.6	26.6	9.3	9.6	10.8	12.2	12.1
GEORGIA	21.2	20.9	20.1	20.3	(3)	11.3	12.1	12.2	12.4	(3)
Colored	22.9	21.9	21.1	20.0	(3)	15.1	16.1	15.8	15.9	(3)
White	20.3	20.3	19.6	20.5	(3)	9.2	9.8	10.0	10.3	(3)
Cities	19.7	20.4	20.4	21.5	(3)	16.5	17.3	17.7	18.5	(3)
Colored	20.1	20.5	20.3	20.5	(3)	23.2	24.8	24.7	25.5	(3)
White	19.5	20.4	20.4	22.1	(3)	12.7	12.9	13.6	14.3	(3)
Rural	21.7	21.0	20.1	20.0	(3)	9.8	10.5	10.6	10.8	(3)
Colored	23.7	22.3	21.3	19.9	(3)	12.6	13.5	13.4	13.4	(3)
White	20.5	20.2	19.3	20.1	(3)	8.1	8.8	9.0	9.2	(3)
ILLINOIS	15.4	16.7	17.0	17.4	18.3	11.1	10.9	11.6	12.1	11.3
Colored	17.2	16.3	18.2	19.6	20.3	16.8	16.2	19.7	21.2	19.8
White	15.3	16.8	17.0	17.3	18.2	10.8	10.6	11.3	11.7	11.0
Cities	15.9	17.8	18.4	18.8	19.5	10.9	10.9	11.8	12.5	11.6
Colored	17.5	17.3	19.0	20.3	21.1	15.5	15.3	18.5	20.2	18.6
White	15.8	17.9	18.4	18.7	19.4	10.6	10.6	11.4	12.1	11.2
Rural	14.4	14.7	14.7	15.3	16.2	11.5	10.9	11.4	11.4	10.8
Colored	15.3	9.4	12.5	14.2	14.6	28.5	22.1	28.2	28.2	27.8
White	14.4	14.8	14.8	15.3	16.2	11.3	10.7	11.1	11.2	10.6
INDIANA	17.2	18.3	18.3	18.9	19.7	11.9	12.1	12.7	12.7	11.9
Colored	14.7	16.1	18.0	18.3	20.7	16.2	18.8	20.2	19.5	19.2
White	17.3	18.3	18.3	18.9	19.7	11.7	11.8	12.5	12.5	11.7
Cities	17.9	19.9	20.0	20.1	21.2	11.7	12.4	13.1	13.1	12.5
Colored	15.3	16.6	18.6	19.2	22.0	15.0	17.6	19.1	18.6	18.5
White	18.1	20.1	20.1	20.1	21.1	11.5	12.0	12.7	12.7	12.1
Rural	16.5	16.9	16.9	18.0	18.6	12.0	11.8	12.5	12.4	11.5
Colored	9.3	12.2	13.4	11.9	12.7	27.0	28.9	27.5	25.3	23.8
White	16.6	16.9	16.9	18.1	18.7	11.9	11.7	12.3	12.3	11.4
IOWA	16.9	17.3	17.1	17.6	18.2	10.4	10.6	10.4	10.3	10.0
Colored	10.9	12.5	13.9	13.4	13.9	14.2	15.8	17.3	17.3	17.9
White	17.0	17.3	17.1	17.7	18.3	10.3	10.6	10.4	10.2	9.9
Cities	19.9	20.5	19.8	19.6	20.2	13.3	13.8	13.9	13.7	13.1
Colored	12.6	14.1	14.7	13.7	15.2	14.5	16.6	15.1	16.5	15.6
White	20.0	20.7	20.0	19.7	20.3	13.3	13.8	13.8	13.6	13.0
Rural	15.7	15.9	16.0	16.9	17.5	9.2	9.3	9.1	9.0	8.9
Colored	6.3	8.4	10.7	12.2	9.3	13.3	13.6	26.0	20.2	25.4
White	15.8	16.0	16.0	16.9	17.5	9.1	9.3	9.1	9.0	8.8

See footnotes at end of table.

TABLE 16.—COMPARISON OF BIRTH AND DEATH RATES FOR COLORED[1] AND WHITE POPULATION IN SELECTED REGISTRATION STATES: 1927 TO 1931—Continued

["Rural" includes incorporated places]

AREA	RATE PER 1,000 POPULATION									
	Births (exclusive of stillbirths)					Deaths (exclusive of stillbirths)				
	1931	1930	1929	1928	1927	1931	1930	1929	1928	1927
SELECTED REGISTRATION STATES—Continued										
KANSAS	17.4	17.9	17.4	18.2	18.8	9.9	10.4	10.4	11.2	10.0
Colored	16.8	17.3	13.1	15.2	13.8	12.9	12.4	18.3	19.8	17.5
White	17.4	17.9	17.6	18.3	18.9	9.7	10.3	10.1	10.9	9.8
Cities	18.8	20.0	19.4	19.8	20.3	11.8	13.0	12.9	14.1	12.6
Colored	16.6	17.5	13.0	15.4	15.0	13.5	13.7	17.6	18.5	17.2
White	19.1	20.3	20.0	20.2	20.9	11.6	12.9	12.4	13.7	12.1
Rural	16.8	17.0	16.7	17.6	18.2	9.0	9.3	9.4	10.2	9.1
Colored	17.1	16.9	13.5	14.7	11.4	11.7	10.2	19.9	22.6	17.9
White	16.7	17.0	16.8	17.6	18.3	9.0	9.3	9.2	10.0	9.0
KENTUCKY	21.7	22.6	21.7	23.0	24.3	11.0	11.3	12.0	11.8	10.6
Colored	14.4	15.0	15.6	16.1	17.7	20.1	21.0	21.3	20.8	19.3
White	22.4	23.4	22.3	23.7	25.0	10.1	10.4	11.1	10.9	9.8
Cities	17.7	19.4	20.4	20.9	21.6	14.9	15.3	15.9	16.0	14.4
Colored	13.8	14.3	15.0	14.7	16.3	23.8	25.1	24.5	24.7	23.7
White	18.3	20.3	21.3	21.9	22.5	13.4	13.6	14.4	14.6	12.8
Rural	22.9	23.6	22.1	23.6	25.1	9.8	10.1	10.9	10.7	9.6
Colored	14.8	15.4	15.9	16.8	18.4	17.8	18.5	19.7	18.8	17.1
White	23.5	24.2	22.6	24.2	25.6	9.2	9.5	10.3	10.0	9.0
LOUISANA	20.4	20.3	20.3	20.5	22.9	11.1	11.7	11.9	12.2	11.8
Colored	21.6	21.3	21.2	21.1	23.0	14.3	15.4	15.7	15.9	15.8
White	19.7	19.8	19.7	20.1	22.8	9.2	9.5	9.7	10.0	9.4
Cities	19.9	20.6	20.3	21.5	23.0	16.1	17.2	17.7	18.3	17.8
Colored	22.7	22.7	22.2	23.1	24.5	22.5	24.0	25.2	25.6	25.4
White	18.6	19.6	19.4	20.8	22.3	13.3	14.2	14.3	15.1	14.4
Rural	20.6	20.2	20.3	20.0	22.8	8.7	9.2	9.4	9.6	9.3
Colored	21.2	20.8	20.8	20.4	22.5	11.3	12.3	12.5	12.7	12.7
White	20.3	19.8	19.9	19.8	23.1	7.9	7.1	7.4	7.5	7.0
MARYLAND	17.5	18.5	18.5	19.9	20.5	13.2	13.2	13.5	13.6	13.3
Colored	22.3	23.1	23.4	24.3	24.4	19.3	18.9	18.9	19.5	19.6
White	16.5	17.6	17.5	19.0	19.8	12.0	12.0	12.4	12.4	12.0
Cities	18.1	19.1	19.0	20.3	21.1	14.4	14.1	14.4	15.0	14.6
Colored	21.7	22.9	22.9	24.2	24.8	20.1	19.9	20.5	21.6	22.0
White	17.3	18.4	18.3	19.5	20.4	13.2	12.9	13.2	13.8	13.2
Rural	16.8	17.7	17.8	19.4	19.8	11.8	12.0	12.4	11.8	11.8
Colored	23.1	23.3	23.9	24.4	23.8	18.4	17.7	17.0	17.1	17.0
White	15.5	16.5	16.5	18.3	18.9	10.4	10.8	11.4	10.6	10.6
MASSACHUSETTS	16.2	17.3	17.5	18.9	19.9	11.3	11.6	12.3	12.2	11.9
Colored	18.4	18.1	19.4	20.1	22.4	15.7	15.9	16.6	17.9	17.0
White	16.1	17.3	17.5	18.9	19.8	11.3	11.5	12.2	12.1	11.8
Cities	17.4	18.6	19.0	20.4	21.3	11.2	11.5	12.3	12.2	11.9
Colored	18.8	18.9	20.1	20.2	22.6	15.7	16.6	16.8	18.2	17.1
White	17.4	18.6	19.0	20.4	21.3	11.2	11.4	12.2	12.1	11.8
Rural	10.3	10.9	11.3	12.6	13.6	11.9	11.9	12.3	12.3	11.9
Colored	15.5	13.6	15.2	19.5	21.4	15.7	12.5	15.4	15.8	16.1
White	10.3	10.8	11.3	12.5	13.5	11.9	11.9	12.2	12.3	11.8
MICHIGAN	18.4	20.4	20.8	21.1	22.1	10.0	10.6	11.8	11.8	11.2
Colored	17.5	20.0	20.5	20.0	22.3	14.4	15.8	20.3	19.4	17.8
White	18.5	20.4	20.9	21.1	22.1	9.8	10.4	11.5	11.5	11.0
Cities	18.6	21.8	23.3	23.3	24.4	9.0	10.1	11.9	11.9	11.3
Colored	17.0	20.0	21.2	20.8	23.0	12.6	14.7	19.8	18.4	17.2
White	18.7	21.9	23.4	23.5	24.5	8.8	9.8	11.5	11.6	10.9
Rural	18.1	18.2	17.8	18.3	19.4	11.5	11.4	11.6	11.6	11.1
Colored	24.3	20.5	16.9	15.3	18.8	36.9	25.1	22.7	24.6	20.6
White	18.1	18.1	17.8	18.3	19.4	11.3	11.2	11.5	11.5	11.0
MISSISSIPPI	22.3	23.9	22.9	24.4	25.3	10.9	12.0	13.0	13.1	11.9
Colored	23.1	24.5	23.4	24.6	25.2	13.1	14.7	15.5	15.6	14.5
White	21.5	23.3	22.3	24.3	25.3	8.6	9.1	10.3	10.5	9.2
Cities	22.4	25.1	24.3	25.5	28.0	19.1	20.2	23.0	22.8	23.6
Colored	20.3	23.7	22.8	24.8	26.2	25.0	27.5	28.8	29.6	32.4
White	23.7	26.1	25.4	26.0	29.3	15.3	15.3	18.9	18.0	17.3
Rural	22.3	23.7	22.7	24.3	25.0	9.7	10.9	11.9	12.1	10.8
Colored	23.4	24.6	23.5	24.6	25.2	11.8	13.4	14.4	14.5	13.1
White	21.1	22.8	21.9	24.1	24.8	7.5	8.1	9.2	9.6	8.3
MISSOURI	16.7	17.1	16.9	17.6	18.6	12.1	11.9	12.3	12.6	11.4
Colored	15.9	16.3	16.3	16.9	18.0	20.1	20.1	21.1	21.8	20.7
White	16.7	17.2	17.0	17.7	18.7	11.5	11.3	11.7	12.0	10.8
Cities	15.8	16.9	17.6	17.8	18.6	13.8	13.6	14.5	15.0	13.7
Colored	16.3	17.3	17.7	17.8	78.6	20.9	20.9	22.5	23.4	21.3
White	15.8	16.8	17.5	17.8	18.6	13.0	12.8	13.7	14.1	12.8
Rural	17.3	17.3	16.5	17.5	18.6	10.8	10.5	10.6	10.9	9.8
Colored	14.9	13.9	13.5	15.1	16.8	18.3	18.2	18.1	18.4	19.5
White	17.4	17.4	16.6	17.6	18.7	10.5	10.2	10.3	10.6	9.5
NEBRASKA	19.2	19.6	19.4	20.5	20.5	9.3	9.6	9.8	10.0	9.1
Colored	25.9	25.3	20.1	20.5	21.7	19.9	19.5	19.1	20.4	19.1
White	19.1	19.5	19.4	20.5	20.5	9.1	9.5	9.6	9.9	9.0
Cities	20.1	21.3	19.9	21.1	21.1	12.6	13.2	13.2	13.4	12.4
Colored	19.8	21.1	16.2	18.0	16.9	18.0	18.2	17.0	17.8	17.9
White	20.1	21.3	20.1	21.2	21.3	12.4	13.0	13.0	13.2	12.2
Rural	18.9	19.0	19.2	20.4	20.4	8.1	8.3	8.7	9.0	8.1
Colored	35.8	31.8	31.0	27.4	34.4	23.1	21.5	25.0	27.4	22.3
White	18.7	18.8	19.1	20.3	20.3	8.0	8.2	8.6	8.9	8.0
NEW HAMPSHIRE	16.6	17.9	17.6	18.8	19.2	12.7	13.6	14.1	14.0	13.8
Colored	6.0	10.0	8.6	2.2	14.6	6.0	9.0	8.6	7.7	13.5
White	16.6	17.9	17.6	18.8	19.2	12.7	13.6	14.1	14.0	13.8
Cities	19.3	20.9	20.2	21.9	22.5	12.4	13.4	13.4	13.4	13.3
Colored	8.0	11.7	11.5	1.7	12.3	8.0	10.0	8.2	8.5	12.3
White	19.3	20.9	20.2	22.0	22.5	12.5	13.5	13.4	13.4	13.3
Rural	14.0	15.0	15.5	16.3	16.5	12.9	13.7	14.7	14.4	14.1
Colored	4.0	7.5	3.1	3.1	18.6	4.0	7.5	9.4	6.2	15.5
White	14.0	15.0	15.5	16.3	16.5	12.9	13.7	14.7	14.4	14.1
NEW JERSEY	15.6	16.8	17.2	18.0	19.1	10.8	10.7	11.6	11.6	11.1
Colored	21.5	23.3	24.1	25.1	25.9	16.2	16.6	18.1	18.6	18.2
White	15.3	16.5	16.8	17.6	18.8	10.5	10.4	11.3	11.2	10.7
Cities	17.6	18.8	20.5	21.3	22.1	10.6	10.6	12.1	12.2	11.5
Colored	22.4	24.4	26.8	27.7	28.6	15.0	16.0	18.6	19.4	18.9
White	17.3	18.4	20.1	20.9	21.7	10.3	10.2	11.7	11.7	11.1
Rural	11.0	12.4	12.5	13.3	14.7	11.4	11.1	10.8	10.7	10.4
Colored	18.4	19.9	18.7	19.8	20.3	20.1	18.6	16.9	16.9	16.9
White	10.7	12.1	12.2	13.0	14.5	11.1	10.7	10.6	10.4	10.1
NEW YORK	16.1	17.1	17.5	18.3	19.0	11.7	11.7	12.4	12.4	11.7
Colored	19.8	20.6	21.1	22.9	23.6	16.5	16.2	16.8	17.8	16.5
White	16.0	17.0	17.4	18.1	18.8	11.5	11.5	12.2	12.2	11.6
Cities	16.8	18.1	18.6	19.3	20.0	11.4	11.4	12.1	12.2	11.4
Colored	19.4	20.9	21.4	23.3	24.2	15.9	16.2	16.6	17.8	16.5
White	16.7	18.0	18.4	19.2	19.8	11.2	11.1	11.9	12.0	11.2
Rural	13.4	13.3	13.7	14.6	15.4	13.0	12.8	13.4	13.0	12.8
Colored	25.2	17.7	18.6	19.2	17.9	25.3	16.0	18.1	17.9	16.8
White	13.3	13.3	13.6	14.5	15.4	12.8	12.8	13.3	12.9	12.8
NORTH CAROLINA	23.3	24.1	24.7	26.4	27.7	10.3	11.2	11.8	11.8	10.9
Colored	24.1	24.8	25.9	27.7	28.8	13.7	15.1	15.5	15.1	14.6
White	22.9	23.8	24.2	25.8	27.3	8.9	9.6	10.2	10.4	9.4
Cities	20.9	23.0	23.3	25.6	27.7	14.1	15.1	15.9	16.6	15.9
Colored	19.4	20.8	21.2	23.8	24.8	19.0	20.2	21.3	21.8	21.9
White	21.6	24.1	24.3	26.5	29.1	11.7	12.6	13.2	14.0	12.8
Rural	23.8	24.4	25.0	26.5	27.7	9.4	10.3	11.0	10.9	10.1
Colored	25.4	25.9	27.0	28.6	29.6	12.2	13.7	14.2	13.7	13.1
White	23.2	23.7	24.1	25.7	27.0	8.3	9.0	9.7	9.8	8.8
OHIO	16.1	17.7	17.7	18.5	19.3	11.3	11.4	12.4	12.3	11.5
Colored	15.6	18.8	20.2	21.4	22.8	17.9	18.3	20.1	20.3	19.6
White	16.1	17.7	17.6	18.4	19.1	10.9	11.1	12.0	12.0	11.1
Cities	16.7	18.9	19.2	19.8	20.7	11.4	11.7	12.8	12.8	12.0
Colored	16.4	19.7	21.2	22.1	25.8	17.4	18.3	20.1	20.1	21.2
White	16.7	18.8	19.1	19.6	20.4	10.9	11.3	12.3	12.3	11.4
Rural	15.2	16.1	15.7	16.9	17.4	11.1	11.0	11.8	11.7	10.8
Colored	11.2	14.6	15.7	17.8	13.5	21.0	18.4	19.9	21.3	14.6
White	15.3	16.2	15.7	16.9	17.5	10.9	10.9	11.6	11.5	10.7
OKLAHOMA	17.9	17.7	16.8	18.4	(3)	7.8	8.2	9.0	9.0	(3)
Colored	13.1	11.8	9.0	9.9	(3)	10.8	11.2	12.0	11.4	(3)
White	18.5	18.4	17.7	19.5	(3)	7.4	7.8	8.7	8.7	(3)
Cities	18.7	20.2	17.3	18.3	(3)	11.2	12.7	12.5	12.6	(3)
Colored	14.3	13.5	11.3	11.9	(3)	17.4	20.0	18.8	18.1	(3)
White	19.3	21.0	18.1	19.1	(3)	10.4	11.8	11.7	11.9	(3)
Rural	17.6	16.9	16.6	18.5	(3)	6.7	6.8	8.1	8.1	(3)
Colored	12.8	11.3	8.3	9.4	(3)	8.8	8.6	10.1	9.6	(3)
White	18.2	17.7	17.6	19.6	(3)	6.4	6.6	7.9	7.9	(3)
PENNSYLVANIA	18.4	19.6	19.8	21.2	22.4	11.5	11.6	12.3	12.6	11.9
Colored	19.3	21.5	22.4	24.3	25.6	17.2	17.0	18.5	19.8	19.2
White	18.4	19.5	19.7	21.0	22.2	11.3	11.3	12.0	12.3	11.5
Cities	18.8	20.2	20.3	21.3	22.4	12.3	12.3	13.4	14.0	12.9
Colored	20.3	22.4	23.2	25.1	26.2	16.7	16.9	18.4	19.7	19.2
White	18.6	20.0	20.1	21.0	22.1	12.0	12.0	13.0	13.5	12.4
Rural	18.0	18.9	19.3	21.1	22.4	10.6	10.6	11.1	11.3	10.8
Colored	14.6	17.1	19.0	21.2	23.4	19.2	17.3	18.5	20.3	19.2
White	18.1	19.0	19.3	21.1	22.4	10.4	10.5	11.0	11.1	10.7
RHODE ISLAND	16.3	17.7	18.0	19.3	20.6	11.5	11.6	13.1	12.5	11.9
Colored	18.5	22.2	24.4	22.0	16.7	17.5	21.0	24.1	23.3	22.6
White	16.3	17.6	17.9	19.3	20.6	11.4	11.5	12.9	12.3	11.7
Cities	16.8	18.2	18.7	20.1	21.5	11.5	11.7	13.4	12.8	12.0
Colored	19.8	23.8	25.1	23.0	25.0	18.9	21.4	24.6	23.4	21.7
White	16.8	18.2	18.6	20.1	21.4	11.4	11.5	13.2	12.6	11.9
Rural	12.5	13.7	14.9	15.6	16.7	11.4	11.2	11.7	11.1	11.2
Colored	11.3	12.0	19.7	15.4	11.1	8.8	18.7	20.5	22.8	28.1
White	12.5	13.7	14.9	15.6	16.8	11.5	11.0	11.6	10.9	11.0
SOUTH CAROLINA	22.7	23.3	22.7	25.0	(4)	12.1	12.9	13.3	14.1	(4)
Colored	25.7	25.7	24.9	26.9	(4)	15.7	16.6	17.0	17.4	(4)
White	20.2	21.2	20.9	23.4	(4)	9.1	9.8	10.1	11.3	(4)
Cities	21.7	23.0	24.3	26.2	(4)	20.7	21.2	21.9	24.6	(4)
Colored	22.4	23.5	25.5	26.3	(4)	28.9	29.3	29.8	32.6	(4)
White	21.2	22.7	23.5	26.2	(4)	15.6	16.3	16.9	19.6	(4)
Rural	22.8	23.3	22.5	24.9	(4)	10.7	11.6	12.2	12.8	(4)
Colored	26.1	26.0	24.9	27.0	(4)	14.0	15.0	15.6	15.8	(4)
White	20.0	20.9	20.5	22.9	(4)	7.9	8.6	9.1	10.1	(4)
TENNESSEE	19.8	20.1	19.5	19.6	21.5	10.8	11.4	12.2	12.2	11.4
Colored	16.4	17.0	17.1	16.8	18.8	16.7	18.3	18.7	19.1	18.0
White	20.5	20.8	20.0	20.2	22.1	9.5	9.9	10.7	10.7	9.9
Cities	18.9	20.3	21.9	21.5	23.1	15.0	15.8	17.6	18.2	17.6
Colored	16.4	17.3	18.8	18.4	21.2	20.8	22.9	24.3	25.5	25.2
White	19.9	21.4	23.2	22.8	23.9	12.6	12.9	14.9	15.3	14.6
Rural	20.1	20.0	18.8	19.1	21.1	9.3	9.8	10.6	10.5	9.7
Colored	16.5	16.7	16.1	16.0	17.5	13.6	15.0	15.6	15.7	14.4
White	20.8	20.6	19.2	19.6	21.7	8.6	9.0	9.7	9.6	8.9
VERMONT	18.5	19.3	18.7	19.6	19.6	12.5	13.0	14.7	13.6	13.6
Colored	3.0	11.0	14.0	17.2	2.0	7.0	9.0	9.3	10.9	4.7
White	18.6	19.3	18.7	19.7	19.6	12.5	13.0	14.8	13.6	13.7
Cities	26.8	27.0	25.9	25.2	24.6	15.4	14.7	16.9	15.4	15.9
Colored	20.0	30.0	24.4	19.0	26.3	10.0	15.0	12.2	25.3	----
White	26.9	27.0	25.9	25.2	24.6	15.4	14.7	16.9	15.4	16.0
Rural	17.1	17.9	17.5	18.7	18.8	12.0	12.7	14.4	13.3	13.3
Colored	1.1	6.3	10.4	16.6	18.6	6.7	7.5	8.4	6.2	6.2
White	17.1	17.9	17.5	18.7	18.8	12.0	12.7	14.4	13.3	13.3
VIRGINIA	21.7	22.6	22.4	23.5	24.3	12.4	12.5	13.0	12.6	12.0
Colored	23.1	24.2	24.2	25.2	26.1	17.8	18.0	18.2	17.9	17.0
White	21.2	22.0	21.7	22.9	23.6	10.4	10.5	11.0	10.6	10.1
Cities	19.0	20.1	19.8	20.8	21.4	14.7	14.9	15.7	15.3	14.5
Colored	19.4	20.0	20.5	21.7	22.9	20.9	21.4	22.3	21.8	20.6
White	18.8	20.1	19.5	20.4	20.7	12.1	12.2	12.8	12.4	11.8
Rural	22.7	23.5	23.2	24.4	25.3	11.5	11.6	12.1	11.7	11.2
Colored	24.6	25.8	25.5	26.5	27.4	16.6	16.6	16.7	16.4	15.6
White	22.0	22.6	22.4	23.7	24.6	9.8	9.9	10.4	10.0	9.6
WEST VIRGINIA	22.5	24.0	23.8	25.8	27.1	10.1	10.5	10.6	10.4	10.2
Colored	18.6	21.2	21.0	23.2	24.2	16.0	16.0	15.9	16.5	17.2
White	22.8	24.2	24.0	25.9	27.3	9.7	10.1	10.2	10.0	9.8
Cities	18.8	20.5	20.9	22.9	24.8	13.4	14.1	14.5	14.1	14.4
Colored	14.6	17.6	17.8	17.5	18.6	20.3	20.7	21.4	19.7	21.6
White	19.1	20.7	21.1	23.3	25.3	12.9	13.7	14.0	13.7	13.9
Rural	23.4	24.8	24.5	26.4	27.6	9.2	9.6	9.7	9.5	9.2
Colored	19.6	22.1	21.8	24.6	25.6	14.9	14.8	14.6	15.7	16.1
White	23.7	25.0	24.7	26.6	27.7	8.8	9.2	9.3	9.1	8.8

[1] Includes Negro and other nonwhite races.
[2] Registration States for which data are available and in which Negroes constitute 55 percent or more of the total colored population.
[3] Not added to the registration area until a later date.
[4] Dropped from the birth registration area in 1925; readmitted in 1928.

TABLE 17.—INFANT MORTALITY RATES (DEATHS[1] UNDER 1 YEAR OF AGE PER 1,000 LIVE BIRTHS) FOR COLORED[2] AND WHITE, IN SELECTED REGISTRATION STATES AND CITIES: 1926 TO 1931

AREA AND COLOR	1931	1930	1929	1928	1927	1926
SELECTED REGISTRATION STATES[3]						
ALABAMA	61	72	74	75	64	(4)
Colored	77	94	91	94	82	(4)
White	53	60	64	64	55	(4)
ARKANSAS	49	51	58	67	61	(4)
Colored	51	56	69	86	77	(4)
White	48	50	55	61	56	(4)
CONNECTICUT	54	56	64	59	59	72
Colored	103	110	89	106	72	81
White	52	55	64	57	58	72
DELAWARE	82	78	81	78	71	93
Colored	155	120	129	124	112	157
White	68	70	71	69	62	82
FLORIDA	64	64	65	67	67	75
Colored	91	95	94	95	93	107
White	52	50	52	55	56	62
GEORGIA	68	77	76	82	(4)	(4)
Colored	86	97	93	104	(4)	(4)
White	57	65	66	68	(4)	(4)
ILLINOIS	59	56	61	64	64	69
Colored	87	90	99	105	105	109
White	57	54	60	62	62	68
INDIANA	58	58	64	63	59	72
Colored	91	140	109	102	96	145
White	56	55	62	61	57	70
IOWA	49	54	53	53	55	59
Colored	156	153	71	109	158	124
White	48	53	52	53	55	58
KANSAS	48	53	58	59	55	65
Colored	52	60	118	127	127	152
White	48	52	56	57	53	63
KENTUCKY	65	65	71	70	61	75
Colored	137	122	130	118	109	134
White	61	62	67	66	58	71
LOUISIANA	66	78	74	78	77	(4)
Colored	85	103	98	102	109	(4)
White	53	62	59	64	58	(4)
MARYLAND	81	75	80	80	81	87
Colored	132	121	120	128	134	137
White	66	63	69	67	68	74
MASSACHUSETTS	55	60	62	64	65	73
Colored	81	98	85	97	98	102
White	54	60	61	64	64	73
MICHIGAN	57	63	66	69	68	77
Colored	94	95	109	126	102	124
White	56	61	65	68	66	76
MISSISSIPPI	56	68	72	74	67	70
Colored	67	83	85	86	78	81
White	44	51	58	61	55	59
MISSOURI	63	59	62	66	60	(4)
Colored	108	108	121	123	112	(4)
White	60	55	58	62	57	(4)
NEBRASKA	49	49	52	53	51	59
Colored	105	114	97	118	81	147
White	47	48	51	52	51	58
NEW HAMPSHIRE	57	61	68	69	69	79
Colored	----	100	----	----	77	----
White	57	61	68	69	69	79
NEW JERSEY	57	56	60	65	61	70
Colored	98	99	105	124	113	122
White	54	53	57	61	58	67
NEW YORK	57	59	61	65	59	71
Colored	104	103	111	123	109	132
White	55	57	59	63	57	68
NORTH CAROLINA	73	79	79	86	79	82
Colored	102	105	107	109	109	107
White	60	67	67	75	66	71
OHIO	60	61	69	66	62	76
Colored	106	107	120	113	103	128
White	58	58	66	64	60	73
OKLAHOMA	51	61	70	69	(4)	(4)
Colored	86	107	142	131	(4)	(4)
White	48	57	66	65	(4)	(4)
PENNSYLVANIA	67	68	71	72	69	82
Colored	115	106	106	116	112	139
White	64	66	69	70	67	80
RHODE ISLAND	61	62	72	67	67	82
Colored	69	49	94	157	140	168
White	61	62	72	66	65	81
SOUTH CAROLINA	81	89	91	97	(5)	(5)
Colored	102	108	110	115	(5)	(5)
White	59	69	72	78	(5)	(5)
TENNESSEE	68	76	77	81	71	(4)
Colored	102	115	117	121	107	(4)
White	61	69	69	73	64	(4)
VERMONT	60	65	66	65	70	72
Colored	----	----	----	91	77	----
White	60	65	66	65	70	72
VIRGINIA	76	77	79	76	75	84
Colored	108	107	107	104	106	111
White	64	65	67	64	62	72
WEST VIRGINIA	77	81	78	70	72	82
Colored	111	97	96	95	101	124
White	75	80	76	69	70	79
SELECTED REGISTRATION CITIES						
Akron, Ohio	54	55	64	69	62	82
Colored	87	(6)	(6)	(6)	(6)	(6)
White	52	(6)	(6)	(6)	(6)	(6)
Asheville, N. C	64	92	98	105	112	90
Colored	92	161	191	169	231	118
White	56	73	64	77	68	79
SELECTED REGISTRATION CITIES—Continued						
Atlanta, Ga	84	94	94	100	(4)	(4)
Colored	121	148	128	156	(4)	(4)
White	65	65	75	71	(4)	(4)
Atlantic City, N. J	76	65	72	85	80	78
Colored	98	109	105	130	113	144
White	68	52	61	71	69	61
Augusta, Ga	114	91	95	106	(4)	(4)
Colored	145	108	116	156	(4)	(4)
White	95	81	82	77	(4)	(4)
Baltimore, Md	74	65	73	82	81	83
Colored	111	94	111	124	127	128
White	64	57	62	70	70	71
Baton Rouge, La	53	62	89	72	79	(4)
Colored	49	60	118	94	134	(4)
White	56	63	75	60	51	(4)
Bessemer, Ala	96	94	87	141	77	(4)
Colored	138	115	100	195	111	(4)
White	55	73	73	85	41	(4)
Birmingham, Ala	65	78	88	95	78	(4)
Colored	86	111	124	127	111	(4)
White	53	55	65	74	58	(4)
Boston, Mass	61	70	69	77	76	84
Colored	78	90	92	79	99	117
White	60	69	68	77	76	83
Buffalo, N. Y	66	67	66	74	72	84
Colored	75	(6)	(6)	(6)	(6)	(6)
White	66	(6)	(6)	(6)	(6)	(6)
Camden, N. J	69	69	71	77	68	87
Colored	103	(6)	(6)	(6)	(6)	(6)
White	65	(6)	(6)	(6)	(6)	(6)
Charleston, S. C	119	115	127	117	(5)	(5)
Colored	171	167	197	159	(5)	(5)
White	63	57	46	69	(5)	(5)
Charleston, W. Va	119	128	101	97	113	101
Colored	202	159	129	56	127	237
White	112	125	99	101	112	90
Charlotte, N. C	82	103	96	110	89	108
Colored	142	172	142	160	158	149
White	61	78	79	90	64	93
Chattanooga, Tenn	89	108	83	130	125	(4)
Colored	151	171	150	228	202	(4)
White	72	92	64	102	97	(4)
Chester, Pa	83	78	85	82	85	100
Colored	137	143	99	127	140	120
White	70	63	82	71	72	96
Chicago, Ill	56	54	60	64	63	67
Colored	75	77	86	98	89	94
White	55	51	58	61	61	65
Cincinnati, Ohio	71	65	77	85	73	89
Colored	140	134	127	122	100	131
White	62	56	70	80	69	83
Cleveland, Ohio	53	54	61	60	56	72
Colored	77	100	95	93	84	117
White	51	50	58	57	53	67
Columbia, S. C	108	103	117	113	(5)	(5)
Colored	165	143	147	176	(5)	(5)
White	75	81	100	81	(5)	(5)
Columbus, Ga	98	95	110	116	(4)	(4)
Colored	109	91	106	118	(4)	(4)
White	89	98	112	115	(4)	(4)
Columbus, Ohio	61	71	71	73	64	75
Colored	66	100	123	100	97	122
White	61	67	65	69	59	70
Dayton, Ohio	62	55	66	67	71	84
Colored	118	(6)	(6)	(6)	(6)	(6)
White	57	(6)	(6)	(6)	(6)	(6)
Detroit, Mich	56	65	69	77	70	84
Colored	85	90	106	122	95	114
White	53	62	66	74	68	82
Durham, N. C	82	82	99	98	97	107
Colored	127	129	146	144	144	173
White	59	56	72	71	72	77
East St. Louis, Ill	79	80	88	68	91	101
Colored	203	159	147	100	172	185
White	58	67	79	62	77	85
Fort Smith, Ark	56	64	49	44	99	(4)
Colored	149	98	82	122	156	(4)
White	49	60	46	39	93	(4)
Gary, Ind	63	68	72	70	62	98
Colored	86	(6)	(6)	(6)	(6)	(6)
White	59	(6)	(6)	(6)	(6)	(6)
Greensboro, N. C	82	73	77	92	102	101
Colored	133	126	127	189	183	187
White	67	57	62	65	76	77
Greenville, S. C	101	118	153	102	(5)	(5)
Colored	146	146	177	116	(5)	(5)
White	66	95	134	92	(5)	(5)
High Point, N. C	68	96	93	96	79	98
Colored	93	182	238	152	63	114
White	65	83	71	86	81	95
Indianapolis, Ind	58	64	68	66	62	77
Colored	71	122	110	94	91	123
White	56	55	61	62	57	70
Jackson, Miss	79	77	85	100	77	95
Colored	94	117	100	124	111	126
White	70	52	73	82	51	69
Jacksonville, Fla	56	67	73	67	65	83
Colored	63	105	114	112	95	117
White	53	50	52	46	50	66
Jersey City, N. J	74	72	67	85	63	67
Colored	127	(6)	(6)	(6)	(6)	(6)
White	71	(6)	(6)	(6)	(6)	(6)

See footnotes at end of table.

TABLE 17.—INFANT MORTALITY RATES (DEATHS[1] UNDER 1 YEAR OF AGE PER 1,000 LIVE BIRTHS), FOR COLORED[2] AND WHITE, IN SELECTED REGISTRATION STATES AND CITIES: 1926 TO 1931—Continued

AREA AND COLOR	1931	1930	1929	1928	1927	1926
SELECTED REGISTRATION CITIES—Continued						
Kansas City, Kans	66	66	72	74	75	84
Colored	39	59	140	89	158	122
White	72	68	64	71	63	78
Kansas City, Mo	69	68	74	76	70	(4)
Colored	126	100	98	153	110	(4)
White	63	64	72	69	66	(4)
Knoxville, Tenn	81	81	80	92	77	(4)
Colored	110	93	135	153	146	(4)
White	78	80	75	85	69	(4)
Lexington, Ky	116	86	87	68	89	97
Colored	227	122	166	105	242	158
White	87	78	72	61	54	83
Little Rock, Ark	72	49	77	79	76	(4)
Colored	107	65	137	111	91	(4)
White	62	45	61	71	71	(4)
Louisville, Ky	77	67	72	81	66	94
Colored	144	96	108	129	80	170
White	67	63	66	75	64	83
Lynchburg, Va	81	86	102	82	68	101
Colored	108	114	150	137	137	146
White	73	78	86	65	46	86
Macon, Ga	63	92	76	84	(4)	(4)
Colored	84	120	102	122	(4)	(4)
White	43	71	54	56	(4)	(4)
Memphis, Tenn	102	102	95	90	80	(4)
Colored	137	139	137	130	108	(4)
White	83	81	73	67	64	(4)
Meridian, Miss	104	72	94	86	82	61
Colored	136	119	125	103	102	100
White	89	48	79	74	72	45
Miami, Fla	57	58	48	67	72	88
Colored	101	94	67	106	116	158
White	40	44	39	50	55	60
Mobile, Ala	65	86	97	91	73	(4)
Colored	91	125	132	126	104	(4)
White	51	64	76	71	54	(4)
Monroe, La	90	82	91	108	85	(4)
Colored	109	93	76	111	94	(4)
White	82	79	95	107	81	(4)
Montclair, N. J	34	33	62	61	73	71
Colored	86	53	34	130	74	78
White	30	30	67	52	72	69
Montgomery, Ala	81	99	74	96	69	(4)
Colored	117	141	121	121	108	(4)
White	52	67	40	78	42	(4)
Muskogee, Okla	72	66	62	104	(4)	(4)
Colored	106	101	126	159	(4)	(4)
White	63	57	43	90	(4)	(4)
Nashville, Tenn	87	99	98	100	71	(4)
Colored	120	138	122	138	103	(4)
White	76	87	90	89	61	(4)
Newark, N. J	49	51	58	61	61	70
Colored	84	97	133	127	132	127
White	44	45	48	53	52	64
New Orleans, La	75	88	80	78	88	(4)
Colored	104	120	117	111	135	(4)
White	60	71	61	62	65	(4)
Newport News, Va	65	79	79	80	83	107
Colored	94	127	121	111	117	140
White	46	47	50	58	56	71
New York, N. Y	56	58	59	65	56	68
Colored	106	105	111	128	108	131
White	52	55	56	62	53	65
Norfolk, Va	72	75	87	77	86	90
Colored	126	139	155	125	148	152
White	44	44	51	49	48	50
Oklahoma City, Okla	62	83	66	68	(4)	(4)
Colored	112	(6)	(6)	(6)	(4)	(4)
White	58	(6)	(6)	(6)	(4)	(4)
Omaha, Nebr	54	50	58	57	59	64
Colored	85	47	54	53	40	79
White	52	50	59	57	60	64
Orange, N. J	38	37	44	46	42	50
Colored	89	33	101	72	63	116
White	34	38	38	44	40	44
Pensacola, Fla	68	106	52	77	97	113
Colored	125	232	64	116	152	181
White	54	69	49	66	84	97
Petersburg, Va	111	102	151	141	110	137
Colored	150	113	205	184	152	182
White	77	93	100	103	68	102
Philadelphia, Pa	64	64	62	71	64	78
Colored	103	100	99	117	103	134
White	58	58	56	63	58	70
Pittsburgh, Pa	70	69	73	75	72	82
Colored	114	108	111	111	112	119
White	65	65	70	71	68	78
Portsmouth, Va	106	74	114	108	153	109
Colored	174	104	185	170	223	161
White	51	50	56	58	83	60
Raleigh, N. C	96	105	90	108	94	86
Colored	130	105	110	154	143	133
White	77	105	80	87	68	61
Richmond, Va	78	73	81	85	80	107
Colored	119	119	131	133	113	164
White	57	51	55	59	61	76
Roanoke, Va	80	98	86	102	86	103
Colored	104	168	148	204	116	147
White	75	84	74	80	80	94
St. Louis, Mo	63	54	59	63	57	(4)
Colored	89	89	107	90	93	(4)
White	60	49	52	60	53	(4)
St. Petersburg, Fla	52	55	67	71	67	54
Colored	99	103	103	146	99	69
White	39	40	51	48	55	49
Savannah, Ga	86	84	94	102	(4)	(4)
Colored	134	130	136	143	(4)	(4)
White	52	49	62	74	(4)	(4)
Seattle, Wash	41	38	46	43	41	47
Colored	54	59	48	40	54	39
White	40	37	46	43	41	47
Shreveport, La	89	87	90	100	82	(4)
Colored	119	121	146	155	126	(4)
White	68	67	63	76	63	(4)
Spartanburg, S. C	87	98	88	127	(5)	(5)
Colored	147	158	95	172	(5)	(5)
White	59	75	86	109	(5)	(5)
Springfield, Ohio	59	69	79	67	69	82
Colored	155	92	133	164	116	317
White	48	66	71	57	64	60
Tampa, Fla	66	58	61	53	62	86
Colored	136	127	114	105	93	177
White	50	43	50	41	55	67
Toledo, Ohio	56	56	70	65	62	82
Colored	101	(6)	(6)	(6)	(6)	(6)
White	54	(6)	(6)	(6)	(6)	(6)
Tulsa, Okla	52	76	65	82	(4)	(4)
Colored	99	183	148	190	(4)	(4)
White	48	68	58	73	(4)	(4)
Vicksburg, Miss	89	93	114	100	87	85
Colored	114	128	145	124	95	119
White	67	63	86	77	78	54
Washington, D. C	67	71	71	65	68	85
Colored	115	110	117	107	109	123
White	44	52	48	46	49	67
West Palm Beach, Fla	55	53	(6)	(6)	(6)	(6)
Colored	103	111	(6)	(6)	(6)	(6)
White	30	27	(6)	(6)	(6)	(6)
Wilmington, Del	70	71	75	71	71	87
Colored	105	74	112	122	108	142
White	65	70	70	65	66	81
Wilmington, N. C	108	85	83	114	128	112
Colored	170	92	102	118	183	129
White	71	82	72	112	95	101
Winston-Salem, N. C	109	103	100	110	122	108
Colored	167	159	154	162	178	200
White	69	67	69	79	89	58
Youngstown, Ohio	58	58	72	71	65	85
Colored	76	(6)	(6)	(6)	(6)	(6)
White	56	(6)	(6)	(6)	(6)	(6)

[1] Exclusive of stillbirths.
[2] Includes Negro and other nonwhite races.
[3] States in which the Negro population constitutes 55 percent or more of the total colored population, and cities of such States where data by color are available.
[4] Not added to the birth registration area until a later date.
[5] Dropped from the birth registration area in 1925; readmitted in 1928.
[6] Rate by color not available.

TABLE 18.—COLORED[1] AND WHITE POPULATION, BIRTHS AND DEATHS, INFANT MORTALITY, AND STILLBIRTHS, IN SELECTED REGISTRATION STATES, CITIES, AND COUNTIES: 1931 AND 1930

[Data are included for States in which the Negro population constitutes 55 percent or more of the total colored population, and cities and counties of such States in which data by color are available. "Cities" includes municipalities of 10,000 inhabitants or more in 1930; "Incorporated places" includes minor cities with populations from 2,500 to 10,000 in 1930; the remainder of the State is included in "Rural"]

AREA AND COLOR	POPULATION ESTIMATED AS OF JULY 1		BIRTHS AND DEATHS (Exclusive of stillbirths): Number: Births		Number: Deaths		Rate per 1,000 population: Births		Rate per 1,000 population: Deaths		Excess of births over deaths [2]		Births per 100 deaths		INFANT MORTALITY (Exclusive of stillbirths): Deaths of infants under 1 year of age: Number		Per 1,000 births		STILLBIRTHS: Number		Rate per 100 live births	
	1931	1930	1931	1930	1931	1930	1931	1930	1931	1930	1931	1930	1931	1930	1931	1930	1931	1930	1931	1930	1931	1930
SELECTED STATES																						
ALABAMA	2,669,000	2,654,000	62,743	63,757	28,431	30,422	23.5	24.0	10.7	11.5	34,312	33,335	221	210	3,855	4,599	61.4	72.1	3,065	3,360	4.9	5.3
Colored	949,000	947,000	22,914	22,977	13,315	14,412	24.1	24.3	14.0	15.2	9,599	8,565	172	159	1,757	2,157	76.7	93.9	1,702	1,878	7.4	8.2
White	1,720,009	1,707,000	39,829	40,780	15,116	16,010	23.2	23.9	8.8	9.4	24,713	24,770	263	255	2,098	2,442	52.7	59.9	1,363	1,482	3.4	3.6
Cities	597,800	583,300	11,703	12,014	8,802	9,061	19.6	20.6	14.7	15.5	2,901	2,953	133	133	888	1,014	75.9	84.4	640	745	5.5	6.2
Colored	228,300	223,600	4,288	4,454	4,336	4,516	18.8	19.9	19.0	20.2	−48	−62	99	99	448	542	104.5	121.7	358	431	8.3	9.7
White	369,500	359,700	7,415	7,560	4,466	4,545	20.1	21.0	12.1	12.6	2,949	3,015	166	166	440	472	59.3	62.4	282	314	3.8	4.2
Incorporated places	170,600	165,900	4,400	4,820	2,423	2,733	25.8	29.1	14.2	16.5	1,977	2,087	182	176	249	354	56.6	73.4	219	259	5.0	5.4
Colored	48,000	46,700	1,215	1,273	945	1,082	25.3	27.3	19.7	23.2	270	191	129	118	82	132	67.5	103.7	110	124	9.1	9.7
White	122,600	119,200	3,185	3,547	1,478	1,651	26.0	29.8	12.1	13.9	1,707	1,896	215	215	167	222	52.4	62.6	109	135	3.4	3.8
Rural	1,900,600	1,904,800	46,640	46,923	17,206	18,628	24.5	24.6	9.1	9.8	29,434	28,295	271	252	2,718	3,231	58.3	68.9	2,206	2,356	4.7	5.0
Colored	672,700	676,700	17,411	17,250	8,034	8,814	25.9	25.5	11.9	13.0	9,377	8,436	217	196	1,227	1,483	70.5	86.0	1,234	1,323	7.1	7.7
White	1,227,900	1,228,100	29,229	29,673	9,172	9,814	23.8	24.2	7.5	8.0	20,057	19,859	319	302	1,491	1,748	51.0	58.9	972	1,033	3.3	3.5
ARKANSAS	1,862,000	1,857,000	41,042	41,093	17,847	18,950	22.0	22.1	9.6	10.2	23,195	22,143	230	217	2,013	2,115	49.0	51.5	1,596	1,776	3.9	4.3
Colored	480,000	480,000	9,467	9,093	5,693	6,466	19.7	18.9	11.9	13.5	3,774	2,627	166	141	483	512	51.0	56.3	661	752	7.0	8.3
White	1,382,000	1,377,000	31,575	32,000	12,154	12,484	22.8	23.2	8.8	9.1	19,421	19,516	260	256	1,530	1,603	48.5	50.1	935	1,024	3.0	3.2
Cities	227,300	222,300	3,621	3,934	3,792	4,069	15.9	17.7	16.7	18.3	−171	−135	95	97	251	232	69.3	59.0	181	208	5.0	5.3
Colored	51,900	50,900	727	764	1,195	1,344	14.0	15.0	23.0	26.4	−468	−580	61	57	66	55	90.8	72.0	82	93	11.3	12.2
White	175,400	171,400	2,894	3,170	2,597	2,725	16.5	18.5	14.8	15.9	297	445	111	116	185	177	63.9	55.8	99	115	3.4	3.6
Incorporated places	164,700	162,300	2,930	3,300	2,204	2,285	17.8	20.3	13.4	14.1	726	1,015	133	144	178	183	60.8	55.5	116	157	4.0	4.8
Colored	39,400	38,800	659	767	783	831	16.7	19.8	19.9	21.4	−124	−64	84	92	56	61	85.0	79.5	40	67	6.1	8.7
White	125,300	123,500	2,271	2,533	1,421	1,454	18.1	20.5	11.3	11.8	850	1,079	160	174	122	122	53.7	48.2	76	90	3.3	3.6
Rural	1,470,000	1,472,400	34,491	33,859	11,851	12,596	23.5	23.0	8.1	8.6	22,640	21,263	291	269	1,584	1,700	45.9	50.2	1,299	1,411	3.8	4.2
Colored	388,700	390,300	8,081	7,562	3,715	4,291	20.8	19.4	9.6	11.0	4,366	3,271	218	176	361	396	44.7	52.4	539	592	6.7	7.8
White	1,081,300	1,082,100	26,410	26,297	8,136	8,305	24.4	24.3	7.5	7.7	18,274	17,992	325	317	1,223	1,304	46.3	49.6	760	819	2.9	3.1
CONNECTICUT	1,624,000	1,612,000	25,555	27,693	17,246	17,287	15.7	17.2	10.6	10.7	8,309	10,406	148	160	1,375	1,551	53.8	56.0	692	807	2.7	2.9
Colored	31,000	30,000	687	736	525	523	22.2	24.5	16.9	17.4	162	213	131	141	71	81	103.3	110.1	35	37	5.1	5.0
White	1,593,000	1,582,000	24,868	26,957	16,721	16,764	15.6	17.0	10.5	10.6	8,147	10,193	149	161	1,304	1,470	52.4	54.5	657	770	2.6	2.9
Cities	1,096,700	1,084,600	20,412	22,036	12,255	12,166	18.6	20.3	11.2	11.2	8,157	9,870	167	181	1,124	1,244	55.1	56.5	558	656	2.7	3.0
Colored	25,400	24,900	629	673	452	435	24.8	27.0	17.8	17.5	177	238	139	155	66	67	104.9	99.6	34	32	5.4	4.8
White	1,071,300	1,059,700	19,783	21,363	11,803	11,731	18.5	20.2	11.0	11.1	7,980	9,632	168	182	1,058	1,177	53.5	55.1	524	624	2.6	2.9
Incorporated places	50,200	50,000	1,054	1,077	577	606	21.0	21.5	11.5	12.1	477	471	183	178	45	58	42.7	53.9	41	25	3.9	2.3
Colored	500	400	21	14	7	13	42.0	35.0	14.0	32.5	14	1	(4)	(4)	1	1	47.6	71.4	1	1	4.8	7.1
White	49,700	49,600	1,033	1,063	570	593	20.8	21.4	11.5	12.0	463	470	181	179	44	57	42.6	53.6	40	24	3.9	2.3
Rural	477,100	477,400	4,089	4,580	4,414	4,515	8.6	9.6	9.3	9.5	−325	65	93	101	206	249	50.4	54.4	93	126	2.3	2.8
Colored	5,100	4,700	37	49	66	75	7.3	10.4	12.9	16.0	−29	−26	(4)	(4)	4	13	108.1	265.3	-----	4	-----	8.2
White	472,000	472,700	4,052	4,531	4,348	4,440	8.6	9.6	9.2	9.4	−296	91	93	102	202	236	49.9	52.1	93	122	2.3	2.7
DELAWARE	240,000	239,000	4,237	4,474	3,301	3,256	17.7	18.7	13.8	13.6	936	1,218	128	137	346	351	81.7	78.5	174	194	4.1	4.3
Colored	33,000	33,000	685	728	696	707	20.8	22.1	21.1	21.4	−11	21	98	103	106	87	154.7	119.5	41	57	6.0	7.8
White	207,000	206,000	3,552	3,746	2,605	2,549	17.2	18.2	12.6	12.4	947	1,197	136	147	240	264	67.6	70.5	133	137	3.7	3.7
Cities	106,597	106,597	2,200	2,305	1,479	1,560	20.6	21.6	13.9	14.6	721	745	149	148	153	163	69.5	70.7	75	121	3.4	5.2
Colored	12,138	12,138	228	242	254	280	18.8	19.9	20.9	23.1	−26	−38	90	86	24	18	105.3	74.4	14	34	6.1	14.0
White	94,459	94,459	1,972	2,063	1,225	1,280	20.9	21.8	13.0	13.6	747	783	161	161	129	145	65.4	70.3	61	87	3.1	4.2
Incorporated places	17,000	16,600	407	413	318	297	23.9	24.9	18.7	17.9	89	116	128	139	33	33	81.1	79.9	27	21	6.6	5.1
Colored	3,000	2,900	79	62	83	74	26.3	21.4	27.7	25.5	−4	−12	(4)	(4)	18	10	227.8	161.3	6	5	7.6	8.1
White	14,000	13,700	328	351	235	223	23.4	25.6	16.8	16.3	93	128	140	157	15	23	45.7	65.5	21	16	6.4	4.6
Rural	116,400	115,800	1,630	1,756	1,504	1,399	14.0	15.2	12.9	12.1	126	357	108	126	160	155	98.2	88.3	72	52	4.4	3.0
Colored	17,900	18,000	378	424	359	353	21.1	23.6	20.1	19.6	19	71	105	120	64	59	169.3	139.2	21	18	5.6	4.2
White	98,500	97,800	1,252	1,332	1,145	1,046	12.7	13.6	11.6	10.7	107	286	109	127	96	96	76.7	72.1	51	34	4.1	2.6
FLORIDA	1,506,000	1,480,000	27,033	26,993	18,102	18,229	18.0	18.2	12.0	12.3	8,931	8,764	149	148	1,728	1,733	63.9	64.2	1,523	1,753	5.6	6.5
Colored	440,000	435,000	8,370	8,391	7,045	7,182	19.0	19.3	16.0	16.5	1,325	1,209	119	117	761	801	90.9	95.5	833	1,006	10.0	12.0
White	1,066,000	1,045,000	18,663	18,602	11,057	11,047	17.5	17.8	10.4	10.6	7,606	7,555	169	168	967	932	51.8	50.1	690	747	3.7	4.0
Cities	576,800	562,100	10,105	10,378	7,911	7,869	17.5	18.5	13.7	14.0	2,194	2,509	128	132	627	665	62.0	64.1	613	690	6.1	6.6
Colored	160,400	157,500	2,725	2,745	2,896	2,939	17.0	17.4	18.1	18.7	−171	−194	94	93	265	302	97.2	110.0	324	373	11.9	13.6
White	416,400	404,600	7,380	7,633	5,015	4,930	17.7	18.9	12.0	12.2	2,365	2,703	147	155	362	363	49.1	47.6	289	317	3.9	4.2
Incorporated places	214,500	203,800	4,157	4,028	3,544	3,473	19.4	19.8	16.5	17.0	613	555	117	116	278	253	66.9	62.8	208	235	5.0	5.8
Colored	57,600	54,700	1,167	1,167	1,299	1,290	20.3	21.3	22.6	23.6	−132	−123	90	90	115	114	98.5	97.7	104	143	8.9	12.3
White	156,900	149,100	2,990	2,861	2,245	2,183	19.1	19.2	14.3	14.6	745	678	133	131	163	139	54.5	48.6	104	92	3.5	3.2
Rural	714,700	714,100	12,771	12,587	6,647	6,887	17.9	17.6	9.3	9.6	6,124	5,700	192	183	823	815	64.4	64.7	702	828	5.5	6.6
Colored	222,000	222,800	4,478	4,479	2,850	2,953	20.2	20.1	12.8	13.3	1,628	1,526	157	152	381	385	85.1	86.0	405	490	9.0	10.9
White	492,700	491,300	8,293	8,108	3,797	3,934	16.8	16.5	7.7	8.0	4,496	4,174	218	206	442	430	53.3	53.0	297	338	3.6	4.2

GEORGIA	2,909,000	2,909,000	61,780	60,689	32,992	35,183	21.2	20.9	11.3	12.1	28,788	25,506	187	172	4,217	4,700	68.3	77.4	3,679	3,795	6.0	6.3
Colored	1,061,000	1,068,000	24,265	23,404	16,004	17,190	22.9	21.9	15.1	16.1	8,261	6,214	152	136	2,090	2,259	86.1	96.5	2,255	2,340	9.3	10.0
White	1,848,000	1,841,000	37,515	37,285	16,988	17,993	20.3	20.3	9.2	9.8	20,527	19,292	221	207	2,127	2,441	56.7	65.5	1,424	1,455	3.8	3.9
Cities	677,800	668,000	13,366	13,637	11,198	11,554	19.7	20.4	16.5	17.3	2,168	2,083	119	118	1,129	1,230	84.5	90.2	958	933	7.2	6.8
Colored	249,200	245,600	5,001	5,036	5,773	6,088	20.1	20.5	23.2	24.8	−772	−1,052	87	83	604	641	120.8	127.3	604	585	12.1	11.6
White	428,600	422,400	8,365	8,601	5,425	5,466	19.5	20.4	12.7	12.9	2,940	3,135	154	157	525	589	62.8	68.5	354	348	4.2	4.0
Rural [6]	2,231,200	2,241,000	48,414	47,052	21,794	23,629	21.7	21.0	9.8	10.5	26,620	23,423	222	199	3,088	3,470	63.8	73.7	2,721	2,862	5.6	6.1
Colored	811,800	822,400	19,264	18,368	10,231	11,102	23.7	22.3	12.6	13.5	9,033	7,266	188	165	1,486	1,618	77.1	88.1	1,651	1,755	8.6	9.6
White	1,419,400	1,418,600	29,150	28,684	11,563	12,527	20.5	20.2	8.1	8.8	17,587	16,157	252	229	1,602	1,852	55.0	64.6	1,070	1,107	3.7	3.9
ILLINOIS	7,718,000	7,659,000	118,788	128,121	85,788	83,591	15.4	16.7	11.1	10.9	33,000	44,530	138	153	6,961	7,152	58.6	55.8	4,080	4,311	3.4	3.4
Colored	378,000	369,000	6,519	6,013	6,361	5,961	17.2	16.3	16.8	16.2	158	52	102	101	564	539	86.5	89.6	389	385	6.0	6.4
White	7,340,000	7,290,000	112,269	122,108	79,427	77,630	15.3	16.8	10.8	10.6	32,842	44,478	141	157	6,397	6,613	57.0	54.2	3,691	3,926	3.3	3.2
Cities	5,097,900	4,993,900	81,004	88,993	55,542	54,664	15.9	17.8	10.9	10.9	25,462	34,329	146	163	4,675	4,831	57.7	54.3	2,921	3,147	3.6	3.5
Colored	339,700	323,400	5,934	5,583	5,269	4,941	17.5	17.3	15.5	15.3	665	632	113	113	485	478	81.7	85.6	346	355	5.8	6.4
White	4,758,200	4,670,500	75,070	83,410	50,273	49,713	15.8	17.9	10.6	10.6	24,797	33,697	149	168	4,190	4,353	55.8	52.2	2,575	2,792	3.4	3.3
Incorporated places	683,100	670,100	10,583	11,418	7,742	7,580	15.5	17.0	11.3	11.3	2,841	3,838	137	151	653	694	61.7	60.8	325	363	3.1	3.2
Colored	16,000	15,800	197	167	250	251	12.3	10.6	15.6	15.9	−53	−84	79	67	26	25	132.0	149.7	14	12	7.1	7.2
White	667,100	654,300	10,386	11,251	7,492	7,329	15.6	17.2	11.2	11.2	2,894	3,922	139	154	627	669	60.4	59.5	311	351	3.0	3.1
Rural	1,937,000	1,995,000	27,201	27,710	22,504	21,347	14.0	13.9	11.6	10.7	4,697	6,363	121	130	1,633	1,627	60.0	58.7	834	801	3.1	2.9
Colored	22,300	29,800	388	263	842	759	17.4	8.8	37.8	25.5	−454	−496	46	35	53	36	136.6	136.9	29	18	7.5	6.8
White	1,914,700	1,965,200	26,813	27,447	21,662	20,588	14.0	14.0	11.3	10.5	5,151	6,859	124	133	1,580	1,591	58.9	58.0	805	783	3.0	2.9
INDIANA	3,262,000	3,246,000	55,973	59,278	38,699	39,196	17.2	18.3	11.9	12.1	17,274	20,082	145	151	3,224	3,423	57.6	57.7	1,628	1,754	2.9	3.0
Colored	126,000	123,000	1,856	1,985	2,039	2,313	14.7	16.1	16.2	18.8	−183	−328	91	86	168	278	90.5	140.1	111	114	6.0	5.7
White	3,136,000	3,123,000	54,117	57,293	36,660	36,883	17.3	18.3	11.7	11.8	17,457	20,410	148	155	3,056	3,145	56.5	54.9	1,517	1,640	2.8	2.9
Cities	1,532,900	1,504,600	27,386	29,891	17,974	18,611	17.9	19.9	11.7	12.4	9,412	11,280	152	161	1,645	1,832	60.1	61.3	841	961	3.1	3.2
Colored	113,800	109,800	1,742	1,824	1,709	1,931	15.3	16.6	15.0	17.6	33	−107	102	94	152	249	87.3	136.5	101	106	5.8	5.8
White	1,419,100	1,394,800	25,644	28,067	16,265	16,680	18.1	20.1	11.5	12.0	9,379	11,387	158	168	1,493	1,583	58.2	56.4	740	855	2.9	3.0
Incorporated places	299,200	298,200	5,315	5,968	4,286	4,309	17.8	20.0	14.3	14.5	1,029	1,659	124	139	331	364	62.3	61.0	164	168	3.1	2.8
Colored	3,900	3,900	37	44	72	90	9.5	11.3	18.5	23.1	−35	−46	[4]	[4]	7	11	189.2	250.0	2	3	5.4	6.8
White	295,300	294,300	5,278	5,924	4,214	4,219	17.9	20.1	14.3	14.3	1,064	1,705	125	140	324	353	61.4	59.6	162	165	3.1	2.8
Rural	1,429,900	1,443,200	23,272	23,419	16,439	16,276	16.3	16.2	11.5	11.3	6,833	7,143	142	144	1,248	1,227	53.6	52.4	623	625	2.7	2.7
Colored	8,300	9,300	77	117	258	292	9.3	12.6	31.1	81.4	−181	−175	30	40	9	18	116.9	153.8	8	5	10.4	7.4
White	1,421,600	1,433,900	23,195	23,302	16,181	15,984	16.3	16.3	11.4	11.1	7,014	7,318	143	146	1,239	1,209	53.4	51.9	615	620	2.7	2.7
IOWA	2,476,000	2,473,000	41,943	42,733	25,681	26,228	16.9	17.3	10.4	10.6	16,262	16,505	163	163	2,055	2,303	49.0	53.9	1,333	1,340	3.2	3.1
Colored	23,000	23,000	250	288	326	363	10.9	12.5	14.2	15.8	−76	−75	77	79	39	44	156.0	152.8	14	27	5.6	9.4
White	2,453,000	2,450,000	41,693	42,445	25,355	25,865	17.0	17.3	10.3	10.6	16,338	16,580	164	164	2,016	2,259	48.4	53.2	1,319	1,313	3.2	3.1
Cities	727,000	718,600	14,440	14,763	9,656	9,940	19.9	20.5	13.3	13.8	4,784	4,823	150	149	780	922	54.0	62.5	553	521	3.8	3.5
Colored	16,700	16,600	210	234	242	276	12.6	14.1	14.5	16.6	−32	−42	87	85	26	29	123.8	123.9	11	26	5.2	11.1
White	710,300	702,000	14,230	14,529	9,414	9,664	20.0	20.7	13.3	13.8	4,816	4,865	151	150	754	893	53.0	61.5	542	495	3.8	3.4
Incorporated places	264,600	263,200	5,746	5,864	4,839	4,731	21.7	22.3	18.3	18.0	907	1,133	119	124	351	362	61.1	61.7	226	209	3.9	3.6
Colored	2,300	2,400	16	23	42	31	7.0	9.6	18.3	12.9	−26	−8	[4]	[4]	6	6	375.0	260.9	------	1	------	4.3
White	262,300	260,800	5,730	5,841	4,797	4,700	21.8	22.4	18.3	18.0	933	1,141	119	124	345	356	60.2	60.9	226	208	3.9	3.6
Rural	1,484,400	1,491,200	21,757	22,106	11,186	11,557	14.7	14.8	7.5	7.8	10,571	10,549	195	191	924	1,019	42.5	46.1	554	610	2.5	2.8
Colored	4,000	4,000	24	31	42	56	6.0	7.8	10.5	14.0	−18	−25	[4]	[4]	7	9	291.7	290.3	3	------	12.5	------
White	1,480,400	1,487,200	21,733	22,075	11,144	11,501	14.7	14.8	7.5	7.7	10,589	10,574	195	192	917	1,010	42.2	45.8	551	610	2.5	2.8
KANSAS	1,889,000	1,884,000	32,794	33,707	18,618	19,505	17.4	17.9	9.9	10.4	14,176	14,202	176	173	1,571	1,772	47.9	52.6	952	1,048	2.9	3.1
Colored	89,000	89,000	1,491	1,540	1,144	1,102	16.8	17.3	12.9	12.4	347	438	130	140	77	92	51.6	59.7	69	78	4.6	5.1
White	1,800,000	1,795,000	31,303	32,167	17,474	18,403	17.4	17.9	9.7	10.3	13,829	13,764	179	175	1,494	1,680	47.7	52.2	883	970	2.8	3.0
Cities	551,300	543,200	10,378	10,871	6,520	7,071	18.8	20.0	11.8	13.0	3,858	3,800	159	154	518	632	49.9	58.1	358	378	3.4	3.5
Colored	57,000	55,900	944	979	769	765	16.6	17.5	13.5	13.7	175	214	123	128	52	63	55.1	64.4	57	56	6.0	5.7
White	494,300	487,300	9,434	9,892	5,751	6,306	19.1	20.3	11.6	12.9	3,683	3,586	164	157	466	569	49.4	57.5	301	322	3.2	3.3
Incorporated places	191,100	189,200	4,519	4,575	2,629	2,794	23.6	24.2	13.8	14.8	1,890	1,781	172	164	236	260	52.2	56.8	155	189	3.4	4.1
Colored	7,600	7,600	161	151	81	76	21.2	19.9	10.7	10.0	80	75	[4]	[4]	9	14	55.9	92.7	6	7	3.7	4.6
White	183,500	181,600	4,358	4,424	2,548	2,718	23.7	24.4	13.9	15.0	1,810	1,706	171	163	227	246	52.1	55.6	149	182	3.4	4.1
Rural	1,146,600	1,151,600	17,897	18,261	9,469	9,640	15.6	15.9	8.3	8.4	8,428	8,621	189	189	817	880	45.7	48.2	439	481	2.5	2.6
Colored	24,400	25,500	386	410	294	261	15.8	16.1	12.0	10.2	92	149	131	157	16	15	41.5	36.6	6	15	1.6	3.7
White	1,122,200	1,126,100	17,511	17,851	9,175	9,379	15.6	15.9	8.2	8.3	8,336	8,472	191	190	801	865	45.7	48.5	433	466	2.5	2.6
KENTUCKY	2,630,000	2,619,000	57,120	59,262	28,905	29,562	21.7	22.6	11.0	11.3	28,215	29,700	198	200	3,713	3,876	65.0	65.4	2,027	2,020	3.5	3.4
Colored	226,000	226,000	3,256	3,381	4,549	4,750	14.4	15.0	20.1	21.0	−1,293	−1,369	72	71	445	413	136.7	122.2	258	243	7.9	7.2
White	2,404,000	2,393,000	53,864	55,881	24,356	24,812	22.4	23.4	10.1	10.4	29,508	31,069	221	225	3,268	3,463	60.7	62.0	1,769	1,777	3.3	3.2
Cities	606,400	601,900	10,727	11,700	9,029	9,181	17.7	19.4	14.9	15.3	1,698	2,519	119	127	837	867	78.0	74.1	402	433	3.7	3.7
Colored	87,400	87,300	1,207	1,249	2,076	2,190	13.8	14.3	23.8	25.1	−869	−941	58	57	195	134	161.6	107.3	89	110	7.4	8.8
White	519,000	514,600	9,520	10,451	6,953	6,991	18.3	20.3	13.4	13.6	2,567	3,460	137	149	642	733	67.4	70.1	313	323	3.3	3.1
Rural [6]	2,023,600	2,017,100	46,393	47,562	19,876	20,381	22.9	23.6	9.8	10.1	26,517	27,181	233	233	2,876	3,009	62.0	63.3	1,625	1,587	3.5	3.3
Colored	138,600	138,700	2,049	2,132	2,473	2,560	14.8	15.4	17.8	18.5	−424	−428	83	83	250	279	122.0	130.9	169	133	8.2	6.2
White	1,885,000	1,878,400	44,344	45,430	17,403	17,821	23.5	24.2	9.2	9.5	26,941	27,609	255	255	2,626	2,730	59.2	60.1	1,456	1,454	3.3	3.2
LOUISIANA	2,125,000	2,109,000	43,369	42,890	23,535	24,707	20.4	20.3	11.1	11.7	19,834	18,183	184	174	2,856	3,352	65.9	78.2	2,148	2,243	5.0	5.2
Colored	790,000	785,000	17,058	16,731	11,262	12,086	21.6	21.3	14.3	15.4	5,796	4,645	151	138	1,449	1,730	84.9	103.4	1,204	1,262	7.1	7.5
White	1,335,000	1,324,000	26,311	26,159	12,273	12,621	19.7	19.8	9.2	9.5	14,038	13,538	214	207	1,407	1,622	53.5	62.0	944	981	3.6	3.8
Cities	676,000	663,000	13,454	13,654	10,892	11,434	19.9	20.6	16.1	17.2	2,562	2,220	124	119	1,018	1,197	75.7	87.7	637	732	4.7	5.4
Colored	209,600	205,400	4,763	4,664	4,709	4,937	22.7	22.7	22.5	24.0	54	−273	101	94	489	561	102.7	120.3	312	343	6.6	7.4
White	466,400	457,600	8,691	8,990	6,183	6,497	18.6	19.6	13.3	14.2	2,508	2,493	141	138	529	636	60.9	70.7	325	389	3.7	4.3
Incorporated places	179,600	175,000	4,379	4,858	2,860	2,941	24.4	27.8	15.9	16.8	1,519	1,917	153	165	361	362	82.4	74.5	254	242	5.8	5.0
Colored	56,500	55,100	1,586	1,758	1,431	1,505	28.1	31.9	25.3	27.3	155	253	111	117	200	188	126.1	106.9	135	150	8.5	8.5
White	123,100	119,900	2,793	3,100	1,429	1,436	22.7	25.9	11.6	12.0	1,364	1,664	195	216	161	174	57.6	56.1	119	92	4.3	3.0
Rural	1,269,400	1,271,000	25,536	24,378	9,783	10,332	20.1	19.2	7.7	8.1	15,753	14,046	261	236	1,477	1,793	57.8	73.5	1,257	1,269	4.9	5.2
Colored	523,900	524,500	10,709	10,309	5,122	5,644	20.4	19.7	9.8	10.8	5,587	4,665	209	183	760	981	71.0	95.2	757	769	7.1	7.5
White	745,500	746,500	14,827	14,069	4,661	4,688	19.9	18.8	6.3	6.3	10,166	9,381	318	300	717	812	48.4	57.7	500	500	3.4	3.6

See footnotes at end of table.

TABLE 18.—COLORED [1] AND WHITE POPULATION, BIRTHS AND DEATHS, INFANT MORTALITY, AND STILLBIRTHS, IN SELECTED REGISTRATION STATES, CITIES, AND COUNTIES: 1931 AND 1930—Continued

[See note at head of this table]

AREA AND COLOR	POPULATION ESTIMATED AS OF JULY 1		BIRTHS AND DEATHS (Exclusive of stillbirths)												INFANT MORTALITY (Exclusive of stillbirths)				STILLBIRTHS			
			Number				Rate per 1,000 population				Excess of births over deaths [2]		Births per 100 deaths		Deaths of infants under 1 year of age				Number		Rate per 100 live births	
			Births		Deaths		Births		Deaths						Number		Per 1,000 births					
	1931	1930	1931	1930	1931	1930	1931	1930	1931	1930	1931	1930	1931	1930	1931	1930	1931	1930	1931	1930	1931	1930
SELECTED STATES—Continued																						
MARYLAND	1,645,000	1,636,000	28,782	30,251	21,763	21,567	17.5	18.5	13.2	13.2	7,019	8,684	132	140	2,318	2,279	80.5	75.3	1,912	2,094	6.6	6.9
Colored	279,000	278,000	6,231	6,417	5,397	5,264	22.3	23.1	19.3	18.9	834	1,153	115	122	822	777	131.9	121.1	632	739	10.1	11.5
White	1,366,000	1,358,000	22,551	23,834	16,366	16,303	16.5	17.6	12.0	12.0	6,185	7,531	138	146	1,496	1,502	66.3	63.0	1,280	1,355	5.7	5.7
Cities	922,300	913,600	16,672	17,485	13,253	12,894	18.1	19.1	14.4	14.1	3,419	4,591	126	136	1,270	1,180	76.2	67.5	1,059	1,191	6.4	6.8
Colored	156,500	153,100	3,402	3,506	3,145	3,053	21.7	22.9	20.1	19.9	257	453	108	115	384	344	112.9	98.1	340	404	10.0	11.5
White	765,800	760,500	13,270	13,979	10,108	9,841	17.3	18.4	13.2	12.9	3,162	4,138	131	142	886	836	66.8	59.8	719	787	5.4	5.6
Incorporated places	64,500	63,600	1,408	1,505	1,153	1,116	21.8	23.7	17.9	17.5	255	389	122	135	98	145	69.6	96.3	109	165	7.7	11.0
Colored	8,400	8,200	245	238	287	248	29.2	29.0	34.2	30.2	−42	−10	85	96	33	40	134.7	168.1	22	41	9.0	17.2
White	56,100	55,400	1,163	1,267	866	868	20.7	22.9	15.4	15.7	297	399	134	146	65	105	55.9	82.9	87	124	7.5	9.8
Rural	658,200	658,800	10,702	11,261	7,357	7,557	16.3	17.1	11.2	11.5	3,345	3,704	145	149	950	954	88.8	84.7	744	738	7.0	6.6
Colored	114,100	116,700	2,584	2,673	1,965	1,963	22.6	22.9	17.2	16.8	619	710	132	136	405	393	156.7	147.0	270	294	10.4	11.0
White	544,100	542,100	8,118	8,588	5,392	5,594	14.9	15.8	9.9	10.3	2,726	2,994	151	154	545	561	67.1	65.3	474	444	5.8	5.2
MASSACHUSETTS	4,280,000	4,259,000	69,221	73,616	48,577	49,333	16.2	17.3	11.3	11.6	20,644	24,283	142	149	3,774	4,426	54.5	60.1	2,408	2,568	3.5	3.5
Colored	57,000	57,000	1,046	1,029	894	908	18.4	18.1	15.7	15.9	152	121	117	113	85	101	81.3	98.2	64	59	6.1	5.7
White	4,223,000	4,202,000	68,175	72,587	47,683	48,425	16.1	17.3	11.3	11.5	20,492	24,162	143	150	3,689	4,325	54.1	59.6	2,344	2,509	3.4	3.5
Cities	3,548,000	3,513,200	61,645	65,507	39,841	40,438	17.4	18.6	11.2	11.5	21,804	25,069	155	162	3,373	3,896	54.7	59.5	2,140	2,278	3.5	3.5
Colored	48,600	47,500	916	900	762	789	18.8	18.9	15.7	16.6	154	111	120	114	75	90	81.9	100.0	57	52	6.2	5.8
White	3,499,400	3,465,700	60,729	64,607	39,079	39,649	17.4	18.6	11.2	11.4	21,650	24,958	155	163	3,298	3,806	54.3	58.9	2,083	2,226	3.4	3.4
Incorporated places	331,200	327,600	4,048	4,217	3,185	3,277	12.2	12.9	9.6	10.0	863	940	127	129	189	256	46.7	60.7	150	161	3.7	3.8
Colored	2,300	2,300	35	36	25	21	15.2	15.7	10.9	9.1	10	15	(4)	(4)	3	2	85.7	55.6	2	3	5.7	8.3
White	328,900	325,300	4,013	4,181	3,160	3,256	12.2	12.9	9.6	10.0	853	925	127	128	186	254	46.3	60.8	148	158	3.7	3.8
Rural	400,800	418,200	3,528	3,892	5,551	5,618	8.8	9.3	13.8	13.4	−2,023	−1,726	64	69	212	274	60.1	70.4	118	129	3.3	3.3
Colored	6,100	7,200	95	93	107	98	15.6	12.9	17.5	13.6	−12	−5	89	(4)	7	9	73.7	96.8	5	4	5.3	4.3
White	394,700	411,000	3,433	3,799	5,444	5,520	8.7	9.2	13.8	13.4	−2,011	−1,721	63	69	205	265	59.7	69.8	113	125	3.3	3.3
MICHIGAN	4,931,000	4,871,000	90,929	99,325	49,104	51,620	18.4	20.4	10.0	10.6	41,825	47,705	185	192	5,184	6,224	57.0	62.7	3,232	3,670	3.6	3.7
Colored	201,000	195,000	3,527	3,907	2,897	3,090	17.5	20.0	14.4	15.8	630	817	122	126	333	370	94.4	94.7	209	227	5.9	5.8
White	4,730,000	4,676,000	87,402	95,418	46,207	48,530	18.5	20.4	9.8	10.4	41,195	46,888	189	197	4,851	5,854	55.5	61.4	3,023	3,443	3.5	3.6
Cities	3,067,800	2,959,200	57,124	64,605	27,678	29,921	18.6	21.8	9.0	10.1	29,446	34,684	206	216	3,263	4,076	57.1	63.1	2,143	2,469	3.8	3.8
Colored	185,800	173,900	3,158	3,475	2,336	2,560	17.0	20.0	12.6	14.7	822	915	135	136	272	317	86.1	91.2	180	205	5.7	5.9
White	2,882,000	2,785,300	53,966	61,130	25,342	27,361	18.7	21.9	8.8	9.8	28,624	33,769	213	223	2,991	3,759	55.4	61.5	1,963	2,264	3.6	3.7
Incorporated places	377,400	370,200	7,585	8,252	4,465	4,311	20.1	22.3	11.8	11.6	3,120	3,941	170	191	421	427	55.5	51.7	282	326	3.7	4.0
Colored	4,700	4,600	110	122	73	60	23.4	26.5	15.5	13.0	37	62	(4)	(4)	14	8	127.3	65.6	8	9	7.3	7.4
White	372,700	365,600	7,475	8,130	4,392	4,251	20.1	22.2	11.8	11.6	3,083	3,879	170	191	407	419	54.4	51.5	274	317	3.7	3.9
Rural	1,485,800	1,541,600	26,220	26,468	16,961	17,388	17.6	17.2	11.4	11.3	9,259	9,080	155	152	1,500	1,721	57.2	65.0	807	875	3.1	3.3
Colored	10,500	16,500	259	310	488	470	24.7	18.8	46.5	28.5	−229	−160	53	66	47	45	181.5	145.2	21	13	8.1	4.2
White	1,475,300	1,525,100	25,961	26,158	16,473	16,918	17.6	17.2	11.2	11.1	9,488	9,240	158	155	1,453	1,676	56.0	64.1	786	862	3.0	3.3
MISSISSIPPI	2,026,000	2,015,000	45,211	48,163	22,009	24,099	22.3	23.9	10.9	12.0	23,202	24,064	205	200	2,529	3,261	55.9	67.7	2,061	2,340	4.6	4.9
Colored	1,018,000	1,015,000	23,515	24,880	13,321	14,961	23.1	24.5	13.1	14.7	10,194	9,919	177	166	1,580	2,072	67.2	83.3	1,421	1,687	6.0	6.8
White	1,008,000	1,000,000	21,696	23,283	8,688	9,138	21.5	23.3	8.6	9.1	13,008	14,145	250	255	949	1,189	43.7	51.1	640	653	2.9	2.8
Cities	244,400	238,600	5,465	5,993	4,680	4,815	22.4	25.1	19.1	20.2	462	1,178	109	124	408	452	74.7	75.4	366	395	6.7	6.6
Colored	97,200	94,900	1,970	2,245	2,428	2,610	20.3	23.7	25.0	27.5	−685	−365	74	86	177	223	89.8	99.3	212	259	10.8	11.5
White	147,200	143,700	3,495	3,748	2,252	2,205	23.7	26.1	15.3	15.3	1,147	1,543	149	170	231	229	66.1	61.1	154	136	4.4	3.6
Rural [6]	1,781,600	1,776,400	39,746	42,170	17,329	19,284	22.3	23.7	9.7	10.9	22,740	22,886	234	219	2,121	2,809	53.4	66.6	1,695	1,945	4.3	4.6
Colored	920,800	920,100	21,545	22,635	10,893	12,351	23.4	24.6	11.8	13.4	10,879	10,284	202	183	1,403	1,849	65.1	81.7	1,209	1,428	5.6	6.3
White	860,800	856,300	18,201	19,535	6,436	6,933	21.1	22.8	7.5	8.1	11,861	12,602	287	282	718	960	39.4	49.1	486	517	2.7	2.6
MISSOURI	3,646,000	3,635,000	60,734	62,166	44,120	43,099	16.7	17.1	12.1	11.9	16,614	19,067	138	144	3,814	3,645	62.8	58.6	2,547	2,682	4.2	4.3
Colored	234,000	232,000	3,713	3,770	4,712	4,653	15.9	16.3	20.1	20.1	−999	−883	79	81	402	407	108.3	108.0	334	373	9.0	9.9
White	3,412,000	3,403,000	57,021	58,396	39,408	38,446	16.7	17.2	11.5	11.3	17,613	19,950	145	152	3,412	3,238	59.8	55.4	2,213	2,309	3.9	4.0
Cities	1,608,000	1,589,300	25,448	26,800	22,158	21,648	15.8	16.9	13.8	13.6	3,290	5,152	115	124	1,658	1,573	65.2	58.7	1,189	1,296	4.7	4.8
Colored	161,800	158,500	2,638	2,749	3,388	3,313	16.3	17.3	20.9	20.9	−750	−564	78	83	258	252	97.8	91.7	245	293	9.3	10.7
White	1,446,200	1,430,800	22,810	24,051	18,770	18,335	15.8	16.8	13.0	12.8	4,040	5,716	122	131	1,400	1,321	61.4	54.9	944	1,003	4.1	4.2
Incorporated places	280,700	275,800	5,210	5,324	4,311	4,122	18.6	19.3	15.4	14.9	899	1,202	121	129	307	335	58.9	62.9	211	205	4.0	3.9
Colored	18,600	18,200	246	230	381	388	13.2	12.6	20.5	21.3	−135	−158	65	59	26	35	105.7	152.2	24	20	9.8	8.7
White	262,100	257,600	4,964	5,094	3,930	3,734	18.9	19.8	15.0	14.5	1,034	1,360	126	136	281	300	56.6	58.9	187	185	3.8	3.6
Rural	1,757,300	1,769,900	30,076	30,042	17,651	17,329	17.1	17.0	10.0	9.8	12,425	12,713	170	173	1,849	1,737	61.5	57.8	1,147	1,181	3.8	3.9
Colored	53,600	55,300	829	791	943	952	15.5	14.3	17.6	17.2	−114	−161	88	83	118	120	142.3	151.7	65	60	7.8	7.6
White	1,703,700	1,714,600	29,247	29,251	16,708	16,377	17.2	17.1	9.8	9.6	12,539	12,874	175	179	1,731	1,617	59.2	55.3	1,082	1,121	3.7	3.8

NEBRASKA	1,384,000	1,380,000	26,609	27,004	12,908	13,292	19.2	19.6	9.3	9.6	13,701	13,712	206	203	1,299	1,333	48.8	49.4	766	747	2.9	2.8
Colored	24,000	24,000	621	606	478	467	25.9	25.3	19.9	19.5	143	139	130	130	65	69	104.7	113.9	29	25	4.7	4.1
White	1,360,000	1,356,000	25,988	26,398	12,430	12,825	19.1	19.5	9.1	9.5	13,558	13,573	209	206	1,234	1,264	47.5	47.9	737	722	2.8	2.7
Cities	377,700	369,100	7,595	7,844	4,763	4,878	20.1	21.3	12.6	13.2	2,832	2,966	159	161	391	402	51.5	51.2	242	243	3.2	3.1
Colored	14,900	14,700	295	310	268	267	19.8	21.1	18.0	18.2	27	43	110	116	22	16	74.6	51.6	9	17	3.1	5.5
White	362,800	354,400	7,300	7,534	4,495	4,611	20.1	21.3	12.4	13.0	2,805	2,923	162	163	369	386	50.5	51.2	233	226	3.2	3.0
Incorporated places	120,100	118,500	3,276	3,434	1,686	1,858	27.3	29.0	14.0	15.7	1,590	1,576	194	185	169	207	51.6	60.3	126	113	3.8	3.3
Colored	1,800	1,700	66	69	53	55	36.7	40.6	29.4	32.4	13	14	(4)	(4)	12	19	181.8	275.4	5	3	7.6	4.3
White	118,300	116,800	3,210	3,365	1,633	1,803	27.1	28.8	13.8	15.4	1,577	1,562	197	187	157	188	48.9	55.9	121	110	3.8	3.3
Rural	886,200	892,400	15,738	15,726	6,459	6,556	17.8	17.6	7.3	7.3	9,279	9,170	244	240	739	724	47.0	46.0	398	391	2.5	2.5
Colored	7,300	7,600	260	227	157	145	35.6	29.9	21.5	19.1	103	82	166	157	31	34	119.2	149.8	15	5	5.8	2.2
White	878,900	884,800	15,478	15,499	6,302	6,411	17.6	17.5	7.2	7.2	9,176	9,088	246	242	708	690	45.7	44.5	383	386	2.5	2.5
NEW HAMPSHIRE	467,000	466,000	7,764	8,342	5,923	6,322	16.6	17.9	12.7	13.6	1,841	2,020	131	132	445	512	57.3	61.4	312	348	4.0	4.2
Colored	1,000	1,000	6	10	6	9	6.0	10.0	6.0	9.0	------	1	(4)	(4)	------	1	------	100.0	------	------	------	------
White	466,000	465,000	7,758	8,332	5,917	6,313	16.6	17.9	12.7	13.6	1,841	2,019	131	132	445	511	57.4	61.3	312	348	4.0	4.2
Cities	232,700	230,800	4,482	4,819	2,895	3,103	19.3	20.9	12.4	13.4	1,587	1,716	155	155	268	306	59.8	63.5	172	188	3.8	3.9
Colored	500	600	4	7	4	6	8.0	11.7	8.0	10.0	------	1	(4)	(4)	------	------	------	------	------	------	------	------
White	232,200	230,200	4,478	4,812	2,891	3,097	19.3	20.9	12.5	13.5	1,587	1,715	155	155	268	306	59.8	63.6	172	188	3.8	3.9
Incorporated places	42,800	42,600	946	282	500	483	22.1	6.6	11.7	11.3	446	−201	189	58	31	48	32.8	170.2	35	37	3.7	13.1
Colored	100	------	------	------	2	------	------	------	20.0	------	−2	------	------	------	------	------	------	------	------	------	------	------
White	42,700	42,600	946	282	498	483	22.2	6.6	11.7	11.3	448	−201	190	58	31	48	32.8	170.2	35	37	3.7	13.1
Rural	191,500	192,600	2,336	3,241	2,528	2,736	12.2	16.8	13.2	14.2	−192	505	92	118	146	158	62.5	48.8	105	123	4.5	3.8
Colored	400	400	2	3	------	3	5.0	7.5	------	7.5	2	------	------	(4)	------	1	------	333.3	------	------	------	------
White	191,100	192,200	2,334	3,238	2,528	2,733	12.2	16.8	13.2	14.2	−194	505	92	118	146	157	62.6	48.5	105	123	4.5	3.8
NEW JERSEY	4,109,000	4,063,000	64,054	68,321	44,475	43,597	15.6	16.8	10.8	10.7	19,579	24,724	144	157	3,640	3,858	56.8	56.5	2,519	2,594	3.9	3.8
Colored	220,000	214,000	4,731	4,991	3,556	3,552	21.5	23.3	16.2	16.6	1,175	1,439	133	141	465	495	98.3	99.2	265	332	5.6	6.7
White	3,889,000	3,849,000	59,323	63,330	40,919	40,045	15.3	16.5	10.5	10.4	18,404	23,285	145	158	3,175	3,363	53.5	53.1	2,254	2,262	3.8	3.6
Cities	2,860,100	2,811,900	50,278	52,823	30,181	29,741	17.6	18.8	10.6	10.6	20,097	23,082	167	178	2,781	2,969	55.3	56.2	1,999	2,077	4.0	3.9
Colored	169,600	162,200	3,803	3,960	2,542	2,588	22.4	24.4	15.0	16.0	1,261	1,372	150	153	364	400	95.7	101.0	218	287	5.7	7.2
White	2,690,500	2,649,700	46,475	48,863	27,639	27,153	17.3	18.4	10.3	10.2	18,836	21,710	168	180	2,417	2,569	52.0	52.6	1,781	1,790	3.8	3.7
Incorporated places	563,300	544,300	5,627	6,663	5,523	5,329	10.0	12.2	9.8	9.8	104	1,334	102	125	336	333	59.7	50.0	226	221	4.0	3.3
Colored	17,900	17,300	348	450	399	363	19.4	26.0	22.3	21.0	−51	87	87	124	41	31	117.8	68.9	23	20	6.6	4.4
White	545,400	527,000	5,279	6,213	5,124	4,966	9.7	11.8	9.4	9.4	155	1,247	103	125	295	302	55.9	48.6	203	201	3.8	3.2
Rural	685,600	706,800	8,149	8,835	8,771	8,527	11.9	12.5	12.8	12.1	−622	308	93	104	523	556	64.2	62.9	294	296	3.6	3.4
Colored	32,500	34,500	580	581	615	601	17.8	16.8	18.9	17.4	−35	−20	94	97	60	64	103.4	110.2	24	25	4.1	4.3
White	653,100	672,300	7,569	8,254	8,156	7,926	11.6	12.3	12.5	11.8	−587	328	93	104	463	492	61.2	59.6	270	271	3.6	3.3
NEW YORK	12,756,000	12,643,000	205,677	216,072	149,107	147,453	16.1	17.1	11.7	11.7	56,570	68,619	138	147	11,808	12,696	57.4	58.8	8,529	8,837	4.1	4.1
Colored	455,000	445,000	8,993	9,188	7,517	7,199	19.8	20.6	16.5	16.2	1,476	1,989	120	128	939	949	104.4	103.3	724	753	8.1	8.2
White	12,301,000	12,198,000	196,684	206,884	141,590	140,254	16.0	17.0	11.5	11.5	55,094	66,630	139	148	10,869	11,747	55.3	56.8	7,805	8,084	4.0	3.9
Cities	10,150,100	9,977,700	170,732	180,541	115,324	113,277	16.8	18.1	11.4	11.4	55,408	67,264	148	159	9,683	10,590	56.7	58.7	7,375	7,680	4.3	4.3
Colored	426,200	405,500	8,267	8,489	6,787	6,568	19.4	20.9	15.9	16.2	1,480	1,921	122	129	859	883	103.9	104.0	689	724	8.3	8.5
White	9,723,900	9,572,200	162,465	172,052	108,537	106,709	16.7	18.0	11.2	11.1	53,928	65,343	150	161	8,824	9,707	54.3	56.4	6,686	6,956	4.1	4.0
Incorporated places	602,000	589,800	9,638	9,558	7,384	7,525	16.0	16.2	12.3	12.8	2,254	2,033	131	127	533	552	55.3	57.8	324	370	3.4	3.9
Colored	9,600	9,400	182	180	136	136	19.0	19.1	14.2	14.5	46	44	134	132	15	16	82.4	88.9	12	4	6.6	2.2
White	592,400	580,400	9,456	9,378	7,248	7,389	16.0	16.2	12.2	12.7	2,208	1,989	130	127	518	536	54.8	57.2	312	366	3.3	3.9
Rural	2,003,900	2,075,500	25,307	25,973	26,399	26,651	12.6	12.5	13.2	12.8	−1,092	−678	96	97	1,592	1,554	62.9	59.8	830	787	3.3	3.0
Colored	19,200	30,100	544	519	594	495	28.3	17.2	30.9	16.4	−50	24	92	105	65	50	119.5	96.3	23	25	4.2	4.8
White	1,984,700	2,045,400	24,763	25,454	25,805	26,156	12.5	12.4	13.0	12.8	−1,042	−702	96	97	1,527	1,504	61.7	59.1	807	762	3.3	3.0
NORTH CAROLINA	3,217,000	3,185,000	74,799	76,772	33,116	35,782	23.3	24.1	10.3	11.2	41,683	40,990	226	215	5,455	6,037	72.9	78.6	3,385	3,745	4.5	4.9
Colored	948,000	939,000	22,899	23,310	12,952	14,155	24.1	24.8	13.7	15.1	9,947	9,155	177	165	2,340	2,451	102.2	105.1	1,756	1,940	7.7	8.3
White	2,269,000	2,246,000	51,900	53,462	20,164	21,627	22.9	23.8	8.9	9.6	31,736	31,835	257	247	3,115	3,586	60.0	67.1	1,629	1,805	3.1	3.4
Cities	612,000	596,700	12,791	13,729	8,634	9,010	20.9	23.0	14.1	15.1	4,157	4,719	148	152	1,116	1,297	87.2	94.5	821	901	6.4	6.6
Colored	200,800	196,000	3,896	4,076	3,819	3,959	19.4	20.8	19.0	20.2	77	117	102	103	526	574	135.0	140.8	453	527	11.6	12.9
White	411,200	400,700	8,895	9,653	4,815	5,051	21.6	24.1	11.7	12.6	4,080	4,602	185	191	590	723	66.3	74.9	368	374	4.1	3.9
Incorporated places	225,400	218,700	4,961	5,084	2,720	2,784	22.0	23.2	12.1	12.7	2,241	2,300	182	183	380	406	76.6	79.9	274	326	5.5	6.4
Colored	53,800	52,200	1,052	990	970	971	19.6	19.0	18.0	18.6	82	19	108	102	149	152	141.6	153.5	111	117	10.6	11.8
White	171,600	166,500	3,909	4,094	1,750	1,813	22.8	24.6	10.2	10.9	2,159	2,281	223	226	231	254	59.1	62.0	163	209	4.2	5.1
Rural	2,379,600	2,369,600	57,047	57,959	21,762	23,988	24.0	24.5	9.1	10.1	35,285	33,971	262	242	3,959	4,334	69.4	74.8	2,290	2,518	4.0	4.3
Colored	694,400	690,800	17,951	18,244	8,163	9,225	25.9	26.4	11.8	13.4	9,788	9,019	220	198	1,665	1,725	92.8	94.6	1,192	1,296	6.6	7.1
White	1,685,200	1,678,800	39,096	39,715	13,599	14,763	23.2	23.7	8.1	8.8	25,497	24,952	287	269	2,294	2,609	58.7	65.7	1,098	1,222	2.8	3.1
OHIO	6,714,000	6,668,000	108,150	118,260	75,557	76,226	16.1	17.7	11.3	11.4	32,593	42,034	143	155	6,494	7,177	60.0	60.7	3,755	4,257	3.5	3.6
Colored	325,000	319,000	5,073	5,992	5,818	5,839	15.6	18.8	17.9	18.3	−745	153	87	103	536	644	105.7	107.5	295	399	5.8	6.7
White	6,389,000	6,349,000	103,077	112,268	69,739	70,387	16.1	17.7	10.9	11.1	33,338	41,881	148	160	5,958	6,533	57.8	58.2	3,460	3,858	3.4	3.4
Cities	3,993,600	3,928,400	66,692	74,077	45,460	46,051	16.7	18.9	11.4	11.7	21,232	28,026	147	161	3,992	4,563	59.9	61.6	2,462	2,855	3.7	3.9
Colored	275,800	263,100	4,523	5,174	4,786	4,812	16.4	19.7	17.4	18.3	−263	362	95	108	459	556	101.5	107.5	265	356	5.9	6.9
White	3,717,800	3,665,300	62,169	68,903	40,674	41,239	16.7	18.8	10.9	11.3	21,495	27,664	153	167	3,533	4,007	56.8	58.2	2,197	2,499	3.5	3.6
Incorporated places	603,200	593,500	8,569	9,486	6,701	6,523	14.2	16.0	11.1	11.0	1,868	2,963	128	145	485	488	56.6	51.4	304	312	3.5	3.3
Colored	16,200	15,900	199	270	308	265	12.3	17.0	19.0	16.7	−109	5	65	102	28	28	140.7	103.7	10	7	5.0	2.6
White	587,000	577,600	8,370	9,216	6,393	6,258	14.3	16.0	10.9	10.8	1,977	2,958	131	147	457	460	54.6	49.9	294	305	3.5	3.3
Rural	2,017,200	2,146,100	32,889	34,697	23,396	23,652	15.5	16.2	11.1	11.0	9,493	11,045	141	147	2,017	2,126	61.3	61.3	989	1,090	3.0	3.1
Colored	33,000	40,000	351	548	724	762	10.6	13.7	21.9	19.1	−373	−214	48	72	49	60	139.6	109.5	20	36	5.7	6.6
White	2,084,200	2,106,100	32,538	34,149	22,672	22,890	15.6	16.2	10.9	10.9	9,866	11,259	144	149	1,968	2,066	60.5	60.5	969	1,054	3.0	3.1

See footnotes at end of table.

Table 18.—COLORED [1] AND WHITE POPULATION, BIRTHS AND DEATHS, INFANT MORTALITY, AND STILLBIRTHS, IN SELECTED REGISTRATION STATES, CITIES, AND COUNTIES: 1931 AND 1930—Continued

[See note at head of this table]

AREA AND COLOR	Population estimated as of July 1: 1931	Population estimated as of July 1: 1930	Births and deaths (Exclusive of stillbirths): Number, Births: 1931	Number, Births: 1930	Number, Deaths: 1931	Number, Deaths: 1930	Rate per 1,000 population, Births: 1931	Rate, Births: 1930	Rate, Deaths: 1931	Rate, Deaths: 1930	Excess of births over deaths [2]: 1931	Excess of births over deaths [2]: 1930	Births per 100 deaths: 1931	Births per 100 deaths: 1930	Infant mortality (Exclusive of stillbirths): Deaths of infants under 1 year of age, Number: 1931	Number: 1930	Per 1,000 births: 1931	Per 1,000 births: 1930	Stillbirths, Number: 1931	Stillbirths, Number: 1930	Rate per 100 live births: 1931	Rate per 100 live births: 1930
SELECTED STATES—Continued																						
OKLAHOMA	2,424,000	2,405,000	43,269	42,505	18,802	19,646	17.9	17.7	7.8	8.2	24,467	22,859	230	216	2,228	2,581	51.5	60.7	1,057	1,283	2.4	3.0
Colored	277,000	274,000	3,638	3,225	2,981	3,063	13.1	11.8	10.8	11.2	657	162	122	105	312	346	85.8	107.3	146	170	4.0	5.3
White	2,147,000	2,131,000	39,631	39,280	15,821	16,583	18.5	18.4	7.4	7.8	23,810	22,697	250	237	1,916	2,235	48.3	56.9	911	1,113	2.3	2.8
Cities	577,500	558,200	10,820	11,250	6,471	7,077	18.7	20.2	11.2	12.7	4,349	4,173	167	159	665	917	61.5	81.5	285	348	2.6	3.1
Colored	64,400	62,800	922	845	1,118	1,254	14.3	13.5	17.4	20.0	−196	−409	82	67	100	149	108.5	176.3	50	63	5.4	7.5
White	513,100	495,400	9,898	10,405	5,353	5,823	19.3	21.0	10.4	11.8	4,545	4,582	185	179	565	768	57.1	73.8	235	285	2.4	2.7
Incorporated places	275,300	269,400	8,734	8,493	4,507	4,610	31.7	31.5	16.4	17.1	4,227	3,883	194	184	478	522	54.7	61.5	216	268	2.5	3.2
Colored	23,400	22,900	761	547	621	611	32.5	23.9	26.5	26.7	140	−64	123	90	61	65	80.2	118.8	34	22	4.5	4.0
White	251,900	246,500	7,973	7,946	3,886	3,999	31.7	32.2	15.4	16.2	4,087	3,947	205	199	417	457	52.3	57.5	182	246	2.3	3.1
Rural	1,571,200	1,577,400	23,715	22,762	7,824	7,959	15.1	14.4	5.0	5.0	15,891	14,803	303	286	1,085	1,142	45.8	50.2	556	667	2.3	2.9
Colored	189,200	188,300	1,955	1,833	1,242	1,198	10.3	9.7	6.6	6.4	713	635	157	153	151	132	77.2	72.0	62	85	3.2	4.6
White	1,382,000	1,389,100	21,760	20,929	6,582	6,761	15.7	15.1	4.8	4.9	15,178	14,168	331	310	934	1,010	42.9	48.3	494	582	2.3	2.8
PENNSYLVANIA	9,700,000	9,654,000	178,714	189,458	111,936	111,606	18.4	19.6	11.5	11.6	66,778	77,852	160	170	11,918	12,892	66.7	68.0	6,421	6,861	3.6	3.6
Colored	450,000	443,000	8,699	9,506	7,718	7,511	19.3	21.5	17.2	17.0	981	1,995	113	127	999	1,010	114.8	106.2	531	568	6.1	6.0
White	9,250,000	9,211,000	170,015	179,952	104,218	104,095	18.4	19.5	11.3	11.3	65,797	75,857	163	173	10,919	11,882	64.2	66.0	5,890	6,293	3.5	3.5
Cities	5,334,300	5,274,800	100,034	106,582	65,788	65,126	18.8	20.2	12.3	12.3	34,246	41,456	152	164	6,638	7,066	66.4	66.3	3,759	3,960	3.8	3.7
Colored	375,900	363,400	7,617	8,141	6,295	6,136	20.3	22.4	16.7	16.9	1,322	2,005	121	133	868	844	114.0	103.7	467	483	6.1	5.9
White	4,958,400	4,911,400	92,417	98,441	59,493	58,990	18.6	20.0	12.0	12.0	32,924	39,451	155	167	5,770	6,222	62.4	63.2	3,292	3,477	3.6	3.5
Incorporated places	1,294,700	1,275,900	22,616	24,187	13,401	13,505	17.5	19.0	10.4	10.6	9,215	10,682	169	179	1,475	1,636	65.2	67.6	790	798	3.5	3.3
Colored	20,200	20,000	290	390	306	291	14.4	19.5	15.1	14.6	−16	99	95	134	38	47	131.0	120.5	24	23	8.3	5.9
White	1,274,500	1,255,900	22,326	23,797	13,095	13,214	17.5	18.9	10.3	10.5	9,231	10,583	170	180	1,437	1,589	64.4	66.8	766	775	3.4	3.3
Rural	3,071,000	3,103,300	56,064	58,689	32,747	32,975	18.3	18.9	10.7	10.6	23,317	25,714	171	178	3,805	4,190	67.9	71.4	1,872	2,103	3.3	3.6
Colored	53,900	59,600	792	975	1,117	1,084	14.7	16.4	20.7	18.2	−325	−109	71	90	93	119	117.4	122.1	40	62	5.1	6.4
White	3,017,100	3,043,700	55,272	57,714	31,630	31,891	18.3	19.0	10.5	10.5	23,642	25,823	175	181	3,712	4,071	67.2	70.5	1,832	2,041	3.3	3.5
RHODE ISLAND	694,000	690,000	11,325	12,191	7,973	8,006	16.3	17.7	11.5	11.6	3,352	4,185	142	152	689	753	60.8	61.8	366	413	3.2	3.4
Colored	11,000	11,000	204	244	192	231	18.5	22.2	17.5	21.0	12	13	106	106	14	12	68.6	49.2	13	10	6.4	4.1
White	683,000	679,000	11,121	11,947	7,781	7,775	16.3	17.6	11.4	11.5	3,340	4,172	143	154	675	741	60.7	62.0	353	403	3.2	3.4
Cities	610,800	603,400	10,287	11,007	7,023	7,039	16.8	18.2	11.5	11.7	3,264	3,968	146	156	641	672	62.3	61.1	333	384	3.2	3.5
Colored	9,400	9,500	186	226	178	203	19.8	23.8	18.9	21.4	8	23	104	111	14	12	75.3	53.1	11	10	5.9	4.4
White	601,400	593,900	10,101	10,781	6,845	6,836	16.8	18.2	11.4	11.5	3,256	3,945	148	158	627	660	62.1	61.2	322	374	3.2	3.5
Incorporated places	34,200	33,900	375	387	369	404	11.0	11.4	10.8	11.9	6	−17	102	96	18	37	48.0	95.6	13	15	3.5	3.9
Colored	100	100	1	2	5	9	10.0	20.0	50.0	90.0	−4	−7	(4)	(4)	---	---	---	---	---	---	---	---
White	34,100	33,800	374	385	364	395	11.0	11.4	10.7	11.7	10	−10	103	97	18	37	48.1	96.1	13	15	3.5	3.9
Rural	49,000	52,700	663	797	581	563	13.5	15.1	11.9	10.7	82	234	114	142	30	44	45.2	55.2	20	14	3.0	1.8
Colored	1,500	1,400	17	16	9	19	11.3	11.4	6.0	13.6	8	−3	(4)	(4)	---	---	---	---	2	---	11.8	---
White	47,500	51,300	646	781	572	544	13.6	15.2	12.0	10.6	74	237	113	144	30	44	46.4	56.3	18	14	2.8	1.8
SOUTH CAROLINA	1,743,000	1,740,000	39,515	40,460	21,087	22,433	22.7	23.3	12.1	12.9	18,428	18,027	187	180	3,201	3,589	81.0	88.7	2,448	2,664	6.2	6.6
Colored	789,000	793,000	20,256	20,403	12,369	13,162	25.7	25.7	15.7	16.6	7,887	7,241	164	155	2,067	2,205	102.0	108.1	1,798	1,930	8.9	9.5
White	954,000	947,000	19,259	20,057	8,718	9,271	20.2	21.2	9.1	9.8	10,541	10,786	221	216	1,134	1,384	58.9	69.0	650	734	3.4	3.7
Cities	239,200	234,500	5,187	5,386	4,941	4,968	21.7	23.0	20.7	21.2	246	418	105	108	537	597	103.5	110.8	403	497	7.8	9.2
Colored	90,900	88,200	2,036	2,072	2,628	2,580	22.4	23.5	28.9	29.3	−592	−508	77	80	317	332	155.7	160.2	287	332	14.1	16.0
White	148,300	146,300	3,151	3,314	2,313	2,388	21.2	22.7	15.6	16.3	838	926	136	139	220	265	69.8	80.0	116	165	3.7	5.0
Incorporated places	139,200	136,700	2,702	2,886	1,741	1,920	19.4	21.1	12.5	14.0	961	966	155	150	185	246	68.5	85.2	166	228	6.1	7.9
Colored	50,200	49,300	1,018	1,016	933	1,033	20.3	20.6	18.6	21.0	85	−17	109	98	105	127	103.1	125.0	110	138	10.8	13.6
White	89,000	87,400	1,684	1,870	808	887	18.9	21.4	9.1	10.1	876	983	208	211	80	119	47.5	63.6	56	90	3.3	4.8
Rural	1,364,600	1,368,800	31,626	32,188	14,405	15,545	23.2	23.5	10.6	11.4	17,221	16,643	220	207	2,479	2,746	78.4	85.3	1,879	1,939	5.9	6.0
Colored	647,900	655,500	17,202	17,315	8,808	9,549	26.6	26.4	13.6	14.6	8,394	7,766	195	181	1,645	1,746	95.6	100.8	1,401	1,460	8.1	8.4
White	716,700	713,300	14,424	14,873	5,597	5,996	20.1	20.9	7.8	8.4	8,827	8,877	258	248	834	1,000	57.8	67.2	478	479	3.3	3.2
TENNESSEE	2,638,000	2,623,000	52,234	52,652	28,618	29,987	19.8	20.1	10.8	11.4	23,616	22,665	183	176	3,530	3,988	67.6	75.7	2,198	2,627	4.2	5.0
Colored	480,000	478,000	7,891	8,106	8,019	8,752	16.4	17.0	16.7	18.3	−128	−646	98	93	803	931	101.8	114.9	658	809	8.3	10.0
White	2,158,000	2,145,000	44,343	44,546	20,599	21,235	20.5	20.8	9.5	9.9	23,744	23,311	215	210	2,727	3,057	61.5	68.6	1,540	1,818	3.5	4.1
Cities	720,000	706,600	13,591	14,309	10,776	11,149	18.9	20.3	15.0	15.8	2,815	3,160	126	128	1,205	1,411	88.7	98.6	723	860	5.3	6.0
Colored	205,000	202,000	3,353	3,498	4,270	4,620	16.4	17.3	20.8	22.9	−917	−1,122	79	76	438	496	130.6	141.8	350	401	10.4	11.5
White	515,000	504,600	10,238	10,811	6,506	6,529	19.9	21.4	12.6	12.9	3,732	4,282	157	166	767	915	74.9	84.6	373	459	3.6	4.2
Rural [6]	1,918,000	1,916,400	38,643	38,343	17,842	18,838	20.1	20.0	9.3	9.8	20,801	19,505	217	204	2,325	2,577	60.2	67.2	1,475	1,767	3.8	4.6
Colored	275,000	276,000	4,538	4,608	3,749	4,132	16.5	16.7	13.6	15.0	789	476	121	112	365	435	80.4	94.4	308	408	6.8	8.9
White	1,643,000	1,640,400	34,105	33,735	14,093	14,706	20.8	20.6	8.6	9.0	20,012	19,029	242	229	1,960	2,142	57.5	63.5	1,167	1,359	3.4	4.0

VERMONT	360,000	360,000	6,676	6,934	4,493	4,687	18.5	19.3	12.5	13.0	2,183	2,247	149	148	400	449	59.9	64.8	186	195	2.8	2.8
Colored	1,000	1,000	3	11	7	9	3.0	11.0	7.0	9.0	−4	2	(4)	(4)	----	----	----	----	----	----	----	----
White	359,000	359,000	6,673	6,923	4,486	4,678	18.6	19.3	12.5	13.0	2,187	2,245	149	148	400	449	59.9	64.9	186	195	2.8	2.8
Cities	54,100	53,500	1,452	1,446	835	786	26.8	27.0	15.4	14.7	617	660	174	184	73	99	50.3	68.5	44	40	3.0	2.8
Colored	100	200	2	6	1	3	20.0	30.0	10.0	15.0	1	3	(4)	(4)	----	----	----	----	----	----	----	----
White	54,000	53,300	1,450	1,440	834	783	26.9	27.0	15.4	14.7	616	657	174	184	73	99	50.3	68.8	44	40	3.0	2.8
Rural [6]	305,900	306,500	5,224	5,488	3,658	3,901	17.1	17.9	12.0	12.7	1,566	1,587	143	141	327	350	62.6	63.8	142	155	2.7	2.8
Colored	900	800	1	5	6	6	1.1	6.3	6.7	7.5	−5	−1	(4)	(4)	----	----	----	----	----	----	----	----
White	305,000	305,700	5,223	5,483	3,652	3,895	17.1	17.9	12.0	12.7	1,571	1,588	143	141	327	350	62.6	63.8	142	155	2.7	2.8
VIRGINIA	2,430,000	2,425,000	52,731	54,703	30,029	30,315	21.7	22.6	12.4	12.5	22,702	24,388	176	180	4,026	4,226	76.3	77.3	2,308	2,473	4.4	4.5
Colored	648,000	651,000	14,986	15,732	11,559	11,722	23.1	24.2	17.8	18.0	3,427	4,010	130	134	1,615	1,687	1,078	107.2	1,172	1,220	7.8	7.8
White	1,782,000	1,774,000	37,745	38,971	18,470	18,593	21.2	22.0	10.4	10.5	19,275	20,378	204	210	2,411	2,539	63.9	65.2	1,136	1,253	3.0	3.2
Cities	643,900	638,600	12,205	12,810	9,461	9,528	19.0	20.1	14.7	14.9	2,744	3,282	129	134	1,010	1,059	82.8	82.7	656	748	5.4	5.8
Colored	187,300	186,800	3,637	3,735	3,921	4,001	19.4	20.0	20.9	21.4	−284	−266	93	93	464	480	127.6	128.5	393	394	10.8	10.5
White	456,600	451,800	8,568	9,075	5,540	5,527	18.8	20.1	12.1	12.2	3,028	3,548	155	164	546	579	63.7	63.8	263	354	3.1	3.9
Incorporated places	138,900	136,200	3,688	3,828	2,183	2,021	26.6	28.1	15.7	14.8	1,505	1,807	169	189	260	279	70.5	72.9	202	164	5.5	4.3
Colored	26,400	25,900	604	639	581	492	22.9	24.7	22.0	19.0	23	147	104	130	55	56	91.1	87.6	69	52	11.4	8.1
White	112,500	110,300	3,084	3,189	1,602	1,529	27.4	28.9	14.2	13.9	1,482	1,660	193	209	205	223	66.5	69.9	133	112	4.3	3.5
Rural	1,647,200	1,650,200	36,838	38,065	18,385	18,766	22.4	23.1	11.2	11.4	18,453	19,299	200	203	2,756	2,888	74.8	75.9	1,450	1,561	3.9	4.1
Colored	434,300	438,300	10,745	11,358	7,057	7,229	24.7	25.9	16.2	16.5	3,688	4,129	152	157	1,096	1,151	102.0	101.3	710	774	6.6	6.8
White	1,212,900	1,211,900	26,093	26,707	11,328	11,537	21.5	22.0	9.3	9.5	14,765	15,170	230	231	1,660	1,737	63.6	65.0	740	787	2.8	2.9
WEST VIRGINIA	1,749,000	1,736,000	39,325	41,614	17,620	18,220	22.5	24.0	10.1	10.5	21,705	23,394	223	228	3,036	3,371	77.2	81.0	1,526	1,547	3.9	3.7
Colored	117,000	116,000	2,177	2,462	1,871	1,856	18.6	21.2	16.0	16.0	306	606	116	133	242	239	111.2	97.1	143	145	6.6	5.9
White	1,632,000	1,620,000	37,148	39,152	15,749	16,364	22.8	24.2	9.7	10.1	21,399	22,788	236	239	2,794	3,132	75.2	80.0	1,383	1,402	3.7	3.6
Cities	352,400	345,600	6,620	7,093	4,730	4,888	18.8	20.5	13.4	14.1	1,890	2,205	140	145	606	703	91.5	99.1	340	325	5.1	4.6
Colored	23,900	23,100	348	406	485	479	14.6	17.6	20.3	20.7	−137	−73	72	85	47	54	135.1	133.0	38	28	10.9	6.9
White	328,500	322,500	6,272	6,687	4,245	4,409	19.1	20.7	12.9	13.7	2,027	2,278	148	152	559	649	89.1	97.1	302	297	4.8	4.4
Incorporated places	151,900	148,300	3,713	4,222	2,656	2,794	24.4	28.5	17.5	18.8	1,057	1,428	140	151	323	381	87.0	90.2	205	195	5.5	4.6
Colored	8,500	8,200	143	167	314	316	16.8	20.4	36.9	38.5	−171	−149	46	53	23	17	160.8	101.8	18	15	12.6	9.0
White	143,400	140,100	3,570	4,055	2,342	2,478	24.9	28.9	16.3	17.7	1,228	1,577	152	164	300	364	84.0	89.8	187	180	5.2	4.4
Rural	1,244,700	1,242,100	28,992	30,299	10,234	10,538	23.3	24.4	8.2	8.5	18,758	19,761	283	288	2,107	2,287	72.7	75.5	981	1,027	3.4	3.4
Colored	84,600	84,700	1,686	1,889	1,072	1,061	19.9	22.3	12.7	12.5	614	828	157	178	172	168	102.0	88.9	87	102	5.2	5.4
White	1,160,100	1,157,400	27,306	28,410	9,162	9,477	23.5	24.5	7.9	8.2	18,144	18,933	298	300	1,935	2,119	70.9	74.6	894	925	3.3	3.3
ALABAMA CITIES																						
Anniston	22,900	22,500	498	483	321	306	21.7	21.5	14.0	13.6	177	177	155	158	39	45	78.3	93.2	27	33	5.4	6.8
Colored	7,300	7,200	159	142	136	117	21.8	19.7	18.6	16.3	23	25	117	121	15	17	94.3	119.7	14	19	8.8	13.4
White	15,600	15,300	339	341	185	189	21.7	22.3	11.9	12.4	154	152	183	180	24	28	70.8	82.1	13	14	3.8	4.1
Bessemer	21,000	20,800	332	414	275	293	15.8	19.9	13.1	14.1	57	121	121	141	32	39	96.4	94.2	23	32	6.9	7.7
Colored	11,900	11,700	167	208	174	183	14.0	17.8	14.6	15.6	−7	25	96	114	23	24	137.7	115.4	17	25	10.2	12.0
White	9,100	9,100	165	206	101	110	18.1	22.6	11.1	12.1	64	96	163	187	9	15	54.5	72.8	6	7	3.6	3.4
Birmingham	269,300	261,600	5,135	5,204	3,510	3,548	19.1	19.9	13.0	13.6	1,625	1,656	146	147	336	404	65.4	77.6	251	285	4.9	5.5
Colored	102,600	99,800	1,915	2,134	1,816	1,925	18.7	21.4	17.7	19.3	99	209	105	111	164	236	85.6	110.6	140	171	7.3	8.0
White	166,700	161,800	32,220	3,070	1,694	1,623	19.3	19.0	10.2	10.0	1,526	1,447	190	189	172	168	53.4	54.7	111	114	3.4	3.7
Decatur	16,900	15,900	264	336	194	197	15.6	21.1	11.5	12.4	70	139	136	171	24	18	90.9	53.6	20	15	7.6	4.5
Colored	4,000	3,900	56	61	71	60	14.0	15.6	17.8	15.4	−15	1	(4)	(4)	11	5	196.4	82.0	13	7	23.2	11.5
White	12,900	12,000	208	275	123	137	16.1	22.9	9.5	11.4	85	138	169	201	13	13	62.5	47.3	7	8	3.4	2.9
Dothan	16,500	16,100	237	253	250	222	14.4	15.7	15.2	13.8	−13	31	95	114	13	17	54.9	67.2	23	22	9.7	8.7
Colored	6,300	6,200	72	81	89	66	11.4	13.1	14.1	10.6	−17	15	(4)	(4)	4	5	55.6	61.7	8	13	11.1	16.0
White	10,200	9,900	165	172	161	156	16.2	17.4	15.8	15.8	4	16	102	110	9	12	54.5	69.8	15	9	9.1	5.2
Fairfield	11,800	11,200	542	584	342	333	45.9	52.1	29.0	29.7	200	251	158	175	47	55	86.7	94.2	30	48	5.5	8.2
Colored	6,900	6,500	204	221	210	206	29.6	34.0	30.4	31.7	−6	15	97	107	27	32	132.4	144.8	17	29	8.3	13.1
White	4,900	4,700	338	363	132	127	69.0	77.2	26.9	27.0	206	236	256	286	20	23	59.2	63.4	13	19	3.8	5.2
Florence	11,900	11,800	244	259	172	177	20.5	21.9	14.5	15.0	72	82	142	146	23	22	94.3	84.9	16	20	6.6	7.7
Colored	2,800	2,800	41	51	45	61	14.6	18.2	16.1	21.8	−4	−10	(4)	(4)	3	7	73.2	137.3	4	9	9.8	17.6
White	9,100	9,000	203	208	127	116	22.3	23.1	14.0	12.9	76	92	160	179	20	15	98.5	72.1	12	11	5.9	5.3
Gadsden	24,900	24,200	445	549	346	329	17.9	22.7	13.9	13.6	99	220	129	167	38	40	85.4	72.9	24	27	5.4	4.9
Colored	6,500	6,400	97	109	104	112	14.9	17.0	16.0	17.5	−7	−3	93	97	15	8	154.6	73.4	7	8	7.2	7.3
White	18,400	17,800	348	440	242	217	18.9	24.7	13.2	12.2	106	223	144	203	23	32	66.1	72.7	17	19	4.9	4.3
Huntsville	12,000	11,600	234	243	208	219	19.5	20.9	17.3	18.9	26	24	113	111	20	22	85.5	90.5	16	29	6.8	11.9
Colored	3,900	3,800	72	63	88	94	18.5	16.6	22.6	24.7	−16	−31	(4)	(4)	11	10	152.8	158.7	3	8	4.2	12.7
White	8,100	7,800	162	180	120	125	20.0	23.1	14.8	16.0	42	55	135	144	9	12	55.6	66.7	13	21	8.0	11.7
Mobile	68,900	68,400	1,408	1,490	1,120	1,243	20.4	21.8	16.3	18.2	288	247	126	120	92	128	65.3	85.9	78	83	5.5	5.6
Colored	24,500	24,600	519	526	528	587	21.2	21.4	21.6	23.9	−9	−61	98	90	47	66	90.6	125.5	48	47	9.2	8.9
White	44,400	43,800	889	964	592	656	20.0	22.0	13.3	15.0	297	308	150	147	45	62	50.6	64.3	30	36	3.4	3.7
Montgomery	67,300	66,300	1,218	1,210	1,033	1,138	18.1	18.3	15.3	17.2	185	72	118	106	99	120	81.3	99.2	64	82	5.3	6.8
Colored	30,500	30,100	546	523	612	664	17.9	17.4	20.1	22.1	−66	−141	89	79	64	74	117.2	141.5	47	57	8.6	10.9
White	36,800	36,200	672	687	421	474	18.3	19.0	11.4	13.1	251	213	160	145	35	46	52.1	67.0	17	25	2.5	3.6
Phenix City [7]	14,300	13,900	292	187	208	102	20.4	13.5	14.5	7.3	84	85	140	183	29	16	99.3	85.6	17	10	5.8	5.3
Colored	4,300	4,100	118	30	72	13	27.4	7.3	16.7	3.2	46	17	(4)	(4)	12	5	101.7	166.7	9	7	7.6	23.3
White	10,000	9,800	174	157	136	89	17.4	16.0	13.6	9.1	38	68	128	(4)	17	11	97.7	70.1	8	3	4.6	1.9
Selma	18,300	18,100	450	450	427	468	24.6	24.9	23.3	25.9	23	−18	105	96	63	63	140.0	140.0	33	29	7.3	6.4
Colored	9,400	9,300	216	205	247	282	23.0	22.0	26.3	30.3	−31	−77	87	73	34	40	157.4	195.1	23	18	10.6	8.8
White	8,900	8,800	234	245	180	186	26.3	27.8	20.2	21.1	54	59	130	132	29	23	123.9	93.9	10	11	4.3	4.5
Tuscaloosa	21,800	20,900	404	352	396	486	18.5	16.8	18.2	23.3	8	−134	102	72	33	25	81.7	71.0	18	30	4.5	8.5
Colored	7,400	7,200	106	100	144	146	14.3	13.9	19.5	20.3	−38	−46	74	68	18	13	169.8	130.0	8	13	7.5	13.0
White	14,400	13,700	298	252	252	340	20.7	18.4	17.5	24.8	46	−88	118	74	15	12	50.3	47.6	10	17	3.4	6.7

See footnotes at end of table.

TABLE 18.—COLORED [1] AND WHITE POPULATION, BIRTHS AND DEATHS, INFANT MORTALITY, AND STILLBIRTHS, IN SELECTED REGISTRATION STATES, CITIES, AND COUNTIES: 1931 AND 1930—Continued

[See note at head of this table]

AREA AND COLOR	POPULATION ESTIMATED AS OF JULY 1		BIRTHS AND DEATHS (Exclusive of stillbirths): Number: Births		BIRTHS AND DEATHS: Number: Deaths		BIRTHS AND DEATHS: Rate per 1,000 population: Births		BIRTHS AND DEATHS: Rate per 1,000 population: Deaths		BIRTHS AND DEATHS: Excess of births over deaths [2]		BIRTHS AND DEATHS: Births per 100 deaths		INFANT MORTALITY (Exclusive of stillbirths): Deaths of infants under 1 year of age: Number		INFANT MORTALITY: Deaths of infants under 1 year of age: Per 1,000 births		STILLBIRTHS: Number		STILLBIRTHS: Rate per 100 live births	
	1931	1930	1931	1930	1931	1930	1931	1930	1931	1930	1931	1930	1931	1930	1931	1930	1931	1930	1931	1930	1931	1930
ARKANSAS CITIES																						
Blytheville	10,500	10,200	158	230	124	206	15.0	22.5	11.8	20.2	34	24	127	112	17	26	107.6	113.0	5	11	3.2	4.8
Colored	2,900	2,800	29	49	38	49	10.0	17.5	13.1	17.5	−9	-------	(4)	(4)	4	5	137.9	102.0	4	2	13.8	4.1
White	7,600	7,400	129	181	86	157	17.0	24.5	11.3	21.2	43	24	(4)	115	13	21	100.8	116.0	1	9	.8	5.0
El Dorado	17,900	16,700	269	279	156	251	15.0	16.7	8.7	15.0	113	28	172	111	15	27	55.8	96.8	11	12	4.1	4.3
Colored	4,200	3,900	34	40	62	93	8.1	10.3	14.8	23.8	−28	−53	(4)	(4)	-------	8	-------	200.0	4	1	11.8	2.5
White	13,700	12,800	235	239	94	158	17.2	18.7	6.9	12.3	141	81	(4)	151	15	19	63.8	79.5	7	11	3.0	4.6
Fort Smith	31,700	31,500	642	674	493	499	20.3	21.4	15.6	15.8	149	175	130	135	36	43	56.1	63.8	25	27	3.9	4.0
Colored	3,500	3,500	47	61	76	79	13.4	17.4	21.7	22.6	−29	−18	(4)	(4)	7	6	148.9	98.4	6	9	12.8	14.8
White	28,200	28,000	595	613	417	420	21.1	21.9	14.8	15.0	178	193	143	146	29	37	48.7	60.4	19	18	3.2	2.9
Hot Springs	21,100	20,400	352	323	469	486	16.7	15.8	22.2	23.8	−117	−163	75	66	24	21	68.2	65.0	15	18	4.3	5.6
Colored	4,300	4,200	31	37	114	144	7.2	8.8	26.5	34.3	−83	−107	27	26	5	1	161.3	27.0	5	2	16.1	5.4
White	16,800	16,200	321	286	355	342	19.1	17.7	21.1	21.1	−34	−56	90	84	19	20	59.2	69.9	10	16	3.1	5.6
Jonesboro	10,400	10,300	185	237	190	177	17.8	23.0	18.3	17.2	−5	60	97	134	26	13	140.5	54.9	9	10	4.9	4.2
Colored	1,300	1,300	18	23	21	21	13.8	17.7	16.2	16.2	−3	2	(4)	(4)	2	2	111.1	87.0	2	3	11.1	13.0
White	9,100	9,000	167	214	169	156	18.4	23.8	18.6	17.3	−2	58	99	137	24	11	143.7	51.4	7	7	4.2	3.3
Little Rock	83,700	82,100	1,257	1,360	1,750	1,850	15.0	16.6	20.9	22.5	−493	−490	72	74	91	67	72.4	49.3	63	81	5.0	6.0
Colored	20,000	19,800	289	277	617	693	14.5	14.0	30.9	35.0	−328	−416	47	40	31	18	107.3	65.0	32	46	11.1	16.6
White	63,700	62,300	968	1,083	1,133	1,157	15.2	17.4	17.8	18.6	−165	−74	85	94	60	49	62.0	45.2	31	35	3.2	3.2
North Little Rock	20,100	19,500	274	299	164	139	13.6	15.3	8.2	7.1	110	160	167	215	17	16	62.0	53.5	13	19	4.7	6.4
Colored	6,300	6,100	109	100	77	65	17.3	16.4	12.2	10.7	32	35	(4)	(4)	9	7	82.6	70.0	11	13	10.1	13.0
White	13,800	13,400	165	199	87	74	12.0	14.9	6.3	5.5	78	125	(4)	(4)	8	9	48.5	45.2	2	6	1.2	3.0
Pine Bluff	[5] 20,760	[5] 20,760	356	405	274	317	17.1	19.5	13.2	15.3	82	88	130	128	17	15	47.8	37.0	33	23	9.3	5.7
Colored	6,167	6,167	137	143	110	131	22.2	23.2	17.8	21.2	27	12	125	109	4	6	29.2	42.0	15	13	10.9	9.1
White	14,593	14,593	219	262	164	186	15.0	18.0	11.2	12.7	55	76	134	141	13	9	59.4	34.4	18	10	8.2	3.8
Texarkana	11,100	10,800	128	127	172	144	11.5	11.8	15.5	13.3	−44	−17	74	88	8	4	62.5	31.5	7	7	5.5	5.5
Colored	3,200	3,100	33	34	80	69	10.3	11.0	25.0	22.3	−47	−35	(4)	(4)	4	2	121.2	58.8	3	4	9.1	11.8
White	7,900	7,700	95	93	92	75	12.0	12.1	11.6	9.7	3	18	(4)	(4)	4	2	42.1	21.5	4	3	4.2	3.2
DELAWARE CITIES																						
Wilmington	[5] 106,597	[5] 106,597	2,200	2,305	1,479	1,560	20.6	21.6	13.9	14.6	721	745	149	148	153	163	69.5	70.7	75	121	3.4	5.2
Colored	12,138	12,138	228	242	254	280	18.8	19.9	20.9	23.1	−26	−38	90	86	24	18	105.3	74.4	14	34	6.1	14.0
White	94,459	94,459	1,972	2,063	1,225	1,280	20.9	21.8	13.0	13.6	747	783	161	161	129	145	65.4	70.3	61	87	3.1	4.2
DISTRICT OF COLUMBIA																						
Washington	491,000	488,000	9,353	9,376	7,743	7,387	19.0	19.2	15.8	15.1	1,610	1,989	121	127	627	664	67.0	70.8	430	466	4.6	5.0
Colored	135,000	133,000	2,985	3,054	2,969	2,792	22.1	23.0	22.0	21.0	16	262	101	109	344	337	115.2	110.3	223	242	7.5	7.9
White	356,000	355,000	6,368	6,322	4,774	4,595	17.9	17.8	13.4	12.9	1,594	1,727	133	138	283	327	44.4	51.7	207	224	3.3	3.5
FLORIDA CITIES																						
Daytona Beach	17,800	16,800	276	255	277	265	15.5	15.2	15.6	15.8	−1	−10	100	96	27	8	97.8	31.4	18	32	6.5	12.5
Colored	5,800	5,500	76	75	93	94	13.1	13.6	16.0	17.1	−17	−19	(4)	(4)	11	1	144.7	13.3	9	21	11.8	28.0
White	12,000	11,300	200	180	184	171	16.7	15.9	15.3	15.1	16	9	109	105	16	7	80.0	38.9	9	11	4.5	6.1
Gainesville	10,900	10,600	228	233	230	223	20.9	22.0	21.1	21.0	−2	10	99	104	17	15	74.6	64.4	22	18	9.6	7.7
Colored	4,200	4,200	73	91	115	119	17.4	21.7	27.4	28.3	−42	−28	63	76	5	6	68.5	65.9	13	9	17.8	9.9
White	6,700	6,400	155	142	115	104	23.1	22.2	17.2	16.3	40	38	135	137	12	9	77.4	63.4	9	9	5.8	6.3
Jacksonville	131,900	130,000	2,478	2,448	1,945	1,977	18.8	18.8	14.7	15.2	533	471	127	124	140	164	56.5	67.0	179	196	7.2	8.0
Colored	48,100	48,200	794	759	982	1,014	16.5	15.7	20.4	21.0	−188	−255	81	75	50	80	63.0	105.4	108	129	13.6	17.0
White	83,800	81,800	1,684	1,689	963	963	20.1	20.6	11.5	11.8	721	726	175	175	90	84	53.4	49.7	71	67	4.2	4.0
Key West	[5] 12,831	[5] 12,831	230	264	204	216	17.9	20.6	15.9	16.8	26	48	113	122	18	12	78.3	45.5	4	14	1.7	5.3
Colored	2,283	2,283	56	60	50	55	24.5	26.3	21.9	24.1	6	5	(4)	(4)	7	3	125.0	50.0	1	3	1.8	5.0
White	10,548	10,548	174	204	154	161	16.5	19.3	14.6	15.3	20	43	113	127	11	9	63.2	44.1	3	11	1.7	5.4
Lakeland	19,800	18,700	302	349	231	243	15.3	18.7	11.7	13.0	71	106	131	144	14	16	46.4	45.8	15	16	5.0	4.6
Colored	4,200	4,000	65	55	56	66	15.5	13.8	13.3	16.5	9	−11	(4)	(4)	5	6	76.9	109.1	4	6	6.2	10.9
White	15,600	14,700	237	294	175	177	15.2	20.0	11.2	12.0	62	117	135	166	9	10	38.0	34.0	11	10	4.6	3.4
Miami	112,500	111,000	1,820	2,022	1,286	1,232	16.2	18.2	11.4	11.1	534	790	142	164	104	118	57.1	58.4	93	112	5.1	5.5
Colored	25,300	25,200	505	576	371	382	20.0	22.9	14.7	15.2	134	194	136	151	51	54	101.0	93.8	46	57	9.1	9.9
White	87,200	85,800	1,315	1,446	915	850	15.1	16.9	10.5	9.9	400	596	144	170	53	64	40.3	44.3	47	55	3.6	3.8
Orlando	29,200	27,700	561	538	506	474	19.2	19.4	17.3	17.1	55	64	111	114	36	45	64.2	83.6	39	41	7.0	7.6
Colored	8,100	7,700	114	117	115	118	14.1	15.2	14.2	15.3	−1	−1	99	99	12	19	105.3	162.4	18	20	15.8	17.1
White	21,100	20,000	447	421	391	356	21.2	21.1	18.5	17.8	56	65	114	118	24	26	53.7	61.8	21	21	4.7	5.0

Pensacola	31,600	31,600	659	746	504	518	20.9	23.6	15.9	16.4	155	228	131	144	45	79	68.3	105.9	56	46	8.5	6.2
Colored	9,500	9,600	136	168	190	226	14.3	17.5	20.0	23.5	−54	−58	72	74	17	39	125.0	232.1	23	18	16.9	10.7
White	22,100	22,000	523	578	314	292	23.7	26.3	14.2	13.3	209	286	167	198	28	40	53.5	69.2	33	28	6.3	4.8
St. Augustine	12,800	12,300	244	219	205	227	19.1	17.8	16.0	18.5	39	−8	119	96	9	15	36.9	68.5	9	14	3.7	6.4
Colored	3,500	3,400	61	34	88	87	17.4	10.0	25.1	25.6	−27	−53	(4)	(4)	2	5	32.8	147.1	7	4	11.5	11.8
White	9,300	8,900	183	185	117	140	19.7	20.8	12.6	15.7	66	45	156	132	7	10	38.3	54.1	2	10	1.1	5.4
St. Petersburg	41,900	40,700	553	523	637	669	13.2	12.9	15.2	16.4	−84	−146	87	78	29	29	52.4	55.4	27	30	4.9	5.7
Colored	7,700	7,500	121	126	119	120	15.7	16.8	15.5	16.0	2	6	102	105	12	13	99.2	103.2	18	13	14.9	10.3
White	34,200	33,200	432	397	518	549	12.6	12.0	15.1	16.5	−86	−152	83	72	17	16	39.4	40.3	9	17	2.1	4.3
Sanford	10,700	10,200	211	215	189	106	19.7	21.1	17.7	10.4	22	109	112	203	19	14	90.0	65.1	17	12	8.1	5.6
Colored	5,200	4,900	102	98	113	49	19.6	20.0	21.7	10.0	−11	49	90	(4)	15	7	147.1	71.4	10	8	9.8	8.2
White	5,500	5,300	109	117	76	57	19.8	22.1	13.8	10.8	33	60	(4)	(4)	4	7	36.7	59.8	7	4	6.4	3.4
Tallahassee	11,200	10,800	256	206	139	147	22.9	19.1	12.4	13.6	117	59	184	140	23	16	89.8	77.7	15	15	5.9	7.3
Colored	4,600	4,400	118	94	80	78	25.7	21.4	17.4	17.7	38	16	(4)	(4)	15	9	127.1	95.7	14	15	11.9	16.0
White	6,600	6,400	138	112	59	69	20.9	17.5	8.9	10.8	79	43	(4)	(4)	8	7	58.0	62.5	1	------	.7	----
Tampa	105,000	101,900	1,776	1,830	1,180	1,178	16.9	18.0	11.2	11.6	596	652	151	155	118	106	66.4	57.9	99	116	5.6	6.3
Colored	22,200	21,500	330	330	341	342	14.9	15.3	15.4	15.9	−11	−12	97	96	45	42	136.4	127.3	39	54	11.8	16.4
White	82,800	80,400	1,446	1,500	839	836	17.5	18.7	10.1	10.4	607	664	172	179	73	64	50.5	42.7	60	62	4.1	4.1
West Palm Beach	28,700	27,000	511	530	378	394	17.8	19.6	13.2	14.6	133	136	135	135	28	28	54.8	52.8	20	28	3.9	5.3
Colored	9,700	9,100	174	162	183	189	17.9	17.8	18.9	20.8	−9	−27	95	86	18	18	103.4	111.1	14	16	8.0	9.9
White	19,000	17,900	337	368	195	205	17.7	20.6	10.3	11.5	142	163	173	180	10	10	29.7	27.2	6	12	1.8	3.3
GEORGIA CITIES																						
Albany	14,800	14,600	322	306	248	259	21.8	21.0	16.8	17.7	74	47	130	118	14	14	43.5	45.8	29	22	9.0	7.2
Colored	7,500	7,500	175	164	171	185	23.3	21.9	22.8	24.7	4	−21	102	89	10	11	57.1	67.1	18	14	10.3	8.5
White	7,300	7,100	147	142	77	74	20.1	20.0	10.5	10.4	70	68	(4)	(4)	4	3	27.2	21.1	11	8	7.5	5.6
Athens	18,900	18,300	339	411	323	321	17.9	22.5	17.1	17.5	16	90	105	128	27	36	79.6	87.6	13	27	3.8	6.6
Colored	6,500	6,400	136	143	163	148	20.9	22.3	25.1	23.1	−27	−5	83	97	15	21	110.3	146.9	6	15	4.4	10.5
White	12,400	11,900	203	268	160	173	16.4	22.5	12.9	14.5	43	95	127	155	12	15	59.1	56.0	7	12	3.4	4.5
Atlanta	277,600	271,700	5,237	5,301	4,147	4,205	18.9	19.5	14.9	15.5	1,090	1,096	126	126	439	496	83.8	93.6	332	321	6.3	6.1
Colored	93,200	90,700	1,759	1,808	2,015	2,106	18.9	19.9	21.6	23.2	−256	−298	87	86	212	268	120.5	148.2	191	203	10.9	11.2
White	184,400	181,000	3,478	3,493	2,132	2,099	18.9	19.3	11.6	11.6	1,346	1,394	163	166	227	228	65.3	65.3	141	118	4.1	3.4
Augusta	61,300	60,500	1,197	1,207	1,233	1,212	19.5	20.0	20.1	20.0	−36	−5	97	100	136	110	113.6	91.1	111	86	9.3	7.1
Colored	24,600	24,400	448	453	629	680	18.2	18.6	25.6	27.9	−181	−227	71	67	65	49	145.1	108.2	74	46	16.5	10.2
White	36,700	36,100	749	754	604	532	20.4	20.9	16.5	14.7	145	222	124	142	71	61	94.8	80.9	37	40	4.9	5.3
Brunswick	5 14,022	5 14,022	290	314	222	267	20.7	22.4	15.8	19.1	68	47	131	118	21	23	72.4	73.2	25	38	8.6	12.1
Colored	6,050	6,050	111	122	132	163	18.3	20.3	21.8	27.2	−21	−41	84	75	15	11	135.1	90.2	17	32	15.3	26.2
White	7,972	7,972	179	192	90	104	22.5	24.0	11.3	13.0	89	88	(4)	185	6	12	33.5	62.5	8	6	4.5	3.1
Columbus	43,400	43,200	882	840	767	776	20.3	19.4	17.7	18.0	115	64	115	108	86	80	97.5	95.2	51	35	5.8	4.2
Colored	14,400	14,200	368	330	347	344	25.6	23.2	24.1	24.2	21	−14	106	96	40	30	108.7	90.9	37	23	10.1	7.0
White	29,000	29,000	514	510	420	432	17.7	17.6	14.5	14.9	94	78	122	118	46	50	89.5	98.0	14	12	2.7	2.4
Decatur	14,100	13,500	91	155	107	132	6.5	11.5	7.6	9.8	−16	23	85	117	9	7	98.9	45.2	4	5	4.4	3.2
Colored	2,600	2,600	37	65	38	53	14.2	25.0	14.6	20.4	−1	12	(4)	(4)	8	4	216.2	61.5	3	1	8.1	1.5
White	11,500	10,900	54	90	69	79	4.7	8.3	6.0	7.2	−15	11	(4)	(4)	1	3	18.5	33.3	1	4	1.9	4.4
Griffin	10,600	10,400	334	299	229	285	31.5	28.8	21.6	27.4	105	14	146	105	23	36	68.9	120.4	29	24	8.7	8.0
Colored	3,500	3,400	97	97	127	124	27.7	28.5	36.3	36.5	−30	−27	76	78	13	15	134.0	154.6	12	16	12.4	16.5
White	7,100	7,000	237	202	102	161	33.4	28.9	14.4	23.0	135	41	232	125	10	21	42.2	104.0	17	8	7.2	4.0
La Grange	20,500	20,200	431	525	234	289	21.0	26.0	11.4	14.3	197	236	184	182	30	58	69.6	110.5	14	19	3.2	3.6
Colored	5,600	5,500	110	129	102	130	19.6	23.5	18.2	23.6	8	−1	108	99	13	26	118.2	201.6	6	7	5.5	6.5
White	14,900	14,700	321	396	132	159	21.5	26.9	8.9	10.8	189	237	243	249	17	32	53.0	80.8	8	12	2.5	3.0
Macon	53,900	53,800	1,145	1,198	942	1,061	21.2	22.3	17.5	19.7	203	137	122	113	72	110	62.9	91.8	78	100	6.8	8.3
Colored	23,100	23,100	545	518	529	609	23.6	22.4	22.9	26.4	16	−91	103	85	46	62	84.4	119.7	58	60	10.6	11.6
White	30,800	30,700	600	680	413	452	19.5	22.1	13.4	14.7	187	228	145	150	26	48	43.3	70.6	20	40	3.3	5.9
Rome	22,200	22,100	480	472	321	311	21.6	21.4	14.5	14.1	159	161	150	152	48	46	100.0	97.5	36	33	7.5	7.0
Colored	4,700	4,800	80	61	116	93	17.0	12.7	24.7	19.4	−36	−32	69	(4)	19	9	237.5	147.5	17	15	21.3	24.6
White	17,500	17,300	400	411	205	218	22.9	23.8	11.7	12.6	195	193	195	189	29	37	72.5	90.0	19	18	4.8	4.4
Savannah	5 85,024	5 85,024	1,625	1,615	1,640	1,660	19.1	19.0	19.3	19.5	−15	−45	99	97	139	136	85.5	84.2	129	135	7.9	8.4
Colored	38,954	38,954	674	700	1,016	1,033	17.3	18.0	26.1	26.5	−342	−333	66	68	90	91	133.5	130.0	92	93	13.6	13.3
White	46,070	46,070	951	915	624	627	20.6	19.9	13.5	13.6	327	288	152	146	49	45	51.5	49.2	37	42	3.9	4.6
Thomasville	12,100	11,800	283	289	264	262	23.4	24.5	21.8	22.2	19	27	107	110	27	24	95.4	83.0	31	30	11.0	10.4
Colored	6,200	6,100	163	162	135	155	26.3	26.6	21.8	25.4	28	7	121	105	17	15	104.3	92.6	24	21	14.7	13.0
White	5,900	5,700	120	127	129	107	20.3	22.3	21.9	18.8	−9	20	93	119	10	9	83.3	70.9	7	9	5.8	7.1
Valdosta	13,800	13,500	305	316	266	236	22.1	23.4	19.3	17.5	39	80	115	134	30	28	98.4	88.6	38	23	12.5	7.3
Colored	6,300	6,200	164	164	130	127	26.0	26.5	20.6	20.5	34	37	126	129	22	17	134.1	103.7	29	16	17.7	9.8
White	7,500	7,300	141	152	136	109	18.8	20.8	18.1	14.9	5	43	104	139	8	11	56.7	72.4	9	7	6.4	4.6
Waycross	5 15,510	5 15,510	405	389	255	278	26.1	25.1	16.4	18.1	150	111	159	140	28	26	69.1	66.8	38	35	9.4	9.0
Colored	5,956	5,956	134	120	123	138	22.5	20.7	20.7	23.8	11	−18	109	87	19	12	141.8	100.0	20	23	14.9	19.2
White	9,554	9,554	271	269	132	140	28.4	28.2	13.8	14.6	139	129	205	192	9	14	33.2	52.0	18	12	6.6	4.5
ILLINOIS CITIES																						
Cairo	5 13,532	5 13,532	150	198	217	268	11.1	14.6	16.0	19.8	−67	−70	69	74	19	11	126.7	55.6	13	9	8.7	4.5
Colored	4,584	4,584	43	39	91	111	9.4	8.5	19.9	24.2	−48	−72	(4)	35	8	7	186.0	179.5	5	4	11.6	10.3
White	8,948	8,948	107	159	126	157	12.0	17.8	14.1	17.5	−19	2	85	101	11	4	102.8	25.2	8	5	7.5	3.1
Chicago	3,458,100	3,392,700	52,993	58,083	36,081	35,316	15.3	17.1	10.4	10.4	16,912	22,767	147	164	2,992	3,112	56.5	53.6	1,905	2,072	3.6	3.6
Colored	276,400	262,200	5,023	4,739	4,232	4,045	18.2	18.1	15.3	15.4	791	694	119	117	375	367	74.7	77.4	297	292	5.9	6.2
White	3,181,700	3,130,500	47,970	53,344	31,849	31,271	15.1	17.0	10.0	10.0	16,121	22,073	151	171	2,617	2,745	54.6	51.5	1,608	1,780	3.4	3.3
Chicago Heights	22,700	22,400	406	469	214	227	17.9	20.9	9.4	10.1	192	242	190	207	31	34	76.4	72.5	17	15	4.2	3.2
Colored	2,600	(3)	30	(3)	34	(3)	11.5	(3)	13.1	(3)	−4	(3)	(4)	(3)	4	(3)	133.3	(3)	1	(3)	3.3	(3)
White	20,100	(3)	376	(3)	180	(3)	18.7	(3)	9.0	(3)	196	(3)	209	(3)	27	(3)	71.8	(3)	16	(3)	4.3	(3)
East St. Louis	75,300	74,500	1,292	1,417	908	886	17.2	19.0	12.1	11.9	384	531	142	160	102	114	78.9	80.5	60	58	4.6	4.1
Colored	12,100	11,600	187	208	238	173	15.5	17.9	19.7	14.9	−51	35	79	120	38	33	203.2	158.7	15	19	8.0	9.1
White	63,200	62,900	1,105	1,209	670	713	17.5	19.2	10.6	11.3	435	496	165	170	64	81	57.9	67.0	45	39	4.1	3.2

See footnotes at end of table.

TABLE 18.—COLORED [1] AND WHITE POPULATION, BIRTHS AND DEATHS, INFANT MORTALITY, AND STILLBIRTHS, IN SELECTED REGISTRATION STATES, CITIES, AND COUNTIES: 1931 AND 1930—Continued

[See note at head of this table]

AREA AND COLOR	POPULATION ESTIMATED AS OF JULY 1		BIRTHS AND DEATHS (*Exclusive of stillbirths*)												INFANT MORTALITY (*Exclusive of stillbirths*)				STILLBIRTHS			
			Number				Rate per 1,000 population				Excess of births over deaths [2]		Births per 100 deaths		Deaths of infants under 1 year of age				Number		Rate per 100 live births	
			Births		Deaths		Births		Deaths						Number		Per 1,000 births					
	1931	1930	1931	1930	1931	1930	1931	1930	1931	1930	1931	1930	1931	1930	1931	1930	1931	1930	1931	1930	1931	1930
INDIANA CITIES																						
East Chicago	57,100	55,200	1,152	1,282	490	558	20.2	23.2	8.6	10.1	662	724	235	230	75	102	65.1	79.6	31	47	2.7	3.7
Colored	11,500	(3)	110	(3)	130	(3)	9.6	(3)	11.3	(3)	−20	(3)	85	(3)	23	(3)	209.1	(3)	5	(3)	4.5	(2)
White	45,600	(3)	1,042	(3)	360	(3)	22.9	(3)	7.9	(3)	682	(3)	289	(3)	52	(3)	49.9	(3)	26	(3)	2.5	(3)
Gary	105,900	101,500	2,095	2,301	1,019	975	19.8	22.7	9.6	9.6	1,076	1,326	206	236	132	157	63.0	68.2	71	75	3.4	3.3
Colored	23,400	(3)	338	(3)	285	(3)	14.4	(3)	12.2	(3)	53	(3)	119	(3)	29	(3)	85.8	(3)	17	(3)	5.0	(3)
White	82,500	(3)	1,757	(3)	734	(3)	21.3	(3)	8.9	(3)	1,023	(3)	239	(3)	103	(3)	58.6	(3)	54	(3)	3.1	(3)
Indianapolis	369,800	365,300	6,586	6,806	5,020	5,193	17.8	18.6	13.6	14.2	1,566	1,613	131	131	382	434	58.0	63.8	200	221	3.0	3.2
Colored	45,200	44,300	801	849	782	867	17.7	19.2	17.3	19.6	19	−18	102	98	57	104	71.2	122.5	48	45	6.0	5.3
White	324,600	321,000	5,785	5,957	4,238	4,326	17.8	18.6	13.1	13.5	1,547	1,631	137	138	325	330	56.2	55.4	152	176	2.6	3.0
Jeffersonville	12,200	12,000	185	199	162	200	15.2	16.6	13.3	16.7	23	−1	114	100	11	17	59.5	84.5	9	9	4.9	4.5
Colored	1,300	1,300	16	16	28	30	12.3	12.3	21.5	23.1	−12	−14	(4)	(4)	3	1	187.5	62.5	4	1	25.0	6.3
White	10,900	10,700	169	183	134	170	15.5	17.1	12.3	15.9	35	13	126	108	8	16	47.3	87.4	5	8	3.0	4.4
KANSAS CITIES																						
Atchison	13,100	13,000	280	285	195	199	21.4	21.9	14.9	15.3	85	86	144	143	13	12	46.4	42.1	13	9	4.6	3.2
Colored	1,700	1,600	27	26	29	35	15.9	16.3	17.1	21.9	−2	−9	(4)	(4)	3	2	111.1	76.9	3	1	11.1	3.8
White	11,400	11,400	253	259	166	164	22.2	22.7	14.6	14.4	87	95	152	158	10	10	39.5	38.6	10	8	4.0	3.1
Coffeyville	16,200	16,200	301	341	163	233	18.6	21.0	10.1	14.4	138	108	185	146	9	29	29.9	85.0	6	12	2.0	3.5
Colored	2,100	2,100	31	42	23	42	14.8	20.0	11.0	20.0	8	--------	(4)	(4)	5	8	161.3	190.5	--------	--------	--------	--------
White	14,100	14,100	270	299	140	191	19.1	21.2	9.9	13.5	130	108	193	157	4	21	14.8	70.2	6	12	2.2	4.0
Kansas City	122,900	122,100	2,302	2,362	1,569	1,678	18.7	19.3	12.8	13.7	733	684	147	141	153	156	66.5	66.0	87	91	3.8	3.9
Colored	23,200	22,800	386	409	343	341	16.6	17.9	14.8	15.0	43	68	113	120	15	24	38.9	58.7	28	27	7.3	6.6
White	99,700	99,300	1,916	1,953	1,226	1,337	19.2	19.7	12.3	13.5	690	616	156	146	138	132	72.0	67.6	59	64	3.1	3.3
Lawrence	13,900	13,800	281	278	170	190	20.2	20.1	12.2	13.8	111	88	165	146	14	10	49.8	36.0	6	9	2.1	3.2
Colored	1,500	1,600	30	17	26	29	20.0	10.6	17.3	18.1	4	−12	(4)	(4)	1	1	33.3	58.8	3	2	10.0	11.8
White	12,400	12,200	251	261	144	161	20.2	21.4	11.6	13.2	107	100	174	162	13	9	51.8	34.5	3	7	1.2	2.7
Leavenworth	17,500	17,500	295	298	255	274	16.9	17.0	14.6	15.7	40	24	116	109	22	20	74.6	67.1	15	8	5.1	2.7
Colored	2,200	2,300	24	26	52	45	10.9	11.3	23.6	19.6	−28	−19	(4)	(4)	3	--------	125.0	--------	5	1	20.8	3.8
White	15,300	15,200	271	272	203	229	17.7	17.9	13.3	15.1	68	43	133	119	19	20	70.1	73.5	10	7	3.7	2.6
Parsons	[5] 14,903	[5] 14,903	202	205	194	223	13.6	13.8	13.0	15.0	8	−18	104	92	12	13	59.4	63.4	6	10	3.0	4.9
Colored	1,531	(3)	30	(3)	19	(3)	19.6	(3)	12.4	(3)	11	(3)	(4)	(3)	3	(3)	100.0	(3)	--------	(3)	--------	(3)
White	13,372	(3)	172	(3)	175	(3)	12.9	(3)	13.1	(3)	−3	(3)	98	(3)	9	(3)	52.3	(3)	6	(3)	3.5	(3)
Topeka	65,200	64,300	1,127	1,234	824	898	17.3	19.2	12.6	14.0	303	336	137	137	54	67	47.9	54.3	32	40	2.8	3.2
Colored	7,700	(3)	140	(3)	99	(3)	18.2	(3)	12.9	(3)	41	(3)	(4)	(3)	4	(3)	28.6	(3)	3	(3)	2.1	(3)
White	57,500	(3)	987	(3)	725	(3)	17.2	(3)	12.6	(3)	262	(3)	136	(3)	50	(3)	50.7	(3)	29	(3)	2.9	(3)
KENTUCKY CITIES																						
Bowling Green	12,700	12,400	239	290	213	214	18.8	23.4	16.8	17.3	26	76	112	136	19	17	79.5	58.6	13	11	5.4	3.8
Colored	2,500	2,400	28	44	51	48	11.2	18.3	20.4	20.0	−23	−4	(4)	(4)	1	3	35.7	68.2	1	3	3.6	6.8
White	10,200	10,000	211	246	162	166	20.7	24.6	15.9	16.6	49	80	130	148	18	14	85.3	56.9	12	8	5.7	3.3
Frankfort	11,800	11,700	175	185	224	194	14.8	15.8	19.0	16.6	−49	−9	78	95	15	20	85.7	108.1	10	5	5.7	2.7
Colored	2,200	2,200	21	19	50	58	9.5	8.6	22.7	26.4	−29	−39	(4)	(4)	1	4	47.6	210.5	1	2	4.8	10.5
White	9,600	9,500	154	166	174	136	16.0	17.5	18.1	14.3	−20	30	89	122	14	16	90.9	96.4	9	3	5.8	1.8
Henderson	[5] 11,668	[5] 11,668	224	211	211	212	19.2	18.1	18.1	18.2	13	−1	106	100	15	23	67.0	109.0	8	10	3.6	4.7
Colored	2,346	2,346	42	34	58	75	17.9	14.5	24.7	32.0	−16	−41	(4)	(4)	5	11	119.0	323.5	4	3	9.5	8.8
White	9,322	9,322	182	177	153	137	19.5	19.0	16.4	14.7	29	40	119	129	10	12	54.9	67.8	4	7	2.2	4.0
Hopkinsville	10,900	10,800	195	200	252	254	17.9	18.5	23.1	23.5	−57	−54	77	79	22	11	112.8	55.0	11	9	5.6	4.5
Colored	4,000	4,000	50	54	122	146	12.5	13.5	30.5	36.5	−72	−92	41	37	12	5	240.0	92.6	5	6	10.0	11.1
White	6,900	6,800	145	146	130	108	21.0	21.5	18.8	15.9	15	38	112	135	10	6	69.0	41.1	6	3	4.1	2.1
Lexington	46,000	45,800	876	914	1,140	1,115	19.0	20.0	24.8	24.3	−264	−201	77	82	102	79	116.4	86.4	37	32	4.2	3.5
Colored	12,700	12,800	185	180	379	421	14.6	14.1	29.8	32.9	−194	−241	49	43	42	22	227.0	122.2	15	11	8.1	6.1
White	33,300	33,000	691	734	761	694	20.8	22.2	22.9	21.0	−70	40	91	106	60	57	86.8	77.7	22	21	3.2	2.9
Louisville	308,300	307,900	5,367	5,730	4,314	4,390	17.4	18.6	14.0	14.3	1,053	1,340	124	131	415	385	77.3	67.2	184	208	3.4	3.6
Colored	47,700	47,500	743	727	1,042	1,104	15.6	15.3	21.8	23.2	−299	−377	71	66	107	70	144.0	96.3	49	69	6.6	9.5
White	260,600	260,400	4,624	5,003	3,272	3,286	17.7	19.2	12.6	12.6	1,352	1,717	141	152	308	315	66.6	63.0	135	139	2.9	2.8
Owensboro	23,000	22,800	479	534	336	385	20.8	23.4	14.6	16.9	143	149	143	139	35	46	73.1	86.1	16	21	3.3	3.9
Colored	2,400	2,500	23	41	51	62	9.6	16.4	21.3	24.8	−28	−21	(4)	(4)	3	2	130.4	48.8	3	3	13.0	7.3
White	20,600	20,300	456	493	285	323	22.1	24.3	13.8	15.9	171	170	160	153	32	44	70.2	89.2	13	18	2.9	3.7
Paducah	34,600	33,800	549	708	516	492	15.9	20.9	14.9	14.6	33	216	106	144	50	56	91.1	79.1	26	29	4.7	4.1
Colored	6,900	6,800	50	86	167	141	7.2	12.6	24.2	20.7	−117	−55	30	61	13	12	260.0	139.5	7	6	14.0	7.0
White	27,700	27,000	499	622	349	351	18.0	23.0	12.6	13.0	150	271	143	177	37	44	74.1	70.7	19	23	3.8	3.7

LOUISIANA CITIES																						
Alexandria	23,700	23,200	470	444	301	355	19.8	19.1	12.7	15.3	169	89	156	125	30	38	63.8	85.6	41	39	8.7	8.8
Colored	9,800	9,600	185	159	143	171	18.9	16.6	14.6	17.8	42	−12	129	93	13	19	70.3	119.5	15	23	8.1	14.5
White	13,900	13,600	285	285	158	184	20.5	21.0	11.4	13.5	127	101	180	155	17	19	59.6	66.7	26	16	9.1	5.6
Baton Rouge	31,600	30,900	395	421	289	289	12.5	13.6	9.1	9.4	106	132	137	146	21	26	53.2	61.8	37	43	9.4	10.2
Colored	10,900	10,700	143	151	134	116	13.1	14.1	12.3	10.8	9	35	107	130	7	9	49.0	59.6	20	29	14.0	19.2
White	20,700	20,200	252	270	155	173	12.2	13.4	7.5	8.6	97	97	163	156	14	17	55.6	63.0	17	14	6.7	5.2
Bogalusa	14,700	14,200	307	357	179	177	20.9	25.1	12.2	12.5	128	180	172	202	19	32	61.9	89.6	16	30	5.2	8.4
Colored	5,000	4,800	85	97	83	82	17.0	20.2	16.6	17.1	2	15	(4)	(4)	11	19	129.4	195.9	8	11	9.4	11.3
White	9,700	9,400	222	260	96	95	22.9	27.7	9.9	10.1	126	165	(4)	(4)	8	13	36.0	50.0	8	19	3.6	7.3
Lafayette	15,500	14,800	349	371	146	160	22.5	25.1	9.4	10.8	203	211	239	232	22	32	63.0	86.3	18	22	5.2	5.9
Colored	5,300	5,100	129	143	70	98	24.3	28.0	13.2	19.2	59	45	(4)	(4)	14	19	108.5	132.9	11	15	8.5	10.5
White	10,200	9,700	220	228	76	62	21.6	23.5	7.5	6.4	144	166	(4)	(4)	8	13	36.4	57.0	7	7	3.2	3.1
Lake Charles	16,100	15,900	385	403	263	255	23.9	25.3	16.3	16.0	122	148	146	158	26	49	67.5	121.6	26	23	6.8	5.7
Colored	6,100	6,000	166	167	104	82	27.2	27.8	17.0	13.7	62	85	160	(4)	12	24	72.3	143.7	16	14	9.6	8.4
White	10,000	9,900	219	236	159	173	21.9	23.8	15.9	17.5	60	63	138	136	14	25	63.9	105.9	10	9	4.6	3.8
Monroe	29,100	26,600	557	582	446	499	19.1	21.9	15.3	18.8	111	83	125	117	50	48	89.8	82.5	42	45	7.5	7.7
Colored	11,200	10,300	156	162	204	225	13.9	15.7	18.2	21.8	−48	−63	76	72	17	15	109.0	92.6	21	25	13.5	15.4
White	17,900	16,300	401	420	242	274	22.4	25.8	13.5	16.8	159	146	166	153	33	33	82.3	78.6	21	20	5.2	4.8
New Orleans	467,500	460,500	9,202	9,337	7,673	8,030	19.7	20.3	16.4	17.4	1,529	1,307	120	116	691	821	75.1	87.9	315	392	3.4	4.2
Colored	134,600	131,700	3,176	3,158	3,166	3,289	23.6	24.0	23.5	25.0	10	−131	100	96	329	380	103.6	120.3	126	140	4.0	4.4
White	332,900	328,800	6,026	6,179	4,507	4,741	18.1	18.8	13.5	14.4	1,519	1,438	134	130	362	441	60.1	71.4	189	252	3.1	4.1
Shreveport	77,800	76,900	1,789	1,739	1,595	1,669	23.0	22.6	20.5	21.7	194	70	112	104	159	151	88.9	86.8	142	138	7.9	7.9
Colored	26,700	27,200	723	627	805	874	27.1	23.1	30.1	32.1	−82	−247	90	72	86	76	118.9	121.2	95	86	13.1	13.7
White	51,100	49,700	1,066	1,112	790	795	20.9	22.4	15.5	16.0	276	317	135	140	73	75	68.5	67.4	47	52	4.4	4.7
MARYLAND CITIES																						
Annapolis	12,700	12,600	301	281	183	170	23.7	22.3	14.4	13.5	118	111	164	165	21	16	69.8	56.9	16	22	5.3	7.8
Colored	3,500	3,500	77	72	74	84	22.0	20.6	21.1	24.0	3	−12	(4)	(4)	13	8	168.8	111.1	6	9	7.8	12.5
White	9,200	9,100	224	209	109	86	24.3	23.0	11.8	9.5	115	123	206	(4)	8	8	35.7	38.3	10	13	4.5	6.2
Baltimore	813,500	806,600	14,210	14,994	11,522	11,239	17.5	18.6	14.2	13.9	2,688	3,755	123	133	1,055	981	74.2	65.4	881	989	6.2	6.6
Colored	146,900	143,500	3,159	3,269	2,921	2,815	21.5	22.8	19.9	19.6	238	454	108	116	352	307	111.4	93.9	312	378	9.9	11.6
White	666,600	663,100	11,051	11,725	8,601	8,424	16.6	17.7	12.9	12.7	2,450	3,301	128	139	703	674	63.6	57.5	569	611	5.1	5.2
Frederick	14,800	14,500	321	348	256	269	21.7	24.0	17.3	18.6	65	79	125	129	25	29	77.9	83.3	21	25	6.5	7.2
Colored	1,600	1,600	26	27	18	27	16.3	16.9	11.3	16.9	8	--------	(4)	(4)	5	5	192.3	185.2	3	3	11.5	11.1
White	13,200	12,900	295	321	238	242	22.3	24.9	18.0	18.8	57	79	124	133	20	24	67.8	74.8	18	22	6.1	6.9
Salisbury	11,400	11,100	389	357	256	244	34.1	32.2	22.5	22.0	133	113	152	146	32	42	82.3	117.6	41	33	10.5	9.2
Colored	1,900	1,900	95	94	72	69	50.0	49.5	37.9	36.3	23	25	(3)	(4)	8	19	84.2	202.1	15	10	15.8	10.6
White	9,500	9,200	294	263	184	175	30.9	28.6	19.4	19.0	110	88	160	150	24	23	81.6	87.5	26	23	8.8	8.7
MASSACHUSETTS CITIES																						
Boston	785,200	782,000	17,136	18,062	11,029	11,018	21.8	23.1	14.0	14.1	6,107	7,044	155	164	1,040	1,263	60.7	69.9	528	520	3.1	2.9
Colored	23,000	22,600	500	488	416	452	21.7	21.6	18.1	20.0	84	36	120	108	39	44	78.0	90.2	30	20	6.0	4.1
White	762,200	759,400	16,636	17,574	10,613	10,566	21.8	23.1	13.9	13.9	6,023	7,008	157	166	1,001	1,219	60.2	69.4	498	500	3.0	2.8
MICHIGAN CITIES																						
Detroit	1,653,100	1,585,600	28,778	32,966	13,403	14,729	17.4	20.8	8.1	9.3	15,375	18,237	215	224	1,614	2,134	56.1	64.7	1,059	1,273	3.7	3.9
Colored	140,100	130,900	2,453	2,713	1,851	2,037	17.5	20.7	13.2	15.6	602	676	133	133	208	245	84.8	90.3	137	158	5.6	5.8
White	1,513,000	1,454,700	26,325	30,253	11,552	12,692	17.4	20.8	7.6	8.7	14,773	17,561	228	238	1,406	1,889	53.4	62.4	922	1,115	3.5	3.7
Ecorse	13,700	12,900	220	335	71	74	16.1	26.0	5.2	5.7	149	261	(4)	(4)	10	15	45.5	44.8	5	6	2.3	1.8
Colored	1,600	(3)	18	(3)	13	(3)	11.3	(3)	8.1	(3)	5	(3)	(4)	(3)	3	(3)	166.7	(3)	--------	(3)	--------	(3)
White	12,100	(3)	202	(3)	58	(3)	16.7	(3)	4.8	(4)	144	(3)	(4)	(3)	7	(3)	34.7	(3)	5	(3)	2.5	(3)
Ypsilanti	10,500	10,200	207	230	132	137	19.7	22.5	12.6	13.4	75	93	157	168	10	9	48.3	39.1	6	11	2.9	4.8
Colored	1,400	(3)	23	(3)	16	(3)	16.4	(2)	11.4	(3)	7	(3)	(4)	(3)	(3)	(3)	130.4	(3)	1	(3)	4.3	(3)
White	9,100	(3)	184	(3)	116	(3)	20.2	(3)	12.7	(3)	68	(3)	159	(3)	7	(3)	38.0	(3)	5	(3)	2.7	(3)
MISSISSIPPI CITIES																						
Biloxi	15,300	14,900	350	376	212	214	22.9	25.2	13.9	14.4	138	162	165	176	22	30	62.9	79.8	18	16	5.1	4.3
Colored	2,500	2,400	42	44	37	52	16.8	18.3	14.8	21.7	5	−8	(4)	(4)	3	7	71.4	159.1	8	5	19.0	11.4
White	12,800	12,500	308	332	175	162	24.1	26.6	13.7	13.0	133	170	176	205	19	23	61.7	69.3	10	11	3.2	3.3
Clarksdale	10,400	10,100	244	299	204	176	23.5	29.6	19.6	17.4	40	123	120	170	11	18	45.1	60.2	19	24	7.8	8.0
Colored	5,100	5,000	155	174	160	140	30.4	34.8	31.4	28.0	−5	34	97	124	8	14	51.6	80.5	15	23	9.7	13.2
White	5,300	5,100	89	125	44	36	16.8	24.5	8.3	7.1	45	89	(4)	(4)	3	4	33.7	32.0	4	1	4.5	.8
Columbus	10,800	10,700	293	330	219	236	27.1	30.8	20.3	22.1	74	94	134	140	18	33	61.4	100.0	13	27	4.4	8.2
Colored	4,800	4,800	156	156	135	154	32.5	32.5	28.1	32.1	21	2	116	101	12	24	76.9	153.8	7	20	4.5	12.8
White	6,000	5,900	137	174	84	82	22.8	29.5	14.0	13.9	53	92	(4)	(4)	6	9	43.8	51.7	6	7	4.4	4.0
Greenville	14,900	14,800	364	436	420	458	24.4	29.5	28.2	30.9	−56	−22	87	95	37	36	101.6	82.6	22	24	6.0	5.5
Colored	8,500	8,400	159	206	300	336	18.7	24.5	35.3	40.0	−141	−130	53	61	20	20	125.8	97.1	13	5	8.2	2.4
White	6,400	6,400	205	230	120	122	32.0	35.9	18.8	19.1	85	108	171	189	17	16	82.9	69.6	9	19	4.4	8.3
Greenwood	11,500	11,200	233	341	176	208	20.3	30.4	15.3	18.6	57	133	132	164	10	8	42.9	23.5	5	16	2.1	4.7
Colored	5,500	5,400	125	206	114	144	22.7	38.1	20.7	26.7	11	62	110	143	6	5	48.0	24.3	4	15	3.2	7.3
White	6,000	5,800	108	135	62	64	18.0	23.3	10.3	11.0	46	71	(4)	(4)	4	3	37.0	22.2	1	1	.9	.7
Gulfport	13,100	12,700	252	252	189	227	19.2	19.8	14.4	17.9	63	25	133	111	16	22	63.5	87.3	21	13	8.3	5.2
Colored	3,300	3,200	62	61	67	70	18.8	19.1	20.3	21.9	−5	−9	(4)	(4)	5	8	80.6	131.1	9	8	14.5	13.1
White	9,800	9,500	190	191	122	157	19.4	20.1	12.4	16.5	68	34	156	122	11	14	57.9	73.3	12	5	6.3	2.6
Hattiesburg	19,300	18,700	438	507	283	326	22.7	27.1	14.7	17.4	155	181	155	156	30	53	68.5	104.5	33	33	7.5	6.5
Colored	7,100	6,800	155	173	110	133	21.8	25.4	15.5	19.6	45	40	141	130	15	16	96.8	92.5	15	27	9.7	15.6
White	12,200	11,900	283	324	173	193	23.2	28.1	14.2	16.2	110	141	164	173	15	37	53.0	110.8	18	6	6.4	1.8
Jackson	51,200	48,800	871	958	822	796	17.0	19.6	16.1	16.3	−274	162	76	120	69	74	79.2	77.2	70	90	8.0	9.4
Colored	20,500	19,600	330	367	431	414	16.1	18.7	21.0	21.1	−328	−47	50	89	31	43	93.9	117.2	46	60	13.9	16.3
White	30,700	29,200	541	591	391	382	17.6	20.2	12.7	13.1	54	209	111	155	38	31	70.2	52.5	24	30	4.4	5.1

See footnotes at end of table.

TABLE 18.—COLORED [1] AND WHITE POPULATION, BIRTHS AND DEATHS, INFANT MORTALITY, AND STILLBIRTHS, IN SELECTED REGISTRATION STATES, CITIES, AND COUNTIES: 1931 AND 1930—Continued

[See note at head of this table]

AREA AND COLOR	POPULATION ESTIMATED AS OF JULY 1		BIRTHS AND DEATHS (*Exclusive of stillbirths*)												INFANT MORTALITY (*Exclusive of stillbirths*)				STILLBIRTHS			
			Number				Rate per 1,000 population				Excess of births over deaths [2]		Births per 100 deaths		Deaths of infants under 1 year of age				Number		Rate per 100 live births	
			Births		Deaths		Births		Deaths						Number		Per 1,000 births					
	1931	1930	1931	1930	1931	1930	1931	1930	1931	1930	1931	1930	1931	1930	1931	1930	1931	1930	1931	1930	1931	1930
MISSISSIPPI CITIES—continued																						
Laurel	18,600	18,100	742	695	391	345	39.9	38.4	21.0	19.1	351	350	190	201	42	43	56.6	61.9	50	34	6.7	4.9
Colored	7,100	6,800	178	171	136	142	25.1	25.1	19.2	20.9	42	29	131	120	5	11	28.1	64.3	15	14	8.4	8.2
White	11,500	11,300	564	524	255	203	49.0	46.4	22.2	18.0	309	321	221	258	37	32	65.6	61.1	35	20	6.2	3.8
McComb	10,300	10,100	269	242	204	174	26.1	24.0	19.8	17.2	65	68	132	139	19	16	70.6	66.1	9	11	3.3	4.5
Colored	2,000	2,000	69	57	71	61	34.5	28.5	35.5	30.5	−2	−4	(4)	(4)	5	2	72.5	35.1	5	6	7.2	10.5
White	8,300	8,100	200	185	133	113	24.1	22.8	16.0	14.0	67	72	150	164	14	14	70.0	75.7	4	5	2.0	2.7
Meridian	32,000	32,000	711	789	675	666	22.2	24.7	21.1	20.8	36	123	105	118	74	57	104.1	72.2	53	53	7.5	6.7
Colored	11,400	11,400	228	270	298	294	20.0	23.7	26.1	25.8	−70	−24	77	92	31	32	136.0	118.5	35	38	15.4	14.1
White	20,600	20,600	483	519	377	372	23.4	25.2	18.3	18.1	106	147	128	140	43	25	89.0	48.2	18	15	3.7	2.9
Natchez	13,500	13,400	225	241	223	246	16.7	18.0	16.5	18.4	2	−5	101	98	18	13	80.0	53.9	23	28	10.2	11.6
Colored	7,200	7,100	92	118	139	149	12.8	16.6	19.3	21.0	−47	−31	66	79	11	10	119.6	84.7	18	19	19.6	16.1
White	6,300	6,300	133	123	84	97	21.1	19.5	13.3	15.4	49	26	(4)	(4)	7	3	52.6	24.4	5	9	3.8	7.3
Vicksburg	23,500	23,100	473	527	662	743	20.1	22.8	28.2	32.2	−189	−216	71	71	42	49	88.8	93.0	30	26	6.3	4.9
Colored	12,200	12,000	219	242	430	521	18.0	20.2	35.2	43.4	−211	−279	51	46	25	31	114.2	128.1	22	19	10.0	7.9
White	11,300	11,100	254	285	232	222	22.5	25.7	20.5	20.0	22	63	109	128	17	18	66.9	63.2	8	7	3.1	2.5
MISSOURI CITIES																						
Columbia	15,500	15,100	278	269	208	207	17.9	17.8	13.4	13.7	70	62	134	130	20	14	71.9	52.0	26	23	9.4	8.6
Colored	2,300	2,300	41	30	65	52	17.8	13.0	28.3	22.6	−24	−22	(4)	(4)	5	4	122.0	133.3	2	4	4.9	13.3
White	13,200	12,800	237	239	143	155	18.0	18.7	10.8	12.1	94	84	166	154	15	10	63.3	41.8	24	19	10.1	7.9
Jefferson City	22,200	21,700	377	402	291	246	17.0	18.5	13.1	11.3	86	156	130	163	31	24	82.2	59.7	10	12	2.7	3.0
Colored	2,200	2,200	14	11	36	24	6.4	5.0	16.4	10.9	−22	−13	(4)	(4)	2	1	142.9	90.9	1	1	7.1	9.1
White	20,000	19,500	363	391	255	222	18.2	20.1	12.8	11.4	108	169	142	176	29	23	79.9	58.8	9	11	2.5	2.8
Kansas City	408,900	401,600	6,109	6,501	5,216	5,301	14.9	16.2	12.8	13.2	893	1,200	117	123	419	440	68.6	67.7	215	227	3.5	3.5
Colored	43,100	42,200	564	621	882	922	13.1	14.7	20.5	21.8	−318	−301	64	67	71	62	125.9	99.8	29	33	5.1	5.3
White	365,800	359,400	5,545	5,880	4,334	4,379	15.2	16.4	11.8	12.2	1,211	1,501	128	134	348	378	62.8	64.3	186	194	3.4	3.3
St. Louis	827,900	823,200	13,650	14,496	12,111	11,482	16.5	17.6	14.6	13.9	1,539	3,014	113	126	866	787	63.4	54.3	706	787	5.2	5.4
Colored	98,000	95,700	1,783	1,873	2,126	1,982	18.2	19.6	21.7	20.7	−343	−109	84	95	158	167	88.6	89.2	190	229	10.7	12.2
White	729,900	727,500	11,867	12,623	9,985	9,500	16.3	17.4	13.7	13.1	1,882	3,123	119	133	708	620	59.7	49.1	516	558	4.3	4.4
Sedalia	[5] 20,806	[5] 20,806	318	361	283	278	15.3	17.4	13.6	13.4	35	83	112	130	21	17	66.0	47.1	17	14	5.3	3.9
Colored	2,157	(3)	19	(3)	38	(3)	8.8	(3)	17.6	(3)	−19	(3)	(4)	(3)	5	(3)	263.2	(3)	4	(3)	21.1	(3)
White	18,649	(3)	299	(3)	245	(3)	16.0	(3)	13.1	(3)	54	(3)	122	(3)	16	(3)	53.5	(3)	13	(3)	4.3	(3)
NEBRASKA CITIES																						
Omaha	216,700	214,500	4,367	4,524	2,870	2,819	20.2	21.1	13.2	13.1	1,497	1,705	152	160	235	225	53.8	49.7	125	127	2.9	2.8
Colored	12,500	12,300	259	254	253	223	20.7	20.7	20.2	18.1	6	31	102	114	22	12	84.9	47.2	6	15	2.3	5.9
White	204,200	202,200	4,108	4,270	2,617	2,596	20.1	21.1	12.8	12.8	1,491	1,674	157	164	213	213	51.9	49.9	119	112	2.9	2.6
NEW JERSEY CITIES																						
Asbury Park	15,300	15,000	159	144	134	146	10.4	9.6	8.8	9.7	25	−2	119	99	4	8	25.2	55.6	6	8	3.8	5.6
Colored	3,700	3,500	22	19	23	22	5.9	5.4	6.2	6.3	−1	−3	(4)	(4)	----	2	----	105.3	3	2	13.6	10.5
White	11,600	11,500	137	125	111	124	11.8	10.9	9.6	10.8	26	1	123	101	4	6	29.2	48.0	3	6	2.2	4.8
Atlantic City	68,100	66,600	1,226	1,223	1,156	1,122	18.0	18.4	17.0	16.8	70	101	106	109	93	79	75.9	64.6	44	50	3.6	4.1
Colored	16,300	15,800	328	275	296	268	20.1	17.4	18.2	17.0	32	7	111	103	32	30	97.6	109.1	11	20	3.4	7.3
White	51,800	50,800	898	948	860	854	17.3	18.7	16.6	16.8	38	94	104	111	61	49	67.9	51.7	33	30	3.7	3.2
Burlington	11,100	10,900	124	171	96	88	11.2	15.7	8.6	8.1	28	83	(4)	(4)	5	6	40.3	35.1	3	3	2.4	1.8
Colored	1.500	(3)	14	(3)	13	(3)	9.3	(3)	8.7	(3)	1	(3)	(4)	(3)	1	(3)	71.4	(3)	1	(3)	7.1	(3)
White	9,600	(3)	110	(3)	83	(3)	11.5	(3)	8.6	(3)	27	(3)	(4)	(3)	4	(3)	36.4	(3)	2	(3)	1.8	(3)
Camden	119,000	118,800	3,027	3,013	1,676	1,590	25.4	25.4	14.1	13.4	1,351	1,423	181	189	209	208	69.0	69.0	112	149	3.7	4.9
Colored	11,800	(3)	360	(3)	211	(3)	30.5	(3)	17.9	(3)	149	(3)	171	(3)	37	(3)	102.8	(3)	14	(3)	3.9	(3)
White	107,200	(3)	2,667	(3)	1,465	(3)	24.9	(3)	13.7	(3)	1,202	(3)	182	(3)	172	(3)	64.5	(3)	98	(3)	3.7	(3)
Englewood	18,600	18,000	834	826	356	293	44.8	45.9	19.1	16.3	478	533	234	282	45	39	54.0	47.2	29	25	3.5	3.0
Colored	2,800	(3)	61	(3)	32	(3)	21.8	(3)	11.4	(3)	29	(3)	(4)	(3)	7	(3)	114.8	(3)	4	(3)	6.6	(3)
White	15,800	(3)	773	(3)	324	(3)	48.9	(3)	20.5	(3)	449	(3)	239	(3)	38	(3)	49.2	(3)	25	(3)	3.2	(3)
Hackensack	25,400	24,700	980	1,017	517	461	38.6	41.2	20.4	18.7	463	556	190	221	53	36	54.1	35.4	37	38	3.8	3.7
Colored	2,700	(3)	87	(3)	42	(3)	32.2	(3)	15.6	(3)	45	(3)	(3)	(3)	9	(3)	103.4	(3)	6	(3)	6.9	(3)
White	22,700	(3)	893	(3)	475	(3)	39.3	(3)	20.9	(3)	418	(3)	188	(3)	44	(3)	49.3	(3)	31	(3)	3.5	(3)
Jersey City	319,000	317,200	5,802	5,881	3,567	3,578	18.2	18.5	11.2	11.3	2,235	2,303	163	164	427	421	73.6	71.6	253	275	4.4	4.7
Colored	13,400	(3)	314	(3)	227	(3)	23.4	(3)	16.9	(3)	87	(3)	138	(3)	40	(3)	127.4	(3)	23	(3)	7.3	(3)
White	305,600	(3)	5,488	(3)	3,340	(3)	18.0	(3)	10.9	(3)	2,148	(3)	164	(3)	387	(3)	70.5	(3)	230	(3)	4.2	(3)

Montclair	43,600	42,300	470	485	334	284	10.8	11.5	7.7	6.7	136	201	141	171	16	16	34.0	33.0	18	22	3.8	4.5
Colored	6,800	6,500	35	57	28	43	5.1	8.8	4.1	6.6	7	14	(4)	(4)	3	3	85.7	52.6	4	2	11.4	3.5
White	36,800	35,800	435	428	306	241	11.8	12.0	8.3	6.7	129	187	142	178	13	13	29.9	30.4	14	20	3.2	4.7
Newark	445,700	443,000	9,514	9,821	5,062	5,263	21.3	22.2	11.4	11.9	4,452	4,558	188	187	463	500	48.7	50.9	384	363	4.0	3.7
Colored	42,500	40,300	1,090	1,100	661	759	25.6	27.3	15.6	18.8	429	341	165	145	92	107	84.4	97.3	64	77	5.9	7.0
White	403,200	402,700	8,424	8,721	4,401	4,504	20.9	21.7	10.9	11.2	4,023	4,217	191	194	371	393	44.0	45.1	320	286	3.8	3.3
Orange	35,700	35,500	1,828	1,911	623	612	51.2	53.8	17.5	17.2	1,205	1,299	293	312	70	71	38.3	37.2	53	61	2.9	3.2
Colored	5,300	5,100	157	209	76	87	29.6	41.0	14.3	17.1	81	122	(4)	(4)	14	7	89.2	33.5	9	9	5.7	4.3
White	30,400	30,400	1,671	1,702	547	525	55.0	56.0	18.0	17.3	1,124	1,177	305	324	56	64	33.5	37.6	44	52	2.6	3.1
Plainfield	35,200	34,600	1,002	957	501	460	28.5	27.7	14.2	13.3	501	497	200	208	49	37	48.9	38.7	28	35	2.8	3.7
Colored	3,800	(3)	111	(3)	71	(3)	29.2	(3)	18.7	(3)	40	(3)	(4)	(3)	13	(3)	117.1	(3)	3	(3)	2.7	(3)
White	31,400	(3)	891	(3)	430	(3)	28.4	(3)	13.7	(3)	461	(3)	207	(3)	36	(3)	40.4	(3)	25	(3)	2.8	(3)
Pleasantville	12,300	11,700	132	104	113	114	10.7	8.9	9.2	9.7	19	−10	117	191	5	5	37.9	48.1	1	4	.8	3.8
Colored	2,200	(3)	16	(3)	28	(3)	7.3	(3)	12.7	(3)	−12	(3)	(4)	(3)	3	(3)	187.5	(3)	1	(3)	6.3	(3)
White	10,100	(3)	116	(3)	85	(3)	11.5	(3)	8.4	(3)	31	(3)	(4)	(3)	2	(3)	17.2	(3)	----	(3)	----	(3)
Red Bank	11,900	11,700	166	187	148	151	13.9	16.0	12.4	12.9	18	36	112	124	7	10	42.2	53.5	8	7	4.8	3.7
Colored	1,700	(3)	14	(3)	17	(3)	8.2	(3)	10.0	(3)	−3	(3)	(4)	(3)	1	(3)	71.4	(3)	1	(3)	7.1	(3)
White	10,200	(3)	152	(3)	131	(3)	14.9	(3)	12.8	(3)	21	(3)	116	(3)	6	(3)	39.5	(3)	7	(3)	4.6	(3)
Roselle	13,900	13,200	62	70	59	56	4.5	5.3	4.2	4.2	3	14	(4)	(4)	3	3	48.4	42.9	4	4	6.5	5.7
Colored	1,700	(3)	15	(3)	13	(3)	8.8	(3)	7.6	(3)	2	(3)	(4)	(3)	1	(3)	66.7	(3)	1	(3)	6.7	(3)
White	12,200	(3)	47	(3)	46	(3)	3.9	(3)	3.8	(3)	1	(3)	(4)	(3)	2	(3)	42.6	(3)	3	(3)	6.4	(3)
NEW YORK CITIES																						
Buffalo	581,200	574,700	10,825	11,560	7,382	7,392	18.6	20.1	12.7	12.9	3,443	4,168	147	156	715	779	66.1	67.4	374	473	3.5	4.1
Colored	15,400	(3)	360	(3)	277	(3)	23.4	(3)	18.0	(3)	83	(3)	130	(3)	27	(3)	75.0	(3)	16	(3)	4.4	(3)
White	565,800	(3)	10,465	(3)	7,105	(3)	18.5	(3)	12.6	(3)	3,360	(3)	147	(3)	688	(3)	65.7	(3)	358	(3)	3.4	(3)
Lackawanna	24,700	24,100	742	832	259	250	30.0	34.5	10.5	10.4	483	582	286	333	54	53	72.8	63.7	28	31	3.8	3.7
Colored	2,700	(3)	36	(3)	19	(3)	13.3	(3)	7.0	(3)	17	(3)	(3)	(3)	3	(3)	83.3	(3)	2	(3)	5.6	(3)
White	22,000	(3)	706	(3)	240	(3)	32.1	(3)	10.9	(3)	466	(3)	294	(3)	51	(3)	72.2	(3)	26	(3)	3.7	(3)
New York	7,090,300	6,962,400	115,062	122,273	77,302	74,913	16.2	17.6	10.9	10.8	37,760	47,360	149	163	6,405	7,073	55.7	57.8	5,418	5,554	4.7	4.5
Colored	365,400	347,600	7,090	7,293	5,934	5,630	19.4	21.0	16.2	16.2	1,156	1,663	119	130	749	764	105.6	104.8	625	634	8.8	8.7
White	6,724,900	6,614,800	107,972	114,980	71,368	69,283	16.1	17.4	10.6	10.5	36,604	45,697	151	166	5,656	6,309	52.4	54.9	4,793	4,920	4.4	4.3
Bronx Borough	1,330,300	1,278,300	17,855	18,352	10,726	10,069	13.4	14.4	8.1	7.9	7,129	8,283	166	182	760	748	42.6	40.8	803	753	4.5	4.1
Colored	14,600	13,800	617	370	479	347	42.3	26.8	32.8	25.1	138	23	129	107	48	30	77.8	81.1	50	38	8.1	10.3
White	1,315,700	1,264,500	17,238	17,982	10,247	9,722	13.1	14.2	7.8	7.7	6,991	8,260	168	185	712	718	41.3	39.9	753	715	4.4	4.0
Brooklyn Borough	2,626,600	2,573,600	46,151	49,062	26,456	25,252	17.6	19.1	10.1	9.8	19,695	23,810	174	194	2,560	2,756	55.5	56.2	2,079	2,217	4.5	4.5
Colored	76,700	72,800	1,854	1,912	1,246	1,144	24.2	26.3	16.2	15.7	608	768	149	167	227	207	122.4	108.3	191	195	10.3	10.2
White	2,549,900	2,500,800	44,297	47,150	25,210	24,108	17.4	18.9	9.9	9.6	19,087	23,042	176	196	2,333	2,549	52.7	54.1	1,888	2,022	4.3	4.3
Manhattan Borough	1,816,500	1,857,100	36,145	39,106	29,779	29,680	19.9	21.1	16.4	16.0	6,366	9,426	121	132	2,340	2,767	64.7	70.8	1,885	1,961	5.2	5.0
Colored	250,200	238,400	4,393	4,742	3,790	3,765	17.6	19.9	15.1	15.8	603	977	116	126	440	491	100.2	103.5	362	381	8.2	8.0
White	1,566,300	1,618,700	31,752	34,364	25,989	25,915	20.3	21.2	16.6	16.0	5,763	8,449	122	133	1,900	2,276	59.8	66.2	1,523	1,580	4.8	4.6
Queens Borough	1,153,500	1,094,000	12,328	13,019	8,144	7,717	10.7	11.9	7.1	7.1	4,184	5,302	151	169	601	651	48.8	50.0	524	489	4.3	3.8
Colored	21,100	19,800	184	221	225	215	8.7	11.2	10.7	10.9	−41	6	82	103	24	26	130.4	117.6	15	17	8.2	7.7
White	1,132,400	1,074,200	12,144	12,798	7,919	7,502	10.7	11.9	7.0	7.0	4,225	5,296	153	171	577	625	47.5	48.8	509	472	4.2	3.7
Richmond Borough	163,400	159,400	2,583	2,734	2,197	2,195	15.8	17.2	13.4	13.8	386	539	118	125	144	151	55.7	55.2	127	134	4.9	4.9
Colored	2,800	2,800	42	48	194	159	15.0	17.1	69.3	56.8	−152	−111	22	30	10	10	238.1	208.3	7	3	16.7	6.3
White	160,600	156,600	2,541	2,686	2,003	2,036	15.8	17.2	12.5	13.0	538	650	127	132	134	141	52.7	52.5	120	131	4.7	4.9
NORTH CAROLINA CITIES																						
Asheville	51,800	50,400	1,059	1,005	728	775	20.4	19.9	14.1	15.4	331	230	145	130	68	92	64.2	91.5	63	78	5.9	7.8
Colored	14,900	14,300	239	211	216	244	16.0	14.8	14.5	17.1	23	−33	111	86	22	34	92.1	161.1	30	47	12.6	22.3
White	36,900	36,100	820	794	512	531	22.2	22.0	13.9	14.7	308	263	160	150	46	58	56.1	73.0	33	31	4.0	3.9
Charlotte	83,900	82,900	1,615	1,734	1,037	1,065	19.2	20.9	12.4	12.8	578	669	156	163	133	178	82.4	102.7	88	113	5.4	6.5
Colored	25,200	25,200	422	454	490	481	16.7	18.0	19.4	19.1	−68	−27	86	94	60	78	142.2	171.8	38	65	9.0	14.3
White	58,700	57,700	1,193	1,280	547	584	20.3	22.2	9.3	10.1	646	696	218	219	73	100	61.2	78.1	50	48	4.2	3.8
Concord	12,100	11,900	254	204	137	140	21.0	17.1	11.3	11.8	117	64	185	146	20	15	78.7	73.5	12	8	4.7	3.9
Colored	2,000	2,000	39	27	42	34	19.5	13.5	21.0	17.0	−3	−7	(4)	(4)	8	3	205.1	111.1	3	3	7.7	11.1
White	10,100	9,900	215	177	95	106	21.3	17.9	9.4	10.7	120	71	(4)	167	12	12	55.8	67.8	9	5	4.2	2.8
Durham	54,800	52,600	1,167	1,283	842	822	21.3	24.4	15.4	15.6	325	461	139	156	96	105	82.3	81.8	77	85	6.6	6.6
Colored	20,200	19,000	402	451	406	426	19.9	23.7	20.1	22.4	−4	25	99	106	51	58	126.9	128.6	37	59	9.2	13.1
White	34,600	33,600	765	832	436	396	22.1	24.8	12.6	11.8	329	436	175	210	45	47	58.8	56.5	40	26	5.2	3.1
Elizabeth City	10,200	10,100	205	178	162	149	20.1	17.6	15.9	14.8	43	29	127	119	16	20	78.0	112.4	10	15	4.9	8.4
Colored	3,800	3,800	92	75	88	72	24.2	19.7	23.2	18.9	4	3	(4)	(4)	7	14	76.1	186.7	10	11	10.9	14.7
White	6,400	6,300	113	103	74	77	17.7	16.3	11.6	12.2	39	26	(4)	(4)	9	6	79.6	58.3	----	4	----	3.9
Fayetteville	13,600	13,200	360	394	284	289	26.5	29.8	20.9	21.9	76	105	127	136	23	34	63.9	86.3	21	32	5.8	8.1
Colored	5,600	5,500	128	159	114	120	22.9	28.9	20.4	21.8	14	39	112	133	10	19	78.1	119.5	14	22	10.9	13.8
White	8,000	7,700	232	235	170	169	29.0	30.5	21.3	21.9	62	66	136	139	13	15	56.0	63.8	7	10	3.0	4.3
Gastonia	17,600	17,200	412	555	180	258	23.4	32.3	10.2	15.0	232	297	229	215	27	56	65.5	100.9	23	33	5.6	5.9
Colored	3,300	3,200	59	79	59	70	17.9	24.7	17.9	21.9	----	9	(4)	(4)	6	15	101.7	189.9	9	11	15.3	13.9
White	14,300	14,000	353	476	121	188	24.7	34.0	8.5	13.4	232	288	292	253	21	41	59.5	86.1	14	22	4.0	4.6
Goldsboro	15,400	15,100	325	326	255	233	21.1	21.6	16.6	15.4	70	93	127	140	34	34	104.6	104.3	20	29	6.2	8.9
Colored	7,100	6,900	165	146	143	131	23.2	21.2	20.1	19.0	22	15	115	111	19	20	115.2	137.0	12	19	7.3	13.0
White	8,300	8,200	160	180	112	102	19.3	22.0	13.5	12.4	48	78	143	176	15	14	93.8	77.8	8	10	5.0	5.6
Greensboro	55,400	53,900	1,073	1,158	645	667	19.4	21.5	11.6	12.4	428	491	166	174	88	85	82.0	73.4	41	63	3.8	5.4
Colored	14,500	14,100	249	277	233	254	17.2	19.6	16.1	18.0	16	23	107	109	33	35	132.5	126.4	30	38	12.0	13.7
White	40,900	39,800	824	881	412	413	20.1	22.1	10.1	10.4	412	468	200	213	55	50	66.7	56.8	11	25	1.3	2.8
High Point	39,300	37,300	863	997	385	447	22.0	26.7	9.8	12.0	478	550	224	223	59	96	68.4	96.3	46	44	5.3	4.4
Colored	7,800	7,400	108	137	99	134	13.8	18.5	12.7	18.1	9	3	(4)	102	10	25	92.6	182.5	20	15	18.5	10.9
White	31,500	29,900	755	860	286	313	24.0	28.8	9.1	10.5	469	547	264	275	49	71	64.9	82.6	26	29	3.4	3.4
Kinston	11,600	11,400	286	296	235	199	24.7	26.0	20.3	17.5	51	97	122	149	35	29	122.4	98.0	24	33	8.4	11.1
Colored	5,200	5,100	107	109	105	95	20.6	21.4	20.2	18.6	2	14	102	(4)	16	10	149.5	91.7	15	20	14.0	18.3
White	6,400	6,300	179	187	130	104	28.0	29.7	20.3	16.5	49	83	138	180	19	19	106.1	101.6	9	13	5.0	7.0

See footnotes at end of table.

TABLE 18.—COLORED[1] AND WHITE POPULATION, BIRTHS AND DEATHS, INFANT MORTALITY, AND STILLBIRTHS, IN SELECTED REGISTRATION STATES, CITIES, AND COUNTIES: 1931 AND 1930—Continued

[See note at head of this table]

AREA AND COLOR	POPULATION ESTIMATED AS OF JULY 1		BIRTHS AND DEATHS (Exclusive of stillbirths)												INFANT MORTALITY (Exclusive of stillbirths)				STILLBIRTHS			
			Number				Rate per 1,000 population				Excess of births over deaths[2]		Births per 100 deaths		Deaths of infants under 1 year of age				Number		Rate per 100 live births	
			Births		Deaths		Births		Deaths						Number		Per 1,000 births					
	1931	1930	1931	1930	1931	1930	1931	1930	1931	1930	1931	1930	1931	1930	1931	1930	1931	1930	1931	1930	1931	1930
NORTH CAROLINA CITIES—continued																						
New Bern	[5] 11,981	[5] 11,981	206	255	222	237	17.2	21.3	18.5	19.8	−16	18	93	108	17	27	82.5	105.9	23	17	11.2	6.7
Colored	6,278	6,278	125	149	139	150	19.9	23.7	22.1	23.9	−14	−1	90	99	13	24	104.0	161.1	18	12	14.4	8.1
White	5,703	5,703	81	106	83	87	14.2	18.6	14.6	15.3	−2	19	(4)	(4)	4	3	49.4	28.3	5	5	6.2	4.7
Raleigh	38,600	37,600	654	744	691	769	16.9	19.8	17.9	20.5	−37	−25	95	97	63	78	96.3	104.8	75	52	11.5	7.0
Colored	12,900	12,600	239	266	274	299	18.5	21.1	21.2	23.7	−35	−33	87	89	31	28	129.7	105.3	45	28	18.8	10.5
White	25,700	25,000	415	478	417	470	16.1	19.1	16.2	18.8	−2	8	100	102	32	50	77.1	104.6	30	24	7.2	5.0
Rocky Mount	22,500	21,600	454	567	386	405	20.2	26.3	17.2	18.8	68	162	118	140	50	72	110.1	127.0	36	41	7.9	7.2
Colored	9,200	8,800	186	207	192	197	20.2	23.5	20.9	22.4	−6	10	97	105	26	35	139.8	169.1	28	25	15.1	12.1
White	13,300	12,800	268	360	194	208	20.2	28.1	14.6	16.3	74	152	138	173	24	37	89.6	102.8	8	16	3.0	4.4
Salisbury	17,300	17,000	320	358	242	221	18.5	21.1	14.0	13.0	78	137	132	162	20	26	62.5	72.6	16	24	5.0	6.7
Colored	4,000	4,000	67	45	64	64	16.8	11.3	16.0	16.0	3	−19	(4)	(4)	4	4	59.7	88.9	6	7	9.0	15.6
White	13,300	13,000	253	313	178	157	19.0	24.1	13.4	12.1	75	156	142	199	16	22	63.2	70.3	10	17	4.0	5.4
Shelby	11,700	11,000	239	232	109	94	20.4	21.1	9.3	8.5	130	138	219	(4)	8	6	33.5	25.9	9	8	3.8	3.4
Colored	2,300	2,200	42	30	21	17	18.3	13.6	9.1	7.7	21	13	(4)	(4)	1	------	23.8	------	1	2	2.4	6.7
White	9,400	8,800	197	202	88	77	21.0	23.0	9.4	8.8	109	125	(4)	(4)	7	6	35.5	29.7	8	6	4.1	3.0
Statesville	10,800	10,600	199	249	189	195	18.4	23.5	17.5	18.4	10	54	105	128	24	33	120.6	132.5	15	15	7.5	6.0
Colored	1,700	1,700	16	34	35	31	9.4	20.0	20.6	18.2	−19	3	(4)	(4)	4	6	250.0	176.5	4	1	25.0	2.9
White	9,100	8,900	183	215	154	164	20.1	24.2	16.9	18.4	29	51	119	131	20	27	109.3	125.6	11	14	6.0	6.5
Thomasville	10,600	10,200	264	270	113	98	24.9	26.5	10.7	9.6	151	172	234	(4)	21	20	79.5	74.1	16	9	6.1	3.3
Colored	1,700	1,700	44	46	34	29	25.9	27.1	20.0	17.1	10	17	(4)	(4)	5	3	113.6	65.2	9	5	20.5	10.9
White	8,900	8,500	220	224	79	69	24.7	26.4	8.9	8.1	141	155	(4)	(4)	16	17	72.7	75.9	7	4	3.2	1.8
Wilmington	[5] 32,270	[5] 32,270	800	890	557	627	24.8	27.6	17.3	19.4	243	263	144	142	86	76	107.5	85.4	62	55	7.8	6.2
Colored	13,111	13,111	294	326	306	326	22.4	24.9	23.3	24.9	−12	------	96	100	50	30	170.1	92.0	36	34	12.2	10.4
White	19,159	19,159	506	564	251	301	26.4	29.4	13.1	15.7	255	263	202	187	36	46	71.1	81.6	26	21	5.1	3.7
Wilson	12,900	12,700	360	326	263	253	27.9	25.7	20.4	19.9	97	73	137	129	45	39	125.0	119.6	31	15	8.6	4.6
Colored	6,400	6,300	191	173	171	165	29.8	27.5	26.7	26.2	20	8	112	105	36	26	188.5	150.3	20	11	10.5	6.4
White	6,500	6,400	169	153	92	88	26.0	23.9	14.2	13.8	77	65	(4)	(4)	9	13	53.3	85.0	11	4	6.5	2.6
Winston-Salem	77,600	75,700	1,676	1,708	972	1,067	21.6	22.6	12.5	14.1	704	641	172	160	183	176	109.2	103.0	113	132	6.7	7.7
Colored	33,600	32,800	682	675	588	620	20.3	20.6	17.5	18.9	94	55	116	109	114	107	167.2	158.5	68	92	10.0	13.6
White	44,000	42,900	994	1,033	384	447	22.6	24.1	8.7	10.4	610	586	259	231	69	69	69.4	66.8	45	40	4.5	3.9
OHIO CITIES																						
Akron	263,200	255,600	4,485	5,270	2,037	2,001	17.0	20.6	7.7	7.8	2,448	3,269	220	263	240	291	53.5	55.2	155	177	3.5	3.4
Colored	12,200	(3)	172	(3)	165	(3)	14.1	(3)	13.5	(3)	7	(3)	104	(3)	15	(3)	87.2	(3)	14	(3)	8.1	(3)
White	251,000	(3)	4,313	(3)	1,872	(3)	17.2	(3)	7.5	(3)	2,441	(3)	230	(3)	225	(3)	52.2	(3)	141	(3)	3.3	(3)
Campbell	14,900	14,700	242	296	72	104	16.2	20.1	4.8	7.1	170	192	(3)	285	20	36	82.6	121.6	7	17	2.9	5.7
Colored	2,100	(3)	25	(3)	28	(3)	11.9	(3)	13.3	(3)	−3	(3)	(4)	(3)	6	(3)	240.0	(3)	------	(3)	------	(3)
White	12,800	(3)	217	(3)	44	(3)	17.0	(3)	3.4	(3)	173	(3)	(4)	(3)	14	(3)	64.5	(3)	7	(3)	3.2	(3)
Cincinnati	457,300	452,400	8,254	8,716	7,166	7,005	18.0	19.3	15.7	15.5	1,088	1,711	115	124	587	569	71.1	65.3	299	357	3.6	4.1
Colored	50,200	48,500	952	1,045	1,192	1,139	19.0	21.5	23.7	23.5	−240	−94	80	92	133	140	139.7	134.0	54	88	5.7	8.4
White	407,100	403,900	7,302	7,671	5,974	5,866	17.9	19.0	14.7	14.5	1,328	1,805	122	131	454	429	62.2	55.9	245	269	3.4	3.5
Cleveland	911,900	902,700	16,143	17,906	10,064	9,906	17.7	19.8	11.0	11.0	6,079	8,000	160	181	863	974	53.5	54.4	594	707	3.7	3.9
Colored	78,100	74,300	1,339	1,515	1,345	1,293	17.1	20.4	17.2	17.4	−6	222	100	117	103	151	76.9	99.7	76	94	5.7	6.2
White	833,800	828,400	14,804	16,391	8,719	8,613	17.8	19.8	10.5	10.4	6,085	7,778	170	190	760	823	51.3	50.2	518	613	3.5	3.7
Columbus	295,600	291,500	4,767	5,371	3,951	4,470	16.1	18.4	13.4	15.3	816	901	121	120	293	380	61.5	70.8	189	248	4.0	4.6
Colored	34,300	33,200	558	609	539	608	16.3	18.3	15.7	18.3	19	1	104	100	37	61	66.3	100.2	25	52	4.5	8.5
White	261,300	258,300	4,209	4,762	3,412	3,862	16.1	18.4	13.1	15.0	797	900	123	123	256	319	60.8	67.0	164	196	3.9	4.1
Dayton	204,200	201,500	3,525	3,665	2,404	2,226	17.3	18.2	11.8	11.0	1,121	1,439	147	165	218	202	61.8	55.1	119	109	3.4	3.0
Colored	17,800	(3)	272	(3)	291	(3)	15.3	(3)	16.3	(3)	−19	(3)	93	(3)	32	(3)	117.6	(3)	15	(3)	5.5	(3)
White	186,400	(3)	3,253	(3)	2,113	(3)	17.5	(3)	11.3	(3)	1,140	(3)	154	(3)	186	(3)	57.2	(3)	104	(3)	3.2	(3)
Springfield	69,700	68,900	1,031	1,157	832	872	14.8	16.8	11.9	12.7	199	285	124	133	61	80	59.2	69.1	28	39	2.7	3.4
Colored	8,400	8,300	103	131	136	141	12.3	15.8	16.2	17.0	−33	−10	76	93	16	12	155.3	91.6	7	6	6.8	4.6
White	61,300	60,600	928	1,026	696	731	15.1	16.9	11.4	12.1	232	295	133	140	45	68	48.5	66.3	21	33	2.3	3.2
Toledo	297,100	291,600	4,850	5,553	3,494	3,680	16.3	19.0	11.8	12.6	1,356	1,873	139	151	273	312	56.3	56.2	189	220	3.9	4.0
Colored	15,000	(3)	238	(3)	258	(3)	15.9	(3)	17.2	(3)	−20	(3)	92	(3)	24	(3)	100.8	(3)	11	(3)	4.6	(3)
White	282,100	(3)	4,612	(3)	3,236	(3)	16.3	(3)	11.5	(3)	1,376	(3)	143	(3)	249	(3)	54.0	(3)	178	(3)	3.9	(3)
Xenia	10,600	10,500	190	183	147	164	17.9	17.4	13.9	15.6	43	19	129	112	17	15	89.5	82.0	3	5	1.6	2.7
Colored	2,200	2,100	18	20	27	39	8.2	9.5	12.3	18.6	−9	−19	(4)	(4)	4	3	222.2	150.0	------	1	------	5.0
White	8,400	8,400	172	163	120	125	20.5	19.4	14.3	14.9	52	38	143	130	13	12	75.6	73.6	3	4	1.7	2.5
Youngstown	172,900	170,500	3,396	3,789	1,684	1,782	19.6	22.2	9.7	10.5	1,712	2,007	202	213	198	218	58.3	57.5	152	125	4.5	3.3
Colored	15,900	(3)	328	(3)	228	(3)	20.6	(3)	14.3	(3)	100	(3)	144	(3)	25	(3)	76.2	(3)	17	(3)	5.2	(3)
White	157,000	(3)	3,068	(3)	1,456	(3)	19.5	(3)	9.3	(3)	1,612	(3)	211	(3)	173	(3)	56.4	(3)	135	(3)	4.4	(3)

OKLAHOMA CITIES																					
Ardmore	15,900	15,800	232	194	242	192	14.6	12.3	15.2	12.2	−10	2	96	101	14	18	60.3	92.8	6	3	2.6	1.5
Colored	2,400	2,500	21	16	49	37	8.8	6.4	20.4	14.8	−28	−21	(4)	(4)	2	5	95.2	312.5				
White	13,500	13,300	211	178	193	155	15.6	13.4	14.3	11.7	18	23	109	115	12	13	56.9	73.0	6	3	2.8	1.7
Chickasha	14,600	14,200	310	261	218	240	21.2	18.4	14.9	16.9	92	21	142	109	20	34	64.5	130.3	6	13	1.9	5.0
Colored	1,800	1,700	30	25	22	44	16.7	14.7	12.2	25.9	8	−19	(4)	(4)	4	9	133.3	360.0	2	1	6.7	4.0
White	12,800	12,500	280	236	196	196	21.9	18.9	15.3	15.7	84	40	143	120	16	25	57.1	105.9	4	12	1.4	5.1
McAlester	11,900	11,800	203	168	238	245	17.1	14.2	20.0	20.8	−35	−77	85	69	7	11	34.5	65.5	7	5	3.4	3.0
Colored	2,000	2,000	14	11	50	44	7.0	5.5	25.0	22.0	−36	−33	(4)	(4)	1	2	71.4	181.8				
White	9,900	9,800	189	157	188	201	19.1	16.0	19.0	20.5	1	−44	101	78	6	9	31.7	57.3	7	5	3.7	3.2
Muskogee	32,200	32,100	636	641	548	604	19.8	20.0	17.0	18.8	88	37	116	106	46	42	72.3	65.5	14	14	2.2	2.2
Colored	8,000	8,000	132	119	162	202	16.5	14.9	20.3	25.3	−30	−83	81	59	14	12	106.1	100.8	3	6	2.3	5.0
White	24,200	24,100	504	522	386	402	20.8	21.7	16.0	16.7	118	120	131	130	32	30	63.5	57.5	11	8	2.2	1.5
Oklahoma City	196,800	187,600	3,709	3,735	2,073	2,105	18.8	19.9	10.5	11.2	1,636	1,630	179	177	229	309	61.7	82.7	94	114	2.5	3.1
Colored	17,200	16,500	269	231	286	269	15.6	14.0	16.6	16.3	−17	−38	94	86	30	33	111.5	142.9	18	22	6.7	9.5
White	179,600	171,100	3,440	3,504	1,787	1,836	19.2	20.5	9.9	10.7	1,653	1,668	193	191	199	276	57.8	78.8	76	92	2.2	2.6
Okmulgee	[5] 17,097	[5] 17,097	323	316	214	272	18.9	18.5	12.5	15.9	109	44	151	116	23	27	71.2	85.4	10	11	3.1	3.5
Colored	4,053	4,053	63	37	87	122	15.5	9.1	21.5	30.1	−24	−85	(4)	30	6	12	95.2	324.3	2	3	3.2	8.1
White	13,044	13,044	260	279	127	150	19.9	21.4	9.7	11.5	133	129	205	186	17	15	65.4	53.8	8	8	3.1	2.9
Sapulpa	[5] 10,533	[5] 10,533	260	270	156	151	24.7	25.6	14.8	14.3	104	119	167	179	14	19	53.8	70.4	10	8	3.8	3.0
Colored	1,352	1,352	36	35	25	22	26.6	25.9	18.5	16.3	11	13	(4)	(4)	2	3	55.6	85.7	2	3	5.6	8.6
White	9,181	9,181	224	235	131	129	24.4	25.6	14.3	14.1	93	106	171	182	12	16	53.6	68.1	8	5	3.6	2.1
Tulsa	145,80	142,000	2,293	2,366	1,162	1,409	15.7	16.7	8.0	9.9	1,131	957	197	168	120	179	52.3	75.7	74	87	3.2	3.7
Colored	17,800	17,400	181	164	199	272	10.2	9.4	11.2	15.6	−18	−108	91	60	18	30	99.4	182.9	17	19	9.4	11.6
White	128,000	124,600	2,112	2,202	963	1,137	16.5	17.7	7.5	9.1	1,149	1,065	219	194	102	149	48.3	67.7	57	68	2.7	3.1
Wewoka	11,500	10,600	195	216	140	161	17.0	20.4	12.2	15.2	55	55	139	134	15	28	76.9	129.6	1	5	.5	2.3
Colored	1,900	1,700	12	10	57	42	6.3	5.9	30.0	24.7	−45	−32	(4)	(4)	6	6	500.0	600.0	1	1	8.3	10.0
White	9,600	8,900	183	206	83	119	19.1	23.1	8.6	13.4	100	87	(4)	173	9	22	49.2	106.8		4		1.9
PENNSYLVANIA CITIES																					
Braddock	[5] 19,329	[5] 19,329	530	554	300	293	27.4	28.7	15.5	15.2	230	261	177	189	49	48	92.5	86.6	20	26	3.8	4.7
Colored	2,245	(3)	53	(3)	50	(3)	23.6	(3)	22.3	(3)	3	(3)	(4)	(3)	7	(3)	132.1	(3)	3	(3)	5.7	(3)
White	17,084	(3)	477	(3)	250	(3)	27.9	(3)	14.6	(3)	227	(3)	191	(3)	42	(3)	88.1	(3)	17	(3)	3.6	(3)
Chester	59,300	59,200	1,211	1,290	727	818	20.4	21.8	12.3	13.8	484	472	167	158	100	101	82.6	78.3	66	61	5.5	4.7
Colored	9,500	9,300	226	252	166	212	23.8	27.1	17.5	22.8	60	40	136	119	31	36	137.2	142.9	22	23	9.7	9.1
White	49,800	49,900	985	1,038	561	606	19.8	20.8	11.3	12.1	424	432	176	171	69	65	70.1	62.6	44	38	4.5	3.7
Clairton	15,800	15,400	300	379	89	107	19.0	24.6	5.6	6.9	211	272	(4)	354	27	26	90.0	68.6	9	11	3.0	2.9
Colored	2,300	(3)	39	(3)	19	(3)	17.0	(3)	8.3	(3)	20	(3)	(4)	(3)	7	(3)	179.5	(3)	1	(3)	2.6	(3)
White	13,500	(3)	261	(3)	70	(3)	19.3	(3)	5.2	(3)	191	(3)	(4)	(3)	20	(3)	76.6	(3)	8	(3)	3.1	(3)
Coatesville	14,600	14,600	183	205	103	102	12.5	14.0	7.1	7.0	80	103	178	201	6	11	32.8	53.7	8	7	4.4	3.4
Colored	2,300	2,300	40	41	24	13	17.4	17.8	10.4	5.7	16	28	(4)	(4)	2	4	50.0	97.6	1	2	2.5	4.9
White	12,300	12,300	143	164	79	89	11.6	13.3	6.4	7.2	64	75	(4)	(4)	4	7	28.0	42.7	7	5	4.9	3.0
Farrell	[5] 14,359	[5] 14,359	201	264	72	78	14.0	18.4	5.0	5.4	129	186	(4)	(4)	8	17	39.8	64.4	9	6	4.5	2.3
Colored	1,608	(3)	23	(3)	16	(3)	14.3	(3)	10.0	(3)	7	(3)	(4)	(3)	1	(3)	43.5	(3)	1	(3)	4.3	(3)
White	12,751	(3)	178	(3)	56	(3)	14.0	(3)	4.4	(3)	122	(3)	(4)	(3)	7	(3)	39.3	(3)	8	(3)	4.5	(3)
Homestead	[5] 20,141	[5] 20,141	396	518	252	229	19.7	25.7	12.5	11.4	144	289	157	226	35	30	88.4	57.9	10	22	2.5	4.2
Colored	3,606	(3)	34	(3)	60	(3)	9.4	(3)	16.6	(3)	−26	(3)	(4)	(3)	11	(3)	323.5	(3)		(3)		(3)
White	16,535	(3)	362	(3)	192	(3)	21.9	(3)	11.6	(3)	170	(3)	189	(3)	24	(3)	66.3	(3)	10	(3)	2.8	(3)
Philadelphia	1,966,500	1,954,100	33,793	35,818	25,167	24,516	17.2	18.3	12.8	12.5	8,626	11,302	134	146	2,173	2,287	64.3	63.9	1,202	1,269	3.6	3.5
Colored	233,100	224,700	4,758	4,963	3,701	3,620	20.4	22.1	15.9	16.1	1,057	1,343	129	137	490	495	103.0	99.7	287	294	6.0	5.9
White	1,733,400	1,729,400	29,035	30,855	21,466	20,896	16.8	17.8	12.4	12.1	7,569	9,959	135	148	1,683	1,792	58.0	58.1	915	975	3.2	3.2
Pittsburgh	676,000	671,000	14,244	14,994	9,507	9,312	21.1	22.3	14.1	13.9	4,737	5,682	150	161	991	1,032	69.6	68.8	523	564	3.7	3.8
Colored	57,700	55,900	1,245	1,315	1,202	1,103	21.6	23.5	20.8	19.7	43	212	104	119	142	142	114.1	108.0	76	83	6.1	6.3
White	618,300	615,100	12,999	13,679	8,305	8,209	21.0	22.2	13.4	13.3	4,694	5,470	157	167	849	890	65.3	65.1	447	481	3.4	3.5
Steelton	[5] 13,291	[5] 13,291	171	198	104	104	12.9	14.9	7.8	7.8	67	94	164	190	13	14	76.0	70.7	6	6	3.5	3.0
Colored	2,580	2,580	41	33	24	23	15.9	12.8	9.3	8.9	17	10	(4)	(4)	4	4	97.6	121.2	1		2.4	
White	10,711	10,711	130	165	80	81	12.1	15.4	7.5	7.6	50	84	(4)	(4)	9	10	69.2	60.6	5	6	3.8	3.6
West Chester	12,400	12,300	694	686	362	307	56.0	55.8	29.2	25.0	332	379	192	223	60	68	86.5	99.1	18	31	2.6	4.5
Colored	2,100	2,100	72	88	68	45	34.3	41.9	32.4	21.4	4	43	(4)	(4)	18	10	250.0	113.6	5	9	6.9	10.2
White	10,300	10,200	622	598	294	262	60.4	58.6	28.5	25.7	328	336	212	228	42	58	67.5	97.0	13	22	2.1	3.7
SOUTH CAROLINA CITIES																					
Anderson	14,800	14,500	532	546	355	391	35.9	37.7	24.0	27.0	177	155	150	140	34	69	63.9	126.4	19	33	3.6	6.0
Colored	4,000	3,900	85	104	121	112	21.3	26.7	30.3	28.7	−36	−8	70	93	11	14	129.4	134.6	7	8	8.2	7.7
White	10,800	10,600	447	442	234	279	41.4	41.7	21.7	26.3	213	163	191	158	23	55	51.5	124.4	12	25	2.7	5.7
Charleston	[5] 62,265	[5] 62,265	1,586	1,647	1,442	1,426	25.5	26.5	23.2	22.9	144	221	110	115	188	189	118.5	114.8	168	204	10.6	12.4
Colored	28,088	28,088	814	869	945	927	29.0	30.9	33.6	33.0	−131	−58	86	94	139	145	170.8	166.9	150	173	18.4	19.9
White	34,177	34,177	772	778	497	499	22.6	22.8	14.5	14.6	275	279	155	156	49	44	63.5	56.6	18	31	2.3	4.0
Columbia	52,500	50,300	979	1,034	1,253	1,223	18.6	20.6	23.9	24.3	−274	−189	78	85	106	106	108.3	102.5	88	97	9.0	9.4
Colored	19,900	18,200	363	364	600	554	18.2	20.0	30.2	30.4	−237	−190	61	66	60	52	165.3	142.9	58	65	16.0	17.9
White	32,600	32,100	616	670	653	669	18.9	20.9	20.0	20.8	−37	1	94	100	46	54	74.7	80.6	30	32	4.9	4.8
Florence	15,200	14,900	349	381	342	376	23.0	25.6	22.5	25.2	7	5	102	101	37	55	106.0	144.4	35	35	10.0	9.2
Colored	6,200	6,100	176	148	171	191	28.4	24.3	27.6	31.3	5	−43	103	77	17	29	96.6	195.9	24	23	13.6	15.5
White	9,000	8,800	173	233	171	185	19.2	26.5	19.0	21.0	2	48	101	126	20	26	115.6	111.6	11	12	6.4	5.2
Greenville	29,900	29,300	563	551	485	530	18.8	18.8	16.2	18.1	78	21	116	104	57	65	101.2	118.0	40	46	7.1	8.3
Colored	11,200	10,900	247	246	265	290	22.1	22.6	23.7	26.6	−18	−44	93	85	36	36	145.7	146.3	18	28	7.3	11.4
White	18,700	18,400	316	305	220	240	16.9	16.6	11.8	13.0	96	65	144	127	21	29	66.5	95.1	22	18	7.0	5.9
Greenwood	11,300	11,100	200	187	164	164	17.7	16.8	14.5	14.8	36	23	122	114	20	15	100.0	80.2	8	6	4.0	3.2
Colored	3,600	3,500	57	60	72	81	15.8	17.1	20.0	23.1	−15	−21	(4)	(4)	7	8	122.8	133.3	3	3	5.3	5.0
White	7,700	7,600	143	127	92	83	18.6	16.7	11.9	10.9	51	44	(4)	(4)	13	7	90.9	55.1	5	3	3.5	2.4
Rock Hill	11,600	11,400	195	224	164	142	16.8	19.6	14.1	12.5	31	82	119	158	21	19	107.7	84.8	7	9	3.6	4.0
Colored	2,500	2,500	23	30	77	50	9.2	12.0	30.8	20.0	−54	−20	(4)	(4)	6	6	260.9	200.0	5	1	21.7	3.3
White	9,100	8,900	172	194	87	92	18.9	21.8	9.6	10.3	85	102	(4)	(4)	15	13	87.2	67.0	2	8	1.2	4.1

See footnotes at end of table.

TABLE 18.—COLORED[1] AND WHITE POPULATION, BIRTHS AND DEATHS, INFANT MORTALITY, AND STILLBIRTHS, IN SELECTED REGISTRATION STATES, CITIES, AND COUNTIES: 1931 AND 1930—Continued

[See note at head of this table]

AREA AND COLOR	Population estimated as of July 1, 1931	Population estimated as of July 1, 1930	Births and deaths (Exclusive of stillbirths): Number: Births, 1931	Births, 1930	Deaths, 1931	Deaths, 1930	Rate per 1,000 population: Births, 1931	Births, 1930	Deaths, 1931	Deaths, 1930	Excess of births over deaths[2], 1931	1930	Births per 100 deaths, 1931	1930	Infant mortality (Exclusive of stillbirths): Deaths of infants under 1 year of age: Number, 1931	Number, 1930	Per 1,000 births, 1931	Per 1,000 births, 1930	Stillbirths: Number, 1931	Number, 1930	Rate per 100 live births, 1931	Rate per 100 live births, 1930
SOUTH CAROLINA CITIES—continued																						
Spartanburg	29,500	28,900	541	564	476	478	18.3	19.5	16.1	16.5	65	86	114	118	47	55	86.9	97.5	28	44	5.2	7.8
Colored	10,100	9,900	170	152	212	222	16.8	15.4	21.0	22.4	−42	−70	80	68	25	24	147.1	157.9	17	14	10.0	9.2
White	19,400	19,000	371	412	264	256	19.1	21.7	13.6	13.5	107	156	141	161	22	31	59.3	75.2	11	30	3.0	7.3
Sumter	12,100	11,800	242	252	260	238	20.1	21.4	21.5	20.2	−18	14	93	106	27	24	111.6	95.2	10	23	4.1	9.1
Colored	5,300	5,100	101	99	165	153	19.1	19.4	31.1	30.0	−64	−54	61	65	16	18	158.4	181.8	5	17	5.0	17.2
White	6,800	6,700	141	153	95	85	20.7	22.8	14.0	12.7	46	68	(4)	(4)	11	6	78.0	39.2	5	6	3.5	3.9
TENNESSEE CITIES																						
Chattanooga	122,200	120,100	2,130	2,335	1,661	1,883	17.4	19.4	13.6	15.7	469	452	128	124	190	253	89.2	108.4	159	189	7.5	8.1
Colored	33,600	33,300	456	485	676	825	13.6	14.6	20.1	24.8	−220	−340	67	59	69	83	151.3	171.1	83	96	18.2	19.8
White	88,600	86,800	1,674	1,850	985	1,058	18.9	21.3	11.1	12.2	689	792	170	175	121	170	72.3	91.9	76	93	4.5	5.0
Jackson	22,500	22,200	378	371	361	329	16.8	16.7	16.0	14.8	17	42	105	113	21	34	55.6	91.6	15	40	4.0	10.8
Colored	7,700	7,600	81	81	150	148	10.5	10.7	19.5	19.5	−69	−67	54	55	7	21	86.4	259.3	10	23	12.3	28.4
White	14,800	14,600	297	290	211	181	20.1	19.9	14.3	12.4	86	109	141	160	14	13	47.1	44.8	5	17	1.7	5.9
Knoxville	109,200	106,500	2,078	2,407	1,384	1,500	19.0	22.6	12.7	14.1	694	907	150	160	169	195	81.3	81.0	90	124	4.3	5.2
Colored	17,800	17,300	200	269	300	320	11.2	15.5	16.9	18.5	−100	−51	67	84	22	25	110.0	92.9	20	39	10.0	14.5
White	91,400	89,200	1,878	2,138	1,084	1,180	20.5	24.0	11.9	13.2	794	958	173	181	147	170	78.3	79.5	70	85	3.7	4.0
Memphis	258,800	254,000	4,722	4,903	4,289	4,398	18.2	19.3	16.6	17.3	433	505	110	111	483	500	102.3	102.0	229	270	4.8	5.5
Colored	98,900	96,900	1,693	1,797	2,122	2,274	17.1	18.5	21.5	23.5	−429	−477	80	79	232	249	137.0	138.6	140	162	8.3	9.0
White	159,900	157,100	3,029	3,106	2,167	2,124	18.9	19.8	13.6	13.5	862	982	140	146	251	251	82.9	80.8	89	108	2.9	3.5
Nashville	155,500	154,200	3,339	3,460	2,603	2,510	21.5	22.4	16.7	16.3	736	950	128	138	292	343	87.5	99.1	206	197	6.2	5.7
Colored	42,900	42,900	860	829	959	990	20.0	19.3	22.4	23.1	−99	−161	90	84	103	114	119.8	137.5	95	74	11.0	8.9
White	112,600	111,300	2,479	2,631	1,644	1,520	22.0	23.6	14.6	13.7	835	1,111	151	173	189	229	76.2	87.0	111	123	4.5	4.7
VIRGINIA CITIES																						
Alexandria	[5] 24,149	[5] 24,149	530	540	349	351	21.9	22.4	14.5	14.5	181	189	152	154	53	44	100.0	81.5	21	22	4.0	4.1
Colored	4,919	4,919	95	101	119	107	19.3	20.5	24.2	21.8	−24	−6	80	94	23	15	242.1	148.5	11	7	11.6	6.9
White	19,230	19,230	435	439	230	244	22.6	22.8	12.0	12.7	205	195	189	180	30	29	69.0	66.1	10	15	2.3	3.4
Charlottesville	15,800	15,400	216	230	143	161	13.7	14.9	9.1	10.5	73	69	151	143	20	17	92.6	73.9	7	6	3.2	2.6
Colored	4,200	4,200	29	45	37	49	6.9	10.7	8.8	11.7	−8	−4	(4)	(4)	1	3	34.5	66.7	1	2	3.4	4.4
White	11,600	11,200	187	185	106	112	16.1	16.5	9.1	10.0	81	73	176	165	19	14	101.6	75.7	6	4	3.2	2.2
Danville	22,300	22,300	453	531	419	370	20.3	23.8	18.8	16.6	34	161	108	144	52	51	114.8	96.0	28	32	6.2	6.0
Colored	5,500	5,600	106	113	162	132	19.3	20.2	29.5	23.6	−56	−19	65	86	18	12	169.8	106.2	16	7	15.1	6.2
White	16,800	16,700	347	418	257	238	20.7	25.0	15.3	14.3	90	180	135	176	34	39	98.0	93.3	12	25	3.5	6.0
Hopewell	12,500	11,600	273	258	89	95	21.8	22.2	7.1	8.2	184	163	(4)	(4)	20	25	73.3	96.9	9	17	3.3	6.6
Colored	1,400	1,400	16	19	23	20	11.4	13.6	16.4	14.3	−7	−1	(4)	(4)	2	4	125.0	210.5	2	4	12.5	21.1
White	11,100	10,200	257	239	66	75	23.2	23.4	5.9	7.4	191	164	(4)	(4)	18	21	70.0	87.9	7	13	2.7	5.4
Lynchburg	41,400	40,800	970	999	646	662	23.4	24.5	15.6	16.2	324	337	150	151	79	86	81.4	86.1	51	56	5.3	5.6
Colored	9,900	9,700	240	220	234	252	24.2	22.7	23.6	26.0	6	−32	103	87	26	25	108.3	113.6	27	28	11.3	12.7
White	31,500	31,100	730	779	412	410	23.2	25.0	13.1	13.2	318	369	177	190	53	61	72.6	78.3	24	28	3.3	3.6
Newport News	[5] 34,417	[5] 34,417	790	818	500	477	23.0	23.8	14.5	13.9	290	341	158	171	51	65	64.6	79.5	53	43	6.7	5.3
Colored	13,297	13,297	307	331	279	260	23.1	24.9	21.0	19.6	28	71	110	127	29	42	94.5	126.9	40	26	13.0	7.9
White	21,120	21,120	483	487	221	217	22.9	23.1	10.5	10.3	262	270	219	224	22	23	45.5	47.2	13	17	2.7	3.5
Norfolk	[5] 129,710	[5] 129,710	2,177	2,254	1,711	1,763	16.8	17.4	13.2	13.6	466	491	127	128	156	170	71.7	75.4	94	135	4.3	6.0
Colored	44,196	44,196	738	750	846	902	16.7	17.0	19.1	20.4	−108	−152	87	83	93	104	126.0	138.7	64	90	8.7	12.0
White	85,514	85,514	1,439	1,504	865	861	16.8	17.6	10.1	10.1	574	643	166	175	63	66	43.8	43.9	30	45	2.1	3.0
Petersburg	[5] 28,564	[5] 28,564	540	549	478	525	18.9	19.2	16.7	18.4	62	24	113	105	60	56	111.1	102.0	42	48	7.8	8.7
Colored	12,602	12,602	254	248	266	310	20.2	19.7	21.1	24.6	−12	−62	95	80	38	28	149.6	112.9	33	33	13.0	13.3
White	15,962	15,962	286	301	212	215	17.9	18.9	13.3	13.5	74	86	135	140	22	28	76.9	93.0	9	15	3.1	5.0
Portsmouth	[5] 45,704	[5] 45,704	737	775	698	617	16.1	17.0	15.3	13.5	39	158	106	126	78	57	105.8	73.5	63	79	8.5	10.2
Colored	18,923	18,923	327	336	419	376	17.3	17.8	22.1	19.9	−92	−40	78	89	57	35	174.3	104.2	52	57	15.9	17.0
White	26,781	26,781	410	439	279	241	15.3	16.4	10.4	9.0	131	198	147	182	21	22	51.2	50.1	11	22	2.7	5.0
Richmond	184,300	183,200	3,457	3,580	2,853	2,737	18.8	19.5	15.5	14.9	604	843	121	131	268	263	77.5	73.5	190	193	5.5	5.4
Colored	52,900	53,000	1,158	1,204	1,130	1,132	21.9	22.7	21.4	21.4	28	72	102	106	138	143	119.2	118.8	113	107	9.8	8.9
White	131,400	130,200	2,299	2,376	1,723	1,605	17.5	18.2	13.1	12.3	576	771	133	148	130	120	56.5	50.5	77	86	3.3	3.6
Roanoke	71,200	69,600	1,389	1,545	848	959	19.5	22.2	11.9	13.8	541	586	164	161	111	151	79.9	97.7	56	65	4.0	4.2
Colored	12,700	12,400	250	256	231	276	19.7	20.6	18.2	22.3	19	−20	108	93	26	43	104.0	168.0	14	18	5.6	7.0
White	58,500	57,200	1,139	1,289	617	683	19.5	22.5	10.5	11.9	522	606	185	189	85	108	74.6	83.8	42	47	3.7	3.6

Staunton	12,200	12,000	215	291	344	383	17.6	24.3	28.2	31.9	−129	−92	63	76	24	25	111.6	85.9	14	16	6.5	5.5
Colored	1,900	1,800	28	34	53	36	14.7	18.9	27.9	20.0	−25	−2	(4)	(4)	6	6	214.3	176.5	4	2	14.3	5.9
White	10,300	10,200	187	257	291	347	18.2	25.2	28.3	34.0	−104	−90	64	74	18	19	96.3	73.9	10	14	5.3	5.4
Suffolk	10,400	10,300	187	179	196	216	18.0	17.4	18.8	21.0	−9	−37	95	83	17	22	90.9	122.9	15	20	8.0	11.2
Colored	3,800	3,800	62	57	102	121	16.3	15.0	26.8	31.8	−40	−64	61	47	6	16	96.8	280.7	12	10	19.4	17.5
White	6,600	6,500	125	122	94	95	18.9	18.8	14.2	14.6	31	27	(4)	(4)	11	6	88.0	49.2	3	10	2.4	8.2
WEST VIRGINIA CITIES																						
Bluefield	[5] 19,339	[5] 19,339	395	399	259	324	20.4	20.6	13.4	16.8	136	75	153	123	35	50	88.6	125.3	18	16	4.6	4.0
Colored	3,365	3,365	53	61	63	83	15.8	18.1	18.7	24.7	−10	−22	(4)	(4)	7	11	132.1	180.3	4	2	7.5	3.3
White	15,974	15,974	342	338	196	241	21.4	21.2	12.3	15.1	146	97	174	140	28	39	81.9	115.4	14	14	4.1	4.1
Charleston	62,700	60,800	1,281	1,421	934	956	20.4	23.4	14.9	15.7	347	465	137	149	152	182	118.7	128.1	86	76	6.7	5.3
Colored	7,300	6,800	94	113	147	123	13.4	16.6	21.0	18.1	−53	−10	64	92	19	18	202.1	159.3	13	9	13.8	8.0
White	55,700	54,000	1,187	1,308	787	833	21.3	24.2	14.1	15.4	400	475	151	157	133	164	112.0	125.4	73	67	6.1	5.1
ALABAMA COUNTIES																						
Autauga	19,800	19,700	427	485	199	228	21.6	24.6	10.1	11.6	228	257	215	213	29	29	67.9	59.8	29	27	6.8	5.6
Colored	10,900	10,900	276	294	120	154	25.3	27.0	11.0	14.1	156	140	230	191	19	20	68.8	68.0	22	22	8.0	7.5
White	8,900	8,800	151	191	79	74	17.0	21.7	8.9	8.4	72	117	(4)	(4)	10	9	66.2	47.1	7	5	4.6	2.6
Baldwin	29,200	28,500	692	671	266	324	23.7	23.5	9.1	11.4	426	347	260	207	32	41	46.2	61.1	26	27	3.8	4.0
Colored	7,000	6,900	185	184	90	92	26.4	26.7	12.9	13.3	95	92	------	(4)	10	11	54.1	59.8	10	13	5.4	7.1
White	22,200	21,600	507	487	176	232	22.8	22.5	7.9	10.7	331	255	288	210	22	30	43.4	61.6	16	14	3.2	2.9
Barbour	32,500	32,400	759	741	345	410	23.4	22.9	10.6	12.7	414	331	220	181	48	64	63.2	86.4	51	56	6.7	7.6
Colored	18,600	18,600	479	448	206	251	25.8	24.1	11.1	13.5	273	197	233	178	30	41	62.6	91.5	41	42	8.6	9,4
White	13,900	13,800	280	293	139	159	20.1	21.2	10.0	11.5	141	134	201	184	18	23	64.3	78.5	10	14	3.6	4.8
Bibb	[5] 20,780	[5] 20,780	479	464	181	205	23.1	22.3	8.7	9.9	298	259	265	226	26	35	54.3	75.4	26	23	5.4	5.0
Colored	6,876	6,876	143	141	70	94	20.8	20.5	10.2	13.7	73	47	(4)	(4)	12	18	83.9	127.7	12	10	8.4	7.1
White	13,904	13,904	336	323	111	111	24.2	23.2	8.0	8.0	225	212	303	291	14	17	41.7	52.6	14	13	4.2	4.0
Bullock	[5] 20,016	[5] 20,016	501	487	234	280	25.0	24.3	11.7	14.0	267	207	214	174	32	43	63.9	88.3	44	42	8.8	8.6
Colored	15,754	15,754	427	405	194	230	27.1	25.7	12.3	14.6	233	175	220	176	30	39	70.3	96.3	43	41	10.1	10.1
White	4,262	4,262	74	82	40	50	17.4	19.2	9.4	11.7	34	32	(4)	(4)	2	4	27.0	48.8	1	1	1.4	1.2
Butler	30,300	30,200	612	680	336	366	20.2	22.5	11.1	12.1	276	314	182	186	45	51	73.5	75.0	36	46	5.9	6.8
Colored	14,700	14,700	318	375	182	203	21.6	25.5	12.4	13.8	136	172	175	185	28	32	88.1	85.3	24	30	7.5	8.0
White	15,600	15,500	294	305	154	163	18.8	19.7	9.9	10.5	140	142	191	187	17	19	57.8	62.3	12	16	4.1	5.2
Calhoun	33,700	33,300	873	819	277	321	25.9	24.6	8.2	9.6	596	498	315	255	46	66	52.7	80.6	30	35	3.4	4.3
Colored	5,300	5,300	152	138	69	78	28.7	26.0	13.0	14.7	83	60	(4)	(4)	12	13	78.9	94.2	11	9	7.2	6.5
White	28,400	28,000	721	681	208	243	25.4	24.3	7.3	8.7	513	438	347	280	34	53	47.2	77.8	19	26	2.6	3.8
Chambers	[5] 39,313	[5] 39,313	777	787	342	449	19.8	20.0	8.7	11.4	435	338	227	175	35	59	45.0	75.0	48	51	6.2	6.5
Colored	17,928	17,928	399	376	149	228	22.3	21.0	8.3	12.7	250	148	268	165	13	28	32.6	74.5	30	36	7.5	9.6
White	21,385	21,385	378	411	193	221	17.7	19.2	9.0	10.3	185	190	196	186	22	31	58.2	75.4	18	15	4.8	3.6
Chilton	24,800	24,600	561	523	227	228	22.6	21.3	9.2	9.3	334	295	247	229	23	31	41.0	59.3	22	25	3.9	4.8
Colored	4,000	3,900	86	77	50	53	21.5	19.7	12.5	13.6	36	24	(4)	(4)	5	9	58.1	116.9	6	14	7.0	18.2
White	20,800	20,700	475	446	177	175	22.8	21.5	8.5	8.5	298	271	268	255	18	22	37.9	49.3	16	11	3.4	2.5
Choctaw	[5] 20,513	[5] 20,513	501	476	184	185	24.4	23.2	9.0	9.0	317	291	272	257	27	25	53.9	52.5	29	32	5.8	6.7
Colored	11,237	11,237	288	280	118	119	25.6	24.9	10.5	10.6	170	161	244	235	18	17	62.5	60.7	26	27	9.0	9.6
White	9,276	9,276	213	196	66	66	23.0	21.1	7.1	7.1	147	130	(4)	(4)	9	8	42.3	40.8	3	5	1.4	2.6
Clarke	[5] 26,016	[5] 26,016	677	667	241	297	26.0	25.6	9.3	11.4	436	370	281	225	34	36	50.2	54.0	43	31	6.4	4.6
Colored	13,626	13,626	375	396	143	181	27.5	29.1	10.5	13.3	232	215	262	219	28	25	74.7	63.1	31	26	8.3	6.6
White	12,390	12,390	302	271	98	116	24.4	21.9	7.9	9.4	204	155	(4)	234	6	11	19.9	40.6	12	5	4.0	1.8
Clay	[5] 17,768	[5] 17,768	438	457	158	154	24.7	25.7	8.9	8.7	280	303	277	297	21	19	47.9	41.6	22	21	5.0	4.6
Colored	2,727	2,727	58	55	44	31	21.3	20.2	16.1	11.4	14	24	(4)	(4)	7	3	120.7	54.5	9	4	15.5	7.3
White	15,041	15,041	380	402	114	123	25.3	26.7	7.6	8.2	266	279	333	327	14	16	36.8	39.8	13	17	3.4	4.2
Coffee	32,900	32,600	867	850	282	277	26.4	26.1	8.6	8.5	585	573	307	307	40	52	46.1	61.2	42	44	4.8	5.2
Colored	7,000	6,900	167	158	69	65	23.9	22.9	9.9	9.4	98	93	(4)	(4)	7	15	41.9	94.9	9	14	5.4	8.9
White	25,900	25,700	700	692	213	212	27.0	26.9	8.2	8.2	487	480	329	326	33	37	47.1	53.5	33	30	4.7	4.3
Colbert	[5] 29,860	[5] 29,860	641	711	293	342	21.5	23.8	9.8	11.5	348	369	219	208	57	53	88.9	74.5	42	50	6.6	7.0
Colored	8,483	8,483	132	207	113	136	15.6	24.4	13.3	16.0	19	71	117	152	16	24	121.2	115.9	21	21	15.9	10.1
White	21,377	21,377	509	504	180	206	23.8	23.6	8.4	9.6	329	298	283	245	41	29	80.6	57.5	21	29	4.1	5.8
Conecuh	25,500	25,500	690	655	256	280	27.1	25.7	10.0	11.0	434	375	270	234	47	52	68.1	79.4	41	33	5.9	5.0
Colored	11,100	11,100	338	349	130	155	30.5	31.4	11.7	14.0	208	194	260	225	28	33	82.8	94.6	27	21	8.0	6.0
White	14,400	14,400	352	306	126	125	24.4	21.3	8.8	8.7	226	181	279	245	19	19	54.0	62.1	14	12	4.0	3.9
Coosa	[5] 12,460	[5] 12,460	290	231	93	103	23.3	18.5	7.5	8.3	197	128	(4)	224	16	9	55.2	39.0	11	12	3.8	5.2
Colored	4,640	4,640	145	99	38	51	31.3	21.3	8.2	11.0	107	48	(4)	(4)	9	7	62.1	70.7	7	5	4.8	5.1
White	7,820	7,820	145	132	55	52	18.5	16.9	7.0	6.6	90	80	(4)	(4)	7	2	48.3	15.2	4	7	2.8	5.3
Covington	41,800	41,400	1,032	1,041	369	405	24.7	25.1	7.4	9.8	723	636	334	257	40	62	38.8	59.6	38	49	3.7	4.7
Colored	7,000	7,000	164	153	55	91	23.4	21.9	7.9	13.0	109	62	(4)	(4)	12	10	73.2	65.4	8	20	4.9	13.1
White	34,800	34,400	868	888	254	314	24.9	25.8	7.3	9.1	614	574	342	283	28	52	32.3	58.6	30	29	3.5	3.3
Crenshaw	23,700	23,700	506	572	223	221	21.4	24.1	9.4	9.3	283	351	227	259	27	25	53.4	43.7	23	33	4.5	5.8
Colored	7,300	7,300	190	211	85	79	26.0	28.9	11.6	10.8	105	132	(4)	(4)	18	10	94.7	47.4	17	17	8.9	8.1
White	16,400	16,400	316	361	138	142	19.3	22.0	8.4	8.7	178	219	229	254	9	15	28.5	41.6	6	16	1.9	4.4
Dale	23,200	23,200	563	562	258	237	24.3	24.2	11.1	10.2	305	325	218	237	28	35	49.7	62.3	31	30	5.5	5.3
Colored	5,400	5,400	143	131	62	70	26.5	24.3	11.5	13.0	81	61	(4)	(4)	11	12	76.9	91.6	11	10	7.7	7.6
White	17,800	17,800	420	431	196	167	23.6	24.2	11.0	9.4	224	264	214	258	17	23	40.5	53.4	20	20	4.8	4.6
Dallas	36,800	37,000	1,000	950	452	479	27.2	25.7	12.3	12.9	548	471	221	198	77	82	77.0	86.3	68	70	6.8	7.4
Colored	31,300	31,500	951	891	420	428	30.4	28.3	13.4	13.6	531	463	226	208	77	78	81.0	87.5	66	70	6.9	7.9
White	5,500	5,500	49	59	32	51	8.9	10.7	5.8	9.3	17	8	(4)	(4)	------	4	------	67.8	2	------	4.1	------
Elmore	35,000	34,400	811	885	345	369	23.2	25.7	9.9	10.7	466	516	235	240	48	71	59.2	80.2	34	42	4.2	4.7
Colored	14,400	14,200	388	407	192	199	26.9	28.7	13.3	14.0	196	208	202	205	28	39	72.2	95.8	22	21	5.7	5.2
White	20,600	20,200	423	478	153	170	20.5	23.7	7.4	8.4	270	308	276	281	20	32	47.3	66.9	12	21	2.8	4.4
Escambia	28,600	28,100	715	714	305	329	25.0	25.4	10.7	11.7	410	385	234	217	40	58	55.9	81.2	31	30	4.3	4.2
Colored	9,200	9,000	205	207	119	115	22.3	23.0	12.9	12.8	86	92	172	180	12	21	58.5	101 4	15	14	7.3	6 8
White	19,400	19,100	510	507	186	214	26.3	26.5	9.6	11.2	324	293	274	237	28	37	54.9	73.0	16	16	3.1	3.2

See footnotes at end of table.

TABLE 18.—COLORED [1] AND WHITE POPULATION, BIRTHS AND DEATHS, INFANT MORTALITY, AND STILLBIRTHS, IN SELECTED REGISTRATION STATES, CITIES, AND COUNTIES: 1931 AND 1930—Continued

[See note at head of this table]

AREA AND COLOR	POPULATION ESTIMATED AS OF JULY 1		BIRTHS AND DEATHS (*Exclusive of stillbirths*): Number				Rate per 1,000 population				Excess of births over deaths [2]		Births per 100 deaths		INFANT MORTALITY (*Exclusive of stillbirths*): Deaths of infants under 1 year of age				STILLBIRTHS			
			Births		Deaths		Births		Deaths						Number		Per 1,000 births		Number		Rate per 100 live births	
	1931	1930	1931	1930	1931	1930	1931	1930	1931	1930	1931	1930	1931	1930	1931	1930	1931	1930	1931	1930	1931	1930
ALABAMA COUNTIES—continued																						
Fayette	18,500	18,400	461	496	120	172	24.9	27.0	6.5	9.3	341	324	384	288	18	36	39.0	72.6	14	25	3.0	5.0
Colored	2,700	2,600	55	56	19	24	20.4	21.5	7.0	9.2	36	32	(4)	(4)	4	7	72.7	125.0	5	4	9.1	7.1
White	15,800	15,800	406	440	101	148	25.7	27.8	6.4	9.4	305	292	402	297	14	29	34.5	65.9	9	21	2.2	4.8
Geneva	30,200	30,100	782	770	238	290	25.9	25.6	7.9	9.6	544	480	329	266	42	65	53.7	84.4	37	43	4.7	5.6
Colored	3,800	3,900	121	107	43	63	31.8	27.4	11.3	16.2	78	44	(4)	(4)	9	21	74.4	196.3	9	15	7.4	14.0
White	26,400	26,200	661	663	195	227	25.0	25.3	7.4	8.7	466	436	339	292	33	44	49.9	66.4	28	28	4.2	4.2
Greene	19,900	19,800	519	491	224	263	26.1	24.8	11.3	13.3	295	228	232	187	36	42	69.4	85.5	32	36	6.2	7.3
Colored	16,400	16,300	449	412	193	223	27.4	25.3	11.8	13.7	256	189	233	185	31	36	69.0	87.4	31	32	6.9	7.8
White	3,500	3,500	70	79	31	40	20.0	22.6	8.9	11.4	39	39	(4)	(4)	5	6	71.4	75.9	1	4	1.4	5.1
Hale	26,500	26,300	622	633	314	325	23.5	24.1	11.8	12.4	308	308	198	195	52	55	83.6	86.9	44	57	7.1	9.0
Colored	19,600	19,400	509	510	257	265	26.0	26.3	13.1	13.7	252	245	198	192	45	46	88.4	90.2	42	54	8.3	10.6
White	6,900	6,900	113	123	57	60	16.4	17.8	8.3	8.7	56	63	(4)	(4)	7	9	61.9	73.2	2	3	1.8	2.4
Henry	23,000	22,900	581	557	162	205	25.3	24.3	7.0	9.0	419	352	359	272	28	38	48.2	68.2	22	37	3.8	6.6
Colored	10,900	10,800	294	306	83	103	27.0	28.3	7.6	9.5	211	203	(4)	297	14	24	47.6	78.4	19	23	6.5	7.5
White	12,100	12,100	287	251	79	102	23.7	20.7	6.5	8.4	208	149	(4)	246	14	14	48.8	55.8	3	14	1.0	5.6
Houston	30,500	30,000	766	731	262	260	25.1	24.4	8.6	8.7	504	471	292	281	42	53	54.8	72.5	41	43	5.4	5.9
Colored	7,600	7,400	234	248	78	85	30.8	33.5	10.3	11.5	156	163	(4)	(4)	19	21	81.2	84.7	15	17	6.4	6.9
White	22,900	22,600	532	483	184	175	23.2	21.4	8.0	7.7	348	308	289	276	23	32	43.2	66.3	26	26	4.9	5.4
Jefferson	144,200	140,900	2,524	2,807	1,204	1,257	17.5	19.9	8.3	8.9	1,320	1,550	210	223	134	197	53.1	70.2	115	115	4.6	4.1
Colored	51,200	51,000	975	1,041	650	679	19.0	20.4	12.7	13.3	325	362	150	153	68	98	69.7	94.1	74	74	7.6	7.1
White	93,000	89,900	1,549	1,766	554	578	16.7	19.6	6.0	6.4	995	1,188	280	306	66	99	42.6	56.1	41	41	2.6	2.3
Lamar	[5] 18,001	[5] 18,001	454	526	147	142	25.2	29.2	8.2	7.9	307	384	309	370	19	27	41.9	51.3	13	14	2.9	2.7
Colored	2,851	2,851	84	95	31	32	29.5	33.3	10.9	11.2	53	63	(4)	(4)	8	5	95.2	52.6	4	5	4.8	5.3
White	15,150	15,150	370	431	116	110	24.4	28.4	7.7	7.3	254	321	319	392	11	22	29.7	51.0	9	9	2.4	2.1
Lauderdale	29,400	29,400	762	794	204	210	25.9	27.0	6.9	7.1	558	584	374	378	43	44	56.4	55.4	24	25	3.1	3.1
Colored	4,900	5,000	119	115	62	47	24.3	23.0	12.7	9.4	57	68	(4)	(4)	10	8	84.0	69.6	4	4	3.4	3.5
White	24,500	24,400	643	679	142	163	26.2	27.8	5.8	6.7	501	516	453	417	33	36	51.3	53.0	20	21	3.1	3.1
Lawrence	27,300	27,000	702	800	232	229	25.7	29.6	8.5	8.5	470	571	303	349	34	51	48.4	63.8	26	29	3.7	3.6
Colored	7,100	7,100	137	146	87	84	19.3	20.6	12.3	11.8	50	62	(4)	(4)	7	5	51.1	34.2	9	9	6.6	6.2
White	20,200	19,900	565	654	145	145	28.0	32.9	7.2	7.3	420	509	390	451	27	46	47.8	70.3	17	20	3.0	3.1
Lee	29,700	29,500	704	821	329	429	23.7	27.8	11.1	14.5	375	392	214	191	58	79	82.4	96.2	56	54	8.0	6.6
Colored	17,400	17,400	509	540	201	281	29.3	31.0	11.6	16.1	308	259	253	192	47	56	92.3	103.7	45	48	8.8	8.9
White	12,300	12,100	195	281	128	148	15.9	23.2	10.4	12.2	67	133	152	190	11	23	56.4	81.9	11	6	5.6	2.1
Limestone	37,300	36,800	955	1,018	312	388	25.6	27.7	8.4	10.5	643	630	306	262	61	82	63.9	80.6	41	46	4.3	4.5
Colored	10,100	10,000	266	261	106	147	26.3	26.1	10.5	14.7	160	114	251	178	15	29	56.4	111.1	22	19	8.3	7.3
White	27,200	26,800	689	757	206	241	25.3	28.2	7.6	9.0	483	516	334	314	46	53	66.8	70.0	19	27	2.8	3.6
Lowndes	[5] 22,878	[5] 22,878	662	615	301	285	28.9	26.9	13.2	12.5	361	330	220	216	55	57	83.1	92.7	48	46	7.3	7.5
Colored	19,632	19,632	615	573	268	262	31.3	29.2	13.7	13.3	347	311	229	219	51	56	82.9	97.7	48	44	7.8	7.7
White	3,246	3,246	47	42	33	23	14.5	12.9	10.2	7.1	14	19	(4)	(4)	4	1	85.1	23.8	----	2	----	4.8
Macon	27,500	27,200	744	760	486	541	27.1	27.9	17.7	19.9	258	219	153	140	59	85	79.3	111.8	51	56	6.9	7.4
Colored	22,600	22,400	650	655	445	477	28.8	29.2	19.7	21.3	205	178	146	137	52	80	80.0	122.1	49	53	7.5	8.1
White	4,900	4,800	94	105	41	64	19.2	21.9	8.4	13.3	53	41	(4)	(4)	7	5	74.5	47.6	2	3	2.1	2.9
Madison	54,300	53,300	1,378	1,420	537	598	25.4	26.6	9.9	11.2	841	822	257	237	118	122	85.6	85.9	53	53	3.8	3.7
Colored	15,600	15,500	394	408	181	219	25.3	26.3	11.6	14.1	213	189	218	186	36	42	91.4	102.9	12	16	3.0	3.9
White	38,700	37,800	984	1,012	356	379	25.4	26.8	9.2	10.0	628	633	276	267	82	80	83.3	79.1	41	37	4.2	3.7
Marengo	36,500	36,400	796	831	387	401	21.8	22.8	10.6	11.0	409	430	206	207	39	36	49.0	43.3	54	66	6.8	7.9
Colored	26,400	26,300	600	632	309	324	22.7	24.0	11.7	12.3	291	308	194	195	29	35	48.3	55.4	50	60	8.3	9.5
White	10,100	10,100	196	199	78	77	19.4	19.7	7.7	7.6	118	122	(4)	(4)	10	1	51.0	5.0	4	6	2.0	3.0
Mobile	51,700	50,400	1,007	1,001	745	702	19.5	19.9	14.4	13.9	262	299	135	143	71	64	70.5	63.9	57	55	5.7	5.5
Colored	18,200	17,800	335	399	441	427	18.4	22.4	24.2	24.0	−106	−28	76	93	35	31	104.5	77.7	32	27	9.6	6.8
White	33,500	32,600	672	602	304	275	20.1	18.5	9.1	8.4	368	327	221	219	36	33	53.6	54.8	25	28	3.7	4.7
Monroe	30,200	30,100	825	890	231	288	27.3	29.6	7.6	9.6	594	602	357	309	38	61	46.1	68.5	54	49	6.5	5.5
Colored	15,800	15,800	488	511	124	175	30.9	32.3	7.8	11.1	364	336	394	292	20	35	41.0	68.5	37	39	7.6	7.6
White	14,400	14,300	337	379	107	113	23.4	26.5	7.4	7.9	230	266	315	335	18	26	53.4	68.6	17	10	5.0	2.6
Montgomery	33,500	32,800	643	563	416	365	19.2	17.2	12.4	11.1	227	198	155	154	28	33	43.5	58.6	25	15	3.9	2.7
Colored	22,100	22,100	517	467	338	301	23.4	21.1	15.3	13.6	179	166	153	155	24	26	46.4	55.7	23	14	4.4	3.0
White	11,400	10,700	126	96	78	64	11.1	9.0	6.8	6.0	48	32	(4)	(4)	4	7	31.7	72.9	2	1	1.6	1.0
Morgan	30,000	30,400	737	799	214	285	24.6	26.3	7.1	9.4	523	514	344	280	34	39	46.1	48.8	25	36	3.4	4.5
Colored	4,400	4,400	115	87	47	58	26.1	19.8	10.7	13.2	68	29	(4)	(4)	7	6	60.9	69.0	6	9	5.2	10.3
White	25,600	26,000	622	712	167	227	24.3	27.4	6.5	8.7	455	485	372	314	27	33	43.4	46.3	19	27	3.1	3.8

Perry	26,500	26,400	776	739	260	283	29.3	28.0	9.8	10.7	516	456	298	261	56	54	72.2	73.1	59	41	7.6	5.5
Colored	19,300	19,200	584	569	203	230	30.3	29.6	10.5	12.0	381	339	288	247	44	46	75.3	80.8	55	36	9.4	6.3
White	7,200	7,200	192	170	57	53	26.7	23.6	7.9	7.4	135	117	(4)	(4)	12	8	62.5	47.1	4	5	2.1	2.9
Pickens	5 24,902	5 24,902	645	607	227	240	25.9	24.4	9.1	9.6	418	367	284	253	36	42	55.8	69.2	30	27	4.7	4.4
Colored	11,932	11,932	313	270	145	139	26.2	22.6	12.2	11.6	168	131	216	194	22	29	70.3	107.4	17	18	5.4	6.7
White	12,970	12,970	332	337	82	101	25.6	26.0	6.3	7.8	250	236	(4)	334	14	13	42.2	38.6	13	9	3.9	2.7
Pike	32,300	32,300	725	711	337	360	22.4	22.0	10.4	11.1	388	351	215	198	45	60	62.1	84.4	53	40	7.3	5.6
Colored	14,500	14,600	339	344	180	194	23.4	23.6	12.4	13.3	159	150	188	177	20	40	59.0	116.3	29	26	8.6	7.6
White	17,800	17,700	386	367	157	166	21.7	20.7	8.8	9.4	229	201	246	221	25	20	64.8	54.5	24	14	6.2	3.8
Randolph	5 26,861	5 26,861	594	590	241	230	22.1	22.0	9.0	8.6	353	360	246	257	27	41	45.5	69.5	21	22	3.5	3.7
Colored	5,884	5,884	120	128	63	67	20.4	21.8	10.7	11.4	57	61	(4)	(4)	5	11	41.7	85.9	5	7	4.2	5.5
White	20,977	20,977	474	462	178	163	22.6	22.0	8.5	7.8	296	299	266	283	22	30	46.4	64.9	16	15	3.4	3.2
Russell 7	5 19,877	5 19,877	488	656	204	362	24.6	33.0	10.3	18.2	284	294	239	181	28	42	57.4	64.0	33	63	6.8	9.6
Colored	16,562	16,562	427	511	164	285	25.8	30.9	9.9	17.2	263	226	260	179	23	32	53.9	62.6	25	57	5.9	11.2
White	3,315	3,315	61	145	40	77	18.4	43.7	12.1	23.2	21	68	(4)	(4)	5	10	82.0	69.0	8	6	13.1	4.1
St. Clair	24,600	24,500	621	553	237	249	25.2	22.6	9.6	10.2	384	304	262	222	43	44	69.2	79.6	26	24	4.2	4.3
Colored	4,800	4,800	97	68	47	52	20.2	14.2	9.8	10.8	50	16	(4)	(4)	8	8	82.5	117.6	9	6	9.3	8.8
White	19,800	19,700	524	485	190	197	26.5	24.6	9.6	10.0	334	288	276	246	35	36	66.8	74.2	17	18	3.2	3.7
Shelby	27,600	27,600	661	691	242	251	23.9	25.0	8.8	9.1	419	440	273	275	42	37	63.5	53.5	22	26	3.3	3.8
Colored	6,900	7,000	139	179	97	93	20.1	25.6	14.1	13.3	42	86	(4)	(4)	14	10	100.7	55.9	10	10	7.2	5.6
White	20,700	20,600	522	512	145	158	25.2	24.9	7.0	7.7	377	354	360	324	28	27	53.6	52.7	12	16	2.3	3.1
Sumter	27,100	27,000	761	681	316	345	28.1	25.2	11.7	12.8	445	336	241	197	53	56	69.6	82.2	52	75	6.8	11.0
Colored	21,400	21,300	672	589	260	289	31.4	27.7	12.1	13.6	412	300	258	204	49	54	72.9	91.7	48	71	7.1	12.1
White	5,700	5,700	89	92	56	56	15.6	16.1	9.8	9.8	33	36	(4)	(4)	4	2	44.9	21.7	4	4	4.5	4.3
Talladega	45,800	45,300	1,307	1,231	501	524	28.5	27.2	10.9	11.6	806	707	261	235	74	87	56.6	70.7	51	58	3.9	4.7
Colored	17,200	17,100	512	431	219	235	29.8	25.2	12.7	13.7	293	196	234	183	27	37	52.7	85.8	25	32	4.9	7.4
White	28,600	28,200	795	800	282	289	27.8	28.4	9.9	10.2	513	511	282	277	47	50	59.1	62.5	26	26	3.3	3.3
Tallapoosa	31,400	31,200	719	726	302	346	22.9	23.3	9.6	11.1	417	380	238	210	41	51	57.0	70.2	38	44	5.3	6.1
Colored	9,800	9,700	229	215	101	116	23.4	22.2	10.3	12.0	128	99	227	185	21	16	91.7	74.4	15	21	6.6	9.8
White	21,600	21,500	490	511	201	230	22.7	23.8	9.3	10.7	289	281	244	222	20	35	40.8	68.5	23	23	4.7	4.5
Tuscaloosa	43,600	43,500	1,009	1,017	449	405	23.1	23.4	10.3	9.3	560	612	225	251	45	70	44.6	68.8	38	61	3.8	6.0
Colored	14,400	14,400	326	341	198	178	22.6	23.7	13.8	12.4	128	163	165	192	18	32	55.2	93.8	19	36	5.8	10.6
White	29,200	29,100	683	676	251	227	23.4	23.2	8.6	7.8	432	449	272	298	27	38	39.5	56.2	19	25	2.8	3.7
Walker	60,500	59,700	1,564	1,610	593	599	25.9	27.0	9.8	10.0	971	1,011	264	269	105	126	67.1	78.3	62	73	4.0	4.5
Colored	7,700	7,800	151	115	110	96	19.6	14.7	14.3	12.3	41	19	137	(4)	12	9	79.5	78.3	10	17	6.6	14.8
White	52,800	51,900	1,413	1,495	483	503	26.8	28.8	9.1	9.7	930	992	293	297	93	117	65.8	78.3	52	56	3.7	3.7
Washington	16,600	16,400	424	415	135	148	25.5	25.3	8.1	9.0	289	267	314	280	18	27	42.5	65.1	32	20	7.5	4.8
Colored	6,900	6,800	169	138	67	71	24.5	20.3	9.7	10.4	102	67	(4)	(4)	8	15	47.3	108.7	20	8	11.8	5.8
White	9,700	9,600	255	277	68	77	26.3	28.9	7.0	8.0	187	200	(4)	(4)	10	12	39.2	43.3	12	12	4.7	4.3
Wilcox	5 24,880	5 24,880	745	713	299	337	29.9	28.7	12.0	13.5	446	376	249	212	55	61	73.8	85.6	44	35	5.9	4.9
Colored	19,319	19,319	642	607	262	276	33.2	31.4	13.6	14.3	380	331	245	220	53	59	82.6	97.2	39	34	6.1	5.6
White	5,561	5,561	103	106	37	61	18.5	19.1	6.7	11.0	66	45	(4)	(4)	2	2	19.4	18.9	5	1	4.9	.9
ARKANSAS COUNTIES 8																						
Arkansas	22,400	22,300	469	512	185	222	20.9	23.0	8.3	10.0	284	290	254	231	25	25	53.3	48.8	12	24	2.6	4.7
Colored	4,900	4,900	93	107	56	77	19.0	21.8	11.4	15.7	37	30	(4)	(4)	9	9	96.8	84.1	5	11	5.4	10.3
White	17,500	17,400	376	405	129	145	21.5	23.3	7.4	8.3	247	260	291	279	16	16	42.6	39.5	7	13	1.9	3.2
Ashley	25,400	25,200	757	777	256	260	29.8	30.8	10.1	10.3	501	517	296	299	30	37	39.6	47.6	47	39	6.2	5.0
Colored	12,100	11,900	347	377	136	143	28.7	31.7	11.2	12.0	211	234	255	264	16	18	46.1	47.7	30	30	8.6	8.0
White	13,300	13,300	410	400	120	117	30.8	30.1	9.0	8.8	290	283	342	342	14	19	34.1	47.5	17	9	4.1	2.3
Bradley	17,700	17,500	453	401	146	155	25.6	22.9	8.2	8.9	307	246	310	259	18	11	39.7	27.4	16	18	3.5	4.5
Colored	5,900	5,700	168	128	59	63	28.5	22.5	10.0	11.1	109	65	(4)	(4)	8	2	47.6	15.6	6	10	3.6	7.8
White	11,800	11,800	285	273	87	92	24.2	23.1	7.4	7.8	198	181	(4)	(4)	10	9	35.1	33.0	10	8	3.5	2.9
Calhoun	5 9,752	5 9,752	274	248	53	77	28.1	25.4	5.4	7.9	221	171	(4)	(4)	7	8	25.5	32.3	12	15	4.4	6.0
Colored	2,993	2,993	74	72	20	40	24.7	24.1	6.7	13.4	54	32	(4)	(4)	5	5	67.6	69.4	6	2	8.1	2.8
White	6,759	6,759	200	176	33	37	29.6	26.0	4.9	5.5	167	139	(4)	(4)	2	3	10.0	17.0	6	13	3.0	7.4
Chicot	22,800	22,700	371	374	201	214	16.3	16.5	8.8	9.4	170	160	185	175	9	17	24.3	45.5	30	22	8.1	5.9
Colored	14,000	14,200	236	242	153	158	16.9	17.0	10.9	11.1	83	84	154	153	6	8	25.4	33.1	25	19	10.6	7.9
White	8,800	8,500	135	132	48	56	15.3	15.5	5.5	6.6	87	76	(4)	(4)	3	9	22.2	68.2	5	3	3.7	2.3
Clark	5 24,932	5 24,932	550	497	228	232	22.1	19.9	9.1	9.3	322	265	241	214	15	15	27.3	30.2	14	18	2.5	3.6
Colored	7,293	7,293	201	108	68	83	27.6	14.8	9.3	11.4	133	25	(4)	(4)	5	4	24.9	37.0	9	10	4.5	9.3
White	17,639	17,639	349	389	160	149	19.8	22.1	9.1	8.4	189	240	218	261	10	11	28.7	28.3	5	8	1.4	2.1
Cleveland	12,800	12,800	306	329	74	64	23.9	25.7	5.8	5.0	232	265	(4)	(4)	6	12	19.6	36.5	13	21	4.2	6.4
Colored	3,400	3,500	70	83	38	34	20.6	23.7	11.2	9.7	32	49	(4)	(4)	1	6	14.3	72.3	7	6	10.0	7.2
White	9,400	9,300	236	246	36	30	25.1	26.5	3.8	3.2	200	216	(4)	(4)	5	6	21.2	24.4	6	15	2.5	6.1
Columbia	5 27,320	5 27,320	344	474	150	192	12.6	17.3	5.5	7.0	194	282	229	247	15	18	43.6	[illegible]	10	22	2.9	4.6
Colored	12,728	12,728	148	196	70	106	11.6	15.4	5.5	8.3	78	90	(4)	185	7	9	47.3	[illegible]	5	14	3.4	7.1
White	14,592	14,592	196	278	80	86	13.4	19.1	5.5	5.9	116	192	(4)	(4)	8	9	40.8	32.4	5	8	2.6	2.9
Conway	5 21,949	5 21,949	622	565	202	249	28.3	25.7	9.2	11.3	420	316	308	227	33	38	53.1	67.3	12	17	1.9	3.0
Colored	5,978	5,978	184	144	66	106	30.8	24.1	11.0	17.7	118	38	(4)	136	13	11	70.7	76.4	5	6	2.7	4.2
White	15,971	15,971	438	421	136	143	27.4	26.4	8.5	9.0	302	278	322	294	20	27	45.7	64.1	7	11	1.6	2.6
Crittenden	41,000	40,000	687	801	451	471	16.8	20.0	11.0	11.8	236	330	152	170	56	41	81.5	51.2	54	67	7.9	8.4
Colored	32,200	31,600	572	632	364	405	17.8	20.0	11.3	12.8	208	227	157	156	41	34	71.7	53.8	49	52	8.6	8.2
White	8,800	8,400	115	169	87	66	13.1	20.1	9.9	7.9	28	103	(4)	(4)	15	7	130.4	41.4	5	15	4.3	8.9
Cross	26,600	25,900	559	585	161	219	21.0	22.6	6.1	8.5	398	366	347	267	25	30	44.7	51.3	31	23	5.5	3.9
Colored	11,400	11,100	209	213	74	122	18.3	19.2	6.5	11.0	135	91	(4)	175	8	10	38.3	46.9	14	18	6.7	8.5
White	15,200	14,800	350	372	87	97	23.0	25.1	5.7	6.6	263	275	(4)	(4)	17	20	48.6	53.8	17	5	4.9	1.3
Dallas	14,700	14,700	333	309	116	106	22.7	21.0	7.9	7.2	217	203	287	292	12	13	36.0	42.1	6	10	1.8	3.2
Colored	5,200	5,200	99	111	56	49	19.0	21.3	10.8	9.4	43	62	(4)	(4)	3	4	30.3	36.0	4	4	4.0	3.6
White	9,500	9,500	234	198	60	57	24.6	20.8	6.3	6.0	174	141	(4)	(4)	9	9	38.5	45.5	2	6	.9	3.0
Desha	22,000	21,900	409	400	196	205	18.6	18.3	8.9	9.4	213	195	209	195	11	19	26.9	47.5	31	22	7.6	5.5
Colored	13,800	14,000	267	264	142	153	19.3	18.9	10.3	10.9	125	111	188	173	6	15	22.5	56.8	23	20	8.6	7.6
White	8,200	7,900	142	136	54	52	17.3	17.2	6.6	6.6	88	84	(4)	(4)	5	4	35.2	29.4	8	2	5.6	1.5

See footnotes at end of table.

TABLE 18.—COLORED [1] AND WHITE POPULATION, BIRTHS AND DEATHS, INFANT MORTALITY, AND STILLBIRTHS, IN SELECTED REGISTRATION STATES, CITIES, AND COUNTIES: 1931 AND 1930—Continued

[See note at head of this table]

AREA AND COLOR	POPULATION ESTIMATED AS OF JULY 1		BIRTHS AND DEATHS (Exclusive of stillbirths): Number, Births		Number, Deaths		Rate per 1,000 population, Births		Rate per 1,000 population, Deaths		Excess of births over deaths [3]		Births per 100 deaths		INFANT MORTALITY (Exclusive of stillbirths): Deaths of infants under 1 year of age, Number		Per 1,000 births		STILLBIRTHS: Number		Rate per 100 live births	
	1931	1930	1931	1930	1931	1930	1931	1930	1931	1930	1931	1930	1931	1930	1931	1930	1931	1930	1931	1930	1931	1930
ARKANSAS COUNTIES—continued																						
Drew	[5] 19,928	[5] 19,928	476	465	151	213	23.9	23.3	7.6	10.7	325	252	315	218	19	34	39.9	73.1	20	20	4.2	4.3
Colored	9,152	9,152	214	195	79	107	23.4	21.3	8.6	11.7	135	88	(4)	182	11	9	51.4	46.2	7	12	3.3	6.2
White	10,776	10,776	262	270	72	106	24.3	25.1	6.7	9.8	190	164	(4)	255	8	25	30.5	92.6	13	8	5.0	3.0
Faulkner	28,500	28,400	703	729	239	240	24.7	25.7	8.4	8.5	464	489	294	304	41	47	58.3	64.5	31	31	4.4	4.3
Colored	3,600	3,600	113	97	58	64	31.4	26.9	16.1	17.8	55	33	(4)	(4)	5	11	44.2	113.4	8	6	7.1	6.2
White	24,900	24,800	590	632	181	176	23.7	25.5	7.3	7.1	409	456	326	359	36	36	61.0	57.0	23	25	3.9	4.0
Hempstead	[5] 30,847	[5] 30,847	729	619	297	303	23.6	20.1	9.6	9.8	432	316	245	204	39	44	53.5	71.1	38	39	5.2	6.3
Colored	13,128	13,128	348	243	164	158	26.5	18.5	12.5	12.0	184	85	212	154	23	23	66.1	94.7	24	26	6.9	10.7
White	17,719	17,719	381	376	133	145	21.5	21.2	7.5	8.2	248	231	286	259	16	21	42.0	55.9	14	13	3.7	3.5
Hot Springs	18,100	18,100	395	486	190	187	21.8	26.9	10.5	10.3	205	299	208	260	17	22	43.0	45.3	18	14	4.6	2.9
Colored	2,300	2,300	37	77	33	33	16.1	33.5	14.3	14.3	4	44	(4)	(4)	2	6	54.1	77.9	----	3	----	3.9
White	15,800	15,800	358	409	157	154	22.7	25.9	9.9	9.7	201	255	228	266	15	16	41.9	39.1	18	11	5.0	2.7
Howard	[5] 17,489	[5] 17,489	343	389	127	116	19.6	22.2	7.3	6.6	216	273	270	335	13	5	37.9	12.9	5	9	1.5	2.3
Colored	3,827	3,827	98	57	33	31	25.6	14.9	8.6	8.1	65	26	(4)	(4)	4	2	40.8	35.1	2	6	2.0	10.5
White	13,662	13,662	245	332	94	85	17.9	24.3	6.9	6.2	151	247	(4)	(4)	9	3	36.7	9.0	3	3	1.2	.9
Jackson	28,200	28,000	786	761	269	322	27.9	27.2	9.5	11.5	517	439	292	236	41	50	52.2	65.7	25	22	3.2	2.9
Colored	5,200	5,200	76	64	54	65	14.6	12.3	10.4	12.5	22	−1	(4)	(4)	4	3	52.6	46.9	6	2	7.9	3.1
White	23,000	22,800	710	697	215	257	30.9	30.6	9.3	11.3	495	440	330	271	37	47	52.1	67.4	19	20	2.7	2.9
Jefferson	43,800	43,400	840	828	293	366	19.2	19.1	6.7	8.4	547	462	287	226	32	29	38.1	35.0	55	68	6.5	8.2
Colored	30,600	30,800	628	614	207	291	20.5	19.9	6.8	9.7	421	323	303	211	22	17	35.0	27.7	47	57	7.5	9.3
White	13,200	12,600	212	214	86	75	16.1	17.0	6.5	6.0	126	139	(4)	(4)	10	12	47.2	56.1	8	11	3.8	5.1
Lafayette	17,100	17,000	310	335	123	141	18.1	19.7	7.2	8.3	187	194	252	238	9	13	29.0	38.8	17	14	5.5	4.2
Colored	8,500	8,500	142	170	70	83	16.7	20.0	8.2	9.8	72	87	(4)	(4)	4	5	28.2	29.4	12	10	8.5	5.9
White	8,600	8,500	168	165	53	58	19.5	19.4	6.2	6.8	115	107	(4)	(4)	5	8	29.8	48.5	5	4	3.0	2.4
Lee	[5] 26,637	[5] 26,637	553	520	348	378	20.8	19.5	13.1	14.2	205	142	159	138	43	38	77.8	73.1	40	30	7.2	5.8
Colored	17,427	17,427	344	310	261	279	19.7	17.8	15.0	16.0	83	31	132	111	31	18	90.1	58.1	34	21	9.9	6.8
White	9,210	9,210	209	210	87	99	22.7	22.8	9.4	10.7	122	111	(4)	(4)	12	20	57.4	95.2	6	9	2.9	4.3
Lincoln	20,400	20,300	445	394	154	186	21.8	19.4	7.5	9.2	291	208	289	212	14	21	31.5	53.3	23	14	5.2	3.6
Colored	13,100	13,100	284	233	107	135	21.7	17.8	8.2	10.3	177	98	265	173	7	16	24.6	68.7	16	12	5.6	5.2
White	7,300	7,200	161	161	47	51	22.1	22.4	6.4	7.1	114	110	(4)	(4)	7	5	43.5	31.1	7	2	4.3	1.2
Little River	[5] 15,515	[5] 15,515	299	297	115	101	19.3	19.1	7.4	6.5	184	196	260	294	10	14	33.4	47.1	8	21	2.7	7.1
Colored	6,046	6,046	91	86	51	55	15.1	14.2	8.4	9.1	40	31	(4)	(4)	4	6	44.0	69.8	3	15	3.3	17.4
White	9,469	9,469	208	211	64	46	22.0	22.3	6.8	4.9	144	165	(4)	(4)	6	8	28.8	37.9	5	6	2.4	2.8
Lonoke	33,800	33,800	728	746	264	329	21.5	22.1	7.8	9.7	464	417	276	227	30	41	41.2	55.0	30	51	4.1	6.8
Colored	10,800	11,000	239	257	86	122	22.1	23.4	8.0	11.1	153	135	(4)	211	12	14	50.2	54.5	13	29	5.4	11.3
White	23,000	22,800	489	489	178	207	21.3	21.4	7.7	9.1	311	282	275	236	18	27	36.8	55.2	17	22	3.5	4.5
Miller	20,300	19,900	273	304	112	151	13.4	15.3	5.5	7.6	161	153	244	201	12	11	44.0	36.2	12	15	4.4	4.9
Colored	6,700	6,500	45	50	50	77	6.7	7.7	7.5	11.8	−5	−27	(4)	(4)	1	2	22.2	40.0	2	7	4.4	14.0
White	13,600	13,400	228	254	62	74	16.8	19.0	4.6	5.5	166	180	(4)	(4)	11	9	48.2	35.4	10	8	4.4	3.1
Mississippi	61,500	59,600	1,778	1,755	704	635	28.9	29.4	11.4	10.7	1,074	1,120	253	276	158	146	88.9	83.2	60	72	3.4	4.1
Colored	24,100	23,500	534	529	287	264	22.2	22.5	11.9	11.2	247	265	186	200	33	32	61.8	60.5	22	33	4.1	6.2
White	37,400	56,100	1,244	1,226	417	371	33.3	34.0	11.1	10.3	827	855	298	330	125	114	100.5	93.0	38	39	3.1	3.2
Monroe	[5] 20,651	[5] 20,651	484	464	214	236	23.4	22.5	10.4	11.4	270	228	226	197	23	20	47.5	43.1	28	29	5.8	6.3
Colored	11,503	11,503	267	244	126	153	23.2	21.2	11.0	13.3	141	91	212	159	10	9	37.5	36.9	20	16	7.5	6.6
White	9,148	9,148	217	220	88	83	23.7	24.0	9.6	9.1	129	137	(4)	(4)	13	11	59.9	50.0	8	13	3.7	5.9
Nevada	[5] 20,407	[5] 20,407	455	303	137	127	22.3	14.8	6.7	6.2	318	176	332	239	10	9	22.0	29.7	11	14	2.4	4.6
Colored	7,244	7,244	168	104	50	47	23.2	14.4	6.9	6.5	118	57	(4)	(4)	3	1	17.9	9.6	3	9	1.8	8.7
White	13,163	13,163	287	199	87	80	21.8	15.1	6.6	6.1	200	119	(4)	(4)	7	8	24.4	40.2	8	5	2.8	2.5
Ouachita	31,000	30,100	684	584	264	296	22.1	19.4	8.5	9.8	420	288	259	197	17	31	24.9	53.1	30	39	4.4	6.7
Colored	13,300	13,100	341	283	126	164	25.6	21.6	9.5	12.5	215	119	271	173	7	13	20.5	45.9	19	20	5.6	7.1
White	17,700	17,000	343	301	138	132	19.4	17.7	7.8	7.8	205	169	249	228	10	18	29.2	59.8	11	19	3.2	6.3
Phillips	[5] 40,683	[5] 40,683	793	664	529	630	19.5	16.3	13.0	15.5	264	34	150	105	31	38	39.1	57.2	62	51	7.8	7.7
Colored	27,355	27,355	479	405	410	468	17.5	14.8	15.0	17.1	69	−63	117	87	22	22	45.9	54.3	52	40	10.9	9.9
White	13,328	13,328	314	259	119	162	23.6	19.4	8.9	12.2	195	97	264	160	9	16	28.7	61.8	10	11	3.2	4.2
Poinsett	30,800	29,900	758	784	296	314	24.6	26.2	9.6	10.5	462	470	256	250	58	62	76.5	79.1	29	39	3.8	5.0
Colored	4,400	4,300	105	107	65	52	23.9	24.9	14.8	12.1	40	55	(4)	(4)	5	7	47.6	65.4	10	8	9.5	7.5
White	26,400	25,600	653	677	231	262	24.7	26.4	8.8	10.2	422	415	283	258	53	55	81.2	81.2	19	31	2.9	4.6
Prairie	[5] 15,187	[5] 15,187	295	326	190	164	19.4	21.5	12.5	10.8	105	162	155	199	20	21	67.8	64.4	15	8	5.1	2.5
Colored	3,632	3,632	80	83	62	56	22.0	22.9	17.1	15.5	18	27	(4)	(4)	11	9	137.5	108.4	13	5	16.3	6.0
White	11,555	11,555	215	243	128	108	18.6	21.0	11.1	9.3	87	135	168	225	9	12	41.9	49.4	2	3	.9	1.2

Pulaski	37,400	36,800	718	619	381	384	19.2	16.8	10.2	10.4	337	235	188	161	44	40	61.3	64.6	24	34	3.3	5.5
Colored	14,500	14,400	306	271	192	188	21.1	18.8	13.2	13.1	114	83	159	144	21	28	68.6	103.3	15	23	4.9	8.5
White	22,900	22,400	412	348	189	196	18.0	15.5	8.3	8.8	223	152	218	178	23	12	55.8	34.5	9	11	2.2	3.2
St. Francis	34,000	33,500	755	765	356	395	22.2	22.8	10.5	11.8	399	370	212	194	29	48	38.4	62.7	32	50	4.2	6.5
Colored	22,800	22,600	464	498	265	280	20.4	22.0	11.6	12.4	199	218	175	178	18	29	38.8	58.2	24	46	5.2	9.2
White	11,200	10,900	291	267	91	115	26.0	24.5	8.1	10.6	200	152	(4)	252	11	19	37.8	71.2	8	4	2.7	1.5
Sevier	[5] 16,364	[5] 16,364	398	405	158	185	24.5	24.7	9.7	11.3	240	220	252	219	18	23	45.2	56.8	7	13	1.8	3.2
Colored	1,757	1,757	45	43	16	23	25.6	24.5	9.1	13.1	29	20	(4)	(4)	2	4	44.4	93.0	------	2	------	4.7
White	14,607	14,607	353	362	142	162	24.2	24.8	9.7	11.1	211	200	249	223	16	19	45.3	52.5	7	11	2.0	3.0
Union	41,100	39,700	509	621	143	171	12.4	15.6	3.5	4.5	366	450	356	363	11	17	21.6	27.4	19	12	3.7	1.9
Colored	13,900	13,700	128	183	39	74	9.2	13.4	2.8	5.4	89	109	(4)	(4)	------	7	------	38.5	8	6	6.3	3.3
White	27,200	26,000	381	458	104	97	14.0	16.8	3.8	3.7	277	341	366	(4)	11	10	28.9	22.8	11	6	2.9	1.4
Woodruff	22,800	22,700	483	523	185	228	21.2	23.0	8.1	10.0	298	295	261	229	24	29	49.7	55.4	31	33	6.4	6.3
Colored	9,900	10,000	201	210	100	137	20.3	21.0	10.1	13.7	101	73	201	153	8	17	39.8	81.0	20	24	10.0	11.4
White	12,900	12,700	282	313	85	91	21.9	24.6	6.6	7.2	197	222	(4)	(4)	16	12	56.7	38.3	11	9	3.9	2.9
DELAWARE COUNTIES [8]																						
Kent	31,900	31,900	628	653	512	496	19.7	20.5	16.1	15.5	116	157	123	132	64	62	101.9	94.9	33	20	5.3	3.1
Colored	6,600	6,700	132	135	127	133	20.0	20.1	19.2	19.9	5	2	104	102	26	23	197.0	170.4	7	3	5.3	2.2
White	25,300	25,200	496	518	385	363	19.6	20.6	15.2	14.4	111	155	129	143	38	39	76.6	75.3	26	17	5.2	3.3
New Castle	56,000	54,700	558	660	675	659	10.0	12.1	12.1	12.0	−117	1	83	100	32	47	57.3	71.2	31	21	5.6	3.2
Colored	6,700	6,500	74	125	157	154	11.0	19.2	23.4	23.7	−83	−29	47	81	13	14	175.7	112.0	7	5	9.5	4.0
White	49,300	48,200	484	535	518	505	9.8	11.1	10.5	10.5	−34	30	93	106	19	33	39.3	61.7	24	16	5.0	3.0
Sussex	45,700	45,600	851	856	635	541	18.6	18.8	13.9	11.9	216	315	134	158	97	79	114.0	92.3	35	32	4.1	3.7
Colored	7,500	7,600	251	226	158	140	33.5	29.7	21.1	18.4	93	86	159	161	43	32	171.3	141.6	13	15	5.2	6.6
White	38,200	38,000	600	630	477	401	15.7	16.6	12.5	10.6	123	229	126	157	54	47	90.0	74.6	22	17	3.7	2.7
FLORIDA COUNTIES [8]																						
Alachua	24,200	24,000	395	426	256	297	16.3	17.8	10.6	12.4	139	129	154	143	29	30	73.4	70.4	43	42	10.9	9.9
Colored	11,300	11,200	205	261	151	183	18.1	23.3	13.4	16.3	54	78	136	143	14	20	68.3	76.6	38	29	18.5	11.1
White	12,900	12,800	190	165	105	114	14.7	12.9	8.1	8.9	85	51	181	145	15	10	78.9	60.6	5	13	2.6	7.9
Baker	6,400	6,300	166	162	60	58	25.9	25.7	9.4	9.2	106	104	(4)	(4)	9	12	54.2	74.1	8	11	4.8	6.8
Colored	1,900	1,800	43	55	25	31	22.6	30.6	13.2	17.2	18	24	(4)	(4)	5	6	116.3	109.1	4	5	9.3	9.1
White	4,500	4,500	123	107	35	27	27.3	23.8	7.8	6.0	88	80	(4)	(4)	4	6	32.5	56.1	4	6	3.3	5.6
Bay	12,200	12,100	329	259	174	155	27.0	21.4	14.3	12.8	155	104	189	167	35	20	106.4	77.2	16	24	4.9	9.3
Colored	3,200	3,100	70	66	76	43	21.9	21.3	23.8	13.9	−6	23	(4)	(4)	20	9	285.7	136.4	6	7	8.6	10.6
White	9,000	9,000	259	193	98	112	28.8	21.4	10.9	12.4	161	81	(4)	172	15	11	57.9	57.0	10	17	3.9	8.8
Bradford	9,700	9,400	189	193	88	93	19.5	20.5	9.1	9.9	101	100	(4)	(4)	9	6	47.6	31.1	15	7	7.9	3.6
Colored	2,900	2,700	40	48	38	38	13.8	17.8	13.1	14.1	2	10	(4)	(4)	1	4	25.0	83.3	6	2	15.0	4.2
White	6,800	6,700	149	145	50	55	21.9	21.6	7.4	8.2	99	90	(4)	(4)	8	2	53.7	13.8	9	5	6.0	3.4
Brevard	13,900	13,400	193	198	154	145	13.9	14.8	11.1	10.8	39	53	125	137	12	11	62.2	55.6	6	14	3.1	7.1
Colored	4,500	4,300	75	57	67	57	16.7	13.3	14.9	13.3	8	------	(4)	(4)	8	6	106.7	105.3	3	11	4.0	19.3
White	9,400	9,100	118	141	87	88	12.6	15.5	9.3	9.7	31	53	(4)	(4)	4	5	33.9	35.5	3	3	2.5	2.1
Broward	21,900	20,500	381	324	234	195	17.4	15.8	10.7	9.5	147	129	163	166	27	29	70.9	89.5	17	21	4.5	6.5
Colored	7,300	6,900	184	152	105	78	25.2	22.0	14.4	11.3	79	74	175	(4)	20	19	108.7	125.0	11	18	6.0	11.8
White	14,600	13,600	197	172	129	117	13.5	12.6	8.8	8.6	68	55	153	147	7	10	35.5	58.1	6	3	3.0	1.7
Calhoun	7,300	7,400	166	183	70	82	22.7	24.7	9.6	11.1	96	101	(4)	(4)	12	23	72.3	125.7	12	11	7.2	6.0
Colored	1,200	1,400	29	28	26	27	24.2	20.0	21.7	19.3	3	1	(4)	(4)	3	5	103.4	178.6	7	3	24.1	10.7
White	6,100	6,000	137	155	44	55	22.5	25.8	7.2	9.2	93	100	(4)	(4)	9	18	65.7	116.1	5	8	3.6	5.2
Charlotte	4,200	4,000	49	68	27	43	11.7	17.0	6.4	10.8	22	25	(4)	(4)	3	3	61.2	44.1	2	4	4.1	5.9
Colored	900	800	11	11	9	17	12.2	13.8	10.0	21.3	2	−6	(4)	(4)	------	2	------	181.8	------	3	------	27.3
White	3,300	3,200	38	57	18	26	11.5	17.8	5.5	8.1	20	31	(4)	(4)	3	1	78.9	17.5	2	1	5.3	1.8
Citrus	5,600	5,500	96	78	68	68	17.1	14.2	12.1	12.4	28	10	(4)	(4)	9	3	93.8	38.5	2	4	2.1	5.1
Colored	1,800	1,800	42	23	34	27	23.3	12.8	18.9	15.0	8	−4	(4)	(4)	6	1	142.9	43.5	------	4	------	17.4
White	3,800	3,700	54	55	34	41	14.2	14.9	8.9	11.1	20	14	(4)	(4)	3	2	55.6	36.4	2	------	3.7	------
Clay	7,000	6,900	102	116	72	75	14.6	16.8	10.3	10.9	30	41	(4)	(4)	7	2	68.6	17.2	7	5	6.9	4.3
Colored	1,700	1,800	27	26	29	23	15.9	14.4	17.1	12.8	−2	3	(4)	(4)	4	------	148.1	------	4	4	14.8	15.4
White	5,300	5,100	75	90	43	52	14.2	17.6	8.1	10.2	32	38	(4)	(4)	3	2	40.0	22.2	3	1	4.0	1.1
Collier	3,100	2,900	25	33	23	11	8.1	11.4	7.4	3.8	2	22	(4)	(4)	1	2	40.0	60.6	------	1	------	3.0
Colored	1,000	900	3	2	8	4	3.0	2.2	8.0	4.4	−5	−2	(4)	(4)	------	1	------	500.0	------	------	------	------
White	2,100	2,000	22	31	15	7	10.5	15.5	7.1	3.5	7	24	(4)	(4)	1	1	45.5	32.3	------	1	------	3.2
Columbia	14,700	14,600	322	363	292	283	21.9	24.9	19.9	19.4	30	80	110	128	24	27	74.5	74.4	21	32	6.5	8.8
Colored	5,700	5,700	135	130	114	110	23.7	22.8	20.0	19.3	21	20	118	118	10	8	74.1	61.5	11	20	8.1	15.4
White	9,000	8,900	187	233	178	173	20.8	26.2	19.8	19.4	9	60	105	135	14	19	74.9	81.5	10	12	5.3	5.2
Dade	42,700	34,400	378	412	310	299	8.9	12.0	7.3	8.7	68	113	122	138	24	21	63.5	51.0	14	15	3.7	3.6
Colored	6,900	5,300	70	84	60	76	10.1	15.8	8.7	14.3	10	8	(4)	(4)	7	8	100.0	95.2	2	5	2.9	6.0
White	35,800	29,100	308	328	250	223	8.6	11.3	7.0	7.7	58	105	123	147	17	13	55.2	39.6	12	10	3.9	3.0
De Soto	7,800	7,800	207	187	153	122	26.5	24.0	19.6	15.6	54	65	135	153	29	15	140.1	80.2	10	9	4.8	4.8
Colored	1,400	1,500	21	33	41	32	15.0	22.0	29.3	21.3	−20	1	(4)	(4)	5	6	238.1	181.8	5	3	23.8	9.1
White	6,400	6,300	186	154	112	90	29.1	24.4	17.5	14.3	74	64	166	(4)	24	9	129.0	58.4	5	6	2.7	3.9
Dixie	7,000	6,500	133	131	64	78	19.0	20.2	9.1	12.0	69	53	(4)	(4)	17	8	127.8	61.1	11	12	8.3	9.2
Colored	3,500	3,000	33	37	27	29	9.4	12.3	7.7	9.7	6	8	(4)	(4)	8	3	242.4	81.1	6	9	18.2	24.3
White	3,500	3,500	100	94	37	49	28.6	26.9	10.6	14.0	63	45	(4)	(4)	9	5	90.0	53.2	5	3	5.0	3.2
Duval	28,700	26,500	371	345	219	248	12.9	13.0	7.6	9.4	152	97	169	139	20	24	53.9	69.6	13	18	3.5	5.2
Colored	6,000	5,400	122	112	84	90	20.3	20.7	14.0	16.7	38	22	(4)	(4)	9	9	73.8	80.4	8	9	6.6	8.0
White	22,700	21,100	249	233	135	158	11.0	11.0	5.9	7.5	114	75	184	147	11	15	44.2	64.4	5	9	2.0	3.9
Escambia	22,500	22,100	422	379	237	239	18.8	17.1	10.5	10.8	185	140	178	159	23	28	54.5	73.9	15	23	3.6	6.1
Colored	4,300	4,300	64	59	73	75	14.9	13.7	17.0	17.4	−9	−16	(4)	(4)	5	8	78.1	135.6	5	10	7.8	16.9
White	18,200	17,800	358	320	164	164	19.7	18.0	9.0	9.2	194	156	218	195	18	20	50.3	62.5	10	13	2.8	4.1
Flagler	2,500	2,500	31	42	27	37	12.4	16.8	10.8	14.8	4	5	(4)	(4)	1	3	32.3	71.4	2	5	6.5	11.9
Colored	900	900	14	27	17	22	15.6	30.0	18.9	24.4	−3	5	(4)	(4)	------	2	------	74.1	1	5	7.1	18.5
White	1,600	1,600	17	15	10	15	10.6	9.4	6.3	9.4	7	------	(4)	(4)	1	1	58.8	66.7	1	------	5.9	------

See footnotes at end of table

TABLE 18.—COLORED [1] AND WHITE POPULATION, BIRTHS AND DEATHS, INFANT MORTALITY, AND STILLBIRTHS, IN SELECTED REGISTRATION STATES, CITIES, AND COUNTIES: 1931 AND 1930—Continued

[See note at head of this table]

AREA AND COLOR	POPULATION ESTIMATED AS OF JULY 1		BIRTHS AND DEATHS (Exclusive of stillbirths)												INFANT MORTALITY (Exclusive of stillbirths)				STILLBIRTHS			
			Number				Rate per 1,000 population				Excess of births over deaths [2]		Births per 100 deaths		Deaths of infants under 1 year of age				Number		Rate per 100 live births	
			Births		Deaths		Births		Deaths						Number		Per 1,000 births					
	1931	1930	1931	1930	1931	1930	1931	1930	1931	1930	1931	1930	1931	1930	1931	1930	1931	1930	1931	1930	1931	1930
FLORIDA COUNTIES—continued																						
Franklin	6,400	6,300	111	117	52	72	17.3	18.6	8.1	11.4	59	45	(4)	(4)	5	6	45.0	51.3	10	7	9.0	6.0
Colored	2,500	2,500	44	53	36	47	17.6	21.2	14.4	18.8	8	6	(4)	(4)	3	6	68.2	113.2	5	6	11.4	11.3
White	3,900	3,800	67	64	16	25	17.2	16.8	4.1	6.6	51	39	(4)	(4)	2	-	29.9	-	5	1	7.5	1.6
Gadsden	30,700	30,000	616	666	771	811	20.1	22.2	25.1	27.0	−155	−145	80	82	61	57	99.0	85.6	47	56	7.6	8.4
Colored	17,300	17,000	390	401	397	470	22.5	23.6	22.9	27.6	−7	−69	98	85	36	47	92.3	117.2	39	38	10.0	9.5
White	13,400	13,000	226	265	374	341	16.9	20.4	27.9	26.2	−148	−76	60	78	25	10	110.6	37.7	8	18	3.5	6.8
Gilchrist	4,200	4,100	103	126	40	34	24.5	30.7	9.5	8.3	63	92	(4)	(4)	8	4	77.7	31.7	7	4	6.8	3.2
Colored	800	700	12	12	8	7	15.0	17.1	10.0	10.0	4	5	(4)	(4)	2	-	166.7	-	1	1	8.3	8.3
White	3,400	3,400	91	114	32	27	26.8	33.5	9.4	7.9	59	87	(4)	(4)	6	4	65.9	35.1	6	3	6.6	2.6
Glades	2,800	2,800	29	38	28	16	10.4	13.6	10.0	5.7	1	22	(4)	(4)	3	3	103.4	78.9	5	7	17.2	18.4
Colored	900	900	13	9	13	8	14.4	10.0	14.4	8.9	-	1	(4)	(4)	1	1	76.9	111.1	3	4	23.1	44.4
White	1,900	1,900	16	29	15	8	8.4	15.3	7.9	4.2	1	21	(4)	(4)	2	2	125.0	69.0	2	3	12.5	10.3
Gulf	3,300	3,200	53	51	16	18	16.1	15.9	4.8	5.6	37	33	(4)	(4)	1	2	18.9	39.2	1	3	1.9	5.9
Colored	1,200	1,100	23	16	11	9	19.2	14.5	9.2	8.2	12	7	(4)	(4)	1	1	43.5	62.5	-	-	-	-
White	2,100	2,100	30	35	5	9	14.3	16.7	2.4	4.3	25	26	(4)	(4)	-	1	-	28.6	1	3	3.3	8.6
Hamilton	[5] 9,454	[5] 9,454	217	212	110	110	23.0	22.4	11.6	11.6	107	102	197	193	12	11	55.3	51.9	6	9	2.8	4.2
Colored	3,779	3,779	86	87	57	39	22.8	23.0	15.1	10.3	29	48	(4)	(4)	8	5	93.0	57.5	4	8	4.7	9.2
White	5,675	5,675	131	125	53	71	23.1	22.0	9.3	12.5	78	54	(4)	(4)	4	6	30.5	48.0	2	1	1.5	.8
Hendry	3,800	3,600	58	54	25	27	15.3	15.0	6.6	7.5	33	27	(4)	(4)	-	6	-	111.1	4	3	6.9	5.6
Colored	1,600	1,400	7	6	14	8	4.4	4.3	8.8	5.7	−7	−2	(4)	(4)	-	2	-	333.3	3	-	42.9	-
White	2,200	2,200	51	48	11	19	23.2	21.8	5.0	8.6	40	29	(4)	(4)	-	4	-	83.3	1	3	2.0	6.3
Hernando	5,000	5,000	82	93	68	75	16.4	18.6	13.6	15.0	14	18	(4)	(4)	5	4	61.0	43.0	5	5	6.1	5.4
Colored	1,500	1,600	33	40	26	31	22.0	25.0	17.3	19.4	7	9	(4)	(4)	4	3	121.2	75.0	2	3	6.1	7.5
White	3,500	3,400	49	53	42	44	14.0	15.6	12.0	12.9	7	9	(4)	(4)	1	1	20.4	18.9	3	2	6.1	3.8
Highlands	9,900	9,300	218	184	127	135	22.0	19.8	12.8	14.5	91	49	172	136	7	13	32.1	70.7	5	8	2.3	4.3
Colored	3,200	2,700	43	46	53	41	13.4	17.0	16.6	15.2	−10	5	(4)	(4)	1	4	23.3	87.0	3	7	7.0	15.2
White	6,700	6,600	175	138	74	94	26.1	20.9	11.0	14.2	101	44	(4)	(4)	6	9	34.3	65.2	2	1	1.1	.7
Hillsborough	56,500	53,200	856	769	497	485	15.2	14.5	8.8	9.1	359	284	172	159	39	39	45.6	50.7	37	37	4.3	4.8
Colored	8,500	7,800	114	125	169	154	13.4	16.0	19.9	19.7	−55	−29	67	81	13	10	114.0	80.0	9	15	7.9	12.0
White	48,000	45,400	742	644	328	331	15.5	14.2	6.8	7.3	414	313	226	195	26	29	35.0	45.0	28	22	3.8	3.4
Indian River	7,100	6,800	170	158	69	41	23.9	23.2	9.7	6.0	101	117	(4)	(4)	5	7	29.4	44.3	6	6	3.5	3.8
Colored	2,000	2,000	59	46	25	15	29.5	23.0	12.5	7.5	34	31	(4)	(4)	3	4	50.8	87.0	4	4	6.8	8.7
White	5,100	4,800	111	112	44	26	21.8	23.3	8.6	5.4	67	86	(4)	(4)	2	3	18.0	26.8	2	2	1.8	1.8
Jackson	32,100	32,000	835	798	303	345	26.0	24.9	9.4	10.8	532	453	276	231	51	53	61.1	66.4	40	56	4.8	7.0
Colored	12,500	12,500	361	311	130	178	28.9	24.9	10.4	14.2	231	133	278	175	16	23	44.3	74.0	22	43	6.1	13.8
White	19,600	19,500	474	487	173	167	24.2	25.0	8.8	8.6	301	320	274	292	35	30	73.8	61.6	18	13	3.8	2.7
Jefferson	[5] 13,408	[5] 13,408	312	355	205	228	23.3	26.5	15.3	17.0	107	127	152	156	28	30	89.7	84.5	30	30	9.6	8.5
Colored	9,120	9,120	256	266	154	169	28.1	29.2	16.9	18.5	102	97	166	157	21	27	82.0	101.5	27	25	10.5	9.4
White	4,288	4,288	56	89	51	59	13.1	20.8	11.9	13.8	5	30	(4)	(4)	7	3	125.0	33.7	3	5	5.4	5.6
Lafayette	4,400	4,400	107	90	27	27	24.3	20.5	6.1	6.1	80	63	(4)	(4)	5	6	46.7	66.7	4	5	3.7	5.6
Colored	600	700	4	4	5	4	6.7	5.7	8.3	5.7	−1	-	(4)	(4)	1	1	250.0	250.0	1	1	25.0	25.0
White	3,800	3,700	103	86	22	23	27.1	23.2	5.8	6.2	81	63	(4)	(4)	4	5	38.8	58.1	3	4	2.9	4.7
Lake	24,400	23,400	456	369	289	237	18.7	15.8	11.8	10.1	167	132	158	156	31	19	68.0	51.5	20	21	4.4	5.7
Colored	6,700	6,500	141	106	111	75	21.0	16.3	16.6	11.5	30	31	127	(4)	18	9	127.7	84.9	12	11	8.5	10.4
White	17,700	16,900	315	263	178	162	17.8	15.6	10.1	9.6	137	101	177	162	13	10	41.3	38.0	8	10	2.5	3.8
Lee	15,900	15,200	246	261	169	192	15.5	17.2	10.6	12.6	77	69	146	136	10	17	40.7	65.1	14	15	5.7	5.7
Colored	3,800	3,600	55	50	61	59	14.5	13.9	16.1	16.4	−6	−9	(4)	(4)	6	3	109.1	60.0	7	8	12.7	16.0
White	12,100	11,600	191	211	108	133	15.8	18.2	8.9	11.5	83	78	177	159	4	14	20.9	66.4	7	7	3.7	3.3
Leon	12,900	12,800	247	214	125	118	19.1	16.7	9.7	9.2	122	96	198	181	18	13	72.9	60.7	20	22	8.1	10.3
Colored	9,400	9,400	209	207	105	96	22.2	22.0	11.2	10.2	104	111	199	(4)	15	12	71.8	58.0	20	18	9.6	8.7
White	3,500	3,400	38	7	20	22	10.9	2.1	5.7	6.5	18	−15	(4)	(4)	3	1	78.9	142.9	-	4	-	57.1
Levy	12,800	12,500	222	222	123	153	17.3	17.8	9.6	12.2	99	69	180	145	16	17	72.1	76.6	22	14	9.9	6.3
Colored	4,900	4,800	94	89	59	75	19.2	18.5	12.0	15.6	35	14	(4)	(4)	10	10	106.4	112.4	20	9	21.3	10.1
White	7,900	7,700	128	133	64	78	16.2	17.3	8.1	10.1	64	55	(4)	(4)	6	7	46.9	52.6	2	5	1.6	3.8
Liberty	[5] 4,067	[5] 4,067	98	102	44	42	24.1	25.1	10.8	10.3	54	60	(4)	(4)	9	7	91.8	68.6	6	8	6.1	7.8
Colored	1,421	1,421	39	34	20	12	27.4	23.9	14.1	8.4	19	22	(4)	(4)	3	4	76.9	117.6	4	4	10.3	11.8
White	2,646	2,646	59	68	24	30	22.3	25.7	9.1	11.3	35	38	(4)	(4)	6	3	101.7	44.1	2	4	3.4	5.9
Madison	[5] 15,614	[5] 15,614	427	366	180	184	27.3	23.4	11.5	11.8	247	182	237	199	29	27	67.9	73.8	27	41	6.3	11.2
Colored	8,203	8,203	257	218	93	100	31.3	26.6	11.3	12.2	164	118	(4)	218	16	14	62.3	64.2	22	25	8.6	11.5
White	7,411	7,411	170	148	87	84	22.9	20.0	11.7	11.3	83	64	(4)	(4)	13	13	76.5	87.8	5	16	2.9	10.8

Manatee	23,500	22,700	349	374	210	230	14.9	16.5	8.9	10.1	139	144	166	163	14	24	40.1	64.2	19	30	5.4	8.0
Colored	6,900	6,900	117	131	68	91	17.0	19.0	9.9	13.2	49	40	(4)	(4)	7	13	59.8	99.2	14	18	12.0	13.7
White	16,600	15,800	232	243	142	139	14.0	15.4	8.6	8.8	90	104	163	175	7	11	30.2	45.3	5	12	2.2	4.9
Marion	30,300	29,700	491	488	420	439	16.2	16.4	13.9	14.8	71	49	117	111	35	36	71.3	73.8	38	48	7.7	9.8
Colored	14,700	14,500	265	241	222	231	18.0	16.6	15.1	15.9	43	10	119	104	22	21	83.0	87.1	27	38	10.2	15.8
White	15,600	15,200	226	247	198	208	14.5	16.3	12.7	13.7	28	39	114	119	13	15	57.5	60.7	11	10	4.9	4.0
Martin	5,500	5,200	81	71	57	48	14.7	13.7	10.4	9.2	24	23	(4)	(4)	7	7	86.4	98.6	3	3	3.7	4.2
Colored	2,100	2,000	31	28	32	23	14.8	14.0	15.2	11.5	−1	8	(4)	(4)	7	3	225.8	107.1	2	2	6.5	7.1
White	3,400	3,200	50	43	25	25	14.7	13.4	7.4	7.8	25	15	(4)	(4)	-----	4	-----	93.0	1	1	2.0	2.3
Monroe	[5] 793	[5] 793	-----	-----	2	6	-----	-----	2.5	7.6	−2	−6	-----	(4)	-----	-----	-----	-----	-----	-----	-----	-----
Colored	214	214	-----	-----	-----	2	-----	-----	-----	9.4	-----	−2	-----	(4)	-----	-----	-----	-----	-----	-----	-----	-----
White	579	579	-----	-----	2	4	-----	-----	3.5	6.9	−2	−4	-----	(4)	-----	-----	-----	-----	-----	-----	-----	-----
Nassau	[5] 9,375	[5] 9,375	202	194	122	108	21.5	20.7	13.0	11.5	80	86	166	180	19	16	94.1	82.5	14	6	6.9	3.1
Colored	3,889	3,889	96	74	79	69	24.7	19.0	20.3	17.7	17	5	(4)	(4)	14	10	145.8	135.1	9	4	9.4	5.4
White	5,486	5,486	106	120	43	39	19.3	21.9	7.8	7.1	63	81	(4)	(4)	5	6	47.2	50.0	5	2	4.7	1.7
Okaloosa	10,000	9,900	240	192	87	84	24.0	19.4	8.7	8.5	153	108	(4)	(4)	9	6	37.5	31.3	9	8	3.8	4.2
Colored	1,000	1,000	21	16	13	11	21.0	16.0	13.0	11.0	8	5	(4)	(4)	2	-----	95.2	-----	-----	-----	-----	-----
White	9,000	8,900	219	176	74	73	24.3	19.8	8.2	8.2	145	103	(4)	(4)	7	6	32.0	34.1	9	8	4.1	4.5
Okeechobee	4,400	4,200	60	47	22	21	13.6	11.2	5.0	5.0	38	26	(4)	(4)	3	4	50.0	85.1	1	1	1.7	2.1
Colored	1,400	1,300	2	13	7	7	1.4	10.0	5.0	5.4	−5	6	(4)	(4)	-----	1	-----	76.9	-----	-----	-----	-----
White	3,000	2,900	58	34	15	14	19.3	11.7	5.0	4.8	43	20	(4)	(4)	3	3	51.7	88.2	1	1	1.7	2.9
Orange	24,200	22,800	297	309	181	207	12.3	13.6	7.5	9.1	116	102	164	149	20	14	67.3	45.3	17	22	5.7	7.1
Colored	5,000	4,700	94	127	63	56	18.8	27.0	12.6	11.9	31	71	(4)	(4)	10	4	106.4	31.5	8	13	8.5	10.2
White	19,200	18,100	203	182	118	151	10.6	10.1	6.1	8.3	85	31	172	121	10	10	49.3	54.9	9	9	4.4	4.9
Osceola	11,100	10,800	137	150	151	161	12.3	13.9	13.6	14.9	−14	−11	91	93	10	11	73.0	73.3	8	9	5.8	6.0
Colored	3,300	3,200	41	34	41	49	12.4	10.6	12.4	15.3	-----	−15	(4)	(4)	4	5	97.6	147.1	6	5	14.6	14.7
White	7,800	7,600	96	116	110	112	12.3	15.3	14.1	14.7	−14	4	87	104	6	6	62.5	51.7	2	4	2.1	3.4
Palm Beach	27,300	25,600	294	290	180	175	10.8	11.3	6.6	6.8	114	115	163	166	23	13	78.2	44.8	12	9	4.1	3.1
Colored	8,700	8,000	117	171	64	63	13.4	21.4	7.4	7.9	53	108	(4)	(4)	10	6	85.5	35.1	4	9	3.4	5.3
White	18,600	17,600	177	119	116	112	9.5	6.8	6.2	6.4	61	7	153	106	13	7	73.4	58.8	8	-----	4.5	-----
Pasco	10,800	10,600	191	178	145	134	17.7	16.8	13.4	12.6	46	44	132	133	12	10	62.8	56.2	9	8	4.7	4.5
Colored	1,700	1,800	42	32	35	27	24.7	17.8	20.6	15.0	7	5	(4)	(4)	2	2	47.6	62.5	5	2	11.9	6.3
White	9,100	8,800	149	146	110	107	16.4	16.6	12.1	12.2	39	39	135	136	10	8	67.1	54.8	4	6	2.7	4.1
Pinellas	24,400	22,300	344	301	261	230	14.1	13.5	10.7	10.3	83	71	132	131	17	16	49.4	53.2	15	24	4.4	8.0
Colored	4,100	3,700	57	49	45	47	13.9	13.2	11.0	12.7	12	2	(4)	(4)	2	6	35.1	122.4	5	17	8.8	34.7
White	20,300	18,600	287	252	216	183	14.1	13.5	10.6	9.8	71	69	133	138	15	10	52.3	39.7	10	7	3.5	2.8
Polk	56,600	54,400	1,110	1,100	549	514	19.6	20.2	9.7	9.4	561	586	202	214	59	57	53.2	51.8	60	62	5.4	5.6
Colored	12,600	12,200	251	287	175	180	19.9	23.5	13.9	14.8	76	107	143	159	16	123	63.7	80.1	29	27	11.6	9.4
White	44,000	42,200	859	813	374	334	19.5	19.3	8.5	7.9	485	479	230	243	43	34	50.1	41.8	31	35	3.6	4.3
Putnam	18,500	18,200	325	334	229	293	17.6	18.4	12.4	16.1	96	41	142	114	23	31	70.8	92.8	22	32	6.8	9.6
Colored	7,900	7,900	152	152	123	173	19.2	19.2	15.6	21.9	29	−21	124	88	15	24	98.7	157.9	15	23	9.9	15.1
White	10,600	10,300	173	182	106	120	16.3	17.7	10.0	11.7	67	62	163	152	8	7	46.2	38.5	7	9	4.0	4.9
St. Johns	6,600	6,500	104	105	47	63	15.8	16.2	7.1	9.7	57	42	(4)	(4)	4	10	38.5	95.2	8	6	7.7	5.7
Colored	3,500	3,300	72	83	37	47	20.6	25.2	10.6	14.2	35	36	(4)	(4)	4	6	55.6	72.3	7	5	9.7	6.0
White	3,100	3,200	32	22	10	16	10.3	6.9	3.2	5.0	22	6	(4)	(4)	-----	4	-----	181.8	1	1	3.1	4.5
St. Lucie	7,400	7,100	142	166	86	72	19.2	23.4	11.6	10.1	56	94	(4)	(4)	11	8	77.5	48.2	8	6	5.6	3.6
Colored	1,800	1,900	39	44	23	22	21.7	23.2	12.8	11.6	16	22	(4)	(4)	6	3	153.8	68.2	3	3	7.7	6.8
White	5,600	5,200	103	122	63	50	18.4	23.5	11.3	9.6	40	72	(4)	(4)	5	5	48.5	41.0	5	3	4.9	2.5
Santa Rosa	14,100	14,100	313	273	128	131	22.2	19.4	9.1	9.3	185	142	245	208	21	20	67.1	73.3	9	13	2.9	4.8
Colored	2,100	2,200	44	36	35	45	21.0	16.4	16.7	20.5	9	−9	(4)	(4)	4	5	90.9	138.9	2	7	4.5	19.4
White	12,000	11,900	269	237	93	86	22.4	19.9	7.8	7.2	176	151	(4)	(4)	17	15	63.2	63.3	7	6	2.6	2.5
Sarasota	13,500	12,600	189	192	126	131	14.0	15.2	9.3	10.4	63	61	150	147	8	8	42.3	41.7	6	6	3.2	3.1
Colored	3,300	2,800	47	39	36	32	14.2	13.9	10.9	11.4	11	7	(4)	(4)	4	2	85.1	51.3	4	5	8.5	12.8
White	10,200	9,800	142	153	90	99	13.9	15.6	8.8	10.1	52	54	(4)	(4)	4	6	28.2	39.2	2	1	1.4	.7
Seminole	9,000	8,700	152	141	77	84	16.9	16.2	8.6	9.7	75	57	(4)	(4)	9	6	59.2	42.6	6	9	3.9	6.4
Colored	3,700	3,600	99	119	43	43	26.8	33.1	11.6	11.9	56	76	(4)	(4)	7	4	70.7	33.6	6	8	6.1	6.7
White	5,300	5,100	53	22	34	41	10.0	4.3	6.4	8.0	19	−19	(4)	(4)	2	2	37.7	90.9	-----	1	-----	4.5
Sumter	11,000	10,700	188	223	117	105	17.1	20.8	10.6	9.8	71	118	161	212	10	12	53.2	53.8	7	14	3.7	6.3
Colored	3,400	3,200	73	78	45	37	21.5	24.4	13.2	11.6	28	41	(4)	(4)	5	7	68.5	89.7	7	9	9.6	11.5
White	7,600	7,500	115	145	72	68	15.1	19.3	9.5	9.1	43	77	(4)	(4)	5	5	43.5	34.5	-----	5	-----	3.4
Suwannee	[5] 15,731	[5] 15,731	407	345	207	194	25.9	21.9	13.2	12.3	200	151	197	178	35	24	86.0	69.6	21	32	5.2	9.3
Colored	5,336	5,336	165	126	102	83	30.9	23.6	19.1	15.6	63	43	162	(4)	22	10	133.3	79.4	7	18	4.2	14.3
White	10,395	10,395	242	219	105	111	23.3	21.1	10.1	10.7	137	108	230	197	13	14	53.7	63.9	14	14	5.8	6.4
Taylor	13,400	13,200	181	205	134	136	13.5	15.5	10.0	10.3	47	69	135	151	16	24	88.4	117.1	2	13	1.1	6.3
Colored	5,100	5,000	52	52	71	65	10.2	10.4	13.9	13.0	−19	−13	(4)	(4)	6	14	115.4	269.2	2	11	3.8	21.2
White	8,300	8,200	129	153	63	71	15.5	18.7	7.6	8.7	66	82	(4)	(4)	10	10	77.5	65.4	-----	2	-----	1.3
Union	7,700	7,500	171	134	72	85	22.2	17.9	9.4	11.3	99	49	(4)	(4)	4	8	23.4	59.7	8	5	4.7	3.7
Colored	3,000	2,900	31	30	41	44	10.3	10.3	13.7	15.2	−10	−14	(4)	(4)	-----	2	-----	66.7	2	2	6.5	6.7
White	4,700	4,600	140	104	31	41	29.8	22.6	6.6	8.9	109	63	(4)	(4)	4	6	28.6	57.7	6	3	4.3	2.9
Volusia	27,300	26,400	365	442	334	311	13.4	16.7	12.2	11.8	31	131	109	142	26	22	71.2	49.8	19	17	5.2	3.8
Colored	7,300	7,100	99	145	115	121	13.6	20.4	15.8	17.0	−16	24	86	120	10	10	101.0	69.0	10	6	10.1	4.1
White	20,000	19,300	266	297	219	190	13.3	15.4	11.0	9.8	47	107	121	156	16	12	60.2	40.4	9	11	3.4	3.7
Wakulla	5,500	5,500	107	146	53	64	19.5	26.5	9.6	11.6	54	82	(4)	(4)	8	12	74.8	82.2	4	15	3.7	10.3
Colored	2,200	2,300	49	43	26	24	22.3	18.7	11.8	10.4	23	19	(4)	(4)	2	6	40.8	139.5	2	9	4.1	20.9
White	3,300	3,200	58	103	27	40	17.6	32.2	8.2	12.5	31	63	(4)	(4)	6	6	103.4	58.3	2	6	3.4	5.8
Walton	14,900	14,600	271	303	109	146	18.2	20.8	7.3	10.0	162	157	249	208	12	19	44.3	62.7	11	20	4.1	6.6
Colored	2,800	2,700	46	58	25	38	16.4	21.5	8.9	14.1	21	20	(4)	(4)	1	5	21.7	86.2	3	9	6.5	15.5
White	12,100	11,900	225	245	84	108	18.6	20.6	6.9	9.1	141	137	(4)	227	11	14	48.9	57.1	8	11	3.6	4.5
Washington	12,200	12,200	309	276	106	106	25.3	22.6	8.7	8.7	203	170	292	260	18	11	58.3	39.9	14	13	4.5	4.7
Colored	2,500	2,600	84	79	35	30	33.6	30.4	14.0	11.5	49	49	(4)	(4)	8	3	95.2	38.0	5	5	6.0	6.3
White	9,700	9,600	225	197	71	76	23.2	20.5	7.3	7.9	154	121	(4)	(4)	10	8	44.4	40.6	9	8	4.0	4.1

See footnotes at end of table.

TABLE 18.—COLORED [1] AND WHITE POPULATION, BIRTHS AND DEATHS, INFANT MORTALITY, AND STILLBIRTHS, IN SELECTED REGISTRATION STATES, CITIES, AND COUNTIES: 1931 AND 1930—Continued

[See note at head of this table]

AREA AND COLOR	POPULATION ESTIMATED AS OF JULY 1		BIRTHS AND DEATHS (Exclusive of stillbirths): Number: Births		Number: Deaths		Rate per 1,000 population: Births		Rate per 1,000 population: Deaths		Excess of births over deaths [2]		Births per 100 deaths		INFANT MORTALITY (Exclusive of stillbirths): Deaths of infants under 1 year of age: Number		Per 1,000 births		STILLBIRTHS: Number		Rate per 100 live births	
	1931	1930	1931	1930	1931	1930	1931	1930	1931	1930	1931	1930	1931	1930	1931	1930	1931	1930	1931	1930	1931	1930
GEORGIA COUNTIES [8]																						
Appling	13,600	13,400	312	281	85	77	22.9	21.0	6.3	5.7	227	204	(4)	(4)	12	15	38.5	53.4	11	16	3.5	5.7
Colored	2,800	2,800	77	76	20	28	27.5	27.1	7.1	10.0	57	48	(4)	(4)	2	4	26.0	52.6	4	9	5.2	11.8
White	10,800	10,600	235	205	65	49	21.8	19.3	6.0	4.6	170	156	(4)	(4)	10	11	42.6	53.7	7	7	3.0	3.4
Atkinson	[5] 6,894	[5] 6,894	146	168	37	29	21.2	24.4	5.4	4.2	109	139	(4)	(4)	7	4	47.9	23.8	12	13	8.2	7.7
Colored	1,962	1,962	36	47	11	12	18.3	24.0	5.6	6.1	25	35	(4)	(4)	2	3	55.6	63.8	6	7	16.7	14.9
White	4,932	4,932	110	121	26	17	22.3	24.5	5.3	3.4	84	104	(4)	(4)	5	1	45.5	8.3	6	6	5.5	5.0
Bacon	7,100	7,100	205	212	60	82	28.9	29.9	8.5	11.5	145	130	(4)	(4)	8	16	39.0	75.5	21	13	10.2	6.1
Colored	1,100	1,100	27	28	11	23	24.5	25.5	10.0	20.9	16	5	(4)	(4)	------	5	------	178.6	10	4	37.0	14.3
White	6,000	6,000	178	184	49	59	29.7	30.7	8.2	9.8	129	125	(4)	(4)	8	11	44.9	59.8	11	9	6.2	4.9
Baker	[5] 7,818	[5] 7,818	230	181	65	64	29.4	23.2	8.3	8.2	165	117	(4)	(4)	10	12	43.5	66.3	23	9	10.0	5.0
Colored	4,794	4,794	151	116	35	34	31.5	24.2	7.3	7.1	116	82	(4)	(4)	5	5	33.1	43.1	15	5	9.9	4.3
White	3,024	3,024	79	65	30	30	26.1	21.5	9.9	9.9	49	35	(4)	(4)	5	7	63.3	107.7	8	4	10.1	6.2
Baldwin	23,300	23,000	288	264	519	592	12.4	11.5	22.3	25.7	−231	−328	55	45	10	24	34.7	90.9	13	14	4.5	5.3
Colored	10,700	10,800	199	183	259	280	18.6	16.9	24.2	25.9	−60	−97	77	65	9	14	45.2	76.5	13	12	6.5	6.6
White	12,600	12,200	89	81	260	312	7.1	6.6	20.6	25.6	−171	−231	34	26	1	10	11.2	123.5	------	2	------	2.5
Barrow	[5] 12,401	[5] 12,401	265	241	122	143	21.4	19.4	9.8	11.5	143	98	217	169	30	16	113.2	66.4	9	13	3.4	5.4
Colored	2,068	2,068	56	52	31	36	27.1	25.1	15.0	17.4	25	16	(4)	(4)	7	5	125.0	96.2	4	4	7.1	7.7
White	10,333	10,333	209	189	91	107	20.2	18.3	8.8	10.4	118	82	(4)	177	23	11	110.0	58.2	5	9	2.4	4.8
Bartow	25,500	25,400	609	557	228	287	23.9	21.9	8.9	11.3	381	270	267	194	49	52	80.5	93.4	34	23	5.6	4.1
Colored	4,600	4,600	91	74	68	82	19.8	16.1	14.8	17.8	23	−8	(4)	(4)	12	17	131.9	229.7	8	10	8.8	13.5
White	20,900	20,800	518	483	160	205	24.8	23.2	7.7	9.9	358	278	324	236	37	35	71.4	72.5	26	13	5.0	2.7
Ben Hill	[5] 13,047	[5] 13,047	319	282	190	165	24.5	21.6	14.6	12.6	129	117	168	171	22	10	69.0	35.5	28	18	8.8	6.4
Colored	4,450	4,450	131	126	90	71	29.4	28.3	20.2	16.0	41	55	(4)	(4)	12	4	91.6	31.7	18	14	13.7	11.1
White	8,597	8,597	188	156	100	94	21.9	18.1	11.6	10.9	88	62	188	(4)	10	6	53.2	38.5	10	4	5.3	2.6
Berrien	15,000	14,700	487	462	127	137	32.5	31.4	8.5	9.3	360	325	383	337	25	24	51.3	51.9	22	27	4.5	5.8
Colored	2,400	2,400	57	55	40	29	23.8	22.9	16.7	12.1	17	26	(4)	(4)	6	4	105.3	72.7	7	5	12.3	9.1
White	12,600	12,300	430	407	87	108	34.1	33.1	6.9	8.8	343	299	(4)	377	19	20	44.2	49.1	15	22	3.5	5.4
Bibb	23,800	23,400	253	260	173	185	10.6	11.1	7.3	7.9	80	75	146	141	21	19	83.0	73.1	16	8	6.3	3.1
Colored	9,800	9,800	149	161	101	110	15.2	16.4	10.3	11.2	48	51	148	146	17	15	114.1	93.2	15	6	10.1	3.7
White	14,000	13,600	104	99	72	75	7.4	7.3	5.1	5.5	32	24	(4)	(4)	4	4	38.5	40.4	1	2	1.0	2.0
Bleckley	[5] 9,133	[5] 9,133	236	235	108	125	25.8	25.7	11.8	13.7	128	110	219	188	13	31	55.1	131.9	11	19	4.7	8.1
Colored	3,261	3,261	92	91	50	58	28.2	27.9	15.3	17.8	42	33	(4)	(4)	6	17	65.2	186.8	7	4	7.6	4.4
White	5,872	5,872	144	144	58	67	24.5	24.5	9.9	11.4	86	77	(4)	(4)	7	14	48.6	97.2	4	15	2.8	10.4
Brantley	7,000	6,900	201	198	80	69	28.7	28.7	11.4	10.0	121	129	(4)	(4)	8	16	39.8	80.8	12	21	6.0	10.6
Colored	1,300	1,300	27	34	20	17	20.8	26.2	15.4	13.1	7	17	(4)	(4)	1	1	37.0	29.4	4	6	14.8	17.6
White	5,700	5,600	174	164	60	52	30.5	29.3	10.5	9.3	114	112	(4)	(4)	7	15	40.2	91.5	8	15	4.6	9.1
Brooks	[5] 21,330	[5] 21,330	494	501	174	243	23.2	23.5	8.2	11.4	320	258	284	206	20	46	40.5	91.8	36	46	7.3	9.2
Colored	11,260	11,260	298	298	94	148	26.5	26.5	8.3	13.1	204	150	(4)	201	15	31	50.3	104.0	31	40	10.4	13.4
White	10,070	10,070	196	203	80	95	19.5	20.2	7.9	9.4	116	108	(4)	(4)	5	15	25.5	73.9	5	6	2.6	3.0
Bryan	[5] 5,952	[5] 5,952	136	117	52	81	22.8	19.7	8.7	13.6	84	36	(4)	(4)	6	14	44.1	119.7	15	7	11.0	6.0
Colored	2,666	2,666	61	52	32	51	22.9	19.5	12.0	19.1	29	1	(4)	(4)	5	7	82.0	134.6	11	3	18.0	5.8
White	3,286	3,286	75	65	20	30	22.8	19.8	6.1	9.1	55	35	(4)	(4)	1	7	13.3	107.7	4	4	5.3	6.2
Bulloch	26,600	26,500	680	674	218	218	25.6	25.4	8.2	8.2	462	456	312	309	36	32	52.9	47.5	43	45	6.3	6.7
Colored	10,100	10,100	260	226	99	86	25.7	22.4	9.8	8.5	161	140	(3)	(3)	19	12	73.1	53.1	28	23	10.8	10.2
White	16,500	16,400	420	448	119	132	25.5	27.3	7.2	8.0	301	316	353	339	17	20	40.5	44.6	15	22	3.6	4.9
Burke	[5] 29,224	[5] 29,224	540	554	271	390	18.5	19.0	9.3	13.3	269	164	199	142	21	40	38.9	72.2	44	43	8.1	7.8
Colored	22,700	22,700	428	465	229	322	18.9	20.5	10.1	14.2	199	143	187	144	19	33	44.4	71.0	40	40	9.3	8.6
White	6,524	6,524	112	89	42	68	17.2	13.6	6.4	10.4	70	21	(4)	(4)	2	7	17.9	78.7	4	3	3.6	3.4
Butts	[5] 9,345	[5] 9,345	162	122	98	132	17.3	13.1	10.5	14.1	64	−10	(4)	92	7	13	43.2	106.6	4	10	2.5	8.2
Colored	4,488	4,488	105	70	56	81	23.4	15.6	12.5	18.0	49	−11	(4)	(4)	6	11	57.1	157.1	3	7	2.9	10.0
White	4,857	4,857	57	52	42	51	11.7	10.7	8.6	10.5	15	1	(4)	(4)	1	2	17.5	38.5	1	3	1.8	5.8
Calhoun	10,600	10,600	266	225	130	127	25.1	21.2	12.3	12.0	136	98	205	177	19	26	71.4	115.6	11	18	4.1	8.0
Colored	7,500	7,500	207	180	104	94	27.6	24.0	13.9	12.5	103	86	199	(4)	14	21	67.6	116.7	11	16	5.3	8.9
White	3,100	3,100	59	45	26	33	19.0	14.5	8.4	10.6	33	12	(4)	(4)	5	5	84.7	111.1	------	2	------	4.4
Camden	[5] 6,338	[5] 6,338	163	151	110	121	25.7	23.8	17.4	19.1	53	30	148	125	14	11	85.9	72.8	23	11	14.1	7.3
Colored	3,745	3,745	100	91	82	89	26.7	24.3	21.9	23.8	18	2	(4)	(4)	11	7	110.0	76.9	18	10	18.0	11.0
White	2,593	2,593	63	60	28	32	24.3	23.1	10.8	12.3	35	28	(4)	(4)	3	4	47.6	66.7	5	1	7.9	1.7
Campbell	[5] 9,903	[5] 9,903	120	126	75	81	12.1	12.7	7.6	8.2	45	45	(4)	(4)	5	10	41.7	79.4	5	1	4.2	.8
Colored	2,959	2,959	56	57	28	32	18.9	19.3	9.5	10.8	28	25	(4)	(4)	------	2	------	35.1	4	------	7.1	------
White	6,944	6,944	64	69	47	49	9.2	9.9	6.8	7.1	17	20	(4)	(4)	5	8	78.1	115.9	1	1	1.6	1.4

Candler	[5] 8,991	[5] 8,991	212	207	83	88	23.6	23.0	9.2	9.8	129	119	(4)	(4)	13	13	61.3	62.8	10	12	4.7	5.8
Colored	3,141	3,141	100	93	47	40	31.8	29.6	15.0	12.7	53	53	(4)	(4)	9	8	90.0	86.0	5	8	5.0	8.6
White	5,850	5,850	112	114	36	48	19.1	19.5	6.2	8.2	76	66	(4)	(4)	4	5	35.7	43.9	5	4	4.5	3.5
Carroll	[5] 34,272	[5] 34,272	677	740	266	338	19.8	21.6	7.8	9.9	411	402	255	219	40	54	59.1	73.0	24	41	3.5	5.5
Colored	7,618	7,618	154	164	68	92	20.2	21.5	8.9	12.1	86	72	(4)	(4)	11	19	71.4	115.9	7	17	4.5	10.4
White	26,654	26,654	523	576	198	246	19.6	21.6	7.4	9.2	325	330	264	234	29	35	55.4	60.8	17	24	3.3	4.2
Charlton	4,400	4,400	133	124	51	41	30.2	28.2	11.6	9.3	82	83	(4)	(4)	11	4	82.7	32.3	8	11	6.0	8.9
Colored	1,000	1,000	19	28	16	5	19.0	28.0	16.0	5.0	3	23	(4)	(4)	2	1	105.3	35.7	2	4	10.5	14.3
White	3,400	3,400	114	96	35	36	33.5	28.2	10.3	10.6	79	60	(4)	(4)	9	3	78.9	31.3	6	7	5.3	7.3
Chatham	21,100	20,600	238	239	260	280	11.3	11.6	12.3	13.6	−22	−41	92	85	21	13	88.2	54.4	20	23	8.4	9.6
Colored	10,900	10,900	170	161	195	217	15.6	14.8	17.9	19.9	−25	−56	87	74	18	10	105.9	62.1	18	20	10.6	12.4
White	10,200	9,700	68	78	65	63	6.7	8.0	6.4	6.5	3	15	(4)	(4)	3	3	44.1	38.5	2	3	2.9	3.8
Chattahoochee	9,300	9,000	164	121	44	54	17.6	13.4	4.7	6.0	120	67	(4)	(4)	6	8	36.6	66.1	6	8	3.7	6.6
Colored	2,700	2,700	45	52	20	22	16.7	19.3	7.4	8.1	25	30	(4)	(4)	2	4	44.4	76.9	4	2	8.9	3.8
White	6,600	6,300	119	69	24	32	18.0	11.0	3.6	5.1	95	37	(4)	(4)	4	4	33.6	58.0	2	6	1.7	8.7
Chattooga	15,500	15,400	416	442	145	161	26.8	28.7	9.4	10.5	271	281	287	275	26	34	62.5	76.9	14	19	3.4	4.3
Colored	•1,900	1,900	53	58	25	28	27.9	30.5	13.2	14.7	28	30	(4)	(4)	6	5	113.2	86.2	2	4	3.8	6.9
White	13,600	13,500	363	384	120	133	26.7	28.4	8.8	9.9	243	251	303	289	20	29	55.1	75.5	12	15	3.3	3.9
Clarke	[5] 6,713	[5] 6,713	130	112	60	75	19.4	16.7	8.9	11.2	70	37	(4)	(4)	10	6	76.9	53.6	4	5	3.1	4.5
Colored	3,449	3,449	69	58	43	46	20.0	16.8	12.5	13.3	26	12	(4)	(4)	7	3	101.4	51.7	2	4	2.9	6.9
White	3,264	3,264	61	54	17	29	18.7	16.5	5.2	8.9	44	25	(4)	(4)	3	3	49.2	55.6	2	1	3.3	1.9
Clay	[5] 6,943	[5] 6,943	142	126	71	43	20.5	18.1	10.2	6.2	71	83	(4)	(4)	6	7	42.3	55.6	8	11	5.6	8.7
Colored	4,533	4,533	113	98	50	30	24.9	21.6	11.0	6.6	63	68	(4)	(4)	6	5	53.1	51.0	7	11	6.2	11.2
White	2,410	2,410	29	28	21	13	12.0	11.6	8.7	5.4	8	15	(4)	(4)	----	2	----	71.4	1	----	3.4	----
Clayton	[5] 10,260	[5] 10,260	159	159	107	114	15.5	15.5	10.4	11.1	52	45	149	139	12	7	75.5	44.0	12	10	7.5	6.3
Colored	3,250	3,250	76	53	57	51	23.4	16.3	17.5	15.7	19	2	(4)	(4)	4	5	52.6	94.3	7	4	9.2	7.5
White	7,010	7,010	83	106	50	63	11.8	15.1	7.1	9.0	33	43	(4)	(4)	8	2	96.4	18.9	5	6	6.0	5.7
Clinch	7,200	7,000	155	152	46	31	21.5	21.7	6.4	4.4	109	121	(4)	(4)	7	6	45.2	39.5	19	29	12.3	19.1
Colored	3,200	3,000	58	54	23	18	18.1	18.0	7.2	6.0	35	36	(4)	(4)	5	5	86.2	92.6	16	20	27.6	37.0
White	4,000	4,000	97	98	23	13	24.3	24.5	5.8	3.3	74	85	(4)	(4)	2	1	20.6	10.2	3	9	3.1	9.2
Cobb	36,000	35,500	682	681	364	370	18.9	19.2	10.1	10.4	318	311	187	184	48	53	70.4	77.8	32	31	4.7	4.6
Colored	6,500	6,500	145	134	104	91	22.3	20.6	16.0	14.0	41	43	139	(4)	10	16	69.0	119.4	10	11	6.9	8.2
White	29,500	29,000	537	547	260	279	18.2	18.9	8.8	9.6	277	268	207	196	38	37	70.8	67.6	22	20	4.1	3.7
Coffee	19,900	19,800	405	480	99	147	20.4	24.2	5.0	7.4	306	333	(4)	327	8	21	19.8	43.8	13	33	3.2	6.9
Colored	5,200	5,300	103	107	39	59	19.8	20.2	7.5	11.1	64	48	(4)	(4)	4	4	38.8	37.4	9	12	8.7	11.2
White	14,700	14,500	302	373	60	88	20.5	25.7	4.1	6.1	242	285	(4)	(4)	4	17	13.2	45.6	4	21	1.3	5.6
Colquitt	30,800	30,700	672	627	235	258	21.8	20.4	7.6	8.4	437	369	286	243	30	38	44.6	60.6	29	34	4.3	5.4
Colored	7,700	7,800	173	134	79	89	22.5	17.2	10.3	11.4	94	45	(4)	(4)	15	18	86.7	134.3	15	12	8.7	9.0
White	23,100	22,900	499	493	156	169	21.6	21.5	6.8	7.4	343	324	320	292	15	20	30.1	40.6	14	22	2.8	4.5
Columbia	[5] 8,793	[5] 8,793	185	207	69	65	21.0	23.5	7.8	7.4	116	142	(4)	(4)	6	7	32.4	33.8	16	15	8.6	7.2
Colored	5,536	5,536	130	144	51	42	23.5	26.0	9.2	7.6	79	102	(4)	(4)	4	5	30.8	34.7	12	15	9.2	10.4
White	3,257	3,257	55	63	18	23	16.9	19.3	5.5	7.1	37	40	(4)	(4)	2	2	36.4	31.7	4	----	7.3	----
Cook	11,300	11,300	253	260	73	107	22.4	23.0	6.5	9.5	180	153	(4)	243	5	11	19.8	42.3	12	15	4.7	5.8
Colored	3,000	3,100	47	44	22	37	15.7	14.2	7.3	11.9	25	7	(4)	(4)	2	1	42.6	22.7	5	7	10.6	15.9
White	8,300	8,200	206	216	51	70	24.8	26.3	6.1	8.5	155	146	(4)	(4)	3	10	14.6	46.3	7	8	3.4	3.7
Coweta	[5] 25,127	[5] 25,127	482	493	205	265	19.2	19.6	8.2	10.5	277	228	235	186	30	36	62.2	73.0	23	22	4.8	4.5
Colored	10,829	10,829	198	186	128	156	18.3	17.2	11.8	14.4	70	30	155	119	17	20	85.9	107.5	13	15	6.6	8.1
White	14,298	14,298	284	307	77	109	19.9	21.5	5.4	7.6	207	198	(4)	282	13	16	45.8	52.1	10	7	3.5	2.3
Crawford	[5] 7,020	[5] 7,020	168	154	78	92	23.9	21.9	11.1	13.1	90	62	(4)	(4)	17	15	101.2	97.4	13	8	7.7	5.2
Colored	3,879	3,879	109	100	49	52	28.1	25.8	12.6	13.4	60	48	(4)	(4)	12	13	110.1	130.0	10	7	9.2	7.0
White	3,141	3,141	59	54	29	40	18.8	17.2	9.2	12.7	30	14	(4)	(4)	5	2	84.7	37.0	3	1	5.1	1.9
Crisp	[5] 17,343	[5] 17,343	402	398	227	239	23.2	22.9	13.1	13.8	175	159	177	167	40	39	99.5	98.0	33	29	8.2	7.3
Colored	8,369	8,369	192	204	129	149	22.9	24.4	15.4	17.8	63	55	149	137	24	23	125.0	112.7	29	21	15.1	10.3
White	8,974	8,974	210	194	98	90	23.4	21.6	10.9	10.0	112	104	(4)	(4)	16	16	76.2	82.5	4	8	1.9	4.1
Decatur	23,700	23,600	585	570	248	291	24.7	24.2	10.5	12.3	337	279	236	196	43	45	73.5	78.9	34	51	5.8	8.9
Colored	11,800	11,700	311	302	138	188	26.4	25.8	11.7	16.1	173	114	225	161	28	30	90.0	99.3	25	40	8.0	13.2
White	11,900	11,900	274	268	110	103	23.0	22.5	9.2	8.7	164	165	249	260	15	15	54.7	56.0	9	11	3.3	4.1
De Kalb	32,700	32,300	944	807	434	401	28.9	25.0	13.3	12.4	510	406	218	201	40	50	42.4	62.0	35	44	3.7	5.5
Colored	7,300	7,100	145	151	97	102	19.9	21.3	13.3	14.4	48	49	(4)	148	13	19	89.7	125.8	19	17	13.1	11.3
White	25,400	25,200	799	656	337	299	31.5	26.0	13.3	11.9	462	357	237	219	27	31	33.8	47.3	16	27	2.0	4.1
Dodge	[5] 21,599	[5] 21,599	547	560	182	193	25.3	25.9	8.4	8.9	365	367	301	290	18	36	32.9	64.3	26	32	4.8	5.7
Colored	7,998	7,998	229	254	76	78	28.6	31.8	9.5	9.8	153	176	(4)	(4)	9	15	39.3	59.1	14	20	6.1	7.9
White	13,601	13,601	318	306	106	115	23.4	22.5	7.8	8.5	212	191	300	266	9	21	28.3	68.6	12	12	3.8	3.9
Dooly	[5] 18,025	[5] 18,025	489	444	198	207	27.1	24.6	11.0	11.5	291	237	247	214	30	33	61.3	74.3	24	35	4.9	7.9
Colored	10,064	10,064	305	264	126	140	30.3	26.2	12.5	13.9	179	124	242	189	21	25	68.9	94.7	17	27	5.6	10.2
White	7,961	7,961	184	180	72	67	23.1	22.6	9.0	8.4	112	113	(4)	(4)	9	8	48.9	44.4	7	8	3.8	4.4
Dougherty	7,800	7,800	40	44	44	59	5.1	5.6	5.6	7.6	−4	−15	(4)	(4)	6	10	150.0	227.3	3	4	7.5	9.1
Colored	5,300	5,300	35	35	37	34	6.6	6.6	7.0	6.4	−2	1	(4)	(4)	6	6	171.4	171.4	2	4	5.7	11.4
White	2,500	2,500	5	9	7	25	2.0	3.6	2.8	10.0	−2	−16	(4)	(4)	----	4	----	444.4	1	----	20.0	----
Douglas	[5] 9,461	[5] 9,461	201	187	80	103	21.2	19.8	8.5	10.9	121	84	(4)	182	12	18	59.7	96.3	5	19	2.5	10.2
Colored	2,271	2,271	52	58	35	37	22.9	25.5	15.4	16.3	17	21	(4)	(4)	4	6	76.9	103.4	4	12	7.7	20.7
White	7,190	7,190	149	129	45	66	20.7	17.9	6.3	9.2	104	63	(4)	(4)	8	12	53.7	93.0	1	7	.7	5.4
Early	[5] 18,273	[5] 18,273	492	475	206	196	26.9	26.0	11.3	10.7	286	279	239	242	33	32	67.1	67.4	22	27	4.5	5.7
Colored	9,737	9,737	290	251	134	110	29.8	25.8	13.8	11.3	156	141	216	228	20	21	69.0	83.7	18	21	6.2	8.4
White	8,536	8,536	202	224	72	86	23.7	26.2	8.4	10.1	130	138	(4)	(4)	13	11	64.4	49.1	4	6	2.0	2.7
Echols	[5] 2,744	[5] 2,744	26	17	9	8	9.5	6.2	3.3	2.9	17	9	(4)	(4)	1	----	38.5	----	1	1	3.8	5.9
Colored	845	845	2	2	6	1	2.4	2.4	7.1	1.2	−4	1	(4)	(4)	----	----	----	----	1	----	50.0	----
White	1,899	1,899	24	15	3	7	12.6	7.9	1.6	3.7	21	8	(4)	(4)	1	----	41.7	----	----	1	----	6.7
Effingham	10,200	10,200	180	167	99	114	17.6	16.4	9.7	11.2	81	53	(4)	146	18	13	100.0	77.8	14	15	7.8	9.0
Colored	4,200	4,200	113	87	64	69	26.9	20.7	15.2	16.4	49	18	(4)	(4)	16	8	141.6	92.0	8	12	7.1	13.8
White	6,000	6,000	67	80	35	45	11.2	13.3	5.8	7.5	32	35	(4)	(4)	2	5	29.9	62.5	6	3	9.0	3.8

See footnotes at end of table.

TABLE 18.—COLORED[1] AND WHITE POPULATION, BIRTHS AND DEATHS, INFANT MORTALITY, AND STILLBIRTHS, IN SELECTED REGISTRATION STATES, CITIES, AND COUNTIES: 1931 AND 1930—Continued

[See note at head of this table]

AREA AND COLOR	POPULATION ESTIMATED AS OF JULY 1		BIRTHS AND DEATHS (Exclusive of stillbirths)												INFANT MORTALITY (Exclusive of stillbirths)				STILLBIRTHS			
			Number				Rate per 1,000 population				Excess of births over deaths[2]		Births per 100 deaths		Deaths of infants under 1 year of age				Number		Rate per 100 live births	
			Births		Deaths		Births		Deaths						Number		Per 1,000 births					
	1931	1930	1931	1930	1931	1930	1931	1930	1931	1930	1931	1930	1931	1930	1931	1930	1931	1930	1931	1930	1931	1930
GEORGIA COUNTIES—continued																						
Elbert	[5] 18,485	[5] 18,485	403	335	192	233	21.8	18.1	10.4	12.6	211	102	210	144	25	26	62.0	77.6	13	26	3.2	7.8
Colored	7,536	7,536	210	141	95	118	27.9	18.7	12.6	15.7	115	23	(4)	119	13	15	61.9	106.4	9	19	4.3	13.5
White	10,949	10,949	193	194	97	115	17.6	17.7	8.9	10.5	96	79	(4)	169	12	11	62.2	56.7	4	7	2.1	3.6
Emanuel	[5] 24,101	[5] 24,101	533	507	212	253	22.1	21.0	8.8	10.5	321	254	251	200	43	40	80.7	78.9	34	40	6.4	7.9
Colored	9,111	9,111	230	170	105	123	25.2	18.7	11.5	13.5	125	47	219	138	23	21	100.0	123.5	18	27	7.8	15.9
White	14,990	14,990	303	337	107	130	20.2	22.5	7.1	8.7	196	207	283	259	20	19	66.0	56.4	16	13	5.3	3.9
Evans	7,200	7,100	120	151	69	62	16.7	21.3	9.6	8.7	51	89	(4)	(4)	9	9	75.0	59.6	5	11	4.2	7.3
Colored	2,700	2,600	41	46	41	29	15.2	17.7	15.2	11.2	-----	17	(4)	(4)	4	5	97.6	108.7	5	7	12.2	15.2
White	4,500	4,500	79	105	28	33	17.6	23.3	6.2	7.3	51	72	(4)	(4)	5	4	63.3	38.1	-----	4	-----	3.8
Fayette	[5] 8,665	[5] 8,665	191	205	89	86	22.0	23.7	10.3	9.9	102	119	(4)	(4)	15	17	78.5	82.9	5	10	2.6	4.9
Colored	2,838	2,838	74	79	39	30	26.1	27.8	13.7	10.6	35	49	(4)	(4)	7	6	94.6	75.9	2	4	2.7	5.1
White	5,827	5,827	117	126	50	56	20.1	21.6	8.6	9.6	67	70	(4)	(4)	8	11	68.4	87.3	3	6	2.6	4.8
Floyd	27,500	26,800	617	630	225	238	22.4	23.5	8.2	8.9	392	392	274	265	50	42	81.0	66.7	19	19	3.1	3.0
Colored	3,800	3,800	88	76	57	60	23.2	20.0	15.0	15.8	31	16	(4)	(4)	12	8	136.4	105.3	3	5	3.4	6.6
White	23,700	23,000	529	554	168	178	22.3	24.1	7.1	7.7	361	376	315	311	38	34	71.8	61.4	16	14	3.0	2.5
Franklin	[5] 15,902	[5] 15,902	381	365	167	160	24.0	23.0	10.5	10.1	214	205	228	228	25	29	65.6	79.5	18	17	4.7	4.7
Colored	2,672	2,672	47	73	31	39	17.6	27.3	11.6	14.6	16	34	(4)	(4)	6	6	127.7	82.2	3	1	6.4	1.4
White	13,230	13,230	334	292	136	121	25.2	22.1	10.3	9.1	198	171	246	241	19	23	56.9	78.8	15	16	4.5	5.5
Fulton	78,100	74,100	550	548	692	676	7.0	7.4	8.9	9.1	−142	−128	79	81	61	54	110.9	98.5	24	15	4.4	2.7
Colored	14,600	14,100	87	77	285	277	6.0	5.5	19.5	19.6	−198	−200	31	28	24	12	275.9	155.8	9	3	10.3	3.9
White	63,500	60,000	463	471	407	399	7.3	7.9	6.4	6.7	56	72	114	118	37	42	79.9	89.2	15	12	3.2	2.5
Glascock	4,400	4,400	109	74	52	34	24.8	16.8	11.8	7.7	57	40	(4)	(4)	12	4	110.1	54.1	3	6	2.8	8.1
Colored	1,300	1,300	17	20	16	14	13.1	15.4	12.3	10.8	1	6	(4)	(4)	4	1	253.3	50.0	1	3	5.9	15.0
White	3,100	3,100	92	54	36	20	29.7	17.4	11.6	6.5	56	34	(4)	(4)	8	3	87.0	55.6	2	3	2.2	5.6
Glynn	5,400	5,400	82	91	76	66	15.2	16.9	14.1	12.2	6	25	(4)	(4)	4	7	48.8	76.9	4	11	4.9	12.1
Colored	2,100	2,300	35	49	47	44	16.7	21.3	22.4	19.1	−12	5	(4)	(4)	1	3	28.6	61.2	2	8	5.7	16.3
White	3,300	3,100	47	42	29	22	14.2	13.5	8.8	7.1	18	20	(4)	(4)	3	4	63.8	95.2	2	3	4.3	7.1
Grady	[5] 19,200	[5] 19,200	464	404	182	204	24.2	21.0	9.5	10.6	282	200	255	198	35	45	75.4	111.4	44	37	9.5	9.2
Colored	6,627	6,627	156	146	49	59	23.5	22.0	7.4	8.9	107	87	(4)	(4)	12	12	76.9	82.2	25	25	16.0	17.1
White	12,573	12,573	308	258	133	145	24.5	20.5	10.6	11.5	175	113	252	178	23	33	74.7	127.9	19	12	6.2	4.7
Greene	[5] 12,616	[5] 12,616	311	270	165	177	24.7	21.4	13.1	14.0	146	93	188	153	19	19	61.1	70.4	15	11	4.8	4.1
Colored	6,628	6,628	178	150	92	108	26.9	22.6	13.9	16.3	86	42	(4)	139	12	12	67.4	80.0	9	7	5.1	4.7
White	5,988	5,988	133	120	73	69	22.2	20.0	12.2	11.5	60	51	(4)	(4)	7	7	52.6	58.3	6	4	4.5	3.3
Gwinnett	[5] 27,853	[5] 27,853	592	595	254	249	21.3	21.4	9.1	8.9	338	346	233	239	51	43	86.1	72.3	27	26	4.6	4.4
Colored	3,344	3,344	97	80	57	40	29.0	23.9	17.0	12.0	40	40	(4)	(4)	12	6	123.7	75.0	10	7	10.3	8.8
White	24,509	24,509	495	515	197	209	20.2	21.0	8.0	8.5	298	306	251	246	39	37	78.8	71.8	17	19	3.4	3.7
Hall	30,700	30,400	647	705	318	326	21.1	23.2	10.4	10.7	329	379	203	216	53	63	81.9	89.4	35	31	5.4	4.4
Colored	3,300	3,400	58	55	55	58	17.6	16.2	16.7	17.1	3	−3	(4)	(4)	12	10	206.9	181.8	11	6	19.0	10.9
White	27,400	27,000	589	650	263	268	21.5	24.1	9.6	9.9	326	382	224	243	41	53	69.6	81.5	24	25	4.1	3.8
Hancock	[5] 13,070	[5] 13,070	337	330	112	124	25.8	25.2	8.6	9.5	225	206	301	266	18	14	53.4	42.4	30	19	8.9	5.8
Colored	9,345	9,345	280	254	82	85	30.0	27.2	8.8	9.1	198	169	(4)	(4)	15	11	53.6	43.3	25	15	8.9	5.9
White	3,725	3,725	57	76	30	39	15.3	20.4	8.1	10.5	27	37	(4)	(4)	3	3	52.6	39.5	5	4	8.8	5.3
Harris	[5] 11,140	[5] 11,140	243	205	115	118	21.8	18.4	10.3	10.6	128	87	211	174	10	18	41.2	87.8	15	7	6.2	3.4
Colored	7,693	7,693	200	173	80	86	26.0	22.5	10.4	11.2	120	87	(4)	(4)	9	18	45.0	104.0	15	6	7.5	3.5
White	3,447	3,447	43	32	35	32	12.5	9.3	10.2	9.3	8	-----	(4)	(4)	1	-----	23.3	-----	-----	1	-----	3.1
Hart	[5] 15,174	[5] 15,174	364	355	119	153	24.0	23.4	7.8	10.1	245	202	306	232	22	26	60.4	73.2	13	16	3.6	4.5
Colored	3,893	3,893	92	93	45	54	23.6	23.9	11.6	13.9	47	39	(4)	(4)	9	4	97.8	43.0	9	10	9.8	10.8
White	11,281	11,281	272	262	74	99	24.1	23.2	6.6	8.8	198	163	(4)	(4)	13	22	47.8	84.0	4	6	1.5	2.3
Heard	[5] 9,102	[5] 9,102	209	238	76	72	23.0	26.1	8.3	7.9	133	166	(4)	(4)	21	18	100.5	75.6	11	19	5.3	8.0
Colored	2,369	2,369	71	66	18	22	30.0	27.9	7.6	9.3	53	44	(4)	(4)	8	3	112.7	45.5	5	7	7.0	10.6
White	6,733	6,733	138	172	58	50	20.5	25.5	8.6	7.4	80	122	(4)	(4)	13	15	94.2	87.2	6	12	4.3	7.0
Henry	[5] 15,924	[5] 15,924	346	321	145	158	21.7	20.2	9.1	9.9	201	163	239	203	20	23	57.8	71.7	27	21	7.8	6.5
Colored	7,914	7,914	202	165	88	99	25.5	20.8	11.1	12.5	114	66	(4)	(4)	13	14	64.4	84.8	19	15	9.4	9.1
White	8,010	8,010	144	156	57	59	18.0	19.5	7.1	7.4	87	97	(4)	(4)	7	9	48.6	57.7	8	6	5.6	3.8
Houston	[5] 11,280	[5] 11,280	217	207	126	138	19.2	18.4	11.2	12.2	91	69	172	150	12	7	55.3	33.8	11	15	5.1	7.2
Colored	7,628	7,628	156	166	85	98	20.5	21.8	11.1	12.8	71	68	(4)	(4)	9	6	57.7	36.1	10	14	6.4	8.4
White	3,652	3,652	61	41	41	40	16.7	11.2	11.2	11.0	20	1	(4)	(4)	3	1	49.2	24.4	1	1	1.6	2.4
Irwin	[5] 12,199	[5] 12,199	306	286	106	103	25.1	23.4	8.7	8.4	200	183	289	278	14	20	45.8	69.9	21	17	6.9	5.9
Colored	4,544	4,544	135	127	47	59	29.7	27.9	10.3	13.0	88	68	(4)	(4)	9	8	66.7	63.0	17	12	12.6	9.4
White	7,655	7,655	171	159	59	44	22.3	20.8	7.7	5.7	112	115	(4)	(4)	5	12	29.2	75.5	4	5	2.3	3.1

Jackson	[5] 21,609	[5] 21,609	462	411	177	210	21.4	19.0	8.2	9.7	285	201	261	196	33	35	71.4	85.2	23	22	5.0	5.4
Colored	4,066	4,066	79	50	45	54	19.4	12.3	11.1	13.3	34	−4	(4)	(4)	6	5	75.9	100.0	6	6	7.6	12.0
White	17,543	17,543	383	361	132	156	21.8	20.6	7.5	8.9	251	205	290	231	27	30	70.5	83.1	17	16	4.4	4.4
Jasper	[5] 8,594	[5] 8,594	219	201	113	109	25.5	23.4	13.1	12.7	106	92	194	184	23	6	105.0	29.9	19	12	8.7	6.0
Colored	5,237	5,237	159	135	87	64	30.4	25.8	16.6	12.2	72	71	(4)	(4)	19	4	119.5	29.6	16	11	10.1	8.1
White	3,357	3,357	60	66	26	45	17.9	19.7	7.7	13.4	34	21	(4)	(4)	4	2	66.7	30.3	3	1	5.0	1.5
Jeff Davis	8,200	8,100	184	139	62	48	22.4	17.2	7.6	5.9	122	91	(4)	(4)	13	6	70.7	43.2	6	4	3.3	2.9
Colored	1,700	1,600	30	24	14	20	17.6	15.0	8.2	12.5	16	4	(4)	(4)	3	1	100.0	41.7	1	1	3.3	4.2
White	6,500	6,500	154	115	48	28	23.7	17.7	7.4	4.3	106	87	(4)	(4)	10	5	64.9	43.5	5	3	3.2	2.6
Jefferson	[5] 20,727	[5] 20,727	408	332	167	158	19.7	16.0	8.1	7.6	241	174	244	210	20	19	49.0	57.2	28	32	6.9	9.6
Colored	12,042	12,042	266	200	102	82	22.1	16.6	8.5	6.8	164	118	261	(4)	14	10	52.6	50.0	22	24	8.3	12.0
White	8,685	8,685	142	132	65	76	16.4	15.2	7.5	8.8	77	56	(4)	(4)	6	9	42.3	68.2	6	8	4.2	6.1
Jenkins	[5] 12,908	[5] 12,908	327	311	156	196	25.3	24.1	12.1	15.2	171	115	210	159	22	18	67.3	57.9	20	22	6.1	7.1
Colored	7,465	7,465	199	195	101	126	26.7	26.1	13.5	16.9	98	69	197	155	14	10	70.4	51.3	16	18	8.0	9.2
White	5,443	5,443	128	116	55	70	23.5	21.3	10.1	12.9	73	46	(4)	(4)	8	8	62.5	69.0	4	4	3.1	3.4
Johnson	[5] 12,681	[5] 12,681	334	315	104	133	26.3	24.8	8.2	10.5	230	182	321	237	18	23	53.9	73.0	11	28	3.3	8.9
Colored	4,961	4,961	164	144	52	52	33.1	29.0	10.5	10.5	112	92	(4)	(4)	6	9	36.6	62.5	8	19	4.9	13.2
White	7,720	7,720	170	171	52	81	22.0	22.2	6.7	10.5	118	90	(4)	(4)	12	14	70.6	81.9	3	9	1.8	5.3
Jones	[5] 8,992	[5] 8,992	211	218	95	82	23.5	24.2	10.6	9.1	116	136	(4)	(4)	14	15	66.4	68.8	14	19	6.6	8.7
Colored	5,775	5,775	164	171	73	57	28.4	29.6	12.6	9.9	91	114	(4)	(4)	13	14	79.3	81.9	14	13	8.5	7.6
White	3,217	3,217	47	47	22	25	14.6	14.6	6.8	7.8	25	22	(4)	(4)	1	1	21.3	21.3		6		12.8
Lamar	[5] 9,745	[5] 9,745	206	213	114	127	21.1	21.9	11.7	13.0	92	86	181	168	12	18	58.3	84.5	12	19	5.8	8.9
Colored	4,473	4,473	115	122	70	70	25.7	27.3	15.6	15.6	45	52	(4)	(4)	11	13	95.7	106.6	12	16	10.4	13.1
White	5,272	5,272	91	91	44	57	17.3	17.3	8.3	10.8	47	34	(4)	(4)	1	5	11.0	54.9		3		3.3
Lanier	[5] 5,190	[5] 5,190	89	84	49	37	17.1	16.2	9.4	7.1	40	47	(4)	(4)	10	7	112.4	83.3	5	8	5.6	9.5
Colored	1,940	1,940	46	31	28	20	23.7	16.0	14.4	10.3	18	11	(4)	(4)	7	3	152.2	96.8	3	5	6.5	16.1
White	3,250	3,250	43	53	21	17	13.2	16.3	6.5	5.2	22	36	(4)	(4)	3	4	69.8	75.5	2	3	4.7	5.7
Laurens	[5] 32,693	[5] 32,693	756	722	331	395	23.1	22.1	10.1	12.1	425	327	228	183	38	53	50.5	73.4	44	41	5.8	5.7
Colored	13,536	13,536	340	290	177	185	25.1	21.4	13.1	13.7	163	105	192	157	20	22	58.8	75.8	28	23	8.2	7.9
White	19,157	19,157	416	432	154	210	21.7	22.6	8.0	11.0	262	222	270	206	18	31	43.3	71.9	16	18	3.8	4.2
Lee	[5] 8,328	[5] 8,328	210	200	97	127	25.2	24.0	11.6	15.2	113	73	(4)	157	10	13	47.6	65.0	15	17	7.6	8.5
Colored	6,492	6,492	167	172	85	113	25.7	26.5	13.1	17.4	82	59	(4)	152	8	11	47.9	64.0	14	16	8.4	9.3
White	1,836	1,836	43	28	12	14	23.4	15.3	6.5	7.6	31	14	(4)	(4)	2	2	46.5	71.4	2	1	4.7	3.6
Liberty	[5] 8,153	[5] 8,153	160	147	131	141	19.6	18.0	16.1	17.3	29	6	122	104	19	13	118.8	88.4	8	17	5.0	11.6
Colored	5,532	5,532	118	117	112	114	21.3	21.1	20.2	20.6	6	3	105	103	18	12	152.5	102.6	8	16	6.8	13.7
White	2,621	2,621	42	30	19	27	16.0	11.4	7.2	10.3	23	3	(4)	(4)	1	1	23.8	33.3		1		3.3
Lincoln	[5] 7,847	[5] 7,847	182	165	28	38	23.2	21.0	3.6	4.8	154	127	(4)	(4)	3	3	16.5	18.2	13	6	7.1	3.6
Colored	4,093	4,093	99	85	12	20	24.2	20.8	2.9	4.9	87	65	(4)	(4)	2	3	20.2	35.3	12	6	12.1	7.1
White	3,754	3,754	83	80	16	18	22.1	21.3	4.3	4.8	67	62	(4)	(4)	1		12.0		1		1.2	
Long	[5] 4,180	[5] 4,180	62	72	42	29	14.8	17.2	10.0	6.9	20	43	(4)	(4)	3	3	48.4	41.7	3	7	4.8	9.7
Colored	1,788	1,788	23	37	28	16	12.9	20.7	15.7	8.9	−5	21	(4)	(4)	2	2	87.0	54.1	3	4	13.0	10.8
White	2,392	2,392	39	35	14	13	16.3	14.6	5.9	5.4	25	22	(4)	(4)	1	1	25.6	28.6		3		8.6
Lowndes	16,900	16,600	323	312	112	109	19.1	18.8	6.6	6.6	211	203	288	286	13	21	40.2	67.3	14	17	4.3	5.4
Colored	7,800	7,600	154	149	62	66	19.7	19.6	7.9	8.7	92	83	(4)	(4)	11	13	71.4	87.2	9	11	5.8	7.4
White	9,100	9,000	169	163	50	43	18.6	18.1	5.5	4.8	119	120	(4)	(4)	2	8	11.8	49.1	5	6	3.0	3.7
McDuffie	[5] 9,014	[5] 9,014	200	174	118	118	22.2	19.3	13.1	13.1	82	56	169	147	15	14	75.0	80.5	9	14	4.5	8.0
Colored	4,572	4,572	123	78	63	84	26.9	17.1	13.8	18.4	60	−6	(4)	(4)	9	9	73.2	115.4	5	12	4.1	15.4
White	4,442	4,442	77	96	55	34	17.3	21.6	12.4	7.7	22	62	(4)	(4)	6	5	77.9	52.1	4	2	5.2	2.1
McIntosh	5,800	5,800	118	164	104	121	20.3	28.3	17.9	20.9	14	43	113	136	10	28	84.7	170.7	17	17	14.4	10.4
Colored	3,800	3,900	81	103	85	105	21.3	26.4	22.4	26.9	−4	−2	(4)	98	7	23	86.4	223.3	13	16	16.0	15.5
White	2,000	1,900	37	61	19	16	18.5	32.1	9.5	8.4	18	45	(4)	(4)	3	5	81.1	82.0	4	1	10.8	1.6
Macon	[5] 16,643	[5] 16,643	358	264	181	177	21.5	15.9	10.9	10.6	177	87	198	149	26	31	72.6	117.4	20	25	5.6	9.5
Colored	11,192	11,192	275	186	131	131	24.6	16.6	11.7	11.7	144	55	210	142	22	26	80.0	139.8	19	21	6.9	11.3
White	5,451	5,451	83	78	50	46	15.2	14.3	9.2	8.4	33	32	(4)	(4)	4	5	48.2	64.1	1	4	1.2	5.1
Madison	[5] 14,921	[5] 14,921	381	339	129	163	25.5	22.7	8.6	10.9	252	176	295	208	24	23	63.0	67.8	15	18	3.9	5.3
Colored	2,834	2,834	76	62	43	54	26.8	21.9	15.2	19.1	33	8	(4)	(4)	13	7	171.1	112.9	3	8	3.9	12.9
White	12,087	12,087	305	277	86	109	25.2	22.9	7.1	9.0	219	168	(4)	254	11	16	36.1	57.8	12	10	3.9	3.6
Marion	[5] 6,968	[5] 6,968	180	160	74	79	25.8	23.0	10.6	11.3	106	81	(4)	(4)	8	5	44.4	31.3	13	18	7.2	11.3
Colored	3,915	3,915	116	95	45	46	29.6	24.3	11.5	11.7	71	49	(4)	(4)	4	2	34.5	21.1	8	9	6.9	9.5
White	3,053	3,053	64	65	29	33	21.0	21.3	9.5	10.8	35	32	(4)	(4)	4	3	62.5	46.2	5	9	7.8	13.8
Meriwether	[5] 22,437	[5] 22,437	497	437	248	274	22.2	19.5	11.1	12.2	249	163	200	159	40	39	80.5	89.2	36	21	7.2	4.8
Colored	11,766	11,766	284	247	141	180	24.1	21.0	12.0	15.3	143	67	201	137	20	30	70.4	121.5	28	14	9.9	5.7
White	10,671	10,671	213	190	107	94	20.0	17.8	10.0	8.8	106	96	199	(4)	20	9	93.9	47.4	8	7	3.8	3.7
Miller	[5] 9,076	[5] 9,076	267	214	68	80	29.4	23.6	7.5	8.8	199	134	(4)	(4)	16	10	59.9	46.7	9	14	3.4	6.5
Colored	3,083	3,083	95	81	29	27	30.8	26.3	9.4	8.8	66	54	(4)	(4)	8	2	84.2	24.7	3	7	3.2	8.6
White	5,993	5,993	172	133	39	53	28.7	22.2	6.5	8.8	133	80	(4)	(4)	8	8	46.5	60.2	6	7	3.5	5.3
Mitchell	[5] 23,620	[5] 23,620	606	621	236	325	25.7	26.3	10.0	13.8	370	296	257	191	46	72	75.9	115.9	61	39	10.1	6.3
Colored	11,862	11,862	338	330	148	200	28.5	27.8	12.5	16.9	190	130	228	165	29	47	85.8	142.4	42	30	12.4	9.1
White	11,758	11,758	268	291	88	125	22.8	24.7	7.5	10.6	180	166	(4)	233	17	25	63.4	85.9	19	9	7.1	3.1
Monroe	[5] 11,606	[5] 11,606	252	295	146	164	21.7	25.4	12.6	14.1	106	131	173	180	20	26	79.4	88.1	23	13	9.1	4.4
Colored	6,750	6,750	182	209	101	110	27.0	31.0	15.0	16.3	81	99	180	190	16	18	87.9	86.1	22	11	12.1	5.3
White	4,856	4,856	70	86	45	54	14.4	17.7	9.3	11.1	25	32	(4)	(4)	4	8	57.1	93.0	1	2	1.4	2.3
Montgomery	10,100	10,000	229	239	99	85	22.7	23.9	9.8	8.5	130	154	(4)	(4)	9	17	39.3	71.1	22	27	9.6	11.3
Colored	4,500	4,400	115	148	45	47	25.6	33.6	10.0	10.7	70	101	(4)	(4)	6	11	52.2	74.3	17	23	14.8	15.5
White	5,600	5,600	114	91	54	38	20.4	16.3	9.6	6.8	60	53	(4)	(4)	3	6	26.3	65.9	5	4	4.4	4.4
Morgan	[5] 12,488	[5] 12,488	259	220	129	154	20.7	17.6	10.3	12.3	130	66	201	143	16	13	61.8	59.1	19	16	7.3	7.3
Colored	7,199	7,199	164	124	81	94	22.8	17.2	11.3	13.1	83	30	(4)	(4)	7	5	42.7	40.3	16	12	9.8	9.7
White	5,289	5,289	95	96	48	60	18.0	18.2	9.1	11.3	47	36	(4)	(4)	9	8	94.7	83.3	3	4	3.2	4.2
Muscogee	15,800	14,700	97	89	43	45	6.1	6.1	2.7	3.1	54	44	(4)	(4)	3	4	30.9	44.9	10	7	10.3	7.9
Colored	6,800	6,600	70	59	31	24	10.3	8.9	4.6	3.6	39	35	(4)	(4)	2	2	28.6	33.9	8	6	11.4	10.2
White	9,000	8,100	27	30	12	21	3.0	3.7	1.3	2.6	15	9	(4)	(4)	1	2	37.0	66.7	2	1	7.4	3.3

See footnotes at end of table.

TABLE 18.—COLORED [1] AND WHITE POPULATION, BIRTHS AND DEATHS, INFANT MORTALITY, AND STILLBIRTHS, IN SELECTED REGISTRATION STATES, CITIES, AND COUNTIES: 1931 AND 1930—Continued

[See note at head of this table]

AREA AND COLOR	POPULATION ESTIMATED AS OF JULY 1		BIRTHS AND DEATHS (Exclusive of stillbirths)												INFANT MORTALITY (Exclusive of stillbirths)				STILLBIRTHS			
			Number				Rate per 1,000 population				Excess of births over deaths [2]		Births per 100 deaths		Deaths of infants under 1 year of age				Number		Rate per 100 live births	
			Births		Deaths		Births		Deaths						Number		Per 1,000 births					
	1931	1930	1931	1930	1931	1930	1931	1930	1931	1930	1931	1930	1931	1930	1931	1930	1931	1930	1931	1930	1931	1930
GEORGIA COUNTIES—continued																						
Newton	[5] 17,290	[5] 17,290	331	337	188	203	19.1	19.5	10.9	11.7	143	134	176	166	12	28	36.3	83.1	17	23	5.1	6.8
Colored	6,778	6,778	131	132	98	105	19.3	19.5	14.5	15.5	33	27	(4)	126	6	17	45.8	128.8	13	12	9.9	9.1
White	10,512	10,512	200	205	90	98	19.0	19.5	8.6	9.3	110	107	(4)	(4)	6	11	30.0	53.7	4	11	2.0	5.4
Oconee	[5] 8,082	[5] 8,082	160	132	83	77	19.8	16.3	10.3	9.5	77	55	(4)	(4)	15	10	93.8	75.8	6	8	3.8	6.1
Colored	2,401	2,401	52	44	34	21	21.7	18.3	14.2	8.7	18	23	(4)	(4)	8	3	153.8	68.2	2	4	3.8	9.1
White	5,681	5,681	108	88	49	56	19.0	15.5	8.6	9.9	59	32	(4)	(4)	7	7	64.8	79.5	4	4	3.7	4.5
Oglethorpe	[5] 12,927	[5] 12,927	295	321	145	144	22.8	24.8	11.2	11.1	150	177	203	223	17	19	57.6	59.2	12	16	4.1	5.0
Colored	6,424	6,424	180	173	85	70	28.0	26.9	13.2	10.9	95	103	(4)	(4)	8	11	44.4	63.6	7	16	3.9	9.2
White	6,503	6,503	115	148	60	74	17.7	22.8	9.2	11.4	55	74	(4)	(4)	9	8	78.3	54.1	5		4.3	
Peach	10,400	10,300	218	158	155	125	21.0	15.3	14.9	12.1	63	33	141	126	26	19	119.3	120.3	12	19	5.5	12.0
Colored	6,700	6,600	157	110	106	99	23.4	16.7	15.8	15.0	51	11	148	(4)	15	17	95.5	154.5	10	18	6.4	16.4
White	3,700	3,700	61	48	49	26	16.5	13.0	13.2	7.0	12	22	(4)	(4)	11	2	180.3	41.7	2	1	3.3	2.1
Pierce	12,800	12,600	340	367	131	137	26.6	29.1	10.2	10.9	209	230	260	268	28	27	82.4	73.6	18	33	5.3	9.0
Colored	3,400	3,300	63	84	48	58	18.5	25.5	14.1	17.6	15	26	(4)	(4)	7	7	111.1	83.3	13	16	20.6	19.0
White	9,400	9,300	277	283	83	79	29.5	30.4	8.8	8.5	194	204	(4)	(4)	21	20	75.8	70.7	5	17	1.8	6.0
Pike	[5] 10,853	[5] 10,853	251	252	129	156	23.1	23.2	11.9	14.4	122	96	195	162	17	23	67.7	91.3	16	15	6.4	6.0
Colored	5,401	5,401	151	148	71	103	28.0	27.4	13.1	19.1	80	45	(4)	144	12	19	79.5	128.4	16	7	10.6	4.7
White	5,452	5,452	100	104	58	53	18.3	19.1	10.6	9.7	42	51	(4)	(4)	5	4	50.0	38.5		8		7.7
Polk	25,700	25,300	491	589	262	275	19.1	23.3	10.2	10.9	229	314	187	214	46	62	93.7	105.3	19	15	3.9	2.5
Colored	4,700	4,800	33	64	75	71	7.0	13.3	16.0	14.8	−42	−7	(4)	(4)	14	5	424.2	78.1	6	6	18.2	9.4
White	21,000	20,500	458	525	187	204	21.8	25.6	8.9	10.0	271	321	245	257	32	57	69.9	108.6	13	9	2.8	1.7
Pulaski	[5] 9,005	[5] 9,005	164	159	82	89	18.2	17.7	9.1	9.9	82	70	(4)	(4)	8	6	48.8	37.7	10	13	6.1	8.2
Colored	5,056	5,056	105	106	45	43	20.8	21.0	8.9	8.5	60	63	(4)	(4)	5	2	47.6	18.9	9	10	8.6	9.4
White	3,949	3,949	59	53	37	46	14.9	13.4	9.4	11.6	22	7	(4)	(4)	3	4	50.8	75.5	1	3	1.7	5.7
Putnam	[5] 8,367	[5] 8,367	199	175	105	117	23.8	20.9	12.5	14.0	94	58	190	150	19	14	95.5	80.0	18	5	9.0	2.9
Colored	5,212	5,212	144	131	74	88	27.6	25.1	14.2	16.9	70	43	(4)	(4)	14	11	97.2	84.0	11	5	7.6	3.8
White	3,155	3,155	55	44	31	29	17.4	13.9	9.8	9.2	24	15	(4)	(4)	5	3	90.9	68.2	7		12.7	
Quitman	3,900	3,800	106	111	42	36	27.2	29.2	10.8	9.5	64	75	(4)	(4)	6	12	56.6	108.1	4	7	3.8	6.3
Colored	2,700	2,600	86	88	27	23	31.9	33.8	10.0	8.8	59	65	(4)	(4)	3	11	34.9	125.0	3	6	3.5	6.8
White	1,200	1,200	20	23	15	13	16.7	19.2	12.5	10.8	5	10	(4)	(4)	3	1	150.0	43.5	1	1	5.0	4.3
Randolph	17,200	17,200	386	330	171	178	22.4	19.2	9.9	10.3	215	152	226	185	18	14	46.6	42.4	32	26	8.3	7.9
Colored	11,600	11,600	275	228	116	125	23.7	19.7	10.0	10.8	159	103	237	182	11	11	40.0	48.2	29	23	10.5	10.1
White	5,600	5,600	111	102	55	53	19.8	18.2	9.8	9.5	56	49	(4)	(4)	7	3	63.1	29.4	3	3	2.7	2.9
Richmond	12,800	12,700	202	178	131	153	15.8	14.0	10.2	12.0	71	25	154	116	12	5	59.4	28.1	7	11	3.5	6.2
Colored	6,000	6,000	130	119	65	72	21.7	19.8	10.8	12.0	65	47	(4)	(4)	9	2	69.2	16.8	4	10	3.1	8.4
White	6,800	6,700	72	59	66	81	10.6	8.8	9.7	12.1	6	−22	(4)	(4)	3	3	41.7	50.8	3	1	4.2	1.7
Rockdale	[5] 7,247	[5] 7,247	135	134	81	83	18.6	18.5	11.2	11.5	54	51	(4)	(4)	7	5	51.9	37.3	10	10	7.4	7.5
Colored	2,441	2,441	52	47	28	37	21.3	19.3	11.5	15.2	24	10	(4)	(4)	1	1	19.2	21.3	3	3	5.8	6.4
White	4,806	4,806	83	87	53	46	17.3	18.1	11.0	9.6	30	41	(4)	(4)	6	4	72.3	46.0	7	7	8.4	8.0
Schley	5,400	5,400	108	118	74	72	20.0	21.9	13.7	13.3	34	46	(4)	(4)	16	12	148.1	101.7	5	3	4.6	2.5
Colored	3,400	3,400	82	84	42	37	24.1	24.7	12.4	10.9	40	47	(4)	(4)	11	8	134.1	95.2	3	3	3.7	3.6
White	2,000	2,000	26	34	32	35	13.0	17.0	16.0	17.5	−6	−1	(4)	(4)	5	4	192.3	117.6	2		7.7	
Screven	[5] 20,503	[5] 20,503	519	495	172	203	25.3	24.1	8.4	9.9	347	292	302	244	35	31	67.4	62.6	44	33	8.5	6.7
Colored	11,621	11,621	322	325	108	124	27.7	28.0	9.3	10.7	214	201	298	262	29	21	90.1	64.6	41	31	12.7	9.5
White	8,882	8,882	197	170	64	79	22.2	19.1	7.2	8.9	133	91	(4)	(4)	6	10	30.5	58.8	3	2	1.5	1.2
Seminole	[5] 7,389	[5] 7,389	157	152	72	63	21.2	20.6	9.7	8.5	85	89	(4)	(4)	11	12	70.1	78.9	10	7	6.4	4.6
Colored	2,898	2,898	92	80	31	35	31.7	27.6	10.7	12.1	61	45	(4)	(4)	5	6	54.3	75.0	7	3	7.6	3.8
White	4,491	4,491	65	72	41	28	14.5	16.0	9.1	6.2	24	44	(4)	(4)	6	6	92.3	83.3	3	4	4.6	5.6
Spalding	13,100	13,100	128	139	122	65	9.8	10.6	9.3	5.0	6	74	105	(4)	21	14	164.1	100.7	14	22	10.9	15.8
Colored	4,400	4,700	59	87	54	39	13.4	18.5	12.3	8.3	5	48	(4)	(4)	13	10	220.3	114.9	10	14	16.9	16.1
White	8,700	8,400	69	52	68	26	7.9	6.2	7.8	3.1	1	26	(4)	(4)	8	4	115.9	76.9	4	8	5.8	15.4
Stephens	11,800	11,800	254	250	99	126	21.5	21.2	8.4	10.7	155	124	(4)	198	9	19	35.4	76.0	9	6	3.5	2.4
Colored	2,100	2,100	24	23	12	31	11.4	11.0	5.7	14.8	12	−8	(4)	(4)	1	4	41.7	173.9	4	1	16.7	4.3
White	9,700	9,700	230	227	87	95	23.7	23.4	9.0	9.8	143	132	(4)	(4)	8	15	34.8	66.1	5	5	2.2	2.2
Stewart	[5] 11,114	[5] 11,114	238	250	125	130	21.4	22.5	11.2	11.7	113	120	190	192	20	24	84.0	96.0	15	17	6.3	6.8
Colored	7,930	7,930	195	216	98	104	24.6	27.2	12.4	13.1	97	112	(4)	208	20	20	102.6	92.6	13	17	6.7	7.9
White	3,184	3,184	43	34	27	26	13.5	10.7	8.5	8.2	16	8	(4)	(4)		4		117.6	2		4.7	
Sumter	[5] 26,800	[5] 26,800	530	548	360	379	19.8	20.4	13.4	14.1	170	169	147	145	39	38	73.6	69.3	34	48	6.4	8.8
Colored	17,390	17,390	393	416	249	257	22.6	23.9	14.3	14.8	144	159	158	162	25	32	63.6	76.9	30	45	7.6	10.8
White	9,410	9,410	137	132	111	122	14.6	14.0	11.8	13.0	26	10	123	108	14	6	102.2	45.5	4	3	2.9	2.3

Talbot	[5] 8,458	[5] 8,458	223	210	102	97	26.4	24.8	12.1	11.5	121	113	219	(4)	16	14	71.7	66.7	20	13	9.0	6.2
Colored	5,828	5,828	192	182	75	71	32.9	31.2	12.9	12.2	117	111	(4)	(4)	15	12	78.1	65.9	17	12	8.9	6.6
White	2,630	2,630	31	28	27	26	11.8	10.6	10.3	9.9	4	2	(4)	(4)	1	2	32.3	71.4	3	1	9.7	3.6
Taliaferro	[5] 6,172	[5] 6,172	170	140	90	82	27.5	22.7	14.6	13.3	80	58	(4)	(4)	16	7	91.1	50.0	13	7	7.6	5.0
Colored	4,222	4,222	140	109	67	62	33.2	25.8	15.9	14.7	73	47	(4)	(4)	14	6	100.0	55.0	11	7	7.9	6.4
White	1,950	1,950	30	31	23	20	15.4	15.9	11.8	10.3	7	11	(4)	(4)	2	1	66.7	32.3	2	------	6.7	------
Tattnall	15,500	15,400	333	311	104	115	21.5	20.2	6.7	7.5	229	196	320	270	14	18	42.0	57.9	20	28	6.0	9.0
Colored	3,300	3,300	74	63	35	30	22.4	19.1	10.6	9.1	39	33	(4)	(4)	4	3	54.1	47.6	8	8	10.8	12.7
White	12,200	12,100	259	248	69	85	21.2	20.5	5.7	7.0	190	163	(4)	(4)	10	15	38.6	60.5	12	20	4.6	8.1
Taylor	[5] 10,617	[5] 10,617	196	213	65	82	18.5	20.1	6.1	7.7	131	131	(4)	(4)	9	11	45.9	51.6	6	13	3.1	6.1
Colored	5,242	5,242	118	137	36	48	22.5	26.1	6.9	9.2	82	89	(4)	(4)	7	9	59.3	65.7	5	9	4.2	6.6
White	5,375	5,375	78	76	29	34	14.5	14.1	5.4	6.3	49	42	(4)	(4)	2	2	25.6	26.3	1	4	1.3	5.3
Telfair	[5] 14,997	[5] 14,997	427	391	154	167	28.5	26.1	10.3	11.1	273	224	277	234	25	28	58.5	71.6	27	20	6.3	5.1
Colored	4,859	4,859	169	131	66	61	34.8	27.0	13.6	12.6	103	70	(4)	(4)	14	9	82.8	68.7	13	15	7.7	11.5
White	10,138	10,138	258	260	88	106	25.4	25.6	8.7	10.5	170	154	(4)	245	11	19	42.6	73.1	14	5	5.4	1.9
Terrell	[5] 18,290	[5] 18,290	376	450	206	242	20.6	24.6	11.3	13.2	170	208	183	186	34	41	90.4	91.1	27	28	7.2	6.2
Colored	12,982	12,982	311	373	166	189	24.0	28.7	12.8	14.6	145	184	187	197	32	35	102.9	93.8	26	28	8.4	7.5
White	5,308	5,308	65	77	40	53	12.2	14.5	7.5	10.0	25	24	(4)	(4)	2	6	30.8	77.9	1	------	1.5	------
Thomas	[9] 20,512	[5] 20,812	433	412	179	225	21.1	19.8	8.7	10.8	254	187	242	183	29	37	67.0	89.8	30	56	6.9	13.6
Colored	9,656	9,756	245	275	106	118	25.4	28.2	11.0	12.1	139	157	231	233	21	26	85.7	94.5	19	38	7.8	13.8
White	10,856	11,056	188	137	73	107	17.3	12.4	6.7	9.7	115	30	(4)	138	8	11	42.6	80.3	11	18	5.9	13.1
Tift	16,300	16,100	282	289	189	202	17.3	18.0	11.6	12.5	93	87	149	143	26	38	92.2	131.5	32	25	11.3	8.7
Colored	5,000	4,900	105	98	85	105	21.0	20.0	17.0	21.4	20	−7	(4)	93	11	26	104.8	265.3	14	17	13.3	17.3
White	11,300	11,200	177	191	104	97	15.7	17.1	9.2	8.7	73	94	170	(4)	15	12	84.7	62.8	18	8	10.2	4.2
Toombs	17,600	17,200	353	373	126	139	20.1	21.7	7.2	8.1	227	234	280	268	18	23	51.0	61.7	20	23	5.7	6.2
Colored	5,100	4,900	118	119	47	53	23.1	24.3	9.2	10.8	71	66	(4)	(4)	4	12	33.9	100.8	12	12	10.2	10.1
White	12,500	12,300	235	254	79	86	18.8	20.7	6.3	7.0	156	168	(4)	(4)	14	11	59.6	43.3	8	11	3.4	4.3
Treutlen	[5] 7,488	[5] 7,488	175	190	64	69	23.4	25.4	8.5	9.2	111	121	(4)	(4)	14	15	80.0	78.9	13	13	7.4	6.8
Colored	2,473	2,473	67	58	29	25	27.1	23.5	11.7	10.1	38	33	(4)	(4)	8	7	119.4	120.7	6	4	9.0	6.9
White	5,015	5,015	108	132	35	44	21.5	26.3	7.0	8.8	73	88	(4)	(4)	6	8	55.6	60.6	7	9	6.5	6.8
Troup	16,300	16,600	272	277	182	197	16.7	16.7	11.2	11.9	90	80	149	141	25	27	91.9	97.5	28	25	10.3	9.0
Colored	9,200	9,600	178	188	115	133	19.3	19.6	12.5	13.9	63	55	155	141	16	19	89.9	101.1	16	19	9.0	10.1
White	7,100	7,000	94	89	67	64	13.2	12.7	9.4	9.1	27	25	(4)	(4)	9	8	95.7	89.9	12	6	12.8	6.7
Turner	[5] 11,196	[5] 11,196	287	291	97	102	25.6	26.0	8.7	9.1	190	189	(4)	285	18	19	62.7	65.3	20	17	7.0	5.8
Colored	3,866	3,866	107	103	53	53	27.7	26.6	13.7	13.7	54	50	(4)	(4)	10	10	93.5	97.1	10	11	9.3	10.7
White	7,330	7,330	180	188	44	49	24.6	25.6	6.0	6.7	136	139	(4)	(4)	8	9	44.4	47.9	10	6	5.6	3.2
Twiggs	[5] 8,372	[5] 8,372	222	204	84	94	26.5	24.4	10.0	11.2	138	110	(4)	(4)	13	13	58.6	63.7	13	14	5.9	6.9
Colored	5,335	5,335	164	165	52	64	30.7	30.9	9.7	12.0	112	101	(4)	(4)	10	12	61.0	72.7	11	12	6.7	7.3
White	3,037	3,037	58	39	32	30	19.1	12.8	10.5	9.9	26	9	(4)	(4)	3	1	51.7	25.6	2	2	3.4	5.1
Upson	20,100	19,600	444	417	201	219	22.1	21.3	10.0	11.2	243	198	221	190	26	34	58.6	81.5	23	25	5.2	6.0
Colored	6,900	6,900	128	163	94	98	18.6	23.6	13.6	14.2	34	65	(4)	(4)	8	14	62.5	85.9	16	13	12.5	8.0
White	13,200	12,700	316	254	107	121	23.9	20.0	8.1	9.5	209	133	295	210	18	20	57.0	78.7	7	12	2.2	4.7
Walton	[5] 21,118	[5] 21,118	471	495	219	237	22.3	23.4	10.4	11.2	252	258	215	209	34	39	72.2	78.8	27	24	5.7	4.8
Colored	6,767	6,767	159	185	90	106	23.5	27.3	13.3	15.7	69	79	(4)	175	10	12	62.9	64.9	14	16	8.8	8.6
White	14,351	14,351	312	310	129	131	21.7	21.6	9.0	9.1	183	179	242	237	24	27	76.9	87.1	13	8	4.2	2.6
Ware	[5] 11,048	[5] 11,048	227	232	58	95	20.5	20.8	5.2	8.6	169	137	(4)	(4)	8	11	35.2	47.4	12	12	5.3	5.2
Colored	2,260	2,260	40	50	15	28	17.7	20.7	6.6	12.4	25	22	(4)	(4)	1	2	25.0	40.0	7	3	17.5	6.0
White	8,788	8,788	187	182	43	67	21.3	20.8	4.9	7.6	144	115	(4)	(4)	7	9	37.4	49.5	5	9	2.7	4.9
Warren	[5] 11,181	[5] 11,181	248	255	117	113	22.2	22.8	10.5	10.1	131	142	212	226	11	15	44.4	58.8	24	18	9.7	7.1
Colored	7,351	7,351	181	185	72	77	24.6	25.2	9.8	10.5	109	108	(4)	(4)	7	14	38.7	75.7	13	16	7.2	8.6
White	3,830	3,830	67	70	45	36	17.5	18.3	11.7	9.4	22	34	(4)	(4)	4	1	59.7	14.3	11	2	16.4	2.9
Washington	[5] 25,030	[5] 25,030	463	462	253	290	18.5	18.5	10.1	11.6	210	172	183	159	18	41	38.9	88.7	25	35	5.4	7.6
Colored	14,132	14,132	302	306	160	167	21.4	21.7	11.3	11.8	142	139	189	183	12	27	39.7	88.2	19	23	6.3	7.5
White	10,898	10,898	161	156	93	123	14.8	14.3	8.5	11.3	68	33	(4)	127	6	14	37.3	89.7	6	12	3.7	7.7
Wayne	12,800	12,700	336	313	149	148	26.3	24.6	11.6	11.7	187	165	226	211	29	30	86.3	95.8	23	20	6.8	6.4
Colored	3,000	3,000	59	80	51	60	19.7	26.7	17.0	20.0	8	20	(4)	(4)	9	11	152.5	137.5	7	6	11.9	7.5
White	9,800	9,700	277	233	98	88	28.3	24.0	10.0	9.1	179	145	(4)	(4)	20	19	72.2	81.5	16	14	5.8	6.0
Webster	[5] 5,032	[5] 5,032	114	100	53	68	22.7	19.9	10.5	13.5	61	32	(4)	(4)	11	17	96.5	170.0	6	7	5.3	7.0
Colored	3,038	3,038	76	71	34	44	25.0	23.4	11.2	14.5	42	27	(4)	(4)	10	11	131.6	154.9	6	5	7.9	7.0
White	1,994	1,994	38	29	19	24	19.1	14.5	9.5	12.0	19	5	(4)	(4)	1	6	26.3	206.9	------	2	------	6.9
Wheeler	[5] 9,149	[5] 9,149	200	188	59	87	21.9	20.5	6.4	9.5	141	101	(4)	(4)	16	16	80.0	85.1	14	10	7.0	5.3
Colored	2,938	2,938	66	74	21	34	22.5	25.2	7.1	11.6	45	40	(4)	(4)	4	6	60.6	81.1	10	9	15.2	12.2
White	6,211	6,211	134	114	38	53	21.6	18.4	6.1	8.5	96	61	(4)	(4)	12	10	89.6	87.7	4	1	3.0	0.9
Wilcox	[5] 13,439	[5] 13,439	276	260	83	106	20.5	19.3	6.2	7.9	193	154	(4)	245	13	26	47.1	100.0	12	18	4.3	6.9
Colored	5,473	5,473	142	132	46	61	25.9	24.1	8.4	11.1	96	71	(4)	(4)	7	18	49.3	136.4	6	9	4.2	6.8
White	7,966	7,966	134	128	37	45	16.8	16.1	4.6	5.6	97	83	(4)	(4)	6	8	44.8	62.5	6	9	4.5	7.0
Wilkes	[5] 15,944	[5] 15,944	277	240	171	176	17.4	15.1	10.7	11.0	106	64	162	136	8	10	28.9	41.7	11	18	4.0	7.5
Colored	10,088	10,088	174	171	119	114	17.2	17.0	11.8	11.3	55	57	146	150	7	4	40.2	23.4	5	14	2.9	8.2
White	5,856	5,856	103	69	52	62	17.6	11.8	8.9	10.6	51	7	(4)	(4)	1	6	9.7	87.0	6	4	5.8	5.8
Wilkinson	[5] 10,844	[5] 10,844	216	214	115	141	19.9	19.7	10.6	13.0	101	73	188	152	26	27	120.4	126.2	7	15	3.2	7.0
Colored	5,114	5,114	116	120	66	82	22.7	23.5	12.9	16.0	50	38	(4)	(4)	16	16	137.9	133.3	6	14	5.2	11.7
White	5,730	5,730	100	94	49	59	17.5	16.4	8.6	10.3	51	35	(4)	(4)	10	11	100.0	117.0	1	1	1.0	1.1
Worth	[5] 21,094	[5] 21,094	569	527	243	237	27.0	25.0	11.5	11.2	326	290	234	222	45	47	79.1	89.2	34	28	6.0	5.3
Colored	9,575	9,575	267	242	139	146	27.9	25.3	14.5	15.2	128	96	192	166	29	32	108.6	132.2	23	20	8.6	8.3
White	11,519	11,519	302	285	104	91	26.2	24.7	9.0	7.9	198	194	290	(4)	16	15	53.0	52.6	11	8	3.6	2.8
ILLINOIS COUNTIES [8]																						
Alexander	[5] 9,010	[5] 9,010	174	189	113	104	19.3	21.0	12.5	11.5	61	85	154	182	27	11	155.2	58.2	9	10	5.2	5.3
Colored	2,044	2,044	14	20	44	27	6.8	9.8	21.5	13.2	−30	−7	(4)	(4)	12	1	857.1	50.0	3	4	21.4	20.0
White	6,966	6,966	160	169	69	77	23.0	24.3	9.9	11.1	91	92	(4)	(4)	15	10	93.8	59.2	6	6	3.8	3.6
Massac	14,100	14,100	163	210	166	198	11.6	14.9	11.8	14.0	−3	12	98	106	22	35	135.0	166.7	7	10	4.3	4.8
Colored	1,600	1,700	10	17	38	34	6.3	10.0	23.8	20.0	−28	−17	(4)	(4)	4	7	400.0	411.8	1	------	10.0	------
White	12,500	12,400	153	193	128	164	12.2	15.6	10.2	13.2	25	29	120	118	28	28	117.6	145.1	6	10	3.9	5.2

See footnotes at end of table.

TABLE 18.—COLORED [1] AND WHITE POPULATION, BIRTHS AND DEATHS, INFANT MORTALITY, AND STILLBIRTHS, IN SELECTED REGISTRATION STATES, CITIES, AND COUNTIES: 1931 AND 1930—Continued

[See note at head of this table]

AREA AND COLOR	POPULATION ESTIMATED AS OF JULY 1		BIRTHS AND DEATHS (Exclusive of stillbirths): Number, Births		Number, Deaths		Rate per 1,000 population, Births		Rate per 1,000 population, Deaths		Excess of births over deaths [2]		Births per 100 deaths		INFANT MORTALITY (Exclusive of stillbirths): Deaths of infants under 1 year of age, Number		Per 1,000 births		STILLBIRTHS: Number		Rate per 100 live births	
	1931	1930	1931	1930	1931	1930	1931	1930	1931	1930	1931	1930	1931	1930	1931	1930	1931	1930	1931	1930	1931	1930
ILLINOIS COUNTIES—continued																						
Pulaski	14,900	14,800	232	227	205	174	15.6	15.3	13.8	11.8	27	53	113	130	25	24	107.8	105.7	13	12	5.6	5.3
Colored	5,000	4,900	59	44	104	79	11.8	9.0	20.8	16.1	−45	−35	57	(4)	14	5	237.3	113.6	5	3	8.5	6.8
White	9,900	9,900	173	183	101	95	17.5	18.5	10.2	9.6	72	88	171	(4)	11	19	63.6	103.8	8	9	4.6	4.9
KANSAS COUNTIES [5]																						
Wyandotte	20,600	19,600	193	228	143	152	9.4	11.6	6.9	7.8	50	7.6	135	150	6	15	31.1	65.8	7	9	3.6	3.9
Colored	2,100	2,100	13	8	34	24	6.2	3.8	16.2	11.4	−21	−16	(4)	(4)	1	3	76.9	375.0	1	2	7.7	25.0
White	18,500	17,500	180	220	109	128	9.7	12.6	5.9	7.3	71	92	165	172	5	12	27.8	54.5	6	7	3.3	3.2
KENTUCKY COUNTIES [5]																						
Barren	25,900	25,900	714	601	301	335	27.6	23.2	11.6	12.9	413	266	237	179	39	46	54.6	76.5	27	15	3.8	2.5
Colored	2,700	2,800	62	54	37	56	23.0	19.3	13.7	20.0	25	−2	(4)	(4)	6	9	96.8	166.7	4	2	6.5	3.7
White	23,200	23,100	652	547	264	279	28.1	23.7	11.4	12.1	388	268	247	196	33	37	50.6	67.6	23	13	3.5	2.4
Bourbon	[5] 18,060	[5] 18,060	328	372	275	319	18.2	20.6	15.2	17.7	53	53	119	117	32	31	97.6	83.3	11	20	3.4	5.4
Colored	4,007	4,007	45	55	107	102	11.2	13.7	26.7	25.5	−62	−47	42	54	8	10	177.8	181.8	3	4	6.7	7.3
White	14,053	14,053	283	317	168	217	20.1	22.6	12.0	15.4	115	100	168	146	24	21	84.8	66.2	8	16	2.8	5.0
Boyle	16,400	16,300	304	334	231	269	18.5	20.5	14.1	16.5	73	65	132	124	30	32	98.7	95.8	6	8	2.0	2.4
Colored	3,100	3,200	34	31	61	80	11.0	9.7	19.7	25.0	−27	−49	(4)	(4)	8	4	235.3	129.0	1	1	2.9	3.2
White	13,300	13,100	270	303	170	189	20.3	23.1	12.8	14.4	100	114	159	160	22	28	81.5	92.4	5	7	1.9	2.3
Caldwell	[5] 13,781	[5] 13,781	248	275	169	157	18.0	20.0	12.3	11.4	79	118	14.7	175	19	22	76.6	80.0	45	31	18.1	11.3
Colored	1,722	1,722	16	17	35	30	9.3	9.9	20.3	17.4	−19	−13	(4)	(4)		2		117.6	7	4	43.8	23.5
White	12,059	12,059	232	258	134	127	19.2	21.4	11.1	10.5	98	131	173	203	19	20	81.9	77.5	38	27	16.4	10.5
Christian	[5] 23,383	[5] 23,483	396	372	482	542	16.9	15.8	20.6	23.1	−86	−170	82	69	25	32	63.1	86.0	30	25	7.6	6.7
Colored	7,704	7,704	103	100	147	175	13.4	18.2	19.1	22.7	−44	−35	70	80	8	16	77.7	114.3	16	10	15.5	7.1
White	15,679	15,779	293	232	335	367	18.7	14.7	21.4	23.3	−42	−135	87	63	17	16	58.0	69.0	14	15	4.8	6.5
Clark	[5] 17,640	[5] 17,640	393	338	295	242	22.3	19.2	16.6	13.7	100	96	134	140	30	24	76.3	71.0	15	20	3.8	5.9
Colored	2,842	2,842	28	27	84	65	9.9	9.5	29.6	22.9	−56	−38	(4)	(4)	9	8	321.4	296.3	4	3	14.3	11.1
White	14,798	14,798	365	311	209	177	24.7	21.0	14.1	12.0	156	134	175	176	21	16	57.5	51.4	11	17	3.0	5.5
Fayette	24,200	23,100	187	225	207	176	7.7	9.7	8.6	7.6	−20	49	90	128	24	20	128.3	88.9	12	4	6.4	1.8
Colored	3,800	3,700	29	36	67	53	7.6	9.7	17.6	14.3	−38	−17	(4)	(4)	6	4	206.9	111.1	2	2	6.9	5.6
White	20,400	19,400	158	189	140	123	7.7	9.7	6.9	6.3	18	66	113	154	18	16	113.9	84.7	10	2	6.3	1.1
Fulton	[5] 14,927	[5] 14,927	258	261	176	208	17.3	17.5	11.8	13.9	82	53	147	125	20	25	77.5	95.8	20	14	7.8	5.4
Colored	3,154	3,154	24	37	57	71	7.6	11.7	18.1	22.5	−33	−34	(4)	(4)	6	10	250.0	270.3	7	6	29.2	16.2
White	11,773	11,773	234	224	119	137	19.9	19.0	10.1	11.6	115	87	197	164	14	15	59.8	67.0	13	8	5.6	3.6
Garrard	[5] 11,562	[5] 11,562	252	281	104	147	21.8	24.3	9.0	12.7	148	134	242	191	10	19	39.7	67.6	8	10	3.2	3.6
Colored	1,464	1,464	29	30	18	42	19.8	20.5	12.3	28.7	11	−12	(4)	(4)	4	5	137.9	166.7	2	5	6.9	16.7
White	10,098	10,098	223	251	86	105	22.1	24.9	8.5	10.4	137	146	(4)	239	6	14	26.9	55.8	6	5	2.7	2.0
Henderson	[5] 14,627	[5] 14,627	327	322	163	136	22.4	22.0	11.1	9.3	164	186	201	237	25	29	76.5	90.1	12	12	3.7	3.7
Colored	2,052	2,052	30	43	21	36	14.6	21.0	10.2	17.5	9	7	(4)	(4)	2	6	66.7	139.5	2	1	6.7	2.3
White	12,575	12,575	297	279	142	100	23.6	22.2	11.3	8.0	155	179	209	279	23	23	77.4	82.4	10	11	3.4	3.9
Hickman	[5] 8,725	[5] 8,725	179	166	110	109	20.5	19.0	12.6	12.5	69	57	163	152	17	18	95.0	108.4	8	6	4.5	3.6
Colored	1,048	1,048	15	9	18	22	14.3	8.6	17.2	21.0	−3	−13	(4)	(4)	3	8	200.0	888.9				
White	7,677	7,677	164	157	92	87	21.4	20.5	12.0	11.3	72	70	(4)	(4)	14	10	85.4	63.7	8	6	4.9	3.8
Hopkins	37,900	37,500	756	795	430	408	19.9	21.2	11.3	10.9	326	387	176	195	61	59	80.7	74.2	40	41	5.3	5.2
Colored	5,200	5,200	63	81	101	82	12.1	15.6	19.4	15.8	−38	−1	62	(4)	8	7	127.0	86.4	9	25	14.3	30.9
White	32,700	32,300	693	714	329	326	21.2	22.1	10.1	10.1	364	388	211	219	53	52	76.5	72.8	31	16	4.5	2.2
Jessamine	12,500	12,400	236	254	139	131	18.9	20.5	11.1	10.6	97	123	170	194	12	16	50.8	63.0	6	9	2.5	3.5
Colored	2,000	1,900	20	22	28	42	10.0	11.6	14.0	22.1	−8	−20	(4)	(4)	3	3	150.0	136.4		2		9.1
White	10,500	10,500	216	232	111	89	20.6	22.1	10.6	8.5	105	143	195	(4)	9	13	41.7	56.0	6	7	2.8	3.0
Logan	[5] 21,875	[5] 21,875	516	492	254	256	23.6	22.5	11.6	11.7	262	236	203	192	37	31	71.7	63.0	22	18	4.3	3.7
Colored	3,486	3,486	61	64	63	57	17.5	18.4	18.1	16.4	−2	7	(4)	(4)	10	4	163.9	62.5	5	1	8.2	1.6
White	18,389	18,389	455	428	191	199	24.7	23.3	10.4	10.8	264	229	238	215	27	27	59.3	63.1	17	17	3.7	4.0
Lyon	[5] 8,530	[5] 8,530	91	96	72	68	10.7	11.3	8.4	8.0	19	28	(4)	(4)	4	5	44.0	52.1	3	1	3.3	1.0
Colored	1,200	1,200	2	4	24	19	1.7	3.3	20.0	15.8	−22	−15	(4)	(4)	1	1	500.0	250.0		1		25.0
White	7,330	7,330	89	92	48	49	12.1	12.6	6.5	6.7	41	43	(4)	(4)	3	4	33.7	43.5	3		3.4	
Madison	27,800	27,700	554	607	302	307	19.9	21.9	10.9	11.1	252	300	183	198	42	31	75.8	51.1	18	21	3.2	3.5
Colored	4,300	4,400	59	50	83	78	13.7	11.4	19.3	17.7	−24	−28	(4)	(4)	14	8	237.3	160.0	5	2	8.5	4.0
White	23,500	23,300	495	557	219	229	21.1	23.9	9.3	9.8	276	328	226	243	28	23	56.6	41.3	13	19	2.6	3.4
Mason	19,000	18,900	392	397	289	267	20.6	21.0	15.2	14.1	103	130	136	149	27	30	68.9	75.6	27	25	6.9	6.3
Colored	2,500	2,500	43	51	57	49	17.2	20.4	22.8	19.6	−14	2	(4)	(4)	4	9	93.0	176.5	7	4	16.3	7.8
White	16,500	16,400	349	346	232	218	21.2	21.1	14.1	13.3	117	128	150	159	23	21	65.9	60.7	20	21	5.7	6.1

Mercer	[5] 14,471	[5] 14,471	284	258	168	188	19.6	17.8	11.6	13.0	116	70	169	137	25	20	88.0	77.5	12	12	4.2	4.7
Colored	1,550	1,550	25	27	24	36	16.1	17.4	15.5	23.2	1	−9	(4)	(4)	6	5	240.0	185.2	1	2	4.0	7.4
White	12,921	12,921	259	231	144	152	20.0	17.9	11.1	11.8	115	79	180	152	19	15	73.4	64.9	11	10	4.2	4.3
Montgomery	[5] 11,660	[5] 11,660	277	284	134	177	23.8	24.4	11.5	15.2	143	107	207	160	23	21	83.0	73.9	19	4	6.9	1.4
Colored	1,968	1,968	17	27	31	42	8.6	13.7	15.8	21.3	−14	−15	(4)	(4)	1	5	58.8	185.2	5	1	29.4	3.7
White	9,692	9,692	260	257	103	135	26.8	26.5	10.6	13.9	157	122	252	190	22	16	84.6	62.3	14	3	5.4	1.2
Nelson	16,600	16,600	406	378	155	169	24.5	22.8	9.3	10.2	251	209	262	224	19	14	46.8	37.0	11	7	2.7	1.9
Colored	2,000	2,100	39	28	26	41	19.5	13.3	13.0	19.5	13	−13	(4)	(4)	5	4	128.2	142.9	1	1	2.6	3.6
White	14,600	14,500	367	350	129	128	25.1	24.1	8.8	8.8	238	222	284	273	14	10	38.1	28.6	10	6	2.7	1.7
Scott	[5] 14,400	[5] 14,400	247	295	183	226	17.2	20.5	12.7	15.7	64	69	135	131	17	22	68.8	74.6	20	13	8.1	4.4
Colored	2,511	2,511	35	44	49	64	13.9	17.5	19.5	25.5	−14	−20	(4)	(4)	4	6	114.3	136.4	3	1	8.6	2.3
White	11,889	11,889	212	251	134	162	17.8	21.1	11.3	13.6	78	89	158	155	13	16	61.3	63.7	17	12	8.0	4.8
Shelby	[5] 17,679	[5] 17,679	272	301	225	194	15.4	17.0	12.7	11.0	47	107	121	155	13	14	47.8	46.5	8	17	2.9	5.6
Colored	2,637	2,637	12	15	50	41	4.6	5.7	19.0	15.5	−38	−26	(4)	(4)	3	2	250.0	133.3	1	----	8.3	----
White	15,042	15,042	260	286	175	153	17.3	19.0	11.6	10.2	85	133	149	187	10	12	38.5	42.0	7	17	2.7	5.9
Simpson	11,400	11,300	172	185	153	154	15.1	16.4	13.4	13.6	19	31	112	120	13	20	75.6	108.1	2	5	1.2	2.7
Colored	1,800	1,700	17	24	33	31	9.4	14.1	18.3	18.2	−16	−7	(4)	(4)	2	2	117.6	83.3	----	1	----	4.2
White	9,600	9,600	155	161	120	123	16.1	16.8	12.5	12.8	35	38	129	131	11	18	71.0	111.8	2	4	1.3	2.5
Todd	[5] 13,520	[5] 13,520	281	288	169	185	20.8	21.3	12.5	13.7	112	103	166	156	19	28	67.6	97.2	11	7	3.9	2.4
Colored	3,393	3,393	68	53	61	69	20.0	15.6	18.0	20.3	7	−16	(4)	(4)	10	10	147.1	188.7	4	2	5.9	3.8
White	10,127	10,127	213	235	108	116	21.0	23.2	10.7	11.5	105	119	197	203	9	18	42.3	76.6	7	5	3.3	2.1
Trigg	[5] 12,531	[5] 12,531	271	238	137	128	21.6	19.0	10.9	10.2	134	110	198	186	27	18	99.6	75.6	7	6	2.6	2.5
Colored	2,373	2,373	38	51	33	44	16.0	21.5	13.9	18.5	5	7	(4)	(4)	6	7	157.9	137.3	1	2	2.6	3.9
White	10,158	10,158	233	187	104	84	22.9	18.4	10.2	8.3	129	103	224	(4)	21	11	90.1	58.8	6	4	2.6	2.1
Union	[5] 17,053	[5] 17,053	425	384	196	192	24.9	22.5	11.5	11.3	229	192	217	200	38	32	89.4	83.3	12	11	2.8	2.9
Colored	2,026	2,026	29	40	38	26	14.3	19.7	18.8	12.8	−9	14	(4)	(4)	3	2	103.4	50.0	5	3	17.2	7.5
White	15,027	15,027	396	344	158	166	26.4	22.9	10.5	11.0	238	178	251	207	35	30	88.4	87.2	7	8	1.8	2.3
Warren	21,300	21,300	423	384	250	250	19.9	18.0	11.7	11.7	173	134	169	154	29	38	68.6	99.0	10	12	2.4	3.1
Colored	2,600	2,600	60	62	40	55	23.1	23.8	15.4	21.2	20	7	(4)	(4)	4	5	66.7	80.6	4	2	6.7	3.2
White	18,700	18,700	363	322	210	195	19.4	17.2	11.2	10.4	153	127	173	165	25	33	68.9	102.5	6	10	1.7	3.1
Washington	[5] 12,623	[5] 12,623	277	314	121	114	21.9	24.9	9.6	9.0	156	200	229	275	19	17	68.6	54.1	10	7	3.6	2.2
Colored	1,362	1,362	20	36	16	18	14.7	26.4	11.7	13.2	4	18	(4)	(4)	3	3	150.0	83.3	1	1	5.0	2.8
White	11,261	11,261	257	278	105	96	22.8	24.7	9.3	8.5	152	182	245	(4)	16	14	62.3	50.4	9	6	3.5	2.2
Webster	[5] 20,534	[5] 20,534	372	382	236	250	18.1	18.6	11.5	12.2	136	132	158	153	18	37	48.4	96.9	11	11	3.0	2.9
Colored	3,104	3,104	38	35	41	51	12.2	11.3	13.2	16.4	−3	−16	(4)	(4)	2	7	52.6	200.0	3	2	7.9	5.7
White	17,430	17,430	334	347	195	199	19.2	19.9	11.2	11.4	139	148	171	174	16	30	47.9	86.5	8	9	2.4	2.6
Woodford	[5] 10,981	[5] 10,981	224	279	124	145	20.4	25.4	11.3	13.2	100	134	181	192	19	25	84.8	89.6	11	14	4.9	5.0
Colored	2,207	2,207	30	31	48	59	13.6	14.0	21.7	26.7	−18	−28	(4)	(4)	6	8	200.0	258.1	1	1	3.3	3.2
White	8,774	8,774	194	248	76	86	22.1	28.3	8.7	9.8	118	162	(4)	(4)	13	17	67.0	68.5	10	13	5.2	5.2
LOUISIANA PARISHES [8]																						
Acadia	39,900	39,400	1,026	956	330	344	25.7	24.3	8.3	8.7	696	612	311	278	86	81	83.8	84.7	48	37	4.7	3.9
Colored	8,200	8,100	215	217	122	118	26.2	26.8	14.9	14.6	93	99	176	184	32	30	148.8	138.2	14	15	6.5	6.9
White	31,700	31,300	811	739	208	226	25.6	23.6	6.6	7.2	603	513	390	327	54	51	66.6	69.0	34	22	4.2	3.0
Allen	[5] 15,261	[5] 15,261	379	321	148	106	24.8	21.0	9.7	6.9	231	215	256	303	14	15	36.9	46.7	15	27	4.0	8.4
Colored	4,233	4,233	95	83	52	37	22.4	19.6	12.3	8.7	43	46	(4)	(4)	3	3	31.6	36.1	8	13	8.4	15.7
White	11,028	11,028	284	238	96	69	25.8	21.6	8.7	6.3	188	169	(4)	(4)	11	12	38.7	50.4	7	14	2.5	5.9
Ascension	[5] 18,438	[5] 18,438	380	321	180	215	20.6	17.4	9.8	11.7	200	106	211	149	21	43	55.3	134.0	19	18	5.0	5.6
Colored	7,086	7,086	160	131	114	140	22.6	18.5	16.1	19.8	46	−9	140	94	14	25	87.5	190.8	16	12	10.0	9.2
White	11,352	11,352	220	190	66	75	19.4	16.7	5.8	6.6	154	115	(4)	(4)	7	18	31.8	94.7	3	6	1.4	3.2
Assumption	[5] 15,990	[5] 15,990	403	412	198	182	25.2	25.8	12.4	11.4	205	230	204	226	36	42	89.3	101.9	24	15	6.0	3.6
Colored	6,319	6,319	188	173	116	102	29.8	27.4	18.4	16.1	72	71	162	170	25	26	133.0	150.3	15	10	8.0	5.8
White	9,671	9,671	215	239	82	80	22.2	24.7	8.5	8.3	133	159	(4)	(4)	11	16	51.2	66.9	9	5	4.2	2.1
Avoyelles	[5] 34,926	[5] 34,926	726	628	237	229	20.8	18.0	6.8	6.6	489	399	306	274	27	23	37.2	36.6	36	27	5.0	4.3
Colored	9,916	9,916	268	209	121	102	27.0	21.1	12.2	10.3	147	107	221	205	13	13	48.5	62.2	10	13	3.7	6.2
White	25,010	25,010	458	419	116	127	18.3	16.8	4.6	5.1	342	292	395	330	14	10	30.6	23.9	26	14	5.7	3.3
Beauregard	[5] 14,569	[5] 14,569	272	241	90	88	18.7	16.5	6.2	6.0	182	153	(4)	(4)	9	8	33.1	33.2	13	7	4.8	2.9
Colored	3,253	3,253	47	44	27	34	14.4	13.5	8.3	10.5	20	10	(4)	(4)	2	3	42.6	68.2	1	1	2.1	2.3
White	11,316	11,316	225	197	63	54	19.9	17.4	5.6	4.8	162	143	(4)	(4)	7	5	31.1	25.4	12	6	5.3	3.0
Bienville	24,100	23,900	355	316	161	175	14.7	13.2	6.7	7.3	194	141	220	181	17	20	47.9	63.3	13	17	3.7	5.4
Colored	10,800	10,700	171	119	74	85	15.8	11.1	6.9	7.9	97	34	(4)	(4)	3	6	17.5	50.4	10	5	5.8	4.2
White	13,300	13,200	184	197	87	90	13.8	14.9	6.5	6.8	97	107	(4)	(4)	14	14	76.1	71.1	3	12	1.6	6.1
Bossier	29,100	28,500	246	274	168	188	8.5	9.6	5.8	6.6	78	86	146	146	15	16	61.0	58.4	7	19	2.8	6.9
Colored	18,100	17,900	110	125	111	133	6.1	7.0	6.1	7.4	−1	−8	99	94	7	8	63.6	64.0	3	14	2.7	11.2
White	11,000	10,600	136	149	57	55	12.4	14.1	5.2	5.2	79	94	(4)	(4)	8	8	58.8	53.7	4	5	2.9	3.4
Caddo	51,900	48,800	819	837	396	460	15.8	17.2	7.6	9.4	423	377	207	182	59	63	72.0	75.3	38	65	4.6	7.8
Colored	33,000	30,600	567	578	275	363	17.2	18.9	8.3	11.9	292	215	206	159	47	49	82.9	84.8	31	42	5.5	7.3
White	18,900	18,200	252	259	121	97	13.3	14.2	6.4	5.3	131	162	208	(4)	12	14	47.6	54.1	7	23	2.8	8.9
Calcasieu	27,000	26,300	546	589	182	170	20.2	22.4	6.7	6.5	364	419	300	346	36	34	65.9	57.7	19	29	3.5	4.9
Colored	6,500	6,200	118	122	68	58	18.2	19.7	10.5	9.4	50	64	(4)	(4)	15	13	127.1	106.6	7	26	5.9	21.3
White	20,500	20,100	428	467	114	112	20.9	23.2	5.6	5.6	314	355	375	417	21	21	49.1	45.0	12	3	2.8	0.6
Caldwell	10,500	10,500	239	253	71	91	22.8	24.1	6.8	8.7	168	162	(4)	(4)	4	7	16.7	27.7	11	12	4.6	4.7
Colored	2,900	3,000	81	70	27	31	27.9	23.3	9.3	10.3	54	39	(4)	(4)	2	3	24.7	42.9	4	4	4.9	5.7
White	7,600	7,500	158	183	44	60	20.8	24.4	5.8	8.0	114	123	(4)	(4)	2	4	12.7	21.9	7	8	4.4	4.4
Catahoula	12,600	12,500	294	245	102	77	23.3	19.6	8.1	6.2	192	168	288	(4)	11	11	37.4	44.9	16	16	5.4	6.5
Colored	4,600	4,700	106	75	51	29	23.0	16.0	11.1	6.2	55	46	(4)	(4)	3	4	28.3	53.3	11	9	10.4	12.0
White	8,000	7,800	188	170	51	48	23.5	21.8	6.4	6.2	137	122	(4)	(4)	8	7	42.6	41.2	5	7	2.7	4.1
Claiborne	32,800	32,400	501	549	181	251	15.3	16.9	5.5	7.7	320	298	277	219	19	36	37.9	65.6	27	16	5.4	2.9
Colored	18,400	18,100	333	284	108	152	18.1	15.7	5.9	8.4	225	132	308	187	11	24	33.0	84.5	15	10	4.5	3.5
White	14,400	14,300	168	265	73	99	11.7	18.5	5.1	6.9	95	166	(4)	(4)	8	12	47.6	45.3	12	6	7.1	2.3
Concordia	12,800	12,800	233	242	121	137	18.2	18.9	9.5	10.7	112	105	193	177	8	13	34.3	53.7	21	12	9.0	5.0
Colored	9,100	9,200	177	183	101	113	19.5	19.9	11.1	12.3	76	70	175	162	5	12	28.2	65.6	18	12	10.2	6.6
White	3,700	3,600	56	59	20	24	15.1	16.4	5.4	6.7	36	35	(4)	(4)	3	1	53.6	16.9	3	----	5.4	----

See footnotes at end of table.

TABLE 18.—COLORED[1] AND WHITE POPULATION, BIRTHS AND DEATHS, INFANT MORTALITY, AND STILLBIRTHS, IN SELECTED REGISTRATION STATES, CITIES, AND COUNTIES: 1931 AND 1930—Continued

[See note at head of this table]

AREA AND COLOR	Population estimated as of July 1: 1931	Population estimated as of July 1: 1930	Births and deaths (Exclusive of stillbirths): Number: Births 1931	Number: Births 1930	Number: Deaths 1931	Number: Deaths 1930	Rate per 1,000 population: Births 1931	Births 1930	Deaths 1931	Deaths 1930	Excess of births over deaths[2] 1931	Excess 1930	Births per 100 deaths 1931	Births per 100 deaths 1930	Infant mortality (Exclusive of stillbirths): Deaths of infants under 1 year of age: Number 1931	Number 1930	Per 1,000 births 1931	Per 1,000 births 1930	Stillbirths: Number 1931	Number 1930	Rate per 100 live births 1931	Rate per 100 live births 1930
LOUISIANA PARISHES—continued																						
De Soto	31,200	31,100	696	706	256	291	22.3	22.7	8.2	9.4	440	415	272	243	33	51	47.4	72.2	46	54	6.6	7.6
Colored	19,400	19,300	477	483	159	194	24.6	25.0	8.2	10.1	318	289	300	249	26	38	54.5	78.7	36	45	7.5	9.3
White	11,800	11,800	219	223	97	97	18.6	18.9	8.2	8.2	122	126	(4)	(4)	7	13	32.0	58.3	10	9	4.6	4.0
East Baton Rouge	39,500	37,900	850	877	529	507	21.5	23.1	13.4	13.4	321	370	161	173	55	73	64.7	83.2	50	73	5.9	8.3
Colored	19,300	18,900	340	360	308	306	17.6	19.0	16.0	16.2	32	54	110	118	33	45	97.1	125.0	31	37	9.1	10.3
White	20,200	19,000	510	517	221	201	25.2	27.2	10.9	10.6	289	316	231	257	22	28	43.1	54.2	19	36	3.7	7.0
East Carroll	16,400	15,900	279	241	149	173	17.0	15.2	9.1	10.9	130	68	187	139	13	14	46.6	58.1	19	14	6.8	5.8
Colored	12,100	11,900	197	170	127	141	16.3	14.3	10.5	11.8	70	29	155	121	12	12	60.9	70.6	16	11	8.1	6.5
White	4,300	4,000	82	71	22	32	19.1	17.8	5.1	8.0	60	39	(4)	(4)	1	2	12.2	28.2	3	3	3.7	4.2
East Feliciana	[5] 17,449	[5] 17,449	322	290	385	363	18.5	16.6	22.1	20.8	−63	−73	84	80	16	23	49.7	79.3	32	16	9.9	5.5
Colored	11,881	11,881	266	256	238	237	22.4	21.5	20.0	19.9	28	19	112	108	14	22	52.6	85.9	30	16	11.3	6.3
White	5,568	5,568	56	34	147	126	10.1	6.1	26.4	22.6	−91	−92	38	27	2	1	35.7	29.4	2	----	3.6	----
Evangeline	25,700	25,500	496	461	88	112	19.3	18.1	3.4	4.4	408	349	(4)	412	12	13	24.2	28.2	15	22	3.0	4.8
Colored	5,800	5,700	145	154	20	38	25.0	27.0	3.4	6.7	125	116	(4)	(4)	3	6	20.7	39.0	10	13	6.9	8.4
White	19,900	19,800	351	307	68	74	17.6	15.5	3.4	3.7	283	233	(4)	(4)	9	7	25.6	22.8	5	9	1.4	2.9
Franklin	31,300	30,700	722	732	235	303	23.1	23.8	7.5	9.9	487	429	307	242	21	47	29.1	64.2	37	47	5.1	6.4
Colored	11,400	11,400	268	279	116	169	23.5	24.5	10.2	14.8	152	110	231	165	5	26	18.7	93.2	19	19	7.1	6.8
White	19,900	19,300	454	453	119	134	22.8	23.5	6.0	6.9	335	319	382	338	16	21	35.2	46.4	18	28	4.0	6.2
Grant	15,900	15,700	301	229	121	117	18.9	14.6	7.6	7.5	180	112	249	196	18	13	59.8	56.8	12	5	4.0	2.2
Colored	5,100	4,900	91	77	44	47	17.8	15.7	8.6	9.6	47	30	(4)	(4)	9	7	98.9	90.9	7	2	7.7	2.6
White	10,800	10,800	210	152	77	70	19.4	14.1	7.1	6.5	133	82	(4)	(4)	9	6	42.9	39.5	5	3	2.4	2.0
Iberia	28,400	28,200	664	604	349	361	23.4	21.4	12.3	12.8	315	243	190	167	71	75	106.9	124.2	39	36	5.9	6.0
Colored	10,800	10,700	301	267	184	177	27.9	25.0	17.0	16.5	117	90	164	151	49	36	162.8	134.8	22	25	7.3	9.4
White	17,600	17,500	363	337	165	184	20.6	19.3	9.4	10.5	198	153	220	183	22	39	60.6	115.7	17	11	4.7	3.3
Iberville	[5] 24,638	[5] 24,638	527	552	316	382	21.4	22.4	12.8	15.5	211	170	167	145	50	57	94.9	103.3	42	32	8.0	5.8
Colored	12,738	12,738	268	286	187	236	21.0	22.5	14.7	18.5	81	50	143	121	32	34	119.4	118.9	29	24	10.8	8.4
White	11,900	11,900	259	266	129	146	21.8	22.4	10.8	12.3	130	120	201	182	18	23	69.5	86.5	13	8	5.0	3.0
Jackson	[5] 13,808	[5] 13,808	201	190	65	65	14.6	13.8	4.7	4.7	136	125	(4)	(4)	9	5	44.8	26.3	6	6	3.0	3.2
Colored	3,987	3,987	63	60	24	24	15.8	15.0	6.0	6.0	39	36	(4)	(4)	2	----	31.7	----	1	3	1.6	5.0
White	9,821	9,821	138	130	41	41	14.1	13.2	4.2	4.2	97	89	(4)	(4)	7	5	50.7	38.5	5	3	3.6	2.3
Jefferson	42,300	40,500	550	588	245	245	13.0	14.5	5.8	6.0	305	343	224	240	36	33	65.5	56.1	18	17	3.3	2.9
Colored	8,400	8,200	92	101	116	87	11.0	12.3	13.8	10.6	−24	14	79	(4)	15	7	163.0	69.3	2	5	2.2	5.0
White	33,900	32,300	458	487	129	158	13.5	15.1	3.8	4.9	329	329	355	308	21	26	45.9	53.4	16	12	3.5	2.5
Jefferson Davis	19,900	19,800	560	516	130	129	28.1	26.1	6.5	6.5	430	387	431	400	23	26	41.1	50.4	17	15	3.0	2.9
Colored	5,000	5,000	149	164	53	54	29.8	32.8	10.6	10.8	96	110	(4)	(4)	14	11	94.0	67.1	8	9	5.4	5.5
White	14,900	14,800	411	352	77	75	27.6	23.8	5.2	5.1	334	277	(4)	(4)	9	15	21.9	42.6	9	6	2.2	1.7
Lafayette	24,300	24,200	610	624	206	248	25.1	25.8	8.5	10.2	404	376	296	252	37	68	60.7	109.0	23	22	3.8	3.5
Colored	8,300	8,200	282	304	86	106	34.0	37.1	10.4	12.9	196	198	(4)	287	23	38	81.6	125.0	17	20	6.0	6.6
White	16,000	16,000	328	320	120	142	20.5	20.0	7.5	8.9	208	178	273	225	14	30	42.7	93.8	6	2	1.8	.6
Lafourche	32,700	32,500	978	886	350	352	29.9	27.3	10.7	10.8	628	534	279	252	92	92	94.1	103.8	38	35	3.9	4.0
Colored	5,300	5,300	147	118	92	136	27.7	22.3	17.4	25.7	55	−18	(4)	87	21	35	142.9	296.6	9	13	6.1	11.0
White	27,400	27,200	831	768	258	216	30.3	28.2	9.4	7.9	573	552	322	356	71	57	85.4	74.2	29	22	3.5	2.9
La Salle	11,900	11,700	244	228	94	84	20.5	19.5	7.9	7.2	150	144	(4)	(4)	12	10	49.2	43.9	15	10	6.1	4.4
Colored	2,200	2,100	43	99	29	20	19.5	47.1	13.2	9.5	14	79	(4)	(4)	1	2	23.3	20.2	5	2	11.6	2.0
White	9,700	9,600	201	129	65	64	20.7	13.4	6.7	6.7	136	65	(4)	(4)	11	8	54.7	62.0	10	8	5.0	6.2
Lincoln	23,500	23,000	390	381	172	171	16.6	16.6	7.3	7.4	218	210	227	223	23	19	59.0	49.9	25	24	6.4	6.3
Colored	10,100	9,800	160	158	86	76	15.8	16.1	8.5	7.8	74	82	(4)	(4)	14	8	87.5	50.6	14	15	8.8	9.5
White	13,400	13,200	230	223	86	95	17.2	16.9	6.4	7.2	144	128	(4)	(4)	9	11	39.1	49.3	11	9	4.8	4.0
Livingston	19,000	18,400	362	388	122	119	19.1	21.1	6.4	6.5	240	269	297	326	20	20	55.2	51.5	14	11	3.9	2.8
Colored	4,400	4,200	40	44	38	33	9.1	10.5	8.6	7.9	2	11	(4)	(4)	5	4	125.0	90.9	8	5	20.0	11.4
White	14,600	14,200	322	344	84	86	22.1	24.2	5.8	6.1	238	258	(4)	(4)	15	16	46.6	46.5	6	6	1.9	1.7
Madison	15,300	14,900	240	252	142	148	15.7	16.9	9.3	9.9	98	104	169	170	18	20	75.0	79.4	13	18	5.4	7.1
Colored	9,700	9,600	160	157	101	111	16.5	16.4	10.4	11.6	59	46	158	141	8	11	50.0	70.1	10	17	6.3	10.8
White	5,600	5,300	80	95	41	37	14.3	17.9	7.3	7.0	39	58	(4)	(4)	10	9	125.0	94.7	3	1	3.8	1.1
Morehouse	24,200	23,800	465	541	223	249	19.2	22.7	9.2	10.5	242	292	209	217	24	32	51.6	59.1	30	31	6.5	5.7
Colored	13,700	13,600	284	320	148	168	20.7	23.5	10.8	12.4	136	152	192	190	14	18	49.3	56.3	27	20	9.5	6.3
White	10,500	10,200	181	221	75	81	17.2	21.7	7.1	7.9	106	140	(4)	(4)	10	14	55.2	63.3	3	11	1.7	5.0
Natchitoches	[5] 38,477	[5] 38,477	967	931	386	417	25.1	24.2	10.0	10.8	581	514	251	223	51	70	52.7	75.2	49	52	5.1	5.6
Colored	20,249	20,249	535	492	231	252	26.4	24.3	11.4	12.4	304	240	232	195	37	41	69.2	83.3	36	31	6.7	6.3
White	18,228	18,228	432	439	155	165	23.7	24.1	8.5	9.1	277	274	279	266	14	29	32.4	66.1	13	21	3.0	4.8
Ouachita	28,200	28,300	400	420	167	172	14.2	14.8	5.9	6.1	233	248	240	244	22	15	55.0	35.7	15	22	3.8	5.2
Colored	8,600	8,900	145	159	73	76	16.9	17.9	8.5	8.5	72	83	(4)	(4)	6	3	41.4	18.9	4	10	2.8	6.3
White	19,600	19,400	255	261	94	96	13.0	13.5	4.8	4.9	161	165	(4)	(4)	16	12	62.7	46.0	11	12	4.3	4.6

Plaquemines	[5] 9,608	[5] 9,608	223	249	83	95	23.2	25.9	8.6	9.9	140	154	(4)	(4)	18	24	80.7	96.4	7	6	3.1	2.4
Colored	4,559	4,559	138	145	60	69	30.3	31.8	13.2	15.1	78	76	(4)	(4)	15	19	108.7	131.0	6	5	4.3	3.4
White	5,049	5,049	85	104	23	26	16.8	20.6	4.6	5.1	62	78	(4)	(4)	3	5	35.3	48.1	1	1	1.2	1.0
Pointe Coupee	[5] 21,007	[5] 21,007	499	465	261	265	23.8	22.1	12.4	12.6	238	200	191	175	57	48	114.2	103.2	37	30	7.4	6.5
Colored	12,211	12,211	305	280	175	184	25.0	22.9	14.3	15.1	130	96	174	152	35	38	114.8	135.7	29	25	9.5	8.9
White	8,796	8,796	194	185	86	81	22.1	21.0	9.8	9.2	108	104	(4)	(4)	22	10	113.4	54.1	8	5	4.1	2.7
Rapides	42,500	42,400	749	691	536	617	17.6	16.3	12.6	14.6	213	74	140	112	33	53	44.1	76.7	42	30	5.6	4.3
Colored	15,700	15,800	309	325	242	308	19.7	20.6	15.4	19.5	67	17	128	10[illegible]	18	33	58.3	101.5	26	22	8.4	6.8
White	26,800	26,600	440	366	294	309	16.4	13.8	11.0	11.6	146	57	150	118	15	20	34.1	54.6	16	8	3.6	2.2
Red River	16,200	16,100	319	301	87	95	19.7	18.7	5.4	5.9	232	206	(4)	(4)	14	15	43.9	49.8	13	13	4.1	4.3
Colored	7,700	7,600	147	134	55	54	19.1	17.6	7.1	7.1	92	80	(4)	(4)	7	8	47.6	59.7	10	8	6.8	6.0
White	8,500	8,500	172	167	32	41	20.2	19.6	3.8	4.8	140	126	(4)	(4)	7	7	40.7	41.9	3	5	1.7	3.0
Richland	27,000	26,500	554	577	246	243	20.5	21.8	9.1	9.2	308	334	225	237	26	53	46.9	91.9	34	24	6.1	4.2
Colored	13,300	13,200	278	292	144	163	20.9	22.1	10.8	12.3	134	129	193	179	11	32	39.6	109.6	22	18	7.9	6.2
White	13,700	13,300	276	285	102	80	20.1	21.4	7.4	6.0	174	205	271	(4)	15	21	54.3	73.7	12	6	4.3	2.1
Sabine	24,500	24,200	465	389	123	143	19.0	16.1	5.0	5.9	342	246	378	272	15	23	32.3	59.1	42	16	9.0	4.1
Colored	7,500	7,200	84	59	35	39	11.2	8.2	4.7	5.4	49	20	(4)	(4)	4	4	47.6	67.8	16	5	19.0	8.5
White	17,000	17,000	381	330	88	104	22.4	19.4	5.2	6.1	293	226	(4)	317	11	19	28.9	57.6	26	11	6.8	3.3
St. Bernard	6,700	6,500	96	96	45	37	14.3	14.8	6.7	5.7	51	59	(4)	(4)	3	5	31.3	52.1	2	2	2.1	2.1
Colored	1,300	1,300	20	26	20	17	15.4	20.0	15.4	13.1	------	9	(4)	(4)	2	4	100.0	153.8	2	1	10.0	3.8
White	5,400	5,200	76	70	25	20	14.1	13.5	4.6	3.8	51	50	(4)	(4)	1	1	13.2	14.3	------	1	------	1.4
St. Charles	12,500	12,200	258	297	100	107	20.6	24.3	8.0	8.8	158	190	258	278	21	24	81.4	80.8	9	7	3.5	2.4
Colored	4,100	4,200	73	87	52	70	17.8	20.7	12.7	16.7	21	17	(4)	(4)	7	19	95.9	218.4	1	2	1.4	2.3
White	8,400	8,000	185	210	48	37	22.0	26.3	5.7	4.6	137	173	(4)	(4)	14	5	75.7	23.8	8	5	4.3	2.4
St. Helena	8,500	8,500	169	169	72	65	19.9	19.9	8.5	7.6	97	104	(4)	(4)	5	10	29.6	59.2	15	6	8.9	3.6
Colored	4,700	4,600	101	102	32	48	21.5	22.2	6.8	10.4	69	54	(4)	(4)	1	6	9.9	58.8	11	4	10.9	3.9
White	3,800	3,900	68	67	40	17	17.9	17.2	10.5	4.4	28	50	(4)	(4)	4	4	58.8	59.7	4	2	5.9	3.0
St. James	[5] 15,338	[5] 15,338	389	385	181	188	25.4	25.1	11.8	12.3	208	197	215	205	36	40	92.5	103.9	22	18	5.7	4.7
Colored	7,596	7,596	195	193	129	124	25.7	25.4	17.0	16.3	66	69	151	156	22	28	112.8	145.1	18	11	9.2	5.7
White	7,742	7,742	194	192	52	64	25.1	24.8	6.7	8.3	142	128	(4)	(4)	14	12	72.2	62.5	4	7	2.1	3.6
St. John the Baptist	14,300	14,100	320	338	174	184	22.4	24.0	12.2	13.0	146	154	184	184	32	35	100.0	103.6	18	16	5.6	4.7
Colored	7,000	6,900	168	157	105	123	24.0	22.8	15.0	17.8	63	34	160	128	20	26	119.0	165.6	16	13	9.5	8.3
White	7,300	7,200	152	181	69	61	20.8	25.1	9.5	8.5	83	120	(3)	(3)	12	9	78.9	49.7	2	3	1.3	1.7
St. Landry	61,100	60,300	1,738	1,567	558	624	28.4	26.0	9.1	10.3	1,180	943	311	251	125	163	71.9	104.0	82	70	4.7	4.5
Colored	29,900	29,600	1,006	933	325	389	33.6	31.5	10.9	13.1	681	544	310	240	90	115	89.5	123.3	66	50	6.6	5.4
White	31,200	30,700	732	634	233	235	23.5	20.7	7.5	7.7	499	399	314	270	35	48	47.8	75.7	16	20	2.2	3.2
St. Martin	[5] 21,767	[5] 21,767	587	494	183	167	27.0	22.7	8.4	7.7	404	327	321	296	26	40	44.3	81.0	19	15	3.2	3.0
Colored	7,545	7,545	263	221	85	87	34.9	29.3	11.3	11.5	178	134	(4)	(4)	14	20	53.2	90.5	11	8	4.2	3.6
White	14,222	14,222	324	273	98	80	22.8	19.2	6.9	5.6	226	193	(4)	(4)	12	20	37.0	73.3	8	7	2.5	2.6
St. Mary	[5] 29,397	[5] 29,397	687	631	334	366	23.4	21.5	11.4	12.5	353	265	206	172	44	47	64.0	74.5	46	35	6.7	5.5
Colored	14,362	14,362	340	310	208	244	23.7	21.6	14.5	17.0	132	66	163	127	33	35	97.1	112.9	29	22	8.5	7.1
White	15,035	15,035	347	321	126	122	23.1	21.4	8.4	8.1	221	199	275	263	11	12	31.7	37.4	17	13	4.9	4.0
St. Tammany	21,000	20,900	340	345	211	189	16.2	16.5	10.0	9.0	129	156	161	183	29	20	85.3	58.0	17	17	5.0	4.9
Colored	7,000	7,000	127	126	102	81	18.1	18.0	14.6	11.6	25	45	125	(4)	21	12	165.4	95.2	10	11	7.9	8.7
White	14,000	13,900	213	219	109	108	15.2	15.8	7.8	7.8	104	111	195	203	8	8	37.6	36.5	7	6	3.3	2.7
Tangipahoa	48,000	46,600	797	801	350	350	16.6	17.2	7.3	7.5	447	451	228	229	50	51	62.7	63.7	36	37	4.5	4.6
Colored	16,400	15,800	194	213	147	127	11.8	13.5	9.0	8.0	47	86	132	168	24	20	123.7	93.9	17	22	8.8	10.3
White	31,600	30,800	603	588	203	223	19.1	19.1	6.4	7.2	400	365	297	264	26	31	43.1	52.7	19	15	3.2	2.6
Tensas	15,500	15,200	281	286	182	187	18.1	18.8	11.7	12.3	99	99	154	153	8	15	28.5	52.4	18	33	6.4	11.5
Colored	10,900	10,900	184	204	151	155	16.9	18.7	13.9	14.2	33	49	122	132	5	9	27.2	44.1	11	26	6.0	12.7
White	4,600	4,300	97	82	31	32	21.1	19.1	6.7	7.4	66	50	(4)	(4)	3	6	30.9	73.2	7	7	7.2	8.5
Terrebonne	30,200	29,900	856	830	285	321	28.3	27.8	9.4	10.7	571	509	300	259	70	78	81.8	94.0	47	50	5.5	6.0
Colored	9,400	9,300	269	233	124	154	28.6	25.1	13.2	16.6	145	79	217	151	31	34	115.2	145.9	22	35	8.2	15.0
White	20,800	20,600	587	597	161	167	28.2	29.0	7.7	8.1	426	430	365	357	39	44	66.4	73.7	25	15	4.3	2.5
Union	20,900	20,800	374	443	160	143	17.9	21.3	7.7	6.9	214	300	234	310	21	21	56.1	47.4	12	34	3.2	7.7
Colored	6,700	6,700	113	129	50	37	16.9	19.3	7.5	5.5	63	92	(4)	(4)	10	5	88.5	38.8	5	14	4.4	10.9
White	14,200	14,100	261	314	110	106	18.4	22.3	7.7	7.5	151	208	237	296	11	16	42.1	51.0	7	20	2.7	6.4
Vermilion	34,600	33,900	832	864	326	294	24.0	25.2	9.4	8.7	506	570	255	294	70	68	84.1	78.7	26	49	3.1	5.7
Colored	4,400	4,500	126	127	52	65	28.6	28.2	11.8	14.4	74	62	(4)	(4)	14	16	111.1	126.0	9	10	7.1	7.9
White	30,200	29,400	706	737	274	229	23.4	25.1	9.1	7.8	432	508	258	322	56	52	79.3	70.6	17	39	2.4	5.3
Vernon	[5] 20,047	[5] 20,047	334	348	112	121	16.7	17.4	5.6	6.0	222	227	298	288	20	21	59.9	60.3	19	15	5.7	4.3
Colored	3,664	3,664	25	37	15	24	6.8	10.1	4.1	6.6	10	13	(4)	(4)	4	7	160.0	189.2	------	2	------	5.4
White	16,383	16,383	309	311	97	97	18.9	19.0	5.9	5.9	212	214	(4)	(4)	16	14	51.8	45.0	19	13	6.1	4.2
Washington	15,900	15,800	300	262	81	94	18.9	16.6	5.1	5.9	219	168	(4)	(4)	9	20	30.0	76.3	11	11	3.7	4.2
Colored	5,000	4,900	97	124	38	42	19.4	25.3	7.6	8.6	59	82	(4)	(4)	2	9	20.6	72.6	5	11	5.2	8.9
White	10,900	10,900	203	138	43	52	18.6	12.7	3.9	4.8	160	86	(4)	(4)	7	11	34.5	79.7	6	------	3.0	------
Webster	30,000	29,600	518	632	237	226	17.3	21.4	7.9	7.6	281	406	219	280	31	31	59.8	49.1	18	43	3.5	6.8
Colored	13,300	13,200	213	300	118	111	16.0	22.7	8.9	8.4	95	189	181	270	16	15	75.1	50.0	11	31	5.2	10.3
White	16,700	16,400	305	332	119	115	18.3	20.2	7.1	7.0	186	217	256	289	15	16	49.2	48.2	7	12	2.3	3.6
West Baton Rouge	[5] 9,716	[5] 9,716	180	148	110	97	18.5	15.2	11.3	10.0	70	51	164	(4)	21	12	116.7	81.1	10	10	5.6	6.8
Colored	6,135	6,135	135	96	89	78	22.0	15.6	14.5	12.7	46	18	(4)	(4)	17	11	125.9	114.6	7	9	5.2	9.4
White	3,581	3,581	45	52	21	19	12.6	14.5	5.9	5.3	24	33	(4)	(4)	4	1	88.9	19.2	3	1	6.7	1.9
West Carroll	14,500	14,000	290	273	82	99	20.0	19.5	5.7	7.1	208	174	(4)	(4)	18	18	62.1	65.9	14	12	4.8	4.4
Colored	2,900	2,800	41	43	32	28	14.1	15.4	11.0	10.0	9	15	(4)	(4)	5	2	122.0	46.5	6	5	14.6	11.6
White	11,600	11,200	249	230	50	71	21.5	20.5	4.3	6.3	199	159	(4)	(4)	13	16	52.2	69.6	8	7	3.2	3.0
West Feliciana	[5] 10,924	[5] 10,924	199	221	129	114	18.2	20.2	11.8	10.4	70	107	154	194	5	14	25.1	63.3	17	17	8.5	7.7
Colored	8,356	8,356	177	196	116	102	21.2	23.5	13.9	12.2	61	94	153	192	5	12	28.2	61.2	15	15	8.5	7.7
White	2,568	2,568	22	25	13	12	8.6	9.7	5.1	4.7	9	13	(4)	(4)	------	2	------	80.0	2	2	9.1	8.0
Winn	[5] 14,766	[5] 14,766	240	228	77	99	16.3	15.4	5.2	6.7	163	129	(4)	(4)	12	15	50.0	65.8	15	15	6.3	6.6
Colored	3,697	3,697	56	44	25	36	15.1	11.9	6.8	9.7	31	8	(4)	(4)	2	6	35.7	136.4	9	6	16.1	13.6
White	11,069	11,069	184	184	52	63	16.6	16.6	4.7	5.7	132	121	(4)	(4)	10	9	54.3	48.9	6	9	3.3	4.9

See footnotes at end of table.

TABLE 18.—COLORED [1] AND WHITE POPULATION, BIRTHS AND DEATHS, INFANT MORTALITY, AND STILLBIRTHS, IN SELECTED REGISTRATION STATES, CITIES, AND COUNTIES: 1931 AND 1930—Continued

[See note at head of this table]

AREA AND COLOR	POPULATION ESTIMATED AS OF JULY 1		BIRTHS AND DEATHS (Exclusive of stillbirths): Number: Births		Number: Deaths		Rate per 1,000 population: Births		Rate per 1,000 population: Deaths		Excess of births over deaths [2]		Births per 100 deaths		INFANT MORTALITY (Exclusive of stillbirths): Deaths of infants under 1 year of age: Number		Per 1,000 births		STILLBIRTHS: Number		Rate per 100 live births	
	1931	1930	1931	1930	1931	1930	1931	1930	1931	1930	1931	1930	1931	1930	1931	1930	1931	1930	1931	1930	1931	1930
MARYLAND COUNTIES [8]																						
Anne Arundel	43,900	42,900	690	687	588	547	15.7	16.0	13.4	12.8	102	140	117	126	81	76	117.4	110.6	52	54	7.5	7.9
Colored	11,800	11,700	311	314	317	283	26.4	26.8	26.9	24.2	−6	31	98	111	55	49	176.8	156.1	26	26	8.4	8.3
White	32,100	31,200	379	373	271	264	11.8	12.0	8.4	8.5	108	109	140	141	26	27	68.6	72.4	26	28	6.9	7.5
Baltimore	130,600	125,800	1,554	1,756	1,219	1,172	11.9	14.0	9.3	9.3	335	584	127	150	82	92	52.8	52.4	92	93	5.9	5.3
Colored	12,100	11,900	151	174	101	110	12.5	14.6	8.3	9.2	50	64	150	158	16	14	106.0	80.5	12	20	7.9	11.5
White	118,500	113,900	1,403	1,582	1,118	1,062	11.8	13.9	9.4	9.3	285	520	125	149	66	78	47.0	49.3	80	73	5.7	4.6
Calvert	[5] 9,528	[5] 9,528	247	260	148	142	25.9	27.3	15.5	14.9	99	118	167	183	32	27	129.6	103.8	29	25	11.7	9.6
Colored	4,519	4,519	146	144	80	83	32.3	31.9	17.7	18.4	66	61	(4)	(4)	25	18	171.2	125.0	21	17	14.4	11.8
White	5,009	5,009	101	116	68	59	20.2	23.2	13.6	11.8	33	57	(4)	(4)	7	9	69.3	77.6	8	8	7.9	6.9
Caroline	[5] 17,387	[5] 17,387	302	316	180	239	17.4	18.2	10.4	13.7	122	77	168	132	15	35	49.7	110.8	17	19	5.6	6.0
Colored	3,677	3,677	80	89	57	62	21.8	24.2	15.5	16.9	23	27	(4)	(4)	9	12	112.5	134.8	9	11	11.3	12.4
White	13,710	13,710	222	227	123	177	16.2	16.6	9.0	12.9	99	50	180	128	6	23	27.0	101.3	8	8	3.6	3.5
Cecil	26,100	25,900	435	520	383	403	16.7	20.1	14.7	15.6	52	117	114	129	39	62	89.7	119.2	51	45	11.7	8.7
Colored	2,600	2,600	62	52	55	56	23.8	20.0	21.2	21.5	7	−4	(4)	(4)	8	10	129.0	192.3	3	6	4.8	11.5
White	23,500	23,300	373	468	328	347	15.9	20.1	14.0	14.9	45	121	114	135	31	52	83.1	111.1	48	39	12.9	8.3
Charles	[5] 16,166	[5] 16,166	377	410	184	224	23.3	25.4	11.4	13.9	193	186	205	183	41	42	108.8	102.4	33	40	8.8	9.8
Colored	7,492	7,492	231	233	115	132	30.8	31.1	15.3	17.6	116	101	201	177	35	31	151.5	133.0	23	18	10.0	7.7
White	8,674	8,674	146	177	69	92	16.8	20.4	8.0	10.6	77	85	(4)	(4)	6	11	41.1	62.1	10	22	6.8	12.4
Dorchester	[5] 26,813	[5] 26,813	497	540	427	447	18.5	20.1	15.9	16.7	70	93	116	121	71	68	142.9	125.9	61	66	12.3	12.2
Colored	7,832	7,832	165	172	168	166	21.1	22.0	21.5	21.2	−3	6	98	104	39	39	236.4	226.7	25	26	15.2	15.1
White	18,981	18,981	332	368	259	281	17.5	19.4	13.6	14.8	73	87	128	131	32	29	96.4	78.8	36	40	10.8	10.9
Harford	31,900	31,700	540	612	364	395	16.9	19.3	11.4	12.5	176	217	148	155	47	50	87.0	81.7	25	23	4.6	3.8
Colored	4,000	4,100	97	113	86	72	24.3	27.6	21.5	17.6	11	41	(4)	(4)	16	14	164.9	123.9	8	6	8.2	5.3
White	27,900	27,600	443	499	278	323	15.9	18.1	10.0	11.7	165	176	159	154	31	36	70.0	72.1	17	17	3.8	3.4
Howard	16,200	16,200	263	257	147	164	16.2	15.9	9.1	10.1	116	93	179	157	15	10	57.0	38.9	15	21	5.7	8.2
Colored	3,200	3,300	70	64	43	37	21.9	19.4	13.4	11.2	27	27	(4)	(4)	8	4	114.3	62.5	4	5	5.7	7.8
White	13,000	12,900	193	193	104	127	14.8	15.0	8.0	9.8	89	66	186	152	7	6	36.3	31.1	11	16	5.7	8.3
Kent	[5] 14,242	[5] 14,242	227	229	185	183	15.9	16.1	13.0	12.8	42	46	123	125	23	19	101.3	83.0	18	27	7.9	11.8
Colored	4,438	4,438	91	104	83	74	20.5	23.4	18.7	16.7	8	30	(4)	(4)	15	9	164.8	86.5	6	13	6.6	12.5
White	9,804	9,804	136	125	102	109	13.9	12.7	10.4	11.1	34	16	133	115	8	10	58.8	80.0	12	14	8.8	11.2
Montgomery	50,900	49,600	775	749	514	547	15.2	15.1	10.1	11.0	261	202	151	137	49	67	63.2	89.5	39	49	5.0	6.5
Colored	8,200	8,300	184	188	132	122	22.4	22.7	16.1	14.7	52	66	139	154	21	30	114.1	159.6	19	16	10.3	8.5
White	42,700	41,300	591	561	382	425	13.8	13.6	8.9	10.3	209	136	155	132	28	37	47.4	66.0	20	33	3.4	5.9
Prince Georges	62,100	60,500	795	839	530	528	12.8	13.9	8.5	8.7	265	311	150	159	69	78	86.8	93.0	44	43	5.5	5.1
Colored	14,200	14,100	314	310	161	184	22.1	22.0	11.3	13.0	153	126	195	168	39	43	124.2	138.7	27	23	8.6	7.4
White	47,900	46,400	481	529	369	344	10.0	11.4	7.7	7.4	112	185	130	154	30	35	62.4	66.2	17	20	3.5	3.8
Queen Annes	[5] 14,571	[5] 14,571	232	269	184	213	15.9	18.5	12.6	14.6	48	56	126	126	15	17	64.7	63.2	18	21	7.8	7.8
Colored	4,380	4,380	71	85	64	66	16.2	19.4	14.6	15.1	7	19	(4)	(4)	6	9	84.5	105.9	9	11	12.7	12.9
White	10,191	10,191	161	184	120	147	15.8	18.1	11.8	14.4	41	37	134	125	9	8	55.9	43.5	9	10	5.6	5.4
St. Marys	[5] 15,189	[5] 15,189	384	408	219	208	25.3	26.9	14.4	13.7	165	200	175	196	45	52	117.2	127.5	24	27	6.3	6.6
Colored	5,592	5,592	160	160	117	97	28.6	28.6	20.9	17.3	43	63	137	(4)	28	29	175.0	181.3	16	20	10.0	12.5
White	9,597	9,597	224	248	102	111	23.3	25.8	10.6	11.6	122	137	220	223	17	23	75.9	92.7	8	7	3.6	2.8
Somerset	[5] 23,382	[5] 23,382	436	450	288	329	18.6	19.2	12.3	14.1	148	121	151	137	48	63	110.1	140.0	52	40	11.9	8.9
Colored	8,111	8,111	177	172	137	152	21.8	21.2	16.9	18.7	40	20	129	113	31	36	175.1	209.3	29	21	16.4	12.2
White	15,271	15,271	259	278	151	177	17.0	18.2	9.9	11.6	108	101	172	157	17	27	65.6	97.1	23	19	8.9	6.8
Talbot	18,600	18,600	353	363	342	326	19.0	19.5	18.4	17.5	11	37	103	111	36	43	102.0	118.5	54	55	15.3	15.2
Colored	5,900	6,000	114	115	149	136	19.3	19.2	25.3	22.7	−35	−21	77	85	22	22	193.0	191.3	17	19	14.9	16.5
White	12,700	12,600	239	248	193	190	18.8	19.7	15.2	15.1	46	58	124	131	14	21	58.6	84.7	37	36	15.5	14.5
Wicomico	20,200	20,200	254	270	252	229	12.6	13.4	12.5	11.3	2	41	101	118	34	25	133.9	92.6	9	21	3.5	7.8
Colored	4,900	4,900	84	125	74	56	17.1	25.5	15.1	11.4	10	69	(4)	(4)	15	12	178.6	96.0	2	13	2.4	10.4
White	15,300	15,300	170	145	178	173	11.1	9.5	11.6	11.3	−8	−28	96	84	19	13	111.8	89.7	7	8	4.1	5.5
Worcester	[5] 21,624	[5] 21,624	395	425	290	279	18.3	19.7	13.4	12.9	105	146	136	152	50	43	126.6	101.2	36	38	9.1	8.9
Colored	6,712	6,712	178	190	125	122	26.5	28.3	18.6	18.2	53	68	142	156	33	26	185.4	136.8	26	25	14.6	13.2
White	14,912	14,912	217	235	165	157	14.6	15.8	11.1	10.5	52	78	132	150	17	17	78.3	72.3	10	13	4.6	5.5
MICHIGAN COUNTIES [9]																						
Lake	[5] 4,066	[5] 4,066	63	51	51	48	15.5	12.5	12.5	11.8	12	3	(4)	(4)	3	3	47.6	58.8	4	3	6.3	5.9
Colored	413	(3)	6	(3)	8	(3)	14.5	(3)	19.4	(3)	−2	(3)	(4)	(3)	---	(3)	---	(3)	---	(3)	---	(3)
White	3,653	(3)	57	(3)	43	(3)	15.6	(3)	11.8	(3)	14	(3)	(4)	(3)	3	(3)	52.6	(3)	4	(3)	7.0	(3)

MISSISSIPPI COUNTIES [9]																					
Adams	10,200	10,200	384	346	318	284	37.6	33.9	31.2	27.8	66	62	121	122	33	35	85.9	101.2	33	17	8.6	4.9
Colored	8,200	8,300	262	213	240	212	32.0	25.7	29.3	25.5	22	1	109	100	23	23	87.8	108.0	29	14	11.1	6.6
White	2,000	1,900	122	133	78	72	61.0	70.0	39.0	37.9	44	61	(4)	(4)	10	12	82.0	90.2	4	3	3.3	2.3
Alcorn	23,900	23,700	502	503	194	239	21.0	21.2	8.1	10.1	308	264	259	210	19	24	37.8	47.7	20	16	4.0	3.2
Colored	4,100	4,100	68	75	42	52	16.6	18.3	10.2	12.7	26	23	(4)	(4)	8	7	117.6	93.3	9	4	13.2	5.3
White	19,800	19,600	434	428	152	187	21.9	21.8	7.7	9.5	282	241	286	229	11	17	25.3	39.7	11	12	2.5	2.8
Amite	19,800	19,700	467	493	148	170	23.6	25.0	7.5	8.6	319	323	316	290	22	29	47.1	58.8	6	17	1.3	3.4
Colored	10,500	10,400	280	304	94	102	26.7	29.2	9.0	9.8	186	202	(4)	298	13	19	46.4	62.5	5	10	1.8	3.3
White	9,300	9,300	187	189	54	63	20.1	20.3	5.8	7.3	133	121	(4)	(4)	9	10	48.1	52.9	1	7	.5	3.7
Attala	26,200	26,100	654	709	205	228	25.0	27.2	7.8	8.7	449	481	319	311	26	53	39.8	74.8	23	23	3.5	3.2
Colored	11,000	10,900	314	292	98	115	28.5	26.8	8.9	10.6	216	177	(4)	254	14	27	44.6	92.5	12	9	3.8	3.1
White	15,200	15,200	340	417	107	113	22.4	27.4	7.0	7.4	233	304	318	369	12	26	35.3	62.4	11	14	3.2	3.4
Benton	[5] 9,813	[5] 9,813	253	271	110	97	25.8	27.6	11.2	9.9	143	174	230	(4)	12	19	47.4	70.1	12	20	4.7	7.4
Colored	4,669	4,669	147	145	59	58	31.5	31.1	12.6	12.4	88	87	(4)	(4)	10	7	68.0	48.3	8	10	5.4	6.9
White	5,144	5,144	106	126	51	39	20.6	24.5	9.9	7.6	55	87	(4)	(4)	2	12	18.9	95.2	4	10	3.8	7.9
Bolivar	72,700	71,400	1,193	1,386	891	998	16.4	19.4	12.3	14.0	302	388	134	139	77	118	64.5	85.1	68	89	5.7	6.4
Colored	53,900	53,400	885	1,011	770	853	16.4	18.9	14.3	16.0	115	158	115	119	66	92	74.6	91.0	63	88	7.1	8.7
White	18,800	18,000	308	375	121	145	16.4	20.8	6.4	8.1	187	230	255	259	11	26	35.7	69.3	5	1	1.6	.3
Calhoun	18,200	18,100	432	476	105	112	23.7	26.3	5.8	6.2	327	364	411	425	13	22	30.1	46.2	14	17	3.2	3.6
Colored	3,600	3,600	74	109	17	26	20.6	30.3	4.7	7.2	57	83	(4)	(4)	1	9	13.5	82.6	4	2	5.4	1.8
White	14,600	14,500	358	367	88	86	24.5	25.3	6.0	5.9	270	281	(4)	(4)	12	13	33.5	35.4	10	15	2.8	4.1
Carroll	[5] 19,765	[5] 19,765	461	524	166	171	23.3	26.5	8.4	8.7	295	353	278	306	24	32	52.1	61.1	25	17	5.4	3.2
Colored	11,274	11,274	268	299	94	108	23.8	26.5	8.3	9.6	174	191	(4)	277	11	23	41.0	76.9	16	17	6.0	5.7
White	8,491	8,491	193	225	72	63	22.7	26.5	8.5	7.4	121	162	(4)	(4)	13	9	67.4	40.0	9	----	4.7	----
Chickasaw	[5] 20,835	[5] 20,835	488	500	225	205	23.4	24.0	10.8	9.8	263	295	217	244	21	22	43.0	44.0	15	26	3.1	5.2
Colored	10,461	10,461	230	258	118	117	22.0	24.7	11.3	11.2	112	141	195	221	12	17	52.2	65.9	10	14	4.3	5.4
White	10,374	10,374	258	242	107	88	24.9	23.3	10.3	8.5	151	154	241	(4)	9	5	34.9	20.7	5	12	1.9	5.0
Choctaw	[5] 12,339	[5] 12,339	288	317	76	120	23.3	25.7	6.2	9.7	212	197	(4)	264	6	17	20.8	53.6	11	12	3.8	3.8
Colored	3,473	3,473	100	103	22	40	28.8	29.7	6.3	11.5	78	63	(4)	(4)	2	7	20.0	68.0	7	7	7.0	6.8
White	8,866	8,866	188	214	54	80	21.2	24.1	6.1	9.0	134	134	(4)	(4)	4	10	21.3	46.7	4	5	2.1	2.3
Claiborne	[5] 12,152	[5] 12,152	230	244	127	141	18.9	20.1	10.5	11.6	103	103	181	173	5	15	21.7	61.5	12	16	5.2	6.6
Colored	9,040	9,040	184	183	100	109	20.4	20.2	11.1	12.1	84	74	184	168	5	13	27.2	71.0	12	10	6.5	5.5
White	3,112	3,112	46	61	27	32	14.8	19.6	8.7	10.3	19	29	(4)	(4)	----	2	----	32.8	----	6	----	9.8
Clarke	19,900	19,700	442	480	196	167	22.2	24.4	9.8	8.5	246	313	226	287	30	21	67.9	43.8	16	34	3.6	7.1
Colored	8,200	8,000	211	231	94	101	25.7	28.9	11.5	12.6	117	130	(4)	229	20	16	94.8	69.3	14	28	6.6	12.1
White	11,700	11,700	231	249	102	66	19.7	21.3	8.7	5.6	129	183	226	(4)	10	5	43.3	20.1	2	6	.9	2.4
Clay	18,000	17,900	427	444	194	226	23.7	24.8	10.8	12.6	233	218	220	196	19	25	44.5	56.3	15	18	3.5	4.1
Colored	11,100	11,100	292	317	127	145	26.3	28.6	11.4	13.1	165	172	230	219	12	20	41.1	63.1	13	17	4.5	5.4
White	6,900	6,800	135	127	67	81	19.6	18.7	9.7	11.9	68	46	(4)	(4)	7	5	51.9	39.4	2	1	1.5	.8
Coahoma	36,500	36,300	597	642	403	533	16.4	17.7	11.0	14.7	194	109	148	120	45	88	75.4	137.1	34	54	5.7	8.4
Colored	31,000	31,000	511	629	373	489	16.5	20.3	12.0	15.8	138	140	137	129	41	80	80.2	127.2	29	53	5.7	8.4
White	5,500	5,300	86	13	30	44	15.6	2.5	5.5	8.3	56	−31	(4)	(4)	4	8	46.5	615.4	5	1	5.8	7.7
Copiah	32,000	31,700	717	820	273	337	22.4	25.9	8.5	10.6	444	483	263	243	25	41	34.9	50.0	21	26	2.9	3.2
Colored	15,700	15,600	408	436	158	203	26.0	27.9	10.1	13.0	250	233	258	215	18	26	44.1	59.6	17	17	4.2	3.9
White	16,300	16,100	309	384	115	134	19.0	23.9	7.1	8.3	194	250	269	287	7	15	22.7	39.1	4	9	1.3	2.3
Covington	15,000	15,000	386	307	122	146	25.7	20.5	8.1	9.7	264	161	316	210	20	17	51.8	55.4	4	10	1.0	3.3
Colored	4,300	4,300	154	97	48	58	35.8	22.6	11.2	13.5	106	39	(4)	(4)	13	10	84.4	103.1	1	5	.6	5.2
White	10,700	10,700	232	210	74	88	21.7	19.6	6.9	8.2	158	122	(4)	(4)	7	7	30.2	33.3	3	5	1.3	2.4
De Soto	25,600	25,500	502	570	296	304	19.6	22.4	11.6	11.9	206	266	170	188	41	37	81.7	64.9	21	41	4.2	7.2
Colored	18,800	18,800	389	424	247	243	20.7	22.6	13.1	12.9	142	181	157	174	35	34	90.0	80.2	21	38	5.4	9.0
White	6,800	6,700	113	146	49	61	16.6	21.8	7.2	9.1	64	85	(4)	(4)	6	3	53.1	20.5	----	3	----	2.1
Forrest	11,900	11,600	137	146	36	38	11.5	12.6	3.0	3.3	101	108	(4)	(4)	2	3	14.6	20.5	3	9	2.2	6.2
Colored	2,900	2,900	37	25	8	16	12.8	8.6	2.8	5.5	29	9	(4)	(4)	2	2	54.1	80.0	----	4	----	16.0
White	9,000	8,700	100	121	28	22	11.1	13.9	3.1	2.5	72	99	(4)	(4)	----	1	----	8.3	3	5	3.0	4.1
Franklin	[5] 12,268	[5] 12,268	274	286	116	151	22.3	23.3	9.5	12.3	158	135	236	189	16	23	58.4	80.4	8	18	2.9	6.3
Colored	4,870	4,870	112	121	60	88	23.0	24.8	12.3	18.1	52	33	(4)	(4)	9	13	80.4	107.4	6	10	5.4	8.3
White	7,398	7,398	162	165	56	63	21.9	22.3	7.6	8.5	106	102	(4)	(4)	7	10	43.2	60.6	2	8	1.2	4.8
George	7,800	7,600	195	136	71	70	25.0	17.9	9.1	9.2	124	66	(4)	(4)	17	12	87.2	88.2	7	10	3.6	7.4
Colored	1,300	1,300	22	22	15	17	16.9	16.9	11.5	13.1	7	5	(4)	(4)	1	3	45.5	136.4	2	2	9.1	9.1
White	6,500	6,300	173	114	56	53	26.6	18.1	8.6	8.4	117	61	(4)	(4)	16	9	92.5	78.9	5	8	2.9	7.0
Greene	10,700	10,600	241	201	86	89	22.5	19.0	8.0	8.4	155	112	(4)	(4)	14	17	58.1	84.6	8	8	3.3	4.0
Colored	2,700	2,600	52	88	38	30	19.3	33.8	14.1	11.5	14	58	(4)	(4)	8	4	153.8	45.5	4	5	7.7	5.7
White	8,000	8,000	189	113	48	59	23.6	14.1	6.0	7.4	141	54	(4)	(4)	6	13	31.7	115.0	4	3	2.1	2.7
Grenada	17,200	16,900	399	408	224	229	23.2	24.1	13.0	13.6	175	179	178	178	36	21	90.2	51.5	24	26	6.0	6.4
Colored	10,200	10,000	243	235	148	150	23.8	23.5	14.5	15.0	95	85	164	157	24	14	98.8	59.6	19	26	7.8	11.1
White	7,000	6,900	156	173	76	79	22.3	25.1	10.9	11.4	80	94	(4)	(4)	12	7	76.9	40.5	5	----	3.2	----
Hancock	11,500	11,400	254	224	126	131	22.1	19.6	11.0	11.5	128	93	202	171	13	24	51.2	107.1	5	5	2.0	2.2
Colored	2,800	2,800	52	53	42	46	18.6	18.9	15.0	16.4	10	7	(4)	(4)	2	8	38.5	150.9	----	2	----	3.8
White	8,700	8,600	202	171	84	85	23.2	19.9	9.7	9.9	118	86	(4)	(4)	11	16	54.5	93.6	5	3	2.5	1.8
Harrison	17,100	16,800	271	299	183	168	15.8	17.8	10.7	10.0	88	131	148	178	14	17	51.7	56.9	15	17	5.5	5.7
Colored	4,500	4,500	73	121	46	57	16.2	26.9	10.2	12.7	27	64	(4)	(4)	4	11	54.8	90.9	5	6	6.8	5.0
White	12,600	12,300	198	178	137	111	15.7	14.5	10.9	9.0	61	67	145	160	10	6	50.5	33.7	10	11	5.1	6.2
Hinds	37,300	37,000	802	861	750	842	21.5	23.3	20.1	22.8	375	19	188	102	54	69	67.3	80.1	33	61	4.1	7.1
Colored	27,300	27,200	654	699	571	657	24.0	25.7	20.9	24.2	310	42	190	106	49	60	74.9	85.8	30	58	4.6	8.3
White	10,000	9,800	148	162	179	185	14.8	16.5	17.9	18.9	65	−23	78	88	5	9	33.8	55.6	3	3	2.0	1.9
Holmes	39,000	38,600	939	1,135	466	476	24.1	29.4	11.9	12.3	473	659	202	238	62	84	66.0	74.0	62	50	6.6	4.4
Colored	29,700	29,400	814	972	379	403	27.4	33.1	12.8	13.7	435	569	215	241	57	78	70.0	80.2	59	48	7.2	4.9
White	9,300	9,200	125	163	87	73	13.4	17.7	9.4	7.9	38	90	(4)	(4)	5	6	40.0	36.8	3	2	2.4	1.2
Humphreys	25,400	24,900	519	612	288	306	20.4	24.6	11.3	12.3	231	306	180	200	43	57	82.9	93.1	25	47	4.8	7.7
Colored	17,400	17,300	377	438	231	252	21.7	25.3	13.3	14.6	146	186	163	174	31	48	82.2	109.6	20	43	5.3	9.8
White	8,000	7,600	142	174	57	54	17.8	22.9	7.1	7.1	85	120	(4)	(4)	12	9	84.5	51.7	5	4	3.5	2.3

See footnotes at end of table.

TABLE 18.—COLORED[1] AND WHITE POPULATION, BIRTHS AND DEATHS, INFANT MORTALITY, AND STILLBIRTHS, IN SELECTED REGISTRATION STATES, CITIES, AND COUNTIES: 1931 AND 1930—Continued

[See note at head of this table]

AREA AND COLOR	POPULATION ESTIMATED AS OF JULY 1		BIRTHS AND DEATHS (Exclusive of stillbirths): Number: Births		Number: Deaths		Rate per 1,000 population: Births		Rate per 1,000 population: Deaths		Excess of births over deaths [2]		Births per 100 deaths		INFANT MORTALITY (Exclusive of stillbirths): Deaths of infants under 1 year of age: Number		Per 1,000 births		STILLBIRTHS: Number		Rate per 100 live births	
	1931	1930	1931	1930	1931	1930	1931	1930	1931	1930	1931	1930	1931	1930	1931	1930	1931	1930	1931	1930	1931	1930
MISSISSIPPI COUNTIES—continued																						
Issaquena	[5] 5,734	[5] 5,734	162	128	99	87	28.3	22.3	17.3	15.2	63	41	(4)	(4)	15	18	92.6	140.6	6	13	3.7	10.2
Colored	4,669	4,669	139	113	91	81	29.8	24.2	19.5	17.3	48	32	(4)	(4)	14	17	100.7	150.4	5	13	3.6	11.5
White	1,065	1,065	23	15	8	6	21.6	14.1	7.5	5.6	15	9	(4)	(4)	1	1	43.5	66.7	1	------	4.3	------
Jackson	[5] 15,973	[5] 15,973	345	348	191	193	21.6	21.8	12.0	12.1	154	155	181	180	19	37	55.1	106.3	14	15	4.1	4.3
Colored	3,854	3,854	78	65	84	70	20.2	16.9	21.8	18.2	−6	−5	(4)	(4)	9	10	115.4	153.8	5	9	6.4	13.8
White	12,119	12,119	267	283	107	123	22.0	23.4	8.8	10.1	160	160	250	230	10	27	37.5	95.4	9	6	3.4	2.1
Jasper	18,600	18,600	489	541	132	171	26.3	29.1	7.1	9.2	357	370	370	316	22	32	45.0	59.1	17	23	3.5	4.3
Colored	9,000	9,000	280	292	74	96	31.1	32.4	8.2	10.7	206	196	(4)	(4)	12	23	42.9	78.8	10	18	3.6	6.2
White	9,600	9,600	209	249	58	75	21.8	25.9	6.0	7.8	151	174	(4)	(4)	10	9	47.8	36.1	7	5	3.3	2.0
Jefferson	[5] 14,291	[5] 14,291	345	338	164	173	24.1	23.7	11.5	12.1	181	165	210	195	24	27	69.6	79.9	9	10	2.6	3.0
Colored	10,838	10,838	285	288	129	127	26.3	26.6	11.9	11.7	156	161	221	227	19	23	66.7	79.9	5	10	1.8	3.5
White	3,453	3,453	60	50	35	46	17.4	14.5	10.1	13.3	25	4	(4)	(4)	5	4	83.3	80.0	4	------	6.7	------
Jefferson Davis	14,500	14,300	383	392	118	126	26.4	27.4	8.1	8.8	265	266	325	311	24	16	62.7	40.8	14	11	3.7	2.8
Colored	8,100	7,900	219	226	68	68	27.0	28.6	8.4	8.6	151	158	(4)	(4)	16	8	73.1	35.4	8	6	3.7	2.7
White	6,400	6,400	164	166	50	58	25.6	25.9	7.8	9.1	114	108	(4)	(4)	8	8	48.8	48.2	6	5	3.7	3.0
Jones	23,900	23,600	405	444	115	131	16.9	18.8	4.8	5.6	290	313	352	339	16	17	39.5	38.3	10	15	2.5	3.4
Colored	4,300	4,400	112	121	32	37	26.0	27.5	7.4	8.4	80	84	(4)	(4)	5	4	44.6	33.1	6	8	5.4	6.6
White	19,600	19,200	293	323	83	94	14.9	16.8	4.2	4.9	210	229	(4)	(4)	11	13	37.5	40.2	4	7	1.4	2.2
Kemper	22,200	21,900	601	577	191	211	27.1	26.3	8.6	9.6	410	366	315	273	27	36	44.9	62.4	19	18	3.2	3.1
Colored	13,000	12,800	387	372	128	131	29.8	29.1	9.8	10.2	259	241	302	284	19	22	49.1	59.1	9	11	2.3	3.0
White	9,200	9,100	214	205	63	80	23.3	22.5	6.8	8.8	151	125	(4)	(3)	8	14	37.4	68.3	10	7	4.7	3.4
Lafayette	20,100	20,000	495	494	211	223	24.6	24.7	10.5	11.2	284	271	235	222	22	29	44.4	58.7	22	20	4.4	4.0
Colored	8,300	8,200	216	219	110	138	26.0	26.7	13.3	16.8	106	81	196	159	13	23	60.2	105.0	10	17	4.6	7.8
White	11,800	11,800	279	275	101	85	23.6	23.3	8.6	7.2	178	190	276	(4)	9	6	32.3	21.8	12	3	4.3	1.1
Lamar	[5] 12,848	[5] 12,848	309	305	110	105	24.1	23.7	8.6	8.2	199	200	281	290	12	20	38.8	65.6	19	11	6.1	3.6
Colored	2,729	2,729	80	60	26	24	29.3	22.0	9.5	8.8	54	36	(4)	(4)	8	5	100.0	83.3	11	3	13.8	5.0
White	10,119	10,119	229	245	84	81	22.6	24.2	8.3	8.0	145	164	(4)	(4)	4	15	17.5	61.2	8	8	3.5	3.3
Lauderdale	21,600	20,900	431	482	135	172	20.0	23.1	6.3	8.2	296	310	319	280	19	26	44.1	53.9	24	17	5.6	3.5
Colored	10,200	9,900	259	298	56	99	25.4	30.1	5.5	10.0	203	199	(4)	(4)	12	12	46.3	40.3	18	10	6.9	3.4
White	11,400	11,000	172	184	79	73	15.1	16.7	6.9	6.6	93	111	(4)	(4)	7	14	40.7	76.1	6	7	3.5	3.8
Lawrence	[5] 12,471	[5] 12,471	275	343	114	99	22.1	27.5	9.1	7.9	161	244	241	(4)	14	11	50.9	32.1	6	20	2.2	5.8
Colored	4,696	4,696	96	133	69	49	20.4	28.3	14.7	10.4	27	84	(4)	(4)	9	4	93.8	30.1	3	11	3.1	8.3
White	7,775	7,775	179	210	45	50	23.0	27.0	5.8	6.4	134	160	(4)	(4)	5	7	27.9	33.3	3	9	1.7	4.3
Leake	22,400	21,900	571	676	149	184	25.5	30.9	6.7	8.4	422	492	383	367	21	54	36.8	79.9	26	23	4.6	3.4
Colored	8,300	8,100	249	279	62	85	30.0	34.4	7.5	10.5	187	194	(4)	(4)	10	33	40.2	118.3	11	11	4.4	3.9
White	14,100	13,800	322	397	87	99	22.8	28.8	6.2	7.2	235	298	(4)	(4)	11	21	34.2	52.9	15	12	4.7	3.0
Lee	36,000	35,500	875	904	345	338	24.3	25.5	9.6	9.5	530	566	254	267	27	50	30.9	55.3	32	37	3.7	4.1
Colored	11,400	11,300	285	278	144	122	25.0	24.6	12.6	10.8	141	156	198	228	10	13	35.1	46.8	12	13	4.2	4.7
White	24,600	24,200	590	626	201	216	24.0	25.9	8.2	8.9	389	410	294	290	17	37	28.8	59.1	20	24	3.4	3.8
Leflore	44,000	42,700	767	953	361	413	17.4	22.3	8.2	9.7	406	540	212	231	42	54	54.8	56.7	38	69	5.0	7.2
Colored	36,900	35,800	657	860	307	347	17.8	24.0	8.3	9.7	350	513	214	248	34	46	51.8	53.5	35	65	5.3	7.6
White	7,100	6,900	110	93	54	66	15.5	13.5	7.6	9.6	56	27	(4)	(4)	8	8	72.7	86.0	3	4	2.7	4.3
Lincoln	26,600	26,400	707	667	282	312	26.6	25.3	10.6	11.8	425	355	251	214	51	45	72.1	67.5	36	34	5.1	5.1
Colored	9,600	9,500	299	255	133	149	31.1	26.8	13.9	15.7	166	106	225	171	28	21	93.6	82.4	22	20	7.4	7.8
White	17,000	16,900	408	412	149	163	24.0	24.4	8.8	9.6	259	249	274	253	23	24	56.4	58.3	14	14	3.4	3.4
Lowndes	19,500	19,300	342	344	133	158	17.5	17.8	6.8	8.2	209	186	257	218	25	18	73.1	52.3	14	15	4.1	4.4
Colored	12,500	12,500	249	267	106	127	19.9	21.4	8.5	10.2	143	140	235	210	23	16	92.4	59.9	12	12	4.8	4.5
White	7,000	6,800	93	77	27	31	13.3	11.3	3.9	4.6	66	46	(4)	(4)	2	2	21.5	26.0	2	3	2.2	3.9
Madison	36,600	36,000	801	867	404	395	21.9	24.1	11.0	11.0	397	472	198	219	58	57	72.4	65.7	44	46	5.5	5.3
Colored	28,800	28,300	678	719	335	333	23.5	25.4	11.6	11.8	343	386	202	216	54	48	79.6	66.8	42	46	6.2	6.4
White	7,800	7,700	123	148	69	62	15.8	19.2	8.8	8.1	54	86	(4)	(4)	4	9	32.5	60.8	2	------	1.6	------
Marion	20,300	20,000	457	483	164	204	22.5	24.2	8.1	10.2	293	279	279	237	19	23	41.6	47.6	15	22	3.3	4.6
Colored	7,800	7,700	184	197	74	91	23.6	25.6	9.5	11.8	110	106	(4)	(4)	11	7	59.8	35.5	8	10	4.3	5.1
White	12,500	12,300	273	286	90	113	21.8	23.3	7.2	9.2	183	173	(4)	253	8	16	29.3	55.9	7	12	2.6	4.2
Marshall	[5] 24,869	[5] 24,869	657	629	284	316	26.4	25.3	11.4	12.7	373	313	231	199	49	56	74.6	89.0	30	30	4.6	4.8
Colored	17,776	17,776	503	474	223	258	28.3	26.7	12.5	14.5	280	216	226	184	39	51	77.5	107.6	28	27	5.6	5.7
White	7,093	7,093	154	155	61	58	21.7	21.9	8.6	8.2	93	97	(4)	(4)	10	5	64.9	32.3	2	3	1.3	1.9
Monroe	36,600	36,200	768	828	334	336	21.0	22.9	9.1	9.3	434	492	230	246	35	56	45.6	67.6	28	35	3.6	4.2
Colored	16,200	16,000	367	369	182	176	22.7	23.1	11.2	11.0	185	193	202	210	22	33	59.9	89.4	21	24	5.7	6.5
White	20,400	20,200	401	459	152	160	19.7	22.7	7.5	7.9	249	299	264	287	13	23	32.4	50.1	7	11	1.7	2.4

Montgomery	15,200	15,000	396	377	169	170	26.1	25.1	11.1	11.3	227	207	234	222	23	25	58.1	66.3	20	24	5.1	6.4
Colored	6,700	6,500	197	179	85	97	29.4	27.5	12.7	14.9	112	82	(4)	(4)	17	17	86.3	95.0	11	14	5.6	7.8
White	8,500	8,500	199	198	84	73	23.4	23.3	9.9	8.6	115	125	(4)	(4)	6	8	30.2	40.4	9	10	4.5	5.1
Neshoba	27,600	26,900	617	721	169	195	22.4	26.8	6.1	7.2	448	526	365	370	28	32	45.4	44.4	16	22	2.6	3.1
Colored	6,500	6,300	163	179	47	68	25.1	28.4	7.2	10.8	116	111	(4)	(4)	9	14	55.2	78.2	8	8	4.9	4.5
White	21,100	20,600	454	542	122	127	21.5	26.3	5.8	6.2	332	415	372	427	19	18	41.9	33.2	8	14	1.8	2.6
Newton	23,200	23,000	569	596	163	194	24.5	25.9	7.0	8.4	406	402	349	307	26	36	45.7	60.4	16	23	2.8	3.9
Colored	8,300	8,200	238	254	62	76	28.7	31.0	7.5	9.3	176	178	(4)	(4)	15	18	63.0	70.9	11	18	4.6	7.1
White	14,900	14,800	331	342	101	118	22.2	23.1	6.8	8.0	230	224	328	290	11	18	33.2	52.6	5	5	1.5	1.5
Noxubee	25,800	25,600	725	603	254	307	28.1	23.6	9.8	12.0	471	296	285	196	37	40	51.0	66.3	32	22	4.4	3.6
Colored	20,300	20,200	607	516	206	256	29.9	25.5	10.1	12.7	401	260	295	202	33	37	54.4	71.7	29	20	4.8	3.9
White	5,500	5,400	118	87	48	51	21.5	16.1	8.7	9.4	70	36	(4)	(4)	4	3	33.9	34.5	3	2	2.5	2.3
Oktibbeha	19,400	19,200	442	507	177	202	22.8	26.4	9.1	10.5	265	305	250	251	23	22	52.0	43.4	15	20	3.4	3.9
Colored	11,500	11,400	293	359	117	147	25.5	31.5	10.2	12.9	176	212	250	244	20	17	68.3	47.4	15	11	5.1	3.1
White	7,900	7,800	149	148	60	55	18.9	19.0	7.6	7.1	89	93	(4)	(4)	3	5	20.1	33.8		9		6.1
Panola	28,700	28,700	710	723	366	397	24.7	25.2	12.8	13.8	344	326	194	182	57	70	80.3	96.8	40	33	5.6	4.6
Colored	18,000	18,000	469	502	271	297	26.1	27.9	15.1	16.5	198	205	173	169	46	62	98.1	123.5	33	28	7.0	5.6
White	10,700	10,700	241	221	95	100	22.5	20.7	8.9	9.3	146	121	(4)	221	11	8	45.6	36.2	7	5	2.9	2.3
Pearl River	19,900	19,500	393	439	145	188	19.7	22.5	7.3	9.6	248	251	271	234	15	32	38.2	72.9	13	15	3.3	3.4
Colored	5,300	5,200	79	72	56	68	14.9	13.8	10.6	13.1	23	4	(4)	(4)	5	9	63.3	125.0	8	7	10.1	9.7
White	14,600	14,300	314	367	89	120	21.5	25.7	6.1	8.4	225	247	(4)	306	10	23	31.8	62.7	5	8	1.6	2.2
Perry	[5] 8,197	[5] 8,197	184	156	68	76	22.4	19.0	8.3	9.3	116	80	(4)	(4)	9	12	48.9	76.9	3	12	1.6	7.7
Colored	2,748	2,748	54	47	39	41	19.7	17.1	14.2	14.9	15	6	(4)	(4)	4	6	74.1	127.7	1	7	1.9	14.9
White	5,449	5,449	130	109	29	35	23.9	20.0	5.3	6.4	101	74	(4)	(4)	5	6	38.5	55.0	2	5	1.5	4.6
Pike	22,300	22,200	454	484	155	215	20.4	21.8	7.0	9.7	299	269	293	225	23	29	50.7	59.9	15	16	3.3	3.3
Colored	12,500	12,500	292	318	93	127	23.4	25.4	7.4	10.2	199	191	(4)	250	17	21	58.2	66.0	10	16	3.4	5.0
White	9,800	9,700	162	166	62	88	16.5	17.1	6.3	9.1	100	78	(4)	(4)	6	8	37.0	48.2	5		3.1	
Pontotoc	22,300	22,100	569	576	146	177	25.5	26.1	6.5	8.0	423	399	390	325	20	33	35.1	57.3	12	11	2.1	1.9
Colored	4,200	4,200	96	111	39	67	22.9	26.4	9.3	16.0	57	44	(4)	(4)	5	12	52.1	108.1	4	4	4.2	3.6
White	18,100	17,900	473	465	107	110	26.1	26.0	5.9	6.1	366	355	442	423	15	21	31.7	45.2	8	7	1.7	1.5
Prentiss	19,500	19,300	427	420	162	192	21.9	21.8	8.3	9.9	265	228	264	219	18	18	42.2	42.9	12	11	2.8	2.6
Colored	2,500	2,500	40	58	31	33	16.0	23.2	12.4	13.2	9	25	(4)	(4)	1	1	25.0	17.2	1	5	2.5	8.6
White	17,000	16,800	387	362	131	159	22.8	21.5	7.7	9.5	256	203	295	228	17	17	43.9	47.0	11	6	2.8	1.7
Quitman	26,000	25,400	471	619	240	319	18.1	24.4	9.2	12.6	231	300	196	194	27	44	57.3	71.1	24	19	5.1	3.1
Colored	17,700	17,400	306	391	175	240	17.3	22.5	9.9	13.8	131	151	175	163	18	34	58.8	87.0	21	15	6.9	3.8
White	8,300	8,000	165	228	65	79	19.9	28.5	7.8	9.9	100	149	(4)	(4)	9	10	54.5	43.9	3	4	1.8	1.8
Rankin	20,400	20,400	556	553	209	217	27.3	27.1	10.2	10.6	347	336	266	255	28	26	50.4	47.0	33	23	5.9	4.2
Colored	11,100	11,100	339	336	124	143	30.5	30.3	11.2	12.9	215	193	273	235	17	21	50.1	62.5	26	19	7.7	5.7
White	9,300	9,300	217	217	85	74	23.3	23.3	9.1	8.0	132	143	(4)	(4)	11	5	50.7	23.0	7	4	3.2	1.8
Scott	21,500	21,000	573	593	150	159	26.7	28.2	7.0	7.6	423	434	382	373	20	32	34.9	54.0	15	15	2.6	2.5
Colored	9,000	8,700	272	255	70	89	30.2	29.3	7.8	10.2	202	166	(4)	(4)	10	16	36.8	62.7	5	12	1.8	4.7
White	12,500	12,300	301	338	80	70	24.1	27.5	6.4	5.7	221	268	(4)	(4)	10	16	33.2	47.3	10	3	3.3	.9
Sharkey	[5] 13,877	[5] 13,877	304	354	177	179	21.9	25.5	12.8	12.9	127	175	172	198	16	27	52.6	76.3	21	23	6.9	6.5
Colored	10,282	10,282	241	267	149	153	23.4	26.0	14.5	14.9	92	114	162	175	13	22	53.9	82.4	21	20	8.7	7.5
White	3,595	3,595	63	87	28	26	17.5	24.2	7.8	7.2	35	61	(4)	(4)	3	5	47.6	57.5		3		3.4
Simpson	21,200	21,000	430	530	178	234	20.3	25.2	8.4	11.1	252	296	242	226	9	21	20.5	39.6	16	22	3.7	4.2
Colored	7,000	7,000	175	182	79	97	25.0	26.0	11.3	13.9	96	85	(4)	(4)	2	14	11.4	76.9	9	11	5.1	6.0
White	14,200	14,000	255	348	99	137	18.0	24.9	7.0	9.8	156	211	(4)	254	7	7	27.5	20.1	7	11	2.7	3.2
Smith	18,700	18,500	476	493	107	106	25.5	26.6	5.7	5.7	369	387	445	465	15	19	31.5	38.5	19	22	4.0	4.5
Colored	3,700	3,600	119	99	19	29	32.2	27.5	5.1	8.1	100	70	(4)	(4)	6	8	50.4	80.8	5	6	4.2	6.1
White	15,000	14,900	357	394	88	77	23.8	26.4	5.9	5.2	269	317	(4)	(4)	9	11	25.2	27.9	14	16	3.9	4.1
Stone	[5] 5,704	[5] 5,704	89	109	38	54	15.6	19.1	6.7	9.5	51	55	(4)	(4)	6	5	67.4	45.9	6	4	6.7	3.7
Colored	1,424	1,424	19	21	19	25	13.3	14.7	13.3	17.6		−4	(4)	(4)	3	2	157.9	95.2	1	3	5.3	14.3
White	4,280	4,280	70	88	19	29	16.4	20.6	4.4	6.8	51	59	(4)	(4)	3	3	42.9	34.1	5	1	7.1	1.1
Sunflower	68,800	66,900	1,323	1,553	714	843	19.2	23.2	10.4	12.6	609	710	185	184	82	145	62.0	93.4	94	96	7.1	6.2
Colored	48,300	47,200	944	952	604	696	19.5	20.2	12.5	14.7	340	256	156	137	71	117	75.2	122.9	86	78	9.1	8.2
White	20,500	19,700	379	601	110	147	18.5	30.5	5.4	7.5	269	454	345	409	11	28	29.0	46.6	8	18	2.1	3.0
Tallahatchie	[5] 35,568	[5] 35,568	719	791	375	370	20.2	22.2	10.5	10.4	344	421	192	214	49	51	68.2	64.5	33	28	4.6	3.5
Colored	24,232	24,232	460	476	278	286	19.0	19.6	11.5	11.8	182	190	165	166	41	38	89.1	79.8	27	25	5.9	5.3
White	11,336	11,336	259	315	97	84	22.8	27.8	8.6	7.4	162	231	(4)	(4)	8	13	30.9	41.3	6	3	2.3	1.0
Tate	[5] 17,671	[5] 17,671	370	415	184	212	20.9	23.5	10.4	12.0	186	203	201	196	22	45	59.5	108.4	17	17	4.6	4.1
Colored	10,628	10,628	224	240	132	145	21.1	22.6	12.4	13.6	92	95	170	166	17	34	75.9	141.7	12	11	5.4	4.6
White	7,043	7,043	146	175	52	67	20.7	24.8	7.4	9.5	94	108	(4)	(4)	5	11	34.2	62.9	5	6	3.4	3.4
Tippah	19,100	18,700	466	473	151	172	24.4	25.3	7.9	9.2	315	301	309	275	22	40	47.2	84.6	7	19	1.5	4.0
Colored	3,300	3,100	88	102	39	52	26.7	32.9	11.8	16.8	49	50	(4)	(4)	7	19	79.5	186.3	2	7	2.3	6.9
White	15,800	15,600	378	371	112	120	23.9	23.8	7.1	7.7	266	251	338	309	15	21	39.7	56.6	5	12	1.3	3.2
Tunica	21,300	21,300	327	361	277	344	15.4	16.9	13.0	16.2	50	17	118	105	24	45	73.4	124.7	18	23	5.5	6.4
Colored	18,200	18,300	280	311	263	315	15.4	17.0	14.5	17.2	17	−4	106	99	24	40	85.7	128.6	17	23	6.1	7.4
White	3,100	3,000	47	50	14	29	15.2	16.7	4.5	9.7	33	21	(4)	(4)		5		100.0	1		2.1	
Union	21,400	21,300	489	510	179	204	22.9	23.9	8.4	9.6	310	306	273	250	17	23	34.8	45.1	22	19	4.5	3.7
Colored	4,600	4,500	92	95	49	64	20.0	21.1	10.7	14.2	43	31	(4)	(4)	2	5	21.7	52.6	9	10	9.8	10.5
White	16,800	16,800	397	415	130	140	23.6	24.7	7.7	8.3	267	275	305	296	15	18	37.8	43.4	13	9	3.3	2.2
Walthall	13,900	13,900	394	352	82	98	28.3	25.3	5.9	7.1	312	254	(4)	(4)	16	21	40.6	59.7	7	13	1.8	3.7
Colored	6,100	6,100	214	187	47	49	35.1	30.7	7.7	8.0	167	138	(4)	(4)	12	12	56.1	64.2	4	11	1.9	5.9
White	7,800	7,800	180	165	35	49	23.1	21.2	4.5	6.3	145	116	(4)	(4)	4	9	22.2	54.5	3	2	1.7	1.2
Warren	12,600	12,700	211	166	104	100	16.7	13.1	8.3	7.9	107	66	203	166	10	8	47.4	48.2	8	15	3.8	9.0
Colored	8,700	8,900	169	135	94	86	19.4	15.2	10.8	9.7	75	49	(4)	(4)	8	7	47.3	51.9	7	13	4.1	9.6
White	3,900	3,800	42	31	10	14	10.8	8.2	2.6	3.7	32	17	(4)	(4)	2	1	47.6	32.3	1	2	2.4	6.5
Washington	39,800	39,600	617	656	358	426	15.5	16.6	9.0	10.8	259	230	172	154	25	52	40.5	79.3	47	48	7.6	7.3
Colored	30,800	31,100	502	512	316	381	16.3	16.5	10.3	12.3	186	131	159	134	19	41	37.8	80.1	42	45	8.4	8.8
White	9,000	8,500	115	144	42	45	12.8	16.9	4.7	5.3	73	99	(4)	(4)	6	11	52.2	76.4	5	3	4.3	2.1

See footnotes at end of table.

TABLE 18.—COLORED[1] AND WHITE POPULATION, BIRTHS AND DEATHS, INFANT MORTALITY, AND STILLBIRTHS, IN SELECTED REGISTRATION STATES, CITIES, AND COUNTIES: 1931 AND 1930—Continued

[See note at head of this table]

AREA AND COLOR	POPULATION ESTIMATED AS OF JULY 1		BIRTHS AND DEATHS (Exclusive of stillbirths): Number: Births		Number: Deaths		Rate per 1,000 population: Births		Rate per 1,000 population: Deaths		Excess of births over deaths [2]		Births per 100 deaths		INFANT MORTALITY (Exclusive of stillbirths): Deaths of infants under 1 year of age: Number		Per 1,000 births		STILLBIRTHS: Number		Rate per 100 live births	
	1931	1930	1931	1930	1931	1930	1931	1930	1931	1930	1931	1930	1931	1930	1931	1930	1931	1930	1931	1930	1931	1930
MISSISSIPPI COUNTIES—continued																						
Wayne	[5] 15,295	[5] 15,295	368	421	120	151	24.1	27.5	7.8	9.9	248	270	307	279	10	21	27.2	49.9	5	14	1.4	3.3
Colored	5,369	5,369	135	159	42	70	25.1	29.6	7.8	13.0	93	89	(4)	(4)	2	10	14.8	62.9	3	6	2.2	3.8
White	9,926	9,926	233	262	78	81	23.5	26.4	7.9	8.2	155	181	(4)	(4)	8	11	34.3	42.0	2	8	.9	3.1
Webster	[5] 12,128	[5] 12,128	307	291	80	98	25.3	24.0	6.6	8.1	227	193	(4)	(4)	14	21	45.6	72.2	7	8	2.3	2.7
Colored	2,559	2,559	97	76	14	26	37.9	29.7	5.5	10.2	83	50	(4)	(4)	5	5	51.5	65.8	1	4	1.0	5.3
White	9,569	9,569	210	215	66	72	21.9	22.5	6.9	7.5	144	143	(4)	(4)	9	16	42.9	74.4	6	4	2.9	1.9
Wilkinson	[5] 13,957	[5] 13,957	394	395	148	214	28.2	28.3	10.6	15.3	246	181	266	185	17	20	43.1	50.6	17	21	4.3	5.3
Colored	9,787	9,787	307	312	111	169	31.4	31.9	11.3	17.3	196	143	277	185	17	15	55.4	48.1	15	15	4.9	4.8
White	4,170	4,170	87	83	37	45	20.9	19.9	8.9	10.8	50	38	(4)	(4)	-----	5	-----	60.2	2	6	2.3	7.2
Winston	21,600	21,300	524	582	161	190	24.3	27.3	7.5	8.9	363	392	325	306	21	34	40.1	58.4	9	13	1.7	2.2
Colored	8,300	8,200	225	222	68	75	27.1	27.1	8.2	9.1	157	147	(4)	(4)	8	12	35.6	54.1	6	10	2.7	4.5
White	13,300	13,100	299	360	93	115	22.5	27.5	7.0	8.8	206	245	(4)	313	13	22	43.5	61.1	3	3	1.0	.8
Yalobusha	[5] 17,750	[5] 17,750	389	443	188	198	21.9	25.0	10.6	11.2	201	245	207	224	20	20	51.4	45.1	22	12	5.7	2.7
Colored	8,253	8,253	226	258	104	110	27.4	31.3	12.6	13.3	122	148	217	235	10	11	44.2	42.6	13	6	5.8	2.3
White	9,497	9,497	163	185	84	88	17.2	19.5	8.8	9.3	79	97	(4)	(4)	10	9	61.3	48.6	9	6	5.5	3.2
Yazoo	37,300	37,300	940	918	485	513	25.2	24.6	13.0	13.8	455	405	194	179	73	71	77.7	77.3	55	50	5.9	5.4
Colored	25,100	25,200	671	618	370	391	26.7	24.5	14.7	15.5	301	227	181	158	54	58	80.5	93.9	47	45	7.0	7.3
White	12,200	12,100	269	300	115	122	22.0	24.8	9.4	10.1	154	178	234	246	19	13	70.6	43.3	8	5	3.0	1.7
MISSOURI COUNTIES [8]																						
Callaway	[5] 19,923	[5] 19,923	287	287	370	369	14.4	14.4	18.6	18.5	−83	−82	78	78	15	18	52.3	62.7	9	11	3.1	3.8
Colored	2,506	2,506	38	43	64	80	15.2	17.2	25.5	31.9	−26	−37	(4)	(4)	2	5	52.6	116.3	3	5	7.9	11.6
White	17,417	17,417	249	244	306	289	14.3	14.0	17.6	16.6	−57	−45	81	84	13	13	52.2	53.3	6	6	2.4	2.5
Cooper	19,500	19,500	301	340	239	238	15.4	17.4	12.3	12.2	62	102	126	143	20	19	66.4	55.9	8	13	2.7	3.8
Colored	2,000	2,000	24	29	33	29	12.0	14.5	16.5	14.5	−9	-----	(4)	(4)	5	2	208.3	69.0	3	2	12.5	6.9
White	17,500	17,500	277	311	206	209	15.8	17.8	11.8	11.9	71	102	134	149	15	17	54.2	54.7	5	11	1.8	3.5
Howard	[5] 13,490	[5] 13,490	184	191	171	146	13.6	14.2	12.7	10.8	13	45	108	131	8	6	43.5	31.4	3	9	1.6	4.7
Colored	1,938	1,938	25	30	47	20	12.9	15.5	24.3	10.3	−22	10	(4)	(4)	2	1	80.0	33.3	-----	4	-----	13.3
White	11,552	11,552	159	161	124	126	13.8	13.9	10.7	10.9	35	35	128	128	6	5	37.7	31.1	3	5	1.9	3.1
Mississippi	16,100	15,800	388	389	226	210	24.1	24.6	14.0	13.3	162	179	172	185	53	34	136.6	87.4	16	18	4.1	4.6
Colored	4,300	4,000	90	82	78	71	20.9	20.5	18.1	17.8	12	11	(4)	(4)	14	14	155.6	170.7	5	7	5.6	8.5
White	11,800	11,800	298	307	148	139	25.3	26.0	12.5	11.8	150	168	201	221	39	20	130.9	65.1	11	11	3.7	3.6
New Madrid	30,900	30,400	617	575	390	355	20.0	18.9	12.6	11.7	227	220	158	162	99	85	160.5	147.8	43	49	7.0	8.5
Colored	6,100	(3)	77	(3)	87	(3)	12.6	(3)	14.3	(3)	−10	(3)	(4)	(3)	19	(3)	246.8	(3)	9	(3)	11.7	(3)
White	24,800	(3)	540	(3)	303	(3)	21.8	(3)	12.2	(3)	237	(3)	178	(3)	80	(3)	148.1	(3)	34	(3)	6.3	(3)
Pemiscot	38,600	37,500	664	692	534	453	17.2	18.5	13.8	12.1	130	239	124	153	118	81	177.7	117.1	44	26	6.6	3.8
Colored	10,800	10,200	139	121	183	139	12.9	11.9	16.9	13.6	−44	−18	76	87	27	17	194.2	140.5	17	6	12.2	5.0
White	27,800	27,300	525	571	351	314	18.9	20.9	12.6	11.5	174	257	150	182	91	64	173.3	112.1	27	20	5.1	3.5
Pike	[5] 18,001	[5] 18,001	278	256	246	259	15.4	14.2	13.7	14.4	32	−3	113	99	22	16	79.1	62.5	10	5	3.6	2.0
Colored	2,146	2,146	24	27	36	56	11.2	12.6	16.8	26.1	−12	−29	(4)	(4)	4	5	166.7	185.2	1	2	4.2	7.4
White	15,855	15,855	254	229	210	203	16.0	14.4	13.2	12.8	44	26	121	113	18	11	70.9	48.0	9	3	3.5	1.3
NEBRASKA COUNTIES [8]																						
Thurston	10,600	10,500	305	277	131	121	28.8	26.4	12.4	11.5	174	156	233	229	22	21	72.1	75.8	14	9	4.6	3.2
Colored	2,000	1,900	79	45	55	55	39.5	23.7	27.5	28.9	24	−10	(4)	(4)	10	12	126.6	266.7	6	-----	7.6	-----
White	8,600	8,600	226	232	76	66	26.3	27.0	8.8	7.7	150	166	(4)	(4)	12	9	53.1	38.8	8	9	3.5	3.9
NEW JERSEY COUNTIES [8]																						
Salem	36,900	36,800	552	527	418	447	15.0	14.3	11.3	12.1	134	80	132	118	44	38	79.7	72.1	30	23	5.4	4.4
Colored	4,900	4,800	95	61	57	61	19.4	12.7	11.6	12.7	38	-----	(4)	(4)	7	7	73.7	114.8	-----	6	-----	9.8
White	32,000	32,000	457	466	361	386	14.3	14.6	11.3	12.1	96	80	127	121	37	31	81.0	66.5	30	17	6.6	3.6
NORTH CAROLINA COUNTIES [8]																						
Alamance	43,300	42,400	966	975	413	397	22.3	23.0	9.5	9.4	553	578	234	246	63	59	65.2	60.5	44	32	4.6	3.3
Colored	8,500	8,400	224	210	109	121	26.4	25.0	12.8	14.4	115	89	206	174	15	19	67.0	90.5	20	10	8.9	4.8
White	34,800	34,000	742	765	304	276	21.3	22.5	8.7	8.1	438	489	244	277	48	40	64.7	52.3	24	22	3.2	2.9
Anson	29,500	29,400	606	696	299	382	20.5	23.7	10.1	13.0	307	314	203	182	42	70	69.3	100.6	33	50	5.4	7.2
Colored	15,300	15,300	317	384	173	219	20.7	25.1	11.3	14.3	144	165	183	175	28	43	88.3	112.0	27	46	8.5	12.0
White	14,200	14,100	289	312	126	163	20.4	22.1	8.9	11.6	163	149	229	191	14	27	48.4	86.5	6	4	2.1	1.3

Beaufort	35,500	35,100	840	859	454	492	23.7	24.5	12.8	14.0	386	367	185	175	75	73	89.3	85.0	45	48	5.4	5.6
Colored	13,700	13,500	361	363	227	263	26.4	26.9	16.6	19.5	134	100	159	138	47	38	130.2	104.7	35	45	9.7	12.4
White	21,800	21,600	479	496	227	229	22.0	23.0	10.4	10.6	252	267	211	217	28	35	58.5	70.6	10	3	2.1	.6
Bertie	26,100	25,900	564	592	286	312	21.6	22.9	11.0	12.0	278	280	197	190	54	55	95.7	92.9	19	25	3.4	4.2
Colored	14,800	14,700	377	382	192	191	25.5	26.0	13.0	13.0	185	191	196	200	39	41	103.4	107.3	16	20	4.2	5.2
White	11,300	11,200	187	210	94	121	16.5	18.8	8.3	10.8	93	89	(4)	174	15	14	80.2	66.7	3	5	1.6	2.4
Bladen	22,700	22,500	610	610	195	257	26.9	27.1	8.6	11.4	415	353	313	237	42	52	68.9	85.2	39	26	6.4	4.3
Colored	9,500	9,400	277	257	87	131	29.2	27.3	9.2	13.9	190	126	(4)	196	20	29	72.2	112.8	23	16	8.3	6.2
White	13,200	13,100	333	353	108	126	25.2	26.9	8.2	9.6	225	227	308	280	22	23	66.1	65.2	16	10	4.8	2.8
Brunswick	15,900	15,800	456	482	194	177	28.7	30.5	12.2	11.2	262	305	235	272	26	35	57.0	72.6	28	40	6.1	8.3
Colored	6,000	5,900	182	203	84	84	30.3	34.4	14.0	14.2	98	119	(4)	(4)	16	18	87.9	88.7	17	27	9.3	13.3
White	9,900	9,900	274	279	110	93	27.7	28.2	11.1	9.4	164	186	249	(4)	10	17	36.5	60.9	11	13	4.0	4.7
Cabarrus	33,500	32,700	757	806	268	282	22.6	24.6	8.0	8.6	489	524	282	286	50	55	66.1	68.2	23	24	3.0	3.0
Colored	6,100	6,000	125	132	80	88	20.5	22.0	13.1	14.7	45	44	(4)	(4)	15	13	120.0	98.5	6	17	4.8	12.9
White	27,400	26,700	632	674	188	194	23.1	25.2	6.9	7.3	444	480	336	347	35	42	55.4	62.3	17	7	2.7	1.0
Camden	5,500	5,500	87	88	39	68	15.8	16.0	7.1	12.4	48	20	(4)	(4)	5	6	57.5	68.2	11	5	12.6	5.7
Colored	2,200	2,200	49	44	21	35	22.3	20.0	9.5	15.9	28	9	(4)	(4)	3	5	61.2	113.6	9	2	18.4	4.5
White	3,300	3,300	38	44	18	33	11.5	13.3	5.5	10.0	20	11	(4)	(4)	2	1	52.6	22.7	2	3	5.3	6.8
Carteret	17,100	16,900	352	411	184	197	20.6	24.3	10.8	11.7	168	214	191	209	28	34	79.5	82.7	13	21	3.7	5.1
Colored	2,600	2,500	55	74	33	39	21.2	29.6	12.7	15.6	22	35	(4)	(4)	4	8	72.7	108.1	5	7	9.1	9.5
White	14,500	14,400	297	337	151	158	20.5	23.4	10.4	11.0	146	179	197	213	24	26	80.8	77.2	8	14	2.7	4.2
Caswell	18,500	18,300	423	451	157	160	22.9	24.6	8.5	8.7	266	291	269	282	27	31	63.8	68.7	13	12	3.1	2.7
Colored	8,500	8,500	221	223	92	98	26.0	26.2	10.8	11.5	129	125	(4)	(4)	14	17	63.3	76.2	9	7	4.1	3.1
White	10,000	9,800	202	228	65	62	20.2	23.3	6.5	6.3	137	166	(4)	(4)	13	14	64.4	61.4	4	5	2.0	2.2
Catawba	45,200	44,200	1,010	1,045	346	421	22.3	23.6	7.7	9.5	664	624	292	248	61	70	60.4	67.0	42	36	4.2	3.4
Colored	5,100	4,900	94	119	66	77	18.4	24.3	12.9	15.7	28	42	(4)	(4)	11	17	117.0	142.9	7	11	7.4	9.2
White	40,100	39,300	916	926	280	344	22.8	23.6	7.0	8.8	636	582	327	269	50	53	54.6	57.2	35	25	3.8	2.7
Chatham	24,200	24,200	442	444	234	226	18.3	18.3	9.7	9.3	208	218	189	196	40	26	90.5	58.6	12	20	2.7	4.5
Colored	8,000	8,000	168	187	87	97	21.0	23.4	10.9	12.1	81	90	(4)	(4)	19	11	113.1	58.8	8	12	4.8	6.4
White	16,200	16,200	274	257	147	129	16.9	15.9	9.1	8.0	127	128	186	199	21	15	76.6	58.4	4	8	1.5	3.1
Chowan	11,400	11,300	272	264	151	140	23.9	23.4	13.2	12.4	121	124	180	189	39	32	143.4	121.2	12	21	4.4	8.0
Colored	5,400	5,300	131	130	98	82	24.3	24.5	18.1	15.5	33	48	(4)	(4)	29	20	221.4	153.8	11	20	8.4	15.4
White	6,000	6,000	141	134	53	58	23.5	22.3	8.8	9.7	88	76	(4)	(4)	10	12	70.9	89.6	1	1	.7	.7
Cleveland	42,400	41,300	974	1,080	277	345	23.0	26.2	6.5	8.4	697	735	352	313	49	76	50.3	70.4	41	40	4.2	3.7
Colored	10,500	10,000	198	266	71	95	18.9	26.6	6.8	9.5	127	171	(4)	(4)	7	21	35.4	78.9	18	17	9.1	6.4
White	31,900	31,300	776	814	206	250	24.3	26.0	6.5	8.0	570	564	377	326	42	55	54.1	67.6	23	23	3.0	2.8
Columbus	38,600	37,900	1,077	1,095	372	389	27.9	28.9	9.6	10.3	705	706	290	281	86	91	79.9	83.1	49	66	4.5	6.0
Colored	12,000	11,900	378	335	155	162	31.5	28.2	12.9	13.6	223	173	244	207	43	33	113.8	98.5	26	45	6.9	13.4
White	26,600	26,000	699	760	217	227	26.3	29.2	8.2	8.7	482	533	322	335	43	58	61.5	76.3	23	21	3.3	2.8
Craven	18,900	18,700	494	477	217	219	26.1	25.5	11.5	11.7	277	258	228	218	44	28	89.1	58.7	26	31	5.3	6.5
Colored	8,500	8,500	218	225	125	135	25.6	26.5	14.7	15.9	93	90	174	167	28	18	128.4	80.0	18	20	8.3	8.9
White	10,400	10,200	276	252	92	84	26.5	24.7	8.8	8.2	184	168	(4)	(4)	16	10	58.0	39.7	8	11	2.9	4.4
Cumberland	32,900	32,300	794	805	287	293	24.1	24.9	8.7	9.1	507	512	277	275	58	50	73.0	62.1	33	33	4.2	4.1
Colored	11,900	11,700	310	361	128	108	26.1	30.9	10.8	9.2	182	253	242	334	27	23	87.1	63.7	24	25	7.7	6.9
White	21,000	20,600	484	444	159	185	23.0	21.6	7.6	9.0	325	259	304	240	31	27	64.0	60.8	9	8	1.9	1.8
Currituck	[5] 6,710	[5] 6,710	106	127	68	87	15.8	18.9	10.1	13.0	38	40	(4)	(4)	13	11	122.6	86.6	3	3	2.8	2.4
Colored	2,255	2,255	44	49	24	26	19.5	21.7	10.6	11.5	20	23	(4)	(4)	6	2	136.4	40.8	1	2	2.3	4.1
White	4,455	4,455	62	78	44	61	13.9	17.5	9.9	13.7	18	17	(4)	(4)	7	9	112.9	115.4	2	1	3.2	1.3
Davie	14,500	14,400	365	296	155	172	25.2	20.6	10.7	11.9	210	124	235	172	26	18	71.2	60.8	7	14	1.9	4.7
Colored	2,500	2,400	67	43	32	41	26.8	17.9	12.8	17.1	35	2	(4)	(4)	6	4	89.6	93.0	2	5	3.0	11.6
White	12,000	12,000	298	253	123	131	24.8	21.1	10.3	10.9	175	122	242	193	20	14	67.1	55.3	5	9	1.7	3.6
Duplin	35,700	35,200	856	913	322	370	24.0	25.9	9.0	10.5	534	543	266	247	60	72	70.1	78.9	48	46	5.6	5.0
Colored	13,200	13,000	337	326	152	171	25.5	25.1	11.5	13.2	185	155	222	191	28	38	83.1	116.6	27	29	8.0	8.9
White	22,500	22,200	519	587	170	199	23.1	26.4	7.6	9.0	349	388	305	295	32	34	61.7	57.9	21	17	4.0	2.9
Durham	15,400	15,200	279	331	143	153	18.1	21.8	9.3	10.1	136	178	195	216	16	17	57.3	51.4	8	7	2.9	2.1
Colored	4,500	4,700	117	122	59	66	26.0	26.0	13.1	14.0	58	56	(4)	(4)	11	10	94.0	82.0	6	1	5.1	.8
White	10,900	10,500	162	209	84	87	14.9	19.9	7.7	8.3	78	122	(4)	(4)	5	7	30.9	33.5	2	6	1.2	2.9
Edgecombe	38,600	38,000	903	1,051	420	521	23.4	27.7	10.9	13.7	483	530	215	202	91	115	100.8	109.4	72	82	8.0	7.8
Colored	22,900	22,600	598	683	265	309	26.1	30.2	11.6	13.7	333	374	226	221	69	73	115.4	106.9	60	76	10.0	11.1
White	15,700	15,400	305	368	155	212	19.4	23.9	9.9	13.8	150	156	197	174	22	42	72.1	114.1	12	6	3.9	1.6
Forsyth	38,300	36,800	794	792	320	313	20.7	21.5	8.4	8.5	474	479	248	253	54	41	68.0	51.8	20	18	2.5	2.3
Colored	5,000	4,600	84	111	92	72	16.8	24.1	18.4	15.7	−8	39	(4)	(4)	12	8	142.9	72.1	3	9	3.6	8.1
White	33,300	32,200	710	681	228	241	21.3	21.1	6.8	7.5	482	440	311	283	42	33	59.2	48.5	17	9	2.4	1.3
Franklin	29,800	29,500	718	695	298	368	24.1	23.6	10.0	12.5	420	327	241	189	56	49	78.0	70.5	32	31	4.5	4.5
Colored	13,100	12,900	385	340	149	204	29.4	26.4	11.4	15.8	236	136	258	167	33	34	85.7	100.0	23	26	6.0	7.6
White	16,700	16,600	333	355	149	164	19.9	21.4	8.9	9.9	184	191	223	216	23	15	69.1	42.3	9	5	2.7	1.4
Gaston	63,800	61,500	1,416	1,495	386	453	22.2	24.3	6.1	7.4	1,030	1,042	367	330	81	86	57.2	57.5	44	50	3.1	3.3
Colored	9,500	9,200	132	144	77	103	13.9	15.7	8.1	11.2	55	41	(4)	140	12	10	90.9	69.4	9	14	6.8	9.7
White	54,300	52,300	1,284	1,351	309	350	23.6	25.8	5.7	6.7	975	1,001	416	386	69	76	53.7	56.3	35	36	2.7	2.7
Gates	10,600	10,600	229	227	97	89	21.6	21.4	9.2	8.4	132	138	(4)	(4)	14	12	61.1	52.9	15	11	6.6	4.8
Colored	5,100	5,100	145	121	45	47	28.4	23.7	8.8	9.2	100	74	(4)	(4)	7	7	48.3	57.9	9	8	6.2	6.6
White	5,500	5,500	84	106	52	42	15.3	19.3	9.5	7.6	32	64	(4)	(4)	7	5	83.3	47.2	6	3	7.1	2.8
Granville	29,000	28,800	723	663	317	382	24.9	23.0	10.9	13.3	406	281	228	174	48	41	66.4	61.8	30	49	4.1	7.4
Colored	14,300	14,100	403	383	169	198	28.2	27.2	11.8	14.0	234	185	238	193	29	19	72.0	49.6	21	38	5.2	9.9
White	14,700	14,700	320	280	148	184	21.8	19.0	10.1	12.5	172	96	216	152	19	22	59.4	78.6	9	11	2.8	3.9
Greene	19,000	18,700	542	495	138	169	28.5	26.5	7.3	9.0	404	326	393	293	44	31	81.2	62.6	30	26	5.5	5.3
Colored	9,100	8,900	240	218	67	95	26.4	24.5	7.4	10.7	173	123	(4)	(4)	22	18	91.7	82.6	21	19	8.8	8.7
White	9,900	9,800	302	277	71	74	30.5	28.3	7.2	7.6	231	203	(4)	(4)	22	13	72.8	46.9	9	7	3.0	2.5
Guilford	44,900	43,100	933	998	324	401	20.8	23.2	7.2	9.3	609	597	288	249	58	60	62.2	60.1	29	17	3.1	1.7
Colored	7,800	7,500	183	164	68	111	23.5	21.9	8.7	14.8	115	53	(4)	148	14	22	76.5	134.1	14	2	7.7	1.2
White	37,100	35,600	750	834	256	290	20.2	23.4	6.9	8.1	494	544	293	288	44	38	58.7	45.6	15	15	2.0	1.8

See footnotes at end of table.

TABLE 18.—COLORED[1] AND WHITE POPULATION, BIRTHS AND DEATHS, INFANT MORTALITY, AND STILLBIRTHS, IN SELECTED REGISTRATION STATES, CITIES, AND COUNTIES: 1931 AND 1930—Continued

[See note at head of this table]

AREA AND COLOR	POPULATION ESTIMATED AS OF JULY 1		BIRTHS AND DEATHS (Exclusive of stillbirths): Number, Births		Number, Deaths		Rate per 1,000 population, Births		Rate per 1,000 population, Deaths		Excess of births over deaths [2]		Births per 100 deaths		INFANT MORTALITY (Exclusive of stillbirths): Deaths of infants under 1 year of age, Number		Per 1,000 births		STILLBIRTHS: Number		Rate per 100 live births	
	1931	1930	1931	1930	1931	1930	1931	1930	1931	1930	1931	1930	1931	1930	1931	1930	1931	1930	1931	1930	1931	1930
NORTH CAROLINA COUNTIES—continued																						
Halifax	54,400	53,500	1,357	1,443	577	606	24.9	27.0	10.6	11.3	780	837	235	238	115	109	84.7	75.5	109	92	8.0	6.4
Colored	31,500	31,000	895	874	371	387	28.4	28.2	11.8	12.5	524	487	241	226	85	65	95.0	74.4	84	86	9.4	9.8
White	22,900	22,500	462	569	206	219	20.2	25.3	9.0	9.7	256	350	224	260	30	44	64.9	77.3	25	6	5.4	1.1
Harnett	39,100	38,100	1,030	1,067	358	399	26.3	28.0	9.2	10.5	672	668	288	267	83	82	80.6	76.9	45	35	4.4	3.3
Colored	10,800	10,500	277	297	135	178	25.6	28.3	12.5	17.0	142	119	205	167	33	33	119.1	111.1	15	19	5.4	6.4
White	28,300	27,600	753	770	223	221	26.6	27.9	7.9	8.0	530	549	338	348	50	49	66.4	63.6	30	16	4.0	2.1
Hertford	17,700	17,600	379	412	213	216	21.4	23.4	12.0	12.3	166	196	178	191	49	65	129.3	157.8	19	21	5.0	5.1
Colored	10,400	10,300	271	280	140	139	26.1	27.2	13.5	13.5	131	141	194	201	34	49	125.5	175.0	13	19	4.8	6.8
White	7,300	7,300	108	132	73	77	14.8	18.1	10.0	10.5	35	55	(4)	(4)	15	16	138.9	121.2	6	2	5.6	1.5
Hoke	14,600	14,300	323	379	174	192	22.1	26.5	11.9	13.4	149	187	186	197	26	32	80.5	84.4	17	21	5.3	5.5
Colored	9,300	9,000	233	260	119	128	25.1	28.9	12.8	14.2	114	132	196	203	21	22	90.1	84.6	15	18	6.4	6.9
White	5,300	5,300	90	119	55	64	17.0	22.5	10.4	12.1	35	55	(4)	(4)	5	10	55.6	84.0	2	3	2.2	2.5
Hyde	8,600	8,600	158	166	51	82	18.4	19.3	5.9	9.5	107	84	(4)	(4)	7	13	44.3	78.3	19	13	12.0	7.8
Colored	3,600	3,500	94	88	28	32	26.1	25.1	7.8	9.1	66	56	(4)	(4)	6	6	63.8	68.2	14	10	14.9	11.4
White	5,000	5,100	64	78	23	50	12.8	15.3	4.6	9.8	41	28	(4)	(4)	1	7	15.6	89.7	5	3	7.8	3.8
Iredell	37,000	36,300	746	768	287	324	20.2	21.2	7.8	8.9	459	444	260	237	40	53	53.6	69.0	37	27	5.0	3.5
Colored	7,900	7,600	162	175	90	122	20.5	23.0	11.4	16.1	72	53	(4)	143	16	20	98.8	114.3	11	13	6.8	7.4
White	29,100	28,700	584	593	197	202	20.1	20.7	6.8	7.0	387	391	296	294	24	33	41.1	55.6	26	14	4.5	2.4
Johnston	58,700	57,800	1,430	1,499	562	600	24.4	25.9	9.6	10.4	868	899	254	250	112	122	78.3	81.4	75	77	5.2	5.1
Colored	13,400	13,100	324	289	166	176	24.2	22.1	12.4	13.4	158	113	195	164	33	26	101.9	90.0	23	23	7.1	8.0
White	45,300	44,700	1,106	1,210	396	424	24.4	27.1	8.7	9.5	710	786	279	285	79	96	71.4	79.3	52	54	4.7	4.5
Jones	10,500	10,400	256	311	98	100	24.4	29.9	9.3	9.6	158	211	(4)	311	23	19	89.8	61.1	16	11	6.3	3.5
Colored	4,700	4,600	126	149	50	61	26.8	32.4	10.6	13.3	76	88	(4)	(4)	13	11	103.2	73.8	12	9	9.5	6.0
White	5,800	5,800	130	162	48	39	22.4	27.9	8.3	6.7	82	123	(4)	(4)	10	8	76.9	49.4	4	2	3.1	1.2
Lee	17,400	17,100	371	397	201	186	21.3	23.2	11.6	10.9	170	211	185	213	35	28	94.3	70.5	12	22	3.2	5.5
Colored	5,600	5,500	125	127	61	64	22.3	23.1	10.9	11.6	64	63	(4)	(4)	11	15	88.0	118.1	6	15	4.8	11.8
White	11,800	11,600	246	270	140	122	20.8	23.3	11.9	10.5	106	148	176	221	24	13	97.6	48.1	6	7	2.4	2.6
Lenoir	24,900	24,500	574	557	237	252	23.1	22.7	9.5	10.3	337	305	242	221	62	46	108.0	82.6	25	32	4.4	5.7
Colored	10,600	10,400	251	326	121	121	23.7	31.3	11.4	11.6	130	205	207	269	35	17	139.4	52.1	16	24	6.4	7.4
White	14,300	14,100	323	231	116	131	22.6	16.4	8.1	9.3	207	100	278	176	27	29	83.6	125.5	9	8	2.8	3.5
Lincoln	23,500	23,000	404	423	188	216	17.2	18.4	8.0	9.4	216	207	215	196	34	29	84.2	68.6	9	25	2.2	5.9
Colored	3,500	3,400	51	55	45	53	14.6	16.2	12.9	15.6	6	2	(4)	(4)	5	6	98.0	109.1	2	5	3.9	9.1
White	20,000	19,600	353	368	143	163	17.7	18.8	7.2	8.3	210	205	247	226	29	23	82.2	62.5	7	20	2.0	5.4
Martin	23,700	23,500	658	693	277	244	27.8	29.5	11.7	10.4	381	449	238	284	59	66	89.7	95.2	24	37	3.6	5.3
Colored	11,100	11,100	342	375	157	148	30.8	33.8	14.1	13.3	185	227	218	253	40	38	117.0	101.3	17	27	5.0	7.2
White	12,600	12,400	316	318	120	96	25.1	25.6	9.5	7.7	196	222	263	(4)	19	28	60.1	88.1	7	10	2.2	3.1
Mecklenburg	49,800	46,200	894	860	376	446	18.0	18.6	7.6	9.7	518	414	238	193	40	44	44.7	51.2	27	35	3.0	4.1
Colored	14,200	13,100	296	283	161	211	20.8	21.6	11.3	16.1	135	72	184	134	12	20	40.5	70.7	13	24	4.4	8.5
White	35,600	33,100	598	577	215	235	16.8	17.4	6.0	7.1	383	342	278	246	28	24	46.8	41.6	14	11	2.3	1.9
Montgomery	16,400	16,300	320	317	154	160	19.5	19.4	9.4	9.8	166	157	208	198	21	20	65.6	63.1	8	16	2.5	5.0
Colored	3,800	3,800	86	65	43	51	22.6	17.1	11.3	13.4	43	14	(4)	(4)	10	6	116.3	92.3	3	9	3.5	13.8
White	12,600	12,500	234	252	111	109	18.6	20.2	8.8	8.7	123	143	211	231	11	14	47.0	55.6	5	7	2.1	2.8
Moore	29,000	28,400	616	585	262	243	21.2	20.6	9.0	8.6	354	342	235	241	32	28	51.9	47.9	27	23	4.4	3.9
Colored	10,200	9,900	246	247	98	88	24.1	24.9	9.6	8.9	148	159	(4)	(4)	10	14	40.7	56.7	17	13	6.9	5.3
White	18,800	18,500	370	338	164	155	19.7	18.3	8.7	8.4	206	183	226	218	22	14	59.5	41.4	10	10	2.7	3.0
Nash	42,200	41,600	955	1,003	347	407	22.6	24.1	8.2	9.8	608	596	275	246	78	90	81.7	89.7	48	61	5.0	6.1
Colored	20,000	19,700	488	516	172	223	24.4	26.2	8.6	11.3	316	293	284	231	41	59	84.0	114.3	31	52	6.4	10.1
White	22,200	21,900	467	487	175	184	21.0	22.2	7.9	8.4	292	303	267	265	37	31	79.2	63.7	17	9	3.6	1.8
New Hanover	11,000	10,800	119	126	111	128	10.8	11.7	10.1	11.9	8	−2	107	98	19	22	159.7	174.6	3	11	2.5	8.7
Colored	3,700	3,700	60	58	58	59	16.2	15.7	15.7	15.9	2	−1	(4)	(4)	12	8	200.0	137.9	2	9	3.3	15.5
White	7,300	7,100	59	68	53	69	8.1	9.6	7.3	9.7	6	−1	(4)	(4)	7	14	118.6	205.9	1	2	1.7	2.9
Northampton	27,600	27,300	575	656	264	292	20.8	24.0	9.6	10.7	311	364	218	225	53	54	92.2	82.3	28	34	4.9	5.2
Colored	17,400	17,200	418	496	174	195	24.0	28.8	10.0	11.3	244	301	240	254	44	46	105.3	92.7	24	32	5.7	6.5
White	10,200	10,100	157	160	90	97	15.4	15.8	8.8	9.6	67	63	(4)	(4)	9	8	57.3	50.0	4	2	2.5	1.3
Onslow	15,400	15,300	432	452	159	186	23.1	29.5	10.3	12.2	273	266	272	243	22	47	50.9	104.0	24	23	5.6	5.1
Colored	4,100	4,100	152	135	47	57	37.1	32.9	11.5	13.9	105	78	(4)	(4)	8	13	52.6	96.3	10	16	6.6	11.9
White	11,300	11,200	280	317	112	129	24.8	28.3	9.9	11.5	168	188	250	246	14	34	50.0	107.3	14	7	5.0	2.2
Orange	21,600	21,300	405	425	196	235	18.8	20.0	9.1	11.0	209	190	207	181	26	40	64.2	94.1	16	19	4.0	4.5
Colored	7,100	7,000	149	157	74	101	21.0	22.4	10.4	14.4	75	56	(4)	155	8	21	53.7	133.8	11	14	7.4	8.9
White	14,500	14,300	253	268	122	134	17.7	18.7	8.4	9.4	134	134	210	200	18	19	70.3	70.9	5	5	2.0	1.9

Pamlico	9,300	9,300	258	232	83	96	27.7	24.9	8.9	10.3	175	136	(4)	(4)	16	9	62.0	38.8	10	14	3.9	6.0
Colored	3,100	3,100	116	113	35	41	37.4	36.5	11.3	13.2	81	72	(4)	(4)	11	6	94.8	53.1	8	12	6.9	10.6
White	6,200	6,200	142	119	48	55	22.9	19.2	7.7	8.9	94	64	(4)	(4)	5	3	35.2	25.2	2	2	1.4	1.7
Pasquotank	9,100	9,100	165	196	95	93	18.1	21.5	10.4	10.2	70	103	(4)	(4)	17	23	103.0	117.3	9	16	5.5	8.2
Colored	4,400	4,400	92	140	59	65	20.9	31.8	13.4	14.8	33	75	(4)	(4)	14	18	152.2	128.6	7	15	7.6	10.7
White	4,700	4,700	73	56	36	28	15.5	11.9	7.7	6.0	37	28	(4)	(4)	3	5	41.1	89.3	2	1	2.7	1.8
Pender	15,800	15,700	408	384	158	195	25.8	24.5	10.0	12.4	250	189	258	197	30	39	73.5	101.6	13	15	3.2	3.9
Colored	7,600	7,600	228	214	95	114	30.0	28.2	12.5	15.0	133	100	(4)	188	19	22	83.3	102.8	8	15	3.5	7.0
White	8,200	8,100	180	170	63	81	22.0	21.0	7.7	10.0	117	89	(4)	(4)	11	17	61.1	100.0	5	----	2.8	----
Perquimans	[5] 10,668	[5] 10,668	241	255	120	126	22.6	23.9	11.2	11.8	121	129	201	202	27	24	112.0	94.1	10	9	4.1	3.5
Colored	5,287	5,287	125	140	65	83	23.6	26.5	12.3	15.7	60	57	(4)	(4)	15	19	120.0	135.7	6	4	4.8	2.9
White	5,381	5,381	116	115	55	43	21.6	21.4	10.2	8.0	61	72	(4)	(4)	12	5	103.4	43.5	4	5	3.4	4.3
Person	22,400	22,100	620	570	173	233	27.7	25.8	7.7	10.5	447	337	358	245	31	41	50.0	71.9	22	31	3.5	5.4
Colored	8,800	8,800	260	276	71	95	29.5	31.4	8.1	10.8	189	181	(4)	(4)	21	22	80.8	79.7	15	23	5.8	8.3
White	13,600	13,300	360	294	102	138	26.5	22.1	7.5	10.4	258	156	353	213	10	19	27.8	64.6	7	8	1.9	2.7
Pitt	55,600	54,700	1,477	1,437	560	600	26.6	26.3	10.1	11.0	917	837	264	240	140	137	94.8	95.3	77	98	5.2	6.8
Colored	26,800	26,500	762	728	308	328	28.4	27.5	11.5	12.4	454	400	247	222	84	91	110.2	125.0	51	83	6.7	11.4
White	28,800	28,200	715	709	252	272	24.8	25.1	8.8	9.6	463	437	284	261	56	46	78.3	64.9	26	15	3.6	2.1
Polk	10,400	10,300	243	203	94	123	23.4	19.7	9.0	11.9	149	80	(4)	165	12	28	49.4	137.9	3	5	1.2	2.5
Colored	1,500	1,600	35	27	12	14	23.3	16.9	8.0	8.8	23	13	(4)	(4)	----	----	----	----	1	----	2.9	----
White	8,900	8,700	208	176	82	109	23.4	20.2	9.2	12.5	126	67	(4)	161	12	28	57.7	159.1	2	5	1.0	2.8
Randolph	36,900	36,400	849	850	299	331	23.0	23.4	8.1	9.1	550	519	284	257	49	46	57.7	54.1	19	48	2.2	5.6
Colored	3,900	3,900	68	78	33	50	17.4	20.0	8.5	12.8	35	28	(4)	(4)	5	8	73.5	102.6	2	13	2.9	16.7
White	33,000	32,500	781	772	266	281	23.7	23.8	8.1	8.6	515	491	294	275	44	38	56.3	49.2	17	35	2.2	4.5
Richmond	35,000	34,200	754	768	381	421	21.5	22.5	10.9	12.3	373	347	198	182	62	78	82.2	101.6	39	38	5.2	4.9
Colored	13,600	13,400	268	294	180	190	19.7	21.9	13.2	14.2	88	104	149	155	30	32	111.9	108.8	22	24	8.2	8.2
White	21,400	20,800	486	474	201	231	22.7	22.8	9.4	11.1	285	243	242	205	32	46	65.8	97.0	17	14	3.5	3.0
Robeson	68,000	66,800	1,873	1,766	739	738	27.5	26.4	10.9	11.0	1,134	1,028	253	239	148	134	79.0	75.9	108	109	5.8	6.2
Colored	36,000	35,300	1,097	948	409	395	30.5	26.9	11.4	11.2	688	553	268	240	91	80	83.0	84.4	65	75	5.9	7.9
White	32,000	31,500	776	818	330	343	24.3	26.0	10.3	10.9	446	475	235	238	57	54	73.5	66.0	43	34	5.5	4.2
Rockingham	51,900	51,300	1,230	1,267	515	503	23.7	24.7	9.9	9.8	715	764	239	252	83	94	67.5	74.2	57	39	4.6	3.1
Colored	11,600	11,600	220	220	165	167	19.0	19.0	14.2	14.4	55	53	133	132	25	30	113.6	136.4	28	19	12.7	8.6
White	40,300	39,700	1,010	1,047	350	336	25.1	26.4	8.7	8.5	660	711	289	312	58	64	57.4	61.1	29	20	2.9	1.9
Rowan	40,900	40,000	912	901	311	327	22.3	22.5	7.6	8.2	601	574	293	276	55	62	60.3	68.8	26	15	2.9	1.7
Colored	7,800	7,600	162	142	92	99	20.8	18.7	11.8	13.0	70	43	(4)	(4)	14	16	86.4	112.7	10	7	6.2	4.9
White	33,100	32,400	750	759	219	228	22.7	23.4	6.6	7.0	531	531	342	333	41	46	54.7	60.6	16	8	2.1	1.1
Rutherford	41,600	40,700	1,101	1,079	376	418	26.5	26.5	9.0	10.3	725	661	293	258	67	71	60.9	65.8	34	28	3.1	2.6
Colored	5,500	5,400	126	121	79	68	22.9	22.4	14.4	12.6	47	53	(4)	(4)	17	11	134.9	90.9	9	7	7.1	5.8
White	36,100	35,300	975	958	297	350	27.0	27.1	8.2	9.9	678	608	328	274	50	60	51.3	62.6	25	21	2.6	2.2
Sampson	40,600	40,200	1,098	1,138	412	428	27.0	28.3	10.1	10.6	686	710	267	266	77	74	70.1	65.0	52	49	4.7	4.3
Colored	14,300	14,100	399	436	186	177	27.9	30.9	13.0	12.6	213	259	215	246	39	31	97.7	71.1	30	37	7.5	8.5
White	26,300	26,100	699	702	226	251	26.6	26.9	8.6	9.6	473	451	309	280	38	43	54.4	61.3	22	12	3.1	1.7
Scotland	20,700	20,300	411	412	238	270	19.9	20.3	11.5	13.3	173	142	173	153	51	51	124.1	123.8	16	27	3.9	6.6
Colored	11,500	11,400	230	212	144	160	20.0	18.6	12.5	14.0	86	52	160	133	36	29	156.5	136.8	9	23	3.9	10.8
White	9,200	8,900	181	200	94	110	19.7	22.5	10.2	12.4	87	90	(4)	182	15	22	82.9	110.0	7	4	3.9	2.0
Stanly	30,600	30,300	739	755	282	322	24.2	24.9	9.2	10.6	457	433	262	234	50	56	67.7	74.2	16	30	2.2	4.0
Colored	3,600	3,500	46	74	54	61	12.8	21.1	15.0	17.4	−8	13	(4)	(4)	12	10	260.9	135.1	6	6	13.0	8.1
White	27,000	26,800	693	681	228	261	25.7	25.4	8.4	9.7	465	420	304	261	38	46	54.8	67.5	10	24	1.4	3.5
Stokes	22,500	22,300	513	549	158	165	22.8	24.6	7.0	7.4	355	384	325	333	36	21	70.2	38.3	11	17	2.1	3.1
Colored	2,500	2,400	49	55	28	24	19.6	22.9	11.2	10.0	21	31	(4)	(4)	6	3	122.4	54.5	1	4	2.0	7.3
White	20,000	19,900	464	494	130	141	23.2	24.8	6.5	7.1	334	353	357	350	30	18	64.7	36.4	10	13	2.2	2.6
Swain	[5] 11,568	[5] 11,568	231	226	61	62	20.0	19.5	5.3	5.4	170	164	(4)	(4)	14	10	60.6	44.2	1	12	.4	5.3
Colored	1,253	(3)	10	(3)	9	(3)	8.0	(3)	7.2	(3)	1	(3)	(4)	(3)	2	(3)	200.0	(3)	----	(3)	----	(3)
White	10,315	(3)	221	(3)	52	(3)	21.4	(3)	5.0	(3)	169	(3)	(4)	(3)	12	(3)	54.3	(3)	1	(3)	.5	(3)
Tyrrell	5,200	5,200	145	152	45	55	27.9	29.2	8.7	10.6	100	97	(4)	(4)	9	7	62.1	46.1	3	6	2.1	3.9
Colored	1,700	1,700	64	65	21	21	37.6	38.2	12.4	12.4	43	44	(4)	(4)	7	2	109.4	30.8	2	1	3.1	1.5
White	3,500	3,500	81	87	24	34	23.1	24.9	6.9	9.7	57	53	(4)	(4)	2	5	24.7	57.5	1	5	1.2	5.7
Union	41,600	41,100	940	1,000	374	421	22.6	24.3	9.0	10.2	566	579	251	238	55	72	58.5	72.0	33	47	3.5	4.7
Colored	10,200	10,100	215	224	134	143	21.1	22.2	13.1	14.2	81	81	160	157	20	17	93.0	75.9	12	19	5.6	8.5
White	31,400	31,000	725	776	240	278	23.1	25.0	7.6	9.0	485	498	302	279	35	55	48.3	70.9	21	28	2.9	3.6
Vance	27,800	27,400	664	580	313	340	23.9	21.2	11.3	12.4	351	240	212	171	54	74	81.3	127.6	53	34	8.0	5.9
Colored	12,200	12,000	352	295	170	180	28.9	24.6	13.9	15.0	182	115	207	164	35	41	99.4	139.0	42	27	11.9	9.2
White	15,600	15,400	312	285	143	160	20.0	18.5	9.2	10.4	169	125	218	178	19	33	60.9	115.8	11	7	3.5	2.5
Wake	58,500	57,600	1,288	1,183	548	633	22.0	20.5	9.4	11.0	740	550	235	187	78	88	60.6	74.4	62	77	4.8	6.5
Colored	21,600	21,400	543	546	273	326	25.1	25.5	12.6	15.2	270	220	199	167	41	47	75.5	86.1	40	61	7.4	11.2
White	36,900	36,200	745	637	275	307	20.2	17.6	7.5	8.5	470	330	271	207	37	41	49.7	64.4	22	16	3.0	2.5
Warren	23,600	23,400	647	679	270	292	27.4	29.0	11.4	12.5	377	387	240	233	53	77	81.9	113.4	38	37	5.9	5.4
Colored	15,000	14,900	477	488	189	208	31.8	32.8	12.6	14.0	288	280	252	235	43	63	90.1	129.1	34	34	7.1	7.0
White	8,600	8,500	170	191	81	84	19.8	22.5	9.4	9.9	89	107	(4)	(4)	10	14	58.8	73.3	4	3	2.4	1.6
Washington	11,600	11,600	304	309	163	162	26.2	26.6	14.1	14.0	141	147	187	191	39	29	128.3	93.9	11	14	3.6	4.5
Colored	5,400	5,400	188	184	85	97	34.8	34.1	15.7	18.0	103	87	(4)	(4)	26	21	138.3	114.1	9	13	4.8	7.1
White	6,200	6,200	116	125	78	65	18.7	20.2	12.6	10.5	38	60	(4)	(4)	13	8	112.1	64.0	2	1	1.7	.8
Wayne	38,800	38,100	830	872	556	600	21.4	22.9	14.3	15.7	274	272	149	145	60	77	72.3	88.3	34	41	4.1	4.7
Colored	16,700	16,400	339	343	374	406	20.3	20.9	22.4	24.8	−35	−63	91	84	26	30	76.7	87.5	17	23	5.0	6.7
White	22,100	21,700	491	529	182	194	22.2	24.4	8.2	8.9	309	335	270	273	34	47	69.2	88.8	17	18	3.5	3.4
Wilson	33,000	32,400	795	865	331	334	24.1	26.7	10.0	10.3	464	531	240	259	71	79	89.3	91.3	37	47	4.7	5.4
Colored	13,300	13,100	353	376	139	166	26.5	28.7	10.5	12.7	214	210	254	227	40	43	113.3	114.4	21	37	5.9	9.8
White	19,700	19,300	442	489	192	168	22.4	25.3	9.7	8.7	250	321	230	291	31	36	70.1	73.6	16	10	3.6	2.0

See footnotes at end of table.

TABLE 18.—COLORED [1] AND WHITE POPULATION, BIRTHS AND DEATHS, INFANT MORTALITY, AND STILLBIRTHS, IN SELECTED REGISTRATION STATES, CITIES, AND COUNTIES: 1931 AND 1930—Continued

[See note at head of this table]

AREA AND COLOR	POPULATION ESTIMATED AS OF JULY 1		BIRTHS AND DEATHS (Exclusive of stillbirths): Number: Births		Number: Deaths		Rate per 1,000 population: Births		Rate per 1,000 population: Deaths		Excess of births over deaths [2]		Births per 100 deaths		INFANT MORTALITY (Exclusive of stillbirths): Deaths of infants under 1 year of age: Number		Per 1,000 births		STILLBIRTHS: Number		Rate per 100 live births	
	1931	1930	1931	1930	1931	1930	1931	1930	1931	1930	1931	1930	1931	1930	1931	1930	1931	1930	1931	1930	1931	1930
OKLAHOMA COUNTIES [8]																						
Adair	14,900	14,800	211	268	165	142	14.2	18.1	11.1	9.6	46	126	128	189	18	19	85.3	70.9	7	10	3.3	3.7
Colored	5,100	5,000	19	41	64	52	3.7	8.2	12.5	10.4	−45	−11	(4)	(4)	4	8	210.5	195.1	----	3	----	7.3
White	9,800	9,800	192	227	101	90	19.6	23.2	10.3	9.2	91	137	190	(4)	14	11	72.9	48.5	7	7	3.6	3.1
Atoka	[5] 14,533	[5] 14,533	321	244	108	109	22.1	16.8	7.4	7.5	213	135	297	224	18	16	56.1	65.6	6	10	1.9	4.1
Colored	2,057	(3)	25	(3)	25	(3)	12.2	(3)	12.2	(3)	----	(3)	(4)	(3)	5	(3)	200.0	(3)	1	(3)	4.0	(3)
White	12,476	(3)	296	(3)	83	(3)	23.7	(3)	6.7	(3)	213	(3)	(4)	(3)	13	(3)	43.9	(3)	5	(3)	1.7	(3)
Blaine	21,000	20,600	437	441	154	181	20.8	21.4	7.3	8.8	283	260	284	244	25	29	57.2	65.8	3	15	.7	3.4
Colored	3,000	(3)	44	(3)	38	(3)	14.7	(3)	12.7	(3)	6	(3)	(4)	(3)	9	(3)	204.5	(3)	----	(3)	----	(3)
White	18,000	(3)	393	(3)	116	(3)	21.8	(3)	6.4	(3)	277	(3)	339	(3)	16	(3)	40.7	(3)	3	(3)	.8	(3)
Bryan	[5] 32,277	[5] 32,277	611	573	252	241	18.9	17.8	7.8	7.5	359	332	242	238	38	30	62.2	52.4	7	17	1.1	3.0
Colored	4,218	(3)	24	(3)	11	(3)	5.7	(3)	2.6	(3)	13	(3)	(4)	(3)	----	(3)	----	(3)	----	(3)	----	(3)
White	28,059	(3)	587	(3)	241	(3)	20.9	(3)	8.6	(3)	346	(3)	244	(3)	38	(3)	64.7	(3)	7	(3)	1.2	(3)
Caddo	52,800	51,200	1,072	1,109	338	325	20.3	21.7	6.4	6.3	734	784	317	341	68	63	63.4	56.8	18	31	1.7	2.8
Colored	5,400	(3)	91	(3)	67	(3)	16.9	(3)	12.4	(3)	24	(3)	(4)	(3)	14	(3)	153.8	(3)	2	(3)	2.2	(3)
White	47,400	(3)	981	(3)	271	(3)	20.7	(3)	5.7	(3)	710	(3)	362	(3)	54	(3)	55.0	(3)	16	(3)	1.6	(3)
Cherokee	[5] 17,470	[5] 17,470	331	235	98	97	18.9	13.5	5.6	5.6	233	138	(4)	(4)	11	9	33.2	38.3	6	5	1.8	2.1
Colored	5,046	5,046	51	32	26	32	10.1	6.3	5.2	6.3	25	----	(4)	(4)	2	1	39.2	31.3	3	1	5.9	3.1
White	12,424	12,424	280	203	72	65	22.5	16.3	5.8	5.2	208	138	(4)	(4)	9	8	32.1	39.4	3	4	1.1	2.0
Choctaw	[5] 24,142	[5] 24,142	79	59	27	29	3.3	2.4	1.1	1.2	52	30	(4)	(4)	3	1	38.0	16.9	----	----	----	----
Colored	7,051	7,051	6	9	5	8	.9	1.3	.7	1.1	1	1	(4)	(4)	----	----	----	----	----	----	----	----
White	17,091	17,091	73	50	22	21	4.3	2.9	1.3	1.2	51	29	(4)	(4)	3	1	41.1	20.0	----	----	----	----
Coal	[5] 11,521	[5] 11,521	195	198	40	23	16.9	17.2	3.5	2.0	155	175	(4)	(4)	4	7	20.5	35.4	7	7	3.6	3.5
Colored	1,175	(3)	5	(3)	2	(3)	4.3	(3)	1.7	(3)	3	(3)	(4)	(3)	----	(3)	----	(3)	----	(3)	----	(3)
White	10,346	(3)	190	(3)	38	(3)	18.4	(3)	3.7	(3)	152	(3)	(4)	(3)	4	(3)	21.1	(3)	7	(3)	3.7	(3)
Craig	[5] 18,052	[5] 18,052	374	306	299	357	20.7	17.0	16.6	19.8	75	−51	125	86	13	14	34.8	45.8	7	8	1.9	2.6
Colored	3,149	3,149	16	21	21	36	5.1	6.7	6.7	11.4	−5	−15	(4)	(4)	----	2	----	95.2	1	----	6.3	----
White	14,903	14,903	358	285	278	321	24.0	19.1	18.7	21.5	80	−36	129	89	13	12	36.3	42.1	6	8	1.7	2.8
Creek	53,800	53,700	569	637	317	335	10.6	11.9	5.9	6.2	252	302	179	190	33	41	58.0	64.4	14	23	2.5	3.6
Colored	6,900	6,900	30	29	67	66	4.3	4.2	9.7	9.6	−37	−37	(4)	(4)	2	7	66.7	241.4	1	2	3.3	6.9
White	46,900	46,800	539	608	250	269	11.5	13.0	5.3	5.7	289	339	216	226	31	34	57.5	55.9	13	21	2.4	3.5
Delaware	15,600	15,400	272	204	84	116	17.4	13.2	5.4	7.5	188	88	(4)	176	18	17	66.2	83.3	8	16	2.9	7.8
Colored	4,000	3,800	21	15	8	14	5.3	3.9	2.0	3.7	13	1	(4)	(4)	1	----	47.6	----	1	1	4.8	6.7
White	11,600	11,600	251	189	76	102	21.6	16.3	6.6	8.8	175	87	(4)	185	17	17	67.7	89.9	7	15	2.8	7.9
Hughes	30,900	30,400	700	568	192	174	22.7	18.7	6.2	5.7	508	394	365	326	32	19	45.7	33.5	14	25	2.0	4.4
Colored	4,400	4,200	57	38	43	35	13.0	9.0	9.8	8.3	14	3	(4)	(4)	7	2	122.8	52.6	4	----	7.0	----
White	26,500	26,200	643	530	149	139	24.3	20.2	5.6	5.3	494	391	432	381	25	17	38.9	32.1	10	25	1.6	4.7
Johnston	[5] 13,082	[5] 13,082	262	218	38	44	20.0	16.7	2.9	3.4	224	174	(4)	(4)	5	4	19.1	18.3	1	4	.4	1.8
Colored	1,516	(3)	18	(3)	1	(3)	11.9	(3)	.7	(3)	17	(3)	(4)	(3)	----	(3)	----	(3)	----	(3)	----	(3)
White	11,566	(3)	244	(3)	37	(3)	21.1	(3)	3.2	(3)	207	(3)	(4)	(3)	5	(3)	20.5	(3)	1	(3)	.4	(3)
Kingfisher	16,000	16,000	300	285	120	106	18.8	17.8	7.5	6.6	180	179	250	269	8	11	26.7	38.6	10	8	3.3	2.8
Colored	2,100	2,100	60	50	28	25	28.6	23.8	13.3	11.9	32	25	(4)	(4)	2	2	33.3	40.0	2	1	3.3	2.0
White	13,900	13,900	240	235	92	81	17.3	16.9	6.6	5.8	148	154	(4)	(4)	6	9	25.0	38.3	8	7	3.3	3.0
Lincoln	33,800	33,700	583	629	237	247	17.2	18.7	7.0	7.3	346	382	246	255	33	25	56.6	39.7	21	12	3.6	1.9
Colored	3,600	3,600	13	34	36	27	3.6	9.4	10.0	7.5	−23	7	(4)	(4)	5	3	384.6	88.2	1	----	7.7	----
White	30,200	30,100	570	595	201	220	18.9	19.8	6.7	7.3	369	375	284	270	28	22	49.1	37.0	20	12	3.5	2.0
Logan	27,800	27,800	479	449	310	365	17.2	16.2	11.2	13.1	169	84	155	123	29	39	60.5	86.9	9	17	1.9	3.8
Colored	6,600	6,600	91	60	91	140	13.8	9.1	13.8	21.2	----	−80	(4)	43	11	14	120.9	233.3	3	6	3.3	10.0
White	21,200	21,200	388	389	219	225	18.3	18.3	10.3	10.6	169	164	177	173	18	25	46.4	64.3	6	11	1.5	2.8
McCurtain	[5] 34,759	[5] 34,759	510	392	205	198	14.7	11.3	5.9	5.7	305	194	249	198	22	20	43.1	51.0	15	10	2.9	2.6
Colored	10,132	10,132	132	73	79	61	13.0	7.2	7.8	6.0	53	12	(4)	(4)	4	7	30.3	95.9	7	1	5.3	1.4
White	24,627	24,627	378	319	126	137	15.3	13.0	5.1	5.6	252	182	300	233	18	13	47.6	40.8	8	9	2.1	2.8
McIntosh	[5] 24,924	[5] 24,924	410	421	172	204	16.5	16.9	6.9	8.2	238	217	238	206	24	38	58.5	90.3	13	15	3.2	3.6
Colored	6,590	6,590	67	55	80	62	10.2	8.3	12.1	9.4	−13	−7	(4)	(4)	12	7	179.1	127.3	4	3	6.0	5.5
White	18,334	18,334	343	366	92	142	18.7	20.0	5.0	7.7	251	224	(4)	258	12	31	35.0	84.7	9	12	2.6	3.3
Mayes	18,000	17,900	343	284	104	111	19.1	15.9	5.8	6.2	239	173	330	256	15	21	43.7	73.9	13	5	3.8	1.8
Colored	4,100	4,000	19	18	29	12	4.6	4.5	7.1	3.0	−10	6	(4)	(4)	7	----	368.4	----	2	1	10.5	5.6
White	13,900	13,900	324	266	75	99	23.3	19.1	5.4	7.1	249	167	(4)	(4)	8	21	24.7	78.9	11	4	3.4	1.5
Muskogee	34,800	34,400	401	335	176	193	11.5	9.7	5.1	5.6	225	142	228	174	18	21	44.9	62.7	5	18	1.2	5.4
Colored	13,200	12,800	84	74	73	97	6.4	5.8	5.5	7.6	11	−23	(4)	(4)	6	7	71.4	94.6	2	5	2.4	6.8
White	21,600	21,600	317	261	103	96	14.7	12.1	4.8	4.4	214	165	308	(4)	12	14	37.9	53.6	3	13	.9	5.0
Nowata	[5] 13,611	[5] 13,611	237	217	132	129	17.4	15.9	9.7	9.5	105	88	180	168	13	14	54.9	64.5	2	10	.8	4.6
Colored	3,158	3,158	12	17	42	29	3.8	5.4	13.3	9.2	−30	−12	(4)	(4)	4	2	333.3	117.6	----	1	----	5.9
White	10,453	10,453	225	200	90	100	21.5	19.1	8.6	9.6	135	100	(4)	200	9	12	40.0	60.0	2	9	.9	4.5

Okfuskee	29,500	29,100	549	415	200	215	18.6	14.3	6.8	7.4	349	200	275	193	25	18	45.5	43.4	13	9	2.4	2.2
Colored	8,600	8,700	117	83	70	79	13.6	9.5	8.1	9.1	47	4	(4)	(4)	5	5	42.7	60.2	4	8	3.4	3.6
White	20,900	20,400	432	332	130	136	20.7	16.3	6.2	6.7	302	196	332	244	20	13	46.3	39.2	9	6	2.1	1.8
Okmulgee	39,600	39,600	661	574	239	186	16.7	14.5	6.0	4.7	422	388	277	309	29	24	43.9	41.8	15	16	2.3	2.8
Colored	9,900	9,800	109	71	46	67	11.0	7.2	4.6	6.8	63	4	(4)	(4)	2	8	18.3	112.7	4	5	3.7	7.0
White	29,700	29,800	552	503	193	119	18.6	16.9	6.5	4.0	359	384	286	423	27	16	48.9	31.8	11	11	2.0	2.2
Pittsburg	[11] 38,878	[5] 38,978	640	577	176	247	16.5	14.8	4.5	6.3	464	330	364	234	18	29	28.1	50.3	30	10	4.7	1.7
Colored	5,686	(3)	41	(3)	29	(3)	7.2	(3)	5.1	(3)	12	(3)	(4)	(3)	2	(3)	48.8	(3)	3	(3)	7.3	(3)
White	33,192	(3)	599	(3)	147	(3)	18.0	(3)	4.4	(3)	452	(3)	407	(3)	16	(3)	26.7	(3)	27	(3)	4.5	(3)
Pushmataha	[5] 14,744	[5] 14,744	437	258	116	58	29.6	17.5	7.9	3.9	321	200	377	(4)	13	13	29.7	50.4	7	8	1.6	3.1
Colored	1,645	(3)	37	(3)	15	(3)	22.5	(3)	9.1	(3)	22	(3)	(4)	(3)	1	(3)	27.0	(3)	3	(3)	8.1	(3)
White	13,099	(3)	400	(3)	101	(3)	30.5	(3)	7.7	(3)	299	(3)	396	(3)	12	(3)	30.0	(3)	4	(3)	1.0	(3)
Rogers	19,100	19,000	342	280	181	173	17.9	14.7	9.5	9.1	161	107	189	162	18	22	52.6	78.6	11	6	3.2	2.1
Colored	3,300	3,300	22	9	31	14	6.7	2.7	9.4	4.2	−9	−5	(4)	(4)	4		181.8			1		11.1
White	15,800	15,700	320	271	150	159	20.3	17.3	9.5	10.1	170	112	213	170	14	22	43.8	81.2	11	5	3.4	1.8
Sequoyah	[5] 19,505	[5] 19,505	363	330	137	123	18.6	16.9	7.0	6.3	226	207	265	268	17	12	46.8	36.4	12	11	3.3	3.3
Colored	4,809	4,809	31	39	31	29	6.4	8.1	6.4	6.0		10	(4)	(4)	2	3	64.5	76.9	2	3	6.5	7.7
White	14,696	14,696	332	291	106	94	22.6	19.8	7.2	6.4	226	197	313	(4)	15	9	45.2	30.9	10	8	3.0	2.7
Tillman	24,600	24,400	457	527	178	174	18.6	21.6	7.2	7.1	279	353	257	303	32	23	70.0	43.6	16	21	3.5	4.0
Colored	3,200	(3)	30	(3)	37	(3)	9.4	(3)	11.6	(3)	−7	(3)	(4)	(3)	8	(3)	266.7	(3)	2	(3)	6.7	(3)
White	21,400	(3)	427	(3)	141	(3)	20.0	(3)	6.6	(3)	286	(3)	303	(3)	24	(3)	56.2	(3)	14	(3)	3.3	(3)
Tulsa	51,400	47,500	820	945	337	313	16.0	19.9	6.6	6.6	483	632	243	302	45	56	54.9	59.3	13	27	1.6	2.9
Colored	5,400	(3)	40	(3)	34	(3)	7.4	(3)	6.3	(3)	6	(3)	(4)	(3)	4	(3)	100.0	(3)		(3)		(3)
White	46,000	(3)	780	(3)	303	(3)	17.0	(3)	6.6	(3)	477	(3)	257	(3)	41	(3)	52.6	(3)	13	(3)	1.7	(3)
Wagoner	22,600	22,500	511	439	216	230	22.6	19.5	9.6	10.2	295	209	237	191	31	22	60.7	50.1	21	18	4.1	4.1
Colored	7,600	7,600	126	101	89	111	16.6	13.3	11.7	14.6	37	−10	(4)	91	11	6	87.3	59.4	8	8	6.3	7.9
White	15,000	14,900	385	338	127	119	25.7	22.7	8.5	8.0	258	219	303	284	20	16	51.9	47.3	13	10	3.4	3.0
Washington	13,100	13,000	196	165	65	69	15.0	12.7	5.0	5.3	131	96	(4)	(4)	9	9	45.9	54.5	3	6	1.5	3.6
Colored	1,900	(3)	19	(3)	12	(3)	10.0	(3)	6.3	(3)	7	(3)	(4)	(4)	2	(3)	105.3	(3)		(3)		(3)
White	11,200	(3)	177	(3)	53	(3)	15.8	(3)	4.7	(3)	124	(3)	(4)	(4)	7	(3)	39.5	(3)	3	(3)	1.7	(3)
SOUTH CAROLINA COUNTIES [5]																						
Abbeville	[5] 23,323	[5] 23,323	484	532	205	283	20.8	22.8	8.8	12.1	279	249	236	188	30	46	62.0	86.5	30	18	6.2	3.4
Colored	11,065	11,065	261	284	122	170	23.6	25.7	11.0	15.4	139	114	214	167	20	29	76.6	102.1	21	14	8.0	4.9
White	12,258	12,258	223	248	83	113	18.2	20.2	6.8	9.2	140	135	(4)	219	10	17	44.8	68.5	9	4	4.0	1.6
Aiken	47,600	47,400	898	954	553	584	18.9	20.1	11.6	12.3	345	370	162	163	60	72	66.8	75.5	56	51	6.2	5.3
Colored	21,200	21,400	437	468	284	321	20.6	21.9	13.4	15.0	153	147	154	146	34	41	77.8	87.6	40	45	9.2	9.6
White	26,400	26,000	461	486	269	263	17.5	18.7	10.2	10.1	192	223	171	185	26	31	56.4	63.8	16	6	3.5	1.2
Allendale	[5] 13,294	[5] 13,294	325	306	129	142	24.4	23.0	9.7	10.7	196	164	252	215	18	20	55.4	65.4	25	33	7.7	10.8
Colored	9,761	9,761	280	256	106	116	28.7	26.2	10.9	11.9	174	140	264	221	15	17	53.6	66.4	22	30	7.9	11.7
White	3,533	3,533	45	50	23	26	12.7	14.2	6.5	7.4	22	24	(4)	(4)	3	3	66.7	60.0	3	3	6.7	6.0
Anderson	66,700	66,600	1,274	1,388	467	520	19.1	20.8	7.0	7.8	807	868	273	267	80	105	62.8	75.6	55	46	4.3	3.3
Colored	18,100	18,600	419	406	175	219	23.1	21.8	9.7	11.8	244	187	239	185	19	37	45.3	91.1	23	37	5.5	9.1
White	48,600	48,000	855	982	292	301	17.6	20.5	6.0	6.3	563	681	293	326	61	68	71.3	69.2	32	9	3.7	.9
Bamberg	[5] 19,410	[5] 19,410	452	462	205	241	23.3	23.8	10.6	12.4	247	221	220	192	31	33	68.6	71.4	33	40	7.3	8.7
Colored	12,475	12,475	345	334	148	172	27.7	26.8	11.9	13.8	197	162	233	194	21	26	60.9	77.8	29	34	8.4	10.2
White	6,935	6,935	107	128	57	69	15.4	18.5	8.2	9.9	50	59	(4)	(4)	10	7	93.5	54.7	4	6	3.7	4.7
Barnwell	[5] 21,221	[5] 21,221	573	468	179	186	27.0	22.1	8.4	8.8	394	282	320	252	28	21	48.9	44.9	42	34	7.3	7.3
Colored	13,465	13,465	414	351	128	139	30.7	26.1	9.5	10.3	286	212	323	253	23	18	55.6	51.3	33	28	8.0	8.0
White	7,756	7,756	159	117	51	47	20.5	15.1	6.6	6.1	108	70	(4)	(4)	5	3	31.4	25.6	9	6	5.7	5.1
Beaufort	[5] 21,815	[5] 21,815	485	454	387	386	22.2	20.8	17.7	17.7	98	68	125	118	48	50	99.0	110.1	58	71	12.0	15.6
Colored	15,572	15,572	397	367	348	354	25.5	23.6	22.3	22.7	49	13	114	104	46	47	115.9	128.1	58	69	14.6	18.8
White	6,243	6,243	88	87	39	32	14.1	13.9	6.2	5.1	49	55	(4)	(4)	2	3	22.7	34.5		2		2.3
Berkeley	22,400	22,300	634	678	332	384	28.3	30.4	14.8	17.2	302	294	191	177	73	74	115.1	109.1	40	41	6.3	6.0
Colored	14,900	15,100	485	533	284	328	32.6	35.3	19.1	21.7	201	205	171	163	65	66	134.0	123.8	36	33	7.4	6.2
White	7,500	7,200	149	145	48	56	19.9	20.1	6.4	7.8	101	89	(4)	(4)	8	8	53.7	55.2	4	8	2.7	5.5
Calhoun	[5] 16,707	[5] 16,707	447	490	241	243	26.8	29.3	14.4	14.5	206	247	185	202	53	62	118.6	126.5	55	44	12.3	9.0
Colored	12,408	12,408	375	417	211	215	30.2	33.6	17.0	17.3	164	202	178	194	49	61	130.7	146.3	53	42	14.1	10.1
White	4,299	4,299	72	73	30	28	16.7	17.0	7.0	6.5	42	45	(4)	(4)	4	1	55.6	13.7	2	2	2.8	2.7
Charleston	[5] 38,785	[5] 38,785	824	922	657	639	21.2	23.8	16.9	16.5	167	283	125	144	118	129	143.2	139.9	85	105	10.3	11.4
Colored	26,764	26,764	685	749	582	558	25.6	28.0	21.7	20.8	103	191	118	134	111	121	162.0	161.5	81	97	11.8	13.0
White	12,021	12,021	139	173	75	81	11.6	14.4	6.2	6.7	64	92	(4)	(4)	7	8	50.4	46.2	4	8	2.9	4.6
Cherokee	32,800	32,300	756	798	272	324	23.0	24.7	8.3	10.0	484	474	278	246	45	74	59.5	92.7	39	41	5.2	5.1
Colored	8,500	8,500	208	203	90	122	24.5	23.9	10.6	14.4	118	81	(4)	166	15	29	72.1	142.9	19	20	9.1	9.9
White	24,300	23,800	548	595	182	202	22.6	25.0	7.5	8.5	366	393	301	295	30	45	54.7	75.6	20	21	3.6	3.5
Chester	[5] 31,803	[5] 31,803	773	707	301	355	24.3	22.2	9.5	11.2	472	352	257	199	42	54	54.3	76.4	41	41	5.3	5.8
Colored	16,458	16,458	478	391	197	225	29.0	23.8	12.0	13.7	281	166	243	174	30	41	62.8	104.9	33	37	6.9	9.5
White	15,345	15,345	295	316	104	130	19.2	20.6	6.8	8.5	191	186	284	243	12	13	40.7	41.1	8	4	2.7	1.3
Chesterfield	34,600	34,400	761	801	297	367	22.0	23.3	8.6	10.7	464	434	256	218	61	67	80.2	83.6	29	34	3.8	4.2
Colored	12,700	12,800	344	337	168	175	27.1	26.3	13.2	13.7	176	162	205	193	38	39	110.5	115.7	16	19	4.7	5.6
White	21,900	21,600	417	464	129	192	19.0	21.5	5.9	8.9	288	272	323	242	23	28	55.2	60.3	13	15	3.1	3.2
Clarendon	[5] 30,036	[5] 30,036	711	747	399	452	23.7	24.9	13.3	15.0	312	295	178	165	75	68	105.5	91.0	48	52	6.8	7.0
Colored	21,563	21,563	554	576	324	369	25.7	26.7	15.0	17.1	230	207	171	156	68	57	122.7	99.0	43	45	7.8	7.8
White	8,473	8,473	157	171	75	83	18.5	20.2	8.9	9.8	82	88	(4)	(4)	7	11	44.6	64.3	5	7	3.2	4.1
Colleton	[5] 25,821	[5] 25,821	644	709	348	426	24.9	27.5	13.5	16.5	296	283	185	166	45	65	69.9	91.7	57	59	8.9	8.3
Colored	14,066	14,066	422	455	219	266	30.0	32.3	15.6	18.9	203	189	193	171	36	50	85.3	109.9	53	43	12.6	9.5
White	11,755	11,755	222	254	129	160	18.9	21.6	11.0	13.6	93	94	172	159	9	15	40.5	59.1	4	16	1.8	6.3
Darlington	41,700	41,500	977	998	453	499	23.4	24.0	10.9	12.0	524	499	216	200	81	98	82.9	98.2	73	84	7.5	8.4
Colored	21,500	21,600	541	539	298	346	25.2	25.0	13.9	16.0	243	193	182	156	66	68	122.0	126.2	60	62	11.1	11.5
White	20,200	19,900	436	459	155	153	21.6	23.1	7.7	7.7	281	306	281	300	15	30	34.4	65.4	13	22	3.0	4.8

See footnotes at end of table.

99576—35——27

TABLE 18.—COLORED [1] AND WHITE POPULATION, BIRTHS AND DEATHS, INFANT MORTALITY, AND STILLBIRTHS, IN SELECTED REGISTRATION STATES, CITIES, AND COUNTIES: 1931 AND 1930—Continued

[See note at head of this table]

AREA AND COLOR	POPULATION ESTIMATED AS OF JULY 1		BIRTHS AND DEATHS (Exclusive of stillbirths)												INFANT MORTALITY (Exclusive of stillbirths)				STILLBIRTHS			
			Number				Rate per 1,000 population				Excess of births over deaths [2]		Births per 100 deaths		Deaths of infants under 1 year of age				Number		Rate per 100 live births	
			Births		Deaths		Births		Deaths						Number [3]		Per 1,000 births					
	1931	1930	1931	1930	1931	1930	1931	1930	1931	1930	1931	1930	1931	1930	1931	1930	1931	1930	1931	1930	1931	1930
SOUTH CAROLINA COUNTIES—continued																						
Dillon	25,800	25,700	668	685	309	307	25.9	26.7	12.0	11.9	359	378	216	223	79	82	118.3	119.7	41	39	6.1	5.7
Colored	12,400	12,400	335	364	173	186	27.0	29.4	14.0	15.0	162	178	194	196	46	55	137.3	151.1	28	19	8.4	5.2
White	13,400	13,300	333	321	136	121	24.9	24.1	10.1	9.1	197	200	245	265	33	27	99.1	84.1	13	20	3.9	6.2
Dorchester	[5] 18,956	[5] 18,956	455	445	213	213	24.0	23.5	11.2	11.2	242	232	214	209	36	39	79.1	87.6	41	30	9.0	6.7
Colored	11,168	11,168	311	277	133	139	27.8	24.8	11.9	12.4	178	138	234	199	32	33	102.9	119.1	31	24	10.0	8.7
White	7,788	7,788	144	168	80	74	18.5	21.6	10.3	9.5	64	94	([4])	([4])	4	6	27.8	35.7	10	6	6.9	3.6
Edgefield	[5] 19,326	[5] 19,326	467	503	186	209	24.2	26.0	9.6	10.8	281	294	251	241	27	41	57.8	81.5	19	29	4.1	5.8
Colored	12,271	12,271	337	372	138	160	27.5	30.3	11.2	13.0	199	212	244	233	24	32	71.2	86.0	16	26	4.7	7.0
White	7,055	7,055	130	131	48	49	18.4	18.6	6.8	6.9	82	82	([4])	([4])	3	9	23.1	68.7	3	3	2.3	2.3
Fairfield	[5] 23,287	[5] 23,287	674	659	262	261	28.9	28.3	11.3	11.2	412	398	257	252	49	36	72.7	54.6	24	25	3.6	3.8
Colored	15,690	15,690	460	488	184	186	29.3	31.1	11.7	11.9	276	302	250	262	41	26	89.1	53.3	19	18	4.1	3.7
White	7,597	7,597	214	171	78	75	28.2	22.5	10.3	9.9	136	96	([4])	([4])	8	10	37.4	58.5	5	7	2.3	4.1
Florence	46,900	46,300	1,188	1,148	516	494	25.3	24.8	11.0	10.7	672	654	230	232	112	93	94.3	81.0	70	67	5.9	5.8
Colored	21,600	21,500	612	583	314	283	28.3	27.1	14.5	13.2	298	300	195	206	69	52	112.7	89.2	50	42	8.2	7.2
White	25,300	24,800	576	565	202	211	22.8	22.8	8.0	8.5	374	354	285	268	43	41	74.7	72.6	20	25	3.5	4.4
Georgetown	21,700	21,700	499	571	379	344	23.0	26.3	17.5	15.9	120	227	132	166	57	50	114.2	87.6	28	39	5.6	6.8
Colored	13,900	14,000	352	382	296	278	25.3	27.3	21.3	19.9	56	104	119	137	47	44	133.5	115.2	20	33	5.7	8.6
White	7,800	7,700	147	189	83	66	18.8	24.5	10.6	8.6	64	123	([4])	([4])	10	6	68.0	31.7	8	6	5.4	3.2
Greenville	90,600	88,400	1,551	1,755	785	869	17.1	19.9	8.7	9.8	766	886	198	202	125	132	80.6	75.2	60	66	3.9	3.8
Colored	17,200	17,100	277	307	185	227	16.1	18.0	10.8	13.3	92	80	150	135	24	30	86.6	97.7	21	18	7.6	5.9
White	73,400	71,300	1,274	1,448	600	642	17.4	20.3	8.2	9.0	674	806	212	226	101	102	79.3	70.4	39	48	3.1	3.3
Greenwood	24,800	25,000	550	537	214	291	22.2	21.5	8.6	11.6	336	246	257	185	19	42	34.5	78.2	17	23	3.1	4.3
Colored	11,600	12,000	267	285	131	180	23.0	23.8	11.3	15.0	136	105	204	158	12	17	44.9	59.6	14	13	5.2	4.6
White	13,200	13,000	283	252	83	111	21.4	19.4	6.3	8.5	200	141	([4])	227	7	25	24.7	99.2	3	10	1.1	4.0
Hampton	[5] 17,243	[5] 17,243	401	367	233	219	23.3	21.3	13.5	12.7	168	148	172	168	40	39	99.8	106.3	36	40	9.0	10.9
Colored	9,821	9,821	295	258	161	171	30.0	26.3	16.4	17.4	134	87	183	151	34	32	115.3	124.0	35	34	11.9	13.2
White	7,422	7,422	106	109	72	48	14.3	14.7	9.7	6.5	34	61	([4])	([4])	6	7	56.6	64.2	1	6	.9	5.5
Horry	40,300	39,600	1,284	1,253	364	351	31.9	31.6	9.0	8.9	920	902	353	357	80	70	62.3	55.9	53	55	4.1	4.4
Colored	9,900	9,700	312	320	121	116	31.5	33.0	12.2	12.0	191	204	258	276	32	28	102.6	87.5	23	20	7.4	6.3
White	30,400	29,900	972	933	243	235	32.0	31.2	8.0	7.9	729	698	400	397	48	42	49.4	45.0	30	35	3.1	3.8
Jasper	10,000	10,000	245	261	175	155	24.5	26.1	17.5	15.5	70	106	140	168	32	27	130.6	103.4	29	27	11.8	10.3
Colored	6,700	6,800	167	176	143	126	24.9	25.9	21.3	18.5	24	50	117	140	30	19	179.6	108.0	21	25	12.6	14.2
White	3,300	3,200	78	85	32	29	23.6	26.6	9.7	9.1	46	56	([4])	([4])	2	8	25.6	94.1	8	2	10.3	2.4
Kershaw	32,400	32,100	635	580	290	309	19.6	18.1	9.0	9.6	345	271	219	188	31	40	48.8	69.0	29	22	4.6	3.8
Colored	17,700	17,600	368	346	174	188	20.8	19.7	9.8	10.7	194	158	211	184	21	27	57.1	78.0	17	14	4.6	4.0
White	14,700	14,500	267	234	116	121	18.2	16.1	7.9	8.3	151	113	230	193	10	13	37.5	55.6	12	8	4.5	3.4
Lancaster	[5] 27,980	[5] 27,980	640	561	277	271	22.9	20.1	9.9	9.7	363	290	231	207	43	39	67.2	69.5	24	35	3.8	6.2
Colored	11,010	11,010	221	209	134	125	20.1	19.0	12.2	11.4	87	84	165	167	23	12	104.1	57.4	14	25	6.3	12.0
White	16,970	16,970	419	352	143	146	24.7	20.7	8.4	8.6	276	206	293	241	20	27	47.7	76.7	10	10	2.4	2.8
Laurens	[5] 42,094	[5] 42,094	855	844	482	541	20.3	20.1	11.5	12.9	373	303	177	156	64	89	74.9	105.5	37	34	4.3	4.0
Colored	17,711	17,711	391	375	248	306	22.1	21.2	14.0	17.3	143	69	158	123	36	47	92.1	125.3	13	17	3.3	4.5
White	24,383	24,383	464	469	234	235	19.0	19.2	9.6	9.6	230	234	198	200	28	42	60.3	89.6	24	17	5.2	3.6
Lee	[5] 24,096	[5] 24,096	648	636	254	283	26.9	26.4	10.5	11.7	394	353	255	225	66	66	101.9	103.8	39	62	6.0	9.7
Colored	16,247	16,247	523	504	181	219	32.2	31.0	11.1	13.5	342	285	289	230	57	55	109.0	109.1	35	54	6.7	10.7
White	7,849	7,849	125	132	73	64	15.9	16.8	9.3	8.2	52	68	([4])	([4])	9	11	72.0	83.3	4	8	3.2	6.1
Lexington	36,500	36,500	742	764	399	420	20.3	20.9	10.9	11.5	343	344	186	182	64	66	86.3	86.4	44	48	5.9	6.3
Colored	10,800	11,000	233	243	170	176	21.6	22.1	15.7	16.0	63	67	137	138	29	27	124.5	111.1	23	26	9.9	10.7
White	25,700	25,500	509	521	229	244	19.8	20.4	8.9	9.6	280	277	222	214	35	39	68.8	74.9	21	22	4.1	4.2
McCormick	[5] 11,471	[5] 11,471	306	275	117	157	26.7	24.0	10.2	13.7	189	118	262	175	13	29	42.5	105.5	18	24	5.9	8.7
Colored	7,698	7,698	252	214	74	121	32.7	27.8	9.6	15.7	178	93	([4])	177	10	25	39.7	116.8	17	20	6.7	9.3
White	3,773	3,773	54	61	43	36	14.3	16.2	11.4	9.5	11	25	([4])	([4])	3	4	55.6	65.6	1	4	1.9	6.6
Marion	27,600	27,300	720	734	261	227	26.1	26.9	9.5	8.3	459	507	276	323	42	35	58.3	47.7	48	55	6.7	7.5
Colored	15,100	15,000	415	404	161	146	27.5	26.9	10.7	9.7	254	258	258	277	25	20	60.2	49.5	34	42	8.2	10.4
White	12,500	12,300	305	330	100	81	24.4	26.8	8.0	6.6	205	249	305	([4])	17	15	55.7	45.5	14	13	4.6	3.9
Marlboro	[5] 31,634	[5] 31,634	774	758	448	447	24.5	24.0	14.2	14.1	326	311	173	170	78	94	100.8	124.0	58	66	7.5	8.7
Colored	18,255	18,255	476	448	262	284	26.1	24.5	14.4	15.6	214	164	182	158	49	62	102.9	138.4	40	48	8.4	10.7
White	13,379	13,379	298	310	186	163	22.3	23.2	13.9	12.2	112	147	160	190	29	32	97.3	103.2	18	18	6.0	5.8
Newberry	[5] 34,681	[5] 34,681	678	719	313	389	19.5	20.7	9.0	11.2	365	330	217	185	40	56	59.0	77.9	47	35	6.9	4.9
Colored	16,154	16,154	336	360	193	218	20.8	22.3	11.9	13.5	143	142	174	165	28	33	83.3	91.7	36	24	10.7	6.7
White	18,527	18,527	342	359	120	171	18.5	19.4	6.5	9.2	222	188	285	210	12	23	35.1	64.1	11	11	3.2	3.1

Oconee	33,800	33,400	797	748	330	370	23.6	22.4	9.8	11.1	467	378	242	202	47	68	59.0	90.9	21	26	2.6	3.5
Colored	6,000	5,900	144	140	84	93	24.0	23.7	14.0	15.8	60	47	(4)	(4)	11	19	76.4	135.7	11	9	7.6	6.4
White	27,800	27,500	653	608	246	277	23.5	22.1	8.8	10.1	407	331	265	219	36	49	55.1	80.6	10	17	1.5	2.8
Orangeburg	[5] 63,864	[5] 63,864	1,690	1,614	863	924	26.5	25.3	13.5	14.5	827	690	196	175	148	164	87.6	101.6	121	122	7.2	7.6
Colored	40,777	40,777	1,247	1,131	660	683	30.6	27.7	16.2	16.7	587	448	189	166	133	137	106.7	121.1	111	108	8.9	9.5
White	23,087	23,087	443	483	203	241	19.2	20.9	8.8	10.4	240	242	218	200	15	27	33.9	55.9	10	14	2.3	2.9
Pickens	34,400	33,800	926	916	263	295	26.9	27.1	7.6	8.7	663	621	352	311	56	60	60.5	65.5	25	38	2.7	4.1
Colored	4,900	4,900	140	128	63	59	28.6	26.1	12.9	12.0	77	69	(4)	(4)	11	10	78.6	78.1	12	15	8.6	11.7
White	29,500	28,900	786	788	200	236	26.6	27.3	6.8	8.2	586	552	393	334	45	50	57.3	63.5	13	23	1.7	2.9
Richland	36,300	37,600	678	680	534	598	18.7	18.1	14.7	15.9	144	82	127	114	56	61	82.6	89.7	46	59	6.8	8.7
Colored	18,400	20,000	477	511	366	432	25.9	25.6	19.9	21.6	111	79	130	118	46	45	96.4	88.1	37	54	7.8	10.6
White	17,900	17,600	201	169	168	166	11.2	9.6	9.4	9.4	33	3	120	102	10	16	49.8	94.7	9	5	4.5	3.0
Saluda	[5] 18,148	[5] 18,148	388	374	142	154	21.4	20.6	7.8	8.5	246	220	273	243	12	13	30.9	34.8	25	13	6.4	3.5
Colored	8,823	8,823	189	200	65	79	21.4	22.7	7.4	9.0	124	121	(4)	(4)	5	8	26.5	40.0	13	11	6.9	5.5
White	9,325	9,325	199	174	77	75	21.3	18.7	8.3	8.0	122	99	(4)	(4)	7	5	35.2	28.7	12	2	6.0	1.1
Spartanburg	89,500	88,000	1,565	1,802	640	717	17.5	20.5	7.2	8.1	925	1,085	245	251	102	133	65.2	73.8	55	61	3.5	3.4
Colored	20,300	20,300	374	412	251	258	18.4	20.3	12.4	12.7	123	154	149	160	35	35	93.6	85.0	23	24	6.1	5.8
White	69,200	67,700	1,191	1,390	389	459	17.2	20.5	5.6	6.8	802	931	306	503	67	98	56.3	70.5	32	37	2.7	2.7
Sumter	33,900	34,100	888	873	442	487	26.2	25.6	30.0	14.3	446	386	201	179	100	103	112.6	118.0	67	67	7.5	7.7
Colored	25,600	25,800	759	788	386	412	29.6	30.5	15.1	16.0	373	376	197	191	95	91	125.2	115.5	57	60	7.5	7.6
White	8,300	8,300	129	85	56	75	15.5	10.2	6.7	9.0	73	10	(4)	(4)	5	12	38.8	141.2	10	7	7.8	8.2
Union	31,000	30,900	634	721	220	216	20.5	23.3	7.1	7.0	414	505	288	334	23	38	36.3	52.7	24	35	3.8	4.9
Colored	12,200	12,300	248	306	74	59	20.3	24.9	6.1	4.8	174	247	(4)	(4)	5	9	20.2	29.4	11	17	4.4	5.6
White	18,800	18,600	386	415	146	157	20.5	22.3	7.8	8.4	240	258	264	264	18	29	46.6	69.9	13	18	3.4	4.3
Williamsburg	[5] 34,914	[5] 34,914	923	962	435	451	26.4	27.6	12.5	12.9	488	511	212	213	85	89	92.1	92.5	82	69	8.9	7.2
Colored	23,342	23,342	667	693	336	341	28.6	29.7	14.4	14.6	331	352	199	203	64	69	96.0	99.6	75	58	11.2	8.4
White	11,572	11,572	256	269	99	110	22.1	23.2	8.6	9.5	157	159	(4)	245	21	20	82.0	74.3	7	11	2.7	4.1
York	42,200	42,100	841	915	375	465	19.9	21.7	8.9	11.0	466	450	224	197	50	60	59.5	65.6	51	62	6.1	6.8
Colored	19,400	19,500	390	441	196	236	20.1	22.6	10.1	12.1	194	205	199	187	20	27	51.3	61.2	34	45	8.7	10.2
White	22,800	22,600	451	474	179	229	19.8	21.0	7.9	10.1	272	245	252	207	30	33	66.5	69.6	17	17	3.8	3.6
TENNESSEE COUNTIES [3]																						
Bedford	[5] 21,077	[5] 21,077	347	404	245	269	16.5	19.2	11.6	12.8	102	135	142	150	20	30	57.6	74.3	17	24	4.9	5.9
Colored	3,711	3,711	57	64	60	69	15.4	17.2	16.2	18.6	−3	−5	(4)	(4)	3	7	52.6	109.4	5	4	8.8	6.3
White	17,366	17,366	290	340	185	200	16.7	19.6	10.7	11.5	105	140	157	170	17	23	58.6	67.6	12	20	4.1	5.9
Carroll	26,300	26,200	487	503	209	258	18.5	19.2	7.9	9.8	278	245	233	195	25	35	51.3	69.6	17	17	3.5	3.4
Colored	4,600	4,700	68	70	42	62	14.8	14.9	9.1	13.2	26	8	(4)	(4)	7	10	102.9	142.9	1	2	1.5	2.9
White	21,700	21,500	419	433	167	196	19.3	20.1	7.7	9.1	252	237	251	221	18	25	43.0	57.7	16	15	3.8	3.5
Chester	10,700	10,600	224	223	109	101	20.9	21.0	10.2	9.5	115	122	206	221	20	13	89.3	58.3	15	3	6.7	1.3
Colored	1,900	1,900	31	30	27	19	16.3	15.8	14.2	10.0	4	11	(4)	(4)	3	3	96.8	100.0	2	-------	6.5	------
White	8,800	8,700	193	193	82	82	21.9	22.2	9.3	9.4	111	111	(4)	(4)	17	10	88.1	51.8	13	3	6.7	1.6
Crockett	[5] 17,359	[5] 17,359	316	343	163	180	18.2	19.8	9.4	10.4	153	163	194	191	23	21	72.8	61.2	10	13	3.2	3.8
Colored	3,434	3,434	59	43	46	41	17.2	12.5	13.4	11.9	13	2	(4)	(4)	4	2	67.8	46.5	-------	3	-------	7.0
White	13,925	13,925	257	300	117	139	18.5	21.5	8.4	10.0	140	161	220	216	19	19	73.9	63.3	10	10	3.9	3.3
Davidson	74,100	70,000	957	1,037	847	866	12.9	14.8	11.4	12.4	110	171	113	120	58	64	60.6	61.7	27	43	2.8	4.1
Colored	9,800	9,100	65	80	202	231	6.6	8.8	20.6	25.4	−137	−151	32	35	4	9	61.5	112.5	6	6	9.2	7.5
White	64,300	60,900	892	957	645	635	13.9	15.7	10.0	10.4	247	322	138	151	54	55	60.5	57.5	21	37	2.4	3.9
Dyer	31,600	31,400	694	686	437	391	22.0	21.8	13.8	12.5	257	295	159	175	75	65	108.1	94.8	37	32	5.3	4.7
Colored	5,100	5,100	52	80	86	77	10.2	15.7	16.9	15.1	−34	3	(4)	(4)	13	6	250.0	75.0	4	12	7.7	15.0
White	26,500	26,300	642	606	351	314	24.2	23.0	13.2	11.9	291	292	183	193	62	59	96.6	97.4	33	20	5.1	3.3
Fayette	[5] 28,891	[5] 28,891	636	577	297	300	22.0	20.0	10.3	10.4	339	277	214	192	53	72	83.3	124.8	32	40	5.0	6.9
Colored	21,095	21,095	463	430	223	228	21.9	20.4	10.6	10.8	240	202	208	189	43	54	92.9	125.6	28	35	6.0	8.1
White	7,796	7,796	173	147	74	72	22.2	18.9	9.5	9.2	99	75	(4)	(4)	10	18	57.8	122.4	4	5	2.3	3.4
Franklin	21,900	21,800	458	462	178	242	20.9	21.2	8.1	11.1	280	220	257	191	18	31	39.3	67.1	25	22	5.5	4.8
Colored	2,500	2,500	55	41	34	46	22.0	16.4	13.6	18.4	21	−5	(4)	(4)	3	5	54.5	122.0	2	5	3.6	12.2
White	19,400	19,300	403	421	144	196	20.8	21.8	7.4	10.2	259	225	280	215	15	26	37.2	61.8	23	17	5.7	4.0
Gibson	46,900	46,600	979	923	445	480	20.9	19.8	9.5	10.3	534	443	220	192	64	67	65.4	72.6	16	26	1.6	2.8
Colored	9,900	9,900	164	171	130	133	16.6	17.3	13.1	13.4	34	38	126	129	15	20	91.5	117.0	5	7	3.0	4.1
White	37,000	36,700	815	752	315	347	22.0	20.5	8.5	9.5	500	405	259	217	49	47	60.1	62.5	11	19	1.3	2.5
Giles	[5] 28,016	[5] 28,016	520	550	304	310	18.6	19.6	10.9	11.1	216	240	171	177	40	38	76.9	69.1	17	27	3.3	4.9
Colored	7,563	7,563	146	160	100	112	19.3	21.2	13.2	14.8	46	48	146	143	11	13	75.3	81.3	9	10	6.2	6.3
White	20,453	20,453	374	390	204	198	18.3	19.1	10.0	9.7	170	192	183	197	29	25	77.5	64.1	8	17	2.1	4.4
Hamblen	16,800	16,700	396	359	182	208	23.6	21.5	10.8	12.5	214	151	218	173	25	24	63.1	66.9	17	15	4.3	4.2
Colored	1,700	1,700	22	18	19	26	12.9	10.6	11.2	15.3	3	−8	(4)	(4)	2	1	90.9	55.6	2	-------	9.1	------
White	15,100	15,000	374	341	163	182	24.8	22.7	10.8	12.1	211	159	229	187	23	23	61.5	67.4	15	15	4.0	4.4
Hardeman	[5] 22,193	[5] 22,193	417	419	263	262	18.8	18.9	11.9	11.8	154	157	159	160	22	24	52.8	57.3	12	19	2.9	4.5
Colored	8,532	8,532	182	183	111	124	21.3	21.4	13.0	14.5	71	59	164	148	10	13	54.9	71.0	7	12	3.8	6.6
White	13,661	13,661	235	236	152	138	17.2	17.3	11.1	10.1	83	98	155	171	12	11	51.1	46.6	5	7	2.1	3.0
Haywood	26,100	26,100	416	503	268	293	15.9	19.3	10.3	11.2	148	210	155	172	28	48	67.3	95.4	24	55	5.8	10.9
Colored	17,200	17,300	289	356	184	203	16.8	20.6	10.7	11.7	105	153	157	175	27	32	93.4	89.9	18	41	6.2	11.5
White	8,900	8,800	127	147	84	90	14.3	16.7	9.4	10.2	43	57	(4)	(4)	1	16	7.9	108.8	6	14	4.7	9.5
Henry	[5] 26,432	[5] 26,432	419	398	247	274	15.9	15.1	9.3	10.4	172	124	170	145	23	25	54.9	62.8	19	20	4.5	5.0
Colored	4,997	4,997	71	64	59	67	14.2	12.8	11.8	13.4	12	−3	(4)	(4)	8	4	112.7	62.5	3	6	4.2	9.4
White	21,435	21,435	348	334	188	207	16.2	15.6	8.8	9.7	160	127	185	161	15	21	43.1	62.9	16	14	4.6	4.2
Lake	10,700	10,500	201	209	119	124	18.8	19.9	11.1	11.8	82	85	169	169	25	28	124.4	134.0	18	25	9.0	12.0
Colored	3,900	3,700	27	59	41	50	6.9	15.9	10.5	13.5	−14	9	(4)	(4)	3	4	111.1	67.8	9	8	33.3	13.6
White	6,800	6,800	174	150	78	74	25.6	22.1	11.5	10.9	96	76	(4)	(4)	22	24	126.4	160.0	9	17	5.2	11.3
Lauderdale	23,600	23,500	435	457	240	277	18.4	19.4	10.2	11.8	195	180	181	165	21	34	48.3	74.4	23	31	5.3	6.8
Colored	9,200	9,200	124	144	126	145	13.5	15.7	13.7	15.8	−2	−1	98	99	9	16	72.6	111.1	8	16	6.5	11.1
White	14,400	14,300	311	313	114	132	21.6	21.9	7.9	9.2	197	181	273	237	12	18	38.6	57.5	15	15	4.8	4.8
Lincoln	[5] 25,422	[5] 25,422	544	514	255	269	21.4	20.2	10.0	10.6	289	245	213	191	37	30	68.0	58.4	28	27	5.1	5.3
Colored	4,058	4,058	84	66	63	67	20.7	16.3	15.5	16.5	21	−1	(4)	(4)	7	6	83.3	90.9	7	4	8.3	6.1
White	21,364	21,364	460	448	192	202	21.5	21.0	9.0	9.5	268	246	240	222	30	24	65.2	53.6	21	23	4.6	5.1

See footnotes at end of table.

TABLE 18.—COLORED[1] AND WHITE POPULATION, BIRTHS AND DEATHS, INFANT MORTALITY, AND STILLBIRTHS, IN SELECTED REGISTRATION STATES, CITIES, AND COUNTIES: 1931 AND 1930—Continued

[See note at head of this table]

AREA AND COLOR	POPULATION ESTIMATED AS OF JULY 1		BIRTHS AND DEATHS (Exclusive of stillbirths): Number: Births		Number: Deaths		Rate per 1,000 population: Births		Rate per 1,000 population: Deaths		Excess of births over deaths[2]		Births per 100 deaths		INFANT MORTALITY (Exclusive of stillbirths): Deaths of infants under 1 year of age: Number		Per 1,000 births		STILLBIRTHS: Number		Rate per 100 live births	
	1931	1930	1931	1930	1931	1930	1931	1930	1931	1930	1931	1930	1931	1930	1931	1930	1931	1930	1931	1930	1931	1930
TENNESSEE COUNTIES—continued																						
Madison	29,400	29,000	570	598	212	264	19.4	20.6	7.2	9.1	358	334	269	227	28	38	49.1	63.5	30	32	5.3	5.4
Colored	11,100	11,000	207	251	114	131	18.6	22.8	10.3	11.9	93	120	182	192	16	21	77.3	83.7	17	20	8.2	8.0
White	18,300	18,000	363	347	98	133	19.8	19.3	5.4	7.4	265	214	(4)	261	12	17	33.1	49.0	13	12	3.6	3.5
Marshall	[5] 15,574	[5] 15,574	271	288	150	183	17.4	18.5	9.6	11.8	121	105	181	157	11	17	40.6	59.0	2	8	.7	2.8
Colored	2,380	2,380	39	47	26	38	16.4	19.7	10.9	16.0	13	9	(4)	(4)	2	4	51.3	85.1	1	2	2.6	4.3
White	13,194	13,194	232	241	124	145	17.6	18.3	9.4	11.0	108	96	187	166	9	13	38.8	53.9	1	6	.4	2.5
Maury	[5] 34,016	[5] 34,016	736	707	408	447	21.6	20.8	12.0	13.1	328	260	180	158	36	37	48.9	52.3	31	31	4.2	4.4
Colored	9,808	9,808	182	184	165	175	18.6	18.8	16.8	17.8	17	9	110	105	13	13	71.4	70.7	20	16	11.0	8.7
White	24,208	24,208	554	523	243	272	22.9	21.6	10.0	11.2	311	251	228	192	23	24	41.5	45.9	11	15	2.0	2.9
Montgomery	[5] 30,882	[5] 30,882	685	699	417	385	22.2	22.6	13.5	12.5	268	314	164	182	41	55	59.9	78.7	25	42	3.6	6.0
Colored	10,121	10,121	208	211	163	179	20.6	20.8	16.1	17.7	45	32	128	118	16	23	76.9	109.0	12	24	5.8	11.4
White	20,761	20,761	477	488	254	206	23.0	23.5	12.2	9.9	223	282	188	237	25	32	52.4	65.6	13	18	2.7	3.7
Obion	29,200	29,100	626	533	392	348	21.4	18.3	13.4	12.0	234	185	160	153	54	31	86.3	58.2	15	23	2.4	4.3
Colored	4,100	4,100	65	52	68	74	15.9	12.7	16.6	18.0	−3	−22	(4)	(4)	3	4	46.2	76.9	3	5	4.6	9.6
White	25,100	25,000	561	481	324	274	22.4	19.2	12.9	11.0	237	207	173	176	51	27	90.9	56.1	12	18	2.1	3.7
Robertson	28,500	28,300	593	570	252	292	20.8	20.1	8.8	10.3	341	278	235	195	34	42	57.3	73.7	23	29	3.9	5.1
Colored	5,900	5,900	108	100	79	75	18.3	16.9	13.4	12.7	29	25	(4)	(4)	16	11	148.1	110.0	8	10	7.4	10.0
White	22,600	22,400	485	470	173	217	21.5	21.0	7.7	9.7	312	253	280	217	18	31	37.1	66.0	15	19	3.1	4.0
Rutherford	[5] 32,286	[5] 32,286	633	657	338	417	19.6	20.3	10.5	12.9	295	240	187	158	34	43	53.7	65.4	29	28	4.6	4.3
Colored	7,742	7,742	145	132	104	132	18.7	17.0	13.4	17.0	41	-------	139	100	6	10	41.4	75.8	15	15	10.3	11.4
White	24,544	24,544	488	525	234	285	19.9	21.4	9.5	11.6	254	240	209	184	28	33	57.4	62.9	14	13	2.9	2.5
Shelby	57,800	54,500	686	640	619	643	11.9	11.7	10.7	11.8	67	−3	111	100	45	57	65.6	89.1	43	48	6.3	7.5
Colored	31,900	31,200	428	381	438	452	13.4	12.2	13.7	14.5	−10	−71	98	84	32	45	74.8	118.1	39	43	9.1	11.3
White	25,900	23,300	258	259	181	191	10.0	11.1	7.0	8.2	77	68	143	136	13	12	50.4	46.3	4	5	1.6	1.9
Sumner	28,700	28,600	680	663	289	279	23.7	23.2	10.1	9.8	391	384	235	238	32	27	47.1	40.7	25	22	3.7	3.3
Colored	4,000	4,000	77	66	51	58	19.3	16.5	12.8	14.5	26	8	(4)	(4)	5	5	64.9	75.8	6	3	7.8	4.5
White	24,700	24,600	603	597	238	221	24.4	24.3	9.6	9.0	365	376	253	270	27	22	44.8	36.9	19	19	3.2	3.2
Tipton	[5] 27,498	[5] 27,498	424	453	246	265	15.4	16.5	8.9	9.6	178	188	172	171	35	30	82.5	66.2	14	31	3.3	6.8
Colored	11,276	11,276	135	175	119	127	12.0	15.5	10.6	11.3	16	48	113	138	10	12	74.1	68.6	4	16	3.0	9.1
White	16,222	16,222	289	278	127	138	17.8	17.1	7.8	8.5	162	140	228	201	25	18	86.5	64.7	10	15	3.5	5.4
Trousdale	[5] 5,629	[5] 5,629	95	73	37	47	16.9	13.0	6.6	8.3	58	26	(4)	(4)	3	3	31.6	41.1	4	4	4.2	5.5
Colored	1,267	1,267	25	16	8	14	19.7	12.6	6.3	11.0	17	2	(4)	(4)	2	1	80.0	62.5	1	2	4.0	12.5
White	4,362	4,362	70	57	29	33	16.0	13.1	6.6	7.6	41	24	(4)	(4)	1	2	14.3	35.1	3	2	4.3	3.5
Williamson	[5] 22,845	[5] 22,845	477	496	182	220	20.9	21.7	8.0	9.6	295	276	262	225	20	13	41.9	26.2	17	16	3.6	3.2
Colored	5,274	5,274	107	102	48	88	20.3	19.3	9.1	16.7	59	14	(4)	(4)	2	3	18.7	29.4	4	9	3.7	8.8
White	17,571	17,571	370	394	134	132	21.1	22.4	7.6	7.5	236	262	276	298	18	10	48.6	25.4	13	7	3.5	1.8
Wilson	[5] 23,929	[5] 23,929	380	427	274	274	15.9	17.8	11.5	11.5	106	153	139	156	15	27	39.5	63.2	16	13	4.2	3.0
Colored	4,481	4,481	71	55	55	76	15.8	12.3	12.3	17.0	16	−21	(4)	(4)	3	10	42.3	181.8	5	5	7.0	9.1
White	19,448	19,448	309	372	219	198	15.9	19.1	11.3	10.2	90	174	141	188	12	17	38.8	45.7	11	8	3.6	2.2
VIRGINIA COUNTIES[8]																						
Accomac	36,000	35,900	659	751	424	450	18.3	20.9	11.8	12.5	235	301	155	167	86	75	130.5	99.9	47	46	7.1	6.1
Colored	14,000	14,000	349	403	234	220	24.9	28.8	16.7	15.7	115	183	149	183	67	56	192.0	139.0	36	37	10.3	9.2
White	22,000	21,900	310	348	190	230	14.1	15.9	8.6	10.5	120	118	163	151	19	19	61.3	54.6	11	9	3.5	2.6
Albemarle	27,100	27,000	904	885	599	602	33.4	32.8	22.1	22.3	305	283	151	147	101	109	111.7	123.2	50	39	5.5	4.4
Colored	6,100	6,200	237	214	195	193	38.9	34.5	32.0	31.1	42	21	122	111	20	34	84.4	158.9	14	20	5.9	9.3
White	21,000	20,800	667	671	404	409	31.8	32.3	19.2	19.7	263	262	165	164	81	75	121.4	111.8	36	19	5.4	2.8
Amelia	[5] 8,979	[5] 8,979	247	217	109	100	27.5	24.2	12.1	11.1	138	117	227	217	22	9	89.1	41.5	11	13	4.5	6.0
Colored	4,614	4,614	132	124	71	58	28.6	26.9	15.4	12.6	61	66	(4)	(4)	14	7	106.1	56.5	8	11	6.1	8.9
White	4,365	4,365	115	93	38	42	26.3	21.3	8.7	9.6	77	51	(4)	(4)	8	2	69.6	21.5	3	2	2.6	2.2
Amherst	[5] 19,020	[5] 19,020	443	445	273	246	23.3	23.4	14.4	12.9	170	199	162	181	38	30	85.8	67.4	17	13	3.8	2.9
Colored	5,999	5,999	182	183	86	91	30.3	30.5	14.3	15.2	96	92	(4)	(4)	21	17	115.4	92.9	13	8	7.1	4.4
White	13,021	13,021	261	262	187	155	20.0	20.1	14.4	11.9	74	107	140	169	17	13	65.1	49.6	4	5	1.5	1.9
Appomattox	[5] 8,402	[5] 8,402	151	171	90	87	18.0	20.4	10.7	10.4	61	84	(4)	(4)	13	8	86.1	46.8	5	3	3.3	1.8
Colored	2,296	2,296	53	54	40	30	23.1	23.5	17.4	13.1	13	24	(4)	(4)	4	3	75.5	55.6	4	2	7.5	3.7
White	6,106	6,106	98	117	50	57	16.0	19.2	8.2	9.3	48	60	(4)	(4)	9	5	91.8	42.7	1	1	1.0	.9
Arlington	29,100	27,000	206	191	173	166	7.1	7.1	5.9	6.1	33	25	119	115	12	18	58.3	94.2	8	6	3.9	3.1
Colored	3,700	3,300	49	41	44	47	13.2	12.4	11.9	14.2	5	−6	(4)	(4)	6	10	122.4	243.9	2	2	4.1	4.9
White	25,400	23,700	157	150	129	119	6.2	6.3	5.1	5.0	28	31	122	126	6	8	38.2	53.3	6	4	3.8	2.7

Bath	8,300	8,200	147	155	84	86	17.7	18.9	10.1	10.5	63	69	(4)	(4)	18	20	122.4	129.0	5	4	3.4	2.6
Colored	1,100	1,200	10	14	7	16	9.1	11.7	6.4	13.3	3	−2	(4)	(4)	1	3	100.0	214.3	1	1	10.0	7.1
White	7,200	7,000	137	141	77	70	19.0	20.1	10.7	10.0	60	71	(4)	(4)	17	17	124.1	120.6	4	3	2.9	2.1
Bedford	[5] 29,091	[5] 29,091	602	652	313	327	20.7	22.4	10.8	11.2	289	325	192	199	39	41	64.8	62.9	18	20	3.0	3.1
Colored	6,969	6,969	166	166	99	99	23.8	23.8	14.2	14.2	67	67	(4)	(4)	13	17	78.3	102.4	8	11	4.8	6.6
White	22,122	22,122	436	486	214	228	19.7	22.0	9.7	10.3	222	258	204	213	26	24	59.6	49.4	10	9	2.3	1.9
Botetourt	[5] 15,457	[5] 15,457	363	351	159	167	23.5	22.7	10.3	10.8	204	184	228	210	24	24	66.1	68.4	13	3	3.6	.9
Colored	2,212	2,212	47	45	35	40	21.2	20.3	15.8	18.1	12	5	(4)	(4)	2	6	42.6	133.3	2	-----	4.3	-----
White	13,345	13,245	316	306	124	127	23.9	23.1	9.4	9.6	192	179	255	241	22	18	69.6	58.8	11	3	3.5	1.0
Bristol (city)	9,100	8,900	283	293	149	166	31.1	32.9	16.4	18.7	134	127	190	177	17	34	60.1	116.0	7	17	2.5	5.8
Colored	1,200	1,200	15	20	23	24	12.5	16.7	19.2	20.0	−8	−4	(4)	(4)	2	4	133.3	200.0	-----	-----	-----	-----
White	7,900	7,700	268	273	126	142	33.9	35.5	15.9	18.4	142	131	213	192	15	30	56.0	109.9	7	17	2.6	6.2
Brunswick	[5] 20,486	[5] 20,486	468	570	235	247	22.8	27.8	11.5	12.1	233	323	199	231	41	47	87.6	82.5	30	21	6.4	3.7
Colored	11,492	11,492	285	356	149	154	24.8	31.0	13.0	13.4	136	202	191	231	27	31	94.7	87.1	26	14	9.1	3.9
White	8,994	8,994	183	214	86	93	20.3	23.8	9.6	10.3	97	121	(4)	(4)	14	16	76.5	74.8	4	7	2.2	3.3
Buckingham	[5] 13,315	[5] 13,315	328	336	165	162	24.6	25.2	12.4	12.2	163	174	199	207	27	31	82.3	92.3	10	11	3.0	3.3
Colored	5,802	5,802	144	149	77	89	24.8	25.7	13.3	15.3	67	60	(4)	(4)	14	18	97.2	120.8	7	8	4.9	5.4
White	7,513	7,513	184	187	88	73	24.5	24.9	11.7	9.7	96	114	(4)	(4)	13	13	70.7	69.5	3	3	1.6	1.6
Campbell	23,000	22,900	527	544	237	242	22.9	23.8	10.3	10.6	290	302	222	225	40	48	75.9	88.2	27	20	5.1	3.7
Colored	6,400	6,600	184	179	98	104	28.8	27.1	15.3	15.8	86	75	(3)	172	13	26	70.7	145.3	18	12	9.8	6.7
White	16,600	16,300	343	365	139	138	20.7	22.4	8.4	8.5	204	227	247	264	27	22	78.7	60.3	9	8	2.6	2.2
Caroline	[5] 15,263	[5] 15,263	301	382	174	185	19.7	25.0	11.4	12.1	127	197	173	206	25	32	83.1	83.8	24	12	8.0	3.1
Colored	7,769	7,769	180	226	106	87	23.2	29.1	13.6	11.2	74	139	170	(4)	18	18	100.0	79.6	17	11	9.4	4.9
White	7,494	7,494	121	156	68	98	16.1	20.8	9.1	13.1	53	58	(4)	(4)	7	14	57.9	89.7	7	1	5.8	.6
Charles City	4,900	4,900	108	130	74	75	22.0	26.5	15.1	15.3	34	55	(4)	(4)	10	9	92.6	69.2	4	8	3.7	6.2
Colored	3,900	3,900	93	116	60	63	23.8	29.7	15.4	16.2	33	53	(4)	(4)	9	9	96.8	77.6	3	8	3.2	6.9
White	1,000	1,000	15	14	14	12	15.0	14.0	14.0	12.0	1	2	(4)	(4)	1	-----	66.7	-----	1	-----	6.7	-----
Charlotte	[5] 16,061	[5] 16,061	364	364	152	163	22.7	22.7	9.5	10.1	212	201	239	223	17	24	46.7	65.9	15	14	4.1	3.8
Colored	6,742	6,742	163	176	72	76	24.2	26.1	10.7	11.3	91	100	(4)	(4)	6	12	36.8	68.2	11	13	6.7	7.4
White	9,319	9,319	201	188	80	87	21.6	20.2	8.6	9.3	121	101	(4)	(4)	11	12	54.7	63.8	4	1	2.0	.5
Chesterfield	26,700	26,200	454	477	247	250	17.0	18.2	9.3	9.5	207	227	184	191	29	35	63.9	73.4	24	24	5.3	5.0
Colored	7,100	7,100	149	172	92	113	21.0	24.2	13.0	15.9	57	59	(4)	152	17	21	114.1	122.1	16	11	10.7	6.4
White	19,600	19,100	305	305	155	137	15.6	16.0	7.9	7.2	150	168	197	223	12	14	39.3	45.9	8	13	2.6	4.3
Clarke	7,200	7,200	135	131	103	89	18.8	18.2	14.3	12.4	32	42	131	(4)	16	10	118.5	76.3	7	6	5.2	4.6
Colored	1,500	1,600	34	30	26	28	22.7	18.8	17.3	17.5	8	2	(4)	(4)	8	4	235.3	133.3	4	5	11.8	16.7
White	5,700	5,600	101	101	77	61	17.7	18.0	13.5	10.9	24	40	(4)	(4)	8	6	79.2	59.4	3	1	3.0	1.0
Clifton Forge (city)	6,900	6,900	128	159	121	134	18.6	23.0	17.5	19.4	7	25	106	119	13	12	101.6	75.5	9	6	7.0	3.8
Colored	1,200	1,200	19	25	28	29	15.8	20.8	23.3	24.2	−9	−4	(4)	(4)	2	3	105.3	120.0	3	3	15.8	12.0
White	5,700	5,700	109	134	93	105	19.1	23.5	16.3	18.4	16	29	(4)	128	11	9	100.9	67.2	6	3	5.5	2.2
Culpeper	13,300	13,300	238	277	131	148	17.9	20.8	9.8	11.1	107	129	182	187	11	17	46.2	61.4	6	7	2.5	2.5
Colored	4,300	4,300	94	102	48	70	21.9	23.7	11.2	16.3	46	32	(4)	(4)	3	14	31.9	137.3	2	4	2.1	3.9
White	9,000	9,000	144	175	83	78	16.0	19.4	9.2	8.7	61	97	(4)	(4)	8	3	55.6	17.1	4	3	2.8	1.7
Cumberland	[5] 7,535	[5] 7,535	150	191	104	125	19.9	25.3	13.8	16.6	46	66	144	153	21	10	140.0	52.4	10	8	6.7	4.2
Colored	4,357	4,357	104	130	78	82	23.9	29.8	17.9	18.8	26	48	(4)	(4)	19	9	182.7	69.2	9	6	8.7	4.6
White	3,178	3,178	46	61	26	43	14.5	19.2	8.2	13.5	20	18	(4)	(4)	2	1	43.5	16.4	1	2	2.2	3.3
Dinwiddie	18,600	18,500	312	351	399	507	16.8	19.0	21.5	27.4	−87	−156	78	69	20	25	64.1	71.2	13	6	4.2	1.7
Colored	11,200	11,200	206	222	339	449	18.4	19.8	30.3	40.1	−133	−227	61	49	16	23	77.7	103.6	12	5	5.8	2.3
White	7,400	7,300	106	129	60	58	14.3	17.7	8.1	7.9	46	71	(4)	(4)	4	2	37.7	15.5	1	1	.9	.8
Elizabeth City	20,200	19,900	218	225	304	493	10.8	11.3	15.0	24.8	−86	−268	72	46	29	31	133.0	137.8	7	8	3.2	3.6
Colored	5,200	5,300	61	78	143	201	11.7	14.7	27.5	37.9	−82	−123	43	39	19	17	311.5	217.9	2	2	3.3	2.6
White	15,000	14,600	157	147	161	292	10.5	10.1	10.7	20.0	−4	−145	98	50	10	14	63.7	95.2	5	6	3.2	4.1
Essex	[5] 6,976	[5] 6,976	135	153	87	89	19.4	21.9	12.5	12.8	48	64	(4)	(4)	7	9	51.9	58.8	4	7	3.0	4.6
Colored	3,827	3,827	81	89	43	57	21.2	23.3	11.2	14.9	38	32	(4)	(4)	5	5	61.7	56.2	3	7	3.7	7.9
White	3,149	3,149	54	64	44	32	17.1	20.3	14.0	10.2	10	32	(4)	(4)	2	4	37.0	62.5	1	-----	1.9	-----
Fairfax	25,700	25,400	344	366	216	220	13.4	14.4	8.4	8.7	128	146	159	166	19	21	55.2	57.4	17	15	4.9	4.1
Colored	4,800	4,900	55	87	50	47	11.5	17.8	10.4	9.6	5	40	(4)	(4)	8	7	145.5	80.5	7	8	12.7	9.2
White	20,900	20,500	289	279	166	173	13.8	13.6	7.9	8.4	123	106	174	161	11	14	38.1	50.2	10	7	3.5	2.5
Fauquier	[5] 21,071	[5] 21,071	453	453	293	262	21.5	21.5	13.9	12.4	160	191	155	173	44	41	97.1	90.5	39	26	8.6	5.7
Colored	6,274	6,274	174	146	100	92	27.7	23.3	15.9	14.7	74	54	174	(4)	20	20	114.9	137.0	14	12	8.0	8.2
White	14,797	14,797	279	307	193	170	18.9	20.7	13.0	11.5	86	137	145	181	24	21	86.0	68.4	25	14	9.0	4.6
Fluvanna	[5] 7,466	[5] 7,466	140	138	99	89	18.8	18.5	13.3	11.9	41	49	(4)	(4)	8	6	57.1	43.5	4	4	2.9	2.9
Colored	2,951	2,951	72	80	50	40	24.4	27.1	16.9	13.6	22	40	(4)	(4)	6	5	83.3	62.5	4	2	5.6	2.5
White	4,515	4,515	68	58	49	49	15.1	12.8	10.9	10.9	19	9	(4)	(4)	2	1	29.4	17.2	-----	2	-----	3.4
Franklin	[5] 24,337	[5] 24,337	573	598	246	223	23.5	24.6	10.1	9.2	327	375	233	268	31	42	54.1	70.2	23	21	4.0	3.5
Colored	3,770	3,770	103	91	63	56	27.3	24.1	16.7	14.9	40	35	(4)	(4)	10	15	97.1	164.8	5	7	4.9	7.7
White	20,567	20,567	470	507	183	167	22.9	24.7	8.9	8.1	287	340	257	304	21	27	44.7	53.3	18	14	3.8	2.8
Fredericksburg (city)	6,900	6,800	188	181	167	164	27.2	26.6	24.2	24.1	21	17	113	110	10	15	53.2	82.9	11	9	5.9	5.0
Colored	1,200	1,200	33	31	41	42	27.5	25.8	34.2	35.0	−8	−11	(4)	(4)	2	2	60.6	64.5	5	-----	15.2	-----
White	5,700	5,600	155	150	126	122	27.2	26.8	22.1	21.8	29	28	123	123	8	13	51.6	86.7	6	9	3.9	6.0
Gloucester	[5] 11,019	[5] 11,019	191	184	132	124	17.3	16.7	12.0	11.3	59	60	145	148	14	10	73.3	54.3	5	11	2.6	6.0
Colored	4,349	4,349	66	72	88	62	15.2	16.6	20.2	14.3	−22	10	(4)	(4)	9	6	136.4	83.3	5	8	7.6	11.1
White	6,670	6,670	125	112	44	62	18.7	16.8	6.6	9.3	81	50	(4)	(4)	5	4	40.0	35.7	-----	3	-----	2.7
Goochland	[5] 7,953	[5] 7,953	184	204	95	108	23.1	25.7	11.9	13.6	89	96	(4)	189	16	15	87.0	73.5	11	12	6.0	5.9
Colored	4,114	4,114	106	116	57	68	25.8	28.2	13.9	16.5	49	48	(4)	(4)	10	12	94.3	103.4	9	8	8.5	6.9
White	3,839	3,839	78	88	38	40	20.3	22.9	9.9	10.4	40	48	(4)	(4)	6	3	76.9	34.1	2	4	2.6	4.5
Greene	[5] 5,980	[5] 5,980	103	109	63	46	17.2	18.2	10.5	7.7	40	63	(4)	(4)	8	11	77.7	100.9	6	9	5.8	8.3
Colored	994	994	23	20	22	13	23.1	20.1	22.1	13.1	1	7	(4)	(4)	2	1	87.0	50.0	2	1	8.7	5.0
White	4,986	4,986	80	89	41	33	16.0	17.8	8.2	6.6	39	56	(4)	(4)	6	10	75.0	112.4	4	8	5.0	9.0
Greensville	13,600	13,400	375	329	155	136	27.6	24.6	11.4	10.1	220	193	242	242	29	19	77.3	57.8	15	23	4.0	7.0
Colored	8,300	8,100	277	237	112	98	33.4	29.3	13.5	12.1	165	139	247	(4)	21	15	75.8	63.3	12	19	4.3	8.0
White	5,300	5,300	98	92	43	38	18.5	17.4	8.1	7.2	55	54	(4)	(4)	8	4	81.6	43.5	3	4	3.1	4.3

See footnotes at end of table.

TABLE 18.—COLORED[1] AND WHITE POPULATION, BIRTHS AND DEATHS, INFANT MORATLITY, AND STILLBIRTHS, IN SELECTED REGISTRATION STATES, CITIES, AND COUNTIES: 1931 AND 1930—Continued

[See note at head of this table]

AREA AND COLOR	POPULATION ESTIMATED AS OF JULY 1		BIRTHS AND DEATHS (Exclusive of stillbirths): Number: Births		Number: Deaths		Rate per 1,000 population: Births		Rate per 1,000 population: Deaths		Excess of births over deaths [2]		Births per 100 deaths		INFANT MORTALITY (Exclusive of stillbirths): Deaths of infants under 1 year of age: Number		Per 1,000 births		STILLBIRTHS: Number		Rate per 100 live births	
	1931	1930	1931	1930	1931	1930	1931	1930	1931	1930	1931	1930	1931	1930	1931	1930	1931	1930	1931	1930	1931	1930
VIRGINIA COUNTIES—continued																						
Halifax	[5] 41,283	[5] 41,283	1,063	1,065	444	458	25.7	25.8	10.8	11.1	619	607	239	233	89	79	83.7	74.2	47	51	4.4	4.8
Colored	18,890	18,890	524	539	249	264	27.7	28.5	13.2	14.0	275	275	210	204	49	44	93.5	81.6	34	35	6.5	6.5
White	22,393	22,393	539	526	195	194	24.1	23.5	8.7	8.7	344	332	276	271	40	35	74.2	66.5	13	16	2.4	3.0
Hampton (city)	6,400	6,400	174	193	154	22	27.2	30.2	24.1	3.4	20	171	113	(4)	7	-------	40.2	-------	17	14	9.8	7.3
Colored	2,900	2,800	69	89	84	13	23.8	31.8	29.0	4.6	−15	76	(4)	(4)	1	-------	14.5	-------	17	14	24.6	15.7
White	3,500	3,600	105	104	70	9	30.0	28.9	20.0	2.5	35	95	(4)	(4)	6	-------	57.1	-------	-------	-------	-------	-------
Hanover	[5] 17,009	[5] 17,009	313	343	232	250	18.4	20.2	13.6	14.7	81	93	135	137	24	25	76.7	72.9	13	17	4.2	5.0
Colored	6,228	6,228	150	171	116	111	24.1	27.5	18.6	17.8	34	60	129	154	12	17	80.0	99.4	9	5	6.0	2.9
White	10,781	10,781	163	172	116	139	15.1	16.0	10.8	12.9	47	33	141	124	12	8	73.6	46.5	4	12	2.5	7.0
Harrisonburg (city)	7,400	7,300	232	204	170	156	31.4	27.9	23.0	21.4	62	48	136	131	28	30	120.7	147.1	11	13	4.7	6.4
Colored	900	900	10	16	20	22	11.1	17.8	22.2	24.4	−10	−6	(4)	(4)	-------	4	-------	250.0	-------	4	-------	25.0
White	6,500	6,400	222	188	150	134	34.2	29.4	23.1	20.9	72	54	148	140	28	26	126.1	138.3	11	9	5.0	4.8
Henrico	31,700	30,600	400	423	285	281	12.6	13.8	9.0	9.2	115	142	140	151	30	38	75.0	89.8	12	20	3.0	4.7
Colored	6,600	6,500	129	121	89	102	19.5	18.6	13.5	15.7	40	19	(4)	119	16	18	124.0	148.8	8	8	6.2	6.6
White	25,100	24,100	271	302	196	179	10.8	12.5	7.8	7.4	75	123	138	169	14	20	51.7	66.2	4	12	1.5	4.0
Henry	20,600	20,200	764	595	261	241	37.1	29.5	12.7	11.9	503	354	293	247	60	49	78.5	82.4	16	31	2.1	5.2
Colored	6,200	6,200	224	203	111	92	36.1	32.7	17.9	14.8	113	111	202	(4)	30	13	133.9	64.0	8	12	3.6	5.9
White	14,400	14,000	540	392	150	149	37.5	28.0	10.4	10.6	390	243	360	263	30	36	55.6	91.8	8	19	1.5	4.8
Isle of Wight	[5] 13,409	[5] 13,409	282	293	175	181	21.0	21.9	13.1	13.5	107	112	161	162	27	29	95.7	99.0	14	14	5.0	4.8
Colored	6,923	6,923	172	177	116	101	24.8	25.6	16.8	14.6	56	76	148	175	20	19	116.3	107.3	11	10	6.4	5.6
White	6,486	6,486	110	116	59	80	17.0	17.9	9.1	12.3	51	36	(4)	(4)	7	10	63.6	86.2	3	4	2.7	3.4
James City	7,800	3,800	70	87	36	91	9.0	22.9	4.6	23.9	34	−4	(4)	(4)	4	9	57.1	103.4	10	5	14.3	5.7
Colored	2,900	1,900	52	52	21	35	17.9	27.4	7.2	18.4	31	17	(4)	(4)	1	7	19.2	134.6	5	3	9.6	5.8
White	4,900	1,900	18	35	15	56	3.7	18.4	3.1	29.5	3	−21	(4)	(4)	3	2	166.7	57.1	5	2	27.8	5.7
King and Queen	[5] 7,618	[6] 7,618	130	167	99	96	17.1	21.9	13.0	12.6	31	71	(4)	(4)	13	7	100.0	41.9	6	11	4.6	6.6
Colored	4,175	4,175	89	101	65	65	21.3	24.2	15.6	15.6	24	36	(4)	(4)	12	4	134.8	39.6	6	9	6.7	8.9
White	3,443	3,443	41	66	34	31	11.9	19.2	9.9	9.0	7	35	(4)	(4)	1	3	24.4	45.5	-------	2	-------	3.0
King George	[5] 5,297	[5] 5,297	101	99	78	88	19.1	18.7	14.7	16.6	23	11	(4)	(4)	6	13	59.4	131.3	4	4	4.0	4.0
Colored	1,878	1,878	58	51	51	43	30.9	27.2	27.2	22.9	7	8	(4)	(4)	5	7	86.2	137.3	3	3	5.2	5.9
White	3,419	3,419	43	48	27	45	12.6	14.0	7.9	13.2	16	3	(4)	(4)	1	6	23.3	125.0	1	1	2.3	2.1
King William	[5] 7,929	[5] 7,929	140	169	89	97	17.7	21.3	11.2	12.2	51	72	(4)	(4)	10	17	71.4	100.6	5	13	3.6	7.7
Colored	4,011	4,011	81	100	52	63	20.2	24.9	13.0	15.7	29	37	(4)	(4)	8	10	98.8	100.0	5	12	6.2	12.0
White	3,918	3,918	59	69	37	34	15.1	17.6	9.4	8.7	22	35	(4)	(4)	2	7	33.9	101.4	-------	1	-------	1.4
Lancaster	[5] 8,896	[5] 8,896	172	179	131	113	19.3	20.1	14.7	12.7	41	66	131	158	19	18	110.5	100.6	6	15	3.5	8.4
Colored	3,970	3,970	102	93	88	66	25.7	23.4	22.2	16.6	14	27	(4)	(4)	15	12	147.1	129.0	5	12	4.9	12.9
White	4,926	4,926	70	86	43	47	14.2	17.5	8.7	9.5	27	39	(4)	(4)	4	6	57.1	69.8	1	3	1.4	3.5
Loudoun	19,852	[5] 19,852	409	399	242	229	20.6	20.1	12.2	11.5	167	170	169	174	26	24	63.6	60.2	7	18	1.7	4.5
Colored	4,350	4,350	95	109	61	59	21.8	25.1	14.0	13.6	34	50	(4)	(4)	12	9	126.3	82.6	2	7	2.1	6.4
White	15,502	15,502	314	290	181	170	20.3	18.7	11.7	11.0	133	120	173	171	14	15	44.6	51.7	5	11	1.6	3.8
Louisa	[5] 14,309	[5] 14,309	262	291	186	171	18.3	20.3	13.0	12.0	76	120	141	170	14	14	53.4	48.1	12	8	4.6	2.7
Colored	5,841	5,841	124	133	86	96	21.2	22.8	14.7	16.4	38	37	(4)	(4)	9	9	72.6	67.7	9	4	7.3	3.0
White	8,468	8,468	138	158	100	75	16.3	18.7	11.8	8.9	38	83	138	(4)	5	5	36.2	31.6	3	4	2.2	2.5
Lunenburg	[5] 14,058	[5] 14,058	309	313	141	185	22.0	22.3	10.0	13.2	168	128	219	169	15	25	48.5	79.9	16	17	5.2	5.4
Colored	6,223	6,223	178	183	82	98	28.6	29.4	13.2	15.7	96	85	(4)	(4)	8	19	44.9	103.8	11	13	6.2	7.1
White	7,835	7,835	131	130	59	87	16.7	16.6	7.5	11.1	72	43	(4)	(4)	7	6	53.4	46.2	5	4	3.8	3.1
Madison	[5] 8,952	[5] 8,952	168	201	85	91	18.8	22.5	9.5	10.2	83	110	(4)	(4)	13	20	77.4	99.5	3	9	1.8	4.5
Colored	2,422	2,422	48	58	25	25	19.8	23.9	10.3	10.3	23	33	(4)	(4)	3	4	62.5	69.0	1	3	2.1	5.2
White	6,530	6,530	120	143	60	66	18.4	21.9	9.2	10.1	60	77	(4)	(4)	10	16	83.3	111.9	2	6	1.7	4.2
Martinsville (city)	8,100	7,800	86	249	116	117	10.6	31.9	14.3	15.0	−30	132	74	213	22	14	255.8	56.2	6	8	7.0	3.2
Colored	2,000	2,000	23	66	49	68	11.5	33.0	24.5	34.0	−26	−2	(4)	(4)	7	6	304.3	90.9	2	3	8.7	4.5
White	6,100	5,800	63	183	67	49	10.3	31.6	11.0	8.4	−4	134	(4)	(4)	15	8	238.1	43.7	4	5	6.3	2.7
Mathews	[5] 7,884	[5] 7,884	106	122	76	86	13.4	15.5	9.6	10.9	30	36	(4)	(4)	9	7	84.9	57.4	2	5	1.9	4.1
Colored	1,994	1,994	37	41	17	33	18.6	20.6	8.5	16.5	20	8	(4)	(4)	5	6	135.1	146.3	2	1	5.4	2.4
White	5,890	5,890	69	81	59	53	11.7	13.8	10.0	9.0	10	28	(4)	(4)	4	1	58.0	12.3	-------	4	-------	4.9
Mecklenburg	32,800	32,700	769	894	373	377	23.4	27.3	11.4	11.5	396	517	206	237	53	76	68.9	85.0	57	50	7.4	5.6
Colored	17,300	17,300	450	545	237	245	26.0	31.5	13.7	14.2	213	300	190	222	38	51	84.4	93.6	47	34	10.4	6.2
White	15,500	15,400	319	349	136	132	20.6	22.7	8.8	8.6	183	217	235	264	15	25	47.0	71.6	10	16	3.1	4.6
Middlesex	[5] 7,273	[5] 7,273	116	144	97	120	15.9	19.8	13.3	16.5	19	24	(4)	120	9	17	77.6	118.1	4	2	3.4	1.4
Colored	3,360	3,360	64	86	63	71	19.0	25.6	18.8	21.1	1	15	(4)	(4)	8	12	125.0	139.5	4	1	6.3	1.2
White	3,913	3,913	52	58	34	49	13.3	14.8	8.7	12.5	18	9	(4)	(4)	1	5	19.2	86.2	-------	1	-------	1.7

Montgomery	19,700	19,600	458	441	202	241	23.2	22.5	10.3	12.3	256	200	227	183	30	35	65.5	79.4	16	13	3.5	2.9
Colored	1,900	1,900	28	30	26	40	14.7	15.8	13.7	21.1	2	−10	(4)	(4)	4	7	142.9	233.3	3	3	10.7	10.0
White	17,800	17,700	430	411	176	201	24.2	23.2	9.9	11.4	254	210	244	204	26	28	60.5	68.1	13	10	3.0	2.4
Nansemond	22,800	22,600	474	530	289	310	20.8	23.5	12.7	13.7	185	220	164	171	45	57	94.9	107.5	40	50	8.4	9.4
Colored	15,500	15,300	362	404	234	239	23.4	26.4	15.1	15.6	128	165	155	169	37	52	102.2	128.7	37	45	10.2	11.1
White	7,300	7,300	112	126	55	71	15.3	17.3	7.5	9.7	57	55	(4)	(4)	8	5	71.4	39.7	3	5	2.7	4.0
Nelson	[5] 16,345	[5] 16,345	385	347	188	150	23.6	21.2	11.5	9.2	197	197	205	231	30	31	77.9	89.3	18	12	4.7	3.5
Colored	4,561	4,561	120	120	62	48	26.3	26.3	13.6	10.5	58	72	(4)	(4)	11	12	91.7	100.0	4	5	3.3	4.2
White	11,784	11,784	265	227	126	102	22.5	19.3	10.7	8.7	139	125	210	223	19	19	71.7	83.7	14	7	5.3	3.1
New Kent	[5] 4,300	[5] 4,300	80	83	53	54	18.6	19.3	12.3	12.6	27	29	(4)	(4)	8	10	100.0	120.5	5	10	6.3	12.0
Colored	2,540	2,540	61	59	36	42	24.0	23.2	14.2	16.5	25	17	(4)	(4)	7	9	114.8	152.5	3	10	4.9	16.9
White	1,760	1,760	19	24	17	12	10.8	13.6	9.7	6.8	2	12	(4)	(4)	1	1	52.6	41.7	2	-----	10.5	-----
Norfolk	39,200	29,900	593	564	427	394	15.1	18.9	10.9	13.2	166	170	139	143	[illegible]	68	116.4	120.6	34	33	5.7	5.9
Colored	15,100	13,100	337	345	263	237	22.3	26.3	17.4	18.1	74	108	128	146	54	50	160.2	144.9	32	25	9.5	7.2
White	24,100	16,800	256	219	164	157	10.6	13.0	6.8	9.3	92	62	156	139	15	18	58.6	82.2	2	8	.8	3.7
Northampton	18,700	18,600	417	439	257	223	22.3	23.6	13.7	12.0	160	216	162	197	32	25	76.7	56.9	25	22	6.0	5.0
Colored	10,000	10,000	276	283	177	136	27.6	28.3	17.7	13.6	99	147	156	208	28	16	101.4	56.5	20	21	7.2	7.4
White	8,700	8,600	141	156	80	87	16.2	18.1	9.2	10.1	61	69	(4)	(4)	4	9	28.4	57.7	5	1	3.5	0.6
Northumberland	[5] 11,081	[5] 11,081	179	218	116	125	16.2	19.7	10.5	11.3	63	93	154	174	18	16	100.6	73.4	4	7	2.2	3.2
Colored	4,648	4,648	97	113	70	61	20.9	24.3	15.1	13.1	27	52	(4)	(4)	13	13	134.0	115.0	3	3	3.1	2.7
White	6,433	6,433	82	105	46	64	12.7	16.3	7.2	9.9	36	41	(4)	(4)	5	3	61.0	28.6	1	4	1.2	3.8
Nottoway	15,000	14,900	295	320	250	287	19.7	21.5	16.7	19.3	45	33	118	111	25	20	84.7	62.5	14	16	4.7	5.0
Colored	6,700	6,700	159	189	199	221	23.7	28.2	29.7	33.0	−40	−32	80	86	20	16	125.8	84.7	14	12	8.8	6.3
White	8,300	8,200	136	131	51	66	16.4	16.0	6.1	8.0	85	65	(4)	(4)	5	4	36.8	30.5	-----	4	-----	3.1
Orange	[5] 12,070	[5] 12,070	195	208	140	135	16.2	17.2	11.6	11.2	55	73	139	154	14	8	71.8	38.5	7	9	3.6	4.3
Colored	3,795	3,795	66	77	57	67	17.4	20.3	15.0	17.7	9	10	(4)	(4)	6	5	90.9	64.9	4	6	6.1	7.8
White	8,275	8,275	129	131	83	68	15.6	15.8	10.0	8.2	46	63	(4)	(4)	8	3	62.0	22.9	3	3	2.3	2.3
Pittsylvania	62,000	61,500	1,286	1,517	672	572	20.7	24.7	10.8	9.3	614	945	191	265	101	86	78.5	56.7	53	50	4.1	3.3
Colored	21,200	21,000	505	570	272	262	23.8	27.1	12.8	12.5	233	308	186	218	47	39	93.1	68.4	24	28	4.8	4.9
White	40,800	40,500	781	947	400	310	19.1	23.4	9.8	7.7	381	637	195	305	54	47	69.1	49.6	29	22	3.7	2.3
Powhatan	[5] 6,143	[5] 6,143	99	99	77	51	16.1	16.1	12.5	8.3	22	48	(4)	(4)	14	2	141.4	20.2	6	14	6.1	14.1
Colored	3,155	3,155	62	57	54	33	19.7	18.1	17.1	10.5	8	24	(4)	(4)	10	1	161.3	17.5	5	12	8.1	21.1
White	2,988	2,988	37	42	23	18	12.4	14.1	7.7	6.0	14	24	(4)	(4)	4	1	108.1	23.8	1	2	2.7	4.8
Prince Edward	[5] 14,520	[5] 14,520	264	300	229	184	18.2	20.7	15.8	12.7	35	116	115	163	20	16	75.8	53.3	16	17	6.1	5.7
Colored	7,546	7,546	154	184	145	102	20.4	24.4	19.2	13.5	9	82	106	180	15	10	97.4	54.3	10	15	6.5	8.2
White	6,974	6,974	110	116	84	82	15.8	16.6	12.0	11.8	26	34	(4)	(4)	5	6	45.5	51.7	6	2	5.5	1.7
Prince George	[5] 10,311	[5] 10,311	273	280	129	129	26.5	27.2	12.5	12.5	144	151	212	217	29	25	106.2	89.3	10	12	3.7	4.3
Colored	4,226	4,226	147	152	76	75	34.8	36.0	18.0	17.7	71	77	(4)	(4)	17	17	115.6	111.8	8	10	5.4	6.6
White	6,085	6,085	126	128	53	54	20.7	21.0	8.7	8.9	73	74	(4)	(4)	12	8	95.2	62.5	2	2	1.6	1.6
Princess Anne	16,600	16,300	335	332	360	325	20.2	20.4	21.7	19.9	−25	7	93	102	24	28	71.6	84.3	25	10	7.5	3.0
Colored	7,700	7,600	198	202	217	201	25.7	26.6	28.2	26.4	−19	1	91	100	15	22	75.8	108.9	20	6	10.1	3.0
White	8,900	8,700	137	130	143	124	15.4	14.9	16.1	14.3	−6	6	96	105	9	6	65.7	46.2	5	4	3.6	3.1
Prince William	14,000	14,000	222	270	127	136	15.9	19.3	9.1	9.7	95	134	175	199	12	19	54.1	70.4	4	5	1.8	1.9
Colored	2,500	2,600	49	52	30	42	19.6	20.0	12.0	16.2	19	10	(4)	(4)	2	8	40.8	153.8	1	4	2.0	7.7
White	11,500	11,400	173	218	97	94	15.0	19.1	8.4	8.2	76	124	(4)	(4)	10	11	57.8	50.5	3	1	1.7	0.5
Pulaski	21,000	20,700	523	492	238	227	24.9	23.8	11.3	11.0	285	265	220	217	34	39	65.0	79.3	26	19	5.0	3.9
Colored	2,200	2,300	57	38	57	38	25.9	16.5	25.9	16.5	-----	-----	(4)	(4)	4	4	70.2	105.3	4	2	7.0	5.3
White	18,800	18,400	466	454	181	189	24.8	24.7	9.6	10.3	285	265	257	240	30	35	64.4	77.1	22	17	4.7	3.7
Radford (city)	6,400	6,300	134	137	54	56	20.9	21.7	8.4	8.9	80	81	(4)	(4)	6	7	44.8	51.1	4	8	3.0	5.8
Colored	600	700	19	15	13	15	31.7	21.4	21.7	21.4	6	-----	(4)	(4)	-----	-----	-----	-----	2	1	10.5	6.7
White	5,800	5,600	115	122	41	41	19.8	21.8	7.1	7.3	74	81	(4)	(4)	6	7	52.2	57.4	2	7	1.7	5.7
Rappahannock	[5] 7,717	[5] 7,717	170	176	69	68	22.0	22.8	8.9	8.8	101	108	(4)	(4)	11	8	64.7	45.5	3	10	1.8	5.7
Colored	1,878	1,878	43	42	22	21	22.9	22.4	11.7	11.2	21	21	(4)	(4)	4	2	93.0	47.6	1	1	2.3	2.4
White	5,839	5,839	127	134	47	47	21.8	22.9	8.0	8.0	80	87	(4)	(4)	7	6	55.1	44.8	2	9	1.6	6.7
Richmond	[5] 6,878	[5] 6,878	138	141	88	78	20.1	20.5	12.8	11.3	50	63	(4)	(4)	17	14	123.2	99.3	9	11	6.5	7.8
Colored	2,664	2,664	68	56	38	37	25.5	21.0	14.3	13.9	30	19	(4)	(4)	12	8	176.5	142.9	8	7	11.8	12.5
White	4,214	4,214	70	85	50	41	16.6	20.2	11.9	9.7	20	44	(4)	(4)	5	6	71.4	70.6	1	4	1.4	4.7
Rockbridge	20,900	20,900	475	521	237	258	22.7	24.9	11.3	12.3	238	263	200	202	32	46	67.4	88.3	25	19	5.3	3.6
Colóred	2,200	2,300	14	54	43	52	6.4	23.5	19.5	22.6	−29	2	(4)	(4)	2	5	142.9	92.6	4	2	28.6	3.7
White	18,700	18,600	461	467	194	206	24.7	25.1	10.4	11.1	267	261	238	227	30	41	65.1	87.8	21	17	4.6	3.6
Southampton	[5] 26,870	[5] 26,870	662	693	332	340	24.6	25.8	12.4	12.7	330	353	199	204	62	63	93.7	90.9	46	62	6.9	8.9
Colored	16,395	16,395	477	505	219	235	29.1	30.8	13.4	14.3	258	270	218	215	44	50	92.2	99.0	33	52	6.9	10.3
White	10,475	10,475	185	188	113	105	17.7	17.9	10.8	10.0	72	83	164	179	18	13	97.3	69.1	13	10	7.0	5.3
South Norfolk (city)	7,900	7,900	54	125	75	89	6.8	15.8	9.5	11.3	−21	36	(4)	(4)	13	12	240.7	96.0	7	7	13.0	5.6
Colored	1,700	1,700	12	20	32	37	7.1	11.8	18.8	21.8	−20	−17	(4)	(4)	6	6	500.0	300.0	6	4	50.0	20.0
White	6,200	6,200	42	105	43	52	6.8	16.9	6.9	8.4	−1	53	(4)	(4)	7	6	166.7	57.1	1	3	2.4	2.9
Spotsylvania	[5] 10,056	[5] 10,056	177	200	116	103	17.6	19.9	11.5	10.2	61	97	153	194	20	11	113.0	55.0	3	8	1.7	4.0
Colored	3,113	3,113	66	69	48	55	21.2	22.2	15.4	17.7	18	14	(4)	(4)	8	5	121.2	72.5	2	3	3.0	4.3
White	6,943	6,943	111	131	68	48	16.0	18.9	9.8	6.9	43	83	(4)	(4)	12	6	108.1	45.8	1	5	0.9	3.8
Stafford	[5] 8,050	[5] 8,050	154	171	78	81	19.1	21.2	9.7	10.1	76	90	(4)	(4)	10	14	64.9	81.9	5	3	3.2	1.8
Colored	1,488	1,488	52	44	22	23	34.9	29.6	14.8	15.5	30	21	(4)	(4)	3	5	57.7	113.6	2	2	3.8	4.5
White	6,562	6,562	102	127	56	58	15.5	19.4	8.5	8.8	46	69	(4)	(4)	7	9	68.6	70.9	3	1	2.9	0.8
urry	[5] 7,096	[5] 7,096	154	126	99	96	21.7	17.8	14.0	13.5	55	30	(4)	(4)	11	10	71.4	79.4	8	11	5.2	8.7
Colored	4,265	4,265	114	98	70	68	26.7	23.0	16.4	15.9	44	30	(4)	(4)	11	9	96.5	91.8	5	9	4.4	9.2
White	2,831	2,831	40	28	29	28	14.1	9.9	10.2	9.9	11	-----	(4)	(4)	-----	1	-----	35.7	3	2	7.5	7.1
Sussex	[5] 12,100	[5] 12,100	329	288	146	153	27.2	23.8	12.1	12.6	183	135	225	188	29	23	88.1	79.9	17	23	5.2	8.0
Colored	8,006	8,006	270	234	114	118	33.7	29.2	14.2	14.7	156	116	237	198	28	21	103.7	89.7	15	23	5.6	9.8
White	4,094	4,094	59	54	32	35	14.4	13.2	7.8	8.5	27	19	(4)	(4)	1	2	16.9	37.0	2	-----	3.4	-----
Warwick	[5] 8,829	[5] 8,829	121	134	63	73	13.7	15.2	7.1	8.3	58	61	(4)	(4)	5	6	41.3	44.8	2	2	1.7	1.5
Colored	2,510	2,510	50	56	24	43	19.9	22.3	9.6	17.1	26	13	(4)	(4)	2	5	40.0	89.3	2	2	4.0	3.6
White	6,319	6,319	71	78	39	30	11.2	12.3	6.2	4.7	32	48	(4)	(4)	3	1	42.3	12.8	-----	-----	-----	-----

See footnotes at end of table.

TABLE 18.—COLORED[1] AND WHITE POPULATION, BIRTHS AND DEATHS, INFANT MORTALITY, AND STILLBIRTHS, IN SELECTED REGISTRATION STATES, CITIES, AND COUNTIES: 1931 AND 1930—Continued

[See note at head of this table]

AREA AND COLOR	POPULATION ESTIMATED AS OF JULY 1		BIRTHS AND DEATHS (Exclusive of stillbirths)														INFANT MORTALITY (Exclusive of stillbirths)				STILLBIRTHS			
			Number				Rate per 1,000 population				Excess of births over deaths[2]		Births per 100 deaths		Deaths of infants under 1 year of age				Number		Rate per 100 live births	
			Births		Deaths		Births		Deaths						Number		Per 1,000 births					
	1931	1930	1931	1930	1931	1930	1931	1930	1931	1930	1931	1930	1931	1930	1931	1930	1931	1930	1931	1930	1931	1930
VIRGINIA COUNTIES—continued																						
Westmoreland	[5] 8,497	[5] 8,497	196	231	154	107	23.1	27.2	18.1	12.6	42	124	127	216	29	18	148.0	77.9	5	14	2.6	6.1
Colored	3,723	3,723	116	135	86	65	31.2	36.3	23.1	17.5	30	70	(4)	(4)	20	11	172.4	81.5	4	11	3.4	8.1
White	4,774	4,774	80	96	68	42	16.8	20.1	14.2	8.8	12	54	(4)	(4)	9	7	112.5	72.9	1	3	1.3	3.1
Williamsburg (city)	3,900	3,800	43	56	122	131	11.0	14.7	31.3	34.5	−79	−75	35	43	4	5	93.0	89.3	5	3	11.6	5.4
Colored	900	900	23	25	7	15	25.6	27.8	7.8	16.7	16	10	(4)	(4)	2	3	87.0	120.0	3	------	13.0	------
White	3,000	2,900	20	31	115	116	6.7	10.7	38.3	40.0	−95	−85	17	27	2	2	100.0	64.5	2	3	10.0	9.7
York	[5] 7,693	[5] 7,693	161	161	81	77	20.9	20.9	10.5	10.0	80	84	(4)	(4)	9	12	55.9	74.5	4	11	2.5	6.8
Colored	3,063	3,063	86	74	50	53	28.1	24.2	16.3	17.3	36	21	(4)	(4)	4	10	46.5	135.1	3	9	3.5	12.2
White	4,630	4,630	75	87	31	24	16.2	18.8	6.7	5.2	44	63	(4)	(4)	5	2	66.7	23.0	1	2	1.3	2.3
WEST VIRGINIA COUNTIES[8]																						
Fayette	73,500	72,300	1,988	2,021	881	854	27.0	28.0	12.0	11.8	1,107	1,167	226	237	171	202	86.0	100.0	82	79	4.1	3.9
Colored	11,900	11,600	246	276	234	219	20.7	23.8	19.7	18.9	12	57	105	126	30	42	122.0	152.2	20	17	8.1	6.2
White	61,600	60,700	1,742	1,745	647	635	28.3	28.7	10.5	10.5	1,095	1,110	269	275	141	160	80.9	91.7	62	62	3.6	3.6
Jefferson	15,800	15,800	320	318	222	224	20.3	20.1	14.1	14.2	98	94	144	142	35	32	109.4	100.6	7	15	2.2	4.7
Colored	2,700	2,800	42	45	45	51	15.6	16.1	16.7	18.2	−3	−6	(4)	(4)	2	3	47.6	66.7	3	2	7.1	4.4
White	13,100	13,000	278	273	177	173	21.2	21.0	13.5	13.3	101	100	157	158	33	29	118.7	106.2	4	13	1.4	4.8
Logan	60,700	59,000	1,675	1,865	591	586	27.6	31.6	9.7	9.9	1,084	1,279	283	318	122	121	72.8	64.9	56	53	3.3	2.8
Colored	7,400	7,100	134	155	92	93	18.1	21.8	12.4	13.1	42	62	(4)	(4)	8	10	59.7	64.5	6	8	4.5	5.2
White	53,300	51,900	1,541	1,710	499	493	28.9	32.9	9.4	9.5	1,042	1,217	309	347	114	111	74.0	64.9	50	45	3.2	2.6
McDowell	93,200	91,000	2,494	2,794	955	1,009	26.8	30.7	10.2	11.1	1,539	1,785	261	277	225	262	90.2	93.8	100	97	4.0	3.5
Colored	23,200	22,700	458	523	306	309	19.7	23.0	13.2	13.6	152	214	150	169	59	50	128.8	95.6	37	27	8.1	5.2
White	70,000	68,300	2,036	2,271	649	700	29.1	33.3	9.3	10.2	1,387	1,571	314	324	166	212	81.5	93.4	63	70	3.1	3.1
Mercer	43,500	42,300	1,222	1,180	380	409	28.1	27.9	8.7	9.7	842	771	322	289	81	111	66.3	94.1	31	36	2.5	3.1
Colored	4,500	4,300	86	102	67	57	19.1	23.7	14.9	13.3	19	45	(4)	(4)	9	8	104.7	78.4	1	3	1.2	2.9
White	39,000	38,000	1,136	1,078	313	352	29.1	28.4	8.0	9.3	823	726	363	306	72	103	63.4	95.5	30	33	2.6	3.1
Raleigh	71,200	68,700	2,150	2,180	637	688	30.2	31.7	8.9	10.0	1,513	1,492	338	317	155	171	72.1	78.4	92	83	4.3	3.8
Colored	11,700	11,300	290	318	139	162	24.8	28.1	11.9	14.3	151	156	209	196	20	19	69.0	59.7	10	15	3.4	4.7
White	59,500	57,400	1,860	1,862	498	526	31.3	32.4	8.4	9.2	1,362	1,336	373	354	135	152	72.6	81.6	82	68	4.4	3.7

[1] Includes Negro and other nonwhite races.
[2] A minus (—) sign indicates an excess of deaths over births.
[3] Rate by color not available.
[4] Figures not shown when the number of deaths is less than 100.
[5] Population Apr. 1, 1930; no estimate made.
[6] Includes "Incorporated places."
[7] Figures for Russell County, Ala., for 1930, include 147 births, 102 deaths at all ages, and 8 deaths under 1 year of age which should be included with those for Phenix City, Ala.
[8] Exclusive of muncipalities having 10,000 or more inhabitants on Apr. 1, 1930.
[9] Exclusive of estimated population for Thomasville.
[10] Exclusive of estimated population for Hopkinsville.
[11] Exclusive of estimated population for McAlester

TABLE 19.—COLORED[1] BIRTHS (EXCLUSIVE OF STILLBIRTHS), BY SEX, AND BY AGE OF MOTHER, IN SELECTED REGISTRATION STATES:[2] 1930

AREA AND SEX	Total births	BIRTHS BY AGE OF MOTHER									
		10 to 14 years	15 to 19 years	20 to 24 years	25 to 29 years	30 to 34 years	35 to 39 years	40 to 44 years	45 to 49 years	50 years and over	Unknown
SELECTED STATES											
ALABAMA	22,977	178	5,611	7,465	4,452	2,595	1,911	559	106	-	100
Male	11,595	88	2,836	3,755	2,297	1,305	928	283	53	-	50
Female	11,382	90	2,775	3,710	2,155	1,290	983	276	53	-	50
ARKANSAS	9,093	71	2,278	2,726	1,735	1,064	736	215	26	4	238
Male	4,602	30	1,165	1,358	896	525	390	101	13	2	122
Female	4,491	41	1,113	1,368	839	539	346	114	13	2	116
CONNECTICUT	736	1	147	269	158	98	48	12	1	1	1
Male	375	1	73	140	84	56	15	6	-	-	-
Female	361	-	74	129	74	42	33	6	1	1	1
DELAWARE	728	4	197	182	134	95	71	30	5	-	10
Male	370	2	95	86	74	56	36	18	1	-	2
Female	358	2	102	96	60	39	35	12	4	-	8
DISTRICT OF COLUMBIA	3,054	30	745	1,025	579	331	213	61	6	-	64
Male	1,605	15	389	564	277	170	120	36	4	-	30
Female	1,449	15	356	461	302	161	93	25	2	-	34
FLORIDA	8,391	79	2,136	2,484	1,788	969	632	182	32	1	88
Male	4,293	41	1,089	1,273	903	489	337	100	20	1	40
Female	4,098	38	1,047	1,211	885	480	295	82	12	-	48
GEORGIA	23,401	211	6,430	7,310	4,179	2,510	1,971	604	136	4	49
Male	11,826	115	3,259	3,697	2,137	1,205	1,002	301	79	1	30
Female	11,578	96	3,171	3,613	2,042	1,305	969	303	57	3	19
ILLINOIS	6,013	23	1,304	1,974	1,334	804	447	109	9	-	9
Male	3,080	10	677	982	687	423	235	57	4	-	5
Female	2,933	13	627	992	647	381	212	52	5	-	4
INDIANA	1,985	16	488	547	445	269	165	48	7	-	-
Male	960	6	244	261	198	132	88	27	4	-	-
Female	1,025	10	244	286	247	137	77	21	3	-	-
IOWA	288	-	71	76	66	39	29	6	1	-	-
Male	143	-	37	33	29	17	21	5	1	-	-
Female	145	-	34	43	37	22	8	1	-	-	-
KANSAS	1,540	11	282	416	353	239	162	64	7	-	6
Male	791	7	136	206	196	127	82	30	4	-	3
Female	749	4	146	210	157	112	80	34	3	-	3
KENTUCKY	3,381	30	740	904	710	505	344	120	20	-	8
Male	1,691	11	386	457	342	249	176	56	10	-	4
Female	1,690	19	354	447	368	256	168	64	10	-	4
LOUISIANA	16,731	98	3,632	5,332	3,505	2,065	1,446	472	77	2	102
Male	8,455	49	1,852	2,645	1,794	1,040	744	238	37	1	55
Female	8,276	49	1,780	2,687	1,711	1,025	702	234	40	1	47
MARYLAND	6,417	55	1,548	1,787	1,299	896	573	206	35	1	17
Male	3,155	27	745	887	637	458	281	100	13	1	6
Female	3,262	28	803	900	662	438	292	106	22	-	11
MASSACHUSETTS	1,029	5	156	264	233	183	133	39	4	1	11
Male	511	4	76	136	110	86	74	19	-	1	5
Female	518	1	80	128	123	97	59	20	4	-	6
MICHIGAN	3,907	9	707	1,273	951	567	306	59	6	-	29
Male	1,989	3	355	655	483	300	143	29	4	-	17
Female	1,918	6	352	618	468	267	163	30	2	-	12
MISSISSIPPI	24,880	206	5,945	8,104	4,515	3,013	2,013	645	115	9	315
Male	12,778	97	3,080	4,130	2,288	1,566	1,043	349	65	4	156
Female	12,102	109	2,865	3,974	2,227	1,447	970	296	50	5	159
MISSOURI	3,770	35	989	1,064	775	486	316	85	9	-	11
Male	1,935	17	527	515	391	266	158	50	5	-	6
Female	1,835	18	462	549	384	220	158	35	4	-	5
NEBRASKA	606	4	111	178	133	104	51	19	-	1	5
Male	283	2	50	89	65	45	26	6	-	-	-
Female	323	2	61	89	68	59	25	13	-	1	5
NEW HAMPSHIRE	10	-	1	3	2	1	2	1	-	-	-
Male	4	-	-	1	1	1	-	1	-	-	-
Female	6	-	1	2	1	-	2	-	-	-	-
NEW JERSEY	4,991	19	945	1,672	1,190	655	379	116	11	1	3
Male	2,546	9	453	861	607	350	187	72	4	1	2
Female	2,445	10	492	811	583	305	192	44	7	-	1
NEW YORK	9,188	15	1,510	3,141	2,324	1,368	658	150	10	-	12
Male	4,676	7	765	1,614	1,164	705	327	84	6	-	4
Female	4,512	8	745	1,527	1,160	663	331	66	4	-	8
NORTH CAROLINA	23,310	25	2,806	6,240	4,376	2,925	2,041	651	99	3	4,144
Male	11,877	16	1,440	3,137	2,235	1,509	1,015	329	51	1	2,144
Female	11,433	9	1,366	3,103	2,141	1,416	1,026	322	48	2	2,000
OHIO	5,992	29	1,305	1,863	1,268	830	514	167	13	1	2
Male	3,102	16	668	948	666	431	278	85	8	-	2
Female	2,890	13	637	915	602	399	236	82	5	1	-
OKLAHOMA	3,225	16	701	967	677	439	311	87	12	-	15
Male	1,660	7	369	500	360	223	154	35	6	-	6
Female	1,565	9	332	467	317	216	157	52	6	-	9
PENNSYLVANIA	9,506	65	2,025	2,958	2,171	1,268	767	218	19	1	14
Male	4,819	32	1,002	1,520	1,077	667	389	115	8	1	8
Female	4,687	33	1,023	1,438	1,094	601	378	103	11	-	6
RHODE ISLAND	244	1	39	58	62	37	33	11	-	-	3
Male	114	1	14	22	31	20	20	4	-	-	2
Female	130	-	25	36	31	17	13	7	-	-	1
SOUTH CAROLINA	20,403	86	4,724	6,899	3,872	2,313	1,869	543	88	-	9
Male	10,365	43	2,350	3,486	2,024	1,158	967	287	47	-	3
Female	10,038	43	2,374	3,413	1,848	1,155	902	256	41	-	6
TENNESSEE	8,106	65	2,046	2,480	1,580	982	694	202	41	3	13
Male	4,219	31	1,047	1,281	818	522	390	101	21	-	8
Female	3,887	34	999	1,199	762	460	304	101	20	3	5
VERMONT	11	-	3	3	2	1	2	-	-	-	-
Male	6	-	2	1	-	1	2	-	-	-	-
Female	5	-	1	2	2	-	-	-	-	-	-
VIRGINIA	15,732	108	3,252	4,541	3,103	2,258	1,746	603	79	-	42
Male	7,869	63	1,597	2,292	1,585	1,109	882	292	30	-	19
Female	7,863	45	1,655	2,249	1,518	1,149	864	311	49	-	23
WEST VIRGINIA	2,462	19	500	747	530	372	223	63	8	-	-
Male	1,274	8	248	383	292	181	126	33	3	-	-
Female	1,188	11	252	364	238	191	97	30	5	-	-

[1] Includes Negro and other nonwhite races.
[2] States in which the Negro population constitutes 55 percent or more of the total colored population.

TABLE 20.—COLORED [1] BIRTHS (EXCLUSIVE OF STILLBIRTHS), WITH THE NUMBER OF CHILD IN ORDER OF BIRTH, IN SELECTED REGISTRATION STATES: [2] 1931 AND 1930

NUMBER OF CHILD	ALABAMA		ARKANSAS		CONNECTICUT		DELAWARE		DISTRICT OF COLUMBIA		FLORIDA		GEORGIA		ILLINOIS		INDIANA		IOWA	
	1931	1930	1931	1930	1931	1930	1931	1930	1931	1930	1931	1930	1931	1930	1931	1930	1931	1930	1931	1930
Total births	22, 914	22, 977	9, 467	9, 093	687	736	685	728	2, 985	3, 054	8, 370	8, 391	24, 265	23, 404	6, 519	6, 013	1, 856	1, 985	250	288
First child	7, 017	7, 112	2, 656	2, 708	164	195	183	213	910	1, 027	2, 612	2, 634	8, 541	7, 832	1, 818	1, 952	440	547	66	99
Second child	3, 911	4, 039	1, 646	1, 534	145	164	122	111	690	630	1, 374	1, 396	4, 274	4, 054	1, 294	1, 210	362	378	49	46
Third child	2, 973	2, 830	1, 156	1, 136	107	113	90	93	399	405	1, 061	1, 073	2, 878	2, 820	978	862	270	271	34	35
Fourth child	2, 269	2, 197	929	885	69	70	55	63	286	285	819	773	2, 047	2, 050	721	616	215	200	25	26
Fifth child	1, 579	1, 665	695	620	58	60	43	65	199	210	649	595	1, 564	1, 550	518	448	147	178	26	25
Sixth child	1, 327	1, 297	554	581	41	35	46	38	130	147	459	464	1, 237	1, 276	390	304	138	121	21	16
Seventh child	994	992	481	442	39	32	43	35	89	82	366	356	898	892	312	218	100	87	6	13
Eighth child	813	790	320	341	29	20	31	33	62	59	277	250	750	794	179	123	62	67	9	7
Ninth child	589	597	299	223	10	16	13	14	53	48	197	177	555	576	113	100	36	44	3	8
Tenth child	478	487	176	187	11	10	18	17	30	31	122	160	456	450	74	68	36	28	3	2
Eleventh child	347	323	111	101	4	7	9	8	25	22	99	91	274	303	38	47	19	21	2	4
Twelfth child	229	220	83	54	4	7	6	9	14	16	49	68	194	238	30	25	13	19	2	4
Thirteenth child	137	137	57	48	4	3	4	8	5	12	31	37	121	194	16	20	10	10	1	2
Fourteenth child	83	93	34	26	1	2	3	6	11	7	24	30	87	92	11	5	4	5	1	
Fifteenth child	58	41	14	18	1	1		4	5	3	17	10	59	53	6	4	1	2	1	1
Sixteenth child	26	27	7	9			2	3		2	8	7	22	27	2	4		1		
Seventeenth child	12	14	8	4			1				4	3	13	20	3	1		3		
Eighteenth child	4	7	4	3		1	2			1	3		11	6	2		1	2		
Nineteenth child	5	3		2					1		1	3	5	1	1		1		1	
Twentieth child		2	4										3	7		1				
Twenty-first child	1	1	1										2	2			1			
Twenty-second child	3	1		1									1	1						
Twenty-third child														1						
Twenty-fourth child														1		1				
Twenty-seventh child														1						
Not stated	59	102	232	170			14	8	76	67	198	264	273	163	13	4		1		

NUMBER OF CHILD	KANSAS		KENTUCKY		LOUISIANA		MARYLAND		MASSACHUSETTS [3]		MICHIGAN		MISSISSIPPI		MISSOURI		NEBRASKA		NEW HAMPSHIRE		NEW JERSEY	
	1931	1930	1931	1930	1931	1930	1931	1930	1931	1930	1931	1930	1931	1930	1931	1930	1931	1930	1931	1930	1931	1930
Total births	1, 491	1, 540	3, 256	3, 381	17, 058	16, 731	6, 231	6, 417	1, 046	1, 029	3, 527	3, 907	23, 515	24, 880	3, 713	3, 770	621	606	6	10	4, 731	4, 991
First child	374	372	1, 001	950	4, 722	4, 918	1, 635	1, 645			773	979	6, 384	7, 074	1, 159	1, 182	122	156	2	3	1, 312	1, 344
Second child	238	258	591	599	2, 995	2, 792	1, 053	1, 114			666	770	4, 046	4, 230	691	718	116	93	1	2	977	1, 026
Third child	215	225	434	443	2, 176	2, 096	796	812			531	536	3, 019	3, 197	516	498	69	83	1		632	740
Fourth child	175	145	362	323	1, 772	1, 645	599	638			445	434	2, 342	2, 380	385	355	74	64	1	1	508	522
Fifth child	121	134	241	316	1, 274	1, 250	533	522			312	337	1, 713	1, 880	249	310	51	45		1	383	405
Sixth child	94	107	200	213	1, 101	1, 038	397	394			248	271	1, 483	1, 511	202	212	43	42			285	287
Seventh child	87	108	141	159	823	750	343	328			168	177	1, 083	1, 151	160	141	39	40			206	209
Eighth child	55	66	105	126	602	544	245	298			136	126	871	922	118	123	28	28		2	132	140
Ninth child	45	46	72	96	473	447	214	201			83	84	583	653	78	73	27	27		1	95	110
Tenth child	29	36	40	56	384	382	145	153			53	67	499	524	60	59	21	11			69	64
Eleventh child	23	20	21	34	255	228	106	103			42	28	353	313	31	34	12	7			34	43
Twelfth child	15	9	18	27	171	184	60	75			20	25	266	222	27	27	4	4			26	27
Thirteenth child	11	4	8	18	104	108	34	50			7	8	155	160	16	16	7	3			21	17
Fourteenth child	6	4	9	8	66	64	37	36			7	10	84	97	8	7	1	1			11	13
Fifteenth child	1	2	5	3	43	40	15	15			3	4	52	79	7	4	4				7	12
Sixteenth child		1	1	1	14	22	5	7			3	2	35	29	3	3	2	2			5	3
Seventeenth child		1		2	7	7	4	5				1	20	14	1	1					1	3
Eighteenth child						3	1	4					11	5	1	1	1				1	
Nineteenth child		1				3	1	1					5	3		1						
Twentieth child					2		1	2				1		1		1						1
Twenty-first child				2		3							1	2								
Twenty-second child													1	1								
Twenty-third child			1									1										
Twenty-fourth child					1									1								
Twenty-fifth child													1	3								
Not stated	2	1	6	5	73	207	7	14	1, 046	1, 029	30	46	508	428	1	4			1		26	25

NUMBER OF CHILD	NEW YORK		NORTH CAROLINA		OHIO		OKLAHOMA		PENNSYLVANIA		RHODE ISLAND		SOUTH CAROLINA		TENNESSEE		VERMONT		VIRGINIA		WEST VIRGINIA	
	1931	1930	1931	1930	1931	1930	1931	1930	1931	1930	1931	1930	1931	1930	1931	1930	1931	1930	1931	1930	1931	1930
Total births	8, 993	9, 188	22, 899	23, 310	5, 073	5, 992	3, 638	3, 225	8, 699	9, 506	204	244	20, 256	20, 403	7, 891	8, 106	3	11	14, 986	15, 732	2, 177	2, 462
First child	2, 724	2, 891	6, 525	6, 729	1, 408	1, 721	1, 144	1, 006	2, 439	2, 785	40	52	6, 516	6, 325	2, 444	2, 649		2	4, 096	4, 116	542	588
Second child	2, 090	2, 163	3, 723	3, 835	989	1, 161	691	622	1, 762	1, 844	45	35	3, 691	3, 563	1, 498	1, 485	1	4	2, 495	2, 540	372	435
Third child	1, 349	1, 387	2, 727	2, 722	735	845	467	408	1, 234	1, 325	20	42	2, 391	2, 397	988	1, 000	1	2	1, 773	1, 837	268	305
Fourth child	959	941	2, 209	2, 178	534	663	338	317	934	940	15	27	1, 846	1, 863	759	790		1	1, 412	1, 482	220	265
Fifth child	664	656	1, 767	1, 823	404	486	252	250	669	764	17	24	1, 446	1, 495	534	592	1	1	1, 099	1, 237	185	219
Sixth child	448	396	1, 402	1, 449	305	325	211	169	526	567	18	17	1, 145	1, 195	432	445			1, 040	1, 070	172	171
Seventh child	265	269	1, 146	1, 115	237	259	160	146	369	414	13	18	886	969	339	345			837	790	116	134
Eighth child	181	175	959	936	156	178	130	103	285	318	13	7	685	783	300	238			641	760	95	127
Ninth child	112	123	682	684	112	118	60	69	177	197	4	7	516	577	198	178		1	507	567	69	63
Tenth child	82	74	521	578	67	93	65	52	129	150	4	6	474	443	140	127			385	447	46	48
Eleventh child	47	42	364	322	49	53	38	31	65	76	6	2	257	308	89	80			244	330	34	38
Twelfth child	36	28	267	245	32	44	26	16	41	48	4	4	166	225	62	64			185	212	22	29
Thirteenth child	8	17	144	160	18	19	15	9	30	28	3		111	113	42	38			96	132	20	11
Fourteenth child	9	9	111	109	14	9	13	11	15	20			54	71	21	22			72	85	5	13
Fifteenth child	4	6	62	55	3	5	3	7	5	11		2	26	39	10	11			34	43	4	7
Sixteenth child	2	3	28	31	3	3	2	2	3	4			13	16	8	8			27	22	3	5
Seventeenth child	2		13	8	1	4		1	1	1			10	9	6	6			9	16	3	2
Eighteenth child	1		8	3				1					2	3	1	3			4	9		2
Nineteenth child		1		4				2			1		2	2					1	6		
Twentieth child	1		3	5	1																1	
Twenty-first child			1																2	2		
Twenty-second child			1	1				1											1			
Twenty-third child																						
Twenty-fourth child																			1			
Not stated	9	7	236	318	5	6	23	2	15	14	1	1	19	7	20	25			25	29		

[1] Includes Negro and other nonwhite races.
[2] States in which the Negro population constituted 55 percent or more of the total colored population.
[3] The birth certificate of this State does not require the number of child in order of birth.

Table 21.—CASES OF COLORED[1] PLURAL BIRTHS IN SELECTED REGISTRATION STATES:[2] 1931, 1930, AND 1929

[States having no plural births are omitted]

AREA AND SEX	1931	1930	1929
CASES OF TWINS			
ALABAMA	351	363	361
2 males	105	101	112
Both living	88	76	80
1 living	10	17	16
Both stillborn	7	8	16
1 male, 1 female	129	145	134
Both living	110	117	106
1 living—M	3	13	6
1 living—F	8	6	9
Both stillborn	8	9	13
2 females	116	117	115
Both living	101	95	87
1 living	9	13	20
Both stillborn	6	9	8
Both unknown	1	-----	-----
Both stillborn	1	-----	-----
ARKANSAS	181	209	154
2 males	58	73	45
Both living	44	60	31
1 living	10	10	8
Both stillborn	4	3	6
1 male, 1 female	73	73	52
Both living	60	60	45
1 living—M	2	7	3
1 living—F	3	4	-----
Both stillborn	8	2	4
2 females	49	63	57
Both living	40	49	44
1 living	7	7	8
Both stillborn	2	7	5
Both unknown	1	-----	-----
Both stillborn	1	-----	-----
CONNECTICUT	10	10	8
2 males	5	1	2
Both living	4	1	2
Both stillborn	1	-----	-----
1 male, 1 female	2	4	3
Both living	2	4	3
2 females	3	5	3
Both living	3	5	3
DELAWARE	12	7	4
2 males	5	4	2
Both living	3	4	1
1 living	-----	-----	1
Both stillborn	2	-----	-----
1 male, 1 female	6	2	1
Both living	5	2	-----
1 living	1	-----	-----
Both stillborn	-----	-----	1
2 females	1	1	1
Both living	1	-----	1
1 living	-----	1	-----
DISTRICT OF COLUMBIA	38	40	38
2 males	10	15	17
Both living	9	11	14
1 living	-----	3	2
Both stillborn	1	1	1
1 male, 1 female	15	10	8
Both living	15	10	7
Both stillborn	-----	-----	1
2 females	13	15	13
Both living	12	11	11
1 living	1	4	-----
Both stillborn	-----	-----	2
FLORIDA	101	150	144
2 males	26	52	54
Both living	20	36	41
1 living	1	10	7
Both stillborn	5	6	6
1 male, 1 female	40	48	44
Both living	32	44	39
1 living—M	2	-----	-----
1 living—F	3	-----	-----
Both stillborn	3	4	5
2 females	35	50	46
Both living	25	37	37
1 living	5	8	8
Both stillborn	5	5	1
GEORGIA	358	370	350
2 males	121	128	109
Both living	89	93	69
1 living	12	14	14
Both stillborn	20	21	26
1 male, 1 female	138	132	132
Both living	106	102	107
1 living—M	3	8	6
1 living—F	6	8	4
Both stillborn	23	14	15
CASES OF TWINS—Continued			
GEORGIA—Con.			
2 females	99	110	109
Both living	87	89	97
1 living	4	12	5
Both stillborn	8	9	7
ILLINOIS	82	82	86
2 males	39	23	34
Both living	34	19	24
1 living	1	3	8
Both stillborn	4	1	2
1 male, 1 female	27	37	29
Both living	23	33	26
1 living—M	-----	-----	2
1 living—F	2	3	-----
Both stillborn	2	1	1
2 females	16	22	23
Both living	12	20	18
1 living	1	1	4
Both stillborn	3	1	1
INDIANA	26	33	25
2 males	11	14	17
Both living	10	13	13
1 living	1	1	3
Both stillborn	-----	-----	1
1 male, 1 female	9	7	3
Both living	8	6	2
1 living—F	1	1	-----
Both stillborn	-----	-----	1
2 females	6	12	5
Both living	4	12	5
1 living	2	-----	-----
IOWA	2	2	4
2 males	1	1	2
Both living	1	1	2
1 male, 1 female	-----	1	1
Both living	-----	1	1
2 females	1	-----	1
Both living	-----	-----	1
1 living	1	-----	-----
KANSAS	16	23	8
2 males	1	7	2
Both living	-----	6	1
1 living	1	1	-----
Both stillborn	-----	-----	1
1 male, 1 female	6	8	3
Both living	5	7	3
1 living—F	1	1	-----
2 females	9	8	3
Both living	8	7	2
1 living	1	1	1
KENTUCKY	47	46	54
2 males	11	16	22
Both living	8	11	18
1 living	-----	2	3
Both stillborn	3	3	1
1 male, 1 female	17	11	13
Both living	16	8	13
1 living—M	1	1	-----
Both stillborn	-----	2	-----
2 females	19	19	19
Both living	15	16	16
1 living	2	2	2
Both stillborn	2	1	1
LOUISIANA	306	292	248
2 males	90	80	79
Both living	67	60	64
1 living	13	12	10
Both stillborn	10	8	5
1 male, 1 female	115	106	100
Both living	97	100	95
1 living—M	2	-----	-----
1 living—F	7	-----	-----
Both stillborn	9	6	5
2 females	101	106	69
Both living	89	82	56
1 living	8	16	9
Both stillborn	4	8	4
MARYLAND	89	96	84
2 males	35	37	26
Both living	24	25	19
1 living	3	5	4
Both stillborn	8	7	3
1 male, 1 female	28	34	26
Both living	25	28	21
1 living—M	2	-----	-----
1 living—F	-----	3	1
Both stillborn	1	3	4
CASES OF TWINS—Continued			
MARYLAND—Continued.			
2 females	26	25	32
Both living	21	20	23
1 living	1	3	5
Both stillborn	4	2	4
MASSACHUSETTS	20	11	16
2 males	6	2	11
Both living	4	1	10
1 living	2	-----	1
Both stillborn	-----	1	-----
1 male, 1 female	7	5	3
Both living	6	5	2
1 living—F	1	-----	1
2 females	7	4	2
Both living	6	3	1
1 living	1	1	1
MICHIGAN	55	55	42
2 males	15	16	15
Both living	14	13	14
1 living	-----	1	-----
Both stillborn	1	2	1
1 male, 1 female	16	22	11
Both living	16	20	11
Both stillborn	-----	2	-----
2 females	24	17	16
Both living	22	16	14
1 living	1	-----	1
Both stillborn	1	1	1
MISSISSIPPI	304	360	331
2 males	113	99	94
Both living	95	80	74
1 living	7	4	12
Both stillborn	11	15	8
1 male, 1 female	107	146	120
Both living	93	113	107
1 living—M	3	7	1
1 living—F	4	6	-----
Both stillborn	7	20	12
2 females	84	115	117
Both living	70	93	99
1 living	8	8	10
Both stillborn	6	14	8
MISSOURI	60	43	49
Two males	21	19	18
Both living	19	14	16
One living	1	3	-----
Both stillborn	1	2	2
One male, one female	24	7	16
Both living	21	5	15
One living—M	2	1	-----
One living—F	1	1	-----
Both stillborn	-----	-----	1
Two females	15	17	15
Both living	11	12	11
One living	3	5	4
Both stillborn	1	-----	-----
NEBRASKA	4	5	2
Two males	-----	3	1
Both living	-----	3	1
One male, one female	1	-----	-----
Both living	1	-----	-----
Two females	3	2	1
Both living	3	2	1
NEW JERSEY	50	59	70
Two males	17	21	26
Both living	16	16	18
One living	1	3	4
Both stillborn	-----	2	4
One male, one female	17	19	20
Both living	16	15	18
One living—M	1	1	-----
One living—F	-----	2	1
Both stillborn	-----	1	1
Two females	16	19	24
Both living	15	17	21
One living	-----	2	2
Both stillborn	1	-----	1
NEW YORK	107	126	109
Two males	44	50	47
Both living	40	44	42
One living	-----	-----	1
Both stillborn	4	6	4
One male, one female	30	37	30
Both living	26	34	24
One living—M	1	1	-----
One living—F	1	-----	-----
Both stillborn	2	2	6
CASES OF TWINS—Continued			
NEW YORK—Continued.			
Two females	32	38	32
Both living	28	32	30
One living	-----	2	-----
Both stillborn	4	4	2
Both unknown	1	1	-----
Both stillborn	1	1	-----
NORTH CAROLINA	412	418	433
Two males	124	155	141
Both living	95	121	110
One living	19	24	17
Both stillborn	10	10	14
One male, one female	150	144	159
Both living	121	120	129
One living—M	7	4	9
One living—F	12	8	9
Both stillborn	10	12	12
Two females	138	119	133
Both living	109	95	115
One living	20	14	7
Both stillborn	9	10	11
OHIO	60	79	103
Two males	9	30	42
Both living	9	23	36
One living	-----	1	4
Both stillborn	-----	6	2
One male, one female	25	18	27
Both living	21	15	21
One living—M	1	-----	2
One living—F	2	1	1
Both stillborn	1	2	3
Two females	26	31	34
Both living	24	26	31
One living	2	2	3
Both stillborn	-----	3	-----
OKLAHOMA	52	63	46
Two males	17	26	18
Both living	15	20	13
One living	2	3	3
Both stillborn	-----	3	2
One male, one female	15	22	16
Both living	14	21	15
One living—M	1	-----	-----
Both stillborn	-----	1	1
Two females	20	15	12
Both living	17	14	10
One living	-----	1	1
Both stillborn	3	-----	1
PENNSYLVANIA	155	131	142
Two males	45	39	52
Both living	37	30	44
One living	4	5	2
Both stillborn	4	4	6
One male, one female	55	51	45
Both living	48	44	35
One living—M	1	4	2
One living—F	4	2	4
Both stillborn	2	1	4
Two females	55	41	45
Both living	39	36	40
One living	11	5	3
Both stillborn	5	-----	2
RHODE ISLAND	4	2	3
Two males	1	-----	1
Both living	1	-----	1
One male, one female	1	-----	1
Both living	1	-----	1
Two females	2	2	1
Both living	2	2	1
SOUTH CAROLINA	403	402	419
Two males	125	117	122
Both living	98	94	98
One living	14	12	12
Both stillborn	13	11	12
One male, one female	149	155	151
Both living	125	123	112
One living—M	8	7	4
One living—F	4	8	14
Both stillborn	12	17	21
Two females	129	130	146
Both living	106	104	113
One living	13	16	19
Both stillborn	10	10	14

See footnotes at end of table.

TABLE 21.—CASES OF COLORED[1] PLURAL BIRTHS IN SELECTED REGISTRATION STATES:[2] 1931, 1930, AND 1929—Continued

[States having no plural births are omitted]

AREA AND SEX	1931	1930	1929
CASES OF TWINS—Continued			
TENNESSEE	120	108	121
Two males	38	42	41
Both living	29	31	31
One living	5	6	7
Both stillborn	4	5	3
One male, one female	35	37	39
Both living	29	31	35
One living—M	3	-	-
One living—F	2	-	1
Both stillborn	1	6	3
Two females	47	29	41
Both living	34	21	32
One living	8	5	6
Both stillborn	5	3	3
VIRGINIA	225	264	252
Two males	69	72	80
Both living	49	53	62
One living	16	11	13
Both stillborn	4	8	5
One male, one female	92	100	91
Both living	60	83	73
One living—M	7	6	6
One living—F	13	5	8
Both stillborn	12	6	4
Two females	64	92	81
Both living	55	69	71
One living	6	17	6
Both stillborn	3	6	4
WEST VIRGINIA	30	32	30
Two males	6	9	10
Both living	5	9	7
One living	-	-	2
Both stillborn	1	-	1
One male, one female	14	12	13
Both living	11	12	10
One living—M	-	-	1
One living—F	1	-	1
Both stillborn	2	-	1
Two females	10	11	7
Both living	8	9	6
One living	2	1	1
Both stillborn	-	1	-
CASES OF TRIPLETS			
ALABAMA	3	7	6
Three males	1	3	3
One living	1	3	3
One male, two females	1	-	2
All living	1	-	1
Two living: 1 M., 1 F	-	-	1
Three females	1	4	1
All living	1	1	1
One living	-	3	-
ARKANSAS	2	3	3
Three males	-	1	1
All living	-	1	1
Two males, one female	1	1	-
All living	-	1	-
All stillborn	1	-	-
One male, two females	1	1	1
One living—F	1	-	-
All stillborn	-	1	1
Three females	-	-	1
All living	-	-	1
DISTRICT OF COLUMBIA	1	-	1
One male, two females	1	-	1
All living	1	-	1
CASES OF TRIPLETS—Continued			
FLORIDA	1	3	-
Three males	-	1	-
All living	-	1	-
One male, two females	-	1	-
All living	-	1	-
Three females	1	1	-
One living	-	1	-
All stillborn	1	-	-
GEORGIA	6	10	3
Three males	-	3	-
All living	-	1	-
One living	-	2	-
Two males, one female	4	2	-
All living	2	-	-
All stillborn	2	2	-
One male, two females	1	2	2
All living	-	2	1
Two living—2 F	-	-	1
All stillborn	1	-	-
Three females	1	3	1
All living	1	1	1
One living	-	2	-
ILLINOIS	2	-	1
Three males	1	-	-
One living	1	-	-
Two males, one female	-	-	1
All living	-	-	1
One male, two females	1	-	-
All living	1	-	-
INDIANA	1	-	-
Three females	1	-	-
Two living	1	-	-
IOWA	-	1	-
Three females	-	1	-
All living	-	1	-
KENTUCKY	-	-	1
Three females	-	-	1
All living	-	-	1
LOUISIANA	3	4	3
Three males	2	1	-
All living	2	1	-
Two males, one female	1	1	1
All living	-	-	1
One living—M	1	-	-
All stillborn	-	1	-
Three females	-	2	2
All living	-	-	1
Two living	-	1	-
One living	-	-	1
All stillborn	-	1	-
MARYLAND	3	-	1
Three males	2	-	-
All living	1	-	-
One living	1	-	-
Two males, one female	1	-	-
All living	1	-	-
One male, two females	-	-	1
All stillborn	-	-	1
CASES OF TRIPLETS—Continued			
MICHIGAN	-	2	-
Three females	-	2	-
All living	-	2	-
MISSISSIPPI	5	5	3
Three males	3	2	-
All living	2	1	-
All stillborn	1	1	-
Two males, one female	1	1	1
All living	1	-	-
Two living 1 M., 1 F	-	1	1
One male, two females	1	1	1
All living	1	1	1
Three females	-	1	1
Two living	-	-	1
One living	-	1	-
MISSOURI	1	-	-
Two males, one female	1	-	-
All stillborn	1	-	-
NEW JERSEY	2	2	1
Three males	-	1	1
All living	-	-	1
Two living	-	1	-
Two males, one female	2	1	-
All living	2	1	-
NEW YORK	2	1	-
Three males	1	1	-
All living	1	1	-
One male, two females	1	-	-
All living	1	-	-
NORTH CAROLINA	8	9	5
Three males	-	4	2
All living	-	2	-
Two living	-	1	-
All stillborn	-	1	2
Two males, one female	2	2	-
All living	-	1	-
Two living 1931: 2 M; 1930: 1 M., 1 F	1	1	-
One living—F	1	-	-
One male, two females	3	2	2
All living	3	2	2
Three females	3	1	1
All living	2	1	1
Two living	1	-	-
OHIO	2	1	1
Three males	-	1	-
Two living	-	1	-
Two males, one female	-	-	1
All stillborn	-	-	1
One male, two females	2	-	-
One living—M	1	-	-
All stillborn	1	-	-
OKLAHOMA	1	1	-
Three males	-	1	-
All living	-	1	-
Two males, one female	1	-	-
All living	1	-	-
CASES OF TRIPLETS—Continued			
PENNSYLVANIA	2	2	3
Three males	-	1	-
One living	-	1	-
Two males, one female	1	-	-
All living	1	-	-
One male, two females	1	-	-
All living	1	-	-
Three females	-	1	3
All living	-	-	3
Two living	-	1	-
RHODE ISLAND	1	-	-
One male, two females	1	-	-
All living	1	-	-
SOUTH CAROLINA	5	1	9
Three males	2	1	-
Two living	1	-	-
All stillborn	1	1	-
Two males, one female	2	-	3
All living	2	-	1
Two living—2 M	-	-	1
All stillborn	-	-	1
One male, two females	-	-	1
Two living—2 F	-	-	1
Three females	1	-	5
All living	-	-	4
Two living	-	-	1
One living	1	-	-
TENNESSEE	1	3	5
Three males	-	-	1
Two living	-	-	1
Two males, one female	-	-	3
All living	-	-	1
All stillborn	-	-	2
One male, two females	1	1	1
All living	1	-	1
All stillborn	-	1	-
Three females	-	2	-
All living	-	2	-
VIRGINIA	1	-	3
Three males	-	-	1
All stillborn	-	-	1
One male, two females	-	-	1
All living	-	-	1
Three females	1	-	1
All living	1	-	-
Two living	-	-	1
CASES OF QUADRUPLETS			
ARKANSAS	-	-	1
Two males, two females	-	-	1
All living	-	-	1
VIRGINIA	-	2	-
Two males, two females	-	2	-
All living	-	1	-
All stillborn	-	1	-

[1] Includes Negro and other nonwhite races.
[2] States in which the Negro population constitutes 55 percent or more of the total colored population.

TABLE 22.—NUMBER OF COLORED[1] PLURAL BIRTHS AND PLURAL STILLBIRTHS IN SELECTED REGISTRATION STATES: 1931 AND 1930

AREA AND YEAR	NUMBER OF TWINS							NUMBER OF TRIPLETS								
	Total	Living			Stillborn			Total	Living				Stillborn			
		Total	Both	One	Total	Both	One		Total	All	Two	One	Total	All	Two	One
SELECTED STATES[2]																
Alabama 1931	702	628	598	30	74	44	30	9	7	6	—	1	2	—	2	—
1930	726	625	576	49	101	52	49	21	9	3	—	6	12	—	12	—
Arkansas 1931	362	310	288	22	52	30	22	6	1	—	—	1	5	3	2	—
1930	418	366	338	28	52	24	28	9	6	6	—	—	3	3	—	—
Connecticut 1931	20	18	18	—	2	2	—	—	—	—	—	—	—	—	—	—
1930	20	20	20	—	—	—	—	—	—	—	—	—	—	—	—	—
Delaware 1931	24	19	18	1	5	4	1	—	—	—	—	—	—	—	—	—
1930	14	13	12	1	1	—	1	—	—	—	—	—	—	—	—	—
District of Columbia 1931	76	73	72	1	3	2	1	3	3	3	—	—	—	—	—	—
1930	80	71	64	7	9	2	7	—	—	—	—	—	—	—	—	—
Florida 1931	202	165	154	11	37	26	11	3	—	—	—	—	3	3	—	—
1930	300	252	234	18	48	30	18	9	7	6	—	1	2	—	2	—
Georgia 1931	716	589	564	25	127	102	25	19	9	9	—	—	9	9	—	—
1930	740	610	568	42	130	88	42	30	16	12	—	4	14	6	8	—
Illinois 1931	164	142	138	4	22	18	4	6	4	3	—	1	2	—	2	—
1930	164	151	144	7	13	6	7	—	—	—	—	—	—	—	—	—
Indiana 1931	52	48	44	4	4	—	4	3	2	—	2	—	1	—	—	1
1930	66	64	62	2	2	—	2	—	—	—	—	—	—	—	—	—
Iowa 1931	4	3	2	1	1	—	1	—	—	—	—	—	—	—	—	—
1930	4	4	4	—	—	—	—	3	3	3	—	—	—	—	—	—
Kansas 1931	32	29	26	3	3	—	3	—	—	—	—	—	—	—	—	—
1930	46	43	40	3	3	—	3	—	—	—	—	—	—	—	—	—
Kentucky 1931	94	81	78	3	13	10	3	—	—	—	—	—	—	—	—	—
1930	92	75	70	5	17	12	5	—	—	—	—	—	—	—	—	—
Louisiana 1931	612	536	506	30	76	46	30	9	7	6	—	1	2	—	2	—
1930	584	512	484	28	72	44	28	12	5	3	2	—	7	6	—	1
Maryland 1931	178	146	140	6	32	26	6	9	7	6	—	1	2	—	2	—
1930	192	157	146	11	35	24	11	—	—	—	—	—	—	—	—	—
Massachusetts 1931	40	36	32	4	4	—	4	—	—	—	—	—	—	—	—	—
1930	22	19	18	1	3	2	1	—	—	—	—	—	—	—	—	—
Michigan 1931	110	105	104	1	5	4	1	—	—	—	—	—	—	—	—	—
1930	110	99	98	1	11	10	1	6	6	6	—	—	—	—	—	—
Mississippi 1931	608	538	516	22	70	48	22	15	12	12	—	—	3	3	—	—
1930	720	597	572	25	123	98	25	15	9	6	2	1	6	3	2	1
Missouri 1931	120	109	102	7	11	4	7	3	—	—	—	—	3	3	—	—
1930	86	72	62	10	14	4	10	—	—	—	—	—	—	—	—	—
Nebraska 1931	8	8	8	—	—	—	—	—	—	—	—	—	—	—	—	—
1930	10	10	10	—	—	—	—	—	—	—	—	—	—	—	—	—
New Jersey 1931	100	96	94	2	4	2	2	6	6	6	—	—	—	—	—	—
1930	118	104	96	8	14	6	8	6	5	3	2	—	1	—	—	1
New York 1931	214	190	188	2	24	22	2	6	6	6	—	—	—	—	—	—
1930	252	223	220	3	29	26	3	3	3	3	—	—	—	—	—	—
North Carolina 1931	824	708	650	58	116	58	58	24	20	15	4	1	4	—	2	2
1930	836	722	672	50	114	64	50	27	22	18	4	—	5	3	—	2
Ohio 1931	120	113	108	5	7	2	5	6	1	—	—	1	5	3	2	—
1930	158	132	128	4	26	22	4	3	2	—	2	—	1	—	—	1
Oklahoma 1931	104	95	92	3	9	6	3	3	3	3	—	—	—	—	—	—
1930	126	114	110	4	12	8	4	3	3	3	—	—	—	—	—	—
Pennsylvania 1931	310	268	248	20	42	22	20	6	6	6	—	—	—	—	—	—
1930	262	236	220	16	26	10	16	6	3	—	2	1	3	—	2	1
Rhode Island 1931	8	8	8	—	—	—	—	3	3	3	—	—	—	—	—	—
1930	4	4	4	—	—	—	—	—	—	—	—	—	—	—	—	—
South Carolina 1931	806	697	658	39	109	70	39	15	9	6	2	1	6	3	2	1
1930	804	685	642	43	119	76	43	3	—	—	—	—	3	3	—	—
Tennessee 1931	240	202	184	18	38	20	18	3	3	3	—	—	—	—	—	—
1930	216	177	166	11	39	28	11	9	6	6	—	—	3	3	—	—
Virginia[3] 1931	450	370	328	42	80	38	42	3	3	3	—	—	—	—	—	—
1930	528	449	410	39	79	40	39	—	—	—	—	—	—	—	—	—
West Virginia 1931	60	51	48	3	9	6	3	—	—	—	—	—	—	—	—	—
1930	64	61	60	1	3	2	1	—	—	—	—	—	—	—	—	—

[1] Includes Negro and other nonwhite races.
[2] States in which the Negro population constitutes 55 percent or more of the total colored population.
[3] 8 quadruplets were reported for 1930, 1 case all living; the other, all stillborn.

TABLE 23.—COLORED DEATHS (EXCLUSIVE OF STILLBIRTHS) FROM IMPORTANT CAUSES, BY CERTAIN SUBDIVISIONS OF THE FIRST YEAR OF LIFE, FOR SELECTED STATES AND CITIES: 1931 AND 1930

[Colored deaths include Negro and other nonwhite races. Data are included for States in which the Negro population constitutes 55 percent or more of the total colored population, and cities of such States in which data by color are available. Number after causes of death corresponds to those of the detailed International list]

AREA AND CAUSE OF DEATH	Total deaths under 1 year of age		DEATHS AT AGE OF— Under 1 day		1 to 2 days		3 to 6 days		1 to 3 weeks		Under 1 month		1 to 3 months		4 to 7 months		8 to 11 months	
	1931	1930	1931	1930	1931	1930	1931	1930	1931	1930	1931	1930	1931	1930	1931	1930	1931	1930
ALABAMA																		
All causes	1,757	2,157	402	505	192	224	140	148	263	277	997	1,154	356	441	266	354	138	208
Measles (7)	8	16							1		1		1	6	2	4	4	6
Scarlet fever (8)																		
Whooping-cough (9)	20	69							3	1	3	1	7	25	8	26	2	17
Diphtheria (10)	6	13								2		2	1	3	3	3	2	5
Influenza (11)	55	48							4	4	4	4	16	13	16	18	19	13
Dysentery (13)	9	6								1		1	3	4	3		3	1
Erysipelas (15)	1	1							1	1	1	1						
Epidemic cerebrosphinal meningitis (18)	4	3											2		2	1		2
Tetanus (22)	9	7					2	2	7	5	9	7						
Tuberculosis of the respiratory system (23)	5	6											3	1	2			5
Tuberculosis of the meninges, etc. (24)	4	2													1	1	3	1
Other forms of tuberculosis (25-32)	4												1		2		1	
Syphilis (34)	63	84	10	20	4	7	2	4	7	13	23	44	28	22	6	13	6	5
Convulsions (86)	30	26	1	3	4	1	8	7	9	5	22	16	5	4	1	6	2	
Bronchitis (106)	3	8	1							1	1	1		4	1	1	1	2
Bronchopneumonia (107)	99	131		1	3	3	3	3	8	18	14	25	40	39	29	49	16	18
Lobar and unspecified pneumonia (108, 109)	86	106			2	2	3		11	12	16	14	23	32	38	39	9	21
Diseases of the stomach (117, 118)	12	11				1		1	3	1	3	3	5	3	2	2	2	3
Diarrhea and enteritis (119)	134	189			1			2	4	4	5	6	46	55	49	74	34	54
Intestinal obstruction (122 b)	7	4							2	2	2	2		1	4	1	1	
Congenital malformations (157)	33	36	7	12	7	2	4	4	5	4	23	22	6	5	3	5	1	4
Congenital debility, icterus, sclerema (158, 161 b, c)	70	131	17	37	7	15	5	17	17	21	46	90	18	29	4	7	2	5
Premature birth (159)	417	495	220	294	85	85	35	39	58	56	398	474	16	20	3	1		
Injury at birth (160)	39	68	25	41	6	14	7	4		7	38	66	1	2				
Other diseases of early infancy (161 a, d)	38	50	8	9	8	14	10	12	10	13	36	48	2	2				
External causes (172-198, 201-214)	39	52	3	4		6	3	2	3	8	9	20	11	16	11	8	8	8
Unknown or ill-defined diseases (199, 200)	511	509	109	84	65	73	58	49	101	90	333	296	98	118	62	74	18	21
All other causes	51	86	1			1		2	9	8	10	11	23	37	14	21	4	17
ARKANSAS																		
All causes	483	512	73	68	40	54	23	37	66	68	202	227	123	111	91	108	67	66
Measles (7)	1	1											1	1				
Scarlet fever (8)																		
Whooping-cough (9)	4	15								1		1	2	4	1	2	1	8
Diphtheria (10)	1	3											1	1		1		1
Influenza (11)	23	21						1	2	3	2	4	7	4	9	6	5	7
Dysentery (13)	11	6								1		1	2	2	5	3	4	
Erysipelas (15)																		
Epidemic cerebrospinal meningitis (18)	1														1			
Tetanus (22)		1								1		1						
Tuberculosis of the respiratory system (23)	2	3											1		1	2		1
Tuberculosis of the meninges, etc. (24)																		
Other forms of tuberculosis (25-32)																		
Syphilis (34)	21	15	1	2	1		1	1	2	4	5	7	9	2	4	5	3	1
Convulsions (86)	2	6				1		2	1	1	1	4	1	1				1
Bronchitis (106)		3												2		1		
Bronchopneumonia (107)	24	33				1			3	3	3	4	9	10	6	14	6	5
Lobar and unspecified pneumonia (108, 109)	19	21							3	1	3	1	7	7	4	11	5	2
Diseases of the stomach (117, 118)	4	10					1			1	1	1		4	1	2	2	3
Diarrhea and enteritis (119)	71	60						1	11	6	11	7	18	14	24	20	18	19
Intestinal obstruction (122 b)	4												3		1			
Congenital malformations (157)	10	4	4	1	2	1	1	1			7	3		1	1		2	
Congenital debility, icterus, sclerema (158, 161, b, c)	27	25	10	4	1	3	2	7	3	3	16	17	4	7	4	1	3	
Premature birth (159)	53	72	33	38	11	18	3	8	6	7	53	71		1				
Injury at birth (160)	4	8	2	3	2	3		1		1	4	8						
Other diseases of early infancy (161 a, d)	8	8	1	2	2	3	1	1	3	2	7	8	1					
External causes (172-198, 201-214)	20	20	1		2	3	1		4	2	8	5	6	10	2	2	4	3
Unknown or ill-defined diseases (199, 200)	139	139	21	18	18	19	11	14	26	29	76	80	38	30	17	24	8	5
All other causes	34	38			1	2	2		2	2	5	4	13	10	10	14	6	10
FLORIDA																		
All causes	761	801	176	156	74	90	67	71	108	129	425	446	145	149	109	134	82	72
Measles (7)	2	3													1	3	1	
Scarlet fever (8)																		
Whooping-cough (9)	4	11								1		1	1	2	1	6	2	2
Diphtheria (10)	3	5											2	3	1			2
Influenza (11)	28	22								3		3	11	11	11	6	6	2
Dysentery (13)	4	1							1		1				2	1	1	
Erysipelas (15)	1												1					
Epidemic cerebrospinal meningitis (18)		1														1		
Tetanus (22)	9	8					2	2	6	4	8	6		2			1	
Tuberculosis of the respiratory system (23)	4	2							1		1		1	1	1		1	1
Tuberculosis of the meninges, etc. (24)																		
Other forms of tuberculosis (25-32)		2														2		
Syphilis (34)	35	32	2	2	3	5	5	4	2	2	12	13	13	9	7	5	3	5
Convulsions (86)	7	18		2		1	2	6	5	3	7	12		3		2		1
Bronchitis (106)	5	4					1			1	1	1	2		2	3		
Bronchopneumonia (107)	44	49			1				3	6	4	6	14	12	17	22	9	9
Lobar and unspecified pneumonia (108, 109)	45	28	1			1			4	5	5	6	12	8	11	10	17	4
Diseases of the stomach (117, 118)	5	7								1		1	2	3	2	3	1	
Diarrhea and enteritis (119)	61	93	1	1	1	1		3	3	10	5	15	22	25	20	30	14	23
Intestinal obstruction (122 b)	5	4				1		2	1		1	3	2		2			1
Congenital malformations (157)	24	15	8	2	5	1	2	1	6	3	21	7	1	4	1	3	1	1
Congenital debility, icterus, sclerema (158, 161 b, c)	56	64	18	12	6	9	5	9	11	10	40	40	12	12	3	9	1	3
Premature birth (159)	173	181	88	78	29	37	24	21	19	35	160	171	9	8	4	2		
Injury at birth (160)	34	22	14	10	7	6	7	4	4	2	32	22	2					
Other diseases of early infancy (161 a, d)	24	22	4	3	5	6	6	4	7	6	22	19	2	3				
External causes (172-198, 201-214)	21	20	2	3	1	1	1		4	4	8	8	4	7	6	3	3	2
Unknown or ill-defined diseases (199, 200)	122	125	37	40	14	19	10	13	26	23	87	95	23	18	6	8	6	4
All other causes	45	62	1	3	2	2	2	2	5	10	10	17	9	18	11	15	15	12

TABLE 23.—COLORED DEATHS (EXCLUSIVE OF STILLBIRTHS) FROM IMPORTANT CAUSES, BY CERTAIN SUBDIVISIONS OF THE FIRST YEAR OF LIFE, FOR SELECTED STATES AND CITIES: 1931 AND 1930—Con.

[See note at head of this table]

AREA AND CAUSE OF DEATH	Total deaths under 1 year of age		DEATHS AT AGE OF—															
			Under 1 day		1 to 2 days		3 to 6 days		1 to 3 weeks		Under 1 month		1 to 3 months		4 to 7 months		8 to 11 months	
	1931	1930	1931	1930	1931	1930	1931	1930	1931	1930	1931	1930	1931	1930	1931	1930	1931	1930
GEORGIA																		
All causes	**2,090**	**2,259**	**425**	**412**	**228**	**226**	**181**	**206**	**316**	**315**	**1,150**	**1,159**	**423**	**483**	**306**	**358**	**211**	**259**
Measles (7)	6	8	-	-	-	1	1	-	-	1	1	2	1	2	3	2	1	2
Scarlet fever (8)	1	-	-	-	-	-	-	-	-	-	-	-	-	-	-	-	1	-
Whooping-cough (9)	35	69	-	-	-	-	-	-	2	3	2	3	10	21	8	18	15	27
Diphtheria (10)	13	8	-	-	-	-	-	-	1	2	1	2	8	1	2	3	2	2
Influenza (11)	59	55	-	-	1	-	1	-	5	2	7	2	17	15	21	22	14	16
Dysentery (13)	23	54	-	-	-	-	-	-	2	7	2	7	9	15	7	14	5	18
Erysipelas (15)	3	-	-	-	-	-	-	-	-	-	-	-	3	-	-	-	-	-
Epidemic cerebrospinal meningitis (18)	1	4	-	-	-	-	-	-	-	1	-	1	-	-	1	1	-	2
Tetanus (22)	5	1	-	-	-	-	-	-	3	1	3	1	1	-	-	-	1	-
Tuberculosis of the respiratory system (23)	1	4	-	-	-	-	-	-	-	-	-	-	-	1	1	1	-	2
Tuberculosis of the meninges, etc. (24)	1	4	-	-	-	-	-	1	-	-	-	1	1	2	-	1	-	-
Other forms of tuberculsosis (25–32)	3	1	-	-	-	-	-	-	-	-	-	-	1	-	1	1	1	-
Syphilis (34)	61	44	5	2	2	-	2	6	13	13	22	21	20	9	11	9	8	5
Convulsions (86)	18	30	1	2	2	2	6	5	2	4	11	13	3	11	3	4	1	2
Bronchitis (106)	5	6	-	-	-	-	-	-	1	2	1	2	3	3	1	1	-	-
Bronchopneumonia (107)	122	160	-	-	1	-	3	1	20	13	24	14	35	62	36	50	27	34
Lobar and unspecified pneumonia (108, 109)	111	130	-	1	2	2	5	5	9	15	16	23	41	47	32	37	22	23
Diseases of the stomach (117, 118)	16	19	-	-	1	-	1	1	2	4	4	5	4	7	2	4	6	3
Diarrhea and enteritis (119)	172	180	1	-	-	4	3	3	18	12	22	19	44	51	63	60	43	50
Intestinal obstruction (122 b)	9	6	-	-	-	-	-	-	2	1	2	1	-	2	4	2	3	1
Congenital malformations (157)	38	32	12	4	5	5	6	2	6	8	29	19	5	5	3	6	1	2
Congenital debility, icterus, sclerema (158, 161b, c)	144	162	31	25	16	15	18	20	27	37	92	97	33	33	16	16	3	16
Premature birth (159)	458	468	223	235	93	92	55	63	67	63	438	453	17	14	3	-	-	1
Injury at birth (160)	61	47	24	16	18	13	8	13	10	4	60	46	1	1	-	-	-	-
Other diseases of early infancy (161 a, d)	44	46	7	8	12	13	11	9	14	13	44	43	-	3	-	-	-	-
External causes (172–198, 201–214)	49	47	7	2	4	3	1	4	8	3	20	12	13	19	11	11	5	5
Unknown or ill-defined diseases (199, 200)	527	566	114	115	69	70	57	70	94	94	334	349	116	120	52	64	25	33
All other causes	104	108	-	2	2	6	3	3	10	12	15	23	37	39	25	31	27	15
KENTUCKY																		
All causes	**445**	**413**	**73**	**55**	**34**	**33**	**38**	**31**	**69**	**66**	**214**	**185**	**109**	**94**	**75**	**91**	**47**	**43**
Measles (7)	2	4	-	-	-	-	-	-	-	1	-	1	-	1	-	1	2	1
Scarlet fever (8)	1	-	-	-	-	-	-	-	1	-	1	-	-	-	-	-	-	-
Whooping-cough (9)	11	15	-	-	-	-	-	-	-	1	-	1	3	4	4	3	4	7
Diphtheria (10)	1	1	-	-	-	-	-	-	-	-	-	-	-	-	1	1	-	-
Influenza (11)	9	7	-	-	-	-	-	1	1	-	1	1	4	1	1	2	3	3
Dysentery (13)	3	10	-	-	-	-	-	1	-	1	-	2	-	2	2	6	1	-
Erysipelas (15)	1	1	-	-	-	-	-	-	-	-	-	-	1	-	-	1	-	-
Epidemic cerebrospinal meningitis (18)	1	-	-	-	-	-	-	-	-	-	-	-	1	-	-	-	-	-
Tetanus (22)	1	1	-	-	-	-	1	-	-	1	1	1	-	-	-	-	-	-
Tuberculosis of the respiratory system (23)	3	3	-	-	-	-	-	-	-	-	-	-	1	1	1	-	1	2
Tuberculosis of the meninges, etc. (24)	4	2	-	-	-	-	-	-	-	-	-	-	1	-	3	1	-	1
Other forms of tuberculosis (25–32)	2	1	-	-	-	-	-	-	-	-	-	-	-	-	1	1	1	-
Syphilis (34)	15	8	2	2	-	2	4	-	2	3	8	7	3	-	3	-	1	1
Convulsions (86)	2	4	-	-	-	1	-	-	1	2	1	3	-	1	-	-	1	-
Bronchitis (106)	3	2	-	-	-	-	-	-	-	-	-	-	3	-	-	2	-	-
Bronchopneumonia (107)	67	49	-	2	2	1	-	2	11	3	13	8	28	16	21	18	5	7
Lobar and unspecified pneumonia (108, 109)	28	24	1	-	-	2	-	-	5	4	6	6	8	9	10	8	4	1
Diseases of the stomach (177, 118)	5	4	-	-	-	-	-	-	-	-	-	-	5	-	-	3	-	1
Diarrhea and enteritis (119)	71	65	-	-	-	1	1	2	6	7	7	10	25	25	22	22	17	8
Intestinal obstruction (122 b)	-	1	-	-	-	-	-	-	-	-	-	-	-	-	-	1	-	-
Congenital malformations (157)	5	12	2	1	1	1	1	3	-	1	4	6	1	4	-	2	-	-
Congenital debility, icterus, sclerema (158, 161 b, c)	24	25	2	2	2	1	4	1	7	3	15	7	7	11	1	6	1	1
Premature birth (159)	115	82	52	34	17	16	18	7	23	21	110	78	4	1	-	3	1	-
Injury at birth (160)	24	18	10	8	6	5	4	3	3	2	23	18	1	-	-	-	-	-
Other diseases of early infancy (161 a, d)	8	15	2	2	3	2	2	7	1	3	8	14	-	1	-	-	-	-
External causes (172–198, 201–214)	6	11	-	-	-	-	1	-	-	3	1	3	3	5	-	1	2	2
Unknown or ill-defined diseases (199, 200)	14	15	2	2	3	-	1	1	3	5	9	8	3	3	2	3	-	1
All other causes	19	33	-	2	-	1	1	3	5	5	6	11	7	9	3	6	3	7
LOUISIANA																		
All causes	**1,449**	**1,730**	**278**	**279**	**132**	**166**	**122**	**139**	**187**	**212**	**719**	**796**	**322**	**429**	**255**	**321**	**153**	**184**
Measles (7)	3	9	-	-	-	-	-	-	-	-	-	-	1	2	2	4	-	3
Scarlet fever (8)	-	-	-	-	-	-	-	-	-	-	-	-	-	-	-	-	-	-
Whooping-cough (9)	34	43	-	-	-	-	1	-	-	2	1	2	11	8	11	20	11	13
Diphtheria (10)	7	5	-	-	1	-	-	-	-	-	1	-	2	2	2	1	2	2
Influenza (11)	89	92	1	-	-	-	1	1	6	9	8	10	30	38	28	23	23	21
Dysentery (13)	8	10	-	-	-	1	-	-	-	-	-	1	5	4	2	4	1	1
Erysipelas (15)	1	-	-	-	-	-	-	-	-	-	-	-	1	-	-	-	-	-
Epidemic cerebrospinal meningitis (18)	5	5	-	-	-	-	-	-	-	1	-	1	-	1	3	1	2	2
Tetanus (22)	26	25	-	1	4	-	10	13	11	11	25	25	-	-	1	-	-	-
Tuberculosis of the respiratory system (23)	4	5	-	-	-	-	-	-	-	-	-	-	2	-	1	3	1	2
Tuberculosis of the meninges, etc. (24)	3	1	-	-	-	-	-	-	-	-	-	-	-	-	3	1	-	-
Other forms of tuberculosis (25–32)	1	1	-	-	-	-	-	-	-	-	-	-	1	-	-	1	-	-
Syphilis (34)	71	92	12	8	3	8	4	10	14	17	33	43	22	21	12	20	4	8
Convulsions (86)	9	11	-	-	-	3	4	3	1	2	5	8	2	2	2	-	-	1
Bronchitis (106)	18	24	-	1	-	-	-	1	3	4	3	6	8	10	4	6	3	2
Bronchopneumonia (107)	159	204	-	-	-	1	5	3	20	22	25	26	58	79	48	64	28	35
Lobar and unspecified pneumonia (108, 109)	72	68	-	-	-	2	3	1	10	7	13	10	22	20	22	25	15	13
Diseases of the stomach (117, 118)	9	21	-	-	-	-	-	1	1	1	1	2	4	8	4	7	-	4
Diarrhea and enteritis (119)	171	210	-	-	1	-	3	6	21	18	25	24	52	79	60	70	34	37
Intestinal obstruction (122 b)	10	17	-	-	-	-	2	1	1	-	3	1	4	6	2	6	1	4
Congenital malformations (157)	39	31	11	6	9	3	1	6	6	5	27	20	5	8	7	3	-	-
Congenital debility, icterus, sclerema (158, 161 b, c)	65	89	10	18	4	10	8	7	12	14	34	49	22	32	4	7	5	1
Premature birth (159)	301	292	153	151	57	63	40	27	38	36	288	277	10	10	2	4	1	1
Injury at birth (160)	64	70	33	34	17	15	8	16	6	4	64	69	-	1	-	-	-	-
Other diseases of early infancy (161 a, d)	38	64	13	20	11	20	5	11	9	11	38	62	-	2	-	-	-	-
External causes (172–198, 201–214)	25	29	3	2	2	2	1	1	2	6	8	11	7	11	7	6	3	1
Unknown or ill-defined diseases (199, 200)	141	222	39	38	19	35	21	27	23	36	102	136	30	48	7	26	2	12
All other causes	76	90	3	-	4	3	5	4	3	6	15	13	23	37	21	19	17	21

TABLE 23.—COLORED DEATHS (EXCLUSIVE OF STILLBIRTHS) FROM IMPORTANT CAUSES, BY CERTAIN SUBDIVISIONS OF THE FIRST YEAR OF LIFE, FOR SELECTED STATES AND CITIES: 1931 AND 1930—Con.

[See note at head of this table]

AREA AND CAUSE OF DEATH	Total deaths under 1 year of age		DEATHS AT AGE OF— Under 1 day		1 to 2 days		3 to 6 days		1 to 3 weeks		Under 1 month		1 to 3 months		4 to 7 months		8 to 11 months	
	1931	1930	1931	1930	1931	1930	1931	1930	1931	1930	1931	1930	1931	1930	1931	1930	1931	1930
MARYLAND																		
All causes	**822**	**777**	**108**	**109**	**60**	**70**	**50**	**51**	**76**	**82**	**294**	**312**	**217**	**188**	**168**	**174**	**143**	**103**
Measles (7)	10	-----	-----	-----	-----	-----	-----	-----	-----	-----	-----	-----	2	-----	2	-----	6	-----
Scarlet fever (8)	-----	-----	-----	-----	-----	-----	-----	-----	-----	-----	-----	-----	-----	-----	-----	-----	-----	-----
Whooping-cough (9)	29	11	-----	-----	-----	-----	-----	-----	-----	1	-----	1	8	1	11	4	10	5
Diphtheria (10)	2	1	-----	-----	-----	-----	-----	-----	1	1	1	1	-----	-----	-----	-----	1	-----
Influenza (11)	18	5	1	-----	-----	-----	-----	-----	2	-----	3	-----	5	-----	6	4	4	1
Dysentery (13)	15	9	-----	-----	-----	-----	-----	-----	-----	-----	-----	-----	4	2	7	7	4	-----
Erysipelas (15)	-----	1	-----	-----	-----	-----	-----	-----	-----	-----	-----	-----	-----	-----	-----	1	-----	-----
Epidemic cerebrospinal meningitis (18)	1	2	-----	-----	-----	-----	-----	-----	-----	-----	-----	-----	-----	-----	1	2	-----	-----
Tetanus (22)	2	1	-----	-----	-----	-----	-----	-----	-----	1	-----	1	2	-----	-----	-----	-----	-----
Tuberculosis of the respiratory system (23)	5	6	-----	-----	-----	-----	-----	-----	-----	1	-----	1	1	2	3	1	1	2
Tuberculosis of the meninges, etc. (24)	2	2	-----	-----	-----	-----	-----	-----	-----	-----	-----	-----	-----	1	1	1	1	-----
Other forms of tuberculosis (25–32)	1	6	-----	-----	-----	-----	-----	-----	1	-----	1	-----	-----	-----	-----	3	-----	3
Syphilis (34)	24	26	2	4	2	-----	-----	-----	4	5	8	9	9	11	5	4	2	2
Convulsions (86)	8	7	1	-----	-----	1	1	1	1	-----	3	2	1	3	1	1	3	1
Bronchitis (106)	20	22	-----	-----	-----	-----	1	-----	1	2	2	2	9	7	4	6	5	7
Bronchopneumonia (107)	103	106	1	-----	1	1	3	2	12	4	17	7	24	32	30	43	32	24
Lobar and unspecified pneumonia (108, 109)	76	49	-----	-----	-----	1	-----	-----	6	2	6	3	28	13	17	16	25	17
Diseases of the stomach (117, 118)	4	2	-----	-----	-----	-----	-----	-----	1	1	1	1	3	-----	-----	-----	-----	1
Diarrhea and enteritis (119)	150	141	-----	-----	-----	-----	1	-----	10	8	11	8	54	54	53	54	32	25
Intestinal obstruction (122 b)	3	2	-----	-----	-----	-----	-----	-----	1	1	1	1	1	-----	1	-----	-----	1
Congenital malformations (157)	43	30	4	2	10	2	5	6	4	4	23	14	10	11	8	3	2	2
Congenital debility, icterus, sclerema (158, 161 b, c)	49	59	7	7	3	5	4	5	6	12	20	29	22	19	4	8	3	3
Premature birth (159)	132	170	66	71	30	40	14	22	14	26	124	159	8	7	-----	3	-----	1
Injury at birth (160)	24	18	12	8	5	6	6	4	1	-----	24	18	-----	-----	-----	-----	-----	-----
Other diseases of early infancy (161 a, d)	35	34	10	10	9	11	8	8	1	3	28	32	7	2	-----	-----	-----	-----
External causes (172–198, 201–214)	10	10	-----	2	-----	-----	-----	1	2	-----	2	3	4	5	2	2	2	-----
Unknown or ill-defined diseases (199, 200)	18	21	4	4	-----	1	3	2	2	3	9	10	6	7	2	3	1	1
All other causes	38	36	-----	1	-----	2	4	-----	6	7	10	10	9	11	10	8	9	7
MISSISSIPPI																		
All causes	**1,580**	**2,072**	**269**	**294**	**154**	**245**	**128**	**173**	**197**	**267**	**748**	**979**	**373**	**492**	**287**	**375**	**172**	**226**
Measles (7)	1	8	-----	-----	-----	-----	-----	-----	-----	-----	-----	-----	-----	4	1	2	-----	2
Scarlet fever (8)	-----	2	-----	-----	-----	-----	-----	-----	-----	-----	-----	-----	-----	-----	-----	2	-----	-----
Whooping-cough (9)	23	64	-----	-----	-----	-----	-----	-----	-----	3	-----	3	9	22	9	23	5	16
Diphtheria (10)	8	8	-----	-----	-----	-----	-----	-----	-----	1	-----	1	2	2	4	1	2	4
Influenza (11)	67	66	-----	-----	1	-----	-----	-----	5	6	6	6	17	19	27	29	17	12
Dysentery (13)	15	24	-----	-----	-----	-----	-----	1	1	2	1	3	3	5	5	10	6	6
Erysipelas (15)	-----	-----	-----	-----	-----	-----	-----	-----	-----	-----	-----	-----	-----	-----	-----	-----	-----	-----
Epidemic cerebrospinal meningitis (18)	2	4	-----	-----	-----	-----	-----	-----	-----	-----	-----	-----	1	-----	1	4	-----	-----
Tetanus (22)	1	2	-----	-----	1	-----	-----	1	-----	1	1	2	-----	-----	-----	-----	-----	-----
Tuberculosis of the respiratory system (23)	7	13	-----	-----	-----	-----	-----	-----	1	2	1	2	2	1	2	5	2	5
Tuberculosis of the meninges, etc. (24)	3	1	-----	-----	-----	-----	-----	-----	1	-----	1	-----	-----	-----	1	1	1	-----
Other forms of tuberculosis (25–32)	1	1	-----	-----	-----	-----	-----	-----	-----	-----	-----	-----	-----	1	1	-----	-----	-----
Syphilis (34)	48	65	8	6	2	3	1	7	4	9	15	25	15	29	9	9	9	2
Convulsions (86)	15	28	1	-----	1	1	1	3	2	9	5	13	5	8	3	5	2	2
Bronchitis (106)	4	11	-----	-----	-----	-----	-----	-----	-----	1	-----	1	2	4	2	3	-----	3
Bronchopneumonia (107)	84	99	1	-----	1	-----	1	1	5	14	8	15	34	25	30	33	12	26
Lobar and unspecified pneumonia (108, 109)	87	108	-----	-----	1	3	1	7	7	9	9	19	28	32	29	39	21	18
Diseases of the stomach (117, 118)	4	4	-----	-----	-----	1	-----	-----	-----	1	-----	2	2	-----	2	1	-----	1
Diarrhea and enteritis (119)	140	197	-----	1	-----	1	1	1	9	14	10	17	49	69	46	65	35	46
Intestinal obstruction (122 b)	10	11	-----	-----	-----	-----	2	-----	3	-----	5	-----	2	4	1	4	2	3
Congenital malformations (157)	19	24	5	5	4	2	4	3	3	3	16	13	2	8	1	2	-----	1
Congenital debility, icterus, sclerema (158, 161 b, c)	65	47	15	4	9	5	5	3	9	9	38	21	17	15	7	7	3	4
Premature birth (159)	159	211	83	103	27	46	21	25	23	31	154	205	5	5	-----	-----	-----	1
Injury at birth (160)	26	40	16	13	3	15	5	6	2	5	26	39	-----	1	-----	-----	-----	-----
Other diseases of early infancy (161 a, d)	14	46	3	5	3	16	4	10	3	12	13	43	1	3	-----	-----	-----	-----
External causes (172–198, 201–214)	42	49	7	6	2	1	4	2	4	5	17	14	6	14	15	9	4	12
Unknown or ill-defined diseases (199, 200)	666	841	129	150	96	150	77	98	108	126	410	524	151	188	74	89	31	40
All other causes	69	98	1	1	3	1	1	5	7	4	12	11	20	33	17	32	20	22
NORTH CAROLINA																		
All causes	**2,340**	**2,451**	**409**	**354**	**229**	**228**	**157**	**195**	**343**	**348**	**1,138**	**1,125**	**581**	**583**	**391**	**462**	**230**	**281**
Measles (7)	3	-----	-----	-----	-----	-----	-----	-----	-----	-----	-----	-----	1	-----	-----	-----	2	-----
Scarlet fever (8)	-----	1	-----	-----	-----	-----	-----	-----	-----	-----	-----	-----	-----	-----	-----	-----	-----	1
Whooping-cough (9)	58	65	-----	-----	-----	1	-----	-----	6	1	6	2	18	19	17	21	17	23
Diphtheria (10)	8	6	-----	-----	-----	-----	-----	-----	-----	-----	-----	-----	6	1	2	3	-----	2
Influenza (11)	79	49	2	-----	-----	-----	-----	-----	8	1	10	1	24	12	33	22	12	14
Dysentery (13)	12	21	-----	-----	-----	-----	-----	-----	1	-----	1	-----	4	5	4	10	3	6
Erysipelas (15)	6	3	-----	-----	-----	-----	-----	-----	1	1	1	1	4	1	-----	1	1	-----
Epidemic cerebrospinal meningitis (18)	1	2	-----	-----	-----	-----	-----	-----	-----	1	-----	1	-----	-----	-----	-----	1	1
Tetanus (22)	5	4	-----	-----	-----	-----	1	2	4	2	5	4	-----	-----	-----	-----	-----	-----
Tuberculosis of the respiratory system (23)	3	7	-----	-----	-----	-----	-----	-----	-----	-----	-----	-----	-----	-----	2	3	1	4
Tuberculosis of the meninges, etc. (24)	-----	3	-----	-----	-----	-----	-----	-----	-----	-----	-----	-----	-----	-----	-----	2	-----	1
Other forms of tuberculosis (25–32)	-----	-----	-----	-----	-----	-----	-----	-----	-----	-----	-----	-----	-----	-----	-----	-----	-----	-----
Syphilis (34)	40	55	7	2	4	5	2	2	4	11	17	20	18	18	3	12	2	5
Convulsions (86)	11	21	1	3	-----	3	-----	3	2	4	3	13	5	4	1	3	2	1
Bronchitis (106)	21	31	-----	-----	-----	-----	-----	1	1	1	1	2	7	12	11	13	2	4
Bronchopneumonia (107)	150	148	-----	-----	2	4	2	2	13	12	17	18	48	51	50	53	35	26
Lobar and unspecified pneumonia (108, 109)	111	108	-----	-----	2	2	2	2	13	9	17	13	37	42	40	27	17	26
Diseases of the stomach (117, 118)	7	13	-----	-----	-----	-----	1	-----	-----	1	1	1	4	3	1	5	1	4
Diarrhea and enteritis (119)	245	320	1	-----	-----	2	-----	3	12	20	13	25	89	104	92	122	51	69
Intestinal obstruction (122 b)	3	10	-----	-----	-----	-----	-----	-----	-----	1	-----	1	-----	3	2	3	1	3
Congenital malformations (157)	39	37	5	5	6	4	8	8	9	4	28	21	5	13	1	1	5	2
Congenital debility, icterus, sclerema (158, 161 b, c)	146	121	16	8	6	9	16	16	33	22	71	55	47	39	16	19	12	8
Premature birth (159)	417	454	161	192	94	93	54	49	75	81	384	415	31	30	2	6	-----	3
Injury at birth (160)	50	50	26	25	11	7	4	6	9	10	50	48	-----	2	-----	-----	-----	-----
Other diseases of early infancy (161 a, d)	48	59	13	11	10	12	7	16	15	16	45	55	3	4	-----	-----	-----	-----
External causes (172–198, 201–214)	45	51	1	3	2	2	1	1	4	6	8	12	18	22	9	11	10	6
Unknown or ill-defined diseases (199, 200)	719	704	175	104	87	83	54	82	122	126	438	395	176	164	72	88	33	57
All other causes	113	108	1	1	5	1	5	2	11	18	22	22	36	34	33	37	22	15

TABLE 23.—COLORED DEATHS (EXCLUSIVE OF STILLBIRTHS) FROM IMPORTANT CAUSES, BY CERTAIN SUBDIVISIONS OF THE FIRST YEAR OF LIFE, FOR SELECTED STATES AND CITIES: 1931 AND 1930—Con.

[See note at head of this table]

AREA AND CAUSE OF DEATH	Total deaths under 1 year of age		DEATHS AT AGE OF— Under 1 day		1 to 2 days		3 to 6 days		1 to 3 weeks		Under 1 month		1 to 3 months		4 to 7 months		8 to 11 months	
	1931	1930	1931	1930	1931	1930	1931	1930	1931	1930	1931	1930	1931	1930	1931	1930	1931	1930
OKLAHOMA																		
All causes	**312**	**346**	**34**	**34**	**16**	**19**	**29**	**31**	**50**	**60**	**129**	**144**	**67**	**89**	**61**	**64**	**55**	**49**
Measles (7)	1	2											1			2		
Scarlet fever (8)																		
Whooping-cough (9)	17	18							2	1	2	1	6	6	4	8	5	3
Diphtheria (10)	2	3											1	1	1	1		1
Influenza (11)	11	7					1	1	2	1	3	2	2	2	4	2	2	1
Dysentery (13)	9	8								1		1	6	1	1	6	2	
Erysipelas (15)	2								1		1		1					
Epidemic cerebrospinal meningitis (18)		1								1		1						
Tetanus (22)		1																1
Tuberculosis of the respiratory system (23)	1	1													1	1		
Tuberculosis of the meninges, etc. (24)	4												1		2		1	
Other forms of tuberculosis (25–32)	1														1			
Syphilis (34)	16	7	2	1		1	2		2		6	2	5	5	4		1	
Convulsions (86)	1	4				1				1		2		2	1			
Bronchitis (106)		2								1		1						1
Bronchopneumonia (107)	33	44				1			2	4	2	5	11	16	11	14	9	9
Lobar and unspecified pneumonia (108, 109)	22	31					1		6	7	7	7	4	12	4	4	7	8
Diseases of the stomach (117, 118)	8	7		1		1	1		1	1	2	3		1	1		5	3
Diarrhea and enteritis (119)	41	46					1	1	4	4	5	5	9	15	15	16	12	10
Intestinal obstruction (122 b)	4	1											1		1	1	2	
Congenital malformations (157)	8	6	5	1		1			1	2	6	4		2			2	
Congenital debility, icterus, sclerema (158, 161, b, c)	15	20	2		2		4	3	3	11	11	14	4	5				1
Premature birth (159)	47	49	20	22	4	7	10	7	9	9	43	45	2	4	2			
Injury at birth (160)	9	9	3	1	2	1	3	4	1	2	9	8		1				
Other diseases of early infancy (161 a, d)	8	12	2	3	3	3	1	2	2	1	8	9		3				
External causes (172–198, 201–214)	7	2						1	1		1	1	5	1	1			
Unknown or ill-defined diseases (199, 200)	27	50		5	4	3	3	11	9	10	16	29	6	6	4	6	1	9
All other causes	18	15			1		2	1	4	3	7	4	2	6	3	3	6	2
SOUTH CAROLINA																		
All causes	**2,067**	**2,205**	**327**	**352**	**222**	**211**	**182**	**180**	**299**	**324**	**1,030**	**1,067**	**468**	**517**	**367**	**388**	**202**	**233**
Measles (7)	6	1													4	1	2	
Scarlet fever (8)																		
Whooping-cough (9)	51	78								3		3	20	21	19	30	12	24
Diphtheria (10)	7	11								1		1	2	9	4	1	1	
Influenza (11)	89	74							4	6	4	6	33	28	34	28	18	12
Dysentery (13)	29	30		1			1		3	2	4	3	11	9	8	8	6	10
Erysipelas (15)	2	1							1		1		1					1
Epidemic cerebrospinal meningitis (18)		2												1		1		
Tetanus (22)	8	8		1			3	1	5	4	8	6		2				
Tuberculosis of the respiratory system (23)	5	7											1		1	3	3	4
Tuberculosis of the meninges, etc. (24)		2												2				
Other forms of tuberculosis (25–32)		1																1
Syphilis (34)	69	50	11	5	6	7	8	1	9	6	34	19	23	22	9	4	3	5
Convulsions (86)	20	29			2		4	6	5	4	11	10	5	11	4	6		2
Bronchitis (106)	1	3								1		1		2			1	
Bronchopneumonia (107)	97	114		1	3	2	4	4	18	13	25	20	34	45	24	29	14	20
Lobar and unspecified pneumonia (108, 109)	126	138			2	1	5	8	16	15	23	24	47	49	40	42	16	23
Diseases of the stomach (117, 118)	53	50				1	2	1	7	6	9	8	21	17	15	17	8	8
Diarrhea and enteritis (119)	239	229			1	1	1	4	23	15	25	20	81	75	80	77	53	57
Intestinal obstruction (122 b)	6	5					1		1	1	2	1	3	1		1	1	2
Congenital malformations (157)	17	15		1	2		2	6	2		6	7	5	2	3	2	3	4
Congenital debility, icterus, sclerema (158, 161 b, c)	83	101	7	13	9	9	15	9	18	27	49	58	14	25	16	13	4	5
Premature birth (159)	299	370	141	177	78	75	37	47	32	59	288	358	8	6	3	6		
Injury at birth (160)	28	25	16	17	6	4	2	3	4	1	28	25						
Other diseases of early infancy (161 a, d)	36	37	7	5	8	8	9	9	11	12	35	34	1	3				
External causes (172–198, 201–214)	21	22			1	1	1		1	2	3	3	8	8	10	8		3
Unknown or ill-defined diseases (199, 200)	662	666	145	130	103	100	83	78	121	128	452	436	116	129	59	76	35	25
All other causes	113	136		1	1	2	4	3	18	18	23	24	34	50	34	35	22	27
TENNESSEE																		
All causes	**803**	**931**	**138**	**143**	**63**	**76**	**49**	**57**	**106**	**107**	**356**	**383**	**203**	**240**	**152**	**198**	**92**	**110**
Measles (7)	3	3												2	2		1	1
Scarlet fever (8)	3														1		2	
Whooping-cough (9)	31	24								1		1	6	9	11	6	14	8
Diphtheria (10)	7	7					1			1	1	1	3	3	1	3	2	
Influenza (11)	11	23								3		3	5	8	4	7	2	5
Dysentery (13)	6	6											2	2		3	4	1
Erysipelas (15)	1								1		1							
Epidemic cerebrospinal meningitis (18)	3	12											1	3	1	6	1	3
Tetanus (22)		1								1		1						
Tuberculosis of the respiratory system (23)	5	12											1	1	1	7	3	4
Tuberculosis of the meninges, etc. (24)	4														2		2	
Other forms of tuberculosis (25–32)	6	3					2				2		1		2	1	1	2
Syphilis (34)	51	42	12	10	4	3	2	3	7	8	25	24	16	13	7	4	3	1
Convulsions (86)	11	6					3		1	2	4	2	2	1	4	2	1	1
Bronchitis (106)	2	2							1		1		1	1		1		
Bronchopneumonia (107)	93	125	2		1	2	2	2	9	6	14	10	29	37	40	53	10	25
Lobar and unspecified pneumonia (108, 109)	34	29			1				2	4	3	4	10	7	10	10	11	8
Diseases of the stomach (117, 118)	3	4				1			1		1	1	2	1		1		1
Diarrhea and enteritis (119)	80	105					1		6	5	7	5	28	34	28	40	17	26
Intestinal obstruction (122 b)	7	2			2						2		1		3	1	1	1
Congenital malformations (157)	7	8	1	1	1	3	3			1	5	5	2	3				
Congenital debility, icterus, sclerema (158, 161 b, c)	33	46	5	3	3	7	3	7	7	9	18	26	11	14	4	4		2
Premature birth (159)	140	153	65	85	24	26	11	15	27	21	127	147	13	6				
Injury at birth (160)	26	23	16	12	5	7	4	2	1	1	26	22		1				
Other diseases of early infancy (161 a, d)	15	19	7	6	2	3	2	6	4	2	15	17		2				
External causes (172–198, 201–214)	10	17	2	1		1	1	1	1		4	3	6	8		5		1
Unknown or ill-defined diseases (199, 200)	178	222	28	25	19	22	13	21	30	38	90	106	52	68	26	33	10	15
All other causes	33	37			1	1	1		8	4	10	5	11	16	5	11	7	5

TABLE 23.—COLORED DEATHS (EXCLUSIVE OF STILLBIRTHS) FROM IMPORTANT CAUSES, BY CERTAIN SUBDIVISIONS OF THE FIRST YEAR OF LIFE, FOR SELECTED STATES AND CITIES: 1931 AND 1930—Con.

[See note at head of this table]

AREA AND CAUSE OF DEATH	Total deaths under 1 year of age		DEATHS AT AGE OF— Under 1 day		1 to 2 days		3 to 6 days		1 to 3 weeks		Under 1 month		1 to 3 months		4 to 7 months		8 to 11 months	
	1931	1930	1931	1930	1931	1930	1931	1930	1931	1930	1931	1930	1931	1930	1931	1930	1931	1930
VIRGINIA																		
All causes	1,615	1,687	255	249	122	141	132	118	217	232	726	740	379	408	318	329	192	210
Measles (7)	6	10	1			1			1	1	2	2	2	2	1	1	1	5
Scarlet fever (8)																		
Whooping-cough (9)	48	74					1		3	2	4	2	9	25	19	30	16	17
Diphtheria (10)	5	8					1		1		2			4	3	2		2
Influenza (11)	76	38						1	5		5	1	27	12	24	19	20	6
Dysentery (13)	21	27								1		1	5	8	10	10	6	8
Erysipelas (15)		2								1		1		1				
Epidemic cerebrospinal meningitis (18)	2	3											1	1	1	1		1
Tetanus (22)	1	3					1			3	1	3						
Tuberculosis of the respiratory system (23)	8	6								1		1	1	1	5	1	2	3
Tuberculosis of the meninges, etc. (24)	7	4			1						1		1	1	1	3	4	
Other forms of tuberculosis (25-32)	5	1											1		1	1	3	
Syphilis (34)	53	70	2	2	3	2	6	4	10	12	21	20	18	32	12	12	2	6
Convulsions (86)	29	38	1		2	3	2	4	8	9	13	16	9	9	7	7		6
Bronchitis (106)	14	15					1			5	1	5	4	6	6	3	3	1
Bronchopneumonia (107)	150	150			2	2	2	3	22	10	26	15	47	46	42	44	35	45
Lobar and unspecified pneumonia (108, 109)	96	84			2		6	2	6	7	14	9	32	29	24	27	26	19
Diseases of the stomach (117, 118)	10	13			2		1			3	3	3	5	5	1	3	1	2
Diarrhea and enteritis (119)	180	216					1	1	14	24	15	25	62	69	72	72	31	50
Intestinal obstruction (122 b)	13	6			1		2		4	1	7	1	2	2	4	2		1
Congenital malformations (157)	30	45	1	10	5	8	3	8	9	10	18	36	6	7	5	2	1	
Congenital debility, icterus, sclerema (158, 161 b, c)	152	136	30	16	13	9	13	13	28	32	84	70	38	40	22	20	8	6
Premature birth (159)	330	332	139	140	53	62	56	44	54	62	302	308	23	23	4		1	1
Injury at birth (160)	64	54	42	28	11	13	6	10	4	3	63	54	1					
Other diseases of early infancy (161 a, d)	31	40	9	8	8	13	6	8	5	9	28	38	3	2				
External causes (172-198, 201-214)	28	36	4	7	1	1	1		2	3	8	11	11	13	3	6	6	6
Unknown or ill-defined diseases (199, 200)	171	194	24	38	16	26	21	18	29	26	90	108	46	43	27	29	8	14
All other causes	85	82	2		2	1	2	2	12	7	18	10	25	27	24	34	18	11
BIRMINGHAM, ALA.																		
All causes	164	236	49	88	16	17	11	6	21	35	97	146	32	37	23	37	12	16
Measles (7)	3	1												1	1		2	
Scarlet fever (8)																		
Whooping cough (9)	1	4													1	4		
Diphtheria (10)																		
Influenza (11)	4	5								2		2	1		2	2	1	1
Dysentery (13)																		
Erysipelas (15)																		
Epidemic cerebrospinal meningitis (18)	2												1		1			
Tetanus (22)																		
Tuberculosis of the respiratory system (23)	1												1					
Tuberculosis of the meninges, etc. (24)	2	1															2	1
Other forms of tuberculosis (25-32)																		
Syphilis (34)	11	29	5	10		3		2	1	4	6	19	4	4	1	3		3
Convulsions (86)																		
Bronchitis (106)																		
Bronchopneumonia (107)	18	22			2			1	3	4	5	5	8	7	4	9	1	1
Lobar and unspecified pneumonia (108, 109)	9	14			1	2			3	4	4	6	2	1	3	4		3
Diseases of the stomach (117, 118)																		
Diarrhea and enteritis (119)	8	16								1		1	3	7	3	5	2	3
Intestinal obstruction (122 b)																		
Congenital malformations (157)	4	6	1	4	1		1		1	1	4	5				1		
Congenital debility, icterus, sclerema (158, 161 b, c)	4	7	2	3						1	2	4	1	2	1	1		
Premature birth (159)	59	86	35	59	9	12	6	3	6	10	56	84	3	2				
Injury at birth (160)	5	10	3	8	1		1			1	5	9		1				
Other diseases of early infancy (161 a, d)	6	7	2	3	2		1		1	3	6	6		1				
External causes (172-198, 201-214)	4	1	1						1		2		1	1			1	
Unknown or ill-defined diseases (199, 200)	19	19		1			2		4	3	6	4	6	7	5	6	2	2
All other causes	4	8							1	1	1	1	1	3	1	2	1	2
WASHINGTON, D. C.																		
All causes	344	337	57	57	30	26	21	26	46	44	154	153	77	79	65	71	48	34
Measles (7)																		
Scarlet fever (8)																		
Whooping cough (9)	10	8											3	1	3	3	4	4
Diphtheria (10)	2												1		1			
Influenza (11)	4	3												1	1	1	3	1
Dysentery (13)	1	1													1			1
Erysipelas (15)		1								1		1						
Epidemic cerebrospinal meningitis (18)																		
Tetanus (22)																		
Tuberculosis of the respiratory system (23)	7	5													3	2	4	3
Tuberculosis of the meninges, etc. (24)	2	1													1		1	1
Other forms of tuberculosis (25-32)		2														1		1
Syphilis (34)	12	19		1			1		1	5	2	6	5	7	4	5	1	1
Convulsions (86)																		
Bronchitis (106)	5	2							1		1			1	2	1	2	
Bronchopneumonia (107)	71	60	1	2		1	1		8	5	10	8	26	28	22	17	13	7
Lobar and unspecified penumonia (108, 109)	9	13					1			1	1	1	4	7	2	1	2	4
Diseases of the stomach (117, 118)		1																1
Diarrhea and enteritis (119)	35	45								4		4	13	12	14	23	8	6
Intestinal obstruction (122 b)	1	3							1		1					1		2
Congenital malformations (157)	10	11	1		2	1	1		4	2	8	3	1	4		4	1	
Congenital debility, icterus, sclerema (158, 161 b, c)	12	9	1	1		1		3	2		3	5	6	2	1	2	2	
Premature birth (159)	92	82	37	26	16	14	11	16	19	17	83	73	8	7	1	2		
Injury at birth (160)	34	37	15	23	9	7	4	3	6	4	34	37						
Other diseases of early infancy (161 a, d)	5	13	1	4	1	2	2	3	1	3	5	12		1				
External causes (172-198, 201-214)	4		1		1						2				1		1	
Unknown or ill-defined diseases (199, 200)		1																1
All other causes	28	20			1			1	3	2	4	3	10	8	8	8	6	1

TABLE 23.—COLORED DEATHS (EXCLUSIVE OF STILLBIRTHS) FROM IMPORTANT CAUSES, BY CERTAIN SUBDIVISIONS OF THE FIRST YEAR OF LIFE, FOR SELECTED STATES AND CITIES: 1931 AND 1930—Con.

[See note at head of this table]

AREA AND CAUSE OF DEATH	Total deaths under 1 year of age		DEATHS AT AGE OF— Under 1 day		1 to 2 days		3 to 6 days		1 to 3 weeks		Under 1 month		1 to 3 months		4 to 7 months		8 to 11 months	
	1931	1930	1931	1930	1931	1930	1931	1930	1931	1930	1931	1930	1931	1930	1931	1930	1931	1930
JACKSONVILLE, FLA.																		
All causes	50	80	5	9	1	8	5	6	6	11	17	34	9	13	14	21	10	12
Measles (7)	----	1	----	----	----	----	----	----	----	----	----	----	----	----	----	1	----	----
Scarlet fever (8)	----	----	----	----	----	----	----	----	----	----	----	----	----	----	----	----	----	----
Whooping-cough (9)	----	----	----	----	----	----	----	----	----	----	----	----	----	----	----	----	----	----
Diphtheria (10)	----	1	----	----	----	----	----	----	----	----	----	----	----	1	----	----	----	----
Influenza (11)	4	----	----	----	----	----	----	----	----	----	----	----	2	----	1	----	1	----
Dysentery (13)	2	----	----	----	----	----	----	----	----	----	----	----	----	----	1	----	1	----
Erysipelas (15)	----	----	----	----	----	----	----	----	----	----	----	----	----	----	----	----	----	----
Epidemic cerebrospinal meningitis (18)	----	----	----	----	----	----	----	----	----	----	----	----	----	----	----	----	----	----
Tetanus (22)	1	1	----	----	----	----	----	----	----	1	----	1	----	----	----	----	1	----
Tuberculosis of the respiratory system (23)	2	----	----	----	----	----	----	----	----	----	----	----	----	----	1	----	1	----
Tuberculosis of the meninges, etc. (24)	----	----	----	----	----	----	----	----	----	----	----	----	----	----	----	----	----	----
Other forms of tuberculosis (25–32)	----	2	----	----	----	----	----	----	----	----	----	----	----	----	----	2	----	----
Syphilis (34)	5	8	----	----	----	1	2	----	1	2	3	3	----	1	1	1	1	3
Convulsions (86)	----	3	----	----	----	----	----	1	----	1	----	2	----	----	----	----	----	1
Bronchitis (106)	----	1	----	----	----	----	----	----	----	----	----	----	----	----	----	1	----	----
Bronchopneumonia (107)	6	6	----	----	----	----	----	----	2	2	2	2	2	2	2	1	----	1
Lobar and unspecified pneumonia (108, 109)	8	8	----	----	----	----	----	----	----	----	----	----	3	2	2	5	3	1
Diseases of the stomach (117, 118)	1	----	----	----	----	----	----	----	----	----	----	----	----	----	1	----	----	----
Diarrhea and enteritis (119)	3	11	----	----	----	1	----	----	----	1	----	2	1	2	2	5	----	2
Intestinal obstruction (122 b)	1	----	----	----	----	----	----	----	----	----	----	----	----	----	1	----	----	----
Congenital malformations (157)	2	1	1	----	----	----	----	----	1	----	2	----	----	----	----	1	----	----
Congenital debility, icterus, sclerema (158, 161 b, c)	----	9	----	----	----	2	----	1	----	1	----	4	----	4	----	1	----	----
Premature birth (159)	7	17	4	7	1	4	1	3	----	1	6	15	1	1	----	1	----	----
Injury at birth (160)	----	2	----	1	----	----	----	1	----	----	----	2	----	----	----	----	----	----
Other diseases of early infancy (161 a, d)	1	1	----	----	----	----	1	----	----	1	1	1	----	----	----	----	----	----
External causes (172–198, 201–214)	3	1	----	----	----	----	----	----	1	----	1	----	----	----	1	----	1	1
Unknown or ill-defined diseases (199, 200)	1	1	----	1	----	----	----	----	1	----	1	1	----	----	----	----	----	----
All other causes	3	6	----	----	----	----	1	----	----	1	1	1	----	----	1	2	1	3
MIAMI, FLA.																		
All causes	51	54	14	9	7	6	4	7	10	10	35	32	8	5	6	8	2	9
Measles (7)	----	----	----	----	----	----	----	----	----	----	----	----	----	----	----	----	----	----
Scarlet fever (8)	----	----	----	----	----	----	----	----	----	----	----	----	----	----	----	----	----	----
Whooping-cough (9)	1	1	----	----	----	----	----	----	----	----	----	----	----	----	----	1	1	----
Diphtheria (10)	----	----	----	----	----	----	----	----	----	----	----	----	----	----	----	----	----	----
Influenza (11)	----	1	----	----	----	----	----	----	----	----	----	----	----	1	----	----	----	----
Dysentery (13)	----	----	----	----	----	----	----	----	----	----	----	----	----	----	----	----	----	----
Erysipelas (15)	----	----	----	----	----	----	----	----	----	----	----	----	----	----	----	----	----	----
Epidemic cerebrospinal meningitis (18)	----	----	----	----	----	----	----	----	----	----	----	----	----	----	----	----	----	----
Tetanus (22)	1	----	----	----	----	----	----	----	1	----	1	----	----	----	----	----	----	----
Tuberculosis of the respiratory system (23)	----	----	----	----	----	----	----	----	----	----	----	----	----	----	----	----	----	----
Tuberculosis of the meninges, etc. (24)	----	----	----	----	----	----	----	----	----	----	----	----	----	----	----	----	----	----
Other forms of tuberculosis (25–32)	----	----	----	----	----	----	----	----	----	----	----	----	----	----	----	----	----	----
Syphilis (34)	3	2	----	----	----	----	----	1	----	----	----	1	2	----	1	----	----	1
Convulsions (86)	----	1	----	----	----	----	----	----	----	----	----	----	1	----	----	1	----	----
Bronchitis (106)	1	----	----	----	----	----	----	----	----	----	----	----	1	----	----	----	----	----
Bronchopneumonia (170)	5	5	----	----	1	----	----	----	----	1	1	1	1	----	3	2	----	2
Lobar and unspecified pneumonia (108, 109)	1	1	----	----	----	----	----	----	----	----	----	----	----	----	----	1	1	----
Diseases of the stomach (117, 118)	----	1	----	----	----	----	----	----	----	----	----	----	----	1	----	----	----	----
Diarrhea and enteritis (119)	3	5	----	----	----	----	----	----	----	----	----	----	2	2	1	----	----	3
Intestinal obstruction (122 b)	----	1	----	----	----	----	----	----	----	----	----	----	----	----	----	----	----	1
Congenital malformations (157)	----	2	----	----	----	----	----	----	----	1	----	1	----	----	----	1	----	----
Congenital debility, icterus, sclerema (158, 161 b, c)	6	7	1	2	1	----	1	----	3	2	6	4	----	1	----	1	----	1
Premature birth (159)	21	19	9	6	2	5	2	3	5	5	18	19	2	----	1	----	----	----
Injury at birth (160)	5	4	2	1	3	1	----	2	----	----	5	4	----	----	----	----	----	----
Other diseases of early infancy (161 a, d)	3	2	1	----	----	----	1	1	1	1	3	2	----	----	----	----	----	----
External causes (172–198, 201–214)	----	----	----	----	----	----	----	----	----	----	----	----	----	----	----	----	----	----
Unknown or ill-defined diseases (199, 200)	1	----	1	----	----	----	----	----	----	----	1	----	----	----	----	----	----	----
All other causes	----	2	----	----	----	----	----	----	----	----	----	----	----	----	----	1	----	1
ATLANTA, GA.																		
All causes	212	268	61	53	20	24	11	17	25	44	117	138	36	45	35	48	24	37
Measles (7)	----	2	----	----	----	----	----	----	----	1	----	1	----	1	----	----	----	----
Scarlet fever (8)	----	----	----	----	----	----	----	----	----	----	----	----	----	----	----	----	----	----
Whooping-cough (9)	----	11	----	----	----	----	----	----	----	----	----	----	----	3	----	2	----	6
Diphtheria (10)	1	----	----	----	----	----	----	----	----	----	----	----	1	----	----	----	----	----
Influenza (11)	5	3	----	----	----	----	----	----	----	----	----	----	----	----	3	----	2	3
Dysentery (13)	----	6	----	----	----	----	----	----	----	1	----	1	----	1	----	4	----	----
Erysipelas (15)	----	----	----	----	----	----	----	----	----	----	----	----	----	----	----	----	----	----
Epidemic cerebrospinal meningitis (18)	1	4	----	----	----	----	----	----	----	1	----	1	----	----	1	1	----	2
Tetanus (22)	----	1	----	----	----	----	----	----	----	1	----	1	----	----	----	----	----	----
Tuberculosis of the respiratory system (23)	----	----	----	----	----	----	----	----	----	----	----	----	----	----	----	----	----	----
Tuberculosis of the meninges, etc. (24)	----	----	----	----	----	----	----	----	----	----	----	----	----	----	----	----	----	----
Other forms of tuberculosis (25–32)	1	1	----	----	----	----	----	----	----	----	----	----	----	----	----	1	1	----
Syphilis (34)	12	7	----	1	----	----	----	----	3	1	3	2	3	2	5	3	1	----
Convulsions (86)	----	----	----	----	----	----	----	----	----	----	----	----	----	----	----	----	----	----
Bronchitis (106)	----	1	----	----	----	----	----	----	----	1	----	1	----	----	----	----	----	----
Bronchopneumonia (107)	23	40	----	----	1	----	2	----	3	3	6	3	8	10	3	15	6	12
Lobar and unspecified pneumonia (108, 109)	6	7	----	----	----	----	----	----	----	1	----	1	2	1	2	3	2	2
Diseases of the stomach (117, 118)	----	1	----	----	----	----	----	----	----	----	----	----	----	----	----	1	----	----
Diarrhea and enteritis (119)	28	30	----	----	----	----	----	----	1	3	1	3	7	8	12	11	8	8
Intestinal obstruction (122b)	1	1	----	----	----	----	----	----	1	----	1	----	----	1	----	----	----	----
Congenital malformations (157)	5	2	----	----	----	1	2	----	1	1	3	2	1	----	1	----	----	----
Congenital debility, icterus, sclerema (158, 161 b, c)	5	11	----	1	----	----	----	2	1	1	1	4	4	4	----	2	----	1
Premature birth (159)	89	93	55	45	14	14	5	9	9	24	83	92	5	1	1	----	----	----
Injury at birth (160)	11	13	4	4	4	5	1	3	2	1	11	13	----	----	----	----	----	----
Other diseases of early infancy (161 a, d)	1	5	1	----	----	2	----	1	----	2	1	5	----	----	----	----	----	----
External causes (172–198, 201–214)	10	1	----	----	----	----	----	----	3	----	3	----	----	1	4	----	3	----
Unknown or ill-defined diseases (199, 200)	7	15	1	2	1	2	1	2	1	1	4	7	2	6	1	2	----	----
All other causes	6	13	----	----	----	----	----	----	----	1	----	1	3	6	2	3	1	3

TABLE 23.—COLORED DEATHS (EXCLUSIVE OF STILLBIRTHS) FROM IMPORTANT CAUSES, BY CERTAIN SUBDIVISIONS OF THE FIRST YEAR OF LIFE, FOR SELECTED STATES AND CITIES: 1931 AND 1930—Con.

[See note at head of this table]

AREA AND CAUSE OF DEATH	Total deaths under 1 year of age		DEATHS AT AGE OF— Under 1 day		1 to 2 days		3 to 6 days		1 to 3 weeks		Under 1 month		1 to 3 months		4 to 7 months		8 to 11 months	
	1931	1930	1931	1930	1931	1930	1931	1930	1931	1930	1931	1930	1931	1930	1931	1930	1931	1930
CHICAGO, ILL.																		
All causes	375	367	81	78	48	48	19	29	49	55	197	210	79	64	60	56	39	37
Measles (7)																		
Scarlet fever (8)																		
Whooping-cough (9)	5	5											2	1	1	3	2	1
Diptheria (10)	1	2												1	1			1
Influenza (11)	4	3											2		2	1		2
Dysentery (13)	1														1			
Erysipelas (15)	1												1					
Epidemic cerebrospinal meningitis (18)	2														1		1	
Tetanus (22)																		
Tuberculosis of the respiratory system (23)	6	4											3		1	2	2	2
Tuberculosis of the meninges, etc. (24)	7	1												1	6		1	
Other forms of tuberculosis (25-32)	3	2											1		2	2		
Syphilis (34)	7	25	2	6		2		1	3	3	5	12	2	10		2		1
Convulsions (86)		1														1		
Bronchitis (106)	4	2	1								1		1	2	2			
Bronchopneumonia (107)	99	64	1	1			4		14	9	19	10	34	15	23	21	23	18
Lobar and unspecified pneumonia (108, 109)	13	4							1		1		5	2	5	2	2	
Diseases of the stomach (117, 118)		1												1				
Diarrhea and enteritis (119)	18	25							2	6	2	6	7	5	7	10	2	4
Intestinal obstruction (122 b)	1	2											1	1		1		
Congenital malformations (157)	16	15	1	1	3	1	2	3	6	2	12	7	4	1		3		4
Congenital debility, icterus, sclerema (158, 161 b, c)	8	11						1	1	2	1	3	3	7	2	1	2	
Premature birth (159)	113	131	50	53	31	32	10	20	17	24	108	129	5	2				
Injury at birth (160)	31	30	17	16	9	10	2	2	3	1	31	29		1				
Other diseases of early infancy (161 a, d)	16	7	9	1	4	2	1	2	1	2	15	7	1					
External causes (172-198, 201-214)		4				1						1		1		1		1
Unknown or ill-defined diseases (199, 200)	1	8								1		1	1	3		2		2
All other causes	18	20			1				1	5	2	5	6	10	6	4	4	1
INDIANAPOLIS, IND.																		
All causes	57	104	10	16	8	17	5	2	6	6	29	41	8	25	12	26	8	12
Measles (7)																		
Scarlet fever (8)																		
Whooping-cough (9)	2	2											1	1			1	1
Diphtheria (10)		1														1		
Influenza (11)	1																1	
Dysentery (13)																		
Erysipelas (15)																		
Epidemic cerebrospinal meningitis (18)	2	2													1	2	1	
Tetanus (22)																		
Tuberculosis of the respiratory system (23)																		
Tuberculosis of meninges, etc. (24)	1	1											1					1
Other forms of tuberculosis (25-32)																		
Syphilis (34)	2	2	1	1		1					1	2	1					
Convulsions (86)																		
Bronchitis (106)		1														1		
Bronchopneumonia (107)	11	21							1	2	1	2	2	8	4	8	4	3
Lobar and unspecified pneumonia (108, 109)	6	6					1	1		1	1	2	1		3	3	1	1
Diseases of the stomach (117, 118)		1																1
Diarrhea and enteritis (119)	2	23												10	2	9		4
Intestinal obstruction (122 b)																		
Congenital malformations (157)		4		1		2						3		1				
Congenital debility, icterus, sclerema (158, 161 b, c)	1	1													1	1		
Premature birth (159)	26	21	9	10	8	6	3		4	2	24	18	2	3				
Injury at birth (160)		6		2		3		1				6						
Other diseases of early infancy (161 a, d)	2	7		2		5	1		1		2	7						
External causes (172-198, 201-214)	1	3								1		1		1	1	1		
Unknown or ill-defined diseases (199, 200)																		
All other causes		2												1				1
LOUISVILLE, KY.																		
All causes	107	70	20	14	6	3	7	4	25	14	58	35	25	13	13	16	11	6
Measles (7)																		
Scarlet fever (8)																		
Whooping-cough (9)	5	3											1	2	1		3	1
Diphtheria (10)																		
Influenza (11)		1																1
Dysentery (13)																		
Erysipelas (15)	1												1					
Epidemic cerebrospinal meningitis (18)																		
Tetanus (22)																		
Tuberculosis of the respiratory system (23)	1																1	
Tuberculosis of the meninges, etc. (24)																		
Other forms of tuberculosis (25-32)	1	1													1	1		
Syphilis (34)	8	2	2	1			2		2	1	6	2	2					
Convulsions (86)		1				1						1						
Bronchitis (106)	1	1											1			1		
Bronchopneumonia (107)	31	12			2				10	2	12	2	13	2	4	5	2	3
Lobar and unspecified pneumonia (108, 109)	6	1							1		1		1	1	2		2	
Diseases of the stomach (117, 118)		1														1		
Diarrhea and enteritis (119)	10	8							1		1		4	3	3	5	2	
Intestinal obstruction (122 b)																		
Congenital malformations (157)		5						1				1		3		1		
Congenital debility, icterus, sclerema (158, 161 b, c)		2		1								1		1				
Premature birth (159)	33	19	18	10	2	2	3		10	7	33	19						
Injury at birth (160)	4	2		1	2		1	1	1		4	2						
Other diseases of early infancy (161 a, d)		3		1				1		1		3						
External causes (172-198, 201-214)	1																1	
Unknown or ill-defined diseases (199, 200)	1	1					1	1			1	1						
All other causes	4	7								3		3	2	1	2	2		

TABLE 23.—COLORED DEATHS (EXCLUSIVE OF STILLBIRTHS) FROM IMPORTANT CAUSES, BY CERTAIN SUBDIVISIONS OF THE FIRST YEAR OF LIFE, FOR SELECTED STATES AND CITIES: 1931 AND 1930—Con.

[See note at head of this table]

AREA AND CAUSE OF DEATH	Total deaths under 1 year of age		DEATHS AT AGE OF— Under 1 day		1 to 2 days		3 to 6 days		1 to 3 weeks		Under 1 month		1 to 3 months		4 to 7 months		8 to 11 months	
	1931	1930	1931	1930	1931	1930	1931	1930	1931	1930	1931	1930	1931	1930	1931	1930	1931	1930
NEW ORLEANS, LA.																		
All causes	329	380	77	67	26	25	22	25	35	39	160	156	57	95	69	76	43	53
Measles (7)	-	2	-	-	-	-	-	-	-	-	-	-	-	-	-	1	-	1
Scarlet fever (8)	-	-	-	-	-	-	-	-	-	-	-	-	-	-	-	-	-	-
Whooping-cough (9)	8	8	-	-	-	-	-	-	-	-	-	-	2	1	3	3	3	4
Diphtheria (10)	1	-	-	-	-	-	-	-	-	-	-	-	1	-	-	-	-	-
Influenza (11)	16	29	-	-	-	-	-	-	2	4	2	4	4	14	4	6	6	5
Dysentery (13)	-	-	-	-	-	-	-	-	-	-	-	-	-	-	-	-	-	-
Erysipelas (15)	-	-	-	-	-	-	-	-	-	-	-	-	-	-	-	-	-	-
Epidemic cerebrospinal meningitis (18)	3	3	-	-	-	-	-	-	-	1	-	1	-	-	2	-	1	2
Tetanus (22)	2	2	-	-	-	-	-	2	2	-	2	2	-	-	-	-	-	-
Tuberculosis of the respiratory system (23)	1	1	-	-	-	-	-	-	-	-	-	-	1	-	-	-	-	1
Tuberculosis of the meninges, etc. (24)	2	-	-	-	-	-	-	-	-	-	-	-	-	-	2	-	-	-
Other forms of tuberculosis (25-32)	-	-	-	-	-	-	-	-	-	-	-	-	-	-	-	-	-	-
Syphilis (34)	24	14	2	-	-	-	2	3	1	1	5	4	7	5	9	4	3	1
Convulsions (86)	-	-	-	-	-	-	-	-	-	-	-	-	-	-	-	-	-	-
Bronchitis (106)	2	-	-	-	-	-	-	-	-	-	-	-	-	-	-	-	2	-
Bronchopneumonia (107)	57	96	-	-	-	-	-	2	6	10	6	12	19	33	22	33	10	18
Lobar and unspecified pneumonia (108, 109)	18	14	-	-	-	1	-	-	3	-	3	1	3	4	6	4	6	5
Diseases of the stomach (117, 118)	-	2	-	-	-	-	-	-	-	-	-	-	-	-	-	1	-	1
Diarrhea and enteritis (119)	43	41	-	-	1	-	1	3	8	2	10	5	10	18	15	10	8	8
Intestinal obstruction (122 b)	1	6	-	-	-	-	1	-	-	-	1	-	-	3	-	3	-	-
Congenital malformations (157)	11	8	2	-	3	1	1	2	2	2	8	5	1	2	2	1	-	-
Congenital debility, icterus, sclerema (158, 161 b, c)	2	7	-	-	-	1	-	-	-	-	-	1	2	4	-	2	-	-
Premature birth (159)	94	86	60	48	13	14	13	3	6	15	92	80	2	5	-	-	-	1
Injury at birth (160)	20	20	11	11	4	3	3	5	2	-	20	19	-	1	-	-	-	-
Other diseases of early infancy (161 a, d)	5	17	1	8	3	4	1	2	-	3	5	17	-	-	-	-	-	-
External causes (172-198, 201-214)	3	1	-	-	-	-	-	-	1	-	1	-	1	-	1	1	-	-
Unknown or ill-defined diseases (199, 200)	1	-	-	-	-	-	-	-	-	-	-	-	1	-	-	-	-	-
All other causes	15	23	1	-	2	1	-	3	2	1	5	5	3	5	3	7	4	6
BALTIMORE, MD.																		
All causes	352	307	47	52	29	35	19	22	33	24	128	133	76	63	76	66	72	45
Measles (7)	7	-	-	-	-	-	-	-	-	-	-	-	-	-	1	-	6	-
Scarlet fever (8)	-	-	-	-	-	-	-	-	-	-	-	-	-	-	-	-	-	-
Whooping-cough (9)	17	4	-	-	-	-	-	-	-	-	-	-	5	1	7	1	5	2
Diphtheria (10)	1	-	-	-	-	-	-	-	-	-	-	-	-	-	-	-	1	-
Influenza (11)	4	2	-	-	-	-	-	-	-	-	-	-	1	-	1	1	2	1
Dysentery (13)	11	4	-	-	-	-	-	-	-	-	-	-	2	-	5	4	4	-
Erysipelas (15)	-	1	-	-	-	-	-	-	-	-	-	-	-	-	-	1	-	-
Epidemic cerebrospinal meningitis (18)	-	2	-	-	-	-	-	-	-	-	-	-	-	-	-	2	-	-
Tetanus (22)	-	-	-	-	-	-	-	-	-	-	-	-	-	-	-	-	-	-
Tuberculosis of the respiratory system (23)	4	2	-	-	-	-	-	-	-	-	-	-	1	1	2	1	1	-
Tuberculosis of the meninges, etc. (24)	2	-	-	-	-	-	-	-	-	-	-	-	-	-	1	-	1	-
Other forms of tuberculosis (25-32)	-	5	-	-	-	-	-	-	-	-	-	-	-	-	-	2	-	3
Syphilis (34)	14	15	-	2	-	-	-	-	4	1	4	3	4	7	4	4	2	1
Convulsions (86)	1	-	-	-	-	-	-	-	-	-	-	-	-	-	1	-	-	-
Bronchitis (106)	2	1	-	-	-	-	-	-	1	-	1	-	1	1	-	-	-	-
Bronchopneumonia (107)	48	49	1	-	-	1	-	1	7	1	8	3	9	15	14	21	17	10
Lobar and unspecified pneumonia (108, 109)	46	39	-	-	-	1	-	-	4	1	4	2	15	10	12	14	15	13
Diseases of the stomach (117, 118)	-	-	-	-	-	-	-	-	-	-	-	-	-	-	-	-	-	-
Diarrhea and enteritis (119)	39	31	-	-	-	-	-	-	2	2	2	2	13	11	13	9	11	9
Intestinal obstruction (122 b)	3	2	-	-	-	-	-	-	1	1	1	1	1	-	1	-	-	1
Congenital malformations (157)	21	16	1	1	5	1	1	1	1	1	8	4	7	8	6	2	-	2
Congenital debility, icterus, sclerema (158, 161 b, c)	14	11	2	1	-	1	1	-	1	4	4	6	7	4	1	1	2	-
Premature birth (159)	73	83	33	38	19	19	8	12	8	11	68	80	5	2	-	-	-	1
Injury at birth (160)	8	11	4	4	2	4	1	3	1	-	8	11	-	-	-	-	-	-
Other diseases of early infancy (161 a, d)	20	20	6	6	3	8	7	5	1	1	17	20	3	-	-	-	-	-
External causes (172-198, 201-214)	2	2	-	-	-	-	-	-	-	-	-	-	-	1	2	1	-	-
Unknown or ill-defined diseases (199, 200)	1	-	-	-	-	-	1	-	-	-	1	-	-	-	-	-	-	-
All other causes	14	7	-	-	-	-	-	-	2	1	2	1	2	2	5	2	5	2
DETROIT, MICH.																		
All causes	208	245	49	50	17	16	15	19	27	29	108	114	28	48	39	38	33	45
Measles (7)	-	1	-	-	-	-	-	-	-	-	-	-	-	-	-	1	-	-
Scarlet fever (8)	-	-	-	-	-	-	-	-	-	-	-	-	-	-	-	-	-	-
Whooping-cough (9)	10	4	-	-	-	-	-	-	-	-	-	-	2	2	5	-	3	2
Diphtheria (10)	-	-	-	-	-	-	-	-	-	-	-	-	-	-	-	-	-	-
Influenza (11)	1	1	-	-	-	-	-	-	-	-	-	-	-	-	1	-	-	1
Dysentery (13)	-	-	-	-	-	-	-	-	-	-	-	-	-	-	-	-	-	-
Erysipelas (15)	3	2	-	-	-	-	-	-	1	2	1	2	2	-	-	-	-	-
Epidemic cerebrospinal meningitis (18)	1	2	-	-	-	-	-	-	-	-	-	-	-	1	-	1	1	-
Tetanus (22)	-	-	-	-	-	-	-	-	-	-	-	-	-	-	-	-	-	-
Tuberculosis of the respiratory system (23)	3	4	-	-	-	-	-	-	-	-	-	-	-	-	-	2	3	2
Tuberculosis of the meninges, etc. (24)	-	1	-	-	-	-	-	-	-	-	-	-	-	-	-	-	-	1
Other forms of tuberculosis (25-32)	1	2	-	-	-	-	-	-	-	-	-	-	-	1	1	1	-	-
Syphilis (34)	2	9	1	3	-	-	-	1	-	-	1	4	1	2	-	1	-	2
Convulsions (86)	1	-	-	-	-	-	-	-	-	-	-	-	-	-	-	-	1	-
Bronchitis (106)	-	6	-	-	-	-	-	-	-	-	-	-	-	3	-	2	-	1
Bronchopneumonia (107)	45	52	-	-	-	-	-	2	7	4	7	6	9	16	16	13	13	17
Lobar and unspecified pneumonia (108, 109)	10	7	-	-	-	-	-	-	2	-	2	-	1	2	4	3	3	2
Diseases of the stomach (117, 118)	-	1	-	-	-	-	-	1	-	-	-	1	-	-	-	-	-	-
Diarrhea and enteritis (119)	15	18	-	-	1	-	-	2	1	-	2	2	5	9	6	3	2	4
Intestinal obstruction (122 b)	1	2	-	-	-	-	-	-	-	-	-	-	-	-	1	2	-	-
Congenital malformations (157)	11	8	1	2	-	1	1	2	6	3	8	8	2	-	1	-	-	-
Congenital debility, icterus, sclerema (158, 161 b, c)	2	4	1	1	-	1	-	1	1	-	2	3	-	1	-	-	-	-
Premature birth (159)	52	74	33	35	6	11	5	5	4	17	48	68	3	5	-	1	1	-
Injury at birth (160)	23	9	11	4	7	1	4	2	1	1	23	8	-	1	-	-	-	-
Other diseases of early infancy (161 a, d)	9	10	2	5	3	2	2	3	2	-	9	10	-	-	-	-	-	-
External causes (172-198, 201-214)	1	3	-	-	-	-	-	-	1	-	1	-	-	1	-	1	-	1
Unknown or ill-defined diseases (199, 200)	-	-	-	-	-	-	-	-	-	-	-	-	-	-	-	-	-	-
All other causes	17	25	-	-	-	-	3	-	1	2	4	2	3	4	4	7	6	12

TABLE 23.—COLORED DEATHS (EXCLUSIVE OF STILLBIRTHS) FROM IMPORTANT CAUSES, BY CERTAIN SUBDIVISIONS OF THE FIRST YEAR OF LIFE, FOR SELECTED STATES AND CITIES: 1931 AND 1930—Con.

[See note at head of this table]

AREA AND CAUSE OF DEATH	Total deaths under 1 year of age		DEATHS AT AGE OF—: Under 1 day		1 to 2 days		3 to 6 days		1 to 3 weeks		Under 1 month		1 to 3 months		4 to 7 months		8 to 11 months	
	1931	1930	1931	1930	1931	1930	1931	1930	1931	1930	1931	1930	1931	1930	1931	1930	1931	1930
KANSAS CITY, MO.																		
All causes	71	62	14	4	8	9	3	3	8	5	33	21	17	13	16	16	5	12
Measles (7)																		
Scarlet fever (8)		1																1
Whooping-cough (9)	4	1											2	1	1		1	
Diphtheria (10)																		
Influenza (11)	1	1													1			1
Dysentery (13)																		
Erysipelas (15)																		
Epidemic cerebrospinal meningitis (18)		1														1		
Tetanus (22)																		
Tuberculosis of the respiratory system (23)	1												1					
Tuberculosis of the meninges, etc. (24)																		
Other forms of tuberculosis (25-32)	1														1			
Syphilis (34)	5	1											3	1	2			
Convulsions (86)																		
Bronchitis (106)																		
Bronchopneumonia (107)	15	17				1	1	1			1	2	6	3	7	5	1	7
Lobar and unspecified pneumonia (108, 109)	3	2	1						1	1	2	1				1	1	
Diseases of the stomach (117, 118)																		
Diarrhea and enteritis (119)	5	8					1			1	1	1		1	2	4	2	2
Intestinal obstruction (122 b)	1	1											1	1				
Congenital malformations (157)	4	2	1		1	1			1		3	1	1	1				
Congenital debility, icterus, sclerema (158, 161 b, c)		7						2		1		3		2		1		1
Premature birth (159)	23	10	11	1	5	5	1		4	2	21	8	1	2	1			
Injury at birth (160)	1	2		2	1						1	2						
Other diseases of early infancy (161 a, d)		3		1		2						3						
External causes (172-198, 201-214)	2	1	1						1		2					1		
Unknown or ill-defined diseases (199, 200)																		
All other causes	5	4			1				1		2		2	1	1	3		
ST. LOUIS, MO.																		
All causes	158	167	32	32	13	10	9	13	22	29	76	84	33	31	29	32	20	20
Measles (7)		1																1
Scarlet fever (8)																		
Whooping-cough (9)	2														2			
Diphtheria (10)	2												1				1	
Influenza (11)	2	2												1	1	1	1	
Dysentery (13)																		
Erysipelas (15)		1								1		1						
Epidemic cerebrospinal meningitis (18)		1																1
Tetanus (22)																		
Tuberculosis of the respiratory system (23)		2														2		
Tuberculosis of the meninges, etc. (24)	1	1													1			1
Other forms of tuberculosis (25-32)	3	1							1		1		1	1			1	
Syphilis (34)	16	7	1	1	1		1	2	4	2	7	5	5		4	1		1
Convulsions (86)																		
Bronchitis (106)	4	3					1	1	1	1	2	2	1		1	1		
Bronchopneumonia (107)	38	38		1	2				3	10	5	12	11	8	10	10	12	8
Lobar and unspecified pneumonia (108, 109)	13	8							3		3		2	3	4	1	4	4
Diseases of the stomach (117, 118)		1								1		1						
Diarrhea and enteritis (119)	5	28				1			1	3	1	4	3	11	1	11		2
Intestinal obstruction (122 b)	1														1			
Congenital malformations (157)	2	6	1			1		1			1	2	1	2		1		1
Congenital debility, icterus, sclerema (158, 161 b, c)		3		1				1		1		3						
Premature birth (159)	49	46	25	26	8	4	4	5	7	9	44	44	5	2				
Injury at birth (160)	5	6	2	2	1	3	1	1	1		5	6						
Other diseases of early infancy (161 a, d)	5	4	3	1		1	1	1	1	1	5	4						
External causes (172-198, 201-214)	1	2												1	1	1		
Unknown or ill-defined diseases (199, 200)																		
All other causes	9	6			1		1				2		3	2	3	3	1	1
NEW YORK, N. Y.																		
All causes	749	764	139	141	63	79	56	47	102	102	360	369	169	159	140	139	80	97
Measles (7)		7												1		2		4
Scarlet fever (8)																		
Whooping-cough (9)	12	11											2	1	6	5	4	5
Diphtheria (10)	2	1											2			1		
Influenza (11)	5	3											1		3		1	3
Dysentery (13)																		
Erysipelas (15)	5	3							4		4			3			1	
Epidemic cerebrospinal meningitis (18)	3	1											1		2	1		
Tetanus (22)																		
Tuberculosis of the respiratory system (23)	5	9											1	1		4	4	4
Tuberculosis of the meninges, etc. (24)	2	5														3	2	2
Other forms of tuberculosis (25-32)	3	7												1	1	3	2	3
Syphilis (34)	30	42	5	5			2	1	4	5	11	11	12	19	3	8	4	4
Convulsions (86)		2														2		
Bronchitis (106)	7	4							1		1		5	1		2	1	1
Bronchopneumonia (107)	164	143	3		1	1	3	3	21	17	28	21	52	44	61	46	23	32
Lobar and unspecified pneumonia (108, 109)	45	51				1	1	2	4	3	5	6	8	15	15	13	17	17
Diseases of the stomach (117, 118)																		
Diarrhea and enteritis (119)	68	87				1	1	1	10	10	11	12	27	36	22	30	8	9
Intestinal obstruction (122 b)	4	1											1		3	1		
Congenital malformations (157)	23	14	2	1	1	4	3	2	6	2	12	9	9	3	1	2	1	
Congenital debility, icterus, sclerema (158, 161 b, c)	27	19				2	2		8	9	10	11	15	7	1	1	1	
Premature birth (159)	183	206	86	92	36	45	26	22	25	38	173	197	9	9			1	
Injury at birth (160)	65	56	29	25	17	17	12	5	7	9	65	56						
Other diseases of early infancy (161 a, d)	34	36	13	15	7	8	5	8	7	4	32	35	2	1				
External causes (172-198, 201-214)	9	10	1	3	1				1		3	3	4	2	2	3		2
Unknown or ill-defined diseases (199, 200)																		
All other causes	53	46					1	3	4	5	5	8	18	15	20	12	10	11

TABLE 23.—COLORED DEATHS (EXCLUSIVE OF STILLBIRTHS) FROM IMPORTANT CAUSES, BY CERTAIN SUBDIVISIONS OF THE FIRST YEAR OF LIFE, FOR SELECTED STATES AND CITIES: 1931 AND 1930—Con.

[See note at head of table]

AREA AND CAUSE OF DEATH	Total deaths under 1 year of age		DEATHS AT AGE OF— Under 1 day		1 to 2 days		3 to 6 days		1 to 3 weeks		Under 1 month		1 to 3 months		4 to 7 months		8 to 11 months	
	1931	1930	1931	1930	1931	1930	1931	1930	1931	1930	1931	1930	1931	1930	1931	1930	1931	1930
NEW YORK, N. Y. (BROOKLYN BOROUGH)																		
All causes	**227**	**207**	**35**	**27**	**9**	**20**	**17**	**14**	**20**	**39**	**81**	**100**	**71**	**41**	**50**	**43**	**25**	**23**
Measles (7)		1																1
Scarlet fever (8)																		
Whooping-cough (9)	5	1											1		3	1	1	
Diphtheria (10)	1												1					
Influenza (11)	2	1													2			1
Dysentery (13)																		
Erysipelas (15)																		
Epidemic cerebrospinal meningitis (18)	2												1		1			
Tetanus (22)																		
Tuberculosis of the respiratory system (23)	1	3												1			1	2
Tuberculosis of the meninges, etc. (24)	1																1	
Other forms of tuberculosis (25-32)		4														2		2
Syphilis (34)	12	12					2			1	2	1	7	8	1	1	2	2
Convulsions (86)																		
Bronchitis (106)	3	1											3			1		
Bronchopneumonia (107)	60	44	1				2	1	4	5	7	6	22	13	24	16	7	9
Lobar and unspecified pneumonia (108, 109)	13	14							1	3	1	3	2	3	3	6	7	2
Diseases of the stomach (117, 118)																		
Diarrhea and enteritis (119)	15	23						1	1	6	1	7	6	7	5	8	3	1
Intestinal obstruction (122 b)																		
Congenital malformations (157)	12	4	1			1	2	1	3		6	2	6	2				
Congenital debility, icterus, sclerema (158, 161 b, c)	12	8							1	6	1	6	10	2	1			
Premature birth (159)	43	45	26	15	7	12	6	8	3	10	42	45	1					
Injury at birth (160)	13	17	6	7	1	5	3	1	3	4	13	17						
Other diseases of early infancy (161 a, d)	5	10	1	5		2	1	2	2	1	4	10	1					
External causes (172-198, 201-214)	4	3			1				1		2		1	1	1	2		
Unknown or ill-defined diseases (199, 200)																		
All other causes	23	16					1		1	3	2	3	9	4	9	6	3	3
NEW YORK, N. Y. (MANHATTAN BOROUGH)																		
All causes	**440**	**491**	**87**	**102**	**43**	**51**	**32**	**30**	**68**	**54**	**230**	**237**	**89**	**101**	**76**	**89**	**45**	**64**
Measles (7)		5												1		2		2
Scarlet fever (8)																		
Whooping-cough (9)	4	10											1	1	2	4	1	5
Diphtheria (10)	1	1											1			1		
Influenza (11)	2	1											1				1	1
Dysentery (13)																		
Erysipelas (15)	5	3							4		4			3			1	
Epidemic cerebrospinal meningitis (18)	1	1													1	1		
Tetanus (22)																		
Tuberculosis of the respiratory system (23)	3	5											1			4	2	1
Tuberculosis of the meninges, etc. (24)	1	3														2	1	1
Other forms of tuberculosis (25-32)	2	3												1		1	2	1
Syphilis (34)	16	26	4	4					4	4	8	8	5	11	2	7	1	
Convulsions (86)		2														2		
Bronchitis (106)	3	3							1		1		1	1		1	1	1
Bronchopneumonia (107)	90	87	2		1	1	1	2	15	9	19	12	26	23	30	29	15	23
Lobar and unspecified pneumonia (108, 109)	27	33				1	1	2	2		3	3	6	10	10	6	8	14
Diseases of the stomach (117, 118)																		
Diarrhea and enteritis (119)	51	56				1	1		9	3	10	4	20	27	16	20	5	5
Intestinal obstruction (122 b)	4	1											1		3	1		
Congenital malformations (157)	8	9	1			3		1	2	2	3	6	3	1	1	2	1	
Congenital debility, icterus, sclerema (158, 161 b, c)	11	11				2	2		5	3	7	5	4	5		1		
Premature birth (159)	114	143	49	70	24	28	16	13	17	26	106	137	7	6			1	
Injury at birth (160)	43	33	19	15	13	10	8	4	3	4	43	33						
Other diseases of early infancy (161 a, d)	24	24	11	10	5	5	3	5	5	3	24	23		1				
External causes (172-198, 201-214)	5	5	1	3							1	3	3		1			2
Unknown or ill-defined diseases (199, 200)																		
All other causes	25	26						3	1		1	3	9	10	10	5	5	8
CINCINNATI, OHIO																		
All causes	**133**	**140**	**22**	**24**	**14**	**4**	**4**	**10**	**24**	**30**	**64**	**68**	**20**	**35**	**33**	**25**	**16**	**12**
Measles (7)																		
Scarlet fever (8)																		
Whooping-cough (9)	6												1		1		4	
Diphtheria (10)	1																1	
Influenza (11)	3														3			
Dysentery (13)																		
Erysipelas (15)		1												1				
Epidemic cerebrospinal meningitis (18)		1												1				
Tetanus (22)																		
Tuberculosis of the respiratory system (23)	1	2								1		1			1	1		
Tuberculosis of the meninges, etc. (24)	1	1													1	1		
Other forms of tuberculosis (25-32)	1	1															1	1
Syphilis (34)	3	3		2					2		2	2		1	1			
Convulsions (86)																		
Bronchitis (106)																		
Bronchopneumonia (107)	15	25				1			1	5	1	6	7	6	6	9	1	4
Lobar and unspecified pneumonia (108, 109)	4	14						1		1		2		6	3	3	1	3
Diseases of the stomach (117, 118)	1						1				1							
Diarrhea and enteritis (119)	26	14							1	1	1	1	6	5	13	5	6	3
Intestinal obstruction (122 b)	2	1							1		1				1	1		
Congenital malformations (157)	4	2	1				1	2	1		3	2	1					
Congenital debility, icterus, sclerema (158, 161 b, c)	3	2	1						1	2	2	2			1			
Premature birth (159)	50	48	19	19	10	1	1	3	16	16	46	39	3	8	1	1		
Injury at birth (160)	4	6	1	2	2			3	1	1	4	6						
Other diseases of early infancy (161 a, d)	3	2			2	1	1			1	3	2						
External causes (172-198, 201-214)	3	2											1	2	1		1	
Unknown or ill-defined diseases (199, 200)		2		1		1						2						
All other causes	2	13						1		2		3	1	5		4	1	1

TABLE 23.—COLORED DEATHS (EXCLUSIVE OF STILLBIRTHS) FROM IMPORTANT CAUSES, BY CERTAIN SUBDIVISIONS OF THE FIRST YEAR OF LIFE, FOR SELECTED STATES AND CITIES: 1931 AND 1930—Contd.

[See note at head of this table]

AREA AND CAUSE OF DEATH	Total deaths under 1 year of age		DEATHS AT AGE OF— Under 1 day		1 to 2 days		3 to 6 days		1 to 3 weeks		Under 1 month		1 to 3 months		4 to 7 months		8 to 11 months	
	1931	1930	1931	1930	1931	1930	1931	1930	1931	1930	1931	1930	1931	1930	1931	1930	1931	1930
CLEVELAND, OHIO																		
All causes	**103**	**151**	**36**	**46**	**12**	**22**	**3**	**9**	**14**	**9**	**65**	**86**	**10**	**25**	**14**	**23**	**14**	**17**
Measles (7)	-	-	-	-	-	-	-	-	-	-	-	-	-	-	-	-	-	-
Scarlet fever (8)	-	-	-	-	-	-	-	-	-	-	-	-	-	-	-	-	-	-
Whooping-cough (9)	3	5	-	-	-	-	-	-	-	-	-	-	-	-	3	3	-	2
Diphtheria (10)	-	1	-	-	-	-	-	-	-	-	-	-	-	1	-	-	-	-
Influenza (11)	1	-	-	-	-	-	-	-	-	-	-	-	-	-	-	-	1	-
Dysentery (13)	-	-	-	-	-	-	-	-	-	-	-	-	-	-	-	-	-	-
Erysipelas (15)	1	1	-	-	-	-	-	-	1	-	1	-	-	1	-	-	-	-
Epidemic cerebrospinal meningitis (18)	1	4	-	-	-	-	-	-	-	-	-	-	-	2	1	1	-	1
Tetanus (22)	-	-	-	-	-	-	-	-	-	-	-	-	-	-	-	-	-	-
Tuberculosis of the respiratory system (23)	1	1	-	-	-	-	-	-	-	1	-	1	-	-	1	-	-	-
Tuberculosis of the meninges, etc. (24)	1	1	-	-	-	-	-	-	-	-	-	-	-	-	-	1	1	-
Other forms of tuberculosis (25–32)	-	1	-	-	-	-	-	-	-	-	-	-	-	-	-	1	-	-
Syphilis (34)	2	5	-	-	-	2	-	-	1	-	1	2	1	2	-	1	-	-
Convulsions (86)	-	-	-	-	-	-	-	-	-	-	-	-	-	-	-	-	-	-
Bronchitis (106)	1	1	-	-	-	-	-	-	1	-	1	-	-	1	-	-	-	-
Bronchopneumonia (107)	18	21	-	-	1	-	-	-	2	1	3	1	2	7	4	6	9	7
Lobar and unspecified pneumonia (108, 109)	5	3	-	-	-	1	-	-	1	-	1	1	1	2	2	-	1	-
Diseases of the stomach (117, 118)	-	-	-	-	-	-	-	-	-	-	-	-	-	-	-	-	-	-
Diarrhea and enteritis (119)	6	12	-	-	-	-	-	-	-	2	-	2	3	1	2	5	1	4
Intestinal obstruction (122b)	-	-	-	-	-	-	-	-	-	-	-	-	-	-	-	-	-	-
Congenital malformations (157)	4	4	-	2	1	1	1	-	2	-	4	3	-	1	-	-	-	-
Congenital debility, icterus, sclerema (158, 161b, c)	3	2	-	-	1	-	-	-	1	2	2	2	1	-	-	-	-	-
Premature birth (159)	41	48	30	28	4	10	-	6	5	2	39	46	2	2	-	-	-	-
Injury at birth (160)	12	15	6	8	4	5	2	1	-	-	12	14	-	1	-	-	-	-
Other diseases of early infancy (161 a, d)	1	8	-	3	1	3	-	2	-	-	1	8	-	-	-	-	-	-
External causes (172–198, 201–214)	-	3	-	-	-	-	-	-	-	-	-	-	-	1	-	2	-	-
Unknown or ill-defined diseases (199, 200)	-	6	-	5	-	-	-	-	-	-	-	5	-	1	-	-	-	-
All other causes	2	9	-	-	-	-	-	-	-	1	-	1	-	2	1	3	1	3
PHILADELPHIA, PA.																		
All causes	**490**	**495**	**85**	**83**	**46**	**40**	**26**	**23**	**59**	**86**	**216**	**232**	**101**	**91**	**102**	**111**	**71**	**61**
Measles (7)	2	-	-	-	-	-	-	-	-	-	-	-	1	-	-	-	1	-
Scarlet fever (8)	3	1	-	-	-	-	-	-	-	-	-	-	-	-	2	-	1	1
Whooping-cough (9)	9	7	-	-	-	-	-	-	-	-	-	-	2	2	3	4	4	1
Diphtheria (10)	-	2	-	-	-	-	-	-	-	1	-	1	-	-	-	-	-	1
Influenza (11)	13	10	-	-	1	-	-	-	1	-	2	-	3	3	3	3	5	4
Dysentery (13)	1	1	-	-	-	-	-	-	-	-	-	-	-	1	1	-	-	-
Erysipelas (15)	2	2	-	-	-	-	-	-	1	-	1	-	-	2	-	-	1	-
Epidemic cerebrospinal meningitis (18)	1	2	-	-	1	-	-	-	-	-	1	-	-	-	-	1	-	1
Tetanus (22)	-	-	-	-	-	-	-	-	-	-	-	-	-	-	-	-	-	-
Tuberculosis of the respiratory system (23)	10	11	-	-	-	-	-	-	-	-	-	-	2	1	4	6	4	4
Tuberculosis of the meninges, etc. (24)	1	3	-	-	-	-	-	-	-	-	-	-	-	-	1	1	-	2
Other forms of tuberculosis (25–32)	3	-	-	-	-	-	-	-	1	-	1	-	1	-	1	-	-	-
Syphilis (34)	33	17	5	4	4	1	2	1	2	5	13	11	12	4	5	2	3	-
Convulsions (86)	1	-	-	-	-	-	-	-	-	-	-	-	-	-	-	-	1	-
Bronchitis (106)	4	4	-	-	-	-	1	1	-	1	1	2	1	-	-	2	2	-
Bronchopneumonia (107)	81	90	-	-	1	2	-	1	10	19	11	22	23	23	27	28	20	17
Lobar and unspecified pneumonia (108, 109)	36	34	-	-	-	-	1	-	3	7	4	7	10	6	14	13	8	8
Diseases of the stomach (117, 118)	1	1	-	-	-	-	-	-	-	-	-	-	-	-	-	-	1	1
Diarrhea and enteristis (119)	45	80	-	-	-	-	-	1	4	13	4	14	14	21	21	35	6	10
Intestinal obstruction (122b)	6	4	-	-	-	-	-	-	1	1	1	1	-	-	3	1	2	2
Congenital malformations (157)	26	22	1	3	5	3	2	4	8	5	16	15	6	5	2	2	2	-
Congenital debility, icterus, sclerema (158, 161b, c)	9	9	1	-	-	1	2	-	2	4	5	5	4	3	-	1	-	-
Premature birth (159)	128	108	69	58	25	19	9	8	18	16	121	101	6	4	1	1	-	2
Injury at birth (160)	15	30	6	12	5	5	2	3	2	8	15	28	-	2	-	-	-	-
Other diseases of early infancy (161 a, d)	13	20	3	5	4	9	5	3	1	3	13	20	-	-	-	-	-	-
External causes (172–198, 201–214)	7	7	-	-	-	-	1	-	-	-	1	-	2	1	4	5	-	1
Unknown or ill-defined diseases (199, 200)	-	1	-	-	-	-	-	-	-	1	-	1	-	-	-	-	-	-
All other causes	40	29	-	1	-	-	1	1	5	2	6	4	14	13	10	6	10	6
PITTSBURGH, PA.																		
All causes	**142**	**142**	**25**	**32**	**16**	**10**	**1**	**7**	**19**	**13**	**61**	**62**	**21**	**31**	**39**	**31**	**21**	**18**
Measles (7)	-	-	-	-	-	-	-	-	-	-	-	-	-	-	-	-	-	-
Scarlet fever (8)	-	1	-	-	-	-	-	-	-	-	-	-	-	-	-	-	-	1
Whooping-cough (9)	7	2	-	-	-	-	-	-	-	-	-	-	-	1	4	-	3	1
Diphtheria (10)	-	1	-	-	-	-	-	-	-	-	-	-	-	-	-	-	-	1
Influenza (11)	2	2	-	-	-	-	-	-	-	-	-	-	-	1	2	1	-	-
Dysentery (13)	1	-	-	-	-	-	-	-	-	-	-	-	-	-	-	-	1	-
Erysipelas (15)	1	-	-	-	-	-	-	-	-	-	-	-	1	-	-	-	-	-
Epidemic cerebrospinal meningitis (18)	1	1	-	-	-	-	-	-	-	-	-	-	-	-	1	1	-	-
Tetanus (22)	-	-	-	-	-	-	-	-	-	-	-	-	-	-	-	-	-	-
Tuberculosis of the respiratory system (23)	1	1	-	-	-	-	-	-	-	-	-	-	-	-	-	1	1	-
Tuberculosis of the meninges, etc. (24)	-	-	-	-	-	-	-	-	-	-	-	-	-	-	-	-	-	-
Other forms of tuberculosis (25–32)	-	-	-	-	-	-	-	-	-	-	-	-	-	-	-	-	-	-
Syphilis (34)	6	7	-	3	2	-	-	-	2	1	4	4	2	2	-	1	-	-
Convulsions (86)	-	1	-	-	-	-	-	-	-	-	-	-	-	-	-	1	-	-
Bronchitis (106)	2	1	-	-	-	-	-	-	-	-	-	-	1	-	1	-	-	1
Bronchopneumonia (107)	25	22	-	-	-	-	-	-	1	2	1	2	4	9	14	4	6	7
Lobar and unspecified pneumonia (108, 109)	19	16	-	-	-	-	-	-	3	-	3	-	3	3	6	10	7	3
Diseases of the stomach (117, 118)	-	-	-	-	-	-	-	-	-	-	-	-	-	-	-	-	-	-
Ciarrhea and enteritis (119)	11	13	-	-	-	-	-	-	2	-	2	-	3	2	5	8	1	3
Intestinal obstruction (122b)	-	-	-	-	-	-	-	-	-	-	-	-	-	-	-	-	-	-
Congenital malformations (157)	7	5	1	-	1	-	1	1	3	1	6	2	1	3	-	-	-	-
Congenital debility, icterus, sclerema (158, 161 b, c)	1	1	1	-	-	-	-	-	-	-	1	-	-	1	-	-	-	-
Premature birth (159)	28	38	17	21	4	6	-	2	6	6	27	35	1	2	-	1	-	-
Injury at birth (160)	9	6	2	4	6	-	-	2	-	-	8	6	1	-	-	-	-	-
Other diseases of early infancy (161a, d)	5	6	3	3	2	1	-	1	-	1	5	6	-	-	-	-	-	-
External causes (172–198, 201–214)	1	-	-	-	-	-	-	-	1	-	1	-	-	-	-	-	-	-
Unknown or ill-defined diseases (199, 200)	5	4	-	-	-	-	-	-	1	1	1	1	2	2	2	1	-	-
All other causes	10	14	1	1	1	3	-	1	-	1	2	6	2	5	4	2	2	1

TABLE 23.—COLORED DEATHS (EXCLUSIVE OF STILLBIRTHS) FROM IMPORTANT CAUSES, BY CERTAIN SUBDIVISIONS OF THE FIRST YEAR OF LIFE, FOR SELECTED STATES AND CITIES: 1931 AND 1930—Con.

[See note at head of this table]

AREA AND CAUSE OF DEATH	Total deaths under 1 year of age		DEATHS AT AGE OF— Under 1 day		1 to 2 days		3 to 6 days		1 to 3 weeks		Under 1 month		1 to 3 months		4 to 7 months		8 to 11 months	
	1931	1930	1931	1930	1931	1930	1931	1930	1931	1930	1931	1930	1931	1930	1931	1930	1931	1930
CHATTANOOGA, TENN.																		
All causes	69	83	10	8	11	7	2	1	5	7	28	23	18	21	17	24	6	15
Measles (7)																		
Scarlet fever (8)																		
Whooping-cough (9)	4	4											1	1	1	1	2	2
Diphtheria (10)		1														1		
Influenza (11)	1	1													1	1		
Dysentery (13)	1	2											1	1		1		
Erysipelas (15)																		
Epidemic cerebrospinal meningitis (18)		1														1		
Tetanus (22)																		
Tuberculosis of the respiratory system (23)																		
Tuberculosis of the meninges, etc. (24)																		
Other forms of tuberculosis (25–32)	1														1			
Syphilis (34)	1	2		1								1		1			1	
Convulsions (86)		1																1
Bronchitis (106)																		
Bronchopneumonia (107)	8	13							1	1	1	1	4	3	2	7	1	2
Lobar and unspecified pneumonia (108, 109)	4	2											1		2	1	1	1
Diseases of the stomach (117, 118)																		
Diarrhea and enteritis (119)	14	13					1		1		2		5	3	7	4		6
Intestinal obstruction (122 b)																		
Congenital malformations (157)		2				1						1		1				
Congenital debility, icterus, sclerema (158, 161 b, c)		4												1		1		2
Premature birth (159)	18	13	7	6	8	5			3	2	18	13						
Injury at birth (160)	2	1	1	1			1				2	1						
Other diseases of early infancy (161 a, d)	2	1	2					1			2	1						
External causes (172–198, 201–214)		1														1		
Unknown or ill-defined diseases (199, 200)	10	18			3	1				4	3	5	5	9	2	3		1
All other causes	3	3											1	1	1	2	1	
MEMPHIS, TENN.																		
All causes	232	249	47	51	14	22	7	13	41	27	109	113	56	65	43	51	24	20
Measles (7)	1														1			
Scarlet fever (8)																		
Whooping-cough (9)	9	4											1		5	1	3	3
Diphtheria (10)	1	2								1		1	1			1		
Influenza (11)	1	2												2			1	
Dysentery (13)	4												1				3	
Erysipelas (15)	1								1		1							
Epidemic cerebrospinal meningitis (18)	1	9											1	3		4		2
Tetanus (22)																		
Tuberculosis of the respiratory system (23)		5												1		3		1
Tuberculosis of the meninges, etc. (24)	1																1	
Other forms of tuberculosis (25–32)	1	1														1	1	
Syphilis (34)	28	21	9	5	2	1		3	4	3	15	12	9	6	4	3		
Convulsions (86)	4	1								1		1			4			
Bronchitis (106)																		
Bronchopneumonia (107)	33	47	1			1		1	3	3	4	5	8	12	16	23	5	7
Lobar and unspecified pneumonia (108, 109)	8	8							1	2	1	2	4	2		3	3	1
Diseases of the stomach (117, 118)	1	2				1						1	1					1
Diarrhea and enteritis (119)	20	14							3	1	3	1	8	4	6	7	3	2
Intestinal obstruction (122 b)		1																1
Congenital malformation (157)	3	2			1	1	1			1	2	2	1					
Congenital debility, icterus, scleremia (158, 161 b, c)	8	15	1		1	1		2	2	3	4	6	3	8	1	1		
Premature birth (159)	57	66	23	36	7	9	3	6	15	10	48	61	9	5				
Injury at birth (160)	11	6	8	4	2	1	1				11	5		1				
Other diseases of early infancy (161 a, d)	3	8	1	2		3		1	2	1	3	7		1				
External causes (172–198, 201–214)	2	6	1	1							1	1	1	5				
Unknown or ill-defined diseases (199, 200)	24	22	3	3	1	4	2		8	1	14	8	3	9	5	3	2	2
All other causes	10	7							2		2		5	6	1	1	2	
NASHVILLE, TENN.																		
All causes	103	114	17	25	12	14	8	4	13	12	50	55	20	33	21	16	12	10
Measles (7)	1	1												1	1			
Scarlet fever (8)																		
Whooping-cough (9)	2	1												1			2	
Diphtheria (10)		1														1		
Influenza (11)	3	1											2	1	1			
Dysentery (13)																		
Erysipelas (15)																		
Epidemic cerebrospinal meningitis (18)	2														1		1	
Tetanus (22)																		
Tuberculosis of the respiratory system (23)	2	2											1			1	1	1
Tuberculosis of the meninges, etc. (24)																		
Other forms of tuberculosis (25–32)	1														1			
Syphilis (34)	13	11	2	4	2	2			2	4	6	10	4	1	1		2	
Convulsions (86)																		
Bronchitis (106)																		
Bronchopneumonia (107)	12	16	1								1		4	10	6	2	1	4
Lobar and unspecified pneumonia (108, 109)	2	1											1			1	1	
Diseases of the stomach (117, 118)																		
Diarrhea and enteritis (119)	9	22								1		1	4	9	4	8	1	4
Intestinal obstruction (122 b)	3				1						1				1		1	
Congenital malformations (157)	3						2				2		1					
Congenital debility, icterus, sclerema (158, 161 b, c)	3	4		2	1	1	1		1	1	3	4						
Premature birth (159)	17	24	9	15	4	5	2	1	2	3	17	24						
Injury at birth (160)	4	7	4	1		4		1		1	4	7						
Other diseases of early infancy (161 a, d)	4	4	1	2	2		1	1		1	4	4						
External causes (172–198, 201–214)	1	5				1			1		1	1		1		2		1
Unknown or ill-defined diseases (199, 200)	13	8		1	2		1	1	5		8	2	2	5	3	1		
All other causes	8	6				1	1		2	1	3	2	1	4	2		2	

TABLE 23.—COLORED DEATHS (EXCLUSIVE OF STILLBIRTHS) FROM IMPORTANT CAUSES, BY CERTAIN SUBDIVISIONS OF THE FIRST YEAR OF LIFE, FOR SELECTED STATES AND CITIES: 1931 AND 1930—Con.

[See note at head of this table]

AREA AND CAUSE OF DEATH	Total deaths under 1 year of age		DEATHS AT AGE OF— Under 1 day		1 to 2 days		3 to 6 days		1 to 3 weeks		Under 1 month		1 to 3 months		4 to 7 months		8 to 11 months	
	1931	1930	1931	1930	1931	1930	1931	1930	1931	1930	1931	1930	1931	1930	1931	1930	1931	1930
NORFOLK, VA.																		
All causes	93	104	14	8	7	13	8	9	12	12	41	42	23	34	20	15	9	13
Measles (7)																		
Scarlet fever (8)																		
Whooping-cough (9)	1	3												1		1	1	1
Diphtheria (10)	1														1			
Influenza (11)	2												1		1			
Dysentery (13)																		
Erysipelas (15)																		
Epidemic cerebrospinal meningitis (18)																		
Tetanus (22)																		
Tuberculosis of the respiratory system (23)	1														1			
Tuberculosis of the meninges, etc. (24)																		
Other forms of tuberculosis (25-32)	1														1			
Syphilis (34)	3	10						1	1		1	1	2	5		2		2
Convulsions (86)		1												1				
Bronchitis (106)		1												1				
Bronchopneumonia (107)	32	27			1		1	1	9	4	11	5	8	11	7	4	6	7
Lobar and unspecified pneumonia (108, 109)	5												2		2		1	
Diseases of the stomach (117, 118)																		
Diarrhea and enteritis (119)	14	22					1	1	1	2	2	3	6	11	5	5	1	3
Intestinal obstruction (122 b)	1												1					
Congenital malformations (157)	2	1											1		1	1		
Congenital debility, icterus, sclerema (158, 161 b, c)	1	5				1		1		1		3	1	2				
Premature birth (159)	15	21	7	5	3	7	4	3	1	5	15	20		1				
Injury at birth (160)	3	2	3			1		1			3	2						
Other diseases of early infancy (161 a, d)	6	8	3	3	2	4	1	1			6	8						
External causes (172-198, 201-214)	3	1	1				1				2				1	1		
Unknown or ill-defined diseases (199, 200)	1				1						1							
All other causes	1	2											1	1		1		
RICHMOND, VA.																		
All causes	138	143	20	16	16	12	11	9	15	18	62	55	27	26	32	38	17	24
Measles (7)																		
Scarlet fever (8																		
Whooping-cough (9)	1	6														5	1	1
Diphtheria (10)																		
Influenza (11)	5	2							1		1				3	1	1	1
Dysentery (13)	1																1	
Erysipelas (15)																		
Epidemic cerebrospinal meningitis (18)		2												1				1
Tetanus (22)																		
Tuberculosis of the respiratory system (23)	1	1													1	1		
Tuberculosis of the meninges, etc. (24)	3	1											1		1	1	1	
Other forms of tuberculosis (25-32)		1														1		
Syphilis (34)	12	10	1		1		1		2	3	5	3	3	5	4	1		1
Convulsions (86)	3	7							1	2	1	2	1	1	1	2		2
Bronchitis (106)	1	2								1		1			1	1		
Bronchopneumonia (107)	14	12							2		2		2	2	6	5	4	5
Lobar and unspecified pneumonia (108, 109)	5	9											2	2	2	3	1	4
Diseases of the stomach (117, 118)		1												1				
Diarrhea and enteritis (119)	15	13							1		1		6	2	6	8	2	3
Intestinal obstruction (122 b)	1	1							1		1					1		
Congenital malformations (157)	1	4	1	1				1		1	1	3		1				
Congenital debility, icterus, sclerema (158, 161 b, c)	10	7				1			1	1	1	2	4	1	3	3	2	1
Premature birth (159)	39	33	11	11	11	7	6	5	5	8	33	31	6	2				
Injury at birth (160)	11	7	7	2	3	1	1	3		1	11	7						
Other diseases of early infancy (161 a, d)	3	1			1		2			1	3	1						
External causes (172-198, 201-214)	1	2		1								1		1			1	
Unknown or ill-defined diseases (199, 200)	5	15		1		3	1				1	4	1	6	2	3	1	2
All other causes	6	6							1		1		1	1	2	2	2	3

CHAPTER XVI—VITAL STATISTICS—MORTALITY

The registration area and classification of deaths.—The statistics given here were compiled by the Bureau of the Census from data on transcripts of certificates of death from registration authorities.

The death registration area in continental United States in 1930 and 1931 included 47 States (all States except Texas), the District of Columbia, and 8 cities in Texas. In 1930, the death registration area contained 96.2 percent of the estimated total population as of July 1, and 94.4 percent of the total Negro population of the United States. In 1920, the death registration area included 34 States, the District of Columbia, and 16 cities in nonregistration States.

The classification of deaths by race distinguishes white, Negro, Indian, Chinese, Japanese, and "other races" which includes Mexican, so far as they were reported. The term "colored", as used in many of the tables in this chapter, includes the nonwhite population for which data by race were not separately reported by States, or if reported, were considered by the Bureau to be too deficient to justify a presentation by racial designations such as Negro, Indian, etc. However, in the tables relating to "colored" are included only States in which Negroes constitute at least 55 percent of the total colored population. Consequently, 16 registration States were omitted from tables for the "colored" population, but these States had in 1930 a combined Negro population of only 142,650 or 1.2 percent of the total Negro population of the United States.

When crude death rates from all causes are shown, caution should be exercised in drawing conclusions as to health conditions in the different localities because of race stock, occupations of inhabitants, the sex and age distribution of the population, and the relative number of deaths of nonresidents.

Cities, incorporated places, and rural areas.—Cities include municipalities of 10,000 inhabitants or more in 1930 and in some States certain towns and townships having a population of 10,000 or more with a population density of 1,000 or more per square mile. Incorporated places include minor cities with a population of 2,500 to 10,000 in 1930. Rural areas include all the population outside of cities or incorporated places with less than 2,500 inhabitants.

Deaths in 1920, 1930, and 1931.—A comparison between the number of Negro deaths in 1930 and 1931, the 2 years when the registration areas were identical, shows a decrease of 8,145 deaths for the entire area. as seen in table 5. Decreases in the number of Negro deaths between 1930 and 1931 occurred in 32 States, while increases were shown in the District of Columbia, and 15 States, all of which except Maryland and West Virginia and the District of Columbia, were in the North and West. Among those States included in the registration area in 1920, 1930, and 1931, Colorado, Kansas, Massachusetts, Minnesota, Mississippi, New Hampshire, and Tennessee, showed fewer deaths during 1931 than 1920, even though there was an increase in the Negro population between 1920 and 1930 in each of these States.

Death rates.—In the registration area in 1920 there were 130,147 Negro deaths (exclusive of stillbirths), from all causes, giving a crude death rate of 18.7 per 1,000 Negro population as compared with 185,503 deaths and a crude death rate of 16.5 in 1930.

Decreases in Negro death rates in 1931 over those in 1930 were reported for 31 of the 47 States in the registration area in both years (see table 2).

The District of Columbia and the States in the registration area which reported 50,000 or more Negro population at the 1930 census and which showed increases in death rates in 1931 over 1930, arranged in order of increases were: District of Columbia, Missouri, Maryland, Illinois, Pennsylvania, New York, Kansas, West Virginia, and California. Negro death rates for these States and the District of Columbia varied from 22.4 per 1,000 Negro population for the District of Columbia to 15.3 for California.

The death rates for the Negro population were much higher than for the white population in the District of Columbia and in all States except Maine, New Hampshire, and Vermont in 1931.

The 6 States among those showing 50,000 or more Negro population in 1930, which reported the lowest death rate for 1931, were Oklahoma, Arkansas, Mississippi, Alabama, North Carolina and Louisiana.

Deaths by age and sex.—Significant decreases have taken place during the decade, 1920–30, in the number of Negro deaths in the lower age groups. Table 1 shows that Negro deaths under 1 year of age per 1,000 deaths at all ages declined from 173 in 1920 to 130 in 1930. In the age group, 1 to 4 years, Negro deaths decreased from 70 per 1,000 deaths in 1920 to 45 in 1930. Between 1920 and 1930 decreases for each age group in the number of Negro deaths per 1,000 deaths were reported for all age groups up to and including 29 years. The high peak for Negro deaths of all ages, exclusive of the group under 1 year of age, was in the 20- to 24-year age group in 1920, whereas in 1930 this peak had moved upward to the 50- to 54-year age group.

Of the total 185,503 Negro deaths in 1930, 97,524, or 52.6 percent were males. The number of female deaths per 1,000 deaths of all ages exceeded the proportion of male Negro deaths in the age groups from 10 to 14 years to and including 40 to 44 years, and in the age groups 90 years of age and over. The high peak, in deaths per 1,000 at all ages, exclusive of the group under 1 year of age, for both males and females, was in the same age group, 50 to 54 years.

Death rates in cities, incorporated places, and rural districts in 1930.—The Negro deaths per 1,000 population in cities was 19.8 as compared with 14.2 in rural districts for the registration area in the United States, as shown in table 6.

Disregarding comparisons in the District of Columbia, Idaho, New Hampshire, Texas, and Utah, where Negro death rates for either incorporated places or rural districts, or both, were not shown, there were 19 States in which the death rates in rural districts were lower than in either cities or incorporated places in 1930. In 10 States the death rates were lower in cities than in incorporated places or rural districts, and in 9 States the death rates were lower in incorporated places than in cities or rural districts.

Comparing the Negro death rates in cities, incorporated places, and rural districts, it should be noted that for 5 States with over 500,000 Negro population, namely, Georgia, Mississippi, North Carolina, South Carolina, and Virginia, higher death rates were reported in cities than in incorporated places or rural districts, whereas the death rates in rural districts were higher

GROWTH OF THE REGISTRATION AREA FOR DEATHS: 1880 TO 1931

NOTE.—In addition to the registration States, the registration area for each year included certain cities in nonregistration States

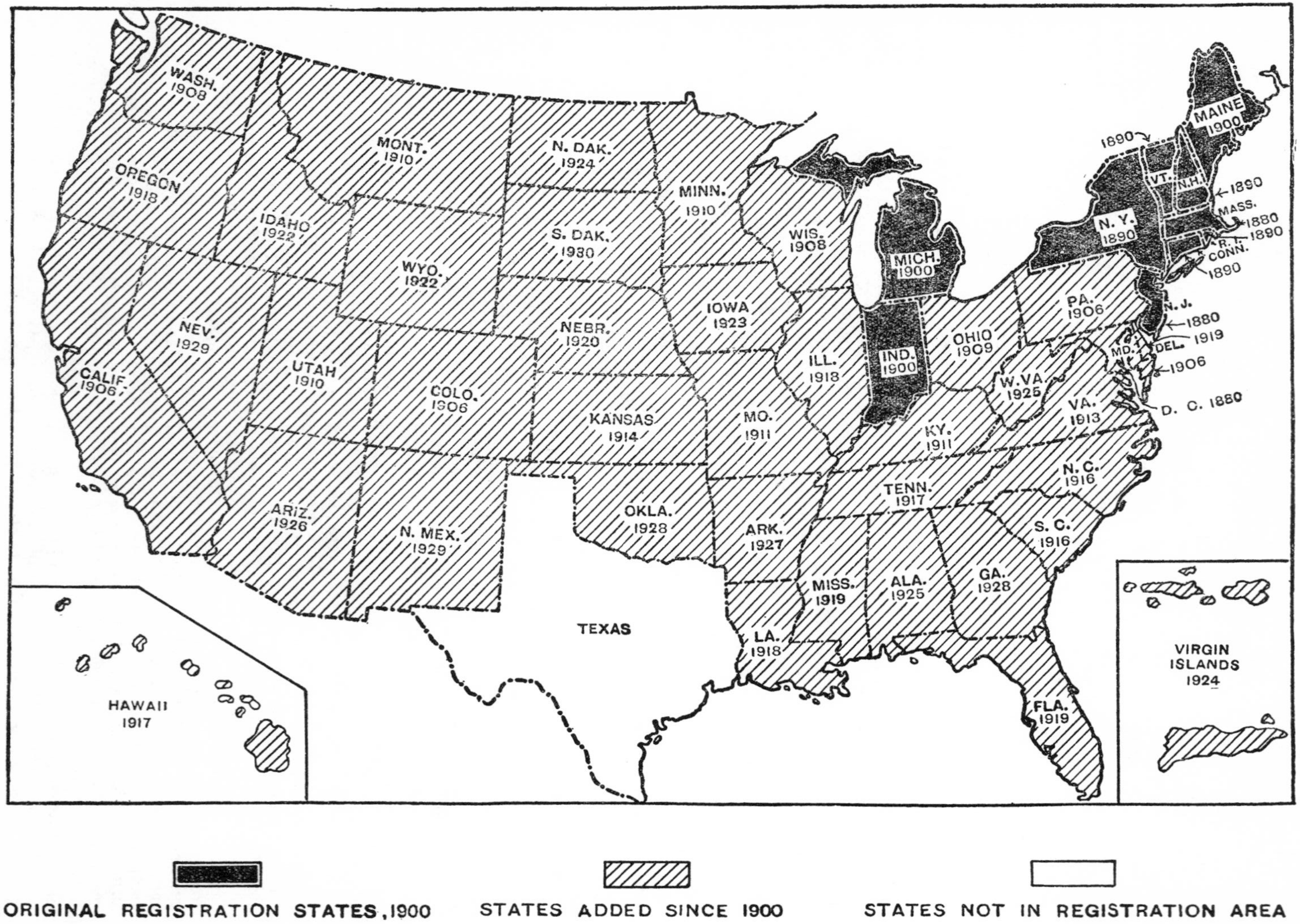

than in incorporated places or cities for the Northern States of New York, Pennsylvania, Illinois, Michigan, and Kansas, and for California.

Colored death rates in cities having 25,000 or more Negro inhabitants.—Among those cities having 25,000 or more Negro inhabitants in 1930, the highest colored death rate for 1931 was reported for Charleston, South Carolina, with a death rate of 33.6 per 1,000 estimated population. The lowest death rate for colored was for Detroit, Mich., with a death rate of 13.2 per 1,000 estimated population. In no instance was the death rate for white persons in these cities equal to or greater than the death rate of colored persons.

Negro deaths from important causes.—The percentages of the total deaths from important causes in 1931 for registration States, including the District of Columbia, were as follows: Tuberculosis of respiratory system, 10.6 percent; chronic nephritis, 6.5 percent; cerebral hemorrhage, 5.9 percent; lobar pneumonia, 5.1 percent; endocarditis, specified as chronic, and other valvular diseases, 4.4 percent; bronchopneumonia, 2.9 percent; chronic myocarditis and myocardial degeneration, 2.8 percent; syphilis, 2.7 percent; homicide, 2.6 percent; premature birth, 2.6 percent; and diarrhea, enteritis (under 2 years of age), 1.8 percent.

TABLE 1.—DEATHS (EXCLUSIVE OF STILLBIRTHS) OF NEGRO, BY AGE, AND SEX, AND WHITE BY AGE, 1930; AND OF NEGRO AND WHITE, BY AGE, 1920, IN THE REGISTRATION AREA OF CONTINENTAL UNITED STATES

AGE	NUMBER					
	1930				1920	
	Negro			White	Negro	White
	Total	Male	Female			
All ages	185, 503	97, 524	87, 979	1, 144, 189	130, 147	1, 007, 117
Under 1 year	24, 178	13, 397	10, 781	118, 134	22, 456	151, 284
1 to 4 years	8, 430	4, 489	3, 941	39, 906	9, 052	64, 118
5 to 9 years	3, 182	1, 692	1, 490	19, 308	3, 139	23, 750
10 to 14 years	3, 066	1, 512	1, 554	14, 232	2, 980	16, 338
15 to 19 years	7, 704	3, 348	4, 356	22, 702	6, 340	24, 724
20 to 24 years	10, 868	5, 158	5, 710	29, 928	9, 275	34, 327
25 to 29 years	11, 031	5, 333	5, 698	30, 205	8, 399	41, 060
30 to 34 years	10, 757	5, 555	5, 202	32, 573	7, 432	42, 314
35 to 39 years	12, 343	6, 282	6, 061	40, 661	8, 663	43, 138
40 to 44 years	12, 564	6, 579	5, 985	47, 861	7, 217	40, 110
45 to 49 years	13, 908	7, 475	6, 433	56, 777	7, 551	44, 185
50 to 54 years	14, 831	8, 125	6, 706	68, 404	7, 194	50, 634
55 to 59 years	11, 445	6, 351	5, 094	79, 146	5, 264	56, 153
60 to 64 years	10, 501	5, 787	4, 714	95, 600	5, 308	67, 183
65 to 69 years	8, 610	4, 746	3, 864	106, 714	4, 978	71, 349
70 to 74 years	7, 020	3, 845	3, 175	114, 833	4, 629	74, 780
75 to 79 years	5, 120	2, 800	2, 320	99, 083	3, 471	70, 398
80 to 84 years	4, 013	2, 161	1, 852	72, 007	2, 671	50, 708
85 to 89 years	2, 396	1, 287	1, 109	39, 078	1, 577	27, 759
90 to 94 years	1, 363	624	739	12, 869	915	9, 425
95 to 99 years	622	276	346	2, 743	411	2, 032
100 years and over	745	264	481	411	601	341
Unknown	806	438	368	1, 014	624	1, 007
NUMBER PER 1,000 DEATHS AT ALL AGES						
All ages	1, 000	1, 000	1, 000	1, 000	1, 000	1, 000
Under 1 year	130	137	123	103	173	150
1 to 4 years	45	46	45	35	70	64
5 to 9 years	17	17	17	17	24	24
10 to 14 years	17	16	18	12	23	16
15 to 19 years	42	34	50	20	49	25
20 to 24 years	59	53	65	26	71	34
25 to 29 years	59	55	65	26	65	41
30 to 34 years	58	57	59	28	57	42
35 to 39 years	67	64	69	36	67	43
40 to 44 years	68	67	68	42	55	40
45 to 49 years	75	77	73	50	58	44
50 to 54 years	80	83	76	60	55	50
55 to 59 years	62	65	58	69	40	56
60 to 64 years	57	59	54	84	41	67
65 to 69 years	46	49	44	93	38	71
70 to 74 years	38	39	36	100	36	74
75 to 79 years	28	29	26	87	27	70
80 to 84 years	22	22	21	63	21	50
85 to 89 years	13	13	13	34	12	28
90 to 94 years	7	6	8	11	7	9
95 to 99 years	3	3	4	2	3	2
100 years and over	4	3	5	(1)	5	(1)
Unknown	4	4	4	1	5	1

[1] Less than 1.

TABLE 2.—NEGRO AND WHITE DEATH RATES FROM ALL CAUSES (EXCLUSIVE OF STILLBIRTHS) PER 1,000 POPULATION: 1931, 1930, AND 1920

AREA AND COLOR	RATE PER 1,000 ENUMERATED POPULATION		
	1931	1930	1920
REGISTRATION STATES			
ALABAMA:			
Negro	14. 1	15. 2	(1)
White	8. 9	9. 4	(1)
ARIZONA:			
Negro	19. 4	19. 2	(1)
White	12. 5	13. 9	(1)
ARKANSAS:			
Negro	11. 9	13. 5	(1)
White	8. 8	9. 1	(1)
CALIFORNIA:			
Negro	15. 3	14. 3	20. 1
White	11. 8	(2)	14. 1
COLORADO:			
Negro	23. 5	25. 5	26. 8
White	12. 0	(2)	14. 6
CONNECTICUT:			
Negro	17. 5	17. 5	23. 3
White	10. 6	10. 6	13. 6
DELAWARE:			
Negro	21. 3	21. 7	22. 0
White	12. 7	12. 4	13. 5
DISTRICT OF COLUMBIA:			
Negro	22. 4	21. 0	20. 8
White	13. 5	13. 0	12. 7
FLORIDA:			
Negro	16. 3	16. 6	15. 6
White	10. 7	10. 7	11. 9
GEORGIA:			
Negro	14. 9	16. 0	(1)
White	9. 2	9. 8	(1)
IDAHO:			
Negro	34. 4	19. 5	(1)
White	8. 8	9. 2	(1)
ILLINOIS:			
Negro	18. 8	17. 7	21. 5
White	10. 9	10. 7	12. 4
INDIANA:			
Negro	17. 5	19. 5	22. 3
White	11. 8	11. 8	13. 2
IOWA:			
Negro	16. 9	17. 1	(1)
White	10. 4	10. 6	(1)
KANSAS:			
Negro	16. 9	16. 3	20. 5
White	9. 7	10. 3	11. 2
KENTUCKY:			
Negro	20. 1	21. 0	19. 3
White	10. 2	10. 4	11. 0
LOUISIANA:			
Negro	14. 5	15. 5	15. 3
White	9. 3	9. 6	9. 9
MAINE:			
Negro	11. 9	16. 4	23. 7
White	13. 2	13. 9	15. 5
MARYLAND:			
Negro	19. 5	19. 0	21. 3
White	12. 1	12. 0	13. 4
MASSACHUSETTS:			
Negro	15. 9	15. 9	21. 8
White	11. 4	11. 5	13. 8
MICHIGAN:			
Negro	15. 8	16. 4	25. 4
White	9. 9	10. 4	13. 8
MINNESOTA:			
Negro	17. 2	20. 8	21. 3
White	9. 9	9. 9	10. 7
MISSISSIPPI:			
Negro	13. 2	14. 8	15. 1
White	8. 7	9. 2	9. 3
MISSOURI:			
Negro	20. 7	20. 6	21. 1
WHITE	11. 6	11. 3	12. 1
MONTANA:			
Negro	19. 1	22. 3	24. 7
White	9. 3	9. 8	9. 3
NEBRASKA:			
Negro	19. 7	18. 5	17. 2
White	9. 2	9. 5	9. 9
NEVADA:			
Negro	32. 9	27. 1	(1)
White	14. 4	12. 3	(1)
NEW HAMPSHIRE:			
Negro	6. 3	8. 9	17. 7
White	12. 7	13. 6	15. 3
NEW JERSEY:			
Negro	16. 9	16. 9	21. 0
White	10. 7	10. 5	12. 8
NEW MEXICO:			
Negro	24. 9	20. 7	(1)
White	17. 4	(2)	(1)
NEW YORK:			
Negro	17. 3	16. 6	19. 8
White	11. 7	11. 5	13. 8
NORTH CAROLINA:			
Negro	13. 9	15. 2	16. 1
White	9. 0	9. 7	11. 3
NORTH DAKOTA:			
Negro	10. 6	13. 3	(1)
White	7. 4	7. 8	(1)
OHIO:			
Negro	18. 7	18. 8	21. 5
White	11. 0	11. 1	12. 6
OKLAHOMA:			
Negro	12. 2	13. 0	(1)
White	7. 5	7. 8	(1)
OREGON:			
Negro	16. 6	24. 6	15. 4
White	10. 6	10. 9	11. 6
PENNSYLVANIA:			
Negro	17. 8	17. 3	21. 3
White	11. 3	11. 3	13. 6
RHODE ISLAND:			
Negro	18. 3	22. 1	26. 9
White	11. 5	11. 5	14. 2
SOUTH CAROLINA:			
Negro	15. 6	16. 6	16. 6
White	9. 2	9. 8	11. 5
SOUTH DAKOTA:			
Negro	9. 3	18. 6	(1)
White	8. 0	7. 9	(1)
TENNESSEE:			
Negro	16. 8	18. 3	18. 1
White	9. 6	9. 9	10. 7
UTAH:			
Negro	18. 1	20. 8	20. 1
White	8. 8	10. 0	11. 5
VERMONT:			
Negro	12. 3	14. 1	10. 5
White	12. 5	13. 0	15. 7
VIRGINIA:			
Negro	17. 8	18. 0	17. 6
White	10. 4	10. 5	11. 3
WASHINGTON:			
Negro	18. 1	21. 1	20. 8
White	10. 4	10. 5	10. 9
WEST VIRGINIA:			
Negro	16. 3	16. 1	(1)
White	9. 8	10. 1	(1)
WISCONSIN:			
Negro	15. 2	18. 7	22. 3
White	10. 2	10. 3	11. 2
WYOMING:			
Negro	16. 0	23. 2	(1)
White	8. 6	8. 7	(1)

[1] Not in registration area.
[2] Death rate not available.

TABLE 3.—GROWTH OF REGISTRATION AREA IN CONTINENTAL UNITED STATES: 1880 TO 1931

STATE	Year	STATE	Year
Massachusetts	[1] 1880	Virginia	1913
New Jersey	[1] 1880	Kansas	1914
District of Columbia [2]	[1] 1880	North Carolina [6]	1916
Connecticut	[1] 1890	South Carolina	1916
Delaware [3]	[1] 1890	Tennessee	1917
New Hampshire	[1] 1890	Illinois	1918
New York	[1] 1890	Louisiana	1918
Rhode Island	[1] 1890	Oregon	1918
Vermont	[1] 1890	Delaware [3]	1919
Maine	[1] 1900	Florida	1919
Michigan	[1] 1900	Mississippi	1919
Indiana	1900	Nebraska	1920
California	1906	Georgia [7]	1922
Colorado	1906	Idaho	1922
Maryland	1906	Wyoming	1922
Pennsylvania	1906	Iowa	1923
South Dakota [4]	1906	North Dakota	1924
Washington	1908	Alabama	1925
Wisconsin	1908	West Virginia	1925
Ohio	1909	Arizona	1926
Minnesota	1910	Arkansas	1927
Montana	1910	Georgia [8]	1928
North Carolina [5]	1910	Oklahoma	1928
Utah	1910	Nevada	1929
Kentucky	1911	New Mexico	1929
Missouri	1911	South Dakota [4]	1930

[1] Census year ending May 31.
[2] Included in States.
[3] Dropped from the area in the census year 1900, readmitted in 1919.
[4] Dropped from the area in 1910, readmitted in 1930.
[5] Included only municipalities having a population of 1,000 or more in 1900; these represented only about 16 percent of the total population.
[6] The remainder of the State of North Carolina was added to the registration area in 1916. (See note 5.)
[7] Dropped from the area in 1925 when the State registration law was declared unconstitutional.
[8] The State was readmitted to the area in 1928 under a new State registration law. (See note 7.)

TABLE 4.—DEATHS (EXCLUSIVE OF STILLBIRTHS), BY COLOR, NATIVITY, AND SEX, IN THE REGISTRATION AREA OF CONTINENTAL UNITED STATES: 1930

COLOR AND NATIVITY	NUMBER			DISTRIBUTION PER 1,000		
	Total	Male	Female	Total	Male	Female
Aggregate	1,343,356	735,600	607,756	1,000.0	1,000.0	1,000.0
Negro	185,503	97,524	87,979	138.1	132.6	144.8
White	1,144,189	629,997	514,192	851.7	856.4	846.1
Native	877,018	475,591	401,427	652.9	646.5	660.5
Foreign born	249,423	141,003	108,420	185.7	191.7	178.4
Unknown	17,748	13,403	4,345	13.2	18.2	7.1
Other races [1]	13,664	8,079	5,585	10.2	11.0	9.2

[1] Includes Indian, Chinese, Japanese, and other colored races.

TABLE 5.—DEATHS OF NEGROES (EXCLUSIVE OF STILLBIRTHS) IN THE REGISTRATION AREA OF CONTINENTAL UNITED STATES: 1931, 1930, AND 1920

STATE	1931			1930			1920		
	Total	Male	Female	Total	Male	Female	Total	Male	Female
The registration area in continental United States	**177,358**	**93,349**	**84,009**	**185,503**	**97,524**	**87,979**	**130,147**	**65,426**	**64,721**
Alabama	13,306	6,871	6,435	14,407	7,376	7,031	[1] 2,723	[1] 1,410	[1] 1,313
Arizona	208	139	69	206	120	86	(2)	(2)	(2)
Arkansas	5,680	2,983	2,697	6,461	3,344	3,117	(2)	(2)	(2)
California	1,239	681	558	1,157	637	520	779	437	342
Colorado	278	151	127	302	178	124	303	172	131
Connecticut	514	254	260	513	290	223	491	253	238
Delaware	696	394	302	706	391	315	668	337	331
District of Columbia	2,958	1,542	1,416	2,780	1,424	1,356	2,289	1,040	1,249
Florida	7,032	3,915	3,117	7,166	4,031	3,135	5,134	2,748	2,386
Georgia	15,994	8,225	7,769	17,182	8,806	8,376	[1] 3,388	[1] 1,619	[1] 1,769
Idaho	23	14	9	13	9	4	(2)	(2)	(2)
Illinois	6,191	3,453	2,738	5,824	3,210	2,614	3,925	2,057	1,868
Indiana	1,959	1,053	906	2,185	1,150	1,035	1,802	944	858
Iowa	293	158	135	298	170	128	(2)	(2)	(2)
Kansas	1,123	611	512	1,082	538	544	1,189	619	570
Kentucky	4,548	2,487	2,061	4,748	2,573	2,175	4,560	2,262	2,298
Louisiana	11,219	5,838	5,381	12,036	6,313	5,723	10,722	5,258	5,464
Maine	13	10	3	18	12	6	31	19	12
Maryland	5,386	2,893	2,493	5,251	2,808	2,443	5,198	2,585	2,613
Massachusetts	832	449	383	834	432	402	993	495	498
Michigan	2,670	1,482	1,188	2,786	1,571	1,215	1,529	925	604
Minnesota	162	89	73	196	107	89	188	110	78
Mississippi	13,296	6,713	6,583	14,910	7,577	7,333	14,092	6,794	7,298
Missouri	4,643	2,506	2,137	4,604	2,538	2,066	3,761	1,868	1,893
Montana	24	14	10	28	17	11	41	25	16
Nebraska	271	145	126	255	151	104	228	138	90
Nevada	17	9	8	14	8	6	(2)	(2)	(2)
New Hampshire	5	1	4	7	4	3	11	6	5
New Jersey	3,526	1,908	1,618	3,519	1,904	1,615	2,460	1,211	1,249
New Mexico	71	45	26	59	34	25	(2)	2,009	(2)
New York	7,137	3,790	3,347	6,841	3,634	3,207	3,938	6,018	1,929
North Carolina	12,797	6,343	6,454	13,976	6,928	7,048	12,315	[1] 2	6,297
North Dakota	4	2	2	5	4	1	[1] 2	2,254	(2)
Ohio	5,787	3,304	2,483	5,803	3,267	2,536	4,010	[1] 86	1,756
Oklahoma	2,106	1,127	979	2,242	1,204	1,038	[1] 170	16	[1] 84
Oregon	37	26	11	55	36	19	33	3,343	17
Pennsylvania	7,664	4,195	3,469	7,459	4,057	3,402	6,065	151	2,722
Rhode Island	181	98	83	219	125	94	270	7,095	119
South Carolina	12,368	6,198	6,170	13,160	6,683	6,477	14,338	(2)	7,243
South Dakota	6	2	4	12	7	5	(2)	3,971	(2)
Tennessee	8,013	4,217	3,796	8,744	4,600	4,144	8,169	952	4,198
Texas [3]	3,335	1,762	1,573	3,482	1,828	1,654	1,866	21	914
Utah	20	8	12	23	18	5	29	6	8
Vermont	7	3	4	8	3	5	6	(2)	(2)
Virginia	11,541	5,939	5,602	11,699	6,074	5,625	12,130	5,985	6,145
Washington	124	74	50	144	82	62	143	85	58
West Virginia	1,871	1,112	759	1,854	1,106	748	[1] 42	[1] 25	[1] 17
Wisconsin	163	104	59	201	124	77	116	75	41
Wyoming	20	12	8	29	21	8	(2)	(2)	(2)

[1] Nonregistration State; data for only those cities with satisfactory registration of deaths.
[2] Not in registration area.
[3] Not a registration State; covers data for 8 cities in 1931 and 1930, and for only 6 cities in 1920.

TABLE 6.—POPULATION, DEATHS (EXCLUSIVE OF STILLBIRTHS), AND DEATH RATES OF NEGROES IN REGISTRATION AREA OF CONTINENTAL UNITED STATES, CITIES, INCORPORATED PLACES, AND RURAL DISTRICTS, AND IN CITIES OF NONREGISTRATION STATE: 1930

AREA	POPULATION				DEATHS							
					Total		Cities		Incorporated places		Rural	
	Total	Cities	Incorporated places	Rural	Number	Rate per 1,000 population	Number	Rate per 1,000 population	Number	Rate per 1,000 population	Number	Rate per 1,000 population
The registration area in continental United States	11,221,472	4,396,775	652,602	6,172,095	185,503	16.5	87,221	19.8	10,424	16.0	87,858	14.2
Alabama	944,834	222,177	46,273	676,384	14,407	15.2	4,515	20.3	1,082	23.4	8,810	13.0
Arizona	10,749	3,369	1,778	5,602	206	19.2	131	38.9	45	25.3	30	5.4
Arkansas	478,463	50,611	38,551	389,301	6,461	13.5	1,344	26.6	828	21.5	4,289	11.0
California	81,048	67,421	3,098	10,529	1,157	14.3	844	12.5	70	22.6	243	23.1
Colorado	11,828	9,829	642	1,357	302	25.5	217	22.1	11	17.1	74	54.5
Connecticut	29,354	24,125	406	4,823	513	17.5	429	17.8	13	32.0	71	14.7
Delaware	32,602	12,080	2,957	17,565	706	21.7	280	23.2	74	25.0	352	20.0
District of Columbia	132,068	132,068	---	---	2,780	21.0	2,780	21.0	---	---	---	---
Florida	431,828	156,397	53,895	221,536	7,166	16.6	2,930	18.7	1,290	23.9	2,946	13.3
Georgia	1,071,125	244,711	71,926	754,488	17,182	16.0	6,085	24.9	(1)	(1)	[1] 11,097	[1] 13.4
Idaho	668	348	154	166	13	19.5	7	20.1	6	39.0	---	---
Illinois	328,972	289,644	14,392	24,936	5,824	17.7	4,834	16.7	246	17.1	744	29.8
Indiana	111,982	99,324	3,718	8,940	2,185	19.5	1,812	18.2	89	23.9	284	31.8
Iowa	17,380	13,657	1,528	2,195	298	17.1	243	17.8	19	12.4	36	16.4
Kansas	66,344	46,155	5,126	15,063	1,082	16.3	758	16.4	73	14.2	251	16.7
Kentucky	226,040	87,015	29,546	109,479	4,748	21.0	2,189	25.2	(1)	(1)	[1] 2,559	[1] 18.4
Louisiana	776,326	202,896	54,567	518,863	12,036	15.5	4,919	24.2	1,502	27.5	[1] 5,615	[1] 10.8
Maine	1,096	574	129	393	18	16.4	8	13.9	(1)	(1)	10	25.4
Maryland	276,379	151,465	8,189	116,725	5,251	19.0	3,041	20.1	248	30.3	1,962	16.8
Massachusetts	52,365	44,194	2,129	6,042	834	15.9	721	16.3	19	8.9	94	15.6
Michigan	169,453	155,889	3,815	9,749	2,786	16.4	2,408	15.4	48	12.6	330	33.8
Minnesota	9,445	8,739	371	335	196	20.8	167	19.1	14	37.7	15	44.8
Mississippi	1,009,718	94,756	39,231	875,731	14,910	14.8	2,607	27.5	(1)	(1)	[1] 12,303	[1] 13.4
Missouri	223,840	151,985	17,969	53,886	4,604	20.6	3,269	21.5	388	21.6	947	17.6
Montana	1,256	856	171	229	28	22.3	10	11.7	4	23.4	14	61.1
Nebraska	13,752	12,512	600	640	255	18.5	230	18.4	12	20.0	13	20.3
Nevada	516	123	241	152	14	27.1	7	56.9	4	16.6	3	19.7
New Hampshire	790	567	27	196	7	8.9	5	8.8	---	---	2	10.2
New Jersey	208,828	158,151	16,834	33,843	3,519	16.9	2,559	16.2	361	21.4	599	17.7
New Mexico	2,850	857	861	1,132	59	20.7	22	25.7	19	22.1	18	15.9
New York	412,814	381,798	8,701	22,315	6,841	16.6	6,296	16.5	123	14.1	422	18.9
North Carolina	918,647	194,436	51,801	672,410	13,976	15.2	3,957	20.4	959	18.5	9,060	13.5
North Dakota	377	168	48	161	5	13.3	2	11.9	1	20.8	2	12.4
Ohio	309,304	256,424	15,548	37,332	5,803	18.8	4,783	18.7	264	17.0	756	20.3
Oklahoma	172,198	52,588	15,213	104,397	2,242	13.0	1,055	20.1	440	28.9	747	7.2
Oregon	2,234	1,727	163	344	55	24.6	46	26.6	4	24.5	5	14.5
Pennsylvania	431,257	354,667	18,913	57,677	7,459	17.3	6,092	17.2	290	15.3	1,077	18.7
Rhode Island	9,913	8,982	97	834	219	22.1	194	21.6	9	92.8	16	19.2
South Carolina	793,681	89,245	49,109	655,327	13,160	16.6	2,579	28.9	1,033	21.0	9,548	14.6
South Dakota	646	251	86	309	12	18.6	5	19.9	2	23.3	5	16.2
Tennessee	477,646	201,252	38,916	237,478	8,744	18.3	4,616	22.9	(1)	(1)	[1] 4,128	[1] 14.9
Texas	[2] 185,293	[2] 185,293	(2)	(2)	[2] 3,482	[2] 18.8	[2] 3,482	[2] 18.8	---	---	---	---
Utah	1,108	913	31	164	23	20.8	22	24.1	1	32.3	---	---
Vermont	568	131	82	355	8	14.1	3	22.9	(1)	(1)	[1] 5	[1] 11.4
Virginia	650,165	187,636	25,765	436,764	11,699	18.0	3,994	21.3	490	19.0	7,215	16.5
Washington	6,840	5,600	218	1,022	144	21.1	105	18.8	11	50.5	28	27.4
West Virginia	114,893	23,040	8,184	83,669	1,854	16.1	478	20.7	316	38.6	1,060	12.7
Wisconsin	10,739	9,678	195	866	201	18.7	131	13.5	4	20.5	66	76.2
Wyoming	1,250	451	408	391	29	23.2	10	22.2	12	29.4	7	17.9

[1] "Incorporated places" included in "Rural."
[2] Nonregistration State in 1930. Statistics given relate to 8 registration cities only: Beaumont, Dallas, El Paso, Fort Worth, Galveston, Houston, San Antonio, and Waco.

TABLE 7.—DEATHS OF COLORED PERSONS (EXCLUSIVE OF STILLBIRTHS), IN CITIES AND RURAL DISTRICTS OF REGISTRATION STATES, BY RACE: 1930

[In this table the term "cities" includes places of 10,000 inhabitants or more; the remainder of the population classed as "rural." Percent not shown where base is less than 100]

AREA	Total	NEGRO		Indian	Chinese	Japanese	Other colored
		Number	Percent of total				
Registration States	**194,082**	**182,021**	**93.79**	**5,384**	**1,331**	**1,109**	**4,237**
Cities	**87,316**	**83,739**	**95.90**	**454**	**1,025**	**682**	**1,416**
Rural	**106,766**	**98,282**	**92.05**	**4,930**	**306**	**427**	**2,821**
ALABAMA:							
Cities	4,516	4,515	99.98	—	1	—	—
Rural	9,896	9,892	99.96	4	—	—	—
ARIZONA:							
Cities	602	131	21.76	39	4	5	423
Rural	2,397	75	3.13	790	11	5	1,516
ARKANSAS:							
Cities	1,344	1,344	100.00	—	—	—	—
Rural	5,122	5,117	99.90	—	4	—	1
CALIFORNIA:							
Cities	2,095	844	40.29	53	430	475	293
Rural	1,542	313	20.30	381	206	291	351
COLORADO:							
Cities	362	217	59.94	1	5	15	124
Rural	689	85	12.34	23	2	12	567
CONNECTICUT:							
Cities	435	429	98.62	1	1	—	4
Rural	88	84	—	3	1	—	—
DELAWARE:							
Cities	280	280	100.00	—	—	—	—
Rural	427	426	99.77	—	—	—	1
FLORIDA:							
Cities	2,939	2,930	99.69	1	4	1	3
Rural	4,243	4,236	99.84	4	—	2	1
GEORGIA:							
Cities	6,088	6,085	99.95	—	3	—	—
Rural	11,102	11,097	99.95	3	2	—	—
IDAHO:							
Cities	16	7	—	3	2	3	1
Rural	145	6	4.14	122	3	10	4
ILLINOIS:							
Cities	4,951	4,834	97.64	6	77	7	27
Rural	1,010	990	98.02	1	6	1	12
INDIANA:							
Cities	1,931	1,812	93.84	1	4	—	114
Rural	382	373	97.64	—	—	—	9
IOWA:							
Cities	276	243	88.04	—	—	—	33
Rural	87	55	—	11	—	—	21
KANSAS:							
Cities	765	758	99.08	6	—	—	1
Rural	337	324	96.14	10	—	—	3
KENTUCKY:							
Cities	2,190	2,189	99.95	—	1	—	—
Rural	2,560	2,559	99.96	1	—	—	—
LOUISIANA:							
Cities	4,937	4,919	99.64	—	10	1	7
Rural	7,149	7,117	99.55	25	4	—	3
MAINE:							
Cities	12	8	—	2	2	—	—
Rural	29	10	—	19	—	—	—
MARYLAND:							
Cities	3,053	3,041	99.61	—	9	—	3
Rural	2,211	2,210	99.95	—	1	—	—
MASSACHUSETTS:							
Cities	789	721	91.38	4	49	4	11
Rural	119	113	94.96	2	3	—	1
MICHIGAN:							
Cities	2,560	2,408	94.06	16	19	1	116
Rural	530	378	71.32	128	2	—	22
MINNESOTA:							
Cities	190	167	87.89	12	8	2	1
Rural	285	29	10.18	252	1	—	3
MISSISSIPPI:							
Cities	2,610	2,607	99.89	—	2	—	1
Rural	12,351	12,303	99.61	27	2	—	19
MISSOURI:							
Cities	3,313	3,269	98.67	4	6	1	33
Rural	1,340	1,335	99.63	2	—	—	3
MONTANA:							
Cities	30	10	—	5	10	1	4
Rural	333	18	5.41	300	8	3	4
NEBRASKA:							
Cities	267	230	86.14	3	1	1	32
Rural	200	25	12.50	90	1	6	78
NEVADA:							
Cities	24	7	—	10	7	—	—
Rural	132	7	5.30	108	9	3	5
NEW HAMPSHIRE:							
Cities	6	5	—	—	1	—	—
Rural	3	2	—	1	—	—	—
NEW JERSEY:							
Cities	2,588	2,559	98.88	2	23	1	3
Rural	964	960	99.59	1	1	1	1
NEW MEXICO:							
Cities	30	22	—	7	—	1	—
Rural	381	37	9.71	341	1	—	2
NEW YORK:							
Cities	6,568	6,296	95.86	35	177	27	33
Rural	631	545	86.37	75	6	2	3
NORTH CAROLINA:							
Cities	3,959	3,957	99.95	1	1	—	—
Rural	10,196	10,019	98.26	176	1	—	—
NORTH DAKOTA:							
Cities	5	2	—	2	—	1	—
Rural	143	3	2.10	137	1	1	1
OHIO:							
Cities	4,812	4,783	99.40	2	16	4	7
Rural	1,027	1,020	99.32	1	2	—	4
OKLAHOMA:							
Cities	1,254	1,055	84.13	154	5	—	40
Rural	1,809	1,187	65.62	581	—	1	40
OREGON:							
Cities	142	46	32.39	10	46	30	10
Rural	166	9	5.42	118	13	16	10
PENNSYLVANIA:							
Cities	6,136	6,092	99.28	2	34	1	7
Rural	1,375	1,367	99.42	4	2	—	2
RHODE ISLAND:							
Cities	203	194	95.57	6	3	—	—
Rural	28	25	—	3	—	—	—
SOUTH CAROLINA:							
Cities	2,580	2,579	99.96	—	—	1	—
Rural	10,582	10,581	99.99	1	—	—	—
SOUTH DAKOTA:							
Cities	9	5	—	2	1	—	1
RURAL	543	7	1.29	530	1	—	5
TENNESSEE:							
Cities	4,620	4,616	99.91	—	3	—	1
Rural	4,132	4,128	99.90	4	—	—	—
UTAH:							
Cities	63	22	—	2	6	10	23
Rural	51	1	—	13	—	14	23
VERMONT:							
Cities	3	3	—	—	—	—	—
Rural	6	5	—	—	—	—	1
VIRGINIA:							
Cities	4,001	3,994	99.83	1	3	1	2
Rural	7,721	7,705	99.79	12	2	1	1
WASHINGTON:							
Cities	307	105	34.20	34	44	85	39
Rural	394	39	9.90	286	8	49	12
WEST VIRGINIA:							
Cities	479	478	99.79	—	—	—	1
Rural	1,377	1,376	99.93	1	—	—	—
WISCONSIN:							
Cities	158	131	82.91	25	1	—	1
Rural	344	70	20.35	269	1	—	4
WYOMING:							
Cities	26	10	—	—	2	—	14
Rural	187	19	10.16	70	1	9	88
DISTRICT OF COLUMBIA	2,792	2,780	99.57	2	4	3	3

TABLE 8.—NEGRO POPULATION OF THE REGISTRATION AREA, AND OF THE NONREGISTRATION AREA, AND PERCENTAGE IN THE AREA, BY SECTIONS, DIVISIONS, AND STATES: 1930, 1920, AND 1910

SECTION, DIVISION, AND STATE	1930		1920			1910			PERCENTAGE IN REGISTRATION AREA		
	Total	Registration area	Total	Registration area	Nonregistration area	Total	Registration area	Nonregistration area	1930	1920	1910
United States [1]	**11,891,143**	**11,221,472**	**10,463,131**	**6,966,516**	**3,496,615**	**9,827,763**	**1,935,976**	**7,891,787**	**94.4**	**66.6**	**19.7**
The North	**2,409,219**	**2,409,219**	**1,472,309**	**1,452,005**	**20,304**	**1,027,674**	**826,551**	**201,123**	**100.0**	**98.6**	**80.4**
The South [1]	**9,361,577**	**8,691,906**	**8,912,231**	**5,452,299**	**3,459,932**	**8,749,427**	**1,066,246**	**7,683,181**	**92.8**	**61.2**	**12.2**
The West	**120,347**	**120,347**	**78,591**	**62,212**	**16,379**	**50,662**	**43,179**	**7,483**	**100.0**	**79.2**	**85.2**
NEW ENGLAND	94,086	94,086	79,051	79,051	-	66,306	66,306	-	100.0	100.0	100.0
Maine	1,096	1,096	1,310	1,310	-	1,363	1,363	-	100.0	100.0	100.0
New Hampshire	790	790	621	621	-	564	564	-	100.0	100.0	100.0
Vermont	568	568	572	572	-	1,621	1,621	-	100.0	100.0	100.0
Massachusetts	52,365	52,365	45,466	45,466	-	38,055	38,055	-	100.0	100.0	100.0
Rhode Island	9,913	9,913	10,036	10,036	-	9,529	9,529	-	100.0	100.0	100.0
Connecticut	29,354	29,354	21,046	21,046	-	15,174	15,174	-	100.0	100.0	100.0
MIDDLE ATLANTIC	1,052,899	1,052,899	600,183	600,183	-	417,870	417,870	-	100.0	100.0	100.0
New York	412,814	412,814	198,483	198,483	-	134,191	134,191	-	100.0	100.0	100.0
New Jersey	208,828	208,828	117,132	117,132	-	89,760	89,760	-	100.0	100.0	100.0
Pennsylvania	431,257	431,257	284,568	284,568	-	193,919	193,919	-	100.0	100.0	100.0
EAST NORTH CENTRAL	930,450	930,450	514,554	514,554	-	300,836	244,137	56,699	100.0	100.0	81.2
Ohio	309,304	309,304	186,187	186,187	-	111,452	111,452	-	100.0	100.0	100.0
Indiana	111,982	111,982	80,810	80,810	-	60,320	60,320	-	100.0	100.0	100.0
Illinois	328,972	328,972	182,274	182,274	-	109,049	52,350	56,699	100.0	100.0	48.0
Michigan	169,453	169,453	60,082	60,082	-	17,115	17,115	-	100.0	100.0	100.0
Wisconsin	10,739	10,739	5,201	5,201	-	2,900	2,900	-	100.0	100.0	100.0
WEST NORTH CENTRAL	331,784	331,784	278,521	258,217	20,304	242,662	98,238	144,424	100.0	92.7	40.5
Minnesota	9,445	9,445	8,809	8,809	-	7,084	7,084	-	100.0	100.0	100.0
Iowa	17,380	17,380	19,005	-	19,005	14,973	-	14,973	100.0	-	-
Missouri	223,840	223,840	178,241	178,241	-	157,452	71,775	85,677	100.0	100.0	45.6
North Dakota	377	377	467	-	467	617	-	617	100.0	-	-
South Dakota	646	646	832	-	832	817	-	817	100.0	-	-
Nebraska	13,752	13,752	13,242	13,242	-	7,689	5,159	2,530	100.0	100.0	67.1
Kansas	66,344	66,344	57,925	57,925	-	54,030	14,220	39,810	100.0	100.0	26.3
SOUTH ATLANTIC	4,421,388	4,421,388	4,325,120	3,032,410	1,292,710	4,112,488	717,203	3,395,285	100.0	70.1	17.4
Delaware	32,602	32,602	30,335	30,335	-	31,181	9,081	22,100	100.0	100.0	29.1
Maryland	276,379	276,379	244,479	244,479	-	232,250	232,250	-	100.0	100.0	100.0
District of Columbia	132,068	132,068	109,966	109,966	-	94,446	94,446	-	100.0	100.0	100.0
Virginia	650,165	650,165	690,017	690,017	-	671,096	102,647	568,449	100.0	100.0	15.3
West Virginia	114,893	114,893	86,345	-	86,345	64,173	1,201	62,972	100.0	-	1.9
North Carolina	918,647	918,647	763,407	763,407	-	697,843	126,566	571,277	100.0	100.0	18.1
South Carolina	793,681	793,681	864,719	864,719	-	835,843	31,056	804,787	100.0	100.0	3.7
Georgia	1,071,125	1,071,125	1,206,365	-	1,206,365	1,176,987	85,148	1,091,839	100.0	-	7.2
Florida	431,828	431,828	329,487	329,487	-	308,669	34,808	273,861	100.0	100.0	11.3
EAST SOUTH CENTRAL	2,658,238	2,658,238	2,523,532	1,622,880	900,652	2,652,513	241,029	2,411,484	100.0	64.3	9.1
Kentucky	226,040	226,040	235,938	235,938	-	261,656	50,037	211,619	100.0	100.0	19.1
Tennessee	477,646	477,646	451,758	451,758	-	473,088	96,602	376,486	100.0	100.0	20.4
Alabama	944,834	944,834	900,652	-	900,652	908,282	94,390	813,892	100.0	-	10.4
Mississippi	1,009,718	1,009,718	935,184	935,184	-	1,009,487	-	1,009,487	100.0	100.0	-
WEST SOUTH CENTRAL [1]	2,281,951	1,612,280	2,063,579	797,009	1,266,570	1,984,426	108,014	1,876,412	70.7	38.6	5.4
Arkansas	478,463	478,463	472,220	-	472,220	442,891	-	442,891	100.0	-	-
Louisiana	776,326	776,326	700,257	700,257	-	713,874	89,262	624,612	100.0	100.0	12.5
Oklahoma	172,198	172,198	149,408	-	149,408	137,612	-	137,612	100.0	-	-
Texas [1]	854,964	185,293	741,694	96,752	644,942	690,049	18,752	671,297	21.7	13.0	2.7
MOUNTAIN	30,225	30,225	30,801	14,422	16,379	21,467	14,431	7,036	100.0	46.8	67.2
Montana	1,256	1,256	1,658	1,658	-	1,834	1,834	-	100.0	100.0	100.0
Idaho	668	668	920	-	920	651	-	651	100.0	-	-
Wyoming	1,250	1,250	1,375	-	1,375	2,235	-	2,235	100.0	-	-
Colorado	11,828	11,828	11,318	11,318	-	11,453	11,453	-	100.0	100.0	100.0
New Mexico	2,850	2,850	5,733	-	5,733	1,628	-	1,628	100.0	-	-
Arizona	10,749	10,749	8,005	-	8,005	2,009	-	2,009	100.0	-	-
Utah	1,108	1,108	1,446	1,446	-	1,144	1,144	-	100.0	100.0	100.0
Nevada	516	516	346	-	346	513	-	513	100.0	-	-
PACIFIC	90,122	90,122	47,790	47,790	-	29,195	28,748	447	100.0	100.0	98.5
Washington	6,840	6,840	6,883	6,883	-	6,058	6,058	-	100.0	100.0	100.0
Oregon	2,234	2,234	2,144	2,144	-	1,492	1,045	447	100.0	100.0	70.0
California	81,048	81,048	38,763	38,763	-	21,645	21,645	-	100.0	100.0	100.0

[1] Includes 669,671 Negroes not in registration area in 1930.

Table 9.—DEATHS (EXCLUSIVE OF STILLBIRTHS), BY AGE, SEX, COLOR, AND NATIVITY OF WHITE: 1931

[Native white includes native born of both parents native, of one or both foreign, and of both unknown or one unknown and one native. Mexicans are included with "other races"]

AREA AND AGE	ALL DEATHS		NEGRO		WHITE						INDIAN		CHINESE		JAPANESE		OTHER RACES	
					Native		Foreign		Unknown									
	Males	Females	Males	Females	Males	Females	Males	Females	Males	Females	Males	Females	Males	Females	Males	Females	Males	Females
THE REGISTRATION AREA IN CONTINENTAL UNITED STATES																		
All ages	726,132	596,455	93,349	84,009	468,822	392,451	141,002	108,543	12,936	4,274	2,597	2,453	1,153	148	756	297	5,517	4,280
Under 1 year	75,558	57,316	12,221	9,799	60,969	45,589	35	16	116	89	543	467	51	28	75	53	1,548	1,275
1 to 4 years	24,700	20,963	4,033	3,540	19,555	16,357	81	47	72	82	299	312	20	17	54	43	586	565
5 to 9 years	12,120	9,768	1,520	1,391	10,155	7,972	128	99	42	49	93	91	15	8	27	20	140	138
10 to 14 years	9,790	7,644	1,496	1,479	7,889	5,775	152	138	40	36	84	91	4	4	24	10	101	111
15 to 19 years	15,993	13,731	3,272	3,967	11,798	9,005	422	327	139	48	142	158	16	9	21	14	183	203
20 to 24 years	20,429	19,631	5,094	5,620	13,552	12,557	1,018	962	237	115	132	150	28	11	16	5	352	211
25 to 29 years	20,513	19,613	5,190	5,468	12,751	12,249	1,755	1,467	319	121	98	102	34	11	21	19	345	176
30 to 34 years	23,043	20,485	5,517	5,365	13,899	12,540	2,737	2,125	382	133	82	99	56	10	38	20	332	193
35 to 39 years	29,560	23,619	6,438	5,802	16,664	14,033	5,322	3,327	668	167	66	80	74	8	28	39	300	163
40 to 44 years	34,991	26,010	6,465	5,869	18,928	15,156	8,336	4,510	805	193	70	81	75	6	53	23	259	172
45 to 49 years	41,925	29,793	6,978	6,132	22,667	17,271	10,635	5,908	1,074	210	86	70	81	9	107	16	297	177
50 to 54 years	48,800	34,797	7,675	6,482	27,047	20,224	12,296	7,601	1,284	245	94	83	86	4	108	13	210	145
55 to 59 years	53,625	38,245	6,212	4,952	32,368	23,639	13,372	9,142	1,174	266	101	81	96	3	89	11	213	151
60 to 64 years	60,626	45,753	5,569	4,576	36,985	28,568	16,190	12,048	1,444	349	126	70	102	4	52	4	158	134
65 to 69 years	63,946	50,351	4,527	3,888	39,222	31,750	18,401	14,056	1,392	416	125	106	125	7	24	1	130	127
70 to 74 years	67,965	56,056	3,718	3,047	45,245	38,209	17,222	14,143	1,409	449	125	105	126	4	12	------	108	99
75 to 79 years	55,800	49,836	2,785	2,212	37,928	34,551	13,845	12,444	935	464	124	84	72	------	6	6	105	75
80 to 84 years	38,264	38,717	2,098	1,788	24,610	25,758	10,694	10,626	664	405	93	86	51	------	1	------	53	54
85 to 89 years	19,587	22,144	1,186	1,052	12,027	14,390	5,964	6,379	292	225	51	49	19	------	------	------	48	49
90 to 94 years	6,123	8,582	565	611	3,574	5,331	1,834	2,492	88	85	29	40	15	3	------	------	18	20
95 to 99 years	1,324	2,042	237	300	639	1,149	407	539	17	20	11	17	3	------	------	------	10	17
100 years and over	410	709	201	382	93	155	81	125	11	9	12	17	3	------	------	------	9	21
Unknown	1,040	650	352	287	257	223	75	22	332	98	11	14	1	2	------	------	12	4
REGISTRATION STATES OF 1920 [1]																		
All ages	622,020	513,273	70,888	63,536	401,628	339,422	132,483	102,941	10,293	3,150	1,228	1,083	1,083	137	719	288	3,698	2,716
Under 1 year	61,660	46,643	9,337	7,564	50,823	37,867	32	15	95	79	239	218	43	25	72	50	1,019	825
1 to 4 years	19,842	16,737	3,079	2,718	16,071	13,429	76	43	45	50	131	105	20	16	52	42	368	334
5 to 9 years	10,056	8,099	1,188	1,077	8,533	6,738	122	95	28	30	50	43	13	8	25	20	97	88
10 to 14 years	8,039	6,216	1,112	1,100	6,629	4,824	139	131	23	20	38	44	4	4	22	10	72	83
15 to 19 years	12,971	10,968	2,342	2,904	9,921	7,509	381	302	93	28	71	57	15	9	21	14	127	145
20 to 24 years	16,561	15,826	3,731	4,129	11,320	10,514	958	904	180	63	59	61	26	11	15	5	272	139
25 to 29 years	16,901	16,024	3,936	4,083	10,697	10,275	1,670	1,392	240	86	40	48	33	11	21	19	264	110
30 to 34 years	19,189	16,984	4,230	3,997	11,682	10,669	2,601	2,030	305	93	34	36	55	9	38	18	244	132
35 to 39 years	25,166	19,781	4,981	4,372	14,196	11,903	5,078	3,200	567	118	33	34	74	7	27	37	210	110
40 to 44 years	30,376	22,020	5,082	4,389	16,264	12,990	8,013	4,335	683	137	37	33	75	6	47	23	175	107
45 to 49 years	36,380	25,521	5,324	4,620	19,542	14,908	10,181	5,685	909	146	44	31	79	9	102	15	199	107
50 to 54 years	42,468	30,262	5,819	4,928	23,432	17,709	11,773	7,316	1,088	184	43	32	83	4	96	13	134	76
55 to 59 years	46,959	33,752	4,761	3,801	28,102	20,807	12,759	8,775	971	206	43	43	92	2	88	11	143	107
60 to 64 years	53,420	40,783	4,258	3,504	32,328	25,271	15,358	11,614	1,166	265	61	39	95	4	51	4	103	82
65 to 69 years	56,405	45,184	3,422	3,039	34,319	28,260	17,288	13,407	1,083	345	73	43	119	5	23	1	78	84
70 to 74 years	59,575	50,095	2,840	2,363	39,337	33,841	16,048	13,452	1,091	331	71	55	111	4	12	------	65	49
75 to 79 years	48,501	44,272	2,106	1,713	32,832	30,516	12,692	11,594	687	355	59	41	67	------	6	6	52	47
80 to 84 years	33,206	34,220	1,540	1,320	21,274	22,617	9,761	9,905	502	301	49	49	45	------	1	------	34	28
85 to 89 years	16,987	19,602	882	789	10,419	12,750	5,390	5,840	230	171	31	22	16	------	------	------	19	30
90 to 94 years	5,273	7,560	411	450	3,117	4,711	1,652	2,289	61	70	10	25	13	1	------	------	9	14
95 to 99 years	1,108	1,772	162	231	546	1,017	372	490	13	18	5	10	3	------	------	------	7	6
100 years and over	293	534	126	268	73	131	76	106	5	5	6	12	2	------	------	------	5	12
Unknown	684	418	219	177	171	166	63	21	228	49	1	2	------	2	------	------	2	1
REGISTRATION STATES [2]																		
All ages	717,630	589,643	91,587	82,436	463,871	388,626	140,179	107,902	12,643	4,180	2,595	2,453	1,146	148	752	297	4,857	3,601
Under 1 year	74,485	56,426	12,049	9,669	60,270	44,999	35	16	115	87	543	467	50	28	75	53	1,348	1,107
1 to 4 years	24,301	20,639	3,967	3,501	19,303	16,147	80	46	72	82	299	312	20	17	54	43	506	491
5 to 9 years	11,977	9,632	1,504	1,376	10,047	7,879	127	98	41	47	93	91	14	8	27	20	124	113
10 to 14 years	9,669	7,544	1,472	1,451	7,803	5,716	149	135	40	36	84	91	4	4	24	10	93	101
15 to 19 years	15,767	13,489	3,209	3,901	11,672	8,870	403	316	138	45	142	158	16	9	21	14	166	176
20 to 24 years	20,071	19,283	4,987	5,514	13,363	12,384	995	935	231	110	132	150	28	11	16	5	319	174
25 to 29 years	20,143	19,222	5,072	5,342	12,561	12,046	1,738	1,442	311	115	98	102	33	11	21	19	309	145
30 to 34 years	22,646	20,126	5,397	5,213	13,683	12,402	2,717	2,092	373	128	82	99	56	10	38	20	300	162
35 to 39 years	29,049	23,240	6,270	5,647	16,412	13,866	5,276	3,297	653	162	66	80	74	8	28	39	270	141
40 to 44 years	34,493	25,611	6,308	5,727	18,666	14,984	8,297	4,463	794	192	70	81	75	6	52	23	231	135
45 to 49 years	41,310	29,349	6,779	5,983	22,369	17,063	10,571	5,867	1,055	202	86	70	79	9	106	16	265	139
50 to 54 years	48,178	34,369	7,518	6,354	26,717	20,015	12,228	7,556	1,254	236	94	83	85	4	106	13	176	108
55 to 59 years	52,980	37,872	6,083	4,853	32,000	23,446	13,286	9,092	1,137	257	101	81	96	3	89	11	188	129
60 to 64 years	60,023	45,344	5,479	4,506	36,613	28,327	16,103	11,988	1,412	341	125	70	102	4	52	4	137	104
65 to 69 years	63,398	49,992	4,458	3,834	38,890	31,530	18,309	14,000	1,356	410	125	106	125	7	24	1	111	104
70 to 74 years	67,436	55,657	3,673	3,003	44,898	37,948	17,131	14,085	1,377	442	125	105	125	4	12	------	95	70
75 to 79 years	55,387	49,487	2,763	2,189	37,648	34,303	13,780	12,386	909	456	124	84	72	------	6	6	85	63
80 to 84 years	38,029	38,470	2,081	1,770	24,468	25,583	10,639	10,585	649	401	92	86	51	------	1	------	48	45
85 to 89 years	19,454	21,995	1,176	1,039	11,950	14,302	5,929	6,342	288	220	51	49	19	------	------	------	41	43
90 to 94 years	6,090	8,527	562	602	3,555	5,298	1,828	2,480	86	84	29	40	15	3	------	------	15	20
95 to 99 years	1,317	2,027	237	300	636	1,142	404	537	16	20	11	17	3	------	------	------	10	11
100 years and over	403	699	197	381	93	154	80	122	10	9	12	17	3	------	------	------	8	16
Unknown	1,024	643	346	281	254	222	74	22	326	98	11	14	1	2	------	------	12	4

[1] See table 3.

[2] Includes the Distict of Columbia.

TABLE 10.—NEGRO AND WHITE DEATHS (EXCLUSIVE OF STILLBIRTHS), BY AGE, AND SEX, IN THE REGISTRATION AREA IN CONTINENTAL UNITED STATES: 1931, 1930, AND 1929

AGE	NEGRO				NATIVE WHITE				FOREIGN WHITE			
	Total	Male	Female	Males per 100 females	Total	Male	Female	Males per 100 females	Total	Male	Female	Males per 100 females
1931												
Total	**177, 358**	**93, 349**	**84, 009**	**111. 1**	**861, 273**	**468, 822**	**392, 451**	**119. 5**	**249, 545**	**141, 002**	**108, 543**	**129. 9**
Under 1 year	22, 020	12, 221	9, 799	124. 7	106, 558	60, 969	45, 589	133. 7	51	35	16	218. 8
1 to 4 years	7, 573	4, 033	3, 540	113. 9	35, 912	19, 555	16, 357	119. 6	128	81	47	172. 3
5 to 9 years	2, 911	1, 520	1, 391	109. 3	18, 127	10, 155	7, 972	127. 4	227	128	99	129. 3
10 to 14 years	2, 975	1, 496	1, 479	101. 1	13, 664	7, 889	5, 775	136. 6	290	152	138	110. 1
15 to 19 years	7, 239	3, 272	3, 967	82. 5	20, 803	11, 798	9, 005	131. 0	749	422	327	129. 1
20 to 24 years	10, 714	5, 094	5, 620	90. 6	26, 109	13, 552	12, 557	107. 9	1, 980	1, 018	962	105. 8
25 to 29 years	10, 658	5, 190	5, 468	94. 9	25, 000	12, 751	12, 249	104. 1	3, 222	1, 755	1, 467	119. 6
30 to 34 years	10, 882	5, 517	5, 365	102. 8	26, 439	13, 899	12, 540	110. 8	4, 862	2, 737	2, 125	128. 8
35 to 39 years	12, 240	6, 438	5, 802	111. 0	30, 697	16, 664	14, 033	118. 7	8, 649	5, 322	3, 327	160. 0
40 to 44 years	12, 334	6, 465	5, 869	110. 2	34, 084	18, 928	15, 156	124. 9	12, 846	8, 336	4, 510	184. 8
45 to 49 years	13, 110	6, 978	6, 132	113. 8	39, 938	22, 667	17, 271	131. 2	16, 543	10, 635	5, 908	180. 0
50 to 54 years	14, 157	7, 675	6, 482	118. 4	47, 271	27, 047	20, 224	133. 7	19, 897	12, 296	7, 601	161. 8
55 to 59 years	11, 164	6, 212	4, 952	125. 4	56, 007	32, 368	23, 639	136. 9	22, 514	13, 372	9, 142	146. 3
60 to 64 years	10, 145	5, 569	4, 576	121. 7	65, 553	36, 985	28, 568	129. 5	28, 238	16, 190	12, 048	134. 4
65 to 69 years	8, 415	4, 527	3, 888	116. 4	70, 972	39, 222	31, 750	123. 5	32, 457	18, 401	14, 056	130. 9
70 to 74 years	6, 765	3, 718	3, 047	122. 0	83, 454	45, 245	38, 209	118. 4	31, 365	17, 222	14, 143	121. 8
75 to 79 years	4, 997	2, 785	2, 212	125. 9	72, 479	37, 928	34, 551	109. 8	26, 289	13, 845	12, 444	111. 3
80 to 84 years	3, 886	2, 098	1, 788	117. 3	50, 368	24, 610	25, 758	95. 5	21, 320	10, 694	10, 626	100. 6
85 to 89 years	2, 238	1, 186	1, 052	112. 7	26, 417	12, 027	14, 390	83. 6	12, 343	5, 964	6, 379	93. 5
90 years and over [1]	2, 935	1, 355	1, 580	85. 8	11, 421	4, 563	6, 858	66. 5	5, 575	2, 397	3, 178	75. 4
1930												
Total	**185, 503**	**97, 524**	**87, 979**	**110. 8**	**877, 018**	**475, 591**	**401, 427**	**118. 5**	**249, 423**	**141, 003**	**108, 420**	**130. 1**
Under 1 year	24, 178	13, 397	10, 781	124. 3	117, 738	67, 142	50, 596	132. 7	92	57	35	162. 9
1 to 4 years	8, 430	4, 489	3, 941	113. 9	39, 588	21, 624	17, 964	120. 4	184	95	89	106. 7
5 to 9 years	3, 182	1, 692	1, 490	113. 6	18, 926	10, 669	8, 257	129. 2	319	175	144	121. 5
10 to 14 years	3, 066	1, 512	1, 554	97. 3	13, 842	7, 994	5, 848	136. 7	325	190	135	140. 7
15 to 19 years	7, 704	3, 348	4, 356	76. 9	21, 543	11, 916	9, 627	123. 8	994	507	487	104. 1
20 to 24 years	10, 868	5, 158	5, 710	90. 3	27, 168	14, 137	13, 031	108. 5	2, 418	1, 319	1, 099	120. 0
25 to 29 years	11, 031	5, 333	5, 698	93. 6	25, 826	13, 139	12, 687	103. 6	3, 924	2, 206	1, 718	128. 4
30 to 34 years	10, 757	5, 555	5, 202	106. 8	26, 503	13, 785	12, 718	108. 4	5, 486	3, 136	2, 350	133. 4
35 to 39 years	12, 343	6, 282	6, 061	103. 6	30, 604	16, 258	14, 346	113. 3	9, 160	5, 682	3, 478	163. 4
40 to 44 years	12, 564	6, 579	5, 985	109. 9	33, 729	18, 585	15, 144	122. 7	13, 106	8, 445	4, 661	181. 2
45 to 49 years	13, 908	7, 475	6, 433	116. 2	39, 180	22, 007	17, 173	128. 1	16, 310	10, 352	5, 958	173. 7
50 to 54 years	14, 831	8, 125	6, 706	121. 2	47, 167	27, 051	20, 116	134. 5	19, 632	12, 174	7, 458	163. 2
55 to 59 years	11, 445	6, 351	5, 094	124. 7	55, 257	31, 616	23, 641	133. 7	22, 401	13, 299	9, 102	146. 1
60 to 64 years	10, 501	5, 787	4, 714	122. 8	65, 286	37, 064	28, 222	131. 3	28, 490	16, 265	12, 225	133. 0
65 to 69 years	8, 610	4, 746	3, 864	122. 8	73, 156	40, 425	32, 731	123. 5	31, 636	17, 921	13, 715	130. 7
70 to 74 years	7, 020	3, 845	3, 175	121. 1	82, 703	44, 715	37, 988	117. 7	30, 274	16, 676	13, 598	122. 6
75 to 79 years	5, 120	2, 800	2, 320	120. 7	71, 151	36, 977	34, 174	108. 2	26, 451	13, 987	12, 464	112. 2
80 to 84 years	4, 013	2, 161	1, 852	116. 7	50, 067	24, 397	25, 670	95. 0	20, 922	10, 401	10, 521	98. 9
85 to 89 years	2, 396	1, 287	1, 109	116. 1	26, 600	11, 732	14, 868	78. 9	11, 956	5, 799	6, 157	94. 2
90 years and over [1]	3, 536	1, 602	1, 934	82. 8	10, 984	4, 358	6, 626	65. 8	5, 343	2, 317	3, 026	76. 6
1929												
Total	**189, 915**	**99, 836**	**90, 079**	**110. 8**	**907, 969**	**488, 351**	**419, 618**	**116. 4**	**261, 647**	**147, 110**	**114, 537**	**128. 4**
Under 1 year	24, 191	13, 479	10, 712	125. 8	123, 191	70, 081	53, 110	132. 0	129	80	49	163. 3
1 to 4 years	9, 368	4, 945	4, 423	111. 8	46, 557	25, 023	21, 534	116. 2	261	141	120	117. 5
5 to 9 years	3, 475	1, 808	1, 667	108. 5	20, 761	11, 583	9, 178	126. 2	407	235	172	136. 6
10 to 14 years	2, 969	1, 556	1, 413	110. 1	15, 133	8, 703	6, 430	135. 3	358	198	160	123. 8
15 to 19 years	7, 811	3, 394	4, 417	76. 8	23, 023	12, 652	10, 371	122. 0	1, 278	673	605	111. 2
20 to 24 years	11, 550	5, 476	6, 074	90. 2	28, 603	14, 484	14, 119	102. 6	3, 051	1, 629	1, 422	114. 6
25 to 29 years	11, 887	5, 714	6, 173	92. 6	27, 353	13, 800	13, 553	101. 8	4, 653	2, 587	2, 066	125. 2
30 to 34 years	10, 749	5, 451	5, 298	102. 9	27, 972	14, 166	13, 806	102. 6	6, 453	3, 667	2, 786	131. 6
35 to 39 years	12, 761	6, 444	6, 317	102. 0	31, 903	16, 833	15, 070	111. 7	10, 468	6, 414	4, 054	158. 2
40 to 44 years	13, 008	6, 801	6, 207	109. 6	34, 602	19, 094	15, 508	123. 1	14, 169	9, 128	5, 041	181. 1
45 to 49 years	13, 781	7, 422	6, 359	116. 7	39, 869	22, 183	17, 686	125. 4	17, 132	10, 999	6, 133	179. 3
50 to 54 years	14, 629	8, 027	6, 602	121. 6	47, 288	26, 752	20, 536	130. 3	19, 800	12, 136	7, 664	158. 4
55 to 59 years	11, 223	6, 245	4, 978	125. 5	55, 892	32, 027	23, 865	134. 2	23, 201	13, 657	9, 544	143. 1
60 to 64 years	10, 370	5, 688	4, 682	121. 5	63, 545	35, 648	27, 897	127. 8	29, 028	16, 648	12, 380	134. 5
65 to 69 years	8, 341	4, 634	3, 707	125. 0	75, 661	41, 425	34, 236	121. 0	32, 624	18, 310	14, 314	127. 9
70 to 74 years	7, 094	3, 971	3, 123	127. 2	82, 551	44, 334	38, 217	116. 0	30, 522	16, 798	13, 724	122. 4
75 to 79 years	5, 715	3, 228	2, 487	129. 8	72, 625	37, 451	35, 174	106. 5	28, 066	14, 709	13, 357	110. 1
80 to 84 years	4, 471	2, 351	2, 120	110. 9	51, 906	25, 271	26, 635	94. 9	21, 854	10, 777	11, 077	97. 3
85 to 89 years	2, 697	1, 441	1, 256	114. 7	27, 928	12, 345	15, 583	79. 2	12, 729	5, 991	6, 738	88. 9
90 years and over [1]	3, 825	1, 761	2, 064	85. 3	11, 606	4, 496	7, 110	63. 2	5, 464	2, 333	3, 131	74. 5

[1] Includes persons of unknown age.

Table 11.—COLORED[1] AND WHITE DEATH RATE (EXCLUSIVE OF STILLBIRTHS) FROM ALL CAUSES, FOR SELECTED CITIES: 1931, 1930, AND 1920

[Includes cities whose Negro population represents 81 percent or more of the colored population, where data by color are available]

CITY AND COLOR	RATE PER 1,000 ESTIMATED POPULATION JULY 1		
	1931	1930	1920
Akron, Ohio	7.7	7.8	11.7
Colored	13.5	(2)	(2)
White	7.5	(2)	(2)
Asheville, N. C	14.1	15.4	25.2
Colored	14.5	17.1	24.3
White	13.9	14.7	25.5
Atlanta, Ga	14.9	15.5	17.1
Colored	21.6	23.2	22.8
White	11.6	11.6	14.6
Atlantic City, N. J	17.0	16.8	17.0
Colored	18.2	17.0	19.0
White	16.6	16.8	16.7
Augusta, Ga	20.1	20.0	21.2
Colored	25.6	27.9	25.4
White	16.5	14.7	18.1
Baltimore, Md	14.2	13.9	15.4
Colored	19.9	19.6	23.3
White	12.9	12.7	14.0
Baton Rouge, La	9.1	9.4	15.1
Colored	12.3	10.8	21.3
White	7.5	8.6	11.1
Bessemer, Ala	13.1	14.1	(3)
Colored	14.6	15.6	(3)
White	11.1	12.1	(3)
Birmingham, Ala	13.0	13.6	16.3
Colored	17.7	19.3	22.6
White	10.2	10.0	12.3
Boston, Mass	14.0	14.1	15.5
Colored	18.1	20.0	25.2
White	13.9	13.9	15.2
Buffalo, N. Y	12.7	12.9	14.7
Colored	18.0	(2)	(2)
White	12.6	(2)	(2)
Camden, N. J	14.1	13.4	14.9
Colored	17.9	(2)	(2)
White	13.7	(2)	(2)
Charleston, S. C	23.2	[4]22.9	23.7
Colored	33.6	[4]33.0	31.6
White	14.5	[4]14.6	16.7
Charlotte, N. C	12.4	12.8	15.6
Colored	19.4	19.1	19.0
White	9.3	10.1	14.0
Chattanooga, Tenn	13.6	15.7	19.4
Colored	20.1	24.8	27.6
White	11.1	12.2	15.5
Chicago, Ill	10.4	10.4	12.7
Colored	15.3	15.4	19.4
White	10.0	10.0	12.4
Cincinnati, Ohio	15.7	15.5	15.0
Colored	23.7	23.5	23.8
White	14.7	14.5	14.3
Cleveland, Ohio	11.0	11.0	12.5
Colored	17.2	17.4	21.0
White	10.5	10.4	12.1
Columbia, S. C	24.6	24.3	34.1
Colored	30.2	30.4	43.7
White	20.0	20.8	28.1
Columbus, Ga	17.7	18.0	(3)
Colored	24.1	24.2	(3)
White	14.5	14.9	(3)
Columbus, Ohio	13.4	15.3	14.8
Colored	15.7	18.3	21.1
White	13.1	15.0	14.1
Dallas, Tex	11.1	11.5	13.3
Colored	20.1	19.0	20.4
White	9.2	9.9	12.0
Dayton, Ohio	11.8	11.0	12.2
Colored	16.3	(2)	(2)
White	11.3	(2)	(2)
Detroit, Mich	8.1	9.3	13.5
Colored	13.2	15.6	22.9
White	7.6	8.7	13.0
Durham, N. C	15.4	15.6	17.0
Colored	20.1	22.4	29.9
White	12.6	11.8	10.0
East St. Louis, Ill	12.1	11.9	12.3
Colored	19.7	14.9	23.4
White	10.6	11.3	10.9
Fort Worth, Tex	10.5	11.0	(3)
Colored	14.7	16.3	(3)
White	9.7	10.0	(3)
Gary, Ind	9.6	9.6	13.8
Colored	12.2	(2)	(2)
White	8.9	(2)	(2)
Greensboro, N. C	11.6	12.4	18.3
Colored	16.1	18.0	24.7
White	10.1	10.4	15.6
Greenville, S. C	16.2	18.1	14.8
Colored	23.7	26.6	19.5
White	11.8	13.0	12.2
Houston, Tex	10.9	12.2	13.5
Colored	15.6	19.1	18.2
White	9.1	9.7	12.0
Indianapolis, Ind	13.6	14.2	14.6
Colored	17.3	19.6	21.1
White	13.1	13.5	13.8
Jackson, Miss	16.1	16.3	33.6
Colored	21.0	21.1	48.5
White	12.7	13.1	22.2
Jacksonville, Fla	14.7	15.2	16.9
Colored	20.4	21.0	20.3
White	11.5	11.8	14.1
Jersey City, N. J	11.2	11.3	14.1
Colored	16.9	(2)	(2)
White	10.9	(2)	(2)
Kansas City, Kans	12.8	13.7	14.5
Colored	14.8	14.9	20.6
White	12.3	13.5	13.5
Kansas City, Mo	12.8	13.2	16.1
Colored	20.5	21.8	24.9
White	11.8	12.2	15.2
Knoxville, Tenn	12.7	14.1	17.0
Colored	16.9	18.5	21.7
White	11.9	13.2	16.2
Lexington, Ky	24.8	24.3	22.9
Colored	29.8	32.9	28.0
White	22.9	21.0	20.8
Little Rock, Ark	20.9	22.5	(3)
Colored	30.9	35.0	(3)
White	17.8	18.6	(3)
Louisville, Ky	14.0	14.3	15.0
Colored	21.8	23.2	21.9
White	12.6	12.6	13.6
Macon, Ga	17.5	19.7	(3)
Colored	22.9	26.4	(3)
White	13.4	14.7	(3)
Memphis, Tenn	16.6	17.3	19.8
Colored	21.5	23.5	26.8
White	13.6	13.5	15.6
Meridian, Miss	21.1	20.8	27.3
Colored	26.1	25.8	36.1
White	18.3	18.1	22.4
Miami, Fla	11.4	11.1	15.0
Colored	14.7	15.2	20.7
White	10.5	9.9	12.5
Mobile, Ala	16.3	18.2	18.3
Colored	21.6	23.9	23.6
White	13.3	15.0	14.9
Monroe, La	15.3	18.8	18.9
Colored	18.2	21.8	23.6
White	13.5	16.8	15.4
Montgomery, Ala	15.3	17.2	20.1
Colored	20.1	22.1	27.0
White	11.4	13.1	14.3
Nashville, Tenn	16.7	16.3	18.1
Colored	22.4	23.1	24.0
White	14.6	13.7	15.5
Newark, N. J	11.4	11.9	12.9
Colored	15.6	18.8	23.3
White	10.9	11.2	12.4
New Orleans, La	16.4	17.4	17.6
Colored	23.5	25.0	26.2
White	13.5	14.4	14.5
Newport News, Va	14.5	[4]13.9	14.7
Colored	21.0	[4]19.6	21.1
White	10.5	[4]10.3	10.5
New York, N. Y	10.9	10.8	12.9
Colored	16.2	16.2	18.8
White	10.6	10.5	12.7
Norfolk, Va	13.2	[4]13.6	15.5
Colored	19.1	[4]20.4	21.1
White	10.1	[4]10.1	12.1
Petersburg, Va	16.7	[4]18.4	19.4
Colored	21.1	[4]24.6	25.9
White	13.3	[4]13.5	14.3
Philadelphia, Pa	12.8	12.5	14.5
Colored	15.9	16.1	20.9
White	12.4	12.1	14.0
Pittsburgh, Pa	14.1	13.9	16.4
Colored	20.8	19.7	22.2
White	13.4	13.3	16.0
Portsmouth, Va	15.3	[4]13.5	14.9
Colored	22.1	[4]19.9	20.9
White	10.4	[4]9.0	10.4
Raleigh, N. C	17.9	20.5	22.8
Colored	21.2	23.7	27.0
White	16.2	18.8	20.6
Richmond, Va	15.5	14.9	16.5
Colored	21.4	21.4	23.3
White	13.1	12.3	13.4
Roanoke, Va	11.9	13.8	16.6
Colored	18.2	22.3	25.2
White	10.5	11.9	14.6
St. Louis, Mo	14.6	13.9	14.1
Colored	21.7	20.7	19.9
White	13.7	13.1	13.5
Savannah, Ga	19.3	19.5	23.6
Colored	26.1	26.5	31.4
White	13.5	13.6	16.7
Shreveport, La	20.5	21.7	25.7
Colored	30.1	32.1	38.3
White	15.5	16.0	15.2
Tampa, Fla	11.2	11.6	13.4
Colored	15.4	15.9	20.8
White	10.1	10.4	11.2
Toledo, Ohio	11.8	12.6	13.9
Colored	17.2	(2)	(2)
White	11.5	(2)	(2)
Tulsa, Okla	8.0	9.9	(3)
Colored	11.2	15.6	(3)
White	7.5	9.1	(3)
Vicksburg, Miss	28.2	32.2	[5]32.1
Colored	35.2	43.4	46.1
White	20.5	20.0	17.6
Washington, D. C	15.8	15.1	14.7
Colored	22.0	21.0	20.6
White	13.4	12.9	12.7
Wilmington, Del	13.9	[4]14.6	14.2
Colored	20.9	[4]23.1	23.0
White	13.0	[4]13.6	13.2
Wilmington, N. C	17.3	[4]19.4	19.6
Colored	23.3	[4]24.9	25.3
White	13.1	[4]15.7	15.8
Winston-Salem, N. C	12.5	14.1	15.5
Colored	17.5	18.9	20.9
White	8.7	10.4	11.4
Youngstown, Ohio	9.7	10.5	13.0
Colored	14.3	(2)	(2)
White	9.3	(2)	(2)

[1] Includes Negro and other nonwhite races.
[2] Figures by color not available.
[3] Not in registration area.
[4] Population Apr. 1, 1930. No estimate made.
[5] Population April 1, 1920. No estimate made.

TABLE 12.—TOTAL COLORED [1] AND WHITE DEATHS (EXCLUSIVE OF STILLBIRTHS), DEATHS OF RESIDENTS, AND DEATH RATES, IN CITIES HAVING 25,000 OR MORE NEGRO INHABITANTS: 1930

CITY AND COLOR	TOTAL DEATHS		DEATHS OF RESIDENTS [2]	
	Number	Rate per 1,000 estimated population, July 1, 1930	Number	Rate per 1,000 estimated population, July 1, 1930
Atlanta, Ga.	4,205	15.5	3,945	14.5
Colored	2,106	23.2	2,068	22.8
White	2,099	11.6	1,877	10.4
Baltimore, Md.	11,239	13.9	10,447	13.0
Colored	2,815	19.6	2,712	18.9
White	8,424	12.7	7,735	11.7
Birmingham, Ala.	3,548	13.6	3,251	12.4
Colored	1,925	19.3	1,841	18.4
White	1,623	10.0	1,410	8.7
Charleston, S. C.	1,426	22.9	(3)	
Colored	927	33.0	(3)	
White	499	14.6	(3)	
Charlotte, N. C.	1,065	12.8	970	11.7
Colored	481	19.1	474	18.8
White	584	10.1	496	8.6
Chattanooga, Tenn.	1,883	15.7	1,841	15.3
Colored	825	24.8	826	24.8
White	1,058	12.2	1,015	11.7
Chicago, Ill.	35,316	10.4	35,545	10.5
Colored	4,045	15.4	4,060	15.5
White	31,271	10.0	31,485	10.1
Cincinnati, Ohio	7,005	15.5	6,439	14.2
Colored	1,139	23.5	1,106	22.8
White	5,866	14.5	5,333	13.2
Cleveland, Ohio	9,906	11.0	9,597	10.6
Colored	1,293	17.4	1,292	17.4
White	8,613	10.4	8,305	10.0
Columbus, Ohio	4,470	15.3	4,002	13.7
Colored	608	18.3	593	17.9
White	3,862	15.0	3,409	13.2
Dallas, Tex.	3,012	11.5	2,625	10.0
Colored	859	19.0	782	17.3
White	2,153	9.9	1,843	8.5
Detroit, Mich.	14,729	9.3	14,947	9.4
Colored	2,037	15.6	2,138	16.3
White	12,692	8.7	12,809	8.8

CITY AND COLOR	TOTAL DEATHS		DEATHS OF RESIDENTS [2]	
	Number	Rate per 1,000 estimated population, July 1, 1930	Number	Rate per 1,000 estimated population, July 1, 1930
Houston, Tex.	3,598	12.2	3,382	11.5
Colored	1,495	19.1	1,449	18.5
White	2,103	9.7	1,933	8.9
Indianapolis, Ind.	5,193	14.2	4,926	13.5
Colored	867	19.6	876	19.8
White	4,326	13.5	4,050	12.6
Jacksonville, Fla.	1,977	15.2	1,802	13.9
Colored	1,014	21.0	978	20.3
White	963	11.8	824	10.1
Kansas City, Mo.	5,301	13.2	4,987	12.4
Colored	922	21.8	930	22.0
White	4,379	12.2	4,057	11.3
Los Angeles, Calif.	14,028	11.2	13,953	11.1
Colored	(4)	(4)	(3)	(3)
White	(4)	(4)	(3)	(3)
Louisville, Ky.	4,390	14.3	(3)	(3)
Colored	1,104	23.2	(3)	(3)
White	3,286	12.6	(3)	(3)
Memphis, Tenn.	4,398	17.3	3,897	15.3
Colored	2,274	23.5	2,159	22.3
White	2,124	13.5	1,738	11.1
Miami, Fla.	1,232	11.1	1,087	9.8
Colored	382	15.2	372	14.8
White	850	9.9	715	8.3
Montgomery, Ala.	1,138	17.2	1,002	15.1
Colored	664	22.1	633	21.0
White	474	13.1	369	10.2
Nashville, Tenn.	2,510	16.3	2,238	14.5
Colored	990	23.1	935	21.8
White	1,520	13.7	1,303	11.7
Newark, N. J.	5,263	11.9	5,210	11.8
Colored	759	18.8	821	20.4
White	4,504	11.2	4,389	10.9
New Orleans, La.	8,030	17.4	6,804	14.8
Colored	3,289	25.0	2,737	20.8
White	4,741	14.4	4,067	12.4

CITY AND COLOR	TOTAL DEATHS		DEATHS OF RESIDENTS [2]	
	Number	Rate per 1,000 estimated population, July 1, 1930	Number	Rate per 1,000 estimated population, July 1, 1930
New York, N. Y.	74,913	10.8	75,341	10.8
Colored	5,630	16.2	5,572	16.0
White	69,283	10.5	69,769	10.5
Norfolk, Va.	1,763	13.6	1,602	12.4
Colored	902	20.4	849	19.2
White	861	10.1	753	8.8
Philadelphia, Pa.	24,516	12.5	24,692	12.6
Colored	3,620	16.1	3,636	16.2
White	20,896	12.1	21,056	12.2
Pittsburgh, Pa.	9,312	13.9	9,002	13.4
Colored	1,103	19.7	1,094	19.6
White	8,209	13.3	7,908	12.9
Richmond, Va.	2,737	14.9	2,439	13.3
Colored	1,132	21.4	1,054	19.9
White	1,605	12.3	1,385	10.6
St. Louis, Mo.	11,482	13.9	10,842	13.2
Colored	1,982	20.7	1,963	20.5
White	9,500	13.1	8,879	12.2
Savannah, Ga.	1,660	19.5	1,453	17.1
Colored	1,033	26.5	948	24.3
White	627	13.6	505	11.0
Shreveport, La.	1,669	21.7	993	12.9
Colored	874	32.1	490	18.0
White	795	16.0	503	10.1
Washington, D. C.	7,387	15.1	6,982	14.3
Colored	2,792	21.0	2,657	20.0
White	4,595	12.9	4,325	12.2
Winston-Salem, N. C.	1,067	14.1	1,019	13.5
Colored	620	18.9	616	18.8
White	447	10.4	403	9.4

[1] Includes Negro, nonwhite, and other races.
[2] The term "residents" excludes all nonresidents and includes residents who died elsewhere in the registration area.
[3] Reliable data for nonresidents are not available.
[4] Deaths and death rates by color not available.

TABLE 13.—COLORED [1] AND WHITE DEATH RATE FROM DISEASES OF THE HEART, IN SELECTED STATES AND CITIES: 1931, 1930, AND 1920

AREA AND COLOR	RATE PER 100,000 ESTIMATED POPULATION JULY 1		
	1931	1930	1920
SELECTED STATES [2]			
ALABAMA	122.5	139.8	(3)
Colored	147.2	177.5	(3)
White	108.9	118.8	(3)
ARKANSAS	111.2	116.8	(3)
Colored	130.8	159.6	(3)
White	104.3	101.9	(3)
CONNECTICUT	258.7	260.9	171.5
Colored	338.7	333.3	(4)
White	257.1	259.5	(4)
DELAWARE	277.5	264.4	174.7
Colored	348.5	339.4	(4)
White	266.2	252.4	(4)
FLORIDA	188.5	193.8	113.3
Colored	187.0	210.1	105.6
White	189.1	187.0	119.6
GEORGIA	142.6	153.8	(3)
Colored	182.6	200.4	(3)
White	119.6	126.8	(3)
ILLINOIS	232.1	223.1	161.9
Colored	283.3	282.9	(4)
White	229.4	220.1	(4)
INDIANA	233.8	241.4	166.6
Colored	285.7	330.9	(4)
White	231.7	237.8	(4)
IOWA	189.6	192.3	(3)
Colored	187.0	217.4	(3)
White	189.6	192.0	(3)
KANSAS	176.0	178.0	128.7
Colored	204.5	214.6	(4)
White	174.6	176.2	(4)

AREA AND COLOR	RATE PER 100,000 ESTIMATED POPULATION JULY 1		
	1931	1930	1920
SELECTED STATES—Continued			
KENTUCKY	159.3	160.4	99.6
Colored	328.8	377.9	210.0
White	143.4	139.9	87.9
LOUISIANA	185.5	197.0	119.6
Colored	227.8	248.2	146.3
White	160.4	166.7	103.4
MARYLAND	259.8	255.9	181.7
Colored	296.1	304.7	232.5
White	252.3	245.9	171.5
MASSACHUSETTS	287.4	281.5	215.9
Colored	331.6	247.4	(4)
White	286.8	282.0	(4)
MICHIGAN	211.3	209.7	176.1
Colored	228.4	249.2	(4)
White	210.5	208.0	(4)
MISSISSIPPI	123.5	135.6	93.2
Colored	127.7	147.7	110.1
White	119.2	123.4	75.9
MISSOURI	218.7	216.3	136.0
Colored	369.7	364.7	(4)
White	208.3	206.2	(4)
NEBRASKA	171.5	166.7	107.6
Colored	245.8	266.7	(4)
White	170.2	164.9	(4)
NEW HAMPSHIRE	295.5	297.9	240.2
Colored	100.0	200.0	(4)
White	295.9	298.1	( )
NEW JERSEY	253.0	245.6	178.5
Colored	278.2	275.7	(4)
White	251.6	243.9	(4)

AREA AND COLOR	RATE PER 100,000 ESTIMATED POPULATION JULY 1		
	1931	1930	1920
SELECTED STATES—Continued			
NEW YORK	287.8	286.3	211.9
Colored	254.7	253.0	(4)
White	289.0	287.5	(4)
NORTH CAROLINA	140.5	154.5	101.7
Colored	164.9	183.9	120.8
White	130.3	142.3	94.1
OHIO	221.5	225.3	160.6
Colored	268.3	285.0	(4)
White	219.1	222.3	(4)
OKLAHOMA	97.8	92.9	(3)
Colored	110.1	105.8	(3)
White	96.2	91.2	(3)
PENNSYLVANIA	247.6	243.5	160.8
Colored	280.4	277.7	(4)
White	246.0	241.9	(4)
RHODE ISLAND	251.4	260.6	182.1
Colored	363.6	581.8	(4)
White	249.6	255.4	(4)
SOUTH CAROLINA	164.7	177.9	109.0
Colored	189.9	206.2	113.0
White	143.9	154.3	104.0
TENNESSEE	128.1	129.2	96.1
Colored	206.7	221.8	154.4
White	110.7	108.6	82.5
VERMONT	281.4	298.3	259.1
Colored	300.0	100.0	(4)
White	281.3	298.9	( )
VIRGINIA	202.6	202.6	138.1
Colored	277.3	283.7	176.7
White	175.4	172.8	121.1

AREA AND COLOR	RATE PER 100,000 ESTIMATED POPULATION JULY 1		
	1931	1930	1920
SELECTED STATES—Continued			
WEST VIRGINIA	116.8	128.0	(3)
Colored	165.8	195.7	(3)
White	113.3	123.1	(3)
SELECTED CITIES OF 100,000 POPULATION OR MORE IN 1930			
Akron	139.8	148.7	109.3
Colored	180.3	(4)	(4)
White	137.8	(4)	(4)
Atlanta	194.2	216.0	147.5
Colored	262.9	285.6	195.3
White	159.4	181.2	125.6
Baltimore	281.4	274.7	194.0
Colored	314.5	345.6	287.3
White	274.1	259.4	177.5
Birmingham	146.7	169.7	153.8
Colored	160.8	230.5	209.3
White	138.0	132.3	118.0
Boston	332.1	311.8	249.4
Colored	395.7	283.2	(4)
White	330.2	312.6	(4)
Buffalo	283.9	273.4	195.3
Colored	259.7	(4)	(4)
White	284.4	(4)	( )
Camden	247.9	250.0	187.2
Colored	245.8	(4)	(4)
White	248.1	(4)	(4)

See footnotes at end of table.

TABLE 13.—COLORED[1] AND WHITE DEATH RATE FROM DISEASES OF THE HEART, IN SELECTED STATES AND CITIES: 1931, 1930, AND 1920—Continued

Area and color	Rate per 100,000 estimated population, July 1: 1931	1930	1920
SELECTED CITIES OF 100,000 POPULATION OR MORE IN 1930—continued			
Chattanooga	130.1	169.9	162.4
Colored	166.7	270.3	226.5
White	116.3	131.3	131.6
Chicago	223.6	218.9	176.4
Colored	260.9	266.6	(4)
White	220.4	214.9	(4)
Cincinnati	284.3	273.0	210.3
Colored	292.8	329.9	257.9
White	283.2	266.2	206.4
Cleveland	195.7	197.2	120.8
Colored	224.1	236.9	(4)
White	193.1	193.6	(4)
Columbus, Ohio	239.5	276.8	161.1
Colored	268.2	322.3	228.0
White	235.7	271.0	154.1
Dallas	160.4	161.5	110.2
Colored	204.3	199.6	157.8
White	151.3	153.6	101.8
Dayton	240.5	252.1	149.1
Colored	275.3	(4)	(4)
White	237.1	(4)	(4)
Detroit	162.0	164.6	126.8
Colored	221.3	240.6	(4)
White	156.5	157.8	(4)
El Paso	126.7	142.9	(4)
Colored	103.3	113.3	(4)
White	161.5	185.7	(4)
Fort Worth	137.4	145.0	(3)
Colored	128.3	163.5	(3)
White	139.1	141.5	(3)
Gary	124.6	119.2	71.2
Colored	111.1	(4)	(4)
White	128.5	(4)	(4)
Houston	130.3	140.2	110.2
Colored	144.8	162.0	128.0
White	125.1	132.3	104.5
Indianapolis	282.6	292.1	190.5
Colored	358.4	367.9	266.8
White	272.0	231.6	181.0
Jacksonville, Fla	238.8	263.1	140.6
Colored	305.6	350.6	144.6
White	200.5	211.5	137.3
Jersey City	253.6	252.2	184.9
Colored	335.8	(4)	(4)
White	250.0	(4)	(4)
Kansas City, Kans	208.3	229.3	134.8
Colored	198.3	205.2	217.9
White	210.6	234.9	120.8
Kansas City, Mo	236.2	224.9	199.3
Colored	408.4	350.7	396.3
White	216.0	210.1	178.6
Knoxville	161.2	163.4	141.4
Colored	241.6	254.3	302.0
White	145.5	145.7	113.9
Louisville	287.1	282.6	183.1
Colored	406.7	482.1	305.5
White	2o5.2	246.2	158.1
Memphis	217.9	216.1	138.3
Colored	266.9	280.7	150.1
White	187.6	176.3	131.1
Miami	175.1	160.4	127.5
Colored	126.5	134.9	124.8
White	139.2	167.8	128.7
Nashville	249.5	209.5	201.0
Colored	361.3	321.7	314.1
White	206.9	166.2	152.5
Newark, N. J	250.4	260.7	183.0
Colored	230.6	280.4	(4)
White	252.5	258.8	(4)
New Orleans	324.5	336.6	226.8
Colored	428 7	445.0	301.8
White	282.4	293.2	200.0
New York	264.6	266.5	186.4
Colored	251.8	253.2	(4)
White	265.3	267.2	(4)
Norfolk	292.2	288.3	163.5
Colored	425.4	445.8	210.9
White	223.4	207.0	135.0
Oklahoma City	126.0	130.6	(4)
Colored	215.1	169.7	(4)
White	117.5	126.8	(4)
Omaha	234.0	216.8	152.6
Colored	344.0	333.3	(4)
White	227.2	209.7	(4)
Philadelphia	316.6	303.1	206.0
Colored	274.6	286.2	213.1
White	322.3	305.3	205.4
Pittsburgh	230.0	228.9	146.6
Colored	221.8	266.5	(4)
White	230.8	225.5	(4)
Richmond, Va	263.7	250.5	177.7
Colored	313.8	324.5	185.0
White	243.5	220.4	174.3
St. Louis	318.3	309.5	177.5
Colored	414.3	423.2	251.9
White	305.4	294.6	169.9
San Antonio	145.8	167.2	107.4
Colored	(4)	(4)	(4)
White	(4)	(4)	(4)
Tampa	202.9	189.4	111.1
Colored	279.3	279.1	126.2
White	182.4	165.4	106.7
Toledo	217.1	279.8	160.0
Colored	246.7	(4)	(4)
White	215.5	(4)	(4)
Tulsa	109.7	116.9	(3)
Colored	44.9	109.2	(3)
White	118.8	118.0	(3)
Washington, D. C	331.0	336.3	210.0
Colored	373.3	400.8	232.6
White	314.9	312.1	202.3
Wilmington, Del	261.7	274.9	140.9
Colored	370.7	321.3	184.3
White	247.7	268.9	136.2
Youngstown	155.6	170.7	92.2
Colored	195.0	(4)	(4)
White	151.6	(4)	(4)

[1] Includes Negro, nonwhite, and other races.
[2] States in registration area whose Negro population represented 55 percent or more of the total colored population in 1930.
[3] Not in registration area.
[4] Death rates by color not available.

TABLE 14.—COLORED[1] AND WHITE DEATH RATE FROM TUBERCULOSIS OF THE RESPIRATORY SYSTEM, IN SELECTED STATES, AND CITIES: 1931, 1930, AND 1920

Area and color	Rate per 100,000 estimated population, July 1: 1931	1930	1920
SELECTED STATES[2]			
ALABAMA	78.3	77.1	(3)
Colored	143.0	136.6	(3)
White	42.7	44.1	(3)
ARKANSAS	68.2	68.0	(3)
Colored	126.0	115.6	(3)
White	48.0	51.3	(3)
CONNECTICUT	49.6	52.5	100.0
Colored	219.4	243.3	(4)
White	46.3	48.9	(4)
DELAWARE	80.0	62.3	126.5
Colored	206.1	166.7	(4)
White	59.9	45.6	(4)
FLORIDA	65.3	63.1	91.2
Colored	135.5	123.0	158.4
White	36.3	38.2	56.9
GEORGIA	68.5	68.9	(3)
Colored	128.6	122.7	(3)
White	34.1	37.8	(3)
ILLINOIS	55.0	55.3	85.4
Colored	228.6	226.0	(4)
White	46.0	46.7	(4)
INDIANA	52.4	58.0	88.6
Colored	186.5	193.5	(4)
White	47.0	52.7	(4)
IOWA	25.8	28.5	(3)
Colored	143.5	226.1	(3)
White	24.7	26.6	(3)
KANSAS	32.4	32.0	39.4
Colored	113.5	112.4	(4)
White	28.4	28.0	(4)
KENTUCKY	83.1	84.5	130.7
Colored	205.8	198.7	309.9
White	71.6	73.7	111.5
LOUISIANA	77.1	78.0	126.8
Colored	131.5	128.2	211.9
White	44.9	48.3	72.6
MARYLAND	86.3	89.1	126.1
Colored	218.6	220.9	271.4
White	59.2	62.1	96.5
MASSACHUSETTS	54.0	57.0	93.8
Colored	226.3	238.6	(4)
White	51.7	54.6	(4)
SELECTED STATES—Continued			
MICHIGAN	47.0	51.0	69.3
Colored	263.7	303.1	(4)
White	37.8	40.5	(4)
MISSISSIPPI	77.7	82.1	119.6
Colored	121.2	128.5	189.0
White	33.8	35.1	43.8
MISSOURI	65.4	63.2	95.5
Colored	252.1	227.6	(4)
White	52.6	52.0	(4)
NEBRASKA	21.7	22.0	33.9
Colored	270.8	250.0	(4)
White	17.3	18.0	(4)
NEW HAMPSHIRE	44.3	44.0	79.2
Colored	------	------	(4)
White	44.4	44.1	(4)
NEW JERSEY	57.5	60.4	97.5
Colored	192.3	222.4	(4)
White	49.9	51.4	(4)
NEW YORK	60.7	63.5	101.4
Colored	262.2	254.4	(4)
White	53.2	56.5	(4)
NORTH CAROLINA	66.6	70.2	102.7
Colored	128.2	129.3	171.4
White	40.9	45.5	73.0
OHIO	54.7	54.9	85.4
Colored	264.9	255.2	(4)
White	44.0	44.8	(4)
OKLAHOMA	43.8	48.7	(3)
Colored	159.9	144.5	(3)
White	34.4	36.4	(3)
PENNSYLVANIA	52.7	55.1	87.3
Colored	224.4	228.2	(4)
White	44.3	46.8	(4)
RHODE ISLAND	53.2	57.2	105.5
Colored	172.7	218.2	(4)
White	51.2	54.6	(4)
SOUTH CAROLINA	69.3	72.9	107.9
Colored	118.3	119.9	155.8
White	28.8	33.5	57.7
TENNESSEE	98.1	106.1	139.1
Colored	205.6	228.9	260.4
White	74.2	78.7	110.2
SELECTED STATES—Continued			
VERMONT	57.2	56.1	65.2
Colored	100.0	------	(4)
White	57.1	56.3	(4)
VIRGINIA	83.3	83.5	124.8
Colored	168.7	164.2	225.6
White	52.2	53.9	82.0
WEST VIRGINIA	54.0	58.6	(3)
Colored	166.7	153.4	(3)
White	45.9	51.9	(3)
SELECTED CITIES OF 100,000 POPULATION OR MORE IN 1930			
Akron	29.6	31.3	48.2
Colored	221.3	(4)	(4)
White	20.3	(4)	(4)
Atlanta	77.8	75.5	85.6
Colored	173.8	153.3	125.0
White	29.3	36.5	67.4
Baltimore	83.7	86.8	126.0
Colored	229.4	218.1	285.4
White	51.6	58.4	97.9
Birmingham	76.9	82.2	130.3
Colored	157.9	172.3	259.6
White	27.0	26.6	46.8
Boston	65.1	69.2	106.4
Colored	239.1	265.5	(4)
White	59.8	63.3	(4)
Buffalo	68.0	70.1	94.9
Colored	428.6	(4)	(4)
White	58.1	(4)	(4)
Camden	37.8	39.6	71.3
Colored	84.7	(4)	(4)
White	32.6	(4)	(4)
Chattanooga	93.3	111.6	162.4
Colored	175.6	225.2	300.3
White	62.1	68.0	96.2
Chicago	57.4	57.3	81.4
Colored	222.1	233.0	(4)
White	43.1	42.6	(4)
SELECTED CITIES OF 100,000 POPULATION OR MORE IN 1930—continued			
Cincinnati	92.9	83.6	133.3
Colored	364.5	317.5	380.3
White	59.4	55.5	112.7
Cleveland	79.0	72.0	91.3
Colored	340.6	314.9	(4)
White	54.4	50.2	(4)
Columbus, Ohio	56.8	57.3	90.8
Colored	139.9	144.6	258.7
White	45.9	46.1	73.1
Dallas	48.0	49.5	90.6
Colored	127.7	130.8	287.3
White	31.4	32.6	55.6
Dayton	53.4	50.6	73.0
Colored	202.2	(4)	(4)
White	39.2	(4)	(4)
Detroit	58.9	68.9	82.5
Colored	261.2	325.4	(4)
White	40.1	45.9	(4)
El Paso	239.0	312.9	611.2
Colored	192.4	259.4	(4)
White	308.8	390.5	(4)
Fort Worth	59.7	54.8	(3)
Colored	135.8	190.1	(3)
White	45.4	29.0	(3)
Gary	58.5	64.0	73.0
Colored	149.6	(4)	(4)
White	32.7	(4)	(4)
Houston	66.8	72.5	92.9
Colored	144.8	150.5	176.4
White	38.6	44.3	66.0
Indianapolis	54.6	66.5	104.9
Colored	177.0	173.8	295.2
White	37.6	51.7	81.1
Jacksonville, Fla	119.8	120.0	140.6
Colored	268.2	236.5	240.9
White	34.6	51.3	58.8
Jersey City	60.5	68.4	94.6
Colored	238.8	(4)	(4)
White	52.7	(4)	(4)

See footnotes at end of table.

Table 14.—COLORED AND WHITE DEATH RATE FROM TUBERCULOSIS OF THE RESPIRATORY SYSTEM, IN SELECTED STATES AND CITIES: 1931, 1930, AND 1920—Continued

AREA AND COLOR	RATE PER 100,000 ESTIMATED POPULATION JULY 1		
	1931	1930	1920
SELECTED CITIES OF 100,000 POPULATION OR MORE IN 1930—continued			
Kansas City, Kans	70.0	68.0	85.6
Colored	150.9	170.3	143.0
White	51.2	44.4	75.9
Kansas City, Mo	73.1	76.4	96.6
Colored	276.1	310.4	361.1
White	49.2	49.0	68.7
Knoxville	39.4	57.3	123.8
Colored	73.0	115.6	146.7
White	32.8	46.0	119.8
Louisville	52.9	58.5	112.1
Colored	146.8	170.5	219.3
White	35.7	38.0	90.1
Memphis	109.4	123.6	152.3
Colored	208.3	236.3	259.9
White	48.2	54.1	87.1
Miami	64.9	70.3	108.9
Colored	158.1	166.7	239.3
White	37.8	42.0	53.2
Nashville	87.5	100.5	166.5
Colored	184.1	223.8	308.5
White	50.6	53.0	105.7
Newark, N. J	50.5	62.3	76.7
Colored	216.5	292.8	(4)
White	33.0	39.2	(4)
New Orleans	132.2	131.6	189.7
Colored	257.8	230.8	316.4
White	81.4	91.8	144.4
New York	62.5	65.1	106.8
Colored	262.5	262.7	(4)
White	51.6	54.8	(4)
Norfolk	72.5	67.1	148.7
Colored	156.1	151.6	261.9
White	29.2	23.4	80.7
Oklahoma City	44.2	50.6	70.0
Colored	133.7	187.9	(4)
White	35.6	37.4	(4)
Omaha	45.7	40.6	63.3
Colored	232.0	219.5	(4)
White	34.3	29.7	(4)
Philadelphia	73.7	73.6	114.9
Colored	220.9	232.3	291.1
White	53.9	53.0	100.3
Pittsburgh	55.6	64.8	92.8
Colored	157.7	186.0	(4)
White	46.1	53.8	(4)
Richmond, Va	89.0	79.7	128.9
Colored	190.9	158.5	203.5
White	47.9	47.6	94.8
St. Louis	75.0	60.5	85.4
Colored	283.7	251.8	249.1
White	47.0	35.3	68.8
San Antonio	135.8	170.2	260.9
Colored	(4)	(4)	338.6
White	(4)	(4)	253.3
Tampa	54.3	72.6	116.7
Colored	112.6	111.6	227.2
White	38.6	62.2	84.9
Toledo	74.4	72.7	121.2
Colored	293.3	(4)	(4)
White	62.7	(4)	(4)
Tulsa	32.2	45.8	(3)
Colored	61.8	97.7	(3)
White	28.1	38.5	(3)
Washington, D. C	107.1	101.8	110.2
Colored	256.3	227.8	215.6
White	50.6	54.6	74.3
Wilmington, Del	48.8	42.2	88.2
Colored	123.6	107.1	212.0
White	39.2	33.9	74.6
Youngstown	23.1	32.8	58.5
Colored	81.8	(4)	(4)
White	17.2	(4)	(4)

[1] Includes Negroes, nonwhite, and other races.
[2] States in registration area whose Negro population represented 55 percent or more of the total colored population in 1930.
[3] Not in registration area.
[4] Death rates by color not available.

Table 15.—COLORED [1] AND WHITE DEATH RATE FROM PNEUMONIA (ALL FORMS) IN SELECTED STATES AND CITIES: 1931, 1930, AND 1920

AREA AND COLOR	RATE PER 100,000 ESTIMATED POPULATION JULY 1		
	1931	1930	1920
SELECTED STATES [2]			
ALABAMA	83.4	85.1	(3)
Colored	102.1	104.4	(3)
White	73.1	74.3	(3)
ARKANSAS	74.4	73.7	(3)
Colored	70.0	79.2	(3)
White	75.9	71.8	(3)
CONNECTICUT	74.8	81.1	156.0
Colored	161.3	160.0	304.9
White	73.1	79.6	153.6
DELAWARE	108.3	106.7	178.8
Colored	242.4	251.5	334.4
White	87.0	83.5	154.2
FLORIDA	56.4	60.8	79.0
Colored	81.1	83.9	96.6
White	46.2	51.2	71.6
GEORGIA	83.9	87.5	(3)
Colored	112.4	125.0	(3)
White	67.5	65.7	(3)
ILLINOIS	71.5	67.5	133.5
Colored	167.5	136.3	302.2
White	66.6	64.1	128.3
INDIANA	76.5	79.6	133.6
Colored	188.9	254.5	344.0
White	72.0	72.7	127.5
IOWA	63.0	78.1	(3)
Colored	139.1	208.7	(3)
White	62.3	76.9	(3)
KANSAS	51.4	55.0	97.4
Colored	89.9	73.0	241.9
White	49.5	54.1	92.2
KENTUCKY	87.7	92.0	121.5
Colored	179.6	186.3	227.5
White	79.0	83.1	110.3
LOUISIANA	81.2	89.1	107.7
Colored	107.1	125.6	132.3
White	65.8	67.5	92.8
MARYLAND	123.2	115.5	153.2
Colored	252.0	228.8	252.5
White	96.9	92.3	133.2
MASSACHUSETTS	83.9	92.2	156.3
Colored	164.9	164.9	276.4
White	82.9	91.2	154.7
MICHIGAN	59.4	70.1	151.8
Colored	145.8	172.3	592.4
White	55.7	65.9	143.0
MISSISSIPPI	66.8	72.8	102.2
Colored	70.7	83.9	122.4
White	62.8	61.4	81.5
MISSOURI	98.7	92.2	163.9
Colored	216.7	202.2	339.3
White	90.6	84.7	154.0
NEBRASKA	56.3	65.9	85.7
Colored	233.3	237.5	378.1
White	53.2	62.9	81.8
NEW HAMPSHIRE	69.6	84.1	130.6
Colored	-----	100.0	394.2
White	69.7	84.1	130.1
NEW JERSEY	81.6	77.5	153.7
Colored	210.9	195.3	335.6
White	74.3	70.9	146.4
SELECTED STATES—Continued			
NEW YORK	99.1	94.8	159.5
Colored	214.3	208.3	353.1
White	94.8	90.7	155.3
NORTH CAROLINA	77.8	84.9	101.4
Colored	109.5	113.7	135.4
White	64.6	72.8	87.4
OHIO	76.5	75.8	136.0
Colored	197.2	189.0	327.6
White	70.4	70.1	129.4
OKLAHOMA	68.1	65.1	(3)
Colored	107.9	114.6	(3)
White	62.9	58.8	(3)
PENNSYLVANIA	102.2	95.9	181.9
Colored	261.3	222.3	404.1
White	94.5	89.8	174.2
RHODE ISLAND	98.6	94.3	162.9
Colored	172.7	190.9	345.5
White	97.4	92.8	159.7
SOUTH CAROLINA	94.9	95.1	110.5
Colored	118.0	121.9	131.5
White	75.8	72.7	87.6
TENNESSEE	85.6	91.0	116.9
Colored	138.3	141.0	187.5
White	73.9	79.9	100.5
VERMONT	73.6	92.8	152.2
Colored	100.0	-----	-----
White	73.5	93.0	152.5
VIRGINIA	89.3	94.6	103.8
Colored	143.8	150.2	154.7
White	69.5	74.1	81.7
WEST VIRGINIA	78.5	84.7	(3)
Colored	149.6	137.1	(3)
White	73.4	80.9	(3)
SELECTED CITIES OF 100,000 POPULATION OR MORE IN 1930			
AKRON	61.9	52.8	239.5
Colored	147.5	(4)	(4)
White	57.8	(4)	(4)
ATLANTA	130.8	122.9	191.3
Colored	225.3	234.8	359.3
White	83.0	66.9	114.1
BALTIMORE	159.7	148.5	185.4
Colored	326.8	308.0	325.3
White	122.9	114.0	160.8
BIRMINGHAM	116.6	122.3	186.1
Colored	190.1	187.4	288.9
White	71.4	82.2	119.8
BOSTON	131.4	144.4	198.2
Colored	221.7	243.4	348.1
White	128.7	141.4	194.6
BUFFALO	91.4	95.4	147.8
Colored	240.3	(4)	(4)
White	87.3	(4)	(4)
CAMDEN	162.2	126.3	218.2
Colored	432.2	(4)	(4)
White	132.5	(4)	(4)
Chattanooga	110.5	140.7	160.7
Colored	199.4	234.2	237.1
White	76.7	104.8	124.0
SELECTED CITIES OF 100,000 POPULATION OR MORE IN 1930—continued			
Chicago	75.0	72.3	160.3
Colored	164.6	136.9	341.1
White	67.3	66.9	152.1
Cincinnati	114.8	108.8	130.6
Colored	243.0	270.1	364.3
White	99.0	89.4	111.1
Cleveland	104.1	92.2	154.7
Colored	217.7	181.7	341.0
White	93.4	84.1	145.8
Columbus, Ohio	79.5	84.0	146.9
Colored	145.8	171.7	350.8
White	70.8	72.8	125.4
Dallas	101.8	100.5	117.6
Colored	300.0	252.8	210.4
White	60.6	69.0	101.0
Dayton	69.0	57.6	122.0
Colored	151.7	(4)	(4)
White	61.2	(4)	(4)
Detroit	65.5	85.7	233.2
Colored	144.2	190.2	743.5
White	58.2	76.3	209.4
El Paso	151.4	131.2	271.2
Colored	194.0	152.7	(4)
White	87.9	100.0	(4)
Fort Worth	73.5	79.2	(3)
Colored	169.8	136.9	(3)
White	55.4	68.2	(3)
Gary	115.2	128.1	286.7
Colored	192.3	(4)	(4)
White	93.3	(4)	(4)
Houston	71.0	79.2	114.4
Colored	130.2	164.5	190.6
White	49.6	48.4	89.8
Indianapolis	99.8	118.5	179.5
Colored	210.2	284.4	346.2
White	84.4	95.6	158.6
Jacksonville, Fla	81.1	82.3	144.9
Colored	133.1	118.3	197.6
White	51.3	61.1	102.0
Jersey City	121.0	116.0	193.0
Colored	335.8	(4)	(4)
White	111.6	(4)	(4)
Kansas City, Kans	95.2	86.0	185.0
Colored	112.1	61.1	245.1
White	91.3	91.7	174.9
Kansas City, Mo	124.5	113.8	247.5
Colored	208.8	208.5	457.0
White	114.5	102.7	225.4
Knoxville	103.5	121.1	161.7
Colored	179.8	185.0	241.6
White	88.6	108.7	147.9
Louisville	130.1	127.6	151.8
Colored	318.7	273.7	305.5
White	95.5	101.0	120.3
Memphis	146.1	111.8	221.1
Colored	200.2	154.8	343.8
White	112.6	85.3	146.8
Miami	57.8	53.2	105.8
Colored	106.7	103.2	166.4
White	43.6	38.5	79.9
Nashville	146.6	137.5	181.6
Colored	184.1	202.8	283.3
White	132.3	112.3	138.1
Newark, N. J	100.5	97.5	177.7
Colored	218.8	245.7	489.3
White	88.0	82.7	163.3
New Orleans	127.1	147.9	185.0
Colored	212.5	282.5	347.6
White	92.5	94.0	127.1
New York	118.7	104.2	183.8
Colored	217.8	220.9	396.1
White	113.3	98.0	177.3
Norfolk	104.1	101.8	140.9
Colored	192.3	194.6	231.7
White	58.5	53.8	86.3
Oklahoma City	100.6	98.1	98.2
Colored	203.5	266.7	(4)
White	90.8	81.8	(4)
Omaha	99.2	103.5	167.6
Colored	168.0	178.9	283.1
White	95.0	98.9	160.9
Philadelphia	110.9	92.5	192.6
Colored	194.3	191.8	388.4
White	99.7	79.6	176.4
Pittsburgh	243.3	203.1	341.5
Colored	669.0	434.7	601.3
White	203.6	182.1	323.1
Richmond, Va	100.4	108.6	183.5
Colored	190.9	181.1	364.5
White	63.9	79.1	100.7
St. Louis	144.7	126.1	212.6
Colored	294.9	252.9	400.3
White	124.5	109.4	193.5
San Antonio	115.4	134.2	118.9
Colored	(4)	(4)	135.4
White	(4)	(4)	117.3
Tampa	59.0	57.9	97.9
Colored	99.1	79.1	151.5
White	48.3	52.2	82.4
Toledo	89.2	83.0	126.1
Colored	266.7	(4)	(4)
White	79.8	(4)	(4)
Tulsa	74.8	87.3	(3)
Colored	179.8	252.9	(3)
White	60.2	64.2	(3)
Washington, D. C	140.5	122.3	185.9
Colored	263.0	218.8	351.5
White	94.1	86.2	129.5
Wilmington, Del	121.0	137.9	215.5
Colored	288.4	346.0	433.1
White	99.5	111.2	191.6
Youngstown	101.8	117.9	267.6
Colored	257.9	(4)	(4)
White	86.0	(4)	(4)

[1] Includes Negro and other nonwhite races.
[2] States in registration area whose Negro population represented 55 percent or more of the total colored population in 1930.
[3] Not in registration area.
[4] Death rates by color not available.

TABLE 16.—COLORED [1] AND WHITE DEATH RATE FROM NEPHRITIS, IN SELECTED STATES AND CITIES: 1931, 1930, AND 1920

AREA AND COLOR	RATE PER 100,000 ESTIMATED POPULATION JULY 1: 1931	1930	1920
SELECTED STATES [2]			
Alabama	87.0	96.8	(3)
Colored	116.9	126.5	(3)
White	70.6	80.3	(3)
Arkansas	71.5	74.3	(3)
Colored	93.3	106.7	(3)
White	64.0	63.0	(3)
Connecticut	80.7	80.7	88.3
Colored	109.7	83.3	139.0
White	80.2	80.7	87.5
Delaware	147.1	161.1	126.0
Colored	178.8	236.4	177.1
White	142.0	149.0	118.0
Florida	112.9	116.0	94.9
Colored	142.0	138.9	96.9
White	100.9	106.5	93.9
Georgia	105.6	117.1	(3)
Colored	128.5	145.5	(3)
White	92.5	100.7	(3)
Illinois	107.2	105.8	90.6
Colored	147.9	148.2	128.9
White	105.1	103.6	89.4
Indiana	109.1	114.9	105.5
Colored	131.7	156.1	136.4
White	108.2	113.3	104.6
Iowa	64.4	66.3	(3)
Colored	95.7	113.0	(3)
White	64.1	65.9	(3)
Kansas	87.3	93.4	82.2
Colored	161.8	152.8	235.3
White	83.6	90.4	76.7
Kentucky	85.2	90.0	78.8
Colored	191.2	219.0	149.8
White	75.2	77.8	71.2
Louisiana	108.3	110.6	86.6
Colored	142.7	146.8	104.5
White	88.0	89.2	75.2
Maryland	135.1	143.5	139.7
Colored	184.9	182.4	189.1
White	125.0	135.6	129.7
Massachusetts	80.2	83.6	75.7
Colored	96.5	129.8	103.6
White	80.0	82.9	75.3
Michigan	58.6	61.4	69.2
Colored	69.7	85.1	83.0
White	58.1	60.4	68.9
Mississippi	104.6	113.2	82.8
Colored	127.3	137.3	95.1
White	81.6	88.6	69.3
Missouri	113.4	115.8	98.2
Colored	192.3	228.0	177.6
White	108.0	108.1	93.8
Nebraska	62.3	65.7	52.1
Colored	112.5	91.7	64.0
White	61.4	65.3	52.0
New Hampshire	99.6	119.5	100.6
Colored	100.0	200.0	131.4
White	99.6	119.4	100.6
New Jersey	94.7	100.1	105.0
Colored	115.0	132.7	154.9
White	93.5	98.3	103.0
SELECTED STATES—continued			
New York	91.0	92.4	110.0
Colored	95.4	97.8	112.0
White	90.8	92.2	109.9
North Carolina	93.4	103.1	74.4
Colored	113.2	133.7	87.6
White	85.1	90.4	68.7
Ohio	76.0	76.4	76.3
Colored	110.5	118.5	110.6
White	74.3	74.3	75.2
Oklahoma	45.2	50.4	(3)
Colored	59.2	71.5	(3)
White	43.4	47.6	(3)
Pennsylvania	95.5	102.3	98.9
Colored	113.1	138.1	128.0
White	94.6	100.6	97.9
Rhode Island	113.8	103.3	96.6
Colored	154.5	136.4	153.6
White	113.2	102.8	95.6
South Carolina	116.8	134.3	84.1
Colored	139.2	155.7	89.2
White	98.3	116.3	78.7
Tennessee	69.9	75.7	65.4
Colored	107.1	128.7	111.4
White	61.6	63.9	54.5
Vermont	111.9	102.5	110.8
Colored	100.0	----	----
White	112.0	102.8	111.0
Virginia	110.9	118.1	90.8
Colored	165.3	171.7	109.5
White	91.2	98.5	82.9
West Virginia	76.3	73.3	(3)
Colored	142.7	145.7	(3)
White	71.6	68.1	(3)
SELECTED CITIES OF 100,000 POPULATION OR MORE IN 1930			
Akron	50.9	46.9	35.3
Colored	90.2	(4)	(4)
White	49.0	(4)	(4)
Atlanta	144.8	164.9	158.8
Colored	186.7	235.9	182.8
White	123.6	129.3	147.8
Baltimore	136.6	144.3	144.7
Colored	187.2	176.3	204.8
White	125.4	137.4	134.1
Birmingham	88.0	100.2	96.3
Colored	127.7	133.3	127.0
White	63.6	79.7	76.6
Boston	77.4	84.1	61.1
Colored	91.3	199.1	112.3
White	77.0	80.7	59.8
Buffalo	112.9	120.6	113.9
Colored	90.9	(4)	(4)
White	113.4	(4)	(4)
Camden	121.0	129.6	136.6
Colored	93.2	(4)	(4)
White	124.1	(4)	(4)
SELECTED CITIES OF 100,000 POPULATION OR MORE IN 1930—continued			
Chattanooga	90.0	92.4	138.5
Colored	157.7	141.1	179.1
White	64.3	73.7	119.0
Chicago	110.1	105.7	96.7
Colored	141.8	138.1	113.7
White	107.3	103.0	95.9
Cincinnati	118.7	125.1	121.6
Colored	95.6	121.6	119.3
White	121.6	125.5	121.8
Cleveland	60.1	61.5	73.6
Colored	105.0	103.6	106.4
White	55.9	57.7	72.1
Columbus, Ohio	91.0	90.6	79.1
Colored	113.7	147.6	78.9
White	88.0	83.2	79.1
Dallas	63.7	65.9	96.2
Colored	131.9	148.6	202.3
White	49.5	48.7	77.2
Dayton	83.7	79.4	73.6
Colored	78.7	(4)	(4)
White	84.2	(4)	(4)
Detroit	42.0	43.8	50.8
Colored	60.0	70.3	52.9
White	40.4	41.5	50.7
El Paso	62.9	62.2	86.6
Colored	62.0	62.4	(4)
White	64.1	61.9	(4)
Fort Worth	68.7	71.3	(3)
Colored	128.3	91.3	(3)
White	57.5	67.5	(3)
Gary	51.9	61.1	55.6
Colored	68.4	(4)	(4)
White	47.3	(4)	(4)
Houston	78.8	80.6	103.3
Colored	113.1	111.0	119.5
White	66.3	69.6	98.1
Indianapolis	115.5	136.1	112.8
Colored	165.9	205.4	136.2
White	108.4	126.5	109.9
Jacksonville, Fla	138.7	170.8	134.1
Colored	180.9	244.8	151.8
White	114.6	127.1	119.7
Jersey City	76.2	92.4	101.7
Colored	67.2	(4)	(4)
White	76.6	(4)	(4)
Kansas City, Kans	135.9	156.4	125.0
Colored	202.6	196.5	299.6
White	120.4	147.2	95.5
Kansas City, Mo	108.6	131.5	110.3
Colored	171.7	258.3	185.4
White	101.1	116.6	102.4
Knoxville	77.8	107.0	87.1
Colored	179.8	190.8	138.1
White	58.0	90.8	78.4
Louisville	113.9	137.7	127.1
Colored	203.4	263.2	165.1
White	97.5	114.8	119.3
SELECTED CITIES OF 100,000 POPULATION OR MORE IN 1930—continued			
Memphis	94.7	115.7	165.1
Colored	118.3	163.1	214.7
White	80.1	86.6	135.0
Miami	88.0	104.5	130.6
Colored	94.9	103.2	72.8
White	86.0	104.9	155.3
Nashville	97.1	108.3	131.2
Colored	158.5	198.1	213.1
White	73.7	73.7	96.1
Newark, N. J	83.2	95.5	102.7
Colored	94.1	124.1	174.0
White	82.1	92.6	99.4
New Orleans	179.3	195.4	172.0
Colored	235.5	280.2	243.4
White	156.5	161.5	146.5
New York	70.6	70.6	106.4
Colored	92.0	92.6	102.7
White	69.4	69.5	106.5
Norfolk	94.1	99.5	99.1
Colored	104.1	126.7	92.7
White	88.9	85.4	103.0
Oklahoma City	54.4	66.1	52.2
Colored	75.6	97.0	(4)
White	52.3	63.1	(4)
Omaha	72.0	84.4	61.2
Colored	104.0	105.7	47.2
White	70.0	83.1	62.1
Philadelphia	120.3	135.4	142.0
Colored	109.4	140.6	145.2
White	121.8	134.7	141.8
Pittsburgh	88.3	90.3	80.4
Colored	78.0	116.3	95.1
White	89.3	88.0	79.4
Richmond, Va	161.2	169.2	139.4
Colored	221.2	237.7	127.7
White	137.0	141.3	144.7
St. Louis	155.1	154.3	136.1
Colored	231.6	250.8	184.7
White	144.8	141.6	131.1
San Antonio	66.2	75.9	81.3
Colored	(4)	(4)	182.8
White	(4)	(4)	71.3
Tampa	118.1	122.7	107.3
Colored	144.1	111.6	151.5
White	111.1	125.6	94.6
Toledo	57.9	65.8	78.8
Colored	40.0	(4)	(4)
White	58.8	(4)	(4)
Tulsa	38.4	61.3	(3)
Colored	78.7	132.2	(3)
White	32.8	51.4	(3)
Washington, D. C	138.7	140.4	110.5
Colored	207.4	186.5	163.7
White	112.6	123.1	92.3
Wilmington, Del	153.9	169.8	109.1
Colored	156.5	247.2	156.7
White	153.5	159.9	103.9
Youngstown	54.9	62.8	39.0
Colored	94.3	(4)	(4)
White	51.0	(4)	(4)

[1] Includes Negro and other nonwhite races.
[2] States in registration area whose Negro population represented 55 percent or more of the total colored population in 1930.
[3] Not in registration area.
[4] Death rates by color not available.

TABLE 17.—COLORED[1] AND WHITE DEATH RATE FROM PUERPERAL CAUSES PER 1,000 LIVE BIRTHS, IN SELECTED STATES AND CITIES: 1931, 1930, AND 1920

[Rates in *italics* are based on less than 5 deaths]

AREA AND COLOR	ALL PUERPERAL CAUSES 1931	ALL PUERPERAL CAUSES 1930	ALL PUERPERAL CAUSES 1920	PUERPERAL SEPTICEMIA 1931	PUERPERAL SEPTICEMIA 1930	PUERPERAL SEPTICEMIA 1920	OTHER PUERPERAL CAUSES 1931	OTHER PUERPERAL CAUSES 1930	OTHER PUERPERAL CAUSES 1920
SELECTED STATES [2]									
Alabama	8.1	9.0	(3)	2.7	2.8	(3)	5.4	6.3	(3)
Colored	10.1	11.7	(3)	3.1	3.6	(3)	7.0	8.1	(3)
White	7.0	7.6	(3)	2.5	2.3	(3)	4.5	5.3	(3)
Arkansas	7.1	9.4	(3)	2.7	3.0	(3)	4.5	6.4	(3)
Colored	10.1	14.5	(3)	3.5	5.3	(3)	6.7	9.2	(3)
White	6.2	7.9	(3)	2.4	2.3	(3)	3.8	5.6	(3)
Florida	10.4	10.2	(4)	3.4	3.1	(4)	7.0	7.1	(4)
Colored	15.4	14.1	(4)	6.0	5.4	(4)	9.4	8.7	(4)
White	8.1	8.5	(4)	2.3	2.1	(4)	5.8	6.4	(4)
Georgia	9.9	10.6	(3)	3.0	3.2	(3)	6.9	7.4	(3)
Colored	12.2	12.4	(3)	3.7	4.0	(3)	8.5	8.4	(3)
White	8.4	9.4	(3)	2.6	2.7	(3)	5.9	6.7	(3)
Kentucky	6.4	6.4	6.4	2.5	2.5	2.8	3.9	4.0	3.7
Colored	13.5	15.4	13.0	5.5	7.7	7.0	8.0	7.7	6.0
White	6.0	5.9	6.0	2.3	2.1	2.5	3.7	3.8	3.5
Louisiana	8.6	10.0	(4)	3.3	2.9	(4)	5.3	7.1	(4)
Colored	10.6	12.5	(4)	4.6	3.9	(4)	6.0	8.5	(4)
White	7.3	8.4	(4)	2.4	2.3	(4)	4.9	6.1	(4)
Maryland	6.1	5.6	7.6	2.3	1.9	2.4	3.8	3.7	5.2
Colored	8.3	6.7	11.8	3.2	2.8	5.0	5.1	3.9	6.8
White	5.5	5.3	6.6	2.1	1.7	1.8	3.5	3.6	4.8
Mississippi	8.0	9.6	(4)	2.5	2.6	(4)	5.5	7.0	(4)
Colored	9.4	12.1	(4)	3.1	3.6	(4)	6.3	8.4	(4)
White	6.5	7.0	(4)	1.9	1.6	(4)	4.6	5.4	(4)
North Carolina	8.0	8.3	10.0	2.2	2.1	2.1	5.8	6.3	7.9
Colored	11.6	12.1	13.2	3.7	3.0	3.1	7.9	9.1	10.1
White	6.4	6.7	8.6	1.5	1.7	1.7	4.9	5.0	6.9
Oklahoma	6.2	6.9	(3)	2.8	3.0	(3)	3.4	3.9	(3)
Colored	15.4	16.4	(3)	7.1	5.0	(3)	8.2	11.5	(3)
White	5.4	6.1	(3)	2.4	2.9	(3)	3.0	3.2	(3)
South Carolina	10.2	11.4	12.2	2.5	2.7	2.8	7.8	8.7	9.4
Colored	12.7	13.1	15.4	3.2	3.2	3.7	9.6	9.9	11.7
White	7.6	9.6	9.0	1.7	2.1	1.8	5.9	7.4	7.1
Tennessee	7.4	8.4	(4)	3.2	3.3	(4)	4.3	5.1	(4)
Colored	13.7	15.8	(4)	6.0	8.4	(4)	7.7	7.4	(4)
White	6.3	7.0	(4)	2.7	2.3	(4)	3.7	4.7	(4)
Virginia	7.5	7.1	8.6	2.4	2.4	2.3	5.1	4.7	6.4
Colored	11.5	11.7	11.1	3.8	3.6	3.1	7.7	8.1	8.0
White	5.9	5.2	7.5	1.9	1.9	1.9	4.0	3.3	5.6
SELECTED CITIES [2]									
Atlanta, Ga	9.5	10.4	(4)	4.6	5.1	(4)	5.0	5.3	(4)
Colored	14.8	14.9	(4)	8.5	8.3	(4)	6.3	6.6	(4)
White	6.9	8.0	(4)	2.6	3.4	(4)	4.3	4.6	(4)
Baltimore, Md	7.7	6.1	7.6	3.0	2.7	2.8	4.8	3.5	4.8
Colored	9.5	8.0	11.5	3.5	3.7	6.3	6.0	4.3	5.2
White	7.2	5.6	6.8	2.8	2.4	2.1	4.4	3.2	4.7
Birmingham, Ala	12.5	11.3	(4)	5.3	5.8	(4)	7.2	5.6	(4)
Colored	19.8	11.7	(4)	7.3	6.6	(4)	12.5	5.2	(4)
White	8.1	11.1	(4)	4.0	5.2	(4)	4.0	5.9	(4)
Chattanooga, Tenn	10.3	13.3	(4)	3.8	6.4	(4)	6.6	6.9	(4)
Colored	17.5	28.9	(4)	*6.6*	20.6	(4)	11.0	*8.2*	(4)
White	8.4	9.2	(4)	3.0	2.7	(4)	5.4	6.5	(4)
Cincinnati, Ohio	7.4	7.0	9.6	3.4	3.1	4.4	4.0	3.9	5.2
Colored	7.4	11.5	22.6	*4.2*	5.7	8.1	*3.2*	5.7	14.5
White	7.4	6.4	8.4	3.3	2.7	4.0	4.1	3.7	4.4
Columbus, Ohio	10.1	10.6	10.0	5.0	4.8	3.6	5.0	5.8	6.4
Colored	12.5	14.8	4.4	*5.4*	*4.9*	4.4	*7.2*	9.9	-----
White	9.7	10.1	10.6	5.0	4.8	3.5	4.8	5.2	7.1
SELECTED CITIES—con.									
Indianapolis, Ind	9.7	6.9	9.6	4.9	2.5	5.3	4.9	4.4	4.4
Colored	8.7	8.2	17.2	*5.0*	*4.7*	10.6	*3.7*	*3.5*	6.6
White	9.9	6.7	8.7	4.8	2.2	4.6	5.0	4.5	4.1
Jacksonville, Fla	9.3	9.8	(4)	5.2	2.9	(4)	4.0	6.9	(4)
Colored	16.4	10.5	(4)	12.6	*5.3*	(4)	*3.8*	*5.3*	(4)
White	5.9	9.5	(4)	*1.8*	*1.8*	(4)	4.2	7.7	(4)
Kansas City, Kans	10.4	8.9	8.9	4.3	4.7	4.0	6.1	4.2	4.9
Colored	20.7	12.2	23.1	*5.2*	12.2	*9.3*	15.5	-----	*13.9*
White	8.4	8.2	7.4	4.2	3.1	3.4	4.2	5.1	3.9
Kansas City, Mo	10.3	8.2	(4)	4.7	3.7	(4)	5.6	4.5	(4)
Colored	*5.3*	16.1	(4)	*3.5*	8.1	(4)	*1.8*	8.1	(4)
White	10.8	7.3	(4)	4.9	3.2	(4)	6.0	4.1	(4)
Knoxville, Tenn	14.0	10.4	(4)	3.8	2.9	(4)	10.1	7.5	(4)
Colored	*15.0*	*11.2*	(4)	*5.0*	*7.4*	(4)	*10.0*	*3.7*	(4)
White	13.8	10.3	(4)	3.7	2.3	(4)	10.1	8.0	(4)
Los Angeles, Calif	9.2	6.5	8.1	3.8	3.1	3.3	5.4	3.3	4.8
Colored	9.0	(5)	12.8	4.0	(5)	6.0	5.0	(5)	6.8
White	9.2	(5)	7.6	3.7	(5)	3.0	5.6	(5)	4.6
Louisville, Ky	8.2	7.7	9.3	3.9	3.1	4.4	4.3	4.5	4.9
Colored	10.8	12.4	20.1	*5.4*	6.9	14.6	*5.4*	*5.5*	*5.5*
White	7.8	7.0	7.9	3.7	2.6	3.1	4.1	4.4	4.8
Memphis, Tenn	10.8	11.4	(4)	7.2	4.3	(4)	3.6	7.1	(4)
Colored	13.6	16.1	(4)	5.9	7.2	(4)	7.7	8.9	(4)
White	9.2	8.7	(4)	7.9	2.6	(4)	*1.3*	6.1	(4)
Miami, Fla	8.8	9.9	(4)	4.4	3.5	(4)	4.4	6.4	(4)
Colored	*7.9*	17.4	(1)	*4.0*	*3.5*	(4)	*4.0*	3.9	(4)
White	9.1	6.9	(4)	4.6	3.5	(4)	4.6	3.5	(4)
Nashville, Tenn	10.5	11.8	(4)	6.6	5.5	(4)	3.9	6.4	(4)
Colored	12.8	25.3	(4)	8.1	15.7	(4)	*4.7*	9.7	(4)
White	9.7	7.6	(4)	6.1	2.3	(4)	3.6	5.3	(4)
New Orleans, La	12.2	11.1	(4)	5.5	4.4	(4)	6.6	6.7	(4)
Colored	16.7	13.6	(4)	9.1	6.6	(4)	7.6	7.0	(4)
White	9.8	9.9	(4)	3.7	3.2	(4)	6.1	6.6	(4)
Norfolk, Va	8.7	12.4	10.8	4.1	5.3	3.1	4.6	7.1	7.7
Colored	13.6	20.0	16.6	9.5	6.7	5.8	*4.1*	13.3	10.7
White	6.3	8.6	7.6	*1.4*	4.7	*1.6*	4.9	4.0	6.0
Philadelphia, Pa	6.8	6.4	7.6	2.8	2.3	2.7	4.1	4.0	4.9
Colored	8.2	7.4	11.1	3.6	3.0	3.2	4.6	4.4	7.9
White	6.6	6.2	7.4	2.6	2.2	2.7	4.0	4.0	4.7
Richmond, Va	12.1	9.2	13.3	5.5	4.2	4.8	6.7	5.0	8.6
Colored	18.1	11.6	20.0	6.9	4.2	7.2	11.2	7.5	12.9
White	9.1	8.0	10.0	4.8	4.2	3.6	4.3	3.8	6.4
St. Louis, Mo	7.0	5.6	(4)	3.9	2.7	(4)	3.2	2.9	(4)
Colored	10.1	8.0	(4)	7.9	5.9	(4)	*2.2*	*2.1*	(4)
White	6.6	5.2	(4)	3.3	2.2	(4)	3.3	3.0	(4)
Tampa, Fla	7.3	7.1	(4)	2.8	3.8	(4)	4.5	3.3	(4)
Colored	*12.1*	*6.1*	(4)	*3.0*	*6.1*	(4)	*9.1*	-----	(4)
White	6.2	7.3	(4)	*2.8*	3.3	(4)	3.5	4.0	(4)
Tulsa, Okla	6.5	10.1	(3)	4.4	5.1	(3)	2.2	5.1	(3)
Colored	27.6	30.5	(3)	*11.0*	*12.2*	(3)	*16.6*	*18.3*	(3)
White	4.7	8.6	(3)	3.8	4.5	(3)	*.9*	4.1	(3)
Washington, D. C	7.1	9.0	8.8	4.1	4.1	2.8	3.0	4.9	6.0
Colored	10.1	17.7	14.4	5.4	7.5	5.2	4.7	10.2	9.2
White	5.7	4.7	6.6	3.5	2.4	1.9	2.2	2.4	4.7
Wilmington, Del	6.4	7.8	(4)	*1.4*	4.3	(4)	5.0	3.5	(4)
Colored	*8.8*	*4.1*	(4)	-----	*4.1*	(4)	*8.8*	-----	(4)
White	6.1	8.3	(4)	*1.5*	4.4	(4)	4.6	3.9	(4)

[1] Includes Negro, nonwhite, and other races.
[2] States and cities for which death rates by color are available.
[3] Not in either birth or death registration area.
[4] Not in birth area.
[5] Death rate by color not available.

TABLE 18.—DEATHS FROM HOMICIDE, BY COLOR, IN CITIES HAVING 25,000 OR MORE NEGRO INHABITANTS: 1930

	Total	Colored[1]	White	PERCENT OF TOTAL: Colored	PERCENT OF TOTAL: White	Percent colored[1] population of total population
Atlanta, Ga	143	115	28	80.4	19.6	33.4
Baltimore, Md	72	41	31	56.9	43.1	17.8
Birmingham, Ala	127	106	21	83.5	16.5	38.1
Charleston, S. C	17	16	1	94.1	5.9	45.1
Charlotte, N. C	31	29	2	93.5	6.5	30.4
Chattanooga, Tenn	64	48	16	75.0	25.0	27.7
Chicago, Ill	488	174	314	35.7	64.3	7.7
Cincinnati, Ohio	87	48	39	55.2	44.8	10.7
Cleveland, Ohio	148	65	83	43.9	56.1	8.2
Columbus, Ohio	34	16	18	47.1	52.9	11.4
Dallas, Tex	66	35	31	53.0	47.0	17.2
Detroit, Mich	207	96	111	46.4	53.6	8.3
Houston, Tex	78	48	30	61.5	38.5	26.5
Indianapolis, Ind	39	19	20	48.7	51.3	12.1
Jacksonville, Fla	45	31	14	68.9	31.1	37.1
Kansas City, Mo	91	50	41	54.9	45.1	10.5
Los Angeles, Calif	87	20	67	23.0	77.0	13.3
Louisville, Ky	54	37	17	68.5	31.5	15.4
Memphis, Tenn	149	121	28	81.2	18.8	38.1
Miami, Fla	42	30	12	71.4	28.6	22.7
Montgomery, Ala	23	17	6	73.9	26.1	45.4
Nashville, Tenn	59	42	17	71.2	28.8	27.8
Newark, N. J	54	27	27	50.0	50.0	9.1
New Orleans, La	107	64	43	59.8	40.2	28.6
New York, N. Y	525	131	394	25.0	75.0	5.0
Norfolk, Va	40	29	11	72.5	27.5	34.1
Philadelphia, Pa	142	68	74	47.9	52.1	11.5
Pittsburgh, Pa	64	23	41	35.9	64.1	8.3
Richmond, Va	29	23	6	79.3	20.7	28.9
St. Louis, Mo	143	68	75	47.6	52.4	11.6
Savannah, Ga	31	29	2	93.5	6.5	45.8
Shreveport, La	36	27	9	75.0	25.0	35.4
Washington, D. C	65	44	21	67.7	32.3	27.3
Winston-Salem, N. C	16	15	1	93.8	6.3	43.3

[1] Includes Negro, and other nonwhite races.

TABLE 19.—COLORED[1] AND WHITE DEATH RATE FROM HOMICIDE, IN SELECTED STATES, AND CITIES: 1931, 1930, AND 1920

[Rates in *italics* are based on less than 5 deaths]

AREA AND COLOR	Rate per 100,000 estimated population July 1		
	1931	1930	1920
SELECTED STATES[2]			
ALABAMA	22.5	19.7	(3)
Colored	42.3	40.0	(3)
White	11.6	8.4	(3)
ARKANSAS	17.6	13.8	(3)
Colored	40.8	28.3	(3)
White	9.5	8.7	(3)
CONNECTICUT	2.8	3.2	3.9
Colored	*12.9*	30.0	(4)
White	2.6	2.7	(4)
DELAWARE	10.4	8.4	4.0
Colored	39.4	36.4	(4)
White	5.8	3.9	(4)
FLORIDA	29.4	24.3	19.9
Colored	66.1	56.1	42.0
White	14.3	11.1	8.7
GEORGIA	20.7	19.9	(3)
Colored	40.0	39.1	(3)
White	9.6	8.7	(3)
ILLINOIS	10.5	10.5	7.3
Colored	66.1	61.0	(4)
White	7.6	7.9	(4)
INDIANA	6.6	6.4	4.7
Colored	44.4	54.5	(4)
White	5.1	4.5	(4)
IOWA	2.5	3.2	(3)
Colored	52.2	39.1	(3)
White	2.1	2.8	(3)
KANSAS	6.9	5.9	4.7
Colored	33.7	40.4	(4)
White	5.6	4.2	(4)
KENTUCKY	17.3	16.8	9.0
Colored	65.9	63.7	31.4
White	12.7	12.3	6.6
LOUISIANA	19.8	18.6	14.0
Colored	37.5	33.4	25.2
White	9.4	9.8	6.9
MARYLAND	9.7	7.8	4.8
Colored	33.0	28.4	16.6
White	5.0	3.5	2.4
MASSACHUSETTS	2.0	1.8	2.1
Colored	5.3	12.3	(4)
White	2.0	1.7	(4)
MICHIGAN	6.0	6.7	5.5
Colored	52.7	58.5	(4)
White	4.0	4.5	(4)
MISSISSIPPI	23.8	22.4	19.7
Colored	35.1	35.7	31.5
White	12.5	8.9	6.7
MISSOURI	11.1	11.3	7.8
Colored	73.9	70.7	(4)
White	6.8	7.2	(4)
NEBRASKA	3.6	3.5	4.2
Colored	75.0	54.2	(4)
White	2.4	2.6	(4)
NEW HAMPSHIRE	2.1	*.9*	1.8
Colored			(4)
White	2.1	*.9*	(4)
NEW JERSEY	5.0	5.5	4.2
Colored	28.6	30.8	(4)
White	3.6	4.1	(4)
NEW YORK	6.4	5.6	4.6
Colored	38.0	33.5	(4)
White	5.3	4.6	(4)
SELECTED STATES—Continued			
NORTH CAROLINA	10.5	11.0	9.7
Colored	21.9	25.0	21.1
White	5.8	5.1	4.8
OHIO	9.0	9.2	6.9
Colored	61.2	68.3	(4)
White	6.3	6.3	(4)
OKLAHOMA	11.1	11.0	(3)
Colored	36.1	30.7	(3)
White	7.8	8.4	(3)
PENNSYLVANIA	4.9	5.1	5.6
Colored	34.2	33.6	(4)
White	3.5	3.7	(4)
RHODE ISLAND	2.2	2.0	1.8
Colored	9.1	18.2	(4)
White	2.0	1.8	(4)
SOUTH CAROLINA	15.5	13.2	15.3
Colored	23.6	18.5	20.9
White	8.8	8.8	9.5
TENNESSEE	20.1	19.3	13.8
Colored	63.1	62.6	42.1
White	10.5	9.7	7.0
VERMONT	*1.1*	1.4	2.3
Colored			(4)
White	1.1	1.4	(4)
VIRGINIA	13.4	12.0	11.2
Colored	28.7	25.7	20.0
White	7.9	6.9	7.5
WEST VIRGINIA	13.7	13.5	(3)
Colored	70.1	64.7	(3)
White	9.7	9.8	(3)
SELECTED CITIES OF 100,000 POPULATION OR MORE IN 1930			
Akron	9.5	11.7	20.0
Colored	90.2	(4)	(4)
White	5.6	(4)	(4)
Atlanta	46.8	52.6	39.8
Colored	113.7	126.8	106.2
White	13.0	15.5	9.3
Baltimore	10.9	8.9	6.4
Colored	36.8	28.6	23.6
White	5.3	4.7	3.3
Birmingham	54.2	48.5	46.5
Colored	105.3	106.2	92.1
White	22.8	13.0	17.1
Boston	3.7	2.3	4.5
Colored	4.3	*17.7*	(4)
White	3.7	1.8	(4)
Buffalo	3.6	4.9	4.9
Colored	*13.0*	(4)	(4)
White	3.4	(4)	(4)
Camden	20.2	13.5	6.0
Colored	84.7	(4)	(4)
White	13.1	(4)	(4)
Chattanooga	55.6	53.3	56.4
Colored	160.7	144.1	121.2
White	15.8	18.4	25.3
Chicago	14.5	14.4	9.7
Colored	61.9	66.4	(4)
White	10.4	10.0	(4)
SELECTED CITIES OF 100,000 POPULATION OR MORE IN 1930—continued			
Cincinnati	16.4	19.2	5.0
Colored	81.7	99.0	29.0
White	8.4	9.7	4.0
Cleveland	13.6	16.4	13.1
Colored	74.3	87.5	(4)
White	7.9	10.0	(4)
Columbus, Ohio	9.5	11.7	6.7
Colored	49.6	48.2	39.5
White	4.2	7.0	3.2
Dallas	24.5	25.1	20.8
Colored	85.1	77.6	76.9
White	11.9	14.3	10.8
Dayton	8.8	9.4	5.2
Colored	67.4	(4)	(4)
White	3.2	(4)	(4)
Detroit	10.5	13.1	13.8
Colored	61.4	73.3	(4)
White	5.8	7.6	(4)
El Paso	19.0	27.2	(4)
Colored	22.3	29.6	(4)
White	14.3	23.8	(4)
Fort Worth	26.3	19.5	(3)
Colored	86.8	72.2	(3)
White	14.9	9.4	(3)
Gary	28.3	28.6	34.8
Colored	72.6	(4)	(4)
White	15.8	(4)	(4)
Houston	26.1	26.4	14.6
Colored	63.3	61.2	45.5
White	12.7	13.8	4.6
Indianapolis	11.1	10.7	5.7
Colored	35.4	42.9	28.4
White	7.7	6.2	2.8
Jacksonville, Fla	47.8	34.6	33.5
Colored	104.0	64.3	57.8
White	15.5	17.1	13.7
Jersey City	2.5	3.2	3.3
Colored	*14.9*	(4)	(4)
White	2.0	(4)	(4)
Kansas City, Kans	21.2	22.9	10.8
Colored	51.7	78.6	54.5
White	14.0	10.1	*3.5*
Kansas City, Mo	23.7	22.7	27.1
Colored	146.2	118.5	76.7
White	9.3	11.4	21.9
Knoxville	19.2	22.5	21.5
Colored	56.2	80.9	60.4
White	12.0	11.2	14.8
Louisville	18.8	17.5	12.1
Colored	79.7	77.9	39.4
White	7.7	6.5	6.5
Memphis	54.5	58.7	62.8
Colored	112.2	124.9	132.4
White	18.8	17.8	20.6
Miami	36.4	37.8	31.1
Colored	118.6	119.0	52.0
White	12.6	14.0	22.2
Nashville	36.7	38.3	13.5
Colored	90.9	97.9	33.7
White	16.0	15.3	*4.8*
SELECTED CITIES OF 100,000 POPULATION OR MORE IN 1930—continued			
Newark, N. J	10.8	12.2	4.1
Colored	51.8	67.0	(4)
White	6.4	6.7	(4)
New Orleans	26.1	23.2	16.1
Colored	61.7	48.6	36.0
White	11.7	13.1	9.0
New York	8.8	7.5	6.2
Colored	43.5	37.7	22.4
White	6.9	6.0	5.7
Norfolk	21.6	30.8	38.3
Colored	52.0	65.6	60.3
White	*5.8*	12.9	25.1
Oklahoma City	22.4	15.5	(4)
Colored	75.6	72.7	(4)
White	17.3	9.9	(4)
Omaha	11.1	8.9	11.4
Colored	88.0	73.2	(4)
White	6.4	4.9	(4)
Philadelphia	6.7	7.3	6.4
Colored	34.3	30.3	24.3
White	3.0	4.3	5.0
Pittsburgh	8.3	9.5	10.3
Colored	41.6	41.1	(4)
White	5.2	6.7	(4)
Richmond, Va	15.7	15.8	7.5
Colored	39.7	43.4	18.5
White	6.1	4.6	*2.5*
St. Louis	15.9	17.4	12.6
Colored	66.3	71.1	26.6
White	9.2	10.3	11.2
San Antonio	23.7	19.3	9.7
Colored	(4)	(4)	33.9
White	(4)	(4)	7.3
Tampa	21.9	27.5	18.8
Colored	58.6	51.2	*33.7*
White	12.1	21.1	14.5
Toledo	17.2	12.0	11.8
Colored	93.3	(4)	(4)
White	13.1	(4)	(4)
Tulsa	17.1	11.3	(3)
Colored	73.0	34.5	(3)
White	9.4	8.0	(3)
Washington, D. C	15.9	13.3	10.5
Colored	37.0	33.1	24.2
White	7.9	5.9	5.8
Wilmington, Del	15.0	12.2	4.5
Colored	57.7	57.7	*18.4*
White	9.5	6.4	*3.0*
Youngstown	13.3	11.1	18.7
Colored	56.6	(4)	(4)
White	8.9	(4)	(4)

[1] Includes Negro and other nonwhite races.
[2] States in registration area whose Negro population represented 55 percent or more of the total colored population in 1930.
[3] Not in registration area.
[4] Death rates not available.

TABLE 20.—COLORED[1] AND WHITE DEATHS (EXCLUSIVE OF STILLBIRTHS) FROM ALL CAUSES AND FROM UNKNOWN OR ILL-DEFINED DISEASES, IN REGISTRATION AREA OF CONTINENTAL UNITED STATES, AND SELECTED REGISTRATION STATES: 1930

AREA	ALL CAUSES		UNKNOWN OR ILL-DEFINED DISEASES			
					Percent of total	
	Colored	White	Colored	White	Colored[1]	White
The registration area in continental United States	**199,167**	**1,144,189**	**12,479**	**12,385**	**6.3**	**1.1**
Selected States[2]	182,232	917,552	11,508	9,487	6.3	1.0
Alabama	14,412	16,010	1,649	670	11.4	4.2
Arkansas	6,466	12,484	654	635	10.1	5.1
Connecticut	523	16,764	2	50	.4	.3
Delaware	707	2,549	5	4	.7	.2
District of Columbia	2,792	4,595	3	2	.1	(3)
Florida	7,182	11,047	396	243	5.5	2.2
Georgia	17,190	17,993	1,403	683	8.2	3.8
Illinois	5,961	77,630	90	416	1.5	.5
Indiana	2,313	36,883	2	26	.1	.1
Iowa	363	25,865	4	130	1.1	.5
Kansas	1,102	18,403	5	131	.5	.7
Kentucky	4,750	24,812	42	395	.9	1.6
Louisiana	12,086	12,621	467	182	3.9	1.4
Maryland	5,264	16,303	43	43	.8	.3
Massachusetts	908	48,425	2	60	.2	.1
Michigan	3,090	48,530	4	162	0.1	0.3
Mississippi	14,961	9,138	2,560	561	17.1	6.1
Missouri	4,653	38,446	35	273	.8	.7
Nebraska	467	12,825	7	70	1.5	.5
New Jersey	3,552	40,045	7	37	.2	.1
New York	7,199	140,254	5	106	.1	.1
North Carolina	14,155	21,627	1,458	1,161	10.3	5.4
Ohio	5,839	70,387	30	241	.5	.3
Oklahoma	3,063	16,583	152	467	5.0	2.8
Pennsylvania	7,511	104,095	44	371	.6	.4
Rhode Island	231	7,775	2	23	.9	.3
South Carolina	13,162	9,271	1,234	259	9.4	2.8
Tennessee	8,752	21,235	752	1,550	8.6	7.3
Virginia	11,722	18,593	442	449	3.8	2.4
West Virginia	1,856	16,364	9	87	.5	.5

[1] Includes Negro and other nonwhite races.
[2] States in the registration area reporting 100 or more colored deaths and whose Negro population in 1930 constituted 55 percent or more of the total colored population.
[3] Less than 1/10 of 1 percent.

TABLE 21.—COLORED [1] AND WHITE DEATHS FROM HOMICIDE, FOR REGISTRATION AREA IN CONTINENTAL UNITED STATES, 1931, 1930, AND 1929, AND LEGAL EXECUTIONS, 1931 AND 1930

AREA AND COLOR	HOMICIDE			LEGAL EXECUTIONS	
	1931	1930	1929	1931	1930
The Registration Area in Continental United States	**11, 160**	**10, 617**	**9, 909**	**142**	**147**
Colored	4, 962	4, 643	4, 446	74	60
White	6, 198	5, 974	5, 463	68	87
Selected States:[2]					
Colored	4, 576	4, 315	4, 216	72	58
White	5, 225	4, 943	4, 491	53	58
ALABAMA:					
Colored	401	379	367	2	4
White	200	144	146	-	1
ARKANSAS:					
Colored	196	136	180	1	9
White	131	120	105	-	1
CONNECTICUT:					
Colored	4	9	7	-	-
White	41	43	34	-	2
DELAWARE:					
Colored	13	12	11	-	1
White	12	8	5	-	1
DISTRICT OF COLUMBIA:					
Colored	50	44	37	1	1
White	28	21	23	-	-
FLORIDA:					
Colored	291	244	251	4	1
White	152	116	118	3	-
GEORGIA:					
Colored	424	418	377	16	6
White	177	161	154	2	1
ILLINOIS:					
Colored	250	225	209	3	4
White	559	576	465	7	2
INDIANA:					
Colored	56	67	52	1	1
White	159	140	172	-	-
IOWA:					
Colored	12	9	9	-	-
White	51	69	55	1	-
KANSAS:					
Colored	30	36	26	-	-
White	100	75	91	-	1
KENTUCKY:					
Colored	149	144	164	-	1
White	306	295	270	-	1
LOUISIANA:					
Colored	296	262	253	6	5
White	125	130	92	1	-
MARYLAND:					
Colored	92	79	80	1	1
White	68	48	51	-	-
MASSACHUSETTS:					
Colored	3	7	8	-	-
White	84	70	62	2	-
MICHIGAN:					
Colored	106	114	141	-	-
White	189	210	251	-	-
MISSISSIPPI:					
Colored	357	362	362	4	-
White	126	89	101	-	1
MISSOURI:					
Colored	173	164	156	-	1
White	232	246	195	-	4
NEBRASKA:					
Colored	18	13	7	-	-
White	32	35	34	-	-
NEW HAMPSHIRE:					
Colored	-	-	-	-	-
White	10	4	7	-	-
NEW JERSEY:					
Colored	63	66	54	1	-
White	141	157	126	5	10
NEW YORK:					
Colored	173	149	125	4	-
White	648	563	535	8	15
NORTH CAROLINA:					
Colored	208	235	189	8	9
White	131	114	140	-	1
OHIO:					
Colored	199	218	218	3	1
White	403	398	325	7	7
OKLAHOMA:					
Colored	100	84	92	2	1
White	168	180	155	1	1
PENNSYLVANIA:					
Colored	154	149	167	4	4
White	325	342	333	12	5
RHODE ISLAND:					
Colored	1	2	-	-	-
White	14	12	16	-	-
SOUTH CAROLINA:					
Colored	186	147	186	8	3
White	84	83	59	1	2
TENNESSEE:					
Colored	303	299	279	1	2
White	227	207	155	-	-
VERMONT:					
Colored	-	-	-	-	-
White	4	5	5	-	-
VIRGINIA:					
Colored	186	167	149	2	3
White	140	123	95	-	-
WEST VIRGINIA:					
Colored	82	75	60	-	-
White	158	159	116	3	2

[1] Includes Negro, nonwhite, and other races.
[2] States in registration area whose Negro population represented 55 percent or more of the total colored population in 1930.

TABLE 22.—COLORED [1] AND WHITE DEATHS (EXCLUSIVE OF STILLBIRTHS) FROM ALL CAUSES AND FROM UNKNOWN OR ILL-DEFINED DISEASES, IN SELECTED REGISTRATION CITIES REPORTING 500 OR MORE COLORED DEATHS IN 1930

CITIES	ALL CAUSES		UNKNOWN OR ILL-DEFINED DISEASES			
	Colored	White	Colored	White	Percent of total	
					Colored	White
Atlanta, Ga	2, 106	2, 099	43	18	2. 0	0. 9
Augusta, Ga	680	532	4	2	. 6	. 4
Baltimore, Md	2, 815	8, 424	-	1	-	(2)
Birmingham, Ala	1, 925	1, 623	218	58	11. 3	3. 6
Charleston, S. C	927	499	2	-	. 2	-
Chattanooga, Tenn	825	1, 058	62	59	7. 5	5. 6
Chicago, Ill	4, 045	31, 271	80	251	2. 0	. 8
Cincinnati, Ohio	1, 139	5, 866	2	4	. 2	. 1
Cleveland, Ohio	1, 293	8, 613	7	29	. 5	. 3
Columbia, S. C	554	669	1	2	. 2	. 3
Columbus, Ohio	608	3, 862	-	4	-	. 1
Dallas, Tex	859	2, 153	-	1	-	(2)
Detroit, Mich	2, 037	12, 692	1	6	(2)	(2)
Houston, Tex	1, 495	2, 103	293	144	19. 6	6. 8
Indianapolis, Ind	867	4, 326	-	-	-	-
Jacksonville, Fla	1, 014	963	6	6	. 6	. 6
Kansas City, Mo	922	4, 379	3	6	. 3	. 1
Little Rock, Ark	693	1, 157	15	7	2. 2	. 6
Los Angeles, Calif	822	13, 206	3	24	. 4	. 2
Louisville, Ky	1, 104	3, 286	2	2	0. 2	0. 1
Macon, Ga	609	452	53	9	8. 7	2. 0
Memphis, Tenn	2, 274	2, 124	95	49	4. 2	2. 3
Mobile, Ala	587	656	2	1	. 3	. 2
Montgomery, Ala	664	474	20	-	3. 0	-
Nashville, Tenn	990	1, 520	49	39	4. 9	2. 6
Newark, N. J	759	4, 504	-	2	-	(2)
New Orleans, La	3, 289	4, 741	1	2	(2)	(2)
New York, N. Y	5, 630	69, 283	-	27	-	(2)
Norfolk, Va	902	861	-	-	-	-
Philadelphia, Pa	3, 620	20, 896	7	10	. 2	(2)
Pittsburgh, Pa	1, 103	8, 209	16	64	1. 5	. 8
Richmond, Va	1, 132	1, 605	39	9	3. 4	. 6
St. Louis, Mo	1, 982	9, 500	1	4	. 1	(2)
Savannah, Ga	1, 033	627	2	-	. 2	-
Shreveport, La	874	795	7	2	. 8	. 3
Vicksburg, Miss	521	222	83	12	15. 9	5. 4
Washington, D. C	2, 792	4, 595	3	2	. 1	(2)
Winston-Salem, N. C	620	447	39	6	6. 3	1. 3

[1] Includes Negro and other nonwhite races.
[2] Less than 1/10 of 1 percent.

TABLE 23.—TOTAL COLORED [1] DEATHS, DEATHS OF RESIDENTS, AND DEATH RATE IN EACH REGISTRATION CITY AND COUNTY IN SELECTED STATES: 1930

AREA	TOTAL DEATHS		DEATHS OF RESIDENTS [2]	
	Number	Rate per 1,000 population	Number	Rate per 1,000 population
ALABAMA CITIES:				
Anniston	117	16.3	113	15.7
Bessemer	183	15.6	192	16.4
Birmingham	1,925	19.3	1,841	18.4
Decatur	60	15.4	57	14.6
Dothan	66	10.6	57	9.2
Fairfield	206	31.7	122	18.8
Florence	61	21.8	55	19.6
Gadsden	112	17.5	108	16.9
Huntsville	94	24.7	90	23.7
Mobile	587	23.9	543	22.1
Montgomery	664	22.1	633	21.0
Phenix City [3]	13	3.2	13	3.2
Selma	282	30.3	209	22.5
Tuscaloosa	146	20.3	129	17.9
ARKANSAS CITIES:				
Blytheville	49	17.5	50	17.9
El Dorado	93	23.8	77	19.7
Fort Smith	79	22.6	78	22.3
Hot Springs	144	34.3	124	29.5
Jonesboro	21	16.2	19	14.6
Little Rock	693	35.0	601	30.4
North Little Rock	65	10.7	81	13.3
Pine Bluff	131	21.2	131	21.2
Texarkana	69	22.3	66	21.3
DELAWARE CITIES:				
Wilmington	280	23.1	289	23.8
DISTRICT OF COLUMBIA:				
Washington	2,792	21.0	2,657	20.0
FLORIDA CITIES:				
Daytona Beach	94	17.1	77	14.0
Gainesville	119	28.3	97	23.1
Jacksonville	1,014	21.0	978	20.3
Key West	55	24.1	52	22.8
Lakeland	66	16.5	66	16.5
Miami	382	15.2	372	14.8
Orlando	118	15.3	106	13.8
Pensacola	226	23.5	221	23.0
St. Augustine	87	25.6	70	20.6
St. Petersburg	120	16.0	110	14.7
Sanford	49	10.0	43	8.8
Tallahassee	78	17.7	70	15.9
Tampa	342	15.9	364	16.9
West Palm Beach	189	20.8	150	16.5
GEORGIA CITIES:				
Albany	185	24.7	170	22.7
Athens	148	23.1	149	23.3
Atlanta	2,106	23.2	2,068	22.8
Augusta	680	27.9	641	26.3
Brunswick	163	27.2	155	25.8
Columbus	344	24.2	328	23.1
Decatur	53	20.4	55	21.2
Griffin	124	36.5	123	36.2
Lagrange	130	23.6	126	22.9
Macon	609	26.4	579	25.1
Rome	93	19.4	86	17.9
Savannah	1,033	26.5	948	24.3
Thomasville	155	25.4	154	25.2
Valdosta	127	20.5	128	20.6
Waycross	138	23.8	128	22.1
ILLINOIS CITIES:				
Cairo	111	24.2	106	23.1
Chicago	4,045	15.4	4,060	15.5
East St. Louis	173	14.9	168	14.5
INDIANA CITIES:				
Indianapolis	867	19.6	876	19.8
Jeffersonville	30	23.1	29	22.3
KANSAS CITIES:				
Atchison	35	21.9	36	22.5
Coffeyville	42	20.0	43	20.5
Kansas City	341	15.0	316	13.9
Lawrence	29	18.1	28	17.5
Leavenworth	45	19.6	50	21.7
KENTUCKY CITIES: [4]				
Bowling Green	48	20.0	------	------
Frankfort	58	26.4	------	------
Henderson	75	32.0	------	------
Hopkinsville	146	36.5	------	------
Lexington	421	32.9	------	------
Louisville	1,104	23.2	------	------
Ownesboro	62	24.8	------	------
Paducah	141	20.7	------	------
LOUISIANA CITIES:				
Alexandria	171	17.8	175	18.2
Baton Rouge	116	10.8	126	11.8
Bogalusa	82	17.1	83	17.3
Lafayette	98	19.2	106	20.8
Lake Charles	82	13.7	86	14.3
Monroe	225	21.8	192	18.6
New Orleans	3,289	25.0	2,737	20.8
Shreveport	874	32.1	490	18.0
MARYLAND CITIES:				
Annapolis	84	24.0	84	24.0
Baltimore	2,815	19.6	2,712	18.9
Frederick	27	16.9	33	20.6
Salisbury	69	36.3	65	34.2
MASSACHUSETTS CITIES:				
Boston	452	20.0	443	19.6
MICHIGAN CITIES:				
Detroit	2,037	15.6	2,138	16.3
MISSISSIPPI CITIES: [4]				
Biloxi	52	21.7	------	------
Clarksdale	140	28.0	------	------
Columbus	154	32.1	------	------
Greenville	336	40.0	------	------
Greenwood	144	26.7	------	------
Gulfport	70	21.9	------	------
Hattiesburg	133	19.6	------	------
Jackson	414	21.1	------	------
Laurel	142	20.9	------	------
McComb	61	30.5	------	------
Meridian	294	25.8	------	------
Natchez	149	21.0	------	------
Vicksburg	521	43.4	------	------
MISSOURI CITIES:				
Columbia	52	22.6	50	21.7
Jefferson City	24	10.9	24	10.9
Kansas City	922	21.8	930	22.0
St. Louis	1,982	20.7	1,963	20.5
NEBRASKA CITIES:				
Omaha	223	18.1	225	18.3
NEW JERSEY CITIES:				
Asbury Park	22	6.3	62	17.7
Atlantic City	268	17.0	260	16.5
Montclair	43	6.6	92	14.2
Newark	759	18.8	821	20.4
Orange	87	17.1	77	15.1
NEW YORK CITIES:				
New York	5,630	16.2	5,572	16.0
NORTH CAROLINA CITIES:				
Asheville	244	17.1	239	16.7
Charlotte	481	19.1	474	18.8
Concord	34	17.0	34	17.0
Durham	426	22.4	395	20.8
Elizabeth City	72	18.9	69	18.2
Fayetteville	120	21.8	118	21.5
Gastonia	70	21.9	64	20.0
Goldsboro	131	19.0	126	18.3
Greensboro	254	18.0	232	16.5
High Point	134	18.1	128	17.3
Kinston	95	18.6	93	18.2
New Bern	150	23.9	146	23.3
Raleigh	299	23.7	263	20.9
Rocky Mount	197	22.4	187	21.3
Salisbury	64	16.0	58	14.5
Shelby	17	7.7	16	7.3
Statesville	31	18.2	32	18.8
Thomasville	29	17.1	29	17.1
Wilmington	326	24.9	296	22.6
Wilson	165	26.2	159	25.2
Winston-Salem	620	18.9	616	18.8
OHIO CITIES:				
Cincinnati	1,139	23.5	1,106	22.8
Cleveland	1,293	17.4	1,292	17.4
Columbus	608	18.3	593	17.9
Springfield	141	17.0	143	17.2
Xenia	39	18.6	39	18.6
OKLAHOMA CITIES: [4]				
Ardmore	37	14.8	------	------
Chickasha	44	25.9	------	------
McAlester	44	22.0	------	------
Muskogee	202	25.3	------	------
Oklahoma City	269	16.3	------	------
Okmulgee	122	30.1	------	------
Sapulpa	22	16.3	------	------
Tulsa	272	15.6	------	------
Wewoka	42	24.7	------	------
PENNSYLVANIA CITIES:				
Chester	212	22.8	208	22.4
Coatesville	13	5.7	14	6.1
Philadelphia	3,620	16.1	3,636	16.2
Pittsburgh	1,103	19.7	1,094	19.6
Steelton	23	8.9	28	10.9
West Chester	45	21.4	40	19.0
SOUTH CAROLINA CITIES: [4]				
Anderson	112	28.7	------	------
Charleston	927	33.0	------	------
Columbia	554	30.4	------	------
Florence	191	31.3	------	------
Greenville	290	26.6	------	------
Greenwood	81	23.1	------	------
Rock Hill	50	20.0	------	------
Spartanburg	222	22.4	------	------
Sumter	153	30.0	------	------
TENNESSEE CITIES:				
Bristol	20	20.0	20	20.0
Chattanooga	825	24.8	826	24.8
Jackson	148	19.5	148	19.5
Johnson City	38	15.8	39	16.3
Kingsport	5	8.3	5	8.3
Knoxville	320	18.5	318	18.4
Memphis	2,274	23.5	2,159	22.3
Nashville	990	23.1	935	21.8
TEXAS CITIES: [5]				
Beaumont	292	15.1	283	14.6
Dallas	859	19.0	782	17.3
El Paso	1,126	18.5	1,067	17.5
Fort Worth	428	16.3	420	16.0
Houston	1,495	19.1	1,449	18.5
Waco	271	24.2	236	21.1
VIRGINIA CITIES:				
Alexandria	107	21.8	103	20.9
Charlottesville	49	11.7	54	12.9
Danville	132	23.6	112	20.0
Hopewell	20	14.3	20	14.3
Lynchburg	252	26.0	228	23.5
Newport News	260	19.6	264	19.9
Norfolk	902	20.4	849	19.2
Petersburg	310	24.6	276	21.9
Portsmouth	376	19.9	384	20.3
Richmond	1,132	21.4	1,054	19.9
Roanoke	276	22.3	270	21.8
Staunton	36	20.0	37	20.6
Suffolk	121	31.8	104	27.4
WASHINGTON CITIES:				
Seattle	197	13.0	183	12.1
WEST VIRGINIA CITIES:				
Bluefield	83	24.7	83	24.7
Charleston	123	18.1	125	18.4
RURAL PART OF REGISTRATION STATES [6]				
ALABAMA COUNTIES:				
Autauga	154	14.1	166	15.2
Baldwin	92	13.3	94	13.6
Barbour	251	13.5	254	13.7
Bibb	94	13.7	102	14.8
Bullock	230	14.6	231	14.7
Butler	203	13.8	205	13.9
Calhoun	78	14.7	80	15.1
Chambers	228	12.7	230	12.8
Chilton	53	13.6	54	13.8
Choctaw	119	10.6	121	10.8
Clarke	181	13.3	189	13.9
Clay	31	11.4	32	11.7
Coffee	65	9.4	64	9.3
Colbert	136	16.0	138	16.3
Conecuh	155	14.0	155	14.0
Coosa	51	11.0	52	11.2
Covington	91	13.0	89	12.7
Crenshaw	79	10.8	79	10.8
Dale	70	13.0	68	12.6
Dallas	428	13.6	442	14.0
Elmore	199	14.0	198	13.9
Escambia	115	12.8	118	13.1
Etowah	49	13.6	51	14.2
Fayette	24	9.2	24	9.2
Geneva	63	16.2	64	16.4
Greene	223	13.7	229	14.0
Hale	265	13.7	266	13.7
Henry	103	9.5	106	9.8
Houston	85	11.5	88	11.9
Jefferson	679	13.3	805	15.8
Lamar	32	11.2	32	11.2
Lauderdale	47	9.4	53	10.6
Lawrence	84	11.8	83	11.7
Lee	281	16.1	283	16.3
Limestone	147	14.7	149	14.9
Lowndes	262	13.3	270	13.8
Macon	477	21.3	473	21.1
Madison	219	14.1	225	14.5
Marengo	324	12.3	336	12.8
Mobile	427	24.0	454	25.5
Monroe	175	11.1	180	11.4
Montgomery	301	13.6	314	14.2
Morgan	58	13.2	59	13.4
Perry	230	12.0	243	12.7
Pickens	139	11.6	140	11.7
Pike	194	13.3	195	13.4
Randolph	67	11.4	67	11.4
Russell [3]	285	17.1	293	17.6
St. Clair	52	10.8	55	11.5
Shelby	93	13.3	101	14.4
Sumter	289	13.6	287	13.5
Talladega	235	13.7	238	13.9
Tallapoosa	116	12.0	117	12.1
Tuscaloosa	178	12.4	190	13.2
Walker	96	12.3	112	14.4
Washington	71	10.4	72	10.6
Wilcox	276	14.3	283	14.6
ARKANSAS COUNTIES:				
Arkansas	77	15.7	80	16.3
Ashley	143	12.0	143	12.0
Bradley	63	11.1	65	11.4
Calhoun	40	13.4	42	14.0
Chicot	158	11.1	160	11.3
Clark	83	11.4	84	11.5
Cleveland	34	9.7	37	10.6
Columbia	106	8.3	105	8.2

See footnotes at end of table.

TABLE 23.—TOTAL COLORED[1] DEATHS, DEATHS OF RESIDENTS, AND DEATH RATE IN EACH REGISTRATION CITY AND COUNTY IN SELECTED STATES: 1930—Continued

AREA	TOTAL DEATHS		DEATHS OF RESIDENTS[2]	
	Number	Rate per 1,000 population	Number	Rate per 1,000 population
RURAL PART OF REGISTRATION STATES—Continued				
ARKANSAS COUNTIES—Continued.				
Conway	106	17.7	108	18.1
Crittenden	405	12.8	422	13.4
Cross	122	11.0	127	11.4
Dallas	49	9.4	50	9.6
Desha	153	10.9	158	11.3
Drew	107	11.7	112	12.2
Faulkner	64	17.8	66	18.3
Hempstead	158	12.0	155	11.8
Hot Spring	33	14.3	33	14.3
Howard	31	8.1	33	8.6
Jackson	65	12.5	65	12.5
Jefferson	291	9.7	296	9.6
Lafayette	83	9.8	85	10.0
Lee	279	16.0	280	16.1
Lincoln	135	10.3	136	10.4
Little River	55	9.1	54	8.9
Lonoke	122	11.1	129	11.7
Miller	77	11.8	77	11.8
Mississippi	264	11.2	272	11.6
Monroe	153	13.3	158	13.7
Nevada	47	6.5	46	6.4
Ouachita	164	12.5	169	12.9
Phillips	468	17.1	465	17.0
Poinsett	52	12.1	53	12.3
Prairie	56	15.5	58	16.0
Pulaski	188	13.1	213	14.8
St. Francis	280	12.4	284	12.6
Sevier	23	13.1	23	13.1
Union	74	5.4	90	6.6
Woodruff	137	13.7	138	13.8
CALIFORNIA COUNTIES:				
Alpine	------	------	1	9.6
Del Norte	6	12.0	6	12.0
Inyo	23	16.8	22	16.1
Mono	4	10.0	5	12.5
DELAWARE COUNTIES:				
Kent	133	19.9	131	19.6
New Castle	154	23.7	138	21.2
Sussex	140	18.4	148	19.5
FLORIDA COUNTIES:				
Alachua	183	16.3	190	17.0
Baker	31	17.2	31	17.2
Bay	43	13.9	46	14.8
Bradford	38	14.1	39	14.4
Brevard	57	13.3	56	13.0
Broward	78	11.3	81	11.7
Calhoun	27	19.3	29	20.7
Charlotte	17	21.3	17	21.3
Citrus	27	15.0	28	15.6
Clay	23	12.8	22	12.2
Collier	4	4.4	5	5.6
Columbia	110	19.3	109	19.1
Dade	76	14.3	76	14.3
De Soto	32	21.3	34	22.7
Dixie	29	9.7	30	10.0
Duval	90	16.7	111	20.6
Escambia	75	17.4	77	17.9
Flagler	22	24.4	22	24.4
Franklin	47	18.8	48	19.2
Gadsden	470	27.6	471	27.7
Gilchrist	7	10.0	7	10.0
Glades	8	8.9	8	8.9
Gulf	9	8.2	9	8.2
Hamilton	39	10.3	37	9.8
Hardee	10	11.1	12	13.3
Hendry	8	5.7	9	6.4
Hernando	31	19.4	32	20.0
Highlands	41	15.2	39	14.4
Hillsborough	154	19.7	118	15.1
Holmes	14	35.0	15	37.5
Indian River	15	7.5	15	7.5
Jackson	178	14.2	180	14.4
Jefferson	169	18.5	169	18.5
Lafayette	4	5.7	4	5.7
Lake	75	11.5	75	11.5
Lee	59	16.4	55	15.3
Leon	96	10.2	109	11.6
Levy	75	15.6	81	16.9
Liberty	12	8.4	12	8.4
Madison	100	12.2	103	12.6
Manatee	91	13.2	93	13.5
Marion	231	15.9	221	15.2
Martin	23	11.5	26	13.0
Monroe	2	9.4	4	18.9
Nassau	69	17.7	73	18.8
Okaloosa	11	11.0	12	12.0
Okeechobee	7	5.4	8	6.2
Orange	56	11.9	68	14.5
Osceola	49	15.3	48	15.0
Palm Beach	63	7.9	97	12.1
RURAL PART OF REGISTRATION STATES—Continued				
FLORIDA COUNTIES—Continued.				
Pasco	27	15.0	29	16.1
Pinellas	47	12.7	50	13.5
Polk	180	14.8	181	14.8
Putnam	173	21.9	170	21.5
St. Johns	47	14.2	61	18.5
St. Lucie	22	11.6	23	12.1
Santa Rosa	45	20.5	45	20.5
Sarasota	32	11.4	30	10.7
Seminole	43	11.9	44	12.2
Sumter	37	11.6	39	12.2
Suwannee	83	15.6	87	16.3
Taylor	65	13.0	69	13.8
Union	44	15.2	45	15.5
Volusia	121	17.0	128	18.0
Wakulla	24	10.4	24	10.4
Walton	38	14.1	38	14.1
Washington	30	11.5	31	11.9
GEORGIA COUNTIES:				
Appling	28	10.0	29	10.4
Atkinson	12	6.1	13	6.6
Bacon	23	20.9	23	20.9
Baker	34	7.1	35	7.3
Baldwin	280	25.9	169	15.6
Banks	39	40.5	22	22.8
Barrow	36	17.4	36	17.4
Bartow	82	17.8	87	18.9
Ben Hill	71	16.0	68	15.3
Berrien	29	12.1	29	12.1
Bibb	110	11.2	132	13.5
Bleckley	58	17.8	59	18.1
Brantley	17	13.1	19	14.6
Brooks	148	13.1	150	13.3
Bryan	51	19.1	60	22.5
Bulloch	86	8.5	88	8.7
Burke	322	14.2	332	14.6
Butts	81	18.0	82	18.3
Calhoun	94	12.5	96	12.8
Camden	89	23.8	96	25.6
Campbell	32	10.8	34	11.5
Candler	40	12.7	40	12.7
Carroll	92	12.1	95	12.5
Charlton	5	5.0	5	5.0
Chatham	217	19.9	254	23.3
Chattahoochee	22	8.1	22	8.1
Chattooga	28	14.7	29	15.3
Clarke	46	13.0	46	13.0
Clay	30	6.6	30	6.6
Clayton	51	15.7	54	16.6
Clinch	18	6.0	18	6.0
Cobb	91	14.0	92	14.2
Coffee	59	11.1	60	11.3
Colquitt	89	11.4	88	11.3
Columbia	42	7.6	48	8.7
Cook	37	11.9	37	11.9
Coweta	156	14.4	158	14.6
Crawford	52	13.4	54	13.9
Crisp	149	17.8	151	18.0
Decatur	188	1o. 1	191	16.3
De Kalb	102	14.4	104	14.6
Dodge	78	9.8	80	10.0
Dooly	140	13.9	145	14.4
Dougherty	34	6.4	43	8.1
Douglas	37	16.3	37	16.3
Early	110	11.3	110	11.3
Echols	1	1.2	2	2.4
Effingham	69	16.4	69	16.4
Elbert	118	15.7	120	15.9
Emanuel	123	13.5	119	13.1
Evans	29	11.2	32	12.3
Fayette	30	10.6	31	10.9
Floyd	60	15.8	64	16.8
Franklin	39	14.6	40	15.0
Fulton	277	19.6	309	21.9
Glascock	14	10.8	14	10.8
Glynn	44	19.1	48	20.9
Grady	59	8.9	61	9.2
Greene	108	16.3	113	17.0
Gwinnett	40	12.0	41	12.3
Hall	58	17.1	59	17.4
Hancock	85	9.1	84	9.0
Haralson	18	13.7	18	13.7
Harris	86	11.2	86	11.2
Hart	54	13.9	54	13.9
Heard	22	9.3	22	9.3
Henry	99	12.5	99	12.5
Houston	98	12.8	99	13.0
Irwin	59	13.0	60	13.2
Jackson	54	13.3	53	13.0
Jasper	64	12.2	69	13.2
Jeff Davis	20	12.5	20	12.5
RURAL PART OF REGISTRATION STATES—Continued				
GEORGIA COUNTIES—Continued.				
Jefferson	82	6.8	86	7.1
Jenkins	126	16.9	124	16.6
Johnson	52	10.5	53	10.7
Jones	57	9.9	59	10.2
Lamar	70	15.6	71	15.9
Lanier	20	10.3	20	10.3
Laurens	185	13.7	186	13.7
Lee	113	17.4	115	17.7
Liberty	114	20.6	118	21.3
Lincoln	20	4.9	22	5.4
Long	16	8.9	16	8.9
Lowndes	66	8.7	70	9.2
McDuffie	84	18.4	84	18.4
McIntosh	105	26.9	113	29.0
Macon	131	11.7	137	12.2
Madison	54	19.1	54	19.1
Marion	46	11.7	46	11.7
Meriwether	180	15.3	179	15.2
Miller	27	8.8	28	9.1
Mitchell	200	16.9	201	16.9
Monroe	110	16.3	111	16.4
Montgomery	47	10.7	48	10.9
Morgan	94	13.1	97	13.5
Muscogee	24	3.6	36	5.5
Newton	105	15.5	109	16.1
Oconee	21	8.7	22	9.2
Oglethorpe	70	10.9	70	10.9
Paulding	15	13.3	15	13.3
Peach	99	15.0	101	15.3
Pierce	58	17.6	59	17.9
Pike	103	19.1	105	19.4
Polk	71	14.8	72	15.0
Pulaski	43	8.5	43	8.5
Putnam	88	16.9	93	17.8
Quitman	23	8.8	24	9.2
Randolph	125	10.8	128	11.0
Richmond	72	12.0	85	14.2
Rockdale	37	15.2	37	15.2
Schley	37	10.9	37	10.9
Screven	124	10.7	135	11.6
Seminole	35	12.1	35	12.1
Spalding	39	8.3	40	8.5
Stephens	31	14.8	31	14.8
Stewart	104	13.1	107	13.5
Sumter	257	14.8	261	15.0
Talbot	71	12.2	74	12.7
Taliaferro	62	14.7	62	14.7
Tattnall	30	9.1	31	9.4
Taylor	48	9.2	50	9.5
Telfair	61	12.6	63	13.0
Terrell	189	14.6	189	14.6
Thomas	118	12.1	119	12.2
Tift	105	21.4	107	21.8
Toombs	53	10.8	55	11.2
Treutlen	25	10.1	26	10.5
Troup	133	13.9	140	14.6
Turner	53	13.7	53	13.7
Twiggs	64	12.0	65	12.2
Upson	98	14.2	98	14.2
Walker	39	16.3	39	16.3
Walton	106	15.7	109	16.1
Ware	28	11.6	31	12.8
Warren	77	10.5	79	10.7
Washington	167	11.8	171	12.1
Wayne	60	20.0	60	20.0
Webster	44	14.5	44	14.5
Wheeler	34	11.6	36	12.3
Wilcox	61	11.1	63	11.5
Wilkes	114	11.3	116	11.5
Wilkinson	82	16.0	85	16.6
Worth	146	15.2	150	15.7
ILLINOIS COUNTIES:				
Alexander	27	13.2	26	12.7
Massac	34	20.0	34	20.0
Pulaski	79	16.1	81	16.5
KANSAS COUNTIES:				
Wyandotte	24	11.4	24	11.4
KENTUCKY COUNTIES:[4]				
Ballard	16	17.2	------	------
Barren	56	20.0	------	------
Bourbon	102	25.5	------	------
Boyle	80	25.0	------	------
Caldwell	30	17.4	------	------
Christian	175	22.7	------	------
Clark	65	22.9	------	------
Fayette	53	14.3	------	------
Franklin	10	25.0	------	------
Fulton	71	22.5	------	------
Garrard	42	28.7	------	------
Henderson	36	17.5	------	------

See footnotes at end of table.

TABLE 23.—TOTAL COLORED[1] DEATHS, DEATHS OF RESIDENTS, AND DEATH RATE IN EACH REGISTRATION CITY AND COUNTY IN SELECTED STATES: 1930—Continued

AREA	TOTAL DEATHS: Number	TOTAL DEATHS: Rate per 1,000 population	DEATHS OF RESIDENTS[2]: Number	DEATHS OF RESIDENTS[2]: Rate per 1,000 population
RURAL PART OF REGISTRATION STATES—Continued				
KENTUCKY COUNTIES—Continued.				
Henry	21	17.8	------	------
Hickman	22	21.0	------	------
Hopkins	82	15.8	------	------
Jessamine	42	22.1	------	------
Lincoln	30	17.6	------	------
Logan	57	16.4	------	------
Lyon	19	15.8	------	------
McCracken	6	6.0	------	------
Madison	78	17.7	------	------
Marion	23	15.7	------	------
Mason	49	19.6	------	------
Mercer	36	23.2	------	------
Montgomery	42	21.3	------	------
Nelson	41	19.5	------	------
Oldham	10	14.0	------	------
Scott	64	25.5	------	------
Shelby	41	15.5	------	------
Simpson	31	18.2	------	------
Taylor	23	20.5	------	------
Todd	69	20.3	------	------
Trigg	44	18.5	------	------
Union	26	12.8	------	------
Warren	55	21.2	------	------
Washington	18	13.2	------	------
Webster	51	16.4	------	------
Woodford	59	26.7	------	------
LOUISIANA PARISHES:				
Acadia	118	14.6	122	15.1
Allen	37	8.7	49	11.6
Ascension	140	19.8	156	22.0
Assumption	102	16.1	111	17.6
Avoyelles	102	10.3	116	11.7
Beauregard	34	10.5	41	12.6
Bienville	85	7.9	100	9.3
Bossier	133	7.4	193	10.8
Caddo	363	11.9	480	15.7
Calcasieu	58	9.4	63	10.2
Caldwell	31	10.3	34	11.3
Cameron	5	8.3	5	8.3
Catahoula	29	6.2	29	6.2
Clairborne	152	8.4	166	9.2
Concordia	113	12.3	112	12.2
De Sota	194	10.1	221	11.5
East Baton Rouge	306	16.2	301	15.9
East Carroll	141	11.8	158	13.3
East Feliciana	237	19.9	222	18.7
Evangeline	38	6.7	40	7.0
Franklin	169	14.8	175	15.4
Grant	47	9.6	53	10.8
Iberia	177	16.5	193	18.0
Iberville	236	18.5	258	20.3
Jackson	24	6.0	31	7.8
Jefferson	87	10.6	131	16.0
Jefferson Davis	54	10.8	56	11.2
Lafayette	106	12.9	108	13.2
Lafourche	136	25.7	157	29.6
La Salle	20	9.5	23	11.0
Lincoln	76	7.8	82	8.4
Livingston	33	7.9	47	11.2
Madison	111	11.6	122	12.7
Morehouse	168	12.4	192	14.1
Natchitoches	252	12.4	271	13.4
Ouachita	76	8.5	104	11.7
Plaquemines	69	15.1	88	19.3
Pointe Coupee	184	15.1	206	16.9
Rapides	308	19.5	312	19.7
Red River	54	7.1	70	9.2
Richland	163	12.3	183	13.9
Sabine	39	5.4	46	6.4
St. Bernard	17	13.1	28	21.5
St. Charles	70	16.7	88	21.0
St. Helena	48	10.4	50	10.9
St. James	124	16.3	140	18.4
St. John the Baptist	123	17.8	141	20.4
St. Landry	389	13.1	413	14.0
St. Martin	87	11.5	89	11.8
St. Mary	244	17.0	266	18.5
St. Tammany	81	11.6	110	15.7
Tangipahoa	127	8.0	162	10.3
Tensas	155	14.2	165	15.1
Terrebonne	154	16.6	167	18.0
Union	37	5.5	45	6.7
Vermilion	65	14.4	71	15.8
Vernon	24	6.6	32	8.7
Washington	42	8.6	52	10.6
Webster	111	8.4	132	10.0
West Baton Rouge	78	12.7	87	14.2
West Carroll	28	10.0	37	13.2
West Feliciana	102	12.2	110	13.2
Winn	36	9.7	38	10.3
MARYLAND COUNTIES:				
Anne Arundel	283	24.2	310	26.5
Baltimore	110	9.2	154	12.9
Calvert	83	18.4	87	19.3
Caroline	62	16.9	71	19.3
Cecil	56	21.5	56	21.5
Charles	132	17.6	149	19.9
Dorchester	166	21.2	170	21.7
Harford	72	17.6	75	18.3
Howard	37	11.2	46	13.9
Kent	74	16.7	80	18.0
Montgomery	122	14.7	143	17.2
Prince Georges	184	13.0	231	16.4
Queen Annes	66	15.1	71	16.2
St. Marys	97	17.3	102	18.2
Somerset	152	18.7	159	19.6
Talbot	136	22.7	127	21.2
Wicomico	56	11.4	57	11.6
Worcester	122	18.2	127	18.9
MINNESOTA COUNTIES:				
Cook	2	6.7	5	16.7
Mahnomen	15	9.3	18	11.2
MISSISSIPPI COUNTIES:[4]				
Adams	212	25.5	------	------
Alcorn	52	12.7	------	------
Amite	102	9.8	------	------
Attala	115	10.6	------	------
Benton	58	12.4	------	------
Bolivar	853	16.0	------	------
Calhoun	26	7.2	------	------
Carroll	108	9.6	------	------
Chickasaw	117	11.2	------	------
Choctaw	40	11.5	------	------
Claiborne	109	12.1	------	------
Clarke	101	12.6	------	------
Clay	145	13.1	------	------
Coahoma	489	15.8	------	------
Copiah	203	13.0	------	------
Covington	58	13.5	------	------
De Soto	243	12.9	------	------
Forrest	16	5.5	------	------
Franklin	88	18.1	------	------
George	17	13.1	------	------
Greene	30	11.5	------	------
Grenada	150	15.0	------	------
Hancock	46	16.4	------	------
Harrison	57	12.7	------	------
Hinds	657	24.2	------	------
Holmes	403	13.7	------	------
Humphreys	252	14.6	------	------
Issaquena	81	17.3	------	------
Itawamba	16	14.5	------	------
Jackson	70	18.2	------	------
Jasper	96	10.7	------	------
Jefferson	127	11.7	------	------
Jefferson Davis	68	8.6	------	------
Jones	37	8.4	------	------
Kemper	131	10.2	------	------
Lafayette	138	16.8	------	------
Lamar	24	8.8	------	------
Lauderdale	99	10.0	------	------
Lawrence	49	10.4	------	------
Leake	85	10.5	------	------
Lee	122	10.8	------	------
Leflore	347	9.7	------	------
Lincoln	149	15.7	------	------
Lowndes	127	10.2	------	------
Madison	333	11.8	------	------
Marion	91	11.8	------	------
Marshall	258	14.5	------	------
Monroe	176	11.0	------	------
Montgomery	97	14.9	------	------
Neshoba	68	10.8	------	------
Newton	76	9.3	------	------
Noxubee	256	12.7	------	------
Oktibbeha	147	12.9	------	------
Panola	297	16.5	------	------
Pearl River	68	13.1	------	------
Perry	41	14.9	------	------
Pike	127	10.2	------	------
Pontotoc	67	16.0	------	------
Prentiss	33	13.2	------	------
Quitman	240	13.8	------	------
Rankin	143	12.9	------	------
Scott	89	10.2	------	------
Sharkey	153	14.9	------	------
Simpson	97	13.9	------	------
Smith	29	8.1	------	------
Stone	25	17.6	------	------
Sunflower	696	14.7	------	------
Tallahatchie	286	11.8	------	------
Tate	145	13.6	------	------
MISSISSIPPI COUNTIES—Continued.				
Tippah	52	16.8	------	------
Tishomingo	12	12.0	------	------
Tunica	315	17.2	------	------
Union	64	14.2	------	------
Walthall	49	8.0	------	------
Warren	86	9.7	------	------
Washington	381	12.3	------	------
Wayne	70	13.0	------	------
Webster	26	10.2	------	------
Wilkinson	169	17.3	------	------
Winston	75	9.1	------	------
Yalobusha	110	13.3	------	------
Yazoo	391	15.5	------	------
MISSOURI COUNTIES:				
Callaway	80	31.9	77	30.7
Cooper	29	14.5	35	17.5
Howard	20	10.3	21	10.8
Mississippi	71	17.8	71	17.8
Pemiscot	139	13.6	143	14.0
Pike	56	26.1	57	26.6
Saline	54	20.0	54	20.0
MONTANA COUNTIES:				
Big Horn	56	23.3	56	23.3
Blaine	27	19.6	27	19.6
Glacier	54	19.3	54	19.3
Missoula	1	3.3	2	6.7
Roosevelt	38	18.1	39	18.6
NEBRASKA COUNTIES:				
Thurston	55	28.9	51	26.8
NEVADA COUNTIES:				
Churchill	5	8.3	5	8.3
Douglas	------	------	------	------
Elko	29	19.3	30	20.0
Humboldt	10	16.7	10	16.7
Lander	2	6.7	2	6.7
Mineral	15	25.0	15	25.0
Ormsby	12	36.9	10	30.8
NEW JERSEY COUNTIES:				
Salem	61	12.7	64	13.3
NEW MEXICO COUNTIES:				
Sandoval	56	18.1	57	18.4
NORTH CAROLINA COUNTIES:				
Alamance	121	14.4	127	15.1
Anson	219	14.3	216	14.1
Beaufort	263	19.5	263	19.5
Bertie	191	13.0	194	13.2
Bladen	131	13.9	134	14.3
Brunswick	84	14.2	89	15.1
Burke	33	12.7	35	13.5
Cabarrus	88	14.7	92	15.3
Camden	35	15.9	38	17.3
Carteret	39	15.6	41	16.4
Caswell	98	11.5	99	11.6
Catawba	77	15.7	80	16.3
Chatham	97	12.1	101	12.6
Chowan	82	15.5	84	15.8
Cleveland	95	9.5	98	9.8
Columbus	162	13.6	166	13.9
Craven	135	15.9	136	16.0
Cumberland	108	9.2	108	9.2
Currituck	26	11.5	28	12.4
Davidson	60	16.7	62	17.2
Davie	41	17.1	40	16.7
Duplin	171	13.2	178	13.7
Durham	66	14.0	66	14.0
Edgecombe	309	13.7	308	13.6
Forsyth	72	15.7	69	15.0
Franklin	204	15.8	214	16.6
Gaston	103	11.2	100	10.9
Gates	47	9.2	49	9.6
Granville	198	14.0	201	14.3
Greene	95	10.7	93	10.4
Guilford	111	14.8	121	16.1
Halifax	387	12.5	390	12.6
Harnett	178	17.0	178	17.0
Hertford	139	13.5	142	13.8
Hoke	128	14.2	115	12.8
Hyde	32	9.1	33	9.4
Iredell	122	16.1	124	16.3
Johnston	176	13.4	178	13.6
Jones	61	13.3	61	13.3
Lee	64	11.6	65	11.8
Lenoir	121	11.6	123	11.8
Lincoln	53	15.6	54	15.9
McDowell	24	12.0	27	13.5
Martin	148	13.3	150	13.5
Mecklenburg	211	16.1	213	16.3
Montgomery	51	13.4	47	12.4
Moore	88	8.9	93	9.4

See footnotes at end of table.

TABLE 23.—TOTAL COLORED[1] DEATHS, DEATHS OF RESIDENTS, AND DEATH RATE IN EACH REGISTRATION CITY AND COUNTY IN SELECTED STATES: 1930—Continued

AREA	TOTAL DEATHS		DEATHS OF RESIDENTS[2]	
	Number	Rate per 1,000 population	Number	Rate per 1,000 population
RURAL PART OF REGISTRATION STATES—Continued				
NORTH CAROLINA COUNTIES—Continued.				
Nash	223	11.3	226	11.5
New Hanover	59	15.9	66	17.8
Northampton	195	11.3	197	11.5
Onslow	57	13.9	58	14.1
Orange	101	14.4	110	15.7
Pamlico	41	13.2	42	13.5
Pasquotank	65	14.8	63	14.3
Pender	114	15.0	118	15.5
Perquimans	83	15.7	86	16.3
Person	95	10.8	98	11.1
Pitt	328	12.4	332	12.5
Polk	14	8.8	14	8.8
Randolph	50	12.8	52	13.3
Richmond	190	14.2	190	14.2
Robeson	395	11.2	398	11.3
Rockingham	167	14.4	174	15.0
Rowan	99	13.0	105	13.8
Rutherford	68	12.6	64	11.9
Sampson	177	12.6	180	12.8
Scotland	160	14.0	161	14.1
Stanly	61	17.4	61	17.4
Stokes	24	10.0	24	10.0
Tyrrell	21	12.4	21	12.4
Union	143	14.2	145	14.4
Vance	180	15.0	178	14.8
Wake	326	15.2	344	16.1
Warren	208	14.0	214	14.4
Washington	97	18.0	98	18.1
Wayne	406	24.8	397	24.2
Wilson	166	12.7	173	13.2
NORTH DAKOTA COUNTIES:				
Rolette	47	13.4	47	13.4
Sioux	26	18.6	26	18.6
OHIO COUNTIES:				
Greene	23	12.1	23	12.1
OKLAHOMA COUNTIES:[4]				
Adair	52	10.4	------	------
Carter	3	1.5	------	------
Cherokee	32	6.3	------	------
Choctaw	8	1.1	------	------
Craig	36	11.4	------	------
Creek	66	9.6	------	------
Delaware	14	3.7	------	------
Hughes	35	8.3	------	------
Kingfisher	25	11.9	------	------
Lincoln	27	7.5	------	------
Logan	140	21.2	------	------
McCurtain	61	6.0	------	------
McIntosh	62	9.4	------	------
Mayes	12	3.0	------	------
Muskogee	97	7.6	------	------
Nowata	29	9.2	------	------
Okfuskee	79	9.1	------	------
Oklahoma	14	4.5	------	------
Okmulgee	67	6.8	------	------
Rogers	14	4.2	------	------
Seminole	26	4.6	------	------
Sequoyah	29	6.0	------	------
Wagoner	111	14.6	------	------
OREGON COUNTIES:				
Jefferson	8	22.6	8	22.6
SOUTH CAROLINA COUNTIES[4]				
Abbeville	170	15.4	------	------
Aiken	321	15.0	------	------
Allendale	116	11.9	------	------
Anderson	219	11.8	------	------
Bamberg	172	13.8	------	------
Barnwell	139	10.3	------	------
Beaufort	354	22.7	------	------
Berkeley	328	21.7	------	------
Calhoun	215	17.3	------	------
Charleston	558	20.8	------	------
Cherokee	122	14.4	------	------
Chester	225	13.7	------	------
Chesterfield	175	13.7	------	------
Clarendon	369	17.1	------	------
Colleton	266	18.9	------	------
Darlington	346	16.0	------	------
Dillon	186	15.0	------	------
Dorchester	139	12.4	------	------
Edgefield	160	13.0	------	------
Fairfield	186	11.9	------	------
Florence	283	13.2	------	------
Georgetown	278	19.9	------	------
Greenville	227	13.3	------	------
Greenwood	180	15.0	------	------
Hampton	171	17.4	------	------
SOUTH CAROLINA COUNTIES—Continued.				
Horry	116	12.0	------	------
Jasper	126	18.5	------	------
Kershaw	188	10.7	------	------
Lancaster	125	11.4	------	------
Laurens	306	17.3	------	------
Lea	219	13.5	------	------
Lexington	176	16.0	------	------
McCormick	121	15.7	------	------
Marion	146	9.7	------	------
Marlboro	284	15.6	------	------
Newberry	218	13.5	------	------
Oconee	9.3	15.8	------	------
Orangeburg	683	16.7	------	------
Pickens	59	12.0	------	------
Richland	432	21.6	------	------
Saluda	79	9.0	------	------
Spartanburg	258	12.7	------	------
Sumter	412	16.0	------	------
Union	59	4.8	------	------
Williamsburg	341	14.6	------	------
York	236	12.1	------	------
SOUTH DAKOTA COUNTIES:				
Bennett	25	19.2	25	19.2
Buffalo	24	34.3	24	34.3
Corson	43	22.6	44	23.2
Dewey	26	15.3	27	15.9
Mellette	36	24.0	37	24.7
Shannon	99	31.9	104	33.5
Todd	26	9.3	25	8.9
Washabaugh	15	16.7	15	16.7
Washington	41	27.3	40	26.7
Ziebach	18	20.0	18	20.0
TENNESSEE COUNTIES:				
Bedford	69	18.6	69	18.6
Carroll	62	13.2	65	13.8
Cheatham	13	15.9	13	15.9
Chester	19	10.0	19	10.0
Crocket	41	11.9	41	11.9
Davidson	231	25.4	242	26.6
Dickson	33	17.9	34	18.4
Dyer	77	15.1	77	15.1
Fayette	228	10.8	231	11.0
Franklin	46	18.4	46	18.4
Gibson	133	13.4	134	13.5
Giles	112	14.8	114	15.1
Hamblen	26	15.3	26	15.3
Hamilton	79	25.5	82	26.5
Hardeman	124	14.5	126	14.8
Hardin	14	9.4	14	9.4
Haywood	203	11.7	205	11.8
Henry	67	13.4	67	13.4
Hickman	21	18.8	22	19.7
Houston	7	13.9	7	13.9
Lake	50	13.5	50	13.5
Lauderdale	145	15.8	147	16.0
Lewis	11	28.3	11	28.3
Lincoln	67	16.5	67	16.5
Madison	131	11.9	132	12.0
Marshall	38	16.0	39	16.4
Maury	175	17.8	177	18.0
Montgomery	179	17.7	179	17.7
Obion	74	18.0	74	18.0
Robertson	75	12.7	82	13.9
Rutherford	132	17.0	135	17.4
Shelby	452	14.5	485	15.5
Sumner	58	14.5	60	15.0
Tipton	127	11.3	131	11.6
Trousdale	14	11.0	15	11.8
Wil iamson	88	16.7	92	17.4
Wilson	76	17.0	78	17.4
UTAH COUNTIES				
San Juan	1	.7	1	.7
Uintah	------	------	------	------
VIRGINIA COUNTIES:				
Accomac	220	15.7	224	16.0
Albemarle	193	31.1	141	22.7
Alleghany	21	10.5	29	14.5
Amelia	58	12.6	59	12.8
Amherst	91	15.2	97	16.2
Appomattox	30	13.1	35	15.2
Arlington	47	14.2	74	22.4
Augusta	68	19.4	72	20.6
Bath	16	13.3	14	11.7
Bedford	99	14.2	104	14.9
Botetourt	40	18.1	35	15.8
Bristol (city)	24	20.0	24	20.0
Brunswick	154	13.4	161	14.0
Buckingham	89	15.3	100	17.2
VIRGINIA COUNTIES—Continued.				
Buena Vista (city)	4	13.3	4	13.3
Campbell	104	15.8	120	18.2
Caroline	87	11.2	93	12.0
Charles City	63	16.2	70	17.9
Charlotte	76	11.3	84	12.5
Chesterfield	113	15.9	120	16.9
Clarke	28	17.5	29	18.1
Clifton Forge (city)	29	24.2	18	15.0
Culpeper	70	16.3	79	18.4
Cumberland	82	18.8	85	19.5
Dinwiddie	449	40.1	452	40.4
Elizabeth City[7]	201	37.9	197	37.2
Essex	57	14.9	61	15.9
Fairfax	47	9.6	64	13.1
Fauquier	92	14.7	94	15.0
Fluvanna	40	13.6	44	14.9
Franklin	56	14.9	57	15.1
Fredericksburg (city)	42	35.0	38	31.7
Gloucester	62	14.3	66	15.2
Goochland	68	16.5	72	17.5
Greene	13	13.1	13	13.1
Greensville	98	12.1	104	12.8
Halifax	264	14.0	268	14.2
Hampton (city)	13	4.6	3	1.1
Hanover	111	17.8	114	18.3
Harrisonburg (city)	22	24.4	20	22.2
Henrico	102	15.7	117	18.0
Henry	92	14.8	93	15.0
Isle of Wight	101	14.6	109	15.7
James City	35	18.4	39	20.5
King and Queen	65	15.6	69	16.5
King George	43	22.9	42	22.4
King William	63	15.7	68	17.0
Lancaster	66	16.6	70	17.6
Loudoun	59	13.6	65	14.9
Louisa	96	16.4	105	18.0
Lunenburg	98	15.7	99	15.9
Madison	25	10.3	27	11.1
Martinsville (city)	68	34.0	67	33.5
Mathews	33	16.5	35	17.6
Mecklenburg	245	14.2	253	14.6
Middlesex	71	21.1	73	21.7
Montgomery	40	21.1	47	24.7
Nansemond	239	15.6	237	15.5
Nelson	48	10.5	61	13.4
New Kent	42	16.5	46	18.1
Norfolk	237	18.1	264	20.2
Northampton	136	13.6	140	14.0
Northumberland	61	13.1	66	14.2
Nottoway	221	33.0	134	20.0
Orange	67	17.7	77	20.3
Pittsylvania	262	12.5	268	12.8
Powhatan	33	10.5	36	11.4
Prince Edward	102	13.5	103	13.6
Prince George	75	17.7	75	17.7
Princess Anne	201	26.4	200	26.3
Prince William	42	16.2	44	16.9
Pulaski	38	16.5	39	17.0
Radford (city)	15	21.4	13	18.6
Rappahannock	21	11.2	26	13.8
Richmond	37	13.9	41	15.4
Roanoke	46	13.5	54	15.9
Rockbridge	52	22.6	52	22.6
Southampton	235	14.3	242	14.8
South Norfolk (city)	37	21.8	37	21.8
Spotsylvania	55	17.7	58	18.6
Stafford	23	15.5	26	17.5
Surry	68	15.9	69	16.2
Sussex	118	14.7	131	16.4
Tazewell	44	16.3	53	19.6
Warren	22	26.6	23	27.8
Warwick	43	17.1	45	17.9
Westmoreland	65	17.5	67	18.0
Williamsburg (city)	15	16.7	15	16.7
York	53	17.3	52	17.0
WASHINGTON COUNTIES:				
Ferry	22	24.4	21	23.3
WEST VIRGINIA COUNTIES:				
Fayette	219	18.9	220	19.0
Jefferson	51	18.2	52	18.6
Logan	93	13.1	94	13.2
McDowell	309	13.6	309	13.6
Mercer	57	13.3	57	13.3
Mingo	60	15.8	60	15.8
Raleigh	162	14.3	162	14.3
Wyoming	31	15.5	32	16.0
WYOMING COUNTIES:				
Fremont	68	35.5	68	35.5

[1] Includes Negro and other nonwhite races.
[2] The term "residents" excludes all nonresidents and includes residents who died elsewhere in the registration area.
[3] Figures for Russell County, Ala., include 102 deaths which should be included with those of Phenix City, Ala.
[4] Reliable data for nonresidents not available.
[5] Nonregistration State, however, cities shown are in registration area.
[6] Exclusive of municipalities having a population of 10,000 or more in 1930.
[7] Includes "National Military Home."

TABLE 24.—NEGRO DEATHS (EXCLUSIVE OF STILLBIRTHS) FROM EACH CAUSE, BY SEX, IN REGISTRATION STATES (INCLUDING DISTRICT OF COLUMBIA): 1931

List no.	CAUSE OF DEATH	Total	Male	Female	List no.	CAUSE OF DEATH	Total	Male	Female
	Total deaths (all causes)	174,023	91,587	82,436		IV.—Diseases of the blood and blood-making organs	425	217	208
	I.—Infectious and parasitic diseases	37,968	19,681	18,287	70	Hemorrhagic conditions	57	32	25
1	Typhoid fever	1,591	843	748	71a	Pernicious anemia	138	58	80
2	Paratyphoid fever	16	6	10	71b	Other anemias	56	19	37
3	Typhus fever	4	1	3	72a	True leukemias	95	54	41
4	Relapsing fever	-------	-------	-------	72b	Pseudoleukemias (Hodgkin's disease)	59	41	18
5	Undulant fever	5	3	2	73	Diseases of the spleen	17	11	6
6	Smallpox	15	10	5	74	Other diseases of blood and blood-making organs	3	2	1
7	Measles	273	146	127		V.—Chronic poisonings and intoxications	452	369	83
8	Scarlet fever	79	45	34	75	Alcoholism (acute or chronic)	428	350	78
9	Whooping cough	909	408	501	76	Chronic poisoning by other organic substances	6	4	2
10	Diphtheria	638	326	312	77a	Chronic lead poisoning	11	11	-------
11a	Influenza, respiratory complications specified	3,531	1,764	1,767	77b,c	Other chronic poisoning by mineral substances	7	4	3
11b	Influenza, respiratory complications not specified	2,027	972	1,055		VI.—Diseases of the nervous system and of the organs of special sense	14,680	7,389	7,291
12	Cholera	-------	-------	-------	78	Encephalitis (nonepidemic)	142	73	69
13	Dysentery	575	288	287	79a	Simple meningitis	339	201	138
14	Plague	-------	-------	-------	79b	Nonepidemic cerebrospinal meningitis	73	43	30
15	Erysipelas	107	63	44	80	Progressive locomotor ataxia (tabes dorsalis)	104	77	27
16	Acute poliomyelitis, acute polioencephalitis	110	59	51	81	Other diseases of spinal cord	223	116	107
17	Lethargic or epidemic encephalitis	71	38	33	82a	Cerebral hemorrhage	10,263	4,827	5,436
18	Epidemic cerebrospinal meningitis	494	309	185	82b	Cerebral embolism and thrombosis	236	120	116
19	Glanders	-------	-------	-------	82c	Softening of brain	24	16	8
20	Anthrax (bacillus anthracis) malignant pustule	-------	-------	-------	82d	Hemiplegia and other paralysis, cause unspecified	1,016	486	530
21	Rabies	4	2	2	83	General paralysis of insane	867	651	216
22	Tetanus	296	200	96	84	Dementia praecox and other psychoses	244	110	134
	Tuberculosis (all forms)	20,683	10,447	10,236	85	Epilepsy	438	271	167
23	Respiratory system	18,511	9,226	9,285	86	Convulsions (under 5 years of age)	224	129	95
24	Meninges and central nervous system	452	270	182	87	Other diseases of nervous system	232	124	108
25	Intestines and peritoneum	684	350	334	88	Diseases of organs of vision	5	3	2
26	Vertebral column	204	141	63	89a	Diseases of ear	159	94	65
27a	Bones (vertebral column excepted)	50	35	15	89b	Diseases of mastoid process	91	48	43
27b	Joints	79	47	32		VII.—Diseases of the circulatory system	26,193	13,735	12,458
28	Skin and subcutaneous cellular tissue	6	2	4	90	Pericarditis	190	116	74
29	Lymphatic system (bronchial, mesenteric, and retroperitoneal glands excepted)	54	29	25	91a	Acute endocarditis	336	150	186
30	Genitourinary system	57	29	28	91b	Endocarditis, unspecified (under 45 years)	137	67	70
31	Other organs	29	16	13	92a	Endocarditis, specified as chronic, and other valvular diseases	7,604	3,897	3,707
32a	Acute disseminated tuberculosis	499	265	234	92b	Endocarditis, unspecified (45 years and over)	473	222	251
32b,c	Other disseminated tuberculosis	58	37	21	93a	Acute myocarditis	559	270	289
33	Leprosy	3	2	1	93b	Myocarditis, unspecified (under 45 years)	463	229	234
34	Syphilis	4,657	2,939	1,718	93c	Chronic myocarditis and myocardial degeneration	4,801	2,612	2,189
35	Gonococcus infection and other venereal diseases	376	54	322	93d	Other diseases of myocardium	2,220	1,126	1,094
36	Purulent infection, septicemia (nonpuerperal)	112	53	59	94a	Angina pectoris	880	483	397
37	Yellow fever	-------	-------	-------	94b	Diseases of coronary arteries	375	218	157
38	Malaria	1,195	593	602	95a	Functional diseases of heart	45	21	24
39	Other diseases due to protozoal parasites	7	2	5	95b	Other and unspecified diseases of heart	5,844	3,085	2,759
40	Ankylostomiasis	5	2	3	96	Aneurysm (except of heart)	396	274	122
41a	Hydatid cysts, liver	2	1	1	97	Arteriosclerosis (coronary arteries excepted)	1,326	686	640
41b	Hydatid cysts, other organs	-------	-------	-------	98	Gangrene	158	84	74
42	Other diseases caused by helminths	47	19	28	99	Other diseases of arteries	68	38	30
43	Mycoses	93	57	36	100	Diseases of veins (varices, hemorrhoids, phlebitis, etc.)	53	23	30
44	Other infectious and parasitic diseases	43	29	14	101	Diseases of lymphatic system (lymphangitis, etc.)	34	21	13
	II.—Cancers and other tumors	7,308	2,225	5,083	102	Idiopathic anomalies of blood pressure	190	88	102
	Cancer and other malignant tumors	6,528	2,150	4,378	103	Other diseases of circulatory system	41	25	16
(45)	Buccal cavity	154	97	57		VIII.—Diseases of the respiratory system	16,734	9,772	6,962
(45)	Pharynx	48	28	20	104a	Diseases of nasal fossae	174	87	87
(46)	Esophagus	70	55	15	104b	Diseases of nasal fossae and annexae	50	28	22
(46)	Stomach and duodenum	1,299	709	590	105	Diseases of larynx	59	32	27
(46)	Liver and biliary passages	410	188	222	106a	Acute bronchitis	201	94	107
(46)	Pancreas	104	57	47	106b	Chronic bronchitis	115	62	53
(46)	Other digestive tract and peritoneum	646	253	393	106c,d	Bronchitis, unspecified	161	91	70
47	Respiratory system	115	73	42	107a	Bronchopneumonia	5,000	2,756	2,244
48	Uterus	1,864	-------	1,864	107b	Capillary bronchitis	79	40	39
49	Other female genital organs	114	-------	114	108	Lobar pneumonia	8,802	5,418	3,384
50	Breast	626	8	618	109	Pneumonia, unspecified	1,238	675	563
51	Male genitourinary organs	422	422	-------	110	Pleurisy	329	182	147
52	Skin	84	41	43	111a	Pulmonary embolism and thrombosis	24	13	11
53	Other or unspecified organs	572	219	353	111b	Pulmonary congestion, edema, hemorrhagic infarct	86	48	38
54a	Nonmalignant tumors, ovary	21	-------	21	112	Asthma	262	148	114
54b	Nonmalignant tumors, uterus	561	-------	561	113	Pulmonary emphysema	11	7	4
54c	Nonmalignant tumors, other female genital organs	-------	-------	-------	114	Other diseases of respiratory system (tuberculosis excepted)	143	91	52
54d,e	Nonmalignant tumors, other organs	67	27	40		IX.—Diseases of the digestive system	11,257	5,991	5,266
55a	Tumors, ovary (nature unspecified)	4	-------	4	115a	Diseases of pharynx and tonsils	529	254	275
55b	Tumors, uterus (nature unspecified)	2	-------	2	115b	Diseases of buccal cavity and annexa	130	59	71
55c	Tumors, other female genital organs (nature unspecified)	1	-------	1	116	Diseases of esophagus	8	4	4
55d,e	Tumors, other organs (nature unspecified)	124	48	76	117a	Ulcer of stomach	516	347	169
	III.—Rheumatic diseases, nutritional diseases, diseases of the endocrine glands, and other general diseases	5,407	1,775	3,632	117b	Ulcer of duodenum	116	88	28
56	Acute rheumatic fever	411	178	233	118	Other diseases of stomach (cancer excepted)	1,188	570	618
57	Chronic rheumatism, osteoarthritis	110	47	63	119	Diarrhea, enteritis (under 2 years of age)	3,049	1,645	1,404
58	Gout	-------	-------	-------	120	Diarrhea, enteritis (2 years and over)	989	486	503
59	Diabetes mellitus	1,465	527	938	121	Appendicitis	1,543	896	647
60	Scurvy	10	4	6	122a	Hernia	393	304	89
61	Beriberi	-------	-------	-------	122b	Intestinal obstruction	1,057	479	578
62	Pellagra	2,832	801	2,031	123	Other diseases of intestines	178	89	89
63	Rickets	138	78	60	124	Cirrhosis of fever	703	412	291
64	Osteomalacia	-------	-------	-------	125a	Yellow atrophy of liver	52	15	37
65	Diseases of pituitary body	1	1	-------	125b	Other diseases of liver	208	114	94
66a	Simple goiter	23	4	19	126	Biliary calculi	120	31	89
66b	Exophthalmic goiter	224	41	183	127	Other diseases of gall-bladder, biliary passages	199	75	124
(66)	Other diseases of thyroid and parathyroid glands	32	18	14	128	Diseases of pancreas	35	19	16
67	Diseases of thymus gland	84	42	42	129	Peritonitis, cause not specified	244	104	140
68	Diseases of adrenals (Addison's disease not specified as tuberculous)	9	2	7					
69	Other general diseases	68	32	36					

TABLE 24.—NEGRO DEATHS (EXCLUSIVE OF STILLBIRTHS) FROM EACH CAUSE, BY SEX, IN REGISTRATION STATES (INCLUDING DISTRICT OF COLUMBIA): 1931—Continued

List no.	CAUSE OF DEATH	Total	Male	Female
	X.—Diseases of the genitourinary system	16,590	9,037	7,553
130	Acute nephritis (including unspecified under 10 years)	1,229	653	576
131	Chronic nephritis	11,246	5,992	5,254
132	Nephritis, unspecified (10 years and over)	2,087	1,219	868
133	Other diseases of kidneys, ureters (puerperal diseases excepted)	523	304	219
134	Calculi of urinary passages	52	33	19
135	Disease of bladder (tumors excepted)	118	93	25
136	Diseases of urethra, urinary abscess, etc	195	193	2
137	Diseases of prostate	522	522	----
138	Diseases of male genital organs, not specified as venereal	28	28	----
139a	Cysts of ovary	60	----	60
139b	Other diseases of ovaries, diseases of tubes and parametrium	410	----	410
139c	Diseases of uterus	86	----	86
139d	Nonpuerperal diseases of breast (cancer excepted)	8	----	8
139e	Other diseases of female genital organs	26	----	26
	XI. Diseases of pregnancy, childbirth, and the puerperal state	2,634	----	2,634
140	Abortion with septic conditions	309	----	309
141	Abortion without mention of septic conditions (includes hemorrhages)	113	----	113
142a	Ectopic gestation, septic conditions specified	20	----	20
142b	Ectopic gestation, septic conditions not mentioned	74	----	74
143	Other accidents of pregnancy (hemorrhage not included)	14	----	14
144a	Placenta praevia	64	----	64
144b	Other puerperal hemorrhages	137	----	137
145a	Puerperal septicemia and pyemia (abortion excluded)	627	----	627
145b	Puerperal tetanus (abortion excluded)	3	----	3
146	Puerperal albuminuria and eclampsia	757	----	757
147	Other toxemias of pregnancy	80	----	80
148	Puerperal phlegmasia alba dolens, embolus, sudden death (not specified as septic)	55	----	55
149	Other accidents of childbirth	372	----	372
150	Other and unspecified conditions of puerperal state	9	----	9
	XII.—Diseases of the skin and cellular tissue	218	105	113
151	Furuncle, carbuncle	50	27	23
152	Phlegmon, acute abscess	94	47	47
153	Other diseases of skin and annexa, and of cellular tissue	74	31	43
	XIII.—Diseases of the bones and organs of locomotion	175	115	60
154	Osteomyelitis	103	70	33
155	Other diseases of bones (tuberculosis excepted)	29	20	9
156	Diseases of joints, other organs of locomotion	43	25	18
	XIV.—Congenital malformations	657	383	274
157a	Congenital hydrocephalus	89	54	35
157b	Spina bifida and meningocele	38	18	20
157c	Congenital malformations of heart	321	194	127
157d	Other congenital malformations	209	117	92
	XV.—Diseases of early infancy	6,859	3,794	3,065
158	Congenital debility	952	537	415
159	Premature birth	4,481	2,394	2,087
160	Injury at birth	759	458	301
161	Other diseases peculiar to early infancy	667	405	262
	XVI.—Senility	2,014	1,009	1,005
162	Senility	2,014	1,009	1,005
	XVII.—Violent and accidental deaths	13,969	10,526	3,443
	Suicide	509	373	136
163	By solid or liquid poisons or by absorption of corrosive substances	106	42	64
164	By poisonous gas	27	22	5
165	By hanging or strangulation	44	38	6
166	By drowning	46	29	17
167	By firearms	206	180	26
168	By cutting or piercing instruments	37	32	5
169	By jumping from high places	23	17	6
170	By crushing	6	6	----
171	By other means	14	7	7

List no.	CAUSE OF DEATH	Total	Male	Female
	XVII.—Violent and accidental deaths—Con.			
	Homicide	4,573	3,708	865
173	By firearms	3,005	2,504	501
174	By cutting or piercing instruments	1,099	860	239
175	By other means	469	344	125
	Accidental, other, or undefined	8,887	6,445	2,412
176	Attack by venomous animals	23	16	7
177	Poisoning by food	157	82	75
178	Absorption of poisonous gas	89	68	21
	Supplemental	1	1	----
179	Other acute accidental poisonings (gas excepted)	252	143	109
180	Conflagration	264	156	108
181	Burns (conflagration excepted)	1,004	396	608
	Supplemental	37	29	8
182	Mechanical suffocation	171	96	75
	Supplemental	10	9	1
183	Drowning	779	705	74
	Supplemental	109	91	18
	Traumatism:	----	----	----
184	By firearms (wounds of war excepted)	527	426	101
185	By cutting or piercing instruments (wounds of war excepted)	130	90	40
	Supplemental	16	13	3
186a	By fall	761	468	293
	Supplemental	306	269	37
186b	By crushing, landslide	58	54	4
	Supplemental	572	487	85
187	Cataclysm	11	8	3
188	Injuries by animals	42	38	4
189	Hunger and thirst	14	9	5
190	Excessive cold	19	15	4
191	Excessive heat	220	172	48
192	Lightning	104	71	33
193	Due to electric currents	32	29	3
	Supplemental	15	14	1
194a	Foreign bodies	54	25	29
	Supplemental	----	----	----
194b	Other accidents	541	422	119
	Supplemental	2,498	1,972	526
195	Violent deaths of unknown nature	----	----	----
196	Wounds of war	2	2	----
197	Execution of civilians by belligerent armies	----	----	----
198	Legal executions	69	69	----
	XVIII.—Ill-defined causes of death	10,483	5,464	5,019
199	Sudden death	763	414	349
200a	Cause of death ill-defined	1,934	1,012	922
200b	Cause of death not specified or unknown	7,786	4,038	3,748

SUPPLEMEMTAL

(This supplemental list is made in accordance with the requirements of the International Conference at Paris, 1929. The deaths shown in this tabulation are supplemental to those reported opposite Titles 178 to 194, inclusive. Comparable figures for titles shown in prior years will be found opposite the International List Titles. To obtain the total number of deaths in 1931 due to any of the accidental causes, the supplemental figures should be added to those reported opposite the International List numbers in the regular table.)

Punch symbol	CAUSE OF DEATH	Total	Male	Female
201	Accidents in mines and quarries	172	172	----
202	Accidents from agricultural machinery	15	14	1
203	Elevator accidents	20	19	1
204	Accidents from machinery used for recreation	1	1	----
205	Other machinery accidents	102	98	4
206	Railroad and automobile collisions	65	46	19
207	Other railroad accidents	537	483	54
208	Street car and automobile collisions	16	8	8
209	Other street car accidents	54	40	14
210	Automobile accidents (primary)	2,381	1,819	562
211	Motorcycle accidents	10	8	2
212	Other land transportation accidents	114	102	12
213	Water transportation accidents	75	73	2
214	Air transportation accidents	2	2	----

TABLE 25.—NEGRO DEATHS (EXCLUSIVE OF STILLBIRTHS) FROM EACH CAUSE, BY SEX, IN REGISTRATION STATES (INCLUDING DISTRICT OF COLUMBIA): 1930

List no.	CAUSE OF DEATH	Total	Male	Female
	Total deaths (all causes)	**182,021**	**95,696**	**86,325**
	I.—Infectious and parasitic diseases	37,629	19,325	18,304
1	Typhoid fever	1,666	892	774
2	Paratyphoid fever	12	7	5
3	Typhus fever			
4	Relapsing fever			
5	Undulant fever	3		3
6	Smallpox	17	10	7
7	Measles	293	155	138
8	Scarlet fever	72	33	39
9	Whooping cough	1,201	562	639
10	Diphtheria	537	284	253
11a	Influenza, respiratory complications specified	2,518	1,336	1,182
11b	Influenza, respiratory complications not specified	1,710	833	877
12	Cholera			
13	Dysentery	739	378	361
14	Plague			
15	Erysipelas	97	52	45
16	Acute poliomyelitis, acute polioencephalitis	115	62	53
17	Lethargic or epidemic encephalitis	65	29	36
18	Epidemic cerebrospinal meningitis	783	511	272
19	Glanders			
20	Anthrax (bacillus anthracis) malignant pustule			
21	Rabies	10	5	5
22	Tetanus	287	196	91
	Tuberculosis (all forms)	20,590	10,207	10,383
23	Respiratory system	18,309	8,978	9,331
24	Meninges and central nervous system	534	291	243
25	Intestines and peritoneum	747	360	387
26	Vertebral column	184	130	54
27a	Bones (vertebral column excepted)	41	28	13
27b	Joints	70	44	26
28	Skin and subcutaneous cellular tissue	4	4	
29	Lymphathic system (bronchial, mesenteric, and retroperitoneal glands excepted)	66	34	32
30	Genitourinary system	51	30	21
31	Other organs	41	25	16
32a	Acute disseminated tuberculosis	493	260	233
32b,c	Other disseminated tuberculosis	50	23	27
33	Leprosy	1	1	
34	Syphilis	4,516	2,747	1,769
35	Gonococcus infection and other venereal diseases	360	69	291
36	Purulent infection, septicemia (nonpuerperal)	170	70	100
37	Yellow fever			
38	Malaria	1,699	795	904
39	Other diseases due to protozoal parasites	2	2	
40	Ankylostomiasis	8	6	2
41a	Hydatid cysts, liver			
41b	Hydatid cysts, other organs			
42	Other diseases caused by helminths	42	16	26
43	Mycoses	68	38	30
44	Other infectious and parasitic diseases	48	29	19
	II.—Cancers and other tumors	7,081	2,189	4,892
	Cancer and other malignant tumors	6,280	2,092	4,188
(45)	Buccal cavity	141	86	55
(45)	Pharynx	33	13	20
(46)	Esophagus	64	48	16
(46)	Stomach and duodenum	1,335	716	619
(46)	Liver and biliary passages	370	193	177
(46)	Pancreas	103	77	26
(46)	Other digestive tract and peritoneum	606	249	357
47	Respiratory system	110	68	42
48	Uterus	1,782		1,782
49	Other female genital organs	94		94
50	Breast	626	6	620
51	Male genitourinary organs	377	377	
52	Skin	93	50	43
53	Other or unspecified organs	546	209	337
54a	Nonmalignant tumors, ovary	14		14
54b	Nonmalignant tumors, uterus	576		576
54c	Nonmalignant tumors, other female genital organs	5		5
54d,e	Nonmalignant tumors, other organs	53	26	27
55a	Tumors, ovary (nature unspecified)	5		5
55b	Tumors, uterus (nature unspecified)	5		5
55c	Tumors, other female genital organs (nature unspecified)	1		1
55d,e	Tumors, other organs (nature unspecified)	142	71	71
	III.—Rheumatic diseases, nutritional diseases, diseases of the endocrine glands, and other general diseases	6,032	1,981	4,051
56	Acute rheumatic fever	469	205	264
57	Chronic rheumatism, osteoarthritis	109	48	61
58	Gout	1		1
59	Diabetes mellitus	1,426	506	920
60	Scurvy	8	4	4
61	Beriberi			
62	Pellagra	3,368	951	2,417
63	Rickets	143	88	55
64	Osteomalacia	1	1	
65	Diseases of pituitary body	1		1
66a	Simple goiter	36	5	31
66b	Exophthalmic goiter	221	31	190
(66)	Other diseases of thyroid and paratyphoid glands	37	18	19
67	Diseases of thymus gland	100	56	44
68	Diseases of adrenals (Addison's disease not specified as tuberculous)	11	8	3
69	Other general diseases	101	60	41
	IV.—Diseases of the blood and blood-making organs	400	186	214
70	Hemorrhagic conditions	40	23	17
71a	Pernicious anemia	135	38	97
71b	Other anemias	56	19	37
72a	True leukemias	96	64	32
72b	Pseudoleukemias (Hodgkin's disease)	57	34	23
73	Diseases of the spleen	14	7	7
74	Other diseases of blood and blood-making organs	2	1	1
	V.—Chronic poisonings and intoxications	462	368	94
75	Alcoholism (acute or chronic)	435	351	84
76	Chronic poisoning by other organic substances	12	5	7
77a	Chronic lead poisoning	8	8	
77b,c	Other chronic poisoning by mineral substances	7	4	3
	VI.—Diseases of the nervous system and of the organs of special sense	15,872	8,122	7,750
78	Encephalitis (nonepidemic)	141	83	58
79a	Simple meningitis	370	226	144
79b	Nonepidemic cerebrospinal meningitis	99	57	42
80	Progressive locomotor ataxia (tabes dorsalis)	100	72	28
81	Other diseases of spinal cord	255	122	133
82a	Cerebral hemorrhage	10,848	5,248	5,600
82b	Cerebral embolism and thrombosis	244	119	125
82c	Softening of brain	27	16	11
82d	Hemiplegia and other paralysis, cause unspecified	1,244	616	628
83	General paralysis of insane	915	653	262
84	Dementia praecox and other psychoses	268	137	131
85	Epilepsy	497	319	178
86	Convulsions (under 5 years of age)	298	161	137
87	Other diseases of nervous system	285	144	141
88	Diseases of organs of vision	11	6	5
89a	Diseases of ear	175	95	80
89b	Diseases of mastoid process	95	48	47
	VII.—Diseases of the circulatory system	27,958	14,724	13,234
90	Pericarditis	213	109	104
91a	Acute endocarditis	374	178	196
91b	Endocarditis, unspecified (under 45 years)	161	70	91
92a	Endocarditis, specified as chronic, and other valvular diseases	8,616	4,471	4,145
92b	Endocarditis, unspecified (45 years and over)	531	278	253
93a	Acute myocarditis	540	285	255
93b	Myocarditis, unspecified (under 45 years)	507	212	295
93c	Chronic myocarditis and myocardial degeneration	4,972	2,628	2,344
93d	Other diseases of myocardium	2,369	1,268	1,101
94a	Angina pectoris	853	461	392
94b	Diseases of coronary arteries	271	170	101
95a	Functional diseases of heart	50	27	23
95b	Other and unspecified diseases of heart	6,071	3,255	2,816
96	Aneurysm (except of heart)	437	302	135
97	Arteriosclerosis (coronary arteries excepted)	1,439	738	701
98	Gangrene	186	77	109
99	Other diseases of arteries	78	46	32
100	Diseases of veins (varices, hemorrhoids, phlebitis, etc.)	47	21	26
101	Diseases of lymphatic system (lymphangitis, etc.)	15	9	6
102	Idiopathic anomalies of blood-pressure	173	91	82
103	Other diseases of circulatory system	55	28	27
	VIII.—Diseases of the respiratory system	17,079	9,950	7,129
104a	Diseases of nasal fossae	162	91	71
104b	Diseases of nasal fossae and annexae	48	30	18
105	Diseases of larynx	59	36	23
106a	Acute bronchitis	242	115	127
106b	Chronic bronchitis	136	63	73
106c,d	Bronchitis, unspecified	208	95	113
107a	Bronchopneumonia	5,268	2,868	2,400
107b	Capillary bronchitis	92	54	38
108	Lobar pneumonia	8,628	5,307	3,321
109	Pneumonia, unspecified	1,274	746	528
110	Pleurisy	354	213	141
111a	Pulmonary embolism and thrombosis	27	19	8
111b	Pulmonary congestion, edema, hemorrhagic infarct	99	48	51
112	Asthma	292	149	143
	Pulmonary emphysema	18	10	8
113 114	Other diseases of respiratory system (tuberculosis excepted)	172	106	66
	IX.—Diseases of the digestive system	12,186	6,412	5,774
115a	Diseases of pharynx and tonsils	501	238	263
115b	Diseases of buccal cavity and annexa	131	67	64
116	Diseases of esophagus	7	5	2
117a	Ulcer of stomach	561	338	223
117b	Ulcer of duodenum	118	86	32
118	Other diseases of stomach (cancer excepted)	1,361	649	712
119	Diarrhea, enteritis (under 2 years of age)	3,628	1,949	1,679
120	Diarrhea, enteritis (2 years and over)	1,143	547	596
121	Appendicitis	1,521	872	649
122a	Hernia	375	281	94
122b	Intestinal obstruction	1,016	459	557
123	Other diseases of intestines	183	92	91
124	Cirrhosis of liver	740	453	287
125a	Yellow atrophy of liver	58	19	39
125b	Other diseases of liver	227	116	111
126	Biliary calculi	111	35	76
127	Other diseases of gall-bladder, biliary passages	206	83	123
128	Diseases of pancreas	36	20	16
129	Peritonitis, cause not specified	263	103	160

TABLE 25.—NEGRO DEATHS (EXCLUSIVE OF STILLBIRTH) FROM EACH CAUSE, BY SEX, IN REGISTRATION STATES (INCLUDING DISTRICT OF COLUMBIA): 1930—Continued

List no.	CAUSE OF DEATH	Total	Male	Female
	X.—Diseases of the genitourinary system	17, 975	9, 757	8, 218
130	Acute nephritis (including unspecified under 10 years)	1, 498	793	705
131	Chronic nephritis	11, 856	6, 418	5, 438
132	Nephritis, unspecified (10 years and over)	2, 487	1, 351	1, 136
133	Other diseases of kidneys, ureters (puerperal diseases excepted)	498	290	208
134	Calculi of urinary passages	54	33	21
135	Diseases of bladder (tumors excepted)	143	113	30
136	Diseases of urethra, urinary abscess, etc	176	169	7
137	Diseases of prostate	554	554	-------
138	Diseases of male genital organs, not specified as venereal	36	36	-------
139a	Cysts of ovary	53	-------	53
139b	Other diseases of ovaries, diseases of tubes and parametrium	508	-------	508
139c	Diseases of uterus	81	-------	81
139d	Nonpuerperal diseases of breast (cancer excepted)	8	-------	8
139e	Other diseases of female genital organs	23	-------	23
	XI.—Diseases of pregnancy, childbirth, and the puerperal state	2, 844	-------	2, 844
140	Abortion with septic conditions	270	-------	270
141	Abortion without mention of septic conditions (includes hemorrhages)	111	-------	111
142a	Ectopic gestation, septic conditions specified	17	-------	17
142b	Ectopic gestation, septic conditions not mentioned	70	-------	70
143	Other accidents of pregnancy (hemorrhage not included)	24	-------	24
144a	Placenta praevia	72	-------	72
144b	Other puerperal hemorrhages	133	-------	133
145a	Puerperal septicemia and pyemia (abortion excluded)	695	-------	695
145b	Puerperal tetanus (abortion excluded)	2	-------	2
146	Puerperal albuminuria and eclampsia	932	-------	932
147	Other toxemias of pregnancy	85	-------	85
148	Puerperal phlegmasia alba dolens, embolus, sudden death (not specified as septic)	61	-------	61
149	Other accidents of childbirth	364	-------	364
150	Other and unspecified conditions of puerperal state	8	-------	8
	XII.—Diseases of the skin and cellular tissue	228	120	108
151	Furuncle, carbuncle	28	17	11
152	Phlegmon, acute abscess	108	61	47
153	Other diseases of skin and annexa, and of cellular tissue	92	42	50
	XIII.—Diseases of the bones and organs of locomotion	139	81	58
154	Osteomyelitis	77	49	28
155	Other diseases of bones (tuberculosis excepted)	21	12	9
156	Diseases of joints, other organs of locomotion	41	20	21
	XIV.—Congenital malformations	638	369	269
157a	Congenital hydrocephalus	113	66	47
157b	Spina bifida and meningocele	31	16	15
157c	Congenital malformations of heart	301	164	137
157d	Other congenital malformations	193	123	70
	XV.—Diseases of early infancy	7, 424	4, 144	3, 280
158	Congenital debility	1, 036	601	435
159	Premature birth	4, 791	2, 551	2, 240
160	Injury at birth	778	491	287
161	Other diseases peculiar to early infancy	819	501	318
	XVI.—Senility	2, 431	1, 128	1, 303
162	Senility	2, 431	1, 128	1, 303
	XVII.—Violent and accidental deaths	14, 236	10, 801	3, 435
	Suicide	458	336	122
163	By solid or liquid poisons or by absorption of corrosive substances	97	42	55
164	By poisonous gas	42	30	12
165	By hanging or strangulation	30	25	5
166	By drowning	48	33	15
167	By firearms	179	159	20
168	By cutting or piercing instruments	34	26	8
169	By jumping from high places	19	14	5
170	By crushing	5	4	1
171	By other means	4	3	1

List no.	CAUSE OF DEATH	Total	Male	Female
	XVII.—Violent and accidental deaths—Con.			
	Homicide	4, 306	3, 460	846
173	By firearms	2, 850	2, 351	499
174	By cutting or piercing instruments	992	762	230
175	By other means	464	347	117
	Accidental, other, or undefined	9, 472	7, 005	2, 467
176	Attack by venomous animals	12	9	3
177	Poisoning by food	207	107	100
178	Absorption of poisonous gas	88	67	21
	Supplemental	3	2	1
179	Other acute accidental poisonings (gas excepted)	248	161	87
180	Conflagration	330	187	143
181	Burns (conflagration excepted)	1, 130	481	649
	Supplemental	44	35	9
182	Mechanical suffocation	202	109	93
	Supplemental	4	4	-------
183	Drowning	906	821	85
	Supplemental	101	81	20
	Traumatism:			
184	By firearms (wounds of war excepted)	660	531	129
185	By cutting or piercing instruments (wounds of war excepted)	86	58	28
	Supplemental	20	16	4
186a	By fall	761	496	265
	Supplemental	263	228	35
186b	By crushing, landslide	77	73	4
	Supplemental	442	400	42
187	Cataclysm	25	12	13
188	Injuries by animals	52	45	7
189	Hunger and thirst	3	2	1
190	Excessive cold	89	70	19
191	Excessive heat	238	178	60
192	Lightning	79	59	20
193	Due to electric currents	28	26	2
	Supplemental	13	13	-------
194a	Foreign bodies	73	48	25
	Supplemental	-------	-------	-------
194b	Other accidents	587	466	121
	Supplemental	2, 644	2, 164	480
195	Violent deaths of unknown nature	1	1	-------
196	Wounds of war	-------	-------	-------
197	Execution of civilians by belligerent armies	-------	-------	-------
198	Legal executions	56	55	1
	XVIII.—Ill-defined causes of death	11, 407	6, 039	5, 368
199	Sudden death	919	483	436
200a	Cause of death ill-defined	2, 080	1, 132	948
200b	Cause of death not specified or unknown	8, 408	4, 424	3, 984

SUPPLEMENTAL

(This supplemental list is made in accordance with the requirements of the International Conference at Paris, 1929. The deaths shown in this tabulation are supplemental to those reported opposite titles 178 to 194, inclusive. Comparable figures for Titles shown in prior years will be found opposite the International List Titles. To obtain the total number of deaths in 1930 due to any of the accidental causes, the supplemental figures should be added to those reported opposite the International List numbers in the regular table.)

Punch symbol	CAUSE OF DEATH	Total	Male	Female
201				
202				
203	Accidents in mines and quarries	238	238	-------
204	Accidents from agricultural machinery	16	15	1
205	Elevator accidents	35	32	3
206	Accidents from machinery used for recreation	1	1	-------
207	Other machinery accidents	120	116	4
208	Railroad and automobile collisions	90	67	23
209	Other railroad accidents	536	495	41
210	Street car and automobile collisions	21	15	6
211	Other street car accidents	41	30	11
212	Automobile accidents (primary)	2, 228	1, 749	479
213	Motorcycle accidents	13	12	1
214	Other land transportation accidents	113	100	13
	Water transportation accidents	79	70	9
	Air transportation accidents	3	3	-------

TABLE 26.—COLORED[1] DEATHS (EXCLUSIVE OF STILLBIRTHS) FROM IMPORTANT CAUSES INCORPORATED PLACES, AND RURAL

[Data are included for States in which the Negro population constitutes 55 percent or more

AREA	All causes	Typhoid and paratyphoid fever	Smallpox	Measles	Scarlet fever	Whooping cough	Diphtheria	Influenza	Erysipelas	Epidemic cerebrospinal meningitis	Tuberculosis of the respiratory system	Tuberculosis of the meninges, etc.	Other forms of tuberculosis	Syphilis	Malaria	Cancer and other malignant tumors	Rheumatism and gout	Diabetes mellitus	Cerebral hemorrhage and softening
The registration area in continental United States	**199,167**	**1,792**	**22**	**524**	**77**	**1,373**	**606**	**4,600**	**125**	**888**	**20,810**	**674**	**1,971**	**4,788**	**1,734**	**6,873**	**621**	**1,545**	**11,426**
ALABAMA	14,412	99	1	41	3	130	47	413	7	17	1,294	27	110	384	179	450	41	83	740
Cities	4,516	31	-	9	2	19	20	150	-	17	354	12	48	131	22	161	12	43	247
Incorporated places	1,082	7	1	-	-	14	4	25	-	-	92	2	10	40	13	37	1	9	63
Rural	8,814	61	-	32	1	97	23	238	7	-	848	13	52	213	144	252	28	31	430
ARKANSAS	6,466	151	1	2	2	23	14	243	2	23	555	5	51	110	325	183	22	29	312
Cities	1,344	20	1	-	1	-	3	40	-	2	145	2	9	37	24	49	1	6	80
Incorporated places	831	21	-	1	-	2	1	38	-	2	84	1	8	17	37	29	3	5	47
Rural	4,291	110	-	1	1	21	10	165	2	19	326	2	34	56	264	105	18	18	185
CONNECTICUT	523	1	-	-	-	1	-	10	-	-	73	5	9	17	-	33	1	7	26
Cities	435	1	-	-	-	1	-	10	-	-	62	3	9	16	-	27	1	5	24
Incorporated places	13	-	-	-	-	-	-	-	-	-	2	-	-	-	-	-	-	-	1
Rural	75	-	-	-	-	-	-	-	-	-	9	2	-	1	-	6	-	2	1
DELAWARE	707	7	-	-	1	3	4	10	-	1	55	5	7	14	-	24	1	10	83
Cities	280	-	-	-	1	-	-	6	-	1	13	2	6	6	-	8	-	4	48
Incorporated places	74	4	-	-	-	1	1	-	-	-	3	-	-	1	-	4	1	3	3
Rural	353	3	-	-	-	2	3	4	-	-	39	3	1	7	-	12	-	3	32
FLORIDA	7,182	41	-	16	2	28	23	177	2	4	535	6	42	303	160	198	24	36	589
Cities	2,939	10	-	9	-	5	6	81	1	2	258	4	29	110	17	104	10	22	239
Incorporated places	1,290	7	-	1	-	8	5	21	-	-	96	2	10	117	21	36	3	5	114
Rural	2,953	24	-	6	2	15	12	75	1	2	181	-	3	76	122	58	11	9	236
GEORGIA	17,190	299	1	36	3	138	38	458	10	46	1,310	14	113	343	253	453	52	113	1,235
Cities	6,088	49	-	15	2	38	6	156	6	43	446	10	76	150	20	152	13	51	508
Rural[2]	11,102	250	1	21	1	100	32	302	4	3	864	4	37	193	233	301	39	62	727
ILLINOIS	5,961	12	-	2	7	24	38	54	6	28	834	37	95	133	4	303	33	71	242
Cities	4,951	9	-	-	7	22	38	40	5	26	681	36	80	107	1	249	23	64	207
Incorporated places	251	-	-	2	-	2	-	3	-	-	24	-	2	5	2	14	3	1	9
Rural	759	3	-	-	-	-	-	11	1	2	129	1	13	21	1	40	7	6	26
NDIANA	2,313	6	-	5	2	11	7	62	1	46	238	7	38	36	-	77	4	18	108
Cities	1,931	4	-	5	1	10	6	51	1	41	194	7	31	28	-	60	4	14	80
Incorporated places	90	2	-	-	1	-	-	3	-	-	8	-	2	2	-	6	-	1	7
Rural	292	-	-	-	-	1	1	8	-	5	36	-	5	6	-	11	-	3	21
IOWA	363	1	-	4	-	3	1	4	2	2	52	2	4	10	-	18	-	6	15
Cities	276	1	-	2	-	1	1	3	1	2	35	1	4	9	-	12	-	6	10
Incorporated places	31	-	-	-	-	-	-	1	-	-	6	-	-	-	-	-	-	-	2
Rural	56	-	-	2	-	2	-	-	1	-	11	1	-	1	-	6	-	-	3
KANSAS	1,102	3	-	3	1	3	2	27	-	6	100	1	10	35	3	50	3	12	92
Cities	765	2	-	2	-	3	2	22	-	6	63	1	7	11	2	40	1	10	62
Incorporated places	76	1	-	-	-	-	-	2	-	-	4	-	-	2	-	4	1	1	4
Rural	261	-	-	1	1	-	-	3	-	-	33	-	3	22	1	6	1	1	26
KENTUCKY	4,750	58	1	10	3	29	7	113	1	23	449	16	63	76	11	210	23	41	336
Cities	2,190	14	-	3	-	12	2	37	-	18	174	7	33	44	3	103	10	25	138
Rural[2]	2,560	44	1	7	3	17	5	76	1	5	275	9	30	32	8	107	13	16	198
LOUISIANA	12,086	138	-	41	-	70	26	376	2	39	1,006	7	64	436	89	466	30	87	655
Cities	4,937	29	-	11	-	23	12	129	1	23	418	4	37	237	11	230	8	37	238
Incorporated places	1,505	12	-	5	-	5	2	44	1	9	136	2	3	41	14	49	4	7	90
Rural	5,644	97	-	25	-	42	12	203	-	7	452	1	24	158	64	187	18	43	327
MARYLAND	5,264	45	-	3	2	27	17	44	2	9	614	28	67	165	1	222	21	43	352
Cities	3,053	20	-	-	2	5	4	22	1	9	324	20	51	125	-	149	18	28	206
Incorporated places	248	6	-	-	-	-	-	1	-	-	20	1	1	7	-	9	1	4	12
Rural	1,963	19	-	3	-	22	13	21	1	-	270	7	15	33	1	64	2	11	134
MASSACHUSETTS	908	-	-	2	-	3	1	6	3	2	136	13	9	22	-	75	2	12	59
Cities	789	-	-	1	-	3	1	4	3	2	96	12	5	18	-	64	2	10	53
Incorporated places	21	-	-	-	-	-	-	2	-	-	5	-	-	-	-	1	-	-	3
Rural	98	-	-	1	-	-	-	-	-	-	35	1	4	4	-	10	-	2	3
MICHIGAN	3,090	6	-	20	2	12	11	34	6	36	591	33	65	95	-	92	9	27	100
Cities	2,560	5	-	18	2	10	10	29	3	34	488	31	58	75	-	71	7	21	72
Incorporated places	60	-	-	-	-	2	-	1	-	-	11	2	1	2	-	4	-	1	4
Rural	470	1	-	2	-	-	1	4	3	2	92	-	6	18	-	17	2	5	24
MISSISSIPPI	14,961	190	2	13	6	104	57	363	6	116	1,304	11	86	356	231	494	19	96	755
Cities	2,610	19	-	2	1	6	7	65	1	43	165	1	15	47	20	94	3	19	169
Rural[2]	12,351	171	2	11	5	98	50	298	5	73	1,139	10	71	309	211	400	16	77	586
MISSOURI	4,653	26	1	8	2	17	4	73	5	34	528	21	51	66	23	223	12	39	286
Cities	3,313	5	-	7	1	3	3	31	3	30	397	18	40	45	1	165	7	26	184
Incorporated places	388	2	-	-	-	1	-	14	-	1	32	-	5	11	4	24	1	4	30
Rural	952	19	1	1	1	13	1	28	2	3	99	3	6	10	18	34	4	9	72
NEBRASKA	467	1	-	5	1	1	1	11	-	2	60	5	11	26	-	29	-	2	12
Cities	267	1	-	-	-	-	1	5	-	1	30	3	9	17	-	23	-	1	9
Incorporated places	55	-	-	1	1	-	-	2	-	-	5	1	-	1	-	1	-	-	-
Rural	145	-	-	4	-	1	-	4	-	1	25	1	2	8	-	5	-	1	3
NEW HAMPSHIRE	9	-	-	-	-	-	-	-	-	-	-	-	-	-	-	-	-	-	1
Cities	6	-	-	-	-	-	-	-	-	-	-	-	-	-	-	-	-	-	-
Rural[4]	3	-	-	-	-	-	-	-	-	-	-	-	-	-	-	-	-	-	1
NEW JERSEY	3,552	10	-	10	3	17	14	33	2	12	476	26	58	93	-	144	10	44	210
Cities	2,588	9	-	8	2	11	12	26	1	12	244	23	44	75	-	99	8	36	150
Incorporated places	363	1	-	1	1	1	2	-	1	-	109	3	5	8	-	20	2	3	17
Rural	601	-	-	1	-	5	-	7	-	-	123	-	9	10	-	25	-	5	43
NEW YORK	7,199	12	-	22	3	32	14	22	10	37	1,132	56	130	315	1	337	27	98	229
Cities	6,568	10	-	19	2	25	14	18	9	37	1,029	54	117	287	-	309	27	88	201
Incorporated places	136	1	-	-	-	3	-	1	-	-	11	2	1	9	-	3	-	5	7
Rural	495	1	-	3	1	4	-	3	1	-	92	-	12	19	1	25	-	5	21
NORTH CAROLINA	14,155	77	4	1	4	127	59	303	7	27	1,214	22	134	236	28	385	45	89	979
Cities	3,959	17	-	-	2	18	11	97	-	7	339	9	53	98	2	119	11	28	312
Incorporated places	971	4	1	1	-	14	4	19	-	2	73	2	4	22	1	35	9	9	76
Rural	9,225	56	3	-	2	95	44	187	7	18	802	11	77	116	25	231	25	52	591

[1] Includes Negro and other nonwhite races.

[2] Includes "Incorporated places."

IN REGISTRATION AREA IN CONTINENTAL UNITED STATES, SELECTED STATES (CITIES, DISTRICTS), AND SELECTED CITIES: 1930

of the total colored population, and cities of such States in which data by color are available]

AREA	Diseases of the heart	Bronchitis	Pneumonia (all forms)	DIARRHEA AND ENTERITIS		Appendicitis	Hernia, intestinal obstruction	Cirrhosis of the liver	Nephritis	Puerperal septicemia	Other puerperal causes	Congenital malformations and diseases of early infancy	Suicide	Homicide	AUTOMOBILE ACCIDENTS		Other external causes	Unknown or ill-defined diseases	All other causes
				Under 2 years	2 years and over										Primary [3]	In collision with railroad trains and street cars			
The registration area in continental United States	26,877	649	17,133	4,547	1,344	1,704	1,524	830	16,592	1,079	2,025	9,041	615	4,643	2,584	149	7,877	12,479	27,026
ALABAMA	1,681	25	989	269	79	103	110	55	1,198	83	186	793	16	379	129	5	597	1,649	2,000
Cities	588	6	425	84	27	59	58	20	395	29	46	232	4	194	53	4	169	299	546
Incorporated places	131	1	64	21	4	13	9	2	114	5	16	47	1	27	8	1	55	83	162
Rural	962	18	500	164	48	31	43	33	689	49	124	514	11	158	68	------	373	1,267	1,292
ARKANSAS	766	18	380	105	52	65	38	28	512	48	84	120	10	136	66	------	284	654	1,047
Cities	218	5	74	8	9	21	16	11	106	6	15	19	2	32	19	------	58	34	271
Incorporated places	79	------	47	10	4	15	4	2	84	8	9	16	1	14	13	------	35	66	128
Rural	469	13	259	87	39	29	18	15	322	34	60	85	7	90	34	------	191	554	648
CONNECTICUT	100	3	48	11	3	3	2	2	25	1	1	36	1	9	13	------	22	2	58
Cities	87	3	40	10	3	3	2	1	21	1	1	29	------	5	10	------	19	1	40
Incorporated places	4	------	2	------	------	------	------	------	------	------	------	1	------	------	------	------	1	------	2
Rural	9	------	6	1	------	------	------	1	4	------	------	6	1	4	3	------	2	1	16
DELAWARE	112	2	83	19	7	3	4	------	78	4	2	30	1	12	8	1	28	5	83
Cities	39	1	42	4	2	3	3	------	30	1	------	6	1	7	1	------	14	------	31
Incorporated places	8	------	9	1	1	------	------	------	11	2	2	4	------	------	3	1	3	1	7
Rural	65	1	32	14	4	------	1	------	37	1	------	20	------	5	4	------	11	4	45
FLORIDA	914	19	365	116	54	81	85	46	604	45	73	312	12	244	135	1	336	396	1,158
Cities	417	10	170	52	18	53	56	22	274	21	26	134	3	114	51	1	111	42	457
Incorporated places	176	4	45	20	8	12	7	13	105	8	15	53	3	37	25	------	52	54	207
Rural	321	5	150	44	28	16	22	11	225	16	32	125	6	93	59	------	173	300	494
GEORGIA	2,140	48	1,335	274	141	124	135	55	1,554	93	197	764	22	418	174	15	649	1,403	2,734
Cities	884	22	539	101	57	75	65	30	641	37	54	280	10	218	78	5	196	191	864
Rural [2]	1,256	26	796	173	84	49	70	25	913	56	143	484	12	200	96	10	453	1,212	1,870
ILLINOIS	1,044	27	503	59	29	66	64	30	547	14	32	270	32	225	84	3	230	90	689
Cities	860	19	447	48	27	59	57	27	439	12	25	246	32	206	70	3	183	84	512
Incorporated places	38	3	21	7	2	------	4	1	41	1	2	11	------	9	1	------	17	3	23
Rural	146	5	35	4	------	7	3	2	67	1	5	13	------	10	13	------	30	3	154
INDIANA	407	8	313	61	19	17	19	17	192	11	13	110	10	67	40	4	78	2	259
Cities	321	8	285	56	19	17	18	14	160	10	11	93	10	65	32	4	67	2	202
Incorporated places	17	------	4	1	------	------	------	------	11	1	1	8	------	1	3	------	2	------	9
Rural	69	------	24	4	------	------	1	3	21	------	1	9	------	1	5	------	9	------	48
IOWA	50	------	48	2	1	6	4	2	26	3	1	17	6	9	8	------	15	4	37
Cities	43	------	37	1	1	5	4	1	24	3	1	12	5	8	7	------	9	------	27
Incorporated places	1	------	6	------	------	------	------	------	2	------	------	3	1	------	------	------	2	1	6
Rural	6	------	5	1	------	1	------	1	------	------	------	2	------	1	1	------	4	3	4
KANSAS	191	4	65	19	8	11	11	6	136	6	8	41	4	36	13	1	45	5	141
Cities	131	2	46	14	6	8	10	5	105	6	5	29	3	27	10	1	29	1	93
Incorporated places	10	2	6	4	------	------	------	------	10	------	------	7	------	3	1	------	5	3	6
Rural	50	------	13	1	2	3	1	1	21	------	3	5	1	6	2	------	11	1	42
KENTUCKY	854	43	421	81	46	32	33	17	495	26	26	154	11	144	51	1	184	42	619
Cities	438	35	213	24	22	19	22	9	249	10	9	54	6	74	29	1	63	5	285
Rural [2]	416	8	208	57	24	13	11	8	246	16	17	100	5	70	22	------	121	37	334
LOUISIANA	1,948	46	986	289	78	86	108	93	1,152	66	143	558	23	262	135	3	475	467	1,636
Cities	826	10	489	87	28	58	65	52	515	38	45	202	14	120	69	3	170	24	674
Incorporated places	257	6	115	39	13	9	7	12	153	5	15	66	1	33	13	------	63	55	219
Rural	865	30	382	163	37	19	36	29	484	23	83	290	8	109	53	------	242	388	743
MARYLAND	847	36	636	155	24	38	41	11	507	18	25	313	15	79	79	6	204	43	525
Cities	525	10	463	44	10	31	35	7	273	16	17	155	7	45	42	5	112	3	269
Incorporated places	45	5	15	5	2	3	2	1	14	1	3	17	1	13	8	------	17	2	32
Rural	277	21	158	106	12	4	4	3	220	1	5	141	7	21	29	1	75	38	224
MASSACHUSETTS	141	------	94	11	1	13	3	3	74	5	8	44	8	7	10	2	30	2	107
Cities	122	------	90	9	1	13	3	2	72	4	8	41	7	7	9	2	26	1	98
Incorporated places	3	------	2	------	------	------	------	------	1	------	------	------	------	------	------	------	1	------	3
Rural	16	------	2	2	------	------	------	1	1	1	------	3	1	------	1	------	3	1	6
MICHIGAN	486	23	336	41	14	38	28	5	166	12	16	167	21	114	57	4	99	4	320
Cities	386	19	302	28	9	38	26	5	136	12	14	146	20	110	50	4	69	1	251
Incorporated places	8	------	8	1	1	------	------	------	4	------	------	2	------	1	------	------	2	------	5
Rural	92	4	26	12	4	------	2	------	26	------	2	19	1	3	7	------	28	3	64
MISSISSIPPI	1,499	26	852	296	94	130	104	44	1,394	90	210	375	19	362	146	1	607	2,560	1,943
Cities	339	8	161	37	22	70	40	13	237	24	30	50	4	72	43	------	134	306	343
Rural [2]	1,160	18	691	259	72	60	64	31	1,157	66	180	325	15	290	103	1	473	2,254	1,600
MISSOURI	846	14	469	87	30	58	37	34	529	24	17	137	17	164	60	7	180	35	489
Cities	634	5	364	45	13	52	25	32	402	19	11	96	11	122	48	2	118	4	344
Incorporated places	54	3	29	7	5	4	4	1	45	2	------	11	3	10	3	1	15	5	57
Rural	158	6	76	35	12	2	8	1	82	3	6	30	3	32	9	4	47	26	88
NEBRASKA	64	1	57	14	5	6	3	2	22	1	6	26	6	13	6	1	19	7	41
Cities	47	------	28	1	2	6	1	2	15	------	2	7	6	10	2	------	13	------	25
Incorporated places	4	------	7	7	------	------	2	------	2	------	1	6	------	2	2	1	------	4	5
Rural	13	1	22	6	3	------	------	------	5	1	3	13	------	1	2	------	6	3	11
NEW HAMPSHIRE	2	------	1	------	------	1	------	------	2	------	------	1	------	------	------	------	------	------	1
Cities	1	------	1	------	------	1	------	------	2	------	------	------	------	------	------	------	------	------	1
Rural	1	------	------	------	------	------	------	------	------	------	------	1	------	------	------	------	------	------	------
NEW JERSEY	590	17	418	60	10	39	26	14	284	19	25	230	12	66	79	7	136	7	351
Cities	429	11	350	46	6	37	24	11	197	16	21	182	9	62	55	1	94	6	271
Incorporated places	69	1	12	1	------	1	2	3	26	3	1	22	------	3	9	1	10	------	25
Rural	92	5	56	13	4	1	------	------	61	------	3	26	3	1	15	5	32	1	55
NEW YORK	1,126	19	927	112	16	75	41	24	435	29	54	419	55	149	120	1	302	5	813
Cities	1,036	18	875	104	10	70	37	22	383	29	52	389	52	144	108	1	268	5	719
Incorporated places	18	------	12	2	1	2	------	2	21	------	2	9	------	1	4	------	5	------	14
Rural	72	1	40	6	5	3	4	------	31	------	------	21	3	4	8	------	29	------	80
NORTH CAROLINA	1,727	53	1,068	464	90	76	94	37	1,255	70	213	731	18	235	146	16	488	1,458	2,175
Cities	523	19	381	101	18	46	47	14	324	25	57	236	9	123	61	2	154	153	543
Incorporated places	119	5	73	22	7	10	8	3	110	4	24	43	2	18	20	3	35	50	139
Rural	1,085	29	614	341	65	20	39	20	821	41	132	452	7	94	65	11	299	1,255	1,493

[3] Excluding collision with railroad trains and street cars.

[4] No deaths in "Incorporative places" in 1930.

TABLE 26.—COLORED[1] DEATHS (EXCLUSIVE OF STILLBIRTHS) FROM IMPORTANT CAUSES, INCORPORATED PLACES AND RURAL

[Data are included for States in which the Negro population constitutes 55 percent or more

AREA	All causes	Typhoid and paratyphoid fever	Smallpox	Measles	Scarlet fever	Whooping cough	Diphtheria	Influenza	Erysipelas	Epidemic cerebrospinal meningitis	Tuberculosis of the respiratory system	Tuberculosis of the meninges, etc.	Other forms of tuberculosis	Syphilis	Malaria	Cancer and other malignant tumors	Rheumatism and gout	Diabetes mellitus	Cerebral hemorrhage and softening
OHIO	5,839	27	1	5	6	20	7	99	6	27	814	45	117	139		261	16	55	365
Cities	4,812	18		5	5	17	6	79	5	27	624	39	105	112		217	13	41	272
Incorporated places	265	3	1			2		5			17	3	2	5		14	2	6	21
Rural	762	6			1	1	1	15	1		173	3	10	22		30	1	8	72
OKLAHOMA	3,063	59	4	17	1	26	10	75	1	4	396	10	48	43	39	90	16	29	117
Cities	1,254	22	1	6		11	3	36		2	126	3	25	21	7	36	7	7	50
Incorporated places	611	8		2		5	1	9	1		100	2	6	9	7	18	2	11	27
Rural	1,198	29	3	9	1	10	6	30		2	170	5	17	13	25	36	7	11	40
PENNSYLVANIA	7,511	11		12	9	29	24	136	4	29	1,011	31	72	223	2	326	25	87	322
Cities	6,136	7		11	7	21	23	108	3	26	729	28	57	187	2	281	21	71	256
Incorporated places	291	2			1	1		10			18	1	5	12		14		8	10
Rural	1,084	2		1	1	7	1	18	1	3	264	2	10	24		31	4	8	56
RHODE ISLAND	231					1	1		1		24	4	4	1		13			14
Cities	203					1	1		1		17	4	4	1		11			12
Incorporated places	9										7								
Rural	19															2			2
SOUTH CAROLINA	13,162	215	1	1	1	122	40	427	4	24	951	20	47	254	290	276	46	62	798
Cities	2,580	20				11	1	92	2	9	176	9	17	79	13	72	6	21	184
Incorporated places	1,033	21	1	1		10	4	29		2	90	2	6	20	14	24	4	5	72
Rural	9,549	174			1	101	35	306	2	13	685	9	24	155	263	180	36	36	542
TENNESSEE	8,752	98		10	2	54	26	283	3	156	1,094	26	107	178	59	241	37	56	535
Cities	4,620	18		3		23	12	110		145	446	17	64	119	21	135	17	39	316
Rural[2]	4,132	80		7	2	31	14	173	3	11	648	9	43	59	38	106	20	17	219
VERMONT	9																	1	
Cities	3																	1	
Rural[4]	6																		
VIRGINIA	11,722	62		21	4	137	44	325	5	17	1,069	36	74	251	11	348	50	113	1,016
Cities	4,001	11		7	2	30	16	108	1	8	289	16	36	93	3	115	19	45	391
Incorporated places	492	6				7	1	20		1	35	2	3	8		23	3	10	37
Rural	7,229	45		14	2	100	27	197	4	8	745	18	35	150	8	210	28	58	588
WEST VIRGINIA	1,856	23		3	2	25	2	35	1	5	178	13	26	47		55	2	17	97
Cities	479	5				2		6		2	38	3	13	7		18		7	27
Incorporated places	316	6		1		3	1	7		3	9	5	3	10		10		5	10
Rural	1,061	12		2	2	20	1	22	1		131	5	10	30		27	2	5	60
CITIES OF 10,000 POPULATION OR MORE																			
ALABAMA:																			
Anniston	117	1						3		1	9		1	1	2	3			6
Bessemer	183	2						20			16		2	2	1	4	1	3	8
Birmingham	1,925	10		5	1	9	10	40		3	172	6	17	70	3	67	5	22	105
Decatur	60				1			5			4			1		3			1
Dothan	66							1			3			4		5	1	1	4
Fairfield	206	2				1	2	4		7	14	1	4	6		9		1	8
Florence	61	1						2			8		2	1		4			4
Gadsden	112					2		5			14	1	1	2		1	1		4
Huntsville	94							7			9			2		1		3	5
Mobile	587	5				3	2	13		4	35	1	5	15	1	26	2	5	32
Montgomery	664	8		4		2	3	29		1	44	1	9	13	12	17	2	5	45
Phenix City	13										1								
Selma	282	2				1	1	12		1	19	1	4	10	2	10		3	19
Tuscaloosa	146					1	2	9			6	1	3	4	1	11			6
ARKANSAS:																			
Blytheville	49	2			1		1	3		2	2		1	1	1			1	1
El Dorado	93	3						8			10			1	3				1
Fort Smith	79	1					1	3			6		1		2				8
Hot Springs	144	1						7			14	1		7		10		2	4
Jonesboro	21										2				2	2			2
Little Rock	693	9	1				1	6			84	1	4	24	4	30	1	3	43
North Little Rock	65							4			5		1		5	2			3
Pine Bluff	131	2						6			17		1	3	6	3			11
Texarkana	69	2						3			5		1	1	1	2			7
DELAWARE:																			
Wilmington	280				1			6		1	13	2	6	6		8		4	48
DISTRICT OF COLUMBIA:																			
Washington	2,792	7			1	12	7	15	2	5	303	12	39	64		155	4	35	140
FLORIDA:																			
Daytona Beach	94	1						2		1	5			2	1	4		1	7
Gainesville	119	1				1		4			9		1	2	2	11			15
Jacksonville	1,014			7			3	20	1		114	1	18	40	4	29	6	4	94
Key West	55										4		1	1				1	4
Lakeland	66						1	2			10		1	3	1	3		1	7
Miami	382					1	1	6		1	42	2	1	16		11		3	27
Orlando	118							5			7		2	4	1	6		2	7
Pensacola	226	1		2		1		10			10	1	1	5	4	11	1	3	17
St. Augustine	87							1			6			3		6	1	1	11
St. Petersburg	120	4						6			3		1	9	2	2			5
Sanford	49							1			2			1	1	2	1		
Tallahassee	78							4			3			1			1	1	8
Tampa	342	2				1	1	15			24		2	17	1	14		2	27
West Palm Beach	189	1				1		5			19		1	6		5		3	10
GEORGIA:																			
Albany	185	1						9			12		1	3	6	5			20
Athens	148	1				1		3		1	11	1		4		1	1		11
Atlanta	2,106	18		4	1	26	2	54	3	28	130	5	50	39		47	2	19	201
Augusta	680	7				2		21	2	6	55	1	6	26	5	15	2	4	56
Brunswick	163							4			18			4	4	3		2	26

[1] Includes Negro and other nonwhite races.

[2] Includes "Incorporated places."

IN REGISTRATION AREA IN CONTINENTAL UNITED STATES, SELECTED STATES (CITIES, DISTRICTS), AND SELECTED CITIES: 1930—Continued

of the total colored population, and cities of such States in which data by color are available]

Area	Diseases of the heart	Bronchitis	Pneumonia (all forms)	Diarrhea and enteritis: Under 2 years	Diarrhea and enteritis: 2 years and over	Appendicitis	Hernia, intestinal obstruction	Cirrhosis of the liver	Nephritis	Puerperal septicemia	Other puerperal causes	Congenital malformations and diseases of early infancy	Suicide	Homicide	Automobile accidents: Primary [3]	Automobile accidents: In collision with railroad trains and street cars	Other external causes	Unknown or ill-defined diseases	All other causes
OHIO	909	13	603	77	29	65	41	33	378	34	36	289	34	218	104	10	255	30	671
Cities	739	10	538	68	25	58	36	26	306	29	33	249	30	206	85	8	200	22	559
Incorporated places	55	1	19	3		4	3	1	24	1		13		5	3	1	16	3	32
Rural	115	2	46	6	4	3	2	6	48	4	3	27	4	7	16	1	39	5	80
OKLAHOMA	290	8	314	69	32	42	19	12	196	16	37	98	10	84	51	1	139	152	508
Cities	122	3	152	28	12	23	9	6	83	5	16	48	2	42	27		56	37	220
Incorporated places	63	3	49	13	4	9	3	2	39	7	7	19	2	14	11	1	22	33	102
Rural	105	2	113	28	16	10	7	4	74	4	14	31	6	28	13		61	82	186
PENNSYLVANIA	1,230	35	985	155	49	73	73	32	612	37	48	401	28	149	100	2	297	44	808
Cities	1,001	27	869	130	37	65	70	25	508	33	41	333	23	125	82		244	27	658
Incorporated places	39	1	42	6		7	2	2	28		1	23	1	3	5	2	12	5	30
Rural	190	7	74	19	12	1	1	5	76	4	6	45	4	21	13		41	12	120
RHODE ISLAND	64	2	21	1		3	1	1	15	2		5	2	2	4		16	2	27
Cities	59	2	20	1		3	1	1	14			5	2	2	3		11	2	25
Incorporated places	1																		1
Rural	4		1						1	2					1		5		1
SOUTH CAROLINA	1,635	19	967	338	83	75	56	28	1,235	65	203	556	16	147	146	6	380	1,234	2,394
Cities	423	4	216	72	29	24	20	9	259	13	31	144	3	46	37	1	73	28	436
Incorporated places	156	4	90	28	3	13	6	1	125	5	23	32	1	13	21		30	32	145
Rural	1,056	11	661	238	51	38	30	18	851	47	149	380	12	88	88	5	277	1,174	1,813
TENNESSEE	1,060	21	674	143	80	78	68	30	615	68	60	252	12	299	92		331	752	1,152
Cities	567	14	367	68	48	58	51	23	333	41	30	171	7	233	64		170	249	641
Rural [2]	493	7	307	75	32	20	17	7	282	27	30	81	5	66	28		161	503	511
VERMONT	1					1									1		1		4
Cities						1													1
Rural [2]	1														1		1		3
VIRGINIA	1,847	46	978	257	74	80	86	45	1,118	56	128	617	22	167	118	14	437	442	1,607
Cities	643	18	408	87	25	49	48	23	383	22	47	179	13	94	53	4	141	68	506
Incorporated places	82	2	31	7	3	8	7	3	39	3	7	20		4	10		22	17	71
Rural	1,122	26	539	163	46	23	31	19	696	31	74	418	9	69	55	10	274	357	1.030
WEST VIRGINIA	227	3	159	73	11	10	17	5	169	4	17	102	8	75	22	1	217	9	196
Cities	56	1	43	13		4	9	2	50	1	4	22	2	22	6		35	2	79
Incorporated places	35		32	9	3	4	3		27		5	6	2	21	10		60	2	24
Rural	136	2	84	51	8	2	5	3	92	3	8	74	4	32	6	1	122	5	93
CITIES OF 10,000 POPULATION OR MORE																			
ALABAMA:																			
Anniston	8	1	20	6		3	3		13	1	3	3		4			4	3	18
Bessemer	37	1	15	1		2	1		6		4	12		10	2		4	17	12
Birmingham	230	1	187	28	5	21	18	7	133	14	11	117	1	106	22	3	60	218	198
Decatur	10		3	3	1	1	1	1	3			2		5			3	1	11
Dothan	9		2	1	1	2	2	1	4		1	1		1	2		4	4	12
Fairfield	12		27	4	2	6	1		32			17	1	7	3		11	8	16
Florence	10	1	4				2		2	2				1	2		2	3	10
Gadsden	10		14	3		2	3		15	1	3	3		7	1		3	6	10
Huntsville	11		11	2		1	1	2	8			2	1	3	2		2	6	15
Mobile	110		60	8	5	1	13	3	84	5	3	29		16	3		26	2	70
Montgomery	89	1	54	21	8	10	9	5	66	4	7	23		17	11		24	20	100
Phenix City	2		1		1				1			3		1			1		2
Selma	39		10	7	3	4	2	1	18	2	10	15	1	6	4	1	12	11	51
Tuscaloosa	11	1	17		1	6	2		10		4	5		10	1		13		21
ARKANSAS:																			
Blytheville	3	1	3	1	1	1	1		3			1		3	1		2	6	6
El Dorado	7	1	8	2	1		1	2	10		3	3		4	2		3	4	16
Fort Smith	14	1	5		1	1	1		9	1		3	1		3		9		8
Hot Springs	34	1	8			6	3	1	12		2		1		1		4	1	24
Jonesboro	3		2						1								2	1	4
Little Rock	113		34	4	2	6	7	5	55	2	8	8		17	9		28	15	169
North Little Rock	13		5	1	2	1	1	2	2	1		1		2			3	3	8
Pine Bluff	15		6		1	2		1	8	1	2	2		5	1		6	3	29
Texarkana	16	1	3		1	4	2		6	1		1		1	2		1	1	7
DELAWARE:																			
Wilmington	39	1	42	4	2	3	3		30	1		6	1	7	1		14		31
DISTRICT OF COLUMBIA:																			
Washington	533	10	291	58	11	36	37	15	248	23	31	153	13	44	34		82	3	369
FLORIDA:																			
Daytona Beach	23	1	3			2	1	2	4	2	1			3	3		6	2	17
Gainesville	17	1	3	3		2	2		13	1	2			6	1		2	1	19
Jacksonville	169	5	57	14	6	11	18	9	118	4	4	32		31	10	1	43	6	135
Key West	13		1	1	1				6			1					1		20
Lakeland	7	1	1				1		10		3	1					3	3	7
Miami	34		26	5	2	13	12	2	26	2	8	34	1	30	12		9	2	53
Orlando	13		6	2	1	3	6		6	5	2	4		6	2		2	10	16
Pensacola	24	2	17	10	7	3	3	2	19		3	18		2	6		7		36
St. Augustine	9		5	1		3		1	6	2		3		2			8	4	14
St. Petersburg	14		11	2	1	6			11	1	2	5		4	1		5	3	22
Sanford	8		7	4		1	1		1		1	2		2	2		2		10
Tallahassee	10		5	3			1		9	1		1		4	2		3	4	17
Tampa	60		17	4		6	10	4	24	2		23	1	11	4		11	6	53
West Palm Beach	16		11	3		3	1	2	21	1		10	1	13	8		9	1	38
GEORGIA:																			
Albany	17		9	6	4	3	3	1	26	1	3	5		6	1		8		35
Athens	30		8	2		3	3		15		1	14		4	2		5	7	19
Atlanta	259	8	213	34	24	22	32	7	214	15	12	126	4	115	33	1	46	43	260
Augusta	122	4	53	6	4	13	2	5	64	4	3	26	1	21	7	1	21	4	111
Brunswick	27		13	3	3	2		2	15	1	2	4		4	2		3	1	20

[3] Excluding collision with railroad trains and street cars.

[4] No deaths in "Incorporated places" in 1930.

TABLE 26.—COLORED[1] DEATHS (EXCLUSIVE OF STILLBIRTHS) FROM IMPORTANT CAUSES, INCORPORATED PLACES, AND RURAL

[Data are included for States in which the Negro population constitutes 55 percent or more

AREA	All causes	Typhoid and paratyphoid fever	Smallpox	Measles	Scarlet fever	Whooping cough	Diphtheria	Influenza	Erysipelas	Epidemic cerebrospinal meningitis	Tuberculosis of the respiratory system	Tuberculosis of the meninges, etc.	Other forms of tuberculosis	Syphilis	Malaria	Cancer and other malignant tumors	Rheumatism and gout	Diabetes mellitus	Cerebral hemorrhage and softening
CITIES OF 10,000 POPULATION OR MORE—con.																			
GEORGIA—Continued.																			
Columbus	344	3	-	1	-	1	-	6	-	4	22	1	3	13	-	8	2	-	16
Decatur	53	-	-	-	-	-	-	2	-	-	4	-	-	2	-	3	-	-	4
Griffin	124	1	-	-	-	-	1	6	-	-	11	-	1	-	-	4	-	2	5
La Grange	130	-	-	-	-	1	-	8	1	-	12	-	-	4	-	5	-	1	3
Macon	609	10	-	7	-	4	-	12	-	2	41	2	4	10	1	21	2	10	35
Rome	93	-	-	-	-	1	-	-	-	2	6	-	-	-	1	-	-	1	4
Savannah	1,033	5	-	-	1	2	3	17	-	-	97	-	8	39	1	22	4	11	93
Thomasville	155	1	-	3	-	-	-	5	-	-	5	-	3	3	-	6	-	1	15
Valdosta	127	2	-	-	-	-	-	6	-	-	9	-	-	2	1	2	-	-	7
Waycross	138	-	-	-	-	-	-	3	-	-	4	-	-	1	1	10	-	-	12
ILLINOIS:																			
Cairo	111	1	-	-	-	-	-	4	-	1	9	-	-	1	1	7	-	1	14
Chicago	4,045	4	-	-	7	18	38	22	4	25	611	32	70	96	-	203	19	54	143
East St. Louis	173	2	-	-	-	2	-	3	1	-	16	-	2	2	-	5	2	3	12
INDIANA:																			
Indianapolis	867	2	-	2	-	6	4	19	1	38	77	4	14	5	-	30	-	10	30
Jeffersonville	30	-	-	-	-	-	-	1	-	-	3	-	1	-	-	2	-	-	1
KANSAS:																			
Atchison	35	-	-	-	-	-	-	7	-	-	1	-	-	-	-	4	-	1	1
Coffeyville	42	-	-	-	-	-	-	1	-	-	4	-	1	-	-	3	-	-	3
Kansas City	341	-	-	-	-	3	1	7	-	6	39	1	4	7	-	16	-	8	21
Lawrence	29	-	-	-	-	-	-	-	-	-	2	-	1	2	-	2	-	-	4
Leavenworth	45	-	-	-	-	-	-	2	-	-	-	-	-	-	-	5	1	-	7
KENTUCKY:																			
Bowling Green	48	1	-	2	-	-	-	2	-	-	2	-	3	-	-	3	-	2	2
Frankfort	58	-	-	-	-	1	-	4	-	-	12	-	5	1	-	3	-	1	3
Henderson	75	-	-	-	-	2	-	-	-	-	7	-	1	-	-	4	1	-	10
Hopkinsville	146	3	-	-	-	-	-	2	-	6	19	-	2	1	-	3	-	1	8
Lexington	421	5	-	1	-	2	-	10	-	6	24	4	5	5	-	22	3	7	22
Louisville	1,104	2	-	-	-	7	2	11	-	6	81	1	12	29	-	50	5	11	66
Owensboro	62	2	-	-	-	-	-	1	-	-	2	1	1	-	-	6	-	1	4
Paducah	141	-	-	-	-	-	-	5	-	-	22	1	2	5	3	5	-	1	10
LOUISIANA:																			
Alexandria	171	1	-	-	-	1	-	3	-	-	4	-	2	4	-	14	-	2	6
Baton Rouge	116	2	-	-	-	-	-	5	-	-	12	1	-	4	-	7	-	-	9
Bogalusa	82	1	-	-	-	2	-	2	-	-	7	-	1	6	-	1	-	-	6
Lafayette	98	1	-	-	-	3	-	1	-	-	9	-	-	3	2	4	-	1	3
Lake Charles	82	-	-	-	-	-	-	1	-	-	3	-	2	3	-	3	-	2	2
Monroe	225	1	-	-	-	-	1	6	1	1	18	-	2	4	2	6	1	-	12
New Orleans	3,289	11	-	11	-	14	6	99	-	21	304	1	21	156	1	165	6	25	165
Shreveport	874	12	-	-	-	3	5	12	-	1	61	2	9	57	6	30	1	7	35
MARYLAND:																			
Annapolis	84	1	-	-	-	-	1	2	-	-	6	1	2	1	-	-	3	-	7
Baltimore	2,815	12	-	-	2	5	3	19	1	9	313	18	48	122	-	139	15	26	187
Frederick	27	-	-	-	-	-	-	-	-	-	1	-	1	-	-	1	-	-	4
Salisbury	69	6	-	-	-	-	-	-	-	-	1	1	-	2	-	3	-	1	3
MASSACHUSETTS:																			
Boston	452	-	-	1	-	2	-	-	3	2	60	7	2	11	-	37	1	5	32
MICHIGAN:																			
Detroit	2,037	4	-	14	2	6	8	19	3	32	426	27	44	62	-	47	6	17	53
MISSISSIPPI:																			
Biloxi	52	-	-	-	-	-	-	2	-	1	-	-	-	2	-	-	-	-	3
Clarksdale	140	2	-	-	-	-	-	2	-	1	11	1	3	3	4	3	-	1	11
Columbus	154	-	-	-	-	2	2	5	-	-	17	-	3	4	-	6	-	4	7
Greenville	336	1	-	-	-	-	1	7	-	30	14	-	2	1	-	10	2	1	31
Greenwood	144	-	-	-	-	-	1	6	-	-	14	-	1	4	3	6	1	1	12
Gulfport	70	-	-	-	-	-	-	1	1	1	2	-	-	3	-	3	-	-	4
Hattiesburg	133	1	-	-	-	1	-	6	-	-	11	-	-	3	-	3	-	2	8
Jackson	414	3	-	-	-	-	2	11	-	-	21	-	2	9	2	19	-	2	14
Laurel	142	1	-	1	1	1	-	4	-	4	10	-	1	2	1	3	-	1	10
McComb	61	2	-	-	-	-	-	-	-	-	4	-	-	2	-	3	-	-	2
Meridian	294	5	-	1	-	1	-	11	-	-	29	-	1	10	4	5	-	1	25
Natchez	149	2	-	-	-	-	1	5	-	-	11	-	-	1	-	10	-	2	11
Vicksburg	521	2	-	-	-	1	-	5	-	6	21	-	2	3	6	23	-	4	31
MISSOURI:																			
Columbia	52	-	-	-	-	-	-	1	-	-	1	-	-	-	-	1	-	-	10
Jefferson City	24	-	-	-	-	-	-	-	-	-	2	-	-	1	-	-	-	-	-
Kansas City	922	-	-	-	1	1	1	6	-	14	131	5	10	10	1	47	-	7	50
St. Louis	1,982	2	-	6	-	1	2	16	3	16	241	11	27	25	-	102	6	18	97
NEBRASKA:																			
Omaha	223	-	-	-	-	-	1	4	-	1	27	3	5	16	-	18	-	1	[illegible]
NEW JERSEY:																			
Asbury Park	22	-	-	-	-	-	-	-	-	-	2	-	-	-	-	1	-	-	2
Atlantic City	268	4	-	-	-	-	-	5	-	-	16	4	3	11	-	11	1	7	21
Montclair	43	-	-	-	-	-	1	-	-	-	4	-	-	-	-	6	1	-	3
Newark	759	-	-	2	1	3	1	6	-	1	118	6	25	9	-	31	3	8	35
Orange	87	1	-	-	-	1	2	-	-	1	9	-	-	1	-	3	-	1	6
NEW YORK:																			
New York	5,630	6	-	18	-	20	14	12	7	33	913	49	91	241	-	261	24	71	153
NORTH CAROLINA:																			
Asheville	244	-	-	-	-	2	-	12	-	-	27	2	5	3	-	10	-	1	30
Charlotte	481	1	-	-	-	4	2	17	-	-	35	-	9	13	-	12	-	2	58
Concord	34	-	-	-	-	1	1	1	-	-	6	-	-	-	-	1	-	-	4
Durham	426	3	-	-	-	1	2	7	-	1	44	1	7	9	-	16	1	1	23

[1] Includes Negro and other nonwhite races.

IN REGISTRATION AREA IN CONTINENTAL UNITED STATES, SELECTED STATES (CITIES, DISTRICTS), AND SELECTED CITIES: 1930—Continued

of the total colored population, and cities of such States in which data by color are available]

AREA	Diseases of the heart	Bronchitis	Pneumonia (all forms)	DIARRHEA AND ENTERITIS		Appendicitis	Hernia, intestinal obstruction	Cirrhosis of the liver	Nephritis	Puerperal septicemia	Other puerperal causes	Congenital malformations and diseases of early infancy	Suicide	Homicide	AUTOMOBILE ACCIDENTS		Other external causes	Unknown or ill-defined diseases	All other causes
				Under 2 years	2 years and over										Primary [2]	In collision with railroad trains and street cars			
CITIES OF 10,000 POPULATION OR MORE—con.																			
GEORGIA—Continued.																			
Columbus	46	1	37	8		2	4	1	30	3	2	6	1	6	5		14	25	73
Decatur	11	1	2		1				3			1	1	1			2	4	11
Griffin	17		5	3	1	1		1	11	3	2	6		2	2		5	14	20
La Grange	15		11	6	2	1	2		24		4	9		3	1	1	5	1	10
Macon	79	3	55	13	2	6	6	2	64	1	6	16	3	16	7	1	23	53	92
Rome	13	1	17			1			14	2		7		5	2		5	2	9
Savannah	189	3	86	13	12	18	9	7	112	6	13	45		29	14	1	36	2	135
Thomasville	27	1	7				3	1	19	1	3	9		2	1		9	3	27
Valdosta	10		6	2	1	2			12		1	3		2			7	31	21
Waycross	22		17	5	3	1	1	3	18		2	3		2	1		7	1	21
ILLINOIS:																			
Cairo	17	1	10		1		3		15	1	1	2		6	2		5	1	7
Chicago	699	12	359	33	16	49	48	21	362	10	20	198	27	174	59	1	132	80	399
East St. Louis	20	2	18	6	3	3	1	1	10	1	1	13	4	12	2		13	1	12
INDIANA:																			
Indianapolis	163	5	126	24	6	9	2	5	91	4	3	39	5	19	13		14		97
Jeffersonville	9		1		2			1	3						1				5
KANSAS:																			
Atchison	2		3	2	2		1		9										2
Coffeyville	10		2	3					3			5		1			1	1	4
Kansas City	47		14	5	3	6	6	2	45	5		14		18	4		19		40
Lawrence	10								3						1				4
Leavenworth	13	1	1			1		1	3					1	2				7
KENTUCKY:																			
Bowling Green	7	1	3	1	2	1			7		1	1		1			1		5
Frankfort	6	3		3	1	1			4								2		8
Henderson	9	1	8	2		1	1		5			3		1			4		15
Hopkinsville	29	1	10	2	3	2	2	1	24	1		1		2	3		3	1	16
Lexington	87		37	6	3	7	5	3	47		2	6	1	20	8		15	2	56
Louisville	229	27	130	8	4	6	13	2	125	5	4	32	5	37	13	1	26	2	152
Owensboro	16		4		2		1	1	11	1	1	2		2			1		2
Paducah	27	2	10	1	2	1			12	2	1	6		2	3		3		15
LOUISIANA:																			
Alexandria	23		17	5	2	2		1	34	1	10	5		8	5		6	1	14
Baton Rouge	22		9		1		1		13			3		3	8		5	2	9
Bogalusa	8	1	10	2	1				9			9		3	1		1	2	9
Lafayette	13	1	9	6		2		3	6		2	3		3	1		1	2	19
Lake Charles	9		5	4		2	3		8	1	3	6					3	9	13
Monroe	31		18	6	1	9	5		16	2	3	4		12	3	2	17		41
New Orleans	586	6	372	53	14	27.	38	46	369	21	22	140	12	64	37	1	97	1	377
Shreveport	134	2	49	11	9	16	18	2	60	13	5	32	2	27	14		40	7	192
MARYLAND:																			
Annapolis	10	4	7	3	1	2			4	1		1		1	3		6		17
Baltimore	496	4	442	35	8	28	35	7	253	12	14	141	7	41	32	5	99		237
Frederick	6		3						1			3			3				4
Salisbury	5		6	5		1			9	3	3	8		2	4		1	2	3
MASSACHUSETTS:																			
Boston	64		55	5	1	7	1	2	45	4	3	18	5	4	5		10	1	59
MICHIGAN:																			
Detroit	315	19	249	20	5	26	21	3	92	11	11	105	15	96	38	4	43	1	193
MISSISSIPPI:																			
Biloxi	6	3	7	2		1			7			1		1	1		5	5	5
Clarksdale	21		6	2	2	2	3	1	13	1				3	3		4	20	17
Columbus	22		13	4	2	1	2		9			3		2	1		7	24	14
Greenville	47		26	4		5	5		27	2	4	6		12	8		19	39	32
Greenwood	14	1	8	2	2	5	3		19	3	1	1	1	7	2		3	7	16
Gulfport	14		5		1		3	1	10	2		4		3	2		2	1	7
Hattiesburg	15		8	1	3	3	1	1	15	3		5		1	2		4	12	24
Jackson	46	1	28	7	3	21	9	2	42	2	7	6	1	8	9		24	47	66
Laurel	10		8	1		8	1		13	2	1	4		4	2		11	7	30
McComb	12		6		2	1			5	1	2			3			5	5	6
Meridian	28	2	17	10	2	3	4	3	14	1	5	7	1	14	5		14	36	35
Natchez	34		5	2	1	1			13	2	1	2		2	1		1	20	21
Vicksburg	70	1	24	2	4	19	9	5	50	5	9	11	1	12	7		35	83	70
MISSOURI:																			
Columbia	16		5				2		1			1	1				2		11
Jefferson City	4		5					1	1			1					4		5
Kansas City	148		88	10	5	13	14	15	109	5	5	24	5	50	23		29	3	92
St. Louis	405	5	242	31	5	33	9	14	240	11	4	65	3	68	23		73	1	177
NEBRASKA:																			
Omaha	41		22		2	4	1	2	13		2	6	5	9	2		12		21
NEW JERSEY:																			
Asbury Park	5		1					1	2			2					2		4
Atlantic City	48		34	3		4	5	1	23	1		11	1	4	11		11	1	27
Montclair	9	1	6	1				1	6			1							3
Newark	113	4	99	15	1	15	4	2	50	5	11	49	2	27	8		21		84
Orange	18		6	2		1	1		7			2	2	1	1		4	1	16
NEW YORK:																			
New York	880	13	768	94	8	63	32	18	322	24	48	333	47	131	92	1	233		610
NORTH CAROLINA:																			
Asheville	37		17	5		6	4		19	3	4	16		6	7		6		22
Charlotte	64		46	12	5	1	5	2	25	1	4	31		29	5		16	4	78
Concord	6		2						3			3					3	2	1
Durham	58	2	42	6	1	3	6	1	32	3	2	22	1	16	6		16	34	59

[2] Excluding collision with railroad trains and street cars.

TABLE 26.—COLORED [1] DEATHS (EXCLUSIVE OF STILLBIRTHS) FROM IMPORTANT CAUSES, INCORPORATED PLACES AND RURAL

[Data are included for States in which the Negro population constitutes 55 percent or more

AREA	All causes	Typhoid and paratyphoid fever	Smallpox	Measles	Scarlet fever	Whooping cough	Diphtheria	Influenza	Erysipelas	Epidemic cerebrospinal meningitis	Tuberculosis of the respiratory system	Tuberculosis of the meninges, etc.	Other forms of tuberculosis	Syphilis	Malaria	Cancer and other malignant tumors	Rheumatism and gout	Diabetes mellitus	Cerebral hemorrhage and softening
CITIES OF 10,000 POPULATION OR MORE—con.																			
NORTH CAROLINA—Con.																			
Elizabeth City	72					1		3			9		2	3		3			2
Fayetteville	120	1			1	3		2			9	2	1	3		1			12
Gastonia	70							1			4		1			4			8
Goldsboro	131							4			8		1	5		5	1	1	8
Greensboro	254					1		3		2	14		1	12		11	3	2	13
High Point	134	1				1		2			9		1	4		5	1	2	12
Kinston	95	1				1		5			11		2			3	1	2	9
New Bern	150						1				15			3					14
Raleigh	299	2			1	1	1	5			30			6		12	2	4	23
Rocky Mount	197							5		1	15	1	3	2		10		3	9
Salisbury	64					2					4			4		2			6
Shelby	17	2									1		1						3
Statesville	31										2			1		1			2
Thomasville	29							2			1			1				1	1
Wilmington	326	1					1	3		1	18	1	7	9	2	8		4	26
Wilson	165	2					1	3			20		3	7				2	7
Winston-Salem	620	3					2	22		2	57	2	9	13		15	2	3	42
OHIO:																			
Cincinnati	1,139			1	1	3		11	1	11	154	11	31	32		51	5	7	65
Cleveland	1,293	3		1	1	9	4	10	2	12	234	9	26	32		55	1	8	70
Columbus	608	2		2		1	1	9			48	7	13	13		32	2	8	37
Springfield	141	1						8			11		1			9	1	1	16
Xenia	39				1			5			3			2		3			3
OKLAHOMA:																			
Ardmore	37	1		1				3			1		1			1			1
Chickasha	44	1						1			3		1				2		3
McAlester	44										4			5		3			1
Muskogee	202	3	1	3				6			21		7		3	11			10
Oklahoma City	269	2		1		2		11		2	31	3	5	5	1	8	3	1	7
Okmulgee	122	4		1		2	1	7			11		2	4		2		2	5
Sapulpa	22	1									4		2	1		1			
Tulsa	272	7				1		6			17		6	2	1	3	1		16
Wewoka	42					2	1	1			8				1	1			1
PENNSYLVANIA:																			
Chester	212	1					1	5			16		2	4		8	1	3	16
Coatesville	13																		
Philadelphia	3,620	1		2	6	7	10	51	3	12	522	14	38	104	2	182	12	47	128
Pittsburgh	1,103			4	1	8	6	16		9	104	7	7	37		43	3	9	51
Steelton	23					1		3			3					1		2	1
West Chester	45	1									2	1		3		3			
SOUTH CAROLINA:																			
Anderson	112	2						5			4					4			6
Charleston	927	4				8	1	13		4	75	5	7	39	4	29	4	4	74
Columbia	554	4				1		27	1	5	34		5	13	6	13		3	41
Florence	191	1						11			13		1	1	2	3		3	22
Greenville	290	2				1		15	1		14		2	19		7		2	23
Greenwood	81	2						4			5	1		1		2	1		3
Rock Hill	50					1		1			10					4			2
Spartanburg	222	3						12			15	2		4		6	1	6	4
Sumter	153	2						4			6	1	2	2	1	4		3	9
TENNESSEE:																			
Chattanooga	825	2		2		11	1	24		35	75	3	13	17	1	19	2	5	51
Jackson	148	1					2	3			17		4	1	4	2			8
Knoxville	320							14		3	20	1	2	9		10		4	20
Memphis	2,274	5				9	7	43		105	229	6	30	68	16	66	11	21	149
Nashville	990	8		1		2	2	23		2	96	7	15	24		36	3	9	84
TEXAS:																			
Beaumont	292					2		7		3	28	1	2	11	5	16	2	4	15
Dallas	859	7		5	1	1	5	14		5	59	1	13	15	5	23		6	58
Fort Worth	428	3		2			1	18		1	50		1	17	2	14		3	16
Galveston	244	3				1		1	1	1	20	2	2	11		18			17
Houston	1,495	4				2	2	43		1	118	2	8	35	9	39	3	22	74
San Antonio	370	1				1		12			44		3	5	1	14		5	20
Waco	271	5					4	8			30		3	7		13		2	18
VIRGINIA:																			
Alexandria	107					5		1			4					3		1	14
Charlottesville	49										8					3		1	2
Danville	132					2		4			7	1	1	2		5		3	12
Hopewell	20										1			1					1
Lynchburg	252	3		3	1	5	3	5	1		13	1		6		7		4	13
Newport News	260	6		1				5			19	1	1	8		3	1	1	30
Norfolk	902	1				6	6	17			67	2	8	20	1	29	5	8	95
Petersburg	310					1	1	12			29	2		4		3	2	2	27
Portsmouth	376					1		17			20	1	5	13	2	9	7	8	57
Richmond	1,132	1			1	6	5	25		8	84	7	16	28		44	3	10	107
Roanoke	276			3		2		18			17		2	10		7		5	19
Staunton	36						1	1			5								2
Suffolk	121					2		3			15	1	3	1		2		2	11
WEST VIRGINIA:																			
Bluefield	83	1				1		1		1	5		2	1		3		1	3
Charleston	123	2				1		1		1	4	1	5	1		3		3	10

[1] Includes Negro and other nonwhite races.

IN REGISTRATION AREA IN CONTINENTAL UNITED STATES, SELECTED STATES (CITIES, DISTRICTS; AND SELECTED CITIES: 1930—Continued

of the total colored population, and cities of such States in which data by color are available]

AREA	Diseases of the heart	Bronchitis	Pneumonia (all forms)	DIARRHEA AND ENTERITIS: Under 2 years	DIARRHEA AND ENTERITIS: 2 years and over	Appendicitis	Hernia, intestinal obstruction	Cirrhosis of the liver	Nephritis	Puerperal septicemia	Other puerperal causes	Congenital malformations and diseases of early infancy	Suicide	Homicide	AUTOMOBILE ACCIDENTS: Primary[2]	AUTOMOBILE ACCIDENTS: In collision with railroad trains and street cars	Other external causes	Unknown or ill-defined diseases	All other causes
CITIES OF 10,000 POPULATION OR MORE—con.																			
NORTH CAROLINA—Con.																			
Elizabeth City	3	1	3	6		2			13	1	1	4	1				5	3	6
Fayetteville	6		11	2	1		1		10	2	2	8	1	7	2	2	6	7	17
Gastonia	9	2	5	4					8		1	3		1			3	7	9
Goldsboro	18	5	6	5	2	2	2	1	8		4	7		5	1		3		29
Greensboro	42		21	4		11	8	2	19	2	3	17		7	7		15		34
High Point	14		27	2	1	2	3	1	6		1	10	1	6	5		3		14
Kinston	15	1	5	1		1			8		1	8			1		4	2	13
New Bern	35		17	9	1			1	18		3	10		5			6		12
Raleigh	39		18	2	2	4	8		19	1	5	16	1	9	7		22	16	43
Rocky Mount	22	4	20	6	1	4		1	17	1	5	16	1	5	4		7	7	27
Salisbury	9		2	1					12	1	2	1			1		3	4	10
Shelby	1								2	1				1			1		4
Statesville	2		4						5		2	2		2			2	3	3
Thomasville	5		2					1	4			2		1				1	7
Wilmington	49	1	28	4		6	5		48	3	8	16	1	5	6		11	4	50
Wilson	12	2	18	8			1		21	2	2	4		3	2		5	20	20
Winston-Salem	77	1	87	24	4	4	4	4	27	4	7	40	2	15	7		17	39	85
OHIO:																			
Cincinnati	160	2	131	16	3	16	7	5	59	6	6	60	5	48	15	3	49	2	162
Cleveland	176	2	135	18	7	10	9	7	77	10	11	77	8	65	21	1	36	7	139
Columbus	107	1	57	7	6	4	7	2	49	3	6	30	6	16	16		41		75
Springfield	22	1	16	5	1	1	1		8	2	1	4	1	4	2	1	4	2	17
Xenia	11								4			1							6
OKLAHOMA:																			
Ardmore	3		5	1	1			2	1			3		1	1		2	1	7
Chickasha	2		7	1	1				1			3		3			2	1	12
McAlester	5		2		1	1			6		1			3			1	4	7
Muskogee	27	3	9	3	1	3	1	1	21	1	4	7	1	4	2		7	6	36
Oklahoma City	28		44	7	1	8	2		16	1	1	6		12	8		11	7	35
Okmulgee	20		8	2	2	1	1		5		2	3		3	4		7	3	20
Sapulpa	1		1					2				2			2		1		4
Tulsa	19		44	7	2	5	4	1	23	2	3	14	1	6	6		17	4	54
Wewoka	2		5			1					1	1		3	1		1	4	8
PENNSYLVANIA:																			
Chester	24	1	31	8	1	1	3	3	22	3		15	1	8	4		8		22
Coatesville	4		1	1								2		1			2		2
Philadelphia	643	18	431	88	21	34	36	13	316	15	22	193	11	68	31		119	7	413
Pittsburgh	149	4	243	16	8	8	15	4	65	10	8	56	5	23	11		50	16	107
Steelton	1		8						3										
West Chester	7		7	1		2	2		3		1	4		2	1		2		3
SOUTH CAROLINA:																			
Anderson	22		13	1	3	1	2		12		2	7		1			2	2	23
Charleston	173	3	91	21	19	4	6	3	88	3	7	65		16	10	1	19	2	125
Columbia	70	1	38	14	2	4	5	4	51	2	5	24	2	13	6		26	1	133
Florence	22		9	10		7	3		22	3	5	8		2	4		5	5	29
Greenville	57		21	8	3	3	1	1	35	2	4	19		4	5		5	1	35
Greenwood	9		11	3		1		1	6		1	2			3		4	1	20
Rock Hill	11		1	4			1		3		2			1	1		2		6
Spartanburg	37		17	4	2	1	2		28	1	2	12		3	5		5	10	40
Sumter	22		15	7		3			14	2	3	7	1	6	3		5	6	25
TENNESSEE:																			
Chattanooga	90	7	78	17	7	11	7	2	47	10	4	22		48	12		40	62	100
Jackson	16		11	3		2	1		6	2	1	4		8			3	24	25
Knoxville	44	1	32	6	10	2	1	1	33	2	1	8	1	14	5		14	15	47
Memphis	272	3	150	17	19	28	34	16	158	13	16	97	3	121	26		82	95	359
Nashville	138	3	87	23	9	15	8	4	85	13	8	40	3	42	21		31	49	99
TEXAS:																			
Beaumont	41	1	23	9		3	3	2	20	3	4	22		6	3		16	4	36
Dallas	90	7	114	28	12	11	11	5	67	3	12	40	2	35	12		45		147
Fort Worth	43		36	16	7	9	3	3	24	6	5	18		19	9		18	11	73
Galveston	31		14	2	1	1	2	1	25	3	4	12		7	5		5	4	50
Houston	127	6	129	43	12	17	16	15	87	15	10	50	5	48	26	3	50	293	181
San Antonio	46	3	27	9	3	6	6	6	36	3	3	11		12	1		6	18	68
Waco	28		13	4		11	4		20	2	2	12		8	4		8	3	62
VIRGINIA:																			
Alexandria	19	1	14	4		1			13		1	5	1	5	1		5	2	7
Charlottesville	9		7	1	1				8			1			1		1	2	4
Danville	26	1	9	2		4	5		4	1	3	4		3	2		6	12	13
Hopewell			3	2		1			1		1	2			1		2		4
Lynchburg	47		22	5		1	1	4	32	1	7	8		8	4		7	1	39
Newport News	38	1	35	9	1	4	2		27	1	2	18	1	5	3	1	14	1	21
Norfolk	197	6	86	25	9	9	11	4	56	5	10	37		29	5		35		113
Petersburg	36		46	8	3	8	4	4	37		5	12	2	8	6		9		39
Portsmouth	39		44	4	2	1	4	3	39	6	4	15	1	2	6	1	11	2	52
Richmond	172	6	96	15	5	13	11	7	126	5	9	53	6	23	15	1	35	39	150
Roanoke	34	1	35	8	4	3	5		28	1	3	13	2	7	3		6	6	34
Staunton	7		2				1	1	5	1		4		1	1			1	3
Suffolk	16	2	6	3		3	2		4	1	2	4		3	3	1	10	2	19
WEST VIRGINIA:																			
Bluefield	7		8	1		2	1		7			2		4	2		14		16
Charleston	15	1	12	4		1	4		12	1		8		6	2		7	1	17

[2] Excluding collision with railroad trains and street cars.

TABLE 27.—COLORED[1] DEATHS (EXCLUSIVE OF STILLBIRTHS), BY AGE, IN THE REGISTRATION AREA OF RURAL DIS

AREA	All deaths	Under 1 year	1 year	2 years	3 years	4 years	5 to 9 years	10 to 14 years	15 to 19 years	20 to 24 years	25 to 29 years	30 to 34 years	35 to 39 years
The registration area in continental United States	**199, 167**	**27, 240**	**5, 096**	**2, 334**	**1, 408**	**1, 082**	**3, 648**	**3, 420**	**8, 288**	**11, 587**	**11, 801**	**11, 340**	**12, 935**
Registration cities in nonregistration States [2]	5, 085	805	156	59	29	28	90	70	189	316	359	388	391
Selected registration States [3]	182, 250	24, 096	4, 347	2, 013	1, 240	919	3, 177	3, 066	7, 627	10, 711	10, 817	10, 452	11, 971
Cities [4]	83, 245	9, 498	1, 693	814	536	401	1, 339	1, 149	3, 154	4, 955	5, 799	5, 951	6, 704
Rural [5]	99, 005	14, 598	2, 654	1, 199	704	518	1, 838	1, 917	4, 473	5, 756	5, 018	4, 501	5, 267
ALABAMA	14, 412	2, 157	313	138	99	71	231	231	649	863	785	747	882
Cities	4, 516	542	92	43	31	18	66	59	223	301	324	309	324
Incorporated places	1, 082	132	28	10	5	7	18	17	57	62	46	55	64
Rural	8, 814	1, 483	193	85	63	46	147	155	369	500	415	383	494
ARKANSAS	6, 466	512	158	78	47	40	113	135	319	423	399	316	391
Cities	1, 344	55	14	10	7	6	16	12	62	76	92	93	121
Incorporated places	831	61	18	8	5	4	15	15	37	55	55	42	54
Rural	4, 291	396	126	60	35	30	82	108	220	292	252	181	216
CONNECTICUT	523	81	8	3	4	1	9	3	16	29	42	34	28
Cities	435	67	7	1	4	1	7	2	11	26	37	31	25
Incorporated places	13	1	----	----	----	----	----	1	1	1	----	3	1
Rural	75	13	1	2	----	----	2	----	4	2	5	----	2
DELAWARE	707	87	20	9	1	2	11	9	20	20	25	25	32
Cities	280	18	6	5	1	1	5	2	8	6	12	11	19
Incorporated places	74	10	1	----	----	----	3	1	4	2	3	2	5
Rural	353	59	13	4	----	1	3	6	8	12	10	12	8
DISTRICT OF COLUMBIA	2, 792	337	69	20	14	7	34	28	97	139	169	164	203
FLORIDA	7, 182	801	135	79	44	26	104	118	263	431	516	439	575
Cities	2, 939	302	53	24	18	10	43	46	113	198	253	224	287
Incorporated places	1, 290	114	29	14	8	3	14	21	42	61	89	90	95
Rural	2, 953	385	53	41	18	13	47	51	108	172	174	125	193
GEORGIA	17, 190	2, 259	428	198	99	92	304	332	786	1, 077	1, 025	887	1, 071
Cities	6, 088	641	129	73	30	28	89	99	272	411	454	402	465
Rural [5]	11, 102	1, 618	299	125	69	64	215	233	514	666	571	485	606
ILLINOIS	5, 961	539	101	68	49	14	101	58	196	348	423	456	503
Cities	4, 951	478	89	63	44	14	96	42	162	297	373	388	428
Incorporated places	251	25	5	3	2	----	1	3	13	12	7	15	8
Rural	759	36	7	2	3	----	4	13	21	39	43	53	67
INDIANA	2, 313	278	43	19	12	13	24	32	86	122	144	152	185
Cities	1, 931	249	39	19	11	13	23	27	73	102	129	137	168
Incorporated places	90	11	1	----	----	----	----	1	4	6	4	2	2
Rural	292	18	3	----	1	----	1	4	9	14	11	13	15
IOWA	363	44	12	5	2	5	8	8	15	12	18	18	22
Cities	276	29	7	5	2	3	7	5	8	9	13	14	20
Incorporated places	31	6	1	----	----	----	----	----	3	1	2	2	1
Rural	56	9	4	----	----	2	1	3	4	2	3	2	1
KANSAS	1, 102	92	16	10	6	4	14	11	33	40	33	67	72
Cities	765	63	11	10	5	3	13	6	26	26	24	50	48
Incorporated places	76	14	4	----	----	----	1	1	2	2	1	2	5
Rural	261	15	1	----	1	1	----	4	5	12	8	15	19
KENTUCKY	4, 750	413	91	40	18	19	66	57	164	229	240	233	253
Cities	2, 190	134	29	13	10	8	22	17	66	107	122	128	139
Rural [5]	2, 560	279	62	27	8	11	44	40	98	122	118	105	114
LOUISIANA	12, 086	1, 730	286	120	79	69	196	188	478	695	688	650	763
Cities	4, 937	561	103	48	30	31	67	76	182	326	321	305	385
Incorporated places	1, 505	188	31	11	6	8	20	21	67	80	97	81	78
Rural	5, 644	981	152	61	43	30	109	91	229	289	270	264	300
MARYLAND	5, 264	777	120	52	35	21	91	85	170	300	277	290	304
Cities	3, 053	344	61	21	18	14	55	44	92	165	188	205	212
Incorporated places	248	40	2	4	2	----	3	6	10	13	12	12	16
Rural	1, 963	393	57	27	15	7	33	35	68	122	77	73	76
MASSACHUSETTS	908	101	11	8	3	7	20	9	19	27	35	49	56
Cities	789	90	9	6	1	7	16	7	17	20	31	39	46
Incorporated places	21	2	----	----	----	----	----	1	----	2	----	----	1
Rural	98	9	2	2	2	----	4	1	2	5	4	10	9
MICHIGAN	3, 090	370	87	47	35	26	69	66	113	208	293	265	328
Cities	2, 560	317	71	42	30	25	61	55	91	182	260	235	289
Incorporated places	60	8	2	2	----	----	1	----	4	3	2	3	1
Rural	470	45	14	3	5	1	7	11	18	23	31	27	38
MISSISSIPPI	14, 961	2, 072	360	186	127	82	309	291	743	1, 037	840	695	821
Cities	2, 610	223	42	25	22	15	44	40	123	202	189	166	177
Rural [5]	12, 351	1, 849	318	161	105	67	265	251	620	835	651	529	644
MISSOURI	4, 653	407	87	34	25	16	62	63	150	224	273	278	293
Cities	3, 313	252	54	22	15	14	33	43	89	169	214	214	241
Incorporated places	388	35	9	1	1	----	4	6	6	18	10	17	19
Rural	952	120	24	11	9	2	25	14	55	37	49	47	33
NEBRASKA	467	69	16	11	8	4	13	8	14	25	26	27	34
Cities	267	16	4	3	3	1	7	1	7	18	16	18	20
Incorporated places	55	19	6	2	1	----	1	----	----	1	5	3	6
Rural	145	34	6	6	4	3	5	7	7	6	5	6	8
NEW HAMPSHIRE	9	1	----	----	----	----	----	----	----	1	----	----	----
Cities	6	----	----	----	----	----	----	----	----	1	----	----	----
Rural [5] [6]	3	1	----	----	----	----	----	----	----	----	----	----	----
NEW JERSEY	3, 552	495	106	30	23	14	71	59	145	202	218	237	237
Cities	2, 588	400	88	24	20	12	53	36	87	132	156	182	191
Incorporated places	363	31	5	1	1	----	4	12	32	33	21	25	14
Rural	601	64	13	5	2	2	14	11	26	37	41	30	32
NEW YORK	7, 199	949	152	83	41	36	125	90	223	407	564	642	686
Cities	6, 568	883	143	78	38	35	113	79	206	375	525	601	636
Incorporated places	136	16	2	1	----	1	4	1	1	4	10	8	12
Rural	495	50	7	4	3	----	8	10	16	28	29	33	38
NORTH CAROLINA	14, 155	2, 451	468	207	95	77	258	289	697	877	784	702	805
Cities	3, 959	574	90	44	15	15	72	69	206	294	318	270	282
Incorporated places	971	152	18	13	5	2	16	18	45	52	57	51	67
Rural	9, 225	1, 725	360	150	75	60	170	202	446	531	409	381	456

[1] Includes Negro and other nonwhite races.
[2] Includes 8 cities in Texas.
[3] States in which the Negro population constitutes 55 percent or more of the total colored population.

CONTINENTAL UNITED STATES, SELECTED REGISTRATION STATES, CITIES, INCORPORATED PLACES, AND TRICTS: 1930

AREA	40 to 44 years	45 to 49 years	50 to 54 years	55 to 59 years	60 to 64 years	65 to 69 years	70 to 74 years	75 to 79 years	80 to 84 years	85 to 89 years	90 to 94 years	95 to 99 years	100 years and over	Deaths at unknown age
The registration area in continental United States	**13,133**	**14,505**	**15,456**	**11,976**	**11,069**	**9,099**	**7,567**	**5,522**	**4,301**	**2,581**	**1,452**	**676**	**798**	**853**
Registration cities in nonregistration States [2]	363	419	390	282	223	169	113	75	71	41	19	11	21	8
Selected registration States [3]	12,173	13,469	14,451	11,142	10,292	8,438	6,948	5,056	3,965	2,373	1,349	616	737	805
Cities [4]	6,928	7,295	7,409	5,429	4,586	3,376	2,389	1,542	992	569	296	132	142	167
Rural [5]	5,245	6,174	7,042	5,713	5,706	5,062	4,559	3,514	2,973	1,804	1,053	484	595	638
ALABAMA	840	975	1,147	790	808	680	589	452	383	215	144	85	87	51
Cities	350	398	439	277	257	175	119	68	49	17	15	7	9	4
Incorporated places	71	73	98	71	69	55	34	34	28	23	7	6	3	9
Rural	419	504	610	442	482	450	436	350	306	175	122	72	75	38
ARKANSAS	390	543	572	409	372	284	231	189	178	106	61	30	29	141
Cities	103	135	140	85	86	55	55	34	32	13	12	6	3	21
Incorporated places	63	85	83	46	52	36	25	19	18	10	6	5	6	8
Rural	224	323	349	278	234	193	151	136	128	83	43	19	20	112
CONNECTICUT	29	34	41	28	40	27	20	21	16	5	4	-	-	-
Cities	21	33	35	25	36	20	19	11	11	1	4	-	-	-
Incorporated places	1	-	1	-	1	1	-	-	1	-	-	-	-	-
Rural	7	1	5	3	3	6	1	10	4	4	-	-	-	-
DELAWARE	48	44	57	54	67	62	36	28	22	13	7	4	1	3
Cities	26	21	27	26	26	21	12	11	5	5	2	2	1	1
Incorporated places	6	3	7	5	7	6	2	2	-	3	1	1	-	-
Rural	16	20	23	23	34	35	22	15	17	5	4	1	-	2
DISTRICT OF COLUMBIA	221	219	232	202	196	168	121	73	38	23	9	4	5	-
FLORIDA	604	639	642	443	366	290	196	136	117	59	49	19	23	68
Cities	285	267	282	165	121	96	39	44	31	12	14	4	3	5
Incorporated places	119	123	127	90	80	52	36	22	21	10	3	3	3	21
Rural	200	249	233	188	165	142	121	70	65	37	32	12	17	42
GEORGIA	1,128	1,233	1,486	1,041	943	724	659	444	408	223	140	67	75	61
Cities	524	557	603	440	301	211	137	84	61	22	23	8	15	9
Rural [5]	604	676	883	601	642	513	522	360	347	201	117	59	60	52
ILLINOIS	507	556	538	386	357	277	193	126	63	52	18	10	20	2
Cities	439	479	452	303	284	197	138	82	41	33	11	7	10	1
Incorporated places	12	20	20	17	18	24	18	12	5	5	2	2	2	-
Rural	56	57	66	66	55	56	37	32	17	14	5	1	8	1
INDIANA	171	204	194	142	122	128	94	66	36	18	11	7	4	6
Cities	157	171	152	119	98	77	69	44	22	12	10	4	4	2
Incorporated places	2	8	9	6	6	15	3	4	3	2	-	-	-	1
Rural	12	25	33	17	18	36	22	18	11	4	1	3	-	3
IOWA	29	18	33	21	22	22	18	9	9	9	3	1	-	-
Cities	24	16	26	18	20	14	12	7	8	6	3	-	-	-
Incorporated places	1	-	2	1	1	6	2	1	-	1	-	-	-	-
Rural	4	2	5	2	1	2	4	1	1	2	-	1	-	-
KANSAS	75	80	73	89	91	77	59	58	42	32	12	6	10	-
Cities	60	57	49	63	59	57	42	38	25	16	9	2	3	-
Incorporated places	4	6	2	3	10	7	-	4	4	3	-	1	-	-
Rural	11	17	22	23	22	13	17	16	13	13	3	3	7	-
KENTUCKY	292	376	371	360	392	329	285	201	148	89	50	12	16	6
Cities	169	198	223	201	185	132	124	68	47	29	12	1	5	1
Rural [5]	123	178	148	159	207	197	161	133	101	60	38	11	11	5
LOUISIANA	765	871	880	718	676	566	465	376	300	173	139	60	80	75
Cities	434	422	449	331	264	208	139	92	56	34	24	16	13	20
Incorporated places	86	123	117	85	88	71	69	57	47	28	19	8	10	9
Rural	245	326	314	302	324	287	257	227	197	111	96	36	57	46
MARYLAND	385	407	438	342	355	265	207	122	101	59	20	12	8	21
Cities	284	295	298	197	203	140	93	47	39	21	6	5	2	4
Incorporated places	20	18	20	17	19	8	12	4	3	3	2	-	-	2
Rural	81	94	120	128	133	117	102	71	59	35	12	7	6	15
MASSACHUSETTS	66	67	79	84	72	68	48	40	22	10	6	-	1	-
Cities	57	60	71	72	65	64	40	35	20	9	6	-	1	-
Incorporated places	-	2	2	2	3	2	2	1	1	-	-	-	-	-
Rural	9	5	6	10	4	2	6	4	1	1	-	-	-	-
MICHIGAN	240	237	177	126	114	90	72	55	33	15	12	4	4	4
Cities	205	203	140	97	84	62	46	29	18	7	7	1	3	-
Incorporated places	2	5	5	4	4	3	5	4	1	-	-	1	-	-
Rural	33	29	32	25	26	25	21	22	14	8	5	2	1	4
MISSISSIPPI	794	937	1,008	850	840	719	664	464	412	279	152	55	117	107
Cities	191	223	222	186	145	114	79	53	45	28	16	10	12	18
Rural [5]	603	714	786	664	695	605	585	411	367	251	136	45	105	89
MISSOURI	403	412	451	318	298	245	184	159	108	68	20	15	15	45
Cities	329	331	362	240	214	168	102	78	52	30	5	6	7	29
Incorporated places	24	25	35	30	24	21	34	27	18	10	6	3	1	4
Rural	50	56	54	48	60	56	48	54	38	28	9	6	7	12
NEBRASKA	33	29	38	30	18	22	13	15	3	5	3	2	-	1
Cities	27	18	30	24	14	19	7	10	1	1	1	1	-	-
Incorporated places	3	1	2	1	-	1	-	-	1	1	1	-	-	-
Rural	3	10	6	5	4	2	6	5	1	3	1	1	-	1
NEW HAMPSHIRE	-	1	2	1	1	1	-	-	1	-	-	-	-	-
Cities	-	1	1	1	-	1	-	-	1	-	-	-	-	-
Rural [5] [6]	-	-	1	-	1	-	-	-	-	-	-	-	-	-
NEW JERSEY	262	257	292	229	197	161	124	72	50	37	15	12	7	-
Cities	199	201	214	167	139	103	73	44	29	19	9	8	2	-
Incorporated places	27	21	27	26	21	14	22	5	5	9	3	2	2	-
Rural	36	35	51	36	37	44	29	23	16	9	3	2	3	-
NEW YORK	623	623	535	408	309	254	170	135	69	44	20	4	4	3
Cities	569	569	483	372	276	223	143	108	56	34	15	3	3	2
Incorporated places	17	11	13	7	6	7	5	2	2	4	2	-	-	-
Rural	37	43	39	29	27	24	22	25	11	6	3	1	1	1
NORTH CAROLINA	734	834	907	736	696	620	586	436	379	187	132	51	66	81
Cities	290	302	296	211	190	135	96	61	52	26	17	4	14	16
Incorporated places	55	75	67	50	60	38	53	28	17	11	6	4	4	7
Rural	389	457	544	475	446	447	437	347	310	150	109	43	48	58

[4] Includes District of Columbia.
[5] Includes "Incorporated places."
[6] No deaths in "Incorporated places." in 1930.

TABLE 27.—COLORED[1] DEATHS (EXCLUSIVE OF STILLBIRTHS), BY AGE, IN THE REGISTRATION AREA OF CONTINENTAL UNITED STATES, SELECTED REGISTRATION STATES, CITIES, INCORPORATED PLACES, AND RURAL DISTRICTS: 1930—Continued

AREA	All deaths	Under 1 year	1 year	2 years	3 years	4 years	5 to 9 years	10 to 14 years	15 to 19 years	20 to 24 years	25 to 29 years	30 to 34 years	35 to 39 years
OHIO	5,839	644	101	47	29	19	97	85	213	347	379	474	468
Cities	4,812	556	87	44	28	19	85	70	157	277	329	418	416
Incorporated places	265	28	4	1			3	4	5	6	11	11	12
Rural	762	60	10	2	1		9	11	51	64	39	45	40
OKLAHOMA	3,063	346	94	41	25	24	60	93	192	205	201	157	202
Cities	1,254	149	44	12	9	7	18	44	78	86	84	80	104
Incorporated places	611	65	16	3	3	3	10	19	32	53	51	34	35
Rural	1,198	132	34	26	13	14	32	30	82	66	66	43	63
PENNSYLVANIA	7,511	1,010	160	59	55	33	129	87	244	374	517	562	632
Cities	6,136	844	137	53	47	28	113	67	190	313	417	459	521
Incorporated places	291	47	8	1	2	2	5	9	12	7	13	18	21
Rural	1,084	119	15	5	6	3	11	11	42	54	87	85	90
RHODE ISLAND	231	12	6	3	2	1	5	2	3	6	12	16	15
Cities	203	12	6	1	2	1	5	2	3	3	11	10	13
Incorporated places	9									2		2	1
Rural	19			2						1	1	4	1
SOUTH CAROLINA	13,162	2,205	419	187	107	90	288	265	641	790	685	684	751
Cities	2,580	332	50	27	22	20	30	36	131	175	170	201	200
Incorporated places	1,033	127	39	11	8	6	23	22	55	62	53	55	59
Rural	9,549	1,746	330	149	77	64	235	207	455	553	462	428	492
TENNESSEE	8,752	931	190	70	45	33	141	165	454	603	568	487	567
Cities	4,620	496	86	33	24	18	72	80	213	301	338	317	362
Rural[5]	4,132	435	104	37	21	15	69	85	241	302	230	170	205
VERMONT	9								1		1		
Cities	3												
Rural[5]	6								1		1		
VIRGINIA	11,722	1,687	242	140	92	64	202	179	420	562	515	548	637
Cities	4,001	480	68	40	30	23	68	51	148	199	200	245	312
Incorporated places	492	56	12	1	2	2	9	9	24	28	21	13	21
Rural	7,229	1,151	162	99	60	39	125	119	248	335	294	290	304
WEST VIRGINIA	1,856	239	48	21	19	9	22	20	63	88	122	151	155
Cities	479	54	5	5	5	4	6	4	13	19	30	35	50
Incorporated places	316	17	4	6	6	2	3	3	12	24	31	40	25
Rural	1,061	168	39	10	8	3	13	13	38	45	61	76	80

AREA	40 to 44 years	45 to 49 years	50 to 54 years	55 to 59 years	60 to 64 years	65 to 69 years	70 to 74 years	75 to 79 years	80 to 84 years	85 to 89 years	90 to 94 years	95 to 99 years	100 years and over	Deaths at unknown age
OHIO	492	478	492	363	257	254	225	150	109	59	29	9	12	7
Cities	427	421	416	301	193	194	156	87	66	32	17	9	4	3
Incorporated places	18	16	22	23	21	17	18	21	11	6	3		2	2
Rural	47	41	54	39	43	43	51	42	32	21	9		6	2
OKLAHOMA	156	195	205	174	148	130	130	86	76	51	18	13	24	17
Cities	68	89	85	83	45	49	37	20	25	13	6	3	5	11
Incorporated places	32	45	42	35	39	22	24	20	13	7	1	2	3	2
Rural	56	61	78	56	64	59	69	46	38	31	11	8	16	4
PENNSYLVANIA	598	646	625	498	444	307	197	152	83	67	20	9	3	
Cities	512	533	518	417	366	234	142	106	50	51	13	4	1	
Incorporated places	15	18	21	14	21	16	14	10	8	3	4	1	1	
Rural	71	95	86	67	57	57	41	36	25	13	3	4	1	
RHODE ISLAND	14	15	24	14	19	15	17	8	11	7	3	1		
Cities	11	15	24	13	17	14	15	7	9	6	2	1		
Incorporated places	3										1			
Rural				1	2	1	2	1	2	1				
SOUTH CAROLINA	875	924	966	716	667	528	441	306	275	159	93	41	42	17
Cities	234	237	230	155	122	82	49	30	23	10	2	4	3	5
Incorporated places	76	80	88	66	47	52	39	24	15	14	6	2	3	1
Rural	565	607	648	495	498	394	353	252	237	135	85	35	36	11
TENNESSEE	528	653	719	568	511	425	353	251	188	125	58	31	37	51
Cities	345	434	409	295	272	167	157	85	42	31	17	7	11	8
Rural[5]	183	219	310	273	239	258	196	166	146	94	41	24	26	43
VERMONT	2	2		1									1	1
Cities	2	1												
Rural[5]		1		1									1	1
VIRGINIA	701	806	1,103	886	802	609	505	395	257	154	91	46	43	36
Cities	322	350	468	309	278	156	112	79	29	16	6	3	2	7
Incorporated places	32	47	42	36	34	32	26	15	15	5	3	1	4	2
Rural	347	409	593	541	490	421	367	301	213	133	82	42	37	27
WEST VIRGINIA	168	154	124	115	92	91	46	31	28	30	10	6	3	1
Cities	43	39	33	34	30	20	16	7	9	12	3	2	1	
Incorporated places	29	37	16	21	15	11	6	2	3	1	1	1		
Rural	96	78	75	60	47	60	24	22	16	17	6	3	2	1

[5] Includes "Incorporated places."

TABLE 28.—COLORED DEATHS (EXCLUSIVE OF STILLBIRTHS) FROM IMPORTANT CAUSES, BY MONTHS, IN SELECTED STATES: 1930

[Colored deaths include Negro, nonwhite, and other races. Numbers after causes of death correspond to those of the 1929 revision of the detailed International List]

AREA AND CAUSE OF DEATH	All deaths	January	February	March	April	May	June	July	August	September	October	November	December
Alabama, all causes	**14,412**	**1,271**	**1,165**	**1,327**	**1,222**	**1,234**	**1,371**	**1,253**	**1,110**	**1,049**	**1,079**	**1,100**	**1,231**
Typhoid and paratyphoid fever (1, 2)	99	2	3	6	2	4	10	18	13	15	16	8	2
Smallpox (6)	1	---	---	---	1	---	---	---	---	---	---	---	---
Measles (7)	41	1	3	4	8	11	4	2	2	---	1	---	5
Scarlet fever (8)	3	---	---	---	---	---	---	---	---	---	---	2	1
Whooping cough (9)	130	9	9	20	19	11	21	17	7	5	4	4	4
Diphtheria (10)	47	4	6	4	1	2	---	---	2	4	6	13	5
Influenza (11)	413	68	63	77	48	27	19	12	7	11	15	27	39
Dysentery (13)	37	---	3	2	2	8	6	4	3	5	1	---	3
Erysipelas (15)	7	1	1	1	---	---	---	1	1	---	1	1	---
Lethargic encephalitis (17)	8	---	1	---	1	1	2	---	1	---	1	---	1
Epidemic cerebrospinal meningitis (18)	17	3	2	1	1	1	2	1	1	---	2	2	1
Tuberculosis of the respiratory system (23)	1,294	113	91	127	125	126	106	115	109	95	95	82	110
Other forms of tuberculosis (24–32)	137	11	7	13	8	16	16	15	10	11	12	10	8
Malaria (38)	179	6	4	4	9	10	16	24	25	29	29	16	7
Diabetes mellitus (59)	83	6	9	9	3	7	7	6	4	6	7	6	13
Cerebral hemorrhage and softening (82a, 82c)	740	68	64	64	58	55	77	79	60	32	58	65	60
Diseases of the heart (90–95)	1,681	137	138	161	150	144	170	148	130	117	135	125	126
Bronchitis (106)	25	2	4	3	2	7	1	2	---	---	1	1	2
Bronchopneumonia (107)	284	38	40	30	26	21	19	10	16	13	16	28	27
Lobar and unspecified pneumonia (108, 109)	705	102	86	76	103	69	39	18	24	30	29	71	58
Diarrhea and enteritis [under 2 years] (119)	269	6	7	9	10	25	85	40	24	26	18	13	6
Diarrhea and enteritis [2 years and over] (120)	79	5	3	2	3	9	14	13	9	5	8	5	3
Nephritis (130–132)	1,198	110	91	105	114	107	105	106	92	90	97	83	98
Puerperal septicemia (140, 145)	83	6	3	4	13	8	8	5	6	5	6	7	12
Other puerperal causes (141–144, 146–150)	186	21	15	20	8	16	17	20	11	12	18	12	16
Suicide (163–171)	16	1	1	2	2	1	3	1	---	1	2	1	1
Automobile accidents [1]	129	10	11	8	5	11	14	5	16	12	13	10	14
Automobile—railroad-train and street-car collisions	5	---	---	1	---	---	---	---	2	---	2	---	---
Other external causes	976	87	86	87	70	57	82	99	103	70	63	74	98
All other causes	5,540	454	414	487	430	480	528	492	432	455	423	434	511
Arkansas, all causes	**6,466**	**588**	**534**	**579**	**562**	**531**	**607**	**637**	**519**	**470**	**503**	**438**	**498**
Typhoid and paratyphoid fever (1, 2)	151	---	6	3	3	4	18	29	27	26	15	9	11
Smallpox (6)	1	---	---	---	1	---	---	---	---	---	---	---	---
Measles (7)	2	---	---	---	1	---	---	---	---	1	---	---	---
Scarlet fever (8)	2	---	1	---	---	---	---	---	1	---	---	---	---
Whooping cough (9)	23	2	5	---	6	1	2	4	---	---	2	1	---
Diphtheria (10)	14	2	3	1	1	2	---	---	---	1	2	2	---
Influenza (11)	243	52	39	46	31	16	5	6	3	3	4	13	25
Dysentery (13)	43	1	2	1	2	7	11	6	4	5	2	1	1
Erysipelas (15)	2	---	---	---	---	---	1	1	---	---	---	---	---
Lethargic encephalitis (17)	1	---	---	---	---	1	---	---	---	---	---	---	---
Epidemic cerebrospinal meningitis (18)	23	3	4	5	4	1	4	---	---	---	1	---	1
Tuberculosis of the respiratory system (23)	555	44	59	39	60	63	54	42	43	39	43	40	29
Other forms of tuberculosis (24–32)	56	4	4	6	3	8	4	11	2	10	1	2	1
Malaria (38)	325	15	9	11	16	23	46	46	60	29	36	20	14
Diabetes mellitus (59)	29	2	1	4	5	5	1	2	2	2	2	1	2
Cerebral hemorrhage and softening (82a, 82c)	312	30	17	30	26	26	26	25	26	24	27	21	34
Diseases of the heart (90–95)	766	71	44	76	83	68	77	58	51	49	72	44	73
Bronchitis (106)	18	2	2	3	2	---	3	---	---	1	---	4	1
Bronchopneumonia (107)	130	18	17	17	17	6	4	9	3	3	7	12	17
Lobar and unspecified pneumonia (108, 109)	250	42	49	44	29	15	8	4	6	5	8	17	23
Diarrhea and enteritis [under 2 years] (119)	105	1	2	4	3	8	23	22	6	9	17	6	4
Diarrhea and enteritis [2 years and over] (120)	52	---	1	4	2	2	6	12	4	8	8	3	2
Nephritis (130–132)	512	44	43	35	37	52	54	45	48	40	40	31	43
Puerperal septicemia (140, 145)	48	6	3	4	6	3	3	4	4	4	2	4	5
Other puerperal causes (141–144, 146–150)	84	6	8	4	9	10	3	13	10	7	4	6	4
Suicide (163–171)	10	---	1	---	1	1	1	1	1	2	2	---	---
Automobile accidents [1]	66	5	10	4	5	2	3	4	13	3	5	8	4
Automobile—railroad-train and street-car collisions	---	---	---	---	---	---	---	---	---	---	---	---	---
Other external causes	420	42	33	43	31	44	29	59	24	25	34	30	26
All other causes	2,223	196	171	195	178	163	221	234	181	174	169	163	178
Florida, all causes	**7,182**	**689**	**591**	**639**	**561**	**586**	**609**	**591**	**562**	**550**	**614**	**599**	**591**
Typhoid and paratyphoid fever (1, 2)	41	3	2	4	2	4	6	3	7	6	2	1	1
Smallpox (6)	---	---	---	---	---	---	---	---	---	---	---	---	---
Measles (7)	16	---	3	1	5	3	---	3	---	---	1	---	---
Scarlet fever (8)	2	---	---	---	---	1	---	---	---	---	1	---	---
Whooping-cough (9)	28	3	---	3	4	1	6	4	3	1	1	1	1
Diphtheria (10)	23	1	3	2	---	1	4	1	1	1	4	4	1
Influenza (11)	177	29	28	25	20	8	10	7	6	4	10	14	16
Dysentery (13)	21	4	---	3	---	4	3	1	---	3	---	2	1
Erysipelas (15)	2	1	---	---	1	---	---	---	---	---	---	---	---
Lethargic encephalitis (17)	1	---	---	1	---	---	---	---	---	---	---	---	---
Epidemic cerebrospinal meningitis (18)	4	1	1	1	---	---	---	---	---	1	---	---	---
Tuberculosis of the respiratory system (23)	535	38	42	48	46	45	44	47	51	38	52	48	36
Other forms of tuberculosis (24–32)	48	3	2	3	6	10	3	5	---	5	6	3	2
Malaria (38)	160	7	7	4	8	10	16	25	23	22	22	13	3
Diabetes mellitus (59)	36	6	2	5	3	1	4	4	2	1	4	2	2
Cerebral hemorrhage and softening (82a, 82c)	589	73	56	49	43	37	50	44	36	39	43	57	62
Diseases of the heart (90–95)	914	86	83	73	77	73	76	80	51	71	97	75	72
Bronchitis (106)	19	3	1	1	---	1	2	4	2	---	2	3	---
Bronchopneumonia (107)	139	13	13	22	12	14	15	4	11	2	8	9	16
Lobar and unspecified pneumonia (108, 109)	226	37	17	27	22	14	15	13	10	11	15	24	21
Diarrhea and enteritis [under 2 years] (119)	116	11	10	12	14	13	10	8	9	5	8	7	9
Diarrhea and enteritis [2 years and over] (120)	54	10	3	7	2	6	4	3	4	3	4	4	4
Nephritis (130–132)	604	58	54	35	45	47	58	45	44	46	52	57	63
Puerperal septicemia (140, 145)	45	5	4	2	2	6	2	4	5	3	3	4	5
Other puerperal causes (141–144, 146–150)	73	7	12	7	2	3	3	2	7	8	12	6	4
Suicide (163–171)	12	2	---	2	---	3	---	1	---	2	---	1	1
Automobile accidents [1]	135	11	8	19	8	6	14	14	8	12	11	9	15
Automobile—railroad-train and street-car collisions	1	---	1	---	---	---	---	---	---	---	---	---	---
Other external causes	580	52	42	44	36	60	48	47	57	55	46	37	56
All other causes	2,581	225	197	239	203	215	216	222	225	211	210	218	200

[1] Excludes collision with railroad trains and street cars.

TABLE 28.—COLORED DEATHS (EXCLUSIVE OF STILLBIRTHS) FROM IMPORTANT CAUSES, BY MONTHS, IN SELECTED STATES: 1930—Continued

[Colored deaths include Negro, nonwhite, and other races. Numbers after causes of death correspond to those of the 1929 revision of the detailed International List]

AREA AND CAUSE OF DEATH	All deaths	January	February	March	April	May	June	July	August	September	October	November	December
Georgia, all causes	**17,190**	**1,547**	**1,397**	**1,593**	**1,533**	**1,485**	**1,599**	**1,468**	**1,268**	**1,221**	**1,430**	**1,333**	**1,316**
Typhoid and paratyphoid fever (1, 2)	299	2	4	12	10	20	31	45	47	60	32	21	15
Smallpox (6)	1			1									
Measles (7)	36	1	3	6	6	7	6	2	2	1		1	1
Scarlet fever (8)	3						1	2					
Whooping-cough (9)	138	6	12	8	13	13	19	24	15	9	9	3	7
Diphtheria (10)	38	4	5	3		1		1	5	5	5	4	5
Influenza (11)	458	84	77	82	55	21	10	9	8	11	22	27	52
Dysentery (13)	148	5	2	6	11	32	29	22	18	9	4	9	1
Erysipelas (15)	10	2	1		1	1	1	1	1		1		1
Lethargic encephalitis (17)	1										1		
Epidemic cerebrospinal meningitis (18)	46	9	6	9	4	7	1		2		2	3	3
Tuberculosis of the respiratory system (23)	1,310	110	104	120	98	144	109	112	105	96	100	102	110
Other forms of tuberculosis (24–32)	127	14	12	11	13	11	9	17	14	9	3	6	8
Malaria (38)	253	14	7	11	8	17	29	37	30	36	32	23	9
Diabetes mellitus (59)	113	16	13	10	11	8	3	8	8	7	10	13	6
Cerebral hemorrhage and softening (82a, 82c)	1,235	100	105	108	115	107	121	104	77	86	114	94	104
Diseases of the heart (90–95)	2,140	184	175	186	191	203	191	178	161	153	183	172	163
Bronchitis (106)	48	6	6	2	4	3	4	6	3	4	2	5	3
Bronchopneumonia (107)	398	46	54	49	45	34	24	22	15	18	27	33	31
Lobar and unspecified pneumonia (108, 109)	937	140	123	135	109	73	53	29	30	24	46	89	86
Diarrhea and enteritis [under 2 years] (119)	274	4	7	10	11	37	55	38	35	34	25	11	7
Diarrhea and enteritis [2 years and over] (120)	141	7	7	6	7	13	27	14	19	13	12	6	10
Nephritis (130–132)	1,554	140	120	158	155	126	165	119	115	115	115	108	118
Puerperal septicemia (140, 145)	93	9	2	9	8	5	9	6	6	7	14	9	9
Other puerperal causes (141–144, 146–150)	197	10	15	19	14	21	18	20	19	16	12	19	14
Suicide (163–171)	22	1	1	3	4	1	1	2	1	2	3	2	1
Automobile accidents [1]	174	22	11	8	12	7	10	17	17	12	23	16	19
Automobile—railroad train and street car collisions	15	1			2		6				5	1	
Other external causes	1,067	90	85	90	88	75	85	123	78	79	90	83	101
All other causes	5,914	520	440	531	538	498	582	510	437	415	538	473	432
Kentucky, all causes	**4,750**	**403**	**418**	**432**	**373**	**372**	**404**	**445**	**384**	**327**	**392**	**401**	**399**
Typhoid and paratyphoid fever (1, 2)	58		1	1	4	1	4	10	11	11	10	4	1
Smallpox (6)	1							1					
Measles (7)	10	1	1	1	3		1				1		2
Scarlet fever (8)	3		1									1	1
Whooping-cough (9)	29	2	2	6	1	2	3	4	4	2	2		1
Diphtheria (10)	7		1				1		1	1		2	1
Influenza (11)	113	22	19	24	12	4	6	3		4	3	9	7
Dysentery (13)	29			1		3	3	6	10	4	1	1	
Erysipelas (15)	1								1				
Lethargic encephalitis (17)													
Epidemic cerebrospinal meningitis (18)	23		4	7	4		1	1	1	1		2	2
Tuberculosis of the respiratory system (23)	449	31	30	34	41	44	42	41	46	27	42	30	41
Other forms of tuberculosis (24–32)	79	5	6	11	7	7	7	8	6	4	4	4	10
Malaria (38)	11				1	1	2	5	2				
Diabetes mellitus (59)	41	2		5	1	3	2	6	7	6	3	3	3
Cerebral hemorrhage and softening (82a, 82c)	336	29	25	30	24	21	36	31	33	24	23	28	32
Diseases of the heart (90–95)	854	66	84	83	78	68	69	75	55	67	76	66	67
Bronchitis (106)	43	3	4	2		6	6	1	4	5	5	5	2
Bronchopneumonia (107)	142	15	27	14	17	6	11	5	1	6	10	12	18
Lobar and unspecified pneumonia (108, 109)	279	35	38	32	26	14	11	12	9	13	27	22	40
Diarrhea and enteritis [under 2 years] (119)	81	6	2	2	4	4	9	18	9	10	14	3	
Diarrhea and enteritis [2 years and over] (120)	46	2	1	2	4	3	6	11	2	6	5	3	1
Nephritis (130–132)	495	40	35	47	36	49	39	31	48	36	35	64	35
Puerperal septicemia (140, 145)	26	1		4	1	1	2	3	4	3	3	2	2
Other puerperal causes (141–144, 146–150)	26	1	3		4	6	2	3		1	2	4	
Suicide (163–171)	11	1	1				1	1	1	1	2	2	1
Automobile accidents [1]	51	2	1	5	2	5	2	5	7	5	1	8	8
Automobile—railroad train and street car collisions	1							1					
Other external causes	328	30	32	25	21	31	25	36	32	15	25	27	29
All other causes	1,177	109	100	96	82	93	113	127	90	75	98	99	95
Louisiana, all causes	**12,086**	**1,146**	**1,079**	**1,084**	**1,053**	**1,054**	**1,161**	**944**	**840**	**828**	**976**	**947**	**974**
Typhoid and paratyphoid fever (1, 2)	138	4	5	6	8	16	16	13	18	12	11	18	11
Smallpox (6)													
Measles (7)	41	3	2	10	8	7	8	1	1				1
Scarlet fever (8)													
Whooping-cough (9)	70	7	4	5	6	8	8	4	8	6	6	5	3
Diphtheria (10)	26	2	2	3	3	2	2	1	2		2	5	2
Influenza (11)	376	65	89	68	31	22	12	12	4	3	15	22	33
Dysentery (13)	66	5	4	2	5	9	14	7	6	4	8	2	
Erysipelas (15)	2			1		1							
Lethargic encephalitis (17)	2			1				1					
Epidemic cerebrospinal meningitis (18)	39	7	3	3	7	4	1	4	3	1		1	5
Tuberculosis of the respiratory system (23)	1,006	91	87	87	111	100	102	81	76	66	68	64	73
Other forms of tuberculosis (24–32)	71	7	3	7	8	6	4	7	8	10	5	3	3
Malaria (38)	89		1	3	1	7	19	14	12	14	5	8	5
Diabetes mellitus (59)	87	16	8	10	14	4	3	5	3	2	9	6	7
Cerebral hemorrhage and softening (82a, 82c)	655	57	58	54	65	47	57	61	39	58	57	47	55
Diseases of the heart (90–95)	1,948	194	170	194	168	153	174	129	147	141	153	165	160
Bronchitis (106)	46	8	4	5	4	2	2	1	2	2	7	2	7
Bronchopneumonia (107)	423	65	50	54	36	37	34	16	18	24	20	28	41
Lobar and unspecified pneumonia (108, 109)	563	79	91	67	51	42	32	18	20	16	31	49	67
Diarrhea and enteritis [under 2 years] (119)	289	11	12	13	14	31	48	26	31	27	41	23	12
Diarrhea and enteritis [2 years and over] (120)	78	4	4	8	2	13	13	8	5	6	8	6	1
Nephritis (130–132)	1,152	91	94	102	108	102	118	82	76	102	112	94	71
Puerperal septicemia (140, 145)	66	2	2	6	6	7	5	4	4	2	8	7	13
Other puerperal causes (141–144, 146–150)	143	13	7	16	9	5	16	20	18	10	11	7	11
Suicide (163–171)	23	1		1	7	4	3			3	2	1	1
Automobile accidents [1]	135	13	10	11	6	15	17	6	8	10	15	9	15
Automobile—railroad train and street car collisions	3					1					2		
Other external causes	737	65	43	55	48	72	80	85	59	45	54	45	86
All other causes	3,812	336	326	292	327	337	373	338	272	264	326	330	291

[1] Excludes collision with railroad trains and street cars.

TABLE 28.—COLORED DEATHS (EXCLUSIVE OF STILLBIRTHS) FROM IMPORTANT CAUSES, BY MONTHS, IN SELECTED STATES: 1930—Continued

[Colored deaths include Negro, nonwhite, and other races. Numbers after causes of death correspond to those of the 1929 revision of the detailed International List]

AREA AND CAUSE OF DEATH	All deaths	January	February	March	April	May	June	July	August	September	October	November	December
Maryland, all causes	**5,264**	**427**	**436**	**463**	**507**	**431**	**376**	**536**	**429**	**405**	**451**	**396**	**407**
Typhoid and paratyphoid fever (1, 2)	45	1	1	1	1	1	2	6	5	9	12	6	
Smallpox (6)													
Measles (7)	3						2		1				
Scarlet fever (8)	2	1			1								
Whooping-cough (9)	27	2	2	5	2	3	4	2	3	2		1	1
Diphtheria (10)	17	2	3	2		1		1		1	3	3	1
Influenza (11)	44	4	8	6	8	4	2	1	1			3	7
Dysentery (13)	16				1		1	6		4	3	1	
Erysipelas (15)	2		2										
Lethargic encephalitis (17)													
Epidemic cerebrospinal meningitis (18)	9	2	3		1	1	1						1
Tuberculosis of the respiratory system (23)	614	61	45	52	63	55	48	69	59	36	53	31	42
Other forms of tuberculosis (24–32)	95	4	8	9	12	10	8	11	11	11	5	4	2
Malaria (38)	1						1						
Diabetes mellitus (59)	43	1	4	4	4	8	5	4	2	4		3	4
Cerebral hemorrhage and softening (82a, 82c)	352	23	30	37	29	31	26	26	37	24	30	22	37
Diseases of the heart (90–95)	847	77	68	70	89	69	71	84	55	60	75	64	65
Bronchitis (106)	36	4	1	11	2	4		5	1		1	1	6
Bronchopneumonia (107)	273	27	27	38	32	19	12	21	10	15	23	20	29
Lobar and unspecified pneumonia (108, 109)	363	45	45	45	59	36	15	6	12	14	24	30	32
Diarrhea and enteritis [under 2 years] (119)	155	5	1	7	1	7	11	45	22	20	20	12	4
Diarrhea and enteritis [2 years and over] (120)	24			3	2		1	6	5	2	1	4	
Nephritis (130–132)	507	33	58	35	46	49	38	50	31	34	47	48	38
Puerperal septicemia (140, 145)	18		1	3	3	1	3	3		2		1	1
Other puerperal causes (141–144, 146–150)	25	2	2	1	4	2	2		3	5	2		2
Suicide (163–171)	15	4				1	1	3	1	2	2	1	
Automobile accidents [1]	79	3	4	4	5	5	5	10	6	7	11	10	9
Automobile—railroad train and street car collisions	6				3				2		1		
Other external causes	283	16	18	18	22	23	24	37	34	35	24	12	20
All other causes	1,363	110	105	112	117	101	93	140	128	118	114	119	106
Mississippi, all causes	**14,961**	**1,428**	**1,242**	**1,404**	**1,294**	**1,220**	**1,465**	**1,364**	**1,076**	**1,017**	**1,144**	**1,132**	**1,175**
Typhoid and paratyphoid fever (1, 2)	190	7	5	6	6	9	16	35	28	21	21	28	8
Smallpox (6)	2				1		1						
Measles (7)	13	3	1	2	2	2				1	2		
Scarlet fever (8)	6			2		1	1			2			
Whooping-cough (9)	104	8	13	9	20	13	11	14	3	5	1	4	3
Diphtheria (10)	57	7	4	3	2	1	3	3	4	3	6	13	8
Influenza (11)	363	68	71	56	46	22	15	7	5	6	12	28	27
Dysentery (13)	79	2		2	4	12	17	14	6	3	13	3	3
Erysipelas (15)	6	1	2		1						2		
Lethargic encephalitis (17)	2											1	1
Epidemic cerebrospinal meningitis (18)	116	10	30	34	13	8	6	2	3	1	4	2	3
Tuberculosis of the respiratory system (23)	1,304	95	92	117	123	129	119	127	123	103	84	101	91
Other forms of tuberculosis (24–32)	97	7	4	10	8	10	8	11	5	7	10	8	9
Malaria (38)	231	5	4	4	14	16	30	42	36	30	23	16	11
Diabetes mellitus (59)	96	14	7	10	6	4	13	6	6	8	10	6	6
Cerebral hemorrhage and softening (82a, 82c)	755	66	63	70	53	66	72	68	61	56	63	54	63
Diseases of the heart (90–95)	1,499	125	107	120	133	127	151	153	109	106	125	120	123
Bronchitis (106)	26	3	1	4	3		1	3	1	1	2	5	2
Bronchopneumonia (107)	216	26	39	30	31	17	11	6	6	9	11	11	19
Lobar and unspecified pneumonia (108, 109)	636	106	116	90	71	38	30	18	20	16	26	45	60
Diarrhea and enteritis [under 2 years] (119)	296	12	4	8	16	30	80	41	18	25	45	11	6
Diarrhea and enteritis [2 years and over] (120)	94	1	3	5	3	10	22	11	11	11	6	7	4
Nephritis (130–132)	1,394	120	100	129	137	124	138	125	103	92	100	122	104
Puerperal septicemia (140, 145)	90	12	8	5	11	3	9	9	12	7	7	3	4
Other puerperal causes (141–144, 146–150)	210	19	14	25	24	14	17	23	21	15	9	10	19
Suicide (163–171)	19	3	1	2	1	2	1	1	1	3	2	1	1
Automobile accidents [1]	146	9	14	16	15	12	14	8	10	15	9	10	14
Automobile—railroad train and street car collisions	1							1					
Other external causes	969	101	72	88	77	72	106	86	75	66	67	67	92
All other causes	5,944	598	467	557	473	478	573	550	409	405	484	456	494
North Carolina, all causes	**14,155**	**1,180**	**1,213**	**1,275**	**1,249**	**1,350**	**1,411**	**1,320**	**1,043**	**906**	**1,027**	**1,083**	**1,098**
Typhoid and paratyphoid fever (1, 2)	77	2		1	4	6	10	20	9	12	7	2	4
Smallpox (6)	4		1		1	1	1						
Measles (7)	1			1									
Scarlet fever (8)	4	1			1	1							1
Whooping-cough (9)	127	10	12	18	15	14	13	22	6	9	5	3	
Diphtheria (10)	59	4	3		5	1	1	1	12	6	13	5	8
Influenza (11)	303	44	66	57	41	15	10	10	1	8	9	24	18
Dysentery (13)	53	1		1	1	15	18	8	3	3	2	1	
Erysipelas (15)	7			1	1	1		1	1		1	1	
Lethargic encephalitis (17)	6					3		2	1				
Epidemic cerebrospinal meningitis (18)	27	3	3	6	6	3	3	2					1
Tuberculosis of the respiratory system (23)	1,214	102	108	108	109	114	117	107	85	86	103	92	83
Other forms of tuberculosis (24–32)	156	9	13	12	16	20	12	19	15	9	10	10	11
Malaria (38)	28		2			1	4	5	8	1	6	1	
Diabetes mellitus (59)	89	10	10	4	3	9	6	4	9	6	11	8	9
Cerebral hemorrhage and softening (82a, 82c)	979	84	82	86	90	69	107	82	79	64	70	94	72
Diseases of the heart (90–95)	1,727	149	166	159	148	157	165	175	137	131	113	125	102
Bronchitis (106)	53	4	9	8	5	5	5	1		3	2	3	8
Bronchopneumonia (107)	349	45	40	41	44	31	15	15	10	10	22	26	50
Lobar and unspecified pneumonia (108, 109)	719	90	100	88	76	79	25	25	28	21	33	76	78
Diarrhea and enteritis [under 2 years] (119)	464	10	11	9	26	86	126	82	39	26	33	10	6
Diarrhea and enteritis [2 years and over] (120)	90	3	4	3	4	18	20	13	11	5	2	4	3
Nephritis (130–132)	1,255	96	95	109	108	92	124	109	110	86	115	102	109
Puerperal septicemia (140, 145)	70	9	4	5	8	5	5	9	7	4	4	6	4
Other puerperal causes (141–144, 146–150)	213	12	23	24	26	19	20	10	9	12	21	15	22
Suicide (163–171)	18	1		5	1	2	2	1	1	2	2	1	
Automobile accidents [1]	146	13	4	12	17	20	8	12	5	14	16	19	6
Automobile—railroad train and street car collisions	16	1	1	3		3			2		2	1	3
Other external causes	723	74	47	69	56	50	51	65	51	61	53	71	75
All other causes	5,178	403	409	445	437	510	543	520	404	327	372	383	425

[1] Excludes collision with railroad trains and street cars.

TABLE 28.—COLORED DEATHS (EXCLUSIVE OF STILLBIRTHS) FROM IMPORTANT CAUSES, BY MONTHS, IN SELECTED STATES: 1930—Continued

[Colored deaths include Negro, nonwhite, and other races. Numbers after causes of death correspond to those of the 1929 revision of the detailed International List]

AREA AND CAUSE OF DEATH	All deaths	January	February	March	April	May	June	July	August	September	October	November	December
Oklahoma, all causes	**3,063**	**299**	**238**	**263**	**257**	**255**	**228**	**287**	**260**	**260**	**241**	**228**	**247**
Typhoid and paratyphoid fever (1, 2)	59		2				2	4	12	17	7	5	10
Smallpox (6)	4			1		1	1	1					
Measles (7)	17	1	1	2	6	3	3	1					
Scarlet fever (8)	1												1
Whooping-cough (9)	26	4	1	3	4	2	1	3	3	1	1	3	
Diphtheria (10)	10	1	1				1	1		2		1	3
Influenza (11)	75	18	17	8	5	4	3	6	1	1	3	4	5
Dysentery (13)	25					1	3	5	5	5	4	1	1
Erysipelas (15)	1				1								
Lethargic encephalitis (17)													
Epidemic cerebrospinal meningitis (18)	4	1				2						1	
Tuberculosis of the respiratory system (23)	396	45	27	46	36	40	24	39	37	16	24	28	34
Other forms of tuberculosis (24–32)	58	5	4	2	8	2	10	2	8	5	5	3	4
Malaria (38)	39		2	2	2	1	3	8	9	3	4	4	1
Diabetes mellitus (59)	29	4	2	2	6	1	2	1	1	4	2	2	2
Cerebral hemorrhage and softening (82a, 82c)	117	10	11	8	11	7	16	10	10	6	6	13	9
Diseases of the heart (90–95)	290	23	25	21	19	30	17	30	27	26	25	21	26
Bronchitis (106)	8		1	3	1					1	1		1
Bronchopneumonia (107)	105	19	14	12	16	5	7	5	1	8	6	4	8
Lobar and unspecified pneumonia (108, 109)	209	37	31	30	20	15	6	4	2	6	12	17	29
Diarrhea and enteritis [under 2 years] (119)	69			5	1	1	4	18	10	11	13	2	4
Diarrhea and enteritis [2 years and over] (120)	32		1	1	3	2	7	7	2	5	3		1
Nephritis (130–132)	196	18	18	14	10	15	13	28	19	16	15	16	14
Puerperal septicemia (140, 145)	16	2			2	2	1	2		5	2		
Other puerperal causes (141–144, 146–150)	37	4	5	2	5	1	2	2	3	4	5	1	3
Suicide (163–171)	10			2	2	1	1	1	2				1
Automobile accidents [1]	51	4	2	5	2	2	9	3	6	5	9	2	2
Automobile—railroad train and street car collisions	1									1			
Other external causes	223	22	14	12	18	26	20	19	19	22	11	24	16
All other causes	955	81	59	82	79	91	72	87	83	90	83	76	72
South Carolina, all causes	**13,162**	**1,136**	**968**	**1,155**	**1,106**	**1,301**	**1,272**	**1,199**	**996**	**949**	**998**	**1,003**	**1,079**
Typhoid and paratyphoid fever (1, 2)	215	8	5	6	7	10	26	49	29	36	18	13	8
Smallpox (6)	1					1							
Measles (7)	1										1		
Scarlet fever (8)	1						1						
Whooping-cough (9)	122	16	9	12	6	24	17	14	3	7	5	4	5
Diphtheria (10)	40	6	2	3		3	2		4	2	8	3	7
Influenza (11)	427	76	48	86	52	29	15	11	5	3	9	38	55
Dysentery (13)	90	2	4	3	7	24	26	14	3	3	1	1	2
Erysipelas (15)	4		1		3								
Lethargic encephalitis (17)	4	1	1	1			1						
Epidemic cerebrospinal meningitis (18)	24	6	4	1	1	3	2	2		1	1	1	2
Tuberculosis of the respiratory system (23)	951	91	71	80	94	117	90	72	88	68	42	68	70
Other forms of tuberculosis (24–32)	67	7	2	3	5	11	3	6	7	9	3	5	6
Malaria (38)	290	4	5	6	13	20	29	47	35	49	43	28	11
Diabetes mellitus (59)	62	3	9	4	10	4	4	11	1	1	3	7	5
Cerebral hemorrhage and softening (82a, 82c)	798	72	56	70	60	61	69	68	62	64	64	84	68
Diseases of the heart (90–95)	1,635	132	139	136	169	158	148	136	108	115	152	114	128
Bronchitis (106)	19		1	2	2	1	1	1	3	1	1	2	4
Bronchopneumonia (107)	236	39	22	26	17	22	12	13	8	8	21	17	31
Lobar and unspecified pneumonia (108, 109)	731	88	101	99	85	46	44	29	20	18	43	58	100
Diarrhea and enteritis [under 2 years] (119)	338	5	8	7	12	83	73	60	28	20	23	13	6
Diarrhea and enteritis [2 years and over] (120)	83	1	6	3	9	13	18	6	4	8	3	9	3
Nephritis (130–132)	1,235	108	89	111	96	115	119	98	94	89	118	107	91
Puerperal septicemia (140, 145)	65	4	5	7	8	9	4	6	3	7	6	5	1
Other puerperal causes (141–144, 146–150)	203	9	13	22	14	25	22	23	9	20	14	18	14
Suicide (163–171)	16	2	1	1	2	2	1	1	2		2	2	
Automobile accidents [1]	146	6	9	14	6	9	11	11	18	16	18	12	16
Automobile—railroad train and street car collisions	6			3			3						
Other external causes	527	48	41	47	29	48	47	64	40	32	42	36	53
All other causes	4,825	402	316	402	399	463	484	457	422	372	357	358	393
Tennessee, all causes	**8,752**	**757**	**714**	**852**	**794**	**736**	**773**	**834**	**732**	**556**	**683**	**631**	**690**
Typhoid and paratyphoid fever (1, 2)	98	1	2	2	2	2	5	28	18	15	10	8	5
Smallpox (6)													
Measles (7)	10				2	1	3	1		2		1	
Scarlet fever (8)	2				2								
Whooping-cough (9)	54	3	3	7	5	1	10	7	7	4	3	3	1
Diphtheria (10)	26		5	1	1	2		3	1	1	5	4	3
Influenza (11)	283	41	51	59	44	19	6	7	2	3	8	17	26
Dysentery (13)	33	1	1		1	4	5	8	1	4	4	3	1
Erysipelas (15)	3			1	2								
Lethargic encephalitis (17)	6		2		1	2				1			
Epidemic cerebrospinal meningitis (18)	156	17	17	40	42	12	7	4	3	2	3	5	4
Tuberculosis of the respiratory system (23)	1,094	95	81	114	120	96	98	113	89	85	76	64	63
Other forms of tuberculosis (24–32)	133	10	7	16	9	11	14	14	12	5	13	9	13
Malaria (38)	59	2			2	11	3	12	11	6	7	4	1
Diabetes mellitus (59)	56	3	2	9	6	6	6	6	4	2	4	3	5
Cerebral hemorrhage and softening (82a, 82c)	535	40	38	51	32	51	48	56	56	35	46	32	50
Diseases of the heart (90–95)	1,060	80	73	82	96	89	99	101	92	79	94	86	89
Bronchitis (106)	21	3	2	1	2	3	3	2	3		1	1	
Bronchopneumonia (107)	281	27	36	32	31	15	29	10	10	7	26	22	36
Lobar and unspecified pneumonia (108, 109)	393	55	46	63	46	21	16	15	15	11	25	33	47
Diarrhea and enteritis [under 2 years] (119)	143	1	5	5	6	8	33	20	20	16	19	6	4
Diarrhea and enteritis [2 years and over] (120)	80		2	8	5	10	13	13	8	8	3	5	5
Nephritis (130–132)	615	52	44	61	44	52	53	56	48	35	63	54	53
Puerperal septicemia (140, 145)	68	6	3	6	7	2	8	9	5	4	8	4	6
Other puerperal causes (141–144, 146–150)	60	9	3	4	3	8	4	7	4	5	2	5	6
Suicide (163–171)	12		2			1		3	2			1	3
Automobile accidents [1]	92	8	5	8	4	6	9	5	7	7	8	15	10
Automobile—railroad train and street car collisions													
Other external causes	630	50	41	47	50	65	40	69	72	43	46	59	48
All other causes	2,749	253	243	235	229	238	261	265	242	176	209	187	211

[1] Excludes collision with railroad trains and street cars.

TABLE 28.—COLORED DEATHS (EXCLUSIVE OF STILLBIRTHS) FROM IMPORTANT CAUSES, BY MONTHS, IN SELECTED STATES: 1930—Continued

[Colored deaths include Negro, nonwhite, and other races. Numbers after causes of death correspond to those of the 1929 revision of the detailed International List]

AREA AND CAUSE OF DEATH	All deaths	January	February	March	April	May	June	July	August	September	October	November	December
Virginia, all causes	**11,722**	**1,039**	**947**	**1,042**	**1,036**	**992**	**1,030**	**1,113**	**860**	**844**	**890**	**928**	**1,001**
Typhoid and paratyphoid fever (1, 2)	62	2	2	---	1	3	6	9	12	17	4	1	5
Smallpox (6)	---	---	---	---	---	---	---	---	---	---	---	---	---
Measles (7)	21	---	2	1	6	6	3	2	1	---	---	---	---
Scarlet fever (8)	4	---	---	---	---	1	---	---	---	1	1	---	1
Whooping-cough (9)	137	20	10	15	17	8	16	15	6	9	6	5	10
Diphtheria (10)	44	6	4	2	4	2	1	1	1	2	10	6	5
Influenza (11)	325	57	52	57	32	27	9	6	7	13	10	17	38
Dysentery (13)	70	1	3	2	1	6	22	15	11	2	3	3	1
Erysipelas (15)	5	---	1	---	---	---	1	1	1	---	---	---	1
Lethargic encephalitis (17)	9	---	2	1	2	2	---	---	1	---	---	1	---
Epidemic cerebrospinal meningitis (18)	17	4	2	2	3	2	1	---	1	---	1	---	1
Tuberculosis of the respiratory system (23)	1,069	90	79	106	82	105	89	88	88	87	88	84	83
Other forms of tuberculosis (24–32)	110	6	6	12	10	13	12	7	15	11	6	7	5
Malaria (38)	11	---	---	1	---	1	1	---	1	4	1	2	---
Diabetes mellitus (59)	113	12	6	12	8	10	10	13	4	7	7	9	15
Cerebral hemorrhage and softening (82a, 82c)	1,016	71	72	111	92	83	91	118	67	63	68	77	103
Diseases of the heart (90–95)	1,847	173	149	162	167	160	173	153	138	131	159	126	156
Bronchitis (106)	46	3	6	5	3	4	3	3	4	1	2	7	5
Bronchopneumonia (107)	347	47	46	46	28	29	10	15	10	10	28	44	34
Lobar and unspecified pneumonia (108, 109)	631	76	91	79	90	36	35	23	20	27	35	54	65
Diarrhea and enteritis [under 2 years] (119)	257	3	6	7	8	28	49	55	34	34	19	8	6
Diarrhea and enteritis [2 years and over] (120)	74	2	2	---	2	10	12	11	13	5	11	4	2
Nephritis (130–132)	1,118	87	72	87	113	98	102	101	82	89	100	107	80
Puerperal septicemia (140, 145)	56	2	3	6	6	7	3	3	5	3	8	7	3
Other puerperal causes (141–144, 146–150)	128	5	8	15	11	6	15	18	14	9	7	8	12
Suicide (163–171)	22	2	3	3	1	1	3	2	1	---	1	1	4
Automobile accidents [1]	118	12	4	9	10	4	5	15	11	15	9	8	16
Automobile—railroad train and street car collisions	14	---	---	---	---	1	---	---	1	---	2	10	---
Other external causes	604	51	54	42	40	48	43	67	60	47	44	55	53
All other causes	3,447	307	262	259	299	291	315	372	251	257	260	277	297

[1] Excludes collision with railroad trains and street cars.

TABLE 29.—COLORED DEATHS (EXCLUSIVE OF STILLBIRTHS) FROM IMPORTANT CAUSES, BY AGE, IN THE 15 CITIES HAVING 50,000 OR MORE NEGRO INHABITANTS: 1930

[Colored deaths include Negro, nonwhite, and other races. Numbers after causes of death correspond to those of the 1929 revision of the detailed International List]

AREA AND CAUSE OF DEATH	All deaths	Under 1 year	1 year	2 years	3 years	4 years	5 to 9 years	10 to 14 years	15 to 19 years	20 to 24 years	25 to 29 years	30 to 34 years	35 to 44 years	45 to 54 years	55 to 64 years	65 to 74 years	75 years and over	Age unknown
Atlanta, Ga., all causes	**2,106**	**268**	**42**	**36**	**14**	**8**	**36**	**36**	**99**	**138**	**165**	**157**	**345**	**388**	**221**	**98**	**54**	**1**
Typhoid and paratyphoid fever (1, 2)	18			2		1	3	1	2	2	4	3						
Measles (7)	4	2	2															
Scarlet fever (8)	1			1														
Whooping-cough (9)	26	11	5	7	1	1	1											
Diphtheria (10)	2						1	1										
Influenza (11)	54	3			1			1	2	6	5	3	12	9	9		3	
Epidemic cerebrospinal meningitis (18)	28	4		6			5	1	2	2	4		2	2				
Tuberculosis of the respiratory system (23)	139				2		3	4	18	26	22	22	30	8	2	2		
Other forms of tuberculosis (24–32)	55	1	2	2	1		5	2	4	5	9	8	10	3	3			
Syphilis (34)	39	7	1						1	4	3	8	7	7	1			
Cancer and other malignant tumors (45–53)	47								1	1	2	3	13	15	9	3		
Diabetes mellitus (59)	19							1			3			6	5	2	2	
Cerebral hemorrhage and softening (82a, 82c)	201			1						2	6	13	42	75	38	13	11	
Diseases of the heart (90–95)	259				1		1	1	1	9	12	12	58	76	48	30	9	1
Bronchitis (106)	8	1					1		3		2			1				
Bronchopneumonia (107)	87	40	12	5	1	1	3	2	3	1	1	3	5	3	3	3	1	
Lobar and unspecified pneumonia (108, 109)	126	7	7	4	1	1	3	4	11	13	9	8	18	24	10	5	1	
Diarrhea and enteritis (119, 120)	58	30	4	3	1	1		1		1	4	4	2	2	3	1	1	
Appendicitis (121)	22							4	2	1	4	3	7	1				
Hernia, intestinal obstruction (122)	32	1						1			2	5	6	12	2	3		
Cirrhosis of the liver (124)	7												3	3		1		
Nephritis (130–132)	214	1					1		3	3	8	16	41	67	44	17	13	
Diseases of the female genital organs (139)	3								1	1	1							
Puerperal septicemia (140, 145)	15								6	4	3	1	1					
Other puerperal causes (141–144, 146–150)	12								3	3	4	2						
Suicide (163–171)	4								1	1	1		1					
Homicide (172–175)	115							2	13	27	27	21	18	4	2		1	
Automobile accidents [1]	33			1		2	1	2	1	5	2		6	8	4		1	
Automobile—railroad train and street car collisions	1							1										
Other external causes	46	1	1	2	4		2	2	3	3	4	4	10	7	3			
All other causes	431	159	8	2	1	1	6	5	18	18	23	18	53	55	35	18	11	
Baltimore, Md., all causes	**2,815**	**307**	**56**	**20**	**17**	**14**	**48**	**41**	**81**	**154**	**167**	**193**	**481**	**553**	**372**	**210**	**101**	
Typhoid and paratyphoid fever (1, 2)	12			1			1	1	2	2	2	1	2					
Measles (7)																		
Scarlet fever (8)	2				1					1								
Whooping-cough (9)	5	4	1															
Diphtheria (10)	3		1		1		1											
Influenza (1)	19	2					1		1			2	5	3	4	1		
Epidemic cerebrospinal meningitis (18)	9	2					2			2	1		1	1				
Tuberculosis of the respiratory system (23)	313	2	2		1	2	7	12	30	59	52	33	64	32	9	8		
Other forms of tuberculosis (24–32)	66	5	9	3	1		5	7	8	5	8	1	7	5	2			
Syphilis (34)	122	15				1			1	4	10	15	33	27	10	5	1	
Cancer and other malignant tumors (45–53)	139			1						2	5	8	22	49	36	12	4	
Diabetes mellitus (59)	26						1			1			5	7	10	1	1	
Cerebral hemorrhage and softening (82a, 82c)	187										4	5	41	61	44	22	10	
Diseases of the heart (90–95)	496					1		6	2	4	9	30	77	142	113	76	36	
Bronchitis (106)	4	1	1										1			1		
Bronchopneumonia (107)	156	49	19	3	4	2	3		3	5	1	5	12	21	13	9	7	
Lobar and unspecified pneumonia (108, 109)	286	39	6	6	2	2	8	5	11	20	15	25	56	49	31	6	5	
Diarrhea and enteritis (119, 120)	43	31	4		2	1	1							3	1			
Appendicitis (121)	28			1				2	3	5	2	5	6	2	1	1		
Hernia, intestinal obstruction (122)	35	2	3				1	1			2		5	11	4	6		
Cirrhosis of the liver (124)	7												2	5				
Nephritis (130–132)	253						1		1	3	8	8	43	59	67	43	20	
Diseases of the female genital organs (139)	4								1	1			1	1				
Puerperal septicemia (140, 145)	12								5		1	4	2					
Other puerperal causes (141–144, 146–150)	14							1		3	3	4	3					
Suicide (163–171)	7									1	1	1	2	1	1			
Homicide (172–175)	41								2	7	13	10	7	2				
Automobile accidents [1]	32						6	1	2	4	2	1	4	8	1	3		
Automobile—railroad train and street car collisions	5									1	1		1	2				
Other external causes	99	2	6	1	2	1	5	3	2	7	10	7	17	22	4	6	4	
All other causes	390	153	4	4	3	4	5	2	7	17	17	28	62	40	21	10	13	
Birmingham, Ala., all causes	**1,925**	**236**	**40**	**15**	**9**	**9**	**27**	**21**	**97**	**129**	**154**	**130**	**292**	**363**	**231**	**105**	**67**	
Typhoid and paratyphoid fever (1, 2)	10						2		2		2	1	2		1			
Measles (7)	5	1	2		1			1										
Scarlet fever (8)	1				1													
Whooping-cough (9)	9	4	3	2														
Diphtheria (10)	10		1	2	1	3	2				1							
Influenza (11)	40	5	2	1					2	4	3	2	9	6	4	1	1	
Epidemic cerebrospinal meningitis (18)	3								1	1		1						
Tuberculosis of the respiratory system (23)	172			1		1	1	1	28	29	35	26	27	17	5		1	
Other forms of tuberculosis (24–32)	23	1	1	1			2	1	1	6	4	1	3	2				
Syphilis (34)	70	29	1						2		3	3	15	9	6	2		
Cancer and other malignant tumors (45–53)	67								1		5	2	18	25	13	2	1	
Diabetes mellitus (59)	22						1				1	1	7	7	3	1	1	
Cerebral hemorrhage and softening (82a, 82c)	105								1		1	2	13	43	16	18	11	
Diseases of the heart (90–95)	230						2	2	6	8	2	15	35	70	51	28	11	
Bronchitis (106)	1															1		
Bronchopneumonia (107)	51	22	3	1			1	1	2	5	2		2	3	4	2	3	
Lobar and unspecified pneumonia (108, 109)	136	14	4	1	2	1	2	1	9	15	16	11	19	28	6	5	2	
Diarrhea and enteritis (119, 120)	33	16	12	1										1	3			
Appendicitis (121)	21						2		2	4	4	1	5	3				
Hernia, intestinal obstruction (122)	18		1								1	1	4	6	3	2		
Cirrhosis of the liver (124)	7									1			2	2	2			
Nephritis (130–132)	133						1	1	1	4	3	2	26	31	40	15	9	
Diseases of the female genital organs (139)	9								2	1		2	2	2				
Puerperal septicemia (140, 145)	14								6	3	1	2	2					
Other pureperal causes (141–144, 146–150)	11									2	5	1	3					
Suicide (163–171)	1									1								
Homicide (172–175)	106								12	21	26	11	24	9	1	1	1	
Automobile accidents [1]	22						1	2	3	4	2	3	2	3	1	1		
Automobile—railroad train and street car collisions	3								2					1				
Other external causes	60	1	1			1	2	2	2	6	3	7	10	12	10	3		
All other causes	532	143	9	5	4	3	8	9	12	14	34	35	62	83	62	23	26	

[1] Excludes collision with railroad trains and street cars.

TABLE 29.—COLORED DEATHS (EXCLUSIVE OF STILLBIRTHS) FROM IMPORTANT CAUSES, BY AGE, IN THE 15 CITIES HAVING 50,000 OR MORE NEGRO INHABITANTS: 1930—Continued

[See note at head of this table]

AREA AND CAUSE OF DEATH	All deaths	Under 1 year	1 year	2 years	3 years	4 years	5 to 9 years	10 to 14 years	15 to 19 years	20 to 24 years	25 to 29 years	30 to 34 years	35 to 44 years	45 to 54 years	55 to 64 years	65 to 74 years	75 years and over	Age unknown
Chicago, Ill., all causes	**4,045**	**367**	**74**	**51**	**39**	**12**	**82**	**34**	**137**	**264**	**324**	**327**	**734**	**780**	**474**	**242**	**103**	**1**
Typhoid and paratyphoid fever (1, 2)	4								2	1		1						
Measles (7)																		
Scarlet fever (8)	7			1			1		2	1	1		1					
Whooping-cough (9)	18	5	7	2	2		2											
Diphtheria (10)	38	2	3	4	9	3	10	3	1	2	1							
Influenza (11)	22	3	1						2	1		3	5	4	1	2		
Epidemic cerebrospinal meningitis (18)	25			4	1	1	2	1	2	2	3	1	3	4	1			
Tuberculosis of the respiratory system (23)	611	4	3	3	1		15	14	61	109	111	90	112	66	20	1	1	
Other forms of tuberculosis (24–32)	102	3	7	9	5	2	13	4	6	8	12	10	13	6	4			
Syphilis (34)	96	25	3					1			3	12	19	23	6	4		
Cancer and other malignant tumors (45–53)	203								1	2	5	10	47	61	49	20	8	
Diabetes mellitus (59)	54									2		3	11	19	9	5	5	
Cerebral hemorrhage and softening (82a, 82c)	143	1									5	3	24	50	40	17	3	
Diseases of the heart (90–95)	699	1	1	2	2	1	5	1	9	24	26	42	150	188	137	80	30	
Bronchitis (106)	12	2	1		1	1	2		1				1	1	1	1		
Bronchopneumonia (107)	160	64	24	11	5		5		2	3	1	5	13	14	5	4	4	
Lobar and unspecified pneumonia (108, 109)	199	4	6	3	1	1	1	1	4	16	23	17	50	52	14	4	2	
Diarrhea and enteritis (119, 120)	49	25	8	3	2	1	5				1		1	1	2			
Appendicitis (121)	49				2		3	2	7	5	6	4	11	4	4	1		
Hernia, intestinal obstruction (122)	48	2	1							1	4	4	14	16	3	3		
Cirrhosis of the liver (124)	21											2	3	11	3	1	1	
Nephritis (130–132)	362			1				1	3	6	8	12	66	103	86	47	29	
Diseases of the female genital organs (139)	18								4	1	6	3	2	1	1			
Puerperal septicemia (140, 145)	10								5	2	1	1	1					
Other puerperal causes (141–144, 146–150)	20								2	3	3	7	5					
Suicide (163–171)	27								1	2	6	6	4	4	4			
Homicide (172–175)	174	1						1	6	27	37	31	48	14	8		1	
Automobile accidents [1]	59				2	2	3	2	3	2	5	2	11	14	6	6	1	
Automobile—railroad-train and street-car collisions	1											1						
Other external causes	132	3	3	2	5		4	2	3	12	15	16	27	21	9	8	2	
All other causes	682	222	6	6	1		11	1	10	32	41	41	92	103	61	38	16	1
Cleveland, Ohio, all causes	**1,293**	**151**	**22**	**12**	**4**	**9**	**23**	**20**	**46**	**87**	**103**	**114**	**267**	**234**	**111**	**64**	**26**	
Typhoid and paratyphoid fever (1, 2)	3						1						2					
Measles (7)	1			1														
Scarlet fever (8)	1		1															
Whooping-cough (9)	9	5	3			1												
Diphtheria (10)	4	1	1			1		1										
Influenza (11)	10										1	2	3	4				
Epidemic cerebrospinal meningitis (18)	12	4	1			1	2	1		2			1					
Tuberculosis of the respiratory system (23)	234	1		5			4	2	26	41	43	27	50	27	3	5		
Other forms of tuberculosis (24–32)	35	2	4	1	1		2	3	5	6	1	3	4	2	1			
Syphilis (34)	32	5	1							3	3	2	7	7	3	1		
Cancer and other malignant tumors (45–53)	55					1			1		1	4	16	17	10	4	1	
Diabetes mellitus (59)	8											1	5	2				
Cerebral hemorrhage and softening (82a, 82c)	70									1			14	24	18	8	5	
Diseases of the heart (90–95)	176						1	3	1	3	8	7	41	52	31	25	4	
Bronchitis (106)	2	1								1								
Bronchopneumonia (107)	56	21	1		2						4	4	6	9	7	1	1	
Lobar and unspecified pneumonia (108, 109)	79	3	1				1		2	6	8	8	21	19	8	1	1	
Diarrhea and enteritis (119, 120)	25	12	6	2		1	2			1				1				
Appendicitis (121)	10									1	1	3	3	2				
Hernia, intestinal obstruction (122)	9						1					2	4	2				
Cirrhosis of the liver (124)	7											1	2	1	3			
Nephritis (130–132)	77	1					1	2		3	2	7	17	11	14	9	10	
Diseases of the female genital organs (139)	7									1		2	4					
Puerperal septicemia (140, 145)	10								2	2	3		3					
Other puerperal causes (141–144, 146–150)	11									2	3	3	3					
Suicide (163–171)	8									2	1	1	1	3				
Homicide (172–175)	65								5	4	14	12	19	9	2			
Automobile accidents [1]	21			1		2	2	1	1	1	3	1	3	3	1	2		
Automobile—railroad-train and street-car collisions	1			1														
Other external causes	36	3		1		2	3	2	1	1	1	4	6	7	2	2	1	
All other causes	219	92	3		1		3	5	2	6	6	20	32	32	8	6	3	
Detroit, Mich, all causes	**2,037**	**245**	**57**	**34**	**24**	**20**	**52**	**46**	**74**	**150**	**213**	**206**	**417**	**259**	**133**	**70**	**37**	
Typhoid and paratyphoid fever (1, 2)	4											1	2	1				
Measles (7)	14	1	8	1	3	1												
Scarlet fever (8)	2				1								1					
Whooping-cough (9)	6	4	2															
Diphtheria (10)	8			3		1	3				1							
Influenza (11)	19	1				2	2		1	1	3	1	3	2	3			
Epidemic cerebrospinal meningitis (18)	32	2	3	1	3		7	3		2	4	5	1	1				
Tuberculosis of the respiratory system (23)	426	4	6	8	1	2	5	13	45	74	77	59	83	37	8	2	2	
Other forms of tuberculosis (24–32)	71	3	5	5	2	5	10	6	6	5	6	4	11	3				
Syphilis (34)	62	9							1	1	2	13	30	1	3	2		
Cancer and other malignant tumors (45–53)	47									1		6	12	12	8	7	1	
Diabetes mellitus (59)	17											2	3	4	4	4		
Cerebral hemorrhage and softening (82a, 82c)	53						1		1		1		10	15	15	4	6	
Diseases of the heart (90–95)	315	2	1	1			3	4	2	10	24	22	82	93	30	27	14	
Bronchitis (106)	19	6	2				1			3	1		1		3		2	
Bronchopneumonia (107)	102	52	16	5	3	2	1	2		2	2	3	5	4	4	1		
Lobar and unspecified pneumonia (108, 109)	147	7	5		2	2	4	3	2	10	24	12	42	20	12	1	1	
Diarrhea and enteritis (119, 120)	25	18	2	1			1			1		1		1				
Appendicitis (121)	26				1		2	1	1	3	2	3	9	2	1	1		
Hernia, intestinal obstruction (122)	21	2			1			1			5	4	5		2	1		
Cirrhosis of the liver (124)	3											1	1		1			
Nephritis (130–132)	92								1	1	9	8	18	19	22	12	2	
Diseases of the female genital organs (139)	16								1	3	5	5	2					
Puerperal septicemia (140, 145)	11								1	1	5	3	1					
Other puerperal causes (141–144, 146–150)	11								1	6	2		2					
Suicide (163–171)	15								1	2		6	4			1	1	
Homicide (172–175)	96							3	6	13	14	19	31	9	1			
Automobile accidents [1]	38				1	1	2	4	1	3	4	4	10	6	1	1		
Automobile—railroad-train and street-car collisions	4									1	1	1			1			
Other external causes	43	3	1	3	3	1	1	3		2	3	8	9	4	1	1		
All other causes	292	131	6	6	3	3	9	3	3	5	18	15	39	25	13	5	8	

[1] Excludes collision with railroad trains and street cars.

TABLE 29.—COLORED DEATHS (EXCLUSIVE OF STILLBIRTHS) FROM IMPORTANT CAUSES, BY AGE, IN THE 15 CITIES HAVING 50,000 OR MORE NEGRO INHABITANTS: 1930—Continued

[See note at head of this table]

AREA AND CAUSE OF DEATH	All deaths	Under 1 year	1 year	2 years	3 years	4 years	5 to 9 years	10 to 14 years	15 to 19 years	20 to 24 years	25 to 29 years	30 to 34 years	35 to 44 years	45 to 54 years	55 to 64 years	65 to 74 years	75 years and over	Age unknown
Houston, Tex., all causes	**1,495**	**205**	**26**	**14**	**8**	**5**	**16**	**14**	**56**	**83**	**124**	**132**	**246**	**292**	**151**	**75**	**48**	
Typhoid and paratyphoid fever (1, 2)	4						1		1	1		1						
Measles (7)																		
Scarlet fever (8)																		
Whooping-cough (9)	2		2															
Diphtheria (10)	2	1	1															
Influenza (11)	43	6	1	1			1			2	4	4	8	8	5	2	1	
Epidemic cerebrospinl meningitis (18)	1						1											
Tuberculosis of the respiratory system (23)	118	2	1					2	11	19	31	18	19	13	2			
Other forms of tuberculosis (24–32)	10	1		1				1		1	2	1	2	1				
Syphilis (34)	35	4			1				1		2	4	9	8	1	5		
Cancer and other malignant tumors (45–53)	39						1			1		3	5	14	11	4		
Diabetes mellitus (59)	22						1		1	1			5	11	2	1		
Cerebral hemorrhage and softening (82a, 82c)	74									2	1	5	15	30	13	6	2	
Diseases of the heart (90–95)	127	1							2	2	6	14	18	40	23	10	11	
Bronchitis (106)	6	1							1					1	1	1	1	
Bronchopneumonia (107)	32	16	3	2	2	1	1			1			2	2	2			
Lobar and unspecified pneumonia (108, 109)	97	14	2						4	6	15	10	22	11	7	5	1	
Diarrhea and enteritis (119, 120)	55	33	10	3	2		1					1	1			2	2	
Appendicitis (121)	17							1	2	2	4	5	1	1	1			
Hernia, intestinal obstruction (122)	16	1		1		1			1		1		2	7	1		1	
Cirrhosis of the liver (124)	15							1					2	5	5	2		
Nephritis (130–132)	87							1		1	1	6	20	26	22	6	4	
Diseases of the female genital organs (139)	10									1	3	3	2	1				
Puerperal septicemia (140, 145)	15								4	3	2	2	4					
Other puerperal causes (141–144, 146–150)	10							1	2	1	2	2	2					
Suicide (163–171)	5							1	2	1		1						
Homicide (172–175)	48								2	9	15	10	6	5	1			
Automobile accidents [1]	26							2	6	2	2	3	4	2	4	1		
Automobile—railroad train and street car collisions	3						1		1				1					
Other external causes	50			1	1	1	1	2	3	7	9	5	9	1	8	1	1	
All other causes	526	125	6	5	2	2	7	2	12	20	24	34	87	105	42	29	24	
Memphis, Tenn., all causes	**2,274**	**249**	**33**	**18**	**14**	**11**	**32**	**37**	**112**	**173**	**175**	**147**	**337**	**440**	**272**	**134**	**86**	**4**
Typhoid and paratyphoid fever (1, 2)	5		1							1	1	1	1					
Mealses (7)																		
Scarlet fever (8)																		
Whooping-cough (9)	9	4	4		1													
Diphtheria (10)	7	2		2		1	2											
Influenza (11)	43	2		1					2		6	2	10	9	9	1		1
Epidemic cerebrospinal meningitis (18)	105	9	5	5	2	1	10	13	14	16	14	3	3	9	1			
Tuberculosis of the respiratory system (23)	229	5	1	1	1		2	4	33	53	32	29	28	28	8	3		1
Other forms of tuberculosis (24–32)	36	1	1	1		2	2		4	10	5	3	5	1	1			
Syphilis (34)	68	21	1	1					1	1	4	7	12	13	5		2	
Cancer and other malignant tumors (45–53)	66							1	1	3	1	4	17	20	11	6	2	
Diabetes mellitus (59)	21								2				3	7	6	3		
Cerebral hemorrhage and softening (82a, 82c)	149	1							1	3	3	3	27	42	37	22	10	
Diseases of the heart (90–95)	272						1	5	2	11	12	12	48	73	53	34	20	1
Bronchitis (106)	3									1	1	1						
Bronchopneumonia (107)	75	47	5	1	5	2			1			1	2	6	5			
Lobar and unspecified pneumonia (108, 109)	75	8	3			1			3	6	5	8	18	12	7	2	2	
Diarrhea and enteritis (119, 120)	36	14	3		2	1	1		2	2		1	2	4	2	1	1	
Appendicitis (121)	28							2	5	3	1	5	6	3	2	1		
Hernia, intestinal obstruction (122)	34	1						1	1	3	3	4	5	8	4	4		
Cirrhosis of the liver (124)	16										1	2	1	6	4	2		
Nephritis (130–132)	158					1	1	2		1	10	5	23	47	39	20	9	
Diseases of the female genital organs (139)	12								2	1	3	2	2	2				
Puerperal septicemia (140, 145)	13								6	3	2		2					
Other puerperal causes (141–144, 146–150)	16								2	5	6	3						
Suicide (163–171)	3												1	2				
Homicide (172–175)	121							1	11	24	25	16	30	11	3			
Automobile accidents [1]	26				1		1	1	1	3	2	4	4	3	3	3		
Automobile—railroad train and street car collisions																		
Other external causes	82	6		1		1	4	3	5	2	4	5	16	14	10	4	6	1
All other causes	566	128	9	5	2	1	8	4	13	21	34	26	71	120	62	28	34	
New Orleans, La., all causes	**3,289**	**380**	**77**	**38**	**26**	**18**	**41**	**46**	**85**	**191**	**197**	**184**	**556**	**612**	**434**	**242**	**149**	**13**
Typhoid and paratyphoid fever (1, 2)	11						1	1	3	2	3		1					
Measles (7)	11	2	2	2	2	1	2											
Scarlet fever (8))																		
Whooping-cough (9)	14	8	5		1													
Diphtheria (10)	6		2	2			1						1					
Influenza (11)	99	29	6	1	2	2	2	2		4	6	3	17	11	7	6	1	
Epidemic cerebrospinal meningitis (18)	21	3	1	1	1		4	1	3	1	3	1	1	1				
Tuberculosis of the respiratory system (23)	304	1	1				2	8	30	55	46	40	69	43	9			
Other forms of tuberculosis (24–32)	22		1				1	1	3	5	2	2	4	3				
Syphilis (34)	156	14		1			1	1	4	10	10	14	47	26	20	6	2	
Cancer and other malignant tumors (45–53)	165			1			1	1		2	5	8	29	54	41	17	6	
Diabetes mellitus (59)	25											3	4	8	4	5	1	
Cerebral hemorrhage and softening (82a, 82c)	165									2	3	6	18	51	48	23	14	
Diseases of the heart (90–95)	586	2		1				3	3	8	20	23	118	148	124	71	61	4
Bronchitis (106)	6			1						1		1	1		1	1		
Bronchopneumonia (107)	190	96	22	7	4	3	6	3	1	2	2		15	12	6	7	3	1
Lobar and unspecified pneumonia (108, 109)	182	14	13	7	2	1	2	3	5	17	17	9	25	37	21	5	3	1
Diarrhea and enteritis (119, 120)	67	41	12	4	1		2		1	1		2		2	1			
Appendicitis (121)	27					1	3	4	2	2	3	2	4	6				
Hernia, intestinal obstruction (122)	38	6	1		1	1			2	2	3	4	6	6	3	2	1	
Cirrhosis of the liver (124)	46	1		2						3		2	8	17	7	4	1	1
Nephritis (130–132)	369	2		1	1			1	3	6	13	14	64	96	74	58	34	2
Diseases of the female genital organs (139)	19							1	1	3	4	4	3	2	1			
Puerperal septicemia (140, 145)	21							1	1	7	7	2	3					
Other puerperal causes (141–144, 146–150)	22								3	4	5	3	7					
Suicide (163–171)	12									3	2	3	2				2	
Homicide (172–175)	64							1	2	15	12	11	15	6	1	1		
Automobile accidents [1]	37				1		4	1	2	2	5	4	5	5	5	2	1	
Automobile—railroad train and street car collisions	1												1					
Other external causes	97	1	7	3	5	5	1	5	6	10	2	4	15	13	8	8	4	
All other causes	506	160	4	4	5	4	8	8	10	24	24	19	73	65	53	26	15	4

[1] Excludes collision with railroad trains and street cars

TABLE 29.—COLORED DEATHS (EXCLUSIVE OF STILLBIRTHS) FROM IMPORTANT CAUSES, BY AGE, IN THE CITIES 15 HAVING 50,000 OR MORE NEGRO INHABITANTS: 1930—Continued

AREA AND CAUSE OF DEATH	All deaths	Under 1 year	1 year	2 years	3 years	4 years	5 to 9 years	10 to 14 years	15 to 19 years	20 to 24 years	25 to 29 years	30 to 34 years	35 to 44 years	45 to 54 years	55 to 64 years	65 to 74 years	75 years and over	Age unknown
New York, N. Y., all causes	**5,630**	**764**	**122**	**70**	**31**	**31**	**93**	**67**	**182**	**337**	**459**	**519**	**1,055**	**904**	**541**	**292**	**160**	**3**
Typhoid and paratyphoid fever (1, 2)	6								1	2	1	1	1					
Measles (7)	18	7	6	3	2													
Scarlet fever (8)																		
Whooping-cough (9)	20	11	6	2			1											
Diphtheria (10)	14	1	2	1	3	2	3					1		1				
Influenza (11)	12	3		1						1	1		4	2				
Epidemic cerebrospinal meningitis (18)	33	1	1	2	1		3	2	3	3	5	3	6	2				1
Tuberculosis of the respiratory system (23)	913	9	12	6	5	2	8	21	88	137	157	121	196	104	34	9	4	
Other forms of tuberculosis (24-32)	140	12	7	9	6	7	12	8	9	18	10	14	13	14	1			
Syphilis (34)	241	42	3	3				1	4	10	18	29	57	53	13	7	1	
Cancer and other malignant tumors (45-53)	261			1			1	3	1	4	13	10	62	52	66	39	9	
Diabetes mellitus (59)	71		1			1		1	1	2	3	3	8	31	13	6	1	
Cerebral hemorrhage and softening (82a, 82c)	153						1				1	2	31	60	32	18	8	
Diseases of the heart (90-95)	880	3		2	1	1	11	4	12	17	30	43	170	222	183	105	75	1
Bronchitis (106)	13	4	2								1	1	2		1		2	
Bronchopneumonia (107)	266	143	41	15	2	1	3		1	2	6	8	15	11	8	6	4	
Lobar and unspecified pneumonia (108, 109)	502	51	21	6	1	3	4	4	13	24	51	59	112	91	45	13	4	
Diarrhea and enteritis (119, 120)	102	87	7	2		1			1	1		1	1		1			
Appendicitis (121)	63	1		2	1	1	6	3	7	11	6	7	12	4	1	1		
Hernia, intestinal obstruction (122)	32	3		1			1		2	2	2	1	6	7	3	1	3	
Cirrhosis of the liver (124)	18												4	4	6	3	1	
Nephritis (130-132)	322	1						2	1	5	14	23	73	74	58	49	22	
Diseases of the female genital organs (139)	55								2	9	7	17	11	6	2	1		
Puerperal septicemia (140, 145)	24								4	3	6	7	4					
Other puerperal causes (141-144, 146-150)	48								4	9	11	13	10	1				
Suicide (163-171)	47								1	7	6	8	17	6	1		1	
Homicide (162-175)	131	4							4	14	32	27	28	18	4			
Automobile accidents [1]	92				2	4	10	5	3	5	6	11	15	13	13	4	1	
Automobile—railroad train and street car collisions	1												1					
Other external causes	233	6	2	2	2	2	12	2	11	18	29	34	61	30	11	5	5	1
All other causes	919	375	11	12	5	6	17	11	9	33	43	75	135	98	45	25	19	
Philadelphia, Pa., all causes	**3,620**	**495**	**81**	**34**	**21**	**15**	**48**	**32**	**111**	**200**	**251**	**271**	**630**	**626**	**463**	**228**	**114**	
Typhoid and paratyphoid fever (1, 2)	1								1									
Measles (7)	2		2															
Scarlet fever (8)	6	1	1				3				1							
Whooping-cough (9)	7	7																
Diphtheria (10)	10	2	3	2	1		1						1					
Influenza (11)	51	10	8	1	1			1		1	3	5	7	8	5	1		
Epidemic cerebrospinal meningitis (18)	12	2					1		3	2	1	1	1	1				
Tuberculosis of the respiratory system (23)	522	11	7	8	2	5	9	13	50	90	84	56	111	47	17	8	4	
Other forms of tuberculosis (24-32)	52	3	3	2	3	2	2	1	9	7	7	2	7	2	2			
Syphilis (34)	104	17			1				1	5	5	13	27	21	11	2	1	
Cancer and other malignant tumors (45-53)	182						1		1	3	4	13	36	57	43	18	6	
Diabetes mellitus (59)	47				1			1		1	1	2	9	14	16	2		
Cerebral hemorrhage and softening (82a, 82c)	128									1	3	5	20	33	35	22	9	
Diseases of the heart (90-95)	643	3	2	1	1	1	3	3	6	10	28	31	112	169	140	97	36	
Bronchitis (106)	18	4	1	1	1			1			2		3	2	2	1		
Bronchopneumonia (107)	168	90	14	5		2	1	4	2	3		2	10	14	9	8	4	
Lobar and unspecified pneumonia (108, 109)	263	34	17	5			4		8	14	24	37	54	32	26	4	4	
Diarrhea and enteritis (119, 120)	109	80	8	2	2		2			1	1	1	3	5	2	2		
Appendicitis (121)	34					1	1		8	4	4	3	9	2	1	1		
Hernia, intestinal obstruction (122)	36	6	1						1	1	1	6	4	7	7	2		
Cirrhosis of the liver (124)	13										1	2		5	4		1	
Nephritis (130-132)	316		1				1	1		8	6	22	58	87	72	35	25	
Diseases of the female genital organs (139)	11								1	3	1		4	1	1			
Puerperal septicemia (140, 145)	15								2	5	1	5	2					
Other puerperal causes (141-144, 146-150)	22								2	4	5	2	9					
Suicide (163-171)	11								1	1	5	1	1	1	1			
Homicide (172-175)	68								1	13	15	10	20	4	5			
Automobile accidents [1]	31			1			4	1	2	1	1	5	4	7	4		1	
Automobile—railroad train and street car collisions																		
Other external causes	119	7	2	3	1	2	6	2	6	6	13	9	26	20	8	6	2	
All other causes	619	218	11	3	7	2	9	4	6	16	34	38	92	87	52	19	21	
Pittsburgh, Pa., all causes	**1,103**	**142**	**31**	**8**	**9**	**7**	**30**	**15**	**41**	**53**	**72**	**95**	**197**	**190**	**129**	**49**	**35**	
Typhoid and paratyphoid fever (1, 2)																		
Measles (7)	4		2	1			1											
Scarlet fever (8)	1	1																
Whooping-cough (9)	8	2	4			1	1											
Diphtheria (10)	6	1				1	3						1					
Influenza (11)	16	2						1	1	2	1	2	2	2	2		1	
Epidemic cerebrospinal meningitis (18)	9	1			1	1	2		1	2		1						
Tuberculosis of the respiratory system (23)	104	1	2	1	1		3	3	14	14	15	17	15	11	5	1	1	
Other forms of tuberculosis (24-32)	14					2	2	1	2	1	1	1	1	2	1			
Syphilis (34)	37	7								1	5	6	4	9	4		1	
Cancer and other malignant tumors (45-53)	43									1	2		10	16	9	3	2	
Diabetes mellitus (59)	9								1			1	1	2	2	2		
Cerebral hemorrhage and softening (82a, 82c)	51				1							5	6	15	18	5	1	
Diseases of the heart (90-95)	149						3	2	1	2	5	10	26	35	35	17	13	
Bronchitis (106)	4	1			1										1		1	
Bronchopneumonia (107)	54	22	6				2	1	2	1	1	1	7	5	5		1	
Lobar and unspecified pneumonia (108, 109)	189	16	4	1	2		4	1	10	8	16	20	54	32	16	3	2	
Diarrhea and enteritis (119, 120)	24	13	3		2					1	1		1	3				
Appendicitis (121)	8						1				1	2	1	3				
Hernia, intestinal obstruction (122)	15	1	1							3			4	3	3			
Cirrhosis of the liver (124)	4												1	3				
Nephritis (130-132)	65			1			1				4	2	7	19	15	8	8	
Diseases of the female genital organs (139)	8										1	1	5	1				
Puerperal septicemia (140, 145)	10								1	3	1		5					
Other puerperal causes (141-144, 146-150)	8								2	2	1	1	2					
Suicide (163-171)	5								1	1		2		1				
Homicide (172-175)	23								2	1	3	5	7	5				
Automobile accidents [1]	11							2	2	1	2		2		2			
Automobile—railroad train and street car collisions																		
Other external causes	50		1	1	1	2	5	3	1	3	4	7	13	4	2	2	1	
All other causes	174	74	8	3			2	1		6	8	11	22	19	9	8	3	

[1] Excludes collision with railroad trains and street cars.

TABLE 29.—COLORED DEATHS (EXCLUSIVE OF STILLBIRTHS) FROM IMPORTANT CAUSES, BY AGE, IN THE 15 CITIES HAVING 50,000 OR MORE NEGRO INHABITANTS: 1930—Continued

[See note at head of this table]

AREA AND CAUSE OF DEATH	All deaths	Under 1 year	1 year	2 years	3 years	4 years	5 to 9 years	10 to 14 years	15 to 19 years	20 to 24 years	25 to 29 years	30 to 34 years	35 to 44 years	45 to 54 years	55 to 64 years	65 to 74 years	75 years and over	Age unknown
Richmond, Va., all causes	**1,132**	**143**	**24**	**7**	**10**	**9**	**19**	**12**	**34**	**51**	**60**	**50**	**170**	**235**	**171**	**97**	**39**	**1**
Typhoid and paratyphoid fever (1, 2)	1										1							
Measles (7)																		
Scarlet fever (8)	1				1													
Whooping-cough (9)	6	6																
Diphtheria (10)	5			1	1	2	1											
Influenza (11)	25	2	2	1						1		2		8	5	2	1	1
Epidemic cerebrospinal meningitis (18)	8	2						1	1		2		1		1			
Tuberculosis of the respiratory system (23)	84	1	1			1	1	1	7	10	14	8	16	17	6	1		
Other forms of tuberculosis (24–32)	23	2	6		1	1	2	1	3	1	2	3		1				
Syphilis (34)	28	10	1				1		1	2	2		4	3	1	3		
Cancer and other malignant tumors (45–53)	44					1					3		9	13	12	5	1	
Diabetes mellitus (59)	10									1			1	6	1	1		
Cerebral hemorrhage and softening (82a, 82c)	107									1		1	13	30	37	17	8	
Diseases of the heart (90–95)	172	1					1		2	3	3	8	34	52	41	15	12	
Bronchitis (106)	6	2												1	1	1	1	
Bronchopneumonia (107)	30	12	5	1			1					1	3	4	1	1	1	
Lobar and unspecified pneumonia (108, 109)	66	9	3		1		3		2	8	5	3	12	10	6	3	1	
Diarrhea and enteritis (119, 120)	20	13	2		1		2						1	1				
Appendicitis (121)	13					1	1	1	1		1		5	1	2			
Hernia, intestinal obstruction (122)	11	2						1					3	2	2	1		
Cirrhosis of the liver (124)	7											1		4	1	1		
Nephritis (130–132)	126	1					1	1		2	2	5	23	39	26	19	7	
Diseases of the female genital organs (139)	6								1		2		1	2				
Puerperal septicemia (140, 145)	5								1	1	2	1						
Other puerperal causes (141–144, 146–150)	9								1	2		1	5					
Suicide (163–171)	6											1	3	1	1			
Homicide (172–175)	23	1							3	3	7	4	3	2				
Automobile accidents [1]	15						1	1	1	1	2	2	1	4	1	1		
Automobile—railroad train and street car collisions	1													1				
Other external causes	35	1	1		1	2		2	4	4	1	5	2	4	4	4		
All other causes	239	78	3	4	4	1	4	3	6	11	11	4	30	29	22	22	7	
St. Louis, Mo., all causes	**1,982**	**167**	**40**	**12**	**8**	**11**	**21**	**30**	**45**	**102**	**137**	**133**	**358**	**397**	**281**	**149**	**91**	
Typhoid and paratyphoid fever (1, 2)	2										1			1				
Measles (7)	6	1	2				3											
Scarlet fever (8)																		
Whooping-cough (9)	1		1															
Diphtheria (10)	2					1		1										
Influenza (11)	16	2	2								1		2	2	5	1	1	
Epidemic cerebrospinal meningitis (18)	16	1	1	2				1	3	3	1	1	1	1	1			
Tuberculosis of the respiratory system (23)	241	2	1	2		3	3	8	20	36	45	27	44	32	9	6	3	
Other forms of tuberculosis (24–32)	38	2	4	2		1	2	2	2	7	2	4	6	2			2	
Syphilis (34)	25	7					1				3		5	4	4		1	
Cancer and other malignant tumors (45–53)	102										4	5	25	37	22	6	3	
Diabetes mellitus (59)	18							1				1	6	4	4		2	
Cerebral hemorrhage and softening (82a, 82c)	97											2	16	35	28	13	3	
Diseases of the heart (90–95)	405							7	2	1	12	21	67	98	93	65	39	
Bronchitis (106)	5	3	2															
Bronchopneumonia (107)	91	38	16	3	3	2	3		1	4	2	3	3	7	3	3		
Lobar and unspecified pneumonia (108, 109)	151	8	5		1			3	2	8	13	18	29	35	21	7	1	
Diarrhea and enteritis (119, 120)	36	28	3	1	1	1						1			1			
Appendicitis (121)	33					1	1	1	3	5	6	5	4	3	3		1	
Hernia, intestinal obstruction (122)	9							1	1				4	2	1			
Cirrhosis of the liver (124)	14								1		1	1	3	4	3	1		
Nephritis (130–132)	240		1		1		1	1		2	8	7	41	70	47	37	24	
Diseases of the female genital organs (139)	5											1	2	2				
Puerperal septicemia (140, 145)	11								2	5	2		2					
Other puerperal causes (141–144, 146–150)	4								1	1		2						
Suicide (163–171)	3													2	1			
Homicide (172–175)	68							1	2	16	13	12	13	8	3			
Automobile accidents [1]	23			2			3		1	3	1	4	4	1	2	1	1	
Automobile—railroad train and street car collisions																		
Other external causes	73	2				1	1	1	1	3	5	5	19	17	8	4	6	
All other causes	247	73	2		2	1	3	2	3	8	17	13	62	30	22	5	4	
Washington, D. C., all causes	**2,792**	**337**	**69**	**20**	**14**	**7**	**34**	**28**	**97**	**139**	**169**	**164**	**424**	**451**	**398**	**289**	**152**	
Typhoid and paratyphoid fever (1, 2)	7						2		1		1		2			1		
Measles (7)																		
Scarlet fever (8)	1			1														
Whooping-cough (9)	12	8	3	1														
Diphtheria (10)	7		3		2							2						
Influenza (11)	15	3							1			3	2		2	3	1	
Epidemic cerebrospinal meningitis (18)	5			1			1		1		2							
Tuberculosis of the respiratory system (23)	303	5	4			1	4	3	35	56	51	31	63	33	12	2	3	
Other forms of tuberculosis (24–32)	51	3	13	2	4		4	3	5	3	1	1	5	4	2	1		
Syphilis (34)	64	19							2	4	5	4	14	8	4	4		
Cancer and other malignant tumors (45–53)	155								3		4	6	21	37	51	24	9	
Diabetes mellitus (59)	35									1	2	1	6	12	7	6		
Cerebral hemorrhage and softening (82a, 82c)	140									1		2	20	33	30	37	17	
Diseases of the heart (90–95)	533	2					3	3	3	11	13	31	84	127	128	84	44	
Bronchitis (106)	10	2									1		1	4	1		1	
Bronchopneumonia (107)	142	60	13	5	2	2	5	2	2	4	3	2	8	8	12	9	5	
Lobar and unspecified pneumonia (108, 109)	149	13	4		2	2	1		4	14	22	11	22	34	12	6	2	
Diarrhea and enteritis (119, 120)	69	45	13	1			1					1	3		2	2	1	
Appendicitis (121)	36		1	1			5	1	4	3	2	4	7	6		2		
Hernia, intestinal obstruction (122)	37	5		1			1			3		1	8	12	4	1	1	
Cirrhosis of the liver (124)	15						1			1		1	4	4	2	1	1	
Nephritis (130–132)	248		1					1	1	5	7	7	35	47	64	49	31	
Diseases of the female genital organs (139)	13								1	1	2	1	5	3				
Puerperal septicemia (140, 145)	23							1	6	3	7	4	2					
Other puerperal causes (141–144, 146–150)	31								7	6	5	5	8					
Suicide (163–171)	13								1	1		3	4	1	2	1		
Homicide (172–175)	44								2	3	7	14	14	3	1			
Automobile accidents [1]	34				2		1	2	2	3	6	2	6	4	2	2	2	
Automobile—railroad train and street car collisions																		
Other external causes	82		3	5		2	2	9	5	7	2	7	17	10	7	5	1	
All other causes	518	172	11	2	2		3	3	11	9	26	20	63	61	53	49	33	

[1] Excludes collision with railroad trains and street cars.

Table 30.—COLORED DEATHS (EXCLUSIVE OF STILLBIRTHS) FROM IMPORTANT CAUSES, BY MONTHS, IN CITIES HAVING 50,000 OR MORE NEGRO INHABITANTS: 1930

[Colored deaths include Negro, nonwhite and other races. Numbers after causes of death correspond to those of the 1929 revision of the detailed International List]

AREA AND CAUSE OF DEATH	All deaths	January	February	March	April	May	June	July	August	September	October	November	December
Atlanta, Ga., all causes	**2,106**	**209**	**195**	**203**	**192**	**162**	**189**	**179**	**147**	**157**	**153**	**150**	**170**
Typhoid and paratyphoid fever (1, 2)	18					1		1	3	8	4	1	
Smallpox (6)													
Measles (7)	4				1	2							1
Scarlet fever (8)	1							1					
Whooping-cough (9)	26	1	4	3	3	2	4	3	3	2	1		
Diphtheria (10)	2											1	1
Influenza (11)	54	9	7	8	5	3	3	2	1	1	3	6	6
Dysentery (13)	14	2			2	1	1	4	2	1	1		
Erysipelas (15)	3	1	1			1							
Lethargic encephalitis (17)													
Epidemic cerebrospinal meningitis (18)	28	7	5	6	4	1			1			3	1
Tuberculosis of the respiratory system (23)	139	8	14	8	8	18	13	8	11	11	11	14	15
Other forms of tuberculosis (24–32)	55	9	5	5	7	2	5	4	7	5	2		4
Malaria (38)													
Diabetes mellitus (59)	19	2	5		3	3		2	2				2
Cerebral hemorrhage and softening (82a, 82c)	201	14	20	22	15	12	18	23	11	18	14	11	23
Diseases of the heart (90–95)	259	31	19	20	25	22	22	14	18	16	22	26	24
Bronchitis (106)	8				2	1		2	2			1	
Bronchopneumonia (107)	87	10	10	10	10	8	8	7	2	4	5	7	6
Lobar and unspecified pneumonia (108, 109)	126	18	13	22	16	11	12	6	6	3	8	6	5
Diarrhea and enteritis [under 2 years] (119)	34					3	6	6	6	5	5	3	
Diarrhea and enteritis [2 years and over] (120)	24	2	1	1	1	1	2	1	6	4	1	1	3
Nephritis (130–132)	214	19	16	28	27	13	22	19	6	18	12	12	22
Puerperal septicemia (140, 145)	15	1	1	1		3	2		2		2	2	1
Other puerperal causes (141–144, 146–150)	12	1		1			1	1	3		1	3	1
Suicide (163–171)	4				1	1			1			1	
Automobile accidents [1]	33	5	3	2	3		1	3	2	2	5	3	4
Automobile—railroad train and street-car collisions	1										1		
Other external causes	161	18	14	12	17	10	9	16	11	16	10	12	16
All other causes	564	51	57	54	42	43	60	56	41	43	45	37	35
Baltimore, Md., all causes	**2,815**	**243**	**223**	**245**	**296**	**233**	**185**	**257**	**223**	**210**	**258**	**218**	**224**
Typhoid and paratyphoid fever (1, 2)	12		1	1				1	1	3	4	1	
Smallpox (6)													
Measles (7)													
Scarlet fever (8)	2	1			1								
Whooping-cough (9)	5		1			1	1		1	1			
Diphtheria (10)	3			1							1	1	
Influenza (11)	19	4	4	2	3	2							4
Dysentery (13)	9				1			2		3	2	1	
Erysipelas (15)	1		1										
Lethargic encephalitis (17)													
Epidemic cerebrospinal meningitis (18)	9	2	3		1	1	1						1
Tuberculosis of the respiratory system (23)	313	31	19	27	35	27	27	31	31	16	28	19	22
Other forms of tuberculosis (24–32)	66	2	6	6	7	8	6	7	7	9	3	3	2
Malaria (38)													
Diabetes mellitus (59)	26	1	3	2	2	6	3	2	2	3		1	1
Cerebral hemorrhage and softening (82a, 82c)	187	10	15	17	18	16	13	17	15	12	21	9	24
Diseases of the heart (90–95)	496	44	42	40	51	41	36	52	33	38	43	41	35
Bronchitis (106)	4	1				1					1		1
Bronchopneumonia (107)	156	18	15	14	21	9	9	15	7	10	12	9	17
Lobar and unspecified pneumonia (108, 109)	286	36	28	37	44	30	10	5	9	12	21	25	29
Diarrhea and enteritis [under 2 years] (119)	35	1		5		2	2	6	6	2	8	1	2
Diarrhea and enteritis [2 years and over] (120)	8						1	2	4			1	
Nephritis (130–132)	253	15	27	16	29	21	18	21	14	19	28	29	16
Puerperal septicemia (140, 145)	12		1	3	3	1	2	1		1			
Other puerperal causes (141–144, 146–150)	14		1	1	2	1	1		3	3	1		1
Suicide (163–171)	7	2				1				1	2	1	
Automobile accidents [1]	32	1	1	1	4	1	1	4	3	4	6	1	5
Automobile—railroad train and street-car collisions	5				3				2				
Other external causes	140	10	5	10	14	14	9	14	16	16	13	6	13
All other causes	715	64	50	62	57	50	45	77	69	57	64	69	51
Birmingham, Ala., all causes	**1,925**	**150**	**163**	**196**	**156**	**165**	**180**	**165**	**142**	**141**	**144**	**153**	**170**
Typhoid and paratyphoid fever (1, 2)	10		1	2		1	2	1	1	1	1		
Smallpox (6)													
Measles (7)	5				1				1				3
Scarlet fever (8)	1												1
Whooping-cough (9)	9		2	2	1	1	1			1	1		
Diphtheria (10)	10		2	1	1						1	3	2
Influenza (11)	40	4	3	9	4	3	4		1	2	2	4	4
Dysentery (13)													
Erysipelas (15)													
Lethargic encephalitis (17)	5				1		2		1				1
Epidemic cerebrospinal meningitis (18)	3			1		1					1		
Tuberculosis of the respiratory system (23)	172	11	16	15	13	26	14	14	13	10	12	9	19
Other forms of tuberculosis (24–32)	23	1	2	2	1	3	2	4		1	1	3	3
Malaria (38)	3							2		1			
Diabetes mellitus (59)	22	1	3	3	2	1	1	1	1	2	2	3	2
Cerebral hemorrhage and softening (82a, 82c)	105	11	6	13	6	5	9	14	9	3	7	12	10
Diseases of the heart (90–95)	230	14	15	25	16	21	31	22	19	16	15	18	18
Bronchitis (106)	1				1								
Bronchopneumonia (107)	51	6	10	5	6	2	4	2	1	3	5	3	4
Lobar and unspecified pneumonia (108, 109)	136	11	12	8	20	14	15	4	7	10	8	18	9
Diarrhea and enteritis [under 2 years] (119)	28	1	1	2	2	1	4	4	4	3	3	2	1
Diarrhea and enteritis [2 years and over] (120)	5		1				2			1	1		
Nephritis (130–132)	133	9	12	11	12	14	11	10	7	4	16	13	14
Puerperal septicemia (140, 145)	14	1			2	3	3	1	1	1			2
Other puerperal causes (141–144, 146–150)	11			1	1	1		3		1	1	1	2
Suicide (163–171)	1											1	
Automobile accidents [1]	22	4	2	1		1	2	2	2	3	1	1	3
Automobile—railroad train and street-car collisions	3			1							2		
Other external causes	166	19	14	23	11	7	15	12	22	11	10	8	14
All other causes	716	57	61	71	55	60	58	69	52	67	54	54	58

[1] Excludes collision with railroad trains and street cars.

TABLE 30.—COLORED DEATHS (EXCLUSIVE OF STILLBIRTHS) FROM IMPORTANT CAUSES, BY MONTHS, IN CITIES HAVING 50,000 OR MORE NEGRO INHABITANTS: 1930—Continued

[Colored deaths include Negro, nonwhite and other races. Numbers after causes of death correspond to those of the 1929 revision of the detailed International List]

AREA AND CAUSE OF DEATH	All deaths	January	February	March	April	May	June	July	August	September	October	November	December
Chicago, Ill., all causes	**4,045**	**369**	**358**	**356**	**370**	**333**	**303**	**352**	**321**	**305**	**290**	**343**	**345**
Typhoid and paratyphoid fever (1, 2)	4							2			1	1	
Smallpox (6)													
Measles (7)													
Scarlet fever (8)	7	2	1	2								2	
Whooping-cough (9)	18	2						2	2	4	3	3	2
Diphtheria (10)	38	5	2	4	6	2	2		1	1	1	6	8
Influenza (11)	22	6	3	6	2			1	1				3
Dysentery (13)	2								1		1		
Erysipelas (15)	4			1				2	1				
Lethargic encephalitis (17)	2		2										
Epidemic cerebrospinal meningitis (18)	25	4	5		5	1	4		2	1		1	2
Tuberculosis of the respiratory system (23)	611	55	46	53	57	60	41	59	50	56	40	49	45
Other forms of tuberculosis (24–32)	102	5	3	8	8	11	12	9	10	9	11	6	10
Malaria (38)													
Diabetes mellitus (59)	54	2	7	4	5	1	3	3	7	4	8	2	8
Cerebral hemorrhage and softening (82a, 82c)	143	9	12	6	10	10	9	14	15	16	16	13	13
Diseases of the heart (90–95)	699	60	62	74	63	53	60	70	50	53	46	55	53
Bronchitis (106)	12		3		3		1	1	1	1	1	1	
Bronchopneumonia (107)	160	14	17	20	15	22	11	7	8	10	9	11	16
Lobar and unspecified pneumonia (108, 109)	199	35	27	23	20	17	14	7	3	7	12	21	13
Diarrhea and enteritis [under 2 years] (119)	33	2	4		3	6	3	2	4	7		2	
Diarrhea and enteritis [2 years and over] (120)	16	1			3			1	5	5		1	
Nephritis (130–132)	362	35	29	32	37	34	34	29	28	24	24	28	28
Puerperal septicemia (140, 145)	10	2	2		1					3		1	1
Other puerperal causes (141–144, 146–150)	20	1	1	2	2	6		2	2		1	2	1
Suicide (163–171)	27		3		5	3	1	1	4	2	1	3	4
Automobile accidents [1]	59	4	7	1	5	1	8	3	8	2	5	5	10
Automobile—railroad train and street car collisions	1			1									
Other external causes	306	25	34	30	29	22	19	33	29	18	17	21	29
All other causes	1,109	100	88	89	91	84	81	104	89	82	93	109	99
Cleveland, Ohio, all causes	**1,293**	**108**	**131**	**134**	**130**	**105**	**125**	**89**	**89**	**81**	**97**	**106**	**98**
Typhoid and paratyphoid fever (1, 2)	3	1				1	1						
Smallpox (6)													
Measles (7)	1							1					
Scarlet fever (8)	1			1									
Whooping-cough (9)	9	1	1			2	1	1	1	1	1		
Diphtheria (10)	4				2	1				1			
Influenza (11)	10	1	4	2	1	1							1
Dysentery (13)													
Erysipelas (15)	2		2										
Lethargic encephalitis (17)	1					1							
Epidemic cerebrospinal meningitis (18)	12	2		3	4	1	1				1		
Tuberculosis of the respiratory system (23)	234	17	18	21	24	20	28	24	15	12	12	25	18
Other forms of tuberculosis (24–32)	35	5	4	5	3	1	2	6	1	3		1	4
Malaria (38)													
Diabetes mellitus (59)	8			2	3			1		1			1
Cerebral hemorrhage and softening (82a, 82c)	70	11	9	3	3	5	13	1	2	2	5	7	9
Diseases of the heart (90–95)	176	11	15	24	14	12	14	6	19	10	15	20	16
Bronchitis (106)	2			1									1
Bronchopneumonia (107)	56	4	9	9	6	2	8	1	3	5	2	5	2
Lobar and unspecified pneumonia (108, 109)	79	11	10	7	9	6	4	1	6	4	10	8	3
Diarrhea and enteritis [under 2 years] (119)	18	1	1	1	1	1		2	1	2	7	1	
Diarrhea and enteritis [2 years and over] (120)	7		1				2	2	1				1
Nephritis (130–132)	77	8	7	10	2	11	4	7	3	5	6	8	6
Puerperal septicemia (140, 145)	10	1	2	2	2						1	1	1
Other puerperal causes (141–144, 146–150)	11	1	2		1	2	1		1		1		2
Suicide (163–171)	8		1	1	1	1	3				1		
Automobile accidents [1]	21	1	2		1	3	4	1	1	2	1	1	4
Automobile—railroad train and street car collisions	1								1				
Other external causes	101	5	10	8	11	10	9	9	9	8	7	6	9
All other causes	336	27	33	34	42	24	30	26	25	25	27	23	20
Detroit, Mich., all causes	**2,037**	**162**	**208**	**212**	**186**	**183**	**177**	**152**	**141**	**147**	**156**	**147**	**166**
Typhoid and paratyphoid fever (1, 2)	4			1				2				1	
Smallpox (6)													
Measles (7)	14		2	3	5	4							
Scarlet fever (8)	2			1									1
Whooping-cough (9)	6				1			1	2		1	1	
Diphtheria (10)	8		3			1		1	1		1	1	
Influenza (11)	19	4	2		5	2		1	1	1		3	
Dysentery (13)													
Erysipelas (15)	3		1			1				1			
Lethargic encephalitis (17)	2		1	1									
Epidemic cerebrospinal meningitis (18)	32	5	10	6	2	3	5						1
Tuberculosis of the respiratory system (23)	426	22	36	45	49	44	44	35	43	29	24	27	28
Other forms of tuberculosis (24–32)	71	2	4	12	5	6	9	6	8	5	3	4	7
Malaria (38)													
Diabetes mellitus (59)	17	2	3	1	2		1	2	1	1		3	1
Cerebral hemorrhage and softening (82a, 82c)	53	6	7	2	4	7	4	6	3	3	6	4	1
Diseases of the heart (90–95)	315	31	26	22	23	30	31	25	14	24	36	26	27
Bronchitis (106)	19	3	1	3	1	1	1	2		1	1	3	2
Bronchopneumonia (107)	102	6	19	22	11	7	4	2	5	8	4	5	9
Lobar and unspecified pneumonia (108, 109)	147	12	21	23	23	13	11		4	12	11	8	9
Diarrhea and enteritis [under 2 years] (119)	20	1	5	1				1	2	2	6	1	1
Diarrhea and enteritis [2 years and over] (120)	5	1	1	1				1					1
Nephritis (130–132)	92	7	4	5	12	12	11	3	8	8	6	5	11
Puerperal septicemia (140, 145)	11	1		1	1	1		1	1	1		2	2
Other puerperal causes (141–144, 146–150)	11			2	1	1	2	3			1	1	
Suicide (163–171)	15		2	3	1	1	1	4			1	1	1
Automobile accidents [1]	38	1	3	4	2	3	3	3	2	7	3	3	4
Automobile—railroad train and street car collisions	4							2		1	1		
Other external causes	139	16	12	14	11	9	10	13	8	12	13	9	12
All other causes	462	42	45	39	27	37	40	38	38	31	38	39	48

[1] Excludes collision with railroad trains and street cars.

TABLE 30.—COLORED DEATHS (EXCLUSIVE OF STILLBIRTHS) FROM IMPORTANT CAUSES, BY MONTHS, IN CITIES HAVING 50,000 OR MORE NEGRO INHABITANTS: 1930—Continued

[Colored deaths include Negro, nonwhite and other races. Numbers after causes of death correspond to those of the 1929 revision of the detailed International List]

AREA AND CAUSE OF DEATH	All deaths	January	February	March	April	May	June	July	August	September	October	November	December
Houston, Texas, all causes	**1,495**	**148**	**127**	**139**	**132**	**142**	**131**	**118**	**101**	**107**	**98**	**130**	**122**
Typhoid and paratyphoid fever (1, 2)	4				1			1	1			1	
Smallpox (6)													
Measles (7)													
Scarlet fever (8)													
Whooping-cough (9)	2							1				1	
Diphtheria (10)	2	1					1						
Influenza (11)	43	12	7	7	7	3	1				1	2	3
Dysentery (13)	4				1				1	1	1		
Erysipelas (15)													
Lethargic encephalitis (17)													
Epidemic cerebrospinal meningitis (18)	1					1							
Tuberculosis of the respiratory system (23)	118	18	10	11	11	15	9	9	9	6	7	8	5
Other forms of tuberculosis (24-32)	10	1			1			1	2	1		3	1
Malaria (38)	9	1					2	2	2	1			1
Diabetes mellitus (59)	22	3		6	2		5	1	1	1		2	1
Cerebral hemorrhage and softening (82a, 82c)	74	6	7	8	10	5	8	7	4	4	4	7	4
Diseases of the heart (90-95)	127	10	8	13	20	12	10	11	7	6	9	8	13
Bronchitis (106)	6			1		1		1				3	
Bronchopneumonia (107)	32	4	6	4	4	1	2	1	1	2	1	3	3
Lobar and unspecified pneumonia (108, 109)	97	13	10	12	9	5	10	2	4	4	6	11	11
Diarrhea and enteritis (under 2 years) (119)	43		2	2		10	4	6	9	3	3	1	3
Diarrhea and enteritis [2 years and over] (120)	12		2	1	1	3	2			2		1	
Nephritis (130-132)	87	11	8	7	3	8	5	11	4	7	3	10	10
Puerperal septicemia (140, 145)	15	2	3	4		1		1	2	1	1		
Other puerperal causes (141-144, 146-150)	10		2			2	1		3		1	1	
Suicide (163-171)	5					2		1	1				1
Automobile accidents [1]	26	3		1		2	2	4	1	1	3	6	3
Automobile—railroad train and street car collisions	3									3			
Other external causes	98	10	12	7	8	7	8	7	10	7	6	7	9
All other causes	645	53	50	55	54	64	61	51	39	57	52	55	54
Memphis, Tenn, all causes	**2,274**	**191**	**196**	**223**	**201**	**212**	**196**	**217**	**183**	**128**	**176**	**166**	**185**
Typhoid and paratyphoid fever (1, 2)	5					1		1	2				1
Smallpox (6)													
Measles (7)													
Scarlet fever (8)													
Whooping-cough (9)	9	1		1			2	2			2	1	
Diphtheria (10)	7		3							1	1	2	
Influenza (11)	43	7	4	11	5	5				1	2	2	6
Dysentery (13)	7	1	1				2	2		1			
Erysipelas (15)													
Lethargic encephalitis (17)	1									1			
Epidemic cerebrospinal meningitis (18)	105	3	9	30	33	10	7	4	2	1		3	3
Tuberculosis of the respiratory system (23)	229	19	16	25	27	22	18	24	16	20	17	10	15
Other forms of tuberculosis (24-32)	36	5	3	2	3	3	4	1	4	2	2	4	3
Malaria (38)	16	2			1	5	1	1	3	1	1	1	
Diabetes mellitus (59)	21		1	4	2	2	5	4	2	1			
Cerebral hemorrhage and softening (82a, 82c)	149	12	13	14	7	10	15	20	14	7	12	5	20
Diseases of the heart (90-95)	272	28	21	18	28	22	25	23	21	14	26	30	16
Bronchitis (106)	3	2				1							
Bronchopneumonia (107)	75	4	7	10	11	3	9	5	3	1	11	6	5
Lobar and unspecified pneumonia (108, 109)	75	10	7	15	6	3		1	3	1	10	5	14
Diarrhea and enteritis [under 2 years] (119)	17			2	2		2		4	3	2		2
Diarrhea and enteritis [2 years and over] (120)	19		1	2		4	4	3	1	1	2	1	
Nephritis (130-132)	158	14	15	13	6	17	8	14	16	10	17	13	15
Puerperal septicemia (140, 145)	13	1			3		2	1	2	1	2	1	
Other puerperal causes (141-144, 146-150)	16	3	1			2	1	2	3	3			1
Suicide (163-171)	3							1				1	1
Automobile accidents [1]	26	3	2	4		2	2	2		2	2	5	2
Automobile—railroad train and street car collisoins													
Other external causes	203	17	18	12	12	22	10	26	21	13	13	21	18
All other causes	766	59	74	60	55	78	79	80	66	43	54	55	63
New Orleans, La., all causes	**3,289**	**325**	**293**	**305**	**297**	**285**	**278**	**242**	**224**	**214**	**274**	**257**	**295**
Typhoid and paratyphoid fever (1, 2)	11			1	1	1	2	1			2		3
Smallpox (6)													
Measles (7)	11	2	1	5	2			1					
Scarlet fever (8)													
Whooping-cough (9)	14			1		1	1	1	1	1	5	3	
Diphtheria (10)	6			2			1		1			1	1
Influenza (11)	99	18	17	13	11	6	3	5	1	1	7	6	11
Dysentery (13)	5	2			1			1	1				
Erysipelas (15)													
Lethargic encephalitis (17)													
Epidemic cerebrospinal meningitis (18)	21	1	1	2	4	1	1	4	1	1		1	4
Tuberculosis of the respiratory system (23)	304	28	24	31	27	36	26	30	27	20	18	15	22
Other forms of tuberculosis (24-32)	22	4	1	2		3	1	1	1	5	1	2	1
Malaria (38)	1						1						
Diabetes mellitus (59)	25	7	4		4			1	1		3	1	4
Cerebral hemorrhage and softening (82a, 82c)	165	21	15	10	18	13	15	14	10	12	10	11	16
Diseases of the heart (90-95)	586	58	57	53	52	39	55	33	35	41	56	45	62
Bronchitis (106)	6			1			1		1	1	1		1
Bronchopneumonia (107)	190	32	24	17	13	19	17	7	13	7	11	13	17
Lobar and unspecified pneumonia (108, 109)	182	21	25	24	12	15	12	7	6	5	15	15	25
Diarrhea and enteritis [under 2 years] (119)	53	5	3	8	4	5	6	2	6	5	7	2	
Diarrhea and enteritis [2 years and over] (120)	14		1	1	2	2	3	2	1	2			
Nephritis (130-132)	369	25	35	35	37	38	33	26	28	22	33	31	26
Puerperal septicemia (140, 145)	21	1		3	3	2	3	1	1		2	1	4
Other puerperal causes (141-144, 146-150)	22	1	2	2		3	1	4	4	1		3	1
Suicide (163-171)	12	1			4	2				2	2	1	
Automobile accidents [1]	37	4	3	5	3	5	2	3		2	3	4	3
Automobile—railroad train and street car collisions	1					1							
Other external causes	161	14	4	17	14	15	15	15	9	13	14	8	23
All other causes	951	80	76	72	85	78	79	83	76	73	84	94	71

[1] Excludes collision with railroad trains and street cars.

TABLE 30.—COLORED DEATHS (EXCLUSIVE OF STILLBIRTHS) FROM IMPORTANT CAUSES, BY MONTHS, IN CITIES HAVING 50,000 OR MORE NEGRO INHABITANTS: 1930—Continued

[Colored deaths include Negro, nonwhite and other races. Numbers after causes of death correspond to those of the 1929 revision of the detailed International List]

AREA AND CAUSE OF DEATH	All deaths	January	February	March	April	May	June	July	August	September	October	November	December
New York, N. Y., all causes	**5,630**	**485**	**441**	**586**	**566**	**514**	**436**	**440**	**426**	**348**	**446**	**441**	**501**
Typhoid and paratyphoid fever (1, 2)	6		1		1			1			2		1
Smallpox (6)													
Measles (7)	18			1	3	10	2	1					1
Scarlet fever (8)													
Whooping-cough (9)	20	1		1			1	5	3	2	1	3	3
Diphtheria (10)	14	3	1	2	3				2	2			1
Influenza (11)	12	2	1	2	2		1		1		1		2
Dysentery (13)	1										1		
Erysipelas (15)	7			1	2	3	1						
Lethargic encephalitis (17)	4					2		1					1
Epidemic cerebrospinal meningitis (18)	33	2	1	5	5	2	3	2	2	1	4	3	3
Tuberculosis of the respiratory system (23)	913	66	58	104	79	93	67	81	90	77	61	62	75
Other forms of tuberculosis (24–32)	140	8	12	11	19	14	9	14	13	13	8	6	13
Malaria (38)													
Diabetes mellitus (59)	71	11	6	6	8	5	4	4	3	7	4	6	7
Cerebral hemorrhage and softening (82a, 82c)	153	15	8	14	15	14	14	8	9	7	16	18	15
Diseases of the heart (90–95)	880	74	75	99	94	71	73	55	51	56	76	64	92
Bronchitis (106)	13	3	1	1	1	1					2	1	3
Bronchopneumonia (107)	266	22	34	34	25	22	22	10	15	9	22	23	28
Lobar and unspecified pneumonia (108, 109)	502	55	54	64	75	67	33	18	16	15	27	41	37
Diarrhea and enteritis [under 2 years] (119)	94	3	8	9	12	7	6	10	11	5	8	12	3
Diarrhea and enteritis [2 years and over] (120)	8				1		2		3		1		1
Nephritis (130–132)	322	31	27	32	27	18	20	29	18	17	34	29	40
Puerperal septicemia (140, 145)	24	2	4	1	3	3	3	2	1		2	2	1
Other puerperal causes (141–144, 146–150)	48	3	3	3	5	2	5	5	6	4	4	2	6
Suicide (163–171)	47	6	5	5	5	2	3	4	5	3	2	4	3
Automobile accidents [1]	92	4	5	7	5	8	7	9	11	5	8	8	15
Automobile—railroad train and street car collisions	1								1				
Other external causes	364	29	34	36	21	22	29	39	33	30	31	31	29
All other causes	1,577	145	103	148	155	148	131	142	132	95	131	126	121
Philadelphia, Pa., all causes	**3,620**	**311**	**282**	**363**	**344**	**335**	**284**	**291**	**285**	**246**	**278**	**284**	**317**
Typhoid and paratyphoid fever (1, 2)	1												1
Smallpox (6)													
Measles (7)	2				1	1							
Scarlet fever (8)	6	1	1	1	3								
Whooping-cough (9)	7					2		2		1	1	1	
Diphtheria (10)	10	1	2	2	1	1	1	1					1
Influenza (11)	51	7	5	7	7	3	1	3	3	1	3	3	8
Dysentery (13)	2									1	1		
Erysipelas (15)	3				1	1							1
Lethargic encephalitis (17)	2			1								1	
Epidemic cerebrospinal meningitis (18)	12	1	2	1	3	1	1	2		1			
Tuberculosis of the respiratory system (23)	522	43	36	60	53	55	54	47	32	23	33	51	35
Other forms of tuberculosis (24–32)	52	3	2	1	10	5	3	5	10	2	4	4	3
Malaria (38)	2				1				1				
Diabetes mellitus (59)	47	5	4	2	4	4	3	5	3	2	5	4	6
Cerebral hemorrhage and softening (82a, 82c)	128	8	9	17	9	16	14	11	5	4	9	10	16
Diseases of the heart (90–95)	643	50	52	74	61	57	36	43	52	51	54	46	67
Bronchitis (106)	18	1	3	3	2		2	2		3	1	1	
Bronchopneumonia (107)	168	19	25	17	13	14	5	14	18	9	11	13	10
Lobar and unspecified pneumonia (108, 109)	263	30	32	36	31	27	10	11	8	9	13	28	28
Diarrhea and enteritis [under 2 years] (119)	88	1	4	2	7	2	3	7	11	18	15	12	6
Diarrhea and enteritis [2 years and over] (120)	21	3	2	1	1	1	2	6	1	3			1
Nephritis (130–132)	316	26	23	30	29	25	26	24	30	23	24	21	35
Puerperal septicemia (140, 145)	15		2	3	3		1	1	3	1	1		
Other puerperal causes (141–144, 146–150)	22	2	3		3	5	2		3		1	2	1
Suicide (163–171)	11			1	3		3	1		1		1	1
Automobile accidents [1]	31	5	2		2	3		2	1	2	3	4	7
Automobile—railroad train and street car collisions													
Other external causes	187	14	9	14	19	15	22	23	20	13	13	14	11
All other causes	990	91	64	90	77	97	95	81	84	78	86	68	79
Pittsburgh, Pa., all causes	**1,103**	**95**	**98**	**110**	**97**	**96**	**81**	**88**	**77**	**71**	**92**	**97**	**101**
Typhoid and paratyphoid fever (1, 2)													
Smallpox (6)													
Measles (7)	4			2		1	1						
Scarlet fever (8)	1				1								
Whooping-cough (9)	8		1	2		1	1	1	1		1		
Diphtheria (10)	6		3		1					1	1		
Influenza (11)	16	4	2	2	3	1					1		3
Dysentery (13)													
Erysipelas (15)													
Lethargic encephalitis (17)	1						1						
Epidemic cerebrospinal meningitis (18)	9	1	1		3		1	2					1
Tuberculosis of the respiratory system (23)	104	12	8	11	10	10	3	9	6	7	7	11	10
Other forms of tuberculosis (24–32)	14			1	3	1	1	1	1		1	3	2
Malaria (38)													
Diabetes mellitus (59)	9		2		1		1	1		2		2	
Cerebral hemorrhage and softening (82a, 82c)	51	6	3	7	4	2	1	4	3	7	4	4	6
Diseases of the heart (90–95)	149	8	10	14	14	19	7	16	9	7	16	15	14
Bronchitis (106)	4	1			1		1						1
Bronchopneumonia (107)	54	5	9	7	4	5	3	3	4	4	3	2	5
Lobar and unspecified pneumonia (108, 109)	189	20	19	23	18	13	20	8	13	11	15	16	13
Diarrhea and enteritis [under 2 years] (119)	16	1	1			1		1	3	3	4	1	1
Diarrhea and enteritis [2 years and over] (120)	8			1	1	1		1	2				2
Nephritis (130–132)	65	3	5	5	6	4	2	10	7	5	4	6	8
Puerperal septicemia (140, 145)	10	1	1	1	2						1	2	2
Other puerperal causes (141–144, 146–150)	8	1		1		1	1	1	1	1		1	
Suicide (163–171)	5	2				1				1	1		
Automobile accidents [1]	11	1			3	2	1	1	1			1	1
Automobile—railroad train and street car collisions													
Other external causes	73	9	10	4	4	8	4	7	7	4	2	7	7
All other causes	288	20	23	29	18	25	32	22	19	18	31	26	25

[1] Excludes collision with railroad trains and street cars.

TABLE 30.—COLORED DEATHS (EXCLUSIVE OF STILLBIRTHS) FROM IMPORTANT CAUSES, BY MONTHS, IN CITIES HAVING 50,000 OR MORE NEGRO INHABITANTS: 1930—Continued

[Colored deaths include Negro, nonwhite and other races. Numbers after causes of death correspond to those of the 1929 revision of the detailed International List]

AREA AND CAUSE OF DEATH	All deaths	January	February	March	April	May	June	July	August	September	October	November	December
Richmond, Va., all causes	**1,132**	**116**	**97**	**107**	**92**	**85**	**92**	**97**	**85**	**84**	**93**	**93**	**91**
Typhoid and paratyphoid fever (1, 2)	1								1				
Smallpox (6)													
Measles (7)													
Scarlet fever (8)	1									1			
Whooping-cough (9)	6	1		1	1					1	2		
Diphtheria (10)	5	1	2					1					1
Influenza (11)	25	5	4	5	2	2			1		1	1	4
Dysentery (13)													
Erysipelas (15)													
Lethargic encephalitis (17)	2		1		1								
Epidemic cerebrospinal meningitis (18)	8	1	1	1	1	1	1		1				1
Tuberculosis of the respiratory system (23)	84	4	4	9	2	10	11	8	6	10	9	5	6
Other forms of tuberculosis (24–32)	23	1	2	4	3		3	1	2	2	3	2	
Malaria (38)													
Diabetes mellitus (59)	10	2	1	1		1		1	1				3
Cerebral hemorrhage and softening (82a, 82c)	107	6	6	14	7	12	10	17	9	7	5	4	10
Diseases of the heart (90–95)	172	20	10	19	14	10	14	14	15	17	14	15	10
Bronchitis (106)	6	1	1		1			1	1		1		
Bronchopneumonia (107)	30	7	3	5	1	1		3		1		7	2
Lobar and unspecified pneumonia (108, 109)	66	11	13	9	7	6	3	3	2	1	2	4	5
Diarrhea and enteritis [under 2 years] (119)	15				1		2	3		3	3	2	1
Diarrhea and enteritis [2 years and ovr] (120)	5	1					2				1	1	
Nephritis (130–132)	126	7	11	12	14	8	12	11	11	5	8	16	11
Puerperal septicemia (140, 145)	5	1		1		2	1						
Other puerperal causes (141–144, 146–150)	9	2	1		2		1		2				1
Suicide (163–171)	6	1	1	1				1					2
Automobile accidents [1]	15		1	1			2	2	2	2	1	1	3
Automobile—railroad train and street car collisions	1								1				
Other external causes	58	2	10	2	7	5	1	4	9	7	8	2	1
All other causes	346	42	25	22	28	27	29	27	21	27	35	33	30
St. Louis, Mo., all causes	**1,982**	**165**	**160**	**182**	**181**	**170**	**172**	**198**	**156**	**136**	**153**	**146**	**163**
Typhoid and paratyphoid fever (1, 2)	2			1					1				
Smallpox (6)													
Measles (7)	6										1	2	3
Scarlet fever (8)													
Whooping-cough (9)	1						1						
Diphtheria (10)	2			1								1	
Influenza (11)	16	1	2	4	3	1	1			1	1	2	
Dysentery (13)													
Erysipelas (15)	3	2	1										
Lethargic encephalitis (17)	3	2	1										
Epidemic cerebrospinal meningitis (18)	16	4	2	2		3		1	3		1		
Tuberculosis of the respiratory system (23)	241	19	22	20	21	23	16	22	12	24	18	22	22
Other forms of tuberculosis (24–32)	38	4	6	5	1	8	3	2	1	1	5		2
Malaria (38)													
Diabetes mellitus (59)	18	1	2	1	3	2	2		2		1		4
Cerebral hemorrhage and softening (82a, 82c)	97	7	9	8	13	10	9	10	5	7	4	6	9
Diseases of the heart (90–95)	405	35	35	47	25	46	50	36	23	25	23	25	35
Bronchitis (106)	5	1						2					2
Bronchopneumonia (107)	91	5	7	10	11	8	6	11	6	4	9	8	6
Lobar and unspecified pneumonia (108, 109)	151	11	22	19	23	11	12	6	4	8	10	11	14
Diarrhea and enteritis [under 2 years] (119)	31	2	2	4	5		3	4	4	1	4	1	1
Diarrhea and enteritis [2 years and over] (120)	5				1				2	1	1		
Nephritis (130–132)	240	12	13	14	20	13	16	22	28	24	28	26	24
Puerperal septicemia (140, 145)	11	3				1	1	2		1	1	2	
Other puerperal causes (141–144, 146–150)	4			1	1							2	
Suicide (163–171)	3		1						2				
Automobile accidents [1]	23		1	1	2	4	2	4	2	3	2	1	1
Automobile—railroad train and street car collisions													
Other external causes	141	15	8	14	11	8	10	31	17	7	10	4	6
All other causes	429	41	26	30	41	32	40	45	44	29	34	33	34
Washington, D. C., all causes	**2,792**	**228**	**214**	**265**	**261**	**213**	**224**	**276**	**219**	**182**	**229**	**242**	**239**
Typhoid and paratyphoid fever (1, 2)	7					1		2	2	2			
Smallpox (6)													
Measles (7)													
Scarlet fever (8)	1												1
Whooping-cough (9)	12		2	2	3		2		1	2			
Diphtheria (10)	7	1	2						1		1		2
Influenza (11)	15	2	2	2				2			1	1	5
Dysentery (13)	3							1		1	1		
Erysipelas (15)	2		1	1									
Lethargic encephalitis (17)	1		1										
Epidemic cerebrospinal meningitis (18)	5					1	1				1	2	
Tuberculosis of the respiratory system (23)	303	17	23	23	29	26	34	30	30	15	29	24	23
Other forms of tuberculosis (24–32)	51	4	4	4	2	3	6	5	7	4	4	4	4
Malaria (38)													
Diabetes mellitus (59)	35	4	3	1	1	5	4	6	2	2	1	2	4
Cerebral hemorrhage and softening (82a, 82c)	140	14	14	10	16	8	10	17	13	12	8	8	10
Diseases of the heart (90–95)	533	51	37	53	50	51	44	44	38	34	40	42	49
Bronchitis (106)	10	2	1	1	3					1	1	1	
Bronchopneumonia (107)	142	16	12	18	23	10	7	6	9	4	8	20	9
Lobar and unspecified pneumonia (108, 109)	149	17	17	20	23	5	4	5	2	6	13	16	21
Diarrhea and enteritis [under 2 years] (119)	58				2	5	2	10	6	13	9	8	3
Diarrhea and enteritis [2 years and over] (120)	11	1	1	1			1	2	4	1			
Nephritis (130–132)	248	26	21	27	17	20	14	20	23	12	24	21	23
Puerperal septicemia (140, 145)	23	1	3	2		5	2	1		6	1	2	
Other puerperal causes (141–144, 146–150)	31	2	4	3	6	3	3	5	1			3	1
Suicide (163–171)	13		2		1	3		3		2	2		
Automobile accidents [1]	34	1	1	1	4	4	2	5	5	1	3	3	4
Automobile—railroad train and street car collisions													
Other external causes	126	7	6	6	10	15	19	15	10	8	5	11	14
All other causes	832	62	57	90	71	48	69	97	65	56	77	74	66

[1] Excludes collision with railroad trains and street cars.

CHAPTER XVII.—RETAIL BUSINESS

Negro proprietorship in retail business.—In this chapter are presented data collected at the first Nation-wide census of retail business in 1930 for the 1929 business operations of retail stores conducted by Negro proprietors in the United States. At the request of a number of organizations of colored people, stores operated by Negro proprietors are classified separately, and in all States in which there are enough such stores to justify analysis, the stores are classified by kind of business.

This census shows in the United States 25,701 stores operated by Negroes whose sales aggregate $101,146,043. The principal classifications are:

Grocery stores.
Filling stations.
Restaurants and lunch rooms.
Cigar stores and cigar stands.
Drug stores.

The figures given will form a basis by which the progress of the Negro in retail business may be measured from time to time. It is particularly fortunate that the base or reporting year was 1929, for no subsequent year to date would have provided what might be described as a normal comparison of the various kinds of business. The data will be particularly useful to retailers, wholesalers, manufacturers, publishers, advertisers, and students of retail business.

Scope of the retail census.—Retail business, as covered in this census, is the process of purveying goods to ultimate consumers for consumption or utilization, together with services incidental to the sale of goods. The function of the retailer is primarily to anticipate the wants of the consumer and to make available, at the right time and at a convenient place, a reasonable selection of goods capable of satisfying those wants. The distinguishing characteristic of a retailer is that the business is done in a retail manner, in a place of business open to the general public. The census does not include wholly service businesses, such as laundries, dry cleaners, barber shops, and the like, nor does it include the professions, such as medicine and law, nor does it include public utilities, such as water, gas, and electricity. Some semiservice businesses, such as garages, which sell a substantial amount of merchandise in addition to service, are included. In such cases the service income is included in the same total with the sale of merchandise. Bakeries, planing mills, power laundries, and cleaning and dyeing establishments for many years have been included in the census of manufactures, and therefore they were not reported by the enumerators as part of the retail census. Bakery-goods stores shown in the retail reports are those which do not produce their own goods, or which produce them in quantities too small to be included in the census of manufactures. Lumber yards which manufacture their own lumber and millwork are likewise excluded, as are hotel dining rooms.

How stores are classified.—The information in this report is shown under kind-of-business classifications. The business classification, although usually related broadly to the kind of merchandise carried, is not synonymous with a merchandise or commodity classification. For instance, grocery-store sales are not exclusively sales of groceries; ready-to-wear stores sell accessories and sometimes shoes in addition to outer apparel; drug stores sell many lines other than drugs; furniture stores sell floor coverings and electric household appliances, and department stores sell furniture. Stores are classified according to their principal commodities or according to their popular designation.

Analyzing a $12,000 store.—In most kinds of business the gross margin on a $12,000 volume of sales ranges between $2,500 and $3,500, and the average does not exceed $3,000. That is, the cost of the merchandise which must be replaced as it is sold is about $9,000, and $3,000 is left to cover all expenses.

About $750 of this $3,000 is required for insurance, taxes, repairs, and upkeep of premises, light, heat, power, communication, occasional advertising, and other essential and unavoidable operating expenses, before taking into consideration the largest items of expense, which are pay roll and rent. Rent averages more than 4 percent of sales, or about $500 a year for a business doing $12,000. It makes little difference in this expense whether the premises are leased and the expense is actually in the form of rent, or whether the premises are owned by the proprietor and the equivalent of rent must be met in the form of fixed charges, depreciation, and interest. More than 72 percent of the total business in the country is done in leased premises.

The $500 for rent and $750 for essential operating expenses leave a margin of about $1,750 for pay roll and possible profit. A store doing $12,000 of business requires at least two sales people. If the proprietor and members of his family are competent to serve in this capacity, it is possible for them jointly to realize from the business a total income of the full $1,750. If the proprietor alone works in the store, he must reinforce his own services with services of one full-time employee and usually one part-timer. The proprietor then realizes, for his own services and as a profit on his working capital, only that part of the $1,750, which is left after paying the wages of his employees.

It is evident, therefore, that even an efficiently operated $12,000 store can provide but a limited wage for any of the people employed in it, whether they are employees or members of the family or the proprietor himself.

Why very small stores can survive.—Competition in the retail business is severe, and as in any kind of merchandise there is just enough margin between the average purchase price and the retail price to cover the necessary operating expenses of the average store. Stores making a profit are those which can purchase below the average price or can operate below the average ratio of expense. The very small retailer who is merely turning over goods bought in the same form in which they are sold is restrained by competition

SALES OF EACH GROUP OF STORES

SALES OF EACH GROUP OF STORES IN PROPORTION TO THE SALES OF ALL STORES IN THE UNITED STATES

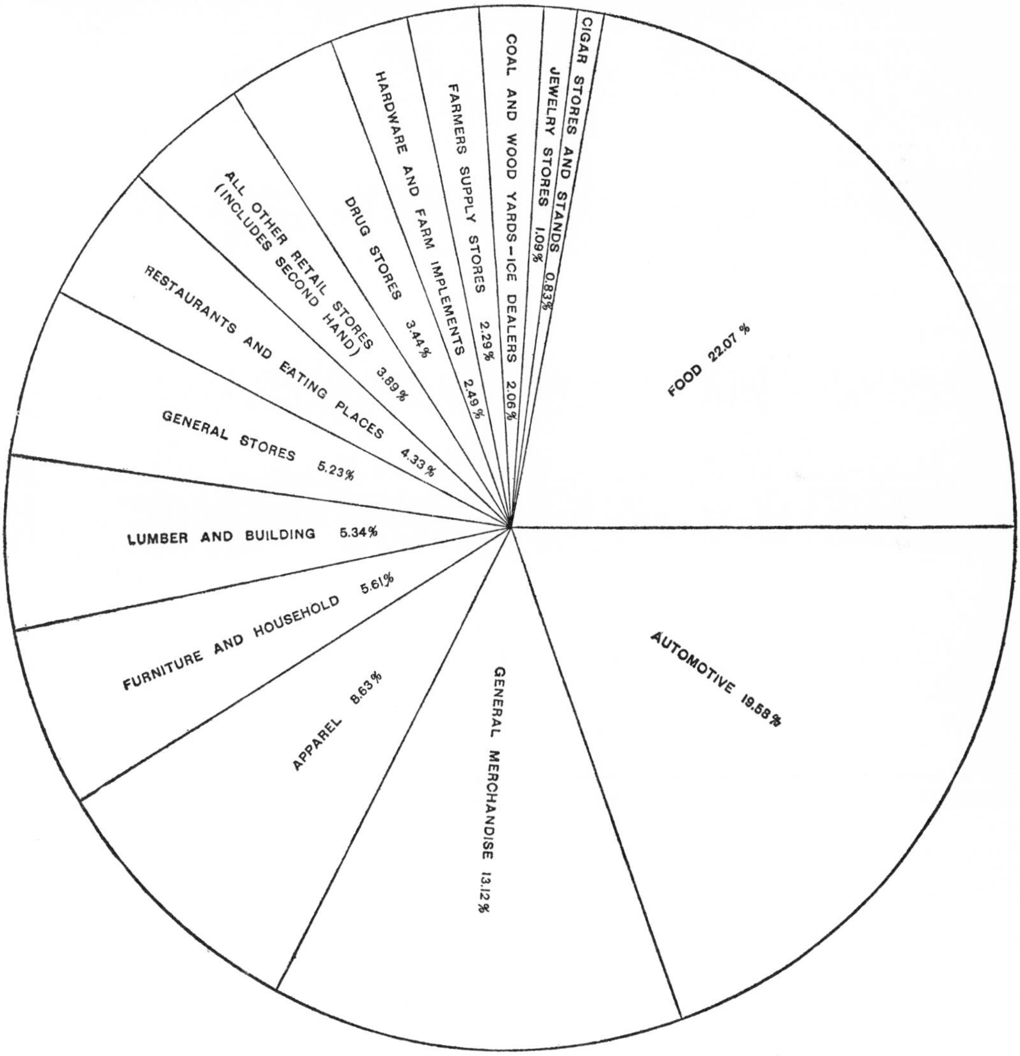

(1,543,158 STORES WITH SALES OF $49,114,653,269)

NEGRO PROPRIETORSHIP—SALES OF EACH GROUP OF STORES

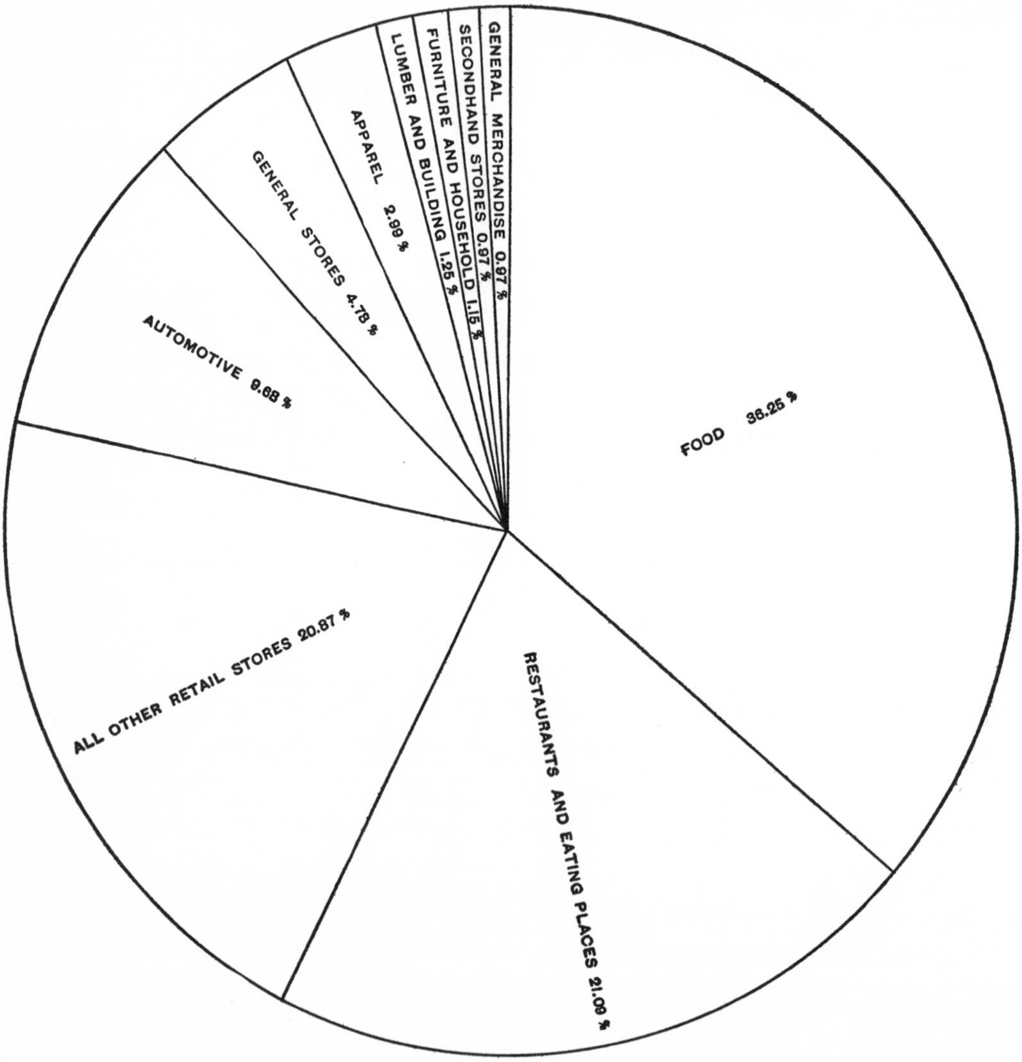

25,701 STORES WITH SALES OF $101,146,043

to about the average selling price, unless he operates in noncompetitive neighborhood locations or in hours when competing stores are closed. But there is nothing except his own ingenuity and sound credit standing to hold down the cost of the goods which he must purchase, and nothing but his own ability to hold down operating expenses.

Every mistake in buying or in selling, and every expense incurred, necessarily must be met from the slim margin between the selling price and the replacement cost of the goods, when nothing but merchandise is sold. But when the selling price includes a margin for processing or converting the goods into a form other than that in which they are bought, or when the income consists of the sale of services primarily, and supplies incidentally, the business provides a much larger margin for the services of the proprietor. The heavy mortality in small stores comes from the other class—those who depend solely upon the sale of merchandise in the same form in which it is bought.

TABLE 1.—RETAIL BUSINESS, BY SPECIFIED RACIAL CLASSES, FOR THE UNITED STATES: 1929

POPULATION, NUMBER OF STORES, PERSONNEL, PAY ROLL, STOCKS, AND SALES

CLASS OR RACE	Population [1]	Number of stores	Proprietors and firm members (*not on pay roll*)	Number of employees (*full time*)	Total pay roll (*including part time*)	Stocks on hand, end of year (*at cost*)	Net sales
United States	122,775,046	1,543,158	1,510,607	3,833,581	$5,189,669,960	$7,262,582,920	$49,114,653,269
Negro	11,891,143	25,701	28,243	12,561	8,528,306	10,657,000	101,146,043
Oriental mutuals [2]	213,788	3,865	6,432	8,926	9,022,555	10,165,470	88,578,405
White [3]	110,670,115	1,513,592	1,475,932	3,812,094	5,172,119,099	7,241,760,450	48,924,928,821
	PERCENT DISTRIBUTION						
United States	100.00	100.00	100.00	100.00	100.00	100.00	100.00
Negro	9.69	1.67	1.87	.33	.16	.15	.21
Oriental mutuals [2]	.17	.25	.43	.23	.17	.14	.18
White [3]	90.14	98.08	97.70	99.44	99.67	99.71	99.61

[1] Enumerated Apr. 1, 1930. [2] Chinese and Japanese proprietors only. [3] Includes all other races.

TABLE 2.—STORES OPERATED BY NEGRO PROPRIETORS, FOR THE UNITED STATES, BY SECTIONS AND DIVISIONS: 1929

POPULATION, NUMBER OF STORES, PERSONNEL, PAY ROLL, STOCKS, AND SALES

SECTION AND DIVISION	Negro population [1]	Number of stores	Proprietors and firm members (*not on pay roll*)	Number of employees (*full time*)	Total pay roll (*including part time*)	Stocks on hand, end of year (*at cost*)	Net sales
United States	11,891,143	25,701	28,243	12,561	$8,528,306	$10,657,000	$101,146,043
THE SOUTH	9,361,577	18,864	20,753	7,762	4,333,477	6,335,200	57,036,307
South Atlantic	4,421,388	9,622	10,412	3,516	2,097,912	3,175,340	27,347,636
East South Central	2,658,238	4,359	4,839	2,050	1,046,500	1,351,960	13,248,290
West South Central	2,281,951	4,883	5,502	2,196	1,189,065	1,807,900	16,440,381
THE NORTH	2,409,219	6,475	7,081	4,371	3,760,864	4,025,100	40,335,397
New England	94,086	232	254	143	173,286	231,710	1,929,224
Middle Atlantic	1,052,899	2,514	2,709	1,464	1,364,432	1,609,400	14,883,293
East North Central	930,450	2,728	3,009	1,980	1,640,070	1,471,150	17,191,719
West North Central	331,784	1,001	1,109	784	583,076	712,840	6,331,161
THE WEST	120,347	362	409	428	433,965	296,700	3,774,339
Mountain	30,225	68	79	71	62,201	47,870	557,044
Pacific	90,122	294	330	357	371,764	248,830	3,217,295
	PERCENT DISTRIBUTION						
United States	100.00	100.00	100.00	100.00	100.00	100.00	100.00
THE SOUTH	78.73	73.40	73.48	61.79	50.81	59.45	56.39
South Atlantic	37.18	37.44	36.87	27.99	24.60	29.80	27.04
East South Central	22.35	16.96	17.13	16.32	12.27	12.69	13.10
West South Central	19.19	19.00	19.48	17.48	13.94	16.96	16.25
THE NORTH	20.26	25.19	25.07	34.80	44.10	37.77	39.88
New England	.79	.90	.90	1.14	2.03	2.17	1.91
Middle Atlantic	8.85	9.78	9.59	11.66	16.00	15.10	14.71
East North Central	7.82	10.61	10.65	15.76	19.23	13.80	17.00
West North Central	2.79	3.89	3.93	6.24	6.84	6.69	6.26
THE WEST	1.01	1.41	1.45	3.41	5.09	2.78	3.73
Mountain	.25	.26	.28	.57	.73	.45	.55
Pacific	.76	1.14	1.17	2.84	4.36	2.33	3.18

[1] Enumerated Apr. 1, 1930

TABLE 3.—NET SALES OF STORES OPERATED BY NEGRO PROPRIETORS, FOR THE UNITED STATES, BY SECTIONS, AND DIVISIONS: 1929

SECTION AND DIVISION	Number of stores	NET SALES	
		Amount	Average per store
United States	**25, 701**	**$101, 146, 043**	**$3, 935**
THE SOUTH	18, 864	57, 036, 307	3, 024
South Atlantic	9, 622	27, 347, 636	2, 842
East South Central	4, 359	13, 248, 290	3, 039
West South Central	4, 883	16, 440, 381	3, 367
THE NORTH	6, 475	40, 335, 397	6, 229
New England	232	1, 929, 224	8, 316
Middle Atlantic	2, 514	14, 883, 293	5, 920
East North Central	2, 728	17, 191, 719	6, 302
West North Central	1, 001	6, 331, 161	6, 325
THE WEST	362	3, 774, 339	10, 426
Mountain	68	557, 044	8, 192
Pacific	294	3, 217, 295	10, 943

TABLE 4.—PAY ROLL AND WAGE COST (PERCENT OF TOTAL SALES) IN RETAIL STORES OPERATED BY NEGRO PROPRIETORS, FOR THE UNITED STATES, BY SECTIONS, AND DIVISIONS: 1929

SECTION AND DIVISION	Total annual pay roll	Wage cost (*percent of total sales*)
United States	**$8, 528, 306**	**8. 43**
THE SOUTH	4, 333, 477	7. 60
South Atlantic	2, 097, 912	7. 67
East South Central	1, 046, 500	7. 90
West South Central	1, 189, 065	7. 23
THE NORTH	3, 760, 864	9. 32
New England	173, 286	8. 98
Middle Atlantic	1, 364, 432	9. 17
East North Central	1, 640, 070	9. 54
West North Central	583, 076	9. 21
THE WEST	433, 965	11. 50
Mountain	62, 201	11. 17
Pacific	371, 764	11. 56

TABLE 5.—STORES OPERATED BY NEGRO PROPRIETORS BY STATES: 1929

STATE	RANKED BY—				
	Population [1]	Number of stores	Stocks on hand, end of year (*at cost*)	NET SALES: Per capita of Negro population	NET SALES: Average per store
Georgia	1	1	7	44	47
Mississippi	2	6	12	46	43
Alabama	3	9	11	45	42
North Carolina	4	2	2	40	41
Texas	5	4	4	38	36
South Carolina	6	10	21	48	49
Louisiana	7	5	13	42	44
Virginia	8	3	1	39	45
Arkansas	9	13	15	43	46
Tennessee	10	12	16	37	35
Florida	11	7	8	33	38
Pennsylvania	12	8	3	26	29
New York	13	16	6	30	13
Illinois	14	11	5	19	23
Ohio	15	14	9	29	25
Maryland	16	20	25	41	39
Kentucky	17	15	18	35	40
Missouri	18	18	17	28	26
New Jersey	19	17	14	31	30
Oklahoma	20	19	10	24	28
Michigan	21	21	19	17	19
District of Columbia	22	25	27	32	22
West Virginia	23	23	22	34	37
Indiana	24	22	24	23	24
California	25	24	20	11	6
Kansas	26	26	23	22	27
Massachusetts	27	27	26	18	10
Delaware	28	29	35	36	33
Connecticut	29	30	31	27	20
Iowa	30	31	32	12	7

TABLE 5.—STORES OPERATED BY NEGRO PROPRIETORS BY STATES: 1929—Continued

STATE	RANKED BY—				
	Population [1]	Number of stores	Stocks on hand, end of year (*at cost*)	NET SALES: Per capita of Negro population	NET SALES: Average per store
Nebraska	31	32	29	13	14
Colorado	32	34	37	14	17
Arizona	33	40	48	47	32
Wisconsin	34	33	30	7	11
Rhode Island	35	35	33	20	31
Minnesota	36	28	28	6	16
Washington	37	36	40	16	9
New Mexico	38	49	49	49	48
Oregon	39	38	34	3	2
Montana	40	41	43	9	15
Wyoming	41	46	44	21	18
Utah	42	42	39	5	3
Maine	43	43	46	8	5
New Hampshire	44	44	42	10	21
Idaho	45	47	45	15	12
South Dakota	46	39	36	2	8
Vermont	47	45	41	4	1
Nevada	48	48	47	25	34
North Dakota	49	37	38	1	4

[1] Enumerated April 1, 1930.

TABLE 6.—PAY ROLL AND WAGE COST (PERCENT OF TOTAL SALES) IN RETAIL STORES OPERATED BY NEGRO PROPRIETORS, BY KIND OF BUSINESS, FOR THE UNITED STATES: 1929

KIND OF BUSINESS	Total annual pay roll	Wage cost (*percent of total sales*)
Total	**$8, 528, 306**	**8. 43**
Food group	1, 341, 671	3. 66
Candy and confectionery stores	124, 841	4. 83
Grocery stores (without meats)	336, 608	2. 29
Combination stores (groceries and meats)	520, 643	3. 81
Meat markets (including sea foods)	188, 200	6. 65
Other food stores	171, 379	5. 95
General stores—groceries with dry goods, apparel, or general merchandise	151, 947	3. 15
General-merchandise group	67, 496	6. 89
Dry-goods stores	27, 418	7. 19
General-merchandise stores	31, 048	6. 81
Variety, 5-and-10, and to-a-dollar stores	9, 030	6. 34
Automotive group	1, 058, 269	10. 81
Motor-vehicle dealers (new and used)	245, 535	7. 80
Filling stations	258, 220	7. 53
Garages and repair shops	481, 317	18. 92
Other automotive establishments	73, 197	10. 93
Apparel group	322, 620	10. 65
Men's and boys' clothing and furnishings stores	59, 816	6. 53
Family clothing stores—men's, women's, and children's	29, 295	6. 86
Women's ready-to-wear specialty stores—apparel and accessories	28, 237	8. 94
Women's accessories stores	32, 649	10. 58
Other apparel stores	139, 385	19. 47
Shoe stores	33, 238	9. 62
Furniture and household group	133, 500	11. 51
Furniture stores	56, 410	14. 07
Floor coverings, drapery, curtain, and upholstery stores	3, 588	18. 45
Household-appliances stores	500	6. 41
Other home-furnishings and appliances stores	15, 414	19. 42
Radio and music stores	57, 588	8. 83
Restaurants and eating places	2, 727, 883	12. 79
Restaurants, cafeterias, and lunch rooms	2, 358, 331	13. 64
Lunch counters, refreshment stands, etc	369, 552	9. 13
Lumber and building group	202, 778	15. 99
Lumber and building-material dealers	73, 175	12. 42
Electrical shops (without radio)	36, 565	22. 87
Heating and plumbing shops	69, 147	19. 50
Paint and glass stores	23, 891	14. 53
Other retail stores	2, 411, 120	11. 42
Hardware stores	34, 606	7. 27
Hardware and farm-implement stores	20, 286	6. 05
Farmers' supplies	45, 880	4. 94
Book stores	4, 933	9. 37
Cigar stores and cigar stands	236, 597	11. 52
Coal and wood yards—ice dealers	250, 079	11. 81
Drug stores	790, 465	10. 90
Jewelry stores	45, 596	11. 74
Miscellaneous classifications (combined)	982, 678	13. 09
Second-hand stores	111, 022	11. 29

TABLE 7.—KIND OF RETAIL BUSINESS, REPORTING NET SALES OF $1,000,000 AND OVER, OPERATED BY NEGRO PROPRIETORS IN THE UNITED STATES: 1929

NUMBER OF STORES, PERSONNEL, PAY ROLL, STOCKS, AND SALES

KIND OF BUSINESS	Number of stores	Proprietors and firm members (*not on pay roll*)	Number of employees (*full time*)	Total pay roll (*including part time*)	Stocks on hand, end of year (*at cost*)	NET SALES: Amount	NET SALES: Percent of total	NET SALES: Average per store
United States, total	**25,701**	**28,243**	**12,561**	**$8,528,306**	**$10,657,000**	**$101,146,043**	**100.0**	**$3,935**
Principal kinds of business, total	22,969	24,979	10,398	6,483,714	7,541,310	83,372,335	82.4	3,630
Grocery stores	8,450	9,118	1,475	857,251	2,857,690	28,369,178	28.0	3,357
Restaurants, cafeterias, and lunch rooms	5,729	6,209	4,742	2,358,331	431,950	17,284,126	17.1	3,017
Drug stores	712	852	955	790,465	1,566,750	7,253,921	7.2	10,188
General stores—groceries with dry goods, apparel, or general merchandise	761	892	229	151,947	1,161,880	4,828,700	4.8	6,345
Lunch counters, refreshment stands, etc.	2,189	2,321	683	369,552	140,100	4,049,072	4.0	1,850
Filling stations (automobile)	799	869	302	258,220	217,100	3,429,826	3.4	4,293
Motor-vehicle dealers (automobile—new and used)	39	46	166	245,535	331,750	3,149,837	3.1	80,765
All other food stores	631	707	182	171,379	107,290	2,880,145	2.8	4,564
Meat markets (including sea foods)	537	576	252	188,200	68,150	2,829,147	2.8	5,268
Candy and confectionery stores	1,137	1,193	230	124,841	207,480	2,584,053	2.6	2,273
Garages and repair shops	732	838	525	481,317	184,310	2,543,898	2.5	3,475
Coal and wood yards—ice dealers	549	594	337	250,079	125,900	2,117,474	2.1	3,857
Cigar stores and cigar stands	704	764	320	236,597	140,960	2,052,958	2.0	2,916

TABLE 8.—STORES OPERATED BY NEGRO PROPRIETORS, BY KIND OF BUSINESS, FOR THE UNITED STATES: 1929

NUMBER OF STORES, PERSONNEL, PAY ROLL, STOCKS, AND SALES

KIND OF BUSINESS	Number of stores	Proprietors and firm members (*not on pay roll*)	Number of employees (*full time*)	Total pay roll (*including part-time*)	Stocks on hand end of year (*at cost*)	NET SALES: Amount	NET SALES: Percent of total
Total	**25,701**	**28,243**	**12,561**	**$8,528,306**	**$10,657,000**	**$101,146,043**	**100.00**
Food group	10,755	11,594	2,139	1,341,671	3,240,610	36,662,523	36.25
Candy and confectionery stores	1,137	1,193	230	124,841	207,480	2,584,053	2.55
Grocery stores (without meats)	6,248	6,690	707	336,608	1,709,750	14,714,500	14.55
Combination stores (groceries and meats)	2,202	2,428	768	520,643	1,147,940	13,654,678	13.50
Meat markets (including sea foods)	537	576	252	188,200	68,150	2,829,147	2.80
All other food stores	631	707	182	171,379	107,290	2,880,145	2.85
General stores—groceries with dry goods, apparel, or general merchandise	761	892	229	151,947	1,161,880	4,828,700	4.78
General merchandise group	128	153	81	67,496	323,790	979,799	.97
Dry goods stores	61	76	33	27,418	165,900	381,111	.38
General merchandise stores	37	47	37	31,048	139,270	456,156	.45
Variety, 5-and-10, and to-a-dollar stores	30	30	11	9,030	18,620	142,532	.14
Automotive group	1,679	1,873	1,059	1,058,269	819,040	9,793,196	9.68
Motor-vehicle dealers (new and used)	39	46	166	245,535	331,750	3,149,837	3.11
Filling stations	799	869	302	258,220	217,100	3,429,826	3.39
Garages and repair shops	732	838	525	481,317	184,310	2,543,898	2.52
Other automotive establishments	109	120	66	73,197	85,880	669,635	.66
Apparel group	477	519	355	322,620	698,830	3,027,917	2.99
Men's and boys' clothing and furnishings stores	66	71	59	59,816	266,660	915,500	.90
Family clothing stores—men's, women's, and children's	32	37	27	29,295	149,040	426,756	.42
Women's ready-to-wear specialty stores—apparel and accessories	57	62	33	28,237	72,290	315,762	.31
Women's accessories stores	54	57	28	32,649	56,080	308,710	.31
Other apparel stores	220	240	176	139,385	62,960	715,764	.71
Shoe stores	48	52	32	33,238	91,800	345,425	.34
Furniture and household group	149	174	125	133,500	240,290	1,160,120	1.15
Furniture stores	54	62	53	56,410	104,250	401,056	.40
Floor coverings, drapery, curtain, and upholstery stores	7	7	6	3,588	2,220	19,450	.02
Household appliances stores	3	3	1	500	1,030	7,800	.01
Other home furnishings and appliances stores	30	33	19	15,414	25,770	79,364	.08
Radio and music stores	55	69	46	57,588	107,020	652,450	.64
Restaurants and eating places	7,918	8,530	5,425	2,727,883	572,050	21,333,198	21.09
Restaurants, cafeterias, and lunch rooms	5,729	6,209	4,742	2,358,331	431,950	17,284,126	17.09
Lunch counters, refreshment stands, etc.	2,189	2,321	683	369,552	140,100	4,049,072	4.00
Lumber and building group	96	112	170	202,778	180,380	1,268,024	1.25
Lumber and building material dealers	26	31	72	73,175	98,070	589,155	.58
Electrical shops (without radio)	23	29	30	36,565	18,010	159,862	.16
Heating and plumbing shops	26	30	45	69,147	29,020	354,537	.35
Paint and glass stores	21	22	23	23,891	35,280	164,470	.16
Other retail stores	3,365	3,994	2,858	2,411,120	3,231,540	21,109,630	20.87
Hardware stores	40	49	22	34,606	179,110	476,048	.47
Hardware and farm implement stores	11	16	22	20,286	92,160	335,348	.33
Farmers' supplies	107	123	50	45,880	97,850	927,859	.92
Book stores	8	9	9	4,933	22,120	52,661	.05
Cigar stores and cigar stands	704	764	320	236,597	140,960	2,052,958	2.03
Coal and wood yards—ice dealers	549	594	337	250,079	125,900	2,117,474	2.09
Drug stores	712	852	955	790,465	1,566,750	7,253,921	7.17
Jewelry stores	67	74	33	45,596	231,650	388,282	.39
Miscellaneous classifications (combined)	1,167	1,513	1,110	982,678	775,040	7,505,079	7.42
Second-hand stores	373	402	120	111,022	188,590	982,936	.97

TABLE 9.—STORES OPERATED BY NEGRO PROPRIETORS, BY SECTIONS, DIVISIONS, AND STATES: 1929

POPULATION, NUMBER OF STORES, PERSONNEL, PAY ROLL, STOCKS, AND SALES

[An (x) indicates that the amount must be withheld to avoid disclosure of individual operations, but it is included in the totals]

DIVISION OR STATE	Negro population[1]	Number of stores	Proprietors and firm members (*not on pay roll*)	Number of employees (*full time*)	Total pay roll (*including part time*)	Stocks on hand, end of year (*at cost*)	NET SALES			
							Amount	Percent distribution	Per capita of Negro population	Average per store
United States	**11,891,143**	**25,701**	**28,243**	**12,561**	**$8,528,306**	**$10,657,000**	**$101,146,043**	**100.00**	**$8.51**	**$3,935**
The North	2,409,219	6,475	7,081	4,371	3,760,864	4,025,100	40,335,397	39.88	16.74	6,229
The South	9,361,577	18,864	20,753	7,762	4,333,477	6,335,200	57,036,307	56.39	6.09	3,024
The West	120,347	362	409	428	433,965	296,700	3,774,339	3.73	31.36	10,426
GEOGRAPHIC DIVISIONS:										
New England	94,086	232	254	143	173,286	231,710	1,929,224	1.91	20.50	8,316
Middle Atlantic	1,052,899	2,514	2,709	1,464	1,364,432	1,609,400	14,883,293	14.71	14.14	5,920
East North Central	930,450	2,728	3,009	1,980	1,640,070	1,471,150	17,191,719	17.00	18.48	6,302
West North Central	331,784	1,001	1,109	784	583,076	712,840	6,331,161	6.26	19.08	6,325
South Atlantic	4,421,388	9,622	10,412	3,516	2,097,912	3,175,340	27,347,636	27.04	6.19	2,842
East South Central	2,658,238	4,359	4,839	2,050	1,046,500	1,351,960	13,248,290	13.10	4.98	3,039
West South Central	2,281,951	4,883	5,502	2,196	1,189,065	1,807,900	16,440,381	16.25	7.20	3,367
Mountain	30,225	68	79	71	62,201	47,870	557,044	.55	18.43	8,192
Pacific	90,122	294	330	357	371,764	248,830	3,217,295	3.18	35.70	10,943
NEW ENGLAND:										
Maine	1,096	4	5	2	4,689	2,300	46,917	.05	42.81	11,729
New Hampshire	790	4	4	5	4,005	5,950	26,791	.03	33.91	6,698
Vermont	568	3	5	4	4,286	9,830	76,462	.08	134.62	25,487
Massachusetts	52,365	121	135	86	98,139	123,380	1,149,686	1.14	21.96	9,502
Rhode Island	9,913	41	43	16	22,485	39,310	194,469	.19	19.62	4,743
Connecticut	29,354	59	62	30	39,682	50,940	434,899	.43	14.82	7,371
MIDDLE ATLANTIC:										
New York	412,814	611	682	510	500,533	564,790	5,625,743	5.56	13.63	9,207
New Jersey	208,828	577	624	294	264,386	349,900	2,737,685	2.71	13.11	4,745
Pennsylvania	431,257	1,326	1,403	660	599,513	694,710	6,519,865	6.45	15.12	4,917
EAST NORTH CENTRAL:										
Ohio	309,304	790	870	498	415,958	433,170	4,411,775	4.36	14.26	5,585
Indiana	111,982	342	383	260	189,328	131,350	2,021,677	2.00	18.05	5,911
Illinois	328,972	1,058	1,136	696	602,798	622,740	6,466,323	6.39	19.66	6,112
Michigan	169,453	488	563	465	379,949	229,970	3,817,530	3.77	22.53	7,823
Wisconsin	10,739	50	57	61	52,037	53,920	474,414	.47	44.18	9,488
WEST NORTH CENTRAL:										
Minnesota	9,445	71	86	72	54,410	100,870	585,676	.58	62.01	8,249
Iowa	17,380	57	64	54	44,543	48,630	573,577	.57	33.00	10,063
Missouri	223,840	575	628	453	315,947	290,470	3,200,109	3.16	14.30	5,565
North Dakota	377	15	16	11	9,735	17,920	198,584	.20	526.75	13,239
South Dakota	646	13	14	15	18,319	23,940	129,862	.13	201.02	9,989
Nebraska	13,752	52	60	55	34,782	86,160	435,433	.43	31.66	8,374
Kansas	66,344	218	241	124	105,340	144,850	1,207,920	1.19	18.21	5,541
SOUTH ATLANTIC:										
Delaware	32,602	61	62	27	[1] 18,811	27,780	260,766	.26	8.00	4,275
Maryland	276,379	515	525	198	164,492	125,700	1,690,747	1.67	6.12	3,283
District of Columbia	132,068	244	284	195	162,063	102,820	1,495,854	1.48	11.33	6,131
Virginia	650,165	1,878	2,043	645	378,446	885,720	4,986,347	4.93	7.67	2,655
West Virginia	114,893	310	344	177	117,419	160,070	1,169,006	1.16	10.17	3,771
North Carolina	918,647	1,907	2,077	577	369,369	707,720	5,770,830	5.71	6.28	3,026
South Carolina	793,681	1,230	1,320	350	180,739	201,010	2,298,672	2.27	2.90	1,869
Georgia	1,071,125	2,099	2,253	763	380,600	525,970	5,147,040	5.09	4.81	2,452
Florida	431,828	1,378	1,504	584	325,973	438,550	4,528,374	4.48	10.49	3,286
EAST SOUTH CENTRAL:										
Kentucky	226,040	683	778	310	191,080	260,760	2,144,159	2.12	9.49	3,139
Tennessee	477,646	973	1,100	537	311,748	327,960	3,728,674	3.69	7.81	3,832
Alabama	944,834	1,297	1,406	643	264,895	393,280	3,566,565	3.53	3.77	2,750
Mississippi	1,009,718	1,406	1,555	560	278,777	369,960	3,808,892	3.77	3.77	2,709
WEST SOUTH CENTRAL:										
Arkansas	478,463	933	1,029	300	144,416	343,450	2,468,727	2.44	5.16	2,646
Louisiana	776,326	1,668	1,884	577	262,787	369,770	4,504,809	4.45	5.80	2,701
Oklahoma	172,198	546	626	320	211,888	419,040	2,833,144	2.80	16.45	5,189
Texas	854,964	1,736	1,963	999	569,974	675,640	6,633,701	6.56	7.76	3,821
MOUNTAIN:										
Montana	1,256	6	7	7	6,036	5,730	49,497	.05	39.41	8,250
Idaho	668	2	(x)	(x)	(x)	(x)	(x)	(x)	(x)	(x)
Wyoming	1,250	3	3	4	4,678	3,250	24,176	.02	19.34	8,059
Colorado	11,828	41	49	44	39,827	20,100	335,893	.33	28.40	8,193
New Mexico	2,850	1	(x)	(x)	(x)	(x)	(x)	(x)	(x)	(x)
Arizona	10,749	8	9	11	7,754	670	34,283	.03	3.19	4,285
Utah	1,108	5	6	5	2,951	14,500	83,945	.08	75.76	16,789
Nevada	516	2	(x)	(x)	(x)	(x)	(x)	(x)	(x)	(x)
PACIFIC:										
Washington	6,840	18	21	18	17,899	10,440	175,521	0.17	25.66	9,751
Oregon	2,234	14	16	27	34,036	34,310	329,541	0.33	147.51	23,539
California	81,048	262	293	312	319,829	204,080	2,712,233	2.68	33.46	10,352

[1] Enumerated Apr. 1, 1930.

TABLE 10.—KIND OF RETAIL BUSINESS OPERATED BY NEGRO PROPRIETORS, FOR STATES REPORTING NET SALES OF $500,000 AND OVER: 1929

STATE AND KIND OF BUSINESS	NET SALES	
	Amount	Percent of total
TEXAS		
All business, total	$6,633,701	100.0
Principal kinds of business	3,559,382	53.7
Grocery stores	1,714,933	25.9
Restaurants, cafeterias, and lunch rooms	1,300,351	19.6
Drug stores	544,098	8.2
PENNSYLVANIA		
All business, total	6,519,865	100.0
Principal kinds of business	2,801,063	42.9
Restaurants, cafeterias, and lunch rooms	1,032,603	15.8
Motor-vehicle dealers (automobile—new and used)	996,095	15.3
Grocery stores	772,365	11.8
ILLINOIS		
All business, total	6,466,323	100.0
Principal kinds of business	2,893,301	44.8
Grocery stores	1,309,911	20.3
Restaurants, cafeterias, and lunch rooms	905,149	14.0
Drug stores	678,241	10.5
NORTH CAROLINA		
All business, total	5,770,830	100.0
Principal kinds of business	2,970,540	51.5
Grocery stores	2,290,317	39.7
Restaurants, cafeterias, and lunch rooms	680,223	11.8
NEW YORK		
All business, total	5,625,743	100.0
Principal kinds of business	2,343,692	41.7
Grocery stores	1,028,109	18.3
Restaurants, cafeterias, and lunch rooms	1,315,583	23.4
GEORGIA		
All business, total	5,147,040	100.0
Principal kinds of business	2,849,982	55.4
Grocery stores	2,120,587	41.2
Restaurants, cafeterias, and lunch rooms	729,395	14.2
VIRGINIA		
All business, total	4,986,347	100.0
Principal kinds of business	2,341,082	46.9
Grocery stores	1,660,710	33.3
General stores—groceries with dry goods, apparel, or general merchandise	680,372	13.6
FLORIDA		
All business, total	4,528,374	100.0
Principal kinds of business	2,590,385	57.2
Grocery stores	1,833,213	40.5
Restaurants, cafeterias, and lunch rooms	757,172	16.7
LOUISIANA		
All business, total	4,504,809	100.0
Principal kinds of business	2,044,715	45.4
Grocery stores	1,253,535	27.8
Restaurants, cafeterias, and lunch rooms	791,180	17.6
OHIO		
All business, total	4,411,775	100.0
Principal kinds of business	1,769,381	40.1
Grocery stores	1,005,504	22.8
Restaurants, cafeterias, and lunch rooms	763,877	17.3
MICHIGAN		
All business, total	3,817,530	100.0
Principal kinds of business	1,832,657	48.0
Grocery stores	1,027,960	26.9
Restaurants, cafeterias, and lunch rooms	804,697	21.1
MISSISSIPPI		
All business, total	$3,808,892	100.0
Principal kinds of business	2,304,791	60.5
Grocery stores	1,729,751	45.4
Restaurants, cafeterias, and lunch roooms	575,040	15.1
TENNESSEE		
All business, total	3,728,674	100.0
Principal kinds of business	2,156,281	57.8
Grocery stores	1,368,391	36.7
Restaurants, cafeterias, and lunch rooms	787,890	21.1
ALABAMA		
All business, total	3,566,565	100.0
Principal kinds of business	2,029,895	56.9
Grocery stores	1,450,036	40.7
Restaurants, cafeterias, and lunch rooms	579,859	16.3
MISSOURI		
All business, total	3,200,109	100.0
Principal kinds of business	1,569,030	49.1
Grocery stores	901,420	28.2
Restaurants, cafeterias, and lunch rooms	667,610	20.9
OKLAHOMA		
All business, total	2,833,144	100.0
Principal kinds of business	964,790	34.1
Grocery stores	964,790	34.1
NEW JERSEY		
All business, total	2,737,685	100.0
Principal kinds of business	584,287	21.3
Restaurants, cafeterias, and lunch rooms	584,287	21.3
CALIFORNIA		
All business, total	2,712,233	100.0
Principal kinds of business	1,379,663	51.0
Motor-vehicle dealers (automobile—new and used)	707,771	26.1
Restaurants, cafeterias, and lunch rooms	671,892	24.8
ARKANSAS		
All business, total	2,468,727	100.0
Principal kinds of business	1,143,804	46.3
Grocery stores	1,143,804	46.3
SOUTH CAROLINA		
All business, total	2,298,672	100.0
Principal kinds of business	923,767	40.2
Grocery stores	923,767	40.2
KENTUCKY		
All business, total	2,144,159	100.0
Principal kinds of business	507,894	23.7
Grocery stores	507,894	23.7
INDIANA		
All business, total	2,021,677	100.0
Principal kinds of business	562,587	27.8
Grocery stores	562,587	27.8

Table 11.—STORES OPERATED BY NEGRO PROPRIETORS, BY STATES: 1929

Number of Stores, Personnel, Pay Roll, Stocks, and Sales

[An (x) indicates that the amount must be withheld to avoid disclosure of individual operations, but it is included in the totals]

KIND OF BUSINESS	Number of stores	Proprietors and firm members (*not on pay roll*)	Number of employees (*full time*)	Total pay roll (*including part time*)	Stocks on hand, end of year (*at cost*)	NET SALES	
						Amount	Percent of total
ALABAMA							
Total	1,297	1,406	643	$264,895	$393,280	$3,566,565	100.00
Food group	616	667	154	60,137	180,760	1,598,656	44.83
Candy and confectionery stores	29	31	5	1,741	3,280	27,693	.78
Grocery stores (without meats)	405	435	69	26,004	105,580	847,286	23.76
Combination stores (groceries and meats)	136	155	55	24,123	65,760	602,750	16.90
Meat markets (including sea foods)	42	42	22	7,809	5,940	114,387	3.21
Other food stores	4	4	3	460	200	6,540	.18
General stores—groceries with dry goods or apparel	56	62	16	11,012	69,940	354,854	9.95
General merchandise group	6	8	5	3,366	21,140	28,939	.81
Dry goods stores—piece goods stores	3	5	2	1,766	14,580	17,104	.48
General merchandise stores	3	3	3	1,600	6,560	11,835	.33
Automotive group	50	57	23	15,028	5,200	126,146	3.54
Filling stations	21	22	5	2,186	2,940	33,999	.95
Garages and repair shops	23	28	15	11,426	1,330	69,057	1.94
Other automotive establishments	6	7	3	1,416	930	23,090	.65
Apparel group	16	17	15	10,253	11,250	65,375	1.83
Men's and boys' clothing and furnishings stores	2	(x)	(x)	(x)	(x)	(x)	(x)
Family clothing stores—men's, women's, and children's	1	(x)	(x)	(x)	(x)	(x)	(x)
Other apparel stores	9	10	9	5,126	2,020	29,275	.82
Shoe stores	4	4	2	2,220	1,280	12,400	.35
Restaurants, cafeterias, and eating places	452	482	297	83,989	21,720	762,644	21.38
Restaurants, cafeterias, and lunch rooms	294	318	248	68,607	14,240	579,859	16.26
Lunch counters, refreshment stands, etc	158	164	49	15,382	7,480	182,785	5.12
Lumber and building group	4	6	10	9,836	4,750	53,417	1.50
Lumber and building material dealers	1	(x)	(x)	(x)	(x)	(x)	(x)
Electrical shops (without radio)	1	(x)	(x)	(x)	(x)	(x)	(x)
Heating and plumbing shops	2	(x)	(x)	(x)	(x)	(x)	(x)
Other retail stores [1]	91	101	120	69,537	77,780	566,484	15.88
Farmers' supplies	3	3	----	----	1,050	3,960	.11
Cigar stores and cigar stands	3	3	7	2,642	1,100	14,256	.40
Coal and wood yards—ice dealers	16	18	21	12,663	3,780	89,178	2.50
Drug stores	25	28	47	25,282	46,150	256,510	7.19
Miscellaneous classifications (combined)	42	47	45	28,950	24,800	200,930	5.64
Second-hand stores	6	6	3	1,737	740	10,050	.28
ARIZONA							
Total	8	9	11	$7,754	$670	$34,283	100.00
ARKANSAS							
Total	933	1,029	300	$144,416	$343,450	$2,463,727	100.00
Food group	448	485	84	37,614	145,600	1,189,147	48.17
Candy and confectionery stores	26	26	4	1,292	1,930	22,289	.90
Grocery stores (without meats)	320	351	40	16,320	92,960	642,342	26.02
Combination stores (groceries and meats)	93	99	37	18,672	49,540	501,462	20.31
Meat markets (including sea foods)	6	6	3	1,330	900	19,890	.81
All other food stores	3	3	----	----	270	3,164	.13
General stores	44	50	13	9,677	63,700	309,548	12.54
Automotive group	57	65	22	14,886	39,320	140,184	5.68
Filling stations	37	41	7	3,412	5,420	55,631	2.25
Garages and repair shops	20	24	15	11,474	33,900	84,553	3.43
Apparel group	6	7	8	5,367	3,300	23,556	.95
Restaurants, cafeterias, and eating places	306	326	124	40,223	23,550	466,769	18.91
Restaurants, cafeterias and lunch rooms	237	254	105	31,327	19,830	379,765	15.38
Lunch counters, refreshment stands, etc	69	72	19	8,896	3,720	87,004	3.53
Lumber and building group	3	3	7	4,310	5,720	28,500	1.15
Lumber and building material dealers	1	(x)	(x)	(x)	(x)	(x)	(x)
Heating and plumbing shops	2	(x)	(x)	(x)	(x)	(x)	(x)
Other retail stores	65	89	39	30,389	59,490	306,931	12.43
Farmers' supplies	5	6	----	----	3,150	25,046	1.01
Cigar stores and cigar stands	10	11	2	700	1,300	11,740	.48
Drug stores	19	27	15	11,721	30,040	124,119	5.03
Miscellaneous classifications	31	45	22	17,968	25,000	146,026	5.91
Second-hand stores	4	4	3	1,950	2,770	4,092	.17
CALIFORNIA							
Total	262	293	312	$319,829	$204,080	$2,712,233	100.00
Food group	56	63	12	10,201	29,210	327,343	12.07
Candy and confectionery stores	6	6	4	2,704	910	18,071	.67
Grocery stores (without meats)	36	41	1	1,148	16,870	148,815	5.49
Combination stores (groceries and meats)	9	9	4	3,200	10,650	114,236	4.21
All other food stores	5	7	3	3,149	780	46,221	1.70
General merchandise group	3	4	4	3,399	15,710	24,075	.89
Dry goods stores—piece goods stores	3	4	4	3,399	15,710	24,075	.89
Automotive group	40	48	52	95,728	46,890	975,649	35.97
Motor-vehicle dealers (new and used)	4	6	25	58,699	37,450	707,771	26.10
Filling stations	11	10	15	20,510	4,810	165,297	6.09
Garages and repair shops	18	24	10	13,440	1,260	77,151	2.84
Other automotive establishments	7	8	2	3,079	3,370	25,430	.94

(See footnotes at end of table.)

TABLE 11.—STORES OPERATED BY NEGRO PROPRIETORS, BY STATES: 1929—Continued

NUMBER OF STORES, PERSONNEL, PAY ROLL, STOCKS, AND SALES—Continued

[See note at head of table]

CALIFORNIA—Continued

KIND OF BUSINESS	Number of stores	Proprietors and firm members (*not on pay roll*)	Number of employees (*full time*)	Total pay roll (*including part time*)	Stocks on hand, end of year (*at cost*)	NET SALES Amount	NET SALES Percent of total
Apparel group	14	15	13	$13,181	$41,950	$134,891	4.97
Men's and boys' clothing and furnishings stores	6	6	9	9,543	34,110	74,901	2.76
Family clothing stores—men's, women's, and children's	3	3	1	1,058	2,700	20,224	.75
Women's ready-to-wear specialty stores—apparel and accessories	2	(x)	(x)	(x)	(x)	(x)	(x)
Other apparel stores	2	(x)	(x)	(x)	(x)	(x)	(x)
Shoe stores	1	(x)	(x)	(x)	(x)	(x)	(x)
Furniture and household group	3	4	1	1,690	6,320	33,392	1.23
Furniture stores	2	(x)	(x)	(x)	(x)	(x)	(x)
Radio and music stores	1	(x)	(x)	(x)	(x)	(x)	(x)
Restaurants, cafeterias, and eating places	55	58	164	130,811	9,510	714,156	26.33
Restaurants, cafeterias, and lunch rooms	47	48	154	125,801	9,130	671,892	24.77
Lunch counters, refreshment stands, etc	8	10	10	5,010	380	42,264	1.56
Lumber and building group	4	7	17	14,054	1,850	85,313	3.15
Lumber and building material dealers	1	(x)	(x)	(x)	(x)	(x)	(x)
Electrical shops (without radio)	2	(x)	(x)	(x)	(x)	(x)	(x)
Heating and plumbing shops	1	(x)	(x)	(x)	(x)	(x)	(x)
Other retail stores	70	76	42	42,844	34,710	367,922	13.57
General stores	2	(x)	(x)	(x)	(x)	(x)	(x)
Farmers' supplies stores (including feeds and fertilizers)	1	(x)	(x)	(x)	(x)	(x)	(x)
Cigar stores and cigar stands	45	48	22	17,957	4.410	111,727	4.12
Drug stores	3	3	10	14,404	10,680	71,320	2.63
Jewelry stores	1	(x)	(x)	(x)	(x)	(x)	(x)
Miscellaneous classifications (combined)	18	20	8	8,829	6,110	104,982	3.87
Second-hand stores	17	18	7	7,921	17,930	49,492	1.82

COLORADO

KIND OF BUSINESS	Number of stores	Proprietors and firm members (*not on pay roll*)	Number of employees (*full time*)	Total pay roll (*including part time*)	Stocks on hand, end of year (*at cost*)	NET SALES Amount	NET SALES Percent of total
Total	**41**	**49**	**44**	**$39,827**	**$20,100**	**$335,893**	**100.00**
Food group	5	5	-	-	630	19,245	5.73
Candy and confectionery stores	2	(x)	(x)	(x)	(x)	(x)	(x)
Grocery stores (without meats)	1	(x)	(x)	(x)	(x)	(x)	(x)
Combination stores (groceries and meats)	1	(x)	(x)	(x)	(x)	(x)	(x)
Other food stores	1	(x)	(x)	(x)	(x)	(x)	(x)
Automotive group	10	14	12	12,735	9,560	150,779	44.89
Motor-vehicle dealers (new and used)	3	3	8	8,412	8,460	109,010	32.46
Garages and repair shops	5	8	3	3,348	350	27,757	8.26
All other automotive establishments	2	3	1	975	750	14,012	4.17
Restaurants, cafeterias, and eating places	11	13	20	12,085	270	65,241	19.42
Other retail stores	15	17	12	15,007	9,640	100,628	29.96
Hardware stores	1	(x)	(x)	(x)	(x)	(x)	(x)
Farmers' supplies stores, including feed and fertilizer	1	(x)	(x)	(x)	(x)	(x)	(x)
Cigar stores and cigar stands	1	(x)	(x)	(x)	(x)	(x)	(x)
Coal and wood yards—ice dealers	6	7	4	4,800	550	40,904	12.18
Drug stores	1	(x)	(x)	(x)	(x)	(x)	(x)
Miscellaneous classifications (combined)	3	4	-	-	850	2,910	.87
Second-hand stores	2	(x)	(x)	(x)	(x)	(x)	(x)

CONNECTICUT

KIND OF BUSINESS	Number of stores	Proprietors and firm members (*not on pay roll*)	Number of employees (*full time*)	Total pay roll (*including part time*)	Stocks on hand, end of year (*at cost*)	NET SALES Amount	NET SALES Percent of total
Total	**59**	**[2]62**	**30**	**$39,682**	**$50,940**	**$434,899**	**100.00**
Food group	24	-	3	4,652	15,220	179,928	41.37
Candy and confectionery stores	2	-	-	-	180	2,785	.64
Grocery stores (without meats)	15	-	2	1,970	9,140	100,655	23.14
Combination stores (groceries and meats)	5	-	1	2,500	5,700	66,245	15.23
Meat markets (including sea foods)	2	-	-	182	200	10,243	2.36
Automotive group	9	-	8	9,215	3,760	40,475	9.31
Garages and repair shops	6	-	5	2,955	1,130	14,644	3.37
Other automotive establishments	3	-	3	6,260	2,630	25,831	5.94
Miscellaneous apparel, including shoes	2	-	3	6,000	1,950	52,500	12.07
Radios and home furnishings	2	-	3	3,330	6,770	18,759	4.31
Restaurants, cafeterias, and eating places	11	-	5	4,770	1,020	43,423	9.98
Restaurants, cafeterias, and lunch rooms	10	-	5	4,770	870	40,323	9.27
Lunch counters, refreshment stands, etc	1	-	-	-	150	3,100	.71
Other retail stores	11	-	8	11,715	22,220	99,814	22.95
Drug stores	4	-	5	8,415	17,790	81,288	18.69
All other stores (including 2 cigar stands and 2 second-hand stores)	7	-	3	3,300	4,430	18,526	4.26

DELAWARE[3]

KIND OF BUSINESS	Number of stores	Proprietors and firm members (*not on pay roll*)	Number of employees (*full time*)	Total pay roll (*including part time*)	Stocks on hand, end of year (*at cost*)	NET SALES Amount	NET SALES Percent of total
Total	**61**	**62**	**27**	**[4]$18,811**	**$27,780**	**$260,766**	**100.00**
Food group:							
Candy and confectionery stores	3	3	1	800	180	6,286	2.41
Grocery stores (without meats)	5	5	-	-	2,400	15,650	6.00
Combination stores (groceries and meats)	1	(x)	(x)	(x)	(x)	(x)	(x)
Meat markets (including sea foods)	2	(x)	(x)	(x)	(x)	(x)	(x)
Other food stores	2	(x)	(x)	(x)	(x)	(x)	(x)
Dry-goods stores—piece-goods stores	1	(x)	(x)	(x)	(x)	(x)	(x)
Automotive group:							
Motor-vehicle dealers (new and used)	1	(x)	(x)	(x)	(x)	(x)	(x)
Filling stations	7	7	-	-	1,310	12,650	4.85
Garages and repair shops	2	(x)	(x)	(x)	(x)	(x)	(x)
Restaurants, cafeterias, and eating places:							
Restaurants, cafeterias, and lunch rooms	15	15	7	3,108	1,230	32,351	12.41
Lunch counters and refreshment stands	2	(x)	(x)	(x)	(x)	(x)	(x)
Other retail stores:							
Cigar stores and cigar stands	11	11	4	1,806	840	24,471	9.38
Drug stores	4	5	5	5,263	7,610	39,350	15.09
Miscellaneous classifications	3	3	1	1,280	1,300	20,800	7.98
Second-hand stores	2	(x)	(x)	(x)	(x)	(x)	(x)

(See footnotes at end of table.)

Table 11.—STORES OPERATED BY NEGRO PROPRIETORS, BY STATES: 1929—Continued

Number of Stores, Personnel, Pay Roll, Stocks, and Sales—Continued

[See note at head of table]

KIND OF BUSINESS	Number of stores	Proprietors and firm members (*not on pay roll*)	Number of employees (*full time*)	Total pay roll (*including part time*)	Stocks on hand, end of year (*at cost*)	NET SALES Amount	NET SALES Percent of total
DISTRICT OF COLUMBIA							
Total	**244**	**284**	**195**	**$162,063**	**$102,820**	**$1,495,854**	**100.00**
Food group	71	80	15	10,509	12,590	289,590	19.36
Candy and confectionery stores	9	10	2	1,766	1,330	12,895	.86
Grocery stores (without meats)	17	18	---	---	3,640	46,511	3.11
Combination stores (groceries and meats)	16	17	1	770	4,530	84,035	5.62
Meat markets (including sea foods)	17	20	9	6,285	1,760	103,362	6.91
Other food stores	12	15	3	1,688	1,330	42,787	2.86
Automotive group	15	18	12	12,893	4,770	68,815	4.60
Filling stations	3	3	3	2,160	480	20,900	1.40
Garages and repair shops	8	10	6	7,453	960	25,575	1.71
Other automotive establishments	4	5	3	3,280	3,330	22,340	1.49
Apparel group	6	7	5	5,740	10,200	35,595	2.38
Men's and boys' clothing and furnishings stores	1	(x)	---	---	(x)	(x)	(x)
Women's ready-to-wear specialty stores—apparel and accessories	1	(x)	---	---	(x)	(x)	(x)
Women's accessories stores	1	(x)	---	---	(x)	(x)	(x)
Other apparel stores	3	3	5	5,740	4,100	16,920	1.13
Furniture and household group	5	7	---	---	1,180	10,620	.71
Floor coverings, draperies, curtains, and upholstery stores	1	(x)	---	---	(x)	(x)	(x)
Other home furnishings and appliances stores	2	(x)	---	---	(x)	(x)	(x)
Radio and music stores	2	(x)	---	---	(x)	(x)	(x)
Restaurants, cafeterias, and eating places	68	83	108	64,703	6,260	481,812	32.21
Restaurants, cafeterias	62	77	106	63,507	5,950	475,152	31.76
Lunch counters and refreshment stands	6	6	2	1,196	310	6,660	.45
Other retail stores	72	82	52	65,563	66,360	597,452	39.94
Farmers' supplies	1	(x)	---	---	(x)	(x)	(x)
Cigar stores and cigar stands	10	10	4	2,520	1,830	25,530	1.71
Coal and wood yards—ice dealers	16	18	11	8,836	3,880	106,316	7.11
Drug stores	23	24	16	18,654	45,160	238,281	15.93
Jewelry stores	1	(x)	---	---	(x)	(x)	(x)
Miscellaneous classifications (combined)	21	26	21	35,553	15,150	217,365	14.53
Second-hand stores	7	7	3	2,655	1,460	11,970	.80
FLORIDA							
Total	**1,378**	**1,504**	**584**	**$325,973**	**$438,550**	**$4,528,374**	**100.00**
Food group	662	716	145	82,543	189,000	2,243,167	49.54
Candy and confectionery stores	66	67	16	6,444	12,560	180,118	3.98
Grocery stores (without meats)	379	408	41	17,486	83,320	791,900	17.49
Combination stores (groceries and meats)	160	182	63	41,502	87,780	1,041,313	23.00
Meat markets (including sea foods)	45	47	17	11,642	2,710	192,990	4.26
All other food stores	12	12	8	5,469	2,630	36,846	.81
General stores (groceries with clothing and dry goods)	41	45	19	12,233	54,470	263,950	5.83
General merchandise group	8	7	7	5,460	19,970	55,636	1.23
Dry goods stores—piece goods stores	4	3	4	3,680	13,300	36,011	.80
General merchandise stores	2	(x)	(x)	(x)	(x)	(x)	(x)
Variety, 5-and-10, and to-a-dollar stores	2	(x)	(x)	(x)	(x)	(x)	(x)
Automotive group [1]	70	75	43	33,305	18,020	294,140	6.50
Filling stations	43	47	16	10,614	7,620	179,860	3.97
Garages and repair shops	26	27	24	21,074	5,450	83,626	1.85
Apparel group	18	19	18	10,100	23,270	86,717	1.92
Men's and boys' clothing and furnishings stores	3	3	4	2,444	6,530	20,343	.45
Family clothing stores—men's, women's, and children's	2	(x)	(x)	(x)	(x)	(x)	(x)
Women's ready-to-wear specialty stores—apparel and accessories	2	(x)	(x)	(x)	(x)	(x)	(x)
Women's accessories stores	1	(x)	(x)	(x)	(x)	(x)	(x)
Other apparel stores	8	9	8	3,836	1,460	26,642	.59
Shoe stores	2	(x)	(x)	(x)	(x)	(x)	(x)
Furniture and household group [1]	5	7	6	6,206	4,900	58,132	1.28
Furniture stores	3	5	4	4,306	3,040	30,388	.67
Restaurants, cafeterias, and eating places	419	450	211	88,258	24,660	938,480	20.72
Restaurants, cafeterias, and lunch rooms	294	322	186	77,554	16,060	757,172	16.72
Lunch counters, refreshment stands, etc.	125	128	25	10,704	8,600	181,308	4.00
Lumber and building group	3	3	2	1,194	440	4,746	.10
Lumber and building material dealers	1	(x)	(x)	(x)	(x)	(x)	(x)
Electrical shops (without radio)	1	(x)	(x)	(x)	(x)	(x)	(x)
Paint and glass stores	1	(x)	(x)	(x)	(x)	(x)	(x)
Other retail stores	152	182	133	86,674	103,820	583,406	12.88
Hardware stores	1	(x)	(x)	(x)	(x)	(x)	(x)
Farmers' supplies (including feeds and fertilizers)	2	(x)	(x)	(x)	(x)	(x)	(x)
Bookstores	2	(x)	(x)	(x)	(x)	(x)	(x)
Cigar stores and cigar stands	20	22	4	3,666	2,050	34,891	.77
Coal and wood yards—ice dealers	32	35	24	14,783	18,970	51,769	1.14
Drug stores	50	58	43	28,391	45,880	260,328	5.75
Jewelry stores	4	4	---	---	1,470	4,633	.10
Miscellaneous classifications	39	54	60	37,734	23,430	202,600	4.48
Second-hand stores	2	(x)	(x)	(x)	(x)	(x)	(x)
GEORGIA							
Total	**2,099**	**2,253**	**763**	**$380,600**	**$525,970**	**$5,147,040**	**100.00**
Food group	1,005	1,069	176	74,788	242,990	2,493,500	48.45
Candy and confectionery stores	65	65	9	2,361	7,870	112,483	2.19
Grocery stores (without meats)	713	759	84	29,740	158,120	1,342,548	26.08
Combination stores (groceries and meats)	154	165	55	25,976	70,460	778,039	15.12
Meat markets (including sea foods)	46	50	20	12,935	5,090	173,799	3.38
Other food stores	27	30	8	3,776	1,450	86,631	1.68
General stores—groceries with dry goods or apparel	31	38	7	3,165	25,030	109,738	2.13

(See footnotes at end of table.)

TABLE 11.—STORES OPERATED BY NEGRO PROPRIETORS, BY STATES: 1929—Continued

NUMBER OF STORES, PERSONNEL, PAY ROLL, STOCKS, AND SALES—Continued

[See note at head of table]

KIND OF BUSINESS	Number of stores	Proprietors and firm members (*not on pay roll*)	Number of employees (*full time*)	Total pay roll (*including part time*)	Stocks on hand, end of year (*at cost*)	NET SALES	
						Amount	Percent of total
GEORGIA—Continued							
General merchandise group	10	13	11	$6,702	$56,010	$125,125	2.43
Dry goods stores	7	10	6	3,066	15,500	39,425	.77
General merchandise stores	2	(x)	(x)	(x)	(x)	(x)	(x)
Variety, 5-and-10, and to-a-dollar stores	1	(x)	(x)	(x)	(x)	(x)	(x)
Automotive group [1]	80	84	44	30,649	11,590	294,374	5.72
Filling stations	44	44	13	8,579	3,990	129,964	2.53
Garages and repair shops	28	31	17	11,607	1,600	47,908	.93
Other automotive establishments	6	5	6	4,233	1,350	32,448	.63
Apparel group [1]	10	10	19	14,250	5,050	51,629	1.00
Other apparel stores	9	9	17	13,386	4,450	45,451	.88
Furniture and household group [1]	5	5	2	1,664	3,700	8,780	.17
Other home furnishings and appliances stores	4	4	2	1,664	3,200	7,280	.14
Restaurants, cafeterias, and eating places	775	807	307	98,911	35,210	1,115,491	21.67
Restaurants, cafeterias, and lunch rooms	473	497	242	74,802	19,870	729,395	14.17
Lunch counters, refreshment stands, etc	302	310	65	24,109	15,340	386,096	7.50
Other retail stores [1]	176	219	193	146,709	144,400	921,487	17.91
Farmers' supplies	4	6	6	4,958	4,950	63,000	1.22
Cigar stores and cigar stands	9	9	7	3,188	510	16,080	.31
Coal and wood yards—ice dealers	38	39	26	12,334	2,710	50,232	.98
Drug stores	30	33	59	40,090	66,550	321,494	6.25
Jewelry stores	9	10	4	1,685	2,150	19,220	.38
Miscellaneous classifications (combined)	84	120	86	82,654	63,680	435,961	8.47
Second-hand stores	7	8	4	3,762	1,990	26,916	.52
IDAHO							
Total	**2**	(x)	(x)	(x)	(x)	(x)	(x)
ILLINOIS							
Total	**1,058**	**1,136**	**696**	**$602,798**	**$622,740**	**$6,466,323**	**100.00**
Food group	318	337	67	59,333	156,660	1,911,409	29.56
Candy and confectionery stores	35	37	7	5,166	6,890	85,046	1.32
Grocery stores (without meats)	114	122	14	11,858	50,700	532,041	8.23
Combination stores (groceries and meats)	88	93	31	26,201	64,180	777,870	12.03
Meat markets (including sea foods)	8	8	1	1,600	3,580	59,552	.92
Other food stores	73	77	14	14,508	31,310	456,900	7.06
General stores	4	5	2	1,960	15,110	58,700	.91
General merchandise group [1]	13	15	9	10,582	18,640	103,084	1.59
General merchandise stores	3	5	6	8,206	9,140	75,709	1.17
Variety, 5-and-10, and to-a-dollar stores	8	8	2	1,776	3,720	18,735	.29
Automotive group	49	57	50	57,755	13,730	329,435	5.09
Filling stations	8	8	7	7,240	1,290	89,651	1.39
Garages and repair shops	31	36	37	44,323	5,350	201,361	3.11
All other automotive establishments	10	13	6	6,192	7,090	38,423	.59
Apparel group [1]	64	68	35	39,100	94,410	456,065	7.06
Men's and boys' clothing and furnishings stores	6	6	4	5,539	25,480	84,137	1.30
Family clothing stores—men's, women's, and children's	4	4	7	11,268	28,400	135,200	2.09
Women's ready-to-wear specialty stores—apparel and accessories	14	17	9	7,620	14,800	63,048	.98
Women's accessories stores	10	11	3	2,460	7,150	43,045	.67
Other apparel stores	29	29	11	11,013	6,580	94,635	1.46
Furniture and household group	13	17	17	23,639	33,490	287,314	4.44
Furniture stores	4	5	4	3,099	3,640	23,154	.36
Floor coverings, draperies, curtains, and upholstery stores	2	(x)	(x)	(x)	(x)	(x)	(x)
Other home furnishings and appliances stores	1	(x)	(x)	(x)	(x)	(x)	(x)
Radio and music stores	6	9	10	18,772	29,380	256,260	3.95
Restaurants, cafeterias, and eating places	274	290	281	168,858	23,970	1,114,172	17.23
Restaurants, cafeterias, and lunch rooms	199	214	239	132,771	12,220	905,149	14.00
Lunch counters, refreshment stands, etc	75	76	42	36,087	11,750	209,023	3.23
Lumber and building group	10	11	13	12,971	7,540	65,826	1.02
Lumber and building material dealers	3	3	4	3,845	1,330	17,876	.28
Electrical shops (without radio)	3	4	1	576	810	7,300	.11
Heating and plumbing shops	2	(x)	(x)	(x)	(x)	(x)	(x)
Paint and glass stores	2	(x)	(x)	(x)	(x)	(x)	(x)
Other retail stores [1]	242	259	208	211,738	223,830	1,942,302	30.04
Hardware stores	3	3	-----	-----	3,500	7,000	.11
Farmers' supplies stores (including feeds and fertilizers)	8	8	4	4,656	3,500	54,995	.85
Cigar stores and cigar stands	39	40	41	31,902	5,550	164,889	2.55
Coal and wood yards—ice dealers	35	38	12	16,075	3,690	113,981	1.76
Drug stores	50	53	77	83,263	140,700	678,241	10.49
Jewelry stores	3	4	-----	-----	5,630	7,870	.12
Miscellaneous classifications (combined)	102	110	72	73,618	50,560	894,826	13.84
Second-hand stores	71	77	14	16,862	35,360	198,016	3.06
INDIANA							
Total	**342**	**383**	**260**	**$189,328**	**$131,350**	**$2,021,677**	**100.00**
Food group	97	105	16	8,844	29,760	621,973	30.76
Candy and confectionery stores	9	10	3	1,974	1,380	29,880	1.48
Grocery stores (without meats)	28	29	-----	-----	6,320	88,794	4.39
Combination stores (groceries and meats)	50	55	9	5,491	19,930	473,793	23.43
Other food stores	10	11	4	1,379	2,130	29,506	1.46
Automotive group	22	24	16	14,529	3,580	91,767	4.54
Motor-vehicle dealers (new and used)	1	(x)	(x)	(x)	(x)	(x)	(x)
Filling stations	2	(x)	(x)	(x)	(x)	(x)	(x)
Garages and repair shops	15	17	11	10,141	1,740	35,356	1.75
Other automotive establishments	4	4	4	2,628	1,280	16,965	.84

(See footnotes at end of table.)

TABLE 11.—STORES OPERATED BY NEGRO PROPRIETORS, BY STATES: 1929—Continued

NUMBER OF STORES, PERSONNEL, PAY ROLL, STOCKS, AND SALES—Continued

[See note at head of table]

KIND OF BUSINESS	Number of stores	Proprietors and firm members (*not on pay roll*)	Number of employees (*full time*)	Total pay roll (*including part time*)	Stocks on hand, end of year (*at cost*)	NET SALES	
						Amount	Percent of total
INDIANA—Continued							
Apparel group	10	12	4	$2,106	$3,380	$31,897	1.58
Men's and boys' clothing and furnishings stores	1	(x)	(x)	(x)	(x)	(x)	(x)
Family clothing stores—men's, women's, and children's	1	(x)	(x)	(x)	(x)	(x)	(x)
Women's ready-to-wear specialty stores—apparel and accessories	1	(x)	(x)	(x)	(x)	(x)	(x)
Women's accessories stores	1	(x)	(x)	(x)	(x)	(x)	(x)
Other apparel stores	6	8	2	1,020	380	13,873	.69
Furniture and household group	3	3	2	2,236	1,250	11,400	.56
Furniture stores	1	(x)	(x)	(x)	(x)	(x)	(x)
Other home furnishings and appliances stores	2	(x)	(x)	(x)	(x)	(x)	(x)
Restaurants, cafeterias, and eating places	116	131	112	47,220	4,910	367,914	18.20
Restaurants, cafeterias, and lunch rooms	89	103	99	39,146	3,600	298,869	14.79
Lunch counters, refreshment stands, etc	27	28	13	8,074	1,310	69,045	3.41
Lumber and building group	3	3	27	40,771	5,580	129,952	6.43
Lumber and building material dealers	1	(x)	(x)	(x)	(x)	(x)	(x)
Electrical shops (without radio)	1	(x)	(x)	(x)	(x)	(x)	(x)
Heating and plumbing shops	1	(x)	(x)	(x)	(x)	(x)	(x)
Other retail stores	77	91	78	68,110	74,490	692,852	34.27
Hardware stores	2	(x)	(x)	(x)	(x)	(x)	(x)
Hardware and farm implement stores	1	(x)	(x)	(x)	(x)	(x)	(x)
Farmers' supplies stores (including feeds and fertilizers)	3	4	3	3,594	7,180	121,550	6.01
Cigar stores and cigar stands	42	49	29	24,581	5,030	125,164	6.19
Coal and wood yards—ice dealers	6	7	22	14,603	11,380	259,409	12.83
Drug stores	9	10	9	11,116	23,600	80,130	3.97
Miscellaneous classifications (combined)	14	17	12	12,436	6,080	78,854	3.90
Second-hand stores	14	14	5	5,512	8,400	73,922	3.66
IOWA							
Total	57	64	54	$44,543	$48,630	$573,577	100.00
Food group	9	13	6	4,379	14,450	210,694	36.73
Grocery stores (without meats)	4	5	5	3,935	12,190	134,105	23.38
Combination stores (groceries and meats)	4	7	1	314	1,530	26,589	4.63
Other food stores	1	1	—	130	730	50,000	8.72
General stores—groceries with dry goods or apparel	3	4	3	1,940	10,200	66,400	11.58
Automotive group	4	4	2	2,622	3,680	46,342	8.08
Apparel group	5	6	1	2,476	2,400	12,786	2.23
Restaurants, cafeterias, and eating places	23	24	32	15,004	1,430	97,926	17.07
Other retail stores	13	13	10	18,122	16,470	139,429	24.31
Radio and music stores	2	(x)	(x)	(x)	(x)	(x)	(x)
Heating and plumbing shops	2	(x)	(x)	(x)	(x)	(x)	(x)
Hardware and farm implement stores	1	(x)	(x)	(x)	(x)	(x)	(x)
Farmers' supplies	1	(x)	(x)	(x)	(x)	(x)	(x)
Cigar stores and cigar stands	4	5	—	—	370	8,300	1.45
Coal and wood yards—ice dealers	1	(x)	(x)	(x)	(x)	(x)	(x)
Drug stores	2	(x)	(x)	(x)	(x)	(x)	(x)
KANSAS							
Total	218	241	124	$105,340	$144,850	$1,207,920	100.00
Food group	83	92	22	17,047	29,710	379,899	31.45
Candy and confectionery stores	11	11	4	1,239	1,920	19,590	1.62
Grocery stores (without meats)	30	32	3	1,864	5,990	84,738	7.01
Combination stores (groceries and meats)	41	48	14	13,224	21,650	272,971	22.60
All other food stores	1	1	1	720	150	2,600	.22
General stores	3	3	7	5,500	45,100	97,800	8.10
Automotive group	19	20	19	20,613	23,570	209,482	17.34
Motor-vehicle dealers (new and used)	1	(x)	(x)	(x)	(x)	(x)	(x)
Filling stations	4	4	3	3,447	1,690	51,100	4.23
Garages and repair shops	12	13	9	9,772	3,520	41,213	3.41
Other automotive establishments	2	(x)	(x)	(x)	(x)	(x)	(x)
Apparel group	5	6	2	2,570	10,350	24,652	2.04
Women's ready-to-wear specialty stores—apparel and accessories	2	(x)	(x)	(x)	(x)	(x)	(x)
Women's accessories stores	1	(x)	(x)	(x)	(x)	(x)	(x)
Other apparel stores	1	(x)	(x)	(x)	(x)	(x)	(x)
Shoe stores	1	(x)	(x)	(x)	(x)	(x)	(x)
Furniture and household group	3	4	—	—	600	2,900	.24
Furniture stores	2	(x)	(x)	(x)	(x)	(x)	(x)
Other home furnishings and appliances stores	1	(x)	(x)	(x)	(x)	(x)	(x)
Restaurants, cafeterias, and eating places	65	72	32	19,909	4,890	203,533	16.85
Restaurants, cafeterias, and lunch rooms	50	56	29	17,849	3,860	150,372	12.45
Lunch counters, refreshment stands, etc	15	16	3	2,060	1,030	53,161	4.40
Other retail stores	40	44	42	39,701	30,630	289,654	23.98
Electrical shops (without radio)	1	(x)	(x)	(x)	(x)	(x)	(x)
Hardware stores	1	(x)	(x)	(x)	(x)	(x)	(x)
Hardware and farm implement stores	1	(x)	(x)	(x)	(x)	(x)	(x)
Farmers' supplies stores (including feeds and fertilizers)	6	6	2	1,388	670	12,213	1.01
Cigar stores and cigar stands	6	6	1	1,791	1,430	22,950	1.90
Coal and wood yards—ice dealers	10	11	15	12,663	12,470	78,138	6.47
Drug stores	12	14	17	16,489	3,910	91,528	7.58
Miscellaneous classifications (combined)	3	3	1	1,900	2,150	8,600	.71

(See footnotes at end of table.)

TABLE 11.—STORES OPERATED BY NEGRO PROPRIETORS, BY STATES: 1929—Continued

NUMBER OF STORES, PERSONNEL, PAY ROLL, STOCKS, AND SALES—Continued

[See note at head of table]

KIND OF BUSINESS	Number of stores	Proprietors and firm members (*not on pay roll*)	Number of employees (*full time*)	Total pay roll (*including part time*)	Stocks on hand, end of year (*at cost*)	NET SALES	
						Amount	Percent of total
KENTUCKY							
Total	683	778	310	$191,080	$260,760	$2,144,159	100.00
Food group	201	230	38	20,907	63,600	601,372	28.05
Candy and confectionery stores	19	21	5	2,726	2,400	36,568	1.70
Grocery stores (without meats)	114	132	13	4,970	38,520	277,749	12.96
Combination stores (groceries and meats)	57	65	15	9,625	21,320	230,145	10.73
Meat markets (including sea foods)	4	4	2	1,300	340	28,450	1.33
Other food stores	7	8	3	2,286	1,020	28,460	1.33
General stores	18	19	8	4,850	37,750	113,493	5.29
General merchandise group	4	5	-----	-----	8,010	9,725	.45
Dry goods stores	2	(x)	(x)	(x)	(x)	(x)	(x)
General merchandise stores	1	(x)	(x)	(x)	(x)	(x)	(x)
Variety, 5-and-10, and to-a-dollar stores	1	(x)	(x)	(x)	(x)	(x)	(x)
Automotive group	28	29	12	8,888	10,720	103,010	4.81
Filling stations	4	4	3	1,250	310	29,510	1.38
Garages and repair shops	21	22	5	2,838	1,020	19,800	.92
All other automotive establishments	3	3	4	4,800	9,390	53,700	2.51
Apparel group	11	11	6	2,898	20,440	62,269	2.90
Men's and boys' clothing and furnishings stores	1	(x)	(x)	(x)	(x)	(x)	(x)
Family clothing stores—men's, women's, and children's	1	(x)	(x)	(x)	(x)	(x)	(x)
Women's accessories stores	1	(x)	(x)	(x)	(x)	(x)	(x)
Other apparel stores	5	5	4	1,658	2,280	15,542	.72
Shoe stores	3	3	1	720	2,400	9,727	.45
Furniture and household group	3	3	1	500	1,850	8,391	.39
Furniture stores	2	(x)	(x)	(x)	(x)	(x)	(x)
Radio and music stores	1	(x)	(x)	(x)	(x)	(x)	(x)
Restaurants, cafeterias, and eating places	274	298	142	68,500	20,410	544,818	25.41
Restaurants, cafeterias	185	201	102	50,819	16,050	389,035	18.14
Lunch counters, refreshment stands, etc	89	97	40	17,681	4,360	155,783	7.27
Lumber and building group	3	3	1	850	2,500	13,000	.61
Lumber and building material dealers	2	(x)	(x)	(x)	(x)	(x)	(x)
Heating and plumbing shops	1	(x)	(x)	(x)	(x)	(x)	(x)
Other retail stores	133	170	102	83,687	93,700	683,356	31.87
Farmers' supplies stores (including feed and fertilizers)	3	3	-----	-----	580	11,560	.54
Cigar stores and cigar stands	11	12	12	5,198	1,720	34,607	1.61
Coal and wood yards—ice dealers	48	51	8	4,344	1,320	35,181	1.64
Drug stores	16	21	35	23,971	47,360	198,812	9.27
Miscellaneous classifications (combined)	55	83	47	50,174	42,720	403,196	18.81
Second-hand stores	8	10	-----	-----	1,780	4,725	.22
LOUISIANA							
Total	1,668	1,884	577	$262,787	$369,770	$4,504,809	100.00
Food group	810	905	94	41,359	147,690	2,126,708	47.21
Candy and confectionery stores	38	45	3	1,080	3,160	47,651	1.06
Grocery stores (without meats)	423	458	41	19,361	110,370	992,471	22.03
Combination stores (groceries and meats)	61	68	12	5,070	24,350	261,064	5.80
Meat markets (including sea foods)	34	40	13	6,868	2,160	115,915	2.57
Other food stores	254	294	25	8,980	7,650	709,607	15.75
General stores (groceries with apparel or dry goods)	43	52	17	6,499	54,120	231,216	5.13
Automotive group	59	70	27	15,706	9,990	179,479	3.98
Filling stations	33	39	11	6,662	7,150	121,344	2.69
Garages and repair shops	24	29	16	9,044	2,140	53,040	1.18
Other automotive establishments	2	2	-----	-----	700	5,095	.11
Apparel group	18	20	9	7,522	10,660	51,421	1.14
Men's and boys' clothing and furnishings stores	1	(x)	(x)	(x)	(x)	(x)	(x)
Family clothing stores—men's, women's, and children's	2	(x)	(x)	(x)	(x)	(x)	(x)
Women's accessories stores	2	(x)	(x)	(x)	(x)	(x)	(x)
Other apparel stores	11	12	5	4,818	2,080	21,365	.47
Shoe stores	2	(x)	(x)	(x)	(x)	(x)	(x)
Furniture and household group	7	8	9	6,600	3,660	30,936	.69
Furniture stores	6	7	7	5,300	2,660	24,324	.54
Other home furnishings and appliances stores	1	1	2	1,300	1,000	6,612	.15
Restaurants, cafeterias, and eating places	567	622	293	103,260	28,490	1,134,580	25.19
Restaurants, cafeterias, and lunch rooms	329	353	254	84,717	18,790	791,180	17.56
Lunch counters, refreshment stands, etc	238	269	39	18,543	9,700	343,400	7.63
Other retail stores	161	204	116	75,341	109,710	728,359	16.17
Paint and glass stores	1	(x)	(x)	(x)	(x)	(x)	(x)
Farmers' supplies stores (including feeds and fertilizers)	2	(x)	(x)	(x)	(x)	(x)	(x)
Cigar stores and cigar stands	18	19	9	5,964	950	25,201	.56
Coal and wood yards—ice dealers	74	93	14	4,823	7,260	172,038	3.82
Drug stores	41	54	48	27,957	74,750	316,570	7.03
Jewelry stores	4	5	-----	-----	780	7,715	.17
Miscellaneous classifications (combined)	21	30	43	34,917	23,470	188,585	4.19
Second-hand stores	3	3	12	6,500	5,450	22,110	.49
MAINE							
Total	4	5	2	$4,689	$2,300	$46,917	100.00
MARYLAND							
Total	515	525	198	$164,492	$125,700	$1,690,747	100.00
Food group	236	241	41	39,351	54,580	720,732	42.63
Candy and confectionery stores	66	67	8	4,450	7,380	130,902	7.74
Grocery stores (without meats)	96	96	11	6,241	29,450	213,942	12.66
Combination stores (groceries and meats)	44	47	7	3,240	12,100	166,215	9.83
Meat markets (including sea foods)	11	11	2	1,578	3,490	59,186	3.50
Other food stores	19	20	13	23,842	2,160	150,487	8.90

(See footnotes at end of table.)

TABLE 11.—STORES OPERATED BY NEGRO PROPRIETORS, BY STATES: 1929—Continued

NUMBER OF STORES, PERSONNEL, PAY ROLL, STOCKS, AND SALES—Continued

[See note at head of table]

KIND OF BUSINESS	Number of stores	Proprietors and firm members (*not on pay roll*)	Number of employees (*full time*)	Total pay roll (*including part time*)	Stocks on hand, end of year (*at cost*)	NET SALES	
						Amount	Percent of total
MARYLAND—Continued							
General stores (groceries with apparel or dry goods)	19	19	4	$2,929	$18,700	$111,092	6.57
Automotive group	20	24	12	8,136	5,770	79,568	4.70
Motor-vehicle dealers (new and used)	1	(x)	(x)	(x)	(x)	(x)	(x)
Filling stations	6	(x)	(x)	(x)	(x)	(x)	(x)
Garages and repair shops	12	14	5	2,267	700	24,198	1.43
Other automotive establishments	1	(x)	(x)	(x)	(x)	(x)	(x)
Apparel group	4	4	2	624	1,470	7,075	.42
Men's and boys' clothing and furnishings stores	1	(x)	(x)	(x)	(x)	(x)	(x)
Women's accessories stores	1	(x)	(x)	(x)	(x)	(x)	(x)
Other apparel stores	2	(x)	(x)	(x)	(x)	(x)	(x)
Restaurants and eating places	120	121	64	31,211	8,480	280,287	16.58
Restaurants, cafeterias, and lunch rooms	99	100	60	29,745	7,070	260,551	15.41
Lunch counters, refreshment stands, etc	21	21	4	1,466	1,410	19,736	1.17
Other retail stores	101	101	74	81,825	33,450	458,183	27.10
Household appliances stores	1	(x)	(x)	(x)	(x)	(x)	(x)
Radio and music stores	1	(x)	(x)	(x)	(x)	(x)	(x)
Heating and plumbing shops	2	(x)	(x)	(x)	(x)	(x)	(x)
Hardware stores	1	(x)	(x)	(x)	(x)	(x)	(x)
Farmers' supplies	1	(x)	(x)	(x)	(x)	(x)	(x)
Cigar stores and cigar stands	11	12	4	1,690	690	26,234	1.55
Coal and wood yards—ice dealers	44	44	6	3,825	2,130	84,783	5.02
Drug stores	15	15	26	21,643	16,560	104,697	6.19
Miscellaneous classifications (combined)	25	25	25	27,107	12,320	122,265	7.23
Second-hand stores	15	15	1	416	3,250	33,810	2.00
MASSACHUSETTS							
Total	**121**	**135**	**86**	**$98,139**	**$123,380**	**$1,149,686**	**100.00**
Food group	49	56	12	11,419	23,760	285,969	24.87
Candy and confectionery stores	6	7	1	680	680	14,660	1.28
Grocery stores (without meats)	32	38	3	2,578	14,060	114,839	9.99
Combination stores (groceries and meats)	8	8	7	6,853	8,630	137,095	11.92
Other food stores	3	3	1	1,308	390	19,375	1.69
Automotive group	21	21	15	22,700	8,720	231,094	20.10
Filling stations	12	12	5	3,350	1,370	65,444	5.69
Garages and repair shops	6	6	3	5,350	420	19,800	1.72
Other automotive establishments	3	3	7	14,000	6,930	145,850	12.69
Apparel group	9	9	10	13,858	59,270	244,179	21.24
Men's and boys' clothing and furnishings stores	5	3	7	11,058	56,570	214,064	18.62
Other apparel and furnishings stores	4	6	3	2,800	2,700	30,115	2.62
Furniture and household group	2	3	----	----	5,120	54,830	4.77
Home furnishings and appliances stores	2	3	----	----	5,120	54,830	4.77
Restaurants, cafeterias, and eating places	21	24	39	36,143	2,230	178,942	15.56
Restaurants, cafeterias, and lunch rooms	14	16	32	30,755	1,340	142,950	12.43
Lunch counters, refreshment stands, etc	7	8	7	5,388	890	35,992	3.13
Other retail stores	15	17	8	12,644	23,150	146,572	12.75
Cigar stores and cigar stands	3	3	----	312	900	8,880	.77
Drug stores	3	4	4	5,052	15,500	70,506	6.13
Miscellaneous classifications	9	10	4	7,280	6,750	67,186	5.84
Second-hand stores	4	5	2	1,375	1,130	8,100	.70
MICHIGAN							
Total	**488**	**563**	**465**	**$379,949**	**$229,970**	**$3,817,530**	**100.00**
Food group	182	200	59	51,898	58,220	1,296,837	33.97
Candy and confectionery stores	56	60	12	6,320	10,240	170,311	4.46
Grocery stores (without meats)	53	60	10	8,020	15,420	262,103	6.87
Combination stores (groceries and meats)	64	70	26	24,160	31,070	765,857	20.06
Meat markets (including sea foods)	4	4	2	2,628	430	46,340	1.21
Other food stores	5	6	9	10,770	1,060	52,226	1.37
General merchandise group	3	4	----	----	8,370	22,360	.59
Dry-goods stores—piece-goods stores	1	(x)	(x)	(x)	(x)	(x)	(x)
Variety, 5-and-10, to-a-dollar stores	2	(x)	(x)	(x)	(x)	(x)	(x)
Automotive group	53	65	39	53,842	23,140	543,319	14.23
Filling stations	27	33	25	33,851	12,630	407,432	10.67
Garages and repair shops	14	17	8	13,061	1,060	55,647	1.46
Other automotive establishments	12	15	6	6,930	9,450	80,240	2.10
Apparel group [1]	15	16	14	9,737	9,220	72,988	1.91
Women's ready-to-wear specialty stores—apparel and accessories	3	3	----	364	790	9,365	.24
Women's accessories stores	3	3	----	----	660	3,770	.10
Other apparel stores	7	8	13	8,341	5,420	32,003	.84
Furniture and household group	4	4	2	1,291	1,160	18,640	.49
Furniture stores	1	(x)	(x)	(x)	(x)	(x)	(x)
Other home furnishings and appliances stores	1	(x)	(x)	(x)	(x)	(x)	(x)
Radio and music stores	2	(x)	(x)	(x)	(x)	(x)	(x)
Restaurants and eating places	136	161	279	183,398	10,340	993,888	26.04
Restaurants, cafeterias, and lunch rooms	104	125	225	148,594	9,110	804,697	21.08
Lunch counters, refreshment stands, etc	32	36	54	34,804	1,230	189,191	4.96
Other retail stores	79	95	66	73,088	115,130	804,826	21.08
General stores	2	(x)	(x)	(x)	(x)	(x)	(x)
Hardware stores	2	(x)	(x)	(x)	(x)	(x)	(x)
Farmers' supplies	2	(x)	(x)	(x)	(x)	(x)	(x)
Cigar stores and cigar stands	29	35	14	8,928	5,270	81,647	2.14
Coal and wood yards—ice dealers	4	4	5	7,129	6,730	69,594	1.82
Drug stores	26	31	35	43,777	81,150	430,466	11.28
Jewelry stores	2	(x)	(x)	(x)	(x)	(x)	(x)
Miscellaneous classifications (combined)	12	16	6	5,826	6,540	72,770	1.90
Second-hand stores	16	18	6	6,695	4,390	64,672	1.69

(See footnotes at end of table.)

TABLE 11.—STORES OPERATED BY NEGRO PROPRIETORS, BY STATES: 1929—Continued

NUMBER OF STORES, PERSONNEL, PAY ROLL, STOCKS, AND SALES—Continued

[See note at head of table]

KIND OF BUSINESS	Number of stores	Proprietors and firm members (*not on pay roll*)	Number of employees (*full time*)	Total pay roll (*including part time*)	Stocks on hand, end of year (*at cost*)	NET SALES Amount	NET SALES Percent of total
MINNESOTA							
Total	71	86	72	$54,410	$100,870	$585,676	100.00
Food group	12	13	9	6,512	6,870	116,743	19.93
Candy and confectionery stores	2	(x)	(x)	(x)	(x)	(x)	(x)
Grocery stores (without meats)	4	5	2	1,212	1,770	27,140	4.63
Combination stores (groceries and meats)	4	4	5	4,370	4,250	63,353	10.82
Meat markets (including sea foods)	1	(x)	(x)	(x)	(x)	(x)	(x)
Other food stores	1	(x)	(x)	(x)	(x)	(x)	(x)
General stores—groceries with dry goods or apparel	3	4	5	2,592	23,240	61,707	10.54
Automotive group	4	4	6	7,945	13,250	53,400	9.12
Motor-vehicle dealers (new and used)	2	(x)	(x)	(x)	(x)	(x)	(x)
Garages and repair shops	1	(x)	(x)	(x)	(x)	(x)	(x)
Other automotive establishments	1	(x)	(x)	(x)	(x)	(x)	(x)
Apparel group	5	5	1	500	8,760	34,055	5.82
Men's and boys' clothing and furnishing stores	2	(x)	(x)	(x)	(x)	(x)	(x)
Women's accessories stores	1	(x)	(x)	(x)	(x)	(x)	(x)
Other apparel stores	1	(x)	(x)	(x)	(x)	(x)	(x)
Shoe stores	1	(x)	(x)	(x)	(x)	(x)	(x)
Restaurants, cafeterias, and eating places	22	28	39	25,919	5,400	152,419	26.02
Restaurants, cafeterias, and lunch rooms	15	18	29	17,774	4,990	104,073	17.77
Lunch counters, refreshment stands, etc.	7	10	10	8,145	410	48,346	8.25
Other retail stores	25	32	12	10,942	43,350	167,352	28.57
Furniture stores	1	(x)	(x)	(x)	(x)	(x)	(x)
Radio and music stores	1	(x)	(x)	(x)	(x)	(x)	(x)
Hardware stores	2	(x)	(x)	(x)	(x)	(x)	(x)
Farmers' supplies	2	(x)	(x)	(x)	(x)	(x)	(x)
Cigar stores and cigar stands	4	5	4	2,938	1,600	14,329	2.45
Coal and wood yards—ice dealers	7	8	2	3,263	1,620	28,954	4.94
Drug stores	3	4	3	2,090	10,200	31,989	5.46
Miscellaneous classifications (combined)	3	4	1	340	3,780	18,835	3.21
Second-hand stores	2	(x)	(x)	(x)	(x)	(x)	(x)
MISSISSIPPI							
Total	1,406	1,555	560	$278,777	$369,960	$3,808,892	100.00
Food group	697	753	148	78,264	165,070	1,850,049	48.57
Candy and confectionery stores	9	9	6	5,853	890	26,153	.69
Grocery stores (without meats)	554	592	81	38,675	115,120	1,194,041	31.35
Combination stores (groceries and meats)	93	111	46	27,172	45,030	535,710	14.06
Meat markets (including sea foods)	37	37	15	6,539	3,960	92,295	2.42
Other food stores	4	4	----------	25	70	1,850	.05
General stores—groceries with dry goods or apparel	74	97	22	13,490	68,560	338,228	8.88
General merchandise group [1]	6	7	2	1,109	1,890	42,350	1.11
General merchandise stores	5	6	2	1,109	1,860	42,300	1.11
Automotive group [1]	72	79	48	37,012	45,030	339,078	8.90
Filling stations	33	34	8	3,911	6,620	80,601	2.12
Garages and repair shops	38	44	28	14,923	4,100	73,603	1.93
Apparel group [1]	15	19	11	6,961	4,040	28,160	.74
Other apparel stores	9	13	5	2,630	2,700	10,310	.27
Shoe stores	4	4	4	3,023	980	16,100	.42
Restaurants, cafeterias, and eating places	472	503	225	70,983	23,840	699,342	18.36
Restaurants, cafeterias, and lunch rooms	343	364	204	65,461	17,860	575,040	15.10
Lunch counters, refreshment stands, etc.	129	139	21	5,522	5,980	124,302	3.26
Lumber and building group	4	4	1	600	930	4,070	.11
Lumber and building material dealers	2	(x)	(x)	(x)	(x)	(x)	(x)
Electrical shops (without radio)	1	(x)	(x)	(x)	(x)	(x)	(x)
Heating and plumbing shops	1	(x)	(x)	(x)	(x)	(x)	(x)
Other retail stores	63	89	99	69,160	59,690	499,665	13.12
Furniture stores	1	(x)	(x)	(x)	(x)	(x)	(x)
Farmers' supplies	5	5	7	3,894	4,780	71,082	1.87
Cigar stores and cigar stands	2	(x)	(x)	(x)	(x)	(x)	(x)
Coal and wood yards—ice dealers	2	(x)	(x)	(x)	(x)	(x)	(x)
Drug stores	19	24	22	13,738	23,090	136,062	3.57
Jewelry stores	2	(x)	(x)	(x)	(x)	(x)	(x)
Miscellaneous classifications (combined)	32	52	65	48,708	29,760	257,869	6.77
Second-hand stores	3	4	4	1,198	910	7,950	.21
MISSOURI							
Total	575	628	453	$315,947	$290,470	$3,200,109	100.00
Food group	165	182	69	61,222	72,170	1,072,134	33.50
Candy and confectionery stores	57	61	14	6,502	5,620	137,459	4.30
Grocery stores (without meats)	49	56	8	4,808	15,040	188,658	5.89
Combination stores (groceries and meats)	50	53	43	47,208	49,880	712,762	22.27
Other food stores	9	12	4	2,704	1,630	33,255	1.04
General stores	6	7	3	3,080	11,960	70,289	2.20
General merchandise group	5	4	----------	----------	6,400	29,071	.91
Dry-goods stores—piece-goods stores	3	3	----------	----------	4,850	11,037	.35
Automotive group	34	40	39	34,127	29,960	297,901	9.31
Motor-vehicle dealers (new and used)	2	(x)	(x)	(x)	(x)	(x)	(x)
Filling stations	9	9	8	7,252	4,040	64,154	2.00
Garages and repair shops	22	28	26	23,995	9,370	164,667	5.15
Other automotive establishments	1	(x)	(x)	(x)	(x)	(x)	(x)

(See footnotes at end of table.)

TABLE 11.—STORES OPERATED BY NEGRO PROPRIETORS, BY STATES: 1929—Continued

NUMBER OF STORES, PERSONNEL, PAY ROLL, STOCKS, AND SALES—Continued

[See note at head of table]

KIND OF BUSINESS	Number of stores	Proprietors and firm members (*not on pay roll*)	Number of employees (*full time*)	Total pay roll (*including part time*)	Stocks on hand, end of year (*at cost*)	NET SALES	
						Amount	Percent of total
MISSOURI—Continued							
Apparel group	14	16	10	$6,283	$11,710	$74,060	2.31
Family clothing stores—men's, women's, and children's	1	(x)	(x)	(x)	(x)	(x)	(x)
Women's ready-to-wear specialty stores—apparel and accessories	5	6	4	3,113	7,000	53,400	1.67
Women's accessories stores	1	(x)	(x)	(x)	(x)	(x)	(x)
Other apparel stores	6	7	5	2,650	700	12,750	.40
Shoe stores	1	(x)	(x)	(x)	(x)	(x)	(x)
Furniture and household group [1]	6	8	5	4,528	13,150	39,750	1.24
Radio and music stores	5	7	2	1,818	2,670	15,250	.48
Restaurants, cafeterias, and eating places	229	245	219	111,853	16,630	876,534	27.39
Restaurants, cafeterias, and lunch rooms	166	179	186	93,735	12,440	667,610	20.86
Lunch counters, refreshment stands, etc.	63	66	33	18,118	4,190	208,924	6.53
Other retail stores	107	117	103	89,020	122,110	702,090	21.94
Hardware stores	3	3	2	1,340	5,300	13,339	.42
Hardware and farm implement stores	1	(x)	(x)	(x)	(x)	(x)	(x)
Farmers' supplies stores (including feeds and fertilizers)	5	5	2	2,000	3,200	30,700	.96
Book stores	1	(x)	(x)	(x)	(x)	(x)	(x)
Cigar stores and cigar stands	14	15	7	5,442	1,090	43,850	1.37
Coal and wood yards—ice dealers	30	31	19	20,552	9,150	114,404	3.57
Drug stores	22	25	41	33,571	65,320	311,623	9.74
Jewelry stores	2	(x)	(x)	(x)	(x)	(x)	(x)
Miscellaneous classifications (combined)	29	35	25	19,002	18,440	143,146	4.47
Second-hand stores	9	9	5	5,834	6,380	38,280	1.20
MONTANA							
Total	6	7	7	$6,036	$5,730	$49,497	100.00
NEBRASKA							
Total	52	60	55	$34,782	$86,160	$435,433	100.00
Food group	11	13	7	3,444	7,380	87,136	20.01
Grocery stores (without meats)	4	5	1	420	600	5,002	1.15
Combination stores (groceries and meats)	5	6	5	2,520	6,700	76,500	17.57
All other food stores	2	2	1	504	80	5,634	1.29
Automotive group	4	4	5	2,070	6,500	25,634	5.89
Apparel group	4	6	1	520	1,760	6,000	1.38
Men's and boys' clothing and furnishings stores	1	(x)	(x)	(x)	(x)	(x)	(x)
Family clothing stores—men's, women's, and children's	2	(x)	(x)	(x)	(x)	(x)	(x)
Other apparel stores	1	(x)	(x)	(x)	(x)	(x)	(x)
Furniture and household group	3	3	-	-	1,000	3,650	.84
Restaurants, cafeterias, and eating places	18	21	31	17,263	1,970	114,593	26.31
Restaurants, cafeterias, and lunch rooms	15	18	30	16,315	1,450	104,438	23.98
Lunch counters, refreshment stands, etc.	3	3	1	948	520	10,155	2.33
Other retail stores	12	13	11	11,485	67,550	198,420	45.57
General stores	2	(x)	(x)	(x)	(x)	(x)	(x)
Lumber and building material dealers	1	(x)	(x)	(x)	(x)	(x)	(x)
Farmers' supplies (including feeds and fertilizers)	2	(x)	(x)	(x)	(x)	(x)	(x)
Cigar stores and cigar stands	3	3	3	1,948	650	10,640	2.44
Drug stores	3	5	3	3,841	20,570	68,964	15.84
Jewelry stores	1	(x)	(x)	(x)	(x)	(x)	(x)
NEVADA							
Total	2	(x)	(x)	(x)	(x)	(x)	100.00
NEW HAMPSHIRE							
Total	4	4	5	$4,005	$5,950	$26,791	100.00
NEW JERSEY							
Total	577	624	294	$264,386	$349,900	$2,737,685	100.00
Food group	216	228	28	29,337	82,350	868,861	31.74
Candy and confectionery stores	56	58	11	9,149	18,270	178,163	6.51
Grocery stores (without meats)	108	114	6	5,972	46,380	371,661	13.58
Combination stores (groceries and meats)	19	22	2	2,832	9,830	125,360	4.58
Meat markets (including sea foods)	13	13	4	2,730	1,360	77,517	2.83
Other food stores	20	21	5	8,654	6,510	116,160	4.24
General merchandise group	5	5	-	-	7,850	13,420	.49
Dry goods stores—piece goods stores	5	5	-	-	7,850	13,420	.49
Automotive group	37	41	39	38,326	14,490	222,061	8.11
Filling stations	14	14	6	5,240	4,630	55,252	2.02
Garages and repair shops	20	24	29	28,110	3,360	146,309	5.34
Other automotive establishments	3	3	4	4,976	6,500	20,500	.75
Apparel group	20	23	6	8,635	43,790	110,282	4.03
Men's and boys' clothing and furnishings stores	7	8	3	3,267	30,600	67,498	2.47
Family clothing stores—men's, women's, and children's	1	(x)	(x)	(x)	(x)	(x)	(x)
Women's ready-to-wear specialty stores—apparel and accessories	2	(x)	(x)	(x)	(x)	(x)	(x)
Women's accessories stores	2	(x)	(x)	(x)	(x)	(x)	(x)
Other apparel stores	7	9	2	3,764	1,090	21,669	.79
Shoe stores	1	(x)	(x)	(x)	(x)	(x)	(x)

(See footnotes at end of table.)

TABLE 11.—STORES OPERATED BY NEGRO PROPRIETORS, BY STATES: 1929—Continued

NUMBER OF STORES, PERSONNEL, PAY ROLL, STOCKS, AND SALES—Continued

[See note at head of table]

KIND OF BUSINESS	Number of stores	Proprietors and firm members (*not on pay roll*)	Number of employees (*full time*)	Total pay roll (*including part time*)	Stocks on hand, end of year (*at cost*)	NET SALES Amount	NET SALES Percent of total
NEW JERSEY—Continued							
Furniture and household group	11	13	10	$7,312	$30,800	$86,074	3.15
Floor coverings, draperies, curtains, and upholstery stores	3	3	2	1,100	650	5,250	.19
Other home furnishings and appliances stores	3	4	2	1,196	6,700	20,444	.75
Radio and music stores	5	6	6	5,016	23,450	60,380	2.21
Restaurants, cafeterias, and eating places	133	146	134	94,403	20,020	608,301	22.22
Restaurants, cafeterias, and lunch rooms	118	129	134	94,385	18,910	584,287	21.34
Lunch counters, refreshment stands, etc	15	17	----------	18	1,110	24,014	.88
Lumber and building group	7	7	9	18,977	22,350	123,840	4.52
Electrical shops (without radio)	3	2	3	3,975	6,310	37,247	1.36
Heating and plumbing shops	2	(x)	(x)	(x)	(x)	(x)	(x)
Paint and glass stores	2	(x)	(x)	(x)	(x)	(x)	(x)
Other retail stores [1]	132	144	62	62,236	123,250	666,411	24.34
Hardware stores	4	4	----------	----------	12,000	23,800	.87
Farmers' supplies	3	5	----------	----------	1,500	6,700	.24
Cigar stores and cigar stands	61	65	25	19,356	13,340	178,701	6.53
Coal and wood yards—ice dealers	14	15	9	8,890	2,870	76,070	2.78
Drug stores	19	22	14	18,557	71,370	238,634	8.72
Miscellaneous classifications (combined)	29	31	14	15,433	20,970	138,306	5.05
Second-hand stores	16	17	6	5,160	5,000	38,435	1.40
NEW MEXICO							
Total	1	(x)	(x)	(x)	(x)	(x)	100.00
NEW YORK							
Total	611	682	510	$500,533	$564,790	$5,625,743	100.00
Food group	196	213	79	95,102	151,620	1,970,031	35.02
Candy and confectionery stores	64	65	12	9,306	29,620	278,771	4.96
Grocery stores (without meats)	69	77	14	13,641	70,270	652,154	11.59
Combination stores (groceries and meats)	16	19	15	22,152	26,180	375,955	6.68
Meat markets (including sea foods)	16	17	15	22,862	4,510	319,000	5.67
Other food stores	31	35	23	27,141	21,040	344,151	6.12
General-merchandise group	6	6	2	4,100	27,340	53,180	.94
Dry-goods stores—piece-goods stores	2	(x)	(x)	(x)	(x)	(x)	(x)
General-merchandise stores	3	3	1	1,500	11,500	12,600	.22
Variety, 5-and-10, and to-a-dollar stores	1	(x)	(x)	(x)	(x)	(x)	(x)
Automotive group [1]	48	55	45	54,743	50,790	520,402	9.25
Filling stations	10	11	10	14,014	18,790	189,517	3.37
Garages and repair shops	25	29	25	33,026	15,850	249,275	4.43
Other automotive establishments	11	13	6	5,453	11,980	67,356	1.20
Apparel group	27	29	12	12,844	38,210	157,571	2.80
Men's and boys' clothing and furnishings stores	5	6	1	2,500	12,500	53,300	.95
Family clothing stores—men's, women's, and children's	2	(x)	(x)	(x)	(x)	(x)	(x)
Women's ready-to-wear specialty stores—apparel and accessories	8	8	6	3,716	8,160	29,680	.53
Women's accessories stores	2	(x)	(x)	(x)	(x)	(x)	(x)
Other apparel stores	8	9	3	2,624	1,700	22,700	.40
Shoe stores	2	(x)	(x)	(x)	(x)	(x)	(x)
Furniture and household group	10	11	8	13,590	10,170	58,526	1.04
Other home furnishings and appliances stores	1	(x)	(x)	(x)	(x)	(x)	(x)
Radio and music stores	9	(x)	(x)	(x)	(x)	(x)	(x)
Restaurants, cafeterias, and eating places	150	173	274	210,325	23,370	1,441,387	25.62
Restaurants, cafeterias, and lunch rooms	128	149	254	194,593	18,470	1,315,583	23.39
Lunch counters, refreshment stands, etc	22	24	20	15,732	4,900	125,804	2.23
Lumber and building group	10	14	21	23,671	59,680	331,263	5.89
Lumber and building-material dealers	3	4	14	16,054	49,750	249,074	4.43
Electrical shops (without radio)	4	6	4	3,897	1,930	27,030	.48
Heating and plumbing shops	1	(x)	(x)	(x)	(x)	(x)	(x)
Paint and glass stores	2	(x)	(x)	(x)	(x)	(x)	(x)
Other retail stores	146	162	65	82,558	191,520	1,052,078	18.70
Hardware stores	2	(x)	(x)	(x)	(x)	(x)	(x)
Farmers' supplies	1	(x)	(x)	(x)	(x)	(x)	(x)
Cigar stores and cigar stands	44	50	19	21,578	25,350	216,940	3.85
Coal-and-wood yards—ice dealers	7	7	1	1,280	2,240	49,346	.88
Drug stores	10	11	22	31,088	89,340	236,205	4.20
Jewelry stores	7	7	1	520	11,100	60,268	1.07
Miscellaneous classifications (combined)	75	84	17	19,622	50,750	337,550	6.00
Second-hand stores	18	19	4	3,600	12,090	41,305	.74
NORTH CAROLINA							
Total	1,907	2,077	577	$369,369	$707,720	$5,770,830	100.00
Food group	956	1,009	144	91,256	279,590	2,679,821	46.44
Candy and confectionery stores	48	49	1	913	3,630	55,187	.96
Grocery stores (without meats)	640	669	59	27,326	158,810	1,183,944	20.51
Combination stores (groceries and meats)	210	227	60	45,078	111,410	1,106,373	19.17
Meat markets (including sea foods)	54	60	22	17,239	5,260	324,787	5.63
Other food stores	4	4	2	700	480	9,530	.17
General stores	62	65	12	6,475	89,040	337,699	5.85
General merchandise group	8	17	6	7,842	22,130	98,226	1.70
Dry goods stores—piece goods stores	4	7	2	2,164	4,790	17,325	.30
General merchandise stores	2	(x)	(x)	(x)	(x)	(x)	(x)
Variety, 5-and-10, and to-a-dollar stores	2	(x)	(x)	(x)	(x)	(x)	(x)

See footnotes at end of table.)

TABLE 11.—STORES OPERATED BY NEGRO PROPRIETORS, BY STATES: 1929—Continued

NUMBER OF STORES, PERSONNEL, PAY ROLL, STOCKS, AND SALES—Continued

[See note at head of table]

KIND OF BUSINESS	Number of stores	Proprietors and firm members (*not on pay roll*)	Number of employees (*full time*)	Total pay roll (*including part time*)	Stocks on hand, end of year (*at cost*)	NET SALES	
						Amount	Percent of total
NORTH CAROLINA—Continued							
Automotive group	192	204	46	$33, 639	$27, 220	$495, 799	8. 60
Filling stations	143	154	25	20, 824	22, 450	414, 770	7. 19
Garages and repair shops	46	47	21	12, 815	4, 240	77, 738	1. 35
Other automotive establishments	3	3	-	-	530	3, 291	. 06
Apparel group	22	25	11	11, 088	13, 160	70, 650	1. 22
Men's and boys' clothing and furnishings stores	1	(x)	(x)	(x)	(x)	(x)	(x)
Women's ready-to-wear specialty stores—apparel and accessories	1	(x)	(x)	(x)	(x)	(x)	(x)
Women's accessories stores	2	(x)	(x)	(x)	(x)	(x)	(x)
Other apparel stores	14	16	8	8, 228	6, 270	53, 885	. 93
Shoe stores	4	5	3	2, 860	3, 690	9, 200	. 16
Furniture and household group	3	4	9	12, 910	23, 900	95, 200	1. 65
Furniture stores	3	4	9	12, 910	23, 900	95, 200	1. 65
Restaurants, cafeterias, and eating places	487	521	206	89, 781	37, 120	911, 935	15. 80
Restaurants, cafeterias, and lunch rooms	336	362	182	73, 520	25, 480	680, 223	11. 79
Lunch counters, refreshment stands, etc	151	159	24	16, 261	11, 640	231, 712	4. 01
Lumber and building group	3	4	4	4, 268	3, 900	24, 150	. 42
Lumber and building material dealers	1	(x)	(x)	(x)	(x)	(x)	(x)
Electrical shops (without radio)	1	(x)	(x)	(x)	(x)	(x)	(x)
Paint and glass stores	1	(x)	(x)	(x)	(x)	(x)	(x)
Other retail stores	161	213	136	109, 939	204, 900	1, 034, 140	17. 92
Cigar stores and cigar stands	9	10	3	1, 396	1, 440	17, 775	. 31
Coal and wood yards—ice dealers	23	24	9	5, 131	3, 970	38, 163	. 66
Drug stores	48	57	61	42, 137	88, 420	404, 776	7. 01
Jewelry stores	3	3	-	-	3, 300	4, 390	. 08
Miscellaneous classifications (combined)	78	119	63	61, 275	107, 770	569, 036	9. 86
Second-hand stores	13	15	3	2, 171	6, 760	23, 210	. 40
NORTH DAKOTA							
Total	**15**	**16**	**11**	**$9, 735**	**$17, 920**	**$198, 584**	**100. 00**
OHIO							
Total	**790**	**870**	**498**	**$415, 958**	**$433, 170**	**$4, 411, 775**	**100. 00**
Food group	262	281	62	56, 199	91, 750	1, 435, 613	32. 54
Candy and confectionery stores	67	70	12	6, 190	11, 200	174, 086	3. 95
Grocery stores (without meats)	96	101	10	8, 165	29, 970	392, 546	8. 90
Combination stores (groceries and meats)	68	77	21	16, 671	43, 200	612, 958	13. 89
Meat markets (including sea foods)	16	17	11	11, 483	2, 280	135, 677	3. 08
Other food stores	15	16	8	13, 690	5, 100	120, 346	2. 73
General stores	5	5	1	570	4, 800	29, 060	. 66
General merchandise group	5	6	3	2, 380	14, 930	81, 865	1. 86
Dry-goods stores—piece-goods stores	2	(x)	(x)	(x)	(x)	(x)	(x)
General merchandise stores	1	(x)	(x)	(x)	(x)	(x)	(x)
Variety, 5-and-10, and to-a-dollar stores	2	(x)	(x)	(x)	(x)	(x)	(x)
Automotive group	93	104	84	97, 822	111, 920	691, 506	15. 67
Motor-vehicle dealers (new and used)	5	7	22	32, 477	45, 180	317, 732	7. 20
Filling stations	20	23	20	18, 781	40, 480	148, 911	3. 38
Garages and repair shops	54	59	39	42, 164	15, 070	166, 378	3. 77
Other automotive establishments	14	15	3	4, 400	11, 190	58, 485	1. 33
Apparel group [1]	18	19	7	10, 256	47, 630	122, 822	2. 78
Women's ready-to-wear specialty stores—apparel and accessories	4	5	1	1, 500	1, 270	10, 700	. 24
Women's accessories stores	3	3	2	1, 900	3, 200	10, 200	. 23
Other apparel stores	4	4	-	200	2, 400	11, 255	. 26
Shoe stores	5	5	1	1, 800	29, 400	60, 185	1. 36
Furniture and household groups	5	6	6	6, 950	18, 750	59, 700	1. 35
Furniture stores	2	(x)	(x)	(x)	(x)	(x)	(x)
Household-appliances stores	1	(x)	(x)	(x)	(x)	(x)	(x)
Other home furnishings and appliances stores	1	(x)	(x)	(x)	(x)	(x)	(x)
Radio and music stores	1	(x)	(x)	(x)	(x)	(x)	(x)
Restaurants, cafeterias, and eating places	217	239	206	119, 902	23, 900	876, 036	19. 86
Restaurants, cafeterias, and lunch rooms	188	209	193	111, 067	22, 060	763, 877	17. 31
Lunch counters, refreshment stands, etc	29	30	13	8, 835	1, 840	112, 159	2. 54
Lumber and building group	7	8	7	6, 818	11, 420	45, 995	1. 04
Lumber and building material dealers	2	(x)	(x)	(x)	(x)	(x)	(x)
Electrical shops (without radio)	1	(x)	(x)	(x)	(x)	(x)	(x)
Heating and plumbing shops	1	(x)	(x)	(x)	(x)	(x)	(x)
Paint and glass stores	3	3	5	5, 818	6, 470	20, 845	. 47
Other retail stores [1]	152	173	114	107, 304	95, 520	1, 003, 646	22. 75
Farmers' supplies	3	4	5	2, 506	2, 500	8, 921	. 20
Cigar stores and cigar stands	51	62	24	18, 843	5, 820	164, 803	3. 74
Coal and wood yards—ice dealers	31	32	26	21, 416	5, 520	161, 602	3. 66
Drug stores	23	29	21	20, 643	46, 510	278, 192	6. 31
Jewelry stores	5	5	1	408	3, 250	15, 050	. 34
Miscellaneous classifications (combined)	38	40	36	41, 672	26, 920	362, 458	8. 22
Second-hand stores	26	29	8	7, 757	12, 550	65, 532	1. 49
OKLAHOMA							
Total	**546**	**626**	**320**	**$211, 888**	**$419, 040**	**$2, 833, 144**	**100. 00**
Food group	199	228	66	40, 015	90, 090	1, 001, 775	35. 36
Candy and confectionery stores	14	18	6	2, 508	2, 710	36, 985	1. 31
Grocery stores (without meats)	92	105	8	4, 123	26, 660	254, 338	8. 98
Combination stores (groceries and meats)	93	105	52	33, 384	60, 720	710, 452	25. 07
General stores—Groceries with dry goods or apparel	43	45	14	10, 774	90, 100	306, 951	10. 84

(See footnotes at end of table.)

Table 11.—STORES OPERATED BY NEGRO PROPRIETORS, BY STATES: 1929—Continued

Number of Stores, Personnel, Pay Roll, Stocks, and Sales—Continued

[See note at head of table]

KIND OF BUSINESS	Number of stores	Proprietors and firm members (*not on pay roll*)	Number of employees (*full time*)	Total pay roll (*including part time*)	Stocks on hand, end of year (*at cost*)	NET SALES Amount	NET SALES Percent of total
OKLAHOMA—Continued							
General merchandise group	9	10	5	$4,120	$29,590	$71,128	2.51
Dry goods stores	6	7	2	1,740	25,790	40,462	1.43
General merchandise stores	3	3	3	2,380	3,800	30,666	1.08
Automotive group	50	56	21	20,053	19,690	197,551	6.97
Filling stations	33	35	11	13,073	6,140	141,652	5.00
Garages and repair shops	16	20	7	5,780	12,550	50,899	1.80
Other automotive establishments	1	1	3	1,200	1,000	5,000	.17
Apparel group	7	7	11	9,888	49,900	104,642	3.69
Men's and boys' clothing and furnishings stores	1	(x)	(x)	(x)	(x)	(x)	(x)
Family clothing stores—men's, women's, and children's	3	3	8	7,400	46,600	88,192	3.11
Women's accessories stores	2	(x)	(x)	(x)	(x)	(x)	(x)
Other apparel stores	1	(x)	(x)	(x)	(x)	(x)	(x)
Furniture and household group [1]	5	6	3	1,375	3,050	9,260	.33
Radio and music stores	3	4	1	220	1,800	4,660	.17
Restaurants, cafeterias, and eating places	170	195	142	74,033	13,900	593,358	20.94
Restaurants, cafeterias, and lunch rooms	129	148	124	64,035	11,410	474,899	16.76
Lunch counters, refreshment stands, etc	41	47	18	9,998	2,490	118,459	4.18
Other retail stores	63	79	58	51,630	122,720	548,479	19.36
Lumber and building material dealers	1	(x)	(x)	(x)	(x)	(x)	(x)
Electrical shops (without radio)	1	(x)	(x)	(x)	(x)	(x)	(x)
Hardware stores	3	4	1	1,860	9,620	16,989	.60
Hardware and farm implement stores	2	(x)	(x)	(x)	(x)	(x)	(x)
Farmers' supplies stores	7	7	5	5,168	9,150	65,132	2.30
Book stores	1	(x)	(x)	(x)	(x)	(x)	(x)
Cigar stores and cigar stands	9	12	12	7,783	1,890	38,866	1.37
Coal and wood yards—ice dealers	1	(x)	(x)	(x)	(x)	(x)	(x)
Drug stores	20	23	21	18,766	57,820	214,032	7.55
Jewelry stores	1	(x)	(x)	(x)	(x)	(x)	(x)
Miscellaneous classifications (including 2 second-hand stores)	17	22	13	11,438	9,340	79,470	2.81
OREGON							
Total	**14**	**16**	**27**	**$34,036**	**$34,310**	**$329,541**	**100.00**
PENNSYLVANIA							
Total	**1,326**	**1,403**	**660**	**$599,513**	**$694,710**	**$6,519,865**	**100.00**
Food group	416	437	74	66,755	139,590	1,541,262	23.64
Candy and confectionery stores	152	155	25	19,050	37,170	359,107	5.51
Grocery stores (without meats)	176	185	14	9,169	73,030	590,165	9.05
Combination stores (groceries and meats)	29	29	9	8,082	16,330	182,200	2.80
Meat markets (including sea foods)	28	31	15	16,685	6,130	257,691	3.95
Other food stores	31	37	11	13,769	6,930	152,099	2.33
General merchandise group	5	5	2	2,580	19,500	58,000	.89
Dry goods stores—piece goods stores	2	(x)	(x)	(x)	(x)	(x)	(x)
General merchandise stores	2	(x)	(x)	(x)	(x)	(x)	(x)
Variety, 5-and-10, and to-a-dollar stores	1	(x)	(x)	(x)	(x)	(x)	(x)
Automotive group	74	80	89	125,200	122,050	1,356,699	20.81
Motor-vehicle dealers (new and used)	5	4	36	66,076	93,410	996,095	15.28
Filling stations	20	21	10	12,876	14,740	160,764	2.47
Garages and repair shops	42	48	40	42,769	7,710	172,439	2.64
Other automotive establishments	7	7	3	3,479	6,190	27,401	.42
Apparel group	46	46	28	32,762	39,160	234,868	3.60
Men's and boys' clothing and furnishings stores	3	3	-----	300	9,500	19,785	.30
Family clothing stores—men's, women's, and children's	3	3	2	2,892	9,660	45,529	.70
Women's ready-to-wear specialty stores—apparel and accessories	6	6	3	2,420	7,960	31,885	.49
Women's accessories stores	6	6	1	1,095	1,620	23,749	.36
Other apparel stores	25	25	19	22,895	5,920	101,495	1.56
Shoe stores	3	3	3	3,160	4,500	12,425	.19
Furniture and household group	23	25	15	11,483	39,860	99,114	1.52
Furniture stores	9	9	6	4,295	15,180	39,555	.61
Other home furnishings and appliances stores	7	8	3	1,500	8,300	8,600	.13
Radio and music stores	7	8	6	5,688	16,380	50,959	.78
Restaurants, cafeterias, and eating places	331	346	255	154,332	35,090	1,140,012	17.49
Restaurants, cafeterias, and lunch rooms	281	294	243	146,024	27,930	1,032,603	15.84
Lunch counters, refreshments stands, etc	50	52	12	8,308	7,160	107,409	1.65
Lumber and building group [1]	8	9	5	4,106	4,560	31,448	.48
Heating and plumbing shops	3	4	4	3,106	3,300	18,143	.28
Paint and glass stores	3	3	-----	400	660	9,295	.14
Other retail stores	359	386	186	197,555	269,170	1,954,072	29.97
General stores—groceries with dry goods and apparel	2	(x)	(x)	(x)	(x)	(x)	(x)
Hardware stores	3	5	-----	-----	9,700	30,908	.47
Hardware and farm implement stores	1	(x)	(x)	(x)	(x)	(x)	(x)
Farmers' supplies	2	(x)	(x)	(x)	(x)	(x)	(x)
Cigar stores and cigar stands	191	198	23	18,803	45,270	454,578	6.97
Coal and wood yards—ice dealers	15	14	28	30,633	12,240	196,454	3.01
Drug stores	40	48	45	54,072	109,720	413,167	6.34
Jewelry stores	7	8	3	3,659	13,140	35,841	.55
Miscellaneous classifications (combined)	98	106	84	88,267	60,140	759,405	11.65
Second-hand stores	64	69	6	4,740	25,730	104,390	1.60

(See footnotes at end of table.)

TABLE 11.—STORES OPERATED BY NEGRO PROPRIETORS, BY STATES: 1929—Continued

NUMBER OF STORES, PERSONNEL, PAY ROLL, STOCKS, AND SALES—Continued

[See note at head of table]

KIND OF BUSINESS	Number of stores	Proprietors and firm members (*not on pay roll*)	Number of employees (*full time*)	Total pay roll (*including part time*)	Stocks on hand, end of year (*at cost*)	NET SALES	
						Amount	Percent of total
RHODE ISLAND							
Total	41	43	16	$22,485	$39,310	$194,469	100.00
Food group	14	14	4	1,976	7,750	60,610	31.17
Grocery stores (without meats)	9	9	2	1,040	5,450	45,240	23.27
Combination stores (groceries and meats)	4	4	2	936	2,250	14,590	7.50
Other food stores	1	1	----	----	50	780	.40
Automotive group	5	5	2	3,120	2,600	26,067	13.40
Filling stations	1	(x)	(x)	(x)	(x)	(x)	(x)
Garages and repair shops	4	(x)	(x)	(x)	(x)	(x)	(x)
Restaurants, cafeterias, and eating places	8	8	3	5,588	2,430	23,172	11.92
Restaurants, cafeterias, and lunch rooms	8	8	3	5,588	2,430	23,172	11.92
Other retail stores	14	16	7	11,801	26,530	84,620	43.51
Dry goods stores—piece goods stores	1	(x)	(x)	(x)	(x)	(x)	(x)
General merchandise stores	1	(x)	(x)	(x)	(x)	(x)	(x)
Paint and glass stores	1	(x)	(x)	(x)	(x)	(x)	(x)
Hardware stores	1	(x)	(x)	(x)	(x)	(x)	(x)
Drug stores	3	4	1	625	13,500	31,750	16.33
Jewelry stores	1	(x)	(x)	(x)	(x)	(x)	(x)
Miscellaneous classifications (combined)	4	4	1	2,670	[illegible],030	27,520	14.15
Second-hand stores	2	(x)	(x)	(x)	(x)	(x)	(x)
SOUTH CAROLINA							
Total	1,230	1,320	350	$180,739	$201,010	$2,298,672	100.00
Food group	671	704	69	33,023	92,860	1,065,240	46.34
Candy and confectionery stores	16	17	4	2,625	1,200	18,207	.79
Grocery stores (without meats)	505	527	39	14,819	70,020	692,035	30.11
Combination stores (groceries and meats)	101	106	13	8,000	18,740	231,732	10.08
Meat markets (including sea foods)	41	45	11	7,219	2,630	114,042	4.96
Other food stores	8	9	2	360	270	9,224	.40
General stores	48	50	8	3,245	19,260	119,396	5.19
General merchandise group [1]	4	4	3	2,387	4,660	14,285	.62
Dry goods stores—piece goods stores	3	3	3	2,387	4,580	13,685	.59
Automotive group	93	104	31	19,781	12,450	168,828	7.35
Filling stations	56	62	13	7,554	10,010	108,912	4.74
Garages and repair shops	37	42	18	12,227	2,440	59,916	2.61
Apparel group [1]	13	14	18	12,376	1,420	33,875	1.47
Apparel stores	12	12	16	11,960	1,070	32,425	1.41
Restaurants, cafeterias, and eating places	278	291	90	30,831	7,870	316,041	13.75
Restaurants, cafeterias, and lunch rooms	219	228	77	24,777	5,770	233,064	10.14
Lunch counters, refreshment stands, etc	59	63	13	6,054	2,100	82,977	3.61
Other retail stores [1]	116	145	127	77,412	60,860	572,888	24.93
Farmers' supplies	3	4	2	1,742	3,550	38,480	1.67
Coal and wood yards—ice dealers	21	21	19	5,635	850	44,251	1.93
Drug stores	20	24	16	7,961	17,320	113,748	4.95
Miscellaneous classifications (combined)	70	94	84	55,643	33,220	325,440	14.16
Second-hand stores	7	8	4	1,684	1,630	8,119	.35
SOUTH DAKOTA							
Total	13	14	15	$18,319	$23,940	$129,862	100.00
TENNESSEE							
Total	973	1,100	537	$311,748	$327,960	$3,728,674	100.00
Food group	360	394	89	48,164	138,790	1,489,115	39.94
Candy and confectionery stores	8	8	9	3,704	810	27,700	.75
Grocery stores (without meats)	196	216	25	11,896	66,070	592,021	15.88
Combination stores (groceries and meats)	136	145	40	21,490	69,450	776,370	20.82
Meat markets (including sea foods)	17	22	9	7,330	2,120	79,584	2.13
Other food stores	3	3	6	3,744	340	13,440	.36
General stores	18	26	4	2,126	17,600	84,800	2.27
General merchandise group	3	6	2	1,200	3,200	11,840	.32
Dry goods stores—piece goods stores	3	6	2	1,200	3,200	11,840	.32
Automotive group [1]	55	66	[illegible]	43,757	9,560	217,890	5.84
Filling stations	15	13	15	12,931	5,950	89,973	2.41
Garages and repair shops	39	47	32	30,826	3,580	127,517	3.42
Apparel group	8	10	8	6,072	15,490	61,578	1.65
Men's and boys' clothing and furnishings stores	1	(x)	(x)	(x)	(x)	(x)	(x)
Family clothing stores—men's, women's, and children's	1	(x)	(x)	(x)	(x)	(x)	(x)
Other apparel stores	4	4	4	2,452	2,800	22,418	.60
Shoe stores	2	x)	(x)	(x)	(x)	(x)	(x)
Furniture and household group	4	4	4	2,462	1,020	14,340	.39
Furniture stores	2	x)	(x)	(x)	(x)	(x)	(x)
Other home furnishings and appliances stores	2	(x)	(x)	(x)	(x)	(x)	(x)
Restaurants, cafeterias, and eating places	427	449	233	99,202	30,350	1,006,873	27.00
Restaurants, cafeterias, and lunch rooms	291	310	206	89,364	23,040	787,890	21.13
Lunch counters, refreshment stands, etc	136	139	27	9,838	7,310	218,983	5.87
Other retail stores	92	139	150	108,765	109,500	834,883	22.39
Hardware stores	1	(x)	(x)	(x)	(x)	(x)	(x)
Hardware and farm implement stores	2	(x)	(x)	(x)	(x)	(x)	(x)
Farmers' supplies (including feeds and fertilizers)	1	(x)	(x)	(x)	(x)	(x)	(x
Coal and wood yards—ice dealers	1	(x)	(x)	(x)	(x)	(x)	(x)
Drug stores	35	47	60	40,8[illegible]	53,610	345,201	9.26
Jewelry stores	1	(x)	(x)	(x)	(x)	(x)	(x)
Miscellaneous classifications (combined)	51	83	84	[illegible],679	4[illegible],[illegible]00	441,358	11.84
Second-hand stores	6	6	----	----	2,450	7,355	.20

(See footnotes at end of table.)

Table 11.—STORES OPERATED BY NEGRO PROPRIETORS, BY STATES: 1929—Continued

Number of Stores, Personnel, Pay Roll, Stocks, and Sales—Continued

[See note at head of table]

KIND OF BUSINESS	Number of stores	Proprietors and firm members (*not on pay roll*)	Number of employees (*full time*)	Total pay roll (*including part time*)	Stocks on hand, end of year (*at cost*)	NET SALES Amount	NET SALES Percent of total
TEXAS							
Total	**1,736**	**1,963**	**999**	**$569,974**	**$675,640**	**$6,633,701**	**100.00**
Food group	610	674	137	70,662	178,420	2,060,579	31.06
Candy and confectionery stores	65	70	19	7,931	7,920	106,526	1.61
Grocery stores (without meats)	351	377	43	16,473	89,050	775,330	11.69
Combination stores (groceries and meats)	156	186	58	32,780	75,840	939,603	14.16
Meat markets	14	14	11	9,808	1,540	118,160	1.76
Other food stores	24	27	6	3,670	4,070	120,960	1.82
General stores—groceries with dry goods or apparel	28	31	8	8,092	107,980	459,192	6.92
Automotive group [1]	149	165	85	63,453	57,670	728,937	10.99
Filling stations	84	89	34	22,398	11,770	326,737	4.93
Garages and repair shops	60	71	37	26,688	27,950	188,003	2.83
Other automotive establishments	4	4	3	2,823	2,180	19,660	.30
Apparel group [1]	32	35	36	32,909	72,480	312,411	4.71
Men's and boys' clothing and furnishings stores	4	4	6	5,888	20,670	63,996	.96
Women's accessories stores	7	7	15	15,576	25,260	132,346	2.00
Other apparel stores	16	18	9	6,145	2,060	47,019	.71
Shoe stores	3	3	1	600	300	4,050	.06
Furniture and household group [1]	4	4	3	4,111	3,180	44,104	.67
Furniture stores	3	3	3	4,111	2,680	41,554	.63
Restaurants, cafeterias, and eating places	707	785	488	238,496	39,610	1,736,710	26.18
Restaurants, cafeterias, and lunch rooms	520	586	410	191,932	28,020	1,300,351	19.60
Lunch counters, refreshment stands, etc	187	199	78	46,564	11,590	436,359	6.58
Other retail stores	195	257	234	145,805	203,670	1,259,209	18.98
Dry goods stores	2	(x)	(x)	(x)	(x)	(x)	(x)
General merchandise stores	1	(x)	(x)	(x)	(x)	(x)	(x)
Electrical shops (without radio)	1	(x)	(x)	(x)	(x)	(x)	(x)
Heating and plumbing shops	2	(x)	(x)	(x)	(x)	(x)	(x)
Paint and glass stores	1	(x)	(x)	(x)	(x)	(x)	(x)
Hardware and farm implement stores	1	(x)	(x)	(x)	(x)	(x)	(x)
Farmers' supplies	7	9	2	964	3,880	27,091	.41
Cigar stores and cigar stands	12	13	17	8,882	1,290	63,148	.95
Coal and wood yards—ice dealers	25	28	21	10,044	3,890	75,424	1.14
Drug stores	77	99	114	61,786	106,610	544,098	8.20
Jewelry stores	3	3	1	1,980	7,320	13,350	.20
Miscellaneous classifications	63	93	63	48,036	43,110	385,933	5.82
Second-hand stores	11	12	8	6,446	12,630	32,559	.49
UTAH							
Total	**5**	**6**	**5**	**$2,951**	**$14,500**	**$83,945**	**100.00**
VERMONT							
Total	**3**	**5**	**4**	**$4,286**	**$9,830**	**$76,462**	**100.00**
VIRGINIA							
Total	**1,878**	**2,043**	**645**	**$378,446**	**$885,720**	**$4,986,347**	**100.00**
Food group	964	1,015	165	85,863	276,000	2,128,400	42.68
Candy and confectionery stores	103	109	21	7,548	19,120	180,688	3.62
Grocery stores (without meats)	562	595	49	21,814	161,960	926,487	18.58
Combination stores (groceries and meats)	197	205	47	29,309	88,480	734,223	14.72
Meat markets (including sea foods)	73	78	40	21,787	3,830	199.317	4.00
Other food stores	29	28	8	5,405	2,610	87,685	1.76
General stores	185	231	27	11,534	213,850	680,372	13.65
General merchandise group [1]	11	12	11	5,107	11,270	24,149	.48
General merchandise stores	6	7	11	5,107	10,550	20,600	.41
Variety, 5-and-10, and to-a-dollar stores	3	3	----------	----------	270	2,549	.05
Automotive group [1]	130	147	44	28,342	32,680	351,598	7.05
Filling stations	85	99	19	7,442	14,280	151,199	3.03
Garages and repair shops	43	45	18	12,757	5,030	72,790	1.46
Apparel group	16	16	21	14,046	7,810	54,686	1.10
Men's and boys' clothing and furnishings stores	2	(x)	(x)	(x)	(x)	(x)	(x)
Family clothing stores—men's, women's, and children's	1	(x)	(x)	(x)	(x)	(x)	(x)
Women's ready-to-wear specialty stores—apparel and accessories	1	(x)	(x)	(x)	(x)	(x)	(x)
Women's accessories stores	1	(x)	(x)	(x)	(x)	(x)	(x)
Other apparel stores	9	9	17	10,402	2,900	32,174	.64
Shoe stores	2	(x)	(x)	(x)	(x)	(x)	(x)
Furniture and household group	6	7	10	11,868	5,070	35,862	.72
Furniture stores	3	4	3	4,652	3.370	19,662	.40
Other home furnishings and appliances stores	2	(x)	(x)	(x)	(x)	(x)	(x)
Radio and music stores	1	(x)	(x)	(x)	(x)	(x)	(x)
Restaurants, cafeterias, and eating places	355	365	172	61,134	28,890	529,306	10.62
Restaurants, cafeterias, and lunch rooms	296	305	166	58,920	24,970	483,407	9.70
Lunch counters, refreshment stands, etc	59	60	6	2,214	3,920	45,899	.92
Lumber and building group	6	6	9	4,963	7,600	18,150	.36
Lumber and building material dealers	1	(x)	(x)	(x)	(x)	(x)	(x)
Electrical shops (without radio)	2	(x)	(x)	(x)	(x)	(x)	(x)
Paint and glass stores	3	3	6	3,178	1,900	8,050	.16

(See footnotes at end of table.)

TABLE 11.—STORES OPERATED BY NEGRO PROPRIETORS, BY STATES: 1929—Continued

NUMBER OF STORES, PERSONNEL, PAY ROLL, STOCKS, AND SALES—Continued

[See note at head of table]

KIND OF BUSINESS	Number of stores	Proprietors and firm members (*not on pay roll*)	Number of employees (*full time*)	Total pay roll (*including part time*)	Stocks on hand, end of year (*at cost*)	NET SALES	
						Amount	Percent of total
VIRGINIA—Continued							
Other retail stores [1]	197	236	184	$154,645	$297,680	$1,148,568	23.03
Farmers' supplies	21	22	1	1,016	13,240	65,867	1.32
Cigar stores and cigar stands	16	16	12	6,868	1,440	32,096	.64
Coal and wood yards—ice dealers	37	38	23	11,919	4,640	92,304	1.85
Drug stores	21	23	26	17,989	60,120	215,376	4.32
Jewelry stores	4	4	13	26,070	152,920	140,718	2.82
Miscellaneous classifications (combined)	96	131	108	89,823	60,320	583,207	11.70
Second-hand stores	8	8	2	944	4,870	15,256	.31
WASHINGTON							
Total	18	21	18	$17,899	$10,440	$175,521	100.00
WEST VIRGINIA							
Total	310	344	177	$117,419	$160,070	$1,169,006	100.00
Food group [1]	92	103	21	10,183	37,670	260,486	22.28
Candy and confectionery stores	17	19	3	1,173	3,380	36,078	3.09
Grocery stores (without meats)	41	44	6	3,090	17,610	94,145	8.05
Combination stores (groceries and meats)	24	30	9	4,902	13,700	100,713	8.62
Other food stores	8	8	3	1,018	2,220	27,173	2.32
General stores—groceries with dry goods or apparel	18	26	10	5,526	36,580	211,981	18.13
Automotive group	13	14	9	6,008	3,040	40,218	3.44
Filling stations	4	4	1	600	370	6,600	.56
Garages and repair shops	9	10	8	5,408	2,670	33,618	2.88
Apparel group [1]	10	10	3	2,436	4,970	25,334	2.17
Men's and boys' clothing and furnishings stores	3	3	1	300	890	5,350	.46
Women's ready-to-wear stores	3	3	-----	-----	1,100	8,500	.73
Shoe stores	3	3	1	936	1,980	8,984	.77
Restaurants, cafeterias, and eating places	149	157	100	55,643	24,820	381,533	32.64
Restaurants, cafeterias, and lunch rooms	107	114	92	49,728	19,990	320,041	27.38
Lunch counters, refreshment stands, etc.	42	43	8	5,915	4,830	61,492	5.26
Other retail stores	25	31	33	36,923	52,340	245,154	20.97
General merchandise stores	1	(x)	(x)	(x)	(x)	(x)	(x)
Furniture stores	1	(x)	(x)	(x)	(x)	(x)	(x)
Other home furnishings and appliances stores	1	(x)	(x)	(x)	(x)	(x)	(x)
Hardware stores	1	(x)	(x)	(x)	(x)	(x)	(x)
Cigar stores and cigar stands	6	7	3	2,016	1,800	13,056	1.12
Coal and wood yards—ice dealers	1	(x)	(x)	(x)	(x)	(x)	(x)
Drug stores	11	15	21	22,479	29,960	148,903	12.74
Miscellaneous classifications (combined)	3	4	2	2,050	1,410	22,853	1.95
Second-hand stores	3	3	1	700	650	4,300	.37
WISCONSIN							
Total	50	57	61	$52,037	$53,920	$474,414	100.00
Food group	10	11	5	5,554	5,790	118,416	24.96
Candy and confectionery stores	3	4	1	596	570	10,865	2.29
Grocery stores (without meats)	2	(x)	(x)	(x)	(x)	(x)	(x)
Combination stores—grocery stores with meats	3	2	1	1,371	3,400	24,165	5.09
Meat markets (including sea foods)	2	(x)	(x)	(x)	(x)	(x)	(x)
Automotive group	4	5	1	1,080	4,360	22,677	4.78
Motor-vehicle dealers (new and used)	2	(x)	(x)	(x)	(x)	(x)	(x)
Garages and repair shops	2	(x)	(x)	(x)	(x)	(x)	(x)
Restaurants, cafeterias, and eating places	17	21	31	17,376	2,050	92,604	19.52
Restaurants, cafeterias, and lunch rooms	11	14	24	13,162	1,250	61,831	13.03
Lunch counters, refreshment stands, etc.	6	7	7	4,214	800	30,773	6.49
Other retail stores	19	20	24	28,027	41,720	240,717	50.74
Variety, 5-and-10, and to-a-dollar stores	2	(x)	(x)	(x)	(x)	(x)	(x)
Men's and boys' clothing and furnishings stores	1	(x)	(x)	(x)	(x)	(x)	(x)
Women's accessories stores	1	(x)	(x)	(x)	(x)	(x)	(x)
Radio and music stores	1	(x)	(x)	(x)	(x)	(x)	(x)
Heating and plumbing shops	1	(x)	(x)	(x)	(x)	(x)	(x)
Book stores	1	(x)	(x)	(x)	(x)	(x)	(x)
Cigar stores and cigar stands	3	3	3	2,704	150	3,995	.84
Coal and wood yards—ice dealers	1	(x)	(x)	(x)	(x)	(x)	(x)
Drug stores	4	5	6	6,619	18,230	95,526	20.14
Miscellaneous classifications (combined)	3	3	-----	-----	1,170	5,677	1.20
Second-hand stores	1	(x)	(x)	(x)	(x)	(x)	(x)
WYOMING							
Total	3	3	4	$4,678	$3,250	$24,176	100.00

[1] This total includes 1 classification in which the number of stores is less than 3, and concerning which no information can be disclosed.
[2] Data by kind of business not available.
[3] Group totals withheld in order to avoid disclosure of individual operations.
[4] This total is for full-time employees only.
[5] This total includes classifications in which the number of stores is less than 3, and concerning which no information can be disclosed.

TABLE 12.—STORES OPERATED BY NEGRO PROPRIETORS, BY KIND OF BUSINESS, FOR CITIES HAVING 50,000 OR MORE NEGRO INHABITANTS: 1929

NUMBER OF STORES, PERSONNEL, PAY ROLL, STOCKS, AND SALES

KIND OF BUSINESS	Number of stores	Proprietors and firm members (*not on pay roll*)	NUMBER OF EMPLOYEES		Total pay roll (*including part time*)	Stocks on hand, end of year (*at cost*)	NET SALES	
			Full time	Part time			Amount	Percent of total
Total	**5,741**	**5,979**	**3,576**	**770**	**$2,674,564**	**$2,151,758**	**$27,862,020**	**100.0**
Food group	1,923	2,002	420	183	335,248	566,530	9,366,532	33.6
Candy and confectionery stores	378	367	79	16	46,464	76,340	1,073,339	3.9
Grocery stores (without meats)	650	650	88	31	61,872	230,420	2,682,498	9.6
Combination stores (groceries and meats)	363	388	108	47	87,959	178,630	2,929,856	10.5
Meat markets (including sea foods)	112	122	54	19	49,416	17,980	849,169	3.1
Bakeries—bakery goods stores (except manufacturing bakeries)	17	24	25	44	38,962	2,840	179,508	.6
Coffee, tea, and spice dealers	3	4	4	----------	2,312	1,350	30,520	.1
Dairy products stores (including ice cream)	29	41	15	2	6,112	5,750	132,329	.5
Delicatessen stores	88	90	10	5	9,077	38,660	447,084	1.6
Egg and poultry dealers	17	19	7	2	6,908	1,840	145,820	.5
Fruit stores and vegetable markets	266	297	30	17	26,166	12,720	896,409	3.2
General stores—groceries with dry goods, apparel, or general merchandise	5	5	----------	----------	----------	2,370	16,098	.1
General merchandise group	33	38	8	----------	8,611	63,990	154,389	.6
Dry goods stores	12	16	6	----------	6,695	45,960	109,886	.4
General merchandise stores	7	8	1	----------	1,500	11,900	20,435	.1
Variety, 5-and-10, and to-a-dollar stores	14	14	1	----------	416	6,130	24,068	.1
Automotive group	262	301	246	44	250,178	114,320	1,679,327	6.0
Filling stations:								
Filling stations—gasoline and oil	34	36	36	10	39,991	11,610	439,714	1.6
Filling stations with tires and accessories	26	28	34	4	34,285	49,010	354,947	1.3
Filling stations with other merchandise	10	12	10	3	6,869	1,820	39,055	.1
Garages and repair shops	142	166	137	23	141,114	20,520	613,240	2.2
Other automotive establishments	50	59	29	4	27,919	31,360	232,371	.8
Apparel group	191	202	119	31	108,594	179,640	951,592	3.4
Men's and boys' clothing and furnishings stores	15	16	10	3	9,145	43,270	156,484	.6
Family clothing stores—men's, women's, and children's	8	9	2	1	1,760	11,980	47,661	.2
Women's ready-to-wear specialty stores—apparel and accessories	34	37	20	2	15,988	29,500	137,184	.5
Women's accessories stores	26	27	18	10	20,490	36,820	186,489	.7
Other apparel stores	95	100	59	14	51,547	27,250	321,328	1.1
Shoe stores	13	13	10	1	9,664	30,820	102,446	.3
Furniture and household group	69	77	46	12	38,074	56,070	275,074	1.0
Furniture stores	15	16	11	----------	7,230	6,770	37,583	.1
Floor coverings, drapery, curtain, and upholstery stores	2 }	5	3	1	1,324	1,480	10,700	.1
Household appliances stores	3 }							
Other home furnishings and appliances stores	11	12	9	4	7,318	12,270	23,507	.1
Radio and music stores	38	44	23	7	22,202	35,550	203,284	.7
Restaurants and eating places	1,898	1,890	1,804	212	1,028,931	140,023	7,371,584	26.5
Restaurants, cafeterias, and lunch rooms:								
Cafeterias	6	6	34	1	24,209	1,040	170,127	.6
Lunch rooms	1,058	999	817	104	441,955	69,533	3,728,269	13.4
Restaurants with table service	225	227	714	67	415,897	26,815	2,056,455	7.4
Lunch counters, refreshment stands, etc.:								
Lunch counters	345	370	199	35	125,707	30,165	1,011,052	3.6
Refreshment stands	142	158	21	2	12,004	5,810	220,957	.8
Soft-drink stands	122	130	19	3	9,159	6,660	184,724	.7
Lumber and building group	28	33	45	2	59,651	26,940	329,156	1.2
Lumber and building material dealers	6	8	10	1	7,286	6,000	51,499	.2
Electrical shops (without radio)	7	9	8	----------	6,773	2,640	40,930	.2
Heating and plumbing shops	8	8	21	----------	34,826	4,980	150,976	.5
Paint and glass stores	7	8	6	1	10,766	13,320	85,751	.3
Other retail stores	1,132	1,216	834	271	800,156	925,055	7,230,335	26.0
Hardware stores	10	12	3	----------	2,300	19,640	52,348	.2
Farmers' supplies	15 }	20	8	3	6,424	5,480	101,627	.4
Book stores	2 }							
Cigar stores and cigar stands:								
Cigar stores without fountains	163	154	34	12	31,568	47,940	529,985	1.9
Cigar stores with fountains	15	16	3	1	2,570	3,085	31,717	.1
Cigar stands (hotel lobbies, pool rooms, etc.)	94	99	66	8	46,382	13,960	284,999	1.0
Coal and wood yards—ice dealers	241	264	98	46	82,784	34,010	825,573	3.0
Drug stores:								
Drug stores without fountains	60	66	74	16	65,991	162,510	673,421	2.4
Drug stores with fountains	161	187	241	78	243,382	420,970	2,116,165	7.6
Jewelry stores	31	33	5	4	4,368	23,150	125,294	.5
Miscellaneous classifications (combined)	340	365	302	103	314,387	194,310	2,489,206	8.9
Second-hand stores	200	215	54	15	45,121	76,820	487,933	1.7

Table 13.—STORES OPERATED BY NEGRO PROPRIETORS FOR CITIES HAVING 50,000 OR MORE NEGRO INHABITANTS: 1929

Number of Stores, Personnel, Pay Roll, Stocks, and Sales

CITIES	Negro population [1]	Number of stores	Proprietors and firm members (*not on pay roll*)	NUMBER OF EMPLOYEES		Total pay roll (*including part time*)	Stocks on hand, end of year (*at cost*)	NET SALES			
				Full time	Part time			Amount	Percent of total	Per capita of Negro population	Average per store
Total	**1,927,569**	**5,741**	**5,979**	**3,576**	**770**	**$2,674,564**	**$2,151,758**	**$27,862,020**	**100.0**	**$14**	**$4,853**
Atlanta, Ga.	90,075	391	424	192	70	95,636	56,710	1,151,850	4.1	13	2,946
Baltimore, Md.	142,106	282	283	132	76	123,198	48,135	1,062,946	3.8	7	3,769
Birmingham, Ala.	99,077	200	228	144	6	64,044	43,790	601,916	2.2	6	3,010
Chicago, Ill.	233,903	815	866	576	147	497,349	435,130	4,826,897	17.3	21	5,923
Cleveland, Ohio	71,899	215	240	161	34	108,666	108,810	1,156,859	4.1	16	5,381
Detroit, Mich.	120,066	358	413	369	38	304,713	154,963	2,951,471	10.6	25	8,244
Houston, Tex.	63,337	259	272	259	22	155,511	82,000	1,343,588	4.8	21	5,188
Memphis, Tenn.	96,550	379	304	217	32	132,858	97,300	1,552,583	5.6	16	4,097
New Orleans, La.	129,632	771	906	238	22	126,252	130,140	2,300,374	8.3	18	2,984
New York, N. Y.	327,706	391	245	313	63	293,482	346,240	3,322,274	11.9	10	8,497
Bronx Borough	12,930	19	19	15	2	14,750	50,110	316,112	1.1	24	16,637
Brooklyn Borough	68,921	94	62	48	2	43,043	52,090	543,047	2.0	8	5,777
Manhattan Borough	224,670	258	142	243	56	227,414	229,990	2,261,677	8.1	10	8,766
Queens Borough	18,609	17	19	7	2	8,125	13,400	190,838	.7	10	11,226
Richmond Borough	2,576	3	3	---	1	150	650	10,600	(2)	4	3,533
Philadelphia, Pa.	219,599	787	819	337	96	300,747	266,480	3,150,007	11.3	14	4,003
Pittsburgh, Pa.	54,983	150	168	128	20	99,327	94,810	830,013	3.0	15	5,533
Richmond, Va.	52,988	189	199	102	36	61,202	67,760	657,961	2.4	12	3,481
St. Louis, Mo.	93,580	310	328	213	45	149,516	116,670	1,457,427	5.2	16	4,701
Washington, D. C.	132,068	244	284	195	63	162,063	102,820	1,495,854	5.4	11	6,131

[1] Enumerated Apr. 1, 1930.

[2] Less than 1/10 of 1 percent.

Table 14.—NET SALES OF SELECTED KIND OF BUSINESS COMPARED, BY CITIES OF 50,000 OR MORE NEGRO INHABITANTS: 1929

CITY	Net sales in order of size	Percent of total
RESTAURANTS AND EATING PLACES		
Total	**$7,371,584**	**100.00**
New York, N. Y.	1,003,713	13.62
Chicago, Ill.	989,569	13.42
Detroit, Mich.	813,454	11.03
Philadelphia, Pa.	678,769	9.21
New Orleans, La.	551,713	7.48
Memphis, Tenn.	495,847	6.73
Washington, D. C.	481,812	6.54
Atlanta, Ga.	467,974	6.35
Houston, Tex.	466,624	6.33
St. Louis, Mo.	432,391	5.86
Cleveland, Ohio	343,383	4.66
Baltimore, Md.	216,387	2.94
Pittsburgh, Pa.	191,843	2.60
Birmingham, Ala.	172,563	2.34
Richmond, Va.	65,542	.89
COMBINATION STORES (GROCERIES AND MEATS)		
Total	**$2,929,856**	**100.00**
Detroit, Mich.	626,242	21.37
Chicago, Ill.	498,924	17.03
Memphis, Tenn.	419,481	14.32
Atlanta, Ga.	266,064	9.08
St. Louis, Mo.	248,470	8.48
Houston, Tex.	147,961	5.05
Richmond, Va.	142,431	4.86
Cleveland, Ohio	138,286	4.72
Washington, D. C.	84,035	2.87
Philadelphia, Pa.	80,460	2.75
Birmingham, Ala.	75,440	2.57
Baltimore, Md.	74,900	2.56
New Orleans, La.	66,100	2.26
New York, N. Y.	32,880	1.12
Pittsburgh, Pa.	28,182	.96

CITY	Net sales in order of size	Percent of total
DRUG STORES		
Total	**$2,789,586**	**100.00**
Chicago, Ill.	632,063	22.66
Detroit, Mich.	392,044	14.05
St. Louis, Mo.	270,885	9.71
Washington, D. C.	238,281	8.54
Philadelphia, Pa.	220,407	7.90
New York, N. Y.	212,705	7.63
Memphis, Tenn.	152,724	5.48
New Orleans, La.	147,804	5.30
Houston, Tex.	106,336	3.81
Pittsburgh, Pa.	99,645	3.57
Baltimore, Md.	87,537	3.14
Atlanta, Ga.	80,670	2.89
Richmond, Va.	68,375	2.45
Birmingham, Ala.	58,680	2.10
Cleveland, Ohio	21,430	.77
GROCERY STORES (WITHOUT MEATS)		
Total	**$2,682,498**	**100.00**
New York, N. Y.	534,598	19.93
Chicago, Ill.	430,434	16.05
New Orleans, La.	377,493	14.07
Philadelphia, Pa.	279,520	10.42
Detroit, Mich.	214,607	8.00
Cleveland, Ohio	171,163	6.38
Memphis, Tenn.	161,537	6.02
Atlanta, Ga.	119,801	4.47
Houston, Tex.	90,533	3.38
Birmingham, Ala.	60,009	2.24
St. Louis, Mo.	54,140	2.02
Baltimore, Md.	53,410	1.99
Pittsburgh, Pa.	48,400	1.80
Washington, D. C.	46,511	1.73
Richmond, Va.	40,342	1.50

Table 15.—KIND OF RETAIL BUSINESS OPERATED BY NEGRO PROPRIETORS, REPORTING NET SALES OF $100,000 AND OVER IN CITIES HAVING 50,000 OR MORE NEGRO INHABITANTS: 1929

CITY AND KIND OF BUSINESS	NET SALES	
	Amount	Percent of total
CHICAGO, ILL.		
All business, total	$4,826,897	100.0
Principal kinds of business	3,477,951	72.1
Grocery stores	929,358	19.3
Restaurants, cafeterias, and lunch rooms	802,179	16.6
Drug stores	632,063	13.1
Delicatessen stores	334,980	6.9
Lunch counters, refreshment stands, etc	187,390	3.9
Second-hand stores	182,216	3.8
Garages and repair shops	156,250	3.2
Cigar stores and cigar stands	139,534	2.9
Coal and wood yards—ice dealers	113,981	2.4
NEW YORK, N. Y.		
All business, total	3,322,274	100.0
Principal kinds of business	2,211,779	66.5
Restaurants, cafeterias, and lunch rooms	930,169	28.0
Grocery stores	567,478	17.1
Drug stores	212,705	6.4
Meat markets (including sea foods)	193,538	5.8
Candy and confectionery stores	187,627	5.6
Cigar stores and cigar stands	120,262	3.6
PHILADELPHIA, PA.		
All business, total	3,150,007	100.0
Principal kinds of business	1,956,779	62.1
Restaurants, cafeterias, and lunch rooms	627,892	19.9
Grocery stores	359,980	11.4
Cigar stores and cigar stands	325,857	10.3
Drug stores	220,407	7.0
Coal and wood yards—ice dealers	178,383	5.7
Meat markets (including sea foods)	122,875	3.9
Candy and confectionery stores	121,385	3.9
DETROIT, MICH.		
All business, total	2,951,471	100.0
Principal kinds of business	2,482,645	84.1
Grocery stores	840,849	28.5
Restaurants, cafeterias, and lunch rooms	638,687	21.6
Drug stores	392,044	13.3
Filling stations	273,747	9.3
Lunch counters, refreshment stands, etc	174,767	5.9
Candy and confectionery stores	162,551	5.5
NEW ORLEANS, LA.		
All business, total	2,300,374	100.0
Principal kinds of business	1,912,769	83.2
Fruit stores and vegetable markets	604,321	26.3
Grocery stores	443,593	19.3
Restaurants, cafeterias, and lunch rooms	300,425	13.1
Lunch counters, refreshment stands, etc	251,288	10.9
Coal and wood yards—ice dealers	165,338	7.2
Drug stores	147,804	6.4
MEMPHIS, TENN.		
All business, total	1,552,583	100.0
Principal kinds of business	1,229,589	79.1
Grocery stores	581,018	37.4
Restaurants, cafeterias, and lunch rooms	353,834	22.8
Drug stores	152,724	9.8
Lunch counters, refreshment stands, etc	142,013	9.1
WASHINGTON, D. C.		
All business, total	$1,495,854	100.0
Principal kinds of business	1,053,657	70.4
Restaurants, cafeterias, and lunch rooms	475,152	31.8
Drug stores	238,281	15.9
Grocery stores	130,546	8.7
Coal and wood yards—ice dealers	106,316	7.1
Meat markets (including sea foods)	103,362	6.9
ST. LOUIS, MO.		
All business, total	1,457,427	100.0
Principal kinds of business	1,045,276	71.7
Restaurants, cafeterias, and lunch rooms	351,597	24.1
Grocery stores	302,610	20.8
Drug stores	270,885	18.6
Candy and confectionery stores	120,184	8.2
HOUSTON, TEX.		
All business, total	1,343,588	100.0
Principal kinds of business	934,750	69.6
Restaurants, cafeterias, and lunch rooms	305,336	22.7
Grocery stores	238,494	17.8
Lunch counters, refreshment stands, etc	161,288	12.0
Women's accessories stores	123,296	9.2
Drug stores	106,336	7.9
CLEVELAND, OHIO		
All business, total	1,156,859	100.0
Principal kinds of business	606,912	52.4
Grocery stores	309,449	26.7
Restaurants, cafeterias, and lunch rooms	297,463	25.7
ATLANTA, GA.		
All business, total	1,151,850	100.0
Principal kinds of business	692,839	60.2
Grocery stores	385,865	33.5
Restaurants, cafeterias, and lunch rooms	306,974	26.7
BALTIMORE, MD.		
All business, total	1,062,946	100.0
Principal kinds of business	332,395	31.3
Restaurants, cafeterias, and lunch rooms	204,085	19.2
Grocery stores	128,310	12.1
PITTSBURGH, PA.		
All business, total	830,013	100.0
Principal kinds of business	288,624	34.8
Restaurants, cafeterias, and lunch rooms	173,179	20.9
Candy and confectionery stores	115,445	13.9
RICHMOND, VA.		
All business, total	657,961	100.0
Principal kind of business	182,773	27.8
Grocery stores	182,773	27.8
BIRMINGHAM, ALA.		
All business, total	601,916	100.0
Principal kinds of business	261,486	43.4
Grocery stores	135,449	22.5
Restaurants, cafeterias, and lunch rooms	126,037	20.9

Table 16.—STORES OPERATED BY NEGRO PROPRIETORS IN CITIES HAVING 50,000 OR MORE NEGRO INHABITANTS: 1929

Ranked by Population, Number of Stores, Stocks, and Sales Per Capita and Per Store

CITIES	RANKED BY—				
	Population [1]	Number of stores	Stocks on hand, end of year (*at cost*)	Net sales: Per capita of Negro population	Net sales: Average per store
New York, N. Y	1	5	2	13	1
Chicago, Ill	2	1	1	2	4
Philadelphia, Pa	3	2	3	9	10
Baltimore, Md	4	9	14	14	11
Washington, D. C	5	11	8	12	3
New Orleans, La	6	3	5	4	14
Detroit, Mich	7	7	4	1	2
Birmingham, Ala	8	13	15	15	13
Memphis, Tenn	9	6	9	6	9
St. Louis, Mo	10	8	6	7	8
Atlanta, Ga	11	4	13	10	15
Cleveland, Ohio	12	12	7	5	6
Houston, Tex	13	10	11	3	7
Pittsburgh, Pa	14	15	10	8	5
Richmond, Va	15	14	12	11	12

[1] Enumerated Apr. 1, 1930.

TABLE 17.—STORES OPERATED BY NEGRO PROPRIETORS, BY KIND OF BUSINESS, FOR CITIES HAVING 50,000 OR MORE NEGRO INHABITANTS: 1929

NUMBER OF STORES, PERSONNEL, PAY ROLL, STOCKS, AND SALES

[An (x) indicates that the amount must be withheld to avoid disclosure of individual operations, but it is included in the totals]

KIND OF BUSINESS	Number of stores	Proprietors and firm members (*not on pay roll*)	NUMBER OF EMPLOYEES: Full time	NUMBER OF EMPLOYEES: Part time	Total pay roll (*including part time*)	Stocks on hand, end of year (*at cost*)	NET SALES: Amount	NET SALES: Percent of total
ATLANTA, GA.								
Total	391	424	192	70	$95,636	$56,710	$1,151,850	100.00
Food group	110	123	24	20	14,299	26,240	430,233	37.35
Grocery stores (without meats)	59	64	6	6	3,818	11,350	119,801	10.40
Combination stores (groceries and meats)	35	43	16	10	9,420	12,040	266,064	23.10
Candy and confectionery stores	14	} 16	2	4	1,061	2,850	44,368	3.85
Delicatessen stores	1							
Meat markets (including sea foods)	1							
Automotive group	13	16	19	2	12,559	1,850	87,629	7.61
Filling stations	4	5	4	1	2,575	280	38,220	3.32
Bicycle shops	3	2	5	1	3,692	1,100	24,500	2.13
Garages and repair shops	6	9	10	----------	6,292	470	24,909	2.16
Apparel group [1]	4	4	7	1	8,726	850	29,551	2.57
Restaurants, and eating places	241	254	113	35	43,824	10,840	467,974	40.63
Restaurants, cafeterias, and lunch rooms:								
Lunch rooms	130	136	59	15	21,093	4,510	220,035	19.10
Restaurants with table service	19	22	32	7	12,744	870	86,939	7.55
Lunch counters, refreshment stands, etc.:								
Lunch counters	43	44	16	8	7,509	2,220	80,050	6.95
Refreshment stands	40	42	6	2	2,146	2,100	67,639	5.87
Soft-drink stands	9	10	----------	3	332	1,140	13,311	1.16
Other retail stores	23	27	29	12	16,228	16,930	136,463	11.85
Cigar stores and cigar stands	4	4	5	2	2,392	310	7,740	.67
Coal and wood yards—ice dealers	4	3	3	3	3,510	180	8,220	.71
Drug stores	4	7	12	6	6,255	10,080	80,670	7.00
Jewelry stores	6	7	2	----------	1,205	1,250	12,255	1.06
Miscellaneous classification (combined)[2]	5	6	7	1	2,866	5,110	27,578	2.39
BALTIMORE, MD.								
Total	282	283	132	76	$123,198	$48,135	$1,062,946	100.00
Food group	100	99	19	51	27,086	14,935	403,217	37.93
Candy and confectionery stores	43	43	4	1	2,111	3,820	94,348	8.88
Grocery stores (without meats)	23	23	1	3	683	2,825	53,410	5.02
Combination stores (groceries and meats)	10	10	----------	1	60	2,980	74,900	7.05
Meat markets (including sea foods)	9	9	2	1	1,578	3,390	58,190	5.47
Fruit stores and vegetable markets	4	4	----------	----------	----------	260	14,665	1.38
Bakeries—bakery goods stores (except manufacturing bakeries)	5	} 5	8	44	19,254	810	81,883	7.70
Caterers	1							
All other food stores:								
Coffee, tea, and spice dealers	1	} 5	4	1	3,400	850	25,821	2.43
Dairy products stores (including ice cream)	1							
Delicatessen stores	1							
Egg and poultry dealers	2							
Automotive group	5	6	2	1	550	620	12,323	1.16
Filling stations	1	} 6	2	1	550	620	12,323	1.16
Garages and repair shops	4							
Apparel group	3	3	2	----------	624	1,320	5,250	.49
Men's and boys' clothing and furnishings stores	1	} 3	2	----------	624	1,320	5,250	.49
Women's accessories stores	1							
Other apparel stores	1							
Furniture and household group [3]	2	(x)	(x)	----------	(x)	(x)	(x)	(x)
Restaurants and eating places	78	79	48	9	21,143	3,310	216,387	20.36
Restaurants, cafeterias, and lunch rooms:								
Lunch rooms	60	61	34	4	13,711	2,290	170,168	16.01
Restaurants with table service	9	9	13	5	6,756	690	33,917	3.19
Lunch counters, refreshment stands, etc.:								
Refreshment stands	2	} 9	1	----------	676	330	12,302	1.16
Soft-drink stands	7							
Lumber and building group [4]	2	(x)	(x)	----------	(x)	(x)	(x)	(x)
Other retail stores	78	79	47	15	45,819	23,500	279,925	26.33
Cigar stores and cigar stands	4	5	----------	1	260	210	15,434	1.45
Coal and wood yards	37	37	5	5	3,424	1,350	67,270	6.33
Ice dealers	4	4	1	----------	45	100	8,785	.83
Drug stores with fountains	12	12	20	7	17,731	13,320	87,537	8.24
Miscellaneous classifications (combined)[5]	21	21	21	2	24,359	8,520	100,899	9.49
Second-hand stores	14	14	1	----------	416	3,150	29,810	2.80
BIRMINGHAM, ALA.								
Total	200	228	144	6	$64,044	$43,790	$601,916	100.00
Food group	64	75	13	2	5,086	12,000	150,434	24.99
Candy and confectionery stores	11	12	3	----------	1,271	2,060	14,985	2.49
Grocery stores (without meats)	33	37	6	----------	2,286	5,090	60,009	9.97
Combination stores (groceries and meats)	20	26	4	2	1,529	4,850	75,440	12.53
General stores—groceries with dry goods or apparel	1	(x)	(x)	(x)	(x)	(x)	(x)	(x)
General merchandise group	4	6	1	----------	1,678	13,380	19,439	3.23
Dry goods stores	2	(x)	(x)	----------	(x)	(x)	(x)	(x)
General merchandise stores	2	(x)	(x)	----------	(x)	(x)	(x)	(x)
Automotive group	14	17	12	----------	6,352	1,210	43,280	7.19
Garages and repair shops	8	10	8	----------	4,456	320	18,940	3.15
All other automotive establishments	6	7	4	----------	1,896	890	24,340	4.04

(See footnotes at end of table.)

TABLE 17.—STORES OPERATED BY NEGRO PROPRIETORS, BY KIND OF BUSINESS, FOR CITIES HAVING 50,000 OR MORE NEGRO INHABITANTS: 1929—Continued

NUMBER OF STORES, PERSONNEL, PAY ROLL, STOCKS, AND SALES—Continued

[See note at head of table]

KIND OF BUSINESS	Number of stores	Proprietors and firm members (*not on pay roll*)	NUMBER OF EMPLOYEES		Total pay roll (*including part time*)	Stocks on hand, end of year (*at cost*)	NET SALES	
			Full time	Part time			Amount	Percent of total
BIRMINGHAM, ALA.—Continued								
Apparel group	4	4	4	----------	$1,898	$370	$7,000	1.16
Apparel stores	3	4	4	----------	1,898	370	7,000	1.16
Shoe stores	1							
Restaurants and eating places	92	99	70	1	21,244	2,790	172,563	28.67
Restaurants, cafeterias, and lunch rooms:								
Lunch rooms	43	48	32	----------	8,326	1,310	73,775	12.26
Restaurants with table service	7	7	29	----------	10,166	230	52,262	8.68
Lunch counters, refreshments stands, etc.:								
Lunch counters	18	18	8	1	2,544	660	28,048	4.66
Refreshment stands	20	22	1	----------	208	470	16,063	2.67
Soft-drink stands	4	4	----------	----------	----------	120	2,415	.40
Lumber and building group	3	5	8	----------	8,101	4,500	49,187	8.17
Lumber and building material dealers	1	(x)	(x)	----------	(x)	(x)	(x)	(x)
Electrical shops (without radio)	1	(x)	(x)	----------	(x)	(x)	(x)	(x)
Heating and plumbing shops	1	(x)	(x)	----------	(x)	(x)	(x)	(x)
Other retail stores	15	18	34	3	18,645	8,050	149,895	24.90
Coal and wood yards—ice dealers	4	5	10	2	7,375	1,700	56,800	9.44
Drug stores	4	4	6	1	2,768	1,550	58,680	9.75
Cigar stores and cigar stands	2	9	18	----------	8,502	4,800	34,415	5.72
Miscellaneous classifications (combined) [6]	5							
Second-hand stores	3	(x)	(x)	(x)	(x)	(x)	(x)	(x)
CHICAGO, ILL.								
Total	**815**	**866**	**576**	**147**	**$497,349**	**$435,130**	**$4,826,897**	**100.00**
Food group	213	222	46	14	46,110	107,040	1,441,241	29.86
Candy and confectionery stores	16	16	3	----------	1,548	5,660	48,451	1.00
Grocery stores (without meats)	76	81	11	3	10,048	37,680	430,434	8.92
Combination stores (groceries and meats)	44	44	19	8	19,056	31,760	498,924	10.34
Meat markets (including sea foods)	8	8	1	----------	2,600	3,580	59,552	1.23
Delicatessen stores	66	70	5	3	5,541	28,130	334,980	6.94
All other food stores	3	3	7	----------	7,317	230	68,900	1.43
General merchandise group	9	9	2	----------	1,016	9,200	21,775	.45
Dry goods stores	2	9	2	----------	1,016	9,200	21,775	.45
Variety, 5-and-10, and to-a-dollar stores	7							
Automotive group	35	42	39	7	47,351	9,410	250,584	5.19
Garages and repair shops	25	29	29	6	34,893	2,440	156,250	3.24
Filling stations	2	13	10	1	12,458	6,970	94,334	1.95
All other automotive establishments	8							
Apparel group	58	61	28	9	27,264	64,310	308,365	6.39
Men's and boys' clothing and furnishings stores	6	8	6	2	7,159	38,180	122,137	2.53
Family clothing stores—men's, women's, and children's	1							
Shoe stores	1							
Women's ready-to-wear specialty stores—apparel and accessories	14	17	9	1	7,620	14,800	63,048	1.31
Women's accessories stores	9	9	3	2	2,460	5,550	36,045	.75
Other apparel stores	27	27	10	4	10,025	5,780	87,135	1.81
Furniture and household group	13	15	12	2	13,089	11,230	87,635	1.82
Furniture stores	1	15	12	2	13,089	11,230	87,635	1.82
Draperies, curtains, and upholstery stores	1							
Radio and music stores	11							
Restaurants and eating places	**207**	**218**	**247**	**39**	**153,736**	**20,070**	**989,569**	**20.50**
Restaurants, cafeterias, and lunch rooms:								
Lunch rooms	**140**	**150**	**132**	**29**	**78,237**	**7,545**	**613,461**	**12.71**
Restaurants with table service	**14**	**14**	**74**	**1**	**40,666**	**1,870**	**188,718**	**3.91**
Lunch counters, refreshment stands, etc.:								
Lunch counters	**46**	**47**	**40**	**9**	**34,353**	**10,105**	**175,100**	**3.63**
Refreshment stands	**2**	**7**	**1**	----------	**480**	**550**	**12,290**	**.25**
Soft-drink stands	**5**							
Lumber and building group	9	10	11	1	11,621	7,180	63,226	1.31
Electrical shops (without radio)	3	4	2	----------	576	810	7,300	.15
Roofing (including tinner)	3	3	6	1	3,845	1,330	17,876	.37
Heating and plumbing shops	2	(x)	(x)	----------	(x)	(x)	(x)	(x)
Paint and glass stores	1	(x)	(x)	----------	(x)	(x)	(x)	(x)
Other retail stores	206	219	177	71	181,000	173,580	1,482,286	30.71
Hardware stores	2	(x)	----------	(x)	(x)	(x)	(x)	(x)
Farmers' supplies stores	6	6	4	1	4,556	410	37,445	.78
Book stores	1	(x)	----------	(x)	(x)	(x)	(x)	(x)
Cigar stores and cigar stands:								
Cigar stores without fountains	9	10	4	1	3,770	1,560	22,680	.47
Cigar stores with fountains	1							
Cigar stands (hotel lobbies, pool rooms, etc.)	21	22	32	1	24,532	3,470	116,854	2.42
Coal and wood yards—ice dealers	35	38	12	25	16,075	3,690	113,981	2.36
Drug stores:								
Drug stores without fountains	13	15	18	6	17,835	35,590	162,395	3.36
Drug stores with fountains	30	30	53	11	59,032	90,390	469,668	9.73
Jewelry stores	2	(x)	----------	(x)	(x)	(x)	(x)	(x)
Miscellaneous classifications (combined) [7]	86	93	54	25	55,056	34,640	546,793	11.33
Second-hand stores	65	70	14	4	16,162	33,110	182,216	3.78
Clothing and shoes	19	16	4	----------	5,610	6,390	32,110	.67
Furniture stores	34	40	7	3	6,496	16,760	117,303	2.43
All other second-hand dealers	12	14	3	1	4,056	9,960	32,803	.68

(See footnotes at end of table.)

TABLE 17.—STORES OPERATED BY NEGRO PROPRIETORS, BY KIND OF BUSINESS, FOR CITIES HAVING 50,000 OR MORE NEGRO INHABITANTS: 1929—Continued

NUMBER OF STORES, PERSONNEL, PAY ROLL, STOCKS, AND SALES—Continued

[See note at head of table]

KIND OF BUSINESS	Number of stores	Proprietors and firm members (*not on pay roll*)	NUMBER OF EMPLOYEES: Full time	NUMBER OF EMPLOYEES: Part time	Total pay roll (*including part time*)	Stocks on hand, end of year (*at cost*)	NET SALES: Amount	NET SALES: Percent of total
CLEVELAND, OHIO								
Total	215	240	161	34	$108,666	$108,810	$1,156,859	100.00
Food group	65	69	24	9	17,550	23,080	470,429	40.66
Candy and confectionery stores	9	10	7	---	2,668	3,040	53,414	4.62
Grocery stores (without meats)	28	29	5	2	4,125	9,680	171,163	14.80
Combination stores (groceries and meats)	15	16	7	1	5,968	7,280	138,286	11.95
Meat markets (including sea foods)	9	10	3	5	2,687	1,060	62,766	5.43
All other food stores	4	4	2	1	2,102	2,020	44,800	3.87
Automotive group	15	17	14	4	11,752	42,790	64,393	5.57
Filling stations	3	3	2	1	2,388	30,250	16,413	1.42
Garages and repair shops	7	8	11	3	7,774	7,360	27,930	2.41
All other automotive establishments	5	6	1	---	1,590	5,180	20,050	1.73
Apparel group	9	9	3	1	3,560	5,120	25,195	2.18
Women's ready-to-wear specialty stores—apparel and accessories	3	3	1	---	1,500	1,220	8,200	.71
Women's accessories stores	1 }							
Shoe stores	2 }	3	2	---	1,800	1,650	7,640	.66
All other apparel stores	3	3	---	1	260	2,250	9,355	.81
Furniture and household group	3	3	1	1	250	2,300	16,500	1.43
Household appliances stores	1 }							
Radio and music stores	2 }	3	1	1	250	2,300	16,500	1.43
Restaurants and eating places	73	85	91	13	48,262	13,750	343,383	29.68
Restaurants, cafeterias, and lunch rooms:								
Lunch rooms	35	41	20	7	12,261	7,570	98,468	8.51
Restaurants with table service	28	33	65	5	33,940	5,460	198,995	17.20
Lunch counters, refreshment stands, etc.:								
Lunch counters	8 }							
Soft-drink stands	2 }	11	6	1	2,061	720	45,920	3.97
Other retail stores	35	40	21	3	21,536	18,600	201,417	17.41
Cigar stores and cigar stands:								
Cigar stores without fountains	8	11	2	---	3,380	1,470	36,900	3.19
Cigar stands (hotel lobbies, pool rooms, etc.)	7	7	3	---	2,776	1,020	37,990	3.28
Coal and wood yards—ice dealers	7	8	2	2	2,672	920	21,200	1.83
Drug stores	3	3	5	---	1,860	5,200	21,430	1.85
Jewelry stores	4	4	1	---	468	1,750	13,300	1.15
Miscellaneous classifications (combined) [8]	6	7	8	1	10,380	8,240	70,597	6.10
Second-hand stores	15	17	7	3	5,756	3,170	35,542	3.07
Automobile parts, tires, and batteries	6	7	5	1	4,394	1,090	15,452	1.34
Clothing and shoes	4	4	2	2	1,362	700	5,130	.44
Furniture	5	6	---	---	---	1,380	14,960	1.29
DETROIT, MICH.								
Total	358	413	369	38	$304,713	$154,963	$2,951,471	100.00
Food group	147	162	50	17	44,321	44,585	1,101,766	37.33
Candy and confectionery stores	52	55	12	1	6,320	9,540	162,551	5.51
Grocery stores (without meats)	39	44	9	2	7,072	9,695	214,607	7.27
Combination stores (groceries and meats)	48	54	18	8	17,531	23,870	626,242	21.22
Meat markets (including sea foods)	4	4	2	2	2,628	430	46,340	1.57
All other food stores	4	5	9	4	10,770	1,050	52,026	1.76
General merchandise group	3	4	---	---	---	8,370	22,360	.76
Dry goods stores	1	(x)	---	---	---	(x)	(x)	(x)
Variety, 5-and-10, and to-a-dollar stores	2	(x)	---	---	---	(x)	(x)	(x)
Automotive group	28	32	27	4	38,811	12,110	348,679	11.81
Filling stations:								
Filling stations—gasoline and oil	5	6	7	1	10,315	2,750	132,475	4.49
Filling stations with tires and accessories	7	6	9	---	14,176	5,210	141,272	4.79
Garages and repair shops	7	9	5	1	7,390	320	31,662	1.07
All other automotive establishments	9	11	6	2	6,930	3,830	43,270	1.47
Apparel group	12	12	6	2	2,532	4,140	45,927	1.56
Men's and boys' clothing and furnishings stores	2	(x)	(x)	(x)	(x)	(x)	(x)	(x)
Women's ready-to-wear specialty stores—apparel and accessories	3	3	---	1	364	790	9,365	.32
Women's accessories stores	2	(x)	---	---	---	(x)	(x)	(x)
All other apparel stores	5	5	5	---	1,136	350	5,092	.17
Furniture and household group	4	4	2	---	1,291	1,050	24,700	.84
Furniture stores	1 }							
Radio and music stores	3 }	4	2	---	1,291	1,050	24,700	.84
Restaurants and eating places	97	116	233	8	161,426	7,893	813,454	27.56
Restaurants, cafeterias, and lunch rooms:								
Lunch rooms	58	71	101	6	72,706	5,913	408,399	13.84
Restaurants with table service	14	16	82	---	56,792	990	230,288	7.80
Lunch counters, refreshment stands, etc.:								
Lunch counters	21	25	48	2	29,708	760	164,232	5.56
Refreshments	2	(x)	(x)	---	(x)	(x)	(x)	(x)
Soft-drink stands	2	(x)	(x)	---	(x)	(x)	(x)	(x)
Other retail stores	54	68	46	6	51,237	73,005	531,938	18.02
Paint and glass stores	1	(x)	(x)	---	(x)	(x)	(x)	(x)
Hardware stores	1	(x)	---	---	---	(x)	(x)	(x)
Feed stores (flour, feed, grain, fertilizer)	2	(x)	(x)	---	(x)	(x)	(x)	(x)
Cigar stores and cigar stands:								
Cigar stores without fountains	4 }							
Cigar stores with fountains	1 }	6	3	---	2,360	475	15,665	.53
Cigar stands (hotel lobbies, pool rooms, etc.)	15	18	8	3	5,508	3,490	41,529	1.41
Ice dealers	1	(x)	---	---	---	---	(x)	(x)
Drug stores:								
Drug stores without fountains	7	8	7	1	8,536	15,830	115,314	3.91
Drug stores with fountains	15	19	23	2	30,153	44,680	276,730	9.38
Jewelry stores	2	(x)	---	---	---	(x)	(x)	(x)
Miscellaneous classifications (combined) [9]	5	8	3	---	3,640	3,490	37,870	1.28
Second-hand stores	13	15	5	1	5,095	3,810	62,647	2.12

(See footnotes at end of table.)

TABLE 17.—STORES OPERATED BY NEGRO PROPRIETORS, BY KIND OF BUSINESS, FOR CITIES HAVING 50,000 OR MORE NEGRO INHABITANTS: 1929—Continued

NUMBER OF STORES, PERSONNEL, PAY ROLL, STOCKS, AND SALES—Continued

[See note at head of table]

KIND OF BUSINESS	Number of stores	Proprietors and firm members (*not on pay roll*)	NUMBER OF EMPLOYEES		Total pay roll (*including part time*)	Stocks on hand, end of year (*at cost*)	NET SALES	
			Full time	Part time			Amount	Percent of total
HOUSTON, TEX.								
Total	**259**	**272**	**259**	**22**	**$155,511**	**$82,000**	**$1,343,588**	**100.00**
Food group	73	74	22	2	12,652	22,420	357,914	26.64
Candy and confectionery stores	8	8	4	1	3,284	1,430	24,120	1.80
Grocery stores (without meats)	21	21	6		2,400	4,480	90,533	6.74
Combination stores (groceries and meats)	28	28	8	1	4,544	14,430	147,961	11.01
Fruit stores and vegetable markets	11	11				1,570	50,900	3.79
Meat markets (including sea foods)	2	6	4		2,424	510	44,400	3.30
All other food stores	3							
Automotive group	22	25	21	3	12,602	3,490	143,833	10.71
Filling stations:								
Filling stations—gasoline and oil	5	6	3		2,120	810	33,688	2.51
Filling stations with tires and accessories	6	6	8	2	5,580	1,200	70,750	5.27
Filling stations with other merchandise	3	4	5	1	3,128	210	10,750	.80
Garages and repair shops	7	9	5		1,774	1,270	28,645	2.13
All other automotive establishments	1							
Apparel group	12	14	18	9	17,945	24,600	156,348	11.64
Women's accessories stores	3	3	12	6	14,226	23,260	123,296	9.18
All other apparel stores	6	8	5	3	3,119	1,040	29,002	2.16
Shoe stores	3	3	1		600	300	4,050	.30
Furniture and household group	1	(x)	(x)	(x)	(x)	(x)	(x)	(x)
Restaurants and eating places	113	117	160	4	86,317	8,320	466,624	34.73
Restaurants, cafeterias, and lunch rooms:								
Cafeterias	1	50	63	3	32,368	4,590	180,746	13.45
Lunch rooms	50							
Restaurants with table service	18	20	62		30,569	1,280	124,590	9.27
Lunch counters, refreshment stands, etc.:								
Lunch counters	22	25	30	1	21,344	1,540	124,545	9.27
Refreshment stands	16	16	5		2,036	610	29,318	2.18
Soft-drink stands	6	6				300	7,425	.55
Other retail stores	38	42	38	4	25,995	23,170	218,869	16.29
Cigar stores and cigar stands	1	(x)	(x)	(x)	(x)	(x)	(x)	(x)
Coal and wood yards	11	11	6		3,312	1,020	31,550	2.35
Ice dealers	3	3				150	4,324	.32
Drug stores:								
Drug stores without fountains	3	3	3		2,000	1,950	16,780	1.25
Drug stores with fountains	12	13	16	1	10,586	8,770	89,556	6.67
Jewelry stores	1	(x)	(x)	(x)	(x)	(x)	(x)	(x)
Miscellaneous classifications (combined) [10]	7	9	10	1	7,517	7,260	65,177	4.85
MEMPHIS, TENN.								
Total	**379**	**304**	**217**	**32**	**$132,858**	**$97,300**	**$1,552,583**	**100.00**
Food group	121	126	24	9	12,531	44,310	598,073	38.52
Candy and confectionery stores	1	(x)	(x)		(x)	(x)	(x)	(x)
Grocery stores (without meats)	50	51	6	1	3,321	12,860	161,537	10.40
Combination stores (groceries and meats)	62	65	15	8	7,826	30,850	419,481	27.02
Meat markets (including sea foods)	6	7	2		1,020	290	9,655	.62
All other food stores	2	(x)	(x)		(x)	(x)	(x)	(x)
General stores—groceries with dry goods	1	(x)	(x)	(x)	(x)	(x)	(x)	(x)
Automotive group	22	26	20	5	23,489	5,810	97,480	6.28
Filling stations:								
Filling stations—gasoline and oil	5	4	6	3	5,841	3,800	45,770	2.95
Filling stations with tires and accessories	1	5	4	1	2,992	1,180	22,393	1.44
Filling stations with other merchandise	3							
Garages and repair shops	12	17	10	1	14,656	830	29,317	1.89
All other automotive establishments	1							
Apparel group	5	6	7		4,402	4,390	28,848	1.86
Men's and boys' clothing and furnishings stores	1							
Family clothing stores—men's, women's, and children's	1	6	7		4,402	4,390	28,848	1.86
All other apparel stores	3							
Furniture and household group	1	(x)	(x)	(x)	(x)	(x)	(x)	(x)
Restaurants and eating places	200	103	106	10	45,985	9,660	495,847	31.94
Restaurants, cafeterias, and lunch rooms:								
Lunch rooms	113	14	80	5	35,272	5,870	322,809	20.79
Restaurants with table service	3	3	11		5,472	490	31,025	2.00
Lunch counters, refreshment stands, etc.:								
Lunch counters	69	70	12	5	3,945	2,780	118,835	7.65
Refreshment stands	5	6				210	8,816	.57
Soft-drink stands	10	10	3		1,296	310	14,362	.93
Other retail stores	29	43	60	8	46,451	33,130	332,335	21.41
Hardware stores	1	(x)	(x)	(x)	(x)	(x)	(x)	(x)
Farmers' supplies stores	1	(x)	(x)	(x)	(x)	(x)	(x)	(x)
Coal and wood yards—ice dealers	1	(x)	(x)	(x)	(x)	(x)	(x)	(x)
Drug stores:								
Drug stores without fountains	3	4	7		4,340	2,820	33,624	2.17
Drug stores with fountains	10	13	16	6	13,117	19,770	119,100	7.67
Miscellaneous classifications (combined) [11]	12	19	35		27,592	7,060	159,407	10.27
Second-hand stores	1	(x)	(x)	(x)	(x)	(x)	(x)	(x)

(See footnotes at end of table.)

TABLE 17.—STORES OPERATED BY NEGRO PROPRIETORS, BY KIND OF BUSINESS, FOR CITIES HAVING 50,000 OR MORE NEGRO INHABITANTS: 1929—Continued

NUMBER OF STORES, PERSONNEL, PAY ROLL, STOCKS, AND SALES—Continued

[See note at head of table]

KIND OF BUSINESS	Number of stores	Proprietors and firm members (*not on pay roll*)	NUMBER OF EMPLOYEES		Total pay roll (*including part time*)	Stocks on hand, end of year (*at cost*)	NET SALES	
			Full time	Part time			Amount	Percent of total
NEW ORLEANS, LA.								
Total	**771**	**906**	**238**	**22**	**$126, 252**	**$130, 140**	**$2, 300, 374**	**100. 00**
Food group	376	438	42	8	22, 826	43, 700	1, 201, 996	52. 25
Candy and confectionery stores	10	14	1	—	600	890	18, 095	. 79
Grocery stores (without meats)	99	116	13	—	10, 476	31, 640	377, 493	16. 41
Combination stores (groceries and meats)	13	13	—	—	—	3, 800	66, 100	2. 87
Meat markets (including sea foods)	9	11	4	—	3, 060	200	41, 278	1. 79
Fruit stores and vegetable markets	219	245	11	7	4, 262	6, 160	604, 321	26. 27
All other food stores:								
Dairy products stores	24	39	13	1	4, 428	1, 010	94, 709	4. 12
Bakeries—bakery goods stores (except manufacturing bakeries)	2							
General stores—groceries with dry goods or apparel	1	(x)	—	—	—	(x)	(x)	(x)
General merchandise group [12]	1	(x)	—	—	—	(x)	(x)	(x)
Automotive group	13	16	9	2	5, 073	2, 900	55, 284	2. 40
Filling stations	7	10	8	—	4, 453	2, 430	42, 384	1. 84
Garages and repair shops	5	6	1	2	620	470	12, 900	. 56
Bicycle shops	1							
Apparel group	10	11	9		7, 354	10, 270	39, 995	1. 74
Family clothing stores—men's, women's, and children's	1	(x)	(x)	—	(x)	(x)	(x)	(x)
Women's accessories stores	1	(x)	(x)	—	(x)	(x)	(x)	(x)
All other apparel stores	7	8	5	—	4, 650	2, 070	18, 595	. 81
Shoe stores	1	(x)	(x)	—	(x)	(x)	(x)	(x)
Furniture and household group	5	6	8	—	6, 300	2, 510	24, 107	1. 05
Furniture stores	4	6	8	—	6, 300	2, 510	24, 107	1. 05
Other home furnishings and appliances stores	1							
Restaurants, and eating places	260	302	114	5	45, 423	12, 400	551, 713	23. 98
Restaurants, cafeterias, and lunch rooms:								
Lunch rooms	79	91	46	5	15, 318	4, 290	207, 722	9. 03
Restaurants with table service	9	10	42	—	18, 010	670	92, 703	4. 03
Lunch counters, refreshment stands, etc.:								
Lunch counters	56	67	7	—	1, 566	2, 960	82, 436	3. 58
Refreshment stands	51	62	6	—	4, 738	1, 870	76, 719	3. 34
Soft-drink stands	65	72	13	—	5, 791	2, 610	92, 133	4. 01
Lumber and building group [13]	1	(x)	—	—	—	(x)	(x)	(x)
Other retail stores	104	130	56	7	39, 276	56, 960	412, 984	17. 95
Cigar stores and cigar stands	4	5	3	—	1, 480	100	3, 666	. 16
Coal and wood yards—ice dealers	71	90	13	—	4, 567	7, 090	165, 338	7. 19
Drug stores:								
Drug stores without fountains	10	11	8	—	5, 856	26, 470	66, 454	2. 89
Drug stores with fountains	8	13	8	2	5, 743	13, 990	81, 350	3. 54
Jewelry stores	2	11	24	5	21, 630	9, 310	96, 176	4. 18
Miscellaneous classifications (combined) [14]	9							
NEW YORK, N. Y.								
Total	**391**	**245**	**313**	**63**	**$293, 482**	**$346, 240**	**$3, 322, 274**	**100. 00**
Food group	127	58	40	10	44, 458	90, 540	1, 186, 432	35. 71
Candy and confectionery stores	40	11	5	—	3, 610	14, 210	187, 627	5. 65
Grocery stores (without meats)	51	6	12	8	11, 281	57, 320	534, 598	16. 09
Combination stores (groceries and meats)	3	4	—	—	—	2, 700	32, 880	. 99
Meat markets (including sea foods)	12	13	7	—	10, 676.	2, 210	193, 538	5. 83
Fruit stores and vegetable markets	7	9	1	1	522	980	37, 015	1. 11
All other food stores:								
Bakeries—bakery goods stores (except manufacturing bakeries)	4	5	10	—	13, 832	1, 120	59, 487	1. 79
Dairy products stores	3	3	1	—	824	4, 600	39, 200	1. 18
Coffee, tea, and spice dealers	1	(x)	(x)	—	(x)	(x)	(x)	(x)
Delicatessen stores	4	3	1	1	968	6, 900	46, 567	1. 40
Egg and poultry dealers	2	(x)	(x)	—	(x)	(x)	(x)	(x)
General merchandise group	5	5	2	—	4, 100	23, 340	50, 580	1. 52
Dry goods stores	2	(x)	(x)	—	(x)	(x)	(x)	(x)
General merchandise stores	2	(x)	(x)	—	(x)	(x)	(x)	(x)
Variety, 5-and-10, and to-a-dollar stores	1	(x)	(x)	—	(x)	(x)	(x)	(x)
Automotive group	22	18	16	3	20, 219	16, 340	187, 889	5. 66
Garages and repair shops	13	7	10	2	13, 886	3, 440	85, 043	2. 56
Filling stations	1	11	6	1	6, 333	12, 900	102, 846	3. 10
All other automotive establishments	8							
Apparel group	20	22	7	3	7, 200	27, 800	100, 077	3. 01
Men's and boys' clothing and furnishings stores	2	(x)	(x)	(x)	(x)	(x)	(x)	(x)
Family clothing stores—men's, women's, and children's	2	(x)	(x)	(x)	(x)	(x)	(x)	(x)
Women's ready-to-wear specialty stores—apparel and accessories	6	6	5	—	3, 196	4, 930	22, 386	. 67
Women's accessories stores	2	(x)	(x)	(x)	(x)	(x)	(x)	(x)
All other apparel stores	6	7	—	—	—	1, 520	12, 500	. 38
Shoe stores	2	(x)	(x)	(x)	(x)	(x)	(x)	(x)
Furniture and household group	10	11	6	3	5, 028	8, 600	26, 398	. 79
All other home furnishings and appliances stores	1	11	6	3	5, 028	8, 600	26, 398	. 79
Radio and music stores	9							
Restaurants and eating places	81	32	193	26	151, 486	15, 780	1, 003, 713	30. 21
Restaurants, cafeterias, and lunch rooms:								
Cafeterias	2	(x)	(x)	—	(x)	(x)	(x)	(x)
Lunch rooms	46	12	89	5	62, 392	6, 190	482, 836	14. 53
Restaurants with table service	24	6	77	20	66, 838	6, 190	361, 604	10. 88
Lunch counters, refreshment stands, etc.:								
Lunch counters	7	9	13	1	9, 856	2, 890	56, 544	1. 70
Soft-drink stands	2	(x)	—	—	—	(x)	(x)	(x)
Lumber and building group	5	7	7	—	7, 147	5, 330	58, 430	1. 76
Lumber and building material dealers	1							
Electrical shops (without radio)	3	7	7	—	7, 147	5, 330	58, 430	1. 76
Paint and glass stores	1							

(See footnotes at end of table.)

TABLE 17.—STORES OPERATED BY NEGRO PROPRIETORS, BY KIND OF BUSINESS, FOR CITIES HAVING 50,000 OR MORE NEGRO INHABITANTS: 1929—Continued

NUMBER OF STORES, PERSONNEL, PAY ROLL, STOCKS, AND SALES—Continued

[See note at head of table]

KIND OF BUSINESS	Number of stores	Proprietors and firm members (*not on pay roll*)	NUMBER OF EMPLOYEES		Total pay roll (*including part time*)	Stocks on hand, end of year (*at cost*)	NET SALES	
			Full time	Part time			Amount	Percent of total
NEW YORK, N. Y.—Continued								
Other retail stores	106	76	40	17	$53,004	$152,200	$682,610	20.55
Hardware stores	1	(x)	---	(x)	(x)	(x)	(x)	(x)
Cigar stores and cigar stands:								
Cigar stores without fountains	20	3	8	3	9,268	15,120	105,915	3.19
Cigar stores with fountains	2							
Cigar stands (hotel lobbies, pool rooms, etc.)	5	6	1	---	1,300	640	14,347	.43
Coal and wood yards—ice dealers	2	(x)	---	(x)	(x)	(x)	(x)	(x)
Drug stores	9	10	18	2	26,928	83,840	212,705	6.40
Jewelry stores	5	5	---	---	---	9,800	56,450	1.70
Miscellaneous classifications (combined) [15]	62	48	13	11	15,008	38,520	277,763	8.36
Second-hand stores	15	16	2	1	840	6,310	26,145	.79
Bronx Borough								
Total	19	19	15	2	$14,750	$50,110	$316,112	100.00
Food group	7	7	4	1	4,104	10,000	135,292	42.80
Candy and confectionery stores	2	(x)	(x)	(x)	(x)	(x)	(x)	(x)
Grocery stores (without meats)	2	(x)	(x)	(x)	(x)	(x)	(x)	(x)
All other food stores	3	3	2	---	1,604	4,300	56,400	17.84
Automotive group	1	(x)	(x)	---	(x)	(x)	(x)	(x)
Apparel group [16]	2	(x)	---	---	---	(x)	(x)	(x)
Furniture and household group	1	(x)	---	---	---	(x)	(x)	(x)
Restaurants and eating places	2	(x)	(x)	---	(x)	(x)	(x)	(x)
Other retail stores	5	4	5	1	5,866	22,000	82,700	26.16
Hardware stores	1							
Drug stores	3	4	5	1	5,866	22,000	82,700	26.16
Miscellaneous classifications (combined) [17]	1							
Second-hand stores	1	(x)	---	---	---	(x)	(x)	(x)
Brooklyn Borough								
Total	94	62	48	2	$43,043	$52,090	$543,047	100.00
Food group	31	11	8	1	5,616	18,930	240,752	44.33
Candy and confectionery stores	7	7	---	---	---	1,960	23,408	4.31
Grocery stores (without meats)	20	1	6	1	4,492	14,780	166,144	30.59
Meat markets (including sea foods)	2	(x)	(x)	---	(x)	(x)	(x)	(x)
All other food stores	2	(x)	(x)	---	(x)	(x)	(x)	(x)
General merchandise group [18]	2	(x)	(x)	---	(x)	(x)	(x)	(x)
Automotive group	13	8	10	---	12,369	4,000	83,739	15.42
Garages and repair shops	9	3	8	---	10,676	2,620	59,987	11.05
All other automotive establishments	4	5	2	---	1,693	1,380	23,752	4.37
Apparel group	4	4	---	---	---	970	4,600	.85
Men's and boys' clothing and furnishings stores	1	(x)	---	---	---	(x)	(x)	(x)
Women's ready-to-wear specialty stores—apparel and accessories	1	(x)	---	---	---	(x)	(x)	(x)
All other apparel stores	2	(x)	---	---	---	(x)	(x)	(x)
Furniture and household group [19]	1	(x)	---	---	---	(x)	(x)	(x)
Restaurants and eating places	16	8	22	---	16,283	1,960	109,823	20.22
Restaurants, cafeterias, and lunch rooms:								
Cafeterias	1	(x)	(x)	---	(x)	(x)	(x)	(x)
Lunch rooms	9	---	8	---	6,642	670	45,994	8.47
Restaurants with table service	4	4	10	---	6,953	330	33,479	6.17
Lunch counters, refreshment stands, etc.:								
Lunch counters	2	(x)	(x)	---	(x)	(x)	(x)	(x)
Lumber and building group [20]	2	(x)	(x)	---	(x)	(x)	(x)	(x)
Other retail stores	16	16	3	1	3,575	5,890	41,238	7.59
Cigar stores and cigar stands	2	(x)	(x)	---	(x)	(x)	(x)	(x)
Jewelry stores	2	(x)	(x)	---	(x)	(x)	(x)	(x)
Miscellaneous classifications (combined) [21]	12	12	2	1	2,275	2,230	30,368	5.59
Second-hand stores	9	10	2	---	800	4,200	17,440	3.21
Manhattan Borough								
Total	258	142	243	56	$227,414	$229,990	$2,261,677	100.00
Food group	81	31	26	7	33,373	53,850	705,302	31.18
Candy and confectionery stores	29	---	2	---	1,270	10,470	124,467	5.50
Grocery stores (without meats)	28	2	5	5	5,264	36,590	289,445	12.80
Combination stores (groceries and meats)	2							
Meat markets (including sea foods)	7	10	6	---	10,052	2,790	152,968	6.76
Fruit stores and vegetable markets	7	9	1	1	522	980	37,015	1.64
All other food stores:								
Bakeries—bakery goods stores (except manufacturing bakeries)	4	5	10	---	13,832	1,120	59,487	2.63
Coffee, tea, spice dealers	1							
Delicatessen stores	2	5	2	1	2,433	1,900	41,920	1.85
Egg and poultry dealers	1							
General-merchandise group	3	3	1	---	1,500	10,000	14,500	.64
Dry goods stores	1	(x)	(x)	---	(x)	(x)	(x)	(x)
General-merchandise stores	2	(x)	(x)	---	(x)	(x)	(x)	(x)
Automotive group	5	6	2	2	2,290	4,620	24,854	1.10
Garages and repair shops	1							
All other automotive establishments	4	6	2	2	2,290	4,620	24,854	1.10

(See footnotes at end of table.)

TABLE 17.—STORES OPERATED BY NEGRO PROPRIETORS, BY KIND OF BUSINESS, FOR CITIES HAVING 50,000 OR MORE NEGRO INHABITANTS: 1929—Continued

NUMBER OF STORES, PERSONNEL, PAY ROLL, STOCKS, AND SALES—Continued

[See note at head of table]

KIND OF BUSINESS	Number of stores	Proprietors and firm members (not on pay roll)	NUMBER OF EMPLOYEES		Total pay roll (including part time)	Stocks on hand, end of year (at cost)	NET SALES	
			Full time	Part time			Amount	Percent of total
Manhattan Borough—Continued								
Apparel group	14	15	7	3	$7,200	$16,430	$68,917	3.05
Family clothing stores—men's, women's, and children's	1	(x)	(x)	(x)	(x)	(x)	(x)	(x)
Women's ready-to-wear specialty stores—apparel and accessories	5	7	6	1	4,900	8,380	29,486	1.30
Women's accessories stores	2							
All other apparel stores	4	5	----------	----------	----------	1,100	9,800	.43
Shoe stores	2	(x)	(x)	(x)	(x)	(x)	(x)	(x)
Furniture and household group	8	9	6	3	5,028	5,700	22,803	1.01
Radio and electrical shops	8	9	6	3	5,028	5,700	22,803	1.01
Restaurants and eating places	61	19	164	25	129,073	13,260	846,790	37.44
Restaurants, cafeterias, and lunch rooms:								
Cafeterias	1	(x)	(x)	----------	(x)	(x)	(x)	(x)
Lunch rooms	33	7	74	4	49,620	4,960	389,742	17.23
Restaurants with table service	20	2	67	20	59,885	5,860	328,125	14.51
Lunch counters, refreshment stands, etc.:								
Lunch counters	5	6	11	1	8,568	1,990	41,944	1.85
Soft-drink stands	2	(x)	(x)	----------	(x)	(x)	(x)	(x)
Lumber and building group	3	5	5	----------	5,347	5,030	49,830	2.20
Electrical shops (without radio)	2	(x)	(x)	----------	(x)	(x)	(x)	(x)
Paint and glass stores	1	(x)	(x)	----------	(x)	(x)	(x)	(x)
Other retail stores	79	50	32	15	43,563	119,640	524,776	23.20
Cigar stores and cigar stands:								
Cigar stores without fountains	20	3	8	3	9,268	15,120	105,915	4.68
Cigar stores with fountains	1	3	----------	----------	----------	280	5,337	.24
Cigar stands (hotel lobbies, pool rooms, etc.)	2							
Drug stores	6	7	14	1	22,752	69,840	153,505	6.79
Coal and wood yards—ice dealers	2	5	----------	1	500	6,330	54,200	2.40
Jewelry stores	3							
Miscellaneous classifications (combined) [22]	45	32	10	10	11,043	28,070	205,819	9.10
Second-hand stores	4	4	----------	1	40	1,460	3,905	.17
Queens Borough								
Total	**17**	**19**	**7**	**2**	**$8,125**	**$13,400**	**$190,838**	**100.00**
Food group	7	8	2	1	1,365	7,460	102,486	53.70
Candy and confectionery stores	2	(x)	(x)	(x)	(x)	(x)	(x)	(x)
Grocery stores (without meats)	1	(x)	(x)	(x)	(x)	(x)	(x)	(x)
Combination stores (groceries and meats)	1	(x)	(x)	(x)	(x)	(x)	(x)	(x)
Meat markets (including sea foods)	2	(x)	(x)	(x)	(x)	(x)	(x)	(x)
All other food stores	1	(x)	(x)	(x)	(x)	(x)	(x)	(x)
Automotive group [23]	3	(x)	(x)	(x)	(x)	(x)	(x)	(x)
Restaurants and eating places	1	(x)	(x)	(x)	(x)	(x)	(x)	(x)
Other retail stores	5	5	----------	----------	----------	4,370	27,396	14.36
Cigar stores and cigar stands	1	5	----------	----------	----------	4,370	27,396	14.36
Miscellaneous classifications (combined) [24]	4							
Second-hand stores	1	(x)	----------	----------	----------	(x)	(x)	(x)
Richmond Borough								
Total	**3**	**3**	----------	**1**	**$150**	**$650**	**$10,600**	**100.00**
Meat markets (including sea foods)	1	(x)	----------	(x)	(x)	(x)	(x)	(x)
Restaurants, cafeterias, and lunch rooms	1	(x)	----------	(x)	(x)	(x)	(x)	(x)
Cigar stores and cigar stands	1	(x)	----------	(x)	(x)	(x)	(x)	(x)
PHILADELPHIA, PA.								
Total	**787**	**819**	**337**	**96**	**$300,747**	**$266,480**	**$3,150,007**	**100.00**
Food group	210	218	26	8	21,037	54,550	733,718	23.29
Candy and confectionery stores	64	64	6	1	2,501	12,450	121,385	3.85
Grocery stores (without meats)	97	102	3	1	1,958	30,330	279,520	8.87
Combination stores (groceries and meats)	14	12	3	----------	2,040	5,060	80,460	2.55
Meat markets (including sea foods)	12	12	5	1	4,480	2,660	122,875	3.90
Fruit stores and vegetable markets	13	15	8	4	8,398	1,530	59,156	1.88
All other food stores:								
Bakeries—bakery goods stores (except manufacturing bakeries)	2	9	----------	1	360	2,070	33,804	1.07
Delicatessen stores	4							
Egg and poultry dealers	4	4	1	----------	1,300	450	36,518	1.16
General merchandise group	3	3	1	----------	985	1,350	11,000	.35
Dry goods stores	1	3	1	----------	985	1,350	11,000	.35
General merchandise stores	1							
Variety, 5-and-10, and to-a-dollar stores	1							
Automotive group	33	36	29	8	29,549	8,870	129,923	4.12
Filling stations	6	6	4	2	4,256	3,010	19,358	.61
Garages and repair shops	22	25	23	6	23,653	1,860	97,683	3.10
All other automotive establishments	5	5	2	----------	1,640	4,000	12,882	.41
Apparel group	36	36	14	2	15,695	17,160	127,486	4.05
Men's and boys' clothing and furnishings stores	2	6	3	----------	3,440	9,680	40,006	1.27
Family clothing stores—men's, women's, and children's	2							
Shoe stores	2							
Women's ready-to-wear specialty stores—apparel and accessories	5	5	2	----------	1,280	1,960	11,885	.38
Women's accessories stores	5	5	----------	1	300	1,250	7,805	.25
Other apparel stores	20	20	9	1	10,675	4,270	67,790	2.15

(See footnotes at end of table.)

Table 17.—STORES OPERATED BY NEGRO PROPRIETORS, BY KIND OF BUSINESS, FOR CITIES HAVING 50,000 OR MORE NEGRO INHABITANTS: 1929—Continued

Number of Stores, Personnel, Pay Roll, Stocks, and Sales—Continued

[See note at head of table]

KIND OF BUSINESS	Number of stores	Proprietors and firm members (*not on pay roll*)	NUMBER OF EMPLOYEES		Total pay roll (*including part time*)	Stocks on hand, end of year (*at cost*)	NET SALES	
			Full time	Part time			Amount	Percent of total
PHILADELPHIA, PA.—Continued								
Furniture and household group	17	18	10	2	$6,696	$15,600	$45,455	1.44
Furniture stores	8	8	3	----------	756	3,000	9,355	.30
All other home furnishings and appliances stores	5	6	3	1	2,500	7,800	6,100	.19
Radio and music stores	4	4	4	1	3,440	4,800	30,000	.95
Restaurants and eating places	183	188	141	26	94,952	16,060	678,769	21.55
Restaurants, cafeterias, and lunch rooms:								
Lunch rooms	130	133	52	8	32,868	9,610	373,014	11.84
Restaurants with table service	31	33	85	16	57,384	3,240	254,878	8.09
Lunch counters, refreshment stands, etc.:								
Lunch counters	20	22	4	2	4,700	3,210	50,877	1.62
Soft-drink stands	2							
All other retail stores	250	261	112	45	128,268	136,690	1,336,785	42.44
Lumber and building material dealers	1	4	----------	----------	----------	700	8,960	.28
Paint and glass stores	1							
Hardware stores	1							
Farmers' supplies stores	1							
Cigar stores and cigar stands:								
Cigar stores without fountains	102	105	7	8	7,092	27,220	279,305	8.87
Cigar stores with fountains	8	8	----------	----------	----------	2,070	17,042	.54
Cigar stands (hotel lobbies, pool rooms, etc.)	25	25	3	1	2,570	2,520	29,510	.94
Coal and wood yards	5	4	19	----------	25,063	11,180	171,675	5.45
Ice dealers	4	4	1	1	860	160	6,708	.21
Drug stores:								
Drug stores without fountains	4	4	4	2	4,232	10,300	26,100	.83
Drug stores with fountains	20	24	24	9	29,569	44,310	194,307	6.17
Jewelry stores	4	4	----------	1	155	1,450	14,885	.47
Miscellaneous classifications (combined) [25]	74	79	54	23	58,727	36,780	588,293	18.68
Second-hand stores	55	59	4	5	3,565	16,200	86,871	2.76
Automobile parts	1	7	----------	----------	----------	1,930	10,175	.32
Clothing and shoe stores	6							
Furniture stores	41	43	4	----------	2,315	10,390	67,876	2.15
All other second-hand dealers	7	9	----------	5	1,250	3,880	8,820	.28
PITTSBURGH, PA.								
Total	150	168	128	20	$99,327	$94,810	$830,013	100.00
Food group	58	61	20	4	19,492	22,560	265,699	32.01
Candy and confectionery stores	33	36	13	3	11,318	11,160	115,445	13.91
Grocery stores (without meats)	15	15	2	1	1,514	7,030	48,400	5.83
Combination stores (groceries and meats)	4	4	1	----------	520	3,090	28,182	3.40
Meat markets (including sea foods)	5	6	4	----------	6,140	1,280	73,672	8.88
Fruit stores and vegetable markets	1							
Automotive group	5	7	8	3	12,970	1,880	98,619	11.88
Filling stations	1	7	8	3	12,970	1,880	98,619	11.88
Garages and repair shops	4							
Apparel group	1	(x)	(x)	----------	(x)	(x)	(x)	(x)
Furniture and household group [26]	3	4	2	----------	1,248	9,580	20,959	2.53
Restaurants and eating places	50	55	60	1	27,622	4,170	191,843	23.11
Restaurants, cafeterias, and lunch rooms:								
Lunch rooms	32	34	24	----------	10,700	1,860	89,783	10.82
Restaurants with table service	13	15	32	1	16,106	1,850	83,396	10.05
Lunch counters, refreshment stands, etc.:								
Lunch counters	5	6	4	----------	816	460	18,664	2.25
Lumber and building group	4	5	4	1	3,506	3,860	22,838	2.75
Heating and plumbing shops	3	5	4	1	3,506	3,860	22,838	2.75
Paint and glass stores	1							
Other retail stores	26	32	33	10	33,489	51,710	221,493	26.69
Farmers' supplies stores	1	(x)	(x)	----------	(x)	(x)	(x)	(x)
Cigar stores and cigar stands	7	8	4	----------	2,940	1,230	14,692	1.77
Drug stores	7	9	8	4	9,273	32,320	99,645	12.01
Jewelry stores	1	(x)	(x)	----------	(x)	(x)	(x)	(x)
Miscellaneous classifications (combined) [27]	10	11	19	6	20,196	15,190	98,994	11.93
Second-hand stores	3	4	1	1	1,000	1,050	8,562	1.03

(See footnotes at end of table.)

TABLE 17.—STORES OPERATED BY NEGRO PROPRIETORS, BY KIND OF BUSINESS, FOR CITIES HAVING 50,000 OR MORE NEGRO INHABITANTS: 1929—Continued

NUMBER OF STORES, PERSONNEL, PAY ROLL, STOCKS, AND SALES—Continued

[See note at head of table]

KIND OF BUSINESS	Number of stores	Proprietors and firm members (*not on pay roll*)	NUMBER OF EMPLOYEES		Total pay roll (*including part time*)	Stocks on hand, end of year (*at cost*)	NET SALES	
			Full time	Part time			Amount	Percent of total
RICHMOND, VA.								
Total	**189**	**199**	**102**	**36**	**$61,202**	**$67,760**	**$657,961**	**100.00**
Food group	106	113	28	17	13,964	22,670	304,996	46.35
Candy and confectionery stores	18	21	5	2	2,508	3,890	54,396	8.27
Grocery stores (without meats)	28	29	6	3	1,490	3,320	40,342	6.13
Combination stores (groceries and meats)	35	36	4	3	3,134	14,340	142,431	21.65
Meat markets (including sea foods)	18	20	12	7	6,078	910	49,163	7.47
Fruit stores and vegetable markets	4	4	1	2	754	150	16,580	2.52
Bakeries—bakery goods stores (except manufacturing bakeries)	3	3	-	-	-	60	2,084	.32
General stores—groceries with dry goods or apparel	2	(x)	-	-	-	(x)	(x)	(x)
General merchandise group	4	5	-	-	-	3,270	6,164	.94
Dry goods stores	1	(x)	-	-	-	(x)	(x)	(x)
General merchandise stores	2	(x)	-	-	-	(x)	(x)	(x)
Variety, 5-and-10, and to-a-dollar stores	1	(x)	-	-	-	(x)	(x)	(x)
Automotive group	3	3	2	-	1,356	130	9,831	1.49
Filling stations	2	(x)	(x)	-	(x)	(x)	(x)	(x)
Garages and repair shops	1	(x)	(x)	-	(x)	(x)	(x)	(x)
Apparel group [28]	1	(x)	(x)	(x)	(x)	(x)	(x)	(x)
Furniture and household group [29]	2	(x)	(x)	(x)	(x)	(x)	(x)	(x)
Restaurants and eating places	35	36	23	5	8,394	1,650	65,542	9.96
Restaurants, cafeterias, and lunch rooms:								
Lunch rooms	25	26	11	1	3,942	950	36,689	5.58
Restaurants with table service	8	(x)	(x)	(x)	(x)	(x)	(x)	(x)
Lunch counters, refreshment stands, etc	2	(x)	(x)	(x)	(x)	(x)	(x)	(x)
Other retail stores	33	34	46	10	34,404	35,340	254,308	38.65
Hardware stores	1	(x)	(x)	-	(x)	(x)	(x)	(x)
Cigar stores	1	(x)	(x)	-	(x)	(x)	(x)	(x)
Coal and wood yards—ice dealers	14	14	8	1	2,362	1,160	17,157	2.61
Drug stores:								
Drug stores without fountains	1	8	7	2	4,756	21,600	68,375	10.39
Drug stores with fountains	6							
Jewelry stores	1	(x)	(x)	-	(x)	(x)	(x)	(x)
Miscellaneous classifications (combined) [30]	9	10	30	7	26,326	10,680	156,526	23.79
Second-hand stores	3	3	1	-	312	1,730	5,070	.77
ST. LOUIS, MO.								
Total	**310**	**328**	**213**	**45**	**$149,516**	**$116,670**	**$1,457,427**	**100.00**
Food group	80	82	26	7	23,015	24,830	422,794	29.01
Candy and confectionery stores	50	52	12	2	6,054	4,300	120,184	8.25
Grocery stores (without meats)	14	14	2	1	1,400	3,480	54,140	3.71
Combination stores (groceries and meats)	16	16	12	4	15,561	17,050	248,470	17.05
General merchandise group	3	3	-	-	-	3,400	10,918	.75
Dry-goods stores	2	3	-	-	-	3,400	10,918	.75
Variety, 5-and-10, and to-a-dollar stores	1							
Automotive group	17	22	16	-	14,652	2,140	80,765	5.54
Filling stations	4	4	4	-	3,780	1,680	36,425	2.50
Garages and repair shops	13	18	12	-	10,872	460	44,340	3.04
Apparel group	10	11	8	1	4,678	7,710	33,760	2.32
Family clothing stores—men's, women's, and children's	1	4	3	-	2,028	7,010	21,010	1.44
Women's ready-to-wear specialty stores—apparel and accessories	2							
Women's accessories stores	1							
All other apparel stores	6	7	5	1	2,650	700	12,750	.87
Restaurants and eating places	120	123	97	24	54,414	7,070	432,391	29.67
Restaurants, cafeterias, and lunch rooms:								
Cafeterias	1	72	26	12	12,259	2,795	162,315	11.14
Lunch rooms	70							
Restaurants with table service	15	17	60	8	34,956	1,505	189,282	12.99
Lunch counters, refreshment stands, etc.:								
Lunch counters	24	24	9	4	5,959	1,870	58,976	4.05
Refreshment stands	3	3	1	-	1,000	190	7,980	.55
Soft-drink stands	7	7	1	-	240	710	13,838	.95
Other retail stores	75	82	64	13	50,977	70,430	466,399	32.00
Hardware stores	2	4	2	1	1,580	5,950	14,149	.97
Jewelry stores	2							
Farmers' supplies stores	3	3	-	-	-	240	8,700	.60
Cigar stores and cigar stands	11	12	7	-	5,130	950	40,890	2.81
Coal and wood yards—ice dealers	22	21	7	3	3,943	1,200	40,124	2.75
Drug stores:								
Drug stores without fountains	7	8	14	-	10,630	31,200	96,825	6.64
Drug stores with fountains	10	11	22	7	19,519	24,340	174,060	11.94
Miscellaneous classifications (combined) [31]	18	23	12	2	10,175	6,550	91,651	6.29
Second-hand stores	5	5	2	-	1,780	1,090	10,400	.71

(See footnotes at end of table.)

TABLE 17.—STORES OPERATED BY NEGRO PROPRIETORS, BY KIND OF BUSINESS, FOR CITIES HAVING 50,000 OR MORE NEGRO INHABITANTS: 1929—Continued

NUMBER OF STORES, PERSONNEL, PAY ROLL, STOCKS, AND SALES—Continued

[See note at head of table]

KIND OF BUSINESS	Number of stores	Proprietors and firm members (*not on pay roll*)	NUMBER OF EMPLOYEES		Total pay roll (*including part time*)	Stocks on hand, end of year (*at cost*)	NET SALES	
			Full time	Part time			Amount	Percent of total
WASHINGTON, D. C.								
Total	244	284	195	63	$162, 063	$102, 820	$1, 495, 854	100. 00
Food group	71	80	15	5	10, 509	12, 590	289, 590	19. 36
Candy and confectionery stores	9	10	2	1	1, 766	1, 330	12, 895	. 86
Grocery stores (without meats)	17	18	----	----	----	3, 640	46, 511	3. 11
Combination stores (groceries and meats)	16	17	1	1	770	4, 530	84, 035	5. 62
Meat markets (including sea foods)	17	20	9	3	6, 285	1, 760	103, 362	6. 91
All other food stores	12	15	3	----	1, 688	1, 330	42, 787	2. 86
Automotive group	15	18	12	2	12, 893	4, 770	68, 815	4. 60
Filling stations	3	3	3	----	2, 160	480	20, 900	1. 40
Garages and repair shops	8	10	6	2	7, 453	960	25, 575	1. 71
All other automotive establishments	4	5	3	----	3, 280	3, 330	22, 340	1. 49
Apparel group	6	7	5	2	5, 740	10, 200	35, 595	2. 38
Men's and boys' clothing and furnishings stores	1	(x)	----	----	----	(x)	(x)	(x)
Women's ready-to-wear specialty stores—apparel and accessories	1	(x)	----	----	----	(x)	(x)	(x)
Women's accessories stores	1	(x)	----	----	----	(x)	(x)	(x)
All other apparel stores	3	3	5	2	5, 740	4, 100	16, 920	1. 13
Furniture and household group	5	7	----	----	----	1, 180	10, 620	. 71
Floor coverings, drapery, and upholstery	1	(x)	----	----	----	(x)	(x)	(x)
All other home furnishings and appliances stores	2	(x)	----	----	----	(x)	(x)	(x)
Radio and music stores	2	(x)	----	----	----	(x)	(x)	(x)
Restaurants and eating places	68	83	108	6	64, 703	6, 260	481, 812	32. 21
Restaurants, cafeterias, and lunch rooms	62	77	106	6	63, 507	5, 950	475, 152	31. 76
Lunch counters, refreshment stands, etc	6	6	2	----	1, 196	310	6, 660	. 45
Other retail stores	72	82	52	48	65, 563	66, 360	597, 452	39. 94
Farmers' supplies stores	1	(x)	----	----	----	(x)	(x)	(x)
Cigar stores and cigar stands	10	10	4	1	2, 520	1, 830	25, 530	1. 71
Coal and wood yards—ice dealers	16	18	11	2	8, 836	3, 880	106, 316	7. 11
Drug stores	23	24	16	25	18, 654	45, 160	238, 281	15. 93
Jewelry stores	1	(x)	----	----	----	(x)	(x)	(x)
Miscellaneous classifications (combined) [32]	21	26	21	20	35, 553	15, 150	217, 365	14. 53
Second-hand stores	7	7	3	----	2, 655	1, 460	11, 970	. 80

[1] Includes 4 custom tailors.
[2] Includes 1 book store, 1 dry goods store, 2 florists, and 1 household appliances store.
[3] Includes 1 household appliance store, and 1 radio and music store.
[4] Includes 2 heating and plumbing shops.
[5] Includes 1 beauty and barber shop, 5 florists, 1 hardware store, 1 locksmith, 1 monument and tombstone shop, 1 news dealer, and 11 undertakers' and funeral supplies stores.
[6] Includes 1 photographer and illustrator, 4 undertakers' and funeral supplies stores.
[7] Includes 1 toy shop, 1 beauty and barber shop, 2 toilet articles shops, 3 florists, 1 malt products supplies store, 33 news dealers, 1 novelty and souvenir shop, 5 patent medicine stores, 1 pet shop (animals, birds, and fish), 2 printers and lithographers, 1 regalia, badges, and emblems shop, 1 religious goods store, 2 sanitary supplies stores, 2 sign shops, 30 undertakers' and funeral supplies stores.
[8] Includes 1 glass and mirror store, 1 patent medicine store, 1 printer and lithographer, and 3 undertakers' and funeral supplies stores.
[9] Includes 1 florist, 1 art and gift shop, 1 malt products supplies store, 1 printer and lithographer, and 1 janitors' supplies store.
[10] Includes 1 florist, 1 printer, 2 toilet articles shops, and 3 undertakers' and funeral supplies stores.
[11] Includes 1 novelty and souvenir shop, 3 patent medicine stores, and 8 undertakers' and funeral supplies stores.
[12] Includes 1 variety, 5-and-10, and to-a-dollar store.
[13] Includes 1 paint and glass store.
[14] Includes 1 chemicals store, 2 florists, 1 photographer and illustrator, 2 printers and lithographers, 1 second-hand store, and 2 undertakers' and funeral supplies stores.
[15] Includes 30 news dealers, 5 florists, 1 barbers' supplies store, 2 opticians, 3 malt products supplies stores, 5 patent medicine stores, 6 printers and lithographers, 2 regalia, badges, and emblems stores, 2 stationers and engravers, 1 typewriter shop, and 5 undertakers' and funeral supplies stores.
[16] Includes 1 men's and boys' clothing and furnishings store and 1 family-clothing store.
[17] Includes 1 news dealer.
[18] Includes 1 dry goods store and 1 variety, 5-and-10, and to-a-dollar store.
[19] Includes 1 antique shop.
[20] Includes 1 electrical shop (without radio), and 1 lumber and building material dealer.
[21] Includes 2 florists, 1 news dealer, 1 optician, 3 patent medicine stores, 4 printers and lithographers, and 1 undertakers' and funeral supplies store.
[22] Includes 1 barbers' supplies store, 3 florists, 3 malt products supplies stores, 24 news dealers, 1 optician, 2 patent medicine stores, 2 printers and lithographers, 2 regalia, badges, and emblems stores, 2 stationers and engravers, 1 typewriter shop, and 4 undertakers' and funeral supplies stores.
[23] Includes 3 garages and repair shops.
[24] Includes 4 news dealers.
[25] Includes 4 beauty and barber shops, 2 toilet articles shops, 1 embroidery and needle work shop, 9 florists, 7 news dealers, 3 novelty and souvenir shops, 3 opticians and optometrists, 4 patent medicine stores, 2 sanitary supplies stores, 1 stationer and engraver, 38 undertakers' and funeral supplies stores.
[26] Includes 3 radio and music stores.
[27] Includes 1 beauty shop, 1 news dealer, 1 novelty and souvenir shop, and 7 undertakers' and funeral supplies stores.
[28] Includes 1 apparel store.
[29] Includes 1 furniture store, 1 other household appliance store.
[30] Includes 1 florist and 1 news dealer, 7 undertakers' and funeral supplies stores.
[31] Includes 2 florists, 2 foods stores, 5 printers and lithographers, 2 radio and music stores, 1 sanitary supplies store, and 6 undertakers' and funeral supplies stores.
[32] Includes 1 beauty shop, 4 florists, 2 news dealers, 1 novelty shop, 1 optical shop, 1 patent medicine shop, 2 printers and lithographers, and 9 undertakers' and funeral supplies stores.

CHAPTER XVIII.—RELIGIOUS BODIES

The census of religious bodies.—A census of religious bodies has been taken once every 10 years since 1906. The statistics given here relate to the last census which was taken for 1926, or to the church-record year most nearly conforming to the end of that year. These data were obtained from persons connected with local church organizations either by mail or by special agent.

The statistics presented here include, besides the number of live churches with their membership, statistics of church edifices and parsonages, value of property and the amount of debt thereon, expenditures classified under two heads—local expenses and benevolences, missions, denominational support, etc., and statistics of Sunday schools conducted by local churches. In 1926 the information on the schedule was tabulated separately for urban and rural churches. Urban churches were those located in cities or other incorporated places which had 2,500 inhabitants or more on January 1, 1920. Rural churches were those located outside such incorporated places.

Number of churches.—Of the 213 religious bodies represented in the 1926 census, 24 were exclusively Negro, while 30 which were primarily white denominations had one or more Negro churches among their number. Following the plan used in 1906 and 1916, no effort was made in 1926 to enumerate the individual Negro members belonging to local white churches. The total number of Negro churches reported was 42,585 in 1926, of which the Negro Baptists had 22,081; the African Episcopal Church, 6,708; the colored Methodist Episcopal Church, 2,518; and the African Methodist Episcopal Zion Church, 2,466. Among white denominations, having a certain number of Negro congregation, the Methodist Episcopal Church had by far the most, 3,743. These five bodies had 88.1 percent of all the Negro churches in the United States.

In 1926 there were 37,790 Negro churches in the South, or 88.7 percent of the total. The States with the largest number of churches were Georgia, Alabama, Mississippi, Texas, North Carolina, and South Carolina.

Growth of churches.—The number of churches included in the tables showing comparative data was the number reporting membership figures.

The net increase or decrease in the number of churches of a particular denomination may not indicate actual growth or decline, becuase certain denominations have been influenced by organic changes. These changes, together with changes in name, are:

Negro Baptists—Returned as National Baptist Convention in 1916 and 1906.

United American Free Will Baptist Church (Colored)—Returned as Colored Free Will Baptists in 1916.

Colored Primitive Baptists—Returned as Colored Primitive Baptists in America in 1906.

Christian Church (General Convention of the Christian Church)—Returned as Christian Church (American Christian Convention) in 1916, and as Christians (Christian Connection) in 1906.

Church of God—Returned as Churches of God, General Assembly, 1916.

Church of the Living God[4] "The Pillar and Ground of Truth"—Church of the Living God, and Church of the Living God, General Assembly, (returned as the Apostolic Church in 1906), reorganized as one body in 1926.

Congregational Churches— Evangelical Protestant Church of North American annexed in 1925.

Independent Churches—Formerly included the Federated Churches.

United Lutheran Churches—Formed by the merger in 1918 of the General Synod, the General Council (exclusive of the Augustina Synod), and the United Synod in the South.

Evangelical Lutheran Synodical Conference of America—This body represents the federation of the four separate synods: The Missouri Synod, the Joint Wisconsin Synod, the Slovak Synod, and the Norwegian Synod.

The number of Negro churches reported was 36,563 in 1906, 39,592 in 1916, and 42,585 in 1926, or an increase of 8.3 percent between 1906 and 1916 and an increase of 7.6 percent between 1916 and 1926.

Church membership.—The Negro membership reported in 1926 totaled 5,203,487, or 9.5 percent of all church members in the United States. The distribution by membership was as follows: Negro Baptists, 61.4 percent; African Methodist Episcopal Church, 10.5 percent; African Methodist-Episcopal Zion Church, 8.8 percent; Methodist Episcopal Church, 6.4 percent; Colored Methodist Episcopal Church, 3.9 percent; Roman Catholic Church, 2.4 percent; Protestant Episcopal Church, 1 percent; and all other denominations, 5.6 percent.

The average number of members to a Negro church was decidedly below the average for all churches. The excess of females among the membership of Negro churches was pronounced. In 1926, there were only 61.9 males for every 100 females.

Negro church membership during the last two decades has been growing at the same rate as the population. There were 3,691,844 Negro church members in 1906; 4,602,805 in 1916; and 5,203,487 in 1926.

The figures for the several denominations for 1906, 1916, and 1926 do not adequately portray membership growth in the various decades; not only because of organic denominational changes, but also because of basic changes in the definition of a "member" adopted within these dates by certain denominations. Between 1916 and 1926 the Protestant Episcopal Church and the Lutheran bodies changed their definition of membership.

Prior to 1916 most Episcopal churches limited the term "members" to persons who were communicants, while after that date the definition was extended to include all baptized persons in the congregation. The effect of this change was a great increase in the number of members under 13 years of age. The same situation prevailed for the Lutheran denominations.

In 1906, in order to put the figures for all different bodies on a comparable basis, it was decided to exclude baptized children who were members. For the Roman Catholic Church, it was necessary to estimate the number of children who had not been confirmed to full membership and deduct this number from the membership reported. However, at later censuses, conditions changed and the number of members as presented in the tables for the year 1906, include all members without regard to age, whether or not they had been confirmed to full membership.

Sunday schools.—Denominational Sunday schools were reported by 85.4 percent of all Negro churches in 1926. Of the 54 denominations having one or more Negro churches, only 3 very small bodies reported no Negro Sunday school. Colored Sunday school officers and teachers numbered 298,283 and scholars, 2,144,553, an average of approximately 7 scholars per teacher.

Value of church edifices and debt.—The value of 37,347 Negro church edifices reported in 1926 was $205,782,628 or an average of $5,510 per church. Certain Negro churches of white denominations had higher values than churches of exclusively Negro denominations.

Debts on church edifices were reported on 23.5 percent of all the Negro churches reporting edifices in 1926. The average debt was $2,496.

Value of parsonages and debt.—In 1926, 15.4 percent of all Negro churches reported the value of the parsonage. The average value of the parsonage per church was $2,770. Of the 6,543 Negro churches reporting parsonages, 21.4 percent reported debts. The average debt was $1,304.

Church expenditures.—The average amount of expenditures per Negro church was $1,096 in 1926. Of this amount, 83.1 percent went for current expenses and improvements, 14.3 percent for benevolences and missions, and 2.6 percent was unclassified.

Urban and rural churches.—Approximately 75 percent of the Negro churches were rural in 1926. The statistics for urban and rural churches, separately, bring out the striking contrasts between these two types of churches. The average country Negro church had 91 members who worshiped in a church building valued at $2,115 and expended annually, $561; while the average city church had 220 members, a church edifice worth $16,279, and yearly expenditures of $2,738 per church.

TABLE 1.—PERCENT DISTRIBUTION OF URBAN AND RURAL NEGRO CHURCHES AND MEMBERSHIP FOR DENOMINATIONS HAVING 50,000 OR MORE MEMBERS: 1926

DENOMINATION	CHURCHES [1]		MEMBERSHIP [2]	
	Urban	Rural	Urban	Rural
Negro Baptists	20.0	80.0	39.0	61.0
African Methodist Episcopal Church	23.8	76.2	50.0	50.0
African Methodist Episcopal Zion Church	26.4	73.6	42.5	57.5
Methodist Episcopal Church	21.5	78.5	45.0	55.0
Colored Methodist Episcopal Church	22.5	77.5	39.1	60.9
Roman Catholic Church	79.6	20.4	85.9	14.1
Protestant Episcopal Church	71.4	28.6	89.7	10.3

[1] Includes only organizations reporting members.
[2] Membership as defined by the particular denomination.

TABLE 2.—NEGRO CHURCHES—MEMBERSHIP BY SEX, WITH NUMBER OF MALES PER 100 FEMALES FOR DENOMINATIONS HAVING 50,000 OR MORE MEMBERS, FOR THE UNITED STATES: 1926

[Figures to be used with due consideration of the number of members not reported by sex]

DENOMINATION	Total	Male	Female	Sex not reported	Males per 100 females
Negro Baptists	3,196,623	1,050,062	1,661,183	485,378	63.2
African Methodist Episcopal Church	545,814	165,615	295,137	85,062	56.1
African Methodist Episcopal Zion Church	456,813	167,432	289,381		57.9
Methodist Episcopal Church	332,347	117,176	192,905	22,266	60.7
Colored Methodist Episcopal Church	202,713	65,781	107,807	29,125	61.0
Roman Catholic Church	124,324	50,732	64,523	9,069	78.6
Protestant Episcopal Church	51,502	17,846	26,422	7,234	67.5

TABLE 3.—NEGRO CHURCHES—AVERAGE VALUE OF CHURCH EDIFICES, AND AVERAGE DEBT, FOR DENOMINATIONS HAVING 50,000 OR MORE MEMBERS, FOR THE UNITED STATES: 1926

DENOMINATION	AVERAGE VALUE OF CHURCH EDIFICE [1]			AVERAGE DEBT OF CHURCH EDIFICE [1]		
	Total	Urban	Rural	Total	Urban	Rural
All denominations	**$5,510**	**$16,279**	**$2,115**	**$2,496**	**$4,959**	**$515**
Selected denominations:						
Negro Baptists	5,217	17,309	2,150	2,814	5,438	569
African Methodist Episcopal Church	5,506	16,850	1,838	1,747	3,822	466
African Methodist Episcopal Zion Church	7,813	21,873	2,886	3,575	6,542	872
Methodist Episcopal Church	5,332	17,037	2,156	2,182	5,551	470
Colored Methodist Episcopal Church	3,935	11,115	1,879	1,625	3,587	383
Roman Catholic Church	37,043	44,397	7,330	19,801	20,578	3,875
Protestant Episcopal Church	16,072	21,054	2,881	5,687	6,252	611

[1] Averages based on number of churches reporting value and debt.

TABLE 4.—NUMBER OF NEGRO CHURCHES AND MEMBERSHIP CLASSIFIED BY SEX, WITH SEPARATE FIGURES FOR URBAN AND RURAL CHURCHES, BY DENOMINATIONS: 1926

[Urban territory includes all cities and other incorporated places which had 2,500 inhabitants or more in 1920, rural territory comprises the remainder of the country]

DENOMINATION	Total number of churches[1] in denominations wholly or in part Negro	NUMBER OF NEGRO CHURCHES [1]			NUMBER OF MEMBERS [2]			AVERAGE MEMBERS PER CHURCH			MEMBERSHIP BY SEX [3]			
		Total	Urban	Rural	Total	Urban	Rural	Total	Urban	Rural	Male	Female	Sex not reported	Males per 100 females
All denominations	**141, 753**	**42, 585**	**10, 158**	**32, 427**	**5, 203, 487**	**2, 238, 871**	**2, 964, 616**	**122**	**220**	**91**	**1, 726, 347**	**2, 789, 749**	**687, 391**	**61. 9**
Adventist bodies:														
Advent Christian Church	444	6	1	5	164	22	142	27	--------	28	83	81	--------	(4)
Seventh-day Adventist Denomination	1, 981	93	88	5	5, 133	5, 052	81	55	57	16	1, 272	3, 831	30	33. 2
African Orthodox Church	13	13	13	--------	1, 568	1, 568	--------	121	121	--------	689	879	--------	78. 4
African Orthodox Church of New Yrok	3	3	3	--------	717	717	--------	239	239	--------	262	355	100	73. 8
Apostolic Overcoming Holy Church of God	16	16	8	8	1, 047	581	466	65	73	58	352	695	--------	50. 6
Baptist Bodies:														
Negro Baptists	22, 081	22, 081	4, 409	17, 672	3, 196, 623	1, 246, 327	1, 950, 296	145	283	110	1, 050, 062	1, 661, 183	485, 378	63. 2
United American Free Will Baptist Church	166	166	11	155	13, 396	1, 804	11, 592	81	164	75	5, 079	8, 236	81	61. 7
Regular Baptists	349	1	--------	1	38	--------	38	--------	--------	--------	16	22	--------	(4)
Colored Primitive Baptists	925	925	76	849	43, 978	4, 637	39, 341	48	61	46	2, 346	4, 856	36, 776	48. 3
Christian and Missionary Alliance	332	10	9	1	535	510	25	54	57	--------	198	337	--------	58. 8
Christian Church (General Convention of the Christian Church)	1, 044	68	18	50	7, 312	1, 705	5, 607	108	95	112	2, 690	4, 622	--------	58. 2
Church of Christ (Holiness) United States of America	82	82	46	36	4, 919	3, 002	1, 917	60	65	53	1, 589	2, 942	388	54. 0
Church of Christ, Scientist	1, 913	1	1	--------	274	274	--------	--------	--------	--------	70	204	--------	34. 3
Church of God	644	29	7	22	887	318	569	31	45	26	296	591	--------	50. 1
Church of God (Headquarters, Anderson, Ind)	932	98	54	44	3, 165	2, 404	761	32	45	17	1, 072	2, 093	--------	51. 2
Church of God and Saints of Christ	112	112	101	11	6, 741	6, 055	686	60	60	62	2, 539	4, 202	--------	60. 4
Church of God in Christ	733	733	405	328	30, 263	20, 805	9, 458	41	51	29	9, 077	20, 873	313	43. 5
Churches of Christ	6, 226	214	80	134	8, 155	3, 580	4, 575	38	45	34	3, 296	4, 839	20	68. 1
Churches of God, Holiness	29	29	24	5	2, 278	1, 929	349	79	80	70	830	1, 410	38	58. 9
Churches of God in North America (General Eldership	428	7	2	5	274	55	219	39	28	44	103	171	--------	60. 2
Churches of the Living God:														
Church of the Living God, Christian Workers for Fellowship	149	149	82	67	11, 558	7, 289	4, 269	78	89	64	3, 964	7, 594	--------	52. 2
Church of the Living God, "The Pillar and Ground of Truth"	81	81	45	36	5, 844	3, 886	1, 958	72	86	54	3, 247	2, 597	--------	125. 0
Congregational Churches	5, 028	155	96	59	16, 000	13, 139	2, 861	103	137	48	6, 081	9, 782	137	62. 2
Disciples of Christ	7, 648	487	160	327	37, 325	14, 938	22, 387	77	93	68	12, 016	18, 459	6, 850	65. 1
Free Christian Zion Church of Christ	5	5	1	4	187	60	127	37	--------	32	94	93	--------	(4)
Free Church of God in Christ	19	19	15	4	874	797	77	46	53	19	300	574	--------	52. 3
Independent Churches	259	7	7	--------	1, 542	1, 542	--------	220	220	--------	401	1, 021	120	39. 3
Lutherans:														
United Lutheran Church in America	3, 650	1	1	--------	126	126	--------	--------	--------	--------	73	53	--------	(4)
Evangelical Lutheran Synodical Conference of America:														
Evangical Lutheran Synod of Missouri, Ohio, and Other States	3, 917	69	33	36	5, 871	3, 596	2, 275	85	109	63	2, 480	3, 308	83	75. 0
Methodist bodies:														
Methodist Episcopal Church	26, 130	3, 743	805	2, 938	332, 347	149, 559	182, 788	89	186	62	117, 176	192, 905	22, 266	60. 7
Methodist Protestant Church	2, 239	46	9	37	2, 529	305	2, 224	55	34	60	725	1, 164	640	62. 3
Wesleyan Methodist Connection (or Church) of America	619	26	10	16	1, 215	672	543	47	67	34	424	791	--------	53. 6
African Methodist Episcopal Church	6, 708	6, 708	1, 599	5, 109	545, 814	272, 765	273, 049	81	171	53	165, 615	295, 137	85, 062	56. 1
African Methodist Episcopal Zion Church	2, 466	2, 466	650	1, 816	456, 813	193, 926	262, 887	185	298	145	167, 432	289, 381	--------	57. 9
Colored Methodist Protestant Church	3	3	3	--------	533	533	--------	178	178	--------	194	339	--------	57. 2
Union American Methodist Episcopal Church	73	73	37	36	10, 169	7, 043	3, 126	139	190	87	4, 223	5, 946	--------	71. 0
African Union Methodist Protestant Church	43	43	23	20	4, 086	2, 707	1, 379	95	118	69	1, 255	1, 786	1, 045	70. 3
Colored Methodist Episcopal Church	2, 518	2, 518	567	1, 951	202, 713	79, 183	123, 530	81	140	63	65, 781	107, 807	29, 125	61. 0
Reformed Zion Union Apostolic Church	48	48	5	43	4, 538	651	3, 887	95	130	90	1, 876	2, 544	118	73. 7
Reformed Methodist Union Episcopal Church	25	25	7	18	2, 265	486	1, 779	91	69	99	764	1, 501	--------	50. 9
Independent African Methodist Episcopal Church	29	29	8	21	1, 003	424	579	35	53	28	351	652	--------	53. 8
Moravian bodies:														
Moravian Church in America	127	1	1	--------	694	694	--------	--------	--------	--------	250	444	--------	56. 3
The (Original) Church of God	50	1	1	--------	12	12	--------	--------	--------	--------	--------	--------	12	--------
Presbyterian bodies:														
Presbyterian Church in the United States of America	8, 947	450	195	255	37, 090	21, 503	15, 587	82	110	61	14, 048	21, 376	1, 666	65. 7
Colored Cumberland Presbyterian Church	178	178	60	118	10, 868	3, 911	6, 957	61	65	59	4, 410	6, 373	85	69. 2
United Presbyterian Church of North America	901	14	6	8	1, 202	602	600	86	100	75	421	668	113	63. 0
Presbyterian Church in the United States	3, 469	52	17	35	2, 134	907	1, 227	41	53	35	817	1, 303	14	62. 7
Protestant Episcopal Church	7, 299	287	205	82	51, 502	46, 201	5, 301	179	225	65	17, 846	26, 422	7, 234	67. 5
Reformed Episcopal Church	69	36	7	29	2, 753	1, 158	1, 595	76	165	55	926	1, 827	--------	50. 7
Roman Catholic Church	18, 940	147	117	30	124, 324	106, 839	17, 485	846	913	583	50, 732	64, 523	9, 069	78. 6
Salvation Army	1, 052	5	5	--------	495	495	--------	99	99	--------	140	355	--------	39. 4
Spiritualists:														
National Spiritualist Association	543	17	17	--------	904	904	--------	53	53	--------	100	176	628	56. 8
Progressive Spiritual Church	9	1	1	--------	500	500	--------	--------	--------	--------	200	300	--------	66. 7
National Spiritual Alliance of the United States of America	59	8	7	1	190	173	17	24	25	--------	64	126	--------	50. 8

[1] Includes only organizations reporting members.
[2] Membership as defined by the particular denomination.
[3] Figures are to be used with due consideration of the number of members not so reported.
[4] Ratio not shown where number of females is less than 100.

TABLE 5.—VALUE OF NEGRO CHURCH EDIFICES AND DEBT, WITH SEPARATE FIGURES FOR URBAN AND RURAL CHURCHES, BY DENOMINATIONS: 1926

[Urban territory includes all cities and other incorporated places which had 2,500 inhabitants or more in 1920; rural territory comprises the remainder of the country]

DENOMINATION	ALL CHURCHES						URBAN CHURCHES						RURAL CHURCHES					
	Number of church edifices	Value of church edifices			Debt on church edifices		Number of church edifices	Value of church edifices			Debt on church edifices		Number of church edifices	Value of church edifices			Debt on church edifices	
		Churches reporting	Amount	Average per church	Churches reporting	Amount		Churches reporting	Amount	Average per church	Churches reporting	Amount		Churches reporting	Amount	Average per church	Churches reporting	Amount
All denominations	37,749	37,347	$205,782,628	$5,510	8,884	$22,178,581	9,124	8,952	$145,730,958	$16,279	3,961	$19,642,007	28,625	28,395	$60,051,670	$2,115	4,923	$2,536,574
Adventist bodies:																		
Advent Christian Church	5	3	4,950	1,650	-	-	1	1	4,000	-	-	-	4	2	950	475	-	-
Seventh-day Adventist Denomination	81	78	789,400	10,121	33	155,215	77	74	785,100	10,609	33	155,215	4	4	4,300	1,075	-	-
African Orthodox Church	2	2	30,000	15,000	2	9,000	2	2	30,000	15,000	2	9,000	-	-	-	-	-	-
African Orthodox Church of New York	1	1	50,000	-	1	12,100	1	1	50,000	-	1	12,100	-	-	-	-	-	-
Apostolic Overcoming Holy Church of God	10	10	16,950	1,695	5	1,975	6	6	12,100	2,017	2	1,600	4	4	4,850	1,213	3	375
Baptist bodies:																		
Negro Baptists	20,011	19,833	103,465,759	5,217	3,743	10,533,174	4,072	4,012	69,444,724	17,309	1,726	9,385,537	15,939	15,821	34,021,035	2,150	2,017	1,147,637
United American Free Will Baptist Church	144	142	308,425	2,172	39	7,962	9	9	53,960	5,989	3	1,243	135	133	254,525	1,914	36	6,719
Colored Primitive Baptists	91	87	171,518	1,971	15	9,793	27	26	93,870	3,610	8	7,259	64	61	77,648	1,273	7	2,534
Christian and Missionary Alliance	6	6	57,625	9,604	3	23,050	5	5	55,625	11,125	3	23,050	1	1	2,000	-	-	-
Christian Church (General Convention of the Christian Church)	56	56	285,100	5,091	15	15,401	8	8	168,000	21,000	3	11,000	48	48	117,100	2,440	12	4,401
Church of Christ (Holiness) United States of America	69	68	326,850	4,807	20	79,224	37	36	274,750	7,632	13	76,153	32	32	52,100	1,628	7	3,071
Church of Christ, Scientist	1	1	254,061	-	1	233,561	1	1	254,061	-	1	233,561	-	-	-	-	-	-
Church of God	15	15	78,015	5,201	10	19,737	5	5	57,000	11,400	2	15,240	10	10	21,015	2,102	8	4,497
Church of God (Headquarters, Anderson, Ind.)	81	77	343,450	4,460	29	66,367	48	45	305,150	6,781	21	64,702	33	32	38,300	1,197	8	1,665
Church of God and Saints of Christ	49	48	149,210	3,109	20	30,219	43	42	138,860	3,306	19	30,130	6	6	10,350	1,725	1	89
Church of God in Christ	531	516	1,508,079	2,923	234	261,611	300	288	1,274,353	4,425	160	242,061	231	228	233,726	1,025	74	19,550
Church of Christ	141	141	139,919	992	21	4,816	49	49	90,010	1,837	7	3,301	92	92	49,909	542	14	1,515
Churches of God, Holiness	16	16	159,700	9,981	7	71,375	11	11	152,500	13,864	6	71,350	5	5	7,200	1,440	1	25
Churches of God in North America (General Eldership)	5	3	8,000	2,667	-	-	3	1	6,200	-	-	-	2	2	1,800	900	-	-
Churches of the Living God:																		
Church of the Living God, Christian Workers for Fellowship	141	139	368,935	2,654	27	26,460	77	75	268,750	3,583	21	24,240	64	64	100,185	1,565	6	2,220
Church of the Living God, "The Pillar and Ground of Truth"	84	81	170,547	2,106	45	29,277	48	45	126,665	2,815	30	24,960	36	36	43,882	1,219	15	4,217
Congregational Churches	145	139	1,896,415	13,643	59	230,470	90	85	1,733,700	20,396	38	224,025	55	54	162,715	3,013	21	6,445
Disciples of Christ	421	411	1,495,568	3,639	94	210,410	147	140	1,058,900	7,564	57	196,119	274	271	436,668	1,611	37	14,291
Free Christian Zion Church of Christ	4	4	22,000	5,500	1	275	1	1	16,000	-	1	275	3	3	6,000	2,000	-	-
Free Church of God in Christ	11	11	23,700	2,155	8	7,200	10	10	23,200	2,320	7	7,000	1	1	500	-	1	200
Independent Churches	2	2	67,000	33,500	2	30,100	2	2	67,000	33,500	2	30,100	-	-	-	-	-	-
Lutherans:																		
United Lutheran Church in America	1	1	13,000	-	-	-	1	1	13,000	-	-	-	-	-	-	-	-	-
Evangelical Lutheran Synodical Conference of America:																		
Evangelical Lutheran Synod of Missouri, Ohio, and Other States	57	55	339,650	6,175	5	13,790	25	23	293,500	12,761	4	13,640	32	32	46,150	1,442	1	150
Methodist bodies:																		
Methodist Episcopal Church	3,572	3,552	18,938,246	5,332	1,095	2,389,675	769	758	12,914,353	17,037	369	2,048,398	2,803	2,794	6,023,893	2,156	726	341,277
Methodist Protestant Church	44	44	91,650	2,083	9	4,998	9	9	26,000	2,889	3	3,155	35	35	65,650	1,876	6	1,843
Wesleyan Methodist Connection (or Church) of America	22	22	83,100	3,777	1	3,600	9	9	67,300	7,478	1	3,600	13	13	15,800	1,215	-	-
African Methodist Episcopal Church	5,927	5,829	32,092,549	5,506	1,908	3,332,972	1,446	1,424	23,994,224	16,850	728	2,782,754	4,481	4,405	8,098,325	1,838	1,180	550,218
African Methodist Episcopal Zion Church	2,370	2,370	18,515,723	7,813	514	1,837,352	615	615	13,451,618	21,873	245	1,602,747	1,755	1,755	5,064,105	2,886	269	234,605
Colored Methodist Protestant Church	3	3	36,000	12,000	1	1,200	3	3	36,000	12,000	1	1,200	-	-	-	-	-	-
Union American Methodist Episcopal Church	65	64	478,951	7,484	23	42,294	33	32	380,150	11,880	15	39,464	32	32	98,801	3,088	8	2,830
African Union Methodist Protestant Church	43	40	476,269	11,907	17	21,925	21	20	381,483	19,074	14	20,675	22	20	94,786	4,739	3	1,250
Colored Methodist Episcopal Church	2,346	2,341	9,211,437	3,935	591	960,124	524	521	5,791,115	11,115	229	821,462	1,822	1,820	3,420,322	1,879	362	138,662
Reformed Zion Union Apostolic Church	46	45	184,075	4,091	17	11,681	3	3	57,000	19,000	3	9,000	43	42	127,075	3,026	14	2,681
Reformed Methodist Union Episcopal Church	28	21	74,800	3,562	5	3,710	9	4	29,450	7,363	2	2,800	19	17	45,350	2,668	3	910
Independent African Methodist Episcopal Church	29	28	98,050	3,502	14	35,619	8	7	74,000	10,571	6	31,297	21	21	24,050	1,145	8	4,322
Moravian bodies:																		
Moravian Church in America	1	1	30,000	-	-	-	1	1	30,000	-	-	-	-	-	-	-	-	-
Presbyterian bodies:																		
Presbyterian Church in the United States of America	418	398	3,285,860	8,256	103	263,743	186	171	2,718,550	15,898	61	243,029	232	227	567,310	2,499	42	20,714
Colored Cumberland Presbyterian Church	164	162	353,825	2,184	35	25,095	54	52	167,920	3,229	20	20,710	110	110	185,905	1,690	15	4,385
United Presbyterian Church of North America	13	12	189,300	15,775	-	-	7	6	126,000	21,000	-	-	6	6	63,300	10,550	-	-
Presbyterian Church in the United States	47	46	138,140	3,003	10	2,102	16	15	92,175	6,145	4	1,670	31	31	45,965	1,483	6	432
Protestant Episcopal Church	263	259	4,162,735	16,072	50	284,374	192	188	3,958,210	21,054	45	281,321	71	71	204,525	2,881	5	3,053
Reformed Episcopal Church	36	36	59,850	1,663	8	2,694	7	7	29,500	4,214	3	753	29	29	30,350	1,047	6	1,941
Roman Catholic Church	129	126	4,667,378	37,043	43	851,461	104	101	4,484,128	44,397	41	843,711	25	25	183,250	7,330	2	7,750
Salvation Army	1	1	67,064	-	1	21,400	1	1	67,064	-	1	21,400	-	-	-	-	-	-
Spiritualists:																		
Progressive Spiritual Church	1	1	3,800	-	-	-	1	1	3,800	-	-	-	-	-	-	-	-	-

TABLE 6.—NEGRO CHURCH EXPENDITURES DURING YEAR, WITH SEPARATE FIGURES FOR URBAN AND RURAL CHURCHES, BY DENOMINATIONS: 1926

[Urban territory includes all cities and other incorporated places which had 2,500 inhabitants or more in 1920; rural territory comprises the remainder of the country]

DENOMINATION	EXPENDITURES—ALL CHURCHES						EXPENDITURES—URBAN CHURCHES					EXPENDITURES—RURAL CHURCHES				
	Churches reporting	Total amount	For current expenses and improvements	For benevolences, missions, etc.	Not classified	Average per church	Churches reporting	Total amount (including not classified)	For current expenses and improvements	For benevolences, missions, etc.	Average per church	Churches reporting	Total amount (including not classified)	For current expenses and improvements (dollars)	For benevolences, missions, etc.	Average per church
All denominations	39, 245	$43, 024, 259	$35, 749, 951	$6, 152, 905	$1, 121, 403	$1, 096	9, 642	$26, 402, 536	$22, 292, 954	$3, 455, 369	$2, 738	29, 603	$16, 621, 723	$13, 456, 997	$2, 697, 536	$561
Adventist bodies:																
Advent Christian Church	4	240	25	215	----	60	1	100	----	100	----	3	140	25	115	47
Seventh-day Adventist Denomination	85	261, 975	94, 525	167, 450	----	3, 082	80	260, 938	94, 294	166, 644	3, 262	5	1, 037	231	806	207
African Orthodox Church	13	19, 368	18, 211	1, 157	----	1, 490	13	19, 368	18, 211	1, 157	1, 490	----	----	----	----	----
African Orthodox Church of New York	2	18, 900	15, 200	3, 700	----	9, 450	2	18, 900	15, 200	3, 700	9, 450	----	----	----	----	----
Apostolic Overcoming Holy Church of God	16	17, 198	15, 010	2, 188	----	1, 075	8	11, 187	9, 935	1, 252	1, 398	8	6, 011	5, 075	936	751
Baptist bodies:																
Negro Baptists	20, 209	19, 475, 981	16, 210, 952	2, 444, 042	820, 987	964	4, 186	11, 553, 870	9, 804, 889	1, 265, 608	2, 760	16, 023	7, 922, 111	6, 406, 063	1, 178, 434	494
United American Free Will Baptist Church	158	67, 773	46, 494	13, 090	8, 189	429	11	12, 975	10, 056	1, 467	1, 180	147	54, 798	36, 438	11, 623	373
Colored Primitive Baptists	111	39, 419	26, 874	12, 052	493	355	30	19, 362	13, 630	5, 389	645	81	20, 057	13, 244	6, 663	248
Christian and Missionary Alliance	10	19, 177	12, 907	6, 270	----	1, 918	9	18, 977	12, 707	6, 270	2, 109	1	200	200	----	----
Christian Church (General Convention of the Christian Church)	68	45, 739	38, 267	7, 038	434	673	18	23, 465	21, 253	1, 778	1, 304	50	22, 274	17, 014	5, 260	445
Church of Christ (Holiness) United States of America	64	48, 968	36, 532	8, 191	4, 245	765	33	36, 006	27, 776	4, 718	1, 091	31	12, 962	8, 756	3, 473	418
Church of Christ, Scientist	1	38, 995	32, 397	6, 598	----	----	1	38, 995	32, 397	6, 598	----	----	----	----	----	----
Church of God	25	39, 064	34, 555	3, 909	600	1, 563	6	21, 644	19, 750	1, 894	3, 607	19	17, 420	14, 805	2, 015	917
Church of God (Headquarters, Anderson, Ind.)	82	86, 094	75, 573	9, 030	1, 491	1, 050	46	77, 258	68, 591	7, 206	1, 680	36	8, 836	6, 982	1, 824	245
Church of God and Saints of Christ	100	137, 345	76, 414	53, 917	7, 014	1, 373	91	129, 220	72, 297	52, 716	1, 420	9	8, 125	4, 117	1, 201	903
Church of God in Christ	624	516, 011	394, 773	90, 384	30, 854	827	359	417, 906	322, 234	70, 874	1, 164	265	98, 105	72, 539	19, 510	370
Churches of Christ	212	40, 996	34, 886	5, 595	515	193	80	26, 373	22, 069	4, 304	330	132	14, 623	12, 817	1, 291	111
Churches of God, Holiness	26	35, 878	27, 878	8, 000	----	1, 380	21	34, 693	26, 769	7, 924	1, 652	5	1, 185	1, 109	76	237
Churches of God in North America (General Eldership)	7	2, 380	2, 066	249	65	340	2	1, 609	1, 428	116	805	5	771	638	133	154
Churches of the Living God:																
Church of the Living God, Christian Workers for Fellowship	144	50, 515	45, 989	4, 526	----	351	80	36, 626	33, 164	3, 462	458	64	13, 889	12, 825	1, 064	217
Church of the Living God, "The Pillar and Ground of Truth"	81	64, 555	51, 284	13, 271	----	797	45	43, 338	32, 682	10, 656	963	36	21, 217	18, 602	2, 615	589
Congregational Churches	144	316, 444	295, 446	20, 388	610	2, 198	91	276, 793	258, 576	17, 607	3, 042	53	39, 651	36, 870	2, 781	748
Disciples of Christ	447	289, 721	239, 279	33, 125	17, 317	648	145	189, 315	165, 795	17, 524	1, 306	302	100, 406	73, 484	15, 601	332
Free Christian Zion Church of Christ	5	2, 481	2, 006	475	----	496	1	1, 806	1, 506	300	----	4	675	500	175	169
Free Church of God in Christ	18	19, 540	12, 505	7, 035	----	1, 086	15	16, 440	10, 805	5, 635	1, 096	3	3, 100	1, 700	1, 400	1, 033
Independent Churches	6	34, 904	32, 044	2, 860	----	5, 817	6	34, 904	32, 044	2, 860	5, 817	----	----	----	----	----
Lutherans:																
United Luthern Church in America	1	306	211	95	----	----	1	306	211	95	----	----	----	----	----	----
Evangelical Lutheran Synodical Conference of America:																
Evangelical Lutheran Synod of Missouri, Ohio, and other States	67	72, 197	62, 421	7, 096	2, 680	1, 078	32	54, 634	48, 081	5, 417	1, 707	35	17, 563	14, 340	1, 679	502
Methodist bodies:																
Methodist Episcopal Church	3, 682	3, 694, 508	3, 138, 411	550, 561	5, 536	1, 003	793	2, 112, 660	1, 797, 791	314, 869	2, 664	2, 889	1, 581, 848	1, 340, 620	235, 692	548
Methodist Protestant Church	44	11, 495	8, 946	2, 299	250	261	9	2, 772	2, 370	402	308	35	8, 723	6, 576	1, 897	249
Wesleyan Methodist Connection (or Church) of America	25	16, 679	13, 781	2, 898	----	667	10	11, 777	10, 422	1, 355	1, 178	15	4, 902	3, 359	1, 543	327
African Methodist Episcopal Church	6, 492	7, 600, 161	6, 205, 632	1, 257, 397	137, 132	1, 171	1, 532	4, 803, 582	3, 993, 308	726, 635	3, 135	4, 960	2, 796, 579	2, 212, 324	530, 762	564
African Methodist Episcopal Zion Church	2, 464	4, 757, 066	4, 091, 023	662, 993	3, 050	1, 931	649	2, 576, 570	2, 284, 192	292, 378	3, 970	1, 815	2, 180, 496	1, 806, 831	370, 615	1, 201
Colored Methodist Protestant Church	3	6, 685	5, 660	1, 025	----	2, 228	3	6, 685	5, 660	1, 025	2, 228	----	----	----	----	----
Union American Methodist Episcopal Church	68	222, 621	202, 075	20, 546	----	3, 274	35	159, 514	145, 485	14, 029	4, 558	33	63, 107	56, 590	6, 517	1, 912
African Union Methodist Protestant Church	43	99, 563	88, 272	11, 291	----	2, 315	23	64, 186	56, 738	7, 448	2, 791	20	35, 377	31, 534	3, 843	1, 769
Colored Methodist Episcopal Church	2, 477	2, 428, 234	1, 934, 540	417, 038	76, 656	980	558	1, 191, 659	962, 220	189, 414	2, 136	1, 919	1, 236, 575	972, 320	227, 624	644
Reformed Zion Union Apostolic Church	44	37, 601	24, 267	13, 334	----	855	5	10, 292	7, 264	3, 028	2, 058	39	27, 309	17, 003	10, 306	700
Reformed Methodist Union Episcopal Church	24	17, 282	14, 744	2, 538	----	720	6	7, 064	6, 255	809	1, 177	18	10, 218	8, 489	1, 729	568
Independent African Methodist Episcopal Church	27	11, 704	9, 958	1, 746	----	433	8	7, 837	7, 374	463	980	19	3, 867	2, 584	1, 283	204
Moravian bodies:																
Moravian Church in America	1	4, 475	3, 555	920	----	----	1	4, 475	3, 555	920	----	----	----	----	----	----
Presbyterian bodies:																
Presbyterian Church in United States of America	438	604, 179	536, 923	66, 356	900	1, 379	192	468, 451	425, 149	42, 402	2, 440	246	135, 728	111, 774	23, 954	552
Colored Cumberland Presbyterian Church	167	80, 304	70, 437	9, 867	----	481	56	38, 569	34, 049	4, 520	689	111	41, 735	36, 388	5, 347	376
United Presbyterian Church of North America	12	20, 211	14, 043	6, 168	----	1, 684	5	10, 167	7, 692	2, 475	2, 033	7	10, 044	6, 351	3, 693	1, 435
Presbyterian Church in the United States	51	27, 846	22, 005	5, 826	15	546	17	18, 771	14, 287	4, 484	1, 104	34	9, 075	7, 718	1, 342	267
Protestant Episcopal Church	272	572, 108	483, 912	87, 826	370	2, 103	198	547, 923	465, 947	81, 714	2, 767	74	24, 185	17, 965	6, 112	327
Reformed Episcopal Church	35	18, 417	12, 470	5, 947	----	526	7	10, 794	7, 197	3, 597	1, 542	28	7, 623	5, 273	2, 350	272
Roman Catholic Church	129	1, 005, 645	913, 914	89, 731	2, 000	7, 796	105	946, 469	858, 990	85, 479	9, 014	24	59, 176	54, 924	4, 252	2, 466
Salvation Army	5	15, 118	12, 345	2, 773	----	3, 024	5	15, 118	12, 345	2, 773	3, 024	----	----	----	----	----
Spiritualists:																
National Spiritualist Association	9	7, 655	6, 114	1, 541	----	851	9	7, 655	6, 114	1, 541	851	----	----	----	----	----
Progressive Spiritual Church	1	2, 125	2, 000	125	----	----	1	2, 125	2, 000	125	----	----	----	----	----	----
National Spiritual Alliance of the United States of America	2	413	200	213	----	207	2	413	200	213	207	----	----	----	----	----

TABLE 7.—VALUE OF NEGRO PARSONAGES AND DEBT, AND STATISTICS OF SUNDAY SCHOOLS DISTINGUISHED AS URBAN AND RURAL, BY DENOMINATIONS: 1926

(Urban territory includes all cities and other incorporated places which had 2,500 inhabitants or more in 1920; rural territory comprises the remainder of the country)

DENOMINATION	Total number of churches	VALUE OF PARSONAGES: Churches reporting	VALUE OF PARSONAGES: Amount	VALUE OF PARSONAGES: Average per church	DEBT ON PARSONAGES: Churches reporting	DEBT ON PARSONAGES: Amount	ALL SUNDAY SCHOOLS[1]: Churches reporting	ALL SUNDAY SCHOOLS[1]: Officers and teachers	ALL SUNDAY SCHOOLS[1]: Scholars	ALL SUNDAY SCHOOLS[1]: Average scholars per church	URBAN SUNDAY SCHOOLS[1]: Churches reporting	URBAN SUNDAY SCHOOLS[1]: Officers and teachers	URBAN SUNDAY SCHOOLS[1]: Scholars	URBAN SUNDAY SCHOOLS[1]: Average scholars per church	RURAL SUNDAY SCHOOLS[1]: Churches reporting	RURAL SUNDAY SCHOOLS[1]: Officers and teachers	RURAL SUNDAY SCHOOLS[1]: Scholars	RURAL SUNDAY SCHOOLS[1]: Average scholars per church
All denominations	**42,585**	**6,543**	**$18,122,240**	**$2,770**	**1,399**	**$1,824,255**	**36,378**	**298,283**	**2,144,553**	**59**	**9,028**	**100,486**	**866,068**	**96**	**27,350**	**197,797**	**1,278,485**	**47**
Adventist bodies:																		
Advent Christian Church	6						4	20	94	24	1	4	15		3	16	79	26
Seventh-day Adventist Denomination	93	6	27,200	4,533	2	5,700	67	575	3,402	51	63	557	3,321	53	4	18	81	20
African Orthodox Church	13	1	5,000		1	2,000	11	49	445	40	11	49	445	40				
African Orthodox Church of New York	3	1	15,000		1	11,000	3	26	220	73	3	26	220	73				
Apostolic Overcoming Holy Church of God	16	1	3,000				15	67	1,068	71	7	38	583	83	8	29	485	61
Baptist bodies:																		
Negro Baptists	22,081	1,325	4,451,057	3,359	376	634,369	18,755	148,067	1,121,362	60	3,918	45,039	402,416	103	14,837	103,028	718,946	48
United American Free Will Baptist Church	166	2	1,300	650	1	40	144	836	5,077	35	11	80	709	64	133	756	4,368	33
Regular Baptists	1																	
Colored Primitive Baptists	925						24	179	2,278	95	10	70	780	78	14	109	1,498	107
Christian and Missionary Alliance	10	1	1,875		1	1,250	8	57	490	61	7	54	465	66	1	3	25	
Christian Church (General Convention of the Christian Church)	68	1	5,000				64	433	3,348	52	16	123	955	60	48	310	2,393	50
Church of Christ (Holiness) U. S. A.	82	11	30,500	2,773	6	4,222	72	460	2,511	35	40	249	1,482	37	32	211	1,029	32
Church of Christ, Scientist	1						1	72	395		1	72	395					
Church of God	29	2	6,000	3,000			24	138	901	38	7	40	246	35	17	98	655	39
Church of God (headquarters, Anderson, Ind.)	98	9	60,200	6,689	2	13,700	89	499	3,131	35	52	350	2,296	44	37	149	835	23
Church of God and Saints of Christ	112	23	68,450	2,976	9	17,439	67	303	2,010	30	60	262	1,751	29	7	41	259	37
Church of God in Christ	733	48	85,000	1,771	25	22,941	585	3,216	19,282	33	331	2,011	12,666	38	254	1,205	6,616	26
Churches of Christ	214						177	505	5,905	33	71	233	2,819	40	106	272	3,086	29
Churches of God, Holiness	29	2	16,700	8,350	1	10,000	27	174	1,246	46	22	148	1,066	48	5	26	180	36
Churches of God in North America (General Eldership)	7						7	33	298	43	2	13	109	55	5	20	189	38
Churches of the Lving God:																		
Church of the Living God, Christian Workers for Fellowship	149	4	6,300	1,575	2	1,700	140	444	3,465	25	77	285	2,171	28	63	159	1,294	21
Church of the Living God, "The Pillar and Ground of Truth"	81	14	25,100	1,793	2	3,350	26	169	1,468	56	19	132	1,177	62	7	37	291	42
Congregational Churches	155	59	262,150	4,443	22	49,827	140	1,082	8,899	64	86	815	6,862	80	54	267	2,037	38
Disciples of Christ	487	30	93,300	3,100	8	16,600	397	2,081	14,848	37	133	876	6,179	46	264	1,205	8,669	33
Free Christian Zion Church of Christ	5						5	22	97	19	1	5	35		4	17	62	16
Free Church of God in Christ	19	1	2,000		1	1,000	17	100	633	37	14	87	568	41	3	13	65	22
Independent Churches	7						6	45	491	82	6	45	491	82				
Lutherans:																		
United Lutheran Church in America	1						1	8	90		1	8	90					
Evangelical Lutheran Synodical Conference of America:																		
Evangelical Lutheran Synod of Missouri, Ohio, and Other States	69	13	20,700	1,592			61	210	3,314	54	26	107	1,801	69	35	103	1,513	43
Methodist bodies:																		
Methodist Episcopal Church	3,743	1,419	2,922,791	2,060	312	282,053	3,527	25,846	196,496	56	778	8,712	83,357	107	2,749	17,134	113,139	41
Methodist Protestant Church	46	3	2,100	700	1	700	42	207	1,283	31	8	34	203	25	34	173	1,080	32
Wesleyan Methodist Connection (or Church) of America	26	4	4,600	1,150			26	196	1,084	42	10	96	578	58	16	100	506	32
African Methodist Episcopal Church	6,708	2,134	4,857,996	2,276	354	357,137	5,884	43,383	288,247	49	1,454	16,544	139,608	96	4,430	26,839	148,639	34
African Methodist Episcopal Zion Church	2,466	478	1,916,950	4,010	72	111,973	2,429	45,087	267,141	110	640	14,200	103,542	162	1,789	30,887	163,599	91
Colored Methodist Protestant Church	3						3	18	98	33	3	18	98	33				
Union American Methodist Episcopal Church	73	15	57,100	3,807	11	14,144	69	428	4,240	61	37	268	3,019	82	32	160	1,221	38
African Union Methodist Protestant Church	43	15	44,050	2,937	3	3,273	42	273	2,851	68	22	142	1,724	78	20	131	1,127	56
Colored Methodist Episcopal Church	2,518	530	984,660	1,858	109	93,929	2,351	15,666	103,523	44	540	4,413	34,571	64	1,811	11,253	68,952	38
Reformed Zion Union Apostolic Church	48	1	500		1	200	42	325	2,882	69	5	37	394	79	37	288	2,488	67
Reformed Methodist Union Episcopal Church	25	6	7,500	1,250			19	107	673	35	3	21	78	26	16	86	595	37
Independent African Methodist Episcopal Church	29	3	7,500	2,500	2	1,750	26	141	663	26	8	44	280	35	18	97	383	21
Moravian bodies:																		
Moravian Church in America	1	1	10,000				1	21	208		1	21	208					
The (Original) Church of God	1																	
Presbyterian bodies:																		
Presbyterian Church in the United States of America	450	137	539,455	3,938	34	35,236	400	3,137	27,817	70	181	1,727	15,598	86	219	1,410	12,219	56
Colored Cumberland Presbyterian Church	178	10	9,700	970	2	450	152	840	5,223	34	51	295	1,763	35	101	545	3,460	34
United Presbyterian Church of North America	14	5	22,300	4,460			14	126	1,587	113	6	64	764	127	8	62	823	103
Presbyterian Church in the United States	52	15	31,850	2,123	4	6,900	43	231	1,569	36	16	98	777	49	27	133	792	29
Protestant Episcopal Church	287	116	636,250	5,485	19	58,225	260	1,717	19,075	73	190	1,450	15,704	83	70	267	3,371	48
Reformed Episcopal Church	36	1	1,200				28	160	1,216	43	7	48	450	64	21	112	766	36
Roman Catholic Church	147	96	879,906	9,166	15	63,147	76	462	11,406	150	65	434	10,736	165	11	28	670	61
Salvation Army	5						5	39	470	94	5	39	470	94				
Spiritualists:																		
National Spiritualist Association	17						1	1	10		1	1	10					
Progressive Spiritual Church	1																	
National Spiritual Alliance of the United States of America	8						1	2	23		1	2	23					

[1] The statistics given relate only to the Sunday schools reported by individual church and do not include undenominational or union Sunday schools; nor do they include the parochial or week-day schools that are maintained by a number of bodies, particularly the Roman Catholic Church and certain Lutheran bodies.

TABLE 8.—NUMBER OF NEGRO CHURCHES AND MEMBERSHIP IN THE URBAN AND RURAL AREAS, MEMBERSHIP CLASSIFIED BY SEX, AND SUNDAY SCHOOLS, BY SECTIONS, DIVISIONS, AND STATES: 1926

[Urban territory includes all cities and other incorporated places which had 2,500 inhabitants or more in 1920; rural territory comprises the remainder of the country]

SECTIONS, DIVISION, AND STATE	NUMBER OF CHURCHES [1]			NUMBER OF MEMBERS [2]			AVERAGE MEMBERS PER CHURCH			TOTAL MEMBERSHIP BY SEX [3]			SUNDAY SCHOOLS [4]		
	Total	Urban	Rural	Total	Urban	Rural	Total	Urban	Rural	Male	Female	Sex not reported	Churches reporting	Officers and teachers	Scholars
United States	42, 585	10, 158	32, 427	5, 203, 487	2, 238, 871	2, 964, 616	122	220	91	1, 726, 347	2, 789, 749	687, 391	36, 378	298, 283	2, 144, 553
The North	4, 442	3, 343	1, 099	875, 748	816, 608	59, 140	197	244	54	267, 354	420, 953	187, 441	3, 769	40, 970	337, 957
The South	37, 790	6, 515	31, 275	4, 288, 621	2, 385, 148	2, 903, 473	113	213	93	1, 447, 031	2, 348, 037	493, 553	32, 332	254, 748	1, 789, 095
The West	353	300	53	39, 118	37, 115	2, 003	111	124	38	11, 962	20, 759	6, 397	277	2, 565	17, 501
NEW ENGLAND	164	153	11	28, 048	27, 395	653	171	179	59	10, 462	17, 421	165	151	1, 761	15, 059
Maine	1	1	—	45	45	—	—	—	—	11	34	—	1	7	28
New Hampshire	1	1	—	63	63	—	—	—	—	13	50	—	1	9	49
Massachusetts	72	70	2	13, 882	13, 806	76	193	197	38	4, 898	8, 819	165	68	752	7, 766
Rhode Island	21	19	2	3, 465	3, 292	173	165	173	87	1, 374	2, 091	—	19	265	1, 800
Connecticut	69	62	7	10, 593	10, 189	404	154	164	58	4, 166	6, 427	—	62	728	5, 416
MIDDLE ATLANTIC	1, 470	1, 142	328	363, 296	338, 710	24, 586	247	297	75	124, 526	185, 804	52, 966	1, 302	16, 139	140, 490
New York	352	313	39	114, 543	112, 406	2, 137	325	359	55	42, 000	65, 720	6, 823	320	4, 361	38, 692
New Jersey	412	275	137	71, 221	61, 181	10, 040	173	222	73	24, 049	39, 437	7, 735	367	3. 588	30, 985
Pennsylvania	706	554	152	177, 532	165, 123	12, 409	251	298	82	58, 477	80, 647	38, 408	615	8, 190	70, 813
EAST NORTH CENTRAL	1, 676	1, 368	308	356, 294	340, 255	16, 039	213	249	52	88, 941	142, 973	124, 380	1, 411	15, 041	130, 625
Ohio	622	465	157	119, 529	112, 308	7, 221	192	242	46	19, 874	32, 513	67, 142	483	5, 596	46, 996
Indiana	326	280	46	49, 704	46, 751	2, 953	152	167	64	16, 298	26, 984	6, 422	281	2, 646	18, 139
Illinois	523	433	90	137, 131	132, 033	5, 098	262	305	57	35, 292	56, 744	45, 095	466	4, 779	48, 116
Michigan	186	171	15	46, 231	45, 464	767	249	266	51	16, 213	25, 036	4, 982	169	1, 918	16, 328
Wisconsin	19	19	—	3, 699	3, 699	—	195	195	—	1, 264	1, 696	739	12	102	1, 046
WEST NORTH CENTRAL	1, 132	680	452	128, 110	110, 248	17, 862	113	162	40	43, 425	74, 755	9, 930	905	8, 029	51, 783
Minnesota	23	22	1	3, 702	3, 688	14	161	168	—	1, 424	2, 264	14	22	195	1, 643
Iowa	89	81	8	8, 577	8, 102	475	96	100	59	2, 987	5, 443	147	79	797	5, 083
Missouri	645	319	326	82, 207	68, 463	13, 744	127	215	42	27, 354	47, 495	7, 358	498	4, 512	30, 174
North Dakota	3	3	—	27	27	—	9	9	—	1	1	25	—	—	—
South Dakota	4	4	—	142	142	—	36	36	—	65	77	—	3	21	55
Nebraska	40	38	2	5, 163	5, 097	66	129	134	33	1, 200	2, 302	1, 661	29	234	1, 580
Kansas	328	213	115	28, 292	24, 729	3, 563	86	116	31	10, 394	17, 173	725	274	2, 270	13, 248
SOUTH ATLANTIC	17, 023	2, 733	14, 290	2, 159, 295	674, 620	1, 484, 675	127	247	104	715, 277	1, 132, 963	311, 055	13, 708	110, 957	860, 878
Delaware	152	43	109	12, 459	6, 702	5, 757	82	156	53	4, 126	6, 532	1, 801	138	960	7, 687
Maryland	654	169	485	97, 025	62, 915	34, 110	148	372	70	34, 150	51, 484	11, 391	606	5, 202	43, 678
District of Columbia	147	147	—	72, 382	72, 382	—	492	492	—	24, 455	38, 662	9, 265	138	1, 889	20, 953
Virginia	2, 255	361	1, 894	378, 742	105, 546	273. 196	168	292	144	147, 751	219, 591	11, 400	2, 062	17, 553	137, 019
West Virginia	480	100	380	32, 754	12, 585	20, 169	68	126	53	11, 713	16, 406	4, 635	412	3, 337	20, 042
North Carolina	3, 203	547	2, 656	431, 333	114, 556	316, 777	135	209	119	158, 055	252, 660	20, 618	2, 801	28, 653	213, 700
South Carolina	2, 838	371	2, 467	405. 614	78, 603	327, 011	143	212	133	148, 679	240, 964	15, 971	2, 641	21, 376	183, 161
Georgia	5, 201	618	4, 583	538, 093	136, 145	401, 948	103	220	88	119, 791	195, 411	222. 891	3, 172	19, 466	141, 582
Florida	2, 093	377	1, 716	190, 893	85, 183	105, 707	91	226	62	66, 557	111, 253	13, 083	1, 738	12, 521	93, 056
EAST SOUTH CENTRAL	11, 379	1, 788	9, 591	1, 259, 605	374, 129	885, 476	111	209	92	417, 963	695, 864	145, 778	10, 326	81, 705	537, 196
Kentucky	1, 103	311	792	127, 126	71, 583	55, 543	115	230	70	46, 903	75. 751	4, 472	957	7, 630	50, 136
Tennessee	1, 958	536	1, 422	226, 823	112, 981	113, 842	116	211	80	80, 561	140, 799	5, 463	1, 714	13, 226	87, 706
Alabama	4, 284	534	3, 750	557, 231	132, 777	424, 454	130	249	113	155, 249	269, 112	132, 870	3, 864	31, 467	237, 265
Mississippi	4, 034	407	3, 627	348, 425	56. 788	291, 637	86	140	80	135, 250	210, 202	2, 973	3, 791	29, 382	162, 089
WEST SOUTH CENTRAL	9, 388	1, 994	7, 394	869, 721	336, 399	533, 322	93	169	72	313, 791	519, 210	36, 720	8, 298	62, 086	391, 021
Arkansas	2, 411	292	2, 119	201, 240	44, 395	156, 845	83	152	74	72, 756	118, 761	9, 723	2, 216	16, 740	101, 375
Louisiana	2, 077	405	1, 672	248, 797	98, 398	150, 399	120	243	90	91, 353	149, 289	8, 155	1, 843	13, 304	87, 867
Oklahoma	990	325	665	68, 379	34, 733	33, 646	69	107	51	25, 352	42, 132	895	863	5, 745	34, 586
Texas	3, 910	972	2, 938	351, 305	158, 873	192, 432	90	163	65	124, 330	209, 028	17, 947	3, 376	26, 297	167, 193
MOUNTAIN	133	106	27	10, 243	9, 137	1, 106	77	86	41	2, 301	4, 035	3, 907	89	607	3, 607
Montana	9	9	—	228	228	—	25	25	—	82	146	—	9	49	183
Idaho	5	5	—	205	205	—	41	41	—	90	115	—	4	24	123
Wyoming	11	11	—	398	398	—	36	36	—	60	111	227	4	18	108
Colorado	55	42	13	6, 188	5, 711	477	113	136	37	1, 260	2, 204	2, 724	39	254	1, 692
New Mexico	17	14	3	710	548	162	42	39	54	182	290	238	9	67	326
Arizona	30	20	10	2, 199	1, 753	446	73	88	45	575	1, 069	555	21	176	1, 056
Utah	4	4	—	269	269	—	67	67	—	38	68	163	2	15	101
Nevada	2	1	1	46	25	21	23	—	—	14	32	—	1	4	18
PACIFIC	220	194	26	28, 875	27, 978	897	131	144	35	9, 661	16, 724	2, 490	188	1, 958	13, 894
Washington	23	22	1	2, 280	2, 271	9	99	103	—	812	1, 468	—	21	178	1, 207
Oregon	5	5	—	832	832	—	166	166	—	202	330	300	4	69	371
California	192	167	25	25, 763	24, 875	888	134	149	36	8, 647	14, 926	2, 190	163	1, 711	12, 316

[1] Includes only organizations reporting members.
[2] Membership as defined by the particular denomination.
[3] Figures are to be used with due consideration of the number of members not so reported.
[4] The statistics given relate only to the Sunday schools reported by individual churches and do not include undenominational or union Sunday schools; nor do they include the parochial or week-day schools that are maintained by a number of bodies, particularly the Roman Catholic Church and certain Lutheran bodies.

TABLE 9.—VALUE OF NEGRO CHURCH PROPERTY, CHURCH DEBT, AND EXPENDITURES, BY SECTIONS, DIVISIONS, AND STATES: 1926

SECTION, DIVISION, AND STATE	Total number of churches	Number of church edifices	VALUE OF CHURCH EDIFICES			DEBT ON CHURCH EDIFICES		VALUE OF PARSONAGES		DEBT ON PARSONAGES		EXPENDITURES DURING YEAR					
			Churches reporting	Amount	Average per church	Churches reporting	Amount	Churches reporting	Amount	Churches reporting	Amount	Churches reporting	Total amount	For current expenses and improvements	For benevolences, missions, etc.	Not classified	Average per church
United States	42,585	37,749	37,347	$205,782,628	$5,510	8,884	$22,178,581	6,543	$18,122,240	1,399	$1,824,255	39,245	$43,024,259	$35,749,951	$6,152,905	$1,121,403	$1,096
The North	4,442	3,746	3,665	70,328,433	19,189	1,739	11,267,594	1,445	6,932,994	429	948,028	4,141	13,132,873	11,154,281	1,564,873	413,719	3,171
The South	37,790	33,725	33,409	132,285,237	3,960	7,007	10,451,596	4,978	10,788,596	939	837,819	34,799	29,225,266	24,029,159	4,493,938	701,169	840
The West	353	278	273	3,168,958	11,608	138	459,391	120	400,650	31	38,408	305	686,120	566,511	94,094	5,515	2,184
NEW ENGLAND	164	141	136	3,093,850	22,749	62	390,349	55	422,900	23	77,950	162	530,409	462,099	68,310		3,274
Maine	1	1	1	15,000		1	2,100	1	8,000			1	1,635	1,500	135		
New Hampshire	1	1	1	10,000								1	2,150	2,109	41		
Vermont																	
Massachusetts	72	61	60	1,201,100	20,018	27	175,129	22	174,500	12	49,300	71	251,967	221,349	30,618		3,549
Rhode Island	21	20	19	410,300	21,595	8	45,050	7	42,000	4	11,750	21	67,809	61,044	6,765		3,229
Connecticut	69	58	55	1,457,450	26,499	26	168,070	25	198,400	7	16,900	68	206,848	176,097	30,751		3,042
MIDDLE ATLANTIC	1,470	1,233	1,200	34,197,990	28,498	675	5,419,901	499	3,410,294	184	525,306	1,396	6,389,469	5,486,782	768,382	134,305	4,577
New York	352	279	274	11,615,049	42,391	150	2,300,302	123	1,059,700	39	182,359	336	2,048,710	1,750,092	258,203	40,415	6,097
New Jersey	412	370	354	7,220,587	20,397	211	971,640	132	870,550	50	112,009	392	1,588,821	1,387,760	161,267	39,794	4,053
Pennsylvania	706	584	572	15,362,354	26,857	314	2,147,959	244	1,480,044	95	230,938	668	2,751,938	2,348,930	348,912	54,096	4,120
EAST NORTH CENTRAL	1,676	1,385	1,361	24,119,779	17,722	664	4,205,558	485	2,089,204	142	263,534	1,549	4,689,535	3,919,940	569,482	200,113	3,027
Ohio	622	523	513	9,113,989	17,766	226	1,362,271	156	766,400	38	89,239	572	1,800,095	1,528,371	188,059	83,665	3,147
Indiana	326	281	278	3,568,814	12,837	140	679,821	107	270,108	35	38,761	297	652,558	556,797	70,186	25,575	2,197
Illinois	523	405	399	7,774,032	19,484	196	1,496,332	154	652,549	41	77,582	487	1,485,297	1,211,496	183,176	90,625	3,050
Michigan	186	160	155	3,362,044	21,691	92	606,184	62	375,147	25	51,452	178	691,181	571,774	119,159	248	3,883
Wisconsin	19	16	16	300,900	18,806	10	60,950	6	25,000	3	6,500	15	60,404	51,502	8,902		4,027
WEST NORTH CENTRAL	1,132	987	968	8,916,814	9,212	338	1,251,786	406	1,010,596	80	81,238	1,034	1,523,460	1,285,460	158,699	79,301	1,473
Minnesota	23	24	20	269,001	13,450	9	26,656	14	73,306	5	10,500	23	72,790	61,976	8,014	2,800	3,165
Iowa	89	82	81	565,135	6,977	41	62,541	39	96,600	8	4,415	87	130,241	105,780	18,728	5,733	1,497
Missouri	645	541	533	5,112,613	9,592	153	807,321	198	520,625	37	36,928	580	846,458	741,794	85,533	19,131	1,459
North Dakota	3	2	2	3,250	1,625	1	150	1	750	1	150	1	258			258	
South Dakota	4	3	2	6,500	3,250	1	90	1	2,000			4	3,579	2,081	261	1,237	895
Nebraska	40	35	33	474,215	14,370	23	77,087	18	68,985	6	11,855	36	90,489	74,754	11,054	4,681	2,514
Kansas	328	300	297	2,486,100	8,371	110	277,941	135	248,330	23	17,390	303	379,645	299,075	35,109	45,461	1,253
SOUTH ATLANTIC	17,023	14,903	14,726	73,377,432	4,983	3,302	5,867,373	2,253	6,137,036	449	482,742	14,985	14,642,047	11,920,310	2,291,398	430,339	977
Delaware	152	146	131	944,380	7,209	74	71,002	57	132,340	16	17,816	149	244,173	211,004	29,719	3,450	1,639
Maryland	654	629	617	5,765,535	9,344	250	1,021,392	253	750,015	75	83,430	641	1,199,001	975,869	183,642	39,490	1,871
District of Columbia	147	128	123	6,589,258	53,571	60	874,460	34	320,200	14	45,800	144	838,212	715,557	121,255	1,400	5,821
Virginia	2,255	2,148	2,137	14,134,101	6,614	397	1,253,979	240	827,721	58	97,462	2,188	2,280,137	1,896,073	354,991	38,073	1,046
West Virginia	480	321	309	2,434,526	7,879	100	166,183	67	258,140	22	27,237	449	499,104	414,546	63,266	21,292	1,112
North Carolina	3,203	2,936	2,914	13,670,308	4,691	643	662,086	337	1,071,815	72	104,340	2,862	3,060,556	2,517,798	450,267	92,491	1,069
South Carolina	2,838	2,729	2,699	9,005,446	3,337	514	617,231	369	771,305	51	24,312	2,783	1,943,809	1,621,003	302,382	20,424	698
Georgia	5,201	4,133	4,085	12,380,886	3,031	805	636,704	462	794,245	64	32,685	3,874	2,434,130	1,827,849	420,702	185,579	628
Florida	2,093	1,733	1,711	8,452,992	4,940	459	564,336	434	1,211,255	77	49,660	1,895	2,133,925	1,740,611	365,174	28,140	1,126
EAST SOUTH CENTRAL	11,379	10,411	10,332	34,227,172	3,313	1,515	1,946,977	1,289	2,410,042	189	111,104	10,851	8,176,840	6,776,926	1,288,737	111,177	754
Kentucky	1,103	994	985	6,602,894	6,703	205	480,883	230	495,631	43	39,252	1,051	1,178,944	1,044,500	125,985	8,459	1,122
Tennessee	1,958	1,763	1,745	7,752,853	4,443	302	443,325	240	497,461	43	22,989	1,831	1,647,742	1,426,234	208,383	13,125	900
Alabama	4,284	3,817	3,799	12,737,558	3,353	593	774,066	455	918,075	57	35,655	4,041	3,480,988	2,838,602	595,514	46,872	861
Mississippi	4,034	3,837	3,803	7,133,867	1,876	413	248,703	364	498,875	46	13,208	3,928	1,869,166	1,467,590	358,855	42,721	476
WEST SOUTH CENTRAL	9,388	8,411	8,351	24,680,633	2,955	2,190	2,637,246	1,436	2,241,518	301	243,973	8,963	6,406,379	5,331,923	913,803	160,653	715
Arkansas	2,411	2,125	2,117	5,340,465	2,523	479	406,647	263	356,293	43	22,320	2,320	1,512,378	1,267,026	215,762	29,590	652
Louisiana	2,077	1,888	1,877	6,514,176	3,471	389	633,819	356	660,305	58	72,799	1,966	1,539,644	1,295,678	219,082	24,884	783
Oklahoma	990	859	851	2,238,849	2,631	228	192,569	141	183,925	20	26,799	943	617,605	519,983	86,809	10,813	655
Texas	3,910	3,539	3,506	10,587,143	3,020	1,094	1,404,211	676	1,040,995	180	122,055	3,734	2,736,752	2,249,236	392,150	95,366	733
MOUNTAIN	133	83	83	409,200	4,930	45	67,946	38	85,450	12	9,383	95	136,400	108,658	22,242	5,500	1,436
Montana	9	9	9	36,400	4,044	5	2,039	7	12,300	1	93	8	7,125	5,669	1,456		891
Idaho	5	4	4	12,500	3,125	2	1,450	2	5,900	1	2,700	4	8,165	6,965	1,200		2,041
Wyoming	11	5	5	21,000	4,200	5	4,200	1	500			6	4,211	3,036	975	200	702
Colorado	55	33	33	215,300	6,524	19	52,386	13	41,300	4	4,200	40	71,853	57,377	12,906	1,570	1,796
New Mexico	17	11	11	25,600	2,327	8	2,270	6	8,900	3	1,000	11	8,968	7,872	1,096		815
Arizona	30	18	18	76,900	4,272	5	5,351	7	14,250	2	690	23	33,716	25,802	4,184	3,730	1,466
Utah	4	2	2	16,500	8,250	1	250	2	2,300	1	700	2	1,962	1,612	350		981
Nevada	2	1	1	5,000								1	400	325	75		
PACIFIC	220	195	190	2,759,758	14,525	93	391,445	82	315,200	19	29,025	210	529,720	457,853	71,852	15	2,522
Washington	23	21	21	172,700	8,224	10	9,185	11	41,100	1	1,000	20	45,146	39,918	5,228		2,257
Oregon	5	4	4	98,510	24,628	4	11,700	2	3,800			5	17,175	13,295	3,880		3,435
California	192	170	165	2,488,548	15,082	79	370,560	69	270,300	18	28,025	185	467,399	404,640	62,744	15	2,526

TABLE 10.—NEGRO CHURCHES—NUMBER OF CHURCHES, MEMBERSHIP, NUMBER AND VALUE OF CHURCH EDIFICES, DEBT, EXPENDITURES, AND SUNDAY SCHOOLS, BY DENOMINATIONS, BY STATES: 1926

[The 17 Negro churches in the States of Maine, Nevada, New Hampshire, Oregon, South Dakota, and Utah are not shown separate presentation being limited to States and denominations in which 3 or more churches reported values or expenditures.]

DENOMINATION	Total number of churches in denominations wholly or in part Negro	Number of Negro churches [1]	MEMBERS [2]		Number of church edifices	VALUE OF CHURCH EDIFICES			DEBT ON CHURCH EDIFICES		EXPENDITURES DURING YEAR			SUNDAY SCHOOLS [3]		
			Total number	Average per church		Churches reporting	Amount	Average per church	Churches reporting	Amount	Churches reporting	Amount	Average per church	Churches reporting	Officers and teachers	Scholars
ALABAMA																
All denominations	**5,649**	**4,284**	**557,231**	**130**	**3,817**	**3,799**	**$12,737,558**	**$3,353**	**595**	**$774,066**	**4,041**	**$3,480,988**	**$861**	**3,864**	**31,467**	**237,265**
Adventist bodies:																
Seventh-day Adventist Denomination	20	7	233	33	5	5	12,000	2,400	1	350	5	10,004	2,001	4	28	117
Apostolic Overcoming Holy Church of God	13	13	847	65	8	8	14,150	1,769	4	1,175	13	13,243	1,019	13	57	853
Baptist bodies:																
Negro Baptists	2,415	2,415	364,565	151	2,267	2,254	7,603,818	3,373	292	423,345	2,361	1,791,325	759	2,258	15,231	135,174
United American Free Will Baptist Church	6	6	300	50	5	5	9,200	1,840	2	593	6	2,397	400	5	20	102
Colored Primitive Baptists	188	188	15,177	81	27	27	76,050	2,817	6	4,550	28	16,421	586	20	151	2,008
Church of Christ (Holiness) United States of America	3	3	130	43	4	3	18,000	6,000	2	2,153	3	1,249	416	3	24	82
Church of God (Headquarters, Anderson, Ind.)	24	7	165	24	7	7	9,050	1,293	2	958	6	2,299	383	7	33	186
Church of God in Christ	24	24	773	32	17	17	21,150	1,244	7	4,714	18	8,335	463	15	81	434
Churches of Christ	460	22	921	42	19	19	18,560	977	-----	-----	22	7,197	327	19	67	813
Churches of the Living God:																
Church of the Living God, Christian Workers for Fellowship	8	8	535	67	8	7	19,050	2,721	1	400	8	4,733	592	8	30	143
Congregational Churches	57	16	1,084	68	14	14	103,400	7,386	3	1,775	16	20,419	1,276	15	98	738
Disciples of Christ	78	23	1,489	65	19	19	41,328	2,175	3	1,121	20	6,690	335	20	103	654
Lutherans:																
Evangelical Lutheran Synodical Conference of America:																
Evangelical Lutheran Synod of Missouri, Ohio, and other States	38	25	1,721	69	18	18	27,400	1,522	-----	-----	25	14,938	598	24	68	1,214
Methodist bodies:																
Methodist Episcopal Church	349	172	12,422	72	165	165	532,100	3,225	56	43,468	171	111,927	655	169	1,079	6,888
Methodist Protestant Church	96	6	322	54	6	6	9,850	1,642	2	685	6	966	161	6	24	147
African Methodist Episcopal Church	524	524	45,330	87	463	461	1,367,092	2,965	108	125,674	518	384,136	742	482	3,317	22,461
African Methodist Episcopal Zion Church	420	420	80,446	192	393	393	1,509,165	3,840	35	81,660	420	740,240	1,762	415	8,845	49,389
Union American Methodist Episcopal Church	8	8	750	94	5	5	4,200	840	3	800	8	4,501	563	7	29	205
Colored Methodist Episcopal Church	300	300	20,983	70	282	282	841,550	2,984	54	73,565	298	229,972	772	294	1,746	11,697
Presbyterian bodies:																
Presbyterian Church in the United States of America	64	4	233	58	4	4	77,500	19,375	-----	-----	4	4,527	1,132	4	27	247
Colored Cumberland Presbyterian Church	58	58	5,153	89	52	52	118,500	2,279	13	6,280	54	27,841	516	52	274	2,294
United Presbyterian Church of North America	6	6	415	69	4	4	35,000	8,750	-----	-----	4	7,291	1,823	6	44	568
Presbyterian Church in the United States	213	9	355	39	8	7	12,395	1,771	1	800	9	4,955	551	7	44	337
Protestant Episcopal Church	99	4	383	96	3	3	79,500	26,500	-----	-----	4	3,465	866	3	12	130
Roman Catholic Church	119	13	2,361	182	12	12	176,150	14,679	-----	-----	12	61,104	5,092	6	22	327
All other denominations	59	3	138	46	2	2	1,400	700	-----	-----	2	813	407	2	13	57
ARIZONA																
All denominations	**30**	**30**	**2,199**	**73**	**18**	**18**	**$76,900**	**$4,272**	**5**	**$5,351**	**23**	**$33,716**	**$1,466**	**21**	**176**	**1,056**
Baptist bodies:																
Negro Baptists	12	12	817	68	9	9	40,100	4,456	2	4,000	10	18,550	1,855	9	66	496
Church of God in Christ	3	3	102	34	1	1	3,500	-----	-----	-----	3	1,490	497	3	17	51
Methodist bodies:																
African Methodist Episcopal Church	6	6	515	86	-----	-----	-----	-----	-----	-----	1	410	-----	-----	-----	-----
African Methodist Episcopal Zion Church	3	3	475	158	2	2	23,000	11,500	-----	-----	3	6,925	2,308	3	66	291
Colored Methodist Episcopal Church	5	5	245	49	5	5	8,300	1,660	2	551	5	6,041	1,208	5	25	198
All other denominations	1	1	45	-----	1	1	2,000	-----	1	800	1	300	-----	1	2	20

See footnotes at end of table.

TABLE 10.—NEGRO CHURCHES—NUMBER OF CHURCHES, MEMBERSHIP, NUMBER AND VALUE OF CHURCH EDIFICES, DEBT, EXPENDITURES, AND SUNDAY SCHOOLS, BY DENOMINATIONS, BY STATES: 1926—Con.

[See note at head of this table]

DENOMINATION	Total number of churches in denominations wholly or in part Negro	Number of Negro churches [1]	MEMBERS [2]: Total number	MEMBERS [2]: Average per church	Number of church edifices	VALUE OF CHURCH EDIFICES: Churches reporting	VALUE OF CHURCH EDIFICES: Amount	VALUE OF CHURCH EDIFICES: Average per church	DEBT ON CHURCH EDIFICES: Churches reporting	DEBT ON CHURCH EDIFICES: Amount	EXPENDITURES DURING YEAR: Churches reporting	EXPENDITURES DURING YEAR: Amount	EXPENDITURES DURING YEAR: Average per church	SUNDAY SCHOOLS [3]: Churches reporting	SUNDAY SCHOOLS [3]: Officers and teachers	SUNDAY SCHOOLS [3]: Scholars
ARKANSAS																
All denominations	**3,601**	**2,411**	**201,240**	**83**	**2,125**	**2,117**	**$5,340,465**	**$2,523**	**479**	**$406,647**	**2,320**	**$1,512,378**	**$652**	**2,216**	**16,740**	**101,375**
Baptist bodies:																
Negro Baptists	1,375	1,375	134,720	98	1,253	1,252	3,077,433	2,458	207	148,800	1,331	784,151	589	1,289	9,448	62,568
Colored Primitive Baptists	25	25	1,441	58	1	1	500	------	------	------	3	755	252	------	------	------
Church of Christ (Holiness) United States of America	7	7	287	41	7	7	14,750	2,107	2	975	7	4,758	680	7	50	205
Church of God (Headquarters, Anderson, Ind.)	31	9	113	13	2	2	1,100	550	1	57	7	476	68	9	29	157
Church of God in Christ	63	63	2,305	37	45	44	72,875	1,656	13	4,677	54	30,202	559	51	256	1,576
Churches of Christ	626	15	412	27	5	5	2,049	410	1	250	15	1,603	107	12	32	379
Churches of God in North America (general eldership)	15	4	203	51	1	1	1,000	------	------	------	4	728	182	4	18	168
Churches of the Living God:																
Church of the Living God, Christian Workers for Fellowship	23	23	1,683	73	22	22	36,550	1,661	------	------	23	4,877	212	22	57	447
Disciples of Christ	153	22	1,001	46	14	14	14,200	1,014	------	------	19	5,894	310	18	76	464
Free Christian Zion Church of Christ	5	5	187	37	4	4	22,000	5,500	1	275	5	2,481	496	5	22	97
Methodist bodies:																
Methodist Episcopal Church	170	118	6,176	52	110	110	375,280	3,412	33	47,576	116	89,834	774	109	736	4,257
African Methodist Episcopal Church	404	404	25,249	62	364	359	886,337	2,469	140	131,686	397	317,483	800	379	3,026	14,726
African Methodist Episcopal Zion Church	89	89	14,344	161	85	85	184,850	2,175	20	23,907	89	72,371	813	89	1,627	8,542
Colored Methodist Episcopal Church	220	220	10,887	49	188	188	453,891	2,414	55	46,061	219	139,285	636	203	1,282	7,121
Presbyterian bodies:																
Presbyterian Church in the United States of America	111	14	464	33	12	12	35,000	2,917	3	993	14	5,385	385	11	54	410
Protestant Episcopal Church	67	7	279	40	6	6	42,900	7,150	1	35	7	4,731	676	5	14	114
Roman Catholic Church	144	3	347	116	2	2	34,000	17,000	------	------	3	24,521	8,174	------	------	------
All other denominations	73	8	1,142	143	4	3	85,750	28,583	2	1,355	7	22,843	3,263	3	13	144
CALIFORNIA																
All denominations	**1,634**	**192**	**25,763**	**134**	**170**	**165**	**$2,488,548**	**$15,082**	**79**	**$370,560**	**185**	**$467,399**	**$2,526**	**163**	**1,711**	**12,316**
Baptist bodies:																
Negro Baptists	75	75	10,454	139	69	68	1,230,270	18,092	33	219,015	72	190,392	2,644	62	535	4,444
Church of Christ (Holiness) United States of America	7	7	538	77	4	4	12,700	3,175	2	1,850	6	5,766	961	7	47	325
Church of God in Christ	10	10	724	72	7	7	84,600	12,086	4	20,500	10	24,055	2,406	7	47	415
Churches of Christ	68	3	130	43	2	2	7,000	3,500	------	------	3	1,506	502	3	12	131
Churches of the Living God:																
Churches of the Living God, Christian Workers for Fellowship	4	4	28	7	4	4	4,850	1,213	1	200	3	443	148	3	9	27
Disciples of Christ	179	4	259	65	4	4	52,500	13,125	1	7,000	4	8,042	2,011	4	24	174
Methodist bodies:																
African Methodist Episcopal Church	38	38	6,183	163	36	35	566,700	16,191	18	37,295	38	105,952	2,788	33	314	2,457
African Methodist Episcopal Zion Church	29	29	4,614	159	22	22	262,568	11,935	9	33,050	29	86,036	2,967	24	586	3,076
Colored Methodist Episcopal Church	12	12	1,434	120	14	12	178,860	14,905	7	38,800	12	29,032	2,419	11	72	694
Protestant Episcopal Church	287	4	786	197	3	3	47,500	15,833	3	11,850	3	5,908	1,969	4	21	158
All other denominations	925	6	613	102	5	4	41,000	10,250	1	1,000	5	10,267	2,053	5	44	415
COLORADO																
All denominations	**480**	**55**	**6,188**	**113**	**33**	**33**	**$215,300**	**$6,524**	**19**	**$52,386**	**40**	**$71,853**	**$1,796**	**39**	**254**	**1,692**
Baptist bodies:																
Negro Baptists	15	15	2,298	153	15	15	110,800	7,387	9	17,209	15	33,830	2,255	14	131	1,003
Church of God in Christ	14	14	394	28	7	7	23,000	3,286	3	15,027	11	9,547	868	12	41	238
Free Church of God in Christ	6	6	184	31	4	4	6,700	1,675	3	2,800	5	5,700	1,140	6	29	165
Methodist bodies:																
Methodist Episcopal Church	217	3	389	130	3	3	34,000	11,333	1	2,500	3	11,155	3,718	3	27	112
African Methodist Episcopal Church	13	13	2,195	169	1	1	800	------	------	------	3	1,820	607	1	2	7
All other denominations	215	4	728	182	3	3	40,000	13,333	3	14,850	3	9,801	3,267	3	24	167

See footnotes at end of table.

TABLE 10.—NEGRO CHURCHES—NUMBER OF CHURCHES, MEMBERSHIP, NUMBER AND VALUE OF CHURCH EDIFICES, DEBT, EXPENDITURES, AND SUNDAY SCHOOLS, BY DENOMINATIONS, BY STATES: 1926—Con.

[See note at head of this table]

DENOMINATION	Total number of churches in denominations wholly or in part Negro	Number of Negro churches[1]	MEMBERS[2]		Number of church edifices	VALUE OF CHURCH EDIFICES			DEBT ON CHURCH EDIFICES		EXPENDITURES DURING YEAR			SUNDAY SCHOOLS[3]		
			Total number	Average per church		Churches reporting	Amount	Average per church	Churches reporting	Amount	Churches reporting	Amount	Average per church	Churches reporting	Officers and teachers	Scholars
CONNECTICUT																
All denominations	584	69	10,593	154	58	55	$1,457,450	$26,499	26	$168,070	68	$206,848	$3,042	62	728	5,416
Baptist bodies:																
Negro Baptists	26	26	5,518	212	27	25	742,000	29,680	14	83,100	26	92,393	3,554	24	312	2,637
Church of God and Saints of Christ	6	6	381	64							6	6,746	1,124	6	25	143
Church of God in Christ	4	4	144	36							3	2,511	837	3	15	89
Methodist bodies:																
African Methodist Episcopal Church	7	7	1,062	152	6	6	87,000	14,500	4	16,000	7	30,750	4,393	6	69	402
African Methodist Episcopal Zion Church	18	18	2,032	113	17	17	507,250	29,838	5	61,400	18	37,651	2,092	18	243	1,596
All other denominations	523	8	1,456	182	8	7	121,200	17,314	3	7,570	8	36,797	4,600	5	64	549
DELAWARE																
All denominations	394	152	12,459	82	146	131	$944,380	$7,209	74	$71,002	149	$244,173	$1,639	138	960	7,687
Baptist bodies:																
Negro Baptists	8	8	1,575	197	6	5	139,500	27,900	4	18,000	8	15,727	1,966	7	57	352
Methodist bodies:																
Methodist Episcopal Church	192	48	3,717	77	48	48	294,580	6,137	26	17,200	48	63,307	1,319	47	435	3,318
African Methodist Episcopal Church	63	63	2,994	48	61	50	152,325	3,046	36	15,122	61	64,543	1,058	53	257	1,770
African Methodist Episcopal Zion Church	3	3	347	116	3	3	38,000	12,667	1	2,000	3	5,467	1,822	3	43	198
Union American Methodist Episcopal Church	10	10	1,763	176	9	9	65,300	7,256	1	580	10	53,553	5,355	10	69	830
African Union Methodist Protestant Church	13	13	1,678	129	13	11	175,675	15,970	4	4,100	13	28,346	2,180	13	78	1,087
All other denominations	105	7	385	55	6	5	79,000	15,800	2	14,000	6	13,230	2,205	5	21	132
DISTRICT OF COLUMBIA																
All denominations	294	147	72,382	492	128	123	$6,589,258	$53,571	60	$874,460	144	$838,212	5,821	138	1,889	20,953
Baptist bodies:																
Negro Baptists	83	83	41,262	497	72	69	3,068,458	44,470	36	462,035	82	433,492	5,286	81	995	10,450
Congregational Churches	7	3	1,405	468	3	3	255,000	85,000			3	14,963	4,988	3	47	326
Methodist bodies:																
Methodist Episcopal Church	40	13	5,282	406	11	11	239,200	21,745	5	52,475	13	56,751	4,365	13	176	2,670
African Methodist Episcopal Church	7	7	2,179	311	8	7	716,000	102,286	5	43,550	7	44,079	6,297	7	84	1,245
African Methodist Episcopal Zion Church	7	7	6,448	921	7	7	704,000	100,571	2	44,000	7	87,900	12,557	7	226	2,565
Colored Methodist Episcopal Church	4	4	1,012	253	4	4	230,000	57,500	1	13,500	4	13,725	3,431	4	46	475
Protestant Episcopal Church	43	7	3,063	438	7	7	263,000	37,571			7	18,885	2,698	7	50	719
Roman Catholic Church	42	7	9,893	1,413	7	7	864,000	123,429	6	219,400	7	102,117	14,588	4	134	1,370
All other denominations	61	16	1,838	115	9	8	249,600	31,200	5	39,500	14	66,300	4,736	12	131	1,133
FLORIDA																
All denominations	2,882	2,093	190,893	91	1,733	1,711	$8,452,992	$4,940	459	$564,336	1,895	$2,133,925	$1,126	1,738	12,521	93,056
Adventist bodies:																
Seventh-Day Adventist denomination	44	9	383	43	10	9	29,340	3,260	3	847	9	16,841	1,871	5	30	259
Baptist bodies:																
Negro Baptists	884	884	98,194	111	785	777	3,485,974	4,486	138	222,885	839	762,256	909	803	5,544	44,893
Colored Primitive Baptists	126	126	7,086	56	17	17	48,950	2,879	1	1,500	35	13,422	383	3	20	240
Church of God	84	21	674	32	13	13	76,115	5,855	9	19,037	19	35,592	1,873	18	115	728
Church of God (headquarters, Anderson, Ind.)	21	7	351	50	7	7	58,000	8,286	1	400	6	6,756	1,126	5	30	200
Church of God in Christ	27	27	1,080	40	21	21	51,545	2,455	14	15,987	23	14,962	651	23	109	803
Churches of the Living God:																
Church of the Living God, Christian Workers for Fellowship	4	4	192	48	4	4	8,300	2,075	1	700	4	1,063	266	4	8	64
Disciples of Christ	71	7	226	32	6	6	7,800	1,300	2	1,300	5	2,432	486	6	14	116
Methodist bodies:																
Methodist Episcopal Church	223	143	8,897	62	121	121	802,130	6,629	32	40,647	127	148,895	1,172	127	753	5,721
African Methodist Episcopal Church	694	694	47,541	69	600	588	2,599,135	4,420	213	186,248	668	786,123	1,177	598	4,256	25,908
African Methodist Episcopal Zion Church	47	47	13,647	290	44	44	453,825	10,314	5	15,500	47	138,567	2,948	47	990	8,426
Colored Methodist Episcopal Church	68	68	5,111	75	60	60	437,873	7,298	28	39,833	62	111,589	1,800	57	421	3,088
Independent African Methodist Episcopal Church	15	15	459	31	15	15	14,300	953	4	2,427	13	2,331	179	13	72	315
Presbyterian bodies:																
Presbyterian Church in the United States of America	51	4	301	75	2	2	10,000	5,000	1	45	4	4,747	1,187	4	41	239
Presbyterian Church in the United States	135	4	81	20	2	2	800	400	1	100	4	430	108	1	2	8
Protestant Episcopal Church	154	19	4,500	237	18	17	255,205	15,012	2	4,150	19	54,570	2,872	15	92	1,371
Roman Catholic Church	115	6	1,657	276	6	6	95,500	15,917	2	5,500	6	20,979	3,497	5	9	510
Spiritualists:																
National Spiritual Alliance of the United States of America	3	3	60	20												
All other denominations	116	5	453	91	2	2	18,200	9,100	2	7,230	5	12,370	2,474	4	15	167

See footnotes at end of table.

TABLE 10.—NEGRO CHURCHES—NUMBER OF CHURCHES, MEMBERSHIP, NUMBER AND VALUE OF CHURCH EDIFICES, DEBT, EXPENDITURES, AND SUNDAY SCHOOLS, BY DENOMINATIONS, BY STATES: 1926—Con.

[See note at head of this table]

DENOMINATION	Total number of churches in denominations wholly or in part Negro	Number of Negro churches [1]	MEMBERS [2]		Number of church edifices	VALUE OF CHURCH EDIFICES			DEBT ON CHURCH EDIFICES		EXPENDITURES DURING YEAR			SUNDAY SCHOOLS [3]		
			Total number	Average per church		Churches reporting	Amount	Average per church	Churches reporting	Amount	Churches reporting	Amount	Average per church	Churches reporting	Officers and teachers	Scholars
GEORGIA																
All denominations	5,978	5,201	538,093	103	4,133	4,085	$12,380,886	$3,031	805	$636,704	3,874	$2,434,130	$628	3,172	19,466	141,582
Adventist bodies:																
Seventh-Day Adventist Denomination	19	6	333	56	6	6	19,100	3,183	1	140	6	15,055	2,509	4	47	275
Baptist bodies:																
Negro Baptists	2,900	2,900	381,312	131	2,236	2,202	6,650,906	3,020	285	206,062	1,797	1,010,077	562	1,339	7,568	63,622
United American Free Will Baptist Church	31	31	1,391	45	24	24	29,150	1,215	2	803	30	7,324	244	25	105	521
Colored Primitive Baptists	199	199	9,251	46	17	15	14,073	938	2	511	16	3,796	237			
Church of God (Headquarters, Anderson, Ind.)	15	8	238	30	7	7	18,000	2,571	1	50	6	1,820	303	5	23	156
Church of God and Saints of Christ	4	4	392	98	1	1	1,200				4	2,210	553	1	4	26
Church of God in Christ	21	21	763	36	15	15	26,100	1,740	7	1,940	20	10,646	532	12	50	345
Churches of God, Holiness	3	3	749	250	2	2	66,000	33,000	1	23,000	3	11,750	3,917	3	30	430
Congregational Churches	50	18	1,510	84	17	17	214,100	12,594	4	12,655	18	35,293	1,961	15	96	804
Disciples of Christ	149	25	985	39	22	22	19,700	895	4	560	24	3,860	161	19	72	404
Methodist bodies:																
Methodist Episcopal Church	348	271	21,280	79	261	258	930,273	3,606	66	43,858	269	153,876	572	257	1,797	11,396
Methodist Protestant Church	51	17	615	36	17	17	32,500	1,912	3	183	17	2,757	162	14	77	445
Wesleyan Methodist Connection (or Church) of America	31	8	253	32	8	8	9,700	1,213			8	3,449	431	8	48	263
African Methodist Episcopal Church	1,173	1,173	74,149	63	1,004	995	2,720,683	2,734	316	233,822	1,149	743,393	647	984	5,886	38,047
African Methodist Episcopal Zion Church	83	83	7,887	95	77	77	177,680	2,308	22	10,144	82	57,558	702	77	1,107	4,852
Colored Methodist Episcopal Church	366	366	31,292	85	360	360	1,057,191	2,937	78	40,555	362	294,022	812	349	2,204	16,177
Independent African Methodist Episcopal Church	3	3	174	58	3	3	4,800	1,600	2	480	3	1,449	483	3	20	111
Presbyterian bodies:																
Presbyterian Church in the United States of America	32	30	2,008	67	24	24	138,400	5,767	5	6,230	27	27,149	1,006	27	192	1,938
Presbyterian Church in the United States	250	6	199	33	6	6	9,500	1,583			6	2,733	456	6	35	204
Protestant Episcopal Church	107	21	2,015	96	20	20	122,680	6,134	3	25,100	20	22,451	1,123	19	86	980
Roman Catholic Church	73	5	1,203	241	5	5	118,200	23,640	3	30,611	5	22,193	4,439	3	11	558
All other denominations	70	3	94	31	1	1	950				2	1,269	635	2	8	28
IDAHO																
All denominations	5	5	205	41	4	4	$12,500	3,125	2	$1,450	4	$8,165	$2,041	4	24	123
Baptist bodies:																
Negro Baptists	3	3	105	35	2	2	9,000	4,500	1	750	2	3,650	1,825	2	12	50
All other denominations	2	2	100	50	2	2	3,500	1,750	1	700	2	4,515	2,258	2	12	73
ILLINOIS																
All denominations	5,682	523	137,131	262	405	399	$7,774,032	$19,484	196	$1,496,332	487	$1,485,297	$3,050	466	4,779	48,116
Baptist bodies:																
Negro Baptists	259	259	83,839	324	203	199	3,880,540	19,500	84	696,723	238	740,262	3,110	227	2,369	22,918
Church of Christ (Holiness) United States of America	3	3	571	190	2	2	60,000	30,000	1	42,000				2	10	100
Church of God in Christ	38	38	1,939	51	20	19	111,905	5,890	12	18,695	33	31,748	962	31	201	1,215
Churches of Christ	146	5	103	21							5	539	108	5	8	95
Churches of the Living God:																
Church of the Living God, Christian Workers for Fellowship	8	8	644	81	8	8	27,300	3,413	3	3,480	8	2,647	331	8	32	372
Disciples of Christ	635	8	626	78	8	7	118,000	16,857	3	75,600	8	24,158	3,020	7	58	488
Independent Churches	24	3	492	164							3	4,089	1,363	2	17	205
Lutherans:																
Evangelical Lutheran Synodical Conference of America:																
Evangelical Lutheran Synod of Missouri, Ohio, and other States	400	3	185	62	3	3	35,700	11,900	1	2,000	3	1,532	511	2	12	96
Methodist bodies:																
Methodist Episcopal Church	1,723	14	6,092	435	12	12	261,000	21,750	9	32,178	14	47,531	3,395	14	186	2,274
African Methodist Episcopal Church	113	113	19,366	171	95	95	1,704,387	17,941	49	231,039	110	359,532	3,268	107	1,074	13,801
African Methodist Episcopal Zion Church	13	13	5,972	459	12	12	342,400	28,533	7	99,100	13	78,126	6,010	13	327	1,964
Colored Methodist Episcopal Church	26	26	6,395	246	22	22	520,000	23,636	17	123,782	25	73,022	2,921	26	218	2,010
Presbyterian bodies:																
Presbyterian Church in the United States of America	543	3	874	291	3	3	115,000	38,333			3	15,349	5,116	3	53	628
Colored Cumberland Presbyterian Church	3	3	162	54	3	3	7,000	2,333	2	1,035	3	970	323	3	19	84
Protestant Episcopal Church	224	4	1,990	498	4	4	57,500	14,375	1	6,000	4	11,470	2,868	4	57	389
Spiritualists:																
National Spiritualist Association	57	4	178	45							4	2,071	518			
All other denominations	1,467	16	7,703	481	10	10	533,300	53,330	7	164,700	13	92,251	7,096	12	138	1,477

See footnotes at end of table.

TABLE 10.—NEGRO CHURCHES—NUMBER OF CHURCHES, MEMBERSHIP, NUMBER AND VALUE OF CHURCH EDIFICES, DEBT, EXPENDITURES, AND SUNDAY SCHOOLS, BY DENOMINATIONS, BY STATES: 1926—Con.

[See note at head of this table]

DENOMINATION	Total number of churches in denominations wholly or in part Negro	Number of Negro churches [1]	MEMBERS [2]		Number of church edifices	VALUE OF CHURCH EDIFICES			DEBT ON CHURCH EDIFICES		EXPENDITURES DURING YEAR			SUNDAY SCHOOLS [3]		
			Total number	Average per church		Churches reporting	Amount	Average per church	Churches reporting	Amount	Churches reporting	Amount	Average per church	Churches reporting	Officers and teachers	Scholars
INDIANA																
All denominations	**3,639**	**326**	**49,704**	**152**	**281**	**278**	**$3,568,814**	**$12,837**	**140**	**$679,821**	**297**	**$652,558**	**$2,197**	**281**	**2,646**	**18,139**
Adventist bodies:																
Seventh-Day Adventist Denomination	55	3	32	11	1	1	3,000				3	1,514	505	3	9	50
Baptist bodies:																
Negro Baptists	161	161	30,388	189	136	134	1,734,664	12,945	71	406,805	136	284,248	2,090	133	1,250	9,176
Church of God (Headquarters, Anderson, Ind.)	69	3	170	57	3	3	17,000	5,667	1	2,700	3	4,930	1,643	3	27	142
Church of God in Christ	12	12	589	49	9	9	37,500	4,167	4	12,766	12	18,974	1,581	10	73	493
Churches of Christ	236	5	173	35	1	1	600				5	891	178	4	11	140
Churches of the Living God:																
Church of the Living God, Christian Workers for Fellowship	4	4	183	46	4	4	11,300	2,825	2	2,300	4	2,147	537	4	13	67
Church of the Living God, "The Pillar and Ground of Truth"	3	3	475	158	3	3	12,300	4,100	2	4,100	3	3,740	1,247			
Methodist bodies:																
Methodist Episcopal Church	1,449	25	3,758	150	23	23	349,500	15,196	12	29,350	25	66,024	2,641	23	195	1,450
African Methodist Episcopal Church	67	67	7,486	112	65	64	716,250	11,191	23	98,168	65	170,799	2,628	61	552	3,445
African Methodist Episcopal Zion Church	19	19	3,867	204	19	19	422,250	22,224	16	70,920	19	62,145	3,271	19	396	2,362
Colored Methodist Episcopal Church	11	11	1,505	137	7	7	149,100	21,300	6	45,112	11	17,154	1,559	9	50	323
All other denominations	1,553	13	1,078	83	10	10	115,350	11,535	3	7,600	11	19,992	1,817	12	70	491
IOWA																
All denominations	**1,463**	**89**	**8,577**	**96**	**82**	**81**	**$565,135**	**$6,977**	**41**	**$62,541**	**87**	**$130,241**	**$1,497**	**79**	**797**	**5,083**
Baptist bodies:																
Negro Baptists	39	39	3,701	95	37	36	237,150	6,588	21	41,033	38	49,962	1,315	35	356	2,089
Church of God in Christ	4	4	114	29	1	1	2,000		1	500	4	2,142	536	3	10	113
Methodist bodies:																
Methodist Episcopal Church	1,102	6	268	45	5	5	19,000	3,800	3	2,575	6	6,075	1,013	6	36	216
African Methodist Episcopal Church	27	27	2,598	96	26	26	229,835	8,840	10	13,673	27	59,644	2,209	23	206	1,551
African Methodist Episcopal Zion Church	8	8	1,647	206	8	8	47,150	5,894	4	2,660	8	7,114	889	8	171	1,003
All other denominations	283	5	249	50	5	5	30,000	6,000	2	2,100	4	5,304	1,326	4	18	111
KANSAS																
All denominations	**2,358**	**328**	**28,292**	**86**	**300**	**297**	**$2,486,100**	**$8,371**	**110**	**$277,941**	**303**	**$379,645**	**$1,253**	**274**	**2,270**	**13,248**
Baptist bodies:																
Negro Baptists	136	136	15,243	112	133	133	1,353,850	10,179	43	124,097	129	186,083	1,443	117	1,115	6,819
Colored Primitive Baptists	10	10	114	11	2	1	1,620				2	800	400			
Church of God (Headquarters, Anderson, Ind.)	15	3	102	34	3	3	6,500	2,167	1	700	3	3,273	1,091	3	15	119
Church of God and Saints of Christ	3	3	47	16	3	3	10,060	3,353	1	46	3	1,913	638	1	5	17
Church of God in Christ	22	22	968	44	16	15	70,070	4,671	7	7,920	16	20,956	1,310	18	93	572
Churches of Christ	143	4	56	14							4	136	34	3	3	49
Churches of the Living God:																
Church of the Living God, Christian Workers for Fellowship	3	3	134	45	2	2	2,300	1,150			3	245	82	2	5	28
Disciples of Christ	369	13	668	51	13	12	77,500	6,458	4	5,415	12	8,995	750	8	50	260
Free Church of God in Christ	3	3	106	35	3	3	4,000	1,333	2	400	3	2,250	750	3	17	90
Methodist bodies:																
Methodist Episcopal Church	1,028	26	1,614	62	23	23	165,600	7,200	13	17,748	25	21,992	880	22	126	828
African Methodist Episcopal Church	77	77	6,336	82	77	77	664,200	8,626	26	101,300	77	92,435	1,200	72	601	3,078
African Methodist Episcopal Zion Church	6	6	953	159	6	6	30,500	5,083	6	9,975	6	5,515	919	6	128	726
Colored Methodist Episcopal Church	15	15	1,166	78	15	15	74,100	4,940	6	7,340	15	26,672	1,778	15	95	573
Protestant Episcopal Church	98	4	281	70	3	3	11,800	3,933			3	3,268	1,089	3	10	79
All other denominations	400	3	504	168	1	1	14,000		1	3,000	2	5,112	2,556	1	7	10

See footnotes at end of table.

TABLE 10.—NEGRO CHURCHES—NUMBER OF CHURCHES, MEMBERSHIP, NUMBER AND VALUE OF CHURCH EDIFICES, DEBT, EXPENDITURES, AND SUNDAY SCHOOLS, BY DENOMINATIONS, BY STATES: 1926—Con.

[See note at head of this table]

DENOMINATION	Total number of churches in denominations wholly or in part Negro	Number of Negro churches [1]	MEMBERS [2]		Number of church edifices	VALUE OF CHURCH EDIFICES			DEBT ON CHURCH EDIFICES		EXPENDITURES DURING YEAR			SUNDAY SCHOOLS [3]		
			Total number	Average per church		Churches reporting	Amount	Average per church	Churches reporting	Amount	Churches reporting	Amount	Average per church	Churches reporting	Officers and teachers	Scholars
							KENTUCKY									
All denominations	**3,146**	**1,103**	**127,126**	**115**	**994**	**985**	**$6,602,894**	**$6,703**	**205**	**$480,883**	**1,051**	**$1,178,944**	**$1,122**	**957**	**7,630**	**50,136**
Adventist bodies:																
Seventh-day Adventist Denomination	20	3	68	23	3	3	4,500	1,500	-----	-----	3	2,494	831	3	17	85
Baptist bodies:																
Negro Baptists	589	589	83,837	142	529	527	3,570,184	6,775	80	233,392	577	616,110	1,068	525	4,275	30,140
Colored Primitive Baptists	14	14	559	40	1	1	800	-----	-----	-----	1	130	-----	-----	-----	-----
Church of God in Christ	12	12	384	32	6	6	16,900	2,817	3	1,950	6	4,547	758	7	44	232
Churches of Christ	367	12	517	43	10	10	34,660	3,466	-----	-----	11	7,601	691	11	28	392
Churches of the Living God:																
Church of the Living God, Christian Workers for Fellowship	5	5	868	174	5	5	39,250	7,850	1	800	5	2,907	581	5	19	238
Disciples of Christ	783	51	4,448	87	47	46	233,400	5,074	11	26,046	37	35,631	963	35	194	1,246
Methodist bodies:																
Methodist Episcopal Church	350	84	6,693	80	80	79	588,100	7,444	24	67,834	81	107,146	1,323	74	497	3,550
African Methodist Episcopal Church	130	130	10,492	81	121	119	891,900	7,495	45	45,180	130	137,264	1,056	121	866	5,517
African Methodist Episcopal Zion Church	63	63	7,174	114	60	60	430,100	7,168	11	51,021	63	101,528	1,612	60	1,000	4,027
Colored Methodist Episcopal Church	97	97	7,715	80	92	92	459,450	4,994	20	30,160	97	118,942	1,226	86	540	3,675
Presbyterian bodies:																
Presbyterian Church in the United States of America	139	7	230	33	7	6	23,400	3,900	2	2,500	7	4,683	669	5	26	146
Colored Cumberland Presbyterian Church	19	19	1,214	64	18	18	45,650	2,536	3	2,560	18	7,945	441	17	85	517
Protestant Episcopal Church	78	5	368	74	6	5	103,000	20,600	2	4,440	5	6,459	1,292	4	13	111
Roman Catholic Church	281	4	2,068	517	3	3	98,000	32,667	2	13,000	3	19,330	6,443	1	1	50
All other denominations	199	8	491	61	6	5	63,600	12,720	1	2,000	7	6,227	890	3	25	210
							LOUISIANA									
All denominations	**2,776**	**2,077**	**248,797**	**120**	**1,888**	**1,877**	**$6,514,176**	**$3,471**	**389**	**$633,819**	**1,966**	**$1,539,644**	**$783**	**1,843**	**13,304**	**87,867**
Baptist bodies:																
Negro Baptists	1,311	1,311	132,743	101	1,200	1,194	3,275,174	2,743	195	207,830	1,251	668,825	535	1,184	9,038	55,287
United American Free Will Baptist Church	7	7	404	58	5	5	12,000	2,400	-----	-----	7	2,675	382	6	29	125
Colored Primitive Baptists	19	19	994	52	1	1	4,000	-----	-----	-----	2	257	129	-----	-----	-----
Church of Christ (Holiness) United States of America	6	6	393	66	6	6	20,700	3,450	-----	-----	6	4,089	682	6	45	230
Church of God (Headquarters, Anderson, Ind.)	22	3	79	26	3	3	3,000	1,000	1	485	3	1,524	508	2	12	70
Church of God in Christ	52	52	1,661	32	37	37	63,418	1,714	10	8,434	44	20,197	459	44	202	953
Churches of Christ	45	3	57	19	1	1	500	-----	-----	-----	3	306	102	3	5	50
Congregational Churches	25	15	973	65	15	14	132,565	9,469	5	8,639	15	20,614	1,374	15	85	661
Lutherans:																
Evangelical Lutheran Synodical Conference of America:																
Evangelical Lutheran Synod of Missouri, Ohio, and other States	41	8	1,123	140	7	7	61,500	8,786	1	150	8	9,593	1,199	8	26	714
Methodist bodies:																
Methodist Episcopal Church	244	220	16,738	76	211	209	907,625	4,343	71	66,063	207	194,156	938	195	1,235	9,686
African Methodist Episcopal Church	206	206	12,464	61	188	186	631,319	3,394	54	103,665	204	206,066	1,010	185	1,155	7,233
African Methodist Episcopal Zion Church	26	26	7,671	295	25	25	275,250	11,010	9	31,850	25	70,069	2,803	25	385	3,004
Colored Methodist Episcopal Church	154	154	11,374	74	150	150	316,475	2,110	29	24,853	153	92,090	602	146	940	6,054
Presbyterian bodies:																
Presbyterian Church in the United States	115	8	324	41	7	7	35,850	5,121	1	100	7	3,145	449	8	42	271
Roman Catholic Church	414	35	61,615	1,760	29	29	768,150	26,488	13	181,750	27	253,669	9,025	12	72	3,427
All other denominations	89	4	184	46	3	3	6,650	2,217	-----	-----	4	2,369	592	4	33	102
							MARYLAND									
All denominations	**1,858**	**654**	**97,025**	**148**	**629**	**617**	**$5,765,535**	**$9,344**	**250**	**$1,021,392**	**641**	**$1,199,001**	**$1,871**	**606**	**5,202**	**43,678**
Baptist bodies:																
Negro Baptists	99	99	33,062	334	87	83	1,503,046	18,109	45	396,480	90	306,628	3,407	77	715	6,115
Christian Church (General Convention of the Christian Church)	7	4	619	155	1	1	40,000	-----	-----	-----	4	7,568	1,892	4	36	308
Church of God and Saints of Christ	6	6	255	43	1	1	1,000	-----	1	89	6	5,053	842	3	8	43
Disciples of Christ	36	3	475	158	2	2	17,500	8,750	2	1,700	3	5,594	1,865	3	25	224
Methodist bodies:																
Methodist Episcopal Church	936	370	35,272	95	368	367	2,214,135	6,033	137	368,535	370	481,143	1,300	358	2,873	24,293
African Methodist Episcopal Church	100	100	11,478	115	100	95	1,110,243	11,687	48	123,956	100	225,947	2,259	94	868	7,808
African Methodist Episcopal Zion Church	26	26	3,014	116	24	24	195,300	8,138	6	17,275	26	51,073	1,964	26	416	2,023
Union American Methodist Episcopal Church	11	11	1,015	92	12	11	71,551	6,505	3	5,050	10	14,123	1,412	8	61	606
African Union Methodist Protestant Church	9	9	439	49	9	9	50,500	5,611	1	500	9	8,544	949	9	54	307
Colored Methodist Episcopal Church	5	5	363	73	5	5	20,000	4,000	2	607	4	6,726	1,682	5	21	147
Presbyterian bodies:																
Presbyterian Church in the United States of America	99	3	709	236	3	3	49,000	16,333	-----	-----	3	9,696	3,232	3	40	474
Protestant Episcopal Church	253	7	2,155	308	6	6	54,260	9,043	-----	-----	7	12,814	1,831	7	16	411
Roman Catholic Church	240	5	7,520	1,504	5	5	286,500	57,300	2	66,000	4	42,597	10,649	5	26	629
All other denominations	31	6	649	108	6	5	152,500	30,500	3	41,200	5	21,495	4,299	4	43	290

See footnotes at end of table.

TABLE 10.—NEGRO CHURCHES—NUMBER OF CHURCHES, MEMBERSHIP, NUMBER AND VALUE OF CHURCH EDIFICES, DEBT, EXPENDITURES, AND SUNDAY SCHOOLS, BY DENOMINATIONS, BY STATES: 1926—Con.

[See note at head of this table]

DENOMINATION	Total number of churches in denominations wholly or in part Negro	Number of Negro churches [1]	MEMBERS [2]: Total number	MEMBERS [2]: Average per church	Number of church edifices	VALUE OF CHURCH EDIFICES: Churches reporting	VALUE OF CHURCH EDIFICES: Amount	VALUE OF CHURCH EDIFICES: Average per church	DEBT ON CHURCH EDIFICES: Churches reporting	DEBT ON CHURCH EDIFICES: Amount	EXPENDITURES DURING YEAR: Churches reporting	EXPENDITURES DURING YEAR: Amount	EXPENDITURES DURING YEAR: Average per church	SUNDAY SCHOOLS [3]: Churches reporting	SUNDAY SCHOOLS [3]: Officers and teachers	SUNDAY SCHOOLS [3]: Scholars
MASSACHUSETTS																
All denominations	**1,325**	**72**	**13,882**	**193**	**61**	**60**	**$1,201,100**	**$20,018**	**27**	**$175,129**	**71**	**$251,967**	**$3,549**	**68**	**752**	**7,766**
African Orthodox Church	3	3	378	126							3	3,922	1,307	3	12	83
Baptist bodies:																
Negro Baptists	25	25	5,396	216	24	24	477,500	19,896	13	59,604	25	101,003	4,040	25	296	2,937
Church of God and Saints of Christ	3	3	188	63	2	2	7,900	3,950			3	3,765	1,255	2	10	66
Congregational Churches	570	6	1,059	177	7	6	94,000	15,667	2	6,800	6	17,671	2,945	6	69	599
Methodist bodies:																
African Methodist Episcopal Church	16	16	1,662	104	14	14	277,700	19,836	8	77,425	16	59,510	3,719	14	135	1,212
African Methodist Episcopal Zion Church	8	8	3,127	391	8	8	246,000	30,750	3	27,300	8	34,140	4,268	8	123	2,006
All other denominations	700	11	2,072	188	6	6	98,000	16,333	1	4,000	10	31,956	3,196	10	107	863
MICHIGAN																
All denominations	**2,981**	**186**	**46,231**	**249**	**160**	**155**	**$3,362,044**	**$21,691**	**92**	**$606,184**	**178**	**$691,181**	**$3,883**	**169**	**1,918**	**16,328**
Baptist bodies:																
Negro Baptists	81	81	24,883	307	70	67	1,703,455	25,425	34	288,874	77	292,454	3,798	76	1,054	8,403
Church of God in Christ	17	17	1,253	74	14	13	116,600	8,969	11	24,618	17	31,201	1,835	14	117	577
Churches of Christ	21	4	229	57	2	2	10,400	5,200	1	2,500	4	3,756	939	4	17	232
Churches of the Living God:																
Church of the Living God, Christian Workers for Fellowship	4	4	293	73	3	3	10,000	3,333	2	5,500	3	1,388	463	3	12	76
Methodist bodies:																
Methodist Episcopal Church	1,093	7	1,615	231	5	5	52,500	10,500	3	17,200	7	15,986	2,284	7	64	546
African Methodist Episcopal Church	42	42	10,818	258	40	39	1,054,364	27,035	21	196,842	41	210,214	5,127	39	368	4,085
African Methodist Episcopal Zion Church	8	8	2,017	252	8	8	149,500	18,688	7	20,700	8	43,169	5,396	8	103	943
Colored Methodist Episcopal Church	9	9	1,946	216	8	8	115,600	14,450	8	31,600	9	35,609	3,957	9	64	562
Protestant Episcopal Church	202	3	1,190	397	3	3	55,000	18,333	2	6,700	3	15,697	5,232	3	42	402
All other denominations	1,504	11	1,987	181	7	7	94,625	13,518	3	11,650	9	41,707	4,634	6	77	502
MINNESOTA																
All denominations	**1,736**	**23**	**3,702**	**161**	**24**	**20**	**$269,001**	**$13,450**	**9**	**$26,656**	**23**	**$72,790**	**$3,165**	**22**	**195**	**1,643**
Baptist bodies:																
Negro Baptists	8	8	1,436	180	9	8	81,600	10,200	4	3,550	8	23,399	2,925	8	87	648
Methodist bodies:																
African Methodist Episcopal Church	8	8	1,402	175	6	5	101,500	20,300	4	21,306	8	34,885	4,361	7	69	631
All other denominations	1,720	7	864	123	9	7	85,901	12,272	1	1,800	7	14,506	2,072	7	39	364
MISSISSIPPI																
All denominations	**4,782**	**4,034**	**348,425**	**86**	**3,837**	**3,803**	**$7,133,867**	**$1,876**	**413**	**$248,703**	**3,928**	**$1,869,166**	**$476**	**3,791**	**29,382**	**162,089**
Adventist bodies:																
Seventh-day Adventist Denomination	18	3	83	28	3	3	13,150	4,383	1	525	3	4,726	1,575	3	21	99
Baptist bodies:																
Negro Baptists	2,314	2,314	226,989	98	2,263	2,239	3,641,884	1,627	106	56,853	2,281	872,817	383	2,225	17,626	92,839
United American Free Will Baptist Church	5	5	189	38	5	5	8,600	1,720	2	171	5	1,756	351	5	27	135
Colored Primitive Baptists	37	37	1,443	39	4	4	2,550	638	1	93	3	715	238	1	8	30
Church of Christ (Holiness), United States of America	25	25	1,632	65	25	25	80,750	3,230	3	1,274	21	11,245	535	21	161	867
Church of God (Headquarters, Anderson, Ind.)	24	6	114	19	6	6	5,600	933	1	245	5	1,567	313	5	20	82
Church of God in Christ	86	86	3,314	39	62	61	88,360	1,449	21	7,651	73	31,240	428	69	387	2,159
Churches of Christ	125	16	617	39	8	8	2,808	351	3	205	16	1,605	100	14	36	475
Churches of the Living God:																
Church of the Living God, Christian Workers for Fellowship	5	5	145	29	4	4	9,150	2,228			4	1,345	336	3	6	46
Congregational Churches	5	5	277	55	5	4	24,150	6,038	1	71	4	2,756	689	3	21	332
Disciples of Christ	106	39	2,185	56	26	22	36,750	1,670	6	3,830	37	13,784	373	22	113	822
Methodist bodies:																
Methodist Episcopal Church	528	526	41,165	78	510	508	1,328,593	2,615	111	75,546	522	318,399	610	509	3,620	25,237
African Methodist Episcopal Church	397	397	22,439	57	384	383	710,800	1,856	53	49,292	393	183,422	467	381	2,484	12,409
African Methodist Episcopal Zion Church	162	162	18,461	114	154	154	366,680	2,381	41	22,379	162	126,459	781	159	2,238	10,422
Colored Methodist Episcopal Church	370	370	25,659	69	346	346	642,347	1,856	57	17,531	364	239,657	658	347	2,495	15,030
Presbyterian bodies:																
Presbyterian Church in the United States of America	53	8	247	31	8	8	10,700	1,338	2	850	8	1,841	230	8	52	204
Presbyterian Church in the United States	279	12	310	26	11	11	8,995	818	3	187	12	3,992	333	9	42	299
Protestant Episcopal Church	91	5	133	27	3	3	41,000	13,667			4	920	230	2	9	165
Roman Catholic Church	112	10	2,956	296	9	9	111,000	12,333	1	12,000	10	50,723	5,072	4	11	415
All other denominations	40	3	67	22	1						1	197		1	5	22

See footnotes at end of table.

TABLE 10.—NEGRO CHURCHES—NUMBER OF CHURCHES, MEMBERSHIP, NUMBER AND VALUE OF CHURCH EDIFICES, DEBT, EXPENDITURES, AND SUNDAY SCHOOLS, BY DENOMINATIONS, BY STATES: 1926—Con.

[See note at head of this table]

DENOMINATION	Total number of churches in denominations wholly or in part Negro	Number of Negro churches [1]	MEMBERS [2]		Number of church edifices	VALUE OF CHURCH EDIFICES			DEBT ON CHURCH EDIFICES		EXPENDITURES DURING YEAR			SUNDAY SCHOOLS [3]		
			Total number	Average per church		Churches reporting	Amount	Average per church	Churches reporting	Amount	Churches reporting	Amount	Average per church	Churches reporting	Officers and teachers	Scholars
MISSOURI																
All denominations	**3,863**	**645**	**82,207**	**127**	**541**	**533**	**$5,112,613**	**$9,592**	**153**	**$807,321**	**580**	**$846,458**	**$1,459**	**498**	**4,512**	**30,174**
Baptist bodies:																
Negro Baptists	244	244	42,299	173	226	223	2,373,919	10,645	58	248,254	236	340,436	1,443	196	1,877	13,409
Church of Christ (Holiness), United States of America	3	3	189	63	1	1	10,000							1	10	75
Church of God in Christ	35	35	1,768	51	31	29	99,065	3,416	15	12,323	26	24,302	935	28	152	842
Churches of Christ	272	5	78	16							5	80	16	2	3	30
Churches of the Living God:																
Church of the Living God, Christian Workers for Fellowship	3	3	193	64	3	3	18,200	6,067	1	3,500	3	2,994	998	3	11	46
Disciples of Christ	857	14	1,172	84	13	13	101,550	7,812	3	10,462	12	13,254	1,105	12	92	471
Methodist bodies:																
Methodist Episcopal Church	690	109	9,143	84	102	101	565,518	5,599	28	65,691	108	103,924	962	91	635	4,056
African Methodist Episcopal Church	155	155	11,179	72	102	101	611,800	6,057	19	78,169	115	107,619	936	101	750	4,271
African Methodist Episcopal Zion Church	17	17	6,873	404	17	17	327,700	19,276	11	26,700	17	55,866	3,286	17	539	3,326
Colored Methodist Episcopal Church	33	33	5,520	167	24	24	296,000	12,333	9	66,561	33	80,203	2,430	29	237	1,921
Presbyterian bodies:																
Presbyterian Church in the United States of America	348	3	531	177	3	3	105,000	35,000	1	9,000	3	8,376	2,792	3	28	260
Colored Cumberland Presbyterian Church	7	7	96	14	4	4	3,100	775			6	1,106	184	2	10	37
Protestant Episcopal Church	106	3	772	257	3	3	147,000	49,000	2	26,500	3	9,300	3,100	2	40	248
Roman Catholic Church	534	3	1,272	424	2	2	47,000	23,500			3	13,695	4,565	2	8	195
All other denominations	559	11	1,122	102	10	9	406,761	45,196	6	260,161	10	85,303	8,530	9	120	987
MONTANA																
All denominations	**9**	**9**	**228**	**25**	**9**	**9**	**$36,400**	**$4,044**	**5**	**$2,039**	**8**	**$7,125**	**$891**	**9**	**49**	**183**
Methodist bodies:																
African Methodist Episcopal Church	7	7	200	29	7	7	33,200	4,743	4	1,339	6	5,599	933	7	42	157
All other denominations	2	2	28	14	2	2	3,200	1,600	1	700	2	1,526	763	2	7	26
NEBRASKA																
All denominations	**1,480**	**40**	**5,163**	**129**	**35**	**33**	**$474,215**	**$14,370**	**23**	**$77,087**	**36**	**$90,489**	**$2,514**	**29**	**234**	**1,580**
Baptist bodies:																
Negro Baptists	11	11	2,062	187	11	10	223,950	22,395	8	42,305	10	28,115	2,812	7	66	464
Church of God in Christ	4	4	170	43	4	4	16,050	4,013	3	2,300	4	6,500	1,625	2	10	52
Churches of the Living God:																
Church of the Living God, Christian Workers for Fellowship	4	4	369	92	3	3	6,000	2,000	1	290	4	1,028	257	4	19	91
Methodist bodies:																
Methodist Episcopal Church	569	4	228	57	4	4	10,200	2,550	2	400	4	3,017	754	3	18	69
African Methodist Episcopal Church	10	10	1,540	154	6	6	115,315	19,219	5	15,127	7	25,440	3,634	6	81	607
All other denominations	882	7	794	113	7	6	102,700	17,117	4	16,665	7	26,389	3,770	7	40	297
NEW JERSEY																
All denominations	**1,826**	**412**	**71,221**	**173**	**370**	**354**	**$7,220,587**	**$20,397**	**211**	**$971,640**	**392**	**$1,558,821**	**$4,053**	**367**	**3,588**	**30,985**
Adventist bodies:																
Seventh-day Adventist Denomination	42	4	193	48	3	3	41,560	13,853	3	21,080	4	10,142	2,536	2	17	84
Baptist bodies:																
Negro Baptists	159	159	41,129	259	152	146	3,473,222	23,789	93	471,018	149	824,234	5,532	137	1,379	12,188
Christian Church (General Convention of the Christian Church)	15	3	184	61	1	1	3,500		1	600	3	4,093	1,364	3	22	191
Church of God and Saints of Christ	7	7	458	65	3	3	29,500	9,833	3	16,940	5	12,059	2,412	2	10	78
Church of God in Christ	14	14	517	37	5	5	14,500	2,900	4	4,715	11	17,024	1,548	12	75	403
Methodist bodies:																
Methodist Episcopal Church	671	29	3,525	122	28	38	549,500	19,625	17	65,588	29	100,332	3,460	29	303	3,363
African Methodist Episcopal Church	101	101	11,415	113	88	85	1,341,484	15,782	48	153,743	101	310,345	3,073	92	792	7,021
African Methodist Episcopal Zion Church	32	32	5,625	176	29	29	870,500	30,017	15	177,500	32	160,440	5,014	31	536	3,713
Union American Methodist Episcopal Church	20	20	2,337	117	18	18	106,650	5,925	6	3,850	17	35,312	2,077	20	107	724
African Union Methodist Protestant Church	10	10	1,192	119	11	10	128,371	12,837	5	4,607	10	33,458	3,346	10	78	904
Colored Methodist Episcopal Church	8	8	433	54	4	4	14,700	3,675	4	7,175	8	8,460	1,058	7	31	171
Independent African Methodist Episcopal Church	4	4	95	24	4	4	9,200	2,300	3	765	4	1,591	398	4	19	90
Presbyterian bodies:																
Presbyterian Church in the United States of America	403	10	2,172	217	16	10	455,800	45,580	4	17,800	10	49,431	4,943	10	159	1,570
Protestant Episcopal Church	325	8	1,847	231	7	7	178,250	25,464	4	24,500	8	21,591	2,699	8	60	485
All other denominations	15	3	99	33	1	1	3,850		1	1,759	1	309				

See footnotes at end of table.

TABLE 10.—NEGRO CHURCHES—NUMBER OF CHURCHES, MEMBERSHIP, NUMBER AND VALUE OF CHURCH EDIFICES, DEBT, EXPENDITURES, AND SUNDAY SCHOOLS, BY DENOMINATIONS, BY STATES, 1926—Con.

[See note at head of this table]

DENOMINATION	Total number of churches in denominations wholly or in part Negro	Number of Negro churches [1]	MEMBERS [2]		Number of church edifices	VALUE OF CHURCH EDIFICES			DEBT ON CHURCH EDIFICES		EXPENDITURES DURING YEAR			SUNDAY SCHOOLS [3]		
			Total number	Average per church		Churches reporting	Amount	Average per church	Churches reporting	Amount	Churches reporting	Amount	Average per church	Churches reporting	Officers and teachers	Scholars
NEW MEXICO																
All denominations	**17**	**17**	**710**	**42**	**11**	**11**	**$25,600**	**$2,327**	**8**	**$2,270**	**11**	**$8,968**	**$815**	**9**	**67**	**326**
Baptist bodies:																
Negro Baptists	9	9	408	45	8	8	16,000	2,000	6	1,520	9	7,743	860	7	44	251
Methodist bodies:																
African Methodist Episcopal Church	5	5	238	48	-------	-------	-------	-------	-------	-------	-------	-------	-------	-------	-------	-------
Colored Methodist Episcopal Church	3	3	64	21	3	3	9,600	3,200	2	750	2	2,225	613	2	23	75
NEW YORK																
All denominations	**6,437**	**352**	**114,543**	**325**	**279**	**274**	**$11,615,049**	**$42,391**	**150**	**$2,300,302**	**336**	**$2,048,710**	**$6,097**	**320**	**4,361**	**38,692**
African Orthodox Church	6	6	916	153	1	1	15,000	-------	1	2,000	6	13,027	2,171	5	26	283
African Orthodox Church of New York	3	3	717	239	1	1	50,000	-------	1	12,100	2	18,900	9,450	3	26	220
Baptist bodies:																
Negro Baptists	111	111	46,823	422	94	93	4,868,435	52,349	68	1,048,862	107	672,530	6,285	102	1,390	11,960
Christian Church (General Convention of the Christian Church)	62	6	208	35	1	1	35,000	-------	1	9,500	6	5,454	909	4	24	167
Church of God (Headquarters, Anderson, Ind.)	16	3	165	55	1	1	8,000	-------	1	3,000	3	8,832	2,944	3	26	189
Church of God and Saints of Christ	13	13	711	55	4	4	20,500	5,125	1	1,200	10	8,126	813	6	33	290
Church of God in Christ	6	6	180	30	2	2	4,000	2,000	2	3,200	5	5,913	1,183	5	20	123
Congregational Churches	280	5	1,884	377	5	5	275,000	55,000	5	97,150	5	51,370	10,274	5	82	1,054
Methodist bodies:																
Methodist Episcopal Church	1,930	14	5,531	395	11	11	1,111,500	101,045	6	374,250	14	121,861	8,704	14	242	3,115
African Methodist Episcopal Church	58	58	10,516	181	51	48	1,144,800	23,850	19	82,980	56	262,324	4,684	53	463	4,050
African Methodist Episcopal Zion Church	74	74	19,797	268	70	70	2,315,000	33,071	23	380,820	73	495,752	6,699	73	1,458	11,095
Union American Methodist Episcopal Church	4	4	613	153	4	4	46,750	11,688	2	8,000	4	20,425	5,106	4	23	195
African Union Methodist Protestant Church	3	3	129	43	3	3	19,500	6,500	2	540	3	6,378	2,126	3	12	126
Colored Methodist Episcopal Church	3	3	920	307	3	3	82,000	27,333	2	16,500	3	24,100	8,033	3	31	285
Presbyterian bodies:																
Presbyterian Church in the United State of America	813	7	2,371	339	7	6	181,000	30,167	4	46,800	7	30,570	4,367	7	108	923
Protestant Episcopal Church	882	15	10,375	692	14	14	903,500	64,536	8	98,000	14	141,239	10,089	15	284	3,255
Roman Catholic Church	1,783	4	10,805	2,701	4	4	420,000	105,000	2	84,000	4	131,591	32,898	3	22	510
Salvation Army	95	3	376	125	1	1	67,064	-------	1	21,400	3	10,679	3,560	3	24	358
Spiritualists:																
National Spiritualist Association	83	6	361	60	-------	-------	-------	-------	-------	-------	2	4,446	2,,223	1	1	10
All other denominations	212	8	1,145	143	2	2	48,000	24,000	1	10,000	8	15,193	1,899	8	66	484
NORTH CAROLINA																
All denominations	**4,662**	**3,203**	**431,333**	**135**	**2,936**	**2,914**	**$13,670,308**	**$4,691**	**643**	**$662,086**	**2,862**	**$3,060,556**	**$1,069**	**2,801**	**28,653**	**213,700**
Adventist bodies:																
Seventh-day Adventist Denomination	33	13	413	32	11	11	41,100	3,736	2	3,180	13	21,446	1,650	10	65	293
Baptist bodies:																
Negro Baptist	1,316	1,316	206,807	157	1,212	1,201	4,920,298	4,097	254	257,127	1,107	944,629	853	1,114	8,380	77,019
United American Free Will Baptist Church	117	117	11,112	95	105	103	249,475	2,422	33	6,395	110	53,621	487	103	655	4,194
Colored Primitive Baptists	102	102	2,626	26	2	2	1,875	938	-------	-------	2	94	47	-------	-------	-------
Christian Church (General Convention of the Christian Church)	161	50	5,684	114	48	48	194,900	4,060	12	5,295	50	27,473	549	48	316	2,350
Church of God (Headquarters, Anderson, Ind.)	18	5	160	32	6	4	14,000	3,500	3	405	5	3,912	782	5	30	214
Church of God and Saints of Christ	14	14	692	49	7	7	9,600	1,371	3	1,544	14	10,431	745	6	21	94
Church of God in Christ	8	8	213	27	6	6	11,400	1,900	3	2,558	8	3,869	484	7	24	152
Churches of God, Holiness	4	4	135	34	3	3	4,500	1,500	1	850	4	3,214	804	4	20	90
Congregational Churches	65	52	3,370	65	48	48	242,400	5,050	36	16,250	46	40,226	874	47	279	2,221
Disciples of Christ	309	123	12,059	98	115	115	243,750	2,120	22	18,219	119	51,858	436	108	523	3,941
Lutherans:																
Evangelical Lutheran Synodical Conference of America:																
Evangelical Lutheran Synod of Missouri, Ohio, and other States	38	24	1,403	58	22	21	71,550	3,407	1	140	22	5,374	244	20	79	809
Methodist bodies:																
Methodist Episcopal Church	372	174	13,466	77	171	169	973,900	5,763	44	38,581	170	150,185	883	169	1,293	9,917
African Methodist Episcopal Church	205	205	18,453	90	199	197	1,045,200	5,306	77	72,931	203	202,640	998	193	1,512	11,183
African Methodist Episcopal Zion Church	769	769	135,698	176	768	768	4,276,150	5,568	111	168,538	769	1,256,074	1,633	767	14,025	87,469
Colored Methodist Episcopal Church	37	37	4,867	132	34	34	218,660	6,431	13	29,360	36	55,859	1,552	35	263	2,416
Reformed Zion Union Apostolic Church	3	3	234	78	3	3	7,650	2,550	1	100	2	360	180	2	16	102
Presbyterian bodies:																
Presbyterian Church in the United States of America	151	134	9,822	73	127	126	744,675	5,910	29	35,535	131	175,527	1,340	114	901	7,881
Protestant Episcopal Church	266	41	3,129	76	38	37	234,025	6,325	4	688	39	33,961	871	39	199	2,586
Roman Catholic Church	66	5	676	135	5	5	139,600	27,920	1	4,000	5	17,893	3,579	4	17	411
All other denominations	608	7	314	45	6	6	25,600	4,267	3	390	7	1,910	273	6	35	358

See footnotes at end of table.

TABLE 10.—NEGRO CHURCHES—NUMBER OR CHURCHES, MEMBERSHIP, NUMBER AND VALUE OF CHURCH EDIFICES, DEBT, EXPENDITURES, AND SUNDAY SCHOOLS, BY DENOMINATIONS, BY STATES: 1926—Con.

[See note at head of this table]

DENOMINATION	Total number of churches in denominations wholly or in part Negro	Number of Negro churches [1]	MEMBERS [2]		Number of church edifices	VALUE OF CHURCH EDIFICES			DEBT ON CHURCH EDIFICES		EXPENDITURES DURING YEAR			SUNDAY SCHOOLS [3]		
			Total number	Average per church		Churches reporting	Amount	Average per church	Churches reporting	Amount	Churches reporting	Amount	Average per church	Churches reporting	Officers and teachers	Scholars
NORTH DAKOTA																
All denominations	**3**	**3**	**27**	**9**	**2**	**2**	**$3,250**	**$1,625**	**1**	**$150**	**1**	**$258**				
Baptist bodies:																
Negro Baptists	3	3	27	9	2	2	3,250	1,625	1	150	1	258				
OHIO																
All denominations	**5,604**	**622**	**119,529**	**192**	**523**	**513**	**$9,113,989**	**$17,766**	**226**	**$1,362,271**	**572**	**$1,800,095**	**$3,147**	**483**	**5,596**	**46,996**
Adventist bodies:																
Seventh-day Adventist Denomination	66	5	381	76	5	5	134,000	26,800	4	50,000	4	36,884	9,221	2	14	149
Baptist bodies:																
Negro Baptists	272	272	73,922	272	246	241	4,244,636	17,613	95	638,852	252	942,546	3,740	183	2,259	19,949
Colored Primitive Baptists	7	7	126	18	2	2	2,300	1,150	1	600	2	399	200			
Church of God (Headquarters, Anderson, Ind.)	70	7	234	33	4	4	39,000	9,750	3	15,200	6	7,752	1,292	7	47	317
Church of God and Saints of Christ	8	8	356	45	2	2	2,600	1,300	1	600	6	12,563	2,094	5	18	118
Church of God in Christ	7	7	447	64	4	4	27,718	6,930	2	14,000	6	8,744	1,457	6	35	369
Churches of Christ	161	3	43	14							3	195	65	3	3	36
Churches of the Living God:																
Church of the Living God, Christian Workers for Fellowship	4	4	659	165	4	4	25,000	6,250	1	3,000	4	1,645	411	4	13	143
Disciples of Christ	485	10	1,248	125	9	9	107,400	11,933	4	21,650	10	23,234	2,323	10	88	779
Methodist bodies:																
Methodist Episcopal Church	2,108	54	8,773	162	51	50	899,000	17,980	22	146,968	54	132,941	2,462	52	501	5,997
Wesleyan Methodist Connection (or Church) of America	39	13	773	59	11	11	47,400	4,309			13	9,268	713	13	113	666
African Methodist Episcopal Church	149	149	16,578	111	121	120	1,791,060	14,926	55	221,599	134	355,698	2,654	124	1,703	11,812
African Methodist Episcopal Zion Church	25	25	7,678	307	19	19	480,975	25,314	11	53,050	25	80,504	3,220	23	381	3,057
Colored Methodist Episcopal Church	26	26	2,789	107	19	18	415,500	23,083	15	77,122	25	85,108	3,404	26	213	1,470
Presbyterian bodies:																
Presbyterian Church in the United States of America	635	5	833	167	5	4	105,000	26,250	3	24,500	5	16,234	3,247	5	65	563
Protestant Episcopal Church	214	7	1,794	256	7	7	170,400	24,343	2	10,250	7	21,798	3,114	7	52	464
Roman Catholic Church	862	4	1,411	353	4	3	457,000	152,333	1	16,000	3	29,772	9,924	3	15	587
All other denominations	466	16	1,484	93	10	10	165,000	16,500	6	68,880	13	34,810	2,678	10	76	520
OKLAHOMA																
All denominations	**2,624**	**990**	**68,379**	**69**	**859**	**851**	**$2,238,849**	**$2,631**	**228**	**$192,569**	**943**	**$617,605**	**$655**	**863**	**5,745**	**34,586**
Adventist bodies:																
Seventh-day Adventist Denomination	47	5	114	23	5	5	14,150	2,830	4	2,150	4	2,854	714	3	18	69
Baptist bodies:																
Negro Baptists	559	559	47,363	85	480	476	1,385,419	2,911	106	100,494	532	344,862	648	497	3,527	22,527
Colored Primitive Baptists	3	3	44	15	2	2	2,300	1,150			1	120				
Church of God in Christ	59	59	1,700	29	48	48	79,750	1,661	22	8,940	51	33,702	661	45	247	1,290
Churches of Christ	559	9	201	22	5	5	3,050	610	2	225	9	829	92	9	17	150
Churches of the Living God:																
Church of the Living God, Christian Workers for Fellowship	20	20	1,396	70	21	20	31,585	1,579	4	1,780	20	5,319	266	20	52	363
Church of the Living God, "The Pillar and Ground of Truth"	18	18	1,100	61	20	18	45,685	2,538	14	10,215	18	20,290	1,127	14	79	686
Congregational Churches	30	3	378	126	3	3	23,000	7,667	1	1,200	3	8,210	2,737	2	15	90
Disciples of Christ	327	15	707	47	13	13	33,950	2,612	4	3,090	13	6,742	519	12	70	398
Methodist bodies:																
Methodist Episcopal Church	348	52	2,029	39	42	41	88,900	2,168	11	19,305	48	26,530	553	47	239	1,287
African Methodist Episcopal Church	107	107	5,918	55	96	96	303,835	3,165	27	19,824	106	92,186	870	97	631	3,439
African Methodist Episcopal Zion Church	15	15	1,729	115	15	15	18,050	1,203	1	750	15	10,020	668	15	238	1,113
Colored Methodist Episcopal Church	85	85	3,834	45	77	77	149,825	1,946	26	16,996	85	51,090	601	75	486	2,427
Presbyterian bodies:																
Presbyterian Church in the United States of America	182	26	603	23	22	22	33,050	1,502	5	4,600	26	8,034	309	19	91	547
Roman Catholic Church	182	8	1,100	138	7	7	20,200	2,886	1	3,000	7	5,511	787	2	7	104
All other denominations	83	6	163	27	3	3	6,100	2,033			5	1,306	261	6	28	96

See footnotes at end of table.

TABLE 10.—NEGRO CHURCHES—NUMBER OF CHURCHES, MEMBERSHIP, NUMBER AND VALUE OF CHURCH EDIFICES, DEBT, EXPENDITURES, AND SUNDAY SCHOOLS, BY DENOMINATIONS, BY STATES: 1926—Con.

[See note at head of this table]

DENOMINATION	Total number of churches in denominations wholly or in part Negro	Number of Negro churches [1]	MEMBERS [2]		Number of church edifices	VALUE OF CHURCH EDIFICES			DEBT ON CHURCH EDIFICES		EXPENDITURES DURING YEAR			SUNDAY SCHOOLS [3]		
			Total number	Average per church		Churches reporting	Amount	Average per church	Churches reporting	Amount	Churches reporting	Amount	Average per church	Churches reporting	Officers and teachers	Scholars
PENNSYLVANIA																
All denominations	**6,726**	**706**	**177,532**	**251**	**584**	**572**	**$15,362,354**	**$26,857**	**314**	**$2,147,959**	**668**	**$2,751,938**	**$4,120**	**615**	**8,190**	**70,813**
Baptist bodies:																
Negro Baptists	303	303	100,202	331	235	231	7,411,419	32,084	141	1,061,452	283	1,218,270	4,305	251	3,116	29,919
Colored Primitive Baptists	8	8	368	46							1	689				
Church of God (headquarters, Anderson, Ind.)	38	3	306	102	3	3	42,500	14,167	2	11,000	3	8,273	2,758	3	44	305
Church of God and Saints of Christ	6	6	472	79	4	3	18,200	6,067	2	1,250	6	26,980	4,497	4	16	146
Church of God in Christ	11	11	1,073	98	6	6	36,450	6,075	5	8,600	11	26,960	2,451	8	75	657
Methodist bodies:																
Methodist Episcopal Church	2,167	31	12,747	411	28	27	1,109,700	41,100	21	351,190	30	174,102	5,803	31	529	8,347
African Methodist Episcopal Church	174	174	23,208	133	159	157	3,064,972	19,522	84	304,070	170	641,160	3,772	158	1,943	14,378
African Methodist Episcopal Zion Church	75	75	20,919	279	72	72	1,870,675	25,982	28	224,950	75	297,780	3,970	74	1,672	9,312
Union American Methodist Episcopal Church	17	17	3,289	193	15	15	162,500	10,833	7	20,514	16	82,253	5,141	17	113	1,513
African Union Methodist Protestant Church	6	6	430	72	6	6	84,223	14,037	4	2,178	6	20,432	3,405	6	44	372
Colored Methodist Episcopal Church	15	15	1,510	101	8	8	207,275	25,909	5	25,605	15	38,409	2,561	13	96	630
Presbyterian bodies:																
Presbyterian Church in the United States of America	1,177	17	3,371	198	16	15	390,500	26,033	6	52,000	17	69,927	4,113	16	236	2,223
Protestant Episcopal Church	535	17	5,314	313	16	16	668,290	41,768	5	36,350	17	71,820	4,225	17	197	1,988
Roman Catholic Church	1,730	5	3,095	619	4	3	140,000	46,667			4	43,573	10,893	5	26	438
Spiritualists:																
National Spiritual Alliance of the United States of America	17	4	70	18							1	108				
All other denominations	447	14	1,158	83	12	10	155,650	15,565	4	48,800	13	31,202	2,400	12	83	585
RHODE ISLAND																
All denominations	**122**	**21**	**3,465**	**165**	**20**	**19**	**$410,300**	**$21,595**	**8**	**$45,050**	**21**	**$67,809**	**$3,229**	**19**	**265**	**1,800**
Baptist bodies:																
Negro Baptists	8	8	1,621	203	9	8	164,000	20,500	4	7,550	8	28,048	3,506	7	143	1,046
Methodist bodies:																
African Methodist Episcopal Church	5	5	645	129	5	5	95,000	19,000	2	12,000	5	13,935	2,787	5	44	232
All other denominations	109	8	1,199	150	6	6	151,300	25,217	2	25,500	8	25,826	3,228	7	78	522
SOUTH CAROLINA																
All denominations	**3,349**	**2,838**	**405,614**	**143**	**2,729**	**2,699**	**$9,005,446**	**$3,337**	**514**	**$617,231**	**2,783**	**$1,943,809**	**$698**	**2,641**	**21,376**	**183,161**
Adventist bodies:																
Seventh-day Adventist Denomination	17	8	174	22	4	4	10,000	2,500			7	5,317	760	7	36	187
Baptist bodies:																
Negro Baptists	1,364	1,364	235,224	172	1,323	1,312	4,615,947	3,518	210	375,459	1,337	796,448	596	1,265	10,014	96,532
Church of God (headquarters, Anderson, Ind.)	28	22	565	26	20	19	38,400	2,021	4	3,402	18	5,166	287	22	106	609
Churches of God (Holiness) United States of America	7	7	631	90	5	5	10,200	2,040	3	1,525	7	4,528	647	7	44	315
Congregational Churches	6	3	284	95	2	2	19,000	9,500			3	6,670	2,223	3	15	145
Disciples of Christ	52	21	2,184	104	19	19	16,025	843	7	330	21	5,408	258	19	77	556
Methodist bodies:																
Methodist Episcopal Church	398	395	47,638	121	392	388	1,268,470	3,269	101	49,480	395	292,334	740	388	2,774	24,177
Methodist Protestant Church	23	9	908	101	8	8	17,400	2,175	1	500	9	3,642	405	9	48	354
African Methodist Episcopal Church	546	546	59,372	109	512	510	1,466,659	2,876	85	104,861	533	437,046	820	491	3,757	27,722
African Methodist Episcopal Zion Church	185	185	38,225	207	182	182	599,820	3,296	49	46,812	185	192,541	1,041	183	3,101	20,754
Colored Methodist Episcopal Church	78	78	4,778	61	79	78	289,740	3,715	21	12,190	78	46,410	595	70	386	2,759
Reformed Methodist Union Episcopal Church	23	23	2,176	95	27	20	73,850	3,693	5	3,710	22	16,013	728	18	100	650
Independent African Methodist Episcopal Church	3	3	77	26	2	2	1,500	750	2	747	3	287	96	3	9	43
Presbyterian bodies:																
Presbyterian Church in the United States of America	99	99	6,994	71	86	82	272,485	3,323	16	15,121	94	84,073	894	92	586	5,504
Presbyterian Church in the United States	287	8	418	52	8	8	31,000	3,875	2	400	8	3,488	436	7	37	235
Protestant Episcopal Church	130	27	2,711	100	22	22	207,100	9,414			25	22,285	891	25	108	1,106
Reformed Episcopal Church	36	36	2,753	76	36	36	59,850	1,663	8	2,694	35	18,417	526	28	160	1,216
All other denominations	67	4	502	126	2	2	8,000	4,000			3	3,736	1,245	4	18	207

See footnotes at end of table.

TABLE 10.—NEGRO CHURCHES—NUMBER OF CHURCHES, MEMBERSHIP, NUMBER AND VALUE OF CHURCH EDIFICES, DEBT, EXPENDITURES, AND SUNDAY SCHOOLS, BY DENOMINATIONS, BY STATES: 1926—Con.

[See note at head of this table]

DENOMINATION	Total number of churches in denominations wholly or in part Negro	Number of Negro churches [1]	MEMBERS [2]: Total number	MEMBERS [2]: Average per church	Number of church edifices	VALUE OF CHURCH EDIFICES: Churches reporting	VALUE OF CHURCH EDIFICES: Amount	VALUE OF CHURCH EDIFICES: Average per church	DEBT ON CHURCH EDIFICES: Churches reporting	DEBT ON CHURCH EDIFICES: Amount	EXPENDITURES DURING YEAR: Churches reporting	EXPENDITURES DURING YEAR: Amount	EXPENDITURES DURING YEAR: Average per church	SUNDAY SCHOOLS [3]: Churches reporting	SUNDAY SCHOOLS [3]: Officers and teachers	SUNDAY SCHOOLS [3]: Scholars
							TENNESSEE									
All denominations	**4,121**	**1,958**	**226,823**	**116**	**1,763**	**1,745**	**$7,752,853**	**$4,443**	**302**	**$443,325**	**1,831**	**$1,647,742**	**$900**	**1,714**	**13,226**	**87,706**
Adventist bodies:																
Advent Christian Church	3	3	98	33	2	2	4,800	2,400	-----	-----	3	190	63	3	15	69
Seventh-day Adventist denomination	38	4	231	58	4	3	12,300	4,100	2	374	4	8,485	2,121	4	41	208
Baptist bodies:																
Negro Baptists	896	896	138,605	155	834	833	3,845,974	4,617	118	212,261	873	741,851	850	830	6,194	44,212
Colored Primitive Baptists	85	85	2,485	29	6	5	3,350	670	1	180	7	499	71	-----	-----	-----
Church of Christ (Holiness) United States of America	4	4	123	31	2	2	5,500	2,750	-----	-----	-----	-----	-----	4	10	80
Church of God in Christ	32	32	1,258	39	28	26	69,250	2,663	12	6,088	30	22,922	764	29	139	812
Churches of Christ	978	69	2,748	40	57	57	41,867	735	2	200	69	9,609	139	55	164	1,882
Churches of the Living God:																
Church of the Living God, Christian Workers for Fellowship	9	9	1,044	116	9	9	48,400	5,378	1	200	9	3,937	437	9	33	415
Congregational Churches	19	5	647	129	5	4	187,000	46,750	2	8,500	5	33,402	6,680	5	47	297
Disciples of Christ	165	20	1,614	81	18	17	81,600	4,800	6	7,300	18	14,387	799	18	119	704
Methodist bodies:																
Methodist Episcopal Church	693	177	12,072	68	168	168	660,230	3,930	35	26,265	174	124,732	717	162	1,067	6,955
African Methodist Episcopal Church	233	233	19,109	82	226	218	924,422	4,240	53	82,194	232	195,536	843	210	1,445	9,221
African Methodist Episcopal Zion Church	96	96	15,176	158	91	91	610,255	6,706	19	43,268	96	172,418	1,796	94	1,940	9,439
Colored Methodist Episcopal Church	211	211	25,198	119	206	206	872,980	4,238	28	38,435	206	248,010	1,204	199	1,483	10,094
Presbyterian bodies:																
Presbyterian Church in the United States of America	200	23	1,326	58	23	22	152,400	6,927	8	9,375	23	21,599	939	20	114	829
Colored Cumberland Presbyterian Church	67	67	3,182	47	66	65	142,125	2,187	12	8,500	63	30,556	485	54	314	1,609
United Presbyterian Church of North America	8	3	248	83	3	3	18,800	6,267	-----	-----	3	6,070	2,023	3	35	407
Protestant Episcopal Church	93	10	425	43	8	8	29,600	3,700	2	165	8	3,831	479	8	27	221
Roman Catholic Church	87	4	661	165	2	1	25,000	-----	-----	-----	2	4,878	2,439	2	3	86
All other denominations	204	7	573	82	5	5	17,000	3,400	1	20	6	4,830	805	5	36	166
							TEXAS									
All denominations	**7,449**	**3,910**	**351,305**	**90**	**3,539**	**3,506**	**$10,587,143**	**$3,020**	**1,094**	**$1,404,211**	**3,734**	**$2,736,752**	**$733**	**3,376**	**26,297**	**167,193**
Baptist bodies:																
Negro Baptists	2,071	2,071	234,056	113	1,964	1,955	5,965,272	3,051	580	825,770	2,023	1,398,713	691	1,861	16,469	110,425
Colored Primitive Baptists	61	61	1,590	26	1	1	1,000	-----	-----	-----	1	174	-----	-----	-----	-----
Church of God in Christ	126	126	5,430	43	103	99	307,109	3,102	41	39,820	105	84,245	802	103	596	3,667
Churches of Christ	1,286	26	1,399	54	24	24	10,925	455	9	1,111	25	2,388	96	22	70	749
Churches of the Living God:																
Church of the Living God, Christian Workers for Fellowship	38	38	3,107	82	36	36	69,700	1,936	7	3,510	36	13,380	372	35	117	839
Church of the Living God, "The Pillar and Ground of Truth"	54	54	3,203	59	55	54	89,512	1,658	26	11,807	54	34,625	641	11	70	482
Congregational Churches	31	10	442	44	7	7	50,000	7,143	4	5,850	8	18,004	2,251	9	57	311
Disciples of Christ	489	62	4,302	69	48	47	159,915	3,402	8	15,487	59	40,759	691	52	254	2,198
Free Church of God in Christ	5	5	297	59	1	1	3,000	-----	1	1,500	5	4,929	986	3	21	187
Methodist bodies:																
Methodist Episcopal Church	550	441	31,204	71	416	415	1,405,700	3,387	152	228,461	437	342,220	783	412	2,966	16,625
Methodist Protestant Church	92	14	684	49	13	13	31,900	2,454	3	3,630	12	4,130	344	13	58	337
African Methodist Episcopal Church	640	640	33,985	53	534	519	1,472,390	2,837	171	143,920	619	441,382	713	529	3,317	16,760
African Methodist Episcopal Zion Church	13	13	1,463	113	13	13	14,750	1,135	3	1,420	13	10,042	772	13	222	959
Colored Methodist Episcopal Church	312	312	22,737	73	289	288	751,770	2,610	81	69,305	301	298,582	992	283	1,922	11,818
Presbyterian bodies:																
Colored Cumberland Presbyterian Church	18	18	835	46	18	17	28,100	1,653	3	820	18	7,510	417	18	101	539
Protestant Episcopal Church	218	3	139	46	3	3	13,500	4,500	-----	-----	3	2,071	690	2	7	36
Roman Catholic Church	742	9	6,120	680	9	9	191,500	21,278	4	51,300	8	26,605	3,326	6	32	1,139
All other denominations	703	7	312	45	5	5	21,100	4,220	1	500	7	6,993	999	4	18	122
							VIRGINIA									
All denominations	**3,394**	**2,255**	**378,742**	**168**	**2,148**	**2,137**	**$14,134,101**	**$6,614**	**397**	**$1,253,979**	**2,188**	**$2,289,137**	**$1,046**	**2,062**	**17,553**	**137,019**
Adventist bodies:																
Seventh-day Adventist denomination	29	5	85	17	5	5	9,700	1,940	2	569	4	1,490	373	4	22	58
Baptist bodies:																
Negro Baptists	1,610	1,610	316,095	196	1,563	1,557	10,491,231	6,738	216	763,218	1,584	1,536,569	970	1,492	12,744	103,115
Colored Primitive Baptists	30	30	436	15	5	5	2,300	460	1	30	4	55	14	-----	-----	-----
Christian Church (General Convention of the Christian Church)	74	5	617	123	5	5	11,700	2,340	1	6	5	1,151	230	5	35	332

See footnotes at end of table.

TABLE 10.—NEGRO CHURCHES—NUMBER OF CHURCHES, MEMBERSHIP, NUMBER AND VALUE OF CHURCH EDIFICES, DEBT, EXPENDITURES, AND SUNDAY SCHOOLS, BY DENOMINATIONS, BY STATES: 1926—Con.

[See note at head of this table]

DENOMINATION	Total number of churches in denominations wholly or in part Negro	Number of Negro churches [1]	MEMBERS [2]		Number of church edifices	VALUE OF CHURCH EDIFICES			DEBT ON CHURCH EDIFICES		EXPENDITURES DURING YEAR			SUNDAY SCHOOLS [3]		
			Total number	Average per church		Churches reporting	Amount	Average per church	Churches reporting	Amount	Churches reporting	Amount	Average per church	Churches reporting	Officers and teachers	Scholars
VIRGINIA—Continued																
Church of Christ (Holiness) United States of America	17	17	733	43	13	13	$64,850	$4,988	8	$28,197	17	$18,074	$1,063	15	76	396
Church of God (Headquarters, Anderson, Ind.)	27	3	34	11	2	2	3,600	1,800	1	1,000	1	1,100	------	2	9	58
Church of God and Saints of Christ	19	19	1,298	68	13	13	32,250	2,481	4	4,200	16	14,783	924	15	77	488
Church of God in Christ	14	14	677	48	11	10	29,864	2,986	6	9,388	14	13,401	957	12	75	491
Churches of Christ	19	4	137	34	3	3	3,800	1,267	2	225	4	754	189	2	8	60
Disciples of Christ	294	20	1,189	59	19	19	51,700	2,721	2	800	19	8,447	445	18	87	651
Methodist bodies:																
Methodist Episcopal Church	306	141	9,872	70	136	136	693,612	5,100	31	79,676	140	125,712	898	125	897	6,254
African Methodist Episcopal Church	108	108	14,635	136	106	105	1,079,537	10,281	53	157,961	107	186,798	1,746	107	835	7,420
African Methodist Episcopal Zion Church	108	108	17,592	163	106	106	588,880	5,555	27	61,783	108	175,793	1,628	108	1,678	8,264
Colored Methodist Episcopal Church	32	32	2,175	68	31	31	283,400	9,142	8	32,255	32	35,580	1,112	31	209	1,299
Reformed Zion Union Apostolic Church	45	45	4,304	96	43	42	176,425	4,201	16	11,581	42	37,241	887	40	309	2,780
Presbyterian bodies:																
Presbyterian Church in the United States of America	45	36	2,167	60	33	33	113,950	3,453	9	20,894	35	24,247	693	32	209	1,883
Protestant Episcopal Church	453	45	3,968	88	43	42	206,125	4,908	6	14,796	43	35,703	830	42	215	2,566
Roman Catholic Church	140	4	1,172	293	2	2	68,677	34,339	------	------	4	31,350	7,838	3	11	207
All other denominations	24	9	1,556	173	9	8	222,500	27,813	4	67,400	9	40,889	4,543	9	57	697
WASHINGTON																
All denominations	**292**	**23**	**2,280**	**99**	**21**	**21**	**$172,700**	**$8,224**	**10**	**$9,185**	**20**	**$45,146**	**$2,257**	**21**	**178**	**1,207**
Baptist bodies:																
Negro Baptists	7	7	681	97	7	7	79,000	11,286	2	3,475	5	16,515	3,303	6	63	391
Methodist bodies:																
African Methodist Episcopal Church	8	8	947	118	8	8	49,700	6,213	4	1,390	7	21,069	3,010	8	60	439
Protestant Episcopal Church	102	3	140	47	2	2	7,000	3,500	------	------	3	1,510	503	2	3	32
All other denominations	175	5	512	102	4	4	37,000	9,250	4	4,320	5	6,052	1,210	5	52	345
WEST VIRGINIA																
All denominations	**1,954**	**480**	**32,754**	**68**	**321**	**309**	**$2,434,526**	**$7,879**	**100**	**$166,183**	**449**	**$499,104**	**$1,112**	**412**	**3,337**	**20,042**
Baptist bodies:																
Negro Baptists	299	299	24,166	81	194	190	1,516,281	7,980	54	115,415	282	309,311	1,097	265	2,187	13,812
Colored Primitive Baptists	5	5	119	24	1	1	1,500	------	------	------	1	50	------	------	------	------
Church of God and Saints of Christ	5	5	182	36	1	1	1,400	------	------	------	4	1,646	412	3	11	53
Methodist bodies:																
Methodist Episcopal Church	1,039	71	4,131	58	63	63	458,400	7,276	23	19,067	70	91,511	1,307	66	489	3,501
Wesleyan Methodist Connection (or Church) of America	9	4	131	33	2	2	18,000	9,000	1	3,600	3	2,462	821	4	25	120
African Methodist Episcopal Church	64	64	2,298	36	37	31	293,095	9,455	14	15,531	58	58,559	1,010	47	369	1,430
African Methodist Episcopal Zion Church	13	13	900	69	8	8	40,500	5,063	2	700	13	17,366	1,336	10	151	526
Colored Methodist Episcopal Church	5	5	134	27	3	3	9,250	3,083	2	2,270	5	2,468	494	4	20	79
Presbyterian bodies:																
Presbyterian Church in the United States of America	71	4	210	53	4	3	64,500	21,500	3	9,500	4	7,048	1,762	4	34	216
All other denominations	444	10	483	48	8	7	31,600	4,514	1	100	9	8,683	965	9	51	305
WISCONSIN																
All denominations	**1,697**	**19**	**3,699**	**195**	**16**	**16**	**$300,900**	**$18,806**	**10**	**$60,950**	**15**	**$60,404**	**$4,027**	**12**	**102**	**1,046**
Baptist bodies:																
Negro Baptists	8	8	2,184	273	8	8	145,500	18,188	5	28,400	5	31,576	6,315	5	57	742
Methodist bodies:																
African Methodist Episcopal Church	5	5	728	146	3	3	27,000	9,000	2	8,400	5	10,708	2,142	2	10	50
All other denominations	1,684	6	787	131	5	5	128,400	25,680	3	24,150	5	18,120	3,624	5	35	254
WYOMING																
All denominations	**11**	**11**	**398**	**36**	**5**	**5**	**$21,000**	**$4,200**	**5**	**$4,200**	**6**	**$4,211**	**$702**	**4**	**18**	**108**
Baptist bodies:																
Negro Baptists	5	5	157	31	4	4	15,000	3,750	4	2,200	5	3,406	681	3	16	93
Methodist bodies:																
African Methodist Episcopal Church	6	6	241	40	1	1	6,000	------	1	2,000	1	805	------	1	2	15

[1] Includes only organizations reporting members.
[2] Membership as defined by the particular denomination.
[3] The statistics given relate only to the Sunday schools reported by individual churches and do not include undenominational or union Sunday schools; nor do they include the parochial or week-day schools that are maintained by a number of bodies, particularly the Roman Catholic Church and certain Lutheran bodies.

TABLE 11.—NUMBER OF NEGRO CHURCHES, MEMBERSHIP, AND SUNDAY SCHOOLS, BY DENOMINATIONS, FOR THE UNITED STATES: 1926, 1916, AND 1906

DENOMINATION	NUMBER OF CHURCHES [1]			NUMBER OF MEMBERS [2]			AVERAGE MEMBERS PER CHURCH			SUNDAY SCHOOLS [3]: Churches reporting			SUNDAY SCHOOLS [3]: Number of scholars			SUNDAY SCHOOLS [3]: Average scholars per church		
	1926	1916	1906	1926	1916	1906	1926	1916	1906	1926	1916	1906	1926	1916	1906	1926	1916	1906
All denominations	42, 585	39, 592	36, 563	5, 203, 487	4, 602, 805	[4] 3, 691, 844	122	116	101	36, 378	36, 797	33, 538	2, 144, 553	2, 153, 843	1, 740, 099	59	59	52
Adventist bodies:																		
Advent Christian Church	6	10	2	164	317	72	27	32	36	4	8	2	94	248	27	24	31	14
Seventh-day Adventist Denomination	93	54	29	5, 133	2, 553	562	55	47	19	67	51	25	3, 402	2, 610	539	51	51	22
African Orthodox Church	13	-	-	1, 568	-	-	121	-	-	11	-	-	445	-	-	40	-	-
African Orthodox Church of New York	3	-	-	717	-	-	239	-	-	3	-	-	220	-	-	73	-	-
Apostolic Overcoming Holy Church of God	16	-	-	1, 047	-	-	65	-	-	15	-	-	1, 068	-	-	71	-	-
Baptist bodies:																		
Northern Baptist Convention [5]	-	142	108	-	53, 842	32, 639	-	379	302	-	137	102	-	20, 705	12, 827	-	151	126
Negro Baptists [5]	22, 081	21, 071	18, 492	3, 196, 623	2, 938, 579	2, 261, 607	145	139	122	18, 755	19, 909	17, 478	1, 121, 362	1, 181, 270	924, 665	60	59	53
Free Baptists [5]	-	-	195	-	-	10, 876	-	-	56	-	-	168	-	-	5, 732	-	-	34
United American Free Will Baptist Church [5]	166	169	247	13, 396	13, 362	14, 489	81	79	59	144	87	100	5, 077	4, 168	3, 307	35	48	33
Regular Baptists	1	1	-	38	23	-	-	-	-	-	-	-	-	-	-	-	-	-
Primitive Baptists	-	-	4	-	-	102	-	-	26	-	-	-	-	-	-	-	-	-
Colored Primitive Baptists [5]	925	336	787	43, 978	15, 144	35, 076	48	45	45	24	87	166	2, 278	3, 201	6, 224	95	37	37
Christian and Missionary Alliance	10	-	-	535	-	-	54	-	-	8	-	-	490	-	-	61	-	-
Christian Church (General Convention of the Christian Church). [5]	68	111	91	7, 312	10, 120	7, 545	108	91	83	64	105	87	3, 348	6, 834	4, 001	52	65	46
Church of Christ (Holiness) United States of America	82	-	-	4, 919	-	-	60	-	-	72	-	-	2, 511	-	-	35	-	-
Church of Christ, Scientist	1	(6)	-	274	(6)	-	-	-	-	1	-	-	395	-	-	-	-	-
Church of God [5]	29	1	-	887	24	-	31	-	-	24	1	-	901	25	-	38	-	-
Church of God (Headquarters, Anderson, Ind.)	98	-	-	3, 165	-	-	32	-	-	89	-	-	3, 131	-	-	35	-	-
Church of God and Saints of Christ	112	92	48	6, 741	3, 311	1, 823	60	36	38	67	57	1	2, 010	1, 526	150	30	27	-
Church of God in Christ	733	-	-	3, 263	-	-	41	-	-	585	-	-	19, 282	-	-	33	-	-
Churches of Christ	214	87	41	8, 155	2, 813	1, 528	38	32	37	177	59	23	5, 905	2, 127	597	33	36	26
Churches of God, Holiness	29	-	-	2, 278	-	-	79	-	-	27	-	-	1, 246	-	-	46	-	-
Churches of God in North America (General Eldership)	7	7	14	274	189	329	39	27	24	7	7	7	298	248	270	43	35	39
Churches of the Living God:																		
Church of the Living God, Christian Workers for Fellowship. [5]	149	154	44	11, 558	9, 626	2, 676	78	63	61	140	99	43	3, 465	2, 328	886	25	24	21
Church of Christ in God [5]	-	-	9	-	-	848	-	-	94	-	-	5	-	-	289	-	-	58
Church of the Living God, "The Pillar and Ground of Truth"	81	-	-	5, 844	-	-	72	-	-	26	-	-	1, 468	-	-	56	-	-
Church of the Living God [5]	-	28	-	-	1, 743	-	-	62	-	-	26	-	-	491	-	-	19	-
Church of the Living God, General Assembly. [5]	-	10	14	-	266	752	-	27	54	-	10	13	-	168	585	-	17	45
Congregational Churches [5]	155	154	156	16, 000	13, 209	11, 960	103	86	77	140	148	150	8, 899	10, 352	10, 339	64	70	69
Disciples of Christ	487	156	129	37, 325	11, 478	9, 705	77	74	75	397	149	111	14, 848	7, 219	4, 319	37	48	39
Evangelistic associations:																		
Voluntary Missionary Society in America	-	4	3	-	855	425	-	214	142	-	4	3	-	386	390	-	97	130
Free Christian Zion Church of Christ	5	35	14	187	6, 225	1, 835	37	178	131	5	35	7	97	3, 411	340	19	97	49
Free Church of God in Christ	19	-	-	874	-	-	46	-	-	17	-	-	633	-	-	37	-	-
Independent Churches	7	6	12	1, 542	428	490	220	71	41	6	6	12	491	198	435	82	33	36
Lutherans:																		
United Lutheran Church in America [5]	1	-	-	126	-	-	-	-	-	1	-	-	90	-	-	-	-	-
General Council of the Evangelical Lutheran Church in North America	-	-	1	-	-	15	-	-	-	-	-	1	-	-	25	-	-	-
Evangelical Lutheran Synodical Conference of America	-	-	-	-	-	-	-	-	-	-	-	-	-	-	-	-	-	-
Evangelical Lutheran Synod of Missouri, Ohio, and Other States	69	31	6	5, 871	1, 525	224	85	49	37	61	28	5	3, 314	2, 158	254	54	77	51
Methodist bodies:																		
Methodist Episcopal Church	3, 743	3, 704	3, 682	332, 347	320, 025	308, 551	89	86	84	3, 527	3, 490	3, 522	196, 496	214, 982	204, 810	56	62	58
Methodist Protestant Church	46	49	62	2, 529	2, 869	2, 612	55	59	42	42	44	48	1, 283	1, 861	1, 650	31	42	34
Wesleyan Methodist Connection (or Church) of America	26	16	19	1, 215	819	1, 258	47	51	66	26	14	16	1, 084	688	769	42	49	48
African Methodist Episcopal Church	6, 708	6, 633	6, 608	545, 814	548, 355	494, 777	81	83	75	5, 884	6, 084	6, 056	288, 247	311, 051	292, 689	49	51	48
African Methodist Episcopal Zion Church	2, 466	2, 716	2, 197	456, 813	257, 169	184, 542	185	95	84	2, 429	2, 535	2, 060	267, 141	135, 102	107, 692	110	53	52
Colored Methodist Protestant Church	3	26	-	533	1, 967	-	178	76	-	3	24	-	98	870	-	33	36	-
Union American Methodist Episcopal Church	73	67	77	10, 169	3, 624	4, 347	139	54	56	69	54	76	4, 240	1, 982	3, 372	61	37	44
African Union Methodist Protestant Church	43	58	69	4, 086	3, 751	5, 592	95	65	81	42	49	66	2, 851	2, 813	5, 266	68	57	80
Colored Methodist Episcopal Church	2, 518	2, 621	2, 365	202, 713	245, 749	172, 996	81	94	73	2, 351	2, 541	2, 207	103, 523	167, 880	92, 457	44	66	42
Reformed Zion Union Apostolic Church	48	47	45	4, 538	3, 977	3, 059	95	85	68	42	42	35	2, 882	2, 505	1, 508	69	60	43
African American Methodist Episcopal Church [7]	-	28	-	-	1, 310	-	-	47	-	-	6	-	-	200	-	-	33	-
Reformed Methodist Union Episcopal Church	25	27	57	2, 265	2, 196	4, 397	91	81	77	19	25	54	673	699	1, 792	35	28	33
Independent African Methodist Episcopal Church	729	-	-	1, 003	-	-	35	-	-	26	-	-	663	-	-	26	-	-
Moravian bodies:																		
Moravian Church in America [5]	1	1	2	694	419	351	-	-	176	1	1	2	208	178	217	-	-	109
The (Original) Church of God	1	-	-	12	-	-	-	-	-	-	-	-	-	-	-	-	-	-

See footnotes at end of table.

TABLE 11.—NUMBER OF NEGRO CHURCHES, MEMBERSHIP, AND SUNDAY SCHOOLS, BY DENOMINATIONS, FOR THE UNITED STATES: 1926, 1916, AND 1906—Continued

DENOMINATION	NUMBER OF CHURCHES [1]			NUMBER OF MEMBERS [2]			AVERAGE MEMBERS PER CHURCH			SUNDAY SCHOOLS [3]								
										Churches reporting			Number of scholars			Average scholars per church		
	1926	1916	1906	1926	1916	1906	1926	1916	1906	1926	1916	1906	1926	1916	1906	1926	1916	1906
Presbyterian bodies:																		
Presbyterian Church in the United States of America[5]	450	434	417	37,090	31,957	27,799	82	74	67	400	414	405	27,817	27,618	24,904	70	67	61
Cumberland Presbyterian Church			1			50			50			1			75			
Colored Cumberland Presbyterian Church	178	136	196	10,868	13,077	18,066	61	96	92	153	133	192	5,223	7,471	6,952	34	56	36
United Presbyterian Church of North America	14			1,202			86			14			1,587			113		
Presbyterian Church in the United States	52	36	40	2,134	1,429	1,183	41	40	30	43	30	36	1,569	1,417	1,166	36	47	32
Associate Reformed Presbyterian Church[5]			1			18						1			35			
Protestant Episcopal Church	287	216	193	51,502	23,775	19,098	179	110	99	260	194	180	19,075	15,932	13,779	73	82	• 77
Reformed bodies:																		
Reformed Church in America			2			59			30			1			52			
Reformed Episcopal Church	36	35	38	2,753	3,017	2,252	76	86	59	28	30	33	1,216	1,266	1,326	43	42	40
Roman Catholic Church	147	83	36	124,324	51,688	[4] 44,982	846	623	1,250	76	74	30	11,406	9,655	3,151	150	130	105
Salvation Army	5			495			99			5			470			94		
Spiritualists:																		
National Spiritualist Association[5]	17			904			53			1			10					
Progressive Spiritual Church[5]	1			500														
National Spiritual Alliance of the United States of America	8			190			24			1			23					
United Brethren bodies:																		
Church of the United Brethren in Christ			10			277			28			8			236			30

[1] Includes only organizations reporting members.
[2] Membership as defined by the particular denomination.
[3] The statistics given relate only to the Sunday schools reported by individual churches and do not include undenominational or union Sunday schools; nor do they include the parochial or week-day schools that are maintained by a number of bodies, particularly the Roman Catholic Church and certain Lutheran bodies.
[4] Corrected figures; see explanation on p. 531 for change in the number of members of the Roman Catholic Church.
[5] For changes in denominations for earlier censuses see text.
[6] Not reported.
[7] So far as can be learned organic denominational existence has ceased, any organization formerly belonging to this group being included among the independent churches.

Table 12.—NEGRO CHURCHES—EXPENDITURES, 1926 AND 1916, AND VALUE OF CHURCH EDIFICES, 1926, 1916, AND 1906, BY DENOMINATIONS, FOR THE UNITED STATES

[Percent not shown where base is less than 100]

DENOMINATION	EXPENDITURES DURING YEAR								VALUE OF CHURCH EDIFICES										
	Churches reporting				Amount		Average per church		Churches reporting					Amount			Average per church		
	1926	1916	Percent of all churches		1926	1916	1926	1916	Number			Percent of all churches		1926	1916	1906	1926	1916	1906
			1926	1916					1926	1916	1906	1926	1916						
All denominations	39,245	37,660	92.2	95.1	$43,024,259	$18,529,827	$1,096	$492	37,347	37,083	34,648	87.7	93.7	$205,782,628	$86,809,970	$56,636,159	$5,510	$2,341	$1,635
Adventist bodies:																			
Advent Christian Church	4	6			240	2,310	60	385	3	6	2			4,950	10,000	3,800	1,650	1,667	1,900
Seventh-day Adventist Denomination	85	43			261,975	41,365	3,082	962	78	29	9			789,400	108,755	6,474	10,121	3,750	719
African Orthodox Church	13				19,368		1,490		2					30,000			15,000		
African Orthodox Church of New York	2				18,900		9,450		1					50,000					
Apostolic Overcoming Holy Church of God	16				17,198		1,075		10					16,950			1,695		
Baptist bodies:																			
Northern Baptist Convention [1]		136		95.8		381,457		2,805		138	97		97.2		2,779,199	1,561,326		20,139	16,096
Negro Baptists [1]	20,209	19,988	91.5	94.9	19,475,981	8,361,919	964	418	19,833	20,117	17,890	89.8	95.5	103,465,759	41,184,920	24,437,272	5,217	2,047	1,366
Free Baptists [1]											173					186,130			1,076
United American Free Will Baptist Church [1]	158	168	95.2	99.4	67,773	36,647	429	218	142	164	151	85.5	97.0	308,425	178,385	79,278	2,172	1,088	525
Regular Baptists		1				1													
Primitive Baptists											4					2,300			575
Colored Primitive Baptists [1]	111	170	12.0	50.6	39,419	22,881	355	135	87	164	501	9.4	48.8	171,518	154,690	296,539	1,971	943	592
Christian and Missionary Alliance	10				19,177		1,918		6					57,625			9,604		
Christian Church (General Convention of the Christian Church)[1]	68	103		92.8	45,739	36,338	673	353	56	107	90		96.4	285,100	156,226	69,505	5,091	1,460	772
Church of Christ (Holiness) U. S. A.	64				48,968		765		68					326,850			4,807		
Church of Christ, Scientist	1				38,995				1					254,061					
Church of God [1]	25	1			39,064	200	1,563		15	1				78,015	1,000		5,201		
Church of God (Headquarters, Anderson, Ind.)	82				86,094		1,050		77					343,450			4,460		
Church of God and Saints of Christ	100	45	89.3		137,345	18,674	1,373	415	48	26	1	42.9		149,210	43,746	6,000	3,109	1,683	
Church of God in Christ	624		85.1		516,011		827		516			70.4		1,508,079			2,923		
Churches of Christ	212	6	99.1		40,996	189	193	32	141	63	25	65.9		139,919	52,925	14,950	992	840	598
Churches of God, Holiness	26				35,878		1,380		16					159,700			9,981		
Churches of God in North America (General Eldership)	7	7			2,380	1,088	340	155	3	5	5			8,000	4,185	5,500	2,667	837	1,100
Churches of the Living God:																			
Church of the Living God, Christian Workers for Fellowship [1]	144	62	96.6	40.3	50,515	18,812	351	303	139	60	27	93.3	39.0	368,935	78,955	23,175	2,654	1,316	858
Church of Christ in God [1]											6					9,700			1,617
Church of the Living God, "The Pillar and Ground of Truth" [1]	81				64,555		797		81					170,547			2,106		
Church of the Living God [1]		27				6,199		230		27					23,875			884	
Church of the Living God, General Assembly [1]		9				3,704		412		6	12				12,700	25,700		2,117	2,142
Congregational Churches [1]	144	139	92.9	90.3	316,444	99,503	2,198	716	139	137	137	89.7	89.0	1,896,415	843,518	459,497	13,643	6,157	3,354
Disciples of Christ	447	96	91.8	61.5	289,721	53,798	648	560	411	95	115	84.4	60.9	1,495,568	246,730	170,265	3,639	2,597	1,481
Evangelistic associations:																			
Voluntary Missionary Society in America [2]		4				2,199		550		4	2				2,580	2,400		645	1,200
Free Christian Zion Church of Christ	5	35			2,481	19,154	496	547	4	35	13			22,000	35,900	5,975	5,500	1,026	460
Free Church of God in Christ	18				19,540		1,086		11					23,700			2,155		
Independent Churches	6	6			34,904	1,128	5,817	188	2	4	12			67,000	8,130	2,750	33,500	2,033	229
Lutherans:																			
United Lutheran Church in America [1]	1				306				1					13,000					
General Council of the Evangelical Lutheran Church in North America											1					5,000			
Evangelical Lutheran Synodical Conference of America:																			
Evangelical Lutheran Synod of Missouri, Ohio, and other States	67	27			72,197	13,134	1,078	486	55	26	6			339,650	57,332	10,000	6,175	2,205	1,667
Methodist bodies:																			
Methodist Episcopal Church	3,682	3,639	98.4	98.2	3,694,508	1,670,407	1,003	459	3,552	3,601	3,585	94.9	97.2	18,938,246	8,047,197	6,104,379	5,332	2,235	1,703
Methodist Protestant Church	44	47			11,495	9,282	261	197	44	44	50			91,650	44,146	62,651	2,083	1,003	1,253
Wesleyan Methodist Connection (or Church) of America	25	13			16,679	4,655	667	358	22	14	14			83,100	33,100	21,000	3,777	2,364	1,500
African Methodist Episcopal Church	6,492	6,516	96.8	98.2	7,600,161	3,413,395	1,171	524	5,829	6,232	6,299	86.9	94.0	32,092,549	14,631,792	11,303,489	5,506	2,348	1,794
African Methodist Episcopal Zion Church	2,464	2,641	99.9	97.2	4,757,066	1,700,737	1,931	644	2,370	2,475	2,104	96.1	91.1	18,515,723	7,591,393	4,833,207	7,813	3,067	2,297
Colored Methodist Protestant Church	3	23			6,685	12,129	2,228	527	3	16				36,000	52,733		12,000	3,296	

See footnotes at end of table.

TABLE 12.—NEGRO CHURCHES—EXPENDITURES, 1926 AND 1916, AND VALUE OF CHURCH EDIFICES, 1926, 1916, AND 1906, BY DENOMINATIONS, FOR THE UNITED STATES—Continued

[Percent not shown where base is less than 100]

DENOMINATION	Expenditures during year: Churches reporting 1926	Expenditures: Churches reporting 1916	Expenditures: Percent of all churches 1926	Expenditures: Percent of all churches 1916	Expenditures: Amount 1926	Expenditures: Amount 1916	Expenditures: Average per church 1926	Expenditures: Average per church 1916	Value of church edifices: Churches reporting, Number 1926	Value: Number 1916	Value: Number 1906	Value: Percent of all churches 1926	Value: Percent of all churches 1916	Value: Amount 1926	Value: Amount 1916	Value: Amount 1906	Value: Average per church 1926	Value: Average per church 1916	Value: Average per church 1906
Methodist bodies—Continued.																			
Union American Methodist Episcopal Church	68	65			222, 621	40, 664	3, 274	626	64	59	59			478, 951	182, 305	170, 150	7, 484	3, 090	2, 884
African Union Methodist Protestant Church	43	53			99, 563	47, 231	2, 315	891	40	53	68			476, 269	205, 825	183, 697	11, 907	3, 883	2, 701
Colored Methodist Episcopal Church	2, 477	2, 613	98. 4	99. 7	2, 428, 234	1, 736, 692	980	665	2, 341	2, 490	2, 264	93. 0	95. 0	9, 211, 437	5, 619, 862	3, 017, 849	3, 935	2, 257	1, 333
Reformed Zion Union Apostolic Church	44	41			37, 610	13, 156	855	321	45	47	41			184, 075	79, 325	37, 875	4, 091	1, 688	924
African American Methodist Episcopal Church [2]		28				13, 455		481		1					6, 280				
Reformed Methodist Union Episcopal Church	24	26			17, 282	3, 420	720	132	21	27	57			74, 800	35, 500	36, 965	3, 562	1, 315	649
Independent African Methodist Episcopal Church	27				11, 704		433		28					98, 050			3, 502		
Moravian bodies:																			
Moravian Church in America [1]	1	1			4, 475	1, 042			1		1			30, 000		8, 000			
The (Original) Church of God																			
Presbyterian bodies:																			
Presbyterian Church in the United States of America [1]	438	414	97. 3	95. 4	604, 179	204, 944	1, 379	495	398	353	365	88. 4	81. 3	3, 285, 860	1, 276, 148	752, 387	8, 256	3, 615	2, 061
Cumberland Presbyterian Church											1					1, 000			
Colored Cumberland Presbyterian Church	167	127	93. 8	93. 4	80, 304	39, 497	481	311	162	130	192	91. 0	95. 6	353, 825	230, 426	203, 778	2, 184	1, 773	1, 061
United Presbyterian Church of North America	12				20, 211		1, 684		12					189, 300			15, 775		
Presbyterian Church in the United States	51	29			27, 846	8, 154	546	281	46	32	33			138, 140	43, 185	32, 850	3, 003	1, 350	995
Associate Reformed Presbyterian Church [1]											1					200			
Protestant Episcopal Church	272	200	94. 8	92. 6	572, 108	218, 912	2, 103	1, 095	259	188	159	90. 2	87. 0	4, 162, 735	1, 527, 768	1, 773, 279	16, 072	8, 126	11, 153
Reformed bodies:																			
Reformed Church in America																			
Reformed Episcopal Church	35	35			18, 417	9, 243	526	264	36	34	38			59, 850	45, 862	28, 287	1, 663	1, 349	744
Roman Catholic Church	129	70	87. 8		1, 005, 645	262, 112	7, 796	3, 744	126	73	32	85. 7		4, 667, 378	1, 173, 372	678, 480	37, 043	16, 074	21, 203
Salvation Army	5				15, 118		3, 024		1					67, 064					
Spirtualists:																			
National Spiritualist Association [1]	9				7, 655		851												
Progressive Spiritual Church [1]	1				2, 125				1					3, 800					
National Spiritual Alliance of the United States of America	2				413		207												
United Brethren bodies:																			
Church of the United Brethren in Christ											6					3, 100			517

[1] For changes in denominations, see text.
[2] So far as can be learned organic denominational existence has ceased, any organization formerly belonging to this group being included among the independent churches.

CHAPTER XIX.—PERSONS IN STATE AND FEDERAL PRISONS AND REFORMATORIES

Scope.—This report presents statistics for persons in State and Federal penal institutions and reformatories for the calendar years 1930, 1931, and 1932. The data on which this report is based were obtained from prison officials, who entered the desired information on schedules furnished them by the Bureau of the Census. Reports were received in 1932 from the 7 Federal prisons and reformatories, the 6 Federal prison camps, and 100 of the 104 State prisons and reformatories. No reports were received for the State penitentiaries in Alabama, Georgia, or Idaho, in 1930, or from the State Penitentiary of Mississippi in 1931, or from the State penitentiaries in Mississippi and South Carolina in 1932. The data from the State penitentiaries in Alabama and in Georgia, being incomplete, were not used in either 1931 or 1932.

Statistics for State and Federal prisons and reformatories for adults do not cover the entire field of imprisonment in the United States. Prisoners are also confined in county and municipal jails and workhouses, in Army and Navy prisons, in institutions for juvenile delinquents, etc. The State and Federal prisons and reformatories undoubtedly contain the majority of those imprisoned for serious offenses, but there is sufficient variation in the laws and judicial practices, as between one State and another, to make comparisons between States on the basis of State prison figures alone rather difficult and sometimes unsatisfactory.

In some States—Ohio, for instance, prisoners sentenced for over 1 year cannot be committed to county institutions; in other States—Pennsylvania, for example, prisoners may be committed to serve long-term sentences in county penal institutions. In States of the first type, therefore, State prison commitments represent all commitments for terms of over 1 year, while in States of the second type only a part of such commitments are to State prisons, and an indeterminate number are to county jails or workhouses.

Prison statistics, furthermore, even if obtained from all classes of penal institutions, cannot be taken as a complete index either of the extent of crime or of the punishment of crime. Many offenders are never arrested, many of those arrested are never brought to trial, and a large proportion of those tried are not convicted. Then, other forms of punishment and other methods of treating convicted criminals furnish alternatives which may be employed in place of imprisonment. Many of those convicted are given suspended sentences, placed on probation, or are punished by fines rather than by imprisonment. Moreover, suspension of sentence, probation, the fine, etc., are not uniformly employed in the different States at a given time, or in the same State at different times. When they are infrequently used for serious crimes, a large proportion of those convicted will be punished by imprisonment; when they are frequently used, the number of prison commitments will be thereby reduced, even though the number of persons convicted of crime may be on the increase. During recent years, probation has been used to a constantly increasing extent, with the evident result that prisoners have represented a constantly decreasing percentage of all convicted offenders.

Prisoners received from courts.—Negroes constituted approximately one-fifth of all prisoners received from courts in 1930, 1931, and 1932. The number of Negroes received from courts per 100,000 population indicates that over three times as many Negro males as native white males were committed to prisons and reformatories. The ratio for Negro females was four times that for native white females.

The high commitment rate shown for Negroes is probably in some degree due to the combination of lower economic status, less frequent use of other forms of penal treatment for Negroes, and unfavorable race attitudes on the part of the white race. Proportion of the general population in the so-called "criminal ages" is another factor to be considered when comparing races. It is hardly possible, therefore, to draw any conclusions from the data presented in this chapter, regarding the comparative criminality of race groups.

Age and sex.—Statistics presented here do not show the extent to which crimes are committed by offenders under 21 years of age, because these offenders are likely to be sent to juvenile training schools and reformatories.

Over two-thirds of the Negro prisoners committed in 1930, 1931, and 1932 were between 20 and 40 years of age. The largest number committed was for the age group 21 to 24 years of age.

Less than 6 percent of the Negroes committed in 1930, 1931, and 1932 were females.

Offense.—The offense of each prisoner received under sentence from the courts was reported the same as given in the commitment papers. Prisoners were assigned to the several broad groups on the basis of the legal designation of the offense for which they were committed.

The principal offenses of male Negroes, arranged in accordance with the largest number of prisoners committed, were: Burglary, larceny, and auto theft, robbery, homicide, assault, and violation of liquor laws. The principal offenses of female Negroes were: Homicide, larceny, and auto theft, assault, sex offenses, and violation of liquor laws. The numerically preponderant offenses of which Negro prisoners received from courts in 1932 were convicted, were as follows: Males under 25 years of age, burglary, larceny; males, 25 to 34 years of age, burglary, larceny, assault, homicide, and violation of liquor laws; males, 35 years and over, burglary, larceny, and violation of liquor laws; females under 25 years of age, sex offenses, larceny, and homicide; females, 25 to 44 years of age, homicide, larceny; and females, 45 years old and over, homicide and larceny.

Length of sentence.—The average definite sentence of Negro males received from courts in 1931 was less than that for native whites and foreign-born whites for homicide, robbery, assault, forgery, and larceny and greater than the average definite sentence given native white males for rape, burglary, sex offenses, except rape, and for violation of drug laws.

Prisoners received from courts under penalty of death and prisoners executed.—The number of executions shown in the tables in this chapter exceeds the number committed under the penalty of death, since some of those executed had not been committed to State and Federal institutions. More Negroes were executed in 1932 than whites, but more whites than Negroes were executed in 1930.

Table 1.—PRISONERS RECEIVED FROM COURTS, BY RACE, NATIVITY, AND SEX, FOR THE UNITED STATES: 1932, 1931, AND 1930

[Ratios based upon estimated population as of July 1 of each year]

RACE AND NATIVITY	1932			1931			1932			NUMBER PER 100,000 OF POPULATION 15 YEARS OLD AND OVER					
										1932		1931		1930	
	Total	Male	Female	Total	Male	Female	Total	Male	Female	Male	Female	Male	Female	Male	Female
Total	**67, 477**	**64, 546**	**2, 931**	**71, 520**	**68, 483**	**3, 037**	**66, 013**	**62, 957**	**3, 056**	**153. 1**	**7. 1**	**161. 8**	**7. 4**	**149. 5**	**7. 4**
Negro	14, 613	13, 822	791	15, 441	14, 605	836	14, 771	13, 908	863	483. 8	27. 2	478. 8	26. 7	416. 3	25. 2
White	50, 889	48, 805	2, 084	54, 160	51, 995	2, 165	49, 331	47, 178	2, 153	128. 0	5. 6	136. 2	5. 8	124. 0	5. 8
Native	47, 488	45, 574	1, 914	50, 265	48, 265	2, 000	45, 495	43, 510	1, 985	146. 2	6. 1	154. 7	6. 4	140. 0	6. 4
Foreign born	3, 401	3, 231	170	3, 895	3, 730	165	3, 836	3, 668	168	46. 3	2. 8	53. 4	2. 7	52. 6	2. 8
Mexican	1, 311	1, 291	20	1, 274	1, 255	19	1, 332	1, 315	17	253. 2	10. 4	252. 6	6. 8	256. 1	7. 7
Indian	402	370	32	420	403	17	387	364	23						
Chinese	152	150	2	126	126	-------	103	103	-------						
Japanese	23	21	2	22	22	-------	12	12	-------						
Other races	87	87	-------	77	77	-------	77	77	-------						

Table 2.—MARITAL CONDITION OF PRISONERS RECEIVED FROM COURTS, BY RACE, NATIVITY, AND SEX, FOR THE UNITED STATES: 1932

MARITAL CONDITION	Total	Negro	WHITE			Other races	PERCENT DISTRIBUTION		
			Total	Native	Foreign-born		Negro	White	Other races
	TOTAL								
Total	**67, 477**	**14, 613**	**50, 889**	**47, 488**	**3, 401**	**1, 975**	**100. 0**	**100. 0**	**100. 0**
Single	33, 786	7, 030	25, 612	24, 232	1, 380	1, 144	48. 1	50. 3	57. 9
Married	25, 097	5, 480	18, 904	17, 445	1, 459	713	37. 5	37. 1	36. 1
Widowed	2, 240	465	1, 730	1, 465	265	45	3. 2	3. 4	3. 2
Divorced	2, 221	215	1, 969	1, 823	146	37	1. 5	3. 9	1. 9
Legally separated	1, 641	361	1, 246	1, 148	98	34	2. 5	2. 4	1. 7
Unknown	2, 492	1, 062	1, 428	1, 375	53	2	7. 3	2. 8	. 1
	MALE								
Total	**64, 546**	**13, 822**	**48, 805**	**45, 574**	**3, 231**	**1, 919**	**100. 0**	**100. 0**	**100. 0**
Single	32, 824	6, 720	24, 978	23, 626	1, 352	1, 126	48. 6	51. 2	58. 7
Married	23, 739	5, 158	17, 895	16, 535	1, 360	636	37. 3	36. 7	35. 7
Widowed	2, 008	406	1, 561	1, 323	238	41	2. 9	3. 2	2. 1
Divorced	2, 062	195	1, 832	1, 697	135	35	1. 4	3. 8	1. 8
Legally separated	1, 516	335	1, 152	1, 055	97	29	2. 4	2. 4	1. 5
Unknown	2, 397	1, 008	1, 387	1, 338	49	2	7. 3	2. 8	. 1
	FEMALE								
Total	**2, 931**	**791**	**2, 084**	**1, 914**	**170**	**56**	**100. 0**	**100. 0**	**100. 0**
Single	962	310	634	606	28	18	39. 2	30. 4	32. 1
Married	1, 358	322	1, 009	910	99	27	40. 7	48. 4	48. 2
Widowed	232	59	169	142	27	4	7. 5	8. 1	7. 1
Divorced	159	20	137	126	11	2	2. 5	6. 6	3. 6
Legally separated	125	26	94	93	1	5	3. 3	4. 5	8. 9
Unknown	95	54	41	37	4	---------	6. 8	2. 0	---------

Table 3.—AVERAGE LENGTH OF SENTENCE OF MALE PRISONERS RECEIVED FROM COURTS, BY RACE, NATIVITY, AND OFFENSE, FOR THE UNITED STATES: 1931

[Average not shown where less than 50 prisoners were received]

RACE AND TYPE OF SENTENCE	All offenses	Homicide	Rape	Robbery	Assault	Burglary	Forgery	Larceny	Sex offenses, except rape	Violating liquor laws	Violating drug laws
Total:	*Months*	*Months*	*Months*	*Months*	*Months*	*Months*	*Months*	*Months*	*Months*	*Months*	*Months*
Definite	40. 4	135. 7	75. 2	108. 9	29. 0	37. 3	31. 6	24. 8	35. 0	19. 1	26. 4
Indeterminate:											
Minimum	27. 8	74. 4	39. 0	55. 8	26. 0	21. 7	17. 2	14. 7	21. 8	12. 3	9. 1
Maximum	112. 7	180. 2	153. 5	176. 0	98. 1	108. 0	119. 2	82. 8	102. 4	35. 1	66. 2
Negro:											
Definite	42. 1	131. 1	82. 5	91. 9	24. 8	38. 4	30. 1	20. 7	37. 9	17. 6	26. 6
Indeterminate:											
Minimum	36. 2	67. 1	55. 2	66. 0	28. 6	27. 0	20. 8	18. 0	---------	14. 9	---------
Maximum	122. 6	177. 5	176. 6	193. 9	99. 0	108. 0	140. 3	81. 6	---------	37. 2	---------
Native white:											
Definite	39. 7	134. 8	70. 1	114. 4	34. 6	36. 2	31. 1	26. 5	34. 8	19. 6	26. 4
Indeterminate:											
Minimum	25. 7	76. 3	35. 6	53. 7	25. 3	20. 2	16. 8	14. 1	20. 5	11. 8	---------
Maximum	111. 3	174. 3	151. 5	173. 4	101. 7	108. 3	118. 7	83. 8	100. 1	34. 8	---------
Foreign-born white:											
Definite	44. 7	159. 3	---------	115. 1	48. 0	60. 2	46. 5	36. 2	---------	16. 7	34. 6
Indeterminate:											
Minimum	31. 8	90. 6	38. 6	56. 5	24. 8	25. 1	19. 5	14. 3	21. 9	12. 6	---------
Maximum	111. 3	188. 8	122. 4	175. 1	89. 7	115. 9	121. 5	79. 8	97. 9	34. 7	---------
Other races:											
Definite	32. 8	---------	---------	---------	---------	32. 5	---------	25. 4	---------	16. 3	21. 4
Indeterminate:											
Minimum	28. 8	80. 2	---------	52. 9	18. 9	23. 5	16. 7	16. 8	---------	---------	---------
Maximum	99. 1	222. 0	---------	124. 9	76. 9	89. 2	91. 3	64. 6	---------	---------	---------

TABLE 4.—PRISONERS RECEIVED FROM COURTS, UNDER SENTENCE OF DEATH, BY RACE, AND AGE, BY STATES: 1932 AND 1930

STATE	1932									1930						
	Total	Negro				White				Total	Negro			White		
		Total	Under 18 years	18 to 24 years	25 years and over	Total	Under 18 years	18 to 24 years	25 years and over		Total	18 to 24 years	25 years and over	Total	18 to 24 years	25 years and over
United States	[1] 107	[2] 27		9	17	77	1	22	54	[1] 112	22	2	20	82	24	58
Vermont	1					1			1							
Massachusetts	1					1		1								
Connecticut	1					1			1	1				1		1
New York	34	5		4	1	28		13	15	19	2		2	17	8	9
New Jersey	3	2			2	1			1	16				15	6	9
Ohio	12	6		2	4	6		2	4	14	2		2	12	1	11
Indiana	5	1			1	4		1	3	2	1		1	1	1	
Illinois	3	1		1		2		1	1	1				1		1
Iowa										2				2	1	1
Maryland	3	[2] 3			2					3	3		3			
West Virginia	3	1			1	2			2	4				4	1	3
South Carolina										6	3	1	2	3		3
Florida	5	1			1	4		1	3	1	1		1			
Kentucky	5	1			1	4			4	4	1		1	3	1	2
Arkansas										9	8	1	7	1		1
Oklahoma	12	2		1	1	9		2	7	3	1		1	1		1
Wyoming	1					1			1							
Colorado	2	1		1		1			1	4				3	2	1
Arizona	1					1			1	1				1		1
Utah	1					1		1		1				1	1	
Nevada										1						
Washington	2					2	1		1	3				3		3
Oregon	1	1			1											
California	11	2			2	8			8	17				13	2	11

[1] Includes 3 prisoners of other races in 1932 and 8 prisoners of other races in 1930.
[2] Includes 1 Negro, age unknown.

TABLE 5.—PRISONERS EXECUTED, BY RACE, AND AGE, BY STATES: 1932 AND 1930

STATE	1932									1930							
	Total	Negro				White				Total	Negro				White		
		Total	Under 18 years	18 to 24 years	25 years and over	Total	Under 18 years	18 to 24 years	25 years and over		Total	Under 18 years	18 to 24 years	25 years and over	Total	18 to 24 years	25 years and over
United States	[1] 140	75	1	26	48	60	1	13	46	[1 2] 155	[3] 65	2	21	41	[2] 85	24	[2] 61
Vermont	1					1			1								
Massachusetts	1	1			1												
Connecticut										2					2		2
New York	20	1			1	18		9	9	15					15	6	9
New Jersey	4	1		1		3		1	2	10					10	6	4
Pennsylvania	5	2			2	3		1	2	9	4		1	3	5	1	4
Ohio	7	3		1	2	4			4	8	1	1			7	1	6
Indiana	2	1			1	1			1	1	1			1			
Illinois	5	3		2	1	2			2	6	4			4	2		2
Missouri	3	1			1	2			2	5	1			1	4	2	2
Delaware										2	1			1	1	1	
Maryland	2	2			2					1	1			1			
District of Columbia	4	4		1	3					1	1			1			
Virginia	2	2		1	1					3	3		2	1			
West Virginia	2	1			1	1			1	2					2		2
North Carolina	8	7		4	3	1			1	10	9	1	5	3	1		1
South Carolina	6	5		1	4	1			1	5	4		2	2	1		1
Georgia	12	8	1	4	3	4			4	7	6		3	3	1	1	
Florida	1	1		1						1	[3] 1						
Kentucky	4	4		1	3					2	1			1	1		1
Tennessee										2	2		2				
Alabama	4	4		1	3					5	4			4	1		1
Mississippi	8	6		2	4	2			2	1					1		1
Arkansas	2	2			2					10	9		2	7	1		1
Louisiana	13	8		3	5	5		2	3	5	5		1	4			
Oklahoma	4	1			1	3			3	2	1		1		1		1
Texas	9	7		3	4	1			1	8	5		2	3	2		2
Wyoming										2					1		1
Colorado	2					1			1	7					5		5
Arizona										2					1		1
Nevada	1					1			1	1					1		1
Washington	2					2	1		1	4					4		4
California	6					4			4	15	1			1	14	6	8

[1] Includes 5 prisoners of other races.
[2] Includes 1 white prisoner reported in "Federal prisons and Reformatories."
[3] Includes 1 Negro, age unknown.

TABLE 6.—NEGRO AND WHITE PRISONERS RECEIVED FROM COURTS, BY STATES: 1932, 1931, AND 1930

STATE	TOTAL [1]			NEGRO			WHITE			PERCENT					
										Negro			White		
	1932	1931	1930	1932	1931	1930	1932	1931	1930	1932	1931	1930	1932	1931	1930
United States	**67,477**	**71,520**	**66,013**	**14,613**	**15,441**	**14,771**	**50,889**	**54,160**	**49,331**	**21.7**	**21.6**	**22.4**	**75.4**	**75.7**	**74.7**
Federal prisons and camps	9,652	10,615	9,800	997	1,140	1,211	8,202	8,968	8,110	10.3	10.7	12.4	85.0	84.5	82.8
State prisons and reformatories	57,825	60,905	56,213	13,616	14,301	13,560	42,687	45,192	41,221	23.5	23.5	24.1	73.8	74.2	73.3
NEW ENGLAND:															
Maine	314	316	216	1	4	----	312	311	214	.3	1.3	----	99.4	98.4	99.1
New Hampshire	93	77	107	1	----	----	92	77	107	1.1	----	----	98.9	100.0	100.0
Vermont	358	417	389	3	5	2	355	412	385	.8	1.2	0.5	99.2	98.8	99.0
Massachusetts	1,133	929	972	54	42	60	1,076	885	911	4.8	4.5	6.2	95.0	95.3	93.7
Rhode Island	198	216	179	20	15	11	177	201	168	10.1	6.9	6.1	89.4	93.1	93.9
Connecticut	651	604	679	44	43	54	605	561	625	6.8	7.1	8.0	92.9	92.9	92.0
MIDDLE ATLANTIC:															
New York	3,629	3,679	3,349	644	579	528	2,957	3,086	2,800	17.7	15.7	15.8	81.5	83.9	83.6
New Jersey	1,743	1,977	1,761	441	474	475	1,295	1,501	1,280	25.3	24.0	27.0	74.3	75.9	72.7
Pennsylvania	2,248	2,572	2,397	450	469	520	1,797	2,100	1,877	20.0	18.2	21.7	79.9	81.6	78.3
EAST NORTH CENTRAL:															
Ohio	3,235	3,511	3,712	740	838	882	2,491	2,671	2,825	22.9	23.9	23.8	77.0	76.1	76.1
Indiana	1,864	2,062	1,942	233	302	304	1,625	1,754	1,627	12.5	14.6	15.7	87.2	85.1	83.8
Illinois	2,582	2,629	2,658	487	479	615	2,078	2,142	2,029	18.9	18.2	23.1	80.5	81.5	76.3
Michigan	3,258	3,733	3,949	528	620	590	2,685	3,044	3,301	16.2	16.6	14.9	82.4	81.5	83.6
Wisconsin	1,247	1,285	1,258	18	28	29	1,208	1,224	1,187	1.4	2.2	2.3	96.9	95.3	94.4
WEST NORTH CENTRAL:															
Minnesota	1,129	1,166	864	27	12	20	1,072	1,134	825	2.4	1.0	2.3	95.0	77.3	95.5
Iowa	930	1,047	976	62	49	47	862	994	926	6.7	4.7	4.8	92.7	94.9	94.9
Missouri	1,932	2,249	1,950	486	540	560	1,446	1,703	1,382	25.2	24.0	28.7	74.8	75.7	70.9
North Dakota	216	268	233	2	5	3	201	248	221	.9	1.9	1.3	93.1	92.5	94.8
South Dakota	380	391	308	1	3	3	343	357	277	.3	.8	1.0	90.3	91.3	89.9
Nebraska	664	723	636	47	33	38	606	680	573	7.1	4.6	6.0	91.3	94.1	90.1
Kansas	1,246	1,246	1,545	170	195	202	1,062	1,039	1,318	13.6	15.7	13.1	85.2	83.4	85.3
SOUTH ATLANTIC:															
Delaware	403	336	(2)	199	193	(2)	204	143	(2)	49.4	57.4	(2)	50.6	42.6	(2)
Maryland	2,873	2,831	2,899	1,590	1,587	1,588	1,281	1,240	1,309	55.3	56.1	54.8	44.6	43.8	45.2
District of Columbia	606	475	(2)	418	296	(2)	187	179	(2)	69.0	62.3	(2)	30.9	37.7	(2)
Virginia	1,849	1,419	1,336	1,005	807	755	844	612	581	54.4	56.9	56.5	45.6	43.1	43.5
West Virginia	1,498	1,388	1,171	244	206	168	1,254	1,180	1,001	16.3	14.8	14.3	83.7	85.0	85.5
North Carolina	1,211	1,591	1,362	543	736	555	665	853	804	44.8	46.3	40.7	54.9	53.6	59.0
South Carolina	(3)	664	554	(3)	317	200	(3)	347	352	(3)	47.7	36.1	(3)	52.3	63.5
Georgia [4]	----	----	----	----	----	----	----	----	----	----	----	----	----	----	----
Florida	1,336	1,315	1,042	752	677	555	584	638	487	56.3	51.5	53.3	43.7	48.5	46.7
EAST SOUTH CENTRAL:															
Kentucky	2,671	2,421	2,260	743	690	696	1,927	1,731	1,564	27.8	28.5	30.8	72.1	71.5	69.2
Tennessee	1,422	1,652	1,459	521	633	604	901	1,019	855	36.6	38.3	41.4	63.4	61.7	58.6
Alabama [4]	----	----	----	----	----	----	----	----	----	----	----	----	----	----	----
Mississippi	(3)	(3)	991	(3)	(3)	703	(3)	(3)	288	(3)	(3)	70.9	(3)	(3)	29.1
WEST SOUTH CENTRAL:															
Arkansas	1,145	1,430	1,266	416	633	529	725	794	729	36.3	44.3	41.8	63.3	55.5	57.6
Louisiana	1,316	1,320	1,070	784	827	697	532	493	373	59.6	62.7	65.1	40.4	37.3	34.9
Oklahoma	2,517	2,853	2,137	510	646	462	1,928	2,116	1,588	20.3	22.6	21.6	76.6	74.2	74.3
Texas	3,300	3,196	2,607	1,081	1,012	828	1,922	1,894	1,504	32.8	31.7	31.8	58.2	59.3	57.7
MOUNTAIN:															
Montana	315	328	398	11	13	8	261	278	352	3.5	4.0	2.0	82.9	84.8	88.4
Idaho	172	222	(3)	----	2	(3)	166	208	(3)	----	.9	(3)	96.5	93.7	(3)
Wyoming	107	151	135	3	2	11	93	134	106	2.8	1.3	8.1	86.9	88.7	78.5
Colorado	911	1,067	872	43	40	31	683	866	738	4.7	3.7	3.6	75.0	81.2	84.6
New Mexico	1,304	378	280	6	11	15	160	206	141	2.0	2.9	5.4	52.6	54.5	50.4
Arizona	368	362	369	32	29	34	203	228	226	8.7	8.0	9.2	55.2	63.0	61.2
Utah	192	217	223	3	6	3	175	203	203	1.6	2.8	1.3	91.1	93.5	91.0
Nevada	121	165	125	5	3	4	101	136	103	4.1	1.8	3.2	83.5	82.4	82.4
PACIFIC:															
Washington	1,031	1,227	1,053	33	43	37	958	1,146	977	3.2	3.5	3.5	92.9	93.4	92.8
Oregon	493	482	501	8	7	10	470	465	479	1.6	1.5	2.0	95.3	96.5	95.6
California	2,614	2,318	2,023	207	150	124	2,118	1,959	1,603	7.9	6.5	6.1	81.0	84.5	79.2

[1] Includes all other races. [2] No State prison in Delaware or the District of Columbia in 1930. [3] No report received. [4] Data incomplete; not used.

TABLE 7.—NEGRO AND WHITE PRISONERS RECEIVED FROM COURTS, BY AGE, AND SEX, FOR THE UNITED STATES: 1932, 1931, AND 1930

AGE	TOTAL[1]			NEGRO		WHITE		PERCENT DISTRIBUTION			
								Negro		White	
	Total	Male	Female	Male	Female	Male	Female	Male	Female	Male	Female
1932											
Total	**67,477**	**64,546**	**2,931**	**13,822**	**791**	**48,805**	**2,084**	**100.0**	**100.0**	**100.0**	**100.0**
Under 15 years	18	17	1	12	1	4	----------	.1	.1	(2)	----------
15 to 17 years	2,644	2,464	180	538	57	1,900	120	3.9	7.2	3.9	5.8
18 years	3,291	3,130	161	611	34	2,456	127	4.4	4.3	5.0	6.1
19 years	4,158	3,987	171	851	33	3,043	137	6.2	4.2	6.2	6.6
20 years	3,800	3,655	145	701	41	2,851	103	5.1	5.2	5.8	4.9
21 to 24 years	14,891	14,334	557	3,031	180	10,867	364	21.9	22.8	22.3	17.5
25 to 29 years	13,020	12,448	572	2,915	179	9,089	381	21.1	22.6	18.6	18.3
30 to 34 years	9,027	8,660	367	2,068	106	6,271	253	15.0	13.4	12.8	12.1
35 to 39 years	6,055	5,744	311	1,281	67	4,290	234	9.3	8.5	8.8	11.2
40 to 44 years	4,148	3,936	212	764	47	3,061	162	5.5	5.9	6.3	7.8
45 to 49 years	2,678	2,555	123	484	23	2,018	97	3.5	2.9	4.1	4.7
50 to 54 years	1,726	1,669	57	285	11	1,346	44	2.1	1.4	2.8	2.1
55 to 59 years	947	919	28	144	3	749	25	1.0	.4	1.5	1.2
60 to 64 years	573	557	16	76	3	471	13	.5	.4	1.0	.6
65 years and over	459	448	11	55	----------	373	11	.4	----------	.8	.5
Not reported	42	23	19	6	6	16	13	(2)	.8	(2)	.6
1931											
Total	**71,520**	**68,483**	**3,037**	**14,605**	**836**	**51,995**	**2,165**	**100.0**	**100.0**	**100.0**	**100.0**
Under 15 years	17	15	2	12	2	3	----------	.1	.2	(2)	(2)
15 to 17 years	3,208	3,021	187	649	39	2,336	147	4.4	4.7	4.5	6.8
18 years	3,635	3,477	158	700	42	2,727	115	4.8	5.0	5.2	5.3
19 years	4,386	4,184	202	817	41	3,270	161	5.6	4.9	6.3	7.4
20 years	4,385	4,219	166	785	27	3,353	137	5.4	3.2	6.4	6.3
21 to 24 years	15,765	15,173	592	3,143	174	11,563	408	21.5	20.8	22.2	18.8
25 to 29 years	13,443	12,936	507	3,046	172	9,466	327	20.9	20.6	18.2	15.1
30 to 34 years	8,991	8,641	350	2,055	107	6,271	235	14.1	12.8	12.1	10.9
35 to 39 years	6,393	6,111	282	1,394	65	4,562	216	9.5	7.8	8.8	10.0
40 to 44 years	4,096	3,923	173	729	40	3,088	130	5.0	4.8	5.9	6.0
45 to 49 years	2,767	2,661	106	561	21	2,051	85	3.8	2.5	3.9	3.9
50 to 54 years	1,773	1,729	44	310	11	1,377	33	2.1	1.3	2.6	1.5
55 to 59 years	1,065	1,041	24	183	5	833	19	1.3	.6	1.6	.9
60 to 64 years	640	633	7	88	1	534	6	.6	.1	1.0	.3
65 years and over	475	468	7	65	1	382	6	.4	.1	.7	.3
Not reported	481	251	230	68	88	179	140	.5	10.5	.3	6.5
1930											
Total	**66,013**	**62,957**	**3,056**	**13,908**	**863**	**47,178**	**2,153**	**100.0**	**100.0**	**100.0**	**100.0**
Under 15 years	25	23	2	14	1	9	1	.1	.1	(2)	(2)
15 to 17 years	3,043	2,809	234	652	55	2,124	177	4.7	6.4	4.5	8.2
18 years	3,430	3,256	174	713	40	2,479	132	5.1	4.6	5.3	6.1
19 years	4,122	3,964	158	784	42	3,075	115	5.6	4.9	6.5	5.3
20 years	3,956	3,817	139	724	45	3,004	93	5.2	5.2	6.4	4.3
21 to 24 years	14,068	13,557	511	2,868	146	10,268	358	20.6	16.9	21.8	16.6
25 to 29 years	11,926	11,517	409	2,803	146	8,246	257	20.2	16.9	17.5	11.9
30 to 34 years	7,955	7,692	263	1,873	98	5,570	162	13.5	11.4	11.8	7.5
35 to 39 years	5,725	5,524	201	1,212	45	4,137	153	8.7	5.2	8.8	7.1
40 to 44 years	3,782	3,664	118	743	30	2,831	88	5.3	3.5	6.0	4.1
45 to 49 years	2,607	2,536	71	505	22	1,960	49	3.6	2.5	4.2	2.3
50 to 54 years	1,585	1,546	39	287	12	1,222	26	2.1	1.4	2.6	1.2
55 to 59 years	984	970	14	163	3	787	9	1.2	.3	1.7	.4
60 to 64 years	549	544	5	69	----------	458	5	.5	----------	1.0	.2
65 years and over	487	481	6	73	1	387	5	.5	.1	.8	.2
Not reported	1,769	1,057	712	425	177	621	523	3.1	20.5	1.3	24.3

[1] Includes all other races.

[2] Less than 1/10 of 1 percent.

TABLE 8.—PRISONERS RECEIVED FROM COURTS, BY RACE, SEX, AND CLASSIFICATION OF OFFENSE, FOR THE UNITED STATES: 1932, 1931, AND 1930

OFFENSE	Total	NEGRO			WHITE			OTHER RACES			PERCENT		
		Total	Male	Female	Total	Male	Female	Total	Male	Female	Negro	White	Other races
1932													
All offenses	**67,477**	**14,613**	**13,822**	**791**	**50,889**	**48,805**	**2,084**	**1,975**	**1,919**	**56**	**21.7**	**75.4**	**2.9**
Homicide	3,736	1,513	1,377	136	2,077	1,996	81	146	140	6	40.5	55.6	3.9
Robbery	8,247	1,586	1,555	31	6,555	6,495	60	106	103	3	19.2	79.5	1.3
Aggravated assault	2,029	888	817	71	1,034	1,015	19	107	104	3	43.8	51.0	5.3
Other assault	1,044	540	500	40	491	477	14	13	12	1	51.7	47.0	1.2
Burglarly	15,354	3,960	3,918	42	10,934	10,854	80	460	458	2	25.8	71.2	3.0
Larceny, except auto theft	10,694	2,558	2,430	128	7,820	7,613	207	316	311	5	23.9	73.1	3.0
Auto theft	3,378	376	373	3	2,967	2,945	22	35	35	----	11.1	87.8	1.0
Embezzlement and fraud	2,196	131	128	3	1,923	1,840	83	142	138	4	6.0	87.6	6.5
Stolen property	576	154	143	11	411	393	18	11	11	----	26.7	71.4	1.9
Forgery	4,011	396	376	20	3,514	3,375	139	101	98	3	9.9	87.6	2.5
Rape	1,287	227	227	----	1,010	1,010	----	50	50	----	17.6	78.5	3.9
Other sex offenses	1,959	283	151	132	1,628	1,176	452	48	36	12	14.4	83.1	2.5
Violating drug laws	1,615	224	187	37	1,203	1,029	174	188	183	5	13.9	74.5	11.6
Violating liquor laws	6,377	902	851	51	5,314	5,097	217	161	157	4	14.1	83.3	2.5
Other offenses	4,974	875	789	86	4,008	3,490	518	91	83	8	17.6	80.6	1.8
1931													
All offenses	**71,520**	**15,441**	**14,605**	**836**	**54,160**	**51,995**	**2,165**	**1,919**	**1,883**	**36**	**21.6**	**75.7**	**2.7**
Homicide	3,804	1,650	1,462	188	2,010	1,925	85	144	141	3	43.4	52.8	3.8
Robbery	8,611	1,600	1,561	39	6,925	6,850	75	86	85	1	18.6	80.4	1.0
Aggravated assault Other assault	3,146	1,578	1,473	105	1,474	1,451	23	94	92	2	50.2	46.9	3.0
Burglarly	14,275	3,755	3,726	29	10,169	10,108	61	351	349	2	26.3	71.2	2.5
Larceny Auto theft	13,662	3,066	2,923	143	10,268	10,022	246	328	323	5	22.4	75.2	2.4
Embezzlement and fraud	1,503	115	106	9	1,381	1,327	54	7	7	----	7.7	91.9	.5
Stolen property	2,257	344	329	15	1,887	1,846	41	26	23	3	15.2	83.6	1.2
Forgery	4,598	487	464	23	4,003	3,845	158	108	108	----	10.6	87.1	2.3
Rape	1,796	304	304	----	1,415	1,415	----	77	77	----	16.9	78.8	4.3
Other sex offenses	1,802	160	98	62	1,610	1,078	532	32	26	6	8.9	89.3	1.8
Violating drug laws	1,798	261	225	36	1,307	1,164	143	230	227	3	14.5	72.7	12.8
Violating liquor laws	7,810	970	885	85	6,620	6,343	277	220	217	3	12.4	84.8	2.8
Other offenses	6,458	1,151	1,049	102	5,091	4,621	470	216	208	8	17.8	78.8	3.3
1930													
All offenses	**66,013**	**14,771**	**13,908**	**863**	**49,331**	**47,178**	**2,153**	**1,911**	**1,871**	**40**	**22.4**	**74.7**	**2.9**
Homicide	3,547	1,647	1,466	181	1,768	1,705	63	132	129	3	46.4	49.8	3.7
Robbery	6,988	1,475	1,439	36	5,419	5,377	42	94	92	2	21.1	77.5	1.3
Aggravated assault Other assault	2,886	1,395	1,299	96	1,378	1,343	35	113	112	1	48.3	47.7	3.9
Burglary	12,368	3,477	3,433	44	8,589	8,537	52	302	301	1	28.1	69.4	2.4
Larceny Auto theft	12,511	2,775	2,650	125	9,426	9,233	193	310	309	1	22.2	75.3	2.5
Embezzlement and fraud	1,420	98	93	5	1,306	1,275	31	16	16	----	6.9	92.0	1.1
Stolen property	2,109	307	286	21	1,788	1,752	36	14	14	----	14.6	84.8	.7
Forgery	4,220	464	445	19	3,640	3,504	136	116	114	2	11.0	86.3	2.7
Rape	1,876	302	302	----	1,512	1,512	----	62	62	----	16.1	80.6	3.3
Other sex offenses	1,692	216	129	87	1,446	925	521	30	27	3	12.8	85.5	1.8
Violating drug laws	1,684	395	345	50	1,106	974	132	183	176	7	23.5	65.7	10.9
Violating liquor laws	7,864	1,095	1,032	63	6,454	6,194	260	315	308	7	13.9	82.1	4.0
Other offenses	6,848	1,125	989	136	5,499	4,847	652	224	211	13	16.4	80.3	3.3

TABLE 9.—PRISONERS RECEIVED FROM COURTS, BY AGE, SEX, RACE, NATIVITY, AND OFFENSE, FOR THE UNITED STATES: 1930

OFFENSE, RACE, AND NATIVITY	ALL AGES			UNDER 15 YEARS		15 TO 17 YEARS		18 YEARS		19 YEARS		20 YEARS		21 TO 24 years		25 TO 29 YEARS	
	Total	Male	Female	Male	Female	Male	Female	Male	Female	Male	Female	Male	Female	Male	Female	Male	Female
All offenses	**66,013**	**62,957**	**3,056**	**23**	**2**	**2,809**	**234**	**3,256**	**174**	**3,964**	**158**	**3,817**	**139**	**13,557**	**511**	**11,517**	**409**
Negro	14,771	13,908	863	14	1	652	55	713	40	784	42	724	45	2,868	146	2,803	146
Native white	45,495	43,510	1,985	9	1	2,063	168	2,390	126	2,978	110	2,882	89	9,840	330	7,727	236
Foreign-born white	3,836	3,668	168			61	9	89	6	97	5	122	4	428	28	519	21
All other	1,911	1,871	40			33	2	64	2	105	1	89	1	421	7	468	6
Homicide:																	
Negro	1,647	1,466	181	5	1	42	3	47	5	47	8	45	8	226	38	291	38
Native white	1,552	1,494	58	3		48	1	39		52	1	65	2	271	5	266	11
Foreign-born white	216	211	5					1				1	1	15		26	
Rape:																	
Negro	302	302				19		9		19		8		61		58	
Native white	1,317	1,317				33		65		76		77		278		232	
Foreign-born white	195	195				1		4		4		8		19		28	
Robbery:																	
Negro	1,475	1,439	36	1		75	1	106	1	124	2	113	2	376	13	316	12
Native white	5,047	5,009	38			268	3	352	4	499	5	512	2	1,580	11	971	8
Foreign-born white	372	368	4			13	1	26		37	1	24		106	1	69	1
Assault:																	
Negro	1,395	1,299	96			21	2	37	6	53	6	57	4	264	24	239	24
Native white	1,146	1,118	28			39	1	36	1	64	3	58	1	255	4	197	4
Foreign-born white	232	225	7			1		1				4		15	2	25	
Burglary:																	
Negro	3,477	3,433	44	5		249	5	242	2	248	5	212	3	791	9	713	5
Native white	8,145	8,095	50	2	1	649	3	707	4	790	5	731	3	2,096	13	1,325	6
Foreign-born white	444	442	2			15		24		22		29		92		73	1
Forgery:																	
Negro	464	445	19	1		11	1	21	2	25	1	30	2	99	5	75	2
Native white	3,477	3,347	130			68	5	96	6	163	8	200	5	784	28	652	25
Foreign-born white	163	157	6			3		3		1		2		18		26	3
Larceny, etc.:																	
Negro	3,180	3,029	151	2		187	7	198	11	205	8	197	9	666	22	570	37
Native white	11,855	11,611	244	2		778	20	849	23	988	16	852	8	2,796	63	2,011	27
Foreign-born white	665	649	16			22		22	1	22	1	33		99	2	94	1
Embezzlement:																	
Negro	34	33	1					2		1		1		3		7	
Native white	445	437	8					5	1	6		9		41	3	71	1
Foreign-born white	32	32												2		5	
Fraud:																	
Negro	64	60	4					1		1	1	1		6	1	10	1
Native white	733	710	23			5	1	5		12		12	1	99	8	134	1
Foreign-born white	96	96						1		1				7		5	
Having stolen property:																	
Negro	307	286	21			29	3	31	2	29		15		69	1	51	5
Native white	1,723	1,687	36			113	2	129	1	163	4	133		479	5	302	4
Foreign-born white	65	65				1		3		2		3		8		17	
Larceny:																	
Negro	2,775	2,650	125	2		158	4	164	9	174	7	180	9	588	20	502	31
Native white	8,954	8,777	177	2		660	17	710	21	807	12	698	7	2,177	47	1,504	21
Foreign-born white	472	456	16			21		18	1	19	1	30		82	2	67	1
Sex offenses except rape:																	
Negro	216	129	87			7	9	1	3	4	7	4	6	19	24	19	12
Native white	1,284	813	471	1		7	57	14	57	20	37	31	33	139	120	170	81
Foreign-born white	162	112	50			3	4		2		2		2	4	18	15	5
Violating liquor laws:																	
Negro	1,095	1,032	63			7		7		18		16	2	129	3	207	4
Native white	5,773	5,533	240	1		15	1	65	1	126	1	158	1	829	16	1,001	17
Foreign-born white	681	661	20							1		4		11		57	1
Violating drug laws:																	
Negro	395	345	50					1		1		3		31	1	82	1
Native white	993	866	127					2		2		4		52	9	137	10
Foreign-born white	113	108	5											4		16	
Carrying weapons:																	
Negro	164	161	3			4		6		5		7		45	1	38	1
Native white	214	212	2			11	1	8		8		13		66		40	1
Foreign-born white	33	33						1		2		1		5		4	
Nonsupport or neglect:																	
Negro	82	67	15				6	1			2	1		9		13	2
Native white	721	677	44				2	2		6		16	3	73	13	147	14
Foreign-born white	73	65	8											1	1	9	2
Other and not reported:																	
Negro	879	761	118			30	21	37	10	35	3	31	9	152	6	132	8
Native white	3,971	3,418	553			147	74	155	30	184	34	165	31	621	48	578	32
Foreign-born white	487	442	45			3	4	7	3	8	1	16	1	39	4	77	7

TABLE 9.—PRISONERS RECEIVED FROM COURTS, BY AGE, SEX, RACE, NATIVITY, AND OFFENSE, FOR THE UNITED STATES: 1930—Continued

OFFENSE, RACE, AND NATIVITY	30 TO 34 YEARS		35 TO 39 YEARS		40 TO 44 YEARS		45 TO 49 YEARS		50 TO 54 YEARS		55 TO 59 YEARS		60 TO 64 YEARS		65 YEARS AND OVER		AGE UNKNOWN	
	Male	Female	Male	Female	Male	Female	Male	Female	Male	Female	Male	Female	Male	Female	Male	Female	Male	Female
All offenses	**7,692**	**263**	**5,524**	**201**	**3,664**	**118**	**2,536**	**71**	**1,546**	**39**	**970**	**14**	**544**	**5**	**481**	**6**	**1,057**	**712**
Negro	1,873	98	1,212	45	743	30	505	22	287	12	163	3	69	----	73	1	425	177
Native white	5,073	147	3,550	126	2,365	70	1,617	40	1,020	20	668	7	385	3	330	3	613	509
Foreign-born white	497	15	587	27	466	18	343	9	202	6	119	2	73	2	57	2	8	14
All other	249	3	175	3	90	----	71	----	37	1	20	2	17	----	21	----	11	12
Homicide:																		
Negro	231	26	162	11	94	9	79	6	43	1	32	----	15	----	9	1	98	26
Native white	206	11	127	11	123	7	70	2	60	1	56	1	25	1	24	1	59	3
Foreign-born white	34	----	35	3	34	----	22	1	17	----	8	----	10	----	8	----	----	----
Rape:																		
Negro	41	----	23	----	21	----	9	----	12	----	7	----	3	----	1	----	11	----
Native white	133	----	138	----	70	----	61	----	49	----	41	----	32	----	25	----	7	----
Foreign-born white	23	----	29	----	17	----	27	----	12	----	9	----	9	----	5	----	----	----
Robbery:																		
Negro	154	1	80	----	31	1	12	1	6	----	3	----	----	----	2	----	40	2
Native white	421	1	195	1	82	1	47	----	16	----	8	----	2	----	2	----	54	2
Foreign-born white	38	----	31	----	9	----	8	----	3	----	2	----	1	----	1	----	----	----
Assault:																		
Negro	194	9	136	9	98	1	61	5	35	----	20	----	11	----	3	----	20	6
Native white	119	3	104	3	72	6	60	1	41	----	30	----	21	----	17	1	5	----
Foreign-born white	39	----	43	4	31	----	31	----	17	----	9	----	4	----	5	----	----	1
Burglary:																		
Negro	391	8	229	2	118	----	68	----	38	----	18	----	7	----	12	----	92	5
Native white	737	4	423	4	255	3	155	1	73	----	27	1	12	----	21	----	92	2
Foreign-born white	47	----	55	1	38	----	28	----	11	----	7	----	----	----	1	----	----	----
Forgery:																		
Negro	71	4	47	----	19	----	20	1	6	----	4	----	----	----	1	----	15	1
Native white	508	20	302	19	220	5	145	1	71	----	39	----	32	----	17	----	50	8
Foreign-born white	19	1	31	1	22	----	11	----	8	1	6	----	4	----	3	----	----	----
Larceny, etc.:																		
Negro	364	22	222	8	127	5	83	----	48	3	17	1	10	----	7	----	126	18
Native white	1,219	24	757	16	465	8	309	7	186	1	112	3	56	1	42	1	189	26
Foreign-born white	78	3	93	2	69	4	48	1	35	1	19	----	9	----	6	----	----	----
Embezzlement:																		
Negro	9	----	5	----	----	----	1	----	----	----	2	----	----	----	1	----	1	1
Native white	79	1	66	----	64	1	41	----	22	----	16	----	8	----	9	----	----	1
Foreign-born white	6	----	3	----	8	----	5	----	2	----	1	----	----	----	----	----	----	----
Fraud:																		
Negro	9	1	8	----	10	----	3	----	5	----	3	----	1	----	1	----	1	----
Native white	140	3	86	4	78	----	58	2	31	1	16	----	18	----	8	----	8	2
Foreign-born white	10	----	24	----	18	----	11	----	10	----	5	----	3	----	1	----	----	----
Having stolen property:																		
Negro	24	1	12	2	9	1	4	----	3	1	----	----	3	----	1	----	6	5
Native white	171	3	90	2	40	1	32	2	11	----	7	1	3	----	3	----	11	11
Foreign-born white	12	----	8	----	6	----	2	----	1	----	2	----	----	----	----	----	----	----
Larceny:																		
Negro	322	20	197	6	108	4	75	----	40	2	12	1	6	----	4	----	118	12
Native white	829	17	515	10	283	6	178	3	122	----	73	2	27	1	22	1	170	12
Foreign-born white	50	3	58	2	37	4	30	1	22	1	11	----	6	----	5	----	----	----
Sex offenses except rape:																		
Negro	26	13	15	7	9	2	12	----	5	----	3	----	2	----	2	----	1	4
Native white	112	26	93	24	73	8	59	3	33	4	26	----	10	----	17	----	8	21
Foreign-born white	21	5	21	8	23	2	15	----	3	1	5	----	----	1	2	----	----	----
Violating liquor laws::																		
Negro	173	3	163	2	110	6	81	5	56	1	31	1	10	----	16	----	8	36
Native white	852	21	740	19	544	12	424	11	312	6	217	1	125	1	100	----	24	132
Foreign-born white	86	2	148	1	116	2	96	3	62	2	34	1	25	1	19	----	2	7
Violating drug laws:																		
Negro	82	3	46	3	50	2	31	3	10	1	5	1	1	----	2	----	----	35
Native white	176	15	208	9	119	4	78	3	45	2	28	----	10	----	5	----	----	75
Foreign-born white	32	1	20	1	21	----	7	----	3	----	3	----	2	----	----	----	----	3
Carrying weapons:																		
Negro	26	1	16	----	3	----	3	----	4	----	4	----	----	----	----	----	----	----
Native white	32	----	15	----	8	----	4	----	4	----	1	----	2	----	----	----	----	----
Foreign-born white	6	----	4	----	3	----	2	----	3	----	----	----	2	----	----	----	----	----
Nonsupport or neglect:																		
Negro	19	4	9	----	9	----	3	1	1	----	----	----	----	----	2	----	----	----
Native white	132	6	133	4	84	2	56	----	15	----	10	----	2	----	----	----	1	----
Foreign-born white	7	1	12	----	15	3	13	----	5	----	2	----	1	----	----	----	----	1
Other and not reported:																		
Negro	101	4	64	3	54	4	43	----	23	6	19	----	10	----	16	----	14	44
Native white	426	16	315	16	250	14	149	11	115	6	73	1	56	----	60	----	124	240
Foreign-born white	67	2	65	6	68	7	35	4	23	1	15	1	6	----	7	2	6	2

TABLE 10.—PRISONERS RECEIVED FROM COURTS, BY AGE, SEX, RACE, NATIVITY, AND OFFENSE, FOR THE UNITED STATES: 1932

OFFENSE, RACE, AND NATIVITY	ALL AGES			UNDER 15 YEARS		15 TO 17 YEARS		18 YEARS		19 YEARS		20 YEARS		21 TO 24 YEARS		25 TO 29 YEARS	
	Total	Male	Female	Male	Female	Male	Female	Male	Female	Male	Female	Male	Female	Male	Female	Male	Female
All offenses	**67,477**	**64,546**	**2,931**	**17**	**1**	**2,464**	**180**	**3,130**	**161**	**3,987**	**171**	**3,655**	**145**	**14,334**	**557**	**12,448**	**572**
Negro	14,613	13,822	791	12	1	538	57	611	34	851	33	701	41	3,031	180	2,915	179
Native white	47,488	45,574	1,914	3		1,856	120	2,403	124	2,934	130	2,765	101	10,482	348	8,660	365
Foreign-born white	3,401	3,231	170	1		44		53	3	109	7	86	2	385	16	429	16
All other	1,975	1,919	56	1		26	3	63		93	1	103	1	436	13	444	12
Homicide:																	
Negro	1,513	1,377	136	2		43	5	32	7	58	7	42	5	252	30	300	36
Native white	1,829	1,754	75			44		57		71	1	80	1	323	12	308	19
Foreign-born white	248	242	6					1		2		2		9		18	
Robbery:																	
Negro	1,586	1,555	31	1		73	2	87		128	1	100	6	446	5	340	6
Native white	6,159	6,099	60			308	4	411	3	508	6	490	5	1,818	12	1,250	18
Foreign-born white	396	396				8		10		31		24		111		87	
Aggravated assault:																	
Negro	888	817	71			10	5	19	6	27	2	27	5	166	10	202	21
Native white	931	912	19			17	1	35		49		50	1	190	3	170	3
Foreign-born white	103	103								1		1		3		9	
Other assault:																	
Negro	540	500	40			8	3	17	2	15	2	25	2	100	12	110	8
Native white	414	402	12			19		15	1	20	1	19	1	100	4	83	3
Foreign-born white	77	75	2							3				6		4	
Burglary:																	
Negro	3,960	3,918	42	6		192	8	222	1	309		251	1	941	9	809	5
Native white	10,439	10,361	78			638	2	811	2	979	3	832	5	2,806	15	1,926	19
Foreign-born white	495	493	2			18		22		35		24		86		79	
Larceny, except auto theft:																	
Negro	2,558	2,430	128			124	4	123	9	166	5	146	6	562	33	502	34
Native white	7,476	7,297	179	1		438	9	512	23	626	15	572	5	1,826	31	1,327	39
Foreign-born white	344	316	28			7		12		15	3	14	1	44	2	35	2
Auto theft:																	
Negro	376	373	3	1		36		36		45		25		108	1	67	
Native white	2,866	2,845	21			212		254	4	284		249	3	809	6	532	3
Foreign-born white	101	100	1			9		4		8		6		29		22	
Embezzlement and fraud:																	
Negro	131	128	3			1	1			5		4		17	1	24	1
Native white	1,706	1,635	71			6	1	14		15	2	24	5	162	6	259	15
Foreign-born white	217	205	12	1				1		2		2	1	21	2	31	1
Stolen property:																	
Negro	154	143	11			5	1	7	2	10		9		34	1	28	1
Native white	387	370	17			12		20	1	15	3	19		79	1	80	4
Foreign-born white	24	23	1													4	1
Forgery:																	
Negro	396	376	20	1	1	4	3	15	3	18	3	15	1	72	1	84	3
Native white	3,287	3,154	133			43	2	82	5	105	7	117	9	605	21	684	27
Foreign-born white	227	221	6			1		1		2		1		16	2	44	
Rape:																	
Negro	227	227				14		6		17		7		38		55	
Native white	926	926				24		34		52		59		203		176	
Foreign-born white	84	84				1				1		1		10		7	
Other sex offenses:																	
Negro	283	151	132			7	11	6	2	8	10	1	12	26	52	30	29
Native white	1,424	1,006	418			17	25	18	38	33	41	31	35	178	116	180	78
Foreign-born white	204	170	34						1	2	2	2		9	4	18	3
Violating drug laws:																	
Negro	224	187	37							1		3		16	3	27	4
Native white	1,138	970	168					3	1	3	2	9	1	66	20	145	33
Foreign-born white	65	59	6									2		3		5	2
Carrying weapons:																	
Negro	143	139	4			2	1	5		3		6		38		37	1
Native white	244	240	4	1		6		14		14		12		66	1	60	1
Foreign-born white	36	36						1		1		3		4		7	
Nonsupport or neglect:																	
Negro	29	23	6								1		1	3		4	2
Native white	455	422	33					2			1	7	1	67	6	86	10
Foreign-born white	47	35	12					1						1	2	4	2
Violating liquor laws:																	
Negro	902	851	51			1		8		20	1	19		98	6	190	11
Native white	4,927	4,730	197			13	1	47	1	86	3	100	4	760	19	947	38
Foreign-born white	387	367	20							1		2		10		22	2
Other offenses:																	
Negro	703	627	76	1		18	13	28	2	21	1	21	2	114	16	106	17
Native white	2,880	2,451	429	1		59	75	74	45	74	45	95	25	424	75	447	55
Foreign-born	346	306	40						2	5	2	2		23	4	33	3

TABLE 10.—PRISONERS RECEIVED FROM COURTS, BY AGE, SEX, RACE, NATIVITY, AND OFFENSE, FOR THE UNITED STATES: 1932—Continued

OFFENSE, RACE, AND NATIVITY	30 TO 34 YEARS		35 TO 39 YEARS		40 TO 44 YEARS		45 TO 49 YEARS		50 TO 54 YEARS		55 TO 59 YEARS		60 TO 64 YEARS		65 YEARS AND OVER		AGE UNKNOWN	
	Male	Female	Male	Female	Male	Female	Male	Female	Male	Female	Male	Female	Male	Female	Male	Female	Male	Female
All offenses	**8,660**	**367**	**5,744**	**311**	**3,936**	**212**	**2,555**	**123**	**1,669**	**57**	**919**	**28**	**557**	**16**	**448**	**11**	**23**	**19**
Negro	2,068	106	1,281	67	764	47	484	23	285	11	144	3	76	3	55	-----	6	6
Native white	5,849	227	3,797	208	2,619	130	1,664	81	1,164	36	642	19	410	9	310	4	16	12
Foreign-born white	422	26	493	26	442	32	354	16	182	8	107	6	61	4	63	7	-----	1
All other	321	8	173	10	111	3	53	3	38	2	26	-----	10	-----	20	-----	1	-----
Homicide:																		
Negro	207	19	175	13	95	9	70	4	50	-----	22	-----	12	-----	13	-----	4	1
Native white	226	9	185	9	142	12	92	4	100	2	47	5	41	1	37	-----	1	-----
Foreign-born white	30	-----	45	-----	46	2	34	-----	29	1	16	1	3	-----	7	2	-----	-----
Robbery:																		
Negro	203	5	93	1	46	1	20	2	13	1	2	1	1	-----	1	-----	1	-----
Native white	659	7	321	4	176	1	82	-----	41	-----	16	-----	10	-----	6	-----	3	-----
Foreign-born white	56	-----	29	-----	26	-----	6	-----	2	-----	4	-----	-----	-----	2	-----	-----	-----
Aggravated assault:																		
Negro	128	9	101	7	60	3	35	3	21	-----	11	-----	8	-----	2	-----	-----	-----
Native white	116	2	85	3	58	1	44	3	42	-----	29	1	18	-----	9	-----	-----	1
Foreign-born white	9	-----	12	-----	24	-----	26	-----	11	-----	-----	-----	4	-----	3	-----	-----	-----
Other assault:																		
Negro	85	7	64	2	37	1	18	1	8	-----	4	-----	5	-----	4	-----	-----	-----
Native white	56	-----	37	1	25	-----	10	-----	7	1	4	-----	4	-----	3	-----	-----	-----
Foreign-born white	8	1	12	-----	14	1	15	-----	5	-----	4	-----	3	-----	1	-----	-----	-----
Burglary:																		
Negro	524	6	307	6	157	3	91	1	59	1	28	-----	15	-----	6	-----	1	1
Native white	1,066	12	546	10	341	7	193	2	112	1	54	-----	32	-----	23	-----	2	-----
Foreign-born white	71	1	50	1	49	-----	29	-----	16	-----	6	-----	5	-----	3	-----	-----	-----
Larceny, except auto theft:																		
Negro	356	15	195	11	131	5	68	2	29	4	17	-----	7	-----	4	-----	-----	-----
Native white	805	17	484	16	290	15	197	5	124	3	52	-----	34	1	9	-----	-----	-----
Foreign-born white	46	7	50	4	37	3	28	3	16	1	7	1	3	-----	2	1	-----	-----
Auto theft:																		
Negro	35	-----	8	1	6	1	4	-----	-----	-----	1	-----	-----	-----	1	-----	-----	-----
Native white	282	2	130	2	50	1	23	-----	14	-----	3	-----	3	-----	-----	-----	-----	-----
Foreign-born white	4	1	12	-----	1	-----	5	-----	-----	-----	-----	-----	-----	-----	-----	-----	-----	-----
Embezzlement and fraud:																		
Negro	25	-----	21	-----	11	-----	11	-----	7	-----	2	-----	-----	-----	-----	-----	-----	-----
Native white	310	8	251	18	22	10	134	2	110	2	68	-----	30	-----	30	-----	-----	2
Foreign-born white	34	1	35	1	25	3	26	2	13	1	8	-----	2	-----	4	-----	-----	-----
Stolen property:																		
Negro	22	4	8	2	10	-----	5	-----	2	-----	3	-----	-----	-----	-----	-----	-----	-----
Native white	52	2	33	2	17	3	16	1	11	-----	11	-----	4	-----	1	-----	-----	-----
Foreign-born white	6	-----	2	-----	5	-----	5	-----	-----	-----	-----	-----	1	-----	-----	-----	-----	-----
Forgery:																		
Negro	71	3	39	-----	33	1	12	1	4	-----	5	-----	2	-----	1	-----	-----	-----
Native white	540	26	353	20	269	7	151	8	99	1	54	-----	23	-----	28	-----	1	-----
Foreign-born white	33	1	40	1	30	2	31	-----	12	-----	3	-----	4	-----	3	-----	-----	-----
Rape:																		
Negro	39	-----	24	-----	8	-----	11	-----	3	-----	3	-----	1	-----	1	-----	-----	-----
Native white	98	-----	76	-----	44	-----	52	-----	39	-----	25	-----	25	-----	18	-----	1	-----
Foreign-born white	6	-----	11	-----	12	-----	14	-----	8	-----	5	-----	2	-----	6	-----	-----	-----
Other sex offenses:																		
Negro	32	10	11	1	5	3	12	2	6	-----	5	-----	1	-----	1	-----	-----	-----
Native white	140	36	123	23	104	12	64	9	41	2	33	1	26	1	18	-----	-----	1
Foreign-born white	14	7	30	8	29	5	23	2	10	-----	12	1	8	-----	13	-----	-----	1
Violating drug laws:																		
Negro	38	9	39	8	27	6	17	2	10	1	6	1	2	1	1	-----	-----	2
Native white	216	42	192	28	137	21	96	10	55	5	24	1	16	-----	7	-----	1	4
Foreign-born white	13	1	21	2	6	1	4	-----	3	-----	2	-----	-----	-----	-----	-----	-----	-----
Carrying weapons:																		
Negro	23	1	15	-----	7	1	1	-----	-----	-----	2	-----	-----	-----	-----	-----	-----	-----
Native white	33	1	13	1	7	-----	4	-----	8	-----	2	-----	-----	-----	-----	-----	-----	-----
Foreign-born white	7	-----	6	-----	3	-----	2	-----	1	-----	-----	-----	1	-----	-----	-----	-----	-----
Nonsupport or neglect:																		
Negro	6	1	3	-----	4	-----	1	-----	1	-----	1	-----	-----	-----	-----	-----	-----	1
Native white	101	10	64	4	48	-----	27	-----	9	-----	8	-----	2	-----	1	1	-----	-----
Foreign-born white	4	2	7	2	7	1	6	2	5	1	-----	-----	-----	-----	-----	-----	-----	-----
Violating liquor laws:																		
Negro	177	8	109	10	75	9	68	2	43	1	16	1	14	1	13	-----	-----	1
Native white	812	27	634	35	475	20	318	21	224	14	138	6	94	3	77	2	5	3
Foreign-born white	46	1	81	2	78	5	62	3	30	2	17	2	10	2	8	1	-----	-----
Other offenses:																		
Negro	97	9	69	5	52	4	40	3	29	3	16	-----	8	1	7	-----	-----	-----
Native white	337	26	270	32	214	20	161	16	128	5	74	5	48	3	43	1	2	1
Foreign-born white	35	3	50	5	50	9	38	4	21	2	23	1	15	2	11	3	-----	-----

TABLE 11.—MARITAL CONDITION OF PRISONERS RECEIVED FROM COURTS, BY OFFENSE, RACE, NATIVITY, AND SEX, FOR THE UNITED STATES: 1932

OFFENSE, RACE, AND NATIVITY	MALE							FEMALE						
	Total	Single	Married	Widowed	Divorced	Legal separation	Unknown	Total	Single	Married	Widowed	Divorced	Legal separation	Unknown
Total	**64,546**	**32,824**	**23,739**	**2,008**	**2,062**	**1,516**	**2,397**	**2,931**	**962**	**1,358**	**232**	**159**	**125**	**95**
Negro	13,822	6,720	5,158	406	195	335	1,008	791	310	322	59	20	26	54
Native white	45,574	23,626	16,535	1,323	1,697	1,055	1,338	1,914	606	910	142	126	93	37
Foreign-born white	3,231	1,352	1,360	238	135	97	49	170	28	99	27	11	1	4
Other races	1,919	1,126	686	41	35	29	2	56	18	27	4	2	5	-------
Homicide	3,513	1,344	1,535	262	99	68	205	223	54	101	37	9	3	19
Negro	1,377	534	569	90	29	31	124	136	38	59	18	3	2	16
Native white	1,754	680	796	122	50	31	75	75	14	36	16	5	1	3
Foreign-born white	242	63	106	44	17	6	6	6	-------	2	3	1	-------	-------
Robbery	8,153	4,784	2,511	180	200	164	314	94	26	50	3	6	5	4
Negro	1,555	810	540	34	21	38	112	31	13	14	2	1	-------	1
Native white	6,099	3,679	1,818	130	159	115	198	60	11	36	-------	5	5	3
Foreign-born white	396	227	127	13	17	8	4	-------	-------	-------	-------	-------	-------	-------
Aggravated assault	1,936	830	809	68	62	46	121	93	28	41	6	4	1	13
Negro	817	315	370	24	15	19	74	71	25	31	3	1	-------	11
Native white	912	426	343	34	41	23	45	19	2	8	3	3	1	2
Foreign-born white	103	28	57	8	5	3	2	-------	-------	-------	-------	-------	-------	-------
Other assault	989	543	311	26	13	23	13	55	27	25	1	1	-------	1
Negro	500	266	206	8	2	8	10	40	20	18	1	-------	-------	1
Native white	402	238	137	7	9	8	3	12	6	5	-------	1	-------	-------
Foreign-born white	75	30	25	11	2	7	-------	2	-------	2	-------	-------	-------	-------
Burglary	15,230	9,316	4,148	372	352	247	795	124	28	66	8	8	3	11
Negro	3,918	2,077	1,211	96	42	80	412	42	16	13	4	-------	1	8
Native white	10,361	6,596	2,711	247	283	155	369	78	11	52	3	7	2	3
Foreign-born white	493	299	128	25	19	8	14	2	-------	1	1	-------	-------	-------
Larceny, except auto theft	10,354	5,876	3,467	169	265	224	353	340	112	170	18	24	8	8
Negro	2,430	1,267	896	45	27	52	143	128	44	65	7	4	4	4
Native white	7,297	4,276	2,336	104	219	158	204	179	59	90	7	16	4	3
Foreign-born white	316	143	130	14	13	10	6	28	8	12	4	3	-------	1
Auto theft	3,353	2,157	815	64	127	80	110	25	5	16	-------	1	1	2
Negro	373	228	93	9	10	7	26	3	1	2	-------	-------	-------	-------
Native white	2,845	1,842	685	52	114	70	82	21	4	13	-------	1	1	2
Foreign-born white	100	69	22	2	3	3	1	1	-------	1	-------	-------	-------	-------
Embezzlement and fraud	2,106	594	1,240	84	86	57	45	90	20	46	5	10	7	2
Negro	128	54	52	2	2	7	11	3	1	1	-------	-------	1	-------
Native white	1,635	389	1,025	68	75	44	34	71	16	35	3	10	5	2
Foreign-born white	205	67	115	12	7	4	-------	12	2	8	2	-------	-------	-------
Stolen property	547	236	227	16	22	19	27	29	7	18	1	2	1	-------
Negro	143	68	52	2	1	8	12	11	5	5	1	-------	-------	-------
Native white	370	158	154	12	21	10	15	17	2	12	-------	2	1	-------
Foreign-born white	23	6	14	2	-------	1	-------	1	-------	1	-------	-------	-------	-------
Forgery	3,849	1,618	1,604	116	252	115	144	162	39	82	11	16	10	4
Negro	376	152	166	8	11	9	30	20	6	8	-------	2	2	2
Native white	3,154	1,326	1,303	96	223	93	113	133	32	70	10	12	7	2
Foreign-born white	221	86	100	11	14	9	1	6	1	2	1	2	-------	-------
Rape	1,287	564	496	86	53	46	42	-------	-------	-------	-------	-------	-------	-------
Negro	227	102	85	11	3	11	15	-------	-------	-------	-------	-------	-------	-------
Native white	926	411	356	63	46	27	23	-------	-------	-------	-------	-------	-------	-------
Foreign-born white	84	21	38	11	3	7	4	-------	-------	-------	-------	-------	-------	-------
Other sex offenses	1,363	597	523	92	66	51	34	596	273	240	30	20	25	8
Negro	151	88	44	8	3	3	5	132	80	38	5	3	6	-------
Native white	1,006	428	391	61	56	42	28	418	185	174	18	15	18	8
Foreign-born white	170	63	73	21	7	5	1	34	5	21	6	2	-------	-------
Violating drug laws	1,399	587	605	63	61	80	3	216	25	130	23	15	23	-------
Negro	187	69	84	18	3	13	-------	37	8	20	4	1	4	-------
Native white	970	394	421	37	54	61	3	168	14	105	17	14	18	-------
Foreign-born white	59	28	25	2	3	1	-------	6	2	3	1	-------	-------	-------
Violating liquor laws	6,105	1,806	3,633	256	207	149	54	272	45	138	44	20	18	7
Negro	851	259	503	34	16	35	4	51	16	21	5	4	3	2
Native white	4,730	1,412	2,810	185	175	100	48	197	27	106	34	14	13	3
Foreign-born white	367	92	214	35	12	12	2	20	1	10	4	2	1	2
Other offenses	4,362	1,972	1,755	154	197	147	137	612	273	235	45	23	20	16
Negro	789	431	287	17	10	14	30	86	37	27	9	1	3	9
Native white	3,113	1,371	1,249	105	172	118	98	466	223	168	31	21	17	6
Foreign-born white	377	130	186	27	13	13	8	52	9	36	5	1	-------	1

TABLE 12.—PRISONERS COMMITTED FOR LIFE, BY RACE, AND SEX, BY STATES: 1932, 1931, AND 1930

[Def.=Definite sentence, life; I. M.=Indeterminate maximum sentence, life]

State and type of sentence		1932								1931								1930							
			Negro			White					Negro			White					Negro			White			
		Total	Total	Male	Female	Total	Male	Female	All other races	Total	Total	Male	Female	Total	Male	Female	All other races	Total	Total	Male	Female	Total	Male	Female	All other races
United States	**Def.**	**891**	**301**	**293**	**8**	**566**	**557**	**9**	**24**	**1,029**	**341**	**328**	**13**	**663**	**651**	**12**	**25**	**1,011**	**389**	**374**	**15**	**598**	**581**	**17**	**24**
	I. M.	**1,504**	**197**	**195**	**2**	**1,254**	**1,239**	**15**	**53**	**1,593**	**174**	**168**	**6**	**1,356**	**1,339**	**17**	**63**	**1,470**	**283**	**279**	**4**	**1,141**	**1,131**	**10**	**46**
Federal prisons and camps	Def.	8	1	1	-	4	4	-	3	5	-	-	-	3	3	-	2	5	-	-	-	2	2	-	3
State prisons and reformatories	Def.	883	300	292	8	562	553	9	21	1,024	341	328	13	660	648	12	23	1,006	389	374	15	596	579	17	21
	I. M.	1,504	197	195	2	1,254	1,239	15	53	1,593	174	168	6	1,366	1,339	17	63	1,470	283	279	4	1,141	1,131	10	46
NEW ENGLAND:																									
Maine	Def.	3	-	-	-	3	3	-	-	1	-	-	-	1	1	-	-	3	-	-	-	3	3	-	-
New Hampshire	Def.	-	-	-	-	-	-	-	-	1	-	-	-	1	1	-	-	-	-	-	-	-	-	-	-
Vermont	Def.	-	-	-	-	-	-	-	-	2	-	-	-	2	2	-	-	-	-	-	-	-	-	-	-
Massachusetts	Def.	7	2	2	-	5	5	-	-	12	-	-	-	12	12	-	-	8	2	2	-	6	6	-	-
Rhode Island	Def.	8	6	6	-	2	2	-	-	-	-	-	-	-	-	-	-	5	1	1	-	4	4	-	-
Connecticut	Def.	9	-	-	-	9	9	-	-	3	-	-	-	3	3	-	-	8	-	-	-	8	8	-	-
MIDDLE ATLANTIC:																									
New York	Def.	19	3	3	-	16	16	-	-	41	7	7	-	34	34	-	-	37	5	4	1	32	30	2	-
	I. M.	84	16	15	1	66	65	1	2	52	8	8	-	43	42	1	1	36	9	9	-	27	25	2	-
New Jersey	Def.	15	4	4	-	11	11	-	-	13	6	5	1	7	7	-	-	17	4	4	-	13	13	-	-
Pennsylvania	Def.	40	15	14	1	25	25	-	-	51	15	15	-	35	33	2	1	56	22	20	2	34	33	1	-
EAST NORTH CENTRAL:																									
Ohio	Def.	80	36	36	-	44	44	-	-	97	27	26	1	70	69	1	-	52	18	18	-	34	34	-	-
	I. M.	22	2	2	-	20	20	-	-	12	2	-	2	10	7	3	-	12	1	-	1	11	11	-	-
Indiana	Def.	28	6	6	-	21	20	1	1	43	11	11	-	31	30	1	1	38	8	8	-	30	29	1	-
Illinois	Def.	35	10	10	-	24	23	1	1	36	5	5	-	30	29	1	1	33	16	16	-	17	17	-	-
	I. M.	668	115	115	-	550	543	7	3	783	132	129	3	650	646	4	1	948	237	234	3	710	707	3	1
Michigan	Def.	2	-	-	-	2	2	-	-	77	23	23	-	52	52	-	2	84	19	19	-	63	63	-	2
	I. M.	2	-	-	-	2	2	-	-	1	-	-	-	1	1	-	-	5	-	-	-	5	5	-	-
Wisconsin	Def.	9	-	-	-	9	9	-	-	14	-	-	-	14	14	-	-	15	2	2	-	13	12	1	-
WEST NORTH CENTRAL:																									
Minnesota	Def.	24	-	-	-	24	24	-	-	13	2	2	-	11	11	-	-	14	1	1	-	13	13	-	-
	I. M.	-	-	-	-	-	-	-	-	1	-	-	-	1	1	-	-	5	1	1	-	4	4	-	-
Iowa	Def.	16	2	2	-	14	14	-	-	14	3	3	-	11	11	-	-	34	3	2	1	31	30	1	-
	I. M.	-	-	-	-	-	-	-	-	1	-	-	-	1	1	-	-	-	-	-	-	-	-	-	-
Missouri	Def.	39	11	11	-	28	27	1	-	40	8	7	1	32	31	1	-	49	17	16	1	31	29	2	1
North Dakota	Def.	2	-	-	-	1	1	-	1	6	1	1	-	5	5	-	-	5	-	-	-	4	4	-	1
South Dakota	Def.	6	-	-	-	6	6	-	-	3	-	-	-	3	3	-	-	2	-	-	-	1	1	-	1
	I. M.	-	-	-	-	-	-	-	-	-	-	-	-	-	-	-	-	1	-	-	-	-	-	-	1
Nebraska	Def.	4	-	-	-	3	3	-	1	7	1	1	-	6	5	1	-	1	-	-	-	1	1	-	-
Kansas	Def.	34	8	8	-	26	26	-	-	38	11	11	-	26	25	1	1	26	2	2	-	24	24	-	-
	I. M.	5	2	2	-	3	3	-	-	-	-	-	-	-	-	-	-	-	-	-	-	-	-	-	-
SOUTH ATLANTIC:																									
Delaware [1]	Def.	5	5	4	1	-	-	-	-	1	-	-	-	1	1	-	-	-	-	-	-	-	-	-	-
Maryland	Def.	9	9	7	2	-	-	-	-	19	10	8	2	9	9	-	-	5	4	4	-	1	1	-	-
District of Columbia [1]	Def.	2	1	1	-	1	1	-	-	2	1	1	-	1	1	-	-	-	-	-	-	-	-	-	-
Virginia	Def.	22	16	16	-	6	6	-	-	22	11	11	-	11	11	-	-	12	7	7	-	5	5	-	-
West Virginia	Def.	37	8	8	-	29	27	2	-	29	12	12	-	17	17	-	-	24	7	7	-	17	17	-	-
North Carolina	Def.	7	5	5	-	2	2	-	-	7	6	6	-	1	1	-	-	14	13	13	-	1	1	-	-
South Carolina [2]	Def.	-	-	-	-	-	-	-	-	25	13	11	2	12	11	1	-	20	10	9	1	10	8	2	-
Georgia [3]	Def.	-	-	-	-	-	-	-	-	-	-	-	-	-	-	-	-	-	-	-	-	-	-	-	-
Florida	Def.	55	27	26	1	28	38	-	-	58	38	35	3	20	20	-	-	38	24	22	2	14	14	-	-
EAST SOUTH CENTRAL:																									
Kentucky	Def.	82	27	27	-	55	55	-	-	75	22	22	-	53	50	3	-	64	24	24	-	40	40	-	-
	I. M.	6	-	-	-	6	5	1	-	-	-	-	-	-	-	-	-	-	-	-	-	-	-	-	-
Tennessee	Def.	12	7	7	-	5	5	-	-	34	22	22	-	12	12	-	-	13	7	7	-	6	6	-	-
	I. M.	-	-	-	-	-	-	-	-	1	-	-	-	1	1	-	-	-	-	-	-	-	-	-	-
Alabama [3]	Def.	-	-	-	-	-	-	-	-	-	-	-	-	-	-	-	-	-	-	-	-	-	-	-	-
Mississippi [2]	Def.	-	-	-	-	-	-	-	-	-	-	-	-	-	-	-	-	104	86	80	6	18	17	1	-
WEST SOUTH CENTRAL:																									
Arkansas	Def.	36	15	15	-	21	21	-	-	32	15	14	1	17	17	-	-	33	21	21	-	12	12	-	-
Louisiana	Def.	83	56	53	3	27	27	-	-	60	47	45	2	13	13	-	-	47	38	38	-	9	9	-	-
Oklahoma	Def.	32	4	4	-	28	28	-	-	37	13	13	-	23	23	-	1	32	8	7	1	23	22	1	1
Texas	Def.	22	10	10	-	10	10	-	2	8	4	4	-	4	4	-	-	27	10	10	-	14	14	-	3
	I. M.	11	3	3	-	5	4	1	3	22	3	3	-	10	10	-	9	12	4	4	-	6	6	-	2
MOUNTAIN:																									
Montana	Def.	2	-	-	-	2	2	-	-	2	1	1	-	1	1	-	-	16	-	-	-	16	16	-	-
Idaho [2]	Def.	2	-	-	-	2	2	-	-	3	-	-	-	3	3	-	-	-	-	-	-	-	-	-	-
	I. M.	2	-	-	-	2	2	-	-	2	-	-	-	2	2	-	-	-	-	-	-	-	-	-	-
Wyoming	Def.	3	-	-	-	2	2	-	1	3	-	-	-	3	3	-	-	2	-	-	-	1	1	-	1
Colorado	Def.	11	1	1	-	10	9	1	-	9	1	1	-	8	8	-	-	7	1	1	-	5	4	1	1
	I. M.	7	1	1	-	4	4	-	2	9	1	1	-	5	5	-	3	1	-	-	-	1	1	-	-
New Mexico	Def.	5	1	1	-	2	2	-	2	13	1	1	-	11	11	-	1	1	-	-	-	-	-	-	1
Arizona	Def.	7	1	1	-	3	3	-	3	11	-	-	-	6	6	-	5	4	1	1	-	1	1	-	2
	I. M.	4	-	-	-	3	3	-	1	3	-	-	-	2	1	1	1	-	-	-	-	-	-	-	-
Utah	Def.	5	-	-	-	5	4	1	-	-	-	-	-	-	-	-	-	-	-	-	-	-	-	-	-
	I. M.	32	-	-	-	32	32	-	-	34	-	-	-	33	33	-	1	30	-	-	-	27	27	-	3
Nevada	Def.	3	-	-	-	3	3	-	-	2	-	-	-	1	1	-	1	2	-	-	-	2	2	-	-
	I. M.	3	-	-	-	3	3	-	-	1	-	-	-	-	-	-	1	1	-	-	-	1	1	-	-
PACIFIC:																									
Washington	Def.	7	-	-	-	7	6	1	-	12	-	-	-	11	11	-	1	5	1	1	-	4	3	1	-
Oregon	Def.	11	-	-	-	11	11	-	-	6	-	-	-	5	5	-	1	12	1	1	-	11	11	-	-
California	Def.	43	4	4	-	30	29	1	9	42	4	4	-	31	31	-	7	37	6	6	-	24	21	3	7
	I. M.	658	58	57	1	558	553	5	42	671	28	27	1	597	589	8	46	419	31	31	-	349	344	5	39

[1] No State prison in Delaware or the District of Columbia in 1930.
[2] No report received for South Carolina, 1932; Mississippi, 1932 and 1931; and Idaho, 1930.
[3] Data incomplete; not used.

TABLE 13.—PRISONERS COMMITTED FOR LIFE, BY OFFENSE, AGE, RACE, AND SEX, FOR THE UNITED STATES: 1932, 1931, AND 1930

[Def.=Definite sentence, life; I. M.=Indeterminate maximum sentence, life]

OFFENSE, TYPE OF SENTENCE, AND AGE		1932									1931									1930								
		Total	Negro			White			All other races	Total	Negro			White			All other races	Total	Negro			White			All other races
			Total	Male	Female	Total	Male	Female			Total	Male	Female	Total	Male	Female			Total	Male	Female	Total	Male	Female	
Total	**Def.**	**891**	**301**	**293**	**8**	**566**	**557**	**9**	**24**	**1,029**	**341**	**328**	**13**	**663**	**651**	**12**	**25**	**1,011**	**389**	**374**	**15**	**598**	**581**	**17**	**24**
	I. M.	**1,504**	**197**	**195**	**2**	**1,254**	**1,239**	**15**	**53**	**1,593**	**174**	**168**	**6**	**1,356**	**1,339**	**17**	**63**	**1,470**	**283**	**279**	**4**	**1,141**	**1,131**	**10**	**46**
BY OFFENSE:																									
Homicide	Def.	656	236	228	8	398	389	9	22	820	296	283	13	502	490	12	22	782	327	313	14	434	420	14	21
	I. M.	108	21	20	1	77	74	3	10	107	14	11	3	77	71	6	16	61	16	15	1	38	37	1	7
Robery	Def.	98	24	24	---	73	73	---	1	78	10	10	---	67	67	---	1	106	19	19	---	87	87	---	---
	I. M.	848	105	104	1	718	712	6	25	932	94	92	2	805	799	6	33	784	151	148	3	610	603	7	23
Assault	Def.	7	4	4	---	3	3	---	---	9	2	2	---	7	7	---	---	3	2	2	---	1	1	---	---
	I. M.	12	2	2	---	9	9	---	1	---	---	---	---	---	---	---	---	---	---	---	---	---	---	---	---
Burglary	Def.	47	20	20	---	26	26	---	1	34	13	13	---	21	21	---	---	32	13	13	---	19	19	---	---
	I. M.	458	64	64	---	383	377	6	11	499	66	65	1	423	418	5	10	564	114	114	---	438	436	2	12
Larceny	Def.	11	2	2	---	9	9	---	---	9	1	1	---	8	8	---	---	21	4	3	1	16	14	2	1
	I. M.	11	1	1	---	10	10	---	---	3	---	---	---	3	3	---	---	2	---	---	---	2	2	---	---
Embezzlement and fraud	Def.	1	---	---	---	1	1	---	---	---	---	---	---	---	---	---	---	---	---	---	---	---	---	---	---
Stolen property	Def.	1	---	---	---	1	1	---	---	1	---	---	---	1	1	---	---	---	---	---	---	---	---	---	---
Forgery	Def.	6	---	---	---	6	6	---	---	13	2	2	---	11	11	---	---	4	---	---	---	4	4	---	---
	I. M.	4	---	---	---	4	4	---	---	---	---	---	---	---	---	---	---	2	---	---	---	2	2	---	---
Rape	Def.	35	14	14	---	21	21	---	---	46	14	14	---	30	30	---	2	43	20	20	---	21	21	---	2
	I. M.	5	---	---	---	2	2	---	3	8	---	---	---	5	5	---	3	47	1	1	---	43	43	---	3
Other sex offenses	Def.	3	---	---	---	3	3	---	---	1	1	1	---	---	---	---	---	3	1	1	---	2	2	---	---
	I. M.	51	3	3	---	45	45	---	3	37	---	---	---	36	36	---	1	4	---	---	---	4	4	---	---
Violating drug laws	Def.	---	---	---	---	---	---	---	---	1	---	---	---	1	1	---	---	1	---	---	---	1	1	---	---
Carrying weapons	Def.	1	---	---	---	1	1	---	---	3	---	---	---	3	3	---	---	1	---	---	---	1	1	---	---
Violating liquor laws	Def.	---	---	---	---	---	---	---	---	1	---	---	---	1	1	---	---	---	---	---	---	---	---	---	---
Other offenses and not reported	Def.	25	1	1	---	24	24	---	---	13	2	2	---	11	11	---	---	15	3	3	---	12	11	1	---
	I. M.	7	1	1	---	6	6	---	---	7	---	---	---	7	7	---	---	6	1	1	---	4	4	---	1
BY AGE:																									
Under 18 years	Def.	16	7	7	---	9	9	---	---	31	12	12	---	18	18	---	1	37	19	19	---	18	18	---	---
	I. M.	60	11	11	---	49	48	1	---	72	12	12	---	60	60	---	---	100	25	24	1	75	75	---	---
18 to 24 years	Def.	220	69	68		146	145	1	5	278	94	89	5	178	177	1	6	272	98	91	7	165	162	3	9
	I. M.	658	87	87	---	553	547	6	18	750	76	74	2	648	642	6	26	671	132	130	2	523	515	8	16
25 to 24 years	Def.	311	128	123	5	175	172	3	8	312	117	113	4	185	182	3	10	364	158	154	4	200	194	6	6
	I. M.	507	65	65	---	416	414	2	26	527	64	62	2	434	427	7	29	456	89	88	1	346	345	1	21
35 to 44 years	Def.	188	64	63	1	118	116	2	6	221	71	70	1	144	141	3	6	174	56	53	3	114	108	6	4
	I. M.	181	20	19	1	156	152	4	5	144	21	19	2	117	115	2	6	167	31	31	---	129	128	1	7
45 years and over [1]	Def.	156	33	32	1	118	115	3	5	187	47	44	3	138	133	5	2	164	58	57	1	101	99	2	5
	I. M.	98	14	13	1	80	78	2	4	100	1	1	---	97	95	2	2	76	6	6	---	68	68	---	2

[1] Includes age not reported.

CHAPTER XX.—AGRICULTURE

Scope.—The statistics presented in this chapter relate only to farm operators. Negroes employed on farms as laborers or wage hands, domestic servants, etc., are not included.

In some of the tables, statistics are presented for farms operated by colored operators. The value of these statistics relating to the aggregate colored, as statistical indicators of conditions and tendencies among Negro farm operators, varies from State to State, as the proportion of colored other than Negro varies in the aggregate of colored farm operators.

However, in the United States as a whole, 96.4 percent of all colored farm operators were Negro in 1930. In the South as a whole and in each Southern State, with the exception of Oklahoma, the colored other than Negro constitute a negligible proportion among colored farm operators. In 1930, Negroes constituted 98.8 percent of all the colored farm operators in the South. In no Southern State, except Oklahoma, was the proportion of Negroes in the aggregate of colored farm operators less than 97 percent.

Statistics in some of the tables relate only to the South. Of all Negro farm operators, 98.7 percent were in the South in 1930.

Number of farm operators.—In 1930, there were 882,850 Negro farm operators in the United States. Negro farm operators constituted 14 percent of all farm operators while the Negro population represented 9.7 percent of the total population. There were Negro farmers in every State and in more than two-thirds of all the counties in 1930. Of the 882,850 Negro farm operators, 98.7 percent were in the South, 1.3 percent in the North, and 0.1 percent in the West.

Between 1920 and 1930, the number of Negro farm operators decreased 4.6 percent. The number of Negro farm operators in the North and West increased but decreased in the South. Within the South itself, there was a decrease of 22.6 percent in the number in the South Atlantic division and increases of 12.4 percent and 4.4 percent in the West South Central and East South Central divisions, respectively.

Farm acreage in 1930.—Negroes operated 3.8 percent of all land in farms in the United States. The acreage in farms operated by Negroes decreased 9.3 percent during the decade, 1920–30. The average acreage per farm operated by Negroes was 42.6 as compared with 176 for white farm operators.

In the South, the acreage in farms operated by Negroes represented 10.7 percent of all land in farms and acreage from which crops were harvested on farms operated by colored operators constituted 18.9 percent of the total crop land from which crops were harvested.

Value of farm land and buildings.—The value of land and buildings for farms operated by Negroes in 1930 was $1,402,945,799. This value was 37.9 percent less than the value reported for farms operated by Negroes in 1920. The average value of land and buildings per farm was $1,589 in 1930 as compared with $2,439 in 1920. The average value per acre of land and buildings on farms operated by Negroes decreased from $54.49 in 1920 to $37.32 in 1930, or a decrease of 31.5 percent. The average value per acre in 1930 was greater in the North and West than in the South.

Value of farm implements and machinery.—The value of implements and machinery on farms operated by Negroes was $60,327,856 or an average of $68 per farm.

Value of farm dwelling.—The value of the dwelling on farms operated by Negroes and for which value of dwelling was reported was less than $500 on 82.9 percent of the farms, between $500 and $999 on 13.7 percent of the farms, and between $1,000 and $1,999 on 2.8 percent of the farms.

Term of occupancy of colored farm operators.—In 1930, of the colored farm operators in the South who reported the number of years they had been operating the farm, 23.6 percent had been on the farm which they were operating less than 1 year; 16.7 percent had been on the farm, 1 year; 22.1 percent, 2 to 4 years; 14.4 percent, 5 to 9 years; and 23.1 percent, 10 years and over.

Farm facilities on farms operated by colored operators.—Telephones were reported on 0.5 percent of all farms operated by colored operatores; electric lights, 0.3 percent; and water piped into dwellings, 0.3 percent, in 1930. There was an average of 4.7 colored farm operators for every automobile reported on farms operated by colored operators in the South in 1930.

Selected farm expenditures on farms operated by colored operators.—In 1930, of all colored operators in the South, 32.3 percent reported expenditures for feed, 18.2 percent reported expenditures for farm labor, 14.1 percent reported expenditures for farm implements and machinery, and 50.7 percent reported expenditures for fertilizer for 1929.

Cooperative sales and purchases on farms operated by colored operators.—In the South, 1.1 percent of the colored farm operators reported sales through farmers' cooperative organizations in 1929. The average sales of products per farm reporting was $674. Approximately 0.6 percent of the colored farm operators in the South reported purchases through farmers' cooperative organizations. The average value of the products purchased was $129.

Livestock on farms operated by colored operators.—In the South, of the farms operated by colored operators 73.9 percent reported horses and/or mules. 47.1 percent reported cattle, and 57.8 percent reported swine in 1930. There were almost three times as many mules as horses on farms of colored operators in the South in 1930. Milk was reported as produced on only 13.1 percent of the farms operated by colored operators in the South.

Production of cotton, tobacco, and other crops on farms operated by colored operators.—In 1929 there was produced on farms operated by colored operators 32.4 percent of the total cotton produced in the South, 24.9 percent of the sweetpotatoes, 18.9 percent of the tobacco produced, 16.4 percent of the total corn harvested for grain, 10.1 percent of Irish potatoes produced, 2.2 percent of the oats threshed for grain, and 1.7 percent wheat threshed. Cotton was reported as produced on 83.5 percent of all the farms operated by colored operators in the South, corn for grain on 78.8 percent, sweetpotatoes and yams on 34.2 percent, wheat on 3.5 percent, Irish potatoes on 16.5 percent, tobacco on 8 percent, and oats threshed on 0.8 percent.

Number of farms by type.—Type of farm was based on sources of income. Value of products from a particular source in relation to the value of products from all sources was a primary basis used in classifying farms by types. "Source" relates to the product or products from which the income is derived, resulting, in certain cases, from the sale of the single product or, in other cases, from the sale of a group of products. Products used on the farm itself are not included except those which are used by the family of the farm operator. The total value of all farm products includes the value of crops, livestock and livestock products, sold or traded, forest products sold, and the value of the products used by the operator's family; but excludes receipts from boarders, lodgers, campers, etc.

For each of the types shown, sales or anticipated sales of the following products, or groups of products, had to represent 40 percent or more of the total value of all products of the farm in order to be so classified.

Cash grain.—Corn, wheat, oats, barley, flax, rye, emmer and spelt, buckwheat, rice, and grain sorghum.

Cotton.—Cotton (lint) and cottonseed.

Crop specialty.—Sweet sorghum for sirup, sugarcane, sugar beets, maple sugar and sirup, soybeans, cowpeas, velvet beans, ripe field peas and beans, tobacco, hay, peanuts, potatoes (Irish or white), sweetpotatoes, mushrooms, hops, broomcorn, and other field crops.

Fruit.—Small fruits, tree fruits, nuts, and grapes.

Truck.—All vegetables sold.

Dairy.—Milk, cream, butterfat, butter, and dairy cows and calves.

Poultry.—Chickens, ducks, geese, turkeys, and eggs.

Animal specialty and stock ranch.—All classes of meat animals, such as beef cattle, sheep, and hogs; also wool, mohair, and slaughtered animals.

The chief distinction between "stock-ranch" and "animal-specialty" farms lies in the ratio of the pasture land to the crop land.

General.—Farms were classified as "general" where the value of products from any one source did not represent as much as 40 percent of the total value of all products of the farm. If the value of products from each of two sources represented 40 percent or more of the total, the farm was classified as "general" except for specialized combination types, such as cotton-tobacco, fruit-truck, dairy-poultry, and other similar combinations, when it was classified as one or the other of these types, depending upon which was dominant in the locality.

Self-sufficing.—Where the value of the farm products used by the family was 50 percent or more of the total value of all products of the farm, it was classified as "self-sufficing."

Abnormal farms.—This type includes five subtypes:

1. Institutions or country estate.
   Institution.—Farms operated by public or semi-public agency.
   Country estate.—Farms over 10 acres in size, on which the value of residence was $25,000 or more.
2. *Part-time.*—Farms on which the value of products did not exceed $750 and the operator spent 150 days or more at work not connected with the farm or reported an occupation other than farming.
3. *Boarding and lodging.*—Farms on which receipts from boarders and lodgers represented 50 percent or more of the value of farm products.
4. *Forest products.*—Farms on which the value of forest products represented 50 percent or more of the value of all farm products.
5. Horse farms, feed lots, and livestock dealers.

More than three-quarters of the farms operated by Negroes in 1930 were classified as cotton farms, 7.5 percent as crop specialty (mostly tobacco farms), and 7.3 percent as abnormal farms (mostly part-time farms).

Value of all farm products.—Value of all farm products includes the value of crops sold or traded, the value of livestock sold or traded, the value of livestock products sold or traded, the value of forest products sold, and the value of farm products used by the family of the farm operator.

The total value of farm products on farms operated by Negroes in the South, was $646,641,216, in 1929, or an average value of $732 per farm. Since a large portion of the farms operated by Negroes was rented, only a part of the value of all farm products produced on farms operated by Negroes was received by Negroes. Of the total value of all farm products, 78.7 percent was derived from crops sold and traded, 16.6 percent was derived from products used by family of the farm operator, 2.4 percent from the value of livestock products sold or traded, 1.6 percent from the value of livestock sold or traded, and 0.6 percent from the value of forest products sold.

Tenure.—Farm operators are classified, according to the tenure under which they operate their farms, into four general classes, as follows:

Full owners.—Farm operators who own all the land which they operate.
Part owners.—Farm operators who own part of the land which they operate, and rent and operate additional land.
Managers.—Farm operators who operate farms or ranches for the owners, receiving wages or salaries for their services.
Tenants.—Farm operators who operate hired land only. In this report separate figures are shown for three classes of tenants, namely, (1) cash tenants who pay a cash rental, as $7 per acre for crop land or $500 for the use of the whole farm; (2) croppers who are defined as share tenants, to whom landlords furnish all the work animals; and (3) all other tenants, including those giving a share of the products for the use of the land or a share for part and cash for part.

Number of farms by tenure.—Of the total Negro farm operators in the United States in 1930, 15.8 percent were owners, 4.7 percent part owners, 11.1 percent cash tenants, 44.7 percent croppers, 23.5 percent other tenants, and 0.1 percent managers. Over 79 percent of the Negro farm operators were tenants in 1930. In the South, more than two-fifths of the Negro farm operators were croppers.

Farm acreage by tenure.—In the South in 1930, the average size of farms operated by colored full owners was 64.1 acres; by colored part owners, 59.5 acres; by colored cash tenants, 41.8 acres; and by colored other tenants, 36.6 acres. The average acreage from which crops were harvested in 1929 was for colored full owners, 21.4 acres; for colored part owners, 26.8 acres; colored cash tenants, 23.5 acres; and colored other tenants, 23.7 acres.

Term of occupancy of colored farm operators by tenure.—Of the 174,626 colored owners and managers reporting years on the farm in the South, 4.2 percent reported occupancy of less than 1 year, 4.7 percent occupancy of 1 year, 11.8 percent occupancy of 2 to 4 years, 15.5 percent occupancy of 5 to 9 years, and 63.7 percent occupancy of 10 years and over. In 1930, of the colored tenants, 28.6 percent reported occupancy of less than 1 year, 19.8 percent occupancy of 1 year, 24.8 percent occupancy of 2 to 4 years, 14.2 percent occupancy of 5 to 9 years, and 12.7 percent occupancy of 10 years and over.

Value of land and buildings, and farm implements and machinery, by tenure.—The average value in the United States of farms operated by Negro owners was $1,848, and by Negro tenants, $1,503 in 1930. The average value per acre was, for Negro owners, $29.86; and for Negro tenants, $40.29. The average value of implements and machinery on farms operated by Negro owners was $109 and by Negro tenants, $57.

Mortgage indebtedness on farms owned by colored operators.—Of the 140,496 farms operated by colored full owners in the South in 1930, 60.4 percent were reported as free from farm mortgage debt, 29.9 percent were reported as mortgaged, and for 9.7 percent there was no report as to mortgage status. The farms operated by full owners on which mortgage debt was reported were larger in size, and had a greater value of land and buildings than those operated by full owners, reported free from mortgage debt.

The average charges (interest, commissions, bonuses, and premiums charged) were $62 per farm in 1929 and the ratio of such charges to the mortgage debt was 7.3 percent. The average amount of debt per farm was $844 and the owner's equity averaged $1,449 in 1930.

Crops by tenure of colored farm operators.—In 1929, 28.6 percent of the cotton crop of the South was produced on farms operated by colored tenants and 3.8 percent on farms operated by colored owners. Over 17.6 percent of the total sweetpotato and yam crop of the South in 1929 was produced on farms operated by colored tenants and over 7.2 percent on farms operated by colored owners. Almost 15 percent of the tobacco crop produced in the South in 1929 was produced on farms operated by colored tenants and 4 percent was produced on farms operated by colored owners. Of the total amount of corn harvested for grain in the South in 1929, 12.3 percent was produced on farms operated by colored tenants and 4.1 percent on farms operated by colored owners.

Negro farmers constitute a national asset.—The data presented in this chapter conclusively show that as farm owners, tenants, and managers, Negroes constitute an appreciable but diminishing national asset. While Negro farmers, like those of most racial groups, materially decreased in number during the decade 1920 to 1930, their fields of operation have been widely extended throughout the States. The figures further show that 20 years (1910 to 1930) of migration from the rural districts, particularly of the South, has not increased the number of Negro farmers in the North; has reduced the number in the South, and has increased only to a small extent the number in the West.

Ten years' losses.—As reported at the Census of 1920 there were 925,708 Negro farmers operating 41,432,182 acres, with land and buildings valued at $2,257,645,325, and a 23.6 percent ownership consisting of 218,612 farms, 13,948,512 acres, with land and buildings valued at $554,158,003. As reported 10 years later, at the Census of 1930, the number of Negro farm operators had decreased to 882,850; their land in farms to 37,597,132 acres; the value of the land and buildings to $1,402,945,799. Their ownership had dropped to 20.5 percent; farms owned decreased to 181,016, and the value of their owned land and buildings fell to $334,451,396.

Improved agricultural credit system encourages ownership.—The acreage loss of Negro farm owners during the 10 years, 1920 to 1930, was most significant. Their loss of 2,749,619 acres was equivalent to 4,296 square miles, or an area more than twice that of the combined area of Delaware and the District of Columbia. Due, however, to a reorganized and greatly improved governmental agricultural credit system with a more comprehensive and liberal administrative policy, and to the further fact that slightly in excess of 28 percent of the colored owners in the South were under 45 years of age, and 58 percent under 55 years, increases in the number of Negro farm owners and in owned acreage is now a possibility.

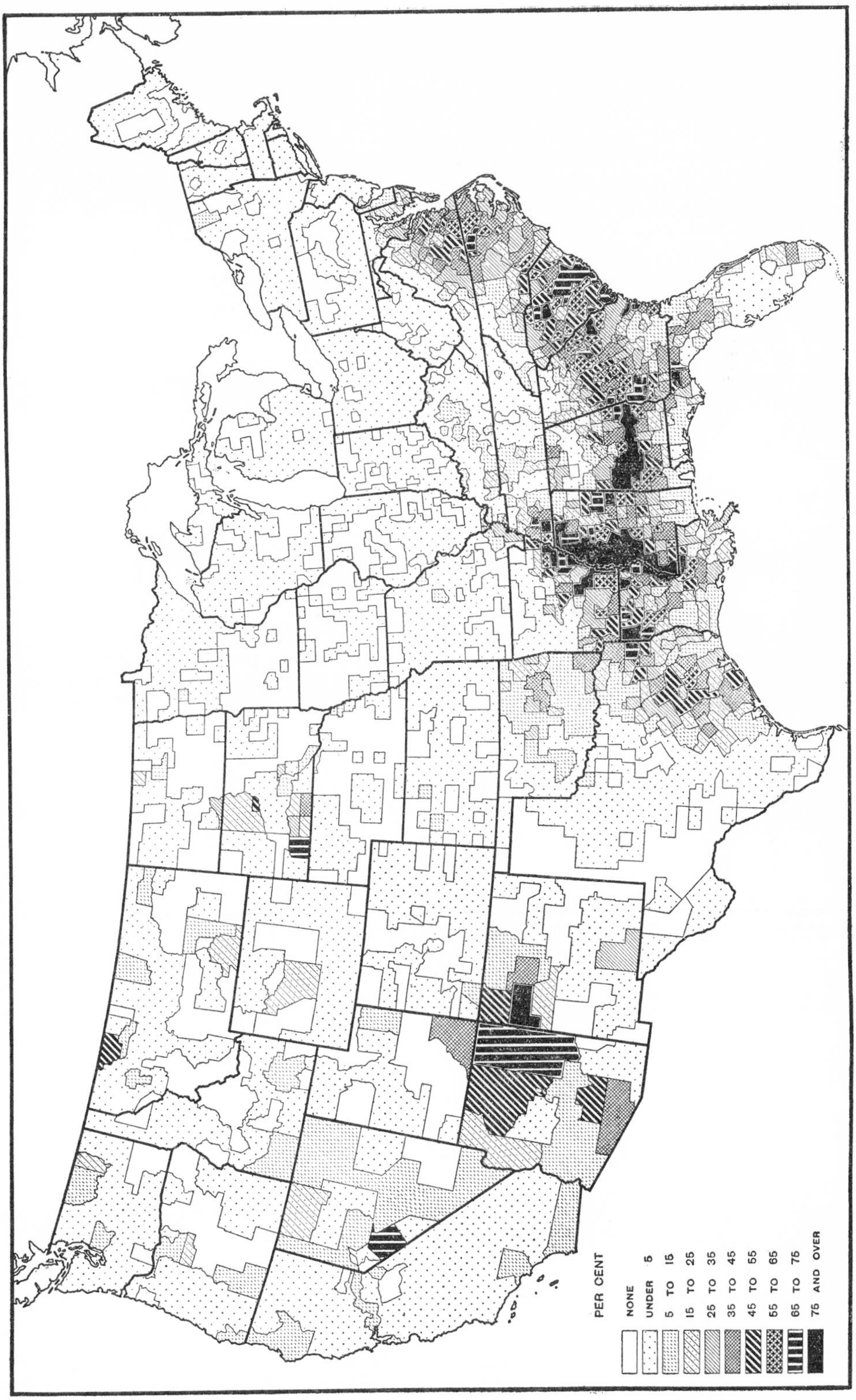

PERCENTAGE OF ALL FARMS OPERATED BY COLORED FARMERS, BY COUNTIES: 1930

Number of Farms, Percent Distribution, by Color of Operator, by States: 1930 and 1920

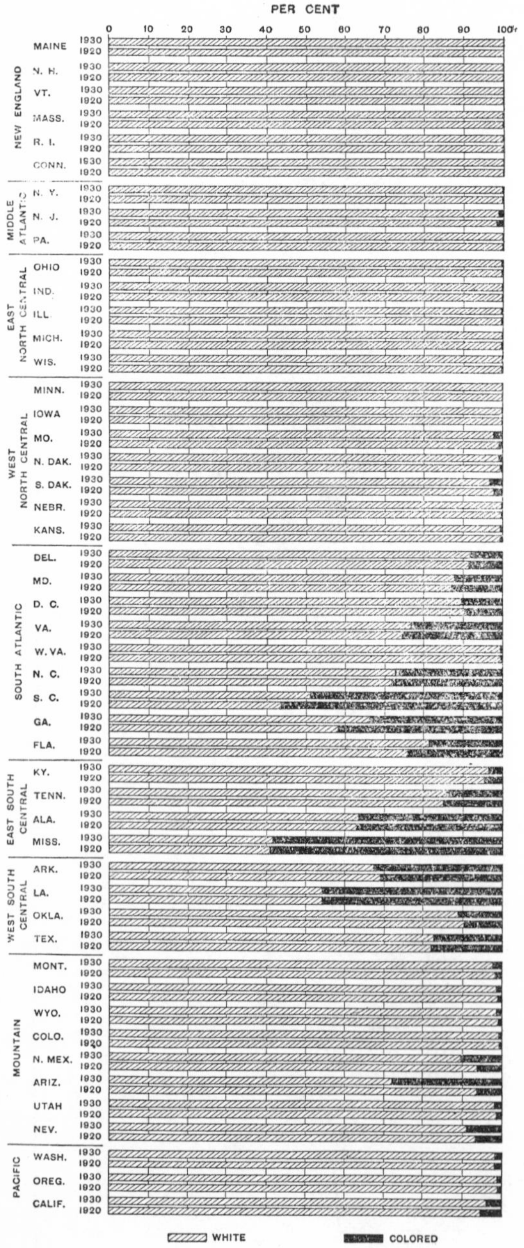

All Land in Farms, Percent Distribution, by Color of Operator, by States: 1930 and 1920

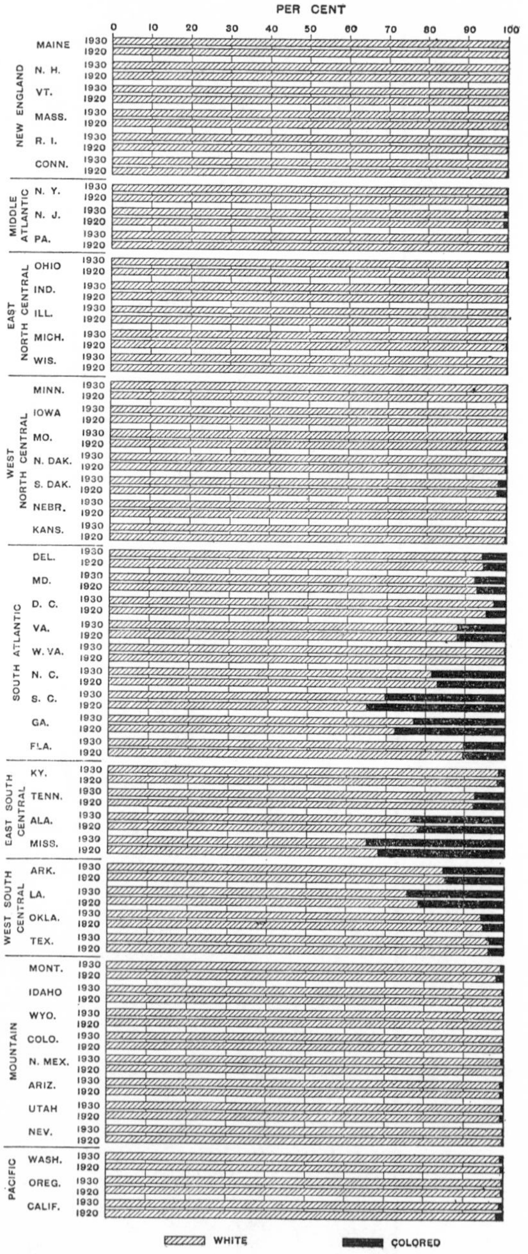

PERCENTAGE OF TOTAL NUMBER OF FARMS OPERATED BY NEGRO FARMERS, BY STATES: 1930

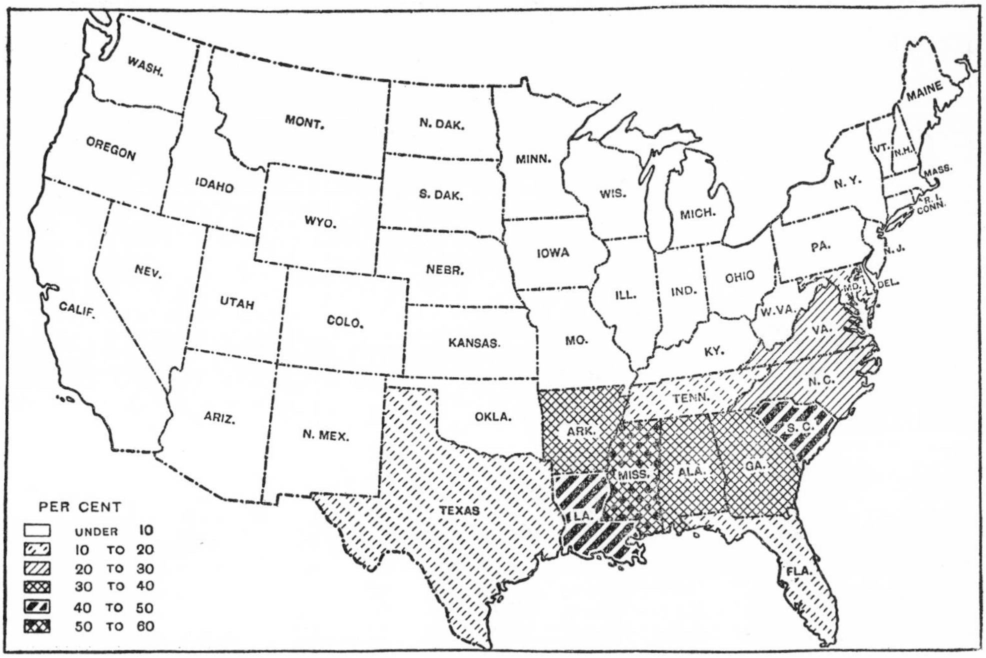

PERCENTAGE OF ALL LAND IN FARMS OPERATED BY NEGRO FARMERS, BY STATES: 1930

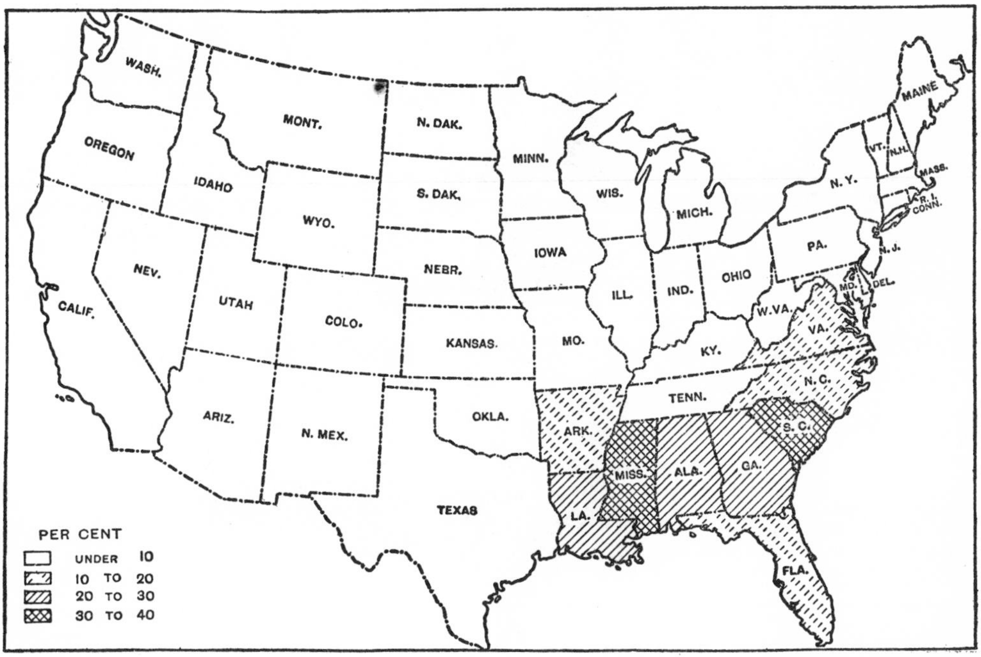

Percentage Negro Owners Are of All Negro Farm Operators (Southern States Only): 1930

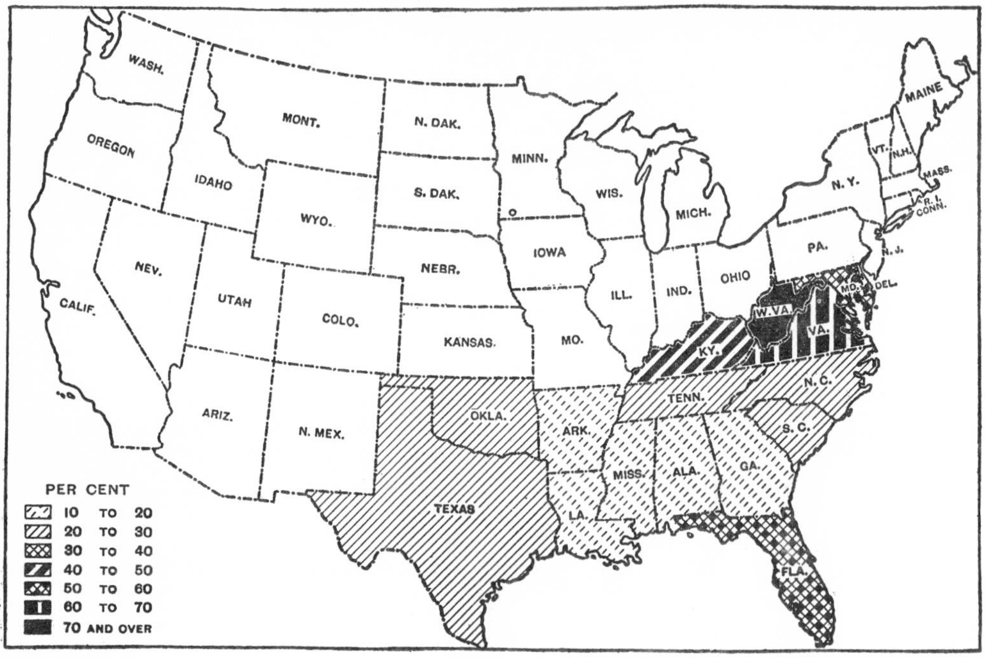

Percentage Negro Tenants Are of All Negro Farm Operators, By States: 1930

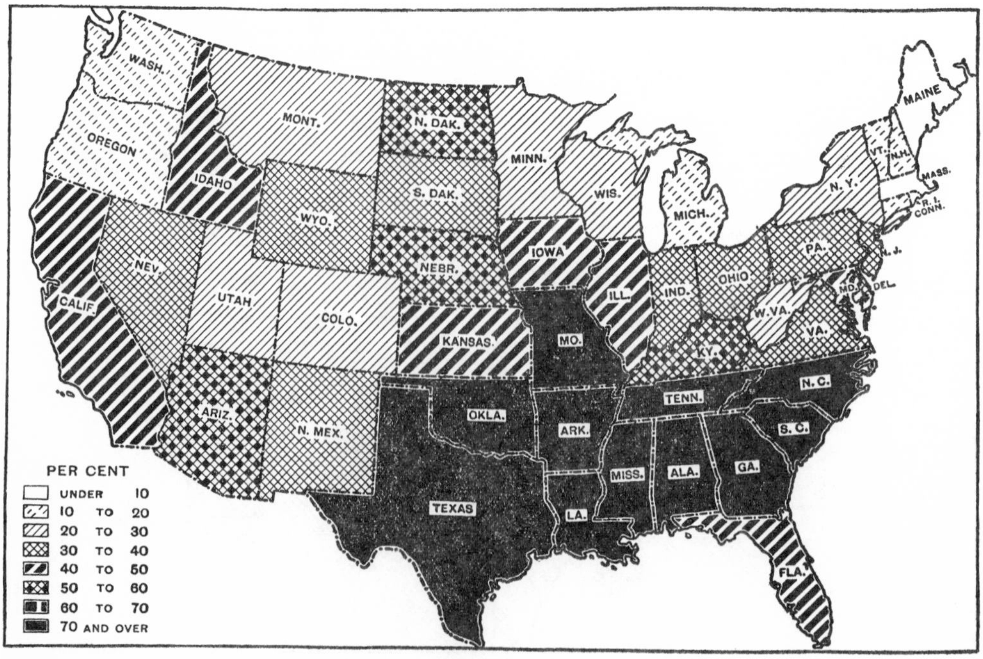

TABLE 1.—TOTAL NEGRO POPULATION, WITH PERCENTAGES, BY SECTIONS: 1930 AND 1920

SECTION	1930	1920	INCREASE, 1920–30	
			Number	Percent
United States	**11, 891, 143**	**10, 463, 131**	**1, 428, 012**	**13. 6**
The South	9, 361, 577	8, 912, 231	449, 346	5. 0
The North	2, 409, 219	1, 472, 309	936, 910	63. 6
The West	120, 347	78, 591	41, 756	53. 1
	PERCENT DISTRIBUTION			
United States	**100. 0**	**100. 0**	**100. 0**	--------
The South	78. 7	85. 2	31. 5	--------
The North	20. 3	14. 1	65. 6	--------
The West	1. 0	. 8	2. 9	--------

TABLE 2.—NEGRO RURAL POPULATION, BY SECTIONS: 1930 AND 1920

SECTION	1930	1920	INCREASE OR DECREASE (−) 1920–30	
			Number	Percent
	RURAL POPULATION			
United States	**6, 697, 230**	**6, 903, 658**	**−206, 428**	**−3. 0**
The South	6, 395, 252	6, 661, 262	−266, 010	−4. 0
The North	280, 890	221, 997	58, 893	26. 5
The West	21, 088	20, 399	689	3. 4
	RURAL FARM			
United States	**4, 680, 523**	**5, 099, 963**	**−419, 440**	**−8. 2**
The South	4, 608, 786	5, 034, 343	−425, 557	−8. 5
The North	65, 601	61, 865	3, 736	6. 0
The West	6, 136	3, 755	2, 381	63. 4
	RURAL NONFARM			
United States	**2, 016, 707**	**1, 803, 695**	**213, 012**	**11. 8**
The South	1, 786, 466	1, 626, 919	159, 547	9. 8
The North	215, 289	160, 132	55, 157	34. 4
The West	14, 952	16, 644	−1, 692	−10. 2

TABLE 3.—POPULATION AND FARM OPERATORS, BY RACIAL CLASSES, FOR THE UNITED STATES: 1930 AND 1920

RACIAL CLASS	POPULATION		FARM OPERATORS	
	1930	1920	1930	1920
	NUMBER			
All classes	**122, 770, 046**	**105, 710, 620**	**6, 288, 648**	**6,448,343**
Negro	11, 891, 143	10, 463, 131	882, 850	925, 708
White [1]	110, 289, 870	94, 823, 422	5, 372, 578	5, 498, 454
Indian	332, 397	244, 437	26, 817	16, 680
Japanese	138, 834	111, 010	5, 840	6, 892
Chinese	74, 954	61, 639	476	609
All other nonwhite	47, 848	6, 981	87	----------
	PERCENT DISTRIBUTION			
All classes	**100. 0**	**100. 0**	**100. 0**	**100. 0**
Negro	9. 7	9. 9	14. 0	14. 4
White [1]	89. 8	89. 7	85. 4	85. 3
Indian	. 3	. 2	. 4	. 3
Japanese	. 1	. 1	. 1	. 1
Chinese	. 1	. 1	(2)	(2)
All other nonwhite	(2)	(2)	(2)	----------

[1] Iucludes Mexicans and Hindus.
[2] Less than 1/10 of 1 percent.

TABLE 4.—INCREASE IN POPULATION AND NUMBER OF FARM OPERATORS, BY RACIAL CLASSES, WITH NUMBER OF OPERATORS PER 1,000 POPULATION OF EACH CLASS, FOR THE UNITED STATES: 1930 AND 1920

RACIAL CLASS	INCREASE OR DECREASE (−) 1920–30				FARM OPERATORS PER 1,000 POPULATION	
	Number		Percent			
	Population	Farm operators	Population	Farm operators	1930	1920
All classes	**17, 064, 426**	**−159, 695**	**16. 1**	**−2. 5**	**51**	**61**
Negro	1, 428, 012	−42, 858	13. 6	−4. 6	74	88
White [1]	15, 466, 448	−125, 876	16. 3	−2. 3	49	58
Indian	87, 960	10, 137	36. 0	60. 8	81	68
Japanese	27, 824	−1, 052	25. 1	−15. 3	42	62
Chinese	13, 315	−133	21. 6	−21. 8	6	10
All other nonwhite	40, 867	87	585. 4	--------	2	--------

[1] Includes Mexicans and Hindus.

TABLE 5.—NUMBER OF COUNTIES REPORTING NEGRO INHABITANTS AND NEGRO FARMERS, BY STATES: 1930

STATE	Total number of counties	COUNTIES REPORTING	
		Negro inhabitants	Negro farmers
United States	**[1] 3, 100**	**2, 855**	**2, 119**
Alabama	67	67	66
Arizona	14	13	9
Arkansas	75	72	63
California	58	57	36
Colorado	63	54	20
Connecticut	8	8	8
Delaware	3	3	3
District of Columbia	1	1	1
Florida	67	67	65
Georgia	161	160	158
Idaho	44	30	9
Illinois	102	96	60
Indiana	92	86	60
Iowa	99	87	32
Kansas	105	99	78
Kentucky	120	120	114
Louisiana	64	64	64
Maine	16	16	8
Maryland	24	24	22
Massachusetts	14	14	11
Michigan	83	76	56
Minnesota	87	71	18
Mississippi	82	82	82
Missouri	115	103	83
Montana	56	45	14
Nebraska	93	65	21
Nevada	17	15	3
New Hampshire	10	10	5
New Jersey	21	21	18
New Mexico	31	28	9
New York	62	62	44
North Carolina	100	100	99
North Dakota	53	33	10
Ohio	88	87	82
Oklahoma	77	73	71
Oregon	36	32	6
Pennsylvania	67	66	44
Rhode Island	5	5	4
South Carolina	46	46	46
South Dakota	69	45	23
Tennessee	95	95	92
Texas	254	243	189
Utah	29	13	2
Vermont	14	13	11
Virginia	124	124	106
Washington	39	33	20
West Virginia	55	54	39
Wisconsin	71	55	27
Wyoming	24	22	8

[1] Includes Baltimore city, St. Louis city, 24 independent cities in Virginia, and that part of Yellowstone National Park located in Wyoming.

TABLE 6.—NUMBER OF FARMS AND FARM ACREAGE OF NEGRO AND WHITE OPERATORS, BY SECTIONS, AND SOUTHERN DIVISIONS: 1930 AND 1920

SECTION AND DIVISION	NEGRO 1930	NEGRO 1920	WHITE[1] 1930	WHITE[1] 1920
	NUMBER OF FARMS			
United States	**882,850**	**925,708**	**5,372,578**	**5,498,454**
THE SOUTH	870,936	915,595	2,342,129	2,283,750
South Atlantic	295,934	382,278	760,089	775,144
East South Central	320,600	307,006	741,255	744,368
West South Central	254,402	226,311	840,785	764,238
THE NORTH	11,104	9,380	2,545,829	2,750,203
THE WEST	810	733	484,620	464,501
	PERCENT DISTRIBUTION			
United States	**100.0**	**100.0**	**100.0**	**100.0**
THE SOUTH	98.7	98.9	43.6	41.5
South Atlantic	33.5	41.3	14.1	14.1
East South Central	36.3	33.2	13.8	13.5
West South Central	28.8	24.4	15.6	13.9
THE NORTH	1.3	1.0	47.4	50.0
THE WEST	.1	.1	9.0	8.4
	LAND IN FARMS (*acres*)			
United States	**37,597,132**	**41,432,182**	**945,683,034**	**910,939,194**
THE SOUTH	36,758,484	40,544,241	305,280,653	308,803,337
South Atlantic	14,550,451	18,151,071	71,704,181	79,550,302
East South Central	11,918,057	12,104,977	60,886,302	66,783,791
West South Central	10,289,976	10,288,193	172,690,170	162,469,244
THE NORTH	720,872	767,953	423,963,841	430,365,628
THE WEST	117,776	119,988	216,438,540	171,770,229
	PERCENT DISTRIBUTION			
United States	**100.0**	**100.0**	**100.0**	**100.0**
THE SOUTH	97.8	97.9	32.3	33.9
South Atlantic	38.7	43.8	7.6	8.7
East South Central	31.7	29.2	6.4	7.3
West South Central	27.4	24.8	18.3	17.8
THE NORTH	1.9	1.9	44.8	47.2
THE WEST	.3	.3	22.9	18.9

[1] Includes Mexicans and Hindus.

TABLE 7.—INCREASE IN NUMBER OF NEGRO AND WHITE FARM OPERATORS, 1920 TO 1930, WITH NUMBER OF OPERATORS PER 1,000 POPULATION, BY SECTIONS, AND SOUTHERN DIVISIONS: 1930 AND 1920

SECTION AND DIVISION	INCREASE OR DECREASE (−) 1920–30: Farm operators, Negro	Farm operators, White[1]	Percent, Negro	Percent, White[1]	FARM OPERATORS PER 1,000 POPULATION: Negro 1930	Negro 1920	White[1] 1930	White[1] 1920
United States	**−42,858**	**−125,876**	**−4.6**	**−2.3**	**74**	**88**	**49**	**58**
THE SOUTH	−44,659	58,379	−4.9	2.6	93	103	85	95
South Atlantic	−86,344	−15,055	−22.6	−1.9	67	88	67	80
East South Central	13,594	−3,113	4.4	−.4	121	122	103	117
West South Central	28,091	76,547	12.4	10.0	111	110	92	94
THE NORTH	1,724	−204,374	18.4	−7.4	5	6	36	44
THE WEST	77	20,119	10.5	4.3	7	9	45	54

[1] Includes Mexicans and Hindus.

TABLE 8.—ALL LAND IN FARMS, BY SECTIONS AND SOUTHERN DIVISIONS: 1930 AND 1920

SECTION AND DIVISION	LAND IN FARMS (ACRES) 1930	LAND IN FARMS (ACRES) 1920	INCREASE OR DECREASE (−) Acres	INCREASE OR DECREASE (−) Per-cent	PERCENT DISTRIBUTION 1930	PERCENT DISTRIBUTION 1920
	TOTAL					
United States	**986,771,016**	**955,883,715**	**30,887,301**	**3.2**	**100.0**	**100.0**
THE SOUTH	343,086,418	350,121,833	−7,035,415	−2.0	34.8	36.6
South Atlantic	86,362,715	97,775,243	−11,412,528	−11.7	8.8	10.2
East South Central	72,817,357	78,897,463	−6,080,106	−7.7	7.4	8.3
West South Central	183,906,346	173,449,127	10,457,219	6.0	18.6	18.1
THE NORTH	425,709,428	432,271,951	−6,562,523	−1.5	43.1	45.2
THE WEST	217,975,170	173,489,931	44,485,239	25.6	22.1	18.1
	NEGRO					
United States	**37,597,132**	**41,432,182**	**−3,835,050**	**−9.3**	**100.0**	**100.0**
THE SOUTH	36,758,484	40,544,241	−3,785,757	−9.3	97.8	97.9
South Atlantic	14,550,451	18,151,071	−3,600,620	−19.8	38.7	43.8
East South Central	11,918,057	12,104,977	−186,920	−1.5	31.7	29.2
West South Central	10,289,976	10,288,193	1,783	([1])	27.4	24.8
THE NORTH	720,872	767,953	−47,081	−6.1	1.9	1.9
THE WEST	117,776	119,988	−2,212	−1.8	.3	.3

[1] Less than 1/10 of 1 percent.

TABLE 9.—AVERAGE ACREAGE PER FARM OF NEGRO AND WHITE OPERATORS, BY SECTIONS, SOUTHERN DIVISIONS, AND STATES: 1930 AND 1920

SECTION, DIVISION, AND STATE	AVERAGE ACREAGE PER FARM OPERATED BY— Negroes 1930	Negroes 1920	Negroes Increase or decrease (−)	White[1] 1930	White[1] 1920	White[1] Increase or decrease (−)
United States	**42.6**	**44.8**	**−2.2**	**176.0**	**165.7**	**10.3**
THE SOUTH	42.2	44.3	−2.1	130.3	135.2	−4.9
South Atlantic	49.2	47.5	1.7	94.3	102.6	−8.3
East South Central	37.2	39.4	−2.2	82.1	89.7	−7.6
West South Central	40.4	45.5	−5.1	205.4	212.6	−7.2
THE NORTH	64.9	81.9	−17.0	166.5	156.5	10.0
THE WEST	145.4	163.7	−18.3	446.6	369.8	76.8
THE SOUTH						
SOUTH ATLANTIC:						
Delaware	67.9	62.9	5.0	95.1	96.0	−0.9
Maryland	65.6	56.6	9.0	106.2	105.7	.5
District of Columbia	8.6	14.4	−5.8	32.0	29.2	2.8
Virginia	51.5	47.3	4.2	112.1	117.7	−5.6
West Virginia	57.2	54.7	2.5	106.8	110.0	−3.2
North Carolina	44.2	45.0	−.8	72.3	85.7	−13.4
South Carolina	41.0	40.2	.8	89.7	96.2	−6.5
Georgia	58.8	54.3	4.5	100.6	101.7	−1.1
Florida	46.7	49.2	−2.5	94.1	131.8	−37.7
EAST SOUTH CENTRAL:						
Kentucky	37.5	33.8	3.7	82.5	82.1	.4
Tennessee	38.6	39.9	−1.3	79.1	83.8	−4.7
Alabama	44.3	45.7	−1.4	81.9	94.6	−12.7
Mississippi	33.2	36.1	−2.9	86.8	111.7	−24.9
WEST SOUTH CENTRAL:						
Arkansas	31.2	36.3	−5.1	83.3	92.5	−9.2
Louisiana	31.4	35.2	−3.8	80.3	106.8	−26.5
Oklahoma	70.0	78.0	−8.0	175.9	174.5	1.4
Texas	51.5	56.5	−5.0	293.7	306.7	−13.0

[1] Includes Mexicans and Hindus.

TABLE 10.—PERCENT DISTRIBUTION BY TYPE OF FARM OPERATED BY NEGROES, BY SECTIONS, AND SOUTHERN DIVISIONS: 1930

SECTION AND DIVISION	Total number of farms	PERCENT OF TOTAL REPORTED AS— Cotton	Crop specialty	Abnormal	Self sufficing	General	All other
United States	**882, 850**	**75. 4**	**7. 5**	**7. 3**	**4. 9**	**3. 0**	**2. 0**
THE SOUTH	870, 936	75. 9	7. 6	7. 1	4. 8	2. 9	1. 7
South Atlantic	295, 934	55. 4	19. 2	10. 1	8. 1	4. 8	2. 3
East South Central	320, 600	85. 5	2. 3	5. 2	3. 6	2. 1	1. 3
West South Central	254, 402	87. 8	. 6	6. 1	2. 4	1. 7	1. 4
THE NORTH	11, 104	32. 4	2. 3	16. 7	11. 4	14. 3	23. 0
New England	148	------	3. 4	31. 1	14. 2	9. 5	41. 9
Middle Atlantic	873	------	3. 7	27. 9	9. 2	15. 6	43. 6
East North Central	3, 065	2. 3	4. 1	22. 5	16. 8	24. 3	29. 9
West North Central	7, 018	50. 2	1. 3	12. 4	9. 2	9. 8	17. 0
THE WEST	810	26. 4	6. 3	28. 6	4. 7	6. 8	27. 2
Mountain	304	32. 6	7. 2	26. 3	5. 6	10. 2	18. 1
Pacific	506	22. 7	5. 7	30. 0	4. 2	4. 7	32. 6

TABLE 11.—NUMBER OF ACRES IN FARMS OPERATED BY NEGRO FARMERS, BY TENURE, BY SECTIONS: 1930 AND 1920

TENURE	ACRES IN FARMS 1930	ACRES IN FARMS 1920	INCREASE OR DECREASE (—) Number	INCREASE OR DECREASE (—) Percent	PERCENT DISTRIBUTION 1930	PERCENT DISTRIBUTION 1920
	United States					
Total	**37, 597, 132**	**41, 432, 182**	**−3, 835, 050**	**−9. 3**	**100. 0**	**100. 0**
Owners	11, 198, 893	13, 948, 512	−2, 749, 619	−19. 7	29. 8	33. 7
Tenants	26, 149, 167	27, 077, 582	−928, 415	−3. 4	69. 6	65. 4
Managers	249, 072	406, 088	−157, 016	−38. 7	. 7	1. 0
	THE SOUTH					
Total	36, 758, 484	40, 544, 241	−3, 785, 757	−9. 3	100. 0	100. 0
Owners	10, 785, 312	13, 434, 106	−2, 648, 794	−19. 7	29. 3	33. 1
Tenants	25, 743, 234	26, 754, 386	−1, 011, 152	−3. 8	70. 0	66. 0
Managers	229, 938	355, 749	−125, 811	−35. 4	. 6	. 9
	THE NORTH					
Total	720, 872	767, 953	−47, 081	−6. 1	100. 0	100. 0
Owners	332, 520	435, 075	−102, 555	−23. 6	46. 1	56. 7
Tenants	373, 214	294, 543	78, 671	26. 7	51. 8	38. 4
Managers	15, 138	38, 335	−23, 197	−60. 5	2. 1	5. 0
	THE WEST					
Total	117, 776	119, 988	−2, 212	−1. 8	100. 0	100. 0
Owners	81, 061	79, 331	1, 730	2. 2	68. 8	66. 1
Tenants	32, 719	28, 653	4, 066	14. 2	27. 8	23. 9
Managers	3, 996	12, 004	−8, 008	−66. 7	3. 4	10. 0

TABLE 12.—NUMBER OF FARM OPERATORS, BY COLOR, AND TENURE, BY SECTIONS: 1930

TENURE	NUMBER Total	NUMBER Colored Negro	NUMBER Colored Indian	NUMBER Colored Other [1]	NUMBER White [2]	PERCENT DISTRIBUTION Colored Negro	PERCENT DISTRIBUTION Colored Indian	PERCENT DISTRIBUTION Colored Other [1]	PERCENT DISTRIBUTION White [2]
	United States								
Total	**6, 288, 648**	**882, 850**	**26, 817**	**6, 403**	**5, 372, 578**	**100. 0**	**100. 0**	**100. 0**	**100. 0**
Owners	3, 568, 394	181, 016	20, 658	1, 046	3, 365, 674	20. 5	77. 0	16. 3	62. 6
Tenants	2, 664, 365	700, 911	6, 091	3, 226	1, 954, 137	79. 4	22. 7	50. 4	36. 4
Managers	55, 889	923	68	2, 131	52, 767	. 1	. 3	33. 3	1. 0
	THE SOUTH								
Total	3, 223, 816	870, 936	10, 637	114	2, 342, 129	100. 0	100. 0	100. 0	100. 0
Owners	1, 415, 675	176, 130	5, 850	39	1, 233, 656	20. 2	55. 0	34. 2	52. 7
Tenants	1, 790, 783	694, 001	4, 766	72	1, 091, 944	79. 7	44. 8	63. 2	46. 6
Managers	17, 358	805	21	3	16, 529	. 1	. 2	2. 6	. 7
	THE NORTH								
Total	2, 561, 785	11, 104	4, 753	99	2, 545, 829	100. 0	100. 0	100. 0	100. 0
Owners	1, 768, 206	4, 424	3, 929	35	1, 759, 818	39. 8	82. 7	35. 4	69. 1
Tenants	768, 486	6, 588	807	64	761, 027	59. 3	17. 0	64. 6	29. 9
Managers	25, 093	92	17	------	24, 984	. 8	. 4	------	1. 0
	THE WEST								
Total	503, 047	810	11, 427	6, 190	484, 620	100. 0	100. 0	100. 0	100. 0
Owners	384, 513	462	10, 879	972	372, 200	57. 0	95. 2	15. 7	76. 8
Tenants	105, 096	322	518	3, 090	101, 166	39. 8	4. 5	49. 9	20. 9
Managers	13, 438	26	30	2, 128	11, 254	3. 2	. 3	34. 4	2. 3

[1] Includes 5,840 Japanese, 476 Chinese, 56 Filipinos, 30 Koreans, and 1 Hawaiian.
[2] Includes Mexicans and Hindus.

TABLE 13.—NUMBER OF NEGRO OPERATORS BY TENURE, BY SECTIONS: 1930, 1920, AND 1910

TENURE	NUMBER OF FARM OPERATORS 1930	1920	1910	INCREASE OR DECREASE (—) 1920–30 Number	1920–30 Percent	1910–20 Number	1910–20 Percent	PERCENT DISTRIBUTION 1930	1920	1910
	United States									
Total	**882, 850**	**925, 708**	**893, 370**	**−42, 858**	**−4. 6**	**32, 338**	**3. 6**	**100. 0**	**100. 0**	**100.0**
Owners	181, 016	218, 612	218, 972	−37, 596	−17. 2	−360	−. 2	20. 5	23. 6	24. 5
Tenants	700, 911	705, 070	672, 964	−4, 159	−. 6	32, 106	4. 8	79. 4	76. 2	75. 3
Managers	923	2, 026	1, 434	−1, 103	−54. 4	592	41. 3	. 1	. 2	. 2
	THE SOUTH									
Total	870, 936	915, 595	880, 836	−44, 659	−4. 9	34, 759	3. 9	100. 0	100. 0	100.0
Owners	176, 130	212, 365	211, 087	−36, 235	−17. 1	1, 278	. 6	20. 2	23. 2	24. 0
Tenants	694, 001	701, 471	668, 559	−7, 470	−1. 1	32, 912	4. 9	79. 7	76. 6	75. 9
Managers	805	1, 759	1, 190	−954	−54. 2	569	47. 8	. 1	. 2	. 1
	THE NORTH									
Total	11, 104	9, 380	12, 052	1, 724	18. 4	−2, 672	−22. 2	100. 0	100. 0	100.0
Owners	4, 424	5, 749	7, 498	−1, 325	−23. 0	−1, 749	−23. 3	39. 8	61. 3	62. 2
Tenants	6, 588	3, 389	4, 330	3, 199	94. 4	−941	−21. 7	59. 3	36. 1	35. 9
Managers	92	242	224	−150	−62. 0	18	8. 0	. 8	2. 6	1. 9
	THE WEST									
Total	810	733	482	77	10. 5	251	52. 1	100. 0	100. 0	100.0
Owners	462	498	387	−36	−7. 2	111	28. 7	57. 0	67. 9	80. 3
Tenants	322	210	75	112	53. 3	135	180. 0	39. 8	28. 6	15. 6
Managers	26	25	20	1	4. 0	5	25. 0	3. 2	3. 4	4. 1

TABLE 14.—ALL FARM LAND IN SQUARE MILES, AND SQUARE MILES OPERATED BY NEGRO AND WHITE FARMERS, BY SECTIONS, AND SOUTHERN DIVISIONS: 1930 AND 1920

SECTION AND DIVISION	ALL LAND IN FARMS (SQUARE MILES) 1930	1920	Increase or decrease (—)	SQUARE MILES OPERATED BY— Negroes 1930	Negroes 1920	Whites [1] 1930	Whites [1] 1920	Increase or decrease (—) Negroes	Increase or decrease (—) Whites [1]
United States	**1, 541, 830**	**1, 493, 568**	**48, 262**	**58, 745**	**64, 737**	**1, 477, 630**	**1, 423, 343**	**—5, 992**	**54, 287**
THE SOUTH	536, 073	547, 065	—10, 992	57, 435	63, 350	477, 001	482, 505	—5, 915	—5, 504
South Atlantic	134, 942	152, 774	—17, 832	22, 735	28, 361	112, 038	124, 297	—5, 626	—12, 259
East South Central	113, 777	123, 277	—9, 500	18, 622	18, 914	95, 135	104, 350	—292	—9, 215
West South Central	287, 354	271, 014	16, 340	16, 078	16, 075	269, 828	253, 858	3	15, 970
THE NORTH	665, 171	675, 425	—10, 254	1, 126	1, 200	662, 444	672, 447	—74	—10, 003
THE WEST	340, 586	271, 078	69, 508	184	187	338, 185	268, 391	—3	69, 794

[1] Includes Mexicans and Hindus.

TABLE 15.—VALUE OF LAND AND BUILDINGS FOR FARMS OPERATED BY NEGROES, BY TENURE, BY SECTIONS: 1930 AND 1920

TENURE	VALUE OF LAND AND BUILDINGS 1930	1920	INCREASE OR DECREASE (—) Amount	Per-cent	PERCENT DISTRIBUTION 1930	1920
	UNITED STATES					
Total	**$1, 402, 945, 799**	**$2, 257, 645, 325**	**—$859, 699, 526**	**—37. 9**	**100. 0**	**100. 0**
Owners	334, 451, 396	554, 158, 003	—219, 706, 607	—39. 6	23. 8	24. 5
Tenants	1, 053, 649, 636	1, 676, 315, 864	—622, 666, 228	—37. 1	75. 1	74. 3
Managers	14, 844, 767	27, 171, 458	—12, 326, 691	—45. 4	1. 1	1. 2
	THE SOUTH					
Total	$1, 355, 181, 667	$2, 191, 005, 642	—$835, 823, 975	—38. 1	100. 0	100. 0
Owners	314, 100, 432	522, 178, 137	—208, 077, 705	—39. 8	23. 2	23. 8
Tenants	1, 028, 371, 428	1, 647, 447, 607	—619, 076, 179	—37. 6	75. 9	75. 2
Managers	12, 709, 807	21, 379, 898	—8, 670, 091	—40. 6	. 9	1. 0

TENURE	VALUE OF LAND AND BUILDINGS 1930	1920	INCREASE OR DECREASE (—) Amount	Per-cent	PERCENT DISTRIBUTION 1930	1920
	THE NORTH					
Total	$41, 668, 222	$59, 832, 464	—$18, 164, 242	—30. 4	100. 0	100. 0
Owners	17, 684, 979	28, 481, 761	—10, 796, 782	—37. 9	42. 4	47. 6
Tenants	22, 327, 483	26, 258, 443	—3, 930, 960	—15. 0	53. 6	43. 9
Managers	1, 655, 760	5, 092, 260	—3, 436, 500	—67. 5	4. 0	8. 5
	THE WEST					
Total	$6, 095, 910	$6, 807, 219	—711, 309	—10. 4	100. 0	100. 0
Owners	2, 665, 985	3, 498, 105	—832, 120	—23. 8	43. 7	51. 4
Tenants	2, 950, 725	2, 609, 814	340, 911	13. 1	48. 4	38. 3
Managers	479, 200	699, 300	—220, 100	—31. 5	7. 9	10. 3

TABLE 16.—PERCENT DISTRIBUTION OF OWNED AND TENANT FARMS OPERATED BY NEGROES, BY SECTIONS, AND STATES: 1930, 1920, AND 1910

SECTION AND STATE	PERCENT OF FARMS OPERATED BY— Owners 1930	Owners 1920	Owners 1910	Tenants 1930	Tenants 1920	Tenants 1910
United States	**20. 5**	**23. 6**	**24. 5**	**79. 4**	**76. 2**	**75. 3**
The North	**39. 8**	**61. 3**	**62. 2**	**59. 3**	**36. 1**	**35. 9**
The South	**20. 2**	**23. 2**	**24. 0**	**79. 7**	**76. 6**	**75. 9**
The West	**57. 0**	**67. 9**	**80. 3**	**39. 8**	**28. 6**	**15. 6**
NEW ENGLAND:						
Maine	93. 3	100. 0	85. 7	6. 7	--------	10. 7
New Hampshire	83. 3	85. 7	78. 6	16. 7	7. 1	14. 3
Vermont	77. 3	75. 0	85. 0	18. 2	14. 3	10. 0
Massachusetts	93. 7	86. 4	86. 4	4. 8	6. 8	9. 7
Rhode Island	88. 9	68. 4	70. 0	--------	26. 3	30. 0
Connecticut	75. 8	67. 7	67. 6	15. 2	24. 6	21. 0
MIDDLE ATLANTIC:						
New York	75. 7	62. 0	65. 4	22. 3	29. 0	30. 5
New Jersey	62. 4	53. 5	55. 5	33. 9	42. 9	38. 8
Pennsylvania	63. 5	57. 9	62. 2	32. 6	32. 2	32. 0
EAST NORTH CENTRAL:						
Ohio	63. 5	65. 2	67. 3	35. 6	32. 6	31. 3
Indiana	59. 7	53. 5	58. 1	39. 9	44. 0	40. 0
Illinois	51. 4	59. 8	55. 3	47. 9	39. 2	43. 4
Michigan	78. 9	73. 4	78. 4	19. 9	25. 3	20. 2
Wisconsin	74. 5	87. 2	81. 3	25. 5	12. 8	16. 7
WEST NORTH CENTRAL:						
Minnesota	70. 4	72. 7	55. 2	29. 6	27. 3	41. 4
Iowa	56. 8	67. 9	65. 2	43. 2	31. 2	33. 7
Missouri	19. 9	58. 2	57. 5	79. 8	40. 1	41. 3
North Dakota	50. 0	42. 3	81. 8	50. 0	50. 0	18. 2
South Dakota	65. 0	70. 2	85. 1	32. 5	27. 7	14. 9
Nebraska	42. 1	49. 2	78. 1	57. 9	44. 4	21. 9
Kansas	57. 4	62. 5	63. 8	41. 6	36. 0	34. 9

SECTION AND STATE	PERCENT OF FARMS OPERATED BY— Owners 1930	Owners 1920	Owners 1910	Tenants 1930	Tenants 1920	Tenants 1910
SOUTH ATLANTIC:						
Delaware	46. 2	40. 7	44. 0	51. 4	57. 8	54. 2
Maryland	55. 8	57. 2	62. 0	41. 9	40. 4	36. 6
District of Columbia	72. 7	45. 0	66. 7	18. 2	50. 0	25. 0
Virginia	61. 6	64. 8	67. 0	38. 2	34. 8	32. 7
West Virginia	75. 9	80. 0	78. 8	22. 7	18. 5	20. 2
North Carolina	25. 4	29. 0	32. 1	74. 5	70. 9	67. 8
South Carolina	20. 7	20. 9	21. 0	79. 3	79. 0	78. 8
Georgia	12. 8	12. 3	12. 8	87. 2	87. 5	87. 1
Florida	50. 5	48. 8	49. 6	48. 7	50. 4	49. 7
EAST SOUTH CENTRAL:						
Kentucky	45. 9	42. 1	50. 5	54. 0	57. 6	49. 1
Tennessee	22. 3	25. 8	27. 9	77. 6	74. 1	71. 9
Alabama	17. 0	18. 1	15. 4	83. 0	81. 8	84. 5
Mississippi	12. 4	14. 4	15. 2	87. 6	85. 5	84. 8
WEST SOUTH CENTRAL:						
Arkansas	14. 4	21. 3	23. 1	85. 6	78. 6	76. 9
Louisiana	14. 2	17. 7	19. 5	85. 7	82. 2	80. 4
Oklahoma	22. 8	37. 0	36. 5	77. 1	62. 4	63. 4
Texas	23. 9	29. 9	30. 3	76. 0	69. 9	69. 5
MOUNTAIN:						
Montana	71. 4	83. 9	75. 9	28. 6	12. 9	17. 2
Idaho	43. 8	69. 6	100. 0	43. 8	30. 4	--------
Wyoming	66. 7	100. 0	89. 5	33. 3	--------	3. 5
Colorado	69. 2	77. 7	71. 6	29. 5	18. 9	27. 2
New Mexico	64. 6	75. 0	85. 4	35. 4	25. 0	6. 3
Arizona	46. 0	59. 4	83. 3	50. 6	31. 3	16. 7
Utah	80. 1	31. 1	100. 0	20. 0	67. 2	--------
Nevada	66. 7	30. 0	66. 7	33. 3	40. 0	16. 7
PACIFIC:						
Washington	83. 6	82. 3	83. 1	13. 7	17. 7	14. 3
Oregon	88. 9	73. 3	81. 5	11. 1	13. 3	14. 8
California	49. 5	63. 1	78. 6	46. 2	32. 4	16. 4

TABLE 17.—VALUE OF IMPLEMENTS AND MACHINERY ON FARMS OPERATED BY NEGROES, BY TENURE, BY SECTIONS, DIVISIONS, AND STATES: 1930

SECTION, DIVISION, AND STATE	Total	Owners	Tenants	Managers	Average value per owned farm
United States	$60,327,856	$19,784,411	$39,920,395	$623,050	$109
The North	1,971,346	1,042,391	855,340	73,615	236
The South	58,072,123	18,598,940	38,945,123	528,060	106
The West	284,387	143,080	119,932	21,375	310
NEW ENGLAND	57,730	44,105	4,625	9,000	345
Maine	6,075	4,575	1,500	--------	327
New Hampshire	2,050	1,800	250	--------	360
Vermont	18,525	12,525	1,000	5,000	737
Massachusetts	19,320	16,645	275	2,400	282
Rhode Island	2,025	825	--------	1,200	103
Connecticut	9,735	7,735	1,600	400	309
MIDDLE ATLANTIC	414,576	235,976	154,140	24,460	415
New York	95,725	61,065	30,260	4,400	545
New Jersey	173,223	88,123	69,750	15,350	380
Pennsylvania	145,628	86,788	54,130	4,710	387
EAST NORTH CENTRAL	584,661	348,235	211,791	24,635	184
Ohio	217,013	118,645	85,743	12,625	152
Indiana	77,162	37,982	38,330	850	138
Illinois	126,810	63,677	54,683	8,450	139
Michigan	137,755	106,595	28,450	2,710	316
Wisconsin	25,921	21,336	4,585	--------	520
WEST NORTH CENTRAL	914,379	414,075	484,784	15,520	226
Minnesota	18,965	17,475	1,490	--------	920
Iowa	46,001	20,271	25,730	--------	303
Missouri	493,459	143,101	339,083	11,275	123
North Dakota	7,875	3,175	4,700	--------	635
South Dakota	32,570	22,920	8,650	1,000	882
Nebraska	28,434	21,178	7,256	--------	1,324
Kansas	287,075	185,955	97,875	3,245	344
SOUTH ATLANTIC	$19,328,688	$7,388,829	$11,648,568	$291,291	$93
Delaware	224,010	100,745	107,075	16,190	270
Maryland	945,402	423,994	440,104	81,304	144
District of Columbia	1,225	100	125	1,000	13
Virginia	3,865,540	2,586,923	1,213,240	65,377	106
West Virginia	47,007	26,570	15,287	5,150	71
North Carolina	5,155,245	1,697,834	3,439,906	17,505	89
South Carolina	4,081,739	1,262,222	2,791,449	28,068	79
Georgia	4,320,997	880,607	3,392,733	47,657	79
Florida	687,523	409,834	248,649	29,040	74
EAST SOUTH CENTRAL	19,776,031	5,560,624	14,087,943	127,464	110
Kentucky	605,430	315,392	281,988	8,050	76
Tennessee	2,978,809	941,349	2,016,755	20,705	120
Alabama	5,091,581	1,549,249	3,516,133	26,199	97
Mississippi	11,100,211	2,754,634	8,273,067	72,510	122
WEST SOUTH CENTRAL	18,967,404	5,649,487	13,208,612	109,305	123
Arkansas	4,769,956	1,298,051	3,455,510	16,395	113
Louisiana	4,870,550	1,198,264	3,648,111	24,175	114
Oklahoma	1,595,879	569,728	1,005,601	20,550	165
Texas	7,731,019	2,583,444	5,099,390	48,185	126
MOUNTAIN	112,654	63,502	42,252	6,900	347
Montana	15,590	14,390	1,200	--------	959
Idaho	14,125	6,725	2,400	5,000	961
Wyoming	7,925	6,025	1,900	--------	753
Colorado	23,097	12,835	10,262	--------	238
New Mexico	18,187	9,277	8,910	--------	175
Arizona	32,175	12,945	17,330	1,900	324
Utah	305	305	--------	--------	76
Nevada	1,250	1,000	250	--------	500
PACIFIC	171,733	79,578	77,680	14,475	285
Washington	22,740	15,615	5,125	2,000	256
Oregon	2,667	2,617	50	--------	327
California	146,326	61,346	72,505	12,475	292

TABLE 18.—AVERAGE VALUE OF LAND AND BUILDINGS ON FARMS OPERATED BY NEGROES, BY TENURE, BY SECTIONS, AND SOUTHERN DIVISIONS: 1930 AND 1920

SECTION, DIVISION, AND TENURE	AVERAGE VALUE PER FARM				AVERAGE VALUE PER ACRE			
	1930	1920	Increase or decrease (—)		1930	1920	Increase or decrease (—)	
			Amount	Per cent			Amount	Per cent
United States	$1,589	$2,439	—$850	—34.9	$37.32	$54.49	—$17.17	—31.5
Owners	1,848	2,535	—687	—27.1	29.86	39.73	—9.87	—24.8
Tenants	1,503	2,378	—875	—36.8	40.29	61.91	—21.62	—34.9
Managers	16,083	13,411	2,672	19.9	59.60	66.91	—7.31	—10.9
THE SOUTH	1,556	2,393	—837	—35.0	36.87	54.04	—17.17	—31.8
Owners	1,783	2,459	—676	—27.5	29.12	38.87	—9.75	—25.1
Tenants	1,482	2,349	—867	—36.9	39.95	61.58	—21.63	—35.1
Managers	15,789	12,155	3,634	29.9	55.27	60.10	—4.83	—8.0
SOUTH ATLANTIC	1,637	2,568	—931	—36.3	33.29	54.08	—20.79	—38.4
Owners	1,703	2,323	—620	—26.7	32.20	43.24	—11.04	—25.5
Tenants	1,585	2,626	—1,041	—39.6	33.43	58.57	—25.14	—42.9
Managers	14,250	11,662	2,588	22.2	62.30	76.39	—14.09	—18.4
EAST SOUTH CENTRAL	1,330	2,104	—774	—36.8	35.79	53.35	—17.56	—32.9
Owners	1,634	2,296	—662	—28.8	23.45	32.41	—8.96	—27.6
Tenants	1,263	2,046	—783	—38.3	40.83	63.52	—22.69	—35.0
Managers	22,237	11,453	10,784	94.2	62.27	54.17	8.10	15.0
WEST SOUTH CENTRAL	1,746	2,490	—744	—29.9	43.17	54.77	—11.60	—21.2
Owners	2,087	2,876	—789	—27.4	31.41	39.22	—7.81	—19.9
Tenants	1,659	2,339	—680	—29.1	48.22	65.14	—16.92	—26.0
Managers	14,890	14,059	831	5.9	39.52	45.02	—5.50	—12.2
THE NORTH	3,753	6,379	—2,626	—41.2	57.80	77.91	—20.11	—25.8
Owners	3,998	4,954	—956	—19.3	53.18	65.46	—12.28	—18.8
Tenants	3,389	7,748	—4,359	—56.3	59.82	89.15	—29.33	—32.9
Managers	17,997	21,042	—3,045	—14.5	109.38	132.84	—23.46	—17.7
THE WEST	7,526	9,287	—1,761	—19.0	51.76	56.73	—4.97	—8.8
Owners	5,771	7,024	—1,253	—17.8	32.89	44.10	—11.21	—25.4
Tenants	9,164	12,428	—3,264	—26.3	90.18	91.08	—.90	—1.0
Managers	18,431	27,972	—9,541	—34.1	119.92	58.26	61.66	105.8

TABLE 19.—VALUE OF LAND IN FARMS AND VALUE OF ALL BUILDINGS ON FARMS OPERATED BY NEGROES, BY TENURE, BY SECTIONS, AND DIVISIONS: 1930

SECTION AND DIVISION	VALUE OF LAND ALONE				VALUE OF ALL BUILDINGS			
	Total	Owners	Tenants	Managers	Total	Owners	Tenants	Managers
United States	**$1,062,536,439**	**$228,709,700**	**$823,005,516**	**$10,821,223**	**$340,409,360**	**$105,741,696**	**$230,644,120**	**$4,023,544**
THE SOUTH	1,026,877,643	214,907,952	802,581,553	9,388,138	328,304.024	99,192,480	225,789,875	3,321,669
South Atlantic	342,118,722	85,227,015	252,300,365	4,591,342	142,325,221	50,497,142	89,622,060	2,206,019
East South Central	323,130,648	57,360,605	263,328,563	2,441,480	103,398,196	25,092,461	77,634,070	671,665
West South Central	361,628,273	72,320,332	286,952,625	2,355,316	82,580,607	23,602,877	58,533,745	443,985
THE NORTH	30,366,748	11,611,190	17,726,373	1,029,185	11,301,474	6,073,789	4,601,110	626,575
New England	406,290	302,565	31,725	72,000	503,105	348,760	35,345	119,000
Middle Atlantic	2,687,260	1,095,865	1,282,195	309,200	2,452,995	1,326,810	883,685	242,505
East North Central	9,130,656	4,265,786	4,602,325	262,545	4,174,095	2,530,750	1,490,320	153,020
West North Central	18,142,542	5,946,974	11,810,128	385,440	4,171,279	1,867,469	2,191,760	112,050
THE WEST	5,292,048	2,190,558	2,697,590	403,900	803,862	475,427	253,135	75,300
Mountain	1,792,685	802,065	919,620	71,000	244,825	141,620	93,205	10,000
Pacific	3,499,363	1,388,493	1,777,970	332,900	559,037	333,807	159,930	65,300
	PERCENT DISTRIBUTION							
United States	**100.0**	**100.0**	**100.0**	**100.0**	**100.0**	**100.0**	**100.0**	**100.0**
The South	96.6	94.0	97.5	86.8	96.4	93.8	97.9	82.6
The North	2.9	5.1	2.2	9.5	3.3	5.7	2.0	15.6
The West	.5	1.0	.3	3.7	.2	.5	.1	1.9

TABLE 20.—MORTGAGED FARMS OPERATED BY COLORED FULL OWNERS REPORTING BOTH AMOUNT OF DEBT AND CHARGES—NUMBER OF FARMS, ACREAGE, VALUE, MORTGAGE INDEBTEDNESS, AND CHARGES, BY SOUTHERN DIVISIONS, AND STATES, AND SELECTED NORTHERN STATES: 1930

[Colored farmers include Negroes, Indians, Chinese, Japanese, and all other nonwhite races]

DIVISION AND STATE	Number	Land in farms (acres)	Value of land and buildings	Amount of mortgage indebtedness	All charges 1929 [1]	Ratio of charges to debt percent	Average charges per farm	AVERAGE VALUE, DEBT, AND EQUITY PER FARM		
								Value of land and buildings	Amount of mortgage debt	Owners' equity
The South	**39,555**	**3,157,969**	**$90,681,315**	**$33,372,640**	**$2,436,459**	**7.30**	**$62**	**$2,293**	**$344**	**$1,449**
SOUTH ATLANTIC	15,021	1,096,515	34,386,847	12,502,573	847,907	6.78	56	2,289	832	1,457
Delaware	119	5,710	302,550	130,671	7,867	6.02	66	2,542	1,098	1,444
Maryland	789	38,607	2,278,995	771,836	46,578	6.03	59	2,888	978	1,910
District of Columbia	3	6	20,000	4,550	298	6.55	99	6,667	1,517	5,150
Virginia	4,007	260,932	8,847,433	2,878,651	182,947	6.36	46	2,208	718	1,490
West Virginia	45	3,409	153,950	43,811	2,724	6.22	61	3,421	974	2,447
North Carolina	4,009	265,433	10,254,093	4,077,374	257,271	6.31	64	2,558	1,017	1,541
South Carolina	3,119	237,909	6,363,949	2,470,693	189,439	7.67	61	2,040	792	1,248
Georgia	2,361	240,359	4,798,877	1,805,196	134,074	7.43	57	2,033	765	1,268
Florida	569	44,150	1,367,000	319,791	26,709	8.35	47	2,402	562	1,840
EAST SOUTH CENTRAL	14,159	1,219,653	27,579,239	10,636,390	783,696	7.37	55	1,948	751	1,197
Kentucky	638	40,350	1,539,473	588,701	35,654	6.06	56	2,413	923	1,490
Tennessee	1,544	105,603	3,424,674	1,378,001	98,850	7.17	64	2,218	892	1,326
Alabama	3,928	379,142	7,731,384	2,927,931	229,050	7.82	58	1,968	745	1,223
Mississippi	8,049	694,558	14,883,708	5,741,757	420,142	7.32	52	1,849	713	1,136
WEST SOUTH CENTRAL	10,375	841,801	28,715,229	10,233,677	804,856	7.86	78	2,768	986	1,782
Arkansas	3,305	225,160	7,182,025	2,681,799	228,659	8.53	69	2,173	811	1,362
Louisiana	2,485	168,734	5,590,514	1,910,978	146,939	7.69	59	2,250	769	1,481
Oklahoma	1,538	170,888	6,794,808	2,404,508	169,899	7.07	110	4,418	1,563	2,855
Texas	3,047	277,019	9,147,882	3,236,392	259,359	8.01	85	3,002	1,062	1,940
SELECTED NORTHERN STATES [2]	1,214	80,235	5,010,504	2,051,511	128,578	6.27	106	4,127	1,690	2,437
New Jersey	102	3,891	480,050	157,475	9,584	6.09	94	4,706	1,544	3,162
Pennsylvania	113	5,817	578,340	206,621	12,317	5.96	109	5,118	1,829	3,289
Ohio	253	13,935	1,043,175	431,358	26,100	6.05	103	4,123	1,705	2,418
Indiana	92	4,892	323,150	138,879	8,684	6.25	94	3,513	1,510	2,003
Illinois	135	8,406	403,369	178,070	11,904	6.69	88	2,988	1,319	1,669
Missouri	356	24,894	1,054,525	513,698	33,160	6.46	93	2,962	1,443	1,519
Kansas	163	18,400	1,127,895	425,410	26,829	6.31	165	6,920	2,610	4,310

[1] Interest, commissions, bonuses, and premiums charged.
[2] States having 200 or more Negro farmers who constitute 90 percent or more of the colored farmers in the State.

TABLE 21.—NUMBER OF DWELLINGS ON FARMS OPERATED BY NEGROES, BY VALUE GROUPS, AND BY TENURE, BY SECTIONS, AND SOUTHERN DIVISIONS: 1930

SECTION AND DIVISION	Total number of farms	REPORTING VALUE OF DWELLINGS: Total	Under $500	$500 to $999	$1,000 to $1,999	$2,000 to $2,999	$3,000 to $4,999	$5,000 to $7,499	$7,500 to $9,999	$10,000 and over	Not reporting value
	TOTAL DWELLINGS										
United States	**882, 850**	**806, 074**	**668, 018**	**110, 267**	**22, 231**	**3, 619**	**1, 384**	**364**	**85**	**106**	**76, 776**
THE SOUTH	870, 936	795, 342	661, 788	108, 094	20, 792	3, 129	1, 102	278	69	90	75, 594
South Atlantic	295, 934	274, 914	209, 368	49, 640	12, 851	2, 051	729	175	41	59	21, 020
East South Central	320, 600	292, 475	254, 097	33, 702	3, 847	550	192	54	19	14	28, 125
West South Central	254, 402	227, 953	198, 323	24, 752	4, 094	528	181	49	9	17	26, 449
THE NORTH	11, 104	9, 988	5, 820	2, 016	1, 325	452	263	83	15	14	1, 116
THE WEST	810	744	410	157	114	38	19	3	1	2	66
	PERCENT DISTRIBUTION										
United States	100. 0	100. 0	100. 0	100. 0	100. 0	100. 0	100. 0	100. 0	100. 0	100. 0	100. 0
THE SOUTH	98. 7	98. 7	99. 1	98. 0	93. 5	86. 5	79. 6	76. 4	81. 2	84. 9	98. 5
South Atlantic	33. 5	34. 1	31. 3	45. 0	57. 8	56. 7	52. 7	48. 1	48. 2	55. 7	27. 4
East South Central	36. 3	36. 3	38. 0	30. 6	17. 3	15. 2	13. 9	14. 8	22. 4	13. 2	36. 6
West South Central	28. 8	28. 3	29. 7	22. 4	18. 4	14. 6	13. 1	13. 5	10. 6	16. 0	34. 4
THE NORTH	1. 3	1. 2	. 9	1. 8	6. 0	12. 5	19. 0	22. 8	17. 6	13. 2	1. 5
THE WEST	. 1	. 1	. 1	. 1	. 5	1. 1	1. 4	. 8	1. 2	1. 9	. 1
	DWELLINGS OF OWNERS [1]										
United States	**181, 939**	**176, 373**	**120, 634**	**39, 320**	**12, 819**	**2, 318**	**923**	**243**	**55**	**61**	**5, 566**
THE SOUTH	176, 935	171, 580	118, 633	38, 091	11, 858	2, 001	721	179	46	51	5, 355
South Atlantic	80, 160	77, 890	49, 690	19, 309	6, 995	1, 264	462	109	27	34	2, 270
East South Central	50, 615	49, 129	36, 555	9, 686	2, 337	369	129	31	15	7	1, 486
West South Central	46, 160	44, 561	32, 388	9, 096	2, 526	368	130	39	4	10	1, 599
THE NORTH	4, 516	4, 334	1, 753	1, 142	882	289	189	62	8	9	182
THE WEST	488	459	248	87	79	28	13	2	1	1	29
	PERCENT DISTRIBUTION										
United States	100. 0	100. 0	100. 0	100. 0	100. 0	100. 0	100. 0	100. 0	100. 0	100. 0	100. 0
THE SOUTH	97. 2	97. 3	98. 3	96. 9	92. 5	86. 3	78. 1	73. 7	83. 6	83. 6	96. 2
South Atlantic	44. 1	44. 2	41. 2	49. 1	54. 6	54. 5	50. 1	44. 9	49. 1	55. 7	40. 8
East South Central	27. 8	27. 9	30. 3	24. 6	18. 2	15. 9	14. 0	12. 8	27. 3	11. 5	26. 7
West South Central	25. 4	25. 3	26. 8	23. 1	19. 7	15. 9	14. 1	16. 0	7. 3	16. 4	28. 7
THE NORTH	2. 5	2. 5	1. 5	2. 9	6. 9	12. 5	20. 5	25. 5	14. 5	14. 8	3. 3
THE WEST	. 3	. 3	. 2	. 2	. 6	1. 2	1. 4	. 8	1. 8	1. 6	. 5
	DWELLINGS OF TENANTS										
United States	**700, 911**	**629, 701**	**547, 384**	**70, 947**	**9, 412**	**1, 301**	**461**	**121**	**30**	**45**	**71, 210**
THE SOUTH	694, 001	623, 762	543, 155	70, 003	8, 934	1, 128	381	99	23	39	70, 239
South Atlantic	215, 774	197, 024	159, 678	30, 331	5, 856	787	267	66	14	25	18, 750
East South Central	269, 985	243, 346	217, 542	24, 016	1, 510	181	63	23	4	7	26, 639
West South Central	208, 242	183, 392	165, 935	15, 656	1, 568	160	51	10	5	7	24, 850
THE NORTH	6, 588	5, 654	4, 067	874	443	163	74	21	7	5	934
THE WEST	322	285	162	70	35	10	6	1	----------	1	37
	PERCENT DISTRIBUTION										
United States	100. 0	100. 0	100. 0	100. 0	100. 0	100. 0	100. 0	100. 0	100. 0	100. 0	100. 0
THE SOUTH	99. 0	99. 1	99. 2	98. 7	94. 9	86. 7	82. 6	81. 8	76. 7	86. 7	98. 6
South Atlantic	30. 8	31. 3	29. 2	42. 8	62. 2	60. 5	57. 9	54. 5	46. 7	55. 6	26. 3
East South Central	38. 5	38. 6	39. 7	33. 9	16. 0	13. 9	13. 7	19. 0	13. 3	15. 6	37. 4
West South Central	29. 7	29. 1	30. 3	22. 1	16. 7	12. 3	11. 1	8. 3	16. 7	15. 6	34. 9
THE NORTH	. 9	. 9	. 7	1. 2	4. 7	12. 5	16. 1	17. 4	23. 3	11. 1	1. 3
THE WEST	(2)	(2)	(2)	. 1	. 4	. 8	1. 3	. 8	----------	2. 2	. 1

[1] Includes 923 managers, 805 in the South, 92 in the North, and 26 in the West.
[2] Less than 1/10 of 1 percent.

TABLE 22.—FARMS OPERATED BY COLORED FULL OWNERS, CLASSIFIED ACCORDING TO MORTGAGE STATUS, BY SOUTHERN DIVISIONS, AND STATES, AND SELECTED NORTHERN STATES: 1930

[Figures relate only to farms wholly owned by their operators. Colored farmers include Negroes, Chinese, Japanese, and all other nonwhite races]

DIVISION AND STATE	Total	Reported free from mortgage	Reported mortgaged	Unknown (no report)	PERCENT DISTRIBUTION: Reported free from mortgage	Reported mortgaged	Unknown (no report)
The South	**140, 496**	**84, 861**	**41, 964**	**13, 671**	**60. 4**	**29. 9**	**9. 7**
SOUTH ATLANTIC	60, 714	39, 887	15, 860	4, 967	65. 7	26. 1	8. 2
Delaware	309	162	124	23	52. 4	40. 1	7. 4
Maryland	2, 362	1, 449	814	99	61. 3	34. 5	4. 2
District of Columbia	7	2	3	2	28. 6	42. 9	28. 6
Virginia	19, 200	14, 077	4, 184	939	73. 3	21. 8	4. 9
West Virginia	328	258	48	22	78. 7	14. 6	6. 7
North Carolina	13, 198	7, 671	4, 258	1, 269	58. 1	32. 3	9. 6
South Carolina	11, 937	7, 745	3, 263	929	64. 9	27. 3	7. 8
Georgia	9, 014	5, 311	2, 541	1, 162	58. 9	28. 2	12. 9
Florida	4, 359	3, 212	625	522	73. 7	14. 3	12. 0
EAST SOUTH CENTRAL	39, 420	20, 659	15, 087	3, 674	52. 4	38. 3	9. 3
Kentucky	3, 055	1, 898	682	475	62. 1	22. 3	15. 5
Tennessee	5, 687	3, 456	1, 639	592	60. 8	28. 8	10. 4
Alabama	11, 417	6, 140	4, 135	1, 142	53. 8	36. 2	10. 0
Mississippi	19, 261	9, 165	8, 631	1, 465	47. 6	44. 8	7. 6
WEST SOUTH CENTRAL	40, 362	24, 315	11, 017	5, 030	60. 2	27. 3	12. 5
Arkansas	9, 058	4, 521	3, 496	1, 041	49. 9	38. 6	11. 5
Louisiana	8, 786	5, 080	2, 659	1, 047	57. 8	30. 3	11. 9
Oklahoma	6, 550	3, 682	1, 604	1, 264	56. 2	24. 5	19. 3
Texas	15, 968	11, 032	3, 258	1, 678	69. 1	20. 4	10. 5
SELECTED NORTHERN STATES [1]	2, 790	1, 369	1, 270	151	49. 1	45. 5	5. 4
New Jersey	217	103	107	7	47. 5	49. 3	3. 2
Pennsylvania	221	91	121	9	41. 2	54. 8	4. 1
Ohio	640	324	265	51	50. 6	41. 4	8. 0
Indiana	207	95	97	15	45. 9	46. 9	7. 2
Illinois	309	150	140	19	48. 5	45. 3	6. 1
Missouri	815	416	370	29	51. 0	45. 4	3. 6
Kansas	381	190	170	21	49. 9	44. 6	5. 5

[1] States having 200 or more Negro farmers who constitute 90 percent or more of the colored farm operators in the State.

TABLE 23.—NUMBER OF COLORED FARM OPERATORS BY RACE, BY SECTIONS, DIVISIONS, AND STATES: 1930

SECTION, DIVISION, AND STATE	Total	Negro	Indian	Japanese	Chinese	Other nonwhite [1]	Percent Negro of total colored
United States	**916, 070**	**882, 850**	**26, 817**	**5, 840**	**476**	**87**	**96. 37**
The North	**15, 956**	**11, 104**	**4, 753**	**83**	**13**	**3**	**69. 59**
The South	**881, 687**	**870, 936**	**10, 637**	**87**	**26**	**1**	**98. 78**
The West	**18, 427**	**810**	**11, 427**	**5, 670**	**437**	**83**	**4. 39**
NEW ENGLAND	159	148	7	1	2	1	93. 08
Maine	17	15	2				88. 23
New Hampshire	8	6	1		1		75. 00
Vermont	22	22					100. 00
Massachusetts	64	63				1	98. 43
Rhode Island	11	9	2				81. 81
Connecticut	37	33	2	1	1		89. 18
MIDDLE ATLANTIC	1, 207	873	314	10	10		72. 32
New York	460	148	303	6	3		32. 17
New Jersey	384	372	2	4	6		96. 87
Pennsylvania	363	353	9		1		97. 24
EAST NORTH CENTRAL	3, 483	3, 065	406	10	1	1	87. 99
Ohio	1, 237	1, 229	6	2			99. 35
Indiana	475	461	10	4			97. 05
Illinois	894	893	1				99. 88
Michigan	561	427	131	1	1	1	76. 11
Wisconsin	316	55	258	3			17. 40
WEST NORTH CENTRAL	11, 107	7, 018	4, 026	62		1	63. 18
Minnesota	245	27	217	1			11. 02
Iowa	154	118	35	1			76. 62
Missouri	5, 861	5, 844	14	2		1	99. 70
North Dakota	801	10	791				1. 24
South Dakota	2, 740	40	2, 698	2			1. 45
Nebraska	270	38	176	56			14. 07
Kansas	1, 036	941	95				90. 83

[1] Includes 56 Filipinos, 30 Koreans, and 1 Hawaiian.

TABLE 23.—NUMBER OF COLORED FARM OPERATORS BY RACE, BY SECTIONS, DIVISIONS, AND STATES: 1930—Continued

SECTION, DIVISION, AND STATE	Total	Negro	Indian	Japanese	Chinese	Other nonwhite	Percent Negro of total colored
SOUTH ATLANTIC	298, 379	295, 934	2, 408	23	13	1	99. 18
Delaware	807	807					100. 00
Maryland	5, 267	5, 264	3				99. 94
District of Columbia	11	11					100. 00
Virginia	39, 673	39, 598	74	1			99. 81
West Virginia	491	490	1				99. 79
North Carolina	76, 873	74, 636	2, 235		2		97. 09
South Carolina	77, 425	77, 331	90	2	2		99. 87
Georgia	86, 789	86, 787	1	1			99. 99
Florida	11, 043	11, 010	4	19	9	1	99. 70
EAST SOUTH CENTRAL	320, 959	320, 600	356	2	1		99. 88
Kentucky	9, 104	9, 104					100. 00
Tennessee	35, 138	35, 123	14		1		99. 95
Alabama	93, 829	93, 795	32	2			99. 96
Mississippi	182, 888	182, 578	310				99. 83
WEST SOUTH CENTRAL	262, 349	254, 402	7, 873	62	12		96. 97
Arkansas	79, 579	79, 556	20	3			99. 97
Louisiana	73, 770	73, 734	31	1	4		99. 95
Oklahoma	22, 937	15, 172	7, 760	5			66. 14
Texas	86, 063	85, 940	62	53	8		99. 85
MOUNTAIN	10, 923	304	9, 601	926	65	27	2. 78
Montana	1, 184	21	1, 135	12	7	9	1. 77
Idaho	698	16	511	149	20	2	2. 29
Wyoming	263	12	217	32	1	1	4. 56
Colorado	601	78	126	390		7	12. 97
New Mexico	3, 345	82	3, 245	14	3	1	2. 45
Arizona	3, 953	87	3, 735	121	8	2	2. 20
Utah	568	5	343	193	23	4	. 88
Nevada	311	3	289	15	3	1	. 96
PACIFIC	7, 504	506	1, 826	4, 744	372	56	6. 74
Washington	1, 349	73	700	523	44	9	5. 41
Oregon	683	9	368	265	36	5	1. 31
California	5, 472	424	758	3, 956	292	42	7. 74

TABLE 24.—AVERAGE VALUE OF LAND AND BUILDINGS PER FARM AND PER ACRE OF FARMS OPERATED BY COLORED FULL OWNERS, BY MORTGAGE STATUS, BY SOUTHERN DIVISIONS, AND STATES, AND SELECTED NORTHERN STATES: 1930

[Colored farmers include Negroes, Indians, Chinese, Japanese, and all other nonwhite races. All averages based on figures in tables 23, 24, and 26]

DIVISION AND STATE	AVERAGE VALUE OF LAND AND BUILDINGS PER FARM: Total	Reporting farms free from mortgage	Reporting farms mortgaged	Unknown (no report)	AVERAGE VALUE OF LAND AND BUILDINGS PER ACRE: Total	Reporting farms free from mortgage	Reporting farms mortgaged	Unknown (no report)
The South	**$1, 872**	**$1, 692**	**$2, 271**	**$1, 766**	**$29. 19**	**$29. 24**	**$28. 65**	**$31. 24**
SOUTH ATLANTIC	1, 746	1, 564	2, 265	1, 554	31. 98	32. 38	31. 23	32. 39
Delaware	2, 143	1, 810	2, 542	2, 330	59. 91	69. 66	54. 02	53. 33
Maryland	2, 286	1, 919	2, 863	2, 913	61. 63	63. 40	58. 25	76. 97
District of Columbia	4, 071	2, 150	6, 667	2, 100	2, 192. 31	1, 433. 33	3, 333. 33	1, 050. 00
Virginia	1, 739	1, 613	2, 188	1, 612	35. 62	36. 13	33. 99	38. 51
West Virginia	2, 260	2, 054	3, 318	2, 359	47. 08	48. 42	45. 79	39. 41
North Carolina	2, 044	1, 810	2, 533	1, 816	38. 70	38. 60	38. 54	40. 07
South Carolina	1, 464	1, 252	2, 025	1, 261	28. 34	28. 92	26. 77	34. 09
Georgia	1, 590	1, 436	2, 009	1, 380	19. 74	19. 66	19. 76	20. 07
Florida	1, 610	1, 508	2, 313	1, 394	31. 45	31. 17	31. 10	34. 32
EAST SOUTH CENTRAL	1, 651	1, 467	1, 939	1, 498	22. 64	22. 25	22. 68	24. 82
Kentucky	1, 744	1, 621	2, 366	1, 345	38. 55	37. 08	38. 00	49. 84
Tennessee	1, 802	1, 594	2, 241	1, 806	33. 07	33. 05	32. 37	35. 87
Alabama	1, 594	1, 398	1, 950	1, 355	19. 85	19. 57	20. 27	19. 30
Mississippi	1, 625	1, 434	1, 843	1, 533	20. 74	19. 51	21. 60	22. 71
WEST SOUTH CENTRAL	2, 278	2, 095	2, 733	2, 170	32. 59	31. 37	33. 99	34. 91
Arkansas	1, 915	1, 762	2, 165	1, 740	30. 93	29. 50	31. 89	33. 84
Louisiana	1, 863	1, 716	2. 218	1, 678	31. 94	31. 37	32. 66	32. 47
Oklahoma	3, 610	3, 315	4, 365	3, 511	37. 94	35. 63	39. 87	42. 24
Texas	2, 167	1, 998	2, 958	1, 734	30. 75	30. 08	33. 00	29. 11
SELECTED NORTHERN STATES [1]	3, 480	2, 948	4, 070	3, 352	62. 20	60. 52	62. 71	72. 11
New Jersey	4, 297	3, 667	4, 633	8, 429	145. 35	165. 01	124. 15	443. 61
Pennsylvania	4, 192	3, 446	4, 921	1, 933	96. 51	92. 56	99. 27	81. 69
Ohio	3, 244	2, 648	4, 078	2, 699	59. 43	47. 50	74. 09	60. 16
Indiana	2, 901	2, 331	3, 544	2, 353	70. 69	74. 68	68. 27	71. 31
Illinois	2, 831	2, 666	2, 954	3, 224	55. 11	62. 34	47. 84	75. 43
Missouri	2, 776	2, 558	2, 952	3, 666	47. 20	50. 24	42. 88	82. 47
Kansas	5, 346	4, 214	6, 747	4, 248	62. 00	64. 70	61. 38	49. 89

[1] States having 200 or more Negro farmers who constitute 90 percent or more of the colored farmers in the State.

Table 25.—NUMBER OF FARMS OPERATED BY NEGROES, BY TENURE, BY SECTIONS, DIVISIONS, AND STATES: 1930

[Percent not shown when less than 1/10 of 1 percent]

SECTION, DIVISION, AND STATE	Total number	OWNERS		TENANTS			Managers	PERCENT DISTRIBUTION					
								Owners		Tenants			Managers
		Full	Part	Cash	Cropper	Other		Full	Part	Cash	Cropper	Other	
United States	882, 850	139, 114	41, 902	98, 246	394, 928	207, 737	923	15. 8	4. 7	11. 1	44. 7	23. 5	0. 1
The North	11, 104	3, 335	1, 089	669	3, 310	2, 609	92	30. 0	9. 8	6. 0	29. 8	23. 5	. 8
The South	870, 936	135, 394	40, 736	97, 495	391, 547	204, 959	805	15. 5	4. 7	11. 2	45. 0	23. 5	. 1
The West	810	385	77	82	71	169	26	47. 5	9. 5	10. 2	8. 8	20. 9	3. 2
NEW ENGLAND	148	119	9	9	2	3	6	80. 4	6. 1	6. 1	1. 4	2. 0	4. 1
Maine	15	13	1	1				86. 7	6. 7	6. 7			
New Hampshire	6	5		1				83. 3		16. 7			
Vermont	22	13	4	2	1	1	1	59. 1	18. 2	9. 1	4. 5	4. 5	4. 5
Massachusetts	63	57	2	2		1	1	90. 5	3. 2	3. 2		1. 6	1. 6
Rhode Island	9	8					1	88. 9					11. 1
Connecticut	33	23	2	3	1	1	3	69. 7	6. 1	9. 1	3. 0	3. 0	9. 1
MIDDLE ATLANTIC	873	527	41	111	39	124	31	60. 4	4. 7	12. 7	4. 5	14. 2	3. 6
New York	148	106	6	14	2	17	3	71. 6	4. 1	9. 5	1. 4	11. 5	2. 0
New Jersey	372	209	23	40	16	70	14	56. 2	6. 2	10. 8	4. 3	18. 8	3. 8
Pennsylvania	353	212	12	57	21	37	14	60. 1	3. 4	16. 1	5. 9	10. 5	4. 0
EAST NORTH CENTRAL	3, 065	1, 453	439	259	192	698	24	47. 4	14. 3	8. 5	6. 3	22. 8	. 8
Ohio	1, 229	637	143	121	54	263	11	51. 8	11. 6	9. 8	4. 4	21. 4	. 9
Indiana	461	199	76	38	31	115	2	43. 2	16. 5	8. 2	6. 7	24. 9	. 4
Illinois	893	308	151	65	95	268	6	34. 5	16. 9	7. 3	10. 6	30. 0	. 7
Michigan	427	274	63	28	11	46	5	64. 2	14. 8	6. 6	2. 6	10. 8	1. 2
Wisconsin	55	35	6	7	1	6		63. 6	10. 9	12. 7	1. 8	10. 9	
WEST NORTH CENTRAL	7, 018	1, 236	600	290	3, 077	1, 784	31	17. 6	8. 5	4. 1	43. 8	25. 4	. 4
Minnesota	27	14	5	5	1	2		51. 9	18. 5	18. 5	3. 7	7. 4	
Iowa	118	55	12	18	2	31		46. 6	10. 2	15. 3	1. 7	26. 3	
Missouri	5, 844	809	354	185	3, 015	1, 461	20	13. 8	6. 1	3. 2	51. 6	25. 0	. 3
North Dakota	10	3	2	1		4		30. 0	20. 0	10. 0		40. 0	
South Dakota	40	8	18	5		8	1	20. 0	45. 0	12. 5		20. 0	2. 5
Nebraska	38	14	2	11		11		36. 8	5. 3	28. 9		28. 9	
Kansas	941	333	207	65	59	267	10	35. 4	22. 0	6. 9	6. 3	28. 4	1. 1
SOUTH ATLANTIC	295, 934	60, 017	19, 666	29, 277	123, 478	63, 019	477	20. 3	6. 6	9. 9	41. 7	21. 3	. 2
Delaware	807	309	64	54	60	301	19	38. 3	7. 9	6. 7	7. 4	37. 3	2. 4
Maryland	5, 264	2, 359	579	213	597	1, 396	120	44. 8	11. 0	4. 0	11. 3	26. 5	2. 3
District of Columbia	11	7	1	2			1	63. 6	9. 1	18. 2			9. 1
Virginia	39, 598	19, 157	5, 242	1, 764	6, 791	6, 568	76	48. 4	13. 2	4. 5	17. 1	16. 6	. 2
West Virginia	490	327	45	38	23	50	7	66. 7	9. 2	7. 8	4. 7	10. 2	1. 4
North Carolina	74, 636	12, 581	6, 397	2, 512	34, 169	18, 954	23	16. 9	8. 6	3. 4	45. 8	25. 4	
South Carolina	77, 331	11, 920	4, 055	11, 756	30, 998	18, 531	71	15. 4	5. 2	15. 2	40. 1	24. 0	. 1
Georgia	86, 787	9, 013	2, 067	10, 532	49, 449	15, 654	72	10. 4	2. 4	12. 1	57. 0	18. 0	. 1
Florida	11, 010	4, 344	1, 216	2, 406	1, 391	1, 565	88	39. 5	11. 0	21. 9	12. 6	14. 2	. 8
EAST SOUTH CENTRAL	320, 600	39, 311	11, 164	53, 365	150, 075	66, 545	140	12. 3	3. 5	16. 6	46. 8	20. 8	
Kentucky	9, 104	3, 055	1, 120	140	3, 116	1, 658	15	33. 6	12. 3	1. 5	34. 2	18. 2	. 2
Tennessee	35, 123	5, 683	2, 145	2, 863	16, 556	7, 842	34	16. 2	6. 1	8. 2	47. 1	22. 3	. 1
Alabama	93, 795	11, 408	4, 512	32, 052	27, 554	18, 247	22	12. 2	4. 8	34. 2	29. 4	19. 5	
Mississippi	182, 578	19, 165	3, 387	18, 310	102, 849	38, 798	69	10. 5	1. 9	10. 0	56. 3	21. 3	
WEST SOUTH CENTRAL	254, 402	36, 066	9, 906	14, 853	117, 994	75, 395	188	14. 2	3. 9	5. 8	46. 4	29. 6	. 1
Arkansas	79, 556	9, 055	2, 397	6, 102	45, 460	16, 519	23	11. 4	3. 0	7. 7	57. 1	20. 8	
Louisiana	73, 734	8, 772	1, 716	6, 687	32, 205	24, 300	54	11. 9	2. 3	9. 1	43. 7	33. 0	. 1
Oklahoma	15, 172	2, 319	1, 135	692	4, 094	6, 908	24	15. 3	7. 5	4. 6	27. 0	45. 5	. 2
Texas	85, 940	15, 920	4, 658	1, 372	36, 235	27, 668	87	18. 5	5. 4	1. 6	42. 2	32. 2	. 1
MOUNTAIN	304	142	41	19	34	62	6	46. 7	13. 5	6. 3	11. 2	20. 4	2. 0
Montana	21	8	7	1		5		38. 1	33. 3	4. 8		23. 8	
Idaho	16	6	1	2		5	2	37. 5	6. 3	12. 5		31. 3	12. 5
Wyoming	12	7	1	2		2		58. 3	8. 3	16. 7		16. 7	
Colorado	78	36	18	3	4	16	1	46. 2	23. 1	3. 8	5. 1	20. 5	1. 3
New Mexico	82	46	7	3	17	9		56. 1	8. 5	3. 7	20. 7	11. 0	
Arizona	87	34	6	7	13	24	3	39. 1	6. 9	8. 0	14. 9	27. 6	3. 4
Utah	5	3	1	1				60. 0	20. 0	20. 0			
Nevada	3	2				1		66. 7				33. 3	
PACIFIC	506	243	36	63	37	107	20	48. 0	7. 1	12. 5	7. 3	21. 1	4. 0
Washington	73	56	5	3	2	5	2	76. 7	6. 8	4. 1	2. 7	6. 8	2. 7
Oregon	9	6	2	1				66. 7	22. 2	11. 1			
California	424	181	29	59	35	102	18	42. 7	6. 8	13. 9	8. 3	24. 1	4. 2

TABLE 26.—VALUE OF FARMS (LAND AND BUILDINGS) OPERATED BY COLORED FULL OWNERS, BY MORTGAGE STATUS, WITH PERCENT DISTRIBUTION, BY SOUTHERN DIVISIONS, AND STATES, AND SELECTED NORTHERN STATES: 1930

[Figures relate only to farms wholly owned by their operators. Colored farmers include Negroes, Indians, Chinese, Japanese, and all other nonwhite races]

DIVISION AND STATE	Total	Reporting farms free from mortgage	Reporting farms mortgaged	Unknown (no report)	PERCENT DISTRIBUTION BY MORTGAGE STATUS: Reporting farms free from mortgage	Reporting farms mortgaged	Unknown (no report)	PERCENT DISTRIBUTION OF TOTAL FOR SOUTH AND SELECTED NORTHERN STATES: Total	Reporting farms free from mortgage	Reporting farms mortgaged	Unknown (no report)
The South	**$263, 039, 069**	**$143, 615, 598**	**$95, 284, 776**	**$24, 138, 695**	**54. 6**	**36. 2**	**9. 2**	**100. 0**	**100. 0**	**100. 0**	**100. 0**
SOUTH ATLANTIC	106, 007, 752	62, 365, 265	35, 921, 883	7, 720, 604	58. 8	33. 9	7. 3	40. 3	43. 4	37. 7	32. 0
Delaware	662, 040	293, 190	315, 250	53, 600	44. 3	47. 6	8. 1	. 3	. 2	. 3	. 2
Maryland	5, 398, 599	2, 779, 909	2, 330, 295	288, 395	51. 5	43. 2	5. 3	2. 1	1. 9	2. 4	1. 2
District of Columbia	28, 500	4, 300	20, 000	4, 200	15. 1	70. 2	14. 7	(1)	(1)	(1)	(1)
Virginia	33, 379, 503	22, 711, 801	9, 153, 708	1, 513, 994	68. 0	27. 4	4. 5	12. 7	15. 8	9. 6	6. 3
West Virginia	741, 153	530, 003	159, 250	51, 900	71. 5	21. 5	7. 0	. 3	. 4	. 2	. 2
North Carolina	26, 970, 344	13, 881, 607	10, 783, 688	2, 305, 049	51. 5	40. 0	8. 5	10. 3	9. 7	11. 3	9. 5
South Carolina	17, 475, 762	9, 695, 157	6, 608, 797	1, 171, 808	55. 5	37. 8	6. 7	6. 6	6. 8	6. 9	4. 9
Georgia	14, 334, 112	7, 624, 588	5, 105, 455	1, 604, 069	53. 2	35. 6	11. 2	5. 4	5. 3	5. 4	6. 6
Florida	7, 017, 739	4, 844, 710	1, 445, 440	727, 589	69. 0	20. 6	10. 4	2. 7	3. 4	1. 5	3. 0
EAST SOUTH CENTRAL	65, 075, 305	30, 315, 560	29, 257, 867	5, 501, 878	46. 6	45. 0	8. 5	24. 7	21. 1	30. 7	22. 8
Kentucky	5, 329, 070	3, 076, 391	1, 613, 623	639, 056	57. 7	30. 3	12. 0	2. 0	2. 1	1. 7	2. 6
Tennessee	10, 249, 910	5, 507, 619	3, 673, 042	1, 069, 249	53. 7	35. 8	10. 4	3. 9	3. 8	3. 9	4. 4
Alabama	18, 197, 589	8, 586, 348	8, 064, 201	1, 547, 040	47. 2	44. 3	8. 5	6. 9	6. 0	8. 5	6. 4
Mississippi	31, 298, 736	13, 145, 202	15, 907, 001	2, 246, 533	42. 0	50. 8	7. 2	11. 9	9. 2	16. 7	9. 3
WEST SOUTH CENTRAL	91, 956, 012	50, 934, 773	30, 105, 026	10, 916, 213	55. 4	32. 7	11. 9	35. 0	35. 5	31. 6	45. 2
Arkansas	17, 344, 877	7, 965, 016	7, 568, 610	1, 811, 251	45. 9	43. 6	10. 4	6. 6	5. 5	7. 9	7. 5
Louisiana	16, 371, 105	8, 717, 070	5, 897, 131	1, 756, 904	53. 2	36. 0	10. 7	6. 2	6. 1	6. 2	7. 3
Oklahoma	23, 645, 210	12, 205, 700	7, 001, 598	4, 437, 912	51. 6	29. 6	18. 8	9. 0	8. 5	7. 3	18. 4
Texas	34, 594, 820	22, 046, 987	9, 637, 687	2, 910, 146	63. 7	27. 9	8. 4	13. 2	15. 4	10. 1	12. 1
SELECTED NORTHERN STATES [2]	9, 709, 768	4, 035, 360	5, 168, 308	506, 100	41. 6	53. 2	5. 2	100. 0	100. 0	100. 0	100. 0
New Jersey	932, 450	377, 700	495, 750	59, 000	40. 5	53. 2	6. 3	9. 6	9. 4	9. 6	11. 7
Pennsylvania	926, 480	313, 580	595, 500	17, 400	33. 8	64. 3	1. 9	9. 5	7. 8	11. 5	3. 4
Ohio	2, 076, 060	857, 845	1, 080, 575	137, 640	41. 3	52. 0	6. 6	21. 4	21. 3	20. 9	27. 2
Indiana	600, 490	221, 440	343, 750	35, 300	36. 9	57. 2	5. 9	6. 2	5. 5	6. 7	7. 0
Illinois	874, 714	399, 895	413, 569	61, 250	45. 7	47. 3	7. 0	9. 0	9. 9	8. 0	12. 1
Missouri	2, 262, 724	1, 064, 245	1, 092, 169	106, 310	47. 0	48. 3	4. 7	23. 3	26. 4	21. 1	21. 0
Kansas	2, 036, 850	800, 655	1, 146, 995	89, 200	39. 3	56. 3	4. 4	21. 0	19. 8	22. 2	17. 6

[1] Less than 1/10 of 1 percent.   [2] States having 200 or more Negro farmers who constitute 90 percent or more of the colored farmers in the State.

TABLE 27.—ALL LAND IN FARMS OPERATED BY COLORED FULL OWNERS, BY MORTGAGE STATUS, WITH AVERAGE ACREAGE PER FARM, AND PERCENT DISTRIBUTION, BY SOUTHERN DIVISIONS, AND STATES, AND SELECTED NORTHERN STATES: 1930

[Figures relate only to farms wholly owned by their operators. Colored farmers include Negroes, Indians, Japanese, Chinese, and other nonwhite races]

DIVISION AND STATE	ALL LAND IN FARMS (ACRES): Total	Reporting farms free from mortgage	Reporting farms mortgaged	Unknown (no report)	AVERAGE ACREAGE PER FARM: Total	Reporting farms free from mortgage	Reporting farms mortgaged	Unknown (no report)	PERCENT DISTRIBUTION OF LAND, BY MORTGAGE STATUS: Reporting farms free from mortgage	Reporting farms mortgaged	Unknown (no report)	PERCENT DISTRIBUTION OF LAND OPERATED BY FULL OWNERS: Total	Reporting farms free from mortgage	Reporting farms mortgaged	Unknown (no report)
The South	**9, 010, 320**	**4, 911, 661**	**3, 325, 882**	**772, 777**	**64. 4**	**57. 9**	**79. 3**	**56. 5**	**54. 5**	**36. 9**	**8. 6**	**100. 0**	**100. 0**	**100. 0**	**100. 0**
SOUTH ATLANTIC	3, 314, 342	1, 925, 835	1, 150, 108	238, 399	54. 6	48. 3	72. 5	48. 0	58. 1	34. 7	7. 2	36. 8	39. 2	34. 6	30. 8
Delaware	11, 050	4, 209	5, 836	1, 005	35. 8	26. 0	47. 1	43. 7	38. 1	52. 8	9. 1	. 1	. 1	. 2	. 1
Maryland	87, 593	43, 844	40, 002	3, 747	37. 1	30. 3	49. 1	37. 8	50. 1	45. 7	4. 3	1. 0	. 9	1. 2	. 5
District of Columbia	13	3	6	4	1. 9	1. 5	2. 0	2. 0	23. 1	46. 2	30. 8	(1)	(1)	(1)	(1)
Virginia	937, 215	628, 624	269, 279	39, 312	48. 8	44. 7	64. 4	41. 9	67. 1	28. 7	4. 2	10. 4	12. 8	8. 1	5. 1
West Virginia	15, 741	10, 946	3, 478	1, 317	48. 0	42. 4	72. 5	59. 9	69. 5	22. 1	8. 4	. 2	. 2	. 1	. 2
North Carolina	696, 930	359, 621	279, 781	57, 528	52. 8	46. 9	65. 7	45. 3	51. 6	40. 1	8. 3	7. 7	7. 3	8. 4	7. 4
South Carolina	616, 579	335, 284	246, 917	34, 378	51. 7	43. 3	75. 7	37. 0	54. 4	40. 0	5. 6	6. 8	6. 8	7. 4	4. 4
Georgia	726, 112	387, 879	258, 326	79, 907	80. 6	73. 0	101. 7	68. 8	53. 4	35. 6	11. 0	8. 1	7. 9	7. 8	10. 3
Florida	223, 109	155, 425	46, 483	21, 201	51. 2	48. 4	74. 4	40. 6	69. 7	20. 8	9. 5	2. 5	3. 2	1. 4	2. 7
EAST SOUTH CENTRAL	2, 874, 227	1, 362, 388	1, 290, 141	221, 698	72. 9	65. 9	85. 5	60. 3	47. 4	44. 9	7. 7	31. 9	27. 7	38. 8	28. 7
Kentucky	138, 252	82, 965	42, 464	12, 823	45. 3	43. 7	62. 3	27. 0	60. 0	30. 7	9. 3	1. 5	1. 7	1. 3	1. 7
Tennessee	309, 906	166, 647	113, 454	29, 805	54. 5	48. 2	69. 2	50. 3	53. 8	36. 6	9. 6	3. 4	3. 4	3. 4	3. 9
Alabama	916, 880	438, 853	397, 886	80, 141	80. 3	71. 5	96. 2	70. 2	47. 9	43. 4	8. 7	10. 2	8. 9	12. 0	10. 4
Mississippi	1, 509, 189	673, 923	736, 337	98, 929	78. 4	73. 5	85. 3	67. 5	44. 7	48. 8	6. 6	16. 7	13. 7	22. 1	12. 8
WEST SOUTH CENTRAL	2, 821, 751	1, 623, 438	885, 633	312, 680	69. 9	66. 8	80. 4	62. 2	57. 5	31. 4	11. 1	31. 3	33. 1	26. 6	40. 5
Arkansas	560, 843	269, 983	237, 339	53, 521	61. 9	59. 7	67. 9	51. 4	48. 1	42. 3	9. 5	6. 2	5. 5	7. 1	6. 9
Louisiana	512, 572	277, 887	180, 582	54, 103	58. 3	54. 7	67. 9	51. 7	54. 2	35. 2	10. 6	5. 7	5. 7	5. 4	7. 0
Oklahoma	623, 258	342, 557	175, 631	105, 070	95. 2	93. 0	109. 5	83. 1	55. 0	28. 2	16. 9	6. 9	7. 0	5. 3	13. 6
Texas	1, 125, 078	733, 011	292, 081	99, 986	70. 5	66. 4	89. 7	59. 6	65. 2	26. 0	8. 9	12. 5	14. 9	8. 8	12. 9
SELECTED NORTHERN STATES [2]	156, 104	66, 673	82, 413	7, 018	56. 0	48. 7	64. 9	46. 5	42. 7	52. 8	4. 5	100. 0	100. 0	100. 0	100. 0
New Jersey	6, 415	2, 289	3, 993	133	29. 6	22. 2	37. 3	19. 0	35. 7	62. 2	2. 1	4. 1	3. 4	4. 8	1. 9
Pennsylvania	9, 600	3, 388	5, 999	213	43. 4	37. 2	49. 6	23. 7	35. 3	62. 5	2. 2	6. 1	5. 1	7. 3	3. 0
Ohio	34, 933	18, 060	14, 585	2, 288	54. 6	55. 7	55. 0	44. 9	51. 7	41. 8	6. 5	22. 4	27. 1	17. 7	32. 6
Indiana	8, 495	2, 965	5, 035	495	41. 0	31. 2	51. 9	33. 0	34. 9	59. 3	5. 8	5. 4	4. 4	6. 1	7. 1
Illinois	15, 871	6, 415	8, 644	812	51. 4	42. 8	61. 7	42. 7	40. 4	54. 5	5. 1	10. 2	9. 6	10. 5	11. 6
Missouri	47, 940	21, 182	25, 469	1, 289	58. 8	50. 9	68. 8	44. 4	44. 2	53. 1	2. 7	30. 7	31. 8	30. 9	18. 4
Kansas	32, 850	12, 374	18, 688	1, 788	86. 2	65. 1	109. 9	85. 1	37. 7	56. 9	5. 4	21. 0	18. 6	22. 7	25. 5

[1] Less than 1/10 of 1 percent.   [2] States having 200 or more Negro farmers who constitute 90 percent or more of the colored farm operators in each State.

TABLE 28.—MORTGAGE STATUS OF COLORED FULL OWNERS AND PERCENT DISTRIBUTION, BY AGE, BY SOUTHERN DIVISIONS, AND STATES, AND SELECTED NORTHERN STATES: 1930 AND 1920

[Colored farmers include Negros, Indians, Chinese, Japanese, and all other nonwhite races]

DIVISION AND STATE	ALL COLORED FULL OWNERS					UNDER 25 YEARS					25 TO 34 YEARS					35 TO 44 YEARS				
	1930			1920		1930			1920		1930			1920		1930			1920	
	Reporting farms free from mortgage	Reporting farms mortgaged	Unknown (no report)	Reporting farms free from mortgage [1]	Reporting farms mortgaged	Reporting farms free from mortgage	Reporting farms mortgaged	Unknown (no report)	Reporting farms free from mortgage [1]	Reporting farms mortgaged	Reporting farms free from mortgage	Reporting farms mortgaged	Unknown (no report)	Reporting farms free from mortgage [1]	Reporting farms mortgaged	Reporting farms free from mortgage	Reporting farms mortgaged	Unknown (no report)	Reporting farms free from mortgage [1]	Reporting farms mortgaged
	NUMBER																			
The South	84,861	41,964	13,671	135,944	42,614	1,643	636	406	3,447	928	6,572	3,298	1,297	13,440	5,166	13,900	7,648	2,333	26,529	9,757
SOUTH ATLANTIC	39,887	15,860	4,967	65,960	17,062	681	170	115	1,590	303	2,903	1,026	432	6,496	1,962	6,938	2,861	845	13,634	4,011
Delaware	162	124	23	178	127	1	-----	1	2	2	7	6	-----	10	12	20	25	3	32	25
Maryland	1,449	814	99	2,170	921	6	4	-----	30	10	80	61	9	152	86	235	168	14	380	224
District of Columbia	2	3	2	6	2	-----	-----	-----	-----	-----	-----	-----	-----	-----	-----	-----	-----	-----	1	-----
Virginia	14,077	4,184	939	20,996	4,524	191	51	17	381	91	981	277	73	1,907	573	2,537	884	167	4,452	1,078
West Virginia	258	48	22	316	50	7	-----	-----	3	1	23	4	-----	22	9	44	9	3	66	9
North Carolina	7,671	4,258	1,269	12,616	3,749	138	44	36	242	52	586	318	126	1,196	429	1,282	779	215	2,439	940
South Carolina	7,745	3,263	929	14,820	3,458	195	40	34	529	72	695	203	92	1,841	420	1,578	574	202	3,520	877
Georgia	5,311	2,541	1,162	10,309	3,375	92	23	20	277	66	318	127	83	943	360	736	325	164	1,894	688
Florida	3,212	625	522	4,549	856	51	8	7	126	9	213	30	49	425	73	506	97	77	850	170
EAST SOUTH CENTRAL	20,659	15,087	3,674	33,375	12,427	355	249	111	642	252	1,433	1,207	340	2,828	1,406	2,887	2,632	558	5,698	2,664
Kentucky	1,898	682	475	3,126	1,054	13	8	22	52	26	105	40	54	207	128	242	114	81	495	252
Tennessee	3,456	1,639	592	6,177	1,694	42	23	16	102	36	192	101	38	415	194	438	259	66	881	333
Alabama	6,140	4,135	1,142	9,933	3,730	116	52	25	182	54	379	262	95	812	385	813	580	162	1,553	620
Mississippi	9,165	8,631	1,465	14,139	5,949	184	166	48	306	136	757	804	153	1,394	699	1,394	1,679	249	2,769	1,459
WEST SOUTH CENTRAL	24,315	11,017	5,030	36,609	13,125	607	217	180	1,215	373	2,236	1,065	525	4,116	1,798	4,075	2,155	930	7,197	3,082
Arkansas	4,521	3,496	1,041	8,041	4,825	84	69	31	204	106	355	248	63	809	555	721	613	173	1,475	1,093
Louisiana	5,080	2,659	1,047	7,527	1,946	104	48	33	169	47	465	230	119	828	251	952	545	212	1,621	462
Oklahoma	3,682	1,604	1,264	5,813	2,189	152	31	59	418	116	613	232	193	977	396	722	333	259	1,376	480
Texas	11,032	3,258	1,678	15,228	4,165	267	69	57	424	104	803	355	150	1,502	596	1,680	664	286	2,725	1,047
SELECTED NORTHERN STATES [2]	1,369	1,270	151	2,199	1,658	5	9	1	35	19	62	58	8	137	152	153	220	21	332	307
New Jersey	103	107	7	145	114	1	-----	-----	1	2	10	5	1	7	10	13	24	2	26	28
Pennsylvania	91	121	9	110	128	1	2	-----	2	2	5	4	3	5	18	11	26	-----	15	15
Ohio	324	265	51	626	276	1	1	1	12	3	13	16	2	37	29	39	56	8	111	50
Indiana	95	97	15	109	103	-----	-----	-----	1	1	2	3	-----	5	8	9	14	3	17	20
Illinois	150	140	19	214	168	-----	1	-----	5	1	4	3	-----	18	10	19	24	3	37	38
Missouri	416	370	29	693	612	1	2	-----	11	9	16	18	2	37	52	36	50	2	82	100
Kansas	190	170	21	302	257	1	3	-----	3	1	12	9	-----	28	25	26	26	3	44	56
	PERCENT DISTRIBUTION																			
The South	60.4	29.9	9.7	76.1	23.9	61.2	23.6	15.1	78.8	21.2	58.9	29.5	11.6	72.2	27.8	58.2	32.0	9.8	73.1	26.9
SOUTH ATLANTIC	65.7	26.1	8.2	79.4	20.6	70.5	17.6	11.9	84.0	16.0	66.6	23.5	9.9	76.8	23.2	65.2	26.9	7.9	77.3	22.7
Delaware	52.4	40.1	7.4	58.4	41.6	50.0	-----	50.0	50.0	50.0	53.8	46.2	-----	45.5	54.5	41.7	52.1	6.3	56.1	43.9
Maryland	61.3	34.5	4.2	70.2	29.8	60.0	40.0	-----	75.0	25.0	53.3	40.7	6.0	63.9	36.1	56.4	40.3	3.4	62.9	37.1
District of Columbia	28.6	42.9	28.6	75.0	25.0	-----	-----	-----	-----	-----	-----	-----	-----	-----	-----	-----	-----	-----	100.0	-----
Virginia	73.3	21.8	4.9	82.3	17.7	73.7	19.7	6.6	80.7	19.3	73.7	20.8	5.5	76.9	23.1	70.7	24.6	4.7	80.5	19.5
West Virginia	78.7	14.6	6.7	86.3	13.7	100.0	-----	-----	75.0	25.0	85.2	14.8	-----	71.0	29.0	78.6	16.1	5.4	88.0	12.0
North Carolina	58.1	32.3	9.6	77.1	22.9	63.3	20.2	16.5	82.3	17.7	56.9	30.9	12.2	73.6	26.4	56.3	34.2	9.4	72.2	27.8
South Carolina	64.9	27.3	7.8	81.1	18.9	72.5	14.9	12.6	88.0	12.0	70.2	20.5	9.3	81.4	18.6	67.0	24.4	8.6	80.1	19.9
Georgia	58.9	28.2	12.9	75.3	24.7	68.1	17.0	14.8	80.8	19.2	60.2	24.1	15.7	72.4	27.6	60.1	26.5	13.4	73.4	26.6
Florida	73.7	14.3	12.0	84.2	15.8	77.3	12.1	10.6	93.3	6.7	72.9	10.3	16.8	85.3	14.7	74.4	14.3	11.3	83.3	16.7
EAST SOUTH CENTRAL	52.4	38.3	9.3	72.9	27.1	49.7	34.8	15.5	71.8	28.2	48.1	40.5	11.4	66.8	33.2	47.5	43.3	9.2	68.1	31.9
Kentucky	62.1	22.3	15.5	74.8	25.2	30.2	18.6	51.2	66.7	33.3	52.8	20.1	27.1	61.8	38.2	55.4	26.1	18.5	66.3	33.7
Tennessee	60.8	28.8	10.4	78.5	21.5	51.9	28.4	19.8	73.9	26.1	58.0	30.5	11.5	68.1	31.9	57.4	33.9	8.7	72.6	27.4
Alabama	53.8	36.2	10.0	72.7	27.3	60.1	26.9	13.0	77.1	22.9	51.5	35.6	12.9	67.8	32.2	52.3	37.3	10.4	71.5	28.5
Mississippi	47.6	44.8	7.6	70.4	29.6	46.2	41.7	12.1	69.2	30.8	44.2	46.9	8.9	66.6	33.4	42.0	50.5	7.5	65.5	34.5
WEST SOUTH CENTRAL	60.2	27.3	12.5	73.6	26.4	60.5	21.6	17.9	76.5	23.5	58.4	27.8	13.7	69.6	30.4	56.9	30.1	13.0	70.0	30.0
Arkansas	49.9	38.6	11.5	62.5	37.5	45.7	37.5	16.8	65.8	34.2	53.3	37.2	9.5	59.3	40.7	47.8	40.7	11.5	57.4	42.6
Louisiana	57.8	30.3	11.9	79.5	20.5	56.2	25.9	17.8	78.2	21.8	57.1	28.3	14.6	76.7	23.3	55.7	31.9	12.4	77.8	22.2
Oklahoma	56.2	24.5	19.3	72.6	27.4	62.8	12.8	24.4	78.3	21.7	59.1	22.4	18.6	71.2	28.8	54.9	25.3	19.7	74.1	25.9
Texas	69.1	20.4	10.5	78.5	21.5	67.9	17.6	14.5	80.3	19.7	61.4	27.1	11.5	71.6	28.4	63.9	25.2	10.9	72.2	27.8
SELECTED NORTHERN STATES [2]	49.1	45.5	5.4	57.0	43.0	33.3	60.0	6.7	64.8	35.2	48.4	45.3	6.3	47.4	52.6	38.8	55.8	5.3	52.0	48.0
New Jersey	47.5	49.3	3.2	56.0	44.0	100.0	-----	-----	33.3	66.7	62.5	31.3	6.3	41.2	58.8	33.3	61.5	5.1	48.1	51.9
Pennsylvania	41.2	54.8	4.1	46.2	53.8	33.3	66.7	-----	50.0	50.0	41.7	33.3	25.0	21.7	78.3	29.7	70.3	-----	50.0	50.0
Ohio	50.6	41.4	8.0	69.4	30.6	33.3	33.3	33.3	80.0	20.0	41.9	51.6	6.5	56.1	43.9	37.9	54.4	7.8	68.9	31.1
Indiana	45.9	46.9	7.2	51.4	48.6	-----	-----	-----	50.0	50.0	40.0	60.0	-----	38.5	61.5	34.6	53.8	11.5	45.9	54.1
Illinois	48.5	45.3	6.1	56.0	44.0	-----	100.0	-----	83.3	16.7	57.1	42.9	-----	64.3	35.7	41.3	52.2	6.5	49.3	50.7
Missouri	51.0	45.4	3.6	53.1	46.9	33.3	66.7	-----	55.0	45.0	44.4	50.0	56.6	41.6	58.4	40.9	56.8	2.3	45.1	54.9
Kansas	49.9	44.6	5.5	54.0	46.0	25.0	75.0	-----	75.0	25.0	57.1	42.9	-----	52.8	47.2	47.3	47.3	5.5	44.0	56.0

[1] Includes full owners whose mortgage status was not reported.
[2] States having 200 or more Negro farmers who constitute 90 percent or more of the colored farmers in the State.

TABLE 28.—MORTGAGE STATUS OF COLORED FULL OWNERS AND PERCENT DISTRIBUTION, BY AGE, BY SOUTHERN DIVISIONS, AND STATES, AND SELECTED NORTHERN STATES: 1930 AND 1920—Continued

[Colored farmers include Negroes, Indians, Chinese, Japanese, and all other nonwhite races]

DIVISION AND STATE	45 TO 54 YEARS					55 TO 64 YEARS					65 YEARS AND OVER					AGE NOT REPORTED				
	1930			1920		1930			1920		1930			1920		1930			1920	
	Reporting farms free from mortgage	Reporting farms mortgaged	Unknown (no report)	Reporting farms free from mortgage [1]	Reporting farms mortgaged	Reporting farms free from mortgage	Reporting farms mortgaged	Unknown (no report)	Reporting farms free from mortgage [1]	Reporting farms mortgaged	Reporting farms free from mortgage	Reporting farms mortgaged	Unknown (no report)	Reporting farms free from mortgage [1]	Reporting farms mortgaged	Reporting farms free from mortgage	Reporting farms mortgaged	Unknown (no report)	Reporting farms free from mortgage [1]	Reporting farms mortgaged
	NUMBER																			
The South	**22, 353**	**12, 753**	**3, 480**	**38, 106**	**13, 786**	**20, 640**	**10, 493**	**2, 980**	**28, 693**	**7, 992**	**17, 779**	**6, 230**	**2, 665**	**24, 226**	**4, 530**	**1, 974**	**906**	**510**	**1, 503**	**455**
SOUTH ATLANTIC	10, 601	4, 812	1, 319	18, 238	5, 375	9, 613	4, 139	1, 089	13, 935	3, 344	8, 198	2, 523	977	11, 401	1, 872	953	329	190	666	195
Delaware	45	35	7	50	36	39	36	7	48	29	46	20	5	36	21	4	2	-----	-----	2
Maryland	347	245	20	611	296	418	211	27	557	193	332	104	21	419	104	31	21	8	21	8
District of Columbia	1	1	1	3	1	1	1	1	1	1	-----	1	-----	1	-----			-----		-----
Virginia	3, 857	1, 270	247	5, 917	1, 402	3, 290	1, 017	183	4, 381	830	2, 887	604	215	3, 770	497	334	81	37	188	53
West Virginia	61	10	7	73	14	54	12	9	78	13	60	11	3	68	4	9	2	-----	6	-----
North Carolina	1, 869	1, 229	317	3, 204	1, 113	1, 861	1, 084	262	2, 853	741	1, 716	697	266	2, 510	439	219	107	47	172	35
South Carolina	2, 154	1, 022	236	3, 925	1, 079	1, 666	862	193	2, 734	625	1, 279	510	148	2, 164	347	178	52	24	107	38
Georgia	1, 423	823	347	3, 087	1, 150	1, 435	733	286	2, 309	712	1, 220	462	230	1, 689	351	87	48	32	110	48
Florida	844	177	137	1, 368	284	849	183	121	974	200	658	114	89	744	109	91	16	42	62	11
EAST SOUTH CENTRAL	5, 497	4, 641	918	9, 525	4, 080	5, 228	3, 785	848	7, 456	2, 440	4, 844	2, 269	765	6, 785	1, 461	415	304	134	441	124
Kentucky	441	194	90	818	305	472	170	86	706	196	570	140	119	778	130	55	16	23	70	17
Tennessee	833	465	140	1, 671	531	895	434	159	1, 565	378	986	313	149	1, 457	195	70	44	24	86	27
Alabama	1, 902	1, 457	324	3, 174	1, 433	1, 483	1, 057	287	2, 152	766	1, 360	650	213	1, 931	428	87	77	36	129	44
Mississippi	2, 321	2, 525	364	3, 862	1, 811	2, 378	2, 124	316	3, 033	1, 100	1, 928	1, 166	284	2, 619	708	203	167	51	156	36
WEST SOUTH CENTRAL	6, 255	3, 300	1, 243	10, 343	4, 331	5, 799	2, 569	1, 043	7, 302	2, 208	4, 737	1, 438	923	6, 040	1, 197	606	273	186	396	136
Arkansas	1, 281	1, 145	294	2, 623	1, 701	1, 126	844	228	1, 651	820	834	507	224	1, 201	488	120	70	28	78	62
Louisiana	1, 348	797	270	2, 073	646	1, 182	656	210	1, 475	329	918	328	183	1, 267	195	111	55	20	94	16
Oklahoma	870	404	297	1, 399	612	693	353	230	861	390	518	209	150	675	173	114	42	76	107	22
Texas	2, 756	954	382	4, 248	1, 372	2, 798	716	375	3, 315	669	2, 467	394	366	2, 897	341	261	106	62	117	36
SELECTED NORTHERN STATES [2]	297	342	34	476	446	367	325	38	588	410	456	281	43	578	306	29	35	6	53	18
New Jersey	24	35	1	32	41	34	26	-----	46	26	18	16	3	31	7	3	1	-----	2	-----
Pennsylvania	27	42	2	28	39	19	32	3	29	27	28	12	1	29	27	-----	3	-----	2	-----
Ohio	69	61	10	152	75	92	66	11	154	71	102	56	17	149	45	8	9	2	11	3
Indiana	21	28	3	22	23	26	25	3	23	27	34	25	2	38	23	3	2	4	3	1
Illinois	37	38	7	47	41	41	40	4	52	42	45	26	5	52	33	4	8	-----	3	3
Missouri	80	90	8	129	165	119	92	6	214	156	155	110	11	196	119	9	8	-----	24	11
Kansas	39	48	3	66	62	36	44	11	70	61	74	36	4	83	52	2	4	-----	8	-----
	PERCENT DISTRIBUTION																			
The South	**57. 9**	**33. 1**	**9. 0**	**73. 4**	**26. 6**	**60. 5**	**30. 8**	**8. 7**	**78. 2**	**21. 8**	**66. 7**	**23. 4**	**10. 0**	**84. 2**	**15. 8**	**58. 2**	**26. 7**	**15. 0**	**76. 8**	**23. 2**
SOUTH ATLANTIC	63. 4	28. 8	7. 9	77. 2	22. 8	64. 8	27. 9	7. 3	80. 6	19. 4	70. 1	21. 6	8. 4	85. 9	14. 1	64. 7	22. 4	12. 9	77. 4	22. 6
Delaware	51. 7	40. 2	8. 0	58. 1	41. 9	47. 6	43. 9	8. 5	62. 3	37. 7	64. 8	28. 2	7. 0	63. 2	36. 8	66. 7	33. 3	-----	-----	100. 0
Maryland	56. 7	40. 0	3. 3	67. 4	32. 6	63. 7	32. 2	4. 1	74. 3	25. 7	72. 6	22. 8	4. 6	80. 1	19. 9	51. 7	35. 0	13. 3	72. 4	27. 6
District of Columbia	33. 3	33. 3	33. 3	75. 0	25. 0	33. 3	33. 3	33. 3	50. 0	50. 0	-----	100. 0	-----	100. 0	-----	-----	-----	-----	-----	-----
Virginia	71. 8	23. 6	4. 6	80. 8	19. 2	73. 3	22. 7	4. 1	84. 1	15. 9	77. 9	16. 3	5. 8	88. 4	11. 6	73. 9	17. 9	8. 2	78. 0	22. 0
West Virginia	78. 2	12. 8	9. 0	83. 9	16. 1	72. 0	16. 0	12. 0	85. 7	14. 3	81. 1	14. 9	4. 1	94. 4	5. 6	81. 8	18. 2	-----	100. 0	-----
North Carolina	54. 7	36. 0	9. 3	74. 2	25. 8	58. 0	33. 8	8. 2	79. 4	20. 6	64. 1	26. 0	9. 9	85. 1	14. 9	58. 7	28. 7	12. 6	83. 1	16. 9
South Carolina	63. 1	30. 0	6. 9	78. 4	21. 6	61. 2	31. 7	7. 1	81. 4	18. 6	66. 0	26. 3	7. 6	86. 2	13. 8	70. 1	20. 5	9. 4	73. 8	26. 2
Georgia	54. 9	31. 7	13. 4	72. 9	27. 1	58. 5	29. 9	11. 7	76. 4	23. 6	63. 8	24. 2	12. 0	82. 8	17. 2	52. 1	28. 7	19. 2	69. 6	30. 4
Florida	72. 9	15. 3	11. 8	82. 8	17. 2	73. 6	15. 9	10. 5	83. 0	17. 0	76. 4	13. 2	10. 3	87. 2	12. 8	61. 1	10. 7	28. 2	84. 9	15. 1
EAST SOUTH CENTRAL	49. 7	42. 0	8. 3	70. 0	30. 0	53. 0	38. 4	8. 6	75. 3	24. 7	61. 5	28. 8	9. 7	82. 3	17. 7	48. 7	35. 6	15. 7	78. 1	21. 9
Kentucky	60. 8	26. 8	12. 4	72. 8	27. 2	64. 8	23. 4	11. 8	78. 3	21. 7	68. 8	16. 9	14. 4	85. 7	14. 3	58. 5	17. 0	24. 5	80. 5	19. 5
Tennessee	57. 9	32. 3	9. 7	75. 9	24. 1	60. 1	29. 2	10. 7	80. 5	19. 5	68. 1	21. 6	10. 3	88. 2	11. 8	50. 7	31. 9	17. 4	76. 1	23. 9
Alabama	51. 6	39. 6	8. 8	68. 9	31. 1	52. 5	37. 4	10. 2	73. 7	26. 3	61. 2	29. 2	9. 6	81. 9	18. 1	43. 5	38. 5	18. 0	74. 6	25. 4
Mississippi	44. 5	48. 5	7. 0	68. 1	31. 9	49. 4	44. 1	6. 6	73. 4	26. 6	57. 1	34. 5	8. 4	78. 7	21. 3	48. 2	39. 7	12. 1	81. 3	18. 8
WEST SOUTH CENTRAL	57. 9	30. 6	11. 5	70. 5	29. 5	61. 6	27. 3	11. 1	76. 8	23. 2	66. 7	20. 3	13. 0	83. 5	16. 5	56. 9	25. 6	17. 5	74. 4	25. 6
Arkansas	47. 1	42. 1	10. 8	60. 7	39. 3	51. 2	38. 4	10. 4	66. 8	33. 2	53. 3	32. 4	14. 3	71. 1	28. 9	55. 0	32. 1	12. 8	55. 7	44. 3
Louisiana	55. 8	33. 0	11. 2	76. 2	23. 8	57. 7	32. 0	10. 3	81. 8	18. 2	64. 2	23. 0	12. 8	86. 7	13. 3	59. 7	29. 6	10. 8	85. 5	14. 5
Oklahoma	55. 4	25. 7	18. 9	69. 6	30. 4	54. 3	27. 7	18. 0	68. 8	31. 2	59. 1	23. 8	17. 1	79. 6	20. 4	49. 1	18. 1	32. 8	82. 9	17. 1
Texas	67. 4	23. 3	9. 3	75. 6	24. 4	71. 9	18. 4	9. 6	83. 2	16. 8	76. 4	12. 2	11. 3	89. 5	10. 5	60. 8	24. 7	14. 5	76. 5	23. 5
SELECTED NORTHERN STATES [2]	44. 1	50. 8	5. 1	51. 6	48. 4	50. 3	44. 5	5. 2	58. 9	41. 1	58. 5	36. 0	5. 5	65. 4	34. 6	41. 4	50. 0	8. 6	74. 6	25. 4
New Jersey	40. 0	58. 3	1. 7	43. 8	56. 2	56. 7	43. 3	-----	63. 9	36. 1	48. 6	43. 2	8. 1	81. 6	18. 4	75. 0	25. 0	-----	100. 0	-----
Pennsylvania	38. 0	59. 2	2. 8	41. 8	58. 2	35. 2	59. 3	5. 6	51. 8	48. 2	68. 3	29. 3	2. 4	51. 8	48. 2	-----	100. 0	-----	100. 0	-----
Ohio	49. 3	43. 6	7. 1	67. 0	33. 0	54. 4	39. 1	6. 5	68. 4	31. 6	58. 3	32. 0	9. 7	76. 8	23. 2	42. 1	47. 4	10. 5	78. 6	21. 4
Indiana	40. 4	53. 8	5. 8	48. 9	51. 1	48. 1	46. 3	5. 6	46. 0	54. 0	55. 7	41. 0	3. 3	62. 3	37. 7	33. 3	22. 2	44. 4	75. 0	25. 0
Illinois	45. 1	46. 3	8. 5	53. 4	46. 6	48. 2	47. 1	4. 7	55. 3	44. 7	59. 2	34. 2	6. 6	61. 2	38. 8	33. 3	66. 7	-----	50. 0	50. 0
Missouri	44. 9	50. 6	4. 5	43. 9	56. 1	54. 8	42. 4	2. 8	57. 8	42. 2	56. 2	39. 9	4. 0	62. 2	37. 8	52. 9	47. 1	-----	68. 6	31. 4
Kansas	43. 3	53. 3	3. 3	51. 6	48. 4	39. 6	48. 4	12. 1	53. 4	46. 6	64. 9	31. 6	3. 5	61. 5	38. 5	33. 3	66. 7	-----	100. 0	-----

[1] Includes full owners whose mortgage status was not reported.
[2] States having 200 or more Negro farmers who constitute 90 percent or more of the colored farmers in the State.

TABLE 29.—NUMBER OF FARMS OPERATED BY NEGROES, BY TYPE OF FARM, BY SECTIONS, DIVISIONS, AND STATES: 1930

SECTION, DIVISION, AND STATE	Total number of farms	Self-sufficing	Abnormal	Truck	Fruit	Cash-grain	Cotton	General	Crop-specialty	Dairy	Stock-ranch	Poultry	Animal specialty
United States	**882, 850**	**42, 987**	**64, 250**	**7, 041**	**2, 904**	**3, 256**	**665, 255**	**26, 822**	**66, 246**	**1, 520**	**123**	**846**	**1, 600**
The North	**11, 104**	**1, 266**	**1, 849**	**356**	**113**	**783**	**3, 593**	**1, 585**	**256**	**438**	**6**	**253**	**606**
The South	**870, 936**	**41, 683**	**62, 169**	**6, 661**	**2, 739**	**2, 448**	**661, 448**	**25, 182**	**65, 939**	**1, 028**	**100**	**560**	**979**
The West	**810**	**38**	**232**	**24**	**52**	**25**	**214**	**55**	**51**	**54**	**17**	**33**	**15**
NEW ENGLAND	148	21	46	7	23	------	------	14	5	21	------	11	------
Maine	15	4	4	------	1	------	------	1	1	4	------	------	------
New Hampshire	6	1	3	------	------	------	------	1	------	1	------	------	------
Vermont	22	3	10	------	1	------	------	------	------	8	------	------	------
Massachusetts	63	7	16	5	21	------	------	5	------	2	------	7	------
Rhode Island	9	------	3	------	------	------	------	4	------	2	------	------	------
Connecticut	33	6	10	2	------	------	------	3	4	4	------	4	------
MIDDLE ATLANTIC	873	80	244	173	9	7	------	136	32	135	------	51	6
New York	148	15	38	3	2	------	------	27	11	40	------	10	2
New Jersey	372	20	78	160	6	1	------	37	11	30	------	28	1
Pennsylvania	353	45	128	10	1	6	------	72	10	65	------	13	3
EAST NORTH CENTRAL	3, 065	516	691	135	69	230	69	746	126	217	------	76	190
Ohio	1, 229	220	285	41	16	98	------	285	58	92	------	43	91
Indiana	461	61	116	22	------	41	------	106	34	26	------	12	43
Illinois	893	187	175	63	39	80	69	215	2	12	------	11	40
Michigan	427	39	108	9	14	11	------	128	32	61	------	10	15
Wisconsin	55	9	7	------	------	------	------	12	------	26	------	------	1
WEST NORTH CENTRAL	7, 018	649	868	41	12	546	3, 524	689	93	65	6	115	410
Minnesota	27	2	7	1	1	1	------	4	3	5	------	2	1
Iowa	118	22	19	2	------	9	------	26	1	4	------	3	32
Missouri	5, 844	508	681	8	3	287	3, 471	447	43	34	------	88	274
North Dakota	10	------	------	1	------	4	------	4	1	------	------	------	------
South Dakota	40	------	4	4	------	9	------	10	2	2	3	------	6
Nebraska	38	3	7	1	1	8	------	5	2	1	1	------	9
Kansas	941	114	150	24	7	228	53	193	41	19	2	22	88
SOUTH ATLANTIC	295, 934	24, 044	29, 822	3, 847	1, 189	860	164, 026	14, 226	56, 929	276	7	323	385
Delaware	807	101	159	133	46	40	------	240	31	18	------	39	------
Maryland	5, 264	650	1, 171	731	160	169	------	690	1, 570	56	------	50	17
District of Columbia	11	2	3	4	------	------	------	1	------	------	------	1	------
Virginia	39, 598	11, 488	7, 694	514	125	218	2, 131	4, 316	12, 788	65	------	154	105
West Virginia	490	264	131	------	2	8	------	59	1	14	------	5	6
North Carolina	74, 636	3, 641	4, 390	262	341	118	31, 132	2, 444	32, 228	30	------	15	35
South Carolina	77, 331	3, 131	6, 736	456	10	187	58, 909	2, 312	5, 511	28	2	13	36
Georgia	86, 787	2, 373	7, 640	358	98	76	69, 985	2, 401	3, 714	49	4	10	79
Florida	11, 010	2, 394	1, 898	1, 389	407	44	1, 869	1, 763	1, 086	16	1	36	107
EAST SOUTH CENTRAL	320, 600	11, 518	16, 706	2, 176	176	635	274, 092	6, 738	7, 490	612	15	83	359
Kentucky	9, 104	1, 731	1, 529	26	21	129	276	851	4, 390	53	1	15	82
Tennessee	35, 123	3, 117	2, 808	269	41	471	23, 933	1, 736	2, 440	101	------	46	161
Alabama	93, 795	3, 499	5, 031	68	100	8	82, 457	1, 938	503	118	8	15	50
Mississippi	182, 578	3, 171	7, 338	1, 813	14	27	167, 426	2, 213	157	340	6	7	66
WEST SOUTH CENTRAL	254, 402	6, 121	15, 641	638	1, 374	953	223, 330	4, 218	1, 520	140	78	154	235
Arkansas	79, 556	994	4, 312	38	29	82	73, 395	603	69	23	------	1	10
Louisiana	73, 734	1, 915	4, 072	355	1, 263	252	63, 209	1, 326	1, 235	44	5	21	37
Oklahoma	15, 172	1, 002	1, 275	11	28	317	11, 494	838	66	20	5	34	82
Texas	85, 940	2, 210	5, 982	234	54	302	75, 232	1, 451	150	53	68	98	106
MOUNTAIN	304	17	80	4	3	17	99	31	22	12	10	6	3
Montana	21	1	2	------	------	7	------	8	------	------	3	------	------
Idaho	16	------	4	------	------	4	------	1	5	2	------	------	------
Wyoming	12	4	1	------	------	1	------	3	1	------	2	------	------
Colorado	78	4	28	1	------	5	------	13	11	9	3	2	2
New Mexico	82	6	25	2	------	------	44	1	3	------	1	------	------
Arizona	87	2	16	1	1	------	55	4	1	1	1	4	1
Utah	5	------	2	------	2	------	------	1	------	------	------	------	------
Nevada	3	------	2	------	------	------	------	------	1	------	------	------	------
PACIFIC	506	21	152	20	49	8	115	24	29	42	7	27	12
Washington	73	2	28	------	6	2	------	13	3	3	3	11	2
Oregon	9	4	1	------	1	1	------	------	------	1	------	1	------
California	424	15	123	20	42	5	115	11	26	38	4	15	10

TABLE 30.—ALL LAND, AND CROP LAND HARVESTED, IN FARMS OF COLORED AND WHITE OWNERS, BY SOUTHERN DIVISIONS, AND STATES, AND SELECTED NORTHERN STATES: CENSUS OF 1930

[Colored farmers include Negroes, Indians, Chinese, Japanese, and all other nonwhite races. White includes Mexicans and Hindus]

DIVISION AND STATE	ALL LAND IN FARMS, 1930		CROP LAND HARVESTED, 1929			
			Number of acres		Percent "All land in farms"	
					Percent	
	Colored	White	Colored	White	Colored	White
The South	11, 478, 898	178, 621, 215	4, 122, 806	45, 035, 636	35. 9	25. 2
SOUTH ATLANTIC	4, 258, 325	47, 393, 132	1, 508, 634	12, 119, 693	35. 4	25. 6
Delaware	13, 781	466, 704	6, 039	207, 770	43. 8	44. 5
Maryland	107, 935	2, 532, 361	34, 273	993, 600	31. 8	39. 2
District of Columbia	28	697	11	416	39. 3	59. 7
Virginia	1, 183, 134	11, 066, 532	331, 379	2, 484, 959	28. 0	22. 5
West Virginia	18, 542	7, 126, 681	3, 772	1, 348, 521	20. 3	18. 9
North Carolina	982, 111	10, 090, 169	371, 689	2, 563, 366	37. 8	25. 4
South Carolina	787, 551	4, 440, 414	323, 781	1, 299, 537	41. 1	29. 3
Georgia	883, 324	8, 971, 316	323, 737	2, 447, 112	36. 6	27. 3
Florida	281, 919	2, 698, 258	113, 953	774, 412	40. 4	28. 7
EAST SOUTH CENTRAL	3, 522, 790	41, 765, 792	1, 138, 893	10, 627, 197	32. 3	25. 4
Kentucky	183, 148	14, 427, 710	54, 756	3, 606, 586	29. 9	25. 0
Tennessee	419, 211	11, 309, 984	156, 685	3, 264, 382	37. 4	28. 9
Alabama	1, 189, 873	8, 214, 031	420, 125	2, 218, 415	35. 3	27. 0
Mississippi	1, 730, 558	7, 814, 067	507, 327	1, 537, 814	29. 3	19. 7
WEST SOUTH CENTRAL	3, 697, 783	89, 462, 291	1, 475, 279	22, 338, 746	39. 9	25. 0
Arkansas	705, 156	8, 285, 121	292, 899	2, 458, 312	41. 5	29. 7
Louisiana	602, 967	4, 157, 573	239, 030	1, 229, 294	39. 6	29. 6
Oklahoma	914, 689	15, 556, 837	325, 508	6, 764, 319	35. 6	43. 5
Texas	1, 474, 971	61, 462, 760	617, 842	11, 886, 821	41. 9	19. 3
SELECTED NORTHERN STATES [1]	275, 792	104, 858, 240	115, 117	48, 495, 136	41. 7	46. 2
New Jersey	7, 682	1, 227, 874	3, 251	546, 553	42. 3	44. 5
Pennsylvania	10, 256	11, 945, 213	4, 018	4, 953, 985	39. 2	41. 5
Ohio	45, 504	14, 364, 938	16, 476	6, 384, 757	36. 2	44. 4
Indiana	14, 607	12, 271, 620	6, 245	6, 015, 323	42. 8	49. 0
Illinois	27, 641	15, 198, 903	12, 025	8, 628, 302	43. 5	56. 8
Missouri	76, 296	22, 141, 050	29, 205	8, 217, 867	38. 3	37. 1
Kansas	93, 806	27, 708, 642	43, 897	13, 748, 349	46. 8	49. 6

[1] States having 200 or more Negro farmers who constitute 90 percent or more of the colored farmers in the State.

TABLE 31.—VALUE OF FARM PRODUCTS SOLD, TRADED, OR USED BY THE FAMILY OF COLORED OPERATORS, BY TENURE, BY SOUTHERN DIVISIONS, AND STATES, AND SELECTED NORTHERN STATES: 1929

[Colored farmers include Negroes, Indians, Chinese, Japanese, and all other nonwhite races]

DIVISION AND STATE	VALUE OF PRODUCTS REPORTED BY—						
					Percent distribution		
	Total	Owners	Tenants	Managers	Owners	Tenants	Managers
The South	$646,641,216	$119,415,311	$524,974,053	$2,251,852	18. 5	81. 2	0. 3
SOUTH ATLANTIC	222, 454, 239	49, 111, 473	172, 103, 916	1, 239, 150	22. 1	77. 4	. 6
Delaware	764, 973	288, 057	431, 807	45, 109	37. 7	56. 4	5. 9
Maryland	4, 791, 394	1, 937, 047	2, 574, 103	280, 244	40. 4	53. 7	5. 8
District of Columbia	11, 460	3, 720	1, 850	5, 890	32. 5	16. 1	51. 4
Virginia	27, 130, 851	13, 462, 260	13, 435, 870	232, 721	49. 6	49. 5	. 9
West Virginia	267, 361	193, 621	66, 517	7, 223	72. 4	24. 9	2. 7
North Carolina	67, 810, 383	14, 107, 815	53, 623, 883	78, 685	20. 8	79. 1	. 1
South Carolina	52, 240, 775	8, 823, 166	43, 276, 542	141, 067	16. 9	82. 8	. 3
Georgia	63, 489, 255	7, 370, 780	55, 910, 339	208, 136	11. 6	88. 1	. 3
Florida	5, 948, 087	2, 925, 007	2, 783, 005	240, 075	49. 2	46. 8	4. 0
EAST SOUTH CENTRAL	239, 301, 592	35, 025, 231	203, 868, 996	407, 365	14. 6	85. 2	. 2
Kentucky	6, 195, 476	2, 616, 064	3, 553, 811	25, 601	42. 2	57. 4	. 4
Tennessee	25, 147, 620	4, 990, 850	20, 081, 668	75, 102	19. 8	79. 9	. 3
Alabama	57, 954, 853	10, 670, 736	47, 149, 048	135, 069	18. 4	81. 4	. 2
Mississippi	150, 003, 643	16, 747, 581	133, 084, 469	171, 593	11. 2	88. 7	. 1
WEST SOUTH CENTRAL	184, 885, 085	35, 278, 607	149, 001, 141	605, 337	19. 1	80. 6	. 3
Arkansas	61, 721, 444	8, 479, 772	53, 182, 042	59, 630	13. 7	86. 2	. 1
Louisiana	54, 729, 926	7, 440, 862	47, 181, 923	107, 141	13. 6	86. 2	. 2
Oklahoma	16, 068, 774	6, 457, 086	9, 377, 480	234, 208	40. 2	58. 4	1. 5
Texas	52, 364, 941	12, 900, 887	39, 259, 696	204, 358	24. 6	75. 0	. 4
SELECTED NORTHERN STATES [1]	9, 225, 358	3, 090, 587	5, 896, 362	238, 409	33. 5	63. 9	2. 6
New Jersey	692, 803	342, 050	276, 034	74, 719	49. 4	39. 8	10. 8
Pennsylvania	391, 810	203, 648	157, 293	30, 869	52. 0	40. 1	7. 9
Ohio	1, 017, 640	542, 097	451, 735	23, 808	53. 3	44. 4	2. 3
Indiana	365, 305	183, 459	174, 589	7, 257	50. 2	47. 8	2. 0
Illinois	665, 389	323, 620	327, 782	13, 987	48. 6	49. 3	2. 1
Missouri	4, 992, 925	844, 463	4, 076, 005	72, 457	16. 9	81. 6	1. 5
Kansas	1, 099, 486	651, 250	432, 924	15, 312	59. 2	39. 4	1. 4

[1] States having 200 or more Negro farmers who constitute 90 percent or more of the colored farmers in the State.

TABLE 32.—PRODUCTION OF COTTON AND COTTONSEED, BY SELECTED STATES: 1929

[Colored farmers include Negroes, Indians, Chinese, Japanese, and all other nonwhite races]

STATE	ALL FARM OPERATORS REPORTING—		COLORED FARM OPERATORS REPORTING—			
					Percent of total	
	Lint cotton (bales)	Cotton-seed (tons)	Lint cotton (bales)	Cot seed (tons)	Lint cotton (bales)	Cotton seed (tons)
Total	14, 080, 231	6, 672, 232	4, 535, 323	2, 175, 434	32. 2	32. 6
Virginia	52, 442	25, 266	25, 791	12, 371	49. 2	49. 0
North Carolina	764, 328	354, 164	297, 838	137, 679	39. 0	38. 9
South Carolina	835, 963	381, 260	390, 999	177, 807	46. 8	46. 6
Georgia	1, 344, 488	625, 735	479, 031	223, 884	35. 6	35. 8
Florida	34, 426	17, 093	7, 726	3, 846	22. 4	22. 5
Kentucky	8, 955	4, 465	3, 893	1, 942	43. 5	43. 5
Tennessee	503, 816	240, 613	163, 440	78, 648	32. 4	32. 7
Alabama	1, 312, 963	629, 410	423, 198	203, 214	32. 2	32. 3
Mississippi	1, 875, 108	914, 893	1, 234, 841	606, 612	65. 9	66. 3
Arkansas	1, 398, 475	685, 902	540, 522	267, 657	38. 7	39. 0
Louisiana	798, 828	385, 476	425, 386	204, 952	53. 3	53. 2
Oklahoma	1, 130, 415	534, 123	88, 017	43, 021	7. 8	8. 1
Texas	3, 793, 392	1, 762, 736	412, 125	193, 023	10. 9	11. 0
Illinois	826	419	544	284	65. 9	67. 8
Missouri	225, 351	110, 449	41, 619	20, 317	18. 5	18. 4
Kansas	455	228	353	177	77. 6	77. 6

TABLE 33.—TOBACCO—ACREAGE AND PRODUCTION, BY STATES REPORTING 10,000 POUNDS OR MORE PRODUCED BY COLORED FARMERS: 1929

[Colored farmers include Negroes, Indians, Chinese, Japanese, and all other nonwhite races]

STATE	ALL FARM OPERATORS REPORTING—		COLORED FARM OPERATORS REPORTING—			
					Percent of total	
	Acreage	Production (pounds)	Acreage	Production (pounds)	Acreage	Production
Total	1, 814, 170	1, 366, 693, 200	365, 798	239, 049, 788	20. 2	17. 5
North Carolina	685, 074	454, 222, 610	212, 144	132, 096, 917	31. 0	29. 1
Virginia	172, 134	115, 825, 610	52, 501	32, 073, 630	30. 5	27. 7
South Carolina	112, 852	83, 302, 706	39, 190	26, 767, 233	34. 7	32. 1
Kentucky	466, 118	376, 648, 533	25, 420	20, 389, 130	5. 5	5. 4
Tennessee	129, 973	112, 236, 961	13, 359	10, 611, 826	10. 3	9. 5
Georgia	90, 170	82, 363, 722	11, 572	9, 910, 692	12. 8	12. 0
Maryland	32, 974	21, 624, 127	9, 400	5, 326, 232	28. 5	24. 6
Florida	10, 302	9, 248, 190	1, 618	1, 410, 717	15. 7	15. 3
Ohio	49, 575	39, 828, 515	303	227, 580	. 6	. 6
Indiana	19, 372	15, 901, 768	184	141, 414	. 9	. 9
Alabama	547	357, 093	64	51, 820	11. 7	14. 5
Pennsylvania	40, 040	50, 584, 276	21	25, 630	. 1	. 1
Missouri	5, 039	4, 549, 089	22	16, 967	. 4	. 4

TABLE 34.—SWEETPOTATOES AND YAMS—ACREAGE AND PRODUCTION, BY STATES REPORTING 10,000 BUSHELS OR MORE PRODUCED BY COLORED FARMERS: 1929

[Colored farmers include Negroes, Indians, Chinese, Japanese, and all other nonwhite races]

STATE	ALL FARM OPERATORS REPORTING—		COLORED FARM OPERATORS REPORTING—			
					Percent of total	
	Acreage	Production (bushels)	Acreage	Production (bushels)	Acreage	Production
Total	618, 356	61, 979, 860	166, 520	14, 998, 766	26. 9	24. 2
Alabama	68, 105	6, 601, 508	27, 533	2, 361, 303	40. 4	35. 8
Mississippi	53, 412	6, 141, 197	20, 881	2, 135, 310	39. 1	34. 8
Georgia	84, 855	7, 889, 447	24, 440	2, 127, 760	28. 8	27. 0
South Carolina	46, 776	5, 011, 099	21, 473	1, 968, 343	45. 9	39. 3
Virginia	35, 720	5, 042, 596	11, 617	1, 545, 236	32. 5	30. 6
Louisiana	66, 579	4, 953, 138	20, 952	1, 443, 584	31. 5	29. 1
North Carolina	60, 352	6, 716, 596	13, 132	1, 292, 998	21. 8	19. 3
Texas	44, 652	3, 392, 764	8, 237	563, 153	18. 4	16. 6
Tennessee	53, 842	5, 498, 467	5, 072	445, 664	9. 4	8. 1
Florida	19, 753	1, 796, 764	4, 888	362, 281	24. 7	20. 2
Arkansas	22, 235	1, 863, 240	4, 174	315, 324	18. 8	16. 9
Maryland	8, 984	1, 629, 673	996	173, 956	11. 1	10. 7
Oklahoma	15, 998	1, 334, 798	1, 864	124, 672	11. 7	9. 3
Delaware	6, 106	884, 527	484	61, 178	7. 9	6. 9
Kentucky	14, 076	1, 266, 724	392	37, 004	2. 8	2. 9
New Jersey	12, 147	1, 498, 799	242	28, 850	2. 0	1. 9
Illinois	4, 764	458, 523	143	12, 150	3. 0	2. 6

TABLE 35.—SALES AND PURCHASES BY COLORED FARM OPERATORS THROUGH FARMERS' COOPERATIVE ORGANIZATIONS, AND VALUE OF ALL PRODUCTS[1] ON FARMS REPORTING COOPERATIVE SALES, BY SOUTHERN DIVISIONS, AND STATES, AND SELECTED NORTHERN STATES: 1929

[Colored farmers include Negroes, Indians, Chinese, Japanese, and all other nonwhite races]

DIVISION AND STATE	Total colored farm operators	Farms reporting cooperative sales	VALUE OF ALL PRODUCTS[1] ON FARMS REPORTING COOPERATIVE SALES, 1929		VALUE OF PRODUCTS SOLD COOPERATIVELY			Farms reporting coöperative purchases	VALUE OF PRODUCTS PURCHASED COOPERATIVELY	
			Amount	Average per farm reporting	Amount	Percent of total product	Average per farm reporting		Amount	Average per farm reporting
The South	**881, 687**	**9, 616**	**$10, 941, 241**	**$1, 138**	**$6, 479, 795**	**59. 2**	**$874**	**5, 263**	**$680, 048**	**$129**
SOUTH ATLANTIC	298, 379	3, 436	4, 891, 412	1, 424	2, 781, 747	56. 9	810	958	175, 261	183
Delaware	807									
Maryland	5, 267	611	697, 437	1, 141	354, 089	50. 8	580	229	18, 850	82
District of Columbia	11									
Virginia	39, 673	575	1, 772, 013	3, 082	1, 331, 252	75. 1	2, 315	161	64, 053	398
West Virginia	491							6	87	15
North Carolina	76, 873	761	936, 973	1, 231	443, 681	47. 4	583	220	36, 412	166
South Carolina	77, 425	530	475, 221	897	250, 462	52. 7	473	75	14, 196	189
Georgia	86, 789	737	797, 128	1, 082	280, 933	35. 2	381	207	28, 502	138
Florida	11, 043	222	212, 640	958	121, 330	57. 1	547	60	13, 161	219
EAST SOUTH CENTRAL	320, 959	3, 812	3, 800, 838	997	2, 348, 197	61. 8	616	2, 464	251, 841	102
Kentucky	9, 104	164	172, 715	1, 053	42, 984	24. 9	262	70	4, 155	59
Tennessee	35, 138	129	116, 609	904	39, 026	33. 5	303	127	9, 255	73
Alabama	93, 829	1, 202	1, 071, 272	891	334, 790	31. 3	279	1, 223	152, 028	124
Mississippi	182, 888	2, 317	2, 440, 242	1, 053	1, 931, 397	79. 1	834	1, 044	86, 403	83
WEST SOUTH CENTRAL	262, 349	2, 368	2, 248, 991	950	1, 349, 851	60. 0	570	1, 841	252, 946	137
Arkansas	79, 579	347	328, 635	947	215, 455	65. 6	621	168	27, 287	162
Louisiana	73, 770	1, 538	1, 254, 949	816	802, 631	64. 0	522	1, 548	213, 025	138
Oklahoma	22, 937	377	497, 132	1, 319	210, 953	42. 4	560	47	4, 441	94
Texas	86, 063	106	168, 275	1, 588	120, 812	71. 8	1, 140	78	8, 193	105
SELECTED NORTHERN STATES[2]	10, 250	452	671, 524	1, 486	237, 757	35. 4	526	216	25, 504	118
New Jersey	384	10	29, 237	2, 924	9, 012	30. 8	901	9	2, 372	264
Pennsylvania	363	8	14, 599	1, 825	8, 720	59. 7	1, 090	9	1, 267	141
Ohio	1, 237	74	159, 540	2, 156	61, 510	38. 6	831	32	5, 820	182
Indiana	475	19	21, 599	1, 137	8, 582	39. 7	452	11	846	77
Illinois	894	51	80, 861	1, 586	4, 197	17. 6	278	13	953	73
Missouri	5, 861	230	223, 021	970	77, 647	34. 8	338	110	8, 526	78
Kansas	1, 036	60	142, 667	2, 378	58, 089	40. 7	968	32	5, 720	179

[1] Sold, traded or consumed by the farm operator's family.
[2] States having 200 or more Negro farmers who constitute 90 percent or more of the colored farmers in the State.

TABLE 36.—NUMBER OF SWINE ON FARMS OF COLORED OPERATORS, BY TENURE OF FARMER, BY SOUTHERN DIVISIONS, AND STATES, AND SELECTED NORTHERN STATES: 1930

[Colored farmers include Negroes, Indians, Chinese, Japanese, and all other nonwhite races]

DIVISION AND STATE	Total	SWINE REPORTED BY— Owners		Tenants		Managers	
		Number	Percent	Number	Percent	Number	Percent
The South	**2, 152, 882**	**660, 865**	**30. 7**	**1, 481, 563**	**68. 8**	**10, 454**	**0. 5**
SOUTH ATLANTIC	789, 273	271, 882	34. 4	512, 293	64. 9	5, 098	. 6
Delaware	1, 942	758	39. 0	1, 079	55. 6	105	5. 4
Maryland	11, 851	5, 449	46. 0	5, 500	46. 4	902	7. 6
District of Columbia	6	6	100. 0				
Virginia	100, 892	61, 859	61. 3	38, 018	37. 7	1, 015	1. 0
West Virginia	1, 881	930	49. 4	851	45. 2	100	5. 3
North Carolina	166, 725	54, 428	32. 6	111, 863	67. 1	434	. 3
South Carolina	152, 173	49, 999	32. 9	101, 734	66. 9	440	. 3
Georgia	282, 131	58, 937	20. 9	221, 967	78. 7	1, 227	. 4
Florida	71, 672	39, 516	55. 1	31, 281	43. 6	875	1. 2
EAST SOUTH CENTRAL	732, 165	173, 346	23. 7	556, 372	76. 0	2, 447	. 3
Kentucky	23, 534	12, 686	53. 9	10, 650	45. 3	198	. 8
Tennessee	78, 880	24, 924	31. 6	53, 307	67. 6	649	. 8
Alabama	273, 970	61, 977	22. 6	211, 080	77. 0	913	. 3
Mississippi	355, 781	73, 759	20. 7	281, 335	79. 1	687	. 2
WEST SOUTH CENTRAL	631, 444	215, 637	34. 1	412, 898	65. 4	2, 909	. 5
Arkansas	154, 192	43, 588	28. 3	110, 347	71. 6	257	. 2
Louisiana	202, 896	47, 554	23. 4	154, 895	76. 3	447	. 2
Oklahoma	89, 416	49, 114	54. 9	38, 875	43. 5	1, 427	1. 6
Texas	184, 940	75, 381	40. 8	108, 781	58. 8	778	. 4
SELECTED NORTHERN STATES[1]	52, 011	24, 649	47. 4	25, 294	48. 6	2, 068	4. 0
New Jersey	2, 242	1, 331	59. 4	865	38. 6	46	2. 1
Pennsylvania	1, 027	405	39. 4	468	45. 6	154	15. 0
Ohio	10, 353	4, 453	43. 0	5, 704	55. 1	196	1. 9
Indiana	4, 194	1, 860	44. 3	2, 253	53. 7	81	1. 9
Illinois	4, 870	2, 382	48. 9	2, 372	48. 7	116	2. 4
Missouri	21, 681	9, 412	43. 4	11, 349	52. 3	920	4. 2
Kansas	7, 644	4, 806	62. 9	2, 283	29. 9	555	7. 3

[1] States having 200 or more Negro farmers who constitute 90 percent or more of the colored farmers in the State.

TABLE 37.—COLORED FARM OPERATORS REPORTING SPECIFIED CLASSES OF LIVESTOCK, BY SECTIONS, DIVISIONS, AND STATES: 1930

[Colored farmers include Negroes, Indians, Chinese, Japanese, and all other nonwhite races]

SECTION, DIVISION, AND STATE	Total colored farm operators	HORSES AND (OR) MULES		CATTLE		SWINE	
		Farms reporting	Percent	Farms reporting	Percent	Farms reporting	Percent
The South	**881, 687**	**651, 750**	**73. 9**	**415, 172**	**47. 1**	**510, 016**	**57. 8**
SOUTH ATLANTIC	881, 687	651, 750	73. 9	415, 172	47. 1	510, 016	57. 80
Delaware	807	718	89. 0	394	48. 8	539	66. 8
Maryland	5, 267	4, 247	80. 6	2, 441	46. 3	2, 788	52. 9
District of Columbia	11	7	63. 6	3	27. 3	3	27. 3
Virginia	39, 673	30, 265	76. 3	23, 006	58. 0	27, 619	69. 6
West Virginia	491	315	64. 2	342	69. 7	315	64. 2
North Carolina	76, 873	59, 012	76. 8	27, 212	35. 4	45, 552	59. 3
South Carolina	77, 425	57, 346	74. 1	37, 073	47. 9	45, 425	58. 7
Georgia	86, 789	74, 684	86. 1	41, 999	48. 4	55, 476	63. 9
Florida	11, 043	8, 468	76. 7	5, 089	46. 1	7, 344	66. 5
EAST SOUTH CENTRAL	320, 959	210, 410	65. 6	165, 602	51. 6	187, 388	58. 4
Kentucky	9, 104	5, 258	57. 8	4, 964	54. 5	4, 219	46. 3
Tennessee	35, 138	22, 990	65. 4	19, 652	55. 9	20, 411	58. 1
Alabama	93, 829	73, 410	78. 2	58, 579	62. 4	63, 971	68. 2
Mississippi	182, 888	108, 752	59. 5	82, 407	45. 1	98, 787	54. 0
WEST SOUTH CENTRAL	262, 349	206, 278	78. 6	112, 011	42. 7	137, 567	52. 4
Arkansas	79, 579	65, 059	81. 8	28, 853	36. 3	39, 011	49. 0
Louisiana	73, 770	54, 196	73. 5	31, 210	42. 3	40, 866	55. 4
Oklahoma	22, 937	19, 165	83. 6	12, 446	54. 3	13, 029	56. 8
Texas	86, 063	67, 858	78. 8	39, 502	45. 9	44, 661	51. 9
SELECTED NORTHERN STATES[1]	10, 250	6, 951	67. 8	4, 651	45. 4	5, 051	49. 3
New Jersey	384	263	68. 5	164	42. 7	153	39. 8
Pennsylvania	363	264	72. 7	230	63. 4	149	41. 0
Ohio	1, 237	941	76. 1	904	73. 1	729	58. 9
Indiana	475	353	74. 3	291	61. 3	269	56. 6
Illinois	894	765	85. 6	479	53. 6	535	59. 8
Missouri	5, 861	3, 511	59. 9	1, 880	32. 1	2, 597	44. 3
Kansas	1, 036	854	82. 4	703	67. 9	619	59. 7

[1] States having 200 or more Negro farmers who constitute 90 percent or more of the colored farm operators in the State.

TABLE 38.—VALUE OF FARM PRODUCTS SOLD, TRADED, OR USED BY COLORED OPERATOR'S FAMILY, BY SOUTHERN DIVISIONS, AND STATES, AND SELECTED NORTHERN STATES: 1929

[Colored farmers include Negroes, Indians, Chinese, Japanese, and all other nonwhite races]

DIVISION AND STATE	Total value of farm products	CROPS SOLD OR TRADED		LIVESTOCK SOLD OR TRADED		LIVESTOCK PRODUCTS SOLD OR TRADED		FOREST PRODUCTS SOLD		PRODUCTS USED BY FAMILY	
		Value	Percent	Value	Percent	Value	Percent	Value	Percent	Value	Percent
The South	**$646, 641, 216**	**$509, 171, 918**	**78. 7**	**$10, 429, 511**	**1. 6**	**$15, 618, 421**	**2. 4**	**$3, 809, 793**	**0. 6**	**$107, 611, 573**	**16. 6**
SOUTH ATLANTIC	222, 454, 539	168, 121, 953	75. 6	2, 831, 544	1. 3	6, 823, 015	3. 1	1, 825, 566	0. 8	42, 852, 461	19. 3
Delaware	764, 973	408, 129	53. 4	18, 816	2. 5	140, 739	18. 4	3, 233	0. 4	194, 056	25. 4
Maryland	4, 791, 394	3, 069, 474	64. 1	159, 176	3. 3	485, 263	10. 1	67, 478	1. 4	1, 010, 003	21. 1
District of Columbia	11, 460	5, 095	44. 5	----------	----------	3, 935	34. 3	190	1. 7	2, 240	19. 5
Virginia	27, 130, 851	15, 278, 648	56. 3	719, 922	2. 7	1, 950, 272	7. 2	512, 724	1. 9	8, 669, 285	32. 0
West Virginia	267, 361	37, 771	14. 1	29, 997	11. 2	47, 615	17. 8	8, 982	3. 4	142, 996	53. 5
North Carolina	67, 810, 383	54, 366, 347	80. 2	433, 890	0. 6	1, 389, 758	2. 0	370, 044	0. 5	11, 250, 344	16. 6
South Carolina	52, 240, 775	41, 432, 909	79. 3	455, 310	0. 9	1, 109, 133	2. 1	327, 119	0. 6	8, 916, 304	17. 1
Georgia	63, 489, 255	49, 906, 288	78. 6	762, 588	1. 2	1, 272, 578	2. 0	484, 710	0. 8	11, 063, 091	17. 4
Florida	5, 948, 087	3, 617, 292	60. 8	251, 845	4. 2	423, 722	7. 1	51, 086	0. 9	1, 604, 142	27. 0
EAST SOUTH CENTRAL	239, 301, 592	192, 358, 242	80. 4	3, 311, 494	1. 4	4, 942, 579	2. 1	912, 162	0. 4	37, 777, 115	15. 8
Kentucky	6, 195, 476	3, 806, 127	61. 4	469, 632	7. 6	481, 015	7. 8	22, 581	0. 4	1, 416, 121	22. 9
Tennessee	25, 147, 620	18, 331, 716	72. 9	660, 292	2. 6	1, 001, 564	4. 0	75, 598	0. 3	5, 078, 450	20. 2
Alabama	57, 954, 853	42, 441, 023	73. 2	1, 076, 382	1. 9	1, 540, 167	2. 7	353, 290	0. 6	12, 543, 991	21. 6
Mississippi	150, 003, 643	127, 779, 376	85. 2	1, 105, 188	0. 7	1, 919, 833	1. 3	460, 693	0. 3	18, 738, 553	12. 5
WEST SOUTH CENTRAL	184, 885, 085	148, 691, 723	80. 4	4, 286, 473	2. 3	3, 852, 827	2. 1	1, 072, 065	0. 6	26, 981, 997	14. 6
Arkansas	61, 721, 444	53, 832, 645	87. 2	393, 267	0. 6	467, 868	0. 8	246, 133	0. 4	6, 781, 531	11. 0
Louisiana	54, 729, 926	45, 319, 226	82. 8	593, 580	1. 1	854, 217	1. 6	194, 735	0. 4	7, 768, 168	14. 2
Oklahoma	16, 068, 774	9, 110, 311	56. 7	2, 062, 307	12. 8	1, 143, 154	7. 1	196, 330	1. 2	3, 556, 672	22. 1
Texas	52, 364, 941	40, 429, 541	77. 2	1, 237, 319	2. 4	1, 387, 588	2. 6	434, 867	0. 8	8, 875, 626	16. 9
SELECTED NORTHERN STATES [1]	9, 225, 358	5, 426, 178	58. 8	1, 257, 911	13. 6	1, 167, 248	12. 7	48, 974	0. 5	1, 325, 047	14. 3
New Jersey	692, 803	405, 826	58. 6	25, 371	3. 7	186, 714	27. 0	1, 127	0. 2	73, 765	10. 6
Pennsylvania	391, 810	96, 935	24. 7	49, 287	12. 6	160, 004	40. 8	5, 716	1. 5	79, 868	20. 4
Ohio	1, 017, 640	288, 313	28. 3	257, 257	25. 3	232, 572	22. 9	9, 867	1. 0	229, 631	22. 6
Indiana	365, 305	115, 815	31. 7	92, 984	25. 5	86, 499	23. 7	1, 897	0. 5	68, 110	18. 6
Illinois	665, 389	283, 282	42. 6	144, 791	21. 8	89, 874	13. 5	11, 697	1. 8	135, 745	20. 4
Missouri	4, 992, 925	3, 666, 920	73. 4	490, 269	9. 8	262, 140	5. 3	15, 036	0. 3	558, 560	11. 2
Kansas	1, 099, 486	569, 087	51. 8	197, 952	18. 0	149, 445	13. 6	3, 634	0. 3	179, 368	16. 3

[1] States having 200 or more Negro farmers who constitute 90 percent or more of the colored farmers in the State.

TABLE 39.—NUMBER AND VALUE OF HORSES AND MULES ON FARMS OF COLORED OPERATORS, BY SOUTHERN DIVISIONS, AND STATES, AND SELECTED NORTHERN STATES: 1930

[Colored farmers include Negroes, Indians, Chinese, Japanese, and all other nonwhite races]

DIVISION AND STATE	Total number of horses and mules	NUMBER		VALUE		AVERAGE VALUE PER HEAD	
		Horses	Mules	Horses	Mules	Horses	Mules
The South	**1, 247, 749**	**320, 750**	**926, 999**	**$19, 032, 769**	**$81, 306, 636**	**$59. 34**	**$87. 71**
SOUTH ATLANTIC	371, 389	79, 813	291, 576	6, 437, 466	30, 602, 643	80. 66	104. 96
Delaware	1, 832	1, 201	631	114, 683	75, 670	95. 49	119. 92
Maryland	10, 397	7, 739	2, 658	788, 759	326, 456	101. 92	122. 82
District of Columbia	7	7	----------	753	----------	107. 61	----------
Virginia	51, 517	28, 120	23, 397	2, 335, 085	2, 596, 833	83. 04	110. 99
West Virginia	589	534	55	48, 055	5, 101	89. 99	92. 74
North Carolina	94, 909	14, 691	80, 218	1, 185, 270	9, 255, 553	80. 68	115. 38
South Carolina	85, 167	13, 450	71, 717	966, 114	7, 293, 619	71. 83	101. 70
Georgia	114, 584	9, 009	105, 575	612, 972	10, 272, 448	68. 04	97. 30
Florida	12, 387	5, 062	7, 325	385, 775	776, 963	76. 21	106. 07
EAST SOUTH CENTRAL	394, 730	93, 721	301, 009	5, 980, 369	27, 718, 619	63. 81	92. 09
Kentucky	12, 509	6, 239	6, 270	423, 940	543, 546	67. 95	86. 69
Tennessee	52, 289	17, 702	34, 587	1, 154, 347	3, 123, 898	65. 21	90. 32
Alabama	123, 699	22, 584	101, 115	1, 521, 710	9, 858, 713	67. 38	97. 50
Mississippi	206, 233	47, 196	159, 037	2, 880, 372	14, 192, 462	61. 03	89. 24
WEST SOUTH CENTRAL	481, 630	147, 216	334, 414	6, 614, 934	22, 985, 374	44. 93	68. 73
Arkansas	118, 474	19, 825	98, 649	870, 912	6, 782, 119	43. 93	68. 75
Louisiana	111, 167	39, 229	71, 938	2, 092, 475	5, 534, 910	53. 34	76. 94
Oklahoma	69, 531	36, 727	32, 804	1, 449, 615	1, 866, 220	39. 47	56. 89
Texas	182, 458	51, 435	131, 023	2, 201, 932	8, 802, 125	42. 81	67. 18
SELECTED NORTHERN STATES [1]	21, 631	12, 517	9, 114	891, 368	709, 509	71. 21	77. 85
New Jersey	663	584	79	68, 211	9, 531	116. 80	120. 65
Pennsylvania	705	592	113	68, 483	14, 571	115. 68	128. 95
Ohio	2, 585	2, 383	202	244, 258	21, 283	102. 50	105. 36
Indiana	1, 043	764	279	61, 105	24, 516	79. 98	87. 87
Illinois	2, 274	1, 121	1, 153	83, 055	100, 461	74. 09	87. 13
Missouri	10, 343	3, 985	6, 358	219, 175	478, 948	55. 00	75. 33
Kansas	4, 018	3, 088	930	147, 081	60, 199	47. 63	64. 73

[1] States having 200 or more Negro farmers who constitute 90 percent or more of the colored farmers in the State.

Table 40.—NUMBER OF FARMS OF COLORED OPERATORS CLASSIFIED BY KIND OF ROAD ON WHICH LOCATED, BY SOUTHERN DIVISIONS, AND STATES, AND SELECTED NORTHERN STATES: 1930

[Colored farmers include Negroes, Indians, Chinese, Japanese, and all other nonwhite races]

DIVISION AND STATE	All farms	NUMBER OF FARMS LOCATED ON— Concrete road	Brick road	Asphalt road	Macadam road	Gravel road	Sand-clay road	Improved dirt road	Unimproved dirt road	All other (*including not reported*)
The South	**881,687**	**14,380**	**242**	**9,283**	**7,282**	**145,964**	**51,595**	**219,951**	**380,914**	**52,076**
SOUTH ATLANTIC	298,379	7,297	145	4,106	3,459	15,464	38,638	78,748	131,937	18,585
Delaware	807	94	-	-	40	43	1	188	380	61
Maryland	5,267	368	1	2	404	693	49	791	2,666	293
District of Columbia	11	-	-	-	4	2	-	1	4	-
Virginia	39,673	662	6	518	1,548	3,977	4,136	7,871	18,977	1,978
West Virginia	491	13	-	12	49	21	20	74	265	37
North Carolina	76,873	3,029	97	1,657	883	5,299	10,922	19,705	28,889	6,392
South Carolina	77,425	1,998	13	824	239	2,829	12,718	18,670	36,741	3,393
Georgia	86,789	991	2	606	112	2,353	9,676	29,567	38,046	5,436
Florida	11,043	142	26	487	180	247	1,116	1,881	5,969	995
EAST SOUTH CENTRAL	320,959	3,746	91	1,090	2,676	86,199	9,132	75,156	126,444	16,425
Kentucky	9,104	34	-	119	1,524	2,024	13	1,028	3,385	977
Tennessee	35,138	909	1	537	1,051	7,806	174	7,001	15,293	2,366
Alabama	93,829	535	-	315	95	14,515	6,556	22,718	43,492	5,603
Mississippi	182,888	2,268	90	119	6	61,854	2,389	44,409	64,274	7,479
WEST SOUTH CENTRAL	262,349	3,337	6	4,087	1,147	44,301	3,825	66,047	122,533	17,066
Arkansas	79,579	1,238	1	2,071	183	11,886	771	15,666	41,651	6,112
Louisiana	73,770	848	-	270	390	23,092	250	15,499	29,970	3,451
Oklahoma	22,937	239	2	77	9	1,366	275	8,604	10,200	2,165
Texas	86,063	1,012	3	1,669	565	7,957	2,529	26,278	40,712	5,338
SELECTED NORTHERN STATES [1]	10,250	548	25	35	366	1,843	43	2,964	3,932	494
New Jersey	384	30	-	8	43	137	1	28	116	21
Pennsylvania	363	24	4	1	34	31	2	43	201	23
Ohio	1,237	21	16	3	206	460	-	65	400	66
Indiana	475	16	-	2	43	262	1	18	103	30
Illinois	894	47	1	1	6	222	-	134	429	54
Missouri	5,861	370	1	5	18	668	22	2,270	2,232	275
Kansas	1,036	40	3	15	16	63	17	406	451	25

[1] States having 200 or more Negro farmers who constitute 90 percent or more of the colored farmers in the State.

Table 41.—FARMS OF COLORED OPERATORS REPORTING TELEPHONES, DWELLINGS LIGHTED BY ELECTRICITY, WATER PIPED INTO DWELLINGS AND INTO BATHROOMS, BY TENURE OF OPERATOR, WITH TOTAL FARM MOTOR EQUIPMENT, BY SOUTHERN DIVISIONS, AND STATES, AND SELECTED NORTHERN STATES: 1930

[Colored farmers include Negroes, Indians, Chinese, Japanese, and all other nonwhite races]

DIVISION AND STATE	FARMS REPORTING— Telephones: Total	Telephones: Owners	Telephones: Tenants	Telephones: Managers	Electric lights: Total	Electric lights: Owners	Electric lights: Tenants	Electric lights: Managers	Water piped into dwellings: Total	Water piped into dwellings: Owners	Water piped into dwellings: Tenants	Water piped into dwellings: Managers	Water piped into bathrooms: Total	Water piped into bathrooms: Owners	Water piped into bathrooms: Tenants	Water piped into bathrooms: Managers	NUMBER OF— Automobiles	Motor trucks	Tractors	Electric motors for farm work	Stationary gas engines	Farmers per automobile
The South	**4,775**	**2,750**	**1,844**	**181**	**2,816**	**1,712**	**965**	**139**	**2,600**	**1,160**	**1,264**	**176**	**1,376**	**717**	**520**	**139**	**186,518**	**11,062**	**2,533**	**363**	**1,681**	**4.7**
SOUTH ATLANTIC	1,015	515	406	94	1,359	846	439	74	902	379	429	94	482	201	207	74	78,764	5,101	1,221	137	1,008	3.8
Delaware	22	12	5	5	16	12	-	4	9	4	1	4	6	4	-	2	524	81	36	1	35	1.5
Maryland	167	75	65	27	113	74	24	15	96	32	37	27	65	23	22	20	2,629	413	157	20	118	2.0
District of Columbia	5	3	1	1	6	4	1	1	3	2	-	1	3	2	-	1	-	-	1	-	-	-
Virginia	270	192	64	14	288	222	50	16	180	115	46	19	120	67	34	19	13,870	1,357	291	30	396	2.9
West Virginia	41	30	8	3	29	20	5	4	20	14	2	4	10	5	1	4	149	29	6	2	9	3.3
North Carolina	199	93	96	10	403	258	138	7	116	52	59	5	68	26	37	5	23,859	1,072	373	22	131	3.2
South Carolina	107	44	51	12	239	121	109	9	136	59	69	8	69	30	33	6	18,901	641	100	28	93	4.1
Georgia	164	46	109	9	188	77	104	7	277	67	195	15	103	22	70	11	16,757	865	182	20	163	5.2
Florida	40	20	7	13	77	58	8	11	65	34	20	11	38	22	10	6	2,075	643	75	14	63	5.3
EAST SOUTH CENTRAL	1,276	619	612	45	618	319	267	32	605	207	358	40	278	104	144	30	56,039	2,673	514	55	213	5.7
Kentucky	392	205	179	8	86	55	30	1	39	15	20	4	27	10	15	2	2,384	83	53	1	29	3.8
Tennessee	356	188	150	18	137	78	47	12	86	33	39	14	56	19	27	10	7,762	269	94	13	41	4.5
Alabama	145	70	72	3	206	106	94	6	152	65	80	7	68	32	30	6	12,534	730	124	25	66	7.5
Mississippi	383	156	211	16	189	80	96	13	328	94	219	15	127	43	72	12	33,359	1,591	243	16	77	5.5
WEST SOUTH CENTRAL	2,484	1,616	826	42	839	547	259	33	1,093	574	477	42	616	412	169	35	51,715	3,288	798	171	460	5.1
Arkansas	398	243	148	7	121	62	54	5	75	37	35	3	43	20	20	3	11,197	618	124	24	63	7.1
Louisiana	164	79	82	3	133	65	60	8	212	67	133	12	98	44	43	11	10,933	684	137	15	89	6.7
Oklahoma	1,129	832	283	14	389	321	60	8	394	320	63	11	311	269	33	9	7,246	669	295	103	189	3.2
Texas	793	462	313	18	196	99	85	12	412	150	246	16	164	79	73	12	22,339	1,317	242	29	119	3.9
SELECTED NORTHERN STATES [1]	1,297	847	420	30	420	305	91	24	299	184	87	28	130	76	35	19	3,708	677	403	59	359	2.8
New Jersey	63	38	19	6	66	47	12	7	47	28	12	7	26	15	6	5	249	173	41	15	67	1.5
Pennsylvania	79	54	22	3	50	27	19	4	56	27	23	6	22	9	9	4	203	68	33	6	46	1.8
Ohio	321	214	103	4	92	67	22	3	83	56	21	6	21	13	5	3	663	127	96	12	66	1.9
Indiana	124	84	39	1	30	20	10	-	23	11	12	-	8	4	4	-	245	50	42	4	29	1.9
Illinois	97	61	34	2	36	27	8	1	17	11	6	-	11	8	3	-	253	62	31	6	29	3.5
Missouri	297	184	105	8	62	47	10	5	29	18	5	6	20	11	3	6	1,461	81	60	3	57	4.0
Kansas	316	212	98	6	84	70	10	4	44	33	8	3	22	16	5	1	634	116	100	13	65	1.6

[1] States having 200 or more Negro farmers who constitute 90 percent or more of the colored farm operators in the State.

TABLE 42.—NEGRO FARM OWNERS IN COUNTIES AND PARISHES HAVING 1,000 OR MORE NEGRO FARM OPERATORS: 1930

COUNTY OR PARISH AND STATE	Total number of farms operated by Negroes	OWNED FARMS		COUNTY OR PARISH AND STATE	Total number of farms operated by Negroes	OWNED FARMS		COUNTY OR PARISH AND STATE	Total number of farms operated by Negroes	OWNED FARMS	
		Number	Per cent			Number	Per cent			Number	Per cent
Bolivar, Miss	13,236	455	3.4	Monroe, Ala	2,091	584	27.9	Dillon, S. C	1,468	99	6.8
Sunflower, Miss	11,644	194	1.7	Chester, S. C	2,077	260	12.5	Charleston, S. C	1,465	995	67.9
Leflore, Miss	8,778	129	1.5	Cass, Tex	2,073	602	29.0	Wilkes, Ga	1,465	141	9.7
Coahoma, Miss	8,440	127	1.5	Jefferson, Miss	2,068	243	11.8	Hardeman, Tenn	1,446	195	13.5
Washington, Miss	7,652	219	2.9	Pulaski, Ark	2,040	433	21.2	Union, S. C	1,441	144	10.0
Crittenden, Ark	7,003	248	3.5	Leon, Tex	2,028	397	19.6	Leake, Miss	1,422	466	32.8
Jefferson, Ark	6,739	631	9.4	Lee, Miss	2,011	227	11.3	McLennan, Tex	1,422	214	15.0
Dallas, Ala	6,405	484	7.6	Clay, Miss	2,006	328	16.4	Yalobusha, Miss	1,420	214	15.1
Caddo, La	6,154	591	9.6	Madison, Tenn	1,997	362	18.1	Sumter, Ga	1,419	73	5.1
Holmes, Miss	5,660	650	11.5	Lee, Ala	1,992	318	16.0	Jasper, Miss	1,418	562	39.6
Madison, Miss	5,572	623	11.2	Greenville, S. C	1,988	290	14.6	Barnwell, S. C	1,416	198	14.0
Shelby, Tenn	5,548	542	9.8	Bowie, Tex	1,962	403	20.5	Miller, Ark	1,407	205	14.6
Tallahatchie, Miss	5,523	141	2.6	Attala, Miss	1,952	494	25.3	Kaufman, Tex	1,403	97	6.9
Yazoo, Miss	5,388	379	7.0	East Feliciana, La	1,933	261	13.5	Wharton, Tex	1,394	266	19.1
Hinds, Miss	5,362	646	12.0	Limestone, Ala	1,929	236	12.2	Lawrence, Ala	1,393	176	12.6
Marengo, Ala	5,314	651	12.3	Autauga, Ala	1,924	364	18.9	Cleveland, N. C	1,389	136	9.8
Mississippi, Ark	5,089	111	2.2	Greenwood, S. C	1,917	231	12.1	Ouachita, La	1,384	196	14.2
St. Francis, Ark	5,083	407	8.0	Bertie, N. C	1,914	483	25.2	Ouachita, Ark	1,375	674	49.0
Harrison, Tex	4,990	1,443	28.9	Talladega, Ala	1,912	426	22.3	East Baton Rouge, La	1,367	329	24.1
Tunica, Miss	4,942	123	2.5	Southampton, Va	1,909	429	22.5	Mecklenburg, N. C	1,360	129	9.5
Phillips, Ark	4,920	540	11.0	Webster, La	1,904	387	20.3	Mitchell, Ga	1,352	107	7.9
Orangeburg, S. C	4,693	821	17.5	Warren, N. C	1,896	772	40.7	Dooly, Ga	1,351	73	5.4
Fayette, Tenn	4,432	432	9.7	Rankin, Miss	1,893	555	29.3	Muskogee, Okla	1,349	331	24.5
Quitman, Miss	4,382	152	3.5	Pemiscot, Mo	1,891	58	3.1	Okmulgee, Okla	1,347	168	12.5
Humphreys, Miss	4,364	234	5.4	Amite, Miss	1,888	457	24.2	Saluda, S. C	1,332	183	13.7
De Soto, Miss	4,312	378	8.8	Falls, Tex	1,885	272	14.4	Henry, Ala	1,331	125	9.4
Lee, Ark	4,134	697	16.9	Oktibbeha, Miss	1,879	519	27.6	Brunswick, Va	1,329	752	56.6
Panola, Miss	4,007	381	9.5	Drew, Ark	1,876	365	19.5	Upshur, Tex	1,326	321	24.2
Noxubee, Miss	3,973	416	10.5	Robertson, Tex	1,869	324	17.3	Newton, Miss	1,323	429	32.4
Bossier, La	3,874	479	12.4	Cherokee, Tex	1,862	486	26.1	Winston, Miss	1,319	469	35.6
Hale, Ala	3,873	653	16.9	Bienville, La	1,858	500	26.9	Burleson, Tex	1,313	325	24.8
Sumter, Ala	3,812	444	11.6	Avoyelles, La	1,840	182	9.9	Milam, Tex	1,307	168	12.9
De Soto, La	3,752	735	19.6	Elmore, Ala	1,837	413	22.5	Meriwether, Ga	1,299	98	7.5
St. Landry, La	3,736	576	15.4	Woodruff, Ark	1,831	201	11.0	Little River, Ark	1,298	206	15.9
Marshall, Miss	3,704	452	12.2	Aiken, S. C	1,826	397	21.7	Red River, Tex	1,297	278	21.4
Wilcox, Ala	3,620	416	11.5	Fort Bend, Tex	1,824	361	19.8	McCurtain, Okla	1,290	241	18.7
Lincoln, Ark	3,598	362	10.1	Pike, Miss	1,803	678	37.6	Bamberg, S. C	1,282	210	16.4
Lowndes, Ala	3,527	333	9.4	Rapides, La	1,802	185	10.3	McCormick, S. C	1,274	138	10.8
Haywood, Tenn	3,512	433	12.3	Beaufort, S. C	1,800	1,609	89.4	Walker, Tex	1,266	370	29.2
Perry, Ala	3,435	480	14.0	Madison, La	1,795	24	1.3	Caswell, N. C	1,265	311	24.6
Natchitoches, La	3,362	423	12.6	Newberry, S. C	1,784	160	9.0	Leon, Fla	1,259	356	28.3
Halifax, N. C	3,305	717	21.7	Washington, Ga	1,782	97	5.4	Lancaster, S. C	1,253	132	10.5
Claiborne, La	3,233	516	16.0	Clarke, Ala	1,772	799	45.1	Johnston, N. C	1,252	222	17.7
Montgomery, Ala	3,178	376	11.8	Anderson, Tex	1,765	561	31.8	Marion, S. C	1,252	216	17.3
Greene, Ala	3,168	326	10.3	Chickasaw, Miss	1,751	302	17.2	Macon, Ga	1,245	86	6.9
Smith, Tex	3,120	941	30.2	Red River, La	1,750	115	6.6	Brazos, Tex	1,237	191	15.4
Clarendon, S. C	3,118	375	12.0	Edgefield, S. C	1,749	207	11.8	Calhoun, Ga	1,227	34	2.8
Macon, Ala	3,114	473	15.2	Darlington, S. C	1,748	202	11.6	Gregg, Tex	1,220	426	34.9
Williamsburg, S. C	3,043	805	26.5	Limestone, Tex	1,740	232	13.3	Issaquena, Miss	1,215	73	6.0
Chicot, Ark	3,036	283	9.3	Wilson, N. C	1,725	137	7.9	Henry, Ga	1,213	82	6.8
Burke, Ga	3,036	217	7.1	Fairfield, S. C	1,724	359	20.8	Scotland, N. C	1,211	132	10.9
Pitt, N. C	2,985	226	7.6	Wayne, N. C	1,722	254	14.8	Hertford, N. C	1,205	295	24.5
Anderson, S. C	2,957	222	7.5	Sampson, N. C	1,719	651	37.9	Hancock, Ga	1,205	174	14.4
Richland, La	2,934	155	5.3	Abbeville, S. C	1,714	172	10.0	Shelby, Tex	1,196	232	19.4
East Carroll, La	2,881	133	4.6	Jefferson Davis, Miss	1,706	528	30.9	Walthall, Miss	1,188	336	28.3
York, S. C	2,876	214	7.4	Butler, Ala	1,695	257	15.2	Cumberland, N. C	1,180	373	31.6
Sumter, S. C	2,865	505	17.6	Freestone, Tex	1,689	463	27.4	Union, N. C	1,178	135	11.5
Desha, Ark	2,843	226	7.9	Calhoun, S. C	1,683	183	10.9	Worth, Ga	1,175	98	8.3
Monroe, Miss	2,842	392	13.8	Pointe Coupee, La	1,679	123	7.3	Ellis, Tex	1,174	32	2.7
Morehouse, La	2,815	224	8.0	Navarro, Tex	1,661	170	10.2	Person, N. C	1,173	211	18.0
Rusk, Tex	2,784	867	31.1	Terrell, Ga	1,658	62	3.7	West Feliciana, La	1,173	77	6.6
Madison, Ala	2,772	404	14.6	Lee, S. C	1,654	187	11.3	Okfuskee, Okla	1,172	254	21.7
Tate, Miss	2,687	214	8.0	Claiborne, Miss	1,643	198	12.1	Tangipahoa, La	1,167	405	34.7
Robeson, N. C	2,685	378	14.1	Warren, Miss	1,642	255	15.5	Tallapoosa, Ala	1,161	165	14.2
Sharkey, Miss	2,657	107	4.0	Anson, N. C	1,635	264	16.1	Scott, Miss	1,158	430	37.1
Carroll, Miss	2,652	320	12.1	Early, Ga	1,624	175	10.8	Vance, N. C	1,153	262	22.7
Houston, Tex	2,627	550	20.9	Lauderdale, Tenn	1,618	149	9.2	Wagoner, Okla	1,146	226	19.7
Spartanburg, S. C	2,623	307	11.7	Franklin, N. C	1,616	240	14.9	Hoke, N. C	1,145	151	13.2
Nash, S. C	2,575	240	9.3	Choctaw, Ala	1,611	543	33.7	Bastrop, Tex	1,139	270	23.7
Copiah, Miss	2,521	510	20.2	Grenada, Miss	1,585	215	13.6	Coweta, Ga	1,134	91	8.0
Franklin, La	2,521	135	5.4	Wilkinson, Miss	1,578	194	12.3	Simpson, Miss	1,123	375	33.4
Lowndes, Miss	2,510	365	14.5	Granville, N. C	1,575	374	23.7	Nevada, Ark	1,117	231	20.7
Tensas, La	2,492	59	2.4	Kershaw, S. C	1,575	355	22.5	Lamar, Tex	1,098	207	18.9
Bullock, Ala	2,473	213	8.6	Washington, Tex	1,573	397	25.2	Brooks, Ga	1,095	227	20.7
Northampton, N. C	2,442	392	16.1	Jackson, Fla	1,566	587	37.5	Lincoln, Miss	1,093	305	27.9
Chambers, Ala	2,431	187	7.7	Richland, S. C	1,561	413	26.5	Gibson, Tenn	1,088	226	20.8
Cross, Ark	2,416	139	5.8	Screven, Ga	1,561	150	9.6	Marion, Tex	1,085	495	45.6
Lonoke, Ark	2,382	238	10.0	Lenoir, N. C	1,559	110	7.1	Union, La	1,082	254	23.5
Halifax, Va	2,380	899	37.8	Laurens, Ga	1,558	143	9.2	Carroll, Ga	1,080	73	6.8
Columbia, Ark	2,374	587	24.7	Lafayette, Ark	1,554	214	13.8	Montgomery, Miss	1,073	209	19.5
Laurens, S. C	2,282	143	6.3	Tuscaloosa, Ala	1,545	414	26.8	Bladen, N. C	1,070	768	71.8
Edgecombe, N. C	2,282	132	5.8	Concordia, La	1,543	30	1.9	Troup, Ga	1,067	105	9.8
Kemper, Miss	2,281	488	21.4	Lincoln, La	1,541	325	21.1	Gonzales, Tex	1,065	264	24.8
Mecklenburg, Va	2,275	853	37.5	Berkeley, S. C	1,521	1,193	78.4	Emanuel, Ga	1,064	122	11.5
Monroe, Ark	2,272	374	16.5	Colleton, S. C	1,515	748	49.4	Giles, Tenn	1,061	209	29.1
Barbour, Ala	2,262	303	13.4	Lafayette, Miss	1,510	315	20.9	Benton, Miss	1,053	127	12.1
Wake, N. C	2,244	549	24.5	Duplin, N. C	1,509	603	40.0	Fayette, Tex	1,045	219	21.0
Russell, Ala	2,243	357	15.9	Pike, Ala	1,506	110	7.3	Martin, N. C	1,043	233	22.3
Hempstead, Ark	2,212	524	23.7	Randolph, Ga	1,502	77	5.1	Chesterfield, S. C	1,030	276	26.8
Florence, S. C	2,207	398	18.0	Jefferson, Ga	1,497	152	10.2	Crenshaw, Ala	1,030	174	16.9
Ashley, Ark	2,189	207	9.5	Union, Ark	1,493	465	31.1	Dorchester, S. C	1,028	474	46.1
Pittsylvania, Va	2,162	557	25.8	Lauderdale, Miss	1,492	481	32.2	Lafayette, La	1,026	109	10.6
Marlboro, S. C	2,147	171	8.0	Conecuh, Ala	1,476	579	39.2	Montgomery, Tenn	1,022	323	31.6
Tipton, Tenn	2,144	295	13.8	Adams, Miss	1,476	218	14.8	Morgan, Ga	1,019	79	7.8
Pickens, Ala	2,119	260	12.3	Greene, N. C	1,473	103	7.0	Harris, Ga	1,014	157	15.5
Panola, Tex	2,117	427	20.2	Grimes, Tex	1,471	271	18.4	Cherokee, S. C	1,006	131	13.0

TABLE 43.—NUMBER OF NEGRO AND WHITE FARM OPERATORS WITH ACREAGE, BY TENURE, BY SECTIONS, DIVISIONS, AND STATES: 1930 AND 1920

SECTION, DIVISION, AND STATE	NEGRO OWNERS			WHITE OWNERS [1]			LAND IN FARMS (ACRES)					
							Negro owners			White owners [1]		
	1930	1920	Increase or decrease (−)	1930	1920	Increase or decrease (−)	1930	1920	Increase or decrease (−)	1930	1920	Increase or decrease (−)
United States	**181, 016**	**218, 612**	**−37, 596**	**3, 365, 674**	**3, 691, 868**	**−326, 194**	**11, 198, 893**	**13, 948, 512**	**−2, 749, 619**	**604, 595, 531**	**620, 070, 823**	**−15, 475, 292**
The North	**4, 424**	**5, 749**	**−1, 325**	**1, 759, 818**	**1, 936, 053**	**−176, 235**	**332, 520**	**435, 075**	**−102, 555**	**272, 174, 162**	**287, 317, 789**	**−15, 143, 627**
The South	**176, 130**	**212, 365**	**−36, 235**	**1, 233, 656**	**1, 379, 636**	**−145, 980**	**10, 785, 312**	**13, 434, 106**	**−2, 648, 794**	**178, 621, 215**	**206, 525, 033**	**−27, 903, 818**
The West	**462**	**498**	**−36**	**372, 200**	**376, 179**	**−3, 979**	**81, 061**	**79, 331**	**1, 730**	**153, 800, 154**	**126, 228, 001**	**27, 572, 153**
NEW ENGLAND	128	192	−64	113, 968	139, 942	−25, 974	7, 297	10, 121	−2, 824	12, 584, 539	14, 693, 218	−2, 108, 679
Maine	14	13	1	36, 732	45, 424	−8, 692	738	953	−215	4, 337, 078	5, 072, 903	−735, 825
New Hampshire	5	12	−7	13, 749	18, 592	−4, 843	574	1, 121	−547	1, 734, 960	2, 295, 262	−560, 302
Vermont	17	21	−4	21, 992	25, 100	−3, 108	3, 211	3, 075	136	3, 321, 892	3, 517, 824	−195, 932
Massachusetts	59	89	−30	23, 138	27, 980	−4, 842	1, 791	3, 003	−1, 212	1, 688, 387	2, 018, 142	−329, 755
Rhode Island	8	13	−5	2, 799	3, 231	−432	121	630	−509	220, 294	248, 296	−28, 002
Connecticut	25	44	−19	15, 558	19, 615	−4, 057	862	1, 339	−477	1, 281, 928	1, 540, 791	−258, 863
MIDDLE ATLANTIC	568	697	−129	298, 227	326, 129	−27, 902	26, 758	28, 516	−1, 758	27, 720, 458	28, 969, 267	−1, 248, 809
New York	112	152	−40	135, 646	151, 288	−15, 642	9, 625	9, 366	259	14, 547, 371	15, 054, 158	−506, 787
New Jersey	232	284	−52	20, 531	21, 604	−1, 073	7, 276	8, 963	−1, 687	1, 227, 874	1, 415, 789	−187, 915
Pennsylvania	224	261	−37	142, 050	153, 237	−11, 187	9, 857	10, 187	−330	11, 945, 213	12, 499, 320	−554, 107
EAST NORTH CENTRAL	1, 892	2, 335	−443	691, 646	763, 702	−72, 056	114, 748	138, 109	−23, 361	72, 222, 278	76, 345, 020	−4, 122, 742
Ohio	780	1, 053	−273	159, 066	176, 933	−17, 867	45, 446	55, 526	−10, 080	14, 364, 938	14, 944, 527	−579, 589
Indiana	275	305	−30	125, 234	136, 904	−11, 670	14, 325	17, 284	−2, 959	12, 271, 620	12, 853, 162	−581, 542
Illinois	459	533	−74	119, 432	132, 040	−12, 608	27, 635	33, 451	−5, 816	15, 198, 903	16, 231, 619	−1, 032, 716
Michigan	337	403	−66	141, 197	158, 843	−17, 646	23, 952	28, 372	−4, 420	13, 575, 675	14, 506, 732	−931, 057
Wisconsin	41	41	----------	146, 717	158, 982	−12, 265	3, 390	3, 476	−86	16, 811, 142	17, 808, 980	−997, 838
WEST NORTH CENTRAL	1, 836	2, 525	−689	655, 977	706, 280	−50, 303	183, 717	258, 329	−74, 612	159, 646, 887	167, 310, 284	−7, 663, 397
Minnesota	19	24	−5	126, 370	132, 567	−6, 197	1, 469	1, 657	−188	19, 550, 952	20, 996, 110	−1, 445, 158
Iowa	67	74	−7	111, 231	121, 814	−10, 583	3, 775	5, 140	−1, 365	16, 438, 618	18, 045, 981	−1, 607, 363
Missouri	1, 163	1, 643	−480	164, 148	183, 386	−19, 238	75, 686	111, 946	−36, 260	22, 141, 050	24, 574, 801	−2, 433, 751
North Dakota	5	11	−6	49, 481	56, 448	−6, 967	1, 405	4, 711	−3, 306	26, 293, 378	26, 684, 516	−391, 138
South Dakota	26	33	−7	43, 323	46, 350	−3, 027	10, 744	14, 205	−3, 461	21, 802, 785	23, 364, 878	−1, 562, 093
Nebraska	16	31	−15	67, 269	69, 418	−2, 149	4, 454	13, 556	−9, 102	25, 711, 462	26, 384, 910	−673, 448
Kansas	540	709	−169	94, 155	96, 297	−2, 142	86, 184	107, 114	−20, 930	27, 708, 642	27, 259, 088	449, 554
SOUTH ATLANTIC	79, 683	102, 056	−22, 373	459, 427	504, 426	−44, 999	4, 214, 663	5, 483, 254	−1, 268, 591	47, 393, 132	56, 279, 975	−8, 886, 843
Delaware	373	355	18	5, 887	5, 655	232	13, 781	12, 512	1, 269	466, 704	438, 964	27, 740
Maryland	2, 938	3, 548	−610	27, 882	29, 256	−1, 374	107, 590	119, 225	−11, 635	2, 532, 361	2, 631, 595	−99, 234
District of Columbia	8	9	−1	51	91	−40	28	25	3	697	1, 704	−1, 007
Virginia	24, 399	30, 908	−6, 509	96, 656	105, 414	−8, 758	1, 179, 824	1, 371, 333	−191, 509	11, 066, 532	12, 387, 142	−1, 320, 610
West Virginia	372	403	−31	66, 200	91, 698	−5, 498	18, 470	19, 052	−582	7, 126, 681	7, 794, 290	−667, 609
North Carolina	18, 978	21, 714	−2, 736	121, 734	129, 099	−7, 365	943, 506	1, 126, 751	−183, 245	10, 090, 169	12, 282, 645	−2, 192, 476
South Carolina	15, 975	22, 759	−6, 784	38, 478	44, 965	−6, 487	786, 893	1, 146, 396	−359, 503	4, 440, 414	5, 570, 841	−1, 130, 427
Georgia	11, 080	16, 040	−4, 960	68, 721	86, 081	−17, 360	883, 284	1, 331, 278	−440, 994	8, 971, 316	11, 469, 031	−2, 497, 715
Florida	5, 560	6, 320	−760	33, 818	32, 167	1, 651	281, 287	356, 682	−75, 395	2, 698, 258	3, 703, 763	−1, 005, 505
EAST SOUTH CENTRAL	50, 475	55, 488	−5, 013	414, 760	470, 268	−55, 508	3, 516, 640	3, 930, 410	−413, 770	41, 765, 792	50, 088, 549	−8, 322, 757
Kentucky	4, 175	5, 318	−1, 143	153, 228	174, 008	−20, 780	183, 148	239, 997	−56, 849	14, 427, 710	16, 551, 588	−2, 123, 878
Tennessee	7, 828	9, 839	−2, 011	123, 694	138, 242	−14, 548	419, 069	535, 265	−116, 196	11, 309, 984	13, 243, 529	−1, 933, 545
Alabama	15, 920	17, 201	−1, 281	74, 441	89, 887	−15, 446	1, 189, 355	1, 332, 621	−143, 266	8, 214, 031	10, 784, 790	−2, 570, 759
Mississippi	22, 552	23, 130	− 578	63, 397	68, 131	−4, 734	1, 725, 068	1, 822, 527	−97, 459	7, 814, 067	9, 508, 642	−1, 694, 575
WEST SOUTH CENTRAL	45, 972	54, 821	−8, 849	359, 469	404, 942	−45, 473	3, 054, 009	4, 020, 442	−966, 433	89, 462, 291	100, 156, 509	−10, 694, 218
Arkansas	11, 452	15, 369	−3, 917	77, 554	97, 274	−19, 720	704, 790	1, 042, 047	−337, 257	8, 285, 121	10, 767, 826	−2, 482, 705
Louisiana	10, 488	10, 975	−487	42, 656	46, 268	−3, 612	601, 423	746, 701	−145, 278	4, 157, 573	5, 507, 512	−1, 349, 939
Oklahoma	3, 454	4, 958	−1, 504	69, 380	83, 729	−14, 349	283, 805	438, 567	−154, 762	15, 556, 837	17, 442, 221	−1, 885, 384
Texas	20, 578	23, 519	−2, 941	169, 879	177, 671	−7, 792	1, 463, 991	1, 793, 127	−329, 136	61, 462, 760	66, 438, 950	−4, 976, 190
MOUNTAIN	183	239	−56	169, 354	198, 153	−28, 799	59, 689	54, 574	5, 115	113, 405, 424	90, 040, 400	23, 365, 024
Montana	15	26	−11	34, 332	49, 286	−14, 954	7, 524	8, 759	−1, 235	33, 787, 665	28, 346, 665	5, 441, 000
Idaho	7	16	−9	30, 044	34, 284	−4, 240	326	1, 523	−1, 197	7, 013, 439	6, 762, 649	250, 790
Wyoming	8	17	−9	12, 018	13, 280	−1, 262	9, 855	6, 702	3, 153	18, 901, 807	9, 341, 381	9, 560, 426
Colorado	54	115	−61	38, 215	45, 043	−6, 828	18, 684	28, 267	−9, 583	19, 502, 254	18, 574, 947	927, 307
New Mexico	53	24	29	21, 451	24, 113	−2, 662	18, 135	5, 103	13, 032	21, 634, 475	17, 794, 166	3, 840, 309
Arizona	40	19	21	7, 556	7, 316	240	4, 432	2, 178	2, 254	5, 951, 090	3, 765, 468	2, 185, 622
Utah	4	19	−15	23, 246	22, 340	906	33	1, 804	−1, 771	4, 471, 974	4, 046, 688	425, 286
Nevada	2	3	−1	2, 492	2, 491	1	700	238	462	2, 142, 720	1, 408, 436	734, 284
PACIFIC	279	259	20	202, 846	178, 026	24, 820	21, 372	24, 757	−3, 385	40, 394, 730	36, 187, 601	4, 207, 129
Washington	61	65	−4	56, 778	52, 184	4, 594	4, 704	5, 803	−1, 099	9, 273, 631	9, 190, 187	83, 444
Oregon	8	11	−3	44, 079	39, 505	4, 574	808	1, 401	−593	12, 816, 895	9, 927, 903	2, 888, 992
California	210	183	27	101, 989	86, 337	15, 652	15, 860	17, 553	−1, 693	18, 304, 204	17, 069, 511	1, 234, 693

[1] Includes Mexicans and Hindus.

TABLE 43.—NUMBER OF NEGRO AND WHITE FARM OPERATORS WITH ACREAGE, BY TENURE, BY SECTIONS, DIVISIONS, AND STATES: 1930 AND 1920—Continued

SECTION, DIVISION, AND STATE	NEGRO TENANTS			WHITE TENANTS [1]			LAND IN FARMS (ACRES)					
							Negro tenants			White tenants [1]		
	1930	1920	Increase or decrease (−)	1930	1920	Increase or decrease (−)	1930	1920	Increase or decrease (−)	1930	1920	Increase or decrease (−)
United States	700,911	705,070	−4,159	1,954,137	1,740,363	213,774	26,149,167	27,077,582	−928,415	279,537,920	237,214,893	42,323,027
The North	6,588	3,389	3,199	761,027	775,431	−14,404	373,214	294,543	78,671	142,733,476	131,244,422	11,489,054
The South	694,001	701,471	−7,470	1,091,944	887,566	204,378	25,743,324	26,754,386	−1,011,152	99,363,713	80,204,960	19,158,753
The West	322	210	112	101,166	77,366	23,800	32,719	28,653	4,066	37,440,731	25,765,511	11,675,220
NEW ENGLAND	14	33	−19	7,868	11,567	−3,699	1,025	5,221	−4,196	938,127	1,300,337	−362,210
Maine	1		1	1,754	2,004	−250	80		80	172,498	206,319	−33,821
New Hampshire	1	1		794	1,372	−578	240	30	210	101,246	153,035	−51,789
Vermont	4	4		2,405	3,382	−977	251	961	−710	418,491	563,754	−145,263
Massachusetts	3	7	−4	1,439	2,280	−841	122	601	−479	99,777	158,861	−59,084
Rhode Island		5	−5	414	628	−214		224	−224	41,404	52,650	−11,246
Connecticut	5	16	−11	1,062	1,901	−839	332	3,405	−3,073	104,711	165,718	−61,007
MIDDLE ATLANTIC	274	444	−170	52,153	87,719	−35,566	24,874	34,933	−10,059	5,975,035	9,594,304	−3,619,269
New York	33	71	−38	21,056	37,006	−15,950	4,473	7,174	−2,701	2,774,266	4,607,110	−1,832,844
New Jersey	126	228	−102	3,819	6,596	−2,777	10,396	15,175	−4,779	368,169	634,063	−265,894
Pennsylvania	115	145	−30	27,278	44,117	−16,839	10,005	12,584	−2,579	2,832,600	4,353,131	−1,520,531
EAST NORTH CENTRAL	1,149	1,273	−124	262,768	303,085	−40,317	96,208	93,247	2,961	36,339,304	38,254,768	−1,915,464
Ohio	438	527	−89	57,162	75,117	−17,955	44,627	40,353	4,274	6,662,366	7,913,758	−1,251,392
Indiana	184	251	−67	54,385	65,335	−10,950	13,734	16,965	−3,231	7,028,357	7,702,957	−674,600
Illinois	428	350	78	92,054	100,846	−8,792	29,414	23,168	6,246	14,927,489	14,973,681	−46,192
Michigan	85	139	−54	26,089	34,561	−8,472	6,528	12,169	−5,641	3,043,269	3,890,472	−847,203
Wisconsin	14	6	8	33,078	27,226	5,852	1,905	592	1,313	4,677,823	3,773,900	903,923
WEST NORTH CENTRAL	5,151	1,639	3,512	438,238	373,060	65,178	251,107	161,142	89,965	99,481,010	82,095,013	17,385,997
Minnesota	8	9	−1	57,593	44,109	13,484	1,223	700	523	11,034,070	8,762,304	2,271,766
Iowa	51	34	17	101,563	89,030	12,533	6,227	3,457	2,770	17,093,900	14,851,232	2,242,668
Missouri	4,661	1,133	3,528	84,405	74,593	9,812	176,385	67,365	109,020	10,835,328	9,356,054	1,479,274
North Dakota	5	13	−8	27,223	19,846	7,377	1,160	5,565	−4,405	11,828,161	8,533,116	3,295,045
South Dakota	13	13		36,647	25,904	10,743	2,974	5,314	−2,340	12,939,786	9,538,258	3,401,528
Nebraska	22	28	−6	60,899	53,304	7,595	4,762	11,648	−6,886	17,513,097	14,295,311	3,217,786
Kansas	391	409	−18	69,908	66,274	3,634	58,376	67,093	−8,717	18,236,668	16,758,738	1,477,930
SOUTH ATLANTIC	215,774	279,266	−63,492	292,177	261,876	30,301	10,226,681	12,521,869	−2,295,188	20,670,173	19,014,267	1,655,906
Delaware	415	504	−89	2,867	3,482	−615	37,631	41,082	−3,451	353,233	430,468	−77,235
Maryland	2,206	2,509	−303	9,235	11,332	−2,097	215,756	210,220	5,536	1,289,949	1,537,483	−247,534
District of Columbia	2	10	−8	22	75	−53	7	168	−161	418	1,820	−1,402
Virginia	15,123	16,585	−1,462	32,822	31,105	1,717	836,999	855,326	−18,327	2,983,964	3,118,095	−134,131
West Virginia	111	93	18	15,236	14,005	1,231	8,574	6,972	1,602	1,391,587	1,393,393	−1,806
North Carolina	55,635	53,040	2,595	80,476	63,542	16,934	2,346,755	2,230,592	116,163	4,323,337	3,928,067	395,270
South Carolina	61,285	86,063	−24,778	41,406	38,163	3,243	2,359,643	3,196,378	−836,735	2,365,051	2,088,404	276,647
Georgia	75,635	113,929	−38,294	98,754	93,016	5,738	4,197,605	5,710,627	−1,513,022	7,094,548	6,003,167	1,091,381
Florida	5,362	6,533	−1,171	11,359	7,156	4,203	223,711	270,504	−46,793	868,086	513,370	354,716
EAST SOUTH CENTRAL	269,985	251,112	18,873	323,738	271,001	52,747	8,351,425	8,088,733	262,692	17,882,827	15,252,588	2,630,239
Kentucky	4,914	7,271	−2,357	83,507	83,056	451	156,178	182,068	−25,890	4,964,349	4,369,095	595,254
Tennessee	27,261	28,289	−1,028	86,248	75,596	10,652	931,482	979,252	−47,770	5,135,552	4,531,916	603,636
Alabama	77,853	77,873	−20	88,545	70,395	18,150	2,953,534	2,983,328	−29,794	4,864,294	4,020,869	843,425
Mississippi	159,957	137,679	22,278	65,448	41,954	23,494	4,310,231	3,944,085	366,146	2,918,632	2,330,708	587,924
WEST SOUTH CENTRAL	208,242	171,093	37,149	476,019	354,689	121,330	7,165,128	6,143,784	1,021,344	60,810,713	45,938,105	14,872,608
Arkansas	68,081	56,811	11,270	84,590	62,407	22,183	1,774,095	1,568,630	205,465	4,995,049	3,725,808	1,269,241
Louisiana	63,192	50,969	12,223	44,338	26,400	17,938	1,691,610	1,419,717	271,893	2,026,288	1,444,076	582,212
Oklahoma	11,694	8,368	3,326	110,770	88,684	22,086	770,501	593,468	177,033	15,325,030	11,894,947	3,430,083
Texas	65,275	54,945	10,330	236,321	177,198	59,123	2,928,922	2,561,969	366,953	38,464,346	28,873,274	9,591,072
MOUNTAIN	115	100	15	57,535	36,420	21,115	15,989	12,445	3,544	25,005,449	13,359,385	11,646,064
Montana	6	4	2	11,469	6,439	5,030	2,280	1,195	1,085	7,461,936	3,217,098	4,244,838
Idaho	7	7		10,335	6,556	3,779	1,610	1,205	405	1,840,414	1,179,619	660,795
Wyoming	4		4	3,435	1,922	1,513	1,070		1,070	2,496,901	979,109	1,517,792
Colorado	23	28	−5	20,304	13,464	6,840	6,133	5,989	144	7,125,546	4,206,226	2,919,320
New Mexico	29	8	21	6,274	3,425	2,849	1,748	971	777	3,592,825	2,688,145	904,680
Arizona	44	10	34	2,185	1,713	472	2,984	740	2,244	996,480	586,417	410,063
Utah	1	41	−40	3,115	2,615	500	4	2,332	−2,328	494,149	362,211	131,938
Nevada	1	2	−1	418	286	132	160	13	147	997,198	140,560	856,638
PACIFIC	207	110	97	43,631	40,946	2,685	16,730	16,208	522	12,435,282	12,406,126	29,156
Washington	10	14	−4	11,726	11,679	47	4,610	1,012	3,598	3,577,470	3,413,196	164,274
Oregon	1	2	−1	9,576	9,220	356	18	214	−196	2,822,629	2,678,005	144,624
California	196	94	102	22,329	20,047	2,282	12,102	14,982	−2,880	6,035,183	6,314,925	−279,742

[1] Includes Mexicans and Hindus.

TABLE 43.—NUMBER OF NEGRO AND WHITE FARM OPERATORS WITH ACREAGE, BY TENURE, BY SECTIONS, DIVISIONS, AND STATES: 1930 AND 1920—Continued

SECTION, DIVISION, AND STATE	NEGRO MANAGERS			WHITE MANAGERS [1]			LAND IN FARMS (ACRES)					
							Negro managers			White managers [1]		
	1930	1920	Increase or decrease (−)	1930	1920	Increase or decrease (−)	1930	1920	Increase or decrease (−)	1930	1920	Increase or decrease (−)
United States	923	2,026	−1,103	52,767	66,223	−13,456	249,072	406,088	−157,016	61,549,583	53,653,478	7,896,105
The North	92	242	−150	24,984	38,719	−13,735	15,138	38,335	−13,197	9,056,203	11,803,417	−2,747,214
The South	805	1,759	−954	16,529	16,548	−19	229,938	355,749	−125,811	27,295,725	22,073,344	5,222,381
The West	26	25	1	11,254	10,956	298	3,996	12,004	−8,008	25,197,655	19,776,717	5,420,938
NEW ENGLAND	6	17	−11	2,930	4,784	−1,854	1,075	3,910	−2,835	750,125	976,421	−226,296
Maine				503	786	−283				129,357	145,793	−16,436
New Hampshire		1	−1	355	545	−190		325	−325	122,953	154,033	−31,080
Vermont	1	3	−2	479	565	−86	350	414	−64	151,902	149,783	2,119
Massachusetts	1	7	−6	957	1,620	−663	150	1,211	−1,061	215,220	311,884	−96,664
Rhode Island	1	1		98	204	−106	450	90	360	16,969	29,702	−12,733
Connecticut	3	5	−2	538	1,064	−526	125	1,870	−1,745	113,724	185,226	−71,502
MIDDLE ATLANTIC	31	86	−55	6,016	9,763	−3,747	4,176	9,448	−5,272	1,272,151	1,913,201	−641,050
New York	3	22	−19	2,644	4,351	−1,707	796	3,455	−2,659	620,611	928,660	−308,049
New Jersey	14	19	−5	644	967	−323	1,626	1,830	−204	141,891	206,413	−64,522
Pennsylvania	14	45	−31	2,728	4,445	−1,717	1,754	4,163	−2,409	409,649	778,128	−268,479
EAST NORTH CENTRAL	24	66	−42	8,605	13,480	−4,875	3,640	8,427	−4,787	2,090,899	2,857,754	−766,855
Ohio	11	36	−25	1,831	3,029	−1,198	2,010	4,533	−2,523	393,951	557,191	−163,240
Indiana	2	14	−12	1,476	2,315	−839	395	2,419	−2,024	359,626	470,497	−110,871
Illinois	6	9	−3	2,117	3,402	−1,285	756	1,077	−321	511,136	711,773	−200,637
Michigan	5	7	−2	1,525	2,310	−785	479	398	81	461,616	587,044	−125,428
Wisconsin				1,656	2,424	−768				364,570	531,249	−166,679
WEST NORTH CENTRAL	31	73	−42	7,433	10,692	−3,259	6,247	16,550	−10,303	4,943,028	6,056,041	−1,113,013
Minnesota				1,047	1,595	−548				307,216	443,065	−135,849
Iowa		1	−1	1,980	2,486	−506		250	−250	475,550	568,836	−93,286
Missouri	20	48	−28	1,526	2,199	−673	3,552	11,057	−7,505	509,625	653,390	−143,765
North Dakota		2	−2	470	853	−383		800	−800	386,587	810,667	−424,080
South Dakota	1	1		447	771	−324	510	80	430	936,951	883,213	53,738
Nebraska		4	−4	1,020	1,311	−291		1,913	−1,913	1,453,888	1,478,572	−24,684
Kansas	10	17	−7	943	1,477	−534	2,185	2,450	−265	873,211	1,218,298	−345,087
SOUTH ATLANTIC	477	956	−479	8,485	8,842	−357	109,107	145,948	−36,841	3,640,876	4,256,070	−615,184
Delaware	19	13	6	146	131	15	3,344	1,294	2,050	26,122	20,191	5,931
Maryland	120	151	−31	819	1,111	−292	21,878	22,082	−204	206,519	237,344	−30,825
District of Columbia	1	1		20	18	2	60	95	−35	1,861	1,856	5
Virginia	76	197	−121	1,459	1,937	−478	22,833	31,294	−8,461	632,096	792,456	−160,360
West Virginia	7	8	−1	714	1,082	−368	969	1,520	−551	255,995	354,563	−98,568
North Carolina	23	95	−72	625	832	−207	6,184	12,848	−6,664	249,062	373,582	−124,520
South Carolina	71	183	−112	622	555	67	21,362	37,095	−15,733	415,672	387,427	28,245
Georgia	72	207	−135	1,334	1,448	−114	23,563	29,038	−5,475	908,107	896,951	11,156
Florida	88	101	−13	2,746	1,728	1,018	8,914	10,682	−1,768	945,442	1,191,690	−246,248
EAST SOUTH CENTRAL	140	406	−266	2,747	3,099	−352	49,992	85,834	−35,842	1,236,683	1,442,654	−204,971
Kentucky	15	35	−20	660	934	−274	2,507	4,709	−2,202	193,394	265,130	−71,736
Tennessee	34	53	−19	577	754	−177	6,132	9,271	−3,139	200,331	211,608	−11,277
Alabama	22	126	−104	580	614	−34	14,162	32,069	−17,907	317,701	422,952	−105,251
Mississippi	69	192	−123	930	797	133	27,191	39,785	−12,594	526,257	542,964	−16,707
WEST SOUTH CENTRAL	188	397	−209	5,297	4,607	690	70,839	123,967	−53,128	22,417,166	16,374,630	6,042,536
Arkansas	23	95	−72	611	641	−30	6,741	13,211	−6,470	285,030	338,354	−53,324
Louisiana	54	92	−38	681	736	−55	20,305	14,465	5,840	856,174	885,656	−29,482
Oklahoma	24	77	−53	779	850	−71	7,035	13,008	−5,973	943,198	901,363	41,835
Texas	87	133	−46	3,226	2,380	846	36,758	83,283	−46,525	20,332,764	14,249,257	6,083,507
MOUNTAIN	6	10	−4	3,502	4,089	−587	1,550	10,230	−8,680	18,035,018	12,939,972	5,095,046
Montana		1	−1	510	889	−379		320	−320	3,010,791	2,855,278	155,513
Idaho	2		2	597	758	−161	880		880	435,728	385,718	50,010
Wyoming				295	377	−82				2,083,992	1,465,993	617,999
Colorado	1	5	−4	836	874	−38	320	2,260	−1,940	2,166,711	1,593,463	573,248
New Mexico				334	431	−97				5,350,383	3,862,963	1,487,420
Arizona	3	3		479	300	179	350	330	20	3,459,969	1,389,819	2,070,150
Utah		1	−1	230	293	−63		7,320	−7,320	607,579	590,341	17,238
Nevada				221	167	54				919,865	796,397	123,468
PACIFIC	20	15	5	7,752	6,867	885	2,446	1,774	672	7,162,637	6,836,745	325,892
Washington	2		2	1,051	1,159	−108	111		111	553,344	539,938	13,406
Oregon		2	−2	815	908	−93		510	−510	836,373	836,557	−184
California	18	13	5	5,886	4,800	1,086	2,335	1,264	1,071	5,772,920	5,460,250	312,670

[1] Includes Mexicans and Hindus.

TABLE 44.—FARMS OPERATED BY NEGROES—NUMBER, FARM ACREAGE, AND VALUE OF

SECTION, DIVISION, AND STATE	NUMBER OF NEGRO FARM OPERATORS								LAND IN FARMS (ACRES)			
	Total		Owner		Tenants		Managers		Total		Owners	
	1930	1920	1930	1920	1930	1920	1930	1920	1930	1920	1930	1920
United States	882, 850	925, 708	181, 016	218, 612	700, 911	705, 070	923	2, 026	37, 597, 132	41, 432, 182	11, 198, 893	13, 948, 512
The North	11, 104	9, 380	4, 424	5, 749	6, 588	3, 389	92	242	720, 872	767, 953	332, 520	435, 075
The South	870, 936	915, 595	176, 130	212, 365	694, 001	701, 471	805	1, 759	36, 758, 484	40, 544, 241	10, 785, 312	13, 434, 106
The West	810	733	462	498	322	210	26	25	117, 776	119, 988	81, 061	79, 331
NEW ENGLAND	148	242	128	192	14	33	6	17	9, 397	19, 252	7, 297	10, 121
Maine	15	13	14	13	1	-	-	-	818	953	738	953
New Hampshire	6	14	5	12	1	1	-	1	814	1, 476	574	1, 121
Vermont	22	28	17	21	4	4	1	3	3, 812	4, 450	3, 211	3, 075
Massachusetts	63	103	59	89	3	7	1	7	2, 063	4, 815	1, 791	3, 003
Rhode Island	9	19	8	13	-	5	1	1	571	944	121	630
Connecticut	33	65	25	44	5	16	3	5	1, 319	6, 614	862	1, 339
MIDDLE ATLANTIC	873	1, 227	568	697	274	444	31	86	55, 808	72, 897	26, 758	28, 516
New York	148	245	112	152	33	71	3	22	14, 894	19, 995	9, 625	9, 366
New Jersey	372	531	232	284	126	228	14	19	19, 298	25, 968	7, 276	8, 963
Pennsylvania	353	451	224	261	115	145	14	45	21, 616	26, 934	9, 857	10, 187
EAST NORTH CENTRAL	3, 065	3, 674	1, 892	2, 335	1, 149	1, 273	24	66	214, 596	239, 783	114, 748	138, 109
Ohio	1, 229	1, 616	780	1, 053	438	527	11	36	92, 083	100, 412	45, 446	55, 526
Indiana	461	570	275	305	184	251	2	14	28, 454	36, 668	14, 325	17, 284
Illinois	893	892	459	533	428	350	6	9	57, 805	57, 696	27, 635	33, 451
Michigan	427	549	337	403	85	139	5	7	30, 959	40, 939	23, 952	28, 372
Wisconsin	55	47	41	41	14	6	-	-	5, 295	4, 068	3, 390	3, 476
WEST NORTH CENTRAL	7, 018	4, 237	1, 836	2, 525	5, 151	1, 639	31	73	441, 071	436, 021	183, 717	258, 329
Minnesota	27	33	19	24	8	9	-	-	2, 692	2, 357	1, 469	1, 657
Iowa	118	109	67	74	51	34	-	1	10, 002	8, 847	3, 775	5, 140
Missouri	5, 844	2, 824	1, 163	1, 643	4, 661	1, 133	20	48	255, 623	190, 368	75, 686	111, 946
North Dakota	10	26	5	11	5	13	-	2	2, 565	11, 076	1, 405	4, 711
South Dakota	40	47	26	33	13	13	1	1	14, 228	19, 599	10, 744	14, 205
Nebraska	38	63	16	31	22	28	-	4	9, 216	27, 117	4, 454	13, 556
Kansas	941	1, 135	540	709	391	409	10	17	146, 745	176, 657	86, 184	107, 114
SOUTH ATLANTIC	295, 934	382, 278	79, 683	102, 056	215, 774	279, 266	477	956	14, 550, 451	18, 151, 071	4, 214, 663	5, 483, 254
Delaware	807	872	373	355	415	504	19	13	54, 756	54, 888	13, 781	12, 512
Maryland	5, 264	6, 208	2, 938	3, 548	2, 206	2, 509	120	151	345, 224	351, 527	107, 590	119, 225
District of Columbia	11	20	8	9	2	10	1	1	95	288	28	25
Virginia	39, 598	47, 690	24, 399	30, 908	15, 123	16, 585	76	197	2, 039, 656	2, 257, 953	1, 179, 824	1, 371, 333
West Virginia	490	504	372	403	111	93	7	8	28, 013	27, 544	18, 470	19, 052
North Carolina	74, 636	74, 849	18, 978	21, 714	55, 635	53, 040	23	95	3, 296, 445	3, 370, 191	943, 506	1, 126, 751
South Carolina	77, 331	109, 005	15, 975	22, 759	61, 285	86, 063	71	183	3, 167, 898	4, 379, 869	786, 893	1, 146, 396
Georgia	86, 787	130, 176	11, 080	16, 040	75, 635	113, 929	72	207	5, 104, 452	7, 070, 943	883, 284	1, 331, 278
Florida	11, 010	12, 954	5, 560	6, 320	5, 362	6, 533	88	101	513, 912	637, 868	281, 287	356, 682
EAST SOUTH CENTRAL	320, 600	307, 006	50, 475	55, 488	269, 985	251, 112	140	406	11, 918, 057	12, 104, 977	3, 516, 640	3, 930, 410
Kentucky	9, 104	12, 624	4, 175	5, 318	4, 914	7, 271	15	35	341, 833	426, 774	183, 148	239, 997
Tennessee	35, 123	38, 181	7, 828	9, 839	27, 261	28, 289	34	53	1, 356, 683	1, 523, 788	419, 069	535, 265
Alabama	93, 795	95, 200	15, 920	17, 201	77, 853	77, 873	22	126	4, 157, 051	4, 348, 018	1, 189, 355	1, 332, 621
Mississippi	182, 578	161, 001	22, 552	23, 130	159, 957	137, 679	69	192	6, 062, 490	5, 806, 397	1, 725, 068	1, 822, 527
WEST SOUTH CENTRAL	254, 402	226, 311	45, 972	54, 821	208, 242	171, 093	188	397	10, 289, 976	10, 288, 193	3, 054, 009	4, 020, 442
Arkansas	79, 556	72, 275	11, 452	15, 369	68, 081	56, 811	23	95	2, 485, 626	2, 623, 888	704, 790	1, 042, 047
Louisiana	73, 734	62, 036	10, 488	10, 975	63, 192	50, 969	54	92	2, 313, 338	2, 180, 883	601, 423	746, 701
Oklahoma	15, 172	13, 403	3, 454	4, 958	11, 694	8, 368	24	77	1, 061, 341	1, 045, 043	283, 805	438, 567
Texas	85, 940	78, 597	20, 578	23, 519	65, 275	54, 945	87	133	4, 429, 671	4, 438, 379	1, 463, 991	1, 793, 127
MOUNTAIN	304	349	183	239	115	100	6	10	77, 228	77, 249	59, 689	54, 574
Montana	21	31	15	26	6	4	-	1	9, 804	10, 274	7, 524	8, 759
Idaho	16	23	7	16	7	7	2	-	2, 816	2, 728	326	1, 523
Wyoming	12	17	8	17	4	-	-	-	10, 925	6, 702	9, 855	6, 702
Colorado	78	148	54	115	23	28	1	5	25, 137	36, 516	18, 684	28, 267
New Mexico	82	32	53	24	29	8	-	-	19, 883	6, 074	18, 135	5, 103
Arizona	87	32	40	19	44	10	3	3	7, 766	3, 248	4, 432	2, 178
Utah	5	61	4	19	1	41	-	1	37	11, 456	33	1, 804
Nevada	3	5	2	3	1	2	-	-	860	251	700	238
PACIFIC	506	384	279	259	207	110	20	15	40, 548	42, 739	21, 372	24, 757
Washington	73	79	61	65	10	14	2	-	9, 425	6, 815	4, 704	5, 803
Oregon	9	15	8	11	1	2	-	2	826	2, 125	808	1, 401
California	424	290	210	183	196	94	18	13	30, 297	33, 799	15, 860	17, 553

LAND AND BUILDINGS, BY TENURE, BY SECTIONS, DIVISIONS, AND STATES: 1930 AND 1920

SECTION, DIVISION, AND STATE	LAND IN FARMS (ACRES)—continued				VALUE OF LAND AND BUILDINGS							
	Tenants		Managers		Total		Owners		Tenants		Managers	
	1930	1920	1930	1920	1930	1920	1930	1920	1930	1920	1930	1920
United States	**26, 149, 167**	**27, 077, 582**	**249, 072**	**406, 088**	**$1,402,945,799**	**$2,257,645,325**	**$334, 451, 396**	**$554, 158, 003**	**$1,053,649,636**	**$1,676,315,864**	**$14, 844, 767**	**$27, 171, 458**
The North	**373, 214**	**294, 543**	**15, 138**	**38, 335**	**41, 668, 222**	**59, 832, 464**	**17, 684, 979**	**28, 481, 761**	**22, 327, 483**	**26, 258, 443**	**1, 655, 760**	**5, 092, 260**
The South	**25, 743, 234**	**26, 754, 386**	**229, 938**	**355, 749**	**1, 355, 181, 667**	**2, 191, 005, 642**	**314, 100, 432**	**522, 178, 137**	**1, 028, 371, 428**	**1, 647, 447, 607**	**12, 709, 807**	**21, 379, 898**
The West	**32, 719**	**28, 653**	**3, 996**	**12, 004**	**6, 095, 910**	**6, 807, 219**	**2, 665, 985**	**3, 498, 105**	**2, 950, 725**	**2, 609, 814**	**479, 200**	**699, 300**
NEW ENGLAND	1, 025	5, 221	1, 075	3, 910	909, 395	1, 076, 815	651, 325	617, 165	67, 070	234, 750	191, 000	224, 900
Maine	80	-	-	-	41, 400	54, 400	28, 400	54, 400	13, 000	-	-	-
New Hampshire	240	30	-	325	18, 000	29, 400	16, 000	18, 200	2, 000	1, 200	-	10, 000
Vermont	251	961	350	414	118, 700	116, 725	85, 700	87, 125	8, 000	20, 700	25, 000	8, 900
Massachusetts	122	601	150	1, 211	376, 595	345, 800	342, 525	243, 350	11, 070	20, 450	23, 000	82, 000
Rhode Island	-	224	450	90	40, 000	31, 500	32, 000	16, 900	-	7, 600	8, 000	7, 000
Connecticut	332	3, 405	125	1, 870	314, 700	498, 990	146, 700	197, 190	33, 000	184, 800	135, 000	117, 000
MIDDLE ATLANTIC	24, 874	34, 933	4, 176	9, 448	5, 140, 255	6, 937, 600	2, 422, 675	2, 294, 225	2, 165, 880	2, 854, 710	551, 700	1, 788, 665
New York	4, 473	7, 174	796	3, 455	875, 575	1, 558, 950	548, 095	619, 600	230, 980	483, 710	96, 500	455, 640
New Jersey	10, 396	15, 175	1, 626	1, 830	2, 070, 400	2, 117, 590	998, 500	755, 715	755, 400	1, 107, 375	316, 500	254, 500
Pennsylvania	10, 005	12, 584	1, 754	4, 163	2, 194, 280	3, 261, 060	876, 080	918, 910	1, 179, 500	1, 263, 625	138, 700	1, 078, 525
EAST NORTH CENTRAL	96, 208	93, 247	3, 640	8, 427	13, 304, 751	22, 308, 742	6, 796, 536	10, 433, 924	6, 092, 645	10, 528, 018	415, 570	1, 346, 800
Ohio	44, 627	40, 353	2, 010	4, 533	5, 434, 735	9, 126, 482	2, 641, 920	4, 173, 124	2, 649, 595	4, 215, 998	143, 220	737, 360
Indiana	13, 734	16, 965	395	2, 419	1, 947, 915	4, 254, 030	949, 485	1, 831, 910	975, 555	2, 157, 980	22, 875	264, 140
Illinois	29, 414	23, 168	756	1, 077	3, 704, 618	6, 082, 675	1, 562, 898	2, 541, 000	1, 972, 745	3, 297, 075	168, 975	244, 600
Michigan	6, 528	12, 169	479	398	1, 874, 378	2, 566, 855	1, 401, 728	1, 643, 890	392, 150	822, 265	80, 500	100, 700
Wisconsin	1, 905	592	-	-	343, 105	278, 700	240, 505	244, 000	102, 600	34, 700	-	-
WEST NORTH CENTRAL	251, 107	161, 142	6, 247	16, 550	22, 313, 821	29, 509, 307	7, 814, 443	15, 136, 447	14, 001, 888	12, 640, 965	497, 490	1, 731, 895
Minnesota	1, 223	700	-	-	187, 325	134, 670	141, 675	75, 320	45, 650	59, 350	-	-
Iowa	6, 227	3, 457	-	250	878, 234	1, 330, 600	350, 814	683, 250	527, 420	596, 350	-	51, 000
Missouri	176, 385	67, 365	3, 552	11, 057	14, 498, 297	16, 524, 007	3, 429, 544	8, 449, 937	10, 706, 493	6, 797, 975	362, 260	1, 276, 095
North Dakota	1, 160	5, 565	-	800	62, 700	285, 740	40, 700	85, 140	22, 000	177, 600	-	23, 000
South Dakota	2, 974	5, 314	510	80	285, 425	623, 515	163, 295	357, 315	101, 730	242, 200	20, 400	24, 000
Nebraska	4, 762	11, 648	-	1, 913	308, 080	1, 095, 040	149, 530	445, 540	158, 550	549, 500	-	100, 000
Kansas	58, 376	67, 093	2, 185	2, 450	6, 093, 760	9, 515, 735	3, 538, 885	5, 039, 945	2, 440, 045	4, 217, 990	114, 830	257, 800
SOUTH ATLANTIC	10, 226, 681	12, 521, 869	109, 107	145, 948	484, 443, 943	981, 677, 765	135, 724, 157	237, 088, 264	341, 922, 425	733, 440, 819	6, 797, 361	11, 148, 682
Delaware	37, 631	41, 082	3, 344	1, 294	2, 628, 590	2, 885, 445	804, 240	681, 300	1, 509, 675	2, 060, 495	314, 675	143, 650
Maryland	215, 756	210, 220	21, 878	22, 082	18, 896, 282	21, 651, 121	6, 695, 319	7, 959, 597	10, 442, 663	11, 354, 874	1, 758, 300	2, 836, 650
District of Columbia	7	168	60	95	82, 000	233, 300	43, 500	40, 300	8, 500	87, 300	30, 000	105, 700
Virginia	836, 999	855, 326	22, 833	31, 294	71, 722, 401	100, 839, 641	41, 743, 427	57, 004, 473	28, 629, 746	41, 502, 119	1, 349, 228	2, 333, 049
West Virginia	8, 574	6, 972	969	1, 520	1, 480, 628	1, 727, 890	832, 553	956, 562	415, 575	547, 628	232, 500	223, 700
North Carolina	2, 346, 755	2, 230, 592	6, 184	12, 848	153, 882, 635	223, 666, 166	36, 881, 352	56, 113, 060	116, 568, 229	166, 525, 511	433, 054	1, 027, 550
South Carolina	2, 359, 643	3, 196, 378	21, 362	37, 095	105, 693, 220	290, 406, 115	22, 788, 137	59, 839, 583	82, 319, 129	228, 355, 704	585, 954	2, 210, 898
Georgia	4, 197, 605	5, 710, 627	23, 563	29, 038	114, 688, 230	322, 706, 709	17, 528, 122	45, 465, 436	96, 253, 338	275, 484, 273	906, 770	1, 757, 020
Florida	223, 711	270, 504	8, 914	10, 682	15, 369, 957	17, 561, 378	8, 407, 507	9, 027, 953	5, 775, 570	7, 522, 915	1, 186, 880	1, 010, 501
EAST SOUTH CENTRAL	8, 351, 425	8, 088, 733	49, 992	85, 834	426, 528, 844	645, 828, 371	82, 453, 066	127, 401, 052	340, 962, 633	513, 777, 358	3, 113, 145	4, 649, 961
Kentucky	156, 178	182, 068	2, 507	4, 709	16, 157, 593	36, 067, 878	7, 348, 683	16, 389, 797	8, 430, 710	18, 993, 535	378, 200	684, 546
Tennessee	931, 482	979, 252	6, 132	9, 271	56, 339, 610	90, 427, 645	14, 169, 523	25, 276, 745	41, 395, 987	64, 349, 200	774, 100	801, 700
Alabama	2, 953, 534	2, 983, 328	14, 162	32, 069	104, 726, 209	116, 894, 012	24, 945, 906	29, 021, 680	79, 029, 593	86, 821, 727	750, 710	1, 050, 605
Mississippi	4, 310, 231	3, 944, 085	27, 191	39, 785	249, 305, 432	402, 438, 836	35, 988, 954	56, 712, 830	212, 106, 343	343, 612, 896	1, 210, 135	2, 113, 110
WEST SOUTH CENTRAL	7, 165, 128	6, 143, 784	70, 839	123, 967	444, 208, 880	563, 499, 506	95, 923, 209	157, 688, 821	345, 486, 370	400, 229, 430	2, 799, 301	5, 581, 255
Arkansas	1, 774, 095	1, 568, 630	6, 741	13, 211	118, 180, 961	182, 378, 759	21, 790, 174	45, 536, 138	96, 062, 087	135, 655, 066	328, 700	1, 187, 555
Louisiana	1, 691, 610	1, 419, 717	20, 305	14, 465	108, 668, 818	107, 615, 718	19, 567, 276	25, 438, 223	88, 375, 116	81, 324, 185	726, 426	853, 310
Oklahoma	770, 501	593, 468	7, 035	13, 008	37, 967, 113	48, 640, 707	9, 954, 907	19, 227, 142	27, 725, 473	28, 681, 300	286, 733	732, 265
Texas	2, 928, 922	2, 561, 969	36, 758	83, 283	179, 391, 988	224, 864, 322	44, 610, 852	67, 487, 318	133, 323, 694	154, 568, 879	1, 457, 442	2, 808, 125
MOUNTAIN	15, 989	12, 445	1, 550	10, 230	2, 037, 510	2, 523, 814	943, 685	1, 273, 200	1, 012, 825	916, 214	81, 000	334, 400
Montana	2, 280	1, 195	-	320	115, 084	240, 310	84, 084	197, 350	31, 000	39, 760	-	3, 200
Idaho	1, 610	1, 205	880	-	107, 200	134, 900	41, 700	83, 200	47, 500	51, 700	18, 000	-
Wyoming	1, 070	-	-	-	139, 020	131, 410	119, 660	131, 410	19, 360	-	-	-
Colorado	6, 133	5, 989	320	2, 260	445, 540	944, 405	263, 910	544, 115	178, 430	223, 090	3, 200	177, 200
New Mexico	1, 748	971	-	-	400, 956	124, 894	182, 881	88, 380	218, 075	36, 514	-	-
Arizona	2, 984	740	350	330	761, 510	277, 700	195, 250	117, 500	506, 460	86, 200	59, 800	74, 000
Utah	4	2, 332	-	7, 320	24, 200	651, 045	20, 200	94, 245	4, 000	476, 800	-	80, 000
Nevada	160	13	-	-	44, 000	19, 150	36, 000	17, 000	8, 000	2, 150	-	-
PACIFIC	16, 730	16, 208	2, 446	1, 774	4, 058, 400	4, 283, 405	1, 722, 300	2, 224, 905	1, 937, 900	1, 693, 600	398, 200	364, 900
Washington	4, 610	1, 012	111	-	356, 705	538, 480	268, 155	378, 960	77, 950	159, 520	10, 600	-
Oregon	18	214	-	510	32, 420	119, 400	26, 420	57, 400	6, 000	18, 000	-	44, 000
California	12, 102	14, 982	2, 335	1, 264	3, 669, 275	3, 625, 525	1, 427, 725	1, 788, 545	1, 853, 950	1, 516, 080	387, 600	320, 900

Table 45.—FARMS OPERATED BY NEGROES—INCREASE OR DECREASE (−) IN NUMBER, FARM ACREAGE,

SECTION, DIVISION, AND STATE	NUMBER OF FARMS								LAND IN FARMS (ACRES)			
	Total		Owners		Tenants		Managers		Total		Owners	
	Number	Percent	Number	Percent	Number	Percent	Number	Percent	Acres	Percent	Acres	Percent
United States	−42, 858	−4. 6	−37, 596	−17. 2	−4, 159	−0. 6	−1, 103	−54. 4	−3, 835, 050	−9. 3	−2, 749, 619	−19. 7
The North	1, 724	18. 4	−1, 325	−23. 0	3, 199	94. 4	−150	−62. 0	−47, 081	−6. 1	−102, 555	−23. 6
The South	−44, 659	−4. 9	−36, 235	−17. 1	−7, 470	−1. 1	−954	−54. 2	−3, 785, 757	−9. 3	−2, 648, 794	−19. 7
The West	77	10. 5	−36	−7. 2	112	53. 3	1	4. 0	−2, 212	−1. 8	1, 730	2. 2
New England	−94	−38. 8	−64	−33. 3	−19	−57. 6	−11	−64. 7	−9, 855	−51. 2	−2, 824	−27. 9
Maine	2	15. 4	1	7. 7	1				−135	−14. 2	−215	−22. 6
New Hampshire	−8	−57. 1	−7	−58. 3			−1	−100. 0	−662	−44. 9	−547	−48. 8
Vermont	−6	−21. 4	−4	−19. 0			−2	−66. 7	−638	−14. 3	136	4. 4
Massachusetts	−40	−38. 8	−30	−33. 7	−4	−57. 1	−6	−85. 7	−2, 752	−57. 2	−1, 212	−40. 4
Rhode Island	−10	−52. 6	−5	−38. 5	−5	−100. 0			−373	−39. 5	−509	−80. 8
Connecticut	−32	−49. 2	−19	−43. 2	−11	−68. 8	−2	−40. 0	−5, 295	−80. 1	−477	−35. 6
Middle Atlantic	−354	−28. 9	−129	−18. 5	−170	−38. 3	−55	−64. 0	−17, 089	−23. 4	−1, 758	−6. 2
New York	−97	−39. 6	−40	−26. 3	−38	−53. 5	−19	−86. 4	−5, 101	−25. 5	259	2. 8
New Jersey	−159	−29. 9	−52	−18. 3	−102	−44. 7	−5	−26. 3	−6, 670	−25. 7	−1, 687	−18. 8
Pennsylvania	−98	−21. 7	−37	−14. 2	−30	−20. 7	−31	−68. 9	−5, 318	−19. 7	−330	−3. 2
East North Central	−609	−16. 6	−443	−19. 0	−124	−9. 7	−42	−63. 6	−25, 187	−10. 5	−23, 361	−16. 9
Ohio	−387	−23. 9	−273	−25. 9	−89	−16. 9	−25	−69. 4	−8, 329	−8. 3	−10, 080	−18. 2
Indiana	−109	−19. 1	−30	−9. 8	−67	−26. 7	−12	−85. 7	−8, 214	−22. 4	−2, 959	−17. 1
Illinois	1	1	−74	−13. 9	78	22. 3	−3	−33. 3	109	. 2	−5, 816	−17. 4
Michigan	−122	−22. 2	−66	−16. 4	−54	−38. 8	−2	−28. 6	−9, 980	−24. 4	−4, 420	−15. 6
Wisconsin	8	17. 0			8	133. 3			1, 227	30. 2	−86	−2. 5
West North Central	2, 781	65. 6	−689	−27. 3	3, 512	214. 3	−42	−57. 5	5, 050	1. 2	−74, 612	−28. 9
Minnesota	−6	−18. 2	−5	−20. 8	−1	−11. 1			335	14. 2	−188	−11. 3
Iowa	9	8. 3	−7	−9. 5	17	50. 0	−1	−100. 0	1, 155	13. 1	−1, 365	−26. 6
Missouri	3, 020	106. 9	−480	−29. 2	3, 528	311. 4	−28	−58. 3	65, 255	34. 3	−36, 260	−32. 4
North Dakota	−16	−61. 5	−6	−54. 5	−8	−61. 5	−2	−100. 0	−8, 511	−76. 8	−3, 306	−70. 2
South Dakota	−7	−14. 9	−7	−21. 2					−5, 371	−27. 4	−3, 461	−24. 4
Nebraska	−25	−39. 7	−15	−48. 4	−6	−21. 4	−4	−100. 0	−17, 901	−66. 0	−9, 102	−67. 1
Kansas	−194	−17. 1	−169	−23. 8	−18	−4. 4	−7	−41. 2	−29, 912	−16. 9	−20, 930	−19. 5
South Atlantic	−86, 344	−22. 6	−22, 373	−21. 9	−63, 492	−22. 7	−479	−50. 1	−3, 600, 620	−19. 8	−1, 268, 591	−23. 1
Delaware	−65	−7. 5	18	5. 1	−89	−17. 7	6	46. 2	−132	−0. 2	1, 269	10. 1
Maryland	−944	−15. 2	−610	−17. 2	−303	−12. 1	−31	−20. 5	−6, 303	−1. 8	−11, 635	−9. 8
District of Columbia	−9	−45. 0	−1	−11. 1	−8	−80. 0			−193	−67. 0	3	12. 0
Virginia	−8, 092	−17. 0	−6, 509	−21. 1	−1, 462	−8. 8	−121	−61. 4	−218, 297	−9. 7	−191, 509	−14. 0
West Virginia	−14	−2. 8	−31	−7. 7	18	19. 4	−1	−12. 5	469	1. 7	−582	−3. 1
North Carolina	−213	−1. 3	−2, 736	−12. 6	2, 595	4. 9	−72	−75. 8	−73, 746	−2. 2	−183, 245	−16. 3
South Carolina	−31, 674	−29. 1	−6, 784	−29. 8	−24, 778	−28. 8	−112	−61. 2	−1, 211, 971	−27. 7	−359, 503	−31. 4
Georgia	−43, 389	−33. 3	−4, 960	−30. 9	−38, 294	−33. 6	−135	−65. 2	−1, 966, 491	−27. 8	−447, 994	−33. 7
Florida	−1, 944	−15. 0	−760	−12. 0	−1, 171	−17. 9	−13	−12. 9	−123, 956	−19. 4	−75, 395	−21. 1
East South Central	13, 594	4. 4	−5, 013	−9. 0	18, 873	7. 5	−266	−65. 5	−186, 920	−1. 5	−413, 770	−10. 5
Kentucky	−3, 520	−27. 9	−1, 143	−21. 5	−2, 357	−32. 4	−20	−57. 1	−84, 941	−19. 9	−56, 849	−23. 7
Tennessee	−3, 058	−8. 0	−2, 011	−20. 4	−1, 028	−3. 6	−19	−35. 8	−167, 105	−11. 0	−116, 196	−21. 7
Alabama	−1, 405	−1. 5	−1, 281	−7. 4	−20	(1)	−104	−82. 5	−190, 967	−4. 4	−143, 266	−10. 8
Mississippi	21, 577	13. 4	−578	−2. 5	22, 278	16. 2	−123	−64. 1	256, 093	4. 4	−97, 459	−5. 3
West South Central	28, 091	12. 4	−8, 849	−16. 1	37, 149	21. 7	−209	−52. 6	1, 783	(1)	−966, 433	−24. 0
Arkansas	7, 281	10. 1	−3, 917	−25. 5	11, 270	19. 8	−72	−75. 8	−138, 262	−5. 3	−337, 257	−32. 4
Louisiana	11, 698	18. 9	−487	−4. 4	12, 223	24. 0	−38	−41. 3	132, 455	6. 1	−145, 278	−19. 5
Oklahoma	1, 769	13. 2	−1, 504	−30. 3	3, 326	39. 7	−53	−68. 8	16, 298	1. 6	−154, 762	−35. 3
Texas	7, 343	9. 3	−2, 941	−12. 5	10, 330	18. 8	−46	−34. 6	−8, 708	−. 2	−329, 136	−18. 4
Mountain	−45	−12. 9	−56	−23. 4	15	15. 0	−4	−40. 0	−21	(1)	5, 115	9. 4
Montana	−10	−32. 3	−11	−42. 3	2	50. 0	−1	−100. 0	−470	−4. 6	−1, 235	−14. 1
Idaho	−7	−30. 4	−9	−56. 3			2		88	3. 2	−1, 197	−78. 6
Wyoming	−5	−29. 4	−9	−52. 9	4				4, 223	63. 0	3, 153	47. 0
Colorado	−70	−47. 3	−61	−53. 0	−5	−17. 9	−4	−80. 0	−11, 379	−31. 2	−9, 583	−33. 9
New Mexico	50	156. 3	29	120. 8	21	262. 5			13, 809	227. 3	13, 032	255. 4
Arizona	55	171. 9	21	110. 5	34	340. 0			4, 518	139. 1	2, 254	103. 5
Utah	−56	−91. 8	−15	−78. 9	−40	−97. 6	−1	−100. 0	−11, 419	−99. 7	−1, 771	−98. 2
Nevada	−2	−40. 0	−1	−33. 3	−1	−50. 0			609	242. 6	462	194. 1
Pacific	122	31. 8	20	7. 7	97	88. 2	5	33. 3	−2, 191	−5. 1	−3, 385	−13. 7
Washington	−6	−7. 6	−4	−6. 2	−4	−28. 6	2		2, 610	38. 3	−1, 099	−18. 9
Oregon	−6	−40. 0	−3	−27. 3	−1	−50. 0	−2	−100. 0	−1, 299	−61. 1	−593	−42. 3
California	134	46. 2	27	14. 8	102	108. 5	5	38. 5	−3, 502	−10. 4	−1, 693	−9. 6

[1] Less than 1/10 of 1 percent.

AND VALUE OF LAND AND BUILDINGS, BY TENURE, BY SECTIONS, DIVISIONS, AND STATES: 1920 TO 1930

SECTION, DIVISION, AND STATE	LAND IN FARMS (ACRES)—continued				VALUE OF LAND AND BUILDINGS							
	Tenants		Managers		Total		Owners		Tenants		Managers	
	Acres	Percent	Acres	Percent	Value	Percent	Value	Percent	Value	Percent	Value	Percent
United States	−928, 415	−3. 4	−157, 016	−38. 7	−$854, 699, 526	−37. 9	−$219, 706, 607	−39. 6	−$622, 666, 228	−37. 1	−$12, 326, 691	−45. 4
The North	78, 671	26. 7	−23, 197	−60. 5	−18, 164, 242	−30. 4	−10, 796, 782	−37. 9	−3, 930, 960	−15. 0	−3, 436, 500	−67. 5
The South	−1, 011, 152	−3. 8	−125, 811	−35. 4	−835, 823, 975	−38. 1	−208, 077, 705	−39. 8	−619, 076, 179	−37. 6	−8, 670, 091	−40. 6
The West	4, 066	14. 2	−8, 008	−66. 7	−711, 309	−10. 4	−832, 120	−23. 8	340, 911	13. 1	−220, 100	−31. 5
NEW ENGLAND	−4, 196	−80. 4	−2, 835	−72. 5	−167, 420	−15. 5	34, 160	5. 5	−167, 680	−71. 4	−33, 900	−15. 1
Maine	80	-------	-------	-------	−13, 000	−23. 9	−26, 000	−47. 8	13, 000	-------	-------	-------
New Hampshire	210	700. 0	−325	−100. 0	−11, 400	−38. 8	−2, 200	−12. 1	800	66. 7	−10, 000	−100. 0
Vermont	−710	−73. 9	−64	−15. 5	1, 975	1. 7	−1, 425	−1. 6	−12, 700	−61. 4	16, 100	180. 9
Massachusetts	−479	−79. 7	−1, 061	−87. 6	30, 795	8. 9	99, 175	40. 8	−9, 380	−45. 9	−59, 000	−72. 0
Rhode Island	−224	−100. 0	360	400. 0	8, 500	27. 0	15, 100	89. 3	−7, 600	−100. 0	1, 000	14. 3
Connecticut	−3, 073	−90. 2	−1, 745	−93. 3	−184, 290	−36. 9	−50, 490	−25. 6	−151, 800	−82. 1	18, 000	15. 4
MIDDLE ATLANTIC	−10, 059	−28. 8	−5, 272	−55. 8	−1, 797, 345	−25. 9	128, 450	5. 6	−688, 830	−24. 1	−1, 236, 965	−69. 2
New York	−2, 701	−37. 6	−2, 659	−77. 0	−683, 375	−43. 8	−71, 505	−11. 5	−252, 730	−52. 2	−359, 140	−78. 8
New Jersey	−4, 779	−31. 5	−204	−11. 1	−47, 190	−2. 2	242, 785	32. 1	−351, 975	−31. 8	62, 000	24. 4
Pennsylvania	−2, 579	−20. 5	−2, 409	−57. 9	−1, 066, 780	−32. 7	−42, 830	−4. 7	−84, 125	−6. 7	−939, 825	−87. 1
EAST NORTH CENTRAL	2, 961	3. 2	−4, 787	−56. 8	−9, 003, 991	−40. 4	−3, 637, 388	−34. 9	−4, 435, 373	−42. 1	−931, 230	−69. 1
Ohio	4, 274	10. 6	−2, 523	−55. 7	−3, 691, 747	−40. 5	−1, 531, 204	−36. 7	−1, 566, 403	−37. 2	−594, 140	−80. 6
Indiana	−3, 231	−19. 0	−2, 024	−83. 7	−2, 306, 115	−54. 2	−882, 425	−48. 2	−1, 182, 425	−54. 8	−241, 265	−91. 3
Illinois	6, 246	27. 0	−321	−29. 8	−2, 378, 057	−39. 1	−978, 102	−38. 5	−1, 324, 330	−40. 2	−75, 625	−30. 9
Michigan	−5, 641	−46. 4	81	20. 4	−692, 477	−27. 0	−242, 162	−14. 7	−430, 115	−52. 3	−20, 200	−20. 1
Wisconsin	1, 313	221. 8	-------	-------	64, 405	23. 1	−3, 495	−1. 4	67, 900	195. 7	-------	-------
WEST NORTH CENTRAL	89, 965	55. 8	−10, 303	−62. 3	−7, 195, 486	−24. 4	−7, 322, 004	−48. 4	1, 360, 923	10. 8	−1, 234, 405	−71. 3
Minnesota	523	74. 7	-------	-------	52, 655	39. 1	66, 355	88. 1	−13, 700	−23. 1	-------	-------
Iowa	2, 770	80. 1	−250	−100. 0	−452, 366	−34. 0	−332, 436	−48. 7	−68, 930	−11. 6	−51, 000	−100. 0
Missouri	109, 020	161. 8	−7, 505	−67. 9	−2, 025, 710	−12. 3	−5, 020, 393	−59. 4	3, 908, 518	57. 5	−913, 835	−71. 6
North Dakota	−4, 405	−79. 2	−800	−100. 0	−223, 040	−78. 1	−44, 440	−52. 2	−155, 600	−87. 6	−23, 000	−100. 0
South Dakota	−2, 340	−44. 0	430	537. 5	−338, 090	−54. 2	−194, 020	−54. 3	−140, 470	−58. 0	−3, 600	−15. 0
Nebraska	−6, 886	−59. 1	−1, 913	−100. 0	−786, 960	−71. 9	−296, 010	−66. 4	−390, 950	−71. 1	−100, 000	−100. 0
Kansas	−8, 717	−13. 0	−265	−10. 8	−3, 421, 975	−36. 0	−1, 501, 060	−29. 8	−1, 777, 945	−42. 2	−142, 970	−55. 5
SOUTH ATLANTIC	−2, 295, 188	−18. 3	−36, 841	−25. 2	−497, 233, 822	−50. 7	−101, 364, 107	−42. 8	−391, 518, 394	−53. 4	−4, 351, 321	−39. 0
Delaware	−3, 451	−8. 4	2, 050	158. 4	−256, 855	−8. 9	122, 940	18. 0	−550, 820	−26. 7	171, 025	119. 1
Maryland	5, 536	2. 6	−204	−. 9	−2, 754, 839	−12. 7	−1, 264, 278	−15. 9	−912, 211	−8. 0	−578, 350	−24. 8
District of Columbia	−161	−95. 8	−35	−36. 8	−151, 300	−64. 9	3, 200	7. 9	−78, 800	−90. 3	−75, 700	−71. 6
Virginia	−18, 327	−2. 1	−8, 461	−27. 0	−29, 117, 240	−28. 9	−15, 261, 046	−26. 8	−12, 872, 373	−31. 0	−983, 821	−42. 2
West Virginia	1, 602	23. 0	−551	−36. 3	−247, 262	−14. 3	−124, 009	−13. 0	−132, 053	−24. 1	8, 800	3. 9
North Carolina	116, 163	5. 2	−6, 664	−51. 9	−69, 783, 531	−31. 2	−19, 231, 708	−34. 3	−49, 957, 282	−30. 0	−594, 541	−57. 9
South Carolina	−836, 735	−26. 2	−15, 733	−42. 4	−184, 712, 895	−63. 6	−37, 051, 446	−61. 9	−146, 036, 575	−64. 0	−1, 624, 874	−73. 5
Georgia	−1, 513, 022	−26. 5	−5, 475	−18. 9	−208, 018, 479	−64. 5	−27, 937, 314	−61. 4	−179, 230, 935	−65. 1	−850, 230	−48. 4
Florida	−46, 793	−17. 3	−1, 768	−16. 6	−2, 191, 421	−12. 5	−620, 446	−6. 9	−1, 747, 345	−23. 2	176, 370	17. 5
EAST SOUTH CENTRAL	262, 692	3. 2	−35, 842	−41. 8	−219, 299, 527	−34. 0	−44, 947, 986	−35. 3	−172, 814, 725	−33. 6	−1, 536, 816	−33. 1
Kentucky	−25, 890	−14. 2	−2, 202	−46. 8	−19, 910, 285	−55. 2	−9, 041, 114	−55. 2	−10, 562, 825	−55. 6	−306, 346	−44. 8
Tennessee	−47, 770	−4. 9	−3, 139	−33. 9	−34, 088, 035	−37. 7	−11, 107, 222	−43. 9	−22, 953, 213	−35. 7	−27, 600	−3. 4
Alabama	−29, 794	−1. 0	−17, 907	−55. 8	−12, 167, 803	−10. 4	−4, 075, 774	−14. 0	−7, 792, 134	−9. 0	−299, 895	−28. 5
Mississippi	366, 146	9. 3	−12, 594	−31. 7	−153, 133, 404	−38. 1	−20, 723, 876	−36. 5	−131, 506, 553	−38. 3	−902, 975	−42. 7
WEST SOUTH CENTRAL	1, 021, 344	16. 6	−53, 128	−42. 9	−119, 290, 626	−21. 2	−61, 765, 612	−39. 2	−54, 743, 060	−13. 7	−2, 781, 954	−49. 8
Arkansas	205, 465	13. 1	−6, 470	−49. 0	−64, 197, 798	−35. 2	−23, 745, 964	−52. 1	−39, 592, 979	−29. 2	−858, 855	−72. 3
Louisiana	271, 893	19. 2	5, 840	40. 4	1, 053, 100	1. 0	−5, 870, 947	−23. 1	7, 050, 931	8. 7	−126, 884	−14. 9
Oklahoma	177, 033	29. 8	−5, 973	−45. 9	−10, 673, 594	−21. 9	−9, 272, 235	−48. 2	−955, 827	−3. 3	−445, 532	−60. 8
Texas	366, 953	14. 3	−46, 525	−55. 9	−45, 472, 334	−20. 2	−22, 876, 466	−33. 9	−21, 245, 185	−13. 7	−1, 350, 683	−48. 1
MOUNTAIN	3, 544	28. 5	−8, 680	−84. 8	−486, 304	−19. 3	−329, 515	−25. 9	96, 611	10. 5	−253, 400	−75. 8
Montana	1, 085	90. 8	−320	−100. 0	−125, 226	−52. 1	−113, 266	−57. 4	−8, 760	−22. 0	−3, 200	−100. 0
Idaho	405	33. 6	880	-------	−27, 700	−20. 5	−41, 500	−49. 9	−4, 200	−8. 1	18, 000	-------
Wyoming	1, 070	-------	-------	-------	7, 610	5. 8	−11, 750	−8. 9	19, 360	-------	-------	-------
Colorado	144	2. 4	−1, 940	−85. 8	−498, 865	−52. 8	−280. 205	−51. 5	−44, 660	−20. 0	−174, 000	−98. 2
New Mexico	777	80. 0	-------	-------	276, 062	221. 0	94, 501	106. 9	181, 561	497. 2	-------	-------
Arizona	2, 244	303. 2	20	6. 1	483, 810	174. 2	77, 750	66. 2	420, 260	487. 5	−14, 200	−19. 2
Utah	−2, 328	−99. 8	−7, 320	−100. 0	−626, 845	−96. 3	−74, 045	−78. 6	−472, 800	−99. 2	−80, 000	−100. 0
Nevada	147	1, 130. 8	-------	-------	24, 850	129. 8	19, 000	111. 8	5, 850	272. 1	-------	-------
PACIFIC	522	3. 2	672	37. 9	−225, 005	−5. 3	−502, 605	−22. 6	244, 300	14. 4	33, 300	9. 1
Washington	3, 598	355. 5	111	-------	−181, 775	−33. 8	−110, 805	−29. 2	−81, 570	−51. 1	10, 600	-------
Oregon	−196	−91. 6	−510	−100. 0	−86, 980	−72. 8	−30, 980	−54. 0	−12, 000	−66. 7	−44, 000	−100. 0
California	−2, 880	−19. 2	1, 071	84. 7	43, 750	1. 2	−360, 820	−20. 1	337, 870	22. 3	66, 700	20. 8

TABLE 46.—AVERAGE SIZE OF FARM, AND AVERAGE VALUE OF SPECIFIED CLASSES OF FARM PROPERTY OF NEGRO FARM OPERATORS, BY TENURE, BY SECTIONS, DIVISIONS, AND STATES: 1930

SECTION, DIVISION, AND STATE	AVERAGE SIZE OF FARM (ACRES)		AVERAGE VALUE—															
			Land and buildings				Land alone				Buildings				Implements and machinery			
			Per farm		Per acre		Per farm		Per acre		Per farm		Per acre		Per farm		Per acre	
	Owners	Tenants	Owners	Tenants	Owners	Tenants	Owners	Tenants	Owners	Tenants	Owners	Tenants	Owners	Tenants	Owners	Tenants	Owners	Tenants
United States	**61.9**	**37.3**	**$1,848**	**$1,503**	**$29.86**	**$40.29**	**$1,263**	**$1,174**	**$20.42**	**$31.47**	**$584**	**$329**	**$9.44**	**$8.82**	**$109**	**$57**	**$1.77**	**$1.53**
The North	**75.2**	**56.7**	**3,998**	**3,389**	**53.18**	**59.82**	**2,625**	**2,691**	**34.92**	**47.50**	**1,373**	**698**	**18.27**	**12.33**	**236**	**130**	**3.13**	**2.29**
The South	**61.2**	**37.1**	**1,783**	**1,482**	**29.12**	**39.95**	**1,220**	**1,156**	**19.93**	**31.18**	**563**	**325**	**9.20**	**8.77**	**106**	**56**	**1.72**	**1.51**
The West	**175.5**	**101.6**	**5,771**	**9,164**	**32.89**	**90.18**	**4,741**	**8,378**	**27.02**	**82.45**	**1,029**	**786**	**5.87**	**7.74**	**310**	**372**	**1.77**	**3.67**
NEW ENGLAND	57.0	73.2	5,088	4,791	89.26	65.43	2,364	2,266	41.46	30.95	2,725	2,525	47.79	34.48	345	330	6.04	4.51
Maine	52.7	80.0	2,029	13,000	38.48	162.50	664	6,400	12.60	80.00	1,364	6,600	25.88	82.50	327	1,500	6.20	18.75
New Hampshire	114.8	240.0	3,200	2,000	27.87	8.33	990	1,000	8.62	4.17	2,210	1,000	19.25	4.17	360	250	3.14	1.04
Vermont	188.9	62.8	5,041	2,000	26.69	31.87	2,524	744	13.36	11.85	2,518	1,256	13.33	20.02	737	250	3.90	3.98
Massachusetts	30.4	40.7	5,806	3,690	191.25	90.74	2,975	1,950	98.02	47.95	2,830	1,740	93.23	42.79	282	92	9.29	2.25
Rhode Island	15.1		4,000		264.46		1,250		82.64		2,750		181.82		103		6.82	
Connecticut	34.5	66.4	5,868	6,600	170.19	99.40	2,395	3,100	69.45	46.69	3,473	3,500	100.74	52.71	309	320	8.97	4.82
MIDDLE ATLANTIC	47.1	90.8	4,265	7,905	90.54	87.07	1,929	4,680	40.95	51.55	2,336	3,225	49.59	35.53	415	563	8.82	6.20
New York	85.9	135.5	4,894	6,999	56.94	51.64	2,060	3,363	23.97	24.81	2,834	3,636	32.98	26.83	545	917	6.34	6.77
New Jersey	31.4	82.5	4,304	5,995	137.23	72.66	2,180	3,572	69.50	43.29	2,124	2,423	67.74	29.37	380	554	12.11	6.71
Pennsylvania	44.0	87.0	3,911	10,257	88.88	117.89	1,605	6,271	36.47	72.08	2,306	3,985	52.41	45.81	387	471	8.80	5.41
EAST NORTH CENTRAL	60.6	83.7	3,592	5,303	59.23	63.33	2,255	4,006	37.18	47.84	1,338	1,297	22.05	15.49	184	184	3.03	2.20
Ohio	58.3	101.9	3,387	6,049	58.13	59.37	2,011	4,358	34.51	42.77	1,376	1,691	23.62	16.60	152	196	2.61	1.92
Indiana	52.1	74.6	3,453	5,302	66.28	71.03	2,318	3,818	44.49	51.15	1,135	1,484	21.79	19.88	138	208	2.65	2.79
Illinois	60.2	68.7	3,405	4,609	56.56	67.07	2,466	3,935	40.95	57.26	939	674	15.60	9.80	139	128	2.30	1.86
Michigan	71.1	76.8	4,159	4,614	58.52	60.07	2,303	2,711	32.40	35.31	1,856	1,902	26.12	24.77	316	335	4.45	4.36
Wisconsin	82.7	136.1	5,866	7,329	70.95	53.86	3,714	5,439	44.92	39.97	2,152	1,889	26.02	13.88	520	328	6.29	2.41
WEST NORTH CENTRAL	100.1	48.7	4,256	2,718	42.54	55.76	3,239	2,293	32.37	47.03	1,017	426	10.16	8.73	226	94	2.25	1.93
Minnesota	77.3	152.9	7,457	5,706	96.44	37.33	3,788	4,456	49.00	29.15	3,668	1,250	47.45	8.18	920	186	11.90	1.22
Iowa	56.3	122.1	5,236	10,342	92.93	84.70	3,503	8,354	62.17	68.42	1,733	1,987	30.77	16.28	303	505	5.37	4.13
Missouri	65.1	37.8	2,949	2,297	45.31	60.70	2,156	1,928	33.13	50.94	793	369	12.18	9.76	123	73	1.89	1.92
North Dakota	281.0	232.0	8,140	4,400	28.97	18.97	5,740	3,720	20.43	16.03	2,400	680	8.54	2.93	635	940	2.26	4.05
South Dakota	413.2	228.8	6,281	7,825	15.20	34.21	5,010	6,222	12.12	27.20	1,270	1,604	3.07	7.01	882	665	2.13	2.91
Nebraska	278.4	216.5	9,346	7,207	33.57	33.29	7,205	5,723	25.88	26.44	2,141	1,484	7.69	6.85	1,324	330	4.75	1.52
Kansas	159.6	149.3	6,553	6,241	41.06	41.80	5,293	5,466	33.17	36.61	1,260	774	7.90	5.19	344	250	2.16	1.68
SOUTH ATLANTIC	52.9	47.4	1,703	1,585	32.20	33.43	1,070	1,169	20.22	24.67	634	415	11.98	8.76	93	54	1.75	1.14
Delaware	36.9	90.7	2,156	3,638	58.36	40.12	1,031	2,360	27.91	26.02	1,125	1,278	30.44	14.09	270	258	7.31	2.85
Maryland	36.6	97.8	2,279	4,734	62.23	48.40	1,224	3,225	33.41	32.97	1,055	1,509	28.82	15.43	144	200	3.94	2.04
District of Columbia	3.5	3.5	5,438	4,250	1,553.57	1,214.29	3,466	1,500	990.18	428.57	1,972	2,750	563.39	785.71	13	63	3.57	17.86
Virginia	48.4	55.3	1,711	1,893	35.38	34.21	948	1,273	19.60	22.99	763	620	15.78	11.21	106	80	2.19	1.45
West Virginia	49.7	77.2	2,238	3,744	45.08	48.47	1,380	2,451	27.79	31.74	858	1,292	17.29	16.73	71	138	1.44	1.78
North Carolina	49.7	42.2	1,943	2,095	39.09	49.67	1,300	1,575	26.15	37.34	643	520	12.94	12.33	89	62	1.80	1.47
South Carolina	49.3	38.5	1,426	1,343	28.96	34.89	945	1,014	19.19	26.33	481	330	9.77	8.56	79	46	1.60	1.18
Georgia	79.7	55.5	1,582	1,273	19.84	22.93	1,066	931	13.38	16.77	516	342	6.47	6.16	79	45	1.00	.81
Florida	50.6	41.7	1,512	1,077	29.89	25.82	1,077	848	21.29	20.32	435	229	8.60	5.50	74	46	1.46	1.11
EAST SOUTH CENTRAL	69.7	30.9	1,634	1,263	23.45	40.83	1,136	975	16.31	31.53	497	288	7.14	9.30	110	52	1.58	1.69
Kentucky	43.9	31.8	1,760	1,716	40.12	53.98	1,136	1,286	25.90	40.48	624	429	14.22	13.50	76	57	1.72	1.81
Tennessee	53.5	34.2	1,810	1,519	33.81	44.44	1,248	1,186	23.31	34.70	562	333	10.50	9.75	120	74	2.25	2.17
Alabama	74.7	37.9	1,567	1,015	20.97	26.75	1,092	764	14.62	20.14	475	251	6.35	6.61	97	45	1.30	1.19
Mississippi	76.5	26.9	1,596	1,326	20.86	49.21	1,129	1,033	14.76	38.33	467	293	6.11	10.88	122	52	1.60	1.92
WEST SOUTH CENTRAL	66.4	34.4	2,087	1,659	31.41	48.22	1,573	1,378	23.68	40.05	513	281	7.73	8.17	123	63	1.85	1.84
Arkansas	61.5	26.1	1,903	1,411	30.92	54.15	1,417	1,143	23.03	43.87	485	268	7.89	10.28	113	51	1.84	1.95
Louisiana	57.3	26.8	1,866	1,399	32.53	52.24	1,370	1,131	23.89	42.29	496	268	8.65	10.00	114	58	1.99	2.16
Oklahoma	82.2	65.9	2,882	2,371	35.08	35.98	2,275	2,068	27.68	31.38	607	303	7.39	4.60	165	86	2.01	1.31
Texas	71.1	44.9	2,168	2,042	30.47	45.52	1,646	1,739	23.13	38.75	522	304	7.34	6.77	126	78	1.76	1.74
MOUNTAIN	326.2	139.0	5,157	8,807	15.81	63.35	4,383	7,997	13.44	57.52	774	810	2.37	5.83	347	367	1.06	2.64
Montana	501.6	380.0	5,606	5,167	11.18	13.60	4,835	4,029	9.64	10.60	771	1,138	1.54	2.99	959	200	1.91	.53
Idaho	46.6	230.0	5,957	6,786	127.91	29.50	4,143	5,436	88.96	23.63	1,814	1,350	38.96	5.87	961	343	20.63	1.49
Wyoming	1,231.9	267.5	14,958	4,840	12.14	18.09	13,308	4,353	10.80	16.27	1,650	488	1.34	1.82	753	475	.61	1.78
Colorado	346.0	266.7	4,887	7,758	14.12	29.09	3,955	6,745	11.43	25.29	932	1,013	2.69	3.80	238	446	.69	1.67
New Mexico	342.2	60.3	3,451	7,520	10.08	124.76	3,147	6,840	9.20	113.47	303	680	.89	11.28	175	307	.51	5.10
Arizona	110.8	67.8	4,881	11,510	44.05	169.73	4,146	10,859	37.42	160.12	736	651	6.64	9.60	324	394	2.92	5.81
Utah	8.3	4.0	5,050	4,000	612.12	1,000.00	4,275	3,000	518.18	750.00	775	1,000	93.94	250.00	76		9.24	
Nevada	350.0	160.0	18,000	8,000	51.43	50.00	15,400	5,700	44.00	35.63	2,600	2,300	7.43	14.38	500	250	1.43	1.56
PACIFIC	76.6	80.8	6,173	9,362	80.59	115.83	4,977	8,589	64.97	106.27	1,196	773	15.62	9.56	285	375	3.72	4.64
Washington	77.1	461.0	4,396	7,795	57.01	16.91	3,108	6,275	40.31	13.61	1,287	1,520	16.70	3.30	256	513	3.32	1.11
Oregon	101.0	18.0	3,303	6,000	32.70	333.33	2,284	4,400	22.61	244.44	1,019	1,600	10.09	88.89	327	50	3.24	2.78
California	75.5	61.7	6,799	9,459	90.02	153.19	5,622	8,729	74.44	141.37	1,177	730	15.58	11.83	292	370	3.87	5.99

TABLE 47.—FARMS OPERATED BY NEGROES—NUMBER, FARM ACREAGE, AND VALUE OF LAND AND BUILDINGS, BY SECTIONS, DIVISIONS, AND STATES: 1930 AND 1910

SECTION, DIVISION, AND STATE	NUMBER OF NEGRO FARM OPERATORS				LAND IN FARMS (ACRES)				VALUE OF LAND AND BUILDINGS			
	1930	1910	Increase or decrease (−) 1910–30		1930	1910	Increase or decrease (−) 1910–30		1930	1910	Increase or decrease (−) 1910–30	
			Number	Percent			Number	Percent			Amount	Percent
United States	882, 850	893, 370	10, 520	−1. 2	37, 597, 132	42, 279, 510	−4, 682, 378	−11. 1	$1,402,945,799	$922, 717, 703	$480, 228, 096	52. 0
The North	11, 104	12, 052	−948	−7. 9	720, 872	868, 630	−147, 758	−17. 0	41, 668, 222	45, 256, 388	−3, 588, 166	−7. 9
The South	870, 936	880, 836	−9, 900	−1. 1	36, 758, 484	41, 284, 471	−4, 525, 987	−11. 0	1, 355, 181, 667	873, 582, 410	481, 599, 257	55. 1
The West	810	482	328	68. 0	117, 776	126, 409	−8, 633	−6. 8	6, 095, 910	3, 878, 905	2, 217, 005	57. 2
NEW ENGLAND	148	310	−162	−52. 3	9, 397	14, 759	−5, 362	−36. 3	909, 395	802, 360	107, 035	13. 3
Maine	15	28	−13	−46. 4	818	1, 280	−462	−36. 1	41, 400	36, 850	4, 550	12. 3
New Hampshire	6	14	−8	−57. 1	814	923	−109	−11. 8	18, 000	61, 300	−43, 300	−70. 6
Vermont	22	20	2	10. 0	3, 812	1, 917	1, 895	98. 9	118, 700	42, 350	76, 350	180. 3
Massachusetts	63	103	−40	−38. 8	2, 063	3, 535	−1, 472	−41. 6	376, 595	258, 065	118, 530	45. 9
Rhode Island	9	40	−31	−77. 5	571	1, 664	−1, 093	−65. 7	40, 000	62, 600	−22, 600	−36. 1
Connecticut	33	105	−72	−68. 6	1, 319	5, 440	−4, 121	−75. 8	314, 700	341, 195	−26, 495	−7. 8
MIDDLE ATLANTIC	873	1, 310	−437	−33. 4	55, 808	74, 849	−19, 041	−25. 4	5, 140, 255	5, 299, 347	−159, 092	−3. 0
New York	148	295	−147	−49. 8	14, 894	22, 552	−7, 658	−34. 0	875, 575	1, 234, 530	−358, 955	−29. 1
New Jersey	372	472	−100	−21. 2	19, 298	22, 200	−2, 902	−13. 1	2, 070, 400	1, 689, 737	380, 663	22. 5
Pennsylvania	353	543	−190	−35. 0	21, 616	30, 097	−8, 481	−28. 2	2, 194, 280	2, 375, 080	−180, 800	−7. 6
EAST NORTH CENTRAL	3, 065	4, 843	−1, 778	−36. 7	214, 596	287, 513	−72, 917	−25. 4	13, 304, 751	17, 477, 649	−4, 172, 898	−23. 9
Ohio	1, 229	1, 948	−719	−36. 9	92, 083	106, 742	−14, 659	−13. 7	5, 434, 735	5, 989, 075	−554, 340	−9. 3
Indiana	461	785	−324	−41. 3	28, 454	43, 627	−15, 173	−34. 8	1, 947, 915	3, 317, 747	−1, 369, 832	−41. 3
Illinois	893	1, 422	−529	−37. 2	57, 805	87, 784	−29, 979	−34. 2	3, 704, 618	5, 972, 592	−2, 267, 974	−38. 0
Michigan	427	640	−213	−33. 3	30, 959	45, 331	−14, 372	−31. 7	1, 874, 378	2, 024, 685	−150, 307	−7. 4
Wisconsin	55	48	7	14. 6	5, 295	4, 029	1, 266	31. 4	343, 105	173, 550	169, 555	97. 7
WEST NORTH CENTRAL	7, 018	5, 589	1, 429	25. 6	441, 071	491, 509	−50, 438	−10. 3	22, 313, 821	21, 677, 032	636, 789	2. 9
Minnesota	27	29	−2	−6. 9	2, 692	2, 362	330	14. 0	187, 325	123, 915	63, 410	51. 2
Iowa	118	187	−69	−36. 9	10, 002	13, 617	−3, 615	−26. 5	878, 234	1, 054, 495	−176, 261	−16. 7
Missouri	5, 844	3, 656	2, 188	59. 8	255, 623	229, 255	26, 368	11. 5	14, 498, 297	12, 006, 443	2, 491, 854	20. 8
North Dakota	10	22	−12	−54. 5	2, 565	5, 484	−2, 919	−53. 2	62, 700	154, 100	−91, 400	−59. 3
South Dakota	40	67	−27	−40. 3	14, 228	20, 753	−6, 525	−31. 4	285, 425	507, 405	−221, 980	−43. 7
Nebraska	38	96	−58	−60. 4	9, 216	36, 585	−27, 369	−74. 8	308, 080	513, 360	−205, 280	−40. 0
Kansas	941	1, 532	−591	−38. 6	146, 745	183, 453	−36, 708	−20. 0	6, 093, 760	7, 317, 314	−1, 223, 554	−16. 7
SOUTH ATLANTIC	295, 934	354, 530	−58, 596	−16. 5	14, 550, 451	17, 605, 488	−3, 055, 037	−17. 4	484, 443, 943	365, 068, 245	119, 375, 698	32. 7
Delaware	807	922	−115	−12. 5	54, 756	56, 973	−2, 217	−3. 9	2, 628, 590	1, 981, 716	646, 874	32. 6
Maryland	5, 264	6, 370	−1, 106	−17. 4	345, 224	358, 509	−13, 285	−3. 7	18, 896, 282	10, 267, 284	8, 628, 998	84, 0
District of Columbia	11	12	−1	−8. 3	95	95	----------	------	82, 000	89, 400	−7, 400	−8. 3
Virginia	39, 598	48, 039	−8, 441	−17. 6	2, 039, 656	2, 233, 883	−194, 227	−8. 7	71, 722, 401	45, 143, 291	26, 579, 110	58. 9
West Virginia	490	707	−217	−30. 7	28, 013	34, 520	−6, 507	−18. 8	1, 480, 628	1, 075, 204	405, 424	37. 7
North Carolina	74, 636	64, 456	10, 180	15. 8	3, 296, 445	3, 121, 827	174, 618	5. 6	153, 882, 635	66, 793, 591	87, 089, 044	130. 4
South Carolina	77, 331	96, 772	−19, 441	−20. 1	3, 167, 898	3, 939, 592	−771, 694	−19. 6	105, 693, 220	98, 966, 444	6, 726, 776	6. 8
Georgia	86, 787	122, 554	−35, 767	−29. 2	5, 104, 452	7, 091, 949	−1, 987, 497	−28. 0	114, 688, 230	128, 877, 032	−14, 188, 802	−11. 0
Florida	11, 010	14, 698	−3, 688	−25. 1	513, 912	768, 140	−254, 228	−33. 1	15, 369, 957	11, 874, 283	3, 495, 674	29. 4
EAST SOUTH CENTRAL	320, 600	324, 884	−4, 284	−1. 3	11, 918, 057	13, 573, 980	−1, 655, 923	−12. 2	426, 528, 844	279, 431, 194	147, 097, 650	52. 6
Kentucky	9, 104	11, 709	−2, 605	−22. 2	341, 833	439, 657	−97, 824	−22. 3	16, 157, 593	15, 017, 228	1, 140, 365	7. 6
Tennessee	35, 123	38, 300	−3, 177	−8. 3	1, 356, 683	1, 605, 694	−249, 011	−15. 5	56, 339, 610	42, 183, 226	14, 156, 384	33. 6
Alabama	93, 795	110, 387	−16, 592	−15. 0	4, 157, 051	5, 083, 552	−926, 501	−18. 2	104, 726, 209	73, 834, 072	30, 892, 137	41. 8
Mississippi	182, 578	164, 488	18, 090	11. 0	6, 062, 490	6, 445, 077	−382, 587	−5. 9	249, 305, 432	148, 396, 668	100, 908, 764	68. 0
WEST SOUTH CENTRAL	254, 402	201, 422	52, 980	26. 3	10, 289, 976	10, 105, 003	184, 973	1. 8	444, 208, 880	229, 082, 971	215, 125, 909	93. 9
Arkansas	79, 556	63, 578	15, 978	25. 1	2, 485, 626	2, 652, 684	−167, 058	−6. 3	118, 180, 961	68, 978, 464	49, 202, 497	71. 3
Louisiana	73, 734	54, 819	18, 915	34. 5	2, 313, 338	2, 121, 258	192, 080	9. 1	108, 668, 818	44, 891, 918	63, 776, 900	142. 1
Oklahoma	15, 172	13, 209	1, 963	14. 9	1, 061, 341	1, 066, 863	−5, 522	−0. 5	37, 967, 113	24, 552, 515	13, 414, 598	54. 6
Texas	85, 940	69, 816	16, 124	23. 1	4, 429, 671	4, 264, 198	165, 473	3. 9	179, 391, 988	90. 660, 074	88, 731, 914	97. 9
MOUNTAIN	304	219	85	38. 8	77, 228	62, 807	14, 421	23. 0	2, 037, 510	1, 155, 995	881, 515	76. 3
Montana	21	29	−8	−27. 6	9, 804	7, 918	1, 886	23. 8	115, 084	114, 680	404	0. 4
Idaho	16	13	3	23. 1	2, 816	1, 043	1, 773	170. 0	107, 200	54, 250	52, 950	97. 6
Wyoming	12	19	−7	−36. 8	10, 925	6, 202	4, 723	76. 2	139, 020	129, 200	9, 820	7. 6
Colorado	78	81	−3	−3. 7	25, 137	32, 003	−6, 866	−21. 5	445, 540	477, 520	−31, 980	−6. 7
New Mexico	82	48	34	70. 8	19, 883	11, 633	8, 250	70. 9	400, 956	199, 245	201, 711	101. 2
Arizona	87	12	75	625. 0	7, 766	1, 222	6, 544	535. 5	761, 510	30, 100	731, 410	2, 429. 9
Utah	5	11	−6	−54. 5	37	506	−469	−92. 7	24, 200	80, 500	−56, 300	−69. 9
Nevada	3	6	−3	−50. 0	860	2, 280	−1, 420	−62. 3	44, 000	70, 500	−26, 500	−37. 6
PACIFIC	506	263	243	92. 4	40, 548	63, 602	−23, 054	−36. 2	4, 058, 400	2, 722, 910	1, 335, 490	49. 0
Washington	73	77	−4	−5. 2	9, 425	7, 651	1, 774	23. 2	356, 705	470, 625	−113, 920	−24. 2
Oregon	9	27	−18	−66. 7	826	3, 021	−2, 195	−72. 7	32, 420	151, 350	−118, 930	−78. 6
California	424	159	265	166. 7	30, 297	52, 930	−22, 633	−42. 8	3, 669, 275	2, 100, 935	1, 568, 340	74. 6

TABLE 48.—NUMBER OF FARMS OF COLORED OPERATORS, BY SIZE, AND TENURE, BY SOUTHERN DIVISIONS, AND STATES, AND SELECTED NORTHERN STATES: 1930

[Colored farmers include Negroes, Indians, Chinese, Japanese, and all other nonwhite races]

DIVISION AND STATE	All farms	UNDER 20 ACRES				20 to 49 acres	50 to 99 acres	100 to 174 acres	175 TO 499 ACRES			500 to 999 acres	1,000 ACRES AND OVER			
		Total	Under 3 acres	3 to 9 acres	10 to 19 acres				Total	175 to 259 acres	260 to 499 acres		Total	1,000 to 4,999 acres	5,000 to 9,999 acres	10,000 acres and over
ALL OWNERS																
The South	182, 019	36, 698	279	13, 206	23, 213	63, 322	48, 820	24, 260	8, 382	5, 814	2, 568	440	97	85	8	4
SOUTH ATLANTIC	80, 503	22 358	142	7, 963	14, 253	27, 674	18, 919	8, 479	2, 928	2, 077	851	132	13	13	-	-
Delaware	373	154	-	66	88	124	71	20	4	2	2	-	-	-	-	-
Maryland	2, 941	1, 489	8	733	748	793	390	194	74	57	17	1	-	-	-	-
District of Columbia	8	8	5	2	1	-	-	-	-	-	-	-	-	-	-	-
Virginia	24, 448	7, 270	22	2, 574	4, 674	8, 660	5, 612	2, 206	667	495	172	29	4	4	-	-
West Virginia	373	129	2	54	73	119	84	28	11	7	4	2	-	-	-	-
North Carolina	19, 711	4, 912	8	1, 596	3, 308	7, 516	4, 990	1, 817	459	333	126	15	2	2	-	-
South Carolina	15, 992	5, 119	13	1, 614	3, 492	5, 385	3, 422	1, 513	524	376	148	26	3	3	-	-
Georgia	11, 081	1, 714	39	669	1, 006	2, 830	3, 284	2, 204	997	674	323	48	4	4	-	-
Florida	5, 576	1, 563	45	655	863	2, 247	1, 066	497	192	133	59	11	-	-	-	-
EAST SOUTH CENTRAL	50, 588	8, 034	63	3, 064	4, 907	17, 226	14, 426	7, 834	2, 896	1, 999	897	151	21	20	1	-
Kentucky	4, 175	1, 649	15	896	738	1 215	860	333	114	84	30	4	-	-	-	-
Tennessee	7, 832	1, 768	13	659	1, 096	2, 770	2, 231	838	219	177	42	6	-	-	-	-
Alabama	15, 931	2, 238	11	757	1, 470	5, 540	4, 379	2, 583	1, 104	750	354	73	14	14	-	-
Mississippi	22, 650	2, 379	24	752	1, 603	7, 701	6, 956	4, 080	1, 459	988	471	68	7	6	1	-
WEST SOUTH CENTRAL	50, 928	6, 306	74	2, 179	4, 053	18, 422	15, 475	7, 947	2, 558	1, 738	820	157	63	52	7	4
Arkansas	11, 455	1, 246	9	355	882	5, 052	3, 341	1, 400	407	292	115	8	1	1	-	-
Louisiana	10, 503	1, 909	23	765	1, 121	4, 463	2, 610	1, 135	361	247	114	20	5	5	-	-
Oklahoma	8, 334	651	21	223	407	2, 311	2, 463	1, 985	795	474	321	91	38	31	5	2
Texas	20, 636	2, 500	21	836	1, 643	6, 596	7, 061	3, 427	995	725	270	38	19	15	2	2
SELECTED NORTHERN STATES [1]	3, 776	996	30	468	498	1, 105	882	518	232	120	112	31	12	12	-	-
New Jersey	240	127	5	57	65	65	30	16	2	-	2	-	-	-	-	-
Pennsylvania	233	100	3	41	56	50	51	26	6	4	2	-	-	-	-	-
Ohio	783	200	5	99	96	222	224	109	28	20	8	-	-	-	-	-
Indiana	283	93	-	50	43	90	64	24	11	7	4	1	-	-	-	-
Illinois	460	97	1	39	57	177	107	60	18	8	10	-	1	1	-	-
Missouri	1, 107	233	5	114	114	389	306	179	61	41	20	2	-	-	-	-
Kansas	607	146	11	68	67	112	100	104	106	40	66	28	11	11	-	-
FULL OWNERS																
The South	140, 496	27, 750	272	10, 962	16, 516	47, 123	38, 305	20, 123	6, 783	4, 742	2, 041	346	61	57	4	-
SOUTH ATLANTIC	60, 714	16, 935	139	6, 584	10, 212	19, 506	14, 785	6, 965	2, 406	1, 722	684	108	9	9	-	-
Delaware	309	138	-	61	77	95	55	18	3	2	1	-	-	-	-	-
Maryland	2, 362	1, 222	8	648	566	589	323	163	64	50	14	1	-	-	-	-
District of Columbia	7	7	5	2		-	-	-	-	-	-	-	-	-	-	-
Virginia	19, 200	5, 931	20	2, 297	3, 614	6, 336	4, 509	1, 843	558	422	136	21	2	2	-	-
West Virginia	328	115	2	48	65	105	75	23	8	5	3	2	-	-	-	-
North Carolina	13, 198	3, 176	8	1, 191	1, 977	4, 644	3, 612	1, 411	339	242	97	14	2	2	-	-
South Carolina	11, 937	3, 700	13	1, 189	2, 498	3, 820	2, 679	1, 274	443	320	123	19	2	2	-	-
Georgia	9, 014	1, 347	38	560	749	2, 232	2, 735	1, 830	826	565	261	41	3	3	-	-
Florida	4, 359	1, 299	45	588	666	1, 685	797	403	165	116	49	10	-	-	-	-
EAST SOUTH CENTRAL	39, 420	5, 692	61	2, 466	3, 165	12, 951	11, 481	6, 705	2, 450	1, 692	758	124	17	16	1	-
Kentucky	3, 055	1, 223	14	737	472	809	653	279	88	63	25	3	-	-	-	-
Tennessee	5, 687	1, 332	12	573	747	1, 850	1, 673	665	162	131	31	5	-	-	-	-
Alabama	11, 417	1, 385	11	567	807	3, 756	3 183	2, 112	913	619	294	57	11	11	-	-
Mississippi	19, 261	1, 752	24	589	1, 139	6, 536	5, 972	3, 649	1, 287	879	408	59	6	5	1	-
WEST SOUTH CENTRAL	40, 362	5, 123	72	1, 912	3, 139	14, 671	12, 039	6, 453	1, 927	1, 328	599	114	35	32	3	-
Arkansas	9, 058	965	9	299	657	4, 129	2, 499	1, 117	340	244	96	7	1	1	-	-
Louisiana	8, 786	1, 575	23	660	892	3, 748	2, 150	976	313	212	101	19	5	5	-	-
Oklahoma	6, 550	559	21	202	336	1, 953	1, 920	1, 560	482	288	194	57	19	18	1	-
Texas	15, 968	2, 024	19	751	1, 254	4, 841	5, 470	2, 800	792	584	208	31	10	8	2	-
SELECTED NORTHERN STATES [1]	2, 790	873	29	438	406	854	612	334	112	65	47	3	2	2	-	-
New Jersey	217	118	5	55	58	58	28	12	1	-	1	-	-	-	-	-
Pennsylvania	221	96	3	40	53	47	49	25	4	3	1	-	-	-	-	-
Ohio	640	177	5	94	78	187	180	75	21	15	6	-	-	-	-	-
Indiana	207	84	-	46	38	65	43	9	6	3	3	-	-	-	-	-
Illinois	309	80	1	38	41	128	55	40	5	4	1	-	1	1	-	-
Missouri	815	198	5	103	90	283	185	114	34	23	11	1	-	-	-	-
Kansas	381	120	10	62	48	86	72	59	41	17	24	2	1	1	-	-

Footnote at end of table.

TABLE 48.—NUMBER OF FARMS OF COLORED OPERATORS, BY SIZE, AND TENURE, BY SOUTHERN DIVISIONS, AND STATES, AND SELECTED NORTHERN STATES: 1930—Continued

[See note at head of table]

DIVISION AND STATE	All farms	UNDER 20 ACRES				20 to 49 acres	50 to 99 acres	100 to 174 acres	175 TO 499 ACRES			500 to 999 acres	1,000 ACRES AND OVER			
		Total	Under 3 acres	3 to 9 acres	10 to 19 acres				Total	175 to 259 acres	260 to 499 acres		Total	1,000 to 4,999 acres	5,000 to 9,999 acres	10,000 acres and over
PART OWNERS																
The South	41,523	8,948	7	2,244	6,697	16,194	10,515	4,137	1,599	1,072	527	94	36	28	4	4
SOUTH ATLANTIC	19,789	5,423	3	1,379	4,041	8,168	4,134	1,514	522	355	167	24	4	4		
Delaware	64	16		5	11	29	16	2	1		1					
Maryland	579	267		85	182	204	67	31	10	7	3					
District of Columbia	1	1			1											
Virginia	5,248	1,339	2	277	1,060	2,324	1,103	363	109	73	36	8	2	2		
West Virginia	45	14		6	8	14	9	5	3	2	1					
North Carolina	6,513	1,736		405	1,331	2,872	1,378	406	120	91	29	1				
South Carolina	4,055	1,419		425	994	1,565	743	239	81	56	25	7	1	1		
Georgia	2,067	367	1	109	257	598	549	374	171	109	62	7	1	1		
Florida	1,217	264		67	197	562	269	94	27	17	10	1				
EAST SOUTH CENTRAL	11,168	2,342	2	598	1,742	4,275	2,945	1,129	446	307	139	27	4	4		
Kentucky	1,120	426	1	159	266	406	207	54	26	21	5	1				
Tennessee	2,145	436	1	86	349	920	558	173	57	46	11	1				
Alabama	4,514	853		190	663	1,784	1,196	471	191	131	60	16	3	3		
Mississippi	3,389	627		163	464	1,165	984	431	172	109	63	9	1	1		
WEST SOUTH CENTRAL	10,566	1,183	2	267	914	3,751	3,436	1,494	631	410	221	43	28	20	4	4
Arkansas	2,397	281		56	225	923	842	283	67	48	19	1				
Louisiana	1,717	334		105	229	715	460	159	48	35	13	1				
Oklahoma	1,784	92		21	71	358	543	425	313	186	127	34	19	13	4	2
Texas	4,668	476	2	85	389	1,755	1,591	627	203	141	62	7	9	7		2
SELECTED NORTHERN STATES [1]	986	123	1	30	92	251	270	184	120	55	65	28	10	10		
New Jersey	23	9		2	7	7	2	4	1		1					
Pennsylvania	12	4		1	3	3	2	1	2	1	1					
Ohio	143	23		5	18	35	44	34	7	5	2					
Indiana	76	9		4	5	25	21	15	5	4	1	1				
Illinois	151	17		1	16	49	52	20	13	4	9					
Missouri	355	35		11	24	106	121	65	27	18	9	1				
Kansas	226	26	1	6	19	26	28	45	65	23	42	26	10	10		
ALL TENANTS																
The South	698,839	203,418	302	39,366	163,750	358,768	94,960	30,931	9,966	6 711	3,255	670	126	125	1	
SOUTH ATLANTIC	217,397	45,613	201	13,682	31,730	106,074	43,595	15,817	5,779	3,915	1,864	451	68	68		
Delaware	415	46		20	26	78	141	101	48	37	11	1				
Maryland	2,206	470	2	176	292	406	409	570	333	211	122	15	3	3		
District of Columbia	2	2	1	1												
Virginia	15,148	4,212	16	1,209	2,987	5,493	3,043	1,613	710	461	249	69	8	8		
West Virginia	111	34		20	14	31	16	15	14	8	6	1				
North Carolina	57,139	15,251	25	3,668	11,558	26,546	10,770	3,549	971	683	288	46	6	6		
South Carolina	61,362	17,341	6	6,130	11,205	30,682	9,498	2,753	981	636	345	91	16	16		
Georgia	75,636	6,830	37	1,752	5,041	40,105	18,878	6,954	2,616	1,811	805	219	34	34		
Florida	5,378	1,427	114	706	607	2,733	840	262	106	68	38	9	1	1		
EAST SOUTH CENTRAL	270,230	93,064	58	16,034	76,972	142,358	25,689	6,806	2,169	1,413	756	119	25	25		
Kentucky	4,914	2,617	31	1,075	1,511	1,542	410	230	110	77	33	4	1	1		
Tennessee	27,272	7,850	6	1,409	6,435	14,722	3,467	976	248	178	70	4	5	5		
Alabama	77,875	17,328	5	4,881	12,442	44,615	11,923	2,959	984	637	347	55	11	11		
Mississippi	160,169	65,269	16	8,669	56,584	81,479	9,889	2,641	827	521	306	56	8	8		
WEST SOUTH CENTRAL	211,212	64,741	43	9,650	55,048	110,336	25,676	8,308	2,018	1,383	635	100	33	32	1	
Arkansas	68,101	28,160	9	3,535	24,616	35,057	3,844	812	215	131	84	8	5	5		
Louisiana	63,213	24,947	25	4,388	20,534	33,226	3,858	889	270	175	95	19	4	4		
Oklahoma	14,559	1,533		363	1,170	5,814	4,171	2,507	510	339	171	19	5	4	1	
Texas	65,339	10,101	9	1,364	8,728	36,239	13,803	4,100	1,023	738	285	54	19	19		
SELECTED NORTHERN STATES [1]	6,394	1,909	6	423	1,480	2,571	980	603	309	188	121	22				
New Jersey	129	22	1	11	10	25	35	39	8	6	2					
Pennsylvania	116	21	2	10	9	17	29	39	10	6	4					
Ohio	442	65		24	41	82	114	111	66	43	23	4				
Indiana	190	48	1	27	20	37	52	38	14	11	3	1				
Illinois	428	80	1	18	61	170	87	56	34	20	14	1				
Missouri	4,671	1,638	1	319	1,318	2,152	556	218	102	71	31	5				
Kansas	418	35		14	21	88	107	102	75	31	44	11				

Footnote at end of table.

TABLE 48.—NUMBER OR FARMS OF COLORED OPERATORS, BY SIZE, AND TENURE, BY SOUTHERN DIVISIONS, AND STATES, AND SELECTED NORTHERN STATES: 1930—Continued

[See note at head of table]

DIVISION AND STATE	All farms	UNDER 20 ACRES				20 to 49 acres	50 to 99 acres	100 to 174 acres	175 TO 499 ACRES			500 to 999 acres	1,000 ACRES AND OVER			
		Total	Under 3 acres	3 to 9 acres	10 to 19 acres				Total	175 to 259 acres	260 to 499 acres		Total	1,000 to 4,999 acres	5,000 to 9,999 acres	10,000 acres and over
	CASH TENANTS															
The South	**97,920**	**25,805**	**96**	**9,689**	**16,020**	**49,881**	**14,471**	**5,384**	**2,154**	**1,385**	**769**	**179**	**46.**	**45**	**1**	-
SOUTH ATLANTIC	29,327	8,985	59	4,842	4,084	11,219	5,377	2,436	1,171	752	419	117	22	22	-	-
Delaware	54	21	-	10	11	16	11	4	2	1	1	-	-	-	-	-
Maryland	213	119	2	71	46	46	20	17	11	6	5	-	-	-	-	-
District of Columbia	2	2	1	1	-	-	-	-	-	-	-	-	-	-	-	-
Virginia	1,767	490	7	209	274	518	382	243	121	82	39	13	-	-	-	-
West Virginia	38	17	-	13	4	11	3	3	3	3	-	1	-	-	-	-
North Carolina	2,545	625	2	200	423	950	640	228	94	58	36	7	1	1	-	-
South Carolina	11,759	6,033	5	3,634	2,394	4,030	1,173	355	147	94	53	17	4	4	-	-
Georgia	10,532	1,066	31	395	640	4,409	2,771	1,449	747	481	266	74	16	16	-	-
Florida	2,417	612	11	309	292	1,239	377	137	46	27	19	5	1	1	-	-
EAST SOUTH CENTRAL	53,371	12,654	9	3,815	8,830	30,398	7,305	2,178	774	498	276	48	14	14	-	-
Kentucky	140	73	1	47	25	33	20	7	7	5	2	-	-	-	-	-
Tennessee	2,863	453	-	128	325	1,496	624	235	50	38	12	3	2	2	-	-
Alabama	32,055	8,329	4	2,966	5,359	17,459	4,542	1,216	462	289	173	36	11	11	-	-
Mississippi	18,313	3,799	4	674	3,121	11,410	2,119	720	255	166	89	9	1	1	-	-
WEST SOUTH CENTRAL	15,222	4,166	28	1,032	3,106	8,264	1,789	770	209	135	74	14	10	9	1	-
Arkansas	6,106	1,305	6	209	1,090	3,846	724	182	45	28	17	2	2	2	-	-
Louisiana	6,692	2,374	16	653	1,705	3,534	531	185	62	44	18	4	2	2	-	-
Oklahoma	1,029	144	-	60	84	253	277	293	54	32	22	4	4	3	1	-
Texas	1,395	343	6	110	227	631	257	110	48	31	17	4	2	2	-	-
SELECTED NORTHERN STATES[1]	587	173	5	88	80	186	121	83	24	18	6	-	-	-	-	-
New Jersey	42	13	1	7	5	14	7	8	-	-	-	-	-	-	-	-
Pennsylvania	58	17	2	9	6	11	11	16	3	2	1	-	-	-	-	-
Ohio	122	27	-	10	17	36	25	26	8	7	1	-	-	-	-	-
Indiana	41	23	-	15	8	8	7	2	1	1	-	-	-	-	-	-
Illinois	65	21	1	7	13	24	15	3	2	1	1	-	-	-	-	-
Missouri	188	59	1	33	25	71	38	14	6	5	1	-	-	-	-	-
Kansas	71	13	-	7	6	22	18	14	4	2	2	-	-	-	-	-
	CROPPERS															
The South	**392,897**	**139,870**	**147**	**22,774**	**116,949**	**201,208**	**39,177**	**9,772**	**2,697**	**1,875**	**822**	**147**	**26**	**26**	-	-
SOUTH ATLANTIC	124,171	26,800	108	6,047	20,645	66,459	22,532	6,388	1,863	1,315	548	114	15	15	-	-
Delaware	60	8	-	3	5	11	19	20	2	2	-	-	-	-	-	-
Maryland	597	173	-	48	125	145	91	118	65	49	16	5	-	-	-	-
Virginia	6,797	2,409	6	628	1,775	2,685	1,039	475	176	105	71	12	1	1	-	-
West Virginia	23	7	-	3	4	7	5	1	3	2	1	-	-	-	-	-
North Carolina	34,805	11,136	19	2,589	8,528	16,772	5,327	1,292	266	196	70	10	2	2	-	-
South Carolina	31,046	8,104	-	1,581	6,523	17,484	4,063	1,055	315	204	111	21	4	4	-	-
Georgia	49,450	4,609	3	1,029	3,577	28,685	11,722	3,355	1,006	738	268	65	8	8	-	-
Florida	1,393	354	80	166	108	670	266	72	30	19	11	1	-	-	-	-
EAST SOUTH CENTRAL	150,239	66,646	31	10,094	56,521	73,846	7,777	1,532	418	277	141	16	4	4	-	-
Kentucky	3,116	1,889	17	753	1,119	972	149	67	39	23	16	-	-	-	-	-
Tennessee	16,559	6,046	4	1,002	5,040	9,127	1,082	247	55	39	16	1	1	1	-	-
Alabama	27,572	6,295	-	1,319	4,976	16,757	3,643	686	185	127	58	6	-	-	-	-
Mississippi	102,992	52,416	10	7,020	45,386	46,990	2,903	532	139	88	51	9	3	3	-	-
WEST SOUTH CENTRAL	118,487	46,424	8	6,633	39,783	60,903	8,868	1,852	416	283	133	17	7	7	-	-
Arkansas	45,465	23,068	1	2,843	20,224	21,132	1,108	119	38	21	17	-	-	-	-	-
Louisiana	32,214	15,587	5	2,879	12,703	15,293	1,083	187	57	38	19	6	1	1	-	-
Oklahoma	4,560	763	-	146	617	2,405	972	350	68	40	28	2	-	-	-	-
Texas	36,248	7,006	2	765	6,239	22,073	5,705	1,196	253	184	69	9	6	6	-	-
SELECTED NORTHERN STATES[1]	3,300	1,478	1	262	1,215	1,483	227	72	40	21	19	-	-	-	-	-
New Jersey	16	1	-	-	1	3	4	7	1	-	1	-	-	-	-	-
Pennsylvania	21	-	-	-	-	-	6	10	5	2	3	-	-	-	-	-
Ohio	55	13	-	5	8	5	11	12	14	9	5	-	-	-	-	-
Indiana	31	16	1	8	7	5	5	4	1	1	-	-	-	-	-	-
Illinois	95	24	-	3	21	40	17	11	3	1	2	-	-	-	-	-
Missouri	3,017	1,423	-	245	1,178	1,399	162	25	8	5	3	-	-	-	-	-
Kansas	65	1	-	1	-	31	22	3	8	3	5	-	-	-	-	-

Footnote at end of table.

TABLE 48.—NUMBER OF FARMS OF COLORED OPERATORS, BY SIZE, AND TENURE, BY SOUTHERN DIVISIONS, AND STATES, AND SELECTED NORTHERN STATES: 1930—Continued

[See note at head of table]

DIVISION AND STATE	All farms	UNDER 20 ACRES				20 to 49 acres	50 to 99 acres	100 to 174 acres	175 TO 499 ACRES			500 to 999 acres	1,000 ACRES AND OVER			
		Total	Under 3 acres	3 to 9 acres	10 to 19 acres				Total	175 to 259 acres	260 to 499 acres		Total	1,000 to 4,999 acres	5,000 to 9,999 acres	10,000 acres and over
OTHER TENANTS																
The South	**208,022**	**37,743**	**59**	**6,903**	**30,781**	**107,679**	**41,312**	**15,775**	**5,115**	**3,451**	**1,664**	**344**	**54**	**54**	-------	-------
SOUTH ATLANTIC	63,899	9,828	34	2,793	7,001	28,396	15,686	6,993	2,745	1,848	897	220	31	31	-------	-------
Delaware	301	17	-------	7	10	51	111	77	44	34	10	1	-------	-------	-------	-------
Maryland	1,396	178	-------	57	121	215	298	435	257	156	101	10	3	3	-------	-------
District of Columbia	-------	-------	-------	-------	-------	-------	-------	-------	-------	-------	-------	-------	-------	-------	-------	-------
Virginia	6,584	1,313	3	372	938	2,290	1,622	895	413	274	139	44	7	7	-------	-------
West Virginia	50	10	-------	4	6	13	8	11	8	3	5	-------	-------	-------	-------	-------
North Carolina	19,789	3,490	4	879	2,607	8,824	4,803	2,029	611	429	182	29	3	3	-------	-------
South Carolina	18,557	3,204	1	915	2,288	9,168	4,262	1,343	519	338	181	53	8	8	-------	-------
Georgia	15,654	1,155	3	328	824	7,011	4,385	2,150	863	592	271	80	10	10	-------	-------
Florida	1,568	461	23	231	207	824	197	53	30	22	8	3	-------	-------	-------	-------
EAST SOUTH CENTRAL	66,620	13,764	18	2,125	11,621	38,114	10,607	3,096	977	638	339	55	7	7	-------	-------
Kentucky	1,658	655	13	275	367	537	241	156	64	49	15	4	1	1	-------	-------
Tennessee	7,850	1,351	2	279	1,070	4,099	1,761	494	143	101	42	-------	2	2	-------	-------
Alabama	18,248	2,704	1	596	2,107	10,399	3,738	1,057	337	221	116	13	-------	-------	-------	-------
Mississippi	38,864	9,054	2	975	8,077	23,079	4,867	1,389	433	267	166	38	4	4	-------	-------
WEST SOUTH CENTRAL	77,503	14,151	7	1,985	12,159	41,169	15,019	5,686	1,393	965	428	69	16	16	-------	-------
Arkansas	16,530	3,787	2	483	3,302	10,079	2,012	511	132	82	50	6	3	3	-------	-------
Louisiana	24,307	6,986	4	856	6,126	14,399	2,244	517	151	93	58	9	1	1	-------	-------
Oklahoma	8,970	626	-------	157	469	3,156	2,922	1,864	388	267	121	13	1	1	-------	-------
Texas	27,696	2,752	1	489	2,262	13,535	7,841	2,794	722	523	199	41	11	11	-------	-------
SELECTED NORTHERN STATES[1]	2,507	258	-------	73	185	902	632	448	245	149	96	22	-------	-------	-------	-------
New Jersey	71	8	-------	4	4	8	24	24	7	6	1	-------	-------	-------	-------	-------
Pennsylvania	37	4	-------	1	3	6	12	13	2	2	-------	-------	-------	-------	-------	-------
Ohio	265	25	-------	9	16	41	78	73	44	27	17	4	-------	-------	-------	-------
Indiana	118	9	-------	4	5	24	40	32	12	9	3	1	-------	-------	-------	-------
Illinois	268	35	-------	8	27	106	55	42	29	18	11	1	-------	-------	-------	-------
Missouri	1,466	156	-------	41	115	682	356	179	88	61	27	5	-------	-------	-------	-------
Kansas	282	21	-------	6	15	35	67	85	63	26	37	11	-------	-------	-------	-------
MANAGERS																
The South	**829**	**63**	**3**	**20**	**40**	**130**	**130**	**172**	**216**	**113**	**103**	**62**	**56**	**52**	**3**	**1**
SOUTH ATLANTIC	479	44	1	15	28	87	62	109	132	73	59	29	16	16	-------	-------
Delaware	19	-------	-------	-------	-------	4	1	9	3	1	2	2	-------	-------	-------	-------
Maryland	120	2	1	-------	1	12	14	39	50	29	21	3	-------	-------	-------	-------
District of Columbia	1	-------	-------	-------	-------	-------	1	-------	-------	-------	-------	-------	-------	-------	-------	-------
Virginia	77	1	-------	1	-------	7	12	22	25	13	12	6	4	4	-------	-------
West Virginia	7	-------	-------	-------	-------	3	-------	-------	4	3	1	-------	-------	-------	-------	-------
North Carolina	23	2	-------	1	1	7	3	1	8	5	3	1	1	1	-------	-------
South Carolina	71	9	-------	4	5	15	12	13	12	9	3	5	5	5	-------	-------
Georgia	72	3	-------	2	1	4	9	20	22	11	11	9	5	5	-------	-------
Florida	89	27	-------	7	20	35	10	5	8	2	6	3	1	1	-------	-------
EAST SOUTH CENTRAL	141	7	-------	1	6	15	28	23	40	18	22	15	13	13	-------	-------
Kentucky	15	2	-------	-------	2	-------	3	4	6	3	3	-------	-------	-------	-------	-------
Tennessee	34	2	-------	1	1	5	10	6	6	4	2	5	-------	-------	-------	-------
Alabama	23	-------	-------	-------	-------	1	3	4	5	2	3	3	7	7	-------	-------
Mississippi	69	3	-------	-------	3	9	12	9	23	9	14	7	6	6	-------	-------
WEST SOUTH CENTRAL	209	12	2	4	6	28	40	40	44	22	22	18	27	23	3	1
Arkansas	23	1	1	-------	-------	3	1	6	8	3	5	3	1	1	-------	-------
Louisiana	54	4	-------	2	2	6	16	9	9	7	2	4	6	5	1	-------
Oklahoma	44	1	-------	1	-------	2	5	12	9	4	5	4	11	9	1	1
Texas	88	6	1	1	4	17	18	13	18	8	10	7	9	8	1	-------
SELECTED NORTHERN STATES[1]	80	7	1	4	2	9	16	23	21	14	7	3	1	1	-------	-------
New Jersey	15	1	-------	-------	1	1	6	3	4	2	2	-------	-------	-------	-------	-------
Pennsylvania	14	2	-------	1	1	4	1	5	1	1	-------	1	-------	-------	-------	-------
Ohio	12	-------	-------	-------	-------	1	2	3	5	4	1	1	-------	-------	-------	-------
Indiana	2	-------	-------	-------	-------	-------	-------	1	1	1	-------	-------	-------	-------	-------	-------
Illinois	6	-------	-------	-------	-------	1	2	2	1	-------	1	-------	-------	-------	-------	-------
Missouri	20	2	-------	2	-------	2	2	5	8	5	3	1	-------	-------	-------	-------
Kansas	11	2	1	1	-------	-------	3	4	1	1	-------	-------	1	1	-------	-------

[1] States having 200 or more Negro farmers who constitute 90 percent or more of the colored farmers in the State.

TABLE 49.—COLORED FARM OWNERS AND TENANTS BY AGE, BY SOUTHERN DIVISIONS, AND STATES, AND SELECTED NORTHERN STATES: 1930

[Colored farmers include Negroes, Indians, Chinese, Japanese, and all other nonwhite races]

DIVISION AND STATE	AGE OF COLORED FARM OPERATORS													
								Percent distribution						
	Total number reporting	Under 25 years	25 to 34 years	35 to 44 years	45 to 54 years	55 to 64 years	65 years and over	Total	Under 25 years	25 to 34 years	35 to 44 years	45 to 54 years	55 to 64 years	65 years and over
	OWNERS													
The South	**177,604**	**3,393**	**14,915**	**33,111**	**52,540**	**43,036**	**30,609**	**100.0**	**1.9**	**8.4**	**18.6**	**29.6**	**24.2**	**17.2**
SOUTH ATLANTIC	78,552	1,231	5,968	15,125	23,409	19,175	13,644	100.0	1.6	7.6	19.3	29.8	24.4	17.4
Delaware	367	3	19	67	101	97	80	100.0	.8	5.2	18.3	27.5	26.4	21.8
Maryland	2,871	16	183	541	815	788	528	100.0	.6	6.4	18.8	28.4	27.4	18.4
District of Columbia	8	-	-	-	4	3	1	100.0	-	-	-	50.0	37.5	12.5
Virginia	23,897	309	1,636	4,794	7,183	5,720	4,255	100.0	1.3	6.8	20.1	30.1	23.9	17.8
West Virginia	360	7	31	70	89	84	79	100.0	1.9	8.6	19.4	24.7	23.3	21.9
North Carolina	19,150	311	1,615	3,748	5,633	4,552	3,291	100.0	1.6	8.4	19.6	29.4	23.8	17.2
South Carolina	15,652	337	1,402	3,394	4,717	3,527	2,275	100.0	2.2	9.0	21.7	30.1	22.5	14.5
Georgia	10,862	169	692	1,578	3,310	2,959	2,154	100.0	1.6	6.4	14.5	30.5	27.2	19.8
Florida	5,385	79	390	933	1,557	1,445	981	100.0	1.5	7.2	17.3	28.9	26.8	18.2
EAST SOUTH CENTRAL	49,477	919	3,881	8,256	14,924	12,411	9,086	100.0	1.9	7.8	16.7	30.2	25.1	18.4
Kentucky	4,045	56	270	689	1,059	976	995	100.0	1.4	6.7	17.0	26.2	24.1	24.6
Tennessee	7,652	118	482	1,150	2,163	2,028	1,711	100.0	1.5	6.3	15.0	28.3	26.5	22.4
Alabama	15,628	270	1,086	2,328	5,425	3,853	2,666	100.0	1.7	6.9	14.9	34.7	24.7	17.1
Mississippi	22,152	475	2,043	4,089	6,277	5,554	3,714	100.0	2.1	9.2	18.5	28.3	25.1	16.8
WEST SOUTH CENTRAL	49,575	1,243	5,066	9,730	14,207	11,450	7,879	100.0	2.5	10.2	19.6	28.7	23.1	15.9
Arkansas	11,170	239	905	2,080	3,605	2,615	1,726	100.0	2.1	8.1	18.6	32.3	23.4	15.5
Louisiana	10,271	221	1,001	2,160	2,949	2,386	1,554	100.0	2.2	9.7	21.0	28.7	23.2	15.1
Oklahoma	8,056	293	1,346	1,716	2,069	1,625	1,007	100.0	3.6	16.7	21.3	25.7	20.2	12.5
Texas	20,078	490	1,814	3,774	5,584	4,824	3,592	100.0	2.4	9.0	18.8	27.8	24.0	17.9
SELECTED NORTHERN STATES [1]	3,684	19	191	587	938	997	952	100.0	.5	5.2	15.9	25.5	27.1	25.8
New Jersey	236	1	19	43	68	64	41	100.0	.4	8.1	18.2	28.8	27.1	17.4
Pennsylvania	230	3	12	41	75	58	41	100.0	1.3	5.2	17.8	32.6	25.2	17.8
Ohio	761	3	39	128	172	211	208	100.0	.4	5.1	16.8	22.6	27.7	27.3
Indiana	272	-	8	37	65	75	87	100.0	-	2.9	13.6	23.9	27.6	32.0
Illinois	442	2	16	76	124	122	102	100.0	.5	3.6	17.2	28.1	27.6	23.1
Missouri	1,144	6	57	155	276	315	335	100.0	.5	5.0	13.5	24.1	27.5	29.3
Kansas	599	4	40	107	158	152	138	100.0	.7	6.7	17.9	26.4	25.4	23.0
	TENANTS													
The South	**675,104**	**95,352**	**153,331**	**152,101**	**151,208**	**84,971**	**38,141**	**100.0**	**14.1**	**22.7**	**22.5**	**22.4**	**12.6**	**5.6**
SOUTH ATLANTIC	208,436	24,065	42,035	49,616	49,719	29,726	13,275	100.0	11.5	20.2	23.8	23.9	14.3	6.4
Delaware	400	13	55	105	125	64	38	100.0	3.3	13.8	26.3	31.3	16.0	9.5
Maryland	2,085	89	400	538	595	311	152	100.0	4.3	19.2	25.8	28.5	14.9	7.3
District of Columbia	2	-	-	-	1	1	-	100.0	-	-	-	50.0	50.0	-
Virginia	14,495	1,469	2,927	3,825	3,520	1,821	933	100.0	10.1	20.2	26.4	24.3	12.6	6.4
West Virginia	107	3	15	24	30	19	16	100.0	2.8	14.0	22.4	28.0	17.8	15.0
North Carolina	53,987	6,401	12,778	13,120	12,199	6,651	2,838	100.0	11.9	23.7	24.3	22.6	12.3	5.3
South Carolina	59,084	7,000	11,574	15,465	13,290	8,059	3,696	100.0	11.8	19.6	26.2	22.5	13.6	6.3
Georgia	73,132	8,763	13,399	15,292	18,529	11,978	5,171	100.0	12.0	18.3	20.9	25.3	16.4	7.1
Florida	5,144	327	887	1,247	1,430	822	431	100.0	6.4	17.2	24.2	27.8	16.0	8.4
EAST SOUTH CENTRAL	262,315	39,313	60,588	55,624	58,327	32,922	15,541	100.0	15.0	23.1	21.2	22.2	12.6	5.9
Kentucky	4,673	510	980	1,178	1,010	648	347	100.0	10.9	21.0	25.2	21.6	13.9	7.4
Tennessee	26,265	4,061	5,820	5,500	5,817	3,530	1,537	100.0	15.5	22.2	20.9	22.1	13.4	5.9
Alabama	76,119	8,551	15,048	14,268	21,721	10,851	5,680	100.0	11.2	19.8	18.7	28.5	14.3	7.5
Mississippi	155,258	26,191	38,740	34,678	29,779	17,893	7,977	100.0	16.9	25.0	22.3	19.2	11.5	5.1
WEST SOUTH CENTRAL	204,353	31,974	50,708	46,861	43,162	22,323	9,325	100.0	15.6	24.8	22.9	21.1	10.9	4.6
Arkansas	66,091	10,701	15,972	14,405	14,958	7,288	2,767	100.0	16.2	24.2	21.8	22.6	11.0	4.2
Louisiana	61,240	8,667	14,678	14,478	12,820	7,279	3,318	100.0	14.2	24.0	23.6	20.9	11.9	5.4
Oklahoma	14,126	1,671	3,393	3,305	3,260	1,812	685	100.0	11.8	24.0	23.4	23.1	12.8	4.8
Texas	62,896	10,935	16,665	14,673	12,124	5,944	2,555	100.0	17.4	26.5	23.3	19.3	9.5	4.1
SELECTED NORTHERN STATES [1]	6,281	614	1,190	1,587	1,531	940	419	100.0	9.8	18.9	25.3	24.4	15.0	6.7
New Jersey	121	2	24	42	32	18	3	100.0	1.7	19.8	34.7	26.4	14.9	2.5
Pennsylvania	110	4	13	27	32	27	7	100.0	3.6	11.8	24.5	29.1	24.5	6.4
Ohio	420	8	53	99	121	86	53	100.0	1.9	12.6	23.6	28.8	20.5	12.6
Indiana	187	7	215	48	49	37	21	100.0	3.7	13.4	25.7	26.2	19.8	11.2
Illinois	411	10	47	86	133	92	43	100.0	2.4	11.4	20.9	32.4	22.4	10.5
Missouri	4,619	553	959	1,163	1,066	616	262	100.0	12.0	20.8	25.2	23.1	13.3	5.7
Kansas	413	30	69	122	98	64	30	100.0	7.3	16.7	29.5	23.7	15.5	7.3

[1] States having 200 or more Negro farmers who constitute 90 percent or more of the colored farmers in the State.

TABLE 50.—COLORED FARM OPERATORS, BY YEARS ON FARM, AND BY TENURE, BY SOUTHERN DIVISIONS, AND STATES, AND SELECTED NORTHERN STATES: 1930

[Colored farmers include Negroes, Indians, Chinese, Japanese, and all other nonwhite races]

DIVISION AND STATE	All colored farm operators	NUMBER REPORTING YEARS ON FARM: Total: Number	Total: Percent of all farms	Less than 1 year	1 year	2 to 4 years	5 to 9 years	10 years and over	PERCENT DISTRIBUTION BY YEARS ON FARM: Total	Less than 1 year	1 year	2 to 4 years	5 to 9 years	10 years and over
ALL OPERATORS														
The South	**881,687**	**852,232**	**96.7**	**201,039**	**142,526**	**188,416**	**123,066**	**197,185**	**100.0**	**23.6**	**16.7**	**22.1**	**14.4**	**23.1**
SOUTH ATLANTIC	298,379	288,210	96.6	62,243	43,823	58,757	42,902	80,485	100.0	21.6	15.2	20.4	14.9	27.9
Delaware	807	777	96.3	98	91	178	139	271	100.0	12.6	11.7	22.9	17.9	34.9
Maryland	5,267	5,026	95.4	492	530	940	865	2,199	100.0	9.8	10.5	18.7	17.2	43.8
District of Columbia	11	10	90.9			1	3	6	100.0			10.0	30.0	60.0
Virginia	39,673	38,132	96.1	3,224	3,645	6,100	5,897	19,266	100.0	8.5	9.6	16.0	15.5	50.5
West Virginia	491	476	96.9	34	36	60	91	255	100.0	7.1	7.6	12.6	19.1	53.6
North Carolina	76,873	73,723	95.9	17,947	12,045	14,688	10,531	18,512	100.0	24.3	16.3	19.9	14.3	25.1
South Carolina	77,425	75,260	97.2	15,382	11,458	16,815	11,876	19,729	100.0	20.4	15.2	22.3	15.8	26.2
Georgia	86,789	84,329	97.2	23,643	14,810	18,243	11,940	15,693	100.0	28.0	17.6	21.6	14.2	18.6
Florida	11,043	10,477	94.9	1,423	1,208	1,732	1,560	4,554	100.0	13.6	11.5	16.5	14.9	43.5
EAST SOUTH CENTRAL	320,959	310,752	96.8	71,152	54,091	74,619	46,586	64,304	100.0	22.9	17.4	24.0	15.0	20.7
Kentucky	9,104	8,734	95.9	1,588	1,345	1,601	1,136	3,064	100.0	18.2	15.4	18.3	13.0	35.1
Tennessee	35,138	33,485	95.3	8,116	6,052	7,628	4,358	7,331	100.0	24.2	18.1	22.8	13.0	21.9
Alabama	93,829	91,097	97.1	16,492	12,881	21,412	16,333	23,979	100.0	18.1	14.1	23.5	17.9	26.3
Mississippi	182,888	177,436	97.0	44,956	33,813	43,978	24,759	29,930	100.0	25.3	19.1	24.8	14.0	16.9
WEST SOUTH CENTRAL	262,349	253,270	96.5	67,644	44,612	55,040	33,578	52,396	100.0	26.7	17.6	21.7	13.3	20.7
Arkansas	79,579	77,355	97.2	24,312	16,172	16,277	8,691	11,903	100.0	31.4	20.9	21.0	11.2	15.4
Louisiana	73,770	70,938	96.2	15,960	11,891	16,767	10,818	15,502	100.0	22.5	16.8	23.6	15.2	21.9
Oklahoma	22,937	21,889	95.4	6,251	3,276	4,116	2,873	5,373	100.0	28.6	15.0	18.8	13.1	24.5
Texas	86,063	83,088	96.5	21,121	13,273	17,880	11,196	19,618	100.0	25.4	16.0	21.5	13.5	23.6
SELECTED NORTHERN STATES [1]	10,250	10,033	97.9	2,835	1,454	1,760	1,258	2,726	100.0	28.3	14.5	17.5	12.5	27.2
New Jersey	384	370	96.4	30	43	90	79	128	100.0	8.1	11.6	24.3	21.4	34.6
Pennsylvania	363	351	96.7	39	37	69	82	124	100.0	11.1	10.5	19.7	23.4	35.3
Ohio	1,237	1,200	97.0	173	118	207	176	526	100.0	14.4	9.8	17.3	14.7	43.8
Indiana	475	463	97.5	60	58	75	64	206	100.0	13.0	12.5	16.2	13.8	44.5
Illinois	894	856	95.7	101	129	144	132	350	100.0	11.8	15.1	16.8	15.4	40.9
Missouri	5,861	5,781	98.6	2,307	963	1,022	553	936	100.0	39.9	16.7	17.7	9.6	16.2
Kansas	1,036	1,012	97.7	125	106	153	172	456	100.0	12.4	10.5	15.1	17.0	45.1
OWNERS AND MANAGERS														
The South	**182,848**	**174,626**	**95.5**	**7,418**	**8,273**	**20,665**	**27,019**	**111,251**	**100.0**	**4.2**	**4.7**	**11.8**	**15.5**	**63.7**
SOUTH ATLANTIC	80,982	77,430	95.6	2,781	3,274	8,028	11,648	51,699	100.0	3.6	4.2	10.4	15.0	66.8
Delaware	392	375	95.7	13	19	56	69	218	100.0	3.5	5.1	14.9	18.4	58.1
Maryland	3,061	2,903	94.8	106	138	328	458	1,873	100.0	3.7	4.8	11.3	15.8	64.5
District of Columbia	9	8	88.9				2	6	100.0				25.0	75.0
Virginia	24,525	23,537	96.0	584	788	2,122	3,293	16,750	100.0	2.5	3.3	9.0	14.0	71.2
West Virginia	380	368	96.8	9	20	38	69	232	100.0	2.4	5.4	10.3	18.8	63.0
North Carolina	19,734	18,761	95.1	726	914	2,094	3,059	11,968	100.0	3.9	4.9	11.2	16.3	63.8
South Carolina	16,063	15,463	96.3	575	626	1,619	2,476	10,167	100.0	3.7	4.0	10.5	16.0	65.8
Georgia	11,153	10,681	95.8	557	498	1,207	1,442	6,977	100.0	5.2	4.7	11.3	13.5	65.3
Florida	5,665	5,334	94.2	211	271	564	780	3,508	100.0	4.0	5.1	10.6	14.6	65.8
EAST SOUTH CENTRAL	50,729	48,621	95.8	2,116	2,404	6,457	8,014	29,630	100.0	4.4	4.9	13.3	16.5	60.9
Kentucky	4,190	4,004	95.6	189	192	469	600	2,554	100.0	4.7	4.8	11.7	15.0	63.8
Tennessee	7,866	7,410	94.2	369	411	910	1,114	4,606	100.0	5.0	5.5	12.3	15.0	62.2
Alabama	15,954	15,305	95.9	668	639	1,929	2,513	9,556	100.0	4.4	4.2	12.6	16.4	62.4
Mississippi	22,719	21,902	96.4	890	1,162	3,149	3,787	12,914	100.0	4.1	5.3	14.4	17.3	59.0
WEST SOUTH CENTRAL	51,137	48,575	95.0	2,521	2,595	6,180	7,357	29,922	100.0	5.2	5.3	12.7	15.1	61.6
Arkansas	11,478	11,044	96.2	555	587	1,394	1,601	6,907	100.0	5.0	5.3	12.6	14.5	62.5
Louisiana	10,557	9,995	94.7	431	512	1,375	1,540	6,137	100.0	4.3	5.1	13.8	15.4	61.4
Oklahoma	8,378	7,789	93.0	596	495	1,088	1,348	4,262	100.0	7.7	6.4	14.0	17.3	54.7
Texas	20,724	19,747	95.3	939	1,001	2,323	2,868	12,616	100.0	4.8	5.1	11.8	14.5	63.9
SELECTED NORTHERN STATES [1]	3,856	3,727	96.7	194	187	461	594	2,291	100.0	5.2	5.0	12.4	15.9	61.5
New Jersey	255	247	96.9	10	17	47	60	113	100.0	4.0	6.9	19.0	24.3	45.7
Pennsylvania	247	236	95.5	13	18	35	60	110	100.0	5.5	7.6	14.8	25.4	46.6
Ohio	795	774	97.4	55	34	93	128	464	100.0	7.1	4.4	12.0	16.5	59.9
Indiana	285	276	96.8	13	15	29	41	178	100.0	4.7	5.4	10.5	14.9	64.5
Illinois	466	446	95.7	20	20	52	61	293	100.0	4.5	4.5	11.7	13.7	65.7
Missouri	1,190	1,146	96.3	55	53	140	149	749	100.0	4.8	4.6	12.2	13.0	65.4
Kansas	618	602	97.4	28	30	65	95	384	100.0	4.7	5.0	10.8	15.8	63.8

See footnote at end of table.

TABLE 50.—COLORED FARM OPERATORS, BY YEARS ON FARM, AND BY TENURE, BY SOUTHERN DIVISIONS AND STATES, AND SELECTED NORTHERN STATES: 1930—Continued

[See note at head of table]

DIVISION AND STATE	All colored farm operators	NUMBER REPORTING YEARS ON FARM: Total: Number	Total: Percent of all farms	Less than 1 year	1 year	2 to 4 years	5 to 9 years	10 years and over	PERCENT DISTRIBUTION BY YEARS ON FARM: Total	Less than 1 year	1 year	2 to 4 years	5 to 9 years	10 years and over
	ALL TENANTS													
The South	**698, 839**	**677, 606**	**97. 0**	**193, 621**	**134, 253**	**167, 751**	**96, 047**	**85, 934**	**100. 0**	**28. 6**	**19. 8**	**24. 8**	**14. 2**	**12. 7**
SOUTH ATLANTIC	217, 397	210, 780	97. 0	59, 462	40, 549	50, 729	31, 254	28. 786	100. 0	28. 2	19. 2	24. 1	14. 8	13. 7
Delaware	415	402	96. 9	85	72	122	70	53	100. 0	21. 1	17. 9	30. 3	17. 4	13. 2
Maryalnd	2, 206	2, 123	96. 2	386	392	612	407	326	100. 0	18. 2	18. 5	28. 8	19. 2	15. 4
District of Columbia	2	2	100. 0			1	1		100. 0			50. 0	50. 0	
Virginia	15, 148	14, 595	96. 3	2, 640	2, 857	3, 978	2, 604	2, 516	100. 0	18. 1	19. 6	27. 3	17. 8	17. 2
West Virginia	111	108	97. 3	25	16	22	22	23	100. 0	23. 1	14. 8	20. 4	20. 4	21. 3
North Carolina	57, 139	54, 962	96. 2	17, 221	11, 131	12, 594	7, 472	6, 544	100. 0	31. 3	20. 3	22. 9	13. 6	11. 9
South Carolina	61, 362	59, 797	97. 4	14, 807	10, 832	15, 196	9, 400	9, 562	100. 0	24. 8	18. 1	25. 4	15. 7	16. 0
Georgia	75, 636	73, 648	97. 4	23, 086	14, 312	17, 036	10, 498	8, 716	100. 0	31. 3	19. 4	23. 1	14. 3	11. 8
Florida	5, 378	5, 143	95. 6	1, 212	937	1, 168	780	1, 046	100. 0	23. 6	18. 2	22. 7	15. 2	20. 3
EAST SOUTH CENTRAL	270. 230	262, 131	97. 0	69, 036	51, 687	68, 162	38, 572	34, 674	100. 0	26. 3	19. 7	26. 0	14. 7	13. 2
Kentucky	4, 914	4, 730	96. 3	1, 399	1, 153	1, 132	536	510	100. 0	29. 6	24. 4	23. 9	11. 3	10. 8
Tennessee	27, 272	26, 075	95. 6	7, 747	5, 641	6, 718	3, 244	2, 725	100. 0	29. 7	21. 6	25. 8	12. 4	10. 5
Alabama	77, 875	75, 792	97. 3	15, 824	12, 242	19, 483	13, 820	14, 423	100. 0	20. 9	16. 2	25. 7	18. 2	19. 0
Mississippi	160, 169	155, 534	97. 1	44, 066	32, 651	40, 829	20, 972	17, 016	100. 0	28. 3	21. 0	26. 3	13. 5	10. 9
WEST SOUTH CENTRAL	211, 212	204, 695	96. 9	65, 123	42, 017	48, 860	26, 221	22, 474	100. 0	31. 8	20. 5	23. 9	12. 8	11. 0
Arkansas	68, 101	66, 311	97. 4	23, 757	15, 585	14, 883	7, 090	4, 996	100. 0	35. 8	23. 5	22. 4	10. 7	7. 5
Louisiana	63, 213	60, 943	96. 4	15, 529	11, 379	15, 392	9, 278	9, 365	100. 0	25. 5	18. 7	25. 3	15. 2	15. 4
Oklahoma	14, 559	14, 100	96. 8	5, 655	2, 781	3, 028	1, 525	1, 111	100. 0	40. 1	19. 7	21. 5	10. 8	7. 9
Texas	65, 339	63, 341	96. 9	20, 182	12, 272	15, 557	8, 328	7, 002	100. 0	31. 9	19. 4	24. 6	13. 1	11. 1
SELECTED NORTHERN STATES [1]	6, 394	6, 306	98. 6	2, 641	1, 267	1, 299	664	435	100. 0	41. 9	20. 1	20. 6	10. 5	6. 9
New Jersey	129	123	95. 3	20	26	43	19	15	100. 0	16. 3	21. 1	35. 0	15. 4	12. 2
Pennsylvania	116	115	99. 1	26	19	34	22	14	100. 0	22. 6	16. 5	29. 6	19. 1	12. 2
Ohio	442	426	96. 4	118	84	114	48	62	100. 0	27. 7	19. 7	26. 8	11. 3	14. 6
Indiana	190	187	98. 4	47	43	46	23	28	100. 0	25. 1	23. 0	24. 6	12. 3	15. 0
Illinois	428	410	95. 8	81	109	92	71	57	100. 0	19. 8	26. 6	22. 4	17. 3	13. 9
Missouri	4, 671	4, 635	99. 2	2, 252	910	882	404	187	100. 0	48. 6	19. 6	19. 0	8. 7	4. 0
Kansas	418	410	98. 1	97	76	88	77	72	100. 0	23. 7	18. 5	21. 5	18. 8	17. 6

[1] States having 200 or more Negro farmers who constitute 90 percent or more of the colored farmers in the State.

TABLE 51.—SELECTED FARM EXPENDITURES OF COLORED FARM OPERATORS, WITH FARMS REPORTING, BY TENURE, BY SOUTHERN DIVISIONS, AND STATES, AND SELECTED NORTHERN STATES: 1930

[Colored farmers include Negroes, Indians, Chinese, Japanese, and all other nonwhite races]

DIVISION AND STATE	All colored farm operators	Total selected expenditures	FEED: Farms reporting	FEED: Amount expended	ELECTRIC CURRENT: Farms reporting	ELECTRIC CURRENT: Amount expended	FARM LABOR: Farms reporting	FARM LABOR: Amount expended	FARM IMPLEMENTS AND MACHINERY: Farms reporting	FARM IMPLEMENTS AND MACHINERY: Amount expended	FERTILIZER: Farms reporting	FERTILIZER: Quantity (tons)	FERTILIZER: Amount expended
	ALL OPERATORS												
The South	**881, 687**	**$79, 777, 157**	**284, 668**	**$18, 063, 402**	**1, 535**	**$66, 270**	**160, 460**	**$10, 534, 357**	**124, 442**	**$6, 464, 666**	**447, 424**	**1, 354, 339**	**$44, 648, 462**
SOUTH ATLANTIC	298, 379	42, 935, 633	92, 062	4, 856, 476	841	27, 816	68, 531	4, 981, 573	58, 473	2, 283, 872	244, 620	969, 099	30, 785, 896
Delaware	807	209, 322	451	52, 708	12	668	253	60, 474	168	36, 875	540	1, 957	58, 597
Maryland	5, 267	1, 006, 941	2, 917	233, 182	73	2, 870	1, 781	325, 281	893	143, 113	3, 721	9, 803	302, 495
District of Columbia	11	8, 834	11	3, 465	5	81	2	4, 760	1	528			
Virginia	39, 673	4, 337, 510	14, 724	664, 305	171	6, 965	7, 796	855, 729	5, 683	511, 528	25, 646	73, 361	2, 298, 983
West Virginia	491	48, 551	262	19, 439	27	1, 879	114	16, 366	43	5, 510	218	250	5, 357
North Carolina	76, 873	14, 364, 765	28, 723	1, 722, 734	271	7, 154	18, 770	1, 127, 379	12, 384	527, 274	68, 000	344, 842	10, 980, 224
South Carolina	77, 425	10, 530, 517	19, 549	841, 864	125	2, 548	16, 199	938, 726	14, 497	413, 428	66, 690	269, 033	8, 333, 951
Georgia	86, 789	11, 147, 580	22, 485	1, 101, 127	105	3, 047	20, 672	1, 254, 535	22, 908	553, 033	74, 346	254, 796	8, 235, 838
Florida	11, 043	1, 281, 613	2, 940	217, 652	52	2, 604	2, 944	398, 323	1, 896	92, 583	5, 459	15, 057	570, 451
EAST SOUTH CENTRAL	320, 959	20, 705, 322	95, 458	6, 268, 837	354	12, 305	43, 780	2, 144, 224	36, 612	1, 975, 165	143, 525	289, 574	10, 304, 791
Kentucky	9, 104	435, 146	2, 879	161, 515	43	1, 658	1, 943	168, 995	535	60, 742	2, 061	1, 587	42, 236
Tennessee	35, 138	1, 339, 838	10, 515	506, 848	85	3, 214	5, 357	250, 542	3, 191	258, 312	7, 830	9, 580	320, 922
Alabama	93, 829	8, 657, 022	33, 371	1, 630, 281	135	4, 296	16, 593	703, 493	19, 735	569, 879	65, 802	173, 029	5, 749, 073
Mississippi	182, 888	10, 273, 316	48, 693	3, 970, 193	91	3, 137	19, 887	1, 021, 194	13, 151	1, 086, 232	67, 832	105, 378	4, 192, 560
WEST SOUTH CENTRAL	262, 349	16, 136, 202	97, 148	6, 938, 089	340	26, 149	48, 149	3, 408, 560	29, 357	2, 205, 629	59, 279	95, 666	3, 557, 775
Arkansas	79, 579	5, 034, 344	32, 220	2, 828, 447	56	6, 422	14, 461	810, 878	8, 186	572, 507	13, 263	21, 179	816, 090
Louisiana	73, 770	4, 388, 016	25, 760	1, 656, 867	41	1, 557	10, 761	749, 677	8, 577	470, 863	24, 865	40, 470	1, 509, 052
Oklahoma	22, 937	1, 889, 480	7, 533	647, 212	164	15, 140	5, 783	649, 155	2, 824	561, 133	292	579	16, 840
Texas	86, 063	4, 824, 362	31, 635	1, 805, 563	79	3, 030	17, 144	1, 198, 850	9, 770	601, 126	20, 859	33, 438	1, 215, 793
SELECTED NORTHERN STATES [1]	10, 250	1, 425, 442	4, 091	551, 115	268	10, 210	2, 407	508, 332	1, 046	232, 727	1, 009	3, 163	123, 058
New Jersey	384	301, 870	276	99, 523	50	2, 045	170	101, 465	104	28, 115	258	1, 678	70, 722
Pennsylvania	363	130, 102	244	54, 135	30	1, 435	122	35, 611	79	20, 671	163	446	18, 250
Ohio	1, 237	189, 387	630	61, 458	56	2, 002	309	67, 916	157	37, 602	395	680	20, 409
Indiana	475	68, 319	260	33, 319	22	843	117	16, 949	39	10, 101	96	207	7, 107
Illinois	894	107, 229	474	45, 974	21	679	242	43, 485	95	13, 899	27	50	3, 192
Missouri	5, 861	421, 910	1, 682	201, 016	41	1, 400	1, 048	170, 812	329	46, 079	58	92	2, 603
Kansas	1, 036	206, 625	525	55, 690	48	1, 806	399	72, 094	243	76, 260	12	10	775

See footnote at end of table.

TABLE 51.—SELECTED FARM EXPENDITURES OF COLORED FARM OPERATORS, WITH FARMS REPORTING, BY TENURE, BY SOUTHERN DIVISIONS, AND STATES, AND SELECTED NORTHERN STATES: 1930—Continued

[See note at head of table]

	All colored farm operators	Total selected expenditures	FEED		ELECTRIC CURRENT		FARM LABOR		FARM IMPLEMENTS AND MACHINERY		FERTILIZER		
			Farms reporting	Amount expended	Farms reporting	Amount expended	Farms reporting	Amount expended	Farms reporting	Amount expended	Farms reporting	Quantity (tons)	Amount expended
	OWNERS (FULL AND PART)												
The South	**182,019**	**$19,731,900**	**87,919**	**$5,086,770**	**993**	**$43,890**	**46,874**	**$3,348,313**	**34,198**	**$2,838,920**	**101,795**	**255,383**	**$8,414,007**
SOUTH ATLANTIC	80,503	10,003,811	35,137	1,766,071	546	17,670	21,756	1,654,214	15,089	1,061,579	57,485	173,107	5,504,277
Delaware	373	81,606	242	26,663	9	353	108	15,173	83	21,509	253	555	17,908
Maryland	2,941	449,690	1,908	142,896	51	1,533	1,029	120,744	492	70,248	2,072	3,529	114,269
District of Columbia	8	1,381	8	845	3	36	1	500	-	-	-	-	-
Virginia	24,448	2,091,051	10,814	464,740	140	5,607	5,132	387,608	3,512	376,823	14,310	28,810	856,273
West Virginia	373	23,424	206	12,691	19	1,163	80	5,158	25	1,720	175	129	2,692
North Carolina	19,711	3,262,539	9,652	509,146	173	4,617	5,545	340,817	3,372	232,993	16,994	67,635	2,174,966
South Carolina	15,992	1,986,527	5,555	232,780	62	1,394	4,749	335,840	3,332	157,868	12,134	40,069	1,258,645
Georgia	11,081	1,458,203	4,831	234,026	50	1,557	3,594	257,847	3,247	138,779	8,798	25,685	825,994
Florida	5,576	649,390	1,921	142,284	39	1,410	1,518	190,527	1,026	61,639	2,749	6,695	253,530
EAST SOUTH CENTRAL	50,588	4,630,441	24,662	1,366,045	202	7,263	11,318	592,210	9,341	283,391	28,128	56,101	1,946,532
Kentucky	4,175	234,229	2,028	109,859	37	1,473	1,007	69,983	322	32,889	1,070	761	20,025
Tennessee	7,832	475,899	4,326	206,284	53	1,637	1,833	85,802	1,074	104,139	2,227	2,402	78,037
Alabama	15,931	1,839,879	7,926	404,175	76	2,711	4,376	237,208	4,316	200,544	12,334	29,661	995,241
Mississippi	22,650	2,080,434	10,382	645,727	36	1,442	4,102	199,217	3,629	380,819	12,497	23,277	853,229
WEST SOUTH CENTRAL	50,928	5,097,648	28,120	1,954,654	245	18,957	13,800	1,101,889	9,768	1,058,950	16,182	26,175	963,198
Arkansas	11,455	1,247,018	7,617	615,098	27	1,620	3,502	214,805	2,522	194,214	3,838	5,952	221,281
Louisiana	10,503	1,000,119	5,527	318,649	27	1,033	2,278	177,883	2,086	164,514	5,342	9,155	338,040
Oklahoma	8,334	1,183,186	3,329	379,381	144	14,422	2,598	362,243	1,379	416,467	170	363	10,673
Texas	20,636	1,667,325	11,647	641,526	47	1,882	5,422	346,958	3,781	283,755	6,832	10,705	393,204
SELECTED NORTHERN STATES [1]	3,776	671,583	2,289	282,016	203	6,593	1,060	197,347	566	135,297	628	1,301	50,330
New Jersey	240	142,333	184	58,486	36	1,491	89	40,219	64	15,466	154	590	26,671
Pennsylvania	233	67,552	162	26,956	20	771	74	18,028	48	14,762	110	209	7,035
Ohio	783	107,903	455	43,807	43	1,440	175	30,607	93	21,526	254	351	10,523
Indiana	283	33,135	167	18,269	16,	528	69	7,468	20	4,571	53	76	2,299
Illinois	460	56,651	278	24,151	17	413	143	22,659	54	7,268	18	31	2,160
Missouri	1,170	125,559	708	72,953	32	791	252	31,008	134	19,860	29	34	947
Kansas	607	138,450	335	37,394	39	1,159	258	47,358	153	51,844	10	10	695
	ALL TENANTS												
The South	**698,839**	**$58,973,561**	**196,339**	**$12,778,593**	**472**	**$16,715**	**113,067**	**$6,617,486**	**89,968**	**$3,511,479**	**345,147**	**1,093,285**	**$36,049,288**
SOUTH ATLANTIC	217,397	32,287,473	56,702	3,011,845	247	5,927	46,446	2,980,123	43,224	1,165,230	186,759	791,109	25,124,348
Delaware	415	102,004	199	22,131	-	-	135	29,768	79	12,976	278	1,247	37,129
Maryland	2,206	417,658	949	77,318	12	784	663	117,096	366	63,460	1,554	5,193	159,000
District of Columbia	2	340	2	320	1	20	-	-	-	-	-	-	-
Virginia	15,148	2,126,252	3,874	189,020	24	608	2,610	397,134	2,145	120,151	11,280	43,875	1,419,339
West Virginia	111	14,886	51	5,147	4	82	28	4,963	16	2,941	36	93	1,753
North Carolina	57,139	11,072,506	19,059	1,206,266	92	2,184	13,209	774,673	9,003	293,132	50,983	276,884	8,796,251
South Carolina	61,362	8,479,256	13,971	602,230	60	1,009	11,407	572,530	11,138	250,692	54,500	228,217	7,052,795
Georgia	75,636	9,563,024	17,620	853,072	50	931	17,028	931,633	19,627	398,409	65,489	228,154	7,378,979
Florida	5,378	511,547	977	56,341	4	309	1,366	152,326	850	23,469	2,639	7,446	279,102
EAST SOUTH CENTRAL	270,230	15,846,638	70,716	4,842,112	138	4,046	32,379	1,438,165	27,215	1,226,399	115,332	232,844	8,335,916
Kentucky	4,914	195,019	846	49,806	5	175	931	96,117	209	26,853	986	820	22,068
Tennessee	27,272	823,115	6,167	289,843	23	936	3,506	142,045	2,105	148,444	5,591	7,148	241,847
Alabama	77,875	6,736,657	25,432	1,214,656	56	1,280	12,198	416,546	15,403	363,119	53,451	142,970	4,741,056
Mississippi	160,169	8,091,847	38,271	3,287,807	54	1,655	15,744	783,457	9,498	687,983	55,304	81,906	3,330,945
WEST SOUTH CENTRAL	211,212	10,839,450	68,921	4,924,636	87	6,742	34,242	2,199,198	19,529	1,119,850	43,056	69,332	2,589,024
Arkansas	68,101	3,761,974	24,590	2,207,504	27	4,687	10,949	583,623	5,654	372,788	9,418	15,183	593,372
Louisiana	63,213	3,329,919	20,207	1,322,426	13	454	8,453	538,735	6,473	299,299	19,506	31,260	1,169,005
Oklahoma	14,459	646,304	4,178	248,646	19	688	3,155	252,309	1,432	138,761	117	207	5,900
Texas	65,339	3,101,253	19,946	1,146,060	28	913	11,685	824,531	5,970	309,002	14,015	22,682	820,747
SELECTED NORTHERN STATES [1]	6,394	624,004	1,754	217,036	51	2,617	1,306	260,699	459	84,800	350	1,604	58,852
New Jersey	129	105,848	83	25,174	9	218	69	36,063	33	7,817	92	894	36,576
Pennsylvania	116	49,377	74	24,659	10	664	44	11,743	28	5,695	46	223	6,616
Ohio	442	68,285	166	15,826	11	367	125	31,229	60	12,126	133	300	8,737
Indiana	190	34,117	92	14,820	6	315	47	8,856	18	5,455	42	127	4,671
Illinois	428	42,488	194	17,573	4	266	98	16,986	41	6,631	9	19	1,032
Missouri	4,671	259,846	960	101,313	5	294	786	133,556	191	23,543	26	41	1,140
Kansas	418	64,043	185	17,671	6	493	137	22,266	88	23,533	2	(2)	80

See footnotes at end of table.

TABLE 51.—SELECTED FARM EXPENDITURES OF COLORED FARM OPERATORS, WITH FARMS REPORTING BY TENURE, BY SOUTHERN DIVISIONS, AND STATES, AND SELECTED NORTHERN STATES: 1930—Continued

[See note at head of table]

DIVISION AND STATE	All colored farm operators	Total selected expenditures	FEED: Farms reporting	FEED: Amount expended	ELECTRIC CURRENT: Farms reporting	ELECTRIC CURRENT: Amount expended	FARM LABOR: Farms reporting	FARM LABOR: Amount expended	FARM IMPLEMENTS AND MACHINERY: Farms reporting	FARM IMPLEMENTS AND MACHINERY: Amount expended	FERTILIZER: Farms reporting	FERTILIZER: Quantity (tons)	FERTILIZER: Amount expended
	MANAGERS												
The South	829	$1,071,696	410	$198,039	70	$5,665	519	$568,558	276	$114,267	482	5,671	$185,167
SOUTH ATLANTIC	479	644,349	223	78,560	48	4,219	329	347,236	160	57,063	376	4,883	157,271
Delaware	19	25,712	10	3,914	3	315	10	15,533	6	2,390	9	155	3,560
Maryland	120	139,593	60	12,968	10	553	89	87,441	35	9,405	95	1,081	29,226
District of Columbia	1	7,113	1	2,300	1	25	1	4,260	1	528	------	------	------
Virginia	77	120,207	36	10,545	7	750	54	70,987	26	14,554	56	676	23,371
West Virginia	7	10,241	5	1,601	4	634	6	6,245	2	849	7	28	912
North Carolina	23	29,720	12	7,322	6	353	16	11,889	9	1,149	23	323	9,007
South Carolina	71	64,734	23	6,854	3	145	43	30,356	27	4,868	56	747	22,511
Georgia	72	126,353	34	14,029	5	559	50	65,055	34	15,845	59	957	30,865
Florida	89	120,676	42	19,027	9	885	60	55,470	20	7,475	71	916	37,819
EAST SOUTH CENTRAL	141	228,243	80	60,680	14	996	83	113,849	56	30,375	65	629	22,343
Kentucky	15	5,898	5	1,850	1	10	5	2,895	4	1,000	5	6	143
Tennessee	34	40,824	22	10,721	9	641	18	22,695	12	5,729	12	30	1,038
Alabama	23	80,486	13	11,450	3	305	19	49,739	16	6,216	17	398	12,776
Mississippi	69	101,035	40	36,659	1	40	41	38,520	24	17,430	31	195	8,386
WEST SOUTH CENTRAL	209	199,104	107	58,799	8	450	107	107,473	60	26,829	41	159	5,553
Arkansas	23	25,352	13	5,845	2	115	10	12,450	10	5,505	7	44	1,437
Louisiana	54	57,978	26	15,792	1	70	30	33,059	18	7,050	17	55	2,007
Oklahoma	44	59,990	26	19,185	1	30	30	34,603	13	5,905	5	9	267
Texas	88	55,784	42	17,977	4	235	37	27,361	19	8,369	12	51	1,842
SELECTED NORTHERN STATES [1]	80	129,855	48	52,063	14	1,000	41	50,286	21	12,630	31	258	13,876
New Jersey	15	53,689	9	15,863	5	336	12	25,183	7	4,832	12	194	7,475
Pennsylvania	14	13,173	8	2,520	------	------	4	5,840	3	214	7	14	4,599
Ohio	12	13,199	9	1,825	2	195	9	6,080	4	3,950	8	29	1,149
Indiana	2	1,067	1	230	------	------	1	625	1	75	1	4	137
Illinois	6	8,090	2	4,250	------	------	1	3,840	------	------	------	------	------
Missouri	20	36,505	14	26,750	4	315	10	6,248	4	2,676	3	17	516
Kansas	11	4,132	5	625	3	154	4	2,470	2	883	------	------	------

[1] States having 200 or more Negro farmers who constitute 90 percent or more of the colored farmers in the State. [2] Less than 1 ton per farm reported.

TABLE 52.—NUMBER OF FARMS, AND FARM ACREAGE, 1930, 1925, AND 1920; AND SPECIFIED CLASSES OF LAND ACCORDING TO USE IN 1929 AND 1924; BY TENURE OF COLORED OPERATORS, BY SOUTHERN DIVISIONS, AND STATES

[Colored farmers include Negroes, Indians, Chinese, Japanese, and all other nonwhite races]

DIVISION OR STATE, USE OF LAND, AND YEAR	Total	OWNERS: Full owners	OWNERS: Part owners	Managers	TENANTS: Cash	TENANTS: Other
THE SOUTH						
Number of farms 1930	881,687	140,496	41,523	829	97,920	600,919
1925	831,455	159,651	34,889	667	78,760	557,488
1920	922,914	178,558	39,031	1,770	100,275	603,280
All land in farms 1930	37,805,765	9,010,320	2,468,578	266,752	4,095,292	21,964,823
1925	33,894,038	9,828,895	1,855,972	185,195	3,003,423	19,020,553
1920	41,318,496	11,950,158	2,126,465	367,820	4,010,599	22,863,454
Crop land harvested. 1929	20,726,437	3,011,824	1,110,982	55,636	2,299,938	14,248,057
1924	19,211,420	3,135,684	867,676	41,306	1,877,098	13,289,656
Plowable pasture. 1929	1,770,492	660,890	162,416	27,087	185,150	734,949
Other pasture [1] 1929	1,265,072	449,438	150,243	49,598	95,913	519,880
SOUTH ATLANTIC						
Number of farms 1930	298,379	60,714	19,789	479	29,327	188,070
1925	326,058	78,941	18,228	417	25,841	202,631
1920	383,832	83,022	19,641	957	26,909	253,303
All land in farms 1930	14,658,534	3,314,342	943,983	109,719	1,471,813	8,818,677
1925	14,078,112	3,870,347	755,737	82,553	1,054,382	8,315,093
1920	18,224,941	4,586,201	932,194	145,967	1,205,317	11,355,262
Crop land harvested. 1929	7,077,341	1,068,812	439,822	31,410	681,489	4,855,808
1924	7,075,075	1,178,310	356,530	24,451	583,161	4,932,623
Plowable pasture. 1929	518,160	182,481	39,557	8,696	43,969	243,457
Other pasture [1] 1924	317,615	88,471	18,255	2,903	27,302	180,684
EAST SOUTH CENTRAL						
Number of farms 1930	320,959	39,420	11,168	141	53,371	216,859
1925	280,827	38,928	9,281	124	44,231	188,263
1920	307,232	45,802	9,738	407	56,556	194,729
All land in farms 1930	11,931,055	2,874,227	648,563	50,042	2,025,059	6,333,164
1925	10,251,014	2,820,995	516,955	46,326	1,623,154	5,243,584
1920	12,113,672	3,425,539	507,707	85,911	2,144,662	5,949,853
Crop land harvested. 1929	6,936,999	861,953	276,940	11,548	1,265,786	4,520,772
1924	6,183,290	788,764	228,859	9,765	1,092,528	4,063,374
Plowable pasture. 1929	724,404	270,480	59,508	7,838	111,291	275,287
Other pasture [1] 1929	398,588	162,596	26,036	2,496	50,861	156,599
WEST SOUTH CENTRAL						
Number of farms 1930	262,349	40,362	10,566	209	15,222	195,990
1925	224,570	41,782	7,380	126	8,688	166,594
1920	231,850	49,734	9,652	406	16,810	155,248
All land in farms 1930	11,216,176	2,821,751	876,032	106,991	598,420	6,812,982
1925	9,564,912	3,137,553	583,280	56,316	325,887	5,461,876
1920	10,979,883	3,938,418	686,564	135,942	660,620	5,558,339
Crop land harvested. 1929	6,712,097	1,081,059	394,220	12,678	352,663	4,871,477
1924	5,953,055	1,168,610	282,287	7,090	201,409	4,293,659
Plowable pasture. 1929	527,928	207,929	63,351	10,553	29,890	216,205
Other pasture [1] 1929	548,869	198,371	105,952	44,199	17,750	182,597
SOUTH ATLANTIC						
DELAWARE						
Number of farms 1930	807	309	64	19	54	361
1925	831	334	28	10	39	420
1920	872	305	50	13	38	466
All land in farms 1930	54,756	11,050	2,731	3,344	2,403	35,228
1925	50,388	11,255	805	1,076	1,126	36,126
1920	54,888	10,689	1,823	1,294	1,368	39,714
Crop land harvested. 1929	21,825	4,513	1,526	1,177	731	13,878
1924	22,253	4,770	556	665	344	15,918
Plowable pasture. 1929	4,312	1,024	107	203	149	2,829
Other pasture [1] 1929	1,054	242	17	106	54	635
MARYLAND						
Number of farms 1930	5,267	2,362	579	120	213	1,993
1925	6,721	3,711	395	105	253	2,257
1920	6,209	3,091	458	151	297	2,212
All land in farms 1930	345,569	87,593	20,342	21,878	8,862	206,894
1925	356,385	105,494	14,633	16,129	10,099	210,030
1920	351,577	100,690	18,585	22,082	12,076	198,144
Crop land harvested. 1929	104,074	25,334	8,939	8,859	2,109	58,833
1924	108,119	31,135	6,066	5,953	2,784	62,181
Plowable pasture. 1929	43,918	10,737	2,247	2,760	733	27,441
Other pasture [1] 1929	7,328	1,563	436	393	477	4,459

[1] Other than plowable or woodland pasture.

TABLE 52.—NUMBER OF FARMS, AND FARM ACREAGE, 1930, 1925, AND 1920; AND SPECIFIED CLASSES OF LAND ACCORDING TO USE IN 1929 AND 1924; BY TENURE OF COLORED OPERATORS, BY SOUTHERN DIVISIONS, AND STATES—Continued

[See note at head of table]

DIVISION OR STATE, USE OF LAND, AND YEAR	Total	OWNERS: Full owners	OWNERS: Part owners	Managers	TENANTS: Cash	TENANTS: Other
SOUTH ATLANTIC—Con.						
DISTRICT OF COLUMBIA						
Number of farms 1930	11	7	1	1	2	-
1925	9	5	-	1	2	1
1920	20	8	1	1	6	4
All land in farms 1930	95	13	15	60	7	-
1925	104	24	-	60	12	8
1920	288	20	5	95	89	79
Crop land harvested 1929	66	8	3	49	6	-
1924	101	21	-	60	12	8
Plowable pasture 1929	7	-	-	7	-	-
Other pasture [1] 1929	-	-	-	-	-	-
VIRGINIA						
Number of farms 1930	39,673	19,200	5,248	77	1,767	13,381
1925	50,147	28,515	4,628	76	1,643	15,285
1920	47,786	25,520	5,429	197	2,239	14,401
All land in farms 1930	2,046,028	937,215	245,919	23,433	114,512	724,949
1925	2,100,147	1,130,363	181,690	16,903	90,447	680,744
1920	2,263,419	1,145,964	227,797	31,294	116,004	742,360
Crop land harvested 1929	606,316	238,415	92,964	4,946	28,203	241,788
1924	613,090	273,724	69,506	3,821	20,456	245,583
Plowable pasture 1929	154,509	85,270	19,629	2,663	4,893	42,054
Other pasture [1] 1929	51,706	26,054	5,826	762	2,303	16,761
WEST VIRGINIA						
Number of farms 1930	491	328	45	7	38	73
1925	714	504	31	5	77	97
1920	504	366	37	8	35	58
All land in farms 1930	8,085	15,741	2,801	969	2,173	6,401
1925	20,006	18,982	1,147	2,050	1,235	6,592
1920	37,544	16,701	2,351	1,520	1,922	5,050
Crop land harvested 1929	26,664	3,113	659	416	404	2,072
1924	7,990	4,549	413	314	341	2,373
Plowable pasture 1929	5,068	2,779	648	260	261	1,120
Other pasture [1] 1929	4,452	2,943	359	17	531	602
NORTH CAROLINA						
Number of farms 1930	76,873	13,198	6,513	23	2,545	54,594
1925	80,966	15,325	6,756	20	2,632	56,233
1920	76,290	16,365	5,912	96	3,213	50,704
All land in farms 1930	3,392,535	696,930	285,181	6,184	137,959	2,266,281
1925	3,240,664	777,126	271,360	5,599	136,360	2,050,219
1920	3,437,442	908,763	250,101	12,867	168,196	2,097,515
Crop land harvested 1929	1,631,695	233,521	138,168	1,395	51,743	1,206,868
1924	1,600,124	241,672	130,538	962	52,448	1,174,504
Plowable pasture 1929	51,537	14,980	4,466	778	1,532	29,781
Other pasture [1] 1929	40,938	12,135	3,327	12	1,381	24,083
SOUTH CAROLINA						
Number of farms 1930	77,425	11,937	4,055	71	11,759	49,603
1925	90,581	14,476	3,892	34	11,389	60,790
1920	109,010	18,278	4,481	183	11,027	75,041
All land in farms 1930	3,171,976	616,579	170,972	21,362	338,850	2,024,213
1925	3,219,753	721,300	144,023	9,718	285,196	2,059,516
1920	4,380,003	967,067	179,329	37,095	326,449	2,870,063
Crop land harvested 1929	1,744,142	231,844	91,937	4,224	195,361	1,220,776
1924	1,945,147	261,994	78,297	2,271	200,682	1,401,903
Plowable pasture 1929	66,564	19,725	4,078	297	4,420	38,044
Other pasture [1] 1929	80,038	18,880	3,112	542	3,487	54,017
GEORGIA						
Number of farms 1930	86,789	9,014	2,067	72	10,532	65,104
1925	84,077	10,032	1,715	124	7,722	64,484
1920	130,187	13,684	2,358	207	7,460	106,478
All land in farms 1930	5,104,659	726,112	157,212	23,563	763,459	3,434,313
1925	4,553,159	823,125	105,906	28,522	445,514	3,150,092
1920	7,071,912	1,124,847	206,981	29,038	470,492	5,240,554
Crop land harvested 1929	2,712,692	252,717	71,020	7,693	338,044	2,043,218
1924	2,527,112	264,692	51,347	9,391	248,406	1,953,276
Plowable pasture 1929	160,987	30,457	5,526	1,045	27,698	96,261
Other pasture [1] 1929	125,304	23,644	4,570	875	17,750	78,465
FLORIDA						
Number of farms 1930	11,043	4,359	1,217	89	2,417	2,961
1925	12,012	6,039	783	42	2,084	3,064
1920	12,954	5,405	915	101	2,594	3,939
All land in farms 1930	514,831	223,109	58,810	8,926	103,588	120,398
1925	527,506	282,678	36,173	2,496	84,393	121,766
1920	637,868	311,460	45,222	10,682	108,721	161,783
Crop land harvested 1929	249,867	79,347	34,606	2,651	64,888	68,375
1924	251,139	95,753	19,807	1,014	57,688	76,877
Plowable pasture 1929	31,258	17,509	2,856	683	4,283	5,927
Other pasture [1] 1929	6,795	3,010	608	196	1,319	1,662
EAST SOUTH CENTRAL						
KENTUCKY						
Number of farms 1930	9,104	3,055	1,120	15	140	4,774
1925	10,717	3,818	1,136	16	146	5,601
1920	12,628	4,180	1,139	35	236	7,038
All land in farms 1930	341,833	138,252	44,896	2,507	5,230	150,948
1925	362,920	167,627	44,480	2,499	5,042	143,272
1920	426,959	200,377	39,750	4,709	8,885	173,238
Crop land harvested 1929	131,173	37,252	17,504	654	1,781	73,982
1924	158,781	39,727	20,287	757	1,586	96,424
Plowable pasture 1929	87,481	39,592	12,551	877	773	33,688
Other pasture [1] 1929	14,306	7,089	2,155	192	184	4,686
EAST SOUTH CENTRAL—Continued						
TENNESSEE						
Number of farms 1930	35,138	5,687	2,145	34	2,863	24,409
1925	34,647	7,086	2,131	18	2,568	22,754
1920	38,182	7,871	1,969	53	4,850	23,439
All land in farms 1930	1,357,374	309,906	109,305	6,132	136,795	795,237
1925	1,228,111	366,755	101,019	4,198	103,724	652,415
1920	1,523,803	441,332	93,948	9,271	219,898	759,354
Crop land harvested 1929	760,844	106,121	50,564	2,204	71,969	529,986
1924	738,932	115,206	50,584	863	63,930	508,349
Plowable pasture 1929	123,323	39,474	11,937	1,558	13,027	57,327
Other pasture [1] 1929	44,628	15,408	4,568	363	5,169	19,120
ALABAMA						
Number of farms 1930	93,829	11,417	4,514	23	32,055	45,820
1925	85,310	10,953	3,771	58	28,403	42,136
1920	95,203	13,663	3,539	127	30,819	47,055
All land in farms 1930	4,158,609	916,880	272,993	14,212	1,197,896	1,756,628
1925	3,705,294	881,968	230,159	25,696	1,036,852	1,530,619
1920	4,348,245	1,131,592	201,109	32,146	1,149,313	1,834,085
Crop land harvested 1929	2,417,565	294,124	126,001	3,509	767,535	1,226,396
1924	2,255,527	267,611	103,494	5,346	719,732	1,159,344
Plowable pasture 1929	181,565	57,046	15,389	2,860	55,177	51,093
Other pasture [1] 1929	96,113	37,167	6,702	570	23,263	28,411
MISSISSIPPI						
Number of farms 1930	182,888	19,261	3,389	69	18,313	141,856
1925	150,142	17,071	2,243	32	13,024	117,772
1920	161,219	20,088	3,091	192	20,651	117,197
All land in farms 1930	6,073,239	1,509,189	221,369	27,191	685,139	3,630,351
1925	4,954,689	1,404,645	141,297	13,933	477,536	2,917,278
1920	5,814,665	1,865,223	172,900	39,785	766,566	3,183,176
Crop land harvested 1929	3,625,417	424,456	82,871	5,181	424,501	2,690,408
1924	3,030,050	366,220	54,494	2,799	307,280	2,299,257
Plowable pasture 1929	332,035	134,368	19,631	2,543	42,314	133,179
Other pasture [1] 1929	243,541	102,392	12,611	1,371	22,245	100,382
WEST SOUTH CENTRAL						
ARKANSAS						
Number of farms 1930	79,579	9,058	2,397	23	6,106	61,995
1925	63,283	9,495	1,568	39	2,692	49,489
1920	72,282	12,866	2,507	95	8,896	47,918
All land in farms 1930	2,487,762	560,843	144,313	6,741	220,119	1,555,746
1925	2,048,450	665,599	99,874	9,653	91,359	1,181,865
1920	2,624,762	901,045	141,526	13,211	312,841	1,256,139
Crop land harvested 1929	1,706,670	220,004	72,895	1,755	154,335	1,257,678
1924	1,335,912	228,573	47,383	3,118	6,947	991,891
Plowable pasture	60,969	26,957	5,873	370	4,414	22,345
Other pasture [1] 1929	31,730	13,648	3,723	886	1,570	11,903
LOUISIANA						
Number of farms 1930	73,770	8,786	1,717	54	6,692	56,521
1925	59,513	8,494	1,076	30	4,314	45,599
1920	62,059	9,473	1,513	92	5,547	45,434
All land in farms 1930	2,315,402	512,572	90,395	20,305	205,148	1,486,982
1925	1,839,934	546,913	63,635	9,578	119,876	1,099,932
1920	2,182,578	677,378	70,365	14,465	180,870	1,239,500
Crop land harvested 1929	1,527,644	190,877	48,153	2,776	129,732	1,156,106
1924	1,203,550	177,254	30,919	1,213	84,257	909,907
Plowable pasture 1929	98,280	40,108	5,218	966	9,481	42,507
Other pasture [1] 1924	47,859	18,465	2,328	6,497	2,476	18,093
OKLAHOMA						
Number of farms 1930	22,937	6,550	1,784	44	1,029	13,530
1925	20,048	7,612	1,076	12	603	10,745
1920	18,725	8,002	1,486	85	1,026	8,126
All land in farms 1930	1,965,752	623,258	291,431	43,037	102,713	905,013
1925	1,616,230	710,676	171,695	10,273	53,258	670,328
1920	1,713,403	830,004	199,468	24,663	98,148	561,120
Crop land harvested 1929	861,507	217,302	108,206	3,552	37,702	494,745
1924	785,729	282,274	69,269	691	25,603	407,892
Plowable pasture 1929	126,632	47,945	23,189	2,942	8,709	43,847
Other pasture [1] 1929	246,786	87,721	65,593	30,235	10,455	52,780
TEXAS						
Number of farms 1930	86,063	15,968	4,668	88	1,395	63,944
1925	81,726	16,181	3,660	45	1,079	60,761
1920	78,784	19,393	4,146	134	1,341	53,770
All land in farms 1930	4,447,260	1,125,078	349,893	36,908	70,440	2,864,941
1925	4,060,298	1,214,365	248,076	26,712	61,394	2,509,751
1920	4,459,140	1,529,991	275,205	83,603	68,761	2,501,580
Crop land harvested 1929	2,616,279	452,876	164,966	4,595	30,894	1,962,948
1924	2,627,864	480,509	134,716	2,068	26,602	1,983,969
Plowable pasture 1929	242,057	92,919	29,071	6,275	6,286	107,506
Other pasture [1] 1929	222,494	78,537	34,308	6,581	3,249	99,819

[1] Other than plowable or woodland pasture.

TABLE 53.—AVERAGE ACREAGE PER FARM, AND PERCENT DISTRIBUTION OF ALL LAND IN FARMS 1930, 1925, AND 1920; AND OF SPECIFIED CLASSES OF LAND ACCORDING TO USE IN 1929 AND 1924 (BASED ON ALL FARMS), BY TENURE OF COLORED OPERATORS, BY SOUTHERN DIVISIONS, AND STATES

[Colored farmers include Negroes, Indians, Chinese, Japanese, and all other nonwhite races]

DIVISION OR STATE, USE OF LAND, AND YEAR	AVERAGE ACREAGE PER FARM						PERCENT DISTRIBUTION BY TENURE				
	All colored operators	Full owners	Part owners	Managers	Cash tenants	Other tenants	Full owners	Part owners	Managers	Cash tenants	Other tenants
THE SOUTH											
All land in farms..1930..	42.9	64.1	59.5	321.8	41.8	36.6	23.8	6.5	0.7	10.8	58.1
1925..	40.8	61.6	53.2	277.7	38.1	34.1	29.0	5.5	.5	8.9	56.1
1920..	44.8	66.9	54.5	207.8	40.0	37.9	28.9	5.1	.9	9.7	55.3
Crop land harvested. 1929..	23.5	21.4	26.8	67.1	23.5	23.7	14.5	5.4	.3	11.1	68.7
1924..	23.1	19.6	24.9	61.9	23.8	23.8	16.3	4.5	.2	9.8	69.2
Plowable pasture. 1929..	2.0	4.7	3.9	32.7	1.9	1 2	37.3	9.2	1.5	10.5	41.5
Other pasture [1]..1929..	1.4	3.2	3.6	59.8	1.0	.9	35.5	11.9	3.9	7.6	41.1
SOUTH ATLANTIC											
All land in farms..1930..	49.1	54.6	47.7	229.1	50.2	46.9	22.6	6.4	.7	10.0	60.2
1925..	43.2	49.0	41.5	198.0	40.8	41.0	27.5	5.4	.6	7.5	59.1
1920..	47.5	55.2	47.5	152.5	44.8	44.8	25.2	5.1	.8	6.6	62.3
Crop land harvested. 1929..	23.7	17.6	22.2	65.6	23.2	25.8	15.1	6.2	.4	9.6	68.6
1924..	21.7	14.9	19.6	58.6	22.6	24.3	16.7	5.0	.3	8.2	69.7
Plowable pasture. 1929..	1.7	3.0	2.0	18.2	1.5	1.3	35.2	7.6	1.7	8.5	47.0
Other pasture [1]..1929..	1.1	1.5	.9	6.1	.9	1.0	27.9	5.7	.9	8.6	56.9
EAST SOUTH CENTRAL											
All land in farms..1930..	37.2	72.9	58.1	354.9	37.9	29.2	24.1	5.4	.4	17.0	53.1
1925..	36.5	72.5	55.7	373.6	36.7	27.9	27.5	5.0	.5	15.8	51.2
1920..	39.4	74.8	52.1	211.1	37.9	30.6	28.3	4.2	.7	17.7	49.1
Crop land harvested. 1929..	21.6	21.9	24.8	81.9	23.7	20.8	12.4	4.0	.2	18.2	65.2
1924..	22.0	20.3	24.7	78.8	24.7	21.6	12.8	3.7	.2	17.7	65.7
Plowable pasture. 1929..	2.3	6.9	5.3	55.6	2.1	1.3	37.3	8.2	1.1	15.4	38.0
Other pasture [1]..1929..	1.2	4.1	2.3	17.7	1.0	.7	40.8	6.5	.6	12.8	39.3
WEST SOUTH CENTRAL											
All land in farms..1930..	42.8	69.9	82.9	511.9	39.3	34.8	25.2	7.8	1.0	5.3	60.7
1925..	42.6	75.1	79.0	447.0	37.5	27.9	32.8	6.1	.6	3.4	57.1
1920..	47.4	79.2	71.1	334.8	39.3	35.8	35.9	6.3	1.2	6.0	50.6
Crop land harvested. 1929..	25.6	26.8	37.3	60.7	23.2	24.9	16.1	5.9	.2	5.3	72.6
1924..	26.5	28.0	38.3	56.3	23.2	25.8	19.6	4.7	.1	3.4	72.1
Plowable pasture. 1929..	2.0	5.2	6.0	50.5	2.0	1.1	39.4	12.0	2.0	5.7	41.0
Other pasture [1]..1929..	2.1	4.9	10.0	211.5	1.2	.9	36.1	19.3	8.1	3.2	33.3
SOUTH ATLANTIC											
DELAWARE											
All land in farms..1930..	67.9	35.8	42.7	176.0	44.5	97.6	20.2	5.0	6.1	4.4	64.3
1925..	60.6	33.7	28.8	107.6	28.9	86.0	22.3	1.6	2.1	2.2	71.7
1920..	62.9	35.0	36.5	99.5	36.0	85.2	19.5	3.3	2.4	2.5	72.4
Crop land harvested. 1929..	27.0	14.6	23.8	61.9	13.5	38.4	20.7	7.0	5.4	3.3	63.6
1924..	26.8	14.3	19.9	66.5	8.8	37.9	21.4	2.5	3.0	1.5	71.5
Plowable pasture. 1929..	5.3	3.3	1.7	10.7	2.8	7.8	23.7	2.5	4.7	3.5	65.6
Other pasture [1]..1929..	1.3	.8	.3	5.6	1.0	1.8	23.0	1.6	10.1	5.1	60.2
MARYLAND											
All land in farms..1930..	65.6	37.1	35.1	182.3	41.3	103.8	25.3	5.9	6.3	2.6	59.9
1925..	53.0	28.4	37.0	153.6	39.9	93.1	29.6	4.1	4.5	2.8	58.9
1920..	56.6	32.6	40.6	146.2	40.7	89.6	28.6	5.3	6.3	3.4	56.4
Crop land harvested. 1929..	19.8	10.7	15.4	73.8	9.9	29.5	24.3	8.6	8.5	2.0	56.5
1924..	16.1	8.4	15.4	56.7	11.0	27.6	28.8	5 6	5.5	2.6	57.5
Plowable pasture. 1929..	8.3	4.5	3.9	23.0	3.4	13.8	24.4	5.1	6.3	1.7	62.5
Other pasture [1]..1929..	1.4	.7	.8	3.3	2.2	2.2	21.3	5.9	5.4	6.5	60.8
DISTRICT OF COLUMBIA											
All land in farms..1930..	8.6	1.9	15.0	60.0	3.5	-----	13.7	15.8	63.2	7.4	-----
1925..	11.6	4.8	-----	60.0	6.0	8.0	23.1	-----	57.7	11.5	7.7
1920..	14.4	2.5	5.0	95.0	14.8	19.8	6.9	1.7	33.0	30.9	27.4
Crop land harvested. 1929..	6.0	1.1	3.0	49.0	3.0	-----	12.1	4.5	74.2	9.1	-----
1924..	11.2	4.2	-----	60.0	6.0	8.0	20.8	-----	59.4	11.9	27.9
Plowable pasture. 1929..	.6	-----	-----	7.0	-----	-----	-----	-----	100.0	-----	-----
Other pasture [1]..1929..	-----	-----	-----	-----	-----	-----	-----	-----	-----	-----	-----
VIRGINIA											
All land in farms..1930..	51.6	48.8	46.9	304.3	64.8	54.2	45.8	12.0	1.1	5.6	35.4
1925..	41.9	39.6	39.3	222.4	55.0	44.5	53.8	8 7	.8	4.3	32.4
1920..	47.4	44.9	42.0	158.9	51.8	51.5	50.6	10.1	1.4	5.1	32.8
Crop land harvested. 1929..	15.3	12.4	17.7	64.2	16.0	18.1	39.3	15.3	.8	4.7	39.9
1924..	12.2	9.6	15.0	50.3	12.5	16.1	44.6	11.3	.6	3.3	40.1
Plowable pasture. 1929..	3.9	4.4	3.7	34.6	2.8	3.1	55.2	12.7	1.7	3.2	27.2
Other pasture [1]..1929..	1.3	1.4	1.1	9.9	1.3	1.3	50.4	11.3	1.5	4.5	32.4
WEST VIRGINIA											
All land in farms..1930.	57.2	48.0	62.2	138.4	57.2	87.7	56.0	10.0	3.5	7.7	22.8
1925.	42.0	37.7	37.0	410.0	16.0	68.0	63.3	3.8	6.8	4.1	22.0
1920.	54.7	45.6	63.5	190.0	54.9	87.1	60.6	8.5	5.5	7.0	18.3
Crop land harvested. 1929.	13.6	9.5	14.6	59.4	10.6	28.4	46.7	9.9	6.2	6.1	31.1
1924.	11.2	9.0	13.3	62.8	4.4	24.5	56.9	5.2	3.9	4.3	29.7
Plowable pasture. 1929.	10.3	8.5	14.4	37.1	6.9	15.3	54.8	12.8	5.1	5.1	22.1
Other pasture [1]..1929.	9.1	9.0	8.0	2.4	14.0	8.2	66.1	8.1	.4	11.9	13.5
NORTH CAROLINA											
All land in farms..1930.	44.1	52.8	43.8	268.9	54.2	41.5	20.5	8.4	.2	4.1	66.8
1925.	40.0	50.7	40.2	280.0	51.8	36.5	24.0	8.4	.2	4.2	63.3
1920.	45.1	55.5	42.3	134.0	52.3	41.4	26.4	7.3	.4	4.9	61.0
Crop land harvested. 1929.	21.2	17.7	21.2	60.7	20.3	22.1	14.3	8.5	.1	3.2	74.0
1924.	19.8	15.8	19.3	48.1	19.9	20.9	15.1	8.2	.1	3.3	73.4
Plowable pasture. 1929.	.7	1.1	.7	33.8	.6	.5	29.1	8.7	1.5	3.0	57.8
Other pasture [1]..1929.	.5	.9	.5	.5	.5	.4	29.6	8.1	([2])	3.4	58.8
SOUTH CAROLINA											
All land in farms..1930.	41.0	51.7	42.2	300.9	28.8	40.8	19.4	5.4	.7	10.7	63.8
1925.	35.5	49.8	37.0	285.8	25.0	33.9	22.4	4.5	.3	8.9	64.0
1920.	40.2	52.9	40.0	202.7	29.6	38.2	22.1	4.1	.8	7.5	65.5
Crop land harvested. 1929.	22.5	19.4	22.7	59.5	16.6	24.6	13.3	5.3	.2	11.2	70.0
1924.	21.5	18.1	20.1	66.8	17.6	23.1	13.5	4.0	.1	10.3	72.1
Plowable pasture. 1929.	.9	1.7	1.0	4.2	.4	.8	29.6	6.1	.4	6.6	57.2
Other pasture [1]..1929.	1.0	1.6	.8	7.6	.3	1.1	23.6	3.9	.7	4.4	67.5
GEORGIA											
All land in farms..1930.	58.8	80.6	76.1	327.3	72.5	52.8	14.2	3.1	.5	15.0	67.3
1925.	54.2	82.0	61.8	230.0	57.7	48.9	18.1	2.3	.6	9.8	69.2
1920.	54.3	82.2	87.8	140.3	63.1	49.2	15.9	2.9	.4	6.7	74.1
Crop land harvested. 1929.	31.3	28.0	34.4	106.8	32.1	31.4	9.3	2.6	.3	12.5	75.3
1924.	30.1	26.4	29.9	75.7	32.2	30.3	10.5	2.0	.4	9.8	77.3
Plowable pasture. 1929.	1.9	3.4	2.7	14.5	2.6	1.5	18.9	3.4	.6	17.2	59.8
Other pasture [1]..1929.	1.4	2.6	2.2	12.2	1.7	1.2	18.9	3.6	.7	14.2	62.6
FLORIDA											
All land in farms..1930.	46.6	51.2	48.3	100.3	42.9	40.7	43.3	11.4	1.7	20.1	23.4
1925.	43.9	46.8	46.2	59.4	40.5	39.7	53.6	6.9	.5	16.0	23.1
1920.	49.2	57.6	49.4	105.8	41.9	41.1	48.8	7.1	1.7	17.0	25.4
Crop land harvested. 1929.	22.6	18.2	28.4	29.8	26.8	23.1	31.8	13.8	1.1	26.0	27.4
1924.	20.9	15.9	25.3	24.1	27.7	25.1	38.1	7.9	.4	23.0	30.6
Plowable pasture. 1929.	2.8	4.0	2.3	7.7	1.8	2.0	56.0	9.1	2.2	13.7	19.0
Other pasture [1]..1929.	.6	.7	.5	2.2	.5	.6	44.3	8.9	2.9	19.4	24.5
EAST SOUTH CENTRAL											
KENTUCKY											
All land in farms..1930.	37.5	45.3	40.1	167.1	37.4	31.6	40.4	13.1	.7	1.5	44.2
1925.	33.9	43.9	39.2	156.2	34.5	25.6	46.2	12.3	.7	1.4	39.5
1920.	33.8	47.9	34.9	134.5	37.6	24.6	46.9	9.3	1.1	2.1	40.6
Crop land harvested. 1929	14.4	12.2	15.6	43.6	12.7	15.5	28.4	13.3	.5	1.4	56.4
1924.	14.8	10.4	17.9	47.3	10.9	17.2	25.0	12.8	.5	1.0	60.7
Plowable pasture. 1929.	9.6	13.0	11.2	58.5	5.5	7.1	45.3	14.3	1.0	.9	38.5
Other pasture [1]..1929.	1.6	2.3	1.9	12.8	1.3	1.0	49.6	15.1	1.3	1.3	32.8
TENNESSEE											
All land in farms..1930.	38.6	54.5	51.0	180.4	47.8	32.6	22.8	8.1	.5	10.1	58.6
1925.	35.4	51.8	47.4	233.2	39.0	28.7	29.9	8.2	.3	8.4	53.1
1920.	39.9	56.1	47.7	174.9	45.3	32.4	29.0	6.2	.6	14.4	49.8
Crop land harvested. 1929.	21.7	18.7	23.6	64.8	25.1	21.7	13.9	6.6	.3	9.5	69.7
1924.	21.3	16.3	23.7	47.9	24.1	22.3	15.6	6.8	.1	8.7	68.8
Plowable pasture. 1929.	3.5	6.9	5.6	45.8	4.6	2.3	32.0	9.7	1.3	10.6	46.5
Other pasture [1]..1929.	1.3	2.7	2.1	10.7	1.8	.8	34.5	10.2	.8	11.6	42.8

[1] Other than plowable or woodland pasture.

[2] Less than one-tenth of 1 percent.

TABLE 53.—AVERAGE ACREAGE PER FARM, AND PERCENT DISTRIBUTION OF ALL LAND IN FARMS 1930, 1925, AND 1920; AND OF SPECIFIED CLASSES OF LAND ACCORDING TO USE IN 1929 AND 1924 (BASED ON ALL FARMS), BY TENURE OF COLORED OPERATORS, BY SOUTHERN DIVISIONS, AND STATES—Continued

[See note at head of table]

DIVISION OR STATE, USE OF LAND, AND YEAR	AVERAGE ACREAGE PER FARM						PERCENT DISTRIBUTION BY TENURE				
	All colored operators	Full owners	Part owners	Managers	Cash tenants	Other tenants	Full owners	Part owners	Managers	Cash tenants	Other tenants
EAST SOUTH CENTRAL—Continued											
ALABAMA											
All land in farms..1930	44.3	80.3	60.5	617.9	37.4	38.3	22.0	6.6	0.3	28.8	42.2
1925	43.4	80.5	61.0	443.0	36.5	36.3	23.8	6.2	.7	28.0	41.3
1920	45.7	82.8	56.8	253.1	37.3	39.0	26.0	4.6	.7	26.4	42.2
Crop land harvested. 1929	25.8	25.8	27.9	152.6	23.9	26.8	12.2	5.2	.1	31.7	50.7
1924	26.4	24.4	27.4	92.2	25.3	27.5	11.9	4.6	.2	31.9	51.4
Plowable pasture. 1929	1.9	5.0	3.4	124.3	1.7	1.1	31.4	8.5	1.6	30.4	28.1
Other pasture [1]..1929	1.0	3.3	1.5	24.8	.7	.6	38.7	7.0	.6	24.2	29.6
MISSISSIPPI											
All land in farms..1930	33.2	78.4	65.3	394.1	37.4	25.6	24.8	3.6	.4	11.3	59.8
1925	33.0	82.3	63.0	435.4	36.7	24.8	28.3	2.9	.3	9.6	58.9
1920	36.1	82.3	55.9	207.2	37.1	27.2	28.4	3.0	.7	13.2	54.7
Crop land harvested. 1929	19.8	22.0	24.5	75.1	23.2	19.0	11.7	2.3	.1	11.7	74.2
1924	20.2	21.5	24.3	87.5	23.6	19.5	12.1	1.8	.1	10.1	75.9
Plowable pasture 1929	1.8	7.0	5.8	36.9	2.3	.9	40.5	5.9	.8	12.7	40.1
Other pasture [1]..1929	1.3	5.3	3.7	19.9	1.2	.7	4.32	5.2	.6	9.1	42.9
WEST SOUTH CENTRAL											
ARKANSAS											
All land in farms..1930	31.3	61.9	60.2	293.1	36.0	25.1	22.5	5.8	.3	8.8	62.5
1925	32.4	70.1	63.7	250.1	33.9	23.9	32.5	4.9	.5	4.5	57.7
1920	36.3	70.0	56.5	139.1	35.1	26.2	34.3	5.4	.5	11.9	47.9
Crop land harvested. 1929	21.4	24.3	30.4	76.3	25.3	20.3	12.9	4.3	.1	9.0	73.7
1924	21.1	24.1	30.2	79.9	24.1	20.0	17.1	3.5	.2	4.9	74.2
Plowable pasture. 1929	.8	3.0	2.5	16.1	.9	.4	44.2	9.6	.6	8.9	36.7
Other pasture [1]..1929	.4	1.5	1.6	38.5	.3	.2	43.0	11.7	2.8	4.9	37.5
WEST SOUTH CENTRAL—Continued											
LOUISIANA											
All land in farms..1930	31.4	58.3	52.6	376.0	30.7	26.3	22.1	3.9	0.9	8.9	64.2
1925	30.9	64.4	59.1	319.3	27.8	24.1	29.7	3.5	.5	6.5	59.8
1920	35.2	71.5	46.5	157.2	32.6	27.3	31.0	3.2	.7	8.3	56.8
Crop land harvested. 1929	20.7	21.7	28.0	51.4	19.4	20.5	12.5	3.2	.2	8.5	75.7
1924	20.2	20.9	28.7	40.4	19.5	20.0	14.7	2.6	.1	7.0	75.6
Plowable pasture. 1929	1.3	4.6	3.0	17.9	1.4	.8	40.8	5.3	1.0	9.6	43.3
Other pasture [1]..1929	.6	2.1	1.4	120.3	.4	.3	38.6	4.9	13.6	5.2	37.8
OKLAHOMA											
All land in farms..1930	85.7	95.2	163.4	978.1	99.8	66.9	31.7	14.8	2.2	5.2	46.1
1925	80.6	93.4	159.6	856.1	88.3	62.4	44.0	10.6	.6	3.3	41.5
1920	91.5	103.7	134.2	290.2	95.7	69.1	48.4	11.6	1.4	5.7	32.7
Crop land harvested. 1929	37.6	33.2	60.7	80.7	36.6	36.6	25.2	12.6	.4	4.4	57.4
1924	39.2	37.1	64.4	57.6	42.5	38.0	35.9	8.8	.1	3.3	51.9
Plowable pasture. 1929	5.5	7.3	13.0	66.9	8.5	3.2	37.9	18.3	2.3	6.9	34.6
Other pasture [1]..1929	10.8	13.4	36.8	687.2	10.2	3.9	35.5	26.6	12.3	4.2	21.4
TEXAS											
All land in farms..1930	51.7	70.5	75.0	419.4	50.5	44.8	25.3	7.9	.8	1.6	64.4
1925	49.7	75.0	67.8	593.6	56.9	41.3	29.9	6.1	.7	1.5	61.8
1920	56.6	78.9	66.4	623.9	51.3	46.5	34.3	6.2	1.9	1.5	56.1
Crop land harvested. 1929	30.4	28.4	35.3	52.2	22.1	30.7	17.3	6.3	.2	1.2	75.0
1924	32.2	29.7	36.8	46.0	24.7	32.7	18.3	5.1	.1	1.0	75.5
Plowable pasture. 1929	2.8	5.8	6.2	71.3	4.5	1.7	38.4	12.0	2.6	2.6	44.4
Other pasture [1]..1929	2.6	4.9	7.3	74.8	2.3	1.6	35.5	15.4	3.0	1.5	44.9

[1] Other than plowabie or woodland pasture.

[2] Less than one-tenth of 1 percent.

TABLE 54.—NUMBER OF FARMS REPORTING ACREAGE IN CROPS, AND PRODUCTION, AND VALUE OF SPECIFIED CROPS ON ALL FARMS, AND ON FARMS OPERATED BY COLORED FARMERS, BY SOUTHERN DIVISIONS, AND STATES, AND SELECTED NORTHERN STATES: 1929

[Colored farmers include Negroes, Indians, Chinese, Japanese, and all other nonwhite races]

DIVISION AND STATE	NUMBER OF FARMS REPORTING			ACREAGE IN CROPS			PRODUCTION OF CROPS			VALUE OF CROPS		
	Total	Colored farmers		All farmers	Colored farmers		All farmers	Colored farmers		All farmers	Colored farmers	
		Number	Percent		Number	Percent		Number	Percent		Amount	Percent
OATS THRESHED FOR GRAIN												
The South	**142, 545**	**6, 983**	**4. 9**	**2, 413, 864**	**62, 980**	**2. 6**	*Bushels* 54, 252, 531	*Bushels* 1, 175, 912	2. 2	**$27, 807, 581**	**$675, 219**	**2. 4**
South Atlantic	58, 373	4, 831	8. 3	363, 932	22, 210	6. 1	8, 219, 765	403, 548	4. 9	5, 695, 996	301, 569	5. 3
East South Central	10, 473	387	3. 7	98, 889	2, 470	2. 5	1, 720, 423	40, 684	2. 4	1, 092, 245	27, 973	2. 6
West South Central	73, 699	1, 765	2. 4	1, 951, 043	28, 300	2. 0	44, 312, 343	731, 680	1. 7	21, 019, 340	345, 677	1. 6
SOUTH ATLANTIC:												
Delaware	287	5	1. 7	1, 862	25	1. 3	52, 947	830	1. 6	32, 283	506	1. 6
Maryland	6, 593	60	. 9	41, 734	249	. 6	1, 164, 583	5, 538	. 5	650, 922	3, 095	. 5
District of Columbia	-	-	-	-	-	-	-	-	-	-	-	-
Florida	-	-	-	-	-	-	-	-	-	-	-	-
Virginia	9, 696	425	4. 4	54, 338	1, 473	2. 7	1, 127, 824	22, 365	2. 0	730, 282	14, 482	2. 0
West Virginia	11, 522	56	. 5	62, 857	210	. 3	1, 514, 150	4, 348	. 3	970, 247	2, 786	. 3
North Carolina	11, 602	754	6. 5	49, 831	2, 612	5. 2	949, 082	40, 508	4. 3	709, 619	30, 287	4. 3
South Carolina	11, 393	2, 503	22. 0	94, 137	12, 440	13. 2	2, 229, 914	245, 692	11. 0	1, 666, 953	183, 665	11. 0
Georgia	7, 185	1, 020	14. 2	58, 051	5, 139	8. 9	1, 165, 731	83, 278	7. 1	923, 346	65, 962	7. 1
Florida	95	8	8. 4	1, 122	62	5. 5	15, 534	989	6. 4	12, 344	786	6. 4
EAST SOUTH CENTRAL:												
Kentucky	4, 734	43	. 9	45, 966	366	. 8	731, 543	4, 980	. 7	424, 087	2, 887	. 7
Tennessee	3, 935	85	2. 2	30, 660	678	2. 2	478, 230	9, 434	2. 0	300, 153	5, 921	2. 0
Alabama	1, 267	207	16. 3	12, 299	1, 123	9. 1	245, 616	20, 243	8. 2	180, 923	14, 911	8. 2
Mississippi	537	52	9. 7	9, 964	308	3. 1	265, 034	6, 027	2. 3	187, 082	4, 254	2. 3
WEST SOUTH CENTRAL:												
Arkansas	2, 407	29	1. 2	32, 394	207	. 6	653, 887	6, 219	1. 0	362, 006	3, 443	1. 0
Louisiana	325	30	9. 2	7, 716	251	3. 3	201, 315	6, 991	3. 5	134, 153	4, 659	3. 5
Oklahoma	33, 544	1, 126	3. 4	762, 823	25, 833	3. 4	16, 196, 880	439, 616	2. 7	7, 546, 828	204, 836	2. 7
Texas	37, 423	580	1. 5	1, 148, 110	12, 009	1. 0	27, 260, 261	278, 854	1. 0	12, 976, 353	132, 739	1. 0
WHEAT												
The South	**263, 536**	**30, 677**	**11. 6**	**9, 873, 808**	**200, 816**	**2. 0**	*Bushels* 125, 944, 868	*Bushels* 2, 140, 135	1. 7	**$132, 035, 012**	**$2, 590, 448**	**2. 0**
South Atlantic	166, 091	29, 084	17. 5	1, 826, 267	151, 557	8. 3	25, 543, 757	1, 605, 538	6. 3	31, 633, 951	2, 040, 079	6. 4
East South Central	34, 646	797	2. 3	485, 922	9, 721	2. 0	4, 985, 794	87, 519	1. 8	6, 223, 874	110, 698	1. 8
West South Central	62, 799	796	1. 3	7, 561, 619	39, 538	. 5	95, 415, 317	447, 078	. 5	94, 177, 187	439, 671	. 5
SOUTH ATLANTIC:												
Delaware	4, 127	210	5. 1	105, 735	4, 536	4. 3	1, 975, 161	71, 616	3. 6	2, 322, 411	84, 201	3. 6
Maryland	19, 378	1, 141	5. 9	506, 499	23, 038	4. 5	9, 095, 169	356, 027	3. 9	10, 757, 043	421, 060	3. 9
District of Columbia	-	-	-	-	-	-	-	-	-	-	-	-
Virginia	59, 390	12, 061	20. 3	656, 968	60, 875	9. 3	8, 575, 461	642, 705	7. 5	10, 536, 082	789, 648	7. 5
West Virginia	9, 999	87	. 9	104, 282	901	. 9	1, 360, 285	11, 518	. 8	1, 704, 684	14, 433	. 8
North Carolina	49, 070	7, 089	14. 4	352, 634	35, 934	10. 2	3, 623, 003	314, 927	8. 7	5, 017, 966	436, 183	8. 7
South Carolina	14, 063	5, 579	39. 7	52, 129	16, 395	31. 5	505, 206	137, 111	27. 1	703, 654	190, 969	27. 1
Georgia	10, 064	2, 917	29. 0	48, 020	9, 878	20. 6	409, 472	71, 634	17. 5	592, 111	103, 585	17. 5
Florida	-	-	-	-	-	-	-	-	-	-	-	-
EAST SOUTH CENTRAL:												
Kentucky	12, 553	203	1. 6	204, 131	2, 623	1. 3	2, 483, 443	28, 654	1. 2	3, 018, 620	35, 347	1. 2
Tennessee	21, 804	562	2. 6	279, 885	6, 997	2. 5	2, 480, 846	57, 803	2. 3	3, 178, 701	74, 061	2. 3
Alabama	277	29	10. 5	1, 524	70	4. 6	15, 070	477	3. 2	18, 959	600	3. 2
Mississippi	12	3	25. 0	382	31	8. 1	6, 435	585	9. 1	7, 594	690	9. 1
WEST SOUTH CENTRAL:												
Arkansas	1, 048	3	. 3	16, 535	22	. 1	153, 281	180	. 1	173, 362	204	. 1
Louisiana	5	-	-	15	-	-	144	-	-	179	-	-
Oklahoma	38, 688	606	1. 6	4, 575, 558	29, 002	. 6	51, 184, 128	292, 105	. 6	49, 844, 440	284, 375	. 6
Texas	23, 058	187	. 8	2, 969, 511	10, 514	. 4	44, 077, 764	154, 793	. 4	44, 159, 206	155, 092	. 4
COTTON												
The South	**1, 958, 927**	**736, 070**	**37. 6**	**42, 222, 592**	**12, 215, 136**	**28. 9**	*Bales* 13, 853, 599	*Bales* 4, 492, 807	32. 4	**$1, 183, 023, 630**	**$384, 333, 320**	**32. 5**
South Atlantic	516, 006	213, 773	41. 4	7, 231, 976	3, 088, 846	42. 7	3, 031, 647	1, 201, 385	39. 6	250, 819, 547	99, 382, 834	39. 6
East South Central	603, 592	287, 715	47. 7	8, 636, 981	4, 422, 648	51. 2	3, 700, 842	1, 825, 372	49. 3	320, 960, 920	159, 567, 989	49. 7
West South Central	839, 329	234, 582	27. 9	26, 353, 635	4, 703, 642	17. 8	7, 121, 110	1, 466, 050	20. 6	611, 234, 163	125, 382, 497	20. 5
SOUTH ATLANTIC:												
Virginia	14, 005	7, 646	54. 6	88, 446	45, 768	51. 7	52, 442	25, 791	49. 2	4, 330, 566	2, 129, 774	49. 2
North Carolina	151, 664	57, 975	38. 2	1, 640, 398	694, 436	42. 3	764, 328	297, 838	39. 0	61, 975, 646	24, 150, 237	39. 0
South Carolina	131, 426	67, 673	51. 5	1, 973, 228	980, 312	49. 7	835, 963	390, 999	46. 8	69, 383, 426	32, 452, 214	46. 8
Georgia	206, 734	76, 221	36. 9	3, 406, 443	1, 335, 211	39. 2	1, 344, 488	479, 031	35. 6	112, 329, 292	40, 022, 085	35. 6
Florida	12, 177	4, 258	35. 0	123, 461	33, 119	26. 8	34, 426	7, 726	22. 4	2, 800, 617	628, 524	22. 4
EAST SOUTH CENTRAL:												
Kentucky	1, 247	299	24. 0	15, 898	6, 940	43. 7	8, 955	3, 893	43. 5	709, 819	308, 579	43. 5
Tennessee	88, 346	26, 164	29. 6	1, 045, 051	376, 634	36. 0	503, 816	163, 440	32. 4	43, 391, 627	14, 076, 424	32. 4
Alabama	231, 824	88, 329	38. 1	3, 566, 498	1, 444, 553	40. 5	1, 312, 963	423, 198	32. 2	110, 484, 056	35, 611, 537	32. 2
Mississippi	282, 175	172, 923	61. 3	4, 009, 534	2, 594, 521	64. 7	1, 875, 108	1, 234, 841	65. 9	166, 384, 418	109, 571, 449	65. 9
WEST SOUTH CENTRAL:												
Arkansas	192, 209	75, 122	39. 1	3, 446, 485	1, 327, 729	38. 5	1, 398, 475	540, 522	38. 7	121, 193. 069	46, 842, 110	38. 7
Louisiana	128, 537	65, 823	51. 2	1, 945, 354	1, 026, 379	52. 8	798, 828	425, 386	53. 3	66, 265, 947	35, 287, 454	53. 3
Oklahoma	123, 477	16, 207	13. 1	4, 148, 228	380, 089	9. 2	1, 130, 415	88, 017	7. 8	90, 551, 892	7, 050, 602	7. 8
Texas	395, 106	77, 430	19. 6	16, 813, 568	1, 969, 445	11. 7	3, 793, 392	412, 125	10. 9	333, 223, 255	36, 202, 331	10. 9

TABLE 54.—NUMBER OF FARMS REPORTING ACREAGE IN CROPS, AND PRODUCTION, AND VALUE OF SPECIFIED CROPS ON ALL FARMS, AND ON FARMS OPERATED BY COLORED FARMERS, BY SOUTHERN DIVISIONS, AND STATES, AND SELECTED NORTHERN STATES: 1929—Continued

[See note at head of table]

DIVISION AND STATE	FARMS OPERATED BY COLORED—											
	Owners				Tenants				Managers			
	Farms reporting	Acres	Production	Value	Farms reporting	Acres	Production	Value	Farms reporting	Acres	Production	Value
	OATS THRESHED FOR GRAIN											
The South	**2,459**	**23,219**	*Bushels* **405,386**	**$218,440**	**4,476**	**38,781**	*Bushels* **749,596**	**$443,296**	**48**	**980**	*Bushels* **20,930**	**$13,483**
South Atlantic	1,586	6,021	99,778	72,724	3,215	15,636	291,872	220,198	30	553	11,898	8,647
East South Central	155	869	13,187	8,945	227	1,494	24,750	17,153	5	107	2,747	1,875
West South Central	718	16,329	292,421	136,771	1,034	21,651	432,974	205,945	13	320	6,285	2,961
SOUTH ATLANTIC:												
Delaware	3	13	185	113	1	2	20	12	1	10	625	381
Maryland	32	112	2,699	1,508	22	99	1,955	1,093	6	38	884	494
District of Columbia	-	-	-	-	-	-	-	-	-	-	-	-
Virginia	333	1,089	16,310	10,561	89	332	4,955	3,208	3	52	1,100	713
West Virginia	45	158	3,047	1,953	10	50	1,171	750	1	2	130	83
North Carolina	301	886	14,157	10,585	453	1,726	26,351	19,702	-	-	-	-
South Carolina	660	2,816	49,406	36,933	1,832	9,318	190,026	142,052	11	306	6,260	4,689
Georgia	207	902	13,101	10,377	805	4,092	67,278	53,289	8	145	2,899	2,206
Florida	5	45	873	694	3	17	116	92	-	-	-	-
EAST SOUTH CENTRAL:												
Kentucky	24	172	2,360	1,368	19	194	2,620	1,519	-	-	-	-
Tennessee	38	233	3,055	1,918	45	405	5,349	3,357	2	35	1,030	646
Alabama	59	330	5,627	4,145	146	761	14,076	10,368	2	32	540	398
Mississippi	34	134	2,145	1,514	17	134	2,705	1,909	1	40	1,177	831
WEST SOUTH CENTRAL:												
Arkansas	16	81	643	356	13	126	5,576	3,087	-	-	-	-
Louisiana	10	38	653	435	20	213	6,338	4,224	-	-	-	-
Oklahoma	600	14,812	258,114	120,266	520	10,859	178,432	83,139	6	162	3,070	1,431
Texas	92	1,398	33,011	15,714	481	10,453	242,628	115,495	7	158	3,215	1,530
	WHEAT											
The South	**14,331**	**85,737**	*Bushels* **863,329**	**$1,040,025**	**16,207**	**110,030**	*Bushels* **1,195,830**	**$1,454,708**	**139**	**5,049**	*Bushels* **80,976**	**$95,715**
South Atlantic	13,618	64,725	656,282	830,202	15,341	82,408	874,706	1,121,123	125	4,424	74,550	88,754
East South Central	361	3,242	28,012	35,341	431	6,289	57,096	72,344	5	190	2,411	3,013
West South Central	352	17,770	179,035	174,482	435	21,333	264,028	261,241	9	435	4,015	3,948
SOUTH ATLANTIC:												
Delaware	60	728	9,626	11,318	143	3,497	55,514	65,269	7	311	6,476	7,614
Maryland	390	4,463	63,594	75,210	675	15,235	234,938	277,853	76	3,340	57,495	67,997
District of Columbia	-	-	-	-	-	-	-	-	-	-	-	-
Virginia	8,239	38,795	412,241	506,492	3,792	21,435	221,596	272,260	30	645	8,868	10,896
West Virginia	62	327	3,640	4,561	23	509	6,779	8,495	2	65	1,099	1,377
North Carolina	3,055	14,771	124,356	172,237	4,032	21,136	190,366	263,662	2	27	205	284
South Carolina	1,228	3,658	28,974	40,355	4,348	12,728	108,089	150,547	3	9	48	67
Georgia	584	1,983	13,851	20,029	2,328	7,868	57,424	83,037	5	27	359	519
Florida	-	-	-	-	-	-	-	-	-	-	-	-
EAST SOUTH CENTRAL:												
Kentucky	120	1,169	11,325	13,970	82	1,364	15,729	19,403	1	90	1,600	1,974
Tennessee	219	2,021	16,313	20,901	339	4,876	40,679	52,121	4	100	811	1,039
Alabama	21	51	364	458	8	19	113	142	-	-	-	-
Mississippi	1	1	10	12	2	30	575	678	-	-	-	-
WEST SOUTH CENTRAL:												
Arkansas	2	8	50	57	1	14	130	147	-	-	-	-
Louisiana	-	-	-	-	-	-	-	-	-	-	-	-
Oklahoma	326	17,284	172,764	168,192	274	11,368	116,676	113,588	6	350	2,665	2,595
Texas	24	478	6,221	6,233	160	9,951	147,222	147,506	3	85	1,350	1,335
	COTTON											
The South	**120,939**	**1,748,577**	*Bales* **533,141**	**$45,408,734**	**614,833**	**10,455,728**	*Bales* **3,955,698**	**$338,586,565**	**298**	**10,831**	*Bales* **3,968**	**$338,021**
South Atlantic	39,183	411,737	148,277	12,226,024	174,466	2,674,024	1,051,809	87,048,937	124	3,085	1,299	107,873
East South Central	39,730	534,383	184,518	16,025,193	247,913	3,885,374	1,639,401	143,415,573	72	2,891	1,453	127,223
West South Central	42,026	802,457	200,346	17,157,517	192,454	3,896,330	1,264,488	108,122,055	102	4,855	1,216	102,925
SOUTH ATLANTIC:												
Virginia	3,261	16,729	9,073	749,232	4,379	28,992	16,689	1,378,147	6	47	29	2,395
North Carolina	13,253	121,711	49,522	4,015,498	44,703	572,446	248,178	20,123,549	19	279	138	11,190
South Carolina	12,488	135,201	46,492	3,858,752	55,135	843,895	344,031	28,553,955	50	1,216	476	39,507
Georgia	8,549	126,767	40,505	3,384,112	67,626	1,206,954	437,882	36,584,168	46	1,490	644	53,805
Florida	1,632	11,329	2,685	218,430	2,623	21,737	5,029	409,118	3	53	12	976
EAST SOUTH CENTRAL:												
Kentucky	11	37	19	1,506	288	6,903	3,874	307,073	-	-	-	-
Tennessee	4,073	49,195	20,592	1,773,505	22,086	327,368	142,805	12,299,215	5	71	43	3,704
Alabama	14,671	215,577	64,088	5,392,918	73,641	1,228,086	358,762	30,189,335	17	890	348	29,284
Mississippi	20,975	269,574	99,819	8,857,264	151,898	2,323,017	1,133,960	100,619,950	50	1,930	1,062	94,235
WEST SOUTH CENTRAL:												
Arkansas	10,730	180,371	58,157	5,039,937	64,372	1,146,754	482,124	41,781,288	20	604	241	20,885
Louisiana	8,548	130,660	44,146	3,662,086	57,261	895,346	381,037	31,608,528	14	373	203	16,840
Oklahoma	4,702	93,412	20,277	1,624,289	11,480	285,512	67,402	5,399,237	25	1,165	338	27,076
Texas	18,046	398,014	77,766	6,831,205	59,341	1,568,718	333,925	29,333,002	43	2,713	434	38,124

TABLE 54.—NUMBER OF FARMS REPORTING ACREAGE IN CROPS, AND PRODUCTION, AND VALUE OF SPECIFIED CROPS ON ALL FARMS, AND ON FARMS OPERATED BY COLORED FARMERS, BY SOUTHERN DIVISIONS, AND STATES, AND SELECTED NORTHERN STATES: 1929—Continued

[See note at head of table]

DIVISION AND STATE	NUMBER OF FARMS REPORTING			ACREAGE IN CROPS			PRODUCTION OF CROPS			VALUE OF CROPS		
	Total	Colored farmers		All farmers	Colored farmers		All farmers	Colored farmers		All farmers	Colored farmers	
		Number	Percent		Number	Percent		Number	Percent		Amount	Percent
							COTTON SEED					
The South	----	----	----	----	----	----	*Tons* 6,651,136	*Tons* 2,154,656	32.8	$199,782,253	$65,606,244	32.8
South Atlantic	----	----	----	----	----	----	1,403,518	555,587	39.6	39,205,354	15,515,287	39.6
East South Central	----	----	----	----	----	----	1,789,381	890,416	49.8	56,087,373	28,351,562	50.5
West South Central	----	----	----	----	----	----	3,368,237	708,653	21.0	104,489,526	21,739,395	20.8
SOUTH ATLANTIC:												
Virginia	----	----	----	----	----	----	25,266	12,371	49.0	757,980	371,130	49.0
North Carolina	----	----	----	----	----	----	354,164	137,679	38.9	10,217,684	3,972,060	38.9
South Carolina	----	----	----	----	----	----	381,260	177,807	46.6	10,458,453	4,877,475	46.6
Georgia	----	----	----	----	----	----	625,735	223,884	35.8	17,290,675	6,186,493	35.8
Florida	----	----	----	----	----	----	17,093	3,846	22.5	480,562	108,129	22.5
EAST SOUTH CENTRAL:												
Kentucky	----	----	----	----	----	----	4,465	1,942	43.5	125,020	54,376	43.5
Tennessee	----	----	----	----	----	----	240,613	78,648	32.7	7,275,654	2,378,158	32.7
Alabama	----	----	----	----	----	----	629,410	203,214	32.3	18,702,817	6,038,471	32.3
Mississippi	----	----	----	----	----	----	914,893	606,612	66.3	29,983,882	19,880,557	66.3
WEST SOUTH CENTRAL:												
Arkansas	----	----	----	----	----	----	685,902	267,657	39.0	20,850,910	8,136,573	39.0
Louisiana	----	----	----	----	----	----	385,476	204,952	53.2	11,654,412	6,196,482	53.2
Oklahoma	----	----	----	----	----	----	534,123	43,021	8.1	16,440,681	1,324,217	8.1
Texas	----	----	----	----	----	----	1,762,736	193,023	11.0	55,543,523	6,082,123	11.0
							SWEETPOTATOES AND YAMS					
The South	**1,021,397**	**301,844**	**29.6**	**602,573**	**166,141**	**27.6**	*Bushels* **60,127,194**	*Bushels* **14,958,279**	**24.9**	**$60,486,855**	**$14,731,655**	**24.4**
South Atlantic	424,820	135,270	31.8	263,674	77,036	29.2	29,075,358	7,532,265	25.9	27,738,266	7,097,510	25.6
East South Central	392,655	109,733	27.9	189,435	53,878	28.4	19,507,896	4,979,281	25.5	19,759,145	4,933,163	25.0
West South Central	203,922	56,841	27.9	149,464	35,227	23.6	11,543,940	2,446,733	21.2	12,989,444	2,700,982	20.8
SOUTH ATLANTIC:												
Delaware	4,150	367	8.8	6,106	484	7.9	884,527	61,178	6.9	850,932	58,854	6.9
Maryland	8,148	1,176	14.4	8,984	996	11.1	1,629,673	173,956	10.7	1,599,256	170,709	10.7
District of Columbia	39	3	7.7	77	3	3.9	7,880	310	3.9	12,214	481	3.9
Virginia	58,473	18,259	31.2	35,720	11,617	32.5	5,042,596	1,545,236	30.6	4,646,629	1,423,897	30.6
West Virginia	7,959	16	.2	1,051	3	.3	96,776	203	.2	158,326	332	.2
North Carolina	130,585	31,434	24.1	60,352	13,132	21.8	6,716,596	1,292,998	19.3	6,223,560	1,198,085	19.3
South Carolina	78,092	38,558	49.4	46,776	21,473	45.9	5,011,099	1,968,343	39.3	4,307,912	1,692,133	39.3
Georgia	116,702	39,584	33.9	84,855	24,440	28.8	7,889,447	2,127,760	27.0	8,064,572	2,174,991	27.0
Florida	20,672	5,873	28.4	19,753	4,888	24.7	1,796,764	362,281	20.2	1,874,865	378,028	20.2
EAST SOUTH CENTRAL:												
Kentucky	61,262	1,326	2.2	14,076	392	2.8	1,266,724	37,004	2.9	1,560,182	45,577	2.9
Tennessee	98,125	9,232	9.4	53,842	5,072	9.4	5,498,467	445,664	8.1	5,642,747	457,358	8.1
Alabama	126,125	49,410	39.2	68,105	27,533	40.4	6,601,508	2,361,303	35.8	6,447,166	2,306,096	35.8
Mississippi	107,143	49,765	46.4	53,412	20,881	39.1	6,141,197	2,135,310	34.8	6,109,050	2,124,132	34.8
WEST SOUTH CENTRAL:												
Arkansas	56,417	12,732	22.6	22,235	4,174	18.8	1,863,240	315,324	16.9	2,290,935	387,705	16.9
Louisiana	65,316	26,433	40.5	66,579	20,952	31.5	4,953,138	1,443,584	29.1	5,168,424	1,506,329	29.1
Oklahoma	22,388	3,534	15.8	15,998	1,864	11.7	1,334,798	124,672	9.3	1,528,837	142,795	9.3
Texas	59,801	14,142	23.6	44,652	8,237	18.4	3,392,764	563,153	16.6	4,001,248	664,153	16.6
							POTATOES (*Irish or white*)					
The South	**1,134,838**	**145,642**	**12.8**	**544,308**	**55,598**	**10.2**	*Bushels* **54,710,592**	*Bushels* **5,502,606**	**10.1**	**$69,312,331**	**$6,841,755**	**9.9**
South Atlantic	442,363	70,451	15.9	291,075	35,207	12.1	34,947,918	4,297,774	12.3	45,020,629	5,307,023	11.8
East South Central	372,342	32,531	8.7	118,202	6,956	5.9	10,089,080	431,652	4.3	12,861,351	599,069	4.7
West South Central	320,133	42,660	13.3	135,031	13,435	9.9	9,673,594	773,180	8.0	11,430,351	935,663	8.2
SOUTH ATLANTIC:												
Delaware	6,755	553	8.2	4,234	292	6.9	340,738	19,480	5.7	484,876	27,720	5.7
Maryland	29,755	2,723	9.2	29,958	1,712	5.7	3,366,152	190,965	5.7	4,611,931	261,639	5.7
District of Columbia	39	4	10.3	61	3	4.9	3,973	261	6.6	5,761	378	6.6
Virginia	114,740	23,493	20.5	102,656	19,579	19.1	15,244,216	2,961,579	19.4	18,642,804	3,621,841	19.4
West Virginia	69,086	322	.5	35,924	150	.4	3,745,941	12,503	.3	5,057,826	16,882	.3
North Carolina	132,771	23,951	18.0	61,507	7,935	12.9	6,072,709	701,753	11.6	6,992,206	808,009	11.6
South Carolina	32,422	10,331	31.9	20,323	2,931	14.4	2,580,248	226,571	8.8	3,202,698	281,228	8.8
Georgia	49,682	8,289	16.7	12,952	1,793	13.8	879,618	97,727	11.1	1,219,568	135,496	11.1
Florida	7,113	785	11.0	23,460	812	3.5	2,714,323	86,935	3.2	4,802,959	153,830	3.2
EAST SOUTH CENTRAL:												
Kentucky	136,618	2,625	1.9	49,250	631	1.3	4,651,948	47,998	1.0	5,700,661	58,818	1.0
Tennessee	129,948	9,119	7.0	38,651	1,954	5.1	3,129,990	113,363	3.6	3,760,125	136,185	3.6
Alabama	66,431	9,424	14.2	21,256	2,015	9.5	1,609,525	121,638	7.6	2,331,052	176,167	7.6
Mississippi	39,345	11,363	28.9	9,045	2,356	26.0	697,617	148,653	21.3	1,069,513	227,899	21.3
WEST SOUTH CENTRAL:												
Arkansas	101,154	13,293	13.1	29,215	2,783	9.5	2,516,745	183,958	7.3	2,818,434	206,010	7.3
Louisiana	36,092	10,629	29.4	27,466	4,496	16.4	1,478,967	239,655	16.2	2,056,651	333,264	16.2
Oklahoma	85,488	7,283	8.5	38,564	3,154	8.2	2,904,666	197,378	6.8	2,803,165	190,481	6.8
Texas	97,399	11,455	11.8	39,786	3,002	7.5	2,773,216	152,189	5.5	3,752,101	205,908	5.5

TABLE 54.—NUMBER OF FARMS REPORTING ACREAGE IN CROPS, AND PRODUCTION, AND VALUE OF SPECIFIED CROPS ON ALL FARMS, AND ON FARMS OPERATED BY COLORED FARMERS, BY SOUTHERN DIVISIONS, AND STATES, AND SELECTED NORTHERN STATES: 1929—Continued

[See note at head of table]

DIVISION AND STATE	FARMS OPERATED BY COLORED—											
	Owners				Tenants				Managers			
	Farms reporting	Acres	Production	Value	Farms reporting	Acres	Production	Value	Farms reporting	Acres	Production	Value
	COTTON SEED											
			Tons				*Tons*				*Tons*	
The South	-----	-----	253, 622	$7, 686, 122	-----	-----	1, 899, 135	$57, 862, 612	-----	-----	1, 899	$57, 510
South Atlantic	-----	-----	69, 336	1, 950, 616	-----	-----	485, 645	13, 547, 860	-----	-----	606	16, 811
East South Central	-----	-----	89, 072	2, 799, 961	-----	-----	800, 631	25, 528, 794	-----	-----	713	22, 807
West South Central	-----	-----	95, 214	2, 935, 545	-----	-----	612, 859	18, 785, 958	-----	-----	580	17, 892
SOUTH ATLANTIC:												
Virginia	-----	-----	4, 346	130, 380	-----	-----	8, 012	240, 360	-----	-----	13	390
North Carolina	-----	-----	23, 072	665, 631	-----	-----	114, 543	3, 304, 583	-----	-----	64	1, 846
South Carolina	-----	-----	21, 583	592, 050	-----	-----	155, 998	4, 279, 226	-----	-----	226	6, 199
Georgia	-----	-----	18, 994	524, 853	-----	-----	204, 593	5, 653, 433	-----	-----	297	8, 207
Florida	-----	-----	1, 341	37, 702	-----	-----	2, 499	70, 258	-----	-----	6	169
EAST SOUTH CENTRAL:												
Kentucky	-----	-----	10	280	-----	-----	1, 932	54, 096	-----	-----	-----	-----
Tennessee	-----	-----	9, 925	300, 112	-----	-----	68, 702	2, 077, 411	-----	-----	21	635
Alabama	-----	-----	30, 735	913, 285	-----	-----	172, 313	5, 120, 253	-----	-----	166	4, 933
Mississippi	-----	-----	48, 402	1, 586, 284	-----	-----	557, 684	18, 277, 034	-----	-----	526	17, 239
WEST SOUTH CENTRAL:												
Arkansas	-----	-----	28, 598	869, 358	-----	-----	238, 925	7, 263, 142	-----	-----	134	4, 073
Louisiana	-----	-----	20, 071	606, 823	-----	-----	184, 792	5, 586, 968	-----	-----	89	2, 691
Oklahoma	-----	-----	9, 958	306, 514	-----	-----	32, 896	1, 012, 562	-----	-----	167	5, 141
Texas	-----	-----	36, 587	1, 152, 850	-----	-----	156, 246	4, 923, 286	-----	-----	190	5, 987
	SWEETPOTATOES AND YAMS											
			Bushels				*Bushels*				*Bushels*	
The South	89, 277	50, 801	4, 302, 500	$4, 258, 937	212, 307	114, 732	10, 602, 109	$10, 418, 946	260	608	53, 670	$53, 772
South Atlantic	44, 499	24, 813	2, 115, 723	1, 981, 466	90, 606	51, 932	5, 384, 258	5, 085, 015	165	291	32, 284	31, 029
East South Central	27, 010	14, 693	1, 406, 754	1, 399, 128	82, 676	39, 062	3, 561, 106	3, 522, 716	47	123	11, 421	11, 319
West South Central	17, 768	11, 295	780, 023	878, 343	39, 025	23, 738	1, 656, 745	1, 811, 215	48	194	9, 965	11, 424
SOUTH ATLANTIC:												
Delaware	184	149	16, 527	15, 899	179	334	44, 571	42, 878	4	1	80	77
Maryland	712	395	48, 123	47, 225	447	561	119, 217	116, 992	17	40	6, 616	6, 492
District of Columbia	1	1	60	93	1	1	50	78	1	1	200	310
Virginia	11, 679	3, 541	360, 625	332, 307	6, 555	7, 997	1, 174, 357	1, 082, 141	25	79	10, 254	9, 449
West Virginia	8	1	91	149	6	1	85	139	2	1	27	44
North Carolina	10, 643	5, 275	477, 072	442, 052	20, 773	7, 828	813, 371	753, 665	18	29	2, 555	2, 368
South Carolina	11, 238	7, 871	617, 665	530, 990	27, 284	13, 566	1, 346, 945	1, 157, 934	36	36	3, 733	3, 209
Georgia	6, 918	5, 065	408, 871	417, 947	32, 630	19, 320	1, 713, 147	1, 751, 174	36	55	5, 742	5, 870
Florida	3, 116	2, 515	186, 689	194, 804	2, 731	2, 324	172, 515	180, 014	26	49	3, 077	3, 210
EAST SOUTH CENTRAL:												
Kentucky	832	254	24, 323	29, 958	491	136	12, 548	15, 455	3	2	133	164
Tennessee	2, 959	1, 483	123, 450	126, 689	6, 262	3, 570	320, 879	329, 299	11	19	1, 335	1, 370
Alabama	10, 337	6, 123	546, 125	533, 357	39, 060	21, 341	1, 808, 751	1, 766, 462	13	69	6, 427	6, 277
Mississippi	12, 882	6, 833	712, 856	709, 124	36, 863	14, 015	1, 418, 928	1, 411, 500	20	33	3, 526	3, 508
WEST SOUTH CENTRAL:												
Arkansas	4, 032	1, 676	124, 161	152, 661	8, 693	2, 474	189, 318	232, 775	7	24	1, 845	2, 269
Louisiana	5, 742	4, 913	338, 653	353, 373	20, 674	15, 986	1, 102, 808	1, 150, 741	17	53	2, 123	2, 215
Oklahoma	1, 557	763	52, 682	60, 340	1, 967	1, 010	68, 088	77, 986	10	91	3, 902	4, 469
Texas	6, 437	3, 943	264, 527	311, 969	7, 691	4, 268	296, 531	349, 713	14	26	2, 095	2, 471
	POTATOES (*Irish or white*)											
			Bushels				*Bushels*				*Bushels*	
The South	54, 894	19, 141	1, 642, 792	$2, 050, 441	90, 501	35, 802	3, 791, 887	$4, 704, 727	247	655	67, 927	$86, 587
South Atlantic	29, 398	11, 693	1, 184, 295	1, 481, 329	40, 892	23, 048	3, 056, 689	3, 753, 234	161	466	56, 790	72, 460
East South Central	10, 630	2, 462	164, 027	223, 625	21, 866	4, 446	263, 467	370, 091	35	48	4, 158	5, 353
West South Central	14, 866	4, 986	294, 470	345, 487	27, 743	8, 308	471, 731	581, 402	51	141	6, 979	8, 774
SOUTH ATLANTIC:												
Delaware	284	142	9, 564	13, 610	261	143	9, 441	13, 434	8	7	475	676
Maryland	1, 602	765	64, 928	88, 957	1, 066	857	116, 916	160, 185	55	90	9, 121	12, 497
District of Columbia	2	1	43	62	1	-----	18	26	1	2	200	290
Virginia	15, 448	6, 181	716, 844	876, 659	8, 006	13, 164	2, 210, 167	2, 702, 907	39	234	34, 568	42, 275
West Virginia	259	118	9, 701	13, 099	59	27	2, 307	3, 115	4	5	495	668
North Carolina	7, 142	2, 421	197, 779	227, 726	16, 790	5, 476	499, 044	574, 607	19	38	4, 930	5, 676
South Carolina	2, 692	1, 244	113, 757	141, 199	7, 622	1, 652	109, 325	135, 698	17	35	3, 489	4, 331
Georgia	1, 497	326	17, 801	24, 681	6, 779	1, 458	79, 489	110, 209	13	9	437	606
Florida	472	495	53, 878	95, 336	308	271	29, 982	53, 053	5	46	3, 075	5, 441
EAST SOUTH CENTRAL:												
Kentucky	1, 635	407	30, 395	37, 247	985	220	16, 940	20, 759	5	4	663	812
Tennessee	3, 091	708	44, 669	53, 662	6, 012	1, 221	66, 427	79, 800	16	25	2, 267	2, 723
Alabama	2, 648	675	43, 305	62, 718	6, 770	1, 328	77, 564	112, 335	6	12	769	1, 114
Mississippi	3, 256	672	45, 658	69, 998	8, 099	1, 677	102, 536	157, 197	8	7	459	704
WEST SOUTH CENTRAL:												
Arkansas	4, 230	1, 037	65, 991	73, 902	9, 057	1, 741	117, 261	131, 317	6	5	706	791
Louisiana	2, 573	1, 137	60, 497	84, 127	8, 041	3, 283	175, 274	243, 736	15	76	3, 884	5, 401
Oklahoma	3, 394	1, 564	102, 644	99, 057	3, 870	1, 541	93, 057	89, 805	19	49	1, 677	1, 619
Texas	4, 669	1, 248	65, 338	88, 401	6, 775	1, 743	86, 139	116, 544	11	11	712	963

TABLE 54.—NUMBER OF FARMS REPORTING ACREAGE IN CROPS, AND PRODUCTION, AND VALUE OF SPECIFIED CROPS ON ALL FARMS, AND ON FARMS OPERATED BY COLORED FARMERS, BY SOUTHERN DIVISIONS, AND STATES, AND SELECTED NORTHERN STATES: 1929—Continued

[See note at head of table]

DIVISION AND STATE	NUMBER OF FARMS REPORTING			ACREAGE IN CROPS			PRODUCTION OF CROPS			VALUE OF CROPS		
	Total	Colored farmers		All farmers	Colored farmers		All farmers	Colored farmers		All farmers	Colored farmers	
		Number	Percent		Number	Percent		Number	Percent		Amount	Percent
CORN HARVESTED FOR GRAIN												
							Bushels	*Bushels*				
The South	**2,486,625**	**694,986**	**27.9**	**29,333,688**	**5,996,875**	**20.4**	**512,909,843**	**84,364,162**	**16.4**	**$482,378,609**	**$81,084,039**	**16.8**
South Atlantic	886,379	264,285	29.8	9,509,689	2,470,836	26.0	163,486,667	32,780,540	20.1	160,883,833	32,027,901	19.9
East South Central	867,155	250,087	28.8	9,907,990	2,003,184	20.2	192,673,904	30,958,390	16.1	183,184,844	30,405,281	16.6
West South Central	733,091	180,614	24.6	9,916,009	1,522,855	15.4	156,749,272	20,625,232	13.2	138,309,932	18,650,857	13.5
SOUTH ATLANTIC:												
Delaware	8,405	698	8.3	129,283	8,925	6.9	3,466,565	208,388	6.0	3,037,740	182,610	6.0
Maryland	34,629	4,246	12.3	463,293	41,630	9.0	14,543,218	894,786	6.2	13,305,214	818,617	6.2
District of Columbia	19	1	5.3	77	10	13.0	2,595	125	4.8	2,517	121	4.8
Virginia	143,601	35,551	24.8	1,352,992	260,476	19.3	32,772,810	4,906,425	15.0	33,709,612	5,046,674	15.0
West Virginia	65,682	372	.6	409,984	2,287	.6	11,656,200	60,684	.5	12,614,701	65,674	.5
North Carolina	241,622	67,832	28.1	1,892,416	459,029	24.3	35,608,833	7,503,924	21.1	36,578,861	7,708,340	21.1
South Carolina	136,161	68,719	50.5	1,339,340	532,034	39.7	19,325,825	6,744,183	34.9	19,393,750	6,767,887	34.9
Georgia	223,783	77,993	34.9	3,309,096	1,024,223	31.0	39,492,897	11,108,328	28.1	36,461,260	10,255,606	28.1
Florida	32,477	8,873	27.3	613,208	142,222	23.2	6,617,724	1,353,697	20.5	5,780,178	1,182,372	20.5
EAST SOUTH CENTRAL:												
Kentucky	196,145	6,392	3.3	2,644,643	66,528	2.5	61,008,387	1,592,438	2.6	55,704,705	1,454,001	2.6
Tennessee	206,090	29,754	14.4	2,693,141	266,317	9.9	61,045,986	5,264,668	8.6	56,518,050	4,874,174	8.6
Alabama	231,669	85,497	36.9	2,591,322	778,792	30.1	35,683,874	9,675,069	27.1	36,851,908	9,991,761	27.1
Mississippi	233,251	128,444	55.1	1,978,884	891,547	45.1	34,935,657	14,426,215	41.3	34,110,181	14,085,345	41.3
WEST SOUTH CENTRAL:												
Arkansas	167,168	49,360	29.5	1,756,968	312,055	17.8	27,388,105	4,667,152	17.0	26,522,188	4,519,593	17.0
Louisiana	121,912	55,544	45.6	1,169,698	409,869	35.0	18,279,702	5,813,687	31.8	17,199,004	5,469,981	31.8
Oklahoma	137,213	17,747	12.9	2,913,137	284,872	9.8	44,830,439	3,824,686	8.5	35,884,585	3,061,475	8.5
Texas	306,798	57,963	18.9	4,076,206	516,059	12.7	66,251,026	6,319,707	9.5	58,704,155	5,599,808	9.5
TOBACCO												
							Pounds	*Pounds*				
The South	**386,021**	**70,729**	**18.3**	**1,707,806**	**365,278**	**21.4**	**1,261,395,143**	**238,642,303**	**18.9**	**$225,181,352**	**$42,832,333**	**19.0**
South Atlantic	210,744	61,704	29.3	1,110,687	326,428	29.4	771,948,663	207,587,101	26.9	140,764,200	37,448,486	26.6
East South Central	174,187	8,989	5.2	596,644	38,843	6.5	489,247,190	31,053,096	6.3	84,371,800	5,383,398	6.4
West South Central	1,090	36	3.3	475	7	1.5	199,290	2,106	1.1	45,352	449	1.0
SOUTH ATLANTIC:												
Delaware												
Maryland	5,477	1,676	30.6	32,974	400	28.5	21,624,127	5,326,232	24.6	5,846,647	1,440,086	24.6
District of Columbia												
Virginia	40,631	11,912	29.3	172,134	52,501	30.5	115,825,610	32,073,630	27.7	20,341,061	5,632,706	27.7
West Virginia	4,641	3	1	7,181	3	(1)	5,361,698	1,680	(1)	1,129,045	354	(1)
North Carolina	117,222	35,568	30.3	685,074	212,144	31.0	454,222,610	132,096,917	29.1	82,296,099	23,933,333	29.1
South Carolina	22,519	9,406	41.8	112,852	39,190	34.7	83,302,706	26,767,233	32.1	12,933,344	4,155,805	32.1
Georgia	18,578	2,732	14.7	90,170	11,572	12.8	82,363,722	9,910,692	12.0	15,297,926	1,840,774	12.0
Florida	1,676	407	24.3	10,302	1,618	15.7	9,248,190	1,410,717	15.3	2,920,078	445,428	15.3
EAST SOUTH CENTRAL:												
Kentucky	123,455	5,795	4.7	466,118	25,420	5.5	376,648,533	20,389,130	5.4	64,253,896	3,478,259	5.4
Tennessee	50,478	3,152	6.2	129,973	13,359	10.3	112,236,961	10,611,826	9.5	20,056,786	1,896,337	9.5
Alabama	234	37	15.8	547	64	11.7	357,093	51,820	14.5	60,235	8,741	14.5
Mississippi	20	5	25.0	6			4,603	320	7.0	883	61	6.9
WEST SOUTH CENTRAL:												
Arkansas	929	23	2.5	232	2	.9	94,750	753	.8	20,233	161	.8
Louisiana	39			189			81,047			20,095		
Oklahoma	104	12	11.5	37	4	10.8	15,909	853	5.4	3,488	187	5.4
Texas	18	1	5.6	17	1	5.9	7,584	500	6.6	1,536	101	6.6
CORN HARVESTED FOR GRAIN												
							Bushels	*Bushels*				
SELECTED NORTHERN STATES [2]	933,534	6,384	0.7	25,928,876	110,074	0.4	746,875,409	2,427,687	0.3	$563,495,919	$1,889,981	0.3
New Jersey	13,348	248	1.9	130,616	2,149	1.6	4,978,926	62,374	1.3	4,948,944	61,998	1.3
Pennsylvania	112,654	252	.2	950,074	1,861	.2	35,294,020	60,946	.2	35,047,460	60,520	.2
Ohio	171,005	957	.6	2,911,424	14,856	.5	102,177,194	466,769	.5	76,826,103	350,959	.5
Indiana	142,248	368	.3	3,675,946	6,722	.2	114,871,320	180,983	.2	83,041,558	130,834	.2
Illinois	180,919	739	.4	7,774,070	13,011	.2	275,850,367	306,681	.1	199,346,073	221,626	.1
Missouri	192,019	3,036	1.6	4,837,812	45,628	.9	112,348,071	951,204	.8	92,165,022	780,323	.8
Kansas	121,341	784	.6	5,648,934	25,847	.5	101,355,511	398,730	.4	72,120,759	283,721	.4
TOBACCO												
							Pounds	*Pounds*				
SELECTED NORTHERN STATES [2]	34,710	230	0.7	114,343	530	0.5	111,131,393	411,726	0.4	$16,250,677	$67,564	0.4
New Jersey												
Pennsylvania	7,770	10	.1	40,040	21	.1	50,584,276	25,630	.1	6,072,423	3,077	.1
Ohio	15,220	131	.9	49,575	303	.6	39,828,515	227,580	.6	6,439,674	36,796	.6
Indiana	8,847	61	.7	19,372	184	.9	15,901,768	141,414	.9	2,689,149	23,915	.9
Illinois	276	3	1.1	184			144,552	75	.1	18,364	10	.1
Missouri	2,560	24	.9	5,039	22	.4	4,549,089	16,967	.4	1,006,428	3,754	.4
Kansas	37	1	2.7	133			123,193	60	(1)	24,639	12	(1)

[1] Less than 1/10 of 1 percent.
[2] States having 200 or more Negro farmers who constitute 90 percent or more of the colored farmers in the State.

TABLE 54.—NUMBER OF FARMS REPORTING ACREAGE IN CROPS, AND PRODUCTION, AND VALUE OF SPECIFIED CROPS ON ALL FARMS, AND ON FARMS OPERATED BY COLORED FARMERS, BY SOUTHERN DIVISIONS, AND STATES, AND SELECTED NORTHERN STATES: 1929—Continued

[See note at head of table]

DIVISION AND STATE	FARMS OPERATED BY COLORED— Owners: Farms reporting	Owners: Acres	Owners: Production	Owners: Value	Tenants: Farms reporting	Tenants: Acres	Tenants: Production	Tenants: Value	Managers: Farms reporting	Managers: Acres	Managers: Production	Managers: Value
CORN HARVESTED FOR GRAIN												
The South	**162, 793**	**1, 517, 864**	*Bushels* **20, 830, 659**	**$19, 972, 366**	**531, 530**	**4, 460, 845**	*Bushels* **63, 192, 383**	**$60, 789, 922**	**663**	**18, 166**	*Bushels* **341, 120**	**$321, 751**
South Atlantic	73, 468	627, 601	8, 758, 639	8, 679, 613	190, 416	1, 833, 793	23, 856, 129	23, 189, 740	401	9, 442	165, 772	158, 548
East South Central	45, 777	435, 826	6, 511, 433	6, 360, 553	204, 191	1, 562, 725	24, 358, 955	23, 959, 546	119	4, 633	88, 002	85, 182
West South Central	43, 548	454, 437	5, 560, 587	4, 932, 200	136, 923	1, 064, 327	14, 977, 299	13, 640, 636	143	4, 091	87, 346	78, 021
SOUTH ATLANTIC:												
Delaware	329	2, 816	67, 478	59, 131	355	5, 882	136, 400	119, 527	14	227	4, 510	3, 952
Maryland	2, 268	14, 462	309, 528	283, 179	1, 875	25, 002	536, 535	490, 862	103	2, 166	48, 723	44, 576
District of Columbia									1	10	125	121
Virginia	22, 249	154, 944	2, 795, 366	2, 875, 271	13, 233	104, 057	2, 076, 836	2, 136, 202	69	1, 475	34, 223	35, 201
West Virginia	287	1, 331	35, 960	38, 917	80	891	22, 745	24, 615	5	65	1, 979	2, 142
North Carolina	18, 243	126, 227	1, 980, 891	2, 034, 853	49, 559	332, 261	5, 513, 308	5, 663, 497	30	541	9, 725	9, 990
South Carolina	15, 066	123, 220	1, 552, 059	1, 557, 514	53, 585	407, 389	5, 169, 939	5, 188, 110	68	1, 425	22, 185	22, 263
Georgia	10, 287	136, 967	1, 379, 797	1, 273, 878	67, 632	884, 704	9, 696, 229	8, 951, 906	74	2, 552	32, 302	29, 822
Florida	4, 739	67, 634	637, 560	556, 870	4, 097	73, 607	704, 137	615, 021	37	981	12, 000	10, 481
EAST SOUTH CENTRAL:												
Kentucky	3, 113	28, 923	613, 167	559, 862	3, 269	37, 291	969, 541	885, 255	10	314	9, 730	8, 884
Tennessee	6, 741	64, 592	1, 257, 293	1, 164, 036	22, 987	200, 829	3, 986, 040	3, 690, 385	26	896	21, 335	19, 753
Alabama	15, 056	154, 423	1, 869, 037	1, 930, 216	70, 416	623, 019	7, 789, 116	8, 044, 075	25	1, 350	16, 916	17, 470
Mississippi	20, 867	187, 888	2, 771, 936	2, 706, 439	107, 519	701, 586	11, 614, 258	11, 339, 831	58	2, 073	40, 021	39, 075
WEST SOUTH CENTRAL:												
Arkansas	9, 954	86, 517	1, 064, 938	1, 031, 268	39, 385	224, 742	3, 586, 036	3, 472, 658	21	796	16, 178	15, 667
Louisiana	9, 263	81, 637	1, 051, 729	989, 551	46, 247	327, 388	4, 739, 292	4, 459, 104	34	844	22, 000	21, 326
Oklahoma	6, 831	119, 504	1, 637, 531	1, 310, 764	10, 877	164, 096	2, 164, 397	1, 732, 494	39	1, 272	22, 758	18, 217
Texas	17, 500	166, 779	1, 806, 389	1, 600, 617	40, 414	348, 101	4, 487, 574	3, 976, 380	49	1, 179	25, 744	22, 811
TOBACCO												
The South	**19, 808**	**80, 410**	*Pounds* **50, 460, 761**	**$9, 129, 909**	**50, 881**	**284, 563**	*Pounds* **187, 964, 469**	**$33, 654, 970**	**40**	**305**	*Pounds* **217, 073**	**47, 454**
South Atlantic	16, 022	68, 569	41, 749, 990	7, 623, 913	45, 652	257, 596	165, 656, 371	29, 783, 415	30	263	180, 740	41, 158
East South Central	3, 768	11, 836	8, 709, 464	1, 505, 720	5, 211	26, 965	22, 307, 299	3, 871, 382	10	42	36, 333	6, 296
West South Central	18	5	1, 307	276	18	2	799	173				
SOUTH ATLANTIC:												
Delaware												
Maryland	691	2, 829	1, 572, 189	425, 082	979	6, 542	3, 731, 543	1, 008, 920	6	29	22, 500	6, 084
District of Columbia												
Virginia	5, 504	19, 246	11, 947, 909	2, 098, 268	6, 403	33, 236	20, 114, 621	3, 532, 489	5	19	11, 100	1, 949
West Virginia	3	3	1, 680	354								
North Carolina	7, 168	36, 392	21, 261, 291	3, 852, 123	28, 394	175, 683	110, 814, 286	20, 077, 344	6	69	21, 340	3, 866
South Carolina	1, 876	7, 108	4, 478, 279	695, 285	7, 521	31, 994	22, 230, 654	3, 451, 469	9	88	58, 300	9, 051
Georgia	569	2, 201	1, 791, 998	332, 839	2, 161	9, 363	8, 110, 194	1, 506, 356	2	8	8, 500	1, 579
Florida	211	790	696, 644	219, 962	194	778	655, 073	206, 837	2	50	59, 000	18, 629
EAST SOUTH CENTRAL:												
Kentucky	2, 558	8, 370	6, 246, 516	1, 065, 617	3, 232	17, 021	14, 118, 314	2, 408, 496	5	29	24, 300	4, 146
Tennessee	1, 196	3, 459	2, 459, 833	439, 573	1, 951	9, 887	8, 139, 960	1, 454, 614	5	13	12, 033	2, 150
Alabama	11	7	2, 920	493	26	57	48, 900	8, 248				
Mississippi	3		195	37	2		125	24				
WEST SOUTH CENTRAL:												
Arkansas	9	1	314	67	14	1	439	94				
Louisiana												
Oklahoma	8	3	493	108	4	1	360	79				
Texas	1	1	500	101								
CORN HARVESTED FOR GRAIN												
SELECTED NORTHERN STATES [2]	2, 893	45, 335	*Bushels* 918, 839	$705, 698	3, 422	63, 262	*Bushels* 1, 463, 791	$1, 147, 509	69	1, 477	*Bushels* 45, 057	$36, 774
New Jersey	149	840	23, 549	23, 407	91	1, 205	34, 025	33, 820	8	104	4, 800	4, 771
Pennsylvania	155	828	26, 552	26, 366	81	873	28, 912	28, 710	16	160	5, 482	5, 444
Ohio	600	6, 351	173, 061	130, 123	346	8, 351	287, 758	216, 362	11	154	5, 950	4, 474
Indiana	209	3, 049	78, 939	57, 066	156	3, 591	99, 744	72, 106	3	82	2, 300	1, 662
Illinois	385	5, 886	130, 996	94, 666	347	6, 879	166, 045	119, 994	7	246	9, 640	6, 966
Missouri	929	13, 639	261, 364	214, 411	2, 090	31, 441	676, 585	555, 038	17	548	13, 255	10, 874
Kansas	466	14, 742	224, 378	159, 659	311	10, 922	170, 722	121, 479	7	183	3, 630	2, 583
TOBACCO												
SELECTED NORTHERN STATES [2]	140	250	*Pounds* 195, 874	$32, 424	90	280	*Pounds* 215, 852	$35, 140			*Pounds*	
New Jersey												
Pennsylvania	4	6	7, 330	880	6	15	18, 300	2, 197				
Ohio	87	158	120, 545	19, 490	44	145	107, 035	17, 306				
Indiana	32	73	57, 249	9, 682	29	111	84, 165	14, 233				
Illinois	1	(3)	60	8	2	(3)	15	2				
Missouri	15	13	10, 630	2, 352	9	9	6, 337	1, 402				
Kansas	1		60	12								

[2] States having 200 or more Negro farmers who constitute 90 percent or more of the colored farmers in the State.
[3] Reported in small fractions.

TABLE 54.—NUMBER OF FARMS REPORTING ACREAGE IN CROPS, AND PRODUCTION, AND VALUE OF SPECIFIED CROPS ON ALL FARMS, AND ON FARMS OPERATED BY COLORED FARMERS, BY SOUTHERN DIVISIONS, AND STATES, AND SELECTED NORTHERN STATES: 1929—Continued

[See note at head of table]

DIVISION AND STATE	NUMBER OF FARMS REPORTING			ACREAGE IN CROPS			PRODUCTION OF CROPS			VALUE OF CROPS		
	Total	Colored farmers		All farmers	Colored farmers		All farmers	Colored farmers		All farmers	Colored farmers	
		Number	Percent		Number	Percent		Number	Percent		Amount	Percent
						SWEETPOTATOES AND YAMS						
							Bushels	*Bushels*				
SELECTED NORTHERN STATES [2]	100,133	1,186	1.2	34,727	570	1.6	3,780,577	59,740	1.6	$5,240,341	$82,209	1.6
New Jersey	3,454	80	2.3	12,147	242	2.0	1,498,799	28,850	1.9	2,181,959	42,000	1.9
Pennsylvania	6,839	12	.2	929	----------	----------	87,189	167	.2	145,697	279	.2
Ohio	5,790	55	.9	662	7	1.1	55,829	725	1.3	80,301	1,043	1.3
Indiana	11,159	58	.5	3,160	9	.3	388,843	1,085	.3	563,255	1,572	.3
Illinois	19,341	319	1.6	4,764	143	3.0	458,523	12,150	2.6	560,577	14,854	2.6
Missouri	49,008	582	1.2	9,482	100	1.1	858,010	8,858	1.0	1,099,419	11,350	1.0
Kansas	4,542	80	1.8	3,583	69	1.9	433,384	7,905	1.8	609,133	11,111	1.8
						OATS THRESHED FOR GRAIN						
							Bushels	*Bushels*				
SELECTED NORTHERN STATES [2]	521,611	872	0.2	10,006,724	13,673	0.1	284,767,855	302,084	0.1	$121,867,533	$133,134	0.1
New Jersey	3,215	6	.2	32,193	43	.1	815,609	593	.1	465,196	338	.1
Pennsylvania	101,178	117	.1	866,704	762	.1	22,921,194	19,702	.1	12,911,629	11,098	.1
Ohio	108,379	286	.3	1,542,574	5,050	.3	44,730,590	115,927	.3	19,603,793	50,807	.3
Indiana	77,709	97	.1	1,661,155	1,452	.1	47,465,387	38,864	.1	18,949,308	15,515	.1
Illinois	118,553	89	.1	3,856,217	1,954	.1	128,257,740	49,142	(1)	51,420,401	19,702	(1)
Missouri	56,336	169	.3	1,006,794	2,699	.3	19,050,770	50,196	.3	8,800,699	23,189	.3
Kansas	56,241	108	.2	1,041,087	1,713	.2	21,526,565	27,660	.1	9,716,507	12,485	.1
						POTATOES (*Irish or white*)						
							Bushels	*Bushels*				
SELECTED NORTHERN STATES [2]	751,362	3,923	0.5	523,415	2,337	0.4	51,284,921	177,413	0.3	$76,493,225	$242,631	0.3
New Jersey	9,097	132	1.5	36,963	315	.9	4,733,520	33,417	.7	7,621,482	53,805	.7
Pennsylvania	133,120	186	.1	193,426	206	.1	20,756,447	13,641	.1	32,765,012	21,533	.1
Ohio	138,581	653	.5	104,490	260	.2	10,031,954	21,272	.2	15,477,956	32,820	.2
Indiana	100,786	204	.2	49,642	73	.1	4,145,446	4,501	.1	6,244,311	6,780	.1
Illinois	128,459	858	.7	46,721	504	1.1	3,920,986	33,350	.9	5,304,782	45,120	.9
Missouri	153,664	1,497	1.0	49,863	369	.7	3,926,305	22,659	.6	4,837,150	27,916	.6
Kansas	87,655	393	.4	42,310	610	1.4	3,770,263	48,573	1.3	4,242,532	54,657	1.3
						WHEAT						
							Bushels	*Bushels*				
SELECTED NORTHERN STATES [2]	457,228	1,033	0.2	19,845,401	39,456	0.2	267,741,806	491,611	0.2	$286,956,356	$527,345	0.2
New Jersey	4,836	43	.9	53,579	486	.9	1,100,937	10,587	1.0	1,377,105	13,243	1.0
Pennsylvania	84,496	119	.1	987,100	1,318	.1	17,410,853	25,655	.1	20,982,618	30,895	.1
Ohio	97,387	230	.2	1,563,740	4,040	.3	30,289,579	65,987	.2	35,055,308	76,361	.2
Indiana	65,187	73	.1	1,533,031	1,895	.1	25,190,384	26,537	.1	28,101,520	29,598	.1
Illinois	66,836	76	.1	2,093,399	2,054	.1	30,150,949	25,933	.1	34,094,069	29,354	.1
Missouri	50,166	253	.5	1,533,531	7,231	.5	15,116,509	64,388	.4	16,818,409	71,624	.4
Kansas	88,320	239	.3	12,081,021	22,432	.2	148,482,595	272,524	.2	150,527,327	276,270	.2

[1] Less than 1/10 of 1 percent.

[2] States having 200 or more Negro farmers who constitute 90 percent or more of the colored farmers in the State.

TABLE 54.—NUMBER OF FARMS REPORTING ACREAGE IN CROPS, AND PRODUCTION, AND VALUE OF SPECIFIED CROPS ON ALL FARMS, AND ON FARMS OPERATED BY COLORED FARMERS, BY SOUTHERN DIVISIONS, AND STATES, AND SELECTED NORTHERN STATES: 1929—Continued

[See note at head of table]

DIVISION AND STATE	FARMS OPERATED BY COLORED—											
	Owners				Tenants				Managers			
	Farms reporting	Acres	Production	Value	Farms reporting	Acres	Production	Value	Farms reporting	Acres	Production	Value
	SWEETPOTATOES AND YAMS											
SELECTED NORTHERN STATES [2]	603	293	*Bushels* 30,042	$41,377	575	271	*Bushels* 28,887	$39,737	8	6	*Bushels* 811	$1,095
New Jersey	61	116	14,070	20,483	19	126	14,780	21,517	------	------	------	------
Pennsylvania	10	(3)	97	162	1	(3)	10	17	1	(3)	60	100
Ohio	42	5	489	704	12	2	176	253	1	(3)	60	86
Indiana	35	6	550	797	22	3	515	746	1	(3)	20	29
Illinois	196	88	7,466	9,128	123	55	4,684	5,726	------	------	------	------
Missouri	198	26	2,060	2,640	380	69	6,292	8,062	4	5	506	648
Kansas	61	52	5,310	7,463	18	16	2,430	3,416	1	1	165	232
	OATS THRESHED FOR GRAIN											
SELECTED NORTHERN STATES [2]	437	5,253	*Bushels* 112,019	$49,908	408	7,915	*Bushels* 177,734	$77,680	27	505	*Bushels* 12,331	$5,546
New Jersey	4	17	313	179	1	19	200	114	1	7	80	45
Pennsylvania	68	398	10,464	5,894	40	296	7,304	4,114	9	68	1,934	1,090
Ohio	140	1,739	36,643	16,059	139	3,138	74,133	32,490	7	173	5,151	2,258
Indiana	52	602	16,093	6,425	43	817	22,001	8,783	2	33	770	307
Illinois	39	657	14,883	5,967	46	1,168	31,434	12,602	4	129	2,825	1,133
Missouri	77	1,011	19,569	9,040	91	1,655	30,242	13,971	1	33	385	178
Kansas	57	829	14,054	6,344	48	822	12,420	5,606	3	62	1,186	535
	POTATOES (*Irish or white*)											
SELECTED NORTHERN STATES [2]	1,920	1,045	*Bushels* 77,745	$106,856	1,963	1,233	*Bushels* 95,754	$130,241	40	59	*Bushels* 3,914	$5,534
New Jersey	83	134	14,209	22,878	44	162	18,153	29,228	5	19	1,055	1,699
Pennsylvania	120	114	7,964	12,572	59	87	5,242	8,275	7	5	435	686
Ohio	447	165	13,378	20,640	198	88	7,351	11,342	8	7	543	838
Indiana	126	42	2,496	3,760	76	30	1,945	2,930	2	1	60	90
Illinois	270	101	6,511	8,809	584	401	26,749	36,189	4	2	90	122
Missouri	603	124	7,992	9,846	884	227	13,244	16,317	10	18	1,423	1,753
Kansas	271	365	25,195	28,351	118	238	23,070	25,960	4	7	308	346
	WHEAT											
SELECTED NORTHERN STATES [2]	522	19,866	*Bushels* 231,040	$243,840	485	19,069	*Bushels* 252,376	$273,987	26	521	*Bushels* 8,195	$9,518
New Jersey	12	122	2,490	3,115	26	286	6,116	7,650	5	78	1,981	2,478
Pennsylvania	66	534	9,508	11,450	45	711	14,900	17,943	8	73	1,247	1,502
Ohio	113	1,307	20,148	23,316	113	2,660	43,961	50,872	4	73	1,878	2,173
Indiana	35	693	8,901	9,928	35	1,142	16,806	18,744	3	60	830	926
Illinois	39	1,001	12,429	14,069	36	1,043	13,254	15,002	1	10	250	283
Missouri	109	2,394	19,845	22,075	141	4,705	43,334	48,204	3	132	1,209	1,345
Kansas	148	13,815	157,719	159,887	89	8,522	114,005	115,572	2	95	800	811

[2] States having 200 or more Negro farmers who constitute 90 percent or more of the colored farmers in the State.
[3] Reported in small fractions.

TABLE 55.—CATTLE ON FARMS—NUMBER BY CLASSES APRIL 1, 1930, WITH NUMBER OF FARMS REPORTING, BY TENURE OF COLORED OPERATORS, BY SOUTHERN DIVISIONS, AND STATES, AND SELECTED NORTHERN STATES

[Colored farmers include Negroes, Indians, Chinese, Japanese, and all other nonwhite races]

DIVISION AND STATE	ALL CATTLE		CALVES BORN BETWEEN JAN. 1, AND APR. 1, 1930		STEERS AND BULLS BORN IN 1929 (YEARLINGS)		HEIFERS BORN IN 1929 (YEARLINGS)		BULLS BORN BEFORE 1929		STEERS BORN IN 1928 (2-YEAR-OLDS)		STEERS BORN BEFORE 1928		HEIFERS BORN IN 1928 (2-YEAR-OLDS): Kept mainly for milk production		HEIFERS BORN IN 1928 (2-YEAR-OLDS): Kept mainly for beef production		COWS AND HEIFERS BORN BEFORE 1928: Kept mainly for milk production		COWS AND HEIFERS BORN BEFORE 1928: Kept mianly for beef production	
	Farms reporting	Number	Farms reporting	Number	Farms reporting	Number	Farms reporting	Number	Farms reporting	Number	Farms reporting	Number	Farms reporting	Number	Farms reporting	Number	Farms reporting	Number	Farms reporting	Number	Farms reporting	Number
ALL OWNERS																						
The South	**127, 175**	**503, 816**	**46, 921**	**78, 918**	**24, 014**	**41, 914**	**39, 498**	**66, 065**	**6, 703**	**8, 794**	**3, 074**	**8, 787**	**2, 039**	**6, 989**	**12, 775**	**21, 201**	**3, 634**	**11, 195**	**115, 178**	**223, 566**	**5, 805**	**36, 387**
SOUTH ATLANTIC	49, 106	124, 614	12, 053	16, 726	4, 823	7, 362	10, 776	14, 759	1, 731	2, 136	876	1, 577	977	1, 458	3, 691	4, 976	1, 037	2, 242	43, 612	64, 817	2, 106	8, 561
Delaware	171	659	53	87	8	19	55	103	12	17	3	8	1	3	19	42	6	11	158	364	3	5
Maryland	1, 240	3, 423	326	465	59	83	224	344	40	51	19	33	43	90	122	185	24	40	1, 094	2, 063	42	69
District of Columbia	1	1																	1	1		
Virginia	15, 976	31, 400	2, 950	3, 646	605	991	2, 388	2, 990	260	280	114	283	83	148	920	1, 162	217	303	14, 909	21, 164	317	433
West Virginia	276	866	77	114	35	67	81	115	4	4	5	12	3	7	30	38	9	11	257	463	9	35
North Carolina	10, 133	18, 742	1, 904	2, 182	674	802	2, 118	2, 449	310	336	86	106	77	100	730	849	163	229	9, 010	11, 393	210	296
South Carolina	10, 271	22, 379	2, 452	3, 016	1, 009	1, 235	2, 183	2, 657	416	486	238	278	478	541	843	1, 032	183	280	8, 786	11, 901	484	953
Georgia	8, 143	33, 291	2, 978	4, 815	1, 700	2, 910	2, 685	4, 318	481	692	300	639	189	372	752	1, 176	280	973	7, 056	12, 894	649	4, 502
Florida	2, 895	13, 853	1, 313	2, 401	733	1, 255	1, 042	1, 783	208	270	111	218	103	197	275	492	155	395	2, 341	4, 574	392	2, 268
EAST SOUTH CENTRAL	40, 184	168, 037	16, 910	27, 866	8, 854	13, 906	14, 225	23, 140	2, 388	3, 049	901	1, 773	475	1, 104	4, 311	7, 330	1, 155	2, 803	37, 267	80, 153	1, 345	6, 913
Kentucky	2, 855	8, 691	946	1, 437	186	446	527	981	67	86	48	119	11	79	200	357	61	83	2, 605	4, 890	96	213
Tennessee	5, 944	19, 123	2, 403	3, 581	760	1, 238	1, 680	2, 533	222	281	97	212	37	85	556	889	150	234	5, 340	9, 678	195	392
Alabama	12, 814	51, 074	4, 456	6, 936	3, 272	4, 917	4, 859	7, 492	828	1, 111	391	703	275	624	1, 399	2, 293	349	957	11, 896	23, 639	393	2, 402
Mississippi	18, 571	89, 149	9, 105	15, 912	4, 636	7, 305	7, 159	12, 134	1, 271	1, 571	365	739	152	316	2, 156	3, 791	595	1, 529	17, 426	41, 946	661	3, 906
WEST SOUTH CENTRAL	37, 885	211, 165	17, 958	34, 326	10, 337	20, 646	14, 497	28, 166	2, 584	3, 609	1, 297	5, 437	587	4, 427	4, 773	8, 895	1, 442	6, 150	34, 299	78, 596	2, 354	20, 913
Arkansas	8, 692	33, 093	3, 923	5, 850	2, 170	3, 156	3, 183	4, 758	430	558	244	434	112	240	999	1, 513	201	384	8, 051	15, 618	198	572
Louisiana	7, 951	38, 687	3, 848	6, 593	2, 087	3, 479	2, 969	4, 960	584	638	254	605	121	381	923	1, 712	310	902	7, 200	16, 049	538	3, 368
Oklahoma	5, 522	52, 976	2, 932	8, 388	1, 357	5, 437	2, 178	7, 029	542	907	226	3, 184	84	3, 158	897	2, 076	286	2, 687	4, 995	13, 844	388	6, 266
Texas	15, 720	86, 409	7, 255	13, 495	4, 723	8, 564	6, 167	11, 419	1, 028	1, 506	573	1, 214	270	648	1, 954	3, 594	645	2, 177	14, 053	33, 085	1, 230	10, 707
SELECTED NORTHERN STATES [1]	2, 551	14, 119	1, 058	2, 332	331	905	856	1, 897	177	207	65	277	14	100	411	879	84	306	2, 275	6, 168	176	1, 048
New Jersey	84	419	19	36	6	7	16	39	8	8					15	28			76	281	4	20
Pennsylvania	149	850	62	122	14	19	60	107	14	19	2	2	2	12	38	69	2	2	137	498		
Ohio	583	2, 572	217	393	57	131	197	378	19	23	22	36	3	21	93	162	6	6	522	1, 372	18	50
Indiana	179	719	55	97	15	28	51	92	11	15	2	3	1	3	22	42	6	11	162	416	4	12
Illinois	289	1, 190	102	187	36	64	81	149	12	15	2	4	2	48	34	58	9	21	268	585	15	59
Missouri	825	3, 947	382	725	102	267	246	468	43	45	19	105	1	1	110	211	30	61	724	1, 679	80	385
Kansas	442	4, 422	221	772	101	389	205	664	70	82	18	127	5	15	99	309	31	205	386	1, 337	55	522
ALL TENANTS																						
The South	**287, 453**	**777, 277**	**97, 935**	**131, 421**	**43, 297**	**60, 076**	**73, 457**	**96, 987**	**8, 134**	**9, 802**	**3, 047**	**6, 443**	**1, 746**	**3, 908**	**19, 012**	**26, 522**	**5, 604**	**9, 843**	**263, 393**	**405, 051**	**7, 363**	**27, 224**
SOUTH ATLANTIC	88, 164	179, 566	19, 413	23, 567	8, 126	10, 164	18, 619	22, 593	2, 309	2, 696	610	1, 022	549	912	5, 278	6, 825	1, 320	2, 096	79, 518	103, 921	1, 916	5, 770
Delaware	211	1, 161	65	138	12	29	73	176	22	25	4	6	2	4	38	98	9	26	183	652	4	7
Maryland	1, 113	4, 748	397	695	62	107	242	426	102	116	26	51	42	111	145	330	22	40	996	2, 762	31	110
District of Columbia	1	1																			1	1
Virginia	6, 971	11, 740	1, 060	1, 266	212	373	830	1, 015	91	96	36	149	22	162	269	350	96	118	6, 445	7, 974	143	237
West Virginia	62	286	25	55	8	13	12	33	4	5	3	13			7	9	5	17	54	131	3	10
North Carolina	17, 067	27, 299	2, 804	3, 080	835	927	2, 959	3, 284	278	312	73	90	55	73	885	1, 061	257	315	15, 192	17, 757	295	400
South Carolina	26, 765	47, 541	5, 041	5, 623	1, 991	2, 216	5, 295	6, 021	691	771	162	197	225	244	1, 549	1, 868	360	462	24, 064	17, 757	525	920
Georgia	33, 806	78, 707	9, 167	11, 401	4, 481	5, 707	8, 527	10, 654	1, 000	1, 225	260	445	117	198	2, 225	2, 893	504	921	30, 776	42, 220	719	3, 043
Florida	2, 168	8, 083	854	1, 309	525	792	681	984	121	146	46	71	86	120	160	216	67	197	1, 808	3, 206	195	1, 042

East South Central	125, 310	369, 099	48, 320	65, 739	22, 073	30, 480	35, 553	47, 425	3, 933	4, 701	1, 401	2, 422	792	1, 354	8, 511	12, 046	2, 464	4, 238	116, 646	191, 719	2, 530	8, 975
Kentucky	2, 099	5, 057	613	855	91	272	251	429	27	27	6	28	5	19	101	175	47	102	1, 890	3, 050	61	100
Tennessee	13, 684	36, 028	5, 369	7, 132	1, 455	2, 897	3, 251	4, 260	295	362	115	316	31	57	793	1, 131	296	490	12, 454	18, 438	505	945
Alabama	45, 745	136, 358	15, 378	20, 767	9, 385	11, 975	14, 557	19, 235	1, 847	2, 203	748	1, 256	555	929	3, 385	4, 677	796	1, 459	42, 803	70, 066	660	3, 791
Mississippi	63, 782	191, 656	26, 960	36, 985	11, 142	15, 336	17, 494	23, 501	1, 764	2, 109	532	822	201	349	4, 232	6, 063	1, 325	2, 187	59, 499	100, 165	1, 304	4, 139
West South Central	73, 979	228, 612	30, 202	42, 115	13, 098	19, 432	19, 285	26, 969	1, 892	2, 405	1, 036	2, 999	405	1, 642	5, 223	7, 651	1, 820	3, 509	67, 229	109, 411	2, 917	12, 479
Arkansas	20, 143	48, 637	7, 407	9, 166	2, 799	3, 452	4, 825	6, 028	455	532	204	270	83	130	1, 249	1, 613	314	445	18, 531	26, 436	264	565
Louisiana	23, 230	71, 246	10, 176	13, 888	4, 421	5, 818	6, 178	8, 257	576	712	354	615	115	267	1, 628	2, 333	718	1, 276	20, 581	34, 012	1, 413	4, 068
Oklahoma	6, 886	27, 581	2, 863	4, 834	1, 127	2, 039	1, 873	3, 223	218	286	105	1, 170	31	416	630	1, 145	162	396	6, 333	11, 998	226	2, 074
Texas	23, 720	81, 148	9, 756	14, 227	4, 751	8, 123	6, 409	9, 461	643	875	373	944	176	829	1, 716	2, 560	626	1, 392	21, 784	36, 965	1, 014	5, 772
Selected Northern States [1]	2, 041	9, 726	811	1, 679	208	511	548	1, 117	128	154	44	143	12	93	252	568	50	116	1, 861	4, 884	105	461
New Jersey	72	595	25	73	2	4	34	75	16	19	-------	-------	-------	-------	22	56	-------	-------	63	363	1	5
Pennsylvania	73	891	34	91	10	17	30	81	20	32	3	26	2	43	19	70	-------	-------	69	530	1	1
Ohio	310	1, 967	141	344	35	78	103	249	24	25	9	29	4	40	62	143	9	48	292	953	11	58
Indiana	110	656	44	96	14	64	30	81	4	9	2	3	-------	-------	16	34	6	9	101	348	6	12
Illinois	186	728	52	114	18	42	46	86	11	14	4	10	-------	-------	20	36	3	5	173	393	5	28
Missouri	1, 037	3, 382	400	671	90	200	206	340	28	28	18	52	5	9	76	149	19	30	950	1, 642	58	261
Kansas	253	1, 507	115	290	39	106	99	205	25	27	8	23	1	1	37	80	13	24	213	655	23	96
MANAGERS																						
The South	**544**	**17, 728**	**280**	**2, 126**	**153**	**1, 512**	**244**	**1, 620**	**155**	**309**	**43**	**1, 360**	**25**	**2, 006**	**136**	**502**	**53**	**1, 223**	**470**	**2, 752**	**86**	**4, 318**
South Atlantic	289	3, 584	136	443	73	298	134	507	76	131	16	101	11	150	78	254	18	115	261	1, 347	27	238
Delaware	12	152	6	17	4	9	6	20	3	3	-------	-------	-------	-------	5	19	2	4	12	80	-------	-------
Maryland	88	956	53	149	16	37	43	101	33	35	4	14	2	21	28	86	2	8	84	471	5	34
District of Columbia	1	23	-------	-------	-------	-------	1	3	1	5	-------	-------	-------	-------	1	2	-------	-------	1	13	-------	-------
Virginia	59	853	28	94	15	96	22	118	12	34	7	31	3	93	17	56	6	59	52	221	9	51
West Virginia	4	46	3	8	1	4	1	1	2	2	1	1	1	13	1	1	-------	-------	4	16	-------	-------
North Carolina	12	215	5	14	2	25	6	30	3	6	1	14	1	4	2	17	-------	-------	11	86	2	19
South Carolina	37	317	12	35	11	56	15	48	5	8	-------	-------	2	2	11	21	3	11	31	96	3	40
Georgia	50	768	19	93	16	45	26	152	12	30	3	41	2	17	9	44	3	28	46	264	3	54
Florida	26	254	10	33	8	26	14	34	5	8	-------	-------	-------	-------	4	8	2	5	20	100	5	40
East South Central	108	2, 608	59	253	32	259	49	259	29	68	10	147	3	53	26	120	8	86	95	697	22	666
Kentucky	10	198	6	24	2	26	3	7	1	1	-------	-------	1	46	1	2	1	4	10	47	2	41
Tennessee	24	854	16	71	10	114	16	81	10	25	3	109	-------	-------	10	53	1	2	23	333	4	66
Alabama	20	851	15	87	9	44	14	82	10	30	2	14	1	5	8	56	2	20	17	118	7	395
Mississippi	54	705	22	71	11	75	16	89	8	12	5	24	1	2	7	9	4	60	45	199	9	164
West South Central	147	11, 536	85	1, 430	48	955	61	854	50	110	17	1, 112	11	1, 803	32	128	27	1, 022	114	708	37	3, 414
Arkansas	18	647	9	61	6	50	5	38	6	11	2	7	-------	-------	4	17	2	31	15	82	1	350
Louisiana	29	935	13	107	8	26	11	147	6	8	2	6	2	15	6	13	5	93	21	111	5	409
Oklahoma	38	4, 548	29	385	14	550	17	384	14	26	7	880	5	1, 171	11	69	3	275	33	306	12	502
Texas	62	5, 406	34	877	20	329	28	285	24	65	6	219	4	617	11	29	17	623	45	209	19	2, 153
Selected Northern States [1]	59	1, 256	33	148	18	116	27	132	12	13	7	237	3	66	19	82	2	10	50	327	10	125
New Jersey	8	160	2	27	2	7	3	17	2	2	1	2	-------	-------	6	24	-------	-------	4	78	1	3
Pennsylvania	8	148	7	23	3	8	4	29	3	3	1	1	-------	-------	2	4	-------	-------	12	80	-------	-------
Ohio	11	240	7	23	7	36	8	32	1	1	1	27	2	36	4	15	2	10	10	57	1	3
Indiana	2	45	1	2	-------	-------	1	5	-------	-------	1	30	-------	-------	-------	-------	-------	-------	2	8	-------	-------
Illinois	4	75	-------	-------	1	37	-------	-------	-------	-------	-------	-------	1	30	-------	-------	-------	-------	4	8	-------	-------
Missouri	18	455	11	46	4	27	6	27	4	5	3	177	-------	-------	4	30	-------	-------	11	63	6	80
Kansas	8	133	5	27	1	1	5	22	2	2	-------	-------	-------	-------	3	9	-------	-------	7	33	2	39

[1] States having 200 or more Negro farmers who constitute 90 percent or more of the colored farmers in the State.

Table 55a.—SPECIFIED DAIRY PRODUCTS PRODUCED AND SOLD IN 1929, WITH NUMBER OF FARMS REPORTING, BY TENURE OF COLORED OPERATORS, BY SOUTHERN DIVISIONS, AND STATES, AND SELECTED NORTHERN STATES

[Colored farmers include Negroes, Indians, Chinese, Japanese, and all other nonwhite races]

DIVISION AND STATE	COWS AND HEIFERS MILKED DAILY, APRIL 1, 1930		TOTAL MILK PRODUCED		TOTAL MILK SOLD		CREAM SOLD AS BUTTERFAT		CREAM SOLD NOT AS BUTTERFAT		BUTTER CHURNED		BUTTER SOLD	
	Farms reporting	Number	Farms reporting	Gallons	Farms reporting	Gallons	Farms reporting	Pounds	Farms reporting	Gallons	Farms reporting	Pounds	Farms reporting	Pounds
	ALL OWNERS													
The South	**91, 231**	**148, 086**	**115, 197**	**63, 846, 334**	**5, 522**	**3, 983, 914**	**5, 305**	**1, 430, 523**	**345**	**49, 876**	**97, 679**	**13, 552, 501**	**18, 012**	**1, 547, 924**
SOUTH ATLANTIC	34, 547	46, 368	43, 992	20, 410, 060	1, 630	893, 944	751	192, 328	89	21, 091	36, 392	4, 718, 244	10, 133	813, 226
Delaware	134	272	156	121, 150	31	58, 618	-	-	-	-	83	8, 273	34	2, 804
Maryland	793	1, 301	1, 108	674, 802	173	232, 862	4	1, 161	1	250	770	69, 835	230	21, 790
District of Columbia	1	1	1	750	1	300	-	-	-	-	1	50	-	-
Virginia	11, 992	15, 053	15, 257	7, 511, 082	353	225, 660	328	107, 820	35	17, 299	14, 453	1, 926, 248	5, 265	402, 719
West Virginia	196	310	264	188, 902	39	20, 570	12	5, 035	-	-	230	38, 422	98	11, 105
North Carolina	7, 048	8, 410	9, 001	4, 186, 404	315	86, 161	58	8, 312	13	650	7, 955	1, 115, 024	1, 880	152, 202
South Carolina	6, 736	8, 343	8, 599	3, 358, 333	319	123, 601	33	10, 015	20	1, 022	5, 404	617, 248	1, 054	78, 824
Georgia	5, 881	9, 565	7, 276	3, 430, 969	264	67, 199	304	59, 058	17	1, 543	5, 920	828, 885	1, 339	130, 335
Florida	1, 766	3, 113	2, 330	937, 668	135	78, 973	12	927	3	327	1, 576	114, 259	233	13, 447
EAST SOUTH CENTRAL	29, 761	52, 660	37, 075	22, 406, 976	2, 514	2, 033, 829	2, 770	669, 410	143	14, 998	32, 486	4, 641, 098	4, 203	392, 683
Kentucky	2, 071	3, 511	2, 689	2, 035, 854	209	144, 032	874	208, 296	31	2, 075	2, 268	264, 611	387	50, 906
Tennessee	4, 370	6, 978	5, 591	3, 604, 021	348	252, 161	662	155, 026	45	5, 238	5, 019	760, 689	1, 010	104, 866
Alabama	9, 397	15, 219	11, 811	6, 245, 505	577	328, 058	214	77, 662	30	5, 362	10, 849	1, 643, 832	1, 645	131, 464
Mississippi	13, 923	26, 952	16, 984	10, 521, 596	1, 380	1, 309, 578	1, 020	228, 426	37	2, 323	14, 350	1, 971, 966	1, 161	105, 447
WEST SOUTH CENTRAL	26, 923	49, 058	34, 130	21, 029, 298	1, 378	1, 056, 141	1, 784	568, 785	113	13, 787	28, 801	4, 193, 159	3, 676	342, 015
Arkansas	6, 089	9, 798	7, 963	4, 359, 075	310	116, 067	204	37, 524	18	3, 044	7, 426	1, 226, 494	1, 037	89, 134
Louisiana	5, 290	9, 201	6, 760	3, 464, 682	197	242, 228	81	22, 141	4	513	4, 550	549, 849	377	28, 508
Oklahoma	4, 312	9, 736	5, 132	4, 924, 624	319	405, 513	1, 054	396, 721	48	6, 691	4, 277	614, 795	590	72, 198
Texas	11, 232	20, 323	14, 275	8, 280, 917	552	292, 333	445	112, 399	43	3, 539	12, 548	1, 802, 021	1, 672	152, 175
SELECTED NORTHERN STATES [1]	2, 050	4, 789	2, 437	2, 856, 385	389	826, 210	870	278, 612	29	1, 911	1, 626	186, 883	339	51, 031
New Jersey	65	230	81	191, 062	37	160, 722	-	-	-	-	19	1, 515	4	330
Pennsylvania	116	407	132	247, 520	68	177, 211	3	1, 124	1	60	65	12, 815	28	6, 068
Ohio	462	1, 067	553	646, 850	97	190, 040	242	74, 058	4	392	287	39, 215	64	13, 211
Indiana	147	316	171	239, 902	47	96, 366	63	23, 749	2	62	90	10, 883	24	3, 894
Illinois	237	458	282	257, 178	42	47, 187	89	24, 924	3	240	193	23, 621	70	9, 813
Missouri	661	1, 220	791	667, 098	48	49, 212	283	73, 925	14	976	663	64, 640	106	10, 715
Kansas	362	1, 091	427	606, 775	50	105, 472	190	80, 832	5	181	399	34, 194	43	7, 000
	ALL TENANTS													
The South	**195, 982**	**264, 827**	**253, 358**	**111, 024, 905**	**6, 442**	**4, 284, 921**	**4, 810**	**1, 008, 579**	**286**	**24, 288**	**208, 533**	**25, 146, 030**	**18, 219**	**1, 314, 832**
SOUTH ATLANTIC	60, 296	73, 422	77, 867	32, 733, 545	1, 461	989, 687	834	161, 456	66	4, 092	65, 245	8, 208, 872	8, 696	603, 929
Delaware	153	464	182	227, 445	61	161, 358	-	-	-	-	78	7, 391	26	2, 331
Maryland	716	1, 766	1, 014	892, 642	198	460, 735	11	3, 623	-	-	667	55, 734	103	10, 175
District of Columbia	-	-	-	-	-	-	-	-	-	-	-	-	-	-
Virginia	4, 787	5, 692	6, 508	2, 824, 720	60	44, 082	46	18, 648	6	1, 476	6, 091	798, 829	1, 107	75, 217
West Virginia	45	118	55	63, 557	9	11, 700	12	6, 405	-	-	45	8, 666	17	2, 701
North Carolina	11, 612	13, 037	14, 898	6, 412, 567	236	55, 398	48	5, 075	9	323	12, 754	1, 672, 726	1, 675	111, 932
South Carolina	18, 067	20, 723	23, 326	8, 971, 156	386	51, 503	54	7, 038	22	422	18, 639	2, 145, 358	2, 147	127, 692
Georgia	23, 624	29, 534	30, 214	12, 735, 762	478	172, 530	648	118, 719	27	1, 846	25, 979	3, 451, 871	3, 513	267, 608
Florida	1, 292	2, 088	1, 670	605, 296	33	32, 381	15	1, 948	2	25	992	68, 297	108	6, 273
EAST SOUTH CENTRAL	86, 808	122, 756	111, 617	49, 345, 777	3, 712	2, 775, 162	2, 833	540, 982	138	11, 529	94, 373	11, 055, 571	6, 077	444, 650
Kentucky	1, 512	2, 310	1, 878	1, 225, 759	121	151, 646	449	101, 156	17	1, 480	1, 540	169, 901	176	15, 745
Tennessee	9, 841	13, 064	12, 276	6, 336, 316	305	217, 367	456	87, 509	37	1, 942	11, 079	1, 522, 639	1, 060	82, 396
Alabama	32, 130	44, 567	41, 717	17, 691, 541	1, 448	745, 750	647	116, 443	36	4, 006	37, 645	4, 618, 998	3, 117	226, 880
Mississippi	43, 325	62, 815	55, 746	24, 092, 161	1, 838	1, 660, 399	1, 281	235, 874	48	4, 101	44, 109	4, 744, 033	1, 724	119, 629
WEST SOUTH CENTRAL	48, 878	68, 649	63, 874	28, 945, 983	1, 269	520, 072	1, 143	306, 141	82	8, 667	48, 915	5, 881, 587	3, 446	266, 253
Arkansas	12, 940	16, 519	17, 568	7, 450, 533	479	81, 158	114	17, 576	16	638	15, 027	2, 027, 456	1, 113	71, 427
Louisiana	14, 477	19, 919	18, 477	6, 968, 131	201	76, 367	55	7, 899	4	2, 242	10, 684	972, 418	473	23, 614
Oklahoma	5, 098	8, 441	6, 335	4, 289, 824	258	191, 969	665	204, 864	38	3, 216	5, 175	688, 480	539	54, 144
Texas	16, 363	23, 770	21, 494	10, 237, 495	331	170, 578	309	75, 802	24	2, 571	18, 029	2, 193, 233	1, 321	117, 068
SELECTED NORTHERN STATES [1]	1, 616	3, 781	1, 880	2, 231, 608	266	809, 253	419	163, 408	12	1, 870	1, 161	137, 408	167	19, 965
New Jersey	59	290	65	200, 247	39	175, 616	-	-	-	-	11	764	1	10
Pennsylvania	68	410	68	301, 730	48	267, 267	2	2, 700	-	-	13	3, 167	7	2, 046
Ohio	268	767	283	411, 496	76	166, 489	104	44, 103	2	533	107	11, 656	13	1, 288
Indiana	82	277	102	174, 726	26	74, 484	37	10, 725	1	20	48	7, 311	9	2, 952
Illinois	150	305	167	184, 581	26	60, 814	33	11, 305	4	1, 121	103	12, 158	34	3, 195
Missouri	793	1, 273	961	665, 124	35	41, 928	144	37, 904	4	96	740	90, 066	95	9, 709
Kansas	196	459	234	293, 697	16	22, 655	99	49, 671	1	100	139	12, 286	8	765
	MANAGERS													
The South	**421**	**1, 979**	**481**	**1, 114, 656**	**120**	**684, 975**	**26**	**21, 713**	**5**	**1, 287**	**295**	**69, 654**	**83**	**28, 496**
SOUTH ATLANTIC	230	979	270	592, 396	70	366, 959	10	9, 037	2	620	149	34, 930	47	15, 561
Delaware	11	62	13	42, 911	6	31, 506	-	-	-	-	2	125	-	-
Maryland	69	317	84	162, 959	28	111, 339	-	-	1	520	27	5, 770	15	3, 579
District of Columbia	1	9	1	7, 300	1	7, 300	-	-	-	-	-	-	-	-
Virginia	49	178	56	129, 915	10	65, 820	6	4, 330	-	-	46	13, 277	16	7, 087
West Virginia	4	15	4	8, 418	2	5, 434	1	130	-	-	2	485	1	285
North Carolina	9	69	11	48, 930	5	38, 690	-	-	1	100	7	1, 828	2	505
South Carolina	32	78	37	44, 943	7	21, 360	-	-	-	-	20	4, 786	6	1, 930
Georgia	39	187	45	112, 490	6	63, 310	3	4, 577	-	-	33	6, 529	6	1, 275
Florida	16	64	19	34, 530	5	22, 200	-	-	-	-	12	2, 130	1	900

[1] States having 200 or more Negro farmers who constitute 90 percent or more of the colored farmers in the State.

TABLE 55a.—SPECIFIED DAIRY PRODUCTS PRODUCED AND SOLD IN 1929, WITH NUMBER OF FARMS REPORTING, BY TENURE OF COLORED OPERATORS, BY SOUTHERN DIVISIONS, AND STATES, AND SELECTED NORTHERN STATES—Continued

[Colored farmers include Negroes, Indians, Chinese, Japanese, and all other nonwhite races]

DIVISION AND STATE	COWS AND HEIFERS MILKED DAILY, APRIL 1, 1930		TOTAL MILK PRODUCED		TOTAL MILK SOLD		CREAM SOLD AS BUTTERFAT		CREAM SOLD NOT AS BUTTERFAT		BUTTER CHURNED		BUTTER SOLD	
	Farms reporting	Number	Farms reporting	Gallons	Farms reporting	Gallons	Farms reporting	Pounds	Farms reporting	Gallons	Farms reporting	Pounds	Farms reporting	Pounds
							MANAGERS—continued							
EAST SOUTH CENTRAL	85	509	91	272, 239	28	184, 724	6	2, 516	2	597	64	19, 946	22	10, 490
Kentucky	10	43	10	20, 930	3	9, 100	3	1, 371	1	50	6	1, 358	4	830
Tennessee	22	226	23	125, 055	11	107, 457	1	50			13	3, 985	3	1, 300
Alabama	17	104	16	64, 175	5	38, 852	1	95	1	547	14	6, 212	6	6, 460
Mississippi	36	136	42	62, 079	9	29, 315	1	1, 000			31	8, 391	9	1, 900
WEST SOUTH CENTRAL	106	491	120	250, 021	22	133, 292	10	10, 160	1	70	82	14, 778	14	2, 445
Arkansas	13	54	14	19, 012	3	8, 757					10	2, 480	3	886
Louisiana	18	76	23	36, 740	5	23, 565			1	70	13	1, 123	1	25
Oklahoma	33	221	34	117, 473	7	58, 120	9	10, 010			25	5, 526	5	1, 030
Texas	42	140	49	76, 796	7	42, 850	1	150			34	5, 649	5	504
SELECTED NORTHERN STATES [1]	50	291	57	223, 012	25	178, 981	4	1, 580			23	5, 569	3	2, 610
New Jersey	6	73	7	64, 241	5	58, 866					1	108		
Pennsylvania	11	67	12	42, 961	6	37, 710					1	200		
Ohio	10	46	10	29, 405	5	21, 801	2	1, 030			4	505		
Indiana	2	8	2	3, 900	1	3, 300					1	80	1	40
Illinois	3	6	5	8, 800	2	6, 400					2	195		
Missouri	12	62	14	50, 846	4	33, 052					10	4, 226	2	2, 570
Kansas	6	29	7	22, 859	2	17, 852	2	550			4	255		

[1] States having 200 or more Negro farmers who constitute 90 percent or more of the colored farmers in the State.

TABLE 56.—NUMBER AND VALUE OF CATTLE ON FARMS OF COLORED OPERATORS, BY TENURE OF FARMER, 1930, WITH SPECIFIED DAIRY PRODUCTS PRODUCED AND SOLD, 1929

[Colored farmers include Negroes, Indians, Chinese, Japanese, and all other nonwhite farmers]

DIVISION AND STATE	CATTLE ON FARMS, 1930								DAIRY PRODUCTS, 1929					
	Total		Owners		Tenants		Managers		Milk		Cream		Butter	
	Number	Value	Number	Value	Number	Value	Number	Value	Produced (gallons)	Sold (gallons)	Cream sold as butterfat (pounds)	Cream sold not as butterfat (gallons)	Churned (pounds)	Sold (pounds)
The South	1,298,821	$54,332,234	503, 816	$21,634,000	777, 277	$31,868,718	17, 728	$829,516	175,986,295	8,953,810	2,460,815	75, 451	38,768,185	2, 891, 252
SOUTH ATLANTIC	307, 764	13, 864, 958	124, 614	5, 818, 662	179, 566	7, 842, 450	3, 584	203, 846	53, 736, 001	2,250,590	362, 821	25, 803	12,962,046	1, 432, 716
Delaware	1, 972	171, 446	659	57, 294	1, 161	100, 937	152	13, 215	391, 506	251, 482			15, 789	5, 135
Maryland	9, 127	720, 485	3, 423	270, 211	4, 748	374, 807	956	75, 467	1, 730, 403	804, 936	4, 784	770	131, 339	35, 544
District of Columbia	25	1, 785	1	71	1	71	23	1, 643	8, 450	7, 600			50	
Virginia	43, 993	2, 558, 633	31, 400	1, 826, 224	11, 740	682, 798	853	49, 611	10, 465, 717	335, 562	130, 798	18, 775	2, 738, 354	485, 023
West Virginia	1, 198	71, 053	866	51, 362	286	16, 963	46	2, 728	260, 877	37, 704	11, 570		47, 573	14, 091
North Carolina	46, 256	2, 326, 214	18, 742	942, 535	27, 299	1, 372, 867	215	10, 812	10, 647, 901	180, 249	13, 387	1, 073	2, 789, 578	264, 63
South Carolina	70, 237	3, 240, 033	22, 379	1, 032, 343	47, 541	2, 193, 067	317	14, 623	12, 374, 432	196, 464	17, 053	1, 444	2, 767, 392	208, 446
Georgia	112, 766	4, 079, 874	33, 291	1, 204, 469	78, 707	2, 847, 619	768	27, 786	16, 279, 221	303, 039	182, 354	3, 389	4, 287, 285	399, 218
Florida	22, 190	695, 435	13, 853	434, 153	8, 083	253, 321	254	7, 961	1, 577, 494	133, 554	2, 875	352	184, 686	20, 620
EAST SOUTH CENTRAL	539, 744	21, 406, 087	168, 037	6, 738, 385	369, 099	14, 557, 463	2, 608	110, 239	72, 024, 992	4,993,715-	1,212,908	27, 124	15,716,615	847, 823
Kentucky	13, 946	762, 986	8, 691	475, 485	5, 057	276, 668	198	10, 833	3, 282, 543	304, 778	310, 823	3, 605	435, 870	.67, 481
Tennessee	56, 005	2, 566, 709	19, 123	876, 407	36, 028	1, 651, 163	854	39, 139	10, 065, 392	576, 985	242, 585	7, 180	2, 287, 313	188, 562
Alabama	188, 283	7, 440, 944	51, 074	2, 018, 444	136, 358	5, 388, 868	851	33, 632	24, 001, 221	1,112,660	194, 200	9, 915	6, 271, 042	364, 804
Mississippi	281, 510	10, 635, 448	89, 149	3, 368, 049	191, 656	7, 240, 764	705	26, 635	34, 675, 836	2,999,292	465, 300	6, 424	6, 722, 390	226, 976
WEST SOUTH CENTRAL	451, 313	19, 061, 189	211, 165	9, 076, 953	228, 612	9, 468, 805	11, 536	515, 431	50, 225, 302	1,709,505	885, 086	22, 524	10,089,524	610, 713
Arkansas	82, 377	3, 116, 322	33, 093	1, 251, 908	48, 637	1, 839, 938	647	24, 476	11, 828, 620	205, 982	55, 100	3, 682	3, 256, 430	161, 447
Louisiana	110, 868	4, 117, 638	38, 687	1, 436, 835	71, 246	2, 646, 077	935	34, 726	10, 469, 553	324, 960	30, 040	2, 825	1, 523, 390	52, 147
Oklahoma	85, 105	3, 902, 064	52, 976	2, 428, 949	27, 581	1, 264, 589	4, 548	208, 526	9, 331, 921	655, 602	611, 595	9, 907	1, 308, 801	127, 372
Texas	172, 963	7, 925, 165	86, 409	3, 959, 261	18, 148	3, 718, 201	5, 406	247, 703	18, 595, 208	505, 761	188, 351	6, 110	4, 000, 903	269, 747
SELECTED NORTHERN STATES [1]	25, 101	1, 568, 755	14, 119	862, 542	9, 726	621, 169	1, 256	85, 044	5, 311, 005	1,814,444	443, 600	3, 781	329, 860	73, 606
New Jersey	1, 174	130, 067	419	46, 421	595	65, 920	160	17, 726	455, 550	395, 204			2, 387	340
Pennsylvania	1, 889	148, 967	850	67, 031	891	70, 264	148	11, 672	592, 218	482, 188	3, 824	60	16, 182	8, 114
Ohio	4, 779	312, 069	2, 572	167, 952	1, 967	128, 445	240	15, 672	1, 087, 751	378, 330	119, 191	925	51, 376	14, 499
Indiana	1, 420	87, 486	719	44, 298	656	40, 416	45	2, 772	418, 528	174, 150	41, 474	82	18, 274	6, 886
Illinois	1, 993	132, 315	1, 190	79, 004	728	48, 332	75	4, 979	450, 559	114, 401	36, 229	1, 361	35, 974	13, 008
Missouri	7, 784	427, 108	3, 947	216, 572	3, 382	185, 570	455	24, 966	1, 383, 068	124, 192	111, 829	1, 072	158, 932	22, 994
Kansas	6, 062	330, 743	4, 422	241, 264	1, 507	82, 222	133	7, 257	923, 331	145, 979	131, 053	281	46, 735	7, 765

[1] States having 200 or more Negro farmers who constitute 90 percent or more of the colored farmers in the State.

TABLE 57.—FARMS OPERATED BY NEGROES—NUMBER, ACREAGE, VALUE OF LAND AND BUILDINGS, AND VALUE OF IMPLEMENTS AND MACHINERY, BY TENURE, BY STATES, AND COUNTIES: 1930

[Counties in which no farms operated by Negroes were reported, are omitted]

COUNTY	NUMBER OF FARMS				ALL LAND IN FARMS (ACRES)				VALUE OF LAND AND BUILDINGS			
	Total	Owners	Tenants	Managers	Total	Owners	Tenants	Managers	Total	Owners	Tenants	Managers
	ALABAMA											
Total	**93, 795**	**15, 920**	**77, 853**	**22**	**4, 157, 051**	**1, 189, 355**	**2, 953, 534**	**14, 162**	**$104, 726, 209**	**$24, 945, 906**	**$79, 029, 593**	**$750, 710**
Autauga	1, 924	364	1, 560		77, 169	28, 618	48, 551		1, 763, 200	449, 592	1, 313, 608	
Baldwin	320	244	76		9, 661	7, 914	1, 747		280, 150	216, 710	63, 440	
Barbour	2, 262	303	1, 956	3	155, 085	38, 441	115, 335	1, 309	2, 398, 743	483, 764	1, 909, 079	5, 900
Bibb	668	189	479		24, 606	10, 476	14, 130		703, 095	205, 569	497, 526	
Blount	86	37	49		4, 115	2, 080	2, 035		105, 860	48, 660	57, 200	
Bullock	2, 473	213	2, 259	1	131, 304	22, 476	108, 628	200	1, 980, 007	336, 376	1, 641, 631	2, 000
Butler	1, 695	257	1, 436	2	82, 713	23, 717	56, 886	2, 110	1, 822, 222	505, 276	1, 281, 946	35, 000
Calhoun	461	103	358		21, 864	6, 727	15, 137		633, 055	169, 610	463, 445	
Chambers	2, 431	187	2, 244		145, 408	16, 980	128, 428		2, 810, 492	329, 249	2, 481, 243	
Cherokee	274	67	207		15, 179	4, 353	10, 826		511, 077	106, 685	404, 392	
Chilton	575	179	396		28, 250	12, 297	15, 953		629, 481	237, 806	391, 675	
Choctaw	1, 611	543	1, 068		79, 538	45, 912	33, 626		1, 382, 777	701, 285	681, 492	
Clarke	1, 772	799	973		82, 377	55, 759	26, 618		1, 452, 771	730, 021	722, 750	
Clay	359	77	282		19, 391	5, 659	13, 732		383, 554	73, 505	310, 049	
Cleburne	67	7	60		3, 175	631	2, 544		67, 192	10, 600	56, 592	
Coffee	732	73	659		43, 997	7, 168	36, 829		1, 256, 612	188, 515	1, 068, 097	
Colbert	931	184	747		37, 433	9, 479	27, 954		2, 752, 667	577, 350	2, 175, 317	
Conecuh	1, 476	579	897		66, 149	33, 534	32, 615		1, 659, 735	772, 640	887, 095	
Coosa	677	201	476		59, 560	21, 502	38, 058		666, 912	256, 020	410, 892	
Covington	520	142	378		25, 032	9, 069	15, 963		297, 315	220, 300	577, 015	
Crenshaw	1, 030	174	856		54, 909	14, 181	40, 728		1, 526, 495	330, 310	1, 196, 185	
Cullman	76	40	36		4, 575	3, 122	1, 453		137, 575	87, 700	49, 875	
Dale	515	82	433		31, 546	9, 154	22, 392		919, 210	205, 950	713, 260	
Dallas	6, 405	484	5, 921		210, 683	32, 195	178, 488		5, 048, 579	741, 275	4, 307, 304	
De Kalb	58	12	46		2, 748	813	1, 935		102, 430	25, 750	76, 680	
Elmore	1, 837	413	1, 424		76, 502	25, 867	50, 635		2, 635, 426	771, 055	1, 864, 371	
Escambia	404	191	213		15, 919	7, 818	8, 101		680, 920	295, 080	385, 840	
Etowah	152	48	104		6, 602	2, 445	4, 157		248, 432	106, 150	142, 282	
Fayette	327	118	209		22, 205	12, 060	10, 145		337, 670	131, 770	205, 900	
Franklin	113	41	72		5, 495	2, 689	2, 806		190, 320	79, 850	110, 470	
Geneva	302	65	237		16, 889	4, 339	12, 550		687, 926	140, 655	547, 271	
Greene	3, 168	326	2, 842		121, 010	24, 852	96, 158		2, 557, 493	499, 748	2, 057, 745	
Hale	3, 873	653	3, 219	1	128, 902	41, 360	86, 142	1, 400	4, 363, 062	1, 129, 634	3, 152, 428	81, 000
Henry	1, 331	125	1, 206		84, 132	16, 819	67, 313		2, 394, 010	343, 534	2, 050, 476	
Houston	971	116	854	1	49, 275	8, 156	40, 019	1, 100	2, 177, 345	217, 670	1, 952, 675	7, 000
Jackson	281	91	190		12, 265	4, 540	7, 725		530, 730	178, 680	352, 050	
Jefferson	327	117	210		8, 823	3, 380	5, 443		1, 082, 505	307, 920	774, 585	
Lamar	410	128	282		32, 371	14, 775	17, 596		427, 502	148, 485	279, 017	
Lauderdale	959	178	781		39, 046	9, 231	29, 815		2, 034, 431	432, 748	1, 601, 683	
Lawrence	1, 393	176	1, 217		52, 458	10, 348	42, 110		2, 463, 289	472, 273	1, 991, 016	
Lee	1, 992	318	1, 673	1	138, 258	31, 979	106, 035	244	2, 377, 692	575, 269	1, 795, 923	6, 500
Limestone	1, 929	236	1, 693		65, 315	9, 973	55, 342		2, 979, 006	477, 005	2, 502, 001	
Lowndes	3, 527	333	3, 193	1	124, 653	25, 229	99, 124	300	2, 923, 121	529, 707	2, 387, 414	6, 000
Macon	3, 114	473	2, 639	2	145, 173	38, 861	104, 417	1, 895	3, 417, 057	890, 480	2, 327, 017	199, 560
Madison	2, 772	404	2, 367	1	106, 212	22, 728	83, 349	135	4, 345, 764	910, 011	3, 415, 503	20, 250
Marengo	5, 314	651	4, 662	1	158, 890	46, 715	111, 780	395	3, 918, 964	797, 895	3, 109, 069	12, 000
Marion	70	45	25		5, 439	3, 968	1, 471		65, 735	43, 520	22, 215	
Marshall	102	22	80		3, 764	927	2, 837		151, 670	31, 050	120, 620	
Mobile	149	93	56		5, 224	2, 382	2, 842		268, 247	150, 612	117, 635	
Monroe	2, 091	584	1, 507		93, 129	46, 660	46, 469		1, 951, 440	777, 371	1, 174, 069	
Montgomery	3, 178	376	2, 797	5	120, 675	21, 155	96, 856	2, 664	4, 056, 209	796, 561	3, 017, 648	242, 000
Morgan	659	161	498		23, 452	7, 117	16, 335		1, 225, 220	335, 500	889, 720	
Perry	3, 435	480	2, 955		128, 949	36, 610	92, 339		2, 976, 587	640, 180	2, 336, 407	
Pickens	2, 119	260	1, 859		103, 188	26, 218	76, 970		2, 096, 577	408, 197	1, 688, 380	
Pike	1, 506	110	1, 396		90, 462	11, 313	79, 149		2, 164, 001	204, 256	1, 959, 745	
Randolph	791	186	605		45, 800	16, 308	29, 492		819, 633	251, 713	567, 920	
Russell	2, 243	357	1, 886		135, 972	42, 189	93, 783		2, 037, 429	552, 627	1, 484, 802	
St. Clair	348	104	244		23, 201	7, 291	15, 910		542, 080	151, 545	390, 535	
Shelby	392	121	271		16, 802	6, 576	10, 226		456, 065	169, 790	286, 275	
Sumter	3, 812	444	3, 368		150, 050	40, 117	109, 933		3, 180, 102	677, 444	2, 502, 658	
Talladega	1, 912	426	1, 485	1	102, 239	32, 249	69, 190	800	2, 346, 943	621, 045	1, 625, 898	100, 000
Tallapoosa	1, 161	165	996		74, 812	15, 656	59, 156		1, 432, 890	311, 621	1, 121, 269	
Tuscaloosa	1, 545	414	1, 131		69, 635	31, 503	38, 132		1, 904, 740	594, 964	1, 309, 776	
Walker	92	38	54		2, 557	1, 515	1, 042		63, 020	31, 850	31, 170	
Washington	676	377	299		32, 126	24, 368	7, 758		523, 834	316, 879	206, 955	
Wilcox	3, 620	416	3, 202	2	102, 713	28, 812	72, 291	1, 610	1, 899, 916	433, 044	1, 433, 372	33, 500
	ARIZONA											
Total	**87**	**40**	**44**	**3**	**7, 766**	**4, 432**	**2, 984**	**350**	**$761, 510**	**$195, 250**	**$506, 460**	**$59. 800**
Cochise	4	4			423	423			8, 150	8, 150		
Graham	5	4	1		600	520	80		13, 000	11, 000	2, 000	
Maricopa	51	20	30	1	2, 709	785	1, 764	160	552, 010	135, 350	384, 660	32, 000
Navajo	1	1			160	160			1, 600	1, 600		
Pima	3	3			173	173			11, 200	11, 200		
Pinal	2	2			11	11			4, 300	4, 300		
Santa Cruz	4	3	1		1, 950	1, 920	30		7, 350	5, 850	1, 500	
Yavapai	1	1			160	160			4, 000	4, 000		
Yuma	16	2	12	2	1, 580	280	1, 110	190	159, 900	13, 800	118, 300	27, 800

TABLE 57.—FARMS OPERATED BY NEGROES—NUMBER, ACREAGE, VALUE OF LAND AND BUILDINGS, AND VALUE OF IMPLEMENTS AND MACHINERY, BY TENURE, BY STATES, AND COUNTIES: 1930—Continued

[Counties in which no farms operated by Negroes were reported, are omitted]

COUNTY	VALUE OF LAND ALONE				VALUE OF BUILDINGS				VALUE OF IMPLEMENTS AND MACHINERY			
	Total	Owners	Tenants	Managers	Total	Owners	Tenants	Managers	Total	Owners	Tenants	Managers
	ALABAMA											
Total	**$77,521,909**	**$17,391,688**	**$59,493,361**	**$636,860**	**$27,204,300**	**$7,554,218**	**$19,536,232**	**$113,850**	**$5,091,581**	**$1,549,249**	**$3,516,133**	**$26,199**
Autauga	1,282,270	315,227	967,043	----	480,930	134,365	346,565	----	84,461	23,122	61,339	----
Baldwin	192,630	143,360	49,270	----	87,520	73,350	14,170	----	15,483	12,753	2,730	----
Barbour	1,604,377	344,549	1,255,678	4,150	794,366	139,215	653,401	1,750	110,646	26,898	83,548	200
Bibb	525,140	134,410	390,730	----	177,955	71,159	106,796	----	31,720	15,042	16,678	----
Blount	70,725	30,745	39,980	----	35,135	17,915	17,220	----	6,349	3,298	3,051	----
Bullock	1,285,947	217,261	1,067,186	1,500	694,060	119,115	574,445	500	134,411	31,186	103,225	----
Butler	1,286,131	369,166	886,465	30,500	536,091	136,110	395,481	4,500	74,207	29,689	43,518	1,000
Calhoun	459,969	116,495	343,474	----	173,086	53,115	119,971	----	28,512	8,652	19,860	----
Chambers	1,960,380	214,984	1,745,396	----	850,112	114,265	735,847	----	103,711	20,979	82,732	----
Cherokee	421,679	77,590	344,089	----	89,398	29,095	60,303	----	31,766	10,360	21,406	----
Chilton	458,536	165,216	293,320	----	170,945	72,590	98,355	----	27,215	12,900	14,315	----
Choctaw	883,986	426,155	457,831	----	498,791	275,130	223,661	----	55,903	32,269	23,634	----
Clarke	1,007,386	469,814	537,572	----	445,385	260,207	185,178	----	57,909	38,996	18,913	----
Clay	238,084	43,455	194,629	----	145,470	30,050	115,420	----	15,720	4,369	11,351	----
Cleburne	49,682	7,675	42,007	----	17,510	2,925	14,585	----	4,133	592	3,541	----
Coffee	978,217	136,540	841,677	----	278,395	51,975	226,420	----	37,067	7,731	29,336	----
Colbert	2,447,924	470,992	1,976,932	----	304,743	106,358	198,385	----	85,114	20,859	64,255	----
Conecuh	1,046,575	468,965	577,610	----	613,160	303,675	309,485	----	71,196	40,173	31,023	----
Coosa	417,085	159,125	257,960	----	249,827	96,895	152,932	----	32,344	15,355	16,989	----
Covington	537,750	145,685	392,065	----	259,565	74,615	184,950	----	40,210	9,589	30,621	----
Crenshaw	1,134,275	224,350	909,925	----	392,220	105,960	286,260	----	48,040	14,307	33,733	----
Cullman	104,130	64,625	39,505	----	33,445	23,075	10,370	----	5,550	4,000	1,550	----
Dale	756,360	164,400	591,960	----	162,850	41,550	121,300	----	23,921	7,815	16,106	----
Dallas	3,470,624	510,250	2,960,374	----	1,577,955	231,025	1,346,930	----	335,482	58,470	277,012	----
De Kalb	78,430	19,950	58,480	----	24,000	5,800	18,200	----	4,811	580	4,231	----
Elmore	1,950,520	549,970	1,400,550	----	684,906	221,085	463,821	----	75,609	30,068	45,541	----
Escambia	472,515	185,010	287,505	----	208,405	110,070	98,335	----	25,260	14,295	10,965	----
Etowah	190,857	73,485	117,372	----	57,575	32,665	24,910	----	13,435	5,841	7,594	----
Fayette	249,615	92,550	157,065	----	88,055	39,220	48,835	----	20,493	10,341	10,152	----
Franklin	138,995	55,750	83,245	----	51,325	24,100	27,225	----	13,745	6,595	7,150	----
Geneva	571,591	109,390	462,201	----	116,335	31,265	85,070	----	17,321	5,950	11,371	----
Greene	1,912,930	354,578	1,558,352	----	644,563	145,170	499,393	----	126,117	33,571	92,546	----
Hale	3,415,927	828,404	2,512,023	75,500	947,135	301,230	640,405	5,500	249,260	88,237	160,023	1,000
Henry	1,903,030	256,534	1,646,496	----	490,980	87,000	403,980	----	83,329	17,605	65,724	----
Houston	1,767,810	159,520	1,603,290	5,000	409,535	58,150	349,385	2,000	77,246	17,006	60,140	100
Jackson	424,745	132,225	292,520	----	105,985	46,455	59,530	----	21,514	6,932	14,582	----
Jefferson	911,090	236,925	674,165	----	171,415	70,995	100,420	----	16,699	7,267	9,432	----
Lamar	304,247	100,500	203,747	----	123,255	47,985	75,270	----	31,017	15,322	15,695	----
Lauderdale	1,650,804	342,038	1,308,766	----	383,627	90,710	292,917	----	113,898	23,124	90,774	----
Lawrence	2,056,784	377,893	1,678,891	----	406,505	94,380	312,125	----	98,778	23,936	74,842	----
Lee	1,636,312	376,789	1,256,523	3,000	741,380	198,480	539,400	3,500	106,634	42,103	63,981	550
Limestone	2,459,830	364,100	2,095,730	----	519,176	112,905	406,271	----	153,918	28,856	125,062	----
Lowndes	2,034,590	362,489	1,669,101	3,000	888,531	167,218	718,313	3,000	188,567	38,271	148,796	1,500
Macon	2,385,340	596,240	1,623,540	165,560	1,031,717	294,240	703,477	34,000	203,260	65,479	126,477	11,304
Madison	3,552,389	683,271	2,852,368	16,750	793,375	226,740	563,135	3,500	193,445	65,974	126,471	1,000
Marengo	2,791,210	538,679	2,243,031	9,500	1,127,754	259,216	866,038	2,500	272,583	69,701	202,382	500
Marion	42,745	27,255	15,490	----	22,990	16,265	6,725	----	4,422	3,317	1,105	----
Marshall	131,262	25,420	105,842	----	20,408	5,630	14,778	----	6,108	1,650	4,458	----
Mobile	197,650	98,952	98,698	----	70,597	51,660	18,937	----	11,546	7,457	4,089	----
Monroe	1,285,809	485,871	799,938	----	665,631	291,500	374,131	----	118,304	62,486	55,818	----
Montgomery	3,096,339	561,570	2,314,369	220,400	959,870	234,991	703,279	21,600	157,403	44,008	108,375	5,020
Morgan	1,005,380	248,885	756,495	----	219,840	86,615	133,225	----	69,399	23,497	45,902	----
Perry	2,349,690	453,241	1,896,449	----	626,897	186,939	439,958	----	152,797	42,227	110,570	----
Pickens	1,403,036	246,537	1,156,499	----	693,541	161,660	531,881	----	105,753	23,089	82,664	----
Pike	1,668,776	148,056	1,520,720	----	495,225	56,200	439,025	----	63,859	6,925	56,934	----
Randolph	554,803	163,273	391,530	----	264,830	88,440	176,390	----	37,498	16,370	21,128	----
Russell	1,452,191	409,198	1,042,993	----	585,238	143,429	441,809	----	123,278	40,344	82,934	----
St. Clair	418,525	113,655	304,870	----	123,555	37,890	85,665	----	27,136	8,098	19,038	----
Shelby	282,495	104,150	178,345	----	173,570	65,640	107,930	----	25,532	9,151	16,381	----
Sumter	2,307,911	475,854	1,832,057	----	872,191	201,590	670,601	----	203,069	51,823	151,246	----
Talladega	1,700,858	424,920	1,205,938	70,000	646,085	196,125	419,960	30,000	125,346	47,190	76,156	2,000
Tallapoosa	987,647	207,551	780,096	----	445,243	104,070	341,173	----	62,264	16,549	45,715	----
Tuscaloosa	1,525,087	447,461	1,077,626	----	379,653	147,503	232,150	----	57,748	23,532	34,216	----
Walker	42,305	19,825	22,480	----	20,715	12,025	8,690	----	2,956	1,697	1,259	----
Washington	350,993	209,181	141,812	----	172,841	107,698	65,143	----	30,398	20,502	9,896	----
Wilcox	1,238,984	303,509	903,475	32,000	660,932	129,535	529,897	1,500	138,756	32,879	103,852	2,025
	ARIZONA											
Total	**$698,930**	**$165,825**	**$477,805**	**$55,300**	**$62,580**	**$29,425**	**$28,655**	**$4,500**	**$32,175**	**$12,945**	**$17,330**	**$1,900**
Cochise	6,800	6,800	----	----	1,350	1,350	----	----	1,085	1,085	----	----
Graham	11,565	9,665	1,900	----	1,435	1,335	100	----	715	565	150	----
Maricopa	515,475	119,350	364,625	31,500	36,535	16,000	20,035	500	19,025	5,495	13,030	500
Navajo	1,300	1,300	----	----	300	300	----	----	100	100	----	----
Pima	5,500	5,500	----	----	5,700	5,700	----	----	2,200	2,200	----	----
Pinal	2,550	2,550	----	----	1,750	1,750	----	----	200	200	----	----
Santa Cruz	7,240	5,760	1,480	----	110	90	20	----	----	----	----	----
Yavapai	2,500	2,500	----	----	1,500	1,500	----	----	600	600	----	----
Yuma	146,000	12,400	109,800	23,800	13,900	1,400	8,500	4,000	8,250	2,700	4,150	1,400

TABLE 57.—FARMS OPERATED BY NEGROES—NUMBER, ACREAGE, VALUE OF LAND AND BUILDINGS, AND VALUE OF IMPLEMENTS AND MACHINERY, BY TENURE, BY STATES, AND COUNTIES: 1930—Continued

[Counties in which no farms operated by Negroes were reported, are omitted]

COUNTY	NUMBER OF FARMS				ALL LAND IN FARMS (ACRES)				VALUE OF LAND AND BUILDINGS			
	Total	Owners	Tenants	Managers	Total	Owners	Tenants	Managers	Total	Owners	Tenants	Managers
ARKANSAS												
Total	**79,556**	**11,452**	**68,081**	**23**	**2,485,626**	**704,790**	**1,774,095**	**6,741**	**$118,180,961**	**$21,790,174**	**$96,062,087**	**$328,700**
Arkansas	605	167	437	1	29,289	13,473	15,656	160	611,710	219,750	388,760	3,200
Ashley	2,189	207	1,981	1	60,827	10,556	49,761	510	3,106,415	358,638	2,722,777	25,000
Bradley	606	234	371	1	28,302	14,202	14,098	2	610,324	291,950	318,174	200
Calhoun	444	207	237		27,030	15,389	11,641		505,370	277,155	228,215	
Chicot	3,036	283	2,752	1	71,870	11,065	59,194	1,611	4,449,538	649,972	3,724,566	75,000
Clark	835	266	569		39,865	19,759	20,106		992,096	397,145	594,951	
Cleveland	656	234	422		31,065	15,169	15,896		524,600	244,040	280,560	
Columbia	2,374	587	1,787		118,641	47,579	71,062		3,160,206	1,157,522	2,002,684	
Conway	964	437	527		52,035	30,896	21,139		1,401,760	713,205	688,555	
Craighead	68	11	57		2,242	458	1,784		162,885	33,250	129,635	
Crawford	54	30	24		2,966	1,798	1,168		89,250	49,850	39,400	
Crittenden	7,003	248	6,751	4	162,667	10,832	150,448	1,387	12,038,354	795,320	11,185,834	57,200
Cross	2,416	139	2,277		62,344	9,031	53,313		4,446,282	356,560	4,089,722	
Dallas	452	240	212		24,280	15,456	8,824		452,725	280,665	172,060	
Desha	2,843	226	2,617		67,542	10,787	56,755		3,491,636	489,088	3,002,548	
Drew	1,876	365	1,510	1	67,674	25,540	41,634	500	2,282,423	660,957	1,609,466	12,000
Faulkner	483	170	313		25,633	12,169	13,464		736,300	278,860	457,440	
Franklin	33	11	22		1,827	613	1,214		62,850	24,250	38,600	
Garland	21	12	9		1,067	773	294		31,850	20,700	11,150	
Grant	115	66	49		7,971	5,924	2,047		115,250	77,565	37,685	
Hempstead	2,212	524	1,688		93,393	36,192	57,201		2,466,348	793,387	1,672,961	
Hot Spring	62	41	21		2,081	1,505	576		100,100	70,400	29,700	
Howard	745	139	606		22,879	8,008	14,871		929,000	293,360	635,640	
Independence	52	28	24		2,173	1,320	853		84,757	41,677	43,080	
Izard	33	8	24	1	1,951	940	811	200	30,550	12,000	13,550	5,000
Jackson	694	67	627		27,275	5,966	21,309		1,621,960	207,650	1,414,310	
Jefferson	6,739	631	6,103	5	160,186	27,172	131,936	1,078	9,606,268	1,247,235	8,294,783	64,250
Johnson	19	9	10		526	337	189		12,978	7,930	5,048	
Lafayette	1,554	214	1,340		52,062	13,568	38,494		2,176,897	385,285	1,791,612	
Lawrence	19	7	12		823	342	481		31,450	13,900	17,550	
Lee	4,134	697	3,437		121,122	33,923	87,199		5,773,548	1,406,093	4,367,455	
Lincoln	3,598	362	3,234	2	84,332	18,318	65,614	400	4,372,286	747,195	3,585,091	40,000
Little River	1,298	206	1,092		43,067	12,433	30,634		1,581,660	328,590	1,253,070	
Logan	65	20	45		2,626	1,227	1,399		171,700	68,450	103,250	
Lonoke	2,382	238	2,143	1	59,678	11,642	47,586	450	3,569,851	440,315	3,126,036	3,500
Madison	3	3			318	318			500	500		
Miller	1,407	205	1,202		41,181	10,842	30,339		2,338,470	538,910	1,799,560	
Mississippi	5,089	111	4,978		111,614	4,365	107,249		10,445,541	331,820	10,113,721	
Monroe	2,272	374	1,897	1	72,779	20,455	52,194	130	3,611,123	732,897	2,874,026	4,200
Montgomery	26	14	12		1,780	912	868		27,950	15,400	12,550	
Nevada	1,117	231	886		63,467	21,275	42,192		1,180,920	349,025	831,895	
Ouachita	1,375	674	700	1	86,670	53,393	33,197	80	1,891,087	1,084,514	804,173	2,400
Perry	85	19	65	1	3,732	1,587	2,110	35	120,600	32,600	87,000	1,000
Phillips	4,920	540	4,378	2	128,693	26,041	102,454	198	6,237,448	1,171,773	5,029,925	35,750
Pike	115	32	83		4,795	2,383	2,412		144,630	65,940	78,690	
Poinsett	726	28	698		17,705	1,385	16,320		1,412,550	81,020	1,331,530	
Pope	151	50	101		6,482	3,046	3,436		253,005	109,030	143,975	
Prairie	511	100	411		18,960	5,579	13,381		645,195	153,850	491,345	
Pulaski	2,040	433	1,607		54,109	19,430	34,679		3,824,281	972,741	2,851,540	
Randolph	35	13	22		1,561	714	847		80,880	28,100	52,780	
St. Francis	5,083	407	4,676		142,473	25,068	117,405		7,622,035	808,080	6,813,955	
Saline	32	20	12		1,212	787	425		46,140	27,340	18,800	
Scott	1	1			280	280			2,500	2,500		
Sebastian	40	9	31		1,437	366	1,071		51,070	12,670	38,400	
Sevier	247	90	157		13,018	6,446	6,572		312,615	146,215	166,400	
Sharp	6	4	2		457	421	36		4,700	3,800	900	
Stone	3	3			412	412			3,700	3,700		
Union	1,493	465	1,028		75,370	35,374	39,996		2,027,262	1,000,595	1,026,667	
Van Buren	19	7	12		1,415	749	666		16,850	8,800	8,050	
Washington	16	9	7		562	365	197		15,710	7,810	7,900	
White	110	52	58		6,590	3,802	2,788		193,850	114,500	79,350	
Woodruff	1,831	201	1,630		64,657	13,137	51,520		3,657,912	499,075	3,158,837	
Yell	124	26	98		4,586	1,496	3,090		211,260	47,060	164,200	
CALIFORNIA												
Total	**424**	**210**	**196**	**18**	**30,297**	**15,860**	**12,102**	**2,335**	**$3,669,275**	**$1,427,725**	**$1,853,950**	**$387,600**
Alameda	3	2	1		35	25	10		29,400	24,000	5,400	
Butte	4	2	1	1	417	22	35	360	14,950	10,350	1,000	3,600
Contra Costa	2	2			36	36			26,000	26,000		
Eldorado	3	3			421	421			15,000	15,000		
Fresno	38	19	18	1	1,234	388	826	20	185,475	61,775	121,700	2,000
Glenn	2	1	1		40	20	20		20,000	15,000	5,000	
Imperial	80	32	38	10	7,050	2,478	3,112	1,460	729,760	110,810	341,950	277,000
Kern	39	4	34	1	2,029	320	1,629	80	446,150	56,000	380,150	10,000
Kings	11	7	4		702	257	445		91,500	38,500	53,000	
Lake	1	1			5	5			3,000	3,000		
Los Angeles	14	9	4	1	407	356	46	5	179,850	58,850	116,000	5,000
Madera	17		17		1,325		1,325		150,400		150,400	
Mariposa	2	1		1	360	40		320	8,000	3,000		5,000
Mendocino	3	3			459	459			38,000	38,000		
Merced	23	8	15		1,118	267	851		106,750	26,150	80,600	
Monterey	2	2			648	648			11,800	11,800		
Napa	2	1	1		21	18	3		5,200	5,000	200	
Orange	15	11	4		1,433	1,228	205		120,100	102,100	18,000	
Placer	2	1		1	32	2		30	78,000	3,000		75,000
Riverside	42	21	21		1,899	586	1,313		256,640	100,440	156,200	
Sacramento	11	6	4	1	170	55	95	20	51,200	30,700	13,500	7,000
San Bernardino	22	18	3	1	1,082	969	73	40	148,000	86,000	59,000	3,000
San Diego	1		1		110		110		50,000		50,000	
San Joaquin	6	5	1		2,848	2,841	7		197,300	195,300	2,000	

TABLE 57.—FARMS OPERATED BY NEGROES—NUMBER, ACREAGE, VALUE OF LAND AND BUILDINGS, AND VALUE OF IMPLEMENTS AND MACHINERY, BY TENURE, BY STATES, AND COUNTIES: 1930—Continued

[Counties in which no farms operated by Negroes were reported, are omitted]

COUNTY	VALUE OF LAND ALONE				VALUE OF BUILDINGS				VALUE OF IMPLEMENTS AND MACHINERY			
	Total	Owners	Tenants	Managers	Total	Owners	Tenants	Managers	Total	Owners	Tenants	Managers
ARKANSAS												
Total	$94, 312, 157	$16, 232, 397	$77, 827, 700	$252, 060	$23, 868, 804	$5, 557, 777	$18, 234, 387	$76, 640	$4, 769, 956	$1, 298, 051	$3, 455, 510	$16, 395
Arkansas	458, 879	162, 655	293, 224	3, 000	152, 831	57, 095	95, 536	200	44, 250	17, 793	25, 957	500
Ashley	2, 500, 212	269, 713	2, 209, 499	21, 000	606, 203	88, 925	513, 278	4, 000	161, 457	23, 143	137, 314	1, 000
Bradley	421, 688	200, 030	221, 558	100	188, 636	91, 920	96, 616	100	31, 539	14, 691	16, 843	5
Calhoun	401, 532	212, 752	188, 780	100	103, 838	64, 403	39, 435	—	22, 906	14, 651	8, 255	—
Chicot	3, 365, 065	477, 535	2, 827, 530	60, 000	1, 084, 473	172, 437	897, 036	15, 000	227, 909	37, 561	190, 248	100
Clark	811, 319	312, 360	498, 959	—	180, 777	84, 785	95, 992	—	41, 561	17, 346	24, 215	—
Cleveland	350, 950	155, 565	195, 385	—	173, 650	88, 475	85, 175	—	31, 126	15, 994	15, 132	—
Columbia	2, 420, 997	850, 015	1, 570, 982	—	739, 209	307, 507	431, 702	—	132, 908	62, 482	70, 426	—
Conway	1, 081, 616	520, 391	561, 225	—	320, 144	192, 814	127, 330	—	50, 143	30, 109	20, 034	—
Craighead	140, 202	28, 192	112, 010	—	22, 683	5, 058	17, 625	—	5, 650	1, 265	4, 385	—
Crawford	68, 145	36, 325	31, 820	—	21, 105	13, 525	7, 580	—	3, 025	1, 845	1, 180	—
Crittenden	9, 789, 480	631, 093	9, 112, 527	45, 860	2, 248, 874	164, 227	2, 073, 307	11, 340	332, 587	56, 056	273, 531	3, 000
Cross	3, 683, 670	270, 790	3, 412, 880	—	762, 612	85, 770	676, 842	—	182, 639	24, 857	157, 782	—
Dallas	323, 860	199, 030	124, 830	—	128, 865	81, 635	47, 230	—	22, 244	13, 779	8, 465	—
Desha	2, 669, 410	370, 398	2, 299, 012	—	822, 226	118, 690	703, 536	—	255, 786	43, 680	212, 106	—
Drew	1, 669, 668	460, 917	1, 196, 751	12, 000	612, 755	200, 040	412, 715	—	112, 158	35, 985	76, 173	—
Faulkner	578, 365	197, 630	380, 735	—	157, 935	81, 230	76, 705	—	30, 154	13, 195	16, 959	—
Franklin	47, 250	17, 650	29, 600	—	15, 600	6, 600	9, 000	—	1, 060	525	535	—
Garland	24, 505	15, 980	8, 525	—	7, 345	4, 720	2, 625	—	617	332	285	—
Grant	91, 196	63, 441	27, 755	—	24, 054	14, 124	9, 930	—	4, 291	3, 128	1, 163	—
Hempstead	1, 981, 608	599, 257	1, 382, 351	—	484, 740	194, 130	290, 610	—	89, 082	39, 218	49, 864	—
Hot Spring	60, 050	39, 050	21, 000	—	40, 050	31, 350	8, 700	—	5, 355	4, 355	1, 000	—
Howard	739, 120	216, 120	523, 000	—	189, 880	77, 240	112, 640	—	33, 511	11, 465	22, 046	—
Independence	66, 737	31, 507	35, 230	—	18, 020	10, 170	7, 850	—	3, 560	1, 600	1, 960	—
Izard	19, 500	7, 600	8, 900	3, 000	11, 050	4, 400	4, 650	2, 000	4, 045	410	1, 635	2, 000
Jackson	1, 311, 100	157, 675	1, 153, 425	—	310, 860	49, 975	260, 885	—	85, 034	13, 210	71, 824	—
Jefferson	7, 843, 807	930, 135	6, 875, 022	38, 650	1, 762, 461	317, 100	1, 419, 761	25, 600	352, 167	65, 591	281, 776	4, 800
Johnson	9, 778	6, 225	3, 553	—	3, 200	1, 705	1, 495	—	180	100	80	—
Lafayette	1, 785, 892	291, 475	1, 494, 417	—	391, 005	93, 810	297, 195	—	81, 927	17, 854	64, 073	—
Lawrence	25, 730	11, 100	14, 630	—	5, 720	2, 800	2, 920	—	953	465	488	—
Lee	4, 277, 534	1, 001, 708	3, 275, 826	—	1, 496, 014	404, 385	1, 091, 629	—	285, 517	99, 983	185, 534	—
Lincoln	3, 525, 336	601, 045	2, 887, 291	37, 000	846, 950	146, 150	697, 800	3, 000	220, 975	51, 853	166, 122	3, 000
Little River	1, 336, 843	260, 255	1, 076, 588	—	244, 817	68, 335	176, 482	—	57, 163	14, 978	42, 185	—
Logan	150, 175	59, 025	91, 150	—	21, 525	9, 425	12, 100	—	2, 892	1, 225	1, 667	—
Lonoke	2, 987, 894	346, 778	2, 638, 616	2, 500	581, 957	93, 537	487, 420	1, 000	118, 507	19, 295	99, 012	200
Madison	310	310	—	—	190	190	—	—	19	19	—	—
Miller	1, 913, 980	396, 690	1, 517, 290	—	424, 490	142, 220	282, 270	—	104, 441	43, 236	61, 205	—
Mississippi	8, 889, 504	253, 185	8, 636, 319	—	1, 556, 037	78, 635	1, 477, 402	—	194, 913	24, 815	170, 098	—
Monroe	2, 830, 635	531, 857	2, 295, 378	3, 400	780, 488	201, 040	578, 648	800	170, 476	47, 762	122, 414	300
Montgomery	18, 750	10, 500	8, 250	—	9, 200	4, 900	4, 300	—	875	470	405	—
Nevada	913, 225	253, 245	659, 980	—	267, 695	95, 780	171, 915	—	55, 242	16, 310	38, 932	—
Ouachita	1, 399, 825	790, 909	607, 016	1, 900	491, 262	293, 605	197, 157	500	94, 966	56, 626	38, 240	100
Perry	97, 075	24, 900	71, 675	500	23, 525	7, 700	15, 325	500	5, 170	1, 415	3, 755	—
Phillips	5, 035, 244	878, 933	4, 133, 161	23, 150	1, 202, 204	292, 840	896, 764	12, 600	267, 828	85, 402	181, 036	1, 390
Pike	117, 050	51, 365	65, 685	—	27, 580	14, 575	13, 005	—	7, 920	3, 490	4, 430	—
Poinsett	1, 233, 574	57, 320	1, 176, 254	—	178, 976	23, 700	155, 276	—	54, 137	5, 645	48, 492	—
Pope	199, 015	77, 420	121, 595	—	53, 990	31, 610	22, 380	—	7, 847	4, 030	3, 817	—
Prairie	489, 490	108, 995	380, 495	—	155, 705	44, 855	110, 850	—	30, 916	8, 755	22, 161	—
Pulaski	3, 183, 821	768, 301	2, 415, 520	—	640, 460	204, 440	436, 020	—	146, 377	61, 326	85, 051	—
Randolph	69, 955	23, 195	46, 760	—	10, 925	4, 905	6, 020	—	2, 103	1, 042	1, 061	—
St. Francis	5, 740, 512	580, 525	5, 159, 987	—	1, 881, 523	227, 555	1, 653, 968	—	250, 699	51, 939	198, 760	—
Saline	33, 470	21, 020	12, 450	—	12, 670	6, 320	6, 350	—	1, 693	1, 178	515	—
Scott	2, 250	2, 250	—	—	250	250	—	—	75	75	—	—
Sebastian	41, 870	8, 970	32, 900	—	9, 200	3, 700	5, 500	—	1, 255	455	800	—
Sevier	244, 545	109, 670	134, 875	—	68, 070	36, 545	31, 525	—	11, 139	6, 422	4, 717	—
Sharp	3, 800	3, 000	800	—	900	800	100	—	250	190	60	—
Stone	3, 150	3, 150	—	—	550	550	—	—	140	140	—	—
Union	1, 552, 764	754, 000	798, 764	—	474, 498	246, 595	227, 903	—	116, 245	71, 461	44, 784	—
Van Buren	11, 675	5, 875	5, 800	—	5, 175	2, 925	2, 250	—	970	585	385	—
Washington	12, 950	6, 800	6, 150	—	2, 760	1, 010	1, 750	—	1, 282	457	825	—
White	143, 150	85, 975	57, 175	—	50, 700	28, 525	22, 175	—	9, 554	4, 724	4, 830	—
Woodruff	2, 944, 285	379, 850	2, 564, 435	—	713, 627	119, 225	594, 402	—	193, 031	28, 748	164, 283	—
Yell	167, 170	32, 770	134, 400	—	44, 090	14, 290	29, 800	—	5, 515	1, 315	4, 200	—
CALIFORNIA												
Total	$3, 218, 125	$1, 180, 605	$1, 710, 820	$326, 700	$451, 150	$247, 120	$143, 130	$60, 900	$146, 326	$61, 346	$72, 505	$12, 475
Alameda	18, 850	13, 500	5, 350	—	10, 550	10, 500	50	—	—	—	—	—
Butte	8, 700	4, 850	850	3, 000	6, 250	5, 500	150	600	1, 931	181	—	1, 750
Contra Costa	22, 000	22, 000	—	—	4, 000	4, 000	—	—	2, 600	2, 600	—	—
Eldorado	13, 700	13, 700	—	—	1, 300	1, 300	—	—	200	200	—	—
Fresno	153, 975	46, 675	105, 700	1, 600	31, 500	15, 100	16, 000	400	7, 510	4, 050	3, 435	25
Glenn	17, 500	12, 500	5, 000	—	2, 500	2, 500	—	—	1, 300	800	500	—
Imperial	699, 665	102, 050	328, 055	269, 600	30, 095	8, 760	13, 935	7, 400	26, 120	6, 350	10, 470	9, 300
Kern	417, 150	48, 350	359, 050	9, 750	29, 000	7, 650	21, 100	250	16, 155	5, 300	10, 805	50
Kings	76, 550	29, 950	46, 600	—	14, 950	8, 550	6, 400	—	3, 765	3, 175	590	—
Lake	2, 500	2, 500	—	—	500	500	—	—	—	—	—	—
Los Angeles	166, 500	46, 700	114, 950	4, 850	13, 350	12, 150	1, 050	150	3, 625	1, 625	1, 800	200
Madera	142, 925	—	142, 925	—	7, 475	—	7, 475	—	6, 850	—	6, 850	—
Mariposa	6, 000	2, 500	—	3, 500	2, 000	500	—	1, 500	700	500	—	200
Mendocino	35, 000	35, 000	—	—	3, 000	3, 000	—	—	—	—	—	—
Merced	85, 790	20, 890	64, 900	—	20, 960	5, 260	15, 700	—	6, 230	2, 250	3, 980	—
Monterey	10, 000	10, 000	—	—	1, 800	1, 800	—	—	300	300	—	—
Napa	5, 200	5, 000	200	—	—	—	—	—	—	—	—	—
Orange	107, 550	90, 700	16, 850	—	12, 550	11, 400	1, 150	—	2, 075	1, 475	600	—
Placer	26, 000	1, 000	—	25, 000	52, 000	2, 000	—	50, 000	625	125	—	500
Riverside	233, 495	84, 665	148, 830	—	23, 145	15, 775	7, 370	—	19, 850	1, 640	18, 210	—
Sacramento	25, 800	12, 600	6, 800	6, 400	25, 400	18, 100	6, 700	600	4, 520	3, 170	900	450
San Bernadino	119, 625	63, 525	53, 100	3, 000	28, 375	22, 475	5, 900	—	2, 505	2, 110	395	—
San Diego	49, 000	—	49, 000	—	1, 000	—	1, 000	—	1, 000	—	1, 000	—
San Joaquin	188, 400	186, 900	1, 500	—	8, 900	8, 400	500	—	4, 200	4, 000	200	—

TABLE 57.—FARMS OPERATED BY NEGROES—NUMBER, ACREAGE, VALUE OF LAND AND BUILDINGS, AND VALUE OF IMPLEMENTS AND MACHINERY, BY TENURE, BY STATES, AND COUNTIES: 1930—Continued

[Counties in which no farms operated by Negroes were reported, are omitted]

COUNTY	NUMBER OF FARMS				ALL LAND IN FARMS (ACRES)				VALUE OF LAND AND BUILDINGS			
	Total	Owners	Tenants	Managers	Total	Owners	Tenants	Managers	Total	Owners	Tenants	Managers
CALIFORNIA—continued												
Santa Clara	3	1	2		18	4	14		$9,200	$5,000	$4,200	
Santa Cruz	1	1			1	1			4,500	4,500		
Shasta	9	7	2		1,435	1,343	92		61,850	47,850	14,000	
Siskiyou	1	1			13	13			1,000	1,000		
Sonoma	3	3			30	30			25,000	25,000		
Stanislaus	4	4			127	127			22,500	22,500		
Sutter	1	1			10	10			7,000	7,000		
Tehama	3	3			176	176			13,000	13,000		
Trinity	2	2			262	262			11,000	11,000		
Tulare	42	21	21		2,890	1,324	1,566		421,300	190,650	230,650	
Yolo	8	5	3		1,059	734	325		68,450	17,450	51,000	
Yuba	2	2			395	395			62,000	62,000		
COLORADO												
Total	**78**	**54**	**23**	**1**	**25,137**	**18,684**	**6,133**	**320**	**$445,540**	**$263,910**	**$178,430**	**$3,200**
Adams	3	2	1		214	57	157		19,550	6,000	13,550	
Alamosa	1	1			160	160			8,000	8,000		
Arapahoe	5	4	1		2,646	2,546	100		47,350	42,850	4,500	
Baca	1	1			480	480			8,000	8,000		
Crowley	4	2	2		402	222	180		30,700	16,700	14,000	
Custer	2	2			1,860	1,860			21,000	21,000		
El Paso	5	1	4		2,649	400	2,249		36,880	10,000	26,880	
Hinsdale	1	1			420	420			3,000	3,000		
Huerfano	2	2			280	280			3,000	3,000		
Jefferson	2	2			16	16			12,300	12,300		
La Plata	1		1		147		147		2,500		2,500	
Las Animas	9	4	5		2,125	1,010	1,115		35,700	7,400	28,300	
Morgan	4	3	1		1,120	960	160		10,260	9,460	800	
Otero	13	11	2		6,566	6,086	480		99,380	43,780	55,600	
Prowers	2	2			723	723			8,000	8,000		
Pueblo	2	1		1	560	240		320	11,200	8,000		3,200
Rio Blanco	1	1			90	90			1,000	1,000		
Teller	1	1			60	60			1,200	1,200		
Washington	5	3	2		1,200	960	240		9,920	7,320	2,600	
Weld	14	10	4		3,419	2,114	1,305		76,600	46,900	29,700	
CONNECTICUT												
Total	**33**	**25**	**5**	**3**	**1,319**	**862**	**332**	**125**	**$314,700**	**$146,700**	**$33,000**	**$135,000**
Fairfield	6	2	1	3	187	32	30	125	160,000	20,000	5,000	135,000
Hartford	9	7	2		251	239	12		65,300	55,800	9,500	
Litchfield	3	2	1		334	84	250		37,000	22,000	15,000	
Middlesex	4	4			41	41			11,900	11,900		
New Haven	2	2			56	50			16,000	16,000		
New London	3	3			145	145			7,500	7,500		
Tolland	3	3			117	117			5,500	5,500		
Windham	3	2	1		194	154	40		11,500	8,000	3,500	
DELAWARE												
Total	**807**	**373**	**415**	**19**	**54,756**	**13,781**	**37,631**	**3,344**	**$2,628.590**	**$804,240**	**1,509,675**	**$314,675**
Kent	328	139	179	10	23,294	3,773	18,221	1,300	1,101,365	272,340	722,350	106,675
New Castle	75	48	22	5	4,970	1,774	2,122	1,074	404,925	125,950	90,975	188,000
Sussex	404	186	214	4	26,492	8,234	17,288	970	1,122,300	405,950	696,350	20,000
DISTRICT OF COLUMBIA												
Total	**11**	**8**	**2**	**1**	**95**	**28**	**7**	**60**	**$82,000**	**$43,500**	**$8,500**	**$30,000**
FLORIDA												
Total	**11,010**	**5,560**	**5,362**	**88**	**513,912**	**281,287**	**223,711**	**8,914**	**$15,369,957**	**$8,407,507**	**$5,775,570**	**$1,186,880**
Alachua	986	678	305	3	45,665	30,526	13,219	1,920	1,245,017	843,482	354,035	47,500
Baker	36	27	9		1,118	705	413		34,950	24,300	10,650	
Bay	28	20	8		676	489	187		45,680	32,950	12,730	
Bradford	161	118	43		3,868	2,611	1,257		199,650	151,745	47,905	
Brevard	36	25	3	8	703	430	57	216	434,250	299,450	40,800	94,000
Broward	403	35	368		2,254	378	1,876		234,130	43,485	190,645	
Calhoun	50	33	17		2,351	1,616	735		39,555	26,035	13,520	
Charlotte	4	2	2		75	25	50		6,350	3,850	2,500	
Citrus	18	13	5		1,298	932	366		22,850	18,250	4,600	
Clay	28	25	3		1,137	1,011	126		42,325	37,925	4,400	
Columbia	427	213	214		36,226	20,642	15,584		523,265	262,245	261,020	
Dade	69	10	58	1	692	202	330	160	115,525	46,350	48,675	20,500
De Soto	1	1			4	4			1,500	1,500		
Dixie	8	5	3		196	114	82		4,050	2,400	1,650	
Duval	128	99	23	6	2,407	1,766	517	124	236,840	152,755	54,385	29,700
Escambia	89	56	33		2,576	1,373	1,203		124,800	71,910	52,890	
Flagler	3	3			45	45			2,500	2,500		
Gadsden	639	409	229	1	29,764	19,826	9,508	430	738,090	468,380	254,710	15,000
Gilchrist	7	2	5		705	280	425		12,740	4,200	8,540	
Glades	1		1		18		18		1,800		1,800	

TABLE 57.—FARMS OPERATED BY NEGROES—NUMBER, ACREAGE, VALUE OF LAND AND BUILDINGS, AND VALUE OF IMPLEMENTS AND MACHINERY, BY TENURE, BY STATES, AND COUNTIES: 1930—Continued

[Counties in which no farms operated by Negroes were reported, are omitted]

COUNTY	VALUE OF LAND ALONE				VALUE OF BUILDINGS				VALUE OF IMPLEMENTS AND MACHINERY			
	Total	Owners	Tenants	Managers	Total	Owners	Tenants	Managers	Total	Owners	Tenants	Managers
CALIFORNIA—continued												
Santa Clara	$9,200	$5,000	$4,200	-------	-------	-------	-------	-------	$100	-------	$100	-------
Santa Cruz	1,500	1,500	-------	-------	$3,000	$3,000	-------	-------	-------	-------	-------	-------
Shasta	44,900	32,900	12,000	-------	16,950	14,950	$2,000	-------	2,000	$1,350	650	-------
Siskiyou	600	600	-------	-------	400	400	-------	-------	50	50	-------	-------
Sonona	22,500	22,500	-------	-------	2,500	2,500	-------	-------	800	800	-------	-------
Stanislaus	15,300	15,300	-------	-------	7,200	7,200	-------	-------	910	910	-------	-------
Sutter	3,000	3,000	-------	-------	4,000	4,000	-------	-------	50	50	-------	-------
Tehama	7,000	7,000	-------	-------	6,000	6,000	-------	-------	1,900	1,900	-------	-------
Trinity	7,500	7,500	-------	-------	3,500	3,500	-------	-------	345	345	-------	-------
Tulare	366,200	158,700	207,500	-------	55,100	31,950	23,150	-------	13,335	6,815	6,520	-------
Yolo	50,550	13,050	37,500	-------	17,900	4,400	13,500	-------	9,775	4,275	5,500	-------
Yuba	58,000	58,000	-------	-------	4,000	4,000	-------	-------	5,000	5,000	-------	-------
COLORADO												
Total	$371,890	$213,560	$155,130	$3,200	$73,650	$50,350	$23,300	-------	$23,097	$12,835	$10,262	-------
Adams	15,950	3,900	12,050	-------	3,600	2,100	1,500	-------	1,600	400	1,200	-------
Alamosa	7,500	7,500	-------	-------	500	500	-------	-------	1,000	1,000	-------	-------
Arapahoe	42,850	39,850	3,000	-------	4,500	3,000	1,500	-------	2,300	1,300	1,000	-------
Baca	7,800	7,800	-------	-------	200	200	-------	-------	100	100	-------	-------
Crowley	22,500	10,200	12,300	-------	8,200	6,500	1,700	-------	3,400	2,000	1,400	-------
Custer	17,800	17,800	-------	-------	3,200	3,200	-------	-------	225	225	-------	-------
El Paso	27,480	7,000	20,480	-------	9,400	3,000	6,400	-------	2,500	300	2,200	-------
Hinsdale	2,000	2,000	-------	-------	1,000	1,000	-------	-------	800	800	-------	-------
Huerfano	1,950	1,950	-------	-------	1,050	1,050	-------	-------	150	150	-------	-------
Jefferson	7,800	7,800	-------	-------	4,500	4,500	-------	-------	100	100	-------	-------
La Plata	2,350	-------	2,350	-------	150	-------	150	-------	100	-------	100	-------
Las Animas	26,550	3,350	23,200	-------	9,150	4,050	5,100	-------	1,160	115	1,045	-------
Morgan	8,360	7,960	400	-------	1,900	1,500	400	-------	1,500	1,300	200	-------
Otero	92,080	38,130	53,950	-------	7,300	5,650	1,650	-------	3,800	2,000	1,800	-------
Prowers	4,100	4,100	-------	-------	3,900	3,900	-------	-------	1,500	1,500	-------	-------
Pueblo	10,200	7,000	-------	3,200	1,000	1,000	-------	-------	75	75	-------	-------
Rio Blanco	200	200	-------	-------	800	800	-------	-------	100	100	-------	-------
Teller	850	850	-------	-------	350	350	-------	-------	-------	-------	-------	-------
Washington	8,520	6,320	2,200	-------	1,400	1,000	400	-------	567	400	167	-------
Weld	65,050	39,850	25,200	-------	11,550	7,050	4,500	-------	2,120	970	1,150	-------
CONNECTICUT												
Total	$116,365	$59,865	$15,500	$41,000	$198,335	$86,835	$17,500	$94,000	$9,735	$7,735	$1,600	$400
Fairfield	50,000	4,000	5,000	41,000	110,000	16,000	-------	94,000	2,300	1,900	-------	400
Hartford	31,065	29,065	2,000	-------	34,235	26,735	7,500	-------	4,335	3,835	500	-------
Litchfield	14,000	7,000	7,000	-------	23,000	15,000	8,000	-------	1,300	300	1,000	-------
Middlesex	4,600	4,600	-------	-------	7,300	7,300	-------	-------	150	150	-------	-------
New Haven	5,000	5,000	-------	-------	11,000	11,000	-------	-------	500	500	-------	-------
New London	4,700	4,700	-------	-------	2,800	2,800	-------	-------	100	100	-------	-------
Tolland	1,500	1,500	-------	-------	4,000	4,000	-------	-------	800	800	-------	-------
Windham	5,500	4,000	1,500	-------	6,000	4,000	2,000	-------	250	150	100	-------
DELAWARE												
Total	$1,553,810	$384,690	$979,295	$189,825	$1,074,780	$419,550	$530,380	$124,850	$224,010	$100,745	$107,075	$16,190
Kent	702,955	146,260	481,620	75,075	398,410	126,080	240,730	31,600	87,040	30,935	46,165	9,940
New Castle	203,580	42,580	63,000	98,000	201,345	83,370	27,975	90,000	17,720	10,380	1,840	5,500
Sussex	647,275	195,850	434,675	16,750	475,025	210,100	261,675	3,250	119,250	59,430	59,070	750
DISTRICT OF COLUMBIA												
Total	$55,725	$27,725	$3,000	$25,000	$26,275	$15,775	$5,500	$5,000	$1,225	$100	$125	$1,000
FLORIDA												
Total	$11,515,243	$5,989,694	$4,546,154	$979,395	$3,854,714	$2,417,813	$1,229,416	$207,485	$687,523	$409,834	$248,649	$29,040
Alachua	812,092	501,232	269,860	41,000	432,925	342,250	84,175	6,500	57,686	45,791	11,520	375
Baker	26,050	17,225	8,825	-------	8,900	7,075	1,825	-------	1,335	1,180	155	-------
Bay	29,655	19,775	9,880	-------	16,025	13,175	2,850	-------	2,330	875	1,455	-------
Bradford	138,633	102,058	36,575	-------	61,017	49,687	11,330	-------	9,085	6,464	2,621	-------
Brevard	405,080	273,230	40,400	91,450	29,170	26,220	400	2,550	4,215	3,495	135	585
Broward	228,910	39,525	189,385	-------	5,220	3,960	1,260	-------	37,409	7,139	30,270	-------
Calhoun	28,425	18,405	10,020	-------	11,130	7,630	3,500	-------	1,383	885	498	-------
Charlotte	3,650	1,800	1,850	-------	2,700	2,050	650	-------	900	850	50	-------
Citrus	16,690	13,115	3,575	-------	6,160	5,135	1,025	-------	3,535	3,300	235	-------
Clay	31,010	27,610	3,400	-------	11,315	10,315	1,000	-------	2,315	2,270	45	-------
Columbia	395,577	181,195	214,382	-------	127,688	81,050	46,638	-------	23,728	17,805	5,923	-------
Dade	103,575	37,850	46,225	19,500	11,950	8,500	2,450	1,000	15,350	3,650	9,700	2,000
De Soto	1,350	1,350	-------	-------	150	150	-------	-------	75	75	-------	-------
Dixie	2,250	1,400	850	-------	1,800	1,000	800	-------	205	145	60	-------
Duval	177,265	108,425	44,840	24,000	59,575	44,330	9,545	5,700	5,855	4,402	1,058	395
Escambia	87,745	45,030	42,715	-------	37,055	26,880	10,175	-------	5,293	2,663	2,630	-------
Flagler	1,775	1,775	-------	-------	725	725	-------	-------	510	510	-------	-------
Gadsden	445,240	282,060	154,180	9,000	292,850	186,320	100,530	6,000	38,462	25,978	11,984	500
Gilchrist	8,490	2,500	5,990	-------	4,250	1,700	2,550	-------	515	100	415	-------
Glades	1,800	-------	1,800	-------	-------	-------	-------	-------	700	-------	700	-------

TABLE 57.—FARMS OPERATED BY NEGROES—NUMBER, ACREAGE, VALUE OF LAND AND BUILDINGS, AND VALUE OF IMPLEMENTS AND MACHINERY, BY TENURE, BY STATES, AND COUNTIES: 1930—Continued

[Counties in which no farms operated by Negroes were reported, are omitted]

COUNTY	NUMBER OF FARMS				ALL LAND IN FARMS (ACRES)				VALUE OF LAND AND BUILDINGS			
	Total	Owners	Tenants	Managers	Total	Owners	Tenants	Managers	Total	Owners	Tenants	Managers
FLORIDA—continued												
Gulf	15	7	8	-------	579	444	135	-------	$12, 105	$7, 480	$4, 625	-------
Hamilton	220	79	141	-------	18, 571	9, 334	9, 237	-------	255, 816	122, 970	132, 846	-------
Hardee	4	1	3	-------	59	20	39	-------	5, 000	1, 000	4, 000	-------
Hendry	6	1	5	-------	99	40	59	-------	9, 900	4, 000	5, 900	-------
Hernando	88	62	22	4	2, 206	1, 556	423	227	239, 075	123, 375	83, 700	$32, 000
Highlands	1	-------	1	-------	40	-------	40	-------	1, 600	-------	1, 600	-------
Hillsborough	81	50	22	9	1, 771	1, 240	274	257	370, 195	190, 050	34, 145	146, 000
Holmes	21	9	12	-------	1, 412	1, 010	402	-------	27, 220	15, 120	12, 100	-------
Indian River	16	5	11	-------	245	81	164	-------	40, 600	14, 000	26, 600	-------
Jackson	1, 566	587	974	5	96, 875	40, 552	54, 673	1, 650	1, 781, 425	722, 764	987, 831	20, 830
Jefferson	873	286	587	-------	38, 778	18, 574	20, 204	-------	882, 612	398, 357	484, 255	-------
Lafayette	7	3	4	-------	307	30	277	-------	6, 600	1, 400	5, 200	-------
Lake	109	75	28	6	2, 449	1, 828	401	220	379, 135	219, 685	29, 450	130, 000
Lee	9	1	8	-------	123	10	113	-------	16, 300	500	15, 800	-------
Leon	1, 259	356	901	2	52, 349	18, 486	33, 678	185	1, 381, 957	454, 270	901, 487	26, 200
Levy	188	129	59	-------	8, 626	6, 379	2, 247	-------	153, 976	109, 971	44, 005	-------
Liberty	72	58	14	-------	5, 908	5, 636	272	-------	77, 925	67, 750	10, 175	-------
Madison	580	156	421	3	35, 611	13, 113	21, 858	640	673, 865	223, 440	416, 225	34, 200
Manatee	24	2	17	5	322	10	157	155	149, 200	5, 000	47, 200	97, 000
Marion	955	809	141	5	35, 238	29, 858	5, 231	149	1, 235, 326	979, 005	188, 721	67, 600
Martin	23	8	15	-------	337	199	138	-------	47, 340	25, 500	21, 840	-------
Monroe	9	2	7	-------	907	190	717	-------	96, 700	20, 500	76, 200	-------
Nassau	43	40	2	1	1, 594	1, 476	101	17	46, 900	39, 900	6, 000	1, 000
Okaloosa	63	33	29	1	3, 412	1, 982	1, 390	40	105, 100	43, 000	61, 100	1, 000
Okeechobee	4	1	3	-------	33	5	28	-------	3, 000	500	2, 500	-------
Orange	56	52	2	2	1, 365	1, 028	22	315	479, 895	372, 395	13, 500	94, 000
Osceola	9	9	-------	-------	92	92	-------	-------	18, 800	18, 800	-------	-------
Palm Beach	177	37	134	6	1, 625	459	1, 013	153	181, 050	43, 700	121, 750	15, 600
Pasco	20	15	5	-------	361	173	188	-------	41, 850	13, 650	28, 200	-------
Pinellas	1	-------	-------	1	65	-------	-------	65	50, 000	-------	-------	50, 000
Polk	42	26	13	3	647	437	108	102	128, 680	60, 150	22, 880	45, 650
Putnam	190	172	14	4	5, 903	4, 861	941	101	447, 727	332, 707	55, 520	59, 500
St. Johns	33	25	6	2	792	546	96	150	114, 920	80, 420	9, 500	25, 000
St. Lucie	3	1	1	1	102	42	40	20	42, 000	8, 000	4, 000	30, 000
Santa Rosa	28	13	13	2	1, 868	572	544	752	73, 300	20, 700	16, 600	36, 000
Sarasota	3	1	2	-------	134	24	110	-------	44, 500	4, 000	40, 500	-------
Seminole	39	31	7	1	617	403	74	140	134, 500	111, 600	15, 900	7, 000
Sumter	121	100	21	-------	4, 609	4, 184	425	-------	163, 195	135, 125	28, 070	-------
Suwannee	394	175	219	-------	31, 322	16, 035	15, 287	-------	453, 455	222, 765	230, 690	-------
Taylor	14	1	12	1	857	80	457	320	32, 800	1, 000	16, 800	15, 000
Union	78	35	43	-------	4, 297	2, 277	2, 020	-------	98, 700	37, 200	61, 500	-------
Volusia	49	39	6	4	1, 318	1, 153	120	45	399, 500	335, 450	21, 050	43, 000
Wakulla	126	97	28	1	5, 624	4, 122	1, 141	361	115, 296	87, 376	24, 320	3, 600
Walton	109	77	32	-------	4, 598	3, 376	1, 222	-------	101, 570	68, 470	33, 100	-------
Washington	160	120	40	-------	8, 087	6, 395	1, 692	-------	183, 480	120, 750	62, 730	-------
GEORGIA												
Total	**86, 787**	**11, 080**	**75, 635**	**72**	**5, 104, 452**	**883, 284**	**4, 197, 605**	**23, 563**	**$114, 688, 230**	**$17, 528, 122**	**$96, 253, 338**	**$906, 770**
Appling	191	95	96	-------	12, 740	7, 256	5, 484	-------	256, 125	131, 505	124, 620	-------
Atkinson	89	36	53	-------	6, 493	1, 869	4, 624	-------	107, 765	27, 050	80, 715	-------
Bacon	50	9	41	-------	3, 983	336	3, 647	-------	84, 077	9, 100	74, 977	-------
Baker	758	162	594	2	49, 230	20, 917	26, 623	1, 690	820, 940	282, 560	498, 880	39, 500
Baldwin	589	68	519	2	36, 705	6, 990	28, 441	1, 274	546, 172	100, 550	429, 722	15, 900
Banks	148	23	125	-------	7, 934	1, 755	6, 179	-------	184, 925	29, 690	155, 235	-------
Barrow	269	25	244	-------	11, 731	1, 612	10, 119	-------	363, 420	45, 950	317, 470	-------
Bartow	375	39	336	-------	16, 210	2, 165	14, 045	-------	659, 292	54, 190	605, 102	-------
Ben Hill	289	70	219	-------	24, 761	7, 307	17, 454	-------	559, 025	161, 625	397, 400	-------
Berrien	114	12	102	-------	8, 330	811	7, 519	-------	167, 530	24, 000	143, 530	-------
Bibb	370	90	278	2	18, 122	4, 632	13, 205	285	658, 566	149, 055	428, 711	$80, 800
Bleckley	221	15	206	-------	12, 466	1, 697	10, 769	-------	283, 035	31, 200	251, 835	-------
Brantley	34	27	7	-------	914	735	179	-------	19, 375	15, 650	3, 725	-------
Brooks	1, 095	227	868	-------	56, 784	16, 924	39, 860	-------	1, 385, 609	369, 615	1, 015, 994	-------
Bryan	152	76	76	-------	12, 649	6, 889	5, 760	-------	160, 062	76, 095	83, 967	-------
Bulloch	996	130	866	-------	57, 449	11, 948	45, 501	-------	1, 763, 781	254, 340	1, 509, 441	-------
Burke	3, 036	217	2, 809	10	152, 756	25, 389	124, 443	2, 924	3, 542, 106	465, 896	3, 044, 795	71, 415
Butts	608	25	582	1	33, 331	1, 389	31, 817	125	666, 844	31, 465	625, 379	10, 000
Calhoun	1, 227	34	1, 192	1	56, 608	4, 605	49, 701	2, 302	1, 676, 852	82, 552	1, 429, 300	165, 000
Camden	225	208	17	-------	10, 532	9, 711	821	-------	267, 720	247, 000	20, 720	-------
Campbell	362	27	335	-------	23, 681	1, 435	22, 246	-------	557, 035	35, 275	521, 760	-------
Candler	344	41	303	-------	20, 720	3, 755	16, 965	-------	509, 920	73, 150	436, 770	-------
Carroll	1, 080	73	1, 007	-------	47, 355	4, 214	43, 141	-------	1, 618, 292	127, 820	1, 490, 472	-------
Catoosa	44	12	30	2	3, 481	793	1, 268	1, 420	105, 515	22, 990	59, 525	23, 000
Charlton	19	17	2	-------	1, 266	1, 206	60	-------	18, 500	13, 500	5, 000	-------
Chatham	82	44	37	1	6, 027	863	5, 064	100	231, 060	74, 060	149, 000	8, 000
Chattahoochee	172	32	140	-------	21, 788	7, 111	14, 677	-------	154, 836	47, 001	107, 835	-------
Chattooga	249	42	207	-------	18, 616	4, 636	13, 980	-------	399, 976	88, 094	311, 882	-------
Cherokee	72	16	56	-------	3, 432	959	2, 473	-------	96, 695	14, 300	82, 395	-------
Clarke	543	87	456	-------	21, 701	3, 354	18, 347	-------	1, 008, 096	155, 897	852, 199	-------
Clay	645	45	600	-------	37, 849	8, 021	29, 828	-------	837, 305	133, 550	703, 755	-------
Clayton	365	18	347	-------	16, 355	1, 386	14, 969	-------	634, 285	37, 720	596, 565	-------
Clinch	45	20	25	-------	2, 638	1, 155	1, 483	-------	46, 100	20, 100	26, 000	-------
Cobb	536	110	426	-------	22, 533	5, 214	17, 319	-------	930, 835	179, 945	750, 890	-------
Coffee	306	50	256	-------	23, 951	5, 181	18, 770	-------	445, 785	75, 440	370, 345	-------
Colquitt	434	34	399	1	24, 012	3, 969	19, 973	70	1, 079, 899	151, 075	926, 824	2, 000
Columbia	801	116	684	1	41, 072	8, 292	32, 376	404	751, 727	151, 323	596, 064	4, 340
Cook	200	26	174	-------	13, 593	1, 487	12, 106	-------	381, 116	42, 120	338, 996	-------
Coweta	1, 134	91	1, 039	4	74, 205	7, 431	65, 987	787	1, 457, 382	142, 003	1, 298, 019	17, 360
Crawford	477	90	387	-------	44, 250	12, 557	31, 693	-------	539, 519	158, 144	381, 375	-------

TABLE 57.—FARMS OPERATED BY NEGROES—NUMBER, ACREAGE, VALUE OF LAND AND BUILDINGS, AND VALUE OF IMPLEMENTS AND MACHINERY, BY TENURE, BY STATES, AND COUNTIES: 1930—Continued

[Counties in which no farms operated by Negroes were reported, are omitted]

COUNTY	VALUE OF LAND ALONE				VALUE OF BUILDINGS				VALUE OF IMPLEMENTS AND MACHINERY			
	Total	Owners	Tenants	Managers	Total	Owners	Tenants	Managers	Total	Owners	Tenants	Managers
					FLORIDA—continued							
Gulf	$8, 525	$5, 450	$3, 075		$3, 580	$2, 030	$1, 550		$800	$535	$265	
Hamilton	178, 401	82, 935	95, 466		77, 415	40, 035	37, 380		9, 824	7, 113	2, 711	
Hardee	4, 500	800	3, 700		500	200	300		170	75	95	
Hendry	9, 850	4, 000	5, 850		50		50		300		300	
Hernando	200, 065	102, 825	71, 040	$26, 200	39, 010	20, 550	12, 660	$5, 800	5, 330	2, 570	1, 125	$1, 635
Highlands	1, 575		1, 575		25		25		15		15	
Hillsborough	313, 320	156, 400	28, 520	128, 400	56, 875	33, 650	5, 625	17, 600	8, 310	6, 145	1, 365	800
Holmes	19, 870	11, 220	8, 650		7, 350	3, 900	3, 450		1, 017	507	510	
Indian River	37, 100	11, 700	25, 400		3, 500	2, 300	1, 200		350	150	200	
Jackson	1, 381, 094	569, 692	792, 312	19, 090	400, 331	203, 072	195, 519	1, 740	82, 947	41, 700	40, 716	531
Jefferson	614, 549	280, 637	333, 912		268, 063	117, 720	150, 343		40, 751	21, 257	19, 494	
Lafayette	4, 500	700	3, 800		2, 100	700	1, 400		540	65	475	
Lake	313, 920	171, 540	24, 200	118, 180	65, 215	48, 145	5, 250	11, 820	6, 780	3, 420	500	2, 860
Lee	14, 050	450	13, 600		2, 250	50	2, 200		1, 500	10	1, 490	
Leon	1, 067, 206	337, 683	713, 823	15, 700	314, 751	116, 587	187, 664	10, 500	56, 729	20, 740	30, 964	5, 025
Levy	115, 943	77, 813	38, 130		38, 033	32, 158	5, 875		5, 498	4, 503	995	
Liberty	54, 940	48, 315	6, 625		22, 985	19, 435	3, 550		2, 975	2, 820	155	
Madison	448, 805	147, 110	282, 845	18, 850	225, 060	76, 330	133, 380	15, 350	34, 840	13, 772	19, 493	1, 575
Manatee	142, 400	4, 600	45, 100	92, 700	6, 800	400	2, 100	4, 300	2, 310	75	1, 360	875
Marion	868, 729	697, 125	154, 729	16, 875	366, 597	281, 880	33, 992	50, 725	75, 384	65, 697	8, 607	1, 080
Martin	44, 215	23, 125	21, 090		3, 125	2, 375	750		3, 080	895	2, 185	
Monroe	86, 800	14, 000	72, 800		9, 900	6, 500	3, 400		100		100	
Nassau	23, 125	19, 375	3, 000	750	23, 775	20, 525	3, 000	250	3, 945	3, 670	225	50
Okaloosa	82, 595	28, 950	52, 845	800	22, 505	14, 050	8, 255	200	3, 030	1, 750	1, 255	25
Okeechobee	2, 500	300	2, 200		500	200	300		175	50	125	
Orange	386, 345	282, 395	13, 000	90, 950	93, 550	90, 000	500	3, 050	8, 310	6, 860	1, 000	450
Osceola	14, 550	14, 550			4, 250	4, 250			900	900		
Palm Beach	168, 920	36, 500	118, 020	14, 400	12, 130	7, 200	3, 730	1, 200	20, 235	3, 205	14, 955	2, 075
Pasco	36, 565	10, 440	26, 125		5, 285	3, 210	2, 075		1, 165	970	195	
Pinellas	49, 950			49, 950	50			50				
Polk	108, 880	53, 600	20, 630	34, 650	19, 800	6, 550	2, 250	11, 000	2, 255	800	205	1, 250
Putnam	294, 840	212, 020	50, 320	32, 500	152, 887	120, 687	5, 200	27, 000	18, 478	16, 118	1, 360	1, 000
St. Johns	83, 675	57, 975	8, 200	17, 500	31, 245	22, 445	1, 300	7, 500	7, 383	6, 523	625	235
St. Lucie	34, 500	5, 500	3, 000	26, 000	7, 500	2, 500	1, 000	4, 400	1, 100	100	500	500
Santa Rosa	60, 590	15, 915	11, 475	33, 200	12, 710	4, 785	5, 125	2, 800	1, 567	775	317	475
Sarasota	41, 450	1, 500	39, 950		3, 050	2, 500	550		110	100	10	
Seminole	103, 700	83, 100	14, 200	6, 400	30, 800	28, 500	1, 700	600	4, 935	4, 565	220	150
Sumter	116, 300	92, 105	24, 195		46, 895	43, 020	3, 875		14, 995	12, 135	2, 860	
Suwannee	331, 510	156, 865	174, 645		121, 945	65, 900	56, 045		14, 967	8, 811	6, 156	
Taylor	26, 400	600	14, 800	11, 000	6, 400	400	2, 000	4, 000	1, 770	20	250	1, 500
Union	63, 490	25, 525	37, 965		35, 210	11, 675	23, 535		2, 409	1, 477	932	
Volusia	348, 638	294, 688	15, 700	38, 250	50, 862	40, 762	5, 350	4, 750	8, 569	5, 675	300	2, 594
Wakulla	76, 611	56, 076	18, 435	2, 100	38, 685	31, 300	5, 885	1, 500	3, 716	2, 536	680	500
Walton	63, 030	40, 180	22, 850		38, 540	28, 290	10, 250		7, 631	5, 941	1, 690	
Washington	121, 460	77, 855	43, 605		62, 020	42, 895	19, 125		9, 442	7, 227	2, 215	
					GEORGIA							
Total	**$82, 893, 996**	**$11, 815, 238**	**$70, 378, 673**	**$700, 085**	**$81, 794, 234**	**$5, 712, 334**	**$25, 874, 665**	**$206, 685**	**$4, 320, 997**	**$880, 607**	**$3, 392, 733**	**$47, 657**
Appling	193, 495	97, 750	95, 745		62, 630	33, 755	28, 875		7, 427	4, 785	2, 642	
Atkinson	77, 865	16, 075	61, 790		29, 900	10, 975	18, 925		3, 440	1, 475	1, 965	
Bacon	58, 817	5, 725	53, 092		25, 260	3, 375	21, 885		2, 614	365	2, 249	
Baker	630, 655	215, 520	383, 635	31, 500	190, 285	67, 040	115, 245	8, 000	47, 651	18, 989	26, 662	2, 000
Baldwin	396, 622	68, 420	316, 602	11, 600	149, 550	32, 130	113, 120	4, 300	29, 036	4, 696	22, 340	2, 000
Banks	133, 410	17, 660	115, 750		51, 515	12, 030	39, 485		5, 223	1, 715	3, 508	
Barrow	256, 545	32, 545	224, 000		106, 875	13, 405	93, 470		15, 410	1, 360	14, 050	
Bartow	518, 667	38, 630	480, 037		140, 625	15, 560	125, 065		48, 009	4, 520	43, 489	
Ben Hill	402, 640	112, 675	289, 965		156, 385	48, 950	107, 435		25, 195	8, 500	16, 695	
Berrien	129, 670	18, 625	111, 045		37, 860	5, 375	32, 485		5, 069	833	4, 236	
Bibb	465, 857	94, 980	320, 527	$50, 350	192, 709	54, 075	108, 184	$30, 450	19, 134	9, 609	9, 015	510
Bleckley	207, 775	20, 975	186, 800		75, 260	10, 225	65, 035		10, 657	2, 780	7, 877	
Brantley	11, 685	9, 195	2, 490		7, 690	6, 455	1, 235		676	536	140	
Brooks	1, 064, 093	269, 694	794, 399		321, 516	99, 921	221, 595		58, 400	19, 655	38, 745	
Bryan	113, 837	53, 265	60, 572		46, 225	22, 830	23, 395		6, 393	3, 785	2, 608	
Bulloch	1, 309, 826	180, 340	1, 129, 486		453, 955	74, 000	379, 955		52, 228	13, 156	39, 072	
Burke	2, 517, 837	326, 683	2, 137, 914	53, 240	1, 024, 269	139, 213	866, 881	18, 175	134, 892	18, 232	113, 853	2, 807
Butts	452, 010	18, 040	425, 970	8, 000	214, 834	13, 425	199, 409	2, 000	27, 386	1, 124	25, 012	1, 250
Calhoun	1, 246, 227	59, 452	1, 032, 475	154, 300	430, 625	23, 100	396, 825	10, 700	82, 636	4, 490	71, 546	6, 600
Camden	195, 565	178, 970	16, 595		72, 155	68, 030	4, 125		8, 874	8, 439	435	
Campbell	371, 030	23, 030	348, 000		186, 005	12, 245	173, 760		20, 245	1, 884	18, 361	
Candler	385, 950	55, 665	330, 285		123, 970	17, 485	106, 485		9, 840	1, 645	8, 195	
Carroll	1, 147, 522	84, 815	1, 062, 707		470, 770	43, 005	427, 765		50, 587	4, 388	46, 199	
Catoosa	83, 465	16, 360	46, 405	20, 700	22, 050	6, 630	13, 120	2, 300	2, 762	305	2, 007	450
Charlton	12, 475	9, 225	3, 250		6, 025	4, 275	1, 750		946	896	50	
Chatham	196, 270	53, 740	137, 530	5, 000	34, 790	20, 320	11, 470	3, 000	4, 263	2, 163	1, 100	1, 000
Chattahoochee	113, 681	34, 726	78, 955		41, 155	12, 275	28, 880		9, 336	2, 781	6, 555	
Chattooga	306, 010	68, 014	237, 996		93, 966	20, 080	73, 886		24, 466	6, 010	18, 456	
Cherokee	61, 655	8, 200	53, 455		35, 040	6, 100	28, 940		3, 685	410	3, 275	
Clarke	714, 691	98, 587	616, 104		293, 405	57, 310	236, 095		32, 953	7, 314	25, 639	
Clay	603, 570	95, 150	508, 420		233, 735	38, 400	195, 335		34, 006	4, 885	29, 121	
Clayton	467, 670	22, 770	444, 900		166, 615	14, 950	151, 665		15, 234	1, 720	13, 514	
Clinch	28, 295	12, 350	15, 945		17, 805	7, 750	10, 055		2, 260	1, 200	1, 060	
Cobb	693, 200	123, 160	570, 040		237, 635	56, 785	180, 850		26, 993	6, 210	20, 783	
Coffee	313, 790	52, 720	261, 070		131, 995	22, 720	109, 275		19, 844	4, 206	15, 638	
Colquitt	872, 064	112, 425	758, 239	1, 400	207, 835	38, 650	168, 585	600	23, 977	3, 101	20, 776	100
Columbia	464, 942	91, 008	369, 894	4, 040	286, 785	60, 315	226, 170	300	29, 929	8, 112	202, 217	1, 600
Cook	289, 696	29, 595	260, 101		91, 420	12, 525	78, 895		13, 104	1, 630	11, 474	
Coweta	1, 060, 745	97, 648	948, 747	14, 350	396, 637	44, 355	349, 272	3, 010	58, 161	8, 046	48, 165	1, 950
Crawford	364, 904	110, 884	254, 020		174, 615	47, 260	127, 355		20, 258	6, 993	13, 265	

TABLE 57.—FARMS OPERATED BY NEGROES—NUMBER, ACREAGE, VALUE OF LAND AND BUILDINGS, AND VALUE OF IMPLEMENTS AND MACHINERY, BY TENURE, BY STATES, AND COUNTIES: 1930—Continued

[Counties in which no farms operated by Negroes were reported, are omitted]

COUNTY	NUMBER OF FARMS				ALL LAND IN FARMS (ACRES)				VALUE OF LAND AND BUILDINGS			
	Total	Owners	Tenants	Managers	Total	Owners	Tenants	Managers	Total	Owners	Tenants	Managers
	GEORGIA—continued											
Crisp	605	28	577	-----	38, 020	2, 521	35, 499	-----	$1, 083, 827	$61, 840	$1, 021, 987	-----
Dade	10	3	7	-----	536	132	404	-----	13, 680	1, 800	11, 880	-----
Decatur	636	248	388	-----	41, 469	17, 778	23, 691	-----	784, 895	332, 220	452, 675	-----
De Kalb	511	58	453	-----	19, 959	1, 862	18, 097	-----	1, 144, 910	133, 325	1, 011, 585	-----
Dodge	790	140	650	-----	50, 074	11, 179	38, 895	-----	1, 327, 555	296, 700	1, 030, 855	-----
Dooly	1, 351	73	1, 278	-----	72, 572	6, 926	65, 646	-----	1, 906, 413	156, 150	1, 750, 263	-----
Dougherty	459	40	415	4	26, 026	5, 274	20, 077	675	698, 185	141, 430	491, 255	$65, 500
Douglas	302	51	251	-----	18, 795	4, 304	14, 491	-----	435, 696	68, 631	367, 065	-----
Early	1, 624	175	1, 449	-----	79, 056	12, 327	66, 729	-----	2, 141, 161	274, 271	1, 866, 890	-----
Echols	17	8	9	-----	1, 196	690	506	-----	15, 650	10, 150	5, 500	-----
Effingham	257	106	151	-----	9, 271	3, 918	5, 353	-----	205, 986	78, 326	127, 660	-----
Elbert	997	86	911	-----	52, 999	6, 853	46, 146	-----	1, 090, 225	135, 265	954, 960	-----
Emanuel	1, 064	122	942	-----	66, 783	9, 700	57, 083	-----	1, 815, 766	209, 620	1, 606, 146	-----
Evans	210	61	149	-----	13, 699	4, 438	9, 261	-----	350, 165	103, 713	246, 452	-----
Fannin	2	2	-----	-----	15	15	-----	-----	1, 200	1, 200	-----	-----
Fayette	502	21	481	-----	24, 577	1, 786	22, 791	-----	544, 285	29, 550	514, 735	-----
Floyd	506	99	407	-----	28, 130	7, 135	20, 995	-----	690, 081	149, 910	540, 171	-----
Forsyth	4	-----	4	-----	113	-----	113	-----	2, 792	-----	2, 792	-----
Franklin	395	33	362	-----	13, 794	1, 592	12, 202	-----	466, 140	43, 350	422, 790	-----
Fulton	185	52	132	1	5, 906	876	4, 880	150	802, 125	167, 075	610, 050	25, 000
Gilmer	4	1	3	-----	270	45	225	-----	2, 600	200	2, 400	-----
Glascock	183	10	173	-----	11, 922	1, 100	10, 822	-----	213, 410	14, 100	199, 310	-----
Glynn	65	59	6	-----	4, 621	3, 221	1, 400	-----	106, 880	87, 580	19, 300	-----
Gordon	99	22	77	-----	5, 526	1, 569	3, 957	-----	199, 040	36, 620	162, 420	-----
Grady	435	98	337	-----	28, 265	7, 579	20, 686	-----	684, 160	178, 175	505, 985	-----
Greene	942	92	849	1	56, 633	6, 142	50, 091	400	780, 613	83, 133	694, 480	3, 000
Gwinnett	316	48	268	-----	16, 956	2, 906	14, 050	-----	394, 655	62, 550	332, 105	-----
Habersham	31	15	16	-----	2, 121	1, 136	985	-----	58, 300	25, 100	33, 200	-----
Hall	216	39	177	-----	12, 021	2, 355	9, 666	-----	259, 400	46, 470	212, 930	-----
Hancock	1, 205	174	1, 030	1	58, 474	14, 701	43, 573	200	808, 464	178, 207	623, 757	6, 500
Haralson	165	56	109	-----	9, 332	3, 256	6, 076	-----	178, 300	61, 820	116, 480	-----
Harris	1, 014	157	857	-----	93, 074	17, 967	75, 107	-----	1, 078, 035	170, 668	907, 367	-----
Hart	612	42	570	-----	26, 469	1, 835	24, 634	-----	817, 722	58, 760	758, 962	-----
Heard	411	59	352	-----	30, 800	4, 881	25, 919	-----	444, 064	72, 637	371, 427	-----
Henry	1, 213	82	1, 131	-----	58, 713	4, 841	53, 872	-----	1, 345, 854	116, 337	1, 229, 517	-----
Houston	772	95	677	-----	61, 681	9, 632	52, 049	-----	1, 176, 557	214, 267	962, 290	-----
Irwin	471	39	432	-----	32, 846	2, 679	30, 167	-----	871, 135	82, 680	788, 455	-----
Jackson	596	68	528	-----	25, 587	5, 308	20, 279	-----	759, 552	179, 281	580, 271	-----
Jasper	622	55	567	-----	54, 179	6, 440	47, 739	-----	790, 505	89, 800	700, 705	-----
Jeff Davis	125	62	63	-----	7, 631	4, 649	2, 982	-----	158, 718	89, 000	69, 718	-----
Jefferson	1, 497	152	1, 345	-----	93, 831	13, 252	80, 579	-----	1, 689, 193	219, 182	1, 470, 011	-----
Jenkins	958	59	899	-----	43, 600	5, 674	37, 926	-----	1, 100, 080	112, 196	987, 884	-----
Johnson	584	14	570	-----	29, 524	1, 172	28, 352	-----	622, 533	21, 935	600, 598	-----
Jones	472	95	377	-----	45, 417	12, 210	33, 207	-----	516, 208	146, 045	370, 163	-----
Lamar	455	58	395	2	30, 199	4, 610	24, 544	1, 045	773, 980	146, 770	606, 960	20, 250
Lanier	116	46	70	-----	9, 910	4, 043	5, 867	-----	199, 110	65, 410	133, 700	-----
Laurens	1, 558	143	1, 415	-----	82, 690	14, 004	68, 686	-----	1, 824, 855	252, 360	1, 572, 495	-----
Lee	935	81	854	-----	57, 702	10, 242	47, 460	-----	1, 153, 570	210, 880	942, 690	-----
Liberty	834	686	146	2	33, 196	27, 707	5, 322	167	826, 394	698, 789	119, 755	7, 850
Lincoln	777	36	741	-----	35, 037	3, 529	31, 508	-----	652, 229	56, 800	595, 429	-----
Long	152	80	72	-----	9, 186	4, 855	4, 331	-----	158, 130	74, 975	83, 155	-----
Lowndes	739	220	518	1	39, 070	14, 679	24, 316	75	1, 268, 469	371, 560	886, 909	10, 000
Lumpkin	18	5	13	-----	1, 154	453	701	-----	17, 090	4, 900	12, 190	-----
McDuffie	626	30	596	-----	30, 858	2, 401	28, 457	-----	470, 397	29, 153	441, 244	-----
McIntosh	181	175	6	-----	5, 600	4, 753	847	-----	154, 600	129, 000	25, 600	-----
Macon	1, 245	86	1, 151	8	79, 002	7, 912	68, 623	2, 467	2, 054, 503	203, 180	1, 741, 198	110, 125
Madison	398	36	362	-----	19, 035	2, 591	16, 444	-----	479, 225	62, 341	416, 884	-----
Marion	533	70	463	-----	49, 738	11, 185	38, 553	-----	573, 220	105, 628	467, 592	-----
Meriwether	1, 299	98	1, 200	1	101, 264	7, 992	93, 154	118	1, 844, 780	171, 100	1, 663, 680	10, 000
Miller	434	52	382	-----	21, 794	3, 734	18, 060	-----	543, 140	79, 380	463, 760	-----
Milton	69	4	65	-----	2, 509	207	2, 302	-----	100, 467	7, 700	92, 767	-----
Mitchell	1, 352	107	1, 244	1	68, 154	9, 170	58, 916	68	2, 124, 455	271, 525	1, 845, 430	7, 500
Monroe	763	120	638	5	62, 282	11, 828	48, 869	1, 585	758, 956	136, 353	587, 153	35, 450
Montgomery	531	65	466	-----	29, 810	3, 083	26, 727	-----	889, 285	83, 840	805, 445	-----
Morgan	1, 019	79	939	1	51, 353	4, 721	46, 299	333	1, 039, 573	116, 782	918, 491	4, 300
Murray	47	3	44	-----	2, 029	219	1, 810	-----	74, 314	5, 100	69, 214	-----
Muscogee	317	35	282	-----	22, 004	3, 520	18, 484	-----	479, 330	56, 850	422, 480	-----
Newton	835	73	761	1	44, 114	6, 001	37, 913	200	1, 011, 166	159, 000	842, 166	10, 000
Oconee	363	26	337	-----	22, 478	2, 212	20, 266	-----	452, 473	38, 960	413, 513	-----
Oglethorpe	933	76	857	-----	62, 025	6, 372	55, 653	-----	1, 032, 493	113, 590	918, 903	-----
Paulding	186	54	132	-----	9, 790	3, 469	6, 321	-----	186, 815	58, 895	127, 920	-----
Peach	492	37	451	4	19, 027	2, 816	15, 807	404	770, 019	86, 930	661, 339	21, 750
Pickens	8	-----	8	-----	549	-----	549	-----	20, 250	-----	20, 250	-----
Pierce	191	63	128	-----	12, 152	3, 460	8, 692	-----	330, 630	109, 900	220, 730	-----
Pike	710	46	664	-----	38, 767	4, 162	34, 605	-----	1, 007, 015	99, 900	907, 115	-----
Polk	374	74	300	-----	18, 448	4, 948	13, 500	-----	499, 884	118, 075	381, 809	-----
Pulaski	536	47	489	-----	31, 725	3, 613	28, 112	-----	781, 100	75, 805	705, 295	-----
Putnam	632	51	581	-----	48, 569	6, 323	42, 246	-----	717, 121	81, 316	635, 805	-----
Quitman	326	23	299	4	26, 123	4, 084	20, 211	1, 828	404, 875	44, 300	343, 775	16, 800
Rabun	11	10	1	-----	234	229	5	-----	20, 800	19, 800	1, 000	-----
Randolph	1, 502	77	1, 425	-----	91, 991	6, 579	85, 412	-----	2, 249, 739	116, 800	2, 132, 939	-----
Richmond	377	45	331	1	26, 956	3, 337	23, 519	100	580, 415	87, 150	487, 265	6, 000
Rockdale	323	18	305	-----	18, 896	1, 474	17, 422	-----	303, 940	23, 700	280, 240	-----
Schley	419	33	386	-----	31, 594	5, 162	26, 432	-----	567, 902	58, 650	509, 252	-----
Screven	1, 561	150	1, 411	-----	67, 050	11, 986	55, 064	-----	1, 509, 535	235, 570	1, 273, 965	-----
Seminole	319	79	240	-----	18, 823	4, 555	14, 268	-----	482, 085	109, 800	372, 285	-----
Spalding	517	53	463	1	28, 965	3, 568	24, 697	700	737, 514	107, 490	580, 024	50, 000
Stephens	152	27	125	-----	7, 040	1, 589	5, 451	-----	235, 890	48, 215	187, 675	-----
Stewart	874	91	783	-----	96, 080	15, 223	80, 857	-----	1, 208, 350	175, 655	1, 032, 695	-----
Sumter	1, 419	73	1, 343	3	75, 449	6, 595	68, 372	482	2, 137, 388	138, 210	1, 972, 598	26, 580

Table 57.—FARMS OPERATED BY NEGROES—NUMBER, ACREAGE, VALUE OF LAND AND BUILDINGS, AND VALUE OF IMPLEMENTS AND MACHINERY, BY TENURE, BY STATES, AND COUNTIES: 1930—Continued.

[Counties in which no farms operated by Negroes were reported, are omitted]

COUNTY	VALUE OF LAND ALONE				VALUE OF BUILDINGS				VALUE OF IMPLEMENTS AND MACHINERY			
	Total	Owners	Tenants	Managers	Total	Owners	Tenants	Managers	Total	Owners	Tenants	Managers
	GEORGIA—continued											
Crisp	$853, 252	$44, 990	$808, 262		$230, 575	$16, 850	$213, 725		$32, 634	$2, 340	$30, 294	
Dade	11, 105	775	10, 330		2, 575	1, 025	1, 550		460	45	415	
Decatur	584, 525	236, 910	347, 615		200, 370	95, 310	105, 060		31, 939	17, 476	14, 463	
De Kalb	953, 445	97, 240	856, 205		191, 465	36, 085	155, 380		15, 268	3, 670	11, 598	
Dodge	957, 445	207, 245	750, 200		370, 110	89, 455	280, 655		54, 177	12, 411	41, 766	
Dooly	1, 478, 783	118, 490	1, 360, 293		427, 630	37, 660	389, 970		75, 564	8, 570	66, 994	
Dougherty	543, 060	109, 845	388, 815	$44, 400	155, 125	31, 585	102, 440	$21, 100	34, 316	4, 659	26, 757	$2, 900
Douglas	288, 576	45, 031	243, 545		147, 120	23, 600	123, 520		17, 289	4, 000	13, 289	
Early	1, 503, 828	182, 421	1, 321, 407		637, 333	91, 850	545, 483		93, 209	17, 442	75, 767	
Echols	10, 825	7, 275	3, 550		4, 825	2, 875	1, 950		935	540	395	
Effingham	150, 546	51, 461	99, 085		55, 440	26, 865	28, 575		5, 379	2, 684	2, 695	
Elbert	741, 908	83, 053	658, 855		348, 317	52, 212	296, 105		56, 188	10, 562	45, 626	
Emanuel	1, 376, 172	143, 120	1, 233, 052		439, 594	66, 500	373, 094		59, 212	8, 067	51, 145	
Evans	244, 365	65, 888	178, 477		105, 800	37, 825	67, 975		9, 438	3, 765	5, 673	
Fannin	650	650			550	550			10	10		
Fayette	385, 635	19, 350	366, 285		158, 650	10, 200	148, 450		22, 449	2, 420	20, 029	
Floyd	521, 966	107, 790	414, 176		168, 115	42, 120	125, 995		33, 381	8, 793	24, 588	
Forsyth	1, 907		1, 907		885		885		55		55	
Franklin	332, 675	26, 695	305, 980		133, 465	16, 655	116, 810		9, 994	1, 544	8, 450	
Fulton	693, 040	124, 875	547, 165	21, 000	109, 085	42, 200	62, 885	4, 000	15, 130	6, 165	8, 165	800
Gilmer	1, 850	125	1, 725		750	75	675		65	5	60	
Glascock	148, 260	10, 250	138, 010		65, 150	3, 850	61, 300		10, 032	512	9, 520	
Glynn	75, 430	58, 430	17, 000		31, 450	29, 150	2, 300		5, 445	4, 920	525	
Gordon	163, 825	24, 680	139, 145		35, 215	11, 940	23, 275		9, 050	2, 130	6, 920	
Grady	513, 625	123, 465	390, 160		170, 535	54, 710	115, 825		21, 359	7, 978	13, 381	
Greene	454, 357	439, 68	408, 389	2, 000	326, 256	39, 165	286, 091	1, 000	38, 724	5, 637	33, 087	
Gwinnett	286, 655	43, 155	243, 500		108, 000	19, 395	88, 605		13, 515	4, 090	9, 425	
Habersham	40, 435	18, 410	22, 025		17, 865	6, 690	11 715		1, 990	710	1, 280	
Hall	186, 045	33, 195	152, 850		73, 355	13, 275	60, 080		7, 297	1, 207	6, 090	
Hancock	550, 617	125, 227	421, 390	4, 000	257, 847	52, 980	202, 367	2, 500	35, 294	8, 796	26, 498	
Haralson	121, 205	40, 440	80, 765		57, 095	21, 380	35, 715		7, 078	2, 928	4, 150	
Harris	695, 595	91, 968	603, 627		382, 440	78, 700	303, 740		36, 727	8, 728	27, 999	
Hart	579, 962	38, 010	541, 952		237, 760	20, 750	217, 010		24, 866	2, 085	22, 781	
Heard	237, 289	38, 102	199, 187		206, 775	34, 535	172, 240		20, 561	7, 180	13, 381	
Henry	926, 179	64, 072	862, 107		419, 675	52, 265	367, 410		46, 945	5, 060	41, 885	
Houston	908, 634	152, 042	756, 592		267, 923	62, 225	205, 698		34, 864	9, 273	25, 591	
Irwin	699, 045	62, 275	636, 770		172, 090	20, 405	151, 685		32, 935	3, 900	29, 035	
Jackson	517, 526	112, 656	404, 870		242. 026	66, 625	175, 401		22, 165	7, 281	14, 884	
Jasper	489, 360	49, 075	440, 285		301, 145	40, 725	260, 420		40, 034	7, 975	32, 059	
Jeff Davis	103, 393	59, 135	44, 258		55, 325	29, 865	25, 460		8, 954	5, 400	3, 554	
Jefferson	1, 205, 557	142, 382	1, 063, 175		483, 636	76, 800	406, 836		70, 315	10, 774	59, 541	
Jenkins	829, 253	82, 621	746, 632		270, 827	29, 575	241, 252		45, 378	5, 769	39, 609	
Johnson	447, 378	14, 710	432, 668		175, 155	7, 225	167, 930		18, 075	1, 747	16, 328	
Jones	362, 468	102, 470	259, 998		153, 740	43, 575	110, 165		11, 775	4, 161	7, 614	
Lamar	504, 290	82, 145	403, 895	18, 250	269, 690	64, 625	203, 065	2, 000	30, 348	8, 072	20, 476	1, 800
Lanier	130, 790	48, 135	82, 655		68, 320	17, 275	51, 045		12, 430	3, 365	9, 065	
Laurens	1, 345, 275	187, 460	1, 157, 815		479, 580	64, 900	414, 680		65, 493	12, 776	52, 717	
Lee	848, 668	153, 430	695, 238		304, 902	57, 450	247, 452		64, 352	18, 225	46, 127	
Liberty	461, 963	399, 128	60, 335	2, 500	364, 431	299, 661	59, 420	5, 350	43, 166	36, 326	3, 740	3, 100
Lincoln	429, 674	34, 295	395, 379		222, 555	22, 505	200, 050		35, 574	5, 369	30, 205	
Long	94, 955	42, 445	52, 510		63, 175	32, 530	30, 645		9, 419	4, 834	4, 585	
Lowndes	988, 158	275, 640	704, 018	8, 500	280. 311	95, 920	182, 891	1, 500	30, 889	11, 894	18, 745	250
Lumpkin	14, 090	3, 675	10, 415		3, 000	1, 225	1, 775		400	160	240	
McDuffie	305, 847	16, 788	289, 059		164, 550	12, 365	152, 185		21, 643	4, 597	17, 046	
McIntosh	89, 690	68. 065	21, 625		64, 910	60, 935	3, 975		7, 453	6, 578	875	
Macon	1, 672, 418	161, 570	1, 416, 273	94, 575	382, 085	41, 610	324, 925	15, 550	63, 569	8, 326	43, 463	11, 780
Madison	346, 235	43, 116	303, 119		132, 990	19, 225	113, 765		14, 052	2, 419	11, 633	
Marion	339, 265	61, 903	277, 362		233, 955	43, 725	190, 230		17, 937	4, 867	13, 070	
Meriwether	1, 193, 600	103, 115	1, 081, 985	8, 500	651, 180	67, 985	581, 695	1, 500	69, 938	9, 527	60, 011	400
Miller	387, 655	54, 655	333, 000		155, 485	24, 725	130, 760		23, 647	3, 400	20, 247	
Milton	76, 137	5, 225	70, 912		24, 330	2, 475	21, 855		2, 140	232	1, 908	
Mitchell	1, 567, 112	200, 370	1, 359, 842	6, 900	557, 343	71, 155	485, 588	600	72, 582	11, 854	60, 428	300
Monroe	514, 638	89, 660	400, 128	24, 850	244, 318	46, 693	187, 025	10, 600	29, 938	6, 263	22, 200	1, 475
Montgomery	712, 610	56, 440	656, 170		176, 675	27, 400	149, 275		20, 593	3, 176	17, 417	
Morgan	627, 983	71, 417	553, 266	3, 300	411, 590	45, 365	365, 225	1, 000	53, 425	5, 151	48, 074	200
Murray	52, 864	3, 900	48, 964		21, 450	1, 200	20, 250		4, 620	170	4, 450	
Muscogee	360, 880	40, 160	320, 720		118, 450	16, 690	101, 760		18, 430	4, 060	14, 370	
Newton	682, 806	98, 090	580, 716	4, 000	328, 360	60, 910	261, 450	6, 000	44, 591	5, 640	38, 651	300
Oconee	300, 923	24, 735	276, 188		151, 550	14, 225	137, 325		22, 190	2, 672	19, 518	
Oglethorpe	678, 417	66, 065	612, 352		354, 076	47, 525	306, 551		46, 283	8, 861	37, 422	
Paulding	114, 790	35, 695	79, 095		72, 025	23, 200	48, 825		7, 805	3, 040	4, 765	
Peach	623, 099	65, 200	539, 649	18, 250	146, 920	21, 730	121, 690	3, 500	20, 292	3, 028	16, 964	300
Pickens	16, 375		16, 375		3, 875		3, 875		222		222	
Pierce	225, 975	67, 780	158, 195		104, 655	42, 120	62, 535		10, 235	3, 615	6, 620	
Pike	669, 794	58, 500	611, 294		337, 221	41, 400	295, 821		35, 908	4, 063	31, 845	
Polk	376, 484	80, 925	295, 559		123, 400	37, 150	86, 250		26, 267	10, 695	15, 572	
Pulaski	593, 060	53, 305	539, 755		188. 040	22, 500	165, 540		33, 181	5, 855	27, 326	
Putnam	469, 871	51, 606	418, 265		247, 250	29, 710	217, 540		24, 559	3, 770	20, 789	
Quitman	277, 780	23, 725	241, 705	12, 350	127, 095	20, 575	102, 070	4, 450	21, 557	2, 925	18, 062	570
Rabun	9, 400	8, 500	900		11, 400	11, 300	100		355	350	5	
Randolph	1, 743, 362	75, 275	1, 668, 087		506, 377	41, 525	464, 852		89, 695	11, 100	78, 595	
Richmond	409, 850	53, 520	352, 330	4, 000	170, 565	33, 630	134, 935	2, 000	28, 602	6, 692	21, 835	75
Rockdale	200, 898	13, 425	187, 473		103, 042	10, 275	92, 767		13, 035	1, 950	11, 085	
Schley	429, 057	41, 615	387, 442		138, 845	17, 035	121, 810		21, 933	5, 365	16, 568	
Screven	1, 103, 306	156, 995	946, 311		406, 229	78, 575	327, 654		37, 111	6, 061	31, 050	
Seminole	345, 925	72, 385	273, 540		136, 160	37, 415	98, 745		20, 881	4, 301	16, 580	
Spalding	458, 768	50, 865	382, 903	$25, 000	278, 746	56, 625	197, 121	25, 000	29, 231	4, 732	23, 199	1, 300
Stephens	179, 330	32, 475	146, 855		56, 560	15, 740	40, 820		5, 529	1, 792	3, 737	
Stewart	897, 865	119, 950	777, 915		310, 485	55, 705	254, 780		58, 864	11, 260	47, 604	
Sumter	1, 656, 123	89, 890	1, 552, 553	13, 680	481, 265	48, 320	420, 045	12, 900	56, 264	9, 271	45, 693	1, 300

TABLE 57—FARMS OPERATED BY NEGROES—NUMBER, ACREAGE, VALUE OF LAND AND BUILDINGS, AND VALUE OF IMPLEMENTS AND MACHINERY, BY TENURE, BY STATES, AND COUNTIES: 1930—Continued

[Counties in which no farms operated by Negroes were reported, are omitted]

COUNTY	NUMBER OF FARMS				ALL LAND IN FARMS (ACRES)				VALUE OF LAND AND BUILDINGS			
	Total	Owners	Tenants	Managers	Total	Owners	Tenants	Managers	Total	Owners	Tenants	Managers
GEORGIA—continued												
Talbot	641	72	569		54,626	9,879	44,747		$707,280	$109,940	$597,340	
Taliaferro	626	103	523		38,892	9,468	29,424		477,980	111,580	366,400	
Tattnall	294	66	228		17,446	4,808	12,638		443,391	85,710	357,681	
Taylor	579	58	520	1	36,090	7,586	27,619	885	628,878	89,103	530,925	$8,850
Telfair	405	131	274		26,402	8,746	17,656		565,281	179,070	386,211	
Terrell	1,658	62	1,596		79,502	4,999	74,503		3,696,058	164,477	3,531,581	
Thomas	960	235	725		57,029	14,658	42,371		1,365,472	315,650	1,049,822	
Tift	253	23	230		12,976	1,211	11,765		483,893	41,413	442,480	
Toombs	434	52	382		23,057	2,382	20,675		767,877	65,197	702,680	
Treutlen	256	45	211		16,820	4,045	12,775		478,924	110,897	368,027	
Troup	1,067	105	962		78,133	10,110	68,023		1,449,970	180,409	1,269,561	
Turner	351	8	343		21,719	724	20,995		627,224	22,665	604,559	
Twiggs	485	61	424		30,010	6,758	23,252		437,359	76,728	360,631	
Upson	457	68	388	1	48,129	8,035	39,994	100	707,275	118,510	568,765	20,000
Walker	217	80	137		8,625	3,957	4,668		306,075	122,675	183,400	
Walton	907	52	855		46,837	3,711	43,126		1,141,465	100,280	1,041,185	
Ware	78	34	44		4,037	1,792	2,245		174,325	58,650	115,675	
Warren	977	54	923		60,955	5,074	55,881		1,015,372	67,715	947,657	
Washington	1,782	97	1,685		88,655	9,655	79,000		1,578,000	128,013	1,449,987	
Wayne	76	23	52	1	6,678	1,654	4,824	200	106,815	26,730	76,085	4,000
Webster	421	51	370		27,845	5,504	22,341		363,480	52,970	310,510	
Wheeler	323	69	254		20,458	5,550	14,908		464,375	113,630	350,745	
White	36	13	23		1,979	468	1,511		42,060	8,610	33,450	
Whitfield	57	22	35		2,980	1,639	1,341		93,800	47,100	46,700	
Wilcox	690	87	603		47,088	6,538	40,550		1,018,675	129,672	889,003	
Wilkes	1,465	141	1,324		77,367	11,201	66,166		1,148,596	196,890	951,706	
Wilkinson	478	51	427		39,142	8,569	30,573		414,895	81,317	333,578	
Worth	1,175	98	1,077		59,818	7,556	52,262		1,722,150	200,570	1,521,580	
IDAHO												
Total	**16**	**7**	**7**	**2**	**2,816**	**326**	**1,610**	**880**	**$107,200**	**$41,700**	**$47,500**	**$18,000**
Bannock	3	1	2		355	5	350		14,500	2,000	12,500	
Benewah	4	1	1	2	1,120	80	160	880	30,000	4,000	8,000	18,000
Bonneville	2		2		640		640		19,000		19,000	
Canyon	2	2			61	61			17,500	17,500		
Elmore	1		1		40		40		3,000		3,000	
Idaho	1		1		420		420		5,000		5,000	
Jefferson	1	1			40	40			7,000	7,000		
Latah	1	1			20	20			10,000	10,000		
Owyhee	1	1			120	120			1,200	1,200		
ILLINOIS												
Total	**893**	**459**	**428**	**6**	**57,805**	**27,635**	**29,414**	**756**	**$3,704,618**	**$1,562,898**	**$1,972,745**	**$168,975**
Adams	2	2			117	117			7,780	7,780		
Alexander	138	33	103	2	6,871	1,630	5,121	120	377,192	65,867	302,350	8,975
Bond	5	4	1		566	338	228		12,495	7,495	5,000	
Carroll	2	1	1		113	25	88		14,800	2,800	12,000	
Champaign	4	2	2		992	612	380		212,000	136,000	76,000	
Christian	3	1	2		411	1	410		59,500	2,500	57,000	
Clay	1	1			115	115			3,500	3,500		
Clinton	3		3		435		435		17,400		17,400	
Cole	2	1	1		25	5	20		3,000	2,000	1,000	
Cook	1		1		80		80		40,000		40,000	
Crawford	1	1			70	70			3,500	3,500		
De Kalb	2	1		1	161	5		156	24,200	1,200		23,000
De Witt	1		1		200		200		12,000		12,000	
Du Page	1		1		100		100		60,000		60,000	
Edwards	1	1			12	12			1,400	1,400		
Fayette	1	1			260	260			7,000	7,000		
Fulton	2	1	1		350	30	320		25,500	3,500	22,000	
Gallatin	3		3		788		788		31,400		31,400	
Hancock	1	1			9	9			2,000	2,000		
Hardin	3	2	1		403	307	96		7,800	4,800	3,000	
Henderson	5	1	4		672	40	632		44,200	5,200	39,000	
Iroquois	1	1			120	120			15,000	15,000		
Jackson	22	12	10		1,658	831	827		68,050	33,350	34,700	
Jasper	4	3	1		264	244	20		14,400	13,400	1,000	
Jefferson	7	5	2		485	265	220		12,150	6,350	5,800	
Jersey	3	1	2		204	80	124		8,900	4,000	4,900	
Johnson	8	1	7		911	60	851		13,000	2,000	11,000	
Kankakee	9	3	6		1,911	516	1,395		76,100	37,100	39,000	
Kendall	1		1		140		140		21,000		21,000	
Lake	3		1	2	378		18	360	153,000		28,000	125,000
Lawrence	14	13	1		1,203	1,123	80		52,700	48,300	4,400	
Logan	3		3		370		370		41,700		41,700	
McLean	4	1	3		1,130	10	1,120		226,000	2,000	224,000	
Macon	2	1	1		13	8	5		8,600	3,800	5,000	
Macoupin	3	2	1		679	519	160		29,500	15,500	14,000	
Madison	45	36	9		2,394	1,699	695		181,865	144,940	36,925	
Marion	5	5			117	117			8,900	8,900		
Marshall	1	1			330	330			49,500	49,500		
Massac	79	54	25		4,804	3,401	1,403		183,960	132,960	61,000	
Montgomery	3		3		166		166		9,900		9,900	

TABLE 57.—FARMS OPERATED BY NEGROES—NUMBER, ACREAGE, VALUE OF LAND AND BUILDINGS, AND VALUE OF IMPLEMENTS AND MACHINERY, BY TENURE, BY STATES, AND COUNTIES: 1930—Continued

[Counties in which no farms operated by Negroes were reported, are omitted]

COUNTY	VALUE OF LAND ALONE				VALUE OF BUILDINGS				VALUE OF IMPLEMENTS AND MACHINERY			
	Total	Owners	Tenants	Managers	Total	Owners	Tenants	Managers	Total	Owners	Tenants	Managers
GEORGIA—continued												
Talbot	$137,305	$72,065	$365,240		$269,975	$37,875	$232,100		$30,900	$5,498	$25,402	
Taliaferro	317,130	70,280	246,850		160,850	41,300	119,550		17,138	7,456	9,682	
Tattnall	324,781	58.730	266,051		118,610	26,980	91,630		12,967	3,946	9,021	
Taylor	457,708	58,258	392,100	$7,350	171,170	30,845	138,825	$1,500	17,307	6,185	11,097	$25
Telfair	427,546	131,005	296,541		137,735	48,065	89,670		20,212	7,398	12,814	
Terrell	2,907,542	118.367	2,789,175		788,516	46,110	742,406		117,906	7,698	110,208	
Thomas	1,014,167	224,110	790,057		351,305	91,540	259,765		34,259	10,200	24,059	
Tift	382,648	29,988	352,660		101,245	11,425	89,820		10,925	1,252	9,673	
Toombs	626,957	51,407	575,550		140,920	13,790	127,130		19,340	2,120	17,220	
Treutlen	344,724	76,372	268,352		134,200	34,525	99,675		18,123	7,684	10,439	
Troup	971,417	109,389	862,028		478,553	71,020	407,533		60,597	8,614	51,983	
Turner	507,769	18,140	489,629		119,455	4,525	114,930		25,169	1,350	23,819	
Twiggs	294.727	48,703	246,024		142,632	28,025	114,607		27,434	4,718	22,716	
Upson	461,530	67,670	374,860	19,000	245,745	50,840	193,905	1,000	29,539	6,980	22,059	500
Walker	230,105	92,365	137,740		75,970	30,310	45,660		11,265	4,816	6,449	
Walton	791,475	62,225	729,250		349,990	38,055	311,935		62,023	8,392	53,631	
Ware	111,375	33,850	77,525		62,950	24,800	38,150		7,785	2,670	5,115	
Warren	736,187	45,775	690,412		279,185	21,940	257,245		40,282	3,195	37,087	
Washington	1,039,308	76,598	962,710		538,692	51,415	487,277		54,595	7,141	47,454	
Wayne	80,380	18,480	58,700	3,200	26,435	8,250	17,385	800	3,740	1,075	2,650	15
Webster	223,932	30,602	193,330		139,548	22,368	117,180		27,783	7,168	20,615	
Wheeler	359,279	87,219	272,060		105,096	26,411	78,685		14,581	5,118	9,463	
White	34,435	6,070	28,365		7,625	2,540	5,085		302	122	180	
Whitfield	70,710	35,885	34,825		23,090	11,215	11,875		5,419	3,960	1,459	
Wilcox	780,710	93,147	687,563		237,965	36,525	201,440		32,899	5,675	27,224	
Wilkes	733,345	124,220	609,125		415,251	72,670	342,581		35,761	7,927	27,834	
Wilkinson	317,625	60,432	257,193		97,270	20,885	76,385		13,278	2,041	11,237	
Worth	1,268,750	131,370	1,137,380		453,400	69,200	384,200		79,171	15,177	63,994	
IDAHO												
Total	**$79,550**	**$29,000**	**$38,050**	**$12,500**	**$27,650**	**$12,700**	**$9,450**	**$5,500**	**$14,125**	**$6,725**	**$2,400**	**$5,000**
Bannock	9,500	1,000	8,500		5,000	1,000	4,000		800	300	500	
Benewah	22,000	3,500	6,000	12,500	8,000	500	2,000	5,500	6,250	500	750	5,000
Bonneville	17,700		17,700		1,300		1,300		600		600	
Canyon	13,000	13,000			4,500	4,500			1,525	1,525		
Elmore	1,000		1,000		2,000		2,000		300		300	
Idaho	4,850		4,850		150		150		250		250	
Jefferson	6,500	6,500			500	500			300	300		
Latah	4,000	4,000			6,000	6,000			4,000	4,000		
Owyhee	1,000	1,000			200	200			100	100		
ILLINOIS												
Total	**$2,926,618**	**$1,131,738**	**$1,684,380**	**$110,500**	**$778,000**	**$431,160**	**$288,365**	**$58,475**	**$126,810**	**$63,677**	**$54,683**	**$8,450**
Adams	5,880	5,880			1,900	1,900			350	350		
Alexander	323,572	53,502	262,070	8,000	53,620	12,365	40,280	975	9,322	3,123	6,049	150
Bond	9,095	4,895	4,200		3,400	2,600	800		525	425	100	
Carroll	9,700	2,200	7,500		5,100	600	4,500		1,050	150	900	
Champaign	188,600	121,000	67,600		23,406	15,000	8,400		5,300	2,500	2,800	
Christian	44,500	500	44,000		15,000	2,000	13,000		2,330	30	2,300	
Clay	2,450	2,450			1,050	1,050			50	50		
Clinton	15,300		15,300		2,100		2,100		900		900	
Coles	1,900	1,300	600		1,100	700	400		120	20	100	
Cook	38,500		38,500		1,500		1,500		800		800	
Crawford	2,500	2,500			1,000	1,000			75	75		
De Kalb	13,700	200		13,500	10,500	1,000		9,500	1,025	25		1,000
De Witt	8,000		8,000		4,000		4,000		50		50	
Du Page	57,700		57,700		2,300		2,300		100		100	
Edwards	1,000	1,000			400	400			100	100		
Fayette	5,500	5,500			1,500	1,500			100	100		
Fulton	23,000	1,500	21,500		2,500	2,000	500		250	100	150	
Gallatin	28,800		28,800		2,600		2,600		720		720	
Hancock	800	800			1,200	1,200			50	50		
Hardin	5,800	3,800	2,000		2,000	1,000	1,000		275	175	100	
Henderson	39,300	4,000	35,300		4,900	1,200	3,700		2,500		2,500	
Iroquois	9,000	9,000			6,000	6,000			1,075	1,075		
Jackson	49,900	23,450	26,450		18,150	9,900	8,250		2,610	885	1,725	
Jasper	10,800	10,500	300		3,600	2,900	700		1,150	1,150		
Jefferson	6,500	3,200	3,300		5,650	3,150	2,500		512	262	250	
Jersey	6,600	3,100	3,500		2,300	900	1,400		545	175	370	
Johnson	8,600	1,200	7,400		4,400	800	3,600		650	200	450	
Kankakee	59,900	22,950	36,950		16,200	14,150	2,050		1,525	1,025	500	
Kendall	14,000		14,000		7,000		7,000		200		200	
Lake	105,000		25,000	80,000	48,000		3,000	45,000	7,075		75	7,000
Lawrence	38,600	35,000	3,600		14,100	13,300	800		1,925	1,775	150	
Logan	39,200		39,200		2,500		2,500		1,825		1,825	
McLean	206,500	1,000	205,500		19,500	1,000	18,500		6,525	25	6,500	
Macon	5,400	1,600	3,800		3,200	2,000	1,200		175	150	25	
Macoupin	18,450	8,450	10,000		11,050	7,050	4,000		1,100	800	300	
Madison	91,350	73,825	17,525		90,515	71,115	19,400		8,520	7,315	1,205	
Marion	3,540	3,540			5,360	5,360			145	145		
Marshall	39,500	39,500			10,000	10,000			2,000	2,000		
Massac	143,095	92,695	50,400		40,865	30,265	10,600		7,065	4,770	2,295	
Montgomery	3,200		3,200		6,700		6,700		55		55	

TABLE 57.—FARMS OPERATED BY NEGROES—NUMBER, ACREAGE, VALUE OF LAND AND BUILDINGS, AND VALUE OF IMPLEMENTS AND MACHINERY, BY TENURE, BY STATES, AND COUNTIES: 1930—Continued

[Counties in which no farms operated by Negroes were reported, are omitted]

COUNTY	NUMBER OF FARMS				ALL LAND IN FARMS (ACRES)				VALUE OF LAND AND BUILDINGS			
	Total	Owners	Tenants	Managers	Total	Owners	Tenants	Managers	Total	Owners	Tenants	Managers
ILLINOIS—continued												
Morgan	3	1	2		767	450	317		$101, 900	$78, 700	$23, 200	
Peoria	3	2	1		26	9	17		18, 700	18, 000	700	
Perry	9	5	4		962	532	430		38, 520	25, 920	12, 600	
Pike	3	1	2		218	34	184		16, 500	2, 500	14, 000	
Pope	23	16	7		1, 750	1, 038	712		40, 435	25, 510	14, 925	
Pulaski	306	160	146		14, 277	7, 606	6, 671		565, 586	326, 686	238, 900	
Randolph	28	17	11		1, 944	1, 320	624		76, 920	56, 925	19, 995	
St. Clair	23	5	18		942	230	712		208, 600	415, 200	193, 400	
Saline	38	28	10		2, 857	1, 977	880		145, 440	105, 040	40, 400	
Sangamon	16	12	4		403	169	234		76, 675	61, 475	15, 200	
Shelby	1		1		192		192		7, 600		7, 600	
Union	1	1			19	19			700	700		
Vermillion	10	7	3		456	269	187		56, 600	39, 600	17, 000	
Warren	2		2		540		540		74, 000		74, 000	
Washington	3	2	1		130	85	45		6, 450	6, 000	450	
White	12	2	10		1, 294	434	860		71, 500	23, 700	47, 800	
Whiteside	1		1		80		80		5, 600		5, 600	
Will	3		2	1	300		180	120	35, 000		23, 000	$12, 000
Williamson	8	6	2		601	544	57		13, 000	9, 500	3, 500	
Winnebago	1	1			20	20			4, 000	4, 000		
INDIANA												
Total	**461**	**275**	**184**	**2**	**28, 454**	**14, 325**	**13, 734**	**395**	**$1, 947, 915**	**$949, 485**	**$975, 555**	**$22, 875**
Adams	1		1		128		128		7, 680		7, 680	
Allen	2		2		130		150		15, 000		15, 000	
Bartholomew	5	1	4		253	120	133		15, 910	2, 435	13, 475	
Benton	2	2			49	49			6, 950	7, 950		
Blackford	1		1		7		7		1, 000		1, 000	
Boone	1	1			120	120			15, 000	15, 000		
Carroll	1		1		164		164		4, 100		4, 100	
Clark	23	13	9	1	767	441	157	169	78, 725	51, 900	15, 950	10, 875
Daviess	11	7	4		670	157	513		60, 450	13, 300	47, 150	
Dearborn	12	3	9		470	191	279		32, 900	10, 750	22, 150	
Delaware	5	2	3		282	72	210		38, 200	11, 500	26, 700	
Dubois	1	1			151	151			1, 000	1, 000		
Fayette	1	1			10	10			1, 000	1, 000		
Floyd	14	13	1		678	669	9		31, 800	30, 800	1, 000	
Fulton	1		1		120		120		5, 000		5, 000	
Gibson	63	36	27		5, 126	2, 738	2, 388		249, 940	126, 800	123, 140	
Grant	20	14	6		1, 141	522	619		124, 890	52, 950	71, 940	
Greene	2	2			92	92			3, 800	3, 800		
Hamilton	18	12	5	1	1, 335	806	303	226	112, 750	72, 350	28, 400	12, 000
Harrison	10	9	1		852	692	160		19, 100	15, 100	4, 000	
Hendricks	4	3	1		226	211	15		18, 000	16, 500	1, 500	
Henry	10	7	3		483	200	283		42, 200	23, 900	18, 300	
Howard	3	2	1		100	13	87		16, 000	4, 000	12, 000	
Huntington	1		1		80		80		6, 800		6, 800	
Jefferson	11	8	3		378	154	224		16, 540	10, 240	6, 300	
Jennings	11	7	4		705	270	435		27, 200	13, 100	14, 100	
Johnson	3	1	2		118	8	110		14, 525	800	13, 725	
Knox	4		4		469		469		18, 100		18, 100	
La Porte	1	1			94	94			10, 000	10, 000		
Lawrence	4	3	1		105	93	12		8, 800	6, 800	2, 000	
Madison	2	2			22	22			4, 200	4, 200		
Marion	29	15	14		1, 020	260	760		201, 800	76, 700	125, 100	
Miami	1		1		130		130		8, 000		8, 000	
Monroe	1	1			160	160			5, 000	5, 000		
Montgomery	1	1			7	7			3, 000	3, 000		
Morgan	1		1		100		100		1, 000		1, 000	
Newton	1	1			836	836			33, 440	33, 440		
Ohio	4	1	3		267	187	80		17, 210	5, 610	11, 600	
Owen	2	2			380	380			13, 000	13, 000		
Parke	3	2	1		238	233	5		4, 900	4, 500	400	
Perry	4	4			140	140			8, 700	8, 700		
Pike	2	2			35	35			1, 500	1, 500		
Porter	1	1			80	80			8, 000	8, 000		
Posey	1		1		87		87		2, 500		2, 500	
Pulaski	2		2		120		120		5, 300		5, 300	
Putnam	3	2	1		113	97	16		5, 000	4, 500	500	
Randolph	17	11	6		821	300	521		46, 195	21, 325	24, 870	
Rush	9	5	4		663	187	476		57, 602	19, 500	38, 120	
St. Joseph	1	1			20	20			15, 000	15, 000		
Shelby	7	3	4		463	97	366		43, 050	10, 150	32, 900	
Spencer	25	13	12		1, 120	397	723		52, 470	19, 740	32, 730	
Starke	4	1	3		250	40	210		14, 500	1, 200	13, 300	
Steuben	2	1	1		167	24	143		10, 800	1, 800	9, 000	
Sullivan	10	7	3		536	416	120		21, 635	16, 235	5, 400	
Switzerland	3	2	1		252	172	80		6, 450	5, 500	950	
Vanderburg	7	4	3		377	247	130		32, 950	22, 950	10, 000	
Vigo	33	26	7		1, 674	1, 139	535		89, 120	75, 420	13, 700	
Warren	2		2		450		450		22, 000		22, 000	
Warrick	6	1	5		315	48	267		15, 600	3, 000	12, 600	
Wayne	31	17	14		2, 288	928	1, 360		194, 615	68, 540	126, 075	

TABLE 57.—FARMS OPERATED BY NEGROES—NUMBER, ACREAGE, VALUE OF LAND AND BUILDINGS, AND VALUE OF IMPLEMENTS AND MACHINERY, BY TENURE, BY STATES, AND COUNTIES: 1930—Continued

[Counties in which no farms operated by Negroes were reported, are omitted]

COUNTY	VALUE OF LAND ALONE				VALUE OF BUILDINGS				VALUE OF IMPLEMENTS AND MACHINERY			
	Total	Owners	Tenants	Managers	Total	Owners	Tenants	Managers	Total	Owners	Tenants	Managers
ILLINOIS—continued												
Morgan	$97,100	$75,700	$21,400		$4,800	$3,000	$1,800		$2,400	$1,800	$600	
Peoria	9,900	9,300	600		8,800	8,700	100		250	200	50	
Perry	24,720	16,820	7,900		13,800	9,100	4,700		1,602	1,392	210	
Pike	13,100	1,300	11,800		3,400	1,200	2,200		1,300	200	1,100	
Pope	31,500	18,475	13,025		8,935	7,035	1,900		1,265	1,030	235	
Pulaski	429,761	245,616	184,145		135,825	81,070	54,755		25,890	16,740	9,150	
Randolph	53,420	38,125	15,295		23,500	18,800	4,700		2,215	1,865	350	
St. Clair	196,225	10,500	185,725		12,375	4,700	7,675		2,232	1,240	992	
Saline	110,215	77,565	32,650		35,225	27,475	7,750		6,822	5,840	982	
Sangamon	49,375	36,775	12,600		27,300	24,700	2,600		1,220	835	385	
Shelby	5,600		5,600		2,000		2,000		300		300	
Union	550	550			150	150			25	25		
Vermilion	44,345	28,925	15,420		12,255	10,675	1,580		1,475	1,050	425	
Warren	67,000		67,000		7,000		7,000		1,750		1,750	
Washington	3,000	2,750	250		3,450	3,250	200		830	800	30	
White	61,900	20,900	41,000		9,600	2,800	6,800		2,445	1,000	1,445	
Whiteside	5,600		5,600						100		100	
Will	27,000		18,000	$9,000	8,000		5,000	$3,000	3,325		3,025	$300
Williamson	8,575	5,400	3,175		4,425	4,100	325		660	600	60	
Winnebago	3,000	3,000			1,000	1,000			35	35		
INDIANA												
Total	$1,358,595	$637,380	$702,540	18,675	$598,320	$312,105	$273,015	$4,200	$77,162	$37,982	$38,330	$850
Adams	4,880		4,880		2,800		2,800		1,000		1,000	
Allen	9,500		9,500		5,500		5,500		510		510	
Bartholomew	14,710	2,135	12,575		1,200	300	900		387	100	287	
Benton	4,900	4,900			2,050	2,050			250	250		
Blackford	500		500		500		500		10		10	
Boone	10,000	10,000			5,000	5,000			300	300		
Carroll	3,600		3,600		500		500		150		150	
Clark	50,900	30,150	11,875	8,875	27,825	21,750	4,075	2,000	2,815	2,310	205	300
Daviess	46,950	9,400	37,550		13,500	3,900	9,600		1,410	160	1,250	
Dearborn	22,750	7,450	15,300		10,150	3,300	6,850		1,215	1,000	215	
Delaware	33,150	8,750	24,400		5,050	2,750	2,300		325	25	300	
Dubois	650	650			350	350			30	30		
Fayette	600	600			400	400			20	20		
Floyd	15,450	14,950	500		16,350	15,850	500		768	743	25	
Fulton	2,700		2,700		2,300		2,300		500		500	
Gibson	191,840	95,600	96,240		58,100	31,200	26,900		10,565	6,065	4,500	
Grant	66,690	30,450	36,240		58,200	22,500	35,700		2,770	1,220	1,550	
Greene	2,900	2,900			900	900			100	100		
Hamilton	68,500	38,350	20,350	9,800	44,250	34,000	8,050	2,200	3,548	2,738	260	550
Harrison	13,550	10,550	3,000		5,550	4,550	1,000		1,057	907	150	
Hendricks	13,200	12,500	700		4,800	4,000	800		575	525	50	
Henry	29,600	15,000	14,600		12,600	8,900	3,700		1,475	1,050	425	
Howard	10,050	2,050	8,000		5,950	1,950	4,000		2,300	300	2,000	
Huntington	4,600		4,600		2,200		2,200		200		200	
Jefferson	9,040	6,040	3,000		7,500	4,200	3,300		390	240	150	
Jennings	16,325	7,625	8,700		10,875	5,475	5,400		1,600	1,245	355	
Johnson	5,825	700	5,125		8,700	100	8,600		575	50	525	
Knox	15,100		15,100		3,000		3,000		550		550	
La Porte	6,500	6,500			3,500	3,500			150	150		
Lawrence	5,025	4,475	550		3,775	2,325	1,450		165	125	40	
Madison	2,500	2,500			1,700	1,700			250	250		
Marion	166,345	54,520	111,825		35,455	22,180	13,275		6,570	3,605	2,965	
Miami	5,000		5,000		3,000		3,000		100		100	
Monroe	4,000	4,000			1,000	1,000			600	600		
Montgomery	1,200	1,200			1,800	1,800			50	50		
Morgan	500		500		500		500		60		60	
Newton	30,940	30,940			2,500	2,500			4,000	4,000		
Ohio	9,110	2,610	6,500		8,100	3,000	5,100		950	500	450	
Owen	11,600	11,600			1,400	1,400			150	150		
Parke	3,760	3,600	160		1,140	900	240		100	100		
Perry	5,100	5,100			3,600	3,600			576	576		
Pike	700	700			800	800			425	425		
Porter	7,300	7,300			700	700			50	50		
Posey	1,500		1,500		1,000		1,000		100		100	
Pulaski	3,500		3,500		1,800		1,800		500		500	
Putnam	3,650	3,500	150		1,350	1,000	350		150	100	50	
Randolph	26,545	11,175	15,370		19,650	10,150	9,500		1,730	855	875	
Rush	47,220	15,900	31,320		10,400	3,600	6,800		2,460	335	2,125	
St. Joseph	13,000	13,000			2,000	2,000						
Shelby	30,050	6,150	23,900		13,000	4,000	9,000		2,670	1,000	1,670	
Spencer	40,295	15,590	24,705		12,175	4,150	8,025		1,550	605	945	
Starke	8,600	700	7,900		5,900	500	5,400		2,026	10	2,016	
Steuben	5,400	900	4,500		5,400	900	4,500		100		100	
Sullivan	15,060	10,960	4,100		6,575	5,275	1,300		515	390	125	
Switzerland	3,850	3,100	750		2,600	2,400	200		320	310	10	
Vanderburg	30,250	21,700	8,550		2,700	1,250	1,450		500	375	125	
Vigo	53,820	44,070	9,750		35,300	31,350	3,950		2,460	1,528	932	
Warren	18,500		18,500		3,500		3,500		750		750	
Warrick	7,900	1,500	6,400		7,700	1,500	6,200		1,175	400	775	
Wayne	121,415	43,340	78,075		73,200	25,200	48,000		10,565	2,115	8,450	

TABLE 57.—FARMS OPERATED BY NEGROES—NUMBER, ACREAGE, VALUE OR LAND AND BUILDINGS, AND VALUE OF IMPLEMENTS AND MACHINERY, BY TENURE, BY STATES, AND COUNTIES: 1930—Continued

[Counties in which no farms operated by Negroes were reported, are omitted]

COUNTY	NUMBER OF FARMS				ALL LAND IN FARMS (ACRES)				VALUE OF LAND AND BUILDINGS			
	Total	Owners	Tenants	Managers	Total	Owners	Tenants	Managers	Total	Owners	Tenants	Managers
IOWA												
Total	**118**	**67**	**51**		**10,002**	**3,775**	**6,227**		**$878,234**	**$350,814**	**$527,420**	
Allamakee	2	1	1		238	88	150		12,500	6,500	6,000	
Appanoose	2	1	1		175	120	55		13,500	8,000	5,500	
Black Hawk	1		1		40		40		3,000		3,000	
Boone	1		1		18		18		5,000		5,000	
Clarke	3	1	2		360	200	160		23,500	14,000	9,500	
Dallas	2		2		59		59		4,780		4,780	
Des Moines	1	1			80	80			5,800	5,800		
Fayette	10	6	4		1,895	873	1,022		117,690	63,900	53,790	
Hancock	2	1	1		198	3	195		29,550	5,000	24,550	
Harrison	1	1			145	145			12,000	12,000		
Henry	2		2		237		237		14,900		14,900	
Jasper	2	2			9	9			4,200	4,200		
Kossuth	1		1		213		213		16,000		16,000	
Lee	24	16	8		1,926	1,107	819		86,845	63,495	23,350	
Linn	1	1			5	5			9,000	9,000		
Lucas	4	1	3		503	66	437		19,480	1,980	17,500	
Mahaska	3	1	2		245	5	240		30,000	2,000	28,000	
Marion	1	1			66	66			1,800	1,800		
Monroe	17	11	6		846	419	427		84,150	39,800	44,350	
Montgomery	1		1		240		240		24,000		24,000	
Muscatine	1	1			22	22			2,200	2,200		
Page	6	3	3		379	79	300		50,500	11,300	39,200	
Polk	15	11	4		219	90	129		55,839	39,739	16,100	
Pottawattamie	1	1			20	20			2,500	2,500		
Poweshiek	2		2		450		450		64,500		64,500	
Shelby	1	1			120	120			21,000	21,000		
Union	2	1	1		497	80	417		78,500	12,000	66,500	
Wapello	2	2			165	165			15,600	15,600		
Warren	4	1	3		529	10	519		49,900	1,000	48,900	
Washington	1		1		20		20		2,000		2,000	
Webster	1	1			3	3			8,000	8,000		
Worth	1		1		80		80		10,000		10,000	
KANSAS												
Total	**941**	**540**	**391**	**10**	**146,745**	**86,184**	**58,376**	**2,185**	**$6,093,760**	**$3,538,885**	**$2,440,045**	**$114,830**
Allen	3	2	1		132	92	40		6,700	5,200	1,500	
Anderson	5	3	2		599	432	167		34,100	27,600	6,500	
Atchison	34	22	11	1	3,800	1,983	1,737	80	247,210	129,210	115,000	3,000
Barber	2	2			31	31			13,000	13,000		
Barton	13	5	8		2,491	811	1,680		147,600	73,600	74,000	
Bourbon	10	5	5		877	329	548		36,400	11,800	24,600	
Brown	4	4			485	485			43,000	43,000		
Butler	4	2	2		748	268	480		26,640	11,840	14,800	
Chase	2	1	1		420	120	300		16,000	4,000	12,000	
Chautauqua	10	5	5		701	165	536		28,550	7,600	20,950	
Cherokee	22	17	5		2,074	1,716	358		96,615	73,815	22,800	
Coffey	5	4	1		191	145	46		10,040	8,400	1,640	
Cowley	5	3	2		364	204	160		16,700	8,200	8,500	
Crawford	9	5	4		353	291	62		11,650	8,400	3,250	
Dickinson	4	4			176	176			14,800	14,800		
Doniphan	25	15	9	1	2,347	972	1,295	80	203,550	88,250	109,300	6,000
Douglas	60	39	21		5,113	2,989	2,124		440,810	257,210	183,600	
Edwards	2	2			225	225			18,500	18,500		
Ellis	1	1			100	100			4,140	4,140		
Ellsworth	2	2			320	320			16,000	16,000		
Finney	8	3	5		2,288	684	1,604		70,300	28,000	42,300	
Franklin	11	11			775	775			59,610	59,610		
Geary	5	3	1	1	427	87	240	100	28,000	6,400	9,600	12,000
Gove	8	8			4,089	4,089			125,070	125,070		
Graham	77	45	31	1	18,198	12,585	5,503	110	420,105	294,250	123,855	2,000
Grant	3	1	2		770	240	530		26,600	7,200	19,400	
Gray	2	1	1		1,760	1,600	160		38,000	32,000	6,000	
Hamilton	2	2			515	515			10,800	10,800		
Harvey	3	3			90	90			14,000	14,000		
Hodgeman	11	5	6		1,878	1,040	838		53,425	27,305	26,120	
Jackson	12	9	3		1,514	964	550		70,200	46,200	24,000	
Jefferson	25	20	5		3,265	2,371	894		174,435	144,935	29,500	
Johnson	22	5	17		1,403	131	1,272		149,900	18,000	131,900	
Kearny	1		1		640		640		10,000		10,000	
Labette	11	4	7		700	339	361		34,830	21,750	13,080	
Leavenworth	37	19	18		2,645	885	1,760		152,345	49,370	102,975	
Lincoln	2	1	1		255	95	160		14,000	7,000	7,000	
Linn	6	3	3		325	144	181		13,900	4,400	9,500	
Logan	31	0	11		22,460	17,950	4,510		236,430	168,810	67,620	
Lyon	16	3	3		1,117	777	340		84,490	68,850	15,640	
Marshall	9	3	6		2,075	720	1,355		114,430	37,530	76,900	
Meade	6	3	3		4,060	1,980	2,080		148,600	64,200	84,400	
Miami	7	2	5		710	120	590		41,800	8,400	33,400	
Montgomery	105	15	89	1	6,661	946	5,635	80	259,510	46,640	210,470	2,400
Morris	14	12	2		800	775	25		31,850	30,450	1,400	
Morton	3	3			760	760			19,500	19,500		
Nemaha	7	1	6		986	10	976		77,850	750	77,100	
Neosho	6	3	3		1,232	842	390		50,560	28,760	21,800	
Norton	2	2			500	500			10,800	10,800		
Osage	11	7	4		890	450	440		36,550	22,600	13,950	

Table 57—FARMS OPERATED BY NEGROES—NUMBER, ACREAGE, VALUE OF LAND AND BUILDINGS, AND VALUE OF IMPLEMENTS AND MACHINERY, BY TENURE, BY STATES, AND COUNTIES: 1930—Continued

[Counties in which no farms operated by Negroes were reported, are omitted]

COUNTY	VALUE OF LAND ALONE				VALUE OF BUILDINGS				VALUE OF IMPLEMENTS AND MACHINERY			
	Total	Owners	Tenants	Managers	Total	Owners	Tenants	Managers	Total	Owners	Tenants	Managers
IOWA												
Total	$660,745	$234,675	$426,070	-	$217,489	$116,139	$101,350	-	$46,001	$20,271	$25,730	-
Allamakee	10,700	4,900	5,800	-	1,800	1,600	200	-	750	350	400	-
Appanoose	9,500	6,000	3,500	-	4,000	2,000	2,000	-	300	-	300	-
Black Hawk	1,900	-	1,900	-	1,100	-	1,100	-	50	-	50	-
Boone	2,000	-	2,000	-	3,000	-	3,000	-	100	-	100	-
Clarke	16,700	10,000	6,700	-	6,800	4,000	2,800	-	2,450	1,800	650	-
Dallas	4,480	-	4,480	-	300	-	300	-	90	-	90	-
Des Moines	5,300	5,300	-	-	500	500	-	-	500	500	-	-
Fayette	90,090	46,300	43,790	-	27,600	17,600	10,000	-	7,700	5,100	2,600	-
Hancock	22,250	1,700	20,550	-	7,300	3,300	4,000	-	900	100	800	-
Harrison	8,000	8,000	-	-	4,000	4,000	-	-	300	300	-	-
Henry	11,400	-	11,400	-	3,500	-	3,500	-	250	-	250	-
Jasper	2,450	2,450	-	-	1,750	1,750	-	-	150	150	-	-
Kossuth	11,000	-	11,000	-	5,000	-	5,000	-	1,000	-	1,000	-
Lee	63,920	45,995	17,925	-	22,925	17,500	5,425	-	4,207	2,992	1,215	-
Linn	3,200	3,200	-	-	5,800	5,800	-	-	1,000	1,000	-	-
Lucas	10,880	1,580	9,300	-	8,600	400	8,200	-	2,250	200	2,050	-
Mahaska	21,000	1,000	20,000	-	9,000	1,000	8,000	-	1,600	-	1,600	-
Marion	1,300	1,300	-	-	500	500	-	-	200	200	-	-
Monroe	62,475	29,150	33,325	-	21,675	10,650	11,025	-	5,310	2,335	2,975	-
Montgomery	21,200	-	21,200	-	2,800	-	2,800	-	1,000	-	1,000	-
Muscatine	2,000	2,000	-	-	200	200	-	-	-	-	-	-
Page	43,600	7,400	36,200	-	6,900	3,900	3,000	-	1,725	475	1,250	-
Polk	43,900	29,900	14,000	-	11,939	9,839	2,100	-	919	769	150	-
Pottawattamie	2,400	2,400	-	-	100	100	-	-	-	-	-	-
Poweshiek	52,500	-	52,500	-	12,000	-	12,000	-	3,700	-	3,700	-
Shelby	7,000	7,000	-	-	14,000	14,000	-	-	2,500	2,500	-	-
Union	71,500	9,000	62,500	-	7,000	3,000	4,000	-	3,250	1,000	2,250	-
Wapello	7,800	7,800	-	-	7,800	7,800	-	-	500	500	-	-
Warren	40,800	800	40,000	-	9,100	200	8,900	-	1,800	-	1,800	-
Washington	1,000	-	1,000	-	1,000	-	1,000	-	1,000	-	1,000	-
Webster	1,500	1,500	-	-	6,500	6,500	-	-	-	-	-	-
Worth	7,000	-	7,000	-	3,000	-	3,000	-	500	-	500	-
KANSAS												
Total	$5,090,775	$2,858,315	$2,137,280	$95,180	$1,002,985	$680,570	$302,765	$19,650	$287,075	$185,955	$97,875	$3,245
Allen	5,550	4,150	1,400	-	1,150	1,050	100	-	400	200	200	-
Anderson	27,600	23,600	4,000	-	6,500	4,000	2,500	-	1,570	1,450	120	-
Atchison	199,085	92,410	104,675	2,000	48,125	36,800	10,325	1,000	7,240	5,070	2,120	50
Barber	7,600	7,600	-	-	5,400	5,400	-	-	1,300	1,300	-	-
Barton	131,825	65,100	66,725	-	15,775	8,500	7,275	-	5,300	1,650	3,650	-
Bourbon	29,400	9,800	19,600	-	7,000	2,000	5,000	-	560	110	450	-
Brown	36,600	36,600	-	-	6,400	6,400	-	-	800	800	-	-
Butler	21,740	8,240	13,500	-	4,900	3,600	1,300	-	2,050	1,000	1,050	-
Chase	13,950	3,450	10,500	-	2,050	550	1,500	-	420	20	400	-
Chatauqua	25,650	6,800	18,850	-	2,900	800	2,100	-	325	50	275	-
Cherokee	74,890	59,340	15,550	-	21,725	14,475	7,250	-	5,755	4,440	1,315	-
Coffey	8,240	6,900	1,340	-	1,800	1,500	300	-	315	240	75	-
Cowley	13,750	6,250	7,500	-	2,950	1,950	1,000	-	1,225	1,100	125	-
Crawford	8,090	5,600	2,490	-	3,560	2,800	760	-	305	200	105	-
Dickinson	9,900	9,900	-	-	4,900	4,900	-	-	720	720	-	-
Doniphan	170,050	61,050	103,200	5,800	33,500	27,200	6,100	200	5,240	3,340	1,800	100
Douglas	348,800	198,100	150,700	-	92,010	59,110	32,900	-	17,500	12,100	5,400	-
Edwards	18,000	18,000	-	-	500	500	-	-	50	50	-	-
Ellis	3,790	3,790	-	-	350	350	-	-	75	75	-	-
Ellsworth	13,300	13,300	-	-	2,700	2,700	-	-	400	400	-	-
Finney	56,900	19,200	37,700	-	13,400	8,800	4,600	-	5,850	2,900	2,950	-
Franklin	52,110	52,110	-	-	7,500	7,500	-	-	770	770	-	-
Geary	22,850	2,950	9,400	10,500	5,150	3,450	200	1,500	2,425	300	1,125	1,000
Gove	108,570	108,570	-	-	16,500	16,500	-	-	7,775	7,775	-	-
Graham	366,230	253,475	111,155	1,600	53,875	40,775	12,700	400	29,015	16,965	12,050	-
Grant	24,000	7,000	17,000	-	2,600	200	2,400	-	800	200	600	-
Gray	32,000	27,000	5,000	-	6,000	5,000	1,000	-	5,600	5,000	600	-
Hamilton	10,475	10,475	-	-	325	325	-	-	550	550	-	-
Harvey	5,200	5,200	-	-	8,800	8,800	-	-	750	750	-	-
Hodgeman	47,375	24,955	22,420	-	6,050	2,350	3,700	-	1,930	1,250	680	-
Jackson	58,225	37,425	20,800	-	11,975	8,775	3,200	-	2,650	1,775	875	-
Jefferson	142,735	116,135	26,600	-	31,700	28,800	2,900	-	7,055	6,405	650	-
Johnson	129,805	12,275	117,530	-	20,095	5,725	14,370	-	1,990	200	1,790	-
Kearny	9,700	-	9,700	-	300	-	300	-	450	-	450	-
Labette	26,840	16,360	10,480	-	7,990	5,390	2,600	-	1,430	725	705	-
Leavenworth	132,770	38,845	93,925	-	19,575	10,525	9,050	-	2,810	1,580	1,230	-
Lincoln	12,300	6,000	6,300	-	1,700	1,000	700	-	575	25	550	-
Linn	11,400	3,400	8,000	-	2,500	1,000	1,500	-	60	50	10	-
Logan	211,555	152,085	59,470	-	24,875	16,725	8,150	-	13,780	10,550	3,230	-
Lyon	62,140	49,100	13,040	-	22,350	19,750	2,600	-	5,555	4,180	1,375	-
Marshall	95,530	31,430	64,100	-	18,900	6,100	12,800	-	2,590	940	1,650	-
Meade	136,400	57,500	78,900	-	12,200	6,700	5,500	-	19,850	11,850	8,000	-
Miami	33,200	7,000	26,200	-	8,600	1,400	7,200	-	675	175	500	-
Montgomery	198,020	29,290	167,330	1,400	61,490	17,350	43,140	1,000	10,200	3,735	6,450	15
Morris	21,800	20,950	850	-	10,050	9,500	550	-	1,545	1,345	200	-
Morton	18,300	18,300	-	-	1,200	1,200	-	-	950	950	-	-
Nemaha	68,600	600	68,000	-	9,250	150	9,100	-	3,480	100	3,380	-
Neosho	41,260	22,060	19,200	-	9,300	6,700	2,600	-	3,400	3,000	400	-
Norton	9,000	9,000	-	-	1,800	1,800	-	-	750	750	-	-
Osage	25,600	14,200	11,400	-	10,950	8,400	2,550	-	1,770	1,245	525	-

TABLE 57.—FARMS OPERATED BY NEGROES—NUMBER, ACREAGE, VALUE OF LAND AND BUILDINGS, AND VALUE OF IMPLEMENTS AND MACHINERY, BY TENURE, BY STATES, AND COUNTIES: 1930—Continued

[Counties in which no farms operated by Negroes were reported, are omitted]

COUNTY	NUMBER OF FARMS				ALL LAND IN FARMS (ACRES)				VALUE OF LAND AND BUILDINGS			
	Total	Owners	Tenants	Managers	Total	Owners	Tenants	Managers	Total	Owners	Tenants	Managers
	KANSAS—continued											
Osborne	2	1	1		195	35	160		$8, 000	$1, 000	$7, 000	
Ottawa	1		1		57		57		3, 585		3, 585	
Pawnee	1	1			320	320			20, 000	20, 000		
Phillips	3	1	2		559	159	400		12, 800	4, 800	8, 000	
Pottawatomie	2	1	1		525	5	520		26, 150	150	26, 000	
Pratt	13	8	5		3, 270	2, 470	800		209, 600	143, 200	66, 400	
Reno	8	7	1		572	342	230		27, 600	23, 800	3, 800	
Rice	3	1	2		505	235	270		42, 200	20, 000	22, 200	
Rooks	5	3	2		1, 140	680	460		27, 900	15, 700	12, 200	
Rush	1	1			480	480			19, 200	19, 200		
Russell	1		1		545		545		18, 000		18, 000	
Saline	4	4			310	310			12, 000	12, 000		
Scott	1	1			640	640			6, 400	6, 400		
Sedgwick	10	2	8		1, 073	280	793		90, 200	22, 500	67, 700	
Seward	1	1			160	160			6, 400	6, 400		
Shawnee	40	32	6	2	2, 975	2, 668	183	124	361, 430	293, 700	29, 800	$37, 930
Smith	1	1			400	400			14, 000	14, 000		
Stafford	8	5	3		1, 730	540	1, 190		114, 730	33, 480	81, 250	
Stevens	20	11	9		7, 688	5, 728	1, 960		143, 760	105, 660	38, 100	
Sumner	5	4	1		1, 088	768	320		84, 500	60, 500	24, 000	
Thomas	2	1	1		1, 735	1, 255	480		36, 000	21, 600	14, 400	
Trego	5	3	2		7, 460	1, 060	6, 400		51, 650	30, 850	20, 800	
Wabaunsee	41	21	18	2	5, 347	2, 006	1, 731	1, 610	271, 360	111, 600	109, 760	50, 000
Wallace	2	1	1		380	160	220		4, 900	1, 600	3, 300	
Washington	1	1			80	80			4, 800	4, 800		
Wichita	1		1		40		40		3, 000		3, 000	
Wilson	1		1		160		160		5, 600		5, 600	
Wyandotte	73	58	14	1	1, 976	1, 085	890	1	458, 100	337, 800	118, 800	1, 500
	KENTUCKY											
Total	9, 104	4, 175	4, 914	15	341, 833	183, 148	156, 178	2, 507	$16, 157, 593	$7, 348, 683	$8, 430, 710	$378, 200
Adair	115	72	43		5, 282	3, 797	1, 485		97, 585	58, 050	39, 535	
Allen	53	27	26		2, 021	1, 201	820		42, 945	21, 900	21, 045	
Anderson	8	4	4		123	51	72		9, 415	5, 000	4, 415	
Ballard	131	41	90		5, 361	2, 194	3, 167		158, 600	54, 670	103, 930	
Barren	324	171	153		10, 897	6, 442	4, 455		468, 360	273, 685	194, 675	
Bath	53	29	24		1, 125	579	546		109, 410	46, 260	63, 150	
Bell	5	4	1		71	47	24		7, 600	5, 600	2, 000	
Boone	41	14	26	1	3, 901	1, 431	2, 098	372	203, 750	69, 900	117, 850	$16, 000
Bourbon	171	85	86		2, 334	1, 256	1, 078		365, 795	201, 785	164, 010	
Boyd	1	1			4	4			1, 200	1, 200		
Boyle	92	56	36		1, 623	1, 152	471		110, 715	76, 500	34, 215	
Bracken	7	1	6		197	60	137		21, 000	2, 500	18, 500	
Breathitt	8	3	5		214	107	107		9, 000	3, 100	5, 900	
Breckinridge	47	21	26		3, 751	2, 452	1, 299		67, 950	47, 450	20, 500	
Bullitt	36	18	18		2, 444	812	1, 632		91, 538	32, 188	59, 350	
Butler	28	21	7		1, 559	1, 324	235		18, 925	11, 625	7, 300	
Caldwell	80	35	45		4, 363	2, 628	1, 735		100. 170	47, 600	52, 570	
Calloway	39	24	15		2, 486	1, 754	732		55, 635	31, 900	23, 735	
Campbell	1	1			7	7			1, 600	1, 600		
Carlisle	9	5	4		421	289	132		13, 850	10, 400	3, 450	
Carroll	18	1	17		523	62	461		38, 850	2, 000	36, 850	
Casey	22	18	4		659	627	32		13, 550	12, 100	1, 450	
Christian	677	203	473	1	35, 485	14, 906	20, 494	85	1, 127, 555	345, 355	773, 700	8, 500
Clark	84	63	21		1, 916	1, 622	294		123, 405	90, 275	33, 130	
Clay	39	31	8		1, 288	1, 085	203		31, 950	27, 550	4, 400	
Clinton	14	11	3		601	540	61		6, 615	5, 490	1, 125	
Crittenden	14	10	4		425	341	84		9, 400	7, 600	1, 800	
Cumberland	98	46	52		3, 437	2, 528	909		120, 500	59, 750	60, 750	
Daviess	204	70	134		6, 484	3, 790	2, 694		342, 485	154, 550	187, 935	
Edmonson	30	28	2		1, 948	1, 906	42		38, 450	35, 550	2, 900	
Estill	1		1		5		5		500		500	
Fayette	175	85	87	3	4, 950	1, 857	2, 479	[illegible]	1, 038, 735	340, 185	508, 350	190, 200
Fleming	41	14	27		807	419	388		70, 590	30, 980	39, 610	
Floyd	13	12	1		564	557	7		18, 000	17, 500	500	
Franklin	20	10	10		651	260	391		43, 115	22, 615	20, 500	
Fulton	313	10	303		10, 722	497	10, 225		953, 915	23, 910	930, 005	
Gallatin	18	10	8		708	596	112		27, 140	22, 300	4, 840	
Garrard	208	124	84		4, 526	3, 306	1, 220		346, 995	233, 990	113, 005	
Grant	8	1	7		52	4	48		6, 500	1, 200	5, 300	
Graves	143	45	98		6, 087	2, 467	3, 620		219, 475	72, 935	146, 540	
Grayson	2	1	1		128	123	5		1, 600	1, 500	100	
Green	184	81	103		6, 473	3, 812	2, 661		185, 405	102, 300	83, 105	
Greenup	5	4	1		148	118	30		9, 400	4, 900	4, 500	
Hancock	15	3	12		344	195	149		35, 055	20, 550	14, 505	
Hardin	48	29	19		2, 373	1, 848	525		87, 675	64, 675	23, 000	
Harlan	7	5	2		417	305	112		10, 400	7, 400	3, 000	
Harrison	58	33	25		2, 250	1, 690	560		164, 039	114, 944	49, 095	
Hart	190	80	110		5, 590	3, 251	2, 339		221, 605	96, 935	124, 670	
Henderson	312	82	227	3	13, 052	4, 056	8, 607	389	610, 475	164, 070	409, 905	36, 500
Henry	79	34	45		1, 650	632	1, 018		[illegible]	73, 200	102, 590	

TABLE 57.—FARMS OPERATED BY NEGROES—NUMBER, ACREAGE, VALUE OF LAND AND BUILDINGS, AND VALUE OF IMPLEMENTS AND MACHINERY, BY TENURE, BY STATES, AND COUNTIES: 1930—Continued

[Counties in which no farms operated by Negroes were reported, are omitted]

COUNTY	VALUE OF LAND ALONE				VALUE OF BUILDINGS				VALUE OF IMPLEMENTS AND MACHINERY			
	Total	Owners	Tenants	Managers	Total	Owners	Tenants	Managers	Total	Owners	Tenants	Managers
KANSAS—continued												
Osborne	$7,700	$350	$6,850		$300	$150	$150		$300	$100	$200	
Ottawa	3,585		3,585						100		100	
Pawnee	16,000	16,000			4,000	4,000			1,200	1,200		
Phillips	10,750	4,000	6,750		2,050	800	1,250		525	50	475	
Pottawatomie	24,515	115	24,400		1,635	35	1,600		275	25	250	
Pratt	191,650	130,600	61,050		17,950	12,600	5,350		16,950	11,475	5,475	
Reno	22,150	18,850	3,300		5,450	4,950	500		1,210	810	400	
Rice	37,700	18,000	19,700		4,500	2,000	2,500		1,050	500	550	
Rooks	24,200	13,650	10,550		3,700	2,050	1,650		4,250	2,600	1,650	
Rush	15,200	15,200			4,000	4,000			5,000	5,000		
Russell	17,400		17,400		600		600		200		200	
Saline	10,150	10,150			1,850	1,850			775	775		
Scott	6,000	6,000			400	400			850	850		
Sedgwick	85,230	21,800	63,430		4,970	700	4,270		2,225	600	1,625	
Seward	5,400	5,400			1,000	1,000			200	200		
Shawnee	288,980	237,900	27,500	$23,580	72,450	55,800	2,300	$14,350	8,605	7,480	575	$550
Smith	12,500	12,500			1,500	1,500			1,000	1,000		
Stafford	100,200	20,500	79,700		14,530	12,980	1,550		8,565	1,815	6,750	
Stevens	125,010	89,660	35,350		18,750	16,000	2,750		9,600	7,600	2,000	
Sumner	77,600	54,100	23,500		6,900	6,400	500		3,500	3,400	100	
Thomas	34,900	21,300	13,600		1,100	300	800		8,000	6,000	2,000	
Trego	46,300	29,100	17,200		5,350	1,750	3,600		1,125	350	775	
Wabaunsee	206,410	77,900	79,510	49,000	64,950	33,700	30,250	1,000	12,750	5,385	5,865	1,500
Wallace	3,825	1,525	2,300		1,075	75	1,000		250	50	200	
Washington	2,800	2,800			2,000	2,000			300	300		
Wichita	1,000		1,000		2,000		2,000		50		50	
Wilson	3,600		3,600		2,000		2,000		500		500	
Wyandotte	371,320	257,545	112,475	1,300	86,780	80,255	6,325	200	9,140	8,035	1,075	30
KENTUCKY												
Total	$11,325,769	$4,744,259	$6,321,810	$259,700	$4,831,824	$2,604,424	$2,108,900	$118,500	$605,430	$315,392	$281,988	$8,050
Adair	68,164	40,204	27,960		29,421	17,846	11,575		3,656	2,600	1,056	
Allen	27,530	12,375	15,155		15,415	9,525	5,890		985	585	400	
Anderson	6,645	3,750	2,895		2,770	1,250	1,520		714	400	314	
Ballard	116,120	37,100	79,020		42,480	17,570	24,910		8,133	2,708	5,425	
Barren	326,140	184,890	141,250		142,220	88,795	53,425		15,612	9,770	5,842	
Bath	66,110	25,360	40,750		43,300	20,900	22,400		3,490	635	2,855	
Bell	2,650	1,450	1,200		4,950	4,150	800		250	220	30	
Boone	138,225	42,625	86,600	9,000	65,525	27,275	31,250	7,000	6,540	4,830	1,710	
Bourbon	247,610	118,600	129,010		118,185	83,185	35,000		16,988	9,975	7,013	
Boyd	400	400			800	800			60	60		
Boyle	77,490	48,950	28,540		33,225	27,550	5,675		3,290	2,765	525	
Bracken	10,700	1,700	9,000		10,300	800	9,500		735	75	660	
Breathitt	6,700	1,375	5,325		2,300	1,725	575		235	40	195	
Breckinridge	34,175	22,750	11,425		35,775	24,700	9,075		1,743	1,305	438	
Bullitt	70,508	24,028	46,480		21,030	8,160	12,870		1,953	1,633	320	
Butler	12,470	7,020	5,450		6,455	4,605	1,850		896	466	430	
Caldwell	72,895	33,475	39,420		27,275	14,125	13,150		2,990	1,505	1,485	
Calloway	37,985	21,950	16,035		17,650	9,950	7,700		1,695	1,215	480	
Campbell	1,000	1,000			600	600			50	50		
Carlisle	9,185	7,200	1,985		4,665	3,200	1,465		308	285	23	
Carroll	28,250	1,500	26,750		10,600	500	10,100		1,010	100	910	
Casey	10,000	9,200	800		3,550	2,900	650		1,025	1,010	15	
Christian	807,115	230,525	571,590	5,000	320,440	114,830	202,110	3,500	53,033	13,031	39,202	800
Clark	77,510	52,180	25,330		45,895	38,095	7,800		4,835	3,800	1,035	
Clay	19,955	17,155	2,800		11,995	10,395	1,600		741	671	70	
Clinton	5,815	4,740	1,075		800	750	50		260	210	50	
Crittenden	6,010	4,500	1,510		3,390	3,100	290		420	365	55	
Cumberland	89,785	43,260	46,525		30,715	16,490	14,225		4,170	1,924	2,246	
Daviess	240,820	99,900	140,920		101,665	54,650	47,015		9,827	5,392	4,435	
Edmonson	28,645	26,245	2,400		9,805	9,305	500		1,730	1,703		
Estill	300		300		200		200		70		70	
Fayette	744,105	206,665	405,740	131,700	294,630	133,520	102,610	58,500	32,170	14,405	14,215	3,550
Fleming	50,605	18,740	31,865		19,985	12,240	7,745		1,918	658	1,260	
Floyd	12,425	12,125	300		5,575	5,375	200		90	85	5	
Franklin	32,810	14,810	18,000		10,305	7,805	2,500		1,575	525	1,050	
Fulton	797,095	16,535	780,560		156,820	7,375	149,445		29,455	690	28,765	
Gallatin	16,765	13,350	3,415		10,375	8,950	1,425		140	100	40	
Garrard	228,110	150,115	77,995		118,885	83,875	35,010		15,113	11,321	3,792	
Grant	5,360	700	4,660		1,140	500	640		50		50	
Graves	162,095	52,265	109,830		57,380	20,670	36,710		6,703	2,483	4,220	
Grayson	1,300	1,200	100		300	300			25	25		
Green	137,660	71,935	65,725		47,745	30,365	17,380		9,205	6,133	3,072	
Greenup	7,400	3,950	3,450		2,000	950	1,050		117	92	25	
Hancock	26,355	14,050	12,305		8,700	6,500	2,200		3,035	650	2,385	
Hardin	56,445	38,110	18,335		31,230	26,565	4,665		3,365	3,040	325	
Harlan	8,250	5,850	2,400		2,150	1,550	600		43	23	20	
Harrison	112,389	77,344	35,045		51,650	37,600	14,050		8,103	6,476	1,627	
Hart	149,450	61,115	88,335		72,155	35,820	36,335		10,955	6,085	4,870	
Henderson	446,000	111,670	306,830	27,500	164,475	52,400	103,075	9,000	21,095	5,190	14,105	1,800
Henry	101,615	35,625	65,990		74,175	37,575	36,600		4,120	2,180	1,940	

TABLE 57.—FARMS OPERATED BY NEGROES—NUMBER, ACREAGE, VALUE OF LAND AND BUILDINGS, AND VALUE OF IMPLEMENTS AND MACHINERY, BY TENURE, BY STATES, AND COUNTIES: 1930—Continued

[Counties in which no farms operated by Negroes were reported, are omitted]

COUNTY	NUMBER OF FARMS				ALL LAND IN FARMS (ACRES)				VALUE OF LAND AND BUILDINGS			
	Total	Owners	Tenants	Managers	Total	Owners	Tenants	Managers	Total	Owners	Tenants	Managers
						KENTUCKY—continued						
Hickman	87	15	72		4, 139	1, 064	3, 075		$133, 270	$32, 585	$100, 685	
Hopkins	70	29	41		2, 448	1, 214	1, 234		115, 645	52, 880	62, 765	
Jackson	1	1			69	69			800	800		
Jefferson	60	33	26	1	1, 720	688	967	65	249, 900	87, 300	157, 600	$5, 000
Jessamine	124	79	44	1	3, 167	1, 903	1, 250	14	365, 640	188, 740	156, 900	20, 000
Kenton	13	8	5		630	579	51		37, 200	30, 500	6, 700	
Knott	17	13	4		580	534	46		18, 060	16, 650	1, 410	
Knox	27	21	6		578	511	67		36, 300	25, 800	10, 500	
Larue	31	21	10		1, 323	1, 104	219		44, 465	36, 865	7, 600	
Laurel	16	15	1		217	209	8		21, 975	21, 675	300	
Lawrence	2	1	1		104	65	39		7, 000	2, 000	5, 000	
Lee	12	6	6		228	160	68		7, 070	3, 380	3, 690	
Leslie	3	1	2		145	75	70		4, 000	2, 000	2, 000	
Lewis	10	7	3		927	756	171		10, 250	7, 950	2, 300	
Lincoln	148	102	46		3, 023	2, 237	786		148, 005	104, 185	43, 820	
Livingston	20	6	14		1, 360	387	973		23, 070	5, 400	17, 670	
Logan	373	129	244		13, 682	6, 729	6, 953		573, 808	211, 513	362, 295	
Lyon	93	48	45		4, 148	2, 667	1, 481		70, 827	38, 108	32, 719	
McCracken	250	212	38		5, 133	4, 141	992		444, 061	391, 161	52, 900	
McLean	24	6	18		1, 211	648	563		43, 810	22, 065	21, 745	
Madison	419	265	154		12, 020	7, 908	4, 112		797, 765	493, 645	304, 120	
Magoffin	5	3	2		408	305	103		10, 200	8, 700	1, 500	
Marion	90	38	52		3, 927	2, 088	1, 839		176, 250	49, 350	126, 900	
Marshall	4	3	1		225	200	25		5, 100	4, 600	500	
Mason	85	25	60		2, 770	1, 260	1, 510		245, 360	107, 440	137, 920	
Meade	55	42	13		6, 213	4, 347	1, 866		102, 553	70, 453	32, 100	
Menifee	3	2	1		275	225	50		1, 650	1, 150	500	
Mercer	53	37	16		1, 805	1, 188	617		127, 400	81, 600	45, 800	
Metcalfe	102	60	42		3, 637	2, 446	1, 191		91, 375	54, 900	36, 475	
Monroe	53	26	27		1, 955	1, 169	786		41, 765	21; 330	20, 435	
Montgomery	67	45	20	2	1, 967	1, 332	304	331	186, 795	98, 535	28, 260	60, 000
Morgan	1	1			8	8			600	600		
Muhlenberg	53	39	14		3, 247	2, 057	1, 190		63, 775	42, 150	21, 625	
Nelson	110	62	48		4, 372	2, 723	1, 649		254, 205	149, 945	104, 260	
Nicholas	45	25	20		693	480	213		60, 690	41, 390	19, 300	
Ohio	35	19	16		2, 263	1, 547	716		39, 410	24, 300	15, 110	
Oldham	15	5	8	2	831	106	412	313	52, 200	6, 200	26, 000	20, 000
Owen	88	27	61		3, 055	1, 678	1, 377		141, 294	71, 010	70, 284	
Owsley	6	3	3		276	190	86		4, 650	2, 600	2, 050	
Pendleton	17	6	11		669	237	432		25, 840	9, 840	16, 000	
Perry	44	38	6		1, 790	1, 630	160		55, 365	48, 550	6, 815	
Pike	6		6		1, 157		1, 157		21, 600		21, 600	
Powell	27	20	7		1, 354	1, 069	285		39, 350	32, 850	6, 500	
Pulaski	38	30	8		1, 093	825	268		42, 075	34, 675	7, 400	
Robertson	5	4	1		322	307	15		18, 300	17, 500	800	
Rockcastle	2	2			75	75			1, 100	1, 100		
Rowan	1		1		26		26		500		500	
Russell	23	15	8		1, 856	1, 625	231		24, 375	16, 250	8, 125	
Scott	119	66	53		2, 276	1, 576	700		282, 060	192, 395	89, 665	
Shelby	120	39	81		2, 917	1, 317	1, 600		255, 016	90, 120	164, 896	
Simpson	173	56	117		8, 325	2, 890	5, 435		294, 625	92, 525	202, 100	
Spencer	35	18	17		1, 312	820	492		84, 955	54, 425	30, 530	
Taylor	122	65	57		4, 444	2, 486	1, 958		153, 035	64, 085	88, 950	
Todd	369	119	250		15, 099	7, 808	7, 291		480, 380	202, 947	277, 433	
Trigg	270	89	181		16, 472	8, 312	8, 160		349, 272	156, 664	192, 608	
Trimble	6	4	2		522	472	50		22, 300	18, 300	4, 000	
Union	42	13	29		1, 271	453	818		52, 425	17, 330	35, 095	
Warren	308	142	165	1	10, 238	5, 205	4, 709	324	474, 370	185, 905	266, 465	22, 000
Washington	155	47	108		4, 850	2, 187	2, 663		261, 655	89, 085	172, 570	
Wayne	54	46	8		1, 953	1, 701	252		50, 300	41, 350	8, 950	
Webster	87	39	48		4, 226	2, 787	1, 439		135, 830	82, 540	53, 290	
Whitley	10	9	1		281	271	10		8, 175	7, 875	300	
Wolfe	1	1			12	12			150	150		
Woodford	111	50	61		2, 067	1, 099	968		232, 135	121, 545	110, 590	
						LOUISIANA						
Total	**73, 734**	**10, 488**	**63, 192**	**54**	**2, 313, 338**	**601, 423**	**1, 691, 610**	**20, 305**	**$108, 668, 818**	**$19, 567, 276**	**$88, 375, 116**	**$726, 426**
Acadia	494	72	421	1	14, 778	2, 373	12, 399	6	852, 951	135, 765	709, 555	7, 631
Allen	116	72	44		3, 801	2, 326	1, 475		130, 120	67, 220	62, 900	
Ascension	306	122	183	1	6, 840	3, 133	3, 637	70	348, 307	173, 577	173, 470	1, 260
Assumption	20	9	9	2	416	106	205	105	30, 055	8, 150	9, 905	12, 000
Avoyelles	1, 840	182	1, 658		35, 691	5, 003	30, 688		2, 555, 854	308, 120	2, 247, 734	
Beauregard	111	44	67		3, 870	1, 243	2, 627		$165, 704	32, 305	133, 399	
Bienville	1, 858	500	1, 358		86, 692	35, 775	50, 917		2, 279, 860	736, 685	1, 543, 175	
Bossier	3, 874	479	3, 391	4	111, 838	30, 093	80, 491	1, 254	6, 492, 333	761, 335	5, 596, 863	134, 135
Caddo	6, 154	591	5, 563		177, 438	33, 371	144, 067		12, 104, 127	1, 192, 487	10, 911, 640	
Calcasieu	300	61	238	1	14, 796	2, 015	12, 621	160	667, 345	90, 720	575, 725	900
Caldwell	319	74	245		9, 471	4, 194	5, 277		483, 448	88, 790	394, 658	
Cameron	85	16	69		3, 220	1, 035	2, 185		160, 950	38, 530	122, 420	
Catahoula	914	45	869		22, 359	4, 052	18, 307		1, 517, 720	179, 080	1, 338, 640	
Claiborne	3, 233	516	2, 717		185, 500	58, 147	127, 353		3, 793, 476	1, 100, 591	2, 692, 885	
Concordia	1, 543	30	1, 513		26, 992	2, 177	24, 815		1, 574, 111	107, 000	1, 467, 111	
De Soto	3, 752	735	3, 017		141, 115	46, 145	94, 970		2, 981, 837	844, 823	2, 137, 014	
East Baton Rouge	1, 367	329	1, 031	7	34, 622	11, 396	21, 836	1, 390	2, 054, 075	706, 685	1, 273, 390	74, 000
East Carroll	2, 881	133	2, 746	2	53, 369	8, 273	44, 825	271	3, 957, 712	489, 820	3, 446, 092	21, 800
East Feliciana	1, 933	261	1, 671	1	67, 666	19, 575	46, 941	1, 150	1, 322, 635	338, 115	961, 520	23, 000
Evangeline	886	55	831		27, 755	2, 222	25, 533		1, 304, 560	83, 400	1, 221, 160	

TABLE 57.—FARMS OPERATED BY NEGROES—NUMBER, ACREAGE, VALUE OF LAND AND BUILDINGS, AND VALUE OF IMPLEMENTS AND MACHINERY, BY TENURE, BY STATES, AND COUNTIES: 1930—Continued

[Counties in which no farms operated by Negroes were reported, are omitted]

COUNTY	VALUE OF LAND ALONE				VALUE OF BUILDINGS				VALUE OF IMPLEMENTS AND MACHINERY			
	Total	Owners	Tenants	Managers	Total	Owners	Tenants	Managers	Total	Owners	Tenants	Managers
KENTUCKY—continued												
Hickman	$101, 395	$23, 160	$78, 235		$31, 875	$9, 425	$22, 450		$4, 700	$890	$3, 810	
Hopkins	78, 695	34, 605	44, 090		36, 950	18, 275	18, 675		4, 650	2, 170	2, 480	
Jackson	600	600			200	200			10	10		
Jefferson	167, 700	53, 900	109, 300	$4, 500	82, 200	33, 400	48, 300	$500	5, 841	3, 121	2, 020	$700
Jessamine	243, 940	109, 790	132, 150	2, 000	121, 700	78, 950	24, 750	18, 000	14, 670	10, 030	4, 640	
Kenton	24, 600	20, 900	3, 700		12, 600	9, 600	3, 000		1, 175	1, 175		
Knott	12, 810	12, 050	760		5, 250	4, 600	650		106	91	15	
Knox	23, 550	15, 550	8, 000		12, 750	10, 250	2, 500		437	385	52	
Larue	23, 565	19, 015	4, 550		20, 900	17, 850	3, 050		2, 090	1, 810	280	
Laurel	16, 485	16, 235	250		5, 490	5, 440	50		284	269	15	
Lawrence	6, 450	1, 650	4, 800		550	350	200		25		25	
Lee	4, 420	1, 705	2, 715		2, 650	1, 675	975		45	20	25	
Leslie	3, 775	1, 875	1, 900		225	125	100					
Lewis	5, 500	4, 200	1, 300		4, 750	3, 750	1, 000		705	430	275	
Lincoln	104, 819	69, 869	34, 950		43, 186	34, 316	8, 870		5, 809	3, 979	1, 830	
Livingston	17, 320	41, 000	13, 220		5, 750	1, 300	4, 450		1, 776	215	1, 561	
Logan	375, 063	135, 223	239, 430		198, 745	76, 290	122, 455		19, 137	7, 040	12, 097	
Lyon	53, 906	29, 352	24, 054		16, 921	8, 256	8, 665		1, 930	911	1, 019	
McCracken	231, 875	248, 325	33, 550		162, 186	142, 836	19, 350		25, 550	22, 830	2, 720	
McLean	35, 685	17, 740	17, 945		8, 125	4, 325	3, 800		3, 060	2, 235	825	
Madison	577, 550	331, 660	245, 890		220, 215	161, 985	58, 230		23, 502	15, 158	8, 344	
Magoffin	8, 900	7, 900	1, 000		1, 300	800	500		140	120	20	
Marion	120, 810	29, 210	91, 600		55, 440	20, 140	35, 300		3, 188	2, 633	555	
Marshall	3, 740	3, 400	340		1, 360	1, 200	160		365	320	45	
Mason	176, 260	76, 990	99, 270		69, 100	30, 450	38, 650		11, 260	3, 990	7, 270	
Meade	69, 643	47, 743	21, 900		32, 910	22, 710	10, 200		5, 660	4, 560	1, 100	
Menifee	1, 150	800	350		500	350	150		140	115	25	
Mercer	79, 600	48, 300	31, 300		47, 800	33, 300	14, 500		3, 695	2, 635	1, 060	
Metcalfe	60, 550	34, 575	25, 975		30, 825	20, 325	10, 500		4, 588	2, 578	2, 010	
Monroe	28, 215	13, 455	14, 760		13, 550	7, 875	5, 675		1, 200	720	480	
Montgomery	129, 745	62, 010	19, 735	48, 000	57, 050	36, 525	8, 525	12, 000	6, 140	5, 370	770	
Morgan	450	450			150	150			10	10		
Muhlenberg	41, 560	23, 605	17, 955		22, 215	18, 545	3, 670		3, 112	2, 452	660	
Nelson	165, 100	102, 515	62, 585		89, 105	47, 430	41, 675		9, 608	4, 773	4, 835	
Nicholas	36, 390	26, 090	10, 300		24, 300	15, 300	9, 000		5, 025	4, 435	590	
Ohio	26, 560	15, 275	11, 285		12, 850	9, 025	3, 825		1, 315	1, 105	210	
Oldham	30, 725	2, 950	15, 775	12, 000	21, 475	3, 250	10, 225	8, 000	2, 785	60	2, 025	700
Owen	97, 474	45, 010	52, 464		43, 820	26, 000	17, 820		4, 226	1, 870	2, 356	
Owsley	3, 775	2, 325	1, 450		875	275	600		27	17	10	
Pendleton	20, 755	7, 955	12, 800		5, 085	1, 885	3, 200		625	200	425	
Perry	21, 415	17, 850	3, 565		33, 950	30, 700	3, 250		1, 420	1, 320	100	
Pike	16, 725		16, 725		4, 875		4, 875		95		95	
Powell	23, 675	20, 275	3, 400		15, 675	12, 575	3, 100		1, 350	1, 195	155	
Pulaski	24, 925	20, 775	4, 150		17, 150	13, 900	3, 250		1, 465	1, 090	375	
Robertson	15, 000	14, 200	800		3, 300	3, 300			525	525		
Rockcastle	600	600			500	500			100	100		
Rowan	500		500						100		100	
Russell	19, 330	12, 805	6, 525		5, 045	3, 445	1, 600		450	330	120	
Scott	187, 515	128, 695	58, 820		94, 545	63, 700	30, 845		12, 615	9, 335	3, 280	
Shelby	158, 536	51, 570	106, 966		96, 480	38, 550	57, 930		9, 321	3, 935	5, 386	
Simpson	209, 505	59, 250	150, 255		85, 120	33, 275	51, 845		13, 025	6, 045	6, 980	
Spencer	57, 880	39, 400	18, 480		27, 075	15, 025	12, 050		3, 844	1, 799	2, 045	
Taylor	113, 390	42, 985	70, 405		39, 645	21, 100	18, 545		6, 585	3, 945	2, 640	
Todd	368, 550	143, 287	225, 263		111, 830	59, 660	52, 170		23, 155	10, 360	12, 795	
Trigg	214, 182	92, 549	121, 633		135, 090	64, 115	70, 975		19, 496	11, 113	8, 383	
Trimble	16, 800	13, 800	3, 000		5, 500	4, 500	1, 000		990	790	200	
Union	36, 980	11, 385	25, 595		15, 445	5, 945	9, 500		2, 320	890	1, 430	
Warren	356, 820	127, 440	209, 380	20, 000	117, 550	58, 465	57, 085	2, 000	14, 867	8, 737	5, 630	500
Washington	189, 130	55, 810	133, 320		72, 525	33, 275	39, 250		5, 695	3, 335	2, 360	
Wayne	35, 185	27, 550	7, 635		15, 115	13, 800	1, 315		1, 336	1, 176	160	
Webster	90, 330	55, 140	35, 190		45, 500	27, 400	18, 100		4, 947	3, 097	1, 850	
Whitley	5, 575	5, 375	200		2, 600	2, 500	100		110	110		
Wolfe	75	75			75	75			50	50		
Woodford	158, 900	69, 320	89, 580		73, 235	52, 225	21, 010		5, 237	2, 867	2, 370	
LOUISIANA												
Total	**$86, 432, 377**	**$14, 387, 487**	**$71, 456, 839**	**$608, 051**	**$22, 236, 441**	**$5, 199, 789**	**$16, 918, 277**	**$118, 375**	**$4, 870, 550**	**$1, 198, 264**	**$3, 648, 111**	**$24, 175**
Acadia	688, 661	106, 355	581, 040	1, 266	164, 290	29, 410	128, 515	6, 365	51, 342	13, 910	37, 032	400
Allen	90, 395	43, 395	47, 000		39, 725	23, 825	15, 900		7, 038	3, 932	3, 106	
Ascension	233, 822	105, 007	127, 815	1, 000	114, 485	68, 570	45, 655	260	12, 969	8, 708	4, 186	75
Assumption	17, 890	3, 685	9, 205	5, 000	12, 165	4, 465	700	7, 000	729	134	345	250
Avoyelles	2, 052, 032	227, 415	1, 824, 617		503, 822	80, 705	423, 117		74, 923	12, 336	62, 587	
Beauregard	125, 579	18, 710	106, 869		40, 125	13, 595	26, 530		7, 650	1, 900	5, 750	
Beienville	1, 625, 550	514, 545	1, 111, 005		654, 310	222, 140	432, 170		135, 049	50, 646	84, 403	
Bossier	5, 628, 283	565, 330	4, 945, 518	117, 435	864, 050	196, 005	651, 345	16, 700	202, 927	42, 703	155, 374	4, 850
Caddo	10, 519, 859	894, 092	9, 625, 767		1, 584, 268	298, 395	1, 285, 873		438, 906	73, 914	364, 992	
Calcasieu	519, 425	58, 340	460, 285	800	147, 920	32, 380	115, 440	100	39, 361	4, 833	34, 403	125
Caldwell	388, 448	54, 570	333, 878		95, 000	34, 220	60, 780		19, 136	3, 939	15, 197	
Cameron	106, 380	24, 110	82, 270		54, 570	14, 420	40, 150		3, 958	552	3, 406	
Catahoula	1, 242, 715	145, 460	1, 097, 255		275, 005	33, 620	241, 385		58, 890	10, 472	48, 418	
Claiborne	2, 882, 712	804, 050	2, 078, 662		910, 764	296, 541	614, 223		172, 903	61, 366	111, 537	
Concordia	1, 215, 211	84, 880	1, 130, 331		358, 900	22, 120	336, 780		53, 944	5, 116	48, 828	
De Soto	2, 227, 624	619, 833	1, 607, 791		754, 213	224, 990	529, 223		171, 264	59, 368	111, 896	
East Baton Rouge	1, 592, 630	513, 045	1, 013, 335	66, 250	461, 445	193, 640	260, 055	7, 750	73, 616	30, 256	40, 875	2, 485
East Carroll	3, 119, 372	400, 770	2, 701, 802	16, 800	838, 340	89, 050	744, 290	5, 000	229, 597	28, 629	198, 718	2, 250
East Feliciana	926, 843	238, 726	668, 117	20, 000	395, 792	99, 389	293, 403	3, 000	103, 762	34, 440	69, 302	60
Evangeline	866, 790	54, 260	812, 530		437, 770	29, 140	408, 630		81, 011	11, 057	69, 954	

TABLE 57.—FARMS OPERATED BY NEGROES—NUMBER, ACREAGE, VALUE OF LAND AND BUILDINGS, AND VALUE OF IMPLEMENTS AND MACHINERY, BY TENURE, BY STATES, AND COUNTIES: 1930—Continued

[Counties in which no farms operated by Negroes were reported, are omitted]

COUNTY	NUMBER OF FARMS				ALL LAND IN FARMS (ACRES)				VALUE OF LAND AND BUILDINGS			
	Total	Owners	Tenants	Managers	Total	Owners	Tenants	Managers	Total	Owners	Tenants	Managers
LOUISIANA—continued												
Franklin	2,521	135	2,386		59,374	6,605	52,769		$3,946,870	$356,120	$3,590,750	
Grant	574	45	529		12,331	1,543	10,788		654,783	52,898	601,885	
Iberia	333	105	225	3	17,393	4,909	11,961	523	1,110,131	307,205	730,326	$72,600
Iberville	250	74	176		7,566	2,406	5,160		362,788	121,073	241,715	
Jackson	511	149	362		28,817	13,901	14,916		473,061	197,375	275,686	
Jefferson	15	2	13		199	24	175		29,080	3,800	25,280	
Jefferson Davis	317	47	270		11,873	2,078	9,795		505,365	80,595	424,770	
Lafayette	1,026	109	917		40,468	5,025	35,443		3,410,150	370,890	3,039,260	
Lafourche	17	12	5		779	336	443		44,025	19,125	24,900	
La Salle	61	41	20		2,094	1,584	510		67,900	52,950	14,950	
Lincoln	1,541	325	1,216		83,557	26,246	57,311		2,405,633	701,148	1,704,485	
Livingston	297	74	223		4,202	1,402	2,800		241,015	65,545	175,470	
Madison	1,795	24	1,769	2	35,245	2,709	32,133	403	2,321,293	113,100	2,191,793	16,400
Morehouse	2,815	224	2,591		75,662	10,507	65,155		4,235,395	510,348	3,725,047	
Natchitoches	3,362	423	2,939		92,553	26,608	65,945		4,993,742	974,880	4,018,862	
Orleans	12	1	11		67	1	66		18,820	2,500	16,320	
Ouachita	1,384	196	1,187	1	43,134	12,243	29,561	1,330	2,371,191	364,895	1,939,796	66,500
Plaquemines	127	96	27	4	4,424	3,286	803	335	314,725	240,800	46,925	27,000
Pointe Coupee	1,679	123	1,555	1	43,371	7,091	35,217	1,063	2,236,209	363,157	1,835,052	38,000
Rapides	1,802	185	1,616	1	40,511	6,914	33,517	80	3,423,726	316,375	3,104,851	2,500
Red River	1,750	115	1,635		45,192	7,538	37,654		2,343,831	229,655	2,114,176	
Richland	2,934	155	2,779		73,235	7,313	65,922		4,293,893	419,751	3,973,142	
Sabine	507	172	335		21,550	10,364	11,186		362,080	175,770	186,310	
St. Bernard	24	10	14		415	273	142		30,900	18,500	12,400	
St. Charles	48	19	29		2,048	526	1,522		110,340	32,600	77,740	
St. Helena	840	255	585		29,849	15,097	14,752		685,220	283,230	401,990	
St. James	94	42	52		5,627	2,432	3,195		243,825	97,950	145,875	
St. John the Baptist	41	17	24		2,432	591	1,841		138,825	72,025	66,800	
St. Landry	3,736	576	3,160		118,446	22,167	96,279		7,429,622	1,359,480	6,070,142	
St. Martin	751	177	574		31,688	7,866	23,822		2,309,777	480,655	1,829,122	
St. Mary	170	72	95	3	5,916	2,227	2,969	720	286,267	142,255	131,612	12,400
St. Tammany	233	165	59	9	16,529	5,765	3,416	7,348	656,465	283,075	266,030	107,360
Tangipahoa	1,167	405	762		22,023	9,283	12,740		1,355,371	492,385	862,986	
Tensas	2,492	59	2,429	4	44,984	5,259	36,640	3,085	2,638,666	242,630	2,339,546	56,490
Terrebone	101	58	37	6	3,971	1,824	1,180	967	174,169	70,431	42,488	51,250
Union	1,082	254	827	1	57,360	21,452	35,863	45	1,146,396	394,430	750,766	1,200
Vermilion	275	88	187		14,223	3,734	10,489		736,510	218,410	518,100	
Vernon	93	52	41		2,960	1,811	1,149		66,215	41,000	25,215	
Washington	743	327	416		31,350	16,718	14,632		835,352	450,957	384,395	
Webster	1,904	387	1,517		83,264	28,383	54,881		2,429,646	806,756	1,622,890	
West Baton Rouge	227	44	183		5,843	1,287	4,556		317,274	64,829	252,445	
West Carroll	596	85	511		13,807	3,297	10,510		950,780	178,170	772,610	
West Feliciana	1,173	77	1,096		33,605	8,843	24,762		798,597	159,455	639,142	
Winn	328	161	167		15,172	9,301	5,871		296,715	154,900	141,815	
MAINE												
Total	15	14	1		818	738	80		$41,400	$28,400	$13,000	
Androscoggin	1	1			7	7			1,400	1,400		
Aroostook	1		1		80		80		13,000		13,000	
Cumberland	2	2			34	34			2,600	2,600		
Knox	2	2			60	60			3,000	3,000		
Oxford	1	1			80	80			1,200	1,200		
Penobscot	6	6			402	402			14,700	14,700		
Washington	1	1			105	105			1,500	1,500		
York	1	1			50	50			4,000	4,000		
MARYLAND												
Total	5,264	2,938	2,206	120	345,224	107,590	215,756	21,878	$18,896,282	$6,695,319	$10,442,663	$1,758,300
Allegany	2	1	1		800	200	600		8,200	6,000	2,200	
Anne Arundel	343	197	138	8	20,992	5,424	14,938	630	1,502,030	562,540	736,290	203,200
Baltimore	63	50	12	1	1,956	1,381	369	206	292,789	211,185	36,604	45,000
Calvert	437	194	242	1	34,352	12,269	22,063	20	1,237,554	436,364	797,190	4,000
Caroline	317	179	134	4	18,042	5,909	11,536	597	817,700	300,850	481,350	35,500
Carroll	26	19	4	3	1,847	763	343	741	109,910	36,810	23,100	50,000
Cecil	34	19	11	4	3,115	830	936	1,349	184,765	58,315	29,450	97,000
Charles	555	276	276	3	50,137	14,931	31,806	400	1,556,785	554,285	986,000	16,500
Dorchester	327	143	180	4	27,337	6,889	19,616	832	1,331,175	297,475	969,100	64,600
Frederick	76	52	22	2	4,235	1,359	2,578	298	246,525	95,225	132,800	18,500
Harford	98	76	19	3	4,188	1,946	1,137	1,105	429,000	218,400	88,100	122,500
Howard	68	51	14	3	3,381	1,973	1,105	303	296,450	159,700	83,750	53,000
Kent	141	88	45	8	7,330	1,254	4,389	1,687	399,220	85,845	191,375	122,000
Montgomery	195	152	40	3	9,627	4,460	4,699	468	1,616,505	496,400	1,043,105	77,000
Prince Georges	581	274	303	4	46,478	12,250	33,525	703	2,873,359	980,164	1,835,095	58,100
Queen Annes	313	190	94	29	19,491	5,028	9,246	5,217	946,780	291,520	423,160	232,100
St. Marys	305	148	153	4	22,245	7,800	13,832	613	993,899	356,930	556,469	80,500
Somerset	458	368	89	1	12,973	8,127	4,614	232	889,390	663,200	217,690	8,500
Talbot	196	106	66	24	13,096	2,359	6,690	4,047	1,146,045	216,245	587,000	342,800
Washington	20	12	8		1,277	228	1,049		85,600	46,700	38,900	
Wicomico	268	149	115	4	11,503	4,571	6,425	507	770,666	304,506	410,160	56,000
Worcester	441	194	240	7	30,822	7,639	21,260	1,923	1,161,935	316,660	773,775	71,500

TABLE 57.—FARMS OPERATED BY NEGROES—NUMBER, ACREAGE, VALUE OF LAND AND BUILDINGS, AND VALUE OF IMPLEMENTS AND MACHINERY, BY TENURE, BY STATES, AND COUNTIES: 1930—Continued

[Counties in which no farms operated by Negroes were reported, are omitted]

COUNTY	VALUE OF LAND ALONE				VALUE OF BUILDINGS				VALUE OF IMPLEMENTS AND MACHINERY			
	Total	Owners	Tenants	Managers	Total	Owners	Tenants	Managers	Total	Owners	Tenants	Managers
					LOUISIANA—continued							
Franklin	$3,304,010	$291,680	$3,012,330		$642,860	$64,440	$578,420		$180,211	$23,725	$156,486	
Grant	535,088	37,163	497,925		119,695	15,735	103,960		25,400	2,808	22,592	
Iberia	909,706	240,345	613,161	$56,200	200,425	66,860	117,165	$16,400	33,013	11,193	21,310	$510
Iberville	264,158	83,283	180,875		98,630	37,790	60,840		16,217	6,134	10,083	
Jackson	331,243	140,200	191,043		141,818	57,175	84,643		26,087	10,513	15,574	
Jefferson	23,205	2,600	20,605		5,875	1,200	4,675		1,880	670	1,210	
Jefferson Davis	377,280	61,090	316,190		128,085	19,505	108,580		33,051	6,770	26,281	
Lafayette	3,017,647	315,915	2,701,732		392,503	54,975	337,528		87,256	17,700	69,556	
Lafourche	32,720	11,920	20,800		11,305	7,205	4,100		1,971	1,363	608	
La Salle	31,200	23,250	7,950		36,700	29,700	7,000		2,736	2,272	464	
Lincoln	1,833,210	511,558	1,321,652		572,423	189,590	382,833		97,149	37,136	60,013	
Livingston	180,265	45,640	134,625		60,750	19,905	40,845		14,590	4,210	10,380	
Madison	1,637,043	84,450	1,537,643	14,950	684,250	28,650	654,150	1,450	180,281	8,850	170,906	525
Morehouse	3,319,801	391,818	2,927,983		915,594	118,530	797,064		216,708	34,926	181,782	
Natchitoches	4,088,622	780,190	3,307,832		905,720	194,690	711,030		208,409	52,729	155,680	
Orleans	11,820	1,000	10,820		7,000	1,500	5,500		800	300	500	
Ouachita	1,955,558	270,855	1,618,603	66,100	415,633	94,040	321,193	400	98,408	16,988	81,270	150
Plaquemines	241,780	174,010	41,220	26,550	72,945	66,790	5,705	450	13,606	9,445	3,661	500
Pointe Coupee	1,640,952	244,427	1,358,775	37,750	595,257	118,730	476,277	250	117,630	29,835	87,720	75
Rapides	2,860,046	228,345	2,630,201	1,500	563,680	88,030	474,650	1,000	114,561	17,420	97,096	45
Red River	1,896,055	179,824	1,716,231		447,776	49,831	397,945		92,768	12,232	80,536	
Richland	3,678,598	351,061	3,327,537		714,295	68,690	645,605		270,455	29,398	241,057	
Sabine	263,602	121,965	141,637		98,478	53,805	44,673		22,693	11,250	11,443	
St. Bernard	21,500	11,350	10,150		9,400	7,150	2,250		3,207	1,340	1,867	
St. Charles	93,905	25,395	68,510		16,435	7,205	9,230		9,245	1,814	7,431	
St. Helena	381,370	165,720	215,650		303,850	117,510	186,340		56,140	32,610	23,530	
St. James	192,745	67,775	124,970		51,080	30,175	20,905		5,497	4,149	1,348	
St. John the Baptist	95,375	48,725	46,650		43,450	23,300	20,150		7,730	4,055	3,675	
St. Landry	5,905,922	1,011,010	4,894,912		1,523,700	348,470	1,175,230		277,264	87,221	190,043	
St. Martin	1,922,690	384,535	1,538,155		387,087	96,120	290,967		75,884	18,156	57,728	
St. Mary	214,530	99,400	104,730	10,400	71,737	42,855	26,882	2,000	14,374	8,128	5,946	300
St. Tammany	425,940	165,460	187,020	73,460	230,525	117,615	79,010	33,900	28,952	15,876	7,076	6,000
Tangipahoa	865,306	310,985	554,321		490,065	181,400	308,665		63,163	26,209	36,954	
Tensas	2,031,424	185,850	1,799,284	46,290	607,242	56,780	540,262	10,200	97,088	11,413	82,175	3,500
Terrebonne	117,609	44,936	27,073	45,600	46,560	25,495	15,415	5,650	9,297	4,547	2,675	2,075
Union	864,775	290,670	573,405	700	281,621	103,760	177,361	500	58,219	27,525	30,694	
Vermilion	643,845	185,050	458,795		92,665	33,360	59,305		38,280	16,518	21,762	
Vernon	38,090	21,750	16,340		28,125	19,250	8,875		4,119	2,520	1,599	
Washington	539,819	275,229	264,590		295,533	175,728	119,805		59,795	32,183	27,612	
Webster	1,811,882	608,591	1,203,291		617,764	198,165	419,599		124,827	59,218	65,609	
West Baton Rouge	228,199	41,614	186,585		89,075	23,215	65,860		17,444	4,620	12,824	
West Carroll	796,752	138,080	658,672		154,028	40,090	113,938		44,140	10,935	33,205	
West Feliciana	540,109	116,580	423,529		258,488	42,875	215,613		57,809	10,190	47,619	
Winn	197,360	99,615	97,745		99,355	55,285	44,070		23,221	12,999	10,222	
					MAINE							
Total	$15,700	$9,300	$6,400		$25,700	$19,100	$6,600		$6,075	$4,575	$1,500	
Androscoggin	400	400			1,000	1,000			100	100		
Aroostook	6,400		6,400		6,600		6,600		1,500		1,500	
Cumberland	500	500			2,100	2,100			510	510		
Knox	1,300	1,300			1,700	1,700			40	40		
Oxford	800	800			400	400			300	300		
Penobscot	4,000	4,000			10,700	10,700			2,900	2,900		
Washington	300	300			1,200	1,200			500	500		
York	2,000	2,000			2,000	2,000			225	225		
					MARYLAND							
Total	$11,746,786	$3,594,643	$7,114,218	$1,037,925	$7,149,496	$3,100,676	$3,323,445	$720,375	$945,402	$423,994	$440,104	$31,304
Allegany	6,600	4,500	2,100		1,600	1,500	100		250	200	50	
Anne Arundel	966,474	307,184	520,840	138,450	535,556	255,356	215,450	64,750	62,631	29,206	31,095	2,330
Baltimore	154,889	112,985	21,904	20,000	137,900	98,200	14,700	25,000	13,968	9,783	3,435	750
Calvert	726,449	251,464	473,785	1,200	511,105	184,900	323,405	2,800	58,512	26,267	32,195	50
Caroline	471,435	157,880	291,055	22,500	346,265	142,970	190,295	13,000	65,844	22,370	41,399	2,075
Carroll	70,585	18,285	11,300	41,000	39,325	18,525	11,800	9,000	5,625	3,375	750	1,500
Cecil	97,380	36,180	15,200	46,000	87,385	22,135	14,250	51,000	8,150	2,485	2,565	3,100
Charles	916,245	289,710	615,635	10,900	640,540	264,575	370,365	5,600	85,074	43,883	40,791	400
Dorchester	989,335	193,295	748,490	47,550	341,840	104,180	220,610	17,050	88,015	26,615	54,900	6,500
Frederick	110,695	52,650	50,545	7,500	135,830	42,575	82,255	11,000	19,362	4,762	14,100	500
Harford	175,800	93,100	39,800	42,900	253,200	125,300	48,300	79,600	20,759	14,037	4,485	2,237
Howard	108,225	61,850	37,700	8,675	188,225	97,850	46,050	44,325	11,275	7,365	3,010	900
Kent	250,745	44,300	128,945	77,500	148,475	41,545	62,430	44,500	18,519	4,975	7,549	5,995
Montgomery	1,248,930	287,225	926,205	35,500	367,575	209,175	116,900	41,500	40,293	22,725	15,868	1,700
Prince Georges	1,799,889	532,594	1,236,195	31,100	1,073,470	447,570	598,900	27,000	99,411	50,470	47,151	1,790
Queen Annes	529,235	139,450	232,585	157,200	417,545	152,070	190,575	74,900	63,809	18,499	28,060	17,250
St. Marys	575,914	201,085	336,929	37,900	417,985	155,845	219,540	42,600	46,192	25,256	18,984	1,952
Somerset	458,510	320,285	134,725	3,500	430,880	342,915	82,965	5,000	67,063	51,650	15,413	
Talbot	752,995	120,580	416,915	215,500	393,050	95,665	170,085	127,300	64,450	13,990	24,835	25,625
Washington	43,525	19,725	23,800		42,075	26,975	15,100		2,495	505	1,990	
Wicomico	508,891	163,003	299,035	46,850	261,775	141,500	111,125	9,150	42,997	23,678	17,919	1,400
Worcester	784,040	187,310	550,530	46,200	377,895	129,350	223,245	25,300	60,708	21,898	33,560	5,250

TABLE 57.—FARMS OPERATED BY NEGROES—NUMBER, ACREAGE, VALUE OF LAND AND BUILDINGS, AND VALUE OF IMPLEMENTS AND MACHINERY, BY TENURE, BY STATES, AND COUNTIES: 1930—Continued

[Counties in which no farms operated by Negroes were reported, are omitted]

COUNTY	NUMBER OF FARMS				ALL LAND IN FARMS (ACRES)				VALUE OF LAND AND BUILDINGS			
	Total	Owners	Tenants	Managers	Total	Owners	Tenants	Managers	Total	Owners	Tenants	Managers
					MASSACHUSETTS							
Total	63	59	3	1	2,063	1,791	122	150	$376,595	$342,525	$11,070	$23,000
Barnstable	17	16	1		183	181	2		72,370	68,200	4,170	
Berkshire	1	1			17	17			3,500	3,500		
Bristol	15	14	1		366	346	20		53,700	49,300	4,400	
Dukes	2	2			290	290			7,500	7,500		
Franklin	1	1			7	7			1,500	1,500		
Hampden	5	4	1		262	162	100		15,625	13,125	2,500	
Hampshire	2	2			131	131			6,100	6,100		
Middlesex	5	5			167	167			43,800	43,800		
Norfolk	4	4			110	110			27,800	27,800		
Plymouth	7	6		1	392	242		150	126,900	103,900		23,000
Worcester	4	4			138	138			17,800	17,800		
					MICHIGAN							
Total	427	337	85	5	30,959	23,952	6,528	479	$1,874,378	$1,401,728	$392,150	$30,500
Alger	1		1		35		35		1,500		1,500	
Allegan	16	12	4		941	703	238		48,000	39,200	8,800	
Antrim	2	2			239	239			6,500	6,500		
Bay	1	1			95	95			15,000	15,000		
Benzie	3	2	1		292	152	140		8,500	5,000	3,500	
Berrien	27	23	4		716	486	230		106,800	89,100	17,700	
Branch	2	1	1		160	40	120		11,000	5,000	6,000	
Calhoun	7	7			392	392			28,000	28,000		
Cass	105	90	15		9,321	7,617	1,704		471,800	369,550	102,250	
Charlevoix	3	2	1		195	95	100		6,200	3,700	2.500	
Cheboygan	2	2			110	110			2,000	2,000		
Chippewa	1	1			80	80			2,500	2,500		
Clare	1	1			160	160			400	400		
Crawford	1	1			40	40			2,000	2,000		
Delta	1		1		40		40		800		800	
Eaton	5	5			231	231			13,700	13,700		
Emmet	1		1		80		80		2,000		2,000	
Genesee	5	5			181	181			15,900	15,900		
Gladwin	1	1			176	176			4,000	4,000		
Grand Traverse	1	1			80	80			500	500		
Gratiot	8	4	4		795	295	500		55,800	31,500	24,300	
Hillsdale	1	1			29	29			7,000	7,000		
Ingham	3	1	2		164	64	100		9,200	2,000	7,200	
Ionia	2	1	1		277	160	117		18,000	6,000	12,000	
Iosco	1		1		80		80		2,000		2,000	
Isabella	15	11	4		1,654	1,188	466		47,500	33,600	13,900	
Jackson	2	2			95	95			6,000	6,000		
Kalamazoo	9	8	1		328	303	25		33,600	32,200	1,400	
Kalkaska	1	1			160	160			3,500	3,500		
Kent	8	5	3		507	367	140		40,300	29,700	10,600	
Lake	13	13			925	925			24,348	24,348		
Lapeer	2	1	1		180	120	60		9,000	6,000	3,000	
Livingston	2	2			49	49			8,500	8,500		
Mackinac	1	1			15	15			5,000	5,000		
Macomb	1		1		10		10		2,000		2,000	
Manistee	5	4	1		274	237	37		8,100	6,900	1,200	
Mecosta	32	26	6		2,628	2,358	270		104,500	98,600	5,900	
Midland	11	9	2		833	613	220		21,850	15,350	6,500	
Monroe	8	3	5		510	276	234		48,800	23,600	25,200	
Montcalm	8	8			666	666			28,300	28,300		
Muskegon	3	2	1		225	195	30		5,100	3,100	2,000	
Newaygo	3	2	1		130	90	40		5,400	4,400	1,000	
Oakland	1		1		120		120		12,000		12,000	
Oceana	4	3	1		459	379	80		19,500	18,000	1,500	
Osceola	1	1			200	200			1,800	1,800		
Ottawa	1	1			60	60			5,000	5,000		
Saginaw	2	2			140	140			4,400	4,400		
St. Clair	5	1	4		430	60	370		27,850	2,850	25,000	
St. Joseph	1	1			60	60			4,000	4,000		
Sanilac	1	1			100	100			3,000	3,000		
Shiawassee	1		1		58		58		2,500		2,500	
Tuscola	1	1			90	90			4,500	4,500		
Van Buren	55	46	6	3	3,270	2,614	410	246	295,530	216,130	21,900	57,500
Washtenaw	22	14	6	2	1,405	881	291	233	203,000	136,000	44,000	23,000
Wayne	5	2	3		269	86	183		45,000	23,000	22,000	
Wexford	2	2			200	200			5,400	5,400		
					MINNESOTA							
Total	27	19	8		2,692	1,469	1,223		$187,325	$141,675	$45,650	
Aitkin	1	1			2	2			2,000	2,000		
Anoka	2	2			300	300			10,075	10,075		
Beltrami	1		1		160		160		3,000		3,000	
Cass	1	1			140	140			1,500	1,500		
Chisago	1	1			40	40			4,000	4,000		
Cook	1	1			240	240			5,000	5,000		
Douglas	1		1		55		55		2,750		2,750	
Hennepin	5	4	1		65	57	8		45,100	35,100	10,000	
Koochiching	2	1	1		175	55	120		4,500	2,500	2,000	
Lake	1	1			28	28			3,100	3,100		

TABLE 57.—FARMS OPERATED BY NEGROES—NUMBER, ACREAGE, VALUE OF LAND AND BUILDINGS, AND VALUE OF IMPLEMENTS AND MACHINERY, BY TENURE, BY STATES, AND COUNTIES: 1930—Continued

[Counties in which no farms operated by Negroes were reported, are omitted]

COUNTY	VALUE OF LAND ALONE				VALUE OF BUILDINGS				VALUE OF IMPLEMENTS AND MACHINERY			
	Total	Owners	Tenants	Managers	Total	Owners	Tenants	Managers	Total	Owners	Tenants	Managers
MASSACHUSETTS												
Total	$201,400	$175,550	$5,850	$20,000	$175,195	$166,975	$5,220	$3,000	$19,320	$16,645	$275	$2,400
Barnstable	26,950	26,100	850		45,420	42,100	3,320		530	345	185	
Berkshire	1,500	1,500			2,000	2,000			500	500		
Bristol	25,700	21,700	4,000		28,000	27,600	400		2,440	2,390	50	
Dukes	4,000	4,000			3,500	3,500			575	575		
Franklin	100	100			1,400	1,400			200	200		
Hampden	8,875	7,875	1,000		6,750	5,250	1,500		400	360	40	
Hampshire	1,300	1,300			4,800	4,800			850	850		
Middlesex	15,800	15,800			28,000	28,000			1,050	1,050		
Norfolk	7,800	7,800			20,000	20,000			2,400	2,400		
Plymouth	105,700	85,700		20,000	21,200	18,200		3,000	8,625	6,225		2,400
Worcester	3,675	3,675			14,125	14,125			1,750	1,750		
MICHIGAN												
Total	$1,045,563	$776,088	$230,475	$39,000	$328,815	$325,640	$161,675	$41,500	$137,755	$106,595	$28,450	$2,710
Alger	800		800		700		700		200		200	
Allegan	22,200	18,400	3,800		25,800	20,800	5,000		6,490	6,050	440	
Antrim	4,500	4,500			2,000	2,000			900	900		
Bay	10,700	10,700			4,300	4,300			200	200		
Benzie	3,900	2,400	1,500		4,600	2,600	2,000		1,325	1,125	200	
Berrien	50,375	42,675	7,700		56,425	46,425	10,000		7,075	2,775	4,300	
Branch	5,000	2,000	3,000		6,000	3,000	3,000		1,500	1,000	500	
Calhoun	12,170	12,170			15,830	15,830			830	830		
Cass	265,700	203,550	62,150		206,100	166,000	40,100		35,330	26,980	8,350	
Charlevoix	4,145	2,845	1,300		2,055	855	1,200		605	305	300	
Cheboygan	900	900			1,100	1,100			450	450		
Chippewa	1,100	1,100			1,400	1,400			1,500	1,500		
Clare	325	325			75	75			75	75		
Crawford	1,450	1,450			550	550			100	100		
Delta	500		500		300		300		40		40	
Eaton	5,950	5,950			7,750	7,750			1,225	1,225		
Emmet	1,000		1,000		1,000		1,000		50		50	
Genesee	7,600	7,600			8,300	8,300			1,200	1,200		
Gladwin	3,000	3,000			1,000	1,000			100	100		
Grand Traverse	350	350			150	150			100	100		
Gratiot	36,400	20,500	15,900		19,400	11,000	8,400		2,850	1,700	1,150	
Hillsdale	5,300	5,300			1,700	1,700			150	150		
Ingham	5,700	1,000	4,700		3,500	1,000	2,500		400	100	300	
Ionia	10,000	3,000	7,000		8,000	3,000	5,000		4,000	1,500	2,500	
Iosco	1,200		1,200		800		800		150		150	
Isabella	27,800	19,375	8,425		19,700	14,225	5,475		4,427	3,767	660	
Jackson	2,100	2,100			3,900	3,900			125	125		
Kalamazoo	9,400	9,200	200		24,200	23,000	1,200		2,945	2,345	600	
Kalkaska	1,650	1,650			1,850	1,850			1,300	1,300		
Kent	20,100	13,700	6,400		20,200	16,000	4,200		1,500	1,120	380	
Lake	16,148	16,148			8,200	8,200			2,930	2,930		
Lapeer	5,500	4,000	1,500		3,500	2,000	1,500		250	250		
Livingston	3,500	3,500			5,000	5,000			655	655		
Mackinac	1,000	1,000			4,000	4,000			25	25		
Macomb	1,000		1,000		1,000		1,000		100		100	
Manistee	4,500	4,000	500		3,600	2,900	700		450	425	25	
Mecosta	65,670	60,970	4,700		38,830	37,630	1,200		7,355	7,300	55	
Midland	13,150	8,750	4,400		8,700	6,600	2,100		1,450	1,250	200	
Monroe	27,900	14,600	13,300		20,900	9,000	11,900		3,050	2,400	650	
Montcalm	14,900	14,900			13,400	13,400			2,050	2,050		
Muskegon	2,900	1,900	1,000		2,200	1,200	1,000		650	150	500	
Newaygo	2,500	2,100	400		2,900	2,300	600		275	175	100	
Oakland	8,000		8,000		4,000		4,000		100		100	
Oceana	9,800	8,800	1,000		9,700	9,200	500		1,830	1,800	30	
Osceola	1,100	1,100			700	700			700	700		
Ottawa	1,500	1,500			3,500	3,500			1,000	1,000		
Saginaw	2,400	2,400			2,000	2,000			130	130		
St. Clair	16,250	2,450	13,800		11,600	400	11,200		960	35	925	
St. Joseph	2,500	2,500			1,500	1,500			100	100		
Sanilac	1,000	1,000			2,000	2,000			100	100		
Shiawassee	2,500		2,500						100		100	
Tuscola	2,700	2,700			1,800	1,800			700	700		
Van Buren	164,530	127,130	13,400	24,000	131,000	89,000	8,500	33,500	22,483	18,398	1,875	2,210
Washtenaw	120,300	81,700	23,600	15,000	82,700	54,300	20,400	8,000	8,320	6,650	1,170	500
Wayne	28,800	13,000	15,800		16,200	10,000	6,200		3,350	850	2,500	
Wexford	4,200	4,200			1,200	1,200			1,500	1,500		
MINNESOTA												
Total	$107,625	$71,975	$35,650		$79,700	$69,700	$10,000		$18,965	$17,475	$1,490	
Aitkin	700	700			1,300	1,300			150	150		
Anoka	8,075	8,075			2,000	2,000			900	900		
Beltrami	2,800		2,800		200		200		500		500	
Cass	700	700			800	800			150	150		
Chisago	2,000	2,000			2,000	2,000			1,000	1,000		
Cook	4,500	4,500			500	500			150	150		
Douglas	2,350		2,350		400		400		80		80	
Hennepin	26,600	18,600	8,000		18,500	16,500	2,000		8,590	8,290	300	
Koochiching	3,200	1,900	1,300		1,300	600	700		150	100	50	
Lake	2,100	2,100			1,000	1,000			100	100		

TABLE 57.—FARMS OPERATED BY NEGROES—NUMBER, ACREAGE, VALUE OF LAND AND BUILDINGS, AND VALUE OF IMPLEMENTS AND MACHINERY, BY TENURE, BY STATES, AND COUNTIES: 1930—Continued

[Counties in which no farms operated by Negroes were reported, are omitted]

COUNTY	NUMBER OF FARMS				ALL LAND IN FARMS (ACRES)				VALUE OF LAND AND BUILDINGS			
	Total	Owners	Tenants	Managers	Total	Owners	Tenants	Managers	Total	Owners	Tenants	Managers
					MINNESOTA—continued							
Otter Tail	1	1	--	--	10	10	--	--	$6, 000	$6, 000	--	--
Pine	2	1	1	--	320	160	160	--	9, 800	4, 800	$5, 000	--
Polk	1	--	1	--	320	--	320	--	6, 000	--	6, 000	--
Ramsey	2	2	--	--	87	87	--	--	39, 900	39, 900	--	--
Rice	1	--	1	--	80	--	80	--	10, 500	--	10, 500	--
St. Louis	2	2	--	--	115	115	--	--	4, 200	4, 200	--	--
Watonwan	1	1	--	--	235	235	--	--	23, 500	23, 500	--	--
Wilkin	1	--	1	--	320	--	320	--	6, 400	--	6, 400	--
					MISSISSIPPI							
Total	182, 578	22, 552	159, 957	69	6, 062, 490	1, 725, 068	4, 310, 231	27, 191	$249, 305, 432	$35, 988, 954	$212, 106, 343	$1, 210, 135
Adams	1, 476	218	1, 258	--	41, 702	11, 416	30, 286	--	1, 509, 799	338, 076	1, 171, 723	--
Alcorn	427	97	330	--	16, 306	5, 534	10, 772	--	518, 565	168, 900	349, 665	--
Amite	1, 888	457	1, 430	1	92, 491	37, 976	54, 352	163	1, 471, 677	519, 792	947, 385	4, 500
Attala	1, 952	494	1, 458	--	93, 640	45, 275	48, 365	--	1, 672, 852	666, 288	1, 006, 564	--
Benton	1, 053	127	926	--	65, 252	15, 723	49, 529	--	900, 965	200, 830	700, 135	--
Bolivar	13, 236	455	12, 773	8	262, 850	14, 430	247, 088	1, 332	25, 134, 819	1, 280, 278	23, 758, 641	95, 900
Calhoun	651	85	566	--	24, 253	7, 710	16, 543	--	598, 764	122, 402	476, 362	--
Carroll	2, 652	320	2, 332	--	109, 287	42, 336	66, 951	--	1, 998, 118	499, 277	1, 498, 841	--
Chickasaw	1, 751	302	1, 448	1	82, 282	25, 009	56, 963	310	1, 754, 970	466, 380	1, 272, 290	16, 300
Choctaw	567	227	340	--	35, 344	21, 442	13, 902	--	359, 707	189, 739	169, 968	--
Claiborne	1, 643	198	1, 440	5	78, 563	31, 896	44, 664	2, 003	1, 478, 178	395, 946	1, 058, 082	24, 150
Clarke	898	428	470	--	42, 395	27, 896	14, 499	--	649, 979	360, 081	289, 898	--
Clay	2, 006	328	1, 677	1	72, 179	20, 556	51, 423	200	1, 846, 210	444, 855	1, 385, 355	16, 000
Coahoma	8, 440	127	8, 302	11	170, 885	5, 933	163, 525	1, 427	18, 029, 568	552, 150	17, 345, 108	132, 310
Copiah	2, 521	510	2, 011	--	88, 654	40, 075	48, 579	--	1, 914, 999	657, 535	1, 257, 464	--
Covington	781	274	507	--	37, 967	19, 930	18, 037	--	873, 167	412, 597	460, 570	--
De Soto	4, 312	378	3, 933	1	155, 850	27, 388	128, 387	75	6, 080, 320	904, 096	5, 174, 724	1, 500
Forrest	224	124	100	--	10, 420	5, 834	4, 586	--	308, 641	170, 696	137, 945	--
Franklin	646	165	481	--	27, 598	14, 859	12, 739	--	466, 578	189, 983	276, 595	--
George	89	75	14	--	4, 546	3, 799	747	--	86, 275	73, 900	12, 375	--
Greene	134	107	27	--	6, 781	5, 836	945	--	112, 618	93, 958	18, 660	--
Grenada	1, 585	215	1, 370	--	80, 694	25, 871	54, 823	--	1, 309, 845	297, 982	1, 011, 863	--
Hancock	49	34	15	--	3, 602	1, 614	1, 988	--	102, 125	54, 075	48, 050	--
Harrison	52	39	13	--	1, 630	1, 071	559	--	94, 225	55, 145	39, 080	--
Hinds	5, 362	646	4, 712	4	181, 797	49, 500	127, 482	4, 815	6, 783, 114	1, 492, 030	5, 015, 084	276, 000
Holmes	5, 660	650	5, 006	4	197, 793	60, 169	136, 518	1, 106	6, 717, 183	1, 159, 943	5, 528, 530	28, 710
Humphreys	4, 364	234	4, 130	--	91, 813	10, 464	81, 349	--	7, 993, 998	792, 346	7, 201, 652	--
Issaquena	1, 215	73	1, 139	3	27, 259	4, 543	21, 872	844	1, 585, 829	225, 850	1, 321, 709	38, 270
Itawamba	158	47	111	--	8, 908	4, 699	4, 209	--	161, 770	63, 470	98, 300	--
Jackson	38	32	5	1	2, 210	1, 724	86	400	54, 200	41, 400	4, 800	8, 000
Jasper	1, 418	562	856	--	79, 825	47, 729	32, 096	--	1, 065, 723	536, 247	529, 476	--
Jefferson	2, 068	243	1, 825	--	86, 359	24, 277	62, 082	--	1, 581, 853	426, 854	1, 154, 999	--
Jefferson Davis	1, 706	528	1, 177	1	81, 925	44, 116	37, 569	240	1, 997, 567	927, 155	1, 060, 912	9, 500
Jones	577	241	336	--	26, 468	14, 074	12, 394	--	689, 820	300, 605	389, 215	--
Kemper	2, 281	488	1, 793	--	115, 666	45, 097	70, 569	--	1, 786, 594	660, 524	1, 126, 070	--
Lafayette	1, 510	315	1, 195	--	88, 576	40, 884	47, 692	--	1, 301, 023	446, 150	854, 873	--
Lamar	95	51	42	2	4, 019	2, 598	941	480	99, 655	55, 900	31, 755	12, 000
Lauderdale	1, 492	481	1, 010	1	81, 179	40, 650	40, 412	117	1, 694, 398	696, 580	988, 218	9, 600
Lawrence	911	338	573	--	42, 774	26, 460	16, 314	--	791, 008	401, 552	389, 456	--
Leake	1, 422	466	956	--	65, 232	37, 034	28, 198	--	1, 335, 622	646, 485	689, 137	--
Lee	2, 011	227	1, 784	--	54, 864	10, 881	43, 983	--	2, 821, 340	440, 685	2, 380, 655	--
Leflore	8, 778	129	8, 645	4	197, 740	6, 226	190, 780	734	18, 398, 663	537, 524	17, 810, 119	51, 020
Lincoln	1, 093	305	788	--	50, 178	22, 200	27, 978	--	741, 180	291, 634	449, 546	--
Lowndes	2, 510	365	2, 145	--	90, 764	22, 878	67, 886	--	2, 683, 049	574, 973	2, 108, 076	--
Madison	5, 572	623	4, 949	--	196, 853	49, 103	147, 750	--	6, 782, 988	1, 316, 021	5, 466, 967	--
Marion	985	430	555	--	38, 197	22, 391	15, 806	--	864, 285	405, 290	458, 995	--
Marshall	3, 704	452	3, 252	--	233, 802	46, 635	187, 167	--	3, 714, 479	708, 762	3, 005, 717	--
Monroe	2, 842	392	2, 450	--	109, 563	23, 739	85, 824	--	3, 804, 340	705, 961	3, 098, 379	--
Montgomery	1, 073	209	864	--	53, 073	23, 073	30, 000	--	1, 190, 338	339, 418	850, 920	--
Neshoba	952	196	756	--	32, 979	13, 453	19, 526	--	847, 574	349, 620	497, 954	--
Newton	1, 323	429	894	--	63, 487	34, 354	29, 133	--	1, 427, 310	646, 225	781, 085	--
Noxubee	3, 973	416	3, 556	1	122, 611	25, 626	95, 657	1, 328	3, 386, 762	571, 171	2, 790, 591	25, 000
Oktibbeha	1, 879	519	1, 360	--	87, 479	37, 878	49, 601	--	1, 797, 460	683, 590	1, 113, 870	--
Panola	4, 007	381	3, 626	--	144, 301	34, 141	110, 160	--	3, 597, 786	605, 936	2, 991, 850	--
Pearl River	120	60	60	--	4, 731	2, 479	2, 252	--	159, 475	66, 400	93, 075	--
Perry	270	174	95	1	17, 330	11, 327	5, 683	320	311, 627	173, 377	128, 250	10, 000
Pike	1, 803	678	1, 124	1	85, 322	46, 784	38, 526	12	1, 763, 714	863, 180	899, 534	1, 000
Pontotoc	818	167	651	--	33, 388	12, 021	21, 367	--	879, 642	258, 731	620, 911	--
Prentiss	421	64	357	--	14, 023	3, 728	10, 295	--	565, 163	108, 315	456, 848	--
Quitman	4, 382	152	4, 230	--	98, 616	6, 429	92, 187	--	7, 502, 706	479, 415	7, 023, 291	--
Rankin	1, 893	555	1, 338	--	82, 359	39, 848	42, 511	--	1, 571, 282	684, 707	886, 575	--
Scott	1, 158	430	728	--	49, 093	31, 052	18, 041	--	941, 650	523, 915	417, 735	--
Sharkey	2, 657	107	2, 549	1	52, 557	6, 019	46, 098	440	4, 692, 869	348, 105	4, 326, 264	18, 500
Simpson	1, 123	375	748	--	49, 947	25, 596	24, 351	--	1, 079, 857	489, 275	590, 582	--
Smith	475	118	357	--	20, 441	9, 296	11, 145	--	444, 865	129, 005	315, 860	--
Stone	127	98	28	1	5, 421	4, 116	1, 225	80	122, 375	76, 875	44, 000	1, 500
Sunflower	11, 644	194	11, 449	1	243, 010	6, 335	236, 465	210	24, 226, 094	577, 729	23, 639, 515	8, 850
Tallahatchie	5, 523	141	5, 379	3	129, 626	8, 313	118, 227	3, 086	9, 888, 853	298, 925	9, 545, 328	44, 600
Tate	2, 687	214	2, 473	--	98, 427	15, 298	83, 129	--	2, 293, 151	295, 516	1, 997, 635	--
Tippah	526	92	434	--	24, 150	8, 674	15, 476	--	498, 110	131, 870	366, 240	--
Tishomingo	128	59	69	--	6, 954	4, 186	2, 768	--	122, 175	74, 020	48, 155	--
Tunica	4, 942	123	4, 817	2	106, 259	6, 055	99, 474	730	9, 213, 651	410, 800	8, 787, 851	15, 000
Union	677	85	592	--	26, 405	5, 557	20, 848	--	949, 015	140, 965	808, 050	--
Walthall	1, 188	336	852	--	48, 959	23, 201	25, 758	--	1, 157, 160	512, 185	644, 975	--
Warren	1, 642	255	1, 385	2	52, 881	18, 928	33, 438	515	1, 544, 430	470, 292	1, 059, 138	15, 000
Washington	7, 652	219	7, 427	6	148, 225	9, 792	133, 250	5, 183	12, 929, 156	602, 365	12, 018, 576	308, 215
Wayne	593	265	328	--	30, 236	17, 516	12, 720	--	551, 728	272, 353	279, 375	--
Webster	412	83	329	--	21, 728	9, 849	11, 879	--	322, 810	99, 945	222, 865	--
Wilkinson	1, 578	194	1, 384	--	55, 328	14, 790	40, 538	--	883, 448	194, 457	688, 991	--
Winston	1, 319	469	850	--	66, 263	37, 284	28, 979	--	1, 009, 151	493, 885	515, 266	--
Yalobusha	1, 420	214	1, 206	--	77, 762	24, 457	53, 305	--	1, 169, 570	256, 045	913, 525	--
Yazoo	5, 388	379	5, 007	2	150, 184	30, 133	119, 010	1, 041	5, 541, 830	791, 440	4, 711, 680	38, 710

TABLE 57.—FARMS OPERATED BY NEGROES—NUMBER, ACREAGE, VALUE OF LAND AND BUILDINGS, AND VALUE OF IMPLEMENTS AND MACHINERY, BY TENURE, BY STATES, AND COUNTIES: 1930—Continued

[Counties in which no farms operated by Negroes were reported, are omitted]

COUNTY	VALUE OF LAND ALONE				VALUE OF BUILDINGS				VALUE OF IMPLEMENTS AND MACHINERY			
	Total	Owners	Tenants	Managers	Total	Owners	Tenants	Managers	Total	Owners	Tenants	Managers
					MINNESOTA—continued							
Otter Tail	$3,000	$3,000			$3,000	$3,000			$350	$350		
Pine	6,600	3,600	$3,000		3,200	1,200	$2,000		210	150	$60	
Polk	5,000		5,000		1,000		1,000		200		200	
Ramsey	9,500	9,500			30,400	30,400			4,035	4,035		
Rice	8,000		8,000		2,500		2,500					
St. Louis	1,800	1,800			2,400	2,400			100	100		
Watonwan	15,500	15,500			8,000	8,000			2,000	2,000		
Wilkin	5,200		5,200		1,200		1,200		300		300	
					MISSISSIPPI							
Total	$191,685,807	$25,455,584	$165,194,753	$1,035,470	$57,619,625	$10,533,370	$46,911,590	$174,665	$11,100,211	$2,754,634	$8,273,067	$72,510
Adams	982,440	229,846	752,594		527,359	108,230	419,129		70,281	16,142	44,139	
Alcorn	376,680	115,590	261,090		141,885	53,310	88,575		26,064	12,030	14,034	
Amite	930,677	317,472	610,205	3,000	541,000	202,320	337,180	1,500	120,375	57,124	63,001	250
Attala	1,196,902	476,213	720,689		475,950	190,075	285,875		124,915	53,540	71,375	
Benton	634,550	143,265	491,285		266,415	57,565	208,850		75,563	16,600	58,963	
Bolivar	20,479,564	978,618	19,425,146	75,800	4,655,255	301,660	4,333,495	20,100	500,237	73,397	418,635	8,205
Calhoun	424,512	87,557	336,955		174,252	34,845	139,407		71,117	11,591	59,526	
Carroll	1,468,900	373,237	1,095,663		529,218	126,040	403,178		170,740	39,824	130,916	
Chickasaw	1,265,742	336,495	913,947	15,300	489,228	129,885	358,343	1,000	159,447	53,254	105,393	800
Choctaw	239,539	123,634	115,905		120,168	66,105	54,063		30,857	17,389	13,468	
Claiborne	948,648	286,321	650,077	12,250	529,530	109,625	408,005	11,900	171,142	40,855	126,887	3,400
Clarke	425,014	240,591	184,423		224,965	119,490	105,475		39,302	26,796	12,506	
Clay	1,340,043	321,549	1,002,494	16,000	506,167	123,306	382,861		110,886	33,784	77,052	50
Coahoma	14,716,657	397,375	14,212,922	106,360	3,312,911	154,775	3,132,186	25,950	209,844	45,771	150,553	13,520
Copiah	1,204,005	436,440	767,565		710,994	221,095	489,899		127,919	54,573	73,346	
Covington	634,642	296,102	338,540		238,525	116,495	122,030		43,880	23,584	20,296	
De Soto	4,655,908	647,214	4,008,194	500	1,424,412	256,882	1,166,530	1,000	357,900	74,524	283,276	100
Forrest	209,370	113,818	95,552		99,271	56,878	42,393		11,780	7,546	4,234	
Franklin	292,273	129,418	162,855		174,305	60,565	113,740		28,990	14,068	14,922	
George	55,585	46,610	8,975		30,690	27,290	3,400		5,372	5,002	370	
Greene	58,248	45,678	12,570		54,370	48,280	6,090		4,721	4,112	609	
Grenada	917,424	214,331	703,093		392,421	83,651	308,770		86,273	18,592	67,681	
Hancock	73,000	41,800	31,200		29,125	12,275	16,850		4,330	2,753	1,577	
Harrison	68,080	35,700	32,380		26,145	19,445	6,700		6,822	2,602	4,220	
Hinds	4,914,146	1,064,240	3,605,406	244,500	1,868,968	427,790	1,409,678	31,500	318,137	96,468	220,519	1,150
Holmes	4,973,813	768,130	4,183,798	21,885	1,743,370	391,813	1,344,732	6,825	384,632	110,252	271,880	2,500
Humphreys	6,525,609	647,756	5,877,853		1,468,389	144,590	1,323,799		334,936	47,668	287,268	
Issaquena	1,086,784	161,300	893,814	31,670	499,045	64,550	427,895	6,600	104,273	21,864	73,109	9,300
Itawamba	128,865	50,245	78,620		32,905	13,225	19,680		10,036	5,868	4,168	
Jackson	31,090	20,500	2,990	7,600	23,110	20,900	1,810	400	3,752	2,612	1,040	100
Jasper	749,400	364,742	384,658		316,323	171,505	144,818		56,026	34,451	21,575	
Jefferson	1,037,450	291,278	746,172		544,403	135,576	408,827		176,843	44,596	132,247	
Jefferson Davis	1,473,612	667,150	799,462	7,000	523,955	260,005	261,450	2,500	94,213	57,282	36,481	450
Jones	462,725	192,965	269,760		227,095	107,640	119,455		37,153	18,024	19,129	
Kemper	1,216,964	470,499	746,465		569,630	190,025	379,605		102,817	47,741	55,076	
Lafayette	924,018	323,040	600,978		377,005	123,110	253,895		120,462	42,357	78,105	
Lamar	66,085	36,735	21,125	8,225	33,570	19,165	10,630	3,775	5,660	3,590	1,420	650
Lauderdale	1,160,786	456,285	696,401	8,100	533,612	240,295	291,817	1,500	78,507	36,219	41,688	600
Lawrence	557,122	273,582	283,540		233,886	127,970	105,916		51,881	29,005	22,876	
Leake	962,797	458,355	504,442		372,825	188,130	184,695		105,314	59,301	46,013	
Lee	2,253,026	333,370	1,919,656		568,314	107,315	460,999		159,535	25,742	133,793	
Leflore	14,990,257	381,669	14,559,038	49,520	3,408,406	155,825	3,251,081	1,500	656,127	38,268	614,659	3,200
Lincoln	483,327	190,724	292,603		257,853	100,910	156,943		31,551	14,979	16,572	
Lowndes	1,955,859	397,891	1,557,968		727,190	177,082	550,108		208,744	60,613	148,131	
Madison	4,914,995	951,444	3,963,551		1,867,993	364,577	1,503,416		474,335	113,652	360,683	
Marion	631,021	284,340	346,681		233,264	120,950	112,314		35,623	18,474	17,149	
Marshall	2,654,016	473,880	2,180,136		1,060,463	234,882	825,581		236,367	64,051	172,316	
Monroe	2,970,974	510,841	2,460,133		833,366	195,120	638,246		242,089	55,482	186,607	
Montgomery	884,972	234,498	650,474		305,366	104,920	200,446		97,576	34,142	63,434	
Neshoba	617,894	247,990	369,904		229,680	101,630	128,050		74,169	30,625	43,544	
Newton	1,066,896	477,870	589,026		360,414	168,355	192,059		105,230	49,970	55,260	
Noxubee	2,375,432	386.071	1,965,061	24,300	1,011,330	185.100	825,530	700	268,141	45,431	221,710	1,000
Oktibbeha	1,161,855	448,060	713,795		635,605	235,530	400,075		147,825	59,802	88,023	
Panola	2,579,658	453,401	2,126,257		1,018,128	152,535	865,593		280,551	56,593	223,958	
Pearl River	90,405	33,560	56,845		69,070	32,840	36,230		7,555	3,770	3,785	
Perry	208,423	110,882	95,541	2,000	103.204	62,495	32,709	8,000	16,631	11,829	4,802	
Pike	1,190,418	561,465	628,553	400	573,296	301,715	270,981	600	93,254	58,268	34,961	25
Pontotoc	667,662	188,301	479,361		211,980	70,430	141,550		55,982	21,412	34,570	
Prentiss	458,238	83,150	375,088		106,925	25,165	81,760		32,656	7,230	25,426	
Quitman	6,141,118	379,880	5,761,238		1,361,588	99,535	1,262,053		162,039	23,448	138,591	
Rankin	1,166,854	515,250	651,604		404,428	169,457	234,971		95,355	49,013	46,342	
Scott	640,587	361,610	278,977		301,063	162,305	138,758		55,933	33,815	22,118	
Sharkey	3,717,754	265,050	3,434,204	18,500	975,115	83,055	892,060		138,827	22,525	116,302	
Simpson	752,538	339,053	413,485		327,319	150,222	177,097		61,821	34,520	27,301	
Smith	322,020	92,505	229,515		122,845	36,500	86,345		21,230	9,040	12,190	
Stone	83,622	48,412	34,010	1,200	38,753	28,463	9,990	300	6,399	4,519	1,855	25
Sunflower	20,251,897	412,159	19,832,388	7,350	3,974,197	165,570	3,807,127	1,500	925,693	44,499	880,194	1,000
Tallahatchie	7,900,567	223,330	7,635,637	41,600	1,988,286	75,595	1,909,691	3,000	170,624	20,640	143,884	6,100
Tate	1,600,246	202,670	1,397,576		692,905	92,846	600,059		158,521	27,094	131,427	
Tippah	357,105	92,745	264,360		141,005	39.125	101,880		32,317	11,000	21,317	
Tishomingo	93,885	57,825	36,060		28,290	16,195	12,095		6,880	4,855	2,025	
Tunica	7,267,067	314,830	6,941,237	11,000	1,946,584	95,970	1,846,614	4,000	116,605	17,145	99,360	100
Union	714,512	98,025	616,487		234,503	42,940	191,563		53,036	11,444	41,592	
Walthall	860,242	371,825	488,417		296,918	140,360	156,558		70,415	38,293	32,122	
Warren	1,085,787	332,252	740,535	13.000	458,653	138,040	318,603	2,000	121,322	28,768	91,879	675
Washington	10,133,603	462,580	9,397,223	273,800	2,795,553	139,785	2,621,353	34,415	498,799	69,987	410,702	18,110
Wayne	367,893	180,982	186,911		183,835	91,371	92,464		32,556	18,958	13,598	
Webster	230,355	69,510	160,845		92,455	30,435	62,020		26,289	6,875	19,414	
Wilkinson	551,544	129,782	421,762		331,904	64,675	267,229		75,798	18,746	57,052	
Winston	641,703	320,305	321,398		367,448	173,580	193,868		86,429	46,934	39,495	
Yalobusha	838,315	181,990	656,325		331,255	74,055	257,200		92,054	25,237	66,817	
Yazoo	3,941,596	571,901	3,335,085	34,610	1,600,234	219,539	1,376,595	4,100	323,929	54,195	268,534	1,200

Table 57.—FARMS OPERATED BY NEGROES—NUMBER, ACREAGE, VALUE OF LAND AND BUILDINGS, AND VALUE OF IMPLEMENTS AND MACHINERY, BY TENURE, BY STATES, AND COUNTIES: 1930—Continued

[Counties in which no farms operated by Negroes were reported, are omitted]

COUNTY	NUMBER OF FARMS				ALL LAND IN FARMS (ACRES)				VALUE OF LAND AND BUILDINGS			
	Total	Owners	Tenants	Managers	Total	Owners	Tenants	Managers	Total	Owners	Tenants	Managers
	MISSOURI											
Total	**5,844**	**1,163**	**4,661**	**20**	**255,623**	**75,686**	**176,385**	**3,552**	**$14,498,297**	**$3,429,544**	**$10,706,493**	**$362,260**
Andrew	3	3			106	106			12,700	12,700		
Audrain	25	9	16		2,101	507	1,594		81,340	16,140	65,200	
Barton	1		1		80		80		3,200		3,200	
Bates	1	1			70	70			2,100	2,100		
Benton	14	11	3		836	644	192		29,900	23,000	6,900	
Boone	71	46	24	1	5,717	3,205	2,112	400	288,700	168,300	100,400	20,000
Buchanan	2	2			25	25			16,000	16,000		
Butler	97	21	76		5,094	998	4,096		140,500	39,755	100,745	
Caldwell	3	3			140	140			5,400	5,400		
Callaway	182	121	60	1	13,510	7,829	5,181	500	326,981	169,300	132,681	25,000
Camden	3	2	1		485	245	240		16,250	12,750	3,500	
Cape Girardeau	40	24	16		2,945	1,718	1,227		100,810	53,300	47,510	
Carroll	18	7	11		2,304	549	1,755		153,850	37,200	116,650	
Cass	5	3	2		73	8	65		12,200	5,700	6,500	
Cedar	1	1			80	80			2,500	2,500		
Chariton	74	41	32	1	5,986	2,719	3,088	179	282,605	133,655	128,950	20,000
Clark	2	2			113	113			4,120	4,120		
Clay	6	4	2		174	89	85		25,100	16,600	8,500	
Clinton	18	14	4		886	633	253		49,980	40,030	9,950	
Cole	11	4	6	1	1,035	408	567	60	75,940	17,540	33,400	25,000
Cooper	105	70	33	2	7,302	3,908	2,843	551	379,900	192,980	147,460	39,460
Crawford	1		1		200		200		5,000		5,000	
Dade	9	4	5		362	136	226		14,850	5,850	9,000	
Daviess	2	1	1		245	85	160		9,000	3,000	6,000	
De Kalb	5	3	2		295	175	120		15,325	9,725	5,600	
Dunklin	46	1	45		1,336	50	1,286		69,880	2,000	67,880	
Franklin	42	25	17		3,180	2,017	1,163		129,930	74,070	55,860	
Gasconade	6	2	4		1,002	225	777		20,500	5,900	14,600	
Greene	46	31	15		1,905	1,052	853		219,100	141,000	78,100	
Grundy	1		1		285		285		21,375		21,375	
Henry	15	6	9		1,520	308	1,212		59,230	12,370	46,860	
Holt	1	1			6	6			1,500	1,500		
Howard	71	31	37	3	7,199	3,131	3,413	655	317,130	109,880	165,250	42,000
Howell	5	4	1		440	280	160		8,700	5,900	2,800	
Iron	5	3	2		233	123	110		10,450	6,650	3,800	
Jackson	15	4	9	2	761	39	522	200	184,800	54,400	79,400	51,000
Jasper	3	2	1		232	132	100		5,400	4,400	1,000	
Jefferson	7	2	5		660	105	555		32,000	7,000	25,000	
Johnson	46	24	20	2	3,237	1,283	1,594	360	140,860	50,320	67,740	22,800
Knox	4	4			342	342			19,600	19,600		
Laclede	7	6	1		927	915	12		19,400	19,000	400	
Lafayette	38	21	17		2,580	998	1,582		196,865	84,180	112,685	
Lawrence	7	3	4		749	299	450		32,190	13,040	19,150	
Lewis	14	7	7		2,585	1,528	1,057		119,440	63,200	56,240	
Lincoln	57	44	13		4,179	3,066	1,113		155,495	112,635	42,860	
Linn	5	2	3		356	155	201		20,860	8,000	12,860	
Livingston	8	7	1		449	441	8		30,970	30,720	250	
Macon	15	14	1		855	848	7		32,255	31,905	350	
Madison	2	2			110	110			5,815	5,815		
Marion	30	16	14		2,449	941	1,508		117,534	58,410	59,124	
Mercer	1	1			20	20			500	500		
Miller	10	8	2		670	397	273		14,640	7,640	7,000	
Mississippi	651	3	648		19,286	280	19,006		1,499,865	26,000	1,473,865	
Moniteau	6	2	3	1	1,175	580	440	155	35,000	12,000	13,000	10,000
Monroe	27	20	7		2,614	1,227	1,387		98,850	41,450	57,400	
Montgomery	33	21	12		3,282	1,729	1,553		93,900	56,550	37,350	
Morgan	13	8	5		1,057	532	525		38,740	17,790	20,950	
New Madrid	998	8	990		30,283	404	29,879		1,727,722	22,825	1,704,897	
Newton	17	9	8		1,034	652	382		47,820	30,320	17,500	
Nodaway	1	1			120	120			15,000	15,000		
Osage	3	3			86	86			2,100	2,100		
Ozark	2	2			740	740			9,000	9,000		
Pemiscot	1,891	58	1,833		43,026	2,206	40,820		3,357,153	163,730	3,193,423	
Perry	7	5	2		356	141	215		10,945	5,945	5,000	
Pettis	61	40	20	1	3,126	1,422	1,464	240	218,365	108,325	98,040	12,000
Phelps	1		1		80		80		1,500		1,500	
Pike	151	100	51		11,217	7,263	3,954		387,169	251,584	135,585	
Platte	6	1	5		725	372	353		48,150	25,000	23,150	
Pulaski	2	2			68	68			2,300	2,300		
Ralls	29	13	15	1	2,644	1,040	1,564	40	116,390	48,590	59,800	8,000
Randolph	54	33	21		3,297	1,781	1,516		145,930	79,520	66,410	
Ray	11	7	4		1,068	572	496		60,200	30,800	29,400	
St. Charles	44	31	13		2,244	1,595	649		117,040	84,240	32,800	
St. Clair	6	5	1		328	288	40		7,300	6,500	800	
St. Louis	21	7	10	4	766	57	497	212	337,900	36,300	214,600	87,000
Ste. Genevieve	9	7	2		785	670	115		26,400	24,000	2,400	
Saline	96	51	45		8,836	3,438	5,398		675,990	252,285	423,705	
Scott	150	3	147		6,738	171	6,567		348,990	8,720	340,270	
Shelby	21	14	7		1,665	905	760		55,635	35,175	20,460	
Stoddard	268	2	266		14,819	395	14,424		860,133	35,675	824,458	
Warren	15	11	4		1,428	825	603		26,940	18,740	8,200	
Washington	7	6	1		425	305	120		7,850	4,850	3,000	
Wright	37	22	15		3,874	2,621	1,253		77,350	56,550	20,800	

TABLE 57.—FARMS OPERATED BY NEGROES—NUMBER, ACREAGE, VALUE OF LAND AND BUILDINGS, AND VALUE OF IMPLEMENTS AND MACHINERY, BY TENURE, BY STATES, AND COUNTIES: 1930—Continued

[Counties in which no farms operated by Negroes were reported, are omitted]

COUNTY	VALUE OF LAND ALONE				VALUE OF BUILDINGS				VALUE OF IMPLEMENTS AND MACHINERY			
	Total	Owners	Tenants	Managers	Total	Owners	Tenants	Managers	Total	Owners	Tenants	Managers
	MISSOURI											
Total	$11,769,862	$2,507,764	$8,985,738	$276,360	$2,728,435	$921,780	$1,720,755	$35,900	$493,459	$143,101	$339,083	$11,275
Andrew	8,690	8,690			4,010	4,010			450	450		
Audrain	51,090	8,690	42,400		30,250	7,450	22,800		4,345	1,450	2,895	
Barton	2,800		2,800		400		400		50		50	
Bates	1,950	1,950			150	150			50	50		
Benton	24,000	18,550	5,450		5,900	4,450	1,450		1,530	1,180	350	
Boone	214,815	115,995	80,820	18,000	73,885	52,305	19,580	2,000	7,475	5,410	2,065	
Buchanan	14,000	14,000			2,000	2,000			380	380		
Butler	105,010	31,490	73,520		35,490	8,265	27,225		7,626	2,140	5,486	
Caldwell	4,000	4,000			1,400	1,400			185	185		
Callaway	215,981	106,270	92,711	17,000	111,000	63,030	39,970	8,000	15,598	7,598	7,700	300
Camden	14,500	11,500	3,000		1,750	1,250	500		800	600	200	
Cape Girardeau	69,890	31,630	38,260		30,920	21,670	9,250		4,245	2,335	1,910	
Carroll	141,900	29,800	112,100		11,950	7,400	4,550		6,205	765	5,440	
Cass	7,950	2,800	5,150		4,250	2,900	1,350		257	32	225	
Cedar	1,500	1,500			1,000	1,000			50	50		
Chariton	215,280	101,180	109,100	5,000	67,325	32,475	19,850	15,000	21,645	7,795	12,350	1,500
Clark	3,120	3,120			1,000	1,000			50	50		
Clay	13,700	6,700	7,000		11,400	9,900	1,500		60		60	
Clinton	38,780	30,880	7,900		11,200	9,150	2,050		1,870	1,570	300	
Cole	64,070	12,770	26,300	25,000	11,870	4,770	7,100		1,032	527	505	
Cooper	291,940	139,170	119,810	32,960	87,960	53,810	27,650	6,500	11,529	7,619	3,010	900
Crawford	4,300		4,300		700		700		100		100	
Dade	10,200	2,950	7,250		4,650	2,900	1,750		690	475	215	
Daviess	7,550	2,750	4,800		1,450	250	1,200		125	25	100	
De Kalb	10,025	5,025	5,000		5,300	4,700	600		740	240	500	
Dunklin	53,745	1,750	51,995		16,135	250	15,885		2,500	25	2,475	
Franklin	99,035	57,795	41,240		30,895	16,275	14,620		3,795	2,915	880	
Gasconade	10,893	3,800	7,093		9,607	2,100	7,507		1,830	400	1,430	
Greene	154,275	93,125	61,150		64,825	47,875	16,950		6,312	5,327	985	
Grundy	17,875		17,875		3,500		3,500		1,650		1,650	
Henry	49,905	9,595	40,310		9,325	2,775	6,550		2,185	530	1,655	
Holt	500	500			1,000	1,000			500	500		
Howard	228,210	76,810	115,400	36,000	88,920	33,070	49,850	6,000	9,475	5,370	3,455	650
Howell	6,350	3,800	2,550		2,350	2,100	250		315	275	40	
Iron	5,550	2,325	3,225		4,900	4,325	575		855	800	55	
Jackson	152,760	40,600	76,960	35,200	32,040	13,800	2,440	15,800	8,945	975	4,670	3,300
Jasper	3,375	2,400	975		2,025	2,000	25		110	105	5	
Jefferson	22,950	5,800	17,150		9,050	1,200	7,850		990	180	810	
Johnson	114,945	39,080	56,665	19,200	25,915	11,240	11,075	3,600	4,735	2,195	2,315	225
Knox	15,025	15,025			4,575	4,575			500	500		
Laclede	13,900	13,500	400		5,500	5,500			580	555	25	
Lafayette	166,005	66,430	99,575		30,860	17,750	13,110		4,170	2,095	2,075	
Lawrence	26,190	10,340	15,850		6,000	2,700	3,300		1,850	400	1,450	
Lewis	90,899	45,859	45,040		28,541	17,341	11,200		6,172	3,277	2,895	
Lincoln	119,800	86,740	33,060		35,695	25,895	9,800		6,502	5,442	1,060	
Linn	17,060	5,500	11,560		3,800	2,500	1,300		550	250	300	
Livingston	17,670	17,620	50		13,300	13,100	200		465	265	200	
Macon	22,,362	22,012	350		9,893	9,893			870	800	70	
Madison	4,615	4,615			1,200	1,200			60	60		
Marion	94,184	45,260	48,924		23,350	13,150	10,200		3,780	2,365	1,415	
Mercer	200	200			300	300			200	200		
Miller	10,840	5,940	4,900		3,800	1,700	2,100		277	197	80	
Mississippi	1,296,525	21,800	1,274,725		203,340	4,200	199,140		50,877	725	50,152	
Moniteau	26,750	10,600	8,150	8,000	8,250	1,400	4,850	2,000	3,000	700	900	1,400
Monroe	64,100	26,850	37,250		34,750	14,600	20,150		3,630	1,930	1,700	
Montgomery	65,610	37,100	28,510		28,290	19,450	8,840		3,945	3,870	1,075	
Morgan	29,330	14,880	14,450		9,410	2,910	6,500		1,765	415	1,350	
New Madrid	1,483,022	17,850	1,465,172		244,700	4,975	239,725		60,165	1,320	58,845	
Newton	39,370	24,295	15,075		8,450	6,025	2,425		1,890	1,620	270	
Nodaway	12,000	12,000			3,000	3,000			700	700		
Osage	1,165	1,165			935	935			29	29		
Ozark	7,250	7,250			1,750	1,750			100	100		
Pemiscot	2,828,611	137,511	2,691,100		528,542	26,219	502,323		97,490	5,970	91,520	
Perry	7,145	3,745	3,400		3,800	2,200	1,600		300	180	120	
Pettis	157,215	71,775	75,440	10,000	61,150	36,550	22,600	2,000	6,430	4,585	1,645	200
Phelps	750		750		750		750					
Pike	271,637	176,642	94,995		115,532	74,942	40,590		15,097	10,350	4,747	
Platte	40,850	23,800	17,050		7,300	1,200	6,100		4,310	3,500	810	
Pulaski	2,050	2,050			250	250			95	95		
Ralls	93,265	40,815	50,450	2,000	23,125	7,775	9,350	6,000	4,035	895	2,140	1,000
Randolph	102,105	57,095	45,010		43,825	22,425	21,400		3,840	2,485	1,355	
Ray	51,140	24,850	26,290		9,060	5,950	3,110		1,320	805	515	
St. Charles	87,055	62,580	24,475		29,985	21,660	8,325		3,598	2,803	795	
St. Clair	4,850	4,350	500		2,450	2,150	300		355	215	140	
St. Louis	297,050	26,400	202,650	68,000	40,850	9,900	11,950	19,000	3,626	425	1,401	1,800
Ste Genevieve	15,025	13,825	1,200		11,375	10,175	1,200		1,755	1,405	350	
Saline	581,550	197,345	384,205		94,440	54,940	39,500		26,414	13,875	12,539	
Scott	286,245	6,720	279,525		62,745	2,000	60,745		10,747	185	10,562	
Shelby	40,635	23,325	17,310		15,000	11,850	3,150		1,900	1,240	660	
Stoddard	739,688	34,275	705,413		130,445	1,400	119,045		21,216	120	21,096	
Warren	15,565	11,065	4,500		11,375	7,675	3,700		1,525	1,005	520	
Washington	4,925	3,425	1,500		2,925	1,425	1,500		300	275	25	
Wright	61,225	44,550	16,675		16,125	12,000	4,125		4,745	4,350	395	

TABLE 57.—FARMS OPERATED BY NEGROES—NUMBER, ACREAGE, VALUE OF LAND AND BUILDINGS, AND VALUE OF IMPLEMENTS AND MACHINERY, BY TENURE, BY STATES, AND COUNTIES: 1930—Continued

[Counties in which no farms operated by Negroes were reported, are omitted]

COUNTY	NUMBER OF FARMS				ALL LAND IN FARMS (ACRES)				VALUE OF LAND AND BUILDINGS			
	Total	Owners	Tenants	Managers	Total	Owners	Tenants	Managers	Total	Owners	Tenants	Managers
MONTANA												
Total	21	15	6		9,804	7,524	2,280		$115,084	$84,084	$31,000	
Cascade	1	1			120	120			2,100	2,100		
Custer	1	1			280	280			1,000	1,000		
Fergus	2	1	1		812	572	240		4,504	4,004	500	
Hill	2	2			1,760	1,760			14,000	14,000		
Jefferson	1	1			246	246			2,230	2,230		
Judith Basin	2	1	1		720	320	400		16,960	960	16,000	
Madison	1		1		200		200		2,500		2,500	
Petroleum	1	1			1,513	1,513			10,590	10,590		
Richland	1	1			90	90			1,500	1,500		
Rosebud	1	1			1,760	1,760			8,880	8,800		
Sheridan	1	1			160	160			2,900	2,900		
Sweet Grass	1		1		880		880		6,000		6,000	
Toole	3	2	1		830	670	160		15,000	13,000	2,000	
Yellowstone	3	2	1		433	33	400		27,000	23,000	4,000	
NEBRASKA												
Total	38	16	22		9,216	4,454	4,762		$308,080	$149,530	$158,550	
Antelope	1		1		160		160		12,000		12,000	
Box Butte	7	2	5		3,241	2,160	1,081		139,500	80,000	59,500	
Boyd	1		1		50		50		2,500		2,500	
Cass	1	1			4	4			1,000	1,000		
Cherry	5	3	2		2,022	1,142	880		17,670	11,520	6,150	
Custer	2	2			25	25			10,000	10,000		
Dakota	2		2		120		120		15,000		15,000	
Dawes	1	1			80	80			1,200	1,200		
Dawson	1		1		480		480		9,600		9,600	
Douglas	3	1	2		57	32	25		15,000	6,500	8,500	
Franklin	1		1		320		320		4,500		4,500	
Furnas	1	1			80	80			2,000	2,000		
Grant	1	1			1,300		1,300		7,800		7,800	
Greeley	1		1		160		160		8,000		8,000	
Hall	1		1		80		80		8,000		8,000	
Harlan	1	1			160	160			12,000	12,000		
Lancaster	2		2		84		84		15,000		15,000	
Logan	1	1			120	120			4,200	4,200		
Otoe	1		1		10		10		1,500		1,500	
Sarpy	3	2	1		112	100	12		16,100	15,600	500	
Sheridan	1	1			551	551			5,510	5,510		
NEVADA												
Total	3	2	1		860	700	160		$44,000	$36,000	$8,000	
Clark	1	1			80	80			20,000	20,000		
Esmeralda	1	1			620	620			16,000	16,000		
Lyon	1		1		160		160		8,000		8,000	
NEW HAMPSHIRE												
Total	6	5	1		814	574	240		$18,000	$16,000	$2,000	
Carroll	1	1			60	60			1,200	1,200		
Grafton	1	1			150	150			800	800		
Hillsborough	2	2			343	343			11,000	11,000		
Merrimack	1	1			21	21			3,000	3,000		
Sullivan	1		1		240		240		2,000		2,000	
NEW JERSEY												
Total	372	232	126	14	19,298	7,276	10,396	1,626	$2,070,400	$998,500	$755,400	$316,500
Atlantic	42	37	5		497	409	88		168,800	154,300	14,500	
Bergen	1	1			5	5			18,000	18,000		
Burlington	26	16	10		1,021	468	553		153,900	81,700	72,200	
Camden	10	8	2		252	107	145		101,800	52,300	49,500	
Cape May	6	5		1	437	137		300	39,200	33,200		6,000
Cumberland	102	52	42	8	7,167	2,219	4,130	818	442,400	171,500	191,400	79,500
Essex	2	1		1	51	1		50	50,000	15,000		35,000
Gloucester	52	31	21		2,521	1,194	1,327		279,500	143,500	136,000	
Hunterdon	3	1	2		106	18	88		9,200	2,500	6,700	
Mercer	11	5	5	1	926	170	656	100	137,200	48,500	76,700	12,000
Middlesex	4	3	1		57	22	35		23,500	13,500	10,000	
Monmouth	24	20	3	1	509	395	104	10	114,400	84,700	23,700	6,000
Morris	3	2	1		261	131	130		36,700	30,500	6,200	
Ocean	4	2	2		127	70	57		8,700	5,000	3,700	
Salem	74	44	29	1	4,794	1,835	2,774	185	268,100	105,600	144,500	18,000
Somerset	6	3	2	1	410	74	173	163	193,000	22,700	10,300	160,000
Union	1	1			21	21			16,000	16,000		
Warren	1		1		136		136		10,000		10,000	

TABLE 57.—FARMS OPERATED BY NEGROES—NUMBER, ACREAGE, VALUE OF LAND AND BUILDINGS, AND VALUE OF IMPLEMENTS AND MACHINERY, BY TENURE, BY STATES, AND COUNTIES: 1930—Continued

[Counties in which no farms operated by Negroes were reported, are omitted]

COUNTY	VALUE OF LAND ALONE				VALUE OF BUILDINGS				VALUE OF IMPLEMENTS AND MACHINERY			
	Total	Owners	Tenants	Managers	Total	Owners	Tenants	Managers	Total	Owners	Tenants	Managers
MONTANA												
Total	**$96,699**	**$72,524**	**$24,175**		**$18,385**	**$11,560**	**$6,825**		**$15,590**	**$14,390**	**$1,200**	
Cascade	1,300	1,300			800	800			100	100		
Custer	1,000	1,000							25	25		
Fergus	2,429	2,004	425		2,075	2,000	75		250	100	150	
Hill	13,300	13,300			700	700			3,800	3,800		
Jefferson	1,930	1,930			300	300			1,200	1,200		
Judith Basin	12,900	900	12,000		4,060	60	4,000		40	40		
Madison	2,300		2,300		200		200		150		150	
Petroleum	9,990	9,990			600	600			800	800		
Richland	1,000	1,000			500	500			300	300		
Rosebud	8,400	8,400			400	400			300	300		
Sheridan	2,600	2,600			300	300			175	175		
Sweet Grass	3,800		3,800		2,200		2,200		400		400	
Toole	13,550	11,600	1,950		1,450	1,400	50		6,450	6,050	400	
Yellowstone	22,200	18,500	3,700		4,800	4,500	300		1,600	1,500	100	
NEBRASKA												
Total	**$241,190**	**$115,280**	**$125,910**		**$66,890**	**$34,250**	**$32,640**		**$28,434**	**$21,178**	**$7,256**	
Antelope	11,200		11,200		800		800		1,000		1,000	
Box Butte	110,150	64,850	45,300		29,350	15,150	14,200		17,575	15,200	2,375	
Boyd	2,350		2,350		150		150		150		150	
Cass	250	250			750	750			50	50		
Cherry	13,420	7,820	5,600		4,250	3,700	550		2,200	1,750	450	
Custer	5,200	5,200			4,800	4,800			1,500	1,500		
Dakota	14,485		14,485		515		515		220		220	
Dawes	700	700			500	500			50	50		
Dawson	9,600		9,600									
Douglas	10,700	6,200	4,500		4,300	300	4,000		201	150	51	
Franklin	2,500		2,500		2,000		2,000		600		600	
Furnas	1,500	1,500			500	500			20	20		
Grant	6,000		6,000		1,800		1,800		635		635	
Greeley	5,500		5,500		2,500		2,500		800		800	
Hall	8,000		8,000						600		600	
Harlan	11,250	11,250			750	750			400	400		
Lancaster	9,000		9,000		6,000		6,000		300		300	
Logan	3,400	3,400			800	800			400	400		
Otoe	1,500		1,500									
Sarpy	9,575	9,200	375		6,525	6,400	125		733	658	75	
Sheridan	4,910	4,910			600	600			1,000	1,000		
NEVADA												
Total	**$36,500**	**$30,800**	**$5,700**		**$7,500**	**$5,200**	**$2,300**		**$1,250**	**$1,000**	**$250**	
Clark	15,000	15,000			5,000	5,000			500	500		
Esmeralda	15,800	15,800			200	200			500	500		
Lyon	5,700		5,700		2,300		2,300		250		250	
NEW HAMPSHIRE												
Total	**$5,950**	**$4,950**	**$1,000**		**$12,050**	**$11,050**	**$1,000**		**$2,050**	**$1,800**	**$250**	
Carroll	300	300			900	900			100	100		
Grafton	400	400			400	400						
Hillsborough	4,000	4,000			7,000	7,000			1,600	1,600		
Merrimack	250	250			2,750	2,750			100	100		
Sullivan	1,000		1,000		1,000		1,000		250		250	
NEW JERSEY												
Total	**$1,142,690**	**$505,650**	**$450,040**	**$187,000**	**$927,710**	**$492,850**	**$305,360**	**$129,500**	**$173,223**	**$88,123**	**$69,750**	**$15,350**
Atlantic	85,750	75,600	10,150		83,050	78,700	4,350		8,640	7,955	685	
Bergen	10,000	10,000			8,000	8,000			100	100		
Burlington	81,800	36,400	45,400		72,100	45,300	26,800		15,300	8,835	6,465	
Camden	67,400	26,600	40,800		34,400	25,700	8,700		3,675	2,075	1,600	
Cape May	25,800	22,800		3,000	13,400	10,400		3,000	1,450	1,350		100
Cumberland	232,900	83,000	103,400	46,500	209,500	88,500	88,000	33,000	46,555	18,505	18,350	9,700
Essex	26,000	3,000		23,000	24,000	12,000		12,000	700	500		200
Gloucester	160,750	90,550	70,200		118,750	52,950	65,800		32,835	13,260	19,575	
Hunterdon	2,200	500	1,700		7,000	2,000	5,000		100		100	
Mercer	99,700	23,000	71,700	5,000	37,500	25,500	5,000	7,000	6,200	3,200	1,500	1,500
Middlesex	12,000	5,000	7,000		11,500	8,500	3,000		1,200	900	300	
Monmouth	62,390	47,300	13,590	1,500	52,010	37,400	10,110	4,500	12,700	10,750	1,600	350
Morris	12,600	10,400	2,200		24,100	20,100	4,000		4,123	3,823	300	
Ocean	3,100	1,800	1,300		5,600	3,200	2,400		150	100	50	
Salem	129,300	45,200	74,100	10,000	138,800	60,400	70,400	8,000	31,995	13,270	16,225	2,500
Somerset	113,500	10,000	5,500	98,000	79,500	12,700	4,800	62,000	5,500	2,500	2,000	1,000
Union	14,500	14,500			1,500	1,500			1,000	1,000		
Warren	3,000		3,000		7,000		7,000		1,000		1,000	

TABLE 57.—FARMS OPERATED BY NEGROES—NUMBER, ACREAGE, VALUE OF LAND AND BUILDINGS, AND VALUE OF IMPLEMENTS AND MACHINERY, BY TENURE, BY STATES, AND COUNTIES: 1930—Continued

[Counties in which no farms operated by Negroes were reported, are omitted]

COUNTY	NUMBER OF FARMS				ALL LAND IN FARMS (ACRES)				VALUE OF LAND AND BUILDINGS			
	Total	Owners	Tenants	Managers	Total	Owners	Tenants	Managers	Total	Owners	Tenants	Managers
NEW MEXICO												
Total	**82**	**53**	**29**		**19, 833**	**13, 135**	**1, 748**		**$400, 956**	**$182, 881**	**$218, 075**	
Bernalillo	1	1			5	5			1, 500	1, 500		
Chaves	2	2			800	800			3, 500	3, 500		
Dona Ana	61	43	18		15, 714	14, 910	804		332, 226	165, 551	166, 675	
Eddy	8		8		244		244		41, 000		41, 000	
Lincoln	2	1	1		600	20	580		3, 250	250	3, 000	
Luna	1		1		75		75		6, 000		6, 000	
Sandoval	1		1		45		45		1, 400		1, 400	
Taos	4	4			1, 600	1, 600			8, 080	8, 080		
Union	2	2			800	800			4, 000	4, 000		
NEW YORK												
Total	**148**	**112**	**33**	**3**	**14, 894**	**9, 625**	**4, 473**	**796**	**$875, 575**	**$548, 095**	**$230, 980**	**$96, 500**
Albany	1		1		90		90		3, 000		3, 000	
Allegany	4	4			484	484			9, 400	9, 400		
Broome	2	2			327	327			7, 500	7, 500		
Cattaraugus	3	2	1		921	281	640		19, 000	12, 000	7, 000	
Cayuga	5	5			524	524			24, 300	24, 300		
Chautauqua	2	1	1		26	14	12		2, 800	600	2, 200	
Chemung	1	1			212	212			4, 000	4, 000		
Chenango	5	5			599	599			22, 100	22, 100		
Clinton	1		1		153		153		5, 000		5, 000	
Columbia	4	3		1	582	52		530	46, 000	5, 500		40, 500
Delaware	5	4		1	969	753		216	28, 400	22, 400		6, 000
Dutchess	20	13	7		2, 841	1, 709	1, 132		180, 580	102, 400	78, 180	
Erie	3	2	1		158	43	115		13, 300	8, 800	4, 500	
Genesee	4	1	3		370	38	332		35, 000	6, 000	29, 000	
Greene	2	2			160	160			6, 500	6, 500		
Herkimer	1		1		242		242		10, 000		10, 000	
Livingston	8	5	3		933	353	580		45, 120	19, 120	26, 000	
Madison	4	3	1		361	297	64		12, 300	10, 500	1, 800	
Monroe	4	4			254	254			32, 000	32, 000		
Niagara	1		1		150		150		15, 000		15, 000	
Oneida	3	2	1		238	134	104		6, 700	4, 200	2, 500	
Onondaga	4	4			231	231			20, 500	20, 500		
Ontario	3	2	1		132	85	47		8, 000	5, 500	2, 500	
Orange	5	5			448	448			24, 800	24, 800		
Orleans	2	2			281	281			22, 000	22, 000		
Oswego	5	5			214	214			6, 775	6, 775		
Otsego	5	4	1		674	414	260		10, 200	9, 200	1, 000	
Putnam	1	1			120	120			30, 000	30, 000		
Rensselaer	2	2			105	105			2, 500	2, 500		
Rockland	1	1			14	14			7, 000	7, 000		
Saratoga	3	2	1		187	155	32		14, 500	2, 000	2, 500	
Schoharie	1	1			138	138			5, 000	15, 000		
Schuyler	2	2			16	16			1, 600	1, 600		
Seneca	2	2			66	66			8, 800	8, 800		
Steuben	1	1			200	200			3, 000	3, 000		
Suffolk	6	3	2	1	120	25	45	50	88, 500	21, 500	17, 000	$50, 000
Sullivan	1	1			50	50			5, 000	5, 000		
Tioga	2	2			55	55			6, 200	6, 200		
Tompkins	6	4	2		486	293	193		19, 400	11, 400	8, 000	
Ulster	4	4			152	152			28, 000	28, 000		
Washington	4	3	1		343	241	102		16, 300	12, 500	3, 800	
Wayne	1		1		107		107		3, 000		3, 000	
Wyoming	2	1	1		139	80	59		10, 000	6, 000	4, 000	
Yates	2	1	1		22	8	14		6, 500	1, 500	5, 000	
NORTH CAROLINA												
Total	**74, 636**	**18, 978**	**55, 635**	**23**	**3, 296, 415**	**943, 503**	**2, 348, 755**	**6, 184**	**$153, 882, 635**	**$36, 881, 352**	**$116, 568, 229**	**$433, 054**
Alamance	631	271	410		36, 272	12, 595	23, 677		1, 194, 238	422, 073	772, 165	
Alexander	92	46	46		3, 927	2, 011	1, 916		132, 005	74, 200	57, 805	
Alleghany	43	40	3		1, 467	1, 413	54		64, 280	61, 830	2, 450	
Anson	1, 635	264	1, 371		95, 441	19, 812	75, 629		2, 523, 532	502, 140	2, 021, 392	
Ashe	84	75	9		2, 830	2, 645	185		95, 214	85, 910	9, 304	
Avery	18	15	3		434	377	57		33, 850	29, 450	4, 400	
Beaufort	865	394	470	1	22, 568	12, 685	9, 668	215	1, 335, 891	638, 021	687, 870	10, 000
Bertie	1, 914	483	1, 431		110, 552	32, 569	77, 983		4, 572, 460	1, 247, 985	3, 324, 475	
Bladen	1, 070	768	302		37, 652	28, 321	9, 331		1, 134, 455	800, 035	334, 420	
Brunswick	404	315	89		19, 072	15, 306	3, 766		385, 975	303, 820	82, 155	
Buncombe	90	66	24		3, 049	1, 909	1, 140		216, 400	149, 360	67, 040	
Burke	176	137	39		6, 139	3, 797	2, 342		219, 908	134, 258	85, 650	
Cabarrus	609	58	551		32, 805	3, 262	29, 543		1, 484, 668	152, 333	1, 332, 335	
Caldwell	105	82	23		3, 421	2, 740	681		108, 310	80, 110	28, 200	
Camden	231	61	169	1	13, 122	2, 897	9, 925	300	791, 150	160, 900	610, 250	20, 000
Carteret	41	23	17	1	2, 085	1, 054	331	700	71, 714	42, 464	14, 250	15, 000
Caswell	1, 265	311	954		85, 461	21, 925	63, 536		2, 293, 312	624, 869	1, 668, 443	
Catawba	304	97	207		12, 318	3, 699	8, 619		498, 723	141, 995	356, 728	
Chatham	937	437	500		59, 369	27, 783	31, 586		1, 123, 331	552, 086	571, 245	
Cherokee	9	4	5		110	45	65		3, 750	1, 150	2, 600	

TABLE 57.—FARMS OPERATED BY NEGROES—NUMBER, ACREAGE, VALUE OF LAND AND BUILDINGS, AND VALUE OF IMPLEMENTS AND MACHINERY, BY TENURE, BY STATES, AND COUNTIES: 1930—Continued

[Counties in which no farms operated by Negroes were reported, are omitted]

COUNTY	VALUE OF LAND ALONE				VALUE OF BUILDINGS				VALUE OF IMPLEMENTS AND MACHINERY			
	Total	Owners	Tenants	Managers	Total	Owners	Tenants	Managers	Total	Owners	Tenants	Managers
					NEW MEXICO							
Total	**$365,146**	**$166,796**	**$198,350**		**$35,810**	**$16,085**	**$19,725**		**$18,187**	**$9,277**	**$8,910**	
Bernalillo	1,100	1,100			400	400			485	485		
Chaves	2,100	2,100			1,400	1,400			150	150		
Dona Ana	304,516	153,016	151,500		27,710	12,535	15,175		13,417	6,792	6,625	
Eddy	38,550		38,550		2,450		2,450		1,985		1,985	
Lincoln	2,550	50	2,500		700	200	500		100		100	
Luna	5,000		5,000		1,000		1,000		200		200	
Sandoval	800		800		600		600					
Taos	6,930	6,930			1,150	1,150			1,300	1,300		
Union	3,600	3,600			400	400			550	550		
					NEW YORK							
Total	**$399,675**	**$230,695**	**$110,980**	**$58,000**	**$475,900**	**$317,400**	**$120,000**	**$38,500**	**$95,725**	**$1,065**	**$30,260**	**$4,400**
Albany	1,500		1,500		1,500		1,500		500		500	
Allegany	3,700	3,700			5,700	5,700			900	900		
Broome	4,000	4,000			3,500	3,500			400	400		
Catteraugus	8,100	5,600	2,500		10,900	6,400	4,500		1,275	975	300	
Cayuga	6,000	6,000			18,300	18,300			3,300	3,300		
Chautauqua	1,450	250	1,200		1,350	350	1,000		110	100	10	
Chemung	1,000	1,000			3,000	3,000			1,000	1,000		
Chenango	6,100	6,100			16,000	16,000			5,475	5,475		
Clinton	1,500		1,500		3,500		3,500		800		800	
Columbia	13,100	2,600		10,500	32,900	2,900		30,000	3,825	825		3,000
Delaware	11,500	9,000		2,500	16,900	13,400		3,500	2,100	1,700		400
Dutchess	80,280	39,100	41,180		100,300	63,300	37,000		20,000	13,350	6,650	
Erie	9,700	7,700	2,000		3,600	1,100	2,500		2,125	125	2,000	
Genesee	13,000	2,000	11,000		22,000	4,000	18,000		2,700		2,700	
Greene	1,700	1,700			4,800	4,800			1,500	1,500		
Herkimer	3,000		3,000		7,000		7,000		1,500		1,500	
Livingston	23,720	11,720	12,000		21,400	7,400	14,000		10,700	2,700	8,000	
Madison	4,950	4,150	800		7,350	6,350	1,000		1,800	1,500	300	
Monroe	13,700	13,700			18,300	18,300			4,200	4,200		
Niagara	8,000		8,000		7,000		7,000		2,170		2,170	
Oneida	4,000	2,000	2,000		2,700	2,200	500		450	250	200	
Onondaga	7,100	7,100			13,400	13,400			1,650	1,650		
Ontario	3,200	2,500	700		4,800	3,000	1,800		700	700		
Orange	14,000	14,000			10,800	10,800			1,910	1,910		
Orleans	17,000	17,000			5,000	5,000			5,500	5,500		
Oswego	2,575	2,575			4,200	4,200			1,000	1,000		
Otsego	3,700	3,400	300		6,500	5,800	700		805	775	30	
Putnam	15,000	15,000			15,000	15,000			400	400		
Rensselaer	900	900			1,600	1,600			1,050	1,050		
Rockland	3,500	3,500			3,500	3,500			200	200		
Saratoga	8,400	7,700	700		6,100	4,300	1,800		875	575	300	
Schoharie	1,500	1,500			3,500	3,500			450	450		
Schuyler	600	600			1,000	1,000						
Seneca	800	800			8,000	8,000			1,800	1,800		
Steuben	900	900			2,100	2,100			2,000	2,000		
Suffolk	71,900	15,500	11,400	45,000	16,600	6,000	5,600	5,000	2,700	700	1,000	1,000
Sullivan	2,000	2,000			3,000	3,000			200	200		
Tioga	700	700			5,500	5,500			20	20		
Tompkins	9,100	4,100	5,000		10,300	7,300	3,000		3,200	1,200	2,000	
Ulster	4,000	4,000			24,000	24,000			575	575		
Washington	7,200	5,500	1,700		9,100	7,000	2,100		1,800	1,500	300	
Wayne	1,000		1,000		2,000		2,000		300		300	
Wyoming	2,600	600	2,000		7,400	5,400	2,000		1,510	510	1,000	
Yates	2,000	500	1,500		4,500	1,000	3,500		250	50	200	
					NORTH CAROLINA							
Total	**$112,647,194**	**$24,674,252**	**$87,638,112**	**$334,830**	**$41,235,441**	**$12,207,100**	**$28,930,117**	**$98,224**	**$5,155,245**	**$1,697,834**	**$3,439,906**	**$17,505**
Alamance	803,368	237,993	565,375		390,870	184,080	206,790		50,344	23,690	26,654	
Alexander	89,800	49,550	40,250		42,205	24,650	17,555		4,979	2,598	2,381	
Alleghany	44,355	42,705	1,650		19,925	19,125	800		2,242	2,212	30	
Anson	1,782,992	329,370	1,453,622		740,540	172,770	567,770		83,332	22,256	61,076	
Ashe	69,764	63,360	6,404		25,450	22,550	2,900		2,675	2,400	275	
Avery	22,850	20,150	2,700		11,000	9,300	1,700		615	500	115	
Beaufort	1,005,256	460,271	535,735	9,250	330,635	177,750	152,135	750	42,313	23,939	17,874	500
Bertie	3,298,389	873,785	2,424,604		1,274,071	374,200	899,871		157,506	50,022	107,484	
Bladen	736,243	500,623	235,620		398,212	299,412	98,800		55,203	43,984	11,219	
Brunswick	246,340	186,565	59,775		139,635	117,255	22,380		13,672	10,402	3,270	
Buncombe	156,300	103,385	52,915		60,100	45,975	14,125		3,912	2,407	1,505	
Burke	144,303	76,233	68,070		75,605	58,025	17,580		6,022	4,312	1,710	
Cabarrus	1,133,353	101,283	1,032,070		351,315	51,050	300,265		56,786	10,315	46,471	
Caldwell	68,385	46,485	21,900		39,925	33,625	6,300		2,621	2,381	240	
Camden	592,525	113,675	463,850	15,000	198,625	47,225	146,400	5,000	33,715	7,585	25,980	150
Carteret	56,664	30,164	12,000	14,500	15,050	12,300	2,250	500	2,190	1,570	320	300
Caswell	1,644,812	402,559	1,242,253		648,500	222,310	426,190		86,072	37,175	48,897	
Catawba	357,095	94,245	262,850		141,628	47,750	93,878		15,736	6,728	9,008	
Chatham	713,026	331,146	381,880		410,305	220,940	189,365		42,227	25,677	16,550	
Cherokee	2,000	550	1,450		1,750	600	1,150		30	20	10	

TABLE 57.—FARMS OPERATED BY NEGROES—NUMBER, ACREAGE, VALUE OF LAND AND BUILDINGS, AND VALUE OF IMPLEMENTS AND MACHINERY, BY TENURE, BY STATES, AND COUNTIES: 1930—Continued

[Counties in which no farms operated by Negroes were reported, are omitted]

COUNTY	NUMBER OF FARMS				ALL LAND IN FARMS (ACRES)				VALUE OF LAND AND BUILDINGS			
	Total	Owners	Tenants	Managers	Total	Owners	Tenants	Managers	Total	Owners	Tenants	Managers
	NORTH CAROLINA—continued											
Chowan	411	154	257		13,572	5,912	7,660		$851,237	$305,295	$545,942	
Clay	11	10	1		493	486	7		15,200	14,700	500	
Cleveland	1,389	136	1,253		48,381	6,421	41.960		3,620,761	439,086	3,181,675	
Columbus	966	550	416		32,138	20,918	11,220		1,387,890	794,885	593.005	
Craven	715	286	429		28,129	14,653	13,476		1,327,195	520,395	806,800	
Cumberland	1,180	373	807		42,659	17,393	25,266		1,952,144	664,125	1,288,019	
Currituck	173	68	105		11,396	3,709	7,687		489,750	179,400	310,350	
Dare	1	1			83	83			3,000	3,000		
Davidson	190	72	118		8,533	2,229	6,304		364,322	113,562	250,760	
Davie	260	86	174		13,469	3,185	10,284		546,819	129,649	417,170	
Duplin	1,509	603	906		45,160	19,355	25,805		2,250,145	898,754	1,351,391	
Durham	523	127	396		29,957	7,282	22,675		1,126,508	250,080	876,428	
Edgecombe	2,282	132	2,149	1	108,768	8,270	100,437	61	5,541,853	458,680	5,079,343	$3,830
Forsyth	314	134	178	2	11,864	4,803	6,986	75	989,818	380,054	517,440	92,324
Franklin	1,616	240	1,374	2	75,402	13,669	61,591	142	2,581,810	492,790	2,058,020	31,000
Gaston	693	114	579		28,201	4,520	23,681		1,931,338	288,210	1,643,128	
Gates	538	283	255		27,215	13,414	13,801		950,737	467.711	483,026	
Granville	1,575	374	1,200	1	91,393	21,761	69,207	425	2,663,593	733,315	1,909,778	20,500
Greene	1,473	103	1,370		42,193	5,628	36,565		3,544,346	364,170	3,180,176	
Guilford	544	280	274		24,984	10,730	14,254		1,408,282	675,027	733,255	
Halifax	3,305	717	2,587	1	181,827	42,482	136,645	2,700	7,006,530	1,735,810	5,216,720	54,000
Harnett	910	271	639		32,730	11,347	21,383		1,848,032	460,522	1,387,510	
Haywood	9	6	3		344	296	48		20,700	14,700	6,000	
Henderson	59	40	19		2,020	1,597	423		116,661	83,761	32,900	
Hertford	1,205	295	910		75,393	20,422	54,971		3,192,490	785,735	2,406,755	
Hoke	1,145	151	991	3	46,087	8,602	36,981	504	3,078,680	466,230	2,577,450	35,000
Hyde	336	82	254		10,989	3,646	7,343		574,958	174,328	400,530	
Iredell	762	219	543		34,203	9,350	24,853		1,417,050	353,675	1,063,375	
Jackson	52	45	7		1,530	1,431	99		66,460	60,910	5,550	
Johnston	1,252	222	1,030		51,101	12,520	38,581		2,938,317	631,995	2,306,322	
Jones	610	92	518		29,296	9,920	19,376		1,076,105	276,495	799,610	
Lee	450	153	297		18,458	5,728	12,730		702,935	209,180	493,755	
Lenoir	1,559	110	1,449		56,158	5,807	50,351		4,117,110	323,220	3,793,890	
Lincoln	399	74	325		14,322	2,791	11,531		698,088	109,380	588,708	
McDowell	63	54	9		3,344	3,003	341		84,270	71,770	12,500	
Macon	43	36	7		1,334	1,097	237		41,550	30,200	11,350	
Madison	22	7	15		239	88	151		16,500	9,400	7,100	
Martin	1,043	233	810		46,057	13,643	32,414		2,289,920	568,140	1,721,780	
Mecklenburg	1,360	129	1,229	2	61,657	6,425	55,150	82	4,482,941	460,194	3,995,247	27,500
Mitchell	6	6			185	185			4,250	4,250		
Montgomery	324	118	206		15,247	5,973	9,274		386,366	122,965	263,401	
Moore	433	198	234	1	21,566	8,761	12,605	200	729,804	249,760	432,644	47,400
Nash	2,575	240	2,335		96,797	12,310	84,487		5,746,500	659,375	5,087,125	
New Hanover	48	33	15		1,933	831	1,102		138,825	71,825	67,000	
Northampton	2,442	392	2,050		110,452	23,671	86,781		5,642,535	1,057,425	4,585,110	
Onslow	518	215	303		20,976	9,541	11,435		813,631	296,501	517,130	
Orange	491	217	274		33,790	13,875	19,915		782,220	338,927	443,293	
Pamlico	203	122	81		6,534	4,777	1,757		285,988	182,023	103,965	
Pasquotank	427	186	240	1	16,732	7,479	9,212	41	1,125,800	373.725	727,075	25,000
Pender	845	620	225		24,086	18,051	6,035		865,579	597,059	268,520	
Perquimans	438	178	260		22,601	9,757	12,844		1,078,805	466,945	611,860	
Person	1,173	211	962		60,688	16,328	44,360		1,751,626	425,331	1,326,295	
Pitt	2,985	226	2,758	1	92,120	12,620	79,459	41	7,383,278	805,915	6,570,363	7,000
Polk	137	40	97		8,615	2,617	5,998		318,096	101,150	216,946	
Randolph	324	208	116		17,695	10.559	7,136		446,675	250,925	195,750	
Richmond	821	225	595	1	50,076	18,167	31,509	400	1,593,843	512,255	1,061,588	20,000
Robeson	2,685	378	2,305	2	92,954	15,750	77,181	23	5,576,296	838,675	4,729,121	8,500
Rockingham	834	207	627		44,251	11,595	32,656		1,462,317	416,715	1,045,602	
Rowan	614	196	418		27,819	8,166	19,643		1,455,850	432,770	1,023,080	
Rutherford	492	189	303		25,418	11,710	13,708		1,049,377	418,260	631,117	
Sampson	1,719	651	1,068		70,233	30,068	40,165		2,832,626	1,031,287	1,801,339	
Scotland	1,211	132	1,079		54,185	7,624	46,561		3,410,910	329,870	3,081,040	
Stanly	158	45	113		8,359	2,240	6,119		245,400	68,205	177,195	
Stokes	295	98	197		14,684	6,025	8,659		498,312	198,612	299,700	
Surry	206	92	114		8,247	4,057	4,190		401,288	179,665	221,623	
Swain	5	5			664	664			11,900	11,900		
Transylvania	3	3			41	41			2,200	2,200		
Tyrrell	97	59	38		4,335	3,103	1,232		160,951	106,580	54,371	
Union	1,178	135	1,043		49,888	7,494	42,394		1,865,417	269,040	1,596,377	
Vance	1,153	262	890	1	56,559	13,429	42,885	245	2,102,099	526,927	1,562,172	13,000
Wake	2,244	549	1,694	1	98,638	28,799	69,809	30	4,517,850	1,295,000	3,219,850	3,000
Warren	1,896	772	1,124		90,973	43,840	47,133		2,560,040	1,251,938	1,308,102	
Washington	296	110	186		11,484	4,625	6,859		489,325	160,500	328,825	
Watauga	12	9	3		620	332	288		17,075	9,575	7,500	
Wayne	1,722	254	1,468		66,248	12,393	53,855		5,268,914	850,840	4,418,074	
Wilkes	241	189	52		9,712	7,431	2,281		353,706	286,650	67,056	
Wilson	1,725	137	1,588		58,194	5,254	52,940		4,726,950	394,400	4,332,550	
Yadkin	114	51	63		3,345	1,632	1,713		167,675	71,465	96,210	
Yancey	16	11	5		328	271	57		13,125	10,300	2,825	

Table 57.—FARMS OPERATED BY NEGROES—NUMBER, ACREAGE, VALUE OF LAND AND BUILDINGS, AND VALUE OF IMPLEMENTS AND MACHINERY, BY TENURE, BY STATES, AND COUNTIES: 1930—Continued

[Counties in which no farms operated by Negroes were reported, are omitted]

COUNTY	VALUE OF LAND ALONE				VALUE OF BUILDINGS				VALUE OF IMPLEMENTS AND MACHINERY			
	Total	Owners	Tenants	Managers	Total	Owners	Tenants	Managers	Total	Owners	Tenants	Managers
	NORTH CAROLINA—continued											
Chowan	$596, 082	$201, 495	$394, 587		$255, 155	$103, 800	$151, 355		$23, 222	$9, 885	$13, 337	
Clay	11, 575	11, 225	350		3, 625	3, 475	150		625	585	40	
Cleveland	3, 016, 190	311, 881	2, 704, 309		604, 571	127, 205	477, 366		88, 897	15, 476	73, 421	
Columbus	970, 635	540, 335	430, 300		417, 255	254, 550	162, 705		45, 503	31, 017	14, 486	
Craven	974, 385	356, 905	617, 480		352, 810	163, 490	189, 320		43, 387	18, 392	24, 995	
Cumberland	1, 365, 244	431, 540	933, 704		586, 900	232, 585	354, 315		70, 672	26, 538	44, 134	
Currituck	363, 510	132, 685	230, 825		126, 240	46, 715	79, 525		15, 174	5, 736	9, 438	
Dare	800	800			2, 200	2, 200			50	50		
Davidson	265, 272	74, 287	190, 985		99, 050	39, 275	59, 775		9, 023	4, 773	4, 250	
Davie	404, 844	86, 814	318, 030		141, 975	42, 835	99, 140		17, 240	5, 684	11, 556	
Duplin	1, 502, 996	550, 259	952, 737		747, 149	348, 495	398, 654		66, 033	36, 073	29, 960	
Durham	801, 393	161, 655	639, 738		325, 115	88, 425	236, 690		30, 879	9, 212	21, 667	
Edgecombe	4, 047, 402	305, 475	3, 740, 097	$1, 830	1, 494, 451	153, 205	1, 339, 246	$2, 000	251, 543	29, 928	221, 575	$10
Forsyth	797, 654	276, 834	430, 320	90, 500	192, 164	103, 220	87, 120	1, 824	28, 821	15, 013	13, 108	700
Franklin	1, 774, 310	314, 865	1, 436, 445	23, 000	807, 500	177, 925	621, 575	8, 000	115, 220	30, 400	83, 820	1, 000
Gaston	1, 498, 958	191, 385	1, 307, 573		432, 380	96, 825	335, 555		53, 525	11, 330	42, 195	
Gates	663, 027	311, 671	351, 356		287, 710	156, 040	131, 670		29, 751	18, 704	11, 047	
Granville	1, 775, 848	442, 420	1, 318, 728	14, 700	887, 745	290, 895	591, 050	5, 800	108, 824	43, 357	63, 667	1, 800
Greene	2, 657, 088	266, 420	2, 390, 668		887, 258	97, 750	789, 508		90, 239	13, 805	76, 434	
Guilford	1, 013, 792	473, 162	540, 630		394, 490	201, 865	192, 625		35, 765	21, 957	13, 808	
Halifax	5, 117, 396	1, 165, 870	3, 901, 126	50, 400	1, 889, 134	569, 940	1, 315, 594	3, 600	362, 935	132, 908	228, 027	2, 000
Harnett	1, 337, 312	300, 797	1, 036, 515		510, 720	159, 725	350, 995		65, 930	20, 521	45, 409	
Haywood	14, 218	10, 818	3, 400		6, 482	3, 882	2, 600		1, 450	1, 070	380	
Henderson	87, 711	61, 536	26, 175		28, 950	22, 225	6, 725		4, 114	3, 134	980	
Hertford	2, 436, 220	553, 525	1, 882, 695		756, 270	232, 210	524, 060		93, 706	33, 841	59, 865	
Hoke	2, 432, 255	336, 830	2, 063, 425	32, 000	646, 425	129, 400	514, 025	3, 000	77, 547	17, 665	57, 632	2, 250
Hyde	484, 319	141, 074	343, 245		90, 639	33, 354	57, 285		20, 580	8, 075	12, 505	
Iredell	1, 086, 322	252, 702	833, 620		330, 728	100, 973	229, 755		40, 679	14, 575	26, 104	
Jackson	44, 905	40, 830	4, 075		21, 555	20, 080	1, 475		1, 307	1, 302	5	
Johnston	2, 162, 488	460, 745	1, 701, 743		775, 829	171, 250	604, 579		101, 285	28, 082	73, 203	
Jones	763, 620	193, 950	569, 670		312, 485	82, 545	229, 940		46, 311	16, 597	29, 714	
Lee	488, 225	132, 790	355, 435		214, 710	76, 390	138, 320		28, 011	8, 928	19, 083	
Lenoir	3, 083, 195	230, 010	2, 853, 185		1, 033, 915	93, 210	940, 705		124, 166	13, 723	110, 443	
Lincoln	550, 768	82, 245	468, 523		147, 320	27, 135	120, 185		17, 537	2, 768	14, 769	
McDowell	57, 385	49, 310	8, 075		26, 885	22, 460	4, 425		2, 960	2, 720	240	
Macon	30, 050	19, 900	10, 150		11, 500	10, 300	1, 200		1, 046	896	150	
Madison	11, 225	5, 000	6, 225		5, 275	4, 400	875		235	195	40	
Martin	1, 697, 265	405, 615	1, 291, 650		592, 655	162, 525	430, 130		65, 675	20, 080	45, 595	
Mecklenburg	3, 825, 819	360, 959	3, 443, 460	21, 400	657, 122	99, 235	551, 787	6, 100	67, 785	10, 451	56, 909	425
Mitchell	3, 130	3, 130			1, 120	1, 120			84	84		
Montgomery	272, 039	77, 183	194, 856		114, 327	45, 782	68, 545		12, 450	4, 934	7, 516	
Moore	477, 689	146, 255	311, 434	20, 000	252, 115	103, 505	121, 210	27, 400	24, 636	14, 988	9, 448	200
Nash	4, 153, 515	441, 440	3, 712, 075		1, 592. 985	217, 935	1, 375, 050		199, 274	30, 730	168, 544	
New Hanover	109, 040	49, 040	60, 000		29, 785	22, 785	7, 000		5, 650	4, 380	1, 270	
Northampton	4, 369, 398	725, 270	3, 644, 128		1, 273, 137	332, 155	940, 982		222, 250	62, 115	160, 135	
Onslow	589, 651	197, 776	391, 875		223, 980	98, 725	125, 255		24, 464	11, 745	12, 719	
Orange	498. 899	191, 163	307, 736		283, 321	147, 764	135, 557		38, 367	24, 645	13, 722	
Pamlico	225, 453	139, 828	85, 625		60, 535	42, 195	18, 340		5, 842	3, 731	2, 111	
Pasquotank	909, 860	284, 155	611, 705	14, 000	215, 940	89, 570	115, 370	11, 000	29, 526	11, 595	17, 531	400
Pender	494, 105	322, 960	171, 145		371, 474	274, 099	97, 375		41, 872	30, 431	11, 441	
Perquimans	788, 160	345, 255	442, 905		290, 645	121, 690	168, 955		32, 011	15, 709	16, 302	
Person	1, 174, 554	265, 934	908, 620		577, 072	159, 397	417, 675		59, 317	18, 106	41, 211	
Pitt	5, 181, 388	558, 200	4, 619, 188	4, 000	2, 201, 890	247, 715	1, 951, 175	3, 000	290, 221	37, 207	252, 324	690
Polk	251, 191	73, 295	177, 896		66, 905	27, 855	39, 050		5, 823	2, 803	3, 020	
Randolph	269, 040	146, 040	123, 000		177, 635	104, 885	72, 750		23, 121	15, 486	7, 635	
Richmond	1, 130, 243	336, 620	781, 123	12, 500	463, 600	175. 635	280, 465	7, 500	44, 621	16, 983	23, 138	4, 500
Robeson	4, 211, 756	575, 970	3. 630, 036	5, 760	1, 364, 540	262, 705	1, 099, 085	2, 750	145, 954	39, 936	105, 518	500
Rockingham	1, 069, 587	279, 265	790, 322		392, 730	137, 450	255, 280		43, 520	17, 036	26, 484	
Rowan	1, 069, 030	293, 790	775, 240		386, 820	138, 980	247, 840		48, 578	22, 791	25. 787	
Rutherford	759, 309	266, 215	493, 094		290. 068	152, 045	138, 023		36, 893	23, 589	13, 304	
Sampson	2, 010, 579	696, 287	1, 314, 292		822, 047	335, 000	487, 047		81, 947	42. 242	39, 705	
Scotland	2, 753, 235	229, 020	2, 524, 215		657, 675	100, 850	556, 825		64, 109	8, 076	56, 033	
Stanly	182, 575	47, 705	134, 870		62, 825	20, 500	42, 325		5, 623	2, 060	3, 563	
Stokes	345, 657	131, 262	214, 395		152, 655	67, 350	85, 305		16, 102	9, 015	7, 087	
Surry	286, 023	116, 770	169, 253		115, 265	62, 895	52, 370		10, 463	6, 005	4, 458	
Swain	8, 650	8, 650			3, 250	3, 250			300	300		
Transylvania	1, 275	1, 275			925	925			30	30		
Tyrrell	122, 841	78, 720	44, 121		38, 110	27, 860	10, 250		4, 894	4, 319	575	
Union	1, 319, 489	172, 605	1, 146, 884		545, 928	96, 435	449, 493		45, 987	10, 541	35, 446	
Vance	1, 428, 819	302, 732	1, 121, 087	5, 000	673, 280	224, 195	441, 085	8. 000	95, 549	30, 549	63, 000	2, 000
Wake	2, 987, 160	827, 660	2, 158. 500	1, 000	1, 530, 690	467, 340	1, 061, 350	2, 000	137, 650	51, 439	86, 161	50
Warren	1, 695, 003	781, 981	913, 022		865, 037	469, 957	395, 080		147, 697	86, 793	60, 904	
Washington	348, 955	106, 025	242, 930		140, 370	54, 475	85, 895		12, 565	5, 368	7, 197	
Watauga	13, 450	7, 200	6, 250		3, 625	2, 375	1, 250		195	150	45	
Wayne	4, 025, 414	602, 015	3, 423, 399		1. 243, 500	248, 825	994, 675		128, 492	36, 846	91, 646	
Wilkes	241, 751	189, 225	52, 526		111, 955	97, 425	14, 530		11. 592	10, 166	1, 426	
Wilson	3, 556, 243	284, 065	3, 272, 178		1, 170, 707	110, 335	1, 060, 372		139, 670	16, 613	123, 057	
Yadkin	124, 715	54, 505	70, 210		42, 960	16, 960	26, 000		7, 713	2, 385	5, 328	
Yancey	8, 800	7, 050	1, 750		4, 325	3, 250	1, 075		349	294	55	

TABLE 57.—FARMS OPERATED BY NEGROES—NUMBER, ACREAGE, VALUE OF LAND AND BUILDINGS, AND VALUE OF IMPLEMENTS AND MACHINERY, BY TENURE, BY STATES, AND COUNTIES: 1930—Continued

[Counties in which no farms operated by Negroes were reported, are omitted]

COUNTY	NUMBER OF FARMS				ALL LAND IN FARMS (ACRES)				VALUE OF LAND AND BUILDINGS			
	Total	Owners	Tenants	Managers	Total	Owners	Tenants	Managers	Total	Owners	Tenants	Managers
	NORTH DAKOTA											
Total	10	5	5		2,565	1,405	1,160		$62,700	$40,700	$22,000	
Benson	1	1			222	222			3,400	3,400		
Burleigh	1		1		160		160		2,400		2,400	
Cass	1		1		160		160		4,000		4,000	
Grant	1		1		320		320		6,000		6,000	
McHenry	1	1			240	240			6,000	6,000		
Mountrail	1	1			293	293			4,500	4,500		
Nelson	1	1			420	420			16,800	16,800		
Pierce	1		1		240		240		4,000		4,000	
Ramsey	1	1			230	230			10,000	10,000		
Sargent	1		1		280		280		5,600		5,600	
	OHIO											
Total	1,229	780	438	11	92,083	45,446	44,627	2,010	$5,434,735	$2,641,920	$2,649,595	$143,220
Adams	6	3	3		552	148	404		18,700	4,200	14,500	
Allen	5	4	1		257	97	160		27,900	11,900	16,000	
Ashland	1			1	105			105	5,000			5,000
Ashtabula	7	6	1		155	136	19		26,100	24,300	1,800	
Athens	25	14	8	3	1,860	616	637	607	57,100	27,950	15,150	14,000
Auglaize	1		1		56		56		4,480		4,480	
Belmont	27	19	8		1,360	988	372		75,700	46,400	29,300	
Brown	68	36	32		3,206	1,635	1,571		162,030	80,660	81,370	
Butler	10	3	7		1,584	322	1,262		195,600	34,500	161,100	
Carroll	4	3	1		295	192	103		14,680	10,680	4,000	
Champaign	40	15	23	2	4,714	779	3,390	545	296,860	53,620	209,240	34,000
Clark	35	24	11		2,486	860	1,626		198,670	92,370	106,300	
Clermont	45	36	9		2,427	1,866	561		177,580	144,480	33,100	
Clinton	18	11	7		1,418	345	1,073		81,080	19,900	61,180	
Columbiana	10	6	4		697	327	370		36,610	22,380	14,230	
Coshocton	1	1			151	151			10,000	10,000		
Crawford	1		1		5		5		5,000		5,000	
Cuyahoga	2	1	1		65	25	40		102,000	88,000	14,000	
Darke	34	25	9		2,347	1,702	645		138,860	97,860	41,000	
Defiance	1	1			54	54			5,400	5,400		
Delaware	12	8	4		1,124	503	621		82,650	44,150	38,500	
Erie	4	2	2		432	27	405		39,800	4,800	35,000	
Fairfield	4	3	1		66	41	25		5,700	2,200	3,500	
Fayette	7	2	4	1	1,053	99	754	200	63,150	7,200	43,950	12,000
Franklin	27	20	7		1,090	656	434		285,340	198,540	86,800	
Fulton	5	2	3		101	31	70		22,300	9,300	13,000	
Gallia	84	58	26		4,427	3,325	1,102		103,220	81,515	21,705	
Geauga	1	1			43	43			5,000	5,000		
Greene	58	30	26	2	3,495	1,362	1,906	227	357,235	141,660	144,575	71,000
Guernsey	6	6			466	466			20,000	20,000		
Hamilton	8	7	1		319	246	73		53,190	46,000	7,190	
Hancock	2	2			201	201			19,600	19,600		
Hardin	11	4	7		941	216	725		56,100	12,200	43,900	
Harrison	18	11	5	2	1,384	443	615	326	37,195	18,000	11,975	7,220
Highland	17	14	3		1,188	1,021	167		61,400	52,200	9,200	
Hocking	5	1	4		747	67	680		27,150	2,300	24,850	
Huron	2	1	1		197	70	127		12,350	6,000	6,350	
Jackson	36	33	3		2,745	2,453	292		86,775	80,050	6,725	
Jefferson	19	8	11		1,580	315	1,265		67,800	21,800	46,000	
Knox	2	2			30	30			4,000	4,000		
Lake	1	1			20	20			4,100	4,100		
Lawrence	33	31	2		1,228	1,138	90		85,800	81,600	4,200	
Licking	2	1	1		277	50	227		8,710	700	8,010	
Logan	21	17	4		1,304	897	407		81,950	56,950	25,000	
Lorain	9	8	1		203	184	19		33,050	30,050	3,000	
Lucas	4	2	2		78	32	46		24,800	5,800	19,000	
Madison	30	9	21		4,569	750	3,819		248,300	57,340	190,960	
Mahoning	5	5			359	359			34,850	34,850		
Marion	1		1		40		40		800		800	
Meigs	29	26	3		749	688	61		38,090	32,490	5,600	
Mercer	5	3	2		312	192	120		21,100	13,000	8,100	
Miami	9	5	4		395	204	191		32,560	15,760	16,800	
Monroe	5	5			187	187			6,120	6,120		
Montgomery	8	3	5		339	115	224		45,000	17,000	28,000	
Morgan	32	19	13		1,989	1,278	711		50,975	34,125	16,850	
Morrow	3	1	2		194	8	186		11,500	2,000	9,500	
Muskingum	14	6	8		889	239	650		63,700	29,600	34,100	
Noble	3	3			171	171			3,800	3,800		
Ottawa	1		1		110		110		14,500		14,500	
Paulding	26	14	12		3,270	1,757	1,513		225,450	123,150	102,300	
Perry	3	3			146	146			6,500	6,500		
Pickaway	16	4	12		3,065	393	2,672		192,360	34,300	158,060	
Pike	49	40	9		5,021	3,744	1,277		144,400	70,400	74,000	
Portage	3	2	1		406	295	111		18,000	8,000	10,000	
Preble	8	5	3		736	353	383		41,410	23,100	18,310	
Richland	2	2			200	200			6,500	6,500		
Ross	60	40	20		5,767	2,876	2,891		320,530	101,445	219,085	
Sandusky	3	2	1		91	83	8		7,600	6,600	1,000	
Scioto	2	2			110	110			4,700	4,700		
Shelby	6	2	4		412	207	205		19,100	10,900	8,200	

Table 57.—FARMS OPERATED BY NEGROES—NUMBER, ACREAGE, VALUE OF LAND AND BUILDINGS, AND VALUE OF IMPLEMENTS AND MACHINERY, BY TENURE, BY STATES, AND COUNTIES: 1930—Continued

[Counties in which no farms operated by Negroes were reported, are omitted]

COUNTY	VALUE OF LAND ALONE				VALUE OF BUILDINGS				VALUE OF IMPLEMENTS AND MACHINERY			
	Total	Owners	Tenants	Managers	Total	Owners	Tenants	Managers	Total	Owners	Tenants	Managers
NORTH DAKOTA												
Total	**$47,300**	**$28,700**	**$18,600**		**$15,400**	**$12,000**	**$3,400**		**$7,875**	**$3,175**	**$4,700**	
Benson	3,100	3,100			300	300			400	400		
Burleigh	2,400		2,400									
Cass	2,200		2,200		1,800		1,800		300		300	
Grant	6,000		6,000						1,900		1,900	
McHenry	3,000	3,000			3,000	3,000			1,000	1,000		
Mountrail	4,300	4,300			200	200			525	525		
Nelson	11,800	11,800			5,000	5,000			1,000	1,000		
Pierce	3,200		3,200		800		800		500		500	
Ramsey	6,500	6,500			3,500	3,500			250	250		
Sargent	4,800		4,800		800		800		2,000		2,000	
OHIO												
Total	**$3,571,445**	**$1,568,295**	**$1,908,780**	**$94,370**	**$1,863,290**	**$1,073,625**	**$740,815**	**$48,850**	**$217,013**	**$118,645**	**$35,743**	**$12,625**
Adams	12,700	2,700	10,000		6,000	1,500	4,500		935	200	735	
Allen	19,600	6,100	13,500		8,300	5,800	2,500		470	370	100	
Ashland	2,500			2,500	2,500			2,500	1,000			1,000
Ashtabula	9,900	9,100	800		16,200	15,200	1,000		1,225	1,215	10	
Athens	28,430	10,330	10,900	7,200	28,670	17,620	4,250	6,800	2,333	1,050	508	775
Auglaize	2,480		2,480		2,000		2,000		200		200	
Belmont	43,100	23,400	19,700		32,600	23,000	9,600		2,963	2,153	810	
Brown	96,220	45,600	50,620		65,810	35,060	30,750		4,780	2,625	2,155	
Butler	123,250	24,250	99,000		72,350	10,250	62,100		5,270	1,600	3,670	
Carroll	5,330	3,330	2,000		9,350	7,350	2,000		1,150	1,100	50	
Champaign	195,460	29,320	137,640	28,500	101,400	24,300	71,600	5,500	11,670	3,345	6,625	1,700
Clark	131,745	50,745	81,000		66,925	41,625	25,300		4,205	2,500	1,705	
Clermont	102,830	79,580	23,250		74,750	64,900	9,850		3,600	3,040	560	
Clinton	45,680	12,100	33,580		35,400	7,800	27,600		3,665	1,080	2,585	
Columbiana	16,960	10,230	6,730		19,650	12,150	7,500		805	240	565	
Coshocton	8,400	8,400			1,600	1,600			1,000	1,000		
Crawford	1,000		1,000		4,000		4,000		275		275	
Cuyahoga	37,000	26,000	11,000		65,000	62,000	3,000		600	500	100	
Darke	82,560	55,560	27,000		56,300	42,300	14,000		7,945	6,515	1,430	
Defiance	3,900	3,900			1,500	1,500			400	400		
Delaware	50,850	26,950	23,900		31,800	17,200	14,600		1,260	1,050	210	
Erie	26,300	2,300	24,000		13,500	2,500	11,000		2,175	175	2,000	
Fairfield	4,400	1,700	2,700		1,300	500	800		300	100	200	
Fayette	48,400	4,700	33,950	9,750	14,750	2,500	10,000	2,250	1,840	140	1,400	300
Franklin	214,860	148,410	66,450		70,480	50,130	20,350		6,540	5,090	1,450	
Fulton	8,500	2,600	5,900		13,800	6,700	7,100		900	650	250	
Gallia	62,095	46,740	15,355		41,125	34,775	6,350		6,620	5,755	865	
Geauga	3,800	3,800			1,200	1,200			200	200		
Greene	210,015	78,860	88,155	43,000	147,220	62,800	56,420	28,000	23,305	8,930	5,675	8,700
Guernsey	15,450	15,450			4,550	4,550			775	775		
Hamilton	41,890	36,200	5,690		11,300	9,800	1,500		1,642	1,642		
Hancock	14,650	14,650			4,950	4,950			900	900		
Hardin	35,525	8,225	27,300		20,575	3,975	16,600		1,760	325	1,435	
Harrison	19,495	9,600	6,475	3,420	17,700	8,400	5,500	3,800	1,560	870	540	150
Highland	39,875	33,475	6,400		21,525	18,725	2,800		3,160	2,360	800	
Hocking	23,300	800	22,500		3,850	1,500	2,350		1,270	125	1,145	
Huron	6,850	2,500	4,350		5,500	3,500	2,000		1,350	750	600	
Jackson	53,525	47,825	5,700		33,250	32,225	1,025		5,210	4,935	275	
Jefferson	44,075	13,375	30,700		23,725	8,425	15,300		1,890	1,055	835	
Knox	1,900	1,900			2,100	2,100			35	35		
Lake	2,000	2,000			2,100	2,100			250	250		
Lawrence	55,200	52,600	2,600		30,600	29,000	1,600		2,370	2,195	175	
Licking	7,210	700	6,510		1,500		1,500					
Logan	43,625	26,125	17,500		38,325	30,825	7,500		2,380	1,980	400	
Lorain	14,850	13,850	1,000		18,200	16,200	2,000		950	925	25	
Lucas	15,700	3,700	12,000		9,100	2,100	7,000		175	115	60	
Madison	199,560	39,200	160,360		48,740	18,140	30,600		7,785	2,160	5,625	
Mahoning	17,700	17,700			17,150	17,150			2,740	2,740		
Marion	800		800						60		60	
Meigs	21,930	17,530	4,400		16,160	14,960	1,200		1,540	1,465	75	
Mercer	16,400	10,800	5,600		4,700	2,200	2,500		1,100	550	550	
Miami	18,910	9,410	9,500		13,650	6,350	7,300		2,385	1,785	600	
Monroe	4,970	4,970			1,150	1,150			80	80		
Montgomery	24,300	6,000	18,300		20,700	11,000	9,700		1,290	800	490	
Morgan	30,845	20,575	10,270		20,130	13,550	6,580		1,735	1,240	495	
Morrow	6,050	550	5,500		5,450	1,450	4,000		300	100	200	
Muskingum	52,500	23,200	29,300		11,200	6,400	4,800		775	350	425	
Noble	2,950	2,950			850	850			80	80		
Ottawa	12,500		12,500		2,000		2,000		25		25	
Paulding	159,050	84,650	74,400		66,400	38,500	27,900		12,300	8,000	4,300	
Perry	3,600	3,600			2,900	2,900			800	800		
Pickaway	156,660	24,400	132,260		35,700	9,900	25,800		8,330	2,505	5,825	
Pike	116,735	50,835	65,900		27,665	19,565	8,100		7,060	3,635	3,425	
Portage	8,200	4,200	4,000		9,800	3,800	6,000		1,150	350	800	
Preble	26,210	13,900	12,310		15,200	9,200	6,000		1,945	520	1,425	
Richland	2,500	2,500			4,000	4,000			425	425		
Ross	255,655	63,620	192,035		64,875	37,825	27,050		14,220	5,665	8,555	
Sandusky	6,200	5,450	750		1,400	1,150	250		135	125	10	
Scioto	2,800	2,800			1,900	1,900			80	80		
Shelby	13,900	7,400	6,500		5,200	3,500	1,700		650	400	250	

TABLE 57.—FARMS OPERATED BY NEGROES—NUMBER, ACREAGE, VALUE OF LAND AND BUILDINGS, AND VALUE OF IMPLEMENTS AND MACHINERY, BY TENURE, BY STATES, AND COUNTIES: 1930—Continued

[Counties in which no farms operated by Negroes were reported, are omitted]

COUNTY	NUMBER OF FARMS				ALL LAND IN FARMS (ACRES)				VALUE OF LAND AND BUILDINGS			
	Total	Owners	Tenants	Managers	Total	Owners	Tenants	Managers	Total	Owners	Tenants	Managers
OHIO—continued												
Stark	7	3	4		256	40	216		$34,500	$8,500	$26,000	
Summit	2		2		289		289		33,900		33,900	
Trumbull	2	1	1		198	18	180		12,000	3,000	9,000	
Tuscarawas	2	2			153	153			7,500	7,500		
Union	6	5	1		420	348	72		29,180	24,200	4,980	
Van Wert	5	3	2		325	225	100		25,400	19,400	6,000	
Vinton	8	7	1		375	349	26		7,200	5,400	1,800	
Warren	28	14	14		2,137	878	1,259		151,480	59,800	91,680	
Washington	100	58	42		9,396	4,859	4,537		246,515	135,625	110,890	
Wayne	3	2	1		143	38	105		11,400	5,700	5,700	
Williams	2		2		236		236		11,300		11,300	
Wood	2	1	1		95	4	91		18,800	800	18,000	
OKLAHOMA												
Total	15,172	3,454	11,694	24	1,061,341	283,805	770,501	7,035	$37,967,113	$9,954,907	$27,725,473	$286,733
Adair	1	1			110	110			1,000	1,000		
Alfalfa	1	1			160	160			14,000	14,000		
Atoka	117	30	87		7,685	1,872	5,813		163,530	43,635	119,895	
Beaver	1	1			320	320			4,000	4,000		
Beckham	47		47		4,164		4,164		180,305		180,305	
Blaine	232	75	157		23,036	9,700	13,336		842,380	368,060	474,320	
Bryan	182	59	123		12,171	4,542	7,629		315,695	104,635	211,060	
Caddo	158	11	147		11,767	1,277	10,490		476,692	40,200	436,492	
Canadian	71	24	47		4,565	1,157	3,408		242,500	78,900	163,600	
Carter	230	112	117	1	16,547	9,148	7,391	8	399,163	227,365	169,495	2,303
Cherokee	89	41	48		5,744	3,640	2,104		122,335	78,620	43,715	
Choctaw	800	199	601		41,266	12,178	29,088		1,106,544	262,429	844,115	
Cleveland	25	7	18		4,997	1,880	3,117		65,710	20,000	45,710	
Coal	64	16	47	1	7,085	1,696	4,192	1,197	121,305	29,410	72,440	19,455
Comanche	43	9	33	1	4,227	1,140	2,927	160	105,312	35,310	67,502	2,500
Cotton	44		44		3,309		3,309		108,390		108,390	
Craig	60	31	29		6,273	3,808	2,465		133,430	89,560	43,870	
Creek	773	88	685		63,971	8,873	55,098		1,849,270	311,800	1,537,470	
Custer	31	4	27		2,480	520	1,960		104,575	24,000	80,575	
Dewey	5	2	3		685	205	480		16,300	3,800	12,500	
Garfield	20	8	12		2,375	1,410	965		108,750	67,000	41,750	
Garvin	157	59	98		12,252	6,564	5,688		326,570	168,380	158,190	
Grady	77	3	74		4,598	250	4,348		264,325	10,500	253,825	
Grant	2	1	1		483	480	3		21,300	20,000	1,300	
Greer	65	2	63		4,194	342	3,852		212,980	18,000	194,980	
Harmon	17		17		731		731		33,740		33,740	
Haskell	29	12	17		1,812	895	917		36,050	21,000	15,050	
Hughes	196	26	170		15,861	3,670	12,191		620,785	135,430	485,355	
Jackson	30		30		2,033		2,033		126,050		126,050	
Jefferson	7		7		660		660		22,400		22,400	
Johnston	53	23	30		3,493	1,250	2,243		62,625	19,185	43,440	
Kay	2		2		70		70		7,000		7,000	
Kingfisher	293	137	156		31,183	15,159	16,024		1,128,700	564,100	564,600	
Kiowa	113	1	112		9,031	160	8,871		516,600	6,000	510,600	
Latimer	30	6	24		913	271	642		19,650	3,200	16,450	
Le Flore	158	65	93		7,686	3,760	3,926		286,522	120,884	165,638	
Lincoln	442	107	335		42,386	11,548	30,838		1,399,940	334,680	1,065,260	
Logan	809	233	574	2	86,141	27,677	57,944	520	3,365,642	1,076,327	2,261,315	28,000
Love	91	20	71		5,678	1,522	4,156		117,890	38,850	79,040	
McClain	80	35	45		4,158	2,014	2,144		186,492	91,085	95,407	
McCurtain	1,290	241	1,048	1	48,004	10,316	37,488	200	2,091,559	391,811	1,693,848	5,900
McIntosh	674	137	536	1	46,407	11,008	34,919	480	1,150,868	307,450	824,443	18,975
Major	8	5	3		2,354	1,544	810		75,000	47,000	28,000	
Marshall	7	2	5		285	92	193		5,609	1,524	4,085	
Mayes	106	51	55		6,057	3,285	2,772		261,250	143,010	118,240	
Murray	17	9	8		1,341	461	880		28,190	12,500	15,690	
Muskogee	1,349	331	1,015	3	86,220	21,750	63,270	1,200	3,579,411	972,565	2,528,846	78,000
Noble	76	13	63		7,708	2,217	5,491		309,295	81,875	227,420	
Nowata	199	90	109		14,564	7,610	6,954		364,990	188,915	176,075	
Okfuskee	1,172	254	915	3	83,327	21,928	60,957	442	3,281,373	1,016,770	2,234,603	30,000
Oklahoma	381	116	265		39,708	14,877	24,831		1,566,690	469,850	1,096,840	
Okmulgee	1,347	168	1,175	4	88,788	10,927	76,888	973	2,805,310	359,995	2,405,315	40,000
Osage	24	1	23		2,007	40	1,967		69,835	3,500	66,335	
Ottawa	1	1			40	40			400	400		
Pawnee	95	2	93		6,582	164	6,418		199,135	5,800	193,335	
Payne	185	12	172	1	15,098	1,343	13,595	160	612,030	62,600	542,430	7,000
Pittsburg	154	57	97		8,339	2,688	5,651		230,454	79,214	151,240	
Pontotoc	72	15	57		4,010	811	3,199		108,810	28,100	80,710	
Pottawatomie	94	30	64		8,130	3,164	4,966		231,060	85,350	145,710	
Pushmataha	38	15	23		2,308	544	1,764		31,530	9,185	22,345	
Roger Mills	8		6	2	1,505		285	1,220	33,450		8,950	24,500
Rogers	49	7	42		3,266	497	2,769		133,185	18,290	114,895	
Seminole	450	128	322		32,154	9,645	22,509		1,363,723	444,325	919,398	
Sequoyah	253	63	190		10,385	3,262	7,123		454,441	119,105	335,336	
Stephens	9		9		1,170		1,170		28,900		28,900	
Tillman	129	1	126	2	7,133	160	6,653	320	421,125	5,000	402,625	13,500
Tulsa	166	26	139	1	10,127	1,716	8,391	20	748,660	142,840	604,220	1,600
Wagoner	1,146	226	920		65,975	13,500	52,475		2,457,083	504,188	1,952,895	
Washington	7	2	4	1	552	160	257	135	30,100	5,800	9,300	15,000
Washita	20	1	19		799	160	639		52,600	12,000	40,600	
Woodward	1	1			698	698			4,600	4,600		

TABLE 57—FARMS OPERATED BY NEGROES—NUMBER, ACREAGE, VALUE OF LAND AND BUILDINGS, AND VALUE OF IMPLEMENTS AND MACHINERY, BY TENURE, BY STATES, AND COUNTIES: 1930—Continued

[Counties in which no farms operated by Negroes were reported, are omitted]

COUNTY	VALUE OF LAND ALONE				VALUE OF BUILDINGS				VALUE OF IMPLEMENTS AND MACHINERY			
	Total	Owners	Tenants	Managers	Total	Owners	Tenants	Managers	Total	Owners	Tenants	Managers
					OHIO—continued							
Stark	$22,200	$5,200	$17,000		$12,300	$3,300	$9,000		$1,900	$200	$1,700	
Summit	26,400		26,400		7,500		7,500		900		900	
Trumbull	7,500	1,500	6,000		4,500	1,500	3,000		400	200	200	
Tuscarawas	3,500	3,500			4,000	4,000			150	150		
Union	12,980	10,400	2,580		16,200	13,800	2,400		1,450	1,250	200	
Van Wert	15,100	11,600	3,500		10,300	7,800	2,500		550	350	200	
Vinton	4,700	4,100	600		2,500	1,300	1,200		175	175		
Warren	100,380	35,600	64,780		51,100	24,200	26,900		6,335	3,470	2,865	
Washington	154,675	78,075	76,600		91,840	57,550	34,290		13,705	8,535	5,170	
Wayne	6,900	2,200	4,700		4,500	3,500	1,000		350	100	250	
Williams	5,600		5,600		5,700		5,700		450		450	
Wood	17,200	200	17,000		1,600	600	1,000		350	100	250	
					OKLAHOMA							
Total	$32,279,927	$7,856,980	$24,178,602	$244,345	$5,687,186	$2,097,927	$3,546,871	$42,388	$1,595,879	$569,728	$1,005,601	$20,559
Adair	700	700			300	300			25	25		
Alfalfa	12,000	12,000			2,000	2,000			1,500	1,500		
Atoka	125,320	33,710	91,610		38,210	9,925	28,285		8,833	3,226	5,607	
Beaver	3,850	3,850			150	150			150	150		
Beckham	166,285		166,285		14,020		14,020		10,635		10,635	
Blaine	738,215	306,300	431,915		104,165	61,760	42,405		60,700	34,265	26,435	
Bryan	269,430	86,420	183,010		46,265	18,215	28,050		14,211	6,386	7,825	
Caddo	429,942	31,710	398,232		46,750	8,490	38,260		17,154	2,165	14,989	
Canadian	217,925	66,600	151,325		24,575	12,300	12,275		8,555	2,415	6,140	
Carter	319,360	184,040	134,480	840	79,803	43,325	35,015	1,463	23,565	12,485	9,630	1,450
Cherokee	96,395	61,625	34,770		25,940	16,995	8,945		3,967	2,545	1,422	
Choctaw	929,048	210,954	718,094		177,496	51,475	126,021		53,384	15,462	37,922	
Cleveland	58,910	16,800	42,110		6,800	3,200	3,600		2,490	1,920	570	
Coal	93,755	20,810	54,990	17,955	27,550	8,600	17,450	1,500	7,590	3,295	3,995	300
Comanche	90,890	29,050	59,540	2,300	14,422	6,260	7,962	200	6,015	2,135	3,780	100
Cotton	95,625		95,625		12,765		12,765		6,995		6,995	
Craig	111,715	75,565	36,150		21,715	13,995	7,720		3,948	2,770	1,178	
Creek	1,578,335	220,560	1,357,775		270,935	91,240	179,695		82,306	18,613	63,693	
Custer	93,685	21,350	72,335		10,890	2,650	8,240		7,550	2,475	5,075	
Dewey	14,100	2,600	11,500		2,200	1,200	1,000		500	350	150	
Garfield	95,625	60,100	35,525		13,125	6,900	6,225		5,685	4,900	785	
Garvin	276,310	134,445	141,865		50,260	33,935	16,325		11,913	7,748	4,165	
Grady	242,565	9,100	233,465		21,760	1,400	20,360		14,425	350	14,075	
Grant	18,550	18,000	550		2,750	2,000	750		260	200	60	
Greer	191,739	7,500	184,239		21,241	10,500	10,741		11,120	2,950	8,170	
Harmon	30,050		30,050		3,690		3,690		1,235		1,235	
Haskell	28,000	15,725	12,275		8,050	5,275	2,775		1,380	720	660	
Hughes	540,580	110,740	429,840		80,205	24,690	55,515		24,257	7,910	16,347	
Jackson	117,650		117,650		8,400		8,400		6,555		6,555	
Jefferson	20,300		20,300		2,100		2,100		425		425	
Johnston	50,275	14,185	36,090		12,350	5,000	7,350		3,045	1,270	1,775	
Kay	6,575		6,575		425		425		250		250	
Kingfisher	961,855	465,535	496,320		166,845	98,565	68,280		59,635	39,460	20,175	
Kiowa	484,400	6,000	478,400		32,200		32,200		30,015		30,015	
Latimer	13,615	2,400	11,215		6,035	800	5,235		2,155	210	1,945	
Le Flore	228,575	97,217	131,358		57,947	23,667	34,280		8,315	3,715	4,600	
Lincoln	1,193,710	260,805	932,905		206,230	73,875	132,355		51,440	17,975	33,465	
Logan	2,838,017	879,072	1,935,945	23,000	527,625	197,255	325,370	5,000	110,454	46,985	61,469	2,000
Love	96,580	31,500	65,080		21,310	7,350	13,960		6,512	2,080	4,432	
McClain	151,232	78,275	82,957		35,260	22,810	12,450		11,049	7,287	3,762	
McCurtain	1,745,875	310,326	1,430,549	5,000	345,684	81,485	263,299	900	90,771	20,842	64,929	5,000
McIntosh	927,873	233,750	680,648	13,475	222,995	73,700	143,795	5,500	47,728	17,746	29,982	
Major	66,700	42,200	24,500		8,300	4,800	3,500		6,780	4,030	2,750	
Marshall	4,409	1,224	3,185		1,200	300	900		220	50	170	
Mayes	216,175	116,035	100,140		45,075	26,975	18,100		7,887	4,792	3,095	
Murray	25,440	10,825	14,615		2,750	1,675	1,075		1,305	320	985	
Muskogee	2,937,386	715,625	2,151,862	69,900	642,025	256,940	376,985	8,100	154,617	59,486	89,506	5,625
Noble	272,195	68,000	204,195		37,100	13,875	23,225		11,238	3,985	7,253	
Nowata	309,400	155,800	153,600		55,590	33,115	22,475		15,994	8,679	7,315	
Okfuskee	2,729,653	779,590	1,929,413	20,650	551,720	237,180	305,190	9,350	146,296	60,342	83,804	2,150
Oklahoma	1,341,095	385,635	955,460		225,595	84,215	141,380		54,512	24,672	29,840	
Okmulgee	2,474,017	295,417	2,140,650	37,950	331,293	64,578	264,665	2,050	103,139	19,067	83,697	375
Osage	51,385	2,500	48,885		18,450	1,000	17,450		3,100	50	3,050	
Ottawa	375	375			25	25			10	10		
Pawnee	174,285	4,350	169,935		24,850	1,450	23,400		7,995	305	7,690	
Payne	547,126	51,300	489,226	6,600	64,904	11,300	53,204	400	15,075	2,770	11,905	400
Pittsburg	171,127	54,472	116,655		59,327	24,742	34,585		7,258	2,890	4,368	
Pontotoc	89,965	22,350	67,615		18,845	5,750	13,095		4,615	1,365	3,250	
Pottawatomie	184,210	62,575	121,635		46,850	22,775	24,075		10,373	5,595	4,778	
Pushmataha	21,760	5,545	16,215		9,770	3,640	6,130		2,023	446	1,577	
Roger Mills	31,275		8,275	23,000	2,175		675	1,500	1,976		1,476	500
Rogers	112,795	14,000	98,795		20,390	4,290	16,100		4,763	1,005	3,758	
Seminole	1,157,633	340,615	817,018		206,090	103,710	102,380		67,483	35,504	31,979	
Sequoyah	378,496	87,905	290,591		75,945	31,200	44,745		11,491	4,668	6,823	
Stephens	25,890		25,890		3,010		3,010		1,550		1,550	
Tillman	382,650	4,550	365,025	13,075	38,475	450	37,600	425	26,650	125	25,075	1,450
Tulsa	682,630	120,305	561,725	600	66,030	22,535	42,495	1,000	13,150	2,735	10,215	200
Wagoner	2,110,494	386,468	1,724,026		346,589	117,720	228,869		91,812	29,682	62,130	
Washington	21,950	4,600	7,350	10,000	8,150	1,200	1,950	5,000	1,325	125	200	1,000
Washita	49,575	11,000	38,575		3,025	1,000	2,025		3,545	1,500	2,045	
Woodward	4,400	4,400			200	200			1,000	1,000		

TABLE 57.—FARMS OPERATED BY NEGROES—NUMBER, ACREAGE, VALUE OF LAND AND BUILDINGS, AND VALUE OF IMPLEMENTS AND MACHINERY, BY TENURE, BY STATES, AND COUNTIES: 1930—Continued

[Counties in which no farms operated by Negroes were reported, are omitted]

COUNTY	NUMBER OF FARMS				ALL LAND IN FARMS (ACRES)				VALUE OF LAND AND BUILDINGS			
	Total	Owners	Tenants	Managers	Total	Owners	Tenants	Managers	Total	Owners	Tenants	Managers
OREGON												
Total	9	8	1		826	808	18		$32,420	$26,420	$6,000	
Clackamas	2	2			58	58			4,920	4,920		
Columbia	1	1			80	80			8,000	8,000		
Harney	2	2			191	191			3,200	3,200		
Jefferson	1	1			460	460			5,000	5,000		
Lane	1	1			18	18			2,500	2,500		
Multnomah	2	1	1		19	1	18		8,800	2,800	6,000	
PENNSYLVANIA												
Total	353	224	115	14	21,616	9,857	10,005	1,754	$2,194,280	$876,080	$1,179,500	$138,700
Adams	5	3	2		364	125	239		14,200	6,200	8,000	
Allegheny	9	4	5		628	180	448		128,200	36,200	92,000	
Armstrong	2	1	1		164	4	160		4,600	600	4,000	
Beaver	10	4	6		1,206	289	917		43,520	13,020	30,500	
Bedford	2	2			140	140			3,400	3,400		
Berks	6	4	2		285	98	187		18,900	10,400	8,500	
Bradford	8	7	1		620	520	100		22,000	18,000	4,000	
Bucks	18	9	5	4	701	208	171	322	131,800	59,800	23,000	49,000
Butler	4	2	2		126	30	96		14,100	4,100	10,000	
Cambria	1	1			112	112			2,000	2,000		
Centre	1		1		33		33		600		600	
Chester	79	50	27	2	3,585	1,504	2,057	24	530,100	212,200	289,900	28,000
Clinton	1		1		160		160		7,000		7,000	
Crawford	10	5	3	2	472	182	222	68	42,700	19,900	17,200	5,600
Cumberland	1	1			160	160			5,000	5,000		
Dauphin	10	7	3		647	437	210		42,000	29,000	13,000	
Delaware	15	9	6		665	154	511		295,800	58,800	237,000	
Erie	5	1	4		333	80	253		19,800	5,000	14,800	
Fayette	20	17	1	2	1,494	618	75	801	66,490	47,490	6,000	13,000
Franklin	6	3	3		450	70	380		22,240	2,240	20,000	
Fulton	1		1		171		171		15,000		15,000	
Greene	4	3	1		347	259	88		16,190	12,190	4,000	
Huntingdon	1	1			100	100			1,700	1,700		
Indiana	3	2	1		286	130	156		8,000	5,000	3,000	
Jefferson	1	1			108	108			2,300	2,300		
Juniata	9	7	2		790	575	215		36,700	25,500	11,200	
Lackawanna	2	2			72	72			12,500	12,500		
Lancaster	16	12	4		731	335	396		60,300	28,600	31,700	
Lawrence	9	8	1		450	370	80		44,400	40,400	4,000	
Lebanon	1	1			19	19			3,000	3,000		
Lycoming	2	2			170	170			11,000	11,000		
Mercer	12	6	6		570	166	404		35,400	13,600	21,800	
Monroe	1	1			72	72			6,000	6,000		
Montgomery	10	5	4	1	382	90	171	121	147,300	28,500	106,700	12,100
Northampton	2	1	1		322	288	34		27,500	25,000	2,500	
Perry	4	3		1	337	189		148	16,300	7,300		9,000
Philadelphia	1		1		56		56		40,000		40,000	
Pike	1		1		120		120		1,000		1,000	
Somerset	1	1			25	25			1,200	1,200		
Susquehanna	1	1			204	204			6,000	6,000		
Washington	27	16	10	1	1,734	869	705	160	162,440	64,440	86,000	12,000
Wayne	1	1			88	88			5,000	5,000		
Westmoreland	5	3	1	1	339	224	5	110	27,200	12,200	5,000	10,000
York	25	17	8		1,778	593	1,185		93,400	31,300	62,100	
RHODE ISLAND												
Total	9	8		1	571	121		450	$40,000	$32,000		$8,000
Kent	1	1			5	5			3,500	3,500		
Newport	3	3			36	36			16,000	16,000		
Providence	2	2			21	21			10,000	10,000		
Washington	3	2		1	509	59		450	10,500	2,500		8,000
SOUTH CAROLINA												
Total	77,331	15,975	61,285	71	3,167,898	786,893	2,359,643	21,362	$105,693,220	$22,788,137	$82,319,129	$585,954
Abbeville	1,714	172	1,542		81,210	11,818	69,392		1,514,875	233,513	1,281,362	
Aiken	1,826	397	1,429		106,134	34,718	71,416		2,507,773	756,758	1,751,015	
Allendale	695	53	642		40,373	6,531	33,842		853,081	116,648	736,433	
Anderson	2,957	222	2,734	1	106,992	12,281	94,637	74	4,554,077	443,412	4,107,665	3,000
Bamberg	1,282	210	1,064	8	71,678	14,418	56,592	668	1,975,417	401,360	1,536,612	37,445
Barnwell	1,416	198	1,217	1	72,075	18,518	53,445	112	1,910,670	357,070	1,547,600	6,000
Beaufort	1,800	1,609	186	5	29,624	26,392	2,389	843	1,694,201	1,551,448	97,469	45,284
Berkeley	1,521	1,193	327	1	40,180	33,884	5,496	800	1,095,068	893,203	200,165	1,700
Calhoun	1,683	183	1,497	3	51,848	10,155	40,985	708	1,401,402	253,324	1,136,393	11,685
Charleston	1,465	995	463	7	22,920	17,698	4,734	488	1,469,812	1,040,997	377,215	51,600

TABLE 57.—FARMS OPERATED BY NEGROES—NUMBER, ACREAGE, VALUE OF LAND AND BUILDINGS, AND VALUE OF IMPLEMENTS AND MACHINERY, BY TENURE, BY STATES, AND COUNTIES: 1930—Continued

[Counties in which no farms operated by Negroes were reported, are omitted]

COUNTY	VALUE OF LAND ALONE				VALUE OF BUILDINGS				VALUE OF IMPLEMENTS AND MACHINERY			
	Total	Owners	Tenants	Managers	Total	Owners	Tenants	Managers	Total	Owners	Tenants	Managers
OREGON												
Total	$22,670	$18,270	$4,400		$9,750	$8,150	$1,600		$2,667	$2,617	$50	
Clackamas	3,670	3,670			1,250	1,250			200	200		
Columbia	5,500	5,500			2,500	2,500			450	450		
Harney	2,100	2,100			1,100	1,100			1,100	1,100		
Jefferson	4,000	4,000			1,000	1,000			717	717		
Lane	1,000	1,000			1,500	1,500			150	150		
Multnomah	6,400	2,000	4,400		2,400	800	1,600		50		50	
PENNSYLVANIA												
Total	$1,144,895	$395,520	$721,175	$64,200	$1,049,385	$516,560	$458,325	$74,500	$145,628	$86,788	$54,130	$4,710
Adams	5,000	2,500	2,500		9,200	3,700	5,500		1,430	530	900	
Allegheny	104,425	18,450	85,975		23,775	17,750	6,025		1,850	1,100	750	
Armstrong	3,100	300	2,800		1,500	300	1,200		520	20	500	
Beaver	23,200	4,400	18,800		20,320	8,620	11,700		4,060	920	3,140	
Bedford	1,800	1,800			1,600	1,600			175	175		
Berks	9,700	4,600	5,100		9,200	5,800	3,400		330	230	100	
Bradford	7,600	6,600	1,000		14,400	11,400	3,000		2,725	2,625	100	
Bucks	42,100	15,100	7,000	20,000	89,700	44,700	16,000	29,000	5,200	2,900	650	1,650
Butler	5,200	1,200	4,000		8,900	2,900	6,000		1,950	350	1,600	
Cambria	1,000	1,000			1,000	1,000			200	200		
Centre	300		300		300		300		50		50	
Chester	228,665	73,115	149,550	6,000	301,435	139,085	140,350	22,000	45,300	27,725	17,375	200
Clinton	3,000		3,000		4,000		4,000		25		25	
Crawford	23,900	9,200	12,100	2,600	18,800	10,700	5,100	3,000	1,520	460	1,000	60
Cumberland	1,000	1,000			4,000	4,000			500	500		
Dauphin	15,700	11,400	4,300		26,300	17,600	8,700		3,345	2,725	620	
Delaware	218,750	39,250	179,500		77,050	19,550	57,500		2,835	1,835	1,000	
Erie	9,000	2,000	7,000		10,800	3,000	7,800		975	200	775	
Fayette	37,390	25,390	2,500	9,500	29,100	22,100	3,500	3,500	4,550	3,350	1,000	200
Franklin	8,990	990	8,000		13,250	1,250	12,000		5,025	125	4,900	
Fulton	5,000		5,000		10,000		10,000		400		400	
Greene	8,990	6,990	2,000		7,200	5,200	2,000		1,670	920	750	
Huntingdon	700	700			1,000	1,000			1,000	1,000		
Indiana	4,500	3,000	1,500		3,500	2,000	1,500		600	200	400	
Jefferson	900	900			1,400	1,400			500	500		
Juniata	15,300	9,850	5,450		21,400	15,650	5,750		6,800	5,200	1,600	
Lackawana	4,300	4,300			8,200	8,200			1,500	1,500		
Lancaster	14,825	5,025	9,800		45,475	23,575	21,900		5,248	3,298	1,950	
Lawrence	19,900	18,400	1,500		24,500	22,000	2,500		4,700	4,700		
Lebanon	1,500	1,500			1,500	1,500			50	50		
Lycoming	6,000	6,000			5,000	5,000			1,500	1,500		
Mercer	14,720	6,420	8,300		20,680	7,180	13,500		4,110	2,450	1,660	
Monroe	1,000	1,000			5,000	5,000			1,500	1,500		
Montgomery	85,700	5,400	73,200	7,100	61,600	23,100	33,500	5,000	2,050	1,700	350	
Northampton	15,500	15,000	500		12,000	10,000	2,000		5,150	4,900	250	
Perry	9,200	2,200		7,000	7,100	5,100		2,000	3,250	1,250		2,000
Philadelphia	37,000		37,000		3,000		3,000		500		500	
Pike	400		400		600		600		10		10	
Somerset	400	400			800	800			100	100		
Susquehanna	3,000	3,000			3,000	3,000			300	300		
Washington	88,240	31,940	48,300	8,000	74,200	32,500	37,700	4,000	10,375	3,950	6,125	300
Wayne	2,000	2,000			3,000	3,000			200	200		
Westmoreland	14,400	8,200	2,200	4,000	12,800	4,000	2,800	6,000	1,575	1,125	150	300
York	41,600	9,000	32,600		51,800	22,300	29,500		9,975	4,475	5,500	
RHODE ISLAND												
Total	$12,000	$10,000		$2,000	$28,000	$22,000		$6,000	$2,025	$825		$1,200
Kent	1,000	1,000			2,500	2,500						
Newport	5,500	5,500			10,500	10,500			600	600		
Providence	2,500	2,500			7,500	7,500						
Washington	3,000	1,000		2,000	7,500	1,500		6,000	1,425	225		1,200
SOUTH CAROLINA												
Total	$77,646,049	$15,102,247	$62,122,863	$420,939	$28,047,171	$7,635,890	$20,196,266	$165,015	$4,081,739	$1,262,222	$2,791,449	$28,068
Abbeville	1,020,550	137,128	883,422		494,325	96,385	397,940		57,636	15,507	42,129	
Aiken	1,693,503	457,068	1,236,435		814,270	299,690	514,580		151,976	55,922	96,054	
Allendale	646,726	84,898	561,828		206,355	31,750	174,605		47,681	10,728	36,953	
Anderson	3,498,557	295,872	3,201,185	1,500	1,055,520	147,540	906,480	1,500	124,214	21,835	101,879	500
Bamberg	1,462,259	271,795	1,165,419	25,045	513,158	129,565	371,193	12,400	89,167	29,268	57,024	2,875
Barnwell	1,362,704	252,185	1,109,519	1,000	547,966	104,885	438,081	5,000	116,291	26,099	90,042	150
Beaufort	898,272	804,682	58,435	35,155	795,929	746,766	39,034	00,129	110,024	101,595	5,858	2,571
Berkeley	711,568	566,678	143,190	1,700	383,500	326,525	56,975		48,919	42,224	6,695	
Calhoun	1,077,076	182,194	884,532	10,350	324,326	71,130	251,861	1,335	80,486	20,759	59,302	425
Charleston	1,039,020	699,851	295,278	43,900	430,783	341,146	81,937	7,700	79,749	59,951	18,493	1,305

Table 57.—FARMS OPERATED BY NEGROES—NUMBER, ACREAGE, VALUE OF LAND AND BUILDINGS, AND VALUE OF IMPLEMENTS AND MACHINERY, BY TENURE, BY STATES, AND COUNTIES: 1930—Continued

[Counties in which no farms operated by Negroes were reported, are omitted]

COUNTY	NUMBER OF FARMS				ALL LAND IN FARMS (ACRES)				VALUE OF LAND AND BUILDINGS			
	Total	Owners	Tenants	Managers	Total	Owners	Tenants	Managers	Total	Owners	Tenants	Managers
	SOUTH CAROLINA—continued											
Cherokee	1,006	131	875		45,018	7,108	37,910		$1,825,206	$255,447	$1,569,759	
Chester	2,077	260	1,816	1	94,471	22,876	71,585	10	2,145,619	434,068	1,706,551	$5,000
Chesterfield	1,030	276	753	1	56,230	18,422	37,801	7	1,779,880	558,635	1,219,245	2,000
Clarendon	3,118	375	2,740	3	86,458	22,584	63,574	300	2,709,039	673,021	2,026,018	10,000
Colleton	1,515	748	765	2	54,771	31,265	23,445	61	1,356,169	697,644	657,035	1,490
Darlington	1,748	202	1,543	3	76,424	11,587	63,713	1,124	3,297,461	473,063	2,801,713	22,685
Dillon	1,466	99	1,367		55,407	4,585	50,822		3,539,624	271,310	3,268,314	
Dorchester	1,028	474	553	1	40,082	18,431	17,651	4,000	904,645	406,750	472,895	25,000
Edgefield	1,749	207	1,542		87,900	18,107	69,793		2,358,808	308,999	2,049,809	
Fairfield	1,724	359	1,361	4	92,075	36,843	53,268	1,964	1,755,720	532,904	1,179,316	43,500
Florence	2,207	398	1,807	2	84,328	21,066	63,047	215	2,939,970	673,741	2,257,829	8,400
Georgetown	535	425	102	8	19,577	12,389	3,958	3,230	388,755	238,250	74,680	75,825
Greenville	1,988	290	1,696	2	71,907	12,813	59,022	72	4,842,477	818,252	4,001,725	22,500
Greenwood	1,917	231	1,685	1	106,386	14,875	91,481	30	2,587,380	437,655	2,134,225	15,500
Hampton	708	194	512	2	26,980	10,322	16,468	190	575,908	197,808	370,600	7,500
Horry	947	450	497		25,376	14,262	11,114		1,177,547	558,445	619,102	
Jasper	650	366	283	1	22,773	15,714	6,259	800	535,403	326,270	199,133	10,000
Kershaw	1,575	355	1,217	3	77,828	27,184	49,636	1,008	1,780,105	516,575	1,210,230	53,300
Lancaster	1,253	132	1,120	1	65,283	10,615	54,568	100	1,473,526	221,410	1,249,616	2,500
Laurens	2,282	143	2,139		121,317	10,329	110,988		3,033,505	287,785	2,745,718	
Lee	1,654	187	1,467		72,758	10,692	62,066		2,870,004	333,370	2,536,634	
Lexington	754	157	596	1	37,583	9,928	24,155	3,500	1,264,439	299,370	915,069	50,000
McCormick	1,274	138	1,136		86,448	11,401	75,047		1,441,344	201,429	1,239,915	
Marion	1,252	216	1,035	1	40,521	9,048	31,343	130	2,384,782	370,966	2,008,816	5,000
Marlboro	2,147	171	1,974	2	90,774	10,160	80,339	275	5,976,932	453,055	5,506,387	17,490
Newberry	1,784	160	1,624		91,920	11,649	80,271		2,125,877	267,953	1,857,924	
Oconee	702	120	582		28,724	5,782	22,942		1,201,511	256,120	945,391	
Orangeburg	4,693	821	3,872		158,298	48,545	109,753		5,042,511	1,233,200	3,809,311	
Pickens	448	87	361		17,478	3,911	13,567		793,660	176,790	616,870	
Richland	1,561	413	1,147	1	52,632	20,976	31,516	140	1,770,505	624,126	1,137,379	9,000
Saluda	1,332	183	1,149		67,239	14,877	52,362		2,069,540	384,105	1,685,435	
Spartanburg	2,623	307	2,315	1	101,861	13,096	88,727	38	6,154,434	818,580	5,325,854	10,000
Sumter	2,865	505	2,360		95,762	26,384	69,378		3,878,995	961,581	2,917,414	
Union	1,441	144	1,297		79,787	14,143	65,644		2,027,325	246,290	1,781,035	
Williamsburg	3,043	805	2,238		88,473	34,707	53,766		2,261,713	837,602	1,424,111	
York	2,876	214	2,658	4	124,015	13,804	109,736	475	4,446,527	387,835	4,026,142	32,550
	SOUTH DAKOTA											
Total	40	26	13	1	14,228	10,744	2,974	510	$285,425	$163,295	$101,730	$20,400
Beadle	1			1	510			510	20,400			20,400
Brown	1	1			240	240			4,800	4,800		
Brule	1		1		6		6		250		250	
Codington	1		1		320		320		22,700		22,700	
Corson	1	1			240	240			960	960		
Custer	1	1			760	760			3,800	3,800		
Deuel	1		1		440		440		18,000		18,000	
Dewey	2	1	1		895	660	235		15,700	13,200	2,500	
Fall River	2	2			452	452			4,820	4,820		
Gregory	1		1		160		160		6,400		6,400	
Hughes	1	1			960	960			5,000	5,000		
Jackson	1	1			474	474			9,000	9,000		
Jones	1	1			160	160			2,000	2,000		
Kingsbury	1		1		5		5		1,500		1,500	
Lawrence	3	2	1		600	440	160		15,800	10,800	5,000	
Lyman	1	1			100	100			1,900	1,900		
Meade	2	2			480	480			4,400	4,400		
Mellette	2	1	1		1,538	1,360	178		26,780	25,000	1,780	
Perkins	1	1			39	39			195	195		
Spink	1		1		640		640		25,600		25,600	
Sully	10	8	2		4,709	4,219	490		72,420	64,420	8,000	
Tripp	1		1		320		320		5,000		5,000	
Yankton	3	2	1		180	160	20		18,000	13,000	5,000	
	TENNESSEE											
Total	35,123	7,828	27,261	34	1,356,683	419,069	931,482	6,132	$56,339,610	$14,169,523	$41,395,987	$774,100
Anderson	21	16	5		1,034	816	218		24,675	20,475	4,200	
Bedford	294	125	168	1	15,202	6,161	8,801	240	533,555	200,335	319,220	14,000
Benton	21	11	10		1,277	922	355		17,750	7,900	9,850	
Bledsoe	15	9	6		866	739	127		16,000	9,800	6,200	
Blount	48	36	12		2,406	1,624	782		136,450	89,950	46,500	
Bradley	52	30	22		2,931	1,422	1,509		90,875	36,600	54,275	
Campbell	6	4	1	1	271	71	50	150	8,900	3,100	2,000	3,800
Cannon	33	14	19		1,141	548	593		39,030	15,575	23,455	
Carroll	670	216	454		31,613	15,010	16,603		792,225	277,945	514,280	
Carter	22	17	5		575	524	51		45,630	37,830	7,800	
Cheatham	90	50	40		3,935	2,958	977		136,195	88,000	48,195	
Chester	311	54	257		13,721	4,518	9,203		416,628	101,931	314,697	
Claiborne	41	26	15		1,834	1,561	273		59,775	44,075	15,700	
Clay	13	10	3		829	743	86		11,750	5,900	5,850	
Cocke	52	40	12		1,764	1,455	309		73,160	56,950	16,210	
Coffee	51	31	20		1,933	1,253	680		35,530	21,740	13,790	
Crockett	565	75	490		18,110	3,435	14,675		909,587	171,605	737,982	
Davidson	264	170	83	11	8,983	5,321	2,621	1,041	1,060,146	514,396	226,450	319,300
Decatur	96	41	55		4,225	2,788	1,437		82,075	39,315	42,760	
De Kalb	42	15	27		1,075	355	720		48,455	12,775	35,680	

Table 57.—FARMS OPERATED BY NEGROES—NUMBER, ACREAGE, VALUE OF LAND AND BUILDINGS, AND VALUE OF IMPLEMENTS AND MACHINERY, BY TENURE, BY STATES, AND COUNTIES: 1930—Continued

[Counties in which no farms operated by Negroes were reported, are omitted]

COUNTY	VALUE OF LAND ALONE				VALUE OF BUILDINGS				VALUE OF IMPLEMENTS AND MACHINERY			
	Total	Owners	Tenants	Managers	Total	Owners	Tenants	Managers	Total	Owners	Tenants	Managers
SOUTH CAROLINA—continued												
Cherokee	$1,358,058	$176,482	$1,181,576		$467,148	$78,965	$388,183		$63,367	$13,191	$50,176	
Chester	1,455,090	294,613	1,155,777	$4,700	690,529	139,455	550,774	$300	75,118	22,107	52,864	$147
Chesterfield	1,252,437	368,990	882,947	500	527,443	189,645	336,298	1,500	57,665	20,505	37,060	100
Clarendon	1,952,892	475,800	1,468,292	8,800	756,147	197,221	557,726	1,200	154,602	48,144	106,333	125
Colleton	910,340	469,263	440,462	615	445,829	228,381	216,573	875	46,747	28,592	18,130	25
Darlington	2,483,816	322,488	2,142,543	18,785	813,645	150,575	659,170	3,900	72,899	14,705	57,649	545
Dillon	2,737,649	196,985	2,540,664		801,975	74,325	727,650		66,509	6,948	59,561	
Dorchester	530,330	235,440	319,890	25,000	324,315	171,310	153,005		30,146	14,855	15,291	
Edgefield	1,687,055	195,874	1,491,181		671,753	113,125	558,628		115,077	19,460	95,617	
Fairfield	1,093,850	335,974	731,376	26,500	661,870	196,930	447,940	17,000	74,085	24,931	47,379	1,775
Florence	2,065,663	460,574	1,597,689	7,400	875,307	213,167	660,140	1,000	109,167	33,849	74,793	525
Georgetown	204,484	129,905	47,730	26,849	184,271	108,345	26,950	48,976	11,044	9,241	1,378	425
Greenville	3,785,828	602,193	3,167,635	16,000	1,056,649	216,059	834,090	6,500	149,854	35,672	113,182	1,000
Greenwood	1,778,996	234,536	1,536,460	8,000	808,384	203,119	597,765	7,500	111,270	25,194	85,576	500
Hampton	390,438	138,488	246,750	5,200	185,470	59,320	123,850	2,300	39,604	14,332	25,072	200
Horry	853,157	403,195	449,962		324,390	155,250	169,140		34,587	20,066	14,521	
Jasper	344,683	212,645	122,538	9,500	190,720	113,625	76,595	500	48,614	31,248	17,166	200
Kershaw	1,238,440	347,810	847,830	42,800	541,665	168,765	362,400	10,500	88,296	28,251	49,995	10,050
Lancaster	1,034,256	148,660	884,596	1,000	439,270	72,750	365,020	1,500	50,414	10,200	39,614	600
Laurens	2,234,458	185,035	2,049,423		799,045	102,750	696,295		147,362	20,795	126,567	
Lee	2,264,383	235,640	2,028,743		605,621	97,730	507,891		103,312	19,551	83,761	
Lexington	932,191	205,452	677,739	49,000	332,248	93,918	237,330	1,000	45,777	16,173	28,629	975
McCormick	983,783	129,439	854,344		457,561	71,990	385,571		66,442	13,176	53,266	
Marion	1,882,625	270,551	1,607,574	4,500	502,157	100,415	410,242	500	79,122	19,765	59,332	25
Marlboro	4,996,863	325,925	4,660,953	9,990	980,064	127,130	845,434	7,500	100,838	16,937	83,276	625
Newberry	1,519,197	167,753	1,351,444		606,880	100,200	506,480		86,124	16,091	70,033	
Oconee	862,966	169,240	693,726		338,545	86,880	251,665		47,569	16,826	30,743	
Orangeburg	3,834,766	904,714	2,930,052		1,207,745	328,486	879,259		235,162	76,990	158,172	
Pickens	607,825	121,315	486,510		185,835	55,475	130,360		21,753	9,163	12,590	
Richland	1,286,187	412,581	865,406	8,200	484,318	211,545	271,973	800	71,430	31,782	38,648	1,000
Saluda	1,537,440	257,860	1,279,580		532,100	126,245	405,855		82,737	20,769	61,968	
Spartanburg	4,804,808	560,940	4,234,668	9,200	1,349,626	257,640	1,091,186	800	231,007	47,932	182,075	1,000
Sumter	2,927,486	673,434	2,254,052		951,509	288,147	663,362		150,941	51,573	99,368	
Union	1,469,859	165,410	1,304,449		557,466	80,880	476,586		90,681	17,042	73,639	
Williamsburg	1,517,619	557,937	959,682		744,094	279,665	464,429		91,775	37,587	54,188	
York	3,365,882	256,755	3,089,377	19,750	1,080,645	131,080	936,765	12,800	124,499	24,691	99,408	400
SOUTH DAKOTA												
Total	$225,045	$130,265	$80,880	$13,900	$60,380	$33,030	$20,850	$6,500	$32,570	$22,920	$8,650	$1,000
Beadle	13,900			13,900	6,500			6,500	1,000			1,000
Brown	2,800	2,800			2,000	2,000			150	150		
Brule	200		200		50		50					
Codington	19,200		19,000		3,500		3,500		800		800	
Corson	760	760			200	200			75	75		
Custer	3,300	3,300			500	500			1,500	1,500		
Deuel	10,000		10,000		8,000		8,000		700		700	
Dewey	13,200	10,700	2,500		2,500	2,500			3,100	1,500	1,600	
Fall River	2,360	2,360			2,460	2,460			1,150	1,150		
Gregory	5,600		5,600		800		800		200		200	
Hughes	3,500	3,500			1,500	1,500			300	300		
Jackson	6,500	6,500			2,500	2,500			3,000	3,000		
Jones	1,600	1,600			400	400			100	100		
Kingsbury	300		300		1,200		1,200		600		600	
Lawrence	12,750	10,250	2,500		3,050	550	2,500		2,300	1,900	400	
Lyman	1,000	1,000			900	900			25	25		
Meade	4,125	4,125			275	275			520	520		
Mellette	19,780	18,500	1,280		7,000	6,500	500		4,200	4,000	200	
Perkins	180	180			15	15			400	400		
Spink	23,800		23,800		1,800		1,800		1,200		1,200	
Sully	62,690	55,190	7,500		9,730	9,230	500		10,050	7,650	2,400	
Tripp	5,000		5,000						200		200	
Yankton	12,500	9,500	3,000		5,500	3,500	2,000		1,000	650	350	
TENNESSEE												
Total	$42,597,163	$9,769,074	$32,318,639	$509,450	$13,742,447	$4,400,449	$9,077,348	$264,650	$2,978,809	$941,349	$2,016,755	$20,705
Anderson	13,315	10,840	2,475		11,360	9,635	1,725		2,487	2,275	212	
Bedford	385,660	132,545	241,115	12,000	147,895	67,790	78,105	2,000	31,424	14,484	14,940	2,000
Benton	12,475	4,925	7,550		5,275	2,975	2,300		1,605	1,105	500	
Bledsoe	10,550	7,100	3,450		5,450	2,700	2,750		875	500	275	
Blount	89,375	54,025	35,350		47,075	35,925	11,150		12,845	8,120	4,725	
Bradley	67,075	24,500	42,575		23,800	12,100	11,700		6,430	4,455	1,975	
Campbell	5,900	1,500	1,400	3,000	3,000	1,600	600	800	455	85	20	350
Cannon	29,205	10,230	18,975		9,825	5,345	4,480		2,997	2,377	620	
Carroll	594,961	195,400	399,561		197,264	82,545	114,719		60,495	23,795	36,700	
Carter	27,055	21,355	5,700		18,575	16,475	2,100		1,726	1,523	203	
Cheatham	100,370	66,645	33,725		35,825	21,355	14,470		7,991	4,680	3,311	
Chester	322,343	78,721	243,622		94,285	23,210	71,075		31,055	8,760	22,295	
Claiborne	42,090	29,600	12,490		17,685	14,475	3,210		1,738	1,448	290	
Clay	8,550	4,500	4,050		3,200	1,400	1,800		345	225	120	
Cocke	53,085	40,075	13,010		20,075	16,875	3,200		2,339	1,865	474	
Coffee	23,850	13,885	9,965		11,680	7,855	3,825		2,293	1,619	674	
Crockett	699,312	120,405	578,907		210,275	51,200	159,075		44,380	11,350	33,030	
Davidson	753,561	366,436	186,925	200,200	306,585	147,960	39,525	119,100	37,689	21,906	10,408	5,375
Decatur	61,650	27,840	33,810		20,425	11,475	8,950		4,506	2,513	1,993	
De Kalb	42,330	9,560	32,770		6,125	3,215	2,910		1,232	490	742	

TABLE 57.—FARMS OPERATED BY NEGROES—NUMBER, ACREAGE, VALUE OF LAND AND BUILDINGS, AND VALUE OF IMPLEMENTS AND MACHINERY, BY TENURE, BY STATES, AND COUNTIES: 1930—Continued

[Counties in which no farms operated by Negroes were reported, are omitted]

COUNTY	NUMBER OF FARMS				ALL LAND IN FARMS (ACRES)				VALUE OF LAND AND BUILDINGS			
	Total	Owners	Tenants	Managers	Total	Owners	Tenants	Managers	Total	Owners	Tenants	Managers
TENNESSEE—continued												
Dickson	202	109	93		7,703	5,126	2,577		$141,260	$89,550	$51,710	
Dyer	314	45	269		9,410	1,594	7,816		583,600	79,840	503,760	
Fayette	4,432	432	4,000		209,739	33,871	175,868		5,325,794	800,505	4,525,289	
Franklin	160	106	54		5,901	3,707	2,194		238,390	143,220	95,170	
Gibson	1,088	226	862		34,828	10,962	23,866		1,899,111	540,793	1,358,318	
Giles	1,061	309	752		43,690	17,684	26,006		1,514,233	524,683	989,550	
Grainger	30	18	12		1,114	612	502		25,730	13,500	12,230	
Greene	65	25	40		1,599	752	847		110,126	38,550	71,576	
Grundy	1	1			31	31			600	600		
Hamblen	75	55	18	2	2,384	1,506	534	344	150,220	85,280	30,940	$34,000
Hamilton	138	85	52	1	5,837	2,918	2,709	210	381,580	167,480	183,100	31,000
Hancock	27	20	7		843	668	175		22,260	16,310	5,950	
Hardeman	1,446	195	1,251		86,636	21,605	65,031		1,502,521	317,950	1,184,571	
Hardin	185	52	133		7,757	3,259	4,498		179,040	66,700	112,340	
Hawkins	85	73	12		2,732	2,261	471		106,325	81,125	25,200	
Haywood	3,512	433	3,079		127,037	27,173	99,864		4,938,844	1,020,446	3,918,398	
Henderson	232	77	155		14,543	7,985	6,558		242,310	102,350	139,960	
Henry	418	171	247		24,052	13,196	10,856		548,693	226,258	322,435	
Hickman	57	31	26		3,228	1,958	1,270		72,855	51,055	21,800	
Houston	46	27	19		2,081	1,529	552		32,805	19,820	12,985	
Humphreys	27	18	9		1,622	1,114	508		51,290	14,740	36,550	
Jackson	9	5	4		323	213	110		13,600	6,900	6,700	
Jefferson	70	56	12	2	2,946	1,960	779	207	180,575	110,635	55,940	14,000
Johnson	20	17	3		408	389	19		39,925	37,725	2,200	
Knox	105	67	35	3	3,882	2,274	1,487	121	334,440	159,430	144,510	30,500
Lake	276	1	275		8,500	31	8,469		737,815	3,800	734,015	
Lauderdale	1,618	149	1,469		47,316	8,472	38,844		2,568,265	428,825	2,139,440	
Lawrence	53	32	21		2,375	1,544	831		48,900	32,800	16,100	
Lewis	9	7	2		471	420	51		6,700	4,200	2,500	
Lincoln	476	99	376	1	19,943	5,423	14,437	83	821,505	199,970	616,535	5,000
Loudon	54	27	27		2,595	770	1,825		75,070	24,100	50,970	
McMinn	109	87	22		4,602	3,640	962		158,380	106,400	51,980	
McNairy	184	52	132		11,244	3,947	7,297		214,885	63,425	151,460	
Macon	53	27	26		1,867	1,191	676		40,900	22,300	18,600	
Madison	1,997	362	1,635		84,264	26,749	57,515		3,464,388	825,465	2,638,923	
Marion	35	21	14		1,342	814	528		43,410	20,160	23,250	
Marshall	199	64	135		9,750	3,271	6,479		332,689	88,969	243,720	
Maury	602	309	288	5	23,337	10,494	11,256	1,587	937,170	356,010	454,160	127,000
Meigs	47	30	17		4,573	3,200	1,373		79,385	39,760	39,625	
Monroe	67	52	15		2,165	1,582	583		87,505	63,655	23,850	
Montgomery	1,022	323	697	2	39,844	18,072	20,403	1,369	1,303,945	458,250	740,695	105,000
Moore	60	16	44		2,272	781	1,491		71,880	21,100	50,780	
Morgan	2	2			79	79			1,100	1,100		
Obion	118	24	93	1	5,542	1,197	3,817	528	370,330	64,000	246,330	60,000
Overton	15	12	3		448	355	93		9,875	9,075	800	
Perry	25	11	14		1,374	832	542		38,150	14,450	23,700	
Pickett	1		1		30		30		300		300	
Polk	16	5	11		940	536	404		28,800	12,300	16,500	
Putnam	59	41	18		1,908	1,316	592		87,575	59,450	28,125	
Rhea	27	20	7		1,034	856	178		40,645	32,300	8,345	
Roane	25	24	1		1,259	1,204	55		21,225	21,025	200	
Robertson	789	136	653		23,839	7,796	16,043		1,209,596	337,429	872,167	
Rutherford	979	392	586	1	34,376	17,307	16,910	159	1,356,430	514,585	833,845	8,000
Scott	1	1			45	45			1,800	1,800		
Sequatchie	2	1	1		90	65	25		2,800	2,000	800	
Sevier	15	9	6		688	324	364		49,750	18,950	30,800	
Shelby	5,548	542	5,003	3	157,088	22,366	134,629	93	12,657,124	1,694,661	10,939,963	22,500
Smith	79	31	48		2,708	1,590	1,118		97,350	43,330	54,020	
Stewart	65	21	44		3,001	1,670	1,331		64,696	27,475	37,221	
Sullivan	9	5	4		131	87	44		15,500	8,900	6,600	
Sumner	397	248	149		13,084	7,818	5,266		644,215	340,890	303,325	
Tipton	2,144	295	1,849		70,017	15,793	54,224		3,265,051	692,552	2,572,499	
Trousdale	138	69	69		4,539	2,663	1,876		201,850	112,040	89,810	
Union	1		1		75		75		1,000		1,000	
Van Buren	7	2	5		627	344	283		14,000	2,000	12,000	
Warren	100	79	21		5,464	4,439	1,025		122,695	98,160	24,535	
Washington	22	10	12		610	273	337		44,485	21,160	23,325	
Wayne	21	2	19		795	62	733		14,475	1,050	13,425	
Weakley	203	68	135		7,184	3,259	3,925		277,800	105,000	172,800	
White	50	32	18		2,729	1,291	1,438		91,995	61,750	30,245	
Williamson	394	197	197		19,491	9,927	9,564		775,715	336,565	439,150	
Wilson	498	248	250		16,977	8,603	8,374		665,973	304,695	361,278	
TEXAS												
Total	85,940	20,578	65,275	87	4,429,671	1,463,991	2,928,922	36,758	$179,391,988	$44,610,852	$133,323,694	$1,457,442
Anderson	1,765	561	1,204		97,801	39,982	57,819		2,227,388	848,324	1,379,064	
Angelina	160	63	97		6,476	1,964	4,512		225,650	72,325	153,325	
Aransas	1	1			2	2			200	200		
Atascosa	20	6	13	1	9,619	362	1,257	8,000	169,310	11,400	37,910	120,000
Austin	847	183	664		36,815	10,908	25,907		2,067,995	511,750	1,556,245	
Bastrop	1,139	270	866	3	76,477	22,973	52,233	1,271	2,725,734	600,785	2,101,209	23,740
Baylor	2		2		620		620		21,000		21,000	
Bee	26	7	19		2,456	564	1,892		120,165	27,110	93,055	
Bell	403	34	367	2	18,284	2,241	15,823	220	1,695,115	160,590	1,515,125	19,400
Bexar	94	42	49	3	5,942	1,996	3,546	400	496,920	89,010	302,710	105,200

Table 57.—FARMS OPERATED BY NEGROES—NUMBER, ACREAGE, VALUE OF LAND AND BUILDINGS, AND VALUE OF IMPLEMENTS AND MACHINERY, BY TENURE, BY STATES, AND COUNTIES: 1930—Continued

[Counties in which no farms operated by Negroes were reported, are omitted]

COUNTY	VALUE OF LAND ALONE				VALUE OF BUILDINGS				VALUE OF IMPLEMENTS AND MACHINERY			
	Total	Owners	Tenants	Managers	Total	Owners	Tenants	Managers	Total	Owners	Tenants	Managers
TENNESSEE—continued												
Dickson	$92,985	$57,465	$35,520	----	$48,275	$32,085	$16,190	----	$7,733	$5,403	$2,330	----
Dyer	479,370	56,215	423,155	----	104,230	23,625	80,605	----	34,960	8,160	26,800	----
Fayette	4,016,274	581,490	3,434,784	----	1,309,520	219,015	1,090,505	----	401,615	79,706	321,909	----
Franklin	161,925	94,170	67,755	----	76,465	49,050	27,415	----	13,035	9,340	3,695	----
Gibson	1,438,676	380,258	1,058,418	----	460,435	160,535	299,900	----	120,042	34,092	85,950	----
Giles	1,095,248	352,013	743,235	----	418,985	172,670	246,315	----	77,184	35,719	41,465	----
Grainger	18,445	9,490	8,955	----	7,285	4,010	3,275	----	1,050	475	575	----
Greene	81,076	28,100	52,976	----	29,050	10,450	18,600	----	7,105	3,280	3,825	----
Grundy	300	300	----	----	300	300	----	----	----	----	----	----
Hamblen	90,595	53,855	19,240	$17,500	59,625	31,425	11,700	$16,500	9,320	5,985	2,545	$790
Hamilton	282,280	107,480	145,300	29,500	99,300	60,000	37,800	1,500	11,819	5,184	5,035	1,600
Hancock	16,810	11,885	4,925	----	5,450	4,425	1,025	----	1,010	765	245	----
Hardeman	1,059,275	210,699	848,576	----	443,246	107,251	335,995	----	112,815	38,020	74,795	----
Hardin	134,390	41,950	92,440	----	44,650	24,750	19,900	----	12,325	6,815	5,510	----
Hawkins	72,815	54,650	18,165	----	33,510	26,475	7,035	----	5,989	5,056	933	----
Haywood	3,456,154	675,591	2,780,563	----	1,482,690	344,855	1,137,835	----	337,514	84,618	252,896	----
Henderson	162,035	66,900	95,135	----	80,275	35,450	44,825	----	19,562	9,462	10,100	----
Henry	387,853	148,993	238,860	----	160,840	77,265	83,575	----	29,622	16,178	13,344	----
Hickman	59,675	40,725	18,950	----	13,180	10,330	2,850	----	4,458	3,368	1,090	----
Houston	21,955	13,170	8,785	----	10,850	6,650	4,200	----	914	574	340	----
Humphreys	44,800	11,100	33,700	----	6,490	3,640	2,850	----	2,195	720	1,475	----
Jackson	10,500	5,700	4,800	----	3,100	1,200	1,900	----	335	55	280	----
Jefferson	128,325	74,835	45,490	8,000	52,250	35,800	10,450	6,000	7,475	5,200	1,650	625
Johnson	14,475	12,275	2,200	----	25,450	25,450	----	----	450	425	25	----
Knox	216,190	93,480	109,710	13,000	118,250	65,950	34,800	17,500	8,933	6,098	2,285	550
Lake	646,473	3,100	643,373	----	91,342	700	90,642	----	23,438	110	23,328	----
Lauderdale	2,025,452	326,407	1,699,045	----	542,813	102,418	440,395	----	115,527	25,779	89,748	----
Lawrence	32,065	18,915	13,150	----	16,835	13,885	2,950	----	2,542	1,927	615	----
Lewis	5,370	2,870	2,500	----	1,330	1,330	----	----	490	415	75	----
Lincoln	590,685	131,735	455,000	3,950	230,820	68,235	161,535	1,050	41,113	12,879	28,084	150
Loudon	55,445	14,200	41,245	----	19,625	9,900	9,725	----	2,470	1,245	1,225	----
McMinn	97,085	60,130	36,955	----	61,295	46,270	15,025	----	10,234	8,654	1,580	----
McNairy	164,150	46,180	117,970	----	50,735	17,245	33,490	----	12,905	4,780	8,125	----
Macon	26,955	14,155	12,800	----	13,945	8,145	5,800	----	2,542	1,190	1,352	----
Madison	2,757,063	606,855	2,150,208	----	707,325	218,610	488,715	----	153,909	47,640	106,269	----
Marion	30,075	12,475	17,600	----	13,335	7,685	5,650	----	2,550	1,445	1,105	----
Marshall	232,859	56,399	176,460	----	99,830	32,570	67,260	----	16,929	6,267	10,662	----
Maury	665,380	232,490	328,790	104,100	271,790	123,520	125,370	22,900	47,742	24,842	19,275	3,625
Meigs	66,545	32,420	34,125	----	12,840	7,340	5,500	----	4,538	2,500	2,038	----
Monroe	58,445	39,495	18,950	----	29,060	24,160	4,900	----	7,488	6,328	1,160	----
Montgomery	814,030	288,810	481,720	43,500	489,915	169,440	258,975	61,500	50,364	19,267	28,147	2,950
Moore	55,195	15,675	39,520	----	16,685	5,425	11,260	----	4,365	1,464	2,901	----
Morgan	1,000	1,000	----	----	100	100	----	----	10	10	----	----
Obion	283,805	42,300	189,505	52,000	86,525	21,700	56,825	8,000	15,690	2,790	10,900	2,000
Overton	7,105	6,455	650	----	2,770	2,620	150	----	395	255	140	----
Perry	27,800	10,000	17,800	----	10,350	4,450	5,900	----	3,193	1,353	1,840	----
Pickett	200	----	200	----	100	----	100	----	25	----	25	----
Polk	20,725	9,700	11,025	----	8,075	2,600	5,475	----	755	570	185	----
Putnam	61,970	40,725	21,245	----	25,605	18,725	6,880	----	3,741	3,056	685	----
Rhea	32,995	25,700	7,295	----	7,650	6,600	1,050	----	1,800	1,550	250	----
Roane	11,625	11,525	100	----	9,600	9,500	100	----	1,113	1,038	75	----
Robertson	869,966	229,529	640,437	----	339,630	107,900	231,730	----	57,180	19,065	38,115	----
Rutherford	1,048,977	367,110	675,867	6,000	307,453	147,475	157,978	2,000	76,335	26,563	49,572	200
Scott	1,300	1,300	----	----	500	500	----	----	20	20	----	----
Sequatchie	1,100	800	300	----	1,700	1,200	500	----	310	300	10	----
Sevier	37,795	9,575	28,220	----	11,955	9,375	2,580	----	2,805	1,895	910	----
Shelby	10,305,371	1,265,123	9,023,548	16,700	2,351,753	429,538	1,916,415	5,800	485,572	99,686	385,396	490
Smith	69,035	26,530	42,505	----	28,315	16,800	11,515	----	3,365	1,550	1,815	----
Stewart	45,491	16,790	28,701	----	19,205	10,685	8,520	----	2,320	1,220	1,100	----
Sullivan	9,740	5,200	4,540	----	5,760	3,700	2,060	----	1,300	1,050	250	----
Sumner	437,730	206,705	231,025	----	206,485	134,185	72,300	----	28,537	17,277	11,260	----
Tipton	2,521,680	479,025	2,042,655	----	743,371	213,527	529,844	----	213,973	63,286	150,687	----
Trousdale	140,985	75,200	65,785	----	60,865	36,840	24,025	----	9,030	4,920	4,110	----
Union	800	----	800	----	200	----	200	----	65	----	65	----
Van Buren	9,300	1,300	8,000	----	4,700	700	4,000	----	580	140	440	----
Warren	85,190	67,305	17,885	----	37,505	30,855	6,650	----	6,211	5,317	894	----
Washington	31,795	15,210	16,585	----	12,690	5,950	6,740	----	2,385	880	1,505	----
Wayne	11,000	600	10,400	----	3,475	450	3,025	----	1,055	125	930	----
Weakley	192,815	64,750	128,065	----	84,985	40,250	44,735	----	11,896	4,560	7,336	----
White	62,345	40,575	21,770	----	29,650	21,175	8,475	----	4,901	3,156	1,745	----
Williamson	582,935	237,345	345,590	----	192,780	99,220	93,560	----	34,049	20,591	13,458	----
Wilson	476,178	206,510	269,668	----	189,795	98,185	91,610	----	28,785	14,121	14,664	----
TEXAS												
Total	**$148,603,812**	**$33,863,468**	**$113,489,484**	**$1,250,860**	**$30,788,176**	**$10,747,384**	**$19,834,210**	**$206,582**	**$7,731,019**	**$2,583,444**	**$5,099,390**	**$48,185**
Anderson	1,065,275	585,583	1,019,692	----	622,113	262,741	359,372	----	149,119	70,186	78,933	----
Angelina	167,45	44,955	122,540	----	58,155	27,370	30,785	----	11,595	5,045	6,550	----
Aransas	50	50	----	----	150	150	----	----	----	----	----	----
Atascosa	160,190	8,580	32,810	118,800	9,120	2,820	5,100	1,200	2,645	925	1,620	100
Austin	1,673,035	392,843	1,280,192	----	394,960	118,907	276,053	----	96,052	34,100	61,952	----
Bastrop	2,312,818	461,990	1,827,768	23,060	412,916	138,795	273,441	680	112,575	26,390	86,160	25
Baylor	18,800	----	18,800	----	2,200	----	2,200	----	350	----	350	----
Bee	106,140	21,500	84,640	----	14,025	5,610	8,415	----	3,154	765	2,389	----
Bell	1,484,710	134,040	1,333,070	17,600	210,405	26,550	182,055	1,800	55,521	8,044	47,067	410
Bexar	424,461	474,492	266,619	83,350	72,459	14,518	36,091	21,850	9,865	2,335	7,255	275

TABLE 57.—FARMS OPERATED BY NEGROES—NUMBER, ACREAGE, VALUE OF LAND AND BUILDINGS, AND VALUE OF IMPLEMENTS AND MACHINERY, BY TENURE, BY STATES, AND COUNTIES: 1930—Continued

[Counties in which no farms operated by Negroes were reported, are omitted]

COUNTY	NUMBER OF FARMS				ALL LAND IN FARMS (ACRES)				VALUE OF LAND AND BUILDINGS			
	Total	Owners	Tenants	Managers	Total	Owners	Tenants	Managers	Total	Owners	Tenants	Managers
	TEXAS—continued											
Blanco	26	18	8		6, 004	5, 127	877		$64, 850	$49, 750	$15, 100	
Bosque	47	12	35		4, 566	1, 882	2, 684		177, 925	44, 300	133, 625	
Bowie	1, 962	403	1, 557	2	72, 671	20, 806	51, 732	133	3, 267, 850	900, 960	2, 355, 090	$11, 800
Brazoria	981	381	597	3	38, 800	13, 700	20, 234	4, 866	2, 006, 959	788, 278	1, 138, 571	80, 110
Brazos	1, 237	191	1, 044	2	65, 486	15, 281	49, 922	283	2, 428, 173	456, 189	1, 960, 984	11, 000
Briscoe	5		5		251		251		18, 225		$18, 225	
Brooks	1	1			100	100			3, 500	3, 500		
Brown	1	1			132	132			6, 600	6, 600		
Burleson	1, 313	325	988		69, 684	26, 350	43, 334		3, 432, 422	1, 042, 048	2, 390, 374	
Burnet	7	3	4		593	238	355		23, 250	9, 500	13, 750	
Caldwell	546	144	401	1	34, 796	11, 415	23, 226	155	1, 767, 000	423, 065	1, 334, 635	9, 300
Calhoun	24	2	22		1, 755	7	1, 748		112, 770	2, 300	110, 470	
Callahan	4	1	3		581	320	261		25, 900	6, 400	19, 500	
Cameron	14		14		530		530		131, 525		131, 525	
Camp	618	205	413		29, 800	12, 330	17, 470		670, 155	274, 988	395, 167	
Cass	2, 073	602	1, 471		109, 161	48. 744	60, 417		2, 219, 951	963, 546	1, 256, 405	
Chambers	155	99	56		28, 878	26, 581	2, 297		519, 109	428, 644	90, 465	
Cherokee	1, 862	486	1, 376		90, 658	30, 485	60, 173		2, 690, 724	960, 357	1, 730, 367	
Childress	17		15	2	1, 676		1, 316	360	121, 560		84, 060	37, 500
Clay	21	17	4		771	648	123		68, 260	56, 660	11, 600	
Coke	4		4		228		228		6, 970		6, 970	
Coleman	16		16		842		842		68, 180		68, 180	
Collin	310	21	289		12, 755	1, 209	11, 546		1, 126, 610	70, 385	1. 056, 225	
Collingsworth	59	2	57		3, 592	170	3, 422		208, 700	3, 600	205, 100	
Colorado	776	117	655	4	37, 918	8, 248	28, 199	1, 471	1, 644, 627	359, 957	1, 241, 190	43, 480
Comal	9	1	8		1, 111	180	931		43, 500	8, 000	35, 500	
Concho	15		15		1, 024		1, 024		61, 040		61, 040	
Cooke	65	10	55		3, 322	573	2, 749		156, 472	29, 723	126, 749	
Coryell	15	9	6		1, 382	899	483		89, 455	51, 955	37, 500	
Cottle	12		12		1, 113		1, 113		54, 360		54, 360	
Crosby	31		31		2, 253		2, 253		118, 625		118, 625	
Dallas	657	76	578	3	27, 118	4, 114	22, 686	318	3, 504, 665	541, 130	2, 920, 785	42, 750
Dawson	30		30		1, 557		1, 557		82, 600		82, 600	
Delta	159	18	141		4, 674	608	4, 066		359, 710	22, 325	337, 385	
Denton	186	37	148	1	12, 597	3, 938	8, 499	160	583, 635	139, 050	429, 585	15, 000
De Witt	397	119	275	3	35, 888	10, 250	22, 948	2, 690	1, 647, 105	441, 100	1, 118, 005	88, 000
Dickens	27	1	26		2, 814	78	2, 736		112, 270	4, 800	107, 470	
Dimmit	1	1			859	859			17, 180	17, 180		
Donley	7		7		98		98		6, 450		6, 450	
Ellis	1, 174	32	1, 138	4	46, 853	1, 368	45, 194	291	4, 560, 068	133, 400	4, 403, 968	22, 700
El Paso	9	4	5		268	105	163		69, 650	32, 050	37, 600	
Erath	12	5	7		892	257	635		28, 750	11, 300	17, 450	
Falls	1, 885	272	1, 610	3	82, 273	13, 134	68, 323	816	5, 390, 450	753, 672	4, 609, 428	27, 350
Fannin	441	94	346	1	23, 101	6, 849	16, 154	98	1, 013, 626	216, 595	791, 031	6, 000
Fayette	1, 045	219	826		59, 300	15, 987	43, 313		2, 612, 361	544, 616	2, 067, 745	
Fisher	48	3	45		4, 350	347	4, 003		226, 915	21, 500	205, 415	
Floyd	8		8		385		385		15, 400		15, 400	
Foard	2		2		105		105		5, 800		5, 800	
Fort Bend	1, 824	361	1, 463		86, 629	22, 704	63, 925		6, 059, 733	1, 363, 801	4, 695, 932	
Franklin	84	20	64		4, 109	1, 265	2, 844		113, 550	34, 580	78, 970	
Freestone	1, 689	463	1, 226		109, 501	36, 560	72, 941		2, 853, 628	935, 601	1, 918, 027	
Frio	10	4	6		2, 430	1, 365	1, 065		59, 935	31, 535	28, 400	
Galveston	60	31	29		1, 199	328	871		159, 100	56, 550	102, 550	
Garza	6		6		123		123		3, 880		3, 880	
Gillespie	8	2	6		463	45	418		23, 000	1, 800	21, 200	
Goliad	103	45	58		6, 367	2, 836	3, 531		233, 865	110, 200	123, 665	
Gonzales	1, 065	264	800	1	68, 523	22, 778	45, 693	52	2, 460, 289	655, 019	1, 803, 970	1, 300
Gray	1		1		100		100		3, 500		3, 500	
Grayson	251	66	184	1	11, 797	2, 531	8, 964	302	624, 300	135, 415	467, 885	21, 000
Gregg	1, 220	426	793	1	62, 996	29, 897	33, 061	38	1, 800, 293	852, 238	946, 555	1, 500
Grimes	1, 471	271	1, 200		73, 659	18, 022	55, 637		2, 461, 360	495, 565	1, 965, 795	
Guadalupe	609	171	436	2	53, 036	17, 833	31, 953	3, 250	2, 546, 540	625, 855	1, 824, 435	96, 250
Hale	4		4		242		242		10, 880		10, 880	
Hall	86	1	85		2, 562	16	2, 546		183, 110	1, 600	181, 510	
Hardeman	35		35		2, 787		2, 787		150 175		150, 175	
Hardin	36	27	8	1	762	587	116	59	49, 630	28, 750	8, 880	12, 000
Harris	651	207	438	6	32, 323	6, 483	25, 399	441	5, 405, 136	841, 761	4, 378, 875	184, 500
Harrison	4, 990	1, 443	3, 554	3	220, 764	94, 967	125, 479	318	5, 873, 158	2, 539, 019	3, 324, 839	9, 300
Haskell	23	1	22		2, 981	190	2, 791		130, 280	16, 000	114, 280	
Hays	69	28	41		3, 874	1, 197	2, 677		263, 895	75, 260	188, 635	
Hemphill	1		1		266		266		7, 980		7, 980	
Henderson	850	217	633		47, 083	16, 749	30, 334		1, 311, 540	395, 170	916, 370	
Hidalgo	7		7		520		520		109, 300		109, 300	
Hill	575	43	532		23, 075	3, 081	19, 994		1, 687, 175	149, 645	1, 537, 530	
Hockley	6	1	5		272	2	270		13, 350	1, 000	12, 350	
Hood	8	5	3		405	175	230		14, 100	5, 000	9, 100	
Hopkins	323	101	222		19, 171	7, 954	11, 217		544. 871	207, 375	337, 496	
Houston	2, 627	550	2, 077		114, 704	43, 474	71, 230		2, 924, 311	905, 172	2, 019, 139	
Howard	2		2		180		180		7, 600		7, 600	
Hudspeth	1	1			1, 640	1, 640			104, 850	104, 850		
Hunt	426	54	372		17, 578	3, 555	14, 023		1, 050. 005	194, 305	855, 700	
Jackson	277	88	189		22, 455	10, 578	11, 877		740, 375	243, 125	497, 250	
Jasper	397	280	117		15, 424	12, 106	3, 318		400, 620	299, 810	100, 810	
Jefferson	103	16	82	5	6, 718	724	4, 922	1, 072	534, 670	67, 400	396, 770	70, 500
Jim Hogg	1		1		100		100		2, 500		2, 500	
Jim Wells	9		9		3, 936		3, 936		140, 645		140, 645	
Johnson	87	17	70		4, 741	952	3, 789		347, 485	49, 320	298, 165	
Jones	20	1	19		1, 894	125	1, 769		124, 050	6, 750	117, 300	
Karnes	95	23	72		10, 532	1, 856	8, 676		446, 795	78, 510	368, 285	
Kaufman	1, 403	97	1, 305	1	71, 028	6, 450	64, 536	42	3, 927, 205	249, 037	3, 670, 168	8, 000

TABLE 57.—FARMS OPERATED BY NEGROES—NUMBER, ACREAGE, VALUE OF LAND AND BUILDINGS, AND VALUE OF IMPLEMENTS AND MACHINERY, BY TENURE, BY STATES, AND COUNTIES: 1930—Continued

[Counties in which no farms operated by Negroes were reported, are omitted]

COUNTY	VALUE OF LAND ALONE				VALUE OF BUILDINGS				VALUE OF IMPLEMENTS AND MACHINERY			
	Total	Owners	Tenants	Managers	Total	Owners	Tenants	Managers	Total	Owners	Tenants	Managers
					TEXAS—continued							
Blanco	$52, 499	$39, 550	$12, 949	-	$12, 351	$10, 200	$2, 151	-	$1, 569	$1, 169	$400	-
Bosque	151, 560	37, 385	114, 175	-	26, 365	6, 915	19, 450	-	8, 685	2, 360	6, 325	-
Bowie	2, 616, 636	697, 998	1, 909, 238	$9, 400	651, 214	202, 962	445, 852	$2, 400	137, 271	36, 061	97, 710	$3, 500
Brazoria	1, 611, 693	599, 338	937, 095	75, 260	395, 266	188, 940	201, 476	4, 850	103, 890	47, 678	52, 712	3, 500
Brazos	1, 962, 651	331, 634	1, 623, 817	7, 200	465, 522	124, 555	337, 167	3, 800	145, 072	34, 011	109, 961	1, 100
Briscoe	$16, 575	-	$16, 575	-	1, 650	-	1, 650	-	1, 250	-	1, 250	-
Brooks	3, 000	3, 000	-	-	500	500	-	-	800	800	-	-
Brown	6, 100	6, 100	-	-	500	500	-	-	100	100	-	-
Burleson	2, 992, 889	877, 995	2, 114, 894	-	439, 533	164, 053	275, 480	-	123, 794	46, 023	77, 771	-
Burnet	17, 050	5, 600	11, 450	-	6, 200	3, 900	2, 300	-	1, 880	705	1, 175	-
Caldwell	1, 524, 175	338, 465	1, 176, 810	8, 900	242, 825	84, 600	157, 825	400	81, 218	25, 540	55, 378	300
Calhoun	102, 770	1, 475	101, 295	-	10, 000	825	9, 175	-	6, 200	25	6, 175	-
Callahan	16, 150	5, 400	10, 750	-	9, 750	1, 000	8, 750	-	675	400	275	-
Cameron	122, 640	-	122, 640	-	8, 885	-	8, 885	-	5, 515	-	5, 515	-
Camp	474, 173	185, 381	288, 792	-	195, 982	89, 607	106, 375	-	35, 108	16, 535	18, 573	-
Cass	1, 597, 274	664, 366	932, 908	-	622, 677	299, 180	323, 497	-	132, 666	67, 025	65, 641	-
Chambers	456, 884	383, 669	73, 215	-	62, 225	44, 975	17, 250	-	19, 030	12, 015	7, 015	-
Cherokee	2, 044, 268	690, 227	1, 354, 041	-	646, 456	270, 130	376, 326	-	181, 160	87, 453	93, 707	-
Childress	99, 960	-	72, 960	27, 000	21, 600	-	11, 100	10, 500	3, 455	-	2, 505	950
Clay	60, 560	49, 360	11, 200	-	7, 700	7, 300	400	-	5, 950	5, 800	150	-
Coke	5, 920	-	5, 920	-	1, 050	-	1, 050	-	650	-	650	-
Coleman	65, 355	-	65, 355	-	2, 825	-	2, 825	-	2, 355	-	2, 355	-
Collin	1, 016, 775	54, 660	962, 115	-	109, 835	15, 725	94, 110	-	28, 945	2, 330	26, 615	-
Collingsworth	198, 255	3, 475	194, 780	-	10, 445	125	10, 320	-	5, 460	-	5, 460	-
Colorado	1, 367, 697	294, 392	1, 034, 475	38, 830	276, 930	65, 565	206, 715	4, 650	91, 556	15, 167	70, 249	6, 140
Comal	38, 150	7, 650	30, 500	-	5, 350	350	5, 000	-	2, 150	350	1, 800	-
Concho	55, 490	-	55, 490	-	5, 550	-	5, 550	-	3, 225	-	3, 225	-
Cooke	132, 038	19, 550	112, 488	-	24, 434	10, 173	14, 261	-	5, 931	879	5, 052	-
Coryell	82, 555	47, 980	34, 575	-	6, 900	3, 975	2, 925	-	2, 700	2, 260	440	-
Cottle	46, 260	-	46, 260	-	8, 100	-	8, 100	-	3, 500	-	3, 500	-
Crosby	111, 050	-	111, 050	-	7, 575	-	7, 575	-	2, 225	-	2, 225	-
Dallas	3, 179, 350	463, 235	2, 674, 715	41, 400	325, 315	77, 895	246, 070	1, 350	61, 832	13, 390	48, 192	250
Dawson	73, 470	-	73, 470	-	9, 130	-	9, 130	-	2, 065	-	2, 065	-
Delta	316, 435	13, 150	303, 285	-	43, 275	9, 175	34, 100	-	12, 785	783	12, 002	-
Denton	503, 685	108, 775	380, 510	14, 400	79, 950	30, 275	49, 075	600	15, 019	4, 375	10, 144	500
De Witt	1, 355, 138	346, 135	922, 103	86, 900	291, 967	94, 965	195, 902	1, 100	77, 701	29, 265	45, 786	2, 650
Dickens	106, 370	4, 500	101, 870	-	5, 900	300	5, 600	-	2, 550	200	2, 350	-
Dimmit	16, 880	16, 880	-	-	300	300	-	-	-	-	-	-
Donley	6, 100	-	6, 100	-	350	-	350	-	500	-	500	-
Ellis	4, 106, 718	111, 525	3, 974, 643	20, 550	453, 350	21, 875	429, 325	2, 150	108, 550	4, 040	103, 515	995
El Paso	56, 350	21, 800	34, 550	-	13, 300	10, 250	3, 050	-	4, 825	3, 350	1, 475	-
Erath	20, 425	6, 250	14, 175	-	8, 325	5, 050	3, 275	-	3, 365	2, 300	1, 065	-
Falls	4, 727, 325	605, 927	4, 099, 498	21, 900	663, 125	147, 745	509, 930	5, 450	175, 270	228, 625	142, 085	4, 560
Fannin	844, 026	156, 800	683, 226	4, 000	169, 600	59, 795	107, 805	2, 000	39, 400	13, 197	26, 103	100
Fayette	2, 178, 206	426, 351	1, 751, 855	-	434, 155	118, 265	315, 890	-	108, 887	33, 098	75, 789	-
Fisher	207, 090	19, 875	187, 215	-	19, 825	1, 625	18, 200	-	9, 075	750	8, 325	-
Floyd	13, 800	-	13, 800	-	1, 600	-	1, 600	-	1, 550	-	1, 550	-
Foard	4, 750	-	4, 750	-	1, 050	-	1, 050	-	250	-	250	-
Fort Bend	5, 225, 705	1, 087, 754	4, 137, 951	-	834, 028	276, 047	557, 981	-	239, 252	71, 004	168, 248	-
Franklin	93, 505	29, 295	64, 210	-	20, 045	5, 285	14, 760	-	4, 466	1, 677	2, 789	-
Freestone	2, 256, 448	702, 371	1, 554, 077	-	597, 180	233, 230	363, 950	-	120, 310	48, 233	72, 077	-
Frio	49, 435	24, 335	25, 100	-	10, 500	7, 200	3, 300	-	2, 250	1, 100	1, 150	-
Galveston	114, 025	37, 450	76, 575	-	45, 075	19, 100	25, 975	-	7, 452	4, 342	3, 110	-
Garza	3, 580	-	3, 580	-	300	-	300	-	125	-	125	-
Gillespie	19, 450	900	18, 550	-	3, 550	900	2, 650	-	1, 540	130	1, 410	-
Goliad	171, 780	71, 425	100, 355	-	62, 085	38, 775	23, 310	-	18, 578	9, 786	8, 792	-
Gonzales	2, 105, 136	531, 164	1, 572, 672	1, 300	355, 153	123, 855	231, 298	-	94, 828	25, 206	69, 572	50
Gray	3, 000	-	3, 000	-	500	-	500	-	150	-	150	-
Grayson	518, 215	100, 865	405, 350	12, 000	106, 085	34, 550	62, 535	9, 000	16, 903	3, 730	13, 173	-
Gregg	1, 388, 198	626, 098	760, 700	1, 400	412, 095	226, 140	185, 855	100	97, 136	55, 927	41, 059	150
Grimes	1, 876, 458	362, 295	1, 514, 163	-	584, 902	133, 270	451, 632	-	124, 938	39, 082	85, 856	-
Guadalupe	2, 252, 106	526, 303	1, 634, 303	91, 500	294, 434	99, 552	190, 132	4, 750	73, 118	25, 400	45, 218	2, 500
Hale	10, 280	-	10, 280	-	600	-	600	-	250	-	250	-
Hall	164, 850	800	164, 050	-	18, 260	800	17, 460	-	7, 908	500	7, 408	-
Hardeman	135, 975	-	135, 975	-	14, 200	-	14, 200	-	5, 655	-	5, 655	-
Hardin	35, 990	17, 885	6, 855	11, 250	13, 640	10, 865	2, 025	750	2, 011	1, 780	231	-
Harris	4, 945, 226	711, 691	4, 084, 535	149, 000	459, 910	130, 070	294, 340	35, 500	80, 873	27, 730	49, 368	3, 775
Harrison	4, 183, 117	1, 720, 729	2, 454, 938	7, 450	1, 690, 041	818, 290	869, 901	1, 850	305, 470	157, 878	146, 462	1, 130
Haskell	118, 380	14, 250	104, 130	-	11, 900	1, 750	10, 150	-	6, 125	100	6, 025	-
Hays	213, 470	55, 260	158, 210	-	50, 425	20, 000	30, 425	-	11, 203	3, 525	7, 678	-
Hemphill	7, 180	-	7, 180	-	800	-	800	-	900	-	900	-
Henderson	1, 023, 430	288, 530	734, 900	-	288, 110	106, 640	181, 470	-	58, 220	21, 556	36, 664	-
Hidalgo	107, 025	-	107, 025	-	2, 275	-	2, 275	-	1, 500	-	1, 500	-
Hill	1, 484, 065	122, 245	1, 361, 820	-	203, 110	27, 400	175, 710	-	58, 184	8, 895	49, 289	-
Hockley	11, 950	450	11, 500	-	1, 400	550	850	-	250	-	250	-
Hood	11, 950	3, 550	8, 400	-	2, 150	1, 450	700	-	260	180	80	-
Hopkins	413, 381	141, 615	271, 766	-	131, 490	65, 760	65, 730	-	22, 715	10, 827	11, 888	-
Houston	2, 301, 281	678, 682	1, 622, 599	-	623, 030	226, 490	396, 540	-	220, 059	63, 343	156, 716	-
Howard	7, 100	-	7, 100	-	500	-	500	-	150	-	150	-
Hudspeth	79, 650	79, 650	-	-	25, 200	25, 200	-	-	20, 000	20, 000	-	-
Hunt	907, 031	158, 540	748, 491	-	142, 974	35, 765	107, 209	-	37, 140	8, 385	28, 755	-
Jackson	596, 647	188, 750	407, 897	-	143, 728	54, 375	89, 353	-	39, 507	15, 285	24, 222	-
Jasper	281, 050	203, 795	77, 255	-	119, 570	96, 015	23, 555	-	23, 159	19, 264	3, 895	-
Jefferson	455, 950	48, 400	343, 100	64, 450	78, 720	19, 000	53, 670	6, 050	15, 500	6, 330	8, 710	460
Jim Hogg	2, 400	-	2, 400	-	100	-	100	-	150	-	151	-
Jim Wells	131, 945	-	131, 945	-	8, 700	-	8, 700	-	1, 555	-	1, 555	-
Johnson	308, 885	37, 720	271, 165	-	38, 600	11, 600	27, 000	-	9, 920	1, 795	8, 125	-
Jones	116, 660	6, 250	110, 410	-	7, 390	500	6, 890	-	3, 165	50	3, 115	-
Karnes	393, 680	65, 735	327, 945	-	53, 115	12, 775	40, 340	-	21, 035	5, 865	15, 170	-
Kaufman	3, 373, 865	184, 167	3, 181, 898	7, 800	553, 340	64, 870	488, 270	200	97, 413	8, 545	88, 748	120

TABLE 57.—FARMS OPERATED BY NEGROES—NUMBER, ACREAGE, VALUE OF LAND AND BUILDINGS, AND VALUE OF IMPLEMENTS AND MACHINERY, BY TENURE, BY STATES, AND COUNTIES: 1930—Continued

[Counties in which no farms operated by Negroes were reported, are omitted]

COUNTY	NUMBER OF FARMS				ALL LAND IN FARMS (ACRES)				VALUE OF LAND AND BUILDINGS			
	Total	Owners	Tenants	Managers	Total	Owners	Tenants	Managers	Total	Owners	Tenants	Managers
TEXAS—continued												
Kendall	1			1	700			700	$22,000			$22,000
Kent	6		6		585		585		20,150		$20,150	
Kerr	2	1	1		116	110	6		2,350	$2,000	350	
King	4		4		440		440		21,500		21,500	
Kinney	1	1			1,184	1,184			9,472	9,472		
Kleberg	5	2	3		307	114	193		18,265	8,190	10,075	
Knox	11		11		463		463		27,060		27,060	
Lamar	1,098	207	890	1	49,982	13,716	35,989	277	2,653,045	508,960	2,119,085	25,000
Lamb	32	1	31		1,539	400	1,139		85,030	24,000	61,030	
Lampasas	6	5	1		737	637	100		25,600	22,600	3,000	
La Salle	3	1	2		657	287	370		31,400	21,350	10,050	
Lavaca	439	122	316	1	30,742	11,304	18,238	1,200	1,186,427	324,747	849,680	12,000
Lee	660	239	421		62,129	25,329	36,800		1,356,455	558,965	797,490	
Leon	2,028	397	1,631		103,154	35,296	67,858		2,215,561	602,319	1,613,242	
Liberty	506	226	280		19,443	9,547	9,896		745,325	341,612	403,713	
Limestone	1,740	232	1,508		80,899	15,887	65,012		4,813,143	862,405	3,950,738	
Live Oak	4	2	2		1,530	1,420	110		28,710	24,000	4,710	
Llano	2		2		135		135		6,000		6,000	
Lubbock	35		35		2,565		2,565		277,390		277,390	
Lynn	26		25	1	1,606		1,326	280	71,540		57,540	14,000
McCulloch	14		14		1,445		1,445		62,100		62,100	
McLennan	1,422	214	1,207	1	66,882	9,670	57,192	20	5,361,406	740,480	4,619,626	1,300
Madison	747	176	571		46,458	15,291	31,167		968,062	284,251	683,811	
Marion	1,085	495	590		60,221	33,708	26,513		1,115,469	643,604	471,865	
Martin	1		1		23		23		690		690	
Mason	3		3		108		108		4,525		4,525	
Matagorda	604	154	450		25,827	5,976	19,851		980,874	191,180	789,694	
Medina	22	10	12		1,878	977	901		63,950	31,850	32,100	
Menard	1		1		40		40		5,000		5,000	
Milam	1,307	168	1,139		71,863	12,334	59,529		3,669,120	452,336	3,216,784	
Mitchell	52	2	50		6,738	1,780	4,958		263,230	30,200	233,030	
Montgomery	684	212	472		31,164	13,106	18,058		684,008	314,933	369,075	
Morris	633	103	529	1	34,305	8,050	26,190	65	721,957	175,527	545,230	1,200
Motley	18	2	16		1,048	200	848		52,660	12,820	39,840	
Nacogdoches	994	234	760		50,474	19,717	30,757		1,339,008	442,566	896,442	
Navarro	1,661	170	1,491		85,144	11,556	73,588		5,725,335	739,915	4,985,420	
Newton	467	358	109		19,164	15,432	3,732		434,408	357,628	76,780	
Nolan	8		8		939		939		38,910		38,910	
Nueces	16	2	14		1,445	442	1,023		130,675	46,750	83,925	
Orange	8	1	6	1	325	2	313	10	14,900	100	12,800	2,000
Panola	2,117	427	1,690		98,215	34,336	63,879		2,469,300	809,258	1,660,042	
Parker	10	8	2		1,031	941	90		35,775	31,875	3,900	
Polk	782	275	507		29,983	14,544	15,439		1,067,848	429,410	638,438	
Rains	153	25	128		6,382	1,912	4,470		175,320	51,055	124,265	
Red River	1,297	278	1,019		58,040	19,380	38,660		2,077,627	485,930	1,591,697	
Reeves	4	1	3		14,390	14,300	90		52,600	45,000	7,600	
Refugio	35	11	24		1,900	1,004	896		79,474	26,930	52,544	
Robertson	1,869	324	1,545		95,266	26,012	69,254		4,365,407	632,477	3,732,930	
Rockwall	250	6	244		7,356	333	7,023		612,351	9,225	603,126	
Runnels	21	1	20		2,956	30	2,926		178,950	3,000	175,950	
Rusk	2,784	867	1,917		157,454	69,902	87,552		3,856,117	1,656,054	2,200,063	
Sabine	288	73	215		13,150	5,820	7,330		380,980	143,800	237,180	
San Augustine	508	132	376		27,400	9,964	17,436		695,036	11,252	493,784	
San Jacinto	962	317	645		35,984	18,066	17,918		946,680	420,236	526,444	
San Patricio	18	2	16		720	44	676		66,975	5,200	61,775	
San Saba	4		4		143		143		10,200		10,200	
Scurry	2		2		545		545		17,850		17,850	
Shackelford	1		1		40		40		2,000		2,000	
Shelby	1,196	232	964		47,644	13,905	33,739		1,329,163	370,774	958,389	
Smith	3,120	941	2,176	3	166,337	68,143	98,018	176	4,834,466	1,983,214	2,828,602	22,650
Stephens	1		1		40		40		1,000		1,000	
Stonewall	18	1	17		1,786	5	1,781		76,550	1,000	75,550	
Sutton	1	1			1,920	1,920			38,400	38,400		
Tarrant	106	37	69		5,191	1,704	3,487		411,095	117,165	293,930	
Taylor	15		15		1,335		1,335		66,400		66,400	
Terry	10		10		381		381		12,990		12,,990	
Titus	315	64	250	1	15,701	4,162	11,129	410	435,313	136,465	286,848	12,000
Tom Green	8		8		525		525		33,375		33,375	
Travis	820	125	690	5	46,814	8,339	37,563	912	3,098,557	441,040	2,585,917	71,600
Trinity	308	117	191		11,763	5,808	5,955		312,790	142,060	170,730	
Tyler	129	56	73		6,570	3,582	2,988		155,475	74,150	81,325	
Upshur	1,326	321	1,002	3	63,804	24,699	38,822	283	1,383,963	538,344	841,269	4,350
Van Zandt	377	100	277		22,666	8,495	14,171		791,425	239,525	551,900	
Victoria	259	111	147	1	24,168	12,122	10,246	1,800	1,088,408	486,463	539,945	62,000
Walker	1,266	370	896		59,569	24,274	35,295		1,399,985	558,714	841,271	
Waller	735	238	495	2	35,376	12,489	21,412	1,475	1,301,487	390,887	837,850	72,750
Ward	5	1	4		76	1	75		10,100	2,500	7,600	
Washington	1,573	397	1,176		81,313	26,500	54,813		3,492,667	1,101,146	2,391,521	
Webb	1		1		40		40		15,000		15,000	
Wharton	1,394	266	1,128		58,506	10,681	47,825		3,627,718	645,158	2,982,560	
Wheeler	12		12		695		695		28,175		28,175	
Wichita	16		13	3	966		846	120	87,275		72,275	15,000
Wilbarger	113		113		5,332		5,332		403,950		403,950	
Williamson	450	42	407	1	27,344	5,571	21,073	700	2,187,971	182,035	1,998,936	7,000
Wilson	76	32	43	1	6,518	2,886	3,252	380	221,900	81,375	125,525	15,000
Wise	10		10		606		606		33,540		33,540	
Wood	533	218	314	1	32,170	15,329	15,997	844	933,427	457,040	446,475	29,912
Young	1		1		50		50		5,000		5,000	
Zavala	1		1		100		100		1,200		1,200	

Table 57.—FARMS OPERATED BY NEGROES—NUMBER, ACREAGE, VALUE OF LAND AND BUILDINGS, AND VALUE OF IMPLEMENTS AND MACHINERY, BY TENURE, BY STATES, AND COUNTIES: 1930—Continued

[Counties in which no farms operated by Negroes were reported, are omitted]

COUNTY	VALUE OF LAND ALONE				VALUE OF BUILDINGS				VALUE OF IMPLEMENTS AND MACHINERY			
	Total	Owners	Tenants	Managers	Total	Owners	Tenants	Managers	Total	Owners	Tenants	Managers
	TEXAS—continued											
Kendall	$7,000	-	-	$7,000	$15,000	-	-	$15,000	$1,000	-	-	$1,000
Kent	19,150	-	$19,150	-	1,000	-	$1,000	-	675	-	$675	-
Kerr	2,100	$1,800	300	-	250	$200	50	-	96	$80	16	-
King	20,500	-	20,500	-	1,000	-	1,000	-	300	-	300	-
Kinney	9,222	9,222	-	-	250	250	-	-	-	-	-	-
Kleberg	16,090	6,090	10,000	-	2,175	2,100	75	-	835	535	300	-
Knox	25,410	-	25,410	-	1,650	-	1,650	-	1,350	-	1,350	-
Lamar	2,249,201	404,110	1,826,591	18,500	403,844	104,850	292,494	6,500	80,484	21,923	53,561	5,000
Lamb	79,655	22,500	57,155	-	5,375	1,500	3,875	-	4,625	1,800	2,825	-
Lampasas	20,500	18,300	2,200	-	5,100	4,300	800	-	1,150	850	300	-
La Salle	28,900	19,850	9,050	-	2,500	1,500	1,000	-	900	600	300	-
Lavaca	972,767	255,172	705,795	11,800	213,660	69,575	143,885	200	34,017	12,565	21,352	100
Lee	1,141,713	459,330	682,383	-	214,742	99,635	115,107	-	56,158	26,946	29,212	-
Leon	1,641,438	416,966	1,224,472	-	574,123	185,353	388,770	-	151,366	53,913	97,453	-
Liberty	570,573	246,852	323,721	-	174,752	94,760	79,992	-	57,352	30,574	26,778	-
Limestone	4,142,066	680,840	3,461,226	-	671,077	181,565	489,512	-	185,707	32,700	153,007	-
Live Oak	27,310	23,500	3,810	-	1,400	500	900	-	545	315	230	-
Llano	5,500	-	5,500	-	500	-	500	-	140	-	140	-
Lubbock	253,395	-	253,395	-	23,995	-	23,995	-	6,630	-	6,630	-
Lynn	66,115	-	53,115	13,000	5,425	-	4,425	1,000	2,670	-	2,170	500
McCulloch	56,750	-	56,750	-	5,350	-	5,350	-	3,020	-	3,020	-
McLennan	4,787,551	598,225	4,188,326	1,000	573,855	142,255	431,300	300	175,648	26,847	148,776	25
Madison	785,215	217,151	568,064	-	182,847	67,100	115,747	-	52,144	19,773	32,371	-
Marion	741,984	418,109	323,875	-	373,485	225,495	147,990	-	73,313	49,296	24,017	-
Martin	590	-	590	-	100	-	100	-	50	-	50	-
Mason	4,125	-	4,125	-	400	-	400	-	300	-	300	-
Matagorda	780,235	145,324	634,911	-	200,639	45,856	154,783	-	69,612	13,216	56,396	-
Medina	53,350	26,200	27,150	-	10,600	5,650	4,950	-	2,080	875	1,205	-
Menard	4,700	-	4,700	-	300	-	300	-	100	-	100	-
Milam	3,131,378	353,041	2,778,337	-	537,742	99,295	438,447	-	130,938	17,911	113,027	-
Mitchell	236,080	29,450	206,630	-	27,150	750	26,400	-	7,695	350	7,345	-
Montgomery	481,025	216,473	264,552	-	202,983	98,460	140,523	-	49,142	21,821	27,321	-
Morris	551,614	125,956	424,658	1,000	170,343	49,571	120,572	200	32,352	9,950	22,402	-
Motley	49,600	12,020	37,040	-	3,600	800	2,800	-	1,940	550	1,390	-
Nacogdoches	1,017,078	318,061	699,017	-	321,930	124,505	197,425	-	87,421	30,693	56,728	-
Navarro	5,063,602	616,225	4,447,377	-	661,733	123,690	538,043	-	212,339	36,210	176,129	-
Newton	307,427	246,192	61,235	-	126,981	111,436	15,545	-	25,914	22,722	3,192	-
Nolan	33,360	-	33,360	-	5,550	-	5,550	-	1,400	-	1,400	-
Nueces	119,750	41,250	78,500	-	10,925	5,500	5,425	-	8,300	1,900	6,400	-
Orange	12,050	50	11,000	1,000	2,850	50	1,800	1,000	878	50	628	200
Panola	1,883,011	615,114	1,267,897	-	586,289	194,144	392,145	-	192,277	53,369	138,908	-
Parker	28,075	24,975	3,100	-	7,700	6,900	800	-	1,520	1,450	70	-
Polk	826,374	315,885	510,489	-	241,474	113,525	127,949	-	57,985	23,442	34,543	-
Rains	126,730	34,030	92,740	-	48,550	17,025	31,525	-	15,705	3,715	11,990	-
Red River	1,698,103	364,900	1,333,203	-	379,524	121,030	258,494	-	71,081	21,062	50,019	-
Reeves	47,250	40,000	7,250	-	5,350	5,000	350	-	500	150	350	-
Refugio	66,349	22,530	43,819	-	13,125	4,400	8,725	-	3,827	2,327	1,500	-
Robertson	3,670,594	459,489	3,211,105	-	694,813	172,988	521,825	-	137,804	32,925	104,879	-
Rockwall	549,786	7,790	541,996	-	62,565	1,435	61,130	-	24,590	390	24,200	-
Runnels	164,250	3,000	161,250	-	14,700	-	14,700	-	2,160	-	2,160	-
Rusk	2,942,914	1,195,364	1,747,550	-	913,203	460,690	452,513	-	292,783	154,615	138,168	-
Sabine	276,320	96,875	179,445	-	104,660	46,925	57,735	-	25,695	11,070	14,625	-
San Augustine	554,896	156,782	398,114	-	140,140	44,470	95,670	-	30,920	12,094	18,826	-
San Jacinto	726,046	309,241	416,805	-	220,634	110,995	109,639	-	51,421	27,226	24,195	-
San Patricio	59,600	3,800	55,800	-	7,375	1,400	5,975	-	3,310	385	2,925	-
San Saba	8,950	-	8,950	-	1,250	-	1,250	-	350	-	350	-
Scurry	15,250	-	15,250	-	2,600	-	2,600	-	600	-	600	-
Shackelford	1,650	-	1,650	-	350	-	350	-	-	-	-	-
Shelby	988,866	267,936	720,930	-	340,297	102,838	237,459	-	61,895	22,675	39,220	-
Smith	3,757,056	1,440,084	2,297,222	19,750	1,077,410	543,130	531,380	2,900	250,007	130,484	119,073	450
Stephens	900	-	900	-	100	-	100	-	18	-	18	-
Stonewall	68,025	250	67,775	-	8,525	750	7,775	-	1,785	100	1,685	-
Sutton	35,000	35,000	-	-	3,400	3,400	-	-	300	300	-	-
Tarrant	366,690	97,840	268,850	-	44,405	19,325	25,080	-	8,075	2,105	5,970	-
Taylor	60,550	-	60,550	-	5,850	-	5,850	-	2,175	-	2,175	-
Terry	12,490	-	12,490	-	500	-	500	-	-	-	-	-
Titus	337,028	100,090	226,438	10,500	98,285	36,375	60,410	1,500	19,241	9,140	10,101	-
Tom Green	30,925	-	30,925	-	2,450	-	2,450	-	625	-	625	-
Travis	2,740,304	353,210	2,323,194	63,900	358,253	87,830	262,723	7,700	120,924	17,731	99,668	3,525
Trinity	242,900	109,060	133,840	-	69,890	33,000	36,890	-	17,542	8,410	9,132	-
Tyler	103,390	45,005	58,385	-	52,085	29,145	22,940	-	9,058	5,958	3,100	-
Upshur	991,673	371,619	616,154	3,900	392,290	166,725	225,115	450	72,420	29,928	42,477	15
Van Zandt	637,400	171,900	465,500	-	154,025	67,625	86,400	-	37,447	11,552	25,895	-
Victoria	957,720	430,853	472,867	54,000	130,688	55,610	67,078	8,000	40,128	17,832	22,096	200
Walker	973,168	390,451	582,717	-	426,817	168,263	258,554	-	90,910	45,060	45,850	-
Waller	1,057,907	300,412	714,095	43,400	243,580	90,475	123,755	29,350	45,779	18,536	25,528	1,715
Ward	7,475	500	6,975	-	2,625	2,000	625	-	250	-	250	-
Washington	2,964,309	901,911	2,062,398	-	528,358	199,235	329,123	-	136,941	55,655	81,286	-
Webb	14,850	-	14,850	-	150	-	150	-	25	-	25	-
Wharton	3,095,321	533,083	2,562,238	-	532,397	112,075	420,322	-	178,155	35,564	142,591	-
Wheeler	25,825	-	25,825	-	2,350	-	2,350	-	1,070	-	1,070	-
Wichita	78,275	-	67,475	10,800	9,000	-	4,800	4,200	1,655	-	1,065	590
Wilbarger	375,620	-	375,620	-	28,330	-	28,330	-	17,485	-	17,485	-
Williamson	1,977,012	152,715	1,818,297	6,000	210,959	29,320	180,639	1,000	71,960	7,209	64,701	50
Wilson	189,510	65,450	109,210	14,850	32,390	15,925	16,315	150	8,220	5,225	2,920	75
Wise	28,490	-	28,490	-	5,050	-	5,050	-	1,098	-	1,098	-
Wood	699,918	319,230	354,928	25,760	233,509	137,810	91,547	4,152	42,734	27,496	14,038	1,200
Young	4,900	-	4,900	-	100	-	100	-	100	-	100	-
Zavala	1,000	-	1,000	-	200	-	200	-	75	-	75	-

TABLE 57.—FARMS OPERATED BY NEGROES—NUMBER, ACREAGE, VALUE OF LAND AND BUILDINGS, AND VALUE OF IMPLEMENTS AND MACHINERY, BY TENURE, BY STATES, AND COUNTIES: 1930—Continued

[Counties in which no farms operated by Negroes were reported, are omitted]

COUNTY	NUMBER OF FARMS				ALL LAND IN FARMS (ACRES)				VALUE OF LAND AND BUILDINGS			
	Total	Owners	Tenants	Managers	Total	Owners	Tenants	Managers	Total	Owners	Tenants	Managers
						UTAH						
Total	5	4	1	—	37	33	4	—	$24,200	$20,200	$4,000	—
Salt Lake	4	3	1	—	27	23	4	—	19,700	51,700	4,000	—
Weber	1	1	—	—	10	10	—	—	4,500	4,500	—	—
						VERMONT						
Total	22	17	4	1	3,812	3,211	251	350	$118,700	$85,700	$8,000	$25,000
Addison	1	1	—	—	258	258	—	—	30,000	30,000	—	—
Bennington	4	2	2	—	110	19	91	—	3,300	1,300	2,000	—
Caledonia	1	1	—	—	60	60	—	—	400	400	—	—
Chittenden	2	2	—	—	177	177	—	—	8,500	8,500	—	—
Franklin	1	—	1	—	10	—	10	—	4,000	—	4,000	—
Orange	3	2	1	—	509	359	150	—	6,500	4,500	2,000	—
Orleans	2	2	—	—	265	265	—	—	9,500	9,500	—	—
Rutland	3	3	—	—	910	910	—	—	9,000	9,000	—	—
Washington	1	1	—	—	163	163	—	—	6,000	6,000	—	—
Windham	1	1	—	—	210	210	—	—	2,500	2,500	—	—
Windsor	3	2	—	1	1,140	790	—	350	39,000	14,000	—	25,000
						VIRGINIA						
Total	39,598	24,399	15,123	76	2,039,656	1,179,824	836,999	22,833	$71,722,401	$41,743,427	$28,629,746	$1,349,228
Accomac	962	148	812	2	43,581	4,950	38,401	230	5,214,000	594,550	4,598,450	21,000
Albemarle	465	414	45	6	15,576	112,370	2,883	1,323	1,030,177	740,517	162,660	127,000
Alleghany	5	4	1	—	172	162	10	—	28,300	24,300	4,000	—
Amelia	726	597	125	4	37,713	27,536	8,181	1,996	1,228,209	982,108	183,201	62,900
Amherst	620	372	248	—	28,261	18,821	9,440	—	877,505	623,225	254,280	—
Appomattox	320	164	155	1	18,291	10,868	7,198	225	388,100	243,090	136,010	9,000
Arlington	2	2	—	—	18	18	—	—	22,000	22,000	—	—
Augusta	99	87	11	1	4,788	3,587	951	250	352,975	267,475	75,500	10,000
Bath	25	23	2	—	1,222	1,105	117	—	48,300	45,800	2,500	—
Bedford	709	507	202	—	36,538	25,182	11,356	—	1,198,164	834,554	363,610	—
Bland	11	11	—	—	1,094	1,094	—	—	16,700	16,700	—	—
Botetourt	90	83	7	—	3,291	3,030	261	—	140,290	128,240	12,050	—
Brunswick	1,329	752	576	1	83,911	47,918	34,493	1,500	1,835,393	1,157,978	637,415	40,000
Buckingham	664	538	126	—	39,370	30,915	8,455	—	851,939	694,711	157,228	—
Campbell	713	424	288	1	36,377	20,930	14,759	688	1,018,050	630,980	347,070	40,000
Caroline	964	781	183	—	53,606	43,495	10,111	—	1,619,985	1,321,910	298,075	—
Carroll	15	11	4	—	720	545	175	—	39,100	30,600	8,500	—
Charles City	372	333	38	1	13,287	10,109	2,578	600	515,270	405,020	85,250	25,000
Charlotte	841	474	365	2	46,177	26,624	19,124	429	1,277,668	743,020	484,045	50,603
Chesterfield	235	204	27	4	9,753	5,797	3,274	682	597,175	404,350	86,700	106,125
Clarke	26	15	10	1	3,018	1,197	1,621	200	226,960	80,860	131,100	15,000
Craig	3	3	—	—	289	289	—	—	6,500	6,500	—	—
Culpeper	286	260	22	4	17,462	14,735	1,874	853	714,290	621,500	59,290	33,500
Cumberland	553	423	130	—	33,140	24,536	8,604	—	708,040	552,570	155,470	—
Dinwiddie	933	589	344	—	63,054	35,587	27,467	—	1,381,040	879,315	501,725	—
Elizabeth City	56	44	10	2	1,236	938	223	75	154,765	131,265	16,000	7,500
Essex	633	535	98	—	30,574	23,990	6,584	—	1,062,090	897,440	164,650	—
Fairfax	85	76	9	—	2,363	1,770	593	—	361,880	323,380	38,500	—
Fauquier	310	269	39	2	19,886	14,288	4,758	840	980,616	641,341	249,275	90,000
Floyd	74	62	12	—	3,835	3,197	638	—	132,546	115,946	16,600	—
Fluvanna	353	309	43	1	14,089	12,120	1,609	360	482,651	418,866	33,785	30,000
Franklin	536	318	218	—	38,190	20,611	17,579	—	830,760	496,725	334,035	—
Frederick	21	13	6	2	1,972	501	1,125	346	191,900	61,900	114,000	16,000
Giles	28	19	9	—	784	573	211	—	37,130	22,850	14,280	—
Gloucester	514	494	19	1	12,918	11,830	883	205	801,730	743,110	46,620	12,000
Goochland	493	444	49	—	22,365	19,253	3,112	—	549,220	490,870	58,350	—
Grayson	78	60	18	—	2,092	1,836	256	—	191,390	160,855	30,535	—
Greene	107	92	14	1	3,098	2,717	347	34	173,100	160,100	11,000	2,000
Greensville	788	338	450	—	50,505	24,431	26,074	—	1,292,010	642,660	649,350	—
Halifax	2,380	899	1,478	3	127,457	53,038	70,094	4,325	3,446,898	1,473,357	1,942,541	31,000
Hanover	559	472	85	2	28,681	19,367	7,267	2,047	1,027,030	697,280	205,750	124,000
Henrico	168	148	20	—	4,878	4,191	687	—	414,195	347,095	67,100	—
Henry	469	259	210	—	28,309	13,511	14,798	—	696,685	414,185	282,500	—
Highland	11	10	1	—	1,715	1,601	114	—	25,800	25,300	500	—
Isle of Wight	469	172	296	1	27,857	11,626	15,856	375	900,083	345,601	542,482	12,000
James City	182	152	30	—	5,762	3,528	2,234	—	336,500	242,965	93,535	—
King and Queen	606	544	62	—	30,059	25,064	4,995	—	794,779	670,749	124,030	—
King George	260	209	51	—	12,731	8,825	3,906	—	482,948	352,703	130,245	—
King William	414	345	69	—	20,289	16,082	4,207	—	540,125	446,205	93,920	—
Lancaster	415	391	24	—	9,069	8,511	558	—	418,355	399,305	19,050	—
Lee	29	17	11	1	1,262	783	179	300	83,125	34,000	9,125	40,000
Loudoun	77	59	17	1	6,017	2,969	2,427	621	401,345	215,445	160,900	25,000
Louisa	740	702	34	4	39,442	35,371	3,626	445	1,042,839	899,229	122,610	21,000
Lunenburg	843	461	382	—	48,993	28,028	20,965	—	1,244,230	778,965	465,265	—
Madison	276	244	32	—	12,584	10,841	1,743	—	488,034	417,859	70,175	—
Mathews	214	201	13	—	2,263	2,148	115	—	273,330	259,930	13,400	—
Mecklenburg	2,275	853	1,422	—	110,539	45,539	65,000	—	3,816,692	1,649,221	2,167,471	—
Middlesex	485	463	22	—	11,978	11,214	764	—	637,390	614,740	22,650	—
Montgomery	98	88	9	1	3,469	2,900	177	392	237,900	190,650	12,250	35,000
Nansemond	918	404	509	5	40,117	18,721	20,807	589	1,865,160	871,835	959,225	34,100

TABLE 57.—FARMS OPERATED BY NEGROES—NUMBER, ACREAGE, VALUE OF LAND AND BUILDINGS, AND VALUE OF IMPLEMENTS AND MACHINERY, BY TENURE, BY STATES, AND COUNTIES: 1930—Continued

[Counties in which no farms operated by Negroes were reported, are omitted]

COUNTY	VALUE OF LAND ALONE				VALUE OF BUILDINGS				VALUE OF IMPLEMENTS AND MACHINERY			
	Total	Owners	Tenants	Managers	Total	Owners	Tenants	Managers	Total	Owners	Tenants	Managers
					UTAH							
Total	$20,100	$17,100	$3,000		$4,100	$3,100	$1,000		$305	$305		
Salt Lake	15,900	12,900	3,000		3,800	2,800	1,000		255	255		
Weber	4,200	4,200			300	300			50	50		
					VERMONT							
Total	$54,875	$42,900	$2,975	$9,000	$63,825	$42,800	$5,025	$16,000	$18,525	$12,525	$1,000	$5,000
Addison	22,000	22,000			8,000	8,000			3,000	3,000		
Bennington	1,875	900	975		1,425	400	1,025		150		150	
Caledonia	300	300			100	100						
Chittenden	3,800	3,800			4,700	4,700			900	900		
Franklin	1,000		1,000		3,000		3,000		50		50	
Orange	3,500	2,500	1,000		3,000	2,000	1,000		1,150	350	800	
Orleans	4,000	4,000			5,500	5,500			1,200	1,200		
Rutland	2,900	2,900			6,100	6,100			3,025	3,025		
Washington	3,000	3,000			3,000	3,000			1,000	1,000		
Windham	700	700			1,800	1,800			50	50		
Windsor	11,800	2,800		9,000	27,200	11,200		16,000	8,000	3,000		5,000
					VIRGINIA							
Total	$43,154,526	$23,125,248	$19,245,935	$783,343	$28,567,875	$18,618,179	$9,383,811	$565,885	$3,865,540	$2,586,923	$1,213,240	$65,377
Accomac	3,735,410	383,210	3,338,200	14,000	1,478,590	211,340	1,260,250	7,000	288,696	36,771	251,175	750
Albemarle	502,792	354,132	87,660	61,000	527,385	386,385	75,000	66,000	40,328	34,730	1,795	3,803
Alleghany	18,200	17,200	1,000		10,100	7,100	3,000		1,002	202	800	
Amelia	683,159	523,993	117,016	42,150	545,050	458,115	66,185	20,750	73,132	60,679	7,353	5,100
Amherst	509,502	350,522	158,980		368,003	272,703	95,300		32,721	26,296	6,425	
Appomattox	210,985	124,275	78,710	8,000	177,115	118,815	57,300	1,000	20,539	13,957	6,282	300
Arlington	5,800	5,800			16,200	16,200			540	540		
Augusta	303,025	156,475	41,550	5,000	149,950	111,000	33,950	5,000	14,950	11,215	2,735	1,000
Bath	31,625	30,025	1,600		16,675	15,775	900		5,145	4,445	700	
Bedford	769,271	498,549	270,722		428,893	336,005	92,888		45,247	34,914	10,333	
Bland	11,600	11,600			5,100	5,100			885	885		
Botetourt	78,940	71,790	7,150		61,350	56,450	4,900		3,173	2,948	225	
Brunswick	987,809	595,343	357,466	35,000	847,584	562,635	279,949	5,000	102,498	69,865	27,633	5,000
Buckingham	493,239	386,251	106,988		358,700	308,460	50,240		46,500	41,333	5,167	
Campbell	548,765	330,160	193,605	25,000	469,285	300,820	153,465	15,000	47,610	35,339	11,571	700
Caroline	910,560	733,635	176,925		709,425	588,275	121,150		88,060	76,115	11,945	
Carroll	29,575	23,275	6,300		9,525	7,325	2,200		2,120	1,915	205	
Charles City	330,580	255,405	60,175	15,000	184,690	149,615	25,075	10,000	43,225	38,685	4,190	350
Charlotte	681,313	384,410	282,300	14,603	596,355	358,610	201,745	36,000	63,033	42,746	19,237	1,050
Chesterfield	307,850	215,445	44,840	47,565	289,325	188,905	41,860	58,560	35,104	21,777	2,580	10,747
Clarke	160,760	53,160	99,600	8,000	66,200	27,700	31,500	7,000	9,300	3,625	4,975	700
Craig	2,900	2,900			3,600	3,600						
Culpeper	396,245	336,350	39,795	20,100	318,045	285,150	19,495	13,400	53,765	51,715	1,375	675
Cumberland	377,278	286,728	90,550		330,762	265,842	64,920		43,672	37,172	6,500	
Dinwiddie	837,256	518,274	318,982		543,784	361,041	182,743		84,859	58,069	26,790	
Elizabeth City	95,553	75,358	14,420	5,775	59,212	55,907	1,580	1,725	9,209	7,801	906	502
Essex	561,373	464,948	96,425		500,717	432,492	68,225		96,089	80,947	15,142	
Fairfax	214,055	190,655	23,400		147,825	132,725	15,100		13,350	12,710	640	
Fauquier	554,091	352,666	161,425	40,000	426,525	288,675	87,850	50,000	35,337	26,272	6,765	2,300
Floyd	97,821	86,021	11,800		34,725	29,925	4,800		5,908	5,707	201	
Fluvanna	237,981	198,836	19,145	20,000	244,670	220,030	14,640	10,000	35,049	32,899	1,650	500
Franklin	523,343	315,078	208,265		307,417	181,647	125,770		28,261	15,659	12,602	
Frederick	142,800	46,900	84,400	11,500	49,100	15,000	29,600	4,500	3,995	1,975	1,520	500
Giles	24,745	13,665	11,080		12,385	9,185	3,200		2,212	1,307	905	
Gloucester	397,480	367,460	28,020	2,000	404,250	375,650	18,600	10,000	64,285	59,895	1,390	3,000
Goochland	290,745	257,020	33,725		258,475	233,850	24,625		23,700	22,763	937	
Grayson	135,455	119,695	15,760		55,935	41,160	14,775		4,982	3,327	1,755	
Greene	98,045	90,795	6,250	1,000	75,055	69,305	4,750	1,000	8,712	8,312	400	
Greensville	782,260	378,700	403,560		509,750	263,960	245,790		87,447	47,872	39,575	
Halifax	2,153,268	858,584	1,273,884	20,800	1,293,630	614,773	668,657	10,200	134,371	68,666	64,795	910
Hanover	530,495	349,470	132,025	49,000	496,535	347,810	73,725	75,000	89,333	74,098	8,535	6,700
Henrico	276,635	223,435	53,200		137,560	123,660	13,900		21,122	19,395	1,727	
Henry	354,535	189,715	164,820		342,150	224,470	117,680		36,125	25,209	10,916	
Highland	18,225	17,775	450		7,575	7,525	50		4,911	4,886	25	
Isle of Wight	643,188	213,101	423,587	6,500	256,895	132,500	118,895	5,500	21,761	13,428	7,933	400
James City	171,711	126,481	45,230		164,789	116,484	48,305		17,941	14,451	3,490	
King and Queen	395,780	318,670	77,110		398,999	352,079	46,920		66,103	58,666	7,437	
King George	254,678	172,833	81,845		228,270	179,870	48,400		38,757	32,285	6,472	
King William	271,355	213,315	58,040		268,770	232,890	35,880		34,312	29,382	4,930	
Lancaster	205,210	194,835	10,375		213,145	204,470	8,675		58,925	57,870	1,055	
Lee	60,725	23,300	7,425	30,000	22,400	10,700	1,700	10,000	1,072	352	220	500
Loudoun	237,090	114,090	104,000	19,000	164,255	101,355	56,900	6,000	17,725	9,575	6,150	2,000
Louisa	552,769	457,174	82,995	12,600	490,070	442,055	39,615	8,400	57,497	54,322	2,470	705
Lunenburg	692,025	427,280	264,745		552,205	351,685	200,520		61,510	43,947	17,563	
Madison	266,289	225,369	40,920		221,745	192,490	29,255		26,192	24,622	1,570	
Mathews	105,735	98,010	7,725		167,595	161,920	5,675		21,546	20,081	1,465	
Mecklenburg	2,263,607	881,871	1,381,736		1,553,085	767,350	785,735		183,058	92,906	90,152	
Middlesex	312,445	299,995	12,450		324,945	314,745	10,200		63,455	61,675	1,780	
Montgomery	133,855	109,380	7,475	17,000	104,045	81,270	4,775	18,000	5,973	4,608	365	1,000
Nansemond	1,263,473	494,208	739,165	30,100	601,687	377,627	220,060	4,000	67,244	44,884	21,120	1,240

TABLE 57.—FARMS OPERATED BY NEGROES—NUMBER, ACREAGE, VALUE OF LAND AND BUILDINGS, AND VALUE OF IMPLEMENTS AND MACHINERY, BY TENURE, BY STATES, AND COUNTIES: 1930—Continued

[Counties in which no farms operated by Negroes were reported, are omitted]

COUNTY	NUMBER OF FARMS				ALL LAND IN FARMS (ACRES)				VALUE OF LAND AND BUILDINGS			
	Total	Owners	Tenants	Managers	Total	Owners	Tenants	Managers	Total	Owners	Tenants	Managers
VIRGINIA—continued												
Nelson	406	280	125	1	17,669	13,771	3,738	160	$710,077	$535,192	$164,885	$10,000
New Kent	147	126	21		8,139	6,450	1,689		222,500	187,850	34,650	
Norfolk	302	154	145	3	11,776	4,879	6,537	360	674,680	316,925	320,755	37,000
Northampton	392	148	244		13,342	3,555	9,787		2,075,320	654,220	1,421,100	
Northumberland	509	480	29		16,590	13,989	2,601		752,861	703,311	49,550	
Nottoway	711	519	192		30,619	20,478	10,141		989,310	750,395	238,915	
Orange	335	292	42	1	14,025	11,861	1,784	380	645,430	549,130	88,300	8,000
Page	42	35	7		1,655	1,037	618		89,250	65,850	23,400	
Patrick	195	97	98		9,559	5,541	4,018		217,770	128,095	89,675	
Pittsylvania	2,162	557	1,605		117,977	35,939	82,038		3,309,367	1,017,575	2,291,792	
Powhatan	373	328	45		23,689	18,057	5,632		763,570	648,355	115,215	
Prince Edward	830	563	267		45,002	30,609	14,393		1,227,430	852,160	375,270	
Prince George	374	214	159	1	23,701	11,179	12,426	96	598,921	274,614	304,307	20,000
Prince William	112	98	14		7,690	5,364	2,326		313,630	249,840	63,790	
Princess Anne	380	221	152	7	12,720	6,434	5,448	838	1,081,330	517,830	425,000	138,500
Pulaski	65	54	11		1,100	973	127		109,150	100,150	9,000	
Rappahannock	154	145	8	1	6,903	5,957	646	300	282,243	252,718	19,025	10,500
Richmond	347	236	110	1	14,100	9,553	4,457	100	454,955	331,950	118,005	5,000
Roanoke	69	62	7		2,796	2,428	368		240,900	213,900	27,000	
Rockbridge	45	32	13		2,188	1,339	849		94,960	56,500	38,460	
Rockingham	22	17	4	1	1,354	780	399	175	69,950	30,350	35,600	4,000
Russell	29	18	11		1,212	631	581		55,010	29,180	25,830	
Scott	11	7	4		403	298	105		21,300	16,000	5,300	
Shenandoah	2	1	1		26	6	20		1,700	900	800	
Smyth	18	18			893	893			35,000	35,000		
Southampton	1,909	429	1,480		125,082	38,722	86,360		3,903,659	1,107,980	2,795,679	
Spotsylvania	463	429	32	2	25,017	22,639	2,164	214	689,536	643,156	34,880	11,500
Stafford	90	80	9	1	6,160	4,000	2,060	100	222,025	139,725	52,300	30,000
Surry	500	311	189		28,345	17,657	10,688		811,553	535,553	276,000	
Sussex	766	327	439		66,824	25,580	41,244		1,350,415	599,275	751,140	
Tazewell	19	17	2		1,384	1,319	65		67,275	65,900	1,375	
Warren	8	7	1		136	133	3		6,400	5,900	500	
Warwick	75	63	12		1,416	867	549		156,323	127,583	28,740	
Washington	37	32	5		1,178	777	401		105,000	66,200	38,800	
Westmoreland	442	321	120	1	24,079	17,592	6,312	175	966,720	690,395	251,325	25,000
Wise	5	4	1		69	67	2		8,900	6,900	2,000	
Wythe	64	58	6		1,235	1,076	159		101,570	87,670	13,900	
York	235	224	11		4,144	3,885	259		405,450	391,000	14,450	
INDEPENDENT CITIES												
Buena Vista	1	1			66	66			3,000	3,000		
Hopewell	1	1			65	65			3,000	3,000		
Lynchburg	4	3	1		26	21	5		16,500	16,000	500	
Newport News	1		1		3		3		2,000		2,000	
Norfolk	7	2	5		142	31	111		37,200	7,900	29,300	
Petersburg	2	1	1		10	2	8		11,000	3,000	8,000	
Portsmouth	2	1	1		34	10	24		25,400	10,000	15,400	
Richmond	3	1	1	1	16	1	10	5	41,500	9,500	2,000	30,000
WASHINGTON												
Total	**73**	**61**	**10**	**2**	**9,425**	**4,704**	**4,610**	**111**	**$356,705**	**$268,155**	**$77,950**	**$10,600**
Benton	1	1			13	13			2,000	2,000		
Clark	2	2			88	88			8,700	8,700		
Douglas	5	4	1		3,892	1,052	2,840		17,905	10,905	7,000	
Ferry	5	1			17	17			500	500		
Franklin	1	1			160	160			1,100	1,100		
Grant	2	2			520	520			2,300	2,300		
King	7	6		1	61	50		11	17,600	16,000		1,600
Kitsap	1	1			17	17			2,000	2,000		
Kittitas	2	1		1	230	130		100	13,800	4,800		9,000
Lewis	10	8	2		285	216	69		33,250	28,750	4,500	
Lincoln	1		1		860		860		30,000		30,000	
Mason	1	1			120	120			10,000	10,000		
Pacific	1	1			5	5			3,000	3,000		
Pierce	4	4			24	24			12,500	12,500		
Snohomish	3	3			53	53			12,000	12,000		
Spokane	3	2	1		915	215	700		24,000	4,000	20,000	
Stevens	4	3	1		708	706	2		13,600	13,400	200	
Thurston	2	2			67	67			11,000	11,000		
Whatcom	1	1			80	80			3,000	3,000		
Yakima	21	17	4		1,310	1,171	139		138,450	122,200	16,250	
WEST VIRGINIA												
Total	**490**	**372**	**111**	**7**	**28,013**	**18,470**	**8,574**	**969**	**$1,480,628**	**$832,553**	**$415,575**	**$232,500**
Barbour	79	67	12		2,768	2,318	450		95,300	79,900	15,400	
Berkeley	15	11	3	1	733	283	406	44	83,400	22,900	23,000	37,500
Boone	5	3	2		231	220	11		17,900	15,700	2,200	
Braxton	9	9			660	660			14,500	14,500		
Cabell	8	3	2	3	486	152	82	252	63,500	9,500	4,000	50,000
Calhoun	2	2			515	515			9,000	9,000		
Fayette	33	32	1		873	847	26		98,300	96,300	2,000	
Grant	6	6			837	837			6,700	6,700		
Greenbrier	24	22	2		1,518	1,310	208		64,700	59,700	5,000	
Hampshire	5	5			234	234			5,000	5,000		

TABLE 57.—FARMS OPERATED BY NEGROES—NUMBER, ACREAGE, VALUE OF LAND AND BUILDINGS, AND VALUE OF IMPLEMENTS AND MACHINERY, BY TENURE, BY STATES, AND COUNTIES: 1930—Continued

[Counties in which no farms operated by Negroes were reported, are omitted]

COUNTY	VALUE OF LAND ALONE				VALUE OF BUILDINGS				VALUE OF IMPLEMENTS AND MACHINERY			
	Total	Owners	Tenants	Managers	Total	Owners	Tenants	Managers	Total	Owners	Tenants	Managers
VIRGINIA—continued												
Nelson	$459,552	$322,882	$127,270	$9,400	$250,525	$212,310	$37,615	$600	$27,326	$24,478	$2,548	$300
New Kent	145,240	117,190	28,050	-	77,260	70,660	6,600	-	13,101	11,941	1,160	-
Norfolk	476,730	197,525	245,505	33,700	197,950	119,400	75,250	3,300	28,802	18,308	9,394	1,100
Northampton	1,531,710	434,195	1,097,515	-	543,610	220,025	323,585	-	114,465	41,115	73,350	-
Northumberland	383,356	359,256	24,100	-	369,505	344,055	25,450	-	52,653	49,893	2,760	-
Nottoway	506,055	363,510	142,545	-	483,255	386,885	96,370	-	60,994	47,920	13,074	-
Orange	329,864	276,914	47,950	5,000	315,566	272,216	40,350	3,000	39,186	32,803	4,883	1,500
Page	54,425	36,175	18,250	-	34,825	29,675	5,150	-	1,900	1,255	645	-
Patrick	150,555	88,195	62,360	-	67,215	39,900	27,315	-	7,206	4,745	2,461	-
Pittsylvania	2,163,842	644,975	1,518,867	-	1,145,525	372,600	772,925	-	144,078	54,941	89,137	-
Powhatan	393,435	319,180	74,255	-	370,135	329,175	40,960	-	67,249	63,069	4,180	-
Prince Edward	685,930	464,515	221,415	-	541,500	387,645	153,855	-	56,150	41,892	14,258	-
Prince George	367,680	159,611	189,469	18,600	231,241	115,003	114,838	1,400	31,907	16,742	14,365	800
Prince William	193,680	150,040	43,640	-	119,950	99,800	20,150	-	11,890	10,850	1,040	-
Princess Anne	729,815	336,835	300,480	92,500	351,515	180,995	124,520	46,000	41,488	20,583	13,210	7,695
Pulaski	60,820	52,995	7,825	-	48,330	47,155	1,175	-	5,009	4,794	215	-
Rappahannock	154,843	134,418	11,925	8,500	127,400	118,300	7,100	2,000	18,944	17,649	795	500
Richmond	256,525	170,280	83,245	3,000	198,430	161,670	34,760	2,000	45,747	34,072	11,675	-
Roanoke	141,200	119,400	21,800	-	99,700	94,500	5,200	-	5,611	5,211	400	-
Rockbridge	54,485	28,075	26,410	-	40,475	28,425	12,050	-	4,740	2,445	2,295	-
Rockingham	49,530	17,600	29,130	2,800	20,420	12,750	6,470	1,200	2,425	1,200	1,225	-
Russell	38,285	19,555	18,730	-	16,725	9,625	7,100	-	905	690	215	-
Scott	16,050	12,050	4,000	-	5,250	3,950	1,300	-	180	80	100	-
Shenandoah	800	300	500	-	900	600	300	-	60	50	10	-
Smyth	27,625	27,625	-	-	7,375	7,375	-	-	540	540	-	-
Southampton	2,680,009	698,055	1,981,954	-	1,223,650	409,925	813,725	-	193,950	71,988	121,962	-
Spotsylvania	357,161	334,601	16,060	6,500	332,375	308,555	18,820	5,000	54,288	51,938	2,100	250
Stafford	111,575	69,375	27,200	15,000	110,450	70,350	25,100	15,000	10,741	9,501	1,040	200
Surry	487,698	317,348	170,350	-	323,855	218,205	105,650	-	47,440	33,885	13,555	-
Sussex	803,676	365,542	438,134	-	546,739	233,733	313,006	-	77,812	36,377	41,435	-
Tazewell	44,425	43,375	1,050	-	22,850	22,525	325	-	755	725	30	-
Warren	3,350	3,150	200	-	3,050	2,750	300	-	155	5	150	-
Warwick	102,799	77,294	25,505	-	53,524	50,289	3,235	-	6,009	5,485	524	-
Washington	76,350	41,200	35,150	-	28,650	25,000	3,650	-	3,012	2,472	540	-
Westmoreland	586,475	412,750	165,725	8,000	380,245	277,645	85,600	17,000	56,675	44,090	11,585	1,000
Wise	7,150	5,950	1,200	-	1,750	950	800	-	25	20	5	-
Wythe	66,322	54,522	11,800	-	35,248	33,148	2,100	-	2,997	2,447	550	-
York	213,395	205,445	7,950	-	192,055	185,555	6,500	-	28,255	27,395	860	-
INDEPENDENT CITIES												
Buena Vista	1,000	1,000	-	-	2,000	2,000	-	-	25	25	-	-
Hopewell	800	800	-	-	2,200	2,200	-	-	2,870	2,870	-	-
Lynchburg	11,150	10,650	500	-	5,350	5,350	-	-	1,210	1,210	-	-
Newport News	300	-	300	-	1,700	-	1,700	-	-	-	-	-
Norfolk	32,800	5,100	27,700	-	4,400	2,800	1,600	-	847	407	440	-
Petersburg	7,200	700	6,500	-	3,800	2,300	1,500	-	125	125	-	-
Portsmouth	22,380	7,500	14,880	-	3,020	2,500	520	-	600	100	500	-
Richmond	23,200	2,000	1,550	19,650	18,300	7,500	450	10,350	1,620	-	20	1,600
WASHINGTON												
Total	**$258,568**	**$189,618**	**$62,750**	**$6,200**	**$98,137**	**$78,537**	**$15,200**	**$4,400**	**$22,740**	**$15,615**	**$5,125**	**$2,000**
Benton	1,970	1,970	-	-	30	30	-	-	100	100	-	-
Clark	4,300	4,300	-	-	4,400	4,400	-	-	700	700	-	-
Douglas	15,580	9,180	6,400	-	2,325	1,725	600	-	1,650	550	1,100	-
Ferry	250	250	-	-	250	250	-	-	150	150	-	-
Franklin	400	400	-	-	700	700	-	-	500	500	-	-
Grant	2,200	2,200	-	-	100	100	-	-	-	-	-	-
King	10,900	9,700	-	1,200	6,700	6,300	-	400	1,480	1,480	-	-
Kitsap	1,200	1,200	-	-	800	800	-	-	-	-	-	-
Kittitas	9,400	4,400	-	5,000	4,400	400	-	4,000	2,100	100	-	2,000
Lewis	18,100	15,100	3,000	-	15,150	13,650	1,500	-	3,900	3,700	200	-
Lincoln	25,000	-	25,000	-	5,000	-	5,000	-	1,400	-	1,400	-
Mason	5,000	5,000	-	-	5,000	5,000	-	-	200	200	-	-
Pacific	2,750	2,750	-	-	250	250	-	-	75	75	-	-
Pierce	7,750	7,750	-	-	4,750	4,750	-	-	55	55	-	-
Snohomish	8,100	8,100	-	-	3,900	3,900	-	-	25	25	-	-
Spokane	20,750	3,750	17,000	-	3,250	250	3,000	-	1,600	100	1,500	-
Stevens	10,500	10,300	200	-	3,100	3,100	-	-	2,300	2,300	-	-
Thurston	7,000	7,000	-	-	4,000	4,000	-	-	200	200	-	-
Whatcom	2,000	2,000	-	-	1,000	1,000	-	-	300	300	-	-
Yakima	105,418	94,268	11,150	-	33,032	27,932	5,100	-	6,005	5,080	925	-
WEST VIRGINIA												
Total	**$905,393**	**$513,278**	**$272,115**	**$120,000**	**$575,235**	**$319,275**	**$143,460**	**$112,500**	**$47,007**	**$26,570**	**$15,287**	**$5,150**
Barbour	75,658	63,818	11,840	-	19,642	16,082	3,560	-	2,345	1,837	508	-
Berkeley	52,600	10,600	12,000	30,000	30,800	12,300	11,000	7,500	2,110	1,110	750	250
Boone	7,800	7,200	600	-	10,100	8,500	1,600	-	525	475	50	-
Braxton	10,600	10,600	-	-	3,900	3,900	-	-	345	345	-	-
Cabell	36,650	7,250	2,400	27,000	26,850	2,250	1,600	23,000	3,257	350	7	2,900
Calhoun	7,200	7,200	-	-	1,800	1,800	-	-	500	500	-	-
Fayette	46,200	44,900	1,300	-	52,100	51,400	700	-	3,485	3,475	10	-
Grant	5,050	5,050	-	-	1,650	1,650	-	-	300	300	-	-
Greenbrier	43,275	39,775	3,500	-	21,425	19,925	1,500	-	1,670	1,570	100	-
Hampshire	2,925	2,925	-	-	2,075	2,075	-	-	100	100	-	-

TABLE 57.—FARMS OPERATED BY NEGROES—NUMBER, ACREAGE, VALUE OF LAND AND BUILDINGS, AND VALUE OF IMPLEMENTS AND MACHINERY, BY TENURE, BY STATES, AND COUNTIES: 1930—Continued

[Counties in which no farms operated by Negroes were reported, are omitted]

COUNTY	NUMBER OF FARMS				ALL LAND IN FARMS (ACRES)				VALUE OF LAND AND BUILDINGS			
	Total	Owners	Tenants	Managers	Total	Owners	Tenants	Managers	Total	Owners	Tenants	Managers
WEST VIRGINIA—continued												
Hancock	1	1			154	154			$5,000	$5,000		
Hardy	4	4			82	82			2,400	2,400		
Harrison	2	2			127	127			7,500	7,500		
Jackson	1	1			81	81			1,600	1,600		
Jefferson	37	13	22	2	3,389	197	2,704	488	383,130	30,730	$232,400	$120,000
Kanawha	31	21	10		1,190	886	304		122,573	94,773	27,800	
Lewis	4	2	2		486	261	225		16,600	12,100	4,500	
McDowell	8	1	7		1,013	4	1,009		25,550	5,000	20,550	
Marion	6	1	5		426	50	376		11,800	1,000	10,800	
Marshall	2		2		50		50		3,700		3,700	
Mason	1	1			50	50			2,500	2,500		
Mercer	23	19	4		677	526	151		39,700	37,300	2,400	
Monongalia	6	3	3		123	15	108		10,400	5,000	5,400	
Monroe	43	33	10		2,192	1,944	248		67,100	57,600	9,500	
Nicholas	1	1			14	14			300	300		
Pendleton	8	8			438	438			12,800	12,800		
Pocahontas	17	16		1	1,282	1,097		185	51,600	26,600		25,000
Preston	1	1			581	581			48,000	48,000		
Putnam	1	1			72	72			2,000	2,000		
Raleigh	6	4	2		512	278	234		11,500	8,000	3,500	
Randolph	3	2	1		186	36	150		4,800	1,800	3,000	
Summers	37	26	11		2,453	1,473	980		61,800	42,200	19,600	
Taylor	43	37	6		2,702	2,040	662		100,125	88,300	11,825	
Upshur	3	2	1		179	95	84		8,650	4,150	4,500	
Wayne	1		1		36		36		1,000		1,000	
Webster	1	1			40	40			1,100	1,100		
Wirt	6	6			434	434			8,800	8,800		
Wood	1	1			7	7			1,500	1,500		
Wyoming	6	4	2		182	112	70		8,800	5,300	3,500	
WISCONSIN												
Total	55	41	14		5,295	3,390	1,905		$343,105	$240,505	$102,600	
Bayfield	3	3			198	198			3,800	3,800		
Burnett	2	1	1		105	65	40		4,850	1,000	3,250	
Chippewa	1	1			80	80			12,000	12,000		
Clark	1	1			80	80			2,700	2,700		
Columbia	1		1		120		120		6,000		6,000	
Dane	1	1			40	40			15,000	15,000		
Douglas	1	1			5	5			4,500	4,500		
Dunn	1		1		120		120		6,000		6,000	
Eau Claire	1	1			20	20			900	900		
Grant	2	1	1		227	8	219		11,605	655	10,950	
Jackson	1	1			40	40			500	500		
Jefferson	1	1			80	80			6,000	6,000		
Juneau	3	3			280	280			17,050	17,050		
Kenosha	1		1		62		62		6,000		6,000	
La Crosse	1		1		280		280		8,000		8,000	
Marinette	1	1			120	120			4,000	4,000		
Monroe	2	1	1		120	10	110		2,400	1,000	1,400	
Price	1	1			52	52			1,100	1,100		
Racine	1	1			80	80			16,000	16,000		
Richland	1	1			18	18			800	800		
Rock	1		1		229		229		12,000		12,000	
Rusk	1	1			120	120			9,000	9,000		
Sauk	4	4			533	533			39,500	39,500		
Taylor	1	1			75	75			8,000	8,000		
Vernon	18	13	5		1,899	1,274	625		126,400	87,400	39,000	
Walworth	2	1	1		112	12	100		13,000	3,000	10,000	
Washburn	1	1			200	200			6,000	6,000		
WYOMING												
Total	12	8	4		10,925	9,855	1,070		$139,020	$119,660	$19,360	
Big Horn	1		1		80		80		4,000		4,000	
Campbell	1	1			80	80			1,500	1,500		
Carbon	1	1			160	160			5,000	5,000		
Crook	2	1	1		405	85	320		4,000	800	3,200	
Lincoln	1	1			764	764			20,000	20,000		
Niobrara	3	2	1		8,206	7,686	520		86,520	82,360	4,160	
Sheridan	2	2			1,080	1,080			10,000	10,000		
Washakie	1		1		150		150		8,000		8,000	

TABLE 57.—FARMS OPERATED BY NEGROES—NUMBER, ACREAGE, VALUE OF LAND AND BUILDINGS, AND VALUE OF IMPLEMENTS AND MACHINERY, BY TENURE, BY STATES, AND COUNTIES: 1930—Continued

[Counties in which no farms operated by Negroes were reported, are omitted]

COUNTY	VALUE OF LAND ALONE				VALUE OF BUILDINGS				VALUE OF IMPLEMENTS AND MACHINERY			
	Total	Owners	Tenants	Managers	Total	Owners	Tenants	Managers	Total	Owners	Tenants	Managers
	WEST VIRGINIA—continued											
Hancock	$2,400	$2,400	----	----	$2,600	$2,600	----	----	$60	$60	----	----
Hardy	1,075	1,075	----	----	1,325	1,325	----	----	1,035	1,035	----	----
Harrison	6,200	6,200	----	----	1,300	1,300	----	----	140	140	----	----
Jackson	1,300	1,300	----	----	300	300	----	----	50	50	----	----
Jefferson	207,530	12,280	$145,250	$50,000	175,600	18,450	$87,150	$70,000	10,435	2,365	$6,570	$1,500
Kanawha	84,295	68,045	16,250	----	38,278	26,728	11,550	----	3,644	912	2,732	----
Lewis	12,200	8,600	3,600	----	4,400	3,500	900	----	550	500	50	----
McDowell	15,500	1,000	14,500	----	10,050	4,000	6,050	----	493	----	493	----
Marion	9,300	800	8,500	----	2,500	200	2,300	----	275	----	275	----
Marshall	2,300	----	2,300	----	1,400	----	1,400	----	----	----	----	----
Mason	1,770	1,770	----	----	730	730	----	----	400	400	----	----
Mercer	25,525	24,025	1,500	----	14,175	13,275	900	----	1,021	1,016	5	----
Monongalia	6,850	2,700	4,150	----	3,550	2,300	1,250	----	210	----	210	----
Monroe	42,375	35,900	6,475	----	24,725	21,700	3,025	----	2,435	2,010	425	----
Nicholas	200	200	----	----	100	100	----	----	----	----	----	----
Pendleton	9,165	9,165	----	----	3,635	3,635	----	----	383	383	----	----
Pocahontas	31,650	18,650	----	13,000	19,950	7,950	----	12,000	985	485	----	500
Preston	17,100	17,100	----	----	30,900	30,900	----	----	2,500	2,500	----	----
Putnam	1,400	1,400	----	----	600	600	----	----	----	----	----	----
Raleigh	7,900	5,800	2,100	----	3,600	2,200	1,400	----	1,610	410	1,200	----
Randolph	4,300	1,600	2,700	----	500	200	300	----	5	5	----	----
Summers	44,925	27,600	17,325	----	16,875	14,600	2,275	----	2,160	775	1,385	----
Taylor	63,200	54,100	9,100	----	36,925	34,200	2,725	----	3,291	3,041	250	----
Upshur	6,100	3,100	3,000	----	2,550	1,050	1,500	----	350	100	250	----
Wayne	500	----	500	----	500	----	500	----	10	----	10	----
Webster	400	400	----	----	700	700	----	----	6	6	----	----
Wirt	4,850	4,850	----	----	3,950	3,950	----	----	120	120	----	----
Wood	900	900	----	----	600	600	----	----	50	50	----	----
Wyoming	6,225	3,000	3,225	----	2,575	2,300	275	----	152	145	7	----
	WISCONSIN											
Total	**$228,435**	**$152,285**	**$76,150**	----	**$114,670**	**$88,220**	**$26,450**	----	**$25,921**	**$21,336**	**$4,585**	----
Bayfield	2,700	2,700	----	----	1,100	1,100	----	----	305	305	----	----
Burnett	2,100	1,000	1,100	----	2,750	600	2,150	----	165	115	50	----
Chippewa	6,000	6,000	----	----	6,000	6,000	----	----	1,000	1,000	----	----
Clark	2,500	2,500	----	----	200	200	----	----	100	100	----	----
Columbia	4,200	----	4,200	----	1,800	----	1,800	----	600	----	600	----
Dane	12,500	12,500	----	----	2,500	2,500	----	----	380	380	----	----
Douglas	500	500	----	----	4,000	4,000	----	----	700	700	----	----
Dunn	5,200	----	5,200	----	800	----	800	----	630	----	630	----
Eau Claire	500	500	----	----	400	400	----	----	100	100	----	----
Grant	10,505	555	9,950	----	1,100	100	1,000	----	500	----	500	----
Jackson	275	275	----	----	225	225	----	----	250	250	----	----
Jefferson	2,500	2,500	----	----	3,500	3,500	----	----	700	700	----	----
Juneau	9,750	9,750	----	----	7,300	7,300	----	----	270	270	----	----
Kenosha	4,000	----	4,000	----	2,000	----	2,000	----	100	----	100	----
La Crosse	3,500	----	3,500	----	4,500	----	4,500	----	200	----	200	----
Marinette	2,000	2,000	----	----	2,000	2,000	----	----	1,000	1,000	----	----
Monroe	1,700	800	900	----	700	200	500	----	150	100	50	----
Price	450	450	----	----	650	650	----	----	100	100	----	----
Racine	6,000	6,000	----	----	10,000	10,000	----	----	1,500	1,500	----	----
Richland	500	500	----	----	300	300	----	----	90	90	----	----
Rock	11,000	----	11,000	----	1,000	----	1,000	----	500	----	500	----
Rusk	8,100	8,100	----	----	900	900	----	----	1,900	1,900	----	----
Sauk	25,800	25,800	----	----	13,700	13,700	----	----	3,321	3,321	----	----
Taylor	5,000	5,000	----	----	3,000	3,000	----	----	800	800	----	----
Vernon	90,155	59,855	30,300	----	36,245	27,545	8,700	----	9,750	8,195	1,555	----
Walworth	6,500	500	6,000	----	6,500	2,500	4,000	----	410	10	400	----
Washburn	4,500	4,500	----	----	1,500	1,500	----	----	400	400	----	----
	WYOMING											
Total	**$123,870**	**$106,460**	**$17,410**	----	**$15,150**	**$13,200**	**$1,950**	----	**$7,925**	**$6,025**	**$1,900**	----
Big Horn	3,500	----	3,500	----	500	----	500	----	400	----	400	----
Campbell	1,000	1,000	----	----	500	500	----	----	125	125	----	----
Carbon	4,000	4,000	----	----	1,000	1,000	----	----	700	700	----	----
Crook	3,650	700	2,950	----	350	100	250	----	200	100	100	----
Lincoln	14,000	14,000	----	----	6,000	6,000	----	----	1,500	1,500	----	----
Niobrara	82,720	79,160	3,560	----	3,800	3,200	600	----	3,100	2,100	1,000	----
Sheridan	7,600	7,600	----	----	2,400	2,400	----	----	1,500	1,500	----	----
Washakie	7,400	----	7,400	----	600	----	600	----	400	----	400	----

APPENDIX

CHARACTERISTICS OF NEGRO POPULATION BY COUNTIES: 1930

[Counties having no Negro inhabitants are omitted. Percent and median size not shown where base is less than 100. Percent not shown where less than 1/10 of 1 percent]

SUBJECT	ALABAMA													
	The State	Autauga	Baldwin	Barbour	Bibb	Blount	Bullock	Butler	Calhoun	Chambers	Cherokee	Chilton	Choctaw
POPULATION BY SEX														
Negro population: 1930	944, 834	10, 907	6, 798	18, 659	6, 876	1, 069	15, 754	14, 682	12, 536	17, 928	1, 831	3, 968	11, 236
Male	457, 144	5, 320	3, 439	8, 914	3, 603	566	7, 458	6, 833	5, 993	8, 562	920	1, 932	5, 660
Female	487, 690	5, 587	3, 359	9, 745	3, 273	503	8, 296	7, 849	6, 543	9, 366	911	2, 036	5, 576
Negro population: 1920	900, 652	10, 696	4, 781	19, 419	7, 817	1, 418	20, 650	14, 580	12, 089	19, 724	2, 079	3, 963	11, 452
Male	439, 779	5, 169	2, 381	9, 199	4, 065	720	9, 911	6, 913	5, 812	9, 575	1, 066	2, 006	5, 686
Female	460, 873	5, 527	2, 400	10, 220	3, 752	698	10, 739	7, 667	6, 277	10, 149	1, 013	1, 957	5, 766
Percent of total population:													
1930	35. 7	55. 4	24. 0	57. 5	33. 1	3. 8	78. 7	48. 6	22. 5	45. 6	9. 1	16. 1	54. 8
1920	38. 4	56. 6	23. 1	60. 6	33. 8	5. 6	81. 5	49. 4	25. 3	47. 9	10. 0	17. 4	55. 2
VOTING AGE: 1930													
Total 21 years old and over	479, 950	5, 182	3, 413	8, 374	3, 475	533	7, 166	6, 680	6, 578	7, 926	754	1, 799	5, 429
Male	229, 903	2, 439	1, 771	3, 844	1, 866	285	3, 232	3, 059	3, 187	3, 729	383	869	2, 749
Female	250, 047	2, 743	1, 642	4, 530	1, 609	248	3, 934	3, 621	3, 391	4, 197	371	930	2, 680
AGE: 1930													
Under 5 years	107, 836	1, 327	840	2, 268	865	122	1, 772	1, 941	1, 409	2, 169	253	489	1, 393
Under 1 year	20, 506	250	124	419	171	24	355	396	319	432	54	107	257
5 to 9 years	117, 708	1, 503	864	2, 724	882	147	2, 139	2, 031	1, 499	2, 528	283	562	1, 445
10 to 14 years	108, 934	1, 340	790	2, 459	742	115	2, 208	1, 940	1, 338	2, 495	269	526	1, 352
15 to 19 years	109, 216	1, 315	768	2, 396	757	132	2, 131	1, 815	1, 434	2, 413	223	502	1, 359
20 to 24 years	97, 073	988	687	1, 730	798	98	1, 297	1, 366	1, 387	1, 685	171	361	1, 245
25 to 29 years	77, 518	757	528	1, 255	582	68	831	990	1, 155	1, 230	133	259	859
30 to 34 years	55, 559	534	346	896	370	55	694	632	768	848	78	169	585
35 to 44 years	104, 262	1, 042	684	1, 732	628	115	1, 567	1, 348	1, 375	1, 566	129	325	1, 017
45 to 54 years	91, 872	1, 138	719	1, 626	724	116	1, 630	1, 390	1, 248	1, 736	153	395	1, 067
55 to 64 years	42, 838	539	306	839	310	53	782	690	527	754	92	213	518
65 to 74 years	20, 936	270	168	489	142	32	434	355	269	340	31	105	230
75 years and over	10, 401	138	96	237	70	15	266	178	126	160	16	59	126
Unknown	681	16	2	8	6	1	3	6	1	4	------	3	40
SCHOOL ATTENDANCE													
Total 7 to 13 years, inclusive	155, 517	1, 948	1, 145	3, 529	1, 075	176	3, 038	2, 762	1, 954	3, 494	387	740	1, 896
Number attending school	125, 450	1, 381	862	1, 797	850	140	2, 317	2, 070	1, 677	2, 798	321	668	1, 566
Percent attending school	80. 7	70. 9	75. 3	50. 9	79. 1	79. 5	76. 3	74. 9	85. 8	80. 1	82. 9	90. 3	82. 6
Total 14 and 15 years, inclusive	44, 844	536	283	1, 020	305	47	999	748	543	1, 004	100	209	556
Number attending school	33, 439	399	206	512	225	34	702	548	396	707	83	177	429
Percent attending school	74. 6	74. 4	72. 8	50. 2	73. 8	------	70. 3	73. 3	72. 9	70. 4	83. 0	84. 7	77. 2
Total 16 and 17 years, inclusive	45, 810	601	325	1, 024	309	54	889	760	603	1, 035	95	228	590
Number attending school	20, 282	284	131	243	128	24	361	313	234	384	54	122	275
Percent attending school	44. 3	47. 3	40. 3	23. 7	41. 4	------	40. 6	41. 2	38. 8	37. 1	------	53. 5	46. 6
Total 18 to 20 years, inclusive	62, 810	702	426	1, 323	455	73	1, 069	958	835	1, 267	130	264	764
Number attending school	7, 712	90	40	57	38	9	113	116	99	148	32	47	102
Percent attending school	12. 3	12. 8	9. 4	4. 3	8. 4	------	10. 6	12. 1	11. 9	11. 7	24. 6	17. 8	13. 4
ILLITERACY													
Total 10 years old and over	719, 290	8, 077	5, 094	13, 667	5, 129	800	11, 843	10, 710	9, 628	12, 231	1, 295	2, 917	8, 398
Number illiterate	188, 673	2, 922	1, 395	5, 345	1, 478	171	3, 160	3, 474	1, 773	3, 583	276	645	2, 422
Percent illiterate	26. 2	36. 2	27. 4	39. 1	28. 8	21. 4	26. 7	32. 4	18. 4	27. 1	21. 3	22. 1	28. 8
Percent illiterate in 1920	31. 3	41. 7	27. 0	39. 4	30. 9	33. 3	34. 9	34. 1	23. 2	29. 1	28. 9	30. 1	25. 9
URBAN AND RURAL													
Urban population	268, 450	------	------	2, 273	------	------	1, 578	1, 983	7, 975	878	------	------	------
Percent urban	28. 4	------	------	12. 2	------	------	10. 0	13. 5	63. 6	4. 9	------	------	------
Rural population	676, 384	10, 907	6, 798	16, 386	6, 876	1, 069	14, 176	12, 699	4, 561	17, 050	1, 831	3, 968	11, 236
Rural-farm	496, 542	9, 134	2, 277	13, 356	3, 504	458	12, 830	9, 345	2, 749	13, 960	1, 571	3, 053	8, 247
Rural-nonfarm	179, 842	1, 773	4, 521	3, 030	3, 372	611	1, 346	3, 354	1, 812	3, 090	260	915	2, 989
Percent rural	71. 6	100. 0	100. 0	87. 8	100. 0	100. 0	90. 0	86. 5	36. 4	95. 1	100. 0	100. 0	100. 0
MARITAL CONDITION													
Males 15 years old and over	290, 079	3, 186	2, 170	5, 179	2, 290	363	4, 382	3, 985	3, 935	4, 982	521	1, 163	3, 554
Single	91, 027	991	654	1, 779	704	109	1, 456	1, 213	1, 187	1, 684	171	391	1, 131
Married	176, 191	1, 977	1, 356	3, 083	1, 336	213	2, 598	2, 472	2, 390	3, 042	313	701	2, 121
Widowed	18, 544	171	134	291	223	31	285	243	303	221	31	64	173
Divorced	3, 912	44	25	24	27	9	42	56	55	34	6	5	55
Unknown	405	3	1	2	------	1	1	1	------	1	------	2	74
Females 15 years old and over	320, 277	3, 551	2, 134	6, 029	2, 097	322	5, 253	4, 785	4, 355	5, 754	505	1, 228	3, 492
Single	77, 161	839	497	1, 732	390	55	1, 561	1, 275	1, 053	1, 701	140	330	854
Married	179, 650	2, 028	1, 313	3, 126	1, 336	209	2, 625	2, 575	2, 375	3, 147	315	708	2, 107
Widowed	55, 127	564	284	1, 088	333	50	961	800	826	807	45	173	400
Divorced	8, 000	117	38	81	37	8	104	134	101	96	5	16	80
Unknown	339	3	2	2	1	------	2	1	------	3	------	1	51
FAMILIES													
Number of families	222, 533	2, 623	1, 537	4, 047	1, 646	261	3, 633	3, 203	2, 950	3, 683	362	827	2, 472
Median size	3. 33	3. 43	3. 50	3. 80	3. 22	2. 94	3. 48	3. 82	3. 31	4. 18	4. 48	4. 09	3. 67
Families having—													
No children under 10	123, 163	1, 375	791	1, 961	875	145	1, 942	1, 541	1, 664	1, 706	154	414	1, 241
1 child under 10	39, 556	474	291	726	313	48	661	600	520	719	65	131	478
2 children under 10	24, 808	328	179	544	187	27	394	403	313	467	47	99	296
3 or more	35, 006	446	276	816	271	41	636	659	453	791	96	183	457

CHARACTERISTICS OF NEGRO POPULATION BY COUNTIES: 1930—Continued

[See note at head of table]

SUBJECT	ALABAMA—Continued												
	Clarke	Clay	Cle-burne	Coffee	Colbert	Conecuh	Coosa	Coving-ton	Cren-shaw	Cull-man	Dale	Dallas	De Kalb
POPULATION BY SEX													
Negro population: 1930	13,625	2,727	766	6,894	8,482	11,095	4,640	7,078	7,301	441	5,410	40,867	851
Male	6,787	1,388	410	3,447	4,074	5,399	2,353	3,469	3,531	229	2,637	19,133	422
Female	6,838	1,339	356	3,447	4,408	5,696	2,287	3,609	3,770	212	2,773	21,734	429
Negro population: 1920	13,906	3,179	735	6,294	11,152	11,103	5,806	7,987	7,115	443	5,031	42,265	771
Male	6,800	1,579	390	3,168	5,759	5,310	2,905	4,105	3,470	243	2,450	19,827	379
Female	7,106	1,600	345	3,126	5,393	5,793	2,901	3,882	3,645	200	2,581	22,438	392
Percent of total population:													
1930	52.4	15.3	5.9	21.2	28.4	43.6	37.2	17.1	30.9	1.1	23.3	74.2	2.1
1920	52.7	14.0	5.5	20.9	34.9	45.1	39.1	21.0	30.9	1.3	22.2	77.3	2.2
VOTING AGE: 1930													
Total 21 years old and over	6,493	1,220	370	3,065	4,392	4,938	1,945	3,520	3,180	200	2,400	20,447	438
Male	3,148	644	194	1,511	2,077	2,365	989	1,709	1,517	110	1,153	9,023	217
Female	3,345	576	176	1,554	2,315	2,573	956	1,811	1,663	90	1,247	11,424	221
AGE: 1930													
Under 5 years	1,683	380	85	911	894	1,467	645	825	960	70	711	4,642	119
Under 1 year	319	75	21	173	152	285	144	150	193	19	140	861	26
5 to 9 years	1,843	363	101	973	1,067	1,588	664	921	1,057	60	765	4,995	104
10 to 14 years	1,686	351	102	931	1,007	1,496	626	791	1,005	45	714	4,791	91
15 to 19 years	1,631	352	89	862	950	1,362	669	887	935	57	687	5,060	80
20 to 24 years	1,386	310	90	662	837	1,016	454	758	721	53	562	3,771	106
25 to 29 years	886	185	62	555	672	705	293	537	500	35	397	2,625	59
30 to 34 years	610	128	45	396	490	482	180	378	302	12	252	2,076	47
35 to 44 years	1,226	202	62	609	941	1,003	364	745	612	34	459	4,532	96
45 to 54 years	1,404	278	68	573	858	1,107	362	727	690	33	460	3,680	64
55 to 64 years	718	99	35	243	449	488	201	307	292	27	221	2,668	45
65 to 74 years	339	50	14	120	193	265	112	132	155	12	113	1,397	23
75 years and over	201	29	13	47	121	116	70	68	70	3	64	604	16
Unknown	12	-	-	12	3	-	-	2	2	-	5	26	1
SCHOOL ATTENDANCE													
Total 7 to 13 years, inclusive	2,408	474	135	1,328	1,425	2,113	887	1,121	1,406	72	1,037	6,641	129
Number attending school	1,926	401	94	905	1,198	1,644	696	772	1,188	60	751	4,720	111
Percent attending school	80.0	84.6	69.6	68.1	84.1	77.8	78.5	68.9	84.5	-	72.4	71.1	86.0
Total 14 and 15 years, inclusive	675	159	43	352	392	607	271	385	412	21	298	2,100	34
Number attending school	538	132	24	207	312	470	189	227	316	14	197	1,530	28
Percent attending school	79.7	83.0	-	58.8	79.6	77.4	69.7	59.0	76.7	-	66.1	72.9	-
Total 16 and 17 years, inclusive	666	159	38	377	398	592	304	367	420	20	279	2,088	43
Number attending school	327	93	9	121	198	306	110	126	181	12	101	998	17
Percent attending school	49.1	58.5	-	32.1	49.7	51.7	36.2	34.3	43.1	-	36.2	47.8	-
Total 18 to 20 years, inclusive	918	185	52	477	538	731	320	463	493	32	384	2,906	42
Number attending school	125	40	5	27	80	124	49	41	49	8	29	403	8
Percent attending school	13.6	21.6	-	5.7	14.9	17.0	15.3	8.9	9.9	-	7.6	13.9	-
ILLITERACY													
Total 10 years old and over	10,099	1,984	580	5,010	6,521	8,040	3,331	5,332	5,284	311	3,934	31,230	628
Number illiterate	2,643	425	169	1,620	1,465	2,426	974	1,318	1,606	56	1,001	10,533	115
Percent illiterate	26.2	21.4	29.1	32.3	22.5	30.2	29.2	24.7	30.4	18.0	25.4	33.7	18.3
Percent illiterate in 1920	33.3	25.3	31.4	33.6	26.2	36.2	29.6	29.9	30.9	13.9	34.2	41.8	24.0
URBAN AND RURAL													
Urban population	-	-	-	1,750	3,047	-	-	2,420	-	5	1,188	9,249	110
Percent urban	-	-	-	25.4	35.9	-	-	34.2	-	1.1	22.0	22.6	12.9
Rural population	13,625	2,727	766	5,144	5,435	11,095	4,640	4,658	7,301	436	4,222	31,618	741
Rural-farm	9,805	2,121	406	4,469	4,579	7,940	3,880	2,700	5,665	407	3,336	30,142	294
Rural-nonfarm	3,820	606	360	675	856	3,155	760	1,958	1,636	29	886	1,476	447
Percent rural	100.0	100.0	100.0	74.6	64.1	100.0	100.0	65.8	100.0	98.9	78.0	77.4	87.1
MARITAL CONDITION													
Males 15 years old and over	4,086	849	254	2,015	2,613	3,125	1,377	2,200	2,018	138	1,538	11,798	265
Single	1,336	314	103	609	781	1,020	524	704	633	46	486	3,717	86
Married	2,466	479	125	1,265	1,615	1,884	752	1,321	1,253	84	931	7,156	155
Widowed	217	47	22	134	176	201	90	133	100	7	100	751	23
Divorced	59	9	4	6	38	18	11	42	31	1	20	166	1
Unknown	8	-	-	1	3	2	-	-	1	-	1	8	-
Females 15 years old and over	4,327	784	224	2,064	2,901	3,419	1,328	2,341	2,261	128	1,682	14,641	272
Single	1,092	230	51	441	679	933	381	583	604	30	437	3,919	69
Married	2,489	456	133	1,235	1,679	1,880	776	1,310	1,274	86	966	7,350	157
Widowed	683	79	33	371	475	541	155	387	324	10	244	2,894	41
Divorced	60	19	7	16	64	60	16	60	57	2	35	468	4
Unknown	3	-	-	1	4	5	-	1	2	-	-	10	1
FAMILIES													
Number of families	3,015	508	158	1,441	2,019	2,365	887	1,626	1,580	95	1,132	10,363	184
Median size	3.68	4.46	3.66	3.93	3.39	3.90	4.42	3.32	3.95	-	4.06	3.16	3.90
Familes having—													
No children under 10	1,523	219	84	638	1,115	1,118	359	859	709	44	517	5,994	96
1 child under 10	566	84	24	288	393	424	187	312	331	17	201	1,804	27
2 children under 10	350	64	19	202	205	305	133	176	227	13	168	1,117	24
3 or more	576	141	31	313	306	518	208	279	313	21	246	1,448	37

CHARACTERISTICS OF NEGRO POPULATION BY COUNTIES: 1930—Continued

[See note at head of table]

SUBJECT	ALABAMA—Continued													
	Elmore more	Escambia	Etowah	Fayette	Franklin	Geneva	Greene	Hale	Henry	Houston	Jackson	Jefferson	Lamar	Lauderdale
POPULATION BY SEX														
Negro population: 1930	14, 182	8, 558	9, 944	2, 630	1, 419	3, 898	16, 263	19, 412	10, 789	13, 529	2, 688	167, 957	2, 851	7, 782
Male	7, 085	4, 325	5, 002	1, 311	677	1, 867	7, 957	9, 442	5, 279	6, 554	1, 355	80, 705	1, 443	3, 688
Female	7, 097	4, 233	4, 942	1, 319	742	2, 031	8, 306	9, 970	5, 510	6, 975	1, 333	87, 252	1, 408	4, 094
Negro population: 1920	11, 944	6, 293	7, 528	2, 481	1, 418	4, 404	15, 043	17, 896	10, 453	10, 421	3, 008	130, 291	2, 850	8, 117
Male	5, 909	3, 065	3, 934	1, 232	691	2, 173	7, 121	8, 572	5, 103	5, 074	1, 472	65, 887	1, 441	4, 254
Female	6, 035	3, 228	3, 594	1, 249	727	2, 231	7, 922	9, 324	5, 350	5, 347	1, 536	64, 404	1, 409	3, 863
Percent of total population:														
1930	41. 4	30. 6	15. 7	14. 3	5. 6	12. 9	82. 4	73. 9	47. 3	29. 5	7. 3	38. 9	15. 8	18. 9
1920	42. 5	28. 0	15. 9	13. 5	6. 4	15. 0	83. 0	73. 7	48. 5	27. 9	8. 4	42. 0	15. 7	20. 5
VOTING AGE: 1930														
Total 21 years old and over	6, 801	4. 320	5, 483	1, 215	720	1, 775	8, 241	9, 424	4, 590	6, 291	1, 288	100, 250	1, 209	3, 893
Male	3, 396	2, 255	2, 800	610	347	842	3, 970	4. 549	2, 287	2, 990	666	48, 812	611	1, 810
Female	3, 405	2, 065	2, 683	605	373	933	4, 271	4, 875	2, 303	3, 301	622	51, 438	598	2, 083
AGE: 1930														
Under 5 years	1, 797	939	987	343	182	472	1, 862	2, 439	1, 534	1, 615	294	16, 257	434	796
Under 1 year	347	165	196	68	41	88	349	432	320	301	67	3, 122	93	172
5 to 9 years	1, 932	1, 061	1, 073	318	183	538	2, 070	2, 526	1, 531	1, 791	362	17, 197	426	1, 000
10 to 14 years	1, 661	991	1, 045	334	159	522	1, 882	2, 275	1, 513	1, 754	332	14, 585	391	1, 013
15 to 19 years	1, 684	1, 060	1, 112	350	141	493	1, 795	2, 330	1, 407	1, 728	357	15, 940	322	903
20 to 24 years	1, 436	903	1, 212	296	132	409	1, 759	1, 853	1, 145	1, 525	268	19, 482	286	736
25 to 29 years	1, 049	623	983	208	99	288	1, 181	1, 346	794	1, 117	162	20, 163	211	540
30 to 34 years	734	533	705	129	76	188	773	874	506	741	156	14, 759	111	454
35 to 44 years	1, 329	966	1, 219	217	142	334	1, 490	1, 723	806	1, 273	229	25, 751	236	836
45 to 54 years	1, 401	824	1, 056	263	161	391	1, 836	2, 025	873	1, 152	260	15, 151	248	810
55 to 64 years	650	394	346	93	80	158	904	965	371	489	149	5, 457	105	386
65 to 74 years	297	176	148	54	42	72	454	652	201	229	83	2, 178	41	197
75 years and over	193	88	53	25	21	28	252	403	100	97	36	925	39	97
Unknown	19	-------	5	-------	1	5	5	1	8	18	-------	112	1	14
SCHOOL ATTENDANCE														
Total 7 to 13 years, inclusive	2, 451	1, 433	1, 433	456	237	733	2, 680	3, 263	2, 107	2, 442	499	22, 021	555	1, 391
Number attending school	1, 792	1, 029	1, 255	392	188	535	1, 698	2, 658	1, 281	1, 908	355	20, 993	510	1, 164
Percent attending school	73. 1	71. 8	87. 6	86. 0	79. 3	73. 0	63. 4	81. 5	60. 8	78. 1	71. 1	95. 3	91. 9	83. 7
Total 14 and 15 years, inclusive	674	392	436	142	63	218	772	936	603	739	125	5, 767	155	405
Number attending school	446	254	304	114	46	146	484	679	302	439	88	4, 782	120	324
Percent attending school	66. 2	64. 8	69. 7	80. 3	-------	67. 0	62. 7	72. 5	50. 1	59. 4	70. 4	82. 9	77. 4	80. 0
Total 16 and 17 years, inclusive	726	444	472	164	56	221	773	978	607	735	160	6, 279	134	377
Number attending school	266	160	130	91	29	92	263	418	149	186	67	3, 009	81	174
Percent attending school	36. 6	36. 0	27. 5	55. 5	-------	41. 6	34. 40	42. 7	24. 5	25. 3	41. 9	47. 9	60. 4	46. 2
Total 18 to 20 years, inclusive	929	623	690	189	87	265	1, 082	1, 307	710	996	187	10, 469	187	517
Number attending school	71	77	40	33	8	19	69	178	43	63	33	1, 189	32	77
Percent attending school	7. 6	12. 4	5. 8	17. 5	-------	7. 2	6. 4	13. 6	6. 1	6. 3	17. 6	11. 4	17. 1	14. 9
ILLITERACY														
Total 10 years old and over	10, 453	6, 558	7, 884	1, 969	1, 054	2, 888	12, 331	14, 447	7, 724	10, 123	2, 032	134, 503	1, 991	5, 986
Number illiterate	3, 377	1, 688	1, 312	353	223	800	5, 234	4, 411	3, 085	2, 835	553	22, 213	447	1, 335
Percent illiterate	32. 3	25. 7	16. 6	17. 9	21. 2	27. 7	42. 4	30. 5	39. 9	28. 0	27. 2	16. 5	22. 5	22. 3
Percent illiterate in 1920	32. 3	35. 0	24. 5	27. 6	32. 8	30. 2	43. 4	38. 6	39. 7	32. 0	29. 4	20. 8	22. 7	22. 6
URBAN AND RURAL														
Urban population	-------	2, 641	8, 018	-------	442	-------	-------	-------	-------	6, 194	-------	120, 353	-------	2, 751
Percent urban	-------	30. 9	80. 6	-------	31. 1	-------	-------	-------	-------	45. 8	-------	71. 7	-------	35. 4
Rural population	14, 182	5, 917	1, 926	2, 630	977	3, 898	16, 263	19, 412	10, 789	7, 335	2, 688	47, 604	2, 851	5, 031
Rural-farm	11, 214	2, 517	854	1, 862	584	2, 286	14, 138	17, 216	8, 649	6, 039	1, 542	1, 878	2, 359	4, 676
Rural-nonfarm	2, 968	3, 400	1, 072	768	393	1, 612	2, 125	2, 196	2, 140	1, 296	1, 146	45, 726	492	355
Percent rural	100. 0	69. 1	19. 4	100. 0	68. 9	100. 0	100. 0	100. 0	100. 0	54. 2	100. 0	28. 3	100. 0	64. 6
MARITAL CONDITION														
Males 15 year old and over	4, 353	2, 842	3, 433	814	419	1, 117	5, 020	5, 811	3, 040	3, 966	868	57, 154	795	2, 329
Single	1, 366	938	1, 094	298	190	327	1, 573	1, 700	911	1, 359	319	16, 551	277	712
Married	2, 690	1, 711	1, 988	456	270	694	3, 005	3, 631	1, 954	2, 306	481	35, 418	474	1, 445
Widowed	261	180	225	51	24	74	373	360	154	225	58	4, 122	39	136
Divorced	32	12	124	7	5	21	66	118	21	67	10	998	5	36
Unknown	4	1	2	2	1	1	3	2	-------	9	-------	65	-------	-------
Females 15 years old and over	4, 439	2, 725	3, 406	821	476	1, 249	5, 429	6, 361	3, 171	4, 403	832	62, 764	805	2, 644
Single	984	670	677	244	117	289	1, 326	1, 480	759	1, 109	223	12, 339	211	636
Married	2, 692	1, 529	1, 994	455	293	730	2, 985	3, 721	1, 941	2, 348	474	36, 600	474	1, 522
Widowed	713	517	581	114	60	182	986	927	420	757	111	11, 965	97	427
Divorced	50	9	153	6	5	48	130	231	51	185	24	1, 803	22	58
Unknown	-------	-------	1	2	1	-------	2	2	-------	4	-------	57	1	1
FAMILIES														
Number of families	3, 082	1, 840	2, 316	527	329	837	3, 988	4, 611	2, 166	2, 880	550	44, 239	548	1, 836
Median size	3. 53	3. 44	3. 19	4. 05	3. 40	3. 72	3. 27	3. 46	4. 26	3. 93	3. 90	2. 90	4. 56	3. 41
Families having—														
No children under 10	1, 532	1, 005	1, 337	265	177	410	2, 195	2, 462	864	1, 344	273	27, 973	212	1, 055
1 child under 10	562	318	432	76	61	169	747	800	473	580	98	7, 632	91	319
2 children under 10	377	187	253	84	34	97	475	571	339	436	76	4, 093	92	180
3 or more	611	330	294	102	57	161	571	778	490	520	103	4, 541	153	282

CHARACTERISTICS OF NEGRO POPULATION BY COUNTIES: 1930—Continued

[See note at head of table]

SUBJECT	Lawrence	Lee	Limestone	Lowndes	Macon	Madison	Marengo	Marion	Marshall	Mobile	Monroe	Montgomery	Morgan	Perry
	ALABAMA—Continued													
POPULATION BY SEX														
Negro population: 1930	7,053	18,629	9,987	19,632	22,320	19,272	26,349	861	1,272	42,255	15,782	52,144	8,311	19,156
Male	3,457	8,839	4,927	9,463	11,111	9,456	12,679	463	665	19,659	7,910	24,230	4,070	9,266
Female	3,596	9,790	5,060	10,169	11,209	9,816	13,670	398	607	22,596	7,872	27,914	4,241	9,890
Negro population: 1920	6,739	18,784	9,628	22,016	19,614	17,483	26,111	621	1,287	39,667	15,945	48,463	7,736	18,258
Male	3,266	9,080	4,769	10,501	9,208	8,512	12,390	297	636	19,322	7,865	22,336	3,777	8,786
Female	3,473	9,704	4,859	11,515	10,406	8,971	13,721	324	651	20,345	8,080	26,127	3,959	9,472
Percent of total population:														
1930	26.2	51.7	27.3	85.8	82.4	29.8	72.3	3.3	3.2	35.7	52.5	52.8	18.0	72.6
1920	27.7	57.2	30.7	86.7	83.2	34.1	72.4	2.8	3.9	39.6	55.2	59.9	19.2	72.0
VOTING AGE: 1930														
Total 21 years old and over	3,390	8,292	4,842	8,981	10,843	9,455	13,225	443	661	25,472	7,123	28,285	4,573	8,889
Male	1,656	3,800	2,352	4,136	5,313	4,496	6,334	253	361	11,757	3,560	12,738	2,236	4,174
Female	1,734	4,492	2,490	4,845	5,530	4,959	6,891	190	300	13,715	3,563	15,547	2,337	4,715
AGE: 1930														
Under 5 years	853	2,382	1,276	2,425	2,387	2,347	3,038	76	111	3,922	2,052	4,817	860	2,568
Under 1 year	177	413	261	470	416	490	538	16	18	718	378	918	177	502
5 to 9 years	915	2,666	1,233	2,654	2,740	2,500	3,389	104	171	4,277	2,319	5,861	911	2,537
10 to 14 years	879	2,496	1,199	2,673	2,923	2,309	3,149	103	137	3,582	2,048	5,658	901	2,404
15 to 19 years	863	2,355	1,207	2,453	2,835	2,216	2,933	115	164	4,066	1,913	6,305	878	2,370
20 to 24 years	738	1,746	1,062	1,713	2,217	1,897	2,625	124	137	4,669	1,541	5,480	854	1,861
25 to 29 years	488	1,305	728	1,144	1,473	1,366	1,932	80	98	4,216	1,076	4,409	721	1,223
30 to 34 years	371	860	542	848	1,269	1,039	1,282	56	82	3,317	733	3,180	539	806
35 to 44 years	727	1,709	975	1,866	2,520	1,930	2,497	82	149	6,022	1,412	6,588	935	1,677
45 to 54 years	661	1,797	905	1,890	2,251	1,868	2,909	69	119	4,665	1,541	5,567	922	1,901
55 to 64 years	333	753	501	1,042	955	1,055	1,466	30	55	2,135	650	2,345	439	934
65 to 74 years	144	381	243	616	501	466	704	13	27	883	327	1,271	224	588
75 years and over	81	160	111	303	237	270	418	7	21	366	152	623	123	275
Unknown	-------	19	5	5	12	9	7	2	1	135	18	40	4	12
SCHOOL ATTENDANCE														
Total 7 to 13 years, inclusive	1,227	3,574	1,703	3,659	3,924	3,287	4,467	139	203	5,398	3,044	7,903	1,283	3,317
Number attending school	1,031	2,457	1,187	3,013	3,136	2,653	3,723	119	140	4,950	2,538	6,827	1,049	2,605
Percent attending school	84.0	68.7	69.7	82.3	79.9	80.7	83.3	85.6	69.0	91.7	83.4	86.4	81.8	78.5
Total 14 and 15 years, inclusive	360	1,030	480	1,093	1,255	976	1,269	45	68	1,478	778	2,513	352	1,032
Number attending school	311	596	309	924	970	745	1,023	37	36	1,141	627	2,091	260	755
Percent attending school	86.4	57.9	64.4	84.5	77.3	76.3	80.6	-------	-------	77.2	80.6	83.2	73.9	73.2
Total 16 and 17 years, inclusive	359	1,024	499	1,072	1,270	887	1,250	43	66	1,555	822	2,581	347	982
Number attending school	214	352	173	679	612	423	582	22	22	607	475	1,342	130	421
Percent attending school	59.6	34.4	34.7	63.3	48.2	47.7	46.6	-------	-------	39.0	57.8	52.0	37.5	42.9
Total 18 to 20 years, inclusive	475	1,254	693	1,343	1,552	1,307	1,722	71	90	2,684	1,037	3,680	548	1,277
Number attending school	74	109	51	282	244	208	230	24	15	196	194	649	49	146
Percent attending school	15.6	8.7	7.4	21.0	15.7	15.9	13.4	-------	-------	7.3	18.7	17.6	8.9	11.4
ILLITERACY														
Total 10 years old and over	5,285	13,581	7,478	14,553	17,193	14,425	19,922	681	990	34,056	11,411	41,466	6,540	14,051
Number illiterate	1,209	4,463	2,564	5,095	3,898	3,449	6,377	136	331	6,956	2,942	10,535	1,530	4,254
Percent illiterate	22.9	32.9	34.3	35.0	22.7	23.9	32.0	20.0	33.4	20.4	25.8	25.4	23.4	30.3
Percent illiterate in 1920	30.2	22.8	38.2	37.7	27.8	28.8	45.6	17.2	26.3	23.8	36.7	29.5	25.1	39.2
URBAN AND RURAL														
Urban population	-------	5,002	853	-------	2,288	3,825	2,365	-------	557	26,573	-------	29,970	3,867	-------
Percent urban	-------	26.9	8.5	-------	10.3	19.8	9.0	-------	43.8	62.9	-------	57.5	46.5	-------
Rural population	7,053	13,627	9,134	19,632	20,032	15,447	23,984	861	715	15,682	15,782	22,174	4,444	19,156
Rural-farm	6,473	12,587	8,572	17,886	17,249	13,584	22,218	418	543	2,224	12,306	18,846	3,267	16,168
Rural-nonfarm	580	1,040	562	1,746	2,783	1,863	1,766	443	172	13,458	3,476	3,328	1,177	2,988
Percent rural	100.0	73.1	91.5	100.0	89.7	80.2	91.0	100.0	56.2	37.1	100.0	42.5	53.5	100.0
MARITAL CONDITION														
Males 15 years old and over	2,116	5,048	3,035	5,526	6,993	5,783	7,995	316	462	13,896	4,671	16,159	2,737	5,491
Single	627	1,607	847	1,799	2,604	1,728	2,294	110	192	4,428	1,574	5,275	787	1,699
Married	1,360	3,101	1,938	3,374	3,930	3,588	5,016	187	219	8,263	2,746	9,602	1,680	3,437
Widowed	109	296	180	331	393	359	532	17	46	1,013	227	1,014	202	309
Divorced	20	43	69	19	56	107	136	2	5	161	35	245	62	46
Unknown	-------	1	1	3	10	1	17	-------	-------	31	89	23	6	-------
Females 15 years old and over	2,290	6,037	3,244	6,354	7,277	6,333	8,778	262	391	16,578	4,692	19,649	2,902	6,156
Single	531	1,684	668	1,732	2,110	1,283	1,969	90	117	3,847	1,293	5,064	568	1,534
Married	1,394	3,173	1,971	3,543	3,827	3,631	5,034	144	202	8,930	2,719	9,866	1,677	3,593
Widowed	337	1,094	480	1,031	1,235	1,196	1,472	26	56	3,400	594	4,071	494	923
Divorced	28	78	123	45	98	221	288	2	13	364	73	611	155	98
Unknown	-------	8	2	3	7	2	15	-------	3	37	13	37	8	8
FAMILIES														
Number of families	1,608	4,092	2,276	4,586	4,792	4,512	6,571	170	245	10,775	3,308	13,354	2,093	4,395
Median size	3.63	3.79	3.68	3.47	3.72	3.46	3.24	3.35	3.78	2.75	3.91	2.96	3.11	3.52
Families having:														
No children under 10	826	2,007	1,121	2,407	2,572	2,436	3,712	84	130	6,942	1,560	8,402	1,282	2,320
1 child under 10	311	736	481	816	848	759	1,148	42	41	1,734	579	2,165	326	746
2 children under 10	193	497	291	533	568	544	699	17	28	981	440	1,224	211	469
3 or more	278	852	383	830	804	773	1,012	27	46	1,118	729	1,563	274	860

CHARACTERISTICS OF NEGRO POPULATION BY COUNTIES: 1930—Continued

[See note at head of table]

SUBJECT	ALABAMA—Continued													
	Pickens	Pike	Ran-dolph	Russell	St. Clair	Shelby	Sumter	Talla-dega	Talla-poosa	Tusca-loosa	Walker	Wash-ington	Wilcox	Win-ston
POPULATION BY SEX														
Negro population: 1930	11, 932	14, 539	5, 884	19, 562	4, 832	6, 973	21, 247	17, 152	9, 773	21, 566	7, 813	6, 813	19, 319	83
Male	5, 775	6, 991	2, 897	9, 209	2, 448	3, 635	10, 173	8, 345	4, 781	10, 525	4, 050	3, 537	9, 368	46
Female	6, 157	7, 548	2, 987	10, 353	2, 384	3, 338	11, 074	8, 807	4, 992	11, 041	3, 763	3, 276	9, 951	37
Negro population: 1920	12, 324	14, 795	5, 936	20, 935	4, 449	7, 044	19, 831	17, 398	10, 070	19, 780	8, 190	5, 856	25, 009	81
Male	6, 030	7, 086	2, 925	9, 855	2, 284	3, 721	9, 517	8, 506	4, 939	9, 827	4, 486	2, 982	12, 017	43
Female	6, 294	7, 709	3, 011	11, 080	2, 165	3, 323	10, 314	8, 892	5, 131	9, 953	3, 704	2, 874	12, 992	38
Percent of total population:														
1930	47. 9	45. 1	21. 9	71. 5	19. 7	25. 3	78. 9	37. 9	31. 3	33. 6	13. 1	41. 6	77. 6	0. 5
1920	48. 6	46. 8	21. 9	76. 3	19. 0	26. 0	77. 6	42. 4	33. 9	36. 8	16. 2	41. 0	80. 5	0. 6
VOTING AGE: 1930														
Total 21 years old and over	5, 623	6, 865	2, 577	8, 383	2, 231	3, 595	10, 210	7, 730	4, 491	11, 541	4, 494	3, 169	8, 991	69
Male	2, 686	3, 193	1, 243	3, 769	1, 229	1, 940	4, 762	3, 690	2, 153	5, 677	2, 443	1, 659	4, 242	36
Female	2, 937	3, 672	1, 334	4, 614	1, 092	1, 655	5, 448	4, 040	2, 338	5, 864	2, 051	1, 510	4, 749	33
AGE: 1930														
Under 5 years	1, 488	1, 639	764	2, 585	596	858	2, 749	2, 129	1, 272	2, 386	873	861	2, 328	3
Under 1 year	304	284	173	430	106	168	478	416	256	459	164	113	435	1
5 to 9 years	1, 647	1, 934	843	2, 937	658	836	2, 871	2, 333	1, 341	2, 449	884	949	2, 630	3
10 to 14 years	1, 534	1, 929	837	2, 785	604	729	2, 515	2, 290	1, 222	2, 225	700	842	2, 590	4
15 to 19 years	1, 396	1, 813	733	2, 464	552	789	2, 484	2, 275	1, 218	2, 442	702	831	2, 354	2
20 to 24 years	1, 077	1, 498	571	1, 659	431	750	1, 964	1, 721	1, 005	2, 486	862	700	1, 692	12
25 to 29 years	818	1, 031	410	1, 294	347	590	1, 496	1, 135	716	2, 036	842	520	1, 088	14
30 to 34 years	623	706	258	888	302	410	1, 110	754	485	1, 257	594	369	759	8
35 to 44 years	1, 088	1, 477	504	1, 655	508	693	2, 095	1, 417	823	2, 498	1, 050	637	1, 749	15
45 to 54 years	1, 151	1, 360	513	1, 832	488	718	1, 655	1, 715	943	2, 155	845	634	2, 085	16
55 to 64 years	624	666	244	871	195	350	1, 358	795	424	981	286	272	1, 114	2
65 to 74 years	328	314	123	408	100	157	631	382	208	445	118	127	590	3
75 years and over	158	151	84	174	50	91	318	201	113	203	48	59	337	1
Unknown	-------	21	-------	10	1	2	1	5	3	3	9	12	3	-------
SCHOOL ATTENDANCE														
Total 7 to 13 years, inclusive	2, 153	2, 612	1, 151	3, 862	889	1, 066	3, 648	3, 198	1, 761	3, 169	1, 061	1, 215	3, 578	5
Number attending school	1, 797	1, 799	936	2, 610	808	996	3, 085	2, 644	1, 438	2, 715	958	795	2, 767	3
Percent attending school	83. 5	68. 9	81. 3	67. 6	90. 9	93. 4	84. 6	82. 7	81. 7	85. 7	90. 3	65. 4	77. 3	-------
Total 14 and 15 years, inclusive	620	815	335	1, 147	231	299	1, 053	952	499	933	253	331	1, 120	1
Number attending school	522	466	252	778	189	257	943	733	368	681	215	187	893	-------
Percent attending school	84. 2	57. 2	75. 2	67. 8	81. 8	86. 0	89. 6	77. 0	73. 7	73. 0	85. 0	56. 5	79. 7	-------
Total 16 and 17 years, inclusive	618	784	292	1, 105	247	324	1, 083	998	544	1, 002	292	361	1, 011	2
Number attending school	329	268	140	431	101	140	679	435	242	431	134	113	518	-------
Percent attending school	53. 2	34. 2	47. 9	39. 0	40. 9	43. 2	62. 7	43. 6	44. 5	43. 0	45. 9	31. 3	51. 2	-------
Total 18 to 20 years, inclusive	745	1, 011	426	1, 256	295	478	1, 306	1, 191	658	1, 514	456	483	1, 211	2
Number attending school	123	111	56	94	20	57	229	153	82	217	52	47	189	-------
Percent attending school	16. 5	11. 0	13. 1	7. 5	6. 8	11. 9	17. 5	12. 8	12. 5	14. 3	11. 4	9. 7	15. 6	-------
ILLITERACY														
Total 10 years old and over	8, 797	10, 966	4, 277	14, 040	3, 578	5, 279	15, 627	12, 690	7, 160	16, 731	6, 056	5, 003	14, 361	77
Number illiterate	3, 040	3, 609	775	4, 872	758	1, 097	5, 073	2, 839	1, 942	3, 947	1, 248	1, 670	5, 198	5
Percent illiterate	34. 6	32. 9	18. 1	34. 7	21. 2	20. 8	32. 5	22. 4	27. 1	23. 6	20. 6	33. 4	36. 2	-------
Percent illiterate in 1920	41. 7	35. 9	22. 8	41. 8	25. 2	32. 3	42. 7	24. 9	31. 2	30. 9	25. 8	37. 9	36. 7	-------
URBAN AND RURAL														
Urban population	-------	3, 115	691	2, 925	-------	-------	-------	3, 630	1, 244	7, 075	1, 615	-------	-------	-------
Percent urban	-------	21. 4	11. 7	15. 0	-------	-------	-------	21. 2	12. 7	32. 8	20. 7	-------	-------	-------
Rural population	11, 932	11, 424	5, 193	16, 637	4, 832	6, 973	21, 247	13, 522	8, 529	14, 491	6, 198	6, 813	19, 319	83
Rural-farm	10, 357	9, 970	4, 738	15, 384	2, 315	3, 007	18, 479	11, 623	6, 765	7, 690	395	4, 037	17, 393	6
Rural-nonfarm	1, 575	1, 454	455	1, 253	2, 517	3, 966	2, 768	1, 899	1, 764	6, 801	5, 803	2, 776	1, 926	77
Percent rural	100. 0	78. 6	88. 3	85. 0	100. 0	100. 0	100. 0	78. 8	87. 3	67. 2	79. 3	100. 0	100. 0	100. 0
MARITAL CONDITION														
Males 15 years old and over	3, 489	4, 220	1, 637	5, 078	1, 552	2, 414	6, 108	4, 993	2, 854	7, 022	2, 852	2, 139	5, 507	39
Single	1, 010	1, 358	544	1, 561	485	780	1, 820	1, 821	981	2, 217	865	749	1, 879	13
Married	2, 237	2, 565	975	3, 193	950	1, 383	3, 837	2, 851	1, 655	4, 239	1, 707	1, 267	3, 258	22
Widowed	201	206	99	282	101	240	334	286	190	478	226	109	307	4
Divorced	41	90	16	40	16	10	117	34	28	82	52	8	62	-------
Unknown	-------	1	3	2	-------	1	-------	1	-------	6	2	6	1	-------
Females 15 years old and over	3, 774	4, 817	1, 803	6, 177	1, 422	2, 136	7, 004	5, 407	3, 084	7, 484	2, 504	2, 022	6, 264	34
Single	850	1, 239	518	1, 639	322	426	1, 713	1, 559	872	1, 662	369	535	2, 022	5
Married	2, 259	2, 631	1, 014	3, 336	947	1, 340	3, 832	2, 913	1, 695	4, 291	1, 654	1, 270	3, 329	22
Widowed	572	735	226	1, 081	143	348	1, 175	812	447	1, 373	386	200	788	7
Divorced	92	209	44	121	10	20	281	121	70	142	94	15	124	-------
Unknown	1	3	1	-------	-------	2	3	2	-------	16	1	2	1	-------
FAMILIES														
Number of families	2, 679	3, 235	1, 171	4, 218	1, 062	1, 577	4, 835	3, 420	2, 027	5, 232	1, 990	1, 455	4, 466	23
Median size	3. 76	3. 68	4. 18	3. 95	3. 52	3. 44	3. 63	4. 24	4. 06	3. 14	2. 88	3. 79	3. 49	-------
Families having—														
No children under 10	1, 311	1, 681	506	1, 982	533	847	2, 455	1, 566	949	3, 042	1, 213	699	2, 371	19
1 child under 10	521	591	239	767	203	288	894	641	347	912	319	267	790	3
2 children under 10	348	383	168	555	131	170	584	485	303	540	180	190	495	-------
3 or more	499	580	258	914	195	272	902	728	428	738	278	299	810	1

CHARACTERISTICS OF NEGRO POPULATION BY COUNTIES: 1930—Continued

[See note at head of table]

SUBJECT	ARIZONA													
	The State	Apache	Cochise	Coconino	Gila	Graham	Greenlee	Maricopa	Navajo	Pima	Pinal	Santa Cruz	Yavapai	Yuma
POPULATION BY SEX														
Negro population: 1930	10,749	338	1,910	115	161	53	28	4,879	98	1,251	234	718	181	783
Male	6,352	189	1,493	55	79	30	22	2,526	48	653	170	568	92	427
Female	4,397	149	417	60	82	23	6	2,353	50	598	64	150	89	356
Negro population: 1920	8,005	14	1,538	53	319	88	60	1,436	46	419	97	3,269	282	382
Male	5,859	10	1,178	25	151	54	28	722	22	210	59	3,031	151	217
Female	2,146	4	360	28	168	34	32	714	24	209	38	238	131	165
Percent of total population:														
1930	2.5	1.9	4.7	0.8	0.5	0.5	0.3	3.2	0.5	2.2	1.1	7.4	0.6	4.4
1920	2.4	0.1	3.3	0.5	1.2	0.9	0.4	1.6	0.3	1.2	0.6	25.8	1.2	2.6
VOTING AGE: 1930														
Total 21 years old and over	7,407	230	1,594	77	100	17	19	3,029	76	918	173	572	123	479
Male	4,591	142	1,295	40	48	10	15	1,595	39	486	133	467	58	263
Female	2,816	88	299	37	52	7	4	1,434	37	432	40	105	65	216
AGE: 1930														
Under 5 years	793	33	60	5	14	7	1	415	5	98	11	43	9	92
Under 1 year	153	4	7	2	2	1		84		22	3	8	2	18
5 to 9 years	831	30	63	10	21	6	4	469	6	84	11	34	18	75
10 to 14 years	727	23	40	9	14	8	3	458	6	60	10	14	13	69
15 to 19 years	788	16	97	11	9	14		432	3	74	21	39	18	54
20 to 24 years	1,128	27	345	10	12	5	3	428	7	98	24	100	13	56
25 to 29 years	1,163	36	281	15	24	3	1	444	13	128	43	89	10	76
30 to 34 years	1,178	53	285	10	22		4	404	13	145	19	136	16	71
35 to 44 years	2,196	84	484	24	26	4	6	864	26	312	42	175	30	119
45 to 54 years	1,236	29	193	13	7	4	4	586	9	165	27	63	37	99
55 to 64 years	460	7	44	5	8	1	1	244	7	51	15	21	8	48
65 to 74 years	163		14	2	4	1		81	2	20	8	3	6	22
75 years and over	60		4	1			1	40	1	6	3		2	2
Unknown	26							14		10		1	1	
SCHOOL ATTENDANCE														
Total 7 to 13 years, inclusive	1,099	35	71	14	27	11	5	661	8	96	19	30	22	100
Number attending school	1,028	35	59	14	27	4	1	625	7	93	18	28	22	95
Percent attending school	93.5							94.6						95.0
Total 14 and 15 years, inclusive	273	6	13	6	3	4		181	2	21	3	7	3	24
Number attending school	239	6	13	6	3	2		155	2	18	3	7	2	22
Percent attending school	87.5							85.6						
Total 16 and 17 years, inclusive	297	7	17	5	2	4		179	1	28	10	11	9	24
Number attending school	165	6	6	4	1	1		99	1	16	4	8	7	12
Percent attending school	55.6							55.3						
Total 18 to 20 years, inclusive	565	14	134	6	9	9	1	243	3	51	17	40	7	31
Number attending school	69		3	2	4	2		31	2	12	1	7	2	3
Percent attending school	12.2		2.2					12.8						
ILLITERACY														
Total 10 years old and over	9,125	275	1,787	100	126	40	23	3,995	87	1,069	212	641	154	616
Number illiterate	366	51	19	13	6	5	1	204	5	11	19	3	4	25
Percent illiterate	4.0	18.5	1.1	13.0	4.8			5.1		1.0	9.0	0.5	2.6	4.1
Percent illiterate in 1920	4.6		2.0		15.3			3.6		3.8		5.1	3.7	5.9
URBAN AND RURAL														
Urban population	5,147		293	100	139			2,499	65	1,003		679	171	198
Percent urban	47.9		15.3	87.0	86.3			51.2		80.2		94.6	94.5	25.3
Rural population	5,602	338	1,617	15	22	53	28	2,380	33	248	234	39	10	585
Rural-farm	1,249	6	97	1	2	36		728	5	50	59	5	5	255
Rural-nonfarm	4,353	332	1,520	14	20	17	28	1,652	28	198	175	34	5	330
Percent rural	52.1	100.0	84.7	13.0	13.7			48.8		19.8	100.0	5.4	5.5	74.7
MARITAL CONDITION														
Males 15 years old and over	5,181	150	1,421	48	53	19	16	1,874	43	525	150	515	70	297
Single	2,381	32	979	16	16	9	8	634	11	186	67	312	25	86
Married	2,373	102	389	28	33	10	7	1,045	29	297	60	161	38	174
Widowed	258	13	20	4	4		1	129	2	25	12	17	5	26
Divorced	157	3	32					56	1	17	11	25	2	10
Unknown	12		1					10						1
Females 15 years old and over	3,217	102	326	43	59	13	4	1,663	38	484	52	112	71	250
Single	450	7	25	5	11	5		254	4	78	8	11	10	32
Married	2,163	82	251	28	33	8	4	1,073	27	312	39	87	40	179
Widowed	481	12	34	9	13			265	6	77	5	12	18	30
Divorced	121	1	16	1	2			71	1	15		2	3	9
Unknown	2									2				
FAMILIES														
Number of families	2,776	107	325	41	46	9	8	1,276	34	394	44	180	60	252
Median size	2.22	2.23	2.01					2.44		1.98		2.06		2.13
Families having—														
No children under 10	2,014	78	256	31	29	5	7	864	28	324	33	129	49	181
1 child under 10	354	12	35	8	8	1	0	193	3	31	6	26	5	26
2 children under 10	179	10	21	1	6	0	0	93	1	12	3	14	1	17
3 or more	229	7	13	1	3	3	1	126	2	27	2	11	5	28

CHARACTERISTICS OF NEGRO POPULATION BY COUNTIES: 1930—Continued

(See note at head of table)

SUBJECT	ARKANSAS													
	The State	Arkansas	Ashley	Baxter	Benton	Bradley	Calhoun	Carroll	Chicot	Clark	Clay	Cleburne	Cleveland	Columbia
POPULATION BY SEX														
Negro population: 1930	478,463	4,916	11,858	1	88	5,752	2,993	25	14,143	7,293	10	3	3,478	12,726
Male	236,909	2,459	6,043		42	2,797	1,449	14	7,050	3,684	8		1,770	6,332
Female	241,554	2,457	5,815	1	46	2,955	1,544	11	7,093	3,609	2	3	1,708	6,394
Negro population: 1920	472,220	5,190	10,443	4	102	4,953	4,240	82	16,060	7,828	3	1	3,719	12,648
Male	236,895	2,718	5,194	3	56	2,503	2,101	62	8,014	3,906	1		1,875	6,219
Female	235,325	2,472	5,249	1	46	2,450	2,139	20	8,046	3,922	2	1	1,844	6,429
Percent of total population:														
1930	25.8	22.0	47.1		0.2	32.9	30.7	0.2	62.5	29.3			27.3	46.6
1920	27.0	24.2	44.6		0.3	31.0	35.9	0.5	73.8	30.5			30.3	45.7
VOTING AGE: 1930														
Total 21 years old and over	257,130	2,640	6,249	1	53	2,900	1,451	20	8,271	3,460	9	2	1,632	5,776
Male	128,795	1,356	3,229		28	1,430	714	11	4,114	1,742	7		826	2,906
Female	128,335	1,284	3,020	1	25	1,470	737	9	4,157	1,718	2	2	806	2,870
AGE: 1930														
Under 5 years	49,957	559	1,365		8	721	346	1	1,224	857		1	423	1,670
Under 1 year	9,709	107	283			143	74	1	220	164			92	362
5 to 9 years	55,233	553	1,350		7	715	396	1	1,482	959	1		478	1,835
10 to 14 years	52,911	559	1,269		13	698	357		1,457	905			432	1,620
15 to 19 years	52,545	497	1,351		3	592	380	2	1,418	933			430	1,540
20 to 24 years	49,256	543	1,304		9	643	302	3	1,396	749	1		391	1,320
25 to 29 years	40,164	437	991		5	467	209	1	1,222	539	3		239	1,043
30 to 34 years	31,431	352	791		8	345	142	2	923	395	2		147	710
35 to 44 years	59,314	585	1,400	1	12	696	286	6	1,938	723			330	1,130
45 to 54 years	49,426	447	1,136		9	502	304	4	1,735	684	1	1	310	1,051
55 to 64 years	23,331	228	562		9	218	161	4	856	306			175	483
65 to 74 years	9,989	99	229		2	104	66	1	323	164			84	215
75 years and over	4,664	55	105		3	51	42		165	77		1	37	103
Unknown	242	2	5				2		4	2	2		2	6
SCHOOL ATTENDANCE														
Total 7 to 13 years, inclusive	74,959	788	1,781		12	979	517		2,043	1,317			650	2,391
Number attending school	65,441	699	1,617		11	883	442		1,833	1,208			551	2,144
Percent attending school	87.3	88.7	90.8			90.2	85.5		89.7	91.7			84.8	89.7
Total 14 and 15 years, inclusive	20,750	176	506		6	245	150		574	354			170	639
Number attending school	17,216	143	448		5	199	112		492	371			133	535
Percent attending school	83.0	81.3	88.5			81.2	74.7		85.7	89.5			78.2	83.7
Total 16 and 17 years, inclusive	20,905	211	534		2	251	148	2	552	381			170	625
Number attending school	11,839	125	328		1	133	93	1	321	265			98	419
Percent attending school	56.6	59.2	61.4			53.0	62.8		58.2	69.6			57.6	67.0
Total 18 to 20 years, inclusive	32,166	308	844		4	359	216	1	879	560			252	874
Number attending school	5,493	37	178			62	53		110	163			36	245
Percent attending school	17.1	12.0	21.1			17.3	24.5		12.5	29.1			14.3	28.0
ILLITERACY														
Total 10 years old and over	373,273	3,804	9,143	1	73	4,316	2,251	23	11,437	5,477	9	2	2,577	9,221
Number illiterate	60,102	550	2,099		8	604	460		2,940	714	3	1	403	1,750
Percent illiterate	16.1	14.5	23.0			14.0	20.4		25.7	13.0			15.6	190
Percent illiterate, 1920	21.8	19.0	28.4			23.1	22.8		31.1	17.1			21.6	27.9
URBAN AND RURAL														
Urban population	89,162	1,179	1,172			319			1,625	575				984
Percent urban	18.6	24.0	9.9			5.5			11.5	7.9				7.7
Rural population	389,301	3,737	10,686	1	88	5,433	2,993	25	12,518	6,718	10	3	3,478	11,742
Rural-farm	324,611	3,115	8,919			3,044	2,343	1	10,523	4,290	2	1	3,006	10,900
Rural-nonfarm	64,690	622	1,767	1	88	2,389	650	24	1,995	2,428	8	2	472	842
Percent rural	81.4	76.0	90.1			94.5	100.0		88.5	92.1			100.0	92.3
MARITAL CONDITION														
Males 15 years old and over	158,239	1,664	4,003		31	1,754	937	12	4,932	2,277	7		1,083	3,744
Single	42,866	471	1,082		10	473	295	3	1,245	745	2		348	1,099
Married	100,470	1,020	2,578		17	1,112	558	9	3,235	1,361	5		658	2,346
Widowed	11,773	101	276		3	107	55		348	132			66	202
Divorced	3,002	72	66		1	62	29		99	37			11	94
Unknown	128		1						5	2				3
Females 15 years old and over	162,123	1,581	3,871	1	29	1,864	957	11	5,048	2,295	2	2	1,082	3,857
Single	30,171	267	689		8	408	236	2	744	549			236	895
Married	101,199	1,029	2,557		14	1,125	567	6	3,274	1,390	1	2	671	2,356
Widowed	25,927	192	556	1	6	255	124	3	840	309	1		125	482
Divorced	4,743	93	66		1	76	30		189	45			30	122
Unknown	83		3						1	2				2
FAMILIES														
Number of families	123,009	1,203	2,931		25	1,339	651	9	4,129	1,594			767	2,752
Median size	3.04	3.10	3.23			3.48	3.81		2.68	3.82			3.64	3.95
Families having—														
No children under 10	73,674	695	1,668		19	692	339	7	2,689	795			386	1,235
1 child under 10	21,391	203	530		2	264	120	2	737	316			143	572
2 children under 10	12,516	135	323		1	156	68		365	196			101	388
3 or more	15,428	170	410		3	227	124		338	287			137	557

CHARACTERISTICS OF NEGRO POPULATION BY COUNTIES: 1930—Continued

(See note at head of table)

SUBJECT	ARKANSAS—Continued													
	Conway	Craighead	Crawford	Crittenden	Cross	Dallas	Desha	Drew	Faulkner	Franklin	Garland	Grant	Greene	Hempstead
POPULATION BY SEX														
Negro population: 1930	5, 977	1, 741	1, 099	31, 366	10, 991	5, 216	13, 903	9, 152	3, 657	352	4, 800	872	22	13, 128
Male	2, 936	823	537	15, 983	5, 493	2, 509	6, 938	4, 471	1, 816	169	2, 193	440	14	6, 419
Female	3, 041	918	562	15, 383	5, 498	2, 707	6, 965	4, 681	1, 841	183	2, 607	432	8	6, 709
Negro population: 1920	6, 652	2, 036	1, 692	24, 650	7, 925	4, 938	15, 257	10, 788	4, 121	305	3, 426	1, 060	32	14, 176
Male	3, 259	968	850	12, 728	4, 026	2, 401	7, 806	5, 319	2, 051	143	1, 515	555	22	6, 997
Female	3, 393	1, 068	842	11, 922	3, 899	2, 537	7, 451	5, 469	2, 070	162	1, 911	505	10	7, 179
Percent of total population:														
1930	27. 2	3. 9	4. 9	79. 0	42. 7	35. 6	63. 7	45. 9	12. 9	2. 2	13. 3	8. 9	0. 1	42. 6
1920	29. 5	5. 4	6. 6	84. 1	42. 7	34. 2	75. 2	49. 4	14. 9	1. 6	13. 3	9. 9	0. 1	44. 9
VOTING AGE: 1930														
Total 21 years old and over	2, 710	1, 051	601	17, 360	5, 702	2, 555	7, 787	4, 674	1, 711	168	3, 359	342	21	6, 237
Male	1, 332	501	286	9, 050	2, 947	1, 243	3, 953	2, 351	827	89	1, 543	169	13	3, 065
Female	1, 378	550	315	8, 310	2, 756	1, 312	3, 834	2, 323	884	79	1, 816	173	8	3, 172
AGE: 1930														
Under 5 years	722	160	92	3, 082	1, 219	596	1, 415	1, 020	427	47	256	122	-------	1, 589
Under 1 year	142	26	9	646	229	129	254	193	89	10	49	22	-------	320
5 to 9 years	851	181	131	3, 501	1, 390	651	1, 560	1, 097	531	39	304	141	-------	1, 749
10 to 14 years	824	183	141	3, 399	1, 198	677	1, 452	1, 079	493	43	348	143	-------	1, 612
15 to 19 years	753	138	118	3, 283	1, 230	638	1, 378	1, 076	411	47	428	108	1	1, 647
20 to 24 years	525	154	74	3, 081	1, 098	502	1, 400	921	356	30	536	69	6	1, 300
25 to 29 years	383	155	89	2, 630	896	386	1, 303	717	276	25	518	47	5	973
30 to 34 years	277	137	67	2, 175	664	275	948	489	205	13	439	45	2	733
35 to 44 years	616	264	140	4, 330	1, 240	563	1, 862	1, 018	351	38	883	73	-------	1, 353
45 to 54 years	483	230	109	3, 527	1, 202	479	1, 451	949	304	29	641	63	2	1, 254
55 to 64 years	284	92	78	1, 555	557	254	692	466	163	20	274	34	3	540
65 to 74 years	169	24	34	566	222	130	319	185	96	17	118	22	2	244
75 years and over	86	22	26	232	72	62	121	134	43	4	48	5	1	124
Unknown	4	1	-------	5	3	3	2	1	1	-------	7	-------	-------	10
SCHOOL ATTENDANCE														
Total 7 to 13 years, inclusive	1, 166	255	189	4, 723	1, 752	923	2, 112	1, 520	714	53	459	197	-------	2, 330
Number attending school	1, 067	213	184	3, 687	1, 501	857	1, 828	1, 379	628	45	441	182	-------	2, 097
Percent attending school	91. 5	83. 5	97. 4	78. 1	85. 7	92. 8	86. 6	90. 7	88. 0	-------	96. 1	92. 4	-------	90. 0
Total 14 and 15 years, inclusive	328	64	59	1, 324	503	265	536	450	174	22	144	47	-------	647
Number attending school	300	45	54	966	404	238	438	389	146	21	133	37	-------	553
Percent attending school	91. 5	-------	-------	73. 0	80. 3	89. 8	81. 7	86. 4	83. 9	-------	92. 4	-------	-------	85. 5
Total 16 and 17 years, esclusive	305	52	55	1, 271	472	270	534	421	179	17	179	48	1	656
Number attending school	236	20	34	581	239	182	258	249	118	11	113	28	1	427
Percent attending school	77. 4	-------	-------	45. 7	50. 6	67. 4	48. 3	59. 1	65. 9	-------	63. 1	-------	-------	65. 1
Total 18 to 20 years, inclusive	387	87	49	2, 128	767	331	883	632	234	27	280	60	-------	949
Number attending school	130	7	9	241	90	102	96	91	65	4	71	16	-------	245
Percent attending school	33. 6	-------	-------	11. 3	11. 7	30. 8	10. 9	14. 4	27. 8	-------	25. 4	-------	-------	25. 8
ILLITERACY														
Total 10 years old and over	4, 404	1, 400	876	24, 783	8, 382	3, 969	10, 928	7, 035	2, 699	266	4, 240	609	22	9, 790
Number illiterate	369	212	76	5, 440	1, 005	396	2, 450	1, 122	328	32	232	104	1	1, 134
Percent illiterate	8. 4	15. 1	8. 7	22. 0	12. 0	10. 0	22. 4	15. 9	12. 2	12. 0	5. 5	17. 1	-------	11. 6
Percent illiterate, 1920	16. 1	16. 8	14. 6	29. 2	17. 9	16. 2	24. 9	21. 6	17. 8	17. 3	10. 0	14. 3	-------	20. 3
URBAN AND RURAL														
Urban population	737	1, 316	578	-------	1, 139	1, 302	1, 236	632	928	-------	4, 194	-------	20	1, 986
Percent urban	12. 3	75. 6	52. 6	-------	10. 4	25. 0	8. 9	6. 9	25. 4	-------	87. 4	-------	-------	15. 1
Rural population	5, 240	425	521	31, 366	9, 852	3, 914	12, 667	8, 520	2, 729	352	606	872	2	11, 142
Rural-farm	4, 765	338	320	27, 794	9, 000	2, 554	10, 368	7, 635	2, 691	160	159	735	2	10, 211
Rural-nonfarm	475	87	201	3, 572	852	1, 360	2, 299	885	38	192	447	137	-------	931
Percent rural	87. 7	24. 4	47. 4	100. 0	89. 6	75. 0	91. 1	93. 1	74. 6	100. 0	12. 6	100. 0	-------	84. 9
MARITAL CONDITION														
Males 15 years old and over	1, 756	570	362	10, 970	3, 615	1, 575	4, 761	2, 927	1, 075	114	1, 772	232	14	3, 953
Single	565	114	123	2, 607	889	484	1, 215	802	334	33	521	79	8	1, 180
Married	1, 021	388	209	7, 427	2, 411	944	3, 071	1, 882	637	70	1, 037	145	4	2, 506
Widowed	152	48	27	743	230	123	352	184	90	10	191	8	2	223
Divorced	16	20	3	171	83	24	122	58	13	1	23	-------	-------	38
Unknown	2	-------	-------	22	2	-------	1	1	1	-------	-------	-------	-------	6
Females 15 years old and over	1, 824	647	373	10, 414	3, 569	1, 717	4, 715	3, 029	1, 131	109	2, 120	234	8	4, 225
Single	479	90	84	1, 510	614	449	706	607	263	32	424	66	4	980
Married	1, 009	393	218	7, 445	2, 426	960	3, 091	1, 888	639	68	1, 064	144	2	2, 558
Widowed	312	111	64	1, 263	433	256	760	443	208	7	561	21	2	612
Divorced	22	53	7	180	96	52	158	91	20	2	68	3	-------	74
Unknown	2	-------	-------	16	-------	-------	-------	-------	1	-------	3	-------	-------	1
FAMILIES														
Number of families	1, 261	479	265	8, 589	2, 824	1, 177	3, 817	2, 299	771	73	1, 401	164	4	2, 99
Median size	4. 04	2. 79	3. 29	2. 87	3. 13	3. 66	2. 77	3. 16	4. 01	-------	2. 31	4. 86	-------	3. 6
Families having—														
No children under 10	604	308	162	5, 410	1, 631	631	2, 449	1, 313	361	39	1, 093	65	4	1, 520
1 child under 10	242	78	37	1, 416	489	205	590	415	141	14	168	28	-------	574
2 children under 10	152	53	36	828	292	138	344	274	117	5	79	25	-------	380
3 or more	263	40	30	935	412	203	434	297	152	15	61	46	-------	517

CHARACTERISTICS OF NEGRO POPULATION BY COUNTIES: 1930—Continued

(See note at head of table)

SUBJECT	Hot Spring	Howard	Independence	Izard	Jackson	Jefferson	Johnson	Lafayette	Lawrence	Lee	Lincoln	Little River	Logan	Lonoke	Madison
	ARKANSAS—Continued														
POPULATION BY SEX															
Negro population: 1930	2, 311	3, 826	894	175	5, 248	37, 116	366	8, 411	430	17, 409	13, 090	6, 013	527	10, 917	16
Male	1, 159	1, 865	422	89	2, 709	18, 113	187	4, 143	203	8, 707	6, 731	2, 980	271	5, 499	5
Female	1, 152	1, 961	472	86	2, 539	19, 003	179	4, 268	227	8, 702	6, 359	3, 033	256	5, 418	11
Negro population: 1920	2, 068	4, 265	1, 075	217	5, 571	39, 493	329	7, 685	625	22, 300	12, 760	6, 006	467	11, 628	40
Male	1, 060	2, 141	520	106	2, 802	19, 376	168	3, 771	325	11, 191	6, 588	3, 070	246	5, 962	20
Female	1, 008	2, 124	555	111	2, 769	20, 117	161	3, 914	300	11, 109	6, 172	2, 936	221	5, 666	20
Percent of total population:															
1930	12. 8	21. 9	3. 7	1. 4	18. 8	57. 9	1. 9	49. 7	2. 0	65. 4	64. 6	38. 8	2. 2	32. 3	0. 1
1920	11. 6	23. 0	4. 5	1. 6	21. 9	65. 5	1. 6	49. 5	2. 8	77. 3	68. 0	36. 8	1. 8	34. 8	0. 3
VOTING AGE: 1930															
Total 21 years old and over	1, 222	1, 741	522	82	2, 968	20, 395	204	4, 249	247	9, 365	7, 181	3, 066	256	5, 471	11
Male	618	857	249	42	1, 575	9, 954	107	2, 106	109	4, 765	3, 807	1, 550	136	2, 782	4
Female	604	884	273	40	1, 393	10, 441	97	2, 143	138	4, 600	3, 374	1, 516	120	2, 689	7
AGE: 1930															
Under 5 years	243	503	77	28	484	3, 703	39	916	39	1, 880	1, 409	646	64	1, 186	1
Under 1 year	51	110	13	5	94	698	12	161	7	384	282	123	12	235	-------
5 to 9 years	276	507	85	14	552	4, 073	39	1, 094	42	2, 048	1, 469	667	83	1, 346	1
10 to 14 years	263	495	90	19	545	4, 102	46	1, 002	46	1, 966	1, 321	713	48	1, 342	2
15 to 19 years	251	493	101	26	596	4, 051	29	953	45	1, 782	1, 385	776	63	1, 304	1
20 to 24 years	259	401	90	23	568	3, 705	38	812	31	1, 678	1, 459	650	51	1, 146	3
25 to 29 years	178	295	54	13	470	2, 972	33	712	43	1, 310	1, 168	527	39	791	1
30 to 34 years	153	235	59	8	344	2, 363	25	498	24	1, 079	872	358	31	569	-------
35 to 44 years	297	375	138	18	678	4, 737	47	973	63	2, 198	1, 560	645	49	1, 190	1
45 to 54 years	210	297	108	12	579	4, 133	31	840	54	1, 761	1, 376	583	49	1, 153	3
55 to 64 years	109	138	40	7	227	2, 004	19	385	17	1, 006	684	264	28	542	2
65 to 74 years	50	55	35	3	138	861	11	155	18	478	275	133	11	244	1
75 years and over	22	31	11	4	62	400	8	65	8	218	105	45	9	100	-------
Unknown	-------	1	6	-------	5	12	1	6	-------	5	7	6	2	4	-------
SCHOOL ATTENDANCE															
Total 7 to 13 years, inclusive	373	695	117	25	759	5, 664	55	1, 455	64	2, 774	1, 903	954	93	1, 862	3
Number attending school	338	646	110	14	691	5, 024	53	1, 116	53	2, 331	1, 756	813	67	1, 561	3
Percent attending school	90. 6	92. 9	94. 0	-------	91. 0	88. 7	-------	76. 7	-------	84. 0	92. 3	85. 2	-------	83. 8	-------
Total 14 to 15 years, inclusive	106	188	41	9	234	1, 652	22	383	19	718	538	297	20	551	-------
Number attending school	82	174	35	7	201	1, 452	17	269	17	560	472	246	13	469	-------
Percent attending school	77. 4	92. 6	-------	-------	85. 9	87. 9	-------	70. 2	-------	78. 0	87. 7	82. 8	-------	85. 1	-------
Total 16 and 17 years, inclusive	104	201	47	12	235	1, 622	11	382	17	713	558	294	26	520	-------
Number attending school	45	146	30	3	120	1, 017	5	192	9	331	362	182	12	290	-------
Percent attending school	43. 3	72. 6	-------	-------	51. 1	62. 7	-------	50. 3	-------	46. 4	64. 9	61. 9	-------	55. 8	-------
Total 18 to 20 years, inclusive	154	295	51	15	342	2, 432	20	592	29	1, 111	882	477	39	779	1
Number attending school	22	75	7	3	64	469	1	94	7	123	138	116	5	107	1
Percent attending school	14. 3	25. 4	-------	-------	18. 7	19. 3	-------	15. 9	-------	11. 1	15. 6	24. 3	-------	13. 7	-------
ILLITERACY															
Total 10 years old and over	1, 792	2, 816	732	133	4, 212	29, 340	288	6, 401	349	13, 481	10, 212	4, 700	380	8, 385	14
Number illiterate	208	121	96	15	345	4, 541	44	1, 307	56	2, 259	2, 143	647	70	1, 373	1
Percent illiterate	11. 6	4. 3	13. 1	11. 3	8. 2	15. 5	15. 3	20. 4	1. 60	16. 8	21. 0	13. 8	18. 4	16. 4	-------
Percent illiterate, 1920	9. 2	17. 7	17. 8	34. 4	17. 6	24. 3	22. 0	25. 2	16. 8	22. 8	26. 9	30. 7	18. 5	22. 0	-------
URBAN AND RURAL															
Urban population	1, 084	-------	431	-------	1, 406	6, 163	184	1, 293	-------	2, 305	-------	-------	42	-------	-------
Percent urban	46. 9	-------	48. 2	-------	26. 8	16. 6	50. 3	15. 4	-------	13. 2	-------	-------	8. 0	-------	-------
Rural population	1, 227	3, 826	463	175	3, 842	30, 953	182	7, 118	430	15, 104	13, 090	6, 013	485	10, 917	16
Rural-farm	362	3, 031	280	160	3, 299	25, 319	99	6, 236	101	14, 744	11, 845	5, 060	409	9, 566	16
Rural-nonfarm	865	795	183	15	543	5, 634	83	882	329	360	1, 245	953	76	1, 351	-------
Percent rural	53. 1	100. 0	51. 8	100. 0	73. 2	83. 4	49. 7	84. 6	100. 0	86. 8	100. 0	100. 0	92. 0	100. 0	-------
MARITAL CONDITION															
Males 15 years old and over	773	1, 138	306	57	1, 918	12, 210	127	2, 655	138	5, 768	4, 619	1, 962	169	3, 539	4
Single	245	332	87	21	535	3, 157	29	723	40	1, 305	1, 150	538	48	1, 008	1
Married	459	716	187	32	1, 175	7, 814	80	1, 733	84	3, 862	3, 086	1, 219	112	2, 150	2
Widowed	49	79	26	4	161	972	12	118	10	529	248	182	8	289	1
Divorced	20	11	5	-------	46	263	6	81	4	71	134	21	1	92	-------
Unknown	-------	-------	1	-------	1	4	-------	-------	-------	1	1	2	-------	-------	-------
Females 15 years old and over	756	1, 183	336	57	1, 749	13, 028	115	2, 744	165	5, 747	4, 272	2, 025	163	3, 504	8
Single	138	268	80	16	332	2, 261	15	548	33	887	667	409	34	641	4
Married	459	717	189	34	1, 077	7, 938	78	1, 770	86	3, 791	2, 871	1, 217	118	2, 183	2
Widowed	121	180	55	7	261	2, 352	18	266	37	968	555	343	11	548	2
Divorced	38	18	12	-------	79	477	4	158	9	99	175	55	-------	130	-------
Unknown	-------	-------	-------	-------	-------	-------	-------	2	-------	2	4	1	-------	2	-------
FAMILIES															
Number of families	570	829	233	39	1, 243	10, 151	91	2, 106	124	4, 817	3, 595	1, 531	113	2, 646	3
Median size	3. 33	3. 99	2. 87	-------	3. 10	2. 90	-------	3. 26	2. 37	2. 86	2. 84	3. 09	3. 89	3. 32	-------
Families having—															
No children under 10	307	395	160	17	774	6, 323	54	1, 204	81	2, 978	2, 219	898	54	1, 484	2
1 child under 10	130	158	33	11	193	1, 770	20	356	26	817	604	273	20	481	1
2 children under 10	66	108	18	6	125	984	6	243	8	410	356	173	13	297	-------
3 or more	67	168	22	5	151	1, 074	11	303	9	612	416	187	26	384	-------

CHARACTERISTICS OF NEGRO POPULATION BY COUNTIES: 1930—Continued

(See note at head of table)

Subject	ARKANSAS—Continued													
	Marion	Miller	Mississippi	Monroe	Montgomery	Nevada	Ouachita	Perry	Phillips	Pike	Poinsett	Polk	Pope	Prairie
POPULATION BY SEX														
Negro population: 1930	1	9, 542	26, 145	11, 501	136	7, 244	12, 987	454	27, 269	1, 122	4, 331	3	1, 320	3, 620
Male	1	4, 650	13, 332	5, 752	70	3, 580	6. 339	210	13, 440	595	2, 189	2	646	1, 849
Female	-------	4, 892	12, 813	5, 749	66	3, 664	6, 648	244	13, 829	527	2, 142	1	674	1, 771
Negro population: 1920	-------	7, 244	19, 907	13, 205	198	7, 115	10, 415	678	32, 929	872	4, 076	9	1, 751	5, 226
Male	-------	3, 567	10, 229	6, 653	102	3, 511	5, 175	351	16, 745	435	2, 149	4	840	2, 654
Female	-------	3, 677	9, 678	6, 552	96	3, 604	5, 240	327	16, 184	437	1, 927	5	911	2, 572
Percent of total population:														
1930	-------	31. 2	37. 7	55. 7	1. 3	35. 5	43. 4	5. 9	67. 0	9. 5	14. 6	-------	5. 0	23. 8
1920	-------	30. 2	42. 1	61. 1	1. 8	32. 4	50. 5	6. 8	73. 9	7. 0	19. 6	0. 1	6. 4	30. 0
VOTING AGE: 1930														
Total 21 years old and over	-------	5, 214	14, 638	6, 222	64	3, 182	6, 277	203	15, 914	631	2, 538	3	676	1, 882
Male	-------	2, 557	7, 754	3, 149	33	1, 596	3, 040	92	7, 938	352	1, 312	2	329	998
Female	-------	2, 657	6, 884	3, 073	31	1, 586	3, 237	111	7, 976	279	1, 226	1	347	884
AGE: 1930														
Under 5 years	-------	932	2, 661	1, 227	13	957	1, 601	67	2, 459	126	474	-------	148	432
Under 1 year	-------	146	525	201	3	200	322	15	445	30	87	-------	23	84
5 to 9 years	-------	1, 111	2, 837	1, 277	19	1, 034	1, 676	83	2, 951	123	420	-------	161	386
10 to 14 years	-------	1, 103	2, 673	1, 285	23	985	1, 594	57	2, 632	115	400	-------	171	432
15 to 19 years	1	975	2, 724	1, 261	14	913	1, 547	40	2, 718	102	403	-------	136	414
20 to 24 years	-------	980	2, 809	1, 176	9	771	1, 377	33	2, 763	127	478	-------	139	354
25 to 29 years	-------	833	2, 424	870	8	550	1, 049	29	2, 381	128	431	-------	100	270
30 to 34 years	-------	683	1, 953	754	6	411	767	26	2, 088	78	353	-------	82	216
35 to 44 years	-------	1, 249	3, 419	1, 402	8	656	1, 254	40	4, 019	168	579	-------	137	426
45 to 54 years	-------	960	2, 897	1, 227	21	537	1, 159	40	3, 033	92	485	-------	131	363
55 to 64 years	-------	458	1, 210	634	11	265	592	21	1, 378	39	214	-------	54	198
65 to 74 years	-------	159	372	260	3	102	228	11	580	14	61	2	43	90
75 years and over	-------	92	159	122	1	63	135	5	265	10	27	1	18	39
Unknown	-------	7	7	6	-------	-------	8	2	2	-------	6	-------	-------	-------
SCHOOL ATTENDANCE														
Total 7 to 13 years, inclusive	-------	1, 534	3, 810	1, 772	30	1, 411	2, 282	96	3, 894	170	581	-------	225	571
Number attending school	-------	1, 285	2, 911	1, 615	23	1, 128	2, 022	86	3, 505	152	468	-------	221	516
Percent attending school	-------	83. 8	76. 4	91. 1	-------	79. 9	88. 6	-------	90. 0	89. 4	80. 6	-------	98. 2	90. 4
Total 14 and 15 years, inclusive	-------	398	1, 061	521	8	351	614	23	998	40	147	-------	70	179
Number attending school	-------	333	753	444	6	271	503	22	825	37	92	-------	61	151
Percent attending school	-------	83. 7	71. 0	85. 2	-------	77. 2	81. 9	-------	82. 7	-------	62. 6	-------	-------	84. 4
Total 16 and 17 years, inclusive	-------	412	1, 085	491	5	382	627	15	1, 044	38	159	-------	55	164
Number attending school	-------	248	444	279	2	206	351	13	556	19	58	-------	22	101
Percent attending school	-------	60. 2	40. 9	56. 8	-------	53. 9	56. 0	-------	53. 3	-------	36. 5	-------	-------	61. 6
Total 18 to 20 years, inclusive	1	602	1, 732	744	8	537	891	18	1, 739	73	265	-------	85	245
Number attending school	-------	107	112	112	3	121	163	3	206	13	18	-------	12	54
Percent attending school	-------	17. 8	6. 5	15. 1	-------	22. 5	18. 3	-------	11. 8	-------	6. 8	-------	-------	22. 0
ILLITERACY														
Total 10 years old and over	1	7, 499	20, 647	8, 997	104	5, 253	9, 710	304	21, 859	873	3, 437	3	1, 011	2, 802
Number illiterate	-------	1, 519	3, 836	1, 613	20	1, 116	1, 658	29	3, 283	144	718	2	109	399
Percent illiterate	-------	20. 3	18. 6	17. 9	19. 2	21. 2	17. 1	9. 5	15. 0	16. 5	20. 9	-------	10. 8	14. 2
Percent illiterate, 1920	-------	25. 8	19. 7	20. 2	12. 6	26. 1	21. 8	14. 8	19. 2	16. 5	21. 7	-------	20. 4	21. 2
URBAN AND RURAL														
Urban population	-------	3, 109	3, 758	1, 507	-------	1, 131	2, 872	-------	6, 593	-------	66	-------	488	-------
Percent urban	-------	32. 6	14. 4	13. 1	-------	15. 6	22. 1	-------	24. 2	-------	1. 5	-------	37. 0	-------
Rural population	1	6, 433	22, 387	9, 994	136	6, 113	10, 115	454	20, 676	1, 122	4, 265	3	832	3, 620
Rural-farm	1	5, 798	20, 579	8, 924	121	5, 669	7, 485	433	18, 134	402	2, 773	2	753	2, 437
Rural-nonfarm	-------	635	1, 808	1, 070	15	444	2, 630	21	2, 542	720	1, 492	1	79	1, 183
Percent rural	-------	67. 4	85. 6	86. 9	100. 0	84. 4	77. 9	100. 0	75. 8	100. 0	98. 5	-------	63. 0	100. 0
MARITAL CONDITION														
Males 15 years old and over	1	3, 087	9, 296	3, 865	44	2, 082	3, 901	109	9, 466	413	1, 526	2	397	1, 236
Single	1	859	2, 316	1, 052	14	691	1, 221	26	2, 542	104	356	2	83	352
Married	-------	1, 919	6, 127	2, 409	28	1, 258	2, 383	68	5, 938	267	1, 056	-------	267	742
Widowed	-------	276	689	252	2	117	214	12	849	18	91	-------	44	118
Divorced	-------	32	152	150	-------	16	83	2	134	24	23	-------	3	24
Unknown	-------	1	12	2	-------	-------	-------	1	3	-------	-------	-------	-------	-------
Females 15 years old and over	-------	3, 309	8, 678	3, 847	37	2, 186	4, 215	138	9, 761	345	1, 511	1	443	1, 134
Single	-------	622	1, 177	669	5	598	1, 014	33	1, 645	44	214	-------	91	205
Married	-------	1, 932	6, 169	2, 421	27	1, 279	2, 439	71	6, 035	259	1, 046	1	271	726
Widowed	-------	693	1, 138	564	2	286	621	28	1, 867	30	212	-------	73	183
Divorced	-------	59	189	190	3	22	140	6	205	12	39	-------	8	20
Unknown	-------	3	5	3	-------	1	1	-------	9	-------	-------	-------	-------	-------
FAMILIES														
Number of families	-------	2, 537	7, 039	2, 930	30	1, 540	2, 906	90	8, 182	278	1, 202	1	320	879
Median size	-------	2. 87	2. 87	3. 11	-------	3. 99	3. 67	-------	2. 47	3. 20	2. 70	-------	3. 40	3. 38
Families having—														
No children under 10	-------	1, 570	4, 348	1, 740	15	703	1, 489	36	5, 511	156	773	1	179	499
1 child under 10	-------	424	1, 252	542	8	309	538	14	1, 252	57	183	-------	54	154
2 children under 10	-------	241	673	282	3	197	358	12	662	28	117	-------	44	101
3 or more	-------	302	766	366	4	331	521	28	757	37	129	-------	43	125

CHARACTERISTICS OF NEGRO POPULATION BY COUNTIES: 1930—Continued

(See note at head of table)

SUBJECT	ARKANSAS—Continued															
	Pulaski	Randolph	St. Francis	Saline	Scott	Searcy	Sebastian	Sevier	Sharp	Stone	Union	Van Buren	Washington	White	Woodruff	Yell
POPULATION BY SEX																
Negro population: 1930	40, 215	271	22, 485	558	13	1	3, 990	1, 753	19	15	17, 484	121	471	1, 872	10, 036	1, 173
Male	18, 953	139	11, 350	290	6	1	1, 871	879	11	6	8, 478	66	225	937	4, 992	578
Female	21, 262	132	11, 135	268	7	—	2, 119	874	8	9	9, 006	55	246	935	5, 044	595
Negro population: 1920	36, 439	294	19, 971	451	10	24	4, 299	2, 282	15	15	12, 355	211	508	1, 971	11, 434	1, 418
Male	17, 963	152	10, 144	252	5	13	2, 075	1, 158	7	7	6, 221	114	255	992	5, 751	709
Female	18, 476	142	9, 827	199	5	11	2, 224	1, 124	8	8	6, 134	97	253	979	5, 683	709
Percent of total population:																
1930	29. 2	1. 6	67. 3	3. 6	0. 1	—	7. 3	10. 7	0. 2	0. 2	31. 3	1. 0	1. 2	4. 9	44. 2	5. 5
1920	33. 3	1. 7	70. 4	2. 7	0. 1	0. 2	7. 6	12. 5	0. 1	0. 2	41. 6	1. 5	1. 4	5. 7	53. 1	5. 5
VOTING AGE: 1930																
Total 21 years old and over	24, 563	133	11, 722	357	6	1	2, 462	812	13	7	8, 864	54	264	982	5, 111	612
Male	11, 453	64	6, 109	189	4	1	1, 150	407	8	2	4, 324	33	131	485	2, 582	308
Female	13, 110	69	5, 613	168	2	—	1, 312	405	5	5	4, 540	21	133	497	2, 529	304
AGE: 1930																
Under 5 years	3, 334	26	2, 410	44	2	—	296	170	1	1	1, 956	20	36	189	1, 111	124
Under 1 year	616	2	463	10	—	—	55	36	—	—	407	5	9	44	214	10
5 to 9 years	3, 814	38	2, 693	52	2	—	347	248	2	4	2, 225	17	51	226	1, 108	129
10 to 14 years	3, 651	45	2, 497	44	2	—	359	243	2	1	2, 106	16	55	203	1, 164	151
15 to 19 years	3, 976	27	2, 620	55	1	—	447	232	1	1	1, 975	12	59	226	1, 283	124
20 to 24 years	4, 107	12	2, 443	51	—	—	377	201	—	2	1, 950	14	41	204	1, 068	143
25 to 29 years	3, 769	16	1, 846	67	2	—	317	117	1	—	1, 765	10	36	127	767	86
30 to 34 years	3, 205	18	1, 469	48	—	—	290	71	1	1	1, 253	9	26	104	548	67
35 to 44 years	6, 117	33	2, 650	77	1	—	640	168	3	1	1, 923	10	56	216	1, 124	131
45 to 54 years	4, 713	22	2, 180	60	—	—	493	151	1	1	1, 379	8	45	194	1, 041	97
55 to 64 years	2, 116	16	1, 072	33	1	—	252	82	5	3	528	4	26	108	455	68
65 to 74 years	915	12	423	15	1	—	110	46	1	—	281	—	20	49	255	34
75 years and over	468	6	180	11	1	1	60	24	1	—	101	1	20	25	103	19
Unknown	30	—	2	1	—	—	2	—	—	—	42	—	—	1	9	—
SCHOOL ATTENDANCE																
Total 7 to 13 years, inclusive	5, 191	62	3, 579	66	4	—	485	353	3	3	2, 982	24	78	289	1, 603	194
Number attending school	4, 983	38	3, 124	56	2	—	467	303	3	—	2, 561	24	66	232	1, 416	161
Percent attending school	96. 0	—	87. 3	—	—	—	96. 3	85. 8	—	—	85. 9	—	—	80. 3	88. 3	83. 0
Total 14 and 15 years, inclusive	1, 459	13	977	14	—	—	158	91	—	1	807	5	29	80	487	58
Number attending school	1, 282	9	858	10	—	—	132	78	—	—	652	5	26	61	435	48
Percent attending school	87. 9	—	87. 8	—	—	—	83. 5	—	—	—	80. 8	—	—	—	89. 3	—
Total 16 and 17 years, inclusive	1, 545	9	1, 024	21	1	—	199	91	1	—	783	6	17	104	499	50
Number attending school	896	5	581	11	—	—	122	58	—	—	434	4	10	53	317	24
Percent attending school	58. 0	—	56. 7	—	—	—	61. 3	—	—	—	55. 4	—	—	51. 0	63. 5	—
Total 18 to 20 years, inclusive	2, 594	15	1, 651	34	—	—	256	144	—	1	1, 177	6	28	130	780	80
Number attending school	541	6	256	8	—	—	50	34	—	—	218	1	—	16	149	7
Percent attending school	20. 9	—	15. 5	—	—	—	19. 5	23. 6	—	—	18. 5	—	—	12. 3	19. 1	—
ILLITERACY																
Total 10 years old and over	33, 067	207	17, 382	462	9	1	3, 347	1, 335	16	10	13, 303	84	384	1, 457	7, 817	920
Number illiterate	3, 617	45	2, 414	80	4	1	378	107	5	1	2, 350	1	70	209	655	60
Percent illiterate	10. 9	21. 7	13. 9	17. 3	—	—	11. 3	8. 0	—	—	17. 7	—	18. 2	14. 3	8. 4	6. 5
Percent illiterate in 1920	15. 7	31. 5	16. 8	24. 7	—	—	15. 7	12. 8	—	—	26. 0	24. 8	20. 4	16. 5	20. 3	14. 9
URBAN AND RURAL																
Urban population	25, 795	—	1, 967	207	—	—	3, 467	143	—	—	4, 293	—	339	597	—	—
Percent urban	64. 1	—	8. 7	37. 1	—	—	86. 9	8. 2	—	—	24. 6	—	72. 0	31. 9	—	—
Rural population	14, 420	271	20, 518	351	13	1	523	1, 610	19	15	13, 191	121	132	1, 275	10, 036	1, 173
Rural-farm	8, 872	191	19, 344	156	10	1	144	1, 272	19	15	8, 207	111	82	582	8, 066	625
Rural-nonfarm	5, 548	80	1, 174	195	3	—	379	338	—	—	4, 984	10	50	693	1, 970	548
Percent rural	35. 9	100. 0	91. 3	62. 9	—	—	13. 1	91. 8	—	—	75. 4	100. 0	28. 0	68. 1	100. 0	100. 0
MARITAL CONDITION																
Males 15 years old and over	13, 615	84	7, 540	221	5	1	1, 378	539	8	3	5, 356	38	160	621	3, 338	384
Single	3, 745	27	1, 961	60	1	1	393	199	1	1	1, 481	10	47	190	1, 061	123
Married	8, 495	47	4, 853	144	3	—	822	297	6	2	3, 310	24	89	336	2, 003	215
Widowed	1, 087	10	644	15	1	—	133	40	1	—	433	4	21	73	230	38
Divorced	275	—	79	2	—	—	29	3	—	—	101	—	2	20	42	8
Unknown	13	—	3	—	—	—	1	—	—	—	31	—	1	2	2	—
Females 15 years old and over	15, 801	78	7, 345	197	2	—	1, 610	553	6	6	5, 841	30	169	633	3, 315	385
Single	3, 124	10	1, 239	28	—	—	365	168	—	2	1, 204	7	39	152	742	99
Married	8, 799	52	4, 848	144	2	—	912	304	5	4	3, 344	23	88	342	2, 005	224
Widowed	3, 231	15	1, 151	21	—	—	285	75	1	—	1, 069	—	36	108	514	53
Divorced	642	1	104	4	—	—	48	6	—	—	215	—	5	30	54	9
Unknown	5	—	3	—	—	—	—	—	—	—	9	—	1	1	—	—
FAMILIES																
Number of families	10, 644	60	5, 762	166	3	—	1, 071	375	7	3	4, 210	24	122	435	2, 315	272
Median size	2. 72	—	3. 12	2. 40	—	—	2. 83	4. 01	—	—	3. 24	—	2. 90	3. 40	3. 49	3. 64
Families having—																
No children under 10	7, 151	33	3, 282	119	2	—	756	174	5	1	2, 274	7	86	246	1, 297	156
1 child under 10	1, 643	8	1, 116	23	—	—	149	90	1	1	815	6	12	78	436	47
2 children under 10	888	7	641	12	—	—	79	48	1	—	508	3	9	45	259	29
3 or more	962	12	723	12	1	—	87	63	—	1	613	8	15	66	323	40

CHARACTERISTICS OF NEGRO POPULATION BY COUNTIES: 1930—Continued

(See note at head of table)

CALIFORNIA

SUBJECT	The State	Alameda	Amador	Butte	Calaveras	Colusa	Contra Costa	Del Norte	Eldorado	Fresno	Glenn	Humboldt	Imperial
POPULATION BY SEX													
Negro population: 1930	81,048	10,150	34	303	8	68	355	3	24	1,363	40	37	1,954
Male	40,052	5,000	33	163	6	45	214	2	14	754	22	20	1,072
Female	40,996	5,150	1	140	2	23	141	1	10	609	18	17	882
Negro population: 1920	38,763	6,320	36	160	11	64	222	3	17	930	30	77	1,648
Male	19,837	3,416	32	89	6	46	146	----	9	468	13	44	947
Female	18,926	2,904	4	71	5	18	76	3	8	462	17	33	701
Percent of total population: 1930	1.4	2.1	0.4	0.9	0.1	0.7	0.5	0.1	0.3	0.9	0.4	0.1	3.2
1920	1.1	1.8	0.5	0.5	0.2	0.7	0.4	0.1	0.3	0.7	0.3	0.2	3.8
VOTING AGE: 1930													
Total 21 years old and over	57,560	7,267	2	224	5	53	259	3	22	862	27	23	1,212
Male	28,628	3,616	2	127	3	38	157	2	14	478	13	13	712
Female	28,932	3,651	----	97	2	15	102	1	8	384	14	10	500
AGE: 1930													
Under 5 years	5,283	627	2	20	----	1	21	----	2	104	3	3	180
Under 1 year	971	93	----	4	----	----	7	----	----	19	1	1	38
5 to 9 years	6,028	706	----	21	1	2	31	----	----	125	2	3	210
10 to 14 years	5,422	698	----	26	2	4	20	----	----	133	4	4	168
15 to 19 years	5,565	696	30	8	----	7	18	----	----	113	4	3	150
20 to 24 years	6,711	811	----	23	----	5	24	----	----	109	4	1	193
25 to 29 years	8,168	938	1	25	----	3	33	----	----	92	1	4	182
30 to 34 years	8,312	1,044	----	28	----	8	52	----	----	119	6	3	181
35 to 44 years	16,361	2,133	1	61	2	11	78	1	6	246	4	8	306
45 to 54 years	11,114	1,466	----	41	2	6	45	----	9	177	7	6	220
55 to 64 years	4,861	578	----	33	1	6	26	2	5	89	3	1	108
65 to 74 years	2,081	274	----	16	----	10	5	----	1	41	2	----	37
75 years and over	863	100	----	1	----	5	2	----	1	14	----	1	18
Unknown	279	79	----	----	----	----	----	----	----	1	----	----	1
SCHOOL ATTENDANCE													
Total 7 to 13 years, inclusive	7,904	971	----	27	3	4	38	----	----	175	5	4	272
Number attending school	7,671	947	----	27	3	4	36	----	----	165	5	4	259
Percent attending school	97.1	97.5	----	----	----	----	----	----	----	94.3	----	----	95.2
Total 14 and 15 years, inclusive	2,141	280	----	8	----	2	4	----	----	59	----	2	55
Number attending school	2,066	273	----	8	----	2	4	----	----	56	----	2	53
Percent attending school	96.5	97.5	----	----	----	----	----	----	----	----	----	----	----
Total 16 and 17 years, inclusive	2,164	270	24	3	----	3	6	----	----	52	2	1	56
Number attending school	1,740	232	5	2	----	2	6	----	----	43	1	----	39
Percent attending school	80.4	85.9	----	----	----	----	----	----	----	----	----	----	----
Total 18 to 20 years, inclusive	3,589	461	6	8	----	4	16	----	----	59	2	2	98
Number attending school	997	145	----	----	----	1	----	----	----	10	2	----	17
Percent attending school	27.8	31.5	----	----	----	----	----	----	----	----	----	----	----
ILLITERACY													
Total 10 years old and over	69,737	8,817	32	262	7	65	303	3	22	1,134	35	31	1,564
Number illiterate	2,148	186	----	13	----	4	14	1	----	36	----	2	114
Percent illiterate	3.1	2.1	----	5.0	----	----	4.6	----	----	3.2	----	----	7.3
Percent illiterate in 1920	4.7	2.8	----	3.4	----	----	5.4	----	----	4.2	----	----	5.9
URBAN AND RURAL													
Urban population	70,519	10,025	----	88	----	----	211	----	----	844	----	37	962
Percent urban	87.0	98.8	----	29.0	----	----	59.4	----	----	61.9	----	----	49.2
Rural population	10,529	125	34	215	8	68	144	3	24	519	40	----	992
Rural-farm	3,461	10	----	10	5	14	12	----	9	344	6	----	622
Rural-nonfarm	7,068	115	34	205	3	54	132	3	15	175	34	----	370
Percent rural	13.0	1.2	----	71.0	----	----	40.6	----	----	38.1	----	----	50.8
MARITAL CONDITION													
Males 15 years old and over	31,749	4,010	32	135	3	42	171	2	14	553	17	16	806
Single	9,889	1,217	31	35	1	23	55	2	7	192	6	7	283
Married	18,490	2,349	1	81	1	11	95	----	6	300	11	8	446
Widowed	1,994	199	----	11	1	6	17	----	----	39	----	1	61
Divorced	1,175	185	----	8	----	2	4	----	1	21	----	----	16
Unknown	201	60	----	----	----	----	----	----	----	1	----	----	----
Females 15 years old and over	32,566	4,109	----	101	2	19	112	1	8	448	14	11	590
Single	5,730	718	----	3	1	4	9	----	1	79	1	----	84
Married	18,870	2,384	----	77	1	10	92	1	7	279	11	7	419
Widowed	6,123	739	----	17	----	3	9	----	----	69	2	2	72
Divorced	1,761	244	----	4	----	2	2	----	----	21	----	2	15
Unknown	82	24	----	----	----	----	----	----	----	----	----	----	----
FAMILIES													
Number of families	22,595	2,848	1	111	3	18	116	2	11	371	11	12	565
Median size	2.35	2.42	----	1.85	----	----	2.30	----	----	2.48	----	----	2.26
Families having— No children under 10	17,050	2,167	----	90	2	16	82	2	10	263	7	11	397
1 child under 10	2,667	343	----	11	1	2	23	----	----	48	3	----	65
2 children under 10	1,474	206	----	3	----	----	6	----	1	25	1	----	38
3 or more	1,404	132	1	7	----	----	5	----	----	35	----	1	65

SUBJECT	Inyo	Kern	Kings	Lake	Lassen	Los Angeles	Madera	Marin	Mariposa	Mendocino	Merced	Modoc	Mono
POPULATION BY SEX													
Negro population: 1930	14	2,142	247	5	38	46,425	416	290	9	49	443	11	3
Male	7	1,112	131	3	22	21,827	223	261	4	33	259	6	3
Female	7	1,030	116	2	16	24,598	193	29	5	16	184	5	----
Negro population: 1920	9	499	180	6	19	18,738	62	101	7	55	48	3	7
Male	4	293	96	3	15	8,868	35	87	5	49	34	2	5
Female	5	206	84	3	4	9,870	27	14	2	6	14	1	2
Percent of total population: 1930	0.2	2.6	1.0	0.1	0.3	2.1	2.4	0.7	0.3	0.2	1.2	0.1	0.2
1920	0.1	0.9	0.8	0.1	0.2	2.0	0.5	0.4	0.3	0.2	0.2	0.1	0.7
VOTING AGE: 1930													
Total 21 years old and over	7	1,258	169	5	19	33,231	211	275	6	45	293	8	3
Male	4	697	93	3	12	15,425	124	246	2	30	180	4	3
Female	3	561	76	2	7	17,806	87	29	4	15	113	4	----
AGE: 1930													
Under 5 years	----	215	14	----	3	2,935	56	----	----	----	40	----	----
Under 1 year	----	34	4	----	----	556	14	----	----	----	11	----	----
5 to 9 years	----	233	15	----	9	3,390	47	----	----	----	32	2	----
10 to 14 years	1	217	24	----	3	3,008	43	1	3	3	32	1	----
15 to 19 years	5	189	22	----	3	3,159	51	9	----	1	38	----	----
20 to 24 years	3	178	19	1	3	4,027	45	50	----	3	34	1	----
25 to 29 years	----	158	19	1	3	4,988	25	52	----	3	37	2	----
30 to 34 years	----	167	15	1	3	4,881	20	50	----	4	32	1	----
35 to 44 years	----	349	45	2	7	9,485	64	67	3	14	85	2	1
45 to 54 years	3	262	41	----	2	6,182	42	41	1	12	67	2	2
55 to 64 years	1	112	16	----	----	2,686	13	17	1	3	34	----	----
65 to 74 years	1	43	12	----	2	1,137	6	----	1	4	7	----	----
75 years and over	----	18	5	----	----	504	3	----	----	1	4	----	----
Unknown	----	1	----	----	----	43	1	3	----	1	1	----	----
SCHOOL ATTENDANCE													
Total 7 to 13 years, inclusive	1	310	32	----	10	4,412	55	----	2	3	40	3	----
Number attending school	1	300	32	----	10	4,280	54	----	2	3	39	3	----
Percent attending school	----	96.8	----	----	----	97.0	----	----	----	----	----	----	----
Total 14 and 15 years, inclusive	1	88	7	----	1	1,197	18	2	2	----	14	----	----
Number attending school	1	80	7	----	1	1,159	17	1	1	----	13	----	----
Percent attending school	----	----	----	----	----	96.8	----	----	----	----	----	----	----
Total 16 and 17 years, inclusive	----	66	13	----	2	1,228	17	1	----	----	16	----	----
Number attending school	----	38	7	----	1	1,054	11	----	----	----	7	----	----
Percent attending school	----	----	----	----	----	85.8	----	----	----	----	----	----	----
Total 18 to 20 years, inclusive	5	111	8	----	2	2,070	33	12	----	1	26	----	----
Number attending school	1	25	3	----	1	626	3	2	----	----	2	----	----
Percent attending school	----	22.5	----	----	----	30.2	----	----	----	----	----	----	----
ILLITERACY													
Total 10 years old and over	14	1,694	218	5	26	40,100	313	290	9	49	371	9	3
Number illiterate	1	84	12	1	4	1,005	17	4	----	----	31	----	----
Percent illiterate	----	5.0	5.5	----	----	2.5	5.4	1.4	----	----	8.4	----	----
Percent illiterate in 1920	----	3.6	3.4	----	----	4.7	----	----	----	----	----	----	----
URBAN AND RURAL													
Urban population	----	907	101	----	----	44,265	105	18	----	6	189	----	----
Percent urban	----	42.3	40.9	----	----	95.3	25.2	6.2	----	----	42.7	----	----
Rural population	14	1,235	146	5	38	2,160	311	272	9	43	254	11	3
Rural-farm	4	745	45	1	----	50	207	----	3	9	161	5	1
Rural-nonfarm	10	490	101	4	38	2,110	104	272	6	34	93	6	2
Percent rural	----	57.7	59.1	----	----	4.7	74.8	93.8	----	----	57.3	----	----
MARITAL CONDITION													
Males 15 years old and over	7	793	104	3	13	17,166	153	260	2	31	199	4	3
Single	3	233	38	3	4	4,917	55	146	1	21	66	1	----
Married	4	476	59	----	7	10,593	91	78	1	7	103	3	1
Widowed	----	62	6	----	1	1,053	5	18	----	3	22	----	1
Divorced	----	22	1	----	1	590	2	18	----	----	8	----	1
Unknown	----	----	----	----	----	13	----	----	----	----	----	----	----
Females 15 years old and over	6	684	90	2	10	19,926	117	29	4	15	140	4	----
Single	2	123	15	----	3	3,562	20	4	1	3	21	1	----
Married	3	465	57	1	5	11,224	91	15	1	5	99	3	----
Widowed	1	81	12	----	1	4,037	4	7	2	4	14	----	----
Divorced	----	14	6	1	1	1,091	2	3	----	3	6	----	----
Unknown	----	1	----	----	----	12	----	----	----	----	----	----	----
FAMILIES													
Number of families	5	571	87	1	10	12,990	95	9	5	9	140	3	1
Median size	----	2.66	----	----	----	2.39	----	----	----	----	2.00	----	----
Families having— No children under 10	3	380	71	1	6	9,801	51	9	5	9	107	2	----
1 child under 10	1	70	9	----	2	1,598	20	----	----	----	17	----	----
2 children under 10	----	52	4	----	1	841	5	----	----	----	7	1	1
3 or more	1	69	3	----	1	750	19	----	----	----	9	----	----

CHARACTERISTICS OF NEGRO POPULATION BY COUNTIES: 1930—Continued

(See note at head of table)

CALIFORNIA—Continued

SUBJECT	Monterey	Napa	Nevada	Orange	Placer	Plumas	Riverside	Sacramento	San Benito	San Bernardino	San Diego	San Francisco
POPULATION BY SEX												
Negro population: 1930	269	77	8	231	66	83	1,303	1,485	40	1,302	2,886	3,803
Male	137	46	6	128	37	60	656	840	21	649	1,411	2,190
Female	132	31	2	103	29	23	647	645	19	653	1,475	1,613
Negro population: 1920	170	40	15	139	52	6	885	873	35	608	1,190	2,414
Male	101	24	10	71	31	4	447	518	15	312	591	1,362
Female	69	16	5	68	21	2	438	355	20	296	599	1,052
Percent of total population:												
1930	0.5	0.3	0.1	0.2	0.3	1.0	1.6	1.0	0.4	1.0	1.4	0.6
1920	0.6	0.2	0.1	0.2	0.3	0.1	1.8	1.0	0.4	0.8	1.1	0.5
VOTING AGE: 1930												
Total 21 years old and over	204	62	8	156	45	75	713	1,072	29	941	2,049	3,152
Male	106	38	6	88	25	58	358	641	17	484	1,006	1,852
Female	98	24	2	68	20	17	355	431	12	457	1,043	1,300
AGE: 1930												
Under 5 years	17	2	----	25	5	2	130	93	1	79	210	150
Under 1 year	6	----	----	5	1	----	26	16	----	12	34	25
5 to 9 years	18	4	----	16	9	1	171	122	----	92	236	165
10 to 14 years	15	4	----	19	5	1	135	98	4	81	192	127
15 to 19 years	10	3	----	11	2	3	142	81	5	86	172	163
20 to 24 years	24	5	2	17	4	8	78	104	4	103	204	288
25 to 29 years	20	7	1	23	6	14	82	167	----	110	277	466
30 to 34 years	24	5	1	20	4	9	62	165	5	104	296	500
35 to 44 years	63	18	2	35	9	29	179	276	10	245	578	957
45 to 54 years	40	12	1	37	6	12	164	234	6	224	388	569
55 to 64 years	25	13	1	21	8	2	92	88	5	110	201	204
65 to 74 years	8	2	----	5	4	----	49	43	----	49	89	72
75 years and over	5	2	----	2	3	----	18	13	----	18	38	25
Unknown	----	----	----	----	1	2	1	1	----	1	5	117
SCHOOL ATTENDANCE												
Total 7 to 13 years, inclusive	22	6	----	22	7	1	211	152	2	119	292	205
Number attending school	20	6	----	22	7	1	207	149	2	118	286	195
Percent attending school	----	----	----	----	----	----	98.1	98.0	----	99.2	97.9	95.1
Total 14 and 15 years, inclusive	5	1	----	7	3	----	55	36	3	35	76	48
Number attending school	4	1	----	6	3	----	54	36	3	34	75	47
Percent attending school	----	----	----	----	----	----	----	----	----	----	----	----
Total 16 and 17 years, inclusive	3	2	----	4	----	----	56	34	2	35	60	56
Number attending school	2	1	----	4	----	----	40	29	2	20	50	42
Percent attending school	----	----	----	----	----	----	----	----	----	----	----	----
Total 18 to 20 years, inclusive	10	3	----	10	1	4	65	50	3	60	103	133
Number attending school	3	2	----	2	----	----	16	16	2	20	23	26
Percent attending school	----	----	----	----	----	----	----	----	----	----	22.3	19.5
ILLITERACY												
Total 10 years old and over	234	71	8	190	52	80	1,002	1,270	39	1,131	2,440	3,488
Number illiterate	10	3	----	6	6	3	50	81	1	119	86	55
Percent illiterate	4.3	----	----	3.2	----	----	5.0	6.4	----	10.5	3.5	1.6
Percent illiterate in 1920	11.3	----	----	----	----	----	6.4	6.0	----	10.2	5.8	3.1
URBAN AND RURAL												
Urban population	194	9	1	187	51	----	632	1,086	34	876	2,809	3,803
Percent urban	72.1	----	----	81.0	----	----	48.5	73.1	----	67.3	97.3	100.0
Rural population	75	68	7	44	15	83	671	399	6	426	77	----
Rural-farm	11	6	----	16	5	----	343	59	3	101	19	----
Rural-nonfarm	64	62	7	28	10	83	328	340	3	325	58	----
Percent rural	27.9	----	----	19.0	----	----	51.5	26.9	----	32.7	2.7	----
MARITAL CONDITION												
Males 15 years old and over	113	42	6	99	26	59	440	678	18	535	1,088	1,961
Single	45	19	3	28	7	21	143	282	11	166	267	823
Married	52	13	3	63	15	33	258	319	7	311	674	854
Widowed	12	9	----	4	2	2	29	44	----	31	92	101
Divorced	3	1	----	4	2	3	9	33	----	24	54	87
Unknown	1	----	----	----	----	----	1	----	----	3	1	96
Females 15 years old and over	106	25	2	72	21	20	427	494	17	515	1,160	1,400
Single	20	5	1	6	1	1	86	98	7	94	176	261
Married	58	15	1	55	15	18	258	284	6	304	692	764
Widowed	22	4	----	10	4	----	70	76	4	92	232	247
Divorced	4	1	----	1	1	1	12	35	----	25	60	101
Unknown	2	----	----	----	----	----	1	1	----	----	----	27
FAMILIES												
Number of families	83	14	2	65	24	24	350	347	13	383	879	988
Median size	----	----	----	----	----	----	2.49	2.28	----	2.22	2.20	1.98
Families having—												
No children under 10	66	12	2	47	20	21	234	255	12	301	672	817
1 child under 10	8	----	----	6	1	3	33	34	1	36	92	99
2 children under 10	5	1	----	3	1	----	33	32	----	26	55	42
3 or more	4	1	----	9	2	----	50	26	----	20	60	30

SUBJECT	San Joaquin	San Luis Obispo	San Mateo	Santa Barbara	Santa Clara	Santa Cruz	Shasta	Sierra	Siskiyou	Solano	Sonoma	Stanislaus	Sutter
POPULATION BY SEX													
Negro population: 1930	572	37	429	581	536	64	78	5	641	376	107	213	16
Male	312	26	220	254	259	35	45	5	350	203	69	108	10
Female	260	11	209	327	277	29	33	----	291	173	38	105	6
Negro population: 1920	419	40	158	224	335	44	76	1	280	420	82	146	13
Male	227	23	99	98	148	29	41	1	167	242	51	80	7
Female	192	17	59	126	187	15	35	----	113	178	31	66	6
Percent of total population:													
1930	0.6	0.1	0.6	0.9	0.4	0.2	0.6	0.2	2.5	0.9	0.2	0.4	0.1
1920	0.5	0.2	0.4	0.5	0.3	0.2	0.6	0.1	1.5	1.0	0.2	0.3	0.1
VOTING AGE: 1930													
Total 21 years old and over	450	31	332	456	405	50	66	5	431	277	61	123	13
Male	258	21	169	200	193	29	41	5	260	156	41	70	9
Female	192	10	163	256	212	21	25	----	171	121	20	53	4
AGE: 1930													
Under 5 years	34	2	21	27	26	6	7	----	55	20	3	18	----
Under 1 year	5	----	2	6	7	2	1	----	8	4	1	7	----
5 to 9 years	36	----	19	35	34	4	1	----	55	22	5	23	1
10 to 14 years	20	2	23	29	33	1	3	----	46	25	10	21	----
15 to 19 years	26	1	27	31	28	2	1	----	47	27	27	23	----
20 to 24 years	35	3	23	34	33	4	3	----	40	28	7	19	3
25 to 29 years	46	6	30	66	52	5	2	----	82	21	9	15	1
30 to 34 years	54	2	70	67	63	5	5	----	86	40	6	10	3
35 to 44 years	124	7	95	146	105	11	21	3	150	64	16	39	3
45 to 54 years	116	8	78	85	88	16	10	2	66	79	11	25	3
55 to 64 years	54	2	29	42	35	8	10	----	8	33	11	14	1
65 to 74 years	19	3	11	13	16	2	12	----	3	14	2	4	1
75 years and over	8	1	1	5	10	----	3	----	3	2	----	2	----
Unknown	----	----	2	1	13	----	----	----	----	1	----	----	----
SCHOOL ATTENDANCE													
Total 7 to 13 years, inclusive	41	2	30	39	52	3	2	----	65	39	12	31	1
Number attending school	40	2	29	39	48	3	2	----	63	39	10	30	1
Percent attending school	----	----	----	----	----	----	----	----	----	----	----	----	----
Total 14 and 15 years, inclusive	12	----	10	9	8	----	2	----	18	7	8	7	----
Number attending school	12	----	9	9	8	----	2	----	17	7	4	7	----
Percent attending school	----	----	----	----	----	----	----	----	----	----	----	----	----
Total 16 and 17 years, inclusive	12	----	10	11	11	----	----	----	15	12	15	8	----
Number attending school	8	----	7	10	8	----	----	----	9	12	4	6	----
Percent attending school	----	----	----	----	----	----	----	----	----	----	----	----	----
Total 18 to 20 years, inclusive	12	2	18	20	23	3	----	----	32	16	7	16	2
Number attending school	2	1	4	7	4	----	----	----	1	5	----	8	----
Percent attending school	----	----	----	----	----	----	----	----	----	----	----	----	----
ILLITERACY													
Total 10 years old and over	502	35	389	519	476	54	70	5	531	334	99	172	15
Number illiterate	23	1	8	15	20	----	4	----	57	6	9	4	1
Percent illiterate	4.6	----	2.1	2.9	4.2	----	----	----	10.7	1.8	----	2.3	----
Percent illiterate in 1920	8.5	----	3.1	2.7	6.4	----	----	----	3.3	6.2	----	3.4	----
URBAN AND RURAL													
Urban population	454	31	344	525	445	52	41	----	34	301	22	171	3
Percent urban	79.4	----	80.2	90.4	83.0	----	----	----	5.3	80.1	20.6	80.3	----
Rural population	118	6	85	56	91	12	37	5	607	75	85	42	13
Rural-farm	33	2	1	8	9	1	22	----	3	12	14	21	10
Rural-nonfarm	85	4	84	48	82	11	15	5	604	63	71	21	3
Percent rural	20.6	----	19.8	9.6	17.0	----	----	----	94.7	19.9	79.4	19.7	----
MARITAL CONDITION													
Males 15 years old and over	278	23	185	213	211	29	41	5	282	167	56	81	10
Single	125	9	65	46	58	6	16	2	88	54	35	26	3
Married	115	8	105	149	125	14	18	3	174	99	17	42	6
Widowed	18	4	8	11	16	5	3	----	14	10	4	8	1
Divorced	13	2	6	4	7	4	3	----	5	4	----	5	----
Unknown	7	----	1	----	5	----	1	----	1	----	----	----	----
Females 15 years old and over	204	10	181	277	232	24	26	----	203	142	33	70	5
Single	23	----	33	42	43	2	2	----	19	24	18	17	1
Married	121	5	108	161	133	16	16	----	167	91	11	38	3
Widowed	36	4	30	55	35	3	7	----	13	22	2	8	1
Divorced	22	1	10	18	11	3	1	----	4	5	2	7	----
Unknown	2	----	----	1	10	----	----	----	----	----	----	----	----
FAMILIES													
Number of families	155	12	103	161	153	26	33	4	177	120	27	54	6
Median size	1.95	----	2.20	2.15	2.18	----	----	----	2.54	2.12	----	----	----
Families having—													
No children under 10	131	10	85	127	118	24	28	4	126	98	24	37	5
1 child under 10	2	2	12	16	23	----	4	----	20	10	2	7	1
2 children under 10	10	----	5	11	7	1	----	----	11	8	----	2	----
3 or more	12	----	1	7	5	1	1	----	20	4	1	8	----

CHARACTERISTICS OF NEGRO POPULATION BY COUNTIES: 1930—Continued

(See note at head of table)

CALIFORNIA—Continued

SUBJECT	Tehama	Trinity	Tulare	Tuolumne	Ventura	Yolo	Yuba
POPULATION BY SEX							
Negro population: 1930	64	6	819	20	125	194	181
Male	38	6	432	14	47	109	93
Female	26	–	387	6	78	85	88
Negro population: 1920	64	3	253	12	123	202	189
Male	29	2	122	10	49	113	101
Female	35	1	131	2	74	89	88
Percent of total population:							
1930	0.5	0.2	1.1	0.2	0.2	0.8	1.6
1920	0.5	0.1	0.4	0.2	0.4	1.2	1.8
VOTING AGE: 1930							
Total 21 years old and over	55	6	459	18	97	107	123
Male	33	6	270	12	42	65	71
Female	22	–	189	6	55	42	52
AGE: 1930							
Under 5 years	–	–	89	2	4	16	13
Under 1 year	–	–	18	–	–	1	2
5 to 9 years	3	–	86	–	5	21	15
10 to 14 years	2	–	79	–	4	32	16
15 to 19 years	3	–	95	–	12	17	14
20 to 24 years	8	1	65	2	13	9	6
25 to 29 years	5	2	57	–	9	15	5
30 to 34 years	6	–	57	1	12	10	5
35 to 44 years	4	1	106	6	27	20	31
45 to 54 years	15	–	99	5	22	26	31
55 to 64 years	8	2	47	2	8	17	25
65 to 74 years	6	–	26	2	6	6	15
75 years and over	4	–	10	–	3	5	5
Unknown	–	–	3	–	–	–	–
SCHOOL ATTENDANCE							
Total 7 to 13 years, inclusive	4	–	112	–	6	38	21
Number attending school	4	–	110	–	6	38	20
Percent attending school	–	–	98.2	–	–	–	–
Total 14 and 15 years, inclusive	–	–	33	–	1	8	10
Number attending school	–	–	31	–	1	8	10
Percent attending school	–	–	–	–	–	–	–
Total 16 and 17 years, inclusive	3	–	32	–	7	11	5
Number attending school	2	–	15	–	5	11	5
Percent attending school	–	–	–	–	–	–	–
Total 18 to 20 years, inclusive	1	–	55	–	8	4	4
Number attending school	–	–	12	–	1	2	2
Percent attending school	–	–	–	–	–	–	–
ILLITERACY							
Total 10 years old and over	61	6	644	18	116	157	153
Number illiterate	2	–	30	–	9	5	5
Percent illiterate	–	–	4.7	–	7.8	3.2	3.3
Percent illiterate in 1920	–	–	7.5	–	5.5	9.2	1.2
URBAN AND RURAL							
Urban population	44	–	265	–	97	87	163
Percent urban	–	–	32.4	–	77.6	44.8	90.1
Rural population	20	6	554	20	28	107	18
Rural-farm	11	–	403	–	14	61	10
Rural-nonfarm	9	6	151	20	14	46	8
Percent rural	–	–	67.6	–	22.4	55.2	9.9
MARITAL CONDITION							
Males 15 years old and over	35	6	312	12	45	78	76
Single	9	1	95	8	16	33	32
Married	19	–	177	3	26	29	27
Widowed	5	–	31	–	1	8	12
Divorced	1	–	7	1	2	6	5
Unknown	1	5	2	–	–	2	–
Females 15 years old and over	24	–	253	6	67	47	61
Single	5	–	53	2	14	7	14
Married	17	–	168	3	26	28	31
Widowed	2	–	26	1	17	12	12
Divorced	–	–	5	–	10	–	4
Unknown	–	–	1	–	–	–	–
FAMILIES							
Number of families	25	1	214	8	46	48	55
Median size	–	–	2.72	–	–	–	–
Families having—							
No children under 10	23	1	141	7	40	30	40
1 child under 10	1	–	24	–	4	8	5
2 children under 10	1	–	17	1	1	1	8
3 or more	–	–	32	–	1	9	2

COLORADO

SUBJECT	The State	Adams	Alamosa	Arapahoe	Baca	Bent	Boulder	Chaffee	Cheyenne	Clear Creek	Conejos	Costilla	Crowley	Custer	Delta	Denver	Douglas	Eagle	Elbert
POPULATION BY SEX																			
Negro population: 1930	11,828	107	49	104	2	15	128	23	1	11	4	1	17	36	1	7,204	2	1	13
Male	5,739	73	27	54	1	7	65	14	1	3	3	1	7	25	–	3,365	2	1	5
Female	6,089	34	22	50	1	8	63	9	–	8	1	–	10	11	1	3,839	–	–	8
Negro population: 1920	11,318	85	45	72	20	37	162	24	20	15	18	–	12	–	4	6,075	1	–	7
Male	5,834	54	28	31	12	28	77	16	13	8	10	–	7	–	3	3,069	–	–	5
Female	5,484	31	17	41	8	9	85	8	7	7	8	–	5	–	1	3,006	1	–	2
Percent of total population:																			
1930	1.1	0.5	0.6	0.5	–	0.2	0.4	0.3	–	0.5	–	–	0.3	1.7	–	2.5	0.1	–	0.2
1920	1.2	0.6	0.9	0.5	0.2	0.4	0.5	0.3	0.5	0.5	0.2	–	0.2	–	–	2.4	–	–	0.1
VOTING AGE: 1930																			
Total 21 years old and over	8,570	76	26	78	2	10	95	17	1	7	1	1	12	25	–	5,305	2	1	5
Male	4,189	59	14	41	1	4	46	9	1	3	1	1	6	18	–	2,485	2	1	3
Female	4,381	17	12	37	1	6	49	8	–	4	–	–	6	7	–	2,820	–	–	2
AGE: 1930																			
Under 5 years	773	5	5	6	–	–	12	–	–	3	1	–	2	2	–	464	–	–	2
Under 1 year	150	1	1	–	–	–	3	–	–	–	–	–	1	1	–	86	–	–	1
5 to 9 years	775	5	7	8	–	–	6	–	–	–	2	–	2	4	–	454	–	–	3
10 to 14 years	757	4	8	7	–	4	4	1	–	–	–	–	1	2	–	423	–	–	3
15 to 19 years	783	16	3	5	–	–	9	3	–	1	–	–	–	3	–	445	–	–	–
20 to 24 years	892	4	1	4	–	1	15	6	–	–	–	1	–	2	1	568	–	–	1
25 to 29 years	995	4	1	7	–	–	15	1	–	–	–	–	2	2	–	622	–	1	1
30 to 34 years	1,049	13	5	9	–	–	3	–	–	–	–	–	1	2	–	712	–	–	–
35 to 44 years	2,249	35	3	16	–	5	17	4	–	1	1	–	5	12	–	1,436	1	–	–
45 to 54 years	1,928	8	13	19	–	4	21	4	–	–	–	–	1	5	–	1,164	–	–	2
55 to 64 years	950	3	2	14	–	1	11	1	1	–	–	–	3	2	–	541	–	–	–
65 to 74 years	478	7	1	6	–	–	11	3	–	2	–	–	–	–	–	275	1	–	–
75 years and over	179	3	–	3	2	–	3	–	–	4	–	–	–	–	–	89	–	–	1
Unknown	20	–	–	–	–	–	1	–	–	–	–	–	–	–	–	11	–	–	–
SCHOOL ATTENDANCE																			
Total 7 to 13 years, inclusive	1,064	8	9	13	–	4	5	1	–	–	2	–	2	5	–	600	–	–	4
Number attending school	1,029	8	9	13	–	4	5	1	–	–	2	–	2	5	–	570	–	–	4
Percent attending school	96.7	–	–	–	–	–	–	–	–	–	–	–	–	–	–	95.0	–	–	–
Total 14 and 15 years, inclusive	284	4	–	2	–	–	3	–	–	–	–	–	–	1	–	161	–	–	1
Number attending school	260	3	–	1	–	–	3	–	–	–	–	–	–	1	–	149	–	–	1
Percent attending school	91.5	–	–	–	–	–	–	–	–	–	–	–	–	–	–	92.5	–	–	–
Total 16 and 17 years, inclusive	319	7	1	–	–	–	3	–	–	–	–	–	–	1	–	182	–	–	–
Number attending school	197	6	1	–	–	–	3	–	–	–	–	–	–	–	–	119	–	–	–
Percent attending school	61.8	–	–	–	–	–	–	–	–	–	–	–	–	–	–	65.4	–	–	–
Total 18 to 20 years, inclusive	506	6	2	3	–	1	8	5	–	1	–	–	–	1	1	307	–	–	–
Number attending school	138	3	2	–	–	–	7	–	–	–	–	–	–	–	–	68	–	–	–
Percent attending school	27.3	–	–	–	–	–	–	–	–	–	–	–	–	–	–	22.1	–	–	–
ILLITERACY																			
Total 10 years old and over	10,280	97	37	90	2	15	110	23	1	8	1	1	13	30	1	6,286	2	1	8
Number illiterate	403	7	2	1	1	–	–	1	–	1	–	1	–	1	–	150	–	–	2
Percent illiterate	3.9	–	–	–	–	–	–	–	–	–	–	–	–	–	–	2.4	–	–	–
Percent illiterate in 1920	6.2	–	–	–	–	–	2.8	–	–	–	–	–	–	–	–	4.1	–	–	–
URBAN AND RURAL																			
Urban population	10,471	5	37	37	–	13	123	18	–	–	–	–	–	–	–	7,204	–	–	–
Percent urban	88.5	4.7	–	35.6	–	–	96.1	–	–	–	–	–	–	–	–	100.0	–	–	–
Rural population	1,357	102	12	67	2	2	5	5	1	11	4	1	17	36	1	–	2	1	13
Rural-farm	360	17	2	28	2	2	–	–	–	1	–	–	15	19	1	–	–	–	13
Rural-nonfarm	997	85	10	39	–	–	5	5	1	10	4	1	2	17	–	–	2	1	–
Percent rural	11.5	95.3	–	64.4	–	–	3.9	–	–	–	–	–	–	–	–	–	–	–	–
MARITAL CONDITION																			
Males 15 years old and over	4,621	65	15	43	1	5	52	13	1	3	1	1	6	20	–	2,730	2	1	3
Single	1,240	22	3	8	–	1	15	8	–	1	–	–	–	6	–	674	1	1	2
Married	2,757	26	10	29	1	3	29	2	–	–	1	1	6	14	–	1,694	–	–	1
Widowed	438	9	2	3	–	–	7	2	1	2	–	–	–	–	–	255	1	–	–
Divorced	173	8	–	3	–	–	1	1	–	–	–	–	–	–	–	102	–	–	–
Unknown	13	–	–	–	–	1	–	–	–	–	–	–	–	–	–	5	–	–	–
Females 15 years old and over	4,902	28	14	40	1	6	54	9	–	5	–	–	6	8	1	3,133	–	–	2
Single	798	10	3	6	–	–	13	2	–	–	–	–	–	1	1	488	–	–	1
Married	2,778	17	10	30	1	4	27	3	–	1	–	–	6	7	–	1,746	–	–	1
Widowed	1,135	1	1	4	–	–	12	4	–	4	–	–	–	–	–	778	–	–	–
Divorced	185	–	–	–	–	2	2	–	–	–	–	–	–	–	–	116	–	–	–
Unknown	6	–	–	–	–	–	–	–	–	–	–	–	–	–	–	5	–	–	–
FAMILIES																			
Number of families	3,538	12	11	29	1	5	43	7	1	7	–	–	6	10	–	2,155	1	–	1
Median size	2.26	–	–	–	–	–	–	–	–	–	–	–	–	–	–	2.28	–	–	–
Families having—																			
No children under 10	2,790	5	6	23	1	5	34	7	1	6	–	–	4	8	–	1,698	1	–	–
1 child under 10	356	4	2	1	–	–	3	–	–	–	–	–	1	–	–	229	–	–	–
2 children under 10	206	1	–	4	–	–	4	–	–	–	–	–	–	1	–	120	–	–	–
3 or more	186	2	3	1	–	–	2	–	–	1	–	–	1	1	–	108	–	–	1

CHARACTERISTICS OF NEGRO POPULATION BY COUNTIES: 1930—Continued

(See note at head of table)

COLORADO—Continued

SUBJECT	El Paso	Fremont	Garfield	Gunnison	Hinsdale	Huerfano	Jefferson	Kiowa	Lake	La Plata	Larimer	Las Animas	Lincoln	Logan	Mesa	Mineral	Moffat	Montezuma	Montrose	Morgan	Otero	Ouray	Pitkin	Prowers	Pueblo	Rio Blanco
POPULATION BY SEX																										
Negro population: 1930	1,096	216	11	13	3	254	64	30	17	35	13	286	1	39	72	1	1	3	8	35	222	3	3	46	1,333	16
Male	489	153	8	9	1	139	29	30	8	19	5	152	----	18	37	1	1	1	4	21	115	2	1	22	647	9
Female	607	63	3	4	2	115	35	----	9	16	8	134	1	21	35	----	----	2	4	14	107	1	2	24	686	7
Negro population: 1920	1,088	254	22	32	3	294	72	3	28	43	20	389	13	26	108	1	6	2	22	48	283	9	2	32	1,455	6
Male	492	157	13	20	2	166	45	3	14	24	12	210	10	15	53	1	4	1	12	26	141	6	1	17	772	3
Female	596	97	9	12	1	128	27	----	14	19	8	179	3	11	55	----	2	1	10	22	142	3	1	15	683	3
Percent of total population:																										
1930	2.2	1.1	0.1	0.2	0.7	1.5	0.3	0.8	0.3	0.3	----	0.8	----	0.2	0.3	0.2	----	----	0.1	0.1	0.9	0.2	0.2	0.3	2.0	0.5
1920	2.5	1.4	0.2	0.6	0.6	1.7	0.5	0.1	0.4	0.4	0.1	1.0	0.2	0.1	0.5	0.1	0.1	----	0.2	0.3	1.3	0.3	0.1	0.2	2.5	0.2
VOTING AGE: 1930																										
Total 21 years old and over	761	175	8	10	2	192	37	30	14	22	10	192	1	22	48	1	1	1	7	19	161	3	3	32	949	6
Male	319	133	5	6	1	108	15	30	6	13	5	106	----	12	25	1	1	----	3	13	85	2	1	17	465	4
Female	442	42	3	4	1	84	22	----	8	9	5	86	1	10	23	----	----	1	4	6	76	1	2	15	484	2
AGE: 1930																										
Under 5 years	66	8	----	----	1	19	----	----	----	3	2	29	----	5	5	----	----	----	----	7	12	----	----	4	82	3
Under 1 year	14	1	----	----	1	4	----	----	----	1	1	8	----	1	----	----	----	----	----	3	3	----	----	----	12	1
5 to 9 years	83	12	----	----	----	12	3	----	----	5	----	18	----	4	10	----	----	1	----	3	14	----	----	4	94	4
10 to 14 years	80	9	----	----	----	10	11	----	3	2	1	26	----	5	8	----	----	1	----	3	18	----	----	3	98	3
15 to 19 years	93	10	3	2	----	18	13	----	----	3	----	20	----	3	1	----	----	----	----	2	14	----	----	2	87	----
20 to 24 years	61	21	----	1	----	24	----	3	----	1	----	13	1	3	5	----	----	----	2	4	22	----	----	6	106	----
25 to 29 years	88	30	----	----	----	13	1	6	2	2	3	17	----	6	6	----	----	----	----	3	22	----	----	3	113	----
30 to 34 years	87	27	1	----	----	21	3	7	----	4	----	17	----	3	4	----	----	----	----	1	17	----	----	1	92	----
35 to 44 years	186	35	----	3	1	46	11	13	6	5	2	53	----	8	8	----	----	----	4	2	30	----	----	7	241	4
45 to 54 years	172	36	3	1	1	49	11	1	2	4	4	50	----	2	8	----	1	----	2	4	37	----	1	9	234	2
55 to 64 years	109	17	1	3	----	25	5	----	3	3	----	32	----	----	7	----	----	----	----	1	23	----	2	5	111	----
65 to 74 years	47	8	2	2	----	13	2	----	----	2	1	8	----	----	6	1	----	----	----	4	12	3	----	1	51	----
75 years and over	23	3	1	1	----	4	4	----	1	1	----	2	----	----	2	----	----	1	----	----	1	----	----	1	23	----
Unknown	1	----	----	----	----	----	----	----	----	----	----	1	----	----	2	----	----	----	----	1	----	----	----	----	1	----
SCHOOL ATTENDANCE																										
Total 7 to 13 years, inclusive	112	14	----	----	----	14	9	----	3	4	1	33	----	5	10	----	----	1	----	5	24	----	----	4	144	4
Number attending school	112	14	----	----	----	14	9	----	3	4	1	33	----	5	10	----	----	1	----	5	24	----	----	4	140	4
Percent attending school	100.0	----	----	----	----	----	----	----	----	----	----	----	----	----	----	----	----	----	----	----	----	----	----	----	97.2	----
Total 14 and 15 years, inclusive	30	3	----	1	----	5	7	----	----	1	----	10	----	1	2	----	----	----	----	1	7	----	----	2	28	1
Number attending school	29	3	----	1	----	4	6	----	----	----	----	8	----	----	2	----	----	----	----	1	7	----	----	2	27	1
Percent attending school	----	----	----	----	----	----	----	----	----	----	----	----	----	----	----	----	----	----	----	----	----	----	----	----	----	----
Total 16 and 17 years, inclusive	39	3	1	----	----	6	9	----	----	2	----	8	----	1	----	----	----	----	----	----	5	----	----	----	39	----
Number attending school	23	1	1	----	----	1	8	----	----	2	----	3	----	----	----	----	----	----	----	----	3	----	----	----	21	----
Percent attending school	----	----	----	----	----	----	----	----	----	----	----	----	----	----	----	----	----	----	----	----	----	----	----	----	----	----
Total 18 to 20 years, inclusive	55	7	2	2	----	12	1	----	----	----	----	8	----	2	1	----	----	----	1	3	8	----	----	2	59	----
Number attending school	23	----	----	1	----	2	----	----	----	----	----	1	----	1	----	----	----	----	----	2	2	----	----	2	22	----
Percent attending school	----	----	----	----	----	----	----	----	----	----	----	----	----	----	----	----	----	----	----	----	----	----	----	----	----	----
ILLITERACY																										
Total 10 years old and over	947	196	11	13	2	223	61	30	17	27	11	239	1	30	57	1	1	2	8	25	196	3	3	38	1,157	9
Number illiterate	56	10	3	1	----	24	2	19	1	1	1	18	----	1	9	----	----	----	----	3	5	1	----	----	68	----
Percent illiterate	5.9	5.1	----	----	----	10.8	----	----	----	----	----	7.5	----	----	----	----	----	----	----	----	2.6	----	----	----	5.9	----
Percent illiterate in 1920	6.4	10.0	----	----	----	12.6	----	----	----	----	----	12.9	----	----	----	----	----	----	----	----	3.7	----	----	----	10.0	----
URBAN AND RURAL																										
Urban population	965	151	----	----	----	90	----	----	17	18	12	144	----	39	58	----	----	----	4	2	169	----	----	38	1,305	----
Percent urban	88.0	69.9	----	----	----	35.4	----	----	----	----	----	50.3	----	----	----	----	----	----	----	----	76.1	----	----	----	97.9	----
Rural population	131	65	11	13	3	164	64	30	----	17	1	142	1	----	14	1	1	3	4	33	53	3	3	8	28	16
Rural-farm	28	1	2	----	3	18	12	7	----	9	1	20	1	----	2	----	1	2	2	19	42	----	----	8	8	1
Rural-nonfarm	103	64	9	13	----	146	52	23	----	8	----	122	----	----	12	1	----	1	2	14	11	3	3	----	20	15
Percent rural	12.0	30.1	----	----	----	64.6	----	----	----	----	----	49.7	----	----	----	----	----	----	----	----	23.9	----	----	----	2.1	----
MARITAL CONDITION																										
Males 15 years old and over	366	140	8	9	1	120	22	30	6	13	5	115	----	13	26	1	1	----	4	15	96	2	1	18	513	4
Single	102	56	6	5	----	27	10	24	2	4	1	29	----	4	8	----	1	----	2	2	24	1	----	5	138	2
Married	219	58	1	3	1	75	10	5	4	8	3	72	----	9	14	----	----	----	2	10	60	----	1	13	303	2
Widowed	32	15	1	1	----	14	1	1	----	1	1	9	----	----	2	1	----	----	----	2	11	1	----	----	48	----
Divorced	12	11	----	----	----	4	1	----	----	----	----	5	----	----	2	----	----	----	----	1	1	----	----	----	18	----
Unknown	1	----	----	----	----	----	----	----	----	----	----	----	----	----	----	----	----	----	----	----	----	----	----	----	6	----
Females 15 years old and over	501	47	3	4	1	93	28	----	8	12	5	98	1	12	23	----	----	1	4	7	82	1	2	17	546	2
Single	99	7	----	1	----	12	8	----	3	3	----	14	----	3	1	----	----	----	1	1	10	----	----	4	87	----
Married	239	31	----	3	1	69	12	----	5	7	4	69	1	9	14	----	----	----	2	6	56	----	1	11	321	2
Widowed	139	6	3	----	----	9	6	----	----	2	1	14	----	----	6	----	----	1	1	----	15	1	1	2	110	----
Divorced	24	3	----	----	----	3	2	----	----	----	----	1	----	----	1	----	----	----	----	----	1	----	----	----	28	----
Unknown	----	----	----	----	----	----	----	----	----	----	----	----	----	----	1	----	----	----	----	----	----	----	----	----	----	----
FAMILIES																										
Number of families	329	39	5	5	1	93	16	1	8	10	6	100	----	9	24	1	----	----	4	10	73	2	2	15	389	3
Median size	2.32	----	----	----	----	----	----	----	----	----	----	2.09	----	----	----	----	----	----	----	----	----	----	----	----	2.34	----
Families having—																										
No children under 10	256	28	5	5	----	76	14	1	8	7	4	83	----	5	19	1	----	----	4	7	59	2	2	11	305	2
1 child under 10	30	6	----	----	1	6	1	----	----	2	1	7	----	----	2	----	----	----	----	----	7	----	----	3	45	----
2 children under 10	27	1	----	----	----	7	1	----	----	----	1	6	----	3	1	----	----	----	----	2	4	----	----	1	18	----
3 or more	16	4	----	----	----	4	----	----	----	1	----	4	----	1	2	----	----	----	----	1	3	----	----	----	21	1

CHARACTERISTICS OF NEGRO POPULATION BY COUNTIES: 1930—Continued

(See note at head of table)

SUBJECT	COLORADO—Continued: Rio Grande	Routt	Saguache	San Juan	San Miguel	Sedgwick	Teller	Washington	Weld	Yuma	CONNECTICUT: The State	Fairfield	Hartford	Litchfield	Middlesex	New Haven	New London	Tolland	Windham	DELAWARE: The State	Kent	New Castle	Sussex
POPULATION BY SEX																							
Negro population: 1930	4	125	2	4	2	4	7	27	111	2	29, 354	8, 193	8, 508	739	540	9, 346	1, 586	167	275	32, 602	6, 612	18, 471	7, 519
Male	3	72	1	1	1	2	3	15	65	1	14, 573	4, 010	4, 163	382	228	4, 765	794	83	148	16, 983	3, 469	9, 643	3, 871
Female	1	53	1	3	1	2	4	12	46	1	14, 781	4, 183	4, 345	357	312	4, 581	792	84	127	15, 619	3, 143	8, 828	3, 648
Negro population: 1920	10	81	---	4	8	13	26	58	238	1	21, 046	5, 043	5, 985	702	324	7, 080	1, 425	142	345	30, 335	6, 753	16, 325	7, 257
Male	7	46	---	2	4	8	11	34	129	---	10, 778	2, 565	3, 122	350	137	3, 662	698	79	165	15, 655	3, 400	8, 562	3, 693
Female	3	35	---	2	4	5	15	24	109	1	10, 268	2, 478	2, 863	352	187	3, 418	727	63	180	14, 680	3, 353	7, 763	3, 564
Percent of total population:																							
1930	---	1. 3	---	0. 2	0. 1	0. 1	0. 2	0. 3	0. 2	---	1. 8	2. 1	2. 0	0. 9	1. 1	2. 0	1. 3	0. 6	0. 5	13. 7	20. 8	11. 5	16. 5
1920	0. 1	0. 9	---	0. 2	0. 2	0. 3	0. 4	0. 5	0. 4	---	1. 5	1. 6	1. 8	0. 9	0. 7	1. 7	1. 4	0. 5	0. 7	13. 6	21. 8	11. 0	16. 6
VOTING AGE: 1930																							
Total 21 years old and over	3	92	2	4	1	4	7	16	70	---	18, 322	5, 403	5, 048	468	313	5, 846	994	90	160	19, 939	3, 675	12, 348	3, 916
Male	3	57	1	1	1	2	3	7	43	---	9, 255	2, 671	2, 511	252	152	3, 046	496	49	78	10, 669	1, 942	6, 661	2, 066
Female	---	35	1	3	---	2	4	9	27	---	9, 067	2, 732	2, 537	216	161	2, 800	498	41	82	9, 270	1, 733	5, 687	1, 850
AGE: 1930																							
Under 5 years	---	8	---	---	---	---	---	2	15	---	2, 969	797	906	65	58	958	143	14	28	2, 787	614	1, 352	821
Under 1 year	---	2	---	---	---	---	---	---	4	---	570	153	174	10	15	189	26	1	2	548	106	252	190
5 to 9 years	---	4	---	---	---	---	---	3	10	---	2, 900	684	960	64	49	932	167	14	30	3, 248	774	1, 541	933
10 to 14 years	---	10	---	---	---	---	---	3	6	---	2, 347	554	742	74	49	755	132	17	24	2, 985	724	1, 401	860
15 to 19 years	1	11	---	---	---	---	---	3	10	2	2, 316	627	697	56	58	700	122	29	27	2, 985	687	1, 470	828
20 to 24 years	1	6	---	1	1	---	---	---	6	---	2, 669	841	734	80	54	810	112	17	21	2, 988	544	1, 762	682
25 to 29 years	1	10	1	1	---	---	---	1	10	---	3, 017	966	869	59	44	900	152	10	17	2, 819	405	1, 899	515
30 to 34 years	1	8	---	---	---	1	---	2	7	---	2, 632	775	787	48	44	813	129	18	18	2, 477	421	1, 615	441
35 to 44 years	---	26	1	2	---	1	---	2	16	---	4, 785	1, 444	1, 325	105	67	1, 555	227	20	42	4, 852	814	3, 183	855
45 to 54 years	---	28	---	---	---	2	1	4	18	---	3, 131	900	827	87	54	1, 019	205	13	26	3, 741	751	2, 256	734
55 to 64 years	---	12	---	---	1	---	1	1	9	---	1, 571	394	412	49	41	541	111	6	17	2, 070	437	1, 181	452
65 to 74 years	---	1	---	---	---	---	2	4	2	---	684	157	162	35	14	239	56	7	14	1, 121	281	549	291
75 years and over	---	---	---	---	---	---	3	2	1	---	308	51	78	16	8	112	30	2	11	509	154	252	103
Unknown	---	1	---	---	---	---	---	---	1	---	25	3	9	1	---	12	---	---	---	20	6	10	4
SCHOOL ATTENDANCE																							
Total 7 to 13 years, inclusive	---	8	---	---	---	---	---	4	12	---	3, 636	865	1, 185	97	68	1, 144	217	24	36	4, 347	1, 063	2, 034	1, 250
Number attending school	---	8	---	---	---	---	---	4	11	---	3, 561	840	1, 175	94	68	1, 120	211	21	32	4, 119	1, 011	1, 917	1, 191
Percent attending school	---	---	---	---	---	---	---	---	---	---	97. 9	97. 1	99. 2	---	---	97. 9	97. 2	---	---	94. 8	95. 1	94. 2	95. 3
Total 14 and 15 years, inclusive	---	7	---	---	---	---	---	1	5	---	856	200	258	26	23	285	42	9	13	1, 146	281	534	331
Number attending school	---	6	---	---	---	---	---	1	4	---	762	177	243	21	21	248	37	6	9	968	239	480	249
Percent attending school	---	---	---	---	---	---	---	---	---	---	89. 0	88. 5	94. 2	---	---	87. 0	---	---	---	84. 5	85. 1	89. 9	75. 2
Total 16 and 17 years, inclusive	---	6	---	---	---	---	---	2	4	---	902	254	27. 3	23	21	270	42	11	8	1, 222	304	573	345
Number attending school	---	2	---	---	---	---	---	2	1	---	372	87	124	13	15	111	17	3	2	516	126	294	96
Percent attending school	---	---	---	---	---	---	---	---	---	---	41. 2	34. 3	45. 4	---	---	41. 1	---	---	---	42. 2	41. 4	51. 3	27. 8
Total 18 to 20 years, inclusive	1	2	---	---	1	---	---	1	1	2	1, 465	401	437	33	37	439	86	16	16	1, 859	395	987	477
Number attending school	---	---	---	---	---	---	---	1	---	1	171	35	48	1	7	66	9	4	1	204	36	135	33
Percent attending school	---	---	---	---	---	---	---	---	---	---	11. 7	8. 7	11. 0	---	---	15. 0	---	---	---	11. 0	9. 1	13. 7	6. 9
ILLITERACY																							
Total 10 years old and over	4	113	2	4	2	4	7	22	86	2	23, 485	6, 712	6, 642	610	433	7, 456	1, 276	139	217	26, 567	5, 224	15, 578	5, 765
Number illiterate	---	10	---	---	---	1	1	---	1	---	1, 157	270	439	22	28	303	63	14	18	3, 496	801	1, 603	1, 092
Percent illiterate	---	8. 8	---	---	---	---	---	---	---	---	4. 9	4. 0	6. 6	3. 6	6. 5	4. 1	4. 9	10. 1	8. 3	13. 2	15. 3	10. 3	18. 9
Percent illiterate in 1920	---	---	---	---	---	---	---	---	7. 5	---	6. 2	6. 8	7. 8	5. 3	3. 6	4. 1	7. 2	8. 7	10. 7	19. 1	23. 9	17. 2	19. 3
URBAN AND RURAL																							
Urban population	2	---	---	---	---	---	---	---	20	---	24, 531	6, 919	7, 219	213	227	8, 449	1, 234	99	171	15, 037	1, 704	13, 184	149
Percent urban	---	---	---	---	---	---	---	---	18. 0	---	83. 6	84. 5	84. 8	28. 8	42. 0	90. 4	77. 8	59. 3	62. 2	46. 1	25. 8	71. 4	2. 0
Rural population	2	125	2	4	2	4	7	27	91	2	4, 823	1, 274	1, 289	526	313	897	352	68	104	17, 565	4, 908	5, 287	7, 370
Rural-farm	---	---	1	---	1	1	1	10	57	2	332	98	81	27	14	30	27	26	29	6, 755	2, 599	851	3, 305
Rural-nonfarm	2	125	1	4	1	3	6	17	34	---	4, 491	1, 176	1, 208	499	299	867	325	42	75	10, 810	2, 309	4, 436	4, 065
Percent rural	---	100. 0	---	---	---	---	---	---	82. 0	---	16. 4	15. 5	15. 2	71. 2	58. 0	9. 6	22. 2	40. 7	37. 8	53. 9	74. 2	28. 6	98. 0
MARITAL CONDITION																							
Males 15 years old and over	3	62	1	1	1	2	3	9	47	1	10, 566	2, 998	2, 921	281	172	3, 465	566	66	97	12, 485	2, 387	7, 527	2, 571
Single	3	19	1	1	---	1	1	2	16	1	3, 457	923	918	101	69	1, 174	200	32	40	4, 971	934	3, 086	951
Married	---	34	---	---	---	1	---	6	26	---	6, 425	1, 912	1, 800	158	95	2, 058	327	28	47	6, 485	1, 213	3, 852	1, 420
Widowed	---	7	---	---	---	---	2	1	5	---	555	129	160	19	7	193	31	6	10	880	214	485	181
Divorced	---	2	---	---	1	---	---	---	---	---	108	28	37	1	1	34	7	---	---	96	23	56	17
Unknwon	---	---	---	---	---	---	---	---	---	---	21	6	6	2	---	6	1	---	---	53	3	48	2
Females 15 years old and over	1	41	1	3	1	2	4	10	33	1	10, 572	3, 160	2, 979	255	212	3, 236	578	56	96	11, 097	2, 113	6, 650	2, 334
Single	1	4	---	2	1	---	2	2	6	1	2, 385	714	642	67	82	675	153	23	29	3, 024	563	1, 831	630
Married	---	33	---	1	---	1	---	6	21	---	6, 507	1, 954	1, 845	155	105	2, 047	331	26	44	6, 424	1, 240	3, 765	1, 419
Widowed	---	4	1	---	---	1	2	2	4	---	1, 486	456	429	31	22	451	89	7	21	1, 544	282	985	277
Divorced	---	---	---	---	---	---	---	---	2	---	185	55	57	2	3	61	5	---	2	82	19	55	8
Unknown	---	---	---	---	---	---	---	---	---	---	9	1	6	---	---	2	---	---	---	23	9	14	---
FAMILIES																							
Number of families	---	51	1	2	---	2	6	8	34	---	7, 174	1, 990	2, 091	166	102	2, 369	369	32	55	7, 682	1, 596	4, 363	1, 723
Median size	---	---	---	---	---	---	---	---	---	---	2. 81	2. 63	3. 11	2. 68	3. 14	2. 69	2. 46	---	---	2. 83	3. 06	2. 52	3. 38
Families having—																							
No children under 10	---	45	1	2	---	2	6	7	24	---	4, 606	1, 332	1, 225	111	57	1, 568	257	19	37	5, 005	987	3, 053	965
1 child under 10	---	2	---	---	---	---	---	---	3	---	1, 070	284	376	23	20	314	42	5	6	1, 134	256	579	299
2 children under 10	---	2	---	---	---	---	---	---	2	---	652	162	224	18	10	204	24	5	5	678	151	342	185
3 or more	---	2	---	---	---	---	---	1	5	---	846	212	266	14	15	283	46	3	7	865	202	389	274

CHARACTERISTICS OF NEGRO POPULATION BY COUNTIES: 1930—Continued

(See note at head of table)

SUBJECT	District of Columbia	FLORIDA: The State	Alachua	Baker	Bay	Bradford	Brevard	Broward	Calhoun	Charlotte	Citrus	Clay	Collier	Columbia	Dade	De Soto	Dixie	Duval	Escambia
POPULATION BY SEX																			
Negro population: 1930	132, 068	431, 828	ı5, 3.3	1, 781	3, 087	2, 730	4, 199	6, 687	1, 361	784	1, 799	1, 767	745	5, 790	29, 894	1, 497	2, 995	53, 411	13, 924
Male	62, 225	215, 148	7, 601	995	1, 593	1, 373	2, 112	3, 498	720	442	936	912	542	2, 888	14, 487	749	1, 722	24, 865	6, 554
Female	69, 843	216, 680	7, 712	786	1, 494	1, 357	2, 087	3, 189	641	342	863	855	203	2, 902	15, 407	748	1, 273	28, 546	7, 370
Negro population: 1920	109, 966	329, 487	14, 573	1, 422	2, 757	3, 492	2, 483	1, 572	2, 408	------	2, 525	2, 072	------	6, 999	12, 680	4, 347	------	47, 989	15, 221
Male	50, 855	167, 156	7, 188	839	1, 445	1, 921	1, 335	869	1, 257	------	1, 333	1, 093	------	3, 491	6, 659	2, 529	------	23, 592	7, 521
Female	59, 111	162, 331	7, 385	583	1, 312	1, 571	1, 148	703	1, 151	------	1, 192	979	------	3, 508	6, 021	1, 820	------	24, 397	7, 700
Percent of total population:																			
1930	27. 1	29. 4	44. 6	28. 4	25. 5	29. 0	31. 6	33. 3	18. 6	19. 5	32. 6	25. 8	25. 8	39. 6	20. 9	19. 3	46. 7	34. 3	26. 0
1920	25. 1	34. 0	46. 0	25. 3	24. 2	27. 9	29. 2	30. 6	27. 4	------	48. 4	36. 9	------	49. 0	29. 7	17. 1	------	42. 3	30. 8
VOTING AGE: 1930																			
Total 21 years old and over	88, 388	251, 025	8, 398	1, 031	1, 659	1, 374	2, 500	3, 662	670	517	1, 010	1, 026	565	2, 963	18, 138	905	1, 984	33, 974	8, 450
Male	41, 584	127, 988	4, 198	619	888	717	1, 332	2, 017	374	301	543	536	426	1, 494	8, 984	478	1, 233	15, 869	3, 985
Female	46, 804	123, 037	4, 200	412	771	657	1, 168	1, 645	296	216	467	490	139	1, 467	9, 154	427	751	18, 105	4, 465
AGE: 1930																			
Under 5 years	10, 006	40, 441	1, 406	198	381	306	404	717	147	59	172	163	34	568	3, 074	118	220	4, 038	1, 217
Under 1 year	1, 847	7, 349	229	37	72	58	67	162	22	8	37	24	5	97	551	20	38	711	240
5 to 9 years	10, 838	45, 450	1, 760	182	361	341	461	757	186	63	201	197	31	726	3, 276	155	255	4, 841	1, 434
10 to 14 years	9, 484	42, 116	1, 684	164	290	337	391	699	157	71	188	189	23	729	2, 419	147	199	4, 516	1, 232
15 to 19 years	10, 675	43, 355	1, 730	167	324	317	350	710	163	63	191	160	70	681	2, 399	143	244	4, 879	1, 283
20 to 24 years	14, 406	48, 402	1, 616	222	382	297	467	752	159	70	171	161	116	575	3, 398	137	488	6, 243	1, 587
25 to 29 years	14, 989	45, 950	1, 267	188	313	245	464	718	110	93	162	134	122	422	4, 375	152	385	6, 667	1, 379
30 to 34 years	12, 360	34, 403	969	134	215	172	345	546	71	57	101	103	81	340	3, 307	112	305	5, 021	1, 030
35 to 44 years	21, 717	61, 584	1, 898	259	366	295	623	959	169	128	227	268	157	640	4, 548	254	478	9, 028	2, 062
45 to 54 years	15, 864	41, 059	1, 521	175	290	234	431	563	100	115	223	202	72	560	2, 159	179	296	5, 220	1, 570
55 to 64 years	6, 786	17, 774	836	57	108	126	172	182	64	46	93	123	30	291	639	62	93	1, 832	698
65 to 74 years	3, 065	7, 610	439	23	34	48	65	65	26	11	47	50	7	184	202	21	25	778	269
75 years and over	1, 226	3, 209	161	12	21	12	20	19	9	7	15	16	2	70	74	8	7	306	147
Unknown	652	475	26	------	2	------	6	------	------	1	8	1	------	4	24	9	------	42	16
SCHOOL ATTENDANCE																			
Total 7 to 13 years, inclusive	14, 112	60, 622	2, 381	222	438	471	584	1, 020	241	93	277	274	33	1, 022	3, 819	212	314	6, 598	1, 874
Number attending school	13, 638	50, 874	1, 706	170	369	322	568	914	105	84	239	182	------	884	3, 672	202	127	6, 111	1, 744
Percent attending school	96. 6	83. 9	71. 7	76. 6	84. 2	68. 4	97. 3	89. 6	43. 6	------	86. 3	66. 4	------	86. 5	96. 2	95. 3	40. 4	92. 6	93. 1
Total 14 and 15 years, inclusive	3, 671	16, 694	715	69	133	151	157	281	66	26	74	73	16	261	888	63	79	1, 736	468
Number attending school	3, 409	11, 794	400	39	89	75	126	190	25	20	55	35	------	225	663	50	18	1, 434	388
Percent attending school	92. 9	70. 6	55. 9	------	66. 9	49. 7	80. 3	67. 6	------	------	------	------	------	86. 2	74. 7	------	------	82. 6	82. 9
Total 16 and 17 years, inclusive	4, 040	17, 081	687	69	108	134	133	27	65	23	63	65	28	285	896	55	90	1, 905	490
Number attending school	2, 292	6, 603	191	19	37	36	65	109	8	10	17	17	------	155	321	18	6	909	259
Percent attending school	56. 7	38. 7	27. 8	------	34. 3	26. 9	48. 9	40. 8	------	------	------	------	------	54. 4	35. 8	------	------	47. 7	52. 9
Total 18 to 20 years, inclusive	7, 489	27, 622	1, 013	112	223	165	236	437	101	41	123	94	53	401	1, 666	85	205	3, 301	876
Number attending school	1, 590	2, 721	97	6	16	12	25	35	7	7	10	4	------	67	114	10	3	414	121
Percent attending school	21. 2	9. 9	9. 6	5. 4	7. 2	7. 3	10. 6	8. 0	6. 9	------	8. 1	------	------	16. 7	6. 8	------	1. 5	12. 5	13. 8
ILLITERACY																			
Total 10 years old and over	111, 224	345, 937	12, 147	1, 401	2, 345	2, 083	3, 334	5, 213	1, 028	662	1, 426	1, 407	680	4, 496	23, 544	1, 224	2, 520	44, 532	11, 273
Number illiterate	4, 591	65, 167	2, 535	414	656	499	463	851	385	113	206	318	306	780	2, 658	311	518	4, 882	1, 827
Percent illiterate	4. 1	18. 8	20. 9	29. 6	28. 0	24. 0	13. 9	16. 3	37. 5	17. 1	14. 4	22. 6	45. 0	17. 3	11. 3	25. 4	20. 6	11. 0	16. 2
Percent illiterate in 1920	8. 6	21. 5	26. 8	31. 8	28. 1	22. 8	9. 2	14. 4	49. 3	------	26. 7	20. 7	------	12. 6	11. 1	27. 4	------	11. 4	18. 6
URBAN AND RURAL																			
Urban population	132, 068	210, 292	4, 106	------	978	------	939	3, 744	------	------	------	------	------	1, 301	25, 988	1, 169	------	48, 788	9, 583
Percent urban	100. 0	48. 7	26. 8	------	31. 7	------	22. 4	56. 0	------	------	------	------	------	22. 5	86. 9	68. 1	------	91. 3	68. 8
Rural population	------	221, 536	11, 207	1, 781	2, 109	2, 730	3, 260	2, 943	1, 361	784	1, 799	1, 767	745	4, 489	3, 906	328	2, 995	4, 623	4, 341
Rural-farm	------	75, 469	5, 272	209	121	979	290	306	247	12	170	159	1	2, 672	570	113	54	629	488
Rural-nonfarm	------	146, 067	5, 935	1, 572	1, 988	1, 751	2, 970	2, 637	1, 114	772	1, 629	1, 608	744	1, 817	3, 336	215	2, 941	3, 994	3, 853
Percent rural	------	51. 3	73. 2	100. 0	68. 3	100. 0	77. 6	44. 0	100. 0	100. 0	100. 0	100. 0	100. 0	77. 5	13. 1	21. 9	100. 0	8. 7	31. 2
MARITAL CONDITION																			
Males 15 years old and over	47, 443	151, 867	5, ı45	719	1, 073	883	1, 531	2, 410	472	343	655	622	490	1, 875	10, 203	554	1, 392	18, 369	4, 635
Single	15, 925	47, 192	1, 695	248	297	274	467	816	130	118	218	192	308	587	2, 974	168	535	5, 074	1, 320
Married	28, 212	90, 572	3, 041	412	668	506	947	1, 447	288	190	344	376	175	1, 085	6, 584	362	766	11, 623	2, 879
Widowed	2, 714	10, 634	335	45	94	84	101	120	50	28	90	46	7	147	534	23	90	1, 425	330
Divorced	342	1, 992	65	13	13	19	16	26	4	6	3	8	------	27	107	1	------	230	102
Unknown	250	1, 477	9	1	1	------	------	1	------	1	------	------	------	29	4	------	1	17	4
Females 15 years old and over	54, 297	151, 954	5, 318	518	982	863	1, 412	2, 104	399	248	583	596	167	1, 892	10, 922	523	929	21, 647	5, 406
Single	14, 058	29, 624	1, 199	69	176	180	244	390	65	23	110	118	42	440	2, 013	81	135	4, 073	1, 133
Married	29, 942	93, 535	3, 151	377	644	523	945	1, 406	268	182	348	391	117	1, 099	7, 081	366	722	12, 667	3, 075
Widowed	9, 556	25, 241	843	62	151	134	208	270	60	33	116	77	8	308	1, 584	72	67	4, 396	1, 036
Divorced	530	3, 115	116	9	10	26	15	38	6	10	9	10	------	43	240	3	1	500	152
Unknown	211	439	9	1	1	------	------	------	------	------	------	------	------	2	4	1	4	11	10
FAMILIES																			
Number of families	29, 995	110, 361	3, 794	486	803	636	1, 142	1, 678	346	255	492	518	127	1, 416	7, 538	432	884	13, 503	3, 812
Median size	2. 84	2. 78	3. 08	2. 41	2. 83	3. 10	2. 60	2. 92	3. 11	2. 10	2. 61	2. 41	2. 04	3. 23	2. 62	2. 49	2. 27	2. 74	2. 71
Families having—																			
No children under 10	20, 630	70, 009	2, 294	309	469	370	745	988	202	191	309	356	97	832	4, 632	293	633	9, 091	2, 521
1 child under 10	4, 253	18, 000	653	74	131	102	173	295	47	37	82	70	15	247	1, 252	65	140	2, 217	601
2 children under 10	2, 428	ı0, 298	402	41	95	63	96	172	47	11	48	32	6	131	721	41	64	1, 150	336
3 or more	2, 684	12, 054	445	62	108	101	128	223	50	16	53	60	9	206	933	33	47	1, 045	354

CHARACTERISTICS OF NEGRO POPULATION BY COUNTIES: 1930—Continued

(See note at head of table)

SUBJECT	FLORIDA—Continued																			
	Flagler	Franklin	Gadsden	Gilchrist	Glades	Gulf	Hamilton	Hardee	Hendry	Hernando	Highlands	Hillsborough	Holmes	Indian River	Jackson	Jefferson	Lafayette	Lake	Lee	Leon
POPULATION BY SEX																				
Negro population: 1930	852	2,469	16,967	803	816	1,096	3,779	931	1,327	1,523	2,677	28,983	449	1,931	12,551	9,120	727	6,442	3,543	13,788
Male	480	1,271	8,276	474	471	590	1,941	496	878	804	1,504	14,067	202	1,066	6,111	4,554	446	3,325	1,904	6,384
Female	372	1,198	8,691	329	345	506	1,838	435	449	719	1,173	14,916	247	865	6,440	4,566	281	3,117	1,639	7,404
Negro population: 1920	958	2,484	14,812	-	-	-	4,263	-	-	1,825	-	16,588	1,034	-	13,320	10,521	1,113	3,817	1,247	12,167
Male	605	1,241	7,047	-	-	-	2,158	-	-	985	-	8,211	540	-	6,488	5,132	601	2,022	663	5,640
Female	353	1,243	7,765	-	-	-	2,105	-	-	840	-	8,377	494	-	6,832	5,389	512	1,795	584	6,527
Percent of total population:																				
1930	34.5	39.3	56.8	19.4	29.5	34.4	40.0	9.0	38.0	30.8	29.1	18.9	3.5	28.7	39.3	68.0	16.7	27.8	23.6	58.7
1920	39.2	46.7	62.9	-	-	-	43.2	-	-	40.1	-	18.8	8.0	-	42.7	72.5	17.8	30.0	13.1	67.4
VOTING AGE: 1930																				
Total 21 years old and over	527	1,493	8,714	488	500	613	1,915	520	983	823	1,715	18,284	249	1,052	5,826	4,353	487	3,656	2,317	6,996
Male	325	799	4,241	314	310	340	1,027	300	693	474	1,055	8,951	118	620	2,659	2,120	324	1,987	1,328	3,129
Female	202	694	4,473	174	190	273	888	220	290	349	660	9,333	131	432	3,167	2,233	163	1,669	989	3,867
AGE: 1930																				
Under 5 years	82	244	1,850	67	63	115	404	92	51	167	224	2,342	33	209	1,468	1,019	56	683	265	1,493
Under 1 year	14	42	383	11	13	22	80	18	15	31	45	392	4	33	286	167	8	120	55	273
5 to 9 years	80	220	2,026	81	69	135	462	104	65	157	249	2,648	53	239	1,516	1,182	50	729	289	1,763
10 to 14 years	70	218	1,991	71	67	105	479	100	63	177	182	2,492	49	174	1,729	1,243	47	574	266	1,715
15 to 19 years	73	237	1,992	70	91	110	418	91	128	163	242	2,597	54	213	1,734	1,123	68	659	319	1,534
20 to 24 years	113	247	1,821	112	124	115	417	88	222	169	325	3,284	45	246	1,230	883	109	726	443	1,329
25 to 29 years	109	244	1,336	89	95	113	287	74	212	142	354	3,473	33	199	762	551	102	700	439	1,100
30 to 34 years	60	178	997	68	74	70	195	63	148	103	284	2,868	15	173	543	440	46	526	353	721
35 to 44 years	150	383	1,866	116	137	140	423	146	235	160	434	4,747	53	217	1,095	964	117	846	642	1,485
45 to 54 years	73	251	1,650	67	70	114	370	116	131	153	262	2,994	64	181	1,122	796	73	541	364	1,260
55 to 64 years	33	162	845	41	21	52	196	40	55	85	82	1,009	30	60	726	481	38	276	115	742
65 to 74 years	4	59	410	14	4	18	94	11	13	30	33	378	19	18	422	265	16	123	37	380
75 years and over	5	25	174	5	1	8	29	6	4	16	4	131	1	2	202	151	5	50	9	222
Unknown	-	1	9	2	-	1	5	-	-	1	2	20	-	-	2	22	-	9	2	44
SCHOOL ATTENDANCE																				
Total 7 to 13 years, inclusive	99	297	2,802	106	97	170	658	139	92	226	309	3,565	70	284	2,221	1,646	59	889	388	2,422
Number attending school	82	170	2,019	51	78	137	314	115	73	195	272	3,291	51	79	1,555	1,226	30	768	349	2,236
Percent attending school	-	57.2	72.1	48.1	-	80.6	47.7	82.7	-	86.3	88.0	92.3	-	27.8	70.0	74.5	-	86.4	89.9	92.3
Total 14 and 15 years, inclusive	22	93	782	25	26	42	189	36	28	69	74	941	22	67	724	484	20	242	102	654
Number attending school	7	44	544	11	8	29	62	28	12	38	54	744	13	23	445	357	3	168	73	530
Percent attending school	-	-	69.6	-	-	-	32.8	-	-	-	-	79.1	-	-	61.5	73.8	-	69.4	71.6	81.0
Total 16 and 17 years, inclusive	29	78	783	27	39	47	190	32	51	61	84	1,049	25	82	757	495	27	241	114	640
Number attending school	3	27	267	6	7	14	39	14	11	10	22	419	9	14	271	237	1	80	32	322
Percent attending school	-	-	34.1	-	-	-	20.5	-	-	-	-	39.9	-	-	35.8	47.9	-	33.2	28.1	50.3
Total 18 to 20 years, inclusive	54	163	1,231	61	64	58	242	69	96	108	181	1,716	31	136	934	598	53	425	241	894
Number attending school	1	14	84	3	1	-	8	5	-	4	4	174	7	12	94	88	-	20	14	152
Percent attending school	-	8.6	6.8	-	-	-	3.3	-	-	3.7	2.2	10.1	-	8.8	10.1	14.7	-	4.7	5.8	17.0
ILLITERACY																				
Total 10 years old and over	690	2,005	13,091	655	684	846	2,913	735	1,211	1,199	2,204	23,993	363	1,483	9,567	6,919	621	5,030	2,989	10,532
Number illiterate	169	487	4,445	208	43	228	1,224	163	329	226	559	2,918	105	303	3,327	2,182	260	931	403	2,841
Percent illiterate	24.5	24.3	34.0	31.8	6.3	27.0	42.0	22.2	27.2	18.8	25.4	12.2	28.9	20.4	34.8	31.5	41.9	18.5	13.5	27.0
Percent illiterate in 1920	36.9	19.4	29.3	-	-	-	38.5	-	-	42.4	-	12.3	33.3	-	36.0	43.1	26.1	22.2	11.1	30.4
URBAN AND RURAL																				
Urban population	-	1,329	3,580	-	-	-	-	15	-	-	1,608	23,263	-	-	1,033	-	-	2,302	2,450	4,401
Percent urban	-	53.8	21.1	-	-	-	-	1.6	-	-	60.1	80.3	-	-	8.2	-	-	35.7	69.2	31.9
Rural population	852	1,140	13,387	803	816	1,096	3,779	916	1,327	1,523	1,069	5,720	449	1,931	11,518	9,120	727	4,140	1,093	9,387
Rural-farm	16	3	6,040	81	452	73	1,608	93	496	490	32	1,166	75	311	8,839	5,361	67	973	74	7,307
Rural-nonfarm	836	1,137	7,347	722	364	1,023	2,171	823	831	1,033	1,037	4,554	374	1,620	2,679	3,759	660	3,167	1,019	2,080
Percent rural	100.0	46.2	78.9	100.0	100.0	100.0	100.0	98.4	100.0	100.0	39.9	19.7	100.0	100.0	91.8	100.0	100.0	64.3	30.8	68.1
MARITAL CONDITION																				
Males 15 year old and over	364	939	5,340	366	372	404	1,252	346	787	576	1,182	10,318	146	752	3,683	2,772	374	2,335	1,497	3,944
Single	130	327	1,640	115	140	108	379	101	363	189	478	3,218	47	276	1,252	876	124	721	480	1,224
Married	215	538	3,104	170	194	269	772	205	354	327	613	6,137	91	417	2,151	1,619	195	1,370	913	2,443
Widowed	14	69	388	55	26	24	86	33	45	38	57	781	8	44	250	243	53	172	64	227
Divorced	5	5	37	26	9	3	9	7	25	22	34	174	-	15	29	13	2	62	29	34
Unknown	-	-	171	-	3	-	6	-	-	-	-	8	-	-	1	21	-	10	11	16
Females 15 years old and over	256	848	5,760	218	245	337	1,182	289	361	446	840	11,183	168	557	4,155	2,904	200	2,121	1,226	4,873
Single	27	159	1,213	26	30	46	228	44	51	73	140	2,100	43	82	1,057	652	19	379	217	1,210
Married	200	529	3,199	159	191	252	761	194	281	317	580	6,656	90	415	2,245	1,667	158	1,414	873	2,615
Widowed	27	154	1,132	26	21	35	183	42	22	51	98	2,093	35	55	789	551	22	272	121	952
Divorced	2	6	47	7	3	4	8	9	7	5	21	332	-	5	64	24	1	52	15	77
Unknown	-	-	169	-	-	-	2	-	-	-	1	2	-	-	-	10	-	4	-	19
FAMILIES																				
Number of families	233	731	3,681	210	219	304	919	253	385	383	755	7,447	119	539	2,879	2,235	285	1,734	949	3,365
Median size	2.32	2.47	3.39	2.48	2.43	2.83	3.13	2.56	2.03	2.83	2.31	2.56	2.98	2.58	3.40	3.20	1.64	2.68	2.32	3.20
Families having—																				
No children under 10	164	498	1,953	131	143	174	528	168	320	245	519	5,086	77	338	1,572	1,274	226	1,091	683	1,941
1 child under 10	28	117	691	41	43	64	150	31	41	48	118	1,104	17	85	506	349	31	268	137	579
2 children under 10	13	54	423	17	18	35	111	26	13	38	59	632	15	50	328	263	17	163	52	341
3 or more	28	62	614	21	15	31	130	28	11	52	59	625	10	66	473	349	11	212	77	504

CHARACTERISTICS OF NEGRO POPULATION BY COUNTIES: 1930—Continued

(See note at head of table)

SUBJECT	Levy	Liberty	Madison	Manatee	Marion	Martin	Monroe	Nassau	Okaloosa	Okeechobee	Orange	Osceola	Palm Beach	Pasco	Pinellas	Polk	Putnam	St. Johns	St. Lucie	Santa Rosa
	FLORIDA—Continued																			
POPULATION BY SEX																				
Negro population: 1930	4,762	1,421	8,203	6,820	14,513	1,984	2,452	3,883	1,016	1,200	12,226	3,056	16,760	1,777	10,974	16,020	7,812	6,689	1,797	2,208
Male	2,519	770	4,072	3,434	7,306	1,080	1,176	1,968	551	692	5,764	1,710	8,856	930	5,018	8,088	3,920	3,242	926	1,128
Female	2,243	651	4,131	3,386	7,207	904	1,276	1,915	465	508	6,462	1,346	7,904	847	5,956	7,932	3,892	3,447	871	1,080
Negro population: 1920	3,960	2,242	8,492	5,804	12,887	-----	4,315	5,029	1,840	211	5,464	1,122	5,512	2,098	4,553	9,359	6,742	4,721	1,895	2,849
Male	2,121	1,243	4,188	3,317	6,448	-----	2,188	2,527	973	133	2,817	578	2,925	1,162	2,227	5,192	3,460	2,314	1,006	1,449
Females	1,839	999	4,304	2,487	6,439	-----	2,127	2,502	867	78	2,647	544	2,587	956	2,326	4,167	3,282	2,407	889	1,400
Percent of total population:																				
1930	38.2	34.9	52.5	30.3	49.1	38.8	18.0	41.4	10.3	29.1	24.6	28.6	32.4	16.8	17.7	22.2	43.2	35.8	25.5	15.7
1920	39.9	44.8	51.4	31.0	53.8	-----	22.1	44.3	19.7	9.9	27.5	15.6	29.5	23.8	16.1	24.2	46.3	36.1	24.0	20.8
VOTING AGE: 1930																				
Total 21 years old and over	2,739	751	3,878	3,751	8,031	1,194	1,390	2,191	531	829	7,289	1,882	10,913	1,060	6,568	9,579	4,439	3,888	1,004	1,212
Male	1,530	436	1,899	1,978	4,164	687	645	1,136	293	507	3,509	1,125	6,017	607	2,984	5,076	2,268	1,881	537	636
Female	1,209	315	1,979	1,773	3,867	507	745	1,055	238	322	3,780	757	4,896	453	3,584	4,503	2,171	2,007	467	576
AGE: 1930																				
Under 5 years	449	168	998	714	1,378	196	246	402	114	93	1,123	277	1,354	153	955	1,480	743	553	207	191
Under 1 year	93	43	200	135	250	29	48	55	25	19	203	45	225	23	152	290	133	93	27	36
5 to 9 years	534	176	1,054	771	1,598	219	263	403	103	107	1,238	307	1,531	181	1,085	1,562	847	670	213	261
10 to 14 years	487	149	1,059	684	1,571	179	283	387	117	84	1,080	246	1,262	154	1,058	1,486	844	670	177	239
15 to 19 years	458	140	1,032	745	1,621	158	237	438	124	70	1,212	277	1,346	186	1,061	1,552	792	758	153	252
20 to 24 years	548	175	893	754	1,484	194	166	380	113	142	1,438	375	2,030	220	1,300	1,822	771	739	192	262
25 to 29 years	486	114	547	653	1,165	218	158	348	77	190	1,454	374	2,375	161	1,350	1,816	714	664	221	219
30 to 34 years	324	90	402	531	924	183	127	235	52	126	1,087	277	1,812	105	978	1,326	525	494	172	116
35 to 44 years	644	160	869	997	1,819	341	279	519	125	192	1,827	449	2,843	297	1,720	2,564	1,098	976	255	261
45 to 54 years	475	120	670	651	1,497	191	318	392	111	145	1,080	304	1,464	189	922	1,565	787	702	152	242
55 to 64 years	211	78	372	224	862	70	200	212	46	34	439	114	534	80	350	570	423	285	42	99
65 to 74 years	84	27	191	69	406	26	116	108	21	8	167	40	151	34	131	179	185	117	9	45
75 years and over	51	24	105	21	174	9	59	53	13	2	76	15	41	13	42	69	71	57	2	21
Unknown	11	-----	11	6	14	-----	-----	6	-----	7	5	1	17	4	22	29	12	4	2	-----
SCHOOL ATTENDANCE																				
Total 7 to 13 years, inclusive	712	220	1,436	1,008	2,215	276	393	552	148	134	1,606	384	1,882	239	1,520	2,108	1,187	937	267	335
Number attending school	461	139	656	805	2,071	191	381	483	117	112	1,483	338	1,678	227	1,457	1,953	1,037	861	241	233
Percent attending school	64.7	63.2	45.7	79.9	93.5	69.2	96.9	87.5	79.1	83.6	92.3	88.0	89.2	95.0	95.9	92.6	87.4	91.9	90.3	69.6
Total 14 and 15 years, inclusive	176	47	423	277	632	67	108	156	55	21	442	97	523	63	417	648	322	266	71	87
Number attending school	91	17	162	167	496	39	94	122	42	10	314	73	398	45	322	518	237	230	51	47
Percent attending school	51.7	-----	38.3	60.3	78.5	-----	87.0	78.2	-----	-----	71.0	-----	76.1	-----	77.2	79.9	73.6	86.5	-----	-----
Total 16 and 17 years, inclusive	192	60	430	273	653	54	90	169	53	27	475	108	513	76	390	571	326	312	56	106
Number attending school	41	11	87	86	314	20	51	74	18	5	173	25	220	27	176	240	124	171	26	26
Percent attending school	21.4	-----	20.2	31.5	48.1	-----	-----	43.8	-----	-----	36.4	23.1	42.9	-----	45.1	42.0	38.0	54.8	-----	24.5
Total 18 to 20 years, inclusive	278	99	593	488	973	104	128	244	69	54	793	189	932	119	701	1,004	462	468	101	156
Number attending school	19	4	40	30	135	5	30	23	7	-----	54	7	70	5	58	106	45	125	22	3
Percent attending school	6.8	-----	6.7	6.1	13.9	4.8	23.4	9.4	-----	-----	6.8	3.7	7.5	4.2	8.3	10.6	9.7	26.7	21.8	1.9
ILLITERACY																				
Total 10 years old and over	3,779	1,077	6,151	5,335	11,537	1,569	1,943	3,078	799	1,000	9,865	2,472	13,875	1,443	8,934	12,978	6,222	5,466	1,377	1,756
Number illiterate	777	454	2,326	965	2,071	304	258	692	238	260	1,479	444	1,762	375	1,147	2,195	958	943	188	437
Percent illiterate	20.6	42.2	37.8	18.1	18.0	19.4	13.3	22.5	29.8	26.0	15.0	18.0	12.7	26.0	12.8	16.9	15.4	17.3	13.7	24.9
Percent illiterate in 1920	16.0	30.0	41.1	17.1	15.7	-----	11.9	21.2	36.3	15.7	14.0	21.0	9.8	29.3	13.5	21.1	18.3	18.6	16.4	34.5
URBAN AND RURAL																				
Urban population	-----	-----	-----	3,890	2,953	-----	2,274	1,484	-----	-----	8,771	759	9,114	-----	10,050	8,994	3,000	3,293	1,226	-----
Percent urban	-----	-----	-----	57.0	20.3	-----	92.7	38.2	-----	-----	71.7	24.8	54.4	-----	91.6	56.1	38.4	49.2	68.2	-----
Rural population	4,762	1,421	8,203	2,930	11,560	1,984	178	2,399	1,016	1,200	3,455	2,297	7,646	1,777	924	7,026	4,812	3,396	571	2,208
Rural-farm	1,262	384	5,068	851	6,017	85	49	271	338	32	678	60	2,979	135	141	912	1,158	505	369	214
Rural-nonfarm	3,500	1,037	3,135	2,079	5,543	1,899	129	2,128	678	1,168	2,777	2,237	4,667	1,642	783	6,114	3,654	2,891	202	1,994
Percent rural	100.0	100.0	100.0	43.0	79.7	100.0	7.3	61.8	100.0	100.0	28.3	75.2	45.6	100.0	8.4	43.9	61.6	50.8	31.8	100.0
MARITAL CONDITION																				
Males 15 years old and over	1,796	526	2,452	2,389	5,105	773	781	1,379	375	548	4,127	1,300	6,810	709	3,528	5,908	2,719	2,298	632	798
Single	555	141	740	767	1,549	282	253	503	135	221	1,185	385	2,376	256	1,119	1,710	809	754	204	301
Married	1,051	329	1,531	1,400	2,954	440	431	743	210	261	2,626	691	3,976	399	2,208	3,694	1,659	1,377	385	458
Widowed	161	49	143	183	478	41	70	129	30	63	258	211	371	40	160	393	204	143	27	33
Divorced	15	7	31	38	117	9	27	3	-----	1	52	11	49	14	39	104	41	22	3	6
Unknown	14	-----	7	1	7	1	-----	1	-----	2	6	2	38	-----	2	7	6	2	13	-----
Females 15 years old and over	1,496	402	2,640	2,262	4,861	617	879	1,312	307	368	4,658	926	5,803	580	4,348	5,584	2,659	2,498	568	719
Single	225	43	607	432	973	81	192	260	59	52	899	94	1,083	122	966	958	500	559	107	150
Married	1,022	306	1,572	1,418	2,932	441	427	775	198	256	2,835	685	3,904	392	2,456	3,678	1,659	1,487	367	453
Widowed	222	48	367	361	814	79	195	266	47	59	790	137	747	62	776	819	462	402	76	100
Divorced	19	5	92	51	137	16	65	11	3	-----	107	9	59	4	148	128	36	50	12	16
Unknown	8	-----	2	-----	5	-----	-----	-----	-----	1	27	1	10	-----	2	1	2	-----	6	-----
FAMILIES																				
Number of families	1,266	382	1,879	1,826	3,677	540	694	974	253	349	3,142	905	4,221	496	2,906	4,399	2,170	1,677	452	553
Median size	2.73	2.79	3.52	2.70	3.00	2.46	2.67	2.91	2.95	2.10	2.79	2.37	2.41	2.37	2.77	2.72	2.77	2.83	2.93	2.97
Families having:																				
No children under 10	786	227	968	1,147	2,282	348	462	609	150	258	2,013	603	2,870	351	1,921	2,863	1,402	1,096	263	339
1 child under 10	231	67	360	274	628	80	97	148	43	37	512	150	615	57	473	753	342	258	74	93
2 children under 10	109	38	225	187	352	46	55	96	30	24	297	80	345	36	226	408	210	150	52	54
3 or more	140	50	326	218	415	66	80	121	30	30	320	72	391	52	286	375	216	173	63	67

CHARACTERISTICS OF NEGRO POPULATION BY COUNTIES: 1930—Continued

(See note at head of table)

SUBJECT	FLORIDA—Continued										GEORGIA								
	Sarasota	Seminole	Sumter	Suwannee	Taylor	Union	Volusia	Wakulla	Walton	Washington	The State	Appling	Atkinson	Bacon	Baker	Baldwin	Banks	Barrow	Bartow
POPULATION BY SEX																			
Negro population: 1930	2,803	8,431	3,217	5,336	4,995	2,846	12,537	2,254	2,724	2,574	1,071,125	2,815	1,962	1,086	4,794	10,736	963	2,068	4,659
Male	1,486	4,238	1,659	2,665	2,858	1,917	6,093	1,207	1,389	1,253	513,451	1,401	1,018	553	2,354	5,226	472	1,012	2,236
Female	1,317	4,193	1,558	2,671	2,137	929	6,444	1,047	1,335	1,321	557,674	1,414	944	533	2,440	5,510	491	1,056	2,423
Negro population: 1920	-------	5,044	2,218	7,947	4,546	-------	8,199	2,361	2,431	2,957	1,206,365	2,312	2,479	852	5,614	11,019	2,548	3,051	5,665
Male	-------	2,594	1,167	3,983	2,585	-------	4,216	1,236	1,205	1,499	590,443	1,179	1,321	448	2,731	5,399	1,245	1,507	2,786
Female	-------	2,450	1,051	3,964	1,961	-------	3,983	1,125	1,226	1,458	615,922	1,133	1,158	404	2,883	5,620	1,303	1,544	2,879
Percent of total population:																			
1930	22.5	45.0	30.2	33.9	38.0	38.3	29.3	41.2	18.7	21.1	36.8	21.1	28.5	15.4	61.3	46.9	9.9	16.7	18.4
1920	-------	45.9	28.3	40.2	40.5	-------	35.1	46.0	20.1	25.0	41.7	21.8	32.4	13.2	67.7	55.7	21.6	23.1	23.1
VOTING AGE: 1930																			
Total 21 years old and over	1,803	4,685	1,654	2,675	3,302	1,918	7,683	1,156	1,396	1,297	528,087	1,284	938	529	2,111	6,128	397	969	2,231
Male	1,023	2,419	926	1,352	2,036	1,419	3,762	648	738	642	248,683	660	498	281	1,029	2,932	193	474	1,073
Female	780	2,266	728	1,323	1,266	499	3,921	508	658	655	279,404	624	440	248	1,082	3,196	204	495	1,158
AGE: 1930																			
Under 5 years	224	843	388	549	379	197	1,030	276	295	317	116,016	368	245	145	654	967	126	260	541
Under 1 year	42	162	84	103	65	39	170	41	54	75	22,042	76	42	34	112	193	28	68	101
5 to 9 years	224	889	382	660	402	224	1,245	255	376	326	134,026	409	266	152	669	1,075	143	270	627
10 to 14 years	236	856	361	677	329	218	1,127	252	312	285	131,393	331	264	113	595	1,120	134	244	574
15 to 19 years	250	971	348	672	451	238	1,188	257	283	295	134,216	345	211	118	637	1,197	137	267	568
20 to 24 years	356	963	330	516	727	411	1,371	254	299	288	112,334	299	202	131	501	1,052	97	240	498
25 to 29 years	352	874	247	410	726	435	1,343	191	236	222	82,252	202	138	106	315	808	56	159	339
30 to 34 years	278	656	195	280	495	283	1,065	120	157	154	61,392	156	128	59	190	715	31	128	255
35 to 44 years	469	1,215	400	551	803	441	1,972	247	297	239	118,235	290	198	111	421	1,591	61	174	461
45 to 54 years	268	738	297	529	469	252	1,266	215	244	242	95,117	228	159	87	382	1,225	78	154	425
55 to 64 years	103	270	150	276	133	99	586	113	133	125	50,024	102	86	39	251	557	64	101	218
65 to 74 years	39	115	73	136	51	38	229	55	64	54	23,939	53	48	13	127	250	18	44	100
75 years and over	4	40	26	78	20	10	90	18	23	26	11,300	26	16	9	48	142	17	27	50
Unknown	-------	1	20	2	10	-------	25	1	5	1	881	6	1	3	4	37	1	-------	3
SCHOOL ATTENDANCE																			
Total 7 to 13 years, inclusive	321	1,193	489	954	503	302	1,635	366	467	421	184,449	483	380	168	864	1,554	186	345	803
Number attending school	288	1,094	347	687	270	191	1,560	264	406	353	153,347	339	270	142	643	1,385	143	275	703
Percent attending school	89.7	91.7	71.0	72.0	53.7	63.2	95.4	72.1	86.9	83.8	83.1	70.2	71.1	84.5	74.4	89.1	76.9	79.7	87.5
Total 14 and 15 years, inclusive	97	377	157	277	134	80	454	92	119	111	53,301	155	88	45	247	460	60	106	247
Number attending school	61	272	99	173	59	42	379	51	82	76	34,378	96	44	33	121	268	47	63	177
Percent attending school	-------	72.1	63.1	62.5	44.0	-------	83.5	-------	68.9	68.5	64.5	61.9	-------	-------	49.0	58.3	-------	59.4	71.7
Total 16 and 17 years, inclusive	85	352	141	286	163	74	503	110	107	112	53,857	139	91	53	247	469	48	99	232
Number attending school	20	141	41	114	22	14	236	28	43	47	17,197	41	19	15	64	116	13	39	63
Percent attending school	-------	40.1	29.1	39.9	13.5	-------	46.9	25.5	40.2	42.0	31.9	29.5	-------	-------	25.9	24.7	-------	-------	27.2
Total 18 to 20 years, inclusive	178	619	223	352	358	179	734	160	188	189	81,719	212	122	79	388	750	83	171	336
Number attending school	10	46	12	50	11	6	101	11	27	26	6,716	17	7	10	19	42	6	10	11
Percent attending school	5.6	7.4	5.4	14.2	3.1	3.4	13.8	6.9	14.4	13.8	8.2	8.0	5.7	-------	4.9	5.6	-------	5.8	3.3
ILLITERACY																			
Total 10 years old and over	2,355	6,699	2,447	4,127	4,214	2,425	10,262	1,723	2,053	1,931	821,083	2,038	1,451	789	3,471	8,694	694	1,538	3,491
Number illiterate	513	1,220	492	1,095	1,536	75	1,585	412	454	439	163,237	400	312	212	922	2,032	133	301	462
Percent illiterate	21.8	18.2	20.1	26.5	36.4	3.1	15.4	23.9	22.1	22.7	19.9	19.6	21.5	26.9	26.6	23.4	19.2	19.6	13.2
Percent illiterate in 1920	-------	16.1	29.7	33.4	35.6	-------	17.4	33.6	21.3	24.9	29.1	21.2	26.5	13.3	47.4	29.0	27.8	25.6	24.2
URBAN AND RURAL																			
Urgan population	2,169	4,884	-------	1,038	1,053	-------	8,190	-------	573	-------	316,637	-------	-------	-------	-------	2,719	-------	546	1,615
Percent urban	77.4	57.9	-------	19.5	21.1	-------	65.3	-------	21.0	-------	29.6	-------	-------	-------	-------	25.3	-------	26.4	34.7
Rural population	634	3,547	3,217	4,298	3,942	2,846	4,347	2,254	2,151	2,574	754,488	2,815	1,962	1,086	4,794	8,017	963	1,522	3,044
Rural-farm	92	1,130	906	2,781	133	442	294	735	679	920	555,764	1,202	569	306	4,082	4,044	859	1,440	2,087
Rural-nonfarm	542	2,417	2,311	1,517	3,809	2,404	4,053	1,519	1,472	1,654	198,724	1,613	1,393	780	712	3,973	104	82	957
Percent rural	22.6	42.1	100.0	80.5	78.9	100.0	34.7	100.0	79.0	100.0	70.4	100.0	100.0	100.0	100.0	74.7	100.0	73.6	65.3
MARITAL CONDITION																			
Males 15 years old and over	1,169	2,940	1,132	1,717	2,315	1,591	4,411	806	900	813	324,068	865	619	352	1,404	3,591	272	633	1,387
Single	418	840	382	545	882	191	1,271	259	302	248	103,281	233	198	101	446	1,290	104	209	413
Married	633	1,891	659	1,011	1,144	354	2,756	474	516	521	196,041	561	362	240	844	2,035	153	382	830
Widowed	94	160	53	143	275	29	295	67	67	38	21,538	66	53	10	100	189	13	32	131
Divorced	21	47	36	14	2	1	76	6	14	6	2,786	1	6	1	13	45	2	10	13
Unknown	3	2	2	4	12	1,016	13	-------	1	-------	422	4	-------	-------	1	32	-------	-------	-------
Females 15 years old and over	950	2,903	954	1,733	1,570	616	4,724	665	841	833	365,622	842	568	324	1,472	3,983	288	661	1,530
Single	157	533	190	380	216	89	897	121	204	188	90,080	161	99	47	345	1,108	99	180	382
Married	641	1,973	640	1,023	1,078	361	2,891	485	490	532	201,168	580	379	246	820	2,142	158	391	843
Widowed	133	343	104	301	271	56	833	57	108	100	67,516	98	88	26	278	656	26	79	285
Divorced	16	52	17	29	4	5	93	2	39	13	6,530	2	2	4	26	63	5	11	19
Unknown	3	2	3	-------	1	105	10	-------	-------	-------	328	1	-------	1	3	14	-------	-------	1
FAMILIES																			
Number of families	714	2,256	764	1,288	1,359	425	3,516	580	605	606	249,942	630	472	267	1,076	1,953	168	463	1,050
Median size	2.40	2.86	3.27	3.29	2.31	3.04	2.55	3.07	3.38	3.22	3.34	3.67	3.25	3.29	3.64	3.45	4.50	3.73	3.56
Families having—																			
No children under 10	505	1,409	428	720	960	230	2,362	325	311	338	137,675	292	250	132	522	1,052	72	222	544
1 child under 10	99	384	134	251	209	93	550	116	118	105	45,917	129	86	55	191	354	29	97	193
2 children under 10	50	224	84	142	98	42	325	62	67	60	28,206	89	62	30	137	227	18	61	115
3 or more	60	239	118	175	92	60	279	77	109	103	38,144	120	74	50	226	320	49	83	198

CHARACTERISTICS OF NEGRO POPULATION BY COUNTIES: 1930—Continued

(See note at head of table)

SUBJECT	GEORGIA—Continued																	
	Ben Hill	Berrien	Bibb	Bleckley	Brantley	Brooks	Bryan	Bulloch	Burke	Butts	Calhoun	Camden	Campbell	Candler	Carroll	Catoosa	Charlton	Chatham
POPULATION BY SEX																		
Negro population: 1930	4, 449	2, 352	32, 906	3, 261	1, 271	11, 259	2, 666	10, 081	22, 698	4, 488	7, 431	3, 745	2, 959	3, 141	7, 617	436	1, 034	49, 707
Male	2, 092	1, 191	14, 858	1, 562	670	5, 393	1, 417	5, 033	10, 914	2, 186	3, 564	1, 872	1, 498	1, 535	3, 783	238	546	22, 582
Female	2, 357	1, 161	18, 048	1, 699	601	5, 866	1, 249	5, 048	11, 784	2, 302	3, 867	1, 873	1, 461	1, 606	3, 834	198	488	27, 125
Negro population: 1920	5, 560	4, 005	33, 025	4, 615	------	14, 247	2, 920	10, 034	24, 775	6, 586	7, 020	4, 273	4, 153	3, 737	7, 265	341	948	49, 238
Male	2, 672	2, 060	15, 712	2, 247	------	6, 918	1, 473	5, 032	12, 069	3, 209	3, 284	2, 080	2, 133	1, 878	3, 596	168	507	23, 654
Female	2, 888	1, 945	17, 313	2, 368	------	7, 329	1, 447	5, 002	12, 706	3, 377	3, 736	2, 193	2, 020	1, 859	3, 669	173	441	25, 584
Percent of total population:																		
1930	34. 1	16. 1	42. 7	35. 7	18. 4	52. 8	44. 8	38. 0	77. 7	48. 0	70. 3	59. 1	29. 9	34. 9	22. 2	4. 6	23. 6	47. 1
1920	38. 1	25. 7	46. 3	43. 8	------	58. 1	46. 0	38. 4	80. 3	53. 4	68. 7	61. 3	35. 5	40. 5	20. 9	5. 1	20. 9	49. 2
VOTING AGE: 1930																		
Total 21 years old and over	2, 157	1, 194	18, 566	1, 569	687	5, 008	1, 213	4, 239	10, 825	2, 021	3, 558	1, 798	1, 304	1, 357	3, 292	213	541	31, 586
Male	994	609	8, 220	721	393	2, 398	664	2, 157	5, 057	979	1, 722	898	649	674	1, 632	116	296	14, 489
Female	1, 163	585	10, 346	848	294	2, 610	549	2, 082	5, 768	1, 042	1, 836	900	655	683	1, 660	97	245	17, 097
AGE: 1930																		
Under 5 years	471	237	3, 004	376	129	1, 422	325	1, 241	2, 437	556	857	398	394	404	1, 044	46	121	3, 663
Under 1 year	81	49	562	70	19	274	60	226	418	122	158	66	79	86	213	11	26	720
5 to 9 years	572	287	3, 499	393	157	1, 566	383	1, 447	3, 018	605	876	508	418	443	1, 004	54	152	4, 445
10 to 14 years	588	293	3, 329	390	123	1, 478	346	1, 431	2, 960	602	887	507	405	417	997	47	95	4, 120
15 to 19 years	559	289	3, 669	440	144	1, 491	339	1, 452	2, 864	580	1, 023	446	371	437	1, 084	66	105	4, 710
20 to 24 years	412	298	3, 676	332	145	1, 191	247	987	2, 232	448	868	291	290	318	795	38	106	6, 088
25 to 29 years	282	178	2, 977	180	123	752	188	665	1, 598	264	554	227	148	217	526	30	100	5, 743
30 to 34 years	247	122	2, 398	189	98	501	119	494	1, 195	222	394	189	112	149	380	25	72	4, 319
35 to 44 years	566	252	4, 785	341	138	970	299	955	2, 349	429	739	374	278	266	651	51	121	8, 270
45 to 54 years	417	214	3, 210	317	93	894	220	749	2, 137	373	620	389	284	256	612	42	91	4, 971
55 to 64 years	184	111	1, 364	156	57	525	114	423	1, 129	218	374	215	152	147	312	16	40	2, 050
65 to 74 years	105	46	646	94	28	293	58	171	515	140	159	131	69	54	154	10	15	916
75 years and over	45	22	275	52	9	153	28	62	223	51	80	64	38	32	58	11	11	350
Unknown	1	3	74	1	27	23	------	4	41	------	------	6	------	1	------	------	5	62
SCHOOL ATTENDANTS																		
Total 7 to 13 years, inclusive	822	386	4, 795	548	193	2, 093	523	1, 965	4, 145	834	1, 204	705	569	610	1, 396	62	163	5, 970
Number attending school	719	319	4, 068	376	177	1, 739	428	1, 363	3, 678	711	919	622	469	440	1, 102	31	64	5, 205
Percent attending school	87. 5	82. 6	84. 8	68. 6	91. 7	83. 1	81. 8	69. 4	88. 7	85. 3	76. 3	88. 2	82. 4	72. 1	78. 9	------	39. 3	87. 2
Total 14 and 15 years, inclusive	215	130	1, 346	153	52	583	117	593	1, 142	254	375	193	160	166	412	28	40	1, 635
Number attending school	166	86	809	59	29	396	77	321	799	169	180	144	107	79	254	13	13	1, 149
Percent attending school	77. 2	66. 2	60. 1	38. 6	------	67. 9	65. 8	54. 1	70. 0	66. 5	48. 0	74. 6	66. 9	47. 6	61. 7	------	------	70. 3
Total 16 and 17 years, inclusive	215	114	1, 441	198	60	619	143	608	1, 139	262	413	188	152	165	438	30	34	1, 755
Number attending school	86	34	410	32	15	223	51	171	361	97	100	80	63	34	141	10	2	643
Percent attending school	40. 0	29. 8	28. 5	16. 2	------	36. 0	35. 7	28. 1	31. 7	37. 0	24. 2	42. 6	41. 4	20. 6	32. 2	------	------	36. 6
Total 18 to 20 years, inclusive	350	166	2, 399	254	88	894	196	823	1, 772	335	656	254	215	262	632	34	72	3, 336
Number attending school	17	10	149	8	5	61	33	61	99	31	66	22	32	12	32	1	5	298
Percent attending school	4. 9	6. 0	6. 2	3. 1	------	6. 8	16. 8	7. 4	5. 6	9. 3	10. 1	8. 7	14. 9	4. 6	5. 1	------	------	8. 9
ILLITERACY																		
Total 10 years old and over	3, 406	1, 828	26, 403	2, 492	985	8, 271	1, 958	7, 393	17, 243	3, 327	5, 698	2, 839	2, 147	2, 294	5, 569	336	761	41, 599
Number illiterate	561	372	4, 068	1, 035	186	2, 170	467	1, 514	5, 082	585	1, 122	439	224	462	780	43	225	7, 901
Percent illiterate	16. 5	20. 4	15. 4	41. 5	18. 9	26. 2	23. 9	20. 5	29. 5	17. 6	19. 7	15. 5	10. 4	20. 1	14. 0	12. 8	29. 6	19. 0
Percent illiterate in 1920	19. 3	37. 4	25. 6	43. 2	------	35. 6	38. 6	19. 7	35. 0	28. 5	41. 4	20. 0	29. 1	20. 3	27. 4	18. 3	26. 0	23. 3
URBAN AND RURAL																		
Urban population	2, 260	------	23, 158	------	------	1, 992	------	1, 301	2, 239	------	------	------	------	------	1, 023	------	------	38, 896
Percent urban	50. 8	------	70. 4	------	------	17. 7	------	12. 9	9. 9	------	------	------	------	------	13. 4	------	------	78. 3
Rural population	2, 189	2, 352	9, 748	3, 261	1, 271	9, 267	2, 666	8, 780	20, 459	4, 488	7, 431	3, 745	2, 959	3, 141	6, 594	436	1, 034	10, 811
Rural-farm	1, 799	831	3, 735	2, 387	179	8, 341	930	7, 108	18, 641	3, 382	6, 013	1, 586	2, 164	2, 443	5, 971	276	252	907
Rural-nonfarm	390	1, 521	6, 013	874	1, 092	926	1, 736	1, 672	1, 818	1, 106	1, 418	2, 159	795	698	623	160	782	9, 904
Percent rural	49. 2	100. 0	29. 6	100. 0	100. 0	82. 3	100. 0	87. 1	90. 1	100. 0	100. 0	100. 0	100. 0	100. 0	86. 6	100. 0	100. 0	21. 7
MARITAL CONDITION																		
Males 15 years old and over	1, 277	781	10, 090	947	492	3, 223	868	2, 972	6, 700	1, 298	2, 279	1, 170	884	916	2, 225	161	358	16, 808
Single	375	250	2, 948	268	159	965	318	1, 022	1, 973	420	610	363	291	309	702	74	103	5, 154
Married	805	466	6, 323	621	309	2, 029	466	1, 745	4, 252	802	1, 497	700	529	548	1, 377	76	228	10, 169
Widowed	85	63	653	53	20	218	67	152	413	73	161	97	59	55	123	10	24	1, 318
Divorced	11	2	154	5	4	9	13	10	56	3	10	9	5	4	21	1	1	152
Unknown	1	------	12	------	------	2	4	43	6	------	1	1	------	------	2	------	2	15
Females 15 years old and over	1, 541	754	12, 984	1, 155	370	3, 570	744	2, 990	7, 583	1, 427	2, 532	1, 162	858	961	2, 347	128	308	20, 671
Single	319	128	3, 045	295	45	907	171	886	1, 690	394	531	254	196	257	627	31	39	5, 153
Married	911	479	6, 717	639	286	2, 077	453	1, 726	4, 333	825	1, 493	710	539	577	1, 391	77	221	10, 565
Widowed	272	131	2, 841	199	37	574	108	360	1, 405	199	473	181	110	121	295	18	41	4, 630
Divorced	39	16	355	21	2	9	9	9	148	9	35	17	13	6	34	2	5	306
Unknown	------	------	20	1	------	3	3	9	7	------	------	------	------	------	------	------	2	17
FAMILIES																		
Number of families	1, 119	556	8, 884	777	347	2, 444	579	2, 036	5, 713	981	1, 825	873	631	642	1, 529	77	276	14, 422
Median size	3. 09	3. 23	2. 87	3. 42	2. 75	3. 80	3. 61	4. 15	3. 17	3. 93	3. 33	3. 55	3. 91	3. 97	4. 07	------	2. 99	2. 45
Families having—																		
No children under 10	630	308	5, 659	420	209	1, 166	284	897	3, 175	452	991	466	284	301	677	36	154	10, 057
1 child under 10	219	118	1, 509	145	62	483	108	408	1, 107	211	364	166	147	116	312	13	44	2, 360
2 children under 10	114	60	808	93	41	307	66	285	646	126	233	98	65	85	216	9	38	1, 046
3 or more	156	70	908	119	35	488	121	446	785	192	237	143	135	140	324	19	40	959

CHARACTERISTICS OF NEGRO POPULATION BY COUNTIES: 1930—Continued

(See note at head of table)

SUBJECT	GEORGIA—Continued																	
	Chattahoochee	Chattooga	Cherokee	Clarke	Clay	Clayton	Clinch	Cobb	Coffee	Colquitt	Columbia	Cook	Coweta	Crawford	Crisp	Dade	Dawson	Decatur
POPULATION BY SEX																		
Negro population: 1930	2,670	1,981	972	9,948	4,533	3,250	3,049	6,540	5,246	7,739	5,536	3,077	10,828	3,879	8,369	206	42	11,812
Male	1,564	1,042	473	4,555	2,148	1,602	1,669	3,168	2,661	3,790	2,762	1,537	5,215	1,949	3,935	111	33	5,693
Female	1,106	939	499	5,393	2,385	1,648	1,380	3,732	2,585	3,949	2,774	1,540	5,613	1,930	4,434	95	9	6,119
Negro population: 1920	1,968	2,299	890	12,191	5,074	5,006	2,957	6,645	5,902	8,457	8,251	3,276	15,599	5,198	9,849	230	------	16,490
Male	968	1,192	442	5,778	2,472	2,506	1,613	3,219	2,960	4,136	4,127	1,650	7,561	2,572	4,718	123	------	7,927
Female	1,000	1,107	448	6,413	2,602	2,500	1,344	3,426	2,942	4,321	4,124	1,626	8,038	2,626	5,131	107	------	8,563
Percent of total population:																		
1930	30.0	12.9	4.9	38.8	65.3	31.7	43.5	18.5	26.6	25.3	63.0	27.2	43.1	55.3	48.3	5.0	1.2	50.0
1920	37.4	16.1	4.8	46.7	67.1	44.9	37.0	21.8	31.6	28.8	70.4	29.3	53.7	58.5	52.1	5.9	------	51.9
VOTING AGE: 1930																		
Total 21 years old and over	1,581	919	481	5,032	2,062	1,383	1,727	3,214	2,456	3,537	2,504	1,452	4,977	1,671	4,190	90	25	5,703
Male	1,051	506	235	2,173	947	676	1,029	1,527	1,261	1,714	1,257	725	2,362	816	1,933	48	22	2,700
Female	530	413	246	2,859	1,115	707	698	1,687	1,195	1,823	1,247	727	2,615	855	2,257	42	3	3,003
AGE: 1930																		
Under 5 years	220	237	116	929	576	358	312	695	599	910	587	357	1,267	490	900	32	1	1,346
Under 1 year	39	51	27	169	101	72	48	151	117	164	121	67	259	93	199	9	1	248
5 to 9 years	278	248	132	1,127	653	471	330	811	654	1,024	792	430	1,433	585	1,012	36	------	1,415
10 to 14 years	267	237	102	1,204	556	514	291	798	671	973	823	377	1,459	541	1,035	24	3	1,466
15 to 19 years	258	286	109	1,386	555	441	317	845	711	1,083	708	391	1,405	490	1,028	19	11	1,554
20 to 24 years	427	233	129	992	494	310	386	668	615	824	503	293	1,030	386	911	21	12	1,270
25 to 29 years	372	141	92	675	354	158	308	464	389	641	304	225	710	235	626	13	10	881
30 to 34 years	269	103	46	591	231	141	225	312	270	383	272	140	536	171	431	17	------	652
35 to 44 years	298	185	79	1,149	416	302	369	694	569	759	527	293	982	314	920	11	3	1,196
45 to 54 years	131	147	78	936	379	268	320	601	393	676	543	269	988	299	828	9	2	1,014
55 to 64 years	88	97	54	556	184	175	115	361	229	285	280	177	630	215	414	14	------	555
65 to 74 years	40	43	20	268	88	84	52	177	84	118	124	72	246	96	192	8	------	286
75 years and over	22	23	15	132	46	27	16	113	52	49	70	36	141	57	71	2	------	153
Unknown	------	1	------	3	1	1	8	1	10	14	3	17	1	------	1	------	------	24
SCHOOL ATTENDANCE																		
Total 7 to 13 years, inclusive	368	331	159	1,648	826	690	431	1,093	891	1,373	1,106	562	2,019	774	1,423	40	2	1,990
Number attending school	339	269	143	1,387	751	572	343	911	593	1,194	937	451	1,771	620	1,253	29	------	1,802
Percent attending school	92.1	81.3	89.9	84.2	90.9	82.9	79.6	83.3	66.6	87.0	84.7	80.2	87.7	80.1	88.1	------	------	90.6
Total 14 to 15 years, inclusive	106	122	43	507	232	207	115	339	288	414	323	159	568	209	427	9	4	583
Number attending school	79	90	31	342	180	148	71	198	151	291	236	103	400	121	248	5	------	439
Percent attending school	74.5	73.8	------	67.5	77.6	71.5	61.7	58.4	52.4	70.3	73.1	64.8	71.4	57.9	58.1	------	------	75.3
Total 16 and 17 years, inclusive	88	104	39	558	233	169	125	351	278	443	299	163	563	200	428	8	2	645
Number attending school	20	52	12	180	110	58	19	86	60	164	113	59	187	59	128	2	1	237
Percent attending school	------	50.0	------	32.3	47.2	34.3	15.2	24.5	21.6	37.0	37.8	36.2	33.2	29.5	29.9	------	------	36.7
Total 18 to 20 years, inclusive	186	159	80	837	336	256	200	509	456	642	387	217	851	297	602	13	8	955
Number attending school	3	19	6	94	40	22	6	27	22	37	69	20	73	14	56	1	1	103
Percent attending school	1.6	11.9	------	11.2	11.9	8.6	3.0	5.3	4.8	5.8	17.8	9.2	8.6	4.7	9.3	------	------	10.8
ILLITERACY																		
Total 10 years old and over	2,172	1,496	724	7,892	3,304	2,421	2,407	5,034	3,993	5,805	4,157	2,290	8,128	2,804	6,457	138	41	9,051
Number illiterate	257	189	84	1,510	484	454	609	665	749	1,344	881	541	1,042	538	1,384	18	15	1,824
Percent illiterate	11.8	12.6	11.6	19.1	14.6	18.8	25.3	13.2	18.8	23.2	21.2	23.6	12.8	19.2	21.4	13.0	------	20.2
Percent illiterate in 1920	26.3	24.4	23.0	24.7	34.9	29.4	26.2	23.9	23.0	24.0	37.7	19.6	25.7	30.3	34.5	22.8	------	28.7
URBAN AND RURAL																		
Urban population	------	30	228	6,378	------	2	------	2,247	1,515	3,078	------	------	2,359	------	3,490	------	------	2,901
Percent urban	------	1.5	23.5	64.1	------	0.1	------	34.4	28.9	39.8	------	------	21.8	------	41.7	------	------	24.6
Rural population	2,670	1,951	744	3,570	4,533	3,248	3,049	4,293	3,731	4,661	5,536	3,077	8,469	3,879	4,879	206	42	8,911
Rural-farm	1,303	1,433	410	2,929	3,713	2,658	564	2,970	2,826	3,303	4,824	1,456	7,297	3,488	4,486	54	42	5,179
Rural-nonfarm	1,367	518	334	641	820	590	2,485	1,323	905	1,358	712	1,621	1,172	391	393	152	------	3,732
Percent rural	100.0	98.5	76.5	35.9	100.0	99.9	100.0	65.6	71.1	60.2	100.0	100.0	78.2	100.0	58.3	100.0	------	75.4
MARITAL CONDITION																		
Males 15 years old and over	1,206	680	301	2,935	1,265	929	1,210	2,011	1,675	2,355	1,673	927	3,133	1,106	2,482	61	30	3,591
Single	661	273	101	1,014	388	316	333	681	586	798	579	263	1,012	372	711	24	22	1,151
Married	501	366	176	1,689	817	551	739	1,147	946	1,409	968	583	1,855	676	1,532	32	7	2,181
Widowed	28	37	22	208	54	60	62	167	112	140	99	61	239	58	212	5	1	241
Divorced	16	4	2	24	6	1	70	15	29	6	26	19	26	------	27	------	------	17
Unknown	------	------	------	------	------	1	6	1	2	2	1	1	1	------	------	------	------	1
Females 15 years old and over	699	579	321	3,753	1,483	978	906	2,225	1,647	2,477	1,661	986	3,536	1,157	2,940	53	8	3,994
Single	210	160	98	1,094	355	291	100	583	404	583	429	216	959	286	602	14	4	931
Married	402	356	163	1,747	830	564	684	1,199	988	1,469	980	589	1,879	680	1,537	30	4	2,184
Widowed	73	57	51	865	274	118	68	398	223	411	215	143	598	189	758	7	------	804
Divorced	13	5	9	47	24	5	50	41	30	13	36	38	99	2	42	2	------	70
Unknown	1	1	------	------	------	------	4	4	2	1	1	------	1	------	1	------	------	5
FAMILIES																		
Number of families	376	369	200	2,555	1,035	643	862	1,508	1,142	1,681	1,204	701	2,342	810	2,147	33	------	2,723
Median size	4.00	4.25	3.80	3.02	3.74	4.40	2.68	3.43	3.52	3.63	3.86	3.52	3.75	4.00	3.07	------	------	3.38
Families having—																		
No children under 10	178	163	93	1,603	488	285	534	834	575	849	603	361	1,191	356	1,255	13	------	1,475
1 child under 10	68	78	39	389	200	132	150	277	241	318	221	134	410	168	384	4	------	532
2 children under 10	42	55	27	257	156	93	90	153	131	222	160	80	319	114	227	3	------	293
3 or more	88	73	41	306	191	133	88	244	195	292	220	126	422	172	281	13	------	423

CHARACTERISTICS OF NEGRO POPULATION BY COUNTIES: 1930—Continued

(See note at head of table)

SUBJECT	GEORGIA—Continued																
	De Kalb	Dodge	Dooly	Dougherty	Douglas	Early	Echols	Effingham	Elbert	Emanuel	Evans	Fannin	Fayette	Floyd	Forsyth	Franklin	Fulton
POPULATION BY SEX																	
Negro population: 1930	12,118	7,998	10,064	12,816	2,271	9,737	845	4,154	7,535	9,111	2,606	72	2,838	8,615	17	2,672	101,505
Male	5,826	3,962	4,927	5,758	1,113	4,658	491	2,090	3,719	4,495	1,320	31	1,441	4,176	8	1,306	46,078
Female	6,292	4,036	5,137	7,058	1,158	5,079	354	2,064	3,816	4,616	1,286	41	1,397	4,439	9	1,366	55,427
Negro population: 1920	9,900	9,015	12,279	13,370	2,951	11,090	1,046	4,010	10,726	10,951	2,412	88	4,153	9,240	30	4,461	70,200
Male	4,986	4,464	5,952	6,275	1,454	5,359	549	2,050	5,422	5,445	1,227	36	2,052	4,475	14	2,210	33,147
Female	4,914	4,551	6,327	7,095	1,497	5,731	497	1,960	5,304	5,506	1,185	52	2,101	4,765	16	2,251	37,053
Percent of total population:																	
1930	17.2	37.0	55.8	57.5	24.0	53.3	30.8	40.9	40.8	37.8	36.7	0.6	32.8	17.7	0.2	16.8	31.9
1920	22.5	40.0	59.8	66.6	28.2	58.4	31.6	40.2	44.9	42.3	36.6	0.7	36.4	23.2	0.3	22.4	30.2
VOTING AGE: 1930																	
Total 21 years old and over	6,089	3,606	4,517	7,390	941	4,491	480	1,969	3,280	4,134	1,191	45	1,225	4,429	10	1,140	60,671
Male	2,859	1,796	2,146	3,144	446	2,101	282	1,018	1,561	2,003	598	17	620	2,152	5	550	26,986
Female	3,230	1,810	2,371	4,246	495	2,390	198	951	1,719	2,131	593	28	605	2,277	5	590	33,685
AGE: 1930																	
Under 5 years	1,273	1,001	1,211	1,105	316	1,169	77	516	859	966	301	7	374	821	------	329	8,109
Under 1 year	263	173	238	224	76	223	12	117	142	177	48	------	80	160	------	70	1,515
5 to 9 years	1,396	1,071	1,369	1,311	324	1,226	92	589	1,094	1,221	383	7	361	1,005	3	384	9,440
10 to 14 years	1,469	1,020	1,353	1,283	350	1,223	75	523	1,074	1,282	334	8	420	1,015	2	376	9,700
15 to 19 years	1,543	1,069	1,361	1,424	296	1,370	96	452	1,024	1,262	332	3	394	1,096	2	378	10,871
20 to 24 years	1,341	875	1,026	1,433	208	1,089	119	414	699	908	277	6	278	997	1	264	12,175
25 to 29 years	1,001	618	697	1,209	137	671	83	294	472	644	203	8	179	717	------	149	11,486
30 to 34 years	746	399	515	850	85	465	57	221	360	465	145	7	127	489	1	126	8,760
35 to 44 years	1,316	769	935	1,620	172	951	111	450	688	855	264	7	247	899	6	237	15,289
45 to 54 years	1,150	626	789	1,372	176	820	72	385	631	785	174	7	235	772	------	185	9,396
55 to 64 years	565	292	478	709	126	424	36	180	373	433	112	7	128	479	------	134	3,739
65 to 74 years	231	190	219	321	43	214	22	84	178	194	55	2	58	212	------	75	1,701
75 years and over	80	67	111	161	37	109	5	40	81	94	25	3	37	112	2	23	756
Unknown	7	1	------	18	1	6	------	6	2	2	1	------	------	1	------	12	83
SCHOOL ATTENDANCE																	
Total 7 to 13 years, inclusive	2,033	1,432	1,900	1,817	481	1,677	119	766	1,510	1,709	489	10	530	1,419	3	513	13,619
Number attending school	1,651	1,067	1,427	1,602	432	1,347	64	566	1,374	1,301	367	8	423	1,126	------	359	12,352
Percent attending school	81.2	74.5	75.1	88.2	89.8	80.3	53.8	73.9	91.0	76.1	75.1	------	79.8	79.4	------	70.0	90.7
Total 14 and 15 years, inclusive	557	428	585	538	127	535	34	182	443	557	133	2	186	414	1	155	3,870
Number attending school	331	252	335	315	86	356	9	103	354	342	73	2	117	256	1	109	2,753
Percent attending school	59.4	58.9	57.3	58.6	67.7	66.5	------	56.6	79.9	61.4	54.9	------	62.9	61.8	------	70.3	71.1
Total 16 and 17 years, inclusive	609	419	550	572	132	549	31	185	400	526	128	1	161	435	1	171	4,187
Number attending school	132	100	126	150	32	169	1	49	159	162	42	------	57	122	1	44	1,800
Percent attending school	21.7	23.9	22.9	26.2	24.2	30.8	------	26.5	39.8	30.8	32.8	------	35.4	28.0	------	25.7	43.0
Total 18 to 20 years, inclusive	993	678	781	877	151	822	72	285	621	713	202	4	217	703	1	197	7,470
Number attending school	69	47	44	64	7	70	------	17	55	38	23	------	19	40	------	5	1,023
Percent attending school	6.9	6.9	5.6	7.3	4.6	8.5	------	6.0	8.9	5.3	11.4	------	8.8	5.7	------	2.5	13.7
ILLITERACY																	
Total 10 years old and over	9,449	5,926	7,484	10,400	1,631	7,342	676	3,049	5,582	6,924	1,922	58	2,103	6,789	14	1,959	83,956
Number illiterate	2,078	1,808	2,052	2,713	101	2,132	262	644	912	1,865	362	7	297	1,281	7	283	9,194
Percent illiterate	22.0	30.5	27.4	26.1	6.2	29.0	38.8	21.1	16.3	26.9	18.8	------	14.1	18.9	------	14.4	11.0
Percent illiterate in 1920	26.3	28.0	38.5	41.1	15.0	29.6	37.5	24.1	24.6	24.6	26.7	------	25.6	27.2	------	26.8	18.2
URBAN AND RURAL																	
Urban population	4,912	1,304	------	7,394	------	------	------	------	1,601	------	------	------	------	4,737	------	------	90,948
Percent urban	40.5	16.3	------	57.7	------	------	------	------	21.2	------	------	------	------	55.0	------	------	89.6
Rural population	7,206	6,694	10,064	5,422	2,271	9,737	845	4,154	5,934	9,111	2,606	72	2,838	3,878	17	2,672	10,557
Rural-farm	3,332	5,527	8,242	3,344	1,809	8,236	120	1,985	5,651	6,892	1,514	7	2,558	2,867	17	2,137	1,189
Rural-nonfarm	3,874	1,167	1,822	2,078	462	1,501	725	2,169	283	2,219	1,092	65	280	1,011	------	535	9,368
Percent rural	59.5	83.7	100.0	42.3	100.0	100.0	100.0	100.0	78.8	100.0	100.0	------	100.0	45.0	------	100.0	10.4
MARITAL CONDITION																	
Males 15 years old and over	3,720	2,450	2,948	3,899	619	2,889	348	1,296	2,172	2,738	799	20	837	2,779	6	759	32,694
Single	1,205	885	945	1,127	226	887	107	422	769	942	323	5	310	833	1	272	10,199
Married	2,240	1,409	1,794	2,428	347	1,794	207	781	1,264	1,615	432	14	473	1,691	5	430	19,773
Widowed	236	141	199	231	39	152	29	83	131	166	39	------	50	227	------	51	2,293
Divorced	31	15	9	103	7	54	5	9	6	13	5	1	4	26	------	5	377
Unknown	8	------	1	10	------	2	------	1	2	2	------	------	------	2	------	1	52
Females 15 years old and over	4,260	2,456	3,183	5,218	662	3,230	253	1,230	2,336	2,904	789	30	846	2,995	6	824	41,562
Single	1,074	586	730	1,065	206	793	26	254	689	746	233	9	274	694	2	253	10,147
Married	2,277	1,396	1,783	2,660	342	1,826	199	777	1,285	1,600	439	12	466	1,733	4	454	20,700
Widowed	808	421	639	1,120	101	515	26	184	339	522	102	8	98	515	------	106	9,454
Divorced	96	52	31	366	13	94	2	14	23	36	15	1	5	50	------	10	1,207
Unknown	5	1	------	7	------	2	------	1	------	------	------	------	3	3	------	1	54
FAMILIES																	
Number of families	2,647	1,785	2,239	3,644	426	2,288	250	969	1,556	2,056	486	20	558	2,047	4	550	25,690
Median size	3.62	3.58	3.66	2.61	4.60	3.51	2.43	3.49	3.93	3.60	3.99	------	4.44	3.26	------	5.15	2.84
Families having;																	
No children under 10	1,429	873	1,100	2,441	188	1,186	173	500	723	1,092	219	13	254	1,200	3	246	16,901
1 child under 10	474	344	462	589	62	463	29	176	321	373	88	2	102	352	------	111	4,270
2 children under 10	339	254	267	285	59	263	23	116	204	247	62	3	80	236	------	79	2,292
3 or more	405	314	410	329	117	376	25	177	308	344	117	2	122	259	1	114	2,227

CHARACTERISTICS OF NEGRO POPULATION BY COUNTIES: 1930—Continued

(See note at head of table)

SUBJECT	GEORGIA—Continued																	
	Gilmer	Glascock	Glynn	Gordon	Grady	Greene	Gwinnett	Habersham	Hall	Hancock	Haralson	Harris	Hart	Heard	Henry	Houston	Irwin	Jackson
POPULATION BY SEX																		
Negro population: 1930	12	1,324	8,296	1,111	6,627	6,628	3,343	685	3,390	9,345	1,313	7,693	3,893	2,369	7,914	7,628	4,544	4,064
Male	3	666	3,964	561	3,259	3,141	1,642	319	1,556	4,616	605	3,825	1,918	1,131	3,923	3,743	2,261	2,030
Female	9	658	4,332	550	3,368	3,487	1,701	366	1,834	4,729	708	3,868	1,975	1,238	3,991	3,885	2,283	2,034
Negro population: 1920	38	1,201	9,850	1,314	7,354	11,200	4,233	615	3,493	13,221	2,022	11,209	5,624	3,370	10,439	14,508	5,719	6,982
Male	20	593	4,909	681	3,656	5,466	2,115	305	1,658	6,519	958	5,453	2,765	1,661	5,234	7,103	2,872	3,458
Female	18	608	4,941	633	3,698	5,734	2,118	310	1,835	6,702	1,064	5,756	2,859	1,709	5,205	7,405	2,847	3,524
Percent of total population:																		
1930	0.2	30.2	42.8	6.6	34.5	52.5	12.0	5.4	11.2	71.5	9.9	69.1	25.7	26.0	49.7	67.6	37.2	18.8
1920	0.5	28.6	50.9	7.4	36.2	59.0	14.0	5.7	13.0	72.0	14.0	71.1	31.3	30.3	51.1	66.1	45.1	28.3
VOTING AGE: 1930																		
Total 21 years old and over	8	514	5,104	512	2,924	3,105	1,517	328	1,665	3,782	601	3,319	1,687	941	3,377	3,501	1,948	1,842
Male	3	245	2,497	245	1,427	1,445	730	158	745	1,776	266	1,593	810	450	1,649	1,688	970	907
Female	5	269	2,607	267	1,497	1,660	787	170	920	2,006	335	1,726	877	491	1,728	1,813	978	935
AGE: 1930																		
Under 5 years	3	156	617	111	791	661	384	70	371	1,211	164	972	441	361	991	975	599	486
Under 1 year	1	31	121	29	157	110	59	12	79	197	231	208	95	70	204	178	121	69
5 to 9 years	------	203	719	145	881	949	466	74	413	1,484	183	1,12[illegible]	552	365	1,101	1,049	613	543
10 to 14 years	------	184	740	154	928	953	451	87	408	1,409	173	1,136	548	359	1,169	1,001	616	547
15 to 19 years	1	231	910	154	922	812	442	103	428	1,235	161	975	568	295	1,081	904	639	544
20 to 24 years	3	108	961	106	686	500	340	69	382	729	100	609	392	169	719	774	491	443
25 to 29 years	------	69	803	73	433	361	220	40	251	448	79	413	230	147	436	519	296	257
30 to 34 years	------	55	622	66	297	342	169	36	157	423	55	325	197	102	322	372	181	186
35 to 44 years	2	114	1,238	108	564	672	294	70	342	797	121	688	331	211	736	780	430	335
45 to 54 years	1	102	939	98	517	659	277	61	306	795	110	670	316	176	705	629	351	338
55 to 64 years	1	62	430	62	353	409	186	50	183	496	100	444	188	100	392	369	200	202
65 to 74 years	1	26	201	21	160	199	72	17	90	212	38	240	79	61	164	181	85	105
75 years and over	------	13	91	13	85	111	38	8	48	102	29	94	42	23	98	74	43	54
Unknown	------	1	25	------	10	------	4	------	11	4	------	5	9	------	------	1	------	24
SCHOOL ATTENDANCE																		
Total 7 to 13 years, inclusive	------	265	1,022	203	1,272	1,315	633	114	571	2,054	257	1,571	758	501	1,619	1,398	855	736
Number attending school	------	244	895	173	1,031	1,079	442	98	493	1,724	226	1,250	637	406	1,339	1,172	746	594
Percent attending school	------	92.1	87.6	85.2	81.1	82.1	69.8	86.0	86.3	83.9	87.9	79.6	84.0	81.0	82.7	83.8	87.3	80.7
Total 14 and 15 years, inclusive	------	93	321	71	397	371	169	46	162	531	66	430	230	137	478	396	267	227
Number attending school	------	69	239	49	216	236	104	36	110	330	50	255	168	79	316	270	192	141
Percent attending school	------	------	74.5	------	54.4	63.6	61.5	------	67.9	62.1	------	59.3	73.0	57.7	66.1	68.2	71.9	62.1
Total 16 and 17 years, inclusive	------	80	349	55	373	343	192	45	175	523	66	414	245	123	433	368	248	218
Number attending school	------	37	138	22	92	116	67	18	51	165	29	90	106	26	128	78	105	86
Percent attending school	------	------	39.5	------	24.7	33.8	34.9	------	29.1	31.5	------	21.7	43.3	21.1	29.6	21.2	42.3	39.4
Total 18 to 20 years, inclusive	1	135	609	97	534	456	250	57	276	671	97	535	305	158	604	549	391	323
Number attending school	------	13	78	8	26	33	15	12	17	75	8	15	37	9	38	16	40	23
Percent attending school	------	9.6	12.8	------	4.9	7.2	6.0	------	6.2	11.2	------	2.8	12.1	5.7	6.3	2.9	10.2	7.1
ILLITERACY																		
Total 10 years old and over	9	965	6,960	855	4,955	5,018	2,493	541	2,606	6,650	966	5,599	2,900	1,643	5,822	5,604	3,332	3,035
Number illiterate	1	235	1,224	79	1,300	1,118	457	76	544	1,291	153	1,078	591	210	906	1,589	661	641
Percent illiterate	------	24.4	17.6	9.2	26.2	22.3	18.3	14.0	20.9	19.4	15.8	19.3	20.4	12.8	15.6	28.4	19.8	21.1
Percent illiterate in 1920	------	48.1	19.0	25.2	36.8	36.2	25.8	17.0	33.2	28.1	24.4	32.9	21.0	33.3	27.4	31.4	25.4	34.4
URBAN AND RURAL																		
Urban population	------	------	6,049	------	1,286	------	777	------	2,051	------	------	------	------	------	------	------	------	419
Percent urban	------	------	72.9	------	19.4	------	23.2	------	60.5	------	------	------	------	------	------	------	------	10.3
Rural population	12	1,324	2,247	1,111	5,341	6,628	2,566	685	1,339	9,346	1,313	7,693	3,893	2,369	7,914	7,628	4,544	3,645
Rural-farm	10	1,105	496	537	3,856	4,966	1,810	207	1,134	7,810	906	5,986	3,244	2,247	6,937	6,422	3,075	3,047
Rural-nonfarm	2	219	1,751	574	1,485	1,662	756	478	205	1,535	407	1,707	649	122	977	1,206	1,169	598
Percent rural	------	100.0	27.1	100.0	80.6	100.0	76.8	100.0	39.5	100.0	100.0	100.0	100.0	100.0	100.0	100.0	100.0	89.7
MARITAL CONDITION																		
Males 15 years old and over	3	370	2,954	349	1,974	1,908	994	210	986	2,484	361	2,175	1,137	621	2,287	2,206	1,357	1,214
Single	------	124	831	129	663	591	354	83	323	838	107	705	402	184	753	664	472	404
Married	3	225	1,831	191	1,211	1,209	581	109	585	1,476	221	1,287	638	409	1,368	1,402	787	720
Widowed	------	19	249	27	95	100	54	16	71	129	29	159	76	28	138	126	93	82
Divorced	------	2	39	2	15	7	2	------	6	8	4	19	14		26	14	5	4
Unknown	------	------	4	------	------	1	3	2	1	33	------	5	7	------	2	------	------	4
Females 15 years old and over	6	411	3,266	352	2,053	2,157	1,048	244	1,212	2,757	432	2,288	1,215	663	2,366	2,397	1,359	1,274
Single	2	120	669	100	503	499	294	85	348	819	118	640	380	156	596	533	319	358
Married	4	228	1,906	201	1,211	1,258	593	124	629	1,515	230	1,[illegible]90	639	406	1,374	1,454	795	724
Widowed	------	47	650	49	307	374	155	26	224	389	72	340	166	98	352	359	223	182
Divorced	------	16	37	2	30	26	6	8	7	23	12	16	22	2	44	50	22	9
Unknown	------	------	4	------	2	------	------	1	4	11	------	2	8	1	------	1	------	1
FAMILIES																		
Number of families	3	272	2,299	236	1,393	1,538	687	155	755	1,846	279	1,610	789	473	1,620	1,765	924	859
Median size	------	4.14	2.65	3.93	3.96	3.61	3.94	3.32	3.67	4.47	3.96	4.08	4.23	4.25	4.11	3.58	3.99	3.95
Families having—																		
No children under 10	2	122	1,592	123	683	824	318	87	395	780	128	751	371	195	739	890	435	412
1 child under 10	------	51	374	41	247	280	143	34	157	352	62	307	155	90	321	329	179	169
2 children under 10	------	44	184	34	186	183	85	12	88	249	36	203	94	57	210	218	101	123
3 or more	1	55	149	38	277	251	141	22	115	465	53	349	169	131	350	328	209	155

CHARACTERISTICS OF NEGRO POPULATION BY COUNTIES: 1930—Continued

(See note at head of table)

SUBJECT	Jasper	Jeff Davis	Jefferson	Jenkins	Johnson	Jones	Lamar	Lanier	Laurens	Lee	Liberty	Lincoln	Long	Lowndes	Lumpkin	McDuffie	McIntosh	Macon
	GEORGIA—Continued																	
POPULATION BY SEX																		
Negro population: 1930	5,237	1,665	12,042	7,464	4,961	5,774	4,473	1,940	13,536	6,489	5,532	4,093	1,788	13,783	188	4,572	3,876	11,192
Male	2,599	816	5,789	3,614	2,431	2,844	2,182	1,013	6,456	3,119	2,721	1,991	919	6,584	93	2,264	1,929	5,338
Female	2,638	849	6,253	3,850	2,530	2,930	2,291	927	7,080	3,370	2,811	2,102	869	7,199	95	2,308	1,947	5,854
Negro population: 1920	11,618	1,615	13,148	8,719	5,665	9,403	—	—	18,601	8,977	7,593	5,152	—	13,535	217	6,140	3,803	12,027
Male	5,712	815	6,375	4,275	2,778	4,650	—	—	8,962	4,398	3,727	2,610	—	6,559	97	3,059	1,872	5,834
Female	5,906	800	6,773	4,444	2,887	4,753	—	—	9,639	4,579	3,866	2,542	—	6,976	120	3,081	1,931	6,193
Percent of total population: 1930	60.9	20.5	58.1	57.8	39.1	64.2	45.9	37.4	41.4	77.9	67.9	52.2	42.8	46.0	3.8	50.7	67.3	67.2
1920	71.0	22.1	58.2	60.9	41.8	70.9	—	—	470	82.3	59.8	52.9	—	51.0	4.1	53.3	74.3	68.1
VOTING AGE: 1930																		
Total 21 years old and over	2,390	771	5,159	3,584	2,184	2,443	1,959	884	6,175	3,173	2,612	1,699	830	6,823	106	2,229	2,012	5,050
Male	1,132	379	2,364	1,732	1,029	1,167	907	478	2,867	1,544	1,294	816	435	3,188	51	1,072	1,033	2,358
Female	1,258	392	2,795	1,852	1,155	1,276	1,052	406	3,308	1,629	1,318	883	395	3,635	55	1,157	979	2,692
AGE: 1930																		
Under 5 years	561	220	1,435	777	638	790	575	266	1,638	722	598	523	227	1,527	24	425	405	1,348
Under 1 year	106	45	252	153	134	143	106	51	291	134	98	91	39	275	4	75	64	272
5 to 9 years	735	232	1,801	995	666	928	662	238	1,781	836	725	624	229	1,760	15	607	453	1,488
10 to 14 years	720	188	1,704	948	668	782	610	264	1,881	793	746	572	214	1,627	15	632	457	1,492
15 to 19 years	696	205	1,628	933	675	721	577	239	1,727	805	728	564	246	1,713	26	571	460	1,507
20 to 24 years	506	204	1,126	814	520	462	360	204	1,318	671	508	387	181	1,370	28	448	406	1,095
25 to 29 years	278	116	763	569	378	352	246	137	934	432	328	259	122	1,054	13	274	234	695
30 to 34 years	222	91	607	429	269	244	229	88	669	305	255	192	84	783	7	262	204	554
35 to 44 years	491	148	1,081	821	422	497	423	199	1,346	650	582	332	201	1,628	19	500	413	1,093
45 to 54 years	469	124	935	594	356	479	374	156	1,134	609	516	319	142	1,252	17	406	421	1,009
55 to 64 years	272	81	535	341	216	274	232	85	658	355	317	181	71	620	14	253	242	547
65 to 74 years	205	42	303	158	116	164	111	44	302	216	144	78	46	311	5	143	117	248
75 years and over	73	14	116	77	37	79	74	16	145	95	85	60	24	132	4	48	60	105
Unknown	9	—	8	8	—	2	—	4	3	—	—	2	1	6	1	3	4	11
SCHOOL ATTENDANCE																		
Total 7 to 13 years, inclusive	1,007	308	2,442	1,349	896	1,192	875	354	2,540	1,128	1,018	805	309	2,359	21	865	641	2,077
Number attending school	778	207	2,113	1,034	520	1,064	717	271	1,735	974	913	565	264	1,949	20	680	559	1,757
Percent attending school	77.3	67.2	86.5	76.6	58.0	89.3	81.9	76.6	68.3	86.3	89.7	70.2	85.4	82.6	—	78.6	87.2	84.6
Total 14 and 15 years, inclusive	273	83	692	369	266	305	233	97	764	303	276	233	81	718	11	243	179	599
Number attending school	150	49	413	230	138	217	141	40	356	194	207	131	50	469	7	150	141	361
Percent attending school	54.9	—	59.7	62.3	51.9	71.1	60.5	—	46.6	64.0	75.0	56.2	—	65.3	—	61.7	78.8	60.3
Total 16 and 17 years, inclusive	297	78	629	369	268	298	250	97	679	328	320	224	102	670	8	229	189	639
Number attending school	79	29	170	91	73	104	84	13	177	85	135	75	20	235	4	72	83	166
Percent attending school	26.6	—	27.0	24.7	27.2	34.9	33.6	—	26.1	25.9	42.2	33.5	19.6	35.1	—	31.4	43.9	26.0
Total 18 to 20 years, inclusive	415	119	954	610	406	379	311	140	1,029	493	398	338	148	1,013	13	337	270	888
Number attending school	41	11	51	26	31	38	26	4	60	43	61	20	7	88	4	13	30	58
Percent attending school	9.9	9.2	5.3	4.3	7.6	10.0	8.4	2.9	5.8	8.7	15.3	5.9	4.7	8.7	—	3.9	11.1	6.5
ILLITERACY																		
Total 10 years old and over	3,941	1,213	8,806	5,692	3,657	4,056	3,236	1,436	10,117	4,931	4,209	2,946	1,332	10,496	149	3,540	3,018	8,356
Number illiterate	968	319	1,537	1,411	1,479	740	546	290	3,450	1,625	463	612	196	1,685	20	1,006	696	2,451
Percent illiterate	24.6	26.3	17.5	24.8	40.4	18.2	16.9	20.2	34.1	33.0	11.0	20.8	14.7	16.1	13.4	28.4	23.1	29.3
Percent illiterate in 1920	42.5	23.0	36.0	40.8	31.6	32.4	—	—	32.7	43.3	23.3	35.7	—	22.0	25.5	33.3	22.2	31.5
URBAN AND RURAL																		
Urban population	—	—	—	1,030	—	—	1,124	—	2,806	—	—	—	—	6,265	—	—	—	—
Percent urban	—	—	—	13.8	—	—	25.1	—	20.7	—	—	—	—	45.5	—	—	—	—
Rural population	5,237	1,665	12,042	6,434	4,961	5,774	3,349	1,940	10,730	6,489	5,532	4,093	1,788	7,518	188	4,572	3,876	11,192
Rural-farm	3,508	811	9,569	6,103	3,797	4,800	3,168	856	9,778	5,590	4,228	3,831	902	5,349	89	3,721	1,048	8,625
Rural-nonfarm	1,729	854	2,473	331	1,164	974	181	1,084	952	899	1,304	262	886	2,169	99	851	2,828	2,567
Percent rural	100.0	100.0	100.0	86.2	100.0	100.0	74.9	100.0	79.3	100.0	100.0	100.0	100.0	54.5	100.0	100.0	100.0	100.0
MARITAL CONDITION																		
Males 15 years old and over	1,538	511	3,315	2,302	1,412	1,602	1,225	635	3,823	1,992	1,686	1,174	580	4,771	63	1,413	1,311	3,225
Single	533	166	1,105	678	426	538	391	206	1,174	538	568	473	195	1,299	24	446	416	934
Married	912	294	2,040	1,417	901	967	739	354	2,415	1,269	993	626	343	2,533	33	861	759	2,004
Widowed	86	46	152	167	80	94	94	73	209	169	108	67	38	286	5	91	102	265
Divorced	4	5	12	35	5	2	1	2	23	16	16	7	4	51	1	14	32	12
Unknown	3	—	6	5	—	1	—	—	2	—	1	2	—	2	—	1	2	10
Females 15 years old and over	1,683	514	3,787	2,442	1,577	1,672	1,401	537	4,413	2,146	1,777	1,200	538	4,698	71	1,495	1,250	3,639
Single	468	119	1,012	493	414	413	355	93	1,128	403	474	385	130	1,032	23	384	269	792
Married	934	305	2,097	1,398	891	985	826	353	2,476	1,274	1,005	628	337	2,663	37	875	749	2,042
Widowed	272	88	648	496	255	269	214	85	735	436	278	177	68	872	7	213	199	764
Divorced	8	2	26	45	15	4	4	6	71	32	20	10	2	131	4	22	32	34
Unknown	1	—	4	10	2	1	2	—	3	1	—	—	1	—	—	1	1	7
FAMILIES																		
Number of families	1,160	373	2,606	1,846	1,151	1,163	972	427	3,130	1,699	1,225	784	421	3,277	44	1,069	981	2,600
Median size	3.75	3.61	4.03	3.17	3.42	4.24	3.83	3.62	3.47	3.11	3.77	4.46	3.40	3.30	—	3.32	3.02	3.43
Families having— No children under 10	601	182	1,175	1,018	558	506	455	203	1,626	961	631	338	217	1,855	27	606	580	1,354
1 child under 10	212	73	539	357	246	211	202	81	595	306	240	141	85	552	6	198	169	491
2 children under 10	139	45	393	213	148	146	110	61	377	213	138	94	54	338	6	112	97	303
3 or more	208	73	499	258	199	300	205	82	532	219	216	211	65	532	5	153	135	452

CHARACTERISTICS OF NEGRO POPULATION BY COUNTIES: 1930—Continued

(See note at head of table)

SUBJECT	GEORGIA—Continued																	
	Madison	Marion	Meriwether	Miller	Milton	Mitchell	Monroe	Montgomery	Morgan	Murray	Muscogee	Newton	Oconee	Oglethorpe	Paulding	Peach	Pickens	Pierce
POPULATION BY SEX																		
Negro population: 1930	2,834	3,915	11,766	3,083	433	11,862	6,750	4,467	7,198	333	20,667	6,777	2,401	6,424	1,124	6,565	795	3,245
Male	1,437	1,960	5,694	1,513	225	5,740	3,253	2,245	3,490	175	9,207	3,271	1,204	3,241	568	3,003	426	1,661
Female	1,397	1,955	6,072	1,570	208	6,122	3,497	2,222	3,708	158	11,460	3,506	1,197	3,183	556	3,562	369	1,584
Negro population: 1920	5,269	4,097	14,594	3,702	477	14,067	12,763	4,348	12,886	432	16,251	10,180	4,719	11,497	1,607	------	324	2,700
Male	2,603	2,005	7,199	1,837	251	6,782	6,248	2,149	6,389	214	7,520	4,935	2,368	5,775	814	------	174	1,433
Female	2,666	2,092	7,395	1,865	226	7,195	6,515	2,199	6,497	218	8,731	5,245	2,351	5,722	793	------	150	1,267
Percent of total population:																		
1930	19.0	56.2	52.4	34.0	6.4	50.2	58.2	44.6	57.6	3.6	35.9	39.2	29.7	49.7	9.1	63.9	8.2	25.9
1920	28.0	53.9	55.8	38.7	6.9	55.0	63.4	47.4	64.0	4.6	36.8	47.0	42.6	56.7	11.5	------	3.9	22.6
VOTING AGE: 1930																		
Total 21 years old and over	1,202	1,733	5,208	1,328	186	5,288	3,001	1,841	3,449	141	11,112	3,135	1,033	2,811	478	3,132	410	1,549
Male	582	859	2,468	644	96	2,467	1,473	937	1,605	74	4,731	1,493	523	1,393	237	1,442	232	818
Female	620	874	2,740	684	90	2,821	1,528	904	1,844	67	6,381	1,642	510	1,418	241	1,690	178	731
AGE: 1930																		
Under 5 years	346	488	1,530	404	49	1,529	834	519	766	53	1,999	702	291	804	146	663	102	385
Under 1 year	85	68	308	72	4	222	170	100	133	10	385	147	51	163	27	135	18	79
5 to 9 years	373	561	1,613	421	56	1,586	905	643	888	49	2,290	905	340	882	153	839	92	400
10 to 14 years	418	520	1,576	390	63	1,564	931	715	923	43	2,247	902	339	898	166	851	57	414
15 to 19 years	409	509	1,526	467	69	1,587	943	633	1,003	37	2,475	947	339	856	150	912	106	405
20 to 24 years	340	369	1,174	290	52	1,186	636	426	606	38	2,483	684	217	637	94	669	110	352
25 to 29 years	170	236	715	226	24	837	362	270	394	16	2,076	402	150	347	71	477	82	205
30 to 34 years	99	197	482	164	19	583	289	207	325	17	1,342	321	91	316	49	347	52	172
35 to 44 years	225	390	1,125	260	36	1,089	549	381	749	35	2,565	684	203	536	91	704	102	379
45 to 54 years	222	319	1,009	214	36	999	628	326	731	26	1,812	627	195	557	84	579	50	314
55 to 54 years	144	184	577	131	19	496	374	212	486	9	846	342	135	331	63	303	24	133
65 to 74 years	56	95	286	75	7	258	194	90	230	6	347	184	66	174	42	153	13	63
75 years and over	29	46	152	39	3	143	104	43	95	4	172	77	35	82	15	68	5	22
Unknown	3	1	1	2	------	5	1	2	2	------	13	------	------	4	------	------	------	1
SCHOOL ATTENDANCE																		
Total 7 to 13 years, inclusive	546	737	2,221	552	81	2,128	1,262	953	1,251	63	3,165	1,286	458	1,251	219	1,182	95	581
Number attending school	422	573	1,976	389	49	1,685	952	772	1,019	59	2,663	1,096	366	1,067	172	920	83	502
Percent attending school	77.3	77.7	89.0	70.5	------	79.2	75.4	81.0	81.5	------	84.1	85.2	79.9	85.3	78.5	77.8	------	86.4
Total 14 and 15 years, inclusive	166	201	614	172	28	679	379	273	417	11	930	354	144	343	65	345	31	176
Number attending school	93	150	467	89	18	414	207	170	268	8	536	229	94	234	45	208	24	118
Percent attending school	56.0	74.6	76.1	51.7	------	61.0	54.6	62.3	64.3	------	57.6	64.7	65.3	68.2	------	60.3	------	67.0
Total 16 and 17 years, inclusive	163	207	603	174	29	614	396	269	416	17	931	413	137	357	75	395	27	167
Number attending school	43	103	209	39	13	178	88	79	126	11	232	122	50	118	32	167	12	58
Percent attending school	26.4	49.8	34.7	22.4	------	29.0	22.2	29.4	30.3	------	24.9	29.5	36.5	33.1	------	42.3	------	34.7
Total 18 to 20 years, inclusive	257	308	942	274	36	973	500	357	543	26	1,620	540	189	505	79	522	87	242
Number attending school	12	54	73	4	3	56	26	21	36	2	140	27	20	28	5	120	8	17
Percent attending school	4.7	17.5	7.7	1.5	------	5.8	5.2	5.9	6.6	------	8.6	5.0	10.6	5.5	------	23.0	------	7.0
ILLITERACY																		
Total 10 years old and over	2,115	2,866	8,623	2,258	328	8,747	5,011	3,305	5,544	231	16,378	5,170	1,770	4,738	825	5,063	601	2,460
Number illiterate	477	768	1,299	738	58	2,426	972	637	851	19	3,034	972	459	1,282	97	1,471	86	329
Percent illiterate	22.6	26.8	15.1	32.7	17.7	27.7	19.4	19.3	15.3	8.2	18.5	18.8	25.9	27.1	11.8	29.1	14.3	13.4
Percent illiterate in 1920	38.1	31.0	31.4	45.5	30.1	39.6	28.2	28.7	33.4	13.9	23.9	31.3	32.2	36.5	23.2	------	4.0	18.1
URBAN AND RURAL																		
Urban population	------	------	716	------	------	852	------	------	------	------	14,157	1,323	------	------	------	2,408	------	------
Percent urban	------	------	6.1	------	------	7.2	------	------	------	------	68.5	19.5	------	------	------	36.7	------	------
Rural population	2,834	3,915	11,050	3,083	433	11,010	6,750	4,467	7,198	333	6,510	5,454	2,401	6,424	1,124	4,157	795	3,245
Rural-farm	2,366	3,060	8,887	2,531	417	9,116	4,787	3,315	5,599	287	2,371	4,773	2,240	5,433	957	3,779	72	1,634
Rural-non farm	468	855	2,163	552	16	1,894	1,963	1,152	1,599	46	4,139	681	161	991	167	378	723	1,611
Percent rural	100.0	100.0	93.9	100.0	100.0	92.8	100.0	100.0	100.0	100.0	31.5	80.5	100.0	100.0	100.0	63.3	100.0	100.0
MARITAL CONDITION																		
Males 15 years old and over	829	1,162	3,378	896	132	3,385	1,986	1,305	2,216	102	5,960	2,035	718	1,919	323	1,913	307	1,075
Single	281	402	1,105	265	52	1,027	659	438	759	41	1,757	706	236	630	118	617	126	349
Married	507	683	2,025	565	72	2,124	1,177	778	1,293	55	3,760	1,149	424	1,141	185	1,188	170	634
Widowed	25	68	223	48	8	203	132	85	159	5	430	159	56	134	19	80	8	83
Divorced	15	9	25	18	------	29	18	1	5	1	13	20	2	13	1	28	3	8
Unknown	1	------	------	------	------	2	------	3	------	------	------	1	------	1	------	------	------	1
Females 15 years old and over	868	1,184	3,669	972	133	3,798	2,094	1,285	2,405	86	8,171	2,233	713	1,921	336	2,299	237	973
Single	242	326	1,009	212	39	850	596	325	576	26	1,969	633	187	499	95	641	59	183
Married	503	659	2,043	581	77	2,212	1,173	768	1,319	51	4,104	1,153	436	1,133	187	1,263	156	616
Widowed	91	155	560	143	17	648	298	186	488	8	2,052	376	88	253	53	331	21	160
Divorced	32	44	55	36	------	84	27	6	19	1	42	70	1	36	1	61	1	12
Unknown	------	------	2	------	------	4	------	------	3	------	4	1	1	------	------	3	------	------
FAMILIES																		
Number of families	571	815	2,460	671	77	2,689	1,392	873	1,773	63	5,051	1,510	488	1,353	219	1,540	150	788
Median size	3.99	4.04	3.95	3.76	------	3.61	4.11	4.37	3.28	------	3.16	3.73	4.12	4.00	4.30	3.29	3.77	3.20
Families having—																		
No children under 10	243	391	1,154	319	33	1,380	666	368	1,043	22	2,972	796	236	652	97	849	70	438
1 child under 10	136	143	489	128	18	487	244	195	267	12	955	265	76	250	41	283	29	131
2 children under 10	81	110	310	100	7	319	186	122	201	11	558	194	71	161	35	200	16	93
3 or more	111	171	507	124	19	503	296	188	262	18	566	255	105	290	46	208	35	126

CHARACTERISTICS OF NEGRO POPULATION BY COUNTIES: 1930—Continued

(See note at head of table)

GEORGIA—Continued

SUBJECT	Pike	Polk	Pulaski	Putnam	Quitman	Rabun	Randolph	Richmond	Rockdale
POPULATION BY SEX									
Negro population: 1930	5, 401	4, 751	5, 056	5, 212	2, 641	164	11, 547	30, 220	2, 441
Male	2, 669	2, 325	2, 371	2, 530	1, 299	91	5, 536	13, 770	1, 188
Female	2, 732	2, 426	2, 685	2, 682	1, 342	73	6, 011	16, 450	1, 253
Negro population: 1920	10, 794	4, 905	7, 164	10, 421	2, 430	289	11, 009	28, 639	3, 534
Male	5, 306	2, 383	3, 478	5, 048	1, 189	171	5, 253	13, 715	1, 769
Female	5, 488	2, 522	3, 686	5, 373	1, 241	118	5, 756	14, 924	1, 765
Percent of total population:									
1930	49. 8	18. 9	56. 1	62. 3	69. 1	2. 6	67. 2	41. 4	33. 7
1920	50. 9	24. 1	61. 8	68. 8	71. 1	5. 0	65. 8	45. 0	37. 1
VOTING AGE: 1930									
Total 21 years old and over	2, 289	2, 176	2, 395	2, 365	1, 116	90	5, 250	17, 788	1, 103
Male	1, 121	1, 048	1, 079	1, 113	554	51	2, 421	7, 997	532
Female	1, 168	1, 128	1, 316	1, 252	562	39	2, 829	9, 791	571
AGE: 1930									
Under 5 years	717	534	567	595	360	14	1, 298	2, 412	293
Under 1 year	142	111	90	118	81	4	232	435	53
5 to 9 years	791	633	653	677	394	15	1, 588	3, 060	340
10 to 14 years	724	614	676	718	352	19	1, 544	2, 977	300
15 to 19 years	736	671	625	736	354	24	1, 557	3, 243	336
20 to 24 years	531	476	495	445	287	11	1, 226	3, 505	254
25 to 29 years	325	309	332	315	177	11	830	3, 072	128
30 to 34 years	250	222	272	212	97	10	601	2, 248	117
35 to 44 years	500	548	577	435	213	28	1, 075	4, 463	213
45 to 54 years	409	413	412	519	219	13	944	3, 040	229
55 to 64 years	225	182	247	300	112	11	563	1, 308	127
65 to 74 years	132	94	137	160	45	5	227	607	75
75 years and over	60	54	63	93	30	3	94	243	28
Unknown	1	1	------	7	1	------	------	42	1
SCHOOL ATTENDANCE									
Total 7 to 13 years, inclusive	1, 065	870	922	967	506	25	2, 180	4, 225	435
Number attending school	908	731	801	694	424	22	1, 987	3, 674	359
Percent attending school	85. 3	84. 0	86. 9	71. 8	83. 8	------	91. 1	87. 0	82. 5
Total 14 and 15 years, inclusive	283	252	284	310	141	8	623	1, 206	139
Number attending school	194	174	190	161	101	6	457	839	86
Percent attending school	68. 6	69. 0	66. 9	51. 9	71. 6	------	73. 4	69. 6	61. 9
Total 16 and 17 years, inclusive	296	272	241	290	151	9	647	1, 224	138
Number attending school	87	106	76	64	49	2	268	431	42
Percent attending school	29. 4	39. 0	31. 5	22. 1	32. 5	------	41. 4	35. 2	30. 4
Total 18 to 20 years, inclusive	436	402	387	401	201	13	917	2, 157	197
Number attending school	32	21	25	25	13	------	121	229	9
Percent attending school	7. 3	5 2	6. 5	6. 2	6. 5	------	13. 2	10. 6	4. 6
ILLITERACY									
Total 10 years old and over	3, 893	3, 584	3, 836	3, 940	1, 887	135	8, 661	24, 748	1, 808
Number illiterate	938	599	997	1, 208	456	12	1, 595	3, 744	435
Percent illiterate	24. 1	16. 7	26. 0	30. 7	24. 2	8. 9	18. 4	15. 1	24. 1
Percent illiterate in 1920	27. 9	26. 1	38. 0	35. 6	35. 2	27. 5	28. 4	24. 9	24. 2
URBAN AND RURAL									
Urban population	------	1, 858	------	------	------	------	1, 963	24, 190	------
Percent urban	------	39. 1	------	------	------	------	17. 0	80. 0	------
Rural population	5, 401	2, 893	5, 056	5, 212	2, 641	164	9, 584	6, 030	2, 441
Rural-farm	4, 781	2, 314	3, 945	3, 772	2, 267	62	8, 579	2, 784	1, 825
Rural-nonfarm	620	579	1, 111	1, 440	374	102	1, 005	3, 246	616
Percent rural	100. 0	60. 9	100. 0	100. 0	100. 0	100. 0	83. 0	20. 0	100. 0
MARITAL CONDITION									
Males 15 years old and over	1, 564	1, 436	1, 432	1, 508	752	64	3, 333	9, 659	734
Single	532	464	451	501	245	22	1, 075	2, 799	255
Married	907	863	885	865	468	34	2, 049	5915	419
Widowed	112	90	90	89	38	5	190	821	52
Divorced	11	19	6	8	1	2	18	114	8
Unknown	2	------	------	45	------	1	1	10	------
Females 15 years old and over	1, 605	1, 534	1 , 728	1, 714	783	52	3, 784	12, 112	774
Single	395	396	413	544	176	12	939	2, 795	212
Married	921	905	918	889	488	25	2, 104	6, 125	425
Widowed	267	209	366	269	110	9	702	2, 930	125
Divorced	20	24	30	12	7	4	39	250	8
Unknown	2	------	1	------	2	2	------	12	4
FAMILIES									
Number of families	1, 100	1, 005	1, 249	1, 133	550	44	2, 609	8, 209	531
Median size	4. 14	3. 91	3. 31	3. 84	3. 80	------	3. 67	2. 81	3. 90
Families—									
No children under 10	476	488	674	576	249	30	1, 314	5, 402	261
1 child under 10	221	209	244	207	100	7	501	1, 409	94
2 children under 10	148	128	166	147	73	2	343	725	70
3 or more	255	180	165	203	128	5	451	673	106

SUBJECT	Schley	Screven	Seminole	Spalding	Stephens	Stewart	Sumter	Talbot	Taliaferro
POPULATION BY SEX									
Negro population: 1930	3, 320	11, 621	2, 898	8, 154	2, 087	7, 930	17, 390	5, 828	4, 222
Male	1, 587	5, 776	1, 366	3, 877	981	3, 901	8, 192	2, 890	2, 024
Female	1, 733	5, 845	1, 532	4, 277	1, 106	4, 029	9, 198	2, 938	2, 198
Negro population: 1920	3, 099	13, 850	------	10, 206	2, 316	8, 644	19, 862	7, 995	6, 230
Male	1, 511	6, 852	------	5, 033	1, 144	4, 117	9, 498	3, 936	2, 993
Female	1, 588	6, 998	------	5, 173	1, 172	4, 527	10, 364	4, 059	3, 237
Percent of total population:									
1930	62. 1	56. 7	39. 2	34. 7	17. 8	71. 4	64. 9	68. 9	68. 4
1920	59. 1	58. 8	------	46. 6	20. 7	71. 5	67. 0	71. 7	70. 5
VOTING AGE: 1930									
Total 21 years old and over	1, 390	5, 073	1, 266	4, 023	918	3, 443	8, 268	2, 423	1, 883
Male	677	2, 500	583	1, 874	411	1, 620	3, 801	1, 181	907
Female	713	2, 573	683	2, 149	507	1, 823	4, 467	1, 242	976
AGE: 1930									
Under 5 years	421	1, 481	341	843	228	985	1, 871	751	539
Under 1 year	79	281	65	143	37	218	386	162	111
5 to 9 years	458	1, 666	403	1, 008	306	1, 109	2, 203	852	596
10 to 14 years	490	1, 646	375	975	301	1, 135	2, 282	831	563
15 to 19 years	491	1, 450	438	1, 089	284	1, 055	2, 310	815	550
20 to 24 years	322	1, 113	291	893	196	788	1, 836	528	371
25 to 29 years	185	779	176	613	125	477	1, 179	345	228
30 to 34 years	161	576	126	443	102	326	868	254	172
35 to 44 years	258	1, 132	247	874	206	699	1, 794	455	387
45 to 54 years	279	901	239	769	180	648	1, 577	482	404
55 to 64 years	154	508	147	380	93	417	848	283	251
65 to 74 years	70	250	76	187	34	193	453	154	109
75 years and over	31	110	36	80	29	98	167	78	51
Unknown	------	9	3	------	3	------	2	------	1
SCHOOL ATTENDANCE									
Total 7 to 13 years, inclusive	668	2, 258	515	1, 391	420	1, 547	3, 144	1, 165	793
Number attending school	610	1, 557	454	1, 063	376	1, 463	2, 774	1, 017	699
Percent attending school	91. 3	69. 0	88. 2	76. 4	89. 5	94. 6	88. 2	87. 3	88. 1
Total 14 and 15 years, inclusive	195	644	165	387	110	463	916	329	226
Number attending school	132	372	132	237	84	370	583	210	161
Percent attending school	67. 7	57. 8	80. 0	61. 2	76. 4	79. 9	63. 6	63. 8	71. 2
Total 16 and 17 years, inclusive	198	564	191	465	122	433	943	343	229
Number attending school	47	154	110	121	40	166	257	78	87
Percent attending school	23. 7	27. 3	57. 6	26. 0	32. 8	38. 3	27. 3	22. 7	38. 0
Total 18 to 20 years, inclusive	275	896	238	650	163	613	1, 375	466	304
Number attending school	9	90	30	43	15	58	77	20	21
Percent attending school	3. 3	14. 0	12. 6	6. 6	9. 2	9. 5	5. 6	4. 3	6. 9
ILLITERACY									
Total 10 years old and over	2, 441	8, 474	2, 154	6, 303	1, 553	5, 836	13, 316	4, 225	3, 087
Number illiterate	270	2, 323	478	1, 045	141	825	3, 427	634	503
Percent illiterate	11. 1	27. 4	22. 2	16. 6	9. 1	14. 1	25. 7	15. 0	16. 3
Percent illiterate in 1920	17. 0	37. 9	------	22. 9	31. 6	33. 2	33. 6	30. 6	32. 9
URBAN AND RURAL									
Urban population	------	------	------	3, 396	1, 139	------	4, 627	39	------
Percent urban	------	------	------	41. 6	54. 6	------	26. 6	. 5	------
Rural population	3, 320	11, 621	2, 898	4, 758	948	7, 930	12, 763	5, 799	4, 222
Rural-farm	2, 858	9, 832	2, 116	4, 126	84. 8	5, 897	11, 477	4, 350	3, 646
Rural-nonfarm	462	1, 789	782	632	100	2, 033	1, 286	1, 449	576
Percent rural	100. 0	100. 0	100. 0	58. 4	45. 4	100. 0	73. 4	99. 5	100. 0
MARITAL CONDITION									
Males 15 years old and over	956	3, 359	828	2, 480	575	2, 230	5, 050	1, 642	1, 212
Single	355	1, 087	283	802	204	754	1, 554	544	357
Married	563	2, 053	513	1, 455	327	1, 341	3, 040	987	755
Widowed	38	197	27	203	43	127	428	109	99
Divorced	------	22	4	20	1	7	27	2	1
Unknown	------	------	1	------	------	1	1	------	------
Females 15 years old and over	995	3, 469	951	2, 848	677	2, 471	5, 984	1, 752	1, 312
Single	273	850	254	668	192	643	1, 405	501	325
Married	564	2, 028	533	1, 505	337	1, 342	3, 095	988	750
Widowed	155	541	150	620	144	470	1, 386	245	233
Divorced	2	48	13	55	4	16	96	18	4
Unknown	1	2	1	------	------	------	2	------	------
FAMILIES									
Number of families	686	2, 550	626	1, 916	429	1, 664	4, 280	1, 225	917
Median size	4. 29	3. 80	3. 72	3. 29	4. 01	3. 93	3. 30	4. 11	3. 96
Families—									
No children under 10	320	1, 216	307	1, 065	198	795	2, 361	548	434
1 child under 10	120	502	116	357	90	308	837	233	183
2 children under 10	97	315	81	224	56	220	488	185	118
3 or more	149	517	122	270	85	341	594	259	182

CHARACTERISTICS OF NEGRO POPULATION BY COUNTIES: 1930—Continued

(See note at head of table)

SUBJECT	GEORGIA—Continued																	
	Tattnall	Taylor	Telfair	Terrell	Thomas	Tift	Toombs	Treutlen	Troup	Turner	Twiggs	Union	Upson	Walker	Walton	Ware	Warren	Washington
POPULATION BY SEX																		
Negro population: 1930	3,328	5,242	4,858	12,982	15,856	4,874	4,890	2,473	15,092	3,866	5,335	47	6,944	2,355	6,767	8,216	7,351	14,132
Male	1,672	2,567	2,437	6,239	7,393	2,364	2,382	1,222	7,171	1,951	2,622	35	3,368	1,178	3,334	3,880	3,542	6,775
Female	1,656	2,675	2,421	6,743	8,463	2,510	2,508	1,251	7,921	1,915	2,713	12	3,576	1,177	3,433	4,336	3,809	7,357
Negro population: 1920	3,550	5,521	5,005	14,055	17,263	4,290	3,828	2,777	16,965	4,924	6,653	46	7,257	2,484	9,715	12,313	7,821	16,404
Male	1,770	2,728	2,444	6,841	8,150	2,061	1,852	1,379	8,333	2,469	3,282	22	3,562	1,261	4,790	7,465	3,783	7,967
Female	1,780	2,793	2,561	7,214	9,113	2,229	1,976	1,398	8,632	2,455	3,371	24	3,695	1,223	4,925	4,848	4,038	8,437
Percent of total population:																		
1930	21.6	49.4	32.4	71.0	48.6	30.3	28.5	33.0	41.1	34.5	63.7	0.7	35.6	9.0	32.0	30.9	65.7	56.5
1920	24.5	48.1	32.7	71.7	52.2	29 6	27.5	36.2	47.0	39.5	63.9	0.7	49.1	10.6	40.1	43.4	66.1	58.3
VOTING AGE: 1930																		
Total 21 years old and over	1,532	2,194	2,214	5,931	7,795	2,485	2,300	1,081	7,179	1,792	2,084	27	3,200	1,126	3,074	4,493	3,120	6,357
Male	780	1,060	1,096	2,749	3,522	1,194	1,105	517	3,271	917	990	23	1,553	564	1,497	2,115	1,471	2,952
Female	752	1,134	1,118	3,182	4,273	1,291	1,195	564	3,908	875	1,094	4	1,647	562	1,577	2,378	1,649	3,405
AGE: 1930																		
Under 5 years	355	714	546	1,498	1,643	532	588	287	1,700	432	776	4	819	263	821	831	865	1,778
Under 1 year	66	128	108	272	311	96	113	46	334	80	131	2	146	52	168	142	173	318
5 to 9 years	465	773	647	1,791	2,019	612	632	331	1,971	478	875	2	966	320	910	987	1,094	2,040
10 to 14 years	439	738	643	1,749	1,963	546	609	361	1,812	535	763	3	873	280	855	875	1,088	1,830
15 to 19 years	445	696	665	1,679	2,054	598	643	354	2,030	533	745	10	924	318	919	873	978	1,768
20 to 24 years	374	450	485	1,375	1,553	506	534	228	1,624	413	398	13	799	218	746	871	740	1,401
25 to 29 years	230	822	329	898	1,072	433	387	181	1,087	238	273	4	492	142	411	777	434	956
30 to 34 years	185	238	234	605	791	281	252	126	793	231	233	4	355	108	295	589	346	734
35 to 44 years	294	498	464	1,250	1,652	543	463	231	1,594	402	472	1	655	244	620	1,026	620	1,335
45 to 54 years	281	412	400	1,143	1,568	451	401	188	1,319	325	374	2	549	207	591	814	643	1,139
55 to 64 years	170	255	244	577	765	236	221	95	639	181	247	4	281	155	376	373	315	636
65 to 74 years	59	95	133	288	479	101	103	53	324	71	125	------	157	67	149	129	136	342
75 years and over	31	48	67	128	278	32	52	36	187	26	54	------	74	33	73	64	86	164
Unknown	------	3	1	1	19	3	5	2	12	1	------	------	------	------	1	7	6	9
SCHOOL ATTENDANCE																		
Total 7 to 13 years, inclusive	639	1,052	903	2,442	2,771	809	872	497	2,620	708	1,108	3	1,282	420	1,227	1,303	1,517	2,647
Number attending school	525	875	742	2,174	2,450	642	625	435	2,109	550	897	3	1,010	350	1,009	1,220	1,266	2,022
Percent attending school	82.2	83.2	82.2	89.0	88.4	79.4	71.7	87.5	80.5	77.7	81.0	------	78.8	83.3	82.2	93.6	83.5	76.4
Total 14 and 15 years, inclusive	172	285	267	709	809	243	279	143	805	205	309	------	369	107	352	362	436	734
Number attending school	105	169	163	498	558	167	151	108	488	115	157	------	199	72	240	266	275	458
Percent attending school	61.0	59.3	61.0	70.2	69.0	68.7	54.1	75.5	60.6	56.1	50.8	------	53.9	67.3	68.2	73.5	63.1	62.4
Total 16 and 17 years, inclusive	184	303	242	700	822	225	234	145	804	230	303	3	360	138	360	354	395	729
Number attending school	55	58	56	207	336	72	62	69	238	52	61	1	80	50	125	151	96	222
Percent attending school	29.9	19.1	23.1	29.6	40.9	32.0	26.5	47.6	29.6	22.6	20.1	------	22.2	36.2	34.7	42.7	24.3	30.5
Total 18 to 20 years, inclusive	262	389	431	983	1,237	338	372	191	1,199	306	384	8	533	171	580	494	587	1,042
Number attending school	14	13	24	61	167	31	26	18	92	24	12	------	23	20	34	64	39	53
Percent attending school	5.3	3.3	5.6	6.2	13.5	9.2	7.0	9.4	7.7	7.8	3.1	------	4.3	11.7	5.9	13.0	6.6	5.1
ILLITERACY																		
Total 10 years old and over	2,508	3,755	3,665	9,693	12,194	3,730	3,670	1,855	11,421	2,956	3,684	41	5,159	1,772	5,036	6,398	5,392	10,314
Number illiterate	295	737	916	2,125	2,651	741	956	396	1,949	656	999	11	955	215	1,246	789	1,097	2,224
Percent illiterate	11.8	19.6	25.0	21.9	21.7	19.9	26.0	21.3	17.1	22.2	27.1	26.8	18.5	12.1	24.7	12.3	20.3	21.6
Percent illiterate in 1920	26.7	32.2	16.1	35.1	29.6	31.7	23.8	29.9	32.6	35.3	36.6	------	31.3	19.9	35.5	17.5	34.8	32.3
URBAN AND RURAL																		
Urban population	------	------	------	2,209	6,074	651	1,298	------	5,471	------	------	------	1,999	304	987	5,956	------	1,556
Percent urban	------	------	------	17.0	38.3	13.4	26.5	------	36.3	------	------	------	28.8	12.9	14.6	72.5	------	11.0
Rural population	3,328	5,242	4,858	10,773	9,782	4,223	3,592	2,473	9,621	3,866	5,335	47	4,945	2,051	5,780	2,260	7,351	12,576
Rural-farm	2,053	3,981	2,794	10,018	7,759	1,843	2,593	1,654	7,130	2,414	4,432	------	4,255	1,082	5,119	486	6,379	10,757
Rural-nonfarm	1,275	1,261	2,064	755	2,023	2,380	999	819	2,491	1,452	903	47	690	969	661	1,774	972	1,819
Percent rural	100.0	100.0	100.0	83.0	61.7	86.6	73.5	100.0	63.7	100.0	100.0	------	71.2	87.1	85.4	27.5	100.0	89.0
MARITAL CONDITION																		
Males 15 years old and over	1,059	1,464	1,511	3,737	4,647	1,544	1,453	732	4,436	1,221	1,384	31	2,037	748	2,044	2,549	2,052	3,956
Single	380	447	519	1,162	1,467	455	448	275	1,478	346	452	18	673	239	673	705	715	1,237
Married	620	903	841	2,311	2,852	945	904	409	2,562	767	840	13	1,228	455	1,208	1,650	1,231	2,506
Widowed	47	80	139	253	279	136	99	35	364	71	88	------	109	46	135	174	97	192
Divorced	12	34	12	11	49	7	2	13	22	37	4	------	25	8	28	16	8	17
Unknown	------	------	------	------	------	1	------	------	10	------	------	------	2	------	------	4	1	4
Females 15 years old and over	1,010	1,553	1,511	4,207	5,584	1,640	1,608	762	5,173	1,200	1,537	7	2,249	744	2,137	2,974	2,252	4,528
Single	248	370	379	931	1,393	279	408	205	1,445	212	455	3	584	189	562	629	641	1,129
Married	618	904	838	2,407	2,927	1,010	943	423	2,627	744	863	3	1,338	455	1,220	1,706	1,251	2,621
Widowed	127	220	259	828	1,145	336	253	109	1,026	167	209	1	284	92	314	584	328	727
Divorced	17	58	35	40	117	15	2	25	68	77	9	------	42	8	41	53	31	50
Unknown	------	1	------	1	2	------	2	------	7	------	1	------	1	------	------	2	1	1
FAMILIES																		
Number of families	715	1,080	1,066	2,900	3,774	1,257	1,032	514	3,334	887	1,054	4	1,401	507	1,447	2,184	1,500	3,103
Median size	3.71	4.09	3.69	3.69	3.29	2.95	3.67	4.06	3.68	3.34	4.32	------	4.11	3.75	3.81	2.88	4.03	3.81
Families having—																		
No children under 10	365	483	553	1,444	2,152	730	497	235	1,715	473	440	1	630	268	706	1,326	688	1,462
1 child under 10	134	188	210	554	687	232	226	112	621	186	194	1	299	86	270	379	297	609
2 children under 10	83	154	108	390	385	119	120	72	420	91	137	1	203	52	189	198	199	411
3 or more	133	255	195	512	550	176	189	95	578	137	283	1	269	101	282	281	316	621

CHARACTERISTICS OF NEGRO POPULATION BY COUNTIES: 1930—Continued

(See note at head of table)

SUBJECT	GEORGIA—Continued									IDAHO							
	Wayne	Webster	Wheeler	White	Whitfield	Wilcox	Wilkes	Wilkinson	Worth	The State	Ada	Bannock	Bear Lake	Benewah	Bingham	Boise	Bonner
POPULATION BY SEX																	
Negro population: 1930	2,995	3,038	2,938	384	1,371	5,473	10,088	5,114	9,575	668	101	293	1	12	7	2	1
Male	1,536	1,478	1,448	192	648	2,722	4,864	2,618	4,750	395	65	161	1	7	5	-	-
Female	1,459	1,560	1,490	192	723	2,751	5,224	2,496	4,825	273	36	132	-	5	2	2	1
Negro population: 1920	3,153	3,080	3,562	396	1,345	7,302	16,093	5,624	12,548	920	82	377	6	24	15	1	4
Male	1,614	1,530	1,818	203	631	3,609	8,036	2,892	6,231	585	47	223	4	15	11	1	2
Female	1,539	1,550	1,744	193	714	3,693	8,057	2,732	6,317	335	35	154	2	9	4	-	2
Percent of total population:																	
1930	23.7	60.4	32.1	6.3	6.6	40.7	63.3	47.2	45.4	0.2	0.3	0.9	-	0.2	-	0.1	-
1920	21.9	57.7	36.3	6.5	8.0	47.1	66.5	49.4	52.6	0.2	0.2	1.4	0.1	0.3	0.1	0.1	-
VOTING AGE: 1930																	
Total 21 years old and over	1,542	1,260	1,217	174	680	2,508	4,645	2,388	4,308	518	88	223	1	10	7	1	1
Male	826	601	611	86	312	1,293	2,181	1,216	2,113	310	57	125	1	7	5	-	-
Female	716	659	606	88	368	1,215	2,464	1,172	2,195	208	31	98	-	3	2	1	1
AGE: 1930																	
Under 5 years	330	394	396	47	169	665	1,060	616	1,167	30	2	19	-	1	-	-	-
Under 1 year	69	80	87	9	36	131	216	123	227	5	-	5	-	-	-	-	-
5 to 9 years	342	457	450	61	167	685	1,450	651	1,320	39	3	18	-	-	-	1	-
10 to 14 years	343	412	412	45	155	764	1,420	669	1,258	35	4	12	-	-	-	-	-
15 to 19 years	369	427	387	49	164	706	1,248	690	1,262	40	2	18	-	1	-	-	-
20 to 24 years	335	304	298	40	147	608	866	505	987	40	9	18	-	1	-	-	-
25 to 29 years	263	170	167	29	83	398	537	369	604	45	15	22	-	1	1	-	-
30 to 34 years	178	133	122	18	91	261	445	286	433	68	11	38	-	2	-	-	-
35 to 44 years	348	230	245	37	134	549	1,036	483	900	167	18	88	1	2	4	-	-
45 to 54 years	242	214	226	25	143	403	986	407	814	105	19	35	-	2	2	-	1
55 to 64 years	143	162	134	14	69	246	622	256	473	58	10	19	-	1	-	-	-
65 to 74 years	73	79	71	10	35	131	272	123	228	22	5	5	-	1	-	-	-
75 years and over	22	56	29	8	13	55	143	53	129	19	2	1	-	-	-	1	-
Unknown	7	-	1	1	1	2	3	6	-	-	-	-	-	-	-	-	-
SCHOOL ATTENDANCE																	
Total 7 to 13 years	491	591	590	69	214	1,009	1,989	910	1,790	49	6	23	-	-	-	-	-
Number attending school	440	528	490	63	182	840	1,718	597	1,377	49	6	23	-	-	-	-	-
Percent attending school	89.6	89.3	83.1	-	85.0	83.3	86.4	65.6	76.9	-	-	-	-	-	-	-	-
Total 14 and 15 years, inclusive	113	160	176	21	75	294	553	282	511	17	2	4	-	1	-	-	-
Number attending school	86	106	100	13	48	198	417	139	291	16	2	4	-	1	-	-	-
Percent attending school	76.1	66.3	56.8	-	-	67.3	75.4	49.3	56.9	-	-	-	-	-	-	-	-
Total 16 and 17 years, inclusive	148	177	149	19	67	306	508	277	500	9	-	6	-	-	-	-	-
Number attending school	53	48	45	4	19	103	226	49	129	4	-	4	-	-	-	-	-
Percent attending school	35.8	27.1	30.2	-	-	33.7	44.5	17.7	25.8	-	-	-	-	-	-	-	-
Total 18 to 20 years, inclusive	235	254	226	25	101	411	762	368	773	29	3	13	-	-	-	-	-
Number attending school	21	8	19	-	5	24	112	12	37	7	-	3	-	-	-	-	-
Percent attending school	8.9	3.1	8.4	-	5.0	5.8	14.7	3.3	4.8	-	-	-	-	-	-	-	-
ILLITERACY																	
Total 10 years old and over	2,323	2,187	2,092	276	1,035	4,123	7,578	3,847	7,088	599	96	256	1	11	7	1	1
Number illiterate	476	319	455	39	85	897	1,610	1,085	1,464	25	1	14	-	-	2	-	-
Percent illiterate	20.5	14.6	21.7	14.1	8.2	21.8	21.2	28.2	20.7	4.2	-	5.5	-	-	-	-	-
Percent illiterate in 1920	21.2	33.1	21.4	18.0	20.2	35.8	34.0	24.7	33.3	5.4	-	2.1	-	-	-	-	-
URBAN AND RURAL																	
Urban population	-	-	-	-	1,028	-	1,766	-	-	502	81	267	-	-	-	-	-
Percent urban	-	-	-	-	75.0	-	17.5	-	-	75.1	80.2	91.1	-	-	-	-	-
Rural population	2,995	3,038	2,938	384	343	5,473	8,322	5,114	9,575	166	20	26	1	12	7	2	1
Rural-farm	500	2,655	2,210	225	254	4,252	7,783	3,135	7,434	70	2	12	-	11	1	-	-
Rural-nonfarm	2,495	383	728	159	89	1,221	539	1,979	2,141	96	18	14	1	1	6	2	1
Percent rural	100.0	100.0	100.0	100.0	25.0	100.0	82.5	100.0	100.0	24.9	19.8	8.9	-	-	-	-	-
MARITAL CONDITION																	
Males 15 years old and over	1,030	857	852	110	413	1,673	2,900	1,627	2,863	338	59	137	1	7	5	-	-
Single	313	296	279	40	134	484	917	580	930	118	20	39	1	3	3	-	-
Married	613	508	527	60	247	1,071	1,791	955	1,721	168	29	79	-	3	1	-	-
Widowed	78	51	42	10	32	111	169	83	201	35	5	15	-	1	-	-	-
Divorced	26	2	4	-	-	6	17	9	9	16	5	4	-	-	-	-	-
Unknown	-	-	-	-	-	1	6	-	2	1	-	-	-	-	1	-	-
Females 15 years old and over	950	918	828	121	467	1,686	3,258	1,551	2,967	226	33	107	-	4	2	1	1
Single	191	266	191	44	108	361	923	387	672	27	3	12	-	1	-	-	-
Married	602	517	539	64	266	1,059	1,871	958	1,746	162	25	78	-	2	2	-	1
Widowed	125	130	91	13	87	247	412	192	521	27	5	12	-	1	-	1	-
Divorced	32	4	7	-	6	18	48	13	28	10	-	5	-	-	-	-	-
Unknown	-	1	-	-	-	1	4	1	-	-	-	-	-	-	-	-	-
FAMILIES																	
Number of families	752	620	578	70	314	1,258	2,329	1,157	2,132	229	31	100	-	3	-	1	-
Median size	2.93	4.09	4.33	-	3.31	3.61	3.47	3.59	3.63	1.90	-	2.03	-	-	-	-	-
Families having—																	
No children under 10	443	279	237	30	164	644	1,227	602	1,049	194	26	80	-	2	-	1	-
1 child under 10	133	116	117	13	61	248	421	218	434	17	5	7	-	1	-	-	-
2 children under 10	84	78	81	7	43	166	287	121	246	11	-	10	-	-	-	-	-
3 or more	92	147	143	20	46	200	394	216	403	7	-	3	-	-	-	-	-

CHARACTERISTICS OF NEGRO POPULATION BY COUNTIES: 1930—Continued

(See note at head of table)

SUBJECT	Bonneville	Boundary	Canyon	Cassia	Clark	Custer	Elmore	Fremont	Gooding	Idaho	Jefferson	Kootenai	Latah	Lincoln	Madison	Minidoka	Nez Perce
	IDAHO—Continued																
POPULATION BY SEX																	
Negro population: 1930	66	1	16	2	1	2	3	27	1	3	3	12	15	2	1	4	35
Male	42	1	11	1	1	2	3	19	1	1	1	6	9	2	1	3	20
Female	24		5	1				8		2	2	6	6			1	15
Negro population: 1920	46	1	36	34		4	7	27	10	6	8	7	29	8	4	10	45
Male	28	1	20	24		4	6	15	6	3	8	5	19	6	3	7	32
Female	18		16	10			1	12	4	3		2	10	2	1	3	13
Percent total population:																	
1930	0.3		0.1		0.1	0.1	0.1	0.3				0.1	0.1	0.1			0.2
1920	0.3		0.1	0.2		0.1	0.1	0.3	0.1	0.1	0.1		0.2	0.2		0.1	0.3
VOTING AGE: 1930																	
Total 21 years old and over	44	1	14	1	1	2	3	6	1	3	3	12	11	2	1	4	27
Male	27	1	10		1	2	3	5	1	1	1	6	6	2	1	3	17
Female	17		4	1				1		2	2	6	5			1	10
AGE: 1930																	
Under 5 years	5							3									
Under 1 year																	
5 to 9 years	5							6									4
10 to 14 years	6							6					2				4
15 to 19 years	6		2	1				5					2				
20 to 24 years						1		2						1		1	1
25 to 29 years	1		2													1	
30 to 34 years	3			1				1				1	3				4
35 to 44 years	18		2		1		1	2	1	2	1		2	1	1	1	6
45 to 54 years	12		2					1		1	2	4	2				12
55 to 64 years	6	1	6				1	1				1	2				2
65 to 74 years	1		2									4				1	1
75 years and over	3					1	1					2	2				1
Unknown																	
SCHOOL ATTENDANCE																	
Total 7 to 13 years, inclusive	4							9					2				3
Number attending school	4							9					2				3
Percent attending school																	
Total 14 and 15 years, inclusive	4							2					2				2
Number attending school	3							2					2				2
Percent attending school																	
Total 16 and 17 years, inclusive	1		1														
Number attending school																	
Percent attending school																	
Total 18 to 20 years, inclusive	4		1	1				5									
Number attending school								3									
Percent attending school																	
ILLITERACY																	
Total 10 years old and over	56	1	16	2	1	2	3	18	1	3	3	12	15	2	1	4	31
Number illiterate	2		2										1				1
Percent illiterate																	
Percent illiterate in 1920																	
URBAN AND RURAL																	
Urban population	47		11	1				14				11	1		1		31
Percent urban																	
Rural population	19	1	5	1	1	2	3	13	1	3	3	1	14	2		4	4
Rural-farm	13		3	1		2	1			2	3		9				3
Rural-nonfarm	6	1	2		1		2	13	1	1		1	5	2		4	1
Percent rural																	
MARITAL CONDITION																	
Male 15 years old and over	32	1	11	1	1	2	3	8	1	1	1	6	7	2	1	3	17
Single	8		6		1	2	1	5	1				3	1	1	1	8
Married	17		3	1				2		1	1	5	4			1	6
Widowed	5		2				1	1						1		1	2
Divorced	2	1					1					1					1
Unknown																	
Females 15 years old and over	18		5	1				4		2	2	6	6			1	10
Single			1	1				3					1				
Married	15		4					1		2	2	6	4			1	6
Widowed	2																2
Divorced	1												1				2
Unknown																	
FAMILIES																	
Number of families	24		6			1	2	3		1	1	5	5		1	3	15
Median size																	
Families having:																	
No children under 10	21		6			1	2	1		1	1	5	5		1	3	13
1 child under 10	1																1
2 children under 10																	1
3 or more	2							2									

CHARACTERISTICS OF NEGRO POPULATION BY COUNTIES: 1930—Continued

(See note at head of table)

SUBJECT	IDAHO—Continued						ILLINOIS										
	Owyhee	Payette	Power	Shoshone	Twin Falls	Washington	The State	Adams	Alexander	Bond	Boone	Brown	Bureau	Carroll	Champaign	Christian	Clark
POPULATION BY SEX																	
Negro population: 1930	4	1	4	12	34	2	328,972	1,344	6,591	65	16	4	90	73	2,040	150	15
Male	2	1	3	6	19	1	164,425	661	3,275	36	10	3	54	37	989	77	6
Female	2		1	6	15	1	164,547	683	3,316	29	6	1	36	36	1,051	73	9
Negro population: 1920		3	13	27	42	6	182,274	1,446	6,436	104	35	5	149	119	1,620	134	25
Male		3	9	20	31	6	93,835	718	3,218	54	16	4	83	80	829	71	12
Female			4	7	11		88,439	728	3,218	50	19	1	66	39	791	63	13
Percent of total population:																	
1930	0.1		0.1	0.1	0.1		4.3	2.1	29.2	0.5	0.1	0.1	0.2	0.4	3.2	0.4	0.1
1920			.3	.2	.1	0.1	2.8	2.3	26.8	.6	.2	.1	.3	.6	2.8	.3	.1
VOTING AGE: 1930																	
Total 21 years old and over	4	1	4	12	28	2	226,692	932	4,198	46	11	3	61	58	1,274	92	14
Male	2	1	3	6	15	1	115,261	468	2,118	23	6	3	37	30	611	45	5
Female	2		1	6	13	1	111,431	464	2,080	23	5		24	28	663	47	9
AGE: 1930																	
Under 5 years							25,378	106	464	3	3		6	3	208	7	1
Under 1 year							4,929	22	92				1		51	1	
5 to 9 years					2		25,760	114	558	8	2	1	9	4	196	14	
10 to 14 years					1		22,111	91	633	3			6	4	156	18	
15 to 19 years					3		23,363	82	621	5			8	4	173	17	
20 to 24 years	1			2	3		33,264	107	557	1		1	3	5	166	6	1
25 to 29 years					2		41,279	109	506	2	4	1	2	8	181	13	
30 to 34 years			1		3		36,531	117	522	3	3		7	11	171	12	4
35 to 44 years	1		1	2	11		61,767	197	1,111	6	2		13	12	352	19	2
45 to 54 years			1	2	6	1	36,442	188	949	10		1	12	13	233	19	2
55 to 64 years	1	1	1	3	2		14,462	110	445	11	1		13	5	118	12	
65 to 74 years	1				1		5,720	63	149	9	1		9	2	60	10	4
75 years and over				3		1	2,354	48	74	4			2	2	23	3	1
Unknown							541	12	2						3		
SCHOOL ATTENDANCE																	
Total 7 to 13 years, inclusive					2		33,053	142	824	5	2		12	5	248	25	
Number attending school					2		31,985	141	768	4	1		11	4	243	25	
Percent attending school							96.8	99.3	93.2						98.0		
Total 14 and 15 years, inclusive							8,417	41	257	2			3	2	59	8	
Number attending school							7,670	36	222				3	2	55	7	
Percent attending school							91.1		86.4								
Total 16 and 17 years, inclusive					1		8,886	23	250	2			3	2	72	9	
Number attending school							4,939	13	124	1			1	2	44	7	
Percent attending school							55.6		49.6								
Total 18 to 20 years, inclusive					2		16,055	58	376	2			3	1	106	7	
Number attending school					1		2,515	4	35	1			1		27	4	
Percent attending school							15.7		9.3						25.5		
ILLITERACY																	
Total 10 years old and over	4	1	4	12	32	2	277,834	1,124	5,569	54	11	3	75	66	1,636	129	14
Number illiterate				2			10,044	113	481	17			5	11	123	3	2
Percent illiterate							3.6	10.1	8.6						7.5	2.3	
Percent illiterate in 1920							6.7	16.1	13.8				11.1	12.5	7.6	9.1	
URBAN AND RURAL																	
Urban population				6	30	1	304,036	1,145	4,575	31	15		75	71	1,992	87	
Percent urban							92.4	85.2	69.4						97.6	58.0	
Rural population	4	1	4	6	4	1	24,936	199	2,016	34	1	4	15	2	48	63	15
Rural-farm	4				2	1	5,479	14	869	21	1	1		2	19	15	1
Rural-nonfarm		1	4	6	2		19,457	185	1,147	13		3	15		29	48	14
Percent rural							7.6	14.8	30.6						2.4	42.0	
MARITAL CONDITION																	
Males 15 years old and over	2	1	3	6	18	1	128,527	521	2,459	27	6	3	43	30	705	57	5
Single	1	1	3	2	6	1	39,768	155	811	7	2	2	18	11	189	16	2
Married	1			2	12		76,887	288	1,436	15	3		18	12	453	33	2
Widowed				1			8,799	55	156	5		1	6	4	40	6	1
Divorced				1			2,866	23	53		1		1	3	23	2	
Unknown							207		3								
Females 15 years old and over	2		1	6	13	1	127,196	512	2,477	24	5		26	32	775	54	9
Single	1		1	2	1		22,349	88	535	3			3	11	133	12	1
Married	1			1	11		77,865	291	1,480	16	4		17	11	481	32	5
Widowed				2	1	1	23,112	115	397	5	1		5	9	139	9	3
Divorced				1			3,722	18	62				1	1	21	1	
Unknown							148		3						1		
FAMILIES																	
Number of families	1	1	3	5	15	2	78,737	413	1,955	21	2	1	35	26	551	39	4
Median size							267	241	244						280		
Families having:																	
No children under 10	1	1	3	5	13	2	55,174	302	1,440	14	1	1	29	22	361	28	3
1 child under 10					2		10,877	55	242	4			2	2	89	4	1
2 children under 10							6,172	32	146	2			1	2	49	6	
3 or more							6,514	24	127	1	1		3		52	1	

CHARACTERISTICS OF NEGRO POPULATION BY COUNTIES: 1930—Continued

(See note at head of table)

SUBJECT	ILLINOIS—Continued																
	Clay	Clinton	Coles	Cook	Crawford	De Kalb	De Witt	Douglas	Du Page	Edgar	Edwards	Effingham	Fayette	Ford	Franklin	Fulton	Gallatin
POPULATION BY SEX																	
Negro population: 1930	13	173	179	246, 992	3	209	56	27	319	258	65	14	64	47	125	124	226
Male	6	90	91	121, 764	2	106	32	15	127	130	35	5	59	19	64	61	117
Female	7	83	88	125, 228	1	103	24	12	192	128	30	9	5	28	61	63	109
Negro population: 1920	11	188	213	115, 238	51	199	111	78	154	298	78	18	10	96	175	168	378
Male	6	99	109	58, 721	27	99	61	41	62	144	46	10	6	43	93	93	201
Female	5	89	104	56, 517	24	100	50	37	92	154	32	8	4	53	82	75	177
Percent of total population:																	
1930	0. 1	0. 8	0. 5	6. 2		0. 6	0. 3	0. 2	0. 3	1. 0	0. 8	0. 1	0. 3	0. 3	0. 2	0. 3	2. 2
1920	0. 1	0. 8	0. 6	3. 8	0. 2	0. 6	0. 6	0. 4	0. 4	1. 2	0. 8	0. 1		0. 6	0. 3	0. 3	2. 9
VOTING AGE: 1930																	
Total 21 years old and over	7	97	112	174, 850	2	118	39	20	219	164	45	5	57	32	79	68	130
Male	3	54	57	87, 502	1	64	23	11	87	83	27	1	52	13	42	35	66
Female	4	43	55	87, 348	1	54	16	9	132	81	18	4	5	19	37	33	64
AGE: 1930																	
Under 5 years	2	17	13	18, 594		20	1		22	14	5	3		2	9	9	23
Under 1 year		3	2	3, 654		4			4	2	3	1		1	2	2	4
5 to 9 years	3	19	15	18, 222	1	21	5	1	28	22	5			2	14	14	24
10 to 14 years	1	21	21	15, 005		27	4	3	20	32	3	5	1	2	15	18	28
15 to 19 years		16	16	16, 076		22	7	3	23	24	7	1	4	9	5	13	19
20 to 24 years	1	16	13	26, 121		12	1		24	17	3	1	12	1	9	8	19
25 to 29 years	2	15	5	33, 911		9	3		32	9	1		9		9	2	14
30 to 34 years		12	9	29, 643		13	3		42	9	6	1	12	2	11	4	13
35 to 44 years	1	15	23	48, 404		26	9	3	57	32	10	3	18	12	24	20	22
45 to 54 years	1	18	32	26, 556	1	33	15	6	39	53	4		5	6	18	22	31
55 to 64 years		11	16	9, 474	1	18	5	7	23	23	9			4	4	9	23
65 to 74 years	2	9	10	3, 428		4	2	3	7	18	5			3	5	4	8
75 years and over		4	6	1, 189		4	1	1	1	5	6		2	4	2	1	2
Unknown				369					1		1		1				
SCHOOL ATTENDANCE																	
Total 7 to 13 years, inclusive	3	32	25	22, 885	1	34	8	2	34	41	7	3	1	2	20	27	32
Number attending school	1	32	25	22, 156	1	32	8	2	34	41	6	3	1	2	20	26	27
Percent attending school				96. 8													
Total 14 and 15 years, inclusive		4	8	5, 566		13	1	2	8	13	4	2		2	4	4	12
Number attending school		3	8	5, 170		12	1	2	7	13	4	2		2	4	4	7
Percent attending school				92. 9													
Total 16 and 17 years, inclusive		4	9	5, 973		8	1	1	6	8	1		3	3	2	6	4
Number attending school		2	7	3, 391		4	1	1	3	6	1			2	2	5	
Percent attending school				56. 8													
Total 18 to 20 years, inclusive		12	6	11, 655		9	5	2	20	13	2	1	3	5	5	7	11
Number attending school		4	2	1, 765		4	2		4	1	1					1	
Percent attending school				15. 1													
ILLITERACY																	
Total 10 years old and over	8	137	151	210, 176	2	168	50	26	269	222	55	11	64	43	102	101	179
Number illiterate		11	8	4, 958		13	4	2	6	9	7		7	4	14	7	38
Percent illiterate		8. 0	5. 3	2. 4		7. 7			2. 2	4. 1					13. 7	6. 9	21. 2
Percent illiterate in 1920		8. 3	8. 8	4. 0		6. 7			7. 6	10. 4					9. 8	6. 5	22. 3
URBAN AND RURAL																	
Urban population			162	244, 871		136	41	26	274	253		5		3		67	
Percent urban			90. 5	99. 1		65. 1			85. 9	98. 1						54. 0	
Rural population	13	173	17	2, 121	3	73	15	1	45	5	65	9	64	44	125	57	226
Rural-farm	11	17	5	9	3	15	5		19	1	5	1	9	2		22	27
Rural-nonfarm	2	156	12	2, 112		58	10	1	26	4	60	8	55	42	125	35	199
Percent rural		100. 0	9. 5	. 9		34. 9			14. 1	1. 9					100. 0	46. 0	100. 0
MARITAL CONDITION																	
Males 15 years old and over	3	66	68	96, 461	1	74	26	13	97	93	30	2	58	18	46	40	77
Single	1	29	18	29, 083		20	12	4	26	25	13	1	31	6	5	14	21
Married	2	25	43	58, 660	1	50	11	7	65	56	13	1	27	11	37	24	51
Widowed		11	6	6, 578		2	3	1	4	8	4			1	2		4
Divorced		1	1	1, 992		2		1	2	4					2	2	1
Unknown				148													
Females 15 years old and over	4	50	62	98, 710	1	67	20	10	152	97	22	4	5	23	41	43	74
Single	1	12	9	16, 723		15	4	1	39	23	5	2	3	5	2	13	13
Married	2	26	42	60, 216	1	43	14	6	71	54	11	2	2	11	33	24	50
Widowed	1	11	10	18, 647		7	2	3	31	19	5			7	5	6	8
Divorced		1	1	3, 020		2			7	1	1				1		3
Unknown				104					4								
FAMILIES																	
Number of families	3	39	51	57, 969	1	50	19	9	54	77	22	1	2	14	41	30	58
Median size				2. 66													
Families having—																	
No children under 10	2	22	38	40, 997		33	17	8	33	56	18		2	12	27	21	36
1 child under 10		5	3	7, 966	1	6		1	8	12	2			1	7	3	8
2 children under 10		7	3	4, 466		3	1		5	7	1	1			5	3	8
3 or more	1	5	7	4, 540		8	1		8	2	1			1	2	3	6

CHARACTERISTICS OF NEGRO POPULATION BY COUNTIES: 1930—Continued

(See note at head of table)

SUBJECT	Greene	Grundy	Hancock	Hardin	Henderson	Henry	Iroquois	Jackson	Jasper	Jefferson	Jersey	Jo Daviess	Johnson	Kane	Kankakee	Kendall	Knox	Lake
	ILLINOIS—Continued																	
POPULATION BY SEX																		
Negro population: 1930	24	29	22	60	38	310	105	2, 608	22	613	55	32	171	1, 787	979	27	1, 108	2, 356
Male	12	15	10	25	18	148	51	1, 282	10	315	29	19	93	937	517	16	567	1, 153
Female	12	14	12	35	20	162	54	1, 326	12	298	26	13	78	850	462	11	541	1, 203
Negro population: 1920	56	47	34	83	28	253	198	2, 733	26	493	60	41	116	1, 015	422	18	955	858
Male	27	19	15	41	17	144	104	1, 383	12	235	29	26	62	534	237	13	496	444
Female	29	28	19	42	11	109	94	1, 350	14	258	31	15	54	481	185	5	459	414
Percent of total population:																		
1930	0. 1	0. 2	0. 1	0. 9	0. 4	0. 7	0. 3	7. 3	0. 2	2. 0	0. 4	0. 2	1. 7	1. 4	2. 0	0. 3	2. 2	2. 3
1920	0. 2	0. 3	0. 1	1. 1	0. 3	0. 6	0. 6	7. 4	0. 2	1. 7	0. 5	0. 2	1. 0	1. 0	0. 9	0. 2	2. 0	1. 2
VOTING AGE: 1930																		
Total, 21 years old and over	15	17	19	38	33	184	61	1, 590	12	402	33	25	101	1, 061	692	19	784	1, 556
Male	8	10	9	18	17	100	33	778	5	210	17	16	54	568	382	11	393	778
Female	7	7	10	20	16	84	28	812	7	192	16	9	47	493	310	8	391	778
AGE: 1930																		
Under 5 years	1	2		4	1	30	7	197	1	43	4	3	13	100	81	1	81	213
Under 1 year		1		2		4	2	41		4	1		2	17	15		17	40
5 to 9 years	1	7		7		25	8	278	3	52	8	1	15	105	70	2	76	228
10 to 14 years	1		2	5	2	34	12	245	2	54	5	1	23	166	62	3	74	171
15 to 19 years	5	3	1	5	2	32	15	244	3	57	4	2	17	340	57	1	73	148
20 to 24 years	3			7	2	26	4	197	3	41	1	2	21	129	81	3	105	214
25 to 29 years	2	1	2	4	1	28	4	189		66	2	3	14	136	106	4	90	305
30 to 34 years		2	1	4	2	14	6	163		51	5	6	5	173	92	3	88	267
35 to 44 years	6	6	8	6	12	50	15	451	3	88	8	6	19	289	194	6	181	392
45 to 54 years	2	4	1	5	4	36	21	308	4	82	9	4	19	191	128	1	179	262
55 to 64 years	1	1		7	12	17	8	197		50	6	2	15	100	61	1	76	87
65 to 74 years		2	3	5		11	4	76	1	21	3	2	6	38	29	2	51	51
75 years and over	2	1	4	1		7	1	42	2	6			4	20	16		32	14
Unknown								21		2					2		2	4
SCHOOL ATTENDANCE																		
Total 7 to 13 years, inclusive	2	3	2	11	1	39	18	361	4	77	8	2	28	160	96	3	105	279
Number attending school	2	3	2	11	1	39	18	341	3	76	6	1	24	151	94	3	105	279
Percent attending school								94. 5						94. 4			100. 0	100. 0
Total 14 and 15 years, inclusive		1	1	3	2	17	5	105	1	22	3		7	144	11	1	32	57
Number attending school			1	3	2	15	5	97	1	17	3		5	106	9	1	27	56
Percent attending school								92. 4						73. 6				
Total 16 and 17 years, inclusive	2	1			1	15	7	116	1	23	1	1	6	173	29		26	57
Number attending school		1			1	10	6	81		12			2	99	19		8	29
Percent attending school								69. 8						57. 2				
Total 18 to 20 years, inclusive	4	1		3		15	6	139	2	27	2	1	10	101	41	2	51	101
Number attending school	1			1		3	1	48	1	8	1			9	7		9	20
Percent attending school								34. 5						8. 9				19. 8
ILLITERACY																		
Total 10 years old and over	22	20	22	49	37	255	90	2, 133	18	518	43	28	143	1, 582	828	24	951	1, 915
Number illiterate	1		4	11	3	26	5	192		47	4	1	25	35	38	3	57	96
Percent illiterate						10. 2		9. 0		9. 1			17. 5	2. 2	4. 6		6. 0	5. 0
Percent illiterate in 1920						9. 5	7. 0	12. 9		12. 8				5. 2	13. 1		7. 8	4. 7
URBAN AND RURAL																		
Urban population		9				300	38	2, 158		560	34	16		1, 562	571		897	2, 015
Percent urban						96. 8	36. 2	82. 7		91. 4				87. 4	58. 3		81. 0	85. 5
Rural population	24	20	22	60	38	10	67	450	22	53	21	16	171	225	408	27	211	341
Rural-farm		2	1	15	22	1	16	109	21	26	21	2	59	4	55	14	1	10
Rural-nonfarm	24	18	21	45	16	9	51	341	1	27		14	112	221	353	13	210	331
Percent rural						3. 2	63. 8	17. 3		8. 6				12. 6	41. 7		19. 0	14. 5
MARITAL CONDITION																		
Males 15 years old and over	11	11	9	21	18	117	43	927	6	241	19	18	65	747	418	12	436	851
Single	5	3	1	9	5	33	20	289	2	84	8	10	25	345	168	6	121	217
Married	6	4	7	11	12	77	18	542	4	135	7	7	37	346	207	6	263	573
Widowed		4	1	1	1	7	5	76		19	4	1	2	36	29		37	45
Divorced								20		2				19	10		15	15
Unknown										1			1	1	4			1
Females 15 years old and over	10	9	11	23	17	104	35	961	10	223	19	9	55	669	348	9	441	893
Single	5	4	3	7	2	13	10	203	5	45	8	3	6	209	54	3	76	148
Married	5	5	5	10	13	81	17	553	4	138	7	4	37	339	232	6	270	589
Widowed			2	4	2	7	7	177	1	35	4	2	12	98	50		88	126
Divorced			1	2		3	1	27		4				22	12		7	30
Unknown								1		1				1				
FAMILIES																		
Number of families	6	8	7	15	15	83	30	745	5	163	13	8	45	321	179	7	334	522
Median size								2. 64		2. 90				2. 73	2. 78		2. 46	2. 95
Families having—																		
No children under 10	5	6	7	10	14	58	24	517	3	108	8	6	31	221	115	5	253	327
1 child under 10				2	1	12		107	1	32	2	1	8	48	23	1	42	74
2 children under 10	1			2		6	4	48		10	1			30	11	1	22	60
3 or more		2		1		7	2	73	1	13	2	1	6	22	30		17	61

CHARACTERISTICS OF NEGRO POPULATION BY COUNTIES: 1930—Continued

(See note at head of table)

SUBJECT	ILLINOIS—Continued																	
	La Salle	Lawrence	Lee	Livingston	Logan	McDonough	McHenry	McLean	Macon	Macoupin	Madison	Marion	Marshall	Massac	Menard	Mercer	Monroe	Montgomery
POPULATION BY SEX																		
Negro population: 1930	313	276	328	540	355	121	35	964	1,976	46	6,750	1,164	10	1,719	49	14	3	235
Male	152	139	190	479	204	62	15	511	984	23	3,462	595	7	840	22	6	2	121
Female	161	137	138	61	151	59	20	453	992	23	3,288	569	3	879	27	8	1	114
Negro population: 1920	332	214	117	346	353	126	24	1,060	1,283	82	3,981	1,054	29	2,057	71	24	18	257
Male	168	112	61	265	183	60	15	528	651	44	2,079	501	18	1,032	38	13	14	129
Female	164	102	56	81	170	66	9	532	632	38	1,902	553	11	1,025	33	11	4	128
Percent of total population:																		
1930	0.3	1.3	1.0	1.4	1.2	0.4	0.1	1.3	2.4	0.1	4.7	3.3	0.1	12.2	0.5	0.1	-	0.7
1920	0.4	1.0	0.4	0.9	1.2	0.5	0.1	1.5	2.0	0.1	3.7	2.8	0.2	15.2	0.6	0.1	0.1	0.6
VOTING AGE: 1930																		
Total 21 years old and over	211	148	163	277	174	65	22	615	1,204	38	4,235	657	8	1,023	31	9	3	128
Male	106	75	95	236	89	37	8	339	623	20	2,265	335	5	506	16	4	2	64
Female	105	73	68	41	85	28	14	276	581	18	1,970	322	3	517	15	5	1	64
AGE: 1930																		
Under 5 years	23	26	6	10	11	12	-	84	180	-	650	129	1	129	9	1	-	33
Under 1 year	7	3	3	2	3	-	-	23	35	-	117	28	-	17	1	-	-	7
5 to 9 years	21	30	25	6	27	13	2	92	204	-	669	131	-	201	2	-	-	27
10 to 14 years	27	37	47	10	57	16	4	63	182	2	548	120	-	171	5	2	-	28
15 to 19 years	28	32	76	158	78	11	6	88	173	4	544	111	1	169	2	2	-	18
20 to 24 years	16	17	37	246	35	11	2	84	168	6	634	91	-	123	1	-	1	11
25 to 29 years	34	14	30	44	18	5	3	65	166	1	720	76	2	82	2	-	-	17
30 to 34 years	27	17	27	5	17	5	1	83	194	-	600	85	2	79	6	1	-	15
35 to 44 years	54	38	39	17	38	15	10	147	317	7	1,114	181	2	251	4	-	1	29
45 to 54 years	46	28	20	17	35	17	5	145	238	8	702	131	-	234	5	4	1	18
55 to 64 years	26	19	12	12	20	7	-	69	106	9	341	58	1	151	9	4	-	26
65 to 74 years	4	10	8	8	16	6	-	22	36	2	134	30	1	83	4	-	-	6
75 years and over	7	8	1	6	3	3	2	22	12	7	87	10	-	46	-	-	-	7
Unknown	-	-	-	1	-	-	-	-	-	-	7	11	-	-	-	-	-	-
SCHOOL ATTENDANCE																		
Total 7 to 13 years, inclusive	30	51	47	13	64	25	5	110	252	2	846	181	-	254	5	2	-	38
Number attending school	29	51	31	13	63	24	5	107	245	2	826	177	-	244	5	2	-	37
Percent attending school	-	-	-	-	-	-	-	97.3	97.2	-	97.6	97.8	-	96.1	-	-	-	-
Total 14 and 15 years, inclusive	15	10	31	4	30	3	1	23	71	1	199	36	1	74	2	1	-	9
Number attending school	11	9	21	4	19	3	1	22	61	1	173	34	1	68	2	1	-	9
Percent attending school	-	-	-	-	-	-	-	-	-	-	86.9	-	-	-	-	-	-	-
Total 16 and 17 years, inclusive	14	10	30	36	29	5	3	43	66	2	201	47	-	75	1	1	-	6
Number attending school	7	8	7	24	10	1	3	20	31	-	80	23	-	37	1	1	-	5
Percent attending school	-	-	-	-	-	-	-	-	-	-	39.8	-	-	-	-	-	-	-
Total 18 to 20 years, inclusive	11	19	42	197	41	8	4	55	109	3	335	63	-	81	1	-	-	9
Number attending school	3	7	3	116	5	2	2	13	10	2	21	15	-	21	1	-	-	2
Percent attending school	-	-	-	58.9	-	-	-	-	9.2	-	6.3	-	-	-	-	-	-	-
ILLITERACY																		
Total 10 years old and over	269	220	297	524	317	96	33	788	1,592	46	5,431	904	9	1,389	38	13	3	175
Number illiterate	21	12	77	14	17	7	-	57	81	1	308	72	-	196	6	3	-	13
Percent illiterate	7.8	5.5	25.9	2.7	5.4	-	-	7.2	5.1	-	5.7	8.0	-	14.1	-	-	-	7.4
Percent illiterate in 1920	6.7	8.9	8.8	16.1	14.9	-	-	9.9	9.7	-	9.0	7.1	-	14.3	-	-	-	11.3
URBAN AND RURAL																		
Urban population	289	107	125	483	309	121	26	903	1,947	8	6,071	1,109	-	613	-	-	-	215
Percent urban	92.3	38.8	38.1	89.4	87.0	100.0	-	93.7	98.5	-	89.9	95.3	-	35.7	-	-	-	91.5
Rural population	24	169	203	57	46	-	9	61	29	38	679	55	10	1,106	49	14	3	20
Rural-farm	-	102	6	2	26	-	2	23	12	25	196	28	5	487	-	-	2	1
Rural-nonfarm	24	67	197	55	20	-	7	38	17	13	483	27	5	619	49	14	1	19
Percent rural	7.7	61.2	61.9	10.6	13.0	-	-	6.3	1.5	-	10.1	4.7	-	64.3	-	-	-	8.5
MARITAL CONDITION																		
Males 15 years old and over	121	94	142	468	149	43	10	388	712	22	2,568	382	6	594	18	5	2	76
Single	43	33	95	360	93	13	5	158	180	8	775	93	2	174	5	1	2	17
Married	65	54	37	100	51	27	5	194	466	9	1,604	265	2	340	9	4	-	48
Widowed	7	4	4	5	5	3	-	24	47	4	150	20	2	68	3	-	-	11
Divorced	6	3	3	3	-	-	-	12	19	-	34	4	-	11	1	-	-	-
Unknown	-	-	3	-	-	-	-	-	-	1	5	-	-	1	-	-	-	-
Females 15 years old and over	121	89	108	46	111	37	19	337	698	22	2,315	402	3	624	15	6	1	71
Single	29	22	61	10	45	7	8	77	121	6	378	73	1	138	2	2	1	9
Married	71	54	35	24	51	27	5	195	479	11	1,582	271	1	359	8	2	-	49
Widowed	18	11	8	12	14	2	6	54	86	5	313	52	1	110	4	2	-	13
Divorced	3	1	3	-	1	1	-	11	12	-	40	5	-	16	1	-	-	-
Unknown	-	1	1	-	-	-	-	-	-	-	2	1	-	1	-	-	-	-
FAMILIES																		
Number of families	90	65	31	35	65	34	7	239	497	14	1,765	314	3	468	18	5	1	62
Median size	-	-	-	-	-	-	-	2.70	2.91	-	2.81	2.95	-	2.65	-	-	-	-
Families having—																		
No children under 10	72	38	24	28	51	23	6	169	326	14	1,141	183	2	319	13	5	1	43
1 child under 10	10	11	2	2	9	5	-	31	76	-	275	65	1	66	2	-	-	5
2 children under 10	2	12	3	2	3	1	1	21	39	-	162	31	-	34	1	-	-	4
3 or more	6	4	2	3	2	5	-	18	56	-	187	35	-	49	2	-	-	10

CHARACTERISTICS OF NEGRO POPULATION BY COUNTIES: 1930—Continued

(See note at head of table)

ILLINOIS—Continued

SUBJECT	Morgan	Ogle	Peoria	Perry	Piatt	Pike	Pope	Pulaski	Putnam	Randolph	Richland	Rock Island	St. Clair	Saline	Sangamon	Schuyler	Scott	Shelby
POPULATION BY SEX																		
Negro population: 1930	1,127	26	3,216	649	9	53	167	4,946	5	1,508	2	1,488	15,550	1,542	3,635	2	18	23
Male	540	16	1,743	319	5	29	89	2,515	3	1,005	1	790	7,772	802	1,814	1	9	14
Female	587	10	1,473	330	4	24	78	2,431	2	503	1	698	7,778	740	1,821	1	9	9
Negro population: 1920	1,232	19	2,334	554	9	88	341	4,969	9	1,592	2	1,553	10,136	1,490	3,256	-	22	64
Male	622	9	1,281	277	3	41	171	2,509	3	1,013	1	865	5,397	800	1,658	-	10	36
Female	610	10	1,053	277	6	47	170	2,460	6	579	1	688	4,739	690	1,598	-	12	28
Percent of total population:																		
1930	3.3	0.1	2.3	2.9	0.1	0.2	2.1	33.3	0.1	5.1	-	1.5	9.9	4.2	3.3	-	0.2	0.1
1920	3.7	0.1	2.1	2.4	0.1	0.3	3.5	34.0	0.1	5.5	-	1.7	7.4	3.9	3.2	-	0.2	0.2
VOTING AGE: 1930																		
Total 21 years old and over	791	20	2,171	405	5	35	104	2,761	3	1,098	2	986	9,420	897	2,400	2	9	19
Male	401	11	1,203	191	2	20	58	1,401	2	809	1	538	4,831	474	1,193	1	3	11
Female	390	9	968	214	3	15	46	1,360	1	289	1	448	4,589	423	1,207	1	6	8
VOTIFG AGE: 1930																		
Under 5 years	58	-	191	47	-	4	12	474	1	76	-	123	1,587	152	279	-	1	-
Under 1 year	8	-	33	4	-	-	3	84	-	17	-	28	300	28	46	-	-	-
5 to 9 years	89	4	253	78	1	5	12	519	1	120	-	129	1,559	179	330	-	-	1
10 to 14 years	93	1	280	57	2	2	14	537	-	111	-	120	1,368	167	284	-	6	1
15 to 19 years	81	1	262	53	1	7	24	560	-	86	-	105	1,322	129	280	-	2	2
20 to 24 years	76	3	302	44	-	1	5	386	-	98	-	121	1,523	100	291	-	-	1
25 to 29 years	64	7	313	46	-	2	5	276	-	165	1	140	1,652	125	312	-	-	-
30 to 34 years	79	1	282	42	-	2	8	263	-	159	-	127	1,446	112	280	-	2	-
35 to 44 years	162	1	661	96	1	4	28	659	1	279	-	235	2,613	221	542	1	3	3
45 to 54 years	183	4	411	89	3	6	23	578	1	203	-	221	1,533	168	515	-	3	7
55 to 64 years	126	3	154	53	-	8	18	400	1	113	-	96	579	95	291	-	-	-
65 to 74 years	55	-	80	31	-	8	15	192	-	56	1	47	234	69	158	1	1	5
75 years and over	36	1	26	11	1	4	3	102	-	37	-	23	89	23	69	-	-	3
Unknown	25	-	1	2	-	-	-	-	-	5	-	1	45	2	4	-	-	-
SCHOOL ATTENDANCE																		
Total 7 to 13 years, inclusive	131	3	369	89	3	5	16	729	1	172	-	176	2,032	238	411	-	5	2
Number attending school	117	3	359	87	3	5	16	703	1	170	-	172	1,979	237	407	-	5	2
Percent attending school	89.3	-	97.3	-	-	-	-	96.4	-	98.8	-	97.7	97.4	99.6	99.0	-	-	-
Total 14 and 15 years, inclusive	32	-	110	23	-	1	11	239	-	37	-	51	503	53	125	-	1	-
Number attending school	27	-	97	22	-	1	10	209	-	33	-	45	453	50	110	-	1	-
Percent attending school	-	-	88.2	-	-	-	-	87.4	-	-	-	-	90.1	-	88.0	-	-	-
Total 16 and 17 years, inclusive	37	-	91	18	-	5	14	221	-	30	-	38	516	59	124	-	1	1
Number attending school	19	-	52	14	-	4	6	114	-	18	-	18	265	40	65	-	1	1
Percent attending school	-	-	-	-	-	-	-	51.6	-	-	-	-	51.4	-	52.4	-	-	-
Total 18 to 20 years, inclusive	45	1	188	35	1	2	5	304	-	53	-	63	864	68	165	-	1	1
Number attending school	10	1	23	9	-	-	3	52	-	8	-	8	104	13	23	-	1	-
Percent attending school	-	-	12.2	-	-	-	-	17.1	-	-	-	-	12.0	-	13.9	-	-	-
ILLITERACY																		
Total 10 years and over	980	22	2,772	524	8	44	143	3,953	3	1,312	2	1,236	12,404	1,211	3,026	2	17	22
Number illiterate	144	1	79	42	1	5	21	561	-	130	-	56	822	115	193	-	-	3
Percent illiterate	14.7	-	2.8	8.0	-	-	14.7	14.2	-	9.9	-	4.5	6.6	9.5	6.4	-	-	-
Percent illiterate in 1920	13.2	-	8.9	6.1	-	-	19.2	14.6	-	11.8	-	5.8	12.7	11.3	10.2	-	-	-
URBAN AND RURAL																		
Urban population	1,053	6	3,046	596	-	-	-	873	-	623	2	1,452	11,715	532	3,324	-	-	15
Percent urban	93.4	-	94.7	91.8	-	-	-	17.7	-	41.3	-	97.6	75.3	34.5	91.4	-	-	-
Rural population	74	20	170	53	9	53	167	4,073	5	885	-	36	3,835	1,010	311	2	18	8
Rural-farm	45	5	16	31	-	19	96	2,149	-	121	-	1	91	250	70	-	6	6
Rural-nonfarm	29	15	154	22	9	34	71	1,924	5	764	-	35	3,744	760	241	2	12	2
Percent rural	6.6	-	5.3	8.2	-	-	100.0	82.3	-	58.7	-	2.4	24.7	65.5	8.6	-	-	-
MARITAL CONDITION																		
Males 15 years old and over	449	12	1,351	218	3	26	69	1,724	2	858	1	596	5,589	550	1,365	1	4	13
Single	185	3	604	66	1	9	23	490	-	326	1	167	1,597	159	391	1	1	6
Married	216	7	587	117	1	11	34	1,048	2	424	-	360	3,528	338	802	-	3	5
Widowed	33	2	63	22	1	5	9	150	-	71	-	51	386	39	107	-	-	2
Divorced	9	-	93	11	-	1	3	36	-	36	-	18	71	14	60	-	-	-
Unknown	6	-	4	2	-	-	-	-	-	1	-	-	7	-	5	-	-	-
Females 15 years and over	438	9	1,141	249	3	16	60	1,692	1	343	1	520	5,447	494	1,377	1	7	8
Single	99	-	331	51	1	2	16	333	-	70	-	81	996	72	258	-	2	2
Married	244	7	577	134	2	8	34	1,062	1	211	-	354	3,528	339	826	-	3	5
Widowed	83	2	166	53	-	6	9	249	-	57	1	76	839	67	234	1	2	1
Divorced	11	-	64	11	-	-	1	48	-	4	-	8	72	16	55	-	-	-
Unknown	1	-	3	-	-	-	-	-	-	1	-	1	12	-	4	-	-	-
FAMILIES																		
Number of families	317	4	62	190	2	21	47	1,293	1	283	1	366	4,059	399	991	1	4	8
Median size	2.35	-	2.53	2.68	-	-	-	2.97	-	2.67	-	2.71	2.81	3.01	2.45	-	-	-
Families having—																		
No children under 10	238	3	480	134	1	18	36	859	-	198	1	246	2,628	256	711	1	3	7
1 child under 10	47	-	77	27	1	1	4	166	-	29	-	58	626	54	126	-	1	1
2 children under 10	18	-	47	10	-	1	5	114	1	28	-	29	371	32	76	-	-	-
3 or more	14	1	58	19	-	1	2	154	-	28	-	33	434	57	78	-	-	-

CHARACTERISTICS OF NEGRO POPULATION BY COUNTIES: 1930—Continued

(See note at head of table)

SUBJECT	ILLINOIS—Continued															INDIANA		
	Stark	Stephenson	Tazewell	Union	Vermilion	Wabash	Warren	Washington	Wayne	White	Whiteside	Will	Williamson	Winnebago	Woodford	The State	Adams	Allen
POPULATION BY SEX																		
Negro population: 1930	6	521	42	157	3,250	4	441	14	1	194	54	3,131	1,358	1,305	2	111,982	5	2,379
Male	5	269	21	90	1,686	2	227	9	1	105	31	2,230	704	675	1	57,068	2	1,247
Female	1	252	21	67	1,564	2	214	5		89	23	901	654	630	1	54,914	3	1,132
Negro population: 1920	7	395	57	188	2,899	5	500	36	7	241	52	1,374	1,825	581	31	80,810		1,471
Male	4	201	27	99	1,511	4	247	20	5	122	28	874	963	319	17	41,817		786
Female	3	194	30	89	1,388	1	253	16	2	119	24	500	862	262	14	38,993		685
Percent of total population:																		
1930	0.1	1.3	0.1	0.8	3.6		2.0	0.1		1.1	0.1	2.8	2.5	1.1		3.5		1.6
1920	0.1	1.0	0.1	0.9	3.4		2.3	0.2		1.2	0.1	1.5	3.0	0.6	0.2	2.8		1.3
VOTING AGE: 1930																		
Total 21 years old and over	4	337	18	147	2,089	4	290	14	1	121	43	2,458	793	858	1	73,642	4	1,578
Male	3	198	9	86	1,141	2	150	9	1	69	25	1,873	405	441		38,250	2	846
Female	1	139	9	61	948	2	140	5		52	18	585	388	417	1	35,392	2	732
AGE: 1930																		
Under 5 years	2	63			252		33			11	2	151	129	109		9,142		208
Under 1 year	1	17			50		9			3		22	18	17		1,654		37
5 to 9 years		42	9	1	275		38			17	3	166	177	114		9,967		225
10 to 14 years		39	8	3	305		33			22	1	130	120	109		8,477		180
15 to 19 years		32	6	4	286		40			20	5	174	120	95	1	8,746	1	155
20 to 24 years		50	3	4	216		33			13	4	372	85	106		10,184		216
25 to 29 years		59		6	206		18			8	8	564	84	135		11,583	1	259
30 to 34 years		53	1	7	261	1	23			8	3	469	77	149		10,802		291
35 to 44 years	2	104	11	21	550		62	2		20	18	583	236	251		19,234		425
45 to 54 years	1	57	4	37	448		58	2		25	2	340	189	149	1	13,123	1	242
55 to 64 years		10		28	279	2	56	6	1	21	2	126	91	50		6,277	2	105
65 to 74 years	1	6		21	96	1	33	1		19	5	37	36	21		2,894		49
75 years and over		4		19	75		14	3		9	1	18	14	11		1,244		17
Unknown		2		6	1					1		1		6		309		7
SCHOOL ATTENDANCE																		
Total 7 to 13 years, inclusive		57	14	4	409		45			28	3	209	191	167		12,781		293
Number attending school		55	14	4	389		44			28	2	196	189	164		12,400		280
Percent attending school					95.1							93.8	99.0	98.2		97.0		95.6
Total 14 and 15 years, inclusive		11	3	1	130		13			8	2	38	52	35		3,276	1	59
Number attending school		10	2	1	110		11			8	2	34	48	34		3,066	1	56
Percent attending school					84.6											93.6		
Total 16 and 17 years, inclusive		12	2	2	108		22			10	3	55	52	47		3,479		62
Number attending school		7	1	1	45		16			7	2	33	35	32		1,921		30
Percent attending school					41.7											55.2		
Total 18 to 20 years, inclusive		21	3	3	151		17			8	1	152	59	50	1	5,674		96
Number attending school		1			21		6			2		11	21	9	1	897		14
Percent attending school					13.9							7.2				15.8		
ILLITERACY																		
Total 10 years old and over	4	416	33	156	2,723	4	370	14	1	166	49	2,814	1,052	1,082	2	92,873	5	1,946
Number illiterate		41	1	64	103		52	2		23	2	142	121	44		5,605		89
Percent illiterate		9.9		41.0	3.8		14.1			13.9		5.0	11.5	4.1		6.0		4.6
Percent illiterate in 1920		8.8		31.6	13.4		11.1			9.6		9.5	13.4	3.7		9.5		8.9
URBAN AND RURAL																		
Urban population		380	6	2	2,782	3	418		1	108	46	1,341	287	1,110		103,042		2,360
Percent urban		72.9		1.3	85.6		94.8			55.7		42.8	21.1	85.1		92.0		99.2
Rural population	6	141	36	155	468	1	23	14		86	8	1,790	1,071	195	2	8,940	5	19
Rural-farm		4	4	1	39	1	10	11		45	1	19	36	12		2,534	5	9
Rural-nonfarm	6	137	32	154	429		13	3		41	7	1,771	1,035	183	2	6,406		10
Percent rural		27.1		98.7	14.4		5.2			44.3		57.2	78.9	14.9		8.0		0.8
MARITAL CONDITION																		
Males 15 years old and over	3	208	12	89	1,295	2	172	9	1	82	27	2,021	473	502	1	43,369	2	945
Single		69	6	32	415		59	1	1	31	14	915	123	141	1	13,259	1	305
Married	1	124	6	36	724	1	89	5		37	12	858	295	330		25,823	1	536
Widowed	2	11		17	107	1	23	2		12	1	88	48	23		3,019		72
Divorced		4			43		1	1		2		159	6	7		1,146		27
Unknown				4	6							1	1	1		122		5
Females 15 years old and over	1	169	13	64	1,123	2	165	5		62	21	663	459	471	1	41,027	3	821
Single		23	7	11	216		31			15	8	107	91	76		7,320	2	125
Married	1	117	6	35	669	1	100	5		36	11	442	299	324		25,491	1	541
Widowed		26		17	206	1	29			11	1	86	63	54	1	7,018		119
Divorced		3			28		5				1	28	6	17		1,127		34
Unknown				1	4											71		2
FAMILIES																		
Number of families	2	121	7	15	840	3	136	7		62	17	482	370	319	1	28,771	1	564
Median size		2.70			2.48		2.53					2.48	2.91	2.93		2.68		2.71
Families having—																		
No children under 10	1	78	3	14	597	3	104	7		47	14	333	236	217	1	19,986	1	387
1 child under 10		19	1	1	111		15			8	2	64	54	48		3,954		77
2 children under 10	1	10	1		60		6			4	1	40	31	26		2,164		30
3 or more		14	2		72		11			3		45	49	28		2,667		70

CHARACTERISTICS OF NEGRO POPULATION BY COUNTIES: 1930—Continued

(See note at head of table)

SUBJECT	INDIANA—Continued																	
	Bartholomew	Benton	Blackford	Boone	Carroll	Cass	Clark	Clay	Clinton	Crawford	Daviess	Dearborn	Decatur	De Kalb	Delaware	Dubois	Elkhart	Fayette
POPULATION BY SEX																		
Negro population: 1930	191	20	10	116	8	288	1, 965	323	96	4	174	168	10	129	2, 678	3	551	449
Male	105	10	7	52	3	140	998	179	53	3	88	91	4	92	1, 363	2	281	242
Female	86	10	3	64	5	148	967	144	43	1	86	77	6	37	1, 315	1	270	257
Negro population: 1920	229	44	9	110	5	306	2, 298	291	81	3	196	122	51	110	2, 103	7	383	504
Male	103	18	7	51	5	182	1, 197	141	39		94	64	18	60	1, 101	3	221	264
Female	126	26	2	59		124	1, 101	150	42	3	102	58	33	50	1, 002	4	162	240
Percent of total population:																		
1930	0. 8	0. 2	0. 1	0. 5	0. 1	0. 8	6. 4	1. 2	0. 4		0. 7	0. 8	0. 1	0. 5	4. 0		0. 8	2. 6
1920	1. 0	0. 4	0. 1	0. 5		0. 8	7. 8	1. 0	0. 3		0. 7	0. 6	0. 3	0. 4	3. 7		0. 7	2. 9
VOTING AGE, 1930																		
Total 21 years old and over	120	16	9	73	3	196	1, 251	196	55	3	101	100	9	99	1, 736	3	345	312
Male	63	9	7	35	2	94	614	106	30	2	51	55	3	80	892	2	179	159
Female	57	7	2	38	1	102	637	90	25	1	50	45	6	19	844	1	166	153
AGE: 1930																		
Under 5 years	20	2		12	1	23	174	19	7	1	11	13		5	218		72	54
Under 1 year	6			4		3	31	2	1			1		3	44		17	6
5 to 9 years	19	2		15	2	21	186	41	15		18	17	1	7	226		44	48
10 to 14 years	14			7	2	20	170	25	9		20	14		9	220		28	41
15 to 19 years	12		1	8		24	168	38	10		20	21		7	229		49	40
20 to 24 years	19	2	1	6		24	139	19	3		12	13		12	237		58	34
25 to 29 years	11	1		7		24	151	22	1		6	6	1	15	264		49	45
30 to 34 years	8	4	1	6	1	19	135	29	8	2	16	7	3	13	228		49	25
35 to 44 years	28		1	22	1	51	281	42	14	1	18	25		29	436	1	91	69
45 to 54 years	26	3	2	19	1	49	246	36	14		28	19	3	21	364		62	64
55 to 64 years	18	3	2	7		22	152	26	9		16	15	1	7	149		29	37
65 to 74 years	11	3	2	6		5	110	12	4		5	11		4	87	1	18	32
75 years and over	5			1		3	51	3	2		4	7	1		20	1	2	8
Unknown						3	2	11										2
SCHOOL ATTENDANCE																		
Total 7 to 13 years, inclusive	20	1		16	3	25	254	44	19		28	21		9	306		50	65
Number attending school	20	1		15	3	24	247	44	19		28	21		9	303		49	64
Percent attending school							97. 2								99. 0			
Total 14 and 15 years, inclusive	7			4		6	68	13	4		7	4		4	80		12	11
Number attending school	6			4		6	56	13	4		7	2		4	78		9	10
Percent attending school																		
Total 16 and 17 years, inclusive	2			2		18	75	17	2		8	8		2	87		21	16
Number attending school	1			1		9	28	15	1		7	4		2	60		9	10
Percent attending school																		
Total 18 to 20 years, inclusive	11		1	4		10	76	18	5		11	13		5	151		31	23
Number attending school	1			2		2	7	4	2		4	1			21		4	6
Percent attending school															13. 9			
ILLITERACY																		
Total 10 years old and over	152	16	10	89	5	244	1, 605	263	74	3	145	138	9	117	2, 234	3	435	397
Number illiterate	13	2	2	4		11	177	10			15	21	1	9	138		13	45
Percent illiterate	8. 6					4. 5	11. 0	3. 8			10. 3	15. 2		7. 7	6. 2		3. 0	11. 3
Percent illiterate in 1920	6. 9					5. 2	15. 0	7. 4			5. 8				12. 3		10. 7	10. 4
URBAN AND RURAL																		
Urban population	146		2	84		240	1, 296	304	90		90	54	8	55	2, 646		541	481
Percent urban	76. 4			72. 4		83. 3	66. 0	94. 1			51. 7	32. 1		42. 6	98. 8		98. 2	96. 4
Rural population	45	20	8	32	8	48	669	19	6	4	84	114	2	74	32	3	10	18
Rural-farm	21	5		22	7	6	139	3	1	4	37	67			15	3	1	14
Rural-nonfarm	24	15	8	10	1	42	530	16	5		47	47	2	74	17		9	4
Percent rural	23. 6			27. 6		16. 7	34. 0	5. 9			48. 3	67. 9		57. 4	1. 2		1. 8	3. 6
MARITAL CONDITION																		
Males 15 years old and over	73	9	7	36	2	108	713	134	36	2	61	72	3	83	1, 035	2	203	182
Single	24	1	3	4	1	36	226	49	11	1	16	28	2	41	298	1	47	50
Married	41	5	2	26	1	62	387	73	23	1	35	31	1	39	643		137	116
Widowed	6	2	1	3		7	66	10	1		8	12		2	51		8	11
Divorced	2		1	3		3	33	2	1		2	1		1	42	1	11	5
Unknown		1					1								1			
Females 15 years old and over	65	7	3	46	1	116	722	104	29	1	64	52	6	25	979	1	204	174
Single	17		1	13		19	123	19	4		19	13	3	7	152	1	29	26
Married	40	6	2	26	1	78	398	69	22	1	38	33	1	16	634		140	121
Widowed	8	1		5		16	150	16	3		7	4	2	2	133		29	22
Divorced				2		3	50					2			60		6	5
Unknown							1											
FAMILIES																		
Number of families	50	5	5	27	2	70	568	83	24		45	40	2	14	698	1	130	127
Median size							2. 61								2. 93		2. 93	3. 00
Families having—																		
No children under 10	33	4	5	17	1	48	405	53	13		29	30	2	8	482	1	87	81
1 child under 10	6			4		12	66	13	6		8	2		2	107		17	21
2 children under 10	5			1		4	44	6	1		5	3		3	46		11	11
3 or more	6	1		5	1	6	53	11	4		3	5		1	63		15	14

CHARACTERISTICS OF NEGRO POPULATION BY COUNTIES: 1930—Continued

(See note at head of table)

SUBJECT	INDIANA—Continued																	
	Floyd	Fountain	Fulton	Gibson	Grant	Greene	Hamilton	Hancock	Harrison	Hendricks	Henry	Howard	Huntington	Jackson	Jasper	Jay	Jefferson	Jennings
POPULATION BY SEX																		
Negro population: 1930	1,399	4	34	789	1,408	13	369	28	130	162	485	1,329	5	67	3	135	420	257
Male	699	2	27	411	749	8	203	16	71	134	137	683	4	35	1	67	234	136
Female	700	2	7	378	659	5	166	12	59	28	248	646	1	32	2	68	186	121
Negro population: 1920	1,535	20	15	965	1,605	48	464	47	201	221	456	913	6	74	11	132	490	247
Male	755	8	6	499	842	26	249	23	103	156	237	472	3	38	5	60	250	116
Female	780	12	9	466	763	22	215	24	98	65	219	441	3	36	6	72	240	131
Percent of total population:																		
1930	4.0	-	0.2	2.7	2.8	-	1.6	0.2	0.8	0.8	1.4	2.8	-	0.3	-	0.6	2.2	2.2
1920	5.0	0.1	0.1	3.3	3.1	0.1	1.9	0.3	1.1	1.1	1.3	2.1	-	0.3	0.1	0.6	2.4	1.9
VOTING AGE: 1930																		
Total 21 years old and over	910	4	29	496	900	12	258	15	85	55	303	830	4	44	3	77	276	138
Male	458	2	26	256	500	8	141	7	44	34	155	427	3	22	1	37	151	76
Female	452	2	3	240	400	4	117	8	41	21	148	403	1	22	2	40	125	62
AGE: 1930																		
Under 5 years	106	-	-	62	137	1	28	1	11	1	42	121	-	6	-	17	29	24
Under 1 year	17	-	-	11	25	-	5	-	2	-	11	13	-	-	-	5	5	7
5 to 9 years	146	-	3	86	111	-	28	5	12	6	48	152	-	5	-	16	40	28
10 to 14 years	98	-	-	68	123	-	17	1	9	50	49	112	1	5	-	12	28	28
15 to 19 years	121	-	1	67	118	-	31	4	10	50	38	104	-	7	-	10	43	34
20 to 24 years	111	-	3	53	114	-	32	4	10	2	29	89	1	12	-	8	26	24
25 to 29 years	126	1	9	56	72	1	30	-	12	2	42	148	-	1	-	14	24	12
30 to 34 years	107	-	6	40	103	1	27	1	4	6	33	126	-	3	-	8	19	12
35 to 44 years	185	-	7	99	250	2	40	1	12	13	60	195	2	12	1	14	52	28
45 to 54 years	203	-	3	100	157	2	53	3	18	18	66	141	1	8	1	16	61	24
55 to 64 years	111	1	1	74	122	1	36	2	14	3	45	83	-	4	1	11	51	22
65 to 74 years	54	2	-	59	51	2	31	3	14	8	19	45	-	3	-	5	30	13
75 years and over	27	-	1	23	34	3	16	3	4	3	13	13	-	1	-	4	15	8
Unknown	4	-	-	1	16	-	-	-	-	-	-	-	-	-	-	-	2	-
SCHOOL ATTENDANCE																		
Total 7 to 13 years, inclusive	169	-	3	110	170	-	27	4	14	33	78	179	1	6	-	21	44	36
Number attending school	167	-	3	108	169	-	25	4	14	32	70	173	1	6	-	20	44	36
Percent attending school	98.8	-	-	98.2	99.4	-	-	-	-	-	-	96.6	-	-	-	-	-	-
Total, 14 and 15 years, inclusive	36	-	-	21	38	-	13	1	4	43	11	42	-	3	-	3	13	8
Number attending school	32	-	-	20	36	-	12	1	3	43	10	39	-	3	-	3	11	8
Percent attending school	-	-	-	-	-	-	-	-	-	-	-	-	-	-	-	-	-	-
Total, 16 and 17 years, inclusive	42	-	-	31	49	-	6	-	4	23	15	43	-	4	-	4	16	17
Number attending school	15	-	-	25	28	-	2	-	2	22	10	22	-	2	-	3	9	9
Percent attending school	-	-	-	-	-	-	-	-	-	-	-	-	-	-	-	-	-	-
Total 18 to 20 years, inclusive	76	-	2	35	71	-	24	5	7	5	21	51	-	1	-	8	24	19
Number attending school	9	-	-	10	13	-	4	-	1	2	2	9	-	-	-	1	3	3
Percent attending school	-	-	-	-	-	-	-	-	-	-	-	-	-	-	-	-	-	-
ILLITERACY																		
Total, 10 years old and over	1,147	4	31	641	1,160	12	313	22	107	155	395	1,056	5	56	3	102	351	205
Number illiterate	107	2	6	62	45	1	26	1	13	7	30	38	1	-	1	2	40	15
Percent illiterate	9.3	-	-	9.7	3.9	-	8.3	-	12.1	4.5	7.6	3.6.	-	-	-	2.0	11.4	7.3
Percent illiterate in 1920	11.8	-	-	11.4	8.5	-	10.9	-	9.0	5.1	9.2	5.7	-	-	-	-	18.1	10.1
URBAN AND RURAL																		
Urban population	1,292	1	2	350	1,056	-	229	18	-	-	326	1,143	1	67	3	129	243	149
Percent urban	92.4	-	-	44.4	75.0	-	62.1	-	-	-	67.2	86.0	-	-	-	95.6	57.9	58.0
Rural population	107	3	32	439	352	13	140	10	130	162	159	186	4	-	-	6	177	108
Rural-farm	61	-	5	342	112	7	90	2	35	15	53	17	4	-	-	-	65	51
Rural-nonfarm	46	3	27	97	240	6	50	8	95	147	106	169	-	-	-	6	112	57
Percent rural	7.6	-	-	55.6	25.0	-	37.9	-	100.0	100.0	32.8	14.0	-	-	-	4.4	42.1	42.0
MARITAL CONDITION																		
Males 15 years old and over	528	2	26	300	570	8	162	11	51	82	171	487	3	24	1	42	179	97
Single	148	1	14	96	196	3	57	4	17	58	53	137	1	8	-	11	74	42
Married	321	1	10	168	301	3	82	4	28	20	96	315	1	12	1	29	82	44
Widowed	38	-	2	23	38	2	18	3	4	3	14	13	-	1	-	2	13	11
Divorced	19	-	-	10	11	-	5	-	2	1	8	22	1	3	-	-	8	-
Unknown	2	-	-	3	24	-	-	-	-	-	-	-	-	-	-	-	2	-
Females 15 years old and over	521	2	5	273	467	4	134	10	47	23	175	457	1	27	2	48	144	80
Single	91	-	1	49	99	-	24	3	13	2	40	62	-	8	1	9	41	17
Married	322	-	4	172	279	3	81	4	28	17	99	316	1	11	1	28	78	44
Widowed	89	2	-	40	80	1	26	3	4	3	29	56	-	7	-	9	19	18
Divorced	19	-	-	10	8	-	3	-	2	1	7	22	-	1	-	2	6	1
Unknown	-	-	-	2	1	-	-	-	-	-	-	1	-	-	-	-	-	-
FAMILIES																		
Number of families	411	3	5	222	355	6	105	5	39	26	124	330	1	19	1	33	96	57
Median size	2.50	-	-	2.81	3.19	-	2.76	-	-	-	2.93	3.25	-	-	-	-	-	-
Families having—																		
No children under 10	299	3	3	148	219	5	76	3	27	20	87	204	1	13	1	21	66	38
1 child under 10	47	-	2	34	44	1	13	1	7	5	14	53	-	4	-	3	11	7
2 children under 10	25	-	-	15	38	-	11	-	1	1	12	36	-	-	-	3	6	7
3 or more	40	-	-	25	34	-	5	1	4	-	11	37	-	2	-	6	13	5

CHARACTERISTICS OF NEGRO POPULATION BY COUNTIES: 1930—Continued

(See note at head of table)

SUBJECT	INDIANA—Continued																	
	Johnson	Knox	Kosciusko	Lagrange	Lake	La Porte	Lawrence	Madison	Marion	Marshall	Martin	Miami	Monroe	Montgomery	Morgan	Newton	Noble	Ohio
POPULATION BY SEX																		
Negro population: 1930	311	337	42	8	23,748	1,284	244	1,699	44,722	123	3	281	541	227	8	9	4	87
Male	160	166	24	8	12,538	910	118	991	21,644	69	3	209	266	113	5	5	2	44
Female	151	171	18	-	11,210	374	126	708	23,078	54	-	72	275	114	3	4	2	43
Negro population: 1920	402	355	40	4	6,918	469	188	1,026	35,634	106	4	173	508	270	51	9	6	103
Male	190	180	26	1	3,995	365	86	529	17,878	71	3	104	254	135	29	6	4	54
Female	212	175	14	3	2,923	104	102	497	17,756	35	1	69	254	135	22	3	2	49
Percent of total population:																		
1930	1.4	0.8	0.2	0.1	9.1	2.1	0.7	2.0	10.6	0.5	-	1.0	1.5	0.8	-	0.1	-	2.3
1920	1.9	0.8	0.1	-	4.3	0.9	0.7	1.5	10.2	0.4	-	0.6	2.1	0.9	0.3	0.1	-	2.6
VOTING AGE: 1930																		
Total 21 years old and over	196	214	30	4	15,543	1,027	145	1,080	29,482	83	3	227	348	135	6	7	4	52
Male	102	108	15	4	8,516	799	72	647	14,332	52	3	177	161	59	4	4	2	24
Female	94	106	5	-	7,027	228	73	433	15,150	31	-	50	187	76	2	3	2	28
AGE: 1930																		
Under 5 years	24	25	1	-	2,266	73	27	140	3,499	11	-	6	45	22	-	-	-	4
Under 1 year	2	5	1	-	397	10	8	24	649	-	-	1	8	6	-	-	-	1
5 to 9 years	24	35	3	-	2,170	65	27	149	3,965	10	-	6	51	28	-	2	-	8
10 to 14 years	27	23	4	-	1,703	43	26	117	3,431	8	-	14	53	20	-	-	-	13
15 to 19 years	37	31	4	1	1,619	59	18	159	3,510	6	-	21	34	22	2	-	-	10
20 to 24 years	22	20	3	3	2,511	95	14	244	3,945	13	2	37	55	14	1	-	-	4
25 to 29 years	19	26	5	-	3,293	176	16	207	4,329	19	1	40	36	10	-	3	-	4
30 to 34 years	20	18	1	2	2,866	228	13	157	4,202	11	-	39	40	11	-	1	1	4
35 to 44 years	38	50	8	-	4,347	338	34	211	7,884	25	-	50	76	28	-	-	1	14
45 to 54 years	36	38	10	-	1,998	142	27	163	5,673	13	-	38	80	30	-	2	1	13
55 to 64 years	36	46	2	1	660	52	25	102	2,561	5	-	15	38	20	5	-	1	4
65 to 74 years	19	18	-	-	187	10	8	26	1,135	2	-	8	18	14	-	1	-	5
75 years and over	9	7	1	1	67	3	9	21	454	-	-	6	12	8	-	-	-	4
Unknown	-	-	-	-	61	-	-	3	134	-	-	1	3	-	-	-	-	-
SCHOOL ATTENDANCE																		
Total 7 to 13 years, inclusive	35	46	4	-	2,652	81	37	180	5,122	12	-	15	75	33	-	1	-	16
Number attending school	35	41	4	-	2,538	77	37	175	4,987	12	-	15	75	32	-	1	-	16
Percent attending school	-	-	-	-	95.7	-	-	97.2	97.4	-	-	-	-	-	-	-	-	-
Total 14 to 15 years, inclusive	13	9	1	-	636	16	11	43	1,320	3	-	5	19	12	-	-	-	5
Number attending school	10	9	1	-	611	14	11	37	1,218	3	-	5	19	11	-	-	-	5
Percent attending school	-	-	-	-	96.1	-	-	-	92.3	-	-	-	-	-	-	-	-	-
Total 16 to 17 years, inclusive	12	11	1	-	643	27	6	54	1,411	3	-	9	14	8	-	-	-	6
Number attending school	6	4	1	-	420	11	2	22	739	2	-	5	11	7	-	-	-	2
Percent attending school	-	-	-	-	65.3	-	-	-	52.4	-	-	-	-	-	-	-	-	-
Total 18 to 20 years, inclusive	19	22	3	4	1,119	40	6	135	2,296	7	-	18	24	9	2	-	-	2
Number attending school	4	6	1	-	149	4	1	32	347	2	-	4	13	3	-	-	-	-
Percent attending school	-	-	-	-	13.3	-	-	23.7	15.1	-	-	-	-	-	-	-	-	-
ILLITERACY																		
Total 10 years old and over	263	277	38	8	19,312	1,146	190	1,410	37,258	102	3	269	445	177	8	7	4	75
Number illiterate	15	21	1	-	880	48	12	122	2,130	1	2	8	20	20	1	1	-	10
Percent illiterate	5.7	7.6	-	-	4.6	4.2	6.3	8.7	5.7	1.0	-	3.0	4.5	11.3	-	-	-	-
Percent illiterate in 1920	13.1	7.9	-	-	7.6	6.4	13.2	11.8	8.5	-	-	8.7	11.9	10.3	-	-	-	-
URBAN AND RURAL																		
Urban population	243	280	39	-	23,720	1,245	214	1,408	43,967	-	-	128	519	225	4	-	-	-
Percent urban	78.1	83.1	-	-	99.9	97.0	87.7	82.9	98.3	-	-	45.6	95.9	99.1	-	-	-	-
Rural population	68	57	3	8	24	39	30	291	755	123	3	153	22	2	4	9	4	87
Rural-farm	24	22	1	2	1	12	16	19	189	-	-	4	4	1	2	8	-	30
Rural-nonfarm	44	35	2	6	23	27	14	272	566	123	3	149	18	1	2	1	4	57
Percent rural	21.9	16.9	-	-	0.1	3.0	12.3	17.1	1.7	100.0	-	54.4	4.1	0.9	-	-	-	-
MARITAL CONDITION																		
Males 15 years old and over	121	130	17	8	9,436	829	79	788	16,306	57	3	195	184	71	5	4	2	30
Single	44	42	5	7	2,848	284	14	326	4,562	27	3	132	56	21	3	1	-	9
Married	66	72	12	1	5,928	401	52	398	10,057	28	-	53	117	41	1	3	2	17
Widowed	10	10	-	-	471	67	6	27	1,279	1	-	6	7	9	1	-	-	4
Divorced	1	6	-	-	177	77	7	37	366	1	-	4	4	-	-	-	-	-
Unknown	-	-	-	-	12	-	-	-	42	-	-	-	-	-	-	-	-	-
Females 15 years old and over	115	124	17	-	8,173	274	85	505	17,521	37	-	60	208	86	3	3	2	32
Single	29	23	6	-	1,171	50	17	86	3,172	5	-	10	49	22	1	-	-	5
Married	64	67	9	-	5,762	189	54	345	10,363	27	-	39	121	42	1	3	2	18
Widowed	19	23	1	-	1,077	27	12	54	3,512	4	-	9	31	20	1	-	-	9
Divorced	3	11	1	-	160	8	2	20	446	-	-	2	6	2	-	-	-	-
Unknown	-	-	-	-	3	-	-	-	28	1	-	-	1	-	-	-	-	-
FAMILIES																		
Number of families	87	100	9	2	5,764	210	71	360	12,023	26	-	46	140	61	2	3	1	25
Median size	-	2.40	-	-	2.83	2.49	-	2.90	2.59	-	-	-	3.08	-	-	-	-	-
Families having—																		
No children under 10	63	73	7	2	3,738	141	45	232	8,540	15	-	39	98	41	2	2	1	19
1 child under 10	12	10	1	-	921	29	11	59	1,570	5	-	5	18	11	-	-	-	4
2 children under 10	5	10	1	-	465	19	8	26	927	4	-	1	8	1	-	1	-	2
3 or more	7	7	-	-	640	21	7	43	986	2	-	1	16	8	-	-	-	-

99576—35——46

CHARACTERISTICS OF NEGRO POPULATION BY COUNTIES: 1930—Continued

(See note at head of table)

SUBJECT	INDIANA—Continued																	
	Orange	Owen	Parke	Perry	Pike	Porter	Posey	Pulaski	Putnam	Randolph	Ripley	Rush	St. Joseph	Shelby	Spencer	Starke	Steuben	Sullivan
POPULATION BY SEX																		
Negro population: 1930	482	42	74	64	51	17	496	5	550	136	10	270	3,525	413	438	19	21	91
Male	303	22	38	22	27	7	263	3	442	67	7	145	1,822	216	215	12	9	49
Female	179	20	36	42	24	10	233	2	108	69	3	125	1,703	197	223	7	12	42
Negro population: 1920	264	57	101	91	137	2	518	9	228	214	7	416	1,304	420	562	22	10	105
Male	131	33	56	30	73	2	279	4	146	117	3	227	731	196	289	12	5	61
Female	133	24	45	61	64		239	5	82	97	4	189	573	224	273	10	5	44
Percent of total population:																		
1930	2.8	0.4	0.4	0.4	0.3	0.1	2.8		2.7	0.5	0.1	1.4	2.2	1.6	2.6	0.2	0.2	0.3
1920	1.6	0.4	0.5	0.5	0.7		2.7	0.1	1.1	0.8		2.2	1.3	1.6	3.1	0.2	0.1	0.3
VOTING AGE: 1930																		
Total, 21 years old and over	438	31	53	40	42	8	297	5	409	97	10	181	2,325	279	281	13	14	62
Male	281	18	27	15	24	3	148	3	339	54	7	99	1,257	142	142	8	7	38
Female	157	13	26	25	18	5	149	2	70	43	3	82	1,068	137	139	5	7	24
AGE: 1930																		
Under 5 years	6	3	1	5	2	3	45		16	4		16	303	29	31	3	1	6
Under 1 year	1	2			1		9		3			3	64	4	5	2		1
5 to 9 years	9	4	8	11	4	5	50		21	12		24	329	38	36		1	9
10 to 14 years	8	1	6	3	2	1	52		16	9		18	258	28	39	2	3	4
15 to 19 years	15	3	6	4	1		40		69	12		28	250	29	44	1	2	8
20 to 24 years	43	4	3	3	2		31		83	9	1	11	332	37	32			6
25 to 29 years	73		2	6	2	3	36		79	3	3	13	400	33	23		2	2
30 to 34 years	50	4	3	3	2	2	23		69	8	2	13	440	32	25		1	3
35 to 44 years	116	5	11	6	12	2	63	3	94	23	3	38	631	61	52	1	2	7
45 to 54 years	103	2	10	9	8	1	60		57	19	1	40	345	56	63	3	3	15
55 to 64 years	43	9	16	4	8		43	2	27	16		31	163	38	40	9	3	17
65 to 74 years	9	6	6	7	5		32		15	15		30	49	26	34		1	9
75 years and over	5	1	2	3	3		20		4	6		8	20	5	18		2	4
Unknown	2						1						5	1	1			1
SCHOOL ATTENDANCE																		
Total, 7 to 13 years, inclusive	12	4	12	13	3	3	71		21	13		32	404	47	57	1		9
Number attending school	12	4	12	12	2	3	69		19	12		31	400	42	54	1		7
Percent attending school													99.0					
Total, 14 and 15 years, inclusive	3	2	1	2	1		21		7	4		5	90	10	13	1	4	2
Number attending school	3	2	1	2	1		21		7	4		5	87	10	13	1	4	2
Percent attending school																		
Total, 16 and 17 years, inclusive	6	1	2				21		30	7		14	96	11	19	1	1	5
Number attending school	6		1				12		10	5		11	45	7	8		1	3
Percent attending school																		
Total, 18 to 20 years, inclusive	14		3	3	1		23		57	5		15	174	21	25			5
Number attending school	3		1		1		3		1	1		9	22	2	4			
Percent attending school													12.6					
ILLITERACY																		
Total, 10 years old and over	467	35	65	48	45	9	401	5	513	120	10	230	2,893	346	371	16	19	76
Number illiterate	15	4	9	8	8		68		41	6		2	160	20	64	2	2	8
Percent illiterate	3.2						17.0		8.0	5.0		0.9	5.5	5.8	17.3			
Percent illiterate in 1920	0.8				13.2		23.2		8.3	6.2		10.1	3.7	14.5	14.6			
URBAN AND RURAL																		
Urban population				27	8	3	455		200	35		161	3,482	345			10	50
Percent urban							91.7		36.4	25.7		59.6	98.8	83.5				
Rural population	482	42	74	37	43	14	41	5	350	101	10	109	43	68	438	19	11	41
Rural-farm	19	7	16	17	7	13	38	5	11	78	1	38		35	101	14	8	31
Rural-nonfarm	463	35	58	20	36	1	3		339	23	9	71	43	33	337	5	3	10
Percent rural	100.0						8.3		63.6	74.3		40.4	1.2	16.5	100.0			
MARITAL CONDITION																		
Males 15 years old and over	291	18	30	15	24	3	173	3	417	60	7	114	1,399	162	166	9	8	40
Single	121	8	11	2	3	1	48		203	25	5	41	375	45	51	4	3	13
Married	141	8	16	11	13	2	95	2	175	27	2	56	910	99	98	4	5	20
Widowed	16	1	3	2	8		27	1	24	5		15	67	16	15	1		7
Divorced	13	1					3		15	3		2	46	1	2			
Unknown													1	1				
Females 15 years old and over	168	16	29	30	19	5	176	2	80	51	3	98	1,236	156	166	5	8	32
Single	30	7	7	12	2	1	35		17	11	1	21	177	35	41		2	7
Married	99	7	17	11	12	2	99	2	44	30	2	59	902	104	100	3	5	19
Widowed	26	2	5	6	5	2	37		19	7		17	132	13	21	2	1	5
Divorced	13			1			5			3		1	25	2	4			1
Unknown														2				
FAMILIES																		
Number of families	98	12	26	17	24	1	135	3	59	41	1	80	823	125	124	6	6	31
Medium size							246						2.89	2.47	2.58			
Families having—																		
No children under 10	87	10	20	10	21		96	3	44	35	1	60	540	92	95	5	5	24
1 child under 10	8	1	4	3	2		12		5	2		12	121	18	10			2
2 children under 10	2		1	2			15		5	2		5	78	6	7		1	3
3 or more	1	1	1	2	1	1	12		5	2		3	84	9	12	1		2

CHARACTERISTICS OF NEGRO POPULATION BY COUNTIES: 1930—Continued

(See note at head of table)

SUBJECT	INDIANA—Continued												IOWA					
	Switzerland	Tippecanoe	Union	Vanderburg	Vermillion	Vigo	Wabash	Warren	Warrick	Wayne	Wells	Whitley	The State	Adair	Adams	Allamakee	Appanoose	Benton
POPULATION BY SEX																		
Negro population: 1930	23	455	98	7,228	69	4,116	128	17	382	2,416	2	12	17,380	32	16	17	341	6
Male	11	240	51	3,577	39	2,039	60	11	201	1,207	1	8	8,987	24	11	12	179	4
Female	12	215	47	3,651	30	2,077	68	6	181	1,209	1	4	8,393	8	5	5	162	2
Negro population: 1920	38	397	143	6,568	235	4,478	174	15	366	1,871	3	4	19,005	11	9	7	426	10
Male	18	199	75	3,282	134	2,268	102	10	196	1,017	2	2	10,121	5	5	5	215	5
Female	20	198	68	3,286	101	2,210	72	5	170	854	1	2	8,884	6	4	2	211	5
Percent of total population:																		
1930	0.3	1.0	1.7	6.4	0.3	4.2	0.5	0.2	2.1	4.4	---	0.1	0.7	0.2	0.2	0.1	1.4	---
1920	0.4	0.9	2.4	7.1	0.9	4.5	0.6	0.2	1.8	3.9	---	---	0.8	0.1	0.1	---	1.4	---
VOTING AGE: 1930																		
Total 21 years old and over	14	302	52	4,964	40	2,668	77	7	217	1,470	1	11	11,330	28	12	8	205	4
Male	6	165	27	2,484	22	1,338	39	7	113	769	1	7	6,010	22	9	5	115	3
Female	8	137	25	2,480	18	1,330	38	---	104	701	---	4	5,320	6	3	3	90	1
AGE: 1930																		
Under 5 years	4	32	10	466	6	293	10	3	51	224	---	---	1,391	---	2	1	25	---
Under 1 year	---	5	1	81	3	53	2	1	6	39	---	---	258	---	---	---	7	---
5 to 9 years	3	46	18	549	7	368	12	3	51	232	---	1	1,563	1	---	2	33	---
10 to 14 years	2	31	9	510	8	349	16	2	31	227	---	---	1,408	---	---	1	38	2
15 to 19 years	---	37	8	614	6	351	10	1	28	224	1	---	1,414	2	2	4	32	---
20 to 24 years	---	35	5	706	3	329	5	1	21	182	---	2	1,363	2	2	2	31	---
25 to 29 years	2	55	5	709	1	316	5	---	23	183	---	5	1,352	4	1	1	18	---
30 to 34 years	2	32	5	621	3	303	5	2	20	175	---	2	1,361	2	1	---	18	---
35 to 44 years	4	64	14	1,246	19	681	17	2	49	394	1	1	2,843	11	3	2	28	1
45 to 54 years	3	50	12	995	5	581	24	---	52	266	---	1	2,352	8	2	2	42	2
55 to 64 years	---	40	8	479	8	303	11	2	31	171	---	---	1,353	1	2	---	48	---
65 to 74 years	2	20	4	197	3	158	11	---	13	92	---	---	638	---	---	1	20	---
75 years and over	1	12	---	114	---	61	2	1	12	44	---	---	310	1	1	1	7	1
Unknown	---	1	---	22	---	23	---	---	---	2	---	---	32	---	---	---	1	---
SCHOOL ATTENDANCE																		
Total 7 to 13 years, inclusive	3	55	16	725	11	520	20	4	54	313	---	---	2,060	---	---	2	47	1
Number attending school	3	55	14	699	11	517	20	4	47	306	---	---	2,014	---	---	2	44	1
Percent attending school	---	---	---	96.4	---	99.4	---	---	---	97.8	---	---	97.8	---	---	---	---	---
Total 14 and 15 years, inclusive	1	8	4	237	3	141	7	1	14	85	---	---	582	---	---	2	16	1
Number attending school	1	7	4	221	3	138	7	1	11	79	---	---	549	---	---	1	14	1
Percent attending school	---	---	---	93.2	---	97.9	---	---	---	---	---	---	94.3	---	---	---	---	---
Total 16 and 17 years, inclusive	---	13	4	228	3	125	4	---	6	102	1	---	580	---	---	1	14	---
Number attending school	---	10	4	119	---	67	2	---	3	49	---	---	358	---	---	---	4	---
Percent attending school	---	---	---	52.2	---	53.6	---	---	---	48.0	---	---	61.7	---	---	---	---	---
Total 18 to 20 years, inclusive	---	26	3	387	4	244	5	1	18	130	---	---	830	3	2	2	20	---
Number attending school	---	10	3	59	1	57	2	---	2	25	---	---	188	---	---	---	4	---
Percent attending school	---	---	---	15.2	---	23.4	---	---	---	19.2	---	---	22.7	---	---	---	---	---
ILLITERACY																		
Total 10 years old and over	16	377	70	6,213	56	3,455	106	11	280	1,960	2	11	14,426	31	14	14	283	6
Number illiterate	1	20	8	547	3	252	4	1	32	80	---	1	777	3	---	1	27	---
Percent illiterate	---	5.3	---	8.8	---	7.3	3.8	---	11.4	4.1	---	---	5.4	---	---	---	9.5	---
Percent illiterate in 1920	---	5.1	10.1	14.6	10.4	8.6	8.6	---	14.1	6.9	---	---	8.1	---	---	---	12.2	---
URBAN AND RURAL																		
Urban population	---	428	---	6,514	67	3,463	125	---	126	2,139	2	---	15,185	---	---	5	257	4
Percent urban	---	94.1	---	90.1	---	84.1	97.7	---	33.0	88.5	---	---	87.4	---	---	---	75.4	---
Rural population	23	27	98	714	2	653	3	17	256	277	---	12	2,195	32	16	12	84	2
Rural-farm	14	1	44	112	1	154	3	16	64	133	---	---	572	1	---	11	19	1
Rural-nonfarm	9	26	54	602	1	499	---	1	192	144	---	12	1,623	31	16	1	65	1
Percent rural	---	5.9	---	9.9	---	15.9	2.3	---	67.0	11.5	---	---	12.6	---	---	---	24.6	---
MARITAL CONDITION																		
Males 15 years old and over	6	184	33	2,829	26	1,550	47	7	131	892	1	7	6,830	23	9	10	132	3
Single	1	64	10	1,026	7	424	14	2	35	265	1	2	2,234	12	2	7	37	2
Married	4	89	22	1,518	15	905	30	4	82	539	---	4	3,841	10	6	2	77	---
Widowed	1	18	1	220	1	146	2	1	14	63	---	---	471	1	1	---	16	1
Divorced	---	13	---	62	3	51	1	---	---	25	---	1	274	---	---	1	2	---
Unknown	---	---	---	3	---	24	---	---	---	---	---	---	10	---	---	---	---	---
Females 15 years old and over	8	162	28	2,874	22	1,556	43	2	118	841	1	4	6,188	8	5	3	113	1
Single	3	38	3	736	3	281	7	1	13	149	1	---	1,137	3	1	---	29	---
Married	4	83	22	1,545	13	892	28	1	85	535	---	4	3,766	3	3	2	71	---
Widowed	1	33	3	516	6	304	6	---	19	128	---	---	1,009	2	---	1	13	1
Divorced	---	8	---	70	---	57	2	---	1	29	---	---	270	---	1	---	---	---
Unknown	---	---	---	7	---	22	---	---	---	---	---	---	6	---	---	---	---	---
FAMILIES																		
Number of families	5	114	24	1,887	22	1,169	30	3	95	605	---	1	4,571	3	4	3	94	1
Median size	---	2.74	---	2.49	---	2.52	---	---	---	2.94	---	---	2.52	---	---	---	---	---
Families having—																		
No children under 10	3	79	12	1,399	15	862	22	2	57	407	---	1	3,239	3	2	2	64	1
1 child under 10	---	16	5	243	4	147	3	---	8	85	---	---	605	---	2	1	15	---
2 children under 10	1	8	3	110	---	60	1	---	11	42	---	---	333	---	---	---	8	---
3 or more	1	11	4	135	3	100	4	1	19	71	---	---	394	---	---	---	7	---

CHARACTERISTICS OF NEGRO POPULATION BY COUNTIES: 1930—Continued

(See note at head of table)

SUBJECT	IOWA—Continued																	
	Black Hawk	Boone	Bremer	Buchanan	Calhoun	Carroll	Cass	Cedar	Cerro Gordo	Cherokee	Clarke	Clay	Clayton	Clinton	Crawford	Dallas	Davis	Decatur
POPULATION BY SEX																		
Negro population: 1930	1,234	49	3	20	21	17	32	2	322	15	37	3	6	233	11	409	28	3
Male	626	26	1	12	7	10	17	1	163	9	19	3	2	113	6	224	17	-
Female	608	23	2	8	14	7	15	1	159	6	18	-	4	120	5	185	11	3
Negro population: 1920	856	142	5	21	33	31	31	9	361	24	34	16	9	338	22	207	27	6
Male	455	83	3	12	8	18	18	7	193	9	15	11	6	185	10	114	13	3
Female	401	59	2	9	25	13	13	2	168	15	19	5	3	153	12	93	14	3
Percent of total population:																		
1930	1.8	0.2	-	0.1	0.1	0.1	0.2	-	0.8	0.1	0.4	-	-	0.5	0.1	1.6	0.3	-
1920	1.5	0.5	-	0.1	0.2	0.1	0.2	0.1	1.0	0.1	0.3	0.1	-	0.8	0.1	0.8	0.2	-
VOTING AGE: 1930																		
Total 21 years old and over	727	35	1	13	19	14	16	2	209	11	27	3	3	161	7	258	20	2
Male	390	18	1	9	5	8	8	1	106	7	12	3	1	80	4	143	14	-
Female	337	17	-	4	14	6	8	1	103	4	15	-	2	81	3	115	6	2
AGE: 1930																		
Under 5 years	127	2	1	-	1	-	1	-	32	-	2	-	1	17	2	37	-	1
Under 1 year	25	1	-	-	-	-	-	-	9	-	-	-	-	4	-	7	-	-
5 to 9 years	146	5	-	-	1	1	3	-	28	1	3	-	-	19	1	39	3	-
10 to 14 years	111	4	-	2	-	-	4	-	26	-	2	-	-	18	-	37	2	-
15 to 19 years	98	3	1	5	-	1	8	-	23	3	3	-	-	14	1	33	2	-
20 to 24 years	110	3	1	1	1	2	1	1	19	1	1	-	2	13	-	37	3	-
25 to 29 years	119	6	-	2	9	-	-	-	29	3	4	-	1	16	1	24	2	1
30 to 34 years	117	2	-	1	1	-	1	-	25	1	2	1	-	21	1	15	1	-
35 to 44 years	202	4	-	5	5	6	9	1	59	1	7	-	1	38	-	55	4	-
45 to 54 years	131	12	-	2	1	6	1	-	47	1	5	-	-	39	2	64	4	-
55 to 64 years	50	4	-	-	1	1	4	-	17	3	1	-	1	19	2	47	1	-
65 to 74 years	15	2	-	-	-	-	-	-	12	-	1	2	-	15	-	14	5	1
75 years and over	8	2	-	1	1	-	-	-	4	1	6	-	-	4	1	7	1	-
Unknown	-	-	-	1	-	-	-	-	1	-	-	-	-	-	-	-	-	-
SCHOOL ATTENDANCE																		
Total 7 to 13 years, inclusive	180	6	-	1	-	1	6	-	38	-	4	-	-	23	1	51	3	-
Number attending school	179	6	-	1	-	1	6	-	38	-	4	-	-	23	1	51	3	-
Percent attending school	99.4	-	-	-	-	-	-	-	-	-	-	-	-	-	-	-	-	-
Total 14 and 15 years, inclusive	50	1	-	2	-	-	1	-	5	1	1	-	-	8	-	15	1	-
Number attending school	48	1	-	2	-	-	1	-	4	1	1	-	-	7	-	14	1	-
Percent attending school	-	-	-	-	-	-	-	-	-	-	-	-	-	-	-	-	-	-
Total 16 and 17 years, inclusive	36	3	1	1	-	-	3	-	10	1	1	-	-	7	1	13	-	-
Number attending school	20	3	-	-	-	-	2	-	6	1	1	-	-	4	-	6	-	-
Percent attending school	-	-	-	-	-	-	-	-	-	-	-	-	-	-	-	-	-	-
Total 18 to 20 years, inclusive	61	-	-	3	-	2	4	-	14	1	1	-	2	9	-	19	2	-
Number attending school	11	-	-	-	-	1	-	-	4	1	1	-	-	3	-	2	1	-
Percent attending school	-	-	-	-	-	-	-	-	-	-	-	-	-	-	-	-	-	-
ILLITERACY																		
Total 10 years old and over	961	42	2	20	19	16	28	2	262	14	32	3	5	197	8	333	25	2
Number illiterate	94	1	-	1	1	-	-	1	10	-	5	1	-	14	-	17	4	-
Percent illiterate	9.8	-	-	-	-	-	-	-	3.8	-	-	-	-	7.1	-	5.1	-	-
Percent illiterate in 1920	7.0	7.1	-	-	-	-	-	-	5.3	-	-	-	-	4.7	-	5.6	-	-
URBAN AND RURAL																		
Urban population	1,222	36	2	2	-	16	20	-	320	13	27	2	-	231	6	109	-	-
Percent urban	99.0	-	-	-	-	-	-	-	99.4	-	-	-	-	99.1	-	26.7	-	-
Rural population	12	13	1	18	21	1	12	2	2	2	10	1	6	2	5	300	28	3
Rural-farm	9	10	1	7	-	1	2	-	1	2	9	-	1	-	-	5	4	3
Rural-nonfarm	3	3	-	11	21	-	10	2	1	-	1	1	5	2	5	295	24	
Percent rural	1.0	-	-	-	-	-	-	-	0.6	-	-	-	-	0.9	-	73.3	-	-
MARITAL CONDITION																		
Males 15 years old and over	450	19	1	10	5	9	11	1	115	8	13	3	2	87	4	164	16	-
Single	162	7	-	7	-	4	4	-	24	4	1	2	-	25	1	46	11	-
Married	257	9	1	-	2	5	6	1	78	4	12	1	2	49	3	104	4	-
Widowed	20	2	-	1	1	-	-	-	8	-	-	-	-	7	-	6	-	-
Divorced	11	1	-	1	2	-	1	-	4	-	-	-	-	6	-	8	1	-
Unknown	-	-	-	1	-	-	-	-	1	-	-	-	-	-	-	-	-	-
Females 15 years old and over	400	19	1	8	14	7	13	1	121	6	17	-	3	92	4	132	7	2
Single	80	3	-	4	1	2	6	-	21	2	2	-	-	13	1	18	4	-
Married	260	8	1	2	9	4	6	1	80	2	10	-	3	53	2	97	2	2
Widowed	46	7	-	-	2	1	1	-	16	1	5	-	-	25	1	12	1	-
Divorced	14	1	-	2	2	-	-	-	4	1	-	-	-	1	-	5	-	-
Unknown	-	-	-	-	-	-	-	-	-	-	-	-	-	-	-	-	-	-
FAMILIES																		
Number of families	263	15	1	1	3	5	7	1	83	1	13	2	-	70	2	125	4	-
Median size	3.28	-	-	-	-	-	-	-	-	-	-	-	-	-	-	2.31	-	-
Families having—																		
No children under 10	152	14	1	1	1	4	6	1	57	1	11	2	-	54	1	92	2	-
1 child under 10	49	-	-	-	2	1	-	-	10	-	1	-	-	7	-	12	1	-
2 children under 10	25	-	-	-	-	-	-	-	8	-	-	-	-	3	-	11	-	-
3 or more	37	1	-	-	-	-	1	-	8	-	1	-	-	6	1	10	1	-

CHARACTERISTICS OF NEGRO POPULATION BY COUNTIES: 1930—Continued

(See note at head of table)

SUBJECT	IOWA—Continued																	
	Delaware	Des Moines	Dickinson	Dubuque	Emmet	Fayette	Floyd	Franklin	Fremont	Greene	Grundy	Guthrie	Hamilton	Hancock	Hardin	Harrison	Henry	Howard
POPULATION BY SEX																		
Negro population: 1930	1	386	2	89	8	104	9	11	17	5	1	1	12	9	120	27	135	1
Male	1	222	1	51	4	60	5	8	11	3	1		6	3	101	15	76	
Female		164	1	38	4	44	4	3	6	2		1	6	6	19	12	59	1
Negro population: 1920	3	337	4	75	42	106	30	13	11	16	1	1	4	9	72	23	212	4
Male	2	188	4	45	17	58	17	9	8	8	1	1	2	3	61	14	114	3
Female	1	149		30	25	48	13	4	3	8			2	6	11	9	98	1
Percent of total population:																		
1930		1.0		0.1	0.1	0.4		0.1	0.1				0.1	0.1	0.5	0.1	0.8	
1920		0.9		0.1	0.3	0.4	0.2	0.1	0.1	0.1				0.1	0.3	0.1	1.2	
VOTING AGE: 1930																		
Total 21 years old and over		295	2	58	8	65	4	6	7	3	1	1	9	6	66	19	105	1
Male		174	1	35	4	41	2	3	5	2	1		4	3	53	11	57	
Female		121	1	23	4	24	2	3	2	1		1	5	3	13	8	48	1
AGE: 1930																		
Under 5 years		19		7		10	1		2					1	1	1	7	
Under 1 year		4		3												1	2	
5 to 9 years		21		3		11		2	2	1			1		7		1	
10 to 14 years		23		7		8	2	2	2				1	1	15	1	14	
15 to 19 years	1	24		14		6	2	1	4	1			1	1	30	6	8	
20 to 24 years		30		7		14			1				1		17	3	2	
25 to 29 years		36	1	5	2	8		1			1		1		10	1	6	
30 to 34 years		29		9	1	7		2		2		1	1		12	1	7	
35 to 44 years		53		14	4	7		3	2				1	1	17	5	13	
45 to 54 years		72		10	1	18	1		1	1			2	1	8	5	33	
55 to 64 years		40		7		7	1		2				1	1	3	3	26	1
65 to 74 years		27	1	5		5	2		1				2	3		1	12	
75 years and over		11		1		3											5	
Unknown		1															1	
SCHOOL ATTENDANCE																		
Total 7 to 13 years, inclusive		35		9		12	1	3	3				2		11	1	11	
Number attending school		35		9		12	1	3	2				2		11	1	11	
Percent attending school																		
Total 14 and 15 years, inclusive		4		3		3	1	1	1					1	15	1	6	
Number attending school		4		3		3	1	1						1	15	1	5	
Percent attending school																		
Total 16 and 17 years, inclusive		11		4		4	2		2				1	1	16	2	4	
Number attending school		9		3		4	2		1				1	1	16	2	3	
Percent attending school																		
Total 18 to 20 years, inclusive	1	15		8		6		1	1	1					8	3	2	
Number attending school		4		2		1		1							7	1		
Percent attending school																		
ILLITERACY																		
Total 10 years old and over	1	346	2	79	8	83	8	9	13	4	1	1	11	8	112	26	127	1
Number illiterate		23	1	2		2			1		1				6	2	21	
Percent illiterate		6.6													5.4		16.5	
Percent illiterate in 1920		7.0															22.6	
URBAN AND RURAL																		
Urban population		377		88	8	33	8	10		2			11		63	15	87	1
Percent urban		97.7				31.7									52.5		64.4	
Rural population	1	9	2	1		71	1	1	17	3	1	1	1	9	57	12	48	
Rural-farm	1	8	1			50		1	2	1	1			6	2	2	2	
Rural-nonfarm		1	1	1		21	1		15	2		1	1	3	55	10	46	
Percent rural		2.3				68.3									47.5		35.6	
MARITAL CONDITION																		
Males 15 years old and over	1	191	1	41	4	46	4	4	8	2	1		4	3	83	14	62	
Single	1	65		23		26	2	3	6	2	1				60	7	23	
Married		90		14	4	16	1	1	1				4	3	23	5	25	
Widowed		22		4		4	1		1							2	8	
Divorced		12	1														6	
Unknown		2																
Females 15 years old and over		123	1	31	4	29	2	3	3	2		1	6	4	14	11	51	1
Single		17		7		12			1	1			2	1	5	5	9	
Married		85	1	17	4	9	1	2	1	1		1	4	3	9	6	29	1
Widowed		25		6		6	1	1	1								11	
Divorced		5		1		2											2	
Unknown																		
FAMILIES																		
Number of families		120		15	2	23	3	4	4	1			4	1	6	6	29	
Median size		2.11																
Families having—																		
No children under 10		100		10	2	17	3	3	3	1			2	1	2	6	24	
1 child under 10		9		3		2		1					2		1		2	
2 children under 10		5		1		2									2		3	
3 or more		6		1		2			1						1			

CHARACTERISTICS OF NEGRO POPULATION BY COUNTIES: 1930—Continued

(See note at head of table)

SUBJECT	IOWA—Continued																	
	Humboldt	Iowa	Jackson	Jasper	Jefferson	Johnson	Jones	Keokuk	Kossuth	Lee	Linn	Louisa	Lucas	Lyon	Mahaska	Marion	Marshall	Mills
POPULATION BY SEX																		
Negro population: 1930	1	3	1	99	63	112	61	19	5	1,353	765	19	45	1	211	146	351	56
Male	1	2	1	55	33	65	60	8	2	721	372	10	24		111	75	176	33
Female		1		44	30	47	1	11	3	632	393	9	21	1	100	71	175	23
Negro population: 1920	5	18	5	144	86	68	67	17	8	1,417	704	8	46	15	352	122	264	57
Male	3	11	3	73	51	40	66	9	3	735	359	6	28	8	183	68	142	28
Female	2	7	2	71	35	28	1	8	5	682	345	2	18	7	169	54	122	29
Percent of total population:																		
1930				0.3	0.4	0.4	0.3	0.1		3.3	0.9	0.2	0.3		0.8	0.6	1.0	0.4
1920		0.1		0.5	0.5	0.3	0.4	0.1		3.6	1.0	0.1	0.3	0.1	1.3	0.5	0.8	0.4
VOTING AGE: 1930																		
Total 21 years old and over	1	3		64	37	81	55	11	4	927	496	11	27		152	75	211	35
Male	1	2		36	21	47	55	6	2	512	254	6	16		83	42	108	19
Female		1		28	16	34		5	2	415	242	5	11		69	33	103	16
AGE: 1930																		
Under 5 years				10	4	13		1		97	57	2	4		17	9	46	3
Under 1 year				2	1	3				12	9		1		4	1	10	
5 to 9 years				10	4	9	1	2		110	70	3	3		8	16	35	6
10 to 14 years				9	8	2		2		93	58	2	3	1	17	24	25	4
15 to 19 years			1	6	8	5	3	3	1	106	69	1	8		16	19	25	8
20 to 24 years				4	5	23	15		2	89	51	3	1		14	9	28	4
25 to 29 years				6	2	10	25	1		88	57	1	2		12	6	20	4
30 to 34 years				5	4	14	9	4		115	58	2	2		19	4	26	5
35 to 44 years		1		15	5	22	5	2		214	148	1	4		28	19	57	11
45 to 54 years				10	12	6	1	2	1	198	115	4	7		20	20	37	6
55 to 64 years	1			14	6	7	1			143	46		7		31	13	26	2
65 to 74 years		1		7	3		1	2	1	60	29		1		21	5	13	2
75 years and over		1		3	2	1				36	7		3		7	2	13	
Unknown										4					1			1
SCHOOL ATTENDANCE																		
Total 7 to 13 years, inclusive				16	8	6		2		137	88	3	5	1	21	33	37	8
Number attending school				16	8	6		2		124	88		5	1	19	33	37	7
Percent attending school										90.5								
Total 14 and 15 years, inclusive				4	6	1		3		45	29	1	4		5	8	12	2
Number attending school				4	6	1		3		44	27		2		1	7	12	1
Percent attending school																		
Total 16 and 17 years, inclusive				1	5					48	29		2		4	8	9	4
Number attending school				1	3					25	21		2		1	2	7	2
Percent attending school																		
Total 18 to 20 years, inclusive			1	3	3	7	5	1	1	55	41	1	2		9	11	20	3
Number attending school				2	2	2	2			15	10		1		1	1	5	3
Percent attending school																		
ILLITERACY																		
Total 10 years old and over	1	3	1	79	55	90	60	16	5	1,146	638	14	38	1	186	121	270	47
Number illiterate	1			9		2	4	1		51	7	11	2		26	7	18	6
Percent illiterate										4.5	1.1				14.0	5.8	6.7	
Percent illiterate in 1920				3.5						9.8	7.8				17.9		15.8	
URBAN AND RURAL																		
Urban population				37	59	110	58			1,209	756		40		171	3	338	50
Percent urban						98.2				89.4	98.8				81.0	2.1	96.3	
Rural population	1	3	1	62	4	2	3	19	5	144	9	19	5	1	40	143	13	6
Rural-farm			1	6	3		1	1	5	138	3	1	5		9	6	1	
Rural-nonfarm	1	3		56	1	2	2	18		6	6	18		1	31	137	12	6
Percent rural						1.8				10.6	1.2				19.0	97.9	3.7	
MARITAL CONDITION																		
Males 15 years old and over	1	2	1	39	26	52	60	7	2	581	300	6	18		92	52	125	24
Single	1	1	1	8	8	23	40	2	1	206	86	4	6		24	15	31	14
Married		1		24	14	25	11	5	1	312	179	2	5		55	30	80	9
Widowed				6	4	1	1			31	15		5		9	7	10	
Divorced				1		3	8			31	20		2		3		3	1
Unknown										1					1		1	
Females 15 years old and over		1		31	21	36		7	3	472	280	6	17		77	45	120	19
Single				4	4	8		2	2	92	49	2	8		14	10	18	6
Married		1		23	11	22		4	1	274	181	4	4		46	30	80	10
Widowed				3	5	5		1		89	34		3		15	5	17	2
Divorced				1	1	1				17	16		2		1		5	1
Unknown															1			
FAMILIES																		
Number of families		1		24	15	27	1	4	1	365	204	4	16		61	39	80	11
Median size										2.43	2.97							
Families having—																		
No children under 10		1		17	11	19	1	3	1	271	138	2	13		48	24	47	8
1 child under 10				4	1	3				43	31		1		8	8	14	2
2 children under 10					2	1				24	21	1	1		2	5	3	
3 or more				3	1	4		1		27	14	1	1		3	2	16	1

CHARACTERISTICS OF NEGRO POPULATION BY COUNTIES: 1930—Continued

(See note at head of table)

SUBJECT	IOWA—Continued																	
	Mitchell	Monona	Monroe	Montgomery	Muscatine	O'Brien	Page	Polk	Pottawattamie	Poweshiek	Sac	Scott	Shelby	Sioux	Story	Tama	Taylor	Union
POPULATION BY SEX																		
Negro population: 1930	2	38	355	58	66	4	225	5,713	684	26	13	865	4	8	55	13	19	59
Male	1	36	191	34	28	4	108	2,803	339	14	4	464	1	5	25	9	9	41
Female	1	2	164	24	38	---	117	2,910	345	12	9	401	3	3	30	4	10	18
Negro population: 1920	7	8	1,652	54	107	18	250	5,837	612	52	23	745	7	14	51	25	34	59
Male	4	6	904	35	57	13	135	2,947	341	25	13	425	4	10	23	14	14	35
Female	3	2	748	19	50	5	115	2,890	271	27	10	320	3	4	28	11	20	24
Percent of total population:																		
1930	---	0.2	2.4	0.3	0.2	---	0.9	3.3	1.0	0.1	0.1	1.1	---	---	0.2	0.1	0.1	0.3
1920	0.1	---	7.0	0.3	0.4	0.1	1.0	3.8	1.0	0.3	0.1	1.0	---	0.1	0.2	0.1	0.2	0.3
VOTING AGE: 1930																		
Total 21 years old and over	2	37	225	33	53	3	155	3,628	460	22	8	558	4	5	34	8	16	45
Male	1	35	122	19	23	3	82	1,779	236	12	3	301	1	3	16	5	8	33
Female	1	2	103	14	30	---	73	1,849	224	10	5	257	3	2	18	3	8	12
AGE: 1930																		
Under 5 years	---	---	31	4	1	1	11	501	52	1	2	72	---	---	2	---	---	---
Under 1 year	---	---	6	1	---	1	1	93	13	---	1	12	---	---	---	---	---	---
5 to 9 years	---	---	37	4	5	---	18	546	78	---	---	80	---	---	6	1	---	5
10 to 14 years	---	---	35	8	1	---	23	491	42	1	---	74	---	2	5	2	1	3
15 to 19 years	---	1	22	6	6	---	14	468	45	2	3	64	---	1	8	2	1	4
20 to 24 years	---	7	14	8	4	---	15	432	47	3	---	95	2	1	3	1	1	3
25 to 29 years	---	3	12	2	2	---	8	440	49	1	---	74	---	---	3	---	2	10
30 to 34 years	---	7	10	2	5	---	21	451	47	2	2	60	---	---	3	---	---	5
35 to 44 years	2	20	46	9	9	2	31	938	136	5	---	142	---	---	13	---	3	10
45 to 54 years	---	---	55	7	17	1	35	750	109	5	2	109	1	2	8	3	2	10
55 to 64 years	---	---	44	5	7	---	22	442	50	3	2	58	1	1	2	1	3	5
65 to 74 years	---	---	28	2	4	---	16	173	20	3	1	24	---	1	2	3	4	1
75 years and over	---	---	21	1	5	---	11	73	5	---	1	13	---	---	---	---	2	3
Unknown	---	---	---	---	---	---	---	8	4	---	---	---	---	---	---	---	---	---
SCHOOL ATTENDANCE																		
Total 7 to 13 years, inclusive	---	---	48	7	5	---	28	732	74	---	---	101	---	2	10	3	1	6
Number attending school	---	---	48	7	5	---	27	717	74	---	---	98	---	2	10	3	1	6
Percent attending school	---	---	---	---	---	---	---	98.0	---	---	---	97.0	---	---	---	---	---	---
Total 14 and 15 years, inclusive	---	---	14	5	1	---	5	181	15	3	---	35	---	---	2	2	---	2
Number attending school	---	---	13	5	1	---	5	176	15	3	---	34	---	---	1	2	---	2
Percent attending school	---	---	---	---	---	---	---	97.2	---	---	---	---	---	---	---	---	---	---
Total 16 and 17 years, inclusive	---	---	10	3	1	---	10	191	17	---	1	22	---	---	3	---	1	2
Number attending school	---	---	6	3	1	---	9	116	12	---	1	11	---	---	2	---	1	2
Percent attending school	---	---	---	---	---	---	---	60.7	---	---	---	---	---	---	---	---	---	---
Total 18 to 20 years, inclusive	---	1	13	4	4	---	7	270	27	---	2	44	---	1	3	---	1	3
Number attending school	---	---	1	---	1	---	1	64	8	---	---	6	---	---	---	---	---	2
Percent attending school	---	---	---	---	---	---	---	23.7	---	---	---	---	---	---	---	---	---	---
ILLITERACY																		
Total 10 years old and over	2	38	287	50	60	3	196	4,666	554	25	11	713	4	8	47	12	19	54
Number illiterate	---	---	37	4	2	---	16	195	11	---	2	35	---	1	---	---	3	4
Percent illiterate	---	---	12.9	---	---	---	8.2	4.2	2.0	---	---	4.9	---	---	---	---	---	---
Percent illiterate in 1920	---	---	12.7	---	---	---	11.0	6.2	9.5	---	---	8.1	---	---	---	---	---	---
URBAN AND RURAL																		
Urban population	2	36	77	54	57	1	150	5,562	669	18	7	811	---	---	54	1	---	31
Percent urban	---	---	21.7	---	---	---	66.7	97.4	97.8	---	---	93.8	---	---	---	---	---	---
Rural population	---	2	278	4	9	3	75	151	15	8	6	54	4	8	1	12	19	28
Rural-farm	---	---	47	4	---	3	19	57	1	5	1	7	4	3	1	---	2	12
Rural-nonfarm	---	2	231	---	9	---	56	94	14	3	5	47	---	5	---	12	17	16
Percent rural	---	---	78.3	---	---	---	33.3	2.6	2.2	---	---	6.2	---	---	---	---	---	---
MARITAL CONDITION																		
Males 15 years old and over	1	36	140	26	27	3	88	2,023	253	12	4	343	1	4	18	6	9	37
Single	1	36	34	11	8	---	34	548	47	4	1	129	1	3	3	2	4	21
Married	---	---	77	14	12	3	44	1,245	168	8	2	183	---	1	15	3	3	10
Widowed	---	---	21	1	4	---	7	154	19	---	1	16	---	---	---	1	2	4
Divorced	---	---	8	---	3	---	3	75	18	---	---	15	---	---	---	---	---	2
Unknown	---	---	---	---	---	---	---	1	1	---	---	---	---	---	---	---	---	---
Females 15 years old and over	1	2	112	16	32	---	85	2,152	259	12	7	296	3	2	24	4	9	14
Single	1	2	14	3	10	---	14	362	41	4	2	45	1	---	8	1	3	4
Married	---	---	76	12	11	---	44	1,275	160	8	3	200	2	2	14	2	2	6
Widowed	---	---	20	---	11	---	19	404	41	---	2	40	---	---	1	---	2	4
Divorced	---	---	2	1	---	---	8	110	17	---	---	11	---	---	1	1	2	---
Unknown	---	---	---	---	---	---	---	1	---	---	---	---	---	---	---	---	---	---
FAMILIES																		
Number of families	---	---	119	14	21	1	56	1,557	199	7	3	215	1	2	13	5	5	10
Median size	---	---	226	---	---	---	---	2.62	2.39	---	---	2.52	---	---	---	---	---	---
Families having—																		
No children under 10	---	---	89	10	17	1	42	1,077	142	6	2	152	1	2	9	5	5	7
1 child under 10	---	---	13	3	2	---	5	209	24	1	1	29	---	---	2	---	---	1
2 children under 10	---	---	6	---	2	---	5	127	13	---	---	15	---	---	---	---	---	2
3 or more	---	---	11	1	---	---	4	144	20	---	---	19	---	---	2	---	---	---

CHARACTERISTICS OF NEGRO POPULATION BY COUNTIES: 1930—Continued

(See note at head of table)

SUBJECT	IOWA—Continued										KANSAS							
	Van Buren	Wapello	Warren	Washington	Wayne	Webster	Winnebago	Winneshiek	Woodbury	Worth	The State	Allen	Anderson	Atchison	Barber	Barton	Bourbon	Brown
POPULATION BY SEX																		
Negro population: 1930	44	447	25	52	5	320	1	10	1,078	85	66,344	527	103	1,777	26	497	835	381
Male	26	241	16	23	4	140	1	6	568	43	33,980	242	56	916	16	275	411	198
Female	18	206	9	29	1	180		4	510	42	32,364	285	47	861	10	222	424	183
Negro population: 1920	49	571	11	108	6	399	12	3	1,147	89	57,925	684	104	1,798	15	396	939	450
Male	25	309	4	54	4	203	6	2	650	52	29,739	334	42	895	7	203	447	219
Female	24	262	7	54	2	196	6	1	497	37	28,186	350	62	903	8	193	492	231
Percent of total population:																		
1930	0.3	1.1	0.1	0.3		0.8			1.1	0.8	3.5	2.5	0.8	7.4	0.3	2.5	3.7	1.9
1920	0.3	1.5	0.1	0.5		1.1	0.1		1.2	0.8	3.3	2.9	0.8	7.7	0.2	2.1	4.0	2.1
VOTING AGE: 1930																		
Total 21 years old and over	40	295	17	30	4	195	1	7	773	41	42,964	319	83	1,188	16	291	518	215
Male	25	167	10	12	3	93	1	4	421	22	22,477	154	45	611	10	160	268	115
Female	15	128	7	18	1	102		3	352	19	20,487	165	38	577	6	131	250	100
AGE: 1930																		
Under 5 years		36	1	1		30			72	9	5,182	53	6	148	4	485	64	39
Under 1 year		6				4			13	1	942	11		29		5	14	9
5 to 9 years	2	34	3	8		35		1	71	17	6,019	53	4	137	3	59	77	39
10 to 14 years	1	39	2	8		22		1	66	10	5,608	45	5	122	2	55	84	36
15 to 19 years	1	36	2	3	1	31		1	72	7	5,434	44	3	143	1	41	78	44
20 to 24 years	4	30	2	4	1	26		2	98	3	5,486	52	12	169	2	35	56	27
25 to 29 years	9	24	2	3	1	26			127	8	5,554	30	11	112	3	46	53	19
30 to 34 years	7	33				24	1		119	13	5,473	35	9	100	4	35	47	25
35 to 44 years	8	62	2	7	1	44		1	247	11	10,731	68	15	245	1	70	113	44
45 to 54 years	4	71	7	6		46		4	131	4	8,353	66	25	263	2	54	117	53
55 to 64 years	5	37	3	8		17			44	2	4,698	54	7	154	3	37	68	33
65 to 74 years	3	28	1	2		9			19	1	2,372	18	2	109	1	5	41	14
75 years and over		16		2	1	7			7		1,376	9	4	71		12	37	8
Unknown		1				3			5		58			4		3		
SCHOOL ATTENDANCE																		
Total 7 to 13 years, inclusive	3	55	3	12		36			96	21	8,117	64	5	181	2	81	118	50
Number attending school	2	55	3	12		36			94	21	7,899	64	5	177	2	81	112	49
Percent attending school											97.3			97.8			94.9	
Total 14 and 15 years, inclusive		15		2		11		1	25	3	2,257	17	2	55		22	32	21
Number attending school		14		2		11		1	23	3	2,042	15	2	44		21	31	18
Percent attending school											90.5							
Total 16 and 17 years, inclusive		18	1	1	1	17		1	29	2	2,115	19	1	57		12	28	18
Number attending school		10	1	1		12		1	14	2	1,364	15	1	34		7	19	13
Percent attending school											64.5							
Total 18 to 20 years, inclusive	1	16	1	4		16			54	4	3,351	31	4	92	1	27	49	24
Number attending school		2		3		6			5	1	847	5		10	1	4	13	11
Percent attending school											25.3							
ILLITERACY																		
Total 10 years old and over	42	377	21	43	5	255	1	9	935	59	55,143	421	93	1,492	19	393	694	303
Number illiterate	8	25			1	17			23	9	3,228	32	9	96	1	24	45	16
Percent illiterate		6.6				6.7			2.5		5.9	7.6		6.4		6.1	6.5	5.3
Percent illiterate in 1920		11.1				8.8			2.5		8.8	10.7		13.5		7.9	10.8	6.7
URBAN AND RURAL																		
Urban population		424	5	49		298		9	1,064		51,281	416	87	1,517		286	729	308
Percent urban		94.9				93.1			98.7		77.3	78.9	84.5	85.4		57.5	87.3	80.8
Rural population	44	23	20	3	5	22	1	1	14	85	15,063	111	16	260	26	211	106	73
Rural-farm		12	18	3	1	9	1	1	11	6	4,392	26	9	184	8	70	72	39
Rural-nonfarm	44	11	2		4	13			3	79	10,671	85	7	76	18	141	34	34
Percent rural		5.1				6.9			1.3		22.7	21.1	15.5	14.6		42.5	12.7	19.2
MARITAL CONDITION																		
Males 15 years old and over	25	187	11	14	4	107	1	4	468	26	25,649	178	46	698	11	189	309	140
Single	8	72	3	3	4	30	1		171	7	7,715	41	11	219	4	64	98	44
Married	13	90	8	9		69		4	270	17	14,746	116	31	363	6	101	161	81
Widowed	4	20		2		6			12	2	2,015	12	3	83	1	13	42	11
Divorced		5				2			14		1,040	9	1	31		10	7	4
Unknown									1		133			2		1	1	
Females 15 years old and over	16	151	8	21	1	126		4	401	23	23,886	198	42	672	6	149	301	127
Single	6	24	2	5		27		1	84	4	4,416	38	3	144	1	22	71	34
Married	7	94	4	11	1	71		3	255	17	14,401	122	30	363	4	99	167	79
Widowed	3	27	2	4		17			45	2	4,130	29	8	138		23	56	14
Divorced		6		1		11			13		920	8	1	27	1	5	7	
Unknown									4		19	1						
FAMILIES																		
Number of families	15	124	7	13		81		3	310	18	17,688	153	34	521	7	123	230	96
Median size		2.63							2.25		2.66	2.88		2.34		3.09	2.76	
Families having—																		
No children under 10	14	87	5	11		54		2	241	8	12,387	101	27	397	4	72	161	62
1 child under 10		21	1	1		12		1	39	4	2,425	19	5	51	1	26	32	12
2 children under 10	1	10	1			6			16	1	1,349	21	1	36	1	12	18	11
3 or more		6		1		9			14	5	1,527	12	1	37	1	13	19	11

CHARACTERISTICS OF NEGRO POPULATION BY COUNTIES: 1930—Continued

(See note at head of table)

SUBJECT	KANSAS—Continued																	
	Butler	Chase	Chautauqua	Cherokee	Clark	Clay	Cloud	Coffey	Cowley	Crawford	Decatur	Dickinson	Doniphan	Douglas	Edwards	Elk	Ellis	Ellsworth
POPULATION BY SEX																		
Negro population: 1930	309	57	136	651	8	54	39	29	930	994	5	223	633	1,796	45	7	63	96
Male	163	29	62	311	5	29	19	15	438	476	3	116	336	875	26	3	30	45
Female	146	28	74	340	3	25	20	14	492	518	2	107	297	921	19	4	33	51
Negro population: 1920	262	90	143	885	11	98	62	57	861	1,548	1	181	597	1,963	56	21	53	122
Male	152	50	74	441	7	49	27	31	436	804	-	86	313	942	31	7	29	69
Female	110	40	69	444	4	49	35	26	425	744	1	95	284	1,021	25	14	24	53
Percent of total population:																		
1930	0.9	0.8	1.3	2.1	0.2	0.4	0.2	0.2	2.3	2.0	0.1	0.9	4.5	7.1	0.6	0.1	0.4	0.9
1920	0.6	1.3	1.2	2.6	0.2	0.7	0.4	0.4	2.4	2.5	-	0.7	4.4	8.2	0.8	0.2	0.4	1.2
VOTING AGE: 1930																		
Total 21 years old and over	176	32	79	418	3	39	25	24	585	595	2	142	387	1,234	25	2	45	67
Male	90	16	39	191	1	21	12	11	290	291	1	76	215	596	14	1	21	35
Female	86	16	40	227	2	18	13	13	295	304	1	66	172	638	11	1	24	32
AGE: 1930																		
Under 5 years	43	7	10	46	1	2	2	1	96	88	-	25	52	106	3	3	5	5
Under 1 year	9	1	4	8	-	-	-	-	17	14	-	8	9	17	1	1	-	1
5 to 9 years	36	7	11	47	1	2	3	-	88	94	-	18	68	124	5	2	4	12
10 to 14 years	30	4	18	69	1	3	5	2	89	124	2	15	68	142	5	-	5	5
15 to 19 years	21	6	15	64	2	6	4	2	59	81	1	20	51	163	6	-	3	5
20 to 24 years	24	2	11	49	-	4	5	1	85	71	-	28	42	142	2	1	4	3
25 to 29 years	32	1	8	29	-	7	1	1	79	61	-	21	31	112	-	-	5	3
30 to 34 years	24	1	9	29	1	-	2	-	98	71	-	14	39	101	2	-	3	11
35 to 44 years	46	11	23	95	-	3	5	7	105	107	1	33	89	256	7	1	20	23
45 to 54 years	30	8	14	89	-	11	10	6	112	145	1	25	87	274	5	-	8	10
55 to 64 years	13	3	11	69	1	10	1	4	58	104	-	13	58	186	3	-	3	8
65 to 74 years	6	6	4	39	1	4	-	2	35	36	-	9	24	110	4	-	3	5
75 years and over	3	1	2	25	-	2	1	3	26	12	-	2	23	77	3	-	-	6
Unknown	1	-	-	1	-	-	-	-	-	-	-	-	1	3	-	-	-	-
SCHOOL ATTENDANCE																		
Total 7 to 13 year, inclusive	44	8	23	77	2	3	5	2	126	160	2	24	82	196	8	-	7	10
Number attending school	43	8	23	76	2	3	5	2	119	157	2	24	82	193	8	-	6	9
Percent attending school	-	-	-	-	-	-	-	-	94.4	98.1	-	-	-	98.5	-	-	-	-
Total 14 and 15 years, inclusive	11	2	5	32	1	3	2	1	29	44	-	5	25	56	2	-	2	1
Number attending school	10	2	5	29	1	3	2	1	25	40	-	5	24	52	2	-	2	1
Percent attending school	-	-	-	-	-	-	-	-	-	-	-	-	-	-	-	-	-	-
Total 16 and 17 years, inclusive	9	2	6	31	-	2	2	-	27	30	1	6	25	65	1	-	-	1
Number attending school	2	1	2	26	-	1	2	-	16	24	-	5	15	51	-	-	-	1
Percent attending school	-	-	-	-	-	-	-	-	-	-	-	-	-	-	-	-	-	-
Total 18 to 20 years, inclusive	10	3	10	29	1	4	1	1	37	43	-	14	27	94	4	-	3	6
Number attending school	2	1	2	6	1	2	-	-	15	25	-	6	5	36	-	-	1	5
Percent attending school	-	-	-	-	-	-	-	-	-	-	-	-	-	-	-	-	-	-
ILLITERACY																		
Total 10 years old and over	230	43	115	558	6	50	34	28	746	812	5	180	513	1,566	37	2	54	79
Number illiterate	12	2	6	49	-	-	-	6	62	66	-	9	53	85	4	-	5	1
Percent illiterate	5.2	-	5.2	8.8	-	-	-	-	8.3	8.1	-	5.0	10.3	5.4	-	-	-	-
Percent illiterate in 1920	11.1	-	17.1	12.8	-	-	-	-	10.7	8.7	-	5.6	8.5	10.4	-	-	-	-
URBAN AND RURAL																		
Urban population	241	-	-	350	-	51	39	-	858	394	-	197	-	1,437	-	-	-	-
Percent urban	78.0	-	-	53.8	-	-	-	-	92.3	39.6	-	88.3	-	80.0	-	-	-	-
Rural population	68	57	136	301	8	3	-	29	72	600	5	26	633	359	45	7	63	96
Rural-farm	28	8	44	111	-	-	-	10	30	43	5	15	158	195	5	7	3	5
Rural-nonfarm	40	49	92	190	8	3	-	19	42	557	-	11	475	164	40	-	60	91
Percent rural	22.0	-	100.0	46.2	-	-	-	-	7.7	60.4	-	11.7	100.0	20.0	-	-	-	-
MARITAL CONDITION																		
Males 15 years old and over	104	21	46	222	3	26	15	12	318	329	2	87	247	680	18	1	24	38
Single	27	7	13	67	2	12	5	6	81	82	1	32	77	220	6	-	8	10
Married	68	13	28	126	1	7	9	3	202	201	1	43	143	370	6	1	15	26
Widowed	8	1	4	19	-	5	1	2	21	35	-	7	25	72	5	-	1	2
Divorced	-	-	1	9	-	2	-	1	14	10	-	5	1	17	1	-	-	-
Unknown	1	-	-	1	-	-	-	-	-	1	-	-	1	1	-	-	-	-
Females 15 years old and over	96	18	51	267	2	21	14	14	339	359	1	78	198	744	14	1	25	36
Single	12	2	12	55	-	5	4	5	65	80	-	18	36	187	4	-	6	5
Married	65	13	27	134	1	8	9	4	210	198	1	43	137	377	7	1	14	26
Widowed	16	3	8	67	-	8	1	5	52	71	-	14	22	159	3	-	4	5
Divorced	3	-	4	10	1	-	-	-	11	10	-	3	3	21	-	-	1	-
Unknown	-	-	-	1	-	-	-	-	1	-	-	-	-	-	-	-	-	-
FAMILIES																		
Number of families	85	15	41	197	1	20	10	12	242	284	-	62	172	563	12	1	19	33
Median size	-	-	-	2.44	-	-	-	-	2.78	2.57	-	-	2.82	2.44	-	-	-	-
Families having—																		
No children under 10	54	9	30	152	-	18	8	11	162	200	-	42	120	441	8	-	15	24
1 child under 10	10	1	5	19	-	2	-	1	33	38	-	11	18	69	2	-	1	4
2 children under 10	9	3	3	14	1	-	1	-	17	17	-	2	15	28	1	-	2	3
3 or more	12	2	3	12	-	-	1	-	30	29	-	7	19	25	1	1	1	2

CHARACTERISTICS OF NEGRO POPULATION BY COUNTIES: 1930—Continued

(See note at head of table)

SUBJECT	KANSAS—Continued																	
	Finney	Ford	Franklin	Geary	Gove	Graham	Grant	Gray	Greeley	Greenwood	Hamilton	Harper	Harvey	Hodgeman	Jackson	Jefferson	Jewell	Johnson
POPULATION BY SEX																		
Negro population: 1930	293	238	576	1,030	39	429	15	9	5	34	15	69	526	55	89	310	6	765
Male	147	121	319	617	21	233	8	6	3	15	7	41	264	30	47	155	2	379
Female	146	117	257	413	18	196	7	3	2	19	8	28	262	25	42	155	4	386
Negro population: 1920	250	134	509	941	58	413	17	19	3	36	27	57	587	108	101	383	7	599
Male	124	63	256	594	38	222	11	11	1	18	14	35	294	60	45	200	5	292
Female	126	71	253	347	20	191	6	8	2	18	13	22	293	48	56	183	2	307
Percent of total population:																		
1930	2.7	1.2	2.6	7.2	0.7	5.5	0.5	0.1	0.3	0.2	0.5	0.5	2.4	1.3	0.6	2.2	-	2.8
1920	3.3	0.9	2.3	7.0	1.2	5.4	1.6	0.4	0.3	0.2	1.0	0.4	2.8	2.9	0.7	2.6	-	3.3
VOTING AGE: 1930																		
Total 21 years old and over	180	154	371	739	20	242	8	7	3	18	9	43	308	29	54	166	4	471
Male	101	77	209	480	12	134	5	5	3	8	3	25	153	16	33	96	2	225
Female	79	77	162	259	8	108	3	2	-	10	6	18	155	13	21	70	2	246
AGE: 1930																		
Under 5 years	20	17	38	67	2	54	1	-	1	2	2	4	57	8	4	15	-	66
Under 1 year	4	2	6	12	1	10	-	-	-	-	-	1	12	2	2	5	-	15
5 to 9 years	35	19	55	60	2	50	-	1	-	6	1	9	48	5	7	27	-	82
10 to 14 years	25	17	48	52	7	44	3	1	-	5	1	6	57	7	6	37	-	70
15 to 19 years	28	26	54	85	6	32	2	-	1	3	-	5	43	5	15	53	2	67
20 to 24 years	26	24	53	149	6	31	2	-	-	5	4	8	35	8	6	23	-	49
25 to 29 years	26	13	43	127	-	28	-	1	-	1	1	6	41	-	3	14	-	53
30 to 34 years	13	21	37	110	1	23	-	1	-	5	-	3	32	-	5	10	-	41
35 to 44 years	50	45	86	202	2	64	2	1	-	3	-	9	85	9	12	38	1	127
45 to 54 years	25	25	68	98	8	31	4	1	1	3	5	11	57	6	16	32	3	88
55 to 64 years	22	17	50	40	2	32	1	1	2	-	-	6	39	-	5	21	-	67
65 to 74 years	18	8	27	29	-	22	-	2	-	-	-	1	19	4	7	25	-	27
75 years and over	5	6	13	9	3	18	-	-	-	1	1	1	13	3	3	15	-	28
Unknown	-	-	4	2	-	-	-	-	-	-	-	-	-	-	-	-	-	-
SCHOOL ATTENDANCE																		
Total 7 to 13 years, inclusive	42	26	71	76	6	69	3	-	-	7	1	11	71	9	7	40	-	110
Number attending school	42	25	70	73	6	66	3	-	-	7	1	10	71	9	7	40	-	110
Percent attending school																		100.0
Total 14 and 15 years, inclusive	7	7	22	19	4	16	1	1	-	3	-	-	23	2	5	24	-	28
Number attending school	7	6	21	19	4	13	1	1	-	3	-	-	11	2	5	23	-	25
Percent attending school																		
Total 16 and 17 years, inclusive	9	16	22	28	1	10	1	-	-	-	-	3	18	2	9	22	1	30
Number attending school	7	8	15	18	-	5	1	-	-	-	-	1	16	1	7	15	1	12
Percent attending school																		
Total 18 to 20 years, inclusive	20	12	32	75	6	20	1	-	1	2	2	4	28	3	7	31	1	33
Number attending school	8	4	9	13	1	4	1	-	-	-	-	-	9	-	4	12	-	7
Percent attending school																		
ILLITERACY																		
Total 10 years old and over	238	202	483	903	35	325	14	8	4	26	12	56	421	42	78	268	6	617
Number illiterate	14	4	18	32	2	19	-	-	1	-	-	-	17	2	2	22	-	29
Percent illiterate	5.9	2.0	3.7	3.5	-	5.8	-	-	-	-	-	-	4.0	-	-	8.2	-	4.7
Percent illiterate in 1920	7.2	7.5	12.2	3.7	-	6.9	-	-	-	-	-	-	6.7	-	-	9.1	-	12.3
URBAN AND RURAL																		
Urban population	252	205	449	493	-	-	-	-	-	25	-	69	518	-	44	-	-	269
Percent urban	86.0	86.1	78.0	47.9	-	-	-	-	-	-	-	-	98.5	-	-	-	-	35.2
Rural population	41	33	127	537	39	429	15	9	5	9	15	-	8	55	45	310	6	496
Rural-farm	40	7	93	20	39	287	9	9	-	1	1	-	8	44	43	145	1	118
Rural-nonfarm	1	26	34	517	-	142	6	-	5	8	14	-	-	11	2	165	5	378
Percent rural	14.0	13.9	22.0	52.1	-	100.0	-	-	-	-	-	-	1.5	-	-	100.0	-	64.8
MARITAL CONDITION																		
Males 15 years old and over	116	94	241	532	16	154	6	5	3	11	5	29	187	18	43	123	2	264
Single	37	28	95	291	8	45	3	2	1	5	1	8	54	6	18	51	-	79
Married	61	56	130	228	6	86	3	2	2	5	3	15	118	8	17	57	2	148
Widowed	15	9	13	11	2	17	-	-	-	1	1	6	9	4	6	15	-	29
Divorced	2	1	3	2	-	6	-	1	-	-	-	-	6	-	2	-	-	7
Unknown	1	-	-	-	-	-	-	-	-	-	-	-	-	-	-	-	-	1
Females 15 years old and over	97	91	194	319	12	127	5	2	1	10	6	21	177	17	29	108	4	283
Single	15	18	47	54	4	19	2	-	-	1	2	1	23	7	9	35	2	64
Married	58	55	114	216	6	89	2	2	-	7	2	15	115	7	19	56	2	155
Widowed	20	14	28	38	2	15	-	-	-	2	2	5	33	2	-	17	-	54
Divorced	3	4	5	11	-	4	1	-	1	-	-	-	6	-	1	-	-	9
Unknown	1	-	-	-	-	-	-	-	-	-	-	-	-	1	-	-	-	1
FAMILIES																		
Number of families	71	79	151	228	9	114	4	2	3	6	4	24	143	13	25	75	1	176
Median size	-	-	2.47	2.47	-	2.97	-	-	-	-	-	-	2.95	-	-	-	-	2.73
Families having—																		
No children under 10	48	59	107	163	7	75	3	1	2	1	3	17	93	7	19	51	1	115
1 child under 10	10	12	21	32	-	13	1	1	1	2	-	5	23	3	3	14	-	23
2 children under 10	3	3	12	20	2	9	-	-	-	3	-	1	10	1	1	6	-	14
3 or more	10	5	11	13	-	17	-	-	-	-	1	1	17	2	2	4	-	24

CHARACTERISTICS OF NEGRO POPULATION BY COUNTIES: 1930—Continued

(See note at head of table)

SUBJECT	KANSAS—Continued																	
	Kearny	Kingman	Kiowa	Labette	Lane	Leavenworth	Lincoln	Linn	Logan	Lyon	McPherson	Marion	Marshall	Meade	Miami	Mitchell	Montgomery	Morris
POPULATION BY SEX																		
Negro population: 1930	5	26	6	1,639	7	4,645	7	235	186	754	4	50	92	36	794	24	3,871	239
Male	3	16	2	812	7	3,138	4	135	100	365	3	27	45	18	418	2	1,941	152
Female	2	10	4	827	-	1,507	3	100	86	389	1	23	47	18	376	22	1,930	87
Negro population: 1920	9	43	4	1,980	1	3,780	15	307	149	739	-	92	161	11	581	27	2,954	247
Male	6	22	2	968	1	2,382	11	159	81	361	-	51	79	8	298	7	1,480	131
Female	3	21	2	1,012	-	1,398	4	148	68	378	-	41	82	3	283	20	1,474	116
Percent of total population: 1930	0.2	0.2	0.1	5.2	0.2	10.9	0.1	1.7	4.5	2.6	-	0.2	0.4	0.5	3.7	0.2	7.5	2.0
1920	0.3	0.4	0.1	5.8	-	9.8	0.2	2.2	4.6	2.8	-	0.4	0.7	0.2	2.9	0.2	6.0	2.1
VOTING AGE: 1930																		
Total 21 years old and over	4	16	5	1,023	7	3,618	6	162	88	469	4	31	59	26	534	2	2,295	159
Male	3	7	2	508	7	2,632	4	96	49	233	3	14	30	15	285	2	1,157	108
Female	1	9	3	515	-	986	2	66	39	236	1	17	29	11	249	-	1,138	51
AGE: 1930																		
Under 5 years	-	-	-	120	-	203	-	16	19	70	-	2	6	2	62	-	345	11
Under 1 year	-	-	-	23	-	50	-	3	3	16	-	-	-	-	9	-	67	-
5 to 9 years	1	4	-	186	-	244	-	18	20	63	-	5	6	4	76	-	414	25
10 to 14 years	-	3	-	139	-	254	-	18	26	67	-	6	9	1	66	12	359	20
15 to 19 years	-	3	1	142	-	251	1	19	26	66	-	4	9	1	44	10	372	22
20 to 24 years	-	-	-	127	1	370	-	11	18	73	-	4	12	5	51	-	367	24
25 to 29 years	-	2	-	110	-	541	-	14	5	54	2	2	3	4	56	-	296	22
30 to 34 years	-	4	-	121	1	598	-	11	8	63	1	5	3	3	49	-	311	17
35 to 44 years	2	7	2	249	5	1,028	2	42	18	111	-	6	12	9	128	-	567	30
45 to 54 years	1	-	-	206	-	559	1	28	26	90	-	7	14	4	105	2	430	30
55 to 64 years	-	2	-	130	-	312	2	22	14	50	-	4	7	1	81	-	251	19
65 to 74 years	1	-	2	69	-	164	1	17	4	23	1	-	8	2	50	-	103	8
75 years and over	-	1	1	39	-	118	-	8	2	24	-	5	3	-	26	-	52	11
Unknown	-	-	-	1	-	3	-	11	-	-	-	-	-	-	-	-	4	-
SCHOOL ATTENDANCE																		
Total 7 to 13 years, inclusive	1	6	-	224	-	349	-	29	30	91	-	8	8	4	96	4	536	32
Number attending school	1	6	-	217	-	335	-	28	30	88	-	8	8	3	95	4	507	27
Percent attending school	-	-	-	96.9	-	96.0	-	-	-	-	-	-	-	-	-	-	94.6	-
Total 14 and 15 years, inclusive	-	1	-	57	-	94	-	6	8	19	-	2	3	1	23	12	141	13
Number attending school	-	1	-	54	-	78	-	5	8	17	-	2	3	-	18	12	126	11
Percent attending school	-	-	-	-	-	-	-	-	-	-	-	-	-	-	-	-	89.4	-
Total 16 and 17 years, inclusive	-	-	-	53	-	92	1	4	13	31	-	1	4	-	13	4	140	6
Number attending school	-	-	-	42	-	53	-	-	9	20	-	1	3	-	7	4	81	3
Percent attending school	-	-	-	-	-	-	-	-	-	-	-	-	-	-	-	-	57.9	-
Total 18 to 20 years, inclusive	-	2	1	88	-	189	-	12	18	45	-	4	7	2	35	2	252	9
Number attending school	-	1	1	38	-	30	-	1	2	15	-	1	4	-	7	1	48	3
Percent attending school	-	-	-	-	-	15.9	-	-	-	-	-	-	-	-	-	-	19.0	-
ILLITERACY																		
Total 10 years old and over	4	22	6	1,333	7	4,198	7	201	147	621	4	43	80	30	656	24	3,112	203
Number illiterate	-	-	2	91	-	307	-	9	1	36	-	8	3	2	47	-	226	16
Percent illiterate	-	-	-	6.8	-	7.3	-	4.5	0.7	5.8	-	-	-	-	7.2	-	7.3	7.9
Percent illiterate in 1920	-	-	-	7.9	-	12.0	-	11.6	3.5	9.5	-	-	2.2	-	12.7	-	10.9	10.1
URBAN AND RURAL																		
Urban population	-	25	-	1,277	-	2,184	-	-	-	564	3	-	9	-	597	2	3,088	75
Percent urban	-	-	-	77.9	-	47.0	-	-	-	74.8	-	-	-	-	75.2	-	79.8	31.4
Rural population	5	1	6	362	7	2,461	7	235	186	190	1	50	83	36	197	22	783	164
Rural-farm	4	-	-	51	-	193	7	33	147	73	1	-	41	19	28	-	598	58
Rural-nonfarm	1	1	6	311	7	2,268	-	202	39	117	-	50	42	17	169	22	185	106
Percent rural	-	-	-	22.1	-	53.0	-	100.0	100.0	25.2	-	-	-	-	24.8	-	20.2	68.6
MARITAL CONDITION																		
Males 15 years old and over	3	10	2	583	7	2,793	4	107	69	269	3	19	36	15	312	2	1,386	121
Single	1	5	1	169	4	1,139	1	30	36	82	1	8	14	2	108	1	384	53
Married	1	5	1	335	3	1,124	2	55	27	152	2	10	21	13	167	1	824	53
Widowed	1	-	-	64	-	148	-	18	3	22	-	1	1	-	23	-	126	11
Divorced	-	-	-	14	-	274	1	2	3	13	-	-	-	-	14	-	51	4
Unknown	-	-	-	1	-	108	-	2	-	-	-	-	-	-	-	-	1	-
Females 15 years old and over	1	9	4	611	-	1,151	3	76	52	285	1	18	35	14	278	10	1,367	62
Single	-	2	1	121	-	233	1	13	16	66	-	4	11	1	40	8	261	13
Married	1	5	2	347	-	670	2	50	31	150	1	10	20	13	163	2	820	39
Widowed	-	2	1	118	-	214	-	11	4	53	-	3	2	-	56	-	221	9
Divorced	-	-	-	24	-	31	-	-	1	16	-	1	2	-	19	-	64	1
Unknown	-	-	-	1	-	3	-	2	-	-	-	-	-	-	-	-	1	-
FAMILIES																		
Number of families	2	7	2	471	-	825	3	77	42	203	1	14	24	12	183	-	1,009	57
Median size	-	-	-	2.59	-	2.22	-	-	-	2.85	-	-	-	-	2.60	-	2.97	-
Familes having— No children under 10	1	5	2	330	-	627	3	64	25	141	1	10	18	9	130	-	643	44
1 child under 10	1	-	-	68	-	97	-	3	5	30	-	1	4	2	19	-	168	3
2 children under 10	-	2	-	25	-	42	-	5	8	11	-	3	-	-	13	-	94	3
3 or more	-	-	-	48	-	59	-	5	4	21	-	-	2	1	21	-	104	7

CHARACTERISTICS OF NEGRO POPULATION BY COUNTIES: 1930—Continued

(See note at head of table)

SUBJECT	KANSAS—Continued																	
	Morton	Nemaha	Neosho	Ness	Norton	Osage	Osborne	Ottawa	Pawnee	Philips	Pottawatomie	Pratt	Reno	Republic	Rice	Riley	Rooks	Rush
POPULATION BY SEX																		
Negro population: 1930	17	112	569	1	14	144	26	26	120	28	57	333	991	2	139	338	70	19
Male	10	59	313	1	8	81	15	16	56	16	27	167	541	2	67	164	34	9
Female	7	53	256	-	6	63	11	11	64	12	30	166	450	-	72	174	36	10
Negro population: 1920	19	142	532	-	10	257	24	34	127	28	83	397	1,052	9	125	354	71	21
Male	12	72	273	-	8	136	16	18	61	15	50	216	566	7	69	194	31	10
Female	7	70	259	-	2	121	8	16	66	13	33	181	486	2	56	160	40	11
Percent of total population:																		
1930	0.4	0.6	2.5	-	0.1	0.8	0.2	0.3	1.1	0.2	0.4	2.5	2.1	-	1.0	1.7	0.7	0.2
1920	0.6	0.8	2.2	-	0.1	1.4	0.2	0.3	1.4	0.2	0.5	3.1	2.4	0.1	0.8	1.7	0.7	0.3
VOTING AGE: 1930																		
Total 21 years old and over	10	65	337	1	9	109	16	20	68	20	30	207	585	2	72	197	43	11
Male	6	33	181	1	6	59	9	12	36	12	19	109	317	2	31	99	17	8
Female	4	32	156	-	3	50	7	8	32	8	11	98	268	-	41	98	26	3
AGE: 1930																		
Under 5 years	-	16	53	-	4	4	1	-	11	1	11	25	60	-	15	31	7	-
Under 1 year	-	2	9	-	1	1	-	-	3	-	3	5	8	-	4	9	1	-
5 to 9 years	3	18	49	-	-	8	2	3	18	4	4	41	100	-	21	46	4	3
10 to 14 years	1	6	49	-	-	8	3	1	13	2	7	37	93	-	15	36	10	3
15 to 19 years	3	5	63	-	1	14	4	3	9	1	3	18	114	-	13	21	5	2
20 to 24 years	1	9	70	-	4	8	-	1	19	5	2	26	120	-	8	33	5	-
25 to 29 years	1	5	54	1	-	10	-	3	7	3	5	22	71	-	8	14	4	-
30 to 34 years	-	11	31	-	1	8	2	2	10	1	4	22	86	-	12	17	2	4
35 to 44 years	-	10	70	-	1	11	6	4	14	4	6	56	128	1	19	46	9	2
45 to 54 years	3	14	70	-	3	31	5	3	10	5	4	43	104	-	15	41	13	4
55 to 64 years	2	8	40	-	-	19	-	5	13	1	3	24	62	1	7	23	7	-
65 to 74 years	1	5	11	-	-	17	1	-	4	-	3	11	35	-	5	20	3	-
75 years and over	2	4	8	-	-	6	2	2	2	1	5	7	18	-	1	10	1	1
Unknown	-	1	1	-	-	-	-	-	-	-	-	1	-	-	-	-	-	-
SCHOOL ATTENDANCE																		
Total 7 to 13 years, inclusive	2	17	69	-	-	12	4	4	21	4	7	52	145	-	25	52	11	5
Number attending school	2	17	67	-	-	12	4	4	21	4	7	52	144	-	25	52	11	5
Percent attending school	-	-	-	-	-	-	-	-	-	-	-	-	99.3	-	-	-	-	-
Total 14 and 15 years, inclusive	1	2	22	-	-	5	-	2	1	1	3	13	28	-	6	16	2	2
Number attending school	1	2	18	-	-	5	-	2	1	1	3	13	27	-	6	15	2	2
Percent attending school	-	-	-	-	-	-	-	-	-	-	-	-	-	-	-	-	-	-
Total 16 and 17 years, inclusive	-	-	26	-	-	4	2	-	4	-	2	6	41	-	4	8	3	1
Number attending school	-	-	16	-	-	2	2	-	3	-	2	5	21	-	2	6	2	1
Percent attending school	-	-	-	-	-	-	-	-	-	-	-	-	-	-	-	-	-	-
Total 18 to 20 years, inclusive	2	5	42	-	1	8	2	1	6	-	2	12	100	-	9	13	2	-
Number attending school	-	1	6	-	-	5	2	-	-	-	-	5	11	-	2	3	-	-
Percent attending school	-	-	-	-	-	-	-	-	-	-	-	-	11.0	-	-	-	-	-
ILLITERACY																		
Total 10 years old and over	14	78	467	1	10	132	23	24	91	23	42	267	831	2	103	261	59	16
Number illiterate	-	11	21	-	-	6	2	3	8	-	6	9	31	-	3	21	2	1
Percent illiterate	-	-	4.5	-	-	4.5	-	-	-	-	-	3.4	3.7	-	2.9	8.0	-	-
Percent illiterate in 1920	-	8.9	7.0	-	-	10.5	-	-	6.9	-	-	13.7	4.5	-	-	3.2	-	-
URBAN AND RURAL																		
Urban population	-	-	507	-	12	-	-	-	100	-	-	254	954	-	58	332	-	-
Percent urban	-	-	89.1	-	-	-	-	-	83.3	-	-	76.3	96.3	-	41.7	98.2	-	-
Rural population	17	112	62	1	2	144	26	27	20	28	57	79	37	2	81	6	79	19
Rural-farm	17	37	21	1	2	24	5	-	5	10	25	55	29	-	8	1	21	4
Rural-nonfarm	-	75	41	-	-	120	21	27	15	18	32	24	8	2	73	5	49	15
Percent rural	-	100.0	10.9	-	-	100.0	-	-	16.7	-	-	23.7	3.7	-	58.3	1.8	-	-
MARITAL CONDITION																		
Males 15 years old and over	8	36	222	1	6	67	12	13	42	13	20	117	424	2	42	112	22	8
Single	4	12	80	1	-	30	7	3	20	8	6	32	171	-	12	33	7	2
Married	3	22	125	-	5	27	5	7	19	5	11	71	213	-	28	65	13	3
Widowed	1	2	13	-	-	5	-	3	1	-	3	7	28	2	1	10	2	2
Divorced	-	-	4	-	1	5	-	-	2	-	-	7	12	-	1	3	-	1
Unknown	-	-	-	-	-	-	-	-	-	-	-	-	-	-	-	1	-	-
Females 15 years old and over	5	36	196	-	4	57	8	10	36	8	15	113	314	-	46	113	27	5
Single	2	7	47	-	-	12	1	2	6	1	4	22	56	-	10	21	6	3
Married	3	18	117	-	4	27	5	7	19	5	8	74	193	-	29	67	14	2
Widowed	-	11	27	-	-	17	2	1	10	2	3	12	54	-	7	20	4	-
Divorced	-	-	5	-	-	1	-	-	1	-	-	5	10	-	-	2	3	-
Unknown	-	-	-	-	-	-	-	-	-	-	-	-	1	-	-	3	-	-
FAMILIES																		
Number of families	2	24	146	-	5	46	6	11	29	7	17	76	249	-	35	92	21	6
Median size	-	-	2.98	-	-	-	-	-	-	-	-	-	2.62	-	-	-	-	-
Families having—																		
No children under 10	1	13	97	-	3	40	5	9	17	4	14	51	169	-	22	60	17	4
1 child under 10	-	3	20	-	-	3	-	1	3	1	-	9	41	-	4	12	1	1
2 children under 10	-	2	12	-	2	2	-	1	5	2	-	6	17	-	2	6	1	1
3 or more	1	6	17	-	-	1	1	-	4	-	3	10	22	-	7	14	2	-

CHARACTERISTICS OF NEGRO POPULATION BY COUNTIES: 1930—Continued

(See note at head of table)

SUBJECT	Russell	Saline	Scott	Sedgwick	Seward	Shawnee	Sheridan	Smith	Stafford	Stevens	Sumner	Thomas	Trego	Wabaunsee	Wallace	Washington	Wichita	Wilson
	KANSAS—Continued																	
POPULATION BY SEX																		
Negro population: 1930	39	540	3	5,726	7	6,785	25	7	37	142	285	13	29	392	66	12	161	132
Male	18	258	2	2,820	5	3,317	11	5	19	79	141	8	15	230	37	8	155	75
Female	21	282	1	2,906	2	3,468	14	2	18	63	144	5	14	162	29	4	6	57
Negro population: 1920	49	661	7	3,627	6	5,176	42	10	114	169	352	13	35	545	84	28	8	150
Male	32	342	4	1,815	4	2,542	22	6	54	100	188	4	21	310	49	15	4	85
Female	17	319	3	1,812	2	2,634	20	4	60	69	164	9	14	235	35	13	4	65
Percent of total population:																		
1930	0.4	1.8	0.1	4.2	0.1	8.0	0.4	0.1	0.4	3.1	1.0	0.2	0.4	3.6	2.3	0.1	6.2	0.7
1920	0.5	2.6	0.2	3.9	0.1	7.5	0.8	0.1	1.0	4.3	1.2	0.2	0.6	4.8	3.5	0.2	0.4	0.7
VOTING AGE: 1930																		
Total 21 years old and over	27	363	3	3,651	6	4,421	14	7	25	68	173	4	26	236	38	8	156	77
Male	13	180	2	1,829	5	2,143	6	5	14	37	86	3	13	133	23	5	153	42
Female	14	183	1	1,822	1	2,278	8	2	11	31	87	1	13	103	15	3	3	35
AGE: 1930																		
Under 5 years	4	44	-	454	-	503	2	-	2	17	23	-	2	33	5	-	3	14
Under 1 year	-	10	-	76	-	92	-	-	-	1	3	-	-	7	-	-	1	2
5 to 9 years	5	55	-	537	-	600	1	-	4	24	27	3	1	42	5	-	-	11
10 to 14 years	2	37	-	486	-	576	2	-	4	14	27	4	-	39	10	2	-	17
15 to 19 years	1	36	-	483	-	578	3	-	2	15	32	2	-	38	4	1	2	10
20 to 24 years	4	35	1	562	1	545	6	2	1	8	20	-	3	26	13	1	53	12
25 to 29 years	6	48	-	642	1	569	1	1	1	8	12	-	3	20	7	-	33	9
30 to 34 years	2	49	-	550	-	509	3	-	2	6	20	-	4	24	5	-	34	11
35 to 44 years	2	78	1	986	1	1,014	4	1	9	22	44	2	3	49	2	6	28	25
45 to 54 years	5	66	1	608	2	844	2	1	7	11	37	1	4	42	7	-	4	14
55 to 64 years	3	57	-	263	1	562	-	1	2	5	20	-	1	48	5	-	3	3
65 to 74 years	4	25	-	106	1	304	1	1	1	9	17	1	7	21	3	1	1	2
75 years and over	1	9	-	49	-	171	-	-	2	3	6	-	1	10	-	1	-	4
Unknown	-	1	-	-	-	10	-	-	-	-	-	-	-	-	-	-	-	-
SCHOOL ATTENDANCE																		
Total 7 to 13 years, inclusive	3	66	-	713	-	797	3	-	6	28	37	5	1	55	12	1	-	19
Number attending school	3	63	-	702	-	780	3	-	6	25	36	4	1	55	12	1	-	17
Percent attending school	-	-	-	98.5	-	97.9	-	-	-	-	-	-	-	-	-	-	-	-
Total 14 and 15 years, inclusive	1	18	-	184	-	272	-	-	1	7	11	1	-	15	-	2	-	6
Number attending school	1	17	-	177	-	228	-	-	1	7	10	1	-	14	-	2	-	6
Percent attending school	-	-	-	96.2	-	83.8	-	-	-	-	-	-	-	-	-	-	-	-
Total 16 and 17 years, inclusive	-	12	-	178	-	230	1	-	2	4	11	1	-	17	3	-	1	4
Number attending school	-	6	-	121	-	143	1	-	1	4	5	1	-	10	2	-	1	3
Percent attending school	-	-	-	68.0	-	62.2	-	-	-	-	-	-	-	-	-	-	-	-
Total 18 to 20 years, inclusive	1	20	-	323	1	325	5	-	-	12	17	1	-	18	5	1	1	8
Number attending school	-	8	-	73	-	68	2	-	-	3	5	1	-	3	1	-	1	2
Percent attending school	-	-	-	22.6	-	20.9	-	-	-	-	-	-	-	-	-	-	-	-
ILLITERACY																		
Total 10 years old and over	30	441	3	4,735	7	5,682	22	7	31	101	235	10	26	317	56	12	158	107
Number illiterate	4	24	-	208	1	369	-	1	1	3	15	-	-	13	2	1	3	7
Percent illiterate	-	5.4	-	4.4	-	6.5	-	-	-	3.0	6.4	-	-	4.1	-	-	1.9	6.5
Percent illiterate in 1920	-	9.8	-	4.5	-	8.3	-	-	-	.9	7.7	-	-	7.3	-	-	-	9.3
URBAN AND RURAL																		
Urban population	-	532	-	5,623	3	5,756	-	-	-	-	185	-	-	-	-	-	-	35
Percent urban	-	98.5	-	98.2	-	84.8	-	-	-	-	64.9	-	-	-	-	-	-	26.5
Rural population	39	8	3	103	4	1,029	25	7	37	142	100	13	29	392	66	12	161	97
Rural-farm	11	8	2	25	2	236	3	5	20	121	23	11	15	144	13	6	2	12
Rural-nonfarm	28	-	1	78	2	793	22	2	17	21	77	2	14	248	53	6	159	85
Percent rural	-	1.5	-	1.8	-	15.2	-	-	-	100.0	35.1	-	-	100.0	-	-	100.0	73.5
MARITAL CONDITION																		
Males 15 years old and over	14	193	2	2,100	5	2,470	9	5	15	48	100	5	13	163	27	7	154	50
Single	3	35	1	551	1	698	4	4	7	17	28	3	4	59	10	4	150	10
Married	10	133	1	1,303	4	1,465	4	1	5	27	63	2	9	80	13	2	4	32
Widowed	1	12	-	162	-	193	1	-	3	4	8	-	-	19	2	-	-	8
Divorced	-	12	-	84	-	114	-	-	-	-	1	-	-	5	2	1	-	-
Unknown	-	1	-	-	-	-	-	-	-	-	-	-	-	-	-	-	-	-
Females 15 years old and over	14	211	1	2,149	2	2,636	11	2	12	39	108	1	13	115	19	3	4	40
Single	2	44	-	378	-	514	5	-	1	8	19	-	1	13	5	-	1	3
Married	10	132	1	1,287	2	1,542	4	2	8	29	70	1	9	79	12	2	3	32
Widowed	2	28	-	402	-	435	2	-	2	2	15	-	3	16	1	-	-	3
Divorced	-	7	-	82	-	144	-	-	1	-	4	-	-	7	1	1	-	2
Unknown	-	-	-	-	-	1	-	-	-	-	-	-	-	-	-	-	-	-
FAMILIES																		
Number of families	11	171	1	1,439	1	1,856	5	1	11	35	76	3	10	105	16	2	2	39
Median size	-	2.28	-	2.79	-	2.70	-	-	-	-	-	-	-	2.78	-	-	-	-
Families having—																		
No children under 10	6	128	1	970	1	1,290	3	1	8	19	56	2	6	71	10	2	1	29
1 child under 10	2	21	-	223	-	264	1	-	2	5	9	-	4	17	4	-	-	4
2 children under 10	2	4	-	122	-	174	1	-	-	3	4	-	-	7	1	-	-	1
3 or more	1	18	-	124	-	128	-	-	1	8	7	1	-	10	1	-	1	5

CHARACTERISTICS OF NEGRO POPULATION BY COUNTIES: 1930—Continued

(See note at head of table)

SUBJECT	KANSAS—Continued Woodson	KANSAS—Continued Wyandotte	KENTUCKY The State	Adair	Allen	Anderson	Ballard	Barren	Bath	Bell	Boone	Bourbon	Boyd	Boyle	Bracken	Breathitt	Breckinridge
POPULATION BY SEX																	
Negro population: 1920	8	21,584	226,040	1,015	482	562	931	2,773	744	1,916	379	4,007	1,081	3,171	222	203	941
Male	4	10,489	113,501	480	225	276	481	1,373	374	928	207	2,044	556	1,566	114	113	488
Female	4	11,095	112,539	535	257	286	450	1,400	370	988	172	1,963	525	1,605	108	90	453
Negro population: 1920	43	16,758	235,938	1,170	798	612	1,386	3,302	1,008	2,445	477	4,898	730	3,190	313	185	1,029
Male	20	8,334	118,548	590	388	306	727	1,637	507	1,294	238	2,475	385	1,572	158	96	533
Female	23	8,424	117,390	580	410	306	659	1,665	501	1,151	239	2,423	345	1,618	155	89	496
Percent of total population:																	
1930	0.1	15.3	8.6	6.2	3.2	6.6	9.4	10.7	6.7	4.9	3.9	22.2	2.5	19.5	2.3	1.0	5.4
1920	0.5	13.7	9.8	6.8	4.8	6.1	11.5	13.0	8.4	7.2	5.0	26.6	2.5	21.3	3.1	0.9	5.2
VOTING AGE: 1930																	
Total 21 years old and over	6	14,009	140,503	504	279	337	521	1,454	401	1,028	228	2,620	683	2,048	145	111	471
Male	2	6,800	71,020	242	140	169	262	703	205	509	130	1,345	358	992	76	64	249
Female	4	7,209	69,483	262	139	168	259	751	196	519	98	1,275	325	1,056	69	47	222
AGE: 1930																	
Under 5 years		1,769	18,587	129	42	56	81	291	71	197	35	292	113	220	20	24	99
Under 1 year		303	3,500	31	13	11	15	62	17	35	9	58	25	36	6	4	19
5 to 9 years	2	2,011	21,824	120	55	66	93	338	89	243	45	371	96	251	17	25	108
10 to 14 years		1,802	20,290	118	50	46	103	330	86	206	34	333	84	267	15	26	118
15 to 19 years		1,687	20,762	124	49	53	121	310	81	201	30	330	86	325	22	17	126
20 to 24 years		1,573	19,816	96	33	42	71	243	54	172	44	275	129	290	14	12	73
25 to 29 years		1,852	18,202	46	30	27	57	179	55	158	24	262	101	228	23	15	48
30 to 34 years		1,884	16,792	44	27	34	39	165	44	122	26	232	89	228	13	12	38
35 to 44 years	1	3,724	33,840	117	71	64	110	310	74	250	49	555	168	454	24	28	100
45 to 54 years	1	2,928	27,707	110	60	68	114	285	74	215	27	619	110	403	30	26	83
55 to 64 years	4	1,404	15,289	51	28	59	69	166	66	88	36	390	67	244	27	12	73
65 to 74 years		631	8,505	41	29	28	45	98	34	42	18	239	26	169	11	6	49
75 years and over		313	4,168	16	8	15	25	57	16	19	10	103	10	88	6		26
Unknown		6	258	3		4	3	1		3	1	6	2	4			
SCHOOL ATTENDANCE																	
Total 7 to 13 years, inclusive	1	2,693	29,041	156	69	79	137	478	116	300	50	476	128	375	24	34	154
Number attending school		2,615	26,450	109	58	77	127	414	113	278	45	437	118	348	23	28	137
Percent attending school		97.1	91.1	69.9			92.7	86.6	97.4	92.7		91.8	92.2	92.8			89.0
Total 14 and 15 years, inclusive		723	8,242	55	24	18	52	120	35	78	18	129	31	126	6	9	50
Number attending school		659	6,702	39	18	16	41	89	32	64	15	109	23	110	5	8	45
Percent attending school		91.1	81.3					74.2				84.5		87.3			
Total 16 and 17 years, inclusive		673	8,509	52	27	21	52	125	32	94	7	142	31	115	9	8	58
Number attending school		439	4,193	22	16	14	25	58	15	57	2	72	16	68	2	2	41
Percent attending school		65.2	49.3					46.4				50.7		59.1			
Total 18 to 20 years, inclusive		949	12,400	69	18	26	51	175	52	117	22	199	58	201	12	7	65
Number attending school		270	2,016	7	4	8	12	28	7	30	2	43	5	40	2		22
Percent attending school		28.5	16.3					16.0		25.6		21.6		19.9			
ILLITERACY																	
Total 10 years old and over	6	17,804	185,629	766	385	440	757	2,144	584	1,476	299	3,344	872	2,700	185	154	734
Number illiterate		959	28,553	129	93	126	133	392	62	193	49	719	73	399	25	42	119
Percent illiterate		5.4	15.4	16.8	24.2	28.6	17.6	18.3	10.6	13.1	16.4	21.5	8.4	14.8	13.5	27.3	16.2
Percent illiterate in 1920		8.2	21.0	24.7	25.2	25.3	20.0	25.4	25.2	18.2	17.1	28.4	12.9	22.6	20.3	24.8	23.3
URBAN AND RURAL																	
Urban population		19,872	116,561					772		1,459		1,533	1,055	1,789			
Percent urban		92.1	51.6					27.8		76.1		38.3	97.6	56.4			
Rural population	8	1,712	109,479	1,015	482	562	931	2,001	744	457	379	2,474	26	1,382	222	203	941
Rural-farm		275	47,849	609	218	43	569	1,617	214	30	222	941	10	455	70	32	411
Rural-nonfarm	8	1,437	61,630	406	264	519	362	384	530	427	157	1,533	16	927	152	171	530
Percent rural		7.9	48.4	100.0	100.0	100.0	100.0	72.2	100.0	23.9	100.0	61.7	2.4	43.6	100.0	100.0	100.0
MARITAL CONDITION																	
Males 15 years old and over	2	7,746	83,165	309	167	192	342	882	256	632	145	1,542	408	1,201	84	77	304
Single		1,790	26,864	110	53	73	117	285	98	196	51	527	127	423	27	31	106
Married	2	5,099	47,225	179	99	100	185	514	138	392	82	838	242	666	47	41	164
Widowed		593	7,242	20	9	18	33	74	19	31	8	134	27	98	10	5	33
Divorced		256	1,722		5	1	7	7	1	12	4	41	12	12			1
Unknown		8	112		1			2		1		2		2			
Females 15 years old and over	4	8,256	82,174	339	168	202	312	932	242	638	120	1,469	380	1,232	86	51	312
Single		1,319	17,585	97	39	57	60	227	61	131	31	318	66	291	19	5	92
Married	2	5,197	47,137	180	98	108	198	522	143	393	77	839	245	678	47	37	168
Widowed	1	1,416	15,349	58	29	37	49	164	37	102	11	263	57	238	20	6	42
Divorced	1	323	2,007	4	2		5	18	1	12	1	48	12	22		2	8
Unknown		1	96					1				1		3		1	2
FAMILIES																	
Number of families	3	6,136	60,672	220	125	160	219	668	178	446	92	1,235	270	903	61	41	220
Median size		2.71	2.69	3.91	3.18	2.48	3.58	3.32	3.31	3.29		2.41	2.90	2.70			3.38
Families having—																	
No children under 10	2	4,312	41,945	111	79	113	131	375	113	253	55	920	171	658	40	23	140
1 child under 10		845	8,146	44	20	14	37	128	19	77	13	135	41	122	11	6	30
2 children under 10	1	463	4,768	26	8	13	25	68	19	39	14	85	31	64	6	2	21
3 or more		516	5,813	39	18	20	26	97	27	77	10	95	27	59	4	10	29

CHARACTERISTICS OF NEGRO POPULATION BY COUNTIES: 1930—Continued

(See note at head of table)

KENTUCKY—Continued

SUBJECT	Bullitt	Butler	Caldwell	Calloway	Campbell	Carlisle	Carroll	Carter	Casey
POPULATION BY SEX									
Negro population: 1930	340	297	1,722	800	1,328	294	385	53	130
Male	177	156	841	404	683	144	214	29	71
Female	163	141	881	396	645	150	171	24	59
Negro population: 1920	442	475	1,908	1,028	934	311	401	59	168
Male	233	234	952	510	443	153	215	27	78
Female	209	241	956	518	491	158	186	32	90
Percent of total population:									
1930	3.8	2.4	12.5	4.5	1.8	4.0	4.7	0.2	0.8
1920	4.7	3.1	13.7	4.9	1.5	3.8	4.8	0.3	1.0
VOTING AGE: 1930									
Total 21 years old and over	201	158	1,003	461	931	162	229	25	67
Male	101	84	496	233	484	78	133	16	36
Female	100	74	507	228	447	84	96	9	31
AGE: 1930									
Under 5 years	32	28	136	61	82	28	34	7	14
Under 1 year	4	6	23	9	14	3	5	2	7
5 to 9 years	32	42	189	79	99	26	40	9	21
10 to 14 years	38	37	187	76	88	36	33	5	16
15 to 19 years	37	28	177	107	105	36	41	7	11
20 to 24 years	22	16	151	74	135	22	37	3	8
25 to 29 years	22	13	119	58	156	18	30	5	6
30 to 34 years	20	16	97	44	136	19	20	5	3
35 to 44 years	40	26	221	125	271	33	51	5	15
45 to 54 years	42	40	194	92	151	27	34	3	11
55 to 64 years	25	17	138	45	68	27	37	2	8
65 to 74 years	20	15	68	27	22	12	20	2	12
75 years and over	10	18	45	12	13	10	8	-----	5
Unknown	-----	1	-----	-----	2	-----	-----	-----	-----
SCHOOL ATTENDANCE									
Total 7 to 13 years, inclusive	52	50	244	101	137	45	48	12	24
Number attending school	41	40	194	92	134	43	44	12	18
Percent attending school	-----	-----	79.5	91.1	97.8	-----	-----	-----	-----
Total 14 and 15 years, inclusive	16	14	80	51	38	15	14	1	5
Number attending school	11	9	44	42	32	14	9	1	4
Percent attending school	-----	-----	-----	-----	-----	-----	-----	-----	-----
Total 16 and 17 years, inclusive	11	12	73	35	38	17	21	4	7
Number attending school	2	9	28	21	18	8	5	2	2
Percent attending school	-----	-----	-----	-----	-----	-----	-----	-----	-----
Total 18 to 20 years inclusive	17	18	101	60	69	17	22	3	4
Number attending school	2	7	21	19	4	4	-----	-----	-----
Percent attending school	-----	-----	20.8	-----	-----	-----	-----	-----	-----
ILLITERACY									
Total 10 years old and over	276	227	1,397	660	1,147	240	311	37	95
Number illiterate	49	40	268	86	149	35	51	1	14
Percent illiterate	17.8	17.6	19.2	13.0	13.0	14.6	16.4	-----	-----
Percent illiterate in 1920	21.8	14.6	26.7	19.6	14.5	18.3	21.6	-----	23.4
URBAN AND RURAL									
Urban population	-----	-----	914	532	1,283	-----	-----	-----	-----
Percent urban	-----	-----	53.1	66.5	96.6	-----	-----	-----	-----
Rural population	340	297	808	268	45	294	385	53	130
Rural-farm	183	120	445	223	13	44	71	9	92
Rural-nonfarm	157	177	363	45	32	250	314	44	38
Percent rural	100.0	100.0	46.9	33.5	3.4	100.0	100.0	-----	100.0
MARITAL CONDITION									
Males 15 years old and over	119	103	595	291	546	96	158	18	43
Single	38	33	203	105	221	27	65	8	15
Married	68	51	333	166	293	59	70	6	23
Widowed	7	19	54	17	21	9	19	4	5
Divorced	6	-----	4	2	11	1	4	-----	-----
Unknown	-----	-----	1	1	-----	-----	-----	-----	-----
Females 15 years old and over	119	87	615	293	513	108	120	14	36
Single	34	23	167	76	119	24	30	7	8
Married	69	50	339	165	292	61	69	6	23
Widowed	15	13	107	47	82	21	16	1	4
Divorced	1	1	2	2	20	2	5	-----	1
Unknown	-----	-----	-----	3	-----	-----	-----	-----	-----
FAMILIES									
Number of families	91	75	449	199	328	72	79	11	30
Median size	-----	-----	2.90	3.20	2.40	-----	-----	-----	-----
Families having—									
No children under 10	62	46	292	128	239	47	48	5	16
1 child under 10	13	9	74	36	44	10	12	1	4
2 children under 10	8	11	34	16	18	8	8	2	3
3 or more	8	9	49	19	27	7	11	3	7

SUBJECT	Christian	Clark	Clay	Clinton	Crittenden	Cumberland	Daviess	Edmonson	Elliott
POPULATION BY SEX									
Negro population: 1930	11,704	2,842	299	55	281	798	3,480	187	1
Male	5,763	1,453	149	26	145	401	1,711	101	1
Female	5,941	1,389	150	29	136	397	1,769	86	-----
Negro population: 1920	12,911	3,691	449	65	470	915	4,533	360	13
Male	6,338	1,888	236	30	240	454	2,244	188	7
Female	6,573	1,803	213	35	230	461	2,289	172	6
Percent of total population:									
1930	34.1	16.1	1.6	0.6	2.4	7.8	7.9	1.6	-----
1920	36.0	20.6	2.3	0.8	3.6	8.6	11.1	3.3	0.1
VOTING AGE: 1930									
Total 21 years old and over	6,840	1,891	150	33	184	400	2,237	108	1
Male	3,355	955	78	14	94	207	1,086	56	1
Female	3,485	936	72	19	90	193	1,151	52	-----
AGE: 1930									
Under 5 years	1,023	174	39	7	25	90	260	8	-----
Under 1 year	189	30	8	2	4	12	50	-----	-----
5 to 9 years	1,225	244	43	8	19	106	300	18	-----
10 to 14 years	1,145	262	32	4	19	109	279	27	-----
15 to 19 years	1,244	224	31	2	31	80	330	22	-----
20 to 24 years	1,058	234	30	5	22	65	290	12	-----
25 to 29 years	830	157	17	4	16	48	201	11	-----
30 to 34 years	759	182	12	4	18	48	212	5	-----
35 to 44 years	1,509	403	22	6	29	94	505	16	-----
45 to 54 years	1,397	416	42	5	37	75	509	29	1
55 to 64 years	802	275	11	5	35	49	321	23	-----
65 to 74 years	462	207	13	3	21	24	186	8	-----
75 years and over	235	64	7	2	8	9	85	8	-----
Unknown	15	-----	-----	-----	1	1	2	-----	-----
SCHOOL ATTENDANCE									
Total 7 to 13 years, inclusive	1,628	377	50	7	27	147	384	35	-----
Number attending school	1,495	366	45	3	23	107	364	34	-----
Percent attending school	91.8	97.1	-----	-----	-----	72.8	94.8	-----	-----
Total 14 and 15 years, inclusive	494	85	14	3	9	39	124	10	-----
Number attending school	405	74	12	-----	7	30	111	10	-----
Percent attending school	82.0	-----	-----	-----	-----	-----	89.5	-----	-----
Total 16 and 17 years, inclusive	509	99	13	1	13	26	154	11	-----
Number attending school	270	57	7	-----	6	7	93	8	-----
Percent attending school	53.0	-----	-----	-----	-----	-----	60.4	-----	-----
Total 18 to 20 years inclusive	721	127	15	2	18	55	196	10	-----
Number attending school	137	31	4	-----	4	9	30	2	-----
Percent attending school	19.0	24.4	-----	-----	-----	-----	15.3	-----	-----
ILLITERACY									
Total 10 years old and over	9,456	2,424	217	40	237	602	2,920	161	1
Number illiterate	1,626	359	24	10	50	146	508	19	-----
Percent illiterate	17.2	14.8	11.1	-----	21.1	24.3	17.4	11.8	-----
Percent illiterate in 1920	23.9	23.4	23.8	-----	20.7	22.3	21.1	16.7	-----
URBAN AND RURAL									
Urban population	3,980	2,007	-----	-----	-----	-----	2,509	-----	-----
Percent urban	34.0	70.6	-----	-----	-----	-----	72.1	-----	-----
Rural population	7,724	835	299	55	281	798	971	187	1
Rural-farm	4,876	525	151	43	81	479	737	136	1
Rural-nonfarm	2,848	310	148	12	200	319	234	51	-----
Percent rural	66.0	29.4	100.0	-----	100.0	100.0	27.9	100.0	-----
MARITAL CONDITION									
Males 15 years old and over	4,054	1,100	97	15	113	253	1,282	72	1
Single	1,257	372	33	3	32	101	399	28	-----
Married	2,311	600	51	10	74	128	718	39	1
Widowed	365	108	12	2	5	21	137	4	-----
Divorced	109	20	1	-----	2	3	27	1	-----
Unknown	12	-----	-----	-----	-----	-----	1	-----	-----
Females 15 years old and over	4,257	1,062	88	21	105	240	1,359	62	-----
Single	966	207	23	6	18	63	339	12	-----
Married	2,370	609	51	11	61	139	736	40	-----
Widowed	801	213	14	4	26	36	265	10	-----
Divorced	113	32	-----	-----	-----	1	18	-----	-----
Unknown	7	1	-----	-----	-----	1	1	-----	-----
FAMILIES									
Number of families	2,952	912	68	16	84	184	1,034	53	-----
Median size	3.09	2.30	-----	-----	-----	3.77	2.48	-----	-----
Families having—									
No children under 10	1,911	697	36	10	63	102	775	40	-----
1 child under 10	445	115	12	1	10	26	113	6	-----
2 children under 10	266	43	5	3	4	21	63	4	-----
3 or more	330	57	15	2	7	35	83	3	-----

CHARACTERISTICS OF NEGRO POPULATION BY COUNTIES: 1930—Continued

(See note at head of table)

SUBJECT	KENTUCKY—Continued																	
	Estill	Fayette	Fleming	Floyd	Franklin	Fulton	Gallatin	Garrard	Grant	Graves	Grayson	Green	Greenup	Hancock	Hardin	Harlan	Harrison	Hart
POPULATION BY SEX																		
Negro population: 1930	145	16, 449	614	857	2, 627	3, 153	184	1, 464	184	2, 194	154	979	298	284	1, 231	5, 879	1, 022	1, 403
Male	83	8, 144	336	477	1, 530	1, 596	95	746	105	1, 091	79	492	195	134	596	3, 194	528	709
Female	62	8, 305	278	380	1, 097	1, 557	89	718	79	1, 103	75	487	103	150	635	2, 685	494	694
Negro population: 1920	204	15, 613	981	428	2, 861	3, 220	241	1, 914	242	2, 600	244	1, 088	206	368	1, 566	2, 901	1, 234	1, 706
Male	105	7, 710	509	240	1, 679	1, 625	125	957	128	1, 281	125	549	110	176	843	1, 798	632	848
Female	99	7, 903	472	188	1, 182	1, 595	116	957	114	1, 319	119	539	96	192	723	1, 103	602	858
Percent of total population:																		
1930	0. 8	24. 0	4. 7	2. 0	12. 5	21. 1	4. 1	12. 7	1. 9	7. 1	0. 9	8. 6	1. 2	4. 6	5. 9	9. 1	6. 9	8. 7
1920	1. 3	28. 6	6. 3	1. 6	14. 8	21. 2	5. 2	15. 3	2. 3	8. 0	1. 2	9. 6	1. 0	5. 3	6. 4	9. 2	7. 8	9. 2
VOTING AGE: 1930																		
Total 21 years old and over	105	10, 888	377	504	1, 927	1, 671	98	842	129	1, 291	91	468	196	157	738	3, 506	689	730
Male	63	5, 384	205	298	1, 180	844	51	429	71	636	49	231	136	75	357	2, 065	368	378
Female	42	5, 504	172	206	747	827	47	413	58	655	42	237	60	82	381	1, 441	321	352
AGE: 1930																		
Under 5 years	10	1, 192	47	85	142	317	23	142	10	172	17	126	23	24	103	641	71	158
Under 1 year	2	233	13	13	23	55	6	25	2	26	3	25	5	8	18	110	10	37
5 to 9 years	3	1, 411	64	113	156	376	21	179	13	212	17	135	31	38	110	640	76	195
10 to 14 years	7	1, 293	61	85	137	347	21	162	15	230	15	128	21	30	121	501	89	146
15 to 19 years	15	1, 401	57	60	211	372	17	124	13	233	12	104	21	30	140	478	84	140
20 to 24 years	16	1, 389	42	82	298	284	16	84	17	238	12	91	46	18	107	654	94	146
25 to 29 years	21	1, 326	34	98	306	273	10	93	16	193	10	47	19	20	95	825	48	102
30 to 34 years	18	1, 329	40	91	267	191	8	94	11	112	9	55	20	16	80	669	52	77
35 to 44 years	19	2, 848	63	131	450	396	17	164	28	282	16	99	52	26	123	939	129	143
45 to 54 years	19	2, 243	79	83	325	312	18	189	25	237	18	85	36	29	155	381	156	129
55 to 64 years	11	1, 161	52	14	187	145	11	118	23	144	9	46	17	24	98	89	103	91
65 to 74 years	4	599	55	9	102	93	12	74	6	91	13	38	11	21	67	33	77	39
75 years and over	2	256	20	6	46	44	10	41	7	45	6	25	1	8	32	17	43	37
Unknown		1				3				5						12		
SCHOOL ATTENDANCE																		
Total 7 to 13 years, inclusive	8	1, 778	80	135	216	489	29	240	22	316	22	184	35	48	175	768	120	226
Number attending school	8	1, 654	68	105	203	386	28	223	18	281	22	128	35	35	163	716	115	166
Percent attending school		93. 0		77. 8	94. 0	78. 9		92. 9		88. 9		69. 6			93. 1	93. 2	95. 8	73. 5
Total 14 and 15 years, inclusive	4	571	32	30	57	141	10	51	3	88	6	51	7	12	43	192	42	67
Number attending school	2	431	27	24	51	103	8	42	2	77	4	33	5	9	36	168	38	45
Percent attending school		75. 5				73. 0										87. 5		
Total 16 and 17 years, inclusive	6	562	22	31	65	174	5	56	5	94	5	39	5	9	62	185	32	50
Number attending school		255	14	7	56	69	2	26	1	52	3	11	2	1	31	96	14	23
Percent attending school		45. 4				39. 7										51. 9		
Total 18 to 20 years, inclusive	10	835	28	28	168	203	12	63	9	155	7	67	18	18	75	310	43	88
Number attending school		132	4		82	18	3	11		24		8		3	12	35	5	8
Percent attending school		15. 8			48. 8	8. 9				15. 5						11. 3		
ILLITERACY																		
Total 10 years old and over	132	13, 846	503	659	2, 329	2, 460	140	1, 143	161	1, 810	120	718	244	222	1, 018	4, 598	875	1, 050
Number illiterate	22	1, 912	98	118	328	491	36	216	44	289	18	158	47	56	133	553	211	276
Percent illiterate	16. 7	13. 8	19. 5	17. 9	14. 1	20. 0	25. 7	18. 9	27. 3	16. 0	15. 0	22. 0	19. 3	25. 2	13. 1	12. 0	24. 1	26. 3
Percent illiterate in 1920	19. 3	23. 0	25. 3	24. 0	21. 1	17. 4	24. 3	18. 8	18. 7	13. 6	18. 9	29. 7	15. 3	20. 6	22. 5	12. 3	27. 2	24. 8
URBAN AND RURAL																		
Urban population	92	12, 759			2, 205	532				1, 147					329	617	659	
Percent urban	63. 4	77. 6			83. 9	16. 9				52. 3					26. 7	10. 5	64. 5	
Rural population	53	3, 690	614	857	422	2, 621	184	1, 464	184	1, 047	154	979	298	284	902	5, 262	363	1, 403
Rural-farm	2	1, 167	97	48	89	1, 926	96	837	44	606	38	757	37	50	256	37	261	871
Rural-nonfarm	51	2, 523	517	809	333	695	88	627	140	441	116	222	261	234	646	5, 225	102	532
Percent rural	36. 6	22. 4	100. 0	100. 0	16. 1	83. 1	100. 0	100. 0	100. 0	47. 7	100. 0	100. 0	100. 0	100. 0	73. 3	89. 5	35. 5	100. 0
MARITAL CONDITION																		
Males 15 years old and over	72	6, 198	241	336	1, 328	1, 063	65	506	82	782	58	292	153	92	436	2, 326	416	464
Single	29	2, 114	75	89	551	319	26	157	29	253	24	99	73	30	158	713	149	160
Married	35	3, 445	129	211	662	625	32	291	42	450	30	167	70	53	230	1, 431	215	259
Widowed	5	501	36	12	87	99	5	48	9	59	2	19	9	7	42	114	46	34
Divorced	3	134	1	24	28	20	2	7	2	20	2	7	1	2	6	64	6	10
Unknown		4						3								4		1
Females 15 years old and over	53	6, 355	201	238	864	1, 050	54	475	64	798	47	298	70	100	461	1, 771	370	440
Single	13	1, 338	41	28	238	212	13	83	9	174	8	75	24	30	107	266	63	105
Married	33	3, 544	121	186	389	621	34	292	41	463	30	167	40	53	244	1, 326	225	271
Widowed	5	1, 294	37	18	202	193	5	91	13	137	9	53	6	15	97	150	77	59
Divorced	2	178	1	6	34	24	2	8	1	22		3		2	12	29	4	5
Unknown		1	1		1			1		2					1		1	
FAMILIES																		
Number of families	41	4, 639	171	201	590	765	45	405	61	573	35	205	50	69	319	1, 282	321	311
Median size		2. 42	2. 99	2. 95	2. 28	3. 19		3. 04		3. 06		3. 57			2. 94	3. 17	2. 32	3. 54
Families having—																		
No children under 10	37	3, 382	116	122	447	452	27	262	48	372	21	103	31	45	213	718	247	170
1 child under 10		586	23	33	61	126	7	60	7	97	3	33	2	6	52	231	35	51
2 children under 10	2	320	18	18	40	77	4	36	4	54	6	26	9	7	30	145	19	30
3 or more	2	351	14	28	42	110	7	47	2	50	5	43	8	11	24	188	20	60

CHARACTERISTICS OF NEGRO POPULATION BY COUNTIES: 1930—Continued

(See note at head of table)

KENTUCKY—Continued

SUBJECT	Henderson	Henry	Hickman	Hopkins	Jackson	Jefferson	Jessamine	Johnson	Kenton	Knott	Knox	Larue	Laurel	Lawrence	Lee	Leslie	Letcher	Lewis
POPULATION BY SEX																		
Negro population: 1930	4,398	1,181	1,048	5,281	18	51,068	1,951	46	3,870	229	595	513	303	124	140	19	2,120	62
Male	2,188	587	530	2,675	8	24,764	1,019	20	1,947	124	317	272	154	72	83	10	1,158	33
Female	2,210	594	518	2,606	10	23,304	932	26	1,923	105	278	241	149	52	57	9	962	29
Negro population: 1920	5,693	1,488	1,248	6,037	4	44,448	2,276	67	3,325	153	677	652	333	156	235	98	1,900	88
Male	2,846	769	629	3,102	4	21,354	1,151	31	1,648	82	360	331	183	90	129	51	1,121	40
Female	2,847	719	619	2,935	—	23,094	1,125	36	1,677	71	317	321	150	66	106	47	779	48
Percent of total population: 1930	16.7	9.4	12.0	14.1	0.2	14.4	15.7	0.2	4.1	1.5	2.3	5.6	1.4	0.7	1.4	0.2	5.9	0.4
1920	20.6	11.1	12.2	17.7	—	15.5	18.6	0.3	4.5	1.3	2.8	6.5	1.7	0.9	2.0	1.0	7.8	0.6
VOTING AGE: 1930																		
Total 21 years old and over	2,668	685	585	3,343	6	35,491	1,197	18	2,760	109	301	265	152	75	85	8	1,218	43
Male	1,317	348	303	1,702	2	17,161	652	9	1,378	66	154	142	73	40	55	5	715	22
Female	1,351	337	282	1,641	4	18,330	545	9	1,382	43	147	123	79	35	30	3	503	21
AGE: 1930																		
Under 5 years	367	113	93	395	4	3,349	159	12	272	30	55	48	33	13	11	—	244	3
Under 1 year	56	26	23	72	2	614	34	7	56	12	10	6	7	1	—	—	49	1
5 to 9 years	446	126	129	463	2	3,906	198	5	253	27	70	57	34	13	17	4	247	6
10 to 14 years	413	119	114	475	2	3,561	184	3	239	32	87	70	40	5	18	3	198	6
15 to 19 years	423	117	109	516	4	3,890	177	7	277	26	73	60	37	17	8	3	171	3
20 to 24 years	358	72	92	442	1	4,624	161	3	312	24	54	54	32	11	11	1	172	3
25 to 29 years	244	69	77	437	—	4,938	124	5	357	12	27	24	14	9	10	—	220	7
30 to 34 years	268	58	54	400	2	4,836	120	3	382	14	30	23	18	10	9	—	230	2
35 to 44 years	602	161	128	946	—	9,436	254	5	805	33	74	45	27	15	16	2	405	8
45 to 54 years	598	154	99	649	2	7,046	245	—	513	19	59	64	30	7	23	4	168	6
55 to 64 years	390	91	73	297	1	3,224	176	1	277	7	38	32	20	11	9	2	44	6
65 to 74 years	194	74	51	169	—	1,485	92	2	131	2	19	26	11	9	4	—	16	6
75 years and over	93	27	26	89	—	690	59	—	48	2	8	10	7	4	4	—	5	6
Unknown	2	—	3	3	—	83	2	—	4	1	1	—	—	—	—	—	—	—
SCHOOL ATTENDANCE																		
Total 7 to 13 years, inclusive	580	173	173	659	3	5,161	264	3	348	41	110	83	52	13	28	3	321	10
Number attending school	548	155	122	598	2	4,998	252	1	335	37	106	72	48	13	18	3	292	7
Percent attending school	94.5	89.6	70.5	90.7	—	96.8	95.5	—	96.3	—	96.4	—	—	—	—	—	91.0	—
Total 14 and 15 years, inclusive	181	46	53	192	1	1,486	66	3	92	9	39	34	15	2	5	1	67	2
Number attending school	151	40	33	160	1	1,297	56	1	74	7	30	24	14	2	3	1	60	1
Percent attending school	83.4	—	—	83.3	—	87.3	—	—	—	—	—	—	—	—	—	—	—	—
Total 16 and 17 years, inclusive	167	52	40	210	2	1,550	73	1	112	16	26	23	11	9	3	2	64	2
Number attending school	89	21	15	107	—	740	39	—	65	10	10	5	6	3	—	1	34	1
Percent attending school	53.3	—	—	51.0	—	47.7	—	—	58.0	—	—	—	—	—	—	—	—	—
Total 18 to 20 years, inclusive	251	67	61	301	1	2,483	107	6	185	13	36	37	30	8	3	2	113	1
Number attending school	44	8	9	52	—	344	15	1	30	2	6	5	6	—	1	—	15	—
Percent attending school	17.5	—	—	17.3	—	13.9	14.0	—	16.2	—	—	—	—	—	—	—	13.3	—
ILLITERACY																		
Total 10 years old and over	3,585	942	826	4,423	12	43,813	1,594	29	3,345	172	470	408	236	98	112	15	1,629	53
Number illiterate	638	253	196	579	4	4,181	449	9	283	22	70	121	14	12	34	4	303	20
Percent illiterate	17.8	26.9	23.7	13.1	—	9.5	28.2	—	8.5	12.8	14.9	29.7	5.9	—	30.4	—	18.6	—
Percent illiterate in 1920	19.4	31.0	20.5	19.1	—	15.4	17.1	—	16.2	—	15.0	24.0	13.0	13.0	25.7	—	36.7	—
URBAN AND RURAL																		
Urban population	2,346	—	—	3,062	—	47,354	709	—	3,689	—	—	—	—	—	—	—	1,386	—
Percent urban	53.3	—	—	58.0	—	92.7	36.3	—	95.3	—	—	—	—	—	—	—	65.4	—
Rural population	2,052	1,181	1,048	2,219	18	3,714	1,242	46	181	229	595	513	303	124	140	19	734	62
Rural-farm	1,462	426	507	332	16	525	604	—	88	109	110	219	58	4	50	14	—	43
Rural-nonfarm	590	755	541	1,887	2	3,189	638	46	93	120	485	294	245	120	90	5	734	19
Percent rural	46.7	100.0	100.0	42.0	—	7.3	63.7	—	4.7	100.0	100.0	100.0	100.0	100.0	100.0	—	34.6	—
MARITAL CONDITION																		
Males 15 years old and over	1,576	413	362	2,008	5	19,318	745	12	1,555	83	198	181	98	53	62	7	812	26
Single	530	127	105	556	3	5,772	248	4	483	37	81	66	37	23	23	3	247	9
Married	874	234	209	1,196	2	11,138	406	8	950	43	100	98	53	18	28	4	497	14
Widowed	148	41	44	233	—	1,851	74	—	84	3	15	17	7	7	9	—	53	3
Divorced	22	11	3	20	—	509	17	—	35	—	2	—	1	5	2	—	13	—
Unknown	2	—	1	3	—	48	—	—	3	—	—	—	—	—	—	—	2	—
Females 15 years old and over	1,596	410	350	1,940	5	20,934	665	14	1,551	57	185	157	98	40	32	5	619	21
Single	370	84	72	355	1	4,276	137	2	287	17	45	43	20	13	2	1	86	5
Married	890	250	209	1,173	2	11,385	389	9	948	36	101	94	55	19	23	4	476	15
Widowed	308	65	63	389	2	4,595	125	1	274	4	35	19	22	6	7	—	46	1
Divorced	28	9	6	20	—	640	14	2	41	—	4	1	1	2	—	—	10	—
Unknown	—	2	—	3	—	38	—	—	1	—	—	—	—	—	—	—	1	—
FAMILIES																		
Number of families	1,217	327	267	1,470	3	14,622	538	10	1,170	44	134	113	73	31	31	3	499	18
Median size	2.62	2.67	2.87	2.71	—	2.37	2.65	—	2.40	—	3.50	3.82	—	—	—	—	2.97	—
Families having—																		
No children under 10	860	223	172	1,047	2	11,128	377	6	889	23	83	68	46	19	20	1	289	12
1 child under 10	140	40	39	180	—	1,677	64	1	146	7	18	14	7	5	4	1	83	4
2 children under 10	91	31	17	138	—	887	45	—	72	3	10	12	11	3	2	—	55	2
3 or more	126	33	39	105	1	930	52	3	63	11	23	19	9	4	5	1	72	—

CHARACTERISTICS OF NEGRO POPULATION BY COUNTIES: 1930—Continued

(See note at head of table)

SUBJECT	KENTUCKY—Continued																	
	Lincoln	Livingston	Logan	Lyon	McCracken	McCreary	McLean	Madison	Magoffin	Marion	Marshall	Martin	Mason	Meade	Menifee	Mercer	Metcalfe	Monroe
POPULATION BY SEX																		
Negro population: 1930	1,762	350	3,486	1,200	7,762	27	315	4,324	44	1,468	62	1	2,471	404	34	1,547	536	484
Male	863	179	1,727	865	3,740	17	161	2,107	25	703	34	1	1,247	212	19	826	274	237
Female	899	171	1,759	335	4,022	10	154	2,217	19	765	28	---	1,224	192	15	721	262	247
Negro population: 1920	2,191	507	4,304	1,184	7,006	28	602	4,910	51	1,701	64	1	2,550	570	50	1,830	654	597
Male	1,068	250	2,149	721	3,381	17	309	2,429	27	835	34	1	1,256	308	28	898	333	300
Female	1,123	257	2,155	463	3,625	11	293	2,481	24	866	30	---	1,294	262	22	932	321	297
Percent of total population:																		
1930	10.0	4.1	15.9	14.1	16.8	0.2	2.8	15.7	0.3	9.5	0.5	---	13.1	5.0	0.7	10.7	5.7	3.7
1920	13.3	5.2	18.2	13.5	18.8	0.2	4.8	18.7	0.4	11.0	0.4	---	14.4	6.0	0.9	12.4	6.5	4.2
VOTING AGE: 1930																		
Total 21 years old and over	958	179	1,960	838	5,098	10	167	2,409	21	773	45	1	1,509	227	11	997	264	241
Male	476	92	985	655	2,452	7	88	1,184	12	364	28	1	763	125	6	550	141	123
Female	482	87	975	183	2,646	3	79	1,225	9	409	17	---	746	102	5	447	123	118
AGE: 1930																		
Under 5 years	165	31	306	64	502	4	20	429	8	167	4	---	229	45	4	122	76	58
Under 1 year	29	9	53	10	77	1	2	73	3	35	1	---	42	10	1	23	10	12
5 to 9 years	214	45	407	83	662	3	30	477	7	189	4	---	237	46	7	141	73	58
10 to 14 years	177	60	383	70	634	6	45	455	5	155	2	---	230	43	5	126	67	56
15 to 19 years	205	34	367	108	707	3	44	464	3	159	6	---	213	37	7	129	48	61
20 to 24 years	149	20	283	186	668	2	27	391	1	127	10	---	206	24	2	155	44	50
25 to 29 years	87	7	240	165	670	1	12	274	3	118	9	---	169	23	---	123	39	29
30 to 34 years	91	16	214	105	596	3	8	252	3	80	3	---	163	21	3	105	37	22
35 to 44 years	204	33	422	175	1,272	3	30	496	2	161	7	---	326	41	3	197	54	49
45 to 54 years	212	45	383	119	1,127	1	43	465	2	125	4	---	284	52	1	181	31	41
55 to 64 years	141	35	260	51	525	1	29	317	4	101	7	---	204	29	1	151	36	30
65 to 74 years	78	11	139	50	262	---	16	203	4	48	4	---	129	27	1	76	21	17
75 years and over	37	11	61	24	127	---	11	94	2	38	2	1	80	16	---	40	10	11
Unknown	2	2	21	---	10	---	---	7	---	---	---	---	1	---	---	1	---	2
SCHOOL ATTENDANCE																		
Total 7 to 13 years, inclusive	278	76	535	106	924	6	52	633	8	237	5	---	316	60	7	181	94	72
Number attending school	255	65	475	97	889	4	52	591	4	191	2	---	304	40	7	160	77	53
Percent attending school	91.7	---	88.8	91.5	96.2	---	---	93.4	---	80.6	---	---	96.2	---	---	88.4	---	---
Total 14 and 15 years, inclusive	59	20	161	30	255	1	16	183	3	58	1	---	99	20	3	44	23	23
Number attending school	48	14	126	17	211	---	12	163	1	42	---	---	89	12	3	36	16	14
Percent attending school	---	---	78.3	---	82.7	---	---	89.1	---	---	---	---	---	---	---	---	---	---
Total 16 and 17 years, inclusive	90	15	155	41	290	1	19	195	---	63	2	---	74	18	3	51	17	28
Number attending school	51	8	57	15	155	1	8	112	---	27	---	---	44	12	3	23	10	11
Percent attending school	---	---	36.8	---	53.4	---	---	57.4	---	---	---	---	---	---	---	---	---	---
Total 18 to 20 years, inclusive	127	12	197	90	447	3	28	276	2	92	4	---	140	16	2	89	30	35
Number attending school	21	1	33	27	100	---	5	54	---	8	---	---	13	5	---	14	1	3
Percent attending school	16.5	---	16.8	---	22.4	---	---	19.6	---	---	---	---	9.3	---	---	---	---	---
ILLITERACY																		
Total 10 years old and over	1,383	274	2,773	1,053	6,598	20	265	3,418	29	1,112	54	1	2,005	313	23	1,284	387	368
Number illiterate	279	52	668	174	778	4	44	490	18	325	17	1	320	58	---	301	114	120
Percent illiterate	20.2	19.0	24.1	16.5	11.8	---	16.6	14.3	---	29.2	---	---	16.0	18.5	---	23.4	29.5	32.6
Percent illiterate in 1920	23.6	17.2	22.4	16.6	19.0	---	18.5	21.1	---	36.0	---	---	22.1	17.0	---	27.5	34.6	25.3
URBAN AND RURAL																		
Urban population	---	---	714	---	6,744	---	---	1,896	---	626	---	---	1,180	---	---	853	---	---
Percent urban		---	20.5		86.9	---	---	43.8	---	42.6	---	---	47.8	---	---	55.1	---	---
Rural population	1,762	350	2,772	1,200	1,018	27	315	2,428	44	842	62	1	1,291	404	34	694	536	484
Rural-farm	771	144	1,988	377	800	---	78	1,838	24	521	27	---	584	270	30	314	496	281
Rural-nonfarm	991	206	784	823	218	27	237	590	20	321	35	1	707	134	4	380	40	203
Percent rural	100.0	100.0	79.5	100.0	13.1	---	100.0	56.2	---	57.4	---	---	52.2	100.0	---	44.9	100.0	100.0
MARITAL CONDITION																		
Males 15 years old and over	586	114	1,196	760	2,871	8	115	1,449	12	449	31	1	901	146	12	630	165	156
Single	187	45	382	310	942	2	49	573	2	161	10	1	320	46	8	255	47	53
Married	342	61	684	354	1,591	4	46	755	6	256	15	---	483	84	3	313	101	93
Widowed	46	8	100	91	302	1	19	106	1	30	6	---	68	15	1	60	16	8
Divorced	10	---	30	5	32	1	1	14	3	2	---	---	29	---	---	1	1	1
Unknown	1	---	---	---	4	---	---	1	---	---	---	---	1	1	---	1	---	1
Females 15 years old and over	620	100	1,194	223	3,093	6	105	1,514	12	508	21	---	874	124	6	528	155	156
Single	159	17	261	47	683	2	31	476	2	148	6	---	200	28	1	120	37	40
Married	354	63	692	130	1,589	4	47	780	7	269	12	---	483	76	3	309	96	89
Widowed	97	19	205	43	752	---	23	230	1	86	2	---	157	19	2	92	20	25
Divorced	10	1	34	3	65	---	2	27	2	4	1	---	34	1	---	7	2	1
Unknown	---	---	2	---	4	---	2	1	---	1	---	---	---	---	---	---	---	1
FAMILIES																		
Number of families	463	81	885	166	2,296	6	80	1,100	7	356	16	---	653	94	5	408	124	109
Median size	2.84	---	3.23	3.40	2.42	---	---	3.14	---	3.20	---	---	2.84	---	---	2.70	3.76	3.55
Families having:																		
No children under 10	286	44	557	95	1,733	2	53	704	2	203	11	---	455	58	1	281	56	58
1 child under 10	64	16	131	31	270	2	14	153	---	67	3	---	77	13	1	60	25	19
2 children under 10	63	6	89	21	145	1	6	98	---	27	1	---	44	11	---	29	20	15
3 or more	50	15	108	19	148	1	7	145	5	59	1	---	77	12	3	38	23	17

CHARACTERISTICS OF NEGRO POPULATION BY COUNTIES: 1930—Continued

(See note at head of table)

KENTUCKY—Continued

SUBJECT	Montgomery	Morgan	Muhlenberg	Nelson	Nicholas	Ohio	Oldham	Owen	Owsley	Pendleton	Perry	Pike	Powell	Pulaski	Robertson	Rockcastle	Rowan	Russell
POPULATION BY SEX																		
Negro population: 1930	1,967	8	2,941	2,045	513	802	716	633	41	205	2,398	1,652	203	861	46	75	27	224
Male	945	5	1,519	1,040	257	393	362	333	19	121	1,328	893	110	410	25	36	14	109
Female	1,022	3	1,422	1,005	256	409	354	300	22	84	1,070	759	93	451	21	39	13	115
Negro population: 1920	2,517	11	2,758	2,069	709	885	1,024	811	56	164	1,687	2,039	111	976	52	70	22	225
Male	1,234	5	1,407	1,039	355	434	521	432	27	90	1,036	1,135	59	445	25	32	9	120
Female	1,283	6	1,351	1,030	354	451	503	379	29	74	651	904	52	531	27	38	13	105
Percent of total population:																		
1930	16.9	0.1	7.8	12.4	6.0	3.3	9.7	5.9	0.6	1.9	5.7	2.6	3.5	2.4	1.4	0.5	0.2	1.9
1920	20.6	0.1	8.3	12.8	7.2	3.3	13.3	6.5	0.7	1.4	6.5	4.1	1.6	2.9	1.3	0.5	0.2	1.9
VOTING AGE: 1930																		
Total 21 years old and over	1,213	6	1,687	1,114	327	477	415	347	18	125	1,306	1,005	101	489	26	42	15	96
Male	582	4	889	565	175	241	223	181	9	73	773	584	56	232	15	18	9	43
Female	631	2	798	549	152	236	192	166	9	52	533	421	45	257	11	24	6	53
AGE: 1930																		
Under 5 years	149	1	247	215	34	76	71	58	5	22	274	191	26	74	2	10	3	33
Under 1 year	16	1	52	42	6	14	15	8	2	5	66	36	7	9	1	2	1	5
5 to 9 years	204		332	246	47	85	68	87	5	29	291	178	28	95	5	8		35
10 to 14 years	205		315	237	46	76	77	67	8	18	246	128	24	86	6	4	3	33
15 to 19 years	173	1	310	196	49	66	72	64	5	10	228	120	22	99	6	10	3	23
20 to 24 years	126	1	254	149	35	76	56	53	3	19	248	171	13	60	5	8	3	11
25 to 29 years	139	1	215	139	25	40	54	34	2	14	243	178	8	49	1	8	2	11
30 to 34 years	118		208	107	26	58	29	32	4	26	180	170	8	57		2		9
35 to 44 years	254		417	223	69	103	84	73	2	15	361	273	17	116	5	10	1	26
45 to 54 years	248	2	351	259	59	83	90	65	2	19	206	137	27	106	7	7	4	14
55 to 64 years	188		152	134	51	68	57	42	3	18	71	63	17	55	4	4	7	13
65 to 74 years	106	1	90	87	41	45	46	37	1	9	33	25	7	40	3	1		7
75 years and over	53	1	48	52	31	26	12	21	1	6	15	7	6	24	2	3	1	7
Unknown	4		2	1							2	11						2
SCHOOL ATTENDANCE																		
Total 7 to 13 years, inclusive	297		442	332	61	117	98	109	11	31	379	203	34	114	8	6	2	44
Number attending school	283		389	307	54	110	83	90	9	30	313	166	32	108	8	3	2	39
Percent attending school	95.3		88.0	92.5		94.0		82.6			82.6	81.8		94.7				
Total 14 and 15 years, inclusive	70		133	89	12	27	27	26		8	78	55	7	45	2	2	1	11
Number attending school	60		96	77	12	23	23	22		5	54	36	5	39	2		1	9
Percent attending school			72.2															
Total 16 and 17 years, inclusive	71	1	119	88	29	29	32	24	3	3	98	46	10	53	4	2	1	16
Number attending school	40	1	57	45	22	12	17	12	2	1	32	15	6	30	1		1	7
Percent attending school			47.9															
Total 18 to 20 years, inclusive	90		175	111	25	45	42	37	2	5	141	73	11	43	3	7	5	10
Number attending school	25		19	29	2	5	5	8		1	9	8	3	13		1	2	2
Percent attending school			10.9	26.1							6.4							
ILLITERACY																		
Total 10 years old and over	1,614	7	2,362	1,584	432	641	577	488	31	154	1,833	1,283	149	692	39	57	24	156
Number illiterate	308	1	355	282	92	93	144	91	8	25	206	185	26	81	6	20	7	19
Percent illiterate	19.1		15.0	17.8	21.3	14.5	25.0	18.6		16.2	11.2	14.4	17.4	11.7				12.2
Percent illiterate in 1920	18.7		18.8	27.6	32.3	22.8	21.5	16.0		33.6	17.1	25.0		21.8				16.7
URBAN AND RURAL																		
Urban population	1,036		449								810	120		434				
Percent urban	52.7		15.3								33.8	7.3		50.4				
Rural population	931	8	2,492	2,045	513	802	716	633	41	205	1,588	1,532	203	427	46	75	27	224
Rural-farm	381	8	226	577	150	116	150	355	40	61	224	43	178	234	39	30	7	140
Rural-nonfarm	550		2,266	1,468	363	686	566	278	1	144	1,364	1,489	25	193	7	45	20	84
Percent rural	47.3		84.7	100.0	100.0	100.0	100.0	100.0		100.0	66.2	92.7	100.0	49.6				100.0
MARITAL CONDITION																		
Males 15 years old and over	683	4	1,073	687	200	289	264	224	9	79	920	648	72	281	20	25	11	59
Single	226	2	330	246	62	97	72	88	2	28	318	185	30	86	8	10	6	19
Married	393	2	629	374	104	161	161	116	7	45	531	415	33	178	11	12	4	35
Widowed	55		81	57	26	21	26	19		6	50	40	6	15	1	3	1	5
Divorced	9		33	10	8	10	5	1			18	8	3	2				
Unknown											3							
Females 15 years old and over	726	3	974	660	186	276	236	197	14	57	667	507	53	325	13	28	10	64
Single	159	1	195	180	36	51	41	42	5	5	93	64	10	83	1	11	3	13
Married	414	2	631	378	104	164	154	118	8	42	510	383	33	182	11	11	6	36
Widowed	144		123	90	37	51	38	31	1	10	55	48	9	54	1	6	1	15
Divorced	9		24	12	9	9	3	6			9	11	1	6				
Unknown			1			1						1						
FAMILIES																		
Number of families	583	1	754	501	165	216	194	157	9	52	526	424	48	224	10	17	6	43
Median size	2.51		3.05	3.31	2.35	3.04	2.40	3.13			3.29	2.92		2.91				
Families having—																		
No children under 10	422	1	472	310	127	142	137	93	5	29	294	260	32	155	7	11	5	17
1 child under 10	71		137	63	16	26	19	25	1	9	82	61	4	27	2	2	1	11
2 children under 10	36		67	52	10	22	14	13	1	6	53	54	2	22		1		3
3 or more	54		78	76	12	26	24	26	2	8	97	49	10	20	1	3		12

CHARACTERISTICS OF NEGRO POPULATION BY COUNTIES: 1930—Continued

(See note at head of table)

SUBJECT	KENTUCKY—Continued															
	Scott	Shelby	Simpson	Spencer	Taylor	Todd	Trigg	Trimble	Union	Warren	Washington	Wayne	Webster	Whitley	Wolfe	Woodford
POPULATION BY SEX																
Negro population: 1930	2,511	2,637	1,751	505	1,121	3,393	2,373	27	2,021	5,057	1,362	524	3,103	299	6	2,206
Male	1,311	1,341	884	261	573	1,686	1,209	12	1,052	2,418	687	263	1,581	153	3	1,126
Female	1,200	1,296	867	244	548	1,707	1,164	15	969	2,639	675	261	1,522	146	3	1,080
Negro population: 1920	3,059	3,266	1,909	673	1,292	4,480	2,947	75	2,193	4,956	1,717	641	2,922	600	18	3,033
Male	1,581	1,672	976	339	638	2,224	1,472	39	1,175	2,373	864	322	1,513	320	10	1,544
Female	1,478	1,594	933	334	654	2,256	1,475	36	1,018	2,583	853	319	1,409	280	8	1,489
Percent of total population:																
1930	17.4	14.9	15.4	7.6	9.3	25.1	18.9	0.5	11.9	15.0	10.8	3.3	15.1	1.0	0.1	20.1
1920	20.0	17.6	17.1	8.6	10.6	28.5	20.7	1.2	12.2	16.1	11.6	4.0	14.1	2.2	0.2	25.7
VOTING AGE: 1930																
Total 21 years old and over	1,619	1,664	949	247	580	1,928	1,198	19	1,218	2,853	680	277	1,912	162	1	1,352
Male	859	859	469	136	286	966	610	11	643	1,334	344	130	982	80		672
Female	760	805	480	111	294	962	588	8	575	1,519	336	147	930	82	1	680
AGE: 1930																
Under 5 years	189	236	148	70	126	321	276	2	184	458	175	41	220	34	1	159
Under 1 year	43	42	20	17	23	65	61	1	38	84	36	8	45	6		33
5 to 9 years	237	268	205	62	151	384	283	4	222	566	184	73	309	38	2	200
10 to 14 years	220	227	207	62	135	343	316	1	182	519	156	57	313	30	1	236
15 to 19 years	211	212	198	53	113	355	246		184	565	145	65	293	35	1	216
20 to 24 years	192	210	148	39	89	301	232	1	165	417	108	52	258	25		150
25 to 29 years	142	210	131	37	51	237	151	3	144	338	106	34	275	16		121
30 to 34 years	147	167	92	34	65	187	123		161	263	69	21	261	18		117
35 to 44 years	354	370	198	45	128	417	241	3	291	616	141	54	500	36		290
45 to 54 years	374	356	198	45	126	371	216	4	239	575	140	50	338	28	1	310
55 to 64 years	215	209	117	24	61	271	158	7	137	377	68	47	172	24		227
65 to 74 years	171	112	70	22	47	130	85	1	66	235	39	23	106	9		131
75 years and over	59	58	38	11	29	74	45	1	44	121	31	7	55	4		49
Unknown		2	1	1		2	1		2	7			3	2		
SCHOOL ATTENDANCE																
Total 7 to 13 years, inclusive	305	348	304	90	195	484	413	3	284	749	238	86	442	50	3	309
Number attending school	281	300	251	74	135	450	387	1	259	702	207	60	397	44		282
Percent attending school	92.1	86.2	82.6		69.2	93.0	93.7		91.2	93.7	87.0		89.8			91.3
Total 14 and 15 years, inclusive	89	70	84	20	59	142	114		74	226	56	18	120	11		103
Number attending school	72	62	59	15	22	124	93		59	192	43	11	93	9		91
Percent attending school						87.3	81.6			85.0			77.5			88.3
Total 16 and 17 years, inclusive	96	87	75	25	40	150	112		71	250	60	31	119	14	1	100
Number attending school	61	41	42	11	8	76	60		25	116	28	8	52	9		56
Percent attending school						50.7	53.6			46.4			43.7			56.0
Total 18 to 20 years, inclusive	110	124	121	29	60	204	144	1	109	303	78	38	168	14		113
Number attending school	31	20	21	5	2	7	20		10	61	8	1	24	3		19
Percent attending school	28.2	16.1	17.4			3.4	13.9		9.2	20.1			14.3			16.8
ILLITERACY																
Total 10 years old and over	2,085	2,133	1,398	373	844	2,688	1,814	21	1,615	4,033	1,003	410	2,574	227	3	1,847
Number illiterate	370	458	409	86	209	599	311	5	350	796	269	94	321	43	2	332
Percent illiterate	17.7	21.5	29.3	23.1	24.8	22.3	17.1		21.7	19.7	26.8	22.9	12.5	18.9		18.0
Percent illiterate in 1920	24.8	26.9	30.0	27.2	25.6	28.7	22.2		28.3	25.7	27.2	21.5	17.6	16.2		20.2
URBAN AND RURAL																
Urban population	1,184	1,123	759						454	2,426			1,014	20		
Percent urban	47.2	42.6	43.3						22.5	48.0			32.7	6.7		
Rural population	1,327	1,514	992	505	1,121	3,393	2,373	27	1,567	2,631	1,362	524	2,089	279	6	2,206
Rural-farm	482	1,021	958	232	651	1,926	1,685	24	313	1,650	749	311	316	36	6	531
Rural-nonfarm	845	493	34	273	470	1,467	688	3	1,254	981	613	213	1,773	243		1,675
Percent rural	52.8	57.4	56.7	100.0	100.0	100.0	100.0		77.5	52.0	100.0	100.0	67.3	93.3		100.0
MARITAL CONDITION																
Males 15 years old and over	985	983	597	169	359	1,176	772	11	755	1,643	427	166	1,148	101	1	801
Single	324	326	199	55	106	352	234	1	227	500	136	48	288	43	1	250
Married	545	546	343	93	209	691	457	9	420	968	261	101	743	48		452
Widowed	98	88	43	18	37	107	61	1	86	143	27	13	88	7		84
Divorced	18	22	11	3	7	26	20		21	31	3	4	28	3		15
Unknown		1	1						1	1			1			
Females 15 years old and over	880	923	594	142	350	1,169	726	9	678	1,871	420	187	1,113	96	1	810
Single	163	195	136	36	71	225	143	1	111	460	84	49	185	24		192
Married	557	540	346	89	215	701	459	8	435	997	263	104	753	47		451
Widowed	151	146	101	15	56	199	87		118	360	71	30	150	19	1	147
Divorced	9	41	11	2	8	42	36		13	53	2	4	24	5		20
Unknown		1				2	1		1	1			1	1		
FAMILIES																
Number of families	753	769	433	115	275	916	553	10	564	1,344	297	128	883	64	1	660
Medium size	2.49	2.47	3.40	4.00	3.23	2.95	3.69		2.75	2.95	3.92	3.38	2.89			2.44
Families having—																
No children under 10	554	545	258	53	157	588	302	7	377	861	153	74	597	31		493
1 child under 10	85	97	73	24	38	136	98	1	86	215	52	24	153	14		76
2 children under 10	53	51	50	17	33	89	64	1	45	116	24	8	68	8		47
3 or more	61	76	52	21	47	103	89	1	56	152	68	22	65	11	1	44

CHARACTERISTICS OF NEGRO POPULATION BY COUNTIES: 1930—Continued

(See note at head of table)

SUBJECT	LOUISIANA: The State	Acadia	Allen	Ascension	Assumption	Avoyelles	Beauregard	Bienville	Bossier	Caddo	Calcasieu	Caldwell	Cameron	Catahoula	Claiborne	Concordia	De Soto
POPULATION BY SEX																	
Negro population: 1930	776,326	8,103	4,103	7,077	6,319	9,915	3,177	10,624	17,846	57,041	12,112	2,937	578	4,651	18,042	9,185	19,215
Male	379,173	3,885	2,045	3,457	3,135	4,942	1,580	5,439	9,003	27,050	5,850	1,496	316	2,327	8,924	4,484	9,343
Female	397,153	4,218	2,058	3,620	3,184	4,973	1,597	5,185	8,843	29,991	6,262	1,441	262	2,324	9,118	4,701	9,872
Negro population: 1920	700,257	7,526	6,352	9,490	7,487	10,353	6,105	8,619	15,730	37,801	8,736	2,983	585	5,122	14,798	9,823	17,914
Male	344,794	3,708	3,422	4,597	3,706	5,143	3,370	4,202	7,808	18,126	4,322	1,511	300	2,571	7,251	4,896	8,653
Female	355,463	3,818	2,930	4,893	3,781	5,210	2,735	4,417	7,922	19,675	4,414	1,472	285	2,551	7,547	4,927	9,261
Percent of total population:																	
1930	36.9	20.6	26.9	38.4	39.5	28.4	21.8	44.7	62.9	45.8	28.9	28.2	9.5	37.4	55.9	71.9	62.0
1920	38.9	21.6	34.6	42.8	41.8	29.3	29.4	41.1	70.6	45.4	26.6	31.4	14.8	46.3	53.1	78.8	61.0
VOTING AGE: 1930																	
Total 21 years old and over	415,047	3,654	2,256	3,755	3,203	4,719	1,844	4,808	9,489	32,580	6,237	1,413	248	2,404	7,915	5,333	8,943
Male	203,259	1,783	1,162	1,799	1,545	2,347	962	2,545	4,886	15,346	3,062	730	133	1,221	3,943	2,629	4,354
Female	211,788	1,871	1,094	1,956	1,658	2,372	882	2,263	4,603	17,234	3,175	683	115	1,183	3,972	2,704	4,589
AGE: 1930																	
Under 5 years	84,986	1,072	414	743	776	1,298	307	1,361	1,960	5,433	1,417	367	100	538	2,467	825	2,400
Under 1 year	16,089	227	81	134	154	259	49	246	289	1,010	270	69	17	119	442	158	411
5 to 9 years	93,082	1,120	503	920	903	1,330	318	1,509	2,140	6,101	1,455	403	80	529	2,549	970	2,793
10 to 14 years	84,800	1,018	465	810	738	1,253	310	1,362	2,006	5,722	1,389	371	70	561	2,507	984	2,534
15 to 19 years	81,293	1,042	374	694	612	1,124	330	1,296	1,843	5,875	1,344	325	70	490	2,172	875	2,119
20 to 24 years	79,550	814	391	586	404	914	293	1,200	1,877	6,426	1,138	273	52	542	1,968	899	1,843
25 to 29 years	69,041	601	359	466	364	696	290	858	1,576	6,206	928	215	35	381	1,519	776	1,470
30 to 34 years	52,188	416	331	362	290	505	264	663	1,120	4,412	802	156	35	295	1,038	639	1,015
35 to 44 years	100,104	814	658	910	813	976	562	1,031	2,186	7,968	1,663	341	53	481	1,707	1,257	2,115
45 to 54 years	71,683	651	409	825	694	899	333	758	1,694	5,057	1,174	263	39	429	1,102	1,020	1,507
55 to 64 years	35,231	335	128	417	384	520	123	361	870	2,275	478	118	20	250	592	563	811
65 to 74 years	15,857	151	48	228	232	241	29	135	362	1,041	191	78	13	95	281	229	385
75 years and over	8,161	69	22	115	107	159	18	89	210	498	130	27	11	59	115	145	210
Unknown	350	------	1	1	2	------	------	1	2	27	3	------	------	1	25	3	13
SCHOOL ATTENDANCE																	
Total 7 to 13 years, inclusive	122,914	1,490	678	1,236	1,114	1,804	450	2,012	2,865	8,156	1,975	549	99	740	3,479	1,353	3,698
Number attending school	102,152	1,058	583	934	930	1,541	410	1,716	2,405	7,280	1,729	485	83	664	3,026	1,209	3,087
Percent attending school	83.1	71.0	86.0	75.6	83.5	85.4	91.1	85.3	83.9	89.3	87.5	88.3	------	89.7	87.0	89.4	83.5
Total 14 and 15 years, inclusive	32,804	408	166	277	270	512	131	487	787	2,289	530	135	32	225	939	403	926
Number attending school	24,007	245	132	164	151	379	100	410	658	1,968	370	116	22	204	779	334	762
Percent attending school	73.2	60.0	79.5	59.2	55.9	74.0	76.3	84.2	83.6	86.0	69.8	85.9	------	90.7	83.0	82.9	82.3
Total 16 and 17 years, inclusive	32,500	432	151	290	235	429	128	569	714	2,308	530	120	27	195	920	332	874
Number attending school	14,078	142	60	88	49	180	60	362	397	1,255	185	65	8	123	548	155	485
Percent attending school	43.3	32.9	39.7	30.3	20.9	42.0	46.9	63.6	55.6	54.4	34.9	54.2	------	63.1	59.6	46.7	55.5
Total 18 to 20 years, inclusive	50,037	609	234	424	342	627	191	808	1,144	3,758	821	190	37	326	1,260	557	1,217
Number attending school	6,811	57	16	48	18	55	29	191	166	553	77	36	2	68	298	55	233
Percent attending school	13.6	9.4	6.8	11.3	5.3	8.8	15.2	23.6	14.5	14.7	9.4	18.9	------	20.9	23.7	9.9	19.1
ILLITERACY																	
Total 10 years old and over	598,258	5,911	3,186	5,414	4,640	7,287	2,552	7,754	13,746	45,507	9,240	2,167	398	3,584	13,026	7,390	14,022
Number illiterate	139,393	2,513	637	1,386	1,503	1,899	312	1,372	3,073	7,817	2,383	388	125	1,125	2,617	1,999	2,540
Percent illiterate	23.3	42.5	20.0	25.6	32.4	26.1	12.2	17.7	22.4	17.2	25.8	17.9	31.4	31.4	20.1	27.1	18.1
Percent illiterate in 1920	38.5	55.4	39.0	48.1	47.4	43.9	26.6	36.3	42.8	28.0	31.9	27.5	59.5	57.2	35.2	44.4	37.6
URBAN AND RURAL																	
Urban population	257,463	3,799	856	1,394	------	------	2,171	------	1,374	27,219	6,768	------	------	------	1,657	1,501	1,446
Percent urban	33.2	46.9	20.9	19.7	------	------	68.3	------	7.7	47.7	55.9	------	------	------	9.2	16.3	7.5
Rural population	518,863	4,304	3,247	5,683	6,319	9,915	1,006	10,624	16,472	29,822	5,344	2,937	578	4,651	16,385	7,684	17,769
Rural-farm	372,496	3,061	785	3,013	2,991	8,153	564	8,624	14,984	25,576	2,132	1,762	497	3,945	15,764	6,278	16,375
Rural-nonfarm	146,367	1,243	2,462	2,670	3,328	1,762	442	2,000	1,488	4,246	3,212	1,175	81	706	621	1,406	1,394
Percent rural	66.8	53.1	79.1	80.3	100.0	100.0	31.7	100.0	92.3	52.3	44.1	100.0	100.0	100.0	90.8	83.7	92.5
MARITAL CONDITION																	
Males 15 years old and over	248,678	2,335	1,356	2,217	1,914	3,019	1,132	3,289	5,993	18,513	3,783	917	174	1,500	5,156	3,118	5,532
Single	76,739	771	386	677	550	951	353	1,143	1,707	5,239	1,092	296	56	436	1,594	856	1,668
Married	153,916	1,455	834	1,325	1,210	1,876	684	1,955	3,763	11,700	2,357	565	109	968	3,278	2,012	3,437
Widowed	14,833	104	106	202	137	161	73	154	420	1,280	223	51	7	87	227	188	377
Divorced	2,855	3	28	10	16	27	22	35	98	287	109	5	2	9	53	56	47
Unknown	335	2	2	3	1	4	------	2	5	7	2	------	------	------	4	6	3
Females 15 years old and over	264,780	2,558	1,365	2,387	1,988	3,015	1,110	3,103	5,747	21,272	4,068	879	154	1,523	5,363	3,288	5,956
Single	59,127	704	255	553	373	683	247	792	1,004	4,383	872	178	36	327	1,279	624	1,429
Married	157,360	1,540	849	1,324	1,224	1,881	731	1,917	3,760	12,067	2,457	573	104	978	3 236	2,010	3,463
Widowed	42,049	298	221	474	353	388	113	353	849	4,159	523	117	12	198	583	571	926
Divorced	5,871	14	39	33	37	61	19	40	129	652	215	11	2	19	174	71	135
Unknown	373	2	1	3	1	2	------	1	5	11	1	------	------	1	1	12	3
FAMILIES																	
Number of families	190,876	1,768	1,041	1,866	1,609	2,222	860	2,278	4,597	15,084	2,887	618	115	1,154	3,855	2,597	4,483
Median size	3.16	3.86	2.97	2.97	3.19	3.81	2.72	3.91	3.06	2.90	3.32	3.81	4.39	3.24	3.91	2.71	3.50
Families having—																	
No children under 10	110,637	867	638	1,137	883	1,100	573	1,030	2,680	9,434	1,589	303	43	645	1,717	1,703	2,243
1 child under 10	33,020	306	173	287	283	419	115	458	837	2,676	527	102	21	234	782	426	860
2 children under 10	20,076	224	93	175	165	263	82	337	447	1,414	339	88	23	119	550	217	532
3 or more	27,143	371	137	267	278	440	90	453	633	1,560	432	125	28	156	806	251	848

CHARACTERISTICS OF NEGRO POPULATION BY COUNTIES: 1930—Continued

(See note at head of table)

SUBJECT	LOUISIANA—Continued																	
	East Baton Rouge	East Carroll	East Feliciana	Evangeline	Franklin	Grant	Iberia	Iberville	Jackson	Jefferson	Jefferson Davis	Lafayette	Lafourche	La Salle	Lincoln	Livingston	Madison	Morehouse
Population by Sex																		
Negro population: 1930	29,424	11,836	11,876	5,772	11,301	4,955	10,733	12,549	3,987	7,900	4,979	13,260	5,313	2,106	9,701	4,147	9,571	13,597
Male	13,639	5,843	5,863	2,882	5,642	2,532	5,281	6,216	2,040	3,896	2,495	6,423	2,674	1,165	4,792	2,098	4,844	6,719
Fenale	15,785	5,993	6,013	2,890	5,659	2,423	5,452	6,333	1,947	4,004	2,484	6,837	2,639	941	4,909	2,049	4,727	6,878
Negro population: 1920	23,098	9,701	12,004	5,681	10,720	4,045	10,898	15,372	4,006	5,880	4,837	10,811	5,888	1,525	6,310	1,667	9,060	13,140
Male	10,951	4,863	5,810	2,923	5,315	2,124	5,442	7,616	2,017	2,948	2,417	5,249	2,914	811	3,083	840	4,625	6,449
Female	12,147	4,838	6,194	2,758	5,405	1,921	5,456	7,756	1,989	2,932	2,420	5,562	2,974	714	3,227	827	4,435	6,691
Percent of total population:																		
1930	43.1	74.8	68.1	22.7	37.0	31.5	38.1	50.9	28.9	19.7	25.2	34.2	16.4	18.0	42.5	22.8	64.5	57.4
1920	51.9	86.4	68.6	24.2	44.5	28.1	40.6	57.3	27.7	27.3	25.5	35.1	19.4	15.5	37.2	14.3	83.7	68.0
Voting Age: 1930																		
Total 21 years old and over	16,824	7,061	5,899	2,281	5,695	2,671	5,258	7,287	1,914	4,510	2,188	5,835	2,747	1,283	4,441	2,131	5,701	7,417
Male	7,716	3,514	2,860	1,161	2,898	1,395	2,603	3,578	1,039	2,252	1,132	2,826	1,392	741	2,247	1,116	2,906	3,700
Female	9,108	3,547	3,039	1,120	2,797	1,276	2,655	3,709	875	2,258	1,056	3,009	1,355	542	2,194	1,015	2,795	3,717
Age: 1930																		
Under 5 years	2,572	1,139	1,401	937	1,417	541	1,231	1,196	453	860	768	1,937	625	187	1,287	450	863	1,327
Under 1 year	453	209	239	189	286	117	235	218	91	179	153	403	119	33	274	75	176	234
5 to 9 years	3,254	1,217	1,534	907	1,420	588	1,409	1,411	514	918	737	1,890	714	217	1,383	489	1,011	1,524
10 to 14 years	2,968	1,129	1,448	815	1,323	548	1,373	1,264	518	766	661	1,661	597	182	1,256	495	922	1,536
15 to 19 years	3,122	1,036	1,316	711	1,201	520	1,254	1,162	495	691	534	1,643	527	190	1,065	470	902	1,471
20 to 24 years	3,070	1,251	1,091	499	1,184	523	949	1,039	453	774	441	1,298	441	259	1,100	507	994	1,492
25 to 29 years	2,759	1,146	797	427	1,050	427	753	875	377	732	355	1,017	335	263	842	407	945	1,204
30 to 34 years	2,091	926	601	347	702	352	561	776	260	562	228	716	265	219	590	283	726	981
35 to 44 years	4,220	1,669	1,291	494	1,281	646	1,238	1,733	449	1,138	540	1,301	714	326	926	496	1,347	1,757
45 to 54 years	2,915	1,232	1,147	328	905	441	1,016	1,574	264	876	414	984	619	163	675	348	992	1,187
55 to 64 years	1,444	675	699	171	475	214	499	871	119	362	170	456	280	62	305	128	529	690
65 to 74 years	679	264	354	90	217	99	302	446	51	143	81	219	135	25	176	59	220	282
75 years and over	328	152	163	46	123	51	144	191	30	70	48	137	61	13	91	14	116	132
Unknown	2	—	29	—	3	5	4	11	4	8	2	1	—	—	5	1	4	14
School Attendance																		
Total 7 to 13 years, inclusive	4,300	1,619	2,069	1,184	1,830	811	1,936	1,855	717	1,155	960	2,466	896	283	1,797	681	1,344	2,122
Number attending school	3,730	1,475	1,769	596	1,575	723	1,537	1,527	591	1,055	678	1,367	591	256	1,508	482	1,070	1,770
Percent attending school	86.7	91.1	85.5	50.3	86.1	9.1	79.4	82.3	82.4	91.3	70.6	55.4	66.0	90.5	83.9	70.8	79.6	83.4
Total 14 and 15 years, inclusive	1,147	395	568	309	524	207	524	468	196	285	239	641	230	75	450	200	301	585
Number attending school	884	304	441	123	411	181	273	286	156	191	142	276	102	58	354	114	221	456
Percent attending school	77.1	77.0	77.6	39.8	78.4	87.4	52.1	61.1	79.6	67.0	59.4	43.1	44.3	—	78.7	57.0	73.4	77.9
Total 16 and 17 years, inclusive	1,281	392	535	298	452	201	502	457	207	277	227	659	208	77	464	193	372	590
Number attending school	643	189	300	71	199	120	115	140	114	64	79	140	39	36	217	60	128	286
Percent attending school	50.2	48.2	56.1	23.8	44.0	59.7	22.9	30.6	55.1	23.1	34.8	21.2	18.8	—	46.8	31.1	34.4	48.5
Total 18 to 20 years, inclusive	1,979	713	783	386	751	306	695	702	299	441	288	959	311	117	667	291	557	941
Number attending school	349	125	90	51	101	75	54	58	53	25	31	69	16	17	126	11	33	168
Percent attending school	17.6	17.5	11.5	13.2	13.4	24.5	7.8	8.3	17.7	5.7	10.8	7.2	5.1	14.5	18.9	3.8	5.9	17.9
Illiteracy																		
Total 10 years old and over	23,598	9,480	8,941	3,928	8,464	3,826	8,093	9,942	3,020	6,122	3,474	9,433	3,974	1,702	7,031	3,208	7,697	10,746
Number illiterate	4,889	1,801	2,139	2,074	1,959	712	2,968	2,853	396	1,554	1,425	5,824	1,193	252	1,423	478	1,823	2,750
Percent illiterate	20.7	19.0	23.9	52.8	23.1	18.6	36.7	28.7	13.1	25.4	41.0	61.7	30.0	14.8	20.2	14.9	23.7	25.6
Percent illiterate in 1920	38.2	36.7	41.6	64.9	56.2	37.9	53.6	52.8	33.7	35.5	51.0	73.6	50.4	18.5	28.9	37.6	43.4	37.2
Urban and Rural																		
Urban population	10,675	1,706	1,299	—	—	—	2,545	1,931	—	2,691	1,146	5,013	1,226	—	1,201	—	1,701	1,604
Percent urban	36.3	14.4	10.9	—	—	—	23.7	15.4	—	34.1	23.0	37.8	23.1	—	12.4	—	17.8	11.8
Rural population	18,749	10,130	10,577	5,772	11,301	4,955	8,188	10,618	3,987	5,209	3,833	8,247	4,087	2,106	8,500	4,147	7,870	11,993
Rural-farm	7,330	9,470	9,600	4,873	10,004	2,728	4,674	3,610	2,520	259	2,442	7,123	2,805	307	7,642	2,725	7,014	10,935
Rural-nonfarm	11,419	660	977	899	1,297	2,227	3,514	7,008	1,467	4,950	1,391	1,124	1,282	1,799	858	1,422	856	1,058
Percent rural	63.7	85.6	89.1	100.0	100.0	100.0	76.3	84.6	100.0	65.9	77.0	62.2	76.9	100.0	87.6	100.0	82.2	88.2
Marital Condition																		
Males 15 years old and over	9,338	4,117	3,638	1,554	3,529	1,679	3,307	4,243	1,311	2,626	1,442	3,773	1,701	847	2,854	1,376	3,387	4,537
Single	2,851	1,029	1,514	460	843	525	1,192	1,318	452	770	428	1,396	502	300	858	525	958	1,206
Married	5,793	2,764	2,082	1,041	2,449	1,017	1,851	2,501	761	1,659	913	2,178	1,077	452	1,822	763	2,207	2,971
Widowed	538	259	185	47	165	86	248	369	92	158	87	186	107	83	151	70	189	272
Divorced	147	63	30	6	70	50	12	48	5	23	12	13	15	12	20	16	32	77
Unknown	9	2	27	—	2	1	4	7	1	16	2	—	—	—	3	2	1	11
Females 15 years old and over	11,292	4,234	3,855	1,559	3,612	1,599	3,413	4,435	1,191	2,730	1,371	3,999	1,676	673	2,921	1,337	3,388	4,673
Single	2,789	631	1,030	364	573	348	940	952	291	521	298	1,206	344	123	677	324	562	873
Married	6,045	2,810	2,248	1,023	2,462	995	1,916	2,514	741	1,680	899	2,264	1,067	424	1,830	856	2,207	2,998
Widowed	2,020	679	510	161	400	205	531	855	145	466	156	479	241	113	361	139	554	649
Divorced	466	113	41	10	170	51	19	110	14	48	17	48	24	12	51	17	65	150
Unknown	2	1	26	1	7	—	7	4	—	15	1	2	—	1	2	1	—	3
Families																		
Number of families	7,586	3,478	2,357	1,152	2,843	1,189	2,446	3,513	882	2,094	1,065	2,707	1,347	537	2,069	876	2,593	3,493
Median size	3.03	2.64	3.94	4.46	3.24	3.05	3.59	2.68	3.57	2.89	3.98	4.23	3.15	2.70	3.81	3.06	2.78	3.13
Families having—																		
No children under 10	4,798	2,306	1,124	412	1,520	698	1,285	2,288	428	1,264	465	1,136	784	345	963	501	1,672	2,098
1 child under 10	1,273	562	417	231	575	199	455	549	192	370	191	531	211	86	393	148	458	642
2 children under 10	711	287	344	180	329	121	280	305	123	196	134	399	126	54	281	97	214	346
3 or more	804	323	472	329	419	171	426	371	139	264	275	641	226	52	432	130	249	407

CHARACTERISTICS OF NEGRO POPULATION BY COUNTIES: 1930—Continued

(See note at head of table)

LOUISIANA—Continued

SUBJECT	Natchitoches	Orleans	Ouachita	Plaquemines	Pointe Coupee	Rapides	Red River	Richland	Sabine	St. Bernard	St. Charles	St. Helena	St. James	St. John the Baptist	St. Landry	St. Martin	St. Mary	St. Tammany
POPULATION BY SEX																		
Negro population: 1930	19,570	129,632	19,041	4,530	12,211	25,126	7,551	13,203	5,237	1,337	4,199	4,611	7,550	6,947	29,516	7,545	14,302	7,066
Male	9.551	59,732	9,312	2,374	5,991	12,146	3,747	6,577	2,710	673	2,208	2,477	3,796	3,597	14,552	3,794	7,112	3,598
Female	10,019	69,900	9,729	2,156	6,220	12,980	3,804	6,626	2,527	664	1,991	2,134	3,754	3,350	14,964	3,751	7,190	3,468
Negro population: 1920	20,697	100,930	13,897	5,393	14,981	24,992	7,589	11,996	4,364	1,597	4,347	4,229	11,602	6,415	26,507	7,902	15,174	7,648
Male	10,224	46,919	6,719	2,799	7,369	12,586	3,765	5,970	2,263	792	2,210	2,085	5,894	3,262	13,082	3,939	7,432	3,844
Female	10,473	54,011	7,178	2,594	7,612	12,406	3,824	6,026	2,101	805	2,137	2,144	5,708	3,153	13,425	3,963	7,742	3,804
Percent of total population:																		
1930	50.9	28.3	35.0	47.1	58.1	38.4	47.0	50.1	21.7	20.5	34.7	54.3	49.2	49.3	49.1	34.7	48.7	33.8
1920	53.6	26.1	45.8	52.9	60.7	42.0	49.6	57.5	21.1	32.1	50.6	50.2	54.7	53.9	51.3	35.9	49.3	37.0
VOTING AGE: 1930																		
Total 21 years old and over	9,542	81,189	11,444	2,051	6,291	13,870	3,809	7,024	2,703	676	2,331	2,044	3,926	3,672	12,549	3e232	7,220	3,717
Male	4,638	36,971	5,675	1,085	3,086	6,748	1,896	3,577	1,441	333	1,249	1,166	1,972	2,006	6,227	1,627	3,567	1,937
Female	4,904	44,218	5,769	966	3,205	7,122	1,913	3,447	1,262	343	1,082	878	1,954	1,666	6,322	1,605	3,653	1,780
AGE: 1930																		
Under 5 years	2,444	11,518	1,634	630	1,341	2,524	934	1,450	585	168	472	587	844	772	4,356	1,035	1,661	849
Under 1 year	503	2,147	291	145	282	495	189	278	109	35	84	84	171	154	967	208	345	141
5 to 9 years	2,570	12,570	1,851	670	1,506	2,893	1,000	1,513	658	179	500	658	956	876	4,357	1,088	1,931	812
10 to 14 years	2,440	10,280	1,764	564	1,500	2,636	846	1,434	608	152	410	635	892	755	4,015	1,057	1,712	736
15 to 19 years	2,157	11,340	1,862	523	1,324	2,656	796	1,438	565	136	400	569	793	700	3,620	965	1,502	789
20 to 24 years	1,864	13,974	2,505	418	1,055	2,562	782	1,554	564	116	398	484	592	686	2,751	697	1,142	721
25 to 29 years	1,496	14,536	2,247	293	827	2,123	622	1,241	489	84	307	343	464	535	2,037	482	958	565
30 to 34 years	1,080	11,700	1,538	235	620	1,668	413	879	358	80	276	220	420	408	1,386	314	759	440
35 to 44 years	2,067	21,395	2,723	443	1,489	3,405	872	1,644	624	160	558	447	963	868	2,804	725	1,692	947
45 to 54 years	1,719	13,511	1,707	373	1,180	2,430	630	1,150	448	154	452	342	858	731	2,141	561	1,514	677
55 to 64 years	994	5,612	681	218	777	1,347	380	548	224	60	243	194	433	387	1,108	333	818	320
65 to 74 years	467	2,174	335	110	361	560	176	224	76	30	119	92	214	158	592	170	395	150
75 years and over	271	953	174	50	229	312	97	123	38	18	62	40	121	61	349	116	215	55
Unknown	1	69	20	3	2	10	3	5	------	------	2	------	------	10	------	2	3	5
SCHOOL ATTENDANCE																		
Total 7 to 13 years, inclusive	3,474	15,559	2,526	858	2,157	3,797	1,262	2,029	880	221	658	919	1,278	1,172	5,792	1,507	2,484	1,055
Number attending school	2,772	14,618	2,315	608	1,434	3,367	900	1,631	730	183	566	739	943	865	3,973	883	2,063	894
Percent attending school	79.8	94.0	91.6	70.9	66.5	88.7	71.3	80.4	83.0	82.8	86.0	80.4	73.8	73.8	68.6	58.6	83.1	84.7
Total 14 and 15 years, inclusive	931	4,202	672	212	536	1,022	314	578	234	58	150	218	356	245	1,574	398	685	308
Number attending school	712	3,337	561	134	307	804	230	463	179	38	88	170	218	111	985	179	412	229
Percent attending school	76.5	79.4	83.5	63.2	57.3	78.7	73.2	80.1	76.5	------	58.7	78.0	61.2	45.3	62.6	45.0	60.1	74.4
Total 16 and 17 years, inclusive	867	4,507	714	188	555	1,046	322	539	240	55	156	228	314	265	1,451	415	614	297
Number attending school	438	1,966	389	41	154	515	139	311	100	17	38	117	85	46	506	89	198	110
Percent attending school	50.5	43.6	54.5	21.8	27.7	49.2	43.2	57.7	41.7	------	24.4	51.3	27.1	17.4	34.9	21.4	32.2	37.0
Total 18 to 29 years, inclusive	1,252	7,536	1,303	323	745	1,661	491	951	335	81	241	339	437	479	2,024	525	842	510
Number attending school	184	960	187	24	56	278	72	214	44	2	14	59	47	27	268	42	85	48
Percent attending school	14.7	12.7	14.4	7.3	7.5	16.7	14.7	22.5	13.1	------	5.8	17.4	10.8	5.6	13.2	8.0	10.1	9.4
ILLITERACY																		
Total 10 years old and over	14,556	105,544	15,556	3,230	9,364	19,709	5,617	10,240	3,994	990	3,227	3,366	5,750	5,299	20,803	5,422	10,710	5,405
Number illiterate	4,945	14,107	3,021	1,427	3,507	3,550	1,991	2,951	826	229	874	409	1,501	1,582	8,659	2,545	2,579	887
Percent illiterate	34.0	13.4	19.4	44.2	37.5	18.0	35.4	28.8	20.7	23.1	27.1	12.2	26.1	29.9	41.6	46.9	24.1	16.4
Percent illiterate in 1920	45.4	15.7	32.7	56.5	58.8	33.7	46.0	41.5	23.5	36.3	47.9	39.5	40.4	43.9	61.0	71.0	46.5	25.7
URBAN AND RURAL																		
Urban population	1,856	129,632	11,098	------	------	10,083	------	------	------	------	------	------	------	------	3,822	------	2,999	1,715
Percent urban	9.5	100.0	58.3	------	------	40.1	------	------	------	------	------	------	------	------	12.9	------	21.0	24.3
Rural population	17,714	------	7,943	4,530	12,211	15,043	7,551	13,203	5,237	1,337	4,199	4,611	7,550	6,947	25,694	7,545	11,303	5,351
Rural-farm	15,521	------	6,196	1,400	8,725	9,180	7,062	11,089	2,507	114	392	4,123	2,144	2,255	21,589	5,478	6,066	1,254
Rural-nonfarm	2,193	------	1,747	3,130	3,486	5,863	489	2,114	2,730	1,223	3,807	488	5,406	4,692	4,105	2,067	5,237	4,097
Percent rural	90.5	------	41.7	100.0	100.0	59.9	100.0	100.0	100.0	100.0	100.0	100.0	100.0	100.0	87.1	100.0	79.0	75.7
MARITAL CONDITION																		
Males 15 years old and over	5,863	42,960	6,721	1,428	3,825	8,227	2,345	4,416	1,756	403	1,506	1,505	2,423	2,430	8,227	2,210	4,406	2,384
Single	1,740	13,141	1,965	526	1,197	2,594	582	1,201	572	130	518	570	776	810	2,818	843	1,336	819
Married	3,696	27,075	4,235	808	2,348	4,874	1,578	2,894	1,084	253	870	850	1,477	1,403	4,968	1,230	2,697	1,364
Widowed	347	2,272	436	80	258	536	153	278	89	20	94	70	163	203	386	123	326	181
Divorced	80	436	81	12	21	115	32	41	10	------	24	9	7	14	50	10	46	15
Unknown	------	36	4	2	1	108	------	2	1	------	------	6	------	------	5	4	1	5
Females 15 years old and over	6,253	52,304	7,071	1,238	4,039	8,846	2,426	4,390	1,630	435	1,311	1,226	2,435	2,114	8,561	2,155	4,592	2,285
Single	1,384	12,167	1,268	301	950	1,911	420	775	346	99	234	357	531	469	2,496	665	996	563
Married	3,741	29,084	4,428	815	2,336	4,996	1,559	2,901	1,077	262	835	723	1,505	1,354	4,993	1,245	2,767	1,356
Widowed	997	10,019	1,220	111	672	1,495	374	636	192	72	203	132	384	285	958	228	757	337
Divorced	129	1,007	153	9	78	281	73	77	15	2	39	7	13	5	111	17	70	26
Unknown	2	27	2	2	3	163	------	1	------	------	------	7	2	1	3	------	2	3
FAMILIES																		
Number of families	4,695	34,461	5,189	903	3,013	6,056	1,923	3,378	1,197	308	1,106	860	1,968	1,713	5,796	1,444	3,480	1,770
Median size	3.43	2.81	2.72	4.46	3.22	3.23	3.16	3.10	3.23	3.53	2.72	4.43	3.08	3.20	4.48	4.82	3.42	2.98
Families having:																		
No children under 10	2,498	22,860	3,410	388	1,771	3,512	1,050	1,968	638	160	693	355	1,159	1,003	2,388	586	1,896	1,047
1 child under 10	841	5,263	884	165	472	1,108	361	656	234	58	150	170	343	273	1,046	259	633	273
2 children under 10	563	3,082	450	114	313	636	226	330	130	33	109	122	177	171	803	232	370	188
3 or more	793	3,256	445	236	457	800	286	424	195	57	154	213	289	266	1,559	367	581	262

CHARACTERISTICS OF NEGRO POPULATION BY COUNTIES: 1930—Continued

(See note at head of table)

SUBJECT	LOUISIANA—Continued												MAINE					
	Tangipahoa	Tensas	Terrebonne	Union	Vermilion	Vernon	Washington	Webster	West Baton Rouge	West Carroll	West Feliciana	Winn	The State	Androscoggin	Aroostook	Cumberland	Franklin	Hancock
POPULATION BY SEX																		
Negro population: 1930	15,644	10,745	8,349	6,634	4,413	3,560	9,719	13,090	6,132	2,840	8,349	3,695	1,096	45	39	384	5	3
Male	7,685	5,294	4,237	3,294	2,216	1,827	4,945	6,487	3,119	1,506	4,440	1,856	597	20	22	207	4	2
Female	7,959	5,501	4,112	3,340	2,197	1,733	4,774	6,603	3,013	1,334	3,909	1,839	499	25	17	177	1	1
Negro population: 1920	8,892	10,314	8,742	6,114	4,560	5,103	7,391	11,387	7,485	2,370	10,187	3,385	1,310	100	61	416	4	15
Male	4,493	5,043	4,372	3,059	2,276	2,786	3,841	5,996	3,699	1,222	5,205	1,665	716	48	37	202	4	10
Female	4,399	5,271	4,370	3,055	2,284	2,317	3,550	5,391	3,786	1,148	4,982	1,720	594	52	24	214	-	5
Percent of total population:																		
1930	33.8	71.5	28.0	32.0	13.1	17.8	32.5	44.4	63.1	20.4	76.4	25.0	0.1	0.1	-	0.3	-	-
1920	28.3	85.3	32.4	31.2	17.2	24.9	30.6	46.1	67.5	26.8	82.8	21.0	0.2	0.2	0.1	0.3	-	-
VOTING AGE: 1930																		
Total 21 years old and over	7,850	6,209	4,108	3,004	1,968	2,013	5,159	6,207	3,388	1,623	4,282	2,002	713	37	26	249	2	3
Male	3,868	3,059	2,087	1,533	1,003	1,088	2,729	3,117	1,716	884	2,411	1,040	391	17	17	134	1	2
Female	3,982	3,150	2,021	1,471	965	925	2,430	3,090	1,672	739	1,871	962	322	20	9	115	1	1
AGE: 1930																		
Under 5 years	1,649	1,032	1,085	952	616	351	1,099	1,559	572	284	934	380	107	1	8	32	1	-
Under 1 year	292	188	176	167	118	72	183	299	110	55	121	62	21	-	1	6	-	-
5 to 9 years	1,998	1,219	1,190	934	600	404	1,192	1,683	786	283	999	446	89	1	2	31	2	-
10 to 14 years	1,926	1,102	943	831	577	366	963	1,675	699	276	989	455	100	3	2	41	-	-
15 to 19 years	1,863	1,022	886	751	553	347	1,075	1,609	572	308	927	350	74	3	1	28	-	-
20 to 24 years	1,693	1,063	654	743	423	350	1,162	1,537	538	326	852	359	56	1	2	23	-	-
25 to 29 years	1,381	918	552	560	343	310	1,039	1,168	439	301	611	319	81	7	1	34	1	1
30 to 34 years	1,014	691	444	393	226	287	716	758	370	210	463	293	70	4	2	29	-	-
35 to 44 years	1,978	1,327	920	610	418	614	1,290	1,347	843	354	948	528	1.67	8	9	57	1	-
45 to 54 years	1,277	1,177	898	437	333	341	659	939	694	293	815	308	160	5	6	52	-	2
55 to 64 years	556	695	483	259	176	136	311	472	372	108	438	154	95	7	3	28	-	-
65 to 74 years	201	325	197	105	90	32	141	239	164	59	237	78	62	3	3	17	-	-
75 years and over	104	209	94	56	52	20	72	102	79	37	135	23	33	2	-	12	-	-
Unknown	4	15	3	3	6	2	-	2	4	1	1	2	2	-	-	-	-	-
SCHOOL ATTENDANCE																		
Total 7 to 13 years, inclusive	2,710	1,602	1,419	1,185	824	553	1,474	2,361	1,047	381	1,372	635	140	2	3	55	-	-
Number attending school	2,194	1,459	1,054	1,025	596	486	1,374	1,961	925	348	1,235	571	135	2	3	52	-	-
Percent attending school	81.0	91.1	74.3	86.5	72.3	87.9	93.2	83.1	88.3	91.3	90.0	89.9	96.4	-	-	-	-	-
Total 14 and 15 years, inclusive	764	444	393	316	228	151	389	643	262	113	374	173	32	2	-	15	-	-
Number attending school	518	358	208	249	142	114	327	515	190	84	237	141	31	2	-	15	-	-
Percent attending school	67.8	80.6	52.9	78.8	62.3	75.5	84.1	80.1	72.5	74.3	63.4	81.5	-	-	-	-	-	-
Total 16 and 17 years, inclusive	758	366	360	302	215	139	435	647	243	112	352	152	28	1	1	9	-	-
Number attending school	252	164	73	175	51	50	255	372	89	61	86	89	23	1	-	8	-	-
Percent attending school	33.2	44.8	20.3	57.9	23.7	36.0	58.6	57.5	36.6	54.5	24.4	58.6	-	-	-	-	-	-
Total 18 to 20 years, inclusive	1,120	628	472	468	311	217	676	1,003	326	206	611	188	46	2	-	17	-	-
Number attending school	69	80	27	107	26	21	130	250	29	22	51	34	17	1	-	8	-	-
Percent attending school	6.2	12.7	5.7	22.9	8.4	9.7	19.2	24.9	8.9	10.7	8.3	18.1	-	-	-	-	-	-
ILLITERACY																		
Total 10 years old and over	11,997	8,544	6,074	4,748	3,197	2,805	7,428	9,848	4,774	2,273	6,416	2,869	900	43	29	321	2	3
Number illiterate	2,410	2,632	1,828	858	1,414	353	772	1,780	1,255	386	1,487	426	43	1	1	20	-	-
Percent illiterate	20.1	30.8	30.1	18.1	44.2	12.6	10.4	18.1	26.3	17.0	23.2	14.8	4.8	-	-	6.2	-	-
Percent illiterate in 1920	33.9	58.0	45.3	35.7	54.3	15.5	24.7	41.6	53.0	30.2	55.0	22.0	5.9	-	-	8.0	-	-
URBAN AND RURAL																		
Urban population	3,988	-	1,244	-	1,115	893	4,751	2,034	-	-	-	1,310	703	36	2	295	-	-
Percent urban	25.5	-	14.9	-	25.3	25.1	48.9	15.5	-	-	-	35.5	64.1	-	-	76.8	-	-
Rural population	11,656	10,795	7,105	6,634	3,298	2,667	4,968	11,056	6,132	2,840	8,349	2,385	393	9	37	89	5	3
Rural-farm	9,336	9,074	2,636	5,361	2,276	510	4,015	9,437	3,767	2,173	6,549	1,702	115	6	11	13	1	1
Rural-nonfarm	2,320	1,721	4,469	1,273	1,022	2,157	953	1,619	2,365	667	1,800	683	278	3	26	76	4	2
Percent rural	74.5	100.0	85.1	100.0	74.7	74.9	51.1	84.5	100.0	100.0	100.0	64.5	35.9	-	-	23.2	-	-
MARITAL CONDITION																		
Males 15 years old and over	4,929	3,619	2,602	1,942	1,327	1,272	3,355	4,050	2,042	1,065	3,001	1,232	442	18	17	152	1	2
Single	1,776	995	774	600	489	382	1,214	1,331	544	322	1,114	358	184	6	9	59	-	1
Married	2,768	2,362	1,622	1,232	748	760	1,903	2,508	1,329	653	1,717	781	210	10	7	77	1	1
Widowed	268	228	160	84	71	105	219	171	132	75	144	72	40	2	1	15	-	-
Divorced	106	31	46	24	16	25	18	39	31	15	22	21	8	-	-	1	-	-
Unknown	11	3	-	2	3	-	1	1	6	-	4	-	-	-	-	-	-	-
Females 15 years old and over	5,142	3,823	2,529	1,975	1,293	1,167	3,110	4,123	2,033	932	2,426	1,182	358	22	10	128	1	1
Single	1,244	662	470	507	381	200	764	993	352	163	627	247	116	9	1	40	1	-
Married	2,891	2,369	1,622	1,221	756	747	1,851	2,562	1,342	650	1,445	774	188	10	8	68	-	1
Widowed	767	708	385	210	127	186	451	504	271	113	320	133	38	1	1	15	-	-
Divorced	229	82	52	35	28	33	42	58	61	6	28	28	15	2	-	5	-	-
Unknown	11	2	-	2	1	1	2	6	7	-	6	-	1	-	-	-	-	-
FAMILIES																		
Number of families	3,699	3,143	1,959	1,388	873	893	2,366	2,963	1,726	767	1,706	872	259	10	7	96	1	1
Median size	3.14	2.62	3.45	4.04	4.24	2.99	3.03	3.56	2.77	2.67	3.64	3.13	2.86	-	-	-	-	-
Families having—																		
No children under 10	2,092	2,069	1,033	606	394	546	1,364	1,490	1,110	505	876	498	171	8	4	66	-	1
1 child under 10	641	492	298	268	139	148	402	611	248	115	320	160	40	2	1	18	-	-
2 children under 10	406	263	230	178	133	97	252	361	158	70	195	89	21	-	1	5	1	-
3 or more	560	319	398	336	207	102	348	501	210	77	315	125	27	-	1	7	-	-

CHARACTERISTICS OF NEGRO POPULATION BY COUNTIES: 1930—Continued

(See note at head of table)

MAINE—Continued

SUBJECT	Kennebec	Knox	Lincoln	Oxford	Penobscot	Piscataquis	Sagadahoc	Somerset	Waldo	Washington	York
POPULATION BY SEX											
Negro population: 1930	69	66	5	35	294	1	57	8	16	25	44
Male	40	40	4	22	152		31	5	11	15	22
Female	29	26	1	13	142	1	26	3	5	10	22
Negro population: 1920	96	52	5	29	250	29	94	6	16	33	104
Male	47	31	1	18	123	26	57	3	12	23	74
Female	49	21	4	11	127	3	37	3	4	10	30
Percent of total population:											
1930	0.1	0.2		0.1	0.3		0.3		0.1	0.1	0.1
1920	0.2	0.2		0.1	0.3	0.1	0.4		0.1	0.1	0.1
VOTING AGE: 1930											
Total 21 years old and over	55	48	3	16	156	1	40	6	13	21	37
Male	36	29	2	10	76		22	3	9	12	21
Female	19	19	1	6	80	1	18	3	4	9	16
AGE: 1930											
Under 5 years	1	5		5	48		4		1		1
Under 1 year		2			11						1
5 to 9 years	2	6		5	27		7	1	1	1	3
10 to 14 years	4	3		6	36		3	1			1
15 to 19 years	6	3	2	3	21		3		1	3	
20 to 24 years	3	4		2	14		2	1		1	3
25 to 29 years	2	3		3	16		4	1	3	3	2
30 to 34 years	4	6		3	16		1	1		1	3
35 to 44 years	13	8		5	42		6	3	3	4	8
45 to 54 years	17	14	2	2	34	1	6		6	4	9
55 to 64 years	10	6		1	20		9		1	3	7
65 to 74 years	3	6			15		8			3	4
75 years and over	4	2	1		5		4			2	1
Unknown											2
SCHOOL ATTENDANCE											
Total 7 to 13 years, inclusive	5	7		8	48		7	2	1		2
Number attending school	5	7		8	47		7	2			2
Percent attending school											
Total 14 and 15 years, inclusive	1	1	1	1	9		2				
Number attending school	1	1	1	1	8		2				
Percent attending school											
Total 16 and 17 years, inclusive	2		1	2	8		2		1	1	
Number attending school	2		1	1	7		2			1	
Percent attending school											
Total 18 to 20 years, inclusive	4	3		1	15					2	2
Number attending school	3			1	3						1
Percent attending school											
ILLITERACY											
Total 10 years old and over	66	55	5	25	219	1	46	7	14	24	40
Number illiterate			2		11		4			2	2
Percent illiterate					5.0						
Percent illiterate in 1920					1.0						
URBAN AND RURAL											
Urban population	42	32			236		35		8	14	3
Percent urban					80.3						
Rural population	27	34	5	35	58	1	22	8	8	11	41
Rural-farm	2	14	2	6	36			5	4	2	12
Rural-nonfarm	25	20	3	29	22	1	22	3	4	9	29
Percent rural					19.7						
MARITAL CONDITION											
Males 15 years old and over	39	31	4	11	94		24	3	10	14	22
Single	21	19	4	2	33		6		7	9	8
Married	11	8		9	52		13	3	3	4	11
Widowed	7	4			6		3			1	1
Divorced					3		2				2
Unknown											
Females 15 years old and over	23	21	1	8	89	1	19	3	4	10	17
Single	8	5	1	3	30	1	4			6	7
Married	10	11		5	46		12	3	3	3	8
Widowed	3	4			8		2		1	1	2
Divorced	1	1			5		1				
Unknown	1										
FAMILIES											
Number of families	14	15	1	8	66		14	1	7	7	11
Median size											
Families having—											
No children under 10	10	10	1	3	37		10		6	7	8
1 child under 10	3	2		2	8		2	1			1
2 children under 10		1		1	9				1		2
3 or more	1	2		2	12		2				

MARYLAND

SUBJECT	The State	Allegany	Anne Arundel	Baltimore	Baltimore city	Calvert	Caroline
POPULATION BY SEX							
Negro population: 1930	276,379	1,454	14,927	11,764	142,106	4,519	3,677
Male	140,506	731	7,822	6,808	70,043	2,358	1,906
Female	135,873	723	7,105	4,956	72,063	2,161	1,771
Negro population: 1920	244,479	1,825	13,411	9,099	108,322	4,789	4,445
Male	123,453	1,073	7,022	4,895	52,889	2,478	2,275
Female	121,026	752	6,389	4,204	55,433	2,311	2,170
Percent of total population:							
1930	16.9	1.8	27.1	9.4	17.7	47.4	21.1
1920	16.9	2.6	30.9	12.2	14.8	49.1	23.8
VOTING AGE: 1930							
Total 21 years old and over	163,464	862	8,267	7,237	92,610	1,990	1,936
Male	84,881	453	4,456	4,457	46,869	1,056	1,018
Female	78,583	409	3,811	2,780	45,741	934	918
AGE: 1930							
Under 5 years	27,006	132	1,614	1,076	12,274	588	353
Under 1 year	5,046	24	286	187	2,244	125	60
5 to 9 years	29,564	169	1,703	1,194	13,053	672	439
10 to 14 years	25,627	157	1,500	1,003	10,423	622	456
15 to 19 years	25,417	113	1,529	959	11,076	539	412
20 to 24 years	27,411	135	1,506	1,542	14,976	392	323
25 to 29 years	25,509	128	1,216	1,269	15,972	235	200
30 to 34 years	21,826	118	983	1,025	13,701	208	182
35 to 44 years	39,659	184	1,859	1,548	24,420	396	396
45 to 54 years	28,546	163	1,545	1,185	15,144	393	410
55 to 64 years	14,372	86	846	579	1,176	250	258
65 to 74 years	7,139	48	421	275	2,702	163	179
75 years and over	2,946	21	175	103	1,001	55	59
Unknown	1,357		30	6	1,188	6	5
SCHOOL ATTENDANCE							
Total 7 to 13 years, inclusive	38,424	237	2,250	1,506	16,322	913	623
Number attending school	35,937	224	2,067	1,426	15,574	840	597
Percent attending school	93.5	94.5	91.9	94.7	95.4	92.0	95.8
Total 14 and 15 years, inclusive	9,586	50	566	355	3,767	231	163
Number attending school	7,102	39	363	295	3,024	137	119
Percent attending school	74.1		64.1	83.1	80.3	59.3	73.0
Total 16 and 17 years, inclusive	10,128	47	576	376	4,231	228	185
Number attending school	3,163	17	128	114	1,597	33	50
Percent attending school	31.2		22.2	30.3	37.7	14.5	27.0
Total 18 to 20 years, inclusive	15,905	63	976	722	7,624	306	234
Number attending school	1,270	5	46	56	741	4	20
Percent attending school	8.0		4.7	7.8	9.7	1.3	8.5
ILLITERACY							
Total 10 years old and over	219,809	1,153	11,610	9,494	116,779	3,259	2,885
Number illiterate	25,073	79	1,707	833	8,194	738	453
Percent illiterate	11.4	6.9	14.7	8.8	7.0	22.6	15.7
Percent illiterate in 1920	18.2	8.6	22.8	13.9	12.9	27.7	20.8
URBAN AND RURAL							
Urban population	159,654	1,370	3,218		142,106		
Percent urban	57.8	94.2	21.6		100.0		
Rural population	116,725	84	11,709	11,764		4,519	3,677
Rural-farm	44,281	5	3,929	1,344		2,896	1,746
Rural-nonfarm	72,444	79	7,780	10,420		1,623	1,931
Percent rural	42.2	5.8	78.4	100.0		100.0	100.0
MARITAL CONDITION							
Males 15 years old and over	99,951	511	5,436	5,168	52,870	1,423	1,279
Single	37,113	178	2,216	2,260	18,440	588	504
Married	55,258	280	2,851	2,633	30,327	751	674
Widowed	6,376	45	281	249	3,291	75	97
Divorced	782	8	32	23	502	4	4
Unknown	422		56	3	310	5	
Females 15 years old and over	94,231	485	4,674	3,323	53,486	1,214	1,150
Single	24,295	131	1,278	832	13,295	325	314
Married	55,009	272	2,783	2,081	30,657	751	679
Widowed	13,466	71	531	377	8,447	130	154
Divorced	1,006	10	52	31	710	7	2
Unknown	455	1	30	2	377	1	1
FAMILIES							
Number of families	61,160	294	2,925	2,029	33,102	876	826
Median size	3.12	3.48	3.56	3.56	2.80	4.33	3.34
Families having—							
No children under 10	37,539	161	1,592	1,148	22,120	395	480
1 child under 10	9,278	65	496	304	4,652	156	150
2 children under 10	5,681	28	291	196	2,771	123	77
3 or more	8,662	40	546	381	3,559	202	119

CHARACTERISTICS OF NEGRO POPULATION BY COUNTIES: 1930—Continued

(See note at head of table)

SUBJECT	MARYLAND—Continued																	
	Carroll	Cecil	Charles	Dorchester	Frederick	Garrett	Harford	Howard	Kent	Montgomery	Prince Georges	Queen Annes	St. Marys	Somerset	Talbot	Washington	Wicomico	Worcester
POPULATION BY SEX																		
Negro population: 1930	1,762	2,595	7,492	7,830	4,713	24	4,023	3,270	4,437	8,266	14,023	4,379	5,592	8,111	5,943	2,010	6,750	6,712
Male	897	1,379	3,896	4,075	2,400	14	2,144	1,733	2,341	4,204	7,333	2,373	2,958	4,217	3,064	978	3,410	3,422
Female	865	1,216	3,596	3,755	2,313	10	1,879	1,537	2,096	4,062	6,690	2,006	2,634	3,894	2,879	1,032	3,340	3,290
Negro population: 1920	1,734	2,908	8,210	8,719	4,764	45	4,604	3,502	5,246	8,282	12,056	5,154	6,437	8,889	6,165	2,242	6,407	7,224
Male	915	1,529	4,275	4,480	2,384	27	2,414	1,839	2,726	4,292	6,308	2,701	3,331	4,513	3,145	1,129	3,209	3,604
Female	819	1,379	3,935	4,239	2,380	18	2,190	1,663	2,520	3,990	5,748	2,453	3,106	4,376	3,020	1,113	3,198	3,620
Percent of total population: 1930	4.9	10.0	46.3	29.2	8.7	0.1	12.7	20.2	31.2	16.8	23.3	30.1	36.8	34.7	32.0	3.1	21.6	31.0
1920	5.1	12.3	46.4	31.3	9.1	.2	15.7	22.1	34.9	23.7	27.8	32.2	40.0	36.1	33.7	3.8	22.7	32.4
VOTING AGE: 1930																		
Total 21 years old and over	975	1,498	3,209	4,240	2,572	17	2,400	1,622	2,508	4,335	6,689	2,396	2,460	4,199	3,368	1,324	3,508	3,242
Male	516	841	1,721	2,215	1,336	12	1,309	881	1,354	2,239	3,485	1,315	1,313	2,172	1,767	630	1,799	1,667
Female	459	657	1,488	2,025	1,236	5	1,091	741	1,154	2,096	3,204	1,081	1,147	2,027	1,601	694	1,709	1,575
AGE: 1930																		
Under 5 years	205	270	1,075	779	507	1	420	428	450	940	1,762	418	737	824	569	117	718	749
Under 1 year	35	50	209	146	102		84	82	96	181	342	78	138	153	114	24	140	146
5 to 9 years	207	309	1,180	884	538	2	432	410	513	1,011	1,853	468	863	1,055	675	176	813	945
10 to 14 years	165	233	1,029	866	524	1	363	382	458	918	1,814	508	774	965	624	170	827	845
15 to 19 years	171	241	882	915	493	3	335	364	440	873	1,665	497	638	910	609	195	747	811
20 to 24 years	176	224	586	670	412	4	351	260	384	762	1,255	394	486	714	536	167	616	535
25 to 29 years	140	209	421	535	326	1	307	188	250	557	943	302	276	548	413	168	487	418
30 to 34 years	105	183	349	482	290		281	190	266	453	785	242	235	456	364	166	407	352
35 to 44 years	170	311	660	949	539	5	502	371	536	942	1,403	527	468	900	789	339	771	674
45 to 54 years	169	282	624	806	461	3	466	287	497	810	1,295	501	500	836	625	248	649	650
55 to 64 years	143	195	379	519	312	2	315	218	357	547	706	312	321	519	407	140	408	377
65 to 74 years	70	91	203	319	195	2	153	114	223	287	322	144	185	271	230	83	233	226
75 years and over	37	47	99	105	113		92	55	66	138	170	66	94	112	101	34	74	129
Unknown	4		5	1	3		3	3		28	50		15	1	1	7		1
SCHOOL ATTENDANCE																		
Total 7 to 13 years, inclusive	270	375	1,528	1,195	720	2	550	535	662	1,346	2,593	680	1,152	1,390	914	247	1,171	1,243
Number attending school	251	333	1,321	1,087	690	2	512	479	602	1,216	2,462	604	1,056	1,313	846	232	1,108	1,095
Percent attending school	93.0	88.8	86.5	91.0	95.8		93.1	89.5	90.9	90.3	94.9	88.8	91.7	94.5	92.6	93.9	94.6	88.1
Total 14 and 15 years, inclusive	61	86	397	385	206		135	156	165	328	700	188	280	399	256	75	310	327
Number attending school	32	50	221	268	151		94	90	132	239	525	148	167	288	194	59	241	226
Percent attending school			55.7	69.6	73.3		69.6	57.7	80.0	72.9	75.0	78.7	59.6	72.2	75.8		77.7	69.1
Total 16 and 17 years, inclusive	65	94	360	354	210	2	120	147	200	386	690	203	281	395	251	72	318	337
Number attending school	12	26	83	79	56		40	22	62	108	194	65	53	122	76	23	113	90
Percent attending school			23.1	22.3	26.7		33.3	15.0	31.0	28.0	28.1	32.0	18.9	30.9	30.3		35.5	26.7
Total 18 to 20 years, inclusive	115	146	435	515	270	1	222	207	240	528	864	305	348	484	327	116	419	438
Number attending school	5	8	29	16	18		12	3	12	22	80	23	18	56	16	12	43	25
Percent attending school	4.3	5.5	6.7	3.1	6.7		5.4	1.4	5.0	4.2	9.3	7.5	5.2	11.6	4.9	10.3	10.3	5.7
ILLITERACY																		
Total 10 years old and over	1,350	2,016	5,237	6,167	3,668	21	3,171	2,432	3,474	6,315	10,408	3,493	3,992	6,232	4,699	1,717	5,219	5,018
Number illiterate	206	268	1,443	920	411	4	438	300	775	794	1,742	664	1,058	1,032	912	240	673	1,189
Percent illiterate	15.3	13.3	27.6	14.9	11.2		13.8	12.3	22.3	12.6	16.7	19.0	26.5	16.6	19.4	14.0	12.9	23.7
Percent illiterate in 1920	17.5	19.8	33.7	23.1	17.9		21.2	23.3	21.5	20.2	20.8	30.5	35.8	22.5	23.7	17.9	18.2	29.8
URBAN AND RURAL																		
Urban population	305	410		2,262	1,682		639		852	203	591			928	1,021	1,517	1,912	638
Percent urban	17.3	15.8		28.9	35.7		15.9		19.2	2.5	4.2			11.4	17.2	75.5	28.3	9.5
Rural population	1,457	2,185	7,492	5,568	3,031	24	3,384	3,270	3,585	8,063	13,432	4,379	5,592	7,183	4,922	493	4,838	6,074
Rural-farm	267	342	5,151	2,145	909	11	1,354	1,273	1,023	2,276	5,341	2,045	2,340	2,692	2,190	112	1,819	3,071
Rural-nonfarm	1,190	1,843	2,341	3,423	2,122	13	2,030	1,997	2,562	5,787	8,091	2,334	3,252	4,491	2,732	381	3,019	3,003
Percent rural	82.7	84.2	100.0	71.1	64.3		84.1	100.0	80.8	97.5	95.8	100.0	100.0	88.6	82.8	24.5	71.7	90.5
MARITAL CONDITION																		
Males 15 years old and over	609	992	2,267	2,812	1,616	12	1,523	1,093	1,607	2,764	4,559	1,664	1,723	2,751	2,145	739	2,248	2,140
Single	226	401	975	1,095	627	6	599	436	595	1,046	1,830	701	740	979	800	292	813	766
Married	323	480	1,139	1,474	869	5	792	587	856	1,489	2,420	828	859	1,544	1,164	370	1,323	1,220
Widowed	53	98	143	220	105	1	119	63	150	205	260	127	123	210	165	67	94	135
Divorced	7	12	4	22	15		12	6	6	21	20	7	1	18	15	10	16	17
Unknown		1	6	1			1	1		3	29	1			1		2	2
Females 15 years old and over	576	791	1,941	2,489	1,528	8	1,285	957	1,409	2,633	4,035	1,321	1,495	2,516	1,930	808	2,144	2,033
Single	167	191	582	651	443	3	300	274	351	766	1,133	329	455	656	479	240	543	557
Married	336	471	1,138	1,472	861	5	757	581	867	1,523	2,436	810	854	1,546	1,173	395	1,335	1,226
Widowed	67	121	212	345	200		218	92	188	320	441	171	183	294	267	157	251	229
Divorced	6	8	2	21	21		10	9	3	18	7	10	2	18	11	15	15	18
Unknown			7		3			1		6	18	1	1	2		1		3
FAMILIES																		
Number of families	349	585	1,386	1,869	1,059	4	933	658	1,050	1,619	2,751	1,009	1,040	1,858	1,482	545	1,487	1,424
Median size	3.61	3.22	4.62	3.14	3.43		3.03	3.77	3.04	3.80	4.03	3.09	4.55	3.56	2.94	2.56	3.74	3.71
Families having—																		
No children under 10	174	351	594	1,130	611	3	568	339	628	863	1,382	623	454	1,039	928	390	815	751
1 child under 10	73	83	220	311	173		148	103	183	250	440	155	177	301	242	78	275	243
2 children under 10	40	59	169	166	117		77	80	91	176	316	97	124	212	120	36	157	158
3 or more	62	92	403	262	158	1	140	136	148	330	613	134	285	306	192	41	240	272

CHARACTERISTICS OF NEGRO POPULATION BY COUNTIES: 1930—Continued

(See note at head of table)

SUBJECT	MASSACHUSETTS: The State	Barnstable	Berkshire	Bristol	Dukes	Essex	Franklin	Hampden	Hampshire	Middlesex	Nantucket	Norfolk	Plymouth	Suffolk	Worcester
POPULATION BY SEX															
Negro population: 1930	52,365	1,642	1,088	5,162	202	1,923	124	3,648	252	10,042	279	1,022	3,943	21,026	2,012
Male	26,097	884	549	2,644	95	943	70	1,824	130	4,772	146	408	2,172	10,451	1,009
Female	26,268	758	539	2,518	107	980	54	1,824	122	5,270	133	614	1,771	10,575	1,003
Negro population: 1920	45,466	740	978	6,221	175	2,059	116	3,149	292	9,953	112	883	1,980	16,880	1,928
Male	22,912	411	473	3,434	80	1,036	67	1,604	136	4,692	58	321	1,073	8,560	967
Female	22,554	329	505	2,787	95	1,023	49	1,545	156	5,261	54	562	907	8,320	961
Percent of total population:															
1930	1.2	5.1	0.9	1.4	4.1	0.4	0.2	1.1	0.3	1.1	7.6	0.3	2.4	2.4	0.4
1920	1.2	2.8	0.9	1.7	4.0	0.4	0.2	1.0	0.4	1.3	4.0	0.4	1.3	2.0	0.4
VOTING AGE: 1930															
Total 21 years old and over	32,898	794	681	2,680	117	1,173	71	2,341	170	6,070	151	781	2,031	14,614	1,224
Male	16,406	452	359	1,389	54	569	41	1,146	88	2,765	88	292	1,204	7,343	616
Female	16,492	342	322	1,291	63	604	30	1,195	82	3,305	63	489	827	7,271	608
AGE: 1930															
Under 5 years	4,708	230	105	631	21	159	16	342	9	850	38	45	451	1,624	187
Under 1 year	859	41	14	107	2	23	4	62	2	174	11	12	92	287	28
5 to 9 years	5,301	229	109	747	19	183	11	325	14	1,081	34	68	547	1,738	196
10 to 14 years	4,698	200	91	641	25	198	10	286	32	967	38	45	518	1,462	185
15 to 19 years	4,018	159	84	399	15	182	14	300	24	916	14	62	349	1,308	192
20 to 24 years	3,798	125	95	284	16	116	9	297	23	769	15	93	241	1,592	123
25 to 29 years	4,035	93	86	267	7	136	8	331	23	660	12	104	182	1,978	148
30 to 34 years	4,421	97	78	301	14	123	10	335	24	844	17	110	222	2,105	141
35 to 44 years	8,785	195	155	756	29	301	20	619	37	1,461	48	200	573	4,095	296
45 to 54 years	6,934	177	121	620	22	256	10	474	27	1,292	44	154	527	2,959	251
55 to 64 years	3,477	76	79	313	18	165	9	196	17	764	6	84	237	1,346	167
65 to 74 years	1,479	38	55	140	12	66	5	107	15	316	10	37	68	528	82
75 years and over	619	18	27	55	4	36	2	29	7	122	3	14	23	236	43
Unknown	92	5	3	8	-------	2	-------	7	-------	-------	-------	6	5	55	1
SCHOOL ATTENDANCE															
Total 7 to 13 years, inclusive	6,946	307	149	973	34	270	17	418	35	1,440	50	70	744	2,182	257
Number attending school	6,768	300	144	925	34	269	16	412	33	1,416	49	69	737	2,109	255
Percent attending school	97.4	97.7	96.6	95.1	-------	99.6	-------	98.6	-------	98.3	-------	-------	99.1	96.7	99.2
Total 14 and 15 years, inclusive	1,742	73	36	191	7	85	3	115	11	369	10	22	173	573	74
Number attending school	1,600	61	30	176	7	82	3	109	11	355	8	22	135	531	70
Percent attending school	91.8	-------	-------	92.1	-------	-------	-------	94.8	-------	96.2	-------	-------	78.0	92.7	-------
Total 16 and 17 years, inclusive	1,574	62	31	165	6	71	3	114	10	346	4	23	137	516	86
Number attending school	911	24	14	60	1	51	2	71	4	225	-------	8	51	343	57
Percent attending school	57.9	-------	-------	36.4	-------	-------	-------	62.3	-------	65.0	-------	-------	37.2	66.5	-------
Total 18 to 20 years, inclusive	2,334	86	47	216	11	96	10	182	13	534	11	49	174	804	101
Number attending school	502	6	7	35	4	23	4	45	-------	160	-------	8	16	174	20
Percent attending school	21.5	-------	-------	16.2	-------	-------	-------	24.7	-------	30.0	-------	-------	9.2	21.6	19.8
ILLITERACY															
Total 10 years old and over	42,356	1,183	874	3,784	162	1,581	97	2,981	229	8,111	207	909	2,945	17,664	1,629
Number illiterate	2,303	194	15	709	14	46	2	89	9	133	37	51	612	328	64
Percent illiterate	5.4	16.4	1.7	18.7	8.6	2.9	-------	3.0	3.9	1.6	17.9	5.6	20.8	1.9	3.9
Percent illiterate in 1920	6.8	26.6	2.6	24.7	11.6	6.1	-------	5.8	7.5	2.4	-------	3.9	17.5	2.3	5.4
URBAN AND RURAL															
Urban population	46,323	546	796	4,826	-------	1,866	94	3,484	203	9,775	279	726	1,115	21,026	1,587
Percent urban	88.5	33.3	73.2	93.5	-------	97.0	75.8	95.5	80.6	97.3	100.0	71.0	28.3	100.0	78.9
Rural population	6,042	1,096	292	336	202	57	30	164	49	267	-------	296	2,828	-------	425
Rural-farm	417	111	6	44	12	5	6	28	9	33	-------	20	124	-------	19
Rural-nonfarm	5,625	985	286	292	190	52	24	136	40	234	-------	276	2,704	-------	406
Percent rural	11.5	66.7	26.8	6.5	100.0	3.0	24.2	4.5	19.4	2.7	-------	29.0	71.7	-------	21.1
MARITAL CONDITION															
Males 15 years old and over	18,702	553	402	1,617	59	669	49	1,334	102	3,286	99	323	1,411	8,081	717
Single	7,006	226	135	604	17	243	17	440	47	1,161	36	138	582	3,079	281
Married	10,304	301	225	934	41	368	26	796	46	1,892	58	163	744	4,338	372
Widowed	1,056	15	34	62	1	46	5	79	8	178	5	15	65	492	51
Divorced	283	10	8	14	-------	12	1	17	1	52	-------	6	18	132	12
Unknown	53	1	-------	3	-------	-------	-------	2	-------	3	-------	1	2	40	1
Females 15 years old and over	18,956	430	381	1,526	78	714	38	1,361	95	3,858	70	541	1,016	8,121	727
Single	5,186	104	99	377	25	212	7	302	41	1,183	13	259	256	2,083	225
Married	10,311	277	215	897	36	367	22	814	39	1,984	51	202	647	4,384	376
Widowed	3,064	45	62	224	16	127	7	215	15	619	5	69	96	1,455	109
Divorced	363	4	5	28	-------	7	1	29	-------	69	1	10	16	177	16
Unknown	32	-------	-------	-------	1	1	1	1	-------	3	-------	1	1	22	1
FAMILIES															
Number of families	12,637	344	277	1,175	52	497	27	962	49	2,288	60	143	897	5,452	414
Median size	2.79	3.60	2.90	3.47	-------	2.72	-------	2.76	-------	3.15	-------	2.56	3.15	2.44	3.19
Families having—															
No children under 10	8,462	175	179	647	36	355	17	640	39	1,516	34	100	533	3,927	264
1 child under 10	1,620	57	39	160	6	58	1	151	3	304	9	17	114	643	58
2 children under 10	1,094	34	31	153	3	31	6	83	2	198	6	11	88	411	37
3 or more	1,461	78	28	215	7	53	3	88	5	270	11	15	162	471	55

CHARACTERISTICS OF NEGRO POPULATION BY COUNTIES: 1930—Continued

(See note at head of table)

SUBJECT	MICHIGAN																	
	The State	Alger	Allegan	Antrim	Baraga	Barry	Bay	Benzie	Berrien	Branch	Calhoun	Cass	Charlevoix	Cheboygan	Chippewa	Clare	Clinton	Crawford
POPULATION BY SEX																		
Negro population: 1930	169,453	17	173	21	1	11	172	47	1,836	49	2,902	1,176	31	33	30	3	9	12
Male	88,936	13	92	8	1	6	94	21	996	30	1,514	629	14	19	16	1	3	6
Female	80,517	4	81	13		5	78	26	840	19	1,388	547	17	14	14	2	6	6
Negro population: 1920	60,082	13	204	26	5	9	136	41	808	40	1,939	1,353	51	25	62	6	7	
Male	34,249	5	113	13	2	3	77	26	428	26	1,037	716	22	10	36	2	3	
Female	25,833	8	91	13	3	6	59	15	380	14	902	637	29	15	26	4	4	
Percent of total population:																		
1930	3.5	0.4	0.4	0.2		0.1	0.2	0.7	2.3	0.2	3.3	5.6	0.3	0.3	0.1			0.4
1920	1.6	0.1	0.5	0.2	0.1		0.2	0.6	1.3	0.2	2.7	6.6	0.3	0.2	0.2	0.1		
VOTING AGE: 1930																		
Total 21 years and over	114,346	13	96	11	1	7	117	33	1,212	24	1,834	754	23	23	23	3	8	8
Male	62,139	10	54	3	1	4	67	14	667	14	988	411	12	13	13	1	2	6
Female	52,207	3	42	8		3	50	19	545	10	846	343	11	10	10	2	6	2
AGE: 1930																		
Under 5 years	15,231		12	2		1	9	2	140	4	289	87		3			1	1
Under 1 year	2,968		4	1			1	1	28		59	21		1			1	
5 to 9 years	14,732	1	15	3		3	11	4	170	6	245	109	3	3	1			2
10 to 14 years	11,387	3	26	1			10	1	147	8	249	117	1	3	1			
15 to 19 years	10,888		21	3			22	6	136	6	238	97	4	1	5			
20 to 24 years	17,731	2	11	2			16	1	154	2	221	81		3	2		1	2
25 to 29 years	24,305	1	9				16	1	150	1	302	55	1	2	4		1	2
30 to 34 years	21,514	1	5				12	1	156	1	278	55		3	1			2
35 to 44 years	31,155	1	16	5	1	4	35	9	335	6	517	139	4	1	4	1	2	2
45 to 54 years	14,470	1	25	2		1	19	13	233	8	352	185	8	10	5		1	
55 to 64 years	5,041	5	21	3			11	6	133	4	120	129	6	1	5		1	1
65 to 74 years	1,860	2	5				4	2	56	1	58	80	1	2	2	2	2	
75 years and over	855		7			2	5	1	26	2	26	42	3	1				
Unknown	284						2				7							
SCHOOL ATTENDANCE																		
Total 7 to 13 years, inclusive	17,741	4	25	3		2	15	4	216	12	339	159	4	3	2			1
Number attending school	17,252	4	21	3		2	14	4	211	12	334	144	4	3	2			1
Percent attending school	97.2								97.7		98.5	90.6						
Total 14 and 15 years, inclusive	4,215		16	1			3	2	64	1	109	44	1	1	1			
Number attending school	3,991		16	1			3	2	56	1	102	39	1	1	1			
Percent attending school	94.7										93.6							
Total 16 and 17 years, inclusive	4,163		9	2			11	3	54	4	99	32	2		1			
Number attending school	2,464		5				7	2	29	3	68	16	1		1			
Percent attending school	59.2																	
Total 18 to 20 years, inclusive	7,616		9	1			12	2	85	3	134	62	1	1	3			1
Number attending school	868		2				4	1	10		28	9						
Percent attending school	11.4										20.9							
ILLITERACY																		
Total 10 years old and over	139,490	16	146	16	1	7	152	41	1,526	39	2,368	980	28	27	29	3	8	9
Number illiterate	4,201		8				6		117	1	80	25		1	1			
Percent illiterate	3.0		5.5				3.9		7.7		3.4	2.6						
Percent illiterate in 1920	4.2		4.8				.9		3.3		3.8	5.1						
URBAN AND RURAL																		
Urban population	159,704	11	47				170		1,298	15	2,774	241	27	4	23		2	
Percent urban	94.2		27.2				98.8		70.7		95.6	20.5						
Rural population	9,749	6	126	21	1	11	2	47	538	34	128	935	4	29	7	3	7	12
Rural-farm	2,364		99	6		7		12	260	17	30	555	4	12	3	3	4	1
Rural-nonfarm	7,385	6	27	15	1	4	2	35	278	17	98	380		17	4		3	11
Percent rural	5.8		72.8				1.2		29.3		4.4	79.5						
MARITAL CONDITION																		
Males 15 years old and over	68,493	10	64	6	1	4	80	18	757	19	1,116	465	13	13	16	1	2	6
Single	21,408	2	23	5	1		27	7	216	10	379	153	3	4	10			1
Married	41,891	4	34	1		4	45	11	470	8	648	262	8	8	4	1	2	4
Widowed	3,492	3	5				4		47		50	40	2	1	1			1
Divorced	1,587	1	2				4		23	1	34	5			1			
Unknown	115								1		5	5						
Females 15 years old and over	59,610	3	56	9		3	62	22	622	12	1,003	398	14	11	12	2	6	3
Single	9,153	1	15	2			18	3	68	4	192	64	3		2		2	
Married	41,061	2	35	3		3	39	13	443	5	627	257	9	10	4	2	3	3
Widowed	7,707		6	4			2	5	87	2	142	67	2	1	6		1	
Divorced	1,630						3	1	24	1	37	8						
Unknown	59										5	2						
FAMILIES																		
Number of families	33,500	4	44	4	1	4	41	16	495	11	671	353	10	9	8	1	4	6
Median size	2.89								2.53		3.00	2.57						
Families having—																		
No children under 10	23,625	4	30	2	1	3	31	12	344	8	432	251	8	8	7	1	3	4
1 child under 10	5,590		7				4	3	76	2	100	53	1		1		1	1
2 children under 10	3,287		4	2			4	1	38		69	20	1					
3 or more	3,998		3			1	2		37	1	70	29		1				

CHARACTERISTICS OF NEGRO POPULATION BY COUNTIES: 1930—Continued

(See note at head of table)

SUBJECT	MICHIGAN—Continued																	
	Delta	Dickinson	Eaton	Emmet	Genesee	Gladwin	Gogebic	Grand Traverse	Gratiot	Hillsdale	Houghton	Huron	Ingham	Ionia	Iosco	Iron	Isabella	Jackson
POPULATION BY SEX																		
Negro population: 1930	27	12	46	63	5,825	6	3	55	75	11	26	9	1,474	339	4	6	120	2,481
Male	15	7	21	32	3,090	5	3	34	45	7	11	4	816	309	2	4	66	1,741
Female	12	5	25	31	2,735	1	-	21	30	4	15	5	658	30	2	2	54	740
Negro population: 1920	38	4	45	26	1,757	31	2	36	90	19	28	17	753	112	11	8	154	840
Male	16	2	27	16	1,149	21	1	15	54	12	15	14	413	87	6	6	76	528
Female	22	2	18	10	608	10	1	21	36	7	13	3	340	25	5	2	78	312
Percent of total population:																		
1930	0.1	-	0.1	0.4	2.8	0.1	-	0.3	0.2	-	-	-	1.3	1.0	0.1	-	0.6	2.7
1920	0.1	-	0.2	0.2	1.4	0.4	-	0.2	0.3	0.1	-	0.1	0.9	0.3	0.1	-	0.7	1.2
VOTING AGE: 1930																		
Total 21 years and over	14	9	26	40	3,836	5	3	44	43	9	15	3	873	256	3	2	58	1,915
Male	9	4	12	25	2,151	4	3	27	28	6	6	1	461	235	2	1	34	1,455
Female	5	5	14	15	1,685	1	-	17	15	3	9	2	412	21	1	1	24	460
AGE: 1930																		
Under 5 years	5	-	7	7	588	-	-	2	2	-	5	2	133	2	-	-	17	150
Under 1 year	1	-	1	-	102	-	-	-	-	-	1	-	23	1	-	-	1	31
5 to 9 years	3	1	11	7	547	-	-	1	10	-	2	1	137	6	-	1	18	138
10 to 14 years	3	-	-	4	411	1	-	3	10	1	2	2	142	2	1	1	15	115
15 to 19 years	1	2	1	2	342	-	-	4	8	1	2	1	166	52	-	2	10	120
20 to 24 years	1	1	3	9	609	-	-	4	5	2	-	-	104	84	-	-	9	317
25 to 29 years	2	1	2	4	808	-	1	4	3	3	-	-	137	63	-	-	5	474
30 to 34 years	5	-	4	1	757	-	-	2	2	1	2	1	146	44	1	-	8	331
35 to 44 years	2	3	6	9	1,031	3	2	14	11	-	4	1	228	41	-	1	9	475
45 to 54 years	1	3	3	13	4811	-	-	10	11	1	2	1	140	26	-	1	8	211
55 to 64 years	3	1	2	4	165	1	-	5	8	1	5	-	71	10	1	-	5	96
65 to 74 years	1	-	5	1	63	1	-	1	5	-	1	-	43	5	1	-	15	29
75 years and over	-	-	2	2	19	-	-	5	-	1	1	-	24	2	-	-	1	24
Unknown	-	-	-	-	4	-	-	-	-	-	-	-	3	2	-	-	-	1
SCHOOL ATTENDANCE																		
Total 7 to 13, years inclusive	5	-	6	6	627	1	-	3	15	1	3	1	198	5	1	2	22	183
Number attending school	5	-	6	6	622	1	-	3	15	1	3	1	190	5	1	2	22	183
Percent attending school	-	-	-	-	99.2	-	-	-	-	-	-	-	96.0	-	-	-	-	100.0
Total 14 and 15 years, inclusive	-	-	1	1	159	-	-	1	4	-	-	2	70	3	-	-	8	38
Number attending school	-	-	1	1	154	-	-	1	4	-	-	1	68	2	-	-	7	38
Percent attending school	-	-	-	-	96.9	-	-	-	-	-	-	-	-	-	-	-	-	-
Total 16 and 17 years, inclusive	1	1	-	1	117	-	-	1	2	1	2	-	82	16	-	2	3	37
Number attending school	1	1	-	-	77	-	-	1	1	-	2	-	67	1	-	2	2	22
Percent attending school	-	-	-	-	65.8	-	-	-	-	-	-	-	-	-	-	-	-	-
Total 18 to 20 years, inclulsve	1	1	1	4	252	-	-	3	6	-	-	-	69	56	-	-	5	110
Number attending school	-	-	1	1	32	-	-	1	2	-	-	-	12	-	-	-	-	2
Percent attending school	-	-	-	-	12.7	-	-	-	-	-	-	-	-	-	-	-	-	1.8
ILLITERACY																		
Total 10 years old and over	19	11	28	49	4,690	6	3	52	63	11	19	6	1,204	331	4	5	85	2,193
Number illiterate	-	-	1	2	113	2	-	7	2	-	-	-	28	21	-	-	1	141
Percent illiterate	-	-	-	-	2.4	-	-	-	-	-	-	-	2.3	6.3	-	-	-	6.4
Percent illiterate in 1920	-	-	-	-	3.7	-	-	-	-	-	-	-	3.3	-	-	-	2.8	4.3
URBAN AND RURAL																		
Urban population	25	7	11	33	5,727	-	2	38	20	10	3	-	1,434	11	-	6	2	1,692
Percent urban	-	-	-	-	98.3	-	-	-	-	-	-	-	97.3	3.2	-	-	1.7	68.2
Rural population	2	5	35	30	98	6	1	17	55	1	23	9	40	328	4	-	118	789
Rural-farm	1	5	28	13	40	5	-	15	43	-	-	9	6	12	4	-	115	10
Rural-nonfarm	1	-	7	17	58	1	1	2	12	1	23	-	34	316	-	-	3	779
Percent rural	-	-	-	-	1.7	-	-	-	-	-	-	-	2.7	96.8	-	-	98.3	31.8
MARITAL CONDITION																		
Males 15 years old and over	10	6	14	27	2,359	4	3	31	32	7	6	1	585	307	2	3	42	1,561
Single	3	3	3	12	740	4	3	15	16	6	2	1	229	199	1	2	15	718
Married	7	3	9	12	1,478	-	-	9	12	-	3	-	310	86	1	1	22	667
Widowed	-	-	2	1	80	-	-	3	3	1	1	-	26	9	-	-	3	96
Divorced	-	-	-	2	59	-	-	2	1	-	-	-	20	11	-	-	2	77
Unknown	-	-	-	-	2	-	-	2	-	-	-	-	-	2	-	-	-	3
Females 15 years old and over	6	5	14	18	1,920	1	-	18	21	3	11	3	477	22	1	1	28	517
Single	-	-	1	4	231	-	-	5	8	1	2	1	76	1	-	-	5	83
Married	6	3	10	11	1,445	-	-	11	13	-	7	2	312	16	1	1	22	332
Widowed	-	2	3	3	184	1	-	1	-	2	2	-	66	5	-	-	1	72
Divorced	-	-	-	-	59	-	-	-	-	-	-	-	23	-	-	-	-	29
Unknown	-	-	-	-	1	-	-	1	-	-	-	-	-	-	-	-	-	1
FAMILIES																		
Number of families	5	3	12	14	1,349	2	-	6	16	2	6	-	342	8	1	1	23	378
Median size	-	-	-	-	2.76	-	-	-	-	-	-	-	2.83	-	-	-	-	2.69
Families having:																		
No children under 10	1	3	7	8	875	2	-	4	10	2	6	-	226	4	1	-	10	249
1 child under 10	2	-	2	4	184	-	-	2	4	-	-	-	53	2	-	1	4	51
2 children under 10	-	-	2	-	122	-	-	-	1	-	-	-	31	-	-	-	4	32
3 or more	2	-	1	2	168	-	-	-	1	-	-	-	32	2	-	-	5	46

CHARACTERISTICS OF NEGRO POPULATION BY COUNTIES: 1930—Continued

(See note at head of table)

MICHIGAN—Continued

SUBJECT	Kalamazoo	Kalkaska	Kent	Lake	Lapeer	Leelanau	Lenawee	Livingston	Luce
POPULATION BY SEX									
Negro population: 1930	1,031	1	2,949	398	105	1	226	77	4
Male	540	1	1,490	208	50	1	107	42	1
Female	491	-	1,459	190	55	-	110	35	3
Negro population: 1920	806	7	1,187	13	38	8	221	33	9
Male	414	4	612	9	23	6	90	17	6
Female	392	3	575	4	15	2	131	16	3
Percent of total population:									
1930	1.1	-	1.2	9.8	0.4	-	0.5	0.4	0.1
1920	1.1	0.1	0.6	0.3	0.1	0.1	0.5	0.2	0.1
VOTING AGE: 1930									
Total 21 years and over	720	1	1,967	278	34	1	129	51	4
Male	381	1	1,032	147	15	1	68	29	1
Female	339	-	935	131	19	-	61	22	3
AGE: 1930									
Under 5 years	69	-	244	27	2	-	20	4	-
Under 1 year	17	-	51	9	-	-	1	-	-
5 to 9 years	88	-	260	33	9	-	19	6	-
10 to 14 years	80	-	211	34	16	-	27	6	-
15 to 19 years	61	-	209	23	38	-	28	6	-
20 to 24 years	90	-	297	13	18	-	14	8	-
25 to 29 years	92	-	314	23	2	-	14	9	-
30 to 34 years	93	-	272	26	3	-	17	3	-
35 to 44 years	156	-	564	55	8	-	28	14	1
45 to 54 years	167	1	337	99	6	-	19	10	2
55 to 64 years	74	-	141	39	1	-	13	9	1
65 to 74 years	40	-	62	18	1	1	22	2	-
75 years and over	21	-	32	8	-	-	5	-	-
Unknown	-	-	6	-	1	-	-	-	-
SCHOOL ATTENDANCE									
Total 7 to 13 years, inclusive	119	-	320	44	19	-	29	9	-
Number attending school	117	-	317	39	19	-	29	9	-
Percent attending school	98.3	-	99.1	-	-	-	-	-	-
Total 14 and 15 years, inclusive	25	-	91	15	10	-	12	1	-
Number attending school	25	-	89	15	10	-	12	1	-
Percent attending school	-	-	-	-	-	-	-	-	-
Total 16 and 17 years, inclusive	23	-	72	10	12	-	19	3	-
Number attending school	17	-	39	5	2	-	14	2	-
Percent attending school	-	-	-	-	-	-	-	-	-
Total 18 to 20 years, inclusive	39	-	148	12	25	-	8	7	-
Number attending school	14	-	30	1	-	-	4	-	-
Percent attending school	-	-	20.3	-	-	-	-	-	-
ILLITERACY									
Total 10 years old and over	874	1	2,445	338	94	1	187	67	4
Number illiterate	31	-	71	13	27	-	4	2	2
Percent illiterate	3.5	-	2.9	3.8	-	-	2.1	-	-
Percent illiterate in 1920	4.5	-	1.9	-	-	-	7.7	-	-
URBAN AND RURAL									
Urban population	967	-	2,812	-	50	-	126	17	-
Percent urban	93.8	-	95.4	-	47.6	-	55.8	-	-
Rural population	64	1	137	398	55	1	100	60	4
Rural-farm	26	1	46	59	3	1	5	27	-
Rural-nonfarm	38	-	91	339	52	-	95	33	4
Percent rural	6.2	-	4.6	100.0	52.4	-	44.2	-	-
MARITAL CONDITION									
Males 15 years old and over	417	1	1,144	160	35	1	76	36	1
Single	123	-	330	37	33	-	17	16	-
Married	248	1	721	107	2	-	43	18	1
Widowed	21	-	59	11	-	1	9	1	-
Divorced	21	-	33	5	-	-	7	1	-
Unknown	4	-	1	-	-	-	-	-	-
Females 15 years old and over	377	-	1,090	144	43	-	84	25	3
Single	62	-	176	17	37	-	29	4	-
Married	252	-	732	104	5	-	42	16	2
Widowed	44	-	138	22	1	-	7	5	-
Divorced	17	-	43	1	-	-	6	-	-
Unknown	2	-	1	-	-	-	-	-	1
FAMILIES									
Number of families	262	1	694	126	3	1	58	18	1
Median size	2.36	-	2.92	2.23	-	-	-	-	-
Families having—									
No children under 10	185	1	450	96	3	1	41	14	1
1 child under 10	33	-	125	16	-	-	5	1	-
2 children under 10	23	-	58	5	-	-	7	2	-
3 or more	21	-	61	9	-	-	5	1	-

SUBJECT	Mackinac	Macomb	Manistee	Marquette	Mason	Mecosta	Menominee	Midland	Missaukee
POPULATION BY SEX									
Negro population: 1930	11	1,513	60	190	40	177	1	71	11
Male	5	735	31	185	18	96	-	35	3
Female	6	778	29	5	22	81	1	36	8
Negro population: 1920	10	240	17	90	25	213	4	108	16
Male	6	121	10	71	13	103	1	56	4
Female	4	119	7	19	12	110	3	52	12
Percent of total population:									
1930	0.1	2.0	0.3	0.4	0.2	1.1	-	0.4	0.2
1920	0.1	0.6	0.1	0.2	0.1	1.2	-	0.6	0.2
VOTING AGE: 1930									
Total 21 years and over	8	858	40	182	22	100	1	43	6
Male	5	447	23	178	8	60	-	23	2
Female	3	411	17	4	14	40	1	20	4
AGE: 1930									
Under 5 years	-	184	7	-	4	17	-	4	1
Under 1 year	-	37	4	-	-	3	-	-	-
5 to 9 years	3	172	3	-	4	21	-	6	1
10 to 14 years	-	148	4	-	7	23	-	8	2
15 to 19 years	-	125	5	2	1	15	-	9	1
20 to 24 years	-	123	8	20	2	7	-	4	-
25 to 29 years	3	110	5	45	5	4	-	-	-
30 to 34 years	-	135	2	48	2	14	-	4	1
35 to 44 years	1	271	5	51	5	18	-	13	2
45 to 54 years	-	145	8	19	5	23	-	8	2
55 to 64 years	2	53	9	4	4	21	-	7	-
65 to 74 years	1	27	4	1	1	12	1	5	-
75 years and over	1	13	-	-	-	4	-	3	1
Unknown	-	7	-	-	-	-	-	-	-
SCHOOL ATTENDANCE									
Total 7 to 13 years, inclusive	1	217	5	-	9	32	-	10	3
Number attending school	-	213	5	-	8	31	-	10	2
Percent attending school	-	98.2	-	-	-	-	-	-	-
Total 14 and 15 years, inclusive	-	54	1	-	1	6	-	4	-
Number attending school	-	51	1	-	1	6	-	4	-
Percent attending school	-	-	-	-	-	-	-	-	-
Total 16 and 17 years, inclusive	-	50	3	-	1	7	-	3	1
Number attending school	-	23	2	-	-	5	-	1	1
Percent attending school	-	-	-	-	-	-	-	-	-
Total 18 to 20 years, inclusive	-	73	2	8	2	7	-	5	-
Number attending school	-	6	-	1	-	-	-	-	-
Percent attending school	-	-	-	-	-	-	-	-	-
ILLITERACY									
Total 10 years old and over	8	1,157	50	190	32	139	1	61	9
Number illiterate	-	96	6	6	3	8	-	-	1
Percent illiterate	-	8.3	-	3.2	-	5.8	-	-	-
Percent illiterate in 1920	-	5.3	-	-	-	7.6	-	-	-
URBAN AND RURAL									
Urban population	-	653	1	188	3	6	-	11	-
Percent urban	-	43.2	-	98.9	-	3.4	-	-	-
Rural population	11	860	59	2	37	171	1	60	11
Rural-farm	-	8	47	-	3	135	1	54	5
Rural-nonfarm	11	852	12	2	34	36	-	6	6
Percent rural	-	56.8	-	1.1	-	96.6	-	-	-
MARITAL CONDITION									
Males 15 years old and over	5	511	27	185	11	68	-	30	3
Single	1	127	12	92	4	29	-	13	1
Married	4	352	11	59	7	25	-	13	2
Widowed	-	23	2	15	-	12	-	3	-
Divorced	-	9	2	19	-	1	-	-	-
Unknown	-	-	-	-	-	1	-	1	-
Females 15 years old and over	3	498	19	5	14	48	1	23	4
Single	-	75	3	1	2	13	-	5	-
Married	3	355	12	4	10	28	1	14	4
Widowed	-	51	3	-	2	7	-	4	-
Divorced	-	17	1	-	-	-	-	-	-
Unknown	-	-	-	-	-	-	-	-	-
FAMILIES									
Number of families	5	379	20	3	11	45	-	18	2
Median size	-	2.99	-	-	-	-	-	-	-
Families having—									
No children under 10	4	232	16	3	9	32	-	14	2
1 child under 10	-	60	2	-	1	3	-	1	-
2 children under 10	1	37	1	-	1	3	-	2	-
3 or more	-	50	1	-	-	7	-	1	-

CHARACTERISTICS OF NEGRO POPULATION BY COUNTIES: 1930—Continued

(See note at head of table)

SUBJECT	MICHIGAN—Continued																	
	Monroe	Montcalm	Muskegon	Newaygo	Oakland	Oceana	Ogemaw	Osceola	Otsego	Ottawa	Presque Isle	Roscommon	Saginaw	St. Clair	St. Joseph	Sanilac	Schoolcraft	Shiawassee
POPULATION BY SEX																		
Negro population: 1930	471	99	1,376	128	4,260	25	1	21	7	56	1	2	2,915	1,133	133	8	3	7
Male	280	55	789	62	2,204	13	1	12	4	30	1	1	1,680	582	77	6	1	6
Female	191	44	587	66	2,056	12		9	3	26		1	1,235	551	56	2	2	1
Negro population: 1920	118	89	254	31	1,148	22		9	6	40	2	20	388	560	79	6	9	14
Male	66	45	141	13	710	14		5	4	22	2	8	213	309	41	5	5	10
Female	52	44	113	18	438	8		4	2	18		12	175	251	38	1	4	4
Percent of total population:																		
1930	0.9	0.4	1.6	0.8	2.0	0.2		0.2	0.1	0.1		0.1	2.4	1.7	0.4			
1920	0.3	0.3	0.4	0.2	1.3	0.1		0.1	0.1	0.1		1.0	0.4	1.0	0.3			
VOTING AGE: 1930																		
Total 21 years and over	334	51	1,009	84	2,808	19	1	15	3	39	1	2	2,160	696	82	5	2	7
Male	209	32	608	44	1,505	10	1	8	2	24	1	1	1,329	372	45	3	1	6
Female	125	19	401	40	1,303	9		7	1	15		1	831	324	37	2	1	1
AGE: 1930																		
Under 5 years	40	19	86	7	463	1		1	1	5			222	121	16		1	
Under 1 year	7	3	18	1	91			1	1	1			48	21	5			
5 to 9 years	36	15	99	9	353	1		3	2	3			201	132	13			
10 to 14 years	27	8	84	14	295	2		2	1	2			149	96	12	1		
15 to 19 years	25	6	79	13	272	2				5			141	76	9	2		
20 to 24 years	62	5	123	4	430					6			322	75	8			
25 to 29 years	66	5	198	6	542	1		2					536	118	17			1
30 to 34 years	61	3	192	13	540	2		2		5			486	106	16		1	3
35 to 44 years	86	11	297	21	757	1		5		15			544	214	15		1	2
45 to 54 years	45	7	142	20	388	3		5	3	7	1		223	110	16	1		
55 to 64 years	15	10	41	15	152	7				6		2	65	64	7	3		1
65 to 74 years	6	3	21	5	37	4	1	1					13	13	4	1		
75 years and over	2	7	12	1	26	1				2			11	8				
Unknown			2		5								2					
SCHOOL ATTENDANCE																		
Total 7 to 13 years, inclusive	42	17	122	18	438	2		2	2	3			251	150	20	1		
Number attending school	42	17	120	17	414	2		2	2	2			214	147	20	1		
Percent attending school			98.4		94.5								85.3	98.0				
Total 14 and 15 years, inclusive	10	2	31	6	112			1		1			52	33	2	1		
Number attending school	8	2	29	5	107			1		1			44	29	2	1		
Percent attending school					95.5					1								
Total 16 to 17 years, inclusive	11	2	29	6	100	1				1			45	39	4	1		
Number attending school	5	1	14		60	1							17	25	3			
Percent attending school					60.0													
Total 18 to 20 years, inclusive	17	2	57	5	190	1				6			108	39	4			
Number attending school			5		23								10	3				
Percent attending school					12.1								9.3					
ILLITERACY																		
Total 10 years old and over	395	65	1,191	112	3,444	23	1	17	4	48	1	2	2,492	880	104	8	2	7
Number illiterate	21	4	36	2	147	3				1	1		40	24	4	1		2
Percent illiterate	5.3		3.0	1.8	4.3								1.6	2.7	3.8			
Percent illiterate in 1920			0.5		9.3								3.1	9.8				
URBAN AND RURAL																		
Urban population	379	26	1,287		2,902					44			2,853	946	99		3	5
Percent urban	80.5		93.5		68.1								97.9	83.5	74.4			
Rural population	92	73	89	128	1,358	25	1	21	7	12	1	2	62	187	34	8		2
Rural-farm	46	51	14	17	24	8		5		5			12	53	8	6		
Rural-nonfarm	46	22	75	111	1,334	17	1	16	7	7	1	2	50	134	26	2		2
Percent rural	19.5		6.5	100.0	31.9								2.1	16.5	25.6			
MARITAL CONDITON																		
Males 15 years old and over	224	35	647	47	1,669	11	1	8	2	27	1	1	1,403	415	50	5	1	6
Single	108	13	233	11	480	2		4		8	1		420	114	17	3		2
Married	111	15	355	34	1,029	7		4	1	17		1	781	266	29	2	1	4
Widowed	4	6	36		94	2	1			1			165	29	3			
Divorced	1	1	23	2	64				1	1			27	6	1			
Unknown					2								10					
Females 15 years old and over	144	22	460	51	1,480	10		7	1	19		1	940	369	42	2	1	1
Single	24	4	74	13	207	1		3	1	5			106	51	7			
Married	99	13	320	32	1,057	6		4		11		1	719	246	27	2	1	1
Widowed	17	4	54	5	160	2				3			103	63	7			
Divorced	4	1	12	1	52	1							11	9	1			
Unknown					4								1					
FAMILIES																		
Number of families	100	23	331	36	921	11	1	6	2	15	1	1	524	276	35	2	1	4
Median size	2.39		2.44		2.88								2.66	2.83				
Families having—																		
No children under 10	69	13	229	29	594	10	1	5	1	10	1	1	366	167	24	2		
1 child under 10	11	2	61	5	114				1	1			73	45	3		1	
2 children under 10	10	4	19	1	99	1				2			39	26	3			
3 or more	10	4	22	1	114			1		2			46	38	5			

CHARACTERISTICS OF NEGRO POPULATION BY COUNTIES: 1930—Continued

(See note at head of table)

SUBJECT	MICHIGAN—Continued					MINNESOTA											
	Tuscola	Van Buren	Washtenaw	Wayne	Wexford	The State	Aitkin	Anoka	Becker	Beltrami	Big Stone	Blue Earth	Brown	Carver	Cass	Chippewa	Chisago
POPULATION BY SEX																	
Negro population: 1930	44	456	2,566	131,747	23	9,445	11	25	1	14	1	6	3	1	16	1	1
Male	27	254	1,375	68,241	12	5,005	5	16		8	1	5	2		10		1
Female	17	202	1,191	63,506	11	4,440	6	9	1	6		1	1	1	6	1	
Negro population: 1920	1	378	1,400	43,720	35	8,809	31	49	3	38	7	5		2	29	3	5
Male		202	678	25,187	18	4,851	16	28	2	21	2	4			18	3	3
Female	1	176	722	18,533	17	3,958	15	21	1	17	5	1		2	11		2
Percent of total population:																	
1930	0.1	1.4	3.9	7.0	0.1	0.4	0.1	0.1		0.1					0.1		
1920		1.2	2.8	3.7	0.2	0.4	0.2	0.3		0.1	0.1				0.2		
VOTING AGE: 1930																	
Total 21 years and over	19	299	1,694	89,212	15	6,805	5	22		9	1	6	2	1	12	1	
Male	13	170	945	47,634	11	3,690	2	14		6	1	5	2		8		
Female	6	129	749	41,578	4	3,115	3	8		3		1		1	4	1	
AGE: 1930																	
Under 5 years	2	31	214	11,947		615	1			2			1				
Under 1 year		7	43	2,321		106				1							
5 to 9 years	9	36	266	11,465	5	675	3	2		3							1
10 to 14 years	6	47	217	8,578		612	1		1						1		
15 to 19 years	7	37	144	8,292	2	614	1	1							3		
20 to 24 years	4	20	205	14,215	2	650	1	1									
25 to 29 years		22	239	19,874		732		2							2		
30 to 34 years	3	20	248	17,373	2	883				1		1					
35 to 44 years	6	52	424	24,587	3	1,925	1	2		3	1	1			3		
45 to 54 years	6	62	305	10,495	5	1,523		6		4		2	1		4	1	
55 to 64 years	1	69	176	3,201	3	761	2	4		1		1			2		
65 to 74 years		46	95	1,024	1	310		4				1		1	1		
75 years and over		14	33	454		134	1	3					1				
Unknown				242		11											
SCHOOL ATTENDANCE																	
Total 7 to 13 years, inclusive	8	62	336	13,580	2	910	3	2	1	2					1		
Number attending school	7	62	332	13,226	1	896	3	2	1	2					1		
Percent attending school			98.8	97.4		98.5											
Total 14 and 15 years, inclusive	3	11	74	3,126		239											
Number attending school	2	11	70	2,964		225											
Percent attending school				94.8		94.1											
Total 16 and 17 years, inclusive	4	18	52	3,163		236	1	1							1		
Number attending school	3	12	40	1,860		148	1	1							1		
Percent attending school				58.8		62.7											
Total 18 to 20 years, inclusive	2	20	89	5,915	3	385									2		
Number attending school		6	12	647	1	102											
Percent attending school				10.9		26.5											
ILLITERACY																	
Total 10 years old and over	33	389	2,086	108,335	18	8,155	7	23	1	9	1	6	2	1	16	1	
Number illiterate	10	11	100	2,967		160	2	4							1		
Percent illiterate		2.8	4.8	2.7		2.0											
Percent illiterate in 1920		3.8	3.6	3.9		3.1											
URBAN AND RURAL																	
Urban population		78	2,234	130,377	4	9,110		22		13		4	2			1	
Percent urban		17.1	87.1	99.0		96.5											
Rural population	44	378	332	1,370	19	335	11	3	1	1	1	2	1	1	16		1
Rural-farm	9	210	94	51	11	193	11	3	1			2		1	11		1
Rural-nonfarm	35	168	238	1,319	8	142				1	1		1		5		
Percent rural		82.9	12.9	1.0		3.5											
MARITAL CONDITION																	
Males 15 years old and over	20	192	1,031	52,384	11	4,033	3	14		6	1	5	2		10		
Single	11	63	313	15,953	4	1,304	2	7		3		2			4		
Married	6	106	590	32,779	5	2,261	1	5		2	1	2	1		3		
Widowed	3	16	72	2,524		283		2		1			1		3		
Divorced		7	56	1,052	2	178						1					
Unknown				76		7											
Females 15 years old and over	7	150	838	47,373	7	3,510	3	9		3		1		1	5	1	
Single	3	20	112	7,303	3	596		1							1		
Married	4	102	554	32,625	3	2,141	2	5		1		1			2	1	
Widowed		27	126	6,184	1	642	1	3		1				1	1		
Divorced		1	46	1,221		126				1					1		
Unknown				40		5											
FAMILIES																	
Number of families	5	126	659	27,916	7	2,592	1	8		5	1	1	1		3		
Median size		2.32	2.52	2.95		2.34											
Families having—																	
No children under 10	1	97	460	17,876	4	1,975		6		3	1	1	1		2		
1 child under 10		14	89	4,364	1	321		2		1							
2 children under 10	2	8	45	2,554	2	144											
3 or more	2	7	65	3,122		152	1			1					1		

CHARACTERISTICS OF NEGRO POPULATION BY COUNTIES: 1930—Continued

(See note at head of table)

SUBJECT	Clay	Clear-water	Cook	Cot-ton-wood	Crow Wing	Dakota	Dodge	Doug-las	Fari-bault	Free-born	Good-hue	Grant	Henne-pin	Hous-ton	Hub-bard	Isanti	Itasca	Jack-son
	MINNESOTA—Continued																	
POPULATION BY SEX																		
Negro population: 1930	20	1	15	5	4	23	3	10	5	15	31	1	4,257	1	1	2	4	2
Male	10	1	10	1	2	14	1	6	4	9	24	1	2,238	----	1	1	3	2
Female	10	----	5	4	2	9	2	4	1	6	7	----	2,019	1	----	1	1	----
Negro population: 1920	18	----	15	3	13	39	2	12	14	10	30	----	3,985	----	1	2	5	----
Male	10	----	11	2	7	30	2	8	9	7	22	----	2,162	----	1	1	4	----
Female	8	----	4	1	6	9	----	4	5	3	8	----	1,823	----	----	1	1	----
Percent of total population:																		
1930	0.1	----	0.6	----	----	0.1	----	0.1	----	0.1	0.1	----	0.8	----	----	----	----	----
1920	0.1	----	0.8	----	0.1	0.1	----	0.1	0.1	----	0.1	----	1.0	----	----	----	----	----
VOTING AGE: 1930																		
Total 21 years old and over	14	1	4	2	3	17	2	7	4	12	5	1	3,102	1	1	1	4	----
Male	8	1	3	----	2	12	1	4	4	7	2	1	1,658	----	1	1	3	----
Female	6	----	1	2	1	5	1	3	----	5	3	----	1,444	1	----	----	1	----
AGE: 1930																		
Under 5 years	2	----	2	----	----	2	1	3	----	2	----	----	292	----	----	----	----	----
Under 1 year	----	----	----	----	----	1	----	2	----	1	----	----	44	----	----	----	----	----
5 to 9 years	----	----	3	----	----	2	----	----	1	1	1	----	307	----	----	----	----	----
10 to 14 years	3	----	3	----	----	----	----	----	----	----	8	----	259	----	----	1	----	----
15 to 19 years	----	----	3	3	1	2	----	----	----	----	17	----	240	----	----	----	----	2
20 to 24 years	2	----	1	----	----	1	----	1	----	----	1	----	317	1	1	----	----	----
25 to 29 years	----	1	----	----	----	2	1	----	----	3	1	----	344	----	----	----	----	----
30 to 34 years	3	----	----	----	----	1	----	----	----	2	----	----	441	----	----	----	----	----
35 to 44 years	3	----	1	----	----	----	1	1	----	3	2	----	912	----	----	----	----	----
45 to 54 years	4	----	2	1	----	5	----	3	2	1	----	----	658	----	----	----	2	----
55 to 64 years	2	----	----	1	2	3	----	2	1	3	1	----	323	----	----	1	1	----
65 to 74 years	1	----	----	----	1	2	----	----	----	----	----	1	114	----	----	----	1	----
75 years and over	----	----	----	----	----	3	----	----	1	----	----	----	45	----	----	----	----	----
Unknown	----	----	----	----	----	----	----	----	----	----	----	----	5	----	----	----	----	----
SCHOOL ATTENDANCE																		
Total 7 to 13 years, inclusive	3	----	4	----	----	----	----	----	1	----	4	----	408	----	----	1	----	----
Number attending school	3	----	4	----	----	----	----	----	1	----	3	----	405	----	----	1	----	----
Percent attending school	----	----	----	----	----	----	----	----	----	----	----	----	99.3	----	----	----	----	----
Total 14 and 15 years, inclusive	----	----	2	----	----	----	----	----	----	----	7	----	105	----	----	----	----	1
Number attending school	----	----	2	----	----	----	----	----	----	----	7	----	100	----	----	----	----	----
Percent attending school	----	----	----	----	----	----	----	----	----	----	----	----	95.2	----	----	----	----	----
Total 16 and 17 years, inclusive	----	----	1	1	1	1	----	----	----	----	10	----	87	----	----	----	----	----
Number attending school	----	----	1	1	----	1	----	----	----	----	4	----	59	----	----	----	----	----
Percent attending school	----	----	----	----	----	----	----	----	----	----	----	----	----	----	----	----	----	----
Total 18 to 20 years, inclusive	1	----	1	2	----	1	----	----	----	----	4	----	153	----	----	----	----	1
Number attending school	----	----	----	----	----	----	----	----	----	----	1	----	41	----	----	----	----	----
Percent attending school	----	----	----	----	----	----	----	----	----	----	----	----	26.8	----	----	----	----	----
ILLITERACY																		
Total, 10 years old and over	18	1	10	5	4	19	2	7	4	12	30	1	3,658	1	1	2	4	2
Number illiterate	----	----	----	----	----	3	1	----	----	----	----	----	62	----	----	----	----	1
Percent illiterate	----	----	----	----	----	----	----	----	----	----	----	----	1.7	----	----	----	----	----
Percent illiterate in 1920	----	----	----	----	----	----	----	----	----	----	----	----	3.6	----	----	----	----	----
URBAN AND RURAL																		
Urban population	20	----	----	----	2	12	----	5	1	14	17	----	4,205	----	----	----	2	----
Percent urban	----	----	----	----	----	----	----	----	----	----	----	----	98.8	----	----	----	----	----
Rural population	----	1	15	5	2	11	3	5	4	1	14	1	52	1	1	2	2	2
Rural-farm	----	----	14	4	2	5	----	4	1	1	11	1	26	1	----	1	----	2
Rural-nonfarm	----	1	1	1	----	6	3	1	3	----	3	----	26	----	1	1	2	----
Percent rural	----	----	----	----	----	----	----	----	----	----	----	----	1.2	----	----	----	----	----
MARITAL CONDITION																		
Males 15 years old and over	8	1	6	1	2	12	1	4	4	7	17	1	1,797	----	1	1	3	2
Single	3	1	5	1	1	5	1	1	1	1	17	----	552	----	1	----	1	2
Married	5	----	1	----	----	6	----	3	----	5	----	1	1,052	----	----	1	2	----
Widowed	----	----	----	----	----	----	----	----	3	1	----	----	124	----	----	----	----	----
Divorced	----	----	----	----	1	----	----	----	----	----	----	----	67	----	----	----	----	----
Unknown	----	----	----	----	----	1	----	----	----	----	----	----	2	----	----	----	----	----
Females 15 years old and over	7	----	1	4	2	7	1	3	----	5	5	----	1,602	1	----	----	1	----
Single	1	----	----	2	1	2	----	----	----	----	2	----	253	1	----	----	----	----
Married	4	----	1	----	1	4	1	3	----	4	2	----	1,013	----	----	----	1	----
Widowed	2	----	----	2	----	1	----	----	----	1	1	----	286	----	----	----	----	----
Divorced	----	----	----	----	----	----	----	----	----	----	----	----	48	----	----	----	----	----
Unknown	----	----	----	----	----	----	----	----	----	----	----	----	2	----	----	----	----	----
FAMILIES																		
Number of families	6	----	2	----	----	4	1	4	3	4	----	----	1,210	----	1	----	2	----
Median size	----	----	----	----	----	----	----	----	----	----	----	----	232	----	----	----	----	----
Families having—																		
No children under 10	5	----	1	----	----	3	1	3	2	2	----	----	928	----	1	----	2	----
1 child under 10	1	----	----	----	----	----	----	----	1	2	----	----	135	----	----	----	----	----
2 children under 10	----	----	----	----	----	----	----	1	----	----	----	----	68	----	----	----	----	----
3 or more	----	----	1	----	----	1	----	----	----	----	----	----	79	----	----	----	----	----

CHARACTERISTICS OF NEGRO POPULATION BY COUNTIES: 1930—Continued

(See note at head of table)

SUBJECT	Kandiyohi	Kittson	Koochiching	Lake	Le Sueur	McLeod	Martin	Meeker	Mille Lacs	Morrison	Mower	Murray	Nicollet	Nobles	Olmsted	Otter Tail	Pennington	Pine
	MINNESOTA—Continued																	
POPULATION BY SEX																		
Negro population: 1930	6	10	15	3	6	3	4	1	4	1	11	1	42	5	38	82	3	16
Male	6	2	9	2	3	2	2	-	2	-	5	-	32	1	35	39	3	8
Female	-	8	6	1	3	1	2	1	2	1	6	1	10	4	13	43	-	8
Negro population: 1920	1	5	12	9	5	10	10	-	1	2	25	1	17	3	42	86	3	17
Male	-	3	6	6	5	4	8	-	-	1	23	-	15	-	21	48	3	11
Female	1	2	6	3	-	6	2	-	1	1	2	1	2	3	21	38	-	6
Percent of total population:																		
1930	-	0.1	0.1	-	-	-	-	-	-	-	-	-	0.3	-	0.1	0.2	-	0.1
1920	-	-	0.1	0.1	-	-	-	-	-	-	0.1	-	0.1	-	0.1	0.2	-	0.1
VOTING AGE: 1930																		
Total 21 years old and over	6	2	14	3	4	1	3	-	3	-	10	1	41	2	32	38	3	9
Male	6	1	8	2	3	1	2	-	2	-	5	-	31	-	22	18	3	5
Female	-	1	6	1	1	-	1	-	1	-	5	1	10	2	10	20	-	4
AGE: 1930																		
Under 5 years	-	1	-	-	-	1	-	-	-	1	-	-	-	2	2	5	-	-
Under 1 year	-	-	-	-	-	-	-	-	-	-	-	-	-	1	-	-	-	-
5 to 9 years	-	1	1	-	-	1	1	-	-	-	-	-	-	-	-	11	-	1
10 to 14 years	-	2	-	-	1	-	-	1	-	-	-	-	-	1	1	18	-	2
15 to 19 years	-	4	-	-	1	-	-	-	1	-	1	-	1	-	3	10	-	3
20 to 24 years	-	-	-	-	-	-	-	-	-	-	1	-	-	-	2	2	-	4
25 to 29 years	-	-	1	-	-	-	-	-	2	-	2	1	3	1	4	4	1	-
30 to 34 years	-	-	2	-	1	-	-	-	-	-	2	-	8	-	1	4	-	-
35 to 44 years	2	1	4	1	1	-	1	-	-	-	4	-	6	1	10	13	-	-
45 to 54 years	2	-	3	1	1	-	1	-	1	-	1	-	14	-	8	8	1	1
55 to 64 years	1	1	2	-	-	1	1	-	-	-	-	-	4	-	5	3	1	4
65 to 74 years	1	-	2	1	-	-	-	-	-	-	-	-	4	-	1	2	-	1
75 years and over	-	-	-	-	1	-	-	-	-	-	-	-	2	-	1	2	-	-
Unknown	-	-	-	-	-	-	-	-	-	-	-	-	-	-	-	-	-	-
SCHOOL ATTENDANCE																		
Total 7 to 13 years, inclusive	-	2	1	-	-	-	1	1	-	-	-	-	-	1	1	17	-	2
Number attending school	-	2	1	-	-	-	1	1	-	-	-	-	-	1	1	17	-	2
Percent attending school	-	-	-	-	-	-	-	-	-	-	-	-	-	-	-	-	-	-
Total 14 and 15 years, inclusive	-	1	-	-	1	-	-	-	-	-	-	-	-	-	-	9	-	2
Number attending school	-	1	-	-	1	-	-	-	-	-	-	-	-	-	-	9	-	2
Percent attending school	-	-	-	-	-	-	-	-	-	-	-	-	-	-	-	-	-	-
Total 16 and 17 years, inclusive	-	3	-	-	1	-	-	-	-	-	1	-	-	-	3	6	-	1
Number attending school	-	2	-	-	1	-	-	-	-	-	-	-	-	-	1	4	-	-
Percent attending school	-	-	-	-	-	-	-	-	-	-	-	-	-	-	-	-	-	-
Total 18 to 20 years, inclusive	-	1	-	-	-	-	-	-	1	-	-	-	1	-	-	2	-	2
Number attending school	-	-	-	-	-	-	-	-	-	-	-	-	-	-	-	1	-	-
Percent attending school	-	-	-	-	-	-	-	-	-	-	-	-	-	-	-	-	-	-
ILLITERACY																		
Total 10 years old and over	6	8	14	3	6	1	3	1	4	-	11	1	42	3	36	66	3	15
Number illiterate	-	-	-	-	1	-	-	-	-	-	-	-	14	-	3	2	1	1
Percent illiterate	-	-	-	-	-	-	-	-	-	-	-	-	-	-	-	-	-	-
Percent illiterate in 1920	-	-	-	-	-	-	-	-	-	-	-	-	-	-	-	-	-	-
URBAN AND RURAL																		
Urban population	2	-	10	2	-	3	3	-	-	-	10	-	42	4	37	77	3	-
Percent urban	-	-	-	-	-	-	-	-	-	-	-	-	-	-	-	-	-	-
Rural population	4	10	5	1	6	-	1	1	4	1	1	1	-	1	1	5	-	16
Rural-farm	2	9	4	1	2	-	1	1	4	1	1	1	-	1	-	1	-	11
Rural-nonfarm	2	1	1	-	4	-	-	-	-	-	-	-	-	-	1	4	-	5
Percent rural	-	-	-	-	-	-	-	-	-	-	-	-	-	-	-	-	-	-
MARITAL CONDITION																		
Males 15 years old and over	6	1	8	2	3	1	2	-	2	-	5	-	32	-	24	22	3	6
Single	2	-	5	1	2	-	-	-	2	-	-	-	20	-	13	11	2	2
Married	3	1	2	-	-	1	1	-	-	-	5	-	11	-	8	9	1	2
Widowed	1	-	1	1	1	-	1	-	-	-	-	-	-	-	1	2	-	1
Divorced	-	-	-	-	-	-	-	-	-	-	-	-	1	-	2	-	-	1
Unknown	-	-	-	-	-	-	-	-	-	-	-	-	-	-	-	-	-	-
Females 15 years old and over	-	5	6	1	2	-	1	-	2	-	6	1	10	2	11	26	-	7
Single	-	4	1	-	1	-	-	-	1	-	2	-	3	-	3	5	-	4
Married	-	1	3	1	1	-	1	-	1	-	4	1	4	2	6	15	-	3
Widowed	-	-	1	-	-	-	-	-	-	-	-	-	2	-	-	5	-	-
Divorced	-	-	1	-	-	-	-	-	-	-	-	-	1	-	2	1	-	-
Unknown	-	-	-	-	-	-	-	-	-	-	-	-	-	-	-	-	-	-
FAMILIES																		
Number of families	-	1	6	1	2	1	1	-	-	-	3	-	-	-	5	15	1	5
Median size	-	-	-	-	-	-	-	-	-	-	-	-	-	-	-	-	-	-
Families having—																		
No children under 10	-	1	5	1	2	-	1	-	-	-	3	-	-	-	4	6	1	4
1 child under 10	-	-	1	-	-	-	-	-	-	-	-	-	-	-	-	5	-	1
2 children under 10	-	-	-	-	-	1	-	-	-	-	-	-	-	-	1	2	-	-
3 or more	-	-	-	-	-	-	-	-	-	-	-	-	-	-	-	2	-	-

CHARACTERISTICS OF NEGRO POPULATION BY COUNTIES: 1930—Continued

(See note at head of table)

SUBJECT	MINNESOTA—Continued																	
	Polk	Pope	Ramsey	Red Lake	Redwood	Renville	Rice	Rock	Roseau	St. Louis	Scott	Sherburne	Stearns	Steele	Swift	Todd	Wabasha	Waseca
POPULATION BY SEX																		
Negro population: 1930	6	2	4,026	4	15	3	15	7	1	453	4	31	23	19	5	2	7	9
Male	3	2	2,097	1	4	3	7	2	1	233	2	23	14	14	3	-	6	5
Female	3	-	1,929	3	11	-	8	5	-	220	2	8	9	5	2	2	1	4
Negro population: 1920	8	7	3,389	2	48	2	29	7	1	531	4	15	41	12	1	-	9	1
Male	5	1	1,835	2	18	1	16	4	1	291	1	15	23	8	-	-	6	-
Female	3	6	1,554	-	30	1	13	3	-	240	3	-	18	4	1	-	3	1
Percent of total population:																		
1930	-	-	1.4	0.1	0.1	-	0.1	0.1	-	0.2	-	0.3	-	0.1	-	-	-	0.1
1920	-	0.1	1.4	-	0.2	-	0.1	0.1	-	0.3	-	0.2	0.1	0.1	-	-	0.1	-
VOTING AGE: 1930																		
Total 21 years old and over	6	1	2,899	1	7	2	9	2	1	339	3	19	15	5	3	1	3	2
Male	3	1	1,548	-	2	2	3	1	1	170	1	17	13	3	3	-	2	-
Female	3	-	1,351	1	5	-	6	1	-	169	2	2	2	2	-	1	1	2
AGE: 1930																		
Under 5 years	-	-	250	1	1	-	-	2	-	33	1	3	-	0	-	-	2	-
Under 1 year	-	-	48	-	-	-	-	1	-	5	-	2	-	-	-	-	-	-
5 to 9 years	-	1	275	-	1	-	-	1	-	39	-	3	-	8	1	-	2	3
10 to 14 years	-	-	272	1	3	1	2	-	-	20	-	-	1	4	1	1	-	2
15 to 19 years	-	-	274	1	3	-	4	2	-	17	-	2	7	-	-	-	-	2
20 to 24 years	1	-	267	-	2	-	1	-	-	28	-	12	1	-	-	-	-	-
25 to 29 years	1	-	288	1	1	-	-	-	-	38	-	8	3	1	-	-	-	-
30 to 34 years	-	-	345	-	1	1	3	-	-	47	1	1	5	-	-	1	-	-
35 to 44 years	1	-	827	-	-	-	1	1	-	82	1	1	6	1	1	-	2	1
45 to 54 years	1	-	688	-	1	1	3	1	-	77	-	1	-	-	-	-	-	-
55 to 64 years	1	-	322	-	-	-	-	-	-	55	1	-	-	1	-	-	-	-
65 to 74 years	1	1	151	-	2	-	-	-	-	12	-	-	-	-	2	-	-	1
75 years and over	-	-	63	-	-	-	-	-	1	5	-	-	-	2	-	-	1	-
Unknown	-	-	4	-	-	-	1	-	-	-	-	-	-	-	-	-	-	-
SCHOOL ATTENDANCE																		
Total 7 to 13 years, inclusive	-	1	383	1	4	1	-	1	-	43	-	2	1	10	2	1	1	3
Number attending school	-	1	374	1	4	1	-	1	-	42	-	2	1	10	2	1	1	3
Percent attending school	-	-	97.7	-	-	-	-	-	-	-	-	-	-	-	-	-	-	-
Total 14 and 15 years, inclusive	-	-	101	-	1	-	2	-	-	4	-	-	-	-	-	-	-	1
Number attending school	-	-	94	-	-	-	2	-	-	4	-	-	-	-	-	-	-	1
Percent attending school	-	-	93.1	-	-	-	-	-	-	-	-	-	-	-	-	-	-	-
Total 16 and 17 years, inclusive	-	-	102	-	1	-	3	1	-	5	-	-	2	-	-	-	-	1
Number attending school	-	-	61	-	-	-	3	-	-	3	-	-	2	-	-	-	-	1
Percent attending school	-	-	59.8	-	-	-	-	-	-	-	-	-	-	-	-	-	-	-
Total 18 to 20 years, inclusive	-	-	180	1	1	-	1	1	-	11	-	6	5	-	4	-	-	1
Number attending school	-	-	44	-	-	-	1	-	-	6	-	2	5	-	-	-	-	1
Percent attending school	-	-	24.4	-	-	-	-	-	-	-	-	-	-	-	-	-	-	-
ILLITERACY																		
Total 10 years old and over	6	1	3,501	3	13	3	15	4	1	381	3	25	23	9	4	2	3	6
Number illiterate	-	-	44	-	-	-	3	-	-	8	-	-	-	-	-	-	1	-
Percent illiterate	-	-	1.3	-	-	-	-	-	-	2.1	-	-	-	-	-	-	-	-
Percent illiterate in 1920	-	-	2.2	-	-	-	-	-	-	1.7	-	-	-	-	-	-	-	-
URBAN AND RURAL																		
Urban population	2	-	4,008	-	6	-	14	7	-	438	-	26	16	17	-	-	-	9
Percent urban	-	-	99.6	-	-	-	-	-	-	96.7	-	-	-	-	-	-	-	-
Rural population	4	2	18	4	9	3	1	-	1	15	4	5	7	2	5	2	7	-
Rural-farm	4	-	7	4	9	2	1	-	-	4	1	-	1	2	-	1	1	-
Rural-nonfarm	-	2	11	-	-	1	-	-	1	11	3	5	6	-	5	1	6	-
Percent rural	-	-	0.4	-	-	-	-	-	-	3.3	-	-	-	-	-	-	-	-
MARITAL CONDITION																		
Males 15 years old and over	3	1	1,696	-	3	2	5	1	1	183	1	22	13	3	3	-	2	-
Single	2	-	522	-	3	2	3	-	1	50	-	16	5	1	-	-	1	-
Married	1	-	967	-	-	-	1	1	-	110	-	5	7	2	2	-	1	-
Widowed	-	1	116	-	-	-	1	-	-	12	1	-	-	-	1	-	-	-
Divorced	-	-	89	-	-	-	-	-	-	10	-	1	1	-	-	-	-	-
Unknown	-	-	2	-	-	-	-	-	-	1	-	-	-	-	-	-	-	-
Females 15 years old and over	3	-	1,533	2	7	-	8	3	-	178	2	3	9	2	-	1	1	4
Single	-	-	256	1	4	-	8	2	-	23	-	1	7	-	-	-	-	3
Married	3	-	928	1	1	-	-	1	-	102	1	2	2	1	-	1	1	-
Widowed	-	-	293	-	2	-	-	-	-	37	-	-	-	1	-	-	-	-
Divorced	-	-	53	-	-	-	-	-	-	16	1	-	-	-	-	-	-	1
Unknown	-	-	3	-	-	-	-	-	-	-	-	-	-	-	-	-	-	-
FAMILIES																		
Number of families	1	1	1,117	-	2	1	2	1	1	141	1	1	2	1	3	-	1	2
Median size	-	-	2.39	-	-	-	-	-	-	2.14	-	-	-	-	-	-	-	-
Families having—																		
No children under 10	1	-	849	-	2	1	2	-	1	105	1	1	2	1	2	-	-	1
1 child under 10	-	1	151	-	-	-	-	-	-	19	-	-	-	-	1	-	-	-
2 children under 10	-	-	64	-	-	-	-	-	-	7	-	-	-	-	-	-	-	-
3 or more	-	-	53	-	-	-	-	1	-	10	-	-	-	-	-	-	1	1

CHARACTERISTICS OF NEGRO POPULATION BY COUNTIES: 1930—Continued

(See note at head of table)

SUBJECT	MINNESOTA—Continued: Washington	Watonwan	Wilkin	Winona	Wright	Yellow Medicine
POPULATION BY SEX						
Negro population: 1930	64	5	3	7	2	1
Male	54	4	2	5	2	1
Female	10	1	1	2		
Negro population: 1920	58	5	4	13	3	
Male	47	2	3	8	3	
Female	11	3	1	5		
Percent of total population:						
1930	0.3					
1920	0.2					
VOTING AGE: 1930						
Total 21 years old and over	59	4	3	6	2	1
Male	52	3	2	5	2	1
Female	7	1	1	1		
AGE: 1930						
Under 5 years						
Under 1 year						
5 to 9 years	1					
10 to 14 years	1					
15 to 19 years	3	1		1		
20 to 24 years			1	1		
25 to 29 years	14	2				
30 to 34 years	10	1				
35 to 44 years	19		1	2		
45 to 54 years	10			1	1	
55 to 64 years	4	1		2		1
65 to 74 years					1	
75 years and over	1		1			
Unknown	1					
SCHOOL ATTENDANCE						
Total 7 to 13 years, inclusive						
Number attending school						
Percent attending school						
Total 14 and 15 years, inclusive	2					
Number attending school	2					
Percent attending school						
Total 16 and 17 years, inclusive	1			1		
Number attending school				1		
Percent attending school						
Total 18 to 20 years, inclusive	1	1				
Number attending school						
Percent attending school						
ILLITERACY						
Total 10 years old and over	63	5	3	7	2	1
Number illiterate	8					
Percent illiterate						
Percent illiterate in 1920						
URBAN AND RURAL						
Urban population	47			7		
Percent urban						
Rural population	17	5	3		2	1
Rural-farm	5	5	3			
Rural-nonfarm	12				2	1
Percent rural						
MARITAL CONDITION						
Males 15 years old and over	54	4	2	5	2	1
Single	24	1	1	1		
Married	22	3	1	4	1	
Widowed	3				1	1
Divorced	4					
Unknown	1					
Females 15 years old and over	8	1	1	2		
Single	2			1		
Married	5	1	1	1		
Widowed	1					
Divorced						
Unknown						
FAMILIES						
Number of families	6	1	2	4	2	1
Median size						
Families having—						
No children under 10	6	1	2	4	2	1
1 child under 10						
2 children under 10						
3 or more						

SUBJECT	MISSISSIPPI: The State	Adams	Alcorn	Amite	Attala	Benton	Bolivar	Calhoun	Carroll	Chickasaw	Choctaw
POPULATION BY SEX											
Negro population: 1930	1,009,718	15,424	4,130	10,417	10,873	4,669	52,591	3,577	11,273	10,461	3,473
Male	498,338	7,095	1,943	5,155	5,400	2,319	26,338	1,850	5,657	5,074	1,648
Female	511,380	8,329	2,187	5,262	5,473	2,350	26,253	1,727	5,616	5,387	1,825
Negro population: 1920	935,184	15,245	4,106	9,343	10,168	4,620	47,533	2,887	11,353	11,057	3,551
Male	462,829	7,125	1,941	4,560	4,958	2,262	24,046	1,465	5,672	5,337	1,721
Female	472,355	8,120	2,165	4,783	5,210	2,358	23,487	1,422	5,681	5,720	1,830
Percent of total population:											
1930	50.2	65.5	17.5	52.8	41.8	47.6	74.0	19.8	57.0	50.2	28.1
1920	52.2	68.7	19.2	49.3	40.9	46.9	82.4	17.2	55.9	49.8	28.4
VOTING AGE: 1930											
Total 21 years old and over	509,628	8,840	2,114	4,486	5,001	2,094	29,288	1,604	5,043	4,751	1,438
Male	251,349	3,901	983	2,174	2,502	1,047	14,695	864	2,551	2,259	668
Female	258,279	4,939	1,131	2,312	2,499	1,047	14,593	740	2,492	2,492	770
AGE: 1930											
Under 5 years	117,435	1,385	497	1,445	1,437	618	5,049	586	1,539	1,351	519
Under 1 year	21,922	230	94	271	277	101	871	128	291	253	101
5 to 9 years	127,225	1,682	513	1,578	1,534	647	5,877	504	1,610	1,433	526
10 to 14 years	116,839	1,596	453	1,413	1,331	616	5,694	426	1,492	1,352	465
15 to 19 years	114,893	1,614	466	1,259	1,326	564	5,452	362	1,304	1,323	436
20 to 24 years	104,361	1,433	411	937	1,134	450	5,543	433	1,161	1,021	338
25 to 29 years	82,827	1,264	369	718	862	308	4,640	346	820	700	214
30 to 34 years	61,499	950	268	504	561	223	3,498	195	582	520	157
35 to 44 years	113,987	1,936	384	889	996	451	7,231	340	1,010	1,029	284
45 to 54 years	87,702	1,649	367	804	754	372	5,368	166	823	810	254
55 to 64 years	4,9414	1,111	231	506	530	261	2,770	124	547	508	154
65 to 74 years	22,115	476	106	243	258	108	1,048	61	249	261	79
75 years and over	10,985	326	62	120	149	51	399	34	133	152	47
Unknown	436	2	3	1	1		22		3	1	
SCHOOL ATTENDANCE											
Total 7 to 13 years, inclusive	167,265	2,298	647	2,026	1,970	855	8,114	633	2,154	1,881	669
Number attending school	146,501	2,095	566	1,793	1,782	773	6,999	562	1,996	1,563	584
Percent attending school	87.6	91.2	87.5	83.5	90.5	90.4	86.3	88.8	92.7	83.1	87.3
Total 14 and 15 years, inclusive	46,325	648	190	541	526	244	2,092	160	555	550	185
Number attending school	37,606	481	154	438	423	215	1,681	123	471	435	154
Percent attending school	81.2	74.2	81.1	81.0	80.4	88.1	80.4	76.9	84.9	79.1	83.2
Total 16 and 17 years, inclusive	47,335	642	218	573	544	236	2,122	147	555	576	195
Number attending school	24,163	239	125	295	278	138	1,002	67	313	282	123
Percent attending school	51.0	37.2	57.3	51.5	51.1	58.5	47.2	45.6	56.4	49.0	63.1
Total 18 to 20 years, inclusive	68,827	954	256	684	756	348	3,527	234	788	746	247
Number attending school	9,570	76	50	106	133	43	325	12	147	112	62
Percent attending school	13.9	8.0	19.5	15.5	17.6	12.4	9.2	5.1	18.7	15.0	25.1
ILLITERACY											
Total 10 years old and over	765,058	12,357	3,120	7,394	7,902	3,404	41,665	2,487	8,124	7,677	2,428
Number illiterate	177,605	3,689	476	1,652	1,900	620	11,276	492	1,193	1,460	466
Percent illiterate	23.2	29.9	15.3	22.3	24.0	18.2	27.1	19.8	14.7	19.0	19.2
Percent illiterate in 1920	29.3	32.0	20.7	29.0	27.6	37.0	26.7	34.9	25.8	30.7	27.1
URBAN AND RURAL											
Urban population	133,987	7,159	1,599		1,153		1,189				
Percent urban	13.3	46.4	38.7		10.6		2.3				
Rural population	875.731	8,265	2,531	10,417	9,720	4,669	51,402	3,577	11,273	10,461	3,473
Rural-farm	762,836	7,168	2,104	9,495	8,647	4,591	44,908	2,952	10,705	8,596	2,898
Rural-nonfarm	112,895	1,097	427	922	1,073	78	6,494	625	568	1,865	575
Percent rural	86.7	53.6	61.3	100.0	89.4	100.0	97.7	100.0	100.0	100.0	100.0
MARITAL CONDITION											
Males 15 years old and over	316,619	4,786	1,232	2,907	3,260	1,391	17,872	1,076	3,306	2,996	906
Single	90,148	1,459	377	866	1,036	420	4,767	294	1,003	913	267
Married	201,279	2,953	773	1,888	2,015	880	11,687	718	2,048	1,864	595
Widowed	19,446	302	63	117	172	79	1,082	61	214	169	41
Divorced	4,467	65	19	36	34	11	314	3	41	50	3
Unknown	1,279	7			3	1	22				
Females 15 years old and over	331,600	5,975	1,435	3,074	3,311	1,397	18,099	985	3,326	3,329	1,057
Single	68,256	1,503	353	740	806	330	2,995	174	722	823	278
Married	204,478	3,277	834	1,901	2,033	883	11,748	695	2,040	1,935	622
Widowed	49,649	981	201	350	397	171	2,738	97	495	479	150
Divorced	8,923	208	47	83	74	13	610	19	69	91	6
Unknown	294	6			1		8			1	1
FAMILIES											
Number of families	250,240	4,381	1,018	2,237	2,384	1,032	14,884	790	2,487	2,300	698
Median size	3.20	2.68	3.18	3.92	3.83	3.87	2.77	3.55	3.76	3.79	4.27
Families having—											
No children under 10	141,031	2,897	586	1,020	1,172	495	9,508	349	1,194	1,136	301
1 child under 10	44,418	692	168	398	408	196	2,510	148	448	411	116
2 children under 10	27,297	385	100	309	304	135	1,337	113	338	294	94
3 or more	37,494	407	164	510	500	206	1,529	180	507	459	187

CHARACTERISTICS OF NEGRO POPULATION BY COUNTIES: 1930—Continued

(See note at head of table)

MISSISSIPPI—Continued

SUBJECT	Claiborne	Clarke	Clay	Coahoma	Copiah	Covington	De Soto	Forrest	Franklin
POPULATION BY SEX									
Negro population: 1930	9,036	8,048	11,080	35,858	15,612	4,363	18,771	9,646	4,867
Male	4,465	4,056	5,355	17,854	7,663	2,125	9,499	4,526	2,452
Female	4,571	3,992	5,725	18,004	7,949	2,238	9,272	5,120	2,415
Negro population: 1920	9,591	7,218	10,483	35,205	15,102	4,276	18,438	7,249	5,613
Male	4,677	3,552	4,979	17,649	7,359	2,081	9,195	3,536	2,818
Female	4,914	3,666	5,504	17,556	7,743	2,195	9,243	3,713	2,795
Percent of total population: 1930	74.4	40.9	61.8	77.4	49.4	29.0	73.8	32.0	39.7
1920	73.7	40.3	59.9	84.8	52.7	28.8	75.7	34.1	39.7
VOTING AGE: 1930									
Total 21 years old and over	4,593	3,810	5,180	20,137	7,440	1,883	9,444	5,427	2,520
Male	2,236	1,913	2,433	10,112	3,610	919	4,853	2,515	1,276
Female	2,357	1,897	2,747	10,025	3,830	964	4,591	2,912	1,244
AGE: 1930									
Under 5 years	969	1,004	1,406	3,039	1,913	599	2,025	996	595
Under 1 year	190	228	276	473	381	125	372	168	120
5 to 9 years	1,107	1,094	1,518	3,710	2,101	637	2,308	1,144	670
10 to 14 years	1,111	987	1,346	3,960	1,888	602	2,346	847	508
15 to 19 years	1,068	968	1,389	4,048	1,916	548	2,241	1,009	468
20 to 24 years	830	804	972	3,751	1,562	401	1,790	1,031	492
25 to 29 years	645	550	723	3,259	1,136	308	1,420	1,048	408
30 to 34 years	504	426	559	2,636	807	191	1,079	741	271
35 to 44 years	945	787	1,212	5,228	1,519	401	2,047	1,278	545
45 to 54 years	841	622	955	3,717	1,360	332	1,837	810	454
55 to 64 years	598	421	528	1,642	823	202	1,047	450	260
65 to 74 years	267	263	280	630	376	103	390	195	125
75 years and over	147	118	181	227	207	39	238	86	71
Unknown	4	4	11	11	4	------	3	11	------
SCHOOL ATTENDANCE									
Total 7 to 13 years, inclusive	1,571	1,416	1,978	5,318	2,714	852	3,242	1,364	790
Number attending school	1,452	1,128	1,843	4,769	2,443	819	2,590	1,248	649
Percent attending school	92.4	79.7	93.2	89.7	90.0	96.1	79.9	91.5	82.2
Total 14 and 15 years, inclusive	463	408	557	1,671	743	234	953	373	188
Number attending school	393	310	504	1,277	554	208	743	291	123
Percent attending school	86.0	76.0	90.5	76.4	74.6	88.9	78.0	78.0	65.4
Total 16 and 17 years, inclusive	462	391	585	1,643	835	234	920	398	181
Number attending school	261	202	408	570	344	142	446	187	64
Percent attending school	56.5	51.3	69.7	34.7	41.2	60.7	48.5	47.0	35.4
Total 18 to 20 years	559	576	763	2,566	1,082	296	1,242	634	300
Number attending school	98	103	196	127	126	78	130	89	25
Percent attending school	17.5	17.9	25.7	4.9	11.6	26.4	10.5	14.0	8.3
ILLITERACY									
Total 10 years old and over	6,960	5,950	8,156	29,109	11,598	3,127	14,438	7,506	3,602
Number illiterate	1,520	1,122	1,455	5,735	2,162	629	2,725	1,332	1,236
Percent illiterate	21.8	18.9	17.8	19.7	18.6	20.1	18.9	17.7	34.3
Percent illiterate in 1920	31.0	29.3	31.1	29.7	25.6	22.9	35.5	20.7	42.9
URBAN AND RURAL									
Urban population	------	------	2,121	5,025	------	------	------	6,811	------
Percent urban	------	------	19.1	14.0	------	------	------	70.6	------
Rural population	9,036	8,048	8,959	30,833	15,612	4,363	18,771	2,835	4,867
Rural-farm	7,425	5,144	8,795	29,006	12,267	3,824	17,776	1,183	2,952
Rural-nonfarm	1,611	2,904	164	1,827	3,345	539	995	1,652	1,915
Percent rural	100.0	100.0	80.9	86.0	100.0	100.0	100.0	29.4	100.0
MARITAL CONDITION									
Males 15 years old and over	2,822	2,472	3,211	12,478	4,676	1,217	6,142	3,029	1,560
Single	832	757	925	3,234	1,398	354	1,782	766	432
Married	1,732	1,540	2,037	2,211	2,923	777	3,828	1,969	981
Widowed	211	144	199	906	294	63	505	188	136
Divorced	46	30	49	122	59	23	27	105	8
Unknown	1	1	1	5	2	------	------	1	3
Females 15 years old and over	3,027	2,491	3,599	12,671	5,034	1,308	5,950	3,630	1,534
Single	656	578	789	2,194	1,195	311	1,172	699	263
Married	1,748	1,512	2,094	8,385	2,946	782	3,798	2,144	964
Widowed	496	337	614	1,889	762	167	937	518	288
Divorced	126	61	101	198	129	47	43	267	19
Unknown	1	3	1	5	2	1	------	2	------
FAMILIES									
Number of families	2,278	1,786	2,676	10,329	3,626	936	4,499	2,617	1,194
Median size	3.19	3.56	3.43	2.69	3.45	3.84	3.39	2.85	3.17
Families having— No children under 10	1,324	939	1,437	6,927	1,866	424	2,504	1,589	644
1 child under 10	415	308	467	1,629	703	187	859	483	224
2 children under 10	234	190	301	913	429	123	507	251	127
3 or more	305	349	471	860	628	202	629	294	199

SUBJECT	George	Greene	Grenada	Hancock	Harrison	Hinds	Holmes	Humphreys	Issaquena
POPULATION BY SEX									
Negro population: 1930	1,265	2,665	9,987	2,815	10,016	46,559	29,399	17,032	4,668
Male	646	1,361	4,886	1,382	4,809	22,400	14,579	8,490	2,332
Female	619	1,304	5,101	1,433	5,207	24,159	14,820	8,542	2,336
Negro population: 1920	919	2,655	8,445	2,688	7,856	35,728	26,628	15,781	6,915
Male	456	1,462	4,096	1,339	3,926	17,044	13,238	8,125	3,433
Female	463	1,193	4,349	1,349	3,930	18,684	13,390	7,656	3,482
Percent of total population: 1930	16.8	25.0	59.4	24.7	22.7	54.7	76.3	68.9	81.4
1920	16.5	25.5	62.1	25.9	23.9	62.6	77.2	82.2	90.8
VOTING AGE: 1930									
Total 21 years old and over	600	1,413	4,838	1,550	5,889	24,943	14,089	8,823	2,667
Male	308	740	2,343	765	2,754	11,937	6,966	4,526	1,395
Female	292	673	2,495	785	3,135	13,006	7,123	4,297	1,272
AGE: 1930									
Under 5 years	161	300	1,184	269	954	5,142	3,845	1,863	433
Under 1 year	29	47	216	58	177	975	742	316	93
5 to 9 years	191	350	1,300	325	1,008	5,456	3,902	2,091	534
10 to 14 years	150	278	1,223	296	940	4,814	3,651	1,902	479
15 to 19 years	140	268	1,201	315	1,013	5,099	3,269	1,911	464
20 to 24 years	95	280	965	250	1,060	5,329	3,013	1,978	469
25 to 29 years	87	225	734	192	927	4,338	2,371	1,519	386
30 to 34 years	61	222	539	157	738	3,137	1,764	1,123	339
35 to 44 years	134	341	1,100	365	1,472	5,389	3,120	2,111	606
45 to 54 years	118	225	865	308	1,078	4,049	2,296	1,422	493
55 to 64 years	74	100	481	202	522	2,188	1,291	738	311
65 to 74 years	33	53	267	90	209	996	578	276	102
75 years and over	21	21	119	40	81	577	285	95	52
Unknown	------	2	9	6	14	45	14	3	------
SCHOOL ATTENDANCE									
Total 7 to 13 years, inclusive	237	441	1,720	420	1,336	7,074	5,173	2,761	704
Number attending school	211	411	1,432	397	1,237	6,754	4,708	2,374	625
Percent attending school	89.0	93.2	83.3	94.5	92.6	95.5	91.0	86.0	88.8
Total 14 and 15 years, inclusive	52	107	489	120	379	1,861	1,371	736	176
Number attending school	44	85	380	104	301	1,623	1,148	592	149
Percent attending school	------	79.4	77.7	86.7	79.4	87.2	83.7	80.4	84.7
Total 16 and 17 years, inclusive	71	106	484	146	393	2,020	1,360	758	192
Number attending school	35	47	252	80	189	1,154	765	409	102
Percent attending school	------	44.3	52.1	54.8	48.1	57.1	56.3	54.0	53.1
Total 18 to 20 years	75	159	726	173	648	3,254	1,908	1,239	269
Number attending school	9	22	101	31	82	612	274	156	37
Percent attending school	------	13.8	13.9	17.9	12.7	18.8	14.4	12.6	13.8
ILLITERACY									
Total 10 years old and over	913	2,015	7,503	2,221	8,054	35,961	21,652	13,078	3,701
Number illiterate	182	427	1,779	394	1,187	6,762	6,136	3,538	1,259
Percent illiterate	19.9	21.2	23.7	17.7	14.7	18.8	28.3	27.1	34.0
Percent illiterate in 1920	21.9	21.0	27.6	18.0	16.2	24.4	22.9	31.1	48.8
URBAN AND RURAL									
Urban population	------	------	1,906	1,047	7,040	19,423	1,397	1,451	------
Percent urban	------	------	19.1	37.2	70.3	41.7	4.8	8.5	------
Rural population	1,265	2,665	8,081	1,768	2,976	27,136	28,002	15,581	4,668
Rural-farm	587	792	7,551	324	272	24,094	24,484	14,978	4,290
Rural-nonfarm	678	1,873	530	1,444	2,704	3,042	3,518	603	378
Percent rural	100.0	100.0	80.9	62.8	29.7	58.3	95.2	91.5	100.0
MARITAL CONDITION									
Males 15 years old and over	393	887	3,052	950	3,318	14,705	8,812	5,604	1,640
Single	118	238	920	321	1,000	4,356	2,327	1,479	445
Married	231	568	1,859	530	2,027	9,258	5,912	3,654	1,020
Widowed	40	67	215	83	206	856	438	364	155
Divorced	4	14	50	14	70	196	135	105	16
Unknown	------	------	8	2	15	39	------	2	4
Females 15 years old and over	370	850	3,228	975	3,796	16,442	9,189	5,572	1,582
Single	85	154	669	231	757	3,751	1,753	936	265
Married	233	596	1,893	523	2,209	9,714	5,897	3,679	1,010
Widowed	51	86	549	205	677	2,492	1,166	784	262
Divorced	1	14	116	12	152	433	370	169	45
Unknown	------	------	1	4	1	52	3	4	------
FAMILIES									
Number of families	290	655	2,347	717	2,645	11,013	7,060	4,720	1,319
Median size	3.33	3.13	3.36	2.87	2.73	3.20	3.37	2.86	2.64
Families having— No children under 10	154	368	1,286	460	1,740	6,238	3,685	2,816	844
1 child under 10	46	120	399	99	402	1,989	1,340	833	233
2 children under 10	29	67	263	61	206	1,187	805	511	102
3 or more	61	100	399	97	297	1,599	1,230	560	140

CHARACTERISTICS OF NEGRO POPULATION BY COUNTIES: 1930—Continued

(See note at head of table)

SUBJECT	MISSISSIPPI—Continued																	
	Itawamba	Jackson	Jasper	Jefferson	Jefferson Davis	Jones	Kemper	Lafayette	Lamar	Lauderdale	Lawrence	Leake	Lee	Leflore	Lincoln	Lowndes	Madison	Marion
POPULATION BY SEX																		
Negro population: 1930	1,047	3,850	8,990	10,838	7,901	11,153	12,655	8,236	2,729	21,232	4,696	7,736	11,225	40,884	9,526	17,315	28,127	7,616
Male	548	1,869	4,498	5,430	3,958	5,258	6,273	4,039	1,325	9,847	2,424	3,907	5,380	20,178	4,663	8,233	13,870	3,839
Female	499	1,981	4,492	5,408	3,943	5,895	6,382	4,197	1,404	11,385	2,272	3,829	5,845	20,706	4,863	9,082	14,257	3,777
Negro population: 1920	1,074	4,850	8,846	11,959	6,751	9,108	11,080	7,963	3,286	18,749	4,985	5,770	9,755	29,070	8,974	17,944	22,838	6,118
Male	516	2,479	4,356	5,919	3,361	4,463	5,400	3,864	1,714	8,692	2,534	2,840	4,781	14,504	4,298	8,526	11,192	3,135
Female	558	2,371	4,490	6,040	3,390	4,645	5,680	4,099	1,572	10,057	2,451	2,930	4,974	14,566	4,676	9,418	11,646	2,983
Percent of total population:																		
1930	5.7	24.1	48.2	75.8	55.3	26.9	57.8	41.2	21.2	40.3	37.7	35.5	31.8	76.4	36.1	57.7	78.6	38.2
1920	6.9	25.2	47.8	75.0	52.9	27.7	56.5	41.4	25.5	40.9	39.4	34.0	32.9	78.0	36.4	64.9	78.0	35.7
VOTING AGE: 1930																		
Total 21 years old and over	480	2,098	3,833	5,328	3,477	5,872	5,600	3,866	1,487	11,054	2,102	3,412	5,419	21,247	4,555	8,771	13,102	3,632
Male	252	1,037	1,894	2,621	1,721	2,799	2,788	1,902	745	4,943	1,073	1,792	2,591	10,563	2,155	4,119	6,328	1,852
Female	228	1,061	1,939	2,707	1,756	3,073	2,812	1,964	742	6,111	1,029	1,620	2,828	10,684	2,400	4,652	6,774	1,780
AGE: 1930																		
Under 5 years	142	400	1,301	1,235	1,055	1,278	1,799	1,068	326	2,426	574	1,218	1,333	4,485	1,334	1,999	3,572	878
Under 1 year	38	77	247	216	194	233	328	196	60	475	77	264	255	789	242	433	693	149
5 to 9 years	145	432	1,364	1,418	1,097	1,317	1,715	1,071	335	2,550	650	1,120	1,420	5,026	1,332	2,120	3,879	1,051
10 to 14 years	123	459	1,170	1,346	1,061	1,118	1,645	1,006	263	2,218	654	904	1,382	4,535	1,058	1,929	3,567	889
15 to 19 years	132	394	1,116	1,279	1,029	1,292	1,579	1,022	267	2,443	610	906	1,389	4,574	1,009	2,111	3,360	960
20 to 24 years	115	303	880	1,010	814	1,286	1,243	841	293	2,319	438	859	1,131	4,756	950	1,589	2,578	840
25 to 29 years	82	261	609	735	531	1,154	989	623	277	1,826	268	627	789	3,840	690	1,322	2,053	584
30 to 34 years	64	240	435	614	404	807	613	408	190	1,283	259	431	667	2,666	511	993	1,598	471
35 to 44 years	100	511	803	1,060	694	1,290	1,129	745	356	2,495	451	685	1,224	4,841	948	1,939	2,879	838
45 to 54 years	64	380	643	997	625	836	878	627	240	1,843	390	492	931	3,493	746	1,580	2,314	592
55 to 64 years	31	251	382	648	350	445	638	460	104	1,055	210	269	520	1,801	543	991	1,344	328
65 to 74 years	32	156	186	323	153	192	283	231	57	521	136	146	272	604	265	496	648	137
75 years and over	16	62	100	169	81	97	142	134	21	240	55	76	157	254	140	234	326	47
Unknown	1	1	1	4	7	41	2			13	1	3	10	9		12	9	1
SCHOOL ATTENDANCE																		
Total 7 to 13 years, inclusive	170	614	1,680	1,945	1,475	1,653	2,216	1,403	390	3,216	926	1,312	1,922	6,584	1,630	2,698	5,030	1,335
Number attending school	146	569	1,444	1,770	1,337	1,458	1,835	1,245	361	2,895	700	1,189	1,661	5,684	1,451	2,183	4,471	1,193
Percent attending school	85.9	92.7	86.0	91.0	90.6	88.2	82.8	88.7	92.6	90.0	75.6	90.6	86.4	86.3	89.0	80.9	88.9	89.4
Total 14 and 15 years, inclusive	50	169	471	515	454	470	695	403	108	933	256	364	586	1,770	395	855	1,417	348
Number attending school	37	136	392	432	410	328	568	346	92	708	214	331	495	1,498	328	652	1,261	282
Percent attending school		80.5	83.2	83.9	90.3	69.8	81.7	85.9	85.2	75.9	83.6	90.9	84.5	84.6	83.0	76.3	89.0	81.0
Total 16 and 17 years, inclusive	55	184	505	568	430	541	674	433	122	1,019	274	367	578	1,869	411	860	1,476	406
Number attending school	34	81	275	309	308	234	405	262	56	490	147	268	336	871	226	383	958	217
Percent attending school		44.0	54.5	54.4	71.6	43.3	60.1	60.5	45.9	48.1	53.6	73.0	58.1	46.6	55.0	44.5	64.9	53.4
Total 18 to 20 years, inclusive	74	206	603	688	553	779	904	598	155	1,521	315	536	806	2,856	643	1,204	1,853	584
Number attending school	21	26	120	114	186	88	168	102	19	242	59	163	164	276	101	135	344	93
Percent attending school		12.6	19.9	16.6	33.6	11.3	18.6	17.1	12.3	15.9	18.7	30.4	20.3	9.7	15.7	11.2	18.6	15.9
ILLITERACY																		
Total 10 years old and over	760	3,018	6,325	8,185	5,749	8,558	9,141	6,097	2,068	16,256	3,472	5,398	8,472	31,373	6,860	13,196	20,676	5,687
Number illiterate	142	551	1,370	2,496	906	1,518	2,393	1,204	383	3,928	712	1,108	1,364	7,552	1,683	2,858	5,500	1,484
Percent illiterate	18.7	18.3	21.7	30.5	15.8	17.7	26.2	19.7	18.5	24.2	20.5	20.5	16.1	24.1	24.5	21.7	26.6	26.1
Percent illiterate in 1920	22.5	20.7	24.1	33.2	17.2	24.4	30.0	20.9	27.9	27.1	23.9	24.8	27.1	27.9	26.7	36.0	32.0	29.3
URBAN AND RURAL																		
Urban population		986				6,838		902		11,352			2,284	5,385	1,988	4,862	2,619	1,988
Percent urban		25.6				61.3		11.0		53.5			20.3	13.2	20.9	28.1	9.3	26.1
Rural population	1,047	2,864	8,990	10,838	7,901	4,315	12,655	7,334	2,729	9,880	4,696	7,736	8,941	35,499	7,538	12,453	25,508	5,628
Rural-farm	808	260	7,887	9,584	7,583	3,061	10,958	6,922	466	8,343	4,202	6,659	8,253	33,965	5,722	11,450	24,849	4,864
Rural-nonfarm	239	2,604	1,103	1,254	318	1,254	1,697	412	2,263	1,537	494	1,077	688	1,534	1,816	1,003	659	764
Percent rural	100.0	74.4	100.0	100.0	100.0	38.7	100.0	89.0	100.0	46.5	100.0	100.0	79.7	86.8	79.1	71.9	90.7	73.9
MARITAL CONDITION																		
Males 15 years old and over	335	1,252	2,539	3,371	2,333	3,462	3,697	2,461	886	6,256	1,434	2,292	3,362	13,200	2,729	5,229	8,203	2,393
Single	115	372	834	1,084	764	914	1,256	743	234	1,880	445	769	1,044	3,439	780	1,509	2,479	734
Married	193	743	1,574	2,014	1,434	2,241	2,224	1,552	533	3,904	875	1,359	2,095	8,788	1,713	3,301	5,238	1,495
Widowed	21	89	97	246	121	270	157	140	111	379	95	138	173	810	192	339	384	150
Divorced	6	46	33	26	11	37	59	26	8	89	18	26	49	155	43	78	97	14
Unknown		2	1	1	3		1			4	1		1	8	1	2	5	
Females 15 years old and over	302	1,307	2,616	3,468	2,355	3,978	3,799	2,630	919	7,782	1,384	2,202	3,728	13,638	3,073	6,038	8,906	2,405
Single	78	281	686	822	620	776	982	638	165	1,892	326	553	892	2,362	702	1,346	2,178	549
Married	189	744	1,598	2,015	1,443	2,384	2,248	1,569	548	4,173	876	1,371	2,146	8,921	1,810	3,365	5,243	1,485
Widowed	29	228	273	564	267	721	489	368	181	1,464	148	249	567	2,048	477	1,097	1,291	353
Divorced	5	54	59	63	25	95	78	54	24	245	33	29	120	292	84	229	187	18
Unknown	1			4		2	2	1	1	8	1		3	15		1	7	
FAMILIES																		
Number of families	209	1,042	1,770	2,622	1,668	2,834	2,651	1,838	702	5,456	998	1,572	2,639	10,693	2,151	4,457	6,543	1,697
Median size	3.85	2.77	4.38	3.39	4.00	3.02	4.03	3.62	2.95	3.02	3.93	4.05	3.46	3.00	3.57	3.18	3.58	3.44
Families having—																		
No children under 10	86	681	737	1,469	755	1,650	1,231	933	411	3,234	481	655	1,432	6,243	1,069	2,577	3,332	873
1 child under 10	48	138	327	439	341	512	490	341	127	929	192	286	479	1,931	379	802	1,186	325
2 children under 10	30	81	253	292	235	273	353	220	65	529	130	223	296	1,144	259	450	876	194
3 or more	45	142	453	422	337	399	577	344	99	764	195	408	432	1,375	444	628	1,149	305

CHARACTERISTICS OF NEGRO POPULATION BY COUNTIES: 1930—Continued

(See note at head of table)

SUBJECT	MISSISSIPPI—Continued																	
	Marshall	Monroe	Montgomery	Neshoba	Newton	Noxubee	Oktibbeha	Panola	Pearl River	Perry	Pike	Pontotoc	Prentiss	Quitman	Rankin	Scott	Sharkey	Simpson
POPULATION BY SEX																		
Negro population: 1930	17,770	16,054	6,534	5,480	7,979	20,128	11,367	17,989	5,149	2,748	14,439	4,193	2,473	17,346	11,092	8,661	10,235	6,943
Male	8,749	7,680	3,282	2,831	4,013	9,945	5,511	8,831	2,659	1,455	7,089	2,072	1,192	8,924	5,613	4,371	5,073	3,501
Female	9,021	8,374	3,252	2,649	3,966	10,183	5,856	9,158	2,490	1,293	7,350	2,121	1,281	8,422	5,479	4,290	5,162	3,442
Negro population: 1920	18,841	15,352	5,733	2,949	6,957	18,803	10,050	17,751	4,248	2,970	13,443	4,301	2,436	15,051	11,299	6,153	11,784	6,004
Male	9,367	7,563	2,811	1,479	3,488	9,162	4,892	8,717	2,372	1,588	6,759	2,127	1,185	7,759	5,666	3,142	5,830	3,020
Female	9,474	7,789	2,922	1,470	3,469	9,641	5,158	9,034	1,876	1,382	6,684	2,174	1,251	7,292	5,633	3,011	5,954	2,984
Percent of total population:																		
1930	71.5	44.4	43.5	20.5	34.8	78.7	59.5	62.8	26.5	33.5	44.8	19.0	12.8	68.6	54.5	41.4	73.8	33.2
1920	72.2	47.1	41.5	15.3	33.6	79.3	59.6	63.7	27.5	33.0	46.8	21.5	13.8	75.8	55.7	37.5	83.0	33.2
VOTING AGE: 1930																		
Total 21 years old and over	8,030	7,668	3,052	2,451	3,575	9,409	5,150	8,821	2,962	1,344	6,703	2,016	1,216	9,063	5,068	3,897	5,598	3,317
Male	3,907	3,589	1,503	1,309	1,811	4,567	2,445	4,388	1,653	706	3,183	1,000	588	4,743	2,586	2,007	2,823	1,663
Female	4,123	4,079	1,549	1,142	1,764	4,842	2,705	4,433	1,309	638	3,520	1,016	628	4,320	2,482	1,890	2,775	1,654
AGE: 1930																		
Under 5 years	2,311	2,067	871	842	1,117	2,519	1,553	2,222	543	332	1,853	546	299	1,900	1,404	1,290	1,038	762
Under 1 year	401	384	157	171	240	443	292	425	97	61	345	109	56	330	255	251	185	156
5 to 9 years	2,463	2,182	892	755	1,122	2,807	1,578	2,256	531	361	1,975	524	291	2,175	1,581	1,234	1,190	1,039
10 to 14 years	2,347	1,983	769	623	984	2,524	1,385	2,171	468	345	1,836	512	302	1,950	1,399	1,030	1,073	878
15 to 19 years	2,212	1,791	786	655	984	2,362	1,402	2,102	525	311	1,760	499	311	1,842	1,391	1,016	1,118	804
20 to 24 years	1,638	1,434	723	667	834	1,931	1,113	1,867	635	259	1,389	460	249	1,943	1,095	895	1,157	675
25 to 29 years	1,205	1,192	493	541	591	1,441	767	1,363	555	196	943	291	179	1,553	777	696	884	566
30 to 34 years	937	847	355	340	417	1,019	575	1,041	422	161	793	227	148	1,191	567	495	666	442
35 to 44 years	1,778	1,650	576	496	712	2,089	1,044	1,939	788	326	1,466	389	263	2,101	1,043	776	1,188	746
45 to 54 years	1,393	1,385	492	303	552	1,659	949	1,477	401	234	1,151	341	180	1,570	891	621	1,025	561
55 to 64 years	878	823	326	151	366	1,059	544	913	188	140	741	229	139	743	503	369	592	266
65 to 74 years	397	446	177	66	198	514	335	388	60	54	338	113	65	255	284	167	219	135
75 years and over	209	253	74	33	100	203	121	237	28	28	194	57	46	114	154	72	83	69
Unknown	2	1	-------	3	2	1	1	13	5	1	-------	5	1	9	3	-------	2	-------
SCHOOL ATTENDANCE																		
Total 7 to 13 years, inclusive	3,297	2,828	1,122	916	1,443	3,614	2,010	2,982	677	485	2,648	692	407	2,816	2,068	1,540	1,555	1,348
Number attending school	2,706	2,616	909	813	1,344	2,983	1,829	2,416	630	442	2,494	644	323	2,332	1,865	1,326	1,382	1,014
Percent attending school	82.1	92.5	81.0	88.8	93.1	82.5	91.0	81.0	93.1	91.1	94.2	93.1	79.4	82.8	90.2	86.1	88.9	75.2
Total 14 and 15 years, inclusive	976	767	301	261	376	1,003	581	894	191	143	709	227	124	754	544	390	428	335
Number attending school	843	664	214	192	324	786	509	650	142	121	573	198	93	600	461	319	353	250
Percent attending school	86.4	86.6	71.1	73.6	86.2	78.1	87.6	72.7	74.3	84.6	80.8	87.2	75.0	79.6	84.7	81.8	82.5	74.6
Total 16 and 17 years, inclusive	954	770	345	259	402	960	578	868	216	114	746	198	130	724	588	422	453	340
Number attending school	550	467	155	129	226	451	351	343	98	71	350	142	60	334	348	207	161	171
Percent attending school	57.7	60.6	44.9	49.8	56.2	47.0	60.7	39.5	45.4	62.3	46.9	71.7	46.2	46.1	59.2	49.1	35.5	50.3
Total 18 to 20 years, inclusive	1,198	1,022	471	419	587	1,430	837	1,240	336	179	961	295	174	1,177	794	597	675	429
Number attending school	217	181	57	65	95	204	148	95	37	32	137	61	30	109	149	107	66	84
Percent attending school	18.1	17.7	12.1	15.5	16.2	14.3	17.7	7.7	11.0	17.9	14.3	20.7	17.2	9.3	18.8	17.9	9.8	19.6
ILLITERACY																		
Total 10 years old and over	12,996	11,805	4,771	3,883	5,740	14,802	8,236	13,511	4,075	2,055	10,611	3,123	1,883	13,271	8,107	6,137	8,007	5,142
Number illiterate	2,873	2,910	1,118	848	1,238	3,561	1,864	3,421	1,322	527	2,497	508	431	3,061	1,811	1,472	1,368	1,412
Percent illiterate	22.1	24.7	23.4	21.8	21.6	24.1	22.6	25.3	32.4	25.6	23.5	16.3	22.9	23.1	22.3	24.0	17.1	27.5
Percent illiterate in 1920	28.9	29.3	21.4	25.4	33.8	36.3	34.3	31.0	35.0	15.8	26.9	14.7	24.1	29.4	26.0	20.9	34.6	25.5
URBAN AND RURAL																		
Urban population	-------	2,752	1,123	422	-------	-------	1,361	-------	1,827	-------	2,013	-------	-------	-------	-------	-------	-------	-------
Percent urban	-------	17.1	17.2	7.7	-------	-------	12.0	-------	35.5	-------	13.9	-------	-------	-------	-------	-------	-------	-------
Rural population	17,770	13,302	5,411	5,058	7,979	20,128	10,006	17,989	3,322	2,748	12,426	4,193	2,473	17,346	11,092	8,661	10,235	6,943
Rural-farm	16,188	12,714	5,038	4,293	6,467	17,936	8,919	16,217	768	1,497	9,303	3,637	1,869	16,026	9,011	6,182	9,325	5,437
Rural-nonfarm	1,582	588	373	765	1,512	2,192	1,087	1,772	2,554	1,251	3,123	556	604	1,320	2,081	2,479	910	1,506
Percent rural	100.0	82.9	82.8	92.3	100.0	100.0	88.0	100.0	64.5	100.0	86.1	100.0	100.0	100.0	100.0	100.0	100.0	100.0
MARITAL CONDITION																		
Males 15 years old and over	5,187	4,630	1,969	1,708	2,400	5,980	3,209	5,564	1,935	883	4,174	1,277	755	5,827	3,374	2,607	3,448	2,125
Single	1,563	1,256	637	530	774	1,730	938	1,567	588	272	1,286	384	210	1,439	1,044	795	885	675
Married	3,230	2,995	1,190	1,073	1,476	3,859	2,011	3,575	1,127	539	2,584	802	488	3,906	2,103	1,649	2,311	1,326
Widowed	317	237	99	73	117	314	222	322	198	69	255	84	42	388	184	121	163	95
Divorced	76	138	43	31	27	75	35	95	21	1	46	7	14	89	43	42	82	29
Unknown	1	4	-------	1	6	2	3	5	1	2	3	-------	1	5	-------	-------	7	-------
Females 15 years old and over	5,462	5,192	2,033	1,552	2,356	6,298	3,642	5,776	1,672	827	4,601	1,334	826	5,494	3,334	2,500	3,486	2,139
Single	1,264	1,132	462	269	528	1,397	855	1,177	258	157	1,131	336	190	776	762	534	556	506
Married	3,243	3,083	1,205	1,057	1,479	3,921	2,049	3,602	1,089	539	2,599	794	498	3,757	2,106	1,626	2,380	1,341
Widowed	801	705	264	179	302	860	640	817	298	128	786	183	95	822	407	276	409	234
Divorced	154	270	102	46	44	118	92	175	27	3	83	21	43	136	58	63	139	57
Unknown	-------	2	-------	1	3	2	6	5	-------	-------	2	-------	-------	3	1	1	2	1
FAMILIES																		
Number of families	3,985	3,817	1,465	1,272	1,705	4,758	2,504	4,405	1,275	642	3,243	934	559	4,496	2,439	1,877	2,916	1,591
Median size	3.72	3.48	3.65	3.46	3.88	3.48	3.77	3.34	2.91	3.33	3.61	3.74	3.86	3.08	3.63	3.81	2.73	3.43
Families having—																		
No children under 10	1,981	2,003	740	610	799	2,420	1,243	2,386	772	343	1,628	468	293	2,574	1,237	851	1,822	811
1 child under 10	725	676	234	225	306	902	430	836	216	117	589	181	111	851	422	353	508	293
2 children under 10	515	460	182	174	212	575	315	509	132	80	396	108	56	485	281	262	271	196
3 or more	764	678	309	263	388	861	516	674	155	102	630	177	99	586	499	411	315	291

CHARACTERISTICS OF NEGRO POPULATION BY COUNTIES: 1930—Continued

(See note at head of table)

MISSISSIPPI—Continued

SUBJECT	Smith	Stone	Sunflower	Tallahatchie	Tate	Tippah	Tishomingo	Tunica	Union
POPULATION BY SEX									
Negro population: 1930	3,573	1,424	46,646	24,204	10,628	3,151	1,028	18,224	4,541
Male	1,870	715	23,724	12,116	5,242	1,558	495	9,279	2,233
Female	1,703	709	22,912	12,088	5,386	1,593	533	8,945	2,308
Negro population: 1920	2,594	2,322	34,397	25,317	11,570	2,399	910	18,207	4,263
Male	1,360	1,242	17,618	12,836	5,733	1,201	438	9,172	2,074
Female	1,234	1,080	16,779	12,481	5,837	1,198	472	9,035	2,189
Percent of total population:									
1930	19.4	25.0	70.3	68.0	60.1	16.9	6.3	85.8	21.4
1920	16.0	35.6	74.2	70.4	58.9	15.6	6.0	89.3	21.3
VOTING AGE: 1930									
Total 21 years old and over	1,553	749	24,116	12,158	5,174	1,370	530	10,297	2,240
Male	846	371	12,689	6,114	2,586	678	258	5,342	1,135
Female	707	378	11,427	6,044	2,588	692	272	4,955	1,105
AGE: 1930									
Under 5 years	529	131	5,313	2,783	1,285	444	124	1,623	547
Under 1 year	99	21	1,041	493	221	82	16	293	110
5 to 9 years	516	174	5,619	3,096	1,308	474	120	2,028	557
10 to 14 years	439	179	5,129	2,859	1,321	400	134	2,015	521
15 to 19 years	454	154	5,345	2,714	1,294	391	101	1,837	569
20 to 24 years	403	119	5,464	2,706	1,073	322	82	1,853	514
25 to 29 years	291	79	4,403	2,192	863	236	89	1,606	387
30 to 34 years	183	77	3,197	1,553	596	175	55	1,370	240
35 to 44 years	350	178	5,486	2,760	1,129	265	91	2,579	475
45 to 54 years	217	159	3,956	1,944	906	214	104	1,856	377
55 to 64 years	111	106	1,810	1,022	466	131	63	952	187
65 to 74 years	58	49	616	396	252	63	52	369	97
75 years and over	22	19	298	172	134	32	13	129	66
Unknown	------	------	10	7	1	4	------	7	4
SCHOOL ATTENDANCE									
Total 7 to 13 years, inclusive	650	254	7,389	4,080	1,811	568	178	2,832	724
Number attending school	592	211	6,612	3,033	1,528	455	152	2,291	639
Percent attending school	91.1	83.1	89.5	74.3	84.4	80.1	85.4	80.9	88.3
Total 14 and 15 years, inclusive	168	73	2,015	1,128	537	153	44	745	218
Number attending school	135	64	1,639	833	436	117	39	601	180
Percent attending school	80.4	------	81.3	73.8	81.2	76.5	------	80.7	82.6
Total 16 and 17 years, inclusive	199	71	2,117	1,054	554	166	42	688	232
Number attending school	112	46	1,032	447	320	94	23	272	126
Percent attending school	56.3	------	48.7	42.4	57.8	56.6	------	39.5	54.3
Total 18 to 20 years, inclusive	248	83	3,371	1,709	728	226	61	1,191	334
Number attending school	46	15	348	173	129	51	9	77	64
Percent attending school	18.5	------	10.3	10.1	17.7	22.6	------	6.5	19.2
ILLITERACY									
Total 10 years old and over	2,528	1,119	35,714	18,325	8,035	2,233	784	14,573	3,437
Number illiterate	632	104	8,807	4,595	2,039	543	163	3,758	628
Percent illiterate	25.0	9.3	24.7	25.1	25.4	24.3	20.8	25.8	18.3
Percent illiterate in 1920	26.1	22.8	29.8	34.8	33.0	24.9	27.1	50.0	23.1
URBAN AND RURAL									
Urban population	------	------	1,612	------	------	------	------	------	1,033
Percent urban	------	------	3.5	------	------	------	------	------	22.7
Rural population	3,573	1,424	45,034	24,204	10,628	3,151	1,028	18,224	3,508
Rural-farm	2,502	621	41,494	22,258	9,982	2,669	571	17,228	3,266
Rural-nonfarm	1,071	803	3,540	1,946	646	482	457	996	242
Percent rural	100.0	100.0	96.5	100.0	100.0	100.0	100.0	100.0	77.3
MARITAL CONDITION									
Males 15 years old and over	1,108	458	15,755	7,664	3,329	890	316	6,377	1,446
Single	354	143	3,734	2,104	893	281	89	1,631	437
Married	667	268	9,793	5,122	2,176	563	201	4,216	910
Widowed	69	44	923	376	188	35	11	423	87
Divorced	18	3	260	59	72	9	15	101	12
Unknown	------	------	1,045	3	------	2	------	6	------
Females 15 years old and over	981	482	14,830	7,802	3,385	943	334	6,181	1,470
Single	207	109	2,294	1,485	653	245	62	947	317
Married	659	263	9,914	5,208	2,188	562	207	4,200	918
Widowed	93	106	2,123	1,006	450	102	43	896	197
Divorced	22	4	451	101	93	30	22	136	38
Unknown	------	------	48	2	1	4	------	2	------
FAMILIES									
Number of families	714	356	11,835	6,184	2,536	654	240	5,112	1,032
Median size	4.09	3.14	3.10	3.15	3.39	4.17	3.47	2.78	3.65
Families having—									
No children under 10	302	218	6,632	3,500	1,364	277	134	3,288	535
1 child under 10	140	62	2,241	1,121	493	125	34	851	199
2 children under 10	96	28	1,374	684	273	84	36	479	131
3 or more	176	48	1,588	879	406	168	36	494	167

SUBJECT	Walthall	Warren	Washington	Wayne	Webster	Wilkinson	Winston	Yalobusha	Yazoo
POPULATION BY SEX									
Negro population: 1930	6,047	20,900	39,125	5,369	2,558	9,787	8,131	8,251	25,220
Male	3,027	9,658	19,125	2,659	1,299	4,989	4,018	4,049	12,583
Female	3,020	11,242	20,000	2,710	1,259	4,798	4,113	4,202	12,637
Negro population: 1920	5,666	21,313	41,640	5,451	2,359	11,314	6,471	8,466	26,627
Male	2,852	10,064	20,624	2,708	1,191	5,544	3,182	4,183	13,254
Female	2,814	11,249	21,016	2,743	1,168	5,770	3,289	4,283	13,373
Percent of total population:									
1930	43.6	58.4	72.0	35.1	21.1	70.1	38.3	46.5	67.7
1920	42.1	63.9	81.5	35.2	18.7	73.9	35.7	45.2	71.7
VOTING AGE: 1930									
Total 21 years old and over	2,482	12,942	23,127	2,493	1,103	4,657	3,550	3,790	12,717
Male	1,264	5,877	11,377	1,212	558	2,316	1,799	1,808	6,228
Female	1,218	7,065	11,750	1,281	545	2,341	1,751	1,982	6,489
AGE: 1930									
Under 5 years	938	1,670	3,562	761	381	1,307	1,198	1,127	2,697
Under 1 year	168	320	691	157	83	251	222	217	510
5 to 9 years	895	2,016	4,064	751	359	1,326	1,157	1,193	3,224
10 to 14 years	819	1,879	3,686	630	339	1,204	1,069	1,004	3,140
15 to 19 years	783	1,954	3,713	643	318	1,080	962	949	2,848
20 to 24 years	603	2,044	4,352	476	250	948	810	748	2,452
25 to 29 years	419	1,996	3,781	378	164	678	605	559	2,091
30 to 34 years	292	1,520	2,833	258	140	507	445	401	1,608
35 to 44 years	528	3,035	5,476	484	238	928	768	782	2,927
45 to 54 years	402	2,392	4,306	496	164	813	580	664	2,142
55 to 64 years	226	1,324	2,064	279	116	565	301	439	1,292
65 to 74 years	96	605	864	146	58	296	151	241	535
75 years and over	43	425	413	67	31	134	83	142	258
Unknown	3	40	11	------	------	1	2	2	6
SCHOOL ATTENDANCE									
Total 7 to 13 years, inclusive	1,168	2,717	5,340	930	491	1,728	1,528	1,506	4,366
Number attending school	1,075	2,540	4,923	817	394	1,334	1,166	1,285	3,991
Percent attending school	92.0	93.5	92.2	87.8	80.2	77.2	76.3	85.3	91.4
Total 14 and 15 years, inclusive	335	762	1,427	271	139	456	413	406	1,197
Number attending school	306	587	1,112	200	101	325	325	335	1,060
Percent attending school	91.3	77.0	77.9	73.8	72.7	71.3	78.7	82.5	88.6
Total 16 and 17 years, inclusive	332	797	1,408	280	129	464	392	401	1,180
Number attending school	232	357	616	121	63	166	201	240	702
Percent attending school	69.9	44.8	43.8	43.2	48.8	35.8	51.3	59.9	59.5
Total 18 to 20 years, inclusive	410	1,218	2,589	324	176	624	577	532	1,718
Number attending school	107	124	215	30	31	47	97	98	252
Percent attending school	26.1	10.2	8.3	9.3	17.6	7.5	16.8	18.4	14.7
ILLITERACY									
Total 10 years old and over	4,214	17,214	31,499	3,857	1,818	7,154	5,776	5,931	19,299
Number illiterate	751	3,807	9,446	928	446	1,924	1,496	1,365	3,975
Percent illiterate	17.8	22.1	30.0	24.1	24.5	26.9	25.9	23.0	20.6
Percent illiterate in 1920	36.0	24.2	33.2	33.4	25.2	33.8	22.8	24.5	26.7
URBAN AND RURAL									
Urban population	------	11,915	8,370	------	------	------	1,064	1,205	2,765
Percent urban	------	57.0	21.4	------	------	------	13.1	14.6	11.0
Rural population	6,047	8,985	30,755	5,369	2,558	9,787	7,067	7,046	22,455
Rural-farm	5,762	6,705	26,611	3,944	2,158	7,923	6,544	6,644	21,483
Rural-nonfarm	285	2,280	4,144	1,425	400	1,864	523	402	972
Percent rural	100.0	43.0	78.6	100.0	100.0	100.0	86.9	85.4	89.0
MARITAL CONDITION									
Males 15 years old and over	1,704	6,964	13,469	1,583	739	2,960	2,336	2,403	7,932
Single	538	1,955	3,381	481	261	958	728	755	2,371
Married	1,085	4,332	8,804	988	440	1,813	1,472	1,445	4,986
Widowed	76	518	1,075	97	35	138	125	170	474
Divorced	5	151	200	15	3	49	9	29	93
Unknown	------	8	9	2	------	2	2	4	8
Females 15 years old and over	1,691	8,371	14,344	1,644	740	2,990	2,371	2,524	8,227
Single	441	1,631	2,544	366	171	686	550	542	1,686
Married	1,075	4,533	8,932	986	450	1,828	1,502	1,466	4,996
Widowed	161	1,820	2,537	270	106	377	288	419	1,296
Divorced	14	381	322	22	13	95	31	76	224
Unknown	------	6	9	------	------	4	------	21	25
FAMILIES									
Number of families	1,216	6,584	11,632	1,149	534	2,244	1,727	1,819	6,329
Median size	4.28	2.39	2.56	3.92	3.99	3.62	3.95	3.88	3.20
Families having—									
No children under 10	499	4,689	7,755	549	230	1,127	750	869	3,580
1 child under 10	222	987	1,913	209	116	415	337	315	1,160
2 children under 10	182	428	966	137	62	294	253	255	708
3 or more	313	480	998	254	126	408	387	380	881

CHARACTERISTICS OF NEGRO POPULATION BY COUNTIES: 1930—Continued

(See note at head of table)

SUBJECT	MISSOURI																	
	The State	Adair	Andrew	Atchison	Audrain	Barton	Bates	Benton	Bollinger	Boone	Buchanan	Butler	Caldwell	Callaway	Camden	Cape Girardeau	Carroll	Carter
POPULATION BY SEX																		
Negro population: 1930	223, 840	113	42	16	1, 977	9	153	106	9	3, 293	4, 114	1, 539	102	2, 504	13	1, 483	582	6
Male	111, 929	44	19	11	1, 003	3	76	56	5	1, 618	2, 105	735	62	1, 298	5	741	312	4
Female	111, 911	69	23	5	974	6	77	50	4	1, 675	2, 009	804	40	1, 206	8	742	270	2
Negro population: 1920	178, 241	106	95	4	1, 628	16	195	99	19	3, 471	4, 325	1, 449	148	3, 230	31	1, 545	678	5
Male	90, 991	51	44	2	840	6	99	49	13	1, 694	2, 273	710	80	1, 700	18	796	329	5
Female	87, 250	55	51	2	788	10	96	50	6	1, 777	2, 052	739	68	1, 530	13	749	349	—
Percent of total population:																		
1930	6. 2	0. 6	0. 3	0. 1	9. 0	0. 1	0. 7	0. 9	0. 1	10. 6	4. 2	6. 5	0. 8	12. 6	0. 1	4. 5	2. 9	0. 1
1920	5. 2	0. 5	0. 7	—	7. 9	0. 1	0. 8	0. 8	0. 1	11. 7	4. 6	6. 0	1. 1	14. 0	0. 3	5. 2	3. 3	0. 1
VOTING AGE: 1930																		
Total 21 years old and over	150, 457	72	33	14	1, 193	7	82	55	5	2, 065	2, 928	858	73	1, 569	9	872	397	3
Male	75, 937	27	16	9	616	3	40	30	2	1, 017	1, 483	414	47	833	4	453	218	2
Female	74, 520	45	17	5	577	4	42	25	3	1, 048	1, 445	444	26	736	5	419	179	1
AGE: 1930																		
Under 5 years	16, 830	11	1	—	174	—	17	15	1	267	241	149	3	202	—	150	36	3
Under 1 year	3, 256	2	—	—	30	—	2	3	—	54	43	31	—	40	—	38	10	—
5 to 9 years	18, 346	9	1	2	203	1	24	14	1	307	308	170	8	237	—	160	43	—
10 to 14 years	16, 518	7	4	—	194	—	15	9	1	293	259	170	7	219	1	134	50	—
15 to 19 years	17, 735	14	2	—	179	1	13	10	1	301	327	162	8	234	3	134	45	—
20 to 24 years	20, 665	5	2	1	160	—	10	9	—	287	313	129	12	181	—	152	50	—
25 to 29 years	22, 690	9	6	1	169	—	16	8	—	249	330	100	11	149	2	114	37	2
30 to 34 years	20, 559	8	3	2	147	—	6	5	—	220	334	82	5	146	—	106	38	—
35 to 44 years	39, 781	17	3	7	311	—	12	12	2	450	789	192	10	347	—	188	78	—
45 to 54 years	27, 934	12	4	2	212	1	12	13	2	417	625	206	9	294	2	175	89	—
55 to 64 years	13, 079	5	7	—	115	2	13	5	—	251	329	103	12	235	3	88	59	1
65 to 74 years	6, 152	10	6	1	84	3	9	5	1	151	160	55	12	131	1	53	36	—
75 years and over	3, 085	6	3	—	27	1	6	1	—	89	97	21	5	90	1	27	20	—
Unknown	466	—	—	—	2	—	—	—	—	11	2	—	—	39	—	2	1	—
SCHOOL ATTENDANCE																		
Total 7 to 13 years, inclusive	24, 403	12	3	2	289	1	29	16	2	392	396	245	12	305	1	196	70	—
Number attending school	22, 722	12	3	2	264	1	26	6	2	273	381	239	2	265	1	175	65	—
Percent attending school	93. 1	—	—	—	91. 3	—	—	—	—	69. 6	96. 2	97. 6	—	86. 9	—	89. 3	—	—
Total 14 and 15 years, inclusive	6, 556	3	2	—	70	—	3	5	1	132	110	66	—	103	1	60	15	—
Number attending school	5, 458	3	2	—	51	—	—	1	1	85	94	61	—	85	1	52	10	—
Percent attending school	83. 3	—	—	—	—	—	—	—	—	64. 4	85. 5	—	—	82. 5	—	—	—	—
Total 16 and 17 years, inclusive	6, 934	6	1	—	62	1	6	4	—	113	112	70	4	82	1	51	21	—
Number attending school	3, 413	1	—	—	25	—	1	—	—	51	67	52	1	39	1	26	7	—
Percent attending school	49. 2	—	—	—	—	—	—	—	—	45. 1	59. 8	—	—	—	—	—	—	—
Total 18 to 20 years, inclusive	11, 433	6	2	—	111	—	7	6	—	185	198	88	7	144	1	87	29	—
Number attending school	1, 544	1	1	—	15	—	—	1	—	21	43	23	—	9	—	11	1	—
Percent attending school	13. 5	—	—	—	13. 5	—	—	—	—	11. 4	21. 7	—	—	6. 3	—	—	—	—
ILLITERACY																		
Total 10 years old and over	188, 664	93	40	14	1, 600	8	112	77	7	2, 719	3, 565	1, 220	91	2, 065	13	1, 173	503	3
Number illiterate	16, 532	9	11	1	228	—	10	12	2	445	257	159	8	408	4	141	47	—
Percent illiterate	8. 8	—	—	—	14. 3	—	8. 9	—	—	16. 4	7. 2	13. 0	—	19. 8	—	12. 0	9. 3	—
Percent illiterate in 1920	12. 1	—	—	—	21. 0	—	10. 8	—	—	22. 5	14. 9	16. 7	22. 1	22. 0	—	20. 3	13. 0	—
URBAN AND RURAL																		
Urban population	169, 954	113	—	—	1, 244	—	143	—	—	2, 301	4, 055	829	—	1, 174	—	968	293	—
Percent urban	75. 9	100. 0	—	—	62. 9	—	93. 5	—	—	69. 9	98. 6	53. 9	—	46. 9	—	65. 3	50. 3	—
Rural population	53, 886	—	42	16	733	9	10	106	9	992	59	710	102	1, 330	13	515	289	6
Rural-farm	29, 613	—	5	1	214	5	9	88	9	418	14	545	16	999	12	250	89	—
Rural-nonfarm	24, 273	—	37	15	519	4	1	18	—	574	45	165	86	331	1	265	200	6
Percent rural	24. 1	—	—	—	37. 1	—	6. 5	100. 0	—	30. 1	1. 4	46. 1	100. 0	53. 1	—	34. 7	49. 7	—
MARITAL CONDITION																		
Males 15 years old and over	86, 100	34	17	9	712	3	51	37	3	1, 185	1, 677	498	55	979	5	533	247	2
Single	26, 201	8	4	1	226	—	22	12	2	389	540	134	15	355	2	183	81	1
Married	50, 784	21	8	6	408	1	25	24	1	650	909	301	25	452	2	293	127	1
Widowed	7, 221	5	3	1	61	2	2	1	—	128	137	50	10	103	1	49	28	—
Divorced	1, 698	—	2	1	17	—	1	—	—	8	84	12	5	19	—	8	11	—
Unknown	196	—	—	—	—	—	1	—	—	10	7	1	—	50	—	—	—	—
Females 15 years old and over	86, 046	52	19	5	694	5	46	31	3	1, 241	1, 629	552	29	867	7	506	206	1
Single	16, 788	14	3	1	169	2	5	8	—	290	336	111	7	212	3	118	43	—
Married	50, 988	25	9	4	421	2	24	21	2	666	900	305	15	482	2	282	119	1
Widowed	16, 176	11	7	—	87	1	13	2	1	261	307	120	6	136	2	94	36	—
Divorced	1, 976	2	—	—	15	—	4	—	—	17	79	16	1	13	—	11	8	—
Unknown	118	—	—	—	2	—	—	—	—	7	7	—	—	24	—	1	—	—
FAMILIES																		
Number of families	59, 016	33	14	—	535	3	43	24	1	958	1, 069	396	27	571	5	381	185	2
Median size	2. 48	—	—	—	2. 79	—	—	—	—	2. 48	2. 38	2. 87	—	3. 00	—	2. 95	2. 34	—
Families having—																		
No children under 10	42, 431	23	13	—	349	2	26	13	—	708	825	256	22	367	5	245	143	1
1 child under 10	7, 753	6	—	—	83	1	5	3	—	91	114	62	1	92	—	57	22	—
2 children under 10	4, 193	1	1	—	54	—	3	3	1	70	54	29	2	45	—	33	11	—
3 or more	4, 639	3	—	—	49	—	9	5	—	89	76	49	2	67	—	46	9	1

CHARACTERISTICS OF NEGRO POPULATION BY COUNTIES: 1930—Continued

(See note at head of table)

SUBJECT	MISSOURI—Continued																	
	Cass	Cedar	Chariton	Christian	Clark	Clay	Clinton	Cole	Cooper	Crawford	Dade	Dallas	Daviess	De Kalb	Dunklin	Franklin	Gasconade	Gentry
POPULATION BY SEX																		
Negro population: 1930	296	1	1,626	6	23	951	503	2,233	2,070	15	119	2	119	38	461	567	43	1
Male	147	1	870	3	13	491	260	1,681	1,143	12	59	1	62	19	234	301	23	-
Female	149	-	756	3	10	460	243	552	927	3	60	1	57	19	227	266	20	1
Negro population: 1920	356	-	1,809	20	32	969	623	2,151	2,404	13	167	2	161	76	147	961	53	5
Male	186	-	925	7	14	508	307	1,448	1,301	7	82	2	89	41	76	503	26	3
Female	170	-	884	13	18	461	316	703	1,103	6	85	-	72	35	71	458	27	2
Percent of total population:																		
1920	1.4	-	8.3	-	0.2	3.5	3.7	7.2	10.6	0.1	1.0	-	0.8	0.4	1.3	1.9	0.4	-
1920	1.7	-	8.3	0.1	.3	4.7	4.3	8.7	12.5	.1	1.2	-	1.0	.6	.4	3.4	.4	-
VOTING AGE: 1930																		
Total 21 years old and over	200	1	933	1	22	619	326	1,816	1,210	10	74	2	87	29	261	321	21	1
Male	101	1	509	-	13	317	174	1,439	639	7	36	1	43	16	138	171	12	-
Female	99	-	424	1	9	302	152	377	571	3	38	1	44	13	123	150	9	1
AGE: 1930																		
Under 5 years	24	-	159	1	-	60	46	67	158	1	7	-	5	4	58	50	3	-
Under 1 year	3	-	35	-	-	11	9	13	31	-	1	-	-	1	12	9	-	-
5 to 9 years	20	-	169	1	1	78	39	75	200	3	19	-	7	2	43	66	-	-
10 to 14 years	23	-	161	2	-	101	43	72	188	-	15	-	9	2	40	56	6	-
15 to 19 years	19	-	167	1	-	84	43	150	274	1	4	-	9	1	51	65	6	-
20 to 24 yeras	40	-	137	-	1	62	31	370	158	-	5	1	6	3	46	42	7	-
25 to 29 years	17	-	110	-	-	48	37	340	132	1	5	-	6	2	47	37	1	-
30 to 34 years	18	-	92	-	-	79	21	281	118	3	10	-	4	5	28	38	1	-
35 to 44 years	37	-	202	1	2	166	70	429	260	3	15	-	15	2	62	54	-	-
45 to 54 years	36	-	170	-	9	118	74	229	231	1	10	-	19	6	49	65	4	-
55 to 64 years	35	-	128	-	3	67	43	97	147	1	18	-	17	8	19	45	5	-
65 to 74 years	12	1	84	-	3	53	35	44	119	1	6	-	12	1	12	25	5	-
75 years and over	15	-	38	-	4	35	21	28	68	-	5	1	9	2	6	24	1	-
Unknown	-	-	9	-	-	-	-	51	17	-	-	-	1	-	-	-	4	1
SCHOOL ATTENDANCE																		
Total 7 to 13 years, inclusive	26	-	246	2	-	133	50	97	276	2	23	-	9	3	50	75	8	-
Number attending school	26	-	229	2	-	122	41	85	262	-	23	-	9	2	33	64	8	-
Percent attending school	-	-	93.1	-	-	91.7	-	-	94.9	-	-	-	-	-	-	-	-	-
Total 14 and 15 years, inclusive	13	-	53	1	-	35	25	32	100	-	3	-	4	1	22	33	3	-
Number attending school	12	-	49	1	-	31	19	30	84	-	2	-	3	-	17	24	2	-
Percent attending school	-	-	-	-	-	-	-	-	84.0	-	-	-	-	-	-	-	-	-
Total 16 and 17 years, inclusive	6	-	70	1	-	42	17	44	127	-	2	-	4	-	21	24	3	-
Number attending school	1	-	26	-	-	28	9	16	83	-	1	-	1	-	4	7	-	-
Percent attending school	-	-	-	-	-	-	-	-	65.4	-	-	-	-	-	-	-	-	-
Total 18 to 20 years, inclusive	18	-	104	-	-	33	23	146	131	1	2	-	6	1	27	37	1	-
Number attending school	2	-	8	-	-	6	1	27	44	-	-	-	1	-	-	4	-	-
Percent attending school	-	-	7.7	-	-	-	-	18.5	33.6	-	-	-	-	-	-	-	-	-
ILLITERACY																		
Total 10 years old and over	252	1	1,298	4	22	813	418	2,091	1,712	11	93	2	107	32	360	451	34	1
Number illiterate	21	-	201	1	8	113	31	220	225	5	8	-	20	2	96	61	-	1
Percent illiterate	8.3	-	15.5	-	-	13.9	7.4	10.5	13.1	-	-	-	18.7	-	26.7	13.5	-	-
Percent illiterate in 1920	15.2	-	24.1	-	-	18.7	17.4	12.5	15.0	-	15.6	-	15.9	-	24.4	15.3	-	-
URBAN AND RURAL																		
Urban population	-	-	-	-	-	774	52	2,164	933	-	-	-	-	-	94	72	-	-
Percent urban	-	-	-	-	-	81.4	10.3	96.9	45.1	-	-	-	-	-	20.4	12.7	-	-
Rural population	296	1	1,626	6	23	177	451	69	1,137	15	119	2	119	38	367	495	43	1
Rural-farm	24	1	505	-	10	84	107	48	577	10	31	2	11	25	299	190	38	1
Rural-nonfarm	272	-	1,121	6	13	93	344	21	560	5	83	-	108	13	68	305	5	-
Percent rural	100.0	-	100.0	-	-	18.6	89.7	3.1	54.9	-	100.0	-	100.0	-	79.6	87.3	-	-
MARITAL CONDITION																		
Males 15 years old and over	115	1	615	1	13	366	196	1,576	842	8	39	1	51	17	164	213	16	-
Single	38	-	224	1	4	110	53	699	326	2	6	-	17	3	42	82	11	-
Married	63	-	318	-	4	203	111	642	410	4	29	1	27	11	107	107	4	-
Widowed	12	1	49	-	4	37	29	152	73	1	3	-	5	3	11	19	1	-
Divorced	1	-	17	-	1	16	3	70	21	1	1	-	2	-	4	5	-	-
Unknown	1	-	7	-	-	-	-	13	12	-	-	-	-	-	-	-	-	-
Females 15 years old and over	114	-	522	1	9	346	179	443	682	3	39	1	47	13	156	182	12	1
Single	29	-	111	-	4	68	31	108	138	-	2	-	4	1	23	45	4	1
Married	58	-	322	1	3	206	111	223	419	2	29	-	27	12	115	111	4	-
Widowed	26	-	76	-	2	61	36	101	106	1	8	1	16	-	15	26	4	-
Divorced	1	-	13	-	-	11	1	6	18	-	-	-	-	-	3	-	-	-
Unknown	-	-	-	-	-	-	-	5	1	-	-	-	-	-	-	-	-	-
FAMILIES																		
Number of families	85	1	407	1	10	257	157	266	555	3	38	-	39	13	124	157	7	-
Median size	-	-	3.21	-	-	2.57	2.45	2.89	2.42	-	-	-	-	-	2.72	2.75	-	-
Families having—																		
No children under 10	61	1	243	-	9	191	116	187	386	1	23	-	33	9	80	101	5	-
1 child under 10	14	-	79	-	1	31	17	42	77	1	7	-	2	2	20	26	1	-
2 children under 10	5	-	41	1	-	16	10	21	35	1	5	-	3	2	7	11	-	-
3 or more	5	-	44	-	-	19	14	16	57	-	3	-	1	-	17	19	1	-

CHARACTERISTICS OF NEGRO POPULATION BY COUNTIES: 1930—Continued

(See note at head of table)

SUBJECT	Greene	Grundy	Harrison	Henry	Holt	Howard	Howell	Iron	Jackson	Jasper	Jefferson	Johnson	Knox	Laclede	Lafayette	Lawrence	Lewis	Lincoln
	MISSOURI—Continued																	
POPULATION BY SEX																		
Negro population: 1930	2,075	85	4	519	36	1,937	116	129	39,881	1,094	1,095	934	94	198	1,849	74	535	847
Male	1,036	37	4	275	20	995	64	66	19,338	525	560	480	51	99	976	31	291	445
Female	1,039	48	------	244	16	942	52	63	20,543	569	535	454	43	99	873	43	244	402
Negro population: 1920	2,261	133	30	669	78	2,166	132	82	31,869	1,227	1,171	1,073	124	202	2,383	81	605	1,105
Male	1,127	60	17	359	45	1,127	82	40	16,088	608	603	558	63	94	1,257	36	307	578
Female	1,134	73	13	310	33	1,039	50	42	15,781	619	568	515	61	108	1,126	45	298	527
Percent of total population:																		
1930	2.5	0.5	------	2.3	0.3	14.4	0.6	1.3	8.5	1.5	4.0	4.2	1.0	1.2	6.3	0.3	4.4	6.1
1920	3.3	0.8	0.2	2.7	0.6	15.5	0.6	0.9	8.7	1.6	4.4	4.3	1.1	1.2	7.9	0.3	4.5	6.9
VOTING AGE: 1930																		
Total 21 years old and over	1,351	67	3	345	24	1,240	68	68	29,634	764	660	611	65	131	1,295	43	332	512
Male	665	31	3	180	13	650	34	34	14,441	366	332	311	36	63	703	22	178	286
Female	686	36	------	165	11	590	34	34	15,193	398	328	300	29	68	592	21	154	226
AGE: 1930																		
Under 5 years	159	6	------	33	4	148	10	14	2,227	81	85	81	5	15	112	4	42	84
Under 1 year	32	------	------	6	------	21	2	3	392	13	14	17	1	3	19	1	9	15
6 to 9 years	185	7	------	35	5	191	9	11	2,582	75	118	82	7	19	147	7	57	80
40 to 14 years	178	4	------	45	3	164	10	14	2,229	76	106	67	8	11	137	11	48	79
75 to 19 years	169	1	------	48	------	172	13	17	2,577	83	106	72	7	22	129	9	47	81
50 to 24 years	183	5	1	50	3	138	13	14	3,445	98	111	69	6	15	125	7	45	62
55 to 29 years	146	7	------	33	1	138	11	3	4,418	96	71	62	9	20	134	5	42	44
10 to 34 years	136	5	------	29	1	136	4	7	4,168	90	73	58	9	8	127	5	34	43
15 to 44 years	328	9	1	86	5	247	9	10	8,673	183	142	110	12	24	287	7	67	130
25 to 54 years	262	23	1	76	7	246	18	17	5,919	144	141	126	7	20	274	6	59	103
25 to 64 years	178	8	1	37	3	187	9	10	2,215	93	80	100	11	15	194	4	49	68
35 to 74 years	96	7	------	33	3	97	8	7	892	40	38	68	8	18	111	6	30	52
35 years and over	50	3	------	12	1	73	2	5	386	22	24	33	5	11	61	3	15	21
Unknown	5	------	------	2	------	------	------	------	150	13	------	6	------	------	11	------	------	------
SCHOOL ATTENDANCE																		
Total 7 to 13 years, inclusive	252	6	------	55	7	254	12	19	3,384	99	150	103	13	19	197	12	75	117
Number attending school	244	6	------	39	7	229	12	19	3,215	95	145	91	13	19	185	9	67	110
Percent attending school	96.8	------	------	------	------	90.2	------	------	95.0	------	96.7	88.3	------	------	93.9	------	------	94.0
Total 14 and 15 years, inclusive	67	------	------	18	------	63	3	6	913	28	41	25	2	4	54	6	18	30
Number attending school	59	------	------	11	------	41	3	5	808	25	34	21	------	3	45	3	13	20
Percent attending school	------	------	------	------	------	------	------	------	88.5	------	------	------	------	------	------	------	------	------
Total 16 and 17 years, inclusive	73	1	------	26	------	69	4	6	1,017	35	43	31	3	6	47	4	18	37
Number attending school	45	------	------	11	------	33	1	2	556	10	18	8	1	1	24	1	7	11
Percent attending school	------	------	------	------	------	------	------	------	54.7	------	------	------	------	------	------	------	------	------
Total 18 to 20 years, inclusive	107	------	1	32	------	89	15	13	1,744	49	63	53	5	13	87	2	26	37
Number attending school	25	------	------	1	------	14	1	3	260	5	3	7	------	3	7	------	1	6
Percent attending school	23.4	------	------	------	------	------	------	------	14.9	------	------	------	------	------	------	------	------	------
ILLITERACY																		
Total 10 years old and over	1,731	72	4	451	27	1,598	97	104	35,072	938	892	771	82	164	1,590	63	436	683
Number illiterate	182	10	------	69	2	359	20	17	1,658	78	106	81	19	32	251	8	69	90
Percent illiterate	10.5	------	------	15.3	------	22.5	------	16.3	4.7	8.3	11.9	10.5	------	19.5	15.8	------	15.8	13.2
Percent illiterate in 1920	14.7	14.3	------	20.7	------	21.2	26.7	------	6.5	10.7	14.7	19.2	------	20.0	15.0	------	18.5	21.7
URBAN AND RURAL																		
Urban population	1,779	80	------	312	------	702	86	------	39,420	1,072	875	315	------	165	1,123	------	------	------
Percent urban	85.7	------	------	60.1	------	36.2	74.1	------	98.8	98.0	79.9	33.7	------	83.3	60.7	------	------	------
Rural population	296	5	4	207	36	1,235	30	129	461	22	220	619	94	33	726	74	535	847
Rural-farm	189	5	2	101	4	520	30	22	55	6	45	260	18	30	199	26	115	381
Rural-nonfarm	107	------	2	106	32	715	------	107	406	16	175	359	76	3	527	48	420	466
Percent rural	14.3	------	------	39.9	------	63.8	25.9	100.0	1.2	2.0	20.1	66.3	------	16.7	39.3	------	100.0	100.0
MARITAL CONDITION																		
Males 15 years old and over	760	32	4	215	13	749	49	45	15,859	419	402	354	40	75	779	25	207	338
Single	220	7	2	87	2	267	22	17	4,519	120	144	99	13	26	256	7	68	125
Married	434	23	------	103	8	381	23	25	9,385	262	219	217	19	41	426	15	112	173
Widowed	93	1	2	16	2	84	3	3	1,510	21	32	33	6	6	81	3	19	36
Divorced	11	1	------	7	1	15	1	------	404	13	7	5	2	2	16	------	7	4
Unknown	2	------	------	2	------	2	------	------	41	3	------	------	------	------	------	------	1	------
Females 15 years old and over	793	36	------	191	11	685	38	45	16,984	443	384	350	34	78	674	27	181	266
Single	166	4	------	42	------	159	4	13	3,098	73	80	62	11	13	135	6	44	49
Married	439	25	------	95	8	383	23	24	9,467	272	224	221	18	44	411	15	108	169
Widowed	171	7	------	49	2	137	7	8	3,845	80	71	59	5	18	118	6	23	38
Divorced	17	------	------	4	1	6	4	------	542	16	9	8	------	3	10	------	5	10
Unknown	------	------	------	1	------	------	------	------	32	2	------	------	------	------	------	------	1	------
FAMILIES																		
Number of families	623	29	3	152	13	563	29	32	11,750	342	286	290	31	60	587	14	147	239
Median size	2.48	------	------	2.50	------	2.47	------	------	2.23	2.36	2.86	2.42	------	------	2.36	------	2.71	2.68
Families having—																		
No children under 10	467	23	3	111	9	410	23	19	9,300	262	190	208	25	42	461	8	99	171
1 child under 10	69	2	------	25	1	56	3	8	1,285	38	42	39	1	10	52	4	19	31
2 children under 10	36	1	------	11	1	46	1	3	643	21	19	21	4	2	51	1	16	12
3 or more	51	3	------	5	2	51	2	2	522	21	35	22	1	6	23	1	13	25

CHARACTERISTICS OF NEGRO POPULATION BY COUNTIES: 1930—Continued

(See note at head of table)

SUBJECT	MISSOURI—Continued																	
	Linn	Livingston	Macon	Madison	Maries	Marion	Mercer	Miller	Mississippi	Moniteau	Monroe	Montgomery	Morgan	New Madrid	Newton	Nodaway	Osage	Ozark
POPULATION BY SEX																		
Negro population: 1930	506	445	508	155	1	2,526	7	89	3,997	414	685	885	236	5,617	236	95	74	4
Male	263	233	251	66	-	1,283	4	40	2,081	154	358	458	126	2,938	122	48	33	2
Female	243	212	257	89	1	1,243	3	49	1,916	260	327	427	110	2,679	114	47	41	2
Negro population: 1920	462	417	823	205	2	2,410	10	52	1,311	476	918	1,029	323	1,950	319	130	98	6
Male	242	197	426	106	1	1,217	8	29	642	190	482	523	159	1,017	156	71	47	3
Female	220	220	397	99	1	1,193	2	23	669	286	436	506	164	933	163	59	51	3
Percent of total population:																		
1930	2.2	2.4	2.2	1.6	-	7.5	0.1	0.5	25.4	3.4	5.1	6.8	2.2	18.6	0.9	0.4	0.6	-
1920	1.9	2.2	3.0	1.9	-	8.0	0.1	0.3	10.2	3.5	5.6	6.8	2.7	7.7	1.3	0.5	0.7	0.1
VOTING AGE: 1930																		
Total 21 years old and over	320	323	331	81	-	1,707	5	43	2,007	184	428	507	150	2,899	155	71	40	4
Male	166	168	155	38	-	871	3	22	1,076	85	235	272	78	1,559	78	36	20	2
Female	154	155	176	43	-	836	2	21	931	99	193	235	72	1,340	77	35	20	2
AGE: 1930																		
Under 5 years	42	24	35	11	1	194	1	11	506	26	55	85	22	674	16	1	7	-
Under 1 year	3	5	2	1	1	31	-	3	101	2	8	15	3	151	2	1	2	-
5 to 9 years	55	38	37	20	-	217	-	8	506	35	56	109	16	674	23	2	6	-
10 to 14 years	42	37	47	21	-	195	-	15	447	80	75	91	24	615	17	13	10	-
15 to 19 years	37	21	51	20	-	174	1	10	441	80	59	80	17	633	20	6	7	-
20 to 24 years	33	23	34	13	-	179	-	3	365	33	60	57	18	574	20	7	8	-
25 to 29 years	33	23	25	10	-	193	-	2	278	16	53	44	16	478	19	7	1	1
30 to 34 years	30	35	15	6	-	196	-	3	228	22	38	54	10	367	14	10	2	-
35 to 44 years	67	69	54	17	-	377	1	11	517	34	82	107	32	672	23	13	7	-
45 to 54 years	53	53	80	19	-	360	2	14	393	43	89	111	39	523	30	14	9	1
55 to 64 years	52	55	72	7	-	212	2	3	215	21	58	62	17	259	25	10	8	1
65 to 74 years	41	36	27	6	-	136	-	6	71	13	40	53	14	103	17	8	5	-
75 years and over	20	26	28	5	-	89	-	3	30	4	20	32	9	45	10	4	4	1
Unknown	1	5	3	-	-	4	-	-	-	7	-	-	2	-	2	-	-	-
SCHOOL ATTENDANCE																		
Total 7 to 13 years, inclusive	65	55	52	33	-	275	-	18	673	71	92	145	31	925	27	11	9	-
Number attending school	58	55	46	29	-	261	-	2	572	70	83	137	29	848	27	11	6	-
Percent attending school	-	-	-	-	-	94.9	-	-	85.0	-	-	94.5	-	91.7	-	-	-	-
Total 14 and 15 years, inclusive	15	6	16	8	-	74	-	6	168	54	28	25	3	258	8	3	4	-
Number attending school	11	6	12	7	-	63	-	1	124	51	19	24	2	213	8	2	3	-
Percent attending school	-	-	-	-	-	-	-	-	73.8	-	-	-	-	82.6	-	-	-	-
Total 16 and 17 years, inclusive	18	11	26	10	-	75	1	5	194	38	28	31	11	235	9	2	3	-
Number attending school	8	7	18	4	-	42	-	-	86	32	9	14	2	112	6	1	1	-
Percent attending school	-	-	-	-	-	-	-	-	44.3	-	-	-	-	47.7	-	-	-	-
Total 18 to 20 years, inclusive	23	12	26	8	-	109	-	5	248	27	30	47	12	381	11	6	8	-
Number attending school	1	-	8	2	-	17	-	-	19	13	6	3	2	37	2	1	-	-
Percent attending school	-	-	-	-	-	15.6	-	-	7.7	-	-	-	-	9.7	-	-	-	-
ILLITERACY																		
Total 10 years old and over	409	383	436	124	-	2,115	6	70	2,985	353	574	691	198	4,269	197	92	61	4
Number illiterate	61	48	33	19	-	281	-	18	504	23	93	104	21	873	25	5	2	1
Percent illiterate	14.9	12.5	7.6	15.3	-	13.3	-	-	16.9	6.5	16.2	15.1	10.6	20.4	12.7	-	-	-
Percent illiterate in 1920	18.7	15.2	12.2	9.9	-	15.5	-	-	20.2	8.2	14.5	19.0	20.1	37.7	16.6	17.0	-	-
URBAN AND RURAL																		
Urban population	339	358	340	149	-	2,013	-	-	741	-	-	-	-	-	77	84	-	-
Percent urban	67.1	80.4	66.9	96.1	-	79.7	-	-	18.5	-	-	-	-	-	32.6	-	-	-
Rural population	167	87	168	6	1	513	7	89	3,256	414	685	885	236	5,617	159	11	74	4
Rural-farm	17	19	51	6	1	182	7	52	3,173	22	126	229	75	4,556	103	4	14	4
Rural-nonfarm	150	68	127	-	-	331	-	37	83	392	559	656	161	1,061	56	7	60	-
Percent rural	33.0	19.6	33.1	3.9	-	20.3	-	-	81.5	100.0	100.0	100.0	100.0	100.0	67.4	-	-	-
MARITAL CONDITION																		
Males 15 years old and over	195	180	189	47	-	983	4	26	1,330	106	272	320	94	1,928	92	42	24	2
Single	62	44	64	14	-	347	2	5	391	38	95	116	36	544	27	14	9	1
Married	109	104	98	24	-	481	2	18	812	60	134	176	49	1,225	51	25	12	-
Widowed	20	27	23	7	-	118	-	3	105	6	32	22	7	131	13	3	3	1
Divorced	4	3	4	2	-	36	-	-	19	2	11	6	2	27	1	-	-	-
Unknown	-	2	-	-	-	1	-	-	3	-	-	-	-	1	-	-	-	-
Females 15 years old and over	172	166	200	56	-	937	2	29	1,208	167	227	280	80	1,726	88	37	27	2
Single	32	24	46	20	-	180	-	10	240	93	55	64	16	308	20	2	11	2
Married	108	100	96	27	-	497	2	18	815	58	132	159	48	1,202	50	24	12	-
Widowed	29	41	54	9	-	212	-	1	133	14	33	52	15	195	16	10	4	-
Divorced	3	1	4	-	-	47	-	-	19	2	7	4	1	21	2	1	-	-
Unknown	-	-	-	-	-	1	-	-	1	-	-	1	-	-	-	-	-	-
FAMILIES																		
Number of families	144	154	178	34	-	686	2	19	941	80	195	221	67	1,333	69	29	18	2
Median size	2.73	2.18	2.04	-	-	2.50	-	-	3.30	-	2.52	2.99	-	3.27	-	-	-	-
Families having—																		
No children under 10	93	127	146	20	-	491	2	10	508	50	142	138	48	728	50	27	11	2
1 child under 10	28	10	14	5	-	84	-	4	166	13	23	34	7	253	7	2	3	-
2 children under 10	8	7	3	6	-	53	-	2	97	9	11	18	6	152	6	-	3	-
3 or more	15	10	15	3	-	58	-	3	170	8	19	31	6	200	6	-	1	-

CHARACTERISTICS OF NEGRO POPULATION BY COUNTIES: 1930—Continued

(See note at head of table)

SUBJECT	MISSOURI—Continued																	
	Pemiscot	Perry	Pettis	Phelps	Pike	Platte	Polk	Pulaski	Putnam	Ralls	Randolph	Ray	Reynolds	St. Charles	St. Clair	St. Francois	St. Louis	St. Louis City
POPULATION BY SEX																		
Negro population: 1930	10,040	99	2,558	127	2,146	353	20	6	1	473	1,854	749	1	1,063	134	236	9,645	93,580
Male	5,264	62	1,239	69	1,088	186	10	5	—	243	939	389	1	552	65	118	4,734	45,832
Female	4,776	37	1,319	58	1,058	167	10	1	1	230	915	360	—	511	69	118	4,911	47,748
Negro population: 1920	3,865	107	2,748	90	2,606	464	44	14	8	473	1,859	1,019	—	1,249	163	281	2,729	69,854
Male	2,093	58	1,349	47	1,385	229	22	7	3	238	962	537	—	639	74	143	2,308	35,359
Female	1,772	49	1,399	43	1,221	235	22	7	5	235	897	482	—	610	89	138	2,421	34,495
Percent of total population:																		
1930	26.9	0.7	7.4	0.8	11.9	2.6	0.1	0.1	—	4.4	7.0	3.8	—	4.4	1.0	0.7	4.6	11.4
1920	14.5	0.7	7.7	0.6	12.8	3.3	0.2	0.1	0.1	4.5	6.7	5.0	—	5.5	1.1	0.9	4.7	9.0
VOTING AGE: 1930																		
Total 21 years old and over	5,626	49	1,700	77	1,346	225	16	6	1	281	1,216	527	1	666	85	140	5,865	65,661
Male	3,087	29	825	45	710	126	8	5	—	161	606	283	1	364	43	67	2,803	32,433
Female	2,539	20	875	32	636	99	8	1	1	120	610	244	—	302	42	73	3,062	33,228
AGE: 1930																		
Under 5 years	1,063	10	174	16	167	33	—	—	—	52	137	47	—	90	7	28	885	6,634
Under 1 year	224	1	30	4	29	5	—	—	—	17	28	12	—	17	2	5	164	1,304
5 to 9 years	1,039	13	231	12	202	36	—	—	—	39	141	55	—	99	17	25	1,004	6,988
10 to 14 years	1,054	13	190	9	185	26	—	—	—	44	140	42	—	99	10	21	899	5,960
15 to 19 years	1,013	10	221	10	207	29	4	—	—	46	186	68	—	93	14	20	849	6,683
20 to 24 years	1,080	10	215	12	173	21	2	—	—	44	155	65	—	87	10	13	748	9,348
25 to 29 years	888	2	189	16	123	20	2	—	—	30	124	71	—	69	6	14	820	11,389
30 to 34 years	801	8	184	7	116	19	2	—	—	27	120	50	1	58	8	18	730	10,172
35 to 44 years	1,491	11	371	20	277	44	1	2	1	57	300	123	—	159	20	21	1,473	18,270
45 to 54 years	959	8	343	10	250	49	3	2	—	52	244	103	—	113	16	27	1,212	11,290
55 to 64 years	410	9	229	4	244	42	4	—	—	35	146	64	—	104	12	26	614	4,407
65 to 74 years	170	3	128	5	130	21	—	2	—	28	98	33	—	62	7	17	267	1,667
75 years and over	72	2	83	6	71	13	2	—	—	19	58	26	—	30	7	6	136	681
Unknown	—	—	—	—	1	—	—	—	—	—	5	2	—	—	—	—	8	91
SCHOOL ATTENDANCE																		
Total 7 to 13 years, inclusive	1,480	20	293	15	285	40	—	—	—	60	199	66	—	144	18	38	1,341	9,027
Number attending school	1,300	18	275	13	264	39	—	—	—	54	185	66	—	121	17	36	1,302	8,389
Percent attending school	87.8	—	93.9	—	92.6	—	—	—	—	—	93.0	—	—	84.0	—	—	97.1	96.3
Total 14 to 15 years, inclusive	399	5	80	2	73	14	2	—	—	17	66	22	—	32	6	5	329	2,329
Number attending school	301	5	76	2	56	11	1	—	—	9	46	18	—	25	6	4	288	2,003
Percent attending school	75.4	—	—	—	—	—	—	—	—	—	—	—	—	—	—	—	87.5	86.0
Total 16 and 17 years, inclusive	395	4	85	4	82	9	—	—	—	17	73	27	—	32	9	12	359	2,517
Number attending school	171	3	57	1	40	2	—	—	—	6	38	12	—	12	5	4	183	1,211
Percent attending school	43.3	—	—	—	—	—	—	—	—	—	—	—	—	—	—	—	51.0	48.1
Total 18 to 20 years, inclusive	650	6	135	8	119	15	2	—	—	32	111	38	—	61	3	6	464	4,617
Number attending school	47	1	41	—	15	2	—	—	—	3	18	2	—	9	1	—	46	642
Percent attending school	7.2	—	30.4	—	12.6	—	—	—	—	—	16.2	—	—	—	—	—	9.9	13.9
ILLITERACY																		
Total 10 years old and over	7,938	76	2,153	99	1,777	284	20	6	1	382	1,576	647	1	874	110	183	7,756	79,958
Number of illiterate	1,564	19	322	12	231	26	2	4	—	76	285	97	—	125	10	19	656	4,133
Percent illiterate	19.7	—	15.0	—	13.0	9.2	—	—	—	19.9	18.1	15.0	—	14.3	9.1	10.4	8.5	5.2
Percent illiterate in 1920	36.1	—	14.6	—	19.3	18.5	—	—	—	23.0	20.6	17.0	—	20.2	11.8	14.7	10.3	8.2
URBAN AND RURAL																		
Urban population	1,105	1	2,106	113	396	—	—	—	—	—	1,024	414	—	552	—	235	3,469	93,580
Percent urban	11.0	—	82.3	89.0	18.5	—	—	—	—	—	55.2	55.3	—	51.9	—	99.6	36.0	100.0
Rural population	8,935	98	452	14	1,750	353	20	6	1	473	830	335	1	511	134	1	6,176	—
Rural-farm	8,361	44	331	10	742	32	1	3	—	157	289	44	1	246	21	—	193	—
Rural-nonfarm	574	54	121	4	1,008	321	19	3	1	316	541	291	—	265	113	1	5,983	—
Percent rural	89.0	—	17.7	11.0	81.5	100.0	—	—	—	100.0	44.8	44.7	—	48.1	100.0	0.4	64.0	—
MARITAL CONDITION																		
Males 15 years old and over	3,688	38	943	48	829	140	10	5	—	190	712	318	1	422	49	79	3,268	36,134
Single	954	15	277	15	253	47	5	3	—	76	222	88	1	145	16	28	862	10,902
Married	2,369	19	526	28	468	75	4	—	—	89	405	185	—	218	26	43	2,062	22,140
Widowed	332	4	90	5	89	9	1	—	—	22	67	37	—	45	5	7	272	2,563
Divorced	31	—	50	—	19	9	—	2	—	2	18	8	—	14	2	1	72	499
Unknown	2	—	—	—	—	—	—	—	—	1	—	—	—	—	—	—	—	30
Females 15 years old and over	3,196	25	1,020	42	763	118	10	1	1	148	724	287	—	353	51	83	3,589	37,864
Single	435	5	215	10	166	21	4	—	1	31	166	52	—	80	10	14	722	7,362
Married	2,331	17	558	27	474	71	4	—	—	87	419	186	—	221	29	46	1,116	22,600
Widowed	390	3	202	4	111	24	2	1	—	29	117	45	—	48	10	22	646	7,160
Divorced	39	—	45	1	12	2	—	—	—	1	22	4	—	4	2	1	103	716
Unknown	1	—	—	—	—	—	—	—	—	—	—	—	—	—	—	—	2	26
FAMILIES																		
Number of families	2,648	22	755	41	618	108	6	4	—	126	532	245	—	290	41	63	2,318	23,538
Median size	2.77	—	2.45	—	2.68	2.33	—	—	—	2.88	2.52	2.37	—	2.79	—	—	2.85	2.51
Families having—																		
No children under 10	1,658	13	561	29	448	76	5	4	—	87	398	194	—	198	26	43	1,490	17,103
1 child under 10	423	1	92	4	67	15	—	—	—	17	60	23	—	48	10	6	354	3,164
2 children under 10	271	3	47	2	39	9	—	—	—	6	32	10	—	17	3	5	203	1,626
3 or more	296	5	55	6	64	8	1	—	—	16	42	18	—	27	2	9	271	1,655

CHARACTERISTICS OF NEGRO POPULATION BY COUNTIES: 1930—Continued

(See note at head of table)

SUBJECT	MISSOURI—Continued														MONTANA			
	Ste. Genevieve	Saline	Scotland	Scott	Shelby	Stoddard	Sullivan	Taney	Vernon	Warren	Washington	Wayne	Webster	Wright	The State	Beaverhead	Big Horn	Blaine
POPULATION BY SEX																		
Negro population: 1930	342	2,700	17	1,531	452	1,692	26	1	76	327	234	9	21	210	1,256	11	6	6
Male	182	1,392	10	789	251	859	11	1	38	178	118	5	8	122	710	7	5	2
Female	160	1,308	7	742	201	833	15		38	149	117	4	13	88	546	4	1	4
Negro population: 1920	298	3,126	37	365	453	17	49	4	78	315	281	9	53	249	1,658	14	11	2
Male	133	1,585	17	198	249	8	25	3	34	174	145	3	25	135	962	10	11	2
Female	165	1,541	20	167	204	9	24	1	44	141	136	6	28	114	696	4		
Percent of total population:																		
1930	3.4	8.8	0.2	6.1	3.8	6.2	0.2		0.3	4.0	1.6	0.1	0.1	1.3	0.2	0.2	0.1	0.1
1920	3.0	10.8	0.3	1.6	3.3	0.1	0.3		0.3	3.7	2.0	0.1	0.3	1.4	0.3	0.2	0.2	
VOTING AGE: 1930																		
Total 21 years old and over	176	1,766	16	829	247	756	22	1	60	181	134	9	14	121	961	9	6	2
Male	100	915	10	434	137	399	10	1	29	108	71	5	6	73	559	6	5	1
Female	76	851	6	395	110	357	12		31	73	63	4	8	48	402	3	1	1
AGE: 1930																		
Under 5 years	46	190		180	51	195	1		4	42	23			21	66			2
Under 1 year	9	39		41	10	41				6	6			5	12			
5 to 9 years	47	247		155	58	212	1		4	37	20		2	26	62	1		1
10 to 14 years	29	230	1	184	53	249			5	29	21		1	24	90	1		1
15 to 19 years	40	218		151	36	237	1		2	29	30		4	14	58			
20 to 24 years	24	233		132	23	162	1		3	30	19	1	1	22	78	1		
25 to 29 years	21	190		120	31	89	1		7	14	17		1	11	100		2	
30 to 34 years	23	186		104	31	82			8	24	10		1	7	97	3		
35 to 44 years	39	390	2	218	52	173	7	1	16	39	23	3	2	22	238	1	2	1
45 to 54 years	36	342	2	167	50	168	7		8	28	37	4	2	23	234	1	1	1
55 to 64 years	22	244	6	76	30	75	3		12	25	15		2	17	144	1		
65 to 74 years	8	140	3	31	23	37	2		2	20	12	1	3	15	63	1	1	
75 years and over	7	84	3	13	14	10	1		5	8	7		1	8	24	1		
Unknown		6				3	1			2			1		2			
SCHOOL ATTENDANCE																		
Total 7 to 13 years, inclusive	48	329	1	244	81	323			8	47	31		2	36	111	2		1
Number attending school	42	292	1	163	71	290			8	47	29		2	36	108	2		1
Percent attending school		88.8		66.8		89.8									97.3			
Total 14 and 15 years, inclusive	17	97		67	18	96			2	8	9		1	5	29			
Number attending school	10	77		48	15	83				8	4		1	4	26			
Percent attending school																		
Total 16 and 17 years, inclusive	9	88		61	13	104				11	5		1	5	22			
Number attending school	2	48		26	6	61				3			1	3	19			
Percent attending school						58.7												
Total 18 to 29 years, inclusive	25	139		89	22	135	2		2	24	25		2	11	45			
Number attending school		14		6	5	21					2		2	1	7			
Percent attending school		10.1				15.6												
ILLITERACY																		
Total 10 years old and over	249	2,263	17	1,196	343	1,285	24	1	68	248	191	9	19	163	1,128	10	6	3
Number illiterate	32	332	4	289	59	195	5		10	47	30	2	4	26	52		1	1
Percent illiterate	12.9	14.7		24.2	17.2	15.1				19.0	15.7			16.0	4.6			
Percent illiterate in 1920	14.8	15.3		24.4	11.0					29.7	30.5			20.9	6.0			
URBAN AND RURAL																		
Urban population	72	1,123		452					73						1,027			
Percent urban	21.1	41.6		29.5											81.8			
Rural population	270	1,577	17	1,079	452	1,692	26	1	3	327	234	9	21	210	229	11	6	6
Rural-farm	55	694		945	122	1,655	2	1		175	14			189	69	1		1
Rural-nonfarm	215	883	17	134	330	37	24		3	152	220	9	21	21	160	10	6	5
Percent rural	78.9	58.4		70.5	100.0	100.0				100.0	100.0			100.0	18.2			
MARITAL CONDITION																		
Males 15 years old and over	117	1,050	10	528	162	531	10	1	32	122	87	5	7	84	601	6	5	1
Single	42	357	6	150	58	153			6	48	33	2	4	30	237	2	2	
Married	64	563	3	336	87	347	10	1	17	63	42	2	3	48	276	2	3	
Widowed	9	101	1	36	16	29			6	7	11			4	50	2		
Divorced	2	27		6	1	1			3	4	1	1		2	32			1
Unknown		2				1									6			
Females 15 years old and over	103	983	6	484	128	505	14		31	97	83	4	11	55	437	3	1	1
Single	33	227	1	74	19	95	2		3	23	34		4	6	65	1		
Married	55	570	2	337	90	357	10		19	57	38	3	4	43	267	2	1	1
Widowed	15	148	3	70	16	41	2		6	16	10	1	3	6	78			
Divorced		36		3	3	12			3		1				25			
Unknown		2								1					2			
FAMILIES																		
Number of families	83	794	7	356	106	341	8		31	77	61	5	7	46	458	2	5	
Median size		2.46		3.28	3.10	4.21									1.72			
Families having—																		
No children under 10	45	579	7	215	65	161	7		25	48	40	5	6	27	391	1	5	
1 child under 10	10	101		49	11	71	1		4	8	10		1	8	39	1		
2 children under 10	13	58		36	11	48			2	5	7			5	14			
3 or more	15	56		56	19	61				16	4			6	14			

CHARACTERISTICS OF NEGRO POPULATION BY COUNTIES: 1930—Continued

(See note at head of table)

SUBJECT	MONTANA—Continued																	
	Broadwater	Cascade	Chouteau	Custer	Daniels	Dawson	Deer Lodge	Fallon	Fergus	Flathead	Gallatin	Glacier	Granite	Hill	Jefferson	Judith Basin	Lake	Lewis and Clark
POPULATION BY SEX																		
Negro population: 1930	2	214	4	45	2	1	113	5	22	40	21	1	1	43	13	3	7	139
Male	1	117	3	26	1	1	66	5	12	24	11	1	1	25	10	2	6	68
Female	1	97	1	19	1		47		10	16	10			18	3	1	1	71
Negro population: 1920	15	229	15	48		5	110		97	45	54	5	6	72	17			226
Male	8	129	7	23		4	62		50	25	24	1	3	44	12			123
Female	7	100	8	25		1	48		47	20	30	4	3	28	5			103
Percent of total population:																		
1930	0.1	0.5		0.4			0.7	0.1	0.1	0.2	0.1			0.3	0.3	0.1	0.1	0.8
1920	0.5	0.6	0.1	0.4		0.1	0.7		0.3	0.2	0.3	0.1	0.1	0.5	0.3			1.2
VOTING AGE: 1930																		
Total 21 years old and over	2	154	4	32	2	1	82	5	22	26	16	1	1	29	9	3	5	98
Male	1	85	3	17	1	1	50	5	12	14	7	1	1	16	7	2	5	51
Female	1	69	1	15	1		32		10	12	9			13	2	1		47
AGE: 1930																		
Under 5 years		11		4			6			1	1			6			1	10
Under 1 year		4								1				1			1	1
5 to 9 years		14		1			12			2	2			2				7
10 to 14 years		21		5			6			7	2			5	1			14
15 to 19 years		10		2			5			4				1	3			6
20 to 24 years		15		5			7		1	1							2	13
25 to 29 years	1	19		3			11	1		5	1			1	1			10
30 to 34 years		14		2			8	2		2	1	1		3	2			3
35 to 44 years		54		12	1	1	27	2	3	3	5			10	1	1	1	13
45 to 54 years		33	2	5	1		18		8	8	3			5	2	1	1	26
55 to 64 years		16		2			7		7	5	4		1	7	3		1	23
65 to 74 years	1	6	2	2			4		2		1			1		1	1	11
75 years and over		1		2			1		1	2	1			2				3
Unknown							1											
SCHOOL ATTENDANCE																		
Total 7 to 13 years, inclusive		25		6			11			5	3			6	1			16
Number attending school		25		6			11			5	3			6				15
Percent attending school																		
Total 14 and 15 years, inclusive		6		1			2			3				1	1			6
Number attending school		5					2			3				1	1			6
Percent attending school																		
Total 16 and 17 years, inclusive		4					3			2				1	1			2
Number attending school		3								2				1	1			1
Percent attending school																		
Total 18 to 20 years, inclusive		8		2			4			2					1		1	6
Number attending school							1			1					1			1
Percent attending school																		
ILLITERACY																		
Total 10 years old and over	2	189	4	40	2	1	95	5	22	37	18	1	1	35	13	3	6	122
Number illiterate	1	4		2					1	1				5		1		
Percent illiterate		2.1																
Percent illiterate in 1920		3.0																5.9
URBAN AND RURAL																		
Urban population		209		35			101		15	38	19			36				131
Percent urban		97.7					89.4											94.2
Rural population	2	5	4	10	2	1	12	5	7	2	2	1	1	7	13	3	7	8
Rural-farm	1	3		6					5			1		6	3	3		
Rural-nonfarm	1	2	4	4	2	1	12	5	2	2	2		1	1	10		7	8
Percent rural		2.3					10.6											5.8
MARITAL CONDITION																		
Males 15 years old and over	1	92	3	20	1	1	54	5	12	17	7	1	1	17	10	2	5	54
Single		34		8		1	22	1	4	7	2	1		5	8		1	17
Married	1	49	2	10	1		26	3	6	8	5			8	2	1	1	29
Widowed		5	1	2			2	1	1	2			1	2			1	7
Divorced		4					1		1					2		1	2	1
Unknown							3											
Females 15 years old and over	1	76	1	15	1		35		10	13	9			13	2	1	1	54
Single		13		2			6		2	1	1			2				10
Married		47	1	8	1		24		6	10	6			9	2	1	1	28
Widowed	1	15		3			3		1	2	2			2				12
Divorced		1		2			1		1									4
Unknown							1											
FAMILIES																		
Number of families	2	68	2	16	1	1	37	2	11	13	7		1	15	4	2	4	53
Median size																		
Families having—																		
No children under 10	2	54	2	11	1	1	27	2	11	11	6		1	12	4	2	3	45
1 child under 10		7		4			6			1				1			1	4
2 children under 10		6		1			2			1				1				1
3 or more		1					2				1			1				3

CHARACTERISTICS OF NEGRO POPULATION BY COUNTIES: 1930—Continued

(See note at head of table)

SUBJECT	MONTANA—Continued																	
	Mc-Cone	Madi-son	Mea-gher	Mis-soula	Mus-selshell	Park	Petro-leum	Phil-lips	Pon-dera	Powell	Prai-rie	Rav-alli	Rich-land	Roose-velt	Rose-bud	San-ders	Sheri-dan	Silver Bow
POPULATION BY SEX																		
Negro population: 1930	2	7	3	121	1	5	3	4	5	28	1	7	3	1	7	7	2	174
Male	2	5	1	63	1	2	2	4	4	24	1	4	1	1	3	6	2	92
Female		2	2	58		3	1		1	4		3	2		4	1		82
Negro population: 1920		8	5	102	2	40		10		39		3	2	18	15	8	12	236
Male		6	2	57		24		7		38		1	1	15	7	8	7	136
Female		2	3	45	2	16		3		1		2	1	3	8		5	100
Percent of total population:																		
1930		0.1	0.1	0.6			0.1		0.1	0.5		0.1			0.1	0.1		0.3
1920		0.1	0.2	0.4		0.4		0.1		0.6				0.2	0.2	0.2	0.1	0.4
VOTING AGE: 1930																		
Total 21 years old and over	2	7	3	80	1	4	3	4	5	27	1	6	3	1	6	6	2	146
Male	2	5	1	42	1	2	2	4	4	24	1	3	1	1	2	6	2	81
Female		2	2	38		2	1		1	3		3	2		4			65
AGE: 1930																		
Under 5 years				11														8
Under 1 year				2														2
5 to 9 years				8		1						1			1			2
10 to 14 years				9														9
15 to 19 years				10														8
20 to 24 years				12				1		2	1				2	2		8
25 to 29 years	1			7						9					1			17
30 to 34 years				15		1				2								24
35 to 44 years	1	3	1	15	1	2		1	1	6		3		1		1		30
45 to 54 years		1	1	18					2	6					2	2	1	35
55 to 64 years		1		12		1	2	2	2	2			2			1	1	19
65 to 74 years		2	1	3						1		2						9
75 years and over				1								1	1		1	1		5
Unknown							1											
SCHOOL ATTENDANCE																		
Total 7 to 13 years, inclusive				12		1						1			1			6
Number attending school				12		1						1			1			6
Percent attending school																		
Total 14 and 15 years, inclusive				2														5
Number attending school				2														4
Percent attending school																		
Total 16 and 17 years, inclusive				3														2
Number attending school				3														2
Percent attending school																		
Total 18 to 20 years, inclusive				9						1						1		5
Number attending school				3														
Percent attending school																		
ILLITERACY																		
Total 10 years old and over	2	7	3	102	1	4	3	4	5	28	1	6	3	1	6	7	2	164
Number illiterate	1			4				1		1		2	3			1	1	3
Percent illiterate				3.9														1.8
Percent illiterate in 1920																		6.2
URBAN AND RURAL																		
Urban population				110	1	1				26								163
Percent urban				90.9														93.7
Rural population	2	7	3	11		4	3	4	5	2	1	7	3	1	7	7	2	11
Rural-farm	1	3				3	2	2				3	3		4		2	
Rural-nonfarm	1	4	3	11		1	1	2	5	2	1	4		1	3	7		11
Percent rural				9.1														6.3
MARITAL CONDITION																		
Males 15 years old and over	2	5	1	50	1	2	2	4	4	24	1	3	1	1	2	6	2	85
Single	1	4	1	18				2	1	18	1	1			1	3	2	35
Married	1			25	1	2	1	1	1	5		2	1	1	1	1		32
Widowed				2				1	2	1						2		11
Divorced		1		5														6
Unknown							1											1
Females 15 years old and over		2	2	43		2	1		1	4		3	2		4	1		70
Single			1	8		1				1		1			2			6
Married		1		21		1	1		1	3		2			2	1		40
Widowed		1	1	11									1					13
Divorced				3									1					10
Unknown																		1
FAMILIES																		
Number of families		3	3	41		1	1	1	1	5		4	3		2	4	1	66
Median size																		
Families having—																		
No children under 10		3	3	32		1	1	1	1	5		3	3		1	4	1	62
1 child under 10				5								1			1			2
2 children under 10				1														
3 or more				3														2

CHARACTERISTICS OF NEGRO POPULATION BY COUNTIES: 1930—Continued

(See note at head of table)

SUBJECT	MONTANA—Continued						NEBRASKA											
	Sweet Grass	Teton	Toole	Valley	Wheatland	Yellowstone	The State	Adams	Antelope	Blaine	Boone	Box Butte	Boyd	Brown	Buffalo	Burt	Butler	Cass
POPULATION BY SEX																		
Negro population: 1930	7	2	12	3	3	149	13,752	102	1	1	1	228	1	1	35	1	14	12
Male	4	2	9	2	3	78	7,063	54	1	1	1	122	1	1	34	1	7	7
Female	3	-	3	1	-	71	6,689	48	-	-	-	106	-	-	1	-	7	5
Negro population: 1920	-	3	5	4	8	130	13,242	91	4	1	11	173	1	-	68	22	16	21
Male	-	2	3	3	4	76	7,309	48	3	1	5	103	1	-	54	12	12	11
Female	-	1	2	1	4	54	5,933	43	1	-	6	70	-	-	14	10	4	10
Percent of total population:																		
1930	0.2	-	0.2	-	0.1	0.5	1.0	0.4	-	-	-	1.9	-	-	0.1	-	0.1	0.1
1920	-	0.1	0.1	-	0.1	0.4	1.0	0.4	-	0.1	0.1	2.1	-	-	0.3	0.2	0.1	0.1
VOTING AGE: 1930																		
Total 21 years old and over	6	2	12	3	3	119	9,521	83	1	1	1	135	1	1	4	1	7	7
Male	4	2	9	2	3	64	4,967	48	1	1	1	75	1	1	3	1	3	4
Female	2	-	3	1	-	55	4,554	35	-	-	-	60	-	-	1	-	4	3
AGE: 1930																		
Under 5 years	-	-	-	-	-	5	1,046	10	-	-	-	23	-	-	-	-	3	1
Under 1 year	-	-	-	-	-	-	217	4	-	-	-	4	-	-	-	-	1	-
5 to 9 years	-	-	-	-	-	7	1,101	1	-	-	-	28	-	-	1	-	2	2
10 to 14 years	-	-	-	-	-	9	930	5	-	-	-	16	-	-	10	-	1	1
15 to 19 years	1	-	-	-	-	8	962	3	-	-	-	25	-	-	18	-	1	1
20 to 24 years	1	-	-	-	-	4	1,122	6	-	-	-	16	-	-	2	-	-	-
25 to 29 years	-	-	-	-	-	10	1,404	8	-	-	-	28	-	-	-	-	-	-
30 to 34 years	-	-	2	-	1	11	1,314	14	-	-	-	14	-	-	1	-	2	-
35 to 44 years	1	-	2	2	-	29	2,697	17	1	-	1	31	-	-	-	1	2	2
45 to 54 years	3	1	6	1	1	38	1,919	19	-	1	-	36	-	1	2	-	2	1
55 to 64 years	1	1	-	-	1	19	762	10	-	-	-	8	-	-	-	-	-	2
65 to 74 years	-	-	2	-	-	9	316	4	-	-	-	1	-	-	1	-	-	2
75 years and over	-	-	-	-	-	-	160	4	-	-	-	2	1	-	-	-	1	-
Unknown	-	-	-	-	-	-	19	1	-	-	-	-	-	-	-	-	-	-
SCHOOL ATTENDANCE																		
Total 7 to 13 years, inclusive	-	-	-	-	-	14	1,400	6	-	-	-	29	-	-	9	-	2	2
Number attending school	-	-	-	-	-	13	1,378	5	-	-	-	29	-	-	9	-	2	2
Percent attending school	-	-	-	-	-	-	98.4	-	-	-	-	-	-	-	-	-	-	-
Total 14 and 15 years, inclusive	-	-	-	-	-	2	360	-	-	-	-	7	-	-	9	-	-	-
Number attending school	-	-	-	-	-	2	340	-	-	-	-	6	-	-	8	-	-	-
Percent attending school	-	-	-	-	-	-	94.4	-	-	-	-	-	-	-	-	-	-	-
Total 16 and 17 years, inclusive	1	-	-	-	-	3	385	2	-	-	-	11	-	-	7	-	-	1
Number attending school	-	-	-	-	-	3	252	1	-	-	-	5	-	-	7	-	-	1
Percent attending school	-	-	-	-	-	-	65.5	-	-	-	-	-	-	-	-	-	-	-
Total 18 to 20 years, inclusive	-	-	-	-	-	5	597	1	-	-	-	11	-	-	6	-	1	-
Number attending school	-	-	-	-	-	-	117	-	-	-	-	6	-	-	5	-	1	-
Percent attending school	-	-	-	-	-	-	19.6	-	-	-	-	-	-	-	-	-	-	-
ILLITERACY																		
Total 10 years old and over	7	2	12	3	3	137	11,605	91	1	1	1	177	1	1	34	1	9	9
Number illiterate	1	1	2	1	1	12	450	13	-	-	1	5	-	-	-	-	1	-
Percent illiterate	-	-	-	-	-	8.8	3.9	-	-	-	-	2.8	-	-	-	-	-	-
Percent illiterate in 1920	-	-	-	-	-	4.2	4.8	-	-	-	-	3.5	-	-	-	-	-	-
URBAN AND RURAL																		
Urban population	-	-	-	-	-	142	13,112	70	-	-	-	203	-	-	5	-	-	-
Percent urban	-	-	-	-	-	95.3	95.3	68.6	-	-	-	89.0	-	-	-	-	-	-
Rural population	7	2	12	3	3	7	640	32	1	1	1	25	1	1	30	1	14	12
Rural-farm	5	1	5	-	-	5	177	1	1	-	-	19	-	-	30	-	1	8
Rural-nonfarm	2	1	7	3	3	2	463	31	-	1	1	6	1	1	-	1	13	4
Percent rural	-	-	-	-	-	4.7	4.7	31.4	-	-	-	11.0	-	-	-	-	-	-
MARITAL CONDITION																		
Males 15 years old and over	4	2	9	2	3	70	5,502	48	1	1	1	86	1	1	23	1	3	5
Single	1	2	4	-	2	25	1,662	13	1	-	1	31	1	1	20	-	1	2
Married	2	-	4	1	-	37	3,159	24	-	-	-	48	-	-	3	-	2	2
Widowed	-	-	1	-	-	3	454	6	-	1	-	2	-	-	-	-	-	1
Divorced	-	-	-	1	1	5	212	3	-	-	-	5	-	-	-	1	-	-
Unknown	1	-	-	-	-	-	15	2	-	-	-	-	-	-	-	-	-	-
Females 15 years old and over	3	-	3	1	-	58	5,173	38	-	-	-	75	-	-	1	-	5	3
Single	1	-	-	-	-	6	845	4	-	-	-	16	-	-	-	-	3	-
Married	2	-	3	1	-	40	3,130	25	-	-	-	47	-	-	1	-	2	2
Widowed	-	-	-	-	-	10	967	7	-	-	-	8	-	-	-	-	-	1
Divorced	-	-	-	-	-	2	219	2	-	-	-	4	-	-	-	-	-	-
Unknown	-	-	-	-	-	-	12	-	-	-	-	-	-	-	-	-	-	-
FAMILIES																		
Number of families	2	1	6	2	1	64	3,700	25	1	1	1	54	1	-	1	-	2	3
Median size	-	-	-	-	-	-	2.41	-	-	-	-	-	-	-	-	-	-	-
Families having:																		
No children under 10	2	1	6	2	1	57	2,688	20	1	1	1	33	1	-	1	-	1	2
1 child under 10	-	-	-	-	-	5	480	1	-	-	-	8	-	-	-	-	-	-
2 children under 10	-	-	-	-	-	1	261	3	-	-	-	6	-	-	-	-	-	-
3 or more	-	-	-	-	-	1	271	1	-	-	-	7	-	-	-	-	1	1

CHARACTERISTICS OF NEGRO POPULATION BY COUNTIES: 1930—Continued

(See note at head of table)

SUBJECT	NEBRASKA—Continued																	
	Cherry	Cheyenne	Clay	Colfax	Custer	Dakota	Dawes	Dawson	Dixon	Dodge	Douglas	Fillmore	Frontier	Furnas	Gage	Garden	Grant	Greeley
POPULATION BY SEX																		
Negro population: 1930	33	15	1	8	17	77	46	13	1	58	11,166	23	5	1	91	1	5	4
Male	17	6	1	4	8	36	23	6		34	5,636	1	1	1	50		2	4
Female	16	9		4	9	41	23	7	1	24	5,530	22	4		41	1	3	
Negro population: 1920	90	18	5	11	33	20	45	13		51	10,341		11	6	87		13	4
Male	48	13	4	8	20	10	20	8		28	5,616		5	4	42		7	3
Female	42	5	1	3	13	10	25	5		23	4,725		6	2	45		6	1
Percent of total population:																		
1930	0.3	0.1		0.1	0.1	0.8	0.4	0.1		0.2	4.8	0.2	0.1		0.3		0.4	
1920	0.8	0.2		0.1	0.1	0.3	0.4	0.1		0.2	5.1		0.1	0.1	0.3		0.9	
VOTING AGE: 1930																		
Total 21 years old and over	18	12	1	5	9	50	35	6	1	46	7,760		1	1	50	1	3	1
Male	11	6	1	3	5	23	17	3		28	3,953			1	27		2	1
Female	7	6		2	4	27	18	3	1	18	3,807		1		23	1	1	
AGE: 1930																		
Under 5 years	3	2			2	7		1			881		1		15			
Under 1 year		1				2					174				4			
5 to 9 years	6	1		2	4	8	7	1		2	897		3		10			
10 to 14 years	4			1		9	1	2		5	733	3			10		1	2
15 to 19 years	2				2	3	2	3		5	738	20			5		1	1
20 to 24 years	1					3	3			7	919				8			
25 to 29 years					1	12	6			4	1,153				9		1	
30 to 34 years	1	2			2	5	1	1		4	1,110				3			
35 to 44 years	5	4		1	2	18	8	4	1	6	2,246		1		14			
45 to 54 years	5	5		1	1	3	6	1		16	1,551				9	1	2	1
55 to 64 years	2		1	2	1	4	4			2	579			1	7			
65 to 74 years	3				1	5	5				234				1			
75 years and over	1	1		1	1		3			7	108							
Unknown											17							
SCHOOL ATTENDANCE																		
Total 7 to 13 years, inclusive	7			2	2	12	5	1		6	1,129	3	2		14		1	2
Number attending school	7			2	2	12	5	1		6	1,111	3	2		14		1	2
Percent attending school											98.4							
Total 14 and 15 years, inclusive					1	1	2	2		1	277	3			3			1
Number attending school					1	1	2	2		1	263	3			3			1
Percent attending school											94.9							
Total 16 and 17 years, inclusive	1					3		2		2	283	5			1		1	
Number attending school	1					2		2		2	186	1						
Per cent attending school											65.7							
Total 18 to 20 years, inclusive	1				1		2			3	479	12			4			
Number attending school	1						1				75	2			1			
Percent attending school											15.7							
ILLITERACY																		
Total 10 years old and over	24	12	1	6	11	62	39	11	1	56	9,388	23	1	1	66	1	5	4
Number illiterate	2	1		1	1	11	4			4	352				5			
Percent illiterate											3.7							
Percent illiterate in 1920											4.5							
URBAN AND RURAL																		
Urban population		8		8	9	72	5			58	11,123				83			
Percent urban											99.6							
Rural population	33	7	1		8	5	41	13	1		43	23	5	1	8	1	5	4
Rural-farm	18		1		7	5	4				5		1	1		1	3	4
Rural-nonfarm	15	7			1		37	13	1		38	23	4		8		2	
Percent rural											0.4							
MARITAL CONDITION																		
Males 15 years old and over	11	6	1	3	5	25	19	5		31	4,361	1		1	29		2	2
Single	2	1		1	2	4	5	2		12	1,250	1		1	7			1
Married	6	5		1	3	18	10	3		16	2,557				19		2	
Widowed	2		1	1		3	4			2	375				2			1
Divorced	1									1	166				1			
Unknown											13							
Females 15 years old and over	9	6		2	6	28	19	4	1	20	4,294	19	1		27	1	2	
Single	2				1	1	1	1		3	663	18	1		7			
Married	6	6		1	3	19	11	3		15	2,586	1			18	1	2	
Widowed	1			1	2	8	5			2	848				1			
Divorced							2		1		185				1			
Unknown											12							
FAMILIES																		
Number of families	7	5		3	4	24	14	3	1	13	3,054		1	1	20		2	1
Median size											2.42							
Families having—																		
No children under 10	4	3		3	2	16	11	2	1	11	2,213			1	11		2	1
1 child under 10	2	1			1	3	2	1		2	393				3			
2 children under 10		1				3					224				1			
3 or more	1				1	2	1				224		1		5			

CHARACTERISTICS OF NEGRO POPULATION BY COUNTIES: 1930—Continued

(See note at head of table)

SUBJECT	NEBRASKA—Continued																	
	Hall	Hamilton	Harlan	Hitchcock	Holt	Howard	Jefferson	Keith	Keya paha	Kimball	Knox	Lancaster	Lincoln	Logan	Madison	Merrick	Morrill	Nemaha
POPULATION BY SEX																		
Negro population: 1930	132	3	9	3	6	1	10	4	1	1	5	1,138	35	10	41	28	2	11
Male	71	3	6	1	3	1	5	4	1	1	3	634	19	5	22	11	2	6
Female	61		3	2	3		5				2	504	16	5	19	17		5
Negro population: 1920	145	27	24	4	21	3	34	17	12	15	42	1,012	71	9	53	41	15	10
Male	85	18	15	2	11	2	19	13	7	15	20	569	53	5	31	16	9	7
Female	60	9	9	2	10	1	15	4	5		22	443	18	4	22	25	6	3
Percent of total population:																		
1930	0.5		0.1				0.1	0.1				1.1	0.1	0.5	0.2	0.3		0.1
1920	0.6	0.2	0.3	0.1	0.1		0.2	0.3	0.3	0.3	0.2	1.2	0.3	0.6	0.2	0.4	0.2	0.1
VOTING AGE: 1930																		
Total 21 years old and over	93	3	7	3	3	1	9	3	1	1	3	795	33	2	31	14	2	10
Male	49	3	4	1	1	1	5	3	1	1	2	461	18	1	15	8	2	5
Female	44		3	2	2		4				1	334	15	1	16	6		5
AGE: 1930																		
Under 5 years	6		1									69		1	1	4		
Under 1 year												13				2		
5 to 9 years	8				1						1	97		1	1	3		
10 to 14 years	14											77	2	3	2	5		
15 to 19 years	9		1		2		1				1	78		2	5	2		1
20 to 24 years	9				1		2	2				105	3	1	3	3	1	
25 to 29 years	13		1	1	1		2	1				118	5		2	2		
30 to 34 years	6	1										99	7		8	1		1
35 to 44 years	32	1	1	2	1		5	1		1	2	192	11	1	4	5	1	3
45 to 54 years	21	1	1			1			1		1	156	5	1	8	1		1
55 to 64 years	9		3									94	1		6	1		2
65 to 74 years	3											39	1					2
75 years and over	2		1									13			1	1		1
Unknown												1						
SCHOOL ATTENDANCE																		
Total 7 to 13 years, inclusive	17				1							110	2	3	2	5		
Number attending school	17				1							109	1	3	2	5		
Percent attending school												99.1						
Total 14 and 15 years, inclusive	5											31		1	3	2		
Number attending school	4											28		1	3	2		
Percent attending school																		
Total 16 and 17 years, inclusive	3		1		2		1				1	40		1	1	1		1
Number attending school	2		1									28		1	1	1		1
Percent attending school																		
Total 18 to 20 years, inclusive	5							1				50		2	3			
Number attending school	1											23						
Percent attending school																		
ILLITERACY																		
Total 10 years old and over	118	3	8	3	5	1	10	4	1	1	4	972	35	8	39	21	2	11
Number illiterate			1					1	1			30			2			3
Percent illiterate												3.1						
Percent illiterate in 1920	7.1											5.3						
URBAN AND RURAL																		
Urban population	120	3					10					997	35		27			7
Percent urban	90.9											87.6						
Rural population	12		9	3	6	1		4	1	1	5	141		10	14	28	2	4
Rural-farm	8		5						1		1	6		10		2		
Rural-nonfarm	4		4	3	6	1		4		1	4	135			14	26	2	4
Percent rural	9.1											12.4						
MARITAL CONDITION																		
Males 15 years old and over	56	3	5	1	2	1	5	4	1	1	3	509	18	3	20	8	2	6
Single	21	1	2		1	1		3	1	1	2	180	7	2	11	2	1	3
Married	31	2	3	1	1		5	1			1	268	10	1	8	6	1	2
Widowed	3											38						1
Divorced	1											23	1		1			
Unknown																		
Females 15 years old and over	48		3	2	3		5				1	386	15	2	17	8		5
Single	13		1		2		1					73	4	1	5	3		1
Married	27		2	2	1		4				1	243	10	1	6	5		1
Widowed	6											52	1		3			3
Divorced	2											18			3			
Unknown																		
FAMILIES																		
Number of families	35	1	5	1	1	1	4	3		1		276	12	1	7	5	2	4
Median size												2.45						
Families having—																		
No children under 10	27	1	4	1		1	4	3		1		196	12		5	2	2	4
1 child under 10	3		1		1							43			2	1		
2 children under 10	4											16		1				
3 or more	1											21				2		

CHARACTERISTICS OF NEGRO POPULATION BY COUNTIES: 1930—Continued

(See note at head of table)

SUBJECT	NEBRASKA—Continued																	
	Nuckolls	Otoe	Phelps	Platte	Red-willow	Rich-ardson	Sarpy	Saun-ders	Scotts Bluff	Sew-ard	Sheri-dan	Sher-man	Stan-ton	Thom-as	Thurs-ton	Wash-ington	Wayne	York
POPULATION BY SEX																		
Negro population: 1930	9	61	4	6	30	54	19	6	99	13	7	1	3	2	4	3	5	24
Male	5	30	3	4	22	28	11	5	64	4	7	-	1	1	3	2	3	12
Female	4	31	1	2	8	26	8	1	35	9	-	1	2	1	1	1	2	12
Negro population, 1920	11	57	19	17	21	57	43	14	79	12	8	-	1	14	9	13	12	25
Male	10	27	11	12	15	32	32	9	48	9	6	-	1	10	6	8	5	16
Female	1	30	8	5	6	25	11	5	31	3	2	-	-	4	3	5	7	9
Percent of total population:																		
1930	0.1	0.3	-	-	0.2	0.3	0.2	-	0.3	0.1	0.1	-	-	0.1	-	-	-	0.1
1920	0.1	0.3	0.2	0.1	0.2	0.3	0.5	0.1	0.4	0.1	0.1	-	-	0.8	0.1	0.1	0.1	0.1
VOTING AGE: 1930																		
Total 21 years old and over	5	39	3	4	21	43	16	6	85	1	5	1	2	2	1	3	5	23
Male	3	19	2	3	16	26	10	5	56	1	5	-	1	1	1	2	3	12
Female	2	20	1	1	5	17	6	1	29	-	-	1	1	1	-	1	2	11
AGE: 1930																		
Under 5 years	-	4	-	1	1	2	-	-	2	5	-	-	-	-	-	-	-	-
Under 1 years	-	1	-	1	1	2	-	-	2	5	-	-	-	-	-	-	-	-
5 to 9 years	1	4	-	-	1	3	1	-	3	-	-	-	-	-	1	-	-	-
10 to 14 years	3	7	1	-	3	3	1	-	2	1	1	-	-	-	-	-	-	1
15 to 19 years	-	6	-	-	4	3	1	-	7	5	1	-	1	-	2	-	-	-
20 to 24 years	-	3	-	2	3	3	2	-	10	1	1	-	-	-	-	1	-	1
25 to 29 years	-	4	-	-	6	6	-	-	18	-	1	-	-	-	-	-	-	1
30 to 34 years	3	2	1	-	3	7	-	1	11	-	-	-	-	-	-	1	-	2
35 to 44 years	-	15	1	2	4	5	2	2	24	-	-	-	2	-	1	-	3	8
45 to 54 years	1	7	1	-	4	14	7	-	14	-	1	1	-	-	-	-	2	5
55 to 64 years	-	4	-	-	-	6	3	1	4	1	2	-	-	-	-	1	-	1
65 to 74 years	1	3	-	1	1	1	1	-	1	-	-	-	-	1	-	-	-	4
75 years and over	-	2	-	-	-	1	1	2	3	-	-	-	-	1	-	-	-	1
Unknown	-	-	-	-	-	-	-	-	-	-	-	-	-	-	-	-	-	-
SCHOOL ATTENDANCE																		
Total 7 to 13 years, inclusive	2	9	-	-	4	3	2	-	4	-	1	-	-	-	1	-	-	-
Number attending school	2	9	-	-	3	3	2	-	4	-	1	-	-	-	1	-	-	-
Percent attending school	-	-	-	-	-	-	-	-	-	-	-	-	-	-	-	-	-	-
Total 14 and 15 years, inclusive	1	4	1	-	-	1	-	-	-	2	-	-	1	-	-	-	-	1
Number attending school	1	4	1	-	-	1	-	-	-	2	-	-	1	-	-	-	-	1
Percent attending school	-	-	-	-	-	-	-	-	-	-	-	-	-	-	-	-	-	-
Total 16 and 17 years, inclusive	-	2	-	-	3	1	1	-	2	3	1	-	-	-	1	-	-	-
Number attending school	-	2	-	-	2	-	-	-	2	2	-	-	-	-	1	-	-	-
Percent attending school	-	-	-	-	-	-	-	-	-	-	-	-	-	-	-	-	-	-
Total 18 to 20 years, inclusive	-	3	-	1	1	2	-	-	5	2	-	-	-	-	1	-	-	-
Number attending school	-	-	-	-	-	1	-	-	-	-	-	-	-	-	-	-	-	-
Percent attending school	-	-	-	-	-	-	-	-	-	-	-	-	-	-	-	-	-	-
ILLITERACY																		
Total 10 years old and over	8	53	4	5	28	49	18	6	94	8	7	1	3	2	3	3	5	24
Number illiterate	-	2	1	-	-	-	4	-	3	-	-	-	-	-	-	-	-	1
Percent illiterate	-	-	-	-	-	-	-	-	-	-	-	-	-	-	-	-	-	-
Percent illiterate in 1920	-	-	-	-	-	-	-	-	-	-	-	-	-	-	-	-	-	-
URBAN AND RURAL																		
Urban population	3	61	4	5	30	51	-	4	86	1	-	-	-	-	-	3	-	21
Percent urban	-	-	-	-	-	-	-	-	-	-	-	-	-	-	-	-	-	-
Rural population	6	-	-	1	-	3	19	2	13	12	7	1	3	2	4	-	5	3
Rural-farm	-	-	-	1	-	1	12	-	-	12	5	-	-	-	-	-	-	3
Rural-nonfarm	6	-	-	-	-	2	7	2	13	-	2	1	3	2	4	-	5	-
Percent rural	-	-	-	-	-	-	-	-	-	-	-	-	-	-	-	-	-	-
MARITAL CONDITION																		
Males 15 years old and over	3	23	2	3	18	27	11	5	60	1	6	-	1	1	3	2	3	12
Single	-	7	-	-	8	11	4	1	23	1	3	-	-	-	2	-	-	3
Married	2	13	1	3	9	15	5	2	32	-	2	-	1	1	1	2	3	7
Widowed	1	2	-	-	-	1	2	2	1	-	-	-	-	-	-	-	-	2
Divorced	-	1	1	-	1	-	-	-	4	-	1	-	-	-	-	-	-	-
Unknown	-	-	-	-	-	-	-	-	-	-	-	-	-	-	-	-	-	-
Females 15 years old and over	2	23	1	2	7	19	6	1	32	6	-	1	2	1	-	1	2	11
Single	-	7	-	-	2	1	1	-	1	6	-	1	1	-	-	-	-	-
Married	2	9	1	1	3	14	5	1	27	-	-	-	1	1	-	1	2	10
Widowed	-	7	-	1	1	4	-	-	4	-	-	-	-	-	-	-	-	1
Divorced	-	-	-	-	1	-	-	-	-	-	-	-	-	-	-	-	-	-
Unknown	-	-	-	-	-	-	-	-	-	-	-	-	-	-	-	-	-	-
FAMILIES																		
Number of families	1	16	2	1	7	18	4	3	32	1	1	-	1	2	1	1	1	7
Median size	-	-	-	-	-	-	-	-	-	-	-	-	-	-	-	-	-	-
Families having—																		
No children under 10	-	11	2	-	6	16	3	3	28	1	1	-	1	2	-	1	1	7
1 child under 10	1	3	-	1	-	1	1	-	4	-	-	-	-	-	1	-	-	-
2 children under 10	-	1	-	-	1	-	-	-	-	-	-	-	-	-	-	-	-	-
3 or more	-	1	-	-	-	1	-	-	-	-	-	-	-	-	-	-	-	-

CHARACTERISTICS OF NEGRO POPULATION BY COUNTIES: 1930—Continued

(See note at head of table)

SUBJECT	NEVADA															
	The State	Churchill	Clark	Douglas	Elko	Esmeralda	Humboldt	Lander	Lincoln	Lyon	Mineral	Nye	Ormsby	Pershing	Washoe	White Pine
POPULATION BY SEX																
Negro population: 1930	516	1	150	2	75	5	36	10	3	7	4	19	13	6	143	42
Male	277	1	77	1	36	3	22	2	2	6	2	9	11	4	79	22
Female	239	--------	73	1	39	2	14	8	1	1	2	10	2	2	64	20
Negro population: 1920	346	12	60	4	34	21	34	10	1	12	4	24	11	7	69	43
Male	196	11	34	4	18	10	16	2	--------	7	4	13	10	3	38	26
Female	150	1	26	--------	16	11	18	8	1	5	--------	11	1	4	31	17
Percent of total population:																
1930	0.6	--------	1.8	0.1	0.8	0.5	0.9	0.6	0.1	0.2	0.2	0.5	0.6	0.2	0.5	0.4
1920	0.4	0.3	1.2	0.2	0.4	0.9	0.9	0.7	--------	0.3	0.2	0.4	0.4	0.2	0.4	0.5
VOTING AGE: 1930																
Total 21 years old and over	439	--------	118	2	66	5	27	6	3	6	3	19	12	5	128	39
Male	242	--------	62	1	31	3	20	1	2	5	2	9	10	3	73	20
Female	197	--------	56	1	35	2	7	5	1	1	1	10	2	2	55	19
AGE: 1930																
Under 5 years	21	--------	12	--------	4	--------	1	2	--------	--------	--------	--------	--------	--------	2	--------
Under 1 year	8	--------	4	--------	1	--------	1	2	--------	--------	--------	--------	--------	--------	--------	--------
5 to 9 years	23	--------	12	--------	1	--------	4	--------	--------	1	1	--------	1	--------	3	--------
10 to 14 years	13	--------	4	--------	--------	--------	1	1	--------	--------	--------	--------	--------	--------	4	3
15 to 19 years	15	--------	4	--------	2	--------	3	--------	--------	--------	--------	--------	--------	1	5	--------
20 to 24 years	29	1	8	--------	4	--------	4	4	1	--------	--------	--------	--------	1	5	1
25 to 29 years	44	--------	11	--------	7	--------	5	2	--------	--------	--------	1	1	--------	15	2
30 to 34 years	50	--------	13	--------	7	--------	2	--------	--------	1	1	1	1	--------	18	6
35 to 44 years	133	--------	42	--------	18	1	8	--------	1	1	--------	4	4	1	43	10
45 to 54 years	102	--------	26	--------	17	4	3	--------	1	2	1	5	2	1	30	10
55 to 64 years	55	--------	11	1	9	--------	4	--------	--------	2	1	3	3	2	12	7
65 to 74 years	21	--------	3	--------	6	--------	1	1	--------	--------	--------	3	--------	--------	4	3
75 years and over	8	--------	2	1	--------	--------	--------	--------	--------	--------	--------	2	1	--------	2	--------
Unknown	2	--------	2	--------	--------	--------	--------	--------	--------	--------	--------	--------	--------	--------	--------	--------
SCHOOL ATTENDANCE																
Total 7 to 13 years, inclusive	24	--------	13	--------	1	--------	2	1	--------	1	--------	--------	--------	--------	4	2
Number attending school	21	--------	10	--------	1	--------	2	1	--------	1	--------	--------	--------	--------	4	2
Percent attending school	--------	--------	--------	--------	--------	--------	--------	--------	--------	--------	--------	--------	--------	--------	--------	--------
Total 14 and 15 years, inclusive	4	--------	1	--------	1	--------	--------	--------	--------	--------	--------	--------	--------	--------	1	1
Number attending school	4	--------	1	--------	1	--------	--------	--------	--------	--------	--------	--------	--------	--------	1	1
Percent attending school	--------	--------	--------	--------	--------	--------	--------	--------	--------	--------	--------	--------	--------	--------	--------	--------
Total 16 and 17 years, inclusive	7	--------	2	--------	--------	--------	2	--------	--------	--------	--------	--------	--------	1	2	--------
Number attending school	4	--------	--------	--------	--------	--------	2	--------	--------	--------	--------	--------	--------	1	1	--------
Percent attending school	--------	--------	--------	--------	--------	--------	--------	--------	--------	--------	--------	--------	--------	--------	--------	--------
Total 18 to 20 years, inclusive	10	1	1	--------	3	--------	1	1	--------	--------	--------	--------	--------	--------	3	--------
Number attending school	1	--------	--------	--------	--------	--------	--------	1	--------	--------	--------	--------	--------	--------	--------	--------
Percent attending school	--------	--------	--------	--------	--------	--------	--------	--------	--------	--------	--------	--------	--------	--------	--------	--------
ILLITERACY																
Total 10 years old and over	472	1	126	2	70	5	31	8	3	6	3	19	12	6	138	42
Number illiterate	7	--------	2	--------	--------	--------	--------	--------	--------	--------	--------	--------	--------	--------	4	1
Percent illiterate	1.5	--------	1.6	--------	--------	--------	--------	--------	--------	--------	--------	--------	--------	--------	2.9	--------
Percent illiterate in 1920	5.1	--------	--------	--------	--------	--------	--------	--------	--------	--------	--------	--------	--------	--------	--------	--------
URBAN AND RURAL																
Urban population	364	--------	144	--------	65	--------	--------	--------	--------	--------	--------	--------	--------	--------	136	19
Percent urban	70.5	--------	96.0	--------	--------	--------	--------	--------	--------	--------	--------	--------	--------	--------	95.1	--------
Rural population	152	1	6	2	10	5	36	10	3	7	4	19	13	6	7	23
Rural-farm	17	1	3	1	2	1	--------	--------	--------	2	1	1	1	1	1	2
Rural-nonfarm	135	--------	3	1	8	4	36	10	3	5	3	18	12	5	6	21
Percent rural	29.5	--------	4.0	--------	--------	--------	--------	--------	--------	--------	--------	--------	--------	--------	4.9	--------
MARITAL CONDITION																
Males 15 years old and over	251	1	63	1	33	3	21	2	2	5	2	9	10	4	75	20
Single	91	1	19	1	14	--------	14	1	2	3	1	3	6	2	23	1
Married	124	--------	39	--------	16	3	5	1	--------	1	1	4	3	2	40	9
Widowed	15	--------	1	--------	2	--------	1	--------	--------	1	--------	--------	1	--------	4	5
Divorced	21	--------	4	--------	1	--------	1	--------	--------	--------	--------	2	--------	--------	8	5
Unknown	--------	--------	--------	--------	--------	--------	--------	--------	--------	--------	--------	--------	--------	--------	--------	--------
Females 15 years old and over	208	--------	59	1	37	2	9	5	1	1	1	10	2	2	59	19
Single	40	--------	7	1	9	--------	4	2	1	--------	--------	1	--------	--------	12	3
Married	123	--------	40	--------	20	2	2	3	--------	1	--------	6	2	2	34	11
Widowed	34	--------	11	--------	4	--------	3	--------	--------	--------	1	3	--------	--------	9	3
Divorced	11	--------	1	--------	4	--------	--------	--------	--------	--------	--------	--------	--------	--------	4	2
Unknown	--------	--------	--------	--------	--------	--------	--------	--------	--------	--------	--------	--------	--------	--------	--------	--------
FAMILIES																
Number of families	194	--------	63	--------	27	2	7	2	1	4	2	13	5	1	45	22
Median size	1.50	--------	--------	--------	--------	--------	--------	--------	--------	--------	--------	--------	--------	--------	--------	--------
Families having—																
No children under 10	170	--------	50	--------	26	2	4	--------	1	4	2	13	4	1	41	22
1 child under 10	17	--------	8	--------	--------	--------	2	2	--------	--------	--------	--------	1	--------	4	--------
2 children under 10	5	--------	3	--------	1	--------	1	--------	--------	--------	--------	--------	--------	--------	--------	--------
3 or more	2	--------	2	--------	--------	--------	--------	--------	--------	--------	--------	--------	--------	--------	--------	--------

CHARACTERISTICS OF NEGRO POPULATION BY COUNTIES: 1930—Continued

(See note at head of table)

SUBJECT	NEW HAMPSHIRE: The State	Belknap	Carroll	Cheshire	Coos	Grafton	Hillsborough	Merrimack	Rockingham	Strafford	Sullivan	NEW JERSEY: The State	Atlantic	Bergen	Burlington	Camden	Cape May	Cumberland
POPULATION BY SEX																		
Negro population: 1930	790	37	15	39	4	60	108	104	378	9	36	208, 828	19, 703	8, 872	6, 762	16, 813	2, 782	4, 748
Male	524	25	7	25	2	29	69	53	292	7	15	102, 929	9, 547	4, 119	3, 473	8, 409	1, 353	2, 445
Female	266	12	8	14	2	31	39	51	86	2	21	105, 899	10, 156	4, 753	3, 289	8, 404	1, 429	2, 303
Negro population: 1920	621	49	9	21	26	74	113	65	208	37	19	117, 132	12, 597	4, 136	4, 493	12, 107	1, 560	3, 094
Male	333	24	5	14	20	40	66	34	106	17	7	57, 432	6, 044	1, 906	2, 266	6, 108	771	1, 600
Female	288	25	4	7	6	34	47	31	102	20	12	59, 700	6, 553	2, 230	2, 227	5, 999	789	1, 494
Percent of total population:																		
1930	0. 2	0. 2	0. 1	0. 1	-	0. 1	0. 1	0. 2	0. 7	-	0. 1	5. 2	15. 8	2. 4	7. 2	6. 7	9. 4	6. 8
1920	0. 1	0. 2	0. 1	0. 1	0. 1	0. 2	0. 1	0. 1	0. 4	0. 1	0. 1	3. 7	15. 0	2. 0	5. 5	6. 4	8. 0	5. 0
VOTING AGE: 1930																		
Total 21 years old and over	566	20	9	29	3	30	77	52	316	9	21	131, 896	14, 199	5, 537	3, 949	10, 091	1, 706	2, 713
Male	409	13	4	19	2	15	53	28	256	7	12	65, 750	6, 851	2, 578	2, 070	5, 111	821	1, 460
Female	157	7	5	10	1	15	24	24	60	2	9	66, 146	7, 348	2, 959	1, 879	4, 980	885	1, 253
AGE: 1930																		
Under 5 years	48	5	3	2	1	9	5	9	9	-	5	19, 790	1, 308	808	699	1, 692	239	521
Under 1 year	10	-	-	-	1	1	3	4	1	-	-	3, 945	244	174	140	333	49	104
5 to 9 years	45	3	2	4	-	6	5	12	11	-	2	19, 824	1, 406	842	773	1, 782	284	490
10 to 14 years	48	3	1	1	-	6	8	16	11	-	2	16, 598	1, 237	716	640	1, 556	277	472
15 to 19 years	63	5	-	1	-	8	9	10	24	-	6	16, 795	1, 275	765	582	1, 417	246	468
20 to 24 years	86	1	2	7	-	7	10	10	45	-	4	21, 295	1, 749	1, 039	601	1, 402	179	420
25 to 29 years	59	1	1	6	-	2	7	3	35	1	3	23, 424	2, 156	1, 026	608	1, 518	192	392
30 to 34 years	71	2	-	3	-	3	15	5	42	1	-	19, 787	2, 011	793	563	1, 378	185	383
35 to 44 years	160	6	2	3	2	6	23	12	98	2	6	33, 874	3, 934	1, 352	999	2, 747	449	651
45 to 54 years	135	5	3	6	1	7	20	14	74	2	3	22, 232	2, 848	941	704	1, 863	392	472
55 to 64 years	43	2	1	3	-	3	4	7	18	1	4	9, 623	1, 118	369	365	897	208	249
65 to 74 years	22	3	-	-	-	2	2	5	7	2	1	3, 678	428	144	151	368	79	143
75 years and over	7	1	-	-	-	1	-	1	4	-	-	1, 505	173	58	65	157	50	65
Unknown	3	-	-	3	-	-	-	-	-	-	-	403	60	19	12	36	2	22
SCHOOL ATTENDANCE																		
Total 7 to 13 years, inclusive	66	5	2	2	-	7	10	22	15	-	3	25, 050	1, 854	1, 046	971	2, 289	406	664
Number attending school	63	5	1	2	-	7	8	22	15	-	3	24, 286	1, 820	1, 026	946	2, 138	395	643
Percent attending school	-	-	-	-	-	-	-	-	-	-	-	97. 0	98. 2	98. 1	97. 4	93. 4	97. 3	96. 8
Total 14 and 15 years, inclusive	25	1	-	1	-	5	5	6	5	-	2	6, 280	442	285	249	593	101	169
Number attending school	22	1	-	1	-	4	5	6	4	-	1	5, 545	397	251	213	516	88	143
Percent attending school	-	-	-	-	-	-	-	-	-	-	-	88. 3	89. 8	88. 1	85. 5	87. 0	87. 1	84. 6
Total 16 and 17 years, inclusive	23	3	-	-	-	3	2	5	10	-	-	6, 605	515	296	248	565	100	199
Number attending school	11	-	-	-	-	2	-	3	6	-	-	2, 971	321	126	110	238	58	76
Percent attending school	-	-	-	-	-	-	-	-	-	-	-	45. 0	62. 3	42. 6	44. 4	42. 1	58. 0	38. 2
Total 18 to 20 years, inclusive	46	2	-	3	-	3	9	7	18	-	4	11, 112	821	538	332	840	132	274
Number attending school	10	-	-	-	-	1	4	1	2	-	2	1, 284	156	49	49	96	31	31
Percent attending school	-	-	-	-	-	-	-	-	-	-	-	11. 6	19. 0	9. 1	14. 8	11. 4	23. 5	11. 3
ILLITERACY																		
Total 10 years old and over	697	29	10	33	3	45	98	83	358	9	29	169, 214	16, 989	7, 222	5, 290	13, 339	2, 259	3, 737
Number illiterate	27	3	-	1	-	3	12	5	1	1	1	8, 711	485	313	366	723	171	375
Percent illiterate	3. 9	-	-	-	-	-	-	-	0. 3	-	-	5. 1	2. 9	4. 3	6. 9	5. 4	7. 6	10. 0
Percent illiterate in 1920	6. 7	-	-	-	-	-	-	-	4. 1	-	-	6. 1	4. 1	4. 6	8. 1	9. 2	7. 2	11. 6
URBAN AND RURAL																		
Urban population	594	9	-	12	-	7	92	69	364	6	35	174, 985	18, 395	7, 869	2, 654	13, 414	1, 624	2, 004
Percent urban	75. 2	-	-	-	-	-	85. 2	66. 3	96. 3	-	-	83. 8	93. 4	88. 7	39. 2	79. 8	58. 4	42. 2
Rural population	196	28	15	27	4	53	16	35	14	3	1	33, 843	1, 308	1, 003	4, 108	3, 399	1, 158	2, 744
Rural-farm	47	2	3	6	1	8	10	15	2	-	-	4, 597	193	17	519	147	78	977
Rural-nonfarm	149	26	12	21	3	45	6	20	12	3	1	29, 246	1, 115	986	3, 589	3, 252	1, 080	1, 767
Percent rural	24. 8	-	-	-	-	-	14. 8	33. 7	3. 7	-	-	16. 2	6. 6	11. 3	60. 8	20. 2	41. 6	57. 8
MARITAL CONDITION																		
Males 15 years old and over	457	17	4	22	2	21	57	35	279	7	13	75, 094	7, 537	2, 975	2, 409	5, 937	957	1, 710
Single	192	8	1	10	1	10	25	18	112	2	5	24, 628	2, 514	879	843	1, 901	278	592
Married	237	7	2	10	1	10	31	14	151	3	8	45, 928	4, 440	1, 958	1, 424	3, 571	609	981
Widowed	18	1	1	2	-	-	-	3	10	1	-	3, 994	515	123	127	432	63	125
Divorced	9	1	-	-	-	1	1	-	5	1	-	432	54	7	13	22	7	12
Unknown	1	-	-	-	-	-	-	-	1	-	-	112	14	8	2	11	-	-
Females 15 years old and over	192	9	5	10	1	18	33	32	68	2	14	77, 522	8, 215	3, 531	2, 241	5, 846	1, 025	1, 555
Single	57	4	1	3	-	4	8	10	20	1	6	18, 041	1, 892	899	536	1, 346	201	404
Married	112	5	4	7	1	11	24	17	36	-	7	47, 247	4, 635	2, 136	1, 402	3, 631	623	964
Widowed	19	-	-	-	-	3	1	3	10	1	1	11, 452	1, 611	467	283	828	193	171
Divorced	4	-	-	-	-	-	-	2	2	-	-	674	63	24	15	34	7	16
Unknown	-	-	-	-	-	-	-	-	-	-	-	108	14	5	5	7	1	-
FAMILIES																		
Number of families	117	5	3	7	1	8	23	18	43	3	6	48, 636	4, 907	1, 817	1, 475	4, 003	750	1, 128
Median size	2. 42	-	-	-	-	-	-	-	-	-	-	2. 92	2. 38	3. 19	3. 31	2. 92	2. 49	2. 96
Families having—																		
No children under 10	85	4	3	4	-	3	18	12	35	3	3	31, 140	3, 654	1, 127	842	2, 565	517	692
1 child under 10	18	-	-	1	1	3	3	5	4	-	1	7, 416	609	274	259	586	114	172
2 children under 10	8	1	-	2	-	2	2	-	-	-	1	4, 449	302	187	144	333	46	125
3 or more	6	-	-	-	-	-	-	1	4	-	1	5, 631	342	229	230	519	73	139

CHARACTERISTICS OF NEGRO POPULATION BY COUNTIES: 1930—Continued

(See note at head of table)

SUBJECT	NEW JERSEY—Continued															NEW MEXICO		
	Essex	Gloucester	Hudson	Hunterdon	Mercer	Middlesex	Monmouth	Morris	Ocean	Passaic	Salem	Somerset	Sussex	Union	Warren	The State	Bernalillo	Chaves
POPULATION BY SEX																		
Negro population: 1930	60,236	6,077	15,970	407	11,949	5,895	13,897	3,269	1,258	5,518	4,763	1,628	119	17,859	303	2,850	554	362
Male	28,663	3,204	7,964	191	6,233	3,238	6,796	1,559	626	2,725	2,568	835	64	8,762	155	1,531	282	178
Female	31,573	2,873	8,006	216	5,716	2,657	7,101	1,710	632	2,793	2,195	795	55	9,097	148	1,319	272	184
Negro population: 1920	28,956	3,154	9,351	359	6,991	2,815	8,938	1,861	566	2,522	3,962	1,221	90	8,087	272	5,733	302	191
Male	13,760	1,589	4,789	152	3,571	1,556	4,197	892	223	1,207	2,132	629	51	3,836	153	4,593	149	93
Female	15,196	1,565	4,562	207	3,420	1,259	4,741	969	343	1,315	1,830	592	39	4,251	119	1,140	153	98
Percent of total population: 1930	7.2	8.6	2.3	1.2	6.4	2.8	9.4	3.0	3.8	1.8	12.9	2.5	0.4	5.9	0.6	0.7	1.2	1.9
1920	4.4	6.5	1.5	1.1	4.4	1.7	8.5	2.3	2.6	1.0	10.8	2.5	0.4	4.0	0.6	1.6	1.0	1.6
VOTING AGE: 1930																		
Total 21 years old and over	38,928	3,340	10,101	233	7,182	3,449	8,958	2,190	849	3,449	2,724	1,019	77	11,005	197	1,768	366	230
Male	18,591	1,839	5,205	88	3,921	1,956	4,346	1,080	432	1,762	1,553	533	41	5,399	113	981	190	116
Female	20,337	1,501	4,896	145	3,261	1,493	4,612	1,110	417	1,687	1,171	486	36	5,606	84	787	176	114
AGE: 1930																		
Under 5 years	5,603	695	1,600	33	1,279	655	1,162	246	121	579	456	155	10	1,905	24	249	42	23
Under 1 year	1,139	128	360	9	236	130	207	53	19	118	88	30	1	379	4	45	9	—
5 to 9 years	5,380	723	1,516	29	1,306	637	1,311	251	106	530	512	141	11	1,764	30	273	52	30
10 to 14 years	4,439	631	1,187	27	983	540	1,124	230	79	378	479	132	8	1,442	26	249	46	34
15 to 19 years	4,672	576	1,243	75	982	522	1,088	278	79	440	494	150	10	1,409	24	259	41	35
20 to 24 years	6,797	550	1,752	41	1,150	574	1,277	347	120	712	480	178	12	1,895	20	236	41	35
25 to 29 years	7,768	499	2,005	34	1,346	699	1,243	384	125	690	361	148	14	2,195	21	245	40	30
30 to 34 years	6,336	400	1,584	32	1,147	582	1,156	322	119	541	370	129	10	1,725	21	223	44	27
35 to 44 years	10,193	850	2,516	56	1,819	861	2,208	516	203	800	687	234	21	2,736	42	516	107	63
45 to 54 years	5,793	690	1,561	37	1,075	505	1,837	395	178	527	487	175	15	1,696	41	364	94	48
55 to 64 years	2,146	315	706	29	529	196	891	195	81	204	261	109	4	721	30	157	28	22
65 to 74 years	767	92	230	7	179	87	383	74	31	71	108	50	2	267	17	50	15	13
75 years and over	291	56	59	7	82	30	159	25	15	44	56	25	2	79	7	23	3	2
Unknown	56	—	11	—	72	7	58	6	1	2	12	2	—	25	—	6	1	—
SCHOOL ATTENDANCE																		
Total 7 to 13 years, inclusive	6,734	944	1,856	38	1,528	809	1,681	330	122	633	704	191	14	2,196	40	374	71	51
Number attending school	6,506	916	1,805	37	1,491	788	1,639	325	117	622	693	183	13	2,145	38	353	67	45
Percent attending school	96.6	97.0	97.3	—	97.6	97.4	97.5	98.5	95.9	98.3	98.4	95.8	—	97.7	—	94.4	—	—
Total 14 and 15 years, inclusive	1,644	237	448	11	408	202	433	102	29	129	184	52	6	546	10	90	12	11
Number attending school	1,494	203	411	8	364	149	396	89	25	121	134	39	4	492	8	81	11	11
Percent attending school	90.9	85.7	91.7	—	89.2	73.8	91.5	87.3	—	93.8	72.8	—	—	90.1	—	—	—	—
Total 16 and 17 years, inclusive	1,782	241	475	33	392	202	429	96	33	177	197	69	3	542	11	115	18	16
Number attending school	753	101	195	5	190	77	216	53	20	79	67	20	—	263	3	63	9	9
Percent attending school	42.3	41.9	41.1	—	48.5	38.1	50.3	—	—	44.6	34.0	—	—	48.5	—	54.8	—	—
Total 18 to 20 years, inclusive	3,338	338	874	47	615	315	697	207	56	345	297	89	6	941	10	153	26	23
Number attending school	308	39	88	3	79	40	99	34	8	26	21	4	—	123	—	29	6	3
Percent attending school	9.2	11.5	10.1	—	12.8	12.7	14.2	16.4	—	7.5	7.1	—	—	13.1	—	19.0	—	—
ILLITERACY																		
Total 10 years old and over	49,253	4,659	12,854	345	9,364	4,603	11,424	2,772	1,031	4,409	3,795	1,332	98	14,190	249	2,328	460	309
Number illiterate	2,327	344	394	15	744	279	522	215	55	296	327	111	6	625	18	140	10	24
Percent illiterate	4.7	7.4	3.1	4.3	7.9	6.1	4.6	7.8	5.3	6.7	8.6	8.3	—	4.4	7.2	6.0	2.2	7.8
Percent illiterate in 1920	4.0	9.8	4.1	11.5	7.8	6.6	6.0	5.2	2.0	4.3	10.1	11.3	—	7.4	11.0	4.3	4.3	6.5
URBAN AND RURAL																		
Urban population	59,489	2,453	15,970	168	9,347	4,759	9,690	2,329	—	5,109	2,244	761	27	16,545	134	1,718	441	343
Percent urban	98.8	40.4	100.0	41.3	78.2	80.7	69.7	71.2	—	92.6	47.1	46.7	22.7	92.6	44.2	60.3	79.6	94.8
Rural population	747	3,624	—	239	2,602	1,136	4,207	940	1,258	409	2,519	867	92	1,314	169	1,132	113	19
Rural-farm	16	899	—	35	218	85	399	50	11	19	792	113	11	14	4	504	3	7
Rural-nonfarm	731	2,725	—	204	2,384	1,051	3,808	890	1,247	390	1,727	754	81	1,300	165	628	110	12
Percent rural	1.2	59.6	—	58.7	21.8	19.3	30.3	28.8	100.0	7.4	52.9	53.3	77.3	7.4	55.8	39.7	20.4	5.2
MARITAL CONDITION																		
Males 15 years old and over	21,080	2,198	5,894	149	4,486	2,297	4,977	1,211	486	1,985	1,861	615	50	6,155	126	1,141	211	143
Single	6,545	777	1,978	88	1,493	868	1,645	390	152	643	839	234	20	1,908	41	364	54	59
Married	13,513	1,294	3,609	53	2,674	1,313	2,919	738	300	1,241	903	343	27	3,943	75	661	139	75
Widowed	874	118	267	8	278	97	371	65	32	86	110	36	3	257	7	75	10	8
Divorced	118	8	38	—	24	13	29	17	1	15	9	2	—	40	3	40	8	1
Unknown	30	1	2	—	17	6	13	1	—	—	—	—	—	7	—	1	—	—
Females 15 years old and over	23,739	1,830	5,773	169	3,895	1,766	5,323	1,331	467	2,046	1,455	585	40	6,593	97	938	203	132
Single	5,631	385	1,170	49	922	319	1,222	349	86	501	391	168	8	1,548	14	158	29	24
Married	14,395	1,247	3,684	83	2,411	1,222	3,085	784	293	1,233	869	349	27	4,103	71	618	137	83
Widowed	3,440	193	862	34	528	196	962	179	84	290	184	66	5	865	11	128	30	21
Divorced	253	5	52	3	23	20	44	17	4	21	9	2	—	61	1	32	7	4
Unknown	20	—	5	—	11	9	10	2	—	1	2	—	—	16	—	2	—	—
FAMILIES																		
Number of families	14,280	1,343	3,878	58	2,410	1,326	3,409	679	321	1,315	1,094	350	24	3,997	72	799	166	102
Median size	2.91	3.24	3.03	—	3.34	3.02	2.66	3.03	2.29	3.05	2.76	3.03	—	3.21	—	2.28	2.29	2.11
Families having—																		
No children under 10	9,193	759	2,447	35	1,338	770	2,333	449	229	798	711	214	15	2,405	47	571	128	75
1 child under 10	2,274	213	619	12	407	213	435	103	38	221	164	57	7	624	14	95	19	10
2 children under 10	1,320	141	375	3	243	145	294	60	19	148	100	37	—	421	6	57	6	7
3 or more	1,493	230	437	8	422	198	347	66	35	148	119	42	2	547	5	76	13	10

CHARACTERISTICS OF NEGRO POPULATION BY COUNTIES: 1930—Continued

(See note at head of table)

SUBJECT	NEW MEXICO—Continued																	
	Colfax	Curry	Dona Ana	Eddy	Grant	Guadalupe	Hidalgo	Lea	Lincoln	Luna	McKinley	Mora	Otero	Quay	Rio Arriba	Roosevelt	Sandoval	San Juan
POPULATION BY SEX																		
Negro population: 1930	170	85	649	239	124	2	14	38	15	56	200	3	93	23	10	3		2
Male	80	41	355	126	74	2	8	23	10	31	113	2	54	11	9	2	3	1
Female	90	44	294	113	50		6	15	5	25	87	1	39	12	1	1	2	1
Negro population: 1920	238	32	78	89	149	3	14	2	9	4,031	177	13	87	20	28	4	9	7
Male	136	20	43	46	108	1	8	2	8	3,642	102	8	44	15	16	1	5	7
Female	102	12	35	43	41	2	6		1	389	75	5	43	5	12	3	4	
Percent of total population:																		
1930	0.9	0.5	2.4	1.5	0.7		0.3	0.6	0.2	0.9	1.0		1.0	0.2				
1920	1.1	0.3	0.5	1.0	0.7		0.3	0.1	0.1	32.9	1.3	0.1	1.1	0.2	0.1	0.1	0.1	0.1
VOTING AGE: 1930																		
Total 21 years old and over	110	65	284	153	94	2	14	29	12	33	125	1	65	20	8	1	5	2
Male	59	33	154	82	61	2	8	16	9	20	72	1	39	10	7	1	3	1
Female	51	32	130	71	33		6	13	3	13	53		26	10	1		2	1
AGE: 1930																		
Under 5 years	12	6	84	15	8			1		7	17	2	15		1			
Under 1 year	4		14	3	2					2	3		3		1			
5 to 9 years	13	3	94	21	10			1		6	22		3		1	1		
10 to 14 years	12	4	91	24	5			2	3	5	14		2					
15 to 19 years	21	6	83	23	3			4		5	20		6	3				
20 to 24 years	12	7	51	22	11		2	4	1	2	14		11	4		2	2	
25 to 29 years	15	22	25	43	10		2	5	1	3	13		8	2				
30 to 34 years	5	10	39	29	9		3	2	2	3	11		10	3	1			
35 to 44 years	35	17	81	33	39	1	4	12	4	12	42	1	21	7	2		2	
45 to 54 years	23	10	69	22	15	1	2	7	2	4	20		12	3	3			2
55 to 64 years	16		25	6	8		1		1	8	20		5	1			1	
65 to 74 years	4		1	1	3					1	3				1			
75 years and over	2		3		3				1		2				1			
Unknown			3								2							
SCHOOL ATTENDANCE																		
Total 7 to 13 years, inclusive	16	4	138	35	8			2	2	8	24		2					
Number attending school	16	3	132	35	8			2	2	7	22		2					
Percent attending school			95.7															
Total 14 and 15 years, inclusive	6	2	34	10	1				1	3	8							
Number attending school	5	2	32	8	1				1	2	6							
Percent attending school																		
Total 16 and 17 years, inclusive	10	3	38	8	1			1		2	6		2	3				
Number attending school	8	2	23	1	1					2	4							
Percent attending school																		
Total 18 to 20 years, inclusive	11	4	40	11	6			4		1	12		6			1		
Number attending school	6		7		2						5							
Percent attending school																		
ILLITERACY																		
Total 10 years old and over	145	76	471	203	106	2	14	36	15	43	161	1	75	23	8	2	5	2
Number illiterate	11	7	30	4	7				1		3		18	2	1	1	1	
Percent illiterate	7.6		6.4	2.0	6.6						1.9							
Percent illiterate in 1920	8.3				8.5					2.1	4.4							
URBAN AND RURAL																		
Urban population	127	85	206	111	52					20	118		78	19				
Percent urban	74.7		31.7	46.4	41.9						59.0							
Rural population	43		443	128	72	2	14	38	15	36	82	3	15	4	10	3	5	2
Rural-farm	3		357	61	4		1		10	13	9	3		3	2	3		
Rural-nonfarm	40		86	67	68	2	13	38	5	23	73		15	1	8		5	2
Percent rural	25.3		68.3	53.6	58.1						41.0							
MARITAL CONDITION																		
Males 15 years old and over	68	36	211	94	64	2	8	20	9	22	80	1	43	11	7	1	3	1
Single	16	4	69	32	22	1	1	8	3	6	27		6	4	2		2	
Married	44	31	124	56	34		7	11	4	13	44	1	31	7	2	1	1	1
Widowed	3	1	14	3	7	1		1	2	1	4		2		3			
Divorced	5		4	3	1					2	4		4					
Unknown																		
Females 15 years old and over	65	36	169	85	37		6	14	3	16	67		30	12	1	1	2	1
Single	13	1	34	16	7			2	1	2	14			2			1	
Married	40	28	116	56	23		6	10	2	11	42		27	7	1	1	1	1
Widowed	11	5	13	10	5			2		1	9		3	2				
Divorced	1	2	5	3	2					2	1			1				
Unknown			1								1							
FAMILIES																		
Number of families	53	29	135	81	33	2	6	16	5	17	60	1	29	9	4	1	1	1
Median size			4.25															
Families having—																		
No children under 10	41	23	71	58	24	2	6	15	4	12	41		19	9	3		1	1
1 child under 10	5	3	20	14	5					1	11		3			1		
2 children under 10	5	3	13	6	4			1		1	2	1	4		1			
3 or more	2		31	3					1	3	6		3					

CHARACTERISTICS OF NEGRO POPULATION BY COUNTIES: 1930—Continued

(See note at head of table)

SUBJECT	NEW MEXICO—Continued: San Miguel	Santa Fe	Sierra	Socorro	Taos	Torrance	Union	Valencia	NEW YORK: The State	Albany	Allegany	Bronx	Broome	Cattaraugus	Cayuga	Chautauqua	Chemung
POPULATION BY SEX																	
Negro population: 1930	40	85	4	26	11	7	26	4	412,814	2,718	169	12,930	797	468	541	471	894
Male	23	59	2	14	8	5	13	2	199,485	1,396	93	6,302	391	236	322	246	538
Female	17	26	2	12	3	2	13	2	213,329	1,322	76	6,628	406	232	219	225	356
Negro population: 1920	127	65	6	26		3	16	7	198,483	1,536	216	4,803	706	371	563	298	615
Male	66	37	5	15		3	8	5	95,418	798	111	2,269	327	208	332	171	351
Female	61	28	1	11			8	2	103,065	738	105	2,534	379	163	231	127	264
Percent of total population:																	
1930	0.2	0.4	0.1	0.3	0.1	0.1	0.2		3.3	1.3	0.4	1.0	0.5	0.6	0.8	0.4	1.2
1920	0.6	0.4	0.1	0.2			0.1	0.1	1.9	0.8	0.6	0.7	0.6	0.5	0.9	0.3	0.9
VOTING AGE: 1930																	
Total 21 years old and over	33	65	4	19	5	6	13	4	287,066	1,964	104	8,062	554	269	384	296	546
Male	20	46	2	10	4	5	8	2	140,078	1,050	64	4,012	281	146	241	153	320
Female	13	19	2	9	1	1	5	2	146,988	914	40	4,050	273	123	143	143	226
AGE: 1930																	
Under 5 years		6		3	2		5		34,116	192	12	1,323	74	48	31	44	64
Under 1 year					1		3		6,616	39	2	210	14	10	9	11	8
5 to 9 years	3	5		3	2		3		31,317	187	21	1,295	63	47	42	46	80
10 to 14 years	2	3					2		24,624	142	15	1,034	57	49	44	42	70
15 to 19 years	1	4			1	1	2		27,472	182	15	968	41	49	34	37	100
20 to 24 years	2	5		3	1	2	2		47,974	262	8	1,335	59	35	39	37	122
25 to 29 years	5	14	1	3	1	1	1		59,075	341	7	1,476	69	31	74	37	87
30 to 34 years	3	14	1	4			1	2	49,742	333	9	1,417	73	38	78	46	78
35 to 44 years	8	15	1	2	1	2	3	1	76,925	519	28	2,124	120	59	79	87	118
45 to 54 years	7	11	1	2	1	1	3	1	39,743	348	12	1,248	110	40	50	44	86
55 to 64 years	4	3		4	2		2		14,002	131	21	434	84	42	31	27	49
65 to 74 years	1	3		2			2		5,210	59	12	185	33	21	23	16	28
75 years and over	4	2							1,931	21	9	57	13	9	15	5	11
Unknown									683	1		34	1		1	3	1
SCHOOL ATTENDANCE																	
Total 7 to 13 years, inclusive	3	5		2			3		38,088	231	24	1,612	87	66	61	60	103
Number attending school	3	5		1			3		36,807	216	24	1,576	85	66	60	59	103
Percent attending school									96.6	93.5		97.8					100.0
Total 14 and 15 years, inclusive	1						1		9,081	57	6	340	18	27	15	18	27
Number attending school	1						1		8,472	51	6	319	18	26	15	18	26
Percent attending school									93.3			93.8					
Total 16 and 17 years, inclusive	1	3				1	2		9,665	68	7	343	18	17	15	17	22
Number attending school		2					2		5,353	30	5	184	9	9	8	11	9
Percent attending school									55.4			53.6					
Total 18 to 20 years, inclusive	1	3		1	2		1		21,606	140	7	717	24	21	18	17	101
Number attending school									2,409	22	2	104	1	3	2	4	6
Percent attending school									11.1	15.7		14.5					5.9
ILLITERACY																	
Total 10 years old and over	37	74	4	20	7	7	18	4	347,381	2,339	136	10,312	660	373	468	381	750
Number illiterate	6	4		9			1		8,604	87	4	133	12	18	11	22	39
Percent illiterate									2.5	3.7	2.9	1.3	1.8	4.8	2.4	5.8	5.2
Percent illiterate in 1920									2.9	4.7	4.0	1.6	5.6	8.2	5.0	9.2	7.9
URBAN AND RURAL																	
Urban population	36	73					9		390,499	2,370	50	12,930	750	330	469	378	830
Percent urban									94.6	87.2	29.6	100.0	94.1	70.5	86.7	80.3	92.8
Rural population	4	12	4	26	11	7	17	4	22,315	481	119		47	138	72	93	64
Rural-farm	4		3		11		7		2,310	15	40		22	13	21	17	11
Rural-nonfarm		12	1	26		7	10	4	20,005	333	79		25	125	51	76	53
Percent rural									5.4	12.8	70.4		5.9	29.5	13.3	19.7	7.2
MARITAL CONDITION																	
Males 15 years old and over	22	51	2	11	5	5	8	2	155,349	1,152	74	4,479	292	177	263	175	415
Single	10	27		5	3	3			55,311	432	30	1,359	106	67	124	52	215
Married	8	15	2	2	1	2	4	1	92,159	654	36	2,944	161	91	116	111	182
Widowed	3	7		2	1		1	1	6,546	55	7	154	19	16	20	6	16
Divorced	1	2		2			3		821	6		14	5	2	3	3	2
Unknown									602	5	1	8	1	1		3	
Females 15 years old and over	13	20	2	9	2	2	8	2	167,408	1,045	47	4,799	311	147	161	164	265
Single	2	6		1		1	2		44,060	224	8	1,319	73	32	43	25	47
Married	7	6	2	2	1	1	6	1	96,475	666	31	2,881	165	91	84	115	169
Widowed	3	5		6	1			1	24,801	147	7	558	70	23	31	21	47
Divorced	1	3							1,520	8	1	30	3	1	3	3	1
Unknown									552			11					1
FAMILIES																	
Number of families	12	17	1	6	4	1	5	2	95,621	719	44	2,883	184	108	83	117	188
Median size									2.63	2.33		3.11	2.60	2.83		2.75	2.99
Families having—																	
No children under 10	11	13	1	3	3	1	4	2	65,401	525	30	1,710	123	74	56	81	123
1 child under 10		1		1	1				14,180	106	4	476	28	11	9	16	32
2 children under 10		2					1		8,327	46	4	349	15	13	2	8	11
3 or more	1	1		2					7,713	42	6	348	18	10	16	12	22

CHARACTERISTICS OF NEGRO POPULATION BY COUNTIES: 1930—Continued

(See note at head of table)

SUBJECT	NEW YORK—Continued																	
	Chenango	Clinton	Columbia	Cortland	Delaware	Dutchess	Erie	Essex	Franklin	Fulton	Genesee	Greene	Hamilton	Herkimer	Jefferson	Kings	Lewis	Livingston
POPULATION BY SEX																		
Negro population: 1930	167	406	1,074	61	119	3,169	16,312	82	71	251	339	496	1	53	115	68,921	20	473
Male	82	368	568	35	62	1,654	8,746	43	36	113	173	269	1	31	59	32,835	8	250
Female	85	38	506	26	57	1,515	7,566	39	35	138	166	227	-	22	56	36,086	12	223
Negro population: 1920	139	218	859	57	143	2,200	4,954	36	47	305	191	389	1	128	116	31,912	14	357
Male	75	183	433	28	72	1,097	2,778	21	24	149	92	201	1	64	59	15,197	11	195
Female	64	35	426	29	71	1,103	2,176	15	23	156	99	188	-	64	57	16,715	3	162
Percent of total population:																		
1930	0.5	0.9	2.6	0.2	0.3	3.0	2.1	0.2	0.2	0.5	0.8	1.9	-	0.1	0.1	2.7	0.1	1.3
1920	0.4	0.5	2.2	0.2	0.3	2.4	0.8	0.1	0.1	0.7	0.5	1.5	-	0.2	0.1	1.6	0.1	1.0
VOTING AGE: 1930																		
Total 21 years old and over	94	365	685	41	69	2,054	11,125	54	40	169	170	335	1	47	78	45,273	11	235
Male	47	344	404	23	36	1,136	6,270	28	18	77	89	184	1	27	42	21,723	6	130
Female	47	21	281	18	33	918	4,855	26	22	92	81	151	-	20	36	23,550	5	105
AGE: 1930																		
Under 5 years	11	12	68	8	13	277	1,538	13	8	22	38	36	-	1	16	6,992	4	50
Under 1 year	2	-	15	2	2	57	304	2	1	5	6	5	-	-	3	1,379	1	9
5 to 9 years	19	8	88	4	11	283	1,332	10	10	19	55	47	-	-	9	6,031	2	66
10 to 14 years	23	7	116	4	16	245	1,055	2	8	12	41	38	-	3	6	4,309	3	63
15 to 19 years	16	8	98	3	9	249	997	1	3	26	32	34	-	2	5	4,821	-	53
20 to 24 years	14	42	87	9	9	285	1,792	6	5	16	21	48	-	5	10	8,431	-	29
25 to 29 years	9	102	115	5	7	284	2,473	13	7	25	19	55	-	7	13	9,530	-	29
30 to 34 years	7	77	106	2	9	282	2,270	11	8	14	27	37	-	2	6	7,593	1	33
35 to 44 years	19	92	148	8	14	539	3,034	14	7	38	52	62	1	10	17	11,488	4	71
45 to 54 years	19	45	115	10	11	408	1,192	7	8	36	25	59	-	8	16	6,176	3	44
55 to 64 years	15	12	75	3	6	194	418	2	3	19	15	38	-	8	11	2,254	-	17
65 to 74 years	12	1	37	4	7	83	140	1	3	13	10	30	-	3	5	829	2	9
75 years and over	3	-	19	1	7	33	55	2	1	10	4	11	-	4	1	331	1	9
Unknown	-	-	2	-	-	7	16	-	-	1	-	1	-	-	-	136	-	-
SCHOOL ATTENDANCE																		
Total 7 to 13 years, inclusive	31	11	138	5	21	362	1,648	5	12	21	65	60	-	3	10	6,929	5	94
Number attending school	31	8	136	5	20	352	1,612	5	9	21	63	55	-	3	8	6,725	5	87
Percent attending school	-	-	98.6	-	-	97.2	97.8	-	-	-	-	-	-	-	-	97.1	-	-
Total 14 and 15 years, inclusive	5	2	52	1	6	88	392	-	2	8	14	12	-	-	4	1,593	-	18
Number attending school	3	2	51	1	6	82	373	-	1	8	13	12	-	-	3	1,445	-	17
Percent attending school	-	-	-	-	-	-	95.2	-	-	-	-	-	-	-	-	90.7	-	-
Total 16 and 17 years, inclusive	6	-	47	1	3	102	354	-	1	6	19	14	-	-	1	1,684	-	28
Number attending school	3	-	31	1	2	41	204	-	1	5	13	9	-	-	-	855	-	16
Percent attending school	-	-	-	-	-	402	57.6	-	-	-	-	-	-	-	-	50.8	-	-
Total 18 to 20 years, inclusive	12	13	48	2	5	169	710	3	3	15	11	22	-	2	4	3,843	-	23
Number attending school	2	2	-	-	-	12	60	-	-	4	2	3	-	-	-	390	-	2
Percent attending school	-	-	-	-	-	7.1	8.5	-	-	-	-	-	-	-	-	10.1	-	-
ILLITERACY																		
Total 10 years old and over	137	386	918	49	95	2,609	13,442	59	53	210	246	413	1	52	90	55,898	14	357
Number illiterate	4	17	73	3	4	156	459	2	10	10	14	25	-	1	7	1,553	-	23
Percent illiterate	2.9	4.4	8.0	-	-	6.0	3.4	-	-	4.8	5.7	6.1	-	-	-	2.8	-	6.4
Percent illiterate in 1920	1.8	8.8	10.2	-	13.3	7.0	3.3	-	-	10.2	5.2	13.6	-	6.3	4.7	2.9	-	8.5
URBAN AND RURAL																		
Urban population	92	354	557	48	5	1,439	15,877	32	32	240	189	283	-	29	90	68,921	13	17
Percent urban	55.1	87.2	51.9	-	4.2	45.4	97.3	-	-	95.6	55.8	57.1	-	-	78.3	100.0	-	3.6
Rural population	75	52	517	13	114	1,730	435	50	39	11	150	213	1	24	25	-	7	456
Rural-farm	35	8	86	8	38	362	29	-	8	3	57	29	-	5	5	-	1	122
Rural-nonfarm	40	44	431	5	76	1,368	406	50	31	8	93	184	1	19	20	-	6	334
Percent rural	44.9	12.8	48.1	-	95.8	54.6	2.7	-	-	4.4	44.2	42.9	-	-	21.7	-	-	96.4
MARITAL CONDITION																		
Males 15 years old and over	58	357	458	24	41	1,275	6,823	29	21	91	105	202	1	29	45	24,330	6	159
Single	28	222	184	8	20	522	2,579	11	7	27	35	67	1	14	14	7,827	1	73
Married	20	121	232	14	19	668	3,929	17	14	53	65	122	-	12	27	15,455	4	78
Widowed	7	10	40	2	2	75	255	-	-	10	5	13	-	3	3	851	1	5
Divorced	2	4	2	-	-	16	56	1	-	1	-	-	-	-	1	99	-	3
Unknown	1	-	-	-	-	4	4	-	-	-	-	-	-	-	-	98	-	-
Females 15 years old and over	56	22	344	21	38	1,089	5,564	28	24	107	100	173	-	20	39	27,259	5	135
Single	19	4	90	3	12	277	942	6	2	22	26	35	-	6	8	6,961	-	49
Married	19	14	209	13	19	660	3,861	18	15	61	60	103	-	13	25	16,149	2	77
Widowed	16	4	44	5	7	138	671	3	6	19	14	35	-	1	6	3,851	3	9
Divorced	2	-	1	-	-	11	86	1	1	5	-	-	-	-	-	202	-	-
Unknown	-	-	-	-	-	3	4	-	-	-	-	-	-	-	-	96	-	-
FAMILIES																		
Number of families	42	12	251	15	22	658	3,818	18	10	68	66	138	-	15	37	17,016	5	86
Median size	-	-	2.33	-	-	2.95	2.68	-	-	-	-	2.40	-	-	-	2.84	-	-
Families having:																		
No children under 10	30	7	183	12	14	421	2,523	10	6	50	31	100	-	15	26	10,805	2	49
1 child under 10	5	2	35	-	5	92	584	4	-	7	15	18	-	-	4	2,779	2	16
2 children under 10	1	2	17	1	-	54	326	-	1	8	4	12	-	-	5	1,767	-	10
3 or more	6	1	16	2	3	91	385	4	3	3	16	8	-	-	2	1,665	1	11

CHARACTERISTICS OF NEGRO POPULATION BY COUNTIES: 1930—Continued

(See note at head of table)

SUBJECT	NEW YORK—Continued																		
	Madison	Monroe	Montgomery	Nassau	New York	Niagara	Oneida	Onondaga	Ontario	Orange	Orleans	Oswego	Otsego	Putnam	Queens	Rensselaer	Richmond	Rockland
POPULATION BY SEX																		
Negro population: 1930	178	2,958	208	7,960	224,670	1,132	936	2,082	293	3,108	84	76	127	113	18,609	715	2,576	2,291
Male	98	1,449	98	3,523	108,229	609	482	1,089	152	1,712	34	33	60	57	8,347	386	1,255	1,194
Female	80	1,509	110	4,437	116,441	523	454	993	141	1,396	50	43	67	56	10,262	329	1,321	1,097
Negro population: 1920	210	1,886	216	3,036	109,133	640	640	1,426	308	2,549	112	112	121	66	5,120	692	1,499	1,471
Male	105	909	106	1,400	51,912	359	330	762	159	1,328	59	66	51	39	2,238	339	735	724
Female	105	977	110	1,636	57,221	281	310	664	149	1,221	53	46	70	27	2,882	353	764	747
Percent of total population:																		
1930	0.4	0.7	0.3	2.6	12.0	0.8	0.5	0.7	0.5	2.4	0.3	0.1	0.3	0.8	1.7	0.6	1.6	3.8
1920	0.5	0.5	0.4	2.4	4.8	0.5	0.4	0.6	0.6	2.1	0.4	0.2	0.3	0.6	1.1	0.6	1.3	3.2
VOTING AGE: 1930																		
Total 21 years old and over	130	2,063	123	5,325	163,079	799	636	1,403	171	2,052	56	45	73	70	12,030	501	1,625	1,319
Male	72	1,001	62	2,332	78,995	447	348	762	96	1,153	22	25	38	35	5,361	274	820	707
Female	58	1,062	61	2,993	84,084	352	288	641	75	899	34	20	35	35	6,669	227	805	612
AGE: 1930																		
Under 5 years	10	231	22	681	16,689	95	59	178	33	266	6	5	10	17	1,663	42	253	219
Under 1 year	3	54	5	125	3,243	19	14	36	7	55		1	3	3	301	8	43	48
5 to 9 years	8	213	19	626	14,986	96	60	178	35	231	9	9	14	8	1,782	54	271	208
10 to 14 years	10	215	26	510	11,662	78	68	149	33	217	3	9	14	9	1,444	62	213	238
15 to 19 years	20	191	15	617	13,822	53	94	136	18	285	8	7	14	6	1,335	47	174	261
20 to 24 years	9	245	14	1,094	26,635	110	90	207	22	344	9	2	7	12	2,014	54	243	248
25 to 29 years	16	346	19	1,092	35,196	124	89	225	23	306	8	2	7	16	2,168	57	291	234
30 to 34 years	9	302	15	884	29,412	129	102	203	26	291	3	5	8	16	1,841	71	270	181
35 to 44 years	23	539	21	1,309	45,146	206	164	334	27	462	9	4	22	12	3,275	119	406	307
45 to 54 years	32	377	29	696	21,389	152	126	264	30	365	13	15	19	9	1,895	107	271	240
55 to 64 years	23	187	12	265	6,583	56	49	124	21	198	7	8	10	7	759	60	102	101
65 to 74 years	12	75	8	122	2,203	26	25	54	15	97	4	9		1	286	31	64	33
75 years and over	6	35	7	41	669	6	9	23	10	40	5	1	2		111	10	16	20
Unknown		2	1	23	278	1	1	7		6					36	1	2	1
SCHOOL ATTENDANCE																		
Total 7 to 13 years, inclusive	10	309	28	786	18,050	127	99	226	45	312	5	14	20	11	2,221	85	345	304
Number attending school	9	307	28	774	17,303	124	94	225	45	304	5	14	20	11	2,172	82	335	265
Percent attending school		99.4		98.5	95.9	97.6		99.6		97.4					97.8		97.1	87.2
Total 14 and 15 years, inclusive	7	72	10	184	4,346	16	23	55	10	79	2	2	8	3	501	18	63	100
Number attending school	7	70	9	174	4,126	16	17	50	10	75	2	2	8	3	471	17	55	70
Percent attending school				94.6	94.9										94.0			70.0
Total 16 and 17 years, inclusive	8	66	3	209	4,749	26	31	53	8	113	5	4	5	3	480	17	63	113
Number attending school	5	41	2	77	2,821	14	9	32	7	49	2	3	2		256	9	40	39
Percent attending school				36.8	59.4					43.4					53.3			34.5
Total 18 to 20 years, inclusive	9	131	10	520	11,389	34	67	94	10	190	4	3	5	6	975	32	122	148
Number attending school	2	22	2	20	1,330	4	5	18	2	16	1	1			119	4	8	9
Percent attending school		16.8		3.8	11.7					8.4					12.2		6.6	6.1
ILLITERACY																		
Total 10 years old and over	160	2,514	167	6,653	192,995	941	817	1,726	225	2,611	69	62	103	88	15,164	619	2,052	1,864
Number illiterate	4	49	3	275	3,611	35	63	83	4	166	1	4	5	3	383	26	42	126
Percent illiterate	2.5	1.9	1.8	4.1	1.9	3.7	7.7	4.8	1.8	6.4			4.9		2.5	4.2	2.0	6.8
Percent illiterate in 1920	5.4	2.6	3.5	5.3	1.8	3.0	7.5	3.8	6.1	10.2	3.0				3.4	5.4	2.7	6.5
URBAN AND RURAL																		
Urban population	64	2,701	169	3,348	224,670	1,099	832	1,902	190	1,856	46	52	72		18,609	658	2,576	1,049
Percent urban	36.0	91.3	81.3	42.1	100.0	97.1	88.9	91.4	64.8	59.7			56.7		100.0	92.0	100.0	45.8
Rural population	114	257	39	4,612		33	104	180	103	1,252	38	24	55	113		57		1,242
Rural-farm	29	29	4	21		16	18	23	22	165	20	13	24	32		9		9
Rural-nonfarm	85	228	35	4,591		17	86	157	81	1,087	18	11	31	81		48		1,233
Percent rural	64.0	8.7	18.8	57.9		2.9	11.1	8.6	35.2	40.3			43.3	100.0		8.0		54.2
MARITAL CONDITION																		
Males 15 years old and over	85	1,103	69	2,642	86,903	470	391	857	104	1,352	26	27	48	39	6,034	299	910	851
Single	34	362	27	795	32,155	159	169	342	39	578	10	6	22	17	1,609	130	333	316
Married	43	664	38	1,731	50,377	284	191	471	57	618	12	18	23	18	4,161	143	510	464
Widowed	6	67	4	86	3,652	22	19	36	7	82	4	3	2	3	230	19	57	54
Divorced	2	8		19	440	5	11	7	1	12			1		26	1	5	4
Unknown		2		11	279		1	1		62				1	8	6	5	13
Females 15 years old and over	65	1,196	72	3,501	94,430	393	358	720	88	1,042	40	26	41	40	7,686	258	929	775
Single	14	263	19	972	25,500	67	123	133	24	238	11	10	18	12	1,893	69	287	226
Married	42	725	43	2,012	53,159	267	189	466	52	631	22	11	18	23	4,562	132	528	449
Widowed	9	198	9	465	14,626	52	40	107	11	156	7	5	4	5	1,159	48	101	85
Divorced		8	1	37	849	7	4	14	1	13			1		65	3	9	4
Unknown		2		15	296		2			4					7	6	4	11
FAMILIES																		
Number of families	52	744	47	1,634	52,387	295	218	526	65	718	18	21	29	15	4,237	205	554	473
Median size		2.45		2.90	2.48	2.43	2.30	2.44		2.56					2.92	2.00	2.90	2.88
Families having—																		
No children under 10	43	536	28	1,037	37,370	207	166	369	42	495	13	14	19	9	2,775	163	358	301
1 child under 10	5	90	9	269	7,478	50	28	79	8	93	2	2	3	2	691	21	73	57
2 children under 10	4	63	5	156	4,171	11	12	38	4	57		4	4	2	395	9	55	58
3 or more		55	5	172	3,368	27	12	40	11	73	3	1	3	2	376	12	68	57

CHARACTERISTICS OF NEGRO POPULATION BY COUNTIES: 1930—Continued

(See note at head of table)

SUBJECT	NEW YORK—Continued																	
	St. Lawrence	Saratoga	Schenectady	Schoharie	Schuyler	Seneca	Steuben	Suffolk	Sullivan	Tioga	Tompkins	Ulster	Warren	Washington	Wayne	Westchester	Wyoming	Yates
POPULATION BY SEX																		
Negro population: 1930	58	617	627	117	109	137	338	5,503	91	146	706	1,339	60	386	122	23,044	76	105
Male	35	314	364	62	61	57	206	2,742	53	77	353	798	36	325	62	10,180	44	52
Female	23	303	263	55	48	80	132	2,760	38	69	353	541	24	61	60	12,864	32	53
Negro population: 1920	143	623	408	166	126	119	299	2,814	60	161	497	985	17	238	135	11,066	94	121
Male	97	307	202	92	70	52	157	1,397	26	85	229	527	10	161	64	4,966	48	60
Female	46	316	206	74	56	67	142	1,417	34	76	268	458	7	77	71	6,100	46	61
Percent of total population:																		
1930	0.1	1.0	0.5	0.6	0.8	0.5	0.4	3.4	0.3	0.6	1.7	1.7	0.2	0.8	0.2	4.4	0.3	0.6
1920	0.2	1.0	0.4	0.8	1.0	0.5	0.4	2.6	0.2	0.7	1.4	1.3	0.1	0.5	0.3	3.2	0.3	0.7
VOTING AGE: 1930																		
Total 21 years old and over	40	466	455	77	83	113	254	3,364	69	100	507	896	50	330	89	15,535	40	73
Male	27	232	263	45	45	48	153	1,712	44	51	252	554	30	295	44	6,819	27	35
Female	13	234	192	32	38	65	101	1,652	25	49	255	342	20	35	45	8,716	13	38
AGE: 1930																		
Under 5 years	3	35	25	7	5	7	19	600	5	18	41	109	3	14	9	1,814	11	17
Under 1 year	1	4	2	-	-	-	4	119	3	4	9	20	-	1	1	379	5	-
5 to 9 years	5	37	48	12	6	5	24	567	5	8	53	102	2	14	4	1,828	8	7
10 to 14 years	7	40	37	9	8	6	22	445	4	10	45	88	2	11	7	1,504	9	6
15 to 19 years	3	31	51	11	6	5	15	436	6	9	47	114	3	10	12	1,822	5	-
20 to 24 years	2	35	70	7	11	3	25	557	13	4	48	152	3	61	7	2,894	9	8
25 to 29 years	8	42	81	11	10	9	19	589	11	6	54	155	7	68	13	2,943	5	10
30 to 34 years	8	54	83	9	5	9	33	459	6	14	60	134	9	65	7	2,457	1	4
35 to 44 years	8	100	121	16	20	25	74	844	18	19	124	193	16	79	20	4,089	11	11
45 to 54 years	5	114	75	14	17	40	47	536	13	24	111	148	11	38	15	2,364	6	16
55 to 64 years	7	76	25	8	11	20	35	278	8	16	76	89	3	17	16	822	7	7
65 to 74 years	2	39	6	7	6	3	11	123	-	9	34	32	1	6	9	282	2	7
75 years and over	-	14	5	6	4	4	14	55	2	9	12	22	-	1	3	123	2	12
Unknown	-	-	-	-	-	1	-	13	-	-	1	1	-	2	-	102	-	-
SCHOOL ATTENDANCE																		
Total 7 to 13 years, inclusive	8	58	63	16	11	10	27	705	6	11	67	123	3	19	6	2,274	12	9
Number attending school	8	57	63	16	11	10	27	682	6	11	60	121	3	18	6	2,236	12	9
Percent attending school	-	-	-	-	-	-	-	96.7	-	-	-	98.4	-	-	-	98.3	-	-
Total 14 and 15 years, inclusive	3	13	19	5	4	-	8	155	-	5	21	40	-	2	4	594	2	2
Number attending school	3	12	19	5	4	-	8	140	-	5	20	39	-	2	4	529	2	2
Percent attending school	-	-	-	-	-	-	-	90.3	-	-	-	-	-	-	-	89.1	-	-
Total 16 and 17 years, inclusive	2	13	9	2	2	2	4	181	1	3	16	42	1	4	4	648	2	-
Number attending school	1	8	6	-	2	1	3	70	1	1	9	19	-	1	3	373	-	-
Percent attending school	-	-	-	-	-	-	-	38.7	-	-	-	-	-	-	-	57.6	-	-
Total 18 to 20 years, inclusive	-	22	40	7	3	4	14	262	7	5	32	84	2	11	8	1,419	5	2
Number attending school	-	4	4	1	-	2	5	16	1	2	11	3	-	2	1	173	-	-
Percent attending school	-	-	-	-	-	-	-	6.1	-	-	-	-	-	-	-	12.2	-	-
ILLITERACY																		
Total 10 years old and over	50	545	554	98	98	125	295	4,335	81	120	612	1,128	55	358	109	19,402	57	81
Number illiterate	3	24	11	7	-	12	11	150	5	3	14	105	3	10	12	661	2	1
Percent illiterate	-	4.4	2.0	-	-	9.6	3.7	3.5	-	2.5	2.3	9.3	-	2.8	11.0	3.4	-	-
Percent illiterate in 1920	22.1	10.1	5.8	3.1	6.4	18.8	2.2	6.9	-	6.1	2.4	13.9	-	7.7	11.1	4.7	-	2.8
URBAN AND RURAL																		
Urban population	50	495	618	42	74	26	182	820	28	135	637	677	46	36	38	20,297	25	55
Percent urban	-	80.2	98.6	35.9	67.9	19.0	53.8	14.9	-	92.5	90.2	50.6	-	9.3	31.1	88.1	-	52.4
Rural population	8	122	9	75	35	111	156	4,682	63	11	69	662	14	350	84	2,747	51	50
Rural-farm	1	21	-	9	5	15	29	509	11	9	29	131	3	19	50	43	40	17
Rural-nonfarm	7	101	9	66	30	96	127	4,173	52	2	40	531	11	331	34	2,704	11	33
Percent rural	-	19.8	1.4	64.1	32.1	81.0	46.2	85.1	-	7.5	9.8	49.4	-	90.7	68.9	11.9	-	47.6
MARITAL CONDITION																		
Males 15 years old and over	27	253	295	55	49	51	166	1,937	48	58	277	653	31	308	51	7,729	34	36
Single	15	92	144	33	17	27	74	657	23	22	80	348	15	166	23	2,423	16	8
Married	9	134	135	15	28	21	76	1,169	21	27	173	264	12	119	24	4,928	14	22
Widowed	2	26	13	7	3	3	11	85	4	9	22	36	3	17	4	273	4	6
Divorced	1	1	2	-	1	-	5	13	-	-	1	3	1	6	-	35	-	-
Unknown	-	-	1	-	-	-	-	13	-	-	1	2	-	-	-	70	-	-
Females 15 years old and over	16	252	222	34	41	68	107	1,953	29	52	290	387	22	39	51	10,169	14	39
Single	7	46	49	7	7	30	22	478	5	8	59	91	6	14	26	3,082	2	9
Married	9	131	137	17	27	28	66	1,224	21	32	169	245	13	19	20	5,436	9	21
Widowed	-	72	34	10	7	10	18	227	3	11	60	47	3	5	5	1,457	2	7
Divorced	-	3	2	-	-	-	1	11	-	1	2	3	-	1	-	118	1	2
Unknown	-	-	-	-	-	-	-	13	-	-	-	1	-	-	-	76	-	-
FAMILIES																		
Number of families	10	191	139	35	33	12	69	1,151	22	44	175	323	16	31	31	4,452	15	31
Median size	-	2.08	2.46	-	-	-	-	2.99	-	-	2.38	2.46	-	-	-	2.91	-	-
Families having—																		
No children under 10	8	158	105	28	25	8	50	690	16	32	131	227	13	21	23	2,884	9	22
1 child under 10	1	14	13	4	5	2	8	172	4	4	23	38	3	2	5	669	1	2
2 children	-	12	12	1	3	-	4	112	2	5	11	27	-	2	2	426	1	3
3 or more	1	7	9	2	-	2	7	177	-	3	10	31	-	6	1	473	4	4

CHARACTERISTICS OF NEGRO POPULATION BY COUNTIES: 1930—Continued

(See note at head of table)

SUBJECT	NORTH CAROLINA																	
	The State	Alamance	Alexander	Alleghany	Anson	Ashe	Avery	Beaufort	Bertie	Bladen	Brunswick	Buncombe	Burke	Cabarrus	Caldwell	Camden	Carteret	Caswell
POPULATION BY SEX																		
Negro population: 1930	918,647	8,354	1,044	343	15,247	419	277	13,535	14,616	9,203	5,928	16,655	2,606	7,907	2,406	2,188	2,534	8,473
Male	446,500	4,129	557	196	7,327	221	153	6,612	7,207	4,499	2,928	7,600	1,228	3,867	1,160	1,099	1,205	4,232
Female	472,147	4,225	487	147	7,920	198	124	6,923	7,409	4,704	3,000	9,055	1,378	4,040	1,246	1,089	1,329	4,241
Negro population: 1920	763,407	7,499	875	333	14,862	502	243	12,093	13,639	8,110	5,373	9,618	2,660	6,347	1,969	2,125	2,385	7,850
Male	373,965	3,603	411	163	7,205	266	125	5,923	6,761	3,966	2,628	4,408	1,329	3,084	967	1,079	1,172	3,899
Female	389,442	3,896	464	170	7,657	236	118	6,170	6,878	4,144	2,745	5,210	1,331	3,263	1,002	1,046	1,213	3,951
Percent of total population:																		
1930	29.0	19.8	8.1	4.8	52.0	2.0	2.3	38.6	56.6	41.1	37.5	17.0	8.9	17.8	8.6	40.1	15.0	46.5
1920	29.8	22.9	7.2	4.5	52.5	2.4	2.4	39.0	56.8	41.0	36.1	15.0	11.4	18.8	9.9	39.5	15.5	49.8
VOTING AGE: 1930																		
Total 21 years old and over	418,975	3,756	472	190	6,097	197	129	6,393	5,723	3,764	2,675	9,854	1,215	3,675	1,149	920	1,200	3,292
Male	200,355	1,821	266	113	2,835	101	71	3,097	2,711	1,776	1,287	4,430	565	1,797	561	465	580	1,684
Female	218,620	1,935	206	77	3,262	96	58	3,296	3,012	1,988	1,388	5,424	650	1,878	588	455	620	1,608
AGE: 1930																		
Under 5 years	114,695	1,027	114	29	2,047	53	30	1,616	2,162	1,239	764	1,474	312	976	306	308	311	1,318
Under 1 year	21,518	217	16	7	375	16	10	320	414	218	144	254	61	195	58	51	64	251
5 to 9 years	130,143	1,204	148	32	2,459	66	33	1,839	2,273	1,431	877	1,689	404	1,119	344	347	355	1,415
10 to 14 years	117,763	1,121	131	39	2,237	53	47	1,689	2,189	1,351	775	1,568	330	994	271	315	305	1,197
15 to 19 years	115,166	1,044	147	36	2,037	43	30	1,681	1,977	1,206	721	1,667	297	957	278	254	310	1,089
20 to 24 years	95,004	842	132	54	1,399	21	34	1,352	1,237	824	559	2,132	249	892	248	183	233	716
25 to 29 years	69,843	597	65	32	937	25	14	984	831	513	414	2,006	169	598	192	150	166	524
30 to 34 years	51,384	454	56	22	723	19	10	733	629	373	262	1,473	146	445	126	111	148	362
35 to 44 years	91,937	787	105	28	1,314	45	25	1,387	1,249	853	599	2,403	257	768	228	194	280	657
45 to 54 years	69,778	618	71	28	1,108	26	17	1,174	1,042	754	487	1,333	194	625	210	155	223	550
55 to 64 years	36,005	367	28	21	587	26	13	599	550	361	267	542	115	324	99	89	114	354
65 to 74 years	17,610	195	26	11	255	32	14	301	328	203	133	244	75	144	65	63	70	199
75 years and over	8,381	95	21	11	133	10	9	174	148	93	66	108	56	57	22	15	18	91
Unknown	938	3	------	------	11	------	1	6	1	2	4	16	2	8	17	4	1	1
SCHOOL ATTENDANCE																		
Total 7 to 13 years, inclusive	170,153	1,600	189	51	3,148	81	52	2,407	3,105	1,920	1,132	2,286	514	1,468	416	457	454	1,799
Number attending school	151,122	1,467	170	38	2,695	65	45	2,105	2,757	1,723	1,086	2,189	470	1,305	374	409	434	1,555
Percent attending school	88.8	90.9	89.9	------	85.6	------	------	87.5	88.8	89.7	95.9	95.8	91.4	88.9	89.9	89.5	95.6	86.4
Total 14 and 15 years, inclusive	46,680	441	51	16	918	24	16	631	828	511	298	613	129	394	103	121	122	457
Number attending school	35,885	337	36	9	747	23	15	441	705	412	255	491	105	295	69	91	101	347
Percent attending school	76.9	76.4	70.6	------	81.4	------	------	69.9	85.1	80.6	85.6	80.1	81.4	74.9	67.0	75.2	82.8	75.9
Total 16 and 17 years, inclusive	46,898	424	58	14	873	18	15	731	835	508	306	639	118	356	115	103	127	456
Number attending school	21,408	192	14	4	493	11	12	282	519	275	181	296	62	138	37	41	55	184
Percent attending school	45.6	45.3	24.1	------	56.5	------	------	38.6	62.2	54.1	59.2	46.3	52.5	38.8	32.2	39.8	43.3	40.4
Total 18 to 20 years, inclusive	67,418	612	102	31	1,118	21	19	962	1,003	661	378	1,131	161	607	175	136	176	554
Number attending school	9,905	76	10	1	266	3	3	102	241	143	49	148	33	76	17	15	34	51
Percent attending school	14.7	12.4	9.8	------	23.8	------	------	10.6	24.0	21.6	13.0	13.1	20.5	12.5	9.7	11.0	19.3	9.2
ILLITERACY																		
Total 10 years old and over	673,809	6,123	782	282	10,741	300	214	10,080	10,181	6,533	4,287	13,492	1,890	5,812	1,756	1,533	1,868	5,740
Number illiterate	139,105	1,100	170	111	2,850	70	55	3,169	1,798	1,425	649	1,450	300	1,232	267	186	177	1,432
Percent illiterate	20.6	18.0	21.7	39.4	26.5	23.3	25.7	31.4	17.7	21.8	15.1	10.7	15.9	21.2	15.2	12.1	9.5	24.9
Percent illiterate in 1920	24.5	27.8	22.4	26.3	31.8	28.7	31.8	22.5	21.9	25.6	23.4	15.5	31.6	23.3	25.6	27.0	21.3	32.9
URBAN AND RURAL																		
Urban population	246,237	972	------	------	1,197	------	------	3,170	------	------	------	14,255	1,018	1,966	1,303	------	1,751	------
Percent urban	26.8	11.6	------	------	7.9	------	------	23.4	------	------	------	85.6	39.1	24.9	54.2	------	69.1	------
Rural population	672,410	7,382	1,044	343	14,050	419	277	10,365	14,616	9,203	5,928	2,400	1,588	5,941	1,103	2,188	783	8,473
Rural-farm	497,496	4,438	575	237	12,178	380	106	6,238	12,267	7,027	2,571	643	1,086	3,776	651	1,683	322	7,786
Rural-nonfarm	174,914	2,944	469	106	1,872	39	171	4,127	2,349	2,176	3,357	1,757	502	2,165	452	505	461	687
Percent rural	73.2	88.4	100.0	100.0	92.1	100.0	100.0	76.6	100.0	100.0	100.0	14.4	60.9	75.1	45.8	100.0	30.9	100.0
MARITAL CONDITION																		
Males 15 years old and over	266,001	2,456	373	144	3,993	134	94	4,046	3,892	2,493	1,696	5,316	723	2,320	717	610	749	2,295
Single	98,885	971	194	73	1,485	54	41	1,489	1,525	982	600	1,743	269	809	251	212	306	884
Married	152,237	1,369	161	64	2,291	70	45	2,346	2,220	1,410	998	3,247	422	1,332	410	372	406	1,288
Widowed	13,023	103	16	6	189	7	7	199	132	96	84	280	29	131	37	25	31	104
Divorced	1,418	13	------	1	12	3	1	12	7	4	14	41	2	14	2	1	6	8
Unknown	438	------	2	------	16	------	------	------	8	1	------	5	1	4	17	------	------	1
Females 15 years old and over	290,045	2,546	278	99	4,511	113	73	4,345	4,100	2,689	1,816	6,608	837	2,498	768	608	814	2,248
Single	90,894	857	99	39	1,613	27	19	1,285	1,348	968	536	1,785	278	818	230	165	255	758
Married	157,643	1,422	143	45	2,332	68	47	2,383	2,264	1,443	1,012	3,593	435	1,354	430	381	430	1,292
Widowed	38,356	242	34	14	508	16	7	629	462	267	257	1,145	113	310	100	60	113	185
Divorced	2,773	24	2	------	32	2	------	44	22	7	10	82	10	12	4	1	14	13
Unknown	379	1	------	1	26	------	------	4	4	4	1	3	1	4	4	1	2	------
FAMILIES																		
Number of families	180,128	1,533	175	61	2,787	92	53	2,800	2,546	1,736	1,224	3,635	515	1,552	477	393	507	1,437
Median size	4.18	4.57	4.58	------	4.82	------	------	4.04	5.21	4.70	4.19	3.12	4.25	4.18	4.08	5.03	4.31	5.57
Families having—																		
No children under 10	81,067	645	66	33	1,023	49	30	1,311	879	679	562	2,171	243	692	225	135	235	484
1 child under 10	33,934	299	42	10	543	14	7	569	483	345	218	652	79	305	74	80	95	236
2 children under 10	24,236	211	25	10	431	8	6	366	387	251	171	394	76	232	67	68	55	206
3 or more	40,891	378	42	8	790	20	10	554	797	461	273	418	117	323	111	110	122	511

CHARACTERISTICS OF NEGRO POPULATION BY COUNTIES: 1930—Continued

(See note at head of table)

SUBJECT	NORTH CAROLINA—Continued																	
	Catawba	Chatham	Cherokee	Chowan	Clay	Cleveland	Columbus	Craven	Cumberland	Currituck	Dare	Davidson	Davie	Duplin	Durham	Edgecombe	Forsyth	Franklin
POPULATION BY SEX																		
Negro population: 1930	4,938	8,018	335	5,323	116	12,067	11,587	14,809	17,049	2,255	404	5,235	2,426	12,987	23,481	27,259	37,182	12,941
Male	2,396	4,055	177	2,571	66	5,996	5,750	7,191	8,202	1,146	199	2,601	1,216	6,325	11,093	13,299	17,623	6,322
Female	2,542	3,963	158	2,752	50	6,071	5,837	7,618	8,847	1,109	205	2,634	1,210	6,662	12,388	13,960	19,559	6,619
Negro population: 1920	3,574	7,818	324	5,297	129	6,024	9,603	15,198	13,961	2,638	399	3,593	2,039	11,116	13,168	22,343	26,121	11,856
Male	1,660	3,867	156	2,670	63	2,954	4,769	7,329	6,822	1,390	203	1,805	998	5,549	6,396	10,956	12,962	5,731
Female	1,914	3,951	168	2,627	66	3,070	4,834	7,869	7,139	1,248	196	1,788	1,041	5,567	6,772	11,387	13,159	6,125
Percent of total population:																		
1930	11.2	33.2	2.1	47.2	2.1	23.2	30.7	48.3	37.7	33.6	7.8	10.9	16.9	37.0	34.9	56.9	33.3	43.9
1920	10.6	32.8	2.1	49.7	2.8	17.6	31.9	52.3	39.8	36.3	7.8	10.2	15.0	36.8	31.2	58.8	33.8	44.5
VOTING AGE: 1930																		
Total 21 years old and over	2,312	3,298	181	2,317	61	5,015	5,011	7,330	7,682	1,057	199	2,652	1,079	5,510	12,916	11,796	21,168	5,318
Male	1,104	1,665	88	1,089	34	2,434	2,449	3,418	3,565	550	103	1,335	534	2,681	6,080	5,615	10,025	2,627
Female	1,208	1,633	93	1,228	27	2,581	2,562	3,912	4,117	507	96	1,317	545	2,829	6,836	6,181	11,143	2,691
AGE: 1930																		
Under 5 years	610	1,156	42	665	6	1,614	1,563	1,680	2,195	266	50	624	306	1,678	2,356	3,626	3,446	1,802
Under 1 year	110	233	4	113	1	331	295	322	398	40	8	116	61	313	441	680	599	352
5 to 9 years	693	1,287	49	777	17	1,831	1,730	1,914	2,377	312	56	650	362	1,989	2,589	4,027	3,980	2,082
10 to 14 years	585	1,143	31	738	9	1,662	1,541	1,734	2,089	295	44	561	320	1,839	2,356	3,736	3,431	1,781
15 to 19 years	616	967	24	718	20	1,654	1,464	1,819	2,267	271	49	611	311	1,689	2,655	3,444	4,096	1,652
20 to 24 years	543	670	36	478	12	1,337	1,192	1,468	1,800	233	31	648	212	1,261	3,076	2,734	5,134	1,202
25 to 29 years	360	481	30	284	14	869	798	1,023	1,290	135	28	434	170	826	2,606	1,988	4,430	831
30 to 34 years	285	395	26	241	5	626	591	836	897	111	22	326	111	643	1,860	1,396	3,394	609
35 to 44 years	451	692	36	534	11	1,012	1,120	1,678	1,701	200	49	562	213	1,247	2,902	2,558	4,785	1,127
45 to 54 years	424	593	26	460	8	792	867	1,404	1,290	232	42	425	175	996	1,739	1,994	2,619	899
55 to 64 years	200	354	15	232	8	421	406	750	616	138	20	218	132	465	816	1,094	1,184	536
65 to 74 years	110	189	13	133	3	172	215	335	314	39	6	115	76	230	352	449	506	274
75 years and over	58	91	7	60	3	72	95	165	193	23	6	60	37	116	145	208	176	142
Unknown	3			3		5	5	3	20		1	1	1	8	29	5	1	4
SCHOOL ATTENDANCE																		
Total 7 to 13 years, inclusive	882	1,677	57	1,038	16	2,383	2,233	2,522	3,065	413	60	846	484	2,595	3,439	5,300	5,123	2,613
Number attending school	799	1,506	54	958	9	2,055	1,801	2,271	2,705	393	57	764	441	2,380	3,269	4,495	4,882	2,343
Percent attending school	90.6	89.8		92.3		86.2	80.7	90.0	88.3	95.2		90.3	91.1	91.7	95.1	84.8	95.3	89.7
Total 14 and 15 years, inclusive	235	444	7	313	5	676	584	727	889	108	23	197	118	769	933	1,453	1,337	717
Number attending school	181	361	6	249	4	493	454	545	687	93	22	143	87	630	704	968	958	555
Percent attending school	77.0	81.3		79.6		72.9	77.7	75.0	77.3	86.1		72.6	73.7	81.9	75.5	66.6	71.7	77.4
Total 16 and 17 years, inclusive	258	388	16	294	6	662	622	703	901	118	18	236	134	699	976	1,440	1,512	680
Number attending school	124	195	10	150	4	286	274	314	460	59	10	81	56	342	379	467	451	328
Percent attending school	48.1	50.3		51.0		43.2	44.1	44.7	51.1	50.0		34.3	41.8	48.9	38.8	32.4	29.8	48.2
Total 18 to 20 years, inclusive	370	546	12	365	15	963	855	1,074	1,346	162	27	413	164	914	1,825	1,919	2,995	915
Number attending school	40	83		47	2	139	105	159	265	16	6	34	19	150	237	183	189	142
Percent attending school	10.8	15.2		12.9		14.4	12.3	14.8	19.7	9.9		8.2	11.6	16.4	13.0	9.5	6.3	15.5
ILLITERACY																		
Total 10 years old and over	3,635	5,575	244	3,881	93	8,622	8,294	11,215	12,477	1,677	298	3,961	1,758	9,320	18,536	19,606	29,756	9,057
Number illiterate	618	920	63	845	24	1,904	1,624	2,648	2,557	265	45	493	417	1,868	2,893	5,814	4,436	1,684
Percent illiterate	17.0	16.5	25.8	21.8		22.1	19.6	23.6	20.5	15.8	15.1	12.4	23.7	20.0	15.6	29.7	14.9	18.6
Percent illiterate in 1920	21.4	24.9	19.6	20.0	30.0	25.3	19.2	22.6	22.4	19.0	23.9	15.8	27.3	26.0	25.3	33.2	19.9	25.2
URBAN AND RURAL																		
Urban population	2,205			1,478		2,810		6,277	5,357			3,205			18,717	7,040	32,566	
Percent urban	44.7			27.8		23.3		42.4	31.4			61.2			79.7	25.8	87.6	
Rural population	2,733	8,018	335	3,845	116	9,257	11,587	8,532	11,692	2,255	404	2,030	2,426	12,987	4,764	20,219	4,616	12,941
Rural-farm	2,128	6,037	46	3,368	67	8,778	7,171	4,540	8,478	1,601	11	1,204	1,714	9,514	3,380	18,400	1,817	10,190
Rural-nonfarm	605	1,981	289	477	49	479	4,416	3,992	3,214	654	393	826	712	3,473	1,384	1,819	2,799	2,751
Percent rural	55.3	100.0	100.0	72.2	100.0	76.7	100.0	57.6	68.6	100.0	100.0	38.8	100.0	100.0	20.3	74.2	12.4	100.0
MARITAL CONDITION																		
Males 15 years old and over	1,444	2,267	103	1,488	48	3,420	3,314	4,485	4,833	700	130	1,708	715	3,609	7,476	7,604	12,264	3,562
Single	527	864	25	494	22	1,268	1,224	1,694	1,894	259	45	684	277	1,367	2,648	2,853	4,525	1,349
Married	850	1,244	69	917	22	1,992	1,929	2,448	2,708	404	80	932	405	2,054	4,357	4,368	7,038	1,975
Widowed	61	145	9	75	4	132	148	306	197	32	5	79	33	152	371	332	650	222
Divorced	5	11		2		26	11	35	19	5		6		27	99	48	48	16
Unknown	1	3				2	2	2	15			7		9	1	3	3	
Females 15 years old and over	1,606	2,165	110	1,655	36	3,540	3,439	4,996	5,555	682	124	1,692	723	3,872	8,704	8,266	14,061	3,714
Single	537	669	23	476	11	1,071	1,042	1,402	1,886	190	32	506	219	1,261	2,607	2,616	4,106	1,256
Married	869	1,239	73	953	21	2,035	1,950	2,558	2,845	418	68	935	407	2,121	4,705	4,488	7,674	1,991
Widowed	190	236	14	222	4	375	435	974	774	69	22	225	92	421	1,216	1,014	2,195	426
Divorced	8	14		4		56	9	60	44	5	2	19	5	56	175	114	80	33
Unknown	2	7				3	3	2	6			7		13	1	34	6	8
FAMILIES																		
Number of families	967	1,434	75	1,057	21	2,174	2,279	3,100	3,335	439	91	1,062	457	2,480	5,055	5,225	8,998	2,364
Median size	4.14	5.01		4.22		4.66	4.42	3.84	4.26	4.66		3.89	4.40	4.63	3.39	4.43	2.93	4.75
Families having—																		
No children under 10	445	502	35	461	8	847	918	1,590	1,469	200	50	546	192	1,028	2,790	2,172	5,517	908
1 child under 10	181	277	13	220	7	417	484	564	651	86	10	177	75	448	982	1,011	1,558	410
2 children under 10	120	229	14	143	3	319	321	350	447	65	10	130	67	348	594	737	911	350
3 or more	221	426	13	233	3	591	556	596	768	88	21	209	123	656	689	1,305	1,012	696

CHARACTERISTICS OF NEGRO POPULATION BY COUNTIES: 1930—Continued

(See note at head of table)

NORTH CAROLINA—Continued

SUBJECT	Gaston	Gates	Graham	Granville	Greene	Guilford	Halifax	Harnett	Haywood	Henderson	Hertford	Hoke	Hyde	Iredell	Jackson	Johnston	Jones	Lee
POPULATION BY SEX																		
Negro population: 1930	12,392	5,042	1	14,045	8,945	28,696	30,845	10,389	695	2,192	10,303	8,635	3,496	9,301	584	13,129	4,680	5,405
Male	5,884	2,509	1	7,026	4,498	13,760	15,170	5,109	337	1,044	5,122	4,233	1,728	4,502	303	6,473	2,307	2,639
Female	6,508	2,533	------	7,019	4,447	14,936	15,675	5,280	358	1,148	5,181	4,402	1,768	4,799	281	6,656	2,373	2,766
Negro population: 1920	9,226	5,082	5	12,722	8,186	17,359	25,893	7,801	711	1,821	9,954	6,485	3,266	7,369	522	11,502	4,455	3,886
Male	4,496	2,494	3	6,291	4,128	8,387	12,838	3,831	355	882	4,911	3,157	1,610	3,550	266	5,690	2,225	1,883
Female	4,730	2,588	2	6,431	4,058	8,972	13,055	3,970	356	939	5,043	3,328	1,656	3,819	256	5,812	2,230	2,003
Percent of total population:																		
1930	15.9	47.8	------	48.9	47.9	21.6	57.9	27.4	2.5	9.4	58.7	60.6	40.9	19.9	3.3	22.8	44.9	31.8
1920	18.0	48.2	0.1	47.4	50.5	21.9	59.2	27.6	3.0	10.0	61.1	55.3	38.9	19.4	3.9	23.5	44.9	29.0
VOTING AGE: 1930																		
Total 21 years old and over	5,907	2,015	1	5,819	3,587	15,634	12,844	4,269	395	1,177	4,188	3,337	1,351	4,373	268	5,538	1,880	2,338
Male	2,742	994	1	2,878	1,790	7,555	6,202	2,078	190	546	2,041	1,578	655	2,047	132	2,668	935	1,120
Female	3,165	1,021	------	2,941	1,797	8,079	6,642	2,191	205	631	2,147	1,759	696	2,326	136	2,870	945	1,218
AGE: 1930																		
Under 5 years	1,381	674	------	1,901	1,237	2,866	4,648	1,543	61	226	1,342	1,233	519	1,063	74	1,742	731	720
Under 1 year	258	114	------	355	232	527	948	284	12	34	253	231	107	223	15	338	151	148
5 to 9 years	1,684	797	------	2,158	1,345	3,178	4,818	1,598	67	258	1,652	1,335	557	1,195	82	1,953	728	805
10 to 14 years	1,466	776	------	1,970	1,338	2,888	4,116	1,410	71	236	1,540	1,248	514	1,199	64	1,846	620	731
15 to 19 years	1,615	684	------	1,870	1,222	3,342	3,759	1,324	88	250	1,371	1,248	480	1,222	80	1,723	600	676
20 to 24 years	1,480	368	------	1,363	918	3,774	2,926	1,061	76	231	922	903	310	970	57	1,244	466	492
25 to 29 years	1,050	261	------	923	615	3,244	1,973	766	65	208	564	515	202	674	35	910	333	382
30 to 34 years	774	216	------	676	393	2,136	1,465	514	46	125	477	365	166	534	28	645	189	285
35 to 44 years	1,241	454	------	1,212	750	3,490	2,641	864	91	271	924	765	251	948	47	1,297	362	509
45 to 54 years	912	360	------	967	612	2,138	2,275	726	65	200	773	554	228	729	49	978	342	403
55 to 64 years	465	241	1	556	316	971	1,298	327	37	119	397	297	161	427	39	458	206	218
65 to 74 years	211	145	------	287	134	447	601	183	22	50	235	122	76	223	14	195	51	129
75 years and over	108	66	------	158	65	201	314	71	4	16	106	47	32	111	15	125	51	53
Unknown	5	------	------	4	------	21	11	2	2	2	------	3	------	6	------	13	1	2
SCHOOL ATTENDANCE																		
Total 7 to 13 years, inclusive	2,175	1,088	------	2,804	1,867	4,156	6,028	2,015	94	358	2,208	1,760	738	1,660	100	2,569	910	1,070
Number attending school	1,956	1,011	------	2,401	1,649	3,907	5,227	1,801	91	299	1,894	1,442	658	1,504	89	2,276	842	951
Percent attending school	89.9	92.9	------	85.6	88.3	94.0	86.7	89.4	------	83.5	85.8	81.9	89.2	90.6	89.0	88.6	92.5	88.9
Total 14 and 15 years, inclusive	599	296	------	784	526	1,182	1,628	544	32	92	599	525	210	523	32	756	238	287
Number attending school	428	264	------	622	429	916	1,224	421	28	70	501	379	150	406	27	615	207	230
Percent attending school	71.5	89.2	------	79.3	81.6	77.5	75.2	77.4	------	------	83.6	72.2	71.4	77.6	------	81.3	87.0	80.1
Total 16 and 17 years, inclusive	641	290	------	704	482	1,282	1,548	550	34	103	572	524	193	507	33	722	252	283
Number attending school	246	169	------	382	246	549	716	278	16	41	356	249	78	233	21	367	145	147
Percent attending school	38.4	58.3	------	48.1	51.0	42.8	46.3	50.5	------	39.8	62.2	47.5	40.4	46.0	------	50.8	57.5	51.9
Total 18 to 20 years, inclusive	992	353	------	1,033	695	2,277	2,090	768	52	141	722	706	265	707	47	995	357	384
Number attending school	90	81	------	144	102	373	322	138	6	17	174	93	43	101	13	173	72	63
Percent attending school	9.1	22.9	------	13.9	14.7	16.4	15.4	18.0	------	12.1	24.1	13.2	16.2	14.3	------	17.4	20.2	16.4
ILLITERACY																		
Total 10 years old and over	9,327	3,571	1	9,986	6,363	22,652	21,379	7,248	567	1,708	7,309	6,067	2,420	7,043	428	9,434	3,221	3,880
Number illiterate	2,014	540	1	2,280	1,766	2,878	5,188	1,581	58	223	1,727	1,443	705	1,486	68	2,011	474	752
Percent illiterate	21.6	15.1	------	22.8	27.8	12.7	24.3	21.8	10.2	13.1	23.6	23.8	29.1	21.1	15.9	21.3	14.7	19.4
Percent illiterate in 1920	25.5	23.8	------	25.9	27.3	17.5	29.5	22.3	16.8	19.1	26.0	27.9	36.8	23.3	21.4	21.7	20.7	20.8
URBAN AND RURAL																		
Urban population	4,358	------	------	1,611	------	21,279	49	1,873	96	1,258	------	------	------	2,347	------	758	------	1,070
Percent urban	35.2	------	------	11.5	------	74.2	0.2	18.0	13.8	57.4	------	------	------	25.2	------	5.8	------	19.8
Rural population	8,034	5,042	1	12,434	8,945	7,417	30,796	8,516	599	934	10,303	8,635	3,496	6,954	584	12,371	4,680	4,335
Rural-farm	4,723	4,158	------	10,205	8,423	4,382	23,992	6,742	15	393	8,014	7,863	2,313	4,700	307	8,958	3,649	3,061
Rural-nonfarm	3,311	884	1	2,229	522	3,035	6,804	1,774	584	541	2,289	772	1,183	2,254	277	3,413	1,031	1,274
Percent rural	64.8	100.0	------	88.5	100.0	25.8	99.8	82.0	86.2	42.6	100.0	100.0	100.0	74.8	100.0	94.2	100.0	80.2
MARITAL CONDITION																		
Males 15 years old and over	3,606	1,398	1	3,990	2,510	9,403	8,388	2,852	241	691	2,829	2,302	916	2,778	184	3,677	1,279	1,519
Single	1,265	547	1	1,593	984	3,593	2,937	1,119	79	257	1,121	913	316	1,041	74	1,456	484	562
Married	2,154	774	------	2,203	1,357	5,288	5,057	1,631	145	387	1,574	1,284	548	1,570	100	2,047	723	863
Widowed	178	74	------	168	156	473	356	93	16	30	119	89	48	139	8	157	66	82
Divorced	4	3	------	25	13	44	22	9	------	13	12	13	4	28	2	16	6	11
Unknown	5	------	------	1	------	5	16	------	1	4	3	3	------	------	------	1	------	1
Females 15 years old and over	4,255	1,397	------	4,026	2,515	10,361	8,875	2,986	255	781	2,940	2,517	990	3,066	180	3,911	1,322	1,630
Single	1,374	460	------	1,289	811	3,183	2,631	990	65	224	1,010	937	324	1,012	54	1,285	470	505
Married	2,321	788	------	2,244	1,375	5,590	5,139	1,674	142	410	1,647	1,288	551	1,608	107	2,108	725	889
Widowed	542	136	------	455	308	1,471	1,045	312	47	121	265	270	111	406	16	491	123	219
Divorced	15	10	------	38	21	113	46	10	------	24	15	18	4	35	3	26	4	16
Unknown	3	3	------	------	------	4	14	------	1	2	3	4	------	5	------	1	------	1
FAMILIES																		
Number of families	2,565	871	------	2,530	1,548	5,772	5,678	1,870	161	485	1,768	1,521	591	1,917	111	2,446	804	1,027
Median size	386	5.26	------	4.76	5.02	3.56	4.83	4.82	3.48	3.41	5.36	5.13	5.51	3.92	4.67	4.66	5.33	4.56
Families having—																		
No children under 10	1,271	311	------	1,007	539	3,090	2,120	691	96	273	594	496	177	944	48	990	255	431
1 child under 10	495	141	------	458	306	1,099	1,030	340	31	83	375	330	118	373	24	472	165	198
2 children under 10	308	154	------	351	260	684	824	285	16	58	275	260	105	246	15	351	123	136
3 or more	491	265	------	714	443	899	1,704	554	18	71	524	435	191	354	24	633	261	262

CHARACTERISTICS OF NEGRO POPULATION BY COUNTIES: 1930—Continued

(See note at head of table)

SUBJECT	NORTH CAROLINA—Continued																	
	Lenoir	Lincoln	McDowell	Macon	Madison	Martin	Mecklenburg	Mitchell	Montgomery	Moore	Nash	New Hanover	Northampton	Onslow	Orange	Pamlico	Pasquotank	Pender
POPULATION BY SEX																		
Negro population: 1930	15,438	3,321	2,001	449	267	11,009	38,023	56	3,730	9,795	23,456	16,779	17,042	4,079	6,904	3,153	8,206	7,567
Male	7,486	1,585	972	238	142	5,358	17,966	28	1,839	4,785	11,497	7,724	8,517	2,033	3,515	1,573	3,985	3,645
Female	7,952	1,736	1,029	211	125	5,651	20,057	28	1,891	5,010	11,959	9,055	8,525	2,046	3,389	1,580	4,221	3,922
Negro population: 1920	13,061	2,231	1,974	465	334	9,764	26,657	56	3,285	6,382	17,413	16,482	13,825	4,439	5,635	3,214	7,838	7,318
Male	6,378	1,063	944	245	179	4,798	12,755	32	1,622	3,086	8,722	7,778	6,815	2,187	2,760	1,618	3,844	3,575
Female	6,683	1,168	1,030	220	155	4,966	13,902	24	1,663	3,296	8,691	8,704	7,010	2,252	2,875	1,596	3,994	3,743
Percent of total population:																		
1930	43.2	14.5	9.8	3.3	1.3	47.0	29.7	0.4	23.0	34.7	44.4	39.0	62.7	26.7	32.6	33.9	42.9	48.2
1920	44.2	12.5	11.8	3.6	1.7	46.9	33.0	0.5	22.5	29.8	42.4	40.6	59.6	30.2	31.5	35.5	44.4	49.5
VOTING AGE: 1930																		
Total 21 years old and over	7,195	1,427	971	231	128	4,360	20,517	34	1,558	4,378	9,823	9,229	6,720	1,662	3,046	1,327	3,785	3,182
Male	3,422	663	463	127	65	2,089	9,618	15	744	2,079	4,850	4,138	3,270	794	1,547	651	1,811	1,487
Female	3,773	764	508	104	63	2,271	10,899	19	814	2,299	4,973	5,091	3,450	868	1,499	676	1,974	1,695
AGE: 1930																		
Under 5 years	1,949	440	217	48	28	1,625	3,677	4	515	1,262	3,145	1,602	2,404	529	923	460	1,030	1,026
Under 1 year	353	93	35	6	5	313	672		103	232	586	295	435	88	177	89	178	204
5 to 9 years	2,107	486	275	56	31	1,775	4,365	6	587	1,472	3,665	1,978	2,731	678	1,033	492	1,157	1,184
10 to 14 years	1,968	431	254	48	40	1,628	4,041	5	491	1,251	3,318	1,764	2,548	569	893	414	1,031	1,028
15 to 19 years	1,848	458	225	53	34	1,364	4,358	4	495	1,210	3,002	1,849	2,246	544	849	393	1,028	975
20 to 24 years	1,674	358	195	48	27	1,014	4,849	9	343	976	2,159	1,719	1,569	343	683	297	764	651
25 to 29 years	1,190	224	112	27	20	657	3,996	5	242	708	1,676	1,421	1,056	243	499	173	529	415
30 to 34 years	873	159	118	33	13	494	2,757	2	174	495	1,268	1,208	741	204	369	149	395	347
35 to 44 years	1,566	274	216	41	22	913	4,538	4	327	970	2,205	2,371	1,440	343	650	244	338	648
45 to 54 years	1,257	239	173	45	16	798	2,951	6	288	748	1,674	1,633	1,177	345	487	251	737	689
55 to 64 years	636	133	98	24	21	410	1,279	4	140	390	839	712	645	159	285	160	427	356
65 to 74 years	244	82	75	20	11	215	596	3	80	209	351	354	343	76	162	74	183	174
75 years and over	119	36	33	6	4	106	281	4	46	89	153	163	138	43	69	45	83	74
Unknown	7	1	10			10	335		2	15	1	5	4	3	2	1	4	
SCHOOL ATTENDANCE																		
Total 7 to 13 years, inclusive	2,855	631	370	70	52	2,322	5,833	8	743	1,863	4,802	2,592	3,603	851	1,308	635	1,498	1,524
Number attending school	2,571	558	317	61	41	2,010	5,367	7	657	1,743	4,244	2,406	2,967	803	1,162	560	1,415	1,335
Percent attending school	90.1	88.4	85.7			86.6	92.0		88.4	93.6	88.4	92.8	82.3	94.4	88.8	88.2	94.5	87.6
Total 14 and 15 years, inclusive	751	167	104	14	15	596	1,641	1	202	510	1,276	737	1,051	240	326	148	430	397
Number attending school	586	124	67	10	10	450	1,173	1	149	388	986	580	820	210	239	110	339	323
Percent attending school	78.0	74.3	64.4			75.5	71.5		73.8	76.1	77.3	78.7	78.0	87.5	73.3	74.3	78.8	81.4
Total 16 and 17 years, inclusive	747	189	89	26	16	561	1,711	1	212	454	1,253	739	911	216	364	149	408	415
Number attending school	374	79	34	15	5	268	605		107	204	549	334	483	107	172	65	200	221
Percent attending school	50.1	41.8				47.8	35.4		50.5	44.9	43.8	45.2	53.0	49.5	47.3	43.6	49.0	53.3
Total 18 to 20 years, inclusive	1,101	262	143	36	18	786	2,894	5	268	709	1,649	1,089	1,210	303	494	234	585	534
Number attending school	168	39	11	6	2	110	245		58	91	183	168	235	43	62	25	92	111
Percent attending school	15.3	14.9	7.7			14.0	8.5		21.6	12.8	11.1	15.4	19.4	14.2	12.6	10.7	15.7	20.8
ILLITERACY																		
Total 10 years old and over	11,382	2,395	1,509	345	208	7,609	29,981	46	2,628	7,061	16,646	13,199	11,907	2,872	4,948	2,201	6,019	5,357
Number illiterate	2,542	429	277	78	49	2,073	6,238	15	605	1,086	3,986	2,333	2,975	600	1,106	318	1,170	1,163
Percent illiterate	22.3	17.9	18.4	22.6	23.6	27.2	20.8		23.0	15.4	23.9	17.7	25.0	20.9	22.4	14.4	19.4	21.7
Percent illiterate in 1920	27.6	22.0	27.1	24.4	25.1	29.7	24.9	42.2	26.1	19.4	27.2	20.8	23.3	25.8	21.7	11.3	27.5	23.1
URBAN AND RURAL																		
Urban population	5,062	524				1,436	25,163			860	3,998	13,106			891		3,722	
Percent urban	32.8	15.8				13.0	66.2			8.8	17.0	78.1			12.9		45.4	
Rural population	10,376	2,797	2,001	449	267	9,573	12,860	56	3,730	8,935	19,458	3,673	17,042	4,079	6,013	3,153	4,484	7,567
Rural-farm	8,883	2,423	412	230	169	7,782	9,193	47	2,480	3,663	16,637	387	14,945	3,178	3,397	1,248	3,296	5,325
Rural-nonfarm	1,493	374	1,589	219	98	1,791	3,667	9	1,250	5,272	2,821	3,286	2,097	901	2,616	1,905	1,185	2,242
Percent rural	67.2	84.2	100.0	100.0	100.0	87.0	33.8		100.0	91.2	83.0	21.9	100.0	100.0	87.1	100.0	54.6	100.0
MARITAL CONDITION																		
Males 15 years old and over	4,469	937	583	165	89	2,856	12,098	17	1,038	2,752	6,528	5,101	4,631	1,120	2,045	871	2,365	2,041
Single	1,601	367	194	58	49	976	3,982	7	401	1,019	2,400	1,906	1,871	438	826	296	574	775
Married	2,572	524	349	98	35	1,720	7,138	8	576	1,599	3,843	2,885	2,619	627	1,113	502	1,436	1,149
Widowed	238	42	35	7	5	127	780	2	52	125	247	284	167	51	100	69	160	110
Divorced	55	4	2	2		27	64		6	8	35	23	22	4	5	4	15	6
Unknown	3		3			6	134		3	1	3	3	6		1			1
Females 15 years old and over	4,945	1,027	672	132	79	3,125	13,842	24	1,099	3,058	6,800	6,334	4,728	1,183	2,010	916	2,623	2,288
Single	1,436	351	227	37	33	939	3,834	10	387	1,003	2,059	1,902	1,564	379	647	255	725	790
Married	2,595	540	354	80	33	1,765	7,522	7	592	1,642	3,893	3,128	2,642	635	1,113	513	1,475	1,170
Widowed	743	131	82	14	13	374	2,328	6	111	377	780	1,250	474	169	241	147	408	314
Divorced	168	4	5	1		45	119	1	9	34	65	50	42		6	1	15	11
Unknown	3	1	4			2	39			2	3	4	6		3			3
FAMILIES																		
Number of families	3,159	620	419	93	54	1,995	8,842	9	695	1,864	4,393	4,159	2,992	770	1,256	626	1,679	1,477
Median size	3.93	4.49	4.01			4.94	3.19		4.77	4.35	4.57	3.04	5.11	4.62	4.78	4.32	4.16	4.62
Families having—																		
No children under 10	1,465	266	220	47	29	710	5,189	3	274	789	1,759	2,452	992	306	507	253	788	596
1 child under 10	620	111	62	15	6	385	1,543	2	130	342	805	772	618	153	218	130	297	279
2 children under 10	434	93	56	15	9	301	951	4	97	265	643	414	474	100	183	88	231	212
3 or more	640	150	81	16	10	599	1,159		194	468	1,186	521	908	211	348	155	363	390

CHARACTERISTICS OF NEGRO POPULATION BY COUNTIES: 1930—Continued

(See note at head of table)

NORTH CAROLINA—Continued

SUBJECT	Perquimans	Person	Pitt	Polk	Randolph	Richmond	Robeson	Rockingham	Rowan	Rutherford	Sampson	Scotland	Stanly	Stokes	Surry	Swain	Transylvania	Tyrrell
POPULATION BY SEX																		
Negro population: 1930	5,287	8,584	26,370	1,530	3,840	13,283	22,784	11,337	11,488	5,362	13,670	10,799	3,531	2,438	2,716	193	644	1,707
Male	2,547	4,268	12,797	740	1,917	6,321	11,005	5,434	5,656	2,560	6,740	5,218	1,774	1,211	1,290	96	291	830
Female	2,740	4,316	13,573	790	1,923	6,962	11,779	5,903	5,832	2,802	6,930	5,581	1,757	1,227	1,426	97	353	877
Negro population: 1920	5,465	7,997	23,025	1,497	3,554	10,545	20,307	10,656	9,233	4,451	12,144	9,210	3,543	2,278	2,381	115	631	1,476
Male	2,712	3,938	11,392	741	1,732	5,118	9,852	5,106	4,552	2,142	5,959	4,453	1,839	1,145	1,135	62	321	718
Female	2,753	4,059	11,633	756	1,822	5,427	10,455	5,550	4,681	2,309	6,185	4,757	1,704	1,133	1,246	53	310	758
Percent of total population:																		
1930	49.6	38.9	48.4	15.0	10.6	39.0	34.3	22.2	20.3	13.3	34.1	53.5	11.7	10.9	6.8	1.7	6.7	33.1
1920	49.1	42.1	50.5	16.9	11.5	41.2	37.1	24.1	21.0	14.2	33.7	59.0	12.9	11.1	7.3	.9	6.8	30.4
VOTING AGE: 1930																		
Total 21 years old and over	2,280	3,410	11,310	696	1,705	5,654	9,399	5,205	5,774	2,276	5,605	4,407	1,780	957	1,237	86	318	712
Male	1,116	1,671	5,328	331	838	2,612	4,427	2,448	2,770	1,076	2,683	2,053	912	487	594	43	144	331
Female	1,164	1,739	5,982	365	867	3,042	4,972	2,757	3,004	1,200	2,922	2,354	868	470	643	43	174	381
AGE: 1930																		
Under 5 years	692	1,256	3,569	175	451	1,583	3,012	1,368	1,163	707	1,950	1,432	405	343	386	22	67	229
Under 1 year	135	270	673	46	88	253	552	263	209	123	390	235	60	66	92	1	15	54
5 to 9 years	775	1,377	3,952	209	539	1,966	3,468	1,564	1,510	834	2,133	1,631	443	389	394	26	104	268
10 to 14 years	720	1,224	3,523	200	549	1,863	3,112	1,424	1,410	717	1,889	1,566	383	355	348	25	68	233
15 to 19 years	709	1,143	3,340	217	504	1,920	3,199	1,486	1,395	701	1,766	1,476	432	332	295	30	73	234
20 to 24 years	435	766	2,739	124	367	1,276	2,266	1,139	1,160	542	1,385	1,029	420	207	248	16	49	151
25 to 29 years	318	518	1,949	107	250	848	1,428	796	937	357	873	670	376	132	193	16	74	97
30 to 34 years	262	370	1,420	79	185	628	1,040	633	735	241	625	471	241	91	154	11	35	87
35 to 44 years	500	702	2,416	156	367	1,296	2,181	1,118	1,346	499	1,198	914	385	200	243	22	69	138
45 to 54 years	440	578	1,930	148	290	1,018	1,615	874	1,028	366	973	751	254	176	198	12	65	140
55 to 64 years	260	339	933	64	175	521	887	476	460	216	499	431	109	100	118	7	19	64
65 to 74 years	117	194	409	36	102	245	408	304	227	120	260	190	50	71	92	5	15	38
75 years and over	57	116	170	15	50	113	156	154	105	58	118	90	28	41	47	1	6	28
Unknown	2	1	20	------	11	6	12	1	12	4	1	148	5	1	------	------	------	------
SCHOOL ATTENDANCE																		
Total 7 to 13 years, inclusive	1,036	1,772	5,135	286	759	2,626	4,494	2,040	2,031	1,081	2,737	2,140	560	510	523	34	110	357
Number attending school	968	1,464	4,706	253	704	2,299	3,763	1,863	1,888	975	2,430	1,392	521	429	475	33	98	332
Percent attending school	93.4	82.6	91.6	88.5	92.8	87.5	83.7	91.3	93.0	90.2	88.8	65.0	93.0	84.1	90.8	------	89.1	93.0
Total 14 and 15 years, inclusive	273	467	1,363	82	208	817	1,222	588	565	284	775	608	158	147	119	16	32	87
Number attending school	241	367	1,016	64	185	614	978	454	436	223	599	386	125	106	94	12	27	77
Percent attending school	88.3	78.6	74.5	------	88.9	75.2	80.0	77.2	77.2	78.5	77.3	63.5	79.1	72.1	79.0	------	------	------
Total 16 and 17 years, inclusive	314	483	1,358	91	211	808	1,331	582	537	285	694	631	168	127	125	13	29	84
Number attending school	199	247	494	46	132	351	705	215	265	131	309	282	84	54	51	5	16	57
Percent attending school	63.4	51.1	36.4	------	62.6	43.4	53.0	36.9	49.3	46.0	44.5	44.7	50.0	42.5	40.8	------	------	------
Total 18 to 20 years, inclusive	380	615	1,978	113	285	996	1,865	891	822	402	1,016	858	270	187	169	13	45	135
Number attending school	106	122	164	23	74	119	355	113	178	53	170	148	43	15	23	2	11	29
Percent attending school	27.9	19.8	8.3	20.4	26.0	11.9	19.0	12.7	21.7	13.2	16.7	17.2	15.9	8.0	13.6	------	------	21.5
ILLITERACY																		
Total 10 years old and over	3,820	5,951	18,849	1,146	2,850	9,734	16,304	8,405	8,815	3,821	9,587	7,736	2,683	1,706	1,936	145	473	1,210
Number illiterate	644	1,735	4,855	209	477	2,355	3,810	1,549	1,521	717	2,016	2,426	359	459	461	18	47	298
Percent illiterate	16.9	29.2	25.8	18.2	16.7	24.2	23.4	18.4	17.3	18.8	21.0	31.4	13.4	26.9	23.8	12.4	9.9	24.6
Percent illiterate in 1920	17.1	30.4	26.5	22.7	20.8	24.7	26.9	29.0	19.5	24.6	24.7	27.7	30.8	33.2	27.8	------	23.0	19.2
URBAN AND RURAL																		
Urban population	------	1,098	4,233	------	802	2,579	1,123	2,333	4,031	630	912	1,258	60	------	477	------	------	------
Percent urban	------	12.8	16.1	------	20.9	19.4	4.9	20.6	35.1	11.7	6.7	11.6	1.7	------	17.6	------	------	------
Rural population	5,287	7,486	22,137	1,530	3,038	10,704	21,661	9,004	7,457	4,732	12,758	9,541	3,471	2,438	2,239	193	644	1,707
Rural-farm	3,571	7,008	17,707	794	2,075	7,435	16,751	5,095	3,819	2,994	10,876	8,538	993	1,891	1,238	31	41	802
Rural-nonfarm	1,716	478	4,430	736	963	3,269	4,910	3,909	3,638	1,738	1,882	1,003	2,478	547	1,001	162	603	905
Percent rural	100.0	87.2	83.9	100.0	79.1	80.6	95.1	79.4	64.9	88.3	93.3	88.4	98.3	100.0	82.4	100.0	100.0	100.0
MARITAL CONDITION																		
Males 15 years old and over	1,497	2,295	7,266	444	1,127	3,670	6,244	3,288	3,598	1,461	3,738	2,924	1,144	673	749	60	186	472
Single	525	914	2,605	165	457	1,370	2,361	1,271	1,339	528	1,413	1,106	403	264	236	28	58	170
Married	880	1,261	4,301	237	615	2,024	3,601	1,791	2,067	866	2,162	1,674	668	361	465	30	122	274
Widowed	84	112	323	38	49	204	257	203	178	65	151	124	67	45	41	1	5	26
Divorced	8	8	34	4	6	8	24	21	14	2	10	16	2	3	7	1	1	2
Unknown	------	------	3	------	------	64	1	2	------	------	2	4	4	------	------	------	------	------
Females 15 years old and over	1,603	2,432	8,060	502	1,174	4,201	6,948	3,693	3,807	1,643	3,960	3,246	1,156	678	839	60	219	505
Single	502	911	2,436	178	413	1,442	2,368	1,273	1,102	538	1,307	1,065	335	243	251	23	62	161
Married	904	1,295	4,488	247	621	2,115	3,726	1,869	2,133	900	2,191	1,725	680	363	488	30	132	272
Widowed	186	214	1,049	71	129	589	798	499	527	201	438	423	135	70	91	7	25	69
Divorced	11	10	81	6	9	19	47	47	41	4	23	31	6	2	8	------	------	2
Unknown	------	2	6	------	2	36	9	5	4	------	1	2	------	------	1	------	------	1
FAMILIES																		
Number of families	1,033	1,457	5,023	315	728	2,607	4,356	2,175	2,546	1,011	2,567	2,041	748	424	546	30	146	294
Median size	4.44	5.15	4.39	4.01	4.42	4.23	4.57	4.24	3.54	4.56	4.69	4.56	3.65	5.18	4.08	------	3.55	5.28
Families having—																		
No children under 10	443	512	1,971	168	337	1,137	1,727	1,004	1,375	424	963	808	367	167	240	15	78	104
1 child under 10	203	254	1,058	55	135	531	886	389	450	185	485	398	167	66	94	3	17	53
2 children under 10	146	227	759	29	76	357	637	291	289	132	408	296	92	51	81	4	23	49
3 or more	241	464	1,235	63	180	582	1,106	491	432	270	711	539	122	140	131	8	28	88

CHARACTERISTICS OF NEGRO POPULATION BY COUNTIES: 1930—Continued

(See note at head of table)

SUBJECT	NORTH CAROLINA—Continued											NORTH DAKOTA						
	Union	Vance	Wake	Warren	Washington	Watauga	Wayne	Wilkes	Wilson	Yadkin	Yancey	The State	Benson	Billings	Bottineau	Bowman	Burleigh	Cass
POPULATION BY SEX																		
Negro population: 1930	10,048	12,009	33,916	14,846	5,441	252	23,205	2,696	19,325	986	163	377	4	1	2	2	60	42
Male	4,974	5,913	16,457	7,246	2,644	158	11,116	1,305	9,401	512	98	243	3	1	1	2	44	28
Female	5,074	6,096	17,459	7,600	2,797	94	12,089	1,391	9,924	474	65	134	1	-	1	-	16	14
Negro population: 1920	8,669	10,171	29,210	13,821	5,570	204	18,995	2,322	16,261	1,102	272	467	1	-	4	2	51	55
Male	4,253	4,951	14,541	6,770	2,694	108	9,193	1,138	8,011	569	153	276	1	-	3	2	33	31
Female	4,416	5,220	14,669	7,051	2,876	96	9,802	1,184	8,250	533	119	191	-	-	1	-	18	24
Percent of total population:																		
1930	24.5	44.0	35.8	63.5	46.9	1.7	43.8	7.5	43.0	5.5	1.1	0.1	-	-	-	-	0.3	0.1
1920	24.1	44.6	38.9	64.0	48.7	1.5	43.5	7.1	44.2	6.7	1.8	.1	-	-	-	-	.3	.1
VOTING AGE: 1930																		
Total 21 years old and over	4,203	5,261	16,292	5,928	2,318	148	11,476	1,186	8,738	450	67	278	3	1	1	1	48	38
Male	2,030	2,550	7,872	2,880	1,099	109	5,404	566	4,179	222	39	177	2	1	1	1	35	25
Female	2,173	2,711	8,420	3,048	1,219	39	6,072	620	4,559	228	28	101	1	-	-	-	13	13
AGE: 1930																		
Under 5 years	1,249	1,562	3,835	2,145	731	28	2,683	337	2,555	121	23	30	1	-	1	-	4	1
Under 1 year	225	297	671	389	144	6	471	59	524	24	1	6	-	-	-	-	1	-
5 to 9 years	1,447	1,816	4,568	2,398	852	25	3,070	398	2,783	136	23	21	-	-	-	-	1	2
10 to 14 years	1,465	1,538	4,235	2,120	729	19	2,768	358	2,491	146	23	15	-	-	-	-	2	-
15 to 19 years	1,443	1,543	4,163	1,959	701	22	2,688	356	2,305	121	23	26	-	-	-	-	3	-
20 to 24 years	987	1,143	3,620	1,233	455	45	2,389	248	2,058	81	13	32	-	-	-	1	6	3
25 to 29 years	654	950	2,746	798	314	44	1,909	189	1,505	62	6	31	-	-	-	-	5	3
30 to 34 years	453	632	2,025	688	255	15	1,426	97	1,136	44	6	32	-	-	-	-	8	7
35 to 44 years	929	1,106	3,668	1,276	462	23	2,652	243	1,937	90	17	74	-	-	-	-	13	7
45 to 54 years	704	831	2,693	1,081	469	12	2,029	208	1,394	66	10	69	3	1	1	1	11	10
55 to 64 years	425	495	1,351	612	260	11	972	136	691	57	4	31	-	-	-	-	3	7
65 to 74 years	200	276	671	355	138	6	384	77	301	41	12	13	-	-	-	-	3	2
75 years and over	89	117	336	177	68	2	201	49	147	20	3	3	-	-	-	-	1	-
Unknown	3	-	5	4	7	-	34	-	22	1	-	-	-	-	-	-	-	-
SCHOOL ATTENDANCE																		
Total 7 to 13 years, inclusive	1,978	2,256	6,114	3,092	1,093	30	4,030	514	3,592	191	34	22	-	-	-	-	2	1
Number attending school	1,595	1,959	5,546	2,844	1,016	26	3,648	458	2,965	147	34	20	-	-	-	-	2	1
Percent attending school	80.6	86.8	90.7	92.0	93.0	-	90.5	89.1	82.5	77.0	-	-	-	-	-	-	-	-
Total 14 and 15 years, inclusive	609	610	1,638	846	295	6	1,039	152	946	53	8	8	-	-	-	-	1	-
Number attending school	391	493	1,324	732	231	6	794	117	645	39	8	6	-	-	-	-	1	-
Percent attending school	64.2	80.8	80.8	86.5	78.3	-	76.4	77.0	68.2	-	-	-	-	-	-	-	-	-
Total 16 and 17 years, inclusive	579	632	1,775	818	314	7	1,067	149	1,003	44	9	13	-	-	-	-	2	-
Number attending school	217	305	925	454	144	1	416	81	347	23	5	7	-	-	-	-	2	-
Percent attending school	37.5	48.3	52.1	55.5	45.9	-	39.0	54.4	34.6	-	-	-	-	-	-	-	-	-
Total 18 to 20 years, inclusive	822	905	2,418	1,009	361	22	1,629	197	1,306	63	15	15	-	-	-	1	2	1
Number attending school	109	172	536	208	56	3	167	53	104	8	3	5	-	-	-	-	-	-
Percent attending school	13.3	19.0	22.2	20.6	15.5	-	10.3	26.9	8.0	-	-	-	-	-	-	-	-	-
ILLITERACY																		
Total 10 years old and over	7,352	8,631	25,513	10,303	3,858	199	17,452	1,961	13,987	729	117	326	3	1	1	2	55	39
Number illiterate	1,818	1,595	4,212	1,476	726	26	3,278	339	3,715	158	9	11	-	1	-	-	2	3
Percent illiterate	24.7	18.5	16.5	14.3	18.8	13.1	18.8	17.3	26.6	21.7	7.7	3.4	-	-	-	-	-	-
Percent illiterate in 1920	26.8	19.2	22.5	18.4	16.3	34.7	22.9	26.6	31.5	29.1	27.8	4.0	-	-	-	-	-	-
URBAN AND RURAL																		
Urban population	1,982	2,843	12,575	-	-	-	7,922	426	6,205	-	-	216	-	-	-	-	45	35
Percent urban	19.7	23.7	37.1	-	-	-	34.1	15.8	32.1	-	-	57.3	-	-	-	-	-	-
Rural population	8,066	9,166	21,341	14,846	5,441	252	15,283	2,270	13,120	986	163	161	4	1	2	2	15	7
Rural-farm	7,128	7,338	15,552	12,655	2,123	48	11,244	1,523	11,477	668	80	78	3	1	-	2	3	5
Rural-nonfarm	938	1,828	5,789	2,191	3,318	204	4,039	747	1,643	318	83	83	1	-	2	-	12	2
Percent rural	80.3	76.3	62.9	100.0	100.0	100.0	65.9	84.2	67.9	100.0	100.0	42.7	-	-	-	-	-	-
MARITAL CONDITION																		
Males 15 years old and over	2,882	3,438	10,219	3,959	1,504	125	6,945	762	5,490	292	58	200	2	1	1	2	38	25
Single	1,057	1,339	3,881	1,491	546	68	2,672	319	2,029	98	27	95	1	-	-	1	17	11
Married	1,702	1,920	5,682	2,273	865	50	3,861	411	3,137	167	29	70	1	-	1	-	12	10
Widowed	106	144	602	170	76	6	343	31	254	24	2	21	-	1	-	-	5	2
Divorced	12	31	46	21	17	1	40	1	69	3	-	13	-	-	-	1	4	2
Unknown	5	4	8	4	-	-	29	-	1	-	-	1	-	-	-	-	-	-
Females 15 years old and over	3,005	3,655	11,059	4,224	1,625	55	7,739	841	6,006	291	36	111	1	-	-	-	15	14
Single	895	1,169	3,558	1,415	462	17	2,392	309	1,785	83	7	22	-	-	-	-	2	1
Married	1,713	1,965	5,734	2,362	907	35	4,197	425	3,198	171	28	68	1	-	-	-	9	9
Widowed	362	462	1,655	422	230	2	1,080	95	825	35	1	17	-	-	-	-	1	4
Divorced	33	58	92	23	26	1	57	9	189	1	-	4	-	-	-	-	3	-
Unknown	2	1	20	2	-	-	13	3	9	1	-	-	-	-	-	-	-	-
FAMILIES																		
Number of families	1,946	2,246	6,673	2,525	1,012	38	4,264	485	3,748	211	30	120	2	-	1	-	16	16
Median size	4.33	4.43	4.04	5.41	4.73	-	4.09	4.62	4.18	3.89	-	1.56	-	-	-	-	-	-
Families having:																		
No children under 10	817	945	3,225	849	396	21	1,923	196	1,624	102	11	103	2	-	-	-	13	15
1 child under 10	396	404	1,194	467	199	2	815	101	732	41	6	8	-	-	1	-	3	1
2 children under 10	299	310	863	392	133	6	568	57	489	25	4	6	-	-	-	-	-	-
3 or more	434	587	1,391	817	284	9	958	131	903	43	9	3	-	-	-	-	-	-

CHARACTERISTICS OF NEGRO POPULATION BY COUNTIES: 1930—Continued

(See note at head of table)

SUBJECT	Cavalier	Dickey	Divide	Eddy	Grand Forks	Grant	Griggs	McHenry	McKenzie	Morton	Mountrail	Nelson	Pembina	Pierce	Ramsey	Ransom	Renville	Richland
	NORTH DAKOTA—Continued																	
POPULATION BY SEX																		
Negro population: 1930	2	3	18	9	19	1	11	10	5	10	5	8	11	6	26	6	1	1
Male	2	1	11	5	10	1	7	6	3	8	5	5	5	3	19	3	1	1
Female	-	2	7	4	9	-	4	4	2	2	-	3	6	3	7	3	-	-
Negro population: 1920	1	4	6	11	30	-	4	8	6	13	10	1	17	17	44	4	10	11
Male	1	4	3	5	19	-	2	6	3	8	5	1	6	8	30	3	5	4
Female	-	-	3	6	11	-	2	2	3	5	5	-	11	9	14	1	5	7
Percent of total population:																		
1930	-	-	0.2	0.1	0.1	-	0.2	0.1	0.1	0.1	-	0.1	0.1	0.1	0.2	0.1	-	-
1920	-	-	0.1	0.2	0.1	-	0.1	0.1	0.1	0.1	0.1	-	0.1	0.2	0.3	-	0.1	0.1
VOTING AGE: 1930																		
Total 21 years old and over	2	-	6	4	12	1	3	7	3	7	5	2	3	3	18	3	1	1
Male	2	-	4	2	7	1	-	4	2	5	5	2	1	2	12	1	1	1
Female	-	-	2	2	5	-	3	3	1	2	-	-	2	1	6	2	-	-
AGE: 1930																		
Under 5 years	-	2	4	4	1	-	3	-	-	-	-	1	2	1	2	1	-	-
Under 1 year	-	-	1	2	-	-	1	-	-	-	-	-	-	1	-	-	-	-
5 to 9 years	-	-	2	1	2	-	2	1	-	-	-	2	2	1	2	2	-	-
10 to 14 years	-	-	3	-	3	-	1	-	-	-	-	2	1	-	1	-	-	-
15 to 19 years	-	-	3	-	1	-	2	2	2	2	-	-	3	1	3	-	-	-
20 to 24 years	-	1	1	1	3	-	-	1	-	1	-	2	1	1	2	1	-	-
25 to 29 years	-	-	1	-	1	-	-	1	-	-	1	-	1	-	2	-	-	-
30 to 34 years	-	-	-	1	1	-	1	-	1	2	-	-	-	-	-	-	-	-
35 to 44 years	1	-	2	-	2	1	1	1	-	2	2	-	1	-	6	1	1	-
45 to 54 years	1	-	2	-	-	-	-	2	2	1	-	1	-	1	6	-	-	-
55 to 64 years	-	-	-	1	4	-	1	1	-	2	1	-	-	-	-	1	-	1
65 to 74 years	-	-	-	1	-	-	-	1	-	-	1	-	-	1	2	-	-	-
75 years and over	-	-	-	-	1	-	-	-	-	-	-	-	-	-	-	-	-	-
Unknown	-	-	-	-	-	-	-	-	-	-	-	-	-	-	-	-	-	-
SCHOOL ATTENDANCE																		
Total 7 to 13 years, inclusive	-	-	4	1	3	-	1	1	-	-	-	4	2	-	1	-	-	-
Number attending school	-	-	4	1	3	-	1	1	-	-	-	4	-	-	1	-	-	-
Percent attending school	-	-	-	-	-	-	-	-	-	-	-	-	-	-	-	-	-	-
Total 14 and 15 years, inclusive	-	-	1	-	1	-	1	1	-	-	-	-	1	-	-	-	-	-
Number attending school	-	-	1	-	1	-	-	1	-	-	-	-	-	-	-	-	-	-
Percent attending school	-	-	-	-	-	-	-	-	-	-	-	-	-	-	-	-	-	-
Total 16 and 17 years, inclusive	-	-	2	-	-	-	1	1	1	-	-	-	3	-	1	-	-	-
Number attending school	-	-	1	-	-	-	1	-	1	-	-	-	-	-	-	-	-	-
Percent attending school	-	-	-	-	-	-	-	-	-	-	-	-	-	-	-	-	-	-
Total 18 to 20 years, inclusive	-	1	-	-	1	-	1	-	1	3	-	1	-	1	2	-	-	-
Number attending school	-	-	-	-	1	-	-	-	-	3	-	-	-	1	-	-	-	-
Percent attending school	-	-	-	-	-	-	-	-	-	-	-	-	-	-	-	-	-	-
ILLITERACY																		
Total 10 years old and over	2	1	12	4	16	1	6	9	5	10	5	5	7	4	22	3	1	1
Number illiterate	-	-	-	-	-	-	-	-	1	-	1	-	1	-	-	-	-	-
Percent illiterate	-	-	-	-	-	-	-	-	-	-	-	-	-	-	-	-	-	-
Percent illiterate in 1920	-	-	-	-	-	-	-	-	-	-	-	-	-	-	-	-	-	-
URBAN AND RURAL																		
Urban population	-	-	-	-	18	-	-	-	-	9	-	-	-	-	24	-	-	1
Percent urban	-	-	-	-	-	-	-	-	-	-	-	-	-	-	-	-	-	-
Rural population	2	3	18	9	1	1	11	10	5	1	5	8	11	6	2	6	1	-
Rural-farm	2	2	2	4	-	1	8	5	2	-	4	8	8	4	1	-	-	-
Rural-nonfarm	-	1	16	5	1	-	3	5	3	1	1	-	3	2	1	6	1	-
Percent rural	-	-	-	-	-	-	-	-	-	-	-	-	-	-	-	-	-	-
MARITAL CONDITION																		
Males 15 years old and over	2	1	4	2	8	1	2	6	3	8	5	2	3	3	15	1	1	1
Single	2	1	1	1	2	1	2	2	2	7	5	1	3	1	7	-	-	-
Married	-	-	3	-	3	-	-	3	1	1	-	1	-	1	6	1	1	-
Widowed	-	-	-	1	1	-	-	1	-	-	-	-	-	1	2	-	-	-
Divorced	-	-	-	-	2	-	-	-	-	-	-	-	-	-	-	-	-	1
Unknown	-	-	-	-	-	-	-	-	-	-	-	-	-	-	-	-	-	-
Females 15 years old and over	-	-	5	2	5	-	3	3	2	2	-	1	3	1	6	2	-	-
Single	-	-	3	-	2	-	1	-	1	-	-	1	2	-	1	-	-	-
Married	-	-	1	1	2	-	2	3	1	2	-	-	1	1	5	1	-	-
Widowed	-	-	1	1	-	-	-	-	-	-	-	-	-	-	-	1	-	-
Divorced	-	-	-	-	1	-	-	-	-	-	-	-	-	-	-	-	-	-
Unknown	-	-	-	-	-	-	-	-	-	-	-	-	-	-	-	-	-	-
FAMILIES																		
Number of families	1	-	3	2	4	1	1	4	1	2	3	1	1	3	9	1	-	1
Median size	-	-	-	-	-	-	-	-	-	-	-	-	-	-	-	-	-	-
Families having—																		
No children under 10	1	-	1	2	2	1	1	3	1	2	3	-	1	2	7	-	-	1
1 child under 10	-	-	-	-	1	-	-	1	-	-	-	-	-	-	-	-	-	-
2 children under 10	-	-	1	-	1	-	-	-	-	-	-	-	-	1	2	-	-	-
3 or more	-	-	1	-	-	-	-	-	-	-	-	1	-	-	-	1	-	-

CHARACTERISTICS OF NEGRO POPULATION BY COUNTIES: 1930—Continued

(See note at head of table)

SUBJECT	NORTH DAKOTA—Continued									OHIO								
	Sargent	Sioux	Stark	Stutsman	Towner	Walsh	Ward	Wells	Williams	The State	Adams	Allen	Ashland	Ashtabula	Athens	Auglaize	Belmont	Brown
POPULATION BY SEX																		
Negro population: 1930	6	1	2	9	2	1	76	2	15	309,304	74	1,686	61	357	1,088	47	2,699	817
Male	4	1	1	6	1	1	45	1	8	159,128	36	887	36	200	592	27	1,456	397
Female	2	-	1	3	1	-	31	1	7	150,176	38	799	25	157	496	20	1,243	420
Negro population: 1920	4	-	6	20	5	2	68	-	20	186,187	79	1,385	34	338	1,350	44	2,029	972
Male	2	-	4	8	3	2	39	-	9	100,160	39	751	21	181	742	23	1,107	483
Female	2	-	2	12	2	-	29	-	11	86,027	40	634	13	157	608	21	922	489
Percent of total population:																		
1930	0.1	-	-	-	-	-	0.2	-	0.1	4.7	0.4	2.4	0.2	0.5	2.5	0.2	2.8	4.1
1920	-	-	-	0.1	0.1	-	0.2	-	0.1	3.2	0.4	2.0	0.1	0.5	2.7	0.1	2.2	4.3
VOTING AGE: 1930																		
Total 21 years old and over	3	1	1	9	2	1	71	2	15	199,291	46	1,122	45	253	624	27	1,662	492
Male	2	1	-	6	1	1	40	1	8	105,736	25	603	26	142	360	15	948	243
Female	1	-	1	3	1	-	31	1	7	93,555	21	519	19	111	264	12	714	249
AGE: 1930																		
Under 5 years	-	-	-	-	-	-	2	-	-	27,845	7	135	2	16	112	4	211	83
Under 1 year	-	-	-	-	-	-	-	-	-	5,326	1	25	-	3	31	-	43	24
5 to 9 years	-	-	-	-	-	-	1	-	-	28,959	7	147	4	27	123	1	278	77
10 to 14 years	2	-	-	-	-	-	-	-	-	24,086	7	121	7	26	90	4	263	80
15 to 19 years	1	-	1	-	-	-	2	-	-	23,758	5	132	2	30	119	9	243	72
20 to 24 years	-	-	-	-	-	-	4	1	2	29,392	8	129	7	26	89	9	196	40
25 to 29 years	-	-	-	-	-	1	14	-	1	34,366	3	146	6	27	73	1	242	38
30 to 34 years	1	-	-	2	-	-	5	-	3	31,179	4	126	2	39	64	2	231	45
35 to 44 years	-	-	-	2	1	-	24	-	6	54,272	8	272	6	81	132	2	443	99
45 to 54 years	-	1	-	2	1	-	19	1	2	32,306	7	250	14	50	120	9	341	90
55 to 64 years	2	-	-	3	-	-	3	-	1	13,967	11	146	6	13	87	4	146	91
65 to 74 years	-	-	1	-	-	-	1	-	-	6,000	3	54	3	10	56	1	72	64
75 years and over	-	-	-	-	-	-	1	-	-	2,741	4	28	2	11	23	1	33	38
Unknown	-	-	-	-	-	-	-	-	-	433	-	-	-	1	-	-	-	-
SCHOOL ATTENDANCE																		
Total 7 to 13 years, inclusive	2	-	-	-	-	-	-	-	-	36,564	9	196	11	45	148	3	385	106
Number attending school	2	-	-	-	-	-	-	-	-	35,493	9	191	11	42	139	3	381	104
Percent attending school	-	-	-	-	-	-	-	-	-	97.1	-	97.4	-	-	93.9	-	99.0	98.1
Total 14 and 15 years, inclusive	1	-	-	-	-	-	1	-	-	9,160	1	54	-	12	37	4	95	33
Number attending school	1	-	-	-	-	-	1	-	-	8,630	1	53	-	10	30	4	89	30
Percent attending school	-	-	-	-	-	-	-	-	-	94.2	-	-	-	-	-	-	-	-
Total 16 and 17 years, inclusive	-	-	1	-	-	-	1	-	-	9,198	3	50	1	13	46	3	96	28
Number attending school	-	-	1	-	-	-	1	-	-	5,618	3	39	1	9	22	1	61	10
Percent attending school	-	-	-	-	-	-	-	-	-	61.1	-	-	-	-	-	-	-	-
Total 18 to 20 years, inclusive	-	-	-	-	-	-	-	-	-	15,486	4	77	2	14	69	6	136	38
Number attending school	-	-	-	-	-	-	-	-	-	2,511	-	21	-	4	15	1	23	13
Percent attending school	-	-	-	-	-	-	-	-	-	16.2	-	-	-	-	-	-	16.9	-
ILLITERACY																		
Total 10 years old and over	6	1	2	9	2	1	73	2	15	252,500	60	1,404	55	314	853	42	2,210	657
Number illiterate	-	-	-	-	-	-	1	1	-	16,213	8	154	1	18	95	1	162	85
Percent illiterate	-	-	-	-	-	-	-	-	-	6.4	-	11.0	-	5.7	11.1	-	7.3	12.9
Percent illiterate in 1920	-	-	-	-	-	-	-	-	-	8.1	-	4.9	-	7.2	7.5	-	8.6	19.9
URBAN AND RURAL																		
Urban population	-	-	2	2	-	1	70	-	9	271,972	-	1,423	53	273	498	38	1,243	-
Percent urban	-	-	-	-	-	-	-	-	-	87.9	-	84.4	-	76.5	45.8	-	46.1	-
Rural population	6	1	-	7	2	-	6	2	6	37,332	74	263	8	84	590	9	1,456	817
Rural-farm	6	1	-	2	-	-	2	1	1	7,441	27	20	5	29	183	9	154	298
Rural-nonfarm	-	-	-	5	2	-	4	1	5	29,891	47	243	3	55	407	-	1,302	519
Percent rural	-	-	-	-	-	-	-	-	-	12.1	-	15.6	-	23.5	54.2	-	53.9	100.0
MARITAL CONDITION																		
Males 15 years old and over	2	1	1	6	1	1	42	1	8	119,402	26	682	29	163	434	22	1,089	284
Single	1	-	1	4	-	1	15	1	4	37,361	10	255	12	60	192	8	361	85
Married	1	-	-	2	1	-	17	-	4	71,922	15	367	14	85	199	13	617	159
Widowed	-	-	-	-	-	-	7	-	-	7,535	1	44	2	14	30	1	90	27
Divorced	-	1	-	-	-	-	3	-	-	2,440	-	16	1	4	10	-	20	10
Unknown	-	-	-	-	-	-	-	-	-	144	-	-	-	-	3	-	1	3
Females 15 years old and over	2	-	1	3	1	-	31	1	7	109,012	27	601	19	125	329	16	858	293
Single	1	-	-	1	-	-	4	1	1	19,662	10	123	2	14	88	5	153	65
Married	1	-	-	2	1	-	20	-	5	70,599	14	370	11	83	198	11	593	159
Widowed	-	-	1	-	-	-	7	-	1	15,863	3	94	3	23	38	-	98	63
Divorced	-	-	-	-	-	-	-	-	-	2,811	-	14	3	5	5	-	14	6
Unknown	-	-	-	-	-	-	-	-	-	77	-	-	-	-	-	-	-	-
FAMILIES																		
Number of families	1	-	1	2	1	-	34	1	7	75,709	20	396	16	110	254	10	725	241
Median size	-	-	-	-	-	-	-	-	-	2.80	-	3.01	-	2.23	3.36	-	2.79	2.64
Families having—																		
No children under 10	1	-	1	2	1	-	32	1	7	50,185	12	279	11	84	155	8	491	171
1 child under 10	-	-	-	-	-	-	1	-	-	10,942	5	38	4	20	34	-	99	30
2 children under 10	-	-	-	-	-	-	1	-	-	6,548	1	36	1	3	31	1	72	13
3 or more	-	-	-	-	-	-	-	-	-	8,034	2	43	-	3	34	1	63	27

CHARACTERISTICS OF NEGRO POPULATION BY COUNTIES: 1930—Continued

(See note at head of table)

SUBJECT	OHIO—Continued																	
	Butler	Carroll	Champaign	Clark	Clermont	Clinton	Columbiana	Coshocton	Crawford	Cuyahoga	Darke	Defiance	Delaware	Erie	Fairfield	Fayette	Franklin	Fulton
POPULATION BY SEX																		
Negro population: 1930	5,614	282	1,157	8,743	830	633	1,533	225	267	74,827	240	26	636	1,150	462	958	35,781	25
Male	2,837	143	598	4,423	427	330	763	109	129	37,417	136	20	263	621	360	488	18,662	11
Female	2,777	139	559	4,320	403	303	770	116	138	37,410	104	6	373	529	102	470	117,119	14
Negro population: 1920	3,465	127	1,251	7,586	793	730	1,401	144	221	35,347	319	28	543	663	396	961	23,917	13
Male	1,900	77	636	3,947	405	392	734	78	136	19,169	162	13	243	345	268	499	12,697	7
Female	1,565	50	615	3,639	388	338	667	66	85	16,178	157	15	300	318	128	462	11,220	6
Percent of total population:																		
1930	4.9	1.8	4.8	9.6	2.8	2.9	1.8	0.8	0.8	6.2	0.6	0.1	2.4	2.7	1.0	4.6	9.9	0.1
1920	4.0	0.8	5.0	9.4	2.8	3.2	1.7	0.5	0.6	3.7	0.7	0.1	2.1	1.7	1.0	4.5	8.4	0.1
VOTING AGE: 1930																		
Total 21 years old and over	3,264	143	734	5,383	496	424	845	129	151	50,093	145	14	330	670	152	591	23,898	14
Male	1,709	80	386	2,797	257	228	430	62	81	25,555	78	11	160	366	80	311	12,905	6
Female	1,555	63	348	2,586	239	196	415	67	70	24,538	67	3	170	304	72	280	10,993	8
AGE: 1930																		
Under 5 years	615	51	96	764	74	48	158	20	29	6,621	21	3	47	112	13	102	2,873	2
Under 1 year	122	11	16	125	11	14	29	1	7	1,266	5	------	8	18	1	16	529	------
5 to 9 years	586	40	107	878	72	64	194	28	36	6,660	25	1	46	129	13	96	3,107	4
10 to 14 years	504	20	117	791	94	47	164	21	27	5,077	26	3	63	115	84	93	2,705	2
15 to 19 years	547	25	90	781	81	42	154	24	21	5,093	19	4	138	100	196	65	2,638	3
20 to 24 years	539	14	75	757	65	40	99	21	19	7,365	17	4	38	101	16	55	3,190	1
25 to 29 years	538	34	57	704	49	46	116	8	23	9,433	11	2	24	106	16	63	3,742	1
30 to 34 years	491	26	61	670	35	37	111	20	28	8,807	10	1	31	94	13	68	3,672	1
35 to 44 years	851	37	169	1,334	104	78	199	39	40	14,865	26	3	79	184	37	116	6,534	5
45 to 54 years	553	22	153	1,085	109	90	188	21	33	7,202	27	1	75	120	27	117	4,391	4
55 to 64 years	247	9	106	552	78	77	95	11	9	2,437	29	2	47	54	28	86	1,827	1
65 to 74 years	87	3	82	279	43	44	38	6	1	827	20	2	31	26	11	62	751	------
75 years and over	55	1	44	145	26	20	17	3	1	270	9	------	16	9	8	35	311	1
Unknown	1	------	------	3	------	------	------	3	------	170	------	------	1	------	------	------	40	------
SCHOOL ATTENDANCE																		
Total 7 to 13 years, inclusive	779	40	160	1,188	117	81	242	38	46	7,999	37	2	65	170	57	124	4,028	4
Number attending school	751	40	159	1,171	116	79	237	38	41	7,787	37	2	63	169	57	124	3,895	4
Percent attending school	96.4	------	99.4	98.6	99	------	97.9	------	------	97.3	------	------	------	99.4	------	100.0	96.7	------
Total 14 and 15 years, inclusive	198	9	40	293	40	19	69	8	10	1,874	6	1	71	39	88	40	1,038	2
Number attending school	182	9	38	278	35	18	67	6	9	1,789	6	1	70	36	86	33	976	2
Percent attending school	91.9	------	------	94.9	------	------	------	------	------	95.5	------	------	------	------	------	------	94.0	------
Total 16 and 17 years, inclusive	229	8	36	295	25	16	70	11	9	1,958	9	2	55	45	121	24	1,041	1
Number attending school	139	4	28	207	18	9	50	7	7	1,181	6	------	46	37	100	13	672	1
Percent attending school	60.7	------	------	70.2	------	------	------	------	------	60.3	------	------	------	------	82.6	------	64.6	------
Total 18 to 20 years, inclusive	317	14	51	478	48	23	69	9	9	3,531	12	3	47	64	27	32	1,670	1
Number attending school	62	1	14	78	8	4	14	1	3	403	2	------	17	4	9	6	304	1
Percent attending school	19.6	------	------	16.3	------	------	------	------	------	11.4	------	------	------	------	------	------	18.2	------
ILLITERACY																		
Total 10 years old and over	4,413	191	954	7,101	684	521	1,181	177	202	61,546	194	22	543	909	436	760	29,801	19
Number illiterate	340	20	57	394	53	29	62	11	29	2,698	2	------	14	68	11	61	2,370	1
Percent illiterate	7.7	10.5	6.0	5.5	7.7	5.6	5.2	6.2	14.4	4.4	1.0	------	2.6	7.5	2.5	8.0	8.0	------
Percent illiterate in 1920	9.5	------	2.9	8.9	11.3	7.8	6.1	10.5	7.3	5.2	0.8	------	5.2	9.5	3.7	10.1	8.2	------
URBAN AND RURAL																		
Urban population	5,075	7	704	8,249	------	398	1,280	159	248	73,592	29	22	442	883	182	548	33,071	3
Percent urban	90.4	2.5	60.8	94.3	------	62.9	83.5	70.7	92.9	98.3	12.1	------	69.5	76.8	39.4	57.2	92.4	------
Rural population	539	275	453	494	830	235	253	66	19	1,235	211	4	194	267	280	410	2,710	22
Rural-farm	44	22	208	194	214	83	74	11	1	16	187	3	67	21	14	119	189	20
Rural-nonfarm	495	253	245	300	616	152	179	55	18	1,219	24	1	137	246	266	291	2,521	2
Percent rural	9.6	97.5	39.2	5.7	100.0	37.1	16.5	29.3	7.1	1.7	87.9	------	30.5	23.2	60.6	42.8	7.6	------
MARITAL CONDITION																		
Males 15 years old and over	2,006	93	437	3,248	302	254	510	74	88	28,437	93	16	192	437	269	347	14,359	8
Single	605	31	131	944	107	82	164	26	21	8,542	28	13	58	152	211	103	4,200	3
Married	1,225	60	261	2,004	174	139	301	40	60	17,601	54	2	112	252	42	207	8,831	5
Widowed	123	2	35	224	20	24	35	7	6	1,693	8	------	17	24	13	30	922	------
Divorced	49	------	9	67	1	9	10	1	1	575	3	1	4	8	3	7	395	------
Unknown	4	------	1	9	------	------	------	------	------	26	------	------	1	1	------	------	11	------
Females 15 years old and over	1,903	78	400	3,062	288	220	507	82	87	28,032	75	3	288	357	83	320	12,737	9
Single	351	18	73	558	63	47	110	23	17	4,983	16	1	129	66	18	56	2,232	3
Married	1,228	57	267	2,007	174	135	309	44	57	17,764	49	2	121	229	44	209	8,228	5
Widowed	271	3	51	442	45	31	75	10	9	4,438	10	------	33	51	16	50	1,789	1
Divorced	52	------	9	49	6	7	13	3	4	824	------	------	5	11	4	5	482	------
Unknown	1	------	------	6	------	------	------	2	------	23	------	------	------	------	1	------	6	------
FAMILIES																		
Number of families	1,383	64	317	2,202	223	182	374	55	69	17,979	58	3	147	256	67	291	8,681	7
Median size	3.09	------	2.81	3.01	2.82	2.64	3.09	------	------	2.76	------	------	2.72	3.15	------	2.40	2.73	------
Families having—																		
No children under 10	831	31	216	1,451	156	131	228	33	44	12,114	37	2	102	151	53	208	5,976	4
1 child under 10	228	8	51	322	27	24	58	9	5	2,515	10	------	22	32	7	28	1,209	2
2 children under 10	144	8	23	201	18	11	38	7	10	1,538	5	------	9	35	2	24	659	------
3 or more	180	17	27	228	22	16	50	6	10	1,812	6	1	14	38	5	31	837	1

CHARACTERISTICS OF NEGRO POPULATION BY COUNTIES: 1930—Continued

(See note at head of table)

SUBJECT	OHIO—Continued																	
	Gallia	Geauga	Greene	Guernsey	Hamilton	Hancock	Hardin	Harrison	Henry	Highland	Hocking	Huron	Jackson	Jefferson	Knox	Lake	Lawrence	Licking
POPULATION BY SEX																		
Negro population: 1930	1,332	90	4,043	571	55,313	282	351	641	12	912	115	438	375	4,391	392	605	1,669	796
Male	690	53	1,982	297	27,783	139	186	334	6	453	70	240	191	2,371	200	350	893	404
Female	642	37	2,061	274	27,530	143	165	307	6	459	45	198	184	2,020	192	255	776	392
Negro population: 1920	1,390	29	3,751	456	33,747	268	355	603	7	1,157	129	238	478	2,063	420	336	1,691	662
Male	757	18	1,849	245	17,079	133	187	294	4	609	65	133	244	1,076	221	186	864	360
Female	633	11	1,902	211	16,668	135	168	309	3	548	64	105	234	987	199	150	827	302
Percent of total population:																		
1930	5.8	0.6	12.2	1.4	9.4	0.7	1.3	3.4	0.1	3.6	0.6	1.3	1.5	5.0	1.3	1.5	3.7	1.3
1920	6.0	0.2	12.0	1.0	6.8	0.7	1.2	3.1	-	4.2	0.6	0.7	1.7	2.7	1.4	1.2	4.3	1.2
VOTING AGE: 1930																		
Total 21 years old and over	774	65	2,484	339	36,346	166	205	318	6	596	70	255	199	2,730	248	411	935	512
Male	406	41	1,208	177	18,724	84	112	168	3	302	44	147	109	1,544	127	246	498	270
Female	368	24	1,276	162	17,622	82	93	150	3	294	26	108	90	1,186	121	165	437	242
AGE: 1930																		
Under 5 years	130	8	291	64	4,740	22	31	86	-	86	13	49	28	440	35	45	152	77
Under 1 year	33	2	57	12	879	2	6	15	-	20	3	12	3	82	9	12	27	18
5 to 9 years	129	5	370	67	4,886	32	38	84	1	86	12	48	45	413	31	57	200	64
10 to 14 years	132	5	404	50	4,144	34	37	80	2	63	11	43	44	393	43	51	194	60
15 to 19 years	141	7	388	45	4,137	21	33	68	3	69	7	38	46	349	28	36	157	67
20 to 24 years	104	6	406	54	5,755	24	28	38	1	65	4	30	35	407	34	41	133	78
25 to 29 years	93	10	239	48	6,504	15	19	40	-	61	11	36	19	520	24	75	113	73
30 to 34 years	72	8	277	47	5,478	22	18	30	-	58	5	42	10	444	21	58	96	62
35 to 44 years	135	18	505	80	9,865	33	36	78	1	103	15	64	27	766	55	108	203	117
45 to 54 years	141	15	486	50	5,896	28	44	64	-	114	14	35	46	390	62	63	186	111
55 to 64 years	127	5	341	44	2,479	28	28	38	1	103	12	23	41	160	36	42	122	51
65 to 74 years	82	1	211	17	976	12	32	20	-	60	6	16	27	75	17	19	72	22
75 years and over	46	2	124	3	391	11	7	15	3	43	5	9	7	33	6	10	40	13
Unknown	-	-	1	2	62	-	-	-	-	1	-	5	-	1	-	-	1	1
CHOOL ATTENDANCE																		
Total 7 to 13 years, inclusive	181	6	542	77	6,178	50	52	116	2	111	18	61	63	564	57	76	285	89
Number attending school	162	6	538	77	5,980	47	50	112	2	108	18	61	62	550	57	75	277	88
Percent attending school	89.5	-	99.3	-	96.8	-	-	96.6	-	97.3	-	-	-	97.5	-	-	97.2	-
Total 14 and 15 years, inclusive	43	5	151	21	1,607	15	20	29	1	27	2	16	21	143	13	15	68	15
Number attending school	37	5	150	21	1,504	15	19	27	1	23	2	15	20	136	13	14	60	15
Percent attending school	-	-	99.3	-	93.6	-	-	-	-	-	-	-	-	95.1	-	-	-	-
Total 16 and 17 years, inclusive	65	4	160	21	1,596	6	12	30	-	29	2	16	24	135	6	19	59	30
Number attending school	33	3	132	11	840	5	8	18	-	13	1	11	13	70	4	10	34	17
Percent attending school	-	-	82.5	-	52.6	-	-	-	-	-	-	-	-	51.9	-	-	-	-
Total 18 to 20 years, inclusive	86	1	269	23	2,832	12	18	29	3	33	6	19	25	216	24	18	96	48
Number attending school	17	-	152	4	334	-	8	11	1	7	-	5	4	29	8	4	18	6
Percent attending school	-	-	56.5	-	11.8	-	-	-	-	-	-	-	-	13.4	-	-	-	-
ILLITERACY																		
Total 10 years old and over	1,073	77	3,382	440	45,687	228	282	471	11	740	90	341	302	3,538	326	503	1,317	655
Number illiterate	111	11	198	25	3,269	9	20	20	2	55	-	18	20	279	9	25	82	69
Percent illiterate	10.3	-	5.9	5.7	7.2	3.9	7.1	4.2	-	7.4	-	5.3	6.6	7.9	2.8	5.0	6.2	10.5
Percent illiterate in 1920	13.2	-	9.8	7.3	10.8	1.0	8.9	5.3	-	15.6	6.7	10.9	10.4	5.9	6.2	5.3	15.0	10.5
URBAN AND RURAL																		
Urban population	609	-	2,166	439	49,941	268	126	345	2	653	36	213	64	3,147	357	485	928	729
Percent urban	45.7	-	53.6	76.9	90.3	95.0	35.9	53.8	-	71.6	31.3	48.6	17.1	71.7	91.1	80.2	55.6	91.6
Rural population	723	90	1,877	132	5,372	14	225	296	10	259	79	225	311	1,244	35	120	741	67
Rural-farm	367	15	393	25	84	14	79	101	3	113	18	14	263	104	5	11	169	13
Rural-nonfarm	356	75	1,484	107	5,288	-	146	195	7	146	61	211	48	1,140	30	109	572	54
Percent rural	54.3	-	46.4	23.1	9.7	5.0	64.1	46.2	-	28.4	68.7	51.4	82.9	28.3	8.9	19.8	44.4	8.4
MARITAL CONDITION																		
Males 15 years old and over	494	44	1,430	202	21,055	96	132	206	6	339	50	171	135	1,734	149	267	604	308
Single	216	14	493	71	6,363	33	44	68	4	82	22	74	64	581	54	81	222	94
Married	228	26	765	116	13,095	53	69	116	1	205	22	88	58	1,017	81	157	335	179
Widowed	38	3	125	11	1,301	9	17	20	1	35	5	6	10	95	11	21	40	22
Divorced	12	1	47	4	285	1	2	2	-	17	1	2	3	41	3	7	7	13
Unknown	-	-	-	-	11	-	-	-	-	-	-	1	-	-	-	1	-	-
Females 15 years old and over	447	28	1,548	188	20,488	98	113	185	3	338	29	127	123	1,411	134	185	519	287
Single	143	4	445	44	3,681	25	30	41	-	72	5	22	49	236	23	17	104	56
Married	216	21	776	113	13,313	56	69	110	2	198	21	88	59	968	82	142	318	185
Widowed	77	3	282	22	3,100	15	12	31	1	51	3	11	13	174	26	20	78	36
Divorced	11	-	45	9	386	2	2	3	-	17	-	6	2	31	1	6	19	10
Unknown	-	-	-	-	8	-	-	-	-	-	-	-	-	2	2	-	-	-
FAMILIES																		
Number of families	320	23	1,055	136	14,483	66	94	124	2	283	31	107	84	1,035	104	153	401	216
Median size	2.92	-	2.75	3.60	2.64	-	-	4.25	-	2.46	-	2.63	-	3.01	3.07	2.49	3.24	2.78
Families having—																		
No children under 10	215	17	745	75	9,928	44	64	62	1	198	23	70	53	644	71	104	254	152
1 child under 10	41	4	136	26	2,102	12	11	16	1	41	3	10	11	169	16	23	50	31
2 children under 10	26	-	87	15	1,149	3	7	14	-	21	1	10	9	102	9	13	35	14
3 or more	38	2	87	20	1,304	7	12	32	-	23	4	17	11	120	8	13	62	19

CHARACTERISTICS OF NEGRO POPULATION BY COUNTIES: 1930—Continued

(See note at head of table)

SUBJECT	OHIO—Continued																	
	Logan	Lorain	Lucas	Madison	Mahoning	Marion	Medina	Meigs	Mercer	Miami	Monroe	Montgomery	Morgan	Morrow	Muskingum	Noble	Ottawa	Paulding
POPULATION BY SEX																		
Negro population: 1930	545	3,334	17,620	972	17,416	435	254	596	55	1,281	37	18,313	275	24	2,111	28	151	276
Male	278	1,713	7,193	607	9,087	227	146	304	28	646	19	9,419	153	12	1,109	13	82	142
Female	267	1,621	6,427	365	8,329	208	108	292	27	635	18	8,894	122	12	1,002	15	69	134
Negro population: 1920	654	1,916	6,096	644	8,509	270	184	631	75	1,115	62	10,115	233	36	1,784	24	110	421
Male	325	989	3,419	337	5,083	148	97	336	38	591	37	5,496	132	17	926	11	71	235
Female	329	927	2,677	307	3,426	122	87	295	37	524	25	4,619	101	19	858	13	39	186
Percent of total population:																		
1930	1.9	3.1	3.9	4.8	7.4	1.0	0.9	2.5	0.2	2.5	0.2	6.7	2.0	0.2	3.1	0.2	0.6	1.8
1920	2.2	2.1	2.2	3.3	4.6	0.6	0.7	2.4	0.3	2.3	0.3	4.8	1.6	0.2	3.1	0.1	0.5	2.2
VOTING AGE: 1930																		
Total 21 years old and over	332	2,060	9,398	644	10,639	273	164	368	26	825	22	11,776	132	18	1,297	15	89	162
Male	176	1,085	5,150	455	5,836	147	102	201	14	435	13	6,306	79	10	702	8	53	90
Female	156	975	4,248	189	4,803	126	62	167	12	390	9	5,470	53	8	595	7	36	72
AGE: 1930																		
Under 5 years	41	345	1,137	78	1,967	41	24	57	8	105	5	1,653	33	2	174	6	15	26
Under 1 year	7	67	237	16	397	11	2	9	3	18	1	326	7	----	33	1	3	5
5 to 9 years	50	345	1,130	84	1,890	49	24	56	7	115	6	1,729	45	1	218	3	22	28
10 to 14 years	60	260	856	84	1,390	41	13	49	10	119	3	1,480	29	1	189	3	10	28
15 to 19 years	55	271	875	71	1,237	26	25	52	4	99	1	1,385	32	2	194	1	12	25
20 to 24 years	34	279	1,370	66	1,666	31	33	44	5	88	4	1,642	18	4	188	2	15	25
25 to 29 years	32	312	1,716	88	2,251	43	25	29	5	109	2	1,966	16	----	178	2	11	11
30 to 34 years	26	301	1,613	90	1,942	40	21	29	1	90	1	1,753	19	----	163	1	11	11
35 to 44 years	62	517	2,651	159	2,928	73	42	73	8	199	6	3,286	25	3	284	5	29	31
45 to 54 years	65	365	1,477	118	1,449	40	26	76	3	164	5	2,024	23	5	236	3	12	37
55 to 64 years	49	205	516	73	455	31	10	61	2	100	2	874	13	4	168	1	12	25
65 to 74 years	44	95	192	40	151	13	6	42	1	58	2	299	16	1	71	1	1	19
75 years and over	27	38	75	21	68	6	5	27	1	34	----	204	6	1	46	----	1	10
Unknown	----	1	12	----	20	1	----	1	----	1	----	18	----	----	2	----	----	----
SCHOOL ATTENDANCE																		
Total 7 to 13 years, inclusive	77	432	1,362	113	2,219	61	26	71	11	160	7	2,226	53	2	262	4	21	42
Number attending school	76	417	1,304	111	2,146	60	25	71	11	154	6	2,168	51	2	255	4	21	42
Percent attending school	----	96.5	95.7	98.2	96.7	----	----	----	----	96.3	----	97.4	----	----	97.3	----	----	----
Total 14 and 15, inclusive	22	101	313	34	527	9	4	21	2	46	----	534	8	----	83	----	6	6
Number attending school	20	99	294	31	507	8	7	21	2	44	----	507	8	----	76	----	6	5
Percent attending school	----	98.0	92.9	----	96.2	----	----	----	----	----	----	94.9	----	----	----	----	----	----
Total 16 and 17 years, inclusive	24	84	309	27	478	9	9	20	2	32	----	545	15	1	71	----	4	12
Number attending school	15	63	197	15	321	5	8	12	1	23	----	331	6	----	38	----	3	6
Percent attending school	----	----	63.8	----	67.2	----	----	----	----	----	----	60.7	----	----	----	----	----	----
Total 18 to 20 years, inclusive	27	183	636	36	797	20	15	34	2	63	1	874	16	1	127	1	8	18
Number attending school	7	50	91	6	83	1	4	10	1	19	1	139	----	1	25	----	3	6
Percent attending school	----	27.3	14.3	----	10.4	----	----	----	----	----	----	15.9	----	----	19.7	----	----	----
ILLITERACY																		
Total 10 years old and over	454	2,644	11,353	810	13,557	345	206	483	40	1,061	26	14,931	197	21	1,719	19	114	222
Number illiterate	27	139	632	84	897	24	21	45	----	38	----	987	18	----	82	1	8	11
Percent illiterate	5.9	5.3	5.6	10.4	6.6	7.0	10.2	9.3	----	3.6	----	6.6	9.1	----	4.8	----	7.0	5.0
Percent illiterate in 1920	3.2	2.7	4.9	8.5	6.2	5.7	8.9	10.9	----	4.6	----	11.0	8.0	----	7.7	----	----	4.1
URBAN AND RURAL																		
Urban population	362	2,974	13,278	352	17,152	387	207	320	----	1,117	----	17,160	----	----	1,776	----	17	----
Percent urban	66.4	89.2	97.5	36.2	98.5	89.0	81.5	53.7	----	87.2	----	93.7	----	----	84.1	----	11.3	----
Rural population	183	360	342	620	264	48	47	276	55	164	37	1,153	275	24	335	28	134	276
Rural-farm	124	23	32	257	40	3	7	66	27	20	28	51	192	9	92	20	24	136
Rural-nonfarm	59	337	310	363	224	45	40	210	28	144	9	1,102	83	15	243	8	110	140
Percent rural	33.6	10.8	2.5	63.8	1.5	11.0	18.5	46.3	----	12.8	----	6.3	100.0	----	15.9	----	88.7	100.0
MARITAL CONDITION																		
Males 15 years old and over	201	1,255	5,641	496	6,526	164	115	229	17	495	13	7,051	95	10	814	8	60	105
Single	67	413	1,608	170	1,966	55	51	79	7	163	5	2,136	41	5	264	2	24	39
Married	106	750	3,480	231	4,058	88	59	115	10	283	7	4,230	47	4	474	5	31	54
Widowed	21	56	441	48	388	17	2	26	----	38	1	495	5	1	67	1	4	10
Divorced	7	35	108	47	110	4	3	9	----	11	----	178	2	----	9	----	1	1
Unknown	----	1	4	----	4	----	----	----	----	----	----	12	----	----	----	----	----	1
Females 15 years and over	193	1,129	4,856	230	5,641	140	78	205	13	447	10	6,400	73	10	716	8	44	89
Single	45	178	683	51	860	20	16	53	2	84	3	1,158	20	3	158	1	6	24
Married	110	739	3,333	141	3,979	96	47	107	10	274	7	4,089	46	3	444	6	32	52
Widowed	31	161	758	31	703	19	14	40	1	74	----	968	7	4	102	1	5	11
Divorced	7	51	79	6	97	5	1	4	----	15	----	178	----	----	12	----	----	2
Unknown	----	----	3	1	2	----	----	1	----	----	----	7	----	----	----	----	1	----
FAMILIES																		
Number of families	143	840	3,267	195	4,234	112	52	176	11	323	9	4,514	50	9	519	6	37	76
Median size	3.00	2.99	2.58	3.02	2.96	2.64	----	2.73	----	2.89	----	2.82	----	----	2.97	----	----	----
Families having—																		
No children under 10	103	516	2,235	125	2,568	78	32	126	6	231	6	2,973	19	7	332	3	23	53
1 child under 10	17	143	469	26	650	12	8	19	----	33	1	649	11	2	94	----	5	8
2 children under 10	10	94	273	15	416	8	5	16	1	25	1	414	5	----	41	1	2	6
3 or more	13	87	290	29	600	14	7	15	4	34	1	478	15	----	52	2	7	9

CHARACTERISTICS OF NEGRO POPULATION BY COUNTIES: 1930—Continued

(See note at head of table)

SUBJECT	**OHIO**—Continued																	
	Perry	Pickaway	Pike	Portage	Preble	Putnam	Richland	Ross	Sandusky	Scioto	Seneca	Shelby	Stark	Summit	Trumbull	Tuscarawas	Union	Van Wert
POPULATION BY SEX																		
Negro population: 1930	421	697	513	760	177	1	1,999	2,469	370	1,993	358	211	5,890	12,480	4,239	987	311	145
Male	254	372	282	412	101	1	1,387	1,370	187	1,091	200	109	3,095	6,463	2,289	542	107	80
Female	167	325	231	348	76	-	612	1,099	183	902	158	102	2,795	6,017	1,950	445	204	65
Negro population: 1920	783	547	510	410	208	28	705	2,232	255	1,348	227	241	2,799	6,577	1,107	514	281	245
Male	432	286	285	239	115	12	542	1,159	130	734	120	116	1,623	4,163	671	326	130	141
Female	351	261	225	171	93	16	163	1,073	125	614	107	125	1,176	2,414	436	188	151	104
Percent of total population:																		
1930	2.2	2.6	3.7	1.8	0.8	-	3.0	5.5	0.9	2.5	0.7	0.8	2.7	3.6	3.4	1.4	1.6	0.6
1920	2.2	2.1	3.6	1.1	0.9	0.1	1.3	5.4	0.7	2.1	0.5	0.9	1.6	2.3	1.3	0.8	1.3	0.9
VOTING AGE: 1930																		
Total 21 years old and over	257	353	268	490	100	1	1,277	1,395	227	1,290	233	123	3,708	7,756	2,505	587	239	97
Male	172	190	151	273	59	1	919	839	122	739	129	66	2,050	4,248	1,407	343	70	54
Female	85	163	117	217	41	-	358	556	105	551	104	57	1,658	3,508	1,098	244	169	43
AGE: 1930																		
Under 5 years	36	49	59	71	21	-	124	267	31	187	33	22	577	1,224	499	98	14	5
Under 1 year	10	7	16	12	3	-	19	65	7	42	6	4	93	229	104	16	2	-
5 to 9 years	43	62	75	70	21	-	130	270	40	192	38	22	558	1,316	498	112	16	15
10 to 14 years	41	89	53	65	15	-	95	236	43	157	27	26	499	989	360	82	14	12
15 to 19 years	40	126	50	49	17	-	254	256	22	135	22	17	465	968	309	92	24	12
20 to 24 years	31	68	31	47	6	-	498	242	34	196	34	12	489	1,279	391	98	35	12
25 to 29 years	28	42	34	58	3	-	344	214	30	243	41	16	703	1,604	457	85	55	6
30 to 34 years	29	41	23	82	11	-	162	147	32	209	32	13	641	1,411	439	100	37	3
35 to 44 years	63	59	55	149	24	-	220	311	70	347	58	36	1,066	2,162	689	155	50	20
45 to 54 years	58	67	50	92	22	-	111	210	43	185	31	20	581	1,009	397	104	18	21
55 to 64 years	30	54	42	56	22	-	36	167	12	77	27	10	189	338	124	40	24	26
65 to 74 years	18	30	24	14	12	-	14	98	8	37	7	11	88	121	40	16	17	8
75 years and over	3	16	17	7	3	1	5	44	5	19	8	6	31	36	21	4	7	5
Unknown	1	-	-	-	-	-	6	7	-	9	-	-	3	23	15	1	-	-
SCHOOL ATTENDANCE																		
Total 7 to 13 years, inclusive	60	94	87	93	24	-	159	350	63	241	41	31	728	1,585	595	135	19	16
Number attending school	59	74	87	91	24	-	159	343	61	234	36	30	700	1,544	567	133	18	16
Percent attending school	-	-	-	-	-	-	100.0	98.0	-	97.1	-	-	96.2	97.4	95.3	98.5	-	-
Total 14 and 15 years, inclusive	19	52	23	21	4	-	33	87	16	60	12	9	183	352	127	35	7	6
Number attending school	19	31	21	21	4	-	30	82	15	57	12	8	163	341	119	30	6	5
Percent attending school	-	-	-	-	-	-	-	-	-	-	-	-	89.1	96.9	93.7	-	-	-
Total 16 and 17 years, inclusive	17	55	18	23	8	-	48	87	6	48	9	11	166	383	114	38	9	6
Number attending school	11	12	7	12	7	-	29	45	5	26	7	7	101	258	59	18	8	3
Percent attending school	-	-	-	-	-	-	-	-	-	-	-	-	60.8	67.4	51.8	-	-	-
Total 18 to 20 years, inclusive	17	63	28	29	9	-	308	167	14	88	14	5	295	655	201	48	15	9
Number attending school	3	2	3	7	6	-	213	18	3	10	2	1	28	85	32	3	3	2
Percent attending school	-	-	-	-	-	-	69.2	10.8	-	-	-	-	9.5	13.0	15.9	-	-	-
ILLITERACY																		
Total 10 years old and over	342	586	379	619	135	1	1,745	1,932	299	1,614	287	167	4,755	9,940	3,242	777	281	125
Number illiterate	33	123	67	81	4	-	85	99	13	145	12	7	348	696	262	56	15	5
Percent illiterate	9.6	21.0	17.7	13.1	3.0	-	4.9	5.1	4.3	9.0	4.2	4.2	7.3	7.0	8.1	7.2	5.3	4.0
Percent illiterate in 1920	10.2	14.8	12.7	6.1	6.4	-	4.2	9.1	4.8	13.2	3.7	2.1	7.4	5.6	11.3	10.3	1.7	5.5
URBAN AND RURAL																		
Urban population	4	374	-	495	50	-	912	1,275	269	1,911	346	146	5,172	12,067	3,048	714	76	91
Percent urban	1.0	53.7	-	65.1	28.2	-	45.6	51.6	72.7	95.9	96.6	69.2	87.8	96.7	71.9	72.3	24.4	62.8
Rural population	417	323	513	265	127	1	1,087	1,194	101	82	12	65	718	413	1,191	273	235	54
Rural-farm	22	105	405	16	35	1	7	608	3	33	3	26	66	21	30	27	38	42
Rural-nonfarm	395	218	108	249	92	-	1,080	586	98	49	9	39	652	392	1,161	246	197	12
Percent rural	99.0	46.3	100.0	34.9	71.8	-	54.4	48.4	27.3	4.1	3.4	30.8	12.2	3.3	28.1	27.7	75.6	37.2
MARITAL CONDITION																		
Males 15 years old and over	197	267	185	302	71	1	1,217	994	133	824	145	75	2,304	4,799	1,605	396	85	65
Single	67	142	65	94	26	1	726	382	44	283	44	24	761	1,519	525	136	37	22
Married	116	101	96	181	35	-	466	508	82	486	82	41	1,399	2,916	982	237	37	36
Widowed	12	18	17	23	8	-	17	69	6	34	12	8	103	250	75	12	9	7
Divorced	2	6	7	4	2	-	8	28	1	20	5	2	39	93	22	11	2	-
Unknown	-	-	-	-	-	-	-	7	-	1	2	-	2	21	1	-	-	-
Females 15 years old and over	104	230	141	252	49	-	433	702	123	633	115	66	1,952	4,152	1,277	299	182	48
Single	20	103	22	40	12	-	79	163	25	103	16	12	323	704	164	50	34	7
Married	73	94	96	169	31	-	278	443	84	449	83	45	1,345	2,867	943	218	113	32
Widowed	10	20	22	39	6	-	59	81	9	67	13	8	241	473	139	21	25	8
Divorced	1	13	1	4	-	-	16	15	5	14	1	1	41	102	31	10	10	1
Unknown	-	-	-	-	-	-	1	-	-	-	2	-	2	6	-	-	-	-
FAMILIES																		
Number of families	91	132	123	170	45	-	313	538	91	476	85	50	1,374	2,791	951	242	59	48
Median size	-	2.61	3.42	3.04	-	-	2.77	3.49	-	2.80	-	-	2.94	3.00	3.13	2.91	-	-
Families having—																		
No children under 10	56	87	66	115	29	-	202	303	61	313	52	29	864	1,699	524	145	45	38
1 child under 10	16	15	21	15	5	-	48	87	10	68	13	10	210	435	174	50	6	5
2 children under 10	8	11	16	17	2	-	25	65	11	41	13	5	137	268	96	16	3	2
3 or more	11	19	20	23	9	-	38	83	9	54	7	6	163	389	157	31	5	3

CHARACTERISTICS OF NEGRO POPULATION BY COUNTIES: 1930—Continued

(See note at head of table)

SUBJECT	OHIO—Continued							OKLAHOMA										
	Vinton	Warren	Washington	Wayne	Williams	Wood	Wyandot	The State	Adair	Alfalfa	Atoka	Beaver	Beckham	Blaine	Bryan	Caddo	Canadian	Carter
POPULATION BY SEX																		
Negro population: 1930	218	741	1,185	308	11	540	11	172,198	2	3	1,139	1	574	2,130	1,192	1,761	970	3,696
Male	118	376	597	174	7	320	6	86,818	2	2	584	1	296	1,097	615	895	505	1,766
Female	100	365	588	134	4	220	5	85,380		1	555		278	1,033	577	866	465	1,930
Negro population: 1920	42	717	1,165	131	7	293	14	149,408	40	22	1,204		3	839	1,829	845	614	4,267
Male	23	358	603	72	5	195	10	76,294	18	12	602		1	439	943	449	307	2,144
Female	19	359	562	59	2	98	4	73,114	22	10	602		2	400	886	396	307	2,123
Percent of total population:																		
1930	2.1	2.7	2.8	0.7		1.1	0.1	7.2			7.8		2.0	10.4	3.7	3.5	3.5	8.9
1920	0.3	2.8	2.7	0.3		0.7	0.1	7.4	0.3	0.1	5.8			5.3	4.5	2.5	2.8	10.6
VOTING AGE: 1930																		
Total 21 years old and over	88	438	654	204	8	337	10	94,162	2	2	609	1	331	1,008	566	907	564	1,983
Male	50	230	342	122	5	213	6	48,364	2	1	310	1	189	544	297	503	306	935
Female	38	208	312	82	3	124	4	45,798		1	299		142	464	269	404	258	1,048
AGE: 1930																		
Under 5 years	27	50	125	26		65		17,337			129		74	257	128	182	94	334
Under 1 year	4	7	19	8		12		3,303			14		18	44	29	35	19	64
5 to 9 years	35	86	156	27	2	55		19,792			129		64	278	174	207	99	475
10 to 14 years	32	98	124	25	1	37		18,296			124		47	260	146	211	93	396
15 to 19 years	32	61	113	19		34	1	18,811		1	121		49	274	145	210	95	425
20 to 24 years	13	41	86	25		47		17,893			111		75	220	89	202	106	363
25 to 29 years	7	35	61	36		59		15,595			70		67	132	63	133	95	283
30 to 34 years	8	44	68	44	2	52		12,469			46		60	114	70	102	75	251
35 to 44 years	19	94	155	65	2	76		21,974	1		147		74	232	127	230	107	421
45 to 54 years	16	75	124	28	3	67	2	16,331		1	135		38	182	123	155	116	414
55 to 64 years	15	84	84	9		18	2	8,207		1	70		19	113	66	86	54	197
65 to 74 years	8	55	64	2	1	9	5	3,504	1		42	1	6	37	38	24	21	85
75 years and over	6	18	24	2		3	1	1,835			15		1	31	23	17	7	49
Unknown			1			18		154								2	8	3
SCHOOL ATTENDANCE																		
Total 7 to 13 years, inclusive	50	129	206	37	2	62		26,443			181		72	369	218	285	138	607
Number attending school	47	125	200	37	2	62		24,173			175		27	341	192	227	123	573
Percent attending school		96.9	97.1					91.4			96.7			92.4	88.1	79.6	89.1	94.4
Total 14 and 15 years, inclusive	11	33	42	9	1	6		7,255			42		15	115	73	84	34	155
Number attending school	9	31	41	8	1	6		6,379			40		7	102	64	61	31	144
Percent attending school								87.9						88.7				92.9
Total 16 and 17 years, inclusive	12	28	44	5		12		7,512			51		18	103	50	92	38	157
Number attending school	3	21	29	3		9		4,789			26		4	65	43	48	22	120
Percent attending school								63.8						63.1				76.4
Total 18 to 20 years, inclusive	19	27	57	17		32	1	11,560		1	72		35	166	89	124	67	272
Number attending school		8	13	4		2		2,635			12		1	36	36	19	12	97
Percent attending school								22.8						21.7		15.3		35.7
ILLITERACY																		
Total 10 years old and over	156	605	904	255	9	420	11	135,069	2	3	881	1	436	1,595	890	1,372	777	2,887
Number illiterate	27	45	58	22		30		12,560	1		96		75	112	130	107	43	340
Percent illiterate	17.3	7.4	6.4	8.6		7.1		9.3			10.9		17.2	7.0	14.6	7.8	5.5	11.8
Percent illiterate in 1920		3.9	8.4	12.3		7.7		12.4			19.9			11.5	16.7	8.9	9.9	14.2
URBAN AND RURAL																		
Urban population		456	286	185	7	54	4	67,801					11		2	486	533	2,069
Percent urban		61.5	24.1	60.1		10.0		39.4					1.9		0.2	27.6	54.9	56.0
Rural population	218	285	899	123	4	486	7	104,397	2	3	1,139	1	563	2,130	1,190	1,275	437	1,627
Rural-farm	86	123	558	19	4	14	5	79,514	1	3	560	1	390	1,416	1,052	973	365	1,357
Rural-nonfarm	132	162	341	104		472	2	24,883	1		579		173	714	138	302	72	270
Percent rural	100.0	38.5	75.9	39.9		90.0		60.6			100.0		98.1	100.0	99.8	72.4	45.1	44.0
MARITAL CONDITION																		
Males 15 years old and over	69	265	402	133	5	241	6	59,193	2	2	383	1	214	718	391	617	354	1,184
Single	33	86	133	40		88	4	17,969		1	113		48	236	123	217	96	388
Married	31	158	236	84	4	125	1	34,965	2	1	239		145	409	224	354	212	684
Widowed	5	20	26	8	1	11	1	4,637			20	1	14	53	39	25	24	86
Divorced		1	7	1		2		1,506			11		7	199	5	20	21	25
Unknown						15		116						1		1	1	1
Females 15 years old and over	55	242	378	97	3	142	5	57,580		1	374		175	617	353	544	330	1,307
Single	17	53	95	12		20	2	11,879			76		18	119	90	117	61	294
Married	34	151	239	81	3	106	2	35,096		1	243		141	416	222	358	212	712
Widowed	4	33	37	4		11	1	8,553			38		15	60	40	60	35	224
Divorced		5	7			5		1,972			17		1	22	1	9	22	76
Unknown								80										1
FAMILIES																		
Number of families	39	195	274	81	3	113	5	40,238	2	1	284	1	152	422	265	435	235	893
Median size		2.64	3.55			3.40		3.13			3.09		2.62	3.94	3.71	3.05	2.69	3.27
Families having—																		
No children under 10	16	137	152	50	1	61	5	23,855	1	1	171	1	90	206	145	259	151	530
1 child under 10	7	25	41	17	2	25		6,654			48		22	82	38	74	34	150
2 children under 10	7	12	36	10		9		4,131			21		26	51	30	40	23	91
3 or more	9	21	45	4		18		5,598	1		44		14	83	52	62	27	122

CHARACTERISTICS OF NEGRO POPULATION BY COUNTIES: 1930—Continued

(See note at head of table)

SUBJECT	OKLAHOMA—Continued																	
	Cherokee	Choctaw	Cleveland	Coal	Comanche	Cotton	Craig	Creek	Custer	Dewey	Ellis	Garfield	Garvin	Grady	Grant	Greer	Harmon	Haskell
Population by Sex																		
Negro population: 1930	610	4,994	624	541	1,458	264	706	6,584	703	22	1	874	1,443	2,247	12	986	555	185
Male	312	2,516	359	270	782	134	351	3,311	359	12	1	426	721	1,143	9	568	305	90
Female	298	2,478	265	271	676	130	355	3,273	344	10	-	448	722	1,104	3	418	250	95
Negro population: 1920	835	5,242	460	729	641	156	771	6,794	135	30	16	591	2,005	1,478	16	179	110	334
Male	419	2,668	237	396	327	92	385	3,538	78	18	10	301	1,031	719	9	111	71	184
Female	416	2,574	223	333	314	64	386	3,256	57	12	6	290	974	759	7	68	39	150
Percent of total population																		
1930	3.5	20.7	2.5	4.7	4.2	1.7	3.9	10.3	2.6	0.2	-	1.9	4.6	4.7	0.1	4.9	4.0	1.1
1920	4.2	16.3	2.4	4.0	2.4	0.9	4.0	10.9	0.7	0.2	0.1	1.6	6.2	4.4	0.1	1.1	1.0	1.7
Voting Age: 1930																		
Total 21 years old and over	337	2,508	506	269	911	136	380	3,208	390	14	1	542	728	1,237	4	512	285	83
Male	170	1,298	280	136	512	75	194	1,629	215	7	1	267	373	640	2	308	155	41
Female	167	1,210	226	133	399	61	186	1,579	175	7	-	275	355	597	2	204	130	42
Age: 1930																		
Under 5 years	80	618	21	63	133	31	93	760	43	2	-	74	154	224	1	109	66	24
Under 1 year	13	112	4	11	27	6	19	140	7	1	-	13	27	48	-	23	11	4
5 to 9 years	77	638	28	69	136	37	76	902	92	2	-	64	209	254	2	76	74	25
10 to 14 years	45	546	19	64	111	33	60	845	80	2	-	82	176	229	2	80	58	29
15 to 19 years	61	595	38	64	132	19	83	711	79	2	-	90	148	259	2	157	57	22
20 to 24 years	45	450	67	52	194	31	57	631	75	5	-	94	129	224	1	174	64	14
25 to 29 years	33	405	60	27	160	27	62	473	61	-	-	101	111	191	-	113	65	6
30 to 34 years	38	247	62	18	133	12	37	413	68	2	-	77	89	163	-	62	42	10
35 to 44 years	63	590	128	50	218	33	74	754	108	4	-	125	143	274	1	120	82	14
45 to 54 years	63	475	110	62	147	20	63	609	59	3	-	85	140	270	1	59	33	21
55 to 64 years	55	276	51	37	58	16	56	328	24	-	-	50	83	98	-	23	11	5
65 to 74 years	25	98	24	22	23	5	28	106	9	-	1	21	35	42	2	12	1	10
75 years and over	20	52	13	13	11	-	16	49	4	-	-	11	26	14	-	1	2	5
Unknown	5	4	3	-	2	-	1	3	1	-	-	-	-	5	-	-	-	-
School Attendance																		
Total 7 to 13 years, inclusive	83	799	29	95	174	49	89	1,227	115	2	-	102	280	325	3	104	86	42
Number attending school	75	702	23	81	152	37	80	1,145	101	2	-	98	270	288	3	64	39	29
Percent attending school	-	87.9	-	-	87.4	-	-	93.3	87.8	-	-	96.1	96.4	88.6	-	61.5	-	-
Total 14 and 15 years, inclusive	23	236	12	16	48	8	32	315	40	-	-	30	57	101	1	42	23	9
Number attending school	21	214	9	11	38	4	26	289	36	-	-	29	50	86	1	19	12	8
Percent attending school	-	90.3	-	-	-	-	-	91.7	-	-	-	-	-	85.1	-	-	-	-
Total 16 and 17 years, inclusive	28	257	13	23	42	8	32	274	27	-	-	39	52	116	1	50	22	9
Number attending school	14	159	5	13	28	1	19	163	13	-	-	25	33	71	1	9	5	7
Percent attending school	-	61.9	-	-	-	-	-	59.5	-	-	-	-	-	61.2	-	-	-	-
Total 18 to 20 years, inclusive	31	307	32	46	97	16	48	450	48	2	-	58	94	143	2	134	41	9
Number attending school	3	74	4	4	20	-	9	124	5	-	-	16	13	44	2	5	-	3
Percent attending school	-	24.1	-	-	-	-	-	27.6	-	-	-	-	-	30.8	-	3.7	-	-
Illiteracy																		
Total 10 years old and over	453	3,738	575	409	1,189	196	537	4,922	568	18	1	736	1,080	1,769	9	801	415	136
Number illiterate	88	553	158	66	76	24	42	4	58	-	-	16	137	212	-	119	89	26
Percent illiterate	19.4	14.8	27.5	16.1	6.4	12.2	7.8	8.5	10.2	-	-	2.2	12.7	12.0	-	14.9	21.4	19.1
Percent illiterate in 1920	22.6	18.3	23.1	10.9	10.4	14.4	11.6	9.7	9.0	-	-	6.4	17.9	11.3	-	13.4	8.0	17.5
Urban and Rural																		
Urban population	-	797	-	-	809	-	415	1,707	434	-	-	763	340	1,625	-	321	145	-
Percent urban	-	16.0	-	-	55.5	-	58.8	25.9	61.7	-	-	87.3	23.6	723	-	32.6	26.1	-
Rural population	610	4,197	624	541	649	264	291	4,877	269	22	1	111	1,103	622	12	665	410	185
Rural-farm	381	3,744	176	348	221	193	272	4,131	195	22	1	111	811	598	12	433	399	160
Rural-nonfarm	229	453	448	193	428	71	19	746	74	-	-	-	292	24	-	232	11	25
Percent rural	100.0	84.0	100.0	100.0	44.5	100.0	41.2	74.1	38.3	-	-	12.7	76.4	27.7	-	67.4	73.9	100.0
Marital Condition																		
Males 15 years old and over	205	1,636	319	177	592	86	234	2,063	259	9	1	318	466	781	4	443	191	56
Single	59	487	172	63	245	20	75	626	94	2	1	85	143	205	2	170	45	19
Married	117	966	120	88	298	63	137	1,241	149	7	-	191	270	452	2	229	136	31
Widowed	24	161	15	21	32	2	19	132	11	-	-	24	47	116	-	24	9	6
Divorced	5	21	1	5	15	1	3	64	5	-	-	17	6	7	-	19	1	-
Unknown	-	1	11	-	2	-	-	-	-	-	-	1	-	1	-	1	-	-
Females 15 years old and over	203	1,556	237	168	486	77	243	2,014	229	7	-	336	438	759	3	278	166	51
Single	42	304	47	39	75	8	63	399	47	1	-	78	75	154	2	36	15	10
Married	119	970	157	92	304	63	134	1,286	153	6	-	194	272	454	1	199	136	30
Widowed	39	252	17	36	64	6	44	247	21	-	-	50	76	137	-	28	12	9
Divorced	3	28	3	1	43	-	2	81	8	-	-	14	15	14	-	15	3	2
Unknown	-	2	13	-	-	-	-	1	-	-	-	-	-	-	-	-	-	-
Families																		
Number of families	160	1,193	33	129	339	69	170	1,469	176	5	-	245	338	531	1	240	160	32
Median size	3.33	3.42	-	3.22	2.55	-	3.25	3.51	2.97	-	-	2.45	3.50	3.10	-	2.46	2.42	-
Families having—																		
No children under 10	89	653	14	80	215	37	99	790	103	2	-	174	186	316	1	152	100	13
1 child under 10	26	183	8	18	59	10	28	238	36	2	-	36	56	88	-	47	26	8
2 children under 10	23	164	3	11	21	13	18	173	25	1	-	19	38	63	-	14	12	3
3 or more	22	193	8	20	44	9	25	268	12	-	-	16	58	64	-	27	22	8

CHARACTERISTICS OF NEGRO POPULATION BY COUNTIES: 1930—Continued

(See note at head of table)

SUBJECT	OKLAHOMA—Continued																	
	Hughes	Jackson	Jefferson	Johnston	Kay	Kingfisher	Kiowa	Latimer	Le Flore	Lincoln	Logan	Love	McClain	McCurtain	McIntosh	Major	Marshall	Mayes
POPULATION BY SEX																		
Negro population: 1930	2,007	1,988	272	458	985	1,927	1,407	385	1,633	3,272	6,487	554	667	7,795	4,448	41	216	531
Male	995	1,018	134	233	523	991	724	186	837	1,657	3,321	300	346	3,945	2,275	21	97	278
Female	1,012	970	138	225	462	936	683	199	796	1,615	3,166	254	321	3,850	2,173	20	119	253
Negro population: 1920	1,746	411	402	659	293	1,623	492	440	2,082	3,955	6,422	746	776	6,914	5,950	45	275	729
Male	887	231	208	340	150	855	261	232	1,082	2,056	3,230	376	399	3,510	3,079	27	135	389
Female	859	180	194	319	143	768	231	208	1,000	1,899	3,192	370	377	3,404	2,871	18	140	340
Percent of total population:																		
1930	6.6	6.9	1.6	3.5	2.0	12.1	4.7	3.4	3.8	9.7	23.4	5.7	3.1	22.4	17.8	0.3	2.0	3.0
1920	6.7	1.9	2.3	3.3	0.8	10.4	2.1	3.2	4.9	11.8	23.3	6.0	4.0	18.2	22.5	0.4	1.9	4.3
VOTING AGE: 1930																		
Total 21 years old and over	966	1,163	163	249	679	985	713	215	855	1,452	3,267	287	348	3,823	2,048	28	109	258
Male	499	639	85	133	369	507	401	101	457	755	1,659	172	177	1,972	1,044	16	52	139
Female	467	524	78	116	310	478	312	114	398	697	1,608	115	171	1,851	1,004	12	57	119
AGE: 1930																		
Under 5 years	256	190	18	56	77	213	159	41	173	398	667	62	81	919	546	-----	23	58
Under 1 year	53	39	4	16	19	46	23	8	36	68	121	14	15	162	110	-----	4	11
5 to 9 years	271	209	29	50	81	259	172	45	201	476	788	67	85	1,002	642	6	29	89
10 to 14 years	235	201	32	44	55	222	166	42	173	458	787	65	78	918	583	2	35	61
15 to 19 years	241	196	28	48	74	210	148	35	205	420	830	61	64	931	543	5	18	58
20 to 24 years	191	232	15	51	143	153	175	31	146	284	633	62	54	838	396	5	19	40
25 to 29 years	159	228	16	37	148	128	131	17	128	180	419	37	34	674	273	4	19	31
30 to 34 years	115	199	18	29	97	92	108	19	82	171	350	32	55	484	228	5	14	26
35 to 44 years	233	301	47	50	164	221	189	51	190	310	686	72	73	860	444	6	27	47
45 to 54 years	166	170	40	42	86	173	103	55	176	287	596	45	64	675	408	3	17	55
55 to 64 years	96	39	17	34	32	108	38	28	105	176	395	34	40	297	225	5	8	31
65 to 74 years	24	18	8	11	20	84	14	11	34	77	206	11	25	126	115	-----	6	18
75 years and over	18	5	4	6	8	63	4	9	20	34	122	5	13	62	45	-----	1	16
Unknown	2	-----	-----	-----	-----	1	-----	1	-----	1	8	1	1	9	-----	-----	-----	1
SCHOOL ATTENDANCE																		
Total 7 to 13 years, inclusive	350	298	45	59	93	330	230	64	271	654	1,115	93	115	1,325	857	4	47	109
Number attending school	319	200	44	46	87	302	155	54	231	587	1,060	91	113	1,182	770	4	30	100
Percent attending school	91.1	67.1	-----	-----	-----	91.5	67.4	-----	85.2	89.8	95.1	-----	98.3	89.2	89.8	-----	-----	91.7
Total 14 and 15 years, inclusive	90	80	10	19	20	97	59	15	70	190	306	25	23	363	220	1	9	27
Number attending school	84	61	6	13	18	90	32	13	53	168	278	21	23	299	190	1	3	19
Percent attending school	-----	-----	-----	-----	-----	-----	-----	-----	-----	88.4	90.8	-----	-----	82.4	86.4	-----	-----	-----
Total 16 and 17 years, inclusive	92	72	11	23	24	92	54	13	83	168	342	17	35	371	223	1	8	22
Number attending school	59	33	1	10	14	72	24	7	43	117	219	9	21	227	163	-----	1	13
Percent attending school	-----	-----	-----	-----	-----	-----	-----	-----	-----	69.6	64.0	-----	-----	61.2	73.1	-----	-----	-----
Total 18 to 20 years, inclusive	142	110	14	31	59	113	120	20	106	233	491	43	32	590	309	3	8	25
Number attending school	28	14	1	-----	8	36	5	6	13	60	177	9	4	106	90	-----	-----	7
Percent attending school	19.7	12.7	-----	-----	-----	31.9	4.2	-----	12.3	25.8	36.0	-----	-----	18.0	29.1	-----	-----	-----
ILLITERACY																		
Total 10 years old and over	1,480	1,589	225	352	827	1,455	1,076	299	1,259	2,398	5,032	425	501	5,874	3,260	35	164	384
Number illiterate	194	222	27	69	60	101	141	47	193	163	309	64	58	823	337	1	36	50
Percent illiterate	13.1	14.0	12.0	19.6	7.3	6.9	13.1	15.7	15.3	6.8	6.1	15.1	11.6	14.0	10.3	-----	22.0	13.0
Percent illiterate in 1920	13.3	6.9	11.0	20.5	4.8	8.9	13.2	21.6	16.8	9.4	10.8	15.6	12.6	19.6	17.6	-----	13.9	9.9
URBAN AND RURAL																		
Urban population	631	992	-----	-----	737	310	276	-----	198	357	1,759	-----	250	628	-----	-----	-----	-----
Percent urban	31.4	49.9	-----	-----	74.8	16.1	19.6	-----	12.1	10.9	27.1	-----	37.5	8.1	-----	-----	-----	-----
Rural population	1,376	996	272	458	248	1,617	1,131	385	1,435	2,915	4,728	554	417	7,167	4,448	41	216	531
Rural-farm	1,058	833	47	309	43	1,439	913	108	920	2,498	3,702	373	410	5,938	3,395	27	67	526
Rural-nonfarm	318	163	225	149	205	178	218	277	515	417	1,026	181	7	1,229	1,053	14	149	5
Percent rural	68.6	50.1	100.0	100.0	25.2	83.9	80.4	100.0	87.9	89.1	72.9	100.0	62.5	91.9	100.0	-----	100.0	100.0
MARITAL CONDITION																		
Males 15 years old and over	624	736	98	165	417	639	493	123	570	977	2,180	208	220	2,507	1,364	17	61	176
Single	197	206	21	45	130	233	127	35	178	331	763	82	72	756	461	7	10	54
Married	366	448	69	99	251	342	325	69	315	568	1,182	103	126	1,561	784	10	42	101
Widowed	46	61	6	19	19	48	21	18	68	64	183	17	19	158	104	-----	8	19
Divorced	14	19	2	2	17	7	19	1	9	14	47	6	3	30	15	-----	1	2
Unknown	1	2	-----	-----	-----	9	1	-----	-----	-----	5	-----	-----	2	-----	-----	-----	-----
Females 15 years old and over	621	652	95	143	355	594	417	134	516	963	2,065	152	203	2,449	1,313	16	68	147
Single	156	89	13	24	57	147	61	25	104	261	525	41	39	515	323	4	12	35
Married	358	438	72	99	225	346	312	75	310	568	1,193	82	123	1,569	806	10	40	97
Widowed	86	96	8	17	44	89	30	33	92	113	315	22	37	318	173	2	16	14
Divorced	21	28	2	3	28	8	14	1	9	21	30	7	3	45	11	-----	-----	1
Unknown	-----	1	-----	-----	1	4	-----	-----	1	-----	2	-----	1	2	-----	-----	-----	-----
FAMILIES																		
Number of families	412	542	75	119	197	453	341	104	404	666	1,536	116	154	1,801	939	12	56	118
Median size	4.01	2.68	-----	3.04	2.57	3.40	3.10	2.56	3.02	3.99	3.30	3.39	3.50	3.45	3.98	-----	-----	4.00
Families having—																		
No children under 10	191	344	51	74	135	256	193	68	229	322	897	68	82	945	460	8	36	56
1 child under 10	82	97	12	16	21	76	64	13	78	116	259	15	32	336	165	3	8	25
2 children under 10	52	47	8	11	17	48	36	7	47	84	168	8	14	213	105	-----	4	10
3 or more	87	54	4	18	24	73	48	16	50	144	212	25	26	307	209	1	8	27

CHARACTERISTICS OF NEGRO POPULATION BY COUNTIES: 1930—Continued

(See note at head of table)

SUBJECT	OKLAHOMA—Continued																	
	Murray	Muskogee	Noble	Nowata	Okfuskee	Oklahoma	Okmulgee	Osage	Ottawa	Pawnee	Payne	Pittsburg	Pontotoc	Pottawatomie	Pushmataha	Roger Mills	Rogers	Seminole
POPULATION BY SEX																		
Negro population: 1930	346	16,059	718	1,542	7,283	17,524	11,014	1,284	2	686	1,924	3,770	1,026	2,072	363	95	679	5,607
Male	155	7,852	379	777	3,697	6,699	5,417	630	2	348	1,026	2,240	519	1,043	183	55	344	2,801
Female	191	8,207	339	765	3,586	8,825	5,597	654	------	338	898	1,530	507	1,029	180	40	335	2,806
Negro population: 1920	339	15,310	362	1,541	8,617	11,401	9,791	788	18	470	1,208	4,005	970	1,916	386	------	550	4,517
Male	165	7,521	175	822	4,374	5,773	5,001	453	11	234	633	2,293	496	942	204	------	305	2,247
Female	174	7,789	187	719	4,243	5,628	4,790	335	7	236	575	1,712	474	974	182	------	245	2,270
Percent of total population:																		
1930	2.8	24.2	4.7	11.3	25.1	7.9	19.5	2.7	------	3.5	5.2	7.4	3.2	3.1	2.5	0.7	3.6	7.0
1920	2.6	24.8	2.7	9.7	34.4	9.8	17.8	2.2	------	2.5	4.0	7.6	3.1	4.2	2.2	------	3.1	19.0
VOTING AGE: 1930																		
Total 21 years old and over	199	8,511	376	852	3,395	11,082	5,389	838	2	338	1,000	2,513	548	1,098	201	57	382	2,932
Male	94	4,162	209	438	1,732	5,584	2,656	417	2	184	533	1,602	279	561	103	35	197	1,490
Female	105	4,349	167	414	1,663	5,498	2,733	421	------	154	467	911	269	537	98	22	185	1,442
AGE: 1930																		
Under 5 years	33	1,501	79	160	790	1,341	1,327	115	------	79	236	268	131	201	38	10	59	575
Under 1 year	10	278	17	35	136	266	258	24	------	16	35	61	30	46	6	3	8	83
5 to 9 years	37	1,860	80	166	932	1,628	1,465	111	------	87	229	310	118	239	41	5	73	679
10 to 14 years	40	1,883	91	181	1,005	1,414	1,324	93	------	83	228	291	109	241	39	9	71	620
15 to 19 years	28	1,970	77	167	999	1,643	1,275	102	------	90	194	312	100	223	37	10	81	662
20 to 24 years	41	1,409	67	104	671	2,240	1,049	152	------	49	202	409	108	266	30	16	59	654
25 to 29 years	31	1,179	57	80	434	2,177	833	137	------	56	151	437	93	203	35	16	44	569
30 to 34 years	26	1,018	43	94	366	1,705	675	115	------	37	144	330	74	144	12	6	39	397
35 to 44 years	37	2,079	82	182	729	2,693	1,224	219	1	76	225	552	126	241	44	8	102	644
45 to 54 years	45	1,681	68	173	679	1,616	1,038	136	------	71	187	449	78	180	41	8	83	418
55 to 64 years	17	894	49	145	390	645	476	58	------	33	77	250	50	81	26	4	39	239
65 to 74 years	6	388	18	61	191	246	211	33	------	19	25	111	26	33	14	2	25	93
75 years and over	5	189	7	28	96	135	116	13	1	6	21	44	12	18	5	------	4	51
Unknown	------	8	------	1	1	41	1	------	------	------	5	7	1	2	1	1	------	6
SCHOOL ATTENDANCE																		
Total 7 to 13 years, inclusive	55	2,629	121	237	1,323	2,071	1,968	134	------	110	324	413	151	346	50	7	105	911
Number attending school	53	2,566	107	220	1,253	1,988	1,865	128	------	96	266	383	136	255	50	2	96	853
Percent attending school	------	96.6	88.4	92.8	94.7	96.0	94.8	95.5	------	87.3	82.1	92.7	90.1	73.7	------	------	91.4	93.6
Total 14 and 15 years, inclusive	11	819	34	66	442	561	476	33	------	38	78	118	41	79	22	5	29	235
Number attending school	11	762	28	59	408	498	444	28	------	29	58	105	37	60	22	------	28	213
Percent attending school	------	93.0	------	------	92.3	88.8	93.3	------	------	------	------	89.0	------	------	------	------	------	90.6
Total 16 and 17 years, inclusive	14	831	26	67	435	635	548	35	------	37	84	126	38	92	14	5	34	241
Number attending school	8	621	16	43	337	356	362	10	------	26	47	82	23	54	11	------	24	163
Percent attending school	------	74.7	------	------	77.5	56.1	66.1	------	------	------	------	65.1	------	------	------	------	------	67.6
Total 18 to 20 years, inclusive	18	1,054	50	91	519	1,156	732	76	------	44	107	204	61	166	22	8	46	434
Number attending school	2	284	13	12	198	245	147	13	------	10	24	43	5	30	9	------	14	121
Percent attending school	------	26.9	------	------	38.2	21.2	20.1	------	------	------	22.4	21.1	------	18.1	------	------	------	27.9
ILLITERACY																		
Total 10 years old and over	276	12,698	557	1,216	5,561	14,555	8,222	1,058	2	520	1,459	3,192	777	1,632	284	80	547	4,353
Number illiterate	29	1,099	57	129	612	695	648	114	1	72	132	365	113	257	47	9	41	439
Percent illiterate	10.5	8.7	10.2	10.6	11.0	4.8	7.9	10.8	------	13.8	9.0	11.4	14.5	15.7	16.5	------	7.5	10.1
Percent illiterate in 1920	13.3	9.8	9.2	13.2	11.0	7.4	11.9	11.9	------	11.5	11.0	15.3	20.6	13.4	17.5	------	9.3	13.1
URBAN AND RURAL																		
Urban population	151	6,576	319	513	94	14,662	3,213	734	------	135	790	1,744	479	1,061	------	------	408	2,440
Percent urban	43.6	40.9	44.4	33.3	1.3	83.7	29.2	57.2	------	19.7	41.1	46.3	46.7	51.2	------	------	60.1	43.5
Rural population	195	9,483	399	1,029	7,189	2,862	7,801	550	2	551	1,134	2,026	547	1,011	363	95	271	3,167
Rural-farm	98	6,564	360	802	5,678	2,359	6,730	153	2	477	1,049	708	481	598	207	42	201	2,758
Rural-nonfarm	97	2,919	39	227	1,511	503	1,071	397	------	74	85	1,318	66	413	156	53	70	409
Percent rural	56.4	59.1	55.6	66.7	98.7	16.3	70.8	42.8	------	80.3	58.9	53.7	53.3	48.8	100.0	------	39.9	56.5
MARITAL CONDITION																		
Males 15 years old and over	112	5,220	255	522	2,319	6,507	3,377	475	2	235	648	1,808	326	709	124	42	248	1,856
Single	34	1,593	86	160	837	1,830	1,028	96	1	64	176	623	76	232	37	9	80	638
Married	64	3,087	140	299	1,296	3,983	2,072	321	------	145	394	938	215	420	70	30	141	1,055
Widowed	11	395	20	49	167	446	219	34	1	16	65	143	22	41	15	2	19	119
Divorced	3	139	8	12	18	200	56	24	------	10	12	102	12	16	2	1	7	43
Unknown	------	6	1	2	1	48	2	------	------	------	1	2	1	------	------	------	1	1
Females 15 years old and over	124	5,595	213	513	2,237	6,634	3,521	490	------	202	583	1,093	342	682	121	29	228	1,877
Single	21	1,324	40	114	596	1,267	799	56	------	34	114	225	61	136	19	2	43	476
Married	64	3,163	135	296	1,336	4,026	2,129	338	------	148	385	621	218	421	72	26	131	1,095
Widowed	36	883	30	89	268	1,004	511	60	------	14	74	229	40	99	29	------	48	244
Divorced	3	222	7	14	37	306	80	34	------	6	9	18	21	24	1	1	6	61
Unknown	------	3	1	------	------	31	2	2	------	------	1	------	2	2	------	------	------	1
FAMILIES																		
Number of families	92	3,866	177	379	1,551	4,103	2,457	346	1	161	451	814	235	486	104	30	155	1,273
Median size	------	3.23	2.88	3.11	3.79	2.77	3.63	2.46	------	3.39	3.21	2.68	3.21	3.07	2.68	------	3.15	3.26
Families having—																		
No children under 10	60	2,324	113	232	814	2,736	1,269	232	1	96	265	545	132	287	66	20	99	697
1 child under 10	13	678	27	62	285	613	442	51	------	19	59	115	35	82	20	6	23	236
2 children under 10	10	383	11	44	167	351	276	38	------	14	51	74	34	55	5	3	10	159
3 or more	9	481	26	41	285	403	470	25	------	32	76	80	34	62	13	1	23	181

CHARACTERISTICS OF NEGRO POPULATION BY COUNTIES: 1930—Continued

(See note at head of table)

SUBJECT	OKLAHOMA—Continued: Sequoyah	Stephens	Tillman	Tulsa	Wagoner	Washington	Washita	Woods	Woodward
POPULATION BY SEX									
Negro population: 1930	1,596	361	2,993	17,817	6,753	1,020	307	1	6
Male	848	176	1,596	8,613	3,426	509	163	1	6
Female	748	185	1,397	9,204	3,327	511	144	-	-
Negro population: 1920	2,766	128	1,371	10,903	7,093	763	11	4	1
Male	1,417	60	798	5,437	3,554	393	7	2	1
Female	1,349	68	573	5,466	3,539	370	4	2	-
Percent of total population: 1930	8.2	1.1	12.3	9.5	30.1	3.7	1.0	-	-
1920	10.3	0.5	6.1	10.0	33.2	2.8	-	-	-
VOTING AGE: 1930									
Total 21 years old and over	772	224	1,675	12,026	3,268	663	182	1	6
Male	394	109	960	5,869	1,724	344	109	1	6
Female	378	115	715	6,157	1,544	319	73	-	-
AGE: 1930									
Under 5 years	183	24	326	1,322	786	95	27	-	-
Under 1 year	39	6	64	278	139	20	7	-	-
5 to 9 years	231	47	337	1,419	892	82	36	-	-
10 to 14 years	188	23	287	1,226	859	66	30	-	-
15 to 19 years	182	40	303	1,428	813	96	25	-	-
20 to 24 years	120	42	329	2,176	603	115	38	-	3
25 to 29 years	97	43	340	2,565	454	126	35	-	2
30 to 34 years	97	38	274	2,021	352	112	35	-	-
35 to 44 years	148	59	426	3,094	676	165	50	1	-
45 to 54 years	170	29	235	1,588	687	105	20	-	1
65 to 64 years	105	6	92	628	372	40	6	-	-
65 to 74 years	40	7	32	231	150	13	2	-	-
75 years and over	33	3	10	111	105	4	3	-	-
Unknown	2	-	2	8	4	1	-	-	-
SCHOOL ATTENDANCE									
Total 7 to 13 years, inclusive	294	48	431	1,828	1,207	99	48	-	-
Number attending school	279	37	297	1,768	1,139	96	18	-	-
Percent attending school	94.9	-	68.9	96.7	94.4	-	-	-	-
Total 14 and 15 years, inclusive	68	16	104	461	354	26	4	-	-
Number attending school	61	13	67	422	327	26	-	-	-
Percent attending school	-	-	64.4	91.5	92.4	-	-	-	-
Total 16 and 17 years, inclusive	82	13	105	528	329	26	14	-	-
Number attending school	58	8	30	338	224	19	2	-	-
Percent attending school	-	-	28.6	64.0	68.1	-	-	-	-
Total 18 to 20 years, inclusive	109	19	207	1,064	446	77	17	-	-
Number attending school	13	5	11	197	119	17	-	-	-
Percent attending school	11.9	-	5.3	18.5	26.7	-	-	-	-
ILLITERACY									
Total 10 years old and over	1,182	290	2,330	15,076	5,075	843	244	1	6
Number illiterate	170	27	353	621	552	66	30	-	1
Percent illiterate	14.4	9.3	15.2	4.1	10.9	7.8	12.3	-	-
Percent illiterate in 1920	17.3	-	14.3	8.1	14.1	10.6	-	-	-
URBAN AND RURAL									
Urban population	-	312	550	15,913	497	610	-	-	5
Percent urban	-	86.4	18.4	89.3	7.4	59.8	-	-	-
Rural population	1,596	49	2,443	1,904	6,256	410	307	1	1
Rural-farm	1,151	43	1,768	790	5,288	56	218	-	1
Rural-nonfarm	445	6	675	1,114	968	354	89	1	-
Percent rural	100.0	13.6	81.6	10.7	92.6	40.2	100.0	-	-
MARITAL CONDITION									
Males 15 years old and over	511	130	1,112	6,650	2,207	392	118	1	6
Single	147	33	298	1,610	705	108	22	-	3
Married	297	80	704	4,128	1,229	243	82	1	3
Widowed	56	10	83	648	236	30	7	-	-
Divorced	11	7	25	259	36	11	6	-	-
Unknown	-	-	2	5	1	-	1	-	-
Females 15 years old and over	483	137	931	7,200	2,009	385	96	-	-
Single	80	26	135	1,198	439	67	6	-	-
Married	313	79	700	4,241	1,230	246	85	-	-
Widowed	82	11	67	1,364	301	51	4	-	-
Divorced	8	21	26	395	39	20	1	-	-
Unknown	-	-	3	2	-	1	-	-	-
FAMILIES									
Number of families	369	100	805	4,370	1,488	308	91	-	1
Median size	3.57	2.86	2.76	2.49	3.77	2.34	-	-	-
Families having— No children under 10	204	65	490	3,052	777	223	61	-	1
1 child under 10	52	18	145	630	257	40	11	-	-
2 children under 10	49	7	77	339	181	21	10	-	-
3 or more	64	10	93	349	273	24	9	-	-

SUBJECT	OREGON: The State	Baker	Benton	Clackamas	Clatsop	Columbia	Coos	Crook	Deschutes	Douglas
POPULATION BY SEX										
Negro population: 1930	2,234	24	9	10	8	72	27	1	8	4
Male	1,210	12	3	5	6	44	12	1	4	1
Female	1,024	12	6	5	2	28	15	-	4	3
Negro population: 1920	2,144	21	15	26	14	4	30	1	17	7
Male	1,197	14	10	15	7	2	18	1	11	4
Female	947	7	5	11	7	2	12	-	6	3
Percent of total population: 1930	0.2	0.1	0.1	-	-	0.4	0.1	-	0.1	-
1920	0.3	0.1	0.1	0.1	0.1	-	0.1	-	0.2	-
VOTING AGE: 1930										
Total 21 years old and over	1,717	18	7	7	8	53	16	1	7	1
Male	978	9	3	3	6	32	7	1	4	-
Female	739	9	4	4	2	21	9	-	3	1
AGE: 1930										
Under 5 years	107	2	1	-	-	8	1	-	-	3
Under 1 year	23	-	-	-	-	-	-	-	-	1
5 to 9 years	127	3	-	2	-	7	2	-	-	-
10 to 14 years	122	1	-	1	-	4	3	-	1	-
15 to 19 years	128	-	1	-	-	-	2	-	-	-
20 to 24 years	161	3	2	-	-	4	3	-	-	1
25 to 29 years	175	1	1	1	-	13	2	-	-	-
30 to 34 years	198	1	1	2	-	8	3	-	-	-
35 to 44 years	522	7	1	-	4	24	5	-	4	-
45 to 54 years	392	3	2	2	3	2	4	1	2	-
65 to 64 years	194	-	-	1	-	2	2	-	1	-
65 to 74 years	75	3	-	1	1	-	-	-	-	-
75 years and over	27	-	-	-	-	-	-	-	-	-
Unknown	6	-	-	-	-	-	-	-	-	-
SCHOOL ATTENDANCE										
Total 7 to 13 years, inclusive	178	3	-	2	-	7	3	-	-	-
Number attending school	172	3	-	2	-	6	3	-	-	-
Percent attending school	96.6	-	-	-	-	-	-	-	-	-
Total 14 and 15 years, inclusive	48	-	-	-	-	-	1	-	1	-
Number attending school	47	-	-	-	-	-	1	-	1	-
Percent attending school	-	-	-	-	-	-	-	-	-	-
Total 16 and 17 years, inclusive	54	-	-	-	-	-	1	-	-	-
Number attending school	40	-	-	-	-	-	-	-	-	-
Percent attending school	-	-	-	-	-	-	-	-	-	-
Total 18 to 20 years, inclusive	85	-	1	-	-	-	4	-	-	-
Number attending school	26	-	-	-	-	-	-	-	-	-
Percent attending school	-	-	-	-	-	-	-	-	-	-
ILLITERACY										
Total 10 years old and over	2,000	19	8	8	8	57	24	1	8	1
Number illiterate	49	1	-	-	-	-	-	-	-	-
Percent illiterate	2.5	-	-	-	-	-	-	-	-	-
Percent illiterate in 1920	4.7	-	-	-	-	-	-	-	-	-
URBAN AND RURAL										
Urban population	1,890	21	7	-	3	-	23	-	8	-
Percent urban	84.6	-	-	-	-	-	-	-	-	-
Rural population	344	3	2	10	5	72	4	1	-	4
Rural-farm	44	1	-	5	-	-	-	1	-	-
Rural-nonfarm	300	2	2	5	5	72	4	-	-	4
Percent rural	15.4	-	-	-	-	-	-	-	-	-
MARITAL CONDITION										
Males 15 years old and over	1,051	9	3	3	6	32	9	1	4	-
Single	367	4	1	1	2	5	2	-	2	-
Married	551	5	2	2	2	24	7	-	2	-
Widowed	85	-	-	-	1	1	-	1	-	-
Divorced	47	-	-	-	1	2	-	-	-	-
Unknown	1	-	-	-	-	-	-	-	-	-
Females 15 years old and over	827	9	5	4	2	21	12	-	3	1
Single	134	-	1	1	1	-	-	-	-	-
Married	512	5	2	2	1	21	8	-	3	1
Widowed	142	4	1	1	-	-	1	-	-	-
Divorced	38	-	1	-	-	-	1	-	-	-
Unknown	1	-	-	-	-	-	-	-	-	-
FAMILIES										
Number of families	674	7	2	4	4	23	11	-	4	-
Median size	2.03	-	-	-	-	-	-	-	-	-
Families having— No children under 10	555	5	2	3	4	16	10	-	4	-
1 child under 10	68	1	-	-	-	4	-	-	-	-
2 children under 10	27	-	-	1	-	1	-	-	-	-
3 or more	24	1	-	-	-	2	1	-	-	-

CHARACTERISTICS OF NEGRO POPULATION BY COUNTIES: 1930—Continued

(See note at head of table)

SUBJECT	OREGON—Continued																	
	Gilliam	Grant	Harney	Hood River	Jackson	Jefferson	Klamath	Lake	Lane	Lincoln	Linn	Malheur	Marion	Morrow	Multnomah	Polk	Sherman	Umatilla
POPULATION BY SEX																		
Negro population: 1930	2	2	9	2	18	4	101	3	16	2	6	5	63	2	1,634	1	6	80
Male	2	1	7	1	9	3	60	3	9	1	5	2	45	2	835	1	5	60
Female		1	2	1	9	1	41		7	1	1	3	18		799		1	20
Negro population: 1920	1	1	14	4	65	5	18		13	1	9	7	72	6	1,627	5	3	84
Male	1	1	8	1	34	3	12		9	1	7	5	38	6	879	4	2	55
Female			6	3	31	2	6		4		2	2	34		748	1	1	29
Percent of total population:																		
1930	0.1		0.2		0.1	0.2	0.3	0.1					0.1		0.5		0.2	0.3
1920			0.4		0.3	0.2	0.2					0.1	0.2	0.1	0.6		0.1	0.3
VOTING AGE: 1930																		
Total 21 years old and over	2	2	9	2	13	3	76	3	10	2	5	3	52	2	1,243	1	5	76
Male	2	1	7	1	8	2	43	3	5	1	4	2	38	2	669	1	4	58
Female		1	2	1	5	1	33		5	1	1	1	14		574		1	18
AGE: 1930																		
Under 5 years					1		7						1		77			1
Under 1 year							1								20			
5 to 9 years							6					2	1		97		1	2
10 to 14 years					4	1	5		4		1		4		85			1
15 to 19 years							3		1				3		111			
20 to 24 years					2	1	9		1		1		6		109			4
25 to 29 years	1				1		12				1		4	1	117	1	2	7
30 to 34 years			1		2		13		1		1		14	1	124		1	9
35 to 44 years	1		5		5		32		3			2	13		364		2	22
45 to 54 years		1	1	1	2	1	12	1	4		1		8		304			22
55 to 64 years		1	1			1		2	2	1	1		4		162			8
65 to 74 years				1			1			1			3		60			1
75 years and over			1		1		1					1	2		20			1
Unknown															4			2
SCHOOL ATTENDANCE																		
Total 7 to 13 years, inclusive					2	1	7		3		1	1	4		134			2
Number attending school					2	1	7		2		1	1	3		131			2
Percent attending school															97.8			
Total 14 and 15 years, inclusive					2		1		1				1		39			
Number attending school					2		1		1				1		38			
Percent attending school																		
Total 16 and 17 years, inclusive							2						1		47			
Number attending school							2						1		34			
Percent attending school																		
Total 18 to 20 years, inclusive							5		2				4		64			
Number attending school							2						1		23			
Percent attending school																		
ILLITERACY																		
Total 10 years old and over	2	2	9	2	17	4	88	3	16	2	6	3	61	2	1,460	1	5	77
Number illiterate			1				4		1			1	8	1	22			6
Percent illiterate															1.5			
Percent illiterate in 1920															5.1			
URBAN AND RURAL																		
Urban population			3	1	7		97		5		5		58		1,559			46
Percent urban							96.0								95.4			
Rural population	2	2	6	1	11	4	4	3	11	2	1	5	5	2	75	1	6	34
Rural-farm	1		6		6	4	1	1	2	1		1			2	1	1	4
Rural-nonfarm	1	2		1	5		3	2	9	1	1	4	5	2	73		5	30
Percent rural							4.0								4.6			
MARITAL CONDITION																		
Males 15 years old and over	2	1	7	1	8	2	47	3	6	1	4	2	42	2	726	1	4	58
Single	1		4	1	2	1	17	3	3	1	2		27		228	1	3	32
Married			2		6	1	26		3		1	2	10	1	399		1	18
Widowed	1	1	1				2				1		4	1	63			4
Divorced							2						1		36			3
Unknown																		1
Females 15 years old and over		1	2	1	5	1	36		6	1	1	1	15		649		1	18
Single							2		1				7		113			1
Married			2		3	1	25		3		1	1	4		393		1	12
Widowed		1		1	2		5		2	1			3		112			5
Divorced							4						1		30			
Unknown															1			
FAMILIES																		
Number of families	1	1	2	1	7	1	32	1	4		2	1	6	1	483			33
Median size															214			
Families having—																		
No children under 10	1	1	2	1	6	1	26	1	3		2		5	1	391			32
1 child under 10					1		2		1						56			
2 children under 10							2					1	1		20			
3 or more							2								16			1

CHARACTERISTICS OF NEGRO POPULATION BY COUNTIES: 1930—Continued

(See note at head of table)

SUBJECT	OREGON—Continued					PENNSYLVANIA												
	Union	Wallowa	Wasco	Washington	Yamhill	The State	Adams	Allegheny	Armstrong	Beaver	Bedford	Berks	Blair	Bradford	Bucks	Butler	Cambria	Cameron
POPULATION BY SEX																		
Negro population: 1930	41	58	8	6	2	431,257	247	83,326	1,136	5,933	280	2,321	1,268	115	2,080	342	2,086	21
Male	23	36	8	3	1	218,412	128	43,408	644	3,132	144	1,262	657	61	1,047	197	1,123	11
Female	18	22	-	3	1	212,845	119	39,918	492	2,801	136	1,059	611	54	1,033	145	963	10
Negro population: 1920	16	1	15	8	8	244,568	295	53,517	1,084	2,897	354	1,165	1,361	137	1,810	387	2,492	46
Male	11	1	10	6	4	148,297	134	29,267	629	1,589	165	636	710	74	927	226	1,777	24
Female	5	-	5	3	4	136,271	161	24,250	455	1,308	189	529	651	63	883	161	715	22
Percent of total population:																		
1930	0.2	0.7	0.1	-	-	4.5	0.7	6.1	1.4	4.0	0.8	1.0	0.9	0.2	2.2	0.4	1.0	0.4
1920	0.1	-	0.1	-	-	3.3	0.9	4.5	1.4	2.6	0.9	0.6	1.1	0.3	2.2	0.5	1.3	0.7
VOTING AGE: 1930																		
Total 21 years old and over	31	44	7	6	2	277,355	143	53,632	670	3,496	184	1,562	755	75	1,100	197	1,202	15
Male	18	33	7	3	1	144,324	75	29,093	404	1,947	95	900	403	34	578	116	663	9
Female	13	11	-	3	1	133,031	68	24,539	266	1,549	89	662	352	38	522	81	539	6
AGE: 1930																		
Under 5 years	1	4	-	-	-	39,345	17	7,905	123	702	14	204	118	12	214	34	271	-
Under 1 year	-	1	-	-	-	7,385	3	1,491	25	111	2	47	20	4	45	6	63	-
5 to 9 years	2	2	-	-	-	40,632	32	7,957	110	646	24	171	144	10	229	35	252	2
10 to 14 years	3	4	-	-	-	33,028	28	6,280	117	487	24	155	114	8	283	37	169	1
15 to 19 years	4	2	1	-	-	33,213	26	6,146	96	495	29	184	113	6	207	38	162	3
20 to 24 years	2	13	-	-	-	41,895	12	7,882	84	544	22	277	90	10	164	14	192	-
25 to 29 years	2	6	2	-	-	50,353	21	9,968	115	714	17	314	111	8	158	22	253	1
30 to 34 years	6	9	1	-	-	44,943	14	9,182	110	631	18	232	92	7	117	25	203	1
35 to 44 years	13	13	-	1	1	74,819	36	14,601	195	937	35	396	185	23	251	58	317	2
45 to 54 years	5	4	1	5	-	45,045	24	8,573	123	487	34	224	171	18	215	49	173	-
55 to 64 years	1	1	2	-	1	18,098	17	3,266	42	202	33	98	64	9	142	22	59	5
65 to 74 years	2	-	1	-	-	6,790	14	1,108	14	67	16	40	30	4	64	5	18	5
75 years and over	-	-	-	-	-	2,569	6	370	7	16	12	10	24	-	27	3	15	1
Unknown	-	-	-	-	-	527	-	88	-	5	2	16	12	-	9	-	2	-
SCHOOL ATTENDANCE																		
Total 7 to 13 years, inclusive	4	4	-	-	-	50,938	41	9,758	159	778	30	228	174	10	378	54	283	3
Number attending school	4	4	-	-	-	48,795	40	9,258	158	754	30	214	169	10	368	52	278	3
Percent attending school	-	-	-	-	-	95.8	-	94.9	99.4	96.9	-	93.9	97.1	-	97.4	-	98.2	-
Total 14 and 15 years, inclusive	1	1	-	-	-	12,139	7	2,353	37	174	14	56	42	5	107	16	55	-
Number attending school	1	1	-	-	-	11,148	7	2,131	32	154	13	50	41	5	101	16	52	-
Percent attending school	-	-	-	-	-	91.8	-	90.6	-	88.5	-	-	-	-	94.4	-	-	-
Total 16 and 17 years, inclusive	2	1	-	-	-	12,873	12	2,401	33	189	10	61	45	1	76	14	81	2
Number attending school	2	1	-	-	-	5,959	5	1,189	15	97	7	28	28	1	42	9	25	2
Percent attending school	-	-	-	-	-	46.3	-	49.5	-	51.3	-	-	-	-	-	-	-	-
Total 18 to 20 years, inclusive	1	3	1	-	-	22,136	12	4,019	67	326	15	135	71	6	124	16	88	1
Number attending school	-	-	-	-	-	2,315	2	465	10	43	4	10	11	3	23	1	3	1
Percent attending school	-	-	-	-	-	10.5	-	11.6	-	13.2	-	7.4	-	-	18.5	-	-	-
ILLITERACY																		
Total 10 years old and over	38	52	8	6	2	351,280	198	67,464	903	4,585	242	1,946	1,006	93	1,637	273	1,563	19
Number illiterate	-	2	1	-	1	14,908	16	2,889	43	254	27	124	60	3	63	11	88	1
Percent illiterate	-	-	-	-	-	4.2	8.1	4.3	4.8	5.5	11.2	6.4	6.0	-	3.8	4.0	5.6	-
Percent illiterate in 1920	-	-	-	-	-	6.1	6.9	5.8	7.4	9.9	13.4	5.0	7.0	4.2	6.9	6.8	8.4	-
URBAN AND RURAL																		
Urban population	39	-	5	3	-	373,580	207	74,924	458	5,179	117	1,996	907	54	515	169	1,734	20
Percent urban	-	-	-	-	-	86.6	83.8	89.9	40.3	87.3	41.8	86.0	71.5	47.0	24.8	49.4	83.1	-
Rural population	2	58	3	3	2	57,677	40	8,402	678	754	163	325	361	61	1,565	173	352	1
Rural-farm	1	-	-	3	2	4,109	24	185	19	49	13	59	7	28	281	45	20	-
Rural-nonfarm	1	58	3	-	-	53,568	16	8,217	659	705	150	266	354	33	1,284	128	332	1
Percent rural	-	-	-	-	-	13.4	16.2	10.1	59.7	12.7	58.2	14.0	28.5	53.0	75.2	50.6	16.9	-
MARITAL CONDITION																		
Males 15 years old and over	22	33	8	3	1	162,770	90	32,563	473	2,232	116	1,009	472	45	691	141	755	11
Single	12	9	3	-	-	55,870	34	11,396	174	737	50	370	177	19	252	51	254	4
Married	7	24	3	2	1	96,793	40	19,154	263	1,376	55	571	267	23	387	75	461	5
Widowed	2	-	1	1	-	8,570	14	1,651	31	93	10	52	22	3	47	12	33	1
Divorced	1	-	1	-	-	1,166	2	308	5	24	1	4	6	-	4	3	5	1
Unknown	-	-	-	-	-	371	-	54	-	2	-	12	-	-	1	-	2	-
Females 15 years old and over	13	15	-	3	1	155,482	80	28,621	313	1,866	102	782	420	40	663	95	639	7
Single	3	2	-	-	-	35,298	17	5,490	39	323	30	160	86	10	191	17	105	2
Married	8	12	-	2	1	96,975	46	18,789	241	1,305	51	535	259	23	380	68	445	5
Widowed	2	-	-	1	-	21,338	17	3,936	27	215	20	72	68	5	90	9	83	-
Divorced	-	1	-	-	-	1,595	-	382	6	23	1	9	7	2	2	1	4	-
Unknown	-	-	-	-	-	276	-	24	-	-	-	6	-	-	-	-	2	-
FAMILIES																		
Number of families	13	23	3	3	1	99,114	60	19,171	282	1,380	76	543	309	28	401	75	504	6
Median size	-	-	-	-	-	2.88	-	2.95	3.00	3.10	-	2.56	3.10	-	3.15	-	3.18	-
Families having—																		
No children under 10	10	21	3	3	1	64,022	35	12,108	186	823	53	375	191	17	239	52	277	5
1 child under 10	3	-	-	-	-	14,798	10	2,997	32	211	15	70	60	5	55	8	81	-
2 children under 10	-	1	-	-	-	9,080	9	1,782	30	130	5	48	19	1	46	3	74	1
3 or more	-	1	-	-	-	11,214	6	2,284	34	216	3	50	39	5	61	12	72	-

CHARACTERISTICS OF NEGRO POPULATION BY COUNTIES: 1930—Continued

(See note at head of table)

SUBJECT	PENNSYLVANIA—Continued																	
	Carbon	Centre	Chester	Clarion	Clearfield	Clinton	Columbia	Crawford	Cumberland	Dauphin	Delaware	Elk	Erie	Fayette	Franklin	Fulton	Greene	Huntingdon
POPULATION BY SEX																		
Negro population: 1930	33	420	13,153	5	319	94	85	801	1,296	10,321	21,842	133	1,330	10,586	1,306	101	516	930
Male	29	336	6,901	4	160	54	39	415	627	5,246	10,818	70	718	5,537	666	50	290	585
Female	4	84	6,252	1	159	40	46	386	669	5,075	11,024	63	612	5,049	640	51	226	345
Negro population: 1920	25	369	11,386	24	511	169	96	695	1,582	8,305	15,717	210	882	6,280	1,457	86	300	717
Male	12	235	6,106	15	304	90	51	353	775	4,406	8,084	124	515	3,377	741	44	161	450
Female	13	134	5,280	9	207	79	45	342	807	3,899	7,633	86	367	2,903	716	42	139	267
Percent of total population:																		
1930	0.1	0.9	10.4	----	0.4	0.3	0.2	1.3	1.9	6.2	7.8	0.4	0.8	5.3	2.0	1.1	1.2	2.4
1920	----	0.8	9.9	0.1	0.5	0.5	0.2	1.1	2.7	5.4	9.1	0.6	0.6	3.3	2.3	0.9	1.0	1.8
VOTING AGE: 1930																		
Total 21 years old and over	29	360	7,542	5	174	68	59	476	808	6,495	13,465	70	880	6,003	776	43	314	447
Male	27	310	4,108	4	92	40	33	255	388	3,405	6,767	38	498	3,325	398	25	187	275
Female	2	50	3,434	1	82	28	26	221	420	3,090	6,698	32	382	2,678	378	18	127	172
AGE: 1930																		
Under 5 years	----	14	1,334	----	38	4	9	89	114	930	2,073	21	113	1,225	118	12	51	107
Under 1 year	----	2	253	----	8	1	----	16	22	163	365	5	23	255	20	2	10	18
5 to 9 years	1	15	1,481	----	34	8	10	88	130	1,004	2,128	17	132	1,290	126	10	63	78
10 to 14 years	2	13	1,331	----	28	5	3	60	106	844	1,824	13	98	1,018	130	20	44	60
15 to 19 years	1	14	1,213	----	36	8	4	76	108	865	1,959	12	87	901	127	12	37	191
20 to 24 years	10	43	1,206	----	23	11	5	60	107	950	2,265	6	119	705	110	14	37	147
25 to 29 years	1	67	1,099	----	22	3	8	68	78	938	2,261	14	152	991	88	3	53	81
30 to 34 years	2	70	1,075	----	23	4	4	65	73	915	1,898	16	159	991	84	7	54	65
35 to 44 years	9	73	1,742	----	39	15	13	114	177	1,717	3,449	15	233	1,686	160	6	74	116
45 to 54 years	6	64	1,448	3	45	13	13	113	177	1,255	2,252	11	145	1,080	154	8	65	51
55 to 64 years	----	26	692	2	14	14	7	45	128	571	1,055	5	64	445	108	7	24	25
65 to 74 years	----	11	366	----	13	5	5	14	62	225	475	3	16	184	69	----	10	3
75 years and over	1	9	136	----	3	4	4	7	36	103	162	----	11	66	32	1	4	5
Unknown	----	1	30	----	1	----	----	2	----	4	41	----	1	4	----	1	----	1
SCHOOL ATTENDANCE																		
Total 7 to 13 years, inclusive	2	19	1,930	----	41	7	6	100	161	1,249	2,696	19	142	1,608	200	21	70	86
Number attending school	2	18	1,852	----	40	6	6	96	155	1,221	2,598	19	133	1,557	186	20	67	82
Percent attending school	----	----	96.0	----	----	----	----	96.0	96.3	97.8	96.4	----	93.7	96.8	93.0	----	----	----
Total 14 and 15 years, inclusive	----	3	538	----	11	3	1	19	33	333	740	8	37	367	54	9	18	23
Number attending school	----	3	497	----	11	3	1	17	30	307	676	8	35	327	46	8	15	22
Percent attending school	----	----	92.4	----	----	----	----	----	----	92.2	91.4	----	----	89.1	----	----	----	----
Total 16 and 17 years, inclusive	----	5	464	----	15	1	2	38	49	360	770	4	42	379	47	4	9	72
Number attending school	----	4	213	----	10	1	1	25	26	186	376	----	22	181	18	----	3	54
Percent attending school	----	----	45.9	----	----	----	----	----	----	51.7	48.8	----	----	47.8	----	----	----	----
Total 18 to 20 years, inclusive	1	12	741	----	24	6	2	40	76	537	1,221	4	55	488	77	9	24	158
Number attending school	----	4	77	----	2	3	1	9	15	91	154	----	5	66	9	----	3	97
Percent attending school	----	----	10.4	----	----	----	----	----	----	16.9	12.6	----	----	13.5	----	----	----	61.4
ILLITERACY																		
Total 10 years old and over	32	391	10,338	5	247	82	66	624	1,052	8,387	17,641	95	1,085	8,071	1,062	79	402	745
Number illiterate	----	13	714	1	16	7	5	26	56	532	1,024	6	70	615	125	7	44	58
Percent illiterate	----	3.3	6.9	----	6.5	----	----	4.2	5.3	6.3	5.8	----	6.5	7.6	11.8	----	10.9	7.8
Percent illiterate in 1920	----	10.4	9.6	----	6.0	6.5	----	4.2	10.1	10.2	7.8	10.8	3.8	9.5	13.4	----	6.9	14.1
URBAN AND RURAL																		
Urban population	21	117	5,601	----	130	43	72	547	1,072	9,232	13,795	8	1,268	2,281	807	----	116	664
Percent urban	----	27.9	42.6	----	40.8	----	----	68.3	82.7	89.4	63.2	6.0	95.3	21.5	61.8	----	22.5	71.4
Rural population	12	303	7,552	5	189	51	13	254	224	1,089	8,047	125	62	8,305	499	101	400	266
Rural-farm	----	2	1,540	1	1	4	----	83	16	36	358	----	21	119	66	23	36	9
Rural-nonfarm	12	301	6,012	4	188	47	13	171	208	1,053	7,689	125	41	8,186	433	78	364	257
Percent rural	----	72.1	57.4	----	59.2	----	----	31.7	17.3	10.6	36.8	94.0	4.7	78.5	38.2	100.0	77.5	28.6
MARITAL CONDITION																		
Males 15 years old and over	28	319	4,866	4	112	43	33	297	451	3,900	7,832	45	544	3,808	474	32	212	458
Single	24	147	1,756	2	31	18	5	94	176	1,390	2,764	14	182	1,132	206	15	82	276
Married	4	127	2,717	2	71	21	23	177	245	2,255	4,540	29	322	2,426	234	14	119	163
Widowed	----	38	324	----	9	4	3	22	29	234	411	1	33	210	32	3	11	17
Divorced	----	7	29	----	1	----	1	2	1	19	57	1	7	34	2	----	----	2
Unknown	----	----	40	----	----	----	1	2	----	2	60	----	----	6	----	----	----	----
Females 15 years old and over	2	59	4,141	1	107	34	30	267	495	3,643	7,985	37	443	3,245	458	27	146	227
Single	----	14	938	----	28	9	6	55	151	800	2,098	4	67	561	138	12	22	60
Married	2	31	2,613	1	66	19	17	170	257	2,304	4,741	30	307	2,338	225	12	109	141
Widowed	----	13	521	----	11	6	7	37	76	502	1,015	3	62	320	95	2	14	26
Divorced	----	1	27	----	1	----	----	3	11	34	93	----	7	23	----	----	1	----
Unknown	----	----	42	----	1	----	----	2	----	3	38	----	----	3	----	1	----	----
FAMILIES																		
Number of families	4	49	2,849	3	79	30	23	197	361	2,496	4,649	30	323	2,605	340	15	133	165
Median size	----	----	3.16	----	----	----	----	2.93	2.78	2.74	3.02	----	2.80	3.03	2.71	----	2.94	3.28
Families having—																		
No children under 10	3	34	1,730	3	53	25	15	122	245	1,664	2,907	19	217	1,544	233	5	84	91
1 child under 10	1	7	420	----	6	2	4	30	52	348	692	4	50	419	41	4	20	26
2 children under 10	----	4	269	----	9	1	1	21	31	210	439	1	20	266	31	2	11	18
3 or more	----	4	430	----	11	2	3	24	33	274	611	6	36	376	35	4	18	30

CHARACTERISTICS OF NEGRO POPULATION BY COUNTIES: 1930—Continued

(See note at head of table)

SUBJECT	PENNSYLVANIA—Continued																	
	Indiana	Jefferson	Juniata	Lackawanna	Lancaster	Lawrence	Lebanon	Lehigh	Luzerne	Lycoming	McKean	Mercer	Mifflin	Monroe	Montgomery	Montour	Northampton	Northumberland
POPULATION BY SEX																		
Negro population: 1930	747	129	69	863	2,593	2,129	329	460	1,056	1,057	217	2,694	283	216	12,572	53	1,334	201
Male	413	75	36	477	1,399	1,129	179	256	547	509	124	1,446	145	130	5,809	26	721	117
Female	334	54	33	386	1,194	1,000	150	204	509	548	93	1,248	138	86	6,763	27	613	84
Negro population: 1920	439	92	95	670	2,166	1,305	304	300	815	1,082	313	2,842	352	149	8,326	53	749	291
Male	246	55	53	362	1,138	733	170	165	450	513	154	1,776	187	69	3,939	26	393	184
Female	193	37	42	308	1,028	572	134	135	365	569	159	1,066	165	80	4,387	27	356	107
Percent of total population:																		
1930	1.0	0.2	0.5	0.3	1.3	2.2	0.5	0.3	0.2	1.1	0.4	2.7	0.7	0.8	4.7	0.4	0.8	0.2
1920	0.5	0.1	0.7	0.2	1.2	1.5	0.5	0.2	0.2	1.3	0.6	3.0	1.1	0.6	4.2	0.4	0.5	0.2
VOTING AGE: 1930																		
Total 21 years old and over	405	78	41	606	1,639	1,284	204	323	739	655	143	1,518	155	159	8,016	43	844	121
Male	234	51	20	343	916	714	116	187	394	312	75	875	84	100	3,755	19	477	69
Female	171	27	21	263	723	570	88	136	345	343	68	643	71	59	4,261	24	367	52
AGE: 1930																		
Under 5 years	92	15	11	50	228	208	18	36	72	93	13	353	48	11	1,064	2	138	15
Under 1 year	19	4	------	10	39	34	3	8	11	17	2	74	9	1	202	------	26	4
5 to 9 years	102	10	8	71	247	236	39	40	97	105	16	282	25	16	1,177	5	141	18
10 to 14 years	81	6	6	61	223	176	33	33	75	93	17	255	30	11	938	2	100	17
15 to 19 years	57	15	2	59	215	194	30	22	58	100	24	248	18	15	1,094	------	92	26
20 to 24 years	60	21	4	65	243	139	29	31	72	63	16	201	21	21	1,372	1	103	10
25 to 29 years	68	18	5	93	230	212	27	53	105	71	19	297	24	16	1,418	2	166	14
30 to 34 years	60	16	6	76	192	218	36	59	132	72	16	267	27	17	1,204	4	153	19
35 to 44 years	109	13	10	163	363	382	57	104	194	149	33	409	45	50	2,033	12	222	36
45 to 54 years	70	12	6	141	315	221	31	46	125	137	26	232	20	34	1,380	12	127	24
55 to 64 years	29	3	5	43	179	97	17	23	77	96	24	103	12	12	567	4	57	13
65 to 74 years	12	------	4	31	101	30	9	10	28	47	7	28	10	9	221	6	23	4
75 years and over	6	------	------	10	55	14	2	2	20	31	6	17	3	4	72	3	8	5
Unknown	1	------	2	------	2	2	1	1	1	------	------	2	------	------	32	------	4	------
SCHOOL ATTENDANCE																		
Total 7 to 13 years, inclusive	130	8	11	101	334	283	51	51	128	142	27	369	43	20	1,432	7	159	25
Number attending school	129	7	10	93	319	272	48	50	126	139	25	365	42	20	1,364	7	152	25
Percent attending school	99.2	------	------	92.1	95.5	96.1	------	------	98.4	97.9	------	98.9	------	------	95.3	------	95.6	------
Total 14 and 15 years, inclusive	28	5	2	23	74	75	9	12	20	29	6	101	7	2	370	------	31	5
Number attending school	26	5	2	23	66	70	7	11	19	27	6	90	6	2	333	------	27	5
Percent attending school	------	------	------	------	------	------	------	------	------	------	------	89.1	------	------	90.0	------	------	------
Total 16 to 17 years, inclusive	22	6	------	19	85	81	9	6	20	42	13	89	9	4	408	------	35	10
Number attending school	14	1	------	10	28	38	5	1	13	29	8	48	4	3	174	------	11	7
Percent attending school	------	------	------	------	------	------	------	------	------	------	------	------	------	------	42.6	------	------	------
Total 18 to 20 years, inclusive	31	11	1	44	137	104	23	16	46	52	12	147	11	14	805	1	65	17
Number attending school	7	------	------	8	15	14	4	------	5	15	7	19	------	2	64	------	4	6
Percent attending school	------	------	------	------	10.9	13.5	------	------	------	------	------	12.9	------	------	8.0	------	------	------
ILLITERACY																		
Total 10 years old and over	553	104	50	742	2,118	1,685	272	384	887	859	188	2,059	210	189	10,331	46	1,055	168
Number illiterate	39	41	------	14	187	115	15	27	35	36	4	140	19	13	543	1	38	6
Percent illiterate	7.1	39.4	------	1.9	8.8	6.8	5.5	7.0	3.9	4.2	2.1	6.8	9.0	6.9	5.3	------	3.6	3.6
Percent illiterate in 1920	14.0	------	------	2.7	13.5	9.1	10.0	6.2	5.8	7.3	3.1	8.2	11.0	9.8	6.5	------	4.9	8.3
URBAN AND RURAL																		
Urban population	241	26	------	768	1,757	1,692	101	425	1,022	990	162	2,310	100	137	9,140	33	1,205	171
Percent urban	32.3	20.2	------	89.0	67.8	79.5	30.7	92.4	96.8	93.7	74.7	85.7	35.3	63.4	72.7	------	90.3	85.1
Rural population	506	103	69	95	836	437	228	35	34	67	55	384	183	79	3,432	20	129	30
Rural-farm	22	1	43	29	155	50	11	2	2	7	3	43	------	8	186	------	16	9
Rural-nonfarm	484	102	26	66	681	387	217	33	32	60	52	341	183	71	3,246	20	113	21
Percent rural	67.7	79.8	------	11.0	32.2	20.5	69.3	7.6	3.2	6.3	25.3	14.3	64.7	36.6	27.3	------	9.7	14.9
MARITAL CONDITION																		
Males 15 years old and over	266	59	21	383	1,056	823	134	200	428	358	92	999	96	111	4,338	19	525	86
Single	79	25	8	163	478	306	52	69	153	106	43	325	31	48	1,505	7	200	38
Married	166	33	11	185	492	457	70	116	256	213	42	601	60	49	2,547	7	281	37
Widowed	20	1	2	25	76	44	10	12	15	34	4	52	4	12	233	2	30	11
Divorced	1	------	------	6	10	13	1	3	3	5	2	20	1	2	29	1	7	------
Unknown	------	------	------	4	------	3	1	------	1	------	1	1	------	------	24	2	7	------
Females 15 years old and over	206	39	23	298	839	686	105	151	384	408	79	805	84	67	5,055	25	430	65
Single	32	6	9	59	205	128	23	24	76	99	18	136	9	13	1,515	10	77	19
Married	155	33	9	171	499	452	67	106	249	220	45	586	56	35	2,759	9	274	37
Widowed	19	------	5	63	123	86	13	18	57	78	15	74	16	14	694	3	70	7
Divorced	------	------	------	4	10	20	2	3	2	11	1	8	3	4	65	1	6	2
Unknown	------	------	------	1	2	------	------	------	------	------	------	1	------	1	22	2	3	------
FAMILIES																		
Number of families	171	34	18	220	622	532	85	107	280	276	53	635	65	47	2,146	10	302	51
Median size	3.38	------	------	2.35	2.55	2.88	------	2.56	2.57	3.03	------	3.21	------	------	3.34	------	2.90	------
Families having—																		
No children under 10	91	26	10	162	429	336	55	75	198	188	38	360	36	33	1,220	7	179	37
1 child under 10	26	3	2	34	68	78	15	13	39	31	7	110	9	10	368	------	46	4
2 children under 10	25	2	6	13	48	47	10	8	19	29	4	69	9	2	223	2	39	5
3 or more	29	3	------	11	77	71	5	11	24	28	4	96	11	2	335	1	38	5

CHARACTERISTICS OF NEGRO POPULATION BY COUNTIES: 1930—Continued

(See note at head of table)

SUBJECT	Perry	Phila-delphia	Pike	Potter	Schuyl-kill	Snyder	Somer-set	Sulli-van	Susque-hanna	Tioga	Union	Ve-nango	War-ren	Wash-ing-ton	Wayne	West-more-land	Wyo-ming	York
	PENNSYLVANIA—Continued																	
POPULATION BY SEX																		
Negro population: 1930	49	219, 599	59	16	583	2	245	4	101	89	32	593	24	10, 933	100	6, 410	13	2, 977
Male	29	108, 483	30	9	344	2	129	1	51	52	11	278	10	5, 979	98	3, 457	7	1, 545
Female	20	111, 116	29	7	239	—	116	3	50	37	21	315	14	4, 954	2	2, 953	6	1, 432
Negro population: 1920	80	134, 229	47	25	253	3	549	1	87	106	28	593	39	7, 428	48	4, 240	19	2, 092
Male	39	67, 132	28	15	154	2	316	1	43	51	10	278	17	3, 991	45	2, 507	14	1, 039
Female	41	67, 097	19	10	99	1	233	—	44	55	18	315	22	3, 437	3	1, 733	5	1, 053
Percent of total population:																		
1930	0. 2	11. 3	0. 8	0. 1	0. 2	—	0. 3	0. 1	0. 3	0. 3	0. 2	0. 9	0. 1	5. 3	0. 4	2. 2	0. 1	1. 8
1920	0. 3	7. 4	0. 7	0. 1	0. 1	—	0. 7	—	0. 3	0. 3	0. 2	1. 0	0. 1	3. 9	0. 2	1. 5	0. 1	1. 4
VOTING AGE: 1930																		
Total 21 years old and over	35	146, 234	44	14	357	1	150	4	67	56	20	331	18	6, 464	99	3, 719	5	1, 719
Male	20	73, 560	23	8	229	1	87	1	34	34	8	169	9	3, 758	97	2, 130	2	918
Female	15	72, 674	21	6	128	—	63	3	33	22	12	162	9	2, 706	2	1, 589	3	801
AGE: 1930																		
Under 5 years	3	18, 658	4	—	68	—	16	—	5	11	1	46	1	1, 116	—	743	4	336
Under 1 year	1	3, 473	1	—	14	—	2	—	2	4	—	14	—	220	—	139	1	71
5 to 9 years	4	19, 300	6	—	66	—	23	—	6	9	—	70	1	1, 215	—	741	—	329
10 to 14 years	4	15, 526	4	1	47	—	28	—	10	7	1	68	3	999	—	590	2	279
15 to 19 years	3	15, 908	1	1	32	1	27	—	11	5	10	66	1	945	—	518	2	257
20 to 24 years	2	22, 527	5	—	57	—	8	—	11	6	3	47	1	850	6	497	—	294
25 to 29 years	2	27, 726	7	—	77	—	21	—	6	9	1	34	—	1, 052	9	645	1	296
30 to 34 years	6	24, 093	6	2	76	—	6	1	7	2	1	41	5	1, 081	16	615	2	272
35 to 44 years	5	40, 281	10	2	86	—	36	1	17	10	2	82	6	1, 775	29	1, 045	—	374
45 to 54 years	8	22, 857	7	6	42	—	37	—	10	22	5	71	5	1, 120	20	626	1	255
55 to 64 years	10	8, 519	5	1	20	—	24	—	10	3	3	45	1	470	15	256	—	164
65 to 74 years	1	2, 941	3	2	10	1	16	1	5	2	5	17	—	192	4	89	—	75
75 years and over	1	1, 029	1	1	2	—	3	1	3	3	—	5	—	99	1	41	1	45
Unknown	—	234	—	—	—	—	—	—	—	—	—	1	—	19	—	4	—	1
SCHOOL ATTENDANCE																		
Total 7 to 13 years, inclusive	5	24, 276	6	—	73	—	38	—	11	11	1	101	4	1, 522	—	907	2	407
Number attending school	4	23, 257	5	—	71	—	37	—	11	11	1	81	4	1, 458	—	880	2	388
Percent attending school	—	95. 8	—	—	—	—	—	—	—	—	—	80. 2	—	95. 8	—	97. 0	—	95. 3
Total 14 and 15 years, inclusive	2	5, 556	1	1	12	—	13	—	4	2	1	24	—	363	—	196	1	101
Number attending school	2	5, 167	1	1	9	—	13	—	4	2	1	22	—	321	—	179	1	92
Percent attending school	—	93. 0	—	—	—	—	—	—	—	—	—	—	—	88. 4	—	91. 3	—	91. 1
Total 16 and 17 years, inclusive	2	6, 039	1	1	16	1	11	—	4	3	2	28	1	391	—	216	—	113
Number attending school	2	2, 605	1	1	2	—	8	—	3	2	2	14	1	192	—	121	—	43
Percent attending school	—	43. 1	—	—	—	—	—	—	—	—	—	—	—	49. 1	—	56. 0	—	38. 1
Total 18 to 20 years, inclusive	—	11, 112	—	—	22	—	10	—	7	2	7	37	—	576	1	312	1	157
Number attending school	—	880	—	—	1	—	2	—	3	—	3	10	—	88	—	37	—	9
Percent attending school	—	7. 9	—	—	—	—	—	—	—	—	—	—	—	15. 3	—	11. 9	—	5. 7
ILLITERACY																		
Total 10 years old and over	42	181, 641	49	16	449	2	206	4	90	69	31	477	22	8, 602	100	4, 926	9	2, 312
Number illiterate	3	5, 432	5	—	38	—	15	—	2	2	1	52	1	632	3	309	—	242
Percent illiterate	—	3. 0	—	—	8. 5	—	7. 3	—	—	—	—	10. 9	—	7. 3	3. 0	6. 3	—	10. 5
Percent illiterate in 1920	—	4. 6	—	—	5. 2	—	11. 1	—	—	—	—	8. 6	—	6. 4	—	7. 4	—	10. 1
URBAN AND RURAL																		
Urban population	—	219, 599	—	9	485	—	127	—	1	24	18	573	2	4, 740	1	3, 391	—	2, 276
Percent urban	—	100. 0	—	—	83. 2	—	51. 8	—	1. 0	—	—	96. 6	—	43. 4	1. 0	52. 9	—	76. 5
Rural population	49	—	59	7	98	2	118	4	100	65	14	20	22	6, 193	99	3, 019	13	701
Rural-farm	22	—	6	1	10	1	12	1	25	—	—	5	—	170	3	37	1	183
Rural-nonfarm	27	—	53	6	88	1	106	3	75	65	14	15	22	6, 023	96	2, 982	12	518
Percent rural	—	—	—	—	16. 8	—	48. 2	—	99. 0	—	—	3. 4	—	56. 6	99. 0	47. 1	—	23. 5
MARITAL CONDITION																		
Males 15 years old and over	23	82, 123	23	9	248	2	95	1	43	37	10	199	10	4, 292	98	2, 436	3	1, 068
Single	10	27, 428	9	5	103	2	41	—	23	13	3	72	3	1, 441	57	807	1	384
Married	10	50, 037	12	4	130	—	41	1	17	22	6	110	6	2, 535	28	1, 444	2	599
Widowed	—	4, 068	2	—	14	—	13	—	3	2	1	14	—	270	13	155	—	78
Divorced	2	458	—	—	1	—	—	—	—	—	—	3	1	40	—	24	—	7
Unknown	1	132	—	—	—	—	—	—	—	—	—	—	—	6	—	6	—	—
Females 15 years old and over	15	83, 992	22	6	154	—	83	3	37	25	20	210	9	3, 311	2	1, 900	4	965
Single	2	20, 124	7	—	29	—	29	—	8	5	11	67	1	609	—	294	—	221
Married	10	51, 046	12	4	108	—	44	—	18	18	5	109	6	2, 329	1	1, 383	2	588
Widowed	3	11, 952	3	2	17	—	10	2	9	2	4	34	2	337	1	206	2	145
Divorced	—	754	—	—	—	—	—	1	2	—	—	—	—	32	—	16	—	10
Unknown	—	116	—	—	—	—	—	—	—	—	—	—	—	4	—	1	—	1
FAMILIES																		
Number of families	11	50, 997	16	7	140	1	55	—	24	24	9	118	4	2, 618	3	1, 554	2	691
Median size	—	2. 79	—	—	2. 63	—	—	—	—	—	—	3. 17	—	2. 99	—	3. 03	—	3. 15
Families having—																		
No children under 10	7	33, 963	13	7	90	1	41	—	19	16	8	78	3	1, 598	3	928	—	412
1 child under 10	3	7, 459	1	—	14	—	3	—	1	3	1	10	—	434	—	240	—	96
2 children under 10	—	4, 520	1	—	13	—	6	—	3	—	—	13	1	244	—	149	2	86
3 or more	1	5, 055	1	—	23	—	5	—	1	5	—	17	—	342	—	237	—	97

CHARACTERISTICS OF NEGRO POPULATION BY COUNTIES: 1930—Continued

(See note at head of table)

SUBJECT	RHODE ISLAND						SOUTH CAROLINA												
	The State	Bristol	Kent	Newport	Providence	Washington	The State	Abbeville	Aiken	Allendale	Anderson	Bamberg	Barnwell	Beaufort	Berkeley	Calhoun	Charleston	Cherokee	Chester
POPULATION BY SEX																			
Negro population: 1930	9,913	69	294	1,734	7,083	733	793,681	11,055	21,530	9,761	22,594	12,475	13,465	15,571	15,051	12,408	54,812	8,472	16,457
Male	4,862	39	155	852	3,432	384	379,300	5,438	10,276	4,656	11,007	5,953	6,468	7,250	7,227	5,959	24,754	4,124	7,826
Female	5,051	30	139	882	3,651	349	414,381	5,617	11,254	5,105	11,587	6,522	6,997	8,321	7,824	6,449	30,058	4,348	8,631
Negro population: 1920	10,036	126	227	1,754	7,151	778	864,719	15,436	23,988	12,497	26,312	14,355	15,583	17,454	16,349	12,604	64,236	8,595	19,338
Male	5,096	78	120	843	3,660	395	422,185	7,553	11,704	6,093	13,082	7,131	7,557	8,226	8,042	6,125	30,193	4,293	9,424
Female	4,940	48	107	911	3,491	383	442,534	7,883	12,284	6,404	13,230	7,224	8,026	9,228	8,307	6,479	34,043	4,302	9,914
Percent of total population:																			
1930	1.4	0.3	0.6	4.2	1.3	2.5	45.6	47.4	45.4	73.4	27.9	64.3	63.5	71.4	67.7	74.3	54.2	26.3	51.7
1920	1.7	0.5	0.6	4.1	1.5	3.1	51.4	56.9	52.6	77.6	34.5	68.5	67.5	78.4	72.5	68.6	59.2	31.2	57.9
VOTING AGE: 1930																			
Total 21 years old and over	5,952	47	185	1,093	4,204	423	343,788	4,858	9,842	4,192	9,977	4,918	5,894	7,523	6,444	4,944	28,404	3,650	7,153
Male	2,937	23	97	496	2,090	231	159,190	2,293	4,688	1,908	4,735	2,294	2,776	3,294	3,043	2,294	12,351	1,702	3,205
Female	3,015	24	88	597	2,114	192	184,598	2,565	5,154	2,284	5,242	2,624	3,118	4,229	3,401	2,650	16,053	1,948	3,948
AGE: 1930																			
Under 5 years	1,008	5	29	149	750	75	96,300	1,263	2,213	1,130	2,528	1,568	1,628	1,606	1,977	1,644	6,002	1,063	1,932
Under 1 year	193	1	5	25	144	18	17,755	243	379	182	498	298	307	296	322	316	1,082	198	358
5 to 9 years	1,069	6	18	181	782	82	116,296	1,471	2,975	1,496	3,256	2,045	2,013	2,132	2,288	1,947	6,972	1,257	2,360
10 to 14 years	938	6	31	159	674	68	111,123	1,629	3,023	1,399	3,158	1,898	1,891	2,066	2,128	1,937	6,181	1,131	2,317
15 to 19 years	807	5	22	128	579	73	106,429	1,608	2,922	1,272	3,054	1,757	1,717	1,887	1,867	1,655	6,035	1,153	2,328
20 to 24 years	674	----	26	114	472	62	76,652	986	2,167	911	2,440	1,166	1,316	1,210	1,327	1,024	5,614	867	1,364
25 to 29 years	690	5	19	129	482	55	51,299	662	1,392	602	1,503	737	889	846	901	694	4,539	595	890
30 to 34 years	718	6	15	120	531	46	38,969	436	1,039	477	1,209	534	675	690	689	550	3,398	393	713
35 to 44 years	1,441	6	54	251	1,041	89	82,019	1,056	2,300	1,004	2,245	1,170	1,385	1,825	1,566	1,254	7,513	797	1,624
45 to 54 years	1,291	14	37	222	927	91	59,982	893	1,759	725	1,644	848	950	1,594	1,252	898	4,787	651	1,435
55 to 64 years	750	10	31	157	501	51	31,956	630	1,023	433	892	468	561	988	622	495	2,274	320	885
65 to 74 years	346	4	4	83	236	19	15,749	280	499	220	447	196	310	513	302	208	1,060	179	434
75 years and over	170	2	8	38	101	21	6,534	140	206	91	203	85	129	214	123	101	410	65	174
Unknown	11	----	----	3	7	1	373	1	12	1	15	3	1	----	9	1	27	1	1
SCHOOL ATTENDANCE																			
Total 7 to 13 years, inclusive	1,389	9	41	247	995	97	157,359	2,153	4,189	2,001	4,408	2,744	2,715	2,958	3,024	2,649	9,178	1,632	3,226
Number attending school	1,354	9	40	245	971	89	125,377	1,705	3,480	1,040	3,539	1,913	1,883	2,478	2,499	2,288	7,900	1,260	2,694
Percent attending school	97.5	----	----	99.2	97.6	----	79.7	79.2	83.1	52.0	80.3	69.7	69.4	83.8	82.6	86.4	86.1	77.2	83.5
Total 14 and 15 years, inclusive	340	1	7	50	252	30	43,962	668	1,216	524	1,258	735	680	814	807	804	2,306	474	1,016
Number attending school	314	1	7	49	230	27	30,923	458	881	253	895	496	438	655	642	636	1,665	296	794
Percent attending school	92.4	----	----	----	91.3	----	70.3	68.6	72.5	48.3	71.1	67.5	64.4	80.5	79.6	79.1	72.2	62.4	78.1
Total 16 and 17 years, inclusive	319	3	11	47	226	32	43,531	689	1,219	546	1,211	739	723	768	778	682	2,348	461	932
Number attending school	149	3	4	28	101	13	18,301	310	479	169	564	342	279	413	389	306	845	189	511
Percent attending school	46.7	----	----	----	44.7	----	42.0	45.0	39.3	31.0	46.6	46.3	38.6	53.8	50.0	44.9	36.0	41.0	54.8
Total 18 to 20 years, inclusive	462	1	17	81	325	38	61,527	820	1,686	756	1,883	957	993	1,074	1,069	873	3,805	665	1,272
Number attending school	62	----	2	19	39	2	8,190	104	209	61	280	126	137	223	185	97	302	91	392
Percent attending school	13.4	----	----	----	12.0	----	13.3	12.7	12.4	8.1	14.9	13.2	13.8	20.8	17.3	11.1	7.9	13.7	30.8
ILLITERACY																			
Total 10 years old and over	7,836	58	247	1,404	5,551	576	581,085	8,321	16,342	7,135	16,810	8,862	9,824	11,833	10,786	8,817	41,838	6,152	12,165
Number illiterate	635	4	17	59	520	35	156,065	2,151	4,365	3,287	3,869	2,277	3,097	3,837	2,934	1,860	12,729	1,790	2,527
Percent illiterate	8.1	----	6.9	4.2	9.4	6.1	26.9	25.9	26.7	46.1	23.0	25.7	31.5	32.4	27.2	21.1	30.4	29.1	20.8
Percent illiterate in 1920	10.2	6.5	10.1	7.3	11.5	6.4	29.3	26.9	28.9	40.8	23.1	25.2	32.4	27.5	49.1	28.2	26.6	31.0	37.6
URBAN AND RURAL																			
Urban population	9,079	69	289	1,554	7,029	138	138,354	1,502	3,489	----	4,120	----	----	1,323	----	----	28,062	1,580	2,159
Percent urban	91.6	----	98.3	89.6	99.2	18.8	17.4	13.6	16.2	----	18.2	----	----	8.5	----	----	51.2	18.6	13.1
Rural population	834	----	5	180	54	595	655,327	9,553	18,041	9,761	18,474	12,475	13,465	14,248	15,051	12,408	26,750	6,892	14,298
Rural-farm	93	----	----	35	3	55	497,954	8,756	12,906	7,531	15,936	9,559	10,661	9,461	10,845	10,288	11,738	5,852	12,311
Rural-nonfarm	741	----	5	145	51	540	157,373	797	5,135	2,230	2,538	2,916	2,804	4,787	4,206	2,120	15,012	1,040	1,987
Percent rural	8.4	----	1.7	10.4	0.8	81.2	82.6	86.4	83.8	100.0	81.8	100.0	100.0	91.5	100.0	100.0	48.8	81.4	86.9
MARITAL CONDITION																			
Males 15 years old and over	3,369	26	114	573	2,386	270	218,367	3,216	6,272	2,648	6,526	3,257	3,744	4,338	4,057	3,209	15,398	2,383	4,517
Single	1,199	9	44	178	852	116	76,557	1,184	2,181	914	2,415	1,181	1,278	1,432	1,260	1,039	4,618	834	1,591
Married	1,855	14	60	329	1,325	127	130,007	1,807	3,680	1,611	3,696	1,963	2,273	2,557	2,600	1,999	9,852	1,413	2,678
Widowed	250	2	5	52	171	20	10,999	214	394	119	389	108	190	333	183	164	817	133	243
Divorced	59	1	5	14	33	6	629	9	17	4	16	2	3	15	12	7	102	3	3
Unknown	6	----	----	----	5	1	175	2	----	----	10	3	----	1	2	----	9	----	2
Females 15 years old and over	3,529	26	102	672	2,491	238	251,595	3,476	7,047	3,088	7,126	3,707	4,189	5,429	4,601	3,671	20,259	2,638	5,331
Single	923	10	27	149	670	67	74,892	1,076	2,034	848	2,239	1,122	1,155	1,490	1,207	989	5,117	836	1,700
Married	1,855	10	63	353	1,299	130	135,531	1,848	3,850	1,641	3,914	2,045	2,362	2,685	2,623	2,091	10,501	1,447	2,857
Widowed	624	5	8	143	434	34	39,385	537	1,130	594	937	528	664	1,213	749	571	4,327	350	766
Divorced	125	1	4	27	86	7	1,579	14	32	5	17	11	8	38	17	18	305	5	5
Unknown	2	----	----	----	2	----	208	1	1	----	19	1	----	3	5	2	9	----	3
FAMILIES																			
Number of families	2,542	20	66	467	1,828	161	168,324	2,395	4,770	2,142	4,683	2,431	3,070	4,011	3,272	2,645	15,351	1,710	3,528
Median size	2.56	----	----	2.38	2.59	3.11	3.95	3.77	3.61	3.90	4.00	4.45	3.72	3.24	4.07	4.16	2.82	4.20	4.00
Families having—																			
No children under 10	1,710	15	52	332	1,209	102	78,089	1,232	2,522	979	2,237	962	1,484	2,171	1,371	1,081	9,051	770	1,762
1 child under 10	311	2	4	57	236	12	33,015	446	823	442	887	501	600	838	722	572	2,805	329	613
2 children under 10	216	----	3	34	153	26	22,510	253	633	294	593	345	412	477	499	303	1,683	217	439
3 or more	305	3	7	44	230	21	34,710	464	792	427	966	623	574	525	680	599	1,812	394	714

CHARACTERISTICS OF NEGRO POPULATION BY COUNTIES: 1930—Continued

(See note at head of table)

SUBJECT	SOUTH CAROLINA—Continued																	
	Chesterfield	Clarendon	Colleton	Darlington	Dillon	Dorchester	Edgefield	Fairfield	Florence	Georgetown	Greenville	Greenwood	Hampton	Horry	Jasper	Kershaw	Lancaster	Laurens
POPULATION BY SEX																		
Negro population: 1930	12,751	21,563	14,063	21,611	12,067	11,166	12,271	15,690	27,573	14,005	27,855	15,608	9,821	9,610	6,785	17,644	11,001	17,709
Male	6,157	10,409	6,848	10,184	5,803	5,261	6,122	7,635	13,038	6,501	13,218	7,505	4,753	4,694	3,339	8,476	5,344	8,727
Female	6,594	11,154	7,215	11,427	6,264	5,905	6,149	8,055	14,535	7,504	14,637	8,103	5,068	4,916	3,446	9,168	5,657	8,982
Negro population: 1920	12,633	25,106	17,366	22,196	12,936	11,439	16,642	20,672	24,924	14,461	23,461	18,912	11,847	7,698	7,112	17,065	13,063	22,105
Male	6,234	12,582	8,885	10,988	6,320	5,573	8,176	10,209	12,410	6,920	11,438	9,352	5,837	3,726	3,547	8,314	6,177	10,951
Female	6,399	12,524	8,481	11,208	6,616	5,866	8,466	10,463	12,514	7,541	12,023	9,560	6,010	3,972	3,565	8,751	6,886	11,154
Percent of total population:																		
1930	37.1	71.8	54.5	52.2	46.9	58.9	63.5	67.4	45.2	64.4	23.8	43.3	57.0	24.4	67.9	55.0	39.3	42.1
1920	39.5	72.0	58.1	56.7	51.2	58.8	69.6	76.1	49.4	66.6	26.5	52.8	60.6	24.0	72.1	58.0	45.6	51.9
VOTING AGE: 1930																		
Total 21 years old and over	4,870	8,345	5,874	8,832	4,846	4,540	4,966	6,171	11,537	6,153	13,544	7,175	4,230	3,928	2,841	6,890	4,354	7,756
Male	2,270	3,997	2,797	4,025	2,290	2,122	2,437	2,885	5,314	2,786	6,236	3,341	1,989	1,912	1,379	3,159	2,034	3,687
Female	2,600	4,348	3,077	4,807	2,556	2,418	2,529	3,286	6,223	3,367	7,308	3,834	2,241	2,016	1,462	3,731	2,320	4,069
AGE: 1930																		
Under 5 years	1,771	2,857	1,845	2,708	1,622	1,427	1,616	2,086	3,386	1,783	2,938	1,671	1,126	1,411	844	2,396	1,409	2,058
Under 1 year	363	490	322	441	309	255	295	413	573	376	583	357	185	296	154	417	269	384
5 to 9 years	2,059	3,484	2,150	3,266	1,957	1,654	1,889	2,499	4,245	2,044	3,564	2,026	1,433	1,456	1,061	2,819	1,670	2,493
10 to 14 years	1,981	3,152	2,009	3,194	1,712	1,681	1,852	2,371	3,979	1,950	3,431	2,095	1,439	1,263	962	2,767	1,644	2,508
15 to 19 years	1,777	3,186	1,858	3,063	1,619	1,605	1,661	2,211	3,724	1,744	3,593	2,212	1,338	1,282	898	2,411	1,610	2,438
20 to 24 years	1,156	2,042	1,325	1,973	1,173	1,008	1,095	1,218	2,799	1,247	3,253	1,588	927	1,048	619	1,421	1,056	1,706
25 to 29 years	755	1,213	785	1,310	763	670	644	767	1,879	851	2,377	1,034	611	688	409	974	590	1,090
30 to 34 years	566	933	619	1,011	585	523	537	634	1,428	658	1,728	741	448	483	300	767	443	856
35 to 44 years	1,155	2,056	1,363	2,239	1,130	1,137	1,124	1,416	2,737	1,581	3,028	1,578	1,117	939	661	1,692	1,037	1,800
45 to 54 years	850	1,432	1,077	1,481	835	774	906	1,205	1,870	1,201	2,090	1,281	792	568	551	1,235	769	1,457
55 to 64 years	376	726	604	794	404	421	536	673	868	555	1,067	831	339	262	261	664	441	733
65 to 74 years	189	335	267	378	191	188	289	401	436	292	498	393	170	150	144	355	224	409
75 years and over	116	128	139	185	76	73	120	203	176	92	228	156	78	56	74	143	106	153
Unknown	------	19	22	9	------	5	2	6	46	7	60	2	3	4	1	------	2	8
SCHOOL ATTENDANCE																		
Total 7 to 13 years, inclusive	2,761	4,580	2,922	4,454	2,504	2,321	2,588	3,321	5,659	2,787	4,845	2,830	2,023	1,844	1,370	3,896	2,284	3,471
Number attending school	2,096	3,215	2,293	3,375	1,944	1,794	2,214	2,442	4,608	2,122	4,318	2,238	1,254	1,588	1,052	3,110	1,912	2,748
Percent attending school	75.9	70.2	78.5	75.8	77.6	77.3	85.5	73.5	81.4	76.1	89.1	79.1	62.0	86.1	76.8	79.8	83.7	79.2
Total 14 and 15 years, inclusive	803	1,279	755	1,280	659	702	748	985	1,579	751	1,391	896	562	491	366	1,068	654	981
Number attending school	553	810	550	813	420	428	588	633	1,131	488	965	608	316	360	270	770	512	668
Percent attending school	68.9	63.3	72.8	63.5	63.7	61.0	78.6	64.3	71.6	65.0	69.4	67.9	56.2	73.3	73.8	72.1	78.3	68.1
Total 16 and 17 years, inclusive	706	1,332	756	1,290	644	648	692	897	1,562	698	1,390	868	552	517	380	989	630	1,028
Number attending school	329	474	383	516	227	195	372	330	634	278	515	319	185	238	142	417	324	394
Percent attending school	46.6	35.6	50.7	40.0	35.2	30.1	53.8	36.8	40.6	39.8	37.1	36.8	33.5	46.0	37.4	42.2	51.4	38.3
Total 18 to 20 years, inclusive	991	1,769	1,064	1,699	963	864	911	1,197	2,117	1,021	2,322	1,330	773	784	537	1,253	976	1,420
Number attending school	139	156	187	207	100	83	204	121	271	109	227	151	61	118	34	198	196	167
Percent attending school	14.0	8.8	17.6	12.2	10.4	9.6	22.4	10.1	12.8	10.7	9.8	11.4	7.9	15.1	6.3	15.8	20.1	11.8
ILLITERACY																		
Total 10 years old and over	8,921	15,222	10,068	15,637	8,488	8,085	8,766	11,105	19,942	10,178	21,353	11,911	7,262	6,743	4,880	12,429	7,922	13,158
Number illiterate	2,441	5,385	2,900	4,929	2,478	2,436	1,840	3,865	4,497	4,075	3,982	2,869	3,091	1,675	1,690	3,140	1,675	3,766
Percent illiterate	27.4	35.4	28.8	31.5	29.2	30.1	21.0	34.8	22.6	40.0	18.6	24.1	42.6	24.8	34.6	25.3	21.1	28.6
Percent illiterate in 1920	28.4	25.7	38.7	26.6	33.1	32.6	29.0	32.0	30.9	40.7	23.7	26.9	31.5	31.3	43.5	23.2	29.4	33.6
URBAN AND RURAL																		
Urban population	1,782	------	908	4,547	931	1,055	------	------	6,067	2,920	10,871	3,512	------	1,290	------	2,457	1,196	3,224
Percent urban	14.0	------	6.5	21.0	7.7	9.4	------	------	22.0	20.8	39.0	22.5	------	13.4	------	13.9	10.9	18.2
Rural population	10,969	21,563	13,155	17,064	11,136	10,111	12,271	15,690	21,506	11,085	16,984	12,096	9,821	8,320	6,785	15,187	9,805	14,485
Rural-farm	7,736	16,247	10,478	14,291	9,600	6,748	10,530	12,838	18,091	5,092	11,702	10,418	6,796	6,300	4,177	12,271	8,345	13,495
Rural-nonfarm	3,233	5,316	2,677	2,773	1,536	3,363	1,741	2,852	3,415	5,993	5,282	1,678	3,025	2,020	2,608	2,916	1,460	990
Percent rural	86.0	100.0	93.5	79.0	92.3	90.6	100.0	100.0	78.0	79.2	61.0	77.5	100.0	86.6	100.0	86.1	89.1	81.8
MARITAL CONDITION																		
Males 15 years old and over	3,275	5,690	3,840	5,691	3,201	2,975	3,378	4,084	7,339	3,673	8,329	4,620	2,773	2,671	1,919	4,463	2,964	5,136
Single	1,223	2,140	1,285	2,021	1,181	1,049	1,199	1,501	2,567	1,137	2,781	1,657	1,050	1,004	710	1,628	1,092	1,790
Married	1,892	3,303	2,354	3,392	1,875	1,780	1,980	2,346	4,404	2,319	4,985	2,673	1,596	1,555	1,112	2,629	1,713	3,042
Widowed	152	234	187	267	134	128	198	229	329	204	528	277	125	96	89	200	156	269
Divorced	7	12	9	8	5	7	1	6	37	12	23	10	2	12	7	2	3	33
Unknown	1	1	5	3	6	11	------	2	2	1	12	3	------	4	1	4		2
Females 15 years old and over	3,665	6,380	4,219	6,752	3,575	3,429	3,536	4,650	8,624	4,555	9,593	5,196	3,050	2,809	1,999	5,199	3,314	5,514
Single	1,176	2,202	1,129	2,136	1,174	1,029	1,020	1,534	2,627	1,242	2,668	1,537	832	859	549	1,612	1,111	1,631
Married	1,961	3,417	2,402	3,523	1,926	1,804	1,992	2,454	4,586	2,427	5,346	2,741	1,669	1,547	1,118	2,770	1,760	3,133
Widowed	517	736	651	1,063	455	558	513	626	1,299	863	1,543	879	539	362	327	794	429	691
Divorced	11	24	31	27	15	16	9	27	110	20	25	31	7	36	4	19	12	56
Unknown	------	1	6	3	5	22	2	9	2	3	11	8	3	5	1	4	2	3
FAMILIES																		
Number of families	2,420	4,082	2,964	4,335	2,348	2,272	2,471	2,951	5,559	3,264	6,376	3,423	2,136	1,775	1,440	3,419	2,050	3,697
Median size	4.57	4.70	4.12	4.24	4.41	4.36	4.24	4.65	4.21	3.66	3.42	3.77	3.90	4.59	4.11	4.56	4.61	4.00
Families having—																		
No children under 10	919	1,535	1,263	1,876	913	973	1,072	1,223	2,356	1,506	3,435	1,732	993	611	649	1,367	844	1,733
1 child under 10	486	803	625	840	471	465	469	502	1,155	724	1,192	722	460	389	276	648	373	756
2 children under 10	350	654	404	603	347	306	328	414	796	438	774	422	281	296	198	499	297	472
3 or more	665	1,090	672	1,016	617	528	602	812	1,252	596	975	547	402	479	317	905	536	736

CHARACTERISTICS OF NEGRO POPULATION BY COUNTIES: 1930—Continued

(See note at head of table)

SUBJECT	SOUTH CAROLINA—Continued																SOUTH DAKOTA	
	Lee	Lexington	McCormick	Marion	Marlboro	Newberry	Oconee	Orangeburg	Pickens	Richland	Saluda	Spartanburg	Sumter	Union	Williamsburg	York	The State	Beadle
POPULATION BY SEX																		
Negro population: 1930	16,246	10,998	7,696	14,911	18,008	16,154	5,999	40,640	4,897	38,127	8,823	30,111	30,974	12,380	23,341	21,932	646	73
Male	7,963	5,540	3,772	7,202	8,602	7,895	2,920	19,530	2,418	17,540	4,361	14,390	14,624	6,071	10,991	10,529	343	36
Female	8,283	5,458	3,924	7,709	9,406	8,259	3,079	21,110	2,479	20,587	4,462	15,721	16,350	6,309	12,350	11,403	303	37
Negro population: 1920	18,050	11,728	11,268	13,147	19,661	20,641	6,398	42,718	4,931	36,499	11,635	27,392	30,508	14,076	25,452	24,230	832	60
Male	8,892	5,801	5,557	6,522	9,617	10,001	3,144	20,874	2,428	17,444	5,654	13,390	14,800	6,912	12,347	11,740	475	32
Female	9,158	5,927	5,711	6,625	10,044	10,640	3,254	21,844	2,503	19,055	5,981	14,002	15,708	7,164	13,105	12,490	357	28
Percent of total population:																		
1930	67.4	30.1	67.1	54.8	56.9	46.6	18.0	63.6	14.5	43.5	48.6	25.9	67.5	40.0	66.9	41.1	0.1	0.3
1920	67.3	32.9	68.5	55.4	59.3	58.1	21.2	65.8	17.4	46.7	52.7	29.1	70.9	46.3	66.0	47.9	0.1	0.3
VOTING AGE: 1930																		
Total 21 years old and over	6,089	4,916	3,169	6,338	7,300	7,233	2,573	16,594	2,114	19,050	3,539	13,806	12,744	5,192	8,834	9,646	420	51
Male	2,891	2,529	1,508	3,036	3,312	3,425	1,237	7,735	1,001	8,504	1,721	6,412	5.809	2,418	4,040	4,369	239	27
Female	3,198	2,387	1,661	3,302	3,988	3,808	1,336	8,859	1,113	10,546	1,818	7,394	6,935	2,774	4,794	5,277	181	24
AGE 1930																		
Under 5 years	2,202	1,264	955	1,981	2,396	1,798	684	5,184	606	3,794	1,159	3,331	4,006	1,516	3,410	2,506	47	6
Under 1 year	358	255	159	383	453	348	132	939	114	666	223	657	731	282	630	464	11	1
5 to 9 years	2,692	1,554	1,218	2,144	2,765	2,345	863	6,270	708	4,811	1,361	4,011	4,738	1,837	3,943	3,055	53	5
10 to 14 years	2,505	1,475	1,176	1,996	2,632	2,185	881	6,034	677	4,691	1,307	4,042	4,519	1,716	4,552	2,987	55	4
15 to 19 years	2,319	1,457	1,005	2,024	2,539	2,206	830	5,615	671	4,808	1,253	4,088	4,168	1,791	3,056	3,114	62	6
20 to 24 years	1,493	1,294	641	1,638	1,599	1,558	572	3,924	480	3,955	742	3,299	2,984	1,161	2,084	2,182	65	12
25 to 29 years	873	766	417	1,077	1,120	975	348	2,565	296	2,998	483	2,260	1,943	742	1,343	1,433	52	6
30 to 34 years	717	490	348	760	874	770	275	1,832	225	2,384	384	1,708	1,459	573	1,091	1,016	51	8
35 to 44 years	1,462	1,131	718	1,502	1,683	1,564	549	3,911	463	4,798	834	3,178	3,055	1,193	2,238	2,211	95	6
45 to 54 years	1,042	760	553	1,010	1,240	1,335	523	2,854	422	3,285	635	2,243	2,224	925	1,465	1,656	80	12
55 to 64 years	552	463	365	470	733	846	266	1,475	199	1,516	400	1,205	1,087	550	655	1,028	45	5
65 to 74 years	281	252	199	225	295	403	142	701	96	736	189	536	612	279	328	518	28	2
75 years and over	106	89	101	81	129	169	63	271	50	298	75	199	179	93	167	221	10	1
Unknown	2	3	------	3	3	------	3	4	4	53	1	11	------	4	9	5	3	------
SCHOOL ATTENDANCE																		
Total 7 to 13 years, inclusive	3,552	2,100	1,660	2,876	3,715	3,148	1,219	8,487	955	6,645	1,876	5,645	6,422	2,487	5,076	4,159	75	6
Number attending school	2,285	1,715	1,438	2,308	2,906	2,625	1,001	6,419	767	5,782	1,611	4,950	4,949	2,116	4,075	3,428	72	6
Percent attending school	64.3	81.7	86.6	80.3	78.2	83.4	82.1	75.6	80.3	87.0	85.9	87.7	77.1	85.1	80.3	82.4	------	------
Total 14 and 15 years, inclusive	984	562	458	791	1,114	866	348	2,341	263	1,849	522	1,609	1,743	660	1,355	1,245	22	2
Number attending school	543	391	357	595	755	664	266	1,618	180	1,382	431	1,119	1,181	499	1,079	871	20	2
Percent attending school	55.2	69.6	77.9	75.2	67.8	76.7	76.4	69.1	68.4	74.7	82.6	69.5	67.8	75.6	79.6	70.0	------	------
Total 16 and 17 years, inclusive	958	611	406	806	1,076	904	352	2,400	264	1,930	522	1,610	1,715	758	1,298	1,246	25	1
Number attending school	279	226	181	383	449	355	152	1,035	92	841	318	597	669	354	716	586	19	1
Percent attending school	29.1	37.0	44.6	47.5	41.7	39.3	43.2	43.1	34.8	43.6	60.9	37.1	39.0	46.7	55.2	47.0	------	------
Total 18 to 20 years, inclusive	1,338	928	549	1,252	1,265	1,267	478	3,058	405	2,963	676	2,529	2,408	1,024	1,678	1,865	35	5
Number attending school	99	95	51	177	179	161	70	425	49	464	129	259	270	154	297	375	10	1
Percent attending school	7.4	10.2	9.3	14.3	14.2	12.7	14.6	13.9	12.1	15.7	19.1	10.2	11.2	15.0	17.7	20.1	------	------
ILLITERACY																		
Total 10 years old and over	11,352	8,180	5,523	10,786	12,847	12,011	4,452	29,186	3,583	29,522	6,303	22,769	22,230	9,027	15,988	16,371	546	62
Number illiterate	3,968	1,960	1,085	3,482	3,901	2,768	849	7,433	867	6,333	1,533	4,692	5,934	2,187	4,039	3,577	12	------
Percent illiterate	35.0	24.0	19.6	32.3	30.4	23.0	19.1	25.5	24.2	21.5	24.3	20.6	26.7	24.2	25.3	21.8	2.2	------
Percent illiterate in 1920	35.9	28.2	29.2	35.4	23.4	30.2	25.2	25.7	27.2	25.4	28.0	27.1	22.4	28.2	30.3	31.2	5.2	------
URBAN AND RURAL																		
Urban population	------	895	------	4,047	1,541	2,679	------	3,952	810	20,097	146	10,305	5,145	2,142	------	3,600	337	68
Percent urban	------	8.1	------	27.1	8.6	16.6	------	9.7	16.5	52.7	1.7	34.2	16.6	17.3	------	16.4	52.2	------
Rural population	16,246	10,103	7,696	10,864	16,467	13,475	5,999	36,688	4,087	18,030	8,677	19,806	25,829	10,238	23,341	18,332	309	5
Rural-farm	10,486	5,153	6,822	8,864	14,653	11,501	4,090	25,609	2,711	12,630	7,951	15,074	16,948	8,681	19,739	15,993	232	5
Rural-nonfarm	5,760	4,950	874	2,000	1,814	1,974	1,909	11,029	1,376	5,400	726	4,732	8,881	1,557	3,602	2,339	77	------
Percent rural	100.0	91.9	100.0	72.9	91.4	83.4	100.0	90.3	83.5	47.3	98.3	65.8	83.4	82.7	100.0	83.6	47.8	------
MARITAL CONDITION																		
Males 15 years old and over	4,178	3,444	2,078	4,201	4,677	4,680	1,697	10,826	1,378	11,032	2,403	8,812	8,000	3,461	5,639	6,275	279	30
Single	1,450	1,356	709	1,524	1,657	1,702	626	3,920	481	3,899	884	3,185	2,693	1,320	1,842	2,367	119	14
Married	2,575	1,888	1,229	2,478	2,778	2,699	955	6,410	823	6,490	1,378	5,100	4,992	1,965	3,601	3,567	131	16
Widowed	150	187	134	149	212	264	106	448	74	594	126	498	288	168	186	326	22	------
Divorced	3	12	5	21	29	13	8	40	------	32	15	17	20	7	10	8	7	------
Unknown	------	1	1	29	1	2	2	8	------	17	------	12	7	1	------	7	------	------
Females 15 years old and over	4,669	3,261	2,269	4,589	5,538	5,146	1,874	12,326	1,528	13,799	2,593	9,915	9,711	3,850	6,797	7,109	212	28
Single	1,408	967	670	1,382	1,721	1,518	654	3,707	463	4,078	855	2,988	2,894	1,300	2,095	2,311	48	7
Married	2,722	1,845	1,246	2,542	2,923	2,745	964	6,582	873	7,109	1,373	5,360	5,251	1,996	3,803	3,757	125	16
Widowed	517	425	336	614	826	854	244	1,926	188	2,469	331	1,516	1,501	534	874	1,019	30	5
Divorced	22	21	14	45	61	27	9	101	4	133	34	40	55	19	22	17	9	------
Unknown	------	3	3	6	7	2	3	10	------	10	------	11	10	1	3	5	------	------
FAMILIES																		
Number of families	3,056	2,206	1,576	3,004	3,632	3,450	1,143	8,318	983	8,128	1,758	6,435	6,284	2,470	4,371	4,520	166	16
Median size	4.69	3.95	4.10	4.23	4.34	3.99	4.52	4.26	4.29	3.42	4.37	3.83	4.25	4.27	4.85	4.12	2.57	------
Families having—																		
No children under 10	1,065	1,049	695	1,284	1,524	1,682	532	3,431	444	4,412	752	3,239	2,617	1,144	1,432	2,165	128	11
1 child under 10	676	402	302	609	714	669	191	1,777	170	1,463	328	1,213	1,316	426	959	866	13	3
2 children under 10	475	289	211	420	521	425	157	1,241	144	947	239	815	900	336	675	598	10	1
3 or more	840	466	368	691	873	674	263	1,869	225	1,306	439	1,168	1,451	564	1,305	891	15	1

CHARACTERISTICS OF NEGRO POPULATION BY COUNTIES: 1930—Continued

(See note at head of table)

SUBJECT	SOUTH DAKOTA—Continued																	
	Bon Homme	Brookings	Brown	Brule	Buffalo	Charles Mix	Codington	Corson	Custer	Davison	Deuel	Dewey	Edmunds	Fall River	Faulk	Grant	Gregory	Haakon
POPULATION BY SEX																		
Negro population: 1930	2	6	15	15	2	2	11	2	7	63	6	12	2	22	1	3	3	1
Male		2	7	7	2	1	7	2	3	37	1	6	1	11	1	2	2	
Female	2	4	8	8		1	4		4	26	5	6	1	11		1	1	1
Negro population: 1920	5	11	27	7		5	19	11	5	15	9	19		30			3	4
Male	2	7	18	5		2	12	8	2	7	6	10		18			2	4
Female	3	4	9	2		3	7	3	3	8	3	9		12			1	
Percent of total population:																		
1930				0.2	0.1		0.1		0.1	0.4	0.1	0.2		0.3				
1920		0.1	0.1	0.1			0.1	0.2	0.1	0.1	0.1	0.4		0.4				0.1
VOTING AGE: 1930																		
Total 21 years old and over	2	6	8	6	2	1	8	2	6	37	2	4	2	16		1	3	
Male		2	5	4	2		4	2	3	22	1	3	1	10		1	2	
Female	2	4	3	2		1	4		3	15	1	1	1	6			1	
AGE: 1930																		
Under 5 years			3	1						10		4						
Under 1 year			1	1						3								
5 to 9 years			2	4		1			1	7		1		1				
10 to 14 years			2	3			1			5	2	1		3		1		
15 to 19 years				1			2			3	2	2		2	1	1		1
20 to 24 years		2	1							7			1					
25 to 29 years		2					1			6		2		1				
30 to 34 years			2	3			2			6		1		2			1	
35 to 44 years	1		1	1	1	1	3		5	14	1			3		1		
45 to 54 years		2	1	2			1	1		3	1			6			2	
55 to 64 years	1				1					1								
65 to 74 years			2				1	1		1				3				
75 years and over									1			1	1	1				
Unknown			1															
SCHOOL ATTENDANCE																		
Total 7 to 13 years, inclusive			3	5			1		1	7	1	1		2		1		
Number attending school			1	5			1		1	7	1	1		2		1		
Percent attending school																		
Total 14 and 15 years, inclusive				1						2	1			2		1		
Number attending school				1						1	1			1		1		
Percent attending school																		
Total 16 and 17 years, inclusive				1			1			1	1	2			1			
Number attending school							1				1	2			1			
Percent attending school																		
Total 18 to 20 years, inclusive							1			2	1			1				1
Number attending school										1				1				
Percent attending school																		
ILLITERACY																		
Total 10 years old and over	2	6	10	10	2	1	11	2	6	46	6	7	2	21	1	3	3	1
Number illiterate							1											
Percent illiterate																		
Percent illiterate in 1920																		
URBAN AND RURAL																		
Urban population		6	8				2			62				4				
Percent urban																		
Rural population	2		7	15	2	2	9	2	7	1	6	12	2	18	1	3	3	1
Rural-farm	2		5	10	1	2	9	1	5	1	6	12	2	5	1	2	3	1
Rural-nonfarm			2	5	1			1	2					13		1		
Percent rural																		
MARITAL CONDITION																		
Males 15 years old and over		2	5	5	2		6	2	3	26	1	4	1	11	1	2	2	
Single		2	1	3	1		2		2	12		1		3	1	2	1	
Married			3	2	1		3		1	13	1	3	1	6				
Widowed			1				1	2										
Divorced										1				2				
Unknown																		
Females 15 years old and over	2	4	3	2		1	4		3	15	3	2	1	7			1	1
Single		2							1		2	1		1				1
Married	2		3	2		1	3		1	14	1	1	1	5				
Widowed		2					1		1	1							1	
Divorced														1				
Unknown																		
FAMILIES																		
Number of families		2	3	3			2	2	2	13	1	3		9			1	
Median size																		
Families having—																		
No children under 10		2	1	2			2	2	2	8	1	1		8			1	
1 child under 10										1		1		1				
2 children under 10			1							1								
3 or more			1	1						3		1						

CHARACTERISTICS OF NEGRO POPULATION BY COUNTIES: 1930—Continued

(See note at head of table)

SUBJECT	Hand	Hughes	Jackson	Jones	Kingsbury	Lake	Lawrence	Lincoln	Lyman	Marshall	Meade	Mellette	Miner	Minnehaha	Pennington	Perkins	Roberts	Shannon
	SOUTH DAKOTA—Continued																	
POPULATION BY SEX																		
Negro population: 1930	2	8	4	8	1	4	28	7	5	1	11	13	1	103	20	1	2	3
Male	2	4	3	6	1	2	15	3	4		5	7		48	11	1		1
Female		4	1	2		2	13	4	1	1	6	6	1	55	9		2	2
Negro population: 1920	4	25	2	7	2	4	50	2	35	2	11	14		83	24	4	4	
Male	4	14	1	2	1	4	20	1	19	1	7	8		47	14	3	2	
Female		11	1	5	1		30	1	16	1	4	6		36	10	1	2	
Percent of total population:																		
1930		0.1	0.2	0.3			0.2	0.1	0.1		0.1	0.2		0.2	0.1			0.1
1920		0.4	0.1	0.2			0.4		0.5		0.1	0.4		0.2	0.2	0.1		
VOTING AGE: 1930																		
Total 21 years old and over	1	6	4	4	1	2	27	4	4		6	7	1	80	14	1	2	3
Male	1	4	3	3	1	1	15	2	4		2	4		38	9	1		1
Female		2	1	1		1	12	2			4	3	1	42	5		2	2
AGE: 1930																		
Under 5 years									1		1			5				
Under 1 year														1				
5 to 9 years										1		2		6	2			
10 to 14 years	1	2		1		2		2			1	2		4	1			
15 to 19 years				3			1	1			3	2		6	3			
20 to 24 years				1		1	5	1						9	1		1	
25 to 29 years							4		1			1		15	2			
30 to 34 years			3				2		2		1			11	1		1	
35 to 44 years		3					5	2			1	2	1	19	3			
45 to 54 years		2		1	1		3	1	1		1	4		14	3			2
55 to 64 years				1			3				3			12	2			1
65 to 74 years	1	1	1				3							1	2	1		
75 years and over				1			2											
Unknown						1								1				
SCHOOL ATTENDANCE																		
Total 7 to 13 years, inclusive	1	2		1		2		1				4		8	3			
Number attending school	1	2		1		2		1				4		7	3			
Percent attending school																		
Total 14 and 15 years, inclusive				1				1			2			1	1			
Number attending school				1				1			2			1	1			
Percent attending school																		
Total 16 and 17 years, inclusive				1				1			1	1		2	1			
Number attending school				1				1				1		2	1			
Percent attending school																		
Total 18 to 20 years, inclusive				1			1				1	1		5	1			
Number attending school				1			1							1				
Percent attending school																		
ILLITERACY																		
Total 10 years old and over	2	8	4	8	1	4	28	7	4		10	11	1	92	18	1	2	3
Number illiterate																		
Percent illiterate																		
Percent illiterate in 1920																		
URBAN AND RURAL																		
Urban population		3				3	16							100	11			
Percent urban																		
Rural population	2	5	4	8	1	1	12	7	5	1	11	13	1	3	9	1	2	3
Rural-farm	1	1	4	8	1	1	9		4	1	9	8	1			1	1	
Rural-nonfarm	1	4					3	7	1		2	5		3	9		1	3
Percent rural																		
MARITAL CONDITION																		
Males 15 years old and over	1	4	3	5	1	1	15	2	4		5	5		43	9	1		1
Single	1		1	4	1		3		2		4	2		13	2	1		
Married		3	1			1	8	2	1		1	3		25	6			1
Widowed		1	1	1			2							4	1			
Divorced							2		1					1				
Unknown																		
Females 15 years old and over		2	1	2		1	13	3			4	4	1	45	8		2	2
Single				1			2	2				1	1	6	4		1	1
Married		2	1			1	9	1			3	3		25	3		1	
Widowed				1			1							10	1			
Divorced							1				1			4				1
Unknown																		
FAMILIES																		
Number of families		3	1	2	1	1	15	2	2		2	3		26	8	1	1	2
Median size																		
Families having—																		
No children under 10		3	1	2	1	1	15	2	1		2	2		21	7	1	1	2
1 child under 10												1		3	1			
2 children under 10														2				
3 or more									1									

CHARACTERISTICS OF NEGRO POPULATION BY COUNTIES: 1930—Continued

(See note at head of table)

SUBJECT	SOUTH DAKOTA—Continued								TENNESSEE									
	Spink	Sully	Todd	Tripp	Turner	Union	Walworth	Yankton	The State	Anderson	Bedford	Benton	Bledsoe	Blount	Bradley	Campbell	Cannon	Carroll
POPULATION BY SEX																		
Negro population: 1930	15	48	1	8	1	3	22	78	477,646	457	3,711	245	690	2,842	1,852	606	314	4,631
Male	11	27	1	7	1	2	8	45	232,569	215	1,792	118	548	1,471	904	283	158	2,296
Female	4	21		1		1	14	33	245,077	242	1,919	127	142	1,371	948	323	156	2,335
Negro population: 1920	15	58	1	15	17	3	11	144	451,758	595	4,358	225	599	2,675	1,732	1,272	430	4,578
Male	9	38	1	12	15	2	6	80	222,639	324	2,109	110	409	1,464	830	656	229	2,272
Female	6	20		3	2	1	5	64	229,119	271	2,249	115	190	1,211	902	616	201	2,306
Percent of total population:																		
1930	0.1	1.2		0.1			0.3	0.5	18.3	2.3	17.6	2.2	9.7	8.4	8.1	2.3	3.5	17.7
1920	0.1	2.0		0.1	0.1		0.1	0.9	19.3	3.3	20.0	1.9	8.3	9.3	9.3	4.5	4.2	18.8
VOTING AGE: 1930																		
Total 21 years old and over	6	25	1	7	1	3	11	42	271,974	258	2,002	118	144	1,661	955	315	153	2,242
Male	4	15	1	7	1	2	6	25	131,776	121	959	52	78	898	458	157	75	1,112
Female	2	10				1	5	17	140,198	137	1,043	66	66	763	497	158	78	1,130
AGE: 1930																		
Under 5 years	5	6					3	2	44,304	44	386	35	33	261	194	68	42	592
Under 1 year	1	2					1		8,399	10	76	10	8	61	32	14	9	118
5 to 9 years	2	7					1	10	50,368	50	417	29	45	317	245	81	39	588
10 to 14 years	2	4					1	10	48,152	50	400	24	161	262	209	59	42	534
15 to 19 years		6					5	11	51,835	49	425	30	298	275	219	73	32	564
20 to 24 years		5		2		1	6	9	49,288	41	326	30	33	339	151	52	21	444
25 to 29 years	2	3		2			2	2	42,349	32	248	13	18	300	147	31	14	331
30 to 34 years		2		1				2	33,608	18	167	12	9	227	121	26	12	232
35 to 44 years		6	1			1	2	11	62,585	47	387	18	34	405	213	63	31	425
45 to 54 years	2	1				1	2	10	49,557	63	420	26	24	255	183	79	35	401
55 to 64 years	2	5		2				6	26,292	32	290	15	23	106	99	41	26	266
65 to 74 years		3		1	1			3	12,311	19	156	8	8	47	53	20	13	174
75 years and over								2	5,929	12	84	5	4	25	18	13	7	78
Unknown									1,068		5			23				2
SCHOOL ATTENDANCE																		
Total 7 to 13 years, inclusive	2	7					1	15	68,398	69	569	37	138	404	311	95	61	777
Number attending school	2	7					1	15	60,824	60	496	33	104	385	278	83	44	632
Percent attending school									88.9		87.2		75.4	95.3	89.4			81.3
Total 14 and 15 years, inclusive		2					1	4	19,653	17	173	8	139	96	96	32	13	205
Number attending school		2					1	4	15,876	17	131	6	104	75	77	25	11	168
Percent attending school									80.8		75.7		74.8					82.0
Total 16 and 17 years, inclusive		2					3	5	20,580	21	176	14	146	121	85	32	13	242
Number attending school		1					2	4	10,036	16	84	6	82	59	49	17	8	124
Percent attending school									48.8		47.7		56.2	48.8				51.2
Total 18 to 20 years, inclusive		3		1			3	7	32,620	28	244	24	80	171	107	30	19	330
Number attending school								3	4,532	2	18	3	31	19	21	8	4	63
Percent attending school									13.9		7.4			11.1	19.6			19.1
ILLITERACY																		
Total 10 years old and over	8	35	1	8	1	3	18	66	382,974	363	2,908	181	612	2,264	1,413	457	233	3,451
Number illiterate	1							10	57,251	38	421	47	46	347	133	82	56	743
Percent illiterate									14.9	10.5	14.5	26.0	7.5	15.3	9.4	17.9	24.0	21.5
Percent illiterate in 1920								10.1	22.4	28.3	22.1	36.2	13.5	24.4	15.0	14.8	45.2	21.6
URBAN AND RURAL																		
Urban population	1						4	49	240,168		1,187			1,950	1,069	240		
Percent urban									50.3		32.0			68.6	57.7	39.6		
Rural population	14	48	1	8	1	3	18	29	237,478	457	2,524	245	690	892	783	366	314	4,631
Rural-farm	12	48	1	2		3	18	25	174,515	116	1,673	114	121	255	398	15	106	3,217
Rural-nonfarm	2			6	1			4	62,963	341	851	131	569	637	385	351	208	1,414
Percent rural									49.7	100.0	68.0	100.0	100.0	31.4	42.3	60.4	100.0	100.0
MARITAL CONDITION																		
Males 15 years old and over	4	18	1	7	1	2	8	35	161,503	144	1,197	72	364	1,074	576	190	97	1,445
Single		10	1	4		1	4	20	49,752	52	368	30	315	326	186	53	32	437
Married	2	7		2		1	4	12	96,330	79	712	36	42	686	343	113	50	878
Widowed	2	1		1	1			3	11,862	11	104	6	7	51	32	20	14	106
Divorced									2,903	2	13			6	15	4	1	24
Unknown									656					5				
Females 15 years old and over	2	13		1		1	9	21	173,319	169	1,311	85	87	928	628	208	94	1,472
Single		4					5	5	38,962	46	322	28	25	153	157	49	24	334
Married	1	7		1		1	4	12	98,188	78	718	35	43	668	362	119	48	894
Widowed	1	1						4	30,642	41	246	19	18	97	81	31	20	224
Divorced		1							4,924	4	24	3	1	10	28	9	2	20
Unknown									603		1							
FAMILIES																		
Number of families	2	11		4		1	3	18	120,402	112	954	50	57	723	436	151	80	998
Median size									2.98	3.40	3.12			2.68	3.36	3.12		3.83
Families having—																		
No children under 10		7		4		1	1	12	76,149	68	581	23	31	472	247	79	48	497
1 child under 10		2						2	19,312	18	157	10	8	95	74	31	9	188
2 children under 10							2	3	11,286	14	89	7	3	64	42	16	7	129
3 or more	2	2						1	13,655	12	127	10	15	92	73	25	16	184

CHARACTERISTICS OF NEGRO POPULATION BY COUNTIES: 1930—Continued

(See note at head of table)

SUBJECT	TENNESSEE—Continued																	
	Carter	Cheatham	Chester	Claiborne	Clay	Cocke	Coffee	Crockett	Cumberland	Davidson	Decatur	De Kalb	Dickson	Dyer	Fayette	Fentress	Franklin	Gibson
POPULATION BY SEX																		
Negro population: 1930	528	817	1,881	573	285	726	1,301	3,433	70	51,797	875	515	1,846	5,117	21,095	53	2,533	9,890
Male	270	407	959	305	147	347	639	1,723	45	24,319	449	237	915	2,529	10,654	53	1,242	4,844
Female	258	410	922	268	138	379	662	1,710	25	27,478	426	278	931	2,588	10,441	-------	1,291	5,046
Negro population: 1920	569	1,127	1,587	563	256	849	1,495	3,632	25	44,528	914	627	2,347	95,432	23,526	42	2,693	9,678
Male	299	563	759	298	122	408	709	1,792	13	20,918	451	315	1,171	2,785	11,798	20	1,341	4,805
Female	270	564	828	265	134	441	786	1,840	12	23,610	463	312	1,176	2,647	11,728	22	1,352	4,873
Percent of total population: 1930	1.8	9.1	17.7	2.4	3.0	3.3	7.7	19.8	0.6	23.2	8.7	3.6	10.0	16.3	73.0	0.5	11.6	21.3
1920	2.6	11.2	16.4	2.4	2.8	4.1	8.6	20.8	0.2	26.5	9.0	4.1	12.1	18.1	74.7	0.4	13.0	22.3
VOTING AGE: 1930																		
Total 21 years old and over	268	395	888	270	149	337	784	1,647	51	33,237	405	293	931	2,801	9,457	22	1,321	5,230
Male	144	189	445	154	82	164	374	819	33	15,563	206	131	454	1,393	4,735	22	641	2,581
Female	124	206	443	116	67	173	410	828	18	17,674	199	162	477	1,408	4,722	-------	680	2,649
AGE: 1930																		
Under 5 years	68	99	234	68	34	102	126	393	5	3,632	124	51	185	410	2,653	-------	264	945
Under 1 year	14	12	53	11	4	23	23	90	1	732	21	12	38	67	524	-------	52	167
5 to 9 years	75	115	232	75	36	97	120	469	1	4,412	121	41	224	535	2,854	-------	306	1,120
10 to 14 years	49	108	234	67	36	86	114	434	3	4,192	104	55	227	572	2,828	-------	314	1,142
15 to 19 years	49	88	234	78	26	84	125	400	9	5,109	107	59	224	675	2,766	24	280	1,201
20 to 24 years	57	52	190	51	32	66	153	351	16	5,614	83	50	161	533	2,151	26	220	997
25 to 29 years	30	50	144	43	24	62	116	225	18	5,201	61	30	127	379	1,309	3	144	776
30 to 34 years	31	46	93	34	22	39	73	202	5	4,172	37	16	94	346	1,067	-------	107	614
35 to 44 years	43	88	210	51	25	69	136	347	7	7,625	76	54	185	693	1,914	-------	265	1,076
45 to 54 years	47	67	124	62	26	62	152	310	5	6,215	66	73	172	535	1,789	-------	267	994
55 to 64 years	48	57	94	25	13	38	101	184	-------	3,134	42	46	145	275	1,042	-------	184	547
65 to 74 years	23	30	54	9	10	15	62	82	-------	1,407	37	25	71	109	465	-------	119	321
75 years and over	7	17	37	9	1	6	22	36	-------	604	17	15	29	49	241	-------	63	149
Unknown	1	-------	1	1	-------	-------	1	-------	1	480	-------	-------	2	6	16	-------	-------	8
SCHOOL ATTENDANCE																		
Total 7 to 13 years, inclusive	79	152	311	100	53	122	161	634	3	6,040	153	68	319	779	3,882	-------	422	1,586
Number attending school	69	138	286	82	47	117	145	555	1	5,534	120	59	240	660	3,488	-------	350	1,384
Percent attending school	-------	90.8	92.0	82.0	-------	95.9	90.1	87.5	-------	91.6	78.4	-------	75.2	84.7	89.9	-------	82.9	87.3
Total 14 and 15 years, inclusive	20	48	98	26	11	35	42	176	1	1,764	51	24	86	229	1,173	-------	124	485
Number attending school	10	40	88	19	5	30	36	148	1	1,488	40	20	64	153	1,014	-------	100	392
Percent attending school	-------	-------	-------	-------	-------	-------	-------	84.1	-------	84.4	-------	-------	-------	66.8	86.4	-------	80.6	80.8
Total 16 and 17 years, inclusive	21	35	91	27	9	32	54	155	3	1,951	36	24	103	273	1,089	1	126	486
Number attending school	5	22	44	8	5	20	29	87	-------	958	16	11	53	130	612	-------	61	253
Percent attending school	-------	-------	-------	-------	-------	-------	-------	56.1	-------	49.1	-------	-------	51.5	47.6	56.2	-------	48.4	52.1
Total 18 to 20 years, inclusive	39	45	158	49	15	59	83	246	6	3,492	52	41	138	415	1,649	30	151	715
Number attending school	7	7	17	8	4	7	10	27	-------	657	7	2	19	53	217	5	17	107
Percent attending school	-------	-------	10.8	-------	-------	-------	-------	11.0	-------	18.8	-------	-------	13.8	12.8	13.2	-------	11.3	15.0
ILLITERACY																		
Total 10 years old and over	385	603	1,415	430	215	527	1,055	2,571	64	43,753	630	423	1,437	4,172	15,588	53	1,963	7,825
Number illiterate	76	112	267	100	40	75	274	535	22	4,869	99	68	321	680	3,191	19	339	1,247
Percent illiterate	19.7	18.6	18.9	23.3	18.6	14.2	26.0	20.8	-------	11.1	15.7	16.1	22.3	16.3	20.5	-------	17.3	15.9
Percent illiterate in 1920	24.3	19.5	16.7	36.0	22.9	18.8	25.4	24.1	-------	18.6	30.0	28.7	20.5	21.8	34.8	-------	22.8	22.6
URBAN AND RURAL																		
Urban population	331	-------	-------	-------	-------	227	689	-------	-------	42,836	-------	-------	222	2,695	-------	-------	-------	3,512
Percent urban	62.7	-------	-------	-------	-------	31.3	53.0	-------	-------	82.7	-------	-------	12.0	52.7	-------	-------	-------	35.5
Rural population	197	817	1,881	573	285	499	612	3,433	70	8,961	875	515	1,624	2,422	21,095	53	2,533	6,378
Rural-farm	101	550	1,490	272	79	281	298	2,810	1	2,262	597	202	917	1,662	20,264	-------	971	5,410
Rural-nonfarm	96	267	391	301	206	218	314	623	69	6,699	278	313	653	760	831	53	1,562	968
Percent rural	37.3	100.0	100.0	100.0	100.0	68.7	47.0	100.0	-------	17.3	100.0	100.0	88.0	47.3	100.0	-------	100.0	64.5
MARITAL CONDITION																		
Males 15 years old and over	178	235	595	194	98	215	460	1,059	40	18,356	271	168	600	1,794	6,478	53	809	3,307
Single	61	69	185	68	36	74	158	304	21	5,858	104	44	214	663	2,044	53	242	1,017
Married	101	138	355	103	56	126	260	665	19	10,566	138	110	330	942	3,904	-------	481	1,976
Widowed	11	22	36	22	6	14	30	75	-------	1,313	27	11	52	175	358	-------	71	268
Divorced	4	6	19	1	-------	1	12	13	-------	378	2	3	4	12	117	-------	14	45
Unknown	1	-------	-------	-------	-------	-------	-------	2	-------	241	-------	-------	-------	2	55	-------	1	1
Females 15 years old and over	158	260	586	169	81	226	481	1,078	21	21,205	255	200	610	1,806	6,282	-------	840	3,376
Single	32	64	135	49	17	74	98	239	2	5,086	73	47	166	441	1,436	-------	199	748
Married	99	143	358	102	52	129	267	663	18	10,621	139	110	343	969	3,894	-------	495	2,026
Widowed	23	48	68	17	11	22	84	158	1	4,387	41	37	95	371	763	-------	126	551
Divorced	4	5	24	-------	-------	1	31	16	-------	884	2	5	6	23	142	-------	20	50
Unknown	-------	-------	1	1	1	-------	1	2	-------	227	-------	1	-------	2	47	-------	-------	1
FAMILIES																		
Number of families	109	184	401	122	67	152	364	773	18	13,643	176	139	442	1,217	4,503	-------	594	2,336
Median size	3.69	3.88	3.86	3.74	-------	4.03	2.78	3.63	-------	2.64	4.10	3.21	3.32	3.31	3.96	-------	3.35	3.47
Families having—																		
No children under 10	57	88	194	58	38	74	239	412	15	9,601	76	93	268	750	2,105	-------	349	1,334
1 child under 10	14	41	98	28	9	25	58	115	1	1,982	36	17	62	227	914	-------	94	432
2 children under 10	11	24	39	12	9	15	37	110	1	1,019	22	19	45	102	610	-------	55	275
3 or more	27	31	70	24	11	38	30	136	1	1,041	42	10	67	138	874	-------	96	295

CHARACTERISTICS OF NEGRO POPULATION BY COUNTIES: 1930—Continued

(See note at head of table)

SUBJECT	Giles	Grainger	Greene	Grundy	Hamblen	Hamilton	Hancock	Hardeman	Hardin	Hawkins	Haywood	Henderson	Henry	Hickman	Houston	Humphreys	Jackson	Jefferson
	TENNESSEE—Continued																	
POPULATION BY SEX																		
Negro population: 1930	7, 563	306	1, 154	155	1, 687	36, 155	162	8, 532	1, 483	1, 069	17, 227	1, 693	4, 997	1, 116	503	725	234	1, 276
Male	3, 737	152	553	89	779	17, 161	74	4, 266	743	546	8, 683	883	2, 486	569	255	386	126	652
Female	3, 826	154	601	66	908	18, 994	88	4, 266	740	523	8, 544	810	2, 511	547	248	339	108	624
Negro population: 1920	9, 431	447	1, 274	145	1, 621	27, 120	256	9, 250	1, 932	1, 201	16, 959	1, 766	5, 558	1, 928	687	867	275	1, 428
Male	4, 652	219	624	74	757	13, 577	119	4, 550	966	607	8, 451	873	2, 770	1, 010	339	447	147	701
Female	4, 779	228	650	71	864	13, 543	137	4, 700	966	594	8508	893	2, 788	918	348	420	128	727
Percent of total population:																		
1930	27. 0	2. 4	3. 3	1. 6	10. 2	22. 7	1. 7	38. 4	9. 1	4. 4	66. 1	9. 6	18. 9	8. 2	9. 1	6. 0	1. 7	7. 1
1920	30. 5	3. 3	3. 9	1. 5	10. 8	23. 4	2. 4	41. 5	11. 2	5. 2	66. 8	9. 6	20. 5	11. 9	11. 1	6. 4	1. 8	8. 1
VOTING AGE: 1930																		
Total 21 years and over	3, 604	149	587	104	903	22, 443	67	4, 044	796	580	7, 974	853	2, 541	560	226	417	105	641
Male	1, 738	75	288	63	403	10, 685	31	2, 014	406	291	3, 958	442	1, 275	280	114	222	58	340
Female	1, 866	74	299	41	500	11, 758	36	2, 030	390	289	4, 016	411	1, 266	280	112	195	47	301
AGE: 1930																		
Under 5 years	876	39	121	16	134	2, 871	26	1, 124	156	113	1, 968	208	533	123	58	77	34	135
Under 1 year	180	7	29	5	26	498	3	220	30	22	366	41	83	23	9	18	9	19
5 to 9 years	970	36	136	12	176	3, 443	26	1, 120	167	129	2, 310	222	623	139	81	76	31	151
10 to 14 years	973	37	143	6	194	3, 116	24	1, 016	149	112	2, 333	192	556	135	76	72	28	149
15 to 19 years	962	37	145	14	236	3, 454	17	1, 012	183	117	2, 216	178	632	138	56	65	30	172
20 to 24 years	698	34	106	22	181	4, 187	15	828	137	88	1, 592	162	489	88	38	78	33	112
25 to 29 years	409	12	70	39	105	4, 111	5	596	105	65	1, 267	125	320	48	23	74	18	72
30 to 34 years	339	11	76	11	105	3, 219	8	485	78	39	961	101	319	38	25	41	12	70
35 to 44 years	728	29	123	15	214	5, 634	16	859	165	130	1, 654	171	538	102	35	82	21	146
45 to 54 years	744	29	103	8	171	3, 770	12	707	158	114	1, 529	137	472	131	56	74	12	124
55 to 64 years	485	24	62	4	98	1, 545	5	424	98	89	792	104	266	80	29	48	9	81
65 to 74 years	247	8	46	7	51	557	7	248	57	42	402	62	160	62	18	24	5	42
75 years and over	127	10	20	1	21	245	1	103	21	29	195	31	85	32	8	14	1	21
Unknown	5	-	3	-	1	3	-	10	9	2	8	-	4	-	-	-	-	1
SCHOOL ATTENDANCE																		
Total 7 to 13 years, inclusive	1, 345	49	192	14	250	4, 619	38	1, 468	216	163	3, 289	291	785	183	98	99	41	209
Number attending school	1, 139	46	148	12	211	4, 377	13	1, 257	183	119	2, 702	205	659	136	84	87	37	192
Percent attending school	84. 7	-	77. 1	-	84. 4	94. 8	-	85. 6	84. 7	73. 0	82. 2	70. 4	83. 9	74. 3	-	-	-	91. 9
Total 14 and 15 years, inclusive	403	16	56	3	85	1, 164	8	431	68	49	875	69	251	52	32	27	13	58
Number attending school	322	14	45	2	67	961	5	327	57	32	639	49	192	36	18	19	11	45
Percent attending school	79. 9	-	-	-	-	82. 6	-	75. 9	-	-	73. 0	-	76. 5	-	-	-	-	-
Total 16 and 17 years, inclusive	390	20	61	4	101	1, 333	9	378	76	49	896	77	280	58	22	29	13	79
Number attending school	192	12	34	1	59	582	1	182	46	23	370	26	138	25	9	10	5	41
Percent attending school	492	-	-	-	58. 4	43. 7	-	48. 1	-	-	41. 3	-	49. 3	-	-	-	-	-
Total 18 to 20 years, inclusive	554	18	87	11	138	2, 377	7	631	106	58	1, 319	106	340	79	28	43	17	95
Number attending school	77	6	17	-	44	279	1	66	25	7	146	19	42	6	2	2	-	20
Percent attending school	13. 9	-	-	-	31. 9	11. 7	-	10. 5	23. 6	-	11. 1	17. 9	12. 4	-	-	-	-	-
ILLITERACY																		
Total 10 years old and over	5, 717	231	897	127	1, 377	29, 841	110	6, 288	1, 160	827	12, 949	1, 263	3, 841	854	364	572	169	990
Number illiterate	1, 056	39	166	27	190	3, 505	35	1, 499	185	161	3, 010	241	821	312	116	126	31	150
Percent illitierate	18. 5	16. 9	18. 5	21. 3	13. 8	11. 7	31. 8	23. 8	15. 9	19. 5	23. 2	19. 1	21. 4	36. 5	31. 9	22. 0	18. 3	15. 2
Percent illiterate in 1920	24. 0	24. 8	23. 2	18. 9	12. 2	13. 9	43. 6	32. 4	19. 5	23. 9	31. 3	24. 3	24. 2	19. 3	23. 4	32. 2	31. 0	22. 0
URBAN AND RURAL																		
Urban population	1, 083	-	575	-	1, 141	33, 289	-	-	-	-	1, 394	-	1, 984	-	-	-	-	-
Percent urban	14. 3	-	49. 8	-	67. 6	92. 1	-	-	-	-	8. 1	-	39. 7	-	-	-	-	-
Rural population	6, 480	306	579	155	546	2, 866	162	8, 532	1, 483	1, 069	15, 833	1, 693	3, 013	1, 116	503	725	234	1, 276
Rural-farm	5, 345	212	425	36	382	789	158	6, 911	722	575	15, 454	1, 175	2, 458	369	276	117	121	583
Rural-nonfarm	1, 135	94	154	119	164	2, 077	4	1, 621	761	494	379	518	555	747	227	608	113	693
Percent rural	85. 7	100. 0	50. 2	100. 0	32. 4	7. 9	100. 0	100. 0	100. 0	100. 0	91. 9	100. 0	60. 3	100. 0	100. 0	100. 0	100. 0	100. 0
MARITAL CONDITION																		
Males 15 years and over	2, 883	94	361	75	517	12, 563	40	2, 631	506	367	5, 288	550	1, 637	357	144	268	76	444
Single	711	32	117	39	189	3, 634	11	848	146	130	1, 655	166	537	122	51	89	27	180
Married	1, 363	51	208	34	300	7, 725	28	1, 509	304	192	3, 252	323	943	202	74	142	45	214
Widowed	159	8	28	1	27	983	-	209	46	38	296	56	137	32	17	29	3	47
Divorced	49	3	8	1	1	212	1	40	7	3	80	5	18	1	2	7	1	1
Unknown	1	-	-	-	-	9	-	25	3	4	5	-	2	-	-	1	-	2
Females 15 years old and over	2, 461	100	393	46	666	14, 162	46	2, 641	505	348	5, 328	521	1, 648	362	144	232	65	397
Single	632	31	108	8	267	2, 821	13	641	121	90	1, 244	125	415	100	48	37	13	131
Married	1, 360	55	215	36	307	8. 100	28	1, 548	311	193	3, 316	311	949	208	74	146	47	208
Widowed	400	13	62	-	87	2, 788	4	387	70	60	650	78	258	52	15	43	4	52
Divorced	68	1	8	2	5	447	-	46	3	4	109	7	23	2	6	6	1	5
Unknown	1	-	-	-	-	6	1	19	-	1	9	-	3	-	1	-	-	1
FAMILIES																		
Number of families	1, 717	59	257	39	358	9, 430	34	1, 765	359	269	3, 709	380	1, 080	257	105	193	49	272
Median size	3. 66	-	3. 70	-	3. 84	2. 77	-	3. 80	3. 54	3. 23	3. 96	3. 80	3. 75	3. 56	4. 19	2. 94	-	3. 88
Families having—																		
No children under 10	928	30	139	28	206	6, 245	12	839	204	162	1, 848	186	561	150	52	121	16	141
1 child under 10	298	8	49	2	64	1, 533	6	351	64	45	675	71	208	32	15	27	12	51
2 children under 10	178	7	30	5	48	885	7	221	46	26	485	59	134	34	17	22	12	37
3 or more	313	14	39	4	40	767	9	354	45	36	701	64	177	41	21	23	9	43

CHARACTERISTICS OF NEGRO POPULATION BY COUNTIES: 1930—Continued

(See note at head of table)

SUBJECT	TENNESSEE—Continued																	
	Johnson	Knox	Lake	Lauderdale	Lawrence	Lewis	Lincoln	Loudon	McMinn	McNairy	Macon	Madison	Marion	Marshall	Maury	Meigs	Monroe	Montgomery
POPULATION BY SEX																		
Negro population: 1930	301	19,198	3,754	9,172	720	389	4,058	677	1,818	1,603	313	18,643	1,524	2,380	9,808	391	974	10,118
Male	151	9,235	2,000	4,639	341	192	2,019	340	880	838	162	9,021	747	1,163	4,728	198	487	4,899
Female	150	9,963	1,754	4,533	379	197	2,039	337	938	765	151	9,622	777	1,217	5,080	193	487	5,219
Negro population: 1920	306	13,310	3,051	8,929	982	668	4,858	1,037	1,923	1,529	476	17,234	1,683	3,089	11,950	449	1,187	11,928
Male	159	6,516	1,601	4,537	498	364	2,434	533	956	767	250	8,430	866	1,518	5,963	224	575	5,771
Female	147	6,794	1,450	4,392	484	304	2,424	504	967	762	226	8,804	817	1,571	5,987	225	612	6,157
Percent of total population:																		
1930	2.5	12.3	35.8	39.2	2.7	7.4	16.0	3.8	6.3	8.1	2.3	36.5	8.7	15.3	28.8	6.4	4.6	32.8
1920	2.5	11.8	33.6	41.5	4.2	11.7	18.8	6.4	7.7	8.3	3.2	39.3	9.7	17.8	33.8	7.4	5.4	37.0
VOTING AGE: 1930																		
Total 21 years old and over	148	12,073	2,088	4,686	373	211	1,973	347	882	805	159	9,864	763	1,203	5,322	177	445	5,380
Male	77	5,816	1,169	2,382	178	111	961	179	426	424	86	4,718	388	568	2,538	87	215	2,597
Female	71	6,257	919	2,304	195	100	1,012	168	456	381	73	5,146	375	635	2,784	90	230	2,783
AGE: 1930																		
Under 5 years	31	1,508	319	913	81	49	455	62	221	182	30	1,861	149	255	951	49	107	1,037
Under 1 year	9	282	70	160	11	12	75	14	44	39	4	328	31	50	182	10	10	184
5 to 9 years	39	1,679	359	1,090	87	41	502	77	257	197	39	2,260	195	291	1,085	51	149	1,135
10 to 14 years	39	1,630	393	1,072	82	28	518	96	226	181	38	2,001	195	314	1,133	57	121	1,162
15 to 19 years	34	1,857	487	1,190	85	52	524	85	204	203	43	2,199	187	276	1,096	50	127	1,177
20 to 24 years	43	2,299	469	861	55	41	331	45	143	171	39	2,062	130	193	834	35	81	876
25 to 29 years	13	2,086	351	688	45	36	255	50	105	127	16	1,538	110	160	561	26	50	650
30 to 34 years	10	1,611	272	552	35	18	240	39	99	80	16	1,171	76	126	522	16	58	572
35 to 44 years	22	2,942	526	1,004	77	33	434	56	205	144	26	2,199	197	255	1,067	33	107	1,138
45 to 54 years	38	2,002	361	952	78	41	402	75	175	147	29	1,736	148	211	1,141	32	84	1,142
55 to 64 years	21	928	138	517	47	28	215	49	99	76	21	953	70	162	730	27	50	696
65 to 74 years	7	409	56	221	30	11	126	23	47	59	10	426	41	97	450	9	20	351
75 years and over	4	164	22	108	18	11	56	18	35	35	6	195	20	40	237	6	20	173
Unknown	---	83	1	4	---	---	---	2	2	1	---	42	6	---	1	---	---	9
SCHOOL ATTENDANCE																		
Total 7 to 13 years, inclusive	52	2,307	537	1,497	103	44	707	128	330	248	53	2,921	271	420	1,570	75	180	1,601
Number attending school	50	2,211	316	1,246	80	44	569	114	279	214	29	2,582	250	366	1,349	71	163	1,432
Percent attending school	---	95.8	58.8	83.2	77.7	---	80.5	89.1	84.5	86.3	---	88.4	92.3	87.1	85.9	---	90.6	89.4
Total 14 and 15 years, inclusive	20	660	160	464	36	20	206	33	93	73	13	828	82	117	443	22	46	486
Number attending school	19	551	66	351	28	19	138	30	83	58	10	669	73	87	335	19	42	389
Percent attending school	---	83.5	41.3	75.6	---	---	67.0	---	---	---	---	80.8	---	74.4	75.6	---	---	80.0
Total 16 and 17 years, inclusive	10	708	193	481	38	19	220	30	81	86	16	892	80	119	422	22	56	497
Number attending school	4	313	36	223	12	13	94	17	47	52	6	493	49	40	193	14	40	209
Percent attending school	---	44.2	18.7	46.4	---	---	42.7	---	---	---	---	55.3	---	33.6	45.7	---	---	42.1
Total 18 to 20 years, inclusive	28	1,269	319	692	44	28	284	46	103	123	27	1,348	106	148	670	28	76	668
Number attending school	3	158	11	112	3	5	46	9	27	17	7	280	24	10	96	8	16	86
Percent attending school	---	12.5	3.4	16.2	---	---	16.2	---	26.2	13.8	---	20.8	22.6	6.8	14.3	---	---	12.9
ILLITERACY																		
Total 10 years old and over	231	16,011	3,076	7,169	552	299	3,101	538	1,340	1,224	244	14,522	1,180	1,834	7,772	291	218	7,946
Number illiterate	20	1,569	811	1,553	100	57	599	75	148	244	77	2,377	163	324	1,736	30	107	1,458
Percent illiterate	8.7	9.8	26.4	21.7	18.1	19.1	19.3	13.9	11.0	19.9	31.6	16.4	13.8	17.7	22.3	10.3	14.9	18.3
Percent illiterate in 1920	25.1	14.7	31.3	32.5	27.9	25.3	23.4	17.6	17.4	24.7	31.0	27.3	18.6	23.1	22.3	18.5	21.5	20.7
URBAN AND RURAL																		
Urban population	---	17,093	---	---	260	---	1,150	133	656	---	---	7,595	---	531	2,507	---	---	3,409
Percent urban	---	89.0	---	---	36.1	---	28.3	19.6	36.1	---	---	40.7	---	22.3	25.6	---	---	33.7
Rural population	301	2,105	3,754	9,172	460	389	2,908	544	1,162	1,603	313	11,048	1,524	1,849	7,301	391	974	6,709
Rural-farm	109	626	3,035	7,240	298	30	2,530	296	612	976	252	9,892	175	1,169	3,595	374	680	5,653
Rural-nonfarm	192	1,479	719	1,932	162	359	378	248	550	627	61	1,156	1,349	680	3,706	17	294	1,056
Percent rural	100.0	11.0	100.0	100.0	63.9	100.0	71.7	80.4	63.9	100.0	100.0	59.3	100.0	77.7	74.4	100.0	100.0	66.3
MARITAL CONDITION																		
Males 15 years old and over	97	6,892	1,448	3,067	230	140	1,280	224	545	551	110	5,983	487	712	3,161	119	283	3,284
Single	35	2,305	429	801	76	49	445	78	187	199	43	1,837	149	228	902	50	104	971
Married	54	4,058	869	1,887	136	80	751	126	314	317	64	3,677	296	431	1,895	59	152	2,000
Widowed	7	391	130	215	13	10	72	16	35	31	3	412	25	43	286	7	21	191
Divorced	1	89	20	47	5	1	11	3	8	4	---	55	15	10	78	1	6	119
Unknown	---	49	---	17	---	---	1	1	1	---	---	2	2	---	---	2	---	3
Females 15 years old and over	95	7,489	1,235	3,030	240	131	1,303	218	569	492	96	6,538	498	808	3,478	115	314	3,500
Single	32	1,761	214	672	64	32	355	62	135	116	24	1,508	130	204	764	33	108	828
Married	53	4,198	855	1,924	142	77	739	125	324	302	61	3,736	294	453	1,968	63	167	2,013
Widowed	6	1,278	146	368	31	22	183	23	97	64	9	1,154	60	134	633	17	34	469
Divorced	4	191	20	59	3	---	21	8	12	8	2	131	14	16	107	1	5	189
Unknown	---	61	---	7	---	---	5	---	1	2	---	9	---	1	6	1	---	1
FAMILIES																		
Number of families	61	4,618	1,129	2,147	165	101	908	148	411	332	70	4,578	346	557	2,604	81	193	2,499
Median size	---	2.91	2,44	3.45	3.56	2.73	3.61	3.81	3.78	3.64	---	3.21	3.39	3.41	2.97	---	4.48	3.29
Families having—																		
No children under 10	35	3,091	769	1,228	95	67	495	85	198	163	36	2,692	189	306	1,641	41	89	1,503
1 child under 10	5	719	171	384	27	13	151	30	87	69	16	779	63	97	412	13	28	407
2 children under 10	8	392	108	238	14	5	116	13	42	46	9	503	43	73	252	11	28	272
3 or more	13	416	81	297	29	16	146	20	84	54	9	604	51	81	299	16	48	317

CHARACTERISTICS OF NEGRO POPULATION BY COUNTIES: 1930—Continued

(See note at head of table)

SUBJECT	Moore	Morgan	Obion	Overton	Perry	Pickett	Polk	Putnam	Rhea	Roane	Robertson	Rutherford	Scott	Sequatchie	Sevier	Shelby	Smith	Stewart
	TENNESSEE—Continued																	
POPULATION BY SEX																		
Negro population: 1930	304	478	4,038	136	239	4	152	573	746	1,453	5,852	7,741	15	11	211	127,324	1,059	626
Male	155	427	1,956	63	114	2	92	284	376	698	2,950	3,780	7	6	130	60,367	527	328
Female	149	51	2,082	73	125	2	60	289	370	755	2,902	3,961	8	5	81	66,957	532	298
Negro population: 1920	388	497	4,103	201	355	6	108	806	901	1,918	5,591	9,786	16	46	318	98,962	1,663	1,215
Male	201	412	2,021	91	193	2	51	409	449	955	2,845	4,697	9	22	165	47,884	845	615
Female	187	85	2,082	110	162	4	57	397	452	963	2,746	5,089	7	24	153	51,078	818	600
Percent of total population:																		
1930	7.5	3.5	13.9	0.8	3.3	0.1	1.0	2.4	5.4	5.9	20.8	24.0	0.1	0.3	1.0	41.5	6.8	4.7
1920	8.6	3.7	14.5	1.1	4.6	0.1	0.8	3.6	6.5	7.8	21.8	29.6	0.1	1.3	1.4	44.3	9.7	8.3
VOTING AGE: 1930																		
Total 21 years old and over	143	402	2,252	72	118	3	82	323	420	734	3,023	4,033	11	11	93	80,592	521	301
Male	79	371	1,086	31	58	1	52	153	207	344	1,544	1,909	5	6	55	38,253	261	152
Female	64	31	1,166	41	60	2	30	170	213	390	1,479	2,124	6	5	38	42,339	260	149
AGE: 1930																		
Under 5 years	31	14	355	15	35	-	15	65	85	168	615	755	1	-	28	10,381	100	86
Under 1 year	8	1	71	4	10	-	3	18	22	36	124	144	-	-	4	1,932	18	19
5 to 9 years	43	10	463	18	32	-	17	61	81	176	728	883	-	-	29	11,416	121	83
10 to 14 years	35	11	427	14	24	-	15	60	62	167	706	940	1	-	30	10,352	147	74
15 to 19 years	46	23	449	14	25	1	17	51	87	167	641	944	2	-	28	11,777	150	77
20 to 24 years	25	114	399	15	21	2	30	64	73	132	545	722	1	2	17	13,760	84	49
25 to 29 years	14	105	310	1	20	-	18	46	46	97	441	469	1	-	11	13,991	63	46
30 to 34 years	13	76	249	7	16	-	11	29	49	59	335	416	-	2	8	10,821	52	33
35 to 44 years	35	68	513	11	21	-	15	58	80	167	658	862	3	-	26	20,258	101	53
45 to 54 years	20	43	415	14	15	-	7	51	70	151	549	785	3	-	10	14,057	119	56
55 to 64 years	25	11	265	11	20	-	4	47	65	98	380	554	1	2	12	6,415	75	35
65 to 74 years	11	1	117	9	7	1	3	25	32	37	169	250	1	5	11	2,581	32	24
75 years and over	6	2	72	7	3	-	-	14	16	34	80	160	1	-	1	1,224	15	10
Unknown	-	-	4	-	-	-	-	2	-	-	5	1	-	-	-	291	-	-
SCHOOL ATTENDANCE																		
Total 7 to 13 years, inclusive	56	16	604	24	42	-	20	78	96	223	995	1,260	-	-	37	15,054	197	108
Number attending school	50	11	529	18	39	-	16	67	89	203	797	1,069	-	-	31	14,206	151	90
Percent attending school	-	-	87.6	-	-	-	-	-	-	91.0	80.1	84.8	-	-	-	94.4	76.6	83.3
Total 14 and 15 years, inclusive	20	4	158	4	4	-	6	27	28	69	270	419	1	-	13	4,216	61	38
Number attending school	14	1	115	2	4	-	3	19	25	57	186	332	1	-	10	3,655	49	32
Percent attending school	-	-	72.8	-	-	-	-	-	-	-	68.9	79.2	-	-	-	86.7	-	-
Total 16 and 17 years, inclusive	15	8	199	5	12	-	7	24	38	83	250	392	1	-	11	4,511	58	30
Number attending school	7	2	91	2	7	-	3	7	19	37	98	194	-	-	4	2,312	39	19
Percent attending school	-	-	45.7	-	-	-	-	-	-	-	39.2	49.5	-	-	-	51.3	-	-
Total 18 to 20 years, inclusive	26	31	268	9	15	1	13	29	46	100	399	528	1	-	15	8,019	76	33
Number attending school	1	-	37	1	2	-	2	5	6	12	43	62	-	-	2	995	19	3
Percent attending school	-	-	13.8	-	-	-	-	-	-	12.0	10.8	11.7	-	-	-	12.4	-	-
ILLITERACY																		
Total 10 years old and over	230	454	3,220	103	172	4	120	447	580	1,109	4,509	6,103	14	11	154	105,527	838	457
Number illiterate	46	81	626	28	23	-	36	78	83	143	1,084	1,093	4	-	25	11,124	168	106
Percent illiterate	20.0	17.8	19.4	27.2	13.4	-	30.0	17.4	14.3	12.9	24.0	17.9	-	-	16.2	10.5	20.0	23.2
Percent illiterate in 1920	20.7	23.0	21.5	29.3	9.8	-	-	23.7	17.1	17.4	18.3	29.2	-	-	21.2	18.8	27.5	27.2
URBAN AND RURAL																		
Urban population	-	-	1,417	-	-	-	-	17	-	801	1,369	2,185	-	-	-	96,550	-	-
Percent urban	-	-	35.1	-	-	-	-	3.0	-	55.1	23.4	28.2	-	-	-	75.8	-	-
Rural population	304	478	2,621	136	239	4	152	556	746	652	4,483	5,556	15	11	211	30,774	1,059	626
Rural-farm	220	2	1,182	66	104	4	93	313	165	181	3,801	4,831	2	9	77	24,891	554	326
Rural-nonfarm	84	476	1,439	70	135	-	59	243	581	471	682	725	13	2	134	5,883	505	300
Percent rural	100.0	100.0	64.9	100.0	100.0	-	100.0	97.0	100.0	44.9	76.6	71.8	-	-	100.0	24.2	100.0	100.0
MARITAL CONDITION																		
Males 15 years old and over	105	403	1,348	40	71	2	68	183	260	443	1,925	2,456	6	6	72	44,529	347	197
Single	34	196	408	14	25	-	40	55	100	155	576	803	1	2	32	12,577	110	74
Married	62	187	773	24	42	1	26	105	143	245	1,151	1,452	5	3	35	27,429	201	105
Widowed	8	12	153	2	4	1	2	15	14	35	162	164	-	1	4	3,419	33	15
Divorced	1	8	14	-	-	-	-	8	3	8	28	33	-	-	1	911	3	3
Unknown	-	-	-	-	-	-	-	-	-	-	8	4	-	-	-	193	-	-
Females 15 years old and over	90	40	1,445	49	77	2	37	204	258	499	1,878	2,707	7	5	52	50,646	344	186
Single	23	6	300	14	26	1	11	56	57	126	437	756	1	-	12	10,295	98	44
Married	57	28	791	26	42	1	23	107	149	267	1,183	1,471	5	3	29	28,406	201	107
Widowed	6	6	344	9	8	-	2	38	44	97	216	423	1	2	10	10,191	38	32
Divorced	4	-	9	-	1	-	1	3	8	9	36	51	-	-	1	1,596	7	3
Unknown	-	-	1	-	-	-	-	-	-	-	6	6	-	-	-	158	-	-
FAMILIES																		
Number of families	69	34	1,028	30	47	1	19	138	175	308	1,390	1,826	5	4	35	36,365	244	130
Median size	-	-	3.12	-	-	-	-	3.31	3.09	3.66	3.34	3.37	-	-	-	2.50	3.50	3.95
Families having—																		
No children under 10	37	20	642	15	15	1	7	76	106	176	759	1,087	4	4	14	25,686	135	61
1 child under 10	14	8	164	6	15	-	3	30	30	39	270	299	1	-	5	5,163	50	20
2 children under 10	5	5	99	5	5	-	5	14	9	36	159	187	-	-	5	2,619	25	21
3 or more	13	1	123	4	12	-	4	18	30	57	202	253	-	-	11	2,897	34	28

CHARACTERISTICS OF NEGRO POPULATION BY COUNTIES: 1930—Continued

(See note at head of table)

SUBJECT	TENNESSEE—Continued														TEXAS			
	Sullivan	Sumner	Tipton	Trousdale	Unicoi	Union	Van Buren	Warren	Washington	Wayne	Weakley	White	Williamson	Wilson	The State	Anderson	Angelina	Aransas
POPULATION BY SEX																		
Negro population: 1930	1,799	4,082	11,275	1,267	13	3	65	1,358	2,798	406	2,590	712	5,274	4,481	854,964	11,485	4,248	48
Male	887	2,077	5,738	660	8	2	38	685	1,415	189	1,279	346	2,683	2,251	422,608	5,584	2,107	25
Female	912	2,005	5,537	607	5	1	27	673	1,383	217	1,311	366	2,591	2,230	432,356	5,901	2,141	23
Negro population: 1920	1,691	4,734	13,139	1,717	4	7	50	1,562	2,250	681	2,896	785	6,546	5,728	741,694	11,162	2,764	89
Male	841	2,350	6,707	865	4	3	27	776	1,130	356	1,422	368	3,255	2,854	371,474	5,533	1,398	43
Female	850	2,384	6,432	852	---	4	23	786	1,120	325	1,474	417	3,291	2,874	370,220	5,629	1,366	46
Percent of total population: 1930	3.5	14.3	41.0	22.5	0.1	---	1.8	6.7	6.1	3.3	8.9	4.6	23.1	18.7	14.7	33.2	15.3	2.2
1920	4.7	17.1	43.4	28.6	---	0.1	1.9	9.0	6.6	5.3	9.3	5.0	28.0	21.8	15.9	32.5	12.4	4.3
VOTING AGE: 1930																		
Total 21 years old and over	1,022	2,242	5,602	658	10	3	21	770	1,665	223	1,414	390	2,661	2,332	469,637	5,718	2,455	37
Male	507	1,118	2,847	335	6	2	11	393	882	104	708	189	1,329	1,135	234,459	2,754	1,290	20
Female	515	1,124	2,755	323	4	1	10	377	783	119	706	201	1,332	1,197	235,178	2,964	1,165	17
AGE: 1930																		
Under 5 years	160	378	1,259	125	1	---	10	143	250	25	249	70	545	420	86,120	1,329	400	3
Under 1 year	39	70	235	18	---	---	---	28	49	3	48	18	110	92	16,622	231	75	1
5 to 9 years	166	439	1,405	161	---	---	11	124	285	55	302	78	649	507	97,509	1,490	345	1
10 to 14 years	205	464	1,334	131	1	---	7	139	278	41	285	78	655	566	89,070	1,315	413	4
15 to 19 years	202	454	1,415	162	---	---	13	150	272	55	289	88	642	551	92,696	1,342	427	1
20 to 24 years	170	359	1,135	126	5	---	3	137	245	45	238	62	480	392	91,569	1,174	460	3
25 to 29 years	151	258	803	68	---	---	3	88	236	28	177	49	364	238	80,192	859	471	8
30 to 34 years	148	228	667	86	---	---	6	71	246	28	138	39	263	239	64,050	676	389	6
35 to 44 years	260	473	1,110	126	3	---	4	144	453	43	314	86	522	504	112,360	1,231	586	8
45 to 54 years	173	446	1,085	114	1	2	3	151	258	42	273	73	516	458	76,240	1,015	402	2
55 to 64 years	100	328	604	90	1	---	4	110	144	21	181	47	371	328	38,014	568	170	4
65 to 74 years	41	170	301	53	1	1	1	74	85	13	89	26	182	183	17,539	330	53	6
75 years and over	22	83	147	24	---	---	---	26	45	10	52	16	83	95	8,585	146	30	2
Unknown	1	2	10	1	---	---	---	1	1	---	3	---	2	---	1,020	10	2	---
SCHOOL ATTENDANCE																		
Total 7 to 13 years, inclusive	264	625	1,944	191	1	---	11	170	402	68	410	113	906	763	130,110	1,972	609	2
Number attending school	245	550	1,748	143	---	---	6	155	340	50	369	103	782	605	114,333	1,661	501	1
Percent attending school	92.8	88.0	89.9	74.9	---	---	---	91.2	84.6	---	90.0	91.2	86.3	79.3	87.9	84.2	82.3	---
Total 14 and 15 years, inclusive	81	188	519	62	---	---	4	60	101	22	119	24	283	218	35,568	512	162	2
Number attending school	70	149	428	47	---	---	2	43	77	19	94	23	202	147	29,972	449	115	---
Percent attending school	---	79.3	82.5	---	---	---	---	---	76.2	---	79.0	---	71.4	67.4	84.3	87.7	71.0	---
Total 16 and 17 years, inclusive	87	189	548	62	---	---	3	57	105	19	121	39	274	221	37,157	556	163	1
Number attending school	53	98	280	30	---	---	3	19	51	11	65	21	120	74	20,048	318	63	---
Percent attending school	---	51.9	51.1	---	---	---	---	---	48.6	---	53.7	---	43.8	33.5	54.0	57.2	38.7	---
Total 18 to 20 years, inclusive	125	287	863	101	1	---	10	95	168	30	162	44	353	335	57,786	808	296	2
Number attending school	27	53	88	15	---	---	2	20	21	4	18	8	41	28	8,031	140	19	---
Percent attending school	21.6	18.5	10.2	14.9	---	---	---	---	12.5	---	11.1	---	11.6	8.4	13.9	17.3	6.4	---
ILLITERACY																		
Total 10 years old and over	1,473	3,265	8,611	981	12	3	44	1,091	2,263	326	2,039	564	4,080	3,554	671,335	8,666	3,403	44
Number illiterate	195	715	1,466	272	3	2	5	167	343	52	355	103	964	496	90,225	1,414	577	5
Percent illiterate	13.2	21.9	17.0	27.7	---	---	---	15.3	15.2	16.0	17.4	18.3	23.6	14.0	13.4	16.3	17.0	---
Percent illiterate in 1920	21.9	28.1	29.8	29.9	---	---	---	22.5	18.0	26.8	19.8	26.2	32.2	28.0	17.8	18.0	17.0	---
URBAN AND RURAL																		
Urban population	1,554	971	1,249	---	11	---	---	688	2,335	---	737	---	1,352	1,174	329,829	3,227	1,349	---
Percent urban	86.4	23.8	11.1	---	---	---	---	50.7	83.5	---	28.5	---	25.6	26.2	38.6	28.1	31.8	---
Rural population	245	3,111	10,026	1,267	2	3	65	670	463	406	1,853	712	3,922	3,307	525,135	8,258	2,899	48
Rural-farm	70	2,013	9,603	692	---	3	58	509	138	88	987	267	3,032	2,348	409,922	7,819	799	10
Rural-nonfarm	175	1,098	423	575	2	---	7	161	325	318	866	445	890	959	115,213	439	2,100	38
Percent rural	13.6	76.2	88.9	100.0	---	---	---	49.3	16.5	100.0	71.5	100.0	74.4	73.8	61.4	71.9	68.2	---
MARITAL CONDITION																		
Males 15 years old and over	621	1,407	3,717	443	7	2	24	483	1,030	136	858	236	1,727	1,468	286,595	3,505	1,530	21
Single	198	472	1,091	157	3	---	14	156	342	55	250	83	600	443	84,217	1,067	447	7
Married	371	773	2,226	258	4	1	10	277	584	74	509	135	964	871	173,426	2,077	905	8
Widowed	43	138	299	22	---	---	---	42	64	6	85	11	128	114	20,281	280	121	6
Divorced	9	23	98	6	---	1	---	8	40	1	13	4	34	36	8,312	80	55	---
Unknown	---	1	3	---	---	---	---	---	---	---	1	3	1	4	359	1	2	---
Females 15 years old and over	647	1,394	3,560	407	4	1	13	469	955	149	896	250	1,698	1,520	295,670	3,846	1,460	19
Single	162	355	670	104	1	---	3	100	230	46	204	78	442	373	60,148	909	239	3
Married	378	775	2,234	252	3	1	9	283	506	76	522	138	967	849	175,844	2,129	916	9
Widowed	98	225	543	41	---	---	1	70	184	24	147	27	238	246	45,658	680	196	6
Divorced	9	38	111	10	---	---	---	16	34	3	22	4	50	50	13,643	127	108	1
Unknown	---	1	2	---	---	---	---	---	1	---	1	3	1	2	377	1	1	---
FAMILIES																		
Number of families	436	1,017	2,568	293	3	1	11	354	587	103	646	166	1,190	1,098	210,795	2,636	1,135	18
Median size	3.19	3.19	3.46	3.58	---	---	---	3.04	3.28	3.35	3.19	3.50	3.57	3.28	3.09	3.49	2.81	---
Families having— No children under 10	269	641	1,391	164	2	1	4	229	344	61	398	81	664	667	127,287	1,404	722	15
1 child under 10	84	160	473	50	1	---	2	50	103	20	105	45	207	170	35,171	464	195	2
2 children under 10	43	87	284	34	---	---	1	27	60	11	61	26	126	125	20,939	315	111	---
3 or more	40	129	420	45	---	---	4	48	80	11	82	14	193	136	27,398	453	107	1

CHARACTERISTICS OF NEGRO POPULATION BY COUNTIES: 1930—Continued

(See note at head of table)

SUBJECT	TEXAS—Continued																	
	Archer	Armstrong	Atascosa	Austin	Bailey	Bandera	Bastrop	Baylor	Bee	Bell	Bexar	Blanco	Borden	Bosque	Bowie	Brazoria	Brazos	Brewster
POPULATION BY SEX																		
Negro population: 1930	19	6	179	4,852	11	11	7,741	102	531	6,334	19,447	133	9	560	15,971	7,341	9,064	53
Male	9	2	96	2,428	7	7	3,816	58	262	3,140	8,850	69	7	281	7,780	4,379	4,323	24
Female	10	4	83	2,424	4	4	3,925	44	269	3,194	10,597	64	2	279	8,191	2,962	4,741	29
Negro population: 1920	16	1	297	5,059	-	18	8,492	43	518	4,886	15,580	169	-	660	12,320	6,574	9,148	33
Male	6	1	144	2,519	-	12	4,153	28	248	2,385	7,478	82	-	340	6,136	3,675	4,552	14
Female	10	-	153	2,540	-	6	4,339	15	270	2,501	8,102	87	-	320	6,184	2,899	4,596	19
Percent of total population:																		
1930	0.2	0.2	1.1	25.7	0.2	0.3	32.4	1.4	3.4	12.7	6.6	3.5	0.6	3.6	32.9	31.8	41.5	0.8
1920	0.3	-	2.3	26.8	-	0.4	31.9	0.6	4.3	10.5	7.7	4.2	-	3.7	31.2	31.9	41.6	0.7
VOTING AGE: 1930																		
Total 21 years old and over	14	4	88	2,421	7	10	3,871	82	291	3,432	12,897	66	6	278	8,394	4,314	4,819	33
Male	7	2	48	1,212	6	6	1,893	47	146	1,727	5,810	34	4	137	4,073	2,757	2,304	17
Female	7	2	40	1,209	1	4	1,978	35	145	1,705	7,087	32	2	141	4,321	1,557	2,515	16
AGE: 1930																		
Under 5 years	1	-	15	560	-	-	826	8	30	651	1,214	17	3	53	1,638	679	946	2
Under 1 year	-	-	2	113	-	-	155	1	1	138	228	2	-	17	306	122	182	2
5 to 9 years	2	1	21	614	1	-	1,006	4	58	741	1,604	22	-	65	2,039	747	1,066	3
10 to 14 years	1	-	29	561	-	-	952	4	63	637	1,461	16	-	74	1,769	663	1,024	8
15 to 19 years	1	1	24	588	2	1	911	1	77	727	1,856	10	-	72	1,803	774	1,017	7
20 to 24 years	1	1	13	451	4	-	716	15	48	685	2,281	11	2	48	1,642	847	964	2
25 to 29 years	7	-	11	344	1	-	492	18	42	557	2,165	5	2	38	1,501	708	783	10
30 to 34 years	2	1	9	266	1	1	426	14	36	496	2,024	3	1	30	1,126	549	582	3
35 to 44 years	3	2	19	524	1	5	866	22	76	846	3,485	19	-	62	1,966	977	1,097	5
45 to 54 years	1	-	12	458	1	3	749	10	51	551	1,977	9	-	55	1,376	673	822	10
55 to 64 years	-	-	14	292	-	1	443	5	26	269	832	9	-	40	661	426	460	3
65 to 74 years	-	-	9	129	-	-	227	1	18	104	357	7	-	18	323	198	197	-
75 years and over	-	-	3	65	-	-	125	-	6	64	177	5	1	5	120	96	102	-
Unknown	-	-	-	-	-	-	2	-	-	6	14	-	-	-	7	4	4	-
SCHOOL ATTENDANCE																		
Total 7 to 13 years, inclusive	1	-	38	813	-	-	1,346	6	87	958	2,148	23	-	99	2,665	973	1,477	6
Number attending school	1	-	21	690	-	-	1,237	-	77	784	2,013	23	-	84	2,417	889	1,346	6
Percent attending school	-	-	-	84.9	-	-	91.9	-	-	81.8	93.7	-	-	-	90.7	91.4	91.1	-
Total 14 and 15 years, inclusive	-	1	13	218	-	-	393	-	37	268	645	8	-	33	728	289	413	4
Number attending school	-	1	6	169	-	-	338	-	32	201	555	7	-	24	622	237	365	3
Percent attending school	-	-	-	77.5	-	-	86.0	-	-	75.0	86.0	-	-	-	85.4	82.0	88.4	-
Total 16 and 17 years, inclusive	1	-	7	236	-	1	398	-	21	284	720	5	-	31	718	285	426	2
Number attending school	-	-	3	96	-	-	244	-	11	135	382	4	-	20	420	117	236	1
Percent attending school	-	-	-	40.7	-	-	61.3	-	-	47.5	53.1	-	-	-	58.5	41.1	55.4	-
Total 18 to 20 years, inclusive	-	-	10	343	3	-	499	4	44	449	1,223	4	-	42	1,039	499	583	4
Number attending school	-	-	1	27	-	-	80	-	6	67	141	1	-	10	167	46	90	2
Percent attending school	-	-	-	7.9	-	-	16.0	-	-	14.9	11.5	-	-	-	16.1	9.2	15.4	-
ILLITERACY																		
Total 10 years old and over	16	5	143	3,678	10	11	5,909	90	443	4,942	16,629	94	6	442	12,294	5,915	7,052	48
Number illiterate	2	1	31	424	1	3	771	13	61	531	958	-	1	84	1,937	1,011	1,452	9
Percent illiterate	-	-	21.7	11.5	-	-	13.0	-	13.8	10.7	5.8	-	-	19.0	15.8	17.1	20.6	-
Percent illiterate in 1920	-	-	18.5	16.6	-	-	17.1	-	13.4	11.9	7.5	5.8	-	16.9	19.8	21.8	19.4	-
URBAN AND RURAL																		
Urban population	-	-	-	-	-	-	800	91	330	3,427	18,185	-	-	-	4,934	183	2,599	27
Percent urban	-	-	-	-	-	-	10.3	89.2	62.1	54.1	93.5	-	-	-	30.9	2.5	28.7	-
Rural population	19	6	179	4,852	11	11	6,941	11	201	2,907	1,262	133	9	560	11,037	7,158	6,465	26
Rural-farm	3	6	110	3,741	11	5	5,537	10	118	2,411	547	132	9	206	9,135	4,286	5,843	13
Rural-nonfarm	16	-	69	1,111	-	6	1,404	1	83	496	715	1	-	354	1,902	2,872	622	13
Percent rural	-	-	100.0	100.0	-	-	89.7	10.8	37.9	45.9	6.5	100.0	-	100.0	69.1	97.5	71.3	-
MARITAL CONDITION																		
Males 15 years old and over	7	2	60	1,557	7	7	2,404	47	188	2,129	6,750	40	4	180	5,034	3,302	2,857	18
Single	-	-	20	492	3	2	771	10	66	637	1,918	11	1	70	1,373	1,190	775	5
Married	7	2	33	940	3	3	1,404	30	104	1,225	4,175	27	3	95	3,200	1,820	1,792	13
Widowed	-	-	7	107	1	1	188	4	9	193	410	1	-	14	339	185	216	-
Divorced	-	-	-	18	-	1	40	3	9	71	246	1	-	1	110	106	72	-
Unknown	-	-	-	-	-	-	1	-	-	3	1	-	-	-	12	1	2	-
Females 15 years old and over	8	3	54	1,560	3	4	2,553	39	192	2,176	8,418	38	2	188	5,491	1,950	3,171	22
Single	-	1	13	373	-	1	658	3	53	442	1,701	9	-	62	1,076	407	585	7
Married	8	2	30	952	3	3	1,429	31	109	1,244	4,406	25	2	91	3,321	1,184	1,829	12
Widowed	-	-	11	197	-	-	403	3	24	367	1,716	3	-	31	844	276	624	3
Divorced	-	-	-	37	-	-	63	2	6	122	591	1	-	4	244	82	133	-
Unknown	-	-	-	1	-	-	-	-	-	1	4	-	-	-	6	1	-	-
FAMILIES																		
Number of families	6	2	47	1,175	3	6	1,737	39	131	1,537	5,175	28	2	128	3,950	1,495	2,317	13
Median size	-	-	-	3.34	-	-	3.71	-	3.07	3.15	2.64	-	-	3.45	3.20	3.07	3.08	-
Families having—																		
No children under 10	3	2	28	655	2	5	957	33	88	895	3,709	15	-	81	2,264	910	1,404	8
1 child under 10	2	-	10	194	1	1	296	3	21	284	754	3	1	16	710	219	373	3
2 children under 10	1	-	3	148	-	-	178	1	8	154	376	2	1	9	430	125	228	1
3 or more	-	-	6	178	-	-	306	2	14	204	336	8	-	22	546	241	312	1

CHARACTERISTICS OF NEGRO POPULATION BY COUNTIES: 1930—Continued

(See note at head of table)

SUBJECT	TEXAS—Continued																	
	Briscoe	Brooks	Brown	Burleson	Burnet	Caldwell	Calhoun	Callahan	Cameron	Camp	Carson	Cass	Castro	Chambers	Cherokee	Childress	Clay	Cochran
POPULATION BY SEX																		
Negro population: 1930	92	18	589	7, 187	139	4, 664	557	38	928	4, 100	15	10, 546	5	1, 369	11, 565	700	216	4
Male	46	10	289	3, 650	68	2, 293	292	26	497	1, 974	7	5, 275	3	746	5, 787	367	106	2
Female	46	8	300	3, 537	71	2, 371	265	12	431	2, 126	8	5, 271	2	623	5, 778	333	110	2
Negro population: 1920	---	17	431	6, 506	175	4, 403	584	20	771	4, 577	2	10, 350	---	1, 083	9, 174	70	127	1
Male	---	11	207	3, 243	97	2, 145	298	14	391	2, 254	---	5, 137	---	598	4, 734	47	65	1
Female	---	6	224	3, 263	78	2, 258	286	6	380	2, 323	2	5, 213	---	485	4, 440	23	62	---
Percent of total population:																		
1930	1. 6	0. 3	2. 2	36. 2	1. 3	14. 9	10. 3	0. 3	1. 2	40. 7	0. 2	35. 1	0. 1	24. 0	26. 8	4. 4	1. 5	0. 2
1920	---	0. 4	2. 0	38. 6	1. 8	17. 5	12. 4	0. 2	2. 1	41. 2	0. 1	34. 5	---	26. 0	24. 4	0. 6	0. 8	---
VOTING AGE: 1930																		
Total 21 years old and over	46	12	411	3, 821	89	2, 457	244	17	621	1, 917	14	4, 699	3	772	5, 900	416	121	2
Male	24	7	200	1, 971	44	1, 220	128	12	342	953	7	2, 404	2	449	3, 033	226	65	1
Female	22	5	211	1, 850	45	1, 237	116	5	279	964	7	2, 295	1	323	2, 867	190	56	1
AGE: 1930																		
Under 5 years	13	4	46	814	7	493	81	9	63	463	---	1, 293	---	129	1, 292	71	12	---
Under 1 year	1	1	9	182	2	114	19	1	5	84	---	272	---	26	271	16	2	---
5 to 9 years	10	---	35	880	12	573	84	7	87	572	1	1, 496	2	145	1, 384	73	18	1
10 to 14 years	10	1	42	773	16	509	71	2	68	516	---	1, 405	---	158	1, 276	56	29	---
15 to 19 years	10	1	43	753	10	527	69	3	72	515	---	1, 362	---	137	1, 417	66	32	1
20 to 24 years	10	1	85	707	18	541	52	3	123	379	7	1, 150	---	126	1, 256	94	21	1
25 to 29 years	5	3	93	561	8	390	35	5	138	300	6	762	2	121	1, 070	86	21	1
30 to 34 years	13	3	58	429	12	293	22	4	120	208	---	562	---	89	818	69	15	---
35 to 44 years	10	1	79	898	22	486	45	2	148	418	---	934	1	165	1, 325	120	34	---
45 to 54 years	8	2	47	749	12	414	66	2	72	356	1	814	---	146	919	45	21	---
55 to 64 years	2	1	35	377	11	221	20	---	21	225	---	426	---	87	471	14	7	---
65 to 74 years	---	1	20	167	10	137	9	1	10	103	---	206	---	35	245	5	6	---
75 years and over	1	---	6	75	1	79	3	---	3	45	---	126	---	24	91	---	---	---
Unknown	---	---	---	4	---	1	---	---	3	---	---	10	---	7	1	1	---	---
SCHOOL ATTENDANCE																		
Total 7 to 13 years, inclusive	15	1	49	1, 143	19	733	118	5	103	754	1	2, 055	2	223	1, 866	77	37	1
Number attending school	14	---	45	896	10	639	98	---	82	629	1	1, 832	2	195	1, 678	47	27	---
Percent attending school	---	---	---	78. 4	---	87. 2	83. 1	---	79. 6	83. 4	---	89. 1	---	87. 4	89. 9	---	---	---
Total 14 and 15 years, inclusive	2	1	19	291	7	210	32	1	30	203	---	533	---	53	516	26	11	1
Number attending school	2	---	18	221	3	171	27	---	19	180	---	446	---	44	445	14	7	---
Percent attending school	---	---	---	75. 9	---	81. 4	---	---	---	88. 7	---	83. 7	---	---	86. 2	---	---	---
Total 16 and 17 years, inclusive	4	---	20	310	3	205	31	1	27	216	---	538	---	49	579	19	13	---
Number attending school	3	---	12	157	1	108	11	---	10	147	---	321	---	14	354	3	1	---
Percent attending school	---	---	---	50. 6	---	52. 7	---	---	---	68. 1	---	59. 7	---	---	61. 1	---	---	---
Total 18 to 20 years, inclusive	8	---	29	455	10	324	27	2	46	311	---	854	---	82	870	55	17	---
Number attending school	---	---	5	49	---	22	1	---	1	81	---	114	---	3	163	1	1	---
Percent attending school	---	---	---	10. 8	---	6. 8	---	---	---	26. 0	---	13. 3	---	---	18. 7	---	---	---
ILLITERACY																		
Total 10 years old and over	69	14	508	5, 493	120	3, 598	392	22	778	3, 065	14	7, 757	3	1, 095	8, 889	556	186	3
Number illiterate	9	2	55	845	29	511	12	8	81	490	---	1, 005	---	248	1, 634	86	10	2
Percent illiterate	---	---	10. 8	15. 4	24. 2	14. 2	3. 1	---	10. 4	16. 0	---	13. 0	---	22. 6	18. 4	15. 5	5. 4	---
Percent illiterate in 1920	---	---	12. 7	16. 2	23. 0	18. 9	9. 6	---	48. 8	22. 3	---	21. 6	---	17. 2	24. 3	---	6. 4	---
URBAN AND RURAL																		
Urban population	---	---	518	---	---	1, 547	---	---	639	970	---	---	---	---	2, 655	333	---	---
Percent urban	---	---	87. 9	---	---	33. 2	---	---	68. 9	23. 7	---	---	---	---	23. 0	47. 6	---	---
Rural population	92	18	71	7, 187	139	3, 117	557	38	289	3, 130	15	10, 546	5	1, 369	8, 910	367	216	4
Rural-farm	70	15	4	5, 895	47	2, 727	238	37	110	3, 080	1	9, 460	5	713	8, 016	317	136	4
Rural-nonfarm	22	3	67	1, 292	92	390	319	1	179	50	14	1, 086	---	656	894	50	80	---
Percent rural	100. 0	---	12. 1	100. 0	100. 0	66. 8	100. 0	---	31. 1	76. 3	---	100. 0	---	100. 0	77. 0	52. 4	100. 0	---
MARITAL CONDITION																		
Males 15 years old and over	31	7	227	2, 388	52	1, 523	169	13	383	1, 252	7	3, 174	2	532	3, 848	257	82	2
Single	6	4	71	670	19	516	59	4	114	430	2	1, 001	---	171	1, 320	71	27	1
Married	23	3	127	1, 448	26	885	93	7	221	748	5	1, 910	2	292	2, 136	165	47	1
Widowed	1	---	27	178	6	86	14	---	27	63	---	189	---	54	313	16	6	---
Divorced	1	---	2	91	1	35	3	2	19	11	---	57	---	15	79	5	2	---
Unknown	---	---	---	1	---	1	---	---	2	---	---	17	---	---	---	---	---	---
Females 15 years old and over	28	6	239	2, 332	52	1, 566	152	7	327	1, 297	7	3, 178	1	405	3, 765	243	75	1
Single	1	3	37	451	10	397	44	---	58	308	---	812	---	63	913	26	15	---
Married	25	3	122	1, 439	26	892	90	7	200	782	7	1, 928	1	280	2, 158	173	46	1
Widowed	---	---	66	340	15	202	14	---	47	187	---	363	---	51	524	30	5	---
Divorced	2	---	14	101	1	75	3	---	22	20	---	65	---	10	170	14	9	---
Unknown	---	---	---	1	---	---	1	---	---	---	---	10	---	1	---	---	---	---
FAMILIES																		
Number of families	22	3	167	1, 844	42	1, 090	115	8	275	927	5	2, 241	2	318	2, 390	208	56	1
Median size	---	---	2. 49	3. 09	---	3. 34	4. 13	---	2. 07	3. 71	---	4. 00	---	2. 97	3. 71	2. 46	---	---
Families having—																		
No children under 10	13	1	128	1, 095	30	625	52	1	199	476	5	1, 033	1	200	1, 204	131	44	---
1 child under 10	4	1	18	288	8	181	21	2	46	175	---	458	---	44	473	40	6	1
2 children under 10	2	---	10	191	1	121	10	3	13	115	---	304	1	33	299	20	2	---
3 or more	3	1	11	270	3	163	32	2	17	161	---	446	---	41	414	17	4	---

CHARACTERISTICS OF NEGRO POPULATION BY COUNTIES: 1930—Continued

(See note at head of table)

SUBJECT	TEXAS—Continued																	
	Coke	Coleman	Collin	Collingsworth	Colorado	Comal	Comanche	Concho	Cooke	Coryell	Cottle	Crane	Crockett	Crosby	Culberson	Dallas	Dawson	Deaf Smith
POPULATION BY SEX																		
Negro population: 1930	66	635	3,979	774	5,955	316	1	82	1,235	506	558	18	40	342	7	47,879	261	12
Male	34	322	2,060	397	2,914	150	-	52	632	338	296	15	22	173	3	22,589	143	8
Female	32	313	1,919	377	3,041	166	1	30	603	168	262	3	18	169	4	25,290	118	4
Negro population: 1920	2	363	3,711	38	6,453	256	35	198	1,398	630	245	-	24	179	2	31,397	23	-
Male	2	195	1,861	25	3,138	127	20	118	710	419	154	-	15	114	1	15,610	17	-
Female	-	168	1,850	13	3,315	129	15	80	688	211	91	-	9	65	1	15,787	6	-
Percent of total population:																		
1930	1.3	2.7	8.6	5.4	31.1	2.6	-	1.1	5.1	2.5	5.9	0.8	1.5	3.1	0.6	14.7	1.9	0.2
1920	-	1.9	7.5	0.4	33.9	2.9	0.1	3.4	5.4	3.1	3.6	-	1.6	2.9	0.2	14.9	0.5	-
VOTING AGE: 1930																		
Total 21 years old and over	40	359	2,086	452	3,251	189	1	55	741	180	314	13	33	186	5	31,419	160	10
Male	22	186	1,095	252	1,603	92	-	35	370	93	181	12	17	95	2	14,894	89	7
Female	18	173	991	200	1,648	97	1	20	371	87	133	1	16	91	3	16,525	71	3
AGE: 1930																		
Under 5 years	13	54	441	73	616	26	-	5	104	33	59	-	2	40	2	3,597	27	1
Under 1 year	4	12	88	16	107	4	-	1	22	10	12	-	-	5	1	669	9	-
5 to 9 years	4	83	449	75	749	37	-	4	102	33	69	2	2	45	-	4,061	34	-
10 to 14 years	2	52	449	70	571	27	-	10	121	89	52	-	-	39	-	3,626	18	-
15 to 19 years	4	66	475	87	634	26	-	7	130	160	54	3	1	23	-	4,083	16	1
20 to 24 years	14	90	406	105	590	32	1	8	128	35	68	4	4	29	1	5,502	44	-
25 to 29 years	10	71	287	86	418	31	-	12	80	30	65	3	9	33	2	6,177	38	4
30 to 34 years	4	59	262	86	383	22	-	9	78	20	57	3	11	26	-	5,137	21	1
35 to 44 years	10	95	491	111	661	42	-	20	155	32	78	3	10	71	-	8,179	36	2
45 to 54 years	2	41	354	55	576	35	-	7	145	32	38	-	1	25	-	4,633	20	2
55 to 64 years	2	14	226	21	417	22	-	-	118	26	10	-	-	8	-	1,761	5	1
65 to 74 years	-	6	92	2	221	10	-	-	49	14	2	-	-	1	-	727	2	-
75 years and over	-	4	41	2	117	6	-	-	22	2	4	-	-	2	2	322	-	-
Unknown	1	-	6	1	2	-	-	-	3	-	2	-	-	-	-	74	-	-
SCHOOL ATTENDANCE																		
Total 7 to 13 years, inclusive	3	86	620	96	915	43	-	11	155	80	87	1	-	57	-	5,297	37	-
Number attending school	-	56	553	59	812	32	-	2	136	73	58	1	-	44	-	4,849	22	-
Percent attending school	-	-	89.2	-	88.7	-	-	-	87.7	-	-	-	-	-	-	91.5	-	-
Total 14 and 15 years, inclusive	-	26	181	35	207	8	-	4	49	66	19	-	-	14	-	1,471	7	-
Number attending school	-	20	160	16	165	4	-	1	41	64	10	-	-	10	-	1,212	4	-
Percent attending school	-	-	88.4	-	79.7	-	-	-	-	-	-	-	-	-	-	82.4	-	-
Total 16 and 17 years, inclusive	2	31	197	28	265	10	-	2	55	81	23	1	-	9	-	1,584	4	1
Number attending school	-	16	111	8	123	-	-	-	29	78	7	-	-	3	-	755	-	-
Percent attending school	-	-	56.3	-	46.4	-	-	-	-	-	-	-	-	-	-	47.7	-	-
Total 18 to 20 years, inclusive	5	43	263	59	398	22	-	3	87	53	32	2	3	16	-	2,881	15	-
Number attending school	-	2	46	2	29	-	-	-	20	33	3	-	-	-	-	271	-	-
Percent attending school	-	-	17.5	-	7.3	-	-	-	-	-	-	-	-	-	-	9.4	-	-
ILLITERACY																		
Total 10 years old and over	49	498	3,089	626	4,590	253	1	73	1,029	440	430	16	36	257	5	40,221	200	11
Number illiterate	25	98	534	104	839	43	-	10	167	43	97	6	4	53	2	3,012	27	-
Percent illiterate	-	19.7	17.3	16.6	18.3	17.0	-	-	16.2	9.8	22.6	-	-	20.6	-	7.5	13.5	-
Percent illiterate in 1920	-	15.4	17.4	-	24.2	17.6	-	20.6	12.2	11.2	34.1	-	-	13.0	-	12.5	-	-
URBAN AND RURAL																		
Urban population	-	405	767	347	-	233	-	-	926	255	221	-	-	-	-	40,166	78	-
Percent urban	-	63.8	19.3	44.8	-	73.7	-	-	75.0	50.4	39.6	-	-	-	-	83.9	29.9	-
Rural population	66	230	3,212	427	5,955	83	1	82	309	251	337	18	40	342	7	7,713	183	12
Rural-farm	60	131	1,880	360	3,699	51	1	75	295	62	332	-	5	179	4	4,322	145	45
Rural-nonfarm	6	99	1,332	67	2,256	32	-	7	14	189	5	18	35	163	3	3,391	38	7
Percent rural	-	36.2	80.7	55.2	100.0	26.3	-	-	25.0	49.6	60.4	-	-	100.0	-	16.1	70.1	-
MARITAL CONDITION																		
Males 15 years old and over	23	226	1,362	293	1,961	110	-	39	456	233	206	14	18	111	2	16,975	99	7
Single	5	73	403	71	568	28	-	13	128	152	55	4	1	20	-	4,200	26	-
Married	16	121	798	193	1,193	73	-	21	267	61	125	8	17	73	2	10,777	63	7
Widowed	2	26	116	14	147	3	-	5	47	8	15	-	-	10	-	1,409	5	-
Divorced	-	6	40	13	52	6	-	-	13	12	11	2	-	8	-	573	5	-
Unknown	-	-	5	2	1	-	-	-	1	-	-	-	-	-	-	16	-	-
Females 15 years old and over	24	220	1,278	263	2,058	116	1	24	452	118	172	2	18	107	3	19,620	83	4
Single	4	42	248	37	446	15	-	2	85	36	30	-	-	11	-	3,261	9	-
Married	18	127	808	194	1,198	74	-	21	264	61	129	2	17	76	2	11,446	62	3
Widowed	2	39	166	26	309	21	1	-	89	9	8	-	1	17	-	3,632	10	-
Divorced	-	11	52	6	103	6	-	1	14	12	5	-	-	3	1	1,261	2	1
Unknown	-	1	4	-	2	-	-	-	-	-	-	-	-	-	-	20	-	-
FAMILIES																		
Number of families	15	153	998	236	1,607	91	-	26	375	83	154	12	19	95	2	12,767	78	3
Median size	-	2.58	3.14	2.29	3.02	-	-	-	2.46	-	2.81	-	-	-	-	2.52	-	-
amilies having—																		
No children under 10	7	94	600	159	970	64	-	19	273	52	95	11	17	60	2	8,971	51	3
1 child under 10	2	23	161	41	277	11	-	6	47	12	26	-	1	13	-	1,886	10	-
2 children under 10	4	14	115	15	146	4	-	-	20	11	15	1	-	7	-	973	7	-
or more	2	22	122	21	214	12	-	1	35	8	18	-	1	15	-	937	10	-

CHARACTERISTICS OF NEGRO POPULATION BY COUNTIES: 1930—Continued

(See note at head of table)

SUBJECT	TEXAS—Continued																	
	Delta	Denton	De Witt	Dickens	Dimmit	Donley	Duval	Eastland	Ector	Edwards	Ellis	El Paso	Erath	Falls	Fannin	Fayette	Fisher	Floyd
POPULATION BY SEX																		
Negro population: 1930	995	2, 159	4, 392	364	18	177	17	701	123	9	12, 610	1, 970	216	12, 515	4, 618	6, 921	443	126
Male	526	1, 107	2, 095	178	13	85	9	323	70	7	6, 407	1, 023	114	6, 254	2, 313	3, 374	234	66
Female	469	1, 052	2, 297	186	5	92	8	378	53	2	6, 203	947	102	6, 261	2, 305	3, 547	209	6
Negro population: 1920	1, 400	2, 580	5, 206	197	31	34	1	665	-	3	12, 662	1, 548	393	11, 555	5, 968	6, 755	314	11
Male	731	1, 298	2, 430	117	20	14	-	391	-	2	6, 441	847	210	5, 761	3, 015	3, 357	180	100
Female	669	1, 282	2, 776	80	11	20	1	274	-	1	6, 221	701	183	5, 794	2, 953	3, 398	134	1
Percent of total population:																		
1930	7. 6	6. 6	16. 0	4. 2	0. 2	1. 7	0. 1	2. 1	3. 1	0. 3	23. 4	1. 5	1. 0	32. 3	11. 2	22. 5	3. 3	1. 0
1920	8. 8	7. 3	18. 6	3. 4	0. 6	0. 4	-	1. 1	-	0. 1	22. 7	1. 5	1. 4	31. 9	12. 4	22. 5	2. 9	0. 1
VOTING AGE: 1930																		
Total 21 years old and over	558	1, 221	2, 437	174	11	105	11	486	93	7	6, 605	1, 399	151	5, 994	2, 546	3, 428	249	74
Male	303	641	1, 147	95	8	54	6	228	53	6	3, 386	726	80	3, 007	1, 301	1, 696	138	45
Female	255	580	1, 290	79	3	51	5	258	40	1	3, 219	673	71	2, 987	1, 245	1, 732	111	29
AGE: 1930																		
Under 5 years	84	215	407	43	-	16	2	49	7	-	1, 271	132	10	1, 499	457	819	46	19
Under 1 year	20	52	82	12	-	5	-	11	1	-	239	39	2	307	96	147	11	4
5 to 9 years	98	221	488	58	6	17	-	50	6	1	1, 511	154	17	1, 700	512	946	53	15
10 to 14 years	110	226	494	41	-	19	2	39	5	-	1, 321	122	19	1, 598	499	788	40	7
15 to 19 years	121	227	469	45	1	18	2	62	10	1	1, 558	133	15	1, 434	506	791	40	9
20 to 24 years	110	206	418	17	-	18	1	73	21	2	1, 297	186	17	1, 228	467	663	48	15
25 to 29 years	101	181	334	40	-	27	2	84	22	1	969	199	19	853	378	514	45	21
30 to 34 years	66	139	304	24	1	17	3	93	20	1	873	188	10	708	298	401	32	13
35 to 44 years	138	251	588	55	1	21	3	147	22	1	1, 625	418	37	1, 442	605	690	84	11
45 to 54 years	77	232	406	27	2	17	2	71	9	1	1, 160	291	33	1, 030	422	595	30	13
55 to 64 years	54	150	255	8	3	4	-	21	1	1	620	89	21	558	243	380	19	3
65 to 74 years	23	80	154	2	3	2	-	9	-	-	288	41	10	320	150	224	4	-
75 years and over	13	30	72	4	1	1	-	3	-	-	113	16	6	145	63	109	2	-
Unknown	-	1	3	-	-	-	-	-	-	-	4	1	2	-	18	1	-	-
SCHOOL ATTENDANCE																		
Total 7 to 13 years, inclusive	149	313	687	72	4	25	2	62	7	1	1, 962	187	26	2, 251	681	1, 224	62	16
Number attending school	132	231	573	41	-	16	2	58	7	-	1, 727	176	25	2, 089	604	1, 110	45	13
Percent attending school	88. 6	73. 8	83. 4	-	-	-	-	-	-	-	88. 0	94. 1	-	92. 8	88. 7	90. 7	-	-
Total 14 and 15 years, inclusive	53	93	211	17	-	7	-	20	3	-	594	42	4	643	211	316	12	1
Number attending school	47	68	186	9	-	5	-	15	2	-	507	38	3	579	176	259	7	-
Percent attending school	-	-	88. 2	-	-	-	-	-	-	-	85. 4	-	-	90. 0	83. 4	82. 0	-	-
Total 16 and 17 years, inclusive	49	89	185	20	1	10	-	28	2	1	640	60	8	593	207	311	19	3
Number attending school	27	37	82	12	-	2	-	7	1	-	316	36	4	346	108	142	9	1
Percent attending school	-	-	44. 3	-	-	-	-	-	-	-	49. 4	-	-	58. 3	52. 2	45. 7	-	-
Total 18 to 20 years, inclusive	67	138	276	19	-	7	2	38	8	-	944	85	11	816	291	455	31	7
Number attending school	9	11	38	2	-	-	-	3	-	-	127	16	4	97	31	47	-	-
Percent attending school	-	8. 0	13. 8	-	-	-	-	-	-	-	13. 5	-	-	11. 9	10. 7	10. 3	-	-
ILLITERACY																		
Total 10 years old and over	813	1, 723	3, 497	263	12	144	15	602	110	8	9, 828	1, 684	189	9, 316	3, 649	5, 156	344	92
Number illiterate	121	222	472	30	5	18	3	35	14	1	1, 306	68	33	1, 284	473	654	59	16
Percent illiterate	14. 9	12. 9	13. 5	11. 4	-	12. 5	-	5. 8	12. 7	-	13. 3	4. 0	17. 5	13. 8	13. 0	12. 7	17. 2	-
Percent illiterate in 1920	19. 3	12. 0	15. 8	21. 0	-	-	-	13. 3	-	-	19. 9	2. 9	19. 2	17. 4	17. 6	17. 0	9. 6	-
URBAN AND RURAL																		
Urban population	-	789	1, 713	-	-	124	-	688	-	-	3, 867	1, 855	128	1, 676	908	-	-	54
Percent urban	-	365	39. 0	-	-	70. 1	-	98. 1	-	-	30. 7	94. 2	59. 3	13. 4	19. 7	-	-	42. 9
Rural population	995	1, 370	2, 679	364	18	53	17	13	123	9	8, 743	115	88	10, 839	3, 710	6, 921	443	72
Rural-farm	631	1, 017	1, 995	186	12	48	8	1	1	4	7, 163	67	43	9, 312	2, 507	5, 148	265	57
Rural-nonfarm	364	353	684	178	6	5	9	12	122	5	1, 580	48	45	1, 527	1, 203	1, 773	178	15
Percent rural	100. 0	63. 5	61. 0	100. 0	-	29. 9	-	1. 9	100. 0	-	69. 3	5. 8	40. 7	86. 6	80. 3	100. 0	100. 0	57. 1
MARITAL CONDITION																		
Males 15 years old and over	374	767	1, 395	117	8	62	6	258	61	7	4, 331	798	88	3, 848	1, 593	2, 124	167	50
Single	106	221	425	36	2	19	1	52	14	2	1, 228	229	22	1, 111	440	671	36	13
Married	232	463	842	68	3	39	5	183	41	3	2, 569	487	56	2, 334	982	1, 281	114	30
Widowed	26	60	91	9	3	3	-	15	1	1	412	52	10	310	112	133	11	3
Divorced	10	23	34	4	-	1	-	7	5	1	121	30	-	92	49	39	6	4
Unknown	-	-	3	-	-	-	-	1	-	-	1	-	-	1	10	-	-	-
Females 15 years old and over	329	730	1, 608	105	4	63	7	305	44	1	4, 176	764	82	3, 870	1, 557	2, 244	137	35
Single	59	140	397	19	2	13	1	50	4	-	768	109	15	767	271	562	11	4
Married	214	454	864	70	1	38	5	196	37	1	2, 553	493	53	2, 335	974	1, 309	107	30
Widowed	46	112	253	12	1	12	1	43	2	-	717	132	13	591	257	307	15	1
Divorced	10	23	92	4	-	-	-	16	1	-	138	29	1	174	48	63	4	-
Unknown	-	1	2	-	-	-	-	-	-	-	-	1	-	3	7	3	-	-
FAMILIES																		
Number of families	279	581	1, 140	83	3	48	4	220	23	1	3, 247	594	73	2, 933	1, 231	1, 564	122	30
Median size	2. 91	2. 98	3. 07	-	-	-	-	2. 22	-	-	3. 05	2. 26	-	3. 47	2. 92	3. 69	2. 54	-
Families having—																		
No children under 10	182	359	722	48	1	29	3	174	16	1	1, 960	458	61	1, 555	792	827	80	14
1 child under 10	57	108	174	8	-	11	1	22	3	-	546	60	6	530	168	269	19	7
2 children under 10	12	59	101	9	1	3	-	9	3	-	327	35	3	346	112	189	8	5
3 or more	28	55	143	18	1	5	-	15	1	-	414	41	3	502	159	279	15	4

CHARACTERISTICS OF NEGRO POPULATION BY COUNTIES: 1930—Continued

(See note at head of table)

SUBJECT	Foard	Fort Bend	Franklin	Freestone	Frio	Gaines	Galveston	Garza	Gillespie	Glasscock	Goliad	Gonzales	Gray	Grayson	Gregg	Grimes	Guadalupe	Hale
	TEXAS—Continued																	
POPULATION BY SEX																		
Negro population: 1930	307	9,787	442	8,776	104	6	14,759	78	128	14	1,040	6,256	306	7,009	8,198	9,700	4,578	320
Male	164	5,167	234	4,368	58	3	7,173	44	77	8	511	3,060	162	3,356	3,944	4,754	2,303	172
Female	143	4,620	208	4,408	46	3	7,586	34	51	6	529	3,196	144	3,653	4,254	4,946	2,275	148
Negro population: 1920	29	9,996	573	9,259	85	-------	11,123	5	57	-------	1,184	7,062	-------	7,694	8,169	9,810	5,259	7
Male	16	5,362	297	4,596	42	-------	5,730	4	31	-------	569	3,464	-------	3,811	3,999	4,818	2,612	5
Female	13	4,634	276	4,663	43	-------	5,393	1	26	-------	615	3,598	-------	3,883	4,170	4,992	2,647	2
Percent of total population:																		
1930	4.9	32.9	5.2	38.9	1.1	0.2	22.9	1.4	1.2	1.1	10.3	22.1	1.4	10.6	52.0	42.8	15.8	1.6
1920	0.6	43.6	6.2	39.8	0.9	-------	20.9	0.1	0.6	-------	12.7	24.8	-------	10.4	48.7	42.5	19.0	0.1
VOTING AGE: 1930																		
Total 21 years old and over	172	5,517	218	4,222	46	3	10,079	50	80	4	561	3,057	241	4,291	3,892	4,907	2,382	232
Male	101	2,945	117	2,116	27	2	4,992	30	49	2	272	1,491	140	2,035	1,856	2,418	1,228	133
Female	71	2,572	101	2,106	19	1	5,087	20	31	2	289	1,566	101	2,256	2,036	2,489	1,154	99
AGE: 1930																		
Under 5 years	31	935	63	1,041	13	2	1,086	7	13	1	91	722	13	564	925	971	474	19
Under 1 year	6	178	11	190	2	1	205	-------	3	-------	21	130	3	111	169	191	98	3
5 to 9 years	30	1,097	37	1,208	15	1	1,183	9	13	2	119	843	8	628	1,118	1,179	584	22
10 to 14 years	27	993	53	1,071	14	-------	964	8	8	2	132	757	11	626	1,079	1,215	510	19
15 to 19 years	32	1,031	59	1,034	12	-------	1,153	3	10	5	112	745	23	759	997	1,204	530	21
20 to 24 years	40	989	45	847	10	-------	1,612	11	26	2	92	562	38	672	763	935	440	49
25 to 29 years	45	782	32	597	8	2	1,933	6	18	-------	69	429	67	544	612	703	309	57
30 to 34 years	25	632	13	474	6	1	1,555	6	10	-------	48	400	53	524	507	580	268	49
35 to 44 years	50	1,326	54	943	9	-------	2,736	19	12	2	132	658	63	1,003	894	1,109	574	49
45 to 54 years	15	1,036	38	722	5	-------	1,579	6	11	-------	102	515	25	905	698	947	444	22
55 to 64 years	11	593	21	486	10	-------	621	1	4	-------	68	302	4	452	340	501	246	8
65 to 74 years	1	239	17	230	-------	-------	205	1	1	-------	52	214	-------	216	168	221	124	3
75 years and over	-------	134	10	123	2	-------	125	-------	2	-------	23	109	-------	87	95	132	72	1
Unknown	-------	-------	-------	-------	-------	-------	7	1	-------	-------	-------	-------	1	29	2	3	3	1
SCHOOL ATTENDANCE																		
Total 7 to 13 years, inclusive	37	1,429	59	1,607	21	-------	1,489	13	16	3	186	1,130	9	889	1,545	1,684	726	27
Number attending school	27	1,279	51	1,439	20	-------	1,416	2	10	-------	160	924	7	831	1,409	1,256	630	17
Percent attending school	-------	89.5	-------	89.5	-------	-------	95.1	-------	-------	-------	86.0	81.8	-------	93.5	91.2	74.6	86.8	-------
Total 14 and 15 years, inclusive	10	395	28	417	5	-------	425	2	2	3	47	316	7	263	409	491	247	9
Number attending school	6	320	24	378	4	-------	379	1	1	-------	37	268	3	229	335	361	202	5
Percent attending school	-------	81.0	-------	90.6	-------	-------	89.2	-------	-------	-------	-------	84.8	-------	87.1	81.9	73.5	81.8	-------
Total 16 and 17 years, inclusive	14	425	25	402	4	-------	444	1	3	1	44	317	6	294	408	478	203	6
Number attending school	3	157	12	286	1	-------	257	-------	-------	-------	22	164	1	197	248	204	111	1
Percent attending school	-------	36.9	-------	71.1	-------	-------	57.9	-------	-------	-------	-------	51.7	-------	67.0	60.8	42.7	54.7	-------
Total 18 to 20 years	29	630	37	616	10	-------	779	2	10	1	68	404	24	457	586	678	306	18
Number attending school	-------	36	5	109	3	-------	104	-------	-------	-------	9	43	-------	99	94	68	50	-------
Percent attending school	-------	5.7	-------	17.7	-------	-------	13.4	-------	-------	-------	-------	10.6	-------	21.7	16.0	10.0	16.3	-------
ILLITERACY																		
Total 10 years old and over	246	7,755	342	6,527	76	3	12,490	62	102	11	830	4,691	285	5,817	6,155	7,550	3,520	279
Number illiterate	45	1,409	60	800	6	1	1,163	12	28	1	96	545	23	698	907	1,409	342	35
Percent illiterate	18.3	18.2	17.5	12.3	-------	-------	9.3	-------	27.5	-------	11.6	11.6	8.1	12.0	14.7	18.7	9.7	12.5
Percent illiterate in 1920	-------	29.7	22.5	15.0	-------	-------	10.4	-------	-------	-------	18.6	18.1	-------	15.4	18.9	24.3	14.4	-------
URBAN AND RURAL																		
Urban population	-------	-------	-------	593	55	-------	13,694	-------	-------	-------	-------	746	267	4,635	1,737	2,483	1,014	241
Percent urban	-------	-------	-------	6.8	52.9	-------	92.8	-------	-------	-------	-------	11.9	87.3	66.1	21.2	25.6	22.1	75.3
Rural population	307	9,787	442	8,183	49	6	1,065	78	128	14	1,040	5,510	39	2,374	6,461	7,217	3,564	79
Rural-farm	155	7,728	377	7,564	49	5	285	51	38	14	608	4,689	10	1,353	5,734	6,791	3,087	60
Rural-nonfarm	152	2,059	65	619	-------	1	780	27	90	-------	432	821	29	1,021	727	426	477	19
Percent rural	100.0	100.0	100.0	93.2	47.1	-------	7.2	-------	100.0	-------	100.0	88.1	12.7	33.9	78.8	74.4	77.9	24.7
MARITAL CONDITION																		
Males 15 years old and over	121	3,597	152	2,686	33	2	5,589	32	58	6	336	1,900	151	2,450	2,425	3,059	1,529	145
Single	39	1,142	53	817	15	1	1,505	4	20	5	110	638	36	674	724	910	520	46
Married	75	2,071	86	1,625	15	1	3,350	17	30	1	197	1,099	104	1,475	1,504	1,801	907	80
Widowed	4	283	13	181	2	-------	338	10	3	-------	23	129	6	218	161	288	71	12
Divorced	3	101	-------	60	1	-------	390	1	5	-------	6	34	5	81	35	59	30	7
Unknown	-------	-------	-------	3	-------	-------	6	-------	-------	-------	-------	-------	-------	2	1	1	1	-------
Females 15 years old and over	98	3,165	137	2,770	29	1	5,937	22	36	3	362	2,034	123	2,741	2,651	3,276	1,481	115
Single	14	634	27	641	8	-------	1,031	3	2	2	107	563	16	532	580	798	371	8
Married	75	1,928	88	1,659	14	1	3,440	16	28	1	197	1,105	95	1,524	1,545	1,833	900	84
Widowed	9	508	16	382	3	-------	922	-------	2	-------	44	321	6	563	418	520	163	20
Divorced	-------	95	6	88	4	-------	535	3	4	-------	13	42	6	121	107	124	44	3
Unknown	-------	-------	-------	-------	-------	-------	9	-------	-------	-------	1	3	-------	1	1	1	3	-------
FAMILIES																		
Number of families	95	2,519	101	1,973	21	1	4,166	26	32	1	253	1,400	94	1,944	1,923	2,408	1,040	97
Median size	-------	2.84	3.65	3.71	-------	-------	2.41	-------	-------	-------	3.29	3.74	-------	2.80	3.54	3.36	3.59	-------
Families having—																		
No children under 10	66	1,607	52	1,005	12	-------	3,020	18	22	-------	145	740	82	1,359	1,023	1,404	585	78
1 child under 10	14	371	21	371	-------	-------	603	1	2	-------	59	240	7	271	363	431	169	10
2 children under 10	8	240	13	230	3	-------	267	6	4	-------	22	166	4	155	223	259	115	4
or more	7	301	15	367	6	1	276	1	4	1	27	254	1	159	314	314	171	5

CHARACTERISTICS OF NEGRO POPULATION BY COUNTIES: 1930—Continued

(See note at head of table)

TEXAS—Continued

SUBJECT	Hall	Hansford	Hardeman	Hardin	Harris	Harrison	Hartley	Haskell	Hays
POPULATION BY SEX									
Negro population: 1930	793	2	608	2, 471	72, 603	29, 409	1	409	1, 289
Male	426	1	332	1, 183	34, 962	14, 262	1	215	600
Female	367	1	276	1, 288	37, 641	15, 147	-	194	689
Negro population: 1920	8	-	188	3, 007	42, 734	26, 858	1	361	1, 679
Male	6	-	129	1, 626	20, 873	13, 071	1	215	788
Female	2	-	59	1, 381	21, 861	13, 787	-	146	891
Percent of total population: 1930	4. 7	0. 1	4. 2	17. 7	20. 2	60. 1	-	2. 5	8. 6
1920	0. 1	-	1. 5	18. 8	22. 9	61. 7	0. 1	2. 5	10. 5
VOTING AGE: 1930									
Total 21 years old and over	458	2	354	1, 428	47, 709	13, 686	1	232	727
Male	250	1	195	692	23, 367	6, 645	1	128	329
Female	208	1	159	736	24, 342	7, 041	-	104	398
AGE: 1930									
Under 5 years	84	-	65	231	5, 589	3, 644	-	45	121
Under 1 year	14	-	17	44	1, 078	687	-	7	25
5 to 9 years	75	-	66	291	6, 145	3, 937	-	49	129
10 to 14 years	80	-	52	229	5, 188	3, 749	-	41	126
15 to 19 years	76	-	59	237	6, 284	3, 614	-	39	163
20 to 24 years	101	-	78	223	9, 008	3, 126	-	25	126
25 to 29 years	92	1	79	229	9, 626	2, 204	-	51	82
30 to 34 years	81	-	83	201	7, 547	1, 630	-	41	71
35 to 44 years	125	1	68	373	12, 075	2, 960	-	61	171
45 to 54 years	53	-	45	289	6, 702	2, 219	-	37	119
55 to 64 years	19	-	9	110	2, 613	1, 362	1	16	94
65 to 74 years	3	-	2	42	1, 002	624	-	3	45
75 years and over	3	-	2	15	486	320	-	1	42
Unknown	1	-	-	1	338	20	-	-	-
SCHOOL ATTENDANCE									
Total 7 to 13 years, inclusive	119	-	80	370	7, 862	5, 435	-	66	170
Number attending school	61	-	26	358	7, 355	4, 900	-	41	131
Percent attending school	51. 3	-	-	96. 8	93. 6	90. 2	-	-	77. 1
Total 14 and 15 years, inclusive	26	-	21	84	2, 057	1, 428	-	15	53
Number attending school	15	-	11	76	1, 736	1, 275	-	11	46
Percent attending school	-	-	-	-	84. 4	89. 3	-	-	-
Total 16 and 17 years, inclusive	28	-	28	96	2, 396	1, 465	-	13	67
Number attending school	8	-	4	59	1, 202	880	-	5	45
Percent attending school	-	-	-	-	50. 2	60. 1	-	-	-
Total 18 to 20 years, inclusive	52	-	35	153	4, 553	2, 234	-	18	94
Number attending school	2	-	1	35	591	404	-	2	30
Percent attending school	-	-	-	22. 9	13. 0	18. 1	-	-	-
ILLITERACY									
Total 10 years old and over	634	2	477	1, 949	60, 869	21, 828	1	315	1, 039
Number illiterate	98	-	66	277	5, 194	2, 983	1	63	115
Percent illiterate	15. 5	-	13. 8	14. 2	8. 5	13. 7	-	20. 0	11. 1
Percent illiterate in 1920	-	-	7. 9	19. 2	12. 4	24. 4	-	19. 0	10. 9
URBAN AND RURAL									
Urban population	239	-	211	-	64, 120	6, 693	-	169	645
Percent urban	30. 1	-	34. 7	-	88. 3	22. 8	-	41. 3	50. 0
Rural population	554	2	397	2, 471	8, 483	22, 716	1	240	644
Rural-farm	445	-	349	138	3, 508	21, 544	-	182	404
Rural-nonfarm	109	2	48	2, 333	4, 975	1, 172	1	58	240
Percent rural	69. 9	-	65. 3	100. 0	11. 7	77. 2	-	58. 7	50. 0
MARITAL CONDITION									
Males 15 years old and over	295	1	219	809	26, 683	8, 684	1	141	409
Single	82	-	54	207	7, 176	2, 664	1	28	131
Married	185	1	144	526	16, 480	5, 331	-	96	234
Widowed	21	-	19	51	1, 964	540	-	11	31
Divorced	7	-	2	25	1, 017	147	-	6	11
Unknown	-	-	-	-	46	2	-	-	2
Females 15 years old and over	259	1	206	911	28, 998	9, 395	-	133	504
Single	25	-	26	156	5, 074	2, 155	-	22	145
Married	193	1	148	573	17, 059	5, 353	-	94	241
Widowed	28	-	23	135	5, 065	1, 575	-	9	98
Divorced	13	-	9	45	1, 763	310	-	8	19
Unknown	-	-	-	2	37	2	-	-	1
FAMILIES									
Number of families	221	1	171	697	19, 340	6, 594	-	125	339
Median size	2. 44	-	2. 43	2. 70	2. 63	3. 73	-	2. 27	3. 11
Families having—									
No children under 10	146	1	110	453	13, 502	3, 341	-	90	221
1 child under 10	30	-	31	102	2, 875	1, 220	-	12	53
2 children under 10	20	-	10	68	1, 522	819	-	6	27
3 or more	25	-	20	74	1, 411	1, 214	-	17	38

SUBJECT	Hemphill	Henderson	Hidalgo	Hill	Hockley	Hood	Hopkins	Houston	Howard
POPULATION BY SEX									
Negro population: 1930	9	5, 792	491	5, 913	92	109	2, 749	12, 374	523
Male	5	2, 876	239	2, 963	51	56	1, 375	6, 374	283
Female	4	2, 916	252	2, 950	41	53	1, 374	6, 000	240
Negro population: 1920	2	4, 860	87	5, 441	-	171	3, 011	10, 793	-
Male	2	2, 447	55	2, 718	-	85	1, 494	5, 472	-
Female	-	2, 413	32	2, 723	-	86	1, 517	5, 321	-
Percent of total population: 1930	0. 2	18. 9	0. 6	13. 7	1. 0	1. 6	9. 3	41. 2	2. 3
1920	-	17. 2	0. 2	12. 6	-	2. 0	8. 7	37. 7	-
VOTING AGE: 1930									
Total 21 years old and over	2	2, 772	363	3, 193	51	69	1, 277	5, 969	378
Male	2	1, 422	186	1, 651	29	38	645	3, 114	213
Female	-	1, 350	177	1, 542	22	31	632	2, 855	165
AGE: 1930									
Under 5 years	-	723	30	651	7	8	322	1, 397	30
Under 1 year	-	149	7	137	2	-	65	208	7
5 to 9 years	2	764	31	663	13	14	356	1, 544	46
10 to 14 years	3	683	23	613	8	3	367	1, 509	23
15 to 19 years	2	704	32	656	11	12	364	1, 588	34
20 to 24 years	-	594	85	611	9	14	260	1, 407	80
25 to 29 years	-	443	97	514	12	7	182	1, 010	86
30 to 34 years	-	363	67	418	7	5	168	710	89
35 to 44 years	2	659	75	777	16	16	264	1, 249	94
45 to 54 years	-	452	38	562	4	12	229	1, 000	31
55 to 64 years	-	245	5	248	4	13	132	632	7
65 to 74 years	-	107	5	121	1	1	67	237	1
75 years and over	-	54	1	71	-	3	34	91	2
Unknown	-	1	2	8	-	1	4	-	-
SCHOOL ATTENDANCE									
Total 7 to 13 years, inclusive	3	1, 001	33	875	16	10	514	2, 115	42
Number attending school	1	859	18	764	6	8	412	1, 547	31
Percent attending school	-	85. 8	-	87. 3	-	-	80. 2	73. 1	-
Total 14 and 15 years, inclusive	1	270	10	241	3	3	148	576	12
Number attending school	-	236	5	194	-	1	128	402	9
Percent attending school	-	87. 4	-	80. 5	-	-	86. 5	69. 8	-
Total 16 and 17 years, inclusive	2	267	12	273	5	3	156	650	15
Number attending school	-	164	-	161	-	-	103	272	2
Percent attending school	-	61. 4	-	59. 0	-	-	66. 0	41. 8	-
Total 18 to 20 years, inclusive	-	445	27	408	6	10	196	1, 034	28
Number attending school	-	79	2	67	-	1	46	97	1
Percent attending school	-	17. 8	-	16. 4	-	-	23. 5	9. 4	-
ILLITERACY									
Total 10 years old and over	7	4, 305	430	4, 599	72	87	2, 071	9, 433	447
Number illiterate	5	581	18	713	8	12	242	1, 996	33
Percent illiterate	-	13. 5	4. 2	15. 5	-	-	11. 7	21. 2	7. 4
Percent illiterate in 1920	-	18. 9	-	19. 8	-	22. 5	19. 2	20. 4	-
URBAN AND RURAL									
Urban population	-	1, 140	375	1, 289	-	-	1, 005	1, 772	490
Percent urban	-	19. 7	76. 4	21. 8	-	-	36. 6	14. 3	93. 7
Rural population	9	4, 652	116	4, 624	92	109	1, 744	10, 602	33
Rural-farm	9	4, 071	45	3, 178	81	40	1, 694	10, 135	26
Rural-nonfarm	-	581	71	1, 446	11	69	50	467	7
Percent rural	-	80. 3	23. 6	78. 2	-	100. 0	63. 4	85. 7	6. 3
MARITAL CONDITION									
Males 15 years old and over	3	1, 805	204	2, 054	36	42	849	4, 132	231
Single	1	565	54	606	10	12	286	1, 586	65
Married	-	1, 068	132	1, 203	24	22	488	2, 241	148
Widowed	2	149	9	177	2	4	60	208	7
Divorced	-	23	9	66	-	4	12	94	10
Unknown	-	-	-	2	-	-	3	3	1
Females 15 years old and over	1	1, 817	203	1, 932	28	42	855	3, 792	193
Single	1	451	30	358	2	10	229	957	23
Married	-	1, 053	132	1, 226	24	24	477	2, 249	143
Widowed	-	272	25	277	1	4	129	438	11
Divorced	-	41	16	69	1	4	19	141	16
Unknown	-	-	-	2	-	-	1	7	-
FAMILIES									
Number of families	1	1, 289	176	1, 524	26	29	591	2, 775	168
Median size	-	3. 61	1. 93	3. 11	-	-	4. 07	3. 56	2. 22
Families having—									
No children under 10	-	649	144	921	17	21	309	1, 522	126
1 child under 10	-	236	17	257	4	2	100	477	24
2 children under 10	1	159	10	159	1	1	65	285	10
3 or more	-	245	5	187	4	5	117	491	8

CHARACTERISTICS OF NEGRO POPULATION BY COUNTIES: 1930—Continued

(See note at head of table)

SUBJECT	TEXAS—Continued																	
	Hudspeth	Hunt	Hutchinson	Irion	Jack	Jackson	Jasper	Jeff Davis	Jefferson	Jim Hogg	Jim Wells	Johnson	Jones	Karnes	Kaufman	Kendall	Kent	Kerr
POPULATION BY SEX																		
Negro population: 1930	20	5, 653	131	6	83	1, 908	5, 005	20	33, 022	20	234	1, 944	863	1, 003	11, 511	66	40	477
Male	10	2, 835	68	3	45	986	2, 590	10	16, 229	9	125	972	421	484	5, 885	34	21	234
Female	10	2, 818	63	3	38	922	2, 415	10	16, 793	11	109	972	442	519	5, 626	32	19	243
Negro population: 1920	11	5, 713	1	5	35	2, 176	4, 982	8	19, 586	13	68	2, 121	568	1, 009	12, 104	136	47	282
Male	6	2, 883	1	4	15	1, 080	2, 655	4	9, 978	8	38	1, 056	319	518	6, 148	64	29	138
Female	5	2, 830	-	1	20	1, 096	2, 327	4	9, 608	5	30	1, 065	249	491	5, 956	72	18	144
Percent of total population:																		
1930	0. 5	11. 5	0. 9	0. 3	0. 9	17. 4	29. 3	1. 1	24. 8	0. 4	1. 7	5. 8	3. 6	4. 3	28. 1	1. 3	1. 0	4. 7
1920	1. 1	11. 3	0. 1	0. 3	0. 4	19. 4	32. 0	0. 6	26. 8	0. 7	1. 0	5. 7	2. 5	5. 3	29. 3	2. 8	1. 4	4. 8
VOTING AGE: 1930																		
Total 21 years old and over	15	2, 924	97	6	51	985	2, 541	9	19, 542	11	126	1, 072	483	502	5, 698	47	24	296
Male	8	1, 468	52	3	27	504	1, 351	5	9, 866	6	66	547	238	259	2, 979	21	14	143
Female	7	1, 456	45	3	24	481	1, 190	4	9, 676	5	60	525	245	243	2, 719	26	10	153
AGE: 1930																		
Under 5 years	3	573	10	-	9	219	553	3	3, 157	1	16	211	105	104	1, 303	2	7	38
Under 1 year	1	111	1	-	2	32	101	1	562	1	4	36	18	21	274	-	2	5
5 to 9 years	1	669	8	-	7	224	654	3	3, 469	3	32	221	104	135	1, 473	3	2	49
10 to 14 years	-	663	8	-	7	229	580	4	2, 993	1	23	186	86	116	1, 391	8	4	39
15 to 19 years	1	684	6	-	6	224	563	1	3, 147	4	33	206	68	132	1, 397	5	2	39
20 to 24 years	1	586	13	-	9	177	533	-	3, 971	1	19	208	88	91	1, 126	4	2	60
25 to 29 years	1	483	26	1	7	148	429	1	4, 146	3	19	178	76	76	929	2	3	55
30 to 34 years	1	404	19	2	12	102	364	2	3, 018	2	18	138	83	67	698	6	2	36
35 to 44 years	6	672	27	2	7	207	540	2	5, 205	3	34	255	142	99	1, 374	8	11	79
45 to 54 years	4	495	10	1	12	182	429	2	2, 613	2	24	169	76	96	990	5	3	43
55 to 64 years	1	256	3	-	3	115	208	-	814	-	11	111	20	38	505	9	4	19
65 to 74 years	1	121	-	-	2	54	106	1	319	-	1	38	10	27	218	9	-	9
75 years and over	-	47	1	-	2	26	41	1	136	-	4	21	5	21	107	5	-	6
Unknown	-	-	-	-	-	1	5	-	34	-	-	2	-	1	-	-	-	5
SCHOOL ATTENDANCE																		
Total 7 to 13 years, inclusive	1	919	13	-	7	317	875	6	4, 463	3	35	297	133	163	2, 027	5	3	63
Number attending school	-	805	9	-	7	271	775	-	4, 134	-	32	265	119	142	1, 616	3	-	61
Percent attending school	-	87. 6	-	-	-	85. 5	88. 6	-	92. 6	-	-	89. 2	89. 5	87. 1	79. 7	-	-	-
Total 14 and 15 years, inclusive	-	285	1	-	2	80	220	-	1, 122	2	13	74	33	56	540	5	1	14
Number attending school	-	244	1	-	2	60	175	-	950	1	9	61	28	53	449	3	-	10
Percent attending school	-	85. 6	-	-	-	-	79. 5	-	84. 7	-	-	-	-	-	83. 1	-	-	-
Total 16 and 17 years, inclusive	1	273	1	-	3	105	226	-	1, 235	1	15	95	25	58	561	3	1	13
Number attending school	-	157	-	-	1	45	123	-	623	-	3	43	16	32	319	1	-	6
Percent attending school	-	57. 5	-	-	-	42. 9	54. 4	-	50. 4	-	-	-	-	-	56. 9	-	-	-
Total 18 to 20 years, inclusive	-	410	7	-	6	109	344	1	2, 070	1	15	120	44	59	798	2	2	37
Number attending school	-	49	-	-	-	17	55	-	284	-	-	26	8	8	113	-	-	-
Percent attending school	-	12. 0	-	-	-	15. 6	16. 0	-	13. 7	-	-	21. 7	-	-	14. 2	-	-	-
ILLITERACY																		
Total 10 years old and over	16	4, 411	113	6	67	1, 465	3, 798	14	26, 396	16	186	1, 512	654	764	8, 735	61	31	390
Number illiterate	-	612	10	-	9	218	517	10	5, 469	-	12	142	79	94	1, 520	12	8	26
Percent illiterate	-	13. 9	8. 8	-	-	14. 9	13. 6	-	20. 7	-	6. 5	9. 4	12. 1	12. 3	17. 4	-	-	6. 7
Percent illiterate in 1920	-	16. 0	-	-	-	16. 9	20. 9	-	22. 2	-	-	11. 8	19. 3	16. 5	18. 4	17. 4	-	5. 9
URBAN AND RURAL																		
Urban population	-	2, 451	122	-	-	-	1, 157	-	28, 554	-	159	867	293	215	2, 239	-	-	408
Percent urban	-	43. 4	93. 1	-	-	-	23. 1	-	86. 5	-	67. 9	44. 6	34. 0	21. 4	19. 5	-	-	85. 5
Rural population	20	3, 202	9	6	83	1, 908	3, 848	20	4, 468	20	75	1, 077	570	788	9, 272	66	40	69
Rural-farm	12	2, 439	-	6	1	1, 406	2, 162	6	826	5	69	669	239	515	7, 615	3	34	41
Rural-nonfarm	8	763	9	-	82	502	1, 686	14	3, 642	15	6	408	331	273	1, 657	63	6	28
Percent rural	-	56. 6	6. 9	-	-	100. 0	76. 9	-	13. 5	-	32. 1	55. 4	66. 0	78. 6	80. 5	-	-	14. 5
MARITAL CONDITION																		
Males 15 years old and over	9	1, 863	54	3	31	634	1, 687	5	11, 510	8	83	677	274	320	3, 764	25	15	170
Single	2	581	12	1	9	209	554	1	3, 125	2	28	249	69	98	1, 153	6	3	41
Married	5	1, 093	36	2	18	381	977	4	7, 221	5	50	371	187	189	2, 165	12	10	111
Widowed	1	151	-	-	2	35	130	-	714	1	5	47	13	27	394	6	2	5
Divorced	1	38	4	-	2	9	25	-	443	-	-	10	4	4	51	1	-	11
Unknown	-	-	2	-	-	-	1	-	7	-	-	-	1	2	1	-	-	2
Females 15 years old and over	7	1, 885	51	3	29	602	1, 531	5	11, 893	7	80	649	294	328	3, 580	28	12	181
Single	-	382	5	-	6	150	339	1	2, 054	1	23	125	47	96	685	7	2	24
Married	5	1, 138	38	3	17	381	972	3	7, 412	5	47	379	212	190	2, 188	12	10	118
Widowed	1	287	7	-	5	56	192	1	1, 654	1	10	121	19	39	628	8	-	23
Divorced	1	77	1	-	1	15	28	-	772	-	-	24	15	2	74	1	-	16
Unknown	-	1	-	-	-	-	-	-	1	-	-	-	1	1	5	-	-	-
FAMILIES																		
Number of families	7	1, 451	44	-	18	434	1, 095	5	8, 640	6	61	473	220	235	2, 609	25	10	119
Median size	-	3. 13	-	-	-	3. 61	3. 58	-	2. 92	-	-	3. 19	3. 01	3. 33	3. 45	-	-	2. 64
Families having—																		
No children under 10	4	847	32	-	12	237	577	2	5, 396	4	37	280	126	138	1, 390	22	7	81
1 child under 10	2	279	8	-	1	79	197	2	1, 505	1	11	75	38	34	512	2	-	14
2 children under 10	1	148	2	-	2	43	147	-	853	1	8	52	24	20	280	1	-	10
3 or more	-	177	2	-	3	75	174	1	886	-	5	66	32	43	427	-	3	14

CHARACTERISTICS OF NEGRO POPULATION BY COUNTIES: 1930—Continued

(See note at head of table)

TEXAS—Continued

SUBJECT	Kimble	King	Kinney	Kleberg	Knox	Lamar	Lamb	Lampasas	La Salle	Lavaca	Lee	Leon	Liberty	Limestone	Live Oak	Llano	Lubbock	Lynn
POPULATION BY SEX																		
Negro population: 1930	10	60	352	554	318	9,382	343	269	76	3,369	3,876	8,362	5,019	10,933	58	63	1,677	222
Male	5	28	165	293	167	4,600	202	132	39	1,692	1,937	4,229	2,559	5,500	37	28	856	129
Female	5	32	187	261	151	4,782	141	137	37	1,677	1,939	4,133	2,460	5,433	21	35	821	93
Negro population: 1920	2	10	223	362	309	12,970	1	274	22	3,975	4,224	7,284	3,828	9,099	4	51	152	13
Male	2	6	108	186	187	6,493	1	132	14	2,007	2,077	3,653	2,003	4,620	3	23	89	9
Female	-	4	115	176	122	6,477	-	142	8	1,968	2,147	3,631	1,825	4,479	1	28	63	4
Percent of total population:																		
1930	0.2	5.0	8.8	4.4	2.8	19.3	2.0	3.1	0.9	12.2	28.9	42.0	25.3	27.7	0.6	1.1	4.3	1.8
1920	0.1	1.5	6.0	4.6	3.3	23.3	0.1	3.1	0.5	13.7	30.1	39.8	26.2	27.3	0.1	1.0	1.4	0.3
VOTING AGE: 1930																		
Total 21 years old and over	6	24	174	380	181	4,954	212	159	42	1,737	1,786	4,107	2,522	5,374	22	36	1,040	132
Male	4	12	79	212	102	2,451	135	78	23	874	874	2,125	1,348	2,733	15	16	546	80
Female	2	12	95	168	79	2,503	77	81	19	863	912	1,982	1,174	2,641	7	20	494	52
AGE: 1930																		
Under 5 years	1	13	44	27	39	949	28	25	12	370	459	983	612	1,219	7	2	153	18
Under 1 year	-	4	8	7	8	159	3	4	3	82	91	177	105	265	1	-	26	3
5 to 9 years	2	9	54	48	45	1,108	40	25	10	424	522	1,037	652	1,418	7	6	149	34
10 to 14 years	-	7	36	42	23	1,043	24	29	2	377	515	981	569	1,307	7	9	131	12
15 to 19 years	1	7	41	48	25	1,118	24	25	8	393	507	1,038	548	1,318	13	7	162	24
20 to 24 years	2	6	30	66	31	1,010	60	22	8	287	376	898	489	1,180	9	6	222	16
25 to 29 years	-	5	26	70	34	771	49	24	10	222	217	669	366	902	1	6	222	33
30 to 34 years	2	3	25	73	22	592	34	24	5	194	196	460	328	706	2	5	191	20
35 to 44 years	2	6	29	102	61	1,168	50	28	11	398	355	900	595	1,273	8	14	260	35
45 to 54 years	-	4	29	51	26	824	28	37	6	315	378	720	422	847	2	3	136	22
55 to 64 years	-	-	18	17	11	451	4	11	4	230	183	436	239	443	-	1	33	7
65 to 74 years	-	-	12	5	-	220	-	15	-	84	111	166	111	213	1	2	13	1
75 years and over	-	-	8	5	1	120	-	4	-	74	56	72	45	102	1	2	3	-
Unknown	-	-	-	-	-	8	2	-	-	1	1	2	43	5	-	-	2	-
SCHOOL ATTENDANCE																		
Total 7 to 13 years, inclusive	-	10	64	73	45	1,533	49	38	7	551	714	1,372	833	1,913	11	11	207	27
Number attending school	-	6	60	71	32	1,287	6	38	2	488	665	1,166	684	1,757	10	11	171	13
Percent attending school	-	-	-	-	-	84.0	-	-	-	88.6	93.1	85.0	82.1	91.8	-	-	8.26	-
Total 14 and 15 years, inclusive	-	4	14	18	7	406	6	9	2	161	206	387	232	538	3	3	52	9
Number attending school	-	2	10	16	6	359	2	9	-	137	184	313	193	480	3	3	43	4
Percent attending school	-	-	-	-	-	88.4	-	-	-	85.1	89.3	80.9	83.2	89.2	-	-	-	-
Total 16 and 17 years, inclusive	-	4	14	19	11	458	9	8	2	159	212	402	224	525	5	4	64	10
Number attending school	-	2	6	14	5	257	-	4	-	80	135	231	106	332	3	4	27	4
Percent attending school	-	-	-	-	-	56.1	-	-	-	50.3	63.7	57.5	47.3	63.2	-	-	-	-
Total 18 to 20 years, inclusive	1	1	22	27	17	677	27	20	7	223	286	675	329	822	8	6	112	10
Number attending school	-	-	4	2	2	78	1	4	-	32	62	85	27	145	-	2	6	1
Percent attending school	-	-	-	-	-	11.5	-	-	-	14.3	21.7	12.6	8.2	17.6	-	-	5.4	-
ILLITERACY																		
Total 10 years old and over	7	38	254	479	234	7,325	275	219	54	2,575	2,895	6,342	3,755	8,298	44	55	1,375	170
Number illiterate	-	5	50	8	32	1,118	37	21	6	322	262	1,132	947	982	4	11	101	16
Percent illiterate	-	-	19.7	1.7	13.7	15.3	13.5	9.6	-	12.5	9.1	17.8	25.2	11.8	-	-	7.3	9.4
Percent illiterate in 1920	-	-	23.2	11.0	19.4	19.6	-	18.9	-	16.8	14.3	205	26.5	13.9	-	-	19.5	-
URBAN AND RURAL																		
Urban population	-	-	-	519	-	3,265	122	237	20	300	-	-	-	1,871	-	-	1,312	-
Percent urban	-	-	-	93.7	-	34.8	35.6	88.1	-	8.9	-	-	-	17.1	-	-	78.2	-
Rural population	10	60	352	35	318	6,117	221	32	56	3,069	3,876	8,362	5,019	9,062	58	63	365	222
Rural-farm	-	56	17	35	93	5,166	207	32	55	2,091	3,342	7,576	2,838	7,955	41	13	337	114
Rural-nonfarm	10	4	335	-	225	951	14	-	1	978	534	786	2,181	1,107	17	50	28	108
Percent rural	-	-	100.0	6.3	100.0	65.2	64.4	11.9	-	91.1	100.0	100.0	100.0	82.9	-	-	21.8	100.0
MARITAL CONDITION																		
Males 15 years old and over	4	14	102	235	115	3,076	149	91	27	1,089	1,160	2,716	1,676	3,505	23	22	627	93
Single	-	2	48	56	27	938	49	25	7	332	418	859	533	1,043	15	5	146	29
Married	4	12	48	148	71	1,827	91	50	19	658	659	1,592	979	2,118	7	13	411	56
Widowed	-	-	5	7	9	222	6	7	1	69	57	198	106	241	1	4	58	7
Divorced	-	-	1	24	8	89	3	9	-	30	26	67	57	98	-	-	11	1
Unknown	-	-	-	-	-	-	-	-	-	-	-	-	1	5	-	-	1	-
Females 15 years old and over	3	17	116	202	96	3,206	102	99	25	1,109	1,220	2,645	1,510	3,484	14	24	617	65
Single	-	4	31	33	10	654	9	22	3	256	340	602	322	754	9	8	78	13
Married	2	11	46	121	66	1,901	84	50	19	659	676	1,582	971	2,132	5	13	441	51
Widowed	-	2	29	20	13	523	4	18	2	145	164	356	142	466	-	3	67	-
Divorced	1	-	10	28	7	126	4	9	1	49	40	104	75	131	-	-	31	1
Unknown	-	-	-	-	-	2	1	-	-	-	-	1	-	1	-	-	-	-
FAMILIES																		
Number of families	3	12	90	144	79	2,346	89	74	19	829	821	2,038	1,173	2,575	7	16	414	60
Median size	-	-	-	2.42	-	3.19	-	-	-	3.24	3.93	3.43	3.30	3.50	-	-	2.42	-
Families having—																		
No children under 10	2	6	49	105	47	1,395	54	48	9	484	419	1,159	648	1,396	2	11	276	40
1 child under 10	-	1	17	22	8	405	16	12	3	135	134	360	198	481	1	2	61	7
2 children under 10	-	1	10	9	11	237	12	9	5	86	98	186	117	279	1	3	40	5
3 or more	1	4	14	8	13	309	7	5	2	124	170	333	210	419	3	-	37	8

CHARACTERISTICS OF NEGRO POPULATION BY COUNTIES: 1930—Continued

(See note at head of table)

SUBJECT	TEXAS—Continued																	
	McCulloch	McLennan	McMullen	Madison	Marion	Martin	Mason	Matagorda	Maverick	Medina	Menard	Midland	Milam	Mills	Mitchell	Montague	Montgomery	Morris
POPULATION BY SEX																		
Negro population: 1930	465	18,697	25	3,456	6,456	116	57	4,520	18	264	72	259	8,772	2	715	3	5,273	3,722
Male	233	9,144	12	1,746	3,248	60	29	2,260	10	139	36	131	4,426	-	377	-	2,656	1,841
Female	232	9,553	13	1,710	3,208	56	28	2,260	8	125	36	128	4,346	2	338	3	2,617	1,881
Negro population: 1920	374	17,575	8	3,127	6,667	-	49	3,974	74	278	23	16	8,973	-	195	1	6,358	3,751
Male	216	8,538	5	1,568	3,307	-	24	2,023	49	138	14	9	4,486	-	112	-	3,239	1,852
Female	158	9,037	3	1,559	3,360	-	25	1,951	25	140	9	7	4,487	-	83	1	3,119	1,899
Percent of total population:																		
1930	3.3	18.9	1.9	28.3	62.3	2.0	1.0	25.6	0.3	1.9	1.6	3.2	23.1	-	5.0	-	36.1	37.1
1920	3.4	21.2	0.8	26.2	61.2	-	1.0	24.0	1.0	2.4	0.7	0.7	23.5	-	2.6	-	36.7	36.5
VOTING AGE: 1930																		
Total 21 years old and over	252	10,484	12	1,596	3,086	71	25	2,327	7	157	47	172	4,250	2	384	1	2,842	1,617
Male	125	5,078	8	802	1,564	38	14	1,175	4	80	23	84	2,154	-	208	-	1,425	791
Female	127	5,406	4	794	1,522	33	11	1,152	3	77	24	88	2,096	2	176	1	1,417	826
AGE: 1930																		
Under 5 years	52	1,773	3	442	756	13	4	489	2	17	8	25	1,065	-	75	-	511	507
Under 1 year	8	351	1	71	134	3	-	86	1	2	1	3	211	-	13	-	83	91
5 to 9 years	64	2,037	4	486	827	15	5	586	5	27	4	30	1,196	-	74	-	625	516
10 to 14 years	47	1,937	3	428	854	10	6	498	1	33	3	10	1,028	-	81	-	607	491
15 to 19 years	42	2,060	2	415	776	6	16	504	2	27	9	19	1,020	-	83	1	570	489
20 to 24 years	47	1,893	4	357	639	14	8	418	1	20	8	23	933	-	83	1	495	392
25 to 29 years	55	1,627	1	261	427	29	5	335	1	30	10	51	640	-	82	-	405	262
30 to 34 years	47	1,350	2	187	332	11	1	271	-	13	5	40	473	-	57	-	352	208
35 to 44 years	56	2,657	2	359	661	12	6	556	1	36	8	43	995	-	85	-	634	313
45 to 54 years	27	1,860	2	278	569	5	2	436	-	25	9	10	722	1	54	-	555	285
55 to 64 years	18	892	-	157	337	1	3	259	3	18	4	6	395	-	26	1	296	152
65 to 74 years	5	412	-	68	171	-	1	112	-	9	3	2	187	1	9	-	133	75
75 years and over	5	192	2	18	84	-	-	55	2	9	1	-	118	-	6	-	80	32
Unknown	-	7	-	-	23	-	-	1	-	-	-	-	-	-	-	-	10	-
SCHOOL ATTENDANCE																		
Total 7 to 13 years, inclusive	85	2,792	6	618	1,212	17	7	764	5	40	5	28	1,545	-	107	-	870	707
Number attending school	60	2,522	2	438	1,077	8	1	723	4	31	1	25	1,335	-	80	-	785	617
Percent attending school	-	90.3	-	70.9	88.9	-	-	94.6	-	-	-	-	86.4	-	74.8	-	90.2	87.3
Total 14 and 15 years, inclusive	16	791	1	164	327	1	5	176	1	15	1	5	428	-	38	-	232	177
Number attending school	14	689	1	117	290	1	2	159	-	11	-	4	379	-	28	-	198	156
Percent attending school	-	86.4	-	71.3	88.7	-	-	90.3	-	-	-	-	88.6	-	-	-	85.3	8.81
Total 16 and 17 years, inclusive	14	834	1	165	312	4	9	210	1	13	3	6	408	-	29	1	243	209
Number attending school	2	512	-	79	196	1	-	97	1	5	-	-	243	-	16	1	166	121
Percent attending school	-	61.4	-	47.9	62.8	-	-	46.2	-	-	-	-	59.6	-	-	-	68.3	57.9
Total 18 to 20 years, inclusive	26	1,225	1	256	444	3	6	335	1	11	6	13	615	-	53	1	338	296
Number attending school	1	201	-	39	82	-	1	39	-	-	-	-	100	-	7	1	47	55
Percent attending school	-	16.4	-	15.2	18.5	-	-	11.6	-	-	-	-	16.3	-	-	-	13.9	18.6
ILLITERACY																		
Total 10 years old and over	349	14,887	18	2,528	4,873	88	48	3,445	11	210	60	204	6,511	2	566	3	4,137	2,699
Number illiterate	21	1,415	12	624	756	13	19	419	2	20	8	11	941	1	101	-	693	434
Percent illiterate	6.0	9.5	-	24.7	15.5	-	-	12.2	-	9.1	-	5.4	14.5	-	17.8	-	16.8	16.1
Percent illiterate in 1920	14.3	14.3	-	18.1	19.7	-	-	13.8	-	12.0	-	-	19.3	-	10.6	-	20.6	25.1
URBAN AND RURAL																		
Urban population	317	10,033	-	-	-	-	-	915	18	-	-	237	1,066	-	414	3	-	-
Percent urban	68.2	53.7	-	-	-	-	-	20.2	-	-	-	91.5	12.2	-	57.9	-	-	-
Rural population	148	8,664	25	3,456	6,456	116	57	3,605	-	264	72	22	7,706	2	301	-	5,273	3,722
Rural-farm	134	6,742	10	3,197	5,112	54	30	2,893	-	223	23	6	6,551	2	291	-	3,005	3,227
Rural-nonfarm	14	1,922	15	259	1,344	62	27	712	-	41	49	16	1,155	-	10	-	2,268	495
Percent rural	31.8	46.3	-	100.0	100.0	100.0	-	79.8	-	100.0	-	8.5	87.8	-	42.1	-	100.0	100.0
MARITAL CONDITION																		
Males 15 years old and over	153	6,260	10	1,045	2,001	41	22	1,472	6	97	29	96	2,739	-	254	-	1,775	1,074
Single	39	1,862	7	301	592	6	13	462	3	37	9	33	808	-	78	-	575	333
Married	98	3,713	-	669	1,240	30	8	860	2	48	16	54	1,679	-	138	-	1,043	649
Widowed	14	445	3	68	132	-	1	98	1	8	1	7	188	-	33	-	114	61
Divorced	2	235	-	7	28	5	-	51	-	3	3	1	63	-	5	-	35	30
Unknown	-	5	-	-	9	-	-	1	-	1	-	1	1	-	-	-	8	1
Females 15 years old and over	149	6,690	5	1,055	2,018	37	20	1,475	4	90	28	98	2,744	2	231	3	1,755	1,134
Single	20	1,359	1	215	454	5	10	336	1	21	3	14	597	1	45	2	388	295
Married	102	3,768	3	676	1,241	29	8	861	2	50	17	59	1,681	1	144	1	1,050	648
Widowed	19	1,111	1	146	291	-	2	185	1	12	5	12	396	-	34	-	266	152
Divorced	8	445	-	17	27	3	-	92	-	7	3	13	70	-	8	-	46	38
Unknown	-	7	-	1	5	-	-	1	-	-	-	-	-	-	-	-	5	1
FAMILIES																		
Number of families	111	4,631	4	810	1,493	34	11	1,100	4	72	19	52	2,041	-	173	-	1,347	764
Median size	3.12	3.08	-	3.68	3.72	-	-	3.13	-	-	-	-	3.48	-	3.06	-	3.11	4.14
Families having—																		
No children under 10	58	2,884	3	395	779	21	6	621	3	48	15	30	1,074	-	107	-	828	351
1 child under 10	20	746	-	162	296	6	3	189	-	12	-	11	351	-	26	-	227	147
2 children under 10	17	429	1	96	167	2	1	128	-	6	2	5	227	-	21	-	124	94
3 or more	16	572	-	157	251	5	1	162	1	6	2	6	389	-	19	-	168	172

CHARACTERISTICS OF NEGRO POPULATION BY COUNTIES: 1930—Continued

(See note at head of table)

SUBJECT	TEXAS—Continued																	
	Motley	Nacogdoches	Navarro	Newton	Nolan	Nueces	Oldham	Orange	Palo Pinto	Panola	Parker	Parmer	Pecos	Polk	Potter	Presidio	Rains	Randall
POPULATION BY SEX																		
Negro population: 1930	358	7,456	15,083	5,172	622	2,640	1	2,447	652	10,269	279	14	31	5,567	1,702	110	531	31
Male	195	3,643	7,667	2,597	306	1,347	1	1,168	300	5,122	132	7	22	2,866	875	72	278	13
Female	163	3,813	7,416	2,575	316	1,293		1,279	352	5,147	147	7	9	2,701	827	38	253	18
Negro population: 1920	40	6,741	12,100	4,601	181	792	5	3,203	732	9,182	337	1	6	5,472	318	29	527	
Male	27	3,304	6,063	2,422	122	391	4	1,671	358	4,493	177	1	5	2,843	162	19	266	
Female	13	3,437	6,037	2,179	59	401	1	1,532	374	4,689	160		1	2,629	156	10	261	
Percent of total population:																		
1930	5.3	24.6	24.9	41.3	3.2	5.1	0.1	16.2	3.7	42.7	1.5	0.2	0.4	31.7	3.7	1.1	7.5	0.4
1920	1.0	23.7	23.9	37.7	1.7	3.5	0.7	20.8	3.1	42.2	1.4	0.1	0.2	32.6	1.9	0.2	6.5	
VOTING AGE: 1930																		
Total 21 years old and over	185	3,396	7,956	2,710	378	1,677	1	1,355	432	4,420	163	11	25	2,806	1,261	91	217	25
Male	106	1,684	4,131	1,446	203	870	1	642	196	2,272	76	5	18	1,480	668	64	120	12
Female	79	1,712	3,825	1,264	175	807		713	263	2,148	87	6	7	1,326	593	27	97	13
AGE: 1930																		
Under 5 years	50	930	1,626	602	63	225		228	60	1,440	19	1		599	85	7	64	2
Under 1 year	15	185	345	133	11	39		54	10	304	1			123	20		13	
5 to 9 years	47	1,092	1,835	673	56	243		298	49	1,528	35	1	2	673	78	6	72	1
10 to 14 years	35	975	1,640	557	52	196		241	45	1,376	32			667	86	1	79	1
15 to 19 years	32	887	1,662	510	59	231		276	55	1,279	25		4	670	131	3	86	2
20 to 24 years	40	747	1,607	516	78	383		243	82	1,039	27	2	3	572	261	19	46	7
25 to 29 years	45	636	1,362	478	95	370	1	214	61	774	13	1	11	435	285	17	35	5
30 to 34 years	16	460	1,104	354	66	254		167	46	531	12	2	3	373	270	15	24	6
35 to 44 years	48	689	1,948	680	90	402		367	120	995	27	3	7	572	330	24	54	5
45 to 54 years	36	560	1,287	452	47	195		260	72	647	37	1		512	129	13	37	1
55 to 64 years	6	265	596	231	10	76		88	41	377	23	2	1	307	31	4	19	
65 to 74 years	2	148	285	87	4	42		42	16	187	20			134	12	1	14	
75 years and over	1	64	130	27	2	17		22	5	94	9	1		50	2		1	
Unknown		3	1	5		6		1		2				3	2			1
SCHOOL ATTENDANCE																		
Total 7 to 13 years, inclusive	56	1,467	2,416	868	74	317		385	66	2,001	50		1	916	114	3	115	1
Number attending school	37	1,277	2,007	820	49	262		349	59	1,768	50			811	87		101	1
Percent attending school		87.0	83.1	94.5		82.6		90.6		88.4				88.5	76.3		87.8	
Total 14 and 15 years, inclusive	16	371	654	188	22	63		98	20	511	14			244	44	1	30	
Number attending school	8	313	556	167	17	41		77	18	447	13			219	36	1	25	
Percent attending school		84.4	85.0	88.8						87.5				89.8				
Total 16 and 17 years, inclusive	10	365	659	193	19	91		108	21	522	11		3	288	48	1	34	
Number attending school	2	216	347	110	7	25		45	12	298	5		1	158	7		13	
Percent attending school		59.2	52.7	57.0				41.7		57.1				54.9				
Total 18 to 20 years, inclusive	23	515	1,035	346	47	171		163	38	747	12	1	1	419	116	4	49	2
Number attending school	2	89	140	64	1	6		13	7	120				67	7		6	
Percent attending school		17.3	13.5	18.5		3.5		8.0		16.1				16.0	6.0			
ILLITERACY																		
Total 10 years old and over	261	5,434	11,622	3,897	503	2,172	1	1,921	543	7,301	225	12	29	4,295	1,539	97	395	28
Number illiterate	38	873	1,403	731	54	131		457	53	1,473	34	9	5	893	49	4	20	2
Percent illiterate	14.6	16.1	12.1	18.8	10.7	6.0		23.8	9.8	20.2	15.1			20.8	3.2		5.1	
Percent illiterate in 1920		26.1	18.6	16.6	13.6	11.8		26.4	15.4	23.3	17.6			24.6	4.8		13.7	
URBAN AND RURAL																		
Urban population		1,362	3,332		539	2,113		2,150	600		220		19		1,570	34		30
Percent urban		18.3	22.1		86.7	80.0		87.9	92.0		78.9				92.2	30.9		
Rural population	358	6,094	11,751	5,172	83	527	1	297	52	10,269	59	14	12	5,567	132	76	531	1
Rural-farm	219	4,985	9,457	2,427	63	329	1	73	12	9,641	57	14	9	3,360			523	1
Rural-nonfarm	139	1,109	2,294	2,745	20	198		224	40	628	2		3	2,207	132	76	8	
Percent rural	100.0	81.7	77.9	100.0	13.3	20.0		12.1	8.0	100.0	21.1			100.0	7.8	69.1	100.0	
MARITAL CONDITION																		
Males 15 years old and over	125	2,191	5,092	1,733	228	1,003	1	790	225	2,970	92	6	21	1,891	747	64	169	12
Single	28	653	1,473	502	77	319	1	201	54	883	35	1	7	586	284	14	65	1
Married	84	1,308	3,084	1,081	138	608		531	141	1,827	48	5	14	1,113	428	43	94	10
Widowed	10	179	372	105	11	42		39	17	199	6			122	21	4	10	
Divorced	3	50	161	44	1	28		19	13	60	3			70	13	3		1
Unknown		1	2	1	1	6				1					1			
Females 15 years old and over	101	2,268	4,890	1,607	223	973		890	273	2,955	101	6	8	1,737	706	32	147	15
Single	7	542	885	338	40	195		154	39	675	16		1	332	159	4	42	1
Married	79	1,328	3,065	1,093	140	635		564	159	1,825	53	4	7	1,095	414	26	85	10
Widowed	13	309	709	130	36	125		123	50	365	28	2		242	101	1	19	
Divorced	2	88	230	46	7	18		48	25	88	4			68	29	1	1	3
Unknown		1	1					1		2					3			1
FAMILIES																		
Number of families	90	1,619	3,727	1,181	178	713		655	166	2,159	80	4	6	1,330	396	31	99	9
Median size		3.82	3.15	3.44	2.11	2.49		2.98	2.81	4.07				3.34	2.31			
Families having—																		
No children under 10	54	752	2,195	643	128	477		407	108	951	50	3	5	744	299	24	41	7
1 child under 10	12	332	611	205	19	118		113	34	395	13			251	63	4	19	1
2 children under 10	8	207	389	123	13	53		62	9	316	12	1	1	133	20	2	16	1
3 or more	16	328	532	210	18	65		73	15	497	5			202	14	1	23	

CHARACTERISTICS OF NEGRO POPULATION BY COUNTIES: 1930—Continued

(See note at head of table)

SUBJECT	TEXAS—Continued																	
	Reagan	Real	Red River	Reeves	Refugio	Robertson	Rockwall	Runnels	Rusk	Sabine	San Augustine	San Jacinto	San Patricio	San Saba	Schleicher	Scurry	Shackelford	Shelby
POPULATION BY SEX																		
Negro population: 1930	64	1	7,442	178	849	11,416	1,955	716	13,944	2,670	3,699	5,117	506	167	36	147	158	7,171
Male	30	1	3,700	98	448	5,697	1,004	357	6,903	1,397	1,798	2,638	263	72	20	93	77	3,642
Female	34	------	3,742	80	401	5,719	951	359	7,041	1,273	1,901	2,479	243	95	16	54	81	3,529
Negro population: 1920	------	1	8,452	17	610	12,474	1,676	478	12,713	2,616	4,152	5,487	176	135	3	128	65	5,852
Male	------	1	4.196	11	310	6,147	818	284	6,285	1,399	2,041	2,717	90	69	2	96	35	2,894
Female	------	------	4,256	6	300	6,327	858	194	6,428	1,217	2,111	2,770	86	66	1	32	30	2,958
Percent of total population:																		
1930	2.1	------	24.1	2.8	11.0	41.9	25.5	3.3	42.9	22.3	29.7	52.7	2.1	1.6	1.1	1.2	2.4	25.0
1920	------	0.1	23.6	.4	15.1	44.7	19.5	2.8	40.1	21.3	30.2	55.6	1.5	1.3	.2	1.4	1.3	21.3
VOTING AGE: 1930																		
Total 21 years old and over	49	1	3,614	97	436	5,753	979	418	6,194	1,364	1,649	2,644	275	90	19	103	99	3,319
Male	27	1	1,815	53	240	2,860	535	216	3,108	755	820	1,363	150	47	11	70	49	1,715
Female	22	------	1,799	44	196	2,893	444	202	3,086	609	829	1,281	125	43	8	33	50	1,604
AGE: 1930																		
Under 5 years	7	------	883	23	97	1,258	248	68	1,774	313	455	497	58	17	5	10	10	861
Under 1 year	2	------	171	6	16	267	49	12	336	56	83	107	9	2	1	3	2	165
5 to 9 years	5	------	958	25	108	1.457	254	81	2,022	339	495	599	65	20	3	14	10	997
10 to 14 years	------	------	864	14	89	1,350	206	68	1,915	316	524	619	60	16	5	9	13	964
15 to 19 years	------	------	924	16	98	1,336	216	66	1,703	266	488	638	36	19	3	9	23	857
20 to 24 years	12	------	746	20	102	1,087	226	81	1,422	320	379	565	58	19	5	21	13	762
25 to 29 years	13	------	572	17	79	777	209	59	1,060	297	256	382	63	13	2	28	19	606
30 to 34 years	6	------	431	19	50	666	133	43	825	184	206	334	50	17	------	18	18	459
35 to 44 years	9	------	797	25	87	1,318	248	123	1,247	300	336	546	62	30	4	24	25	752
45 to 54 years	8	------	670	11	67	1,061	132	79	973	193	282	450	25	12	4	12	10	487
55 to 64 years	3	------	331	6	43	613	48	27	560	95	159	296	19	------	1	1	6	255
65 to 74 years	1	1	181	1	18	328	24	10	278	26	78	120	6	3	------	1	8	126
75 years and over	------	------	81	1	11	163	10	10	164	19	36	67	4	1	------	------	2	45
Unknown	------	------	4	------	------	2	1	1	1	2	5	4	------	------	4	------	1	------
SCHOOL ATTENDANCE																		
Total 7 to 13 years, inclusive	1	------	1,264	23	134	1,976	300	101	2,718	453	752	883	87	23	5	17	18	1,398
Number attending school	------	------	1,180	19	107	1,706	183	82	2,427	346	550	801	68	17	------	9	18	1,181
Percent attending school	------	------	93.4	------	79.9	86.3	61.0	81.2	89.3	76.4	73.1	90.7	------	------	------	------	------	84.5
Total 14 and 15 years, inclusive	------	------	363	8	36	565	81	28	718	112	201	241	12	10	2	3	9	353
Number attending school	------	------	335	4	28	503	53	22	622	83	140	202	10	9	------	1	8	294
Percent attending school	------	------	92.3	------	------	89.0	------	------	86.6	74.1	69.7	83.8	------	------	------	------	------	83.3
Total 16 and 17 years, inclusive	------	------	374	5	38	540	77	25	714	104	210	267	15	7	1	3	8	339
Number attending school	------	------	235	1	14	318	18	10	453	59	98	126	8	5	------	------	3	177
Percent attending school	------	------	62.8	------	------	58.9	------	------	63.4	56.7	46.7	47.2	------	------	------	------	------	52.2
Total 18 to 20 years, inclusive	3	------	551	10	63	779	154	42	972	184	269	366	28	12	3	7	10	527
Number attedning school	------	------	86	2	1	91	5	3	158	30	44	34	3	2	------	------	1	78
Percent attending school	------	------	15.6	------	------	11.7	3.2	------	16.3	16.3	16.4	9.3	------	------	------	------	------	14.8
ILLITERACY																		
Total 10 years old and over	52	1	5,601	130	644	8,701	1,453	567	10,148	2,018	2,749	4,021	383	130	28	123	138	5,313
Number illiterate	2	------	883	17	63	1,592	368	48	1,484	358	645	983	67	18	8	18	6	1,154
Percent illiterate	------	------	15.8	13.1	9.8	18.3	25.3	8.5	14.6	17.7	23.5	24.4	17.5	13.8	------	14.6	4.3	21.7
Percent illiterate in 1920	------	------	21.8	------	14.7	19.8	24.7	15.6	20.6	26.6	28.9	16.8	19.5	20.0	------	13.8	------	25.1
URBAN AND RURAL																		
Urban population	------	------	910	162	------	1,289	------	419	1,006	------	------	------	------	------	------	27	------	453
Percent urban	------	------	12.2	91.0	------	11.3	------	58.5	7.2	------	------	------	------	------	------	18.4	------	6.3
Rural population	64	1	6,532	16	849	10,127	1,955	297	12,938	2,670	3,699	5,117	506	167	36	120	158	6,718
Rural-farm	------	------	5,818	14	337	8,325	1,552	175	12,661	1,407	2,903	3,971	202	27	10	21	15	5,489
Rural-nonfarm	64	1	714	2	512	1,802	403	122	277	1,263	796	1,146	304	140	26	99	143	1,229
Percent rural	------	------	87.8	9.0	100.0	88.7	100.0	41.5	92.8	100.0	100.0	100.0	100.0	100.0	------	81.6	100.0	93.7
MARITAL CONDITION																		
Males 15 years old and over	27	1	2,373	61	306	3,639	656	249	4,088	916	1,090	1,739	172	54	12	76	62	2,214
Single	4	------	727	14	113	1,061	154	55	1,312	278	373	514	53	19	5	30	21	684
Married	20	------	1,457	44	168	2,214	449	171	2,469	535	626	1,028	103	30	6	42	34	1,327
Widowed	1	1	151	2	20	298	34	17	235	98	80	143	11	5	------	1	4	112
Divorced	2	------	37	1	5	66	15	6	72	5	11	52	4	------	1	3	3	91
Unknown	------	------	1	------	------	------	4	------	------	------	------	2	1	------	------	------	------	------
Females 15 years old and over	25	------	2,364	55	249	3,712	591	250	4,145	786	1,135	1,663	151	60	11	38	63	2,135
Single	5	------	507	5	46	763	85	40	1,055	144	337	320	24	19	2	4	14	470
Married	18	------	1,471	41	176	2,248	440	167	2,465	526	621	1,028	104	29	7	29	36	1,324
Widowed	2	------	333	8	19	576	57	30	482	106	156	253	15	12	1	4	9	243
Divorced	------	------	51	1	8	125	9	12	141	10	18	58	8	------	1	1	4	97
Unknown	------	------	2	------	------	------	------	1	2	------	3	4	------	------	------	------	------	1
FAMILIES																		
Number of families	25	------	1,743	47	198	2,788	530	196	2,925	608	777	1,233	128	35	5	25	38	1,615
Median size	------	------	3.57	------	3.28	3.32	2.90	2.69	4.10	3.30	3.97	3.32	2.91	------	------	------	------	3.61
Families having—																		
No children under 10	19	------	937	31	99	1,606	306	130	1,330	315	372	721	75	20	3	13	23	788
1 child under 10	4	------	308	5	48	478	89	29	566	120	147	219	16	6	------	4	11	307
2 children under 10	------	------	207	4	25	269	58	13	404	68	116	123	16	2	------	5	3	238
3 or more	2	------	291	7	26	435	77	24	625	105	142	170	21	7	2	3	1	282

CHARACTERISTICS OF NEGRO POPULATION BY COUNTIES: 1930—Continued

(See note at head of table)

SUBJECT	TEXAS—Continued																	
	Smith	Starr	Stephens	Sterling	Stonewall	Sutton	Swisher	Tarrant	Taylor	Terrell	Terry	Throckmorton	Titus	Tom Green	Travis	Trinity	Tyler	Upshur
POPULATION BY SEX																		
Negro population: 1930	19,128	1	447	2	278	45	50	24,660	1,632	18	69	9	2,700	1,760	15,832	3,181	2,960	6,933
Male	9,630	-----	196	1	147	24	29	11,771	798	11	32	3	1,373	856	7,349	1,602	1,612	3,448
Female	9,498	1	251	1	131	21	21	12,889	834	7	37	6	1,327	904	8,483	1,579	1,348	3,485
Negro population: 1920	17,609	1	62	5	108	5	6	18,730	481	-----	-----	11	3,180	633	13,415	3,420	2,195	6,234
Male	8,707	1	44	5	62	3	5	9,425	242	-----	-----	3	1,618	300	6,303	1,743	1,158	3,050
Female	8,902	-----	18	-----	46	2	1	9,305	239	-----	-----	8	1,562	333	7,112	1,677	1,037	3,184
Percent of total population:																		
1930	36.0	-----	2.7	0.1	4.9	1.6	0.7	12.5	4.0	0.7	0.8	0.2	16.9	4.9	20.4	23.3	25.9	31.1
1920	37.7	-----	0.4	0.5	2.6	0.3	0.1	12.3	2.0	-----	-----	0.3	17.5	4.2	23.3	25.1	21.1	27.7
VOTING AGE: 1930																		
Total 21 years old and over	9,509	1	295	2	149	28	37	16,226	1,066	16	36	2	1,316	1,240	9,144	1,691	1,637	3,058
Male	4,835	-----	129	1	85	15	23	7,823	523	9	21	1	660	605	4,135	859	952	1,529
Female	4,674	1	166	1	64	13	14	8,403	543	7	15	1	656	635	5,009	832	685	1,529
AGE: 1930																		
Under 5 years	2,098	-----	38	-----	38	2	3	1,725	129	-----	14	1	315	138	1,506	296	321	909
Under 1 year	389	-----	8	-----	11	1	1	333	27	-----	3	-----	58	27	311	71	59	161
5 to 9 years	2,407	-----	37	-----	31	5	-----	2,147	147	1	6	1	332	113	1,742	355	314	965
10 to 14 years	2,241	-----	27	-----	25	6	3	1,995	115	-----	4	3	302	116	1,453	378	327	936
15 to 19 years	2,381	-----	40	-----	30	4	3	2,054	141	1	8	1	366	109	1,634	387	286	879
20 to 24 years	2,052	-----	52	-----	31	3	14	2,664	173	2	6	1	302	232	1,669	288	308	697
25 to 29 years	1,588	-----	63	1	24	6	10	2,958	241	2	8	1	206	291	1,354	254	287	521
30 to 34 years	1,202	-----	51	1	28	4	7	2,579	193	1	3	1	177	213	1,102	224	213	365
35 to 44 years	2,075	-----	85	-----	39	9	6	4,501	296	2	11	-----	313	296	2,211	420	397	630
45 to 54 years	1,615	-----	39	-----	24	4	2	2,461	127	4	3	-----	218	158	1,551	324	286	548
55 to 64 years	859	1	11	-----	4	2	2	917	47	4	5	-----	100	53	914	138	121	274
65 to 74 years	411	-----	3	-----	3	-----	-----	402	15	-----	1	-----	43	26	416	69	55	132
75 years and over	198	-----	1	-----	1	-----	-----	176	8	1	-----	-----	26	14	239	46	30	75
Unknown	1	-----	-----	-----	-----	-----	-----	81	-----	-----	-----	-----	-----	1	41	2	15	2
SCHOOL ATTENDANCE																		
Total 7 to 13 years, inclusive	3,242	-----	55	-----	40	10	2	2,926	176	1	8	3	450	162	2,209	505	462	1,303
Number attending school	2,832	-----	48	-----	11	9	-----	2,750	150	-----	-----	-----	362	126	1,988	432	379	1,170
Percent attending school	87.4	-----	-----	-----	-----	-----	-----	94.0	85.2	-----	-----	-----	80.4	77.8	90.0	85.5	82.0	89.8
Total 14 and 15 years, inclusive	900	-----	9	-----	10	1	2	778	49	-----	2	-----	138	42	613	149	118	382
Number attending school	795	-----	8	-----	1	-----	-----	669	38	-----	-----	-----	104	31	544	128	98	331
Percent attending school	88.3	-----	-----	-----	-----	-----	-----	86.0	-----	-----	-----	-----	75.4	-----	88.7	85.9	83.1	86.6
Total 16 and 17 years, inclusive	978	-----	13	-----	10	1	-----	782	55	-----	3	-----	141	39	652	164	105	349
Number attending school	593	-----	5	-----	1	-----	-----	412	27	-----	-----	-----	69	16	391	71	40	239
Percent attending school	60.6	-----	-----	-----	-----	-----	-----	52.7	-----	-----	-----	-----	48.9	-----	60.0	43.3	38.1	68.5
Total 18 to 20 years, inclusive	1,444	-----	29	-----	19	2	6	1,415	99	1	4	2	216	94	1,029	224	199	549
Number attending school	278	-----	3	-----	-----	-----	1	160	12	-----	-----	-----	19	12	217	31	11	127
Percent attending school	19.3	-----	-----	-----	-----	-----	-----	11.3	-----	-----	-----	-----	8.8	-----	21.1	13.8	5.5	23.1
ILLITERACY																		
Total 10 years old and over	14,623	1	372	2	209	38	47	20,788	1,356	17	49	7	2,053	1,509	12,584	2,530	2,325	5,059
Number illiterate	2,276	-----	13	-----	29	2	7	1,591	110	3	19	2	380	70	1,078	438	394	578
Percent illiterate	15.6	-----	3.5	-----	13.9	-----	-----	7.7	8.1	-----	-----	-----	18.5	4.6	8.6	17.3	16.9	11.4
Percent illiterate in 1920	17.6	-----	-----	-----	-----	-----	-----	8.4	9.9	-----	-----	-----	24.1	7.6	13.4	22.4	21.4	21.5
URBAN AND RURAL																		
Urban population	4,092	-----	426	-----	-----	-----	-----	22,536	1,403	-----	-----	-----	979	1,653	9,868	-----	-----	-----
Percent urban	21.4	-----	95.3	-----	-----	-----	-----	91.4	86.0	-----	-----	-----	36.3	93.9	62.3	-----	-----	-----
Rural population	15,036	1	21	2	278	45	50	2,124	229	18	69	9	1,721	107	5,964	3,181	2,960	6,933
Rural-farm	14,124	-----	6	-----	203	26	15	725	128	9	29	4	1,580	57	4,839	1,415	679	6,001
Rural-nonfarm	912	1	15	2	75	19	35	1,399	101	9	40	5	141	50	1,125	1,766	2,281	932
Percent rural	78.6	-----	4.7	-----	100.0	-----	-----	8.6	14.0	-----	-----	-----	63.7	6.1	37.7	100.0	100.0	100.0
MARITAL CONDITION																		
Males 15 years old and over	6,192	-----	149	1	105	17	27	8,942	601	10	25	1	871	666	5,023	1,080	1,123	2,077
Single	1,962	-----	46	-----	28	2	10	2,153	124	4	5	-----	294	152	1,414	378	317	675
Married	3,619	-----	92	1	70	11	16	5,763	433	3	13	1	510	450	3,024	624	629	1,228
Widowed	444	-----	5	-----	4	1	1	727	26	3	7	-----	51	40	335	41	77	145
Divorced	166	-----	6	-----	3	3	-----	282	18	-----	-----	-----	16	24	175	35	82	26
Unknown	1	-----	-----	-----	-----	-----	-----	17	-----	-----	-----	-----	-----	-----	75	2	18	3
Females 15 years old and over	6,190	1	196	1	79	15	17	9,851	640	7	20	3	880	727	6,108	1,072	875	2,046
Single	1,420	-----	39	-----	3	3	2	1,524	93	1	2	-----	209	93	1,359	247	140	500
Married	3,647	-----	110	1	66	12	15	5,991	453	3	15	1	518	443	3,232	633	603	1,234
Widowed	888	1	32	-----	9	-----	-----	1,861	62	1	1	1	127	147	996	145	78	252
Divorced	234	-----	15	-----	1	-----	-----	452	32	2	2	1	26	44	386	45	52	58
Unknown	1	-----	-----	-----	-----	-----	-----	23	-----	-----	-----	-----	-----	-----	135	2	2	2
FAMILIES																		
Number of families	4,328	1	131	1	71	16	15	6,838	415	5	17	1	606	476	3,734	777	729	1,472
Median size	3.60	-----	2.24	-----	-----	-----	-----	2.55	2.59	-----	-----	-----	3.62	2.38	3.17	3.29	3.06	4.05
Families having—																		
No children under 10	2,315	1	91	1	42	13	13	4,838	278	4	8	1	307	345	2,265	459	430	717
1 child under 10	817	-----	23	-----	9	1	2	1,019	63	1	3	-----	120	64	594	147	127	263
2 children under 10	493	-----	8	-----	8	1	-----	505	36	-----	2	-----	89	41	392	84	77	170
3 or more	703	-----	9	-----	12	1	-----	476	38	-----	4	-----	90	26	483	87	95	322

CHARACTERISTICS OF NEGRO POPULATION BY COUNTIES: 1930—Continued

(See note at head of table)

SUBJECT	TEXAS—Continued																	
	Upton	Uvalde	Val Verde	Van Zandt	Victoria	Walker	Waller	Ward	Washington	Webb	Wharton	Wheeler	Wichita	Wilbarger	Willacy	Williamson	Wilson	Winkler
POPULATION BY SEX																		
Negro population: 1930	249	222	243	2,404	2,880	8,531	4,952	58	9,893	153	7,903	316	4,817	1,687	89	7,056	595	273
Male	130	113	111	1,236	1,420	4,312	2,425	31	4,769	79	3,999	168	2,272	868	45	3,500	306	148
Female	119	109	132	1,168	1,460	4,219	2,527	27	5,124	74	3,904	148	2,545	819	44	3,556	289	125
Negro population: 1920	------	152	185	1,516	3,119	9,741	4,967	21	11,646	41	7,884		2,272	374		6,515	767	
Male	------	73	90	804	1,497	5,481	2,440	9	5,624	17	3,960	------	1,278	219	------	3,310	398	------
Female	------	79	95	712	1,622	4,260	2,527	12	6,022	24	3,924	------	994	155	------	3,205	369	------
Percent of total population:																		
1930	4.2	1.7	1.6	7.4	14.4	46.0	49.5	1.3	39.0	0.4	26.6	2.0	6.5	6.9	0.8	16.0	3.4	4.0
1920	------	1.4	1.5	4.9	17.1	52.5	48.3	0.8	43.7	0.1	32.5	------	3.1	2.5	------	15.2	4.4	------
VOTING AGE: 1930																		
Total 21 years old and over	169	116	138	1,176	1,649	4,372	2,736	43	5,165	104	4,231	217	3,218	995	53	3,674	283	187
Male	96	61	68	608	790	2,297	1,315	23	2,441	58	2,141	119	1,532	532	32	1,840	139	104
Female	73	55	70	568	859	2,075	1,421	20	2,724	46	2,090	98	1,686	463	21	1,834	144	83
AGE: 1930																		
Under 5 years	13	19	19	293	225	852	439	2	1,094	13	875	27	359	161	7	766	68	14
Under 1 year	------	4	6	58	41	150	88	------	205	4	182	6	59	37	1	152	12	1
5 to 9 years	34	25	24	276	315	1,066	540	2	1,135	15	958	18	387	177	6	891	79	24
10 to 14 years	13	19	31	309	302	1,024	543	3	1,079	5	841	18	347	153	10	753	80	23
15 to 19 years	18	40	25	281	316	1,008	590	8	1,208	10	829	26	412	163	12	814	73	17
20 to 24 years	35	20	22	302	276	901	477	6	940	19	751	37	630	210	11	736	49	28
25 to 29 years	39	19	26	194	223	687	389	8	694	22	625	50	727	224	6	577	25	41
30 to 34 years	36	19	30	125	221	549	283	9	518	12	490	37	570	187	13	486	29	48
35 to 44 years	35	30	23	246	408	972	586	9	1,129	24	1,014	61	826	245	9	881	59	65
45 to 54 years	18	16	20	182	291	745	503	8	1,026	17	794	27	371	112	8	616	55	8
55 to 64 years	4	5	12	123	184	443	315	3	592	9	410	10	137	32	4	315	45	4
65 to 74 years	4	7	8	49	74	208	168	------	305	3	223	2	33	14	2	148	22	1
75 years and over	------	3	2	23	43	76	89	------	170	4	91	3	16	8	------	65	11	------
Unknown	------	------	1	1	2	------	30	------	3	------	2	------	2	1	1	8	------	------
SCHOOL ATTENDANCE																		
Total 7 to 13 years, inclusive	37	25	43	424	427	1,423	777	5	1,532	12	1,239	21	504	231	12	1,141	108	39
Number attending school	37	19	35	382	358	1,321	721	2	1,404	7	1,094	13	467	163	11	1,004	84	36
Percent attending school	------	------	------	90.1	83.8	92.8	92.8	------	91.6	------	88.3	------	92.7	70.6	------	88.0	77.8	------
Total 14 and 15 years, inclusive	3	14	10	102	130	410	214	2	468	3	340	14	159	67	3	297	32	3
Number attending school	2	14	6	84	110	364	175	1	403	2	278	6	136	45	2	259	27	3
Percent attending school	------	------	------	82.4	84.6	88.8	81.8	------	86.1	------	81.8	------	85.5	------	------	87.2	------	------
Total 16 and 17 years, inclusive	6	13	10	118	139	419	239	3	478	4	357	7	157	70	5	335	30	4
Number attending school	3	8	3	71	67	249	125	1	225	1	178	2	81	25	3	174	16	4
Percent attending school	------	------	------	60.2	48.2	59.4	52.3	------	47.1	------	49.9	------	51.6	------	------	51.9	------	------
Total 18 to 20 years, inclusive	12	24	14	182	188	620	346	3	703	11	484	21	271	97	6	480	42	20
Number attending school	------	5	1	25	19	81	70	------	79	------	43	1	24	4	------	60	3	1
Percent attending school	------	------	------	13.7	10.1	13.1	20.2	------	11.2	------	8.9	------	8.9	------	------	12.5	------	------
ILLITERACY																		
Total 10 years old and over	202	178	200	1,835	2,340	6,613	3,973	54	7,664	125	6,070	271	4,071	1,349	76	5,399	448	235
Number illiterate	4	2	12	267	374	1,073	661	4	995	14	870	50	236	179	9	584	63	19
Percent illiterate	2.0	1.1	6.0	14.6	16.0	16.2	16.6	------	13.0	11.2	14.3	18.5	5.8	13.3	------	10.8	14.1	8.1
Percent illiterate in 1920	------	12.4	9.5	22.1	14.5	23.6	17.6	------	16.2	------	19.3	------	5.9	18.5	------	18.3	16.2	------
URBAN AND RURAL																		
Urban population	222	164	216	------	1,100	1,363	------	------	1,896	72	513	77	4,587	744	------	2,597	------	212
Percent urban	89.2	73.9	88.9	------	38.2	16.0	------	------	19.2	47.1	6.5	24.4	95.2	44.1	------	36.8	------	77.7
Rural population	27	58	27	2,404	1,780	7,168	4,952	58	7,997	81	7,390	239	230	943	89	4,459	595	61
Rural-farm	------	12	10	1,849	1,291	5,516	2,933	15	7,433	18	6,089	94	111	753	23	3,097	409	------
Rural-nonfarm	27	46	17	555	489	1,652	2,019	43	564	63	1,301	145	119	190	66	1,362	186	61
Percent rural	10.8	26.1	11.1	100.0	61.8	84.0	100.0	------	80.8	52.9	93.5	75.6	4.8	55.9	------	63.2	100.0	22.3
MARITAL CONDITION																		
Males 15 years old and over	104	77	77	757	975	2,884	1,644	26	3,103	64	2,637	134	1,733	625	38	2,315	188	115
Single	29	31	20	231	338	888	488	7	982	28	788	27	395	158	17	682	72	43
Married	57	44	48	463	536	1,704	1,014	16	1,873	31	1,607	97	1,176	395	18	1,359	102	63
Widowed	18	2	6	44	63	171	98	1	183	3	148	9	116	55	1	170	11	5
Divorced	------	------	3	19	37	120	43	2	64	2	89	1	46	17	1	102	3	4
Unknown	------	------	------	------	1	1	1	------	1	------	5	------	------	------	1	2	------	------
Females 15 years old and over	85	82	92	769	1,063	2,705	1,786	25	3,482	56	2,592	119	1,991	571	28	2,331	180	97
Single	4	27	17	185	286	625	431	3	912	6	523	10	264	78	6	468	47	21
Married	54	44	51	470	541	1,596	1,016	15	1,905	32	1,623	96	1,273	396	18	1,366	105	58
Widowed	27	8	21	90	179	376	266	5	538	11	315	10	321	79	4	336	26	18
Divorced	------	3	2	24	57	108	71	2	124	7	129	3	133	17	------	158	2	------
Unknown	------	------	1	------	------	------	2	------	3	------	2	------	------	1	------	3	------	------
FAMILIES																		
Number of families	72	52	67	533	803	1,925	1,305	23	2,494	48	2,018	97	1,613	471	18	1,765	129	97
Median size	------	------	------	3.69	2.64	3.42	2.92	------	3.24	------	3.06	------	2.19	2.53	------	3.15	3.82	------
Families having—																		
No children under 10	41	31	42	271	548	1,063	838	20	1,495	31	1,238	74	1,228	312	12	1,016	64	76
1 child under 10	21	9	16	107	117	341	216	3	407	11	303	9	187	70	3	304	26	12
2 children under 10	6	6	5	75	58	222	123	------	259	3	183	8	104	41	2	199	16	5
3 or more	4	6	4	80	80	299	128	------	333	3	294	6	94	48	1	246	23	4

CHARACTERISTICS OF NEGRO POPULATION BY COUNTIES: 1930—Continued

(See note at head of table)

SUBJECT	TEXAS—Continued						UTAH											
	Wise	Wood	Yoakum	Young	Zapata	Zavala	The State	Box Elder	Cache	Carbon	Emery	Grand	Millard	Morgan	Salt Lake	Summit	Tooele	Uintah
POPULATION BY SEX																		
Negro population: 1930	166	4,017	2	324	6	19	1,108	1	1	39	33	24	8	1	740	12	3	4
Male	90	1,960	1	173	2	12	609			22	16	16	5		407	7	3	2
Female	76	2,057	1	151	4	7	499	1	1	17	17	8	3	1	333	5		2
Negro population: 1920	138	3,895		1		1	1,446	31	13	196	64	3	13	2	810	4	1	4
Male	85	1,957		1			834	20	8	114	43	2	9	2	450	1	1	3
Female	53	1,938				1	612	11	5	82	21	1	4		360	3		1
Percent of total population:																		
1930	0.9	16.6	0.2	1.6	0.2	0.2	0.2			0.2	0.5	1.3	0.1		0.4	0.1		
1920	0.6	14.1					0.3	0.2		1.3	0.9	0.2	0.1	0.1	0.5	0.1		
VOTING AGE: 1930																		
Total 21 years old and over	99	1,957	2	259	2	11	806	1		25	24	21	5	1	532	8	3	3
Male	59	978	1	137	1	7	454			12	13	13	2		297	5	3	2
Female	40	979	1	122	1	4	352	1		13	11	8	3	1	235	3		1
AGE: 1930																		
Under 5 years	19	448		16		4	89			7	5	1	1		59	1		
Under 1 year	3	97		1			22			1	1		1		14			
5 to 9 years	18	472		20	2		77			3	1	1			54	1		1
10 to 14 years	15	484		12	2	1	86			1	1	1			61	2		
15 to 19 years	12	538		16		3	44		1	2	2		2		29			
20 to 24 years	28	425		47		2	69			2	2		2		56			
25 to 29 years	10	298		65		4	88			3	2	2	1		53	1		
30 to 34 years	19	232		46	2		101			7	3	7			56	1	1	
35 to 44 years	23	428	2	65		3	228			6	7	9			136	4	2	
45 to 54 years	16	311		25			195	1		5	9	3	1	1	139			
55 to 64 years	2	208		10		2	81			2	1		1		55	2		2
65 to 74 years	2	105		2			33			1					26			1
75 years and over	2	62					16								15			
Unknown		6					1								1			
SCHOOL ATTENDANCE																		
Total 7 to 13 years, inclusive	18	687		25	2		113			2	1	1			80	2		1
Number attending school	17	610		16			109			1	1	1			79	2		1
Percent attending school		88.8					96.5											
Total 14 and 15 years, inclusive	6	185		3	1	2	28			1	1				20			
Number attending school	4	165		1			26				1				20			
Percent attending school		89.2																
Total 16 and 17 years, inclusive	4	211		8			10			2	1				5			
Number attending school	1	135		1			6			1	1				3			
Percent attending school		64.0																
Total 18 to 20 years, inclusive	9	351		7		2	32		1	1			2		23			
Number attending school		91					9								9			
Percent attending school		25.9																
ILLITERACY																		
Total 10 years old and over	129	3,097	2	288	4	15	942	1	1	29	27	22	7	1	627	10	3	3
Number illiterate	12	369		34		3	30	1		3	1		1		16			1
Percent illiterate	9.3	11.9		11.8			3.2								2.6			
Percent illiterate in 1920	4.5	17.2					4.6			6.5					3.5			
URBAN AND RURAL																		
Urban population		856		269		8	944			20					682	10		
Percent urban		21.3		83.0			85.2								92.2			
Rural population	166	3,161	2	55	6	11	164	1	1	19	33	24	8	1	58	2	3	4
Rural-farm	56	2,593	2	9		11	30				1	1	1	1	25			
Rural-nonfarm	110	568		46	6		134	1	1	19	32	23	7		33	2	3	4
Percent rural	100.0	78.7		17.0			14.8								7.8			
MARITAL CONDITION																		
Males 15 years old and over	64	1,291	1	143	1	8	482			15	14	13	4		317	5	3	2
Single	8	444		28	1	1	160			4	4	2	4		104	2	2	1
Married	48	735	1	106		6	267			8	10	10			174	3		1
Widowed	7	81		8		1	28			2		1			20			
Divorced	1	29		1			27			1					19		1	
Unknown		2																
Females 15 years old and over	50	1 322	1	133	1	6	374	1	1	13	12	8	3	1	249	3		1
Single	1	350		17		1	42		1		2		1		30			
Married	46	773	1	96		5	251	1		12	10	8	1	1	154	3		1
Widowed	2	154		12	1		63						1		51			
Divorced		45		8			18			1					14			
Unknown	1																	
FAMILIES																		
Number of families	51	864		100	1	5	331	1		13	14	11	3		213	4		2
Median size		3.74		1.95			2.12								2.21			
Families having:																		
No children under 10	34	443		80		2	255	1		12	12	10	2		158	3		2
1 child under 10	7	172		13		2	31			1			1		23			
2 children under 10	4	118		4	1	1	28					1			20	1		
3 or more	6	131		3			17				2				12			

CHARACTERISTICS OF NEGRO POPULATION BY COUNTIES: 1930—Continued

(See note at head of table)

SUBJECT	UTAH—Con. Utah	Weber	VERMONT The State	Addison	Bennington	Caledonia	Chittenden	Essex	Franklin	Lamoille	Orange	Orleans	Rutland	Washington	Windham	Windsor
POPULATION BY SEX																
Negro population: 1930	9	233	568	29	60	16	156	2	49	2	38	4	82	33	33	64
Male	6	125	310	14	31	9	87	2	25		22	4	43	16	18	39
Female	3	108	258	15	29	7	69		24	2	16		39	17	15	25
Negro population: 1920	17	270	572	36	55	3	175	2	38	5	21	6	68	31	34	97
Male	10	156	320	20	32	2	94	2	19	4	15	3	40	16	18	55
Female	7	114	252	16	23	1	81		19	1	6	3	29	15	16	42
Percent of total population:																
1930		0. 4	0. 2	0. 2	0. 3	0. 1	0. 3		0. 2		0. 2		0. 2	0. 1	0. 1	0. 2
1920		0. 6	0. 2	0. 2	0. 3		0. 4		0. 1		0. 1		0. 1	0. 1	0. 1	0. 3
VOTING AGE: 1930																
Total, 21 years old and over	9	174	319	18	33	7	92		23	2	23	4	47	18	13	39
Male	6	101	197	8	19	5	55		15		15	4	30	9	8	29
Female	3	73	122	10	14	2	37		8	2	8		17	9	5	10
AGE: 1930																
Under 5 years		15	75	1	11	3	18		6		8		10	5	8	5
Under 1 year		5	16		2		5		1		2		4		1	1
5 to 9 years		16	48	1	6	3	13	2	7				6	3	4	3
10 to 14 years		20	54	5	5	1	11		5		1		8	5	4	9
15 to 19 years		8	62	3	3	2	19		7		5		11	1	4	7
20 to 24 years		7	39	1	7		9		2		7		3	2		8
25 to 29 years	1	25	29	2	2	2	6		2		2	1	5	1	1	5
30 to 34 years	1	25	36	2	7	1	6		2		2	1	7	4		4
35 to 44 years	2	62	71	4	6	2	22		7		3		10	5	6	6
45 to 54 years	3	33	76	4	4	2	27		5	2	8	1	11	5	1	6
55 to 64 years	1	17	40	5	2		12		3		1	1	4	2	2	8
65 to 74 years	1	4	22		6		9		1		1		3		1	1
75 years and over		1	16	1	1		4		2				4		2	2
Unknown																
SCHOOL ATTENDANCE																
Total, 7 to 13 years, inclusive		26	69	5	8	3	13	2	8		1		10	7	4	8
Number attending school		24	66	5	7	3	13	2	8		1		9	7	3	8
Percent attending school																
Total, 14 and 15 years, inclusive		6	21	2			6		1		1		4		4	3
Number attending school		5	18	2			5		1		1		2		4	3
Percent attending school																
Total, 16 and 17 years, inclusive		2	25	2	2	1	8		4		1		3		1	3
Number attending school		1	15		1	1	4		3				3		1	2
Percent attending school																
Total, 18 to 20 years, inclusive		5	39	1	3	1	11		4		4		6	2	2	5
Number attending school			5								2		1		1	1
Percent attending school																
ILLITERACY																
Total, 10 years old and over	9	202	445	27	43	10	125		36	2	30	4	66	25	21	56
Number illiterate	2	5	22		5		1		5		1		5		2	3
Percent illiterate		2. 5	4. 9				0. 8									
Percent illiterate in 1920		0. 8	6. 2				5. 9									
URBAN AND RURAL																
Urban population	8	224	213		9	4	117		35			1	27	10	4	6
Percent urban		96. 1	37. 5				75. 0									
Rural population	1	9	355	29	51	12	39	2	14	2	38	3	55	23	29	58
Rural-farm		1	129	5	13	10	26		2	2	19	2	16	5	8	21
Rural-nonfarm	1	8	226	24	38	2	13	2	12		19	1	39	18	21	37
Percent rural		3. 9	62. 5				25. 0									
MARITAL CONDITION																
Males 15 years old and over	6	103	226	10	22	6	63		18		19	4	33	10	9	32
Single	4	33	96	6	10	2	19		8		10	2	16	3	1	19
Married	1	60	109	4	9	3	40		8		8	2	14	5	4	12
Widowed	1	4	12		2	1	1		2				1	1	3	1
Divorced		6	7		1		3				1		1		1	
Unknown			2										1	1		
Females 15 years old and over	3	79	165	12	16	3	51		13	2	10		25	10	8	15
Single	1	7	51	4	3	1	15		2		3		9	2	5	7
Married		60	84	7	6	2	27		7	2	7		10	8	2	6
Widowed	1	10	25	1	4		9		4				4		1	2
Divorced	1	2	5		3								2			
Unknown																
FAMILIES																
Number of families	1	69	135	5	17	3	47		6		9	2	18	6	7	15
Median size			2. 35													
Families having—																
No children under 10	1	54	99	5	13	2	33		4		6	2	15	2	5	12
1 child under 10		6	14				8				1		1	2		2
2 children under 10		6	8		1		3		1					2	1	
3 or more		3	14		3	1	3		1		2		2		1	1

CHARACTERISTICS OF NEGRO POPULATION BY COUNTIES: 1930—Continued

(See note at head of table)

SUBJECT	VIRGINIA: The State	Accomac County	Albemarle County	Charlottesville city	Alleghany County	Clifton Forge city	Amelia County	Amherst County	Appomattox County	Arlington County	Alexandria city	Augusta County	Staunton city	Bath County	Bedford County	Bland County	Botetourt County
POPULATION BY SEX																	
Negro population: 1930	650, 165	13, 925	6, 232	4, 083	2, 005	1, 175	4, 614	5, 721	2, 296	3, 337	4, 912	3, 609	1, 805	1, 150	6, 962	125	2, 212
Male	321, 545	7, 159	3, 146	1, 883	986	553	2, 381	2, 947	1, 173	1, 661	2, 375	1, 813	801	620	3, 510	86	1, 103
Female	328, 620	6, 766	3, 086	2, 200	1, 019	622	2, 233	2, 774	1, 123	1, 676	2, 537	1, 796	1, 004	530	3, 452	39	1, 109
Negro population: 1920	690, 017	13, 213	7, 569	2, 947	2, 528	1, 000	5, 470	6, 840	2, 838	2, 507	4, 112	4, 188	1, 774	931	7, 983	111	2, 971
Male	342, 536	6, 701	3, 752	1, 299	1, 310	475	2, 792	3, 481	1, 428	1, 236	1, 962	2, 030	717	513	3, 994	60	1, 535
Female	347, 481	6, 512	3, 817	1, 648	1, 218	525	2, 678	3, 359	1, 410	1, 271	2, 150	2, 158	1, 057	418	3, 989	51	1, 436
Percent of total population:																	
1930	26. 8	38. 8	23. 1	26. 8	9. 9	17. 2	51. 4	30. 1	27. 3	12. 5	20. 3	9. 5	15. 1	14. 1	23. 9	2. 1	14. 3
1920	29. 9	38. 0	29. 1	27. 6	16. 5	16. 2	55. 8	34. 6	30. 7	15. 6	22. 8	12. 1	16. 7	14. 6	26. 0	2. 0	17. 9
VOTING AGE: 1930																	
Total 21 years old and over	329, 220	6, 385	3, 121	2, 352	1, 067	695	2, 091	2, 539	1, 024	2, 006	2, 962	1, 897	1, 114	721	3, 278	75	1, 059
Male	162, 285	3, 315	1, 544	1, 059	537	331	1, 107	1, 296	508	1, 001	1, 451	969	485	407	1, 657	56	534
Female	166, 935	3, 070	1, 577	1, 293	530	364	984	1, 243	516	1, 005	1, 511	928	629	314	1, 621	19	525
AGE: 1930																	
Under 5 years	70, 662	1, 640	726	373	213	104	565	737	255	322	431	353	156	98	737	6	253
Under 1 year	13, 008	295	132	60	44	15	114	147	45	62	86	67	33	16	142	—	40
5 to 9 years	85, 074	2, 091	843	456	251	118	652	846	319	358	543	459	177	87	981	8	314
10 to 14 years	78, 893	1, 868	766	381	241	107	662	823	351	312	441	441	149	95	972	14	285
15 to 19 years	73, 443	1, 678	668	419	198	124	570	665	301	280	434	391	185	117	882	17	251
20 to 24 years	56, 567	1, 173	477	421	187	108	327	473	168	294	484	320	164	132	550	18	153
25 to 29 years	44, 478	880	307	381	140	85	216	325	126	248	443	229	146	111	401	13	114
30 to 34 years	38, 283	787	339	272	145	83	179	248	85	268	380	209	137	105	335	8	96
35 to 44 years	79, 682	1, 550	622	604	278	190	424	516	232	479	749	409	243	156	699	12	241
45 to 54 years	63, 757	1, 221	647	423	191	144	459	512	186	441	560	389	227	132	600	11	237
55 to 64 years	33, 373	649	462	225	94	63	301	283	140	189	259	213	117	71	359	9	133
65 to 74 years	17, 487	271	247	95	47	43	156	188	84	97	128	131	65	33	294	4	90
75 years and over	8, 058	116	127	32	18	6	103	105	48	45	51	65	39	13	143	5	44
Unknown	408	1	1	1	2	—	—	—	1	4	9	—	—	—	9	—	1
SCHOOL ATTENDANCE																	
Total 7 to 13 years, inclusive	114, 474	2, 758	1, 095	578	353	159	957	1, 153	465	472	686	608	231	132	1, 356	18	421
Number attending school	99, 417	2, 190	988	529	332	144	852	904	393	450	634	529	225	123	1, 161	12	362
Percent attending school	86. 8	79. 4	90. 2	91. 5	94. 1	90. 6	89. 0	78. 4	84. 5	95. 3	92. 4	87. 0	97. 4	93. 2	85. 6	—	86. 0
Total 14 and 15 years, inclusive	30, 662	748	301	145	91	54	248	309	151	115	160	174	59	36	385	7	113
Number attending school	23, 486	500	253	122	77	46	184	217	109	97	119	138	51	31	293	4	82
Percent attending school	76. 6	66. 8	84. 1	84. 1	—	—	74. 2	70. 2	72. 2	84. 3	74. 4	79. 3	—	—	76. 1	—	72. 6
Total 16 and 17 years, inclusive	30, 154	694	264	163	70	43	230	268	119	94	162	170	74	42	388	7	94
Number attending school	12, 767	201	104	86	22	19	103	101	47	39	65	74	40	22	142	—	43
Percent attending school	42. 3	29. 0	39. 4	52. 8	—	—	44. 8	37. 7	39. 5	—	40. 1	43. 5	—	—	36. 6	—	—
Total 18 to 20 years, inclusive	41, 199	888	364	292	110	73	283	375	157	194	299	215	104	87	431	10	153
Number attending school	5, 423	36	28	46	11	7	26	29	18	20	17	38	22	2	33	—	24
Percent attending school	13. 2	4. 1	7. 7	15. 8	10. 0	—	9. 2	7. 7	11. 5	10. 3	5. 7	17. 7	21. 2	—	7. 7	—	15. 7
ILLITERACY																	
Total 10 years old and over	494, 429	10, 194	4, 663	3, 254	1, 541	953	3, 397	4, 138	1, 722	2, 657	3, 938	2, 797	1, 472	965	5, 244	111	1, 645
Number illiterate	95, 148	2, 123	1, 027	287	161	157	847	1, 188	396	264	575	506	195	103	1, 180	28	312
Percent illiterate	19. 2	20. 8	22. 0	8. 8	10. 4	16. 5	24. 9	28. 7	23. 0	9. 9	14. 6	18. 1	13. 2	10. 7	22. 5	25. 2	19. 0
Percent illiterate in 1920	23. 5	35. 1	20. 1	16. 0	12. 6	17. 6	22. 2	32. 2	24. 2	17. 2	16. 4	23. 5	18. 5	11. 8	26. 7	—	26. 2
URBAN AND RURAL																	
Urban population	213, 401	—	—	4, 083	1, 114	1, 175	—	—	—	—	4, 912	688	1, 805	—	908	—	—
Percent urban	32. 8	—	—	100. 0	55. 6	100. 0	—	—	—	—	100. 0	19. 1	100. 0	—	13. 0	—	—
Rural population	436, 764	13, 925	6, 232	—	891	—	4, 614	5, 721	2, 296	3, 337	—	2, 921	—	1, 150	6, 054	125	2, 212
Rural-farm	258, 967	7, 406	2, 867	—	58	—	3, 970	3, 721	1, 978	10	—	835	—	180	4, 435	71	484
Rural-nonfarm	177, 797	6, 519	3, 365	—	833	—	644	2, 000	318	3, 327	—	2, 086	—	970	1, 619	54	1, 728
Percent rural	67. 2	100. 0	100. 0	—	44. 4	—	100. 0	100. 0	100. 0	100. 0	—	80. 9	—	100. 0	87. 0	100. 0	100. 0
MARITAL CONDITION																	
Males 15 years old and over	204, 713	4, 314	1, 968	1, 283	654	397	1, 455	1, 722	696	1, 155	1, 704	1, 190	576	489	2, 160	73	688
Single	75, 076	1, 613	684	421	217	137	548	664	285	361	655	440	189	208	850	40	266
Married	114, 672	2, 431	1, 121	765	387	232	765	926	359	696	961	657	346	227	1, 116	26	361
Widowed	12, 630	227	146	63	39	24	129	118	42	78	62	78	35	33	158	5	57
Divorced	2, 008	41	15	32	11	4	12	11	10	19	26	14	6	21	28	2	4
Unknown	327	2	2	2	—	—	1	3	—	1	—	1	—	—	8	—	—
Females 15 years old and over	210, 823	4, 012	1, 929	1, 590	646	449	1, 280	1, 593	675	1, 190	1, 793	1, 166	747	381	2, 112	24	672
Single	59, 134	1, 109	475	465	139	120	346	440	210	268	453	343	220	112	634	9	200
Married	116, 842	2, 432	1, 144	817	403	244	790	930	369	699	991	659	370	198	1, 153	11	372
Widowed	31, 848	401	300	271	82	76	138	209	86	209	308	151	137	40	305	3	93
Divorced	2, 834	67	9	36	22	9	6	12	10	14	41	12	19	31	17	1	5
Unknown	165	3	1	1	—	—	—	2	—	—	—	1	1	—	3	—	2
FAMILIES																	
Number of families	140, 726	2, 846	1, 313	1, 018	411	292	939	1, 125	457	862	1, 239	750	432	193	1, 430	15	469
Median size	3. 55	4. 13	3. 81	3. 09	3. 73	2. 95	4. 21	4. 35	4. 15	2. 93	2. 87	3. 58	2. 99	3. 68	4. 02	—	3. 85
Families having—																	
No children under 10	76, 556	1, 278	694	621	217	182	455	532	226	557	815	433	292	110	725	9	249
1 child under 10	23, 444	587	215	180	70	51	163	172	85	127	167	118	54	28	243	3	60
2 children under 10	15, 415	398	158	100	55	28	112	137	54	80	108	65	41	27	166	1	56
3 or more	25, 311	583	246	117	69	31	209	284	92	98	149	134	45	28	296	2	104

CHARACTERISTICS OF NEGRO POPULATION BY COUNTIES: 1930—Continued

(See note at head of table)

SUBJECT	VIRGINIA—Continued																	
	Brunswick County	Buchanan County	Buckingham County	Campbell County	Lynchburg city	Caroline County	Carroll County	Charles City County	Charlotte County	Chesterfield County	Clarke County	Craig County	Culpeper County	Cumberland County	Dickenson County	Dinwiddie County	Petersburg city	Elizabeth City County
POPULATION BY SEX																		
Negro population: 1930	11,492	133	5,802	6,650	9,653	7,730	374	3,757	6,742	7,107	1,531	15	4,317	4,357	302	11,192	12,600	5,311
Male	5,770	99	2,932	3,377	4,164	3,897	186	1,916	3,363	3,551	735	6	2,200	2,215	166	5,700	5,734	2,748
Female	5,722	34	2,870	3,273	5,489	3,833	188	1,841	3,379	3,556	796	9	2,117	2,142	136	5,492	6,866	2,563
Negro population: 1920	12,017	-	6,847	8,597	8,329	8,077	207	3,603	7,537	7,084	1,743	95	4,692	5,754	296	10,817	13,608	6,352
Male	6,066	-	3,411	4,188	3,670	4,101	103	1,820	3,718	3,547	873	44	2,306	2,904	172	5,510	6,174	3,161
Female	5,951	-	3,436	4,409	4,659	3,976	104	1,783	3,819	3,537	870	51	2,386	2,850	124	5,307	7,434	3,191
Percent of total population:																		
1930	56.1	0.8	43.6	29.1	23.7	50.6	1.7	77.0	42.0	27.3	21.4	0.4	32.4	57.8	1.9	60.5	44.1	26.8
1920	57.2	-	46.0	32.2	27.7	50.6	1.0	75.2	43.0	34.6	24.3	2.3	35.3	63.2	2.2	60.3	43.9	33.2
VOTING AGE: 1930																		
Total 21 years old and over	4,537	111	2,452	2,901	5,611	3,325	175	1,668	2,805	3,326	765	13	2,070	1,889	171	6,036	7,391	3,271
Male	2,285	86	1,215	1,464	2,324	1,700	88	885	1,373	1,700	389	6	1,054	958	95	3,061	3,285	1,711
Female	2,252	25	1,237	1,437	3,287	1,625	87	783	1,432	1,626	376	7	1,016	931	76	2,975	4,106	1,560
AGE: 1930																		
Under 5 years	1,596	5	721	832	831	992	48	486	931	725	163	-	508	572	36	1,062	1,047	453
Under 1 year	297	1	122	155	154	163	11	79	174	154	23	-	86	100	6	186	177	80
5 to 9 years	1,866	2	938	1,018	963	1,203	51	544	1,125	873	171	1	599	685	53	1,323	1,375	529
10 to 14 years	1,794	-	891	933	928	1,108	48	519	987	842	217	1	574	631	17	1,341	1,235	482
15 to 19 years	1,522	7	701	841	1,075	945	47	462	787	1,115	183	-	487	514	18	1,220	1,270	483
20 to 24 years	804	32	364	498	932	582	30	311	470	794	130	-	335	294	38	832	1,240	425
25 to 29 years	521	36	228	359	773	386	32	225	315	470	92	3	254	194	35	649	1,167	393
30 to 34 years	449	14	226	292	660	328	22	173	254	339	73	-	213	165	28	673	900	389
35 to 44 years	1,074	24	564	637	1,374	750	43	385	653	736	168	1	429	437	49	1,533	1,917	871
45 to 54 years	906	8	506	558	1,078	680	24	343	548	617	159	3	380	383	23	1,288	1,416	686
55 to 64 years	511	4	335	378	546	424	16	187	344	337	100	1	258	262	2	693	608	340
65 to 74 years	313	1	196	207	308	237	10	86	190	177	49	5	196	138	1	412	286	175
75 years and over	135	-	127	97	171	90	3	35	137	81	26	-	103	80	2	165	137	85
Unknown	1	-	5	-	14	5	-	1	1	1	-	-	1	2	-	1	2	-
SCHOOL ATTENDANCE																		
Total 7 to 13 years, inclusive	2,581	1	1,260	1,353	1,317	1,600	71	741	1,453	1,217	269	1	822	920	40	1,872	1,814	704
Number attending school	2,247	1	1,029	1,124	1,227	1,306	63	692	1,081	1,092	238	1	709	691	36	1,565	1,591	666
Percent attending school	87.1	-	81.7	83.1	93.2	81.6	-	93.4	74.4	89.7	88.5	-	86.3	75.1	-	83.6	87.7	94.6
Total 14 and 15 years, inclusive	697	-	356	359	381	442	22	230	376	352	87	1	216	256	7	535	460	194
Number attending school	549	-	277	251	315	320	17	194	258	262	71	1	150	163	3	378	356	171
Percent attending school	78.8	-	77.8	69.9	82.7	72.4	-	84.3	68.6	74.4	-	-	69.4	63.7	-	70.7	77.4	88.1
Total 16 and 17 years, inclusive	653	3	297	356	434	414	15	181	351	421	79	-	213	219	5	511	480	187
Number attending school	284	-	140	127	207	131	9	85	138	206	43	-	69	86	-	165	216	114
Percent attending school	43.5	-	47.1	35.7	47.7	31.6	-	47.0	39.3	48.9	-	-	32.4	39.3	-	32.3	45.0	61.0
Total 18 to 20 years, inclusive	712	12	337	420	717	469	23	241	359	730	96	-	254	230	16	662	849	294
Number attending school	98	-	50	29	124	28	3	43	49	326	17	-	21	12	-	49	146	79
Percent attending school	13.8	-	14.8	6.9	17.3	6.0	-	17.8	13.6	44.7	-	-	8.3	5.2	-	7.4	17.2	26.9
ILLITERACY																		
Total 10 years old and over	8,030	126	4,143	4,800	7,859	5,535	275	2,727	4,686	5,509	1,197	14	3,210	3,100	213	8,807	10,178	4,329
Number illiterate	1,897	30	1,215	1,121	1,468	1,000	47	510	1,514	1,012	84	1	708	1,007	54	2,892	1,671	570
Percent illiterate	23.6	23.8	29.3	23.4	18.7	18.1	17.1	18.7	32.3	18.4	7.0	-	22.1	32.5	25.4	32.8	16.4	13.2
Percent illiterate in 1920	36.8	-	34.6	23.4	20.7	24.0	25.7	21.7	19.4	25.7	24.3	-	24.8	33.2	25.5	37.1	22.5	15.2
URBAN AND RURAL																		
Urban population	-	-	-	-	9,653	-	121	-	-	-	-	-	-	-	-	-	12,600	869
Percent urban	-	-	-	-	100.0	-	32.4	-	-	-	-	-	-	-	-	-	100.0	16.4
Rural population	11,492	133	5,802	6,650	-	7,730	253	3,757	6,742	7,107	1,531	15	4,317	4,357	302	11,192	-	4,442
Rural-farm	9,244	9	4,038	3,934	-	5,912	105	2,322	5,038	1,725	802	15	2,119	3,387	3	6,716	-	225
Rural-nonfarm	2,248	124	1,764	2,716	-	1,818	148	1,435	1,704	5,382	729	-	2,198	970	299	4,476	-	4,217
Percent rural	100.0	100.0	100.0	100.0	-	100.0	67.6	100.0	100.0	100.0	100.0	-	100.0	100.0	100.0	100.0	-	83.6
MARITAL CONDITION																		
Male 15 years old and over	3,153	97	1,639	1,960	2,854	2,262	111	1,155	1,827	2,340	489	6	1,353	1,279	105	3,821	3,946	1,994
Single	1,198	51	619	743	924	950	37	486	676	1,061	187	2	535	496	31	1,848	1,337	663
Married	1,800	42	899	1,093	1,682	1,176	70	612	1,049	1,115	254	4	680	700	73	1,725	2,327	1,101
Widowed	130	4	107	106	205	112	3	48	92	151	47	-	93	72	1	203	260	190
Divorced	25	-	11	17	43	21	1	9	10	13	1	-	8	11	-	44	19	40
Unknown	-	-	3	1	-	3	-	-	-	-	-	-	37	-	-	1	3	-
Females 15 years old and over	3,083	29	1,613	1,907	4,077	2,165	116	1,053	1,872	2,327	491	7	1,283	1,190	91	3,645	4,997	1,853
Single	911	5	458	562	1,288	704	32	343	536	930	170	-	384	318	13	1,234	1,383	482
Married	1,852	24	909	1,102	1,834	1,201	67	607	1,121	1,106	247	6	695	696	71	1,905	2,466	979
Widowed	289	-	226	227	876	244	16	97	203	273	66	1	191	168	7	441	1,072	358
Divorced	30	-	14	15	73	11	1	6	11	18	6	-	12	8	-	64	70	31
Unknown	1	-	6	1	6	5	-	-	1	-	2	-	1	-	-	1	6	3
FAMILIES																		
Number of families	2,059	17	1,165	1,338	2,422	1,451	71	731	1,266	1,283	312	6	870	858	75	1,559	3,472	1,281
Median size	5.01	-	4.35	4.19	2.93	4.78	-	4.59	4.64	4.32	3.83	-	4.01	4.19	-	5.03	2.73	3.02
Families having—																		
No children under 10	790	12	524	614	1,574	607	33	319	531	652	180	5	429	402	35	640	2,303	837
1 child under 10	350	5	226	232	395	261	9	130	198	202	52	1	146	141	19	291	538	199
2 children under 10	283	-	115	178	210	196	9	104	172	150	27	-	114	81	6	196	283	103
3 or more	636	-	300	314	243	387	20	178	365	279	53	-	181	234	15	432	348	142

CHARACTERISTICS OF NEGRO POPULATION BY COUNTIES: 1930—Continued

(See note at head of table)

SUBJECT	VIRGINIA—Continued																	
	Hampton city	Essex County	Fairfax County	Fauquier County	Floyd County	Fluvanna County	Franklin County	Frederick County	Winchester city	Giles County	Gloucester County	Goochland County	Grayson County	Greene County	Greensville County	Halifax County	Hanover County	Henrico County
POPULATION BY SEX																		
Negro population: 1930	2,804	3,816	4,803	6,272	515	2,951	3,770	458	1,043	571	4,349	4,114	695	994	8,129	18,881	6,228	6,506
Male	1,307	1,987	2,896	3,234	267	1,507	1,935	246	488	303	2,255	2,233	341	525	4,021	9,259	3,208	3,212
Female	1,497	1,829	1,907	3,038	248	1,444	1,835	212	555	268	2,094	1,881	354	469	4,108	9,622	3,020	3,294
Negro population: 1920	2,169	4,898	4,546	6,932	675	3,427	4,612	499	934	820	5,581	4,783	901	1,099	6,826	20,053	7,183	5,877
Male	1,019	2,470	2,471	3,546	335	1,701	2,268	275	434	410	2,801	2,485	454	543	3,294	9,791	3,658	2,940
Female	1,150	2,428	2,075	3,386	340	1,726	2,344	224	500	410	2,780	2,298	447	556	3,532	10,262	3,525	2,937
Percent of total population:																		
1930	43.9	54.7	19.0	29.8	4.4	39.5	15.5	3.5	9.6	4.5	39.5	51.7	3.5	16.6	60.7	45.7	36.6	21.5
1920	35.3	57.3	20.7	31.7	5.1	40.1	17.5	4.0	13.6	6.9	46.9	54.0	4.5	17.3	58.8	48.5	39.7	31.0
VOTING AGE: 1930																		
Total 21 years old and over	1,838	1,812	2,828	3,025	238	1,317	1,574	242	618	271	2,175	1,863	300	530	3,502	7,751	2,670	3,399
Male	828	920	1,821	1,582	119	666	786	139	284	150	1,104	1,059	140	277	1,730	3,711	1,302	1,673
Female	1,010	892	1,007	1,443	119	651	788	103	334	121	1,071	804	160	253	1,772	4,040	1,368	1,726
AGE: 1930																		
Under 5 years	211	420	437	742	61	394	448	44	86	52	363	495	83	76	1,118	2,516	684	669
Under 1 year	36	73	84	132	11	68	81	6	18	10	45	107	20	15	214	523	128	119
5 to 9 years	267	495	503	850	68	462	582	58	105	73	562	592	110	102	1,306	3,046	819	818
10 to 14 years	200	553	438	860	69	390	601	52	100	93	592	587	100	116	1,053	2,786	870	764
15 to 19 years	238	461	497	688	68	331	488	53	113	67	576	520	90	145	990	2,435	1,063	721
20 to 24 years	276	260	534	518	45	235	281	35	112	52	302	294	43	113	711	1,414	471	572
25 to 29 years	233	159	471	375	20	118	168	24	88	28	156	207	32	55	595	960	273	466
30 to 34 years	224	163	360	335	14	149	153	27	63	23	162	212	38	55	392	832	222	427
35 to 44 years	470	383	620	653	47	289	322	62	141	68	454	385	58	98	747	1,835	688	814
45 to 54 years	384	412	461	566	39	268	303	44	112	49	550	378	56	102	653	1,528	598	687
55 to 64 years	192	260	266	340	41	155	206	33	62	35	318	222	46	63	350	850	268	323
65 to 74 years	69	177	129	216	23	103	132	15	35	16	210	149	31	44	164	454	170	174
75 years and over	32	71	87	129	18	57	79	71	23	13	102	72	8	25	48	219	94	68
Unknown	8	2	------	------	2	------	7	------	3	2	2	1	------	------	2	6	2	3
SCHOOL ATTENDANCE																		
Total 7 to 13 years, inclusive	319	746	637	1,218	100	585	832	75	144	108	827	826	149	164	1,605	4,059	1,182	1,101
Number attending school	302	659	556	955	88	512	579	61	137	89	723	746	131	135	1,294	3,446	1,031	1,008
Percent attending school	94.7	88.3	87.3	78.4	88.0	87.5	69.6	------	95.1	82.4	87.4	90.3	87.9	82.3	80.6	84.9	87.2	91.6
Total 14 and 15 years, inclusive	88	221	177	313	31	155	238	25	47	46	248	222	36	53	411	1,105	395	304
Number attending school	78	183	131	209	25	117	163	19	37	36	213	172	28	42	301	864	324	217
Percent attending school	------	82.8	74.0	66.8	------	75.5	68.5	------	------	------	85.9	77.5	------	------	73.2	78.2	82.0	71.4
Total 16 and 17 years, inclusive	83	194	179	280	23	130	196	24	41	26	244	224	35	48	418	1,016	497	300
Number attending school	47	103	64	81	12	49	62	17	10	9	138	85	18	21	184	483	293	85
Percent attending school	------	53.1	35.8	28.9	------	37.7	31.6	------	------	------	56.6	37.9	------	------	44.0	47.5	59.0	28.3
Total 18 to 20 years, inclusive	157	240	340	364	38	175	261	26	66	38	282	245	47	86	522	1,205	476	412
Number attending school	48	52	26	29	10	12	30	2	5	1	46	12	9	6	64	143	138	23
Percent attending school	30.6	21.7	7.6	8.0	------	6.9	11.5	------	------	------	16.3	4.9	------	------	10.3	11.9	29.0	5.6
ILLITERACY																		
Total 10 years old and over	2,326	2,901	3,863	4,680	386	2,095	2,740	356	852	446	3,424	3,027	502	816	5,705	13,319	4,725	5,019
Number illiterate	177	658	430	893	90	464	721	55	96	101	556	573	125	186	1,815	2,967	927	892
Percent illiterate	7.6	22.7	11.1	19.1	23.3	22.1	26.3	15.4	11.3	22.6	16.2	18.9	24.9	22.8	31.8	22.3	19.6	17.8
Percent illiterate in 1920	20.4	20.7	13.5	21.6	24.0	28.8	31.1	18.3	18.9	36.0	20.6	29.9	26.2	34.1	37.6	27.4	26.0	19.7
URBAN AND RURAL																		
Urban population	2,804	------	------	------	------	------	------	------	1,043	------	------	------	27	------	------	1,726	------	------
Percent urban	100.0	------	------	------	------	------	------	------	100.0	------	------	------	3.9	------	------	9.1	------	------
Rural population	------	3,816	4,803	6,272	515	2,951	3,770	458	------	571	4,349	4,114	668	994	8,129	17,155	6,228	6,506
Rural-farm	------	3,314	663	3,203	403	2,257	3,193	207	------	191	2,444	2,946	505	569	5,736	13,978	3,932	1,561
Rural-nonfarm	------	502	4,140	3,069	112	694	577	251	------	380	1,905	1,168	163	425	2,393	3,177	2,296	4,945
Percent rural	------	100.0	100.0	100.0	100.0	100.0	100.0	100.0	------	100.0	100.0	100.0	96.1	100.0	100.0	90.9	100.0	100.0
MARITAL CONDITION																		
Males 15 years old and over	957	1,214	2,175	2,015	161	878	1,098	172	347	188	1,470	1,394	198	371	2,291	5,134	1,978	2,102
Single	294	499	876	[illegible]	65	359	473	76	131	76	563	598	76	177	826	1,928	902	765
Married	580	623	1,176	1,041	79	458	551	77	197	100	814	683	112	170	1,343	2,897	970	1,182
Widowed	78	80	99	151	16	55	63	13	16	11	84	97	10	19	100	258	102	124
Divorced	5	12	21	23	1	3	8	6	3	1	8	15	------	5	22	50	2	31
Unknown	------	------	3	1	------	3	3	------	------	------	1	1	------	------	------	1	2	------
Females 15 years old and over	1,169	1,134	1,250	1,805	156	827	1,041	132	405	165	1,362	1,046	204	329	2,361	5,399	1,877	2,153
Single	299	357	306	522	44	220	346	42	132	49	386	293	63	121	661	1,637	656	628
Married	617	619	766	1,019	84	462	557	73	207	98	800	605	118	158	1,381	2,974	987	1,194
Widowed	418	150	162	231	27	140	127	16	61	17	163	139	21	50	292	700	223	300
Divorced	35	5	14	32	1	3	8	1	5	1	12	7	2	------	25	83	11	31
Unknown	------	3	2	1	------	2	3	------	------	------	1	2	------	------	2	5	------	------
FAMILIES																		
Number of families	833	823	885	1,245	109	583	679	99	251	106	995	764	131	203	1,620	3,479	1,160	1,317
Median size	2.48	3.75	3.43	3.97	3.65	4.38	4.60	------	3.04	4.42	3.61	4.41	4.48	3.44	4.35	4.81	4.39	3.72
Families having—																		
No children under 10	589	460	506	625	59	249	301	61	163	50	591	362	58	124	652	1,422	571	707
1 child under 10	126	123	135	216	19	109	112	13	38	21	152	117	22	37	337	635	206	225
2 children under 10	54	83	98	156	8	81	82	8	26	15	96	101	13	15	219	455	125	136
3 or more	64	157	146	248	23	144	184	17	24	20	156	184	38	27	412	967	258	249

CHARACTERISTICS OF NEGRO POPULATION BY COUNTIES: 1930—Continued

(See note at head of table)

SUBJECT	Richmond City	Henry County[1]	Martinsville city[1]	Highland County	Isle of Wight County	James City County	Williamsburg city	King and Queen County	King George County	King William County	Lancaster County	Lee County	Loudoun County	Louisa County	Lunenburg County	Madison Coun.	Mathews County	Mecklenburg County
	VIRGINIA—Continued																	
POPULATION BY SEX																		
Negro population: 1930	52,988	6,167	1,963	153	6,923	2,042	854	4,156	1,878	3,805	3,970	533	4,347	5,841	6,223	2,415	1,993	17,187
Male	24,354	3,024	906	96	3,479	1,072	410	2,134	987	1,939	2,046	301	2,225	2,944	3,144	1,220	1,067	8,638
Female	28,634	3,143	1,057	57	3,444	970	444	2,022	891	1,866	1,924	232	2,122	2,897	3,079	1,195	926	8,549
Negro population: 1920	54,041	7,417	1,512	221	7,149	2,034	686	5,056	2,292	4,603	5,003	671	4,810	7,803	7,141	2,868	2,363	16,586
Male	24,696	3,596	696	107	3,644	(2)	(2)	2,549	1,150	2,357	2,573	378	2,393	3,891	3,635	1,417	1,219	8,242
Female	29,345	3,821	816	114	3,505	(2)	(2)	2,507	1,142	2,246	2,430	293	2,417	3,912	3,506	1,451	1,144	8,344
Percent of total population:																		
1930	29.0	30.7	25.5	3.4	51.6	52.6	22.6	54.6	35.5	48.0	44.6	1.8	21.9	40.8	44.3	27.0	25.3	52.7
1920	31.5	36.6	37.1	4.5	49.5	55.3	27.9	55.2	39.8	52.7	51.3	2.7	23.4	45.7	46.8	29.9	28.0	53.1
VOTING AGE: 1930																		
Total 21 years old and over	32,365	2,558	1,041	99	3,089	961	510	1,841	873	1,768	1,943	285	2,187	2,705	2,548	1,131	1,085	7,005
Male	14,783	1,261	487	65	1,587	534	249	955	459	908	1,034	165	1,151	1,328	1,313	562	564	3,503
Female	17,582	1,297	554	34	1,502	427	261	886	414	860	909	120	1,036	1,377	1,235	569	521	3,502
AGE: 1930																		
Under 5 years	4,576	870	186	10	858	249	76	508	215	421	412	50	499	691	798	285	171	2,188
Under 1 year	811	169	34	1	164	50	18	91	39	71	69	7	87	141	178	54	29	410
5 to 9 years	5,389	975	245	13	1,049	264	73	622	296	518	551	68	567	808	1,036	324	213	2,793
10 to 14 years	4,754	851	196	14	987	255	74	610	260	536	525	62	514	873	983	350	239	2,606
15 to 19 years	4,904	793	230	13	799	261	98	501	204	484	468	50	493	677	753	284	235	2,227
20 to 24 years	5,011	565	248	20	583	208	98	283	119	295	310	72	354	357	449	170	205	1,480
25 to 29 years	4,988	375	186	11	426	127	77	188	87	205	199	46	255	260	287	106	111	920
30 to 34 years	4,444	257	115	11	335	88	61	154	79	151	175	32	211	207	260	90	102	825
35 to 44 years	8,938	518	208	21	737	205	114	424	164	385	457	61	473	611	639	207	233	1,603
45 to 54 years	6,027	466	188	14	577	185	90	395	200	404	386	47	441	605	487	229	203	1,237
55 to 64 years	2,378	243	78	15	343	116	62	223	128	247	270	25	266	397	278	171	148	720
65 to 74 years	1,131	173	45	7	153	52	23	183	94	111	161	14	167	227	155	119	88	409
75 years and over	396	81	38	4	67	32	8	64	32	40	55	6	107	122	97	80	42	177
Unknown	52	-	-	-	9	-	-	1	-	8	1	-	-	6	1	-	3	2
SCHOOL ATTENDANCE																		
Total 7 to 13 years, inclusive	7,161	1,268	310	18	1,444	376	96	838	387	752	742	89	729	1,175	1,416	488	319	3,759
Number attending school	6,724	1,028	272	10	1,265	347	92	755	343	585	651	61	609	1,009	1,221	373	294	3,314
Percent attending school	93.9	81.1	87.7	-	87.6	92.3	-	90.1	88.6	77.8	87.7	-	83.5	85.9	86.2	76.4	92.2	88.2
Total 14 and 15 years, inclusive	1,764	329	69	6	356	98	36	258	98	202	211	22	222	337	352	124	94	969
Number attending school	1,425	217	50	2	286	76	28	219	76	124	168	8	156	244	289	92	81	808
Percent attending school	80.8	66.0	-	-	80.3	-	-	84.9	-	61.4	79.6	-	70.3	72.4	82.1	74.2	-	83.4
Total 16 and 17 years, inclusive	1,940	337	93	1	323	99	40	217	81	192	181	16	211	284	336	118	103	904
Number attending school	839	95	37	-	140	37	23	115	46	60	79	5	66	96	168	60	44	477
Percent attending school	43.2	28.2	-	-	43.3	-	-	53.0	-	31.3	43.6	-	31.3	33.8	50.0	50.8	42.7	52.8
Total 18 to 20 years, inclusive	3,111	428	170	13	446	155	66	244	101	268	251	47	259	327	353	145	138	1,224
Number attending school	461	42	30	1	60	20	15	44	8	9	26	4	17	33	53	34	16	191
Percent attending school	14.8	9.8	17.6	-	13.5	12.9	-	18.0	7.9	3.4	10.4	-	6.6	10.1	15.0	23.4	11.6	15.6
ILLITERACY																		
Total 10 years old and over	43,023	4,322	1,532	130	5,016	1,529	705	3,026	1,367	2,866	3,007	415	3,281	4,342	4,389	1,806	1,609	12,206
Number illiterate	5,389	1,079	294	21	1,170	304	101	572	330	729	785	129	604	881	1,029	317	234	2,723
Percent illiterate	12.5	25.0	19.2	16.2	23.3	19.9	14.3	18.9	24.1	25.4	26.1	31.1	18.4	20.3	23.4	17.6	14.5	22.3
Percent illiterate in 1920	14.9	29.8	24.1	25.7	24.6	(2)	(2)	20.3	33.2	23.0	29.1	28.1	19.3	23.3	25.6	21.7	16.0	28.4
URBAN AND RURAL																		
Urban population	52,988	-	1,963	-	-	-	854	-	-	-	-	-	-	-	-	-	-	-
Percent urban	100.0	-	100.0	-	-	-	100.0	-	-	-	-	-	-	-	-	-	-	-
Rural population	-	6,167	-	153	6,923	2,042	-	4,156	1,878	3,805	3,970	533	4,347	5,841	6,223	2,415	1,993	17,187
Rural-farm	-	3,506	-	59	3,082	1,154	-	3,780	1,577	2,366	2,131	154	1,322	3,802	5,191	1,699	1,012	14,246
Rural-nonfarm	-	2,661	-	94	3,841	888	-	376	301	1,439	1,839	379	3,025	2,039	1,032	716	981	2,941
Percent rural	-	100.0	-	100.0	100.0	100.0	-	100.0	100.0	100.0	100.0	100.0	100.0	100.0	100.0	100.0	100.0	100.0
MARITAL CONDITION																		
Males 15 years old and over	17,230	1,709	618	75	2,049	687	305	1,252	593	1,217	1,325	207	1,450	1,722	1,736	740	729	4,794
Single	5,194	669	235	35	763	273	117	480	211	519	481	82	568	645	601	326	287	1,885
Married	10,665	943	339	36	1,126	359	162	669	335	616	753	113	772	948	1,013	347	400	2,657
Widowed	1,116	84	41	4	145	51	24	93	40	68	82	10	99	123	105	67	40	212
Divorced	248	11	3	-	13	1	2	9	7	14	8	2	8	6	16	-	2	39
Unknown	7	2	-	-	2	3	-	1	-	-	1	-	3	-	1	-	-	1
Females 15 years old and over	21,039	1,762	718	41	1,980	587	326	1,164	514	1,113	1,157	146	1,317	1,747	1,670	716	641	4,806
Single	5,465	570	249	15	562	165	110	339	111	351	280	32	380	497	450	228	154	1,494
Married	11,090	974	346	22	1,151	354	158	676	335	610	731	95	778	974	1,027	371	398	2,704
Widowed	4,075	204	118	4	257	65	51	143	67	141	140	17	148	273	172	116	87	555
Divorced	405	11	5	-	9	1	7	6	1	11	6	2	11	2	21	1	2	52
Unknown	4	3	-	-	1	2	-	-	-	-	-	-	-	1	-	-	-	1
FAMILIES																		
Number of families	13,679	1,108	386	32	1,336	426	191	820	414	768	850	122	894	1,240	1,185	480	458	3,113
Median size	2.74	4.88	3.76	-	4.47	4.02	3.17	4.52	3.63	4.18	3.74	2.97	3.53	3.95	4.59	4.03	3.73	4.85
Families having—																		
No children under 10	8,987	452	209	18	597	221	122	364	202	383	445	74	487	639	481	244	275	1,312
1 child under 10	2,141	175	59	8	239	60	34	159	79	133	162	15	136	219	227	75	78	501
2 children under 10	1,029	148	41	3	166	61	11	119	45	97	89	16	90	141	151	62	51	399
3 or more	1,342	333	77	3	334	84	24	178	88	155	154	17	181	241	326	99	54	901

[1] Martinsville town incorporated as a city and made independent of Henry County, in 1929.

[2] Data not available. Williamsburg city less than 2,500.

CHARACTERISTICS OF NEGRO POPULATION BY COUNTIES: 1930—Continued

(See note at head of table)

VIRGINIA—Continued

SUBJECT	Middlesex County	Montgomery County	Radford city	Nansemond County	Suffolk city	Nelson County	New Kent County	Norfolk County[1]	South Norfolk city[1]	Norfolk city	Portsmouth city	Northampton County	Northumberland County	Nottoway County	Orange County	Page County	Patrick County	Pittsylvania County
POPULATION BY SEX																		
Negro population: 1930	3, 360	1, 965	637	15, 203	3, 806	4, 561	2, 529	13, 307	1, 703	43, 942	18, 849	9, 930	4, 648	6, 659	3, 795	733	1, 373	21, 059
Male	1, 777	1, 006	318	7, 698	1, 665	2, 278	1, 319	6, 753	801	20, 790	8, 941	5, 038	2, 480	3, 315	1, 872	354	707	10, 271
Female	1, 583	959	319	7, 505	2, 141	2, 283	1, 210	6, 554	902	23, 152	9, 908	4, 892	2, 168	3, 344	1, 923	379	666	10, 788
Negro population: 1920	4, 117	2, 078	525	12, 875	3, 616	5, 026	2, 623	22, 765	*2, 015*	43, 392	23, 245	9, 587	4, 873	6, 579	4, 865	894	1, 393	20, 000
Male	2, 134	1, 018	261	6, 391	1, 630	2, 537	1, 334	11, 929	*962*	21, 794	11, 635	4, 767	2, 552	3, 239	2, 497	425	691	9, 726
Female	1, 983	1, 060	264	6, 484	1, 986	2, 489	1, 289	10, 836	*1, 053*	21, 598	11, 610	4, 820	2, 321	3, 340	2, 496	469	702	10, 274
Percent of total population:																		
1930	46. 2	10. 0	10. 2	67. 5	37. 1	27. 9	58. 8	44. 2	21. 7	33. 9	41. 2	53. 5	41. 9	44. 8	31. 4	4. 9	8. 7	34. 3
1920	50. 5	11. 2	11. 3	63. 7	39. 6	29. 1	57. 8	39. 7	*26. 1*	37. 5	42. 7	53. 7	42. 3	46. 5	36. 5	6. 1	8. 3	35. 4
VOTING AGE: 1930																		
Total 21 years old and over	1, 636	1, 026	321	7, 166	2, 130	1, 999	1, 093	6, 599	974	27, 920	11, 482	4, 633	2, 068	2, 950	1, 841	383	600	8, 755
Male	865	533	151	3, 637	909	995	593	3, 430	454	13, 138	5, 467	2, 371	1, 125	1, 434	893	189	319	4, 183
Female	771	493	170	3, 529	1, 221	1, 004	500	3, 169	520	14, 782	6, 015	2, 262	943	1, 516	948	194	281	4, 572
AGE: 1930																		
Under 5 years	370	182	83	1, 726	287	624	323	1, 568	152	3, 378	1, 510	1, 127	536	859	432	87	181	3, 060
Under 1 year	70	32	18	276	49	112	49	290	30	616	247	194	106	158	87	18	41	626
5 to 9 years	479	242	92	2, 075	409	710	379	1, 849	195	4, 171	2, 067	1, 337	722	994	522	96	226	3, 341
10 to 14 years	446	235	77	2, 015	435	613	361	1, 553	179	3, 737	1, 780	1, 302	687	895	510	72	183	2, 820
15 to 19 years	373	242	48	1, 885	459	531	313	1, 450	169	3, 849	1, 649	1, 325	542	825	408	81	164	2, 653
20 to 24 years	233	176	47	1, 418	425	368	210	1, 302	153	4, 359	1, 775	816	387	466	302	58	97	1, 735
25 to 29 years	136	120	49	1, 037	314	232	111	941	126	4, 350	1, 671	622	254	331	173	47	98	1, 253
30 to 34 years	135	113	45	819	278	190	119	752	124	3, 833	1, 573	578	233	349	148	29	60	933
35 to 44 years	356	227	80	1, 630	558	406	245	1, 550	221	7, 812	3, 092	1, 200	481	659	387	77	124	1, 968
45 to 54 years	371	204	64	1, 354	372	349	237	1, 379	213	5, 157	2, 255	848	399	637	407	76	99	1, 625
55 to 64 years	262	105	32	766	159	286	124	608	107	2, 116	976	455	227	373	213	57	61	919
65 to 74 years	138	71	12	335	74	162	78	252	48	797	373	212	128	172	181	46	50	492
75 years and over	61	43	8	126	36	89	29	95	16	294	122	107	50	97	98	7	28	248
Unknown	------	5	------	17	------	1	------	8	------	89	6	1	2	2	14	------	2	12
SCHOOL ATTENDANCE																		
Total 7 to 13 years, inclusive	665	340	124	2, 850	591	920	508	2, 327	273	5, 536	2, 770	1, 827	985	1, 297	744	121	275	4, 231
Number attending school	606	307	115	2, 403	512	653	457	2, 078	265	5, 121	2, 607	1, 573	853	1, 213	666	108	197	3, 435
Percent attending school	91. 1	90. 3	92. 7	84. 3	86. 6	71. 0	90. 0	89. 3	97. 1	92. 5	94. 1	86. 1	86. 6	93. 5	89. 5	89. 3	71. 6	81. 2
Total 14 and 15 years, inclusive	154	96	21	791	172	245	160	561	66	1, 333	606	579	257	387	192	28	73	1, 115
Number attending school	128	85	17	595	108	156	117	396	49	1, 121	480	454	218	308	149	19	48	810
Percent attending school	83. 1	------	------	75. 2	62. 8	63. 7	73. 1	70. 6	------	84. 1	79. 2	78. 4	84. 8	79. 6	77. 6	------	------	72. 6
Total 16 and 17 years, inclusive	162	106	22	805	190	235	116	621	74	1, 530	661	528	227	336	167	35	73	1, 116
Number attending school	64	61	4	380	59	77	40	173	26	765	304	257	123	134	67	12	27	428
Percent attending school	39. 5	57. 5	------	47. 2	31. 1	32. 8	34. 5	27. 9	------	50. 0	46. 0	48. 7	54. 2	39. 9	40. 1	------	------	38. 4
Total 18 to 20 years, inclusive	190	122	33	1, 028	269	260	176	866	99	2, 570	1, 049	699	295	430	223	42	70	1, 424
Number attending school	36	32	3	151	28	21	10	67	9	405	158	109	58	53	17	1	12	115
Percent attending school	18. 9	26. 2	------	14. 7	10. 4	8. 1	5. 7	7. 7	------	15. 8	15. 1	15. 6	19. 7	12. 3	7. 6	------	------	8. 1
ILLITERACY																		
Total 10 years old and over	2, 511	1, 541	462	11, 402	3, 110	3, 227	1, 827	9, 890	1, 356	36, 393	15, 272	7, 466	3, 390	4, 806	2, 841	550	966	14, 658
Number illiterate	460	228	59	2, 134	784	811	331	2, 193	374	4, 135	2, 467	1, 103	580	851	626	130	322	3, 801
Percent illiterate	18. 3	14. 8	12. 8	18. 7	25. 2	25. 1	18. 1	22. 2	27. 6	11. 4	16. 2	14. 8	17. 1	17. 7	22. 0	23. 6	33. 3	25. 9
Percent illiterate in 1920	29. 5	23. 1	23. 9	25. 0	23. 1	25. 0	27. 4	21. 7	*22. 1*	13. 9	21. 3	25. 9	26. 9	21. 4	23. 9	32. 1	25. 5	32. 3
URBAN AND RURAL																		
Urban population	------	------	637	------	3, 806	------	------	------	1, 703	43, 942	18, 849	679	------	------	------	------	------	------
Percent urban	------	------	100. 0	------	100. 0	------	------	------	100. 0	100. 0	100. 0	6. 8	------	------	------	------	------	------
Rural population	3, 360	1, 965	------	15, 203	------	4, 561	2, 529	13, 307	------	------	------	9, 251	4, 648	6, 659	3, 795	733	1, 373	21, 059
Rural-farm	2, 618	453	------	7, 120	------	3, 438	1, 017	3, 524	------	------	------	4, 674	2, 923	4, 032	1, 830	194	1, 129	14, 232
Rural-nonfarm	742	1, 512	------	8, 083	------	1, 123	1, 512	9, 783	------	------	------	4, 577	1, 725	2, 627	1, 965	539	244	6, 827
Percent rural	100. 0	100. 0	------	100. 0	------	100. 0	100. 0	100. 0	------	------	------	93. 2	100. 0	100. 0	100. 0	100. 0	100. 0	100. 0
MARITAL CONDITION																		
Males 15 years old and over	1, 109	665	183	4, 754	1, 108	1, 311	784	4, 272	539	15, 236	6, 368	3, 133	1, 480	1, 928	1, 152	244	426	5, 678
Single	407	261	51	1, 949	371	495	308	1, 514	142	5, 149	2, 080	1, 206	593	714	433	92	183	2, 039
Married	624	341	113	2, 498	649	730	418	2, 448	364	8, 950	3, 649	1, 693	803	1, 071	608	128	217	3, 312
Widowed	72	55	14	269	75	79	55	261	33	959	519	172	77	129	106	23	21	282
Divorced	6	5	5	29	11	2	3	38	------	163	79	62	6	13	5	1	4	44
Unknown	------	3	------	9	2	5	------	11	------	15	41	------	1	1	------	------	1	1
Females 15 years old and over	956	641	202	4, 633	1, 567	1, 303	682	4, 065	638	17, 420	7, 124	3, 031	1, 223	1, 983	1, 179	234	357	6, 160
Single	235	196	51	1, 449	480	383	178	1, 023	160	4, 354	1, 679	882	312	582	309	70	102	1, 835
Married	597	321	115	2, 553	760	751	422	2, 468	362	9, 633	3, 740	1, 701	790	1, 118	626	127	202	3, 417
Widowed	120	114	34	574	299	153	74	527	113	3, 178	1, 531	363	114	242	233	34	51	822
Divorced	4	10	2	52	25	6	8	33	3	246	173	83	7	40	11	3	1	79
Unknown	------	------	------	5	3	10	------	14	------	9	1	2	------	1	------	------	1	7
FAMILIES																		
Number of families	788	438	140	2, 992	937	876	504	2, 907	431	11, 488	5, 096	2, 010	900	1, 310	863	170	250	4, 024
Median size	3. 45	3. 44	3. 50	4. 18	3. 04	4. 46	4. 20	3. 77	3. 01	2. 64	2. 73	4. 06	4. 58	4. 39	3. 36	3. 15	4. 67	4. 53
Families having—																		
No children under 10	435	252	74	1, 444	596	388	216	1, 472	268	7, 886	3, 387	987	380	596	484	103	112	1, 661
1 child under 10	130	74	18	534	154	133	111	513	78	1, 721	794	378	185	233	141	18	33	692
2 children under 10	80	42	17	359	105	126	55	369	34	934	420	239	125	149	79	19	30	519
3 or more	143	70	31	655	82	229	122	553	51	947	495	406	210	332	159	30	75	1, 152

[1] South Norfolk city incorporated as a city and made independent of Norfolk County, in 1921.

CHARACTERISTICS OF NEGRO POPULATION BY COUNTIES: 1930—Continued

(See note at head of table)

SUBJECT	Danville city	Powhatan County	Prince Edward County	Prince George County	Hopewell city	Princess Anne County	Prince William County	Pulaski County	Rappahannock County	Richmond County	Roanoke County	Roanoke city	Rockbridge County	Buena Vista city	Rockingham County	Harrisonburg city	Russell County	Scott County
	VIRGINIA—Continued																	
POPULATION BY SEX																		
Negro population: 1930	5,519	3,155	7,546	4,226	1,318	7,597	2,536	2,248	1,878	2,664	3,269	12,368	2,301	264	890	848	779	277
Male	2,363	1,654	3,718	2,171	718	3,829	1,300	1,147	1,005	1,367	1,574	5,755	1,137	117	473	405	407	157
Female	3,156	1,501	3,828	2,055	600	3,768	1,236	1,101	873	1,297	1,695	6,613	1,164	147	417	443	372	120
Negro population: 1920	5,678	3,942	8,183	5,134	235	6,426	2,741	2,425	2,154	2,957	2,877	9,331	2,670	356	1,012	780	1,282	404
Male	2,517	1,992	4,089	2,507	117	3,175	1,512	1,181	1,119	1,487	1,383	4,455	1,221	169	498	343	744	220
Female	3,161	1,950	4,094	2,627	118	3,251	1,279	1,244	1,035	1,470	1,494	4,876	1,449	187	514	437	538	184
Percent of total population:																		
1930	24.8	51.4	52.0	41.0	11.6	46.7	18.2	10.9	24.3	38.7	9.3	17.9	11.0	6.6	3.0	11.7	3.0	1.1
1920	26.4	60.2	55.4	39.8	16.8	47.2	20.4	14.2	26.7	39.8	12.8	18.4	12.9	9.1	3.4	13.3	4.8	1.6
VOTING AGE: 1930																		
Total 21 years old and over	3,235	1,505	3,324	1,843	789	3,554	1,242	1,223	881	1,153	1,719	7,269	1,288	152	444	489	378	152
Male	1,324	831	1,596	971	466	1,824	633	622	482	614	814	3,381	619	69	234	229	198	88
Female	1,911	674	1,728	872	323	1,730	609	601	399	539	905	3,888	669	83	210	260	180	64
AGE: 1930																		
Under 5 years	525	335	900	512	129	848	306	226	234	293	332	1,144	224	27	116	89	100	26
Under 1 year	88	61	155	83	26	135	57	48	54	53	70	199	42	2	22	13	23	4
5 to 9 years	581	471	1,155	634	127	1,075	336	273	227	417	409	1,252	265	21	119	95	109	28
10 to 14 years	493	424	1,088	640	90	1,040	317	253	273	370	372	1,151	251	27	82	81	109	31
15 to 19 years	563	380	957	505	144	926	302	224	225	369	360	1,280	231	35	101	77	66	34
20 to 24 years	566	210	495	382	202	725	203	205	136	220	305	1,305	189	24	102	81	74	32
25 to 29 years	492	164	332	247	158	463	141	161	116	132	208	1,266	175	13	49	57	59	17
30 to 34 years	410	126	324	222	103	389	132	131	83	121	187	1,126	118	20	42	55	43	14
35 to 44 years	787	332	779	432	175	815	278	265	201	259	397	1,888	268	34	99	115	92	34
45 to 54 years	581	308	737	369	113	692	238	218	137	225	310	1,123	271	38	72	99	52	27
55 to 64 years	317	199	398	175	46	388	151	155	108	145	206	496	179	14	56	44	42	17
65 to 74 years	134	136	253	85	22	160	74	90	91	78	126	203	85	9	32	33	21	10
75 years and over	65	68	126	23	3	71	57	44	46	35	55	121	45	2	20	16	12	7
Unknown	5	2	2	-	6	5	1	3	1	-	2	13	-	-	-	-	-	-
SCHOOL ATTENDANCE																		
Total 7 to 13 years, inclusive	729	608	1,553	898	141	1,499	453	361	370	541	546	1,654	359	36	141	123	159	37
Number attending school	697	535	1,297	814	131	1,300	392	321	314	410	492	1,579	314	34	122	115	137	34
Percent attending school	95.6	88.0	83.5	90.6	92.9	86.7	86.5	88.9	84.9	75.8	90.1	95.5	87.5	-	86.5	93.5	86.2	-
Total 14 and 15 years, inclusive	214	177	439	246	44	394	133	103	90	164	142	492	95	13	29	31	33	10
Number attending school	169	136	337	187	29	299	103	87	66	118	108	408	73	7	17	24	26	9
Percent attending school	79.0	76.8	76.8	76.0	-	75.9	77.4	84.5	-	72.0	76.1	82.9	-	-	-	-	-	-
Total 16 and 17 years, inclusive	208	152	446	228	47	380	123	90	80	161	150	499	82	12	43	30	23	17
Number attending school	80	56	175	71	4	145	43	48	31	55	50	240	38	3	14	19	9	10
Percent attending school	38.5	36.8	39.2	31.1	-	38.2	35.0	-	-	34.2	33.3	48.1	-	-	-	-	-	-
Total 18 to 20 years, inclusive	365	175	430	258	113	523	143	141	138	183	210	802	146	17	71	46	41	21
Number attending school	37	24	48	26	4	40	12	19	14	20	31	145	21	1	4	21	6	6
Percent attending school	10.1	13.7	11.2	10.1	3.5	7.6	8.4	13.5	10.1	10.9	14.8	18.1	14.4	-	-	-	-	-
ILLITERACY																		
Total 10 years old and over	4,413	2,349	5,491	3,080	1,062	5,674	1,894	1,749	1,417	1,954	2,528	9,972	1,812	216	655	664	570	223
Number illiterate	1,063	508	1,409	527	199	1,164	363	263	376	608	386	1,251	250	42	149	71	121	64
Percent illiterate	24.1	21.6	25.7	17.1	18.7	20.5	19.2	15.0	26.5	31.1	15.3	12.5	13.8	19.4	22.7	10.7	21.2	28.7
Percent illiterate in 1920	30.5	29.6	25.5	24.0	35.1	20.4	20.0	18.9	29.1	36.6	24.4	16.9	19.8	27.5	24.1	22.6	26.6	28.4
URBAN AND RURAL																		
Urban population	5,519	-	1,269	-	1,318	-	-	1,045	-	-	992	12,368	1,076	264	-	848	-	-
Percent urban	100.0	-	16.8	-	100.0	-	-	46.5	-	-	30.3	100.0	46.8	100.0	-	100.0	-	-
Rural population	-	3,155	6,277	4,226	-	7,597	2,536	1,203	1,878	2,664	2,277	-	1,225	-	890	-	779	277
Rural-farm	-	2,146	5,164	2,698	-	3,575	667	367	1,336	2,146	606	-	377	-	201	-	185	63
Rural-nonfarm	-	1,009	1,113	1,528	-	4,022	1,869	836	542	518	1,671	-	848	-	689	-	594	214
Percent rural	-	100.0	83.2	100.0	-	100.0	100.0	53.5	100.0	100.0	69.7	-	53.2	-	100.0	-	100.0	100.0
MARITAL CONDITION																		
Males 15 years old and over	1,588	1,071	2,144	1,285	551	2,339	808	764	630	838	1,025	4,024	747	82	308	264	245	107
Single	424	456	781	505	222	826	320	268	241	404	352	1,318	278	29	135	90	75	42
Married	1,039	532	1,220	697	293	1,353	437	439	275	385	604	2,429	408	48	156	158	145	56
Widowed	112	79	127	72	32	142	45	48	46	40	63	216	55	3	15	14	21	9
Divorced	16	9	16	10	3	14	6	8	1	9	5	60	4	2	2	2	2	-
Unknown	7	1	-	1	1	4	-	1	67	-	1	1	2	-	-	-	2	-
Females 15 years old and over	2,332	854	2,259	1,155	421	2,295	769	732	514	746	1,131	4,797	814	107	265	313	216	85
Single	626	239	661	300	102	623	207	198	162	257	321	1,329	246	33	92	95	47	26
Married	1,115	478	1,255	689	270	1,355	450	423	279	384	624	2,530	410	54	139	168	139	47
Widowed	553	134	320	160	44	291	100	104	69	98	174	820	144	18	33	49	29	12
Divorced	30	3	23	6	4	21	11	7	4	7	12	112	14	2	1	1	1	-
Unknown	8	-	-	-	1	5	1	-	-	-	-	6	-	-	-	-	-	-
FAMILIES																		
Number of families	1,427	606	1,545	827	297	1,533	518	484	346	504	726	2,806	559	71	176	201	164	56
Median size	2.88	4.11	4.08	4.23	2.79	4.11	3.99	3.59	4.50	4.39	3.48	3.20	3.18	-	3.85	3.25	3.47	-
Families having—																		
No children under 10	906	306	748	371	177	756	260	271	156	204	417	1,691	345	45	85	126	84	36
1 child under 10	225	90	254	143	48	273	81	78	67	98	100	461	84	13	30	24	24	5
2 children under 10	144	73	195	112	39	172	70	58	42	75	95	311	45	6	27	17	23	5
3 or more	152	137	348	201	33	332	107	77	81	122	114	343	80	7	34	34	33	10

CHARACTERISTICS OF NEGRO POPULATION BY COUNTIES: 1930—Continued

(See note at head of table)

VIRGINIA—Continued

SUBJECT	Shenandoah County	Smyth County	Southampton County	Spotsylvania County	Fredericksburg city	Stafford County	Surry County	Sussex County	Tazewell County	Warren County	Warwick County	Newport News city	Washington County	Bristol city, Va.	Westmoreland County	Wise County	Wythe County	York County
POPULATION BY SEX																		
Negro population: 1930	501	631	16,394	3,113	1,218	1,488	4,265	8,006	2,689	821	2,506	13,281	1,457	1,184	3,723	3,180	1,416	2,985
Male	316	309	8,147	1,606	564	768	2,216	4,022	1,361	396	1,361	6,442	715	563	1,913	1,761	708	1,531
Female	185	322	8,247	1,507	654	720	2,049	3,984	1,328	425	1,145	6,839	742	621	1,810	1,419	708	1,454
Negro population: 1920	434	925	16,919	3,450	1,193	1,530	5,693	8,429	2,894	1,129	4,167	14,077	1,789	1,062	5,042	3,810	1,743	3,445
Male	208	452	8,468	1,747	545	780	2,952	4,250	1,540	571	2,238	7,654	878	496	2,592	2,096	831	1,762
Female	226	473	8,451	1,703	648	750	2,741	4,179	1,354	558	1,929	6,423	911	566	2,450	1,714	912	1,683
Percent of total population:																		
1930	2.4	2.5	61.0	31.0	17.9	18.5	60.1	66.2	8.3	9.8	28.4	38.6	4.3	13.4	43.8	6.2	6.8	39.2
1920	2.1	4.2	61.4	32.6	20.3	18.9	61.2	65.7	10.4	12.8	36.5	39.5	5.5	15.8	49.2	8.2	8.6	42.8
VOTING AGE: 1930																		
Total 21 years old and over	325	343	6,833	1,454	690	670	1,878	3,555	1,468	412	1,301	7,960	773	739	1,652	1,887	714	1,502
Male	224	167	3,425	745	298	341	972	1,819	761	210	722	3,960	377	353	854	1,115	332	794
Female	101	176	3,408	709	392	329	906	1,734	707	202	579	4,000	396	386	798	772	382	708
AGE: 1930																		
Under 5 years	35	56	2,223	361	122	197	486	1,002	301	95	293	1,216	142	88	408	339	168	340
Under 1 year	3	14	419	64	25	41	91	186	51	26	46	228	22	19	62	72	27	77
5 to 9 years	45	55	2,605	440	132	239	635	1,128	327	105	309	1,366	177	108	553	340	178	388
10 to 14 years	39	69	2,407	441	113	189	672	1,108	295	113	271	1,203	156	96	532	277	177	368
15 to 19 years	49	89	2,023	368	134	164	527	1,035	248	82	285	1,246	170	132	502	267	161	336
20 to 24 years	48	60	1,477	211	119	125	270	734	256	67	228	1,359	131	128	270	281	107	258
25 to 29 years	58	37	990	140	113	76	191	481	229	37	179	1,306	87	113	190	317	81	179
30 to 34 years	59	19	788	126	69	70	159	404	184	46	173	1,087	67	96	192	256	58	151
35 to 44 years	67	84	1,553	333	144	157	456	776	350	93	302	2,190	155	169	353	534	154	308
45 to 54 years	61	75	1,214	307	142	149	423	723	242	82	275	1,552	170	146	345	348	142	348
55 to 64 years	23	50	660	219	61	59	243	382	148	51	131	505	114	70	194	142	95	193
65 to 74 years	9	27	310	117	41	39	145	170	73	40	42	188	62	25	138	57	61	91
75 years and over	8	10	142	47	22	24	58	60	35	10	16	62	25	11	43	19	33	25
Unknown	------	------	2	3	1	------	------	3	1	------	2	1	1	2	3	3	1	------
SCHOOL ATTENDANCE																		
Total 7 to 13 years, inclusive	57	80	3,539	613	168	285	915	1,549	428	153	404	1,833	225	152	759	415	248	537
Number attending school	53	74	3,003	544	152	231	804	1,108	386	131	369	1,731	207	141	684	282	223	495
Percent attending school	------	------	84.9	88.7	90.5	81.1	87.9	71.5	90.2	85.6	91.3	94.4	92.0	92.8	90.1	68.0	89.9	92.2
Total 14 and 15 years, inclusive	18	38	911	171	41	73	264	437	106	44	109	403	66	48	207	105	66	141
Number attending school	12	36	690	139	33	61	218	266	84	29	70	335	53	34	171	71	56	95
Percent attending school	------	------	75.7	81.3	------	------	82.6	60.9	79.2	------	64.2	83.1	------	------	82.6	67.6	------	67.4
Total 16 and 17 years, inclusive	19	37	841	154	75	76	226	415	105	42	108	491	75	44	236	112	61	127
Number attending school	5	20	372	73	28	38	107	129	41	10	44	233	39	22	128	33	26	51
Percent attending school	------	------	44.2	47.4	------	------	47.3	31.1	39.0	------	40.7	47.5	------	------	54.2	29.5	------	40.2
Total 18 to 20 years, inclusive	29	54	1,029	187	67	85	243	584	147	35	166	844	106	75	245	180	88	185
Number attending school	2	13	107	18	3	9	29	42	23	1	13	125	16	18	31	22	13	23
Percent attending school	------	------	10.4	9.6	------	------	11.9	7.2	15.6	------	7.8	14.8	15.1	------	12.7	12.2	------	12.4
ILLITERACY																		
Total 10 years old and over	421	520	11,566	2,312	964	1,052	3,144	5,876	2,061	621	1,904	10,699	1,138	988	2,762	2,501	1,070	2,257
Number illiterate	77	79	2,833	349	125	207	747	1,927	370	80	302	1,119	185	101	663	717	173	324
Percent illiterate	18.3	15.2	24.5	15.1	13.0	19.7	23.8	32.8	18.0	12.9	15.9	10.5	16.3	10.2	24.0	28.7	16.2	14.4
Percent illiterate in 1920	30.3	20.6	31.4	19.8	16.3	28.7	24.8	32.6	19.5	25.7	17.9	14.6	22.7	16.7	36.2	31.3	27.3	28.0
URBAN AND RURAL																		
Urban population	------	350	1,351	------	1,218	------	------	------	285	------	------	13,281	597	1,184	------	1,013	474	------
Percent urban	------	55.5	8.2	------	100.0	------	------	------	10.6	------	------	100.0	41.0	100.0	------	31.9	33.5	------
Rural population	501	281	15,043	3,113	------	1,488	4,265	8,006	2,404	821	2,506	------	860	------	3,723	2,167	942	2,985
Rural-farm	20	106	12,854	2,497	------	969	2,958	5,571	171	212	408	------	231	------	2,686	26	401	1,350
Rural-nonfarm	481	175	2,189	616	------	519	1,307	2,435	2,233	609	2,098	------	629	------	1,037	2,141	541	1,635
Percent rural	100.0	44.5	91.8	100.0	------	100.0	100.0	100.0	89.4	100.0	100.0	------	59.0	------	100.0	68.1	66.5	100.0
MARITAL CONDITION																		
Males 15 years old and over	256	223	4,593	976	371	435	1,302	2,421	918	254	892	4,625	474	420	1,173	1,276	426	992
Single	110	100	1,724	371	133	175	511	906	334	88	301	1,572	171	141	478	421	147	364
Married	131	106	2,623	531	209	235	701	1,371	528	148	496	2,608	254	249	579	731	251	557
Widowed	11	15	227	63	28	23	85	129	45	16	78	354	48	20	66	103	25	62
Divorced	3	1	18	11	1	2	5	15	10	2	17	89	------	9	16	19	2	9
Unknown	1	1	1	------	------	------	------	------	1	------	------	2	1	1	34	2	1	------
Females 15 years old and over	126	228	4,566	895	480	428	1,170	2,347	848	254	741	4,871	508	472	1,057	948	467	897
Single	36	80	1,376	261	165	144	297	719	212	71	164	1,147	155	114	333	170	126	210
Married	62	113	2,703	520	224	233	712	1,368	524	149	474	2,684	254	258	587	667	263	552
Widowed	27	33	459	112	79	45	157	248	96	31	91	909	96	80	131	99	68	125
Divorced	1	1	25	2	12	6	4	12	14	3	12	129	3	19	6	11	9	10
Unknown	------	1	3	------	------	------	------	------	2	------	------	2	------	1	------	1	1	------
FAMILIES																		
Number of families	90	140	2,992	643	272	299	884	1,572	587	178	552	3,513	366	295	736	821	324	681
Median size	------	3.70	4.86	3.99	3.36	4.38	4.16	4.53	3.55	3.85	3.53	2.62	3.31	3.09	4.36	2.62	3.50	3.70
Families having—																		
No children under 10	56	84	1,151	318	169	135	431	709	339	92	284	2,320	221	191	330	517	176	359
1 child under 10	17	27	538	116	37	49	162	289	74	26	115	524	61	50	144	121	58	132
2 children under 10	5	13	434	82	25	37	103	208	61	26	55	301	39	33	104	87	33	76
3 or more	12	16	869	127	41	78	188	366	113	34	98	368	45	21	158	96	57	114

CHARACTERISTICS OF NEGRO POPULATION BY COUNTIES: 1930—Continued

(See note at head of table)

SUBJECT	WASHINGTON																	
	The State	Adams	Benton	Chelan	Clallam	Clark	Columbia	Cowlitz	Douglas	Ferry	Franklin	Gray Harbor	Jefferson	King	Kitsap	Kittitas	Klickitat	Lewis
POPULATION BY SEX																		
Negro population: 1930	6,840	5	6	67	56	50	2	80	23	3	9	79	6	3,482	104	209	15	58
Male	3,797	3	5	34	32	37	2	47	10	3	5	39	4	1,936	50	110	10	34
Female	3,043	2	1	33	24	13	------	33	13	------	4	40	2	1,546	54	99	5	24
Negro population: 1920	6,883	48	3	42	87	29	3	19	15	2	19	88	7	3,109	169	328	34	103
Male	3,957	44	2	22	46	14	2	11	13	1	12	61	4	1,801	111	181	19	61
Female	2,926	4	1	20	41	15	1	8	2	1	7	27	3	1,308	58	147	15	42
Percent of total population:																		
1930	0.4	0.1	0.1	0.2	0.3	0.1	------	0.3	0.3	0.1	0.1	0.1	0.1	0.8	0.3	1.2	0.2	0.1
1920	0.5	0.5	------	0.2	0.8	0.1	------	0.2	0.2	------	0.3	0.2	0.1	0.8	0.5	1.8	0.4	0.3
VOTING AGE: 1930																		
Total 21 years old and over	5,061	5	4	43	46	42	2	51	13	2	9	75	6	2,660	71	133	12	33
Male	2,895	3	3	25	26	36	2	32	8	2	5	37	4	1,522	38	73	8	17
Female	2,166	2	1	18	20	6	------	19	5	------	4	38	2	1,138	33	60	4	16
AGE: 1930																		
Under 5 years	400	------	------	4	2	2	------	11	4	1	------	1	------	173	11	16	2	9
Under 1 year	72	------	------	------	------	------	------	4	1	------	------	------	------	36	2	2	------	3
5 to 9 years	448	------	------	9	5	3	------	4	2	------	------	------	------	208	11	19	1	5
10 to 14 years	421	------	------	5	2	------	------	5	------	------	------	------	------	183	8	22	------	8
15 to 19 years	416	------	1	5	------	2	------	8	3	------	------	2	------	208	3	14	------	3
20 to 24 years	459	------	1	5	4	3	------	7	3	------	------	6	------	249	1	12	2	2
25 to 29 years	466	------	------	2	7	7	------	10	------	------	------	6	------	254	6	7	2	3
30 to 34 years	542	------	------	4	3	5	------	7	3	------	------	11	1	279	14	12	------	1
35 to 44 years	1,301	2	1	13	12	6	------	17	2	1	3	28	1	710	18	35	2	7
45 to 54 years	1,288	3	------	14	10	11	------	8	1	------	4	16	3	707	18	24	4	7
55 to 64 years	696	------	3	5	7	6	2	2	2	1	2	6	1	330	11	25	2	5
65 to 74 years	278	------	------	1	4	3	------	1	2	------	------	2	------	115	2	12	------	5
75 years and over	102	------	------	------	------	1	------	------	1	------	------	1	------	47	1	11	------	3
Unknown	23	------	------	------	------	1	------	------	------	------	------	------	------	19	------	------	------	------
SCHOOL ATTENDANCE																		
Total 7 to 13 years, inclusive	590	------	------	9	5	1	------	7	2	------	------	------	------	262	13	27	1	7
Number attending school	569	------	------	8	5	1	------	6	2	------	------	------	------	249	13	26	1	7
P rcent attending school	96.4	------	------	------	------	------	------	------	------	------	------	------	------	95.0	------	------	------	------
Total 14 and 15 years, inclusive	166	------	------	3	------	------	------	3	------	------	------	------	------	71	1	9	------	4
Number attending school	159	------	------	3	------	------	------	3	------	------	------	------	------	66	1	9	------	4
Percent attending school	95.8	------	------	------	------	------	------	------	------	------	------	------	------	------	------	------	------	------
Total 16 and 17 years, inclusive	179	------	------	3	------	1	------	1	1	------	------	------	------	93	2	8	------	2
Number attending school	139	------	------	3	------	1	------	1	1	------	------	------	------	73	2	6	------	2
Percent attending school	77.7	------	------	------	------	------	------	------	------	------	------	------	------	------	------	------	------	------
Total 18 to 20 years, inclusive	255	------	2	2	1	2	------	6	3	------	------	3	------	130	1	9	------	------
Number attending school	61	------	1	1	------	------	------	------	1	------	------	2	------	28	------	1	------	------
Per cent attending school	23.9	------	------	------	------	------	------	------	------	------	------	------	------	21.	------	------	------	------
ILLITERACY																		
Total 10 years old and over	5,992	5	6	54	49	45	2	65	17	2	9	78	6	3,101	82	174	12	44
Number illiterate	174	------	------	3	------	3	------	6	4	1	------	1	------	58	2	10	------	5
Percent illiterate	2.9	------	------	------	------	------	------	------	------	------	------	------	------	1.9	------	5.7	------	------
Percent illiterate in 1920	4.0	------	------	------	------	------	------	------	------	------	------	------	------	2.3	1.9	8.3	------	------
URBAN AND RURAL																		
Urban population	5,818	------	------	67	54	19	1	78	------	------	8	63	6	3,304	84	104	------	13
Percent urban	85.1	------	------	------	------	------	------	------	------	------	------	------	------	94.9	80.8	49.8	------	------
Rural population	1,022	5	6	------	2	31	1	2	23	3	1	16	------	178	20	105	15	45
Rural-farm	268	------	2	------	------	6	------	------	10	3	1	------	------	35	2	4	4	36
Rural-nonfarm	754	5	4	------	2	25	1	2	13	------	------	16	------	143	18	101	11	9
Percent rural	14.9	------	------	------	------	------	------	------	------	------	------	------	------	5.1	19.2	50.2	------	------
MARITAL CONDITION																		
Males 15 years old and over	3,152	3	5	27	27	37	2	38	9	2	5	39	4	1,652	39	80	8	18
Single	1,126	1	4	8	13	21	1	14	3	------	2	15	1	601	11	25	4	3
Married	1,567	2	------	16	10	8	------	20	5	1	2	17	2	812	27	43	3	12
Widowed	264	------	1	1	3	4	------	3	1	1	1	5	1	133	1	7	1	3
Divorced	166	------	------	2	1	3	1	1	------	------	------	2	------	84	------	5	------	------
Unknown	29	------	------	------	------	1	------	------	------	------	------	------	------	22	------	------	------	------
Females 15 years old and over	2,419	2	1	22	20	8	------	22	8	------	4	39	2	1,266	35	72	4	18
Single	376	------	------	5	3	2	------	4	3	------	1	3	1	190	4	13	------	3
Married	1,466	2	1	16	10	4	------	18	5	------	3	18	------	766	26	46	3	10
Widowed	431	------	------	1	3	2	------	------	------	------	------	6	1	235	3	10	1	4
Divorced	143	------	------	------	4	------	------	------	------	------	------	12	------	73	2	2	------	1
Unknown	3	------	------	------	------	------	------	------	------	------	------	------	------	2	------	1	------	------
FAMILIES																		
Number of families	2,059	3	3	20	19	13	2	23	9	2	5	39	2	1,060	34	57	4	17
Median size	2.12	------	------	------	------	------	------	------	------	------	------	------	------	2.12	------	------	------	------
Families having—																		
No children under 10	1,633	3	3	13	17	12	2	14	5	1	5	38	2	867	25	42	3	11
1 child under 10	222	------	------	2	------	------	------	5	2	1	------	------	------	102	5	9	1	3
2 children under 10	102	------	------	4	1	------	------	2	2	------	------	------	------	47	2	1	------	------
3 or more	102	------	------	1	1	1	------	2	------	------	------	1	------	44	2	5	------	3

CHARACTERISTICS OF NEGRO POPULATION BY COUNTIES: 1930—Continued

(See note at head of table)

SUBJECT	WASHINGTON—Continued															
	Lincoln	Mason	Okanogan	Pacific	Pend Oreille	Pierce	Skagit	Snohomish	Spokane	Stevens	Thurston	Wahkiakum	Walla Walla	Whatcom	Whitman	Yakima
POPULATION BY SEX																
Negro population: 1930	2	1	1	2	2	900	24	158	694	8	32	2	115	43	9	593
Male	2		1	2	2	495	16	89	363	6	19	2	88	22	8	321
Female		1				405	8	69	331	2	13		27	21	1	272
Negro population: 1920	5	3	8	16	13	992	23	191	776	13	15	6	107	52	14	529
Male	3	1	5	13	9	541	16	109	407	7	6	4	80	31	9	306
Female	2	2	3	3	4	451	7	82	369	6	9	2	27	21	5	223
Percent total population: 1930						0.5	0.1	0.2	0.5		0.1	0.1	0.4	0.1		0.8
1920		0.1		0.1	0.2	0.7	0.1	0.3	0.5	0.1	0.1	0.2	0.4	0.1		0.8
VOTING AGE: 1930																
Total 21 years old and over	2	1	1	2	2	668	22	112	504	6	19	2	94	38	8	371
Male	2		1	2	2	383	15	60	270	6	11	2	76	19	7	198
Female		1				285	7	52	234	2	8		18	19	1	173
AGE: 1930																
Under 5 years						57		7	43		4		2	1		50
Under 1 year						3		1	6		1			1		12
5 to 9 years						60		9	44		2		6	1		59
10 to 14 years						59		14	54		2		6	1	1	51
15 to 19 years						47	2	11	44		4		5	2		52
20 to 24 years						57	1	12	41		3		8	3	1	38
25 to 29 years						48	1	7	51		1	2	12	2		38
30 to 34 years				1		67	3	13	62		2		17	4		33
35 to 44 years	1					161	6	29	107		4		36	12	5	82
45 to 54 years	1			1	2	183	6	21	134	4	4		12	8		82
55 to 64 years						109	4	21	74	2	3		8	3	1	61
65 to 74 years		1				41	1	9	33	1	3		3	4		35
75 years and over			1			9		4	7	1				2	1	12
Unknown						2		1								
SCHOOL ATTENDANCE																
Total 7 to 13 years, inclusive						92		18	62		3		8	1	1	71
Number attending school						88		18	62		3		8	1	1	70
Percent attending school																
Total 14 and 15 years, inclusive						18	1	5	26		1		1			23
Number attending school						18	1	5	25		1		1			22
Percent attending school																
Total 16 and 17 years, inclusive						21	1	4	17		1		2	1		21
Number attending school						16	1	2	15		1		1			14
Percent attending school																
Total 18 to 20 years, inclusive						27		10	21		3		5	1		29
Number attending school						8		6	8		1		1	1		2
Percent attending school																
ILLITERACY																
Total 10 years old and over	2	1	1	2	2	783	24	142	607	8	26	2	107	41	9	484
Number illiterate	1		1			23	3	4	23		3		1			22
Percent illiterate						2.9		2.8	3.8				0.9			4.5
Percent illiterate in 1920						4.6		1.9	3.9							8.1
URBAN AND RURAL																
Urban population						734	12	121	617		7		111	40	4	371
Percent urban						81.6		76.6	88.9				96.5			62.6
Rural population	2	1	1	2	2	166	12	37	77	8	25	2	4	3	5	222
Rural-farm	2	1	1	1		22		10	19	4	5		1	3	1	95
Rural-nonfarm				1	2	144	12	27	58	4	20	2	3		4	127
Percent rural						18.4		23.4	11.1				3.5			37.4
MARITAL CONDITION																
Males 15 years old and over	2		1	2	2	410	16	71	294	6	13	2	80	20	7	231
Single	1		1		1	137	6	31	100	3	5	2	36	5	4	67
Married	1			1		221	6	31	154	2	6		25	13	2	125
Widowed					1	26	3	7	21		1		16			23
Divorced				1		24	1	2	15	1	1		3	2	1	16
Unknown						2			4							
Females 15 years old and over		1				314	8	57	259	2	11		21	20	1	202
Single						48	3	9	39		3		6	3		33
Married						191	4	33	143	2	5		13	14	1	132
Widowed		1				57	1	12	56		3		2	2		31
Divorced						18		3	21					1		6
Unknown																
FAMILIES																
Number of families	1	1		2	1	249	4	50	216	4	10		16	19	3	171
Median size						2.20			2.27							2.32
Familes having—																
No children under 10		1		2	1	190	4	41	166	4	7		12	17	3	122
1 child under 10						31		8	28		1		2	2		20
2 children under 10						14			14				1			14
3 or more	1					14		1	8		2		1			15

CHARACTERISTICS OF NEGRO POPULATION BY COUNTIES: 1930—Continued

(See note at head of table)

SUBJECT	WEST VIRGINIA																
	The State	Barbour	Berkeley	Boone	Braxton	Brooke	Cabell	Calhoun	Clay	Doddridge	Fayette	Gilmer	Grant	Greenbrier	Hampshire	Hancock	Hardy
POPULATION BY SEX																	
Negro population: 1930	114,893	971	1,583	746	188	1,176	4,803	12	170	20	11,607	21	240	2,329	194	1,073	309
Male	60,873	531	805	419	99	639	2,270	7	91	12	6,424	11	127	1,211	92	588	159
Female	54,020	440	778	327	89	537	2,533	5	79	8	5,183	10	113	1,118	102	485	150
Negro population: 1920	86,345	820	1,816	759	273	494	3,011	36	147	1	9,636	38	232	1,726	196	573	298
Male	47,129	436	902	420	147	284	1,516	16	84	1	5,397	21	123	878	97	404	158
Female	39,216	384	914	339	126	210	1,495	20	63	-------	4,239	17	109	848	99	169	140
Percent of total population:																	
1930	6.6	5.2	5.6	3.0	0.8	4.8	5.3	0.1	1.3	0.2	16.1	0.2	2.8	6.5	1.6	3.8	3.1
1920	5.9	4.5	7.4	5.0	1.1	..0	4.6	0.4	1.3	-------	16.0	0.4	2.6	6.6	1.7	2.9	3.1
VOTING AGE: 1930																	
Total 21 years old and over	67,155	444	938	391	88	705	3,117	9	97	7	6,492	8	111	1,553	113	594	156
Male	37,731	246	488	242	45	408	1,514	6	58	5	3,912	4	57	727	59	363	88
Female	29,424	198	450	149	43	297	1,603	3	39	2	2,580	4	54	626	54	231	68
AGE: 1930																	
Under 5 years	12,104	134	126	88	20	128	408	2	26	2	1,265	2	38	229	23	146	41
Under 1 year	2,280	40	20	17	7	23	76	-------	5	-------	238	-------	10	50	3	23	12
5 to 9 years	12,868	137	157	104	28	145	424	-------	21	3	1,358	5	29	252	25	134	39
10 to 14 years	10,444	121	149	80	26	107	383	-------	16	3	1,161	3	28	213	14	94	32
15 to 19 years	10,109	118	174	75	20	80	393	1	6	5	1,103	3	30	225	17	79	36
20 to 24 years	11,217	72	153	57	15	69	467	-------	13	1	1,049	1	21	232	16	117	25
25 to 29 years	11,681	73	131	73	5	134	508	-------	20	-------	1,085	1	11	179	13	142	26
30 to 34 years	10,546	51	78	64	10	147	467	-------	20	1	1,006	2	13	161	8	122	13
35 to 44 years	18,370	113	207	107	17	217	853	3	20	1	1,762	-------	26	328	22	160	37
45 to 54 years	10,739	84	192	62	19	101	480	3	19	2	1,130	2	19	232	19	49	26
55 to 64 years	4,227	40	119	22	11	25	243	1	7	1	481	2	11	157	23	21	18
65 to 74 years	1,744	26	55	11	12	17	130	-------	2	-------	139	-------	8	86	11	8	11
75 years and over	715	2	34	3	4	5	42	2	-------	1	55	-------	5	34	3	1	4
Unknown	129	-------	8	-------	1	1	5	-------	-------	-------	13	-------	1	1	-------	-------	1
SCHOOL ATTENDANCE																	
Total 7 to 13 years, inclusive	16,136	184	226	132	34	180	592	-------	24	5	1,756	7	47	330	24	152	46
Number attending school	15,080	62	211	128	26	174	558	-------	17	5	1,675	7	41	308	23	147	39
Percent attending school	93.5	33.7	93.4	97.0	-------	96.7	94.3	-------	-------	-------	95.4	-------	-------	93.3	-------	96.7	-------
Total 14 and 15 years, inclusive	3,801	46	58	30	12	32	136	-------	4	1	408	2	11	73	7	32	12
Number attending school	3,279	25	38	24	10	27	123	-------	2	1	356	1	7	63	6	25	9
Percent attending school	86.3	-------	-------	-------	-------	-------	90.4	-------	-------	-------	87.3	-------	-------	-------	-------	-------	-------
Total 16 and 17 years, inclusive	3,988	43	73	34	10	34	154	-------	2	2	455	-------	13	90	5	31	9
Number attending school	2,103	4	30	15	5	17	88	-------	-------	-------	219	-------	5	41	-------	20	3
Percent attending school	52.7	-------	-------	-------	-------	-------	57.1	-------	-------	-------	48.1	-------	-------	-------	-------	-------	-------
Total 18 to 20 years, inclusive	6,444	68	105	33	10	36	242	1	7	2	673	1	12	150	10	62	28
Number attending school	1,399	1	13	6	2	1	56	-------	-------	-------	107	-------	1	17	2	3	4
Percent attending school	21.7	-------	12.4	-------	-------	-------	23.1	-------	-------	-------	15.9	-------	-------	11.3	-------	-------	-------
ILLITERACY																	
Total 10 years old and over	89,921	700	1,300	554	140	903	3,971	10	123	15	8,984	14	173	1,848	146	793	229
Number illiterate	10,173	226	175	43	29	98	244	-------	20	3	1,113	1	36	254	23	58	46
Percent illiterate	11.3	32.3	13.5	7.8	20.7	10.9	6.1	-------	16.3	-------	12.4	-------	20.8	13.7	15.8	7.3	20.1
Percent illiterate in 1920	15.3	15.4	17.2	15.3	18.9	7.3	12.0	-------	26.2	-------	15.2	-------	26.6	16.6	30.2	30.5	40.8
URBAN AND RURAL																	
Urban population	31,224	-------	1,046	-------	-------	311	4,615	-------	-------	-------	402	-------	-------	-------	-------	2	-------
Percent urban	27.2	-------	66.1	-------	-------	26.4	96.1	-------	-------	-------	3.5	-------	-------	-------	-------	0.2	-------
Rural population	83,669	971	537	746	188	865	188	12	170	20	11,205	21	240	2,329	194	1,071	309
Rural-farm	3,815	533	72	27	89	1	49	12	-------	17	193	8	110	181	47	7	70
Rural-nonfarm	79,854	438	465	719	99	864	139	-------	170	3	11,012	13	130	2,148	147	1,064	239
Percent rural	72.8	100.0	33.9	100.0	100.0	73.6	3.9	-------	100.0	-------	96.5	-------	100.0	100.0	100.0	99.8	100.0
MARITAL CONDITION																	
Males 15 years old and over	43,429	318	585	279	64	446	1,686	7	61	8	4,550	5	76	874	68	412	108
Single	15,492	112	238	104	35	138	545	5	19	6	1,601	1	33	330	21	152	51
Married	24,969	182	286	150	23	296	985	2	36	2	2,587	4	39	480	41	239	47
Widowed	2,302	21	54	18	6	10	117	-------	5	-------	303	-------	2	55	6	15	9
Divorced	636	3	6	7	-------	2	37	-------	1	-------	57	-------	1	9	-------	6	1
Unknown	30	-------	1	-------	-------	-------	2	-------	-------	-------	2	-------	1	-------	-------	-------	-------
Females 15 years old and over	36,048	261	566	195	50	350	1,902	3	46	4	3,273	6	69	761	64	287	89
Single	7,602	56	180	40	17	51	479	1	7	2	608	2	24	187	16	38	24
Married	23,838	174	305	136	25	257	1,064	2	36	1	2,278	4	34	472	40	233	47
Widowed	4,045	28	75	14	7	36	303	-------	3	1	357	-------	11	91	8	21	17
Divorced	544	3	2	4	1	5	55	-------	-------	-------	29	-------	-------	10	-------	5	1
Unknown	19	-------	4	1	-------	1	1	-------	-------	-------	1	-------	-------	1	-------	-------	-------
FAMILIES																	
Number of families	26,274	212	371	159	28	294	1,109	2	46	3	2,682	3	46	538	43	223	63
Median size	3.08	3.98	3.07	3.42	-------	2.88	2.86	-------	-------	-------	3.07	-------	-------	3.18	-------	3.39	-------
Families having—																	
No children under 10	15,565	103	234	79	7	181	724	1	28	1	1,578	1	22	326	26	109	32
1 child under 10	4,235	32	68	27	7	40	187	-------	5	1	445	-------	6	81	4	39	11
2 children under 10	2,678	24	33	20	7	28	101	1	7	-------	238	-------	8	54	5	24	7
3 or more	3,796	53	36	33	7	45	97	-------	6	1	421	2	10	77	8	51	13

CHARACTERISTICS OF NEGRO POPULATION BY COUNTIES: 1930—Continued

(See note at head of table)

SUBJECT	Harrison	Jackson	Jefferson	Kanawha	Lewis	Lincoln	Logan	McDowell	Marion	Marshall	Mason	Mercer	Mineral	Mingo	Monongalia	Monroe	Morgan	Nicholas
	WEST VIRGINIA—Continued																	
POPULATION BY SEX																		
Negro population: 1930	2,253	4	2,742	12,671	122	42	6,993	22,558	4,989	882	692	7,587	607	3,768	2,331	547	178	65
Male	1,118	3	1,373	6,272	61	30	3,784	12,119	2,645	704	414	3,830	326	2,106	1,289	264	104	52
Female	1,135	1	1,369	6,399	61	12	3,209	10,439	2,344	178	278	3,757	281	1,662	1,042	283	74	13
Negro population: 1920	2,549	12	3,016	8,929	291	61	4,737	18,157	2,454	502	227	6,427	641	2,191	638	559	159	68
Male	1,331	6	1,482	4,655	161	34	2,794	10,213	1,339	406	114	3,314	350	1,268	341	259	90	31
Female	1,218	6	1,534	4,274	130	27	1,943	7,944	1,115	96	113	3,113	241	923	297	300	69	37
Percent of total population:																		
1930	2.9	------	17.4	8.0	0.6	0.2	11.9	24.9	7.5	2.2	3.3	12.4	3.0	9.8	4.7	4.6	2.1	0.3
1920	3.4	0.1	19.2	7.5	1.4	0.3	11.6	26.5	4.5	1.5	1.1	13.0	3.2	8.3	1.9	4.3	1.9	0.3
VOTING AGE: 1930																		
Total 21 years old and over	1,406	3	1,482	7,694	85	31	4,249	12,524	3,053	758	501	4,312	332	2,405	1,478	302	91	54
Male	724	2	756	3,961	42	27	2,473	7,322	1,728	629	269	2,257	181	1,415	906	146	49	44
Female	682	1	726	3,733	43	4	1,776	5,202	1,325	129	232	2,055	151	990	572	156	42	10
AGE: 1930																		
Under 5 years	169	------	273	1,027	10	6	805	2,680	566	24	19	792	73	387	262	53	27	4
Under 1 year	31	------	53	185	2	1	146	481	119	1	2	167	12	62	50	9	2	1
5 to 9 years	248	------	350	1,199	11	1	786	2,780	583	23	29	829	81	346	232	60	31	1
10 to 14 years	202	------	309	1,065	5	1	562	2,209	408	25	57	743	62	283	157	61	16	1
15 to 19 years	195	1	265	1,333	9	2	491	1,944	317	33	79	759	54	262	164	58	10	3
20 to 24 years	162	------	228	1,504	9	6	662	2,318	412	113	42	778	56	431	186	62	12	15
25 to 29 years	157	------	178	1,156	10	7	862	2,503	636	167	60	668	43	481	284	40	10	7
30 to 34 years	192	------	139	1,052	9	6	726	2,129	551	142	59	639	51	469	276	27	10	12
35 to 44 years	416	1	312	2,052	21	8	1,328	3,448	871	205	110	1,084	59	685	455	48	20	9
45 to 54 years	302	1	312	1,392	18	4	580	1,715	454	113	118	803	55	300	223	57	16	10
55 to 64 years	121	------	185	552	13	------	137	528	132	26	67	331	37	87	64	39	11	3
65 to 74 years	56	1	116	231	5	1	40	176	39	7	34	99	25	29	19	29	9	------
75 years and over	27	------	68	95	2	------	14	58	17	3	17	43	11	8	9	12	6	------
Unknown	6	------	7	13	------	------	------	30	3	1	1	19	------	------	------	1	------	------
SCHOOL ATTENDANCE																		
Total 7 to 13 years, inclusive	313	------	457	1,603	6	1	926	3,417	689	35	54	1,073	101	419	259	88	35	------
Number attending school	301	------	411	1,541	6	1	822	3,220	657	34	41	1,014	101	392	249	76	34	------
Percent attending school	96.2	------	89.9	96.1	------	------	88.8	94.2	95.4	------	------	94.5	100.0	93.6	96.1	------	------	------
Total 14 and 15 years, inclusive	77	------	118	403	4	1	179	763	129	5	33	308	24	116	72	21	5	1
Number attending school	71	------	83	373	3	------	147	677	116	5	28	279	17	96	65	17	5	------
Percent attending school	------	------	70.3	92.6	------	------	82.1	88.7	89.9	------	------	90.6	------	82.8	------	------	------	------
Total 16 and 17 years, inclusive	84	1	115	475	5	------	176	806	117	12	38	306	21	85	57	22	2	1
Number attending school	51	------	39	320	5	------	86	443	65	2	33	179	6	47	25	8	1	------
Percent attending school	------	------	33.9	67.4	------	------	48.9	55.0	55.6	------	------	58.5	------	------	------	------	------	------
Total 18 to 20 years, inclusive	106	------	164	990	5	2	320	1,210	198	39	32	459	27	205	106	37	8	4
Number attending school	30	------	13	466	3	------	46	207	17	4	16	119	4	39	13	11	1	------
Percent attending school	28.3	------	7.9	47.1	------	------	14.4	17.1	8.6	------	------	25.9	------	19.0	12.3	------	------	------
ILLITERACY																		
Total 10 years old and over	1,836	4	2,119	10,445	101	35	5,402	17,098	3,840	835	644	5,966	453	3,035	1,837	434	120	60
Number illiterate	158	1	317	730	10	12	579	2,086	555	143	198	741	54	409	223	70	19	8
Percent illiterate	8.6	------	15.0	7.0	9.9	------	10.7	12.2	14.5	17.1	30.7	12.4	11.9	13.5	12.1	16.1	15.8	------
Percent illiterate in 1920	11.8	------	20.1	10.2	6.5	------	15.2	17.7	14.5	15.2	4.1	15.4	14.7	20.6	10.7	16.2	21.6	------
URBAN AND RURAL																		
Urban population	1,253	------	------	7,037	95	------	242	1,216	2,012	777	161	3,771	160	1,624	334	------	------	12
Percent urban	55.6	------	------	55.5	77.9	------	3.5	5.4	40.3	88.1	23.3	49.7	26.4	43.1	14.3	------	------	------
Rural population	1,000	4	2,742	5,634	27	42	6,751	21,342	2,977	105	531	3,816	447	2,144	1,997	547	178	53
Rural-farm	48	2	641	213	21	3	2	68	53	15	52	133	7	7	34	225	1	4
Rural-nonfarm	952	2	2,101	5,421	6	39	6,749	21,274	2,924	90	479	3,683	440	2,137	1,963	322	177	49
Percent rural	44.4	------	100.0	44.5	22.1	------	96.5	94.6	59.7	11.9	76.7	50.3	73.6	56.9	85.7	100.0	100.0	------
MARITAL CONDITION																		
Males 15 years old and over	827	3	934	4,664	48	27	2,749	8,381	1,898	669	336	2,664	209	1,577	1,002	182	56	48
Single	285	2	350	1,783	20	12	905	2,982	539	297	204	875	82	599	338	77	17	27
Married	490	1	501	2,545	25	14	1,717	4,877	1,220	302	98	1,592	111	859	607	84	28	19
Widowed	41	------	67	263	2	------	93	387	107	51	24	150	12	89	37	15	9	1
Divorced	9	------	13	73	1	1	33	130	[illegible]	19	10	43	3	29	19	5	2	1
Unknown	2	------	3	------	------	------	1	5	1	------	------	4	1	1	1	1	------	------
Females 15 years old and over	807	1	876	4,716	48	7	2,091	6,508	1,534	141	251	2,559	182	1,175	678	191	48	11
Single	197	------	230	1,328	18	2	307	1,226	204	17	71	629	42	214	92	67	7	4
Married	501	------	512	2,678	19	5	1,605	4,585	1,166	112	139	1,592	111	826	528	92	29	7
Widowed	101	1	125	599	11	------	159	607	151	12	34	306	23	111	52	29	9	------
Divorced	8	------	8	111	------	------	19	88	13	------	7	31	4	24	6	3	3	------
Unknown	------	------	1	------	------	------	1	2	------	------	------	1	2	------	------	------	------	------
FAMILIES																		
Number of families	590	1	645	2,833	35	7	1,719	5,073	1,200	71	57	1,807	133	894	609	123	39	4
Median size	2.67	------	3.32	3.04	------	------	2.83	3.22	2.84	------	------	3.21	3.70	2.75	2.42	4.05	------	------
Families having—																		
No children under 10	414	1	380	1,822	25	3	1,036	2,772	719	50	41	1,068	71	568	404	66	21	2
1 child under 10	60	------	102	429	4	2	274	880	193	8	6	313	21	124	76	28	4	------
2 children under 10	53	------	69	273	3	------	160	561	122	7	2	199	20	96	56	15	4	1
3 or more	63	------	94	309	3	1	249	860	166	6	8	227	21	106	68	14	10	1

CHARACTERISTICS OF NEGRO POPULATION BY COUNTIES: 1930—Continued

(See note at head of table)

SUBJECT	WEST VIRGINIA—Continued																	
	Ohio	Pendleton	Pocahontas	Preston	Putnam	Raleigh	Randolph	Ritchie	Roane	Summers	Taylor	Tucker	Tyler	Upshur	Wayne	Webster	Wetzel	Wirt
POPULATION BY SEX																		
Negro population: 1930	2,574	131	558	92	124	11,116	342	7	14	1,369	722	77	35	201	117	9	53	25
Male	1,310	70	295	50	73	6,078	180	1	7	639	372	42	15	91	70	3	25	13
Female	1,264	61	263	42	51	5,038	162	6	7	730	350	35	20	110	47	6	28	12
Negro population: 1920	1,663	112	638	147	397	6,393	431	13	12	1,120	641	210	52	196	142	------	89	35
Male	857	56	345	86	186	3,650	220	5	10	574	359	113	27	94	79	------	44	20
Female	806	56	293	61	211	2,743	211	8	2	546	282	97	25	102	63	------	45	15
Percent of total population:																		
1930	3.6	1.4	3.8	0.3	0.7	16.3	1.4	------	0.1	6.7	3.8	0.6	0.3	1.1	0.4	0.1	0.2	0.4
1920	2.6	1.2	4.3	0.5	2.3	15.0	1.6	0.1	0.1	5.9	3.4	1.3	0.4	1.1	0.5	------	0.4	0.5
VOTING AGE: 1930																		
Total 21 years old and over	1,778	65	313	53	78	6,072	161	6	12	824	347	41	18	114	70	3	32	13
Male	929	35	177	29	54	3,546	80	1	6	362	181	26	6	56	46	1	16	7
Female	849	30	136	24	24	2,526	81	5	6	462	166	15	12	58	24	2	16	6
AGE: 1930																		
Under 5 years	192	20	32	11	10	1,359	41	------	------	133	89	10	1	18	7	2	3	6
Under 1 year	40	5	5	2	3	254	6	------	------	25	15	3	1	3	3	------	1	1
5 to 9 years	191	24	63	15	8	1,440	45	------	------	164	110	6	4	30	12	2	6	3
10 to 14 years	170	13	69	9	15	1,085	43	------	1	110	89	11	7	19	10	2	6	3
15 to 19 years	194	9	68	3	12	971	45	1	------	112	74	9	5	16	16	------	5	------
20 to 24 years	233	11	51	8	9	1,084	20	------	4	119	52	4	1	22	11	------	3	------
25 to 29 years	279	8	45	7	10	1,125	28	------	3	118	45	3	2	10	9	------	1	1
30 to 34 years	268	6	27	6	8	1,059	22	------	3	110	42	3	------	17	8	1	2	2
35 to 44 years	513	15	81	11	15	1,772	47	1	1	223	103	16	6	14	8	------	10	4
45 to 54 years	333	13	58	11	19	850	19	1	2	134	66	7	5	24	19	------	11	2
55 to 64 years	124	6	38	5	10	255	17	1	------	67	30	4	2	17	12	2	4	1
65 to 74 years	54	3	15	2	6	78	6	3	------	57	16	2	2	7	5	------	2	3
75 years and over	23	3	6	4	2	35	5	------	------	22	5	2	------	7	------	------	------	------
Unknown	------	------	5	------	------	3	4	------	------	------	1	------	------	------	------	------	------	------
SCHOOL ATTENDANCE																		
Total 7 to 13 years, inclusive	249	25	87	18	16	1,741	56	------	1	191	138	12	11	36	18	2	10	6
Number attending school	239	24	74	17	16	1,673	53	------	------	178	123	12	11	32	15	2	10	5
Percent attending school	96.0	------	------	------	------	96.1	------	------	------	93.2	89.1	------	------	------	------	------	------	------
Total 14 and 15 years, inclusive	65	5	30	2	4	389	20	------	------	48	34	4	2	5	4	1	2	------
Number attending school	52	4	24	2	3	348	18	------	------	37	25	4	2	4	4	1	1	------
Percent attending school	------	------	------	------	------	89.5	------	------	------	------	------	------	------	------	------	------	------	------
Total 16 and 17 years, inclusive	76	3	23	------	7	400	18	1	------	42	30	5	1	6	4	------	2	------
Number attending school	38	1	11	------	3	205	12	1	------	21	8	3	------	3	2	------	1	------
Percent attending school	------	------	------	------	------	51.3	------	------	------	------	------	------	------	------	------	------	------	------
Total 18 to 20 years, inclusive	139	4	45	2	5	563	25	------	1	70	41	3	2	11	10	------	2	------
Number attending school	26	1	7	------	------	90	12	------	------	23	4	2	------	6	2	------	------	------
Percent attending school	18.7	------	------	------	------	16.0	------	------	------	------	------	------	------	------	------	------	------	------
ILLITERACY																		
Total 10 years old and over	2,191	87	463	66	106	8,317	256	7	14	1,072	523	61	30	153	98	5	44	16
Number illiterate	200	7	74	5	15	686	17	------	2	113	45	10	------	10	13	------	2	1
Percent illiterate	9.1	------	16.0	------	14.2	8.2	6.6	------	------	10.5	8.6	------	------	6.5	------	------	------	------
Percent illiterate in 1920	6.6	------	20.6	16.4	4.4	17.5	10.7	------	------	12.4	11.4	11.7	------	10.4	18.3	------	------	------
URBAN AND RURAL																		
Urban population	2,192	------	------	------	------	1,599	282	------	------	755	247	------	22	152	25	------	5	------
Percent urban	85.2	------	------	------	------	14.4	82.5	------	------	55.1	34.2	------	------	75.6	21.4	------	------	------
Rural population	382	131	558	92	124	9,517	60	7	14	614	475	77	13	49	92	9	48	25
Rural-farm	2	84	93	3	19	38	21	------	4	210	293	1	------	29	5	9	------	25
Rural-nonfarm	380	47	465	89	105	9,479	39	7	10	404	182	76	13	20	87	------	48	------
Percent rural	14.8	100.0	100.0	------	100.0	85.6	17.5	------	------	44.9	65.8	------	------	24.4	78.6	------	------	------
MARITAL CONDITION																		
Males 15 years old and over	1,034	40	218	32	61	4,097	105	1	7	440	229	31	7	64	55	1	18	7
Single	322	11	91	10	26	1,469	39	------	3	158	86	15	1	23	30	------	7	1
Married	643	25	116	20	27	2,425	61	1	3	251	134	13	5	36	21	1	11	5
Widowed	57	4	9	2	7	150	4	------	1	26	8	3	1	5	4	------	------	1
Divorced	12	------	2	------	1	51	1	------	------	5	1	------	------	------	------	------	------	------
Unknown	------	------	------	------	------	2	------	------	------	------	------	------	------	------	------	------	------	------
Females 15 years old and over	987	34	176	25	30	3,135	108	6	6	522	205	19	16	70	33	2	20	6
Single	178	8	55	6	8	557	35	4	------	110	42	4	6	27	13	------	4	------
Married	623	23	101	15	21	2,245	60	1	6	294	142	13	8	34	17	2	15	5
Widowed	159	3	18	4	1	300	10	1	------	85	20	2	1	9	3	------	1	1
Divorced	27	------	2	------	------	32	2	------	------	33	1	------	1	------	------	------	------	------
Unknown	------	------	------	------	------	1	1	------	------	------	------	------	------	------	------	------	------	------
FAMILIES																		
Number of families	688	28	105	22	37	2,404	71	3	1	286	141	23	8	42	21	1	18	6
Median size	2.43	------	3.65	------	------	3.46	------	------	------	3.28	4.12	------	------	------	------	------	------	------
Families having—																		
No children under 10	494	11	58	11	28	1,265	34	3	1	161	67	16	4	24	13	1	13	3
1 child under 10	101	6	23	6	3	412	16	------	------	53	19	3	3	5	2	------	2	------
2 children under 10	47	2	15	1	4	276	10	------	------	22	21	2	1	4	4	------	2	1
3 or more	46	9	9	4	2	451	11	------	------	50	34	2	------	9	2	------	1	2

CHARACTERISTICS OF NEGRO POPULATION BY COUNTIES: 1930—Continued

(See note at head of table)

SUBJECT	WEST VIRGINIA—Continued		WISCONSIN															
	Wood	Wyoming	The State	Barron	Bayfield	Brown	Burnett	Chippewa	Clark	Columbia	Crawford	Dane	Dodge	Door	Douglas	Dunn	Eau Claire	Fond du lac
POPULATION BY SEX																		
Negro population: 1930	893	1,961	10,739	9	10	58	13	14	26	7	2	383	73	1	62	7	16	22
Male	449	1,111	5,811	3	4	36	6	7	19	6	2	202	65	1	29	5	7	11
Female	444	850	4,928	6	6	22	7	7	7	1		181	8		33	2	9	11
Negro population: 1920	783	1,590	5,201	5	8	49	10	24	14	6		341	59	7	117	10	23	59
Male	374	955	2,965	4	4	28	4	16	11	5		178	46	3	68	8	11	29
Female	409	635	2,236	1	4	21	6	8	3	1		163	13	4	49	2	12	30
Percent of total population:																		
1930	1.6	9.4	0.4		0.1	0.1	0.1		0.1			0.3	0.1		0.1			
1920	1.9	10.5	0.2			0.1	0.1	0.1				0.4	0.1		0.2		0.1	0.1
VOTING AGE: 1930																		
Total 21 years old and over	628	1,144	7,265	2	5	32	6	6	12	6		262	68	1	51	6	15	19
Male	329	691	4,133	1	2	21	4	3	9	6		137	62	1	25	4	7	10
Female	299	453	3,132	1	3	11	2	3	3			125	6		26	2	8	9
AGE: 1930																		
Under 5 years	79	236	850	2	4	5	2		5	1	2	36	1		3			
Under 1 year	14	51	176		1	1			1	1	1	7			1			
5 to 9 years	72	222	960	2	1	5	2	1	5			23	3		4		1	
10 to 14 years	45	141	788	3		2	1	4				28			2			1
15 to 19 years	50	175	696			9	1	3	3			28			1			1
20 to 24 years	68	213	1,066			18	2	3	2	1		29	6		3	2		5
25 to 29 years	82	235	1,396			3		1	4	1		33	11		2		1	2
30 to 34 years	81	229	1,206	1	1	3			1			35	17		8		1	1
35 to 44 years	161	324	2,053	1	2	3	3		5	2		75	20		12	2	6	5
45 to 54 years	130	123	1,053		1	5	1	1				45	9		7	2	5	3
55 to 64 years	71	46	425		1	1		1	1	1		28	4		12		1	1
65 to 74 years	39	12	157			2						16	1		4			1
75 years and over	13	3	72			2	1			1		7	1	1	4	1	1	2
Unknown	2	2	17															
SCHOOL ATTENDANCE																		
Total 7 to 13 years, inclusive	80	224	1,235	4		5	3	4	4			34	2		3			1
Number attending school	71	204	1,211	4		5	3	4	4			33	2		3			1
Percent attending school		91.1	98.1															
Total 14 and 15 years, inclusive	12	50	236			1		2	1			10						
Number attending school	11	40	223			1		1	1			10						
Percent attending school			94.5															
Total 16 and 17 years, inclusive	21	66	272			2		1	1			11			1			
Number attending school	14	23	212			2		1				10			1			
Percent attending school			77.9															
Total 18 to 20 years, inclusive	42	127	503			11	2	1	2			19	1		1	1		2
Number attending school	12	12	85			5						10						
Percent attending school		9.4	16.9															
ILLITERACY																		
Total 10 years old and o er	742	1,503	8,929	5	5	48	9	13	16	6		324	69	1	55	7	15	22
Number illiterate	33	258	391				2	1				21	4					3
Percent illiterate	4.4	17.2	4.4									6.5						
Percent illiterate in 1920	13.4	12.1	4.1									4.9			0.9			
URBAN AND RURAL																		
Urban population	875		9,873			21				3		348	63	1	51		11	16
Percent urban	98.0		91.9									90.9						
Rural population	18	1,961	866	9	10	37	13	14	26	4	2	35	10		11	7	5	6
Rural-farm	9	25	377		10	7	4	9	18	3	2	3			7	5	2	1
Rural-nonfarm	9	1,936	489	9		30	9	5	8	1		32	10		4	2	3	5
Percent rural	2.0	100.0	8.1									9.1						
MARTIAL CONDITION																		
Males 15 years old and over	357	804	4,539	1	2	31	5	5	11	6		155	63	1	25	5	7	10
Single	118	297	1,594			25	3	4	7	4		58	29		11	4	1	5
Married	208	474	2,505	1	2	5	2	1	4	2		81	24		11	1	6	2
Widowed	23	28	303			1						10	7	1	1			2
Divorced	8	3	123									6	3		2			
Unknown		2	14															1
Females 15 years old and over	340	558	3,602	1	3	15	3	4	5			141	6		28	2	8	11
Single	79	79	568			4		2	2			25			11			2
Married	181	427	2,383	1	2	5	2	2	3			79	6		9	2	6	5
Widowed	74	51	514		1	5	1					29			7		2	3
Divorced	6		132									8			1			1
Unknown		1	5			1												
FAMILIES																		
Number of families	239	468	2,523	1	3	9	3	1	5	3		99	5	1	21	2	5	6
Median size	2.49	2.86	2.52															
Families having—																		
No children under 10	169	269	1,747		2	6	2		3	3		68	5	1	18	1	4	6
1 child under 10	25	79	362					1				16			2		1	
2 children under 10	20	47	187			1						7				1		
3 or more	25	73	227	1	1	2	1		2			8			1			

CHARACTERISTICS OF NEGRO POPULATION BY COUNTIES: 1930—Continued

(See note at head of table)

SUBJECT	Grant	Green	Iowa	Jackson	Jefferson	Juneau	Kenosha	La Crosse	Lafayette	Langlade	Lincoln	Manitowoc	Marathon	Marinette	Marquette	Milwaukee	Monroe	Oconto
	WISCONSIN—Continued																	
POPULATION BY SEX																		
Negro population: 1930	27	3	3	8	7	13	210	52	1	1	7	2	7	23	1	7,723	21	1
Male	15	-	2	4	4	8	109	34	1	1	2	1	3	16	1	4,188	11	-
Female	12	3	1	4	3	5	101	18	-	-	5	1	4	7	-	3,535	10	1
Negro population: 1920	43	4	8	16	11	4	101	41	30	12	7	10	8	29	12	2,346	28	1
Male	23	1	5	9	6	4	58	20	18	9	6	4	6	16	7	1,316	16	-
Female	20	3	3	7	5	-	43	21	12	3	1	6	2	13	5	1,030	12	1
Percent of total population:																		
1930	0.1	-	-	-	-	0.1	0.3	0.1	-	-	-	-	-	0.1	-	1.1	0.1	-
1920	0.1	-	-	0.1	-	-	0.2	0.1	0.1	0.1	-	-	-	0.1	0.1	0.4	0.1	-
VOTING AGE: 1930																		
Total 21 years old and over	23	3	3	5	7	8	152	35	1	1	5	2	6	7	1	5,291	11	1
Male	13	-	2	3	4	5	83	24	1	1	2	1	3	6	1	3,024	8	-
Female	10	3	1	2	3	3	69	11	-	-	3	1	3	1	-	2,267	3	1
AGE: 1930																		
Under 5 years	-	-	-	-	-	2	23	2	-	-	-	-	-	2	-	584	3	-
Under 1 year	-	-	-	-	-	-	5	-	-	-	-	-	-	1	-	115	1	-
5 to 9 years	-	-	-	1	-	2	17	8	-	-	-	-	-	4	-	696	4	-
10 to 14 years	-	-	-	2	-	-	9	5	-	-	1	-	-	5	-	550	2	-
15 to 19 years	3	-	-	-	-	1	7	2	-	-	1	-	1	5	-	467	1	-
20 to 24 years	3	-	-	-	-	-	19	7	-	1	-	-	1	2	1	798	2	-
25 to 29 years	2	-	-	-	-	2	27	8	1	-	2	-	2	-	-	1,096	1	-
30 to 34 years	5	-	-	-	2	1	27	3	-	-	-	-	1	-	-	916	-	-
35 to 44 years	5	2	1	3	2	1	36	9	-	-	2	-	1	3	-	1,524	1	1
45 to 54 years	3	-	-	-	3	1	27	2	-	-	-	-	-	2	-	732	1	-
55 to 64 years	5	-	2	1	-	2	11	4	-	-	-	1	1	-	-	239	3	-
65 to 74 years	-	-	-	1	-	-	6	1	-	-	1	1	-	-	-	76	1	-
75 years and over	1	1	-	-	-	1	1	1	-	-	-	-	-	-	-	30	2	-
Unknown	-	-	-	-	-	-	-	-	-	-	-	-	-	-	-	15	-	-
SCHOOL ATTENDANCE																		
Total 7 to 13 years, inclusive	-	-	-	3	-	1	18	9	-	-	1	-	-	5	-	881	5	-
Number attending school	-	-	-	3	-	1	17	9	-	-	1	-	-	5	-	865	3	-
Percent attending school	-	-	-	-	-	-	-	-	-	-	-	-	-	-	-	98.2	-	-
Total 14 and 15 years, inclusive	1	-	-	-	-	-	2	1	-	-	-	-	-	2	-	160	1	-
Number attending school	1	-	-	-	-	-	2	1	-	-	-	-	-	2	-	153	1	-
Percent attending school	-	-	-	-	-	-	-	-	-	-	-	-	-	-	-	95.6	-	-
Total 16 and 17 years, inclusive	2	-	-	-	-	1	1	2	-	-	-	-	1	3	-	173	-	-
Number attending school	1	-	-	-	-	1	1	-	-	-	-	-	-	2	-	136	-	-
Percent attending school	-	-	-	-	-	-	-	-	-	-	-	-	-	-	-	78.6	-	-
Total 18 to 20 years, inclusive	1	-	-	-	-	-	7	-	-	-	1	-	-	2	-	366	-	-
Number attending school	-	-	-	-	-	-	1	-	-	-	1	-	-	-	-	56	-	-
Percent attending school	-	-	-	-	-	-	-	-	-	-	-	-	-	-	-	15.3	-	-
ILLITERACY																		
Total 10 years old and over	27	3	3	7	7	9	170	42	1	1	7	2	7	17	1	6,443	14	1
Number illiterate	2	1	1	-	-	1	11	2	-	-	-	-	-	-	-	251	-	1
Percent illiterate	-	-	-	-	-	-	6.5	-	-	-	-	-	-	-	-	3.9	-	-
Percent illiterate in 1920	-	-	-	-	-	-	-	-	-	-	-	-	-	-	-	3.2	-	-
URBAN AND RURAL																		
Urban population	-	1	-	-	2	-	198	38	-	-	6	2	5	15	-	7,516	7	1
Percent urban	-	-	-	-	-	-	94.3	-	-	-	-	-	-	-	-	97.3	-	-
Ruarl population	27	2	3	8	5	13	12	14	1	1	1	-	2	8	1	207	14	-
Rural-farm	8	-	-	5	3	13	12	13	1	1	1	-	-	7	1	1	10	-
Rural-nonfarm	19	2	3	3	2	-	-	1	-	-	-	-	2	1	-	206	4	-
Percent rural	-	-	-	-	-	-	5.7	-	-	-	-	-	-	-	-	2.7	-	-
MARITAL CONDITION																		
Males 15 years old and over	15	-	2	3	4	6	88	26	1	1	2	1	3	9	1	3,297	8	-
Single	10	-	2	-	2	4	26	14	1	1	-	-	1	7	1	1,127	4	-
Married	3	-	-	2	-	2	51	8	-	-	2	1	2	2	-	1,852	2	-
Widowed	2	-	-	1	1	-	6	3	-	-	-	-	-	-	-	228	1	-
Divorced	-	-	-	-	1	-	4	1	-	-	-	-	-	-	-	83	1	-
Unknown	-	-	-	-	-	-	1	-	-	-	-	-	-	-	-	7	-	-
Females 15 years old and over	12	3	1	2	3	3	73	11	-	-	4	1	4	3	-	2,596	4	1
Single	7	1	1	-	1	1	7	1	-	-	1	-	2	2	-	365	2	-
Married	4	-	-	2	2	2	50	5	-	-	2	1	1	1	-	1,764	-	-
Widowed	1	2	-	-	-	-	15	2	-	-	1	-	1	-	-	372	2	-
Divorced	-	-	-	-	-	-	1	3	-	-	-	-	-	-	-	93	-	-
Unknown	-	-	-	-	-	-	-	-	-	-	-	-	-	-	-	2	-	-
FAMILIES																		
Number of families	6	-	1	2	2	3	51	6	-	-	1	1	2	2	-	1,820	4	-
Median size	-	-	-	-	-	-	-	-	-	-	-	-	-	-	-	253	-	-
Families having:																		
No children under 10	6	-	1	1	2	1	37	4	-	-	1	1	2	-	-	1,261	3	-
1 child under 10	-	-	-	1	-	1	2	-	-	-	-	-	-	1	-	271	-	-
2 children under 10	-	-	-	-	-	-	6	1	-	-	-	-	-	-	-	136	1	-
3 or more	-	-	-	-	-	1	6	1	-	-	-	-	-	1	-	152	-	-

CHARACTERISTICS OF NEGRO POPULATION BY COUNTIES: 1930—Continued

(See note at head of table)

SUBJECT	WISCONSIN—Continued																	
	Oneida	Outagamie	Ozaukee	Pierce	Polk	Price	Racine	Richland	Rock	Rusk	Sauk	Shawano	Sheboygan	Taylor	Vernon	Vilas	Walworth	Washburn
POPULATION BY SEX																		
Negro population: 1930	3	4	1	11	7	7	519	11	897	15	34	18	3	19	123	2	81	7
Male	2	2		8	3	4	274	3	441	10	22	11	1	11	74	1	42	4
Female	1	2	1	3	4	3	245	8	456	5	12	7	2	8	49	1	39	3
Negro population: 1920	10	19	1	9	10	3	328	15	880	12	35	29	1	31	54	1	65	9
Male	6	7	1	55	5	3	197	10	509	11	18	21	1	21	27	1	36	5
Female	4	12		4	5		131	5	371	1	17	8		10	27		29	4
Percent of total population:																		
1930				0.1			0.6	0.1	1.2	0.1	0.1	0.1		0.1	0.4		0.3	0.1
1920	0.1						0.4	0.1	1.3	0.1	0.1	0.1		0.2	0.2		0.2	0.1
VOTING AGE: 1930																		
Total 21 years old and over	3	4	1	6	2	2	379	6	546	6	23	6	3	9	48	2	65	2
Male	2	2		4	1	1	212	2	281	4	14	6	1	6	34	1	32	1
Female	1	2	1	2	1	1	167	4	265	2	9		2	3	14	1	33	1
AGE: 1930																		
Under 5 years				3	1		31		87	2	2	2		2	26		2	1
Under 1 year				1			8		22		1			1	6			
5 to 9 years				1	1	2	34	3	91	2	2	4		2	21		4	1
10 to 24 years				1	2	2	31	1	85	3	3	5		3	16		4	1
15 to 19 years					1	1	38	1	73	2	3	1		3	10		6	2
20 to 24 years							46		83	2	5			4	8		3	
25 to 29 years	1			1		1	80		76		1	1	1		10		8	
30 to 34 years	1		1				62		94		1	1			8		7	
35 to 44 years		1			1	1	102	2	161	2	6			1	5		14	1
45 to 54 years	1	1		1			50	2	90	2	5	3	2	1	10	2	11	1
55 to 64 years				3			33	2	36		3	1		1	4		13	
65 to 74 years		2		1	1		9		15		2				5		7	
75 years and over							2		6		1			2			1	
Unknown							1										1	
SCHOOL ATTENDANCE																		
Total 7 to 13 years, inclusive				1	3	4	48	3	122	3	5	6		4	26		7	2
Number attending school				1	3	4	47	3	121	3	5	6		4	24		7	2
Percent attending school									99.2									
Total 14 and 15 years, inclusive					1		9		27	1		2		1	5		1	1
Number attending school					1		9		27	1		1			4			
Percent attending school																		
Total 16 and 17 years, inclusive						1	15		32	1		1		1	5		3	
Number attending school						1	14		27			1			1		2	
Percent attending school																		
Total 18 to 20 years, inclusive							24	1	42	1	4			1	5		2	1
Number attending school							6		5									
Percent attending school																		
ILLITERACY																		
Total 10 years old and over	3	4	1	7	5	5	454	8	719	11	30	12	3	15	76	2	75	
Number illiterate							18	1	58		1	1		1	1			
Percent illiterate							4.0		8.1									
Percent illiterate in 1920							7.7		6.5									
URBAN AND RURAL																		
Urban population	2	3					477		870		19		1		1		59	
Percent urban							91.9		97.0						0.8			
Rural population	1	1	1	11	7	7	42	11	27	15	15	18	2	19	122	2	22	7
Rural-farm				7	2	7	22	3	9	15	13	7		14	115		8	6
Rural-nonfarm	1	1	1	4	5		20	8	18		2	11	2	5	7	2	14	1
Percent rural							8.1		3.0						99.2			
MARITAL CONDITION																		
Males 15 years old and over	2	2		4	2	1	228	2	318	6	17	6	1	7	41	1	35	2
Single	1	1		2	2		70		90	1	11	2		3	19		10	1
Married	1			2		1	142	2	204	2	3	2	1	3	20	1	19	1
Widowed							10		16		1	1		1	2		2	
Divorced		1					6		7		2	1					3	
Unknown									1	3							1	
Females 15 years old and over	1	2	1	2	1	2	195	5	316	2	10	1	2	5	19	1	36	2
Single		1	1			2	34	2	62		2	1		2	4		6	1
Married	1			2			130	2	212	2	7		2	3	15	1	19	1
Widowed		1			1		25		27								8	
Divorced							5		15		1						3	
Unknown							1	1										
FAMILIES																		
Number of families	1	2	1	3	1	1	131	2	227	2	9	4		3	19	1	21	1
Median size							2.32		3.03									
Families having—																		
No children under 10	1	2	1	2			101	1	147	1	7	2		2	6	1	17	
1 child under 10					1	1	18		33		2				2		3	
2 children under 10							7		19			1			3			1
3 or more				1			5	1	28	1		1		1	8		1	

CHARACTERISTICS OF NEGRO POPULATION BY COUNTIES: 1930—Continued

(See note at head of table)

SUBJECT	WISCONSIN—Continued				WYOMING											
	Waukesha	Waupaca	Waushara	Winnebago	The State	Albany	Big Horn	Campbell	Carbon	Converse	Crook	Fremont	Goshen	Hot Springs	Johnson	Laramie
POPULATION BY SEX																
Negro population: 1930	102	1	1	60	1,250	136	12	7	165	8	7	16	4	28	2	327
Male	60	1	1	33	699	75	8	6	107	6	5	6	4	12	1	162
Female	42			27	551	61	4	1	58	2	2	10		16	1	165
Negro population: 1920	66	10	8	55	1,375	66	10	3	141	19	4	31	23	45	8	372
Male	39	6	7	31	863	45	6	3	112	11	3	18	15	22	6	193
Female	27	4	1	24	512	21	4		29	8	1	13	8	23	2	179
Percent of total population:																
1930	0.2			0.1	0.6	1.1	0.1	0.1	1.4	0.1	0.1	0.2		0.5		1.2
1920	0.2			0.1	0.7	0.7	0.1	0.1	1.5	0.2	0.1	0.3	0.3	0.9	0.2	1.8
VOTING AGE: 1930																
Total 21 years old and over	53	1	1	44	962	108	5	6	125	8	4	12	4	28	2	256
Male	29	1	1	25	560	62	3	5	86	6	4	5	4	12	1	133
Female	24			19	402	46	2	1	39	2		7		16	1	123
AGE: 1930																
Under 5 years	9			5	63	4	2		7		1	1				11
Under 1 year	1			1	10	1			1							1
5 to 9 years	11			2	69	4	2		7		2					19
10 to 14 years	10			6	70	7	3	1	8			2				26
15 to 19 years	18			3	68	11			13			1				12
20 to 24 years	6			4	95	17	1		14					1		24
25 to 29 years	10			7	83	9			11			1		1		23
30 to 34 years	7			1	135	14	1	1	21		1	1	1	5		30
35 to 44 years	11		1	17	277	26	1	3	38	5	1	6	2	9		70
45 to 54 years	15	1		5	225	25	1	1	21	2	1	1	1	6	1	63
55 to 64 years	2			7	107	12	1	1	18		1	3		4	1	31
65 to 74 years	2			2	36	6			4							9
75 years and over	1			1	17	1			3	1				2		7
Unknown					5											2
SCHOOL ATTENDANCE																
Total 7 to 13 years, inclusive	11			7	103	10	3		13		1	1				35
Number attending school	11			7	103	10	3		13		1	1				35
Percent attending school					100.0											
Total 14 and 15 years, inclusive	7				29	1	1	1	4			2				8
Number attending school	7				25		1	1	4			2				7
Percent attending school																
Total 16 and 17 years, inclusive	12			2	27	7			5							5
Number attending school	9			2	14				4							4
Percent attending school																
Total 18 to 20 years, inclusive	4			1	45	6			9							8
Number attending school	1				12											5
Percent attending school																
ILLITERACY																
Total 10 years old and over	82	1	1	53	1,118	128	8	7	151	8	4	15	4	28	2	297
Number illiterate	6			3	47	6			19							13
Percent illiterate					4.2	4.7			12.6							4.4
Percent illiterate in 1920					5.3				4.0							8.8
URBAN AND RURAL																
Urban population	84	1		51	859	109			94							305
Percent urban	82.4				68.7	80.1			57.0							93.3
Rural population	18		1	9	391	27	12	7	71	8	7	16	4	28	2	22
Rural-farm	1		1		64	4	9	4	5	2	5					2
Rural-nonfarm	17			9	327	23	3	3	66	6	2	16	4	28	2	20
Percent rural	17.6				31.3	19.9			43.0							6.7
MARITAL CONDITION																
Males 15 years old and over	42	1	1	26	602	69	3	5	99	6	4	5	4	12	1	135
Single	24	1	1	4	240	40	2	3	57	4	1		1	6		31
Married	15			17	292	24	1	1	30	2	3	4		6	1	86
Widowed	3			3	53	4			11			1	2			15
Divorced				2	14			1	1				1			3
Unknown					3	1										
Females 15 years old and over	30			21	446	52	2	1	44	2		8		16	1	136
Single	8			5	73	10			6	1		1		3		20
Married	16			14	278	33	2	1	23	1		6		10	1	85
Widowed	6			1	78	7			12			1		3		27
Divorced				1	16	2			3							4
Unknown					1											
FAMILIES																
Number of families	17	1		11	418	42	2	4	50	2	3	6	4	13	1	107
Median size					1.85											2.15
Families having—																
No children under 10	8	1		8	354	37	1	4	45	2	2	5	4	13	1	90
1 child under 10	4			2	34	3			1			1				9
2 children under 10	2			1	9	1										5
3 or more	3				21	1	1		4		1					3

CHARACTERISTICS OF NEGRO POPULATION BY COUNTIES: 1930—Continued

(See note at head of table)

SUBJECT	WYOMING—Continued										
	Lincoln	Natrona	Niobrara	Park	Platte	Sheridan	Sweet-water	Teton	Uinta	Washa-kie	Weston
POPULATION BY SEX											
Negro population: 1930	17	164	9	6	5	84	194	1	18	31	9
Male	6	83	5	2	2	47	122	1	15	19	5
Female	11	81	4	4	3	37	72		3	12	4
Negro population: 1920	35	166	24	7	2	147	164		80	19	8
Male	21	87	12	5	1	90	120		73	15	4
Female	14	79	12	2	1	57	44		7	4	4
Percent of total population:											
1930	0.2	0.7	0.2	0.1	0.1	0.5	1.1		0.3	0.8	0.2
1920	0.3	1.1	0.4	0.1		0.8	1.2		1.2	0.6	0.2
VOTING AGE: 1930											
Total 21 years old and over	16	126	6	4	3	68	134	1	18	22	6
Male	5	66	3	2	2	40	89	1	15	13	3
Female	11	60	3	2	1	28	45		3	9	3
AGE: 1930											
Under 5 years		7				3	24			2	1
Under 1 year		2					5				
5 to 9 years		12	1			5	17				
10 to 14 years		8		2		3	7			2	1
15 to 19 years	1	10	2		1	4	7			5	1
20 to 24 years	3	7			2	4	18	1		2	1
25 to 29 years	2	5		1		7	19		1	3	
30 to 34 years	3	23	1	1		7	21		1	3	
35 to 44 years	4	35	3	1		15	44		7	5	2
45 to 54 years	4	42	1		2	14	25		6	6	2
55 to 64 years		8	1			13	9		2	1	1
65 to 74 years		4		1		7	3			2	
75 years and over		3									
Unknown						2			1		
SCHOOL ATTENDANCE											
Total 7 to 13 years, inclusive		16	1	2		6	14			1	
Number attending school		16	1	2		6	14			1	
Percent attending school											
Total 14 and 15 years, inclusive		3	1			2	4			1	1
Number attending school		3				2	3			1	1
Percent attending school											
Total 16 and 17 years, inclusive		3	1		1	1	2			2	
Number attending school		3				1	1			1	
Percent attending school											
Total 18 to 20 years, inclusive	1	7			1	2	7			3	1
Number attending school		2				1	3			1	
Percent attending school											
ILLITERACY											
Total 10 years old and over	17	145	8	6	5	76	153	1	18	29	8
Number illiterate		4					4		1		
Percent illiterate		2.8					2.6				
Percent illiterate in 1920		3.1				3.1	6.5				
URBAN AND RURAL											
Urban population		146				50	150		5		
Percent urban		89.0					77.3				
Rural population	17	18	9	6	5	34	44	1	13	31	9
Rural-farm	9	3	8			6				7	
Rural-nonfarm	8	15	1	6	5	28	44	1	13	24	9
Percent rural		11.0					22.7				
MARITAL CONDITION											
Males 15 years old and over	6	72	4	2	2	44	92	1	15	17	4
Single	3	19	2	1		13	35	1	7	12	2
Married	3	45	1	1	2	26	44		6	4	2
Widowed		2	1			2	12		2	1	
Divorced		5				2	1				
Unknown		1				1					
Females 15 years old and over	11	65	4	2	3	29	54		3	10	3
Single	6	7	1	1	1	4	8			3	1
Married	3	40	2	1	2	21	37		3	5	2
Widowed	2	12	1			3	8			2	
Divorced		5				1	1				
Unknown		1									
FAMILIES											
Number of families	6	54	3	1	1	27	71		4	14	3
Median size											
Families having—											
No children under 10	6	46	2	1	1	24	53		4	11	2
1 child under 10		6	1			1	8			3	1
2 children under 10							3				
3 or more		2				2	7				